S0-FME-514

SUBJECT GUIDE TO

Children's Books In Print®

2024

This edition of

SUBJECT GUIDE TO CHILDREN'S BOOKS IN PRINT® 2024

was prepared by R.R. Bowker's Database Publishing Group
in collaboration with the Information Technology Department.

Audrey Marcus, Sr Vice President ProQuest Books
Rob Biter, Vice President Books Operations
Mark Van Orman, Senior Director Content Operations

International Standard Book Number/Standard Address Number Agency

Beat Barblan, General Manager
John Purcell, Operations Manager
Richard Smith, Lead Product Manager
Raymond Reynolds, Publisher Relations Representative
Colleen Margetich, Publisher Relations Representative
John Tabeling, Publisher Relations Representative
Hailey Schumacher, Publisher Relations Representative

Books Content Operations
Margot Cronin, Lisa Heft, Senior Managers, Content Operations
Adrene Allen, Manager, Content Operations
Ila Joseph, Senior Content Data Analysts
Ron Butkiewicz, Latonia Hall, Lynda Keller
Tom Lucas, Charu Mehta, Daniel Smith, Content Data Analysts

Provider Relations
Patricia Payton, Senior Manager Provider Relations
Ralph Coviello, Suzanne Franks, Engagement Managers
Michael Olenick, Content Business Analyst Senior
Matt O'Connell, Content Business Analyst Lead

Data Services Production
Andy K. Haramasz, Manager Data Distribution & QA

Computer Operations Group
John Nesselt, UNIX Administrator

Bowker®

SUBJECT GUIDE TO

Children's Books In Print®

2024

A Subject Index to Books
for Children and Young Adults

SUBJECT GUIDE

- **Subjects J-Z**
- **Publishers**
- **Wholesalers & Distributors**

GREY HOUSE PUBLISHING

ProQuest LLC
789 E. Eisenhower Parkway
P.O. Box 1346
Ann Arbor, MI 48106-1346
Phone: 734-761-4700
Toll-free: l-800-521-0600
E-mail:
customerservice@proquest.com
URL: http://www.proquest.com

Grey House Publishing, Inc.
4919 Route 22
Amenia, NY 12501
Phone: 518-789-8700
Toll-free: 1-800-562-2139
Fax: 518-789-0545
E-mail: books@greyhouse.com
URL: http://www.greyhouse.com

Subject Guide to Children's Books In Print® 2024 is published by Grey House Publishing, Inc. under exclusive license from ProQuest, a Clarivate company.

Publishers may update or add to their listings by accessing one of Bowker's online portals: **BowkerLink** for international publishers at http://www.bowkerlink.com and **MyIdentifiers** for USA publishers at http://www.myidentifiers.com.

No payment is either solicited or accepted for the inclusion of entries in this publication.

R.R. Bowker has used its best efforts in collecting and preparing material for inclusion in **Subject Guide to Children's Books In Print® 2024,** but does not warrant that the information herein is complete or accurate, and does not assume, and hereby disclaims any liability to any person for the loss or damage caused by errors or omissions in **Subject Guide to Children's Books In Print® 2024**, whether such errors or omissions result from negligence, accident or any other cause.

International Standard Book Numbers
ISBN 13: 978-1-63700-643-6 (Set)
ISBN 13: 978-1-63700-644-3 (Vol. 1)
ISBN 13: 978-1-63700-645-0 (Vol. 2)

International Standard Serial Number
0000-0167

Library of Congress Control Number
74-643526

Printed and bound in the United States

CONTENTS

How To Use

SUBJECT GUIDE TO CHILDREN'S BOOKS IN PRINT®

The 55th edition of R.R. Bowker's ***Subject Guide to Children's Books In Print***® was produced from the Books In Print database. This volume only includes books published after 2003. Titles listed in ***Children's Books In Print***® *are included in the Subject Guide edition.* There are approximately 500,000 listings under 10,000 subject categories. These titles are available from approximately 20,000 United States publishers. An index with full contact information for all of the publishers listed in the bibliographic entries is included in this volume, as well as in a separate index to wholesalers and distributors.

RELATED PRODUCTS

In addition to the printed version, the entire Books In Print database (more than 50 million records, including OP/OSI titles, ebooks, audio books and videos) can be searched by customers on Bowker's Web site, *http://www.booksinprint.com.*

The Books In Print database is also available in an array of other formats such as online access through Books In Print site licensing. Database vendors such as OVID Technologies, Inc make the Books In Print database available to their subscribers.

COMPILATION

In order to be useful to subscribers, the information contained in ***Subject Guide to Children's Books In Print***® must be complete and accurate. Publishers are asked to review and correct their entries prior to each publication, providing current price, publication date, availability status, and ordering information, as well as recently published and forthcoming titles. Tens of thousands of entries are added or updated for each edition.

DATA ACQUISITION

Bowker aggregates bibliographic information via ONIX, Excel & Text data feeds from publishers, national libraries, distributors & wholesalers. Publishers may also add to or update their listings using one of Bowker's online portals: **BowkerLink** for international publishers at http://www.bowkerlink.com and **MyIdentifiers** for USA publishers at http://www.myidentifiers.com.

Larger publishing houses can submit their bibliographic information to the Books In Print database from their own databases. Bowker's system accepts publisher data 24 hours a day, 7 days a week via FTP. The benefits to this method are: no paper intervention, reduced costs, increased timeliness, and less chance of human error that can occur when rekeying information.

To communicate new title information to Books In Print, the quality of the publisher's textual data must be up to—or extremely close to—reference book standards. Publishers interested in setting up a data feed are invited to access the Bowker Title Submission Guide at http://www.bowker.com or contact us at Data.Submission@bowker.com.

Updated information or corrections to the listings in *Books In Print* can now be submitted at any time via email at Data.Submission@bowker.com. Publishers can also submit updates and new titles to ***Children's Books In Print***® through one of Bowker's online portals: **BowkerLink** for international publishers at http://www.bowkerlink.com and **MyIdentifiers** for USA publishers at http://www.myidentifiers.com.

To ensure the accuracy, timeliness and comprehensiveness of data in ***Children's Books In Print***®, Bowker has initiated discussions with the major publishers. This outreach entails analyzing the quality of all publisher submissions to the Books In Print database and working closely with the publisher to improve the content and timeliness of the information. This outreach also lays the groundwork for incorporating new valuable information into ***Children's Books In Print***®. We are now collecting cover art, descriptive jacket and catalog copy, tables of contents, and contributor biographies, as well as awards won, bestseller listings, and review citations.

Bowker will make this important additional information available to customers who receive *Books In Print* in specific electronic formats and through subscriptions to *http://www.booksinprint.com*.

HOW THE SUBJECT HEADINGS WERE ASSIGNED

R.R. Bowker's ***Subject Guide to Children's Books In Print***® is based primarily on the Library of Congress Subject Headings. Many headings were consolidated where they seemed too cumbersome for the needs of this *Subject Guide*. Some books have been assigned to a single category, while other books have been assigned two, three, or more headings.

ALPHABETICAL ARRANGEMENT OF SUBJECT CATEGORIES

Headings are filed alphabetically with the following conditions and variations. First, punctuation is not considered:

ART, ANCIENT
ART—FICTION
ART, GREEK

Second, proper nouns precede improper nouns and names of people precede geographical names:

CLEVELAND, GROVER, 1837-1908
CLEVELAND (OHIO)
CLEVELAND BROWNS (FOOTBALL TEAM)

Third, when personal names appear as headings, those without surnames appear first and religious titles precede royal titles:

PETER, THE APOSTLE, SAINT
PETER I, EMPEROR OF RUSSIA, 1672-1725
PETER, SARAH (WORTHINGTON) KING, 1800-1877

ALPHABETICAL ARRANGEMENT OF TITLES WITHIN THE SUBJECT CATEGORIES

Under each subject heading entries are filed alphabetically by contributor's last name if available, and by title when no contributor exists. Please note the following exceptions:

Initial articles of titles in English, French, German, Italian, and Spanish are deleted from both author and title entries.

Numerals, including year dates, are written out in most cases and are filed alphabetically.

U.S., UN, Dr., Mr., and St. are filed in strict alphabetical order unless the author/publisher requests that the title be filed as if it were spelled out.

Proper names beginning with "Mc" and "Mac" are filed in strict alphabetical order. For example, entries for contributor's names such as MacAdam, MacA vory, MacCarthy, MacDonald, and MacLean are located prior to the pages with entries for names such as McAdams, McCarthy, McCoy, and McDermott.

Entries beginning with initial letters (whether authors' given names, or titles) are filed first, e.g., Smith, H.C., comes before Smith, Harold A.; B is for Betsy comes before Babar, etc.

Compound names are listed under the first part of the name, and cross-references appear under the last part of the name.

INFORMATION INCLUDED IN ENTRIES

Entries include the following bibliographic information, when available: author, co-author, editor, co-editor, translator, co-translator, illustrator, co-illustrator, photographer, co-photographer, title, number of volumes, edition, series information, language if other than English, whether or not illustrated, grade range, year of publication, price, International Standard Book Number, publisher's order number, imprint, and publisher abbreviation. Entries new to this edition are indicated by an asterisk (*) before the bolded ISBN. (Information on the International Standard Book Numbering System is available from R.R. Bowker.)

The prices cited are those provided by the publishers and generally refer to either the trade edition or the Publisher's Library Bound edition. The abbreviation "lib. bdg." is used whenever the price cited is for a publisher's library bound edition.

ISBN AGENCY

Each title included in R.R. Bowker's ***Subject Guide to Children's Books In Print***® has been assigned an International Standard Book Number (ISBN) by the publisher. All ISBNs listed in this directory have been validated by using the check digit control, ensuring accuracy. ISBNs allow order transmission and bibliographic information updating using publishing industry supported EDI formats (e.g., ONIX). Publishers not currently participating in the ISBN system may request the assignment of an ISBN Publisher Prefix from the ISBN Agency by calling 877-310-7333, faxing 908-219-0195, or through the ISBN Agency's web site at **http://www.myidentifiers.com**. Please note: The ISBN prefix 0-615 is for decentralized use by the U.S. ISBN Agency and has been assigned to many publishers. It is not unique to one publisher.

SAN AGENCY

Another listing feature in **Subject Guide to Books In Print®** is the Standard Address Number (SAN), a unique identification number assigned to each address of an organization in or served by the publishing industry; it facilitates communications and transactions with other members of the industry.

The SAN identifies either a bill to or ship to address for purchasing, billing, shipping, receiving, paying, crediting, and refunding, and can be used for any other communication or transaction between participating companies and organizations in the publishing supply chain.

To obtain an application or further information on the SAN system, please email the SAN Agency at **SAN@bowker.com,** or visit **www.myidentifiers.com**

Publishers with like or similar names are referenced by a "Do not confuse with ... " notation at the end of the entry. In addition, cross-references

PUBLISHER NAME INDEX

A key to the abbreviated publisher names (e.g., "Middle Atlantic Pr.") used in the bibliographic entries of ***Subject Guide to Children's Books In Print***® is found after the Subject Index. Entries in this index contain each publisher's abbreviated name, followed by its ISBN prefix(es), business affiliation, (e.g., "Div. of International Publishing") when available, ordering address(es), SAN (Standard Address Number), telephone, fax, and toll-free numbers. Editorial address(es) (and associated contact numbers) follow. Addresses without a specific label are for editorial offices rather than ordering purposes.

Abbreviations used to identify publishers' imprints are followed by the full name of the imprint. E-mail and Web site addresses are then supplied. A listing of distributors associated with the publisher concludes each entry; each distributor name is in bold type and may be found in the Wholesaler & Distributor Name Index (see below).

A dagger preceding an entry and the note "CIP" at the end of the entry both indicate that the publisher participates in the Cataloging in Publication Program of the Library of Congress.

Foreign publishers with U.S. distributors are listed, followed by their three-character ISO (International Standards Organization) country code ("GBR," "CAN," etc.), ISBN prefix(es), when available, and a cross-reference to their U.S. distributor, as shown below:

Atrium (GBR) *(0-9535353) Dist by* **Dufour.**

are provided from imprints and former company names to the new name.

WHOLESALER & DISTRIBUTOR NAME

INDEX

Full information on distributors as well as wholesalers is provided in this index. Note that those publishers who also serve as distributors may be listed both here and in the Publisher Name Index.

SAMPLE ENTRY – SUBJECT

1 **BEACH EROSION**
2 **see also Coast Changes; Shore Protection**
3 Akyeampong, Emmanuel. 4 Between the Sea & the Lagoon:
5 An Eco-Social History of the Anlo of Southeastern Ghana: c. 1850 to Recent Times
6 2008 7 (Western African Studies). 8 (Illus.). 9 **256p.** 10 pap. 11 24.95
12 978-0-8214-1409-5(7). 13 Ohio Univ. Pr.
14 __ 15 Between the Sea & the Lagoon:
16 An Eco-Social History of the Anlo of Southeastern Ghana: c. 1850 to Recent Times
17 2008 18 Tchr's Ed. 19 (Western African Studies). 20 (Illus.). 95' 21 256p.

22 34.99 23 978-0-8214-1408-8(9). 24 Ohio Univ. Pr.

BEACH EROSION

see also Coast Changes; Shore Protection

Akyeampong, Emmanuel Kwaku. Between the Sea & the Lagoon : An Eco-Social History of the Anlo of South-eastern Ghana: c. 1850 to Recent Times. 2002. (Western African Studies). (Illus.). 256p. pap. 24.95 978-0-8214-1409-5(7) . Ohio Univ. Pr.

—Between the Sea & the Lagoon : An Eco-Social History of the Anlo of Southeastern Ghana: C. 1850 to Recent Times. 2002. (Western African Studies). (Illus.). 256p. 44.95 978-0-8214-1408-8(9) . Ohio Univ. Pr.

Footnote:
This sample does not include all elements that can be found in an entry.

KEY

1 Subject Heading
2 Subject x-reference information
3 Main Contributor's last name, first, M.I.
4 Title of the Book
5 Subtitle
6 Publication Year
7 Title of the Series
8 Illustration Indicator
9 Total pages
10 Binding - format
11 Price
12 International Standard Book Number - ISBN13 (ISBN10 check digit)
13 Publisher
14 New title under same contributor indicator
15 Title of book
16 Subtitle
17 Publication year
18 Edition Information
19 Title of Series
20 Illustration Indicator
21 Total pages
22 Price
23 International Standard Book Number - ISBN13 (ISBN10 check digit)
24 Publisher

SAMPLE ENTRY PUBLISHER NAME INDEX

1 † 2 **Mosby, Inc.,** 3 *(0-323; 0-7234; 0-8016; 0-8151; 0-88416; 0-941158; 1-55664; 1-56815),* 4 Div. of Harcourt, Inc., A Harcourt Health Sciences Co., 5 Orders Addr.: 6227 Sea Harbor Dr., Orlando, FL 32887 6 Toll Free Fax: 800-235-0256 7 Toll Free: 800-543-1918 8 Edit Addr.: 11830 Westline Industrial Dr., Saint Louis, MO 63146
9 (SAN 200-2280) 10 Toll Free: 800-325-4177
11 Web site: http://www.mosby.com/
12 Dist(s): ***PennWell Corp.*** 13 *CIP.*

KEY

1 CIP Identifier
2 Publisher Name
3 ISBN Prefixes
4 Division of
5 Orders Address
6 Orders Fax
7 Orders Telephone
8 Editorial Address
9 SAN
10 Toll-Free
11 Web site
12 Distributors
13 Cataloging in Publication

SAMPLE ENTRY WHOLESALER & DISTRIBUTOR NAME INDEX

1 **New Leaf Distributing Co., Inc.,** 2 *(0-9627209),* 3 Div. of Al-Wali Corp.,
4 401 Thornton Rd., Lithia Springs, GA 30122-1557 5 (SAN 169-1449)
6 Tel: 770-948-7845; 7 Fax: 770-944-2313; 8 Toll Free Fax: 800-326-1066;
9 Toll Free: 800-326-2665
10 Email: NewLeaf-dist.com
11 Web site: http://www.NewLeaf-dist.com

KEY

1 Distributor name
2 ISBN prefix
3 Division of
4 Editorial address
5 SAN
6 Telephone
7 Fax
8 Toll free fax
9 Toll free
10 E-mail
11 Web site

PUBLISHER COUNTRY CODES

Foreign Publishers are listed with the three letter International Standards Organization (ISO) code for their country of domicile. This is the complete list of ISO codes though not all countries may be represented. The codes are mnemonic in most cases. The country names here may be shortened to a more common usage form.

Code	Country
AFG	AFGHANISTAN
AGO	ANGOLA
ALB	ALBANIA
AND	ANDORRA
ANT	NETHERLANDS ANTILLES
ARE	UNITED ARAB EMIRATES
ARG	ARGENTINA
ARM	ARMENIA
ASM	AMERICAN SAMOA
ATA	ANTARCTICA
ATG	ANTIGUA & BARBUDA
AUS	AUSTRALIA
AUT	AUSTRIA
AZE	AZERBAIJAN
BDI	BURUNDI
BEL	BELGIUM
BEN	BENIN
BFA	BURKINA FASO
BGD	BANGLADESH
BGR	BULGARIA
BHR	BAHRAIN
BHS	BAHAMAS
BIH	BOSNIA & HERZEGOVINA
BLR	BELARUS
BLZ	BELIZE
BMU	BERMUDA
BOL	BOLIVIA
BRA	BRAZIL
BRB	BARBADOS
BRN	BRUNEI DARUSSALAM
BTN	BHUTAN
BWA	BOTSWANA
BWI	BRITISH WEST INDIES
CAF	CENTRAL AFRICAN REP
CAN	CANADA
CH2	CHINA
CHE	SWITZERLAND
CHL	CHILE
CHN	CHINA
CIV	IVORY COAST
CMR	CAMEROON
COD	ZAIRE
COG	CONGO (BRAZZAVILLE)
COL	COLOMBIA
COM	COMOROS
CPV	CAPE VERDE
CRI	COSTA RICA
CS	CZECHOSLOVAKIA
CUB	CUBA
CYM	CAYMAN ISLANDS
CYP	CYPRUS
CZE	CZECH REPUBLIC
DEU	GERMANY
DJI	DJIBOUTI
DMA	DOMINICA
DNK	DENMARK
DOM	DOMINICAN REPUBLIC
DZA	ALGERIA
ECU	ECUADOR
EG	East Germany
EGY	EGYPT
EI	EUROPEAN UNION
EN	England
ESP	SPAIN
EST	ESTONIA
ETH	ETHIOPIA
FIN	FINLAND
FJI	FIJI
FLK	FALKLAND ISLANDS
FRA	FRANCE
FRO	FAEROE ISLANDS
FSM	MICRONESIA
GAB	GABON
GBR	UNITED KINGDOM
GEO	GEORGIA
GHA	GHANA
GIB	GIBRALTAR
GIN	GUINEA
GLP	GUADELOUPE
GMB	GAMBIA
GNB	GUINEA-BISSAU
GNQ	EQUATORIAL GUINEA
GRC	GREECE
GRD	GRENADA
GRL	GREENLAND
GTM	GUATEMALA
GUF	FRENCH GUIANA
GUM	GUAM
GUY	GUYANA
HKG	HONG KONG
HND	HONDURAS
HRV	Croatia
HTI	HAITI
HUN	HUNGARY
IDN	INDONESIA
IND	INDIA
IRL	IRELAND
IRN	IRAN
IRQ	IRAQ
ISL	ICELAND
ISR	ISRAEL
ITA	ITALY
JAM	JAMAICA
JOR	JORDAN
JPN	JAPAN
KAZ	KAZAKSTAN
KEN	KENYA
KGZ	KYRGYZSTAN
KHM	CAMBODIA
KNA	ST. KITTS-NEVIS
KO	Korea
KOR	SOUTH KOREA
KOS	KOSOVA
KWT	KUWAIT
LAO	LAOS
LBN	LEBANON
LBR	LIBERIA
LBY	LIBYA
LCA	ST. LUCIA
LIE	LIECHTENSTEIN
LKA	SRI LANKA
LSO	LESOTHO
LTU	LITHUANIA
LUX	LUXEMBOURG
LVA	LATVIA
MAC	MACAO
MAR	MOROCCO
MCO	MONACO
MDA	MOLDOVA
MDG	MALAGASY REPUBLIC
MDV	MALDIVE ISLANDS
MEX	MEXICO
MHL	MARSHALL ISLANDS
MKD	MACEDONIA
MLI	MALI
MLT	MALTA
MMR	UNION OF MYANMAR
MNE	MONTENEGRO
MNG	MONGOLIA
MOZ	MOZAMBIQUE
MRT	MAURITANIA
MSR	MONTESERRAT
MTQ	MARTINIQUE
MUS	MAURITIUS
MWI	MALAWI
MYS	MALAYSIA
NAM	NAMIBIA
NCL	NEW CALEDONIA
NER	NIGER
NGA	NIGERIA
NIC	NICARAGUA
NLD	THE NETHERLANDS
NOR	NORWAY
NPL	NEPAL
NRU	NAURU
NZL	NEW ZEALAND
OMN	SULTANATE OF OMAN
PAK	PAKISTAN
PAN	PANAMA
PER	PERU
PHL	PHILIPPINES
PNG	PAPUA NEW GUINEA
POL	POLAND
PRI	Puerto Rico
PRK	NORTH KOREA
PRT	PORTUGAL
PRY	PARAGUAY
PYF	FRENCH POLYNESIA
REU	REUNION
ROM	RUMANIA
RUS	RUSSIA
RWA	RWANDA
SAU	SAUDI ARABIA
SC	Scotland
SCG	SERBIA & MONTENEGRO
SDN	SUDAN
SEN	SENEGAL
SGP	SINGAPORE
SLB	SOLOMON ISLANDS
SLE	SIERRA LEONE
SLV	EL SALVADOR
SMR	SAN MARINO
SOM	SOMALIA
STP	SAO TOME E PRINCIPE
SU	Soviet Union
SUR	SURINAM

PUBLISHER COUNTRY CODES

SVK	Slovakia
SVN	SLOVENIA
SWE	SWEDEN
SWZ	SWAZILAND
SYC	SEYCHELLES
SYN	SYNDETICS
SYR	SYRIA
TCA	TURKS NDS
TCD	CHAD
TGO	TOGO
THA	THAILAND
TKM	TURKMENISTAN
TON	TONGA
TTO	TRINIDAD AND TOBAGO
TUN	TUNISIA
TUR	TURKEY
TWN	TAIWAN
TZA	TANZANIA
UGA	UGANDA
UI	UNITED KINGDOM
UKR	UKRAINE
UN	UNITED NATIONS
URY	URUGUAY
USA	UNITED STATES
UZB	UZBEKISTAN
VAT	VATICAN CITY
VCT	ST. VINCENT
VEN	VENEZUELA
VGB	BRITISH VIRGIN ISLANDS
VIR	U.S. VIRGIN ISLANDS
VNM	VIETNAM
VUT	VANUATU
WA	Wales
WSM	WESTERN SAMOA
YEM	REPUBLIC OF YEMEN
YUG	YUGOSLAVIA
ZAF	SOUTH AFRICA
ZMB	ZAMBIA
ZWE	ZIMBABWE

COUNTRY SEQUENCE

Country	Code
AFGHANISTAN	AFG
ALBANIA	ALB
ALGERIA	DZA
AMERICAN SAMOA	ASM
ANDORRA	AND
ANGOLA	AGO
ANGUILLA	AIA
ANTARCTICA	ATA
ANTIGUA & BARBUDA	ATG
ARGENTINA	ARG
ARMENIA	ARM
ARUBA	ABW
AUSTRALIA	AUS
AUSTRIA	AUT
AZERBAIJAN	AZE
BAHAMAS	BHS
BAHRAIN	BHR
BANGLADESH	BGD
BARBADOS	BRB
BELARUS	BLR
BELGIUM	BEL
BELIZE	BLZ
BENIN	BEN
BERMUDA	BMU
BHUTAN	BTN
BOLIVIA	BOL
BOSNIA & HERZEGOVINA	BIH
BOTSWANA	BWA
BOUVET ISLAND	BVT
BRAZIL	BRA
BRITISH INDIAN OCEAN TERRITORY	IOT
BRITISH WEST INDIES	BWI
BRUNEI DARUSSALAM	BRN
BULGARIA	BGR
BURKINA FASO	BFA
BURUNDI	BDI
CAMBODIA	KHM
CAMEROON	CMR
CANADA	CAN
CAPE VERDE	CPV
CAYMAN ISLANDS	CYM
CENTRAL AFRICAN REPUBLIC	CAF
CHAD	TCD
CHILE	CHL
CHINA	CHN
CHRISTMAS ISLAND	CXR
COCOS (KEELING) ISLANDS	CCK
COLOMBIA	COL
COMOROS	COM
CONGO	COG
CONGO, THE DEMOCRATIC REPUBLIC OF THE CONGO	COD
COOK ISLANDS	COK
COSTA RICA	CRI
COTE' D' IVOIRE	CIV
CROATIA	HRV
CUBA	CUB
CYPRUS	CYP
CZECH REPUBLIC	CZE
CZECHOSLOVAKIA	CSK
DENMARK	DNK
DJIBOUTI	DJI
DOMINICA	DMA
DOMINICAN REPUBLIC	DOM
EAST TIMOR	TMP
ECUADOR	ECU
EGYPT (ARAB REPUBLIC OF EGYPT)	EGY
EL SALVADOR	SLV
EQUATORIAL GUINEA	GNQ
ERITREA	ERI
ESTONIA	EST
ETHIOPIA	ETH
EAST GERMANY	DDR
FALKLAND ISLANDS	FLK
FAROE ISLANDS	FRO
FEDERATED STATES OF MICRONESIA	FSM
FIJI	FJI
FINLAND	FIN
FRANCE	FRA
FRENCH GUIANA	GUF
FRENCH POLYNESIA	PYF
FRENCH SOUTHERN TERRITORIES	ATF
GABON	GAB
GAMBIA	GMB
GEORGIA	GEO
GERMANY	DEU
GHANA	GHA
GIBRALTAR	GIB
GREECE	GRC
GREENLAND	GRL
GRENADA	GRD
GUADELOUPE	GLP
GUAM	GUM
GUATEMALA	GTM
GUINEA	GIN
GUINEA-BISSAU	GNB
GUYANA	GUY
HAITI	HTI
HEARD ISLAND & MCDONALD ISLANDS	HMD
HONDURAS	HND
HONG KONG	HKG
HUNGARY	HUN
ICELAND	ISL
INDIA	IND
INDONESIA	IDN
IRAN, ISLAMIC REPUBLIC OF	IRN
IRAQ	IRQ
IRELAND	IRL
ISRAEL	ISR
ITALY	ITA
JAMAICA	JAM
JAPAN	JPN
JORDAN	JOR
KAZAKSTAN	KAZ
KENYA	KEN
KIRIBATI	KIR
KOREA, DEMOCRATIC PEOPLE'S REPUBLIC OF	PRK
KOREA, REPUBLIC OF	KOR
KUWAIT	KWT
KYRGYZSTAN	KGZ
KOSOVA	KOS
LAO PEOPLE'S DEMOCRATIC REPUBLIC	LAO
LATVIA	LVA
LEBANON	LBN
LESOTHO	LSO
LIBERIA	LBR
LIBYAN ARAB JAMAHIRIYA	LBY
LIECHTENSTEIN	LIE
LITHUANIA	LTU
LUXEMBOURG	LUX
MACAU	MAC
MACEDONIA, THE FORMER YUGOSLAV REPUBLIC OF	MKD
MADAGASCAR	MDG
MALAWI	MWI
MALAYSIA	MYS
MALDIVE ISLANDS	MDV
MALI	MLI
MALTA	MLT
MARSHALL ISLANDS	MHL
MARTINIQUE	MTQ
MAURITANIA	MRT
MAURITIUS	MUS
MAYOTTE	MYT
MEXICO	MEX
MOLDOVA, REPUBLIC OF	MDA
MONACO	MCO

COUNTRY SEQUENCE

Country	Code
MONGOLIA	MNG
MONTENEGRO	MNE
MONTSERRAT	MSR
MOROCCO	MAR
MOZAMBIQUE	MOZ
MYANMAR	MMR
NAMIBIA	NAM
NAURU	NRU
NEPAL	NPL
NETHERLANDS	NLD
NETHERLANDS ANTILLES	ANT
NEW CALEDONIA	NCL
NEW ZEALAND	NZL
NICARAGUA	NIC
NIGER	NER
NIGERIA	NGA
NIUE	NIU
NORFOLK ISLAND	NFK
NORTHERN MARIANA ISLANDS	MNP
NORWAY	NOR
OMAN	OMN
OCCUPIED PALESTINIAN TERRITORY	PSE
PAKISTAN	PAK
PALAU	PLW
PANAMA	PAN
PAPUA NEW GUINEA	PNG
PARAGUAY	PRY
PERU	PER
PHILIPPINES	PHL
PITCAIRN	PCN
POLAND	POL
PORTUGAL	PRT
PUERTO RICO	PRI
QATAR	QAT
REUNION	REU
ROMANIA	ROM
RUSSIAN FEDERATION	RUS
RWANDA	RWA
SAINT HELENA	SHN
SAINT KITTS & NEVIS	KNA
SAINT PIERRE & MIQUELON	SPM
SAINT VINCENT & THE GRENADINES	VCT
SAMOA	WSM
SAN MARINO	SMR
SAO TOME E PRINCIPE	STP
SAUDI ARABIA	SAU
SENEGAL	SEN
SERBIA	SRB
SERBIA & MONTENEGRO	SCG
SEYCHELLES	SYC
SIERRA LEONE	SLE
SINGAPORE	SGP
SLOVAKIA	SVK
SLOVENIA	SVN
SOLOMON ISLANDS	SLB
SOMALIA	SOM
SOUTH AFRICA	ZAF
SOUTH GEORGIA & THE SANDWICH ISLANDS	SGS
SPAIN	ESP
SRI LANKA	LKA
ST. LUCIA	LCA
SUDAN	SDN
SURINAME	SUR
SVALBARD & JAN MAYEN	SJM
SWAZILAND	SWZ
SWEDEN	SWE
SWITZERLAND	CHE
SYRIAN ARAB REPUBLIC	SYR
TAIWAN, REPUBLIC OF CHINA	TWN
TAJIKISTAN	TJK
TANZANIA, UNITED REPUBLIC OF	TZA
THAILAND	THA
TOGO	TGO
TOKELAU	TKL
TONGA	TON
TRINIDAD & TOBAGO	TTO
TUNISIA	TUN
TURKEY	TUR
TURKMENISTAN	TKM
TURKS & CAICOS ISLANDS	TCA
TUVALU	TUV
U.S.S.R.	SUN
UGANDA	UGA
UKRAINE	UKR
UNITED ARAB EMIRATES	UAE
UNITED KINGDOM	GBR
UNITED STATES	USA
UNITED STATES MINOR OUTLYING ISLANDS	UMI
URUGUAY	URY
UZBEKISTAN	UZB
VANUATU	VUT
VATICAN CITY STATE (HOLY SEE)	VAT
VENEZUELA	VEN
VIET NAM	VNM
VIRGIN ISLANDS, BRITISH	VGB
VIRGIN ISLANDS, U. S.	VIR
WALLIS & FUTUNA	WLF
WESTERN SAHARA	ESH
West Germany	BRD
YEMEN	YEM
YUGOSLAVIA	YUG
ZAMBIA	ZMB
ZIMBABWE	ZWE
ZAIRE	ZAR

LANGUAGE CODES

Code	Language
ACE	Achioli
AFA	Afro-Asiatic
AFR	Afrikaans
AKK	Akkadian
ALB	Albanian
ALE	Aleut
ALG	Algonquin
AMH	Amharic
ANG	Anglo-Saxon
APA	Apache
ARA	Arabic
ARC	Aramaic
ARM	Armenian
ARN	Araucanian
ARP	Arapaho
ARW	Arawak
ASM	Assamese
AVA	Avar
AVE	Avesta
AYM	Aymara
AZE	Azerbaijani
BAK	Bashkir
BAL	Baluchi
BAM	Bambara
BAQ	Basque
BAT	Baltic
BEJ	Beja
BEL	Belorussian
BEM	Bemba
BEN	Bengali
BER	Berber Group
BIH	Bihari
BLA	Blackfoot
BRE	Breton
BUL	Bulgarian
BUR	Burmese
CAD	Caddo
CAI	Central American
CAM	Cambodian
CAR	Carib
CAT	Catalan
CAU	Caucasian
CEL	Celtic Group
CHB	Chibcha
CHE	Chechen
CHI	Chinese
CHN	Chinook
CHO	Choctaw
CHR	Cherokee
CHU	Church Slavic
CHV	Chuvash
CHY	Cheyenne
COP	Coptic
COR	Cornish
CRE	Cree
CRO	Croatian
CRP	Creoles and Pidgins
CUS	Cushitic
CZE	Czech
DAK	Dakota
DAN	Danish
DEL	Delaware
DIN	Dinka
DOI	Dogri
DRA	Dravidian
DUA	Duala
DUT	Dutch
EFI	Efik
EGY	Egyptian
ELX	Elamite
ENG	English
ENM	English, Middle
ESK	Eskimo
RUM	Romanian
RUN	Rundi
RUS	Russian
SAD	Sandawe
SAG	Sango
SAI	South American
SAM	Samaritan
SAN	Sanskrit
SAO	Sampan
SBC	Serbo-Croatian
SCO	Scots
SEL	Selkup
SEM	Semitic
SER	Serbian
SHN	Shan
SHO	Shona
SID	Sidamo
SIO	Siouan Languages
SIT	Sino-Tibetan
SLA	Slavic
SLO	Slovak
SLV	Slovenian
SMO	Samoan
SND	Sindhi
SNH	Singhalese
SOG	Sogdian
SOM	Somali
SON	Songhai
ESP	Esperanto
EST	Estonian
ETH	Ethiopic
EWE	Ewe
FAN	Fang
FAR	Faroese
FEM	French, Middle
FIJ	Fijian
FIN	Finnish
FIU	Finno-Ugrian
FLE	Flemish
FON	Fon
FRE	French
FRI	Frisian
FRO	French, Old
GAA	Ga
GAE	Gaelic
GAG	Gallegan
GAL	Galla
GEC	Greek, Classical
GEH	German, Middle h
GEM	Germanic
GEO	Georgian
GER	German
GLG	Galician
GOH	German, Old High
GON	Gondi
GOT	Gothic
GRE	Greek
GUA	Guarani
GUJ	Gujarati
HAU	Hausa
HAW	Hawaiian
HEB	Hebrew
HER	Herero
HIL	Hiligaynon
HIN	Hindi
HUN	Hungarian
HUP	Hupa
IBA	Iban
IBO	Igbo
ICE	Icelandic
IKU	Inuktitut
ILO	Ilocano
INC	Indic
IND	Indonesian
INE	Indo-European
INT	Interlingua
IRA	Iranian
IRI	Irish
IRO	Iroquois
ITA	Italian
JAV	Javanese
JPN	Japanese
KAA	Karakalpak
KAC	Kachin
KAM	Kamba
KAN	Kannada
KAR	Karen
KAS	Kashmiri
KAU	Kanuri
KAZ	Kazakh
KHA	Khasi
KHM	Khmer, Central
KIK	Kikuyu
KIN	Kinyarwanda
KIR	Kirghiz
KOK	Konkani
KON	Kongo
KOR	Korean
KPE	Kpelle
KRO	Kru
KRU	Kurukh
SOT	Sotho, Southern
SPA	Spanish
SRD	Sardinian
SRR	Serer
SSA	Sub-Saharan
SUK	Sukuma
SUN	Sundanese
SUS	Susu
SUX	Sumerian
SWA	Swahili
SWE	Swedish
SYR	Syriac
TAG	Tagalog
TAJ	Tajik
TAM	Tamil
TAR	Tatar
TEL	Telugu
TEM	Temne
TER	Tereno
THA	Thai
TIB	Tibetan
TIG	Tigre
TIR	Tigrinya
TOG	Tonga, Nyasa

LANGUAGE CODES

Code	Language
TON	Tonga, Tonga
TSI	Tsimshian
TSO	Tsonga
TSW	Tswana
KUA	Kwanyama
KUR	Kurdish
LAD	Ladino
LAH	Lahnda
LAM	Lamba
LAO	Laotian
LAP	Lapp
LAT	Latin
LAV	Latvian
LIN	Lingala
LIT	Lithuanian
LOL	Lolo
LUB	Luba
LUG	Luganda
LUI	Luiseno
MAC	Macedonian
MAI	Maithili
MAL	Malayalam
MAN	Mandingo
MAO	Maori
MAP	Malayo-Polynesian
MAR	Marathi
MAS	Masai
MAY	Malay
MEN	Mende
MIC	Micmac
MIS	Miscellaneous
MLA	Malagasy
MLT	Malteses
MNO	Manobo
MOL	Moldavian
MON	Mongol
MOS	Mossi
MUL	Multiple Languages
MUS	Muskogee
MYN	Mayan
NAI	North American
NAV	Navaho
NBL	Ndebele, Southern
NDE	Ndebele, Northern
NEP	Nepali
NEW	Newari
NIC	Niger-Congo
NNO	Norwegian
NOB	Norwegian Bokmal
NOR	Norwegian
NSO	Sotho, Northern
NUB	Nubian
NYA	Nyanja
NYM	Nyamwezi
NYO	Nyoro Group
OES	Ossetic
OJI	Ojibwa
ORI	Oriya
OSA	Osage
OTO	Otomi
PAA	Papuan-Australian
PAH	Pahari
PAL	Pahlavi
PAN	Panjabi
PEO	Persian, Old
PER	Persian, Modern
PLI	Pali
POL	Polish
POR	Portuguese
PRA	Prakrit
PRO	Provencal
PUS	Pushto
QUE	Quechua
RAJ	Rajasthani
ROA	Romance
ROH	Romanish
ROM	Romany
TUK	Turkmen
TUR	Turkish
TUT	Turko-Tataric
TWI	Twi
UGA	Ugaritic
UIG	Uigur
UKR	Ukrainian
UMB	Umbundu
UND	Undetermined
URD	Urdu
UZB	Uzbek
VIE	Vietnamese
VOT	Votic
WAL	Walamo
WAS	Washo
WEL	Welsh
WEN	Wendic
WOL	Wolof
XHO	Xhosa
YAO	Yao
YID	Yiddish
YOR	Yoruba
ZAP	Zapotec
ZEN	Zenaga
ZUL	Zulu
ZUN	Zuni

LIST OF ABBREVIATIONS

Abr.	abridged
act. bk.	activity book
adapt.	adapted
aft.	afterword
alt.	alternate
Amer.	American
anniv.	anniversary
anno.	annotated by
annot.	annotation(s)
ans.	answer(s)
app.	appendix
Apple II	Apple II disk
approx.	approximately
assn.	association
audio	analog audio cassette
auth.	author
bd.	bound
bdg.	binding
bds.	boards
bibl(s).	bibliography(ies)
bk(s).	book(s)
bklet(s).	booklet(s)
boxed	boxed set, slipcase or caseboard
Bro.	Brother
C	college audience level
co.	company
comm.	commission, committee
comment.	commentaries
comp.	complied
cond.	condensed
contrib.	contributed
corp.	corporation
dept.	department
des	designed
diag(s).	diagram(s)
digital audio	digital audio cassette
dir.	director
disk	software disk or diskette
dist.	distributed
Div.	Division
doz.	dozen
ea.	each
ed.	edited, edition, editor
eds.	editions, editors
educ.	education
elem.	elementary
ency.	encyclopedia
ENG	English
enl.	enlarged
epil.	epilogue
exp.	expanded
expr.	experiments
expurg.	expurgated
fac.	facsimile
fasc.	fascicule
fict.	fiction
fig(s).	figure(s)
flmstrp.	filmstrip
footn.	
for.	foreign
frwd.	foreword
gen.	general
gr.	grade(s)
hndbk.	handbook
illus.	Illustrated, illustration(s), Illustrator(s)
in prep.	in preparation
incl.	includes, including
info.	information
inst.	institute
intro.	introduction
ISBN	International Standard Book Number
ISO	International Standards Organization
ITA	Italian
i.t.a.	initial teaching alphabet
J.	juvenile audience level
JPN	Japanese
Jr.	Junior
jt. auth.	joint author
jt. ed.	joint editor
k	kindergarten audience level
lab	laboratory
lang(s).	language(s)
LC	Library of Congress
lea.	leather
lib.	library
lib. bdg.	library binding
lit.	literature, literary
lp	record, album, long playing
l.t.	large type
ltd.	limited
ltd. ed.	limited edition
mac hd	144M, Mac
mac ld	800K, Mac
mass mkt.	mass market paperbound
math.	mathematics
mic. film	microfilm
mic form	microform
mod.	modern
MS(S)	manuscript(s)
natl.	national
net	net price
no(s).	number(s)
o.p.	out of print
orig.	original text, not a reprint (paperback)
o.s.i.	out of stock indefinitely
p.	pages
pap.	paper
per.	perfect binding
photos	photographer, photographs
pop. ed.	Popular edition
prep.	preparation
probs.	problems
prog. bk.	programmed books
ps.	preschool audience level
pseud.	pseudonym
pt(s).	part(s)
pub.	published, publisher publishing
pubn.	publication
ref(s).	reference(s)
rep.	reprint
reprod(s).	reproduction(s)
ret.	retold by
rev.	revised
rpm.	revolution per minute (phono records)
SAN	Standard Address Number
S&L	signed and limited
sec.	section
sel.	selected
ser.	series
Soc.	society
sols.	solutions
s.p.	school price
Sr. (after given name)	Senior
Sr. (before given name	Sister
St.	Saint
stu.	student manual, study guide, etc.
subs.	subsidiary
subsc.	subscription
suppl.	supplement
tech.	technical
text ed.	text edition
tr.	translated, translation translator
trans.	transparencies
unabr.	unabridged
unexpurg.	unexpurgated
univ.	university
var.	variorum
vdisk	videodisk
VHS	video, VHS format
vol(s).	volume(s)
wkbk.	workbook
YA	Young adult audience level
yrbk.	yearbook
3.5 hd	1.44M, 3.5 disk, DOS
3.5 ld	720, 3.5 Disk, DOS
5.25 hd	1.2M, 5.25 Disk, DOS
5.25 ld	360K, 5.25 Disk, DOS

SUBJECT INDEX

Volume 2

J – Z

J

JACKSON, ANDREW, 1767-1845

Behrman, Carol H. Andrew Jackson. 2004. (History Maker Biographies Ser.). (ENG., Illus.). 48p. (gr. 3-6). 27.93 *(978-0-8225-1543-2(1))* Lerner Publishing Group.

Byers, Ann. The Trail of Tears: A Primary Source History of the Forced Relocation of the Cherokee Nation. (Primary Sources in American History Ser.). 64p. (gr. 5-8). 2009. 58.50 *(978-1-60851-504-2(4))* 2004. (ENG., Illus.). (J). lib. bdg. 37.13 *(978-0-8239-4007-3(1),* b562ef02-5b3f-4dbd-9ef9-c57bb0cb3bce, Rosen Reference) Rosen Publishing Group, Inc., The.

Frost, J. Old Hickory. reprint ed. 150.00 *(978-0-7222-8720-0(8))* Library Reprints, Inc.

Gregory, Josh. Andrew Jackson: The 7th President. 2015. (First Look at America's Presidents Ser.). (ENG.). 24p. (J). (gr. -1-3). lib. bdg. 26.99 *(978-1-62724-556-2(1))* Bearport Publishing Co., Inc.

Gunderson, Megan M. Andrew Jackson, 1 vol. 2016. (United States Presidents *2017 Ser.). (ENG., Illus.). 40p. (J). (gr. 2-5). 35.64 *(978-1-68078-101-4(4),* 21819, Big Buddy Bks.) ABDO Publishing Co.

Harmon, Daniel E. Andrew Jackson. 2004. (Childhoods of the Presidents Ser.). (Illus.). 48p. (J). (gr. 4-18). lib. bdg. 17.95 *(978-1-59084-274-4(X))* Mason Crest.

Hollar, Sherman, contrib. by. Andrew Jackson, 1 vol. 2012. (Pivotal Presidents: Profiles in Leadership Ser.). (ENG., Illus.). 80p. (gr. 8-8). (J). lib. bdg. 36.47 *(978-1-61530-941-2(1),* 737af3a6-c513-49f6-acf9-24697e25672b); (YA). 72.94 *(978-1-61530-954-2(3),* 02050021-ca99-4165-b09b-f75bed6bd80e) Rosen Publishing Group, Inc., The.

Hunsicker, Jennifer. Young Andrew Jackson in the Carolinas: A Revolutionary Boy. 2014. Orig. Title: Young Andrew Jackson in the Carolinas: a Revolutionary Boy. (ENG., Illus.). 160p. (gr. 4-7). pap. 14.99 *(978-1-62619-359-8(2),* History Pr., The) Arcadia Publishing.

Kanefield, Teri. Andrew Jackson: The Making of America #2. 2019. (ENG., Illus.). 256p. (J). (gr. 5-9). pap. 7.99 *(978-1-4197-3421-2(0),* 1197903, Abrams Bks. for Young Readers) Abrams, Inc.

Marsh, Carole. Andrew Jackson. 2003. 12p. (gr. k-4). 2.95 *(978-0-635-02360-5(1))* Gallopade International.

Marsico, Katie. Andrew Jackson, 1 vol. 2011. (Presidents & Their Times Ser.). (ENG.). 96p. (gr. 6-6). 36.93 *(978-0-7614-4813-6(6),* fd698aa9-6430-4c86-ad70-db96aebfbad4) Cavendish Square Publishing LLC.

Mis, Melody S. How to Draw the Life & Times of Andrew Jackson. (Kid's Guide to Drawing the Presidents of the United States of America Ser.). 32p. (gr. 4-4). 2009. 50.50 *(978-1-61511-131-2(X),* PowerKids Pr.) 2005. (ENG.). (YA). 30.27 *(978-1-4042-2984-6(1),* 9f2575b6-163f-468c-b48f-ad0b5dd3d467) Rosen Publishing Group, Inc., The.

Rajczak, Michael. Before Andrew Jackson Was President, 1 vol. 2017. (Before They Were President Ser.). (ENG.). 24p. (J). (gr. 2-3). pap. 9.15 *(978-1-5382-1060-4(6),* b174df3e-496d-4bd7-8722-4404184e127b) Stevens, Gareth Publishing LLLP.

Rausch, Monica. Andrew Jackson, 1 vol. 2007. (Grandes Personajes (Great Americans) Ser.). 24p. (gr. 2-4). (SPA.). pap. 9.15 *(978-0-8368-7989-6(9),* 17f7e0be-a6fd-4de2-9b75-31ac3cf2329f, Weekly Reader Leveled Readers); (ENG., Illus.). pap. 9.15 *(978-0-8368-7690-1(3),* 510d4909-8d8c-45d2-9052-f8bee0eadc45, Weekly Reader Leveled Readers); (ENG., Illus.). lib. bdg. 24.67 *(978-0-8368-7683-3(0),* 254c7830-155a-43c0-bdc8-699aafed0d92, Weekly Reader Leveled Readers); (SPA., Illus.). lib. bdg. 24.67 *(978-0-8368-7982-7(1),* 3ffc0869-c621-4fff-a0e9-6226247195e8) Stevens, Gareth Publishing LLLP.

Robinson, Peg. Andrew Jackson: Populist President, 1 vol. 2018. (Hero or Villain? Claims & Counterclaims Ser.). (ENG.). 112p. (YA). (gr. 8-8). 45.93 *(978-1-5026-3526-6(7),* b86265d9-7922-4379-8388-727033706c5d) Cavendish Square Publishing LLC.

Stanley, George E. Andrew Jackson: Young Patriot. Henderson, Meryl, illus. 2003. (Childhood of Famous Americans Ser.). (ENG.). 192p. (J). (gr. 3-7). pap. 9.99 *(978-0-689-85744-7(6),* Simon & Schuster/Paula Wiseman Bks.) Simon & Schuster/Paula Wiseman Bks.

Venezia, Mike. Andrew Jackson. Venezia, Mike, illus. 2005. (Getting to Know the U. S. Presidents Ser.). (ENG., Illus.). 32p. (J). (gr. 3-4). 28.00 *(978-0-516-22612-5(6),* Children's Pr.) Scholastic Library Publishing.

Whitelaw, Nancy. Andrew Jackson: Frontier President. 2004. (Notable Americans Ser.). (Illus.). 128p. (J). (gr. 6-12). 23.95 *(978-1-883846-67-1(6),* First Biographies) Reynolds, Morgan Inc.

Wilson, Steve. Andrew Jackson's Presidency: Democracy in Action, 1 vol. 2016. (Spotlight on American History Ser.). (ENG., Illus.). 24p. (J). (gr. 4-6). 27.93 *(978-1-5081-4938-5(0),* 6649632c-035b-4121-ad0c-f1d92c5f188f, PowerKids Pr.) Rosen Publishing Group, Inc., The.

Yomtov, Nel. Andrew Jackson: Heroic Leader or Cold-Hearted Ruler?, 1 vol. 2013. (Perspectives on History Ser.). (ENG., Illus.). 32p. (J). (gr. 3-6). 27.99 *(978-1-4765-0245-8(5),* 122299); pap. 7.95 *(978-1-4765-3409-1(8),* 123540) Capstone.

Zuchora-Walske, Christine. Andrew Jackson's Presidency. 2016. (Presidential Powerhouses Ser.). (ENG., Illus.). 104p. (YA). (gr. 6-12). 35.99 *(978-1-4677-7926-5(1),* 78407cea-eed3-4c5d-9bd1-0b769822ca4e); E-Book 54.65 *(978-1-4677-8548-8(2))* Lerner Publishing Group. (Lerner Pubns.).

JACKSON, JESSE, 1941-

Jacoby, Randolph. Jesse Jackson, Vol. 9. 2018. (Civil Rights Leaders Ser.). 144p. (J). (gr. 7). lib. bdg. 35.93 *(978-1-4222-4006-9(1))* Mason Crest.

Linde, Barbara M. Jesse Jackson, 1 vol. 2011. (Civil Rights Crusaders Ser.). (ENG.). 24p. (gr. 2-3). (J). pap. 9.15 *(978-1-4339-5684-3(5),* d063e89c-99de-44a7-8ee7-161e687fba16, Gareth Stevens Learning Library); (YA). lib. bdg. 25.27 *(978-1-4339-5682-9(9),* a50c4d10-7920-40f4-b6e2-7549dfc3fe47) Stevens, Gareth Publishing LLLP.

Mis, Melody S. Meet Jesse Jackson. (Civil Rights Leaders Ser.). 24p. (gr. 2-3). 2009. 42.50 *(978-1-61511-852-6(7),* PowerKids Pr.) 2007. (ENG., Illus.). (YA). lib. bdg. 26.27 *(978-1-4042-4212-8(0),* 7f13a688-1352-4455-9287-50c573805ee0) Rosen Publishing Group, Inc., The.

Woog, Dan. Jesse Jackson. 2003. (People in the News Ser.). (ENG., Illus.). 118p. (YA). (gr. 6-9). 33.45 *(978-1-56006-631-6(8),* Lucent Bks.) Cengage Gale.

JACKSON, MAHALIA, 1911-1972

Nolan, Nina. Mahalia Jackson: Walking with Kings & Queens. Holyfield, John, illus. 2015. (ENG.). 32p. (J). (gr. -1-3). 17.99 *(978-0-06-087944-0(0),* HarperCollins) HarperCollins Pubs.

Pinkney, Andrea Davis. Martin & Mahalia: His Words, Her Song. 2013. (ENG., Illus.). 40p. (J). (gr. 1-17). 18.99 *(978-0-316-07013-3(0))* Little, Brown Bks. for Young Readers.

JACKSON, STONEWALL, 1824-1863

Brager, Bruce L. There He Stands: The Story of Stonewall Jackson. 2005. (Civil War Leaders Ser.). (Illus.). 176p. (J). (gr. 6-12). 26.95 *(978-1-931798-44-0(3))* Reynolds, Morgan Inc.

Hale, Sarah Elder, ed. Stonewall Jackson: Spirit of the South. 2005. (ENG., Illus.). 48p. (J). (gr. 3-9). 17.95 *(978-0-8126-7907-6(5))* Cobblestone Pr.

McLeese, Don. Stonewall Jackson. 2005. (Civil War Military Leaders Ser.). (Illus.). 32p. (J). (gr. 3-6). lib. bdg. 19.95 *(978-1-59515-477-4(9))* Rourke Educational Media.

Pflueger, Lynda. Stonewall Jackson: General of the Confederate Army. 2015. (J). *(978-0-7660-6495-9(6))* Enslow Publishing, LLC.

Power, J. Tracey. Stonewall Jackson: Hero of the Confederacy. 2009. (Library of American Lives & Times Ser.). 112p. (gr. 5-5). 69.20 *(978-1-60853-507-1(X))* Rosen Publishing Group, Inc., The.

Power, J. Tracy. Stonewall Jackson: Confederate General & American Hero, 1 vol. 2004. (Library of American Lives & Times Ser.). (ENG., Illus.). 112p. (J). (gr. 5-5). lib. bdg. 38.27 *(978-1-4042-2654-8(0),* 053a6843-f802-4993-ad6b-9bf22fdb071b) Rosen Publishing Group, Inc., The.

JACKSON, STONEWALL, 1824-1863—FICTION

Altsheler, Joseph A. The Scouts of Stonewall: The Story of the Great Valley Campaign. 2006. (Civil War Ser.: Vol. 3). 312p. (J). reprint ed. 29.95 *(978-1-4218-1779-8(9))*; pap. 14.95 *(978-1-4218-1879-5(5))* 1st World Publishing, Inc. (1st World Library - Literary Society).

—The Scouts of Stonewall: The Story of the Great Valley Campaign. l.t. ed. (Civil War Ser.: Vol. 3). (J). reprint ed. 2007. (ENG.). 240p. pap. 22.99 *(978-1-4264-1531-9(1))* 2011. 370p. (gr. 4-7). pap. 32.75 *(978-1-245-65787-7(9))* 2008. 244p. 24.99 *(978-0-554-31333-7(2))* 2008. 244p. 27.99 *(978-0-554-22030-7(X))* 2006. 250p. pap. 20.99 *(978-1-4264-1498-5(6))* Creative Media Partners, LLC.

—The Scouts of Stonewall: The Story of the Great Valley Campaign. 2006. (Civil War Ser.: Vol. 3). (J). reprint ed. pap. *(978-1-4065-0820-8(9))* Dodo Pr.

—The Scouts of Stonewall: The Story of the Great Valley Campaign. 2007. (Civil War Ser.: Vol. 3). 184p. (J). reprint ed. per. *(978-1-4068-1684-6(1))* Echo Library.

—The Scouts of Stonewall: The Story of the Great Valley Campaign. 2010. (Civil War Ser.: Vol. 3). (Illus.). 166p. (J). (gr. 4-7). reprint ed. pap. 19.99 *(978-1-153-72009-0(4))* General Bks. LLC.

—The Scouts of Stonewall: The Story of the Great Valley Campaign. reprint ed. 2010. (Civil War Ser.: Vol. 3). 252p. (J). (gr. 4-7). 33.56 *(978-1-169-30265-5(3))* 2010. (Civil War Ser.: Vol. 3). 252p. (J). (gr. 4-7). pap. 21.56 *(978-1-162-70768-6(2))* 2010. (Civil War Ser.: Vol. 3). 252p. (J). 41.95 *(978-1-161-47632-3(6))* 2004. pap. 26.95 *(978-1-4191-8162-7(9))* 2004. (Civil War Ser.: Vol. 3). (J). pap. 1.99 *(978-1-4192-8162-4(3))* Kessinger Publishing, LLC.

—The Scouts of Stonewall: The Story of the Great Valley Campaign. 2011. (Civil War Ser.: Vol. 3). 278p. (J). (gr. 4-7). reprint ed. pap. *(978-3-8424-6100-0(3))* tredition Verlag.

JACKSON, THOMAS JONATHAN, 1824-1863

see Jackson, Stonewall, 1824-1863

JACOB (BIBLICAL PATRIARCH)

Hoak, Benjamin T. Jacob. (Money at its Best: Millionaires of the Old Testament Ser.). 112p. (YA). (gr. 7-12). 2009. 24.95 *(978-1-4222-0470-2(7))* 2007. pap. 14.95 *(978-1-4222-0845-8(1))* Mason Crest.

Larsen, Carolyn. Abraham, Isaac, & Jacob. 2012. (Standard Bible Storybook Ser.). (ENG., Illus.). 32p. (J). 7.99 *(978-0-7847-3563-3(8))* Standard Publishing.

Nakhat, Shamim. The Story of Yaqub & Yusuf: Based on Qur'anic Facts. 2005. (Me & My Holy Qur'ân Ser.). (Illus.). 24p. (J). *(978-81-7231-618-1(6))* Islamic Bk. Service.

Racklin-Siegel, Alison, illus. Jacob's Travels. 2005. (ENG & HEB.). 32p. (J). per. 11.95 *(978-0-939144-53-2(0))* EKS Publishing Co.

JAGUAR

Adamson, Thomas K. Anaconda vs. Jaguar. 2020. (Animal Battles Ser.). (ENG.). 24p. (J). (gr. 3-7). lib. bdg. 26.95 *(978-1-64487-155-3(6),* Torque Bks.) Bellwether Media.

Archer, Claire. Jaguars, 1 vol. 2014. (Big Cats Ser.). (ENG.). 24p. (J). (gr. -1-2). lib. bdg. 32.79 *(978-1-62970-002-1(9),* 1225, Abdo Kids) ABDO Publishing Co.

Arnold, Quinn M. Jaguars. 2016. (Seedlings Ser.). (ENG.). 24p. (J). (gr. -1-k). pap. 7.99 *(978-1-62832-334-4(5),* 20725, Creative Paperbacks); (Illus.). *(978-1-60818-738-6(1),* 20727, Creative Education) Creative Co., The.

Bodden, Valerie. Jaguars. 2013. (Amazing Animals Ser.). (ENG., Illus.). 24p. (J). (gr. 1-4). 25.65 *(978-1-60818-086-8(7),* 21722, Creative Education) Creative Co., The.

Diemer, Lauren. Jaguars. 2014. (J). pap. *(978-1-4896-0919-9(9))* Weigl Pubs., Inc.

Franchino, Vicky. Jaguars. 2013. (ENG.). 48p. (J). 28.00 *(978-0-531-23360-3(X))*; pap. 6.95 *(978-0-531-25158-4(6))* Scholastic Library Publishing.

Gagne, Tammy. Jaguars, 1 vol. 2012. (Big Cats Ser.). (ENG.). 32p. (J). (gr. 3-9). lib. bdg. 28.65 *(978-1-4296-7642-7(6),* 117239, Capstone Pr.) Capstone.

Gates, Margo. Jaguars. 2013. (Animal Safari Ser.). (ENG., Illus.). 24p. (J). (gr. k-3). lib. bdg. 26.95 *(978-1-60014-911-5(1),* Blastoff! Readers) Bellwether Media.

Gish, Melissa. Jaguars. 2011. (Illus.). 46p. (J). 35.65 *(978-1-60818-079-0(4),* Creative Education) Creative Co., The.

Golkar, Golriz. Jaguars. 2018. (Rain Forest Animals Ser.). (ENG., Illus.). 24p. (J). (gr. 1-1). pap. 8.95 *(978-1-63517-822-7(3),* 1635178223) North Star Editions.

—Jaguars. 2018. (Rain Forest Animals (Cody Koala) Ser.). (ENG., Illus.). 24p. (J). (gr. k-3). lib. bdg. 31.36 *(978-1-5321-6027-1(5),* 28686, Pop! Cody Koala) Pop!

Grack, Rachel. Jaguars. 2019. (Animals of the Rain Forest Ser.). (ENG., Illus.). 24p. (J). (gr. k-3). lib. bdg. 26.95 *(978-1-62617-950-9(6),* Blastoff! Readers) Bellwether Media.

Guidone, Julie. Jaguars, 1 vol. 2009. (Animals That Live in the Rain Forest Ser.). (ENG.). 24p. (J). (gr. 1-1). pap. 9.15 *(978-1-4339-0105-8(6),* cdb1c9fe-1be3-496c-97b3-f8c344dab9cb); lib. bdg. 25.27 *(978-1-4339-0023-5(8),* 6cf0749e-2e93-4534-b35a-2c4f41e80065) Stevens, Gareth Publishing LLLP. (Weekly Reader Leveled Readers).

—Jaguars / Jaguares, 1 vol. 2009. (Animals That Live in the Rain Forest / Animales de la Selva Ser.). (SPA & ENG.). 24p. (gr. 1-1). pap. 9.15 *(978-1-4339-0112-6(9),* 4ef6fc98-4aa0-4612-9ed2-4f18b042fd78); lib. bdg. 25.27 *(978-1-4339-0062-4(9),* 587a9f10-b8c9-4a10-ad4f-d8bfeb66cbf6) Stevens, Gareth Publishing LLLP. (Weekly Reader Leveled Readers).

Huntrods, David. Jaguars. 2006. (Amazing Animals Ser.). (Illus.). 24p. (J). (gr. 3-7). pap. 8.95 *(978-1-59036-398-0(1))*; lib. bdg. 24.45 *(978-1-59036-392-8(2))* Weigl Pubs., Inc.

Kenan, Tessa. It's a Jaguar! 2017. (Bumba Books (r) — Rain Forest Animals Ser.). (ENG., Illus.). 24p. (J). (gr. -1-1). E-Book 39.99 *(978-1-5124-3755-3(7),* 9781512437553); E-Book 4.99 *(978-1-5124-3756-0(5),* 9781512437560); E-Book 39.99 *(978-1-5124-2760-8(8))* Lerner Publishing Group. (Lerner Pubns.).

Lawrence, Ellen. Jaguar. 2016. (Apex Predators of the Amazon Rain Forest Ser.). (ENG., Illus.). 24p. (J). (gr. -1-3). 26.99 *(978-1-68402-030-0(1))* Bearport Publishing Co., Inc.

Luna, Tom. The Spots on the Jaguar: A Counting Book. Luna, Tom & Álvarez, Laura, illus. 2005. (SPA & ENG.). 20p. (J). *(978-0-9716580-4-2(8))* Lectura Bks.

Lynette, Rachel. Jaguars. 2013. (Jungle Babies of the Amazon Rain Forest Ser.). 24p. (J). (gr. -1-3). lib. bdg. 25.65 *(978-1-61772-755-9(5))* Bearport Publishing Co., Inc.

Macleod, Steve. Jaguar. 2011. (J). *(978-1-61690-758-7(4))*; pap. *(978-1-61690-851-5(3))* Weigl Pubs., Inc.

—Soy el Jaguar. 2012. (SPA.). (J). *(978-1-61913-177-4(3))* Weigl Pubs., Inc.

Marks, Jennifer L. Jaguars, 1 vol. 2010. (Wildcats Ser.). (ENG.). 24p. (J). (gr. -1-2). lib. bdg. 27.32 *(978-1-4296-4481-5(8),* 102952, Capstone Pr.) Capstone.

Marsico, Katie. Jaguars. 2012. (21st Century Basic Skills Library: Baby Zoo Animals Ser.). (ENG.). 24p. (gr. k-3). pap. 12.79 *(978-1-61080-628-2(X),* 202238); (Illus.). 26.35 *(978-1-61080-454-7(6),* 202064) Cherry Lake Publishing.

Mezzanotte, Jim. The Story of Jaguar, 1 vol. 2004. (Classic Cars Ser.). (ENG., Illus.). 24p. (gr. 2-4). lib. bdg. 25.67 *(978-0-8368-4535-8(8),* 95f41e76-1f1e-4caf-bb38-443023d34ac2, Gareth Stevens Learning Library) Stevens, Gareth Publishing LLLP.

Miller, Reagan & Johnson, Robin. Jaguar. 2010. (ENG., Illus.). 64p. (J). lib. bdg. *(978-0-7787-2143-7(4))* Crabtree Publishing Co.

Morgan, Elizabeth. Jaguar, 1 vol., 1. 2015. (North America's Biggest Beasts Ser.). (ENG., Illus.). 24p. (J). (gr. 3-4). pap. 9.25 *(978-1-5081-4303-1(X),* 02594aff-5863-48c8-961e-3fa6f507ee61, PowerKids Pr.) Rosen Publishing Group, Inc., The.

Murray, Julie. Jaguars. 2019. (Animal Kingdom Ser.). (ENG., Illus.). 32p. (J). (gr. 2-5). lib. bdg. 34.21

(978-1-5321-1640-7(3), 32391, Big Buddy Bks.) ABDO Publishing Co.

Otfinoski, Steven. Jaguars, 1 vol. 2011. (Animals, Animals Ser.). (ENG.). 48p. (gr. 5-5). 32.64 (978-0-7614-4839-6(X), 52e0682d-548d-4b1a-81ff-1013035ab257) Cavendish Square Publishing LLC.

Pallotta, Jerry. Jaguar vs. Skunk. Bolster, Rob, illus. 2017. 32p. (J). (978-1-338-20629-6(X)) Scholastic, Inc.

Ringstad, Arnold. Jaguars. 2014. (Wild Cats Ser.). (ENG., Illus.). 24p. (J). (gr. 1-4). 27.10 (978-1-60753-601-7(3), 16064) Amicus.

Ryndak, Rob. Leopard or Jaguar?, 1 vol. 2015. (Animal Look-Alikes Ser.). (ENG., Illus.). 24p. (J). (gr. 1-2). pap. 9.15 (978-1-4824-2720-2(6), 3c4a7be3-29bd-4c5c-ae24-8282504aba90) Stevens, Gareth Publishing LLLP.

Schuh, Mari. Jaguars. 2014. (Illus.). 24p. (J). lib. bdg. 25.65 (978-1-62031-111-0(9), Bullfrog Bks.) Jump! Inc.

Stacy, Lee. Jaguar. 2004. (Hot Cars Ser.). (Illus.). 32p. (gr. 4-8). lib. bdg. (978-1-59515-211-4(3)) Rourke Educational Media.

Statts, Leo. Jaguars. 2016. (Rain Forest Animals Ser.). (ENG.). 24p. (J). (gr. -1-2). 49.94 (978-1-68079-362-8(4), 22983, Abdo Zoom-Launch) ABDO Publishing Co.

Vail, Grace. Jaguars, 1 vol. 2012. (Killer Cats Ser.). (ENG., Illus.). 24p. (J). (gr. 2-3). pap. 9.15 (978-1-4339-7004-7(X), e127c0f6-5fa8-44b4-96cf-1097b2e76dc4); lib. bdg. 25.27 (978-1-4339-7003-0(1), d1f20d7b-9b31-4745-b091-d9ff028eac7b) Stevens, Gareth Publishing LLLP.

Vink, Amanda. Jaguars, 1 vol. 2019. (Killers of the Animal Kingdom Ser.). (ENG.). 24p. (gr. 3-3). pap. 9.25 (978-1-7253-0609-7(3), 103355e6-74d9-4b41-803f-34904cee8b58, PowerKids Pr.) Rosen Publishing Group, Inc., The.

Vogel, Elizabeth. Jaguars. 2009. (Big Cats (Powerkids Readers) Ser.). 24p. (gr. 1-1). 37.50 (978-1-61511-568-6(4), PowerKids Pr.) Rosen Publishing Group, Inc., The.

Von Zumbusch, Amelie. Jaguars: World's Strongest Cats, 1 vol. 2007. (Dangerous Cats Ser.). (ENG., Illus.). 24p. (J). (gr. 2-3). lib. bdg. 26.27 (978-1-4042-3628-8(7), 7288273e-b016-433c-8e24-34990245e560, PowerKids Pr.) Rosen Publishing Group, Inc., The.

von Zumbusch, Amelie. Jaguars: World's Strongest Cats. 2009. (Dangerous Cats Ser.). 24p. (gr. 2-3). 42.50 (978-1-61512-127-4(7), PowerKids Pr.) Rosen Publishing Group, Inc., The.

Walker, Sally M. Jaguars. 2008. (Nature Watch Ser.). (ENG.). 48p. (gr. 4-8). 27.93 (978-0-8225-7510-8(8), Lerner Pubns.) Lerner Publishing Group.

Williams, Zella. Jaguars & Other Latin American Wild Cats: and Other Latin American Wild Cats, 1 vol. 2009. (Animals of Latin America / Animales de Latinoamérica Ser.). (SPA & ENG., Illus.). 24p. (gr. 2-2). pap. 8.25 (978-1-4358-3378-4(3), 837ab270-6773-4ada-82a7-de6e38ff5d5f, PowerKids Pr.) Rosen Publishing Group, Inc., The.

—Jaguars & Other Latin American Wild Cats: Jaguares y Otros Felinos de Latino América, 1 vol. 2009. (Animals of Latin America / Animales de Latinoamérica Ser.). (SPA & ENG., Illus.). 24p. (J). (gr. 2-2). lib. bdg. 26.27 (978-1-4042-8125-7(8), 03d4beb8-9faf-4bf0-a65a-86c792bdf824, PowerKids Pr.) Rosen Publishing Group, Inc., The.

Woods, Theresa. Jaguars. 2015. (Animals of the Rain Forest Ser.). (ENG.). 24p. (J). (gr. 2-5). 32.79 (978-1-63143-748-9(8), 208577) Child's World, Inc, The.

JAGUAR—FICTION

Cowcher, Helen. Jaguar. (CHI, ENG, URD, TUR & VIE., Illus.). 40p. 16.95 (978-1-84059-009-8(2)) Milet Publishing.

—Jaguar. (J). (gr. 1-2). (978-0-590-36037-1(X)); (SPA., Illus.). pap. 3.96 net. (978-0-590-87599-8(X), SO30738, Scholastic Pr.) Scholastic, Inc.

Driscoll, Laura. Where Is Baby Jaguar? Mangano, Tom & Miller, Victoria, illus. 2011. (Dora & Diego Ser.). (ENG.). 24p. (J). pap. 3.99 (978-1-4424-1398-6(0), Simon Spotlight/Nickelodeon) Simon Spotlight/Nickelodeon.

Eggers, Dave. We Became Jaguars. White, Woodrow, illus. 2021. (ENG.). 44p. (J). (gr. k-3). 18.99 (978-1-4521-8393-0(7)) Chronicle Bks. LLC.

Flor Ada, Alma. Eyes of the Jaguar. Davalos, Felipe, illus. 2004. (Puertas Al Sol / Gateways to the Sun Ser.). 48p. (gr. k-6). pap. 17.95 (978-1-58105-970-0(1)) Santillana USA Publishing Co., Inc.

Gosse, Jim. Jimmy Jaguar: Collection of Stories. 2006. 17.00 (978-0-8059-9373-8(8)) Dorrance Publishing Co., Inc.

Nickelodeon Staff & Nickelodeon / LeapFrog. Go Diego Go! Underwater Mystery. 2008. (J). 13.99 (978-1-59319-925-8(2)) LeapFrog Enterprises, Inc.

Sargent, Pat L. The Jaguar, 8 vols. Lenoir, Jane, illus. 2007. (Barney the Bear Killer Ser.: 8). 164p. (YA). lib. bdg. 26.25 (978-1-59381-424-3(0)) Ozark Publishing.

JAILS

see Prisons

JAM

Heos, Bridget. From Grapes to Jelly. Coleman, Stephanie Fizer, illus. 2018. (Who Made My Lunch? Ser.). (ENG.). 24p. (J). (gr. k-3). pap. 10.99 (978-1-68152-147-3(4), 14769) Amicus.

Spilsbury, Louise. Collins Big Cat Phonics for Letters & Sounds - Blackcurrant Jam: Band 05/Green, Bd. 5. 2018. (Collins Big Cat Ser.). (ENG., Illus.). 24p. (J). pap. 7.99 (978-0-00-823029-6(3)) HarperCollins Pubs. Ltd. GBR. Dist: Independent Pubs. Group.

Zemlicka, Shannon. From Fruit to Jelly. 2004. (Start to Finish Ser.). (J). pap. 5.95 (978-0-8225-0748-2(X)); (Illus.). 24p. 18.60 (978-0-8225-0942-4(3), Lerner Pubns.) Lerner Publishing Group.

JAMAICA

Barraclough, John. Jamaica. (World Focus Ser.). (Illus.). 31p. (J). (gr. 3-7). pap. 3.99 (978-0-431-07266-1(3)) Oxfam Publishing GBR. Dist: Stylus Publishing, LLC.

Bastrya, Judy. Living in Jamaica. 2006. (Living In- Ser.). (Illus.). 32p. (J). (gr. 4-7). lib. bdg. 27.10 (978-1-59771-047-3(4)) Sea-To-Sea Pubns.

Colleen Madonna Flood Williams. Jamaica, Vol. 11. Henderson, James D., ed. 2015. (Discovering the Caribbean: History, Politics, & Culture Ser.). (Illus.). 64p. (J). (gr. 7). lib. bdg. 22.95 (978-1-4222-3313-9(8)) Mason Crest.

Crespi, Jess. Exploring Jamaica with the Five Themes of Geography. (Library of the Western Hemisphere Ser.). 24p. 2009. (gr. 4-4). 42.50 (978-1-60853-927-7(X), PowerKids Pr.) 2004. (ENG., Illus.). (J). (gr. 3-4). lib. bdg. 26.27 (978-1-4042-2674-6(5), 75577d03-0547-4896-976b-32b1b86a7c76, PowerKids Pr.) 2004. (ENG., Illus.). (gr. 3-4). pap. 8.25 (978-0-8239-4634-1(7), d7c9c361-0df0-4dd1-b279-b59ed33cbb22) Rosen Publishing Group, Inc., The.

Hamilton, Janice. Jamaica in Pictures. 2005. (Visual Geography Series, Second Ser.). (ENG., Illus.). 80p. (gr. 5-12). 31.93 (978-0-8225-2394-9(9)) Lerner Publishing Group.

Harris, Devon & Cortés, Ricardo. Yes, I Can! The Story of the Jamaican Bobsled Team. 2008. (Illus.). (978-0-9764082-5-3(2)) Waterhouse Publishing.

Heinrichs, Ann. True Books: Jamaica. 2003. (True Bks.). (ENG., Illus.). 48p. (J). (gr. 3-5). pap. 6.95 (978-0-516-27751-6(0), Children's Pr.) Scholastic Library Publishing.

Irving, Barrington & Peppe, Holly. Touch the Sky. 2012. (J). (978-0-531-22525-7(9)) Scholastic, Inc.

Klepeis, Alicia Z. Jamaica, 1 vol. 2018. (Exploring World Cultures (First Edition) Ser.). (ENG.). 32p. (gr. 3-3). 31.64 (978-1-5026-3805-2(3), 2aefb1d9-711f-44c7-b9ef-b6987225da67) Cavendish Square Publishing LLC.

Kwek, Karen. Welcome to Jamaica, 1 vol. 2004. (Welcome to My Country Ser.). (ENG.). 48p. (gr. 2-4). lib. bdg. 29.67 (978-0-8368-2564-0(0), d32d5de8-d2b0-49a8-a0af-9e1e498b49e8) Stevens, Gareth Publishing LLLP.

Miller, Calvin Craig. Reggae Poet: The Story of Bob Marley. 2007. (Modern Music Masters Ser.). (Illus.). 128p. (YA). (gr. 9-18). lib. bdg. 27.95 (978-1-59935-071-4(8)) Reynolds, Morgan Inc.

Morris, Kerry-Ann. Jamaica, 1 vol. 2003. (Countries of the World Ser.). (ENG., Illus.). 96p. (gr. 6-8). lib. bdg. 33.67 (978-0-8368-2364-6(8), 7237d154-89d0-4c12-9226-3a60680e1586) Stevens, Gareth Publishing LLLP.

Murray, John. Bolt - The Fastest Man on Earth. 2018. (Ultimate Sports Heroes Ser.). (ENG.). 176p. (J). (gr. 4-8). pap. 10.99 (978-1-78606-467-7(7)) Blake, John Publishing, Ltd. GBR. Dist: Independent Pubs. Group.

Owings, Lisa. Jamaica. 2014. (Exploring Countries Ser.). (ENG., Illus.). 32p. (J). (gr. 3-7). lib. bdg. 27.95 (978-1-62617-067-4(3), Blastoff! Readers) Bellwether Media.

Peppas, Lynn. Cultural Traditions in Jamaica. 2015. (Cultural Traditions in My World Ser.). (ENG., Illus.). 32p. (J). (gr. 2-3). (978-0-7787-8062-5(7)) Crabtree Publishing Co.

Rozines Roy, Jennifer & Roy, Gregory. Jamaica, 1 vol. 2006. (Discovering Cultures Ser.). (ENG., Illus.). 48p. (gr. 3-4). 31.21 (978-0-7614-1793-4(1), b7ba0451-e0f1-4aa0-b048-132724b21dec) Cavendish Square Publishing LLC.

Rudolph, Jessica. Jamaica. 2016. (Countries We Come From Ser.). (ENG., Illus.). 32p. (J). (gr. -1-3). 28.50 (978-1-944102-72-2(8)) Bearport Publishing Co., Inc.

Savage, Jeff. Usain Bolt. 2012. (Amazing Athletes Ser.). (ENG., Illus.). 32p. (J). (gr. 2-5). lib. bdg. 26.65 (978-1-4677-1088-6(1), e49a26e2-feb8-4dac-ab1a-01a5b8bfb4d7, Lerner Pubns.) Lerner Publishing Group.

Sheehan, Sean & Black, Angela. Jamaica, 1 vol. 2nd rev. ed. 2006. (Cultures of the World (Second Edition)(r) Ser.). (ENG., Illus.). 144p. (gr. 5-5). 49.79 (978-0-7614-1785-9(0), b4ad8a83-e8d4-4e89-96db-54c18567460d) Cavendish Square Publishing LLC.

Sheehan, Sean, et al. Jamaica, 1 vol. 3rd rev. ed. 2014. (Cultures of the World (Third Edition)(r) Ser.). (ENG., Illus.). 144p. (gr. 5-5). lib. bdg. 48.79 (978-1-5026-0077-6(3), 925d884d-4455-4707-8f47-4f73746096d5) Cavendish Square Publishing LLC.

Sullivan, Laura L. Sir Henry Morgan. 2015. (J). lib. bdg. (978-1-62713-308-1(9)) Cavendish Square Publishing LLC.

Thomas, Naam. Collins Social Studies Atlas Skills for Jamaica Primary Workbook. 2018. (ENG.). 128p. (gr. 4-6). pap. 11.99 (978-0-00-830024-1(0)) HarperCollins Pubs. Ltd. GBR. Dist: Independent Pubs. Group.

Williams, Colleen Madonna Flood. Jamaica. (Caribbean Today Ser.). 64p. (YA). 2010. (Illus.). (gr. 9-12). 21.95 (978-1-4222-0626-3(2)) 2006. (gr. 7-18). pap. 9.95 (978-1-4222-0693-5(9)) Mason Crest.

JAMAICA—FICTION

Angelou, Maya. Cedric of Jamaica. Rockwell, Lizzy, illus. 2005. (Random House Pictureback Book Ser.). (J). (978-0-375-83269-7(6)) Random Hse., Inc.

Berry, James. A Story about Afiya, 1 vol. Cunha, Anna, illus. 2020. (ENG.). 32p. (J). (gr. k-2). 17.99 (978-1-911373-33-9(1), 4323210b-63fd-4a2c-bb37-155b56eb9f96) Lantana Publishing GBR. Dist: Lerner Publishing Group.

Burford, Lorrimer. A Jamaican Storyteller's Tale. 2005. (ENG., Illus.). 197p. pap. 7.99 (978-976-8184-84-9(1)) Penguin Publishing Group.

Curtatone, Raffaello. The Adventures of Mr Greenwood from Jamaic. 2011. 50p. (J). pap. 9.99 (978-0-557-91852-2(9)) Lulu Pr., Inc.

Eights, Melissa Irene. Jamaican Farm Life. 2009. (ENG.). 24p. pap. 15.99 (978-1-4415-2533-8(5)) Xlibris Corp.

Grant Sr, Hector J. Sybil: The Trials & Triumphs of a Jamaican Girl. 2008. 208p. per. 15.95 (978-1-4327-1889-3(4)) Outskirts Pr., Inc.

Hall, Rose. After the Storm. Jazvic, Beryl, illus. 2005. (J). bds. 19.95 (978-0-9770503-0-7(0)) Institute For Behavior Change Incorporated The.

Harris, Angela Brent -. Sweet Jamaican Summertime at Grandma's. 2011. 28p. pap. 21.99 (978-1-4628-7271-8(9)) Xlibris Corp.

Isbell, Tessa J. Animal Adventures: Goosey & Beauty Take a Mystery Magic Carpet Ride to Jamaica. 2013. 48p. pap. 21.99 (978-1-4669-7217-9(3)) Trafford Publishing.

King, A. S. The Dust of 100 Dogs. 2017. 336p. (YA). (gr. 9). pap. 10.99 (978-0-425-29057-6(3), Speak) Penguin Young Readers Group.

Magnus, Kellie. Little Lion Goes to School. Robinson, Michael, illus. l.t. ed. 2003. 16p. (J). 9.99 (978-0-9744211-0-0(3)) Media Magic New York.

McCaulay, Diana. Gone to Drift. 2018. (ENG.). 272p. (J). (gr. 3-7). 16.99 (978-0-06-267296-4(7), HarperCollins) HarperCollins Pubs.

McKnight, Penny. Nix. 2006. (Illus.). 84p. (J). (gr. 3-7). per. 8.99 (978-1-59166-610-3(4)) BJU Pr.

Montague, Chester. Timmy's Vacation. 2008. 40p. pap. 24.95 (978-1-60441-225-3(9)) America Star Bks.

Oldfield, Matt & Oldfield, Tom. Sterling. 2018. (Ultimate Football Heroes Ser.). (ENG.). 176p. (J). (gr. 2-7). pap. 9.99 (978-1-78606-811-8(7)) Blake, John Publishing, Ltd. GBR. Dist: Independent Pubs. Group.

Peacock, Shane. Double You, 1 vol. 2014. (Seven Sequels Ser.: 3). (ENG., Illus.). 272p. (J). (gr. 4-7). pap. 10.95 (978-1-4598-0534-7(8)) Orca Bk. Pubs. USA.

Richmond, Beulah. Anancy & Friends: A Grandmother's Anancy Stories for Her Grandchildren. Brown, Clovis, illus. 2004. (ENG.). 52p. pap. 5.99 (978-976-8184-48-1(5)) Penguin Publishing Group.

Salkey, Andrew. Drought, 1 vol. 2011. (Caribbean Modern Classics Ser.). (ENG., Illus.). 128p. (J). (gr. 7). pap. 13.95 (978-1-84523-183-5(X)) Peepal Tree Pr., Ltd. GBR. Dist: Independent Pubs. Group.

—Earthquake, 1 vol. 2011. (Caribbean Modern Classics Ser.). (ENG., Illus.). 108p. (J). (gr. 7). pap. 13.95 (978-1-84523-182-8(1)) Peepal Tree Pr., Ltd. GBR. Dist: Independent Pubs. Group.

—Hurricane, 1 vol. 2011. (Caribbean Modern Classics Ser.). (ENG., Illus.). 104p. (J). (gr. 7-7). pap. 13.95 (978-1-84523-180-4(5)) Peepal Tree Pr., Ltd. GBR. Dist: Independent Pubs. Group.

—Riot, 1 vol. 2011. (Caribbean Modern Classics Ser.). (ENG., Illus.). 176p. (J). (gr. 7). pap. 14.95 (978-1-84523-181-1(3)) Peepal Tree Pr., Ltd. GBR. Dist: Independent Pubs. Group.

Smith, Vicki. Jamaican Adventure with Tori & Paul. 2012. (ENG., Illus.). 24p. (J). pap. 13.95 (978-1-4327-8578-9(8)) Outskirts Pr., Inc.

Walker, Charmaine. Jon & Alex: Goes to School. 2012. 34p. pap. (978-1-105-62383-7(1)) Lulu.com.

Weathers, Marlon. Henry Baldpate & His Treetop Friends. 2008. 24p. pap. 24.95 (978-1-60672-923-6(3)) America Star Bks.

Wilson, Heather Gemmen. Lydia Barnes & the Escape from Shark Bay. 2008. 160p. (J). 9.99 (978-0-89827-352-6(8)) Wesleyan Publishing Hse.

Wohlt, Julia. Naughty Eddie Larue. Brown, Clovis, illus. 27p. (978-976-610-173-2(6)) Creative Links.

JAMAICA—HISTORY—FICTION

Rees, Celia. Pirates! The True & Remarkable Adventures of Minerva Sharpe & Nancy Kington, Female Pirates. 2005. (Illus.). 379p. (YA). (gr. 9-12). 16.60 (978-0-7569-6304-0(4)) Perfection Learning Corp.

JAMAICAN AMERICANS

Caravantes, Peggy. Marcus Garvey: Black Nationalist. 2004. (Twentieth Century Leaders Ser.). (Illus.). 128p. (YA). (gr. 6-12). 23.95 (978-1-931798-14-3(1)) Reynolds, Morgan Inc.

Kallen, Stuart A. Marcus Garvey & the Back to Africa Movement, 1 vol. 2006. (Lucent Library of Black History Ser.). (ENG., Illus.). 112p. (gr. 7-7). lib. bdg. 41.03 (978-1-59018-838-5(1), fa971f56-845c-43da-881a-1a10b033a0da, Lucent Pr.) Greenhaven Publishing LLC.

Mohamed, Paloma. A Man Called Garvey: The Life & Times of the Great Leader Marcus Garvey. Braithwaithe, Barrington, illus. l.t. ed. 2004. (Majority Press Inc., Wisdom for Children Ser.: No. 1). (ENG.). 36p. (J). 12.95 (978-0-912469-40-9(4)) Majority Pr., The.

JAMAICAN AMERICANS—FICTION

Gunning, Monica. A Shelter in Our Car, 1 vol. 2014. (ENG., Illus.). 32p. (J). (gr. k-2). pap. 11.95 (978-0-89239-308-4(4), leelowcbp, Children's Book Press) Lee & Low Bks., Inc.

Never So Good (Jamaicans) 76p. (YA). (gr. 6-12). pap. 9.95 (978-0-8224-3806-9(2)) Globe Fearon Educational Publishing.

JAMES, JESSE, 1847-1882

Burlingame, Jeff. Jesse James: I Will Never Surrender, 1 vol. 2008. (Americans: the Spirit of a Nation Ser.). (ENG., Illus.). 128p. (gr. 5-6). lib. bdg. 35.93 (978-0-7660-3353-5(8), d2c6626d-19eb-49c0-9525-bdde4d7388ea) Enslow Publishing, LLC.

Collins, Kathleen. Jesse James: Bank Robber of the American West. (Primary Sources of Famous People in American History Ser.). 32p. (gr. 2-3). 2009. 47.90 (978-1-60851-690-2(3)) 2003. (ENG & SPA., Illus.). lib. bdg. 29.13 (978-0-8239-4160-5(4), 1e40f58b-78c2-4e1f-911d-e6cd70abd37f, Editorial Buenas Letras) Rosen Publishing Group, Inc., The.

—Jesse James: Bank Robber of the American West / Legendario bandido del oeste Americano. 2009. (Famous People in American History/Grandes personajes en la historia de los Estados Unidos Ser.). (ENG & SPA.). 32p. (gr. 2-3). 47.90 (978-1-61512-547-0(7), Editorial Buenas Letras) Rosen Publishing Group, Inc., The.

—Jesse James: Legendario Bandido del Oeste Americano, 1 vol. 2003. (Grandes Personajes en la Historia de Los Estados Unidos (Famous People in American History) Ser.). (SPA.). 32p. (gr. 3-4). pap. 10.00 (978-0-8239-4230-5(9), 6e7f9fb2-76bb-47aa-a222-9838d6e7e24b, Rosen Classroom); (Illus.). lib. bdg. 29.13 (978-0-8239-4136-0(1), ba04e6c3-aaa3-4019-8265-115cda3cdf68, Editorial Buenas Letras) Rosen Publishing Group, Inc., The.

—Jesse James: Legendario bandido del oeste americano (Jesse James: Bank Robber of the American West) 2009. (Grandes personajes en la historia de los Estados Unidos (Famous People in American History) Ser.). (SPA.). 32p. (gr. 2-3). 47.90 (978-1-61512-801-3(8), Editorial Buenas Letras) Rosen Publishing Group, Inc., The.

—Jesse James: Western Bank Robber, 1 vol. 2003. (Primary Sources of Famous People in American History Ser.). (ENG., Illus.). 32p. (gr. 3-4). pap. 10.00 (978-0-8239-4184-1(1), ca1bfbb3-f1ce-4abe-b4da-eabcc13ac8e8); lib. bdg. 29.13 (978-0-8239-4112-4(4), 64ea6b9e-e169-4615-8b57-798e12cdd9df, Rosen Reference) Rosen Publishing Group, Inc., The.

Cooke, Tim. Jesse James: A Notorious Bank Robber of the Wild West, 1 vol. 2015. (Wanted! Famous Outlaws Ser.). (ENG., Illus.). 48p. (J). (gr. 6-8). pap. 15.05 (978-1-4824-4259-5(0), 5c82e94b-70dd-4a3b-9df6-f4ad8812d3cb) Stevens, Gareth Publishing LLLP.

Engsberg Cunningham, Meghan. Jesse James: Outlaw, 1 vol. Lapegüe, Matías, illus. 2016. (American Legends & Folktales Ser.). (ENG.). 32p. (gr. 3-3). 30.21 (978-1-5026-2197-9(5), e7040c0a-5b11-44f5-88ee-79d91f517313) Cavendish Square Publishing LLC.

Frisch, Aaron. Jesse James. 2005. (Legends of the West (Creative Education) Ser.). (Illus.). 48p. (J). (gr. 5-9). lib. bdg. 21.95 (978-1-58341-338-8(3), Creative Education) Creative Co., The.

Green, Carl R. & Sanford, William R. Jesse James, 1 vol. rev. ed. 2008. (Outlaws & Lawmen of the Wild West Ser.). (ENG., Illus.). 48p. (J). (gr. 5-7). lib. bdg. 27.93 (978-0-7660-3172-2(1), 5f7068a6-2645-490d-aac7-944c447c791f) Enslow Publishing, LLC.

Randolph, Ryan. A Bank Robber's End: The Death of Jesse James. 2009. (Great Moments in American History Ser.). 32p. (gr. 3-3). 47.90 (978-1-61513-138-9(8)) Rosen Publishing Group, Inc., The.

Randolph, Ryan P. A Bank Robber's End: The Death of Jesse James, 1 vol. 2003. (Great Moments in American History Ser.). (ENG., Illus.). 32p. (J). (gr. 3-3). lib. bdg. 29.13 (978-0-8239-4359-3(3), d0b8bfc2-268f-47e1-8743-de7d5e8bdbd0) Rosen Publishing Group, Inc., The.

Woog, Adam. Jesse James: The Wild West for Kids. 2014. (ENG., Illus.). 128p. (J). (gr. 2-7). pap. 12.95 (978-1-62636-160-7(6), 263160, Sky Pony Pr.) Skyhorse Publishing Co., Inc.

JAMES, WILL, 1892-1942

James, Will. The Will James Cowboy Book, Vol. 1. rev. ed. (Illus.). 128p. (J). (gr. 4). (978-0-87842-469-6(5), 816) Mountain Pr. Publishing Co., Inc.

JAMESTOWN (VA.)—FICTION

Archambault, Jeanne. Larry the Lawnmower. Corey, Victoria, illus. 2004. 32p. (J). 14.95 (978-0-9763031-0-7(8)); per. 10.00 (978-0-9763031-1-4(6)) Jitterbug Bks.

Carbone, Elisa. Blood on the River: James Town 1607. 2007. 272p. (J). (gr. 5-18). 8.99 (978-0-14-240932-9(4), Puffin Books) Penguin Young Readers Group.

—Blood on the River: James Town 1607. 2009. (Illus.). 237p. 17.00 (978-1-60686-385-5(1)) Perfection Learning Corp.

Hall, Lucy. From England to Jamestowne: A Journey to Find My Father. 2007. (J). (978-0-9763706-5-9(4)) Tendril Pr., LLC.

Lapallo, Connie. Dark Enough to See the Stars in a Jamestown Sky. 2006. (YA). (gr. 7-18). pap. 19.95 (978-1-59526-421-3(3)) Aeon Publishing Inc.

Smith, Andrea P. Pocahontas & John Smith, 1 vol. 2011. (Jr. Graphic Colonial America Ser.). (ENG., Illus.). 24p. (J). (gr. 2-3). lib. bdg. 28.93 (978-1-4488-5190-4(4), 7856ab38-7648-4ab9-abab-e8472a2624c3, PowerKids Pr.) Rosen Publishing Group, Inc., The.

Stone, Marie. On Their Own: A Journey to Jamestown. 2006. (Illus.). 166p. (J). (gr. 3-7). per. 8.95 (978-1-57249-385-8(2), White Mane Kids) White Mane Publishing Co., Inc.

JAMESTOWN (VA.)—HISTORY

Becker, Sandra. Pocahontas. 2003. (Folk Heroes Ser.). (Illus.). 24p. (J). lib. bdg. 24.45 (978-1-59036-074-3(5)) Weigl Pubs., Inc.

Benge, Janet & Benge, Geoff. Heroes of History - John Smith: A Foothold in the New World. 2006. (Heroes of History Ser.). (ENG., Illus.). 224p. (YA). (gr. 3-7). pap. 11.99 (978-1-932096-36-1(1)) Emerald Bks.

Benoit, Peter. Cornerstones of Freedom, Third Series: the Jamestown Colony. 2012. (ENG.). 64p. (J). lib. bdg. 30.00 (978-0-531-23058-9(9), Children's Pr.) Scholastic Library Publishing.

Brannon, Barbara. Discover Jamestown. 2005. (J). pap. (978-1-4108-5142-0(7)) Benchmark Education Co.

Braun, Eric. The Story of Jamestown, 1 vol. Erwin, Steve et al, illus. 2005. (Graphic History Ser.). (ENG.). 32p. (J). (gr. 3-9). 31.32 (978-0-7368-4967-8(X), 87151, Capstone Pr.) Capstone.

Brindell Fradin, Dennis. Jamestown, Virginia, 1 vol. 2007. (Turning Points in U. S. History Ser.). (ENG., Illus.). 48p. (gr. 4-4). lib. bdg. 34.07 (978-0-7614-2122-1(X), f90b4dfc-7667-449b-a030-3715f19e4a4f) Cavendish Square Publishing LLC.

Broyles, Janell. A Timeline of the Jamestown Colony. (Timelines of American History Ser.). 32p. (gr. 4-4). 2009. 47.90 (978-1-60854-385-4(4)) 2004. (ENG., Illus.). lib. bdg. 29.13 (978-0-8239-4536-8(7), 340643bf-8e58-4b9f-9b41-c3d1f91e22f6) Rosen Publishing Group, Inc., The. (Rosen Reference).

Bruchac, Joseph. Pocahontas. 2005. (ENG., Illus.). 192p. (YA). (gr. 7-12). pap. 7.99 (978-0-15-205465-6(0), 1196444, Clarion Bks.) HarperCollins Pubs.

—Pocahontas. 2005. (Illus.). 173p. (gr. 7). 15.95 (978-0-7569-5604-2(8)) Perfection Learning Corp.

Cipriano, Jeri. Three Historical Communities of North America: Text Pairs. 2008. (Bridges/Navigators Ser.). (J). (gr. 3). 89.00 (978-1-4108-8375-9(2)) Benchmark Education Co.

Early Jamestown (NCHS) (YA). (gr. 5-8). spiral bd., tchr.'s planning gde. ed. 11.50 (978-0-382-40928-8(0)) Cobblestone Publishing Co.

Harkins, William H. & Harkins, Susan Sales. Jamestown: The First Colony. 2006. (Building America Ser.). (Illus.). 48p. (J). (gr. 3-7). lib. bdg. 29.95 (978-1-58415-458-7(6)) Mitchell Lane Pubs.

Higgins, Melissa. Jamestown Colony, 1 vol. 2013. (Foundations of Our Nation Ser.). (ENG.). 48p. (J). (gr. 4-8). lib. bdg. 35.64 (978-1-61783-710-4(5), 7818); (Illus.). pap. 18.50 (978-1-61783-760-9(1), 8751) ABDO Publishing Co.

Kells, Deanne. The Jamestown Community. 2005. (J). pap. *(978-1-4108-4624-2(5))* Benchmark Education Co.

Kirkman, Marissa. The Life & Times of Pocahontas & the First Colonies. 2016. (Life & Times Ser.). (ENG., Illus.). 24p. (J). (gr. 1-3). lib. bdg. 27.99 *(978-1-5157-2477-3(8)*, 132849, Capstone Pr.) Capstone.

Lange, Karen. 1607: A New Look at Jamestown. 2007. (Illus.). 48p. (J). (gr. 3-7). 17.95 *(978-1-4263-0012-7(3)*, National Geographic Kids) Disney Publishing Worldwide.

Levy, Janey. Life in Jamestown Colony, 1 vol., Vol. 1. 2013. (What You Didn't Know about History Ser.). (ENG.). 24p. (J). (gr. 2-3). 25.27 *(978-1-4824-0586-6(5)*, 2d53cf66-8e71-46bc-bc25-cea7b8d6a4ab) Stevens, Gareth Publishing LLLP.

Loker, Aleck. Fearless Captain: The Adventures of John Smith. 2006. (Founders of the Republic Ser.). (Illus.). 176p. (J). (gr. 6-12). lib. bdg. 26.95 *(978-1-931798-83-9(4))* Reynolds, Morgan Inc.

Lusted, Marcia Amidon. The Jamestown Colony Disaster: A Cause-And-Effect Investigation. 2016. (Cause-And-Effect Disasters Ser.). (ENG., Illus.). 40p. (J). (gr. 4-6). E-Book 46.65 *(978-1-5124-1127-0(2)*, Lerner Pubns.) Lerner Publishing Group.

Marsh, Carole. I'm Reading about Jamestown. 2016. (I'm Reading About Ser.). (ENG., Illus.). (J). lib. bdg. 24.99 *(978-0-635-12187-5(5))*; pap. 7.99 *(978-0-635-12188-2(3))* Gallopade International.

—Jamestown: America's First Permanent English Settlement. 2006. (American Milestones Ser.). (Illus.). 32p. (J). (gr. -1-3). pap. 7.99 *(978-0-635-06323-6(9))* Gallopade International.

McAneney, Caitlin. Uncovering the Jamestown Colony, 1 vol. 2016. (Hidden History Ser.). (ENG., Illus.). 32p. (J). (gr. 4-5). pap. 11.50 *(978-1-4824-5806-0(3)*, 50cd09a8-84db-4827-be1a-a6381d7f1e4c) Stevens, Gareth Publishing LLLP.

McNeese, Tim. Jamestown. 2007. (ENG., Illus.). 112p. (gr. 5-9). lib. bdg. 30.00 *(978-0-7910-9335-1(2)*, P124585, Facts On File) Infobase Holdings, Inc.

Morley, Jacqueline. You Wouldn't Want to Be an American Colonist! A Settlement You'd Rather Not Start. 2013. (You Wouldn't Want To Ser.). lib. bdg. 20.80 *(978-0-606-31628-6(0))* Turtleback.

National Geographic Learning. Reading Expeditions (Social Studies: Seeds of Change in American History): Jamestown & the Virginia Colony. 2007. (ENG., Illus.). 40p. (J). pap. 21.95 *(978-0-7922-4547-6(4))* CENGAGE Learning.

Oney, Yannick. First American Colonies. 2004. (World Discovery History Readers Ser.). (Illus.). 32p. (J). pap. *(978-0-439-66555-1(8))* Scholastic, Inc.

Quasha, Jennifer. Jamestown: Hands-on Projects about One of America's First Communities. 2009. (Great Social Studies Projects Ser.). 24p. (gr. 3-3). 42.50 *(978-1-61513-210-2(4)*, PowerKids Pr.) Rosen Publishing Group, Inc., The.

Ransom, Candice. Why Did English Settlers Come to Virginia? And Other Questions about the Jamestown Settlement. 2011. (Six Questions of American History Ser.). (ENG.). 48p. (gr. 4-6). pap. 56.72 *(978-0-7613-7301-8(2))* Lerner Publishing Group.

Rudolph, Ellen K. Willi Gets a History Lesson: In Virginia's Historic Triangle. Rudolph, Ellen K., photos by. 2007. (ENG., Illus.). 80p. pap. 24.00 *(978-0-9791348-0-7(3))* EKR Pubns.

Ruffin, Frances E. Jamestown, 1 vol. 2005. (Places in American History Ser.). (ENG., Illus.). 24p. (gr. 2-4). lib. bdg. 24.67 *(978-0-8368-6410-6(7)*, 4fa0404b-c119-41de-b270-b4328057ef7b, Weekly Reader Leveled Readers) Stevens, Gareth Publishing LLLP.

Sita, Lisa. Pocahontas: The Powhatan Culture & the Jamestown Colony. (Library of American Lives & Times Ser.). 112p. (gr. 5-5). 2009. 69.20 *(978-1-60853-500-2(2))* 2004. (ENG., Illus.). (J). lib. bdg. 38.27 *(978-1-4042-2653-1(2)*, 0630cc02-b680-457c-b3b0-922753babdca) Rosen Publishing Group, Inc., The.

Solomon, Sharon. Christopher Newport: Jamestown Explorer, 1 vol. Bridy, Dan, illus. 2013. (ENG.). 32p. (J). (gr. k-3). 19.99 *(978-1-4556-1752-4(0)*, Pelican Publishing) Arcadia Publishing.

JAMESTOWN (VA.)—HISTORY—FICTION

Johnston, Tony. The Harmonica. Mazellan, Ron, illus. 2008. (ENG.). 32p. (J). (gr. 2-5). pap. 7.95 *(978-1-57091-489-8(3))* Charlesbridge Publishing, Inc.

Kudlinski, Kathleen V. My Lady Pocahontas, 0 vols. unabr. ed. 2013. (ENG.). 288p. (J). (gr. 4-8). pap. 9.99 *(978-1-4778-1711-7(5)*, 9781477817117, Skyscape) Amazon Publishing.

LeSourd, Nancy. Adventures in Jamestown, 1 vol. 2008. (Liberty Letters Ser.). (ENG., Illus.). 240p. (J). pap. 7.99 *(978-0-310-71392-0(7))* Zonderkidz.

Lincoln Collier, James. The Corn Raid. 2004. 142p. (J). lib. bdg. 16.92 *(978-1-4242-0768-8(1))* Fitzgerald Bks.

Marsh, Carole. The Mystery at Jamestown: First Permanent English Colony in America! 2009. (Real Kids, Real Places Ser.). (Illus.). 137p. (J). lib. bdg. 18.99 *(978-0-635-07023-4(5)*, Marsh, Carole Mysteries) Gallopade International.

Ransom, Candice. Sam Collier & the Founding of Jamestown. Archambault, Matthew, illus. (On My Own History Ser.). 48p. (J). 2007. (ENG.). (gr. 2-4). pap. 8.99 *(978-0-8225-6451-5(3)*, 46f87909-8f65-4124-8208-f52f31597e22, First Avenue Editions) 2006. (gr. 1-2). 25.26 *(978-1-57505-874-0(X)*, Millbrook Pr.) Lerner Publishing Group.

Smith, Andrea P. Pocahontas & John Smith. (Illus.). 24p. (J). 2012. 63.60 *(978-1-4488-5219-2(6))* 2011. (ENG., (gr. 2-3). pap. 11.60 *(978-1-4488-5218-5(8)*, b60ab931-cd98-4c6a-8e80-ee5088d5964a) Rosen Publishing Group, Inc., The. (PowerKids Pr.).

JAMESTOWN (VA.)—SOCIAL LIFE AND CUSTOMS

Quasha, Jennifer. Jamestown: Hands-on Projects about One of America's First Communities. 2009. (Great Social Studies Projects Ser.). 24p. (gr. 3-3). 42.50 *(978-1-61513-210-2(4)*, PowerKids Pr.) Rosen Publishing Group, Inc., The.

JANIE (FICTITIOUS CHARACTER: COONEY)—FICTION

Cooney, Caroline B. The Face on the Milk Carton. 2009. 9.14 *(978-0-7848-0397-4(8)*, Everbind) Marco Bk. Co.

JANSEN, CAM (FICTITIOUS CHARACTER)—FICTION

Adler, David A. Cam Jansen: The Mystery of the Babe Ruth Baseball. (Cam Jansen Ser.: No. 6). 57p. (J). (gr. 2-4). pap. 3.99 *(978-0-8072-1347-6(0)*, Listening Library) Random Hse. Audio Publishing Group.

—Cam Jansen & the Sports Day Mysteries: A Super Special. 2009. (Cam Jansen Ser.). lib. bdg. 16.00 *(978-0-606-00110-6(7))* Turtleback.

—Cam Jansen: Cam Jansen & the Mystery Writer Mystery #27. Allen, Joy, illus. 27th ed. 2008. (Cam Jansen Ser.: 27). (ENG.). 64p. (J). (gr. 2-5). 5.99 *(978-0-14-241194-0(9)*, Puffin Books) Penguin Young Readers Group.

—Cam Jansen: Cam Jansen & the Summer Camp Mysteries: A Super Special. Allen, Joy, illus. 2007. (Cam Jansen Ser.). 128p. (J). (gr. 2-5). 6.99 *(978-0-14-240742-4(9)*, Puffin Books) Penguin Young Readers Group.

—Cam Jansen: Cam Jansen & the Valentine Baby Mystery #25. Natti, Susanna, illus. 25th ed. 2006. (Cam Jansen Ser.: 25). (ENG.). 80p. (J). (gr. 2-5). 4.99 *(978-0-14-240694-6(5)*, Puffin Books) Penguin Young Readers Group.

—Cam Jansen: the Mystery at the Haunted House #13, 13 vols. Natti, Susanna, illus. 2004. (Cam Jansen Ser.: 13). (ENG.). 64p. (J). (gr. 2-5). 4.99 *(978-0-14-240210-8(9)*, Puffin Books) Penguin Young Readers Group.

—Cam Jansen: the Mystery of the Carnival Prize #9, 9 vols. Natti, Susanna, illus. 2004. (Cam Jansen Ser.: 9). (ENG.). 64p. (J). (gr. 2-5). 5.99 *(978-0-14-240018-0(1)*, Puffin Books) Penguin Young Readers Group.

—Cam Jansen: the Mystery of the Circus Clown #7, 7 vols. Natti, Susanna, illus. 2004. (Cam Jansen Ser.: 7). 64p. (J). (gr. 2-5). 5.99 *(978-0-14-240016-6(5)*, Puffin Books) Penguin Young Readers Group.

—Cam Jansen: the Mystery of the Gold Coins #5, 5 vols. Natti, Susanna, illus. 2004. (Cam Jansen Ser.: 5). 64p. (J). (gr. 2-5). 5.99 *(978-0-14-240014-2(9)*, Puffin Books) Penguin Young Readers Group.

—Cam Jansen: the Mystery of the Monkey House #10. Natti, Susanna, illus. 2004. (Cam Jansen Ser.: 10). (ENG.). 64p. (J). (gr. 2-5). 5.99 *(978-0-14-240019-7(X)*, Puffin Books) Penguin Young Readers Group.

—Cam Jansen: the Mystery of the Monster Movie #8, 8 vols. Natti, Susanna, illus. 2004. (Cam Jansen Ser.: 8). (ENG.). 64p. (J). (gr. 2-5). 5.99 *(978-0-14-240017-3(3)*, Puffin Books) Penguin Young Readers Group.

—Cam Jansen: the Mystery of the Stolen Diamonds #1. Natti, Susanna, illus. 2004. (Cam Jansen Ser.: 1). (ENG.). 64p. (J). (gr. 2-5). pap. 5.99 *(978-0-14-240010-4(6)*, Puffin Books) Penguin Young Readers Group.

—Cam Jansen: the Mystery of the Television Dog #4, 4 vols. Natti, Susanna, illus. 2004. (Cam Jansen Ser.: 4). 64p. (J). (gr. 2-5). 5.99 *(978-0-14-240013-5(0)*, Puffin Books) Penguin Young Readers Group.

—Cam Jansen: the Mystery of the U. F. O. #2, 2 vols. Natti, Susanna, illus. 2004. (Cam Jansen Ser.: 2). (ENG.). 64p. (J). (gr. 2-5). 5.99 *(978-0-14-240011-1(4)*, Puffin Books) Penguin Young Readers Group.

—Young Cam Jansen & the 100th Day of School Mystery, 15 vols. Natti, Susanna, illus. 2010. (Young Cam Jansen Ser.: 15). (ENG.). 32p. (J). (gr. 1-3). mass mkt. 4.99 *(978-0-14-241685-3(1)*, Penguin Young Readers) Penguin Young Readers Group.

—Young Cam Jansen & the Circus Mystery. Natti, Susanna, illus. 2013. (Young Cam Jansen Ser.: 17). (ENG.). 32p. (J). (gr. 1-3). pap. 4.99 *(978-0-448-46614-9(7)*, Penguin Young Readers) Penguin Young Readers Group.

—Young Cam Jansen & the Double Beach Mystery. Natti, Susanna, illus. 2003. (Young Cam Jansen Ser.: 8). (ENG.). 32p. (J). (gr. 1-3). mass mkt. 4.99 *(978-0-14-250079-8(8)*, Penguin Young Readers) Penguin Young Readers Group.

—Young Cam Jansen & the Double Beach Mystery. Natti, Susanna, illus. 2003. (Young Cam Jansen — Penguin Young Readers Level 3 Ser.: 8). 30p. (gr. -1-3). lib. bdg. 13.55 *(978-0-613-67477-5(4))* Turtleback.

—Young Cam Jansen & the Knock, Knock Mystery. Natti, Susanna, illus. 2015. (Young Cam Jansen Ser.: 20). (ENG.). 32p. (J). (gr. 1-3). pap. 4.99 *(978-0-14-242225-0(8)*, Penguin Young Readers) Penguin Young Readers Group.

—Young Cam Jansen & the New Girl Mystery. Natti, Susanna, illus. 2005. (Young Cam Jansen Ser.: 10). (ENG.). 32p. (J). (gr. 1-3). mass mkt. 5.99 *(978-0-14-240353-2(9)*, Penguin Young Readers) Penguin Young Readers Group.

JAPAN

Antram, David. Manga Action Figures, 1 vol. 2012. (How to Draw Ser.). (ENG.). 32p. (J). (gr. 4-5). pap. 12.75 *(978-1-4488-6469-0(0)*, 02819a85-666b-4353-9737-05d3b4a4dc2f); lib. bdg. 30.27 *(978-1-4488-6460-7(7)*, be1a5f95-450a-49b8-b49d-0a9e231f9fce) Rosen Publishing Group, Inc., The. (PowerKids Pr.).

Bjorklund, Ruth. Japan (Enchantment of the World) (Library Edition) 2017. (Enchantment of the World. Second Ser.). (ENG., Illus.). 144p. (J). (gr. 5-9). lib. bdg. 40.00 *(978-0-531-23569-0(6)*, Children's Pr.) Scholastic Library Publishing.

Blevins, Wiley. Japan (Follow Me Around) (Library Edition) 2017. (Follow Me Around... Ser.). (ENG., Illus.). 32p. (J). (gr. 3-4). lib. bdg. 27.00 *(978-0-531-23705-2(2)*, Children's Pr.) Scholastic Library Publishing.

Crean, Susan. Discover Japan, 1 vol. 2011. (Discover Countries Ser.). (ENG., Illus.). 32p. (YA). (gr. 4-4). lib. bdg. 30.27 *(978-1-4488-5269-7(2)*, dd12014c-2c80-414a-94e7-1ae892732e9c) Rosen Publishing Group, Inc., The.

Eppard, Jon. Manga. 2012. (You Can Draw It! Ser.). (ENG., Illus.). 24p. (J). (gr. 3-8). pap. 8.99 *(978-1-60014-857-6(3)*, 11977); lib. bdg. 26.95 *(978-1-60014-812-5(3)*, Express Bks.) Bellwether Media.

Freed, Kira. Surviving the 2011 Japanese Earthquake & Tsunami, 1 vol. 2015. (Surviving Disaster Ser.). (ENG., Illus.). 48p. (J). (gr. 5-6). 33.47 *(978-1-4994-3645-7(9)*, 48782b5a-f171-4b26-b777-028c16fc4e72, Rosen Central) Rosen Publishing Group, Inc., The.

Gitlin, Marty. Japan. 2017. (Country Profiles Ser.). (ENG., Illus.). 32p. (J). (gr. 3-8). lib. bdg. 27.95 *(978-1-62617-684-3(1)*, Blastoff! Discovery) Bellwether Media.

Green, Yuko. Let's Learn about JAPAN: Activity & Coloring Book. 2013. (Dover Kids Activity Bks.). (ENG.). 48p. (J). (gr. 1-5). pap. 4.99 *(978-0-486-48993-3(0)*, 489930) Dover Pubns., Inc.

Greene, Meg. Japan: A Primary Source Cultural Guide. (Primary Sources of World Cultures Ser.). 128p. (gr. 4-5). 2009. 79.90 *(978-1-60851-926-2(0))* 2004. (ENG., Illus.). (J). lib. bdg. 43.60 *(978-1-4042-2912-9(4)*, fed58d65-b0b5-4207-8e70-1543860a4ae3) Rosen Publishing Group, Inc., The.

Hardyman, Robyn. Japan. 2009. (Celebrate! (Chelsea Clubhouse) Ser.). (ENG.). 32p. (gr. 4-6). 28.00 *(978-1-60413-268-7(X)*, P169967, Chelsea Clubhse.) Infobase Holdings, Inc.

Hartz, Paula R. Shinto. 3rd rev. ed. 2009. (World Religions Ser.). Orig. Title: Shinto. (ENG., Illus.). 144p. (gr. 6-12). 40.00 *(978-1-60413-113-0(6)*, P163094, Facts On File) Infobase Holdings, Inc.

Juarez, Christine. Japan, 1 vol. 2013. (Countries Ser.). (ENG.). 24p. (J). (gr. -1-2). 27.32 *(978-1-4765-3080-2(7)*, 123053, Capstone Pr.) Capstone.

Kalman, Bobbie. Japan: The Land. 3rd rev. ed. 2008. (Lands, Peoples, & Cultures Ser.). (ENG., Illus.). 32p. (J). (gr. 3-9). pap. *(978-0-7787-9664-0(7))* Crabtree Publishing Co.

—Japan the Land. 3rd rev. ed. 2008. (Lands, Peoples, & Cultures Ser.). (ENG., Illus.). 32p. (J). (gr. 3-9). lib. bdg. *(978-0-7787-9296-3(X))* Crabtree Publishing Co.

—Spotlight on Japan. 2010. (Spotlight on My Country Ser.). (ENG.). 32p. (J). (gr. 2-5). lib. bdg. *(978-0-7787-3459-8(5))* Crabtree Publishing Co.

March, Michael. Japan. 2003. (Country Files Ser.). 32p. (J). lib. bdg. 24.25 *(978-1-58340-237-5(3))* Black Rabbit Bks.

Marsh, Carole. Japan: An Island Country of Endless Intrigue! 2009. (It's Your World Ser.). 48p. (J). (gr. 2-9). pap. 7.99 *(978-0-635-06819-4(2))* Gallopade International.

Mattern, Joanne. Japan, 1 vol. 2018. (Exploring World Cultures (First Edition) Ser.). (ENG.). 32p. (gr. 3-3). pap. 12.16 *(978-1-5026-4338-4(3)*, a8aa18be-637e-41bd-9c79-9716b7f6b56a) Cavendish Square Publishing LLC.

Moon, Walt K. Let's Explore Japan. 2017. (Bumba Books (r) — Let's Explore Countries Ser.). (ENG., Illus.). 24p. (J). (gr. -1-1). 26.65 *(978-1-5124-3008-0(0)*, f11b99d2-aa43-4594-8723-09a4b9a839be); E-Book 4.99 *(978-1-5124-3738-6(7)*, 9781512437386); E-Book 39.99 *(978-1-5124-3020-2(X))*; E-Book 39.99 *(978-1-5124-3737-9(9)*, 9781512437379) Lerner Publishing Group. (Lerner Pubns.).

Nolan, Jennifer & Whelan, Gloria. K Is for Kabuki: A Japan Alphabet. Han, Oki S., illus. 2009. (Discover the World Ser.). (ENG.). 40p. (J). (gr. 1-3). 17.95 *(978-1-58536-444-2(4)*, 202169) Sleeping Bear Pr.

Pipe, Jim. Japan in Our World. 2011. (Countries in Our World Ser.). 32p. (YA). (gr. 4-7). lib. bdg. 28.50 *(978-1-59920-390-4(1))* Black Rabbit Bks.

Popper, Garry. Keito in Japan. Johnson, Andi, illus. 2004. 36p. (gr. -1-7). 4.00 *(978-1-84161-058-0(5))* Ravette Publishing, Ltd. GBR. Dist: Parkwest Pubns., Inc.

Powell, Jillian. Descubramos Japón (Looking at Japan), 1 vol. 2007. (Descubramos Países Del Mundo (Looking at Countries) Ser.). (SPA.). 32p. (gr. 2-4). pap. 11.50 *(978-0-8368-8192-9(3)*, a8bd8e05-fb00-4b90-a524-972d390618e1, Gareth Stevens Learning Library) Stevens, Gareth Publishing LLLP.

—Looking at Japan, 1 vol. 2007. (Looking at Countries Ser.). (ENG.). 32p. (gr. 2-4). pap. 11.50 *(978-0-8368-8178-3(8)*, 2772d988-921c-4653-990d-4d6e3c898fe1); (Illus.). lib. bdg. 28.67 *(978-0-8368-8171-4(0)*, e07764ae-bb1f-4f0d-9280-688362417ec9) Stevens, Gareth Publishing LLLP. (Gareth Stevens Learning Library).

Reiser, Robert. Japan, 1 vol. 2003. (Discovering Cultures Ser.). (ENG.). 48p. (gr. 3-4). 31.21 *(978-0-7614-1177-2(1)*, 70226f6d-cd3b-4742-ae47-193f7b8a104e) Cavendish Square Publishing LLC.

Roberts, Jeremy. Japanese Mythology a to Z. 2nd rev. ed. 2009. (Mythology A to Z Ser.). (ENG., Illus.). 168p. (gr. 5-8). 45.00 *(978-1-60413-435-3(6)*, P173445, Facts On File) Infobase Holdings, Inc.

Roop, Peter & Roop, Connie. Japan. 2nd rev. ed. 2016. (Visit To Ser.). (ENG.). 32p. (J). (gr. k-2). pap. 8.29 *(978-1-4846-3873-6(5)*, 134814, Heinemann) Capstone.

Singh, Asavari. How to Draw the Most Exciting, Awesome Manga, 1 vol. James, Martin et al, illus. 2011. (Drawing Ser.). (ENG.). 48p. (J). (gr. 5-9). lib. bdg. 32.65 *(978-1-4296-6593-3(9)*, 115715) Capstone.

Somervill, Barbara A. It's Cool to Learn about Countries: Japan. 2010. (Explorer Library: Social Studies Explorer Ser.). (ENG., Illus.). 48p. (gr. 4-8). lib. bdg. 34.93 *(978-1-60279-832-8(X)*, 200530) Cherry Lake Publishing.

—Japan. 2011. (Enchantment of the World Ser.). (ENG., Illus.). 144p. (J). (gr. 5-9). lib. bdg. 40.00 *(978-0-531-25354-0(6))* Scholastic Library Publishing.

Southgate, Anna & Sparrow, Keith. Drawing Manga Boys. 2011. (J). 84.30 *(978-1-4488-4807-2(5))*; (ENG.). 80p. (gr. 5-5). pap. 15.05 *(978-1-4488-4803-4(2)*, 99e93c2a-f7a5-4045-a192-bd5d1f5d0711); (ENG.). 80p. (gr. 5-5). lib. bdg. 38.47 *(978-1-4488-4799-0(0)*, 3a9d87e7-39a6-4d55-8fec-08491a3ca4e5) Rosen Publishing Group, Inc., The. (Rosen Reference).

—Drawing Manga Expressions & Poses, 1 vol. 2011. (Manga Magic Ser.). (ENG.). 80p. (J). (gr. 5-5). pap. 15.05 *(978-1-4488-4804-1(0)*, bd1b04e8-4bb1-4ce5-8bed-cad51d1458a5); lib. bdg. 38.47 *(978-1-4488-4800-3(8)*, 54d2b9a8-a981-466b-a72a-50dedf5b7e89) Rosen Publishing Group, Inc., The. (Rosen Reference).

—Drawing Manga Weapons, Vehicles, & Accessories. 2011. (Illus.). 80p. (J). 84.30 *(978-1-4488-4809-6(1))*; (ENG., (gr. 5-5). pap. 15.05 *(978-1-4488-4805-8(9)*, ede0ce1a-9750-4cf5-9eab-bacf691c08de); (ENG., (gr. 5-5). lib. bdg. 38.47 *(978-1-4488-4801-0(6)*, eb244bd9-1943-4c8a-9e27-d234bcbe3104) Rosen Publishing Group, Inc., The. (Rosen Reference).

Stewart, Tobi Stanton. A Primary Source Guide to Japan. 2009. (Countries of the World). 24p. (gr. 2-3). 42.50 *(978-1-61512-037-6(8)*, PowerKids Pr.) Rosen Publishing Group, Inc., The.

Streissguth, Thomas. Japan. 2008. (Country Explorers Ser.). (ENG., Illus.). 48p. (gr. 2-4). lib. bdg. 29.27 *(978-0-8225-8659-3(2))* Lerner Publishing Group.

Streissguth, Tom. Japan. 2008. pap. 40.95 *(978-0-8225-9303-4(3))* Lerner Publishing Group.

Taylor, Des. Cartoons & Manga, 1 vol. 2011. (Master This! Ser.). (ENG., Illus.). 32p. (J). (gr. 4-4). lib. bdg. 28.93 *(978-1-4488-5283-3(8)*, 243908cb-39c1-4e45-9416-4416ba653dce, PowerKids Pr.) Rosen Publishing Group, Inc., The.

Tecco, Betsy Dru. How to Draw Japan's Sights & Symbols. 2009. (Kid's Guide to Drawing the Countries of the World Ser.). 48p. (gr. 4-4). 53.00 *(978-1-61511-116-9(6)*, PowerKids Pr.) Rosen Publishing Group, Inc., The.

Thomas, Mark. The Akashi-Kaikyo Bridge: World's Longest Bridge. 2009. (Record-Breaking Structures Ser.). 24p. (gr. 1-2). 42.50 *(978-1-60852-453-2(1)*, PowerKids Pr.) Rosen Publishing Group, Inc., The.

—El puente Akashi Kaikyo: El puente más largo del mundo (the Akashi-Kaikyo Bridge: World's Longest Bridge) 2009. (Estructuras extraordinarias (Record-Breaking Structures) Ser.). (SPA.). 24p. (gr. 1-2). 42.50 *(978-1-61512-311-7(3)*, Editorial Buenas Letras) Rosen Publishing Group, Inc., The.

Tidmarsh, Celia. Focus on Japan, 1 vol. 2006. (World in Focus Ser.). (ENG., Illus.). 64p. (gr. 5-8). pap. 15.05 *(978-0-8368-6729-9(7)*, 98622b79-77b4-4452-a6dc-863270f721c6); lib. bdg. 36.67 *(978-0-8368-6722-0(X)*, 62a612eb-94a5-45c8-9483-11663a5c1ff7) Stevens, Gareth Publishing LLLP. (Gareth Stevens Secondary Library).

Zocchi, Judy. In Japan. Brodie, Neale, illus. 2005. (Global Adventures II Ser.). 32p. (J). per. 10.95 *(978-1-59646-140-6(3))* Dingles & Co.

—In Japan/en Japón. Brodie, Neale, illus. 2005. (Global Adventures II Ser.).Tr. of En Japón. (ENG & SPA.). 32p. (J). per. 10.95 *(978-1-59646-142-0(X))* Dingles & Co.

JAPAN—BIOGRAPHY

Benge, Janet & Benge, Geoff. Jacob Deshazer: Forgive Your Enemies. 2009. (ENG.). 224p. (YA). pap. 11.99 *(978-1-57658-475-0(5))* YWAM Publishing.

Bloom, Harold, ed. The Tale of Genji: Murasaki Shikibu. 2003. (Bloom's Modern Critical Interpretations Ser.). (ENG., Illus.). 176p. (gr. 9-13). 45.00 *(978-0-7910-7584-5(2)*, P113889, Facts On File) Infobase Holdings, Inc.

Christopher, Matt. At the Plate With... Ichiro. 2003. (ENG., Illus.). 112p. (J). (gr. 5-8). pap. 9.99 *(978-0-316-13679-2(4))* Little, Brown Bks. for Young Readers.

Duffield, Katy S. Ken Kutaragi: PlayStation Developer, 1 vol. 2007. (Innovators Ser.). (ENG., Illus.). 48p. (gr. 4-8). lib. bdg. 34.58 *(978-0-7377-3862-9(6)*, 452f45d5-dcdd-49b9-a151-e9d1511551e1, KidHaven Publishing) Greenhaven Publishing LLC.

Hillenbrand, Laura. Unbroken: An Olympian's Journey from Airman to Castaway to Captive (Young Readers Edition) 2017. lib. bdg. 22.10 *(978-0-606-39867-1(8))* Turtleback.

Levin, Judith. Ichiro Suzuki. 2009. (Baseball Superstars Ser.). (ENG., Illus.). 144p. (gr. 6-12). pap. 11.95 *(978-0-7910-9849-3(4)*, P147497, Checkmark Bks.) Infobase Holdings, Inc.

Mochizuki, Ken. Passage to Freedom: The Sugihara Story. 2004. (Illus.). (J). (gr. k-3). spiral bd. *(978-0-616-03098-1(3))* Canadian National Institute for the Blind/Institut National Canadien pour les Aveugles.

—Passage to Freedom: The Sugihara Story. 2005. 19.45 *(978-0-7569-4773-6(1))* Perfection Learning Corp.

Nobleman, Marc Tyler. Thirty Minutes over Oregon: A Japanese Pilot's World War II Story. Iwai, Melissa, illus. 2018. (ENG.). 40p. (J). (gr. 1-4). 17.99 *(978-0-544-43076-1(X)*, 1595751, Clarion Bks.) HarperCollins Pubs.

Savage, Jeff. Ichiro Suzuki. (Amazing Athletes Ser.). 2007. (J). pap. 6.95 *(978-0-8225-7266-4(4)*, Lerner Pubns.) 2005. (Illus.). 32p. (gr. 3-4). lib. bdg. 22.60 *(978-0-8225-1344-5(7))* Lerner Publishing Group.

Scheff, Matt. Naomi Osaka: Tennis Star. 2020. (Biggest Names in Sports Set 5 Ser.). (ENG., Illus.). 32p. (J). (gr. 3-5). 31.35 *(978-1-64493-054-0(4)*, 1644930544, Focus Readers) North Star Editions.

Stelson, Caren. A Bowl Full of Peace: A True Story. Kusaka, Akira, illus. 2020. (ENG.). 40p. (J). (gr. 1-5). 18.99 *(978-1-5415-2148-3(X)*, 6e68f323-73fa-4b42-adb2-47050749fd75, Carolrhoda Bks.) Lerner Publishing Group.

Thomas, Rachael L. Nintendo Innovator. 2018. (Toy Trailblazers Ser.). (ENG., Illus.). 32p. (J). (gr. 3-6). lib. bdg. 32.79 *(978-1-5321-1712-1(4)*, 30712, Checkerboard Library) ABDO Publishing Co.

Turner, Pamela S. Samurai Rising: The Epic Life of Minamoto Yoshitsune. Hinds, Gareth, illus. 2018. 256p. (J). (gr. 7). pap. 9.99 *(978-1-58089-585-9(9))* Charlesbridge Publishing, Inc.

—Samurai Rising: the Epic Life of Minamoto Yoshitsune. Hinds, Gareth, illus. 2016. 256p. (YA). (gr. 7-12). 16.95 *(978-1-58089-584-2(0))* Charlesbridge Publishing, Inc.

JAPAN—CIVILIZATION

Centore, Michael. Japan, Vol. 12. 2015. (Major Nations in a Global World: Tradition, Culture, & Daily Life Ser.). (Illus.). 64p. (J). (gr. 7). 23.95 *(978-1-4222-3347-4(2))* Mason Crest.

Greene, Meg. The Technology of Ancient Japan. 2009. (Technology of the Ancient World Ser.). 48p. (gr. 6-6). 61.20 *(978-1-60854-241-3(6)*, Rosen Reference) Rosen Publishing Group, Inc., The.

Kalman, Bobbie. Japan: The Culture, 1 vol. 3rd rev. ed. 2008. (ENG., Illus.). 32p. (J). (gr. 3-9). pap. *(978-0-7787-9666-4(3))* Crabtree Publishing Co.

Kaminski, Leah. Konnichiwa, Japan. 2019. (Countries of the World Ser.). (ENG., Illus.). 48p. (J). (gr. 4-8). pap. 17.07 *(978-1-5341-5092-8(7)*, 213675); lib. bdg. 39.21 *(978-1-5341-4806-2(X)*, 213674) Cherry Lake Publishing.

JAPAN—FICTION

Ahdieh, Renée. Flame in the Mist. (Flame in the Mist Ser.: 1). (ENG.). (YA). (gr. 7). 2018. 448p. pap. 11.99 *(978-0-14-751387-8(1)*, Penguin Books) 2017. 416p. 17.99 *(978-0-399-17163-5(0)*, G.P. Putnam's Sons Books for Young Readers) Penguin Young Readers Group.

—Flame in the Mist. 2018. lib. bdg. 22.10 *(978-0-606-40878-3(9))* Turtleback.

—Smoke in the Sun. 2018. (Flame in the Mist Ser.: 2). (ENG.). 432p. (YA). (gr. 7). 18.99 *(978-1-5247-3814-3(X)*, G.P. Putnam's Sons Books for Young Readers) Penguin Young Readers Group.

Amara, Phil & Chin, Oliver. The Discovery of Anime & Manga: The Asian Hall of Fame. Calle, Juan, illus. 2019. (Asian Hall of Fame Ser.). (ENG.). 36p. (J). 16.95 *(978-1-59702-146-3(6))* Immedium.

Ando, Natsumi. Arisa 1. 2012. (Arisa Ser.: 1). (Illus.). 208p. (gr. 8-12). pap. 10.99 *(978-1-61262-335-1(2))* Kodansha America, Inc.

Ann, Dee. Burden of Silence. 2013. 136p. pap. *(978-1-4602-2099-3(4))* FriesenPress.

Asai, Carrie. The Book of the Shadow. Alarcão, Renato, illus. 2013. (Samurai Girl Ser.: 2). (ENG.). 224p. (YA). (gr. 11). pap. 13.99 *(978-1-4814-1540-8(9)*, Simon Pulse) Simon Pulse.

Avila, Kat. Hanako Loves Monsters. 2008. 32p. 14.98 *(978-1-4357-0188-5(7))* Lulu Pr., Inc.

Benwell, Sarah. The Last Leaves Falling. 2015. (ENG., Illus.). 368p. (YA). (gr. 9). 17.99 *(978-1-4814-3065-4(3))* Simon & Schuster Children's Publishing.

Bidoli, Katie. Karate Adventures of Kisho, Hana, & Nobu: Karate Is for Everyone! 2006. (Illus.). 16p. (J). 10.00 *(978-1-60243-029-7(2))* Keen's Martial Arts Academy.

Bradford, Chris. The Ring of Earth: Young Samurai. 4th ed. 2010. (Young Samurai Ser.: 4). (Illus.). 336p. (YA). (gr. 7). pap. 12.99 *(978-0-14-133253-6(0)*, Penguin Global) Penguin Publishing Group.

—The Ring of Fire: Young Samurai. 6th ed. 2011. (Young Samurai Ser.: 6). (Illus.). 352p. (YA). (gr. 7). pap. 12.99 *(978-0-14-133255-0(7))* Penguin Bks., Ltd. GBR. Dist: Independent Pubs. Group.

—The Ring of Sky. 8th ed. 2012. (Young Samurai Ser.: 8). (Illus.). 384p. (YA). (gr. 7). pap. 12.99 *(978-0-14-133972-6(1))* Penguin Bks., Ltd. GBR. Dist: Independent Pubs. Group.

—The Ring of Water: Young Samurai. 5th ed. 2011. (Young Samurai Ser.: 5). (Illus.). 320p. (YA). (gr. 7). pap. 12.99 *(978-0-14-133254-3(9))* Penguin Bks., Ltd. GBR. Dist: Independent Pubs. Group.

—The Ring of Wind. 7th ed. 2012. (Young Samurai Ser.: 7). (Illus.). 368p. (YA). (gr. 7). 12.99 *(978-0-14-133971-9(3)*, Penguin Global) Penguin Publishing Group.

—The Way of the Dragon, 3. 2012. (Young Samurai Ser.). (ENG.). 512p. (J). (gr. 6-8). 22.44 *(978-1-4231-3779-5(5))* Hyperion Bks. for Children.

—The Way of the Dragon. l.t. ed. 2012. (Young Samurai Ser.). (ENG.). 448p. (J). (gr. 9-12). 23.99 *(978-1-4104-4466-0(X))* Thorndike Pr.

—The Way of the Sword. l.t. ed. 2012. (Young Samurai Ser.). (ENG.). 547p. (J). (gr. 6-9). 23.99 *(978-1-4104-4404-2(X))* Thorndike Pr.

—The Way of the Warrior, 1. 2008. (Young Samurai Ser.). (ENG.). 384p. (J). (gr. 6-8). 22.44 *(978-1-4231-1986-9(X))* Hyperion Bks. for Children.

—The Way of the Warrior. l.t. ed. 2011. (Young Samurai Ser.). (ENG.). 328p. (J). 23.99 *(978-1-4104-4329-8(9))* Thorndike Pr.

—Young Samurai: the Way of the Sword, 2. 2011. (Young Samurai Ser.). (ENG.). 448p. (gr. 6-8). 22.44 *(978-1-4231-2937-0(7))* Hyperion Bks. for Children.

—Young Samurai the Way of the Warrior: The Way of the Warrior, Bk. 1. 2008. (Young Samurai Ser.: 1). (Illus.). 352p. (J). (gr. 6-10). pap. 12.99 *(978-0-14-132430-2(9))* Penguin Bks., Ltd. GBR. Dist: Independent Pubs. Group.

Burkinshaw, Kathleen. The Last Cherry Blossom. 2016. (ENG.). 240p. (J). (gr. 5-8). 16.99 *(978-1-63450-693-9(6)*, Sky Pony Pr.) Skyhorse Publishing Co., Inc.

Canning, Charlie. The 89th Temple. 2012. (ENG.). 211p. pap. 14.95 *(978-1-4787-1763-8(7))* Outskirts Pr., Inc.

The Case of the Secret Box. 2007. 56p. pap. 7.75 *(978-0-8341-2288-8(X)*, 083-412-288X) Beacon Hill Pr. of Kansas City.

Chrystyn, Julie. Hachiko: The Story of a Loyal Akita & the Royal Dogs of Japan. 2009. (ENG.). 53p. (J). (gr. k-7). pap. 7.95 *(978-1-59777-629-5(7))* Phoenix Bks., Inc.

Clum, James. Koji's Ninja Secrets. 2010. (ENG.). 35p. pap. 15.96 *(978-0-557-60314-5(5))* Lulu Pr., Inc.

Coatsworth, Elizabeth. The Cat Who Went to Heaven. 2011. 7.64 *(978-0-7848-3455-8(5)*, Everbind) Marco Bk. Co.

—The Cat Who Went to Heaven. Vitale, Raoul, illus. 3rd ed. 2008. (ENG.). 96p. (J). (gr. 3-7). pap. 7.99 *(978-1-4169-4973-2(9)*, Simon & Schuster/Paula Wiseman Bks.) Simon & Schuster/Paula Wiseman Bks.

—Gata Que Se Fue para el Cielo. 2011. (SPA.). 104p. (gr. 5-8). pap. 12.99 *(978-958-04-1530-5(7)*, NR4853) Norma S.A. COL. Dist: Lectorum Pubns., Inc.

Coerr, Eleanor. Circus Day in Japan: Bilingual English & Japanese Text. Matsunari, Yumi, tr. Coerr, Eleanor, illus. 2016. (Illus.). 48p. (J). (gr. -1-3). 9.95 *(978-0-8048-4743-8(6))* Tuttle Publishing.

Dahl, Michael. Monster Hunter, 1 vol. Aime, Luigi, illus. 2012. (Dragonborn Ser.). (ENG.). 72p. (J). (gr. 4-8). pap. 7.10 *(978-1-4342-4256-3(0)*, 120317, Stone Arch Bks.) Capstone.

Dalton, Annie. Budding Star, Book 8. 2008. (Mel Beeby Agent Angel Ser.). (ENG.). 208p. (J). (gr. 4-7). pap. 6.95 *(978-0-00-720478-6(7))* HarperCollins Pubs. Ltd. GBR. Dist: Independent Pubs. Group.

—The Divine Collection: Three Amazing Missions in One Book! 2008. (Mel Beeby Agent Angel Ser.). (ENG., Illus.). 608p. (J). (gr. 4-7). pap. 19.95 *(978-0-00-719074-4(3))* HarperCollins Pubs. Ltd. GBR. Dist: Independent Pubs. Group.

Davisson, Zack. Yokai Stories. D'Onofrio, Eleonora, illus. 2018. (ENG.). 64p. (J). (gr. 2-7). 16.95 *(978-1-63405-914-5(X))* Chin Music Pr.

Egan, Tim. Dodsworth in Tokyo. Egan, Tim, illus. 2014. (Dodsworth Book Ser.). (ENG., Illus.). 48p. (J). (gr. 1-4). pap. 4.99 *(978-0-544-33915-6(0)*, 1584486, Clarion Bks.) HarperCollins Pubs.

Falk, Nick. The Battle for the Golden Egg. Flowers, Tony, illus. 2015. (Samurai vs Ninja Ser.: 1). 96p. (J). (gr. 1-3). pap. 7.99 *(978-0-85798-605-4(8))* Random Hse. Australia AUS. Dist: Independent Pubs. Group.

—Curse of the Oni. Flowers, Tony, illus. 2016. (Samurai vs Ninja Ser.: 4). 96p. (J). (gr. 1-3). pap. 7.99 *(978-0-85798-640-5(6))* Random Hse. Australia AUS. Dist: Independent Pubs. Group.

—The Race for the Shogun's Treasure. Flowers, Tony, illus. 2015. (Samurai vs Ninja Ser.: 2). 96p. (J). (gr. 1-3). pap. 12.99 *(978-0-85798-636-8(8))* Random Hse. Australia AUS. Dist: Independent Pubs. Group.

Friesner, Esther. Spirit's Chosen. 2014. (Princesses of Myth Ser.). (ENG., Illus.). 512p. (YA). (gr. 7). pap. 10.99 *(978-0-375-87316-4(3)*, Ember) Random Hse. Children's Bks.

Friesner, Esther M. Spirit's Princess. 2012. 449p. (YA). *(978-0-375-87315-7(5))* Random Hse., Inc.

Fussell, Sandy. Samurai Kids #2: Owl Ninja. James, Rhian Nest, illus. 2011. (Samurai Kids Ser.: 2). (ENG.). 272p. (J). (gr. 4-7). 15.99 *(978-0-7636-5003-2(X))* Candlewick Pr.

Gerber, Linda. Now & Zen. 2006. (S. A. S. S. Ser.). (Illus.). 224p. (YA). (gr. 7-18). 7.99 *(978-0-14-240657-1(0)*, Speak) Penguin Young Readers Group.

Gerstein, Mordicai, illus. Three Samurai Cats: A Story from Japan. 2004. (J). *(978-0-439-69256-4(3))* Scholastic, Inc.

Gilligan, Shannon. The Mystery of Ura Senke. 2005. (Illus.). 120p. (Orig.). (J). *(978-0-7608-9701-0(8))* Sundance/Newbridge Educational Publishing.

Gollub, Matthew. Ten Oni Drummers. Stone, Kazuko G., illus. 2018. (Ten Oni Drummers Ser.). (ENG.). 32p. (J). (gr. -1-k). 17.95 *(978-1-889910-51-2(1))* Tortuga Pr.

Gollub, Matthew & Stone, Kazuko G. Ten Oni Drummers. 2013. (ENG., Illus.). 32p. (J). (gr. -1-3). 16.95 *(978-1-58430-011-3(6))* Lee & Low Bks., Inc.

Goto, Scott. The Perfect Sword. Goto, Scott, illus. 2010. (ENG., Illus.). 48p. (J). (gr. 1-4). pap. 8.95 *(978-1-57091-698-4(5))* Charlesbridge Publishing, Inc.

Gratz, Alan. Samurai Shortstop. 2006. (ENG.). 280p. (J). (gr. 9-12). 22.44 *(978-0-8037-3075-5(6)*, Dial) Penguin Publishing Group.

Gratz, Alan M. Samurai Shortstop. 2008. 288p. (YA). (gr. 7-18). 9.99 *(978-0-14-241099-8(3)*, Speak) Penguin Young Readers Group.

Haibara, Yak & Haibara, Yak. Sengoku Basara: Samurai Legends Volume 2: Samurai Legends Volume 2, 2 vols. 2013. (ENG., Illus.). 424p. (YA). pap. 19.99 *(978-1-926778-59-4(6)*, d748e1c6-88c3-40b7-ab2f-84ecedb6a598) URON Entertainment Corp. CAN. Dist: Diamond Comic Distributors, Inc.

Haidar, Hanna. Earl's Big Adventure in Japan. Newton, Kimberly, illus. 2012. 26p. (J). *(978-0-9800975-1-1(7))* Old Silver Pr.

Hall, H. Tom. The Golden Tombo. 2011. 42p. 35.95 *(978-1-258-10444-3(X))* Literary Licensing, LLC.

Hamazaki, Tatsuya. . hack //Legend of the Twilight, Volume 1: Kaplan SAT/ACT Vocabulary-Building Manga. Izumi, Rei, illus. 2007. (Kaplan SAT/ACT Score-Raising Manga Ser.). 192p. pap. 9.99 *(978-1-4277-5497-4(7))* Kaplan Publishing.

Hana's Year: Evaluation Guide. 2006. (J). *(978-1-55942-408-0(7))* Witcher Productions.

Hara, Yui. Kiniro Mosaic, Vol. 1. 2016. (Kiniro Mosaic Ser.: 1). (ENG., Illus.). 128p. (J). (gr. 8-17). pap. 17.00 *(978-0-316-50146-0(8))* Yen Pr. LLC.

Harrington, Claudia. My Mom & Dad, 1 vol. Persico, Zoe, illus. 2015. (My Family Ser.). (ENG.). 32p. (J). (gr. -1-3). 32.79 *(978-1-62402-107-7(7)*, 18156, Looking Glass Library) Magic Wagon.

Haugaard, Erik C. The Boy & the Samurai. 2005. (ENG.). 240p. (J). (gr. 5-7). pap. 6.95 *(978-0-618-61511-7(3)*, 484916, Clarion Bks.) HarperCollins Pubs.

—The Revenge of the Forty-Seven Samurai. 2005. (ENG.). 240p. (J). (gr. 5-7). pap. 14.95 *(978-0-618-54896-5(3)*, 487444, Clarion Bks.) HarperCollins Pubs.

—The Samurai's Tale. 2005. (ENG.). 256p. (J). (gr. 5-7). pap. 7.99 *(978-0-618-61512-4(1)*, 484894, Clarion Bks.) HarperCollins Pubs.

Hearn, Lian. Leyendas de los Otori I. 2004. (SPA.). 312p. (YA). (gr. 8-12). pap. 13.95 *(978-956-239-300-3(3))* Santillana USA Publishing Co., Inc.

Heffernan, John. Hotaka: Through My Eyes - Natural Disaster Zones. White, Lyn, ed. 2017. (Through My Eyes Ser.). (ENG.). 224p. (J). (gr. 6-9). pap. 15.99 *(978-1-76011-376-6(X))* Allen & Unwin AUS. Dist: Independent Pubs. Group.

Higgins, Simon. Moonshadow: Rise of the Ninja. 2011. (Moonshadow Ser.: 1). (ENG.). 352p. (J). (gr. 3-7). pap. 18.99 *(978-0-316-05532-1(8))* Little, Brown Bks. for Young Readers.

—Moonshadow: the Nightmare Ninja. 2012. (Moonshadow Ser.: 2). (ENG.). 384p. (J). (gr. 3-7). pap. 19.99 *(978-0-316-05534-5(4))* Little, Brown Bks. for Young Readers.

Hiwatari, Saki. Please Save My Earth, Vol. 17. 2006. (Please Save My Earth Ser.: 17). (ENG., Illus.). 184p. pap. 9.99 *(978-1-4215-0550-3(9))* Viz Media.

—Please Save My Earth, Vol. 18, Vol. 18. 2006. (Please Save My Earth Ser.: 18). (ENG., Illus.). 184p. pap. 9.99 *(978-1-4215-0551-0(7))* Viz Media.

Hoobler, Dorothy & Hoobler, Thomas. The Demon in the Teahouse. 2005. 181p. (J). (gr. 4-7). 13.65 *(978-0-7569-6725-3(2))* Perfection Learning Corp.

—The Ghost in the Tokaido Inn. 2005. 240p. (J). (gr. 3-7). 7.99 *(978-0-14-240541-3(8)*, Puffin Books) Penguin Young Readers Group.

—The Ghost in the Tokaido Inn. 2005. 214p. (J). (gr. 4-7). 14.65 *(978-0-7569-6403-0(2))* Perfection Learning Corp.

—In Darkness, Death. 2005. (Puffin Sleuth Novels Ser.). 195p. (J). (gr. 5-9). 14.65 *(978-0-7569-5457-4(6))* Perfection Learning Corp.

—The Sword That Cut the Burning Grass. 2006. 211p. (gr. 5-9). 17.00 *(978-0-7569-6907-3(7))* Perfection Learning Corp.

Hulme-Cross, Benjamin. The Samurai's Assassin. Rinaldi, Angelo, illus. 2015. (Warrior Heroes Ser.). (ENG.). 160p. (J). (gr. 6). *(978-0-7787-1766-9(6))* Crabtree Publishing Co.

Hunt, Elizabeth Singer. Secret Agent Jack Stalwart: Book 11: the Theft of the Samurai Sword: Japan. 2009. (Secret Agent Jack Stalwart Ser.: 11). (ENG., Illus.). 128p. (J). (gr. 1-4). pap. 5.99 *(978-1-60286-098-8(X))* Hachette Bk. Group.

Ihara, Shigekatsu. Pokémon Diamond & Pearl Adventure!, Vol. 8 Vol. 8. 2010. (ENG., Illus.). 192p. (J). pap. 9.99 *(978-1-4215-3671-2(4))* Viz Media.

Iinuma, Yuuki. Itsuwaribito , Vol. 14. 2015. (ENG.). 192p. pap. 9.99 *(978-1-4215-6525-5(0))* Viz Media.

Ikeda, Daisaku. The Cherry Tree. McCaughrean, Geraldine, tr. from JPN. Wildsmith, Brian, illus. 2013. 6.95 *(978-1-935523-57-4(0))* World Tribune Pr.

Inzer, Christine Mari. Diary of a Tokyo Teen: A Japanese-American Girl Travels to the Land of Trendy Fashion, High-Tech Toilets & Maid Cafes. 2016. (Illus.). 128p. (gr. 6-12). pap. 14.99 *(978-4-8053-1396-1(X))* Tuttle Publishing.

Izumi, Kaneyoshi. Seiho Boys' High School!, Vol. 3. 2010. (Seiho Boys' High School! Ser.: 3). (ENG., Illus.). 192p. pap. 9.99 *(978-1-4215-3733-7(8))* Viz Media.

Kajikawa, Kimiko. Tsunami! Young, Ed, illus. 2009. (ENG.). 32p. (J). (gr. -1-k). 17.99 *(978-0-399-25006-4(9)*, Philomel Bks.) Penguin Young Readers Group.

Kamachi, Kazuma. A Certain Magical Index, Vol. 1 (light Novel), Vol. 1. Haimura, Kiyotaka, illus. 2014. (Certain Magical Index Ser.: 1). (ENG.). 224p. (gr. 8-17). 14.00 *(978-0-316-33912-4(1)*, Yen Pr.) Yen Pr. LLC.

Kann, Victoria. Pinkalicious: Cherry Blossom. Kann, Victoria, illus. 2015. (I Can Read Level 1 Ser.). (ENG., Illus.). 32p. (J). (gr. -1-3). 16.99 *(978-0-06-224593-9(7)*, HarperCollins) HarperCollins Pubs.

—Pinkalicious: Cherry Blossom: A Springtime Book for Kids. Kann, Victoria, illus. 2015. (I Can Read Level 1 Ser.). (ENG., Illus.). 32p. (J). (gr. -1-3). pap. 5.99 *(978-0-06-224594-6(5)*, HarperCollins) HarperCollins Pubs.

Kishimoto, Masashi. Naruto: Chapter Book, Vol. 11: The Tenth Question. 2010. (Naruto: Chapter Bks.: 11). (ENG., Illus.). 80p. (J). pap. 4.99 *(978-1-4215-3041-3(4))* Viz Media.

—Naruto: Chapter Book, Vol. 12: Coward. 2010. (Naruto: Chapter Bks.: 12). (ENG., Illus.). 80p. (J). pap. 4.99 *(978-1-4215-3042-0(2))* Viz Media.

—Naruto: Chapter Book, Vol. 13: Beauty Is the Beast. 2010. (Naruto: Chapter Bks.: 13). (ENG., Illus.). 80p. (J). pap. 4.99 *(978-1-4215-3043-7(0))* Viz Media.

—Naruto: Chapter Book, Vol. 15: The Last Chance. 2010. (Naruto: Chapter Bks.: 15). (ENG., Illus.). 80p. (J). (gr. 1-4). pap. 4.99 *(978-1-4215-3045-1(7))* Viz Media.

—Naruto: Chapter Book, Vol. 16: The Final Battle, 16. 2010. (Naruto: Chapter Bks.: 16). (ENG., Illus.). 80p. (J). (gr. 2-4). pap. 4.99 *(978-1-4215-3046-8(5))* Viz Media.

—Naruto: Chapter Book, Vol. 2: The Tests of a Ninja. 2008. (Naruto: Chapter Bks.: 2). (ENG., Illus.). 80p. (J). (gr. 1-5). pap. 4.99 *(978-1-4215-2213-5(6))* Viz Media.

—Naruto: Chapter Book, Vol. 5: Bridge of Courage. 2009. (Naruto: Chapter Bks.: 5). (ENG., Illus.). 80p. (J). (gr. 1). pap. 4.99 *(978-1-4215-2315-6(9))* Viz Media.

Kline, Spencer. The Adventures of Fujimori-San. Brown, E. Jackie, illus. 2010. 20p. 12.99 *(978-1-4520-6275-4(7))* AuthorHouse.

Kogawa, Joy. Naomi's Tree, 1 vol. Ohi, Ruth, illus. 2011. (ENG.). 32p. (J). (gr. 4-6). pap. 9.95 *(978-1-55455-184-2(6)*, f862ef7e-47dc-47dc-be11-165b1858bc27) Trifolium Bks., Inc. CAN. Dist: Firefly Bks., Ltd.

Krensky, Stephen. Bokuden & the Bully: [a Japanese Folktale]. Noll, Cheryl Kirk, illus. 2009. (On My Own Folklore Ser.). (ENG.). 48p. (J). (gr. 2-4). pap. 8.99 *(978-1-58013-847-5(0)*, bf186838-186f-421e-872e-51de33b9040b, First Avenue Editions) Lerner Publishing Group.

Krulik, Nancy. Don't Mess with the Ninja Puppy! 2014. (Magic Bone Ser.: 6). lib. bdg. 14.75 *(978-0-606-36162-0(6))* Turtleback.

—Don't Mess with the Ninja Puppy! #6, No. 6. Braun, Sebastien, illus. 2014. (Magic Bone Ser.: 6). 128p. (J). (gr. 1-3). 6.99 *(978-0-448-48095-4(6)*, Grosset & Dunlap) Penguin Young Readers Group.

Lake, Nick. Blood Ninja. 2010. (ENG., Illus.). 400p. (YA). (gr. 7). pap. 12.99 *(978-1-4169-8628-7(6)*, Simon & Schuster Bks. For Young Readers) Simon & Schuster Bks. For Young Readers.

—Blood Ninja II: The Revenge of Lord Oda. (ENG., Illus.). (YA). (gr. 7). 2011. 416p. pap. 9.99 *(978-1-4169-8630-0(8))* 2010. 400p. 16.99 *(978-1-4169-8629-4(4))* Simon & Schuster Bks. For Young Readers. (Simon & Schuster Bks. For Young Readers).

—Blood Ninja III: The Betrayal of the Living. 2013. (ENG., Illus.). 368p. (YA). (gr. 9). pap. 9.99 *(978-1-4424-2680-1(2)*, Simon & Schuster Bks. For Young Readers) Simon & Schuster Bks. For Young Readers.

Lane, Dakota. Gothic Lolita: A Mystical Thriller. Lane, Dakota, illus. 2008. (ENG., Illus.). 208p. (YA). (gr. 7-18). 17.99 *(978-1-4169-1396-2(3)*, Atheneum Bks. for Young Readers) Simon & Schuster Children's Publishing.

Leibold, Jay. Secret of the Ninja. Nugent, Suzanne, illus. 2006. (ENG.). 144p. (J). (gr. 4-8). per. 7.99 *(978-1-933390-16-1(6))* Chooseco LLC.

Lemke, Donald. The Awakening, 1 vol. Glass House Graphics, illus. 2011. (Good vs Evil Ser.). (ENG.). 48p. (J). (gr. 5-9). lib. bdg. 23.99 *(978-1-4342-2089-9(3)*, 102835, Stone Arch Bks.) Capstone.

Lendroth, Susan. Maneki Neko: The Tale of the Beckoning Cat. Otoshi, Kathryn, illus. 2010. (J). *(978-1-885008-39-8(2)*, Shen's Bks.) Lee & Low Bks., Inc.

—Natsumi! Burris, Priscilla, illus. 2018. (ENG.). 32p. (J). (gr. -1-3). 18.99 *(978-0-399-17090-4(1)*, G.P. Putnam's Sons Books for Young Readers) Penguin Young Readers Group.

Li, August. Fox-Hat & Neko. 2016. (ENG., Illus.). (YA). 29.99 *(978-1-63533-018-2(1)*, Harmony Ink Pr.) Dreamspinner Pr.

Libster, Bernard. The Bonsai Bear. Cheung, Aries, illus. 2006. 31p. (J). (gr. k-4). reprint ed. 16.00 *(978-1-4223-5857-3(7))* DIANE Publishing Co.

Lifton, Betty Jean. Taka-Chan & I: A Dog's Journey to Japan by Runcible. Hosoe, Eikoh, photos by. 2012. (Illus.). 64p. (J). (gr. k-4). 16.95 *(978-1-59017-502-6(6)*, NYR Children's Collection) New York Review of Bks., Inc., The.

Low, Chen-Chen-Chen. Lizzie May & Oshin. 2009. 46p. pap. 29.99 *(978-1-4092-5740-0(1))* Lulu Pr., Inc.

Lowitz, Leza & Oketani, Shogo. Jet Black & the Ninja Wind. 2013. (ENG., Illus.). 320p. (J). (gr. 7-12). 17.99 *(978-4-8053-1284-1(X))* Tuttle Publishing.

—Jet Black & the Ninja Wind: British Edition. 2017. (ENG.). 320p. (J). (gr. 7-12). pap. 5.99 *(978-0-8048-4884-8(X))* Tuttle Publishing.

Lydia Jane. Fifth Moon: The First Installment in the Gates Trilogy. 2007. 480p. 35.95 *(978-0-595-91408-1(X))*; per. 25.95 *(978-0-595-43671-2(4))* iUniverse, Inc.

Manley, Ruth. The Plum-Rain Scroll. 2005. (UQP Children's Classics Ser.). 378p. (J). pap. *(978-0-7022-3505-4(9))* Univ. of Queensland Pr.

Marriott, Zoë. The Name of the Blade. 2014. (Name of the Blade Ser.: 1). (ENG.). 368p. (YA). (gr. 7). 16.99 *(978-0-7636-6957-7(1))* Candlewick Pr.

Marsh, Carole. The Mystery at Mt. Fuji: Tokyo, Japan. 2009. (Around the World in 80 Mysteries Ser.). 131p. (J). 18.99 *(978-0-635-07016-6(2)*, Marsh, Carole Mysteries) Gallopade International.

Matsumoto, Reiko Odate. The Princess with the Magic Bowl: As retold from the Japanese folk tale By. 2008. 48p. pap. 22.49 *(978-1-4389-1225-7(0))* AuthorHouse.

Matsuno, Masako. A Pair of Red Clogs. Mizumura, Kazue, illus. 2019. (ENG.). 32p. (J). (gr. k-3). pap. 13.95 *(978-1-948959-06-3(2))* Purple Hse. Pr.

Mayer, Mercer. Shibumi & the Kitemaker, 1 vol. 2003. (ENG., Illus.). 32p. (J). (gr. -1-3). pap. 5.95 *(978-0-7614-5145-7(5))* Marshall Cavendish Corp.

McCune, D. J. Fault Lines. 2016. (Death & Co Ser.: 3). (ENG.). 352p. (YA). (gr. 8). pap. 11.99 *(978-1-4714-0271-5(1))* Bonnier Publishing GBR. Dist: Independent Pubs. Group.

Meshon, Aaron. Take Me Out to the Yakyu. Meshon, Aaron, illus. 2013. (ENG., Illus.). 40p. (J). (gr. -1-3). 19.99 *(978-1-4424-4177-4(1)*, Atheneum Bks. for Young Readers) Simon & Schuster Children's Publishing.

Moore, Sandra. The Peace Tree from Hiroshima: The Little Bonsai with a Big Story. Wilds, Kazumi, illus. 2015. 32p. (J). (gr. 2-6). 14.95 *(978-4-8053-1347-3(1))* Tuttle Publishing.

Myers, Tim. The Outfoxed Fox: Based on a Japanese Kyogen, 0 vols. Pang, Ariel, illus. 2013. (ENG.). 32p. (J). (gr. k-3). pap. 9.99 *(978-1-4778-1681-3(X)*, 9781477816813, Two Lions) Amazon Publishing.

Namioka, Lensey. Valley of the Broken Cherry Trees. 2005. (ENG.). 1p. pap. 7.95 *(978-0-8048-3610-4(8))* Tuttle Publishing.

Narita, Ryohgo. Durarara!!, Vol. 5 (light Novel) 2016. (Durarara!! (novel) Ser.: 5). (ENG., Illus.). 192p. (gr. 8-17). pap. 14.00 *(978-0-316-30479-5(4)*, Yen Pr.) Yen Pr. LLC.

—Durarara!!, Vol. 7 (light Novel) 2017. (Durarara!! (novel) Ser.: 7). (ENG., Illus.). 224p. (gr. 8-17). pap. 14.00 *(978-0-316-43968-8(1)*, Yen Pr.) Yen Pr. LLC.

Nelson, Carmen R. Jacob & Katie in Japan: The Adventures of Tcks in a New Home. 2013. 26p. pap. 13.95 *(978-1-935986-38-6(4))* Liberty University Press.

Newman, Leslea. Hachiko Waits: Based on a True Story. Kodaira, Machiyo, illus. 2008. (ENG.). 96p. (J). (gr. 3-5). pap. 8.99 *(978-0-312-55806-2(6)*, 900057661) Square Fish.

Nomura, Mizuki. Book Girl & the Captive Fool (light Novel), Volume 3. 2011. (Book Girl Ser.: 3). (ENG., Illus.). 248p. (YA). (gr. 8-17). pap. 13.00 *(978-0-316-07693-7(7)*, Yen Pr.) Yen Pr. LLC.

—Book Girl & the Corrupted Angel (light Novel), Volume 4. 2012. (Book Girl Ser.: 4). (ENG., Illus.). 248p. (YA). (gr. 8-17). pap. 13.00 *(978-0-316-07694-4(5)*, Yen Pr.) Yen Pr. LLC.

—Book Girl & the Suicidal Mime (light Novel), Volume 1. 2010. (Book Girl Ser.: 1). (ENG., Illus.). 200p. (YA). (gr. 8-17). pap. 13.00 *(978-0-316-07690-6(2)*, Yen Pr.) Yen Pr. LLC.

Ohnogi, Hiroshi. Rahxephon, Vol. 4. 2006. (RahXephon (Dr Masterbook) Ser.). (ENG., Illus.). 200p. (YA). pap. 7.95 *(978-1-59796-003-8(9))* DrMaster Pubns. Inc.

—Rahxephon, Vol. 5. 2006. (RahXephon (Dr Masterbook) Ser.). (ENG., Illus.). 200p. (YA). pap. 7.95 *(978-1-59796-004-5(7))* DrMaster Pubns. Inc.

Ohtaka, Shinobu, creator. Sumomomo, Momomo, Vol. 12: The Strongest Bride on Earth, 12 vols. 2012. (Sumomomo, Momomo Ser.: 12). (ENG., Illus.). 240p. (gr. 11-17). pap. 13.00 *(978-0-316-20470-5(6))* Yen Pr. LLC.

Okei-san: The Girl from Wakamatsu. 2006. (J). pap. 11.95 *(978-0-9642112-8-5(9))* Barsotti Bks.

Orsak, Lane Rockford. Keiko the Fairy, the Kujiki. 2010. (ENG.). 192p. pap. 14.95 *(978-0-557-47206-2(7))* Lulu Pr., Inc.

Osborne, Mary Pope. Dragon of the Red Dawn. Murdocca, Sal, illus. 2008. (Magic Tree House (R) Merlin Mission Ser.: 9). 144p. (J). (gr. 2-5). 6.99 *(978-0-375-83728-9(0)*, Random Hse. Bks. for Young Readers) Random Hse. Children's Bks.

—La Noche de Los Ninjas. 2004. (Casa del Arbol Ser.: 5).Tr. of Night of the Ninjas. (SPA., Illus.). (J). pap. 6.99 *(978-1-930332-66-9(1))* Lectorum Pubns., Inc.

Osborne, Mary Pope, et al. El Dragon Del Amanecer Rojo. Murdocca, Sal, illus. 2018. (SPA.). 132p. (J). (gr. 2-4). pap. 6.99 *(978-1-63245-680-9(X))* Lectorum Pubns., Inc.

Otey Little, Mimi. Yoshiko & the Foreigner. Otey Little, Mimi, illus. 2004. (Illus.). 31p. (J). (gr. 4-8). reprint ed. 16.00 *(978-0-7567-7510-0(8))* DIANE Publishing Co.

Ozaki, Yei. Warriors of Old Japan. 2007. 168p. per. 14.95 *(978-1-59654-553-3(4))* Disruptive Publishing.

Parenteau, Shirley. Dolls of Hope. (Friendship Dolls Ser.). (ENG.). 336p. (J). (gr. 3-7). 2018. pap. 9.99 *(978-1-5362-0026-3(3))* 2015. 16.99 *(978-0-7636-7752-7(3))* Candlewick Pr.

—Dolls of War. (Friendship Dolls Ser.: 3). 320p. (J). (gr. 3-7). 2019. (ENG.). pap. 7.99 *(978-1-5362-0889-4(2))* 2017. 16.99 *(978-0-7636-9069-4(4))* Candlewick Pr.

Paterson, Katherine. The Master Puppeteer. 3rd ed. (J). pap. 3.95 *(978-0-13-800095-0(6))* Prentice Hall (Schl. Div.).

—El Signo del Crisantemo. 2003.Tr. of Sign of the Chrysanthemum. (SPA., Illus.). 142p. (YA). (gr. 5-8). *(978-84-348-6699-7(4)*, SM30544) SM Ediciones ESP. Dist: Lectorum Pubns., Inc.

Pearce, Jacqueline. L' effet Manga, 1 vol. 2010. (Orca Currents en Français Ser.). (FRE.). 136p. (J). (gr. 4-7). pap. 9.95 *(978-1-55469-379-5(9))* Orca Bk. Pubs. USA.

—Manga Touch, 1 vol. 2007. (Orca Currents Ser.). (ENG.). 105p. (J). (gr. 6-8). lib. bdg. 26.19 *(978-1-55143-748-4(1))* Orca Bk. Pubs. USA.

Perkins, Lucy Fitch. The Japanese Twins. 2005. 26.95 *(978-1-4218-0369-2(0)*, 1st World Library - Literary Society) 1st World Publishing, Inc.

—The Japanese Twins. 2004. reprint ed. pap. 15.95 *(978-1-4191-6781-2(2))*; pap. 1.99 *(978-1-4192-6781-9(7))* Kessinger Publishing, LLC.

—The Japanese Twins (Yesterday's Classics) 2006. (J). per. 9.95 *(978-1-59915-058-1(1))* Yesterday's Classics.

Preus, Margi. The Bamboo Sword. (ENG., Illus.). (J). (gr. 5-9). 2016. 368p. pap. 9.99 *(978-1-4197-0824-4(4)*, 1007403) 2015. 335p. 16.95 *(978-1-4197-0807-7(4)*, 1007401) Abrams, Inc. (Amulet Bks.).

—Heart of a Samurai. 2012. (ENG.). 336p. (YA). (gr. 3-7). pap. 9.99 *(978-1-4197-0200-6(9)*, 669703, Amulet Bks.) Abrams, Inc.

—Heart of a Samurai. 2011. (CHI.). (J). (gr. 4-8). pap. *(978-986-216-843-1(9))* Commonwealth Publishing Co., Ltd.

—Heart of a Samurai, 5 vols. (YA). 77.75 *(978-1-4618-0507-6(4))*; 77.75 *(978-1-4618-0343-0(8))*; 2011. 1.25 *(978-1-4618-4275-0(1))*; 2011. 79.75 *(978-1-4618-0358-4(6))* Recorded Bks., Inc.

—Heart of a Samurai. 2012. (J). lib. bdg. 19.60 *(978-0-606-38363-9(8))* Turtleback.

Puccini, Giacomo. Madame Butterfly. Fucíková, Renata, illus. 2005. (ENG.). 40p. (Orig.). (J). 15.95 *(978-1-933327-04-4(9))* Purple Bear Bks., Inc.

Reibstein, Mark. Wabi Sabi. Young, Ed, illus. 2008. (ENG.). 40p. (J). (gr. -1-3). 19.99 *(978-0-316-11825-5(7))* Little, Brown Bks. for Young Readers.

—Wabi Sabi. 2009. (J). 37.75 *(978-1-4407-1924-0(1))*; 37.75 *(978-1-4407-1920-2(9))*; 192.75 *(978-1-4407-1919-6(5))*; 39.75 *(978-1-4407-1922-6(5))*; 1.25 *(978-1-4407-1925-7(X))*; 39.75 *(978-1-4407-1918-9(7))* Recorded Bks., Inc.

Renn, Diana. Tokyo Heist. 2013. (ENG.). 384p. (YA). (gr. 7). pap. 8.99 *(978-0-14-242654-8(7)*, Speak) Penguin Young Readers Group.

Revoy, Antoine. Animus. 2018. (ENG., Illus.). 224p. (YA). pap. 16.99 *(978-1-62672-183-8(1)*, 900143706, First Second Bks.) Roaring Brook Pr.

Ripley's Believe It Or Not! Ripley's Bureau of Investigation 2: Dragon's Triangle. 2010. (Rbi Ser.: 2). (ENG.). 128p. (J). pap. 4.99 *(978-1-893951-53-2(7))* Ripley Entertainment, Inc.

Roberts, Deborah. Mr Otagiri's Promise. Ju-Young Im, Joy & Da-Young Im, Linda, illus. 2012. 40p. pap. *(978-1-77067-719-7(4))* FriesenPress.

Rohan, Jason. The Sword of Kuromori. 2017. 315p. (J). pap. 6.99 *(978-1-61067-355-6(7))* Kane Miller.

Roman, Javier. Adventures of Tinturu & Kumachan the M. 2007. (Illus.). 48p. pap. 16.95 *(978-1-4241-1626-3(0))* PublishAmerica, Inc.

Rooks, Elizabeth. Where Does Santa Go on Vacation after Christmas? 2012. 24p. pap. 17.99 *(978-1-4772-6535-2(X))* AuthorHouse.

Saijyo, Shinji. Iron Wok Jan!, 27 vols. 2005. (ENG., Illus.). (YA). 2nd ed. 190p. pap. 9.95 *(978-1-58899-256-7(X))* Vol. 5. 200p. pap. 9.95 *(978-1-58899-260-4(8))* ComicsOne Corp./Dr. Masters.

Say, Allen. Grandfather's Journey. 2008. (ENG.). 32p. (J). (gr. -1-3). pap. 7.99 *(978-0-547-14178-7(5)*, Sandpiper) Houghton Mifflin Harcourt Trade & Reference Pubs.

—Grandfather's Journey. 2011. (J). (gr. k-5). 18.95 *(978-0-545-12708-0(4))*; 29.95 *(978-0-545-10696-2(6))* Weston Woods Studios, Inc.

—Grandfather's Journey: A Caldecott Award Winner. Say, Allen, illus. 2008. (ENG., Illus.). 32p. (J). (gr. -1-3). 7.99 *(978-0-547-07680-5(0)*, 1042044, Clarion Bks.) HarperCollins Pubs.

—Grandfather's Journey 20th Anniversary: A Caldecott Award Winner. Say, Allen, illus. 20th anniv. ed. 2013. (ENG., Illus.). 32p. (J). (gr. -1-3). 18.99 *(978-0-544-05050-1(9)*, 1532595, Clarion Bks.) HarperCollins Pubs.

—The Ink-Keeper's Apprentice. 2006. 149p. (YA). 14.60 *(978-0-7569-6811-3(9))* Perfection Learning Corp.

—Kamishibai Man. 2005. (ENG., Illus.). 32p. (J). (gr. -1-3). 17.99 *(978-0-618-47954-2(6)*, 598441, Clarion Bks.) HarperCollins Pubs.

—Tea with Milk. 2009. (ENG., Illus.). 32p. (J). (gr. -1-3). pap. 7.99 *(978-0-547-23747-3(2)*, 1083741, Clarion Bks.) HarperCollins Pubs.

—Tree of Cranes: A Christmas Holiday Book for Kids. 2009. (ENG., Illus.). 32p. (J). (gr. -1-3). pap. 7.99 *(978-0-547-24830-1(X)*, 1100745, Clarion Bks.) HarperCollins Pubs.

Scieszka, Jon. Sam Samurai. McCauley, Adam, illus. 2006. (Time Warp Trio Ser.: No. 10). 85p. (gr. 4-7). 15.00 *(978-0-7569-6779-6(1))* Perfection Learning Corp.

—Sam Samurai #10. McCauley, Adam, illus. 2004. (Time Warp Trio Ser.: 10). 96p. (J). (gr. 2-4). pap. 5.99 *(978-0-14-240088-3(2)*, Puffin Books) Penguin Young Readers Group.

See, Jonny. On the Walk Trail - Japan. 2011. 32p. pap. 18.65 *(978-1-4568-9463-4(3))* Xlibris Corp.

Seki, Sunny. The Last Kappa of Old Japan Bilingual English & Japanese Edition: A Magical Journey of Two Friends (English-Japanese) Seki, Sunny, illus. rev. ed. 2016. (Illus.). 32p. (J). (gr. k-8). 12.95 *(978-4-8053-1399-2(4))* Tuttle Publishing.

—The Tale of the Lucky Cat. Seki, Sunny, illus. 2008. (ENG & SPA., Illus.). 32p. (J). 18.95 *(978-0-9669437-9-5(1))* East West Discovery Pr.

—Yuko-Chan & the Daruma Doll: The Adventures of a Blind Japanese Girl Who Saves Her Village - Bilingual English & Japanese Text. 2012. (Illus.). 32p. (J). (gr. -1-3). 15.95 *(978-4-8053-1187-5(8))* Tuttle Publishing.

Seki, Sunny, illus. & retold by. The Tale of the Lucky Cat. Seki, Sunny, retold by. 2008. 32p. (J). *(978-0-9669437-6-4(7))* East West Discovery Pr.

Sento, Atelier, et al. Onibi: Diary of a Yokai Ghost Hunter. Velde, Marie, tr. 2018. (Illus.). 128p. (gr. 6-12). pap. 14.99 *(978-4-8053-1496-8(6))* Tuttle Publishing.

Seven, John. The Terror of the Tengu, 1 vol. Hans, Stephanie, illus. 2014. (Time-Tripping Faradays Ser.). (ENG.). 192p. (J). (gr. 4-8). 26.65 *(978-1-4342-9173-8(1)*, 125643, Stone Arch Bks.) Capstone.

Shakespeare, William. Manga Shakespeare: Romeo & Juliet. Leong, Sonia, illus. 2007. (ENG.). 208p. (J). (gr. 2-8). pap. 16.99 *(978-0-8109-9325-9(2)*, Abrams Bks. for Young Readers) Abrams, Inc.

Shaw, Carol Anne. Hannah & the Wild Woods. 2015. (ENG.). 240p. pap. 11.95 *(978-1-55380-440-6(6))* Ronsdale Pr. CAN. Dist: SPD-Small Pr. Distribution.

Smale, Holly. Geek Girl: Model Misfit. 2016. (Geek Girl Ser.: 2). (ENG.). 416p. (YA). (gr. 8). pap. 11.99 *(978-0-06-233361-2(5)*, HarperTeen) HarperCollins Pubs.

Smith, Lindsay. A Darkly Beating Heart. 2016. (ENG.). 272p. (YA). 34.99 *(978-1-62672-044-2(4)*, 900132964) Roaring Brook Pr.

So-Un, Kim. The Tigers of the Kumgang Mountains: A Korean Folktale. Kyoung-Sim, Jeong, illus. 2005. (ENG.). 1p. (J). (gr. 4-11). 16.95 *(978-0-8048-3653-1(1))* Tuttle Publishing.

Sorachi, Hideaki. Gin Tama, Vol. 4. (JPN., Illus.). 186p. (YA). pap. *(978-4-08-873672-3(9))* Shuei-Sha.

Stilton, Geronimo. Geronimo Stilton Graphic Novels #12: The First Samurai, Vol. 12. 2013. (Geronimo Stilton Graphic Novels Ser.: 12). (ENG., Illus.). 56p. (J). (gr. 2-6). 9.99 *(978-1-59707-385-1(7)*, 900117449, Papercutz) Mad Cave Studios.

Stilton, Gerónimo. The Way of the Samurai. 2012. (Geronimo Stilton Ser.: 49). lib. bdg. 18.40 *(978-0-606-26094-7(3))* Turtleback.

Stokes, Katherine. Motor Maids in Fair Japan. 2006. pap. *(978-1-4068-3090-3(9))* Echo Library.

Stutzman, D. J. The Promise Ring. 2007. (J). pap. 9.00 *(978-0-8059-7365-5(6))* Dorrance Publishing Co., Inc.

Sun, Amanda. Ink. 2013. (Paper Gods Ser.: 2). (ENG., Illus.). 384p. (YA). pap. 9.99 *(978-0-373-21071-8(X)*, Harlequin Teen) Harlequin Enterprises ULC CAN. Dist: HarperCollins Pubs.

—Storm. 2015. (Paper Gods Ser.: 5). (ENG.). 304p. (YA). pap. 9.99 *(978-0-373-21174-6(0)*, Harlequin Teen) Harlequin Enterprises ULC CAN. Dist: HarperCollins Pubs.

Sylvester, Kevin. Neil Flambé & the Tokyo Treasure. Sylvester, Kevin, illus. 2014. (Neil Flambe Capers Ser.: 4). (ENG., Illus.). 368p. (J). (gr. 3-7). pap. 8.99 *(978-1-4424-4289-4(1)*, Simon & Schuster Bks. For Young Readers) Simon & Schuster Bks. For Young Readers.

Takahashi, Rumiko. Inuyasha Ani-Manga, Vol. 15, Vol. 15. 2006. (Inuyasha Ani-Manga Ser.: 15). (ENG., Illus.). 216p. pap. 11.99 *(978-1-4215-0482-7(0))* Viz Media.

—Inuyasha Ani-Manga, Vol. 20, Vol. 20. 2007. (Inuyasha Ani-Manga Ser.: 20). (ENG., Illus.). 216p. pap. 11.99 *(978-1-4215-0904-4(0))* Viz Media.

Tamura, Mitsuhisa. BakéGyamon, Vol. 4, Vol. 4. 2009. (Bakégyamon Ser.: 4). (ENG., Illus.). 216p. (J). pap. 7.99 *(978-1-4215-1882-4(1))* Viz Media.

Tanaka, Shelley. Nobody Knows, 1 vol. 2012. (ENG., Illus.). 144p. (J). (gr. 4-5). 16.95 *(978-1-55498-140-3(9))* Groundwood Bks. CAN. Dist: Publishers Group West (PGW).

Tanigawa, Nagaru. The Boredom of Haruhi Suzumiya (light Novel) 2010. (Haruhi Suzumiya Ser.: 3). (ENG., Illus.). 224p. (YA). (gr. 10-17). 24.00 *(978-0-316-03886-7(5)*, Yen Pr.) Yen Pr. LLC.

—The Sigh of Haruhi Suzumiya. 2009. (Haruhi Suzumiya Ser.: Bk. 1). (ENG., Illus.). 208p. (YA). (gr. 10-18). 14.99 *(978-0-316-03881-2(4))* Hachette Bk. Group.

Tarshis, Lauren. I Survived the Japanese Tsunami 2011. Dawson, Scott, illus. 2013. (I Survived Ser.: No. 8). 83p. (J). *(978-0-545-62981-2(0))* Scholastic, Inc.

—I Survived the Japanese Tsunami 2011. 2013. (I Survived Ser.: No. 8). lib. bdg. 14.75 *(978-0-606-32390-1(2))* Turtleback.

—I Survived the Japanese Tsunami, 2011 (I Survived #8) 2013. (I Survived Ser.: 8). (ENG., Illus.). 112p. (J). (gr. 2-5). pap. 5.99 *(978-0-545-45937-2(0)*, Scholastic Paperbacks) Scholastic, Inc.

Terheyden, Jerry, reader. Crow Boy. 2004. (Illus.). (J). (gr. -1-2). 28.95 incl. audio compact disk *(978-1-59112-802-1(1))* Live Oak Media.

Thompson, Holly. Orchards. 2012. 336p. (YA). (gr. 7-12). (ENG.). lib. bdg. 26.19 *(978-0-385-90806-1(7)*, Delacorte Pr.); pap. 10.99 *(978-0-385-73978-8(8)*, Ember) Random Hse. Children's Bks.

Uegaki, Chieri. Ojiichan's Gift. Simms, Genevieve, illus. 2019. (ENG.). 32p. (J). (gr. -1-2). 19.99 *(978-1-77138-963-1(X))* Kids Can Pr., Ltd. CAN. Dist: Hachette Bk. Group.

Vernon, Ursula. Attack of the Ninja Frogs. 2012. (Dragonbreath Ser.: 2). lib. bdg. 17.20 *(978-0-606-26666-6(6))* Turtleback.

—Dragonbreath #2: Attack of the Ninja Frogs. 2nd ed. (Dragonbreath Ser.: 2). 208p. (J). (gr. 3-7). 2012. pap. 8.99 *(978-0-14-242066-9(2)*, Puffin Books) 2010. 14.99 *(978-0-8037-3365-7(8)*, Dial Bks) Penguin Young Readers Group.

Vinesse, Cecilia. Seven Days of You. 2018. (ENG.). 352p. (YA). (gr. 9-17). pap. 10.99 *(978-0-316-39110-8(7)*, Poppy) Little, Brown Bks. for Young Readers.

Watkins, Yoko Kawashima. So Far from the Bamboo Grove. 2008. (ENG., Illus.). 192p. (J). (gr. 3-7). reprint ed. pap. 9.99 *(978-0-688-13115-9(8)*, HarperCollins) HarperCollins Pubs.

Watson, Mary. The Paper Dragonfly. Watson, Mary, illus. 2007. (ENG., Illus.). 32p. (J). (gr. k-3). 15.95 *(978-0-9726614-3-0(3))* Shenanigan Bks.

Welles, Lee. Gaia Girls Way of Water. Coogan, Carol, illus. 2007. (Gaia Girls Ser.: 2). (ENG.). 336p. (YA). (gr. 4-7). pap. 24.95 *(978-1-933609-03-4(6))* Chelsea Green Publishing.

Wells, Rosemary. Yoko Finds Her Way. 2014. (Yoko Book Ser.). (ENG.). 32p. (J). (gr. -1-3). 16.99 *(978-1-4231-6512-5(8))* Little, Brown Bks. for Young Readers.

Weston Woods Staff, creator. Grandfather's Journey. 2011. 38.75 *(978-0-545-12710-3(6))* Weston Woods Studios, Inc.

Whelan, Gloria. Yuki & the One Thousand Carriers. Nascimbene, Yan, illus. 2008. (Tales of the World Ser.). (ENG.). 40p. (J). (gr. 1-4). 17.95 *(978-1-58536-352-0(9)*, 202139) Sleeping Bear Pr.

Williams, Jan. An Amazing Storytelling Cat. Peecock, Simon & McKissock, Charmaine, illus. 2013. 120p. pap. *(978-0-9568148-6-9(7))* Swift Publishing.

Wynne-Jones, Tim. The Emperor of Any Place. 2015. 336p. (YA). (gr. 9). 17.99 *(978-0-7636-6973-7(3))* Candlewick Pr.

Yashima, Taro. Crow Boy. Yashima, Taro, illus. 2004. (Illus.). 34p. (J). (gr. k-3). reprint ed. pap. 14.00 *(978-0-7567-7102-7(1))* DIANE Publishing Co.

—Crow Boy. Yashima, Taro, illus. (Illus.). pap. 35.95 incl. audio compact disk *(978-1-59112-803-8(X))* Live Oak Media.

Yoshikawa, Sachiko, illus. The Boy from the Dragon Palace: A Folktale from Japan. 2012. (J). *(978-1-61913-110-1(2))* Weigl Pubs., Inc.

JAPAN—FOREIGN RELATIONS—UNITED STATES

Blumberg, Rhoda. Commodore Perry in the Land of the Shogun. 2003. (Illus.). 144p. (gr. 3-7). 20.00 *(978-0-7569-1440-0(X))* Perfection Learning Corp.

—Commodore Perry in the Land of the Shogun: A Newbery Honor Award Winner. 2003. (ENG., Illus.). 144p. (J). (gr. 3-18). pap. 9.99 *(978-0-06-008625-1(4)*, HarperCollins) HarperCollins Pubs.

Burgan, Michael. The Attack on Pearl Harbor: U. S. Entry into World War II, 1 vol. 2012. (Perspectives On Ser.). (ENG., Illus.). 112p. (YA). (gr. 8-8). 42.64 *(978-1-60870-448-4(3)*, 8295e9d5-7add-4634-94de-b5f45c295476) Cavendish Square Publishing LLC.

Dougherty, Steve. Attack on Pearl Harbor: World War II Strikes Home in the USA. 2011. (J). pap. *(978-0-545-32930-9(2))* Scholastic, Inc.

Edwards, Sue Bradford. Bombing of Pearl Harbor, 1 vol. 2015. (Essential Library of World War II Ser.). (ENG.). 112p. (YA). (gr. 6-12). 41.36 *(978-1-62403-791-7(7)*, 17780, Essential Library) ABDO Publishing Co.

Johnson, Robin. Pearl Harbor. 2014. (Crabtree Chrome Ser.). (ENG., Illus.). 48p. (J). (gr. 2-2). *(978-0-7787-1367-8(9))* Crabtree Publishing Co.

McNeese, Tim. The Perry Expedition & the Opening of Japan. 2012. (J). 35.00 *(978-1-60413-924-2(2)*, Facts On File) Infobase Holdings, Inc.

Ross, Stewart & Woodward, Joe. Pearl Harbor. 2011. (Place in History Ser.). (Illus.). 48p. (YA). (gr. 5-9). lib. bdg. 34.25 *(978-1-84837-676-2(6))* Arcturus Publishing GBR. Dist: Black Rabbit Bks.

Samuels, Charlie. The Attack on Pearl Harbor, 1 vol., Vol. 1. 2013. (Turning Points in U. S. Military History Ser.). (ENG.). 48p. (J). (gr. 5-6). 34.61 *(978-1-4824-0409-8(5)*, 24a85a65-96ca-4173-b00a-66c7a0e08511) Stevens, Gareth Publishing LLLP.

Swanson, Jennifer & Larson, Kirby. Pearl Harbor. McMorris, Kelley, illus. 2018. 106p. (J). *(978-1-5444-0721-0(1))* Scholastic, Inc.

Yomtov, Nel. The Attack on Pearl Harbor: December 7 1941, 1 vol. Campidelli, Maurizio, illus. 2014. (24-Hour History Ser.). (ENG.). 48p. (J). (gr. 3-9). pap. 8.95 *(978-1-4329-9299-6(6)*, 124615); lib. bdg. 33.99 *(978-1-4329-9293-4(7)*, 124610) Capstone. (Heinemann).

Zimmerman, Andrea. Eliza's Cherry Trees: Japan's Gift to America, 1 vol. Chen, Ju-Hong, illus. 2011. (ENG.). 32p. (J). (gr. k-3). 16.99 *(978-1-58980-954-3(8)*, Pelican Publishing) Arcadia Publishing.

JAPAN—HISTORY

Allen, John. Anime & Manga. 2014. (Discovering Art). (ENG., Illus.). 80p. (J). lib. bdg. *(978-1-60152-696-0(2))* ReferencePoint Pr., Inc.

Anderson, Dale. Japanese Americans, 1 vol. 2006. (World Almanac(r) Library of American Immigration Ser.). (ENG., Illus.). 48p. (gr. 5-8). pap. 15.05 *(978-0-8368-7326-9(2)*, c3bed7bf-7f23-46f4-beb0-af9e54a3db86); lib. bdg. 33.67 *(978-0-8368-7313-9(0)*, 2a4e375d-d010-4e4c-89f2-0d3f9baf9185) Stevens, Gareth Publishing LLLP. (Gareth Stevens Secondary Library).

Arato, Rona. Fukushima Nuclear Disaster. 2013. (ENG., Illus.). 32p. (J). *(978-0-7787-1192-6(7))*; pap. *(978-0-7787-1194-0(3))* Crabtree Publishing Co.

Ball, Jacqueline A. Himeji Castle: Japan's Samurai Past. 2005. (Castles, Palaces, & Tombs Ser.). 32p. (J). lib. bdg. 28.50 *(978-1-59716-001-8(6))* Bearport Publishing Co., Inc.

Baxter, Roberta. The Dropping of the Atomic Bombs: A History Perspectives Book. 2014. (Perspectives Library). (ENG., Illus.). 32p. (J). (gr. 4-8). 32.07 *(978-1-62431-665-4(4)*, 203224) Cherry Lake Publishing.

Blumberg, Rhoda. Commodore Perry in the Land of the Shogun. 2003. (Illus.). 144p. (gr. 3-7). 20.00 *(978-0-7569-1440-0(X))* Perfection Learning Corp.

—Commodore Perry in the Land of the Shogun: A Newbery Honor Award Winner. 2003. (ENG., Illus.). 144p. (J). (gr. 3-18). pap. 9.99 *(978-0-06-008625-1(4)*, HarperCollins) HarperCollins Pubs.

—Shipwrecked! The True Adventures of a Japanese Boy. 2003. (ENG., Illus.). 80p. (J). (gr. 3-18). pap. 8.99 *(978-0-688-17485-9(X)*, HarperCollins) HarperCollins Pubs.

Bolte, Mari. Harajuku Style: Fun Fashions You Can Sketch, 1 vol. Hagel, Brooke, illus. 2013. (Drawing Fun Fashions Ser.). (ENG.). 32p. (J). (gr. 3-9). lib. bdg. 28.65 *(978-1-62065-034-9(7)*, 120714) Capstone.

Candlewick Press. Japan: Panorama Pops. Smith, Anne, illus. 2015. (Panorama Pops Ser.). (ENG.). 30p. (J). (gr. k-4). 8.99 *(978-0-7636-7504-2(0))* Candlewick Pr.

Chambers, Catherine. A Shogun's Guide. Pentney, Ryan, illus. 2017. (How-To Guides for Fiendish Rulers Ser.). (ENG.). 32p. (J). (gr. 3-6). 27.99 *(978-1-5124-1552-0(9)*, 756551ce-b244-47e9-b8d7-fc7d29135d09); E-Book 42.65 *(978-1-5124-3629-7(1)*, 9781512436297); E-Book 4.99 *(978-1-5124-3630-3(5)*, 9781512436303) Lerner Publishing Group. (Hungry Tomato (r)).

Chant, Christopher. The End of World War II: The Japanese Surrender. 2017. (World War II Ser.: Vol. 5). (ENG., Illus.). 79p. (YA). (gr. 7-12). 24.95 *(978-1-4222-3898-1(9))* Mason Crest.

Cunningham, Mark E. & Zwier, Lawrence J. The End of the Shoguns & the Birth of Modern Japan. 2009. (Pivotal Moments in History Ser.). (ENG.). 160p. (gr. 9-12). 38.60 *(978-0-8225-8747-7(5))* Lerner Publishing Group.

Daniels-Cowart, Catrina. Japan. 2019. (Asian Countries Today Ser.). (Illus.). 96p. (J). (gr. 12). lib. bdg. 34.60 *(978-1-4222-4266-7(8))* Mason Crest.

Duling, Kaitlyn. The Order to Drop the Atomic Bomb 1945, 1 vol. 2018. (America's Most Important Documents: Inquiry into Historical Sources Ser.). (ENG.). 64p. (gr. 6-6). lib. bdg. 37.36 *(978-1-5026-3619-5(0)*, d7ccedcb-4d67-4f2b-96c2-f5700f00e95b) Cavendish Square Publishing LLC.

Fishman, Jon M. Ninja Weapons. 2020. (Lightning Bolt Books (r) — Ninja Mania Ser.). (ENG., Illus.). 24p. (J). (gr. 1-3). pap. 9.99 *(978-1-5415-8917-9(3)*, 899f3989-2a75-4596-a16d-e9da79f73a36); lib. bdg. 29.32 *(978-1-5415-7708-4(6)*, 7fe4e6e9-d672-47e5-802a-7d1ca9cbdbac) Lerner Publishing Group. (Lerner Pubns.).

—Real-Life Ninja. 2020. (Lightning Bolt Books (r) — Ninja Mania Ser.). (ENG., Illus.). 24p. (J). (gr. 1-3). pap. 9.99 *(978-1-5415-8918-6(1)*, 41eb8370-8018-4d11-86a3-52cdfdd4a47b); lib. bdg. 29.32 *(978-1-5415-7706-0(X)*, acd1fef7-a396-47e3-86cc-eec57033aba1) Lerner Publishing Group. (Lerner Pubns.).

Gagne, Tammy. Japanese Gods, Heroes, & Mythology. 2018. (Gods, Heroes, & Mythology Ser.). (ENG., Illus.). 48p. (J). (gr. 4-8). lib. bdg. 35.64 *(978-1-5321-1784-8(1)*, 30856) ABDO Publishing Co.

Giannotta, Andres Bernardo & Drawing Staff. How to Draw Manga. 2010. (Dover How to Draw Ser.). (ENG., Illus.). 64p. (J). (gr. 3-5). pap. 6.99 *(978-0-486-47662-9(6)*, 476626) Dover Pubns., Inc.

Grant, R. G. Why Did Hiroshima Happen?, 1 vol. 2010. (Moments in History Ser.). (ENG., Illus.). 48p. (YA). (gr. 6-8). pap. 15.05 *(978-1-4339-4164-1(3)*, 4285aa00-25dc-4d29-8457-40bedebcfee9, Gareth Stevens Secondary Library); lib. bdg. 34.60 *(978-1-4339-4163-4(5)*, 2b6ea7b6-a641-4b5e-86c9-252c57d25795) Stevens, Gareth Publishing LLLP.

Green, Sara. Sony. 2016. (Brands We Know Ser.). (ENG., Illus.). 24p. (J). (gr. 3-8). 27.95 *(978-1-62617-412-2(1)*, Pilot Bks.) Bellwether Media.

Hale, Nathan. Raid of No Return (Nathan Hale's Hazardous Tales #7) A World War II Tale of the Doolittle Raid. 2017. (Nathan Hale's Hazardous Tales Ser.). (ENG., Illus.). 128p. (J). (gr. 3-7). 14.99 *(978-1-4197-2556-2(4)*, 1128101) Abrams, Inc.

Heppermann, Christine. Samurai. 2013. (Great Warriors Ser.). (ENG., Illus.). 48p. (J). (gr. 4-8). pap. 18.50 *(978-1-61783-777-7(6)*, 10809) ABDO Publishing Co.

Idee, Ari. Delicious Japan by Month. 2013. 40p. pap. 9.49 *(978-0-9798991-1-9(7))* Technology & Imagination Pr.

Jones, Richard & Santillan, Jorge. Manga Animals, 1 vol. 2012. (Learn to Draw Manga Ser.). (ENG., Illus.). 32p. (J). (gr. 4-5). pap. 12.75 *(978-1-4488-7943-4(4)*, ac950444-7abd-4fae-8973-451cbad890d5); lib. bdg. 30.27 *(978-1-4488-7872-7(1)*, f16f71cf-5d1b-4852-8dd2-c26bc2988824) Rosen Publishing Group, Inc., The. (PowerKids Pr.).

—Manga Dragons, 1 vol. 2012. (Learn to Draw Manga Ser.). (ENG., Illus.). 32p. (J). (gr. 4-5). pap. 12.75 *(978-1-4488-7945-8(0)*, bc4bcadf-e3d3-4d37-ac5e-4f21aadcf43f); lib. bdg. 30.27 *(978-1-4488-7874-1(8)*, a285dd41-f414-45cb-80bd-981fbb1315ca) Rosen Publishing Group, Inc., The. (PowerKids Pr.).

—Manga Martial Arts Figures, 1 vol. 2012. (Learn to Draw Manga Ser.). (ENG., Illus.). 32p. (J). (gr. 4-5). pap. 12.75 *(978-1-4488-7946-5(9)*, 5aeedcb5-393e-47d3-a1f7-55539121b638); lib. bdg. 30.27 *(978-1-4488-7875-8(6)*, 9ba79e5c-5e1a-4957-9767-eefa83373931) Rosen Publishing Group, Inc., The. (PowerKids Pr.).

—Manga Superheroes, 1 vol. 2012. (Learn to Draw Manga Ser.). (ENG., Illus.). 32p. (J). (gr. 4-5). pap. 12.75 *(978-1-4488-7948-9(5)*, 278ab01e-bee6-42fa-932a-35d667dabd24); lib. bdg. 30.27 *(978-1-4488-7877-2(2)*, 303b4179-5d3c-4c7f-be11-5f2282130936) Rosen Publishing Group, Inc., The. (PowerKids Pr.).

Kalman, Bobbie. Spotlight on Japan. 2010. (Spotlight on My Country Ser.). (ENG.). 32p. (J). (gr. 2-5). pap. *(978-0-7787-3485-7(4))* Crabtree Publishing Co.

Macdonald, Fiona. Ancient Japan: Step Back to the Time of Shoguns & Samurai, with 15 Step-by-Step Projects & over 330 Exciting Pictures. 2014. (Illus.). 64p. (J). (gr. k-8). pap. 12.99 *(978-1-84322-824-0(6)*, Armadillo) Anness Publishing GBR. Dist: National Bk. Network.

McDowell, Pamela. Japan. 2016. (Illus.). 32p. (J). *(978-1-5105-1903-9(3))* SmartBook Media, Inc.

—Japan. 2014. (J). *(978-1-4896-1018-8(9))* Weigl Pubs., Inc.

McLeese, Don. Samurai. 2009. 32p. pap. 7.99 *(978-0-8249-1444-8(9)*, Ideals Pubns.) Worthy Publishing.

McManus, Lori. Meet Our New Student from Japan. 2009. (Meet Our New Student Ser.). 48p. (J). (gr. 2-5). 29.95 *(978-1-58415-780-9(1))* Mitchell Lane Pubs.

Miller, Karen, ed. Japan, 1 vol. 2009. (Opposing Viewpoints Ser.). (ENG., Illus.). 208p. (gr. 10-12). 50.43 *(978-0-7377-4372-2(7)*, 2b24be5e-38a1-4937-81a9-40bea0e809b8, Greenhaven Publishing) Greenhaven Publishing LLC.

—Japan, 1 vol. 2009. (Opposing Viewpoints Ser.). (ENG., Illus.). 208p. (gr. 10-12). pap. 34.80 *(978-0-7377-4371-5(9)*, 221fbb4c-2418-4574-b4f4-493380640149, Greenhaven Publishing) Greenhaven Publishing LLC.

Miocevich, Grant. Investigating Japan: Prehistory to Postwar. Cheng & Tsui, ed. 2005. (Illus.). 84p. (YA). (gr. 10-12). per. 24.99 *(978-0-7339-0163-8(8))* Pearson Education Australia AUS. Dist: Cheng & Tsui Co.

Miyake, Okiko, ed. Miyake: Japan in English Books for Boys & Girls, 1819-1935. 2008. (ENG.). 2700p. (C). 1510.00 *(978-4-86166-061-0(0)*, RU0610) Synapse, Edition JPN. Dist: Taylor & Francis Group.

Murray, Julie. Japan, 1 vol. 2013. (Explore the Countries Ser.). (ENG.). 40p. (J). (gr. 2-5). lib. bdg. 35.64 *(978-1-61783-815-6(2)*, 6935, Big Buddy Bks.) ABDO Publishing Co.

Murrell, Deborah Jane & Dennis, Peter. Samurai. 2012. (ENG., Illus.). 32p. (gr. 3-5). pap. 8.95 *(978-1-926853-55-0(5))* Saunders Bk. Co. CAN. Dist: RiverStream Publishing.

Obiols, Anna. Japan, 1 vol. 2018. (On the Way to School Ser.). (ENG.). 32p. (gr. 3-3). 28.93 *(978-1-5081-9579-5(X)*, 599d2d54-62b1-478b-9465-54e4d73bb9f1); pap. 11.00 *(978-1-5081-9580-1(3)*, 15496eb3-5ea7-45e8-ac18-de045ba37f22) Rosen Publishing Group, Inc., The. (Windmill Bks.).

Olson, Elsie. Samurai! Strong & Steady Warriors. 2017. (History's Hotshots Ser.). (ENG., Illus.). 32p. (J). (gr. 3-6). lib. bdg. 32.79 *(978-1-5321-1274-4(2)*, 27598, Checkerboard Library) ABDO Publishing Co.

Osborne, Mary Pope & Boyce, Natalie Pope. Ninjas & Samurai: A Nonfiction Companion to Magic Tree House #5:

Night of the Ninjas. Murdocca, Sal, illus. 2014. (Magic Tree House (R) Fact Tracker Ser.: 30). 128p. (J). (gr. 2-5). 6.99 (978-0-385-38632-6(X), Random Hse. Bks. for Young Readers) Random Hse. Children's Bks.

Park, Louise & Love, Timothy. Japanese Samurai, 1 vol. 2010. (Ancient & Medieval People Ser.). (ENG.). 32p. (gr. 5-5). 31.21 (978-0-7614-4448-0(3), 1a1a6f84-5d32-4503-9bb2-f91e7d521053) Cavendish Square Publishing LLC.

Parker, Lewis K. Why Japanese Immigrants Came to America. 2009. (Coming to America Ser.). 24p. (gr. 2-3). 42.50 (978-1-61511-886-1(1), PowerKids Pr.) Rosen Publishing Group, Inc., The.

Persano, Thomas. Japan. 2017. (Countries We Come From Ser.). (ENG., Illus.). 32p. (J). (gr. k-3). 19.95 (978-1-68402-253-3(3)) Bearport Publishing Co., Inc.

Redmond, Shirley Raye. Hiroshima. 2009. (J). (978-1-58415-784-7(4)) Mitchell Lane Pubs.

Reynolds, A. M. Let's Look at Japan. 2019. (Let's Look at Countries Ser.). (ENG., Illus.). 24p. (J). (gr. -1-2). lib. bdg. 27.32 (978-1-9771-0384-0(7), 139355, Capstone Pr.) Capstone.

Richardson, Hazel. Life in Ancient Japan. 2005. (Peoples of the Ancient World Ser.). (ENG., Illus.). 32p. (J). (gr. -1-9). pap. (978-0-7787-2071-3(3)) Crabtree Publishing Co.

Riggs, Kate. Samurai. 2011. (Great Warriors Ser.). 24p. (J). (gr. k-2). 16.95 (978-1-60818-003-5(4), Creative Education) Creative Co., The.

Rissman, Rebecca. Swept Away: The Story of the 2011 Japanese Tsunami. 2017. (Tangled History Ser.). (ENG., Illus.). 112p. (J). (gr. 3-9). lib. bdg. 32.65 (978-1-5157-3605-9(9), 133595, Capstone Pr.) Capstone.

Ross, Stewart. Hiroshima. 2011. (Place in History Ser.). 48p. (YA). (gr. 5-9). lib. bdg. 34.25 (978-1-84837-674-8(X)) Arcturus Publishing GBR. Dist: Black Rabbit Bks.

Shelley, Rex. Japan, 1 vol. 3rd rev. ed. 2012. (Cultures of the World (Third Edition)(r) Ser.). (ENG., Illus.). 144p. (J). (gr. 5-5). 48.79 (978-1-60870-784-3(9), 5e9e5dc0-c3e2-4ea3-a06a-573589f798fa) Cavendish Square Publishing LLC.

Smith-Llera, Danielle. Fukushima Disaster: How a Tsunami Unleashed Nuclear Destruction. 2018. (Captured Science History Ser.). (ENG., Illus.). 64p. (J). (gr. 5-9). lib. bdg. 35.32 (978-0-7565-5742-3(9), 137538, Compass Point Bks.) Capstone.

Stelson, Caren. Sachiko: A Nagasaki Bomb Survivor's Story. 2016. (ENG., Illus.). 144p. (J). (gr. 5-12). E-Book 9.99 (978-1-5124-1884-2(6), 9781512418842); E-Book 30.65 (978-1-5124-0893-5(X)); E-Book 30.65 (978-1-5124-1885-9(4), 9781512418859) Lerner Publishing Group. (Carolrhoda Bks.).

Turnbull, Stephen R. The Most Daring Raid of the Samurai, 1 vol. 2011. (Most Daring Raids in History Ser.). (ENG., Illus.). 64p. (YA). (gr. 7-7). lib. bdg. 37.13 (978-1-4488-1872-3(9), b7b3e90d-ba10-464d-925e-df4a877d580b) Rosen Publishing Group, Inc., The.

Waxman, Laura Hamilton. Ninja Competitions. 2020. (Lightning Bolt Books (r) — Ninja Mania Ser.). (ENG., Illus.). 24p. (J). (gr. 1-3). pap. 9.99 (978-1-5415-8916-2(5), 0ad7bc1d-8113-4512-ba60-ff93601bb746); lib. bdg. 29.32 (978-1-5415-7705-3(1), 599eb8cc-4258-4a9b-8059-f648655ed580) Lerner Publishing Group. (Lerner Pubns.).

Whyte, Harlinah & Frank, Nicole. Welcome to Japan, 1 vol. 2011. (Welcome to My Country Ser.). (ENG.). 48p. (gr. 3-3). 31.21 (978-1-60870-156-8(5), 78a1d1fc-67d9-4006-9ebd-5402102f02ab) Cavendish Square Publishing LLC.

Zocchi, Judy. In Japan. Brodie, Neale, illus. 2005. (Global Adventures I Ser.). 32p. (J). pap. 10.95 (978-1-59646-139-0(X)); lib. bdg. 21.65 (978-1-59646-004-1(0)) Dingles & Co.

—In Japan/en Japón. Brodie, Neale, illus. 2005. (Global Adventures I Ser.).Tr. of En Japón. (ENG & SPA.). 32p. (J). pap. 10.95 (978-1-59646-141-3(1)); lib. bdg. 21.65 (978-1-59646-005-8(9)) Dingles & Co.

JAPAN—HISTORY—1868-1945

Bodden, Valerie. The Bombing of Hiroshima & Nagasaki. 2007. (Days of Change Ser.). (Illus.). 48p. (J). (gr. 4-7). lib. bdg. 31.35 (978-1-58341-545-0(9), Creative Education) Creative Co., The.

King, Margaret. World War II in the Pacific. rev. ed. 2019. (Social Studies: Informational Text Ser.). (ENG., Illus.). 32p. (J). (gr. 4-8). pap. 11.99 (978-1-4258-5071-5(5)) Teacher Created Materials, Inc.

JAPAN—SOCIAL LIFE AND CUSTOMS

Bingham, Jane. Costume Around the World: Japan. 2008. (Costume Around the World Ser.). (ENG., Illus.). 32p. (gr. 4-6). 28.00 (978-0-7910-9770-0(6), P459457, Chelsea Clubhse.) Infobase Holdings, Inc.

Brooks, Susie. Japan, 1 vol. 2016. (Land & the People Ser.). (ENG.). 48p. (gr. 5-5). pap. 15.05 (978-1-4824-5103-0(4), c9715751-5988-405f-887f-7c64e0d853bd) Stevens, Gareth Publishing LLLP.

Centore, Michael. Japan, Vol. 12. 2015. (Major Nations in a Global World: Tradition, Culture, & Daily Life Ser.). (Illus.). 64p. (J). (gr. 7). 23.95 (978-1-4222-3347-4(2)) Mason Crest.

Chambers, Catherine. A Shogun's Guide. Pentney, Ryan, illus. 2017. (How-To Guides for Fiendish Rulers Ser.). (ENG.). 32p. (J). (gr. 3-6). 27.99 (978-1-5124-1552-0(9), 756551ce-b244-47e9-b8d7-fc7d29135d09); E-Book 42.65 (978-1-5124-3629-7(1), 9781512436297); E-Book 4.99 (978-1-5124-3630-3(5), 9781512436303) Lerner Publishing Group. (Hungry Tomato (r)).

Coleman, Miriam. The Culture & Crafts of Japan, 1 vol. 2015. (Cultural Crafts Ser.). (ENG., Illus.). 32p. (J). (gr. 4-6). pap. 12.75 (978-1-4994-1125-6(1), 20353ce2-1a1a-4c35-9a0e-d61576c86f31, PowerKids Pr.) Rosen Publishing Group, Inc., The.

Idee, Ari. Delicious Japan by Month. 2013. 40p. pap. 9.49 (978-0-9798991-1-9(7)) Technology & Imagination Pr.

Kalman, Bobbie. Japan: The Culture, 1 vol. 3rd rev. ed. 2008. (ENG., Illus.). 32p. (J). (gr. 3-9). pap. (978-0-7787-9666-4(3)) Crabtree Publishing Co.

—Japan: The People. 3rd rev. ed. 2008. (Lands, Peoples, & Cultures Ser.). (ENG., Illus.). 32p. (J). (gr. 3-9). lib. bdg. (978-0-7787-9297-0(8)) Crabtree Publishing Co.

—Japan - The People, 1 vol. 3rd rev. ed. 2008. (Lands, Peoples, & Cultures Ser.). (ENG., Illus.). 32p. (J). (gr. 3-9). pap. (978-0-7787-9665-7(5)) Crabtree Publishing Co.

McKay, Susan. Festivals of the World: Japan, 1 vol. 2011. (Festivals of the World Ser.). (ENG.). 32p. (gr. 4-4). 31.21 (978-1-60870-103-2(4), d83a1bbb-ad49-40c7-930f-2c8585ee5a97) Cavendish Square Publishing LLC.

Moore, Willamarie. All about Japan: Stories, Songs, Crafts & Games for Kids. Wilds, Kazumi, illus. 2017. 64p. (J). (gr. 3-6). 14.95 (978-4-8053-1440-1(0)) Tuttle Publishing.

Nakaya, Andrea C. Growin up in Japan. 2017. (ENG., Illus.). 80p. (J). (gr. 5-12). (978-1-68282-219-7(2)) ReferencePoint Pr., Inc.

National Geographic Learning. Reading Expeditions (Social Studies: Civilizations Past to Present): Japan. 2007. (ENG., Illus.). 24p. (J). pap. 15.95 (978-0-7922-4540-7(7)) CENGAGE Learning.

Otowa, Rebecca. My Awesome Japan Adventure: A Diary about the Best 4 Months Ever! 2013. (Illus.). 48p. (J). (gr. 2-6). 14.95 (978-4-8053-1216-2(5)) Tuttle Publishing.

Peppas, Lynn. Cultural Traditions in Japan, 1 vol. 2012. (ENG.). 32p. (J). pap. (978-0-7787-7593-5(3)); lib. bdg. (978-0-7787-7586-7(0)) Crabtree Publishing Co.

Reynolds, Betty. Tokyo Friends. 2nd rev. ed. 2012. (Illus.). 64p. (J). (gr. 1-3). 14.95 (978-4-8053-1075-5(8)) Tuttle Publishing.

Rich, Mari. My Teenage Life in Japan. 2017. (Customs & Cultures of the World Ser.). (ENG., Illus.). 64p. (J). (gr 7-12). 23.95 (978-1-4222-3906-3(3)) Mason Crest.

Rolbin, Cyrus. Art & Life in Rural Japan: Toho Village Throught the Eyes of Its Youth. 2011. 176p. (J). (gr. 3-6). pap. 24.95 (978-0-9815595-3-7(0)) Next Generation Pr.

Sato, Shozo. Tea Ceremony: Explore the Unique Japanese Tradition of Sharing Tea. 2017. (Asian Arts & Crafts for Creative Kids Ser.). (ENG., Illus.). 64p. (J). (gr. 2-6). 9.95 (978-0-8048-4988-3(9)) Tuttle Publishing.

Sexton, Colleen. Japan. 2010. (Exploring Countries Ser.). (ENG., Illus.). 32p. (J). (gr. 3-7). lib. bdg. 27.95 (978-1-60014-486-8(1), Blastoff! Readers) Bellwether Media.

Sexton, Colleen A. Japan. 2011. (ENG., Illus.). 32p. (J). (978-0-531-26467-6(X), Blastoff! Readers) Bellwether Media.

Takabayashi, Mari. I Live in Tokyo. 2004. (ENG., Illus.). 32p. (J). (gr. -1-3). reprint ed. pap. 7.99 (978-0-618-49484-2(7), 490015, Clarion Bks.) HarperCollins Pubs.

Teacher Created Resources Staff. Japan: Come on a Journey of Discovery. 2008. (Qeb Travel Through Ser.). (ENG., Illus.). 32p. (gr. 4-7). pap. 7.99 (978-1-4206-8284-7(9)) Teacher Created Resources, Inc.

Temko, Florence. Traditional Crafts from Japan. Gooch, Randall, illus. 2005. (Culture Crafts Ser.). 64p. (gr. 3-8). 23.93 (978-0-8225-2938-5(6)) Lerner Publishing Group.

West, Patricia. East Meets West: Japan & America. 2005. (ENG., Illus.). 12p. (J). (gr. 3-3). pap. 5.97 net. (978-0-328-13382-6(5), Scott Foresman) Savvas Learning Co.

Zocchi, Judy. In Japan. Brodie, Neale, illus. 2005. (Global Adventures I Ser.). 32p. (J). pap. 10.95 (978-1-59646-139-0(X)); lib. bdg. 21.65 (978-1-59646-004-1(0)) Dingles & Co.

—In Japan/en Japón. Brodie, Neale, illus. 2005. (Global Adventures I Ser.).Tr. of En Japón. (ENG & SPA.). 32p. (J). lib. bdg. 21.65 (978-1-59646-005-8(9)) Dingles & Co.

JAPANESE—UNITED STATES

Aihara, Chris. Nikkei Donburi: A Japanese American Cultural Survival Guide. Iwasaki, Glen, illus. 2004. 124p. (J). (gr. 1-4). pap. 18.95 (978-1-879965-18-8(6)) Polychrome Publishing Corp.

Burgan, Michael. Japanese American Internment. 2017. (Eyewitness to World War II Ser.). (ENG., Illus.). 112p. (J). (gr. 5-9). lib. bdg. 38.65 (978-0-7565-5581-8(7), 135466, Compass Point Bks.) Capstone.

Heinrichs, Ann. The Japanese American Internment: Innocence, Guilt, & Wartime Justice, 1 vol. 2011. (Perspectives On Ser.). (ENG., Illus.). 112p. (J). (gr. 8-8). 42.64 (978-0-7614-4983-6(3), 134471b9-944f-4a56-99ea-d911466205eb) Cavendish Square Publishing LLC.

JAPANESE—UNITED STATES—FICTION

Berry, Eileen M. Haiku on Your Shoes. Regan, Dana, illus. 2005. 56p. (J). (gr. -1-3). per. 7.49 (978-1-59166-374-4(1)) BJU Pr.

Hathaway, Lucinda Churchman. 'Round the World: Takashi Sails Home. 2008. (Illus.). 135p. (J). 12.95 (978-1-59322-034-1(0)) Down The Shore Publishing.

Okei-san: The Girl from Wakamatsu. 2006. (J). pap. 11.95 (978-0-9642112-8-5(9)) Barsotti Bks.

Preus, Margi. Heart of a Samurai. 2012. (ENG.). 336p. (YA). (gr. 3-7). pap. 9.99 (978-1-4197-0200-6(9), 669703, Amulet Bks.) Abrams, Inc.

—Heart of a Samurai. 2011. (CHI.). (J). (gr. 4-8). pap. (978-986-216-843-1(9)) Commonwealth Publishing Co., Ltd.

—Heart of a Samurai, 5 vols. (YA). 77.75 (978-1-4618-0343-0(8)); 77.75 (978-1-4618-0507-6(4)); 2011. 1.25 (978-1-4618-4275-0(1)); 2011. 79.75 (978-1-4618-0358-4(6)) Recorded Bks., Inc.

—Heart of a Samurai. 2012. (J). lib. bdg. 19.60 (978-0-606-38363-9(8)) Turtleback.

Simmons, Andrew & Averdonz, N. R. I Was an Eighth-Grade Ninja, 1 vol., 1. Padilla, Ariel, illus. 2007. (Z Graphic Novels / Tomo Ser.). (ENG.). 160p. (J). (gr. 3-7). pap. 6.99 (978-0-310-71300-5(5)) Zondervan.

Yashima, Taro. Umbrella. unabr. ed. (J). (gr. k-3). 24.95 incl. audio (978-0-670-73864-9(6)) Live Oak Media.

JAPANESE AMERICANS

Anderson, Dale. Japanese Americans, 1 vol. 2006. (World Almanac(r) Library of American Immigration Ser.). (ENG., Illus.). 48p. (gr. 5-8). pap. 15.05 (978-0-8368-7326-9(2), c3bed7bf-7f23-46f4-beb0-af9e54a3db86); lib. bdg. 33.67 (978-0-8368-7313-9(0), 2a4e375d-d010-4e4c-89f2-0d3f9baf9185) Stevens, Gareth Publishing LLLP. (Gareth Stevens Secondary Library).

Atkins, Laura & Yogi, Stan. Fred Korematsu Speaks Up. Houlette, Yutaka, illus. 2017. (Fighting for Justice Ser.: 1). (ENG.). 112p. (J). 20.00 (978-1-59714-368-4(5)) Heyday.

Bailey, Rachel A. The Japanese Internment Camps: A History Perspectives Book. 2014. (Perspectives Library). (ENG., Illus.). 32p. (J). (gr. 4-8). 32.07 (978-1-62431-666-1(2), 203228) Cherry Lake Publishing.

Bjorklund, Ruth. Internment: Japanese Americans in World War II, 1 vol. 2016. (Public Persecutions Ser.). (ENG., Illus.). 128p. (J). (gr. 9-9). 47.36 (978-1-5026-2323-2(4), 8ba43ff0-9098-489a-a112-40427750d362) Cavendish Square Publishing LLC.

Blegen, Daniel. Bob Sakata: American Farmer. 2009. (Now You Know Bio Ser.: 13). (Illus.). 102p. (J). pap. 8.95 (978-0-86541-093-0(3)) Filter Pr., LLC.

Bryan, Nichol. Japanese Americans, 1 vol. 2004. (One Nation Set 2 Ser.). (ENG.). 32p. (gr. k-6). 27.07 (978-1-59197-529-8(8), Checkerboard Library) ABDO Publishing Co.

Burgan, Michael. Japanese American Internment. 2017. (Eyewitness to World War II Ser.). (ENG., Illus.). 112p. (J). (gr. 5-9). lib. bdg. 38.65 (978-0-7565-5581-8(7), 135466, Compass Point Bks.) Capstone.

Cham, Stephanie. Ellison Onizuka. 2018. (Great Asian Americans Ser.). (ENG., Illus.). 24p. (J). (gr. -1-2). lib. bdg. 27.32 (978-1-5157-9956-6(5), 136954, Capstone Pr.) Capstone.

Christopher, Matt. At the Plate with... Ichiro. 2003. (Matt Christopher Sports Bio Bookshelf Ser.). (Illus.). 101p. (J). (gr. 4-7). 12.65 (978-0-7569-1606-0(2)) Perfection Learning Corp.

Duncan, E. E. Ralph Carr: Defender of Japanese Americans. 2011. (ENG & SPA., Illus.). 66p. (J). pap. 8.95 (978-0-86541-116-6(6)) Filter Pr., LLC.

Fremon, David K. The Internment of Japanese Americans in United States History, 1 vol. 2014. (In United States History Ser.). (ENG., Illus.). 96p. (J). (gr. 5-6). 31.61 (978-0-7660-6068-5(3), 9f84f185-a80d-4442-b12c-b74643c95ba5) Enslow Publishing, LLC.

Garstecki, Julia. Go for Broke Regiment. 2016. (All-American Fighting Forces Ser.). (ENG.). 32p. (J). (gr. 4-6). pap. 9.99 (978-1-64466-152-9(7), 10310); (Illus.). 31.35 (978-1-68072-001-3(5), 10309) Black Rabbit Bks. (Bolt).

Goldstein, Margaret J. Japanese in America. 2006. (In America Ser.). (ENG., Illus.). 80p. (gr. 5-8). 27.93 (978-0-8225-3952-0(7), Lerner Pubns.) Lerner Publishing Group.

Grady, Cynthia. Write to Me: Letters from Japanese American Children to the Librarian They Left Behind. Hirao, Amiko, illus. 32p. (J). (gr. -1-3). 2019. (ENG.). pap. 7.99 (978-1-62354-111-8(5)) 2018. 16.99 (978-1-58089-688-7(X)) Charlesbridge Publishing, Inc.

Hale, Christy. The East West House: Noguchi's Childhood in Japan. 2012. (ENG., Illus.). 32p. (J). (gr. 2-7). 17.95 (978-1-60060-363-1(7)) Lee & Low Bks., Inc.

Hasday, Judy L. Japanese Americans. (Successful Americans Ser.). 64p. (YA). 2009. (gr. 9-12). 22.95 (978-1-4222-0519-8(3)) 2007. (gr. 7-18). pap. 9.95 (978-1-4222-0863-2(X)) Mason Crest.

Heinrichs, Ann. The Japanese American Internment: Innocence, Guilt, & Wartime Justice, 1 vol. 2011. (Perspectives On Ser.). (ENG., Illus.). 112p. (J). (gr. 8-8). 42.64 (978-0-7614-4983-6(3), 134471b9-944f-4a56-99ea-d911466205eb) Cavendish Square Publishing LLC.

Hyde, Natalie. Internment Camps. 2016. (Uncovering the Past: Analyzing Primary Sources Ser.). (ENG., Illus.). 48p. (J). (gr. 5-9). (978-0-7787-2860-3(9)) Crabtree Publishing Co.

Kamei, Susan H. When Can We Go Back to America? Voices of Japanese American Incarceration During WWII. (ENG.). 736p. (YA). 2022. pap. 15.99 (978-1-4814-0145-6(9)) 2021. (Illus.). (gr. 7). 22.99 (978-1-4814-0144-9(0)) Simon & Schuster Bks. For Young Readers. (Simon & Schuster Bks. For Young Readers).

Kops, Deborah. Racial Profiling, 1 vol. 2007. (Open for Debate Ser.). (ENG., Illus.). 144p. (J). (gr. 8-8). lib. bdg. 45.50 (978-0-7614-2298-3(6), a4b030ae-e8ea-4a9d-96bc-d9a129f8229e) Cavendish Square Publishing LLC.

MacCarald, Clara. Children in Japanese American Confinement Camps. 2018. (Children in History Ser.). (ENG., Illus.). 48p. (J). (gr. 5-6). pap. 11.95 (978-1-63517-976-7(9), 1635179769); lib. bdg. 34.21 (978-1-63517-875-3(4), 1635178754) North Star Editions. (Focus Readers).

—Japanese Immigrants: In Their Shoes. 2017. (Immigrant Experiences Ser.). (ENG.). 32p. (J). (gr. 3-6). lib. bdg. 35.64 (978-1-5038-2027-2(0), 211849) Child's World, Inc, The.

Marrin, Albert. Uprooted: The Japanese American Experience During World War II. 2016. (Illus.). 256p. (YA). (gr. 7). 32.99 (978-0-553-50936-6(5), Knopf Bks. for Young Readers) Random Hse. Children's Bks.

Mattern, Joanne. Japanese Americans. 2003. (Immigrants in America Ser.). (ENG., Illus.). 112p. (gr. 6-12). 30.00 (978-0-7910-7130-4(8), P113737, Facts On File) Infobase Holdings, Inc.

Moreno, Barry. The Japanese Americans. (Major American Immigration Ser.). (YA). 2010. (Illus.). 64p. (gr. 9-12). 22.95 (978-1-4222-0610-2(6)) 2007. pap. 9.95 (978-1-4222-0677-5(7)) Mason Crest.

Moss, Marissa. Barbed Wire Baseball. Shimizu, Yuko, illus. 2013. (ENG.). 48p. (J). (gr. 1-5). 19.95 (978-1-4197-0521-2(0), 671701, Abrams Bks. for Young Readers) Abrams, Inc.

Nickles, Greg. The Japanese: We Came to North America. 2006. (Illus.). 32p. (J). (gr. 4-8). reprint ed. 19.00 (978-0-7567-9908-3(2)) DIANE Publishing Co.

Oppenheim, Joanne. Dear Miss Breed: True Stories of the Japanese American Incarceration During World War II & a Librarian Who Made a Difference. 2006. (ENG., Illus.). 288p. (J). (gr. 7-7). 27.99 (978-0-439-56992-7(3)) Scholastic, Inc.

Otfinoski, Steven. Japanese American Internment: Prisoners in Their Own Land. 2019. (Tangled History Ser.). (ENG., Illus.). 112p. (J). (gr. 3-9). pap. 6.95 (978-1-5435-7557-6(9), 141089); lib. bdg. 32.65 (978-1-5435-7257-5(X), 140593) Capstone.

Parker, Lewis K. Why Japanese Immigrants Came to America. 2009. (Coming to America Ser.). 24p. (gr. 2-3). 42.50 (978-1-61511-886-1(1), PowerKids Pr.) Rosen Publishing Group, Inc., The.

Perl, Lila. Behind Barbed Wire: The Story of Japanese-American Internment During World War II, 1 vol. 2003. (Great Journeys Ser.). (ENG., Illus.). 112p. (J). (gr. 6-6). 39.79 (978-0-7614-1321-9(9), df488a39-ae2b-4b65-97d6-f35a181fcf6a) Cavendish Square Publishing LLC.

Ruggiero, Adriane. World War II, 1 vol. 2003. (American Voices From Ser.). (ENG., Illus.). 160p. (J). (gr. 6-6). 41.21 (978-0-7614-1206-9(9), fdea97f5-91c3-478b-8640-d66ec601d883) Cavendish Square Publishing LLC.

Sandler, Martin W. Imprisoned: The Betrayal of Japanese Americans During World War II. 2013. (ENG., Illus.). 176p. (J). (gr. 5-8). 24.99 (978-0-8027-2277-5(6), 900074397, Bloomsbury USA Childrens) Bloomsbury Publishing USA.

Say, Allen. Drawing from Memory. 2011. (978-0-545-17687-3(5), Scholastic Pr.) Scholastic, Inc.

—Drawing from Memory. Say, Allen, illus. 2011. (ENG., Illus.). 64p. (J). (gr. 3-7). 24.99 (978-0-545-17686-6(7), Scholastic Pr.) Scholastic, Inc.

Taylor, Charlotte & Kent, Deborah. The Internment of Japanese Americans, 1 vol. 2015. (Our Shared History Ser.). (ENG., Illus.). 128p. (J). (gr. 7-7). lib. bdg. 38.93 (978-0-7660-7008-0(5), 2cb03d49-bd3c-43a8-aa2c-98c8dbbae5af) Enslow Publishing, LLC.

Tunnell, Michael O. Desert Diary: Japanese American Kids Behind Barbed Wire. 2020. (Illus.). 144p. (J). (gr. 4-7). lib. bdg. 19.99 (978-1-58089-789-1(4)) Charlesbridge Publishing, Inc.

Warren, Andrea. Enemy Child: The Story of Norman Mineta, a Boy Imprisoned in a Japanese American Internment Camp During World War II. 2019. (Illus.). 224p. (J). (gr. 5). 22.99 (978-0-8234-4151-8(2), Margaret Ferguson Books) Holiday Hse., Inc.

Welch, Catherine A. Children of the Relocation Camps. 2005. (Picture the American Past Ser.). (Illus.). 48p. (J). (gr. 2-5). lib. bdg. 22.60 (978-1-57505-350-9(0)) Lerner Publishing Group.

Welky, Ali, ed. A Captive Audience: Voices of Japanese American Youth in World War II Arkansas. 2015. (ENG., Illus.). 124p. (J). pap. 21.95 (978-1-935106-86-9(4), P483240) Butler Ctr. for Arkansas Studies.

West, Patricia. East Meets West: Japan & America. 2005. (ENG., Illus.). 12p. (J). (gr. 3-3). pap. 5.97 net. (978-0-328-13382-6(5), Scott Foresman) Savvas Learning Co.

Wukovits, John F. Internment of Japanese Americans, 1 vol. 2012. (World History Ser.). (ENG., Illus.). 120p. (gr. 7-7). lib. bdg. 41.53 (978-1-4205-0824-6(5), 2e07a3d0-03bf-4a0b-8e29-021ac7be5902, Lucent Pr.) Greenhaven Publishing LLC.

JAPANESE AMERICANS—FICTION

Banks, Jacqueline Turner. A Day for Vincent Chin & Me. 2005. (ENG.). 128p. (J). (gr. 5-7). pap. 11.95 (978-0-618-54879-8(3), 481194, Clarion Bks.) HarperCollins Pubs.

Bunting, Eve. So Far from the Sea. Soentpiet, Chris K., illus. 2009. (ENG.). 32p. (J). (gr. 5-7). pap. 7.99 (978-0-547-23752-7(9), 1083866, Clarion Bks.) HarperCollins Pubs.

Cheaney, J. B. My Friend the Enemy. 2007. 266p. (gr. 4-7). 16.50 (978-0-7569-7946-1(3)) Perfection Learning Corp.

Ching, Tokie. Boy's Day in Hawaii. Arai, Setsuo, illus. 2008. 32p. (J). 12.95 (978-1-56647-852-6(9)) Mutual Publishing LLC.

—Girl's Day in Hawaii with Yuki Chan. 2006. 40p. (J). 14.95 (978-1-56647-820-5(0)) Mutual Publishing LLC.

Conkling, Winifred. Sylvia & Aki. 2013. 160p. (J). (gr. 4-7). 7.99 (978-1-58246-345-2(X), Yearling) Random Hse. Children's Bks.

Crilley, Mark. Akiko Flights of Fancy. exp. ed. 2007. (Illus.). 264p. pap. 24.95 (978-1-57989-088-9(1)) Sirius Entertainment, Inc.

—The Battle for Boach's Keep Vol. 7. 2004. (Illus.). 144p. pap. 14.95 (978-1-57989-064-3(4)) Sirius Entertainment, Inc.

Dallas, Sandra. Red Berries, White Clouds, Blue Sky. (ENG., Illus.). 216p. (J). (gr. 3-6). 2015. pap. 9.99 (978-1-58536-907-2(1), 203820) 2014. 15.95 (978-1-58536-906-5(3), 203673) Sleeping Bear Pr.

DeNomme, Donna & Proctor, Tina. Ophelia's Oracle: Discovering the Healthy, Happy, Self-aware, & Competant Girl in the Mirror. 2009. (YA). pap. 16.95 (978-1-61539-958-1(5)) Independent Pub.

Falwell, Cathryn. Butterflies for Kiri. 2003. (ENG., Illus.). 32p. (J). (978-1-58430-100-4(7)); pap. 11.95 (978-1-60060-342-6(4), leelowbooks) Lee & Low Bks., Inc.

Faulkner, Matt. Gaijin: American Prisoner of War. 2014. (ENG., Illus.). 144p. (J). (gr. 3-7). 19.99 (978-1-4231-3735-1(3)) Little, Brown Bks. for Young Readers.

Fein, Eric. Mystery at Manzanar: A WWII Internment Camp Story, 1 vol. Hartman, Kurt, illus. 2008. (Historical Fiction Ser.). (ENG.). 56p. (J). (gr. 3-6). pap. 6.25 (978-1-4342-0847-7(8), 95208, Stone Arch Bks.) Capstone.

Fitzmaurice, Kathryn. A Diamond in the Desert. 2013. 272p. (J). (gr. 4-6). 21.19 (978-0-670-01292-3(0), Viking) Penguin Publishing Group.

Florence, Debbi Michiko. Jasmine Toguchi, Mochi Queen. 2017. (J). pap. (978-0-374-30411-9(4)) Farrar, Straus & Giroux.

—Jasmine Toguchi, Super Sleuth. Vukovic, Elizabet, illus. 2017. (J). pap. (978-0-374-30414-0(9)) Farrar, Straus & Giroux.

Gates, Margo. Into the Clouds. Crowther, Jeff, illus. 2019. (Let's Look at Weather (Pull Ahead Readers — Fiction) Ser.). (ENG.). 16p. (J). (gr. -1-1). 27.99 (978-1-5415-5840-3(5), 502ef064-f1f6-4054-ad17-b5b579637c44, Lerner Pubns.) Lerner Publishing Group.

Harrington, Claudia. My Mom & Dad, 1 vol. Persico, Zoe, illus. 2015. (My Family Ser.). (ENG.). 32p. (J). (gr. -1-3). 32.79 (978-1-62402-107-7(7), 18156, Looking Glass Library) Magic Wagon.

Hesse, Monica. The War Outside. (ENG.). (YA). (gr. 7-17). 2019. 352p. pap. 10.99 (978-0-316-31671-2(7)) 2018. (Illus.). 336p. 34.99 (978-0-316-31669-9(5)) Little, Brown Bks. for Young Readers.

Hirahara, Naomi. 1001 Cranes. 2009. (ENG.). 240p. (J). (gr. 3-7). 7.99 (978-0-440-42234-1(5), Yearling) Random Hse. Children's Bks.

Hughes, Dean. Four-Four-Two. 2016. (ENG., Illus.). 272p. (YA). (gr. 7). 18.99 (978-1-4814-6252-5(0), Atheneum Bks. for Young Readers) Simon & Schuster Children's Publishing.

Kadohata, Cynthia. Kira-Kira. (ENG., Illus.). (J). (gr. 5-9). 2004. 256p. 19.99 (978-0-689-85639-6(3)) 2006. 272p. reprint ed. pap. 8.99 (978-0-689-85640-2(7)) Simon & Schuster Children's Publishing. (Atheneum Bks. for Young Readers).

—A Place to Belong. Kuo, Julia, illus. (ENG.). (J). (gr. 5-9). 2020. 432p. pap. 8.99 (978-1-4814-4665-5(7), Atheneum Bks. for Young Readers) 2019. 416p. 17.99 (978-1-4814-4664-8(9), Atheneum/Caitlyn Dlouhy Books) 2019. 416p. E-Book (978-1-4814-4666-2(5), Atheneum/Caitlyn Dlouhy Books) Simon & Schuster Children's Publishing.

—The Thing about Luck. Kuo, Julia, illus. (ENG.). (J). (gr. 5-9). 2014. 304p. pap. 8.99 (978-1-4424-7465-9(3), Atheneum Bks. for Young Readers) 2013. 288p. 16.99 (978-1-4169-1882-0(5)) Simon & Schuster Children's Publishing.

—The Thing about Luck. 2014. lib. bdg. 18.40 (978-0-606-35798-2(X)) Turtleback.

—Weedflower. 2009. (ENG.). 272p. (J). (gr. 5-9). pap. 7.99 (978-1-4169-7566-3(7), Atheneum Bks. for Young Readers) Simon & Schuster Children's Publishing.

—Weedflower. 2006. (ENG., Illus.). 272p. (J). (gr. 5-9). 22.99 (978-0-689-86574-9(0)) Simon & Schuster, Inc.

Kogawa, Joy. Naomi's Road, 1 vol. Ohi, Ruth, illus. 2005. (ENG.). 120p. (Orig.). (J). (gr. 3-6). pap. 9.95 (978-1-55005-115-5(6), 7f5a7c7d-f192-417e-b65d-89dde3534a89) Fitzhenry & Whiteside, Ltd. CAN. Dist: Firefly Bks., Ltd.

Larson, Kirby. Dash (Dogs of World War II) 2016. (Dogs of World War II Ser.). (ENG.). 256p. (J). (gr. 3-7). pap. 8.99 (978-0-545-41636-8(1), Scholastic Paperbacks) Scholastic, Inc.

—The Fences Between Us: The Diary of Piper Davis. 2010. (Illus.). 313p. (J). pap. (978-0-545-27094-6(4)) Scholastic, Inc.

Lee, Camellia. Lines We Draw: A Story of Imprisoned Japanese Americans. Freeberg, Eric, illus. 2019. (I Am America Ser.). (ENG.). 160p. (J). (gr. 3-4). pap. 8.99 (978-1-63163-280-8(9), 1631632809); lib. bdg. 28.50 (978-1-63163-279-2(5), 1631632795) North Star Editions. (Jolly Fish Pr.).

Lee-Tai, Amy. A Place Where Sunflowers Grow. Hoshino, Felicia, illus. 2006. (JPN & ENG.). 32p. (J). (gr. k-3). 17.95 (978-0-89239-215-5(0)) Lee & Low Bks., Inc.

Lee-Tai, Amy. Place Where Sunflowers Grow, 1 vol. 2015. (ENG., Illus.). 32p. (J). (gr. 2-5). pap. 11.95 (978-0-89239-274-2(6), leelowcbp, Children's Book Press) Lee & Low Bks., Inc.

Lieurance, Suzanne. The Lucky Baseball: My Story in a Japanese-American Internment Camp, 1 vol. 2010. (Historical Fiction Adventures Ser.). (ENG., Illus.). 160p. (J). (gr. 3-5). lib. bdg. 31.93 (978-0-7660-3311-5(2), de535228-7abe-4f5d-92ff-dfd0e351cb79) Enslow Publishing, LLC.

Lorenzi, Natalie Dias. Flying the Dragon. 240p. (J). (gr. 4-7). 2014. (ENG.). pap. 8.95 (978-1-58089-435-7(6)) 2012. 16.95 (978-1-58089-434-0(8)) Charlesbridge Publishing, Inc.

Maetani, Valynne. Ink & Ashes, 1 vol. 2015. (ENG.). 368p. (YA). (gr. 7-12). 19.95 (978-1-62014-211-0(2), leelowtu, Tu Bks.) Lee & Low Bks., Inc.

Maruno, Jennifer. When the Cherry Blossoms Fell: A Cherry Blossom Book. 2009. (Cherry Blossom Book Ser.: 1). (ENG.). 144p. (J). (gr. 4-7). pap. 10.99 (978-1-894917-83-4(9), Napoleon & Co.) Dundurn Pr. CAN. Dist: Publishers Group West (PGW).

May, Kyla. Mika: My New Life. 2013. (Lotus Lane Ser.: 4). lib. bdg. 14.75 (978-0-606-32365-9(1)) Turtleback.

Mazer, Harry. A Boy No More. 2007. 136p. (gr. 5-9). 16.00 (978-0-7569-8112-9(3)) Perfection Learning Corp.

Michiko Florence, Debbi. Jasmine Toguchi, Drummer Girl. Vukovic, Elizabet, illus. 2018. (Jasmine Toguchi Ser.: 3). (ENG.). 128p. (J). pap. 5.99 (978-0-374-30836-0(5), 900185579, Farrar, Straus & Giroux (BYR)) Farrar, Straus & Giroux.

—Jasmine Toguchi, Flamingo Keeper. Vukovic, Elizabet, illus. 2018. (Jasmine Toguchi Ser.: 4). (ENG.). 128p. (J). pap. 5.99 (978-0-374-30837-7(3), 900185590, Farrar, Straus & Giroux (BYR)) Farrar, Straus & Giroux.

—Jasmine Toguchi, Mochi Queen. Vukovic, Elizabet, illus. 2017. (Jasmine Toguchi Ser.: 1). (ENG.). 128p. (J). 15.99 (978-0-374-30410-2(6), 900158910); pap. 5.99 (978-0-374-30834-6(9), 900185577) Farrar, Straus & Giroux. (Farrar, Straus & Giroux (BYR)).

—Jasmine Toguchi, Super Sleuth. Vukovic, Elizabet, illus. 2017. (Jasmine Toguchi Ser.: 2). (ENG.). 128p. (J). 16.99 (978-0-374-30413-3(0), 900158913); pap. 5.99 (978-0-374-30835-3(7), 900185578) Farrar, Straus & Giroux. (Farrar, Straus & Giroux (BYR)).

Mitsui Brown, Janet, illus. Oshogatsu with Obaachan. 2005. (J). (978-1-879965-24-9(0)) Polychrome Publishing Corp.

Mochizuki, Ken. Baseball Saved Us. 97th rev. ed. 2014. (ENG.). 30p. (J). (gr. k-12). 15.65 (978-1-63245-249-8(9)) Lectorum Pubns., Inc.

—Baseball Saved Us. Lee, Dom, illus. (Picture Book Readalong Ser.). pap. 39.95 incl. audio compact disk (978-1-59112-917-2(6)); 2004. (J). (gr. -1-2). 25.95 incl. audio (978-1-59112-456-6(5)) Live Oak Media.

—Beacon Hill Boys. 2004. 200p. 16.00 (978-0-7569-4281-6(0)) Perfection Learning Corp.

Morrill, Stephanie. Within These Lines, 1 vol. 2019. (ENG.). 352p. (YA). 17.99 (978-0-310-76523-3(4)) Blink.

Nagai, Mariko. Dust of Eden. 2018. (ENG.). 144p. (J). (gr. 3-7). pap. 9.99 (978-0-8075-1738-3(0), 807517380) Whitman, Albert & Co.

Noguchi, Rick & Jenks, Deneen. Flowers from Mariko, 1 vol. Kumata, Michelle Reiko, illus. 2016. (ENG.). 32p. (J). (gr. 1-4). pap. 11.95 (978-1-62014-315-5(1), leelowbooks) Lee & Low Bks., Inc.

—Flowers from Mariko. Reiko Kumata, Michelle, illus. 2013. (ENG.). 32p. (J). (gr. 1-18). 16.95 (978-1-58430-032-8(9)) Lee & Low Bks., Inc.

Parkhurst, Liz S. Under One Flag: A Year at Rohwer. Clifton, Tom, illus. 2006. (ENG.). 32p. (J). (gr. 3-7). 16.95 (978-0-87483-759-9(6), 1241971) August Hse. Pubs., Inc.

Patneaude, David. Thin Wood Walls. 2008. (ENG., Illus.). 240p. (J). (gr. 5-7). pap. 7.99 (978-0-618-80915-8(5), 492685, Clarion Bks.) HarperCollins Pubs.

Platt, Randall. Incommunicado. 2017. (ENG.). 352p. (J). (gr. 5-8). pap. 9.99 (978-1-5107-0991-1(6), Sky Pony Pr.) Skyhorse Publishing Co., Inc.

Reece, Colleen L. Last Page in the Diary. 2011. 94p. pap. 8.95 (978-1-61633-179-5(8)) Guardian Angel Publishing, Inc.

Robbins, Trina. The Bark in Space: Book 5, No. 5. Page, Tyler, illus. 2013. (Chicagoland Detective Agency Ser.: 5). (ENG.). 64p. (J). (gr. 4-8). pap. 6.95 (978-1-4677-0725-1(2), 659d0711-80dc-41a4-866d-7c460cfaabf5, Graphic Universe™) Lerner Publishing Group.

—The Drained Brains Caper: Book 1, No. 1. Page, Tyler, illus. 2010. (Chicagoland Detective Agency Ser.: 1). (ENG.). 64p. (J). (gr. 4-8). pap. 8.99 (978-0-7613-5635-6(5), 3b3c032d-e980-466a-9075-55d5ee724833, Graphic Universe™) Lerner Publishing Group.

—Night of the Living Dogs. Page, Tyler, illus. 2012. (Chicagoland Detective Agency Ser.). 64p. (J). (gr. 4-8). pap. 39.62 (978-0-7613-9313-9(7), Graphic Universe™) Lerner Publishing Group.

Salisbury, Graham. House of the Red Fish. 2014. (Prisoners of the Empire Ser.). (ENG.). 320p. (YA). (gr. 7). pap. 9.99 (978-0-385-38657-9(5), Ember) Random Hse. Children's Bks.

—Under the Blood Red Sun. 246p. (YA). 22.00 (978-0-8446-7322-6(6)) Smith, Peter Pub., Inc.

—Under the Blood-Red Sun. 2014. (Prisoners of the Empire Ser.: 1). (ENG.). 272p. (YA). (gr. 7-7). pap. 9.99 (978-0-385-38655-5(9), Ember) Random Hse. Children's Bks.

Say, Allen. The Favorite Daughter. 2013. (J). pap. (978-0-545-17663-7(8), Levine, Arthur A. Bks.) Scholastic, Inc.

—The Favorite Daughter. Say, Allen, illus. 2013. (ENG., Illus.). 32p. (J). (gr. -1-3). 19.99 (978-0-545-17662-0(X), Levine, Arthur A. Bks.) Scholastic, Inc.

—Grandfather's Journey. 2008. (ENG.). 32p. (J). (gr. -1-3). pap. 7.99 (978-0-547-14178-7(5), Sandpiper) Houghton Mifflin Harcourt Trade & Reference Pubs.

—Grandfather's Journey. 2011. (J). (gr. k-5). 29.95 (978-0-545-10696-2(6)); 18.95 (978-0-545-12708-0(4)) Weston Woods Studios, Inc.

—Grandfather's Journey: A Caldecott Award Winner. Say, Allen, illus. 2008. (ENG., Illus.). 32p. (J). (gr. -1-3). 7.99 (978-0-547-07680-5(0), 1042044, Clarion Bks.) HarperCollins Pubs.

—Grandfather's Journey 20th Anniversary: A Caldecott Award Winner. Say, Allen, illus. 20th anniv. ed. 2013. (ENG., Illus.). 32p. (J). (gr. -1-3). 18.99 (978-0-544-05050-1(9), 1532595, Clarion Bks.) HarperCollins Pubs.

Sepahban, Lois. Paper Wishes. 2017. (ENG.). 192p. (J). pap. 8.99 (978-1-250-10414-4(9), 900163680) Square Fish.

—Paper Wishes. 2017. (J). lib. bdg. 18.40 (978-0-606-39942-5(9)) Turtleback.

Shimose Poe, Mayumi. Alice on the Island: A Pearl Harbor Survival Story. Forsyth, Matt, illus. 2019. (Girls Survive Ser.). (ENG.). 112p. (J). (gr. 3-7). pap. 7.95 (978-1-4965-8012-2(5), 139979, Stone Arch Bks.) Capstone.

Sugiura, Misa. It's Not Like It's a Secret. (ENG.). 400p. (YA). (gr. 8). 2018. pap. 10.99 (978-0-06-247342-4(5)) 2017. 18.99 (978-0-06-247341-7(7)) HarperCollins Pubs. (HarperTeen).

—This Time Will Be Different. 2019. (ENG.). 400p. (YA). (gr. 8). 17.99 (978-0-06-247344-8(1), HarperTeen) HarperCollins Pubs.

Terasaki, Stanley Todd. Ghosts for Breakfast. Shinjo, Shelly, illus. 2013. (ENG.). 32p. (J). (gr. k-4). 16.95 (978-1-58430-046-5(9)) Lee & Low Bks., Inc.

Terry, Alana. What, No Sushi? Steffen, Jeremy, illus. 2013. 116p. pap. 7.99 (978-1-937848-04-0(3)) Do Life Right, Inc.

Thompson, Holly. Orchards. 2012. 336p. (YA). (gr. 7). pap. 10.99 (978-0-385-73978-8(8), Ember) Random Hse. Children's Bks.

Uchida, Yoshiko. Samurai of Gold Hill. Forberg, Ati, illus. 2005. 119p. (J). (gr. 2). per. 8.95 (978-1-59714-015-7(5)) Heyday.

Villani, Donna. The Capture of Art. 2008. 244p. pap. 14.95 (978-1-60693-104-2(0), Eloquent Bks.) Strategic Book Publishing & Rights Agency (SBPRA).

Wells, Rosemary. Yoko. Wells, Rosemary, illus. 2009. (Yoko Book Ser.: 1). (ENG., Illus.). 32p. (J). (gr. -1-3). pap. 8.99 (978-1-4231-1983-8(5)) Little, Brown Bks. for Young Readers.

Weston Woods Staff, creator. Grandfather's Journey. 2011. 38.75 (978-0-545-12710-3(6)) Weston Woods Studios, Inc.

Yamasaki, Katie. Fish for Jimmy: Inspired by One Family's Experience in a Japanese American Internment Camp. (Illus.). (J). (gr. 1-4). 2019. 40p. pap. 8.99 (978-0-8234-4431-1(7)) 2013. (ENG., 32p. 16.99 (978-0-8234-2375-0(1)) Holiday Hse., Inc.

—When the Cousins Came. 2018. (ENG., Illus.). 32p. (J). (gr. -1-3). 17.99 (978-0-8234-3457-2(5)) Holiday Hse., Inc.

JAPANESE LANGUAGE

Ace Academics, ed. Japanese: A Whole Course in a Box! 2007. (Exambusters Ser.). 384p. (gr. 7-18). 12.95 (978-1-881374-96-1(3), Exambusters) Ace Academics, Inc.

Brown, Michelle Haney. My First Book of Japanese Words: An ABC Rhyming Book of Japanese Language & Culture. Padron, Aya, illus. 2017. (My First Words Ser.). 32p. (J). (gr. -1-3). 10.95 (978-0-8048-4953-1(6)) Tuttle Publishing.

Cacciapuoti, Aurora. Let's Learn Japanese: First Words for Everyone (Learn Japanese for Kids, Learn Japanese for Adults, Japanese Learning Books) 2019. (ENG., Illus.). 48p. (J). (gr. -1-3). 12.99 (978-1-4521-6625-4(0)) Chronicle Bks. LLC.

Evans, Meg, et al. Mirai Stage 1: Course Book, Stage 2. 2004. (JPN & ENG., Illus.). 158p. (gr. 7-10). tchr. ed., per. 100.00 (978-0-7339-1367-9(9)) Pearson Education Australia AUS. Dist: Cheng & Tsui Co.

—Mirai 2 Student Book Stage 1, 6 vols., Stage 2. 2004. (Illus.). 168p. (gr. 7-10). stu. ed., per. 49.95 (978-0-7339-0929-0(9)) Pearson Education Australia AUS. Dist: Cheng & Tsui Co.

Fedoruk, Dennis, prod. Bilingual Baby - Flashcard Set - Japanese. 2013. (JPN.). (J). 7.99 (978-1-892703-78-1(5)) Small Fry Beginnings.

Green, Yuko. Japanese Word Book. 2004. (JPN., Illus.). 112p. pap. 14.95 (978-1-57306-196-4(4)) Bess Pr., Inc.

Kalz, Jill. My First Japanese Phrases, 1 vol. TransPerfect Translations Staff, tr. Fabbri, Daniele, illus. 2012. (Speak Another Language! Ser.). (ENG.). 32p. (J). (gr. k-3). lib. bdg. 27.32 (978-1-4048-7514-2(X), 119611, Picture Window Bks.) Capstone.

Kardy, Glenn. Kanji de Manga Special Edition: Yoji-Jukugo: Yoji-Jukugo. 2008. (ENG., Illus.). 112p. pap. 9.99 (978-4-921205-22-5(1), a06c6bf5-894a-413a-b157-3a2b7020dacc) Japanime Co., Ltd. JPN. Dist: Diamond Comic Distributors, Inc.

Kids, Lonely Planet. Lonely Planet Kids First Words - Japanese 1: 100 Japanese Words to Learn. Iwohn, Sebastien & Mansfield, Andy, illus. 2018. (Lonely Planet Kids Ser.). (ENG.). 208p. (J). (gr. 1-3). pap. 12.99 (978-1-78701-270-7(0), 5711) Lonely Planet Global Ltd. IRL. Dist: Hachette Bk. Group.

Konda, Cynthia. Okasan & Me: Japanese American Educational Program. 2003. (JPN., Illus.). 26p. (J). (gr. -1-18). spiral bd. 19.99 (978-0-9743613-0-7(5)) Okasan & Me.

Lee, Margaret. Tsumiki 1 Student Book, 2 vols. 2004. (Illus.). 177p. (gr. 7-9). pap., stu. ed. 45.95 (978-0-17-010267-4(X)) Cengage Learning Australia AUS. Dist: Cheng & Tsui Co.

—Tsumiki 1 Teacher Resource Book. 2004. (Illus.). 194p. (gr. 7-9). pap., tchr. ed. 135.00 (978-0-17-010268-1(8)) Cengage Learning Australia AUS. Dist: Cheng & Tsui Co.

Mahoney, Judy. Teach Me Everyday Japanese V 1, Vol 1. Girouard, Patrick, illus. 2008. (ENG.). 32p. (J). (gr. -1). 19.95 (978-1-59972-104-0(X)) Teach Me Tapes, Inc.

McBride, Helen, et al. Kimono, Level 3. (JPN.). 160p. (J). pap., wbk. ed. 29.95 (978-0-8219-1038-2(8), 58653) EMC/Paradigm Publishing.

—Kimono, Level 3. Incl. Level 3. pap., wbk. ed. 29.95 (978-0-8219-1038-2(8), 58653); Level 3. tchr. ed. 189.95 (978-0-8219-1049-8(3), 58653); (J). (gr. k-5). (JPN.). 160p. Set stu. ed. 47.95 (978-0-8219-1037-5(X), 58253) EMC/Paradigm Publishing.

Passport Books Staff, ed. Japanese Picture Dictionary: Elementary Through Junior High. Goodman, Marlene, illus. 2003. (Let's Learn... Picture Dictionary Ser.). (JPN.). 80p. (J). (gr. 4-7). pap. 11.95 (978-0-8442-8494-1(7), 84947) McGraw-Hill Trade.

Peterson, Hiromi & Omizo, Naomi. Adventures in Japanese, Vol. 2. Muronaka, Michael & Kaylor, Emiko, illus. 2004. (JPN & ENG.). 210p. (gr. 7-10). pap., wbk. ed. 19.95 (978-0-88727-321-6(1)) Cheng & Tsui Co.

—Adventures in Japanese: Field Test Edition. 2004. (JPN & ENG., Illus.). (gr. 9-12). 462p. pap. 45.00 (978-0-88727-416-9(1)); 116p. pap., wbk. ed. 21.95 (978-0-88727-417-6(X)) Cheng & Tsui Co.

York, M. J. Learn Japanese Words. Petelinsek, Kathleen, illus. 2014. (Foreign Language Basics Ser.). (ENG & JPN.). 24p. (J). (gr. 2-5). 32.79 (978-1-62687-376-6(3), 207123) Child's World, Inc, The.

JAPANESE LANGUAGE—GRAMMAR

Brenda, Stapleton. Grammar Keys: A Guide for Japanese Students. 3rd ed. 2005. pap. (978-0-9770443-0-6(0)) Top Shelf Publishing.

Evans, Meg, et al. Mirai 1 Student Book Stage 1, 6 vols., Stage 1. 2004. (JPN & ENG., Illus.). 191p. (gr. 6-9). stu. ed., per. 49.95 (978-0-7339-0425-7(4)) Pearson Education Australia AUS. Dist: Cheng & Tsui Co.

—Mirai 1 Teacher's Book Stage 1, Stage 1. 2004. (JPN & ENG., Illus.). 141p. (gr. 6-9). tchr. ed., per. 100.00 (978-0-7339-0504-9(8)) Pearson Education Australia AUS. Dist: Cheng & Tsui Co.

—Mirai 2 Audio CD Stage 1, Stage 2. 2004. (gr. 7-10). audio compact disk 100.00 (978-0-7339-1214-6(1)) Pearson Education Australia AUS. Dist: Cheng & Tsui Co.

Goodman, Marlene. Let's Learn Japanese Picture Dictionary. 2003. (ENG., Illus.). 80p. 18.00 (978-0-07-140827-1(4), 0071408274) McGraw-Hill Education.

Green, Yuko. Japanese Word Book. 2004. (JPN., Illus.). 112p. pap. 14.95 (978-1-57306-196-4(4)) Bess Pr., Inc.

Kardy, Glenn. Kana de Manga: the Fun, Easy Way to Learn the ABCs of Japanese: The Fun, Easy Way to Learn the ABCs of Japanese. 2005. (ENG., Illus.). 144p. (YA). pap. 9.99 (978-4-921205-01-0(9), 3efd3897-096f-4b44-a720-ae549046cd74) Japanime Co., Ltd. JPN. Dist: Diamond Comic Distributors, Inc.

Kudela, Katy R. My First Book of Japanese Words, 1 vol. Translations.com Staff, tr. 2010. (Bilingual Picture Dictionaries Ser.). (MUL.). 32p. (J). (gr. -1-2). pap. 8.10 (978-1-4296-6337-3(5), 115537, Capstone Pr.) Capstone.

—My First Book of Japanese Words. Translations.com, Inc., tr. 2010. (Bilingual Picture Dictionaries Ser.). (MUL.). 32p. (J). (gr. 1-2). pap. 48.60 (978-1-4296-6464-6(9), 16218, Capstone Pr.) Capstone.

Milet Publishing Staff. My First Bilingual Book - Colors. 2011. (My First Bilingual Book Ser.). (ENG.). 24p. (J). (gr. k — 1). bds. 8.99 (978-1-84059-600-7(7)) Milet Publishing.

Stout, Timothy G. Tuttle Japanese for Kids Flash Cards Kit: Includes 64 Flash Cards, Online Audio, Wall Chart & Learning Guide, Kit. 2008. (Tuttle Flash Cards Ser.). (Illus.). 1p. (J). (gr. -1-8). 19.95 (978-4-8053-0904-9(0)) Tuttle Publishing.

Takahashi, Peter X. Jimi's Book of Japanese: A Motivating Method to Learn Japanese (Kanji) Moto, Mikki, ed. Toka, Yumie, illus. 2006. (J). pap. 24.95 (978-0-9723247-5-5(5), PB&J OmniMedia) Takahashi & Black.

—Jimi's Book of Japanese: A Motivating Method to Learn Japanese (Katakana) Moto, Mikki, ed. Toka, Yumie, illus. 2005. (JPN & ENG.). 76p. (J). pap. 18.95 (978-0-9723247-2-4(0), PB&J OmniMedia) Takahashi & Black.

—Jimi's Sumo Stack: A Motivating Method to Memorize Japanese. Toka, Yumie, illus. 2006. pap. 19.95 (978-0-9723247-8-6(X), PB&J OmniMedia) Takahashi & Black.

Uchiyama, Akira & Kodaira, Hiromi. Yubisashi Yubinazori Aiueo. 2011. (JPN., Illus.). 96p. (J). (gr. -1-3). (978-4-564-00493-3(X)) Hikari no Kuni.

JAY, JOHN, 1745-1829

Miller, Chuck. John Jay. 2003. (America's Founders Ser.). (J). pap. (978-1-58417-083-9(2)); lib. bdg. (978-1-58417-020-4(4)) Lake Street Pubs.

White, Casey. John Jay: Diplomat of the American Experiment. (Library of American Thinkers Ser.). 112p. (gr. 6-6). 2009. 66.50 (978-1-60853-515-6(0), Rosen Reference) 2006. (ENG., Illus.). (YA). lib. bdg. 39.80 (978-1-4042-0507-9(1), d02aee73-ee35-409b-89c1-7c009ebf0d42) Rosen Publishing Group, Inc., The.

JAZZ

Allen, Richard, contrib. by. Mysterious Thelonious. abr. ed. 2003. (Illus.). (J). (gr. -1-2). audio compact disk 28.95 (978-1-59112-422-1(0)) Live Oak Media.

Barron, Rachel Stiffler. John Coltrane: Jazz Revolutionary. 2004. (Masters of Music Ser.). (Illus.). 112p. (YA). (gr. 6-12). 23.95 (978-1-883846-57-2(9), First Biographies) Reynolds, Morgan Inc.

Battaglia, Stephen. Mr. Mcsymphony's It's All about Jazz. 2008. (ENG.). 28p. pap. 9.99 (978-1-4196-8086-1(2)) CreateSpace Independent Publishing Platform.

Batten, Jack. Oscar Peterson: The Man & His Jazz. 2012. (Illus.). 192p. (J). (gr. 5). 19.95 (978-1-77049-269-1(0), Tundra Bks.) Tundra Bks. CAN. Dist: Penguin Random Hse. LLC.

Ben-Hur, Roni Amos, text. Talk Jazz: A Comprehensive Collection of Be Bop Studies for All Instrumentalists & Vocalists. Ben-Hur, Roni Amos, . 2003. 54p. (YA). pap. 19.00 net. (978-0-9744943-0-2(5), (201 862-1692) Bohobza Music.

Berman, Kathleen Cornell. Birth of the Cool: How Jazz Great Miles Davis Found His Sound. Brown, Keith Henry, illus. 2019. (ENG.). 40p. (J). 18.99 (978-1-62414-690-9(2), 900197958) Page Street Publishing Co.

Collins, Terry. Louis Armstrong: Jazz Legend. Pope, Richmond, illus. 2012. (American Graphic Ser.). (ENG.). 32p. (J). (gr. 3-4). pap. 48.60 (978-1-4296-9337-0(1), 18560, Capstone Pr.) Capstone.

Hal Leonard Corp. Staff, creator. Jazzy Opera Classix: For Clarinet. 2005. (ENG.). 36p. pap. 23.99 incl. audio compact disk (978-1-902455-29-7(0), 49012965) Schott Music Corp.

—Jazzy Opera Classix: For Violin. 2005. (ENG.). 36p. pap. 23.99 incl. audio compact disk (978-1-902455-32-7(0), 49012968) Schott Music Corp.

Josephson, Judith P. Louis Armstrong. 2008. pap. 52.95 (978-0-8225-9392-8(0)) Lerner Publishing Group.

Lynette, Rachel. Miles Davis: Legendary Jazz Musician, 1 vol. 2010. (Innovators Ser.). (ENG., Illus.). 48p. (gr. 4-8). 36.23 (978-0-7377-5034-8(0), 3294fa0d-68af-4bb1-bd8b-19d4f9a076e8, KidHaven Publishing) Greenhaven Publishing LLC.

McDonough, Yona Zeldis & Who HQ. Who Was Louis Armstrong? O'Brien, John, illus. 2004. (Who Was? Ser.). 112p. (J). (gr. 3-7). pap. 5.99 (978-0-448-43368-4(0), Penguin Workshop) Penguin Young Readers Group.

Orgill, Roxane. Skit-Scat Raggedy Cat: Candlewick Biographies: Ella Fitzgerald. Qualls, Sean, illus. 2012. (Candlewick Biographies Ser.). (ENG.). 48p. (J). (gr. 3-7). pap. 5.99 (978-0-7636-6458-9(8)) Candlewick Pr.

Pinkney, Andrea. Ella Fitzgerald: The Tale of a Vocal Virtuosa. Pinkney, Brian, illus. 2007. (Great Black Performers Ser.: 3). (ENG.). 32p. (J). (gr. 1-3). pap. 6.99 (978-0-7868-1416-9(0), Jump at the Sun) Hyperion Bks. for Children.

Ransom, Candice. Jazz Dance. 2017. (Shall We Dance? Ser.). (ENG., Illus.). 32p. (J). (gr. 2-3). pap. 9.95 (978-1-63517-341-3(8), 1635173418); lib. bdg. 31.35 (978-1-63517-276-8(4), 1635172764) North Star Editions. (Focus Readers).

Raschka, Chris. Mysterious Thelonious. Raschka, Chris, illus. (Illus.). pap. 18.95 incl. audio compact disk (978-1-59112-421-4(2)) Live Oak Media.

Russell-Brown, Katheryn. Little Melba & Her Big Trombone, 1 vol. Morrison, Frank, illus. 2014. (ENG.). 40p. (J). (gr. 1-5). 20.95 (978-1-60060-898-8(1), leelowbooks) Lee & Low Bks., Inc.

Watson, Cindy. Out of Darkness: The Jeff Healey Story. 2010. (ENG., Illus.). 134p. (YA). (gr. k-6). pap. 21.99 (978-1-55488-706-4(2), 9781554887064) Dundurn Pr. CAN. Dist: Ingram Publisher Services.

Weston Woods Staff, creator. Ella Fitzgerald. 2011. 18.95 (978-0-545-02761-8(6)); 38.75 (978-0-545-02763-2(2)) Weston Woods Studios, Inc.

What Jazz & Blues Can I Play - Alto Sax. 20p. 6.95 (978-1-85909-426-6(0), Warner Bros. Pubns.) Alfred Publishing Co., Inc.

What Jazz & Blues Can I Play - Flute. 20p. 6.95 (978-1-85909-422-8(8), Warner Bros. Pubns.) Alfred Publishing Co., Inc.

What Jazz & Blues Can I Play - Trumpet. 20p. 6.95 (978-1-85909-425-9(2), Warner Bros. Pubns.) Alfred Publishing Co., Inc.

What Jazz & Blues Can I Play - Violin. 24p. 6.95 (978-1-85909-424-2(4), Warner Bros. Pubns.) Alfred Publishing Co., Inc.

What Jazz Blues Can I Play. 20p. 6.95 (978-1-85909-423-5(6), Warner Bros. Pubns.) Alfred Publishing Co., Inc.

Winter, Jonah. Dizzy. Qualls, Sean, illus. 2006. (J). 16.99 (978-0-439-50736-3(7), Levine, Arthur A. Bks.) Scholastic, Inc.

JAZZ—FICTION

Alexander, Kwame. Acoustic Rooster & His Barnyard Band. Bowers, Tim, illus. 2011. (ENG.). 32p. (J). (gr. 1-4). lib. bdg. 17.99 (978-1-58536-688-0(9), 202227) Sleeping Bear Pr.

Bell, Krista & Smith, Craig. If the Shoe Fits. 2008. (Illus.). (Orig.). (J). 60p. (gr. -1-3). 14.95 (978-1-58089-338-1(4)); (ENG., 64p. (gr. 4-7). pap. 5.95 (978-1-58089-339-8(2)) Charlesbridge Publishing, Inc.

Calmenson, Stephanie. Jazzmatazz! Degen, Bruce, illus. 2008. 32p. (J). (gr. -1). lib. bdg. 17.89 (978-0-06-077290-1(5)) HarperCollins Pubs.

Carlon, Mick. Riding on Duke's Train. 2011. (LeapKids Ser.). (ENG.). 160p. (J). (gr. k-7). pap. 9.95 (978-1-935248-06-4(5)) Leapfrog Pr.

—Travels with Louis. 2012. (LeapKids Ser.). (ENG.). 240p. (J). (gr. 2-10). pap. 9.95 (978-1-935248-35-4(9)) Leapfrog Pr.

Celenza, Anna Harwell. Duke Ellington's Nutcracker Suite. Tate, Don, illus. 2018. (Once upon a Masterpiece Ser.: 5).

32p. (J). (gr. 1-4). 16.99 (978-1-57091-701-1(9)) Charlesbridge Publishing, Inc.

Ehrhardt, Karen. This Jazz Man. Roth, R. G., illus. 2010. (J). (gr. 1-5). 28.95 incl. audio compact disk (978-1-4301-0740-8(5)) Live Oak Media.

Elvgren, Jennifer. The Edelweiss Pirates. Stamatiadi, Daniela, illus. 2018. (ENG.). 32p. (J). (gr. 3-6). 12.99 (978-1-5124-8360-4(5), 791f516e-7c1a-4768-8987-e9aa55d662c7, Kar-Ben Publishing) Lerner Publishing Group.

Farley, Robin. Mia Jazzes It Up! 2013. (Mia I Can Read Bks.). (J). lib. bdg. 13.55 (978-0-606-32164-8(0)) Turtleback.

Friedman, Carol. Nicky the Jazz Cat. 2004. (Illus.). 32p. (J). (gr. -1-3). 16.95 (978-0-9726092-0-3(2)) Dominick Pictures.

Gollub, Matthew. Jazz Fly 2: The Jungle Pachanga. 2010. (Jazz Fly Ser.). (ENG., Illus.). 32p. (J). (gr. k-2). 18.95 (978-1-889910-44-4(9)) Tortuga Pr.

—Jazz Fly 2: The Jungle Pachanga. Hanke, Karen, illus. 2010. (J). (978-1-889910-45-1(7)) Tortuga Pr.

Mahin, Michael. Stalebread Charlie & the Razzy Dazzy Spasm Band. Tate, Don, illus. 2018. (ENG.). 40p. (J). (gr. -1-3). 17.99 (978-0-547-94201-8(X), 1517145, Clarion Bks.) HarperCollins Pubs.

Miller, William. Rent Party Jazz, 1 vol. Riley-Webb, Charlotte, illus. 2011. (ENG.). 32p. (J). (gr. 1-4). pap. 10.95 (978-1-60060-344-0(0), leelowbooks) Lee & Low Bks., Inc.

Myers, Walter Dean. Jazz. Myers, Christopher, illus. 2006. (ENG.). 48p. (J). (gr. 3-7). 18.95 (978-0-8234-1545-8(7)) Holiday Hse., Inc.

Neftzger, Amy. All That the Dog Ever Wanted. 2005. (Illus.). 32p. (J). lib. bdg. 21.99 (978-0-9746296-1-2(8), FOG104) Fields of Gold Publishing, Inc.

Osborne, Mary Pope. A Good Night for Ghosts. 2010. (Magic Tree House Merlin Missions Ser.: No. 14). (Illus.). 157p. (J). pap. (978-4-8401-3411-8(1)) Fukuinkan Shoten.

—A Good Night for Ghosts. Murdocca, Sal, illus. 2011. (Magic Tree House (R) Merlin Mission Ser.: 14). 144p. (J). (gr. 2-5). 5.99 (978-0-375-85649-5(8), Random Hse. Bks. for Young Readers) Random Hse. Children's Bks.

Pittman, Samuel, II. Alligator Jazz, 1 vol. Bailey, Sheila, illus. 2018. (ENG.). 32p. (J). (gr. -1-3). 16.99 (978-1-4556-2422-5(5), Pelican Publishing) Arcadia Publishing.

Raschka, Chris. John Coltrane's Giant Steps. Raschka, Chris, illus. (Illus.). pap. 16.95 incl. audio (978-0-87499-972-3(3)); pap. incl. audio (978-0-87499-974-7(X)); pap. 18.95 incl. audio compact disk (978-1-59112-416-0(6)); pap. incl. audio compact disk (978-1-59112-603-4(7)) Live Oak Media.

—John Coltrane's Giant Steps. 2003. (Live Oak Readalong Ser.). (Illus.). (J). (gr. -1-2). audio compact disk 28.95 (978-1-59112-417-7(4)) Live Oak Media.

Shahan, Sherry. The Jazzy Alphabet. Thelen, Mary, illus. 2006. 30p. (J). (gr. k-4). reprint ed. 16.00 (978-1-4223-5730-9(9)) DIANE Publishing Co.

Taylor, Debbie A. Sweet Music in Harlem. Morrison, Frank, illus. 2014. 32p. pap. 9.00 (978-1-61003-220-9(9)) Center for the Collaborative Classroom.

—Sweet Music in Harlem, 1 vol. Morrison, Frank, illus. 2004. (ENG.). 32p. (J). 17.95 (978-1-58430-165-3(1)); (gr. 1-4). pap. 11.95 (978-1-62014-080-2(2), leelowbooks) Lee & Low Bks., Inc.

Townley, Roderick. Sky. 2010. (ENG.). 272p. (YA). (gr. 7). pap. 12.99 (978-1-4423-3973-6(X), Atheneum Bks. for Young Readers) Simon & Schuster Children's Publishing.

Volponi, Paul. Hurricane Song. 2009. 160p. (YA). (gr. 7-18). 8.99 (978-0-14-241418-7(2), Speak) Penguin Young Readers Group.

—Hurricane Song: A Novel of New Orleans. 2009. (ENG.). 144p. (YA). (gr. 7-12). 21.19 (978-0-670-06160-0(3), Viking) Penguin Publishing Group.

Weatherford, Carole Boston. Becoming Billie Holiday. Cooper, Floyd, illus. 2008. (ENG.). 120p. (YA). (gr. 4-7). 19.95 (978-1-59078-507-2(X), Wordsong) Highlights Pr., c/o Highlights for Children, Inc.

JAZZ—HISTORY AND CRITICISM

Asirvatham, Sandy. The History of Jazz. 2006. (Illus.). 108p. (J). (gr. 4-8). reprint ed. 25.00 (978-1-4223-5545-9(4)) DIANE Publishing Co.

Handyside, Chris. A History of Jazz. 2006. (J). (978-1-4109-1812-3(2)) Steck-Vaughn.

Kallen, Stuart A. The History of Jazz, 1 vol. 2012. (Music Library). (ENG., Illus.). 128p. (gr. 7-10). lib. bdg. 41.03 (978-1-4205-0820-8(2), 4698a2a7-f1d5-487e-af81-de5f5bbc4f46, Lucent Pr.) Greenhaven Publishing LLC.

Riggs, Kate. Jazz Music. 2008. (World of Music Ser.). (Illus.). 24p. (J). (gr. -1). lib. bdg. 24.25 (978-1-58341-567-2(X), Creative Education) Creative Co., The.

Weatherford, Carole. The Sound That Jazz Makes. 2003. (ENG., Illus.). 32p. (J). (gr. 2-4). pap. 7.95 (978-0-8027-7674-7(4), c621b412-1796-420c-90f6-7495f41e7acb) Fitzhenry & Whiteside, Ltd. CAN. Dist: Firefly Bks., Ltd.

Weatherford, Carole Boston. The Sound That Jazz Makes, 0 vols. Velasquez, Eric, illus. 2012. (ENG.). 34p. (J). (gr. 1-3). pap. 7.99 (978-0-7614-5732-9(1), 9780761457329, Two Lions) Amazon Publishing.

JEALOUSY

Barnham, Kay. Feeling Jealous! Gordon, Mike, illus. 2017. (Everyday Feelings Ser.). (ENG.). 32p. (J). (gr. k-4). 15.99 (978-1-63198-252-1(4), 82521) Free Spirit Publishing Inc.

Beattie, Amy. When I Feel Jealous, 1 vol. 2019. (My Feelings Ser.). (ENG.). 24p. (gr. 1-1). pap. 9.25 (978-1-9785-1167-5(1), 288ac781-7830-421b-9ee7-9e26474d9256) Enslow Publishing, LLC.

Berry, Joy. Let's Talk about Feeling Jealous. Smith, Maggie, illus. 2010. (Let's Talk About Ser.). (ENG.). 32p. (J). (gr. -1-k). pap. 4.99 (978-1-60577-223-3(2)) Berry, Joy Enterprises.

Croft, Priscilla. Dealing with Jealousy/Que Hacer con Los Celos, 1 vol. Velazquez De Leon, Mauricio, tr. 2007. (Conflict Resolution Library / Biblioteca Solución de Conflictos Ser.). (SPA & ENG., Illus.). 24p. (J). (gr. 2-3). lib. bdg. 26.27 (978-1-4042-7662-8(9), ca093948-042a-4c26-9839-4427f86621f4) Rosen Publishing Group, Inc., The.

Hewitt, Sally, et al. Teimlo'n Genfigennus. 2005. (WEL., Illus.). 32p. (978-0-86174-097-0(1)) Drake Educational Assocs. Ltd.

Hill, Z. B. Envy & Jealousy. Croft, Cindy, ed. 2014. (Causes & Effects of Emotions Ser.: 13). 64p. (J). (gr. 7-18). 23.95 (978-1-4222-3072-5(4)) Mason Crest.

Johnston, Marianne. Dealing with Jealousy / Qué hacer con los Celos. 2009. (Conflict Resolution Library / Biblioteca solución de conflictos Ser.). (ENG & SPA.). 24p. (gr. 2-3). 42.50 (978-1-60853-416-6(2), Editorial Buenas Letras) Rosen Publishing Group, Inc., The.

Kravetz, Jonathan. How to Deal with Jealousy. (Let's Work It Out Ser.). 24p. (gr. 2-3). 2009. 42.50 (978-1-61514-264-4(9), PowerKids Pr.) 2006. (ENG., Illus.). (YA). lib. bdg. 26.27 (978-1-4042-3674-5(0), 927c1478-91b5-4e19-a2ad-2b2c31a5aa15) Rosen Publishing Group, Inc., The.

Marcovitz, Hal. A Jealous Guy's Guide: How to Deal, 1 vol. 2014. (Guy's Guide Ser.). (ENG.). 64p. (gr. 5-7). 19.61 (978-1-62293-015-9(0), c1f4bdf3-8dcd-4de3-8433-4c2ffa428f72) Enslow Publishing, LLC.

Marcovitz, Hal & Snyder, Gail. A Guys' Guide to Jealousy; a Girls' Guide to Jealousy, 1 vol. 2009. (Flip-It-Over Guides to Teen Emotions Ser.). (ENG., Illus.). 128p. (gr. 5-6). lib. bdg. 35.93 (978-0-7660-2854-8(2), 215ec03e-5465-43c4-af4c-db7922fe8836) Enslow Publishing, LLC.

Orr, Tamra B. Coping with Breakups & Jealousy, 1 vol. 2017. (Coping (2017-2020) Ser.). (ENG.). 112p. (J). (gr. 7-7). 40.13 (978-1-5081-7388-5(5), 30324d26-9c24-4fd1-97a1-2306e93de9d3, Rosen Young Adult) Rosen Publishing Group, Inc., The.

Smith, Brendan Powell. Joseph & the Colorful Coat: The Brick Bible for Kids. 2015. (Brick Bible for Kids Ser.). (ENG., Illus.). 32p. (J). (gr. -1-k). 12.99 (978-1-63220-409-7(6), Sky Pony Pr.) Skyhorse Publishing Co., Inc.

Snyder, Gail. Jealous Girl? Girls Dealing with Feelings, 1 vol. 2014. (Girls Dealing with Feelings Ser.). (ENG.). 64p. (gr. 5-6). 19.61 (978-1-62293-045-6(2), 02625b79-c016-409c-8929-c38977157e12) Enslow Publishing, LLC.

Thomas, Isabel. Dealing with Feeling Jealous. Elsom, Clare, illus. 2013. (Dealing with Feeling... Ser.). (ENG.). 24p. (J). (gr. 1-2). pap. 6.79 (978-1-4329-7115-1(8), 121116); lib. bdg. 25.99 (978-1-4329-7106-9(9), 121108) Capstone. (Heinemann).

Toner, Jacqueline B. & Freeland, Claire A.B. What to Do When It's Not Fair: A Kid's Guide to Handling Envy & Jealousy. Thompson, David, illus. 2013. 96p. pap. 15.95 (978-1-4338-1341-2(6)) American Psychological Assn.

Wigand, Molly. Jealousy Is Not for Me: A Guide for Freeing Yourself from Envy. Alley, R. W., illus. 2008. (Elf-Help Books for Kids Ser.). 28p. (J). (gr. -1-3). per. 7.95 (978-0-87029-408-2(3)) Abbey Pr.

JEALOUSY—FICTION

Allen, Elise & Stanford, Halle. Winter's Flurry Adventure. Pooler, Paige, illus. 2014. (Enchanted Sisters Ser.: 2). (YA). lib. bdg. 16.00 (978-0-606-36217-7(7)) Turtleback.

Anderson, Derek. What about Harry? Anderson, Derek, illus. 2019. (ENG., Illus.). 32p. (J). (gr. -1-3). 17.99 (978-0-06-240259-2(5), HarperCollins) HarperCollins Pubs.

Atwood, Megan. Olive Becomes Famous (and Hopes She Can Become Un-Famous) Llewhellin, Gareth, illus. 2018. (Dear Molly, Dear Olive Ser.). (ENG.). 96p. (J). (gr. 1-3). lib. bdg. 21.99 (978-1-5158-2922-5(7), 138458, Picture Window Bks.) Capstone.

Barden, Stephanie. Cinderella Smith. Goode, Diane, illus. 2011. (Cinderella Smith Ser.: 1). (ENG.). 160p. (J). (gr. 3-7). 16.99 (978-0-06-196423-7(9), HarperCollins) HarperCollins Pubs.

—Cinderella Smith: the Super Secret Mystery, Vol. 3. Goode, Diane, illus. 2013. (Cinderella Smith Ser.: 3). (ENG.). 144p. (J). (gr. 1-5). 16.99 (978-0-06-200443-7(3), HarperCollins) HarperCollins Pubs.

Benton, Jim. Let's Pretend This Never Happened (Dear Dumb Diary #1) Benton, Jim, illus. 2004. (Dear Dumb Diary Ser.: 1). (ENG., Illus.). 112p. (J). (gr. 4-7). pap. 7.99 (978-0-439-62904-1(7), Scholastic Paperbacks) Scholastic, Inc.

—School. Hasn't This Gone on Long Enough? 2012. (Dear Dumb Diary: Year Two Ser.: 1). lib. bdg. 16.00 (978-0-606-23731-4(3)) Turtleback.

Bowe, Julie. So Much Drama. 2016. (Victoria Torres, Unfortunately Average Ser.). (ENG., Illus.). 160p. (J). (gr. 4-8). pap. 5.95 (978-1-4965-3807-9(2), 133115); lib. bdg. 27.99 (978-1-4965-3799-7(8), 133112) Capstone. (Stone Arch Bks.).

Bowman, Crystal. Little David & His Best Friend, 1 vol. Hartung, Susan Kathleen & Endersly, Frank, illus. 2010. (I Can Read! / Little David Ser.). (ENG.). 32p. (J). pap. 4.99 (978-0-310-71710-2(8)) Zonderkidz.

Bracken, Beth, et al. A Wish in the Woods, 1 vol. Sawyer, Odessa, illus. 2012. (Faerieground Ser.). (ENG.). 96p. (J). (gr. 5-9). lib. bdg. 23.99 (978-1-4342-3303-5(0), 116267, Stone Arch Bks.) Capstone.

Brouwer, Sigmund. Sewer Rats, 1 vol. 2006. (Orca Currents Ser.). (ENG.). 128p. (J). (gr. 4-7). per. 9.95 (978-1-55143-488-9(1)) Orca Bk. Pubs. USA.

—Sewer Rats. 2006. (Orca Currents Ser.). 106p. (gr. 4-7). 19.95 (978-0-7569-6872-4(0)) Perfection Learning Corp.

Bucay, Jorge. The King & the Magician. Gusti, illus. 2014. (ENG.). 52p. (J). (gr. -1). 14.95 (978-0-7892-1204-7(8), 791204, Abbeville Kids) Abbeville Pr., Inc.

Cameron, Jill. Miffy, the Crooked-Eyed Cat. 2009. 28p. pap. 12.99 (978-1-60860-353-4(9), Eloquent Bks.) Strategic Book Publishing & Rights Agency (SBPRA).

Carbone, Courtney. This Makes Me Jealous: Dealing with Feelings. Kushnir, Hilli, illus. 2019. (Rodale Kids Curious Readers/Level 2 Ser.: 6). 32p. (J). (gr. -1-1). pap. 4.99 (978-1-63565-077-8(1), 9781635650778, Rodale Kids) Random Hse. Children's Bks.

Carter, Aimée & Carter, Aimée. The Goddess Inheritance. 2013. (Goddess Test Novel Ser.: 3). (ENG.). 304p. (YA). pap. 11.99 (978-0-373-21067-1(1), Harlequin Teen) Harlequin Enterprises ULC CAN. Dist: HarperCollins Pubs.

Clarke, Kathryn. The Breakable Vow. 2004. 480p. (YA). (gr. 7-18). 16.89 (978-0-06-051822-6(7)) HarperCollins Pubs.

Clarke, Kathryn Ann. The Breakable Vow. 2004. (ENG.). 480p. (YA). (gr. 8-18). pap. 8.99 (978-0-06-051821-9(9), HarperTeen) HarperCollins Pubs.

Cooke, Brandy. You Poked My Heart! Logan, Laura, illus. 2016. (ENG.). 16p. (J). (gr. -1-1). bds. 5.99 (978-1-4998-0310-5(9)) Little Bee Books Inc.

Covey, Sean. Sammy & the Pecan Pie: Habit 4. Curtis, Stacy, illus. (7 Habits of Happy Kids Ser.: 4). (ENG.). 32p. (J). (gr. -1-1). 2018. 6.99 (978-1-5344-1581-2(5)) 2013. 7.99 (978-1-4424-7647-9(8)) Simon & Schuster Bks. For Young Readers. (Simon & Schuster Bks. For Young Readers).

—Sammy & the Pecan Pie: Habit 4 (Ready-To-Read Level 2) Curtis, Stacy, illus. 2019. (7 Habits of Happy Kids Ser.: 4). (ENG.). 32p. (J). (gr. k-2). 17.99 (978-1-5344-4454-6(8)); pap. 4.99 (978-1-5344-4453-9(X)) Simon Spotlight. (Simon Spotlight).

Dadey, Debby & Dadey, Debbie. Secret Sea Horse, Bk. 6. Avakyan, Tatevik, illus. 2015. (Mermaid Tales Ser.). (ENG.). 96p. (J). (gr. 1-4). 31.36 (978-1-61479-327-4(1), 17149, Chapter Bks.) Spotlight.

de la Cruz, Melissa. The Ashley Project. 2014. (Ashley Project Ser.: 1). (ENG., Illus.). 288p. (J). (gr. 4-8). pap. 6.99 (978-1-4424-9033-8(0), Aladdin) Simon & Schuster Children's Publishing.

De la Cruz, Melissa. Jealous? 2008. (Ashleys Ser.: Bk. 2). (ENG.). 256p. (YA). (gr. 4-8). pap. 9.99 (978-1-4169-3407-3(3), Simon & Schuster Bks. For Young Readers) Simon & Schuster Bks. For Young Readers.

de la Cruz, Melissa. Social Order. 2014. (Ashley Project Ser.: 2). (ENG., Illus.). 288p. (J). (gr. 4-8). 16.99 (978-1-4814-0667-3(1), Simon & Schuster/Paula Wiseman Bks.) Simon & Schuster/Paula Wiseman Bks.

DeFelice, Cynthia. The Ghost & Mrs. Hobbs. 2010. (Ghost Mysteries Ser.: 2). (ENG.). 208p. (J). (gr. 3-7). pap. 14.99 (978-0-312-62909-0(5), 900066873) Square Fish.

Elliott, Rebecca. Eva & the New Owl: a Branches Book (Owl Diaries #4) Elliott, Rebecca, illus. 2016. (Owl Diaries: 4). (ENG., Illus.). 80p. (J). (gr. k-2). pap. 5.99 (978-0-545-82559-7(8)) Scholastic, Inc.

Feiffer, Jules. The House Across the Street. Feiffer, Jules, illus. 2003. (Illus.). 28p. (J). (gr. 1-4). reprint ed. 16.00 (978-0-7567-6845-4(4)) DIANE Publishing Co.

Filliozat, Isabelle. Jealousy: A Toy Story Tale. 2020. (J). (978-1-5415-9859-1(8)) Lerner Publishing Group.

Genhart, Michael & Mack, Steve. Peanut Butter & Jellyous: ... sometimes Friendships Get Sticky. 2017. (ENG., Illus.). 32p. (J). (978-1-4338-2337-4(3), Magination Pr.) American Psychological Assn.

Green, Poppy. The Mouse House. Bell, Jennifer A., illus. 2017. (Adventures of Sophie Mouse Ser.: 11). (ENG.). 128p. (J). (gr. k-4). pap. 6.99 (978-1-4814-9435-9(X), Little Simon) Little Simon.

Greene, Stephanie. Princess Posey & the First Grade Play. Roth Sisson, Stephanie, illus. 2017. (Princess Posey, First Grader Ser.: 11). 96p. (J). (gr. k-3). 5.99 (978-0-14-751719-7(2), Puffin Books) Penguin Young Readers Group.

—Princess Posey & the New First Grader. Roth Sisson, Stephanie, illus. 2013. (Princess Posey, First Grader Ser.: 6). 96p. (J). (gr. k-3). pap. 5.99 (978-0-14-242763-7(2), Puffin Books) Penguin Young Readers Group.

Guest, Elissa Haden. Iris & Walter & the Substitute Teacher. Davenier, Christine, illus. 2006. (Iris & Walter Ser.). 44p. (gr. 1-4). 15.95 (978-0-7569-7122-9(5)) Perfection Learning Corp.

Gutknecht, Allison. Sing Like Nobody's Listening. 2018. (Mix Ser.). (ENG.). 256p. (J). (gr. 4-8). 18.99 (978-1-4814-7157-2(0)); (Illus.). pap. 7.99 (978-1-4814-7156-5(2)) Simon & Schuster Children's Publishing. (Aladdin).

Hahn, Mary Downing. The Ghost of Crutchfield Hall. 2011. (ENG.). 160p. (J). (gr. 5-7). pap. 7.99 (978-0-547-57715-9(X), 1458473, Clarion Bks.) HarperCollins Pubs.

Hale, Bruce. Key Lardo: A Chet Gecko Mystery. Hale, Bruce, illus. 2007. (Chet Gecko Ser.: 12). (ENG., Illus.). 128p. (J). (gr. 3-7). pap. 7.99 (978-0-15-205235-5(6), 1195772, Clarion Bks.) HarperCollins Pubs.

Harper, Charise Mericle. Just Grace, Star on Stage. 2014. (Just Grace Ser.: 9). (ENG., Illus.). 208p. (J). (gr. 1-4). pap. 7.99 (978-0-544-22533-6(3), 1563387, Clarion Bks.) HarperCollins Pubs.

Hermes, Patricia. Emma Dilemma & the Camping Nanny. Carter, Abby, illus. 2019. (Emma Dilemma Ser.: 4). (ENG.). 146p. (J). (gr. 3-6). pap. 9.99 (978-1-4778-1079-8(X), 9781477810798, Two Lions) Amazon Publishing.

Hooks, Gwendolyn. Three's a Crowd. Walker, Sylvia, illus. 2004. 32p. (J). lib. bdg. 15.00 (978-1-4242-0240-9(X)) Fitzgerald Bks.

Johnston, Gail. The Shaggy Pony & the Spotted Pup. 2010. 24p. 11.32 (978-1-4520-9653-7(8)) AuthorHouse.

Jones, Jen. The New Ashley. Franco, Paula, illus. 2014. (Sleepover Girls Ser.). (ENG.). 128p. (J). (gr. 3-5). lib. bdg. 22.65 (978-1-4342-9758-7(6), 127106, Stone Arch Bks.) Capstone.

Jones, Patrick. Friend or Foe. 2016. (Unbarred Ser.). (ENG.). 120p. (YA). (gr. 6-12). pap. 7.99 (978-1-5124-0095-3(5), 5b8cb162-38ac-444d-b04f-780ace2a68bf, Darby Creek) Lerner Publishing Group.

—Friend or Foe. 2016. (Unbarred Ser.). (ENG.). 120p. (YA). (gr. 6-12). E-Book 42.65 (978-1-5124-0096-0(3), Darby Creek) Lerner Publishing Group.

Kantorovitz, Sylvie. The Very Tiny Baby. Kantorovitz, Sylvie, illus. 2014. (Illus.). 240p. (J). (gr. -1-2). lib. bdg. 14.95 (978-1-58089-445-6(3)) Charlesbridge Publishing, Inc.

—The Very Tiny Baby. 2014. (J). pap. (978-1-58089-446-3(1)) Charlesbridge Publishing, Inc.

Keene, Carolyn. Princess Mix-Up Mystery, No. 24. Pamintuan, Macky, illus. 2009. (Nancy Drew & the Clue Crew Ser.: 24). (ENG.). 96p. (J). (gr. 1-4). pap. 5.99 (978-1-4169-7811-4(9), Aladdin) Simon & Schuster Children's Publishing.

Kingsley, Kate. Pretty on the Outside. 2010. (Young, Loaded, & Fabulous Ser.: 1). (ENG.). 320p. (YA). (gr. 9-18). pap. 9.99 (978-1-4169-9399-5(1), Simon Pulse) Simon Pulse.

Kowitt, Holly, illus. Revenge of the Loser. 2012. 233p. (J). (978-0-545-42611-4(1), Scholastic Pr.) Scholastic, Inc.

Kreie, Chris. The Superstar. 2018. (Kick! Ser.). (ENG.). 104p. (YA). (gr. 6-12). 25.32 (978-1-5415-0024-2(5), 1b86e765-43e2-4a01-aaa5-a2d1cf2da395, Darby Creek) Lerner Publishing Group.

Krulik, Nancy. Eww! What's on My Shoe? 2013. (George Brown, Class Clown Ser.: 11). lib. bdg. 14.75 (978-0-606-32126-6(8)) Turtleback.

Lamb, Charles & Lamb, Mary. Tales from Shakespeare: "Othello" Strang, Kay, ed. Andrews, Gary, illus. rev. ed. 2005. 36p. pap. 4.95 (978-0-9542905-4-2(2)) Capercaillie Bks., Ltd GBR. Dist: Gatewood Pr.

L'Engle, Madeleine. The Other Dog. Davenier, Christine, illus. 2018. (ENG.). 48p. (J). (gr. -1-k). 17.99 (978-1-4521-7189-0(0)) Chronicle Bks. LLC.

Mackall, Dandi Daley. Natalie Really Very Much Wants to Be a Star, 1 vol. Blakeslee, Lys, illus. 2009. (That's Nat! Ser.: 2). (ENG.). 96p. (J). (gr. 1-4). pap. 4.99 (978-0-310-71567-2(9)) Zonderkidz.

—A Perfect Pony, 1 vol. Wolf, Claudia, illus. 2011. (I Can Read! / a Horse Named Bob Ser.). (ENG.). 32p. (J). pap. 4.99 (978-0-310-71783-6(3)) Zonderkidz.

Maddox, Jake. Soccer Sabotage. 2018. (Jake Maddox JV Ser.). (ENG., Illus.). 96p. (J). (gr. 4-6). lib. bdg. 26.65 (978-1-4965-5932-6(0), 137134, Stone Arch Bks.) Capstone.

Madonna. The English Roses. 10th ed. 2017. (ENG., Illus.). 48p. (J). (gr. 3-5). 24.95 (978-0-935112-10-8(3)) Callaway Editions, Inc.

Manushkin, Fran. Keep Dancing, Katie, 1 vol. Lyon, Tammie, illus. 2014. (Katie Woo Ser.). (ENG.). 32p. (J). (gr. k-2). 21.32 (978-1-4795-5187-3(2), 125541, Picture Window Bks.) Capstone.

Mazer, Anne. Mabel Strikes a Chord, 4. Brown, Bill, illus. 2008. (Sister Magic Ser.). (ENG.). 86p. (J). (gr. 3-6). 17.44 (978-0-439-87249-2(9)) Scholastic, Inc.

Mazer, Norma Fox. Ten Ways to Make My Sister Disappear. (ENG.). 160p. (J). (gr. 4-6). 2012. 21.19 (978-0-439-83984-6(X)) 2007. 16.99 (978-0-439-83983-9(1)) Scholastic, Inc. (Levine, Arthur A. Bks.).

McKee, David. Denver. McKee, David, illus. 2012. (ENG., Illus.). 32p. (J). (gr. -1-k). pap. 10.99 (978-1-84939-389-8(3)) Andersen Pr. GBR. Dist: Independent Pubs. Group.

Metz, Melinda. S. M. A. R. T. S. & the 3-D Danger. McKenzie, Heath, illus. 2015. (S. M. A. R. T. S. Ser.). (ENG.). 128p. (J). (gr. 3-6). 22.65 (978-1-4965-0465-4(8), 128490, Stone Arch Bks.) Capstone.

—S. M. A. R. T. S. & the Mars Mission Mayhem. McKenzie, Heath, illus. 2016. (S. M. A. R. T. S. Ser.). (ENG.). 128p. (J). (gr. 3-6). pap. 9.95 (978-1-4965-3018-9(7), 131905); lib. bdg. 22.65 (978-1-4965-3016-5(0), 131903) Capstone. (Stone Arch Bks.).

Misra, Michelle. Secrets & Sapphires. Chaffey, Samantha, illus. 2016. (Angel Wings Ser.: 3). (ENG.). 128p. (J). (gr. 1-4). pap. 6.99 (978-1-4814-5803-0(5), Aladdin) Simon & Schuster Children's Publishing.

Moonheart, Ella. Kitty's Magic 3: Ruby the Runaway Kitten. 2018. (Kitty's Magic Ser.). (ENG., Illus.). 128p. (J). pap. 5.99 (978-1-68119-389-2(2), 900172064, Bloomsbury Children's Bks.) Bloomsbury Publishing USA.

Myracle, Lauren. Friends of a Feather. Henry, Jed, illus. 2015. (Life of Ty Ser.: 3). (ENG.). 144p. (J). (gr. 1-4). 7.99 (978-0-14-242320-2(3), Puffin Books) Penguin Young Readers Group.

Oates, Joyce Carol. The New Kitten. Mottram, Dave, illus. 2019. (ENG.). 32p. (J). (gr. -1-3). 17.99 (978-0-06-256392-7(0), HarperCollins) HarperCollins Pubs.

Ormerod, Jan. The Baby Swap. Joyner, Andrew, illus. 2015. (ENG.). 32p. (J). (gr. -1-1). 16.99 (978-1-4814-1914-7(5), Little Simon) Little Simon.

Osiyemi, Linda Omonike. The Pot & the Necklace. 2012. (Illus.). 72p. (gr. -1). pap. 13.66 (978-1-4772-3104-3(8)) AuthorHouse.

Pakkala, Christine. Last-But-Not-Least Lola & the Wild Chicken. Hoppe, Paul, illus. 2015. (Last-But-Not-Least Lola Ser.). (ENG.). 216p. (J). (gr. 2-5). pap. 7.95 (978-1-62979-404-4(X), Astra Young Readers) Astra Publishing Hse.

Petrovic, Svetlana. Brown Bear, White Bear. Hardy, Vincent, illus. 2009. 28p. (J). (gr. -1-3). 17.00 (978-0-8028-5353-0(6), Eerdmans Bks For Young Readers) Eerdmans, William B. Publishing Co.

Rippin, Sally. The Best Party Ever. 2014. (ENG., Illus.). 48p. (J). pap. 4.99 (978-1-61067-261-0(5)) Kane Miller.

—The Playground Problem. 2015. (ENG., Illus.). 48p. (J). pap. 4.99 (978-1-61067-260-3(7)) Kane Miller.

Rissi, Anica Mrose. Anna, Banana, & the Recipe for Disaster. Park, Meg, illus. 2018. (Anna, Banana Ser.: 6). (ENG.). 128p. (J). (gr. 1-5). 17.99 (978-1-4814-8672-9(1)); pap. 6.99 (978-1-4814-8673-6(X)) Simon & Schuster Bks. For Young Readers. (Simon & Schuster Bks. For Young Readers).

Roberts, Daniel. Harrison & His Dinosaur Robot & the Super-Fast Race Car. 2009. (Illus.). 32p. pap. 14.95 (978-1-4389-2847-0(5)) AuthorHouse.

Robins, Eleanor. Pay Back, 1 vol. unabr. ed. 2011. (Choices Ser.). (ENG.). 52p. (YA). (gr. 5-12). 9.75 (978-1-61651-594-2(5)) Saddleback Educational Publishing, Inc.

Russo, Marisabina. The Trouble with Baby. Russo, Marisabina, illus. 2003. (Illus.). 32p. (J). (gr. -1-18). 16.89 (978-0-06-008925-2(3)) HarperCollins Pubs.

Sareva, Ibrahim. West of Kilimanjaro 1: Book 1. 2010. 44p. pap. 16.99 (978-1-4520-3006-7(5)) AuthorHouse.

Schraff, Anne E. Bad Blood. 2014. (Urban Underground — Cesar Chavez High School Ser.). (YA). lib. bdg. 20.80 (978-0-606-35591-9(X)) Turtleback.

Sheldon, Dyan. One or Two Things I Learned about Love. 2013. (ENG.). 304p. (YA). (gr. 7). 15.99 (978-0-7636-6665-1(3)) Candlewick Pr.

Shuttlewood, Craig. Awesome! Shuttlewood, Craig, illus. 2018. (ENG., Illus.). 32p. (J). (gr. k-2). 15.95 (978-1-68446-013-7(1), 138906, Capstone Editions) Capstone.

Simon, Coco. Emma Catwalks & Cupcakes! 2018. (Cupcake Diaries: 31). (ENG.). 160p. (J). (gr. 3-7). 17.99 (978-1-5344-1736-6(2)); (Illus.). pap. 6.99 (978-1-5344-1735-9(4)) Simon Spotlight. (Simon Spotlight).

Sommer, Isabell & Reinhardt, Swen. CHIP CHIPS JAM - 4: Der Schatz in der Elbe. 2010. 86p. pap. (978-3-8391-0219-0(7)) Books on Demand GmbH.

Spelman, Cornelia Maude. When I Feel Jealous. Parkinson, Kathy, illus. 2003. (Way I Feel Bks.). (ENG.). 24p. (J). (gr. -1-3). 7.99 (978-0-8075-8902-1(0), 807589020) Whitman, Albert & Co.

Spires, Sharlene. The Grandsisters. 2010. 56p. pap. 15.99 (978-1-4535-3004-7(5)) Xlibris Corp.

Swan, Bill. Corner Kick, 1 vol. 2004. (Lorimer Sports Stories Ser.: 66). (ENG.). 144p. (J). (gr. 4-8). 16.95 (978-1-55028-817-9(2), 817) James Lorimer & Co. Ltd., Pubs. CAN. Dist: Formac Lorimer Bks. Ltd.

Trueit, Trudi. The Sister Solution. 2015. (Mix Ser.). (ENG., Illus.). 240p. (J). (gr. 4-8). pap. 7.99 (978-1-4814-3239-9(7), Aladdin) Simon & Schuster Children's Publishing.

Wesley, Valerie Wilson. How to Fish for Trouble. Roos, Maryn, illus. 2004. 89p. (J). lib. bdg. 15.00 (978-1-4242-0643-8(X)) Fitzgerald Bks.

Wisler, Joelle. Ariana Gold. 2016. (What's Your Dream? Ser.). (ENG., Illus.). 96p. (J). (gr. 4-6). lib. bdg. 25.99 (978-1-4965-3442-2(5), 132564, Stone Arch Bks.) Capstone.

Young, Amy. A New Friend for Sparkle. 2017. (Unicorn Named Sparkle Ser.). (ENG., Illus.). 40p. (J). 18.99 (978-0-374-30553-6(6), 900163984, Farrar, Straus & Giroux (BYR)) Farrar, Straus & Giroux.

JEEPS

see Automobiles; Trucks

JEFFERSON, THOMAS, 1743-1826

Adler, David A. A Picture Book of Thomas Jefferson. Wallner, John & Wallner, Alexandra, illus. 2018. (Picture Book Biography Ser.). (ENG.). 32p. (J). (gr. -1-3). 7.99 (978-0-8234-4049-8(4)) Holiday Hse., Inc.

Albee, Sarah & Benchmark Education Co., LLC. Thomas Jefferson: American Architect. 2014. (Text Connections Ser.). (J). (gr. 3). (978-1-4509-9658-7(2)) Benchmark Education Co.

Anderson, Michael, contrib. by. Thomas Jefferson, 1 vol. 2012. (Pivotal Presidents: Profiles in Leadership Ser.). (ENG.). 80p. (YA). (gr. 8-8). lib. bdg. 36.47 (978-1-61530-940-5(3), 6d704455-cf16-4556-9645-37410ab7e520); (Illus.). 72.94 (978-1-61530-959-7(4), a3e4e882-20c6-4ce3-9198-2e9402760d1f) Rosen Publishing Group, Inc., The.

Behrman, Carol H. Thomas Jefferson. 2004. (Presidential Leaders Ser.). (Illus.). 112p. (J). 29.27 (978-0-8225-0822-9(2), Lerner Pubns.) Lerner Publishing Group.

Bennett, Doraine. Thomas Jefferson. 2012. (Illus.). 24p. (J). (978-1-935884-39-2(5)); pap. (978-1-935884-48-4(4)) State Standards Publishing, LLC.

Bober, Natalie S. Thomas Jefferson: Draftsman of a Nation. 2008. (ENG., Illus.). 376p. per. 16.95 (978-0-8139-2732-9(3), P144204) University of Virginia Pr.

Braun, Eric Mark. The Real Thomas Jefferson: The Truth Behind the Legend. 2019. (Real Revolutionaries Ser.). (ENG., Illus.). 64p. (J). (gr. 5-9). pap. 7.95 (978-0-7565-6127-7(2), 140074); lib. bdg. 34.65 (978-0-7565-5891-8(3), 138696) Capstone. (Compass Point Bks.).

Carr, Aaron. Jefferson Memorial. 2014. (J). (978-1-4896-2898-5(3)) Weigl Pubs., Inc.

Clickard, Carrie. Thomas Jefferson & the Mammoth Hunt: The True Story of the Quest for America's Biggest Bones. Carpenter, Nancy, illus. 2019. (ENG.). 40p. (J). (gr. -1-3). 17.99 (978-1-4814-4268-8(6), Beach Lane Bks.) Beach Lane Bks.

Coddington, Andrew. Thomas Jefferson: Architect of the Declaration of Independence, 1 vol. 2016. (Great American Thinkers Ser.). (ENG., Illus.). 128p. (YA). (gr. 9-9). 47.36 (978-1-5026-1924-2(5), 75a7aea4-6e46-499f-8c25-a7a46fbc5d49) Cavendish Square Publishing LLC.

Collard, Sneed B., III. Thomas Jefferson: Let Freedom Ring!, 1 vol. 2009. (American Heroes Ser.). (ENG.). 48p. (gr. 3-3). lib. bdg. 32.64 (978-0-7614-3067-4(9), 8eac1ebf-a575-4a39-a66b-9e82fcc32ff5) Cavendish Square Publishing LLC.

Elston, Heidi. Thomas Jefferson, 1 vol. 2016. (United States Presidents *2017 Ser.). (ENG., Illus.). 40p. (J). (gr. 2-5). 35.64 (978-1-68078-102-1(2), 21821, Big Buddy Bks.) ABDO Publishing Co.

Ferry, Joseph. Thomas Jefferson. 2004. (Childhood of the Presidents Ser.). (Illus.). 48p. (J). (gr. 4-18). lib. bdg. 17.95 (978-1-59084-271-3(5)) Mason Crest.

Fradin, Dennis Brindell & Fradin, Dennis. Who Was Thomas Jefferson? 2003. (Who Was... ? Ser.). (Illus.). 103p. (J). (gr. 3-7). 16.00 (978-0-613-63486-1(1)) Turtleback.

Fradin, Dennis Brindell & Who HQ. Who Was Thomas Jefferson? O'Brien, John, illus. 2003. (Who Was? Ser.). 112p. (J). (gr. 3-7). pap. 5.99 (978-0-448-43145-1(9), Penguin Workshop) Penguin Young Readers Group.

Furgang, Kathy. The Declaration of Independence & Thomas Jefferson of Virginia. 2009. (Framers of the Declaration of Independence Ser.). 24p. (gr. 3-3). 42.50 (978-1-61512-633-0(3), PowerKids Pr.) Rosen Publishing Group, Inc., The.

Gaines, Ann Graham. Thomas Jefferson. 2004. (Triangle History of the American Revolution Ser.). (Illus.). 104p. (J). 27.45 (978-1-56711-781-3(3), Blackbirch Pr., Inc.) Cengage Gale.

Gosman, Gillian. Thomas Jefferson, 1 vol. 2011. (Life Stories Ser.). (Illus.). 24p. (J). (gr. 3-3). (ENG.). pap. 9.25 (978-1-4488-3180-7(6), aa940604-afba-402c-9f00-9fa5315e3895, PowerKids Pr.); (SPA & ENG., lib. bdg. 26.27 (978-1-4488-3221-7(7), e5e60a96-36ef-45db-b4dc-d760cd59aa5a); (ENG., lib. bdg. 26.27 (978-1-4488-3178-4(4), 6e7e2cdf-68fc-42f2-98e4-ec91f3c5b148, PowerKids Pr.) Rosen Publishing Group, Inc., The.

Gregory, Josh. Thomas Jefferson: The 3rd President. 2015. (First Look at America's Presidents Ser.). (ENG.). 24p. (J). (gr. -1-3). lib. bdg. 26.99 (978-1-62724-553-1(7)) Bearport Publishing Co., Inc.

Harness, Cheryl. Thomas Jefferson. 2007. (Illus.). 48p. (J). (gr. 3-7). per. 7.95 (978-1-4263-0043-1(3), National Geographic Children's Bks.) Disney Publishing Worldwide.

Jeffrey, Gary. Thomas Jefferson & the Declaration of Independence, 1 vol. 2011. (Graphic Heroes of the American Revolution Ser.). (ENG., Illus.). 24p. (J). (gr. 3-3). 26.60 (978-1-4339-6025-3(7), b3ad44c5-2d19-400f-8ba3-6b2e6bef69a2); pap. 9.15 (978-1-4339-6026-0(5), 6bfbc259-f45e-48b1-85a7-4b2b3c1cce56, Gareth Stevens Learning Library) Stevens, Gareth Publishing LLLP.

Jurmain, Suzanne Tripp. Worst of Friends: Thomas Jefferson, John Adams & the True Story of an American Feud. Day, Larry, illus. 2011. (ENG.). 32p. (J). (gr. 1-3). 18.99 (978-0-525-47903-1(1), Dutton Books for Young Readers) Penguin Young Readers Group.

Kalman, Maira. Thomas Jefferson: Life, Liberty & the Pursuit of Everything. Kalman, Maira, illus. 2014. (ENG., Illus.). 40p. (J). (gr. k-3). 17.99 (978-0-399-24040-9(3), Nancy Paulsen Books) Penguin Young Readers Group.

Keppeler, Jill. 20 Fun Facts about Thomas Jefferson. 2017. (Fun Fact File: Founding Fathers Ser.). 32p. (J). (gr. 2-3). pap. 63.00 (978-1-5382-0274-6(3)) Stevens, Gareth Publishing LLLP.

Kerley, Barbara. Those Rebels, John & Tom. Fotheringham, Edwin, illus. 2012. (ENG.). 48p. (J). (gr. 2-5). 17.99 (978-0-545-22268-6(0), Scholastic Pr.) Scholastic, Inc.

Kishel, Ann-Marie. Thomas Jefferson: A Life of Patriotism. 2006. (Pull Ahead Books — Biographies Ser.). (ENG., Illus.). 32p. (J). (gr. k-3). lib. bdg. 22.65 (978-0-8225-3480-8(0), 7e675b82-3fea-41a6-889e-074788415669, Lerner Pubns.) Lerner Publishing Group.

—Thomas Jefferson: Una Vida de Patriotismo. Translations.com Staff, tr. 2006. (Libros para Avanzar-Biografías (Pull Ahead Books-Biographies) Ser.). (ENG & SPA., Illus.). 32p. (gr. k-3). lib. bdg. 22.60 (978-0-8225-6238-2(3), Ediciones Lerner) Lerner Publishing Group.

—Thomas Jefferson: Una vida de patriotismo (A Life of Patriotism) 2006. (Libros para Avanzar-Biografias (Pull Ahead Books-Biographies Ser.). (Illus.). 32p. (J). (gr. 3-7). per. 6.95 (978-0-8225-6554-3(4), Ediciones Lerner) Lerner Publishing Group.

Kit, Oscar. A Timeline of the Life of Thomas Jefferson. (Timelines of American History Ser.). 32p. (gr. 4-4). 2009. 47.90 (978-1-60854-389-2(7)) 2004. (ENG., Illus.). lib. bdg. 29.13 (978-0-8239-4539-9(1), 47a2bcaf-4d4e-4142-9348-ee6f4d4c961c) Rosen Publishing Group, Inc., The. (Rosen Reference).

Kukla, Amy. Thomas Jefferson: Life, Liberty, & the Pursuit of Happiness. 2009. (Library of American Lives & Times Ser.). 112p. (gr. 5-5). 69.20 (978-1-60853-508-8(8)) Rosen Publishing Group, Inc., The.

Kukla, Amy & Kukla, Jon. Thomas Jefferson: Life, Liberty, & the Pursuit of Happiness, 1 vol. 2004. (Library of American Lives & Times Ser.). (ENG., Illus.). 112p. (YA). (gr. 5-5). lib. bdg. 38.27 (978-1-4042-2655-5(9), dc1c3fb6-97ec-4a36-b098-de511a783f4d, PowerKids Pr.) Rosen Publishing Group, Inc., The.

Landau, Elaine. Jefferson's Louisiana Purchase: Would You Make the Deal of the Century?, 1 vol. 2014. (What Would You Do? Ser.). (ENG.). 48p. (gr. 3-4). 27.93 (978-0-7660-6305-1(4), 4a599c69-5c92-4682-95d0-9a93f9891693); pap. 11.53 (978-0-7660-6306-8(2), 0c240e39-3a16-4732-bbd2-78d7c4c61d18, Enslow Elementary) Enslow Publishing, LLC.

—The Louisiana Purchase: Would You Close the Deal?, 1 vol. 2008. (What Would You Do? Ser.). (ENG., Illus.). 48p. (gr. 3-3). pap. 11.53 (978-1-59845-196-2(0), ba81a5a3-263e-4e3c-99e1-1f0721932655); lib. bdg. 27.93 (978-0-7660-2902-6(6), ab076af9-e6df-4809-afdd-7ab429047f40) Enslow Publishing, LLC. (Enslow Elementary).

Lusted, Marcia Amidon. Revolution & the New Nation: 1750-Early 1800s. 2007. (Presidents of the United States Ser.). (Illus.). 48p. (J). (gr. 4-7). lib. bdg. 29.05 (978-1-59036-739-1(1)); per. 10.95 (978-1-59036-740-7(5)) Weigl Pubs., Inc.

Maloof, Torrey. Thomas Jefferson & the Empire of Liberty. rev. ed. 2017. (Social Studies: Informational Text Ser.). (ENG., Illus.). 32p. (gr. 4-8). pap. 11.99 (978-1-4938-3792-2(3)) Teacher Created Materials, Inc.

Manolis, Kay & Leslie, Tonya. Thomas Jefferson: A Life of Patriotism. 2007. (People of Character Ser.). (ENG., Illus.). 24p. (J). (gr. 2-5). lib. bdg. 26.95 (978-1-60014-093-8(9)) Bellwether Media.

McLeese, Don. Thomas Jefferson. 2005. (Heroes of the American Revolution Ser.). (Illus.). 32p. (gr. 2-5). 19.95 (978-1-59515-217-6(2)) Rourke Educational Media.

Miller, Brandon Marie. Thomas Jefferson for Kids: His Life & Times with 21 Activities. 2011. (For Kids Ser.: 37). (ENG., Illus.). 144p. (J). (gr. 4). pap. 16.95 (978-1-56976-348-3(8)) Chicago Review Pr., Inc.

Mis, Melody S. How to Draw the Life & Times of Thomas Jefferson. 2009. (Kid's Guide to Drawing the Presidents of the United States of America Ser.). 32p. (gr. 4-4). 50.50 (978-1-61511-161-9(1), PowerKids Pr.) Rosen Publishing Group, Inc., The.

Mullin, Rita Thievon. Thomas Jefferson: Architect of Freedom. 2007. (Sterling Biographies Ser.). (ENG., Illus.). 124p. (J). (gr. 6-8). 18.69 (978-1-4027-4750-2(0)) Sterling Publishing Co., Inc.

Murphy, Frank. Thomas Jefferson's Feast. Walz, Richard, illus. 2004. (Step into Reading Ser.). 48p. 14.00 (978-0-7569-3235-0(1)) Perfection Learning Corp.

Nelson, Sheila. Thomas Jefferson's America: The Louisiana Purchase (1800-1811) 2006. (How America Became America Ser.). (Illus.). 96p. (YA). lib. bdg. 22.95 (978-1-59084-904-0(3)) Mason Crest.

Oachs, Emily Rose. Thomas Jefferson's Presidency. 2016. (Presidential Powerhouses Ser.). (ENG., Illus.). 104p. (YA). (gr. 6-12). 35.99 (978-1-4677-7923-4(7), f04c63b9-b37c-4da8-81b6-da668eacfffa); E-Book 54.65 (978-1-4677-8602-7(0)) Lerner Publishing Group. (Lerner Pubns.).

O'Donoghue, Sean. Thomas Jefferson & the Louisiana Purchase, 1 vol. 2016. (Spotlight on American History Ser.). (ENG., Illus.). 24p. (J). (gr. 4-6). 27.93 (978-1-5081-4948-4(8), 05df1466-a916-4843-9a6b-54ecd33a7ede, PowerKids Pr.) Rosen Publishing Group, Inc., The.

Pelleschi, Andrea. Thomas Jefferson, 1 vol. 2012. (Jr. Graphic Founding Fathers Ser.). (ENG., Illus.). 24p. (J). (gr. 2-3). pap. 11.60 (978-1-4488-7994-6(9), c5665c08-ef12-44d8-9855-490e1be876af); lib. bdg. 28.93 (978-1-4488-7900-7(0), abe1e8b1-36a7-402f-9565-b3e200393a16) Rosen Publishing Group, Inc., The. (PowerKids Pr.).

Pingry, Patricia A. Meet Thomas Jefferson. Johnson, Meredith, ed. Johnson, Meredith, illus. 2003. 32p. (J). 9.95 (978-0-8249-5459-8(9), Ideals Pubns.) Worthy Publishing.

Raabe, Emily. Thomas Jefferson & the Louisiana Purchase. 2009. (Westward Ho! Ser.). 24p. (gr. 2-3). 42.50 (978-1-60854-763-0(9), PowerKids Pr.) Rosen Publishing Group, Inc., The.

Rajczak, Michael. Before Thomas Jefferson Was President, 1 vol. 2018. (Before They Were President Ser.). (ENG.). 24p. (gr. 2-3). lib. bdg. 24.27 (978-1-5382-2913-2(7), 099a0c98-7425-4e15-86c0-b759e6216a9b) Stevens, Gareth Publishing LLLP.

Ransom, Candice. Bones in the White House: Thomas Jefferson's Mammoth. Christoph, Jamey, illus. 2020. 40p. (J). (gr. -1-2). 17.99 (978-0-525-64607-5(8), Doubleday Bks. for Young Readers) Random Hse. Children's Bks.

—Thomas Jefferson. 2018. (Founding Fathers Ser.). (ENG., Illus.). 24p. (J). (gr. 1-1). pap. 8.95 (978-1-63517-815-9(0), 1635178150) North Star Editions.

—Thomas Jefferson. 2018. (Founding Fathers Ser.). (ENG., Illus.). 24p. (J). (gr. k-3). lib. bdg. 31.36 (978-1-5321-6020-2(8), 28672, Pop! Cody Koala) Pop!

Rausch, Monica. Thomas Jefferson, 1 vol. 2007. (Great Americans Ser.). (Illus.). 24p. (gr. 2-4). (ENG.). pap. 9.15 (978-0-8368-7691-8(1), d67c8373-d0d8-4d03-83af-e3d6765ca2f2, Weekly Reader Leveled Readers); (ENG., lib. bdg. 24.67 (978-0-8368-7684-0(9), ff86d974-794f-4499-8286-be4c3be4e118, Weekly Reader Leveled Readers); (SPA., lib. bdg. 24.67 (978-0-8368-7983-4(X), ed472768-1ea2-495d-b495-d8cd58814b41) Stevens, Gareth Publishing LLLP.

Redmond, Shirley Raye. Lewis & Clark: A Prairie Dog for the President. Manders, John, illus. 2003. (Step into Reading Ser.). 48p. 14.00 (978-0-7569-1697-8(6)) Perfection Learning Corp.

Ribke, Simone T. Rookie Biographies: Thomas Jefferson. 2004. (Rookie Biographies Ser.). (ENG., Illus.). 32p. (J). (gr. 1-2). pap. 4.95 (978-0-516-27927-5(0), Children's Pr.) Scholastic Library Publishing.

—Thomas Jefferson. 2003. (Rookie Biographies Ser.). (Illus.). 32p. (J). 20.50 (978-0-516-25884-3(2), Children's Pr.) Scholastic Library Publishing.

Roberts, Russell. Thomas Jefferson: The Life & Times Of. 2007. (Profiles in American History Ser.). (Illus.). 48p. (J). (gr. 3-7). lib. bdg. 29.95 (978-1-58415-439-6(X)) Mitchell Lane Pubs.

Rosenstock, Barb. Thomas Jefferson Builds a Library. O'Brien, John, illus. 2013. (ENG.). 32p. (J). (gr. 2-5). 17.99 (978-1-59078-932-2(6), Calkins Creek) Highlights Pr., c/o Highlights for Children, Inc.

Roxburgh, Ellis. Thomas Jefferson vs. John Adams: Founding Fathers & Political Rivals, 1 vol. 2015. (History's Greatest Rivals Ser.). (ENG., Illus.). 48p. (J). (gr. 6-8). pap. 15.05 (978-1-4824-4239-7(6), 349f4b41-e98f-45d4-8ece-ef7a1fda66f9) Stevens, Gareth Publishing LLLP.

Ruffin, Frances E. Sally Hemings. 2009. (American Legends Ser.). 24p. (gr. 3-3). 42.50 (978-1-61511-386-6(X), PowerKids Pr.) Rosen Publishing Group, Inc., The.

Saddleback Educational Publishing Staff, ed. Thomas Jefferson, 1 vol. unabr. ed. 2007. (Graphic Biographies Ser.). (ENG., Illus.). 25p. (YA). (gr. 4-12). pap. 9.75 (978-1-59905-229-8(6)) Saddleback Educational Publishing, Inc.

Sandeen, Del. Thomas Jefferson & Sally Hemings, 1 vol. 2018. (Joined by Fate: Intertwined Biographies Ser.). (ENG.). 128p. (J). (gr. 7-7). 40.27 (978-0-7660-9824-4(9), 0f9af01b-f7e8-4bdc-b4b8-3c105c36b48e) Enslow Publishing, LLC.

Sharp, Constance. Thomas Jefferson & the Growing United States (1800-1811) 2012. (J). pap. (978-1-4222-2414-4(7)) Mason Crest.

—Thomas Jefferson & the Growing United States (1800-1811) Rakove, Jack N., ed. 2012. (How America Became America Ser.). 48p. (J). (gr. 3-4). 19.95 (978-1-4222-2400-7(7)) Mason Crest.

Shea, John M. Thomas Jefferson in His Own Words, 1 vol., Vol. 1. 2014. (Eyewitness to History Ser.). (ENG.). 32p. (J). (gr. 4-5). 29.27 (978-1-4339-9873-7(4), 83721893-7690-4eb5-8f24-0b77d0692070); pap. 11.50 (978-1-4339-9933-8(1), f9f6647c-6c19-4b67-a2a0-1619deb0ac5d) Stevens, Gareth Publishing LLLP.

Slepian, Curtis. Hamilton vs. Jefferson (Alexander Hamilton) rev. ed. 2017. (Social Studies: Informational Text Ser.). (ENG., Illus.). 32p. (gr. 4-8). pap. 11.99 (978-1-4258-6354-8(X)) Teacher Created Materials, Inc.

Strain Trueit, Trudi. Thomas Jefferson, 1 vol. 2010. (Presidents & Their Times Ser.). (ENG.). 96p. (gr. 6-6). 36.93 (978-0-7614-3622-5(7), 304d3240-2f53-4dd1-b5f5-16559fd45e72) Cavendish Square Publishing LLC.

Thomas, Peggy. Thomas Jefferson Grows a Nation. Innerst, Stacy, illus. 2015. (ENG.). 48p. (J). (gr. 2-5). 16.95 (978-1-62091-628-5(2), Calkins Creek) Highlights Pr., c/o Highlights for Children, Inc.

Venezia, Mike. Getting to Know the U. S. Presidents: Thomas Jefferson, 3. Venezia, Mike, illus. 2004. (Getting to Know the U. S. Presidents Ser.). (ENG., Illus.). 32p. (J). (gr. 3-6). 22.44 (978-0-516-22608-8(8)) Scholastic Library Publishing.

—Thomas Jefferson: Third President, 1801-1809. Venezia, Mike, illus. 2005. (Getting to Know the U. S. Presidents Ser.). (ENG., Illus.). 32p. (J). (gr. 3-4). pap. 7.95 (978-0-516-27477-5(5), Children's Pr.) Scholastic Library Publishing.

Whitelaw, Nancy. Thomas Jefferson: Philospher & President. 2004. (Notable Americans Ser.). (Illus.). 144p. (YA). (gr. 6-12). 23.95 (978-1-883846-81-7(1), First Biographies) Reynolds, Morgan Inc.

Winter, Jonah. My Name Is James Madison Hemings. Widener, Terry, illus. 2016. (ENG.). 40p. (J). (gr. k-4). 17.99 (978-0-385-38342-4(8), Schwartz & Wade Bks.) Random Hse. Children's Bks.

JEFFERSON, THOMAS, 1743-1826—FICTION

Edwards, Myrtice J. Dirty Sally. 2007. 44p. per. 18.95 (978-1-4327-0774-3(4)) Outskirts Pr., Inc.

Fox, Mary Virginia. Treasure of the Revolution. Cary, illus. 2011. 192p. 42.95 (978-1-258-09675-5(7)) Literary Licensing, LLC.

Goldsmith, Howard. Thomas Jefferson & the Ghostriders: Ready-To-Read Level 2. Rose, Drew, illus. 2008. (Ready-To-Read Childhood of Famous Americans Ser.). (ENG.). 32p. (J). (gr. k-2). pap. 4.99 (978-1-4169-2692-4(5), Simon Spotlight) Simon Spotlight.

Grigsby, Susan. First Peas to the Table: How Thomas Jefferson Inspired a School Garden. Tadgell, Nicole, illus. 2012. (ENG.). 32p. (J). (gr. -1-3). 16.99 (978-0-8075-2452-7(2), 807524522) Whitman, Albert & Co.

Limbaugh, Rush & Adams Limbaugh, Kathryn. Rush Revere & the Presidency. 2016. (Rush Revere Ser.: 5). (ENG., Illus.). 272p. (gr. 4-7). 21.00 (978-1-5011-5689-2(6), Threshold Editions) Threshold Editions.

Roy, Ron. Capital Mysteries #11: the Secret at Jefferson's Mansion. Bush, Timothy, illus. 2009. (Capital Mysteries Ser.: 11). (ENG.). 96p. (J). (gr. 1-4). 6.99 (978-0-375-84533-8(X), Random Hse. Bks. for Young Readers) Random Hse. Children's Bks.

Turner, Ann Warren. When Mr. Jefferson Came to Philadelphia: What I Learned of Freedom 1776. Hess, Mark, illus. 2004. 32p. (J). (gr. -1-3). 15.99 (978-0-06-027579-2(0)) HarperCollins Pubs.

JEKYLL, DOCTOR (FICTITIOUS CHARACTER)—FICTION

Kennedy, Cam, illus. Dr Jekyll & Mr Hyde: RL Stevenson's Strange Case. 2008. (ENG.). 48p. (YA). (gr. 7). pap. 11.95 (978-0-88776-882-8(2), Tundra Bks.) Tundra Bks. CAN. Dist: Penguin Random Hse. LLC.

Novel Units. Dr. Jekyll & Mr. Hyde Novel Units Student Packet. 2019. (ENG.). (YA). (gr. 9-12). pap., stu. ed. 13.99 (978-1-58130-785-6(3), Novel Units, Inc.) Classroom Library Co.

Stevenson, Robert Louis. Classic Starts(r): the Strange Case of Dr. Jekyll & Mr. Hyde: Retold from the Robert Louis Stevenson Original. Akib, Jamel, illus. 2006. (Classic Starts(r) Ser.). 160p. (J). (gr. 2-4). 6.95 (978-1-4027-2667-5(8), 1252057) Sterling Publishing Co., Inc.

—Dr. Jekyll & Mr. Hyde. 2008. (Bring the Classics to Life Ser.). (ENG., Illus.). 72p. (gr. 4-12). pap., act. bk. ed. 10.95 (978-0-931334-50-4(0), EDCTR-402B) EDCON Publishing Group.

—Dr. Jekyll & Mr. Hyde. Gelev, Penko, illus. 2017. (Classic Graphic Fiction Ser.). (ENG.). 48p. (J). (gr. 4). pap. 7.95 (978-1-912006-01-4(4)) Book Hse. GBR. Dist: Sterling Publishing Co., Inc.

—Dr. Jekyll & Mr. Hyde Graphic Novel. 2010. (Illustrated Classics Ser.). (ENG., Illus.). 64p. (YA). (gr. 4-12). per. 11.95 (978-1-56254-894-0(8)) Saddleback Educational Publishing, Inc.

—The Strange Case of Dr. Jekyll & Mr. Hyde. (Classics Illustrated Ser.). (Illus.). 52p. (YA). pap. 4.95 (978-1-57209-008-8(1)) Classics International Entertainment, Inc.

—The Strange Case of Dr. Jekyll & Mr. Hyde. Andrews, Gary, illus. 2008. (Fast Track Classics Ser.). (ENG.). 48p. pap. 10.00 (978-1-4190-5082-4(6)) Steck-Vaughn.

—The Strange Case of Dr. Jekyll & Mr. Hyde (Quality Library Classics) 2008. (YA). pap. 14.95 (978-1-57545-703-1(2)) RP Media.

Stevenson, Robert Louis & Venable, Alan. The Strange Case of Dr. Jekyll & Mr. Hyde. 2005. (Classic Literature Ser.). 108p. pap. 9.95 (978-1-4105-0119-6(1)); pap., E-Book 69.00 incl. audio compact disk (978-1-4105-0117-2(5)) Building Wings LLC.

JELLYFISHES

Allen, Catherine Judge. Corals, Jellyfish, Sponges & Other Simple Animals. Harris, Madeline S. et al, eds. 2005. (Grzimek's Student Animal Life Resource Ser.). (ENG., Illus.). 368p. (J). (gr. 3-7). 129.00 (978-0-7876-9412-8(6), UXL) Cengage Gale.

Bodden, Valerie. Amazing Animals: Jellyfish. 2017. (Amazing Animals Ser.). (ENG., Illus.). 24p. (J). (gr. 1-3). pap. 10.99 (978-1-62832-363-4(9), 20039, Creative Paperbacks) Creative Co., The.

—Jellyfish. 2017. (Amazing Animals Ser.). (ENG., Illus.). 24p. (J). (gr. 1-4). (978-1-60818-755-3(1), 20041, Creative Education) Creative Co., The.

Byerly, Robbie. Jellyfish. 2016. (2G Marine Life Ser.). (ENG., Illus.). 24p. (J). pap. 8.00 (978-1-61406-042-0(8)) American Reading Co.

Cheshire, Gerard. Jellyfish - Scary Creatures. 2008. (Scary Creatures Ser.). (ENG., Illus.). 32p. (J). (gr. 2-7). 27.00 (978-0-531-20446-7(4), Children's Pr.) Scholastic Library Publishing.

Coleman, Clara O. Jellyfish in the Water, 1 vol. 2017. (Critters by the Sea Ser.). (ENG.). 24p. (J). (gr. 3-3). 25.27 (978-1-5383-2515-5(2), a57ba419-3094-41a6-a894-c06c06a75cff, PowerKids Pr.) Rosen Publishing Group, Inc., The.

Douglas, Lloyd G. Jellyfish. 2005. (Ocean Life Ser.). (ENG., Illus.). 24p. (J). (gr. -1-2). per. 4.95 (978-0-516-23738-1(1), Children's Pr.) Scholastic Library Publishing.

Gibbs, Maddie. Jellyfish, 1 vol. 2013. (PowerKids Readers: Fun Fish Ser.). (ENG.). 24p. (J). (gr. k-k). 26.27 (978-1-4777-0759-3(X), f14f2b36-513a-4fb5-bfc6-dac02a692436); pap. 9.25 (978-1-4777-0851-4(0), 485bc6f7-8fe1-482d-9c1d-9e2629e413d1) Rosen Publishing Group, Inc., The. (PowerKids Pr.).

J
K
L

Gibbs, Maddie & Alamán, Eduardo. Jellyfish: Las Medusas, 1 vol. 2013. (PowerKids Readers: Peces Divertidos / Fun Fish Ser.). (SPA & ENG.). 24p. (J). (gr. k-k). lib. bdg. 26.27 (978-1-4777-1217-7(8), a2b19763-a290-40ef-a6a2-b9a2b84440c7, PowerKids Pr.) Rosen Publishing Group, Inc., The.

Gish, Melissa. Jellyfish. (Living Wild Ser.). (J). 2016. (ENG.). 48p. (gr. 5-9). pap. 12.00 (978-1-62832-169-2(5), 20890, Creative Paperbacks) 2015. (Illus.). 46p. (978-1-60818-568-9(0), Creative Education) Creative Co., The.

Gray, Susan H. Australian Spotted Jellyfish. 2010. (21st Century Skills Library: Animal Invaders Ser.). (ENG., Illus.). 32p. (gr. 4-8). lib. bdg. 32.07 (978-1-60279-628-7(9), 200333) Cherry Lake Publishing.

—Jellyfish. 2014. (21st Century Skills Library: Exploring Our Oceans Ser.). (ENG., Illus.). 32p. (J). (gr. 3-6). 32.07 (978-1-62431-600-5(X), 203184) Cherry Lake Publishing.

Gross, Miriam J. The Jellyfish. (Weird Sea Creatures Ser.). 24p. (gr. 3-3). 2009. 42.50 (978-1-60854-751-7(5)) 2005. (ENG., Illus.). (J). lib. bdg. 26.27 (978-1-4042-3192-4(7), 9f01b4ac-bb22-48d4-9590-ef4bbd2e5c28) Rosen Publishing Group, Inc., The. (PowerKids Pr.).

Hansen, Grace. Becoming a Jellyfish, 1 vol. 2016. (Changing Animals Ser.). (ENG., Illus.). 24p. (J). (gr. -1-2). lib. bdg. 32.79 (978-1-68080-511-6(8), 21302, Abdo Kids) ABDO Publishing Co.

—Jellyfish, 1 vol. 2015. (Ocean Life Ser.). (ENG.). 24p. (J). (gr. -1-2). lib. bdg. 32.79 (978-1-62970-709-9(0), 17217, Abdo Kids) ABDO Publishing Co.

—Jellyfish. 2017. (Ocean Life Ser.). (ENG.). 24p. (J). (gr. -1-2). pap. 7.95 (978-1-4966-1253-3(1), 135001, Capstone Classroom) Capstone.

—Medusas (Jellyfish), 1 vol. 2016. (Vida en el Océano (Ocean Life) Ser.). (SPA., Illus.). 24p. (J). (gr. -1-2). lib. bdg. 32.79 (978-1-68080-746-2(3), 22654, Abdo Kids) ABDO Publishing Co.

Herriges, Ann. Jellyfish. 2006. (Oceans Alive Ser.). (ENG., Illus.). 24p. (J). (gr. k-3). lib. bdg. 26.95 (978-1-60014-018-1(1)) Bellwether Media.

Jellyfish. 2013. (PowerKids Readers: Fun Fish Ser.). 24p. (J). (gr. k-2). pap. 49.50 (978-1-4777-0852-1(9), PowerKids Pr.) Rosen Publishing Group, Inc., The.

Kenan, Tessa. Look, a Jellyfish! 2016. (Bumba Books (r) — I See Ocean Animals Ser.). (ENG., Illus.). 24p. (J). (gr. -1-1). 26.65 (978-1-5124-1421-9(2), 01cb9e82-3e3f-42ea-90d0-000f11a62900, Lerner Pubns.) Lerner Publishing Group.

—¡Mira, una Medusa! (Look, a Jellyfish!) 2017. (Bumba Books (r) en Español — Veo Animales Marinos (I See Ocean Animals) Ser.). (SPA., Illus.). 24p. (J). (gr. -1-1). 26.65 (978-1-5124-2866-7(3), c37542de-4615-4686-ac42-2b17e1f10294, Ediciones Lerner) Lerner Publishing Group.

King, David C. Jellyfish, 1 vol. 2007. (Animals, Animals Ser.). (ENG., Illus.). 48p. (gr. 5-5). lib. bdg. 32.64 (978-0-7614-1867-2(9), 2f47b2ba-370f-4178-b5c7-f2e8093db4a8) Cavendish Square Publishing LLC.

Kissock, Heather. Jellyfish. 2017. (Illus.). 24p. (J). (978-1-5105-0584-1(9)) SmartBook Media, Inc.

Laughlin, Kara L. Jellyfish. 2017. (In the Deep Blue Sea Ser.). (ENG.). 24p. (J). (gr. k-3). lib. bdg. 32.79 (978-1-5038-1686-2(9), 211520) Child's World, Inc, The.

Leaf, Christina. Jellyfish. 2016. (Ocean Life up Close Ser.). (ENG., Illus.). 24p. (J). (gr. k-3). 26.95 (978-1-62617-418-4(0)); pap. 7.99 (978-1-61891-266-4(6), 12056) Bellwether Media. (Blastoff! Readers).

Lunis, Natalie. Box Jellyfish: Killer Tentacles. 2009. (Afraid of the Water Ser.). (Illus.). 24p. (YA). (gr. 2-5). lib. bdg. 26.99 (978-1-59716-945-5(5)) Bearport Publishing Co., Inc.

—Gooey Jellyfish. (No Backbone! Marine Invertebrates Ser.). (Illus.). 24p. (J). (gr. k-3). 2016. (ENG.). pap. 7.99 (978-1-59716-776-5(2)) 2007. lib. bdg. 26.99 (978-1-59716-510-5(7)) Bearport Publishing Co., Inc.

—Portuguese Man-Of-War: Floating Misery. 2009. (Afraid of the Water Ser.). (Illus.). 24p. (YA). (gr. 2-5). lib. bdg. 26.99 (978-1-59716-946-2(3)) Bearport Publishing Co., Inc.

Magby, Meryl. Jellyfish, 1 vol. 2012. (Under the Sea Ser.). (ENG., Illus.). 24p. (J). (gr. 2-3). pap. 9.25 (978-1-4488-7476-7(9), 16c56d7e-58da-4dba-9fe5-0c329454f42b); lib. bdg. 26.27 (978-1-4488-7397-5(5), e18e12c0-1a65-4800-98da-17d0a8ed62ce) Rosen Publishing Group, Inc., The. (PowerKids Pr.).

McAneney, Caitie. Why Don't Jellyfish Have Brains? And Other Odd Invertebrate Adaptations, 1 vol. 2018. (Odd Adaptations Ser.). (ENG.). 32p. (gr. 3-4). 28.27 (978-1-5382-2039-9(3), 10921473-98b1-4a84-a72d-ccd246d267ba) Stevens, Gareth Publishing LLLP.

McFee, Shane. Jellyfish. (Poison! Ser.). 24p. (gr. 2-3). 2009. 42.50 (978-1-60851-324-6(6), PowerKids Pr.) 2007. (ENG., Illus.). (J). lib. bdg. 26.27 (978-1-4042-3799-5(2), 350ebada-b874-4d7a-bd1e-ab73dbc62fde) Rosen Publishing Group, Inc., The.

McKenzie, Michelle. Jellyfish Inside Out. 2003. (Illus.). 48p. (J). 14.95 (978-1-878244-43-7(4)) Monterey Bay Aquarium.

Meister, Cari. Jellyfish. 2014. (Illus.). 24p. (J). lib. bdg. 25.65 (978-1-62031-098-4(8), Bullfrog Bks.) Jump! Inc.

Metz, Lorijo. Discovering Jellyfish, 1 vol. 2011. (Along the Shore Ser.). (ENG.). 24p. (J). (gr. 2-3). lib. bdg. 26.27 (978-1-4488-4997-0(7), 4735c300-66a8-4716-b35e-ae04a0301401) Rosen Publishing Group, Inc., The.

Owen, Ruth. Box Jellyfish, 1 vol., 1. 2014. (Real Life Sea Monsters Ser.). (ENG.). 32p. (J). (gr. 3-3). pap. 11.00 (978-1-4777-6269-1(8), bb99ffb5-8c83-4c61-ba68-84448b693d90, PowerKids Pr.) Rosen Publishing Group, Inc., The.

Rajczak, Kristen. Jellyfish, 1 vol. 2014. (Living Fossils Ser.). (ENG., Illus.). 24p. (J). (gr. 2-3). pap. 9.25 (978-1-4777-5827-4(5), 9a1b2fa0-2eab-4151-ad7c-6e4f3005a1ea, PowerKids Pr.) Rosen Publishing Group, Inc., The.

Rake, Jody S. Jellyfish. 2016. (Faceless, Spineless, & Brainless Ocean Animals Ser.). (ENG., Illus.). 24p. (J). (gr. 1-3). lib. bdg. 27.99 (978-1-5157-2141-3(8), 132715, Capstone Pr.) Capstone.

Raum, Elizabeth. Box Jellyfish. 2015. (Poisonous Animals Ser.). (ENG., Illus.). 32p. (J). (gr. 2-5). lib. bdg. 19.95 (978-1-60753-786-1(9), 15302) Amicus.

Roza, Greg. Jellyfish, 1 vol. 2015. (Things That Sting Ser.). (ENG., Illus.). 24p. (J). (gr. 2-3). lib. bdg. 24.27 (978-1-4824-1702-9(2), e79f1e9f-8d62-4a93-9e46-5eb309306d2a) Stevens, Gareth Publishing LLLP.

Schuh, Mari. Jellyfish. 2018. (Spot Ocean Animals Ser.). (ENG.). 16p. (J). (gr. -1-2). pap. 7.99 (978-1-68152-300-2(0), 15002); lib. bdg. (978-1-68151-380-5(3), 14996) Amicus.

Schuh, Mari C. Jellyfish. 2015. (Sea Life Ser.). (ENG., Illus.). 24p. (J). (gr. -1-2). lib. bdg. 27.32 (978-1-4914-6043-6(1), 128957, Capstone Pr.) Capstone.

Sexton, Colleen. The Box Jellyfish. 2011. (Nature's Deadliest Ser.). (ENG., Illus.). 24p. (J). (gr. 3-8). lib. bdg. 27.95 (978-1-60014-664-0(3), Pilot Bks.) Bellwether Media.

Spilsbury, Louise. Jellyfish, 1 vol. 2010. (Day in the Life: Sea Animals Ser.). (ENG.). 24p. (J). (gr. k-2). pap. 6.79 (978-1-4329-4007-2(4), 113127, Heinemann) Capstone.

Stone, Lynn M. Jellyfish. 2005. (Rourke Discovery Library). (Illus.). 24p. (J). (gr. 1-4). lib. bdg. 14.95 (978-1-59515-439-2(6)) Rourke Educational Media.

Strain Trueit, Trudi. Jellyfish, 1 vol. 2011. (Ocean Life Ser.). (ENG.). 24p. (gr. k-1). 25.50 (978-0-7614-4891-4(8), 1f019af4-b571-4e74-9fd9-6f5245306faa) Cavendish Square Publishing LLC.

Sullivan, Laura L. The Box Jellyfish. 2017. (Toxic Creatures Ser.). 32p. (J). (gr. 3-3). pap. 63.48 (978-1-5026-2579-3(2), Cavendish Square) Cavendish Square Publishing LLC.

Vink, Amanda. Jellyfish Are Brainless!, 1 vol. 2019. (Animals Without Brains! Ser.). (ENG.). 24p. (J). (gr. 1-2). pap. 9.15 (978-1-5382-4582-8(5), ca749043-34fd-4a94-8a81-b713f5f59beb) Stevens, Gareth Publishing LLLP.

Wearing, Judy. Jellyfish. 2009. (World of Wonder Ser.). (Illus.). 24p. (J). (gr. k-3). lib. bdg. 24.45 (978-1-60596-100-2(0)) Weigl Pubs., Inc.

—Jellyfish: World of Wonder: Underwater Life. 2009. (Illus.). 24p. (J). pap. 8.95 (978-1-60596-101-9(9)) Weigl Pubs., Inc.

JEMISON, MARY, 1743-1833

Aller, Susan Bivin. Living with the Senecas: A Story about Mary Jemison. Harden, Laurie, illus. 2007. (Creative Minds Biographies Ser.). 64p. (J). (gr. 3-7). lib. bdg. 22.60 (978-0-8225-5989-4(7)) Lerner Publishing Group.

JENGHIS KHAN, 1162-1227

see Genghis Khan, 1162-1227

JERUSALEM

Ashabranner, Brent. Gavriel & Jemal: Two Boys of Jerusalem. Conklin, Paul, photos by. 2005. (Illus.). 94p. (J). (gr. 4-10). reprint ed. 12.00 (978-0-7567-9758-4(6)) DIANE Publishing Co.

Bowden, Rob. Jerusalem, 1 vol. 2005. (Great Cities of the World Ser.). (ENG., Illus.). 48p. (J). (gr. 5-8). lib. bdg. 33.67 (978-0-8368-5051-2(3), 4fd85bcc-857f-45af-901b-550ab2c63f05, Gareth Stevens Secondary Library) Stevens, Gareth Publishing LLLP.

Ford, Nick. Jerusalem under Muslim Rule in the Eleventh Century: Christian Pilgrims under Islamic Government. (Library of the Middle Ages Ser.). 64p. (gr. 5-8). 2009. 58.50 (978-1-60853-899-7(0)) 2003. (ENG., Illus.). lib. bdg. 37.13 (978-0-8239-4216-9(3), 932bfaf4-6148-4296-abc6-a894d46909ef) Rosen Publishing Group, Inc., The. (Rosen Reference).

Furstinger, Nancy. Jerusalem, 1 vol. 2005. (Cities Set 1 Ser.). (Illus.). 32p. (gr. k-6). 27.07 (978-1-59197-860-2(2), Checkerboard Library) ABDO Publishing Co.

Hancock, Lee. Saladin & the Kingdom of Jersusalem: The Muslims Recapture the Holy Land in AD 1187, 1 vol. 2003. (Library of the Middle Ages Ser.). (ENG., Illus.). 64p. (YA). (gr. 5-8). lib. bdg. 37.13 (978-0-8239-4217-6(1), be24bfc6-801b-4c8c-b4c1-4580fc94f0a6, Rosen Reference) Rosen Publishing Group, Inc., The.

Jerusalem 30 A. D. When Yeshua (Jesus) Walked. 2004. (YA). 0.00 net. (978-0-9748424-0-0(0)) Magee, Burke & Glenna.

Levy, Leah. The Waiting Wall. Rosenfeld, D. L. & Leverton, Yossi, eds. 2009. (ENG., Illus.). 26p. (J). (gr. -1-1). 13.99 (978-1-929628-49-0(8)) Hachai Publishing.

Slavik, Diane. Daily Life in Ancient & Modern Jerusalem. Webb, Ray, illus. (Cities Through Time Ser.). 64p. 2005. (gr. 5-12). 25.26 (978-0-8225-3218-7(2)) 2003. (J). 18.95 (978-1-58013-075-2(5), Kar-Ben Publishing) Lerner Publishing Group.

JERUSALEM—FICTION

Benjamin, Amanda. Journey Through Jerusalem. Blumenfeld, Tamar, illus. 2017. (ENG.). 24p. (J). 17.95 (978-1-68115-531-9(1), f58f9449-5f98-48e5-b246-fca39f6395c3) Behrman Hse., Inc.

Breen, Mirka M. G. The Voice of Thunder. 2012. (ENG.). 118p. (J). pap. 12.95 (978-1-937178-17-8(X)) WiDo Publishing.

Busheri, Devora. In the Jerusalem Forest. Kelner, Noa, illus. 2019. (ENG.). 32p. (J). (gr. -1-3). 17.99 (978-1-5415-3472-8(7), 44f7f14e-ddaf-4dfe-9235-7200edce6859, Kar-Ben Publishing) Lerner Publishing Group.

Dateno, Maria Grace. Discovery at Dawn. Cunningham, Paul, illus. 2014. (ENG.). 79p. (J). pap. 5.95 (978-0-8198-1895-9(X)) Pauline Bks. & Media.

Eddy, Daniel. Walter's Tours in the East: Walter in Je. 2005. pap. 16.95 (978-1-59605-437-0(9), Cosimo Classics) Cosimo, Inc.

Emmer, E. R. The Dolphin Project. 2004. (Going to Ser.). (ENG., Illus.). 202p. (J). (gr. 4-8). pap. 6.95 (978-1-893577-12-1(0)) Four Corners Publishing Co., Inc.

Fals, Mary. The Chosen Colt. 2009. 40p. pap. 18.49 (978-1-4389-9417-8(6)) AuthorHouse.

Greene, Janice. The Dark Lady, 1 vol. unabr. ed. 2010. (Q Reads Ser.). (ENG.). 32p. (YA). (gr. 9-12). pap. 8.50 (978-1-61651-215-6(6)) Saddleback Educational Publishing, Inc.

Haggard, H. Rider. Pearl-Maiden. Kou, Christopher D. & McHugh, Michael J., eds. 2003. 372p. (YA). pap. 9.95 (978-1-930367-89-0(9)) Christian Liberty Pr.

Holliday, Bobby. Hamor: The Road to Jerusalem. 2013. (ENG., Illus.). 32p. (J). 18.99 (978-0-9829082-3-5(7)) Lady Hawk Pr.

—A Lump of Clay. Price, Rebecca, illus. 2010. 28p. (J). 18.99 (978-0-9829082-1-1(0)) Lady Hawk Pr.

Hotz, Donna. Aaron's Surprise! 2010. 32p. pap. 14.49 (978-1-4520-4522-1(4)) AuthorHouse.

Hyman, Frieda Clark. Victory on the Walls: A Story of Nehemiah. 2005. (Living History Library). 182p. (YA). (gr. 4-7). pap. 12.95 (978-1-883937-96-6(5)) Bethlehem Bks.

Kimmel, Eric A. Search for the Shamir. Stevanovic, Ivica, illus. 2018. (Scarlett & Sam Ser.). (ENG.). 152p. (J). (gr. 1-3). pap. 6.99 (978-1-5124-2938-1(4), fa05c70d-97fc-4c41-af59-93be9cd9769f, Kar-Ben Publishing) Lerner Publishing Group.

King, Bonnie. Left Behind: Marion's Story. 2005. 57p. pap. 16.95 (978-1-4137-9286-7(3)) PublishAmerica, Inc.

Levy, Marilyn. Checkpoints. 2009. (ENG.). 256p. (gr. 7). pap. 14.95 (978-0-8276-0870-2(5)) Jewish Pubn. Society.

Magni, Aurora. The 10 Marys & the Little Gabriel. Vignaga, Francesca Dafne, illus. 2011. (ENG.). 44p. (J). 16.95 (978-0-8091-6764-7(6)) Paulist Pr.

Mindel, Nissan. Eight Chanukah Tales. Toron, Eli & Graybar, Shmuel, illus. 2007. 78p. (J). 10.95 (978-0-8266-0039-4(5)) Kehot Pubn. Society.

Molina, Maria Isabel. De Victoria para Alejandro. (SPA., Illus.). 136p. (YA). (gr. 5-8). 8.95 (978-84-204-4861-9(3)) Ediciones Alfaguara ESP. Dist: Lectorum Pubns., Inc.

Monson, Marianne. The Enchanted Tunnel Vol. 3: Journey to Jerusalem. Burr, Dan, illus. 2011. 85p. (YA). (gr. 3-6). pap. 7.99 (978-1-60908-068-6(8)) Deseret Bk. Co.

Ofanansky, Allison Maile. Tisha B'Av: A Jerusalem Journey. Alpern, Eliyahu, photos by. 2017. (ENG., Illus.). 32p. (J). (gr. -1-3). E-Book 27.99 (978-1-5124-2719-6(5), 9781512427196, Kar-Ben Publishing) Lerner Publishing Group.

Ogorek, Keith. Eli the Stable Boy. 2009. (ENG.). 28p. pap. 13.99 (978-1-4490-4116-8(7)) AuthorHouse.

Petersen, Alicia. Out of Darkness. 2007. (Illus.). 177p. (J). (gr. 3-7). per. 8.99 (978-1-59166-822-0(0)) BJU Pr.

Rouss, Sylvia A. Tali's Jerusalem Scrapbook. Oppenheimer, Nancy, illus. 2003. 32p. (J). (gr. 1-4). 14.95 (978-1-930143-68-5(0)); pap. 9.95 (978-1-930143-69-2(9)) Simcha Media Group. (Pitspopany Pr.).

Rucinski, Sandra. The Story of Jesus According to Tobin. 2009. 32p. pap. 14.50 (978-1-60860-372-5(5), Eloquent Bks.) Strategic Book Publishing & Rights Agency (SBPRA).

Sachs, Tamar. The Golden Bell. Abolafia, Yossi, illus. 2019. (ENG.). 24p. (J). (gr. -1-3). 12.99 (978-1-5415-2612-9(0), c13ea2fb-6fac-471a-9d3c-b94ff812eeb3, Kar-Ben Publishing) Lerner Publishing Group.

Sandbank, Rachella & Shem-Tov, Tami. A Queen in Jerusalem. Ofer, Avi, illus. 2018. (ENG.). 32p. (J). (gr. -1-2). 12.99 (978-1-5124-4441-4(3), 53662b24-b791-48fe-a9c3-28ad79f7107d, Kar-Ben Publishing) Lerner Publishing Group.

Smith, Chris. One City, Two Brothers. Fronty, Aurélia & Fronty, Aurélia, illus. 2015. (ENG.). 32p. (J). (gr. 1-4). pap. 9.99 (978-1-78285-252-0(2)) Barefoot Bks., Inc.

—One City, Two Brothers. Fronty, Aurélia, illus. 2007. (ENG.). 32p. (J). (gr. -1-3). 16.99 (978-1-84686-042-3(3)) Barefoot Bks., Inc.

Smith, Jimmie. Jonas Little Donkey, Big Job. 2013. 20p. pap. 11.99 (978-1-62509-331-8(4)) Salem Author Services.

star, celina. Paw Prints on the Road. 2008. (ENG.). 79p. pap. 9.96 (978-0-557-02420-9(X)) Lulu Pr., Inc.

Stever, Karen Malloy. Jabin, the Talking Donkey: In Jerusalem. 2012. 24p. pap. 24.95 (978-1-4626-8285-0(5)) America Star Bks.

Tenney, Richard L. Conflict & Calling. 2012. 184p. (978-1-77097-461-6(X)); pap. (978-1-77097-462-3(8)) FriesenPress.

Toska, Mary Lou. The Shepherd Boy. 2013. 32p. pap. 24.95 (978-1-62709-475-7(X)) America Star Bks.

Weber, Elka. Shimri's Big Idea. Bousidan, Gigi, illus. 2019. (ENG.). 32p. (J). 17.95 (978-1-68115-541-8(9), 3ff17ff9-678c-4b6b-b239-c1f8d17226a7, Apples & Honey Pr.) Behrman Hse., Inc.

JESUITS

Rodríguez-Ponga, Pedro. Ignatius of Loyola. 2018. (ENG., Illus.). 48p. pap. 12.95 (978-0-8091-6783-8(2)) Paulist Pr.

JESUS CHRIST

see also Christianity

Adelsperger, Charlotte. Amazing Miracles of Jesus. 2014. (Happy Day Ser.). (ENG.). 16p. (J). pap. 2.49 (978-1-4143-9528-9(0), 4608518, Happy Day) Tyndale Hse. Pubs.

Almquist, Beth, et al. Growing up in Jesus: Weekly Meeting Plans for Voyager Leaders. 2007. (J). 19.95 (978-0-9743503-5-6(4)) Pioneer Clubs.

Amya Penny Anysia Turpin. Jesus & Me. 2009. 52p. pap. 25.49 (978-1-4389-6818-6(3)) AuthorHouse.

Aragon, Quina. Love Gave: A Story of God's Greatest Gift. 2021. (ENG.). 32p. (J). (gr. -1-2). 17.99 (978-0-7369-7438-7(5), 6974387) Harvest Hse. Pubs.

Arch Books, creator. Jesus' First Miracle. 2006. (Arch Bks.). (ENG., Illus.). 16p. (J). (gr. k). pap. 1.99 (978-0-7586-0865-9(9)) Concordia Publishing Hse.

Arthur, Kay & Arndt, Janna. Jesus, to Eternity & Beyond. 2005. (Discover-4-Yourself for Kids Ser.). 143p. (J). pap. 8.99 (978-1-888655-90-2(9)) Precept.

Arthur, Kay & Shearer, Cyndy. Jesus in the Spotlight. (Discover-4-Yourself for Kids Ser.). 128p. (J). 2006. pap. 8.99 (978-1-888655-24-7(0)) 2004. pap. 8.99 (978-1-888655-73-5(9)) Precept.

Arthur, Kay, et al. Jesus, Awesome Power, Awesome Love. 2004. (Discover-4-Yourself for Kids Ser.). 138p. (J). pap. 8.99 (978-1-888655-75-9(5)) Precept.

Bader, Joanne. He's Risen! He's Alive! Heroldt, Richard, illus. 2003. (Arch Bks.). (ENG.). 16p. (J). 1.99 (978-0-570-07583-7(1)) Concordia Publishing Hse.

—Jesus Heals the Centurion's Servant. 2010. (Arch Bks.). (Illus.). 16p. (J). (gr. k-4). pap. 2.49 (978-0-7586-1864-1(6)) Concordia Publishing Hse.

Bagley, Val Chadwick, illus. I Will Trust in Heavenly Father & Jesus. 2006. (J). (978-1-59811-056-2(X)) Covenant Communications.

Balika, Susan. Jesus Is My Special Friend. Bolling, Vickey, illus. 2003. 24p. (J). 2.49 (978-0-7847-1270-2(0)) Standard Publishing.

Balika, Susan S. Jesus Is My Special Friend. Bolling, Vickey, illus. 2013. (Happy Day Ser.). (ENG.). 16p. (J). pap. 2.99 (978-1-4143-9294-3(X), 4608284, Happy Day) Tyndale Hse. Pubs.

Benjamin, M. A. Jesus the Good Shepherd. 2008. 16p. pap. 24.95 (978-1-60441-029-7(9)) America Star Bks.

Bishop, Jennie. Jesus Must Be Really Special. Wummer, Amy, illus. 2006. (Heritage Builders Ser.). 32p. (J). 14.99 (978-0-7847-1379-2(0), 04029) Standard Publishing.

Blyton, Enid. Story of Jesus. 2012. 24p. (J). 9.95 (978-1-84135-744-7(8)) Award Pubns. Ltd. GBR. Dist: Parkwest Pubns., Inc.

Bohnet, Eric C. Arch Books: The Centurion at the Cross. Murphy, Terri, illus. 2007. (Arch Bks.). (J). 1.99 (978-0-7586-1260-1(5)) Concordia Publishing Hse.

Bowman, Crystal. Jesus Feeds the Five Thousand, 1 vol. Sokolova, Valerie, illus. 2011. (I Can Read! / Bible Stories Ser.). (ENG.). 32p. (J). (gr. -1-2). pap. 4.99 (978-0-310-72157-4(1)) Zonderkidz.

—Jesus Raises Lazarus, 1 vol. Sokolova, Valerie, illus. 2011. (I Can Read! / Bible Stories Ser.). (ENG.). 32p. (J). (gr. -1-2). pap. 4.99 (978-0-310-72158-1(X)) Zonderkidz.

Brand, Leonard. God, Science, Friends: Do You Know Jesus? 2019. (Illus.). 185p. (J). pap. (978-0-8163-6518-0(0)) Pacific Pr. Publishing Assn.

Breems, Beau. The Promise. Breems, Beau, illus. 2006. (Illus.). (YA). 10.00 (978-0-9768680-9-5(1)); 20.00 (978-0-9768680-8-8(3)) Burning Bush Creation.

Breems, Beau A. La Gran Historia: The Illustrated Gospel from Creation to Resurrection. Breems, Beau A., illus. 2005.Tr. of His Story. (SPA., Illus.). (J). 10.99 (978-0-9768680-5-7(9)) Burning Bush Creation.

Breems, Beau Alan. His Story: The Illustrated Gospel from Creation to Resurrection. Breems, Beau Alan, illus. 2005. (Illus.). (J). per. 14.95 (978-0-9768680-2-6(4)) Burning Bush Creation.

Brokering, Herbert. The Night Before Jesus. 2018. (ENG., Illus.). 40p. (J). (gr. 1-4). pap. 12.99 (978-0-7586-6029-9(4)) Concordia Publishing Hse.

Brown-Johnson, G. C. O. T. K. A City Called Heaven: Revelations. 2012. 36p. pap. 21.32 (978-1-4691-2616-6(8)) Xlibris Corp.

Bryant, Patricia White. Jesus, Is Your Daddy Mean? 112p. (J). 7.95 (978-1-56794-148-7(6), C-2485) Star Bible & Tract Corp.

Buck, Deanna. My First Story of the First Easter. 2008. (Illus.). 32p. (J). 13.95 (978-1-59038-871-6(2)) Deseret Bk. Co.

Budensiek, Joy. Jesus, My Very Best Friend. 2003. (J). (978-0-9618730-8-0(6)) FEA Ministries.

Buehner, Caralyn. In the Garden. Dorman, Brandon, illus. 2007. (J). 18.95 (978-1-59038-403-9(2)) Deseret Bk. Co.

Burchett, Author Walter, BA. Christian children's questions & answers resurrection of christ Volume 7. 2009. 32p. pap. 14.28 (978-0-557-08245-2(5)) Lulu Pr., Inc.

Burkart, Jeffrey, narrated by. The Week That Led to Easter/Jesus Washes Peter's Feet. 2005. (Arch Books on CD Ser.). (Illus.). 16p. (J). (gr. -1-3). pap. 7.99 incl. audio compact disk (978-5-559-30143-3(4)) Concordia Publishing Hse.

Busch, Melinda Kay. Jesus & the Woman at the Well. Clark, Bill, illus. 2005. (Arch Bks.). (ENG.). 16p. (J). 1.99 (978-0-7586-0675-4(3)) Concordia Publishing Hse.

Carolyn, Berg. Jesus Walks Away. Paris, Pat, illus. 2003. (Arch Bks.). 16p. (J). 2.49 (978-0-7586-0504-7(8)) Concordia Publishing Hse.

Carruth, Jane. More Bible Stories for Children. Cloke, Rene, illus. 2012. (ENG.). 32p. (J). 9.95 (978-0-86163-770-6(4)) Award Pubns. Ltd. GBR. Dist: Parkwest Pubns., Inc.

Choi, Young-Jin. Jesus Feeds Everybody! 2007.Tr. of Jesus' Breadbasket. (Illus.). 26p. bds. 5.95 (978-0-8198-3987-9(6)) Pauline Bks. & Media.

—Mary's Big Surprise. 2007.Tr. of Mary, Crying & Laughing. (Illus.). 26p. (J). (gr. -1-k). bds. 5.95 (978-0-8198-4853-6(0)) Pauline Bks. & Media.

Choi, Young-Jin & Kim, Jung-cho. A Walk on the Waves. 2007. (Illus.). 26p. bds. 5.95 (978-0-8198-8315-5(8)) Pauline Bks. & Media.

Christian Art Gifts, creator. The Miracles of Jesus Puzzle Bible. 2008. (Illus.). 10p. (J). (gr. -1-3). bds. (978-1-86920-787-8(4)) Christian Art Pubs.

Consuegra, Claudio & Consuegra, Pamela. Making Jesus My Best Friend: Baptism Preparation for Younger Children (Ages 8-10) 2005. (Illus.). 95p. (J). (gr. 4-7). per. 8.99 (978-0-8280-1836-4(7)) Review & Herald Publishing Assn.

Cooley, Karen. Jesus Blesses the Children. Julien, Terry, illus. 2015. (Faith That Sticks Bks.). (ENG.). 24p. (J). pap. 3.99 (978-1-4964-0316-2(9), 4611991, Faith that Sticks) Tyndale Hse. Pubs.

Copland, Steve. Just Because. 2007. 224p. per. 14.99 (978-1-60266-916-1(3)) Salem Author Services.

Creek, Lorie. Who Is This Jesus? A Hidden Picture Book. Creek, Chris, illus. 2012. (J). 18.99 (978-1-60908-909-2(X)) Deseret Bk. Co.

Dateno, Maria Grace. The Stations of the Cross for Children. Pompei, Maria Teresa, tr. Richards, Virginia Helen, illus. 2006. (SPA.). 24p. (J). 1.25 (978-0-8198-7095-7(1)) Pauline Bks. & Media.

David C Cook. Noah's Park Children's Church Leader's Guide, Blue Edition. ldr.'s ed. 2003. (Children's Church Kit Ser.). (ENG.). 248p. pap. 49.99 (978-0-7814-3697-7(4), 100745) Cook, David C.

Davidson, Alice Joyce. The Story of the Loaves & Fishes. 2016. (ENG., Illus.). (J). 9.95 (978-0-87029-710-6(4)) Abbey Pr.

Demars, Sue. Jesus Loves You More. 2009. 20p. pap. 10.95 (978-1-60860-695-5(3), Eloquent Bks.) Strategic Book Publishing & Rights Agency (SBPRA).

Demi. Jesus. Demi, illus. 2005. (ENG., Illus.). 48p. (J). (gr. 2-5). 24.99 (978-0-689-86905-1(3), McElderry, Margaret K. Bks.) McElderry, Margaret K. Bks.

dePaola, Tomie. The Miracles of Jesus. 2008. (Illus.). 32p. (J). (gr. -1-3). pap. 8.99 (978-0-14-241068-4(3), Puffin Books) Penguin Young Readers Group.

DeWitt, Becky. Destiny's Closet: Circle of Friends. 2010. 68p. pap. 17.99 *(978-1-4520-8364-3(9))* AuthorHouse.

Dobson, Cynthia Lund. I'm Trying to Be Like Jesus. Dewey, Simon, illus. 2010. (J). 19.99 *(978-1-60641-846-8(7))* Deseret Bk. Co.

Donaghy, Thomas J. Thank You, Jesus: St. Joseph Window Book. 2015. (ENG., Illus.). 12p. (J). bds. 8.95 *(978-1-941243-36-7(3)*, 571/22) Catholic Bk. Publishing Corp.

Doxey, Heidi. Jesus Was Just Like Me. Talbot, Josh, illus. 2017. (ENG.). (J). (gr. -1-k). bds. 12.99 *(978-1-4621-2120-5(9))* Cedar Fort, Inc./CFI Distribution.

—Jesus Was Just Like Me. 2017. (ENG.). (J). bds. 10.99 *(978-1-4621-1925-7(5))* Cedar Fort, Inc./CFI Distribution.

Doyle, Christopher. The Story of Easter. Haysom, John, illus. 2008. 29p. (J). (gr. k-3). pap. 7.49 *(978-0-7586-1495-7(0))* Concordia Publishing Hse.

Dudley, Cathy D. Toddler Theology: Childlike Faith for Everyone. 2012. 24p. pap. 13.99 *(978-1-4685-5728-2(9))* AuthorHouse.

Ellis, Gwen. The Story of Easter, 1 vol. Smallman, Steve, illus. 2008. (Read & Share (Tommy Nelson) Ser.). (ENG.). 32p. (gr. -1-2). 7.99 *(978-1-4003-0855-2(0))* Nelson, Thomas Inc.

Esquinaldo, Virginia. What Did Baby Jesus Do? Esquinaldo, Virginia, illus. 2006. (Illus.). 12p. (J). bds. 6.95 *(978-0-8198-8310-0(7))* Pauline Bks. & Media.

Fawcett, Cheryl & Newman, Robert C. Kids' Questions about God & Jesus. Mazellan, Ron, illus. 2003. 71p. pap. *(978-1-59402-081-0(7))* Regular Baptist Pr.

Fitzgerald, Josephine. Christ, Our Burden Bearer. Skorackiji, Olga et al, eds. 2003. 168p. (YA). pap. 8.95 *(978-0-910487-55-9(3))* Royalty Publishing Co.

Flanagan, Anne. Miracles of Jesus Act/Col Bk. 24p. pap. 1.25 *(978-0-8198-4836-9(0)*, 332-225) Pauline Bks. & Media.

Fogle, Robin. Itty-bitty Bible Activity Book, the Legend of the Candy Cane. 2007. (Illus.). 48p. (J). pap. 1.49 *(978-1-59317-212-1(5))* Warner Pr., Inc.

Frank, Penny & Allsopp, Sophie. The First Easter. Haysom, John, illus. 2nd rev. ed. (ENG.). 24p. pap. 2.99 *(978-0-7459-4123-3(0)*, Lion Books) Lion Hudson PLC GBR. Dist: Trafalgar Square Publishing.

Freeman, Emily Belle & Butler, David. Celebrating a Christ-Centered Easter: Children's Edition. Jeppesen, Ryan, illus. 2018. (ENG.). 32p. (J). (gr. k-3). 17.99 *(978-1-62972-418-8(1)*, 5194501, Ensign Peak) Shadow Mountain Publishing.

Frey, Daniel J., illus. Jacy's Coloring & Activity Book. 2006. 32p. (J). 3.00 *(978-0-9755314-2-6(5))* Majestic Publishing, LLC.

Fryar, Jane L. Jesus Enters Jerusalem. Dorenkamp, Michelle, illus. 2004. (ENG.). 16p. (J). 1.99 *(978-0-7586-0641-9(9))* Concordia Publishing Hse.

Galloway, Tammy. I Am Healed: Praying God's Word for Children. 2010. 28p. 13.95 *(978-1-4497-0428-5(X)*, WestBow Pr.) Author Solutions, LLC.

Galvin, Jennifer. Jesus Loves Me Pre-School Activity Book. 2006. (ENG., Illus.). 32p. (J). pap. 6.95 *(978-0-8091-6734-0(4)*, 6734-4) Paulist Pr.

Ganeri, Anita. The Easter Story. Phillips, Rachael, illus. 2003. (Festival Stories Ser.). 24p. (J). pap. *(978-0-237-52475-3(9))* Evans Brothers, Ltd.

Garris, Norma, illus. The Story of Christmas. 2013. (Happy Day Ser.). (ENG.). 16p. (J). pap. 2.99 *(978-1-4143-9524-1(8)*, 4608514, Happy Day) Tyndale Hse. Pubs.

Gay, Susana & Gay, Owen. First Easter. 2019. (ENG., Illus.). 16p. (J). (gr. -1 — 1). bds. 6.99 *(978-0-8249-1685-5(9)*, Worthy Kids/Ideals) Worthy Publishing.

Glavich, Mary Kathleen. A Child's Book of Miracles. 2004. *(978-0-8294-1038-9(4))* Loyola Pr.

Godfrey, Jan. The Road to Easter Day. Piwowarski, Marcin, illus. 2009. 32p. (J). (gr. -1-1). 14.95 *(978-0-8198-6486-4(2))* Pauline Bks. & Media.

God's Gift: The Birth of Jesus. (Illus.). 16p. (J). pap. 1.50 *(978-0-87162-855-8(4)*, E4573) Warner Pr., Inc.

Grack, Rachel. Easter. 2017. (Celebrating Holidays Ser.). (ENG., Illus.). 24p. (J). (gr. k-3). pap. 7.99 *(978-1-61891-273-2(9)*, 12062, Blastoff! Readers) Bellwether Media.

Greendyk, William, tr. from ENG. El Hijo de la Viuda. l.t. ed. 2004. Orig. Title: The Widow's Son. (SPA., Illus.). 92p. (J). pap. *(978-1-932789-11-9(1))* Editorial Sendas Antiguas, LLC.

Group Publishing Staff, creator. Flip Flops, Pre-K - K: Group's Buzz: the Instant Sunday School Three-Lesson Mini-Kit. 2013. (ENG.). 19.99 incl. audio compact disk *(978-1-4707-0468-1(4))* Group Publishing, Inc.

Gudmundson, C. J. When I Take the Sacrament, I Remember Jesus. Tenney, Shawna J. C., illus. 2012. (J). *(978-1-62108-020-6(X))* Covenant Communications, Inc.

Gunny, Lynn Tuttle. Meet Jesus: The Life & Lessons of a Beloved Teacher. Conteh Morgan, Jane, illus. 2008. (ENG.). 40p. (J). (gr. 3-7). 12.00 *(978-1-55896-524-9(6)*, Skinner Hse. Bks.) Unitarian Universalist Assn.

Gynux. Jesus Loves Me, 1 vol. 2017. (Sing-Along Book Ser.). (ENG., Illus.). 20p. (J). bds. 8.99 *(978-0-310-75894-5(7))* Zonderkidz.

Halpin, D. I Learn about Jesus Col/Act Bk. 32p. pap. 1.25 *(978-0-8198-3686-1(9)*, 332-139) Pauline Bks. & Media.

Handloser, Rick. Sneezy Neezy. Byous, Shawn, illus. 2006. 48p. pap. 19.97 *(978-1-59800-291-1(0))* Outskirts Pr., Inc.

Harman, Debbie G. Jesus Said- 2004. (Illus.). 17.95 *(978-1-59156-091-3(8))* Covenant Communications, Inc.

Hartman, Sara. Mary Magdalene's Easter Story. Koehler, Ed, illus. 2005. (ENG.). 16p. (J). 1.99 *(978-0-7586-0722-5(9))* Concordia Publishing Hse.

Hendricks, Brenda K. Much More to Christmas. Hendricks, Brenda K., illus. 2013. (Illus.). 30p. pap. 9.99 *(978-0-9826582-5-3(7))* Two Small Fish Pubns.

Hendrix, John. Miracle Man: The Story of Jesus. 2016. (ENG., Illus.). 40p. (J). (gr. 1-4). 19.99 *(978-1-4197-1899-1(1)*, 697101, Abrams Bks. for Young Readers) Abrams, Inc.

Hinkle, Cynthia. Star of Wonder. van der Sterre, Johanna, illus. 2005. (Arch Bks.). (ENG.). 16p. (J). 1.99 *(978-0-7586-0724-9(5))* Concordia Publishing Hse.

Hinkle, Cynthia A. The Thankful Leper: The Story of the Ten Lepers: Luke 17:11-19 & 2 Kings 5:1-15 for Children. Collier-Morales, Roberta, illus. 2006. (Arch Bks.). (J). 2.49 *(978-0-7586-1284-7(2))* Concordia Publishing Hse.

Hitchen, Danielle. Jesus Heals: An Anatomy Primer. 2020. (Baby Believer Ser.). (ENG., Illus.). 20p. (J). (— 1). bds. 12.99 *(978-0-7369-7944-3(1)*, 6979443) Harvest Hse. Pubs.

Hite, LaDonna J. I Love to Pray. 2007. 24p. per. 14.45 *(978-0-9765898-9-1(3))* FAITHTOGO.

Hoffa, Darlene. Bible Stories about Jesus. 2004. (Illus.). 96p. (J). (gr. 3-4). pap. 11.95 *(978-0-937282-07-6(3)*, RB36114) Rainbow Pubs. & Legacy Pr.

Holder, Jennifer. My Story of Jesus. Munger, Nancy, illus. 2014. (Happy Day Ser.). (ENG.). 16p. (J). pap. 2.99 *(978-1-4143-9325-4(3)*, 4608315, Happy Day) Tyndale Hse. Pubs.

Hook, Katie Jo. Momma Loves You. Hook, Katie Jo, illus. 2015. (ENG., Illus.). 32p. pap. 9.99 *(978-1-63047-495-9(9))* Morgan James Publishing.

Hudson, Angus. Localiza la Diferencia (Find the Difference) Parabolas Que Jesus Relato. (SPA.). (J). 1.89 *(978-1-56063-965-7(2)*, 497756) Editorial Unilit.

Jakubowsky, Frank. God Looked down & Saw a Baby. 2012. 56p. (gr. 4-6). pap. 9.95 *(978-1-4497-7319-9(2)*, WestBow Pr.) Author Solutions, LLC.

James, Ben, illus. Los Tres Reyes Magos, the Three Wise Men. 2006. (ENG & SPA.). (J). bds. *(978-0-9786863-2-1(2))* ITRON Publishing.

James, Betsy, illus. The Word & Picture Books Set 1: For Year B/C, 6 vols. Incl. Breakfast at the Lake. Wehreim, Carol. bds. 4.95 *(978-0-8298-1186-5(9))*; Come to Jesus. Wehreim, Carol, ed. bds. 4.95 *(978-0-8298-1183-4(4))*; First Church. Wehreim, Carol, ed. bds. 4.95 *(978-0-8298-1188-9(5))*; Jesus, a Special Baby. Wehreim, Carol, ed. bds. 4.95 *(978-0-8298-1184-1(2))*; Jesus Goes Fishing. Wehreim, Carol, ed. bds. 4.95 *(978-0-8298-1185-8(0))*; Loving Shepherd. Wehreim, Carol, ed. bds. 4.95 *(978-0-8298-1187-2(7))*; 12p. (J). (gr. -1-4). 1997. (Word & Picture Bks.). (Illus.). 29.70 *(978-0-8298-1189-6(3))* Pilgrim Pr., The/United Church Pr.

Jeffs, Stephanie. Where's Jesus. Laver, Sarah, 8th, illus. 2004. 32p. 13.95 *(978-0-8294-1728-9(1))* Loyola Pr.

Jesus: A 365-Day Devotional, 1 vol. 2016. (ENG.). 384p. (J). 15.99 *(978-0-310-75809-9(2))* Zonderkidz.

Jesus & His Disciples: Coloring Book. (Illus.). 16p. (J). pap. 1.50 *(978-0-87162-856-5(2)*, E6040) Warner Pr., Inc.

Jesus Is Born. 2004. *(978-0-8294-9909-4(1))* Loyola Pr.

Jesus Is Everything I Need: Challenging Bible Activities on Jesus & All He Is to Us! (Illus.). 16p. (J). pap. 1.50 *(978-0-87162-818-3(X)*, E4512) Warner Pr., Inc.

Jesus, our Righteousness. 2005. (YA). 14.00 *(978-1-59872-121-6(6))* Instant Pub.

Johnson, Alice. Believe & You're There (4 vol. Set), 4 vols. 2009. pap. 24.99 *(978-1-60641-186-5(1))* Deseret Bk. Co.

Johnson, Alice W. & Warner, Allison H. Believe & You're There at the Miracles of Jesus. Nelson, Holly, illus. 2009. 96p. (J). pap. 8.95 *(978-1-59038-722-1(8))* Deseret Bk. Co.

—Believe & You're There When the Stone Was Rolled Away. Nelson, Holly, illus. 2009. 96p. (J). pap. 8.95 *(978-1-59038-723-8(6))* Deseret Bk. Co.

—Believe & You're There When the White Dove Descended. Nelson, Holly, illus. 2009. 96p. (J). pap. 8.95 *(978-1-59038-721-4(X))* Deseret Bk. Co.

Jones, Dennis. First Easter Ever, 1 vol. 2015. (ENG., Illus.). 32p. (J). pap. 2.99 *(978-0-310-74084-1(3))* Zonderkidz.

Jones, Ron, ed. Jesus: Passages from the Gospel Records. 2003. *(978-0-9747452-0-6(0))* ECF Bks.

Julien, Terry & Carter, Nancy, illus. Jesus Loves Me. 2015. (Faith That Sticks Bks.). (ENG.). 24p. (J). pap. 3.99 *(978-1-4964-0315-5(0)*, 4611990, Faith that Sticks) Tyndale Hse. Pubs.

Keable, Ruth. Jesus A True Story. 2006. (Illus.). 108p. per. *(978-0-901860-41-5(7))* Scripture Truth Pubns.

Keating, Susan K. Jesus Christ. 2004. (Great Names Ser.). (Illus.). 32p. (J). (gr. 3-18). lib. bdg. 19.95 *(978-1-59084-138-9(7))* Mason Crest.

KH Pathways. Kindergarten Stepping Stones: Jesus Is God's Best Gift Lapbook. rev. ed. 2013. (ENG.). 32p. 34.50 *(978-1-4652-0019-8(3))* Kendall Hunt Publishing Co.

Knight, Chris. The Body of Jesus. 2010. 24p. pap. 12.99 *(978-1-4520-7413-9(5))* AuthorHouse.

Kovacs, Victoria. Jesus' Miracles/Martha Flip-Over Book. Krome, Mike & Ryley, David, illus. 2015. (Little Bible Heroes(tm) Ser.). (ENG.). 32p. (J). (gr. k-2). pap. 3.99 *(978-1-4336-8714-3(3)*, 005742013, B&H Kids) B&H Publishing Group.

Krenzer, Rolf. Jesus Is Risen. Maloney, Linda M., tr. from GER. Droop, Constanza, illus. 2005. 24p. (gr. -1-3). 14.95 *(978-0-8146-2764-8(1))* Liturgical Pr.

Kueker, Donald, illus. The Easter Story According to Matthew. 2007. 32p. (J). per. 7.49 *(978-0-7586-1008-9(4))* Concordia Publishing Hse.

Lafond, Pascale. The Story of Jesus. Flowerpot Press, ed. 2012. (Illus.). 32p. (J). *(978-1-77093-387-3(5))* Flowerpot Children's Pr. Inc.

Land Fairer Than Day. 7.50 *(978-0-8054-5937-1(5))* B&H Publishing Group.

Lane, Leena. Come to the Party with Jesus. Reynolds, Annette, ed. Saunderson, Chris, illus. 2007. (Action Rhymes Ser.). (ENG.). 16p. (J). (gr. -1-2). pap. 4.99 *(978-0-9789056-5-1(2))* New Day Publishing, Inc.

Larsen, Carolyn. Stories about Jesus for Little Ones. Incrocci, Rick, illus. 2008. 35p. (gr. -1-k). bds. *(978-1-86920-173-9(6))* Christian Art Pubs.

Later Life of Jesus: Pict O Graph. (Pict-O-Graph Ser.). (Illus.). (J). 10.99 *(978-0-7847-1028-9(7)*, 02228) Standard Publishing.

Lee, Otha. Mrs. Lee's Stories about Jesus. 2013. 274p. pap. 19.95 *(978-1-58427-388-2(7))* Truth Publications, Inc.

Lesson in a Bag-Eucharist Lesson 8. 2012. (ENG.). 26.99 *(978-1-59982-394-2(2))* Saint Mary's Press of Minnesota.

Lesson in a Bag-Reconciliation Lesson 2. 2012. (ENG.). 26.99 *(978-1-59982-399-7(3))* Saint Mary's Press of Minnesota.

Lewis, Jan. Baby's First Stories of Jesus. 2015. (Illus.). 24p. (J). (gr. -1-2). bds. 6.99 *(978-1-86147-415-5(6)*, Armadillo) Anness Publishing GBR. Dist: National Bk. Network.

Librado. Thank You Jesus. l.t. ed. 2006. (Illus.). 29p. (J). (gr. -1-3). per. 11.99 *(978-1-59879-209-6(1))* Lifevest Publishing, Inc.

Lloyd-Jones, Sally. Jesus Storybook Bible / Biblia para niños, Historias de Jesús Every Story Whispers His Name / Cada Historia Susurra Su Nombre, 1 vol. 2008. (Jesus Storybook Bible Ser.). Tr. of (Bilingual) (Bilingüe). (SPA.). 352p. (J). 24.99 *(978-0-8297-5606-7(X))* Vida Pubs.

Lord, Jill Roman. If Jesus Lived Inside My Heart. 2014. (ENG., Illus.). 22p. (J). bds. 7.99 *(978-0-8249-1937-5(8)*, Ideals Pubns.) Worthy Publishing.

Lounsbury, Pete. Jesus & the Blind Man. 2007. (J). per. 12.95 *(978-1-59879-408-3(6))* Lifevest Publishing, Inc.

Lucado, Max. Next Door Savior, 1 vol. 2008. (ENG.). 212p. (YA). pap. 14.99 *(978-1-4041-7544-0(X)*, Tommy Nelson) Nelson, Thomas Inc.

MacKenzie, Carine. God, the Ten Commandments & Jesus. rev. ed. 2003. (ENG.). 48p. (J). 12.99 *(978-1-85792-850-1(4)*, f3a73706-7f26-4bdb-b50d-80d41637f069) Christian Focus Pubns. GBR. Dist: Baker & Taylor Publisher Services (BTPS).

—Little Hands Life of Jesus. 2008. (ENG., Illus.). 144p. (J). 10.99 *(978-1-84550-339-0(2)*, b0cf452d-f13c-41b1-aa7f-fd57374339d8) Christian Focus Pubns. GBR. Dist: Baker & Taylor Publisher Services (BTPS).

—My First Book about Jesus. rev. ed. 2014. (My First Bks.). (ENG., Illus.). 64p. (J). pap. 3.99 *(978-1-84550-463-2(1)*, 67606737-a911-442a-ad99-54045f08c29a) Christian Focus Pubns. GBR. Dist: Baker & Taylor Publisher Services (BTPS).

MacKenzie, Catherine. Jesus Christ the Best King of All. 2010. (Colour Bks.). (ENG., Illus.). 64p. (J). 6.99 *(978-1-84550-568-4(9)*, 8e219b87-d418-460f-9e8e-36e393117f1d) Christian Focus Pubns. GBR. Dist: Baker & Taylor Publisher Services (BTPS).

—Jesus Helps His People. 2008. (Sent to Save Ser.). (ENG., Illus.). 16p. (J). (gr. -1-3). bds. 3.99 *(978-1-84550-322-2(8)*, f4add069-dfe0-4c89-9211-00693165f5e1) Christian Focus Pubns. GBR. Dist: Baker & Taylor Publisher Services (BTPS).

—Jesus Rose from the Dead - the Evidence. rev. ed. 2010. (ENG., Illus.). 96p. (J). 7.99 *(978-1-84550-537-0(9)*, a54ebc8d-c70d-477c-b1c1-8eaf69927f9b) Christian Focus Pubns. GBR. Dist: Baker & Taylor Publisher Services (BTPS).

—John Calvin: What Is the Truth? rev. ed. 2013. (Little Lights Ser.). (ENG., Illus.). 24p. (J). 7.99 *(978-1-84550-560-8(3)*, 893a01da-0af7-45de-bf5f-42a078868520) Christian Focus Pubns. GBR. Dist: Baker & Taylor Publisher Services (BTPS).

—Martin Luther: What Should I Do? rev. ed. 2013. (Little Lights Ser.). (ENG., Illus.). 24p. (J). 7.99 *(978-1-84550-561-5(1)*, 73c43d0a-3047-4c73-ae23-2834dd3639b9) Christian Focus Pubns. GBR. Dist: Baker & Taylor Publisher Services (BTPS).

Maier, Paul L. The Very First Easter. 32p. (J). 9.99 *(978-0-570-07195-2(X))* Concordia Publishing Hse.

—The Very First Easter. Ordaz, Francisco, illus. 2004. 32p. (J). pap. 7.49 *(978-0-7586-0627-3(3))*; 13.49 *(978-0-570-07053-5(8))* Concordia Publishing Hse.

Mann, Brooke Malia, illus. Miracles of Jesus. 2019. (J). 16.99 *(978-1-62972-522-2(6))* Deseret Bk. Co.

Marra, Julie M. A Mother's Book of Prayers, Black Pearl. 2012. (ENG., Illus.). 96p. (gr. 8-12). pap. 6.95 *(978-0-88271-091-4(5)*, RG10310) Regina Pr., Malhame & Co.

Marsh, Dilleen, tr. & illus. What Happens When People Die? Marsh, Dilleen, illus. 2003. (J). 12.95 *(978-1-57008-954-1(X))* Deseret Bk. Co.

McClendon, Kimberli A. Have You Heard? Jesus Walks on Water. 2012. 30p. pap. 13.99 *(978-1-4497-4179-2(7)*, WestBow Pr.) Author Solutions, LLC.

McDonough, Andrew. Jesus & the Children. 2019. (Lost Sheep Ser.: 11). (ENG., Illus.). 32p. (J). (gr. k-3). pap. 7.99 *(978-1-910786-95-6(0)*, f9799a7e-8545-42fe-b328-e9d0817e0fca, Sarah Grace Publishing) Malcolm Down Publishing Ltd. GBR. Dist: Baker & Taylor Publisher Services (BTPS).

McGuire, George. God & Me. 2006. 36p. pap. 13.99 *(978-1-4116-9218-3(7))* Lulu Pr., Inc.

Milbourne, Anna & Roberti, Alessandra. The Story of the Nativity. 2010. (Illus.). (J). 10.99 *(978-0-7945-2552-1(0)*, Usborne) EDC Publishing.

Miles, David. Miracles of Jesus, 1 vol. 2014. (I Can Read! / Adventure Bible Ser.). (ENG., Illus.). 32p. (J). pap. 4.99 *(978-0-310-73242-6(5))* Zonderkidz.

Millard, Bart. I Can Only Imagine: A Friendship with Jesus Now & Forever, 1 vol. Collina, Sumiti, illus. 2018. (ENG.). 32p. (J). 16.99 *(978-1-4003-2133-9(6)*, Tommy Nelson) Nelson, Thomas Inc.

Miracles of Jesus. (Pict-O-Graph Ser.). (Illus.). (J). 10.99 *(978-0-7847-1026-5(0)*, 02226) Standard Publishing.

Miracles of Jesus. (Illus.). 16p. (J). pap. 1.50 *(978-0-87162-858-9(9)*, E6039) Warner Pr., Inc.

Moore, Alan & Tavner, Gill. Jesus of Nazareth. Donnelly, Karen, illus. 2014. (New Testament Ser.). (ENG.). 64p. pap. 7.95 *(978-1-906230-24-1(2))* Real Reads Ltd. GBR. Dist: Casemate Pubs. & Bk. Distributors, LLC.

Moore, Angela Hays. Maggie Seeks the Kingdom of God. Kiel, Casey Kizer, illus. 2007. 32p. (J). 19.99 *(978-1-59879-323-9(3))* Lifevest Publishing, Inc.

Mortimer, F. L. More about Jesus. 288p. (J). pap. 7.99 *(978-1-85792-592-0(0))* Christian Focus Pubns. GBR. Dist: Riverside.

My Story of Jesus. 2006. 32p. (J). pap. 2.89 *(978-0-7847-1281-8(6)*, 22094) Standard Publishing.

Neeley, Deta Petersen & Neeley, Nathan Glen. Paul of Tarsus, V2: A Child's Story of the New Testament. 2011. 152p. 41.95 *(978-1-258-07519-4(9))* Literary Licensing, LLC.

Neff, LaVonne. The Jesus Book: 40 Bible Stories. Goffe, Toni, illus. 2004. (Life of Christ for Children Ser.). 84p. (J). (gr. -1-k). 9.95 *(978-0-8294-1373-1(1))* Loyola Pr.

Nielson, Mark S. I Believe in Jesus Too. Stapley, Craig, illus. 2011. (J). 17.99 *(978-1-60908-741-8(0))* Deseret Bk. Co.

Nyland, Richard. Jesus. 2005. 18.99 *(978-1-59467-983-4(5))*; per. 10.99 *(978-1-59467-982-7(7))* Salem Author Services.

Oakes, Loretta. Peek-a-Boo Jesus! Hall, Mary, illus. 2010. (ENG.). 16p. (J). (gr. -1). bds. 9.95 *(978-0-8091-6755-5(7)*, Ambassador Bks.) Paulist Pr.

O'Neill-McGrath, Michael. Jesus A to Z. O'Neill-McGrath, Michael, illus. 2007. (Illus.). 32p. 16.99 *(978-1-58459-332-4(6))* World Library Pubns.

Palmer, Alison. Simply Singing Time. 2009. 96p. (J). pap. 8.99 *(978-0-88290-970-7(3))* Cedar Fort, Inc./CFI Distribution.

Pascucci, Mary Ann. Adventures on Green Pasture Farm Scruff: An Orphan Lamb. 2013. 48p. pap. 20.45 *(978-1-4908-1184-0(2)*, WestBow Pr.) Author Solutions, LLC.

Perez III, Librado. Thank You Jesus. l.t. ed. 2006. (Illus.). 36p. (J). 23.99 *(978-1-59879-317-8(9))* Lifevest Publishing, Inc.

Pingry, Patricia A. Bible Story Cards: The Story of Jesus. 2006. (ENG., Illus.). 10p. 7.95 *(978-0-8249-1704-3(9)*, Ideals Pubns.) Worthy Publishing.

—The Easter Story. 2006. (ENG., Illus.). 32p. (J). (gr. -1-1). per. 4.99 *(978-0-8249-5531-1(5)*, Ideals Pubns.) Worthy Publishing.

—Jesus in the Temple: Based on Luke 2:40/52. Munger, Nancy, illus. 2008. (ENG.). 26p. (J). bds. 6.95 *(978-0-8249-6569-3(8)*, Ideals Pubns.) Worthy Publishing.

—The Story of Easter. Wells, Lorraine, illus. 2006. (ENG.). 26p. (gr. -1-k). 12.95 *(978-0-8249-6649-2(X)*, Ideals Pubns.) Worthy Publishing.

—The Story of Loaves & Fishes. Venturi-Pickett, Stacy, illus. 2003. 26p. (J). bds. 6.95 *(978-0-8249-6518-1(3)*, Ideals Pubns.) Worthy Publishing.

Piper, Sophie. The First Easter, 1 vol. Corke, Estelle, illus. 2009. (Bible Story Time Ser.). 32p. (J). 5.95 *(978-0-8254-7832-1(4)*, Lion Children's) Lion Hudson PLC GBR. Dist: Kregel Pubns.

Pipkin, Evelyn Ruth. The Pretty Little Red Bird. l.t. ed. 2004. 19p. (J). (gr. 1-3). 7.95 *(978-0-9755789-0-2(1))* Two Seed Planters Inc.

Plante, Patty. Joy for Jesus: Friends with God, 1. 2nd ed. 2003. (Joy for Jesus Ser.: 1). Orig. Title: Joy for Jesus: Friends with God. 91p. (J). ring bd. 24.95 *(978-1-889723-31-0(2))* Family Harvest Church.

—Joy for Jesus: Jesus in Me. 2003. (Joy for Jesus Ser.: 2). 78p. (J). ring bd. 24.95 *(978-1-889723-40-2(1))* Family Harvest Church.

—Viviendo Como Jesus, Libro 1. Garcia de Ortiz, Lic. Rosalinda, tr. from ENG. 2003. (SPA.). 71p. (J). ring bd. 24.95 *(978-1-889723-32-7(0))* Family Harvest Church.

Poelman, Heidi. I Can Love Like Jesus. 2017. (ENG., Illus.). (J). (gr. -1-2). 14.99 *(978-1-4621-1940-0(9))* Cedar Fort, Inc./CFI Distribution.

—Jesus Worked Miracles. Pruett, Jason, illus. 2018. (ENG.). 32p. (J). (gr. k-3). 14.99 *(978-1-4621-2277-6(9))* Cedar Fort, Inc./CFI Distribution.

Poole, Susie. The Amazing Journey: Jesus, Creation, Death & Life! 2nd ed. 2007. (ENG., Illus.). 44p. pap. 10.99 *(978-1-904637-43-1(4)*, 1904637434) Authentic Media GBR. Dist: EMI CMG Distribution.

Provencher, Devon. The Gospel. Provencher, Jessica, illus. 2020. (Big Theology for Little Hearts Ser.). (ENG.). 22p. (J). bds. 9.99 *(978-1-4335-6525-0(0))* Crossway.

—Jesus. Provencher, Jessica, illus. 2020. (Big Theology for Little Hearts Ser.). (ENG.). 22p. (J). bds. 9.99 *(978-1-4335-6524-3(2))* Crossway.

Puhalo, Lazar. Twelve Great Feast Days. Date not set. (Illus.). 45p. (J). pap. 5.00 *(978-1-879038-43-1(9)*, 9011) Synaxis Pr.

Pulley, Kelly. The Beginner's Bible All about Jesus Sticker & Activity Book, 1 vol. 2015. (Beginner's Bible Ser.). (ENG., Illus.). 16p. (J). pap. 8.99 *(978-0-310-74693-5(0))* Zonderkidz.

—Jesus & His Friends, 1 vol. 2007. (I Can Read! / the Beginner's Bible Ser.). (ENG., Illus.). 32p. (J). (gr. -1-1). pap. 4.99 *(978-0-310-71461-3(3))* Zonderkidz.

Redding, David Asbury. He Never Spoke Without a Parable: His Kingdom, Your Antagonist, It's up to You, 3 bks, 5 vols. l.t. ed. 2003. pap. 16.00 *(978-0-9671701-3-8(3)*, 0-9671701-3-3) Redding Stenner, Marion.

Redford, Marjorie. My Bible Says. Marlin, Kathryn, illus. 2013. (Happy Day Ser.). (ENG.). 16p. (J). pap. 2.99 *(978-1-4143-9301-8(6)*, 4608291, Happy Day) Tyndale Hse. Pubs.

Reeves, Eira. Jesus & Me Every Day Book 1, 1 vol. 2009. (ENG., Illus.). 64p. (J). pap. *(978-1-85345-518-6(0))* Crusade for World Revival.

—Jesus & Me Every Day Book 2, 1 vol. 2009. (ENG., Illus.). 64p. (J). pap. *(978-1-85345-519-3(9))* Crusade for World Revival.

The Revolutionary Revelation on the Book of Revelation & its all about Jesus. 2005. (YA). per. *(978-1-59872-168-3(2))* Instant Pub.

Rhodes, Karen. Do You Know Jesus? 2005. (J). pap. 1.79 *(978-1-59317-111-7(0))* Warner Pr., Inc.

Rhydderch, Gwyn, et al. Iesu'r Ffrind: 16 Sesiwn Yn Cyflwyno Bywyd Iesu Ar Gyfer Plant Cynradd Yn Seiliedig Ar Efengyl Luc. 2005. (WEL., Illus.). 120p. pap. *(978-1-85994-007-5(2))* Cyhoeddiadau'r Gair.

Risen Today. 7.50 *(978-0-8054-5925-8(1))* B&H Publishing Group.

Robinson, Timothy. What Happens When People Die? Reprint. 2009. 32p. 10.95 *(978-1-60641-114-8(4))* Deseret Bk. Co.

Roche, Maite. The Gospel for Little Ones. 2011. (ENG., Illus.). 30p. (J). (gr. -1-1). bds. 14.99 *(978-1-58617-507-8(6))* Ignatius Pr.

—My First Pictures of Jesus. 2012. (ENG.). 14p. (J). 6.99 *(978-1-58617-651-8(X))* Ignatius Pr.

Rose, Drew, illus. God's Son, Jesus. 2005. (Bible Activity Bks.). 94p. (J). (gr. -1-3). 2.99 *(978-0-7814-4314-2(8)*, 0781443148) Cook, David C.

Rottmann, Erik. The Easter Victory. Billin-Frye, Paige, illus. 2006. (Arch Bks.). (ENG.). 16p. (J). (gr. -1-3). 2.49 *(978-0-7586-0869-7(1))* Concordia Publishing Hse.

—Jesus, My Good Shepherd. Miyake, Yoski, illus. 2005. (ENG.). 16p. (J). 1.99 *(978-0-7586-0725-6(3))* Concordia Publishing Hse.

Saint Mary's Press Staff. Lesson in a Bag-Eucharist Lesson 1. 2012. (ENG.). (J). 60.99 *(978-1-59982-387-4(X))* Saint Mary's Press of Minnesota.

JKL

—Lesson in a Bag-Eucharist Lesson 10. 2012. (ENG.). 26.99 *(978-1-59982-396-6(9))* Saint Mary's Press of Minnesota.

—Lesson in a Bag-Eucharist Lesson 2. 2012. (ENG.). 26.99 *(978-1-59982-388-1(8))* Saint Mary's Press of Minnesota.

—Lesson in a Bag-Eucharist Lesson 3. 2012. (ENG.). (gr. 6-8). 26.99 *(978-1-59982-389-8(6))* Saint Mary's Press of Minnesota.

—Lesson in a Bag-Eucharist Lesson 4. 2012. (ENG.). 26.99 *(978-1-59982-390-4(X))* Saint Mary's Press of Minnesota.

—Lesson in a Bag-Eucharist Lesson 5. 2012. (ENG.). 26.99 *(978-1-59982-391-1(8))* Saint Mary's Press of Minnesota.

—Lesson in a Bag-Eucharist Lesson 6. 2012. (ENG.). 26.99 *(978-1-59982-392-8(6))* Saint Mary's Press of Minnesota.

—Lesson in a Bag-Eucharist Lesson 7. 2012. (ENG.). 26.99 *(978-1-59982-393-5(4))* Saint Mary's Press of Minnesota.

—Lesson in a Bag-Eucharist Lesson 9. 2012. (ENG.). 26.99 *(978-1-59982-395-9(0))* Saint Mary's Press of Minnesota.

—Lesson in a Bag-Reconciliation Lesson 1. 2012. (ENG.). 6p. 26.99 *(978-1-59982-398-0(5))* Saint Mary's Press of Minnesota.

—Lesson in a Bag-Reconciliation Lesson 3. 2012. (ENG.). 26.99 *(978-1-59982-400-0(0))* Saint Mary's Press of Minnesota.

—Lesson in a Bag-Reconciliation Lesson 4. 2012. (ENG.). 26.99 *(978-1-59982-401-7(9))* Saint Mary's Press of Minnesota.

—Lesson in a Bag-Reconciliation Lesson 5. 2012. (ENG.). 26.99 *(978-1-59982-402-4(7))* Saint Mary's Press of Minnesota.

—Lesson in a Bag-Reconciliation Lesson 6. 2012. (ENG.). 26.99 *(978-1-59982-403-1(5))* Saint Mary's Press of Minnesota.

—Lesson in a Bag-Reconciliation Lesson 7. 2012. (ENG.). 26.99 *(978-1-59982-404-8(3))* Saint Mary's Press of Minnesota.

—Lesson in a Bag-Reconciliation Lesson 8. 2012. (ENG.). 26.99 *(978-1-59982-405-5(1))* Saint Mary's Press of Minnesota.

Sanders, Nancy I. Jesus Walks on the Water. Swisher, Elizabeth, illus. 2005. (ENG.). 16p. (J). 1.99 *(978-0-7586-0864-2(0))* Concordia Publishing Hse.

Sanderson, Harvelene. Hello, Jesus Loves You. 2012. 16p. pap. 7.99 *(978-1-4624-0120-8(1)*, Inspiring Voices) Author Solutions, LLC.

Sarell, Nadja, illus. Little Dove & the Story of Easter, 1 vol. 2019. (ENG.). 22p. (J). bds. 7.99 *(978-0-310-76668-1(0))* Zonderkidz.

Schkade, Jonathan. Jesus Shows His Glory. 2008. (Arch Bks.). 16p. (J). (gr. k-4). pap. 1.99 *(978-0-7586-1452-0(7))* Concordia Publishing Hse.

—The Love Bridge. 2017. (ENG., Illus.). 42p. (J). (gr. -1-3). 10.99 *(978-0-7586-5777-0(3))* Concordia Publishing Hse.

—Nicodemus & Jesus. Miyake, Yoshi, illus. 2014. (Arch Bks.). (ENG.). 16p. (J). (gr. k-4). pap. 2.49 *(978-0-7586-4606-4(2))* Concordia Publishing Hse.

Schlitt, D. Celebrate the Names of Jesus. 2004. 52p. 6.99 *(978-0-8054-0825-6(8))* B&H Publishing Group.

Schmertz Navarro, Christine, ed. Student Activity Workbook for Breakthrough! the Bible for Young Catholics: Getting to Know Jesus. 2007. (ENG., Illus.). 32p. pap. 10.50 *(978-0-88489-978-5(0))* Saint Mary's Press of Minnesota.

Seifert, Sheila. Happy Birthday Jesus. 2007. (Discipleship Junction Ser.). (ENG., Illus.). 112p. (J). per. 19.99 *(978-0-7814-4511-5(6)*, 105278) Cook, David C.

Setzer, Lee Ann. Tiny Talks: My Savior, Jesus Christ, Vol. 10. 2009. 86p. (J). pap. 8.99 *(978-1-59955-375-7(9))* Cedar Fort, Inc./CFI Distribution.

Sharpe, Jean Ann. The Saving Name of God the Son. 2009. (ENG., Illus.). 22p. (J). 9.95 *(978-1-932350-30-2(6))* Ignatius Pr.

Shegog, Jakeenya. My Friend Jesus. 2013. 24p. pap. 9.95 *(978-0-9896581-6-4(3))* Kingdom Publishing Group, Inc.

Smart, Dominic. 40 Days with Jesus: A Journey Through Mark's Gospel. rev. ed. 2006. (Daily Readings Ser.). (ENG., Illus.). 144p. (J). per. 10.99 *(978-1-84550-193-8(4)*, 90c8c6bb-b0e2-4fde-8d9c-35fa755f0c38) Christian Focus Pubns. GBR. Dist: Baker & Taylor Publisher Services (BTPS).

Smart Kidz, creator. Jesus Loves the Little Children. 2013. (Bible Sing along Bks.). (ENG., Illus.). 12p. (gr. -1). bds. 12.99 *(978-1-891100-34-5(3)*, Smart Kids) Penton Overseas, Inc.

Smith, Evans. The Christmas Angel. 2009. 40p. pap. 18.49 *(978-1-4490-4056-7(X))* AuthorHouse.

Smith, Judah. Jesus Is Student Edition, 1 vol. 2014. (ENG.). 224p. (J). pap. 14.99 *(978-0-7180-2245-7(9)*, Tommy Nelson) Nelson, Thomas Inc.

Smith, Martina. The Story of Easter: A Spark Bible Story. Grosshauser, Peter & Temple, Ed, illus. 2016. (Spark Bible Stories Ser.). 32p. (J). (gr. -1-2). 12.99 *(978-1-5064-0230-7(5)*, Sparkhouse Family) 1517 Media.

Southall, M. Renee. My Daddy Loves Me & He Can Do Anything. 2012. 28p. pap. 19.99 *(978-1-4772-8221-2(1))* AuthorHouse.

St. Pierre, Stephanie. Jesus, the Good Shepherd. Bolam, Emily, illus. 2003. 14p. (J). bds. 7.99 *(978-0-7847-1272-6(7)*, 04032) Standard Publishing.

Stanton, Sue. Child's Guide to the Stations of the Cross. Blake, Anne Catharine, illus. 32p. (J). 2018. (ENG.). pap. 12.95 *(978-0-8091-6786-9(7))* 2008. 10.95 *(978-0-8091-6739-5(5)*, 6739-5) Paulist Pr.

Stayton, Claudia Grace. Day by Day the Jesus Way: What Jesus Has to Say about Life, Love, & the Way to God. 2003. 144p. per. 5.95 *(978-0-9728900-0-7(9)*, 888-899-3207) Good News Connections.

Steigemeyer, Julie. My Little Easter Book. Regan, Dana, illus. 2008. 20p. (J). (gr. -1-k). bds. 6.49 *(978-0-7586-1444-5(6))* Concordia Publishing Hse.

Stephens Landoll, Mary. A Vision from Heaven. 2013. 50p. pap. 9.95 *(978-1-4908-0604-4(0)*, WestBow Pr.) Author Solutions, LLC.

Stiegemeyer, Julie. Things I See at Christmas. Mitter, Kathryn, illus. 2005. 16p. (J). (gr. -1-17). bds. 5.49 *(978-0-7586-0809-3(8))* Concordia Publishing Hse.

Stohs, Anita Reith. Hush, Little One: A Lullaby for God's Children. Kanzler, John, tr. Kanzler, John, illus. 2004. 32p. (J). 12.99 *(978-0-570-07144-0(5))* Concordia Publishing Hse.

—Hush Little One: A Lullaby for God's Children. Kanzler, John, illus. 2006. 20p. (J). (gr. -1). bds. 5.49 *(978-0-7586-0861-1(6))* Concordia Publishing Hse.

Stoner, Diane. Do You Know My Friend, Jesus? 2012. (ENG.). 20p. (J). pap. 16.95 *(978-1-4327-9049-3(8))* Outskirts Pr., Inc.

Story of Jesus. 2004. 16p. (J). act. bk. ed. 8.99 *(978-0-570-07178-5(X))* Concordia Publishing Hse.

Story of Jesus for Children. 2004. pap. 14.98 *(978-0-7378-0584-0(6))* Brentwood Home Video.

Strobel, Lee. Case for Christ for Kids, 1 vol. enl. ed. 2010. (Case for... Series for Kids Ser.). (ENG., Illus.). 144p. (J). pap. 9.99 *(978-0-310-71990-8(9))* Zonderkidz.

—Case for Miracles for Kids, 1 vol. 2018. (Case for... Series for Kids Ser.). (ENG.). 160p. (J). pap. 8.99 *(978-0-310-74864-9(X))* Zonderkidz.

—The Case for Miracles Student Edition: A Journalist Explores the Evidence for the Supernatural, 1 vol. 2018. (Case for ... Series for Students Ser.). (ENG.). 160p. (YA). pap. 16.99 *(978-0-310-74636-2(1))* Zondervan.

Stuckey, Denise. Jesus, I Feel Close to You. Saroff, Phyllis, illus. 2005. 32p. (J). 10.95 *(978-0-8091-6718-0(2)*, 6718-2) Paulist Pr.

Student Life Staff & Navigators Staff, The. 31 Verses - Community: Every Teenager Should Know. 2009. 80p. (YA). pap. 4.99 *(978-1-935040-16-3(2))* NavPress Publishing Group.

Summerer, Marilyn. The First Christmas Present. van der Sterre, Johanna, illus. 2009. 32p. (J). (gr. -1). 14.99 *(978-0-7586-1663-0(5))* Concordia Publishing Hse.

Szczebak, Patricia & Peterson, Mary Joseph. Jesus Our Savior: The Story of God's Son for Children. 2018. (ENG., Illus.). 64p. (J). pap. 8.95 *(978-0-8198-4023-3(8))* Pauline Bks. & Media.

Tebo, Mary Elizabeth. My First Book about Jesus. Peterson, Mary Joseph, illus. 2008. 64p. (J). (gr. 1-3). pap. 7.95 *(978-0-8198-4865-9(4))* Pauline Bks. & Media.

Thomas-Logan, Sharon. The Miracles of Jesus Christ. 2009. 24p. pap. 12.99 *(978-1-4389-4615-3(5))* AuthorHouse.

Thornborough, Tim. The Fright of Your Life, 25 vols. 2010. 6p. (J). *(978-1-906334-27-7(7))* Good Bk. Co., The.

Thorne, Rick. The Hidden Secrets of Jesus & Other Revelations. 2004. (Illus.). 268p. (YA). pap. 19.95 *(978-0-937327-04-3(2))* Soul Pubns.

Tnt. On the Way 3-9's - Book 2 Vol. 2. 2006. (On the Way Ser.). (ENG.). 96p. (J). pap. 17.99 *(978-1-85792-319-3(7)*, cea731bc-f8a7-4b46-97fe-a5adfaae73fd) Christian Focus Pubns. GBR. Dist: Baker & Taylor Publisher Services (BTPS).

Trafton O'Neal, Debbie. J Is for Jesus: An Easter Alphabet & Activity Book. Bryan-Hunt, Jan, illus. 2005. 32p. (J). (gr. 3-7). per., act. bk. ed. 11.99 *(978-0-8066-5123-1(7)*, Augsburg Bks.) 1517 Media.

True God, True Man. 2004. (Effective Dre Ser.). pap. *(978-0-8294-1499-8(1))* Loyola Pr.

Turton, Karalynn Teresa. The Passion for Children: Bilingual (English & Spanish) Guide to the Passion of Christ, 1 bk. Ruiz, Jeanette, tr. Burnett, Anne, illus. 2005. (J). 3.00 *(978-0-9765180-0-6(7))* Catholic World Mission.

Twin Sisters(r) Staff. The Story of Jesus Handlebox-4books. 2009. 12.99 *(978-1-59922-111-3(X))* Twin Sisters IP, LLC.

Tyndale House Publishers Staff, creator. I Can Follow Jesus. 2014. (Happy Day Ser.). (ENG., Illus.). 16p. (J). pap. 2.99 *(978-1-4143-9419-0(5)*, 4608409, Happy Day) Tyndale Hse. Pubs.

Understanding Scripture: The Genesis Creation Story. 2004. (Our Catholic Tradition Handbooks Ser.). *(978-0-8294-1044-0(9))* Loyola Pr.

ur-Rahim, Muhammad Ata & Thomson, Ahmad. Jesus: Prophet of Islam. rev. ed. 2003. (ENG.). 320p. pap. 12.00 *(978-1-879402-73-7(4))* Tahrike Tarsile Quran, Inc.

Van der Veer, Andrew. Bible Lessons for Juniors, Book 3: The Life of Christ. 2007. (ENG.). 88p. (J). 6.00 *(978-1-60178-014-0(1))* Reformation Heritage Bks.

Van Leeuwen, Wendy. Miracle Man Activity Book. 2007. (Illus.). 16p. (J). pap. 1.89 *(978-1-59317-209-1(5))* Warner Pr., Inc.

Walker, Joni. Jesus Is with Me. Walker, Joni, illus. 2004. (Illus.). 20p. (J). bds. 5.49 *(978-0-7586-0628-0(1))* Concordia Publishing Hse.

—Jesus Knows Me. Walker, Joni, illus. 2003. (Illus.). 14p. (J). (gr. -1-k). bds. 5.49 *(978-0-7586-0507-8(2))* Concordia Publishing Hse.

Warner, Anna Bartlett. Yes Jesus Loves Me. 2006. (Illus.). 36p. (J). 14.99 *(978-0-7847-1512-3(2)*, 04154) Standard Publishing.

Warner Press Staff. Jesus in My Heart Coloring Books Intermediate. 2005. 2.69 *(978-0-87162-939-5(9))* Warner Pr., Inc.

—Jesus Loves Me Coloring Book Pre-K. 2005. (J). pap. 2.69 *(978-1-59317-017-2(3))* Warner Pr., Inc.

Warnes, Tim, illus. Jesus Loves Me! 2008. (ENG.). 26p. (J). (gr. -1-k). bds. 7.99 *(978-1-4169-5367-8(1)*, Little Simon) Little Simon.

—Jesus Loves Me! 2006. (ENG.). 32p. (J). (gr. -1-3). 15.99 *(978-1-4169-0065-8(9)*, Simon & Schuster Bks. For Young Readers) Simon & Schuster Bks. For Young Readers.

Wedeven, Carol. The Easter Cave. 2007. (Illus.). 28p. (J). (gr. -1). per. 7.49 *(978-0-7586-1213-7(3))* Concordia Publishing Hse.

Wesley, Misty Lynn. The Dancing Easter Lilies. 2012. 36p. pap. 16.95 *(978-1-4626-6819-9(4))* America Star Bks.

White, Susan K. Jesus Does Good Things. McQuitty, LaVonia Corbin, illus. 2013. 24p. (J). 15.00 *(978-0-9832570-6-6(X))* Scribe's Closet Pubns., The.

Wildsmith, Brian. The Easter Story. Wildsmith, Brian, illus. 2004. (Illus.). 24p. (gr. -1-7). 18.00 *(978-0-8028-5189-5(4))* Eerdmans, William B. Publishing Co.

—Jesus. Wildsmith, Brian, illus. 2004. (Illus.). 24p. (J). (gr. 3-7). 20.00 *(978-0-8028-5212-0(2))* Eerdmans, William B. Publishing Co.

Wildwood Forest Customizable Outdoor Banner. 2009. (Vacation Bible School Ser.). (J). 35.00 *(978-2-608-00908-1(5))* Cook, David C.

Williams, Lynda Anne. This Is Why I Talk to Jesus. 2005. (J). act. bk. ed. 10.00 *(978-0-9771015-0-4(9))* Let's Learn Library of Knowledge Series.

Wood, Minister Dorothy F. Samuel's New Suit. 2012. 20p. pap. 17.99 *(978-1-4343-7605-3(2))* AuthorHouse.

Woodward, Antonia. The Promised One: The Wonderful Story of Easter. Woodward, Antonia, illus. 2017. (ENG., Illus.). 32p. (J). pap. 10.99 *(978-0-7459-7679-2(4)*, 57148a3b-2061-41ef-9826-6a34cd27ea72, Lion Children's) Lion Hudson PLC GBR. Dist: Baker & Taylor Publisher Services (BTPS).

Wynbeek Rikkers, Doris. Little Jesus, Little Me, 1 vol. 2017. (ENG., Illus.). 14p. (J). bds. 6.99 *(978-0-310-76177-8(8))* Zonderkidz.

Young, Sarah. Jesus Calling: The Story of Easter, 1 vol. Longhi, Katya, illus. 2020. (Jesus Calling(r) Ser.). (ENG.). (J). 32p. 17.99 *(978-1-4002-1032-9(1))*; 24p. bds. 12.99 *(978-1-4002-1034-3(8))* Nelson, Thomas Inc. (Tommy Nelson).

Zobel-Nolan, Allia. Amazing Life of Jesus. Cox, Steve, illus. 2005. 10p. (J). 10.99 *(978-0-8254-5522-3(7))* Kregel Pubns.

Zonderkidz. Let's Meet Jesus, 1 vol. 2018. (Beginner's Bible Ser.). (ENG., Illus.). 16p. (J). bds. 9.99 *(978-0-310-76003-0(8))* Zonderkidz.

—The Very First Easter: The Beginner's Bible, Vol. 1. 2018. (Beginner's Bible Ser.). (ENG., Illus.). 32p. (J). pap. 3.99 *(978-0-310-76301-7(0))* Zonderkidz.

Zondervan Staff. Jesus & His Friends, 1 vol. Pulley, Kelly, illus. 2009. (I Can Read! / the Beginner's Bible / ¡Yo Sé Leer! Ser.). (SPA.). 32p. (J). (gr. -1-2). pap. 4.99 *(978-0-310-71889-5(9))* Zonderkidz.

—Jesus Feeds the People, 1 vol. Pulley, Kelly, illus. 2010. (I Can Read! / the Beginner's Bible Ser.). (ENG.). 32p. (J). pap. 5.99 *(978-0-310-71779-9(5))* Zonderkidz.

—Jesus God's Only Son, 1 vol. Jones, Dennis, illus. 2010. (I Can Read! / Dennis Jones Ser.). (ENG.). 32p. (J). (gr. -1-2). pap. 4.99 *(978-0-310-71880-2(5))* Zonderkidz.

—Jesus Loves Me, 1 vol. Borlasca, Hector, illus. 2008. (I Can Read! / Song Ser.). (ENG.). 32p. (J). (gr. -1-3). pap. 4.99 *(978-0-310-71619-8(5))* Zonderkidz.

—Jesus Loves the Little Children, 1 vol. Trasler, Janee, illus. 2008. (I Can Read! / Song Ser.). (ENG.). 32p. (J). (gr. -1-3). pap. 4.99 *(978-0-310-71620-4(9))* Zonderkidz.

—The Very First Easter, 1 vol. Pulley, Kelly, illus. 2009. (Beginner's Bible Ser.). (ENG.). 32p. (J). pap. 47.76 *(978-0-310-71817-8(1))* Zonderkidz.

JESUS CHRIST—ART

see also Bible—Pictorial Works; Christian Art and Symbolism

Daily, Eileen M. Beyond the Written Word: Exploring Faith Through Christian Art. 2005. (ENG., Illus.). 32p. (YA). pap. 8.25 *(978-0-88489-849-8(0))* Saint Mary's Press of Minnesota.

Newton, Richard. The Life of Jesus Christ for the Young. 2007. (ENG.). 204p. pap. 20.99 *(978-1-4346-2211-2(8))* Creative Media Partners, LLC.

—The Life of Jesus Christ for the Young. 2004. reprint ed. pap. 22.95 *(978-1-4191-6962-5(9))*; pap. 1.99 *(978-1-4192-6962-2(3))* Kessinger Publishing, LLC.

—The Life of Jesus Christ for the Young. 2005. pap. 32.00 *(978-1-932474-89-3(7))*; pap. 30.00 *(978-1-932474-88-6(9))* Solid Ground Christian Bks.

Olsen, Greg. Beautiful Savior. 2004. (Illus.). (J). *(978-1-59156-553-6(7))* Covenant Communications.

JESUS CHRIST—BIOGRAPHY

see also Jesus Christ—Nativity

Award, Anna. The Story of Jesus. 2012. (ENG., Illus.). 24p. (J). pap. 6.50 *(978-1-84135-604-4(2))* Award Pubns. Ltd. GBR. Dist: Parkwest Pubns., Inc.

Boon, Fiona. The Story of Jesus. Ede, Lara, illus. 2014. (ENG.). 22p. (J). (— 1). bds. 6.99 *(978-1-78235-883-1(8))* Make Believe Ideas GBR. Dist: Scholastic, Inc.

Brennan, Gerald T. The Man Who Never Died: The Life & Adventures of St. Peter, the First Pope. 2005. (Illus.). 87p. (J). (gr. 3-7). per. 11.95 *(978-1-933184-09-8(4))* Sophia Institute Pr.

Brierley, Jane. Life of Jesus Puzzle Book. Lebedev, Aleksandr, illus. 2006. (Play & Learn Puzzle Bks.). (J). 12.95 *(978-0-88271-854-5(1))* Regina Pr., Malhame & Co.

Concordia Publishing House. The Story of Jesus Coloring & Activity Book. 2015. (ENG.). 96p. (J). pap. 3.99 *(978-0-7586-5222-5(4))* Concordia Publishing Hse.

Cram101 Textbook Reviews Staff. Studyguide for Jesus of History Christ of Faith by Zanzig, Isbn 9780884895305. 3rd ed. 2014. (ENG.). 184p. (C). pap. 30.95 *(978-1-61812-856-0(6))* Cram101 Inc.

Daily, Eileen M. Beyond the Written Word: Exploring Faith Through Christian Art. 2005. (ENG., Illus.). 32p. (YA). pap. 8.25 *(978-0-88489-849-8(0))* Saint Mary's Press of Minnesota.

Dearmer, Mabel. A Child's Life of Christ. 2006. pap. 30.95 *(978-1-4286-0075-1(2))* Kessinger Publishing, LLC.

Dickens, Charles. The Life of Our Lord: Illustrated 200th Anniversary Edition. Dewey, Simon, illus. 2012. 17.99 *(978-1-60907-185-1(9)*, Shadow Mountain) Shadow Mountain Publishing.

—The Life of Our Lord: The Story of Jesus Told by Charles Dickens. 2009. 144p. 29.99 *(978-1-86118-960-8(5))* Third Millennium Pr., Ltd. GBR. Dist: Send The Light Distribution LLC.

—The Life of Our Lord: Written for His Children During the Years 1846 To 1849. 2004. 60p. pap. 7.95 *(978-1-57646-705-3(8))* Quiet Vision Publishing.

Dumont, C. & Lacoursiere, Suzanne. Jesus: A Story of Love. Merola, Caroline, tr. from FRE. Merola, Caroline, illus. 2003. 32p. (J). mass mkt. 5.95 *(978-0-8198-3977-0(9)*, 332-153) Pauline Bks. & Media.

ED., Stephen Arterburn M. & Brotherton, M. N. Kirby Mccook & the Jesus Chronicles. Zain, Damian, illus. 2019. (ENG.). 224p. (J). 17.99 *(978-1-4964-2977-3(X)*, 20_30075) Tyndale Hse. Pubs.

Foster, Charles. Story of the Gospel. 2004. reprint ed. pap. 33.95 *(978-1-4191-1372-7(0))* Kessinger Publishing, LLC.

Glaser, Rebecca. The Holy Moly Easter Story. Ferenc, Bill & Trihart, Emma, illus. 2016. (Holy Moly Bible Storybooks Ser.). 32p. (J). (gr. k-3). 12.99 *(978-1-5064-0256-7(9)*, Sparkhouse Family) 1517 Media.

—Jesus Feeds 5,000 & Other Bible Stories. Ferenc, Bill, illus. 2015. (Holy Moly Bible Storybooks Ser.). (ENG.). 32p. (J). (gr. k-3). 12.99 *(978-1-5064-0252-9(6)*, Sparkhouse Family) 1517 Media.

Hemenway, Priya. The Little Book of Jesus. 2004. (Illus.). 152p. *(978-0-7607-5447-4(0))* Barnes & Noble, Inc.

Hitchen, Danielle. Holy Week: An Emotions Primer. 2019. (Baby Believer Ser.). (ENG., Illus.). 20p. (J). (— 1). bds. 12.99 *(978-0-7369-7696-1(5)*, 6976961) Harvest Hse. Pubs.

Hook, Richard & Hook, Frances, illus. Jesus the Friend of Children. 6th ed. 2006. (David C Cook Read to Me Bible Stories Ser.). 112p. (J). (gr. 3-7). 14.99 *(978-0-7814-4390-6(3))* Cook, David C.

Hudgins, Ellis A. A Good Man Who Came Out of Nazareth: A Biography of Jesus for Young Teen Readers. 2009. 240p. pap. 15.99 *(978-1-61579-140-8(X))* Salem Author Services.

Humble-Jackson, Sally. The Miracle Maker: The Greatest Story Ever Told. (ENG., Illus.). 48p. (J). pap. *(978-0-340-74958-6(X))* Hodder & Stoughton.

Hunt, Marigold. A Life of Our Lord for Children. 2003. (Illus.). v, 189p. (J). pap. 14.95 *(978-1-928832-64-5(4))* Sophia Institute Pr.

Jeffs, Stephanie. Bywyd Iesu. Wyn, Delyth, tr. Tulip, Jenny, illus. 2005. (WEL.). 94p. *(978-1-85994-496-7(5))* Cyhoeddiadau'r Gair.

—People Jesus Met. Tulip, Jenny, illus. 2004. (My First Find Out about Book Ser.). 24p. (gr. -1-18). pap. 3.95 *(978-0-8294-1731-9(1))* Loyola Pr.

—Things Jesus Did. Tulip, Jenny, illus. 2004. 24p. (gr. -1-18). pap. 3.95 *(978-0-8294-1734-0(6))* Loyola Pr.

Jesus Christ - the Passion: And the Gospels of Matthew, Mark, Luke & John. 2004. mass mkt. 14.95 net. *(978-0-9749755-4-2(0))* Science Pubs.

Keating, Susan. Jesus Christ: Influential Religious Leader. 2013. (People of Importance Ser.: 21). (Illus.). 32p. (J). (gr. 4-18). 19.95 *(978-1-4222-2847-0(9))* Mason Crest.

Kredell, Janine. Jesus, the Brother of James & Jude, & the Savior of the World. 2013. 68p. pap. 13.95 *(978-1-4908-0953-3(8)*, WestBow Pr.) Author Solutions, LLC.

Langford, Norman F. King Nobody Wanted. 2006. 25.95 *(978-1-4218-3214-2(3))*; pap. 10.95 *(978-1-4218-3215-9(1))* 1st World Publishing, Inc.

Larsen, Carolyn. Jesus: His Last Days. 2012. (Standard Bible Storybook Ser.). (ENG., Illus.). 32p. (J). 7.99 *(978-0-7847-3566-4(2))* Standard Publishing.

Laubach, Frank. The Story of Jesus: Part 1. Woodworth, Ralph, ed. Aldredge, Terry Beckham, illus. 2005. per. *(978-0-9749168-6-6(2))* FEA Ministries.

—The Story of Jesus: Part 2. Woodworth, Ralph, ed. Aldredge, Terry Beckham, illus. 2005. per. *(978-0-9749168-8-0(9))* FEA Ministries.

Malone, Jean M. The Miracle of Easter. Langdo, Bryan, illus. 2010. (Penguin Young Readers, Level 3 Ser.). 48p. (J). (gr. 1-3). 4.99 *(978-0-448-45265-4(0)*, Penguin Young Readers) Penguin Young Readers Group.

Mears, Henrietta C. What Jesus Is All About: Meet the Man Whose Life - & Death - Changed the Course of History. 2004. 140p. pap. 9.99 *(978-0-8307-3332-3(9)*, Gospel Light) Gospel Light Pubns.

Moore, Christopher. Lamb: The Gospel According to Biff, Christ's Childhood Pal. 2004. (gr. 7-12). lib. bdg. 26.95 *(978-0-613-70985-9(3))* Turtleback.

Morgan, Ellen. Who Was Jesus? 2015. (Who Was... ? Ser.). lib. bdg. 16.00 *(978-0-606-36593-2(1))* Turtleback.

Morgan, Ellen & Who HQ. Who Was Jesus? Marchesi, Stephen, illus. 2015. (Who Was? Ser.). 112p. (J). (gr. 3-7). 5.99 *(978-0-448-48320-7(3)*, Penguin Workshop) Penguin Young Readers Group.

Murray, David. Meeting with Jesus: A Daily Bible Reading Plan for Kids. Reifsnyder, Scotty, illus. 2020. (ENG.). 208p. pap. 19.99 *(978-1-4335-6595-3(1))* Crossway.

National Gallery of Art Staff. Jesus of Nazareth: The National Gallery of Art, Washington. (ENG., Illus.). 40p. (J). (gr. 1-18). *(978-0-7112-0871-1(9))* ReiseArt Buchhandlung GmbH.

Neff, Merlin L. The Mighty Prince. 2008. (J). *(978-0-8163-2267-1(8))* Pacific Pr. Pubns.

Newton, Richard. The Life of Jesus Christ for the Young. 2007. (ENG.). 204p. pap. 20.99 *(978-1-4346-2211-2(8))* Creative Media Partners, LLC.

—The Life of Jesus Christ for the Young. 2004. reprint ed. pap. 22.95 *(978-1-4191-6962-5(9))*; pap. 1.99 *(978-1-4192-6962-2(3))* Kessinger Publishing, LLC.

—The Life of Jesus Christ for the Young. 2005. pap. 30.00 *(978-1-932474-88-6(9))*; pap. 32.00 *(978-1-932474-89-3(7))* Solid Ground Christian Bks.

O'Reilly, Bill. Los Últimos días de Jesús (the Last Days of Jesus) Uxo, Carlos, tr. Low, William, illus. 2015.Tr. of Last Days of Jesus, His Life & Times. (SPA.). 320p. (J). (gr. 5). 25.99 *(978-1-62779-278-3(3)*, 900145047, Holt, Henry & Co. Bks. For Young Readers) Holt, Henry & Co.

Paris, Pilar, et al. Jesus Grows Up. 2003. (Illus.). 64p. *(978-2-89088-895-1(9))* Novalis Publishing.

Paterson, Katherine. Life of Jesus for Children. Roca, François, illus. 2008. (J). *(978-0-545-01173-0(6)*, Levine, Arthur A. Bks.) Scholastic, Inc.

Piantedosi, John J. The Gospel for Children. Cioffi, Ben, illus. 2011. (J). pap. *(978-1-56548-370-5(7))* New City Community Pr.

Pulley, Kelly & Zondervan Staff. Jesus Saves the World, 1 vol. Pulley, Kelly, illus. 2009. (I Can Read! / the Beginner's Bible / ¡Yo Sé Leer! Ser.). (SPA., Illus.). 32p. (J). (gr. -1-2). pap. 4.99 *(978-0-310-71893-2(7))* Zonderkidz.

Roche, Maite. The Beautiful Story of Jesus. Roche, Maite, illus. 2010.Tr. of belle histoire de Jesus. (Illus.). 64p. (J). (gr. k-2). 14.95 *(978-0-8198-1177-6(7))* Pauline Bks. & Media.

Rock, Lois. Who Is Jesus? 2007. Orig. Title: Tell Me about Jesus. (Illus.). 21p. (J). 12.95 *(978-0-8198-8313-1(1))* Pauline Bks. & Media.

Rokus, Patti. He Is Risen: Rocks Tell the Story of Easter, 1 vol. 2019. (ENG., Illus.). 32p. (J). 17.99 *(978-0-310-76486-1(6))* Zondervan.

Rylant, Cynthia. Nativity. Rylant, Cynthia, illus. 2017. (ENG., Illus.). 40p. (J). (gr. -1-3). 18.99 *(978-1-4814-7041-4(8)*, Beach Lane Bks.) Beach Lane Bks.

Skevington, Andrea. The Story of Jesus. Ruta, Angelo, illus. 2008. (ENG.). 128p. (J). (gr. 2-4). pap. 16.95

(978-0-7459-6121-7(5)) Lion Hudson PLC GBR. Dist: Independent Pubs. Group.

Smith, Brendan Powell. The Miracles of Jesus: The Brick Bible for Kids. 2017. (ENG.). 32p. (J). 12.99 (978-1-5107-2697-0(7), Sky Pony Pr.) Skyhorse Publishing Co., Inc.

Smither, Ethel L. Stories of Jesus. Wiese, Kurt, illus. 2012. 82p. 37.95 (978-1-258-23282-5(0)); pap. 22.95 (978-1-258-24854-3(9)) Literary Licensing, LLC.

Snow, Eliza R. The Story of Jesus. 2011. (978-1-59955-940-7(4)) Cedar Fort, Inc./CFI Distribution.

St. John, P. Historias Que Jesus Conto (Stories That Jesus Told) (SPA.). 56p. (J). 9.99 (978-1-56063-589-5(4), 498751) Editorial Unilit.

Stiegemeyer, Julie. Bright Easter Day. Spellman, Susan, illus. 2005. 32p. (J). 10.49 (978-0-7586-0818-5(7)) Concordia Publishing Hse.

Sturtz, Maria Ester H. La Vida de Jesus. 2005. (Illus.). 32p. (J). (gr. -1-4). pap. 6.99 (978-0-7586-1241-0(9)) Concordia Publishing Hse.

Thomas, Sylvia. Jesus, My Lord. 2012. 36p. pap. 19.99 (978-1-61904-638-2(5)) Salem Author Services.

Unspecified. Jesus: His Life in Verses from the King James Holy Bible, 0 vols. Cuyler, Margery, ed. Spirin, Gennady, illus. 2012. (ENG.). 36p. (J). (gr. 4-6). 21.00 (978-0-7614-5630-8(9), 9780761456308, Two Lions) Amazon Publishing.

Watson, Jane Werner. The Story of Jesus: A Christian Book for Kids. Smath, Jerry, illus. 2007. (Little Golden Book Ser.). 24p. (J). (gr. -1-k). 5.99 (978-0-375-83941-2(0), Golden Bks.) Random Hse. Children's Bks.

White, Ellen Gould Harmon. Story of Jesus. 2003. (Review Kids Ser.). (Illus.). 142p. (J). 19.99 (978-0-8280-1765-7(4), 196-010) Review & Herald Publishing Assn.

Wilder, John Watson. His Name Is Jesus. 2005. pap. 19.95 (978-1-4179-9157-0(7)) Kessinger Publishing, LLC.

Williamson, Karen. My Little Life of Jesus, 1 vol. Enright, Amanda, illus. 2014. (ENG.). 68p. (J). (gr. -1-k). 7.99 (978-1-78128-131-4(9), 6ea863aa-a83e-4352-94d8-33785a017092, Candle Bks.) Lion Hudson PLC GBR. Dist: Baker & Taylor Publisher Services (BTPS).

Zonderkidz. The Beginner's Bible Jesus Saves the World, 1 vol. 2019. (I Can Read! / the Beginner's Bible Ser.). (ENG., Illus.). 32p. (J). pap. 4.99 (978-0-310-76036-8(4)) Zonderkidz.

Zondervan Staff. The Beginner's Bible Jesus Saves the World, 1 vol. 2019. (I Can Read! / the Beginner's Bible Ser.). (ENG., Illus.). 32p. (J). 16.99 (978-0-310-76819-7(5)) Zonderkidz.

JESUS CHRIST—BIRTH

see Jesus Christ—Nativity

JESUS CHRIST—FICTION

Adams, Michelle Medlock. Memories of the Manger. Ettlinger, Doris, illus. 2005. (J). (978-0-8249-5484-0(X), Ideals Pubns.) Worthy Publishing.

Alborghetti, Marci. The Miracle of the Myrrh. Biondon, Herve, illus. 2003. (J). 16.95 (978-0-87946-249-9(3), 708) ACTA Pubns.

Alexander, Florence & Alexander, Stanley. Jesus Child Is Born: Dare to Be Great. l.t. ed. 2003. (Illus.). 32p. (YA). 7.99 net. (978-0-915960-85-9(0)) Ebon Research Systems Publishing, LLC.

Alexander, Janice Marie. Princess Panny - Not Princess Nobody. Arkanov, Elvira, illus. 2013. 46p. pap. 21.95 (978-0-9890410-1-0(8)) Artistic Angels Corp.

Alexander, Marilee. The Wise Man's Last Wish: A Christmas Tale. Nash, Gisele, illus. 2012. (ENG.). 23p. (J). 23.95 (978-1-4327-8307-5(6)); pap. 14.95 (978-1-4327-8040-1(9)) Outskirts Pr., Inc.

Anderson, Ashley. My Day with Jesus. 2010. 26p. pap. 7.99 (978-0-88144-017-1(5), Thorncrown Publishing) Yorkshire Publishing Group.

Anderson, Debby. Jesus Is Alive. 2017. (Cuddle & Sing Ser.). (ENG., Illus.). 18p. (J). bds. 6.99 (978-1-4347-1115-1(3), 139847) Cook, David C.

Aoki, Hisako. Santa's Favorite Story: Santa Tells the Story of the First Christmas. Gantschev, Ivan, illus. 2007. (ENG.). 28p. (J). (gr. -1-3). 9.99 (978-1-4169-5029-5(X), Simon & Schuster Bks. For Young Readers) Simon & Schuster Bks. For Young Readers.

Arroyo, Kritzia. Angel Princess Star. 2008. 18p. 10.28 (978-1-4303-2776-9(6)) Lulu Pr., Inc.

Arroyo, Madeline. What Matthias Found. Vavak, S. Dean, illus. 2005. 32p. (J). (gr. -1-3). 16.95 (978-0-9740061-1-6(4)) Stairway Pubns.

Arruda, Suzanne M. A Stocking for Jesus. Ogden, Betina, illus. 2005. (J). pap. 7.95 (978-0-8198-7076-6(5), 332-372) Pauline Bks. & Media.

Austin, Diane Vaughan. The Hideout: A Child's Conversations with Jesus. 2012. 108p. (gr. -1). pap. 12.00 (978-1-4772-4464-7(6)) AuthorHouse.

Ballou, Bert. Anthony's Amazing Garden. 2011. 20p. pap. 9.99 (978-1-936750-12-2(0)) Yorkshire Publishing Group.

Banks, Celia. Issy's Gift: A Story about Giving. 2006. (Illus.). 41p. 14.99 (978-0-9764460-7-1(3)) HonorNet.

Barker, Alan. The Shepherd Who Couldn't Sing. Baker, Thea, illus. 2018. (ENG.). 32p. (J). pap. 9.99 (978-0-281-07674-1(X), f7244507-7038-4e7b-8686-9785f2e0c12c) SPCK Publishing GBR. Dist: Baker & Taylor Publisher Services (BTPS).

Barnhill, Carla. Rufus & the Very Special Baby: A Frolic Christmas Story. Rimmington, Natasha, illus. 2016. (Frolic First Faith Ser.). 32p. (J). (gr. -1-3). 12.99 (978-1-5064-1762-2(0), Sparkhouse Family) 1517 Media.

Basal, Patricia. Sammy Discovers Jesus. 2008. 28p. per. 24.95 (978-1-4241-8400-2(2)) America Star Bks.

Basye, Dottie. The Angel with Big Feet. 2012. 32p. pap. 13.95 (978-1-4497-3595-1(9), WestBow Pr.) Author Solutions, LLC.

Bauer, Marion Dane. The Christmas Baby. Cowdrey, Richard, illus. 2009. (ENG.). 32p. (J). (gr. -1-k). 15.99 (978-1-4169-7885-5(2), Simon & Schuster Bks. For Young Readers) Simon & Schuster Bks. For Young Readers.

Beatty, Connie. Why Owls Say Who. Beatty, Connie & Phillippi, Faith, illus. 2008. 20p. per. 24.95 (978-1-4137-6715-5(X)) America Star Bks.

Bell, Cheryl. Boy Jesus. 2011. 24p. pap. 10.95 (978-1-4497-1636-3(9), WestBow Pr.) Author Solutions, LLC.

Benoist, Cathy & Gilmore, Cathy. El Conejito de Pascua: El Cuento de un Dia Extraordinario. Sundy, Jonathan, illus. 2014. (SPA.). 40p. (J). (gr. 4-7). 16.99 (978-0-7648-2456-2(2), Libros Liguori) Liguori Pubns.

Benton, Ann. Ferdinand: The Engine Who Went off the Rails. 2009. (Colour Bks.). (ENG., Illus.). 40p. (J). 7.99 (978-1-84550-444-1(5), 3899eafe-6fe6-4c4f-8a1d-ad4cf7894d45) Christian Focus Pubns. GBR. Dist: Baker & Taylor Publisher Services (BTPS).

Berenstain, Jan & Mike. The Berenstain Bears: The Very First Christmas, 1 vol. 2015. (Berenstain Bears/Living Lights: a Faith Story Ser.). (ENG., Illus.). 100p. (J). pap. 4.99 (978-0-310-75102-1(0)) Zonderkidz.

Bertola, Ann Marie, et al, contrib. by. Four in the Afternoon. 2003. 118p. pap. 11.99 (978-0-9743661-0-4(2)) Circle Pr.

Black, Chuck. Kingdom's Reign, 4 bks. Black, Andrea & Black, Brittney, eds. Johnson, Marcella, illus. 2004. 160p. (YA). per. 9.95 (978-0-9679240-3-8(0)) Perfect Praise Publishing.

Bolme, Edward Sarah. Baby Bible Board Books Collection No. 1: Stories of Jesus, 4 vols. Gillette, Tim, illus. l.t. ed. 2003. 20p. (J). bds. 23.99 (978-0-9725546-4-0(5)) CREST Pubns.

—Jesus Feeds the People. Gillette, Tim, illus. l.t. ed. 2003. 20p. (J). bds. 6.99 (978-0-9725546-0-2(2)) CREST Pubns.

—Jesus Heals a Little Girl. Gillette, Tim, illus. l.t. ed. 2003. 20p. (J). bds. 6.99 (978-0-9725546-1-9(0)) CREST Pubns.

—Jesus Helps a Blind Man. Gillette, Tim, illus. l.t. ed. 2003. 20p. (J). bds. 6.99 (978-0-9725546-2-6(9)) CREST Pubns.

—Jesus Stops a Storm. Gillette, Tim, illus. l.t. ed. 2003. 20p. (J). bds. 6.99 (978-0-9725546-3-3(7)) CREST Pubns.

Booth, Anne. Refuge. Usher, Sam, illus. 2016. (ENG.). 32p. (J). (gr. -1-3). 15.99 (978-0-316-36172-9(0)) Little, Brown Bks. for Young Readers.

Booth, Bradley. Adventures in Galilee. 2011. (J). pap. (978-0-8163-2506-1(5)) Pacific Pr. Publishing Assn.

Bostrom, Kathleen. The Secret of the Twelve Days of Christmas. Bostrom, Christopher, illus. 2005. 68p. (gr. -1-7). per. 10.95 (978-1-931195-74-4(9)) KiwE Publishing, Ltd.

Bowman, Crystal. A Star for Jesus, 1 vol. Gevry, Claudine, illus. 2014. (ENG.). 14p. (J). bds. 6.99 (978-0-310-73826-8(1)) Zonderkidz.

Brent, Isabelle. The Christmas Horse & the Three Wise Men. 2016. (Illus.). 28p. (J). (gr. k-3). 17.95 (978-1-937786-61-8(7), Wisdom Tales) World Wisdom, Inc.

Brock Bryant, Anita. Abcs of Advent. 2009. 40p. pap. 16.99 (978-1-4490-3151-0(X)) AuthorHouse.

Broughton, Pamela. Miracles of Jesus. Smath, Jerry, illus. 2009. (Little Golden Book Ser.). 24p. (J). (gr. -1-2). 5.99 (978-0-375-85623-5(4), Golden Inspirational) Random Hse. Children's Bks.

Brown, Donna. Crippled Like Me. 2009. 36p. pap. 14.75 (978-1-60693-986-4(6), Eloquent Bks.) Strategic Book Publishing & Rights Agency (SBPRA).

Brown, Margery W. Baby Jesus Like My Brother. 2008. (Illus.). 32p. 6.95 (978-1-60349-000-9(0), Marimba Bks.) Just Us Bks., Inc.

Buck, Nola. A Christmas Goodnight: A Christmas Holiday Book for Kids. Wright, Sarah Jane, illus. 2011. (ENG.). 24p. (J). (gr. -1-k). 12.99 (978-0-06-166491-5(X), Tegen, Katherine Bks) HarperCollins Pubs.

Burow, Ginger. The Night That Was Christmas, 1 vol. 2009. 21p. pap. 24.95 (978-1-4489-9842-5(5)) America Star Bks.

Bynum, Jeff. Blinky. 2008. 24p. pap. 10.49 (978-1-4389-2331-4(7)) AuthorHouse.

Campbell, Jeffrey. St. Francis & the Christmas Miracle of Greccio. Bianco, Francesca, illus. 2014. (ENG.). 28p. (J). 14.95 (978-0-9796766-3-5(0), Tau Publishing) Vesuvius Pr. Inc.

Campos Eichelberger, Misty. Who Is Santa? & Where Did He Come From? 2009. 16p. pap. 9.49 (978-1-4490-1857-3(2)) AuthorHouse.

Cannon, Sherrill S. Santa's Birthday Gift. 2009. 24p. pap. 11.50 (978-1-60860-824-9(7), Eloquent Bks.) Strategic Book Publishing & Rights Agency (SBPRA).

Carlson, Melody. Benjamin's Box: The Story of the Resurrection Eggs, 1 vol. Stockman, Jack, illus. rev. ed. 2008. (ENG.). 40p. (J). (gr. -1-3). 8.99 (978-0-310-71505-4(9)) Zonderkidz.

Carroll, Harlisha. Miracle Mouse & Jesus Book #3: Short Stories 2. 2013. 32p. pap. 24.95 (978-1-4626-6647-8(7)) America Star Bks.

Chavez, Joe. Benny the Bunny & Jesus. 2013. 136p. (J). pap. 9.99 (978-1-62697-463-0(2)) Salem Author Services.

Chris Hansen. Grandfather's Journal. 2006. (ENG.). 94p. pap. 32.99 (978-1-4257-0258-8(9)) Xlibris Corp.

Christ Legends & Other Stories. 2012. 204p. pap. (978-1-84902-141-8(4)) Benediction Classics.

Christensen, Catherine. Emily's Perfect Christmas Tree. 2015. (Illus.). (J). 14.99 (978-1-4621-1750-5(3)) Cedar Fort, Inc./CFI Distribution.

Church, Peggy Pond. Shoes for the Santo Niño. Carrillo, Charles M., illus. 2013. 64p. 25.95 (978-1-936744-23-7(6), Rio Grande Bks.) LPD Pr.

—Shoes for the Santo Niño: Zapitillos para el Santo Niño: A Bilingual Tale. Carrillo, Charles M., illus. 2009. (SPA & ENG.). 61p. (J). pap. (978-1-890689-64-3(5), Rio Grande Bks.) LPD Pr.

Columbro, Judy. The Gift of Rainbows. Scottorosano, Deborah, illus. 2011. 24p. pap. 24.95 (978-1-4626-0355-8(6)) PublishAmerica, Inc.

Correa, Alvaro. Mountain Miracle: A Navtivity Story. Lorenzo, Gloria, illus. 2008. 94p. (J). (gr. -1). pap. 14.95 (978-1-933271-23-1(X)) Circle Pr.

Cowan, Dolly. Yeehaw, the Chosen Donkey. 2012. 26p. pap. 13.95 (978-1-4497-6675-7(7), WestBow Pr.) Author Solutions, LLC.

Dacey, Richard. Spinner McClock & the Christmas Visit. Gillett, Hallie, illus. 2004. 32p. (J). 13.95 (978-1-929039-24-1(7)) Ambassador Bks., Inc.

Dateno, Maria Grace. Braving the Storm, 6 vols., Vol. 2. Cunningham, Paul, illus. 2013. 70p. (J). pap. 5.95 (978-0-8198-1204-9(8)) Pauline Bks. & Media.

—Courageous Quest. Cunningham, Paul, illus. 2014. 81p. (J). pap. 5.95 (978-0-8198-1628-3(0)) Pauline Bks. & Media.

—Danger at Sea. Cunningham, Paul, illus. 2013. 80p. (J). pap. 5.95 (978-0-8198-1891-1(7)) Pauline Bks. & Media.

—Mystery of the Missing Jars. Cunningham, Paul, illus. 2014. 77p. (J). 5.95 (978-0-8198-4922-9(7)) Pauline Bks. & Media.

—Shepherds to the Rescue, 6 vols., Vol. 1. Cunningham, Paul, illus. 2013. 71p. (J). pap. 5.95 (978-0-8198-7251-7(2)) Pauline Bks. & Media.

David, Juliet. The Midnight Visitors, 1 vol. Parry, Jo, illus. 2015. 32p. (J). 14.99 (978-1-78128-233-5(1), Candle Bks.) Lion Hudson PLC GBR. Dist: Kregel Pubns.

Debecker, Benoit & Benoît, Debecker. La Primera Navidad de los Animales. 2005. (Montana Encantada Ser.). (SPA., Illus.). 48p. (J). (gr. k-2). pap. 8.50 (978-84-241-1675-0(5)) Lectorum Pubns., Inc.

Denger, Monique. Who Colored the Rainbow, Mimi? 2010. 40p. pap. 16.99 (978-1-4490-6166-1(4)) AuthorHouse.

dePaola, Tomie. The Birds of Bethlehem. dePaola, Tomie, illus. 2012. (Illus.). 40p. (J). (gr. -1-k). 18.99 (978-0-399-25780-3(2), Nancy Paulsen Books) Penguin Young Readers Group.

Deseret Book Company Staff, compiled by. A Christmas Journey: Four Classic Stories for the Season. 2013. 29.99 (978-1-60907-715-0(6)) Deseret Bk. Co.

DeStefano, Anthony. Little Star. 2013. (ENG., Illus.). 36p. (J). (gr. k-3). 15.99 (978-0-7369-5859-2(2), 6958592) Harvest Hse. Pubs.

—The Miracle of the Bread, the Fish, & the Boy. 2018. (ENG., Illus.). 32p. (J). (gr. -1-2). 15.99 (978-0-7369-6859-1(8), 6968591) Harvest Hse. Pubs.

Dettmer, Christina. The Secret. 2017. (ENG., Illus.). (J). (gr. k-4). pap. 9.95 (978-1-946977-54-0(3)) Yorkshire Publishing Group.

Deweerd, Jamison. Priceless. 2013. 32p. pap. 13.95 (978-1-4497-9077-6(1), WestBow Pr.) Author Solutions, LLC.

Dineen, Kaite. What Santa Wants You to Know: A Story of Santa's Love for Jesus, 1 vol. 2010. 34p. pap. 24.95 (978-1-4489-7071-1(7)) PublishAmerica, Inc.

Dumont, Claire. Noel: An Unforgettable Night! Keshavarz, Mehrafarin, illus. 2017. (ENG.). 32p. (J). 14.95 (978-0-8091-6780-7(8)) Paulist Pr.

Edwards, Carol. Jacy Faces Evil: Jacy's Search for Jesus Book III. Frey, Daniel J., illus. 2008. 32p. (J). 15.95 (978-0-9755314-3-3(3)) Majestic Publishing, LLC.

—Jacy's Search for Jesus Frey, Daniel J., illus. 2005. 31p. (J). (gr. -1-3). 15.95 (978-0-9755314-0-2(9)) Majestic Publishing, LLC.

Elkins, Christy. Sir Stinks-A-Lot. 2011. (ENG.). 43p. pap. 12.00 (978-0-557-34847-3(1)) Lulu Pr., Inc.

Elliott, Rebecca. Not So Silent Night, 1 vol. 2016. (ENG., Illus.). 5p. (J). (— 1). bds. 7.99 (978-0-7459-6560-4(1), 8b565f41-af2c-41ef-9334-eb623bb83f92, Lion Children's) Lion Hudson PLC GBR. Dist: Baker & Taylor Publisher Services (BTPS).

Entinger, Chad. A Deaf Boy Meets Jesus. Schofield-Farmer, Twila, illus. 2011. 42p. (J). 10.00 (978-1-59799-082-0(5)) Deaf Missions.

Falk, Karen. Tacianna & the Endless Ball of String. 2006. 83p. pap. 19.95 (978-1-4241-3287-4(8)) PublishAmerica, Inc.

Fals, Mary. The Chosen Colt. 2009. 40p. pap. 18.49 (978-1-4389-9417-8(6)) AuthorHouse.

Felden, Georgia. When Jesus Hired Santa. 2006. (J). pap. (978-0-9790444-8-9(0)) Dynasty Publishing, Inc.

Felton, Jerilyn E. The Master's Companion: A Christian Midrash. 2007. (Illus.). 134p. 16.75 (978-0-88489-936-5(5)) Saint Mary's Press of Minnesota.

Fleming, Theresa. Going Home with Jesus, 1 vol. Fleming, Yvonne B., illus. 2009. 22p. pap. 24.95 (978-1-60813-703-9(1)) America Star Bks.

Fletcher, Susan. Alphabet of Dreams. 2008. (ENG., Illus.). 432p. (YA). (gr. 7-12). mass mkt. 7.99 (978-0-689-85152-0(9), Simon Pulse) Simon Pulse.

Flinn, Lisa & Younger, Barbara. The Christmas Garland. Corvino, Lucy, tr. Corvino, Lucy, illus. 2003. 32p. (J). 14.95 (978-0-8249-5460-4(2), Ideals Pubns.) Worthy Publishing.

Fogle, Robin. The Legend of the Candy Cane. 2006. (J). pap. 1.79 (978-1-59317-158-2(7)) Warner Pr., Inc.

Foster, Lisa. 5 Little Tomatoes. 2008. 44p. pap. 17.95 (978-1-4327-2306-4(5)) Outskirts Pr., Inc.

Fox, Ruth M. The Bible, in Story, from the Beginning. 2012. 156p. pap. 53.99 (978-1-4497-7351-9(6), WestBow Pr.) Author Solutions, LLC.

Freddie. The Rooster's Story. 2009. 28p. pap. 13.99 (978-1-4389-8827-6(3)) AuthorHouse.

Freeman, Emily. God Bless Your Way: A Christmas Journey. Burr, Dan, illus. 2007. 32p. (J). (gr. -1-3). 19.95 incl. audio compact disk (978-1-59038-806-8(2)) Deseret Bk. Co.

Gamble, Adam. Good Night Baby Jesus. 2010. (Good Night Our World Ser.). (ENG.). 20p. (J). (gr. -1 — 1). bds. 9.95 (978-1-60219-049-8(6)) Good Night Bks.

Gibson, Beatrice. The Legend of the Sandals. 2008. (ENG.). 26p. pap. 15.99 (978-1-4363-9169-6(5)) Xlibris Corp.

Gilmore, Cathy & Benoist, Carol. Easter Bunny's AMAZING Day. Sundy, Jonathan, illus. 2011. (ENG.). 40p. (J). 15.99 (978-0-9847656-1-4(1)) I.H.S. Pubs.

Ginolfi, Art. The Tiny Star. 2005. 32p. (J). pap. 3.99 (978-1-4003-0683-1(3)) Nelson, Thomas Inc.

Ginolfi, Arthur. The Tiny Star. 2019. (Faith-Based Picture Books for God's ChildrenTM Ser.). (ENG.). 32p. (J). (-1). 14.99 (978-1-68099-525-1(1), Good Bks.) Skyhorse Publishing Co., Inc.

Giordano, Paula J. The Honey Bees Going to a New School. 2012. 30p. 29.99 (978-1-61996-501-0(1)); pap. 19.99 (978-1-61996-500-3(3)) Salem Author Services.

Gloria, Truitt. Baby Jesus Is Born. 2004. (ENG., Illus.). 16p. (J). pap. 1.99 (978-0-7586-0635-8(4)) Concordia Publishing Hse.

Gooch-Anderson, Stacy. The Legend of the Star. 2009. (Illus.). (J). 15.99 (978-1-59955-243-9(4)) Cedar Fort, Inc./CFI Distribution.

Gorla, Stefano. A Donkey's Tale. Marchetti, Angela, illus. 2013. 64p. (J). pap. 9.95 (978-0-8198-1901-7(8)) Pauline Bks. & Media.

Gould, M. & Gould, R. About Gossip: What Would Jesus Do, 1 vol. Hurst, Debbie, illus. 2009. 28p. pap. 24.95 (978-1-60749-680-9(1)) America Star Bks.

Grant, Cindy M. Itty-Bitty Jesus Is Born Christmas Storybook. 2005. (J). pap. 1.29 (978-1-59317-117-9(X)) Warner Pr., Inc.

Grover, Lorie Ann. Bright Night, 1 vol. Parry, Jo, illus. 2017. (ENG.). 16p. (J). bds. 8.99 (978-0-310-75736-8(3)) Zonderkidz.

Guiffre, William. Angelita's Song. Baron, Cheri Ann, illus. 2008. 32p. (J). (gr. -1-3). pap. 9.95 (978-1-931650-36-6(5)) Guiffre Bk. Publishing.

—The First Gift of Christmas. Baron, Cheri Ann, illus. 2008. 32p. (J). (gr. -1-3). pap. 9.95 (978-1-931650-33-5(0)) Guiffre Bk. Publishing.

Guiffre, William A. Angelita's Song. Baron, Cheri Ann, illus. 2008. 32p. (J). (gr. -1-3). lib. bdg. 17.95 (978-1-931650-30-4(6)) Guiffre Bk. Publishing.

Hall, Stephen M. The Shepherd's Son. 2013. 36p. 25.99 (978-1-4808-0112-7(7)); pap. 16.99 (978-1-4808-0078-6(3)) Archway Publishing.

Hallinan, P. K. That's What a Friend Is! 2003. (ENG.). 24p. (J). bds. 6.95 (978-0-8249-5468-0(8), Ideals Pubns.) Worthy Publishing.

Harp, Georgieanna. This Is Your Earthday. 2009. 32p. pap. 14.62 (978-1-4251-7064-6(1)) Trafford Publishing.

Harrast, Tracy. Oh Holy Night. Corke, Estelle, illus. 2006. 10p. (J). (gr. -1-k). bds. 10.49 (978-0-7586-1129-1(3)) Concordia Publishing Hse.

Hartman, Bob & Abel, Simone. Who Frightened the Fishermen? (Illus.). 48p. pap. 6.99 (978-0-7459-4987-1(8)) Lion Hudson PLC GBR. Dist: Trafalgar Square Publishing.

Harvey, Charlene A. The Adventures of the Tiger Club. 2011. 14p. pap. 10.99 (978-1-61215-027-7(6)) Salem Author Services.

Hays, Phillip. Porka-Bella-Snu & the Mystery of the Letters. Spencer, Chip, illus. 2013. 54p. pap. 6.95 (978-1-938679-05-6(9)) Written World Communications.

Hennessey, David G. A Cricket's Christmas: the Bethlehem Story. 2009. 151p. pap. 15.30 (978-0-557-04685-0(8)) Lulu Pr., Inc.

Henry, Juliann. The Little Shepherd Girl: A Christmas Story. Madsen, Jim, illus. 2007. 32p. (J). (gr. -1-3). 14.99 (978-0-7814-4513-9(2)) Cook, David C.

Herzog. Kimberly. All That We Could Give. 2013. 24p. pap. 24.95 (978-1-63000-830-7(3)) America Star Bks.

Heyer, Carol. Humphrey's First Christmas. (ENG., Illus.). (J). (gr. -1-k). 2018. 26p. bds. 7.99 (978-0-8249-1681-7(6)) 2012. 32p. 17.99 (978-0-8249-5559-5(5), Ideals Pubns.) Worthy Publishing.

Hildahl, Melita K. Life Is an Adventure with Ernie. 2008. 156p. per. 15.99 (978-1-60477-139-8(9)) Salem Author Services.

Hopkins, Lee Bennett. Mary's Song. Alcorn, Stephen, illus. 2012. (ENG.). 32p. (J). 17.00 (978-0-8028-5397-4(8), Eerdmans Bks For Young Readers) Eerdmans, William B. Publishing Co.

Horner, Susan. The Mission: An Angel's Most Important Assignment. Allen, Joe, illus. 2006. pap. 10.99 (978-1-59317-148-3(X)) Warner Pr., Inc.

Howie, Vicki. The Easter Swallows. Grudina, Paola Bertolini, illus. 2007. 32p. (J). 10.95 (978-0-8198-2360-1(0)) Pauline Bks. & Media.

Hulslander, Dyan. I Just Love You So Much. Heaton, Jr., illus. 2009. 28p. pap. 14.49 (978-1-4490-0454-5(7)) AuthorHouse.

Ippolito, Eva Marie. The Donkey's Tale. Ippolito, Eva Marie, illus. 2003. (Illus.). III, 15p. (J). (gr. -1-3). pap. 1.95 (978-0-9705350-3-0(1)) Ippolito, Eva Marie.

Jackson, Leona Novy. The Littlest Christmas Kitten. Dupre, Kelly, illus. 2005. (ENG.). 32p. (J). 16.00 (978-0-930643-18-8(6), 1250560) Images Unlimited Publishing.

Jacob's Gift. 2004. (Max Lucado Ser.). 32p. 19.99 incl. DVD (978-1-4003-0182-9(3)) Nelson, Thomas Inc.

Jaeger, Elizabeth. The Little Shepherd. Montano, Irene, illus. 2019. 32p. (J). (gr. -1-k). 16.99 (978-1-5064-4873-2(9), Beaming Books) 1517 Media.

Jaxland, Sheila. Mylo. 2013. 32p. pap. 12.95 (978-0-578-12595-4(1)) Roald Publishing.

Jay, Alison. Song of the Stars, 1 vol. 2015. (ENG., Illus.). 32p. (J). bds. 7.99 (978-0-310-73630-1(7)) Zonderkidz.

Jeanmarie, Michele. Curiosity, Curiosity: Lost in an Array. 2008. 74p. pap. 19.95 (978-1-60610-169-8(2)) America Star Bks.

Jeffs, Stephanie. Llygoden y Nadolig. Wyn, Delyth, tr. Thorne, Jenny, illus. 2005. (WEL.). 28p. (978-1-85994-497-4(3)) Cyhoeddiadau'r Gair.

Jenkins, Barbie. The Legend of the Christmas Kiss. 2010. (ENG.). 32p. pap. 11.99 (978-1-4391-9623-6(0), Howard Bks.) Howard Bks.

Jensen, Kimberly. Always the Elf. Harmon, Glenn, illus. 2007. 38p. (J). (gr. -1-3). 15.99 (978-1-59955-086-2(5)) Cedar Fort, Inc./CFI Distribution.

Johnson-Carrigan, Ettarose. Old Rugged: How the Tree Became the Cross. 2008. 24p. pap. 11.99 (978-1-4389-2781-7(9)) AuthorHouse.

Joslin, Mary. The Fourth Wise Man. Johnson, Richard, illus. 2007. 28p. (J). (gr. -1-2). 14.99 (978-0-7814-4545-0(0)) Cook, David C.

King, Emily. Clopper & the Lost Boy, 1 vol. Olson, Ed, illus. 2009. 32p. (J). 12.99 (978-0-8254-2946-0(3)) Kregel Pubns.

—Clopper & the Night Travelers. Olson, Ed, illus. 2007. 32p. (J). (gr. -1-3). 12.99 (978-0-8254-3066-4(6)) Kregel Pubns.

Koch, Theresa F. The Gift of Laughter. 2007. 16p. per. 24.95 (978-1-4241-8343-2(X)) America Star Bks.

Konecny, Linda. Dave's First Christmas. 2011. (Illus.). 26p. (J). pap. 9.99 (978-1-61379-817-1(2)) Salem Author Services.

Lagerlöf, Selma. Christ Legends. 2004. pap. 14.95 (978-0-8095-9388-0(2)); 196p. 29.95 (978-0-8095-9883-0(3)) Wildside Pr., LLC.

—Christ Legends: & Other Stories. 2010. 200p. pap. 44.50 (978-1-4092-0934-8(2)) Lulu Pr., Inc.

Lamson, Deborah Ann. The Nativity Lighting. 2008. (Illus.). 36p. pap. 15.95 (978-1-4343-9521-4(9)) AuthorHouse.

Lang, Gordon. Everyday Encounters: Face to Face with Jesus. 2003. 115p. per. 14.95 (978-1-932338-19-5(5)) Lifevest Publishing, Inc.

Lingenfelter, Libby. The Watermelon Story. 2010. 36p. pap. 21.99 (978-1-4535-2683-5(8)) Xlibris Corp.

Little Fish Jesus Merchandiser. (J). 128.16 (978-0-8307-2907-4(0), Gospel Light) Gospel Light Pubns.

J
K
L

Liu, Davy. Jordan's Guest. 2016. (ENG., Illus.). (J). 12.99 *(978-1-937212-28-5(9))* Three Sixteen Publishing.

Lloyd-Jones, Sally. The Jesus Storybook Bible, 1 vol. Jago, illus. 2007. (Jesus Storybook Bible Ser.). (ENG.). 352p. (J). (gr. -1-3). 24.99 *(978-0-310-70825-4(7))* Zonderkidz.

Lockhart, Linda J. A Little Angel Dressed in Red. 2006. (J). pap. 8.00 *(978-0-8059-6923-8(3))* Dorrance Publishing Co., Inc.

Long, Mary Evelyn Curton. The First Christmas Gift. 2012. 16p. (-18). pap. 15.99 *(978-1-4772-8836-8(8))* AuthorHouse.

Lord, Jill Roman. Noisy Silent Night. 2018. (J). *(978-0-8198-5188-8(4))* Pauline Bks. & Media.

—That Grand Easter Day! Trunfio, Alessia, illus. 2018. (ENG.). 32p. (J). (gr. -1-2). 16.99 *(978-0-8249-5680-6(X))* Worthy Publishing.

Lozano, Neal. Will You Bless Me? Hatke, Ben, illus. 2009. 32p. (J). lib. bdg. 16.95 *(978-1-883551-32-2(3)*, MCP-323, Maple Corners Press) Attic Studio Publishing Hse.

Lucado, Max. Itsy Bitsy Christmas: You're Never Too Little for His Love, 1 vol. 2013. (ENG., Illus.). 32p. (J). pap. 9.99 *(978-1-4003-2404-0(1))* Nelson, Thomas Inc.

Luther, Martin. Away in a Manger. Julien, Terry, illus. 2015. (Faith That Sticks Bks.). (ENG.). 24p. (J). pap. 3.99 *(978-1-4964-0318-6(5)*, 4611993, Faith that Sticks) Tyndale Hse. Pubs.

Mackall, Dandi Daley. One Small Donkey, 1 vol. 2016. (ENG., Illus.). 32p. (J). 14.99 *(978-0-7180-8747-0(X)*, Tommy Nelson) Nelson, Thomas Inc.

—The Shepherd's Christmas Story. Catalano, Dominic, illus. 2005. 32p. (J). (gr. 1-5). 12.99 *(978-0-7586-0904-5(3))* Concordia Publishing Hse.

Mackall, Dandi Daley, adapted by. El Pastorcito: Para ninos de 4-7 Anos.Tr. of Little Shepherd. (SPA.). 32p. 3.99 *(978-0-7586-0362-3(2))* Concordia Publishing Hse.

MacKenzie, Carine. How God Changes People: Conversion Stories from the Bible. 2012. (ENG., Illus.). 48p. (J). 9.99 *(978-1-84550-822-7(X)*, 133c6037-c25e-4644-a0e2-65867ee8c801) Christian Focus Pubns. GBR. Dist: Baker & Taylor Publisher Services (BTPS).

Marie, Lynne. The Star in the Christmas Play. Hussey, Lorna, illus. 2018. 32p. (J). 16.99 *(978-1-5064-3813-9(X)*, Beaming Books) 1517 Media.

Marsh, Carole. The Legend of the Candy Cane. 2003. 12p. (J). (gr. k-4). pap. 2.95 *(978-0-635-02124-3(2))* Gallopade International.

Marshall, Geraldine Ann. Spider's Gift: A Christmas Story. Sorge, Rebecca, illus. 2016. 40p. (J). pap. 14.95 *(978-0-8198-9058-0(8))* Pauline Bks. & Media.

Martin, Jann. This Babe So Small. 2007. 32p. pap. 11.95 *(978-1-933916-13-2(3))* Nelson Publishing & Marketing.

Martinez, Roland. The Angel with Red Wings. Graphic Manufacture, illus. 2008. 27p. pap. 24.95 *(978-1-60672-713-3(3))* America Star Bks.

Matson, Carole. Jesus Loves Dirt Bikes Too!! 2011. (ENG.). 33p. pap. 15.40 *(978-0-557-15092-2(2))* Lulu Pr., Inc.

McCarthy, Margaret. The Cat Did Not Know. Molloy, Sophie, illus. 2006. (ENG.). 36p. (J). pap. 14.95 *(978-1-85390-923-8(8))* Veritas Pubns. IRL. Dist: Casemate Pubs. & Bk. Distributors, LLC.

McCaughrean, Geraldine. The Jesse Tree. Willey, Bee, illus. 2005. 93p. (J). (gr. k). 20.00 *(978-0-8028-5288-5(2)*, Eerdmans Bks For Young Readers) Eerdmans, William B. Publishing Co.

McCoy, Jacquelyn. The Heavenly Hen. 2010. 28p. 13.54 *(978-1-4269-4606-6(6))* Trafford Publishing.

McCurdy, Steve. Keeper at the Inn. Lohmann, Stephanie, illus. 2007. 36p. 17.95 *(978-0-9761179-2-6(4))* StoryMaster Pr.

McDonough, Andrew. Dave the Donkey. 2019. (Lost Sheep Ser.: 9). (ENG., Illus.). 32p. (J). (gr. -1-k). pap. 7.99 *(978-1-910786-96-3(9)*, f5d5f9ec-dc13-4691-acc3-cb1eb27c61d7, Sarah Grace Publishing) Malcolm Down Publishing Ltd. GBR. Dist: Baker & Taylor Publisher Services (BTPS).

McElligott, Walter Lee. A Blessed Bethlehem Birth: As told by Abraham & Anna Mousenstern. Collier, Kevin Scott, illus. 2006. 28p. (J). E-Book 5.00 incl. cd-rom *(978-1-933090-21-4(9))* Guardian Angel Publishing, Inc.

McGhee, Alison. Star Bright: A Christmas Story. Reynolds, Peter H., illus. 2014. (ENG.). 40p. (J). (gr. -1-3). 17.99 *(978-1-4169-5858-1(4)*, Atheneum Bks. for Young Readers) Simon & Schuster Children's Publishing.

McKissick, Angela Lorraine (Dame). Jonathan & Elizabeth Meet Jesus of Nazareth. 2013. 28p. pap. 24.95 *(978-1-4626-8916-3(7))* America Star Bks.

Metlen, Ryan W. & Metlen, Ryan. Ewe. 2009. (J). *(978-1-58768-054-0(8)*, HiddenSpring) Paulist Pr.

Meyers, David. The Illustrated Life of Jesus: Through the Gospels, Arranged Chronologically. 2005. (Illus.). 304p. *(978-1-59258-125-2(0))* Hylas Publishing.

Milbourne, Anna. Very First Christmas. 2006. 24p. (J). 9.99 *(978-0-7945-1474-7(X)*, Usborne) EDC Publishing.

Monson, Marianne. The Enchanted Tunnel Vol. 3: Journey to Jerusalem. Burr, Dan, illus. 2011. 85p. (YA). (gr. 3-6). pap. 7.99 *(978-1-60908-068-6(8))* Deseret Bk. Co.

Montgomery Gibson, Jane. Jesus Is! Montgomery Gibson, Jane, illus. 2005. (Illus.). (J). bds. 8.99 *(978-1-4183-0033-3(0))* Christ Inspired, Inc.

—Jesus Loves Me. Montgomery Gibson, Jane, illus. 2005. (Illus.). (J). bds. 8.99 *(978-1-4183-0048-7(9))* Christ Inspired, Inc.

Murphy, Patty. I Wonder Who? 2012. 32p. pap. 24.95 *(978-1-4626-6258-6(7))* America Star Bks.

Murphy, Paul. The 13th Apostle. 2004. 224p. pap. 11.99 *(978-1-58169-142-9(4)*, 3000, Evergreen Pr.) Genesis Communications, Inc.

Napoli, Donna Jo. Song of the Magdalene. 2004. (ENG., Illus.). 256p. (YA). (gr. 7). pap. 12.99 *(978-0-689-87396-6(4)*, Simon Pulse) Simon Pulse.

Navillus, Nell. God's Christmas Gift. McCallum, Jodie, illus. 2006. (J). *(978-1-58173-595-6(2))* Sweetwater Pr.

—Happy Birthday, Jesus. McCallum, Jodie, illus. 2007. (J). *(978-1-60261-264-8(1))* Cliff Road Bks.

Nellist, Glenys. 'Twas the Evening of Christmas, 1 vol. Selivanova, Elena, illus. 2017. ('Twas Ser.). (ENG.). 32p. (J). 17.99 *(978-0-310-74553-2(5))* Zonderkidz.

Neuberger, Anne E. That Baby in the Manger. 2017. (ENG., Illus.). 32p. (J). pap. 15.99 *(978-1-61261-946-0(0))* Paraclete Pr., Inc.

Neuhofer, Sheri L. Courageous Warrior. Amory, Deanna & O'Hara, Cynthia, illus. 2010. 28p. pap. 10.95 *(978-0-9787472-7-5(5))* Ajoyin Publishing, Inc.

Novel Units. The Bronze Bow Novel Units Teacher Guide. 2019. (ENG.). (J). pap. 12.99 *(978-1-56137-726-8(0)*, Novel Units, Inc.) Classroom Library Co.

Nunes, Ernest. Oh! How I Wish I Could Play Soccer with Ernie & the Dreamers. 2013. 70p. pap. 12.99 *(978-1-62509-705-7(0))* Salem Author Services.

Obasi, Lucy. My Short Story of Jesus on Earth. 2012. 26p. pap. 10.95 *(978-1-4497-3920-1(2)*, WestBow Pr.) Author Solutions, LLC.

Olsen, Bevan. Bethlehem's Star. 2008. 16p. pap. 2.99 *(978-1-59955-181-4(0))* Cedar Fort, Inc./CFI Distribution.

—The Innkeeper's Christmas. 2010. (Illus.). 12p. (J). pap. 2.99 *(978-1-59955-433-4(X))* Cedar Fort, Inc./CFI Distribution.

—The Magi. 2011. (Illus.). 12p. (J). pap. 2.99 *(978-1-59955-924-7(2)*, Bonneville Bks.) Cedar Fort, Inc./CFI Distribution.

Olson, Kris C. The Shepherd & the Wolf. 2006. 51p. pap. 16.95 *(978-1-4241-1655-3(4))* PublishAmerica, Inc.

Pantelides, Sherry. It's Red Like Me! A Story about the Blood of Jesus. Perez, Debi, illus. 2007. (J). lib. bdg. 12.99 *(978-0-9771076-0-5(4))* Lacey Productions.

Park, Linda Sue. The Third Gift: A Christmas Holiday Book for Kids. Ibatoulline, Bagram, illus. 2011. (ENG.). 32p. (J). (gr. 1-4). 17.99 *(978-0-547-20195-5(8)*, 1058916, Clarion Bks.) HarperCollins Pubs.

Paterson, Katherine. The Night of His Birth. Aisato, Lisa, illus. 2019. (ENG.). 32p. (J). (gr. k-4). 18.00 *(978-1-947888-12-8(9)*, Flyaway Bks.) Westminster John Knox Pr.

Petersen, Alicia. Out of Darkness. 2007. (Illus.). 177p. (J). (gr. 3-7). per. 8.99 *(978-1-59166-822-0(0))* BJU Pr.

—A Sparrow Alone. 2004. 154p. (YA). 8.99 *(978-1-59166-204-4(4))* BJU Pr.

Phillips, Dixie. Angel Eyes. Sponaugle, Kim, illus. 2008. 24p. pap. 10.95 *(978-1-933090-74-0(X))* Guardian Angel Publishing, Inc.

—Baby Jesus Is Missing. Snider, K. C., illus. 2009. 16p. pap. 9.95 *(978-1-61633-000-2(7))* Guardian Angel Publishing, Inc.

Phillips, Dixie & Sharon, et al. Bethlehem's King Size Bed. 2013. 24p. pap. 7.95 *(978-1-61633-423-9(1))* Guardian Angel Publishing, Inc.

Phillips, Shirley. The Best Gift. 2012. 20p. pap. 10.95 *(978-1-4497-4229-4(7)*, WestBow Pr.) Author Solutions, LLC.

Pigman, Shari. Little Frog Finds Jesus. 2005. 23p. (J). 12.67 *(978-1-4116-5779-3(9))* Lulu Pr., Inc.

Piper, Sophie. The Angel & the Dove: A Story for Easter, 1 vol. Stephenson, Kristina, illus. 2010. 32p. (J). 12.99 *(978-0-8254-7897-0(9)*, Lion Children's) Lion Hudson PLC GBR. Dist: Kregel Pubns.

—The Angel & the Lamb: A Story for Christmas, 1 vol. Stephenson, Kristina, illus. 2009. 32p. (J). 12.99 *(978-0-8254-7887-1(1)*, Lion Children's) Lion Hudson PLC GBR. Dist: Kregel Pubns.

Prime, Derek. Sarah & Paul Have a Visitor. 2006. (Sarah & Paul Ser.). (ENG., Illus.). 128p. (J). (gr. 2-5). per. 6.99 *(978-1-84550-158-7(6)*, 1ad56387-6385-442a-b604-98ae55b8f5f4) Christian Focus Pubns. GBR. Dist: Baker & Taylor Publisher Services (BTPS).

Ramos, Peregrina. The Little Clay Jar: La Vasijita de Barro. Graham, Dennis, illus. 2006.Tr. of vasijita de Barro. (SPA & ENG.). (J). per. 15.95 *(978-0-9788381-0-2(6))* Word Gift Pubns.

Ranga, Katherine. Jesus Loves Me: A Bedtime Prayer. Ang, Selvi, illus. 2011. 26p. pap. 11.95 *(978-1-60976-989-5(9)*, Eloquent Bks.) Strategic Book Publishing & Rights Agency (SBPRA).

Rangel, Graciela. Anthony's Christmas Journey. 2006. (ENG.). 80p. pap. 9.95 *(978-1-59526-650-7(X)*, Llumina Christian Bks.) Aeon Publishing Inc.

Raum, Elizabeth. Christmas Crossroads. 2015. 133p. (J). *(978-1-62856-046-6(0)*, Bloomsbury Visual Arts) BJU Pr.

—Crossroads among the Gentiles. 2018. (Illus.). xii, 128p. (J). pap. *(978-1-62856-490-7(3))* BJU Pr.

—Crossroads in Galilee. 2016. (Illus.). xii, 139p. (J). *(978-1-62856-239-2(0))* BJU Pr.

Reeve, Penny. The Back Leg of a Goat. rev. ed. 2008. (Tania Abbey Adventure Ser.). (ENG., Illus.). 96p. (J). pap. 6.99 *(978-1-84550-340-6(6)*, 22e799f1-63ee-4400-99b8-cbf4a68f2655) Christian Focus Pubns. GBR. Dist: Baker & Taylor Publisher Services (BTPS).

—Water or Goo? rev. ed. 2008. (Tania Abbey Adventure Ser.). (ENG., Illus.). 96p. (J). pap. 6.99 *(978-1-84550-341-3(4)*, c15eedb6-2fac-4a7f-93b9-d8d9f4745e42) Christian Focus Pubns. GBR. Dist: Baker & Taylor Publisher Services (BTPS).

Reid, Pamela Carrington. Little One. Tolman, Tom, illus. 2010. (J). *(978-1-59811-574-1(X))* Covenant Communications.

Reyes, Cameron. In Your Heart. DeBroech, Sarah, illus. 2011. 28p. pap. 24.95 *(978-1-4560-1009-6(3))* America Star Bks.

Rhodes, Tiffany. What I Learned This Christmas. 2013. (Illus.). 42p. pap. 15.99 *(978-0-9899099-1-4(3))* Bee Creative, LLC.

—Where the Seeds Fall. 2013. (Illus.). 32p. pap. 9.99 *(978-0-9899099-0-7(5))* Bee Creative, LLC.

Rikkers, Don. Jesus Loves Me. 2009. 16p. 6.95 *(978-1-60349-025-2(6)*, Marimba Bks.) Just Us Bks., Inc.

Robinson, Ella M. Happy Home Stories. 2005. (Illus.). 137p. (J). per. 6.95 *(978-1-57258-313-9(4))* TEACH Services, Inc.

Roesti, Delores. Mareena Maree Mulligan & the Flying Wheel Chair: Book 1: School Days. 2007. 81p. pap. 9.95 *(978-0-7414-4048-8(2))* Infinity Publishing.

Roesti, Delores Anne. Mareena Maree Mulligan & the Flying Wheelchair Book #3: Temptation's Talking, 1 vol. 2010. 93p. pap. 16.95 *(978-1-4489-6692-9(2))* PublishAmerica, Inc.

Rowe, Kysha D. What Creatures Teach Us, 1. 2005. (Illus.). 112p. (J). per. *(978-0-9769339-0-8(X))* Rowe, Kysha.

Rowland, Wilmer. Wise & Silly: The Reason for Christmas. 2012. (Illus.). (J). *(978-1-56722-948-6(4))* Word Aflame Pr.

Rowley, Deborah Pace. Easter Walk: A Treasure Hunt for the Real Meaning of Easter. Burr, Dan, illus. 2010. (J). *(978-1-60641-055-4(5))* Deseret Bk. Co.

RR. Priscilla. 2008. 32p. pap. 24.95 *(978-1-60813-213-3(7))* America Star Bks.

Rucinski, Sandra. The Story of Jesus According to Tobin. 2009. 32p. pap. 14.50 *(978-1-60860-372-5(5)*, Eloquent Bks.) Strategic Book Publishing & Rights Agency (SBPRA).

Sanchez, Elizabeth. Jesus, It's Me Nicholas! Gutierrez, Chris, illus. 2005. 12p. (J). per. 9.99 *(978-1-59879-062-7(5))* Lifevest Publishing, Inc.

Sassi, Laura. Goodnight, Manger, 1 vol. Chapman, Jane, illus. 2015. (ENG.). 32p. (J). 17.99 *(978-0-310-74556-3(X))* Zonderkidz.

Scherm, Deedra. Cinco Panes y un Par de Peces: Una Historia de la Fe y de Dar. Dreyer, Laura, illus. 2008. (SPA.). 20p. (J). (gr. -1-3). bds. 7.99 *(978-1-934789-06-3(2))* Lemon Vision Productions.

Schomberger, Mary. The Adventures of Goldy the Mouse. 2013. 36p. pap. 16.95 *(978-1-4908-0375-3(0)*, WestBow Pr.) Author Solutions, LLC.

Scull, Paul E. Los Animales Cuentan Su Histori. 2011. 20p. pap. *(978-1-4269-7319-2(5))* Trafford Publishing (UK) Ltd.

Sehlin, Gunhild. Mary's Little Donkey, 30 vols. Muller, Helene, illus. 2016. 32p. (J). 17.95 *(978-1-78250-294-4(7))* Floris Bks. GBR. Dist: Consortium Bk. Sales & Distribution.

Sellers, Amy C., ed. Finding Jesus: Contemporary Children's Story. Behan, Rachel A., illus. l.t. ed. 2006. 19p. (J). 24.95 *(978-1-934194-00-3(X))* Olmstead Publishing LLC.

Seres, Frank & Seres, Nancy. The Jacob Series: Book #1 Fearfully & Wonderfully Made. 2009. 24p. (J). pap. 16.95 *(978-1-4327-3862-4(3))* Outskirts Pr., Inc.

Shultz, Carrie. V. I. P. Stepkid. 2013. 24p. pap. 10.95 *(978-1-4908-0831-4(0)*, WestBow Pr.) Author Solutions, LLC.

Sisk, Liza. Clay Birds of Jesus. 2007. 28p. pap. 10.95 *(978-1-59526-897-6(9)*, Llumina Christian Bks.) Aeon Publishing Inc.

Smart Kidz, creator. Jesus Loves Me! 2013. (Bible Sing along Bks.). (ENG., Illus.). 12p. (gr. -1). bds. 12.99 *(978-1-891100-33-8(5)*, Smart Kids) Penton Overseas, Inc.

Speed, Evelyn. Digger Rabbit & the First Easter. 2009. (Illus.). 24p. pap. 11.49 *(978-1-4389-6105-7(7))* AuthorHouse.

Spellman, Rhonda J., as told by. When I Was a Little Boy, by Jesus: Written for Children, Illustrated by Children: Experience the Life Jesus Lived When Jesus Was a Little Boy. l.t. ed. 2003. (Illus.). 32p. (J). per. 19.95 *(978-0-9741009-0-6(0))* Creative Cranium Concept, The.

Stockstill, Gloria McQueen. The Blind Man by the Road. Girouard, Patricia L., illus. 2003. (Listen! Look! Ser.). 20p. (J). bds. 5.49 *(978-0-7586-0144-5(1))* Concordia Publishing Hse.

Stohs, Anita Reith. Oh, Come, Little Children. Huang, Benrei, illus. 2006. 22p. (J). (gr. -1-3). 14.99 *(978-0-7586-1215-1(X))* Concordia Publishing Hse.

Summers, Susan. The Greatest Gift: The Story of the Other Wise Man. Morris, Jackie, illus. 2011. 30p. (J). 16.99 *(978-1-84686-578-7(6))* Barefoot Bks., Inc.

Tangvald, Christine Harder. The Best Thing about Christmas. Nobens, C. A., illus. 2014. (Faith That Sticks Bks.). (ENG.). 24p. (J). pap. 3.99 *(978-1-4964-0087-1(9)*, 4611762, Faith that Sticks) Tyndale Hse. Pubs.

Taylor, Shirley A. The Stable Boy. Hall, Wendell E., illus. 2012. (ENG.). 40p. (J). (gr. 2-17). 17.95 *(978-1-935166-79-5(4))* Parkhurst Brothers, Inc., Pubs.

Tebbs, Victoria. Christmas Story, 1 vol. Mitchell, Melanie, illus. 2009. (See & Say! Ser.). 24p. (J). 6.99 *(978-0-8254-7884-0(7)*, Lion Children's) Lion Hudson PLC GBR. Dist: Kregel Pubns.

Terbay, Susan Handle. Jeremiah & the Man, 6 vols., Vol. 1. Mariants, tr. Children-Oln, illus. 2007. 43p. (J). (gr. 1-6). pap. *(978-0-9628309-8-3(4))* Marianist Pr.

Tewkesbury, Alexa. Topz Gospels: Christmas. 2017. (Topz Ser.). (ENG., Illus.). 112p. (J). pap. 9.99 *(978-1-78259-689-9(5)*, 356b8930-5f40-48fd-a29d-0c38df997a46) Crusade for World Revival GBR. Dist: Baker & Taylor Publisher Services (BTPS).

Tewkesbury, Alexa & Legg, Steve. It's a Boy! 10th ed. 2015. (ENG., Illus.). 48p. (J). pap. 7.99 *(978-1-78259-454-3(X)*, d544f008-2596-4e28-9673-3472b28bff11) Crusade for World Revival GBR. Dist: Baker & Taylor Publisher Services (BTPS).

Thomas, Joan G. If Jesus Came to My House. McElrath-Eslick, Lori, illus. 2008. (ENG.). 40p. (J). (gr. -1-3). 18.99 *(978-0-06-083942-0(2)*, HarperCollins) HarperCollins Pubs.

Thompson, Lauren. One Starry Night. Bean, Jonathan, illus. (ENG.). 32p. (J). 2011. (gr. -1-3). lib. bdg. 17.99 *(978-0-689-82851-5(9))* 2003. 6.99 *(978-0-689-84215-3(5))* McElderry, Margaret K. Bks. (McElderry, Margaret K. Bks.).

Tolan, Stephanie S. Bartholomew's Blessing. Moore, Margie, illus. 2004. 32p. (J). (gr. -1-3). lib. bdg. 16.89 *(978-0-06-001198-7(X))* HarperCollins Pubs.

Tolstoi, Leo. Shoemaker Martin. Watts, Bernadette, illus. 2018. (ENG.). 32p. (J). (gr. -1-3). 17.95 *(978-0-7358-4304-2(X))* North-South Bks., Inc.

Tucker, David J. The Fourth Gift. 2010. 96p. 12.99 *(978-1-59955-438-9(0))* Cedar Fort, Inc./CFI Distribution.

Underhill, Marjorie Fay. Jeremiah. Garrett, Caroline S., tr. Garrett, Caroline S., illus. 2003. (J). 12.00 *(978-1-887905-75-6(8))* Parkway Pubs., Inc.

Van Dyke, Henry. The Other Wise Man. 2004. pap. 11.95 incl. audio compact disk *(978-1-932226-34-8(6))* Wizard Academy Pr.

—The Story of the Other Wise Man. 2007. 52p. per. *(978-1-4065-4728-3(X))* Dodo Pr.

Van Scott, Miriam. Candy Canes in Bethlehem. Van Wagoner, Traci, illus. 2012. (J). 7.95 *(978-0-8198-1606-1(X))* Pauline Bks. & Media.

Vardamaskos, Angela. Everlasting Truth. Bournakis, Maria, illus. 2008. 48p. pap. 24.95 *(978-1-60610-950-2(2))* America Star Bks.

Villarreal, Carlos C. The Light Beneath the Shadow: Sharing God's Love with Your Child as You Read Together: A Bedtime Story Intended to Awaken Your Parental Christian Spirit. 2006. 48p. pap. 16.95 *(978-1-4241-1247-0(8))* PublishAmerica, Inc.

Visconti, Guido. One Night in a Stable. Cimatoribus, Alessandra, illus. 2004. 32p. (J). 16.00 *(978-0-8028-5279-3(3))* Eerdmans, William B. Publishing Co.

Vivas, Julie. The Nativity: A Christmas Holiday Book for Kids. 2006. (ENG., Illus.). 36p. (J). (gr. -1-3). pap. 7.99 *(978-0-15-206085-5(5)*, 1198278, Clarion Bks.) HarperCollins Pubs.

Vonnegut, Kurt. Sun Moon Star. Chermayeff, Ivan, illus. 2016. 64p. (J). (gr. k-4). 22.95 *(978-1-60980-724-5(3)*, Triangle Square) Seven Stories Pr.

Waddell, Martin. Room for a Little One: A Christmas Tale. Cockcroft, Jason, illus. 2008. (ENG.). 26p. (J). (gr. -1-2). bds. 8.99 *(978-1-4169-6177-2(1)*, Little Simon) Little Simon.

—Room for a Little One: A Christmas Tale. Cockcroft, Jason, illus. (ENG.). 32p. (J). (gr. -1-3). 2006. 12.99 *(978-1-4169-2518-7(X))* 2004. 19.99 *(978-0-689-86841-2(3))* McElderry, Margaret K. Bks. (McElderry, Margaret K. Bks.).

Walburg, Lori. The Legend of the Candy Cane: The Inspirational Story of Our Favorite Christmas Candy, 1 vol. Bernardin, James & Cowdrey, Richard, illus. ed. 2012. (ENG.). 32p. (J). 15.99 *(978-0-310-73012-5(0))* Zonderkidz.

Wallace, Lew. Ben-Hur. (SPA., Illus.). (YA). 11.95 *(978-84-7281-099-0(2)*, AF1099) Auriga, Ediciones S.A. ESP. Dist: Continental Bk. Co., Inc.

Wallace, Sally. A Big Secret: A Nativity Story. 2009. 40p. pap. 16.99 *(978-1-4490-1660-9(X))* AuthorHouse.

Warren, G. A. Starr Light & the Christmas Story. Ciesinska, Izabela, illus. 2009. 32p. (J). 14.95 *(978-1-935268-09-3(0))* Halo Publishing International.

Washington, LaVonne & Washington, LaShawn. The Parables of Humpty Dumpty: Volume 1. 2011. 40p. pap. 24.95 *(978-1-4626-0989-5(9))* America Star Bks.

Webber, Jerry. The Game: None. 2007. 52p. per. 9.95 *(978-1-4327-0911-2(9))* Outskirts Pr., Inc.

Weiner-Booth, Patsy. The Day Santa Met Jesus: A Christmas story & Play. 2009. 56p. pap. 10.99 *(978-1-4490-1090-4(3))* AuthorHouse.

Wiersum, Gale. The Animals' Christmas Eve. 2007. (Little Golden Book Ser.). (Illus.). 24p. (J). (gr. -1-k). 4.99 *(978-0-375-83923-8(2)*, Golden Bks.) Random Hse. Children's Bks.

Wright, Boyd. Donkey Tales. 2006. 74p. pap. 16.95 *(978-1-4241-1900-4(6))* PublishAmerica, Inc.

Wright, Sally Ann. Christmas Baby. 2008. 14p. (J). 12.99 *(978-1-4003-1301-3(5))* Nelson, Thomas Inc.

Young, Norman, illus. The Christmas Story. rev. ed. 2006. (Usborne Bible Tales Ser.). 16p. (J). (gr. -1-3). pap. 4.99 *(978-0-7945-1286-6(0)*, Usborne) EDC Publishing.

—The Story of Jesus for Young Children. 2005. (Usborne Bible Tales Ser.). 98p. (J). (gr. -1-k). 14.99 incl. audio compact disk *(978-0-7945-0831-9(6)*, Usborne) EDC Publishing.

Ytreeide, Arnold. Amon's Adventure: A Family Story for Easter, 1 vol. 2010. 192p. (J). (gr. 2-7). pap. 16.99 *(978-0-8254-4171-4(4))* Kregel Pubns.

Zemanick, Patty. A Walk with Papa. Hammack, Sandra, illus. 2006. pap. 14.95 *(978-0-9788289-0-5(9))* Dragonfly Ministries.

Zondervan Staff. Story Early Elementary Curriculum: 31 Lessons, 1 vol. 2011. (Story Ser.). (ENG.). cd-rom 34.99 *(978-0-310-71921-2(6))* Zonderkidz.

—Story Preschool Curriculum: 31 Lessons, 1 vol. 2011. (Story Ser.). (ENG.). (J). cd-rom 34.99 *(978-0-310-71920-5(8))* Zonderkidz.

Zondervan Staff & Walburg, Lori. The Legend of the Candy Cane, 1 vol. Cowdrey, Richard, illus. 2014. (ENG.). 30p. (J). bds. 9.99 *(978-0-310-74672-0(8))* Zonderkidz.

JESUS CHRIST—ICONOGRAPHY

see Jesus Christ—Art

JESUS CHRIST—NATIVITY

see also Christmas

Alexander, Florence & Alexander, Stanley. Jesus Christ Is Born. l.t. ed. 2003. (Dare to Be Great Ser.). (Illus.). 36p. (J). 7.99 *(978-0-915960-02-6(8))* Ebon Research Systems Publishing, LLC.

Arensen, Shel. The First Christmas: Nativity Puzzle Book with 6 Play Pieces. 2003. (Illus.). 16p. (J). 10.99 *(978-0-8254-5509-4(X))* Kregel Pubns.

Armadillo Publishing Staff. Baby's Bible Stories: The Birth of Jesus. Lewis, Jan, illus. 2015. 24p. (J). (gr. -1 — 1). pap. 6.99 *(978-1-86147-484-1(9)*, Armadillo) Anness Publishing GBR. Dist: National Bk. Network.

Aston, Al. The Shepherds' Surprise. Hutchinson, Joy, illus. 2005. 16p. pap., pap. 2.00 *(978-1-84427-178-8(1))* Scripture Union GBR. Dist: Send The Light Distribution LLC.

Baby Jesus. 16p. (J). 1.89 *(978-0-7847-1386-0(3))* Standard Publishing.

Beavers, David R. I Am a Manger. 2007. 48p. per. 14.95 *(978-0-9801674-0-5(X))* Global Education Advance.

Benson, Lyn. Who Were the Magi. Joshua, Benson Benson Joshua, illus. 2007. 56p. pap. 23.99 *(978-0-615-13524-3(2))* Benson, Lyn.

Bible, King James. Christmas Is Here. Castillo, Lauren, illus. 2010. (ENG.). 32p. (J). (gr. -1-2). 12.99 *(978-1-4424-0822-7(7)*, Simon & Schuster Bks. For Young Readers) Simon & Schuster Bks. For Young Readers.

Bierhorst, John. El Nino Espiritu: Una Historia de la Navidad. Aramburu, Francisco Gonzalez, tr. Cooney, Barbara, illus. 2003.Tr. of Spirit Child: A Story of the Nativity. (SPA.). 26p. (J). (gr. 3-7). reprint ed. 20.00 *(978-0-7567-6882-9(9))* DIANE Publishing Co.

Boadt, Lawrence. Stations of the Nativity. 2017. (ENG., Illus.). 32p. (J). pap. 10.95 *(978-0-8091-6778-4(6))* Paulist Pr.

Bowman, Crystal & McKinley, Teri. M Is for Manger. Keay, Claire, illus. 2015. (ENG.). 64p. (J). 7.99 *(978-1-4964-0195-3(6)*, 4611870, Tyndale Kids) Tyndale Hse. Pubs.

Bowman, David, illus. Beyond Bethlehem: A Book of Mormon Christmas. 2008. 32p. (J). pap. 11.95 *(978-1-59038-991-1(3))* Deseret Bk. Co.

Box, Su. Baby Jesus. East, Jacqueline, illus. 2014. (Bible Dial-A-Picture Bks.). (ENG.). 8p. (J). (gr. k-1). bds. 6.99 *(978-0-7641-6694-5(8))* Sourcebooks, Inc.

Brooks, Felicity. Nativity Jigsaw Bk. 2006. 14p. (J). bds. 12.99 *(978-0-7945-1188-3(0)*, Usborne) EDC Publishing.

Burchett, Author Walter, BA. Christian children's questions & answers birth of christ Volume 5. 2009. 33p. pap. 14.32 *(978-0-557-08275-9(7))* Lulu Pr., Inc.

Burrin, Angela M. Jesus Speaks to Me on My First Holy Communion. Lo Cascio, Maria Cristina, illus. 2009. 39p. (J). (gr. 1-5). 12.95 *(978-1-59325-149-9(1))* Word Among Us Pr.

Busch, Melinda Kay. Born on Christmas Morn. Hall, Melanie, illus. 2003. (Arch Bks.). (ENG.). 16p. (J). (gr. k-4). pap. 1.99 *(978-0-570-07584-4(X))* Concordia Publishing Hse.

—Savior of the Nations-Mini BK. Hall, Melanie, illus. 2009. 16p. pap. 2.29 *(978-0-7586-1756-9(9))* Concordia Publishing Hse.

Carter, Jason Andrew. Stations of the Nativity. 2012. (ENG.). (J). pap. *(978-1-4675-4331-6(4))* Independent Pub.

Carton, Gerard. We Four Kings. 2009. (Illus.). 52p. pap. *(978-1-84748-474-1(3))* Athena Pr.

Castor, Rachelle. Christmas Angels. Pace, Alycia, illus. 2018. (ENG.). 32p. (J). (gr. k-3). 14.99 *(978-1-4621-2263-9(9))* Cedar Fort, Inc./CFI Distribution.

Chand, Candy. The Twelve Prayers of Christmas. 2009. (ENG., Illus.). 32p. (J). (gr. -1-2). 16.99 *(978-0-06-077636-7(6))*, HarperCollins) HarperCollins Pubs.

Charette, Beverly. Story of Christmas for Children. 2004. pap. 3.95 *(978-0-8249-5338-6(X))*, Ideals Pubns.) Worthy Publishing.

Che, Akwanwi Mfonyam. The Baby King: Born in a Stable. 2012. (Illus.). 16p. pap. 18.30 *(978-1-4772-4756-3(4))* AuthorHouse.

Christmas Greetings, My Little Friend. 2011. (ENG.). 24p. pap. 12.99 *(978-1-4520-5614-2(5))* AuthorHouse.

Christmas Stable, 1 vol. 2014. (Candle Tiny Tots Ser.). (ENG., Illus.). 16p. (J). 11.99 *(978-1-78128-122-2(X)*, adbd8aec-c73d-44fe-b60a-cb8587021262, Candle Bks.) Lion Hudson PLC GBR. Dist: Baker & Taylor Publisher Services (BTPS).

Clark, Lisa. The Song of Christmas. Dyrud, Chris Wold, illus. 2014. (Arch Bks.). (ENG.). 16p. (J). (gr. k-4). pap. 2.49 *(978-0-7586-4605-7(4))* Concordia Publishing Hse.

Cotten, Cynthia. This Is the Stable. Bettoli, Delana, illus. 2008. (ENG.). 32p. (J). (gr. -1-3). pap. 8.99 *(978-0-312-38421-0(1)*, 900053322) Square Fish.

Crump, Fred, Jr. Three Kings & a Star. Crump, Fred, Jr., illus. 2010. (Illus.). 40p. (J). (gr. -1-3). 12.95 *(978-1-932715-52-1(5))* UMI (Urban Ministries, Inc.).

Dalton, Pamela, illus. The Story of Christmas: Text Based on the King James Version. 2011. (ENG.). 32p. (J). (gr. -1-17). 17.99 *(978-1-4521-0470-6(0))* Chronicle Bks. LLC.

Dardik, Helen, illus. The Story of Christmas. 2017. (ENG.). 24p. (J). (gr. -1 — 1). bds. 9.95 *(978-0-7624-6242-1(6)*, Running Pr. Kids) Running Pr.

David, Juliet. The Christmas Story, 1 vol. Ellis, Elina, illus. 2016. (99 Stories from the Bible Ser.). (ENG.). 24p. (J). (gr. k-3). 7.99 *(978-1-78128-282-3(X)*, 6c214623-2042-49ba-85fc-363e557d832b, Candle Bks.) Lion Hudson PLC GBR. Dist: Baker & Taylor Publisher Services (BTPS).

—Follow the Star, 1 vol. Prole, Helen, illus. 2005. (Poster Sticker Bks.). 8p. (J). (gr. k-2). pap. 6.99 *(978-0-8254-7304-3(7)*, Candle Bks.) Lion Hudson PLC GBR. Dist: Kregel Pubns.

Davidson, Alice Joyce. Baby Blessings Christmas. 2009. (Baby Blessings Ser.). (ENG.). 18p. (J). (gr. -1-k). bds. 12.99 *(978-0-7847-2374-6(5)*, B&H Kids) B&H Publishing Group.

Davidson, Susanna. Story of Baby Jesus. 2015. (Picture Bks.). (ENG.). 24p. (J). 9.99 *(978-0-7945-3419-6(8)*, Usborne) EDC Publishing.

—Story of the Nativity. 2011. (Story of the Nativity Ser.). 24p. (J). ring bd. 9.99 *(978-0-7945-3188-1(1)*, Usborne) EDC Publishing.

Donaghy, Thomas J. My Golden Christmas Book. 2009. (ENG., Illus.). 42p. (J). bds. 14.00 *(978-0-89942-361-6(2)*, 425/97) Catholic Bk. Publishing Corp.

Edwards, Josh. Pull-Out Christmas, 1 vol. Embleton-Hall, Chris, illus. 2014. (Candle Pull-Out Ser.). (ENG.). 10p. (J). (gr. -1-k). bds. 9.99 *(978-1-85985-999-5(2)*, 8e2d1272-478c-46e6-853b-8a5970c418b6, Lion Children's) Lion Hudson PLC GBR. Dist: Baker & Taylor Publisher Services (BTPS).

The First Christmas. 2003. (Illus.). (J). bds. 6.98 *(978-1-4054-0967-4(3))* Parragon, Inc.

The First Christmas. (Illus.). 12p. (J). 4.95 *(978-1-58989-102-9(3))* Thurman Hse., LLC.

Fogle, Robin. A Christmas Story. 2006. (J). pap. 1.79 *(978-1-59317-159-9(5))* Warner Pr., Inc.

Follow That Star. (Hear Me Read Classroom Sets Ser.). 32.00 *(978-0-570-07172-3(0))* Concordia Publishing Hse.

Freeman, Emily Belle & Butler, David. Celebrating a Christ-Centered Christmas: Children's Edition. Jeppesen, Ryan, illus. 2017. (ENG.). 32p. (J). (gr. k-3). 17.99 *(978-1-62972-357-0(6)*, 5182310, Ensign Peak) Shadow Mountain Publishing.

Ganeri, Anita. The Christmas Story. 2003. (Festival Stories Ser.). (Illus.). 24p. (J). pap. *(978-0-237-52468-5(6))* Evans Brothers, Ltd.

Gay, Susana & Gay, Owen. First Christmas. 2018. (ENG., Illus.). 16p. (J). (gr. -1 — 1). bds. 6.99 *(978-0-8249-1679-4(4))* Worthy Publishing.

Gibby, Shauna. Jesus Is Born! A Flashlight Discovery Book. 2018. (Illus.). (J). 16.99 *(978-1-62972-469-0(6))* Deseret Bk. Co.

Glaser, Rebecca. The Holy Moly Christmas Story. Ferenc, Bill, illus. 2015. (Holy Moly Bible Storybooks Ser.). (ENG.). 32p. (J). (gr. k-3). 12.99 *(978-1-5064-0257-4(7)*, Sparkhouse Family) 1517 Media.

Godfrey, Jan. The Road to Christmas Day. Piwowarski, Marcin, illus. 2008. 32p. (J). (gr. -1-1). 14.95 *(978-0-8198-6487-1(0))* Pauline Bks. & Media.

Godwin, Laura. This First Christmas Night. Szabla, Liz, ed. Low, William, illus. 2017. (ENG.). 22p. (J). bds. 7.99 *(978-1-250-12793-8(9)*, 900175582) Feiwel & Friends.

Goodings, Christina. My Nativity Jigsaw Book, 1 vol. Elliott, Rebecca, illus. 2009. 12p. (J). bds. 9.99 *(978-0-8254-7888-8(X)*, Lion Children's) Lion Hudson PLC GBR. Dist: Kregel Pubns.

Grack, Rachel. Christmas. 2017. (Celebrating Holidays Ser.). (ENG., Illus.). 24p. (J). pap. 7.99 *(978-1-61891-271-8(2)*, 12060); lib. bdg. 26.95 *(978-1-62617-592-1(6))* Bellwether Media. (Blastoff! Readers).

Green, Yuko. The Nativity Activity & Coloring Book. 2013. (Dover Christmas Activity Books for Kids Ser.). (ENG.). 48p. (J). (gr. k-4). pap. 5.99 *(978-0-486-49717-4(8)*, 497178) Dover Pubns., Inc.

Grimes, Nikki. Voices of Christmas, 1 vol. Velasquez, Eric, illus. 2009. (ENG.). 32p. (J). (gr. -1-2). 16.99 *(978-0-310-71192-6(4))* Zonderkidz.

Guess Who? Christmas: A Flip-The-Flap Book. 2014. (ENG., Illus.). 6p. (J). (— 1). bds. 9.99 *(978-0-7459-6408-9(7)*, 6d672ab0-8922-4179-915d-ddd3f66f0cfd, Lion Children's) Lion Hudson PLC GBR. Dist: Baker & Taylor Publisher Services (BTPS).

Hall, Hannah C. Star Bright, Christmas Night. Jatkowska, Ag, illus. 2017. (ENG.). 20p. (J). (gr. -1-k). bds. 7.99 *(978-0-8249-1658-9(1))* Worthy Publishing.

Hansen, Janis. Jesus: The Birthday of the King, 5 vols. Francisco, Wendy, illus. 2003. (Bible Adventure Club Ser.). 36p. wbk. ed. 19.99 incl. audio, cd-rom *(978-1-58134-331-1(0))* Crossway.

Harmon, Ruth. The Christmas Story. Date not set. 4.95 *(978-0-88271-132-4(6)*, 1415) Regina Pr., Malhame & Co.

Harrast, Tracy. My Giant Fold-Out Book: Christmas. Doherty, Paula, illus. 2008. 10p. (J). (gr. -1). bds. 13.49 *(978-0-7586-1425-4(X))* Concordia Publishing Hse.

Hartman, Sara. When Jesus Was Born. Mitter, Kathy, illus. 2007. (ENG.). 16p. (J). (gr. k-4). pap. 1.99 *(978-0-7586-1281-6(8))* Concordia Publishing Hse.

Haws, Dona. Are You the Babe of Bethlehem. Moyer, Aubrie, illus. 2018. (ENG.). 32p. (J). (gr. k-3). 14.99 *(978-1-4621-2273-8(6))* Cedar Fort, Inc./CFI Distribution.

Henning, Heather. Christmas. Bull, Nicola, ed. Chapman, Gillian, illus. 2007. (Touch & Feel Ser.). 14p. (J). (gr. -1-3). bds. 10.49 *(978-0-7586-1383-7(0))* Concordia Publishing Hse.

Heyer, Carol, illus. The Christmas Story. (J). 6.95 *(978-0-8249-5347-8(9)*, Ideals Pubns.) Worthy Publishing.

Hoffman, Patricia. Bethlehem Town: Where Jesus Was Born. Munger, Nancy, illus. 2003. 32p. (J). 9.49 *(978-0-7586-0412-5(2))* Concordia Publishing Hse.

Howie, Vicky & MacLean, Moira. Cnoc, Cnoc! Pwy Sy 'Na? Llyfr Fflapiau Stori'r Nadolig. Wyn, Delyth, tr. 2005. (WEL., Illus.). 16p. *(978-1-85994-498-1(1))* Cyhoeddiadau'r Gair.

Hudak, Michal. The Uproar in Bethlehem. 2005. (ENG., Illus.). 24p. (gr. -1-4). 14.95 *(978-0-8146-2774-7(9))* Liturgical Pr.

The Incarnation of Christ: Immanuel l.t. ed. 2004. (CHI., Illus.). 52p. (J). *(978-0-9752775-0-8(2)*, 0-9752775-0-2) Unitrust Design.

Jackson, Antonia. The Lion Nativity Colouring Book. French, Felicity, illus. 2016. (ENG.). 32p. (J). (gr. 2-4). pap. 7.99 *(978-0-7459-7617-4(4)*, 7ea7e858-faf3-4ab4-89aa-67417f414794, Lion Children's) Lion Hudson PLC GBR. Dist: Baker & Taylor Publisher Services (BTPS).

James, Jeana. Gifts of the Nativity. 2017. (ENG.). (J). (gr. 1-4). 14.99 *(978-1-4621-2060-4(1))* Cedar Fort, Inc./CFI Distribution.

Jaroszko, Mike, illus. Away in a Manger Devotional. 2008. pap. 2.29 *(978-0-7586-1449-0(7))* Concordia Publishing Hse.

Jeffs, Stephanie. Baby Jesus. Tulip, Jenny, illus. 2004. (My First Find Out about Book Ser.). 24p. (gr. -1-18). pap. 3.95 *(978-0-8294-1730-2(3))* Loyola Pr.

Jesus' Birth. (Bulletin Board Jumbo Cutouts Ser.). (Illus.). 96p. (J). 9.99 *(978-0-7847-0551-3(8)*, 02588) Standard Publishing.

Johnson, Alice W. & Warner, Allison H. Believe & You're There When the Night Was Bright As Day. Harston, Jerry, illus. 2010. viii, 81p. (J). *(978-1-60641-249-7(3))* Deseret Bk. Co.

—Believe & You're There When the Prince of Peace Was Born. Harston, Jerry, illus. 2009. 74p. (J). *(978-1-60641-200-8(0))* Deseret Bk. Co.

Jones, Sherilyn. Can't Keep up with the Joneses: Created to Be. Jones, Sherilyn, illus. 2015. (ENG., Illus.). (J). pap. 9.99 *(978-0-9864191-0-2(9))* Concept Media Group, LLC, The.

Kennedy, Anne Vittur & Kennedy, Anne V. One Shining Star, 1 vol. 2006. (ENG., Illus.). 22p. (J). (gr. -1). bds. 6.99 *(978-0-310-71029-5(4))* Zonderkidz.

Kinkade, Thomas, illus. Away in a Manger. 2005. 32p. (J). lib. bdg. 17.89 *(978-0-06-078733-2(3))* HarperCollins Pubs.

Kramer, Janice. The Christmas Baby. Rooney, Ronnie, illus. 2008. (Arch Bks.). 16p. (J). (gr. k-4). pap. 1.99 *(978-0-7586-1454-4(3))* Concordia Publishing Hse.

Lafortune, Claude. The Wonderful Story of Christmas. 2003. (Illus.). 48p. act. bk. ed. *(978-2-89507-439-7(9))*; 24p. *(978-2-89507-438-0(0))* Novalis Publishing.

Litchfield, Jo. Usborne Lift-The-Flap Nitivity. Allman, Howard, photos by. 2004. (Illus.). (J). *(978-0-439-68683-9(0))* Scholastic, Inc.

Lloyd-Jones, Sally. My Merry Christmas (padded Board Book) Gianassi, Sara, illus. 2017. (ENG.). 20p. (J). (gr. -1-k). bds. 12.99 *(978-1-4336-4895-3(4)*, 005790558, B&H Kids) B&H Publishing Group.

Lucado, Max. The Christmas Story for Children, 1 vol. 2014. (ENG.). 32p. (J). pap. 6.99 *(978-0-310-73598-4(X))* Zonderkidz.

MacKenzie, Catherine. The Shepherds Find Jesus: Born to Be King 2. 2006. (Board Books Born to Be King Ser.). (ENG., Illus.). 16p. (J). (gr. -1-k). bds. 3.99 *(978-1-84550-185-3(3)*, 29342dd6-6bc9-44c7-9fbe-4f237a28678e, Christian Focus) Christian Focus Pubns. GBR. Dist: Baker & Taylor Publisher Services (BTPS).

Maier, Paul L. The Very First Christmas. 32p. (J). 9.99 *(978-0-570-07186-0(0))* Concordia Publishing Hse.

—The Very First Christmas. Ordaz, Francisco, illus. (J). 2004. 20p. (gr. -1-k). bds. 7.49 *(978-0-7586-0689-1(3))* 2003. 32p. (gr. 1-5). 7.49 *(978-0-7586-0616-7(8))* Concordia Publishing Hse.

Malone, Jean M. No Room at the Inn: The Nativity Story. Langdo, Bryan, illus. 2009. (All Aboard Reading: Station Stop 2 Ser.). 48p. (J). (gr. 1-3). 16.19 *(978-0-448-45217-3(0))* Penguin Young Readers Group.

Martin, Oscar, Jr., creator. Birth of Jesus l.t. ed. 2003. (Illus.). 25p. (J). E-Book 19.95 incl. cd-rom *(978-0-9748416-4-9(1))* Build Your Story.

McCaughrean, Geraldine. The Nativity Story, 1 vol. Williams, Sophy, illus. 2009. 48p. (J). 14.99 *(978-0-8254-7878-9(2)*, Lion Children's) Lion Hudson PLC GBR. Dist: Kregel Pubns.

McDermott, Gerald. The Light of the World. McDermott, Gerald, illus. 2006. (Illus.). 32p. (J). 16.99 *(978-0-525-47488-3(9)*, Dutton Juvenile) Penguin Publishing Group.

McKinley, Teri & Bowman, Crystal. M is for Manger. Keay, Claire, illus. 2016. (ENG.). 32p. (J). bds. 6.99 *(978-1-4964-2004-6(7)*, 20_29070, Tyndale Kids) Tyndale Hse. Pubs.

Michael, Sally. Jesus Is Most Special. Apps, Fred, illus. 2014. (ENG.). 24p. (J). (gr. 4-7). 9.99 *(978-1-62995-029-7(7))* P & R Publishing.

Miller, Claire. The Christmas Message. Dorenkamp, Michelle, illus. 2006. (Arch Bks.). 16p. (J). 1.99 *(978-0-7586-0872-7(1))* Concordia Publishing Hse.

Milligan, Bryce. Brigid's Cloak: An Ancient Irish Story. Cann, Helen, illus. 2004. 32p. (J). (gr. k-18). 16.00 *(978-0-8028-5224-3(6))* Eerdmans, William B. Publishing Co.

Miralles, Jose & McTeigue, Jane, illus. Christmas Star: A Light-up Shadow-Box Book. 2005. 10p. (J). (gr. k-4). reprint ed. 10.00 *(978-0-7567-9559-7(1))* DIANE Publishing Co.

Miras, Christie. The First Christmas Day. 2011. 28p. pap. 15.99 *(978-1-4628-7660-0(9))* Xlibris Corp.

Monge, Marlyn. Christmas: Jesus Is Born! Griffin, Lisa M., illus. 2018. 32p. (J). pap. *(978-0-8198-1670-2(1))* Pauline Bks. & Media.

Monge, Marlyn & Griffin, Lisa M. Navidad: Jesús Ha Nacido. Griffin, Lisa M., illus. 2018. (SPA., Illus.). (J). *(978-0-8198-5192-5(2))* Pauline Bks. & Media.

Mower, Christine Stevens. Little Lamb from Bethlehem. 2017. (Illus.). (J). 26.99 *(978-1-62972-369-3(X))* Deseret Bk. Co.

Neff, Larry M. Ha Nacido Jesus (Vida de Cristo)Tr. of Jesus Is Born. (SPA.). 12p. (J). 5.99 *(978-0-7899-0033-3(5)*, 497759) Editorial Unilit.

Nellist, Glenys. Christmas Love Letters from God: Bible Stories, 1 vol. Clowes, Rachel, illus. 2016. (Love Letters from God Ser.). (ENG.). 32p. (J). 17.99 *(978-0-310-74824-3(0))* Zonderkidz.

—Christmas Stories, 1 vol. Biscoe, Cee, illus. 2017. (Snuggle Time Padded Board Book Ser.). (ENG.). 26p. (J). bds. 9.99 *(978-0-310-76132-7(8))* Zonderkidz.

Noble, Marty. Nativity Stained Glass Coloring Book. 2004. (Dover Christmas Coloring Bks.). (ENG., Illus.). 32p. (J). (gr. -1-5). pap. 7.99 *(978-0-486-43527-5(X)*, 43527X) Dover Pubns., Inc.

Nye, Christopher. The Old Shepherd's Tale. 2004. (Illus.). 32p. (J). 16.95 *(978-0-913098-85-1(X))* Orion Society, The.

Oakes, Loretta. A Peek-a-Boo Christmas! Hall, Mary, illus. 2010. 16p. (J). pap. 9.95 *(978-0-8091-6754-8(9)*, Ambassador Bks.) Paulist Pr.

Parry, Alan & Parry, Linda. The Herald Angels. 2003. (Illus.). 16p. 9.99 *(978-1-85608-253-2(9))* Hunt, John Publishing Ltd. GBR. Dist: Send The Light Distribution LLC.

Peak, Cindy. The Little Star That Shines for Jesus. 2011. (ENG., Illus.). 36p. (J). 19.99 *(978-1-937008-01-7(0))* Heart to Heart Publishing, Inc.

Pingry, Patricia A. The Christmas Story. Edelson, Wendy, illus. 2004. (ENG.). 26p. (J). bds. 6.95 *(978-0-8249-6549-5(3)*, Ideals Pubns.) Worthy Publishing.

Piper, Sophie. Jesus Is Born. Gilbert, Anne Yvonne, illus. 2016. (ENG.). 32p. (J). (gr. -1-3). 16.99 *(978-1-68099-187-1(6)*, Good Bks.) Skyhorse Publishing Co., Inc.

Poole, Susie. A Christmas Journey. Poole, Susie, illus. 2014. (ENG., Illus.). 48p. (gr. -1-3). 12.99 *(978-1-4336-8343-5(1)*, 005617204, B&H Kids) B&H Publishing Group.

Roche, Maite. The First Noel. Roche, Maite, illus. 2009.Tr. of plus belle histoire de Noël. (Illus.). 48p. (J). (gr. -1-1). 16.95 *(978-0-8198-2687-9(1))* Pauline Bks. & Media.

Rock, Lois. Look Inside Nativity, 1 vol. Coloji, Livia, illus. 2016. (ENG.). 12p. (J). (gr. -1 — 1). 11.99 *(978-0-7459-7611-2(5)*, 393911bd-4af2-4e29-b555-344646b2bac9, Lion Books) Lion Hudson PLC GBR. Dist: Baker & Taylor Publisher Services (BTPS).

—On That Christmas Night. Jay, Alison, illus. 2018. (ENG.). 32p. (J). (gr. k-3). pap. 10.99 *(978-0-7459-6509-3(1)*, 045238c6-a54f-43ec-b882-cbec4e3cfb71, Lion Children's) Lion Hudson PLC GBR. Dist: Baker & Taylor Publisher Services (BTPS).

Rokus, Patti. A Savior Is Born: Rocks Tell the Story of Christmas, 1 vol. 2018. (ENG., Illus.). 32p. (J). 17.99 *(978-0-310-76496-0(3))* Zondervan.

Rylant, Cynthia. Nativity. Rylant, Cynthia, illus. 2017. (ENG., Illus.). 40p. (J). (gr. -1-3). 18.99 *(978-1-4814-7041-4(8)*, Beach Lane Bks.) Beach Lane Bks.

Sanderson, Ruth. The Nativity. 2010. (ENG.). 32p. 15.00 *(978-0-8028-5371-4(4)*, Eerdmans Bks For Young Readers) Eerdmans, William B. Publishing Co.

Schuon, Catherine & Fitzgerald, Michael Oren, eds. A King James Christmas: Biblical Selections with Illustrations from Around the World. 2012. (Illus.). 80p. (J). (gr. 3-7). 19.95 *(978-1-937786-03-8(X))* World Wisdom, Inc.

Smith, Martina. La Historia de la Navidad: Un Relato de la Biblia Chispita. Grosshauser, Peter & Temple, Ed, illus. 2016. (SPA.). (J). *(978-1-5064-2102-5(4))* 1517 Media.

—The Story of Christmas: A Spark Bible Story. Grosshauser, Peter & Temple, Ed, illus. 2015. (Spark Bible Stories Ser.). 32p. (J). (gr. -1-2). 12.99 *(978-1-5064-0224-6(0)*, Sparkhouse Family) 1517 Media.

Sumner, Esther Yu. My Nativity 1-2-3s. Davis, Robert, illus. 2018. (ENG.). 32p. (J). 14.99 *(978-1-4621-2246-2(9))* Cedar Fort, Inc./CFI Distribution.

The Metropolitan Museum of Art. The Christmas Story [Deluxe Edition]. deluxe ed. 2017. (ENG., Illus.). 32p. (J). (gr. -1-2). 19.95 *(978-1-4197-2307-0(3)*, 668502, Abrams Bks. for Young Readers) Abrams, Inc.

Tietz, Heather. Rockabye Baby Jesus. Miller, Nancy, illus. 2011. (ENG.). 20p. (J). 12.95 *(978-0-8091-6760-9(3))* Paulist Pr.

Traini, Agostino. The Birth of Jesus: A Christmas Pop-Up Book. 2016. (Agostino Traini Pop-Ups Ser.). (Illus.). 14p. (J). 19.99 *(978-1-5064-1769-1(8)*, Sparkhouse Family) 1517 Media.

Tyrrell, Frances, illus. The Huron Carol. 2004. 32p. 16.00 *(978-0-8028-5263-2(7))* Eerdmans, William B. Publishing Co.

Walker, Joni. Tell Me the Christmas Story. Walker, Joni, illus. 2003. (Illus.). 14p. (J). (gr. -1-k). bds. 5.49 *(978-0-7586-0508-5(0))* Concordia Publishing Hse.

Wallace, Dora J. Twas the Night Before Jesus Was Born. 2012. 36p. pap. 16.99 *(978-1-4497-5807-3(X)*, WestBow Pr.) Author Solutions, LLC.

Wallace, Ian. The Huron Carol, 1 vol. 2013. (ENG., Illus.). 32p. (J). (gr. k). 14.95 *(978-1-55498-394-0(0))* Groundwood Bks. CAN. Dist: Publishers Group West (PGW).

Waltersdorff, Christy J. 25 Days to Jesus. Miller, Mitchell, illus. 2018. (J). *(978-0-87178-258-8(8))* Brethren Pr.

Whitaker-Taylor, Kandice. A Child Is Born. 2012. 20p. pap. 9.99 *(978-1-62419-090-2(1))* Salem Author Services.

Wilkeshuis, Cornelius. The Gift for the Child, 50 vols. Verstegen, Jeska, illus. (ENG.). 28p. (J). 16.95 *(978-0-86315-349-5(6))* Floris Bks. GBR. Dist: SteinerBooks, Inc.

Williamson, Karen. My Little Story of Christmas. Enright, Amanda, illus. 2014. (ENG.). 20p. (J). (gr. -1-k). E-Book 3.99 *(978-1-78128-153-6(X)*, Candle Bks.) Lion Hudson PLC GBR. Dist: Independent Pubs. Group.

Woodward, Antonia. The Extra Special Baby, 1 vol. Woodward, Antonia, illus. 2016. (ENG., Illus.). 32p. (J). (gr. -1-k). 13.99 *(978-0-7459-7699-0(9)*, a5bc0201-d06c-477d-8855-01abef359f9b, Lion Children's) Lion Hudson PLC GBR. Dist: Baker & Taylor Publisher Services (BTPS).

—The Extra Special Baby: The Story of the Christmas Promise. Woodward, Antonia, illus. 2018. (ENG., Illus.). 32p. (J). pap. 10.99 *(978-0-7459-7678-5(6)*, 3ff563e7-6af0-43cd-af27-ee33fd9d22e4, Lion Children's) Lion Hudson PLC GBR. Dist: Baker & Taylor Publisher Services (BTPS).

Yamamoto, Makoto. O Holy Night: The First Christmas. Moritsu, Wakako, illus. 2005. 24p. (J). (gr. -1-3). per. 16.95 *(978-0-8198-5440-7(9))* Pauline Bks. & Media.

Young, Sarah. Jesus Calling: The Story of Christmas, 1 vol. Longhi, Katya, illus. 2018. (Jesus Calling(r) Ser.). (ENG.). 32p. (J). 17.99 *(978-1-4002-1029-9(1)*, Tommy Nelson) Nelson, Thomas Inc.

Zobel-Nolan, Allia. Lift the Flap Nativity. Moroney, Trace, illus. 2015. (Lift-The-Flap Ser.). (ENG.). 20p. (J). (gr. -1-k). 10.99 *(978-0-7944-3527-1(0)*, Studio Fun International) Printers Row Publishing Group.

Zondervan, A. The First Christmas Ever, 1 vol. Jones, Dennis, illus. 2014. (ENG.). 32p. (J). pap. 2.99 *(978-0-310-74083-4(5))* Zonderkidz.

Zondervan Staff. The Beginner's Bible Jesus Is Born, 1 vol. 2019. (I Can Read! / the Beginner's Bible Ser.). (ENG., Illus.). 32p. (J). pap. 4.99 *(978-0-310-76050-4(X))* Zonderkidz.

—Jesus God's Great Gift, 1 vol. Jones, Dennis G., illus. 2010. (I Can Read! / Dennis Jones Ser.). (ENG.). 32p. (J). (gr. -1-2). pap. 5.99 *(978-0-310-71881-9(3))* Zonderkidz.

JESUS CHRIST—NATIVITY—DRAMA

Edwards, Emyr. O Achos y Mab Bychan: Casgliad o Ddramâu I Blant Ar Gyfer y Nadolig. 2005. (WEL.). 150p. pap. *(978-0-86381-601-7(0))* Gwasg Carreg Gwalch.

JESUS CHRIST—PARABLES

Amery, Heather. Little Book of Stories of Jesus. 2007. (ENG., Illus.). 72p. *(978-0-7460-8492-2(7))* Usborne Publishing, Ltd.

Bowman, Crystal. The Prodigal Son, 1 vol. Sokolova, Valerie, illus. 2011. (I Can Read! / Bible Stories Ser.). (ENG.). 32p. (J). (gr. -1-2). pap. 4.99 *(978-0-310-72155-0(5))* Zonderkidz.

Burgdorf, Larry. The Wise & Foolish Builders: A Parable of Jesus, Matthew 7:24-27 & Luke 6:47-49 for Children. Billen-Frye, Paige, illus. 2007. (Arch Bks.). 16p. (J). 2.49 *(978-0-7586-1263-2(X))* Concordia Publishing Hse.

Burgdorf, Larry, et al. Best-Loved Parables of Jesus. Billen-Frye, Paige et al, illus. 2014. (ENG.). 101p. (J). 9.99 *(978-0-7586-4662-0(3))* Concordia Publishing Hse.

Butterworth, Nick. Stories Jesus Told Colouring Book. Inkpen, Mick, illus. 2006. (Stories Jesus Told Ser.). (ENG.). 128p. (J). (gr. -1-k). pap. 5.99 *(978-1-85985-653-6(5)*, 7c361727-f41a-44e2-a6c9-529c437790c9, Candle Bks.) Lion Hudson PLC GBR. Dist: Baker & Taylor Publisher Services (BTPS).

Butterworth, Nick & Inkpen, Mick. Favorite Parables from the Bible: Stories Jesus Told, 1 vol. 2012. (ENG., Illus.). 216p. (J). 9.99 *(978-0-310-72432-2(5))* Zonderkidz.

Carlson, Melody. The Other Brother. Björkman, Steve, illus. 2004. 40p. (gr. -1-3). 9.99 *(978-1-58134-122-5(9))* Crossway.

Clark, Paul. The Good Wagon. Preston, Graham, illus. 2012. (J). lthr. *(978-1-921633-88-1(3)*, Even Before Publishing) Wombat Bks.

David C. Cook Publishing Company Staff. Ring, Robe & Shoes, 10, Pack. 2008. (Pencil Fun Bks). 16p. (J). pap. 9.90 *(978-1-4347-6822-3(8))* Cook, David C.

Dreyer, Nicole E. The Lost Coin. Collier-Morales, Roberta, illus. 2006. (ENG.). 16p. (J). pap. 1.99 *(978-0-7586-0873-4(X))* Concordia Publishing Hse.

—The Parable of the Talents. Morris, Susan, illus. 2007. (ENG.). 16p. (J). (gr. k-4). pap. 1.99 *(978-0-7586-1282-3(6))* Concordia Publishing Hse.

Froeb, Lori. A Child's Book of Parables. Moroney, Tracy, illus. 2003. 32p. (J). 15.99 *(978-0-7847-1278-8(6)*, 04344) Standard Publishing.

Glaser, Rebecca. The Good Samaritan & Other Bible Stories. Ferenc, Bill, illus. 2015. (Holy Moly Bible Storybooks Ser.). (ENG.). 32p. (J). (gr. k-3). 12.99 *(978-1-5064-0251-2(8)*, Sparkhouse Family) 1517 Media.

Glavich, Mary Kathleen. A Child's Book of Parables. 2004. *(978-0-8294-1039-6(2))* Loyola Pr.

Haines, Geri Berger. The Little Lost Lamb. Haines, Geri Berger, illus. 2009. (Illus.). 40p. (J). (gr. -1-k). 8.95 *(978-0-8198-4528-3(0))* Pauline Bks. & Media.

Henley, Claire. Lost Sheep & the Scary Day, 1 vol. 2009. (All Join In Ser.). 18p. (J). bds. 6.99 *(978-0-8254-7882-6(0)*, Lion Children's) Lion Hudson PLC GBR. Dist: Kregel Pubns.

Jeffs, Stephanie. Stories Jesus Told. Tulip, Jenny, illus. 2004. (My First Find Out about Book Ser.). 24p. (gr. -1-18). pap. 3.95 *(978-0-8294-1733-3(8))* Loyola Pr.

JKL

Larsen, Carolyn. Teachings of Jesus. 2012. (Standard Bible Storybook Ser.). (ENG., Illus.). 32p. (J). 7.99 *(978-0-7847-3565-7(4))* Standard Publishing.

Levine, Amy-Jill & Eisenberg Sasso, Sandy. ¿Quién Cuenta? 100 Ovejas, 10 Monedas y 2 Hijos. Meganck, Margaux, illus. 2018. (ENG & SPA.). 40p. (J). (gr. -1-3). pap. 10.00 *(978-0-664-26406-2(9))* Westminster John Knox Pr.

Lindvall, Ella K. Read-Aloud Bible Stories, Vol. 5. 2015. (Read Aloud Bible Stories Ser.: 5). (ENG.). 160p. (J). 15.99 *(978-0-8024-1264-5(5))* Moody Pubs.

Littleton, Mark. Stories Jesus Told. Moroney, Trace, illus. 2004. 20p. (J). bds. 10.99 *(978-0-8254-5519-3(7))* Kregel Pubns.

Lumsden, Colin, illus. Parables of Jesus. 2003. (Bible Colour & Learn Ser.). 32p. pap. 2.50 *(978-1-903087-47-3(3))* DayOne Pubns. GBR. Dist: Send The Light Distribution LLC.

—People in the Life of Jesus. 2003. (Bible Colour & Learn Ser.). 32p. pap. 2.50 *(978-1-903087-49-7(X))* DayOne Pubns. GBR. Dist: Send The Light Distribution LLC.

Make Believe Ideas, Ltd., creator. Read with Me: the Good Samaritan. 2006. (Read with Me (Make Believe Ideas) Ser.). (Illus.). 32p. (J). (gr. -1-3). pap. 8.97 *(978-1-59145-529-5(4))* Nelson, Thomas Inc.

—Read with Me: the Loaves & Fish. 2006. (Read with Me (Make Believe Ideas) Ser.). (Illus.). 32p. (J). (gr. -1-3). pap. 8.97 *(978-1-59145-528-8(6))* Nelson, Thomas Inc.

Mathews, Janice. Jack's Hats. 2013. (Illus.). 31p. (J). *(978-0-8280-2718-2(8))* Review & Herald Publishing Assn.

Miles, David. Father's Love, 1 vol. 2014. (I Can Read! / Adventure Bible Ser.). (ENG., Illus.). 32p. (J). pap. 4.99 *(978-0-310-73240-2(9))* Zonderkidz.

Miller, Claire. La parabola de la oveja perdida (The Parable of the Lost Sheep) 2011. 16p. pap. 2.49 *(978-0-7586-3065-0(4))* Concordia Publishing Hse.

Mills, Charles. Refreshed Parables: Jesus' Stories Retold. 2018. 127p. (J). pap. *(978-0-8163-6349-0(8))* Pacific Pr. Publishing Assn.

Rabbit. Parables That Jesus Told. (J). pap. 19.95 *(978-0-689-80229-4(3)*, Simon & Schuster Bks. For Young Readers) Simon & Schuster Bks. For Young Readers.

Rottmann, Erik. Parable of the Prodigal Son. 2009. (ENG.). 16p. (J). (gr. k-4). pap. 2.49 *(978-0-7586-1613-5(9))* Concordia Publishing Hse.

Schantin, Diane. Parables from Twilight: A Bible Study. 2009. 80p. pap. 10.49 *(978-1-4389-7757-7(3))* AuthorHouse.

Sexton, Clarence. The Parables of Jesus: The Greatest Stories Ever Told. (Complete Junior High Bible Study Resource Bks.: No. 3). (Illus.). (J). (gr. 6-9). pap. 16.99 *(978-0-8307-1699-9(8))* Gospel Light Pubns.

Smouse, Phil. Born Again! 2004. 64p. (J). pap. 4.97 *(978-1-59310-099-5(X))* Barbour Publishing, Inc.

Stockstill, Gloria McQueen. Jesus Rose on Easter Morn: A Listen! Look! Book. Durrell, Julie, illus. 2004. 20p. (J). bds. 5.49 *(978-0-7586-0143-8(3))* Concordia Publishing Hse.

Teresa, Olive. The Story of the Good Samaritan. 2005. (ENG., Illus.). 16p. (J). pap. 1.99 *(978-0-7586-0863-5(2))* Concordia Publishing Hse.

Tnt. On the Way 3-9's - Book 8. 2014. (On the Way Ser.). (ENG.). 100p. (J). pap. 17.99 *(978-1-85792-403-9(7)*, 14255ce1-f0d8-47a2-bba8-313acccdedd6) Christian Focus Pubns. GBR. Dist: Baker & Taylor Publisher Services (BTPS).

Wach, Randy-Lynne. A Child's Collection of Parables. Harston, Jerry, illus. 2007. 13.95 *(978-1-59038-724-5(4))* Deseret Bk. Co.

JESUS CHRIST—POETRY

Butcher, A D. Grandma Can You Tell Me. Dugan, Alan, illus. 2007. 16p. per. 10.95 *(978-1-4327-1316-4(7))* Outskirts Pr., Inc.

Hopkins, Lee Bennett. Manger. Cann, Helen, illus. 2014. (ENG.). 34p. (J). 16.00 *(978-0-8028-5419-3(2)*, Eerdmans Bks For Young Readers) Eerdmans, William B. Publishing Co.

Jeffs, Stephanie. Share Out the Food with Jesus. Reynolds, Annette, ed. Saunderson, Chris, illus. 2007. (Action Rhymes Ser.). (ENG.). 16p. (J). (gr. -1-2). pap. 4.99 *(978-0-9789056-1-3(X))* New Day Publishing, Inc.

Lane, Leena. Sail in the Boat with Jesus. Reynolds, Annette, ed. Saunderson, Chris, illus. 2007. (Action Rhymes Ser.). (ENG.). 16p. (J). (gr. -1-2). pap. 4.99 *(978-0-9789056-0-6(1))* New Day Publishing, Inc.

—Stand up & Walk with Jesus. Reynolds, Annette, ed. Saunderson, Chris, illus. 2007. (Action Rhymes Ser.). (ENG.). 16p. (J). (gr. -1-2). pap. 4.99 *(978-0-9789056-4-4(4))* New Day Publishing, Inc.

pierce, km. The Very First Christmas. 2007. (ENG.). 52p. pap. *(978-0-615-15984-3(2))* Saeligstone.

Stiegemeyer, Julie. Baby in a Manger. Wong, Nicole, illus. 2004. 32p. (J). (gr. k-4). 9.99 *(978-0-7586-0726-3(1))* Concordia Publishing Hse.

JESUS CHRIST—SERMON ON THE MOUNT

see Sermon on the Mount

JESUS CHRIST—TEACHINGS

Buck, Bryant. My First Christian Abc Bk. 2009. 32p. 14.95 *(978-1-58169-322-5(2)*, Evergreen Pr.) Genesis Communications, Inc.

Butler, David. Redeemer: Who He Is & Who He Will Always Be. 2019. (Illus.). 169p. (J). pap. 15.99 *(978-1-62972-574-1(9))* Deseret Bk. Co.

Cantrell, Pete. The Happy Angel: A Fractured Fairy Tale. Farris, Kim, illus. 2010. (ENG.). 32p. (J). 9.95 *(978-1-61005-010-4(X))* BookLogix.

Carmody, Michael A. Life with Jesus: Bible Study Workbook. 2003. 32p. (YA). pap. 10.00 *(978-0-910487-54-2(5))* Royalty Publishing Co.

Craft, Sandra. Jesus Whispers in My Ear. 2013. 20p. pap. 10.95 *(978-1-4497-8083-8(0)*, WestBow Pr.) Author Solutions, LLC.

Fair, Barbara A. Children Following the Teachings of Jesus: An Activity Book for Kids. Date not set. (J). (gr. k-2). pap. *(978-0-9621174-3-5(9))* Fair, Barbara A.

Ficocelli, Elizabeth. The Imitation of Christ for Children: A Guide to Following Jesus. Sabatino, Chris, illus. 2006. (ENG.). 64p. (J). (gr. 3-7). per. 9.95 *(978-0-8091-6733-3(6)*, 6733-6) Paulist Pr.

Flamini, Lorella, illus. Growing in Love: Virtues for Little Ones. 2006. 40p. (J). (gr. -1-k). bds. 11.95 *(978-0-8198-3105-7(0))* Pauline Bks. & Media.

Fogg, Paul, illus. Jesus Said. 2008. 36p. pap. 10.95 *(978-0-9814878-2-3(3))* Little Hands Bk. Co., LLC.

Hendrix, John. Go & Do Likewise! The Parables & Wisdom of Jesus. 2021. (ENG., Illus.). 40p. (J). (gr. -1-3). 18.99 *(978-1-4197-3705-3(8)*, 1156801, Abrams Bks. for Young Readers) Abrams, Inc.

Keefer, Mikal. Notes from Jesus: What Your New Best Friend Wants You to Know. 2018. (ENG.). 64p. 7.99 *(978-1-4707-5029-9(5))* Group Publishing, Inc.

Larsen, Carolyn. Teachings of Jesus. 2012. (Standard Bible Storybook Ser.). (ENG., Illus.). 32p. (J). 7.99 *(978-0-7847-3565-7(4))* Standard Publishing.

Lee, Ella Dolbear, illus. The Wonderful Story of Jesus. 2004. reprint ed. pap. 20.95 *(978-1-4179-3177-4(9))* Kessinger Publishing, LLC.

Maes, Adolfo P. Christ & the Children. 2011. 16p. (gr. -1). pap. 9.99 *(978-1-4567-6217-9(6))* AuthorHouse.

Moran, Mary Y. & Myers, Theresa F. Jesus Teaches Us. 77p. (J). (gr. 3). pap. 2.25 *(978-0-8198-3925-1(6))* Pauline Bks. & Media.

Notto, E. T. Light of God Bible Books: Book 1 (Creation, God's Commandments, Faith) 2008. 52p. pap. 22.49 *(978-1-4389-1702-3(3))* AuthorHouse.

Scherm, Deedra. Five Loaves & a Couple of Fish: A Story of Faith & Giving. Dreyer, Laura, illus. 2007. (ENG.). 20p. 7.99 *(978-1-934789-01-8(1))* Lemon Vision Productions.

Schuon, Catherine & Fitzgerald, Michael Oren, eds. A King James Christmas: Biblical Selections with Illustrations from Around the World. 2012. (Illus.). 80p. (J). (gr. 3-7). 19.95 *(978-1-937786-03-8(X))* World Wisdom, Inc.

Schut, Jessie. Telling Your Friends about Jesus. (Friendship Ser.). stu. ed. 3.25 *(978-1-56212-744-2(6)*, 300550); 55p. mentor's hndbk. ed. 6.25 *(978-1-56212-251-5(7)*, 300555) Faith Alive Christian Resources.

Vanier, Jean. I Meet Jesus: He Tells Me "I Love You" 2014. (ENG., Illus.). 216p. pap. 16.95 *(978-0-8091-4835-6(8))* Paulist Pr.

—I Walk with Jesus. 2014. (ENG., Illus.). 208p. (Orig.). pap. 16.95 *(978-0-8091-4836-3(6))* Paulist Pr.

Young, Sarah. Jesus Always: 365 Devotions for Kids, 1 vol. 2017. (Jesus Always Ser.). (ENG.). 400p. (J). 18.99 *(978-0-7180-9688-5(6)*, Tommy Nelson) Nelson, Thomas Inc.

—Jesus Calling: Family Devotional: 100 Devotions for Families to Enjoy Peace in His Presence. 2017. 205p. *(978-1-4041-0582-9(4))* Nelson, Thomas Inc.

—Jesus Today Devotions for Kids, 1 vol. 2016. (Jesus Today Ser.). (ENG.). 368p. (J). 16.99 *(978-0-7180-3805-2(3)*, Tommy Nelson) Nelson, Thomas Inc.

Zonderkidz. Jesus Loves the World, 1 vol. 2018. (Beginner's Bible Ser.). (ENG., Illus.). 18p. (J). bds. 9.99 *(978-0-310-76004-7(6))* Zonderkidz.

JESUS CHRIST IN ART

see Jesus Christ—Art

JET PLANES

Alvarez, Carlos & Finn, Denny Von. Supersonic Jets. 2009. (World's Fastest Ser.). (ENG., Illus.). 24p. (J). (gr. 3-7). lib. bdg. 26.95 *(978-1-60014-287-1(7))* Bellwether Media.

Amato, William. Supersonic Jets. 2009. (High-Tech Vehicles Ser.). 24p. (gr. 2-3). 42.50 *(978-1-61513-307-9(0)*, PowerKids Pr.) Rosen Publishing Group, Inc., The.

Byers, Ann. The Crash of the Concorde. 2009. (When Disaster Strikes! Ser.). 48p. (gr. 5-8). 53.00 *(978-1-60854-779-1(5)*, Rosen Reference) Rosen Publishing Group, Inc., The.

Cefrey, Holly. Super Jumbo Jets: Inside & Out. 2009. (Technology: Blueprints of the Future Ser.). 48p. (gr. 4-4). 53.00 *(978-1-60853-285-8(2))* Rosen Publishing Group, Inc., The.

—Super Jumbo Jets: Por dentro y por fuera (Super Jumbo Jets: Inside & Out) 2009. (Tecnología: Mapas para el Futuro Ser.). (SPA.). 48p. (gr. 4-4). 53.00 *(978-1-60853-289-6(5)*, Editorial Buenas Letras) Rosen Publishing Group, Inc., The.

Christopher, Maynard. Me pregunto por qué: los aviones tienen alas y otras preguntas sobre los transportes. 2003. (Enciclopedia Me Pregunto Por Que). (SPA., Illus.). 32p. (J). (gr. 3-5). 12.99 *(978-84-241-2169-3(4)*, EV2031) Everest Editora ESP. Dist: Lectorum Pubns., Inc.

David, Jack. F-14 Tomcats. 2008. (Torque Ser.). (ENG.). 24p. (J). (gr. 3-7). 20.00 *(978-0-531-21643-9(8)*, Children's Pr.) Scholastic Library Publishing.

—F-15 Eagles. 2008. (Torque Ser.). (ENG.). 24p. (J). (gr. 3-7). 20.00 *(978-0-531-21644-6(6)*, Children's Pr.) Scholastic Library Publishing.

Doeden, Matt. Air Show Jets. 2009. pap. 52.95 *(978-0-7613-4791-0(7))*; (ENG.). 48p. (gr. 4-7). 26.60 *(978-0-8225-9430-7(7))* Lerner Publishing Group.

Eason, Sarah. How Does a Jet Plane Work?, 1 vol. 2010. (How Does It Work? Ser.). (ENG.). 32p. (J). (gr. 3-4). lib. bdg. 28.67 *(978-1-4339-3471-1(X)*, 9a969deb-4b6c-4cdb-98df-e09339d2522c); (Illus.). pap. 11.50 *(978-1-4339-3472-8(8)*, 2123ba55-43ce-442f-be09-f23a005c59a5) Stevens, Gareth Publishing LLLP. (Gareth Stevens Learning Library).

Editors of Klutz. Straw-Shooter Jets. 2014. (ENG.). 60p. (J). (gr. 3). 16.99 *(978-0-545-64779-3(7))* Klutz.

Fighter Jets. (Mighty MacHines Ser.). 16p. (J). *(978-2-7643-0172-2(3))* Phidal Publishing, Inc./Editions Phidal, Inc.

Finn, Denny Von. F-16 Fighting Falcons. 2013. (Military Vehicles Ser.). (ENG., Illus.). 24p. (J). (gr. 3-7). lib. bdg. 26.95 *(978-1-60014-884-2(0)*, Epic Bks.) Bellwether Media.

Hamilton, John. F-16 Fighting Falcon. 2012. (Xtreme Military Aircraft Ser.). (ENG.). 32p. (J). (gr. 3-9). lib. bdg. 32.79 *(978-1-61783-268-0(5)*, 15672, Abdo & Daughters) ABDO Publishing Co.

—F-35 Lightning II. 2012. (Xtreme Military Aircraft Ser.). (ENG.). 32p. (J). (gr. 3-9). lib. bdg. 32.79 *(978-1-61783-269-7(3)*, 15674, Abdo & Daughters) ABDO Publishing Co.

—F/A-18 Super Hornet. 2012. (Xtreme Military Aircraft Ser.). (ENG., Illus.). 32p. (J). (gr. 3-9). lib. bdg. 32.79 *(978-1-61783-270-3(7)*, 15676, Abdo & Daughters) ABDO Publishing Co.

High Flying: Level P, 6 vols., Vol. 3. (Explorers Ser.). 32p. (gr. 3-6). 44.95 *(978-0-7699-0619-5(2))* Shortland Pubns. (U. S. A.) Inc.

Hill, Lee Sullivan. Jets. 2004. (Pull Ahead Books-Mighty Movers Ser.). (ENG., Illus.). 32p. (gr. k-3). lib. bdg. 22.60 *(978-0-8225-1541-8(5))* Lerner Publishing Group.

Jackson, Robert. Military Jets up Close, 1 vol., 1. Pearson, Colin, illus. 2015. (Military Technology: Top Secret Clearance Ser.). (ENG.). 224p. (YA). (gr. 7-8). 46.80 *(978-1-5081-7080-8(0)*, 1db03d48-96df-49d7-8015-0cb0a7c4a614, Rosen Young Adult) Rosen Publishing Group, Inc., The.

Kennedy, Robert. Would You Dare Fly a Fighter Jet?, 1 vol. 2016. (Would You Dare? Ser.). (ENG., Illus.). 32p. (J). (gr. 1-2). lib. bdg. 28.27 *(978-1-4824-5812-1(8)*, 67d0bd68-db1e-404b-9124-c88e574efeaa) Stevens, Gareth Publishing LLLP.

Mattern, Joanne. Pilotos (Pilots) 2009. (Trabajo en grupo (Working Together) Ser.). (SPA.). 24p. (gr. 1-2). 42.50 *(978-1-60854-577-3(6)*, Editorial Buenas Letras) Rosen Publishing Group, Inc., The.

—Pilots. 2009. (Working Together Ser.). 24p. (gr. 1-2). 42.50 *(978-1-60854-832-3(5)*, PowerKids Pr.) Rosen Publishing Group, Inc., The.

Morey, Allan. Fighter Jets. 2014. (Illus.). 24p. (J). lib. bdg. 25.65 *(978-1-62031-107-3(0)*, Bullfrog Bks.) Jump! Inc.

Mullins, Matt. How Does It Fly? Jet Plane. 2011. (Community Connections: How Does It Fly? Ser.). (ENG., Illus.). 24p. (gr. 2-5). lib. bdg. 29.21 *(978-1-61080-069-3(9)*, 201064) Cherry Lake Publishing.

Peterson, Megan Cooley. F/a-18 Super Hornet. 2019. (Air Power Ser.). (ENG., Illus.). 32p. (J). (gr. 4-6). pap. 9.99 *(978-1-64466-011-9(3)*, 12633); lib. bdg. *(978-1-68072-788-3(5)*, 12632) Black Rabbit Bks. (Bolt).

Riggs, Kate. Jets. (Seedlings Ser.). 24p. (J). (gr. -1-k). 2015. (ENG.). *(978-1-60818-521-4(4)*, 21233) 2010. 16.95 *(978-1-58341-913-7(6))* Creative Co., The. (Creative Education).

Schuh, Mari. Jet Planes, 1 vol. 2013. (Aircraft Ser.). (ENG.). 24p. (J). (gr. -1-2). lib. bdg. 27.32 *(978-1-62065-113-1(0)*, 120808) Capstone.

Silverman, Buffy. How Do Jets Work? 2013. (Lightning Bolt Books (r) — How Flight Works). (ENG., Illus.). 32p. (J). (gr. 1-3). lib. bdg. 29.32 *(978-0-7613-8967-5(9)*, 37217d69-38d4-45f7-a332-204c4d3efdb1, Lerner Pubns.) Lerner Publishing Group.

Zobel, Derek. F-22 Raptors. 2008. (Torque Ser.). (ENG.). 24p. (J). (gr. 3-7). 20.00 *(978-0-531-21645-3(4)*, Children's Pr.) Scholastic Library Publishing.

JET PLANES—FICTION

Biedrzycki, David. Santa's New Jet. Biedrzycki, David, illus. 2011. (Illus.). 32p. (J). (gr. -1-2). pap. 7.95 *(978-1-58089-292-6(2))* Charlesbridge Publishing, Inc.

—Santa's New Jet. 2007. (Illus.). (J). pap. *(978-0-545-00238-7(9))* Scholastic, Inc.

Cook, Sherry & Johnson, Terri. Jazzy Jet, 26 vols. Kuhn, Jesse, illus. l.t. ed. 2006. (Quirkles — Exploring Phonics through Science Ser.: 10). 32p. (J). 7.99 *(978-1-933815-09-1(4)*, Quirkles, The) Creative 3, LLC.

JET STREAM

Randolph, Joanne, ed. Jet Stream Steering the Winds!, 1 vol. 2017. (Weather Report). (ENG.). 32p. (gr. 3-3). pap. 11.52 *(978-0-7660-9017-0(5)*, d21f363a-b4f7-4271-b99e-92bdce070772) Enslow Publishing, LLC.

JETER, DEREK, 1974-

Anniss, Matt. Derek Jeter in the Community, 1 vol., 1. 2013. (Making a Difference: Athletes Who Are Changing the World Ser.). (ENG.). 48p. (J). (gr. 5-5). 29.44 *(978-1-62275-185-3(X)*, f766875a-c097-4a4b-9b76-dcce0130bf08) Rosen Publishing Group, Inc., The.

Bednar, Chuck. Derek Jeter: All-Star Major League Baseball Player. 2012. (Transcending Race Ser.). 64p. (J). (gr. 5). 22.95 *(978-1-4222-2728-2(6))* Mason Crest.

Bradley, Michael. Derek Jeter, 1 vol. 2005. (All-Stars Ser.). (ENG., Illus.). 48p. (gr. 4-4). lib. bdg. 34.07 *(978-0-7614-1626-5(9)*, 481b5234-65a9-4bc8-8888-ddd61610278c) Cavendish Square Publishing LLC.

Donovan, Sandy. Derek Jeter. 2008. pap. 40.95 *(978-1-58013-718-8(0))* 2004. 32p. (J). (gr. 2-5). pap. 6.95 *(978-0-8225-2038-2(9))* 2004. (Illus.). 32p. (J). (gr. 3-4). lib. bdg. 23.93 *(978-0-8225-3674-1(9))* Lerner Publishing Group.

—Derek Jeter, 2nd Edition. rev. ed. 2011. (ENG., Illus.). 32p. (gr. 2-5). E-Book 25.26 *(978-0-7613-7203-5(2))* Lerner Publishing Group.

—Derek Jeter (Revised Edition) 2011. (Amazing Athletes Ser.). 32p. (J). pap. 45.32 *(978-0-7613-7652-1(6))* Lerner Publishing Group.

Edwards, Ethan. Meet Derek Jeter: Baseball's Superstar Shortstop. 2009. (All-Star Players Ser.). 32p. (gr. 4-5). 47.90 *(978-1-61511-279-1(0)*, PowerKids Pr.) Rosen Publishing Group, Inc., The.

—Meet Derek Jeter: Captain of the New York Yankees, 1 vol. 2008. (All-Star Players Ser.). (ENG., Illus.). 32p. (YA). (gr. 4-5). lib. bdg. 28.93 *(978-1-4042-4488-7(3)*, 24d1ceed-b96f-4658-9d25-85ded96adc7f) Rosen Publishing Group, Inc., The.

Feldman, Heather. Derek Jeter: Baseball's Best / Estrella del Béisbol. 2009. (Superstars of Sports/Superestrellas del deporte Ser.). (ENG & SPA.). 24p. (gr. 1-2). 42.50 *(978-1-60853-237-7(2)*, Editorial Buenas Letras) Rosen Publishing Group, Inc., The.

—Derek Jeter: Estrella del Béisbol (Baseball's Best) 2009. (Superestrellas del Deporte (Superstars of Sports) Ser.). (SPA.). 24p. (gr. 1-2). 42.50 *(978-1-60853-225-4(9)*, Editorial Buenas Letras) Rosen Publishing Group, Inc., The.

Gatto, Kimberly. Derek Jeter: A Baseball Star Who Cares, 1 vol. 2014. (Sports Stars Who Care Ser.). (ENG.). 48p. (gr. 3-3). pap. 11.53 *(978-1-4644-0541-9(7)*, 889741a8-df16-47ea-9a56-7687dd70b013); lib. bdg. 27.93 *(978-0-7660-4298-8(7)*, 15eebc90-1c4b-42e9-a264-78c3f80b724d) Enslow Publishing, LLC. (Enslow Elementary).

Greenberg, Keith Elliot. Derek Jeter. 2005. (Sports Heroes & Legends Ser.). (Illus.). 106p. (J). (gr. 3-7). lib. bdg. 27.93 *(978-0-8225-3068-8(6)*, Lerner Pubns.) Lerner Publishing Group.

—Derek Jeter: Spectacular Shortstop. 2011. (USA TODAY Lifeline Biographies Ser.). (ENG.). 112p. (gr. 6-12). 34.60 *(978-0-7613-6422-1(6))* Lerner Publishing Group.

Herman, Gail. Who Is Derek Jeter? 2015. (Who Is... ? Ser.). lib. bdg. 16.00 *(978-0-606-37552-8(X))* Turtleback.

Herman, Gail & Who HQ. Who Is Derek Jeter? Thomson, Andrew, illus. 2015. (Who Was? Ser.). 112p. (J). (gr. 3-7). 6.99 *(978-0-448-48697-0(0)*, Penguin Workshop) Penguin Young Readers Group.

Kennedy, Mike. Derek Jeter, 1 vol. 2009. (Today's Superstars Ser.). (ENG.). 48p. (J). (gr. 3-3). pap. 15.05 *(978-1-4339-2162-9(6)*, bd078773-7353-4dab-8e12-18d2c6e83777); lib. bdg. 34.60 *(978-1-4339-1969-5(9)*, 126f2134-378f-4a30-bd13-b62c8c3f93f9) Stevens, Gareth Publishing LLLP.

Marcovitz, Hal. Derek Jeter. (Modern Role Models Ser.). (Illus.). 64p. (YA). 2010. (gr. 7-12). lib. bdg. 22.95 *(978-1-4222-0482-5(0))* 2007. pap. 9.95 *(978-1-4222-0770-3(6))* Mason Crest.

Mills, Clifford W. Derek Jeter. (Baseball Superstars Ser.). (Illus.). 2008. 128p. (gr. 6-12). pap. 11.95 *(978-0-7910-9846-2(X)*, Checkmark Bks.) 2007. (ENG., 122p. (gr. 7-12). lib. bdg. 30.00 *(978-0-7910-9422-8(7)*, P126610, Facts On File) Infobase Holdings, Inc.

O'Connell, Jack. Derek Jeter: The Yankee Kid. Rains, Rob, ed. 2003. (Super Star Ser.). 96p. (J). pap. 4.95 *(978-1-58261-043-6(5))* Sports Publishing, LLC.

Rappoport, Ken. Derek Jeter: Champion Baseball Star, 1 vol. 2012. (Sports Star Champions Ser.). (ENG., Illus.). 48p. (gr. 5-7). 29.60 *(978-0-7660-4025-0(9)*, e17af628-ea2c-4892-97f5-a81fcbcd36f3) Enslow Publishing, LLC.

Sandler, Michael. Derek Jeter & the New York Yankees: 2000 World Series. 2008. (World Series Superstars). (Illus.). 24p. (J). (gr. 1-4). lib. bdg. 26.99 *(978-1-59716-641-6(3))* Bearport Publishing Co., Inc.

Sheen, Barbara. Derek Jeter, 1 vol. 2008. (People in the News Ser.). (ENG., Illus.). 104p. (gr. 7-7). lib. bdg. 41.03 *(978-1-4205-0089-9(9)*, be53a154-7d48-4bc8-86bc-af65cd18882f, Lucent Pr.) Greenhaven Publishing LLC.

Torres, John Albert. Derek Jeter. 2004. (Blue Banner Biography Ser.). (Illus.). 32p. (J). lib. bdg. 25.70 *(978-1-58415-333-7(4))* Mitchell Lane Pubs.

Torsiello, David P. Read about Derek Jeter, 1 vol. 2011. (I Like Sports Stars! Ser.). (ENG., Illus.). 24p. (gr. k-2). pap. 10.35 *(978-1-59845-301-0(7)*, 14687c3e-cdde-4eef-97fa-307c65104fae, Enslow Elementary); lib. bdg. 25.27 *(978-0-7660-3829-5(7)*, 4e679d40-6839-42d8-89a6-a1d2bd12a8d8) Enslow Publishing, LLC.

JEWELRY

see also Gems

AZ Books Staff. Favorite Jewelry. 2012. (My Collection). (ENG., Illus.). 14p. (J). (gr. 1-3). bds. 12.95 *(978-1-61889-078-8(6))* AZ Bks. LLC.

Chen, D. M. & Sun, Michelle. Tie a Wish with Bracelets: Easy & Fun Chinese Knotting. 2012. (ENG., Illus.). 71p. (J). (gr. 4). pap. 10.95 *(978-1-937489-01-4(9))* StoryRobin Co.

Design your own Jewelry. 2004. (How 2 Kits Ser.). (Illus.). 48p. (J). *(978-1-84229-927-2(1))* Top That! Publishing PLC.

Editors of Klutz. Grow Your Own Crystal Jewelry: 7 Sparkly Projects to Make & Wear. 2016. (ENG.). 48p. (J). (gr. 3-7). 22.99 *(978-1-338-03749-4(8))* Klutz.

—Toolbox Jewelry. 2013. (ENG.). 60p. (J). (gr. 3). 21.99 *(978-0-545-56134-1(5))* Klutz.

Everett, Felicity. Make Your Own Jewelry. (Fashion Guides Ser.). (Illus.). 32p. (YA). (gr. 6-18). pap. 6.95 *(978-0-7460-0077-9(4))* EDC Publishing.

Felix, Rebecca. Mini Wearables. 2017. (Mini Makers Ser.). (ENG., Illus.). 32p. (J). (gr. 2-5). 26.65 *(978-1-5124-2635-9(0)*, 296fd5af-5b1c-42e5-831b-1b54c3341a79); E-Book 39.99 *(978-1-5124-3842-0(1)*, 9781512438420); E-Book 39.99 *(978-1-5124-2813-1(2))*; E-Book 6.99 *(978-1-5124-3843-7(X)*, 9781512438437) Lerner Publishing Group. (Lerner Pubns.).

French, Cathy. Make a Necklace. 2011. (Early Connections Ser.). (J). *(978-1-61672-235-7(5))* Benchmark Education Co.

Holzach, Cornelie. Schatzsuche MIT Schmuckl der Perlsau: Im Schmuckmuseum Pforzheim Für Groß und Klein. 2012. (Illus.). 80p. 35.00 *(978-3-89790-351-7(2))* Arnoldsche Art Pubs. DEU. Dist: Antique Collectors' Club.

Johnson, Anne Akers. Pulseras Rusticas. 2005. (SPA., Illus.). 32p. (J). (gr. 1). 17.95 *(978-968-5528-11-5(X))* Klutz Latino MEX. Dist: Independent Pubs. Group.

Leisure Arts, creator. Rubber Band Loom Fun! 2013. (ENG., Illus.). 48p. (J). (gr. 4-7). pap. 9.99 *(978-1-4647-1578-5(5))* Leisure Arts, Inc.

Macdonald, Fiona. Jewelry & Makeup Through History, 1 vol. 2006. (Why Do We Wear? Ser.). (ENG., Illus.). 32p. (gr. 3-5). lib. bdg. 28.67 *(978-0-8368-6856-2(0)*, c00b0f11-e7e8-4440-9229-bc79ae2cd27f, Gareth Stevens Learning Library) Stevens, Gareth Publishing LLLP.

Schiffer, Nancy N. Rhinestones! A Collector's Handbook & Price Guide, 1 vol. 4th rev. ed. 2003. (ENG., Illus.). 160p. (gr. 10-13). pap. 16.95 *(978-0-7643-1751-4(2)*, 2183) Schiffer Publishing, Ltd.

—Silver Jewelry Treasures, 1 vol. 3rd rev. ed. 2003. (ENG., Illus.). 144p. (gr. 10-13). pap. 16.95 *(978-0-7643-1852-8(7)*, 2184) Schiffer Publishing, Ltd.

Stillerman, Robbie. Glitter Jewelry Sticker Activity Book. 2008. (Dover Little Activity Books Stickers Ser.). (ENG., Illus.). 2p. (J). (gr. 1-4). 1.50 *(978-0-486-46576-0(4))* Dover Pubns., Inc.

Torres, Laura. Brazaletes de la Amistad. 2005. (SPA., Illus.). 57p. (J). (gr. 3). 17.95 *(978-968-5528-05-4(5))* Klutz Latino MEX. Dist: Independent Pubs. Group.

Turnbull, Stephanie. Wardrobe Makeover. 2016. (Sleepover Secrets Ser.). (ENG.). 24p. (J). (gr. 2-5). 28.50 *(978-1-62588-381-0(1)*, 17394) Black Rabbit Bks.

Ward, Charlotte, ed. Gem Care. Ward, Fred, photos by. 2nd ed. 2003. (Fred Ward Gem Book Ser.). (Illus.). 32p. pap. 9.95 (978-1-887651-07-3(1)) Gem Bk. Pubs.

JEWELRY MAKING

Blake, Susannah. Crafts for Accessorizing That Look, 1 vol. 2013. (Eco Chic Ser.). (ENG.). 32p. (gr. 4-6). pap. 10.35 (978-1-4644-0571-6(9), b57edcf1-3d9b-4cf2-9347-3cb23d585b10); lib. bdg. 26.61 (978-0-7660-4313-8(4), 73c37536-5e8d-4ccd-a5a8-c3fa9ad56b45) Enslow Publishing, LLC.

Carlson-Berne, Emma. Jewelry Tips & Tricks. Heschke, Elena, illus. 2015. (Style Secrets Ser.). (ENG.). 32p. (J). (gr. 4-8). lib. bdg. 26.65 (978-1-4677-5220-6(7), 485aca3e-9ea8-45ee-af40-470e45eca329); E-Book 39.99 (978-1-4677-8654-6(3)) Lerner Publishing Group. (Lerner Pubns.).

Dorsey, Colleen. Epic Rubber Band Crafts: Totally Cool Gadget Gear, Never Before Seen Bracelets, Awesome Action Figures, & More! 2014. (ENG., Illus.). 48p. (J). pap. 9.99 (978-1-57421-914-2(6), DO5472, Design Originals) Fox Chapel Publishing Co., Inc.

—Totally Awesome Rubber Band Jewelry: Make Bracelets, Rings, Belts & More with Rainbow Loom(r), Cra-Z-Loom & FunLoom. 2013. lib. bdg. 18.40 (978-0-606-35178-2(7)) Turtleback.

Dybvik, Tina. Trendy Jewelry for the Crafty Fashionista, 1 vol. 2011. (Fashion Craft Studio Ser.). (ENG.). 32p. (J). (gr. 3-9). lib. bdg. 28.65 (978-1-4296-6549-0(1), 115651) Capstone.

Editors of Klutz. Loop Loom Bracelets: Make Super-Stretchy Beaded Bracelets. 2014. (ENG.). 48p. (J). (gr. 3). 21.99 (978-0-545-70318-5(2)) Klutz.

—Safety Pin Bracelets. 2011. (ENG.). (J). (gr. 3-7). 19.99 (978-1-59174-932-5(8)) Klutz.

Editors of Klutz & Phillips, Karen. Shrink Art Jewelry. 2007. (Klutz Ser.). (ENG., Illus.). (J). (gr. 7-12). 24.95 (978-1-59174-437-5(7)) Klutz.

Etchison, Denise. Kids! Picture Yourself Making Jewelry. 2008. (Picture Yourself Ser.). (ENG.). 104p. pap. 12.99 (978-1-59863-526-3(3)) Course Technology.

Hollis, Matthew. Jada Makes Jewelry: Use Place Value Understanding & Properties of Operations to Add & Subtract, 1 vol. 2014. (Math Masters: Number & Operations in Base Ten Ser.). (ENG.). 24p. (J). (gr. 2-2). 25.27 (978-1-4777-6402-2(X), cf151c5c-c94c-4be3-a733-616ea8a4f546); pap. 8.25 (978-1-4777-4742-1(7), e0c5e66a-a3c4-4044-8ab9-97eb6be982c0) Rosen Publishing Group, Inc., The. (Rosen Classroom).

Hove, Carol. Make It Yourself! from Junk to Jewelry. 2017. (Cool Makerspace Ser.). (ENG., Illus.). 32p. (J). (gr. 3-6). lib. bdg. 34.21 (978-1-5321-1070-2(7), 25716, Checkerboard Library) ABDO Publishing Co.

Jewelry. 2013. (From Trash to Treasure Ser.). 32p. (J). (gr. 3-6). pap. 70.50 (978-1-4777-1361-7(1), PowerKids Pr.) Rosen Publishing Group, Inc., The.

Kachidurian, Debbie, et al. Bring on the Bling! Bracelets, Anklets, & Rings for All Occasions. 2016. (Accessorize Yourself! Ser.). (ENG., Illus.). 48p. (J). (gr. 4-8). lib. bdg. 35.32 (978-1-4914-8231-5(1), 130694, Capstone Pr.) Capstone.

Kachidurian, Debbie Prestine, et al. Bring on the Bling! Bracelets, Anklets, & Rings for All Occasions. 2017. (Illus.). 47p. (J). pap. (978-1-4914-8621-4(X)) Capstone.

Kenney, Karen Latchana. Super Simple Jewelry: Fun & Easy-to-Make Crafts for Kids, 1 vol. 2009. (Super Simple Crafts Ser.). (ENG., Illus.). 32p. (J). (gr. -1-4). 34.21 (978-1-60453-625-6(X), 13932, Super SandCastle) ABDO Publishing Co.

Kollmar, Elizabeth. Hooked on Rubber Band Jewelry: 12 off-The-Loom Designs for Bracelets, Necklaces, & Other Accessories. 2014. (ENG., Illus.). 52p. pap. 9.99 (978-1-57421-915-9(4), 9781574219159, Design Originals) Fox Chapel Publishing Co., Inc.

Laughlin, Kara L. Sparkle & Shine! Trendy Earrings, Necklaces, & Hair Accessories for All Occasions. 2016. (Accessorize Yourself! Ser.). (ENG., Illus.). 48p. (J). (gr. 4-8). lib. bdg. 35.32 (978-1-4914-8228-5(1), 130692, Capstone Pr.) Capstone.

Lim, Annalees. Jewelry Crafts, 1 vol., Vol. 1. 2013. (Craft Attack! Ser.). (ENG.). 32p. (J). (gr. 3-3). 29.27 (978-1-4824-0199-8(1), bbf66e2a-a7d9-48c2-981e-debb1c8d888e) Stevens, Gareth Publishing LLLP.

MacFarlane, Katherine. The Jeweler's Art, 1 vol. 2007. (Eye on Art Ser.). (ENG., Illus.). 112p. (gr. 7-7). lib. bdg. 41.03 (978-1-59018-984-9(1), b0e3fecc-8fec-414f-87ee-1a3b1baa042a, Lucent Pr.) Greenhaven Publishing LLC.

Owen, Ruth. Jewelry, 1 vol. 2013. (From Trash to Treasure Ser.). (ENG.). 32p. (J). (gr. 4-5). 30.17 (978-1-4777-1283-2(6), aecbd09a-ed4b-4dca-bca3-d1ed27433eff); pap. 12.75 (978-1-4777-1360-0(3), 7c2a7eb6-5339-462e-ac51-539cb811f27a) Rosen Publishing Group, Inc., The. (PowerKids Pr.).

Petelinsek, Kathleen. Making Jewelry with Rubber Bands. Petelinsek, Kathleen, illus. 2014. (How-To Library). (ENG., Illus.). 32p. (J). (gr. 3-6). 32.07 (978-1-63137-781-5(7), 205367) Cherry Lake Publishing.

Quinn, Amy. Making Electric Jewelry. 2017. (21st Century Skills Innovation Library: Makers As Innovators Junior Ser.). (ENG., Illus.). 24p. (J). (gr. 2-5). lib. bdg. 30.64 (978-1-63472-191-2(8), 209336) Cherry Lake Publishing.

Rau, Dana Meachen. Making Jewelry. 2012. (How-To Library). (ENG.). 32p. (gr. 3-6). pap. 14.21 (978-1-61080-649-7(2), 202259); (Illus.). 32.07 (978-1-61080-475-2(9), 202085) Cherry Lake Publishing.

Ross, Kathy. Jazzy Jewelry, Pretty Purses, & More! Bosch, Nicole in den, illus. 2009. (Girl Crafts Ser.). (ENG.). 48p. (gr. 2-5). 26.60 (978-0-8225-9212-9(6)); pap. 7.95 (978-1-58013-883-3(7), Millbrook Pr.) Lerner Publishing Group.

Sadler, Judy Ann. Beads.Tr. of Perles. (FRE., Illus.). (J). pap. 7.99 (978-0-590-24194-6(X)) Scholastic, Inc.

—Hemp Jewelry. Bradford, June, illus. 2005. (Kids Can Do It Ser.). (ENG.). 40p. (YA). (gr. 3-6). 18.69 (978-1-55337-774-0(5)) Kids Can Pr., Ltd. CAN. Dist: Children's Plus, Inc.

Sadler, Judy Ann & Sadler, Judy. Hemp Jewelry. Bradford, June, illus. 2005. (Kids Can Do It Ser.). 40p. (J). (gr. 3-7). 6.95 (978-1-55337-775-7(3)) Kids Can Pr., Ltd. CAN. Dist: Hachette Bk. Group.

Thomas, Becky & Sweeney, Monica. Loom Magic Charms! 25 Cool Designs That Will Rock Your Rainbow. 2014. (ENG., Illus.). 128p. (J). (gr. k). 12.95 (978-1-63220-259-8(X), Sky Pony Pr.) Skyhorse Publishing Co., Inc.

Warwick, Ellen & Di Salle, Rachel. Junk Drawer Jewelry. Kurisu, Jane, illus. 2006. (Kids Can Do It Ser.). 40p. (J). (gr. 3-7). 6.95 (978-1-55337-966-9(7)) Kids Can Pr., Ltd. CAN. Dist: Hachette Bk. Group.

JEWELS

see Gems; Jewelry; Precious Stones

JEWISH-ARAB RELATIONS

Ellis, Deborah. Three Wishes, 1 vol. 2004. (ENG., Illus.). 112p. (J). (gr. 5-6). pap. 8.95 (978-0-88899-645-9(4)) Groundwood Bks. CAN. Dist: Publishers Group West (PGW).

Ellis, Deborah, ed. Three Wishes: Palestinian & Israeli Children Speak. 2004. (YA). 16.95 (978-0-88899-608-4(X), Libros Tigrillo) Groundwood Bks. CAN. Dist: Publishers Group West (PGW).

Hanel, Rachel. The Israeli-Palestine Conflict. 2007. (Days of Change Ser.). (Illus.). 48p. (YA). (gr. 4-7). lib. bdg. 31.35 (978-1-58341-548-1(3)) Creative Co., The.

Israel & Palestine: The Roots of Conflict; Fight for Peace, 2 cass.; set. 2003. (YA). (gr. 9-12). tchr. ed. 89.95 (978-1-58738-432-5(9)) Discovery Education.

Katz, Samuel M. Jerusalem or Death: Palestinian Terrorism. 72p. (YA). (gr. 9-18). 19.95 (978-1-58013-208-4(1), Kar-Ben Publishing); 2003. (Illus.). (J). (gr. 6-12). 26.60 (978-0-8225-4033-5(9)) Lerner Publishing Group.

Lusted, Marcia Amidon. The Israeli-Palestinian Conflict. 2017. (Special Reports Set 3 Ser.). (ENG., Illus.). 112p. (J). (gr. 6-12). lib. bdg. 41.36 (978-1-5321-1333-8(1), 27541, Essential Library) ABDO Publishing Co.

Luxenberg, Alan. The Palestine Mandate & the Creation of Israel, 1920-1949. 2007. (Making of the Middle East Ser.). (Illus.). 80p. (J). (gr. 3-7). lib. bdg. 22.95 (978-1-4222-0170-1(8)) Mason Crest.

Marx, Trish. Sharing Our Homeland: Palestinian & Jewish Children at Summer Peace Camp, 1 vol. Karp, Cindy, photos by. (ENG., Illus.). 48p. (J). 2017. (gr. 3-8). 12.95 (978-1-62014-581-4(2), leelowbooks) 2010. (gr. 1-6). 19.95 (978-1-58430-260-5(7)) Lee & Low Bks., Inc.

Robson, David. Israeli-Palestinian Conflict, 1 vol. 2010. (World History Ser.). (ENG., Illus.). 96p. (gr. 7-7). 41.53 (978-1-4205-0239-8(5), b4e98fb5-5388-402f-9967-a2fe09a1e259, Lucent Pr.) Greenhaven Publishing LLC.

Ruelle, Karen Gray & Desaix, Deborah Durland. The Grand Mosque of Paris: A Story of How Muslims Rescued Jews During the Holocaust. 2010. (ENG., Illus.). 40p. (J). (gr. 2-18). pap. 8.99 (978-0-8234-2304-0(2)) Holiday Hse., Inc.

Whiting, Jim. The Creation of Isreal. 2007. (Monumental Milestones Ser.). (Illus.). 48p. (YA). (gr. 4-7). lib. bdg. 29.95 (978-1-58415-538-6(8)) Mitchell Lane Pubs.

JEWISH-ARAB RELATIONS—FICTION

Clinton, Cathryn. A Stone in My Hand. 2010. (ENG., Illus.). 208p. (J). (gr. 5). pap. 7.99 (978-0-7636-4772-8(1)) Candlewick Pr.

JEWISH COOKING

Grossman, Chaya. The Cherry on Top: A Kosher Junior Cookbook. 2009. 79p. 16.99 (978-1-58330-310-8(3)) Feldheim Pubs.

Hepker, Sue. This Is the Challah. Wummer, Amy, illus. 2012. (J). (ENG.). 24p. 9.95 (978-0-87441-922-1(0), 066fad9c-5fc9-416f-a6ea-bde1ca4e2650); (978-0-87441-522-3(5)) Behrman Hse., Inc.

House, Behrman. Get Cooking! a Jewish American Family Cookbook & Rockin' Mama Doni Celebration. 2012. (ENG., Illus.). 1p. (J). (gr. 3-7). pap. 19.95 (978-0-87441-948-1(4), b1cc866c-d702-45e8-80fa-476212ca3b21) Behrman Hse., Inc.

Newman, Lesléa. Here Is the World: A Year of Jewish Holidays. Gal, Susan, illus. 2014. (ENG.). 48p. (J). (gr. k-2). 19.99 (978-1-4197-1185-5(7), 1066801) Abrams, Inc.

Rauchwerger, Lisa. Chocolate Chip Challah: And Other Twists on the Jewish Holiday Table. Rauchwerger, Lisa, illus. 2004. (Illus.). 127p. (J). (gr. k-3). pap. 17.95 (978-0-8074-0700-4(3), 510606) URJ Pr.

Schapira, Leah. Kids Cooking Made Easy: Favorite Triple-Tested Recipes. 2013. (ENG., Illus.). 144p. (J). pap. 15.99 (978-1-4226-1435-8(2)) Mesorah Pubns., Ltd.

Sheen, Barbara. Foods of Israel, 1 vol. 2011. (Taste of Culture Ser.). (ENG., Illus.). 64p. (gr. 3-6). 36.83 (978-0-7377-5882-5(1), 83f5626b-687b-4114-a859-b3022d31bde1, KidHaven Publishing) Greenhaven Publishing LLC.

Yolen, Jane & Stemple, Heidi E. Y. Jewish Fairy Tale Feasts: A Literary Cookbook. Shefrin, Sima Elizabeth, illus. 2013. (ENG.). 160p. (J). 25.00 (978-1-56656-909-5(5), Crocodile Bks.) Interlink Publishing Group, Inc.

Zakon, Miriam. Kids' Kosher Cookbook. 2005. (Illus.). 111p. (J). 16.99 (978-1-56871-376-2(2)) Targum Pr., Inc.

JEWISH HOLIDAYS

see Fasts and Feasts—Judaism

JEWISH LANGUAGE

see Hebrew Language

JEWISH LEGENDS

Goldin, Barbara Diamond. The Family Book of Midrash: 52 Jewish Stories from the Sages. 2006. Orig. Title: A Child's Book of Midrash. (ENG.). 128p. per. 37.00 (978-0-7425-5285-2(3)) Rowman & Littlefield Publishers, Inc.

Lumer, Marc, illus. When Miracles Happened- Wondrous Stories of Tzaddikim. 2009. 22p. (J). (978-1-56871-484-4(X)) Targum Pr., Inc.

Paulette (Pesha Razela) Fein Lieberman. Jewish Stories & Ideas for Children: A book for bonding, educational fun, & fund-raising purposes for children & Adults! 2009. 180p. pap. 16.95 (978-1-4401-1914-9(7)) iUniverse, Inc.

Rabbi Yaakov Yosef Reinman. Touched by a Story for Children. 2004. (ArtScroll Youth Ser.). (ENG., Illus.). 48p. (J). (978-1-57819-436-0(9)) Mesorah Pubns., Ltd.

Redmond, Shirley Raye. Golem, 1 vol. 2011. (Monsters Ser.). (ENG., Illus.). 48p. (gr. 4-8). lib. bdg. 36.83 (978-0-7377-5866-5(X), dc381994-d1b2-4c4f-93bb-2f3309cceda5, KidHaven Publishing) Greenhaven Publishing LLC.

Schwartz, Howard. A Journey to Paradise: And Other Jewish Tales. Carmi, Giora, illus. 2005. (Jewish Storyteller Ser.). 48p. (J). (gr. -1-3). 16.95 (978-0-943706-21-4(1)); pap. 9.95 (978-0-943706-16-0(5)) Simcha Media Group. (Devora Publishing).

Sherman, Josepha. Rachel the Clever & Other Jewish Folktales. 2005. (American Storytelling Ser.). (ENG., Illus.). 171p. (J). (gr. 4-17). pap. 12.95 (978-0-87483-307-2(8)) August Hse. Pubs., Inc.

Weber, Vicki L. It's Too Crowded in Here! & Other Jewish Folk Tales. Borlasca, Hector, illus. 2010. (ENG.). 64p. (J). pap. 9.95 (978-0-87441-850-7(X), 35582e25-a982-4076-8355-009ec204b195) Behrman Hse., Inc.

Wein, Berel & Mahr, Aryeh. Of Heaven & Earth: Stories of the Chassidic Masters. 2008. 56p. 18.99 (978-1-58330-953-7(5)) Feldheim Pubs.

JEWISH RELIGION

see Judaism

JEWITT, JOHN RODGERS, 1783-1821—FICTION

Goldfield, Rebecca & Short, Mike. Captive of Friendly Cove: Based on the Secret Journals of John Jewitt. 2015. (ENG., Illus.). 168p. (YA). (gr. 7-7). pap. 25.95 (978-1-936218-11-0(9)) Fulcrum Publishing.

JEWS

see also Discrimination

Byrne, Judy. A New Queen. 2013. 28p. pap. 13.95 (978-1-4908-0887-1(6), WestBow Pr.) Author Solutions, LLC.

Chait, Baruch. The Lost Treasure of Tikkun Hamiddos Island. Pollack, Gadi, illus. (Good Middos Ser.: Vol. 2). 62p. 25.99 (978-1-58330-478-5(9)) Feldheim Pubs.

Dion, L. N. The Opposites of My Jewish Year. Olson, Julie, illus. 2005. (ENG.). 12p. (J). (gr. -1 — 1). bds. 5.95 (978-1-58013-113-1(1), 1926b5c8-6b5f-49bf-bb34-c6d7288a8b2b, Kar-Ben Publishing) Lerner Publishing Group.

Horton, Casey. The Jews: We Came to North America. 2006. (Illus.). 32p. (J). (gr. 4-8). reprint ed. 19.00 (978-0-7567-9905-2(8)) DIANE Publishing Co.

Katz, Yoni, prod. Virtual l'Shana Tovah. 2003. (J). cd-rom 12.00 (978-1-932349-23-8(5), 20,000) Jewish Educational Media.

Lehman-Wilzig, Tami. Keeping the Promise: A Torah's Journey. Orback, Craig, illus. 2004. 32p. (J). (gr. 1-5). 16.95 (978-1-58013-117-9(4), Kar-Ben Publishing) Lerner Publishing Group.

McKay, Jenny. Children of the Holocaust. 2015. (ENG., Illus.). 80p. (J). (gr. 5-12). lib. bdg. (978-1-60152-838-4(8)) ReferencePoint Pr., Inc.

National Geographic Learning. Reading Expeditions (Social Studies: Voices from America's Past): Our New Life in America. 2007. (Nonfiction Reading & Writing Workshops Ser.). (ENG., Illus.). 40p. (J). pap. 21.95 (978-0-7922-8701-8(0)) CENGAGE Learning.

Rosenthal, Zelda B. Precious Jewels: The Roadmap to a Child's Heart - a Delightful Resources for Mothers & Teachers. 2006. (ArtScroll Ser.). (Illus.). 268p. (978-1-4226-0075-7(0)); pap. (978-1-4226-0076-4(9)) Mesorah Pubns., Ltd.

Seidman, Lauren. What Makes Someone a Jew? What Makes Someone a Jew? 2007. (ENG., Illus.). 32p. pap. 8.99 (978-1-58023-321-7(X), 0feeae39-9d4a-484b-94dc-54d6425b9619, Jewish Lights Publishing) LongHill Partners, Inc.

Skolnik, Fred & Berenbaum, Michael. Encyclopedia Judaica, 22 vols., Set. 2nd rev. ed. 2006. (Encyclopaedia Judaica Ser.). (ENG., Illus.). 1000p. 4008.00 (978-0-02-865928-2(7), Macmillan Reference USA) Cengage Gale.

Tsivia Yanofsky. Take Me to Europe: Jewish Life in England, Spain, France & Italy. 2013. (ENG., Illus.). 85p. (J). (978-1-4226-1349-8(6)) Mesorah Pubns., Ltd.

Verzov, Ella & Oirechman, Chana. Moshe of Japan. 2013. (Illus.). 50p. (J). (978-1-61465-171-0(X)) Menucha Pubs. Inc.

—Tamar of Venice. 2013. (Illus.). 54p. (J). (978-1-61465-170-3(1)) Menucha Pubs. Inc.

Zeligs, Dorothy Freda. A Child's History of the Hebrew People: From Nomadic Times to the Destruction of the Second Temple. 2012. 200p. 44.95 (978-1-258-25277-9(5)); pap. 29.95 (978-1-258-25530-5(8)) Literary Licensing, LLC.

JEWS—BIOGRAPHY

see also Rabbis

Abramson, Ann & Who HQ. Who Was Anne Frank? Harrison, Nancy, illus. 2007. (Who Was? Ser.). 112p. (J). (gr. 3-7). pap. 5.99 (978-0-448-44482-6(8), Penguin Workshop) Penguin Young Readers Group.

Agrimbau, Diego. Anne Frank. Trusted Translations, Trusted, tr. 2017. (Graphic Lives Ser.). (ENG., Illus.). 80p. (J). (gr. 3-9). lib. bdg. 32.65 (978-1-5157-9161-4(0), 136603, Capstone Pr.) Capstone.

Alexander, Lori. A Sporting Chance: How Ludwig Guttmann Created the Paralympic Games. Drummond, Allan, illus. 2020. (ENG.). 128p. (J). (gr. 3-7). 17.99 (978-1-328-58079-5(2), 1728624, Clarion Bks.) HarperCollins Pubs.

Amler, Jane Frances. Haym Salomon: Patriot Banker of the American Revolution. 2009. (Library of American Lives & Times Ser.). 112p. (gr. 5-5). 69.20 (978-1-60853-487-6(1)) Rosen Publishing Group, Inc., The.

Ashby, Ruth. Anne Frank: Young Diarist. 2005. 186p. (J). lib. bdg. 18.46 (978-1-4242-2208-7(7)) Fitzgerald Bks.

Avital, Moshe. Not to Forget, Impossible to Forgive: Poignant Reflections on the Holocaust. 2004. (Illus.). 339p. (YA). 29.95 (978-965-90462-4-9(3)) Mazo Pubs.

Bat Zvi, Pnina & Wolfe, Margie. The Promise, 1 vol. Cardinal, Isabelle, illus. 2018. (ENG.). 32p. (J). (gr. 3-6). 18.95 (978-1-77260-058-2(X)) Second Story Pr. CAN. Dist: Orca Bk. Pubs. USA.

Boas, Jacob. We Are Witnesses: Five Diaries of Teenagers Who Died in the Holocaust. 2009. (ENG.). 208p. (YA). (gr. 6-10). pap. 10.99 (978-0-312-53567-4(8), 900054746) Square Fish.

Borden, Louise. The Journey That Saved Curious George: The True Wartime Escape of Margret & H. A. Rey. Drummond, Allan, illus. 2005. (Curious George Ser.). (ENG.). 80p. (J). (gr. 3-7). 17.99 (978-0-618-33924-2(8), 581802, Clarion Bks.) HarperCollins Pubs.

Bornstein, Michael & Holinstat, Debbie Bornstein. Survivors Club: The True Story of a Very Young Prisoner of Auschwitz. 2019. (ENG., Illus.). 368p. (J). pap. 12.99 (978-1-250-11875-2(1), 900169967) Square Fish.

Byers, Ann. Saving Children from the Holocaust: The Kindertransport, 1 vol. 2012. (Holocaust Through Primary Sources Ser.). (ENG., Illus.). 128p. (gr. 6-7). pap. 13.88 (978-1-59845-344-7(0), ef006a13-f6f9-49ac-963c-c8b6cf01445b); lib. bdg. 35.93 (978-0-7660-3323-8(6), 5b209fcd-5b79-4241-b064-3d26a7fc54c7) Enslow Publishing, LLC.

Callahan, Kerry P. Mordechai Anielewicz: Hero of the Warsaw Ghetto Uprising. 2009. (Holocaust Biographies Ser.). 112p. (gr. 7-12). 63.90 (978-1-61513-389-5(5)) Rosen Publishing Group, Inc., The.

Eisenberg, Azriel. Fill a Blank Page: A Biography of Solomon Schechter. (Illus.). (J). (gr. 6-11). 3.75 (978-0-8381-0730-0(3), 10-730) United Synagogue of America Bk. Service.

Frank, Anne. The Diary of a Anne Frank. adapted ed. pap., tchr. ed. 4.95 (978-0-8359-0138-3(6)) Globe Fearon Educational Publishing.

Friedman, Laurie. Angel Girl. Amit, Ofra, illus. 2008. 32p. (J). (gr. 3-7). 16.95 (978-0-8225-8739-2(4), Carolrhoda Bks.) Lerner Publishing Group.

Gertner, Sheina Sachar. The Tree Stood Still. 2006. 96p. per. 9.95 (978-1-58939-886-3(6)) Virtualbookworm.com Publishing, Inc.

Glaser, Linda. Emma's Poem: The Voice of the Statue of Liberty. Nivola, Claire A., illus. 2010. (ENG.). 32p. (J). (gr. -1-3). 17.99 (978-0-547-17184-5(6), 1054295, Clarion Bks.) HarperCollins Pubs.

Golabek, Mona & Cohen, Lee. The Children of Willesden Lane: A True Story of Hope & Survival During World War II (Young Readers Edition) 2017. (ENG., Illus.). 224p. (J). E-Book (978-0-316-55489-3(8)) Little Brown & Co.

Goldman, David J. Jewish Jocks: Athletic Stars Past & Present. 2004. (General Jewish Interest Ser.). (ENG., Illus.). 96p. (J). (gr. 6-18). pap. 8.95 (978-1-58013-085-1(2), Kar-Ben Publishing) Lerner Publishing Group.

—Jewish Sports Stars: Athletic Heroes Past & Present. 2006. (Illus.). 96p. (J). (gr. 6-9). per. 9.95 (978-1-58013-183-4(2), Kar-Ben Publishing) Lerner Publishing Group.

Gruenbaum, Michael. Somewhere There Is Still a Sun: A Memoir of the Holocaust. 2015. (ENG., Illus.). 384p. (J). (gr. 5-9). 19.99 (978-1-4424-8486-3(1), Aladdin) Simon & Schuster Children's Publishing.

—Somewhere There Is Still a Sun: A Memoir of the Holocaust. 2017. (ENG., Illus.). 384p. (J). (gr. 5-9). pap. 9.99 (978-1-4424-8487-0(X), Simon & Schuster/Paula Wiseman Bks.) Simon & Schuster/Paula Wiseman Bks.

Harris, Samuel R. Sammy Child Survivor of the Holocaust. 2005. (Illus.). 128p. pap. 14.95 (978-0-9759253-0-0(X)) Harris, Samuel.

Hillman, Laura. I Will Plant You a Lilac Tree: A Memoir of a Schindler's List Survivor. 2008. (ENG., Illus.). 288p. (YA). (gr. 9-12). mass mkt. 8.99 (978-1-4169-5366-1(3), Simon Pulse) Simon Pulse.

Hoffman, Betty N. Liberation: Stories of Survival from the Holocaust, 1 vol. 2012. (Holocaust Through Primary Sources Ser.). (ENG., Illus.). 128p. (gr. 6-7). pap. 13.88 (978-1-59845-348-5(3), ae8d4f43-e1b6-42c2-badb-93a219f2338f); lib. bdg. 35.93 (978-0-7660-3319-1(8), 5d444e32-dbd3-48fb-83c2-fefb3e94148c) Enslow Publishing, LLC.

Houghton, Sarah. Elie Wiesel: A Holocaust Survivor Cries Out for Peace. 2003. (High Five Reading - Green Ser.). (ENG., Illus.). 48p. (J). (gr. 3-4). per. 9.00 (978-0-7368-2833-8(8)) Capstone.

—Elie Wiesel Set: A Holocaust Survivor Cries Out for Peace, 6. 2003. (High Five Reading - Green Ser.). (ENG.). 48p. (gr. 3-4). pap. 54.00 (978-0-7368-2843-7(5)) Capstone.

Kacer, Kathy. Hiding Edith: A True Story, 1 vol. 2006. (Holocaust Remembrance Series for Young Readers Ser.: 8). (ENG., Illus.). 152p. (J). (gr. 4-8). pap. 14.95 (978-1-897187-06-7(8)) Second Story Pr. CAN. Dist: Orca Bk. Pubs. USA.

Killcoyne, Hope Lourie. Anne Frank: Heroic Diarist of the Holocaust, 1 vol., 1. 2015. (Britannica Beginner Bios Ser.). (ENG., Illus.). 32p. (J). (gr. 2-3). pap. 13.90 (978-1-5081-0061-4(6), 75537ed8-53b8-4d8f-a786-4e37995b2ba7, Britannica Educational Publishing) Rosen Publishing Group, Inc., The.

Koestler-Grack, Rachel. Elie Wiesel: Witness for Humanity, 1 vol. 2009. (Life Portraits Ser.). (ENG., Illus.). 112p. (J). (gr. 6-8). lib. bdg. 38.67 (978-1-4339-0054-9(8), 74f0f7fc-d07c-4729-897a-72060673239c) Stevens, Gareth Publishing LLLP.

Kramer, Ann. World History Biographies: Anne Frank: The Young Writer Who Told the World Her Story. 2009. (National Geographic World History Biographies Ser.). (ENG., Illus.). 64p. (J). (gr. 3-7). 7.99 (978-1-4263-0414-9(5), National Geographic Kids) Disney Publishing Worldwide.

Landau, Abraham, et al. Branded on My Arm & in My Soul: A Holocaust Memoir. 2011. (Illus.). 144p. 50.00 (978-0-932027-20-7(2)) Spinner Pubns., Inc.

—Branded on My Arm & in My Soul: The Holocaust Memoir of Abraham Landau. 2011. (Illus.). 144p. pap. 25.00 (978-0-932027-19-1(9)) Spinner Pubns., Inc.

Lee, Carol Ann. Anne Frank & the Children of the Holocaust. 2008. (ENG., Illus.). 256p. (J). (gr. 5-18). 7.99 (978-0-14-241069-1(1), Puffin Books) Penguin Young Readers Group.

Levy, Max. Brief Jewish Biographies in Biblical, Post-Biblical & Talmudical Times. 2011. 190p. 42.95 (978-1-258-06674-1(2)) Literary Licensing, LLC.

J K L

Leyson, Leon. The Boy on the Wooden Box: How the Impossible Became Possible ... on Schindler's List. (ENG., Illus.). (J). (gr. 4-9). 2015. 256p. pap. 9.99 *(978-1-4424-9782-5(3))* 2013. 240p. 19.99 *(978-1-4424-9781-8(5))* Simon & Schuster Children's Publishing. (Atheneum Bks. for Young Readers).

—The Boy on the Wooden Box: How the Impossible Became Possible ... on Schindler's List. 2015. lib. bdg. 19.65 *(978-0-606-36097-5(2))* Turtleback.

Lobel, Anita. No Pretty Pictures. 2008. (ENG.). 288p. (J). (gr. 5). pap. 7.99 *(978-0-06-156589-2(X)*, Greenwillow Bks.) HarperCollins Pubs.

—No Pretty Pictures: A Child of War. 2008. (J). (gr. 5-8). lib. bdg. 18.40 *(978-0-613-28590-2(5))* Turtleback.

McDowell, Pamela. Anne Frank. 2014. (Illus.). 24p. (J). *(978-1-4896-2456-7(2))* Weigl Pubs., Inc.

Michelson, Richard. As Good As Anybody: Martin Luther King, Jr. , & Abraham Joshua Heschel's Amazing March Toward Freedom. ón, Raul, illus. 2013. (ENG.). 40p. (J). (gr. 1-4). 8.99 *(978-0-385-75387-6(X)*, Dragonfly Bks.) Random Hse. Children's Bks.

—Lipman Pike: America's First Home Run King. Pullen, Zachary, illus. 2011. (ENG.). 32p. (J). (gr. 1-4). 16.95 *(978-1-58536-465-7(7)*, 202186) Sleeping Bear Pr.

Miklowitz, Gloria. Anne Frank. 2009. pap. 13.25 *(978-1-60559-053-0(3))* Hameray Publishing Group, Inc.

Parks, Peggy J. Anne Frank. 2016. (ENG.). 80p. (J). (gr. 5-12). 38.60 *(978-1-60152-946-6(5))* ReferencePoint Pr., Inc.

Poole, Josephine. Anne Frank. Barrett, Angela, illus. 2nd ed. 2020. 40p. (J). pap. 15.99 *(978-0-09-940976-2(3)*, Red Fox) Random House Children's Books GBR. Dist: Independent Pubs. Group.

Rogow, Sally M. Faces of Courage: Young Heroes of World War II. 2008. (ENG., Illus.). 162p. (J). pap. *(978-1-894694-67-4(8))* Granville Island Publishing.

Rose, Or N. Abraham Joshua Heschel: Man of Spirit, Man of Action. 2003. (ENG., Illus.). 80p. pap. 9.95 *(978-0-8276-0758-3(X))* Jewish Pubn. Society.

Rubin, Susan Goldman & Weissberger, Ela. The Cat with the Yellow Star: Coming of Age in Terezin. 2008. (ENG., Illus.). 40p. (J). (gr. 3-7). pap. 8.99 *(978-0-8234-2154-1(6))* Holiday Hse., Inc.

Russo, Marisabina. Always Remember Me: How One Family Survived World War II. Russo, Marisabina, illus. 2005. (ENG., Illus.). 48p. (J). (gr. 1-5). 24.99 *(978-0-689-86920-4(7)*, Atheneum Bks. for Young Readers) Simon & Schuster Children's Publishing.

Sasso, Sandy Eisenberg. Anne Frank & Remembering Tree. Steiskal, Erika, illus. 2015. (ENG.). 32p. (J). 16.00 *(978-1-55896-738-0(9)*, Skinner Hse. Bks.) Unitarian Universalist Assn.

Schloss, Eva & Powers, Barbara. The Promise: The Moving Story of a Family in the Holocaust. Yaron, Sophie, illus. 2006. 160p. (J). (gr. 13-18). 12.99 *(978-0-14-132081-6(8))* Penguin Bks., Ltd. GBR. Dist: Independent Pubs. Group.

Shackleton, Kath, ed. Survivors of the Holocaust: True Stories of Six Extraordinary Children. Whittingham, Zane, illus. 2019. (ENG.). 96p. (J). (gr. 3-7). 19.99 *(978-1-4926-8892-1(4))* Sourcebooks, Inc.

Sherman, Jill. Gal Gadot: Soldier, Model, Wonder Woman. 2018. (Gateway Biographies Ser.). (ENG., Illus.). 48p. (J). (gr. 4-8). 31.99 *(978-1-5415-2358-6(X)*, d2d1310c-1b61-4586-9092-c59559e4db4f, Lerner Pubns.) Lerner Publishing Group.

Singer, Flora M. Flora - I Was but A Child. 2007. 180p. (J). pap. 26.50 *(978-0-9760739-8-7(6))* Yad Vashem Pubns. ISR. Dist: Coronet Bks.

Speregen, Devra Newberger. Ilan Ramon: Jewish Star. 2004. (ENG., Illus.). 120p. pap. 13.00 *(978-0-8276-0769-9(5))* Jewish Pubn. Society.

Spielman, Gloria. Janusz Korczak's Children. Archambault, Matthew, illus. 2007. (Kar-Ben for Older Readers Ser.). (ENG.). 40p. (J). (gr. 3-7). lib. bdg. 17.95 *(978-1-58013-255-8(3)*, Kar-Ben Publishing) Lerner Publishing Group.

Thomson, Ruth. Terezin: Voices from the Holocaust. 2013. (ENG., Illus.). 64p. (YA). (gr. 5-9). pap. 11.99 *(978-0-7636-6466-4(9))* Candlewick Pr.

Van Maarsen, Jacqueline. A Friend Called Anne: One Girl's Story of War, Peace, & a Unique Friendship with Anne Frank. 2007. (Illus.). 163p. (J). (gr. 5-9). 14.65 *(978-0-7569-8146-4(8))* Perfection Learning Corp.

van Maarsen, Jacqueline & Lee, Carol Ann. A Friend Called Anne. 2007. (ENG., Illus.). 176p. (J). (gr. 3-7). 6.99 *(978-0-14-240719-6(4)*, Puffin Books) Penguin Young Readers Group.

Watad, Mahmoud & Grob, Leonard. Teen Voices from the Holy Land: Who Am I to You? 2007. (Illus.). 221p. (gr. 7). per. 21.99 *(978-1-59102-535-1(4))* Prometheus Bks., Pubs.

Waxman, Laura Hamilton. Anne Frank. 2009. (History Maker Biographies Ser.). (ENG.). 48p. (gr. 3-6). 27.93 *(978-0-7613-4221-2(4)*, Lerner Pubns.) Lerner Publishing Group.

Winkelstein, Steven Paul. Brisko: A True Tale of Holocaust Survival. Juliano, Dana, illus. 2014. 104p. (J). *(978-0-9824498-6-8(0))* Winkelstein Studios.

Winter, Jonah. Ruth Bader Ginsburg: The Case of R. B. G. vs. Inequality. Innerst, Stacy, illus. 2017. (ENG.). 48p. (J). (gr. 1-4). 18.95 *(978-1-4197-2559-3(9)*, 1163401, Abrams Bks. for Young Readers) Abrams, Inc.

JEWS—CZECH REPUBLIC—FICTION

Kimmel, Eric A. The Golem's Latkes, 0 vols. Jasinski, Aaron, illus. 2012. (ENG.). 40p. (J). (gr. -1-3). 17.99 *(978-0-7614-5904-0(9)*, 9780761459040, Two Lions) Amazon Publishing.

JEWS—FESTIVALS

see Fasts and Feasts—Judaism

JEWS—FICTION

A. L. O. E. The Triumph over Midian. 2006. 344p. per. 23.99 *(978-1-4255-3466-0(X))* Michigan Publishing.

Aaron, Chester. Gideon. 2009. (ENG., Illus.). 190p. (YA). pap. 12.99 *(978-1-934841-62-4(5)*, Zumaya Thresholds) Zumaya Pubns. LLC.

Abraham, Michelle Shapiro. Good Night, Lilah Tov. Alko, Selina, illus. 2004. pap. 6.95 *(978-0-8074-0784-4(4)*, 101975) URJ Pr.

—My Cousin Tamar Lives in Israel (Paperback) Koffsky, Ann D., illus. 2007. (ENG.). 14p. (J). (gr. -1). pap. 9.95 *(978-0-8074-0989-3(8)*, 8c4402fe-9404-4318-88cf-4a9162fd8179) Behrman Hse., Inc.

Abramson, Susan & Dvorkin, Aaron. Who Hogged the Hallah? A Shabbat Shabang. 2008. (Illus.). 80p. (J). pap. 9.95 *(978-0-9659546-5-5(X))* Oak Leaf Systems.

Adelson, Leone. The Mystery Bear: A Purim Story. Howland, Naomi, tr. Howland, Naomi, illus. 2004. 32p. (J). (gr. -1-2). 15.00 *(978-0-618-33727-9(X)*, Clarion Bks.) HarperCollins Pubs.

Adler, Ella. A Day Full of Mitzvos. 2009. (ENG., Illus.). 26p. (J). *(978-1-4226-0949-1(9))* Mesorah Pubns., Ltd.

Appelfeld, Aharon. Adam & Thomas. Green, Jeffrey M., tr. Dumas, Philippe, illus. 2017. 160p. (J). (gr. 3-7). pap. 14.95 *(978-1-60980-744-3(8)*, Triangle Square) Seven Stories Pr.

—Long Summer Nights. Green, Jeffrey, tr. Mintzi, Vali, illus. 2019. (ENG.). 160p. (J). (gr. 5-9). 18.95 *(978-1-60980-898-3(3)*, Triangle Square) Seven Stories Pr.

Arato, Rona. Mrs. Kaputnik's Pool Hall & Matzo Ball Emporium. 2010. (Illus.). 192p. (J). (gr. 4-7). pap. 9.95 *(978-0-88776-967-2(5)*, Tundra Bks.) Tundra Bks. CAN. Dist: Penguin Random Hse. LLC.

Artscroll Mesorah. The Best of Olomeinu: Stories for All Year 'Round: an Anthology of 20 Exciting, Inspiring & Beautifully Illustrating Stories for Young & Old (ArtScroll Youth) 2003. (ENG.). 136p. 13.99 *(978-1-57819-398-1(2)*, BO1H) Mesorah Pubns., Ltd.

Asner, Anne-Marie. Klutzy Boy. Asner, Anne-Marie, illus. l.t. ed. 2007. (ENG., Illus.). 32p. (J). (gr. -1-2). per. 6.95 *(978-0-9753629-4-5(1))* Matzah Ball Bks.

Balsley, Tilda & Fischer, Ellen. It's a Mitzvah, Grover! Leigh, Tom, illus. 2013. (ENG.). 24p. (J). (gr. -1-1). 6.99 *(978-0-7613-7563-0(5)*, 529dc0d1-53a2-4b4d-a2c2-cb5a36c1bbb3); lib. bdg. 16.95 *(978-0-7613-7562-3(7))* Lerner Publishing Group. (Kar-Ben Publishing).

Baraitser, Marion & Evans, Anna. Home Number One. 2006. (ENG., Illus.). 63p. (YA). pap. *(978-0-9529426-7-2(4))* Loki Books Ltd.

Behar, Ruth. Letters from Cuba. 2020. (ENG., Illus.). 272p. (J). (gr. 5). 17.99 *(978-0-525-51647-7(6)*, Nancy Paulsen Books) Penguin Young Readers Group.

Benenfeld, Rikki. I Go to Eretz Yisroel. Benenfeld, Rikki, illus. 2017. (Toddler Experience Ser.). (ENG., Illus.). 28p. (J). 11.95 *(978-1-929628-92-6(7))* Hachai Publishing.

—Let's Go to the Park. 2015. (ENG., Illus.). 36p. (J). 11.99 *(978-1-929628-82-7(X))* Hachai Publishing.

—Let's Meet Community Helpers. Benenfeld, Rikki, illus. 2013. (ENG., Illus.). 32p. (J). 11.99 *(978-1-929628-75-9(7))* Hachai Publishing.

Benjamin, Amanda. Journey Through Jerusalem. Blumenfeld, Tamar, illus. 2017. (ENG.). 24p. (J). 17.95 *(978-1-68115-531-9(1)*, f58f9449-5f98-48e5-b246-fca39f6395c3) Behrman Hse., Inc.

Berkowitz, Leah Rachel. The World Needs Beautiful Things. Fabbri, Daniele, illus. 2018. (ENG.). 32p. (J). (gr. -1-2). 12.99 *(978-1-5124-4448-3(0)*, b25e07dc-215c-42e1-ae78-a5ae65884f21, Kar-Ben Publishing) Lerner Publishing Group.

Berman, Seryl. Around the Shabbos Table. Binus, Ari, illus. 2008. (ENG.). 40p. (J). (gr. -1-k). pap. 11.99 *(978-1-929628-44-5(7))* Hachai Publishing.

Bietz, Barbara. The Sundown Kid: A Southwestern Shabbat. 2017. (ENG., Illus.). 32p. (J). (gr. k-2). pap. 8.95 *(978-1-939160-94-2(4))* August Hse. Pubs., Inc.

Blanc, Esther Silverstein & Eagle, Godeane. Long Johns for a Small Chicken. Dixon, Tennessee, illus. 2003. (J). 16.95 *(978-1-884244-23-0(8))* volcano pr.

Blankman, Anne. Prisoner of Night & Fog. (ENG.). (YA). (gr. 8). 2015. 432p. pap. 10.99 *(978-0-06-227882-1(7))* 2014. 416p. 17.99 *(978-0-06-227881-4(9))* HarperCollins Pubs. (Balzer & Bray).

Blitz, Shmuel. The Adventures of Aliza & Dovid: Holidays at the Farm. Katz, Tova, illus. 2005. (ArtScroll Youth Ser.). 48p. (J). *(978-1-4226-0021-4(1))* Mesorah Pubns., Ltd.

—Bedtime Stories to Make You Smile (Artscroll Youth Series) 2003. (ArtScroll Youth Ser.). (ENG., Illus.). 47p. (J). 14.99 *(978-1-57819-745-3(7)*, BEDS) Mesorah Pubns., Ltd.

—Every Story Has a Soul. 2006. (ENG., Illus.). 47p. (J). 15.99 *(978-1-4226-0224-9(9))* Mesorah Pubns., Ltd.

Booth, Bradley. The Watchers. 2017. 144p. (J). pap. *(978-0-8163-6278-3(5))* Pacific Pr. Publishing Assn.

Bradley, Kimberly Brubaker. The War I Finally Won. (ENG.). (J). (gr. 4-7). 2018. 416p. 9.99 *(978-0-14-751681-7(1)*, Puffin Books) 2017. 400p. 18.99 *(978-0-525-42920-3(4)*, Dial Bks) Penguin Young Readers Group.

Brightwood, Laura, illus. Wise People of Helm. Brightwood, Laura, . 2006. (J). *(978-0-9779290-4-7(3))* 3-C Institute for Social Development.

Brown, Jason Robert. Tickety Tock. GrandPré, Mary, illus. 2008. 32p. (J). (gr. -1-3). lib. bdg. 18.89 *(978-0-06-078753-0(8)*, Geringer, Laura Book) HarperCollins Pubs.

Carlson, Claudia. Avi & the Snowy Day. Decker, C. B., illus. 2017. (ENG.). 32p. (J). 9.95 *(978-1-68115-528-9(1)*, 6363aae9-476f-492a-a905-b7d889214a40) Behrman Hse., Inc.

—Avi the Ambulance Goes to School. Carlson, Claudia, illus. 2015. (ENG., Illus.). 32p. (J). pap. 9.95 *(978-1-68115-503-6(6)*, 193dd950-0960-428f-9e07-e9f10212d629) Behrman Hse., Inc.

—Avi to the Rescue. Decker, C. B., illus. 2016. (ENG.). 32p. (J). pap. 9.95 *(978-1-68115-512-8(5)*, 1454631d-d406-41ce-8105-6bb363db65a6) Behrman Hse., Inc.

Cerrito, Angela. The Safest Lie. 2018. 192p. (J). (gr. 3-7). pap. 7.99 *(978-0-8234-4046-7(X))* Holiday Hse., Inc.

Chaikin, Miriam. Hardlucky: The Story of a Boy Who Learns How to Think Before He Acts. Lisowski, Gabriel, illus. 2012. (ENG.). 40p. (J). (gr. -1-3). 16.95 *(978-1-61608-963-4(6)*, 608963, Sky Pony Pr.) Skyhorse Publishing Co., Inc.

Chotjewitz, David. Daniel Half Human. Orgel, Doris, tr. 2006. (ENG., Illus.). 336p. (YA). (gr. 7). reprint ed. mass mkt. 11.99 *(978-0-689-85748-5(9)*, Simon Pulse) Simon Pulse.

Ciddor, Anna. The Family with Two Front Doors. 2018. (ENG., Illus.). 208p. (J). (gr. 3-6). 12.99 *(978-1-5415-0011-2(3)*, cde459b6-6cee-4eae-8964-4b6e58cdfefc); pap. 6.99 *(978-1-5415-0012-9(1)*, 7bf0f625-be94-4f2c-aa3e-8be52aaf66e4) Lerner Publishing Group. (Kar-Ben Publishing).

Cleveland, Rob. The Magic Apple: A Middle Eastern Folktale. Hoffmire, Baird, illus. 2006. (Story Cove Ser.). (ENG.). 32p. (J). (gr. -1-3). pap. 4.95 *(978-0-87483-800-8(2))* August Hse. Pubs., Inc.

Cohen, Barbara. The Carp in the Bathtub. 48p. (J). (gr. 2-4). pap. 5.95 *(978-0-8072-1332-2(2)*, Listening Library) Random Hse. Audio Publishing Group.

Cohen, Deborah Bodin. Engineer Ari & the Sukkah Express. Kober, Shahar, illus. 2010. (Sukkot & Simchat Torah Ser.). (ENG.). 32p. (J). (gr. k-3). lib. bdg. 17.95 *(978-0-7613-5126-9(4)*, Kar-Ben Publishing) Lerner Publishing Group.

—Engineer Arielle & the Israel Independence Day Surprise. Orrelle, Yael Kimhi, illus. 2017. (ENG.). 32p. (J). (gr. k-3). pap. 7.99 *(978-1-5124-2095-1(6)*, dd3698d6-6646-4d26-b8b8-9f61ee612b7f, Kar-Ben Publishing) Lerner Publishing Group.

—The Seventh Day. Hall, Melanie, illus. 2005. (ENG.). 24p. (J). (gr. -1-2). 16.95 *(978-0-929371-24-5(0)*, Kar-Ben Publishing) Lerner Publishing Group.

Cohen, Leslie, et al. Jewish Love Stories for Kids: An Anthology of Short Stories. 2005. (Jewish Stories for Kids Ser.). 232p. (J). 16.95 *(978-1-930143-45-6(1)*, 3451); pap. 12.95 *(978-1-930143-46-3(X)*, 346X) Simcha Media Group. (Devora Publishing).

Cohen, R. G. The Place That I Love. Levitas, Alexander, illus. 2006. (ENG.). 30p. (J). 11.99 *(978-1-929628-29-2(3))* Hachai Publishing.

Cooper, Alexandra. Spin the Dreidel! Gévry, Claudine & Gévry, Claudine, illus. 2004. (ENG.). 14p. (J). (gr. -1-2). bds. 8.99 *(978-0-689-86430-8(2)*, Little Simon) Little Simon.

Dauvillier, Loïc. Hidden: a Child's Story of the Holocaust. Lizano, Marc, illus. 2014. (ENG.). 80p. (J). (gr. 1-5). 18.99 *(978-1-59643-873-6(8)*, 900111569, First Second Bks.) Roaring Brook Pr.

Deutsch, Barry. Hereville: How Mirka Got Her Sword. 2012. (Hereville Ser.). (ENG., Illus.). 144p. (J). (gr. 3-7). pap. 12.99 *(978-1-4197-0619-6(5)*, 667403) Abrams, Inc.

Djilmand, Shira Yehudit. The Secret of the Ruined Castle: And Other Stories. 2009. 148p. (J). *(978-1-56871-521-6(8))* Targum Pr., Inc.

Dostis, Isaac & Haddad Ikonomopoulos, Marcia. Ten Gold Medals: Glory or Freedom. 2005. (Illus.). ii, 72p. (J). *(978-0-8197-0770-3(8))* Bloch Publishing Co.

Draus, Naudia Burtwell. My Grandma Wears A Number: How One Girl Survived World War Ii. 2011. 40p. (gr. 4-6). pap. 19.57 *(978-1-4269-3351-6(7))* Trafford Publishing.

Dublin, Anne. The Baby Experiment: A Novel (Large Print 16pt) 2013. 172p. pap. *(978-1-4596-6337-4(3))* ReadHowYouWant.com, Ltd.

—A Cage Without Bars, 1 vol. 2018. (ENG.). 154p. (J). (gr. 5-8). pap. 11.95 *(978-1-77260-069-8(5))* Second Story Pr. CAN. Dist: Orca Bk. Pubs. USA.

Edwards, Michelle. Chicken Man. (ENG.). 32p. (J). 2009. pap. 10.95 *(978-1-58838-237-5(0)*, 8701) 3rd ed. 2007. (Illus.). 16.95 *(978-1-58838-223-8(0)*, 8700) NewSouth, Inc. (NewSouth Bks.).

Elissa, Barbara. The Remarkable Journey of Josh's Kippah. Zaman, Farida, illus. 2010. (ENG.). (J). (gr. -1-2). 24p. lib. bdg. 7.95 *(978-0-8225-9911-1(2)*, 8e962b4b-1989-4e3d-819d-f40ffae64988); 32p. pap. 7.95 *(978-0-8225-9933-3(3))* Lerner Publishing Group. (Kar-Ben Publishing).

Elkeles, Simone. How to Ruin a Summer Vacation. 2006. (How to Ruin a Summer Vacation Novel Ser.: 1). (ENG.). 240p. (YA). (gr. 9-12). pap. 11.99 *(978-0-7387-0961-1(1)*, 0738709611, Flux) North Star Editions.

Fabiyi, Jan Goldin. Where Shabbat Lives. Rubinroit, Sue, illus. 2008. (ENG.). 12p. (J). (gr. -1 — 1). bds. 5.95 *(978-0-8225-8946-4(X)*, 461e912a-547a-4d9c-8255-2c823b815bb4, Kar-Ben Publishing) Lerner Publishing Group.

Flam, Chanie. Erev Shabbos. (Goldie Gold Board Book Ser.: Vol. 2). (Illus.). (J). (gr. -1-1). bds. 4.95 *(978-1-58330-026-8(0))* Feldheim Pubs.

Fleischman, Sid. The Entertainer & the Dybbuk. 2009. (ENG.). 192p. (J). (gr. 4-9). pap. 6.99 *(978-0-06-177140-8(6)*, Greenwillow Bks.) HarperCollins Pubs.

Flor Ada, Alma. Celebrate Hanukkah with Bubbe's Tales. Hayes, Joe & Franco, Sharon, trs. from SPA. Epelbaum, Mariano, illus. 2007. (Cuentos para Celebrar / Stories to Celebrate Ser.). 30p. (J). (gr. k-6). per. 11.95 *(978-1-59820-134-5(4))* Santillana USA Publishing Co., Inc.

Frankel, Valerie Estelle. Chelm for the Holidays. Wimmer, Sonja, illus. 2019. (ENG.). 72p. (J). (gr. 3-9). pap. 8.99 *(978-1-5415-5462-7(0)*, afdf6bb4-341d-400d-b5f2-173f45c6a355, Kar-Ben Publishing) Lerner Publishing Group.

Fridman, Sashi. The Great Friday Clean-up (French Flap) Salem, Iosi, illus. 2009. 32p. 12.95 *(978-1-934440-77-3(9)*, Pitspopany Pr.) Simcha Media Group.

—The Great Friday Clean-up (Hard Cover) Salem, Iosi, illus. 2009. 32p. 17.95 *(978-1-934440-93-3(0)*, Pitspopany Pr.) Simcha Media Group.

Fruchter, Yaakov. Best of Olomeinu - Series 2: Stories for All Year 'Round. 2003. 136p. pap. 10.99 *(978-1-57819-399-8(0)*, BO1P) Mesorah Pubns., Ltd.

Ganz, Yaffa. The Adventures of Jeremy & Heddy Levi. Katz, Avi, illus. 2005. 204p. (J). 16.95 *(978-1-930143-50-0(8)*, 3508); pap. 12.95 *(978-1-930143-51-7(6)*, 3516) Simcha Media Group. (Devora Publishing).

—The Travels & Tales of Dr. Emanuel J. Mitzva. 2003. (J). 15.99 *(978-1-58330-581-2(5))* Feldheim Pubs.

Geller, Beverly. Ellies Shabbat Surprise. 2008. (ENG.). 32p. 13.95 *(978-965-229-390-9(3))* Gefen Publishing Hse., Ltd ISR. Dist: Gefen Bks.

Gellman, Ellie B. Shai's Shabbat Walk. Conger, Holli, illus. 2014. (ENG.). 12p. (J). (gr. -1 — 1). bds. 5.95 *(978-1-4677-4949-7(4)*, 7f8f9e16-92c6-44c5-8d3c-44056cdf0745, Kar-Ben Publishing) Lerner Publishing Group.

Gibbs, Noni & Kahrs, Christina. Rahab's Promise. Vieira, Andrei, illus. 2007. 32p. (J). (gr. -1-2). pap. 9.99 *(978-0-8127-0432-7(0))* Autumn Hse. Publishing Co.

Gidwitz, Adam. The Inquisitor's Tale: Or, the Three Magical Children & Their Holy Dog. Aly, Hatem, illus. (ENG.). (J). (gr. 5). 2018. 400p. 9.99 *(978-0-14-242737-8(3)*, Puffin Books) 2016. 384p. 18.99 *(978-0-525-42616-5(7)*, Dutton Books for Young Readers) Penguin Young Readers Group.

—The Inquisitor's Tale: Or, the Three Magical Children & Their Holy Dog. 2018. lib. bdg. 20.85 *(978-0-606-40873-8(8))* Turtleback.

Gilani-Williams, Fawzia. Yaffa & Fatima: Shalom, Salaam. Fedele, Chiara, illus. 2017. (ENG.). 24p. (J). (gr. -1-3). 17.99 *(978-1-4677-8938-7(0)*, 8b6f0d02-4214-4d99-9d3c-9fb65bc60527, Kar-Ben Publishing) Lerner Publishing Group.

Glaser, Linda. Hannah's Way. Gustavson, Adam, illus. 2012. (ENG.). 32p. (J). (gr. k-3). pap. 7.95 *(978-0-7613-5138-2(8)*, 59392402-0f00-41e2-b7cf-f8230b7c8ebc, Kar-Ben Publishing) Lerner Publishing Group.

—Way Too Many Latkes: A Hanukkah in Chelm. Zolotic, Aleksandar, illus. 2017. (ENG.). 32p. (J). (gr. -1-2). 17.99 *(978-1-5124-2092-0(1)*, 6f2e3963-2317-45ae-963d-a2da005bd7eb, Kar-Ben Publishing) Lerner Publishing Group.

Glasthal, Jacqueline B. Liberty on 23rd Street. Reingold, Alan, illus. 2006. (Adventures in America Ser.). (gr. 4). 14.95 net. *(978-1-893110-45-8(1))* Silver Moon Pr.

Glatshteyn, Yankev. Emil & Karl: A Novel. Shandler, Jeffrey, tr. 2008. (ENG.). 208p. (J). (gr. 4-9). per. 18.99 *(978-0-312-37387-0(2)*, 900045531) Square Fish.

Gleitzman, Morris. Maybe. 2018. (Once/Now/Then/after Ser.). (ENG.). 240p. (J). (gr. 4-6). pap. 13.99 *(978-0-14-138865-6(X))* Penguin Bks., Ltd. GBR. Dist: Independent Pubs. Group.

—Now. 2013. (Once Ser.: 3). (ENG.). 192p. (YA). (gr. 7). pap. 10.99 *(978-1-250-03417-5(5)*, 900120589) Square Fish.

—Once. 2005. 160p. (J). pap. *(978-0-14-330195-0(0)*, Puffin) Penguin Publishing Group.

—Once. 2013. (Once Ser.: 1). (ENG.). 192p. (YA). (gr. 7). pap. 10.99 *(978-0-312-65304-0(2)*, 900069444) Square Fish.

—Then. 2013. (Once Ser.: 2). (ENG.). 224p. (YA). (gr. 7). pap. 11.99 *(978-1-250-00341-6(5)*, 900079882) Square Fish.

Goddu, Krystyna Poray. An Unlikely Ballerina. Kawa, Cosei, illus. 2018. (ENG.). 32p. (J). (gr. k-4). 17.99 *(978-1-5124-8362-8(1)*, 104ccfd2-7f48-4caa-b738-4ff6f233af46, Kar-Ben Publishing) Lerner Publishing Group.

Goelman, Ari. The Path of Names. 2013. (Illus.). 339p. (J). pap. *(978-0-545-47431-3(0)*, Levine, Arthur A. Bks.) Scholastic, Inc.

Gold, R. & Marmorshteyn, M. H. Hershi Lernt Zikh Farmestn MIT Gefiln. Leybler, Nehameh, illus. 2018. (YID.). (J). *(978-1-68091-229-6(1))* Kinder Shpiel USA, Inc.

Goldberg, Barbara. Mindy's Passover Parsley. 2008. 24p. per. 24.95 *(978-1-4241-9779-8(1))* America Star Bks.

Goldberg, Malky. What Else Do I Say? A Lift the Flap Book. Argoff, Patti, illus. 2007. (ENG.). (J). (gr. -1-k). bds. 11.99 *(978-1-929628-34-6(X))* Hachai Publishing.

Goldin, Barbara Diamond. A Mountain of Blintzes, 0 vols. McGrory, Anik, illus. 2012. (ENG.). 32p. (J). (gr. k-3). pap. 6.99 *(978-0-7614-5790-9(9)*, 9780761457909, Two Lions) Amazon Publishing.

Gonzalez, Christina Diaz. A Thunderous Whisper. 2013. (Illus.). 320p. (J). (gr. 5). pap. 8.99 *(978-0-375-87371-3(6)*, Yearling) Random Hse. Children's Bks.

Got, Eli & Gold, D., illus. The Cryptic Script. 2018. 74p. (J). *(978-1-68091-257-9(7))* Kinder Shpiel USA, Inc.

Gratz, Alan, et al. Prisoner B-3087. 2013. (ENG.). 272p. (J). (gr. 5-9). 17.99 *(978-0-545-45901-3(X)*, Scholastic Pr.) Scholastic, Inc.

Graudin, Ryan. Blood for Blood. (Wolf by Wolf Ser.: 2). (ENG.). (YA). (gr. 10-17). 2017. 592p. pap. 10.99 *(978-0-316-40516-4(7))* 2016. 496p. 17.99 *(978-0-316-40515-7(9))* Little, Brown Bks. for Young Readers.

Greenberg, David E. The Ugly Brown Pear. 2010. 40p. pap. 12.96 *(978-0-557-28055-1(9))* Lulu Pr., Inc.

Greenberger, Tehilla. Gifts to Treasure. Toron, Eli, illus. 2007. (Fun to Read Book). (ENG.). 224p. (J). per. 10.95 *(978-1-929628-32-2(3))* Hachai Publishing.

Greenspan, Sophie. Masada Will Not Fall Again: A Novel. 2019. (ENG., Illus.). 186p. (J). (gr. 3-5). pap. 17.95 *(978-0-8276-1469-7(1))* Jewish Pubn. Society.

Grubman, Bonnie. Oy Vey! Life in a Shoe. Mottram, Dave, illus. 2019. *(978-1-68115-556-2(7)*, Apples & Honey Pr.) Behrman Hse., Inc.

—Oy Vey Life in a Shoe. Mottram, Dave, illus. 2016. (ENG.). 32p. (J). 17.95 *(978-1-68115-515-9(X)*, 59dea969-ab96-4880-8181-e7254c0178d3) Behrman Hse., Inc.

Halahmy, Miriam. Saving Hanno: The Story of a Refugee Dog. 2019. (ENG.). 112p. (J). (gr. 3-7). 17.99 *(978-0-8234-4165-5(2))* Holiday Hse., Inc.

Hannigan, Lynne. Sam's Passover. 2004. (Illus.). 32p. pap. 5.95 *(978-0-7136-4084-7(7)*, 93342, A&C Black) Bloomsbury Publishing Plc GBR. Dist: Consortium Bk. Sales & Distribution.

Hecht, Zalmy. My Very Own Letter. Judowitz, Chani, illus. 2016. (ENG.). 20p. (J). 11.95 *(978-1-929628-89-6(7))* Hachai Publishing.

Hering, Marianne & Younger, Marshal. Escape to the Hiding Place. 2012. (AIO Imagination Station Bks.: 9). (ENG., Illus.). 128p. (J). pap. 5.99 *(978-1-58997-693-1(2)*, 4609384) Focus on the Family Publishing.

Herman, Charlotte. My Chocolate Year: A Novel with 12 Recipes. Pham, LeUyen, illus. 2008. (ENG.). 176p. (J). (gr. 3-7). 15.99 *(978-1-4169-3341-0(7)*, Simon & Schuster Bks. For Young Readers) Simon & Schuster Bks. For Young Readers.

Herman, Debbie. Rosie Saves the World. Lyon, Tammie, illus. 2017. (ENG.). 32p. (J). (gr. -1-2). 17.99 *(978-1-5124-2085-2(9)*, 1a26aeae-930a-429d-807d-fd9e48a3eb2b, Kar-Ben Publishing) Lerner Publishing Group.

Herman, Michael. Under the Sabbath Lamp. Massari, Alida, illus. 2017. (ENG.). 32p. (J). (gr. -1-2). 17.99

(978-1-5124-0841-6(7), 9b9c5015-2225-426f-b181-850a9deba823, Kar-Ben Publishing) Lerner Publishing Group.

Hesse, Karen. Letters from Rifka. 2009. 9.00 (978-0-7848-2599-0(8), Everbind) Marco Bk. Co.

—Letters from Rifka. 2008. (ENG.). 148p. 17.00 (978-1-60686-224-7(3)) Perfection Learning Corp.

—Letters from Rifka. 2009. (ENG.). 176p. (J). (gr. 4-6). pap. 7.99 (978-0-312-53561-2(9), 900054737) Square Fish.

Hest, Amy. When Jessie Came Across the Sea. 2003. 17.20 (978-0-613-69484-1(8)) Turtleback.

House, Behrman. Shalom Coloring: Jewish Designs for Contemplation & Calm. 2015. (Illus.). 1p. (J). pap. 11.95 (978-0-87441-941-2(7), e24bf900-15ad-43cc-96e4-4d5edb60565b) Behrman Hse., Inc.

Hyde, Heidi Smith. Feivel's Flying Horses. van der Sterre, Johanna, illus. 2010. (ENG.). 32p. (J). (gr. k-4). lib. bdg. 17.95 (978-0-7613-3957-1(4), Kar-Ben Publishing) Lerner Publishing Group.

Ioannides, Mara W. Cohen. A Shout in the Sunshine. 2007. (ENG.). 120p. (gr. 5). per. 14.95 (978-0-8276-0838-2(1)) Jewish Pubn. Society.

Irenshtain, Hadas. Kligerovke: Aza Shtetele: Mesholim Fun Pirke Oves - in Bilder. Vainreb, M., illus. 2017. (YID.). 73p. (978-1-68091-168-8(6)) Kinder Shpiel USA, Inc.

Ish-Kishor, Sulamith. A Boy of Old Prague. Shahn, Ben, illus. 2008. (Dover Children's Classics Ser.). (ENG.). 96p. (J). (gr. 4-6). pap. 3.99 (978-0-486-46766-5(X), 46766X) Dover Pubns., Inc.

Jablonski, Carla. Resistance: Book 1, Bk. 1. Purvis, Leland, illus. 2010. (Resistance Ser.: 1). (ENG.). 128p. (YA). (gr. 7-12). pap. 19.99 (978-1-59643-291-8(8), 900044619, First Second Bks.) Roaring Brook Pr.

Jane, Yolen. The Devil's Arithmetic. 2014. (ENG.). 176p. (J). 11.24 (978-1-63245-218-4(9)) Lectorum Pubns., Inc.

Joffo, Joseph. A Bag of Marbles: The Graphic Novel. Bailly, Vincent, illus. 2013. (ENG.). 128p. (YA). (gr. 7-12). pap. 12.99 (978-1-4677-1516-4(6), 3cb490f5-e7ac-4c1a-8900-02f6f003202d); E-Book 43.99 (978-1-4677-1651-2(0)) Lerner Publishing Group. (Graphic Universe™).

Johnston, Tony. The Harmonica. Mazellan, Ron, illus. 2004. (ENG.). 32p. (J). (gr. 2-4). 22.44 (978-1-57091-547-5(4)) Charlesbridge Publishing, Inc.

Jules, Jacqueline. The Generous Fish. Tyrrell, Frances, illus. 2020. 40p. (J). (gr. k-3). 16.95 (978-1-937786-79-3(X), Wisdom Tales) World Wisdom, Inc.

—Goodnight Sh'ma. Hall, Melanie, illus. 2008. (ENG.). 12p. (J). (gr. -1 — 1). bds. 6.99 (978-0-8225-8945-7(1), 9f4fe877-880a-412e-aa37-60c81bb615d2, Kar-Ben Publishing) Lerner Publishing Group.

—Happy Hanukkah Lights. Shapiro, Michelle, illus. 2010. (ENG.). 12p. (J). (gr. -1 — 1). 5.95 (978-0-7613-5120-7(5), 6b1d3e67-1a45-4507-8004-6606ea176931, Kar-Ben Publishing) Lerner Publishing Group.

—What a Way to Start a New Year! A Rosh Hashanah Story. Stead, Judy, illus. 2013. (ENG.). 24p. (J). (gr. -1-2). 7.95 (978-0-7613-8117-4(1), f7438181-666c-4652-8821-3d6f7f9a904b, Kar-Ben Publishing) Lerner Publishing Group.

—The Ziz & the Hanukkah Miracle. Kahn, Katherine Janus, illus. 2006. (ENG.). 32p. (J). (gr. -1-2). lib. bdg. 17.95 (978-1-58013-160-5(3), Kar-Ben Publishing) Lerner Publishing Group.

Kacer, Kathy. The Diary of Laura's Twin, 1 vol. 2008. (Holocaust Remembrance Series for Young Readers Ser.: 9). (ENG., Illus.). 202p. (J). (gr. 4-8). pap. 14.95 (978-1-897187-39-5(4)) Second Story Pr. CAN. Dist: Orca Bk. Pubs. USA.

—Masters of Silence. 2019. (Heroes Quartet Ser.: 2). (Illus.). 272p. (J). (gr. 4-7). 18.95 (978-1-77321-262-3(1)); (ENG., pap. 9.95 (978-1-77321-261-6(3)) Annick Pr., Ltd. CAN. Dist: Publishers Group West (PGW).

—Shanghai Escape, 1 vol. 2013. (Holocaust Remembrance Series for Young Readers Ser.: 14). (ENG.). 240p. (J). (gr. 6-8). pap. 14.95 (978-1-927583-10-4(1)) Second Story Pr. CAN. Dist: Orca Bk. Pubs. USA.

—The Sound of Freedom. 2018. (Heroes Quartet Ser.: 1). (ENG.). 256p. (J). (gr. 4-7). pap. 9.95 (978-1-55451-969-9(1)) Annick Pr., Ltd. CAN. Dist: Publishers Group West (PGW).

Kalechofsky, Roberta. A Boy, a Chicken & the Lion of Judah: How Ari Became a Vegetarian. 2012. (ENG., Illus.). 50p. (J). pap. 12.00 (978-0-916288-58-7(7)) Micah Pubns.

Kamin, Rachel & The Association of Jewish Libraries Staff. The 2011 Sydney Taylor Book Award: Quest for the Best. 2011. 228p. (YA). pap. 18.00 (978-0-929262-02-4(6)) Association of Jewish Libraries.

Karlin, Ann Bell. Eight Bedtime Stories for Jewish Children. Mazo, Chaim, ed. 2012. 64p. pap. 11.95 (978-1-936778-67-6(X)) Mazo Pubs.

Kasnett, Yitzchak. The Studen't Guide to the Cohens of Tzefat. (J). pap. 3.99 (978-0-89906-849-7(9), SGCO) Mesorah Pubns., Ltd.

Katies Choice. 2005. (YA). per. (978-1-59872-217-8(4)) Instant Pub.

Kiffel-Alcheh, Jamie. Kol Hakavod: Way tc Go! Mercer, Sarah-Jayne, illus. 2019. (ENG.). 24p. (J). (gr. -1-1). 12.99 (978-1-5415-2211-4(7), b84a0d64-9428-41c8-bd4e-62d67e465030); pap. 7.99 (978-1-5415-3835-1(8), 7e7eff52-94d5-4a87-97c2-47a1b22118b3) Lerner Publishing Group. (Kar-Ben Publishing).

Killeen, Matt. Orphan Monster Spy. 2019. (ENG.). 448p. (YA). (gr. 7). pap. 11.99 (978-0-451-47875-7(4), Penguin Books) Penguin Young Readers Group.

Kimmel, Eric A. Escape from Egypt. Stevanovic, Ivica, illus. 2015. (Scarlett & Sam Ser.). (ENG.). 168p. (J). (gr. 1-3). E-Book 23.99 (978-1-4677-6207-6(5), Kar-Ben Publishing) Lerner Publishing Group.

—Hanukkah Bear. Wohnoutka, Mike, illus. (ENG.). 32p. (J). (gr. -1-3). 2014. 7.99 (978-0-8234-3169-4(X)) 2013. 17.99 (978-0-8234-2855-7(9)) Holiday Hse., Inc.

—Nicanor's Gate. Massari, Alida, illus. 2020. (ENG.). 24p. (J). (gr. -1-2). 17.99 (978-1-5415-7452-6(4), 60c73a83-3fd3-4596-9e96-c021bece5d99, Kar-Ben Publishing) Lerner Publishing Group.

—Onions & Garlic: An Old Tale. Arnold, Katya, illus. 2005. 29p. (J). (gr. k-4). reprint ed. 16.00 (978-0-7567-9638-9(5)) DIANE Publishing Co.

Kimmelman, Leslie. The Little Red Hen & the Passover Matzah. Meisel, Paul, illus. 2011. (ENG.). 32p. (J). (gr. -1-3). pap. 8.99 (978-0-8234-2327-9(1)) Holiday Hse., Inc.

Kimmelman, Leslie. The Rabbi Slurps Spaghetti. Davey, Sharon, illus. 2019. (ENG.). 24p. (J). 17.95 (978-1-68115-543-2(5), cfe9e5c8-3bf9-48b5-83cb-c43c795375ae, Apples & Honey Pr.) Behrman Hse., Inc.

Kimmelman, Leslie. The Shabbat Puppy, 0 vols. Zollars, Jaime, illus. 2012. (ENG.). 32p. (J). (gr. -1-1). 17.99 (978-0-7614-6145-6(0), 9780761461456, Two Lions) Amazon Publishing.

—You're the Cheese in My Blintz. Kaulitzki, Ramona, illus. 2020. (ENG.). 12p. (J). (gr. -1 — 1). bds. 6.99 (978-1-5415-3467-4(0), 3d66852f-012f-48cc-ab8b-c39cc70b188a, Kar-Ben Publishing) Lerner Publishing Group.

Kleinberg, Naomi. Elmo's Little Dreidel (Sesame Street) Moroney, Christopher, illus. 2011. (ENG.). 12p. (J). (gr. k — 1). bds. 5.99 (978-0-375-87396-6(1), Random Hse. Bks. for Young Readers) Random Hse. Children's Bks.

Kohuth, Jane. Who's Got the Etrog? Elissambura, illus. 2018. (ENG.). 32p. (J). (gr. -1-2). 12.99 (978-1-5415-0966-5(8), 27e60bba-90f4-4323-b232-0f10b9b4722d, Kar-Ben Publishing) Lerner Publishing Group.

Korngold, Jamie S. Mazel Tov! It's a Boy: Mazel Tov! It's a Girl. Finkelstein, Jeff, illus. Finkelstein, Jeff, photos by. 2015. (J). 6.99 (978-1-4677-6206-9(7), Kar-Ben Publishing) Lerner Publishing Group.

—Sadie's Sukkah Breakfast. Fortenberry, Julie, illus. 2011. (Sukkot & Simchat Torah Ser.). (ENG.). 24p. (J). (gr. -1-1). lib. bdg. 16.95 (978-0-7613-5647-9(9), Kar-Ben Publishing) Lerner Publishing Group.

Kosofsky, Chaim. Much, Much Better. Schiffman, Jessica, illus. 2006. (ENG.). 32p. (J). (gr. -1-3). 14.95 (978-1-929628-22-3(6)) Hachai Publishing.

Krantz, Hazel. In the Garden of the Caliph. 2012. 132p. (gr. 4-6). 23.14 (978-1-4669-2888-6(3)); (J). pap. 13.14 (978-1-4669-2886-2(7)) Trafford Publishing.

Kranzler, Gershon. Seder in Herlin: And Other Stories. Kotler, Arkady & Kotler, Elina, illus. 2003. 108p. (gr. 5-9). reprint ed. 13.95 (978-0-8266-0343-2(2)) Merkos L'Inyonei Chinuch.

Kubert, Joe. The Adventures of Yaakov & Isaac. 64p. 9.99 (978-1-58330-741-0(9)) Feldheim Pubs.

Kushner, Lawrence & Schmidt, Gary. In God's Hands. Baek, Matthew J., illus. 2005. (ENG.). 32p. (gr. k-3). 16.99 (978-1-58023-224-1(8), a1cc0a97-7f67-4181-af6c-a32ed0d50d1e, Jewish Lights Publishing) LongHill Partners, Inc.

Kviat, Hindy & Lefkowitz, Chaya. Yes I Can. Epstein, Len, illus. 2018. (ENG.). 28p. (J). 11.95 (978-1-945560-05-7(3)) Hachai Publishing.

Lang, Andrew, ed. & compiled by. The Orange Fairy Book. Lang, Andrew, compiled by. 2011. 234p. 27.95 (978-1-4638-9520-4(8)) Rodgers, Alan Bks.

Lanton, Sandy. The Littlest Levine. Keay, Claire, illus. 2014. (ENG.). 24p. (J). (gr. -1-2). 7.95 (978-0-7613-9046-6(4), b497aad7-f252-4a37-8c22-6411450d7d2b, Kar-Ben Publishing) Lerner Publishing Group.

—Lots of Latkes: A Hanukkah Story. Redenbaugh, Vicki Jo, illus. 2003. (ENG.). 32p. (J). (gr. -1-3). 14.95 (978-1-58013-091-2(7), Kar-Ben Publishing) Lerner Publishing Group.

Lawton, Wendy G. Shadow of His Hand: A Story Based on the Life of Holocaust Survivor Anita Dittman. 2004. (Daughters of the Faith Ser.). (ENG.). 160p. (J). (gr. 3-3). pap. 8.99 (978-0-8024-4074-7(6)) Moody Pubs.

Lazewnik, Libby. Out of the Woods a Brave Group of Youngsters, a Thrilling Campaign - & Positive Word Power. 2011. (ENG., Illus.). 320p. (J). (978-1-4226-1176-0(0)) Mesorah Pubns., Ltd.

Lehman, Theodore H. Defying Odds. 2014. (YA). pap. (978-1-935604-63-1(5)) Gaon Bks.

Lehman-Wilzig, Tami. Zvuvi's Israel. Topaz, Ksenia, illus. 2009. (Israel Ser.). (ENG.). 32p. (J). (gr. -1-2). pap. 7.95 (978-0-8225-8760-6(2), Kar-Ben Publishing) Lerner Publishing Group.

Lenhard, Elizabeth. The Ball of Clay That Rolled Away, 0 vols. Wolff, Jason, illus. 2012. (ENG.). 24p. (J). (gr. -1-3). 16.99 (978-0-7614-6142-5(6), 9780761461425, Two Lions) Amazon Publishing.

Lester, Julius. Pharaoh's Daughter: A Novel of Ancient Egypt. 2009. (ENG., Illus.). 192p. (YA). (gr. 7). pap. 7.99 (978-0-15-206662-8(4), 1099001, Clarion Bks.) HarperCollins Pubs.

Levine, Anna. Jodie's Hanukkah Dig. Topaz, Ksenia, illus. 2008. (Hanukkah Ser.). (ENG.). 32p. (J). (gr. k-3). 17.95 (978-0-8225-7391-3(1), Kar-Ben Publishing) Lerner Publishing Group.

—Jodie's Shabbat Surprise. Topaz, Ksenia, illus. 2015. (ENG.). 32p. (J). (gr. k-3). lib. bdg. 17.95 (978-1-4677-3465-3(9), 6e98fe25-b7ef-417b-b29e-cbaacfbdc3bf); E-Book 27.99 (978-1-4677-6204-5(0)) Lerner Publishing Group. (Kar-Ben Publishing).

Levy, Marilyn. Checkpoints. 2009. (ENG.). 256p. (gr. 7). pap. 14.95 (978-0-8276-0870-2(5)) Jewish Pubn. Society.

Levy, Rochel. Moshe Goes to Yeshiva. David, Racheli, illus. 2012. 24p. 11.95 (978-1-60091-212-2(5)) Israel Bookshop Pubns.

Liddiment, Carol, illus. The Wooden Sword: A Jewish Folktale from Afghanistan. 2012. (ENG.). 32p. (J). (gr. -1-3). 16.99 (978-0-8075-9201-4(3), 807592013) Whitman, Albert & Co.

Littlefield, Holly. The Rooftop Adventure of Minnie & Tessa, Factory Fire Survivors. Hammond, Ted & Carbajal, Richard, illus. 2011. (History's Kid Heroes Ser.). 32p. pap. 51.02 (978-0-7613-7639-2(9), Graphic Universe™) Lerner Publishing Group.

Locke, Katherine. The Spy with the Red Balloon. 2019. (Balloonmakers Ser.: 2). (ENG.). 368p. (YA). (gr. 8-12). pap. 9.99 (978-0-8075-2938-6(9), 807529389) Whitman, Albert & Co.

Lois, Lowry. Compte les Etoiles. pap. 16.95 (978-2-211-03436-4(5)) Archimede Editions FRA. Dist: Distribooks, Inc.

—Number the Stars. 2004. 144p. (J). (gr. 5-9). pap. 29.00 incl. audio (978-1-4000-8637-5(X), Listening Library) Random Hse. Audio Publishing Group.

Londner, Renee. The Missing Letters: A Dreidel Story. Bodnaruk, Iryna, illus. 2017. (ENG.). 32p. (J). (gr. -1-3). 12.99 (978-1-4677-8933-2(X), 5a26b3d7-a59a-4eee-9c00-97f890a98ee6, Kar-Ben Publishing) Lerner Publishing Group.

Lowry, Lois. Number the Stars. l.t. ed. 2019. (ENG.). 282p. (J). (gr. 5-7). pap. 12.99 (978-1-4328-6393-7(2), Large Print Pr.) Thorndike Pr.

—Number the Stars: A Newbery Award Winner. 2011. (ENG.). 160p. (J). (gr. 5-7). pap. 9.99 (978-0-547-57709-8(5), 1458457, Clarion Bks.) HarperCollins Pubs.

Mandell, Sherri. The Elephant in the Sukkah. Kuman, Ivana, illus. 2019. (ENG.). 32p. (J). (gr. -1-2). 17.99 (978-1-5415-2212-1(5), 74932875-71e9-4511-bcc7-4c7c08af1988); pap. 7.99 (978-1-5415-2213-8(3), 6f257079-ee4c-48b2-872c-f747f0da82da) Lerner Publishing Group. (Kar-Ben Publishing).

Manushkin, Fran. Many Days, One Shabbat, 0 vols. Monescillo, Maria, illus. 2011. (ENG.). 24p. (J). (gr. -1-3). 12.99 (978-0-7614-5965-1(0), 9780761459651, Two Lions) Amazon Publishing.

Maristella. One Step to Freedom. 2010. 82p. pap. (978-1-84748-756-8(4)) Athena Pr.

Marshall, Linda Elovitz. The Mitzvah Magician. Engel, Christiane, illus. 2012. (ENG.). 24p. (J). (gr. -1-2). lib. bdg. 7.95 (978-0-7613-5655-4(X), 7ba9f681-643a-4044-bd26-5b8cae01eeae, Kar-Ben Publishing) Lerner Publishing Group.

Martinez, Mario X. Abran & Isabella's Hidden Faith. 2015. 103p. (J). pap. (978-1-935604-73-0(2)) Gaon Bks.

Masih, Tara Lynn. My Real Name Is Hanna. 3rd ed. 2018. 224p. (YA). (gr. 6-16). pap. 16.95 (978-1-942134-51-0(7)) Mandel Vilar Pr.

Mazer, Harry. The Last Mission. 192p. (YA). (gr. 7-18). pap. 4.99 (978-0-8072-1366-7(7), Listening Library) Random Hse. Audio Publishing Group.

McDonough, Yona Zeldis. The Bicycle Spy. 2016. (ENG.). 208p. (J). (gr. 3-7). 17.99 (978-0-545-85095-7(9), Scholastic Pr.) Scholastic, Inc.

Medoff, Francine. The Mouse in the Matzah Factory. in den Bosch, Nicole, illus. 2003. (ENG.). 32p. (J). (gr. -1-3). pap. 6.95 (978-1-58013-048-6(8), 4779524e-3c70-401a-b185-08c61229f311, Kar-Ben Publishing) Lerner Publishing Group.

Meir, Tamar. Francesco Tirelli's Ice Cream Shop. Albert, Yael, illus. 2019. (ENG.). 32p. (J). (gr. 3-6). 9.99 (978-1-5415-3465-0(4), 3436a1ef-0e38-40bc-bf54-16acb9a854ee, Kar-Ben Publishing) Lerner Publishing Group.

Meltzer, Amy. A Mezuzah on the Door. Fried, Janice, illus. 2007. (Jewish Identity Ser.). 32p. (J). (gr. -1-3). 17.95 (978-1-58013-249-7(9), Kar-Ben Publishing) Lerner Publishing Group.

—The Shabbat Princess. Avilés, Martha Graciela, illus. 2011. (ENG.). 32p. (J). (gr. -1-2). pap. 7.99 (978-0-7613-5106-1(X), ee9de847-6e71-4330-9fe7-ddde39ce88ee, Kar-Ben Publishing) Lerner Publishing Group.

Mermelstein, Yael. The Stupendous Adventures of Shragi & Shia. 2008. (ENG., Illus.). 93p. (J). pap. (978-1-4226-0865-4(4)) Mesorah Pubns., Ltd.

Meyer, Susan Lynn. Black Radishes. 2011. 240p. (J). (gr. 3-7). 8.99 (978-0-375-85822-2(9), Yearling) Random Hse. Children's Bks.

Miklowitz, Gloria D. The Enemy Has a Face. 2004. (ENG.). 143p. (YA). pap. 8.00 (978-0-8028-5261-8(0)) Eerdmans, William B. Publishing Co.

Miller, David Lee & Rubin, Steven Jay. The Cat Who Lived with Anne Frank. Baddeley, Elizabeth, illus. 2019. (ENG.). 40p. (J). (gr. -1-3). 18.99 (978-1-5247-4150-1(7), Philomel Bks.) Penguin Young Readers Group.

Miller, Deborah U. & Ostrove, Karen. Fins & Scales: A Kosher Tale. Ostrove, Karen, illus. 2004. (Israel Ser.). (Illus.). 32p. (J). (gr. 1-3). pap. 4.95 (978-0-929371-25-2(9), Kar-Ben Publishing) Lerner Publishing Group.

Morgan, Anna. Daughters of the Ark, 1 vol. 2005. (ENG., Illus.). 200p. (J). (gr. 5-12). pap. 9.95 (978-1-896764-92-4(4)) Second Story Pr. CAN. Dist: Orca Bk. Pubs. USA.

Moskowitz-Sweet, Gloria & Smith, Hope Anita. It Rained Warm Bread: Moishe Moskowitz's Story of Hope. Lyon, Lea, illus. 2019. (ENG.). 160p. (J). 16.99 (978-1-250-16572-5(5), 900187113, Holt, Henry & Co. Bks. For Young Readers) Holt, Henry & Co.

Muñiz-Huberman, Angelina & Menton, Seymour. Dreaming of Safed. 2014. 126p. (YA). pap. (978-1-935604-61-7(9)) Gaon Bks.

Naomi, Aunt. Jewish Fairy Tales & Legends. 2006. pap. 28.95 (978-1-4254-9788-0(8)) Kessinger Publishing, LLC.

Nargi, Lela. A Heart Just Like My Mother's. Cis, Valeria, illus. 2018. (ENG.). 32p. (J). (gr. -1-2). pap. 7.99 (978-1-5124-2099-9(9), 862306a5-0512-4e3c-b235-a7651e28407a, Kar-Ben Publishing) Lerner Publishing Group.

Narváez, Concha López. El Tiempo y la Promesa.Tr. of Time & the Promise. (SPA.). (YA). (gr. 5-8). 164p. (978-84-216-2558-3(6), BU7323); 9th ed. (Illus.). 208p. (978-84-216-1538-6(6), BU6188) Bruño, Editorial ESP. Dist: Lectorum Pubns., Inc.

Nayboym, A. Di Ban Fort. 2011. (YID., Illus.). (J). (978-1-63587-096-1(8)) Double Bridge Publishing.

—Di Ban Fort. 2011. (YID., Illus.). (J). (978-1-64204-063-0(0)) Primedia eLaunch LLC.

Newman, Lesléa. Baby's Blessings. Nakata, Hiroe, illus. 2019. (ENG.). 12p. (J). (gr. -1 — 1). bds. 5.99 (978-1-5415-2214-5(1), 040e002c-9875-486d-a397-f12d98022137, Kar-Ben Publishing) Lerner Publishing Group.

Newman, Tracy. Havdalah Is Coming! Garofoli, Viviana, illus. 2020. (ENG.). 12p. (J). (gr. -1 — 1). bds. 6.99 (978-1-5415-2163-6(3), 701faafe-bdd8-4b76-b195-9290a39c1d77, Kar-Ben Publishing) Lerner Publishing Group.

—Sukkot Is Coming! Garofoli, Viviana, illus. 2017. (ENG.). 12p. (J). (gr. -1 — 1). bds. 6.99 (978-1-5124-0828-7(X), 25c6eda2-8813-43b2-8729-5b6ad881b52a, Kar-Ben Publishing) Lerner Publishing Group.

—Tu B'Shevat Is Coming! Garofoli, Viviana, illus. 2017. (ENG.). 12p. (J). (gr. -1 — 1). bds. 5.99 (978-1-5124-2676-2(8), 5e159d59-3c9d-4741-825e-df72a2d6a00e, Kar-Ben Publishing) Lerner Publishing Group.

Newman, Vivian Bonnie. Moti the Mitzvah Mouse. Knopp-Kilpert, Inga, illus. 2017. (ENG.). 24p. (J). (gr. -1-k). 17.99 (978-1-5124-2647-2(4), 11b75fab-3f40-4b46-b9b9-50eea00768f6, Kar-Ben Publishing) Lerner Publishing Group.

Nislick, June Levitt. Zayda Was a Cowboy. 2005. (ENG.). 88p. pap. 11.95 (978-0-8276-0817-7(9)) Jewish Pubn. Society.

North, Phoebe. Starbreak. 2014. (Starglass Sequence Ser.). (ENG., Illus.). 432p. (YA). (gr. 7). 17.99 (978-1-4424-5956-4(5), Simon & Schuster Bks. For Young Readers) Simon & Schuster Bks. For Young Readers.

—Starglass. (Starglass Sequence Ser.). (ENG., Illus.). (YA). (gr. 7). 2014. 464p. pap. 12.99 (978-1-4424-5954-0(9)) 2013. 448p. 17.99 (978-1-4424-5953-3(0)) Simon & Schuster Bks. For Young Readers. (Simon & Schuster Bks. For Young Readers).

Novick, Rona Milch. Mommy, Can You Stop the Rain? Kubaszewska, Anna, illus. 2020. (ENG.). 32p. (J). 17.95 (978-1-68115-555-5(9), 0af463f0-a462-4701-8221-bd14af153516, Apples & Honey Pr.) Behrman Hse., Inc.

Now I Am Thee. (Yoni Gold Board Book Ser.). (J). bds. 4.95 (978-1-58330-153-1(4)) Feldheim Pubs.

Ofanansky, Allison. Sukkot Treasure Hunt. Alpern, Eliyahu, illus. Alpern, Eliyahu, photos by. 2009. (Sukkot & Simchat Torah Ser.). (ENG.). 32p. (J). (gr. -1-5). 15.95 (978-0-8225-8763-7(7), Kar-Ben Publishing) Lerner Publishing Group.

Olswanger, Anna. Shlemiel Crooks. Koz, Paula Goodman, illus. 2005. (ENG.). 36p. (J). (gr. 2-4). 15.95 (978-1-58838-165-1(X), 8993, NewSouth Bks.) NewSouth, Inc.

Ostow, Micol. Emily Goldberg Learns to Salsa. 2007. 208p. (YA). (gr. 7-18). 8.99 (978-1-59514-144-6(8), Razorbill) Penguin Young Readers Group.

Packer, Rachel Orenstein. Sky High Sukkah. Zemke, Deborah, illus. 2016. (ENG.). 32p. (J). 17.95 (978-1-68115-513-5(3), fa1eb525-090c-42a2-b44c-b9fecdbdcf77) Behrman Hse., Inc.

Pearl, Sydelle. Elijah's Tears: Stories for the Jewish Holidays, 1 vol. Skortcheva, Rossitza, illus. 2004. (ENG.). 80p. (J). (gr. 3-7). 14.95 (978-1-58980-178-3(4), Pelican Publishing) Arcadia Publishing.

Penn, Audrey. The Miracle Jar: A Hanukkah Story. Lyon, Lea, illus. 2009. (ENG.). 32p. (J). (gr. -1-3). pap. 8.95 (978-1-933718-26-2(9)) Tanglewood Pr.

Peretz, I. L. & Goldin, Barbara Diamond. The Magician's Visit: A Passover Tale. Parker, Robert Andrew, illus. 2006. 28p. (J). (gr. 4-8). reprint ed. 15.00 (978-1-4223-5408-7(3)); pap. 5.00 (978-1-4223-5400-1(8)) DIANE Publishing Co.

Perl, Erica S. When Life Gives You O. J. 2013. (ENG.). 224p. (J). (gr. 3-7). 8.99 (978-0-375-85902-1(0), Yearling) Random Hse. Children's Bks.

Perl, Lila. Isabel's War. 2014. (ENG.). 224p. (J). (gr. 2-7). pap. 12.95 (978-1-939601-27-8(4)) Ig Publishing, Inc.

Perrin, Randy, et al. Time Like a River. 2004. 144p. (gr. 5-18). 14.95 (978-1-57143-061-8(X)) RDR Bks.

Petersen, Alicia. A Sparrow Alone. 2004. 154p. (YA). 8.99 (978-1-59166-204-4(4)) BJU Pr.

Pfeiffer, Chaviva. Making Hashem Proud: Stories of Kiddush Hashem in Everyday Life. 2014. (ENG., Illus.). 48p. (J). (978-1-4226-1464-8(6)) Mesorah Pubns., Ltd.

Platt, Randall. The Girl Who Wouldn't Die. 2017. (ENG.). 368p. (J). (gr. 8-8). 16.99 (978-1-5107-0809-9(X), Sky Pony Pr.) Skyhorse Publishing Co., Inc.

Polacco, Patricia. The Blessing Cup. Polacco, Patricia, illus. 2013. (ENG., Illus.). 48p. (J). (gr. -1-3). 19.99 (978-1-4424-5047-9(9), Simon & Schuster Bks. For Young Readers) Simon & Schuster Bks. For Young Readers.

—The Butterfly. 2009. 48p. (J). (gr. k-3). pap. 8.99 (978-0-14-241306-7(2), Puffin Books) Penguin Young Readers Group.

—The Keeping Quilt. 2007. 18.00 (978-0-7569-1720-3(4)) Perfection Learning Corp.

—The Keeping Quilt: 25th Anniversary Edition. Polacco, Patricia, illus. 25th ed. 2013. (ENG., Illus.). 64p. (J). (gr. -1-3). 18.99 (978-1-4424-8237-1(0), Simon & Schuster/Paula Wiseman Bks.) Simon & Schuster/Paula Wiseman Bks.

Press, Judy. Bubbe's Got the Beat. Hall, Mary, illus. 2017. (ENG.). 12p. (J). (gr. -1 — 1). bds. 5.99 (978-1-5124-4763-7(3), d4146f28-8c83-4401-8ded-078b05583b54, Kar-Ben Publishing) Lerner Publishing Group.

Pressler, Mirjam. Malka. Murdoch, Brian, tr. 2005. 280p. (YA). (gr. 7-12). 13.65 (978-0-7569-5217-4(4)) Perfection Learning Corp.

Prins, Piet. Hideout in the Swamp. 2006. (Illus.). 136p. (J). pap. (978-1-894666-73-2(9)) Inheritance Pubns.

Propp, Vera W. When the Soldiers Were Gone: A Novel. 2006. 101p. (J). (gr. 4-8). reprint ed. 15.00 (978-1-4223-5310-3(9)) DIANE Publishing Co.

Pryor, Bonnie. Simon's Escape: A Story of the Holocaust, 1 vol. 2011. (Historical Fiction Adventures Ser.). (ENG., Illus.). 160p. (J). (gr. 3-5). 31.93 (978-0-7660-3388-7(0), 77eae799-a832-47e4-96ef-4e05fa560d75); pap. 13.88 (978-1-59845-216-7(9), 5304890e-e1fa-4a41-9faf-e8971ad9e71f) Enslow Publishing, LLC.

Pullman, Philip. The Tiger in the Well: a Sally Lockhart Mystery. 2008. (Sally Lockhart Ser.: Bk. 3). (ENG.). 432p. (YA). (gr. 7). pap. 9.99 (978-0-375-84517-8(8), Ember) Random Hse. Children's Bks.

J
K
L

Rabbi Binyomin Pruzansky. Stories for a Child's Heart. 2009. (ENG., Illus.). 48p. (J). *(978-1-4226-0915-6(4))* Mesorah Pubns., Ltd.

Radding, Alan. Miracles: Stories for Jewish Children & Their Families. 2003. 135p. (J). pap. 13.95 *(978-1-59113-309-4(2))* Booklocker.com, Inc.

Rahlens, Holly-Jane. Prince William, Maximilian Minsky, & Me. 2007. (ENG.). 320p. (YA). (gr. 7-11). per. 7.99 *(978-0-7636-3299-1(6))* Candlewick Pr.

Reinhardt, Dana. The Things a Brother Knows. 2011. 256p. (YA). (gr. 9). pap. 9.99 *(978-0-375-84456-0(2)*, Ember) Random Hse. Children's Bks.

Rocklin, Joanne. Fleabrain Loves Franny. (ENG.). (J). (gr. 3-7). 2015. 281p. pap. 8.95 *(978-1-4197-1676-8(X)*, 1073803) 2014. 288p. 16.95 *(978-1-4197-1068-1(0)*, 1073801) Abrams, Inc. (Amulet Bks.).

Romero, R. M. The Dollmaker of Krakow. 2017. (ENG.). 336p. (J). (gr. 3-7). lib. bdg. 19.99 *(978-1-5247-1540-3(9)*, Delacorte Bks. for Young Readers) Random Hse. Children's Bks.

Rose, Robert. Godintoxicated Becoming Paranoid. 2007. 260p. pap. 29.95 *(978-1-4327-0041-6(3))* Outskirts Pr., Inc.

Rosen, Michael. Happy Harry's Cafe. Holland, Richard, illus. 2012. (ENG.). 32p. (J). (gr. -1-2). 16.99 *(978-0-7636-6239-4(9))* Candlewick Pr.

Rosenbaum, Andrea Warmflash. Hand in Hand. Shleifer, Maya, illus. 2018. (ENG.). 32p. (J). 17.95 *(978-1-68115-538-8(9)*, 3447b1ea-4080-4d17-89e0-66a98406b7fd, Apples & Honey Pr.) Behrman Hse., Inc.

Rosenbaum, Andria Warmflash. A Grandma Like Yours: A Grandpa Like Yours. Björnson, Barbara, illus. 2006. 32p. (J). 16.95 *(978-1-58013-167-4(0)*, Kar-Ben Publishing) Lerner Publishing Group.

Rosenberg, Madelyn. The Schmutzy Family. Meisel, Paul, illus. 2018. 32p. (J). (gr. -1-3). pap. 8.99 *(978-0-8234-4241-6(1))* Holiday Hse., Inc.

Rosenfeld, Dina. A Chanukah Story for Night Number Three. 2009. (Illus.). 32p. (J). 13.99 *(978-1-929628-54-4(4))* Hachai Publishing.

Ross, Susan. Searching for Lottie. 2019. (ENG., Illus.). 176p. (J). (gr. 3-7). 17.99 *(978-0-8234-4166-2(0))* Holiday Hse., Inc.

Rossoff, Donald. The Perfect Prayer. Keiser, Tammy L., illus. 2003. (gr. k-3). 13.95 *(978-0-8074-0853-7(0)*, 164005) URJ Pr.

Rostoker-Gruber, Karen. Farmer Kobi's Hanukkah Match. Decker, C. B., illus. 2015. (ENG.). 32p. (J). 17.95 *(978-1-68115-501-2(X)*, abd78a55-d5db-444d-b9c6-a1870409e3d7) Behrman Hse., Inc.

—Maddie the Mitzvah Clown. Grove, Christine, illus. 2017. (ENG.). 32p. (J). 17.95 *(978-1-68115-523-4(0)*, e191c28c-c839-4584-a784-db033b746a0c) Behrman Hse., Inc.

Rotenberg, Yael. Heldishkeyt Inem Goldenem Land. Tovahleh, illus. 2018. (YID.). 37p. (J). *(978-1-68091-255-5(0))* Kinder Shpiel USA, Inc.

Rouss, Sylvia. Yosef's Dream. Blumenfeld, Tamar, illus. 2016. (ENG.). 36p. (J). 17.95 *(978-1-68115-506-7(0)*, 0f677281-4169-409d-85c9-387bd90c817c) Behrman Hse., Inc.

Rouss, Sylvia A. Aaron's Bar Mitzvah. Dubois, Liz Goulet, tr. Dubois, Liz Goulet, illus. 2003. (J). 14.95 *(978-0-8246-0447-9(4))* David, Jonathan Pubs., Inc.

—The Littlest Candlesticks. Hannon, Holly, illus. 2005. (Littlest Ser.). 32p. (J). 14.95 *(978-1-930143-48-7(6)*, Devora Publishing) Simcha Media Group.

—Sammy Spider's First Day of School. Kahn, Katherine Janus, illus. 2009. (Kar-Ben Favorites Ser.). (ENG.). 32p. (J). (gr. -1-2). 16.95 *(978-0-8225-8583-1(9)*, Kar-Ben Publishing) Lerner Publishing Group.

—Sammy Spider's First Haggadah. Kahn, Katherine Janus, illus. 2007. (ENG.). 32p. (J). (gr. -1-3). per. 7.99 *(978-1-58013-230-5(8)*, a576058b-9534-4121-80bf-9ba351c5c0af, Kar-Ben Publishing) Lerner Publishing Group.

—Sammy Spider's First Shavuot. Kahn, Katherine Janus, illus. 2008. (ENG.). 32p. (J). (gr. -1-3). lib. bdg. 9.99 *(978-0-8225-7224-4(9)*, c79a4b2f-eed5-4ab2-97f9-40e1c8e3bbca, Kar-Ben Publishing) Lerner Publishing Group.

—Sammy Spider's Hanukkah Colors. Kahn, Katherine Janus, illus. 2017. (ENG.). 12p. (J). (gr. -1 — 1). bds. 5.99 *(978-1-4677-5238-1(X)*, 2f9f5071-1e9b-4c00-abb8-936a4314e444, Kar-Ben Publishing) Lerner Publishing Group.

Roy, Jennifer. Yellow Star, 0 vols. 2014. (ENG.). 256p. (J). (gr. 4-6). pap. 9.99 *(978-0-7614-6310-8(0)*, 9780761463108, Two Lions) Amazon Publishing.

Rozen, R. In Trit Fun Di Farkhapte Kinder. Krishevski, E., illus. 2018. (YID.). 58p. (J). *(978-1-68091-243-2(7))* Kinder Shpiel USA, Inc.

Rubens, Michael. Sons of The 613. 2012. (ENG.). 320p. (YA). (gr. 7). 16.99 *(978-0-547-61216-4(8)*, 1464621, Clarion Bks.) HarperCollins Pubs.

Ruby, Lois. Shanghai Shadows. 2006. (ENG.). 256p. (YA). 16.95 *(978-0-8234-1960-9(6))* Holiday Hse., Inc.

Rudetsky, Seth. My Awesome/Awful Popularity Plan. 2013. 224p. (YA). (gr. 7). pap. 8.99 *(978-0-375-89997-3(9)*, Ember) Random Hse. Children's Bks.

Sachs, Marilyn. A Pocket Full of Seeds. Stabl, Ben, illus. 2005. (ENG.). 146p. pap. 10.95 *(978-0-595-33846-7(1)*, Backinprint.com) iUniverse, Inc.

Sachs, Tamar. The Golden Bell. Abolafia, Yossi, illus. 2019. (ENG.). 24p. (J). (gr. -1-3). 12.99 *(978-1-5415-2612-9(0)*, c13ea2fb-6fac-471a-9d3c-b94ff812eeb3, Kar-Ben Publishing) Lerner Publishing Group.

Safran, Faigy. Uncle Moishy Visits Torah Island. Snowden, Linda, illus. (J). pap. 5.99 *(978-0-89906-806-0(5)*, UM1P) Mesorah Pubns., Ltd.

Salem, Iosi, illus. The Mr. Mentch Coloring Book. 2008. (J). (gr. -1-3). 6.95 *(978-1-934440-37-7(X)*, Pitspopany Pr.) Simcha Media Group.

Sandbank, Rachella & Shem-Tov, Tami. A Queen in Jerusalem. Ofer, Avi, illus. 2018. (ENG.). 32p. (J). (gr. -1-2). 12.99 *(978-1-5124-4441-4(3)*, 53662b24-b791-48fe-a9c3-28ad79f7107d, Kar-Ben Publishing) Lerner Publishing Group.

Sasso, Sandy Eisenberg. Butterflies under Our Hats. Rothenberg, Joani Keller, illus. 2014. (ENG.). 32p. (J). (gr. k-5). pap. 15.99 *(978-1-61261-583-7(X)*, 5837) Paraclete Pr., Inc.

—The Shema in the Mezuzah: Listening to Each Other. Rothenberg, Joani Keller, illus. 2012. (ENG.). 32p. (J). 18.99 *(978-1-58023-506-8(9)*, 2d784922-ed10-4d47-9068-9861ce43a990, Jewish Lights Publishing) LongHill Partners, Inc.

Saturen, Myra. Journey to a New World. 2006. (J). pap. 9.99 *(978-0-88092-494-8(2))* Royal Fireworks Publishing Co.

—Journey to a New World: Mystic River of the West. 2006. (J). pap. *(978-0-88092-495-5(0))* Royal Fireworks Publishing Co.

—Julietta. (YA). pap. 9.99 *(978-0-88092-538-9(8))* Royal Fireworks Publishing Co.

Savit, Gavriel. The Way Back. 2020. (ENG.). 368p. (YA). (gr. 7). 18.99 *(978-1-9848-9462-5(5)*, Knopf Bks. for Young Readers) Random Hse. Children's Bks.

Sax, Aline. The War Within These Walls. 2013. (ENG., Illus.). 176p. (YA). 17.00 *(978-0-8028-5428-5(1)*, Eerdmans Bks For Young Readers) Eerdmans, William B. Publishing Co.

Schmidt, Gary D. Mara's Stories: Glimmers in the Darkness. 2008. (ENG.). 160p. (YA). (gr. 5-9). per. 15.99 *(978-0-312-37388-7(0)*, 900045532) Square Fish.

Schotter, Roni. Passover Magic, 0 vols. Hafner, Marylin, illus. 2012. (ENG.). 34p. (J). (gr. -1-3). pap. 7.99 *(978-0-7614-5842-5(5)*, 9780761458425, Two Lions) Amazon Publishing.

Schram, Peninnah. The Magic Pomegranate. Hall, Melanie, illus. 2007. (On My Own Folklore Ser.). 48p. (J). lib. bdg. 17.95 *(978-0-8225-8856-6(0)*, Kar-Ben Publishing) Lerner Publishing Group.

—The Magic Pomegranate: [a Jewish Folktale]. Hall, Melanie, illus. 2008. (On My Own Folklore Ser.). (ENG.). 48p. (J). (gr. 2-4). pap. 8.99 *(978-0-8225-6746-2(6)*, 4f41ed64-2f1b-448e-836e-1dc731e89df0, First Avenue Editions) Lerner Publishing Group.

Schur, Maxine Rose. Sacred Shadows. 2005. (ENG.). 224p. pap. 14.95 *(978-0-595-36793-1(3)*, Backinprint.com) iUniverse, Inc.

Scott, Walter. Ivanhoe. 2017. (ENG., Illus.). (J). pap. 21.95 *(978-1-374-90171-1(7))* Capital Communications, Inc.

Scott, Walter, ed. Ivanhoe. (SPA., Illus.). 176p. (YA). 14.95 *(978-84-7281-096-9(8)*, AF1096) Auriga, Ediciones S.A. ESP. Dist: Continental Bk. Co., Inc.

—Ivanhoe. 2008. (Bring the Classics to Life Ser.). (Illus.). 72p. (gr. 5-12). pap., act. bk. ed. 10.95 *(978-1-55576-099-1(6)*, EDN506B) EDCON Publishing Group.

Segal, Nechamy. The Torah Book of Opposites. Lumer, Marc, illus. 2012. (ENG.). 12p. (J). pap. 8.99 *(978-1-929628-67-4(6))* Hachai Publishing.

Seyforth, Edward L. A Horribly Frightening Deception, 1 vol. 2009. 75p. pap. 19.95 *(978-1-61546-260-5(0))* America Star Bks.

Sharenow, Robert. The Berlin Boxing Club. 2011. (ENG.). 416p. (YA). (gr. 8-18). 17.99 *(978-0-06-157968-4(8)*, Balzer & Bray) HarperCollins Pubs.

—The Berlin Boxing Club. 2012. (YA). lib. bdg. 20.85 *(978-0-606-26871-4(5))* Turtleback.

Shazak. Out of Egypt. 2007. 104p. 24.99 *(978-1-930925-11-3(5))* Feldheim Pubs.

Sher, Steven. Where the Shouting Began. 2008. (J). *(978-1-932727-08-1(6))* Montemayor Pr.

Shmuel, Naomi. Too Far from Home. Katz, Avi, illus. 2020. (ENG.). 96p. (J). (gr. 3-7). 15.99 *(978-1-5415-4671-4(7)*, 15d83bab-1d1f-4e49-9c2f-6edeed30b6ae, Kar-Ben Publishing) Lerner Publishing Group.

Shulman, Lisa. The Matzo Ball Boy. Litzinger, Rosanne, illus. 2007. 32p. (J). (gr. -1-2). pap. 8.99 *(978-0-14-240769-1(0)*, Puffin Books) Penguin Young Readers Group.

Silberman, Shoshana. A Family Haggadah II, Vol. 2. Kahn, Katherine Janus, illus. l.t. ed. 2003. 64p. (J). pap. 6.95 *(978-1-58013-014-1(3)*, Kar-Ben Publishing) Lerner Publishing Group.

Simon, Tanya & Simon, Richard. Oskar & the Eight Blessings. Siegel, Mark, illus. 2015. (ENG.). 40p. (J). (gr. -1-3). 19.99 *(978-1-59643-949-8(1)*, 900123918) Roaring Brook Pr.

Simpson, Lesley. The Purim Surprise. Church, Peter, illus. 2004. (Purim Ser.). (ENG.). 32p. (J). (gr. -1-3). pap. 6.95 *(978-1-58013-090-5(9)*, Kar-Ben Publishing) Lerner Publishing Group.

Simpson, Martha Seif. The Dreidel That Wouldn't Spin: A Toyshop Tale of Hanukkah. Bernhard, Durga Yael, illus. 2014. 32p. (J). (gr. -1-2). 16.95 *(978-1-937786-28-1(5)*, Wisdom Tales) World Wisdom, Inc.

—Esther's Gragger: A Toyshop Tale of Purim. 2019. (Illus.). 40p. (J). (gr. k-3). 16.95 *(978-1-937786-75-5(7)*, Wisdom Tales) World Wisdom, Inc.

Soban Biniashvili, Freidele Galya. There Is a Reason Why. Zimmer, Glenn, illus. 2016. (ENG.). 38p. (J). 13.99 *(978-1-929628-90-2(0))* Hachai Publishing.

Soci Et E de La Faune Et Des Parcs Du Qu Ebec. Sarah de Cordoba. Sanchez, Andres & Tagle, illus. 2003. (la Orilla del Viento Ser.). (SPA.). 136p. (J). per. 8.50 *(978-968-16-7020-7(5))* Fondo de Cultura Economica USA.

Spinelli, Jerry. Milkweed. (ENG.). 240p. (YA). (gr. 7). 2010. pap. 10.99 *(978-0-375-86147-5(5)*, Ember) 2005. mass mkt. 8.99 *(978-0-440-42005-7(9)*, Laurel Leaf) Random Hse. Children's Bks.

Spring, Debbie. The Righteous Smuggler, 1 vol. 2005. (Holocaust Remembrance Series for Young Readers Ser.: 6). (ENG., Illus.). 162p. (J). (gr. 4-7). pap. 9.95 *(978-1-896764-97-9(5))* Second Story Pr. CAN. Dist: Orca Bk. Pubs. USA.

Stamper, Vesper. What the Night Sings. 2018. (Illus.). 272p. (YA). (gr. 7). 21.99 *(978-1-5247-0038-6(X)*, Knopf Bks. for Young Readers) Random Hse. Children's Bks.

Starting First Grade. (Tami & Moishy Ser.: Vol. 4). (J). bds. 6.95 *(978-1-58330-968-1(3))* Feldheim Pubs.

Stavans, Ilan. Golemito. Villegas, Teresa, illus. 2013. (ENG.). 32p. (J). 16.95 *(978-1-58838-292-4(3)*, 8804, NewSouth Bks.) NewSouth, Inc.

Strom, Yale. The Wedding That Saved a Town. Prosmitsky, Jenya, illus. 2008. (J). (gr. -1). 17.95 *(978-0-8225-7376-0(8)*, Kar-Ben Publishing) Lerner Publishing Group.

Stuchner, Joan Betty. Can Hens Give Milk?, 1 vol. Weissmann, Joe, illus. 2013. (ENG.). 32p. (J). (gr. -1-k). 9.95 *(978-1-4598-0427-2(9))* Orca Bk. Pubs. USA.

—The Kugel Valley Klezmer Band. Row, Richard, illus. 2005. 30p. (J). (gr. 2-6). reprint ed. 16.00 *(978-0-7567-8605-2(3))* DIANE Publishing Co.

—The Kugel Valley Klezmer Band. Row, Richard, illus. 2010. (ENG.). 32p. (J). (gr. -1-3). pap. 7.95 *(978-1-56656-782-4(3)*, Crocodile Bks.) Interlink Publishing Group, Inc.

Sugarman, Brynn Olenberg. Rebecca's Journey Home. Shapiro, Michelle, illus. 2006. 32p. (J). (gr. -1-3). lib. bdg. 17.95 *(978-1-58013-157-5(3)*, Kar-Ben Publishing) Lerner Publishing Group.

Sutton, Jane. Esther's Hanukkah Disaster. Rowland, Andrew, illus. 2013. (Hanukkah Ser.). 32p. (J). (gr. -1-3). lib. bdg. 17.95 *(978-0-7613-9043-5(X)*, Kar-Ben Publishing) Lerner Publishing Group.

Swartz, Daniel. Bim & Bom, 2nd Edition: A Shabbat Tale. Iwai, Melissa, illus. 2nd rev. ed. 2011. (ENG.). 24p. (J). (gr. -1-1). pap. 8.95 *(978-0-7613-6717-8(9)*, 17cb14e4-1645-4843-9309-9a4eabea2edc, Kar-Ben Publishing) Lerner Publishing Group.

Tarshis, Lauren. I Survived the Nazi Invasion 1944. 2014. (I Survived Ser.: No. 9). lib. bdg. 14.75 *(978-0-606-35397-7(6))* Turtleback.

—I Survived the Nazi Invasion, 1944 (I Survived #9) 2014. (I Survived Ser.: 9). (ENG., Illus.). 112p. (J). (gr. 3-7). pap. 5.99 *(978-0-545-45938-9(9))* Scholastic, Inc.

Taylor, Sydney. All-Of-a-Kind Family Uptown. 2014. (ENG.). 200p. (J). (gr. 3). pap. 12.95 *(978-1-939601-17-9(7))* Ig Publishing, Inc.

Terwilliger, Kelly. Bubbe Isabella & the Sukkot Cake. Hornung, Phyllis, illus. 2005. 24p. (J). (gr. -1-3). 15.95 *(978-1-58013-187-2(5))*; (gr. 3-8). per. 6.95 *(978-1-58013-128-5(X))* Lerner Publishing Group. (Kar-Ben Publishing).

Tetzner, Annika. Lullabies for Annik. 2012. 120p. pap. 12.33 *(978-1-4669-6581-2(9))* Trafford Publishing.

The Mamas. Meet the Yids: Mr. Mentch. 2007. pap. 18.95 *(978-965-91048-0-2(4)*, Pitspopany Pr.) Simcha Media Group.

Thomas, M. J. The Secret of the Hidden Scrolls: the Shepherd's Stone, Book 5. 2018. (Secret of the Hidden Scrolls Ser.: 5). (ENG., Illus.). 128p. (J). (gr. 1-4). pap. 6.99 *(978-0-8249-5691-2(5)*, Worthy Kids/Ideals) Worthy Publishing.

Thor, Annika. A Faraway Island. Schenck, Linda, tr. 2011. (Faraway Island Ser.: 1). 256p. (J). (gr. 3-7). 7.99 *(978-0-375-84495-9(3)*, Yearling) Random Hse. Children's Bks.

—The Lily Pond. Schenck, Linda, tr. (Faraway Island Ser.). 224p. (J). (gr. 4-7). 2012. 7.99 *(978-0-385-74040-1(9)*, Yearling)2. 2013. (ENG.). lib. bdg. 21.19 *(978-0-385-90838-2(5)*, Delacorte Pr.) Random Hse. Children's Bks.

Toffler-Corrie, Laura. Noah Green Saves the World. Pamintuan, Macky, illus. 2020. (ENG.). 280p. (J). (gr. 4-7). 17.99 *(978-1-5415-6036-9(1)*, 4e539792-d4b9-48b5-a143-9e038eaf9c09, Kar-Ben Publishing) Lerner Publishing Group.

Tonti, Mat. The Book of Secrets. Tonti, Mat, illus. 2020. (ENG., Illus.). 208p. (J). (gr. 3-5). 19.99 *(978-1-5415-7825-8(2)*, 19dcb295-d07f-4fda-99fb-7d14d5741f18, Kar-Ben Publishing) Lerner Publishing Group.

Toro, Sandra. Dona Gracia: Beacon of Hope. 2016. 292p. (YA). pap. *(978-1-935604-75-4(9))* Gaon Bks.

Travis, Lucille. Tirzah. Garber, S. David, ed. 2004. (ENG.). 160p. (YA). (gr. 4-7). pap. 9.99 *(978-0-8361-3546-6(6))* Herald Pr.

Ungar, Richard. Rachel's Library. 2004. 32p. (J). (gr. 2-5). 15.95 *(978-0-88776-678-7(1)*, Tundra Bks.) Tundra Bks. CAN. Dist: Penguin Random Hse. LLC.

Vander Zee, Ruth. Erika's Story. Innocenti, Roberto, illus. 2013. (ENG.). 24p. (J). (gr. 2-5). pap. 10.99 *(978-0-89812-891-8(9)*, 22045, Creative Paperbacks) Creative Co., The.

Vogiel, Eva. Facing the Music. 2003. 284p. 19.95 *(978-1-880582-94-7(5))* Judaica Pr., Inc., The.

Vogiel, Eva & Steinberg, Ruth. A Light for Greytowers. 252p. 11.99 *(978-0-87306-598-6(0))* Feldheim Pubs.

Waldman, Debby. Miriam's Secret, 1 vol. 2017. (ENG.). 208p. (J). (gr. 4-7). pap. 10.95 *(978-1-4598-1425-7(8))* Orca Bk. Pubs. USA.

—A Sack Full of Feathers, 1 vol. Revell, Cindy, illus. 2007. (ENG.). 32p. (J). (gr. -1-k). 9.95 *(978-1-55143-863-4(1))* Orca Bk. Pubs. USA.

Walfish, Miriam. The Jewel & the Journey. 2007. 208p. (J). 16.95 *(978-1-932443-81-3(9))* Judaica Pr., Inc., The.

Wasserman, Mira. Too Much of a Good Thing. Carolan, Christine, illus. 2003. 32p. (J). (gr. -1-3). pap. 6.95 *(978-1-58013-066-0(6))*; (ENG.). 15.95 *(978-1-58013-082-0(8))* Lerner Publishing Group. (Kar-Ben Publishing).

Watts, Irene N. A Telling Time, 1 vol. Shoemaker, Kathryn E., illus. 2004. (ENG.). 32p. (J). (gr. 1-3). pap. 7.95 *(978-1-896580-72-2(6))* Tradewind Bks. CAN. Dist: Orca Bk. Pubs. USA.

Weber, Elka. Shimri's Big Idea. Bousidan, Gigi, illus. 2019. (ENG.). 32p. (J). 17.95 *(978-1-68115-541-8(9)*, 3ff17ff9-678c-4b6b-b239-c1f8d17226a7, Apples & Honey Pr.) Behrman Hse., Inc.

Weber, Ilse. Mendel Rosenbusch: Tales for Jewish Children. Fisher, Hans, tr. from GER. Burden, P. John, illus. 2006. Orig. Title: Mendel Rosenbusch: Geschichen Fur Jud Kinder. 128p. (J). pap. 18.00 *(978-1-933480-05-3(X))* Bunim and Bannigan Ltd.

—Mendel Rosenbusch: Tales for Jewish Children, 1 vol. Fisher, Hans & Fisher, Ruth, trs. Burden, P. John, illus. 2006. Orig. Title: Mendel Rosenbusch: Geschichen Fur Jud Kinder. (ENG.). 58p. (J). lib. bdg. 18.95 *(978-1-933480-04-6(1))* Bunim and Bannigan Ltd.

Whitney, Kim Ablon. The Other Half of Life. 2010. 256p. (YA). (gr. 7). mass mkt. 7.99 *(978-0-375-84422-5(8)*, Laurel Leaf) Random Hse. Children's Bks.

Wigden, Susan & Salem, I. A Mitzva for Zelda. 2008. 32p. 12.95 *(978-1-934440-54-4(X)*, Pitspopany Pr.) Simcha Media Group.

Williams, Laura E. Behind the Bedroom Wall. Goldstein, A. Nancy, illus. 2006. 169p. (gr. -1-7). 17.45 *(978-0-7569-6389-7(3))* Perfection Learning Corp.

Wing, Natasha. The Night Before Hanukkah. 2014. (Night Before Ser.). lib. bdg. 13.55 *(978-0-606-36160-6(X))* Turtleback.

Wiseman, Eva. The World Outside. 2014. (Illus.). 240p. (YA). (gr. 7). 19.99 *(978-0-88776-981-8(0)*, Tundra Bks.) Tundra Bks. CAN. Dist: Penguin Random Hse. LLC.

Wisniewski, David. Golem: A Caldecott Award Winner. 2007. (ENG., Illus.). 32p. (J). (gr. 5-7). 8.99 *(978-0-618-89424-6(1)*, 100586, Clarion Bks.) HarperCollins Pubs.

Wiviott, Meg. Benno & the Night of Broken Glass. Bisaillon, Josée, illus. 2010. (ENG.). (J). (gr. 2-5). 40p. pap. 9.99 *(978-0-8225-9975-3(9)*, 3906c2ec-1130-4778-92de-55739aff7b1a); 32p. lib. bdg. 17.95 *(978-0-8225-9929-6(5))* Lerner Publishing Group. (Kar-Ben Publishing).

Wohl, Lauren L. The Eighth Menorah. Hughes, Laura, illus. 2013. (ENG.). 32p. (J). (gr. -1-3). 16.99 *(978-0-8075-1892-2(1)*, 807518921) Whitman, Albert & Co.

Wulf, Linda Press. The Night of the Burning. 2007. 224p. pap. *(978-0-7475-9051-4(6))* Bloomsbury Publishing Plc.

Yavin, T. S. All-Star Season. 2006. 160p. (J). (gr. 3-7). lib. bdg. 15.95 *(978-1-58013-211-4(1)*, Kar-Ben Publishing) Lerner Publishing Group.

Yehudis Backenroth. The Adventures of PJ Pepperjay. 2014. (ENG., Illus.). 96p. (J). pap. *(978-1-4226-1535-5(9))* Mesorah Pubns., Ltd.

Yerushalmi, Miriam. Feivel the Falafel Ball Who Wanted to Do a Mitzvah. Ginsberg, Dvora, illus. 2007. 28p. (J). 16.50 *(978-0-911643-37-4(0))* Aura Printing, Inc.

—Gedalia the Goldfish Who Wanted Be Just Like the King. Weinberg, Devorah, illus. 2007. 26p. (J). (gr. -1-3). 16.50 *(978-0-911643-36-7(2))* Aura Printing, Inc.

—Let's Go Camping & Discover Our Nature. Perez, Esther Ido, illus. 2007. 28p. (J). (gr. 2-4). 16.50 *(978-0-911643-38-1(9))* Aura Printing, Inc.

—Let's Go Camping & Discover Our Nature. Perez, Esther Ido, illus. 2017. (ENG.). 30p. (J). (gr. 2-4). 22.00 *(978-1-934152-56-0(0))* Sane.

Yolen, Jane. The Devil's Arithmetic (Puffin Modern Classics) 2004. (Puffin Modern Classics Ser.). (ENG.). 208p. (J). (gr. 5-5). pap. 8.99 *(978-0-14-240109-5(9)*, Puffin Books) Penguin Young Readers Group.

Yoon, Salina. My First Menorah. Yoon, Salina, illus. 2005. (ENG., Illus.). 20p. (J). (gr. -1-2). bds. 7.99 *(978-0-689-87746-9(3)*, Little Simon) Little Simon.

Yorinks, Arthur. The Flying Latke. 2004. (Illus.). (J). (gr. k-3). spiral bd. *(978-0-616-03066-0(5))* Canadian National Institute for the Blind/Institut National Canadien pour les Aveugles.

Zirkind, Chaya Sara. Bas Mitzvah X 3. 2008. 156p. (J). *(978-1-56871-448-6(3))* Targum Pr., Inc.

JEWS—FOLKLORE

Here are entered works on post-Biblical Jewish folklore and Jews as a theme in folklore.

Forest, Heather. A Big Quiet House: A Yiddish Folktale from Eastern Empire. Gaber, Susan & Greenstein, Susan, illus. 2005. (ENG.). 32p. (J). (gr. k-3). pap. 7.95 *(978-0-87483-604-2(2))* August Hse. Pubs., Inc.

—A Big Quiet House: A Yiddish Folktale from Eastern Europe. Greenstein, Susan, illus. 2005. (ENG.). 32p. (J). (gr. k-3). 15.95 *(978-0-87483-462-8(7))* August Hse. Pubs., Inc.

Gelfand, Shoshana Boyd. Jewish Tales. Hall, Amanda, illus. 2013. 80p. (J). (gr. 4-6). 19.99 *(978-1-84686-884-9(X))* Barefoot Bks., Inc.

Gilman, Phoebe. Something from Nothing. (J). (gr. k-13). pap. *(978-0-590-47281-4(X)*, SO8818) Scholastic, Inc.

Goldin, Barbara Diamond. The Family Book of Midrash: 52 Jewish Stories from the Sages. 2006. Orig. Title: A Child's Book of Midrash. (ENG.). 128p. per. 37.00 *(978-0-7425-5285-2(3))* Rowman & Littlefield Publishers, Inc.

Labensohn, Judy, et al. Jewish Sports Stories for Kids. 2005. (Illus.). 224p. (J). (gr. 3-7). 16.95 *(978-1-930143-66-1(4))*; pap. 12.95 *(978-1-930143-67-8(2))* Simcha Media Group. (Devora Publishing).

Matov, G. Tales of Tzaddikim. Weinbach, Shaindel, tr. Bardugo, Miriam, illus. (J). pap. 56.99 *(978-0-89906-842-8(1))* Mesorah Pubns., Ltd.

Schwartz, Howard. The Day the Rabbi Disappeared: Jewish Holiday Tales of Magic. 2003. (ENG., Illus.). 80p. pap. 13.00 *(978-0-8276-0757-6(1))* Jewish Pubn. Society.

—A Journey to Paradise: And Other Jewish Tales. Carmi, Giora, illus. 2005. (Jewish Storyteller Ser.). 48p. (J). (gr. -1-3). 16.95 *(978-0-943706-21-4(1))*; pap. 9.95 *(978-0-943706-16-0(5))* Simcha Media Group. (Devora Publishing).

Sherman, Josepha. Rachel the Clever & Other Jewish Folktales. 2005. (American Storytelling Ser.). (ENG., Illus.). 171p. (J). (gr. 4-17). pap. 12.95 *(978-0-87483-307-2(8))* August Hse. Pubs., Inc.

Sokoloff, David. Classic Jewish Tales. 2003. (Illus.). 96p. pap. 8.95 *(978-1-56171-948-8(X))* SPI Bks.

Story of Pnei Yehoshua. (J). 6.99 *(978-0-89906-845-9(6)*, PNYH) Mesorah Pubns., Ltd.

Weston Woods Staff, creator. Joseph Had a Little Overcoat. 2004. 29.95 *(978-1-55592-109-5(4))* Weston Woods Studios, Inc.

JEWS—GERMANY

Bartoletti, Susan Campbell. Hitler Youth: Growing up in Hitler's Shadow (Scholastic Focus) 2019. (ENG.). 384p. (YA). (gr. 7-7). pap. 10.99 *(978-1-338-30984-3(6)*, Scholastic Nonfiction) Scholastic, Inc.

Byers, Ann. Anti-Semitism & the Final Solution: The Holocaust Overview, 1 vol. 2014. (Remembering the Holocaust Ser.). (ENG.). 96p. (gr. 6-7). (J). pap. 13.88 *(978-0-7660-6193-4(0)*, 532be88f-42d9-4ca5-a66a-87fc327ba1b2); (Illus.). 31.61 *(978-0-7660-6192-7(2)*, 96ebda6d-7667-4be6-b077-bda479bfb51d) Enslow Publishing, LLC.

—Kristallnacht & Living in Nazi Germany, 1 vol. 2014. (Documentary History of the Holocaust Ser.). (ENG.). 80p. (YA). (gr. 7-7). 37.47 *(978-1-4777-7595-0(1)*, cc87b96f-89ff-4cc9-a240-2d18fcd0f8ab) Rosen Publishing Group, Inc., The.

Deem, James. Kristallnacht: The Nazi Terror That Began the Holocaust, 1 vol. 2012. (Holocaust Through Primary Sources Ser.). (ENG., Illus.). 128p. (gr. 6-7). pap. 13.88 *(978-1-59845-345-4(9),* 7acf8bff-a445-45c4-a5e2-b68784effa27); lib. bdg. 35.93 *(978-0-7660-3324-5(4),* fafb7391-d3e4-4869-9c4d-462b6e5cfd25) Enslow Publishing, LLC.

Hillman, Laura. I Will Plant You a Lilac Tree: A Memoir of a Schindler's List Survivor. 2005. (ENG., Illus.). 256p. (YA). (gr. 8). 22.99 *(978-0-689-86980-8(0),* Atheneum Bks. for Young Readers) Simon & Schuster Children's Publishing.

Jacobs Altman, Linda. Warsaw, Lodz, Vilna: The Holocaust Ghettos, 1 vol. 2014. (Remembering the Holocaust Ser.). (ENG.). 96p. (J). (gr. 6-7). pap. 13.88 *(978-0-7660-6208-5(2),* ec751daf-6e53-4560-947e-0e7831cc2b92) Enslow Publishing, LLC.

Mara, Wil. Kristallnacht: Nazi Persecution of the Jews in Europe, 1 vol. 2010. (Perspectives On Ser.). (ENG.). 112p. (YA). (gr. 8-8). 42.64 *(978-0-7614-4026-0(7),* 6dd82e89-75ad-4fe7-9850-f03665ccabdd) Cavendish Square Publishing LLC.

Perl, Lila. Four Perfect Pebbles: A True Story of the Holocaust. 2016. (ENG.). 160p. (J). (gr. 7-7). pap. 7.99 *(978-0-06-248996-8(8),* Greenwillow Bks.) HarperCollins Pubs.

Russo, Marisabina. Always Remember Me: How One Family Survived World War II. Russo, Marisabina, illus. 2005. (ENG., Illus.). 48p. (J). (gr. 1-5). 24.99 *(978-0-689-86920-4(7),* Atheneum Bks. for Young Readers) Simon & Schuster Children's Publishing.

Shoup, Kate. Nazi Propaganda: Jews in Hitler's Germany, 1 vol. 2016. (Public Persecutions Ser.). (ENG., Illus.). 128p. (J). (gr. 9-9). 47.36 *(978-1-5026-2321-8(8),* a16e22a3-9ffb-4141-bf8d-6feb6fd658b2) Cavendish Square Publishing LLC.

JEWS—GREAT BRITAIN

Alexander, Lori. A Sporting Chance: How Ludwig Guttmann Created the Paralympic Games. Drummond, Allan, illus. 2020. (ENG.). 128p. (J). (gr. 3-7). 17.99 *(978-1-328-58079-5(2),* 1728624, Clarion Bks.) HarperCollins Pubs.

JEWS—HISTORY

Bader, Joanne. Moses & the Long Walk. von der Sterre, Johanna, illus. 2006. (ENG.). 16p. (J). pap. 1.99 *(978-0-7586-0874-1(8))* Concordia Publishing Hse.

Bartoletti, Susan Campbell. Hitler Youth: Growing up in Hitler's Shadow (Scholastic Focus), 1 vol. 2005. (ENG., Illus.). 176p. (YA). (gr. 7-7). 21.99 *(978-0-439-35379-3(3))* Scholastic, Inc.

Batalion, Judy. The Light of Days Young Readers' Edition: The Untold Story of Women Resistance Fighters in Hitler's Ghettos. (ENG.). 288p. (J). (gr. 5). 2022. pap. 8.99 *(978-0-06-303770-0(X))* 2021. (Illus.). 17.99 *(978-0-06-303769-4(6))* HarperCollins Pubs. (HarperCollins).

Behar, Yvonne. Out of Spain Vol. 3: Celebrating Sephardi Culture. Brooks, Andree Aelion, ed. (Illus.). 58p. (J). (gr. 5-7). pap. 4.95 *(978-0-9702700-3-0(8))* Brooks, Andree Aelion.

Bower, Gary. The Hurry-Up Exit from Egypt. Chotiner, Barbara, illus. 2017. (Faith That God Built Book Ser.). (ENG.). 32p. (J). 14.99 *(978-1-4964-1745-9(3),* 20_28620, Tyndale Kids) Tyndale Hse. Pubs.

Broida, Marian. Ancient Israelites & Their Neighbors: An Activity Guide. 2003. (Cultures of the Ancient World Ser.). (ENG., Illus.). 160p. (J). (gr. 4). pap., act. bk. ed. 19.99 *(978-1-55652-457-8(9))* Chicago Review Pr., Inc.

Brown, Jonatha A. Anne Frank, 1 vol. 2004. (Gente Que Hay Que Conocer (People We Should Know) Ser.). (SPA., Illus.). 24p. (gr. 2-4). lib. bdg. 24.67 *(978-0-8368-4351-4(7),* 7fe331d8-2239-48d7-b26a-bd97a16a9e3e, Weekly Reader Leveled Readers) Stevens, Gareth Publishing LLLP.

Charry, Elias & Segal, Abraham. The Eternal People. (Illus.). 448p. (J). (gr. 9-11). 7.50 *(978-0-8381-0206-0(9),* 10-206) United Synagogue of America Bk. Service.

Draper, Allison Stark. Pastor André Trocmé: Spiritual Leader of the French Village le Chambon. 2009. (Holocaust Biographies Ser.). 112p. (gr. 7-12). 63.90 *(978-1-61513-390-1(9))* Rosen Publishing Group, Inc., The.

Eisenberg, Azriel. Fill a Blank Page: A Biography of Solomon Schechter. (Illus.). (J). (gr. 6-11). 3.75 *(978-0-8381-0730-0(3),* 10-730) United Synagogue of America Bk. Service.

Engel, Barbara, et al. From Ur to Eternity: The Historical Adventures of the Jewish People. 2010. (J). *(978-1-60280-034-2(0));* (Illus.). pap. *(978-1-60280-035-9(9))* Ktav Publishing Hse., Inc.

Goldstein, Jessica & Inker, Inna, eds. Let My People Go! Carol, Racklin-Siegel, illus. 2011. (ENG & HEB.). 32p. (J). pap. 11.95 *(978-0-939144-67-9(0))* EKS Publishing Co.

Heiman, Diane & Suneby, Liz. The Mitzvah Project Book: Making Mitzvah Part of Your Bar/Bat Mitzvah ... & Your Life. 2011. (ENG., Illus.). 224p. (J). pap. 16.99 *(978-1-58023-458-0(5),* 9607fb2a-3be2-44c2-839b-f171f29fdc57, Jewish Lights Publishing) LongHill Partners, Inc.

House, Behrman. Min Ha'aretz. 2016. (ENG.). 1p. pap. 10.95 *(978-0-87441-938-2(7),* 3375f295-7eb6-4671-af10-ef77abd7c21b) Behrman Hse., Inc.

Immell, Myra, ed. The Creation of the State of Israel, 1 vol. 2009. (Perspectives on Modern World History Ser.). (ENG., Illus.). 224p. (gr. 10-12). 49.43 *(978-0-7377-4556-6(8),* 2d04d54d-7c12-4cc2-a77c-863ec3ac2d0c, Greenhaven Publishing) Greenhaven Publishing LLC.

Jones, Graham. How They Lived in Bible Times. Deverell, Richard, illus. 2003. 48p. 6.49 *(978-1-85999-435-1(0))* Scripture Union GBR. Dist: Gabriel Resources.

Kacer, Kathy. To Hope & Back: The Journey of the St. Louis, 1 vol. 2011. (Holocaust Remembrance Series for Young Readers Ser.: 11). (ENG., Illus.). 204p. (J). (gr. 6-8). pap. 14.95 *(978-1-897187-96-8(3))* Second Story Pr. CAN. Dist: Orca Bk. Pubs. USA.

Kor, Eva Mozes & Buccieri, Lisa Rojany. Surviving the Angel of Death: The True Story of a Mengele Twin in Auschwitz. 2012. lib. bdg. 19.60 *(978-0-606-23838-0(7))* Turtleback.

Krohn, Genendel. When We Left Yerushalayim: Stories of the Churban Beis HaMikdash. 2009. 48p. (J). (gr. 1-5). 14.99 *(978-1-59826-393-0(5))* Feldheim Pubs.

Laurel Corona. Jewish Americans. 2004. (Immigrants in America Ser.). (ENG., Illus.). 112p. (J). 30.85 *(978-1-59018-431-8(9))* Cengage Gale.

Lefcourt, Jack. Four Thousand Years of Jewish History: Then & Now. 2009. 108p. (YA). (gr. 6-18). 16.95 *(978-1-60280-132-5(0))* Ktav Publishing Hse., Inc.

Leiman, Sondra. The Atlas of Great Jewish Communities: A Voyage Through History. 2004. (gr. 4-6). pap. 13.95 *(978-0-8074-0801-8(8),* 123941) URJ Pr.

Levinger, Elma Ehrli. The Story of the Jew for Young People. 2005. pap. 30.95 *(978-1-4191-5468-3(0))* Kessinger Publishing, LLC.

Maalos, text. Baruch & Berel. 2011. (YID.). 21.00 *(978-0-9832102-4-5(1))* Roth Pubs.

Nicola, Christos & Taylor, Peter Lane. The Secret of Priest's Grotto: A Holocaust Survival Story. Nicola, Christos & Taylor, Peter Lane, photos by. 2007. (ENG., Illus.). 64p. (YA). (gr. 5-12). per. 8.95 *(978-1-58013-261-9(8),* 7cacf770-a778-4fb5-b90e-a2031c561994, Kar-Ben Publishing) Lerner Publishing Group.

Rappaport, Doreen. Beyond Courage: The Untold Story of Jewish Resistance During the Holocaust. 2012. (ENG., Illus.). 240p. (J). (gr. 5). 22.99 *(978-0-7636-2976-2(6))* Candlewick Pr.

Rosenfield, Geraldine. The Heroes of Masada. Sugarman, S. Allan, illus. 38p. (J). (gr. 6-10). pap. 1.50 *(978-0-8381-0733-1(8),* 10-732) United Synagogue of America Bk. Service.

Sarna, Jonathan D. History of the Jewish People Vol. 2: the Birth of Zionism to Our Time, 2 vols. 2007. (ENG., Illus.). 144p. (J). pap. 15.95 *(978-0-87441-192-8(0),* 57ad7000-fd44-4391-99b6-8459cb644bb5) Behrman Hse., Inc.

Schiffman, Lawrence H. Understanding Second Temple & Rabbinic Judaism. 2003. (Illus.). xviii, 409p. (YA). 29.50 *(978-0-88125-813-4(X))* Ktav Publishing Hse., Inc.

Senker, Cath. Judaism. 2007. (Atlas of World Faiths/Arcturus Ser.). (Illus.). 48p. (YA). (gr. 7-12). lib. bdg. 32.80 *(978-1-59920-056-9(2))* Black Rabbit Bks.

Stadtler, Bea. The Adventures of Gluckel of Hameln. (J). (gr. 6-10). 3.75 *(978-0-8381-0731-7(1),* 10-731) United Synagogue of America Bk. Service.

Weilerstein, Sadie Rose. Jewish Heroes, 2 bks. Cassel, Lili, illus. 208p. (J). (gr. 2-3). Bk. 1. 4.25 *(978-0-8381-0180-3(1))*Bk. 2. 4.25 *(978-0-8381-0177-3(1))* United Synagogue of America Bk. Service.

Yeatts, Tabatha. Wiesel, Wiesenthal, Klarsfeld: The Holocaust Survivors, 1 vol. 2014. (Remembering the Holocaust Ser.). (ENG.). 96p. (gr. 6-7). (J). pap. 13.88 *(978-0-7660-6203-0(1),* 6094e36c-db75-4306-950a-a73e2181ab01); 31.61 *(978-0-7660-6202-3(3),* 9ec1316b-2d0a-4151-8b87-82a52cca4da2) Enslow Publishing, LLC.

JEWS—HISTORY—FICTION

Anton, Maggie. Rashi's Daughter, Secret Scholar. 2008. (ENG.). 160p. (gr. 4-7). pap. 14.00 *(978-0-8276-0869-6(1))* Jewish Pubn. Society.

Benderly, Beryl Lieff. Jason's Miracle: A Hanukkah Story. 2004. 114p. (J). (gr. 4-8). reprint ed. *(978-0-7567-7792-0(5))* DIANE Publishing Co.

Berneger, Marcia. A Dreidel in Time: A New Spin on an Old Tale. Castro, Beatriz, illus. 2019. (ENG.). 88p. (J). (gr. 3-7). 17.99 *(978-1-5415-4672-1(5),* 192e3233-0d85-465d-9d2d-d3070039f409, Kar-Ben Publishing) Lerner Publishing Group.

Booth, Bradley. Escape from Egypt. 2009. (J). pap. 11.99 *(978-0-8163-2305-0(4))* Pacific Pr. Publishing Assn.

—Esther: A Star Is Born. 2009. (J). pap. 12.99 *(978-0-8163-2359-3(3))* Pacific Pr. Publishing Assn.

—Plagues in the Palace. 2006. 159p. (J). 10.99 *(978-0-8163-2143-8(4))* Pacific Pr. Publishing Assn.

—Prince of Dreams. 2008. (J). pap. 10.99 *(978-0-8163-2253-4(8))* Pacific Pr. Publishing Assn.

Chotjewitz, David & Orgel, Doris. Daniel, Half Human: And the Good Nazi. 2004. 298p. (J). *(978-3-551-58045-0(6))* Carlsen Verlag DEU. Dist: Distribooks, Inc.

Deutsch, Barry. Hereville: How Mirka Met a Meteorite. 2012. (Hereville Ser.). (ENG., Illus.). 128p. (J). (gr. 3-7). 17.95 *(978-1-4197-0398-0(6),* 1004001, Amulet Bks.) Abrams, Inc.

Elvgren, Jennifer. The Whispering Town. Santomauro, Fabio, illus. 2014. (ENG.). 32p. (J). (gr. 2-5). 8.99 *(978-1-4677-1195-1(0),* ea7ed36f-d609-41ba-9b7b-1f284ebcad1d, Kar-Ben Publishing) Lerner Publishing Group.

Focus on the Family Staff & Hering, Marianne. Light in the Lions' Den. 2017. (AIO Imagination Station Bks.: 19). (ENG., Illus.). 144p. (J). pap. 5.99 *(978-1-58997-878-2(1),* 20_28513) Focus on the Family Publishing.

Greene, Jacqueline Dembar. The Secret Shofar of Barcelona. Chayka, Doug, illus. 2009. (High Holidays Ser.). (ENG.). 32p. (J). (gr. k-3). 17.95 *(978-0-8225-9915-9(5),* Kar-Ben Publishing) Lerner Publishing Group.

Hernandez, David. Land of the Pharaohs, 1 vol., 1. 2003. (Adventures of Toby Digz Ser.: 1). (ENG., Illus.). 96p. (J). pap. 5.99 *(978-1-4003-0195-9(5),* Tommy Nelson) Nelson, Thomas Inc.

Hesse, Monica. Girl in the Blue Coat. (ENG.). 320p. (YA). (gr. 7-17). 2017. pap. 10.99 *(978-0-316-26063-3(0))* 2016. E-Book 45.00 *(978-0-316-26064-0(9))* Little, Brown Bks. for Young Readers.

—Girl in the Blue Coat. 2017. (YA). lib. bdg. 20.85 *(978-0-606-39918-0(6))* Turtleback.

Kaplan, Kathy Walden. The Dog of Knots. 2005. 139p. (J). pap. 7.50 *(978-0-8028-5274-8(2))* Eerdmans, William B. Publishing Co.

Kerr, Judith. When Hitler Stole Pink Rabbit. (SPA.). 172p. (J). 11.95 *(978-84-204-3201-4(6))* Santillana USA Publishing Co., Inc.

—When Hitler Stole Pink Rabbit. 2009. (gr. 3-6). lib. bdg. 17.20 *(978-0-8085-9123-8(1))* Turtleback.

Kimmel, Eric A. Search for the Shamir. Stevanovic, Ivica, illus. 2018. (Scarlett & Sam Ser.). (ENG.). 152p. (J). (gr. 1-3). pap. 6.99 *(978-1-5124-2938-1(4),* fa05c70d-97fc-4c41-af59-93be9cd9769f, Kar-Ben Publishing) Lerner Publishing Group.

Lawrence, Caroline. The Assassins of Rome. 2005. (Roman Mysteries Ser.). (Illus.). 161p. (J). (gr. 3-7). 14.65 *(978-0-7569-5879-4(2))* Perfection Learning Corp.

Lawton, Wendy. A La Sombra de Su Mano, 1 vol. 2009. Orig. Title: Shadow of His Hand. (SPA.). 160p. pap. 4.99 *(978-0-8254-1379-7(6),* Editorial Portavoz) Kregel Pubns.

Lawton, Wendy G. Shadow of His Hand: A Story Based on the Life of Holocaust Survivor Anita Dittman. 2004. (Daughters of the Faith Ser.). (ENG.). 160p. (J). (gr. 3-3). pap. 8.99 *(978-0-8024-4074-7(6))* Moody Pubs.

Lehmann, R' Marcus, contrib. by. The Family y Aguilar. 12.95 *(978-0-87306-318-0(X))* Feldheim Pubs.

Lois, Lowry. Number the Stars: And Related Readings. 2006. (Literature Connections Ser.). 172p. (gr. 6-12). *(978-0-395-88457-7(8),* 2-70863) Holt McDougal.

Martin, Gary & Zondervan Bibles Staff. The Maiden of Thunder, 1 vol. Cariello, Sergio & Lanphear, Dave, illus. 2008. (Z Graphic Novels / Son of Samson Ser.). (ENG.). 160p. (J). (gr. 4-7). pap. 6.99 *(978-0-310-71281-7(5))* Zondervan.

—The Sword of Revenge, 1 vol., 7. Cariello, Sergio, illus. 2009. (Z Graphic Novels / Son of Samson Ser.). (ENG.). 160p. (J). pap. 6.99 *(978-0-310-71285-5(8))* Zondervan.

Martin, Gary & Zondervan Staff. The Heroes of God, 1 vol., 6. Cariello, Sergio, illus. 2009. (Z Graphic Novels / Son of Samson Ser.). (ENG.). 160p. (J). pap. 6.99 *(978-0-310-71284-8(X))* Zondervan.

Matas, Carol. Dear Canada: Turned Away. 2005. (Dear Canada Ser.). (ENG., Illus.). 208p. (J). *(978-0-439-96946-8(8))* Scholastic Canada, Ltd.

—Lisa's War. 2007. (ENG.). 128p. (J). (gr. 2-7). pap. 11.95 *(978-1-4169-6163-5(1),* Aladdin) Simon & Schuster Children's Publishing.

—Rosie in New York City: Gotcha! 2003. (ENG., Illus.). 128p. (J). (gr. 4-7). pap. 9.95 *(978-0-689-85714-0(4),* Simon & Schuster/Paula Wiseman Bks.) Simon & Schuster/Paula Wiseman Bks.

McKay, Sharon E. Esther. 2004. (ENG.). 336p. (J). pap. *(978-0-14-331204-8(9))* Penguin Canada.

Merritt, Ginny. The Window in the Wall. 2013. 78p. (J). *(978-1-60682-781-9(2))* BJU Pr.

Miklowitz, Gloria D. Masada: The Last Fortress. 2004. 198p. (YA). (gr. 4-7). 16.00 *(978-0-8028-5165-9(7))* Eerdmans, William B. Publishing Co.

—Secrets in the House of Delgado. 2004. (ENG.). 192p. (J). (gr. 4-18). pap. 8.00 *(978-0-8028-5210-6(6))* Eerdmans, William B. Publishing Co.

Morgan-Cole, Trudy J. Esther: Courage to Stand. 2010. 144p. (J). pap. 12.99 *(978-0-8280-2430-3(8))* Review & Herald Publishing Assn.

Napoli, Donna Jo. Daughter of Venice. 2003. (ENG.). 288p. (YA). (gr. 7). mass mkt. 9.99 *(978-0-440-22928-5(6),* Laurel Leaf) Random Hse. Children's Bks.

Novel Units. The Bronze Bow Novel Units Teacher Guide. 2019. (ENG.). (J). pap. 12.99 *(978-1-56137-726-8(0),* Novel Units, Inc.) Classroom Library Co.

Orgad, Dorit. The Boy from Seville. Silverston, Sondra, tr. Katz, Avi, illus. 2007. (Kar-Ben for Older Readers Ser.). (ENG.). 200p. (J). (gr. 5-7). lib. bdg. 16.95 *(978-1-58013-253-4(7),* Kar-Ben Publishing) Lerner Publishing Group.

Petersen, Alicia. Out of Darkness. 2007. (Illus.). 177p. (J). (gr. 3-7). per. 8.99 *(978-1-59166-822-0(0))* BJU Pr.

Shapiro, David L. Sara's Journey. 2005. (ENG.). 224p. (gr. 7-12). per. 16.95 *(978-0-8276-0776-7(8))* Jewish Pubn. Society.

Sharenow, Robert. The Berlin Boxing Club. 2012. (ENG.). 432p. (YA). (gr. 8-12). pap. 11.99 *(978-0-06-157970-7(X),* Balzer & Bray) HarperCollins Pubs.

Silberberg, Alan. Meet the Latkes. 2018. (ENG., Illus.). 36p. (J). (-k). 18.99 *(978-0-451-47912-9(2),* Viking Books for Young Readers) Penguin Young Readers Group.

Silverberg, Selma Kritzer. Naomi's Song. 2009. (ENG.). 142p. (gr. 7-18). pap. 19.95 *(978-0-8276-0886-3(1))* Jewish Pubn. Society.

Weil, Sylvie. Elvina's Mirror. 2009. (ENG.). 150p. (gr. 5-18). pap. 14.00 *(978-0-8276-0885-6(3))* Jewish Pubn. Society.

—My Guardian Angel. Rosner, Gillian, tr. 2014. (ENG., Illus.). 208p. (J). pap. 14.95 *(978-0-8276-1211-2(7))* Jewish Pubn. Society.

Wiseman, Eva. The Last Song. 2012. (Illus.). 232p. (YA). (gr. 7). 17.95 *(978-0-88776-979-5(9),* Tundra Bks.) Tundra Bks. CAN. Dist: Penguin Random Hse. LLC.

—Puppet. 2012. (Illus.). 256p. (YA). (gr. 7). pap. 9.95 *(978-1-77049-296-7(8),* Tundra Bks.) Tundra Bks. CAN. Dist: Penguin Random Hse. LLC.

Yolen, Jane. Miriam at the River. Le, Khoa, illus. 2020. (ENG.). 32p. (J). (gr. k-3). 17.99 *(978-1-5415-4400-0(5),* cefdb840-8803-4757-aaf8-f021c9dc804d, Kar-Ben Publishing) Lerner Publishing Group.

Zusak, Markus. The Book Thief. 2014. (ENG.). 576p. (YA). 17.24 *(978-1-63245-052-4(6))* Lectorum Pubns., Inc.

—The Book Thief. 2009. 12.64 *(978-0-7848-1941-8(6),* Everbind) Marco Bk. Co.

—The Book Thief. 2008. 552p. (gr. 7-12). 23.00 *(978-0-7569-8440-3(8))* Perfection Learning Corp.

—The Book Thief. (ENG., Illus.). (YA). (gr. 7-12). 2007. 608p. pap. 14.99 *(978-0-375-84220-7(9))* 2013. 592p. pap. 14.99 *(978-0-385-75472-9(8))* Random Hse. Children's Bks. (Knopf Bks. for Young Readers).

—The Book Thief. l.t. ed. 2006. (ENG.). 552p. 23.99 *(978-1-4104-6806-2(2));* 757p. (YA). (gr. 7-12). 24.95 *(978-0-7862-9021-5(8))* Thorndike Pr.

—The Book Thief. 2008. (ENG., Illus.). 560p. pap. *(978-0-552-77389-8(1),* Black Swan) Transworld Publishers Ltd.

—The Book Thief. 2007. 552p. lib. bdg. 24.50 *(978-1-4177-9738-7(X))* 2013. lib. bdg. 24.50 *(978-0-606-34656-6(2))* Turtleback.

—The Book Thief (Anniversary Edition) anniv. ed. 2016. (ENG., Illus.). 592p. (YA). (gr. 7-12). 22.99 *(978-1-101-93418-0(2),* Knopf Bks. for Young Readers) Random Hse. Children's Bks.

JEWS—LANGUAGE

see Hebrew Language

JEWS—NETHERLANDS

Abramson, Ann. Who Was Anne Frank? Harrison, Nancy, illus. 2007. (Who Was... ? Ser.). 103p. (gr. 2-6). 15.00 *(978-0-7569-8166-2(2))* Perfection Learning Corp.

—Who Was Anne Frank? Harrison, Nancy, illus. 2007. (Who Was... ? Ser.). 103p. (J). (gr. 4-7). 16.00 *(978-1-4177-6854-7(1))* Turtleback.

Abramson, Ann & Who HQ. Who Was Anne Frank? Harrison, Nancy, illus. 2007. (Who Was? Ser.). 112p. (J). (gr. 3-7). pap. 5.99 *(978-0-448-44482-6(8),* Penguin Workshop) Penguin Young Readers Group.

Agrimbau, Diego. Anne Frank. Trusted Translations, Trusted, tr. 2017. (Graphic Lives Ser.). (ENG., Illus.). 80p. (J). (gr. 3-9). lib. bdg. 32.65 *(978-1-5157-9161-4(0),* 136603, Capstone Pr.) Capstone.

Ashby, Ruth. Anne Frank: Young Diarist. 2005. 186p. (J). lib. bdg. 18.46 *(978-1-4242-2208-7(7))* Fitzgerald Bks.

Brown, Jonatha A. Anne Frank, 1 vol. 2004. (People We Should Know Ser.). (ENG., Illus.). 24p. (gr. 2-4). lib. bdg. 24.67 *(978-0-8368-4309-5(6),* 1756f7e6-d6b1-4106-9097-14cafa3b0b86, Weekly Reader Leveled Readers) Stevens, Gareth Publishing LLLP.

Brown, Jonatha A. & Hudson Goff, Elizabeth. Ana Frank (Anne Frank), 1 vol. 2007. (Biografías Gráficas (Graphic Biographies) Ser.). (SPA., Illus.). 32p. (gr. 3-3). lib. bdg. 29.67 *(978-0-8368-7880-6(9),* 5a383ae8-7aad-4cf3-b321-9bea4df69353) Stevens, Gareth Publishing LLLP.

—Anne Frank, 1 vol. 2005. (Graphic Biographies Ser.). (ENG., Illus.). 32p. (gr. 3-3). pap. 11.50 *(978-0-8368-6248-5(1),* 4389bf4e-ddcf-4c14-9b51-eedd036e4d5a); lib. bdg. 29.67 *(978-0-8368-6196-9(5),* f87809c2-c8f1-4401-9304-f8c4b7eb4908) Stevens, Gareth Publishing LLLP.

Gil, Carmen. Ana Frank. 2010. (Me Llamo... Ser.). (SPA., Illus.). 63p. (J). pap. *(978-84-342-3339-3(8))* Parramon Ediciones S.A.

Hollingsworth, Tamara. Anne Frank: A Light in the Dark, 1 vol. 2nd rev. ed. (TIME for KIDS(r): Informational Text Ser.). (ENG., 48p. (gr. 4-5). 2013. Illus.). (J). lib. bdg. 29.96 *(978-1-4807-1117-4(9))* 2012. pap. 13.99 *(978-1-4333-4865-5(9))* Teacher Created Materials, Inc.

Kramer, Ann. World History Biographies: Anne Frank: The Young Writer Who Told the World Her Story. 2009. (National Geographic World History Biographies Ser.). (ENG., Illus.). 64p. (J). (gr. 3-7). 7.99 *(978-1-4263-0414-9(5),* National Geographic Kids) Disney Publishing Worldwide.

McDowell, Pamela. Anne Frank. 2014. (Illus.). 24p. (J). *(978-1-4896-2456-7(2))* Weigl Pubs., Inc.

Miklowitz, Gloria. Anne Frank. 2009. pap. 13.25 *(978-1-60559-053-0(3))* Hameray Publishing Group, Inc.

Parks, Peggy J. Anne Frank. 2016. (ENG.). 80p. (J). (gr. 5-12). 38.60 *(978-1-60152-946-6(5))* ReferencePoint Pr., Inc.

Poole, Josephine. Ana Frank. Barrett, Angela, illus. 2005. (SPA.). 32p. (J). (gr. 3-4). 17.99 *(978-1-930332-87-4(4))* Lectorum Pubns., Inc.

—Anne Frank. Barrett, Angela, illus. 2nd ed. 2020. 40p. (J). pap. 15.99 *(978-0-09-940976-2(3),* Red Fox) Random House Children's Books GBR. Dist: Independent Pubs. Group.

Reiss, Johanna. The Upstairs Room. 2019. (ENG.). 208p. (J). (gr. 3-7). pap. 9.99 *(978-0-06-284980-9(8),* HarperCollins) HarperCollins Pubs.

Sasso, Sandy Eisenberg. Anne Frank & Remembering Tree. Steiskal, Erika, illus. 2015. (ENG.). 32p. (J). 16.00 *(978-1-55896-738-0(9),* Skinner Hse. Bks.) Unitarian Universalist Assn.

Waxman, Laura Hamilton. Anne Frank. 2009. (History Maker Biographies Ser.). (ENG.). 48p. (gr. 3-6). 27.93 *(978-0-7613-4221-2(4),* Lerner Pubns.) Lerner Publishing Group.

Whiting, Jim. Anne Frank. 2007. (What's So Great About... ? Ser.). (Illus.). 32p. (YA). (gr. 2-4). lib. bdg. 25.70 *(978-1-58415-581-2(7))* Mitchell Lane Pubs.

JEWS—NEW YORK (STATE)—NEW YORK—FICTION

Arato, Rona. Ice Cream Town, 1 vol. 2006. (ENG.). 192p. (J). (gr. 3-4). pap. 12.95 *(978-1-55041-591-9(3),* 3011cf3e-87a3-4d4e-9031-5a5ffd95d187) Trifolium Bks., Inc. CAN. Dist: Firefly Bks., Ltd.

Chayil, Eishes. Hush. 2012. (ENG.). 368p. (YA). (gr. 9-12). pap. 10.99 *(978-0-8027-2332-1(2),* 900076205, Bloomsbury USA Childrens) Bloomsbury Publishing USA.

Crowder, Melanie. Audacity. 2015. 400p. (YA). (gr. 7). bds. 17.99 *(978-0-399-16899-4(0),* Philomel Bks.) Penguin Young Readers Group.

Greene, Jacqueline. Rebecca Story Collection. Hirsch, Jennifer, ed. Hunt, Robert, illus. 2009. (ENG.). 456p. (YA). (gr. 3-18). 29.95 *(978-1-59369-626-9(4))* American Girl Publishing, Inc.

Hest, Amy. When Jessie Came Across the Sea. Lynch, P. J., illus. 2003. (ENG.). 40p. (J). (gr. 1-4). pap. 7.99 *(978-0-7636-1274-0(X))* Candlewick Pr.

Levine, Gail Carson. Dave at Night. 2006. (ENG.). 304p. (J). (gr. 3-7). reprint ed. pap. 9.99 *(978-0-06-440747-2(0),* HarperCollins) HarperCollins Pubs.

—Dave at Night. 2004. 281p. (gr. 3-7). 17.00 *(978-0-7569-4101-7(6))* Perfection Learning Corp.

—Dave at Night. unabr. ed. 2004. 278p. (J). (gr. 4-7). pap. 38.00 incl. audio *(978-0-8072-8379-0(7),* YA174SP, Listening Library) Random Hse. Audio Publishing Group.

Moriarty, Chris. The Watcher in the Shadows. Geyer, Mark Edward, illus. 2014. (ENG.). 336p. (J). (gr. 5-7). pap. 18.99 *(978-0-544-22776-7(X),* 1563388, Clarion Bks.) HarperCollins Pubs.

JEWS—PERSECUTIONS

Brezina, Corona. Nazi Architects of the Holocaust, 1 vol. 2014. (Documentary History of the Holocaust Ser.). (ENG.). 80p. (YA). (gr. 7-7). 37.47 *(978-1-4777-7597-4(8),* 7ce1cc23-25a8-49e4-be0a-852e8780b3d3) Rosen Publishing Group, Inc., The.

Byers, Ann. Anti-Semitism & the Final Solution: The Holocaust Overview, 1 vol. 2014. (Remembering the Holocaust Ser.). (ENG., Illus.). 96p. (J). (gr. 6-7). 31.61 *(978-0-7660-6192-7(2),* 96ebda6d-7667-4be6-b077-bda479bfb51d) Enslow Publishing, LLC.

—Kristallnacht & Living in Nazi Germany, 1 vol. 2014. (Documentary History of the Holocaust Ser.). (ENG.). 80p.

JKL

(YA). (gr. 7-7). 37.47 *(978-1-4777-7595-0(1),* cc87b96f-89ff-4cc9-a240-2d18fcd0f8ab) Rosen Publishing Group, Inc., The.

—Rescuing the Danish Jews: A Heroic Story from the Holocaust, 1 vol. 2012. (Holocaust Through Primary Sources Ser.). (ENG., Illus.). 128p. (gr. 6-7). pap. 13.88 *(978-1-59845-343-0(2),* 92e1f854-298d-4272-889c-57646367b2ed); lib. bdg. 35.93 *(978-0-7660-3321-4(X),* 82ad2f9d-f92e-4294-81a4-3a2bd64d9ad3) Enslow Publishing, LLC.

Darman, Peter, ed. The Holocaust & Life under Nazi Occupation, 1 vol. 2012. (World War II Ser.). (ENG., Illus.). 64p. (YA). (gr. 6-6). lib. bdg. 37.13 *(978-1-4488-9235-8(X),* ccc8b3e4-86a1-4236-9e10-27c64e09e64a) Rosen Publishing Group, Inc., The.

Deem, James. Auschwitz: Voices from the Death Camp, 1 vol. 2012. (Holocaust Through Primary Sources Ser.). (ENG., Illus.). 128p. (gr. 6-7). pap. 13.88 *(978-1-59845-346-1(7),* 7ff561ea-2e36-4e96-85c9-b9c7562ebbd9); lib. bdg. 35.93 *(978-0-7660-3322-1(8),* 55a671b7-eb78-49a3-b7a2-be45729f6fd7) Enslow Publishing, LLC.

—Kristallnacht: The Nazi Terror That Began the Holocaust, 1 vol. 2012. (Holocaust Through Primary Sources Ser.). (ENG., Illus.). 128p. (gr. 6-7). pap. 13.88 *(978-1-59845-345-4(9),* 7acf8bff-a445-45c4-a5e2-b68784effa27); lib. bdg. 35.93 *(978-0-7660-3324-5(4),* fafb7391-d3e4-4869-9c4d-462b6e5cfd25) Enslow Publishing, LLC.

Fitzgerald, Stephanie. Kristallnacht. 2017. (Eyewitness to World War II Ser.). (ENG., Illus.). 112p. (J). (gr. 5-9). lib. bdg. 38.65 *(978-0-7565-5583-2(3),* 135468, Compass Point Bks.) Capstone.

Forest, Jim. Silent As a Stone: Mother Maria of Paris & the Trash Can Rescue. Pancheshnaya, Dasha, illus. 2007. (ENG.). 32p. (J). 18.00 *(978-0-88141-314-4(3))* St. Vladimir's Seminary Pr.

Heing, Bridey. The Persecution of Christians & Religious Minorities by ISIS, 1 vol. 2017. (Crimes of ISIS Ser.). (ENG.). 104p. (gr. 8-8). 38.93 *(978-0-7660-9216-7(X),* 9b809955-9b80-4aec-8640-44247674f520); pap. 20.95 *(978-0-7660-9584-7(3),* 32c73849-47b1-46fc-b5c4-d73d8257cc86) Enslow Publishing, LLC.

Jacobs Altman, Linda. Warsaw, Lodz, Vilna: The Holocaust Ghettos, 1 vol. 2014. (Remembering the Holocaust Ser.). (ENG.). 96p. (gr. 6-7). (J). pap. 13.88 *(978-0-7660-6208-5(2),* ec751daf-6e53-4560-947e-0e7831cc2b92); (Illus.). 31.61 *(978-0-7660-6207-8(4),* 49a7e035-e10e-471b-86ec-fd6d3f19bdb0) Enslow Publishing, LLC.

Lensky, Mordechai. A Physician Inside the Warswa Ghetto. 2009. 257p. (YA). pap. 27.50 *(978-0-9814686-3-1(2))* Yad Vashem Pubns. ISR. Dist: Coronet Bks.

Lombardo, Jennifer & Robson, David. The Horrors of Auschwitz, 1 vol. 2016. (World History Ser.). (ENG.). 104p. (YA). (gr. 7-7). 41.53 *(978-1-5345-6054-3(8),* 9060cc72-3515-4ea6-a50a-71ab4a51a5cc, Lucent Pr.) Greenhaven Publishing LLC.

Lomberg, Michelle & Gillespie, Katie. The Diary of a Young Girl. 2018. (J). *(978-1-5105-3706-4(6))* SmartBook Media, Inc.

Mara, Wil. Kristallnacht: Nazi Persecution of the Jews in Europe, 1 vol. 2010. (Perspectives On Ser.). (ENG.). 112p. (YA). (gr. 8-8). 42.64 *(978-0-7614-4026-0(7),* 6dd82e89-75ad-4fe7-9850-f03665ccabdd) Cavendish Square Publishing LLC.

Nardo, Don. Auschwitz, 1 vol. 2009. (World History Ser.). (ENG., Illus.). 104p. (gr. 7-7). 41.53 *(978-1-4205-0131-5(3),* 954205ab-e2d7-4325-ae99-8bb21b6ba5d1, Lucent Pr.) Greenhaven Publishing LLC.

Norton, James. The Holocaust: Jews, Germany, & the National Socialists. 2009. (Genocide in Modern Times Ser.). 64p. (gr. 6-6). 58.50 *(978-1-61512-677-4(5))* Rosen Publishing Group, Inc., The.

Norton, James R. The Holocaust: Jews, Germany, & the National Socialists, 1 vol. 2008. (Genocide in Modern Times Ser.). (ENG., Illus.). 64p. (YA). (gr. 6-6). lib. bdg. 37.13 *(978-1-4042-1821-5(1),* 6ee55512-c4b4-41da-9e1e-f65f491bb9ba) Rosen Publishing Group, Inc., The.

Russo, Marisabina. Always Remember Me: How One Family Survived World War II. Russo, Marisabina, illus. 2005. (ENG., Illus.). 48p. (J). (gr. 1-5). 24.99 *(978-0-689-86920-4(7),* Atheneum Bks. for Young Readers) Simon & Schuster Children's Publishing.

Thornton, Jeremy. Religious Intolerance: Jewish Immigrants Come to America (1881-1914), 1 vol. 2003. (Primary Sources of Immigration & Migration in America Ser.). (ENG., Illus.). 24p. (J). (gr. 3-4). lib. bdg. 26.27 *(978-0-8239-6834-3(0),* cdb21403-a229-45f0-b107-6287b9669da5) Rosen Publishing Group, Inc., The.

—Religious Intolerance: Jewish Immigrants Come to America, 1890-1924, 1 vol. 2003. (Primary Sources of Immigration & Migration in America Ser.). (ENG., Illus.). 24p. (J). (gr. 3-4). pap. 9.40 *(978-0-8239-8960-7(7),* 4d026f5e-8dcc-4cc9-8e6b-135a92a572b9) Rosen Publishing Group, Inc., The.

Toll, Nelly S. Behind the Secret Window. 2003. 176p. (J). (gr. 3-7). 5.99 *(978-0-14-230241-5(4),* Puffin Books) Penguin Young Readers Group.

Ziemian, Joseph. The Cigarette Sellers of Three Crosses Square. 2005. (Library of Holocaust Testimonies Ser.). (ENG., Illus.). 168p. pap. 19.95 *(978-0-85303-686-9(1))* Vallentine Mitchell Pubs. GBR. Dist: Independent Pubs. Group.

JEWS—POLAND

Beyer, Mark. Emmanuel Ringelblum: Historian of the Warsaw Ghetto. 2009. (Holocaust Biographies Ser.). 112p. (gr. 7-12). 63.90 *(978-1-61513-384-0(4))* Rosen Publishing Group, Inc., The.

Brophy Down, Susan. Irena Sendler: Bringing Life to Children of the Holocaust. 2012. (ENG.). 112p. (J). pap. *(978-0-7787-2556-5(1));* (Illus.). *(978-0-7787-2553-4(7))* Crabtree Publishing Co.

Callahan, Kerry P. Mordechai Anielewicz: Hero of the Warsaw Ghetto Uprising. 2009. (Holocaust Biographies Ser.). 112p. (gr. 7-12). 63.90 *(978-1-61513-389-5(5))* Rosen Publishing Group, Inc., The.

Friedman, Laurie. Angel Girl. Amit, Ofra, illus. 2008. 32p. (J). (gr. 3-7). 16.95 *(978-0-8225-8739-2(4),* Carolrhoda Bks.) Lerner Publishing Group.

Jacobs Altman, Linda. The Warsaw Ghetto Uprising: Striking a Blow Against the Nazis, 1 vol. 2012. (Holocaust Through Primary Sources Ser.). (ENG., Illus.). 128p. (gr. 6-7). pap. 13.88 *(978-1-59845-347-8(5),* 4cf23899-8f03-417e-a3d3-9527718511a7); lib. bdg. 35.93 *(978-0-7660-3320-7(1),* 410c3b67-7f83-48a7-b9cb-5af796e0193f) Enslow Publishing, LLC.

—Warsaw, Lodz, Vilna: The Holocaust Ghettos, 1 vol. 2014. (Remembering the Holocaust Ser.). (ENG.). 96p. (J). (gr. 6-7). pap. 13.88 *(978-0-7660-6208-5(2),* ec751daf-6e53-4560-947e-0e7831cc2b92) Enslow Publishing, LLC.

Lensky, Mordechai. A Physician Inside the Warswa Ghetto. 2009. 257p. (YA). pap. 27.50 *(978-0-9814686-3-1(2))* Yad Vashem Pubns. ISR. Dist: Coronet Bks.

Lobel, Anita. No Pretty Pictures. 2008. (ENG.). 288p. (J). (gr. 5). pap. 7.99 *(978-0-06-156589-2(X),* Greenwillow Bks.) HarperCollins Pubs.

Rubinstein, Robert E. Zishe the Strongman. Miller, Woody, illus. 2010. (Kar-Ben Favorites Ser.). (ENG.). 32p. (J). (gr. k-3). lib. bdg. 17.95 *(978-0-7613-3958-8(2),* Kar-Ben Publishing) Lerner Publishing Group.

Shulevitz, Uri. Chance: Escape from the Holocaust. 2020. (ENG., Illus.). 336p. (J). 34.99 *(978-0-374-31371-5(7),* 900219796, Farrar, Straus & Giroux (BYR)) Farrar, Straus & Giroux.

Vaughan, Marcia. Irena's Jars of Secrets, 1 vol. Mazellan, Ron, illus. 2011. (ENG.). 40p. (J). 18.95 *(978-1-60060-439-3(0))* Lee & Low Bks., Inc.

Ziemian, Joseph. The Cigarette Sellers of Three Crosses Square. 2005. (Library of Holocaust Testimonies Ser.). (ENG., Illus.). 168p. pap. 19.95 *(978-0-85303-686-9(1))* Vallentine Mitchell Pubs. GBR. Dist: Independent Pubs. Group.

JEWS—RELIGION

see Judaism

JEWS—RITES AND CEREMONIES

Chanover, Hyman & Zusman, Evelyn. A Book of Prayer for Junior Congregations: Sabbath & Festivals. (ENG & HEB.). 256p. (J). (gr. 4-7). 4.50 *(978-0-8381-0174-2(7),* 10-174) United Synagogue of America Bk. Service.

Eisenberg, Azriel & Robinson, Jessie B. My Jewish Holidays. 208p. (J). (gr. 5-6). 3.95 *(978-0-8381-0176-6(3),* 10-176) United Synagogue of America Bk. Service.

Kunda, Shmuel. Boruch Learns His Brochos. Kunda, Shmuel, illus. 2005. (Illus.). 40p. (J). 17.95 *(978-1-932443-41-7(X))* Judaica Pr., Inc., The.

Metter, Bert & Friedman, Marvin. Bar Mitzvah, Bat Mitzvah: The Ceremony, the Party, & How the Day Came to Be. Reilly, Joan & Katz, Avi, illus. 2007. (ENG.). 80p. (J). (gr. 5-7). pap. 8.95 *(978-0-618-76773-1(8),* 100540, Clarion Bks.) HarperCollins Pubs.

JEWS—SOVIET UNION

Taybert, Efim. I Kedriy Tojze Plachyt. 2003.Tr. of And Cedars Also Cry. (RUS.). 254p. (YA). pap. *(978-0-9728301-2-6(X))* Publishing Hse. Gelany.

JEWS—SOVIET UNION—FICTION

Blumberg, Margie. Avram's Gift. McGaw, Laurie, illus. 2005. (ENG.). 48p. (YA). pap. 12.95 *(978-0-9624166-3-7(0))* MB Publishing, LLC.

Howland, Naomi. Latkes, Latkes, Good to Eat: A Hanukkah Holiday Book for Kids. 2004. (ENG., Illus.). 32p. (J). (gr. -1-3). pap. 7.99 *(978-0-618-49295-4(X),* 100396, Clarion Bks.) HarperCollins Pubs.

Lasky, Kathryn. The Night Journey. 2005. 151p. (gr. 3-7). 16.00 *(978-0-7569-5062-0(7))* Perfection Learning Corp.

Rosen, Michael J. Chanukah Lights Everywhere. 2010. (ENG.). 22p. (J). pap. 6.00 *(978-1-4379-7172-9(5))* DIANE Publishing Co.

Watts, Irene N. Good-Bye Marianne: A Story of Growing up in Nazi Germany. Shoemaker, Kathryn E., illus. 2008. 128p. (J). (gr. 4-7). pap. 12.95 *(978-0-88776-830-9(X),* Tundra Bks.) Tundra Bks. CAN. Dist: Penguin Random Hse. LLC.

JEWS—UNITED STATES

Amler, Jane Frances. Haym Salomon: Patriot Banker of the American Revolution. 2009. (Library of American Lives & Times Ser.). 112p. (gr. 5-5). 69.20 *(978-1-60853-487-6(1))* Rosen Publishing Group, Inc., The.

Bell, Samantha S. Children in the Holocaust. 2018. (Children in History Ser.). (ENG., Illus.). 48p. (J). (gr. 5-6). pap. 11.95 *(978-1-63517-977-4(7),* 1635179777); lib. bdg. 34.21 *(978-1-63517-876-0(2),* 1635178762) North Star Editions. (Focus Readers).

Borden, Louise. The Journey That Saved Curious George: The True Wartime Escape of Margret & H. A. Rey. Drummond, Allan, illus. 2010. (Curious George Ser.). (ENG.). 80p. (J). (gr. 3-7). pap. 8.99 *(978-0-547-41746-2(2),* 1430026, Clarion Bks.) HarperCollins Pubs.

Bryan, Nichol. Jewish Americans, 1 vol. 2004. (One Nation Set 1 Ser.). (ENG.). 32p. (gr. k-6). 27.07 *(978-1-57765-986-0(4),* Checkerboard Library) ABDO Publishing Co.

Cohon, Rhody & Deutsch, Stacia. Hot Pursuit: Murder in Mississippi. Orback, Craig, illus. 2010. (ENG.). 40p. (J). (gr. 3-5). pap. 7.95 *(978-0-7613-3956-4(6),* 77cdd621-0509-4a81-bddf-ae8d265cd44d, Kar-Ben Publishing) Lerner Publishing Group.

Glaser, Linda. Emma's Poem: The Voice of the Statue of Liberty. Nivola, Claire A., illus. 2013. (ENG.). 32p. (J). (gr. -1-3). pap. 9.99 *(978-0-544-10508-9(7),* 1540808, Clarion Bks.) HarperCollins Pubs.

Laurel Corona. Jewish Americans. 2004. (Immigrants in America Ser.). (ENG., Illus.). 112p. (J). 30.85 *(978-1-59018-431-8(9))* Cengage Gale.

Lewin, Rhoda. Reform Jews of Minneapolis. 2004. (Images of America Ser.). (ENG., Illus.). 128p. pap. 21.99 *(978-0-7385-3217-2(7))* Arcadia Publishing.

Macy, Sue. The Book Rescuer: How a Mensch from Massachusetts Saved Yiddish Literature for Generations to Come. Innerst, Stacy, illus. 2019. (ENG.). 48p. (J). (gr. k-3). 17.99 *(978-1-4814-7220-3(8))* Simon & Schuster.

Michelson, Richard. As Good As Anybody: Martin Luther King, Jr., & Abraham Joshua Heschel's Amazing March Toward Freedom. ón, Raul, illus. 2013. (ENG.). 40p. (J). (gr. 1-4). 8.99 *(978-0-385-75387-6(X),* Dragonfly Bks.) Random Hse. Children's Bks.

Moreno, Barry. The Jewish Americans. (Major American Immigration Ser.). (YA). 2010. (Illus.). 64p. (gr. 9-12). 22.95 *(978-1-4222-0611-9(4))* 2007. pap. 9.95 *(978-1-4222-0678-2(5))* Mason Crest.

Palmer, Bill. Gallup Guides for Youth Facing Persistent Prejudice. 2012. (Gallup Guides for Youth Facing Persistent Prejudice Ser.). 64p. (J). (gr. 7-8). 22.95 *(978-1-4222-2466-3(X))* Mason Crest.

Rubinstein, Robert E. Zishe the Strongman. Miller, Woody, illus. 2010. (Kar-Ben Favorites Ser.). (ENG.). 32p. (J). (gr. k-3). lib. bdg. 17.95 *(978-0-7613-3958-8(2),* Kar-Ben Publishing) Lerner Publishing Group.

Sohn, Ruth H. Crossing Cairo: A Jewish Woman's Encounter with Egypt. 2013. 272p. pap. 18.95 *(978-1-935604-50-1(3))* Gaon Bks.

Stein, Robert. Jewish Americans: Coming to America. 2006. (Illus.). 128p. (J). (gr. 4-8). reprint ed. 15.00 *(978-1-4223-5576-3(4))* DIANE Publishing Co.

Stone, Amy M. Jewish Americans, 1 vol. 2006. (World Almanac(r) Library of American Immigration Ser.). (ENG., Illus.). 48p. (gr. 5-8). pap. 15.05 *(978-0-8368-7327-6(0),* e3f89159-d969-406e-9348-c4ad54e49520); lib. bdg. 33.67 *(978-0-8368-7314-6(9),* b9e6cfa9-f253-4ca8-b5a0-48647b4cd37e) Stevens, Gareth Publishing LLLP. (Gareth Stevens Secondary Library).

Taylor, Peter Lane. The Secret of Priest's Grotto: A Holocaust Survival Story. 2007. (Holocaust Ser.). (Illus.). 64p. (J). (gr. 3-7). lib. bdg. 18.95 *(978-1-58013-260-2(X),* Kar-Ben Publishing) Lerner Publishing Group.

Thornton, Jeremy. Religious Intolerance: Jewish Immigrants Come to America (1881-1914) (Primary Sources of Immigration & Migration in America Ser.). 24p. (gr. 3-4). 2009. 42.50 *(978-1-60851-783-1(7),* PowerKids Pr.) 2003. (ENG., Illus.). (J). lib. bdg. 26.27 *(978-0-8239-6834-3(0),* cdb21403-a229-45f0-b107-6287b9669da5) Rosen Publishing Group, Inc., The.

—Religious Intolerance: Jewish Immigrants Come to America, 1890-1924, 1 vol. 2003. (Primary Sources of Immigration & Migration in America Ser.). (ENG., Illus.). 24p. (J). (gr. 3-4). pap. 9.40 *(978-0-8239-8960-7(7),* 4d026f5e-8dcc-4cc9-8e6b-135a92a572b9) Rosen Publishing Group, Inc., The.

JEWS—UNITED STATES—FICTION

Ades, Audrey. Judah Touro Didn't Want to Be Famous. Mildenberger, Vivien, illus. 2020. (ENG.). 32p. (J). (gr. k-3). 17.99 *(978-1-5415-4561-8(3),* 35256b85-1e87-4c96-b654-f9cca58b6dcc, Kar-Ben Publishing) Lerner Publishing Group.

Adler, David. Hanukkah Cookies with Sprinkles. Ebbeler, Jeffrey, illus. 2015. (ENG.). 32p. (J). 17.95 *(978-1-68115-500-5(1),* 4cebbde7-e454-483a-8bcf-491915b1324f) Behrman Hse., Inc.

—Yom Kippur Shortstop. Ceolin, Andre, illus. 2017. (ENG.). 32p. (J). 17.95 *(978-1-68115-521-0(4),* 49f3280f-23c8-4bfb-b3e9-53590244a34b) Behrman Hse., Inc.

Aldredge, Betsy & DuBois-Shaw, Carrie. Sasquatch, Love, & Other Imaginary Things. 2017. (ENG., Illus.). 272p. (YA). (gr. 9). 19.99 *(978-1-5072-0280-7(6),* Simon Pulse) Simon Pulse.

Andrews, Jesse. Me & Earl & the Dying Girl. 2015. (CHI.). 320p. (YA). (gr. 9-17). pap. *(978-986-344-282-0(8))* Rye Field Publishing, Co.

—Me & Earl & the Dying Girl. 2015. lib. bdg. 20.80 *(978-0-606-37113-1(3))* Turtleback.

—Me & Earl & the Dying Girl (Revised Edition) rev. ed. 2015. (ENG.). 320p. (YA). (gr. 9-17). pap. 11.99 *(978-1-4197-1960-8(2),* 1003806) Abrams, Inc.

Asher, Diana Harmon. Sidetracked. (ENG.). (J). (gr. 3-7). 2018. 256p. pap. 8.99 *(978-1-4197-3139-6(4),* 1153303) 2017. 240p. 16.99 *(978-1-4197-2601-9(3),* 1153301) Abrams, Inc. (Amulet Bks.).

Avrech, Robert J. The Hebrew Kid & the Apache Maiden. 2006. (Illus.). 220p. (J). (gr. 4-7). per. 11.95 *(978-0-9754382-2-0(0))* Seraphic Pr.

Backenroth, Yehudis. More Adventures of PJ Pepperjay, 1 vol. Judowitz, Chani, illus. 2016. (ENG.). 96p. (J). *(978-1-4226-1688-6(6),* ArtScroll Series) Mesorah Pubns., Ltd.

Baer, Julie, illus. & text. I Only Like What I Like. Baer, Julie, text. 2003. 32p. (J). 15.99 *(978-1-932188-00-4(2))* Bollix Bks.

Barash, Chris. One Fine Shabbat. Mai-Wyss, Tatjana, illus. 2016. (ENG.). 12p. (J). (gr. -1 — 1). E-Book 23.99 *(978-1-4677-9614-9(X),* Kar-Ben Publishing) Lerner Publishing Group.

—Wait It's Friday. Grove, Christine, illus. 2019. (ENG.). 24p. (J). 17.95 *(978-1-68115-542-5(7),* 6bc32c17-0b30-46e6-8ae9-a0206e93bcfb, Apples & Honey Pr.) Behrman Hse., Inc.

Barbara, Cohen. Molly's Pilgrim. 97th rev. ed. 2014. (ENG.). 32p. (J). (gr. 1-5). 8.24 *(978-1-63245-244-3(8))* Lectorum Pubns., Inc.

Barnhart, Aaron. Firebrand. 2015. (ENG., Illus.). 168p. (J). 19.95 *(978-0-9669258-6-9(6))* Quindaro Pr.

Baron, Jeff. Sean Rosen Is Not for Sale. 2015. (ENG.). 384p. (J). (gr. 3-7). pap. 6.99 *(978-0-06-218751-2(1),* Greenwillow Bks.) HarperCollins Pubs.

Baskin, Nora Raleigh. My Bat Mitzvah. 2008. (ENG.). 144p. (J). (gr. 6-8). 18.69 *(978-1-4169-3558-2(4))* Simon & Schuster, Inc.

—The Truth about My Bat Mitzvah. 2009. (Mix Ser.). (ENG.). 144p. (J). (gr. 4-8). pap. 7.99 *(978-1-4169-7469-7(5),* Aladdin) Simon & Schuster Children's Publishing.

Benjamin, Ruth. The Lost Treasure of Chelton. 2004. viii, 170p. (J). 13.95 *(978-1-932443-02-8(9))* Judaica Pr., Inc., The.

—The Mysterious Lighthouse of Chelton. 2006. (ENG.). 160p. (J). 14.95 *(978-1-932443-57-8(6))* Judaica Pr., Inc., The.

Bick, Ilsa J. Draw the Dark. (ENG.). 344p. (YA). (gr. 9-12). 2011. pap. 9.95 *(978-0-7613-8131-0(7),* 308f22d6-6abe-45af-b28c-b962f2cb5485) 2010. 16.95 *(978-0-7613-5686-8(X))* Lerner Publishing Group. (Carolrhoda Lab™).

Blume, Judy. Starring Sally J. Freedman As Herself. 2014. (ENG., Illus.). (J). (gr. 3-7). 384p. 18.99 *(978-1-4814-1437-1(2));* 400p. pap. 8.99 *(978-1-4814-1355-8(4))* Simon & Schuster Children's Publishing. (Atheneum Bks. for Young Readers).

Brandeis, Gayle. My Life with the Lincolns. 2010. (ENG.). 256p. (J). (gr. 5-9). 35.99 *(978-0-8050-9013-0(4),* 900059042, Holt, Henry & Co. Bks. For Young Readers) Holt, Henry & Co.

Burkhart, Kiersi & Keyser, Amber J. The Long Trail Home. 2017. (Quartz Creek Ranch Ser.). (ENG.). 240p. (J). (gr. 4-8). E-Book 42.65 *(978-1-5124-2698-4(9),* Darby Creek) Lerner Publishing Group.

Cohen, Barbara. Molly's Pilgrim. Bricking, Jennifer, illus. 2018. (ENG.). 48p. (J). (gr. 1-5). pap. 5.99 *(978-0-06-287094-0(7),* HarperCollins) HarperCollins Pubs.

—Molly's Pilgrim. 97th rev. ed. 2005. (ENG., Illus.). 32p. (J). (gr. 1-5). pap. 3.99 *(978-0-688-16280-1(0),* HarperCollins) HarperCollins Pubs. Ltd. GBR. Dist: HarperCollins Pubs.

—Molly's Pilgrim. (Literature to Go Ser.). pap., tchr. ed. incl. VHS *(978-0-7919-2685-7(0))* Phoenix Films & Video.

Crowder, Melanie. Audacity. 400p. (YA). (gr. 7). 2016. pap. 12.99 *(978-0-14-751249-9(2),* Speak) 2015. bds. 17.99 *(978-0-399-16899-4(0),* Philomel Bks.) Penguin Young Readers Group.

Dembar Greene, Jacqueline. Speak up, Tommy! Melmon, Deborah, illus. 2012. (ENG.). 32p. (J). (gr. -1-3). lib. bdg. 7.99 *(978-0-7613-7497-8(3),* b2cb5815-831a-4c38-bdc1-077c718db263, Kar-Ben Publishing) Lerner Publishing Group.

Edwards, Michelle. A Hat for Mrs. Goldman: A Story about Knitting & Love. Karas, G. Brian, illus. 2016. 40p. (J). (gr. -1-3). 18.99 *(978-0-553-49710-6(3),* Schwartz & Wade Bks.) Random Hse. Children's Bks.

Elkeles, Simone. How to Ruin My Teenage Life. 2007. (How to Ruin a Summer Vacation Novel Ser.: 2). (ENG.). 288p. (YA). (gr. 9-12). per. 11.99 *(978-0-7387-1019-8(9),* 0738710199, Flux) North Star Editions.

Fagan, Cary. Mr. Tempkin Climbs a Tree. Arbat, Carles, illus. 2019. (ENG.). 32p. (J). (gr. -1-2). 17.99 *(978-1-5415-2173-5(0),* 91d22d39-8a82-48ce-a5d1-699b688c7999, Kar-Ben Publishing) Lerner Publishing Group.

Faigen, Anne G. New World Waiting. 2006. iii, 188p. (J). pap. *(978-0-9744715-5-6(0))* Local History Co., The.

Feldman, Eve B. Seymour, the Formerly Fearful. Singh, Parwinder, illus. 2019. (ENG.). 184p. (J). (gr. 3-6). pap. 8.99 *(978-1-5415-3951-8(6),* def5e665-e8c7-4bc2-a8fe-04cb2a223083, Kar-Ben Publishing) Lerner Publishing Group.

Fields, Terri. One Good Deed. Melmon, Deborah, illus. 2015. (ENG.). 24p. (J). (gr. -1-3). E-Book 23.99 *(978-1-4677-8841-0(4),* Kar-Ben Publishing) Lerner Publishing Group.

Fireside, Bryna J. Private Joel & the Sewell Mountain Seder. Costello, Shawn, illus. 2008. (Passover Ser.). 47p. (J). (gr. 3-6). lib. bdg. 16.95 *(978-0-8225-7240-4(0),* Kar-Ben Publishing) Lerner Publishing Group.

Frank, Steven B. Armstrong & Charlie. 2017. (ENG.). 304p. (J). (gr. 5-7). 16.99 *(978-0-544-82608-3(6),* 1644260, Clarion Bks.) HarperCollins Pubs.

Fuks, Menuhah & Tager, Gavriella. Smile with Avigayil #1: Avigayil & the Little Student. Haas, Esti, illus. 2006. 64p. (J). 12.95 *(978-1-932443-60-8(6))* Judaica Pr., Inc., The.

—Smile with Avigayil #2: Avigayil & the Black Cat. Haas, Esti, illus. 2006. (ENG.). 64p. (J). 12.95 *(978-1-932443-58-5(4))* Judaica Pr., Inc., The.

Gadot, A. S. The First Gift. Lafrance, Marie, illus. 2006. (ENG.). 24p. (J). (gr. -1-3). lib. bdg. 15.95 *(978-1-58013-146-9(8),* Kar-Ben Publishing) Lerner Publishing Group.

Gagnon, Mary. Are Those Your Shoes? 2008. 120p. pap. 11.95 *(978-1-4357-2942-1(0))* Lulu Pr., Inc.

Gardner, Sheldon. The Converso Legacy. 2005. 264p. (J). 18.95 *(978-1-932687-18-7(1),* Devora Publishing) Simcha Media Group.

Geras, Adèle. Voyage. 2006. (Illus.). 116p. (J). (gr. 4-7). per. 6.95 *(978-1-903015-00-1(6))* Barn Owl Bks, London GBR. Dist: Independent Pubs. Group.

Glaser, Linda. Hannah's Way. Gustavson, Adam, illus. 2012. (Shabbat Ser.). 32p. (J). (gr. k-3). lib. bdg. 17.95 *(978-0-7613-5137-5(X),* Kar-Ben Publishing) Lerner Publishing Group.

Goldblatt, Mark. Finding the Worm (Twerp Sequel) 2016. (Twerp Ser.: 2). 368p. (J). (gr. 4-7). 7.99 *(978-0-385-39111-5(0),* Yearling) Random Hse. Children's Bks.

Greene, Bette. Summer of My German Soldier (Puffin Modern Classics) 2006. (Puffin Modern Classics Ser.). (ENG.). 240p. (J). (gr. 5-18). 8.99 *(978-0-14-240651-9(1),* Puffin Books) Penguin Young Readers Group.

Griffis, Molly Levite. Simon Says. 2004. vi, 263p. (J). 22.95 *(978-1-57168-836-1(6));* pap. *(978-1-57168-847-7(1))* Eakin Pr. (Eakin Pr.).

Haft, Sheryl. Goodnight Bubbala. Weber, Jill, illus. 2019. (ENG.). 32p. (J). (gr. k-k). 17.99 *(978-0-525-55477-6(7),* Dial Bks) Penguin Young Readers Group.

Heiligman, Deborah. Intentions. 2013. (ENG.). 176p. (J). (gr. 9-12). 26.19 *(978-0-375-96861-7(X),* Knopf Bks. for Young Readers) Random Hse. Children's Bks.

Heller, Linda. The Castle on Hester Street. Kulikov, Boris, illus. 25th ed. 2007. (ENG.). 40p. (J). (gr. -1-3). 19.99 *(978-0-689-87434-5(0),* Simon & Schuster Bks. For Young Readers) Simon & Schuster Bks. For Young Readers.

Herman, Michael. The Cholent Brigade. Harmer, Sharon, illus. 2017. (ENG.). 24p. (J). (gr. -1-2). 17.99 *(978-1-5124-0844-7(1),* b722c6c0-cad2-413d-b91b-0dc341c18f8f, Kar-Ben Publishing) Lerner Publishing Group.

Hesse, Karen. Brooklyn Bridge: A Novel. Sheban, Chris, illus. 2011. (ENG.). 256p. (J). (gr. 6-8). pap. 11.99 *(978-0-312-67428-1(7),* 900072843) Square Fish.

Hilb, Jessie. The Calculus of Change. 2018. (ENG.). 336p. (YA). (gr. 9). 17.99 *(978-0-544-95333-8(9))*, 1660557, Clarion Bks.) HarperCollins Pubs.

Hoberman, Mary Ann. Strawberry Hill. Halperin, Wendy Anderson, illus. 2009. (ENG.). 240p. (J). (gr. 4-6). 21.19 *(978-0-316-04136-2(X))* Little Brown & Co.

—Strawberry Hill. 2010. (ENG., Illus.). 240p. (J). (gr. 3-7). pap. 13.99 *(978-0-316-04135-5(1))* Little, Brown Bks. for Young Readers.

House, Behrman. Lets Talk Now! More Modern Heb for Teens TG. 2015. (ENG., Illus.). 1p. (J). pap. 26.95 *(978-0-87441-918-4(2)*, b7e55376-8e54-47ce-b6d2-c7e994a9764c) Behrman Hse., Inc.

Houston, Julian. New Boy. 2008. (ENG.). 288p. (YA). (gr. 7-12). pap. 7.99 *(978-0-618-88405-6(X)*, 488284, Clarion Bks.) HarperCollins Pubs.

—New Boy. 2007. 282p. (gr. 7-12). 18.00 *(978-0-7569-8139-6(5))* Perfection Learning Corp.

Hubner, Carol Korb. The Devora Doresh Mysteries. 2006. (Illus.). 288p. (J). 16.95 *(978-1-932443-59-2(2))* Judaica Pr., Inc., The.

—The Devora Doresh Mysteries 2. 2007. (Illus.). 280p. (J). 16.95 *(978-1-932443-68-4(1))* Judaica Pr., Inc., The.

Hyde, Heidi Smith. Emanuel & the Whale Oil Lamp. Akib, Jamel, illus. 2012. (Hanukkah Ser.). (ENG.). 32p. (J). (gr. -1-1). lib. bdg. 17.95 *(978-0-7613-6625-6(3)*, Kar-Ben Publishing) Lerner Publishing Group.

—Pavel & the Tree Army. Vavouri, Elisa, illus. 2019. (ENG.). 32p. (J). (gr. k-3). 17.99 *(978-1-5124-4446-9(4)*, 73217719-2ba5-49a0-995a-fcf9635f5470, Kar-Ben Publishing) Lerner Publishing Group.

Jenkins, Emily. All-Of-a-Kind Family Hanukkah. Zelinsky, Paul O., illus. 2018. 40p. (J). (gr. -1-2). 18.99 *(978-0-399-55419-3(X)*, Schwartz & Wade Bks.) Random Hse. Children's Bks.

Karwoski, Gail Langer. When Hurricane Katrina Hit Home. Marshall, Julia, illus. 2013. Orig. Title: When Hurricane Katrina Hit Home. (ENG.). 192p. (gr. 4-7). 29.99 *(978-1-62619-083-2(6)*, History Pr., The) Arcadia Publishing.

Keyser, Amber J. & Burkhart, Kiersi. The Long Trail Home. 2017. (Quartz Creek Ranch Ser.). (ENG.). 240p. (J). (gr. 4-8). 6.99 *(978-1-5124-3090-5(0)*, 237da2bf-d64a-47f5-9377-07661a1f1425, Darby Creek) Lerner Publishing Group.

Koffsky, Ann. Judah Maccabee Goes to the Doctor: a Story for Hanukkah. Shipman, Talitha, illus. 2017. (ENG.). 32p. (J). 17.95 *(978-1-68115-522-7(2)*, 57a5ddfc-cab2-49df-bc22-fafffeb5edf) Behrman Hse., Inc.

—Noah's Swim-A-Thon. 2016. (ENG.). 32p. (J). pap. 9.95 *(978-1-68115-519-7(2)*, 52caebb3-d65b-4e90-b35e-d0a856084982, Apples & Honey Pr.) Behrman Hse., Inc.

Koffsky, Ann D. Noah's Swim-A-Thon. 2010. (J). *(978-0-8074-1168-1(X))* URJ Pr.

Konigsburg, E. L. About the B'nai Bagels. Konigsburg, E. L., illus. 2008. (ENG., Illus.). 208p. (J). (gr. 3-7). pap. 8.99 *(978-1-4169-5798-0(7)*, Atheneum Bks. for Young Readers) Simon & Schuster Children's Publishing.

Korngold, Jamie. Sadie's Lag Ba'Omer Mystery. Fortenberry, Julie, illus. 2014. (ENG.). 32p. (J). (gr. -1-3). 9.99 *(978-0-7613-9048-0(0)*, 034ad977-184b-4135-b7fb-d522d1bc86eb, Kar-Ben Publishing) Lerner Publishing Group.

—Sadie's Snowy Tu B'Shevat. Fortenberry, Julie, illus. 2017. (ENG.). 32p. (J). (gr. -1-1). 17.99 *(978-1-5124-2677-9(6)*, cc2842f7-c68a-4c05-8326-0b0af8b8de00, Kar-Ben Publishing) Lerner Publishing Group.

Kushner, Elisabeth. The Purim Superhero. Byrne, Mike, illus. 2013. (ENG.). 32p. (J). (gr. -1-3). 8.99 *(978-0-7613-9062-6(6)*, e21c8b88-429e-4a15-bf99-c61687205a7d, Kar-Ben Publishing) Lerner Publishing Group.

Lakritz, Deborah. Joey & the Giant Box. Byrne, Mike, illus. 2015. (ENG.). 32p. (J). (gr. -1-2). lib. bdg. 9.99 *(978-1-4677-1953-7(6)*, edd32a84-7290-406d-8c23-7cba166d7843); E-Book 27.99 *(978-1-4677-6205-2(9))* Lerner Publishing Group. (Kar-Ben Publishing).

Lepon, Shoshana. Hillel Builds a House. Ruiz, Ángeles, illus. 2020. (ENG.). 32p. (J). (gr. -1-3). 17.99 *(978-1-5415-4402-4(1)*, 8fa8284d-6dbf-42d7-9020-18bb71a86656, Kar-Ben Publishing) Lerner Publishing Group.

Levinson, Robin K. Shoshana & the Native Rose. Kehl, Drusilla, illus. 2006. 103p. (J). (gr. 3-5). per. 12.00 *(978-0-9773673-2-0(0))* Gali Girls, Inc.

Levy, Debbie. Yiddish Saves the Day. Borlasca, Hector, illus. 2019. (ENG.). 32p. (J). 17.95 *(978-1-68115-544-9(3)*, 563e41f9-3396-4de3-bb96-a74b11225faf, Apples & Honey Pr.) Behrman Hse., Inc.

Lieurance, Suzanne. The Locket: Surviving the Triangle Shirtwaist Fire, 1 vol. 2008. (Historical Fiction Adventures Ser.). (ENG., Illus.). 160p. (J). (gr. 3-5). lib. bdg. 31.93 *(978-0-7660-2928-6(X)*, 22662cfe-5ae4-4ede-affa-913d7a92d0d5) Enslow Publishing, LLC.

Littman, Sarah Darer. Confessions of a Closet Catholic. 2006. 208p. (J). (gr. 5-18). reprint ed. 7.99 *(978-0-14-240597-0(3)*, Puffin Books) Penguin Young Readers Group.

—Life, After. 2010. (ENG.). 288p. (J). (gr. 7-18). 17.99 *(978-0-545-15144-3(9)*, Scholastic Pr.) Scholastic, Inc.

Manushkin, Fran. Sophie & the Shofar. Kaye, Rosalind Charney, illus. 2004. (J). (gr. k-3). 13.95 *(978-0-8074-0751-6(8)*, 101078) URJ Pr.

Markel, Michelle. Hanukkah Hamster. Ceolin, André, illus. 2018. (ENG.). 32p. (J). (gr. k-2). 16.99 *(978-1-58536-399-5(5)*, 204583) Sleeping Bear Pr.

Matas, Carol. Rosie in Los Angeles: Action! 2004. (ENG., Illus.). 128p. (J). (gr. 4-7). pap. 9.95 *(978-0-689-85716-4(0)*, Simon & Schuster/Paula Wiseman Bks.) Simon & Schuster/Paula Wiseman Bks.

Mayer, Pamela. Chicken Soup, Chicken Soup. Melmon, Deborah, illus. 2016. (ENG.). 32p. (J). (gr. -1-3). 17.99 *(978-1-4677-8934-9(8)*, d1826602-2ac3-41a4-ba03-fbb1f5545a02, Kar-Ben Publishing) Lerner Publishing Group.

—Don't Sneeze at the Wedding. Avilés, Martha Graciela, illus. 2013. (ENG.). 32p. (J). (gr. k-3). E-Book 23.99 *(978-1-4677-1641-3(3)*, Kar-Ben Publishing) Lerner Publishing Group.

Mazer, Norma Fox. Good Night, Maman. 2006. 185p. (J). (gr. k-4). reprint ed. 16.00 *(978-1-4223-5862-7(3))* DIANE Publishing Co.

—Good Night, Maman. 2010. (ENG., Illus.). 192p. (J). (gr. 5-7). pap. 12.95 *(978-0-15-206173-9(8)*, 1198532, Clarion Bks.) HarperCollins Pubs.

McDonough, Yona Zeldis. The Cats in the Doll Shop. Maione, Heather, illus. 2012. (ENG.). 128p. (J). (gr. 2-4). 18.69 *(978-0-670-01279-4(3))* Penguin Young Readers Group.

—The Doll Shop Downstairs. Maione, Heather, illus. 2011. 144p. (J). (gr. 2-5). 5.99 *(978-0-14-241691-4(6)*, Puffin Books) Penguin Young Readers Group.

Mermelstein, Yael. A Car That Goes Far. Rosenfeld, Dina, ed. Romanenko, Vitaliy & Romanenko, Vasilisa, illus. 2009. (ENG.). 30p. (J). (gr. 1-3). 13.99 *(978-1-929628-47-6(1))* Hachai Publishing.

Moriarty, Chris. The Inquisitor's Apprentice. Geyer, Mark Edward, illus. 2013. (ENG.). 352p. (J). (gr. 5-7). pap. 7.99 *(978-0-547-85084-9(0)*, 1501042, Clarion Bks.) HarperCollins Pubs.

Napoli, Donna Jo. The King of Mulberry Street. 2007. 245p. (gr. 3-7). 17.00 *(978-0-7569-7945-4(5))* Perfection Learning Corp.

—The King of Mulberry Street. 2007. (ENG.). 256p. (J). (gr. 3-7). 8.99 *(978-0-553-49416-7(3)*, Yearling) Random Hse. Children's Bks.

Newman, Lesléa & Bates, Amy June. Gittel's Journey: An Ellis Island Story. 2019. (ENG., Illus.). 48p. (J). (gr. k-3). 18.99 *(978-1-4197-2747-4(8)*, 1152401, Abrams Bks. for Young Readers) Abrams, Inc.

Newman, Tracy. Shabbat Hiccups. Exelby, Ilana, illus. 2016. (ENG.). 32p. (J). (gr. -1-3). 16.99 *(978-0-8075-7312-9(4)*, 807573124) Whitman, Albert & Co.

Noble, Trinka Hakes. A Fist for Joe Louis & Me. Tadgell, Nicole, illus. 2019. (Tales of Young Americans Ser.). (ENG.). 40p. (J). (gr. 1-4). 17.99 *(978-1-5341-1016-8(X)*, 204748) Sleeping Bear Pr.

Novel Units. Summer of My German Soldier Novel Units Teacher Guide. 2019. (ENG.). (YA). pap. 12.99 *(978-1-56137-113-6(0)*, Novel Units, Inc.) Classroom Library Co.

O'Connell, Rebecca. Penina Levine Is a Hard-Boiled Egg. Lue Sue, Majella, illus. 2009. (ENG.). 192p. (J). (gr. 3-7). pap. 18.99 *(978-0-312-55026-4(X)*, 900055956) Square Fish.

Old Ways, New Ways (Eastern European Jews) 76p. (YA). (gr. 6-12). pap. 9.95 *(978-0-8224-3682-9(5))* Globe Fearon Educational Publishing.

Olswanger, Anna. Greenhorn. Nerlove, Miriam, illus. 2012. (ENG.). (J). 48p. 17.95 *(978-1-58838-235-1(4)*, 8806); E-Book 9.99 *(978-1-60306-159-9(2)*, 8807) NewSouth, Inc. (NewSouth Bks.).

—Shlemiel Crooks. Koz, Paula Goodman, illus. 2009. (ENG.). 36p. (J). pap. 11.95 *(978-1-58838-236-8(2)*, 8994, NewSouth Bks.) NewSouth, Inc.

Oppenheim, Joanne. The Knish War on Rivington Street. Davis, Jon, illus. 2017. (ENG.). 32p. (J). (gr. -1-3). 16.99 *(978-0-8075-4182-1(6)*, 807541826) Whitman, Albert & Co.

Peet, Amanda & Troyer, Andrea. Dear Santa, Love, Rachel Rosenstein. Davenier, Christine, illus. 2015. 40p. (J). (gr. -1-2). 17.99 *(978-0-553-51061-4(4)*, Doubleday Bks. for Young Readers) Random Hse. Children's Bks.

Perl, Erica S. Aces Wild. 2015. (ENG.). 224p. (J). (gr. 3-7). 7.99 *(978-0-307-93173-3(0)*, Yearling) Random Hse. Children's Bks.

—When Life Gives You O. J. 2013. (When Life Gives You O. J. Ser.). (ENG.). 208p. (J). (gr. 4-6). 21.19 *(978-0-375-95924-0(6)*, Knopf Bks. for Young Readers) Random Hse. Children's Bks.

Perlov, Rebecca Rosenberg. Rifka Takes a Bow. Kawa, Cosei, illus. 2013. (ENG.). 32p. (J). (gr. k-3). 9.99 *(978-0-7613-8128-0(7)*, d57777e5-7e97-46e6-9ab1-3e429f027bc8, Kar-Ben Publishing) Lerner Publishing Group.

Pinkham, Mark Amaru. Love Me Later. 2005. 202p. 14.95 *(978-1-932188-02-8(9))* Adventures Unlimited Pr.

Press, Judy. The Case of the Missing Kiddush Cup. 2018. (J). *(978-1-5415-0015-0(6)*, Kar-Ben Publishing) Lerner Publishing Group.

Reinhardt, Dana. A Brief Chapter in My Impossible Life. 2007. (ENG.). 256p. (YA). (gr. 9-12). pap. 8.99 *(978-0-375-84691-5(3)*, Ember) Random Hse. Children's Bks.

Reiss, Kathryn. A Bundle of Trouble: A Rebecca Mystery. Giovine, Sergio, illus. 2011. (American Girl Mysteries Ser.). (ENG.). 192p. (YA). (gr. 4-6). pap. 21.19 *(978-1-59369-754-9(6))* American Girl Publishing, Inc.

Robinson, Sharon. The Hero Two Doors down: Based on the True Story of Friendship Between a Boy & a Baseball Legend. 2017. (ENG.). 208p. (J). (gr. 4-7). pap. 7.99 *(978-0-545-80452-3(3)*, Scholastic Paperbacks) Scholastic, Inc.

Rosen, Michael J. Chanukah Lights. Sabuda, Robert, illus. 2011. (ENG.). 16p. (J). (gr. k-4). 34.99 *(978-0-7636-5533-4(3))* Candlewick Pr.

—Chanukah Lights Everywhere: A Hanukkah Holiday Book for Kids. Iwai, Melissa, illus. 2006. (ENG.). 32p. (J). (gr. -1-3). pap. 7.99 *(978-0-15-205675-9(0)*, 1197061, Clarion Bks.) HarperCollins Pubs.

Rosenbaum, Thane. The Stranger Within Sarah Stein. 2012. (Modern Jewish Literature & Culture Ser.). (ENG., Illus.). 160p. (YA). (gr. 6-12). 19.95 *(978-0-89672-747-2(5)*, P200880) Texas Tech Univ. Pr.

Rosenthal, Betsy R. It's Not Worth Making a Tzimmes Over! Rivers, Ruth, illus. 2006. 32p. (J). (gr. k-3). lib. bdg. 16.99 *(978-0-8075-3677-3(6))* Whitman, Albert & Co.

—Looking for Me: ... in This Great Big Family. 2013. (ENG., Illus.). 176p. (J). (gr. 5-7). pap. 7.99 *(978-0-544-02271-3(8)*, 1528493, Clarion Bks.) HarperCollins Pubs.

Rosenthal, Sally. Matzo Frogs. Sheldon, David, illus. 2014. (ENG.). 32p. (J). 17.95 *(978-1-58838-302-0(4)*, 8911, NewSouth Bks.) NewSouth, Inc.

Ross, Susan. Searching for Lottie. 2019. (ENG., Illus.). 176p. (J). (gr. 3-7). 17.99 *(978-0-8234-4166-2(0))* Holiday Hse., Inc.

Rothenberg, Joan. Matzah Ball Soup. Rothenberg, Joan, illus. 2005. (Illus.). 29p. (J). (gr. -1-2). reprint ed. 15.00 *(978-0-7567-8930-5(3))* DIANE Publishing Co.

Rouss, Sylvia. Holiday for Ari Ant. Kahn, Katherine Janus, illus. 2016. (ENG.). 24p. (J). pap. 9.95 *(978-1-68115-507-4(9)*, ba2f5450-de4f-4717-befc-c9c4ed3658bb) Behrman Hse., Inc.

—Holiday for Ari Ant. 2016. (Illus.). 24p. (J). pap. *(978-965-229-664-1(3))* Gefen Bks.

Rouss, Sylvia A. Sammy Spider's First Mitzvah. Kahn, Katherine Janus, illus. 2014. (ENG.). 24p. (J). (gr. -1-3). 17.95 *(978-1-4677-1947-6(1)*, a8861aa7-d249-435f-ac41-dc242b6e1326, Kar-Ben Publishing) Lerner Publishing Group.

—Sammy Spider's First Sukkot. Kahn, Katherine Janus, illus. 2004. (ENG.). 32p. (J). (gr. -1-3). 17.95 *(978-1-58013-142-1(5)*, Kar-Ben Publishing) Lerner Publishing Group.

—Sammy Spider's First Sukkot. Kahn, Katherine Janus, illus. 2004. (ENG.). 32p. (J). (gr. -1-3). pap. 8.99 *(978-1-58013-083-7(6)*, 30089e0a-abc2-4e86-8e0f-4cc8ea2d1fd6, Kar-Ben Publishing) Lerner Publishing Group.

—Sammy Spider's New Friend. Kahn, Katherine, illus. 2012. (Kar-Ben Favorites Ser.). (ENG.). 32p. (J). (gr. -1-2). lib. bdg. 17.95 *(978-0-7613-6663-8(6)*, Kar-Ben Publishing) Lerner Publishing Group.

Ruby, Laura. York: The Clockwork Ghost. 2019. (Illus.). 464p. (YA). *(978-0-06-293755-1(3)*, Waldon Pond Pr.) HarperCollins Pubs.

—York: the Clockwork Ghost. 2019. (York Ser.: 2). (ENG., Illus.). 464p. (J). (gr. 3-7). 17.99 *(978-0-06-230696-8(0)*, Waldon Pond Pr.) HarperCollins Pubs.

Ruby, Lois. Red Menace. 2020. (ENG., Illus.). 224p. (J). (gr. 6-8). 17.99 *(978-1-5415-5749-9(2)*, 85d52fc4-d672-4bce-a708-5bd9a1658221, Carolrhoda Bks.) Lerner Publishing Group.

Scheerger, Sarah Lynn. Mitzvah Pizza. Melmon, Deborah, illus. 2019. (ENG.). 32p. (J). (gr. k-4). 17.99 *(978-1-5415-2170-4(6)*, cf855a72-f931-4885-a070-ed4d5dcd5c29, Kar-Ben Publishing) Lerner Publishing Group.

Schnur, Susan. Tashlich at Turtle Rock. Schnur-Fishman, Anna & Steele-Morgan, Alexandra, illus. 2010. (High Holidays Ser.). 32p. (J). (gr. k-4). lib. bdg. 17.95 *(978-0-7613-4509-1(4)*, Kar-Ben Publishing) Lerner Publishing Group.

Seidman, Richard. The Secret of Ebbets Field. 2017. (J). mass mkt. 11.95 *(978-1-55571-859-6(0)*, Paloma Bks.) L & R Publishing, LLC.

Sharenow, Robert. The Girl in the Torch. 2015. (ENG.). 304p. (J). (gr. 3-7). 16.99 *(978-0-06-222795-9(5)*, Balzer & Bray) HarperCollins Pubs.

Sheinmel, Alyssa. A Danger to Herself & Others. 2019. (ENG.). 352p. (YA). (gr. 9-12). 17.99 *(978-1-4926-6724-7(2))* Sourcebooks, Inc.

Silverman, Erica. The Hanukkah Hop! D'Amico, Steven, illus. 2011. (ENG.). 32p. (J). (gr. -1-3). 12.99 *(978-1-4424-0604-9(6)*, Simon & Schuster Bks. For Young Readers) Simon & Schuster Bks. For Young Readers.

Silverman, Laura. You Asked for Perfect. 2019. (ENG.). 288p. (YA). (gr. 8-12). pap. 11.99 *(978-1-4926-5827-6(8))* Sourcebooks, Inc.

Simhaee, Rebeka. Sara Finds a Mitzva. Leverton, Yossi, ed. 2010. (ENG., Illus.). 28p. (J). 11.99 *(978-1-929628-46-9(3))* Hachai Publishing.

Singer, Isaac Bashevis. The Parakeet Named Dreidel. Berkson, Suzanne Raphael, illus. 2015. (J). pap. *(978-0-374-30096-8(8))* Farrar, Straus & Giroux.

Snyder, Laurel. Baxter, the Pig Who Wanted to Be Kosher. 2010. (J). pap. 2.46 *(978-1-58246-373-5(5)*, Tricycle Pr.) Ten Speed Pr.

Solomon, Rachel Lynn. Our Year of Maybe. 2019. (ENG., Illus.). 384p. (YA). (gr. 9). 18.99 *(978-1-4814-9776-3(6)*, Simon Pulse) Simon Pulse.

—You'll Miss Me When I'm Gone. 2018. (ENG., Illus.). 384p. (YA). (gr. 9). 19.99 *(978-1-4814-9773-2(1)*, Simon Pulse) Simon Pulse.

Spielman, Gloria. French Toast Sundays. Bousidan, Inbal Gigi, illus. 2018. (ENG.). 32p. (J). 17.95 *(978-1-68115-529-6(X)*, f1013abc-dd12-4f81-ae5c-276a29d1231d, Apples & Honey Pr.) Behrman Hse., Inc.

Steinberg, Jessica. Not This Turkey! 2018. (2019 Av2 Fiction Ser.). (ENG.). 32p. (J). (gr. k-3). lib. bdg. 34.28 *(978-1-4896-8273-4(2)*, AV2 by Weigl) Weigl Pubs., Inc.

—Not This Turkey! Pike, Amanda, illus. 2016. (ENG.). 32p. (J). (gr. -1-3). 16.99 *(978-0-8075-7908-4(4)*, 807579084) Whitman, Albert & Co.

Thompson, Holly. Orchards. 2012. 336p. (YA). (gr. 7). pap. 10.99 *(978-0-385-73978-8(8)*, Ember) Random Hse. Children's Bks.

Vander Zee, Ruth & Sneider, Marian. Eli Remembers. Farnsworth, Bill, illus. 2007. (ENG.). 32p. (J). (gr. -1-3). 18.00 *(978-0-8028-5309-7(9)*, Eerdmans Bks For Young Readers) Eerdmans, William B. Publishing Co.

Vernick, Shirley Reva. The Blood Lie. (ENG.). 144p. (YA). (gr. 9-12). 2015. pap. 16.95 *(978-1-941026-09-0(5)*, 23353382) 2011. 15.95 *(978-1-933693-84-2(3)*, 23353382) Lee & Low Bks., Inc. (Cinco Puntos Press).

Weber, Judith Eichler. Seeking Safety. Martin, John F., illus. 2006. (Adventures in America Ser.). (J). *(978-1-893110-46-5(X))* Silver Moon Pr.

Weissman, Elissa Brent. The Length of a String. 2018. 384p. (J). (gr. 5-9). 17.99 *(978-0-7352-2947-1(3)*, Dial Bks) Penguin Young Readers Group.

Westheimer, Ruth K. Roller-Coaster Grandma: the Amazing Story of Dr. Ruth. Simmons, Mark, illus. 2018. (ENG.). 64p. (J). pap. 12.95 *(978-1-68115-532-6(X)*, 90a0c68d-5266-4ac7-b02d-05c2c85437b2, Apples & Honey Pr.) Behrman Hse., Inc.

Wolff, Ferida. Rachel's Roses. Lucas, Margeaux, illus. 2019. (ENG.). 112p. (J). (gr. 2-5). 15.99 *(978-0-8234-4365-9(5))* Holiday Hse., Inc.

JIUJITSU

see Judo

JOAN, OF ARC, SAINT, 1412-1431

Demi. Joan of Arc, 0 vols. 2012. (ENG.). 56p. (J). (gr. 4-6). 19.99 *(978-0-7614-5953-8(7)*, 9780761459538, Two Lions) Amazon Publishing.

Hilliam, David. Joan of Arc: Heroine of France, 1 vol. 2004. (Leaders of the Middle Ages Ser.). (ENG., Illus.). 112p. (J). (gr. 5-8). lib. bdg. 39.80 *(978-1-4042-0164-4(5)*, 3da45756-c61b-4793-81ad-25b7cecbf6d5) Rosen Publishing Group, Inc., The.

JOAN of ARC. 2010. (ENG., Illus.). 128p. (gr. 6-12). 35.00 *(978-1-60413-710-1(X)*, P179338, Facts On File) Infobase Holdings, Inc.

Macdonald, Fiona. You Wouldn't Want to Be Joan of Arc! A Mission You Might Want to Miss. Antram, David, illus. 2010. (You Wouldn't Want to Ser.). (ENG.). 32p. (J). 29.00 *(978-0-531-20473-3(1))* Scholastic Library Publishing.

Pollack, Pam & Belviso, Meg. Who Was Joan of Arc? Thomson, Andrew, illus. 2016. (Who Was-? Chapters Ser.). (ENG.). 112p. (J). (gr. 3-6). 18.69 *(978-1-4844-7648-2(4)*, Penguin Workshop) Penguin Young Readers Group.

Pollack, Pam, et al. Who Was Joan of Arc? Thomson, Andrew, illus. 2016. (Who Was? Ser.). 112p. (J). (gr. 3-7). pap. 5.99 *(978-0-448-48304-7(1)*, Penguin Workshop) Penguin Young Readers Group.

Pollack, Pamela D. & Belviso, Meg. Who Was Joan of Arc? 2016. (Who Was... ? Ser.). lib. bdg. 16.00 *(978-0-606-38395-0(6))* Turtleback.

Ross, Nancy Wilson. Joan of Arc. 2003. vii, 182p. pap. 29.00 *(978-0-7581-5017-2(2))* Textbook Pubs.

Thiel, Kristin. Joan of Arc, 1 vol. 2017. (Great Military Leaders Ser.). (ENG.). 128p. (YA). (gr. 9-9). 47.36 *(978-1-5026-2791-9(4)*, 61492b8d-dfdd-49d4-9b3c-8b9f9c6129f2) Cavendish Square Publishing LLC.

Whiting, Jim. The Life & Times of Joan of Arc. 2005. (Biography from Ancient Civilizations Ser.). (Illus.). 48p. (J). (gr. 4-8). lib. bdg. 29.95 *(978-1-58415-345-0(8))* Mitchell Lane Pubs.

Wilkinson, Philip. Joan of Arc: The Teenager Who Saved Her Nation. 2009. (National Geographic World History Biographies Ser.). (Illus.). 64p. (J). (gr. 3-7). pap. 7.95 *(978-1-4263-0415-6(3)*, National Geographic Kids) Disney Publishing Worldwide.

Wolny, Philip. Joan of Arc: French Soldier & Saint, 1 vol. 2017. (Women Who Changed History Ser.). (ENG., Illus.). 48p. (J). (gr. 6-7). pap. 15.05 *(978-1-68048-645-2(4)*, 025bb447-f7cc-45bc-a107-9d8c97a0ee00, Britannica Educational Publishing) Rosen Publishing Group, Inc., The.

JOAN, OF ARC, SAINT, 1412-1431—FICTION

Chandler, Pauline. Warrior Girl: A Novel of Joan of Arc. 2006. 354p. (J). (gr. 5-9). 17.89 *(978-0-06-084103-4(6))* HarperCollins Pubs.

Everett-Green, Evelyn. A Heroine of France. 2006. (ENG.). 188p. pap. 19.99 *(978-1-4264-7060-8(6))* Creative Media Partners, LLC.

Hemphill, Stephanie. The Language of Fire: Joan of Arc Reimagined. 2019. (ENG.). 512p. (YA). (gr. 8). 17.99 *(978-0-06-249011-7(7)*, Balzer & Bray) HarperCollins Pubs.

Johnson, Vargie. Joan of Arc the Messenger: What Made Them Famous? 2006. 156p. (J). per. 15.00 *(978-1-931195-95-9(1))* KiwE Publishing, Ltd.

Lee, Tony. Messenger: the Legend of Joan of Arc. Hart, Sam, illus. 2015. (ENG.). 112p. (J). (gr. 5). 21.99 *(978-0-7636-7613-1(6))* Candlewick Pr.

JOB DISCRIMINATION

see Discrimination in Employment

JOB HUNTING

Byers, Ann. Great Resume, Application, & Interview Skills. (Work Readiness Ser.). 64p. (gr. 6-6). 2009. 58.50 *(978-1-60854-827-9(9))* 2008. (ENG., Illus.). (J). lib. bdg. 37.13 *(978-1-4042-1425-5(9)*, a41ac272-036c-4ef2-b086-77c58c032df0) Rosen Publishing Group, Inc., The.

Coon, Nora. Teen Dream Jobs: How to Find the Job You Really Want Now! 2004. (Illus.). 132p. (YA). (gr. 8-12). per. 9.95 *(978-1-58270-093-9(1))* Beyond Words Publishing, Inc.

Currie-McGhee, Leanne. Getting a Job. 2019. (Teen Life Skills Ser.). (ENG.). 64p. (J). (gr. 6-12). 41.27 *(978-1-68282-743-7(7))* ReferencePoint Pr., Inc.

Draper, Allison Stark. World of Work: Exciting World of Careers, 7 bks. Incl. Choosing a Career in the Pulp & Paper Industry. (Illus.). 64p. (YA). (gr. 5-5). 2000. lib. bdg. 37.13 *(978-0-8239-3333-4(4)*, a0e83b07-1053-448a-961c-7a2f22107097); (Illus.). Set lib. bdg. 167.65 *(978-0-8239-9208-9(X))* Rosen Publishing Group, Inc., The.

Ehmann, Mary Pat. Jobs Around the World, 1 vol. 2018. (Adventures in Culture Ser.). (ENG.). 24p. (gr. 1-2). 24.27 *(978-1-5382-1871-6(2)*, 267d46b9-1ba5-499f-9286-e05dc1c1f036) Stevens, Gareth Publishing LLLP.

Essential Careers: Set 3, 12 vols. 2013. (Essential Careers Ser.). (ENG.). 80p. (YA). (gr. 6-6). 224.82 *(978-1-4488-9485-7(9)*, fa82d95b-6e92-4d9b-a86d-62863d2c5a1d) Rosen Publishing Group, Inc., The.

Essential Careers: Set 4, 10 vols. 2013. (Essential Careers Ser.). (ENG.). 80p. (YA). (gr. 6-6). 187.35 *(978-1-4777-1800-1(1)*, fd163d87-3342-42ab-9fc4-5fe051aedcf9) Rosen Publishing Group, Inc., The.

Essential Careers: Sets 1 - 3. 2013. (Essential Careers Ser.). 80p. (YA). (gr. 7-12). 731.50 *(978-1-4777-0615-2(1))* Rosen Publishing Group, Inc., The.

Fischer, James. Earning Money: Jobs. 2010. (Junior Library of Money). 64p. (YA). (gr. 7-18). lib. bdg. 22.95 *(978-1-4222-1763-4(9))* Mason Crest.

Gabler, Laura R., ed. Career Exploration on the Internet: A Student's Guide to More Than 500 Web Sites. 2nd ed. 2006. (ENG., Illus.). 404p. 24.95 *(978-0-89434-305-6(X)*, P101953, Ferguson Publishing Company) Infobase Holdings, Inc.

Gagne, Tammy. Teen Guide to Earning Income. 2014. (ENG., Illus.). 48p. (J). (gr. 4-6). lib. bdg. 29.95 *(978-1-61228-470-5(1))* Mitchell Lane Pubs.

Hagler, Gina. Money-Making Opportunities for Teens Who Are Artistic, 1 vol. 2013. (Make Money Now! Ser.). (ENG., Illus.). 80p. (YA). (gr. 7-7). lib. bdg. 38.41 *(978-1-4488-9387-4(9),* c4f51914-1559-4110-b282-9142951b13c5) Rosen Publishing Group, Inc., The.

Henneberg, Susan. Step-By-Step Guide to Effective Job Hunting & Career Preparedness, 1 vol. 2014. (Winning at Work Readiness Ser.). (ENG.). 64p. (YA). (gr. 6-6). 36.13 *(978-1-4777-7774-9(1),* 15ef561b-2528-4f6f-b7bc-d193de36f89e) Rosen Publishing Group, Inc., The.

Huddleston, Emma. Finding a Job. 2020. (ENG.). 80p. (YA). (gr. 6-12). 41.27 *(978-1-68282-799-4(2),* BrightPoint Pr.) ReferencePoint Pr., Inc.

JAMES MICHAEL FARR TRUST A. Job Search Basics. 3rd ed. 2006. (ENG., Illus.). 256p. wbk. ed. 31.00 *(978-1-59357-313-3(8),* J3138) Kendall Hunt Publishing Co.

Marsh, Carole. Would You Hire This Person? A Look at Getting Hired (or Not!)... from the Point of View of Your (Possible!) Future Employer. 2012. (Carole Marsh's Careers Curriculum Ser.). (ENG., Illus.). 82p. (J). pap. 19.99 *(978-0-635-10553-0(5))* Gallopade International.

Mccormick, Anita Louise. How to Create Digital Portfolios to Showcase Your Achievements & Interests, 1 vol. 2017. (Project Learning Using Digital Portfolios Ser.). (ENG.). 64p. (J). (gr. 7-7). 36.13 *(978-1-5081-7534-6(9),* 06f825bf-1165-4248-9ad3-da45f7e406d1, Rosen Young Adult) Rosen Publishing Group, Inc., The.

Orr, Tamra B. Money-Making Opportunities for Teens Who Like Working Outside, 1 vol. 2013. (Make Money Now! Ser.). (ENG., Illus.). 80p. (YA). (gr. 7-7). lib. bdg. 38.41 *(978-1-4488-9383-6(6),* b870f6ad-bdc8-44e9-9b23-0389cffe871e) Rosen Publishing Group, Inc., The.

Project Learning Using Digital Portfolios, 12 vols. 2017. (Project Learning Using Digital Portfolios Ser.). (ENG.). 64p. (gr. 7-7). 216.78 *(978-1-4994-6635-5(8),* 1ad34bde-10bc-4abe-8d3b-d611bb4d31ba, Rosen Young Adult) Rosen Publishing Group, Inc., The.

Timmons-Hanselka, Angela. How to Create Digital Portfolios to Show What You Know, 1 vol. 2017. (Project Learning Using Digital Portfolios Ser.). (ENG.). 64p. (J). (gr. 7-7). 36.13 *(978-1-5081-7532-2(2),* 848cf8af-2a68-4d88-ad19-c146020a82d0, Rosen Young Adult) Rosen Publishing Group, Inc., The.

Troutman, Kathryn K. Creating Your High School Resume, Second Edition: A Step-by-Step Guide to Preparing an Effective Resume for Jobs, College & Training Programs. 2nd ed. 2003. (Illus.). 160p. pap. 10.95 *(978-1-56370-902-9(3),* JIST Works) JIST Publishing.

Wilkes, Donald & Hamilton-Wilkes, Viola. Teen Guide Job Search: 10 Easy Steps to Your Future. 2006. (ENG., Illus.). 122p. (YA). (gr. 10-12). per. 12.95 *(978-0-595-39696-2(8))* iUniverse, Inc.

World of Work: Choose the Right Career for You!, 7 bks. Incl. Choosing a Career in Child Care. Weintraub, Aileen. (gr. 5-5). lib. bdg. 37.13 *(978-0-8239-3241-2(9),* 10db786d-78a8-4d17-9768-8c6a0428b66f); Choosing a Career in Hotels, Motels & Resorts. rev. ed. Rue, Nancy N. (gr. 7-12). lib. bdg. 27.95 *(978-0-8239-2999-3(X),* WWHOMO); Choosing a Career in Law Enforcement. 2nd rev. ed. Wirths, Claudine G. (gr. 5-5). lib. bdg. 37.13 *(978-0-8239-3282-5(6),* 0662e88c-dc94-4aaf-a254-2db82ecab2da); Choosing a Career in the Restaurant Industry. rev. ed. Beal, Eileen J. (gr. 7-12). lib. bdg. 35.45 *(978-0-8239-3002-9(5),* WWREST); 64p. (YA). 1999. (Illus.). Set lib. bdg. 167.65 *(978-0-8239-9306-2(X))* Rosen Publishing Group, Inc., The.

JOB HUNTING—FICTION

Brundin, Anders & Dranger, Joanna Rubin. Dudley the Daydreamer. Perry, Frank, tr. from SWE. 2008. (ENG., Illus.). 32p. (J). (gr. k-2). pap. 12.95 *(978-1-905341-10-8(5))* WingedChariot Pr. GBR. Dist: Independent Pubs. Group.

Buyer, Robert L. & Coute, Ursula T. Following the North Star. 2013. 52p. pap. 23.95 *(978-1-4624-0611-1(4),* Inspiring Voices) Author Solutions, LLC.

Dufresne, Michèle. A Job for Little Elf: Little Elf Set 1. 2006. (Little Elf Set 1 Ser.). (ENG., Illus.). (J). pap. 7.33 *(978-1-932570-72-4(1))* Pioneer Valley Bks.

Durham, Kathryn. Mom, Can You Buy Me This? Richard Gets a Job 2004. 115p. (YA). spiral bd. 11.95 *(978-0-9703876-2-2(8))* Pen & Paper Publishing.

Elga Learns to Juggle. 2006. (J). 6.99 *(978-0-9770918-0-5(5))* Forelle Graphics.

Kowalski, William. The Way It Works, 1 vol. 2010. (ENG.). 128p. pap. 10.95 *(978-1-55469-367-2(5))* Orca Bk. Pubs. CAN. Dist: Orca Bk. Pubs. USA.

Lynn, Michelle. Sasha Discovers There Is a Job for Everyone. 2013. 28p. pap. 24.95 *(978-1-4241-0153-5(0))* America Star Bks.

Regan, Peter. Riverside: Exit Point. 2009. (ENG., Illus.). 128p. (J). pap. *(978-1-901737-59-2(4),* Anvil Bks.) Mercier Pr., Ltd., The.

Ross, Sonny. Duck Gets a Job. Ross, Sonny, illus. 2018. (ENG., Illus.). 32p. (J). (gr. -1-2). 16.99 *(978-0-7636-9896-6(2),* Templar) Candlewick Pr.

JOBS, STEVE, 1955-2011

Blumenthal, Karen. Steve Jobs: the Man Who Thought Different: A Biography. 2012. (ENG., Illus.). 320p. (YA). (gr. 7-12). pap. 14.99 *(978-1-250-01445-0(X),* 900086311) Square Fish.

Colting, Fredrik & Medina, Melissa. What I Can Learn from the Incredible & Fantastic Life of Steve Jobs. Yoneyama, Natsuko, illus. 2017. 32p. (J). 14.95 *(978-0-9977145-9-3(X))* Moppet Bks.

Corrigan, Jim. Steve Jobs. 2008. (Business Leaders Ser.). 128p. (YA). (gr. 7-12). lib. bdg. 27.95 *(978-1-59935-076-9(9))* Reynolds, Morgan Inc.

Gillam, Scott. Steve Jobs: Apple & iPod Wizard, 1 vol. 2008. (Essential Lives Set 2 Ser.). (ENG., Illus.). 112p. (J). (gr. 6-12). lib. bdg. 41.36 *(978-1-60453-037-7(5),* 6655, Essential Library) ABDO Publishing Co.

—Steve Jobs: Apple ICon, 1 vol. 2008. (Essential Lives Set 2 Ser.). (ENG.). 112p. (YA). (gr. 6-12). lib. bdg. 41.36 *(978-1-60453-997-4(6),* 6649, Essential Library) ABDO Publishing Co.

Goldsworthy, Steve. Steve Jobs. 2011. (J). (gr. 4-6). pap. 12.95 *(978-1-61690-675-7(8),* AV2 by Weigl); (Illus.). 24p. (YA). (gr. 3-6). 27.13 *(978-1-61690-670-2(7))* Weigl Pubs., Inc.

Gould, Jane H. Steve Jobs, 1 vol. 2013. (Jr. Graphic American Inventors Ser.). (ENG., Illus.). 24p. (J). (gr. 2-3). pap. 11.60 *(978-1-4777-0145-4(1),* f98a1be3-cdcf-472f-9d96-1d0f59bc9c61); lib. bdg. 28.93 *(978-1-4777-0080-8(3),* 730827ec-80e6-4264-bf85-33b2c30888e9) Rosen Publishing Group, Inc., The. (PowerKids Pr.).

Green, Sara. Steve Jobs. 2014. (Tech Icons Ser.). (ENG., Illus.). 24p. (J). (gr. 3-8). lib. bdg. 27.95 *(978-1-60014-994-8(4),* Pilot Bks.) Bellwether Media.

Gregory, Josh. Steve Jobs. 2013. (Cornerstones of Freedom™, Third Ser.). (ENG., Illus.). 64p. (J). pap. 8.95 *(978-0-531-21964-5(X))* Scholastic Library Publishing.

—Steve Jobs (a True Book: Biographies) 2013. (True Book (Relaunch) Ser.). (ENG., Illus.). 48p. (J). (gr. 3-5). pap. 6.95 *(978-0-531-23878-3(4),* Children's Pr.) Scholastic Library Publishing.

—A True Book - Biographies: Steve Jobs. 2013. (True Book: Biographies Ser.). (ENG., Illus.). 48p. (J). (gr. 3-5). lib. bdg. 21.19 *(978-0-531-21907-2(0),* Children's Pr.) Scholastic Library Publishing.

Hartland, Jessie. Steve Jobs: Insanely Great. Hartland, Jessie, illus. 2015. (ENG., Illus.). 240p. (YA). (gr. 7). 22.95 *(978-0-307-98295-7(5),* Schwartz & Wade Bks.) Random Hse. Children's Bks.

Honders, Christine. Steve Jobs: Father of the Digital Revolution, 1 vol. 2015. (Britannica Beginner Bios Ser.). (ENG., Illus.). 32p. (J). (gr. 2-3). 26.06 *(978-1-62275-921-7(4),* 42f579f9-275b-48f1-abb4-c6592e086eab, Britannica Educational Publishing) Rosen Publishing Group, Inc., The.

—Steve Jobs: Visionary of the Digital Revolution, 4 vols. 2015. (Britannica Beginner Bios Ser.). (ENG.). 32p. (J). (gr. 2-3). 52.12 *(978-1-62275-924-8(9),* 1afe7d74-2a36-408e-a84e-528dd15bc409, Britannica Educational Publishing) Rosen Publishing Group, Inc., The.

Imbimbo, Anthony. Steve Jobs: the Brilliant Mind Behind Apple, 1 vol. 2009. (Life Portraits Ser.). (ENG., Illus.). 112p. (YA). (gr. 6-8). lib. bdg. 38.67 *(978-1-4339-0060-0(2),* 0d230d17-c4e1-4f87-ad3e-2f38e3957ab2) Stevens, Gareth Publishing LLLP.

Isabella, Jude. Steve Jobs: Visionary Entrepreneur of the Digital Age. 2013. (ENG.). 112p. (J). E-Book *(978-1-4271-8936-3(6));* (Illus.). *(978-0-7787-1189-6(7));* (Illus.). pap. *(978-0-7787-1191-9(9))* Crabtree Publishing Co.

Jackson, Aurelia. Disney's Pixar(r): How Steve Jobs Changed Hollywood. 2014. (Wizards of Technology Ser.: 10). 64p. (J). (gr. 7-18). 23.95 *(978-1-4222-3180-7(1))* Mason Crest.

Kjelle, Marylou Morano. Steve Jobs: Visionary Founder of Apple, 1 vol. 2015. (Newsmakers Ser.). (ENG., Illus.). 48p. (J). (gr. 4-8). lib. bdg. 35.64 *(978-1-62403-642-2(2),* 17183) ABDO Publishing Co.

Klein, Adria F. Steve Jobs. 2009. pap. 13.25 *(978-1-60559-071-4(1))* Hameray Publishing Group, Inc.

La Bella, Laura. Steve Jobs & Steve Wozniak, 1 vol., 1. 2015. (Tech Pioneers Ser.). (ENG.). 112p. (J). (gr. 7-7). 38.80 *(978-1-4994-6286-9(7),* e26659a3-88c1-4a10-a6aa-fb71bc936d44, Rosen Young Adult) Rosen Publishing Group, Inc., The.

Lakin, Patricia. Steve Jobs: Thinking Differently. 2012. (ENG.). 192p. (J). (gr. 3-7). pap. 7.99 *(978-1-4424-5393-7(1),* Aladdin) Simon & Schuster Children's Publishing.

—Steve Jobs: Thinking Differently. 2012. (ENG.). 192p. (J). (gr. 3-7). 17.99 *(978-1-4424-5394-4(X),* Simon & Schuster/Paula Wiseman Bks.) Simon & Schuster/Paula Wiseman Bks.

Mattern, Joanne. Rookie Biographies: Steve Jobs. 2013. (Rookie Biographies(r) Ser.). (ENG., Illus.). 32p. (J). lib. bdg. 23.00 *(978-0-531-24739-6(2))* Scholastic Library Publishing.

—Steve Jobs (Rookie Biographies) 2013. (Rookie Biographies Ser.). (ENG., Illus.). 32p. (J). (gr. 1-2). pap. 5.95 *(978-0-531-24705-1(8),* Children's Pr.) Scholastic Library Publishing.

Nakaya, Andrea C. Steve Jobs & Apple. 2015. (ENG., Illus.). 80p. (J). lib. bdg. *(978-1-60152-880-3(9))* ReferencePoint Pr., Inc.

Pollack, Pam, et al. Who Was Steve Jobs? O'Brien, John, illus. 2012. (Who Was? Ser.). 112p. (J). (gr. 3-7). pap. 5.99 *(978-0-448-46211-0(7),* Penguin Workshop) Penguin Young Readers Group.

Pollack, Pamela & Belviso, Meg. Who Was Steve Jobs? 2012. (Who Was...? Ser.). lib. bdg. 16.00 *(978-0-606-26649-9(6))* Turtleback.

Shea, Therese. Steve Jobs & Apple, 1 vol. 2012. (Internet Biographies Ser.). (ENG., Illus.). 128p. (YA). (gr. 7-7). lib. bdg. 39.80 *(978-1-4488-6910-7(2),* 3ee8d3c5-2cd8-4598-983c-21012af9a75c) Rosen Publishing Group, Inc., The.

Sheen, Barbara. Steve Jobs, 1 vol. 2009. (People in the News Ser.). (ENG., Illus.). 96p. (gr. 7-7). 41.03 *(978-1-4205-0160-5(7),* f11f532a-cab8-4ed2-b6a5-2ad8413693c0, Lucent Pr.) Greenhaven Publishing LLC.

Steve Jobs & Apple. 2011. (Graphic Nonfiction Biographies Ser.). (ENG.). 48p. (YA). (gr. 5-8). *(978-1-4488-5546-9(2));* pap. *(978-1-4488-5645-9(0))* Rosen Publishing Group, Inc., The. (Rosen Reference).

Venezia, Mike. Steve Jobs & Steve Wozniak (Getting to Know the World's Greatest Inventors & Scientists) Venezia, Mike, illus. 2010. (Getting to Know the World's Greatest Inventors & Scientists Ser.). (ENG., Illus.). 32p. (J). (gr. 3-4). pap. 6.95 *(978-0-531-22351-2(5),* Children's Pr.) Scholastic Library Publishing.

Ventura, Marne. Awesome Minds: The Creators of the Iphone(r). Feynman, Drew, illus. 2017. (Awesome Minds Ser.). 56p. (J). (gr. 1-5). 14.99 *(978-1-938093-77-7(1),* 809377) Duo Pr. LLC.

Washburne, Sophie & Sheen, Barbara. Steve Jobs: Computer Visionary, 1 vol. 2016. (People in the News Ser.). (ENG.). 104p. (J). (gr. 7-7). lib. bdg. 41.03 *(978-1-5345-6031-4(9),* 0f17967b-3857-4b1c-95fb-e794800a2c08, Lucent Pr.) Greenhaven Publishing LLC.

Ziller, Amanda. Steve Jobs: American Genius. 2012. (ENG.). 176p. (J). (gr. 3-7). pap. 6.99 *(978-0-06-219765-8(7),* HarperCollins) HarperCollins Pubs.

JOBS

see Occupations; Professions

JOGUES, ISAAC, SAINT, 1607-1646

Pelous, Donald. A Dream Come True: A Story of St. Isaac Jogues. Jagodits, Carolyn Lee, illus. 2011. 94p. 38.95 *(978-1-258-06266-8(6))* Literary Licensing, LLC.

JOHN, THE APOSTLE, SAINT

Woodman, Ros. Bible Detectives John. 2006. (Activity Ser.). (ENG.). 64p. (J). pap., act. bk. ed. 7.99 *(978-1-85792-759-7(1),* 51b6b732-b1ac-49f6-9c83-06b1729968ba) Christian Focus Pubns. GBR. Dist: Baker & Taylor Publisher Services (BTPS).

JOHN, THE BAPTIST, SAINT

Johnson, Alice W. & Warner, Allison H. Believe & You're There When the White Dove Descended. Nelson, Holly, illus. 2009. 96p. (J). pap. 8.95 *(978-1-59038-721-4(X))* Deseret Bk. Co.

Lumsden, Colin, illus. John the Baptist. 2003. (Bible Colour & Learn Ser.). 32p. pap. 2.50 *(978-1-903087-44-2(9))* DayOne Pubns. GBR. Dist: Send The Light Distribution LLC.

MacKenzie, Carine. John: The Baptist. rev. ed. 2013. (Bible Time Ser.). (ENG., Illus.). 32p. (J). (gr. -1-2). pap. 4.50 *(978-1-84550-164-8(0),* 5dceabdb-8e78-47d3-927c-07e75750d968) Christian Focus Pubns. GBR. Dist: Baker & Taylor Publisher Services (BTPS).

JOHN, THE BAPTIST, SAINT—FICTION

Rivera-Ashford, Roni Capin & Johnson, Richard. Hip Hip Hooray, It's Monsoon Day! 2007. (ENG & SPA.). (YA). pap. 15.95 *(978-1-886679-36-8(3))* Arizona Sonora Desert Museum Pr.

JOHN, ELTON, 1947-

Anderson, Kirsten. Who Is Elton John? 2016. (Who Is... ? Ser.). lib. bdg. 16.00 *(978-0-606-38396-7(4))* Turtleback.

O'Mahony, John. Elton John. 2003. (World Musicmakers Ser.). (Illus.). 64p. (J). 26.20 *(978-1-56711-972-5(7),* Blackbirch Pr., Inc.) Cengage Gale.

Schlesinger, Ethan. Elton John. (Pop Rock Ser.). (Illus.). 64p. (YA). (gr. 3-7). 2008. lib. bdg. 22.95 *(978-1-4222-0189-3(9))* 2007. pap. 7.95 *(978-1-4222-0316-3(6))* Mason Crest.

White, Katherine. Elton John. 2009. (Rock & Roll Hall of Famers Ser.). 112p. (gr. 5-8). 63.90 *(978-1-60852-473-0(6),* Rosen Reference) Rosen Publishing Group, Inc., The.

JOHN HENRY (LEGENDARY CHARACTER)

Gould, Jane H. John Henry, 1 vol. 2014. (Jr. Graphic American Legends Ser.). (ENG., Illus.). 24p. (J). (gr. 2-3). lib. bdg. 28.93 *(978-1-4777-7197-6(2),* 6309c37d-3ab4-4017-bb4a-f72459e052ad, PowerKids Pr.) Rosen Publishing Group, Inc., The.

Keats, Ezra Jack. John Henry: An American Legend. 50th anniv. ed. 2014. (Illus.). 32p. (J). (gr. -1-2). 17.99 *(978-0-553-51307-3(9),* Knopf Bks. for Young Readers) Random Hse. Children's Bks.

Krensky, Stephen. John Henry. Oldroyd, Mark, illus. 2006. (On My Own Folklore Ser.). (ENG.). 48p. (J). (gr. 2-4). lib. bdg. 25.26 *(978-1-57505-887-0(1),* Millbrook Pr.) Lerner Publishing Group.

Meister, Cari. John Henry vs. the Mighty Steam Drill, 1 vol. Rivas, Victor, illus. 2014. (American Folk Legends Ser.). (ENG.). 32p. (J). (gr. k-2). 27.99 *(978-1-4795-5430-0(8),* 126078, Picture Window Bks.) Capstone.

JOHNSON, ANDREW, 1808-1875

Gunderson, Megan M. Andrew Johnson, 1 vol. 2016. (United States Presidents *2017 Ser.). (ENG., Illus.). 40p. (J). (gr. 2-5). 35.64 *(978-1-68078-103-8(0),* 21823, Big Buddy Bks.) ABDO Publishing Co.

Havelin, Kate. Andrew Johnson. 2005. (Presidential Leaders Ser.). (Illus.). 112p. (J). (gr. 6-12). lib. bdg. 29.27 *(978-0-8225-1000-0(6))* Lerner Publishing Group.

Powell, Walter. How to Draw the Life & Times of Andrew Johnson. 2009. (Kid's Guide to Drawing the Presidents of the United States of America Ser.). 32p. (gr. 4-4). 50.50 *(978-1-61511-132-9(8),* PowerKids Pr.) Rosen Publishing Group, Inc., The.

Randolph, Ryan P. How to Draw the Life & Times of Andrew Johnson, 1 vol. 2005. (Kid's Guide to Drawing the Presidents of the United States of America Ser.). (ENG.). 32p. (YA). (gr. 4-4). 30.27 *(978-1-4042-2994-5(9),* cbd7b5dc-17ac-4aa1-a539-24dd3ee629b1) Rosen Publishing Group, Inc., The.

Venezia, Mike. Andrew Johnson: Seventeenth President. Venezia, Mike, illus. 2005. (Getting to Know the U. S. Presidents Ser.). (ENG., Illus.). 32p. (J). (gr. 3-7). lib. bdg. 28.00 *(978-0-516-22622-4(3),* Children's Pr.) Scholastic Library Publishing.

JOHNSON, JAMES WELDON, 1871-1938

Shull, Jodie A. Words of Promise: A Story about James Weldon Johnson. Stetz, Ken, illus. 2005. (Creative Minds Biographies Ser.). (ENG.). 64p. (gr. 4-8). lib. bdg. 22.60 *(978-1-57505-755-2(7),* Carolrhoda Bks.) Lerner Publishing Group.

JOHNSON, LADY BIRD, 1912-2007

Appelt, Kathi. Miss Lady Bird's Wildflowers: How a First Lady Changed America. Hein, Joy Fisher, illus. 2005. 40p. (J). lib. bdg. 17.89 *(978-0-06-001108-6(4));* (ENG.). (gr. -1-3). 17.99 *(978-0-06-001107-9(6),* HarperCollins) HarperCollins Pubs.

Collard, Sneed B., III. American Heroes, 6 vols., Group 3. Incl. Cesar Chavez. 32.64 *(978-0-7614-4055-0(0),* abfe4b16-e58b-4817-8708-b7bdbc77951d); George Washington. 32.64 *(978-0-7614-4060-4(7),* 2757fb59-5b7f-48ba-b248-ebe59643b8d1); Jacob Lawrence. 32.64 *(978-0-7614-4058-1(5),* 19d54f3f-2d13-43c3-a7af-77244e0ba9a9); Lady Bird Johnson. 32.64 *(978-0-7614-4056-7(9),* 1b484198-89c3-48ec-b434-f596e2cfb712); Phillis Wheatley. (Illus.). 32.64 *(978-0-7614-4057-4(7),* b5aabf94-bd02-4815-9f30-a3d8be34143b); Sitting Bull. 32.64 *(978-0-7614-4059-8(3),* d331b804-8748-40a1-a55d-cc9e79408f93); 48p. (gr. 3-3). 2010. (American Heroes 3 Ser.). 2009. Set lib. bdg. 179.57 o.p. *(978-0-7614-4054-3(2),* Cavendish Square) Cavendish Square Publishing LLC.

—Lady Bird Johnson, 1 vol. 2010. (American Heroes Ser.). (ENG.). 48p. (gr. 3-3). 32.64 *(978-0-7614-4056-7(9),* 1b484198-89c3-48ec-b434-f596e2cfb712) Cavendish Square Publishing LLC.

Strand, Jennifer. Lady Bird Johnson. 2018. (First Ladies (Launch!) Ser.). (ENG., Illus.). 24p. (J). (gr. -1-2). lib. bdg. 31.36 *(978-1-5321-2284-2(5),* 28335, Abdo Zoom-Launch) ABDO Publishing Co.

Yasuda, Anita. Lady Bird Johnson. 2010. (My Life Ser.). 24p. (J). (gr. 2-4). lib. bdg. 25.70 *(978-1-61690-062-5(8))* Weigl Pubs., Inc.

—Lady Bird Johnson: My Life. 2010. pap. 9.95 *(978-1-61690-063-2(6))* Weigl Pubs., Inc.

JOHNSON, LYNDON B. (LYNDON BAINES), 1908-1973

Baxter, Kathleen & McConnell, Robert L., contrib. by. Assassination & Its Aftermath: How a Photograph Reassured a Shocked Nation, 1 vol. 2013. (Captured History Ser.). (ENG., Illus.). 64p. (J). (gr. 5-9). 35.32 *(978-0-7565-4692-2(3),* Compass Point Bks.) Capstone.

Blake, Kevin. Lyndon B. Johnson. 2016. (First Look at America's Presidents Ser.). (ENG., Illus.). 24p. (J). (gr. -1-3). 26.99 *(978-1-943553-32-7(7))* Bearport Publishing Co., Inc.

Colbert, Nancy A. Great Society: The Story of Lyndon Baines Johnson. 2004. (Notable Americans Ser.). (Illus.). 144p. (YA). (gr. 6-12). 23.95 *(978-1-883846-84-8(6),* First Biographies) Reynolds, Morgan Inc.

Day, Meredith, ed. Lyndon B. Johnson, 1 vol. 2016. (Pivotal Presidents: Profiles in Leadership Ser.). (ENG., Illus.). 80p. (gr. 8-8). lib. bdg. 36.47 *(978-1-68048-527-1(X),* 5e555973-7621-4474-aec5-45e2fe88a7dc) Rosen Publishing Group, Inc., The.

Devera, Czeena. Lyndon B. Johnson. Bane, Jeff, illus. 2017. (My Early Library: My Itty-Bitty Bio Ser.). (ENG.). 24p. (J). (gr. k-1). 30.64 *(978-1-63472-817-1(3),* 209694) Cherry Lake Publishing.

Dudley Gold, Susan. Lyndon B. Johnson, 1 vol. 2009. (Presidents & Their Times Ser.). (ENG.). 96p. (gr. 6-6). lib. bdg. 36.93 *(978-0-7614-2837-4(2),* b7365e2b-017f-4a6b-b790-7837fd51eb6c) Cavendish Square Publishing LLC.

Gunderson, Megan M. Lyndon B. Johnson, 1 vol. 2016. (United States Presidents *2017 Ser.). (ENG., Illus.). 40p. (J). (gr. 2-5). lib. bdg. 35.64 *(978-1-68078-104-5(9),* 21825, Big Buddy Bks.) ABDO Publishing Co.

Hasselius, Michelle M. Lyndon B. Johnson, 1 vol. 2014. (Presidential Biographies Ser.). (ENG.). 24p. (J). (gr. -1-2). lib. bdg. 27.32 *(978-1-4765-9611-2(5),* 125417, Capstone Pr.) Capstone.

Isecke, Harriet. Lyndon B. Johnson: A Texan in the White House, 1 vol. rev. ed. 2012. (Social Studies: Informational Text Ser.). (ENG.). 32p. (gr. 3-5). pap. 11.99 *(978-1-4333-5052-8(1))* Teacher Created Materials, Inc.

—Lyndon B. Johnson: Un Texano en la Casa Blanca / Lyndon B. Johnson - A Texan in the White House. 2013. (Primary Source Readers Ser.). (SPA.). lib. bdg. 19.65 *(978-0-606-31873-0(9))* Turtleback.

Levy, Debbie. Lyndon B. Johnson. 2003. (Presidential Leaders Ser.). (Illus.). 112p. (J). 29.27 *(978-0-8225-0097-1(3),* Lerner Pubns.) Lerner Publishing Group.

Lüsted, Marcia Amidon. Lyndon B. Johnson & the Civil Rights ACT, 1 vol. 2017. (Spotlight on the Civil Rights Movement Ser.). (ENG., Illus.). 48p. (J). (gr. 6-6). 33.47 *(978-1-5383-8048-2(X),* 7e6c6e30-9ee8-43e5-9413-0bf6bf097a92); pap. 12.75 *(978-1-5081-7746-3(5),* cb9830f6-0104-416a-bb10-efb9ad35aa6c) Rosen Publishing Group, Inc., The.

Mis, M. S. How to Draw the Life & Times of Lyndon B. Johnson. 2009. (Kid's Guide to Drawing the Presidents of the United States of America Ser.). 32p. (gr. 4-4). 50.50 *(978-1-61511-154-1(9),* PowerKids Pr.) Rosen Publishing Group, Inc., The.

Mis, Melody S. How to Draw the Life & Times of Lyndon B. Johnson, 1 vol. 2005. (Kid's Guide to Drawing the Presidents of the United States of America Ser.). (ENG., Illus.). 32p. (YA). (gr. 4-4). 30.27 *(978-1-4042-3012-5(2),* d67b7c7f-fbff-4357-a198-f971f81927bc) Rosen Publishing Group, Inc., The.

Porterfield, Jason. How Lyndon B. Johnson Fought the Vietnam War, 1 vol. 2017. (Presidents at War Ser.). (ENG.). 128p. (gr. 8-8). lib. bdg. 38.93 *(978-0-7660-8531-2(7),* d7431810-368e-46b2-bba1-293a64dd0532) Enslow Publishing, LLC.

Venezia, Mike. Lyndon B. Johnson: Thirty-Sixth President, 1963-1969. Venezia, Mike, illus. 2007. (Getting to Know the U. S. Presidents Ser.). (Illus.). 32p. (J). (gr. 3-4). 28.00 *(978-0-516-22640-8(1),* Children's Pr.) Scholastic Library Publishing.

Yasuda, Anita. Lady Bird Johnson. 2010. (My Life Ser.). 24p. (J). (gr. 2-4). lib. bdg. 25.70 *(978-1-61690-062-5(8))* Weigl Pubs., Inc.

—Lady Bird Johnson: My Life. 2010. pap. 9.95 *(978-1-61690-063-2(6))* Weigl Pubs., Inc.

JOHNSTOWN (CAMBRIA COUNTY, PA.)—FLOOD, 1889

see Floods—Pennsylvania—Johnstown (Cambria County)

JOKES

see Wit and Humor

JOLIET, LOUIS, 1645-1700

Donaldson-Forbes, Jeff. Jacques Marquette & Louis Jolliet. 2009. (Primary Source Library of Famous Explorers Ser.). 24p. (gr. 4-4). 42.50 *(978-1-60854-127-0(4),* PowerKids Pr.) Rosen Publishing Group, Inc., The.

Larkin, Tanya. Jacques Marquette & Louis Jolliet: Explorers of the Mississippi. 2009. (Library of Explorers & Exploration Ser.). 112p. (gr. 5-8). 66.50 *(978-1-60853-608-5(4),* Rosen Reference) Rosen Publishing Group, Inc., The.

Zelenyi, Alexander & Zelenyj, Alexander. Marquette & Jolliet: Quest for the Mississippi. 2006. (In the Footsteps of Explorers Ser.). (ENG., Illus.). 32p. (J). (gr. 4-7). pap. *(978-0-7787-2467-4(0));* lib. bdg. *(978-0-7787-2431-5(X))* Crabtree Publishing Co.

JONAH (BIBLICAL PROPHET)

Amery, H. Jonah & the Whale. 2004. (Bible Tales Readers Ser.). 16p. (J). lib. bdg. 12.95 *(978-1-58086-632-3(8),* Usborne); (Illus.). pap. 4.95 *(978-0-7945-0414-4(0))* EDC Publishing.

Arthur, Kay & Domeij, Scott. Wrong Way Jonah. 2006. (Discover-4-Yourself for Kids Ser.). 93p. (J). pap. 8.99 *(978-1-888655-21-6(6))* Precept.
Arthur, Kay, et al. Wrong Way, Jonah! Jonah. 2010. (Discover 4 Yourself Inductive Bible Studies for Kids Ser.). (ENG.). 128p. (J). (gr. 2-6). pap. 11.99 *(978-0-7369-2819-9(7)*, 6928199) Harvest Hse. Pubs.
Balsley, Tilda. Oh No, Jonah! Silver, Jago, illus. 2012. (Bible Ser.). (ENG.). 32p. (J). (gr. k-4). lib. bdg. 17.95 *(978-0-7613-5139-9(6)*, Kar-Ben Publishing) Lerner Publishing Group.
Bishop, Jennie. Jonah & the Big Fish Coloring Book. 2007. (Illus.). 16p. (J). pap. 1.89 *(978-1-59317-206-0(0))* Warner Pr., Inc.
Gressman, Carylee Anne. Draw & Write Through History: Creation Through Jonah. Wolf, Aaron D., ed. Dick, Peggy, illus. 2006. (J). per. 12.95 *(978-0-9778597-0-2(3))* CPR Pubng.
Grosche, Erwin. Jonah & the Whale. Teich, Karsten, illus. 2016. 28p. (J). (gr. k-3). 12.99 *(978-1-5064-0882-8(6)*, Sparkhouse Family) 1517 Media.
Hansen, Janis. Jonah & His Amazing Voyage, 5 vols. Francisco, Wendy, illus. 2003. (Bible Adventure Club Ser.). 36p. wbk. ed. 19.99 incl. audio, cd-rom *(978-1-58134-326-7(4))* Crossway.
Jonah Bible Sticker Book. 2003. (Illus.). 16p. (J). 2.98 *(978-1-4054-1555-2(X))* Parragon, Inc.
MacLean, Ruth. The Man Who Ran: A Puzzle Book about Jonah. rev. ed. 2009. (Puzzle Ser.). (ENG., Illus.). 24p. (J). 4.99 *(978-1-84550-496-0(8)*, 713d8502-5f12-4157-94f2-f74d4237f2d6) Christian Focus Pubns. GBR. Dist: Baker & Taylor Publisher Services (BTPS).
Pingry, Patricia A. Jonah & the Fish: Based on Jonah 1-3:3. Venturi-Pickett, Stacy, illus. 2005. (Stories from the Bible Ser.). (ENG.). 26p. (J). (gr. -1-k). bds. 6.95 *(978-0-8249-6626-3(0)*, Ideals Pubns.) Worthy Publishing.
Piper, Sophie. Jonah & the Whale, 1 vol. Corke, Estelle, illus. 2009. (Bible Story Time Ser.). 32p. (J). 5.95 *(978-0-8254-7836-9(7)*, Lion Children's) Lion Hudson PLC GBR. Dist: Kregel Pubns.
Pulley, Kelly & Zondervan Staff. Jonah & the Big Fish · JonÃ¡s y el Gran Pez: (Bilingual), 1 vol. Pulley, Kelly, illus. 2009. (I Can Read! / the Beginner's Bible / ¡Yo Sé Leer! Ser.).Tr. of (Bilingüe). (SPA., Illus.). 32p. (J). (gr. -1-2). pap. 5.99 *(978-0-310-71887-1(2))* Vida Pubs.
Scherm, Deedra. The Whale & Jonah: A Story of Obedience & Forgiveness. Dreyer, Laura, illus. 2007. (ENG.). 20p. 7.99 *(978-1-934789-00-1(3))* Lemon Vision Productions.
Simon, Mary Manz. Jonah & the Big Fish: Read & Learn the Bible. 2005. (ENG., Illus.). 24p. (J). pap. 2.99 *(978-1-4037-1158-8(5)*, Spirit Pr.) Bendon, Inc.
Smart Kids Publishing Staff. Jonah & the Whale: A Story about Responsibility. Sharp, Chris, illus. 2006. (I Can Read the Bible Ser.). (ENG.). 12p. (J). (gr. -1-3). 14.95 *(978-0-8249-6661-4(9)*, Ideals Pubns.) Worthy Publishing.
Smith, Brendan Powell. Jonah & the Whale: The Brick Bible for Kids. 2014. (Brick Bible for Kids Ser.). (ENG., Illus.). 32p. (J). (gr. -1-k). 3.99 *(978-1-63450-055-5(5))*; 12.95 *(978-1-62873-589-5(9))* Skyhorse Publishing Co., Inc. (Sky Pony Pr.).
Wickenden, Nadine, illus. The Story of Jonah. 2006. 10p. (J). (gr. k-4). reprint ed. 8.00 *(978-0-7567-9923-6(6))* DIANE Publishing Co.
Zonderkidz. The Beginner's Bible Jonah & the Giant Fish, 1 vol. 2019. (I Can Read! / the Beginner's Bible Ser.). (ENG., Illus.). 32p. (J). pap. 4.99 *(978-0-310-76044-3(5))* Zonderkidz.
—Jonah's Big Fish Adventure, 1 vol. 2018. (Beginner's Bible Ser.). (ENG., Illus.). 18p. (J). bds. 9.99 *(978-0-310-75994-2(3))* Zonderkidz.
Zondervan Bibles Staff. Jonah, God's Messenger, 1 vol. Jones, Dennis, illus. 2011. (I Can Read! / Dennis Jones Ser.). (ENG.). 32p. (J). pap. 4.99 *(978-0-310-71835-2(X))* Zonderkidz.

JONATHAN (BIBLICAL FIGURE)

Dietrich, Julie. David & His Friend, Jonathan. Ramsey, Marcy, illus. 2005. (Arch Bks.). (ENG.). 16p. (J). pap. 1.99 *(978-0-7586-0723-2(7))* Concordia Publishing Hse.
MacKenzie, Carine. David the Fugitive: True Friendship. 2009. (Bible Alive Ser.). (ENG., Illus.). 24p. (J). 4.50 *(978-1-84550-487-8(9)*, 203b9477-590f-403b-b69c-ef8ff0959d24) Christian Focus Pubns. GBR. Dist: Baker & Taylor Publisher Services (BTPS).
—Jonathan: The Faithful Friend. 2007. (Bible Wise Ser.). (ENG., Illus.). 32p. (J). (gr. -1-2). 4.50 *(978-1-84550-289-8(2)*, d69b5ff0-2c37-441d-88ea-422d76612620) Christian Focus Pubns. GBR. Dist: Baker & Taylor Publisher Services (BTPS).

JONES, HERCULEAH (FICTITIOUS CHARACTER)—FICTION

Byars, Betsy. The Black Tower. 2007. (Herculeah Jones Mystery Ser.: 7). 144p. (J). (gr. 3-7). 6.99 *(978-0-14-240937-4(5)*, Puffin Books) Penguin Young Readers Group.
—The Dark Stairs. (Herculeah Jones Mystery Ser.). 160p. (J). (gr. 3-5). pap. 4.99 *(978-0-8072-1478-7(7)*, Listening Library) Random Hse. Audio Publishing Group.
—Death's Door. 2006. (Herculeah Jones Mystery Ser.: 4). (ENG.). 144p. (J). (gr. 3-7). 6.99 *(978-0-14-240565-9(5)*, Puffin Books) Penguin Young Readers Group.
—Disappearing Acts. 2006. (Herculeah Jones Mystery Ser.: 5). (ENG.). 144p. (J). (gr. 3-7). 6.99 *(978-0-14-240566-6(3)*, Puffin Books) Penguin Young Readers Group.
—King of Murder. 2007. (Herculeah Jones Mystery Ser.: 6). 144p. (J). (gr. 3-7). 5.99 *(978-0-14-240759-2(3)*, Puffin Books) Penguin Young Readers Group.
—Tarot Says Beware. 2006. (Herculeah Jones Mystery Ser.). 151p. (gr. 3-7). 16.00 *(978-0-7569-6737-6(6))* Perfection Learning Corp.

JONES, INDIANA (FICTITIOUS CHARACTER)—FICTION

Windham, Ryder & Weyn, Suzanne. Indiana Jones Collector's Edition. 2008. (Illus.). 657p. (J). *(978-0-545-09183-1(7))* Scholastic, Inc.

JONES, JOHN PAUL, 1747-1792

Alphin, Elaine Marie & Alphin, Arthur B. I Have Not Yet Begun to Fight: A Story about John Paul Jones. Casale, Paul, tr. Casale, Paul, illus. 2004. (Creative Minds Biography Ser.). 64p. (J). 22.60 *(978-1-57505-601-2(1)*, Carolrhoda Bks.) Lerner Publishing Group.
Bradford, James C. John Paul Jones & the American Navy. 2009. (Library of American Lives & Times Ser.). 112p. (gr. 5-5). 69.20 *(978-1-60853-490-6(1))* Rosen Publishing Group, Inc., The.
Brager, Bruce L. John Paul Jones: America's Sailor. 2006. (Founders of the Republic Ser.). (Illus.). 160p. (J). (gr. 6-12). lib. bdg. 26.95 *(978-1-931798-84-6(2))* Reynolds, Morgan Inc.
Crickard, Sarah. John Paul Jones & the Birth of the American Navy, 1 vol. 2015. (Spotlight on American History Ser.). (ENG., Illus.). 24p. (J). (gr. 4-6). pap. 11.00 *(978-1-4994-1759-3(4)*, 124776b9-9541-49f4-8833-1044127807af, PowerKids Pr.) Rosen Publishing Group, Inc., The.
Egan, Tracie. John Paul Jones, 1 vol. 2003. (Primary Sources of Famous People in American History Ser.). (ENG., Illus.). 32p. (gr. 3-4). pap. 10.00 *(978-0-8239-4185-8(X)*, 4d1e4acb-7c3f-49b6-b241-feedeacf84ff); lib. bdg. 29.13 *(978-0-8239-4113-1(2)*, 64ad2eb6-aa31-4d2f-84d0-69248f6885af) Rosen Publishing Group, Inc., The. (Rosen Reference).
—John Paul Jones: American Naval Hero. 2009. (Primary Sources of Famous People in American History Ser.). 32p. (gr. 2-3). 47.90 *(978-1-60851-693-3(8))* Rosen Publishing Group, Inc., The.
—John Paul Jones: American Naval Hero = Heroe de la Marina Estadounidense, 1 vol. 2003. (Famous People in American History / Grandes personajes en la Historia de Los Estados Unidos Ser.). (ENG & SPA., Illus.). 32p. (gr. 2-3). lib. bdg. 29.13 *(978-0-8239-4161-2(2)*, 225db84f-6c93-473e-8987-a1ec9fabaf6a, Editorial Buenas Letras) Rosen Publishing Group, Inc., The.
—John Paul Jones: American Naval Hero / Héroe de la marina Estadounidense. 2009. (Famous People in American History/Grandes personajes en la historia de los Estados Unidos Ser.). (ENG & SPA.). 32p. (gr. 2-3). 47.90 *(978-1-61512-548-7(5)*, Editorial Buenas Letras) Rosen Publishing Group, Inc., The.
—John Paul Jones: Heroe de la Marina Estadounidense, 1 vol. 2003. (Grandes Personajes en la Historia de Los Estados Unidos (Famous People in American History) Ser.). (SPA.). 32p. (gr. 3-4). pap. 10.00 *(978-0-8239-4231-2(7)*, b3703f85-95f6-4e9f-a095-a83bcc5de34c); (Illus.). lib. bdg. 29.13 *(978-0-8239-4137-7(X)*, 1ffc0fac-3788-416a-99f9-7cc2c66cbb0e, Editorial Buenas Letras) Rosen Publishing Group, Inc., The.
—John Paul Jones: Héroe de la marina estadounidense (John Paul Jones: American Naval Hero) 2009. (Grandes personajes en la historia de los Estados Unidos (Famous People in American History) Ser.). (SPA.). 32p. (gr. 2-3). 47.90 *(978-1-61512-802-0(6)*, Editorial Buenas Letras) Rosen Publishing Group, Inc., The.
Harkins, Susan Sales & Harkins, William H. The Life & Times of John Paul Jones. 2007. (Profiles in American History Ser.). (Illus.). 48p. (J). (gr. 4-8). lib. bdg. 29.95 *(978-1-58415-529-4(9))* Mitchell Lane Pubs.
Sperry, Armstrong. John Paul Jones: The Pirate Patriot. 2017. (Great Leaders & Events Ser.). (ENG.). (J). (gr. 4-8). lib. bdg. 35.99 *(978-1-942875-42-0(8))* Quarto Publishing Group USA.
Waldman, Scott. Victory at Sea: John Paul Jones & the Continental Navy. 2009. (Great Moments in American History Ser.). 32p. (gr. 3-3). 47.90 *(978-1-61513-156-3(6))* Rosen Publishing Group, Inc., The.
Waldman, Scott P. Victory at Sea: John Paul Jones & the Continental Navy, 1 vol. 2003. (Great Moments in American History Ser.). (ENG., Illus.). 32p. (gr. 3-3). lib. bdg. 29.13 *(978-0-8239-4362-3(3)*, 24b16829-525c-4393-99e5-49d67f31656f, Rosen Reference) Rosen Publishing Group, Inc., The.

JONES, JUNIE B. (FICTITIOUS CHARACTER)—FICTION

Park, Barbara. Junie B., First Grader - Boss of Lunch. Brunkus, Denise, illus. 2003. (Junie B., First Grader Ser.: No. 2). 96p. (J). (gr. k-3). lib. bdg. 11.99 *(978-0-375-90294-9(5)*, Golden Bks.) Random Hse. Children's Bks.
—Junie B. Jones: Boss of Lunch. 2003. (Junie B. Jones Ser.: 19). (gr. k-3). lib. bdg. 14.75 *(978-0-613-63168-6(4))* Turtleback.
—Junie B. Jones #20: Toothless Wonder. Brunkus, Denise, illus. 2003. (Junie B. Jones Ser.: 20). (ENG.). 96p. (J). (gr. 1-4). pap. 4.99 *(978-0-375-82223-0(2)*, Random Hse. Bks. for Young Readers) Random Hse. Children's Bks.
—Junie B. Jones #21: Cheater Pants. Brunkus, Denise, illus. 2004. (Junie B. Jones Ser.: 21). 96p. (J). (gr. 1-4). 5.99 *(978-0-375-82302-2(6)*, Random Hse. Bks. for Young Readers) Random Hse. Children's Bks.
—Junie B. Jones #23: Shipwrecked, No. 23. Brunkus, Denise, illus. 2005. (Junie B. Jones Ser.: 23). (ENG.). 96p. (J). (gr. 1-4). mass mkt. 5.99 *(978-0-375-82805-8(2)*, Random Hse. Bks. for Young Readers) Random Hse. Children's Bks.
—Junie B. Jones #24: BOO... & I MEAN It! Brunkus, Denise, illus. 2005. (Junie B. Jones Ser.: 24). (ENG.). 96p. (J). (gr. 1-4). 5.99 *(978-0-375-82807-2(9)*, Random Hse. Bks. for Young Readers) Random Hse. Children's Bks.
—Junie B. Jones & a Little Monkey Business, Vol. 2. unabr. ed. 2004. (Junie B. Jones Ser.: Vol. 2). 68p. (J). (gr. k-3). pap. 17.00 incl. audio *(978-0-8072-0779-6(9)*, LFTR 238 SP, Listening Library) Random Hse. Audio Publishing Group.
—Junie B. Jones & the Mushy Gushy Valentine. unabr. ed. 2004. (Junie B. Jones Ser.: No. 14). 69p. (J). (gr. k-3). pap. 17.00 incl. audio *(978-0-8072-0335-4(1)*, Listening Library) Random Hse. Audio Publishing Group.
—Junie B. Jones & the Stupid Smelly Bus. unabr. ed. 2004. (Junie B. Jones Ser.: Vol. 1). 69p. (J). (gr. k-3). pap. 17.00 incl. audio *(978-0-8072-0778-9(0)*, LFTR 237 SP, Listening Library) Random Hse. Audio Publishing Group.
—Junie B. Jones Fifth Boxed Set Ever! Books 17-20, 4 vols. Brunkus, Denise, illus. 2008. (Junie B. Jones Ser.). (ENG.). (gr. 1-4). 19.96 *(978-0-375-85570-2(X)*, Random Hse. Bks. for Young Readers) Random Hse. Children's Bks.
—Junie B. Jones Fourth Boxed Set Ever! Books 13-16, 4 vols. Brunkus, Denise, illus. 2004. (Junie B. Jones Ser.). (ENG.). (J). (gr. 1-4). 23.96 *(978-0-375-82829-4(X)*, Random Hse. Bks. for Young Readers) Random Hse. Children's Bks.
—Junie B. Jones Has a Monster under Her Bed. unabr. ed. 2004. (Junie B. Jones Ser.: No. 8). 69p. (J). (gr. k-3). pap. 17.00 incl. audio *(978-0-8072-0644-7(X)*, Listening Library) Random Hse. Audio Publishing Group.
—Junie B. Jones Third Boxed Set Ever! Books 9-12, 4 vols., Bks. 9-12. Brunkus, Denise, illus. 2003. (Junie B. Jones Ser.). (ENG.). (J). (gr. 1-4). 19.96 *(978-0-375-82552-1(5)*, Random Hse. Bks. for Young Readers) Random Hse. Children's Bks.
—Toothless Wonder. 2003. (Junie B. Jones Ser.: 20). (gr. k-3). lib. bdg. 14.75 *(978-0-613-71014-5(2))* Turtleback.
—Turkeys We Have Loved & Eaten (and Other Thankful Stuff) 2014. (Junie B. Jones Ser.: 28). lib. bdg. 14.75 *(978-0-606-36015-9(8))* Turtleback.

JONES, MOTHER, 1830-1930

Cole, Peter. Ben Fletcher: The Life & Times of a Black Wobbly: Including Fellow Worker Fletcher's Writings & Speeches. 10th annot. ed. 2006. (Labor Classics Ser.). (Illus.). 149p. per. 15.00 *(978-0-88286-311-5(8))* Kerr, Charles H. Publishing Co.
Gay, Kathlyn. Mother Jones. 2006. (American Workers Ser.). (Illus.). 144p. (J). (gr. 3-7). lib. bdg. 28.95 *(978-1-59935-016-5(5))* Reynolds, Morgan Inc.
Kraft, Betsy Harvey. Mother Jones: One Woman's Fight for Labor. 2006. (Illus.). 116p. (YA). (gr. 6-10). reprint ed. 17.00 *(978-1-4223-5443-8(1))* DIANE Publishing Co.
Miller, Connie Colwell. Mother Jones: Labor Leader, 1 vol. Erwin, Steve & Barnett, Charles, III, illus. 2006. (Graphic Biographies Ser.). (ENG.). 32p. (J). (gr. 3-9). per. 8.10 *(978-0-7368-9662-7(7)*, 93447, Capstone Pr.) Capstone.

JORDAN

Carew-Miller, Anna. Jordan. (Major Muslim Nations Ser.). 112p. 2010. (YA). (gr. 5-18). lib. bdg. 25.95 *(978-1-4222-1383-4(8))* Vol. 13. 2015. (Illus.). (J). (gr. 7). lib. bdg. 25.95 *(978-1-4222-3444-0(4))* Mason Crest.
Etheredge, Laura. Syria, Lebanon, & Jordan, 1 vol. 2011. (Middle East: Region in Transition Ser.). (ENG., Illus.). 248p. (YA). (gr. 10-10). lib. bdg. 43.59 *(978-1-61530-329-8(4)*, b19482da-7bc4-4f09-9f95-b00cd6590743) Rosen Publishing Group, Inc., The.
Hansen, Grace. Petra. 2017. (World Wonders Ser.). (ENG., Illus.). 24p. (J). (gr. -1-2). lib. bdg. 32.79 *(978-1-5321-0443-5(X)*, 26569, Abdo Kids) ABDO Publishing Co.
Kummer, Patricia K. Jordan. 2006. (Enchantment of the World Ser.). (ENG., Illus.). 144p. (J). (gr. 5-9). 39.00 *(978-0-516-24870-7(7)*, Children's Pr.) Scholastic Library Publishing.
Perdew, Laura. Understanding Jordan Today. 2014. (Illus.). 64p. (J). (gr. 3-6). 33.95 *(978-1-61228-654-9(2))* Mitchell Lane Pubs.
Pundyk, Grace. Welcome to Jordan, 1 vol. 2004. (Welcome to My Country Ser.). (ENG., Illus.). 48p. (gr. 2-4). lib. bdg. 29.67 *(978-0-8368-2565-7(9)*, 8c34631d-f7d4-4a44-8b17-cd5fb4b79f04) Stevens, Gareth Publishing LLLP.
Rechner, Amy. Jordan. 2018. (Country Profiles Ser.). (ENG., Illus.). 32p. (J). (gr. 3-8). lib. bdg. 27.95 *(978-1-62617-843-4(7)*, Blastoff! Discovery) Bellwether Media.
Romano, Amy. A Historical Atlas of Jordan. 2009. (Historical Atlases of South Asia, Central Asia, & the Middle East Ser.). 64p. (gr. 6-6). 61.20 *(978-1-61513-322-2(4))* Rosen Publishing Group, Inc., The.
Skinner, Patricia. Jordan, 1 vol. 2003. (Countries of the World Ser.). (ENG., Illus.). 96p. (gr. 6-8). lib. bdg. 33.67 *(978-0-8368-2365-3(6)*, f6148c46-93a4-4ce9-9bc8-e23f807cb5c1) Stevens, Gareth Publishing LLLP.
Sonneborn, Liz. Jordan (Enchantment of the World) (Library Edition) 2019. (Enchantment of the World. Second Ser.). (ENG., Illus.). 144p. (J). (gr. 5-9). lib. bdg. 40.00 *(978-0-531-12698-1(6)*, Children's Pr.) Scholastic Library Publishing.
South, Coleman. Jordan, 1 vol. 2nd rev. ed. 2008. (Cultures of the World (Second Edition)(r) Ser.). (ENG.). 144p. (gr. 5-5). lib. bdg. 49.79 *(978-0-7614-2080-4(0)*, 899f1a9c-8510-4cd8-9244-3d79af93e63e) Cavendish Square Publishing LLC.
South, Coleman & Newsome, Joel. Jordan, 1 vol. 2017. (Cultures of the World (Third Edition)(r) Ser.). (ENG.). 144p. (gr. 5-5). 48.79 *(978-1-5026-2608-0(X)*, 1d155058-6abe-46eb-a2de-1456e2c2ed5e) Cavendish Square Publishing LLC.

JORDAN, MICHAEL, 1963-

Aaseng, Nathan. Michael Jordan: Hall of Fame Basketball Superstar, 1 vol. 2013. (Hall of Fame Sports Greats Ser.). (ENG.). 64p. (gr. 4-6). 30.60 *(978-1-62285-035-8(1)*, 85d629ce-2903-4f99-aaf5-c8e372608e71); pap. 12.71 *(978-1-62285-036-5(X)*, 6d348f16-ac24-4507-b7a5-85e743244267) Enslow Publishing, LLC.
Anderson, Kirsten & Who HQ. Who Is Michael Jordan? Putra, Dede, illus. 2019. (Who Was? Ser.). 112p. (J). (gr. 3-7). 5.99 *(978-0-451-53245-9(7))*; lib. bdg. 15.99 *(978-0-451-53247-3(3))* Penguin Young Readers Group. (Penguin Workshop).
Aretha, David. LeBron vs. Durant vs. Curry vs. Jordan, 1 vol. 2019. (Who's the GOAT? Using Math to Crown the Champion Ser.). (ENG.). 64p. (gr. 5-5). pap. 13.95 *(978-1-7253-4846-2(2)*, 32640532-3703-451d-98aa-c891920bc735) Rosen Publishing Group, Inc., The.
Christopher, Matt. Michael Jordan: Legends in Sports. rev. ed. 2008. (ENG., Illus.). 176p. (gr. 3-7). pap. 6.99 *(978-0-316-02380-1(9))* Little, Brown Bks. for Young Readers.
Hasday, Judy L. Michael Jordan. 2012. (Role Model Athletes Ser.). 64p. (J). (gr. 7). 22.95 *(978-1-4222-2711-4(1))* Mason Crest.
Jordan, Michael. Michael Jordan. 2015. (Quotes from the Greatest Athletes Ser.). (ENG., Illus.). 24p. (J). lib. bdg. 28.55 *(978-1-4896-3368-2(5)*, 1393457); lib. bdg. 12.95 *(978-1-4896-3369-9(3)*, 1393457) Weigl Pubs., Inc. (AV2 by Weigl).
Kirkpatrick, Rob. Michael Jordan: Basketball Superstar. 2009. (Great Record Breakers in Sports Ser.). 24p. (gr. 3-3). 42.50 *(978-1-61513-190-7(6)*, PowerKids Pr.) Rosen Publishing Group, Inc., The.
Levit, Joe. Michael Jordan: Flying High. 2020. (Epic Sports Bios (Lerner (tm) Sports) Ser.). (ENG., Illus.). 32p. (J). (gr. 2-5). 30.65 *(978-1-5415-9743-3(5)*, d2e06fc8-7d24-4514-9b00-e18d7a549b5f); pap. 9.99 *(978-1-7284-1340-2(0)*, 4e9c3663-7584-4cdb-89fb-95bc610a2795) Lerner Publishing Group. (Lerner Pubns.).
Mason, Tyler. Michael Jordan & the Chicago Bulls. 2018. (Sports Dynasties Ser.). (ENG., Illus.). 48p. (J). (gr. 4-4). pap. 11.95 *(978-1-64185-283-8(6)*, 1641852836); (gr. 3-6). lib. bdg. 34.21 *(978-1-5321-1434-2(6)*, 29078) ABDO Publishing Co. (SportsZone).

JORDAN RIVER

Bowman, Crystal. Joshua Crosses the Jordan, 1 vol. Sokolova, Valerie, illus. 2011. (I Can Read! / Bible Stories Ser.). (ENG.). 32p. (J). (gr. -1-2). pap. 4.99 *(978-0-310-72156-7(3))* Zonderkidz.

JOSEPH, NEZ PERCE CHIEF, 1840-1904

Biskup, Agnieszka. Thunder Rolling down the Mountain: The Story of Chief Joseph & the Nez Perce. Zimmerman, Rusty, illus. 2010. (American Graphic Ser.). (ENG.). 32p. (J). (gr. 3-4). pap. 49.60 *(978-1-4296-6437-0(1)*, 16178, Capstone Pr.); pap. 8.10 *(978-1-4296-6270-3(0)*, 115417) Capstone.
Gunther, Vanessa Ann. Chief Joseph: A Biography, 1 vol. 2010. (Greenwood Biographies Ser.). (ENG., Illus.). 200p. 43.00 *(978-0-313-37920-8(3)*, 900297637, Bloomsbury Academic) Bloomsbury Publishing Plc GBR. Dist: Macmillan.
Kiely Miller, Barbara. Chief Joseph, 1 vol. 2007. (Great Americans Ser.). (ENG.). 24p. (gr. 2-4). pap. 9.15 *(978-0-8368-8321-3(7)*, a136fcda-0bc0-4908-b126-4e5c3af596e2); lib. bdg. 24.67 *(978-0-8368-8314-5(4)*, 7059abea-3114-45b1-afbb-d8e0deb55224) Stevens, Gareth Publishing LLLP. (Weekly Reader Leveled Readers).
—Jefe Joseph (Chief Joseph), 1 vol. 2007. (Grandes Personajes (Great Americans) Ser.). (SPA.). 24p. (gr. 2-4). pap. 9.15 *(978-0-8368-8338-1(1)*, 8c723db6-9f06-4a39-9859-167a3637bab5); lib. bdg. 24.67 *(978-0-8368-8331-2(4)*, 2bdc2c31-5a7c-4345-a2bb-d8df4d35901a) Stevens, Gareth Publishing LLLP. (Weekly Reader Leveled Readers).
Sanford, William R. Nez Percé Chief Joseph, 1 vol. 2013. (Native American Chiefs & Warriors Ser.). (ENG.). 48p. (gr. 5-7). pap. 11.53 *(978-1-4644-0251-7(5)*, b030ca92-b0c0-4089-8d60-791cd290daa7); (Illus.). (J). 25.27 *(978-0-7660-4092-2(5)*, da80a29d-110d-4b26-bac1-f90bc184ce7f) Enslow Publishing, LLC.
Schwartz, Heather E. Seeking Freedom: Causes & Effects of the Flight of the Nez Perce. 2015. (Cause & Effect: American Indian History Ser.). (ENG., Illus.). 32p. (J). (gr. 3-6). lib. bdg. 27.99 *(978-1-4914-2034-8(0)*, 127512) Capstone.
Sutcliffe, Jane. Chief Joseph. 2004. (History Maker Bios Ser.). (J). pap. 6.95 *(978-0-8225-2068-9(0))* Lerner Publishing Group.
—Chief Joseph. Parlin, Tim, tr. Parlin, Tim, illus. 2004. (History Maker Bios Ser.). 48p. (J). (gr. 3-5). lib. bdg. 26.60 *(978-0-8225-0696-6(3))* Lerner Publishing Group.

JOSEPH, SAINT

Drake, Tim. From an Angel in a Dream, the Story of Saint Joseph, Marys Husband: De un Angel en un Sueño, la Historia de San José, Esposo de María. Alvarado, Tomas, tr. Webber, John & Cohee, Ron, illus. 2nd ed. 2003. (SPA.). (J). 5.00 *(978-0-9747571-0-0(1))* Catholic World Mission.
Love, Pamela. Staircase for the Sisters: A Story of Prayer & Saint Joseph. 2018. (Illus.). 25p. (J). *(978-0-8198-9097-9(9))* Pauline Bks. & Media.

JOSEPH (SON OF JACOB)

Amery, H. Joseph & the Amazing Coat. 2004. (Bible Tales Readers Ser.). (SPA., Illus.). 16p. (J). pap. 4.95 *(978-0-7945-0417-5(5))* EDC Publishing.
Booth, Bradley. God Said It #2: The Life of Joseph. 2018. (Illus.). 31p. (J). pap. *(978-0-8163-6481-7(8))* Pacific Pr. Publishing Assn.
David, R., illus. Joseph & His Brothers. 2010. 12p. *(978-965-91286-0-0(6))* Sifrei Bet Shearim Ltd.
Gallaudet, Thomas H. Scripture Biography for the Young: Vol. 2 - Joseph. 2009. 220p. pap. 18.00 *(978-1-59925-234-6(1))* Solid Ground Christian Bks.
Hoak, Benjamin T. Joseph. 2007. (Money at its Best: Millionaires of the Old Testament Ser.). 112p. (YA). (gr. 7-18). pap. 14.95 *(978-1-4222-0847-2(8))* Mason Crest.
Joseph: A Bible Story to Color. (Illus.). 16p. (J). pap. 1.50 *(978-0-87162-812-1(0)*, E6026) Warner Pr., Inc.
Joseph & the Colorful Coat: A Little Story in Color. (Illus.). 16p. (J). pap. 1.50 *(978-0-87162-733-9(7)*, E4313) Warner Pr., Inc.
Koralek, Jenny. The Coat of Many Colors. Baynes, Pauline, illus. 2004. 32p. (J). 16.00 *(978-0-8028-5277-9(7))* Eerdmans, William B. Publishing Co.
Kovacs, Victoria. Joseph/the Good Samaritan Flip-Over Book. Krome, Mike, illus. 2015. (Little Bible Heroes(tm) Ser.). (ENG.). 32p. (J). (gr. k-2). pap. 3.99 *(978-1-4336-8715-0(1)*, 005742014, B&H Kids) B&H Publishing Group.
Laff, Becky. Joseph the Dreamer. Laff, Becky, illus. 2016. (ENG., Illus.). 48p. (J). (gr. k-4). 17.99 *(978-1-4677-7845-9(1)*, 0ba032c2-b4b4-4b62-83f1-f362a8415f75, Kar-Ben Publishing) Lerner Publishing Group.
MacKenzie, Carine. Bible Heroes Joseph. 2005. (Bible Art Ser.). (ENG.). 16p. (J). act. bk. ed. 2.50 *(978-1-84550-091-7(1)*, d8cf8fb7-3ba1-4982-9fb3-37b11abd6b5d) Christian Focus Pubns. GBR. Dist: Baker & Taylor Publisher Services (BTPS).
Mendenhall, Cheryl, illus. Joseph & His Coat of Many Colors. 2004. (ENG.). 24p. (J). 2.99 *(978-1-4037-0966-0(1)*, Spirit Pr.) Bendon, Inc.

JKL

Miles, David. Joseph the Dreamer, 1 vol. 2015. (I Can Read! / Adventure Bible Ser.). (ENG., Illus.). 32p. (J). pap. 5.99 *(978-0-310-75084-0(9))* Zonderkidz.
Miles, David, illus. Joseph the Dreamer. 2015. 32p. (J). *(978-1-5182-0994-9(7))* Zonderkidz.
Murdock, Hy. Joseph. (Bible Stories Ser.: No. S846-4). (Illus.). (J). (gr. -1-2). 3.95 *(978-0-7214-5067-4(9)*, Dutton Juvenile) Penguin Publishing Group.
Nakhat, Shamim. The Story of Yaqub & Yusuf: Based on Qur'anic Facts. 2005. (Me & My Holy Qur'ân Ser.). (Illus.). 24p. (J). *(978-81-7231-618-1(6))* Islamic Bk. Service.
Pennington, Jack & Tank, Daniel, illus. Joseph. 2004. 87p. (J). pap. *(978-0-8280-1855-5(3))* Review & Herald Publishing Assn.
Smith, Brendan Powell. Joseph & the Colorful Coat: The Brick Bible for Kids. 2015. (Brick Bible for Kids Ser.). (ENG., Illus.). 32p. (J). (gr. -1-k). 12.99 *(978-1-63220-409-7(6)*, Sky Pony Pr.) Skyhorse Publishing Co., Inc.
Smith, Fiona Veitch. Joseph & the Fearful Family. 2018. (ENG., Illus.). 32p. (J). pap. 12.99 *(978-0-281-07473-0(9)*, ce45791b-1851-4bb1-a171-2c067d51c720) SPCK Publishing GBR. Dist: Baker & Taylor Publisher Services (BTPS).
—Joseph & the Hidden Cup. 2018. (ENG., Illus.). 32p. (J). pap. 12.99 *(978-0-281-07474-7(7)*, 74dde451-a4b2-4770-80da-760cf517666f) SPCK Publishing GBR. Dist: Baker & Taylor Publisher Services (BTPS).
Zondervan Staff. Joseph & His Brothers, 1 vol. Pulley, Kelly, illus. 2009. (I Can Read! / the Beginner's Bible Ser.). (ENG.). 32p. (J). pap. 4.99 *(978-0-310-71731-7(0))* Zonderkidz.

JOURNALISM

Adams, Jonathan S. Internet Journalism & Fake News, 1 vol. 2018. (Fourth Estate: Journalism in North America Ser.). (ENG.). 112p. (gr. 8-8). lib. bdg. 44.50 *(978-1-5026-3495-5(3)*, 182f1d1d-8d84-44ef-8af8-ae97a4b90417) Cavendish Square Publishing LLC.
Adams, Simon. Politics. 2010. (Media Power Ser.). 48p. (YA). (gr. 5-9). 35.65 *(978-1-60753-114-2(3))* Amicus Learning.
Anderson, Judith. Crime. 2010. (Media Power Ser.). 48p. (YA). (gr. 5-9). 35.65 *(978-1-60753-113-5(5))* Amicus Learning.
Barrett Osborne, Linda. Guardians of Liberty: Freedom of the Press & the Nature of News. 2020. (ENG., Illus.). 208p. (YA). (gr. 5-9). 18.99 *(978-1-4197-3689-6(2)*, 1267401, Abrams Bks. for Young Readers) Abrams, Inc.
Bausum, Ann. Muckrackers: How Ida Tarbell, Upton Sinclair, & Lincoln Steffens Helped Expose Scandal, Inspire Reform, & Invent Investigative Journalism (Large P. Lt. ed. 2013. 238p. pap. *(978-1-4596-6718-1(2))* ReadHowYouWant.com, Ltd.
Beutel, Roger & Spencer, Lauren. Writing about Issues. 2011. 77.70 *(978-1-4488-4746-4(X))*; (ENG.). 64p. (gr. 5-5). pap. 13.95 *(978-1-4488-4688-7(9)*, d7f351cb-5cf5-4eb7-8a77-cd30b83b4d29); (ENG.). 64p. (YA). (gr. 5-5). lib. bdg. 37.13 *(978-1-4488-4682-5(X)*, 2ef9bc2c-1ff0-4622-804c-5b74d44f1765) Rosen Publishing Group, Inc., The.
Bodden, Valerie. Journalistic Articles. 2010. (Nonfiction: Writing for Fact & Argument Ser.). (ENG.). 48p. (J). (gr. 5-8). 23.95 *(978-1-58341-934-2(9)*, 22256, Creative Education); pap. 12.99 *(978-0-89812-546-7(4)*, 22259, Creative Paperbacks) Creative Co., The.
Bonnice, Sherry. Journalist. Riggs, Ernestine G. & Gholar, Cheryl, eds. 2013. (Careers with Character Ser.: 18). 96p. (J). (gr. 7-18). 22.95 *(978-1-4222-2758-9(8))* Mason Crest.
Brown, Robin Terry. Breaking the News: What's Real, What's Not, & Why the Difference Matters. 2020. 160p. (J). (gr. 5-9). (ENG.). 29.90 *(978-1-4263-3889-2(9))*; (Illus.). 19.99 *(978-1-4263-3888-5(0))* Disney Publishing Worldwide. (National Geographic Kids).
Burden, Peter. News of the World? Fake Sheikhs & Royal Trappings. Dillon, Julia & Hiscocks, Dan, eds. 2009. (ENG., Illus.). 320p. pap. 13.95 *(978-1-903070-72-7(4))* Eye Bks. GBR. Dist: Independent Pubs. Group.
Dakers, Diane. Health Care Journalism. 2018. (Investigative Journalism That Inspired Change Ser.). (Illus.). 48p. (J). (gr. 6-6). pap. *(978-0-7787-5363-6(8))* Crabtree Publishing Co.
—Information Literacy & Fake News. 2018. (Why Does Media Literacy Matter? Ser.). (ENG., Illus.). 48p. (J). (gr. 6-6). *(978-0-7787-4542-6(2))*; pap. *(978-0-7787-4546-4(5))* Crabtree Publishing Co.
DiConsiglio, John. Reporting Live. 2011. (Illus.). 112p. (J). *(978-0-531-22552-3(6))* Scholastic, Inc.
Duhig, Holly. Media & the News. 2018. (Our Values - Level 3 Ser.). (Illus.). 32p. (J). (gr. 5-6). *(978-0-7787-5434-3(0))* Crabtree Publishing Co.
Emmer, Rae. School Newspaper. 2009. (School Activities Ser.). 24p. (gr. 1-1). 42.50 *(978-1-60852-999-5(1)*, PowerKids Pr.) Rosen Publishing Group, Inc., The.
—School Newspaper / Periódico Escolar. 2009. (School Activities / Actividades escolares Ser.). (ENG & SPA.). 24p. (gr. 1-2). 42.50 *(978-1-60853-005-2(1)*, Editorial Buenas Letras) Rosen Publishing Group, Inc., The.
Fandel, Jennifer. Picture Yourself Writing Nonfiction: Using Photos to Inspire Writing. 2011. (See It, Write It Ser.). (ENG.). 32p. (gr. 3-4). pap. 47.70 *(978-1-4296-7208-5(0)*, Capstone Pr.) Capstone.
—You Can Write a Terrific Opinion Piece, 1 vol. 2012. (You Can Write Ser.). (ENG., Illus.). 24p. (J). (gr. 1-3). pap. 7.29 *(978-1-4296-9316-5(9)*, 120368, Capstone Pr.) Capstone.
—You Can Write a Terrific Opinion Piece. 2012. (You Can Write Ser.). (ENG.). 24p. (J). (gr. 1-2). pap. 43.74 *(978-1-4296-9317-2(7)*, 18548, Capstone Pr.) Capstone.
Fromm, Megan. Accuracy in Media, 1 vol. 2014. (Media Literacy Ser.). (ENG.). 48p. (YA). (gr. 6-6). 33.47 *(978-1-4777-8070-1(X)*, eae4bdeb-578f-45c6-b721-64d9343abd97, Rosen Reference) Rosen Publishing Group, Inc., The.
—Digital Content Creation, 1 vol. 2014. (Media Literacy Ser.). (ENG.). 48p. (YA). (gr. 6-6). 33.47 *(978-1-4777-8060-2(2)*, 6bf7aa61-7eeb-4028-a007-6af96d5cf1ed, Rosen Reference) Rosen Publishing Group, Inc., The.
—Gathering & Sharing Digital Information, 1 vol. 2014. (Media Literacy Ser.). (ENG.). 48p. (YA). (gr. 6-6). 33.47 *(978-1-4777-8062-6(9)*, 92199e94-8489-499b-8204-35689ea99924, Rosen Reference) Rosen Publishing Group, Inc., The.
—Understanding Advertising & Monetization, 1 vol. 2014. (Media Literacy Ser.). (ENG.). 48p. (YA). (gr. 6-6). 33.47 *(978-1-4777-8064-0(5)*, 3d98313f-641a-4831-b282-f98b7855f290, Rosen Reference) Rosen Publishing Group, Inc., The.
Fromowitz, Lori. 12 Great Moments That Changed Newspaper History. 2015. (Great Moments in Media Ser.). (ENG., Illus.). 32p. (J). (gr. 3-6). pap. 9.95 *(978-1-63235-085-5(8)*, 11599, 12-Story Library) Bookstaves, LLC.
Gish, Melissa. A Newspaper Publisher. 2003. 24p. (J). lib. bdg. 21.35 *(978-1-58340-324-2(8))* Black Rabbit Bks.
Gitlin, Martin. Online News. 2019. (21st Century Skills Innovation Library: Disruptors in Tech Ser.). (ENG.). 32p. (J). (gr. 4-8). pap. 14.21 *(978-1-5341-5043-0(9)*, 213479); (Illus.). lib. bdg. 32.07 *(978-1-5341-4757-7(8)*, 213478) Cherry Lake Publishing.
Hall, Homer L. Junior High Journalism. 2009. (Junior High Journalism Ser.). 352p. 73.00 *(978-1-61513-873-9(0))* Rosen Publishing Group, Inc., The.
Hamilton, John. Real-Time Reporting. 2004. (War in Iraq Ser.). (Illus.). 48p. (gr. 4-8). lib. bdg. 27.07 *(978-1-59197-497-0(6)*, Abdo & Daughters) ABDO Publishing Co.
Haynes, Danielle. Opinion vs. News, 1 vol. 2018. (Young Citizen's Guide to News Literacy Ser.). (ENG.). 32p. (J). (gr. 4-5). 27.93 *(978-1-5383-4500-9(5)*, 268ebc76-0a58-4fcb-88bb-64020385bc3d, PowerKids Pr.) Rosen Publishing Group, Inc., The.
—What Is Bias?, 1 vol. 2018. (Young Citizen's Guide to News Literacy Ser.). (ENG.). 32p. (gr. 4-5). pap. 11.00 *(978-1-5383-4620-4(6)*, 83a328b4-2f14-420b-abf8-1ec4d1e8e8e2, PowerKids Pr.) Rosen Publishing Group, Inc., The.
Heitkamp, Kristina Lyn. Fake News & the Factories That Make It, 1 vol. 2018. (Critical Thinking about Digital Media Ser.). (ENG.). 80p. (gr. 7-7). 37.60 *(978-1-9785-0472-1(1)*, b6032ac0-3ce6-4d3f-a253-6dda3deca934) Enslow Publishing, LLC.
Hernandez, Roger E. Teens & the Media. Developed in Association with the Gallup Organization Staff, ed. 2013. (Gallup Youth Survey: Major Issues & Trends Ser.: 14). 112p. (J). (gr. 7-18). 24.95 *(978-1-4222-2954-5(8))* Mason Crest.
Jeffries, Joyce. What's Fake News?, 1 vol. 2018. (What's the Issue? Ser.). (ENG.). 24p. (gr. 3-3). 26.23 *(978-1-5345-2583-2(1)*, b17f2d84-80af-40d9-a48e-7cacec747930, KidHaven Publishing) Greenhaven Publishing LLC.
Jordano, Kimberly & Adsit, Kim. Jumping into Journals: Guided Journaling for Beginning Readers & Writers. Cernek, Kim, ed. Weller, Linda, illus. 2006. 112p. pap. 15.99 *(978-1-59198-227-2(8)*, 2229) Creative Teaching Pr., Inc.
Keppeler, Jill. Newspapers Throughout American History. 2019. (Journey to the Past: Investigating Primary Sources Ser.). (ENG.). 32p. (gr. 4-5). 63.00 *(978-1-5382-4047-2(5))* Stevens, Gareth Publishing LLLP.
—Online Journalists, 1 vol. 2019. (Digital Insiders Ser.). (ENG.). 32p. (gr. 3-4). pap. 11.50 *(978-1-5382-4755-6(0)*, 3a503bfc-6c41-470c-9847-3c23723c43e0) Stevens, Gareth Publishing LLLP.
Kokino, Olga. Journalism Student Activity Book: Student Activities Book. Matthews, Douglas L., ed. 2003. (Illus.). stu. ed., per., wbk. ed. *(978-1-931680-16-5(7)*, Expert Systems for Teachers) Teaching Point, Inc.
Krajna, Cheryl. Blurred Lines: News or Advertisements?, 1 vol. 2018. (Young Citizen's Guide to News Literacy Ser.). (ENG.). 32p. (gr. 4-5). 27.93 *(978-1-5383-4497-2(1)*, 8a994da0-7f70-4eb3-956c-4802d399ab51, PowerKids Pr.) Rosen Publishing Group, Inc., The.
Krasner, Barbara. 12 Great Tips on Writing a Blog. 2017. (Great Tips on Writing Ser.). (ENG., Illus.). 32p. (J). (gr. 3-6). 32.80 *(978-1-63235-273-6(7)*, 11727, 12-Story Library) Bookstaves, LLC.
Macfarlane, Colin. Hit the Headlines: Exciting Journalism Activities for Improving Writing & Thinking Skills. 2012. (ENG., Illus.). 192p. (C). pap. 57.95 *(978-0-415-69511-4(2)*, Y126804) Routledge.
Mahoney, Ellen. Nellie Bly & Investigative Journalism for Kids: Mighty Muckrakers from the Golden Age to Today, with 21 Activities. 2015. (For Kids Ser.: 56). (ENG., Illus.). 144p. (J). (gr. 4). pap. 16.95 *(978-1-61374-997-5(X))* Chicago Review Pr., Inc.
Mara, Wil. Fake News. 2018. (21st Century Skills Library: Global Citizens: Modern Media Ser.). (ENG.). 32p. (J). (gr. 4-7). pap. 14.21 *(978-1-5341-3250-4(3)*, 211765); (Illus.). lib. bdg. 32.07 *(978-1-5341-2930-6(8)*, 211764) Cherry Lake Publishing.
—Mainstream News. 2018. (21st Century Skills Library: Global Citizens: Modern Media Ser.). (ENG.). 32p. (J). (gr. 4-7). pap. 14.21 *(978-1-5341-3251-1(1)*, 211769); (Illus.). lib. bdg. 32.07 *(978-1-5341-2931-3(6)*, 211768) Cherry Lake Publishing.
Mattern, Joanne. Katherine Graham & 20th Century American Journalism. 2009. (Women Who Shaped History Ser.). 24p. (gr. 2-3). 42.50 *(978-1-60854-820-0(1)*, PowerKids Pr.) Rosen Publishing Group, Inc., The.
Minden, Cecilia. Writing a News Article. Herring, Carol, illus. 2019. (Write It Right Ser.). (ENG.). 24p. (J). (gr. 1-4). pap. 12.79 *(978-1-5341-5008-9(0)*, 213339); lib. bdg. 30.64 *(978-1-5341-4722-5(5)*, 213338) Cherry Lake Publishing.
Mooney, Carla. Asking Questions about How the News Is Created. 2015. (21st Century Skills Library: Asking Questions about Media Ser.). (ENG., Illus.). 32p. (J). (gr. 4-8). 32.07 *(978-1-63362-489-4(7)*, 206864) Cherry Lake Publishing.
Morrison, Taylor. Civil War Artist. 2004. (ENG., Illus.). 32p. (J). (gr. -1-3). pap. 5.95 *(978-0-618-49538-2(X)*, 499080, Clarion Bks.) HarperCollins Pubs.
Murray, Laura K. & Harris, Duchess. Uncovering Bias in the News. 2017. (News Literacy Ser.). (ENG., Illus.). 48p. (J). (gr. 4-8). lib. bdg. 35.64 *(978-1-5321-1390-1(0)*, 27688) ABDO Publishing Co.
Pelleschi, Andrea. Olivia & Oscar Build an Opinion Piece. Hu, Caroline, illus. 2014. (Writing Builders Ser.). (ENG.). 32p. (J). (gr. 2-4). pap. 11.94 *(978-1-60357-556-0(1))*; lib. bdg. 25.27 *(978-1-59953-582-1(3))* Norwood Hse. Pr.
Pelusey, Michael & Pelusey, Jane. Newspapers. 2005. (Media Ser.). (ENG., Illus.). 32p. (gr. 5-8). lib. bdg. 21.95 *(978-0-7910-8800-5(6)*, P114421, Facts On File) Infobase Holdings, Inc.
Peters, Jennifer, ed. Critical Perspectives on Media Bias, 1 vol. 2017. (Analyzing the Issues Ser.). (ENG.). 224p. (gr. 8-8). 50.93 *(978-0-7660-9169-6(4)*, 19cef3b9-e6f0-486f-bd11-64599a70ac1a); pap. 26.23 *(978-0-7660-9560-1(6)*, 5f9be1e4-32ff-46a0-8fbd-420dd9986633) Enslow Publishing, LLC.
Pettiford, Rebecca. Reporters. 2015. (Illus.). 24p. (J). lib. bdg. 25.65 *(978-1-62031-159-2(3)*, Bullfrog Bks.) Jump! Inc.
Rice, Dona Herweck. Deception: Real or Fake News? 2018. (TIME(r): Informational Text Ser.). (ENG., Illus.). 48p. (J). (gr. 5-8). pap. 11.99 *(978-1-4258-4994-8(6))* Teacher Created Materials, Inc.
Rustad, Martha E. H. Learning about Fact & Opinion. 2015. (Media Literacy for Kids Ser.). (ENG., Illus.). 24p. (J). (gr. -1-2). lib. bdg. 27.32 *(978-1-4914-1831-4(1)*, 127273, Capstone Pr.) Capstone.
Saenger, Diana. Everyone Wants My Job! The ABCs of Entertainment Writing. Fife, Bruce, ed. unabr. ed. 2003. (Writing & Publishing Ser.). (Illus.). 159p. (YA). (gr. 8-12). pap. 15.00 *(978-0-941599-53-5(1))* Piccadilly Bks., Ltd.
Special Reports, 8 vols. 2015. (Special Reports: 8). (ENG.). 112p. (J). (gr. 6-12). lib. bdg. 330.88 *(978-1-62403-897-6(2)*, 18746, Essential Library) ABDO Publishing Co.
Sullivan, George. Journalists at Risk: Reporting America's Wars. 2005. (People's History Ser.). (ENG., Illus.). 96p. (J). (gr. 5-12). 33.26 *(978-0-7613-2745-5(2))* Lerner Publishing Group.
Thiel, Kristin. Julian Assange: Founder of WikiLeaks, 1 vol. 2018. (Hero or Villain? Claims & Counterclaims Ser.). (ENG.). 112p. (YA). (gr. 8-8). 45.93 *(978-1-5026-3517-4(8)*, 5be1ea0f-2c81-4fce-a120-c8d68cd4e649) Cavendish Square Publishing LLC.
Wright, Adrienne. Hector: A Boy, a Protest, & the Photograph That Changed Apartheid. 2019. (ENG., Illus.). 48p. (J). 18.99 *(978-1-62414-691-6(0)*, 900197957) Page Street Publishing Co.

JOURNALISM—FICTION

Alger, Horatio. Risen from the Ranks. 2005. 28.95 *(978-1-4218-1458-2(7))*; 292p. pap. 13.95 *(978-1-4218-1558-9(3))* 1st World Publishing, Inc. (1st World Library - Literary Society).
Bauer, Joan. Peeled. 2009. (ENG.). 256p. (YA). (gr. 7-18). 10.99 *(978-0-14-241430-9(1)*, Speak) Penguin Young Readers Group.
Buchanan, Paul & Buchanan, P. The Last Place I Want to Be, 1 vol. 2009. 176p. (J). pap. 7.99 *(978-0-8254-2408-3(9))* Kregel Pubns.
Butler, Dori Hillestad. The Truth about Truman School, 1 vol. 2009. (ENG.). 176p. (J). (gr. 3-7). pap. 8.99 *(978-0-8075-8096-7(1)*, 807580961) Whitman, Albert & Co.
Crane, Cheri J. Moment of Truth: A Novel. 2005. 238p. (YA). *(978-1-59156-727-1(0))* Covenant Communications.
Dairman, Tara. Stars So Sweet: An All Four Stars Book. 2016. (All Four Stars Ser.: 3). 288p. (J). (gr. 3-7). 17.99 *(978-1-101-99648-5(X)*, G.P. Putnam's Sons Books for Young Readers) Penguin Young Readers Group.
Devlin, Calla. Right Where You Left Me. 2017. (ENG., Illus.). 256p. (YA). (gr. 9). 17.99 *(978-1-4814-8699-6(3)*, Atheneum Bks. for Young Readers) Simon & Schuster Children's Publishing.
Duff, Hilary. Devoted: An Elixir Novel. 2012. (Elixir Ser.). (ENG.). 368p. (YA). (gr. 9). pap. 9.99 *(978-1-4424-0856-2(1)*, Simon & Schuster Bks. For Young Readers) Simon & Schuster Bks. For Young Readers.
—True: An Elixir Novel. (Elixir Ser.). (ENG., 304p. (YA). (gr. 7). 2014. Illus.). pap. 12.99 *(978-1-4424-0858-6(8))* 2013. 17.99 *(978-1-4424-0857-9(X))* Simon & Schuster Bks. For Young Readers. (Simon & Schuster Bks. For Young Readers).
Feinstein, John. Change-Up: Mystery at the World Series (the Sports Beat, 4) 2010. (Sports Beat Ser.: 4). 336p. (J). (gr. 5). 8.99 *(978-0-375-84759-2(6)*, Yearling) Random Hse. Children's Bks.
—Cover-Up: Mystery at the Super Bowl (the Sports Beat, 3)   2008. (Sports Beat Ser.: 3). (ENG.). 320p. (J). (gr. 5). 8.99 *(978-0-440-42205-1(1)*, Yearling) Random Hse. Children's Bks.
—Last Shot: Mystery at the Final Four (the Sports Beat, 1) 2006. (Sports Beat Ser.: 1). (ENG.). 272p. (J). (gr. 7-9). reprint ed. per. 8.99 *(978-0-553-49460-0(0)*, Yearling) Random Hse. Children's Bks.
—Vanishing Act: Mystery at the U. S. Open (the Sports Beat, 2) 2008. (Sports Beat Ser.: 2). (ENG.). 304p. (J). (gr. 3-7). 9.99 *(978-0-440-42125-2(X)*, Yearling) Random Hse. Children's Bks.
Frampton, David. Beastie ABC. Frampton, David, illus. Date not set. (Illus.). 32p. (J). (gr. -1-1). pap. 5.99 *(978-0-06-443653-3(5))* HarperCollins Pubs.
Goo, Maurene. Since You Asked... 2013. (YA). 262p. pap. *(978-0-545-44822-2(0))*; (ENG.). 272p. (gr. 7). 17.99 *(978-0-545-44821-5(2))* Scholastic, Inc. (Scholastic Pr.).
Halliday, Gemma. Social Suicide. 2012. (Deadly Cool Ser.: 2). (ENG.). 288p. (YA). (gr. 8). pap. 8.99 *(978-0-06-200332-4(1)*, HarperTeen) HarperCollins Pubs.
Hutchins, Hazel. Robyn Makes the News, 1 vol. Cathcart, Yvonne, illus. 2003. (Formac First Novels Ser.: 27). (ENG.). 64p. (J). (gr. 1-5). 4.95 *(978-0-88780-593-6(0)*, 593) Formac Publishing Co., Ltd. CAN. Dist: Formac Lorimer Bks. Ltd.
Ingold, Jeanette. Paper Daughter. 2013. (ENG.). 224p. (YA). (gr. 7). pap. 15.99 *(978-0-544-10484-6(6)*, 1540793, Clarion Bks.) HarperCollins Pubs.
Klingele, Lindsey. The Truth Lies Here. 2018. (ENG.). 416p. (YA). (gr. 8). 17.99 *(978-0-06-238039-5(7)*, HarperTeen) HarperCollins Pubs.
Kraft, Erik P. Lenny & Mel after-School Confidential. Kraft, Erik P., illus. 2012. (Lenny & Mel Ser.). (ENG., illus.). 64p. (J). (gr. 2-5). pap. 6.99 *(978-1-4424-6314-1(7)*, Simon & Schuster/Paula Wiseman Bks.) Simon & Schuster/Paula Wiseman Bks.
Meddaugh, Susan. Martha Speaks: Martha's Nose for News (chapter Book) 2013. (Martha Speaks Ser.). (ENG., Illus.). 96p. (J). (gr. 1-4). 14.99 *(978-0-544-13567-3(9))* Houghton Mifflin Harcourt Publishing Co.
—Nose for News. 2013. (Martha Speaks Ser.). (ENG., Illus.). 96p. (J). (gr. 1-4). pap. 5.99 *(978-0-544-08572-5(8))* Houghton Mifflin Harcourt Publishing Co.
Mendle, Jane. My Ultimate Sister Disaster: A Novel. 2010. (ENG.). 208p. (YA). (gr. 7-18). pap. 18.99 *(978-0-312-36904-0(2)*, 900042729, St. Martin's Griffin) St. Martin's Pr.
Messner, Kate. Breakout. (ENG.). 448p. (J). 2019. pap. 9.99 *(978-1-68119-538-4(0)*, 900176499) 2018. (Illus.). 17.99 *(978-1-68119-536-0(4)*, 900176497) Bloomsbury Publishing USA. (Bloomsbury Children's Bks.).
Miller-Lachmann, Lyn. Gringolandia. 2009. (ENG.). 288p. (gr. 7-17). 18.95 *(978-1-931896-49-8(6))* Curbstone Pr.
Miller, Robin Caroll. Samantha Sanderson at the Movies, 1 vol. 2014. (FaithGirlz / Samantha Sanderson Ser.: 1). (ENG.). 272p. (J). pap. 8.99 *(978-0-310-74245-6(5))* Zonderkidz.
—Samantha Sanderson on the Scene, 1 vol. 2014. (FaithGirlz / Samantha Sanderson Ser.: 2). (ENG.). 256p. (J). pap. 8.99 *(978-0-310-74247-0(1))* Zonderkidz.
Moore, Stephanie Perry. Truth & Nothing But, No. 4. 2014. (Sharp Sisters Ser.: 4). (ENG.). 160p. (YA). (gr. 6-12). pap. 7.95 *(978-1-4677-4489-8(1)*, 5499bf15-c234-411b-a0b7-7f09c055b2b2, Darby Creek) Lerner Publishing Group.
Paige, D. M. Going to Press. (Opportunity Ser.). (ENG.). 104p. (YA). (gr. 6-12). 2013. pap. 7.95 *(978-1-4677-1495-2(X)*, 9781467714952, Darby Creek) 2013. lib. bdg. 27.99 *(978-1-4677-1373-3(2)*, 1c70bf7b-24bf-4cd8-ae36-e34ad0c2c525, Darby Creek) 2015. E-Book 53.32 *(978-1-4677-6016-4(1)*, 9781467760164, Lerner Digital) Lerner Publishing Group.
Peet, Mal. The Penalty. 2016. (ENG.). 272p. (J). (gr. 7). pap. 8.99 *(978-0-7636-8747-2(2))* Candlewick Pr.
Petty, Kate Reed. The Leak. Bell, Andrea & Bell, Andrea, illus. 2021. (ENG.). 240p. (J). 23.99 *(978-1-250-21795-0(4)*, 900207080); pap. 14.99 *(978-1-250-21796-7(2)*, 900207081) Roaring Brook Pr. (First Second Bks.).
Stamper, Phil. The Gravity of Us. 2020. (ENG.). 320p. (YA). 17.99 *(978-1-5476-0014-4(4)*, 900195006, Bloomsbury Young Adult) Bloomsbury Publishing USA.
Stilton, Gerónimo. I'm Too Fond of My Fur! Wolf, Matt, illus. 2004. (Geronimo Stilton Ser.: No. 4). 116p. (J). lib. bdg. 10.00 *(978-1-4242-0698-8(7))* Fitzgerald Bks.
—It's Halloween, You 'Fraidy Mouse! Wolf, Matt, illus. 2004. 113p. (J). lib. bdg. 10.00 *(978-1-4242-0280-5(9))* Fitzgerald Bks.
—Lost Treasure of the Emerald Eye. Wolf, Matt, illus. 2004. (Geronimo Stilton Ser.: No. 1). 116p. (J). lib. bdg. 10.00 *(978-1-4242-0695-7(2))* Fitzgerald Bks.
—The Mona Mousa Code. Wolf, Matt, illus. 2005. (Geronimo Stilton Ser.: No. 15). 113p. (J). lib. bdg. 10.00 *(978-1-4242-0284-3(1))* Fitzgerald Bks.
—The Phantom of the Subway. Wolf, Matt, illus. 2004. (Geronimo Stilton Ser.: No. 13). 112p. (J). lib. bdg. 10.00 *(978-1-4242-0282-9(5))* Fitzgerald Bks.
—Valentine's Day Disaster. Keys, Larry et al, illus. 2006. (Geronimo Stilton Ser.: No. 23). 122p. (J). lib. bdg. 18.46 *(978-1-4242-0292-8(2))* Fitzgerald Bks.
Stilton, Gerónimo, et al. Get the Scoop, Geronimo! Facciotto, Giuseppe & Costa, Alessandro, illus. 2015. 113p. (J). *(978-1-5182-0417-3(1))* Scholastic, Inc.
Whybrow, Ian. Dear Little Wolf. Ross, Tony, illus. 2005. (Little Wolf Adventures Ser.). 64p. (gr. 3-6). pap., lib. bdg. 14.95 *(978-0-87614-902-7(6))* Lerner Publishing Group.
Winerip, Michael. Adam Canfield of the Slash. 2005. (Adam Canfield of the Slash Ser.: 1). (ENG., Illus.). 336p. (J). (gr. 3-7). 15.99 *(978-0-7636-2340-1(7))* Candlewick Pr.
—Adam Canfield: the Last Reporter. 2010. (Adam Canfield of the Slash Ser.: 3). (ENG., Illus.). 384p. (J). (gr. 3-7). 7.99 *(978-0-7636-4838-1(8))* Candlewick Pr.
—Adam Canfield, Watch Your Back! 2009. (Adam Canfield of the Slash Ser.: 2). (ENG., Illus.). 352p. (J). (gr. 3-7). 8.99 *(978-0-7636-4412-3(9))* Candlewick Pr.
Winston, Sherri. President of the Whole Sixth Grade: Girl Code. (President Ser.: 3). (ENG.). (J). (gr. 3-7). 2019. 288p. pap. 8.99 *(978-0-316-50529-1(3))* 2018. 272p. 16.99 *(978-0-316-50528-4(5))* Little, Brown Bks. for Young Readers.
Wise, Rachel. Cast Your Ballot! 2013. (Dear Know-It-All Ser.: 9). (ENG., Illus.). 160p. (J). (gr. 3-7). 15.99 *(978-1-4424-8793-2(3))*; pap. 5.99 *(978-1-4424-8792-5(5))* Simon Spotlight. (Simon Spotlight).
—Texting 1, 2, 3, 8. 2013. (Dear Know-It-All Ser.: 8). (ENG., Illus.). 160p. (J). (gr. 3-7). 16.99 *(978-1-4424-7520-5(X)*, Simon Spotlight) Simon & Schuster Children's Publishing.
—Texting 1, 2, 3. 2013. (Dear Know-It-All Ser.: 8). (ENG., Illus.). 160p. (J). (gr. 3-7). pap. 6.99 *(978-1-4424-7519-9(6)*, Simon Spotlight) Simon Spotlight.
Zielin, Lara. Donut Days. 2010. (ENG.). 256p. (YA). (gr. 6-8). 22.44 *(978-0-399-25066-8(2))* Penguin Young Readers Group.

JOURNALISM—UNITED STATES

Christensen, Bonnie. The Daring Nellie Bly: America's Star Reporter. 2009. (ENG., Illus.). 32p. (J). (gr. k-3). pap. 7.99 *(978-0-375-85118-6(6)*, Dragonfly Bks.) Random Hse. Children's Bks.
Engdahl, Sylvia, ed. Blogs, 1 vol. 2008. (Current Controversies Ser.). (ENG., Illus.). 224p. (gr. 10-12). pap. 33.00 *(978-0-7377-3955-8(X)*, 0f30a8cf-3d13-41cf-b201-ede0b30381e9); lib. bdg. 48.03 *(978-0-7377-3954-1(1)*, 228c1e5c-e5cb-4649-9570-a3adeaef0bf8) Greenhaven Publishing LLC. (Greenhaven Publishing).
Fromowitz, Lori. 12 Great Moments That Changed Newspaper History. 2015. (Great Moments in Media Ser.). (ENG., Illus.). 32p. (J). (gr. 3-6). 32.80 *(978-1-63235-025-1(4)*, 11595, 12-Story Library) Bookstaves, LLC.
Gallagher, Aileen. The Muckrakers: American Journalism During the Age of Reform. 2009. (Progressive Movement 1900-1920: Efforts to Reform America's New Industrial Society Ser.). 32p. (gr. 3-4). 47.90 *(978-1-60854-173-7(8))* Rosen Publishing Group, Inc., The.
Griffin, Brett. Yellow Journalism, Sensationalism, & Circulation Wars, 1 vol. 2018. (Fourth Estate: Journalism in North America Ser.). (ENG.). 112p. (gr. 8-8). lib. bdg. 44.50 *(978-1-5026-3471-9(6)*,

d8f78bff-ca76-4d27-bbed-512e5d87bc81) Cavendish Square Publishing LLC.
Hall, Homer L. High School Journalism. 2009. (High School Journalism Ser.). (ENG.). 464p. (YA). 159.90 (978-1-61513-265-2(1)); 352p. 159.90 (978-1-61513-264-5(3)) Rosen Publishing Group, Inc., The.
—High School Journalism Teacher's Workbook & Guide. 2009. (High School Journalism Ser.). 136p. 53.00 (978-1-61513-266-9(X)) Rosen Publishing Group, Inc., The.
—Student's Workbook for Junior High Journalism. (Junior High Journalism Ser.). 88p. 2009. 53.00 (978-1-61513-874-6(9)) 2003. (ENG., Illus.). (YA). pap., wbk. ed. 26.50 (978-0-8239-4046-2(2)) Rosen Publishing Group, Inc., The.
Hall, Homer L. & Aimone, Logan. Student's Workbook for Junior High Journalism. 2010. (ENG.). 92p. (J). pap. 26.50 (978-1-4042-8188-2(6)) Rosen Publishing Group, Inc., The.
Heing, Bridey, ed. Critical Perspectives on Freedom of the Press & Threats to Journalists, 1 vol. 2018. (Analyzing the Issues Ser.). (ENG.). 224p. (gr. 8-8). 50.93 (978-0-7660-9854-1(0), 238e4a9e-624b-407f-8825-5f91bd9e1dab) Enslow Publishing, LLC.
Sherman, Patrice. Colonial & Early American Journalism, 1 vol. 2018. (Fourth Estate: Journalism in North America Ser.). (ENG.). 112p. (gr. 8-8). 44.50 (978-1-5026-3467-2(8), 642afc25-9da0-488d-bd55-45e31b360b64) Cavendish Square Publishing LLC.
Thiel, Kristin. Watergate & Investigative Journalism, 1 vol. 2018. (Fourth Estate: Journalism in North America Ser.). (ENG.). 112p. (gr. 8-8). lib. bdg. 44.50 (978-1-5026-3487-0(2), 3df255b5-d062-46f5-b0de-6952b8fcf69f) Cavendish Square Publishing LLC.

JOURNALISM—VOCATIONAL GUIDANCE

Alagna, Magdalena. War Correspondents: Life under Fire, 1 vol. 2003. (Extreme Careers Ser.). (ENG., Illus.). 64p. (YA). (gr. 5-5). 37.13 (978-0-8239-3798-1(4), 1425256d-a227-4410-923b-04414b545da1) Rosen Publishing Group, Inc., The.
Roberts, Laura. Careers in Digital Media. 2017. (Exploring Careers Ser.). (ENG.). 80p. (J). (gr. 5-12). (978-1-68282-196-1(X)) ReferencePoint Pr., Inc.
Thomas, William David. Journalist, 1 vol. 2009. (Cool Careers: on the Go Ser.). (ENG., Illus.). 32p. (J). (gr. 3-3). pap. 11.50 (978-1-4339-0168-3(4), 81573464-41f8-447b-8d37-413d6ffb067a); lib. bdg. 28.67 (978-1-4339-0004-4(1), bf374be7-c0dc-4aa8-9064-fec3f0c7c3dc) Stevens, Gareth Publishing LLLP.

JOURNALISTIC PHOTOGRAPHY

see Photojournalism

JOURNALISTS

Abrams, Dennis. Barbara Walters. 2010. (ENG., Illus.). 128p. (J). (gr. 6-12). 35.00 (978-1-60413-686-9(3), P179328, Facts On File) Infobase Holdings, Inc.
Anderson, Kirsten. Who Was Robert Ripley? 2015. (Who Was...? Ser.). lib. bdg. 16.00 (978-0-606-36596-3(6)) Turtleback.
Anderson, Kirsten & Who HQ. Who Was Robert Ripley? Foley, Tim, illus. 2015. (Who Was? Ser.). 112p. (J). (gr. 3-7). 5.99 (978-0-448-48298-9(3), Penguin Workshop) Penguin Young Readers Group.
Caravantes, Peggy. A Great & Sublime Fool: The Story of Mark Twain. 2010. (World Writers Ser.). (Illus.). 176p. (YA). (gr. 8-18). lib. bdg. 28.95 (978-1-59935-088-2(2)) Reynolds, Morgan Inc.
Castaldo, Nancy. The Race Around the World (Totally True Adventures) How Nellie Bly Chased an Impossible Dream... Lowe, Wesley, illus. 2015. (Totally True Adventures Ser.). (ENG.). 112p. (J). (gr. 2-5). 4.99 (978-0-553-52278-5(7), Random Hse. Bks. for Young Readers) Random Hse. Children's Bks.
Christensen, Bonnie. The Daring Nellie Bly: America's Star Reporter. 2009. (ENG., Illus.). 32p. (J). (gr. k-3). pap. 7.99 (978-0-375-85118-6(6), Dragonfly Bks.) Random Hse. Children's Bks.
Cline-Ransome, Lesa. The Power of Her Pen: The Story of Groundbreaking Journalist Ethel L. Payne. Parra, John, illus. 2020. (ENG.). 48p. (J). (gr. -1-3). 18.99 (978-1-4814-6289-1(X), Simon & Schuster Bks. For Young Readers) Simon & Schuster Bks. For Young Readers.
Dublin, Anne. June Callwood: A Life of Action, 1 vol. 2006. (ENG., Illus.). 142p. (J). (gr. 3-12). pap. 14.95 (978-1-897187-14-2(9)) Second Story Pr. CAN. Dist: Orca Bk. Pubs. USA.
Goodman, Tonne. Tonne Goodman: Point of View. 2019. (ENG., Illus.). 356p. 75.00 (978-1-4197-3458-8(X), 1242503) Abrams, Inc.
Hacker, Carlotta. E. Cora Hind, 1 vol. 2003. (Canadians Ser.). (ENG., Illus.). 64p. (J). (gr. 5-8). pap. 6.95 (978-1-55041-834-7(3), 6baff298-406e-48d8-8469-5e003457f3b9) Trifolium Bks., Inc. CAN. Dist: Firefly Bks., Ltd.
Higgins, Melissa. Julian Assange: WikiLeaks Founder, 1 vol. 2011. (Essential Lives Set 7 Ser.). (ENG., Illus.). 112p. (YA). (gr. 6-12). lib. bdg. 41.36 (978-1-61783-001-3(1), 6741, Essential Library) ABDO Publishing Co.
Hoge, Robert. Ugly. 2016. (ENG., Illus.). 208p. (J). (gr. 3-7). 16.99 (978-0-425-28775-0(0), Viking Books for Young Readers) Penguin Young Readers Group.
Hunter-Gault, Charlayne. To the Mountaintop: My Journey Through the Civil Rights Movement. 2014. (New York Times Ser.). (ENG., Illus.). 224p. (YA). (gr. 7). pap. 16.00 (978-1-250-04062-6(0), 900124083) Square Fish.
Jones, Naomi E. Ida B. Wells-Barnett: Suffragette & Social Activist, 1 vol. 2019. (African American Trailblazers Ser.). (ENG.). 128p. (gr. 9-9). pap. 22.16 (978-1-5026-4560-9(2), cb519ffa-ab7a-438d-b1e0-9a25e98d89c7) Cavendish Square Publishing LLC.
Lane, Laura & Harris, Duchess. How Journalists Work. 2017. (News Literacy Ser.). (ENG., Illus.). 48p. (J). (gr. 4-8). lib. bdg. 35.64 (978-1-5321-1389-5(7), 27687) ABDO Publishing Co.
McCully, Emily Arnold. Ida M. Tarbell: The Woman Who Challenged Big Business — And Won! 2014. (ENG., Illus.). 288p. (YA). (gr. 7). 18.99 (978-0-547-29092-8(6), 1412369, Clarion Bks.) HarperCollins Pubs.
Mckissack, Patricia & Mckissack, Fredrick. Ida B. Wells-Barnett: Fighter for Justice, 1 vol. 2013. (Famous African Americans Ser.). (ENG.). 24p. (gr. k-2). pap. 10.35 (978-1-4644-0198-5(5), eb7e9a8e-6b17-4790-bf93-adb0f9aff98b, Enslow Elementary); (Illus.). 25.27 (978-0-7660-4108-0(5), f37a0a7c-6b05-4e1f-9f84-ee2615e0615f) Enslow Publishing, LLC.
Moritz, Rachel. Julian Assange: Founder of WikiLeaks. 2017. (Newsmakers Set 2 Ser.). (ENG., Illus.). 48p. (J). (gr. 4-8). lib. bdg. 35.64 (978-1-5321-1179-2(7), 25934) ABDO Publishing Co.
—Julian Assange: Founder of WikiLeaks. 2017. (Newsmakers Set 2 Ser.). (ENG.). 48p. (J). (gr. 4-8). 55.65 (978-1-68078-964-5(3), 26365) ABDO Publishing Co.
Noyes, Deborah. Ten Days a Madwoman: The Daring Life & Turbulent Times of the Original Girl Reporter, Nellie Bly. 2016. (Illus.). 144p. (J). (gr. 5). 18.99 (978-0-8037-4017-4(4), Viking Books for Young Readers) Penguin Young Readers Group.
Robson, David. Soledad O'Brien. 2009. (Transcending Race in America: Biographies of Biracial Achievers Ser.). (Illus.). 64p. (J). (gr. 5-18). pap. 9.95 (978-1-4222-1631-6(4)) Mason Crest.
Rubini, Julie K. Missing Millie Benson: The Secret Case of the Nancy Drew Ghostwriter & Journalist. 2015. (Biographies for Young Readers Ser.). (ENG., Illus.). 136p. (J). (gr. 1-6). 32.95 (978-0-8214-2183-3(2)) Ohio Univ. Pr.
Sauerwein, Stan. Ma Murray: The Story of Canada's Crusty Queen of Publishing. 2003. (ENG., Illus.). 144p. per. (978-1-55153-979-9(9)) Heritage Hse.
Scarbrough, Mary Hertz. African American Writers & Journalists. 2012. pap. (978-1-4222-2389-5(2)) Mason Crest.
—African American Writers & Journalists. Hill, Marc Lamont, ed. 2012. (Major Black Contributions from Emancipation to Civil Rights Ser.). 64p. (J). (gr. 5). 22.95 (978-1-4222-2376-5(0)) Mason Crest.
Somervill, Barbara A. Ida Tarbell: Pioneer Investigative Reporter. 2004. (World Writers Ser.). (Illus.). 112p. (YA). (gr. 6-12). 23.95 (978-1-883846-87-9(0), First Biographies) Reynolds, Morgan Inc.
Sonneborn, Liz. The Khmer Rouge, 1 vol. 2012. (Great Escapes Ser.). (ENG., Illus.). 80p. (gr. 6-6). 36.93 (978-1-60870-474-3(2), 149e435b-e136-4ed9-b4b5-7f18a6663000) Cavendish Square Publishing LLC.
Towsend, Dana. Lonely Orphan Girl: The Story of Nellie Bly. 2005. (Illus.). 32p. (J). (978-0-7367-2902-4(X)) Zaner-Bloser, Inc.
Walius Sammons, Sandra. The Three Marjories: Marjory Stoneman Douglas, Marjorie Kinnan Rawlings, Marjorie Harris Carr & Their Contributions to Florida. 2019. (Pineapple Press Young Reader Biographies Ser.). (Illus.). 152p. pap. 12.95 (978-1-68334-035-5(3)) Pineapple Pr., Inc.
Whitelaw, Nancy. Joseph Pulitzer & the New York World. rev. exp. ed. 2004. (Makers of the Media Ser.). (Illus.). 128p. (J). lib. bdg. 21.95 (978-1-931798-36-5(2)) Reynolds, Morgan Inc.
Wint, Eleanor. Marcus Teaches Us. 2012. 36p. pap. 15.50 (978-1-4669-5620-9(8)) Trafford Publishing.
Zuchora-Walske, Christine. The Dust Bowl: A History Perspectives Book. 2013. (Perspectives Library). (ENG., Illus.). 32p. (J). (gr. 4-8). 32.07 (978-1-62431-417-9(1), 202788); pap. 14.21 (978-1-62431-493-3(7), 202790) Cherry Lake Publishing.

JOURNEYS

see Voyages and Travels; Voyages around the World

JUAREZ, BENITO, 1806-1872

Flor Ada, Alma & Campoy, F. Isabel, contrib. by. Sonrisas. (Literature Collection of Puertas Al Sol Ser.). (SPA.). 32p. (J). (gr. k-6). pap. 13.95 (978-1-59437-701-3(4)) Santillana USA Publishing Co., Inc.
Kaplan, Leslie. Cinco de Mayo, 1 vol. 2003. (Library of Holidays Ser.). (ENG., Illus.). 24p. (J). (gr. 2-3). lib. bdg. 26.27 (978-0-8239-6662-2(3), 3d73d6db-9a36-4471-b5c1-02020fca16fc, PowerKids Pr.) Rosen Publishing Group, Inc., The.
Kaplan, Leslie C. Cinco de Mayo. 2009. (Library of Holidays Ser.). 24p. (gr. 2-3). 42.50 (978-1-60853-708-2(0), PowerKids Pr.) Rosen Publishing Group, Inc., The.

JUDAISM

see also Jews; Sabbath; Synagogues

Abraham, Michelle Shapiro. The Be a Mensch Campaign. 2004. (gr. 4-6). stu. ed. 5.95 (978-0-8074-0743-1(7), 571206); pap., tchr. ed., tchr.'s training gde. ed. 11.95 (978-0-8074-0745-5(3), 208056) URJ Pr.
Abrams, Judith Z. The Secret World of Kabbalah. 2006. (Illus.). 80p. (J). (gr. 5-9). per. 9.95 (978-1-58013-224-4(3), Kar-Ben Publishing) Lerner Publishing Group.
Adler, David A. The Story of Hanukkah. Weber, Jill, illus. (J). 2018. 24p. (— 1). bds. 7.99 (978-0-8234-4032-0(X)) 2012. (ENG.). 32p. (gr. -1-3). pap. 7.99 (978-0-8234-2547-1(9)) Holiday Hse., Inc.
Aman, Israa. The Monotheistic Faiths: Judaism, Christianity, & Islam, Vol. 8. Pecastaing, Camille, ed. 2016. (Understanding Islam Ser.: Vol. 8). (ENG., Illus.). 112p. (J). (gr. 7-12). 25.95 (978-1-4222-3674-1(9)) Mason Crest.
Amar, Elisheva. One Word Too Many: Stories for Kids about the Life Changing Impact of Words. 2008. 119p. 26.99 (978-1-59826-210-0(6)) Feldheim Pubs.
Ashear, David. Living Emunah for Teens: Achieving a Life of Serenity Through Faith. 2017. 284p. (J). (978-1-4226-1952-0(4)) Mesorah Pubns., Ltd.
Atkinson, Kenneth. Judaism. 2004. (ENG., Illus.). 150p. (gr. 9-13). 35.00 (978-0-7910-7860-0(4), P114029, Facts On File) Infobase Holdings, Inc.
Auerbach, Annie. Eight Chanukah Lights. Iwai, Melissa, illus. 2005. (ENG.). 18p. (J). 10.95 (978-1-58117-326-0(1), Intervisual/Piggy Toes) Bendon, Inc.
Band, Debra. All the World Praises You: An Illuminated Aleph-Bet Book. Band, Arnold J., tr. Band, Debra, illus. 2018. (ENG., Illus.). 32p. (gr. -1). 19.99 (978-0-9857996-7-0(6)) Honeybee in the Garden, LLC.
Bardack, Amy & Naditch, Beth, eds. Halleli Nafshi: A Weekday Siddur for Children. 2011. (Illus.). 144p. 25.00 (978-0-9836623-2-7(0)) Solomon Schechter Day Schl. of Greater Boston.
Bernstein, Jordan. The Bible According to Grandpa. Doehring, Aurora, illus. 2011. 34p. pap. 6.50 (978-0-9743414-3-9(6)) Adventure in Discovery.
Blitz, Shmuel. Jewish Essentials Artscroll Children's Hebrew/English Machzor for Rosh Hashanah & Yom Kippur. 2009. (ENG., Illus.). 96p. (978-1-4226-0910-1(3)) Mesorah Pubns., Ltd.
Blohm, Craig E. Understanding Judaism. 2018. (Understanding World Religions Ser.). (ENG.). 80p. (J). (gr. 6-12). 39.93 (978-1-68282-467-2(5)) ReferencePoint Pr., Inc.
Bobbie, Match. Havdallah Three Stars in the Sky. 2012. (ENG.). (J). pap. 14.99 (978-1-4675-2709-5(2)) Independent Pub.
Carlson Berne, Emma, ed. Judaism, 1 vol. 2008. (Introducing Issues with Opposing Viewpoints Ser.). (ENG., Illus.). 120p. (gr. 7-10). 43.63 (978-0-7377-3976-3(2), ea4e75a4-7622-4441-b426-3cd3da71819f, Greenhaven Publishing) Greenhaven Publishing LLC.
Cato, Vivienne. The Torah & Judaism. 2003. 30p. (J). lib. bdg. 16.95 (978-1-58340-244-3(6)) Black Rabbit Bks.
Ccar, ed. Mishkan T'filah for Youth, 2 vols., Vol. 1. 2013. (J). (978-0-88123-201-1(7)) Central Conference of American Rabbis/CCAR Pr.
Chaikin, Miriam. Menorahs, Mezuzas, & Other Jewish Symbols. Weihs, Erika, illus. 2003. (ENG.). 112p. (J). (gr. 5-7). pap. 7.95 (978-0-618-37835-7(9), 100323, Clarion Bks.) HarperCollins Pubs.
Chait, Baruch. The Terrifying Trap of the Bad Middos Pirates, 2 vols. Pollack, Gadi, illus. (Good Middos Ser.). 96p. 25.99 (978-1-58330-664-2(1)) Feldheim Pubs.
Cisner, Naftali. Get Ready for Shabbos with Mendel. Cisner, Naftali, illus. 2003. (Illus.). 10p. (J). bds. 5.95 (978-1-880582-03-9(1)) Judaica Pr., Inc., The.
Cook, Esky. Jewish Artwork by Esky: Children, Borders, Hebrew Alphabets. (Illus.). 128p. (Orig.). (J). (gr. 1-8). pap. 19.95 (978-1-885143-02-0(8)) Preferred Enterprises.
—Jewish Artwork by Esky: Complete Set of Jewish Graphics. (Illus.). 384p. (Orig.). (J). (gr. 1-8). pap. 59.95 (978-1-885143-00-6(1)) Preferred Enterprises.
—Jewish Artwork by Esky: Mitzvot, Animals, Food & Brachot. Whitman, Jonathan, ed. (Illus.). 128p. (Orig.). (J). (gr. 1-8). pap. 19.95 (978-1-885143-03-7(6)) Preferred Enterprises.
Cooper, Howard. Can I Tell You about Being Jewish? A Helpful Introduction for Everyone. Pape, Catherine, illus. 2019. (Can I Tell You About...? Ser.). 88p. 15.95 (978-1-78592-491-0(5), 696828) Kingsley, Jessica Pubs. GBR. Dist: Hachette UK Distribution.
Dick, Judy. The Seder Activity Book. Dick, Judy, illus. 2004. (Illus.). 39p. (gr. k-3). pap., act. bk. ed. 9.95 (978-0-8074-0728-8(3), 101097) URJ Pr.
Dicker, Katie & Sheldon, Sam. I Belong to the Jewish Faith, 1 vol. 2009. (I Belong Ser.). (ENG., Illus.). 24p. (J). (gr. 2-2). pap. 9.25 (978-1-4358-8622-3(4), 0d02b2a4-ea25-4eb7-b6e7-0f1911777e9d, PowerKids Pr.); lib. bdg. 26.27 (978-1-4358-3034-9(2), b62f5fae-361a-4a38-9521-acba0d1aa696) Rosen Publishing Group, Inc., The.
Dowley, Tim. The Kregel Pictorial Guide to the Tabernacle, 1 vol. Parry, Alan, illus. 2003. (Kregel Pictorial Guide Ser.). 32p. pap. 11.99 (978-0-8254-2468-7(2)) Kregel Pubns.
Feinstein, Edward. Tough Questions Jews Ask 2/e: A Young Adult's Guide to Building a Jewish Life. 2nd ed. 2012. (ENG.). 160p. (YA). pap. 21.99 (978-1-58023-454-2(2), d2041c9f-1c02-43cb-86a8-ab9d480861bb, Jewish Lights Publishing) LongHill Partners, Inc.
Finkelman, Shimon. The Story of Reb Moshe: A Biography for Young Readers. 2015. (Illus.). 308p. (J). (978-1-4226-1665-9(7), ArtScroll Series) Mesorah Pubns., Ltd.
Freedman, E. b., et al. What Does Being Jewish Mean? Read-Aloud Responses to Questions Jewish Children Ask about History, Culture, & Religion. 2003. (ENG.). 160p. pap. 12.95 (978-0-7432-5413-7(9), Touchstone) Touchstone.
Gerner, Katy. Judaism, 1 vol. 2009. (Religions Around the World Ser.). (ENG.). 32p. (gr. 3-3). 21.27 (978-0-7614-3170-1(5), a0bdbba9-a99a-4e69-b79e-842c9143ccb7) Cavendish Square Publishing LLC.
Ginsburgh, Judy. The Complete Jewish Songbook for Children, Vol. 2. 2004. (ENG.). 288p. (gr. k-3). pap. 39.95 (978-0-8074-0822-3(0), 00191475) Transcontinental Music Pubns.
Glazer, Devorah. A Touch of the High Holidays: A Touch & Feel Book. Seva, illus. 2006. 16p. (J). bds. 7.95 (978-0-8266-0020-2(4)) Merkos L'Inyonei Chinuch.
Gold, Avie. Pirkei Avos, Vol. 2. Horen, Michael & Halasz, Andras, illus. (J). pap. 12.99 (978-0-89906-199-3(0), PIYP) Mesorah Pubns., Ltd.
Goldner, Harriet. Please, Don't Pass over the Seder Plate: A Haggadah for the Young & Young-at-Heart. 2006. (978-0-9779676-0-5(3)) Goldner, Harriet LLC.
Graham, Ian. Judaism. (Illus.). 64p. (YA). (gr. 4-18). lib. bdg. 29.95 (978-1-59389-132-9(6)) Chrysalis Education.
Greenberg, Sidney & Silverman, Morris. Siddurenu. (J). (gr. 3-7). 8.95 (978-0-87677-099-3(5)) Prayer Bk. Pr., Inc.
Greenwald, Zee. Loving Kindness: Stories of Chesed from Our Sages. 2008. 48p. 17.99 (978-1-59826-267-4(X)) Feldheim Pubs.
Grinvald, Zeev & Zryl, Laya. Watching My Words: An Illustrated Children's Guide to the Laws of Shemiras Halashon. Baifus, Rut, illus. 2013. 63p. (J). (978-1-56871-539-1(0)) Menucha Pubs. Inc.
Gross, Moshe. The Annotated & Illustrated Masekhet Sukka. 2017. (HEB., Illus.). 106p. 19.95 (978-965-526-214-8(6), Maggid) Toby Pr. LLC, The.
Has, M., illus. Di Zeksling Hagodeh. 2017. (HEB & YID.). 85p. (J). (978-1-68091-246-3(1)) Kinder Shpiel USA, Inc.
Hawker, Frances & Taub, Daniel. Judaism in Israel. Campbell, Bruce, photos by. 2009. (ENG., Illus.). 32p. (J). (gr. 3-6). (978-0-7787-5010-9(8)); pap. (978-0-7787-5027-7(2)) Crabtree Publishing Co.
Head, Honor. Celebrating Yom Kippur: The Jewish New Year, 1 vol. 2009. (We Love Holidays (2008-2009) Ser.). (ENG., Illus.). 24p. (J). (gr. 2-2). pap. 9.25 (978-1-4358-2906-0(9), ba45fb90-3bb8-401a-a578-511932207233) Rosen Publishing Group, Inc., The.
Heiligman, Deborah. Holidays Around the World: Celebrate Rosh Hashanah & Yom Kippur: With Honey, Prayers, & the Shofar. 2016. (Holidays Around the World Ser.). 32p. (J). (gr. 3-7). pap. 7.99 (978-1-4263-2628-8(9), National Geographic Kids) Disney Publishing Worldwide.
Hessel-Mial, Michael. Judaism, 1 vol. 2018. (Let's Find Out! Religion Ser.). (ENG.). 32p. (gr. 2-3). 26.06 (978-1-5081-0687-6(8), 9acdb0a0-e891-4798-b0c5-4f5cb6024dca) Rosen Publishing Group, Inc., The.
Hipps, Amelia. Islam, Christianity, Judaism. 2005. (Introducing Islam Ser.). (Illus.). 112p. (J). lib. bdg. 24.95 (978-1-59084-698-8(2)) Mason Crest.
Hoffman, Lawrence A. & Wolfson, Ron. What You Will See Inside a Synagogue. Aron, Bill, photos by. 2008. (What You Will See Inside ... Ser.). (ENG., Illus.). 32p. (J). pap. 8.99 (978-1-59473-256-0(6), 0206b87d-4ecf-4a43-af2c-3d2eaf77e346, Skylight Paths Publishing) LongHill Partners, Inc.
Horen, Michael, illus. My Blessings for Food. 2003. (ArtScroll Ser.). (ENG., ARC & HEB.). (J). 49.99 (978-0-89906-702-5(6), TCH3) Mesorah Pubns., Ltd.
House, Behrman. The Bar & Bat Mitzvah Manual. 2008. (ENG.). 1p. (J). pap. 11.95 (978-0-87441-812-5(7), 8b33fec8-e6b5-4b63-abe3-06c2f486b8ae) Behrman Hse., Inc.
—Building Jewish Identity 1: Our Community. 2012. (ENG.). 1p. (J). pap. 9.95 (978-0-87441-861-3(5), 684dbd15-52ca-4dc5-a742-56d8dc3f8783) Behrman Hse., Inc.
—Building Jewish Identity 2: Sacred Time. 2012. (ENG.). 1p. (J). pap. 9.95 (978-0-87441-863-7(1), 61c2102b-1738-4f7c-b394-0b3b702558f5) Behrman Hse., Inc.
—Count Me In. 2005. (ENG., Illus.). 1p. (J). pap. 13.95 (978-0-87441-194-2(7), 8879e694-8207-46f6-b8d5-a02743dddeae) Behrman Hse., Inc.
—Judaism's Great Debates. 2012. (ENG., Illus.). 1p. (J). pap. 14.95 (978-0-87441-852-1(6), 0b227744-cfc8-4ac9-957d-aaf5c3537217) Behrman Hse., Inc.
—Machzor Katan: High Holiday Prayer Book for Families with Young Children. 2012. (ENG., Illus.). 1p. (J). pap. 8.95 (978-0-87441-910-8(7), e04b09ef-9793-4534-bea7-f8a0122d13fb) Behrman Hse., Inc.
—Min Ha'aretz. 2016. (ENG.). 1p. pap. 10.95 (978-0-87441-938-2(7), 3375f295-7eb6-4671-af10-ef77abd7c21b) Behrman Hse., Inc.
—The Time of Our Lives. 2003. (ENG., Illus.). 1p. (J). pap. 14.95 (978-0-87441-718-0(X), aef8a532-afc2-470d-bf5b-3cee3581f857) Behrman Hse., Inc.
—100 + Jewish Art Projects for Children. 2005. (ENG., Illus.). 1p. (J). (gr. -1-6). pap. 45.00 (978-0-86705-039-4(X), af8ebd8f-b1de-439a-9dec-df8d49b4a82e) Behrman Hse., Inc.
Keene, Michael. Judaism, 1 vol. 2005. (Religions of the World Ser.). (ENG., Illus.). 48p. (gr. 5-8). pap. 15.05 (978-0-8368-5875-4(1), 5c1d164c-de17-44b7-8695-67004ac65ffd); lib. bdg. 33.67 (978-0-8368-5869-3(7), 4a4136fe-4b07-4683-a42a-9f06a926624a) Stevens, Gareth Publishing LLLP. (Gareth Stevens Secondary Library).
Kimmel, Eric A. Bar Mitzvah: A Jewish Boy's Coming of Age. Weihs, Erika, illus. 2004. 143p. (J). (gr. 6-9). reprint ed. pap. 15.00 (978-0-7567-7261-1(3)) DIANE Publishing Co.
Kripke, Dorothy Karp. Let's Talk about God. Tripp, Christine, tr. Tripp, Christine, illus. 2003. (J). 9.95 (978-1-881283-34-8(8)) Alef Design Group.
Kunda, Shmuel. Boruch Learns His Brochos. Kunda, Shmuel, illus. 2005. (Illus.). 40p. (J). 17.95 (978-1-932443-41-7(X)) Judaica Pr., Inc., The.
Laurel Corona. Jewish Americans. 2004. (Immigrants in America Ser.). (ENG., Illus.). 112p. (J). 30.85 (978-1-59018-431-8(9)) Cengage Gale.
Lefcourt, Jack. Four Thousand Years of Jewish History: Then & Now. 2009. 108p. (YA). (gr. 6-18). 16.95 (978-1-60280-132-5(0)) Ktav Publishing Hse., Inc.
Lehman-Wilzig, Tami. Keeping the Promise: A Torah's Journey. Orback, Craig, illus. 2004. 32p. (J). (gr. 1-5). 16.95 (978-1-58013-117-9(4), Kar-Ben Publishing) Lerner Publishing Group.
Leon, Carol Boyd. Dayenu! A Passover Haggadah for Families & Children. Connelly, Gwen, illus. 2008. 32p. (J). (gr. 1-3). 16.95 incl. audio compact disk (978-1-60280-041-0(3)); pap. 8.95 incl. audio compact disk (978-1-60280-039-7(1)); spiral bd. 16.95 incl. audio compact disk (978-1-60280-040-3(5)); bds. 24.95 incl. audio compact disk (978-1-60280-042-7(1)) Ktav Publishing Hse., Inc.
Levy, Leah. The Waiting Wall. Rosenfeld, D. L. & Leverton, Yossi, eds. 2009. (ENG., Illus.). 26p. (J). (gr. -1-1). 13.99 (978-1-929628-49-0(8)) Hachai Publishing.
Lewinsky, Adam. Judaism. 2017. (Illus.). 64p. (J). (978-1-4222-3820-2(2)) Mason Crest.
Lewis, Andy. Judaism. 2017. (ENG., Illus.). 40p. (J). (gr. 6-9). pap. 15.95 (978-0-00-822771-5(3)) HarperCollins Pubs. Ltd. GBR. Dist: Independent Pubs. Group.
Lewis, Andy & Orme, Robert. World Religions: Judaism, Christianity & Islam. 2017. (ENG.). 120p. (J). (gr. 6-9). pap. 29.99 (978-0-00-822768-5(3)) HarperCollins Pubs. Ltd. GBR. Dist: Independent Pubs. Group.
Maalos, text. Baruch & Berel. 2011. (YID.). 21.00 (978-0-9832102-4-5(1)) Roth Pubs.
Manushkin, Fran. Come, Let Us Be Joyful! The Story of Hava Nagila. Kaye, Rosalind Charney, illus. 2004. (gr. k-3). 13.95 (978-0-8074-0731-8(3), 101073) URJ Pr.
Marx, Trish. Sharing Our Homeland: Palestinian & Jewish Children at Summer Peace Camp, 1 vol. Karp, Cindy, photos by. (ENG., Illus.). 48p. (J). 2017. (gr. 3-8). 12.95 (978-1-62014-581-4(2), leelowbooks) 2010. (gr. 1-6). 19.95 (978-1-58430-260-5(7)) Lee & Low Bks., Inc.

Merkaz le-Inyene hinukh (Brooklyn, New York, N.Y.) Staff, contrib. by. Hagadah Shel Pesah: Haggadah Shel Pesach for Youth: With Explanatory English Translation & Selected Insights from the Rebbe's Haggadah. 2013. (HEB & ENG., Illus.). 135p. (J). (978-0-8266-0632-7(6)) Merkos L'Inyonei Chinuch.

Michels, Dia L. Look What I See! Where Can I Be? At the Synagogue. Bowles, Michael J. N., photos by. 2005. (Look What I See! Where Can I Be? Ser.). (Illus.). 32p. (J). (gr. -1-3). 9.95 (978-1-930775-16-9(4)) Platypus Media, L.L.C.

Miller, Woody, illus. Tefilat Haderech: The Traveler's Prayer. 2012. (ENG.). 32p. (J). 17.95 (978-0-939144-69-3(7)) EKS Publishing Co.

—Tefilat Haderech: The Traveler's Pryaer. 2012. (ENG.). 32p. (J). pap. 11.95 (978-0-939144-68-6(9)) EKS Publishing Co.

Mrowiec, Katia, et al. God, Yahweh, Allah. 2014. (ENG., Illus.). 192p. (J). 19.95 (978-0-8091-6771-5(9)) Paulist Pr.

Musleah, Rahel. Apples & Pomegranates: A Rosh Hashanah Seder. Gier, Judy Jarrett, illus. 2004. (ENG.). 64p. (J). (gr. k-5). pap. 7.95 (978-1-58013-123-0(9), b45762af-fdbd-4900-b333-b3b8df81257e, Kar-Ben Publishing) Lerner Publishing Group.

Night. 2009. (ENG.). 136p. (gr. 9-13). 30.00 (978-1-60413-198-7(5), P161630, Facts On File) Infobase Holdings, Inc.

Ochs, Carol. Reaching Godward: Voices from Jewish Spiritual Guidance. Kofsky, Ann, illus. 2004. 250p. pap. 14.95 (978-0-8074-0866-7(2), 142612) URJ Pr.

Ofanansky, Allison. How It's Made: Hanukkah Menorah. Alpern, Eliyahu, illus. 2018. (ENG.). 32p. (J). 16.95 (978-1-68115-534-0(6), 5f7e9377-7a9d-4824-8dbb-5dd0241ef80a, Apples & Honey Pr.) Behrman Hse., Inc.

—How It's Made: Torah Scroll. Alpern, Eliyahu, illus. 2016. (ENG.). 32p. (J). 16.95 (978-1-68115-516-6(8), 6bea73b8-6776-4423-9e9f-28af7e417c9c) Behrman Hse., Inc.

Oren, Rony. The Animaged Haggadah. 2012. (ENG., Illus.). 48p. (978-965-524-118-1(1), Lambda) Urim Pubns.

Plaut, W. Gunther & Meyer, Michael. The Reform Judaism Reader: North American Documents. 2004. xi, 228p. (gr. 10-12). pap. 15.95 (978-0-8074-0732-5(1), 386054) URJ Pr.

Pollack, Gadi, illus. Trakht Fun Frier: Herlikhe Mesholim Fun Di Gdoyle Ha-Doyres. 2013. (YID.). 55p. (J). (978-1-937637-36-1(0)) Kinder Shpiel USA, Inc.

Rocklin, Joanne. I Say Shehechiyanu. Filipina, Monika, illus. 2015. (ENG.). 24p. (J). (gr. -1-2). E-Book 23.99 (978-1-4677-6203-8(2), Kar-Ben Publishing) Lerner Publishing Group.

Rose, Or N. Abraham Joshua Heschel: Man of Spirit, Man of Action. 2003. (ENG., Illus.). 80p. pap. 9.95 (978-0-8276-0758-3(X)) Jewish Pubn. Society.

Roseman, Kenneth D. Until the Messiah Comes. 2004. (Do-It-Yourself Jewish Adventure Ser.). (Illus.). 145p. (gr. 4-6). pap. 11.95 (978-0-8074-0706-6(2), 140073) URJ Pr.

Rosenberg, concept. Reach Your Goal. 2011. (YID.). 198p. (YA). 21.00 (978-0-9832102-1-4(7)) Roth Pubs.

Rosenthal, Zelda B. Precious Jewels: The Roadmap to a Child's Heart - a Delightful Resources for Mothers & Teachers. 2006. (ArtScroll Ser.). (Illus.). 268p. (978-1-4226-0075-7(0)); pap. (978-1-4226-0076-4(9)) Mesorah Pubns., Ltd.

Rossel, Seymour. The Storybook Haggadah. Zwebner, Janet, illus. 2006. 72p. (J). pap. 9.95 (978-1-932687-84-2(X), Pitspopany Pr.) Simcha Media Group.

—Torah Portion-by-Portion. 2007. (Illus.). 368p. (J). pap. 15.95 (978-1-891662-94-2(5)) Torah Aura Productions.

Sajja, Raja Choudary. The Jews are the Jewels. 2007. (ENG.). 110p. pap. 18.00 (978-1-4116-1486-4(0)) Lulu Pr., Inc.

Salkin, Jeffrey K. For Kids — Putting God on Your Guest List: How to Claim the Spiritual Meaning of Your Bar or Bat Mitzvah. 2nd ed. 2007. (ENG., Illus.). 144p. (J). (gr. 5-8). per. 18.99 (978-1-58023-308-8(2), c0579c8c-9800-45df-ae36-eac2d6605c7a, Jewish Lights Publishing) LongHill Partners, Inc.

Saul, Laya. My Friend Is Jewish. 2015. (ENG., Illus.). 47p. (J). 29.95 (978-1-62469-106-5(4)) Purple Toad Publishing, Inc.

Schiffman, Lawrence H. Understanding Second Temple & Rabbinic Judaism. 2003. (Illus.). xviii, 409p. (YA). 29.50 (978-0-88125-813-4(X)) Ktav Publishing Hse., Inc.

Schwarz, Jacob D., ed. In the Land of Kings & Prophets. 2004. reprint ed. pap. 22.95 (978-1-4179-4135-3(9)) Kessinger Publishing, LLC.

Seidman, Lauren. What Makes Someone a Jew? What Makes Someone a Jew? 2007. (ENG., Illus.). 32p. pap. 8.99 (978-1-58023-321-7(X), 0feeae39-9d4a-484b-94dc-54d6425b9619, Jewish Lights Publishing) LongHill Partners, Inc.

Senker, Cath. Judaism. 2007. (Atlas of World Faiths/Arcturus Ser.). (Illus.). 48p. (YA). (gr. 7-12). lib. bdg. 32.80 (978-1-59920-056-9(2)) Black Rabbit Bks.

—Judaism: Signs, Symbols, Stories, 1 vol. 2009. (Religious Signs, Symbols, & Stories Ser.). (ENG., Illus.). 32p. (J). (gr. 3-3). pap. 11.00 (978-1-4358-3047-9(4), e14e6f00-c63b-4ac2-b4b2-4620b2f1eab4); lib. bdg. 28.93 (978-1-4358-3039-4(3), 3f5bcdd8-4124-46ba-b2c6-0819dfed54a1) Rosen Publishing Group, Inc., The. (PowerKids Pr.).

Sharer, Avigail. Here, There, Everywhere / Kids' True Stories of Finding Hashem in Their Lives. 2012. (ENG.). 159p. (J). pap. (978-1-4226-1179-1(5)) Mesorah Pubns., Ltd.

Shazak Productions Inc. Staff, Shazak Productions. Miracle Lights: The Complete Story of Chanukah... Like You've Never Seen Before! 2004. (Illus.). 64p. (J). 15.95 (978-1-930925-06-9(9)) Torah Excel.

Shmuel Katz. The Artscroll Children's Book of Berachos. 2011. (ENG., Illus.). 48p. (J). (978-1-4226-1170-8(1)) Mesorah Pubns., Ltd.

Simon, Solomon & Bial, Morrison D. The Rabbi's Bible Vol. 1: Torah, 2 pts. (J). (gr. 5-6). wbk. ed. 8.95 (978-0-87441-020-4(7)) Behrman Hse., Inc.

Singer, Howard. With Mind & Heart. (J). (gr. 8-13). 3.95 (978-0-8381-0203-9(4), 10-203) United Synagogue of America Bk. Service.

Sirois, Celia. My Jewish Friend: A Young Catholic Learns about Judaism. Santillan, Mariano, illus. 2008. 47p. (J). (gr. 5-7). 15.95 (978-0-8198-4857-4(3)) Pauline Bks. & Media.

Stone, Amy M. Jewish Americans, 1 vol. 2006. (World Almanac(r) Library of American Immigration Ser.). (ENG., Illus.). 48p. (gr. 5-8). pap. 15.05 (978-0-8368-7327-6(0), e3f89159-d969-406e-9348-c4ad54e49520); lib. bdg. 33.67 (978-0-8368-7314-6(9), b9e6cfa9-f253-4ca8-b5a0-48647b4cd37e) Stevens, Gareth Publishing LLLP. (Gareth Stevens Secondary Library).

Stren, Ariella. Bracha Do You Know? Argoff, Patti, illus. 2015. (ENG.). 28p. (J). 11.95 (978-1-929628-76-6(5)) Hachai Publishing.

Suneby, Liz & Heiman, Diane. It's a ... It's a ... It's a Mitzvah. Molk, Laurel, illus. (ENG.). 38p. (J). 2017. pap. 14.99 (978-1-68336-772-7(3)) 2012. 24.99 (978-1-58023-509-9(3), 2b22e42c-0985-4849-8130-5e5cfadcc977) LongHill Partners, Inc. (Jewish Lights Publishing).

Swamer, Kristina, illus. The Bedtime Sh'ma: A Good Night Book. 2007. (ENG & HEB.). 40p. (J). 17.95 (978-0-939144-55-6(7)); pap. 11.95 (978-0-939144-54-9(9)) EKS Publishing Co.

—The BEDTIME SH'MA, Book & CD Set. 2007. (ENG & HEB.). 40p. (J). 24.95 incl. audio compact disk (978-0-939144-58-7(1)) EKS Publishing Co.

—Modeh Ani: A Good Morning Book. 2010. (HEB & ENG.). 32p. (J). 17.95 (978-0-939144-64-8(6)); pap. 11.95 (978-0-939144-63-1(8)) EKS Publishing Co.

Touger, Malka. A Door That's Never Locked. 2011. (ENG.). 64p. (J). 14.95 (978-0-8266-0131-5(6)) Kehot Pubn. Society.

Walker, Robert. Bar & Bat Mitzvahs. 2012. (ENG., Illus.). 32p. (J). (978-0-7787-4086-5(2), 1340852); pap. (978-0-7787-4091-9(9), 1340852) Crabtree Publishing Co.

Weber, Vicki L. Hillel Takes a Bath. Joven, John, illus. 2019. (ENG.). 24p. (J). 17.95 (978-1-68115-546-3(X), d5fa3a4c-927b-4a3c-ae4e-3900236c400f, Apples & Honey Pr.) Behrman Hse., Inc.

—It's Too Crowded in Here! & Other Jewish Folk Tales. Borlasca, Hector, illus. 2010. (ENG.). 64p. (J). pap. 9.95 (978-0-87441-850-7(X), 35582e25-a982-4076-8355-009ec204b195) Behrman Hse., Inc.

Weiss, Bernard P. I Am Jewish. (Religions of the World Ser.). 24p. (gr. 3-3). 2009. 42.50 (978-1-60852-460-0(4)) 2003. (ENG., Illus.). (J). lib. bdg. 26.27 (978-0-8239-6810-7(3), dac6bb02-4ef0-4340-afa6-01ea3221d502) Rosen Publishing Group, Inc., The. (PowerKids Pr.).

Whitman, Jonathan, ed. Jewish Artwork by Esky: Shabbat & Jewish Holidays. (Illus.). (Orig.). (J). (gr. 1-8). pap. 19.95 (978-1-885143-01-3(X)) Preferred Enterprises.

Wikler, Madeline & Groner, Judyth. Thank You, God! A Jewish Child's Book of Prayers. Haas, Shelly O., illus. 2003. (ENG.). 32p. (J). (gr. -1-2). pap. 8.99 (978-1-58013-101-8(8), 503b5039-5df0-4281-b204-5a29b180a432, Kar-Ben Publishing) Lerner Publishing Group.

Witman, Melissa Buyer. Mishkan HaNefesh for Youth: A Machzor for Youth & Families. Podwal, Mark H., illus. 2018. (HEB & ENG.). (J). (978-0-88123-291-2(2)) Central Conference of American Rabbis/CCAR Pr.

Wood, Angela Gluck. Judaism. 2006. (QEB World of Faiths Ser.). (Illus.). 32p. (J). lib. bdg. 19.95 (978-1-59566-209-5(X)) QEB Publishing Inc.

Yomtov, Nel. Understanding Judaism. 2018. (Understanding World Religions & Beliefs Ser.). (ENG., Illus.). 112p. (J). (gr. 6-12). lib. bdg. 41.36 (978-1-5321-1427-4(3), 28836, Essential Library) ABDO Publishing Co.

Zoldan, Yael. We Can Do Mitzvos from Aleph to Tav. Allen, Shira, illus. 2009. 46p. (J). (gr. -1-2). 14.99 (978-1-59826-395-4(1)) Feldheim Pubs.

JUDGES

see also Courts; Lawyers

Aldred, Lisa. Thurgood Marshall. 2004. (Black Americans of Achievement Legacy Edition Ser.). (ENG., Illus.). 112p. (gr. 6-12). 35.00 (978-0-7910-8163-1(X), P114167, Facts On File) Infobase Holdings, Inc.

Allen, Mitchell. A Job As a Judge: Understanding Government, 1 vol. 2018. (Civics for the Real World Ser.). (ENG.). 12p. (gr. 1-2). pap. (978-1-5383-6430-7(1), fcf053ff-d948-43fd-adf1-c43e4d73941c, Rosen Classroom) Rosen Publishing Group, Inc., The.

Barrington, Richard. Sonia Sotomayor, 1 vol. 2014. (Making a Difference: Leaders Who Are Changing the World Ser.). (ENG.). 48p. (YA). (gr. 5-5). 28.41 (978-1-62275-435-9(2), 643eba7b-a816-4c8e-9c3d-1b628b35c60a) Rosen Publishing Group, Inc., The.

Benson, Michael. William H. Taft. 2004. (Presidential Leaders Ser.). (ENG., Illus.). 112p. (gr. 6-12). 29.27 (978-0-8225-0849-6(4), Lerner Pubns.) Lerner Publishing Group.

Boerst, William J. Galileo Galilei & the Science of Motion. 2004. (Profiles in Science Ser.). (Illus.). 144p. (YA). (gr. 6-12). lib. bdg. 26.95 (978-1-931798-00-6(1)) Reynolds, Morgan Inc.

Branscomb, Leslie Wolf. Earl Warren. 2011. (Supreme Court Justices Ser.). (Illus.). 112p. 28.95 (978-1-59935-158-2(7)) Reynolds, Morgan Inc.

Burton, Dolores T. & Marcellino, Patricia Ann. A Story of Courage: Supreme Court Justice Sonia Sotomoyar. 2017. (ENG.). 146p. (J). (gr. 4-7). pap. 10.00 (978-0-9974421-2-0(3)) Breaklight Pubns.

Byers, Ann. Clarence Thomas: Conservative Supreme Court Justice, 1 vol. 2019. (African American Trailblazers Ser.). (ENG.). 128p. (gr. 9-9). pap. 22.16 (978-1-5026-4554-8(8), ea5122e5-b0a0-4a2b-863b-4b3f321e20c8) Cavendish Square Publishing LLC.

Calkhoven, Laurie. Ruth Bader Ginsburg: Ready-To-Read Level 3. Vukovic, Elizabet, illus. 2019. (You Should Meet Ser.). (ENG.). 48p. (J). (gr. 1-1). 17.99 (978-1-5344-4858-2(6)); pap. 4.99 (978-1-5344-4857-5(8)) Simon Spotlight. (Simon Spotlight).

Carey Rohan, Rebecca. Thurgood Marshall: The First African-American Supreme Court Justice, 1 vol. 2016. (Great American Thinkers Ser.). (ENG.). 128p. (J). (gr. 9-9). 47.36 (978-1-5026-1932-7(6), 756c9265-9225-4c4f-8b5b-6445c19afc2c) Cavendish Square Publishing LLC.

Carmon, Irin. Notorious RGB Young Readers' Edition: The Life & Times of Ruth Bader Ginsburg. 2017. (ENG., Illus.). 208p. (J). (gr. 3-7). 17.99 (978-0-06-274853-9(X), HarperCollins) HarperCollins Pubs.

Chavez, Emilio. Thurgood Marshall: Supreme Court Justice, 1 vol. 2013. (InfoMax Readers Ser.). (ENG.). 24p. (J). (gr. 3-3). pap. 8.25 (978-1-4777-2599-3(7), 11ef806a-272f-4544-86d4-42b9491905cd); pap. 49.50 (978-1-4777-2600-6(4)) Rosen Publishing Group, Inc., The. (Rosen Classroom).

Colins, Luke. Thurgood Marshall, 1 vol. 2014. (Great African-Americans Ser.). (ENG., Illus.). 24p. (J). (gr. -1-2). lib. bdg. 24.65 (978-1-4765-3956-0(1), 123955, Capstone Pr.) Capstone.

Collins, David. Clarence Thomas: Fighter with Words, 1 vol. 2003. (ENG., Illus.). 32p. (gr. 1-3). 16.99 (978-1-56554-862-6(0), Pelican Publishing) Arcadia Publishing.

Corrigan, Jim. John Marshall: The Story of John Marshall. 2011. (Supreme Court Justices Ser.). (Illus.). 112p. (J). 28.95 (978-1-59935-159-9(5)) Reynolds, Morgan Inc.

Cox, Vicki. Clarence Thomas: Supreme Court Justice. 2008. (Black Americans of Achievement Ser.). (ENG., Illus.). 120p. (gr. 7-12). 35.00 (978-1-60413-048-5(2), P159423, Facts On File) Infobase Holdings, Inc.

De Capua, Sarah. Sandra Day O'Connor, 1 vol. 2013. (Leading Women Ser.). (ENG.). 96p. (YA). (gr. 7-7). 42.64 (978-0-7614-4961-4(2), e5bd4eec-f5ac-4615-923a-b14ad1304d8e); pap. 20.99 (978-1-62712-117-0(X), d5c45fcc-aabe-4f9c-84d2-ea7d6e642c32) Cavendish Square Publishing LLC.

Demuth, Patricia Brennan & Who HQ. Who Was Ruth Bader Ginsburg? Murray, Jake, illus. 2019. (Who Was? Ser.). 112p. (J). (gr. 3-7). 5.99 (978-1-5247-9353-1(1)); 15.99 (978-1-5247-9354-8(X)) Penguin Young Readers Group. (Penguin Workshop).

Furgang, Kathy. Ruth Bader Ginsburg: Supreme Court Justice, 1 vol. 2019. (Junior Biographies Ser.). (ENG.). 24p. (gr. 3-4). 24.27 (978-1-9785-0790-6(9), dbce21c1-e875-4a4c-861e-c30ec5685b1a) Enslow Publishing, LLC.

Gagne, Tammy. What Its Like to Be Sonia Sotomayor. de la Vega, Eida, tr. from SPA. 2010. (What It's Like to Be/Que se Siente al Ser Ser.). (ENG & SPA., Illus.). 32p. (J). (gr. -1-2). lib. bdg. 25.70 (978-1-58415-853-0(0)) Mitchell Lane Pubs.

Gitlin, Martin. Sonia Sotomayor: Supreme Court Justice, 1 vol. 2010. (Essential Lives Set 5 Ser.). (ENG.). 112p. (YA). (gr. 6-12). lib. bdg. 41.36 (978-1-61613-518-8(2), 6719, Essential Library) ABDO Publishing Co.

Harris, Nancy. What's the State Judicial Branch? rev. ed. 2016. (First Guide to Government Ser.). (ENG.). 32p. (J). (gr. 1-3). pap. 8.29 (978-1-4846-3691-6(0), 134103, Heinemann) Capstone.

Horn, Geoffrey M. Thurgood Marshall, 1 vol. 2004. (Trailblazers of the Modern World Ser.). (ENG., Illus.). 48p. (gr. 5-8). pap. 15.05 (978-0-8368-5258-5(3), 0eaf0b52-0726-4be3-b1fa-870937b22719); lib. bdg. 33.67 (978-0-8368-5098-7(X), 243d2da1-a59e-4bd5-a401-db59905c50c5) Stevens, Gareth Publishing LLLP. (Gareth Stevens Secondary Library).

Howse, Jennifer. Sandra Day O'Connor. 2007. (Remarkable People Ser.). (Illus.). 24p. (J). (gr. 3-7). pap. 8.95 (978-1-59036-648-6(4)); lib. bdg. 24.45 (978-1-59036-647-9(6)) Weigl Pubs., Inc.

Isle, Mick. A Timeline of the Supreme Court. 2009. (Timelines of American History Ser.). 32p. (gr. 4-4). 47.90 (978-1-60854-391-5(9), Rosen Reference) Rosen Publishing Group, Inc., The.

Jakubiak, David J. What Does a Supreme Court Justice Do? 2010. (How Our Government Works Ser.). 24p. (J). (gr. 3-6). lib. bdg., E-Book 42.50 (978-1-4488-0031-5(5)); (ENG., Illus.). pap. 9.25 (978-1-4358-9818-9(4), e1b03e4f-966f-44ef-b010-eb814dc79290, PowerKids Pr.); (ENG., Illus.). lib. bdg. 26.27 (978-1-4358-9361-0(1), 0b1487b1-e8ca-474e-a67b-59e45e307f29, PowerKids Pr.) Rosen Publishing Group, Inc., The.

Jarrow, Gail. Robert H. Jackson: New Deal Lawyer, Supreme Court Justice, Nuremberg Prosecutor. 2008. (ENG., Illus.). 128p. (J). (gr. 4-7). 22.99 (978-1-59078-511-9(8), Calkins Creek) Highlights Pr., c/o Highlights for Children, Inc.

Jones, Brenn. Learning about Equal Rights from the Life of Ruth Bader Ginsburg. 2009. (Character Building Book Ser.). 24p. (gr. 2-3). 42.50 (978-1-61511-000-1(3), PowerKids Pr.) Rosen Publishing Group, Inc., The.

Kanefield, Teri. Thurgood Marshall: The Making of America #6. 2020. (Making of America Ser.). (ENG., Illus.). 256p. (J). (gr. 5-9). 16.99 (978-1-4197-4104-3(7), 1264101, Abrams Bks. for Young Readers) Abrams, Inc.

Kemp, Kristin. Amazing Americans: Thurgood Marshall, 1 vol. rev. ed. 2014. (Social Studies: Informational Text Ser.). (ENG., Illus.). 32p. (gr. 3-4). pap. 11.99 (978-1-4333-7374-9(2)) Teacher Created Materials, Inc.

Kramer, Barbara. National Geographic: Readers: Sonia Sotomayor. 2016. (Readers Bios Ser.). (Illus.). 48p. (J). (gr. 1-3). pap. 5.99 (978-1-4263-2289-1(5), National Geographic Kids) Disney Publishing Worldwide.

Krull, Kathleen. No Truth Without Ruth: The Life of Ruth Bader Ginsburg. Zhang, Nancy, illus. 2018. (ENG.). 48p. (J). (gr. -1-3). 17.99 (978-0-06-256011-7(5), Quill Tree Bks.) HarperCollins Pubs.

Laks Gorman, Jacqueline. Judge, 1 vol. 2009. (Know Your Government Ser.). (ENG.). 24p. (J). (gr. 3-3). pap. 9.15 (978-1-4339-0120-1(X), 42ede309-2100-404c-ae3c-01e4ea9b36c8); lib. bdg. 24.67 (978-1-4339-0092-1(0), 47543302-1c8a-4a6e-b628-f83895760594) Stevens, Gareth Publishing LLLP. (Weekly Reader Leveled Readers).

—Juez (Judge), 1 vol. 2009. (Conoce Tu Gobierno (Know Your Government) Ser.). (SPA., Illus.). 24p. (gr. 3-3). (J). lib. bdg. 24.67 (978-1-4339-0099-0(8), 81ff6d81-e8fc-431f-bc43-3c99f0e1d99e); pap. 9.15 (978-1-4339-0127-0(7), a4ea216b-b0b2-4687-9aaf-0901dc3ce327) Stevens, Gareth Publishing LLLP. (Weekly Reader Leveled Readers).

Levy, Debbie. Becoming RBG: Ruth Bader Ginsburg's Journey to Justice. Gardner, Whitney, illus. 2019. (ENG.). 208p. (J). (gr. 5). 19.99 (978-1-5344-2456-2(3)); pap. 12.99 (978-1-5344-2455-5(5)) Simon & Schuster Bks. For Young Readers. (Simon & Schuster Bks. For Young Readers).

—I Dissent: Ruth Bader Ginsburg Makes Her Mark. Baddeley, Elizabeth, illus. 2016. (ENG.). 40p. (J). (gr. -1-3). 18.99 (978-1-4814-6559-5(7), Simon & Schuster Bks. For Young Readers) Simon & Schuster Bks. For Young Readers.

Linde, Barbara M. Becoming a Supreme Court Justice, 1 vol. 2015. (Who's Your Candidate? Choosing Government Leaders Ser.). (ENG., Illus.). 32p. (J). (gr. 3-4). pap. 11.50 (978-1-4824-4051-5(2), d4e3a4e2-a86d-4450-ab19-9a846a8ff364) Stevens, Gareth Publishing LLLP.

—Thurgood Marshall, 1 vol. 2011. (Civil Rights Crusaders Ser.). (ENG., Illus.). 24p. (gr. 2-3). (J). pap. 9.15 (978-1-4339-5700-0(0), a763392e-f931-40e5-a06b-9318b2a8cb6e, Gareth Stevens Learning Library); (YA). 25.27 (978-1-4339-5698-0(5), d09a8987-29e0-4a37-8c3b-77d76a0f9247) Stevens, Gareth Publishing LLLP.

Littlefield, Sophie. Oliver Wendell Holmes Jr: The Supreme Court & American Legal Thought. 2009. (Library of American Lives & Times Ser.). 112p. (gr. 5-5). 69.20 (978-1-60853-496-8(0)) Rosen Publishing Group, Inc., The.

Littlefield, Sophie W. & Wiecek, William. Oliver Wendell Holmes Jr: The Supreme Court & American Legal Thought, 1 vol. 2004. (Library of American Lives & Times Ser.). (ENG., Illus.). 112p. (J). (gr. 5-5). lib. bdg. 38.27 (978-1-4042-2652-4(4), 112d9c02-ccea-44bf-881d-3803e12359e3, PowerKids Pr.) Rosen Publishing Group, Inc., The.

Mara, Wil. Thurgood Marshall: Champion for Civil Rights. 2004. (Great Life Stories Ser.). (ENG., Illus.). 128p. (J). 30.50 (978-0-531-12058-3(9), Watts, Franklin) Scholastic Library Publishing.

McElroy, Lisa Tucker. John G. Roberts, Jr: Chief Justice. 2006. (Gateway Biographies Ser.). (ENG., Illus.). 48p. (J). (gr. 4-8). lib. bdg. 26.60 (978-0-8225-6389-1(4), Lerner Pubns.) Lerner Publishing Group.

Mcpherson, Stephanie Sammartino. Sonia Sotomayor: Supreme Court Justice, 1 vol. 2015. (Exceptional Latinos Ser.). (ENG., Illus.). 24p. (gr. 3-4). pap. 10.35 (978-0-7660-6722-6(X), 081c6f85-56a9-4395-96ef-6c779111ff1b) Enslow Publishing, LLC.

Mead, Wendy. William H. Taft, 1 vol. 2012. (Presidents & Their Times Ser.). (ENG.). 96p. (gr. 6-6). 36.93 (978-1-60870-186-5(7), c3f6f76c-90ed-45ce-9fab-680c514e816d) Cavendish Square Publishing LLC.

Meltzer, Brad. I Am Sonia Sotomayor. Eliopoulos, Christopher, illus. 2018. (Ordinary People Change the World Ser.). 40p. (J). (gr. k-4). 15.99 (978-0-7352-2873-3(6), Dial Bks) Penguin Young Readers Group.

Meltzer, Brad. Soy Sonia Sotomayor. Eliopoulos, Christopher, illus. 2023.Tr. of I Am Sonia Sotomayor. (SPA.). 40p. (J). (gr. k-3). pap. 14.99 **(978-1-5433-8606-6(7))** Vista Higher Learning, Inc.

Micklos Jr., John. Ruth Bader Ginsburg: Get to Know the Justice Who Speaks Her Mind. 2019. (People You Should Know Ser.). (ENG., Illus.). 32p. (J). (gr. 3-6). pap. 7.95 (978-1-5435-5926-2(3), 139904, Capstone Pr.) Capstone.

My Children Publishing, prod. I am the Judge. 2008. (Illus.). 154p. (YA). pap. 19.95 (978-0-9799376-0-6(4)) My Children Publishing Inc.

Polinsky, Paige. Sonia Sotomayor: Supreme Court Justice. 2019. (Women Leading the Way Ser.). (ENG., Illus.). 24p. (J). (gr. k-3). pap. 7.99 (978-1-61891-506-1(1), 12156, Blastoff! Readers) Bellwether Media.

Polinsky, Paige V. Sonia Sotomayor: Supreme Court Justice. 2019. (Women Leading the Way Ser.). (ENG., Illus.). 24p. (J). (gr. k-3). lib. bdg. 26.95 (978-1-62617-945-5(X), Blastoff! Readers) Bellwether Media.

Roland, James. Ruth Bader Ginsburg: Iconic Supreme Court Justice. 2016. (Gateway Biographies Ser.). (ENG., Illus.). 48p. (J). (gr. 4-8). E-Book 47.99 (978-1-5124-0597-2(3), Lerner Pubns.) Lerner Publishing Group.

Scirri, Kaitlin. Ruth Bader Ginsburg: Supreme Court Justice, 1 vol. 2019. (Barrier-Breaker Bios Ser.). (ENG.). 32p. (gr. 2-2). pap. 11.58 (978-1-5026-4964-5(0), 36468a8a-5b1d-423f-a4ee-eab76a22d5d6) Cavendish Square Publishing LLC.

Shichtman, Sandra H. Sonia Sotomayor. 2011. (Supreme Court Justices Ser.). (Illus.). 111p. 28.95 (978-1-59935-156-8(0)) Reynolds, Morgan Inc.

Sikora, Frank & Batcheler, Michelle. Frank M. Johnson, Jr: Courageous Judge. 2009. (Illus.). 104p. (978-1-59421-045-7(4)) Seacoast Publishing, Inc.

Sommers, Michael A. A Timeline of the Supreme Court, 1 vol. 2004. (Timelines of American History Ser.). (ENG., Illus.). 32p. (gr. 4-4). lib. bdg. 29.13 (978-0-8239-4541-2(3), de6a6a6c-6ee8-4a0c-aa97-19e64a51d5ff, Rosen Reference) Rosen Publishing Group, Inc., The.

Sotomayor, Sonia. The Beloved World of Sonia Sotomayor. 352p. (J). (gr. 5). 2019. (ENG.). 10.99 (978-1-5247-7117-1(1), Yearling) 2018. (Illus.). 17.99 (978-1-5247-7114-0(7), Delacorte Bks. for Young Readers) Random Hse. Children's Bks.

—Pasando Páginas: La Historia de Mi Vida. Delacre, Lulu, illus. 2018. 40p. (J). (gr. -1-3). 18.99 (978-0-525-51549-4(6), Philomel Bks.) Penguin Young Readers Group.

—Turning Pages: My Life Story. Delacre, Lulu, illus. 2018. 40p. (J). (gr. -1-3). 17.99 (978-0-525-51408-4(2), Philomel Bks.) Penguin Young Readers Group.

Spiller, Sara. Ruth Bader Ginsburg. Bane, Jeff, illus. 2019. (My Early Library: My Itty-Bitty Bio Ser.). (ENG.). 24p. (J). (gr. k-1). pap. 12.79 (978-1-5341-3925-1(7), 212529); lib. bdg. 30.64 (978-1-5341-4269-5(X), 212528) Cherry Lake Publishing.

Stine, Megan. Who Is Sonia Sotomayor? 2017. (Who Is... ? Ser.). lib. bdg. 16.00 (978-0-606-39779-7(5)) Turtleback.

Stine, Megan & Who HQ. Who Is Sonia Sotomayor? Putra, Dede, illus. 2017. (Who Was? Ser.). 112p. (J). (gr. 3-7). 6.99 (978-0-399-54192-6(6), Penguin Workshop) Penguin Young Readers Group.

Tol, Alex Van. Sonia Sotomayor: U.S. Supreme Court Justice. 2010. (Crabtree Groundbreaker Biographies Ser.). (ENG., Illus.). 112p. (J). pap. (978-0-7787-2546-6(4)) Crabtree Publishing Co.

Torres, John A. Sonia Sotomayor: First Latina Supreme Court Justice, 1 vol. 2015. (Influential Latinos Ser.). (ENG., Illus.). 128p. (gr. 7-7). 38.93 *(978-0-7660-7001-1(8),* 651b4c34-0dcb-4d08-b8bc-f31f9a85801e) Enslow Publishing, LLC.

Tyner, Artika R. So You Want to Be a Supreme Court Justice. 2019. (Being in Government Ser.). (ENG., Illus.). 32p. (J). (gr. 3-6). pap. 7.95 *(978-1-5435-7527-9(7),* 141057); lib. bdg. 27.99 *(978-1-5435-7197-4(2),* 140442) Capstone.

Van Tol, Alex. Sonia Sotomayor: U. S. Supreme Court Justice. 2010. (Crabtree Groundbreaker Biographies Ser.). (ENG., Illus.). 112p. (J). (gr. 5-8). lib. bdg. *(978-0-7787-2537-4(5))* Crabtree Publishing Co.

Weakland, Mark. When Bill Gates Memorized the Encyclopedia. Volpari, Daniela, illus. 2018. (Leaders Doing Headstands Ser.). (ENG.). 32p. (J). (gr. 1-4). pap. 7.95 *(978-1-5158-3048-1(9),* 138683, Picture Window Bks.) Capstone.

—When Ruth Bader Ginsburg - Chewed 100 Sticks of Gum. Volpari, Daniela, illus. 2018. (Leaders Doing Headstands Ser.). (ENG.). 32p. (J). (gr. 1-4). lib. bdg. 28.65 *(978-1-5158-3039-9(X),* 138676, Picture Window Bks.) Capstone.

Wetterer, Charles M. & Wetterer, Margaret K. Chief Justice. Walters, Kurt K. C., illus. 2005. 32p. (J). *(978-1-59336-306-2(0));* pap. *(978-1-59336-307-9(9))* Mondo Publishing.

Wheeler, Jill C. Thurgood Marshall. 2003. (Breaking Barriers Ser.). 64p. (gr. 3-8). lib. bdg. 27.07 *(978-1-57765-907-5(4),* Abdo & Daughters) ABDO Publishing Co.

White, Casey. John Jay: Diplomat of the American Experiment. (Library of American Thinkers Ser.). 112p. (gr. 6-6). 2009. 66.50 *(978-1-60853-515-6(0),* Rosen Reference) 2006. (ENG., Illus.). (YA). lib. bdg. 39.80 *(978-1-4042-0507-9(1),* d02aee73-ee35-409b-89c1-7c009ebf0d42) Rosen Publishing Group, Inc., The.

Whitelaw, Nancy. Mr. Civil Rights: The Story of Thurgood Marshall. 2nd rev. exp. ed. 2004. (Notable Americans Ser.). (Illus.). 144p. (YA). (gr. 6-12). 23.95 *(978-1-931798-02-0(8))* Reynolds, Morgan Inc.

—Thurgood Marshall. 2011. (Supreme Court Justices Ser.). (Illus.). 128p. 28.95 *(978-1-59935-157-5(9))* Reynolds, Morgan Inc.

Williams, Zella. Sonia Sotomayor: Supreme Court Justice, 1 vol. 2010. (Hispanic Headliners Ser.). (ENG.). 24p. (J). (gr. 2-3). pap. 9.25 *(978-1-4488-1474-9(X),* cd6f00b6-cddd-427a-aee1-55ce68516c66); lib. bdg. 26.27 *(978-1-4488-1455-8(3),* f4603e2c-aa7e-4852-9dd9-5b56dc9574a2) Rosen Publishing Group, Inc., The. (PowerKids Pr.).

—Sonia Sotomayor: Supreme Court Justice - Sonia Sotomayor: Jueza de la Corte Suprema, 1 vol. 2010. (Hispanic Headliners / Hispanos en Las Noticias Ser.). (ENG & SPA.). 24p. (J). (gr. 2-3). lib. bdg. 26.27 *(978-1-4488-0711-6(5),* 28250fdb-120d-426c-ab26-764866e59bd1) Rosen Publishing Group, Inc., The.

Wilson, Natashya. How to Draw the Life & Times of William Howard Taft. 2009. (Kid's Guide to Drawing the Presidents of the United States of America Ser.). 32p. (gr. 4-4). 50.50 *(978-1-61511-165-7(4),* PowerKids Pr.) Rosen Publishing Group, Inc., The.

Winter, Jonah. Ruth Bader Ginsburg: The Case of R. B. G. vs. Inequality. Innerst, Stacy, illus. 2017. (ENG.). 48p. (J). (gr. 1-4). 18.95 *(978-1-4197-2559-3(9),* 1163401, Abrams Bks. for Young Readers) Abrams, Inc.

—Sonia Sotomayor. Rodriguez, Edel, illus. 2015. 40p. pap. 8.00 *(978-1-61003-616-0(6))* Center for the Collaborative Classroom.

—Sonia Sotomayor: A Judge Grows in the Bronx/la Juez Que Creció en el Bronx. Rodriguez, Edel, illus. 2009. (SPA & ENG.). 40p. (J). (gr. -1-3). 18.99 *(978-1-4424-0303-1(9),* Atheneum Bks. for Young Readers) Simon & Schuster Children's Publishing.

—Thurgood. Collier, Bryan, illus. 2019. 40p. (J). (gr. k-4). 17.99 *(978-1-5247-6533-0(3),* Schwartz & Wade Bks.) Random Hse. Children's Bks.

JUDO

see also Karate

Brousse, Michel & Matsumoto, David. A Century of Dedication, the History of Judo in America. 2003. (YA). pap. 25.00 *(978-0-9729790-0-9(X));* pap. 30.00 *(978-0-9729790-1-6(8))* United States Judo Federation, Inc.

Brown, Heather E. & Martin, Ashley. How to Improve at Judo. 2009. (How to Improve at... Ser.). (ENG., Illus.). 48p. (J). (gr. 3-9). pap. *(978-0-7787-3596-0(6));* (gr. 4-8). lib. bdg. *(978-0-7787-3574-8(5))* Crabtree Publishing Co.

Chesterman, Barnaby. Judo, 1 vol. 2004. (Martial Arts Ser.). (ENG., Illus.). 32p. (gr. 3-5). lib. bdg. 28.67 *(978-0-8368-4192-3(1),* 8624eff5-79a5-4fea-8277-dc7de7ec6ad8, Gareth Stevens Learning Library) Stevens, Gareth Publishing LLLP.

—Judo: Winning Ways. James, Adam, ed. 2015. (Mastering Martial Arts Ser.). 96p. (J). (gr. 5). lib. bdg. 24.95 *(978-1-4222-3236-1(0))* Mason Crest.

Craats, Rennay. Judo. 2019. (For the Love of Sports Ser.). (ENG.). 24p. (J). (gr. 3-6). pap. 12.95 *(978-1-7911-0573-0(4));* (Illus.). lib. bdg. 28.55 *(978-1-7911-0014-8(7))* Weigl Pubs., Inc.

Crossingham, John & Kalman, Bobbie. Judo in Action. 2005. (Sports in Action Ser.). (ENG., Illus.). 32p. (J). (gr. 2-3). lib. bdg. *(978-0-7787-0342-6(8))* Crabtree Publishing Co.

—Judo in Action. Crabtree, Marc, photos by. 2005. (Sports in Action Ser.). (ENG., Illus.). 32p. (J). (gr. 2-3). pap. *(978-0-7787-0362-4(2))* Crabtree Publishing Co.

Crossingham, John, et al. Le Judo. 2010. (Sans Limites! Ser.). (FRE., Illus.). 32p. (J). pap. 9.95 *(978-2-89579-318-2(2))* Bayard Canada Livres CAN. Dist: Crabtree Publishing Co.

Ellis, Carol. Judo & Jujitsu, 1 vol. 2012. (Martial Arts in Action Ser.). (ENG., Illus.). 48p. (J). (gr. 5-5). lib. bdg. 32.64 *(978-0-7614-4933-1(7),* 4b27243f-bdeb-474e-b042-4a4cf4bef2a2) Cavendish Square Publishing LLC.

Ghetti, Roberto. A Complete Guide to Judo, 1 vol. 2017. (Mastering Martial Arts Ser.). (ENG.). 128p. (gr. 6-6). lib. bdg. 38.93 *(978-0-7660-8547-3(3),* 8b0d6ae9-bf82-470c-8b47-b9b52c883030) Enslow Publishing, LLC.

Mason, Paul. Judo. 2010. (Combat Sports Ser.). 32p. lib. bdg. 28.50 *(978-1-59771-274-3(4))* Sea-To-Sea Pubns.

Sander, Hedda & Deling, Bjorn. Judo: From White/Yellow Belt to Brown Belt. 2004. (Illus.). 184p. pap. 17.95 *(978-1-84126-076-1(2))* Meyer & Meyer Sport, Ltd. GBR. Dist: Lewis International, Inc.

Tometich, Annabelle. Judo, 1 vol. 2015. (Inside Martial Arts Ser.). (ENG., Illus.). 48p. (J). (gr. 3-6). lib. bdg. 34.21 *(978-1-62403-602-6(3),* 17071, SportsZone) ABDO Publishing Co.

Wood, Alix. Judo, 1 vol. 2013. (Kid's Guide to Martial Arts Ser.). (ENG., Illus.). 32p. (J). (gr. 2-3). 30.27 *(978-1-4777-0318-2(7),* 39847170-02f7-4826-a8bd-363f6e592b01); pap. 12.75 *(978-1-4777-0358-8(6),* 3abad18f-5aed-4700-9797-feaa9963282e) Rosen Publishing Group, Inc., The. (PowerKids Pr.).

—Jujitsu, 1 vol. 2013. (Kid's Guide to Martial Arts Ser.). (ENG., Illus.). 32p. (J). (gr. 2-3). pap. 12.75 *(978-1-4777-0356-4(X),* 95ea817e-8f19-4454-9866-f249ce26c39e); lib. bdg. 30.27 *(978-1-4777-0317-5(9),* f5cedc92-8210-4f97-a613-c94dc3bdd40d) Rosen Publishing Group, Inc., The. (PowerKids Pr.).

JUGGLING

Beak, Nick Huckleberry. How to Juggle: 25 Fantastic Juggling Tricks & Techniques to Try! 2013. (Illus.). 64p. (J). (gr. 3-7). 9.99 *(978-1-84322-865-3(3),* Armadillo) Anness Publishing GBR. Dist: National Bk. Network.

Cooney, Barbara. The Little Juggler. 2018. (Juggling the Middle Ages Ser.). (ENG., Illus.). 52p. (J). 12.50 *(978-0-88402-436-1(9),* 30448) Dumbarton Oaks.

Juggling. Date not set. 64p. (J). 5.98 *(978-1-4054-0408-2(6))* Parragon, Inc.

Juggling Kid Kit. 2004. (Kid Kits Ser.). (Illus.). 32p. (J). 9.95 *(978-1-58086-417-6(1))* EDC Publishing.

Juggling Skills. 2004. (Formula Fun Ser.). (Illus.). 48p. (J). *(978-1-84229-588-5(8))* Top That! Publishing PLC.

Just Juggling. 2004. (Whizz Kits Ser.). (Illus.). 48p. (J). *(978-1-84229-940-1(9))* Top That! Publishing PLC.

Top That Publishing Staff, ed. Boob Juggling. 2004. (Naughty Shenanigans Ser.). (Illus.). 48p. *(978-1-84510-218-0(5))* Top That! Publishing PLC.

JUNGLE ANIMALS

Alderton, David. Jungle Animals Around the World. 2014. (Animals Around the World Ser.). (ENG., Illus.). 32p. (J). (gr. 2-5). 31.35 *(978-1-62588-194-6(0),* 19259, Smart Apple Media) Black Rabbit Bks.

AZ Books Staff. About Wildlife. Petrovskaya, Olga, ed. 2012. (Million Whys Ser.). (ENG.). 12p. (J). (gr. -1-4). bds. 18.95 *(978-1-61889-059-7(X))* AZ Bks. LLC.

—Forest Animals. Gorojan, Elena, ed. 2012. (My First Library). (ENG.). 12p. (J). (gr. -1-k). bds. 8.95 *(978-1-61889-120-4(0))* AZ Bks. LLC.

—In the Jungle. Efimova, Tatiana, ed. 2012. (Animal Sounds Ser.). (ENG.). 14p. (J). (gr. -1-k). bds. 7.95 *(978-1-61889-125-9(1))* AZ Bks. LLC.

—Jungle Animals. Gorojan, Elena, ed. 2012. (My First Library). (ENG.). 12p. (J). (-k). bds. 8.95 *(978-1-61889-121-1(9))* AZ Bks. LLC.

—Living Book of the Jungle. Gasteva, Julia, ed. 2012. (Our Amazing World Ser.). (ENG.). 12p. (J). (gr. 1-3). bds. 19.95 *(978-1-61889-024-5(7))* AZ Bks. LLC.

—Living Book of the Savanna. Aksimovich, Natalja, ed. 2012. (Our Amazing World Ser.). (ENG.). 12p. (J). (gr. 1-3). bds. 19.95 *(978-1-61889-023-8(9))* AZ Bks. LLC.

—Savanna Animals. Gorojan, Elena, ed. 2012. (My First Library). (ENG.). 12p. (J). (-k). bds. 8.95 *(978-1-61889-118-1(9))* AZ Bks. LLC.

—Scouting the Forest. Vasilkova, Elena, ed. 2012. (Wild Theater Ser.). (ENG.). 8p. (J). (gr. -1-3). bds. 17.95 *(978-1-61889-018-4(2))* AZ Bks. LLC.

—Sounds of the Forest. Sheljagovich, Yana, ed. 2012. (Sounds Around Us Ser.). (ENG.). 16p. (J). (gr. 1-3). bds. 17.95 *(978-1-61889-028-3(X))* AZ Bks. LLC.

—Sounds of the Jungle. Migiz, Anna, ed. 2012. (Sounds Around Us Ser.). (ENG.). 16p. (J). (gr. 1-3). bds. 17.95 *(978-1-61889-030-6(1))* AZ Bks. LLC.

—Sounds of the Savanna & Desert. Migiz, Anna, ed. 2012. (Sounds Around Us Ser.). (ENG.). 16p. (J). (gr. 1-3). bds. 17.95 *(978-1-61889-031-3(X))* AZ Bks. LLC.

—Sounds of Wild Nature. Naumovets, Elena, ed. 2012. (Sounds Around Us Ser.). (ENG.). 16p. (J). (gr. 1-3). bds. 17.95 *(978-1-61889-026-9(3))* AZ Bks. LLC.

Bradley, Timothy J. Terror in the Tropics, 1 vol. 2nd rev. ed. 2013. (TIME for KIDS(r): Informational Text Ser.). (ENG., Illus.). 64p. (J). (gr. 4-8). lib. bdg. 31.96 *(978-1-4333-7421-0(8))* Teacher Created Materials, Inc.

Casado, Dami & Casado, Alicia. Bebes de la Selva. 2003. (Bebes Ser.). (SPA., Illus.). 12p. (J). bds. 7.99 *(978-84-272-6061-0(X))* Molino, Editorial ESP. Dist: Santillana USA Publishing Co., Inc.

Cocoretto, illus. Peekaboo! in the Jungle! 2016. (Peekaboo! Ser.: 4). 12p. (J). spiral bd. *(978-1-84643-866-0(7))* Child's Play International Ltd.

Delafosse, Claude & Broutin, Christian. Let's Look at the Jungle. Broutin, Christian, illus. 2012. (ENG., Illus.). 38p. (J). (gr. k-3). spiral bd. 11.99 *(978-1-85103-332-4(7))* Moonlight Publishing, Ltd. GBR. Dist: Independent Pubs. Group.

Devera, Czeena. Animals of the Jungle. 2019. (Wild Things Ser.). (ENG.). 16p. (J). (gr. -1-2). pap. 11.36 *(978-1-5341-4981-6(3),* 213232, Cherry Blossom Press) Cherry Lake Publishing.

DK. Touch & Feel: Jungle Animals. 2012. (Touch & Feel Ser.). (ENG.). 12p. (J). (gr. -1-k). bds. 6.99 *(978-0-7566-9289-6(X),* DK Children) Dorling Kindersley Publishing, Inc.

Fog City Press Staff, contrib. by. The Wonder of Safari Animals. 2016. (Illus.). 47p. (J). *(978-1-68188-093-8(8))* Fog City Pr.

Gersh, Camilla. DK Readers L1: Jungle Animals: Discover the Secrets of the Jungle! 2016. (DK Readers Level 1 Ser.). (ENG., Illus.). 24p. (J). (gr. -1-1). pap. 4.99 *(978-1-4654-4962-7(0),* DK Children) Dorling Kindersley Publishing, Inc.

Gresham, Jennifer. Jungle Animals. 2013. (Illus.). (J). *(978-1-58865-832-6(5))* Kidsbooks, LLC.

Guettier, Bénédicte. In the Jungle. 2010. (Funny Faces Ser.). (Illus.). 14p. bds. *(978-1-84089-645-9(0))* Zero to Ten, Ltd.

Jungle Animals, 12 vols. 2014. (Jungle Animals Ser.). (ENG.). 24p. (J). (gr. k-k). lib. bdg. 145.62 *(978-1-4824-1630-5(1),* 734c0a46-e08c-4a0c-a9c8-4ceeee2c6eb4) Stevens, Gareth Publishing LLLP.

Jungle Fun. 2017. (Jungle Fun Ser.). 24p. (gr. 4-6). pap. 24.75 *(978-1-5081-6184-4(4),* PowerKids Pr.) Rosen Publishing Group, Inc., The.

Kainen, Dan & Wollard, Kathy. Jungle: A Photicular Book. 2016. (Photicular Ser.). (ENG., Illus.). 24p. 26.99 *(978-0-7611-8953-4(X),* 18953) Workman Publishing Co., Inc.

Look Who's Popping Up: In the Jungle. 2003. (J). (gr. -1-k). 4.98 *(978-0-7525-8902-2(4))* Parragon, Inc.

Marshall, Natalie. Jungle. 2019. (ENG.). 12p. (J). (gr. -1 — 1). bds. 9.99 *(978-1-4380-5070-6(4))* Sourcebooks, Inc.

Martin, Ruth. Noisy Nature: in the Jungle. Pledger, Maurice, illus. 2015. (ENG.). 12p. (J). (gr. -1). 16.95 *(978-1-62686-104-6(8),* Silver Dolphin Bks.) Readerlink Distribution Services, LLC.

Moran, Shelby. Animals of the Jungle. 2017. (Animals in My World Ser.). 24p. (gr. 4-6). 49.50 *(978-1-5383-2141-6(6),* PowerKids Pr.) Rosen Publishing Group, Inc., The.

Ottina, Laura. In the Jungle, 1 vol. 2009. (Learn with Animals Ser.). (ENG., Illus.). 24p. (J). (gr. k-1). pap. 9.15 *(978-1-4339-2090-5(5),* d6510c78-9edb-41f9-a220-e934b231e427); lib. bdg. 24.67 *(978-1-4339-1913-8(3),* 54182daf-5da1-4513-8757-387593d44d7a) Stevens, Gareth Publishing LLLP. (Weekly Reader Leveled Readers).

Pallotta, Jerry. Ultimate Jungle Rumble (Who Would Win?) Bolster, Rob, illus. 2020. (Who Would Win? Ser.: 19). (ENG.). 32p. (J). (gr. 1-4). pap. 4.99 *(978-0-545-94609-4(3))* Scholastic, Inc.

Radley, Gail. Forests & Jungles. Sherlock, Jean, illus. (Vanishing from Ser.). 32p. 2005. (gr. 6-12). lib. bdg. 22.60 *(978-1-57505-405-6(1))* 2003. (J). (gr. 3-5). 6.95 *(978-1-57505-567-1(8))* Lerner Publishing Group.

Reasoner, Charles. Animals in the Jungle. Pitt, Sarah, illus. 2009. (3D Board Bks.). 12p. (J). (gr. -1-k). bds. 9.99 *(978-1-934650-38-7(2))* Just For Kids Pr., LLC.

—Fan-Tab-U-Lus: Jungle Animals. Devaney, Adam, illus. 2011. (Fan-Tab-U-Lus Bks.). (ENG.). 12p. (J). (gr. -1-3). bds. 9.99 *(978-1-935498-55-1(X))* Just For Kids Pr., LLC.

Rice, William B. Endangered Animals of the Jungle, 1 vol. 2nd rev. ed. 2013. (TIME for KIDS(r): Informational Text Ser.). (ENG.). 64p. (gr. 4-8). pap. 14.99 *(978-1-4333-4937-9(X))* Teacher Created Materials, Inc.

Tejido, Jomike. Jumbo Stickers for Little Hands: Jungle Animals: Includes 75 Stickers. 2016. (Jumbo Stickers for Little Hands Ser.). (ENG.). 24p. (J). (gr. -1-k). pap. 7.95 *(978-1-63322-119-2(9),* 223807, Moondance) Quarto Publishing Group USA.

Vetere, Lori. Jungle Wildlife, Vol. 4. 2018. (Into the World's Amazing Jungles Ser.). (Illus.). 80p. (J). (gr. 7). lib. bdg. 33.27 *(978-1-4222-4096-0(7))* Mason Crest.

Watt, Fiona. Jungle. Elkerton, Andy, illus. 2009. (Luxury Touchy-Feely Board Bks). 10p. (J). (gr. -1). bds. 15.99 *(978-0-7945-2433-3(8),* Usborne) EDC Publishing.

West, David. Jungle Animals. 2015. (Safari Sam's Wild Animals Ser.). (ENG.). 24p. (J). (gr. k-3). 28.50 *(978-1-62588-072-7(3),* 19363, Smart Apple Media) Black Rabbit Bks.

Zimmerman, Beverly. Bridal Planner. 2013. (ENG.). 49p. pap. 29.99 *(978-1-932676-80-8(5),* af825778-aace-43c8-a7a9-4f8bd48e4aa9) Vision Pubs., LLC.

Zondervan Staff. Jungle Beasts, 1 vol. 2011. (I Can Read! / Made by God Ser.). (ENG., Illus.). 32p. (J). pap. 4.99 *(978-0-310-72191-8(1))* Zonderkidz.

JUNGLE ANIMALS—FICTION

Adlerman, Danny. Africa Calling, Nighttime Falling, 1 vol. 2018. (ENG., Illus.). 32p. (J). (gr. k-2). pap. 9.95 *(978-1-62014-795-5(5),* leelowbooks) Lee & Low Bks., Inc.

Alborough, Jez. Hug. Alborough, Jez, illus. 2009. (ENG., Illus.). 32p. (J). (gr. -1-k). pap. 5.99 *(978-0-7636-4510-6(9))* Candlewick Pr.

—Hug Lap-Size Board Book. Alborough, Jez, illus. 2005. (ENG., Illus.). 32p. (J). (— 1). bds. 12.99 *(978-0-7636-2893-2(X))* Candlewick Pr.

Alegria, Ciro. Sacha en el Reino de los Arboles. (SPA.). 96p. (YA). (gr. 5-8). *(978-84-204-3693-7(3),* AF1748) Ediciones Alfaguara ESP. Dist: Lectorum Pubns., Inc.

—Sacha en el Reino de los Arboles. (SPA.). (YA). (gr. 5-8). *(978-956-11-0965-0(4),* UV6346) Universitaria, Editorial S.A.

Alexander, Heather. Wallace & Grace & the Cupcake Caper. Zarrin, Laura, illus. 2018. (Wallace & Grace Ser.). (ENG.). 80p. (J). pap. 7.99 *(978-1-68119-011-2(7),* 900154812, Bloomsbury Children's Bks.) Bloomsbury Publishing USA.

Andreae, Giles. Leo, the Lovable Lion. 2004. (Illus.). *(978-0-439-65567-5(6))* Scholastic, Inc.

—Rumble in the Jungle. Wojtowycz, David, illus. 2011. (ENG.). 26p. (J). (-k). bds. 9.99 *(978-1-58925-864-8(9))* Tiger Tales.

AZ Books Staff. Forest Animals Moving & Talking. Dubovik, Ludmila, ed. 2012. (Funny Trails Ser.). (ENG.). 10p. (J). (gr. -1-k). bds. 9.95 *(978-1-61889-176-1(6))* AZ Bks. LLC.

—My Forest. Yaroshevich, Angelica, ed. 2012. (Open the Book-I Am Alive Ser.). (ENG.). 8p. (J). (— 1). bds. 5.95 *(978-1-61889-042-9(5))* AZ Bks. LLC.

—Our Faraway Jungle. Zayceva, Irina, ed. 2012. (Hook-And-Loop-Pictures Ser.). (ENG.). 12p. (J). (-k). bds. 11.95 *(978-1-61889-158-7(8))* AZ Bks. LLC.

—Who Lives in the Jungle? Gridina, Anna, ed. 2012. (Funny Animals Ser.). (ENG.). 10p. (J). (-k). bds. 8.95 *(978-1-61889-048-1(4))* AZ Bks. LLC.

Baena, Gloria. Invitacion a la Fiesta del Gran Gorila. Osorno, Laura, illus. 2003. (SPA.). 32p. (J). 8.95 *(978-958-04-7072-4(3))* Norma S.A. COL. Dist: Distribuidora Norma, Inc.

Baggott, Stella, illus. Baby's Very First Stroller Book Jungle. 2015. (Baby's Very First Stroller Bks.). (ENG.). 8p. (J). 7.99 *(978-0-7945-3533-9(X),* Usborne) EDC Publishing.

Balouch, Kristen. The Little Little Girl with the Big Big Voice. Balouch, Kristen, illus. 2011. (ENG., Illus.). 32p. (J). (gr. -1-k). 14.99 *(978-1-4424-0808-1(1),* Little Simon) Little Simon.

Beaton, Clare & Blackstone, Stella. How Loud Is a Lion? Beaton, Clare, illus. 2007. (Illus.). 24p. (J). (gr. -1-k). bds. 7.99 *(978-1-84686-000-3(8))* Barefoot Bks., Inc.

Bergin, Jennifer J. Jungle Jim & Jungle Jen in the African Savannahs. 2012. 68p. pap. 8.99 *(978-1-4525-5314-6(9))* Balboa Pr.

Blackford, Andy. The Hungry Little Monkey. 2011. (Tadpoles Ser.). (ENG., Illus.). 24p. (J). (gr. k-2). lib. bdg. *(978-0-7787-0581-9(1));* pap. *(978-0-7787-0592-5(7))* Crabtree Publishing Co.

Blackstone, Stella & Beaton, Clare. How Loud Is a Lion? Beaton, Clare, illus. 2011. (Illus.). 24p. (J). (gr. -1-2). pap. 6.99 *(978-1-84686-534-3(4))* Barefoot Bks., Inc.

Bland, Nick. The Very Cranky Bear. Bland, Nick, illus. 2014. (ENG., Illus.). 32p. (J). (gr. -1-k). 17.99 *(978-0-545-61269-2(1),* Orchard Bks.) Scholastic, Inc.

Broach, Elise. Gumption! Egielski, Richard, illus. 2010. (ENG.). 40p. (J). (gr. k-3). 19.99 *(978-1-4169-1628-4(8),* Atheneum Bks. for Young Readers) Simon & Schuster Children's Publishing.

Brooks, David. You Can Count in the Jungle. 2005. (You Can Count Ser.). (ENG., Illus.). 24p. (J). (gr. -1 — 1). bds. 6.95 *(978-1-55971-931-5(1))* Cooper Square Publishing Llc.

Brown, J. A. Hurray for Elephant. 2003. (Funny Faces Ser.). (Illus.). (J). 3.95 *(978-1-58925-717-7(0))* Tiger Tales.

Burgess, Thornton W. Billy Mink. Cady, Harrison, illus. 2012. (Dover Children's Thrift Classics Ser.). (ENG.). 128p. (J). (gr. k-3). pap. 5.00 *(978-0-486-48107-4(7),* 481077) Dover Pubns., Inc.

Butler, John. Bedtime in the Jungle, 1 vol. 2019. (ENG., Illus.). 32p. (J). (gr. -1-k). pap. 7.95 *(978-1-68263-145-4(1))* Peachtree Publishing Co. Inc.

Carle, Eric. "Slowly, Slowly, Slowly," Said the Sloth. Carle, Eric, illus. 2007. (Illus.). (J). (gr. -1-3). 18.00 *(978-0-7569-8002-3(X))* Perfection Learning Corp.

—Slowly, Slowly, Slowly, Said the Sloth. Carle, Eric, illus. 2007. (ENG., Illus.). 32p. (J). (gr. -1-2). pap. 7.99 *(978-0-14-240847-6(6))* Penguin Young Readers Group.

—"Slowly, Slowly, Slowly," Said the Sloth. 2007. 18.40 *(978-1-4177-7475-3(4))* Turtleback.

Carter, Wade. The Adventures of Ernie & Ike: Lessons in Life Series. 2008. 44p. pap. 16.99 *(978-1-4343-9087-5(X))* AuthorHouse.

Chachas, George & Wojtak, James. The Adventures of Dynamic Doolittle: The Problem with Paulie Python. De Soto, Ben, illus. 2011. 31p. (J). pap. 9.95 *(978-0-9793144-1-4(0))* Doolittle Edutainment Corp.

—The Story of Doolittle: An Exceptional Young Gorilla. De Soto, Ben, illus. 2011. 32p. (J). pap. 9.95 *(978-0-9793144-0-7(2))* Doolittle Edutainment Corp.

Chapman, Jason. Who's That Singing? A Pull-The-Tab Book. Chapman, Jason, illus. 2010. (ENG., Illus.). 12p. (J). (gr. -1-1). bds. 9.99 *(978-1-4169-8736-9(3),* Little Simon) Little Simon.

Charles, Faustin & Terry, Michael. The Selfish Crocodile Book of Nursery Rhymes. Terry, Michael, illus. 2008. (Illus.). (J). (gr. -1-k). audio compact disk 25.95 *(978-0-7475-9523-6(2))* Bloomsbury Publishing Plc GBR. Dist: Independent Pubs. Group.

Chichester Clark, Emma, illus. No More Kissing! 2015. (J). *(978-1-4351-5751-4(6))* Barnes & Noble, Inc.

Chukovsky, Kornei. Doctor Ouch. Seabaugh, Jan, tr. from RUS. Seabaugh, Jan, illus. 2004. (Children's International Ser.: 1). Orig. Title: Aibolit. 43p. (J). pap. 6.99 *(978-0-9740551-0-7(7))* Smith, Viveca Publishing.

Clarke, Jane. Who Woke the Baby? Fuge, Charles, illus. 2016. (ENG.). 32p. (J). (gr. -1-2). 12.99 *(978-0-7636-8662-8(X))* Candlewick Pr.

Cole, Babette. Tarzana. 2nd ed. 2003. (Babette Cole Ser.).Tr. of Tarzanna! (SPA., Illus.). 34p. (J). 12.95 *(978-84-233-2274-9(2))* Ediciones Destino ESP. Dist: Planeta Publishing Corp.

Cole, Bob. Power Reading: Classics/Jungle Book. Connor, Robin, illus. 2004. 94p. (J). (gr. 4-18). vinyl bd. 39.95 *(978-1-883186-61-6(7),* PPCL2) National Reading Styles Institute, Inc.

Colleen, Marcie. Going Nuts: Super Happy Party Bears 4. James, Steve, illus. 2017. (Super Happy Party Bears Ser.: 4). (ENG.). 144p. (J). pap. 5.99 *(978-1-250-10049-8(6),* 900162461) Imprint IND. Dist: Macmillan.

Crowson, Andrew. Flip Flap Safari. Crowson, Andrew, illus. 2003. (ENG., Illus.). 12p. (J). bds. *(978-1-85602-473-0(3),* Pavilion Children's Books) Pavilion Bks.

Dahl, Roald. The Enormous Crocodile. 2009. (gr. k-3). lib. bdg. 18.40 *(978-0-613-87826-5(4))* Turtleback.

Daniels, Katie C. Danny's Adventure in Afric. 2009. 24p. pap. 12.99 *(978-1-4389-3404-4(1))* AuthorHouse.

Davies, Gill. A Special Wish: A Story of Confidence, 1 vol. O'Neill, Robert, illus. 2009. (Let's Grow Together Ser.). (ENG.). 32p. (J). (gr. k-1). pap. 11.55 *(978-1-60754-769-3(4),* 1cdf674f-f43e-4704-8354-8024314dd13c); lib. bdg. 27.27 *(978-1-60754-760-0(0),* 7715bb86-8c42-4ae0-b691-d6c361230a9f) Rosen Publishing Group, Inc., The. (Windmill Bks.).

DePrisco, Dorothea. Who's in the Jungle? Gilvan-Cartwright, Chris, illus. 2006. (ENG.). 10p. (J). bds. 4.95 *(978-1-58117-507-3(8),* Intervisual/Piggy Toes) Bendon, Inc.

Derrick, David G., Jr. I'm the Scariest Thing in the Jungle! 2013. (ENG., Illus.). 36p. (J). (gr. -1-3). 15.95 *(978-1-59702-087-9(7))* Immedium.

Desai, Naina. Fun Jungle. 2009. 28p. pap. 13.99 *(978-1-4490-2058-3(5))* AuthorHouse.

Dillingham Pierson, Clara. Among the Forest People. 2008. 92p. pap. 8.15 *(978-1-60459-501-7(9))* Wilder Pubns., Corp.

Disney Storybook Artists Staff, et al, illus. Disney's the Lion King. 2007. (Play-A-Sound Ser.). 16p. (J). (gr. -1-3). 16.98 *(978-1-4127-8776-5(9))* Publications International, Ltd.

Doerrfeld, Cori. Wild Baby. Doerrfeld, Cori, illus. 2019. (ENG., Illus.). 32p. (J). (gr. -1-3). 17.99 *(978-0-06-269894-0(X),* HarperCollins) HarperCollins Pubs.

—Wild Baby Board Book. Doerrfeld, Cori, illus. 2019. (ENG., Illus.). 36p. (J). (gr. -1 — 1). bds. 7.99 *(978-0-06-269893-3(1),* HarperFestival) HarperCollins Pubs.

Donaldson, Julia. Where's My Mom? Scheffler, Axel, illus. 2008. (ENG.). 32p. (J). (gr. -1-2). 18.99 *(978-0-8037-3228-5(7),* Dial Bks) Penguin Young Readers Group.

J K L

Douglas, Babette. Noreen: The Real King of the Jungle. Johnson, John, illus. 2006. (Kiss a Me Teacher Creature Stories Ser.). 20p. (J). (gr. -1-3). 9.99 *(978-1-890343-25-5(0))* Kiss A Me Productions, Inc.

Dufresne, Michèle. The Big Game: Little Dinosaur Chapter Books. 2007. (Little Dinosaur Chapter Ser.). (J). per. 7.67 *(978-1-932570-68-7(3))* Pioneer Valley Bks.

Durant, Alan. If You Go Walking in Tiger Wood. Boon, Debbie, illus. 2005. (ENG.). 24p. (J). (gr. -1-k). pap. 9.99 *(978-0-00-710390-4(5)*, HarperSport) HarperCollins Pubs. Ltd. GBR. Dist: Independent Pubs. Group.

Dutson, Shelly. Jingle Jangle Jungle Jeepers. Christenson, Maren, illus. 2009. 24p. pap. 12.50 *(978-1-4490-1061-4(X))* AuthorHouse.

Edwards, Pamela Duncan. Roar! A Noisy Counting Book. Cole, Henry, illus. Date not set. 32p. (J). (gr. -1-2). pap. 5.99 *(978-0-06-443572-7(5))* HarperCollins Pubs.

Ellery, Amanda. If I Were a Jungle Animal. Ellery, Tom, illus. 2009. (ENG.). 40p. (J). (gr. -1-3). 19.99 *(978-1-4169-3778-4(1)*, Simon & Schuster Bks. For Young Readers) Simon & Schuster Bks. For Young Readers.

Ely, Kosa. The Peaceable Forest: India's Tale of Kindness to Animals. Johansson, Anna, illus. 2012. (ENG.). 32p. (gr. k). 16.99 *(978-1-60887-115-5(0))* Mandala Publishing.

Emmett, Jonathan. Through the Heart of the Jungle. Gomez, Elena, illus. 2003. 32p. (J). tchr. ed. 15.95 *(978-1-58925-029-1(X))*; pap. 5.95 *(978-1-58925-380-3(9))* Tiger Tales.

Flyte, Min. Would You Dare... ? A Lift-The-flap Adventure. Hunt, Matt, illus. 2017. (ENG.). 24p. (J). (gr. -1-2). 14.99 *(978-0-7636-9619-1(6))* Candlewick Pr.

Foster, Claudie. Princess Vanilla of the Amazon Jungle. 2011. 48p. pap. 24.95 *(978-1-60749-297-9(0))* America Star Bks.

Frampton, David. The Whole Night Through. Frampton, David, illus. Date not set. (Illus.). 32p. (J). (gr. -1-1). pap. 5.99 *(978-0-06-443652-6(7))* HarperCollins Pubs.

—The Whole Night Through: A Lullaby. Frampton, David, illus. 2004. (Illus.). 30p. (J). (gr. k-4). reprint ed. *(978-0-7567-7723-4(2))* DIANE Publishing Co.

Freedman, Claire & Cabban, Vanessa. Gooseberry Goose. 2003. (Illus.). 32p. (J). (gr. -1-2). tchr. ed. 15.95 *(978-1-58925-030-7(3))* Tiger Tales.

Friden, Chris. Bedtime Safari. 2008. (Illus.). 27p. (J). bds. 14.99 *(978-0-9758785-4-5(9))* Haydenburri Lane.

—Bedtime Safari. Otoshi, Kathryn & Ciccarelli, Gary, illus. 2007. (J). *(978-0-9758785-3-8(0))* Haydenburri Lane.

—Sleepytime with Rory. 2008. (Illus.). 27p. (J). bds. 14.99 *(978-0-9758785-5-2(7))* Haydenburri Lane.

—Sleepytime with Rory. Zapater Oliva, Carlos & Glazier, Garth, illus. 2008. (J). *(978-0-9801849-1-4(6))* Haydenburri Lane.

George, Joshua. Elepants. Poh, Jennie, illus. 2016. (J). *(978-1-4351-6486-4(5))* Barnes & Noble, Inc.

Gerver, Jane E. Who's at Home? A Lift-The-Flap Book. Davis, Kathryn Lynn, illus. 2010. (ENG.). 14p. (J). (gr. -1 — 1). bds. 6.99 *(978-1-4169-9758-0(X)*, Little Simon) Little Simon.

Gibbs, Edward. Little Bee. 2012. (ENG.). 24p. (J). (gr. -1-17). bds. 8.99 *(978-0-316-12707-3(8))* Little, Brown Bks. for Young Readers.

Guzman, Lila. Kichi in Jungle Jeopardy. Johnson, Regan, illus. (J). 2007. (ENG.). 135p. (gr. 2-7). pap. 8.95 *(978-0-9769417-2-9(4))* 2006. 144p. 13.95 *(978-0-9769417-1-2(6))* Blooming Tree Pr.

Hanton, Sophie. Numbers in the Jungle. 2009. (Mag-NUT-Tics! Ser.). (Illus.). (J). bds. 9.99 *(978-1-934650-75-9(5))* Just For Kids Pr., LLC.

Harris, Patricia. Do You Wonder Why?, 1 vol. 2017. (Jungle Fun Ser.). (ENG.). 24p. (gr. 1-1). pap. 9.25 *(978-1-5383-2132-4(7)*, 2fe061d7-7e26-437a-aaf1-1f379be68a3d, PowerKids Pr.) Rosen Publishing Group, Inc., The.

—Hide & Seek in the Jungle, 1 vol. 2017. (Jungle Fun Ser.). (ENG.). 24p. (gr. 1-1). pap. 9.25 *(978-1-5383-2136-2(X)*, 1178bf53-b2cd-4e61-9bdc-cf477dbd6858, PowerKids Pr.) Rosen Publishing Group, Inc., The.

Harrison, David L. & Yolen, Jane. Rum Pum Pum. Sarkar, Anjan, illus. 2020. 40p. (J). (gr. -1-2). 18.99 *(978-0-8234-4100-6(8))* Holiday Hse., Inc.

Harter, Debbie. Animal Boogie. 2008. (ENG., Illus.). 32p. (J). 16.99 *(978-1-84686-231-1(0))* Barefoot Bks., Inc.

Hartmann, Wendy. This Is the Chick. Rankin, Joan, illus. 2017. (ENG.). 32p. (J). (gr. -1-3). 17.95 *(978-1-56656-039-9(X)*, Crocodile Bks.) Interlink Publishing Group, Inc.

Hicks, Michael Christopher. Tales of Drake: The Tale of the Lost Dog. 2011. 40p. pap. 18.99 *(978-1-4634-1823-6(X))* AuthorHouse.

Holden, Pam. Fire in the Jungle, 1 vol. Hatam, Samer, illus. 2009. (Red Rocket Readers Ser.). (ENG.). 17p. (gr. 2-2). pap. *(978-1-877363-73-3(1))* Flying Start Bks.

I Can Swim, 6 Packs. (Sails Literacy Ser.). 16p. (gr. k-18). 27.00 *(978-0-7635-4399-0(3))* Rigby Education.

Jarkins, Sheila. The Adventures of Marco Flamingo in the Jungle. Jarkins, Sheila, illus. 2012. (Illus.). 32p. (J). 1.99 *(978-1-936299-31-7(3)*, Raven Tree Pr.) Delta Systems Company, Inc.

Jarocki, Martin. The Daily Zoo. 2013. 12p. pap. 12.68 *(978-1-4669-9683-0(8))* Trafford Publishing.

Johnson, Amy. Tales of the Forest. 2011. (Illus.). 64p. pap. 13.95 *(978-1-4670-1976-7(3))* AuthorHouse.

Johnson, Penny, illus. Here Comes Santa! 2016. (J). *(978-1-4351-6387-4(7))* Barnes & Noble, Inc.

Johnson, Sandra, adapted by. Shoobie, 1 vol. 2009. 15p. pap. 24.95 *(978-1-60813-705-3(8))* America Star Bks.

Jones, Vanessa. I Dreamed It Snowed in Afric. 2007. 40p. per. 14.95 *(978-1-4327-1535-9(6))* Outskirts Pr., Inc.

The Jungle: Individual Title Six-Packs. (Sails Literacy Ser.). 16p. (gr. k-18). 27.00 *(978-0-7635-4388-4(8))* Rigby Education.

Kipling, Rudyard. The Jungle Book. 2010. 318p. (gr. 3-7). pap. 30.75 *(978-1-142-79715-7(5))* Creative Media Partners, LLC.

—The Jungle Book. Detmold, Edward J. & Detmold, Maurice, illus. 2010. (Calla Editions Ser.). (ENG.). 192p. 30.00 *(978-1-60660-009-2(5)*, 600095) Dover Pubns., Inc.

—The Jungle Book. 2008. (Bring the Classics to Life Ser.). (ENG., Illus.). 72p. (gr. 1-12). pap., act. bk. ed. 10.95 *(978-1-55576-355-8(3)*, EDCTR-109B) EDCON Publishing Group.

—The Jungle Book. 2009. 122p. (gr. 3-7). pap. 19.99 *(978-1-4589-2084-3(4))* General Bks. LLC.

—The Jungle Book. 2013. (Vintage Children's Classics Ser.). (Illus.). 256p. (J). (gr. 4-7). pap. 10.99 *(978-0-09-957302-9(4))* Penguin Random Hse. GBR. Dist: Independent Pubs. Group.

—The Jungle Book. 2014. (Word Cloud Classics Ser.). (ENG., Illus.). 320p. pap. 14.99 *(978-1-62686-258-6(3)*, Canterbury Classics) Printers Row Publishing Group.

—The Jungle Book. 2011. (Oberon Plays for Young People Ser.). (ENG., Illus.). 64p. (gr. 2). pap. *(978-1-84943-010-4(1)*, 513144) Oberon Bks., Ltd.

—The Jungle Book. Kipling, John Lockwood, illus. 2015. (First Avenue Classics (tm) Ser.). (ENG.). 198p. (J). (gr. 3-8). E-Book 19.99 *(978-1-4677-5836-9(1)*, First Avenue Editions) Lerner Publishing Group.

—The Jungle Book: A Classic Story about Uniqueness. 2003. (Illus.). 32p. per. 3.95 *(978-0-9747133-1-1(7)*, Values to Live By Classic Stories) Thomas, Frederic Inc.

—Jungle Book: The Classic Edition. 2014. (ENG., Illus.). 64p. (J). (gr. -1). 19.99 *(978-1-60433-475-3(4))* Cider Mill Pr. Bk. Pubs., LLC.

—The Jungle Books. 2013. (ENG.). 384p. (gr. 12). mass mkt. 5.95 *(978-0-451-41918-7(9)*, Signet) Penguin Publishing Group.

—The Jungle Books. Nagai, Kaori, ed. 2013. 448p. (gr. 12). 11.00 *(978-0-14-119665-7(3)*, Penguin Classics) Penguin Publishing Group.

Krebs, Laurie. We're Roaming in the Rainforest. Wilson, Anne, illus. 2010. 40p. (J). (gr. -1-5). 16.99 *(978-1-84686-331-8(7))* Barefoot Bks., Inc.

Kroll, Steven. Jungle Bullies, 0 vols. Nguyen, Vincent, illus. 2013. (ENG.). 34p. (J). (gr. -1-2). pap. 7.99 *(978-0-7614-5620-9(1)*, 9780761456209, Two Lions) Amazon Publishing.

Laird, Elizabeth. Beautiful Bananas, 1 vol. Pichon, Liz, illus. 2013. (ENG.). 32p. (J). (gr. -1-3). pap. 7.95 *(978-1-56145-691-8(8))* Peachtree Publishing Co. Inc.

Lang, Suzanne. Grumpy Monkey Oh, No! Christmas. Lang, Max, illus. 2021. (Grumpy Monkey Ser.). (ENG.). 32p. (J). (gr. -1-2). 18.99 *(978-0-593-30609-3(0))* Random Hse. Children's Bks.

Lehrhaupt, Adam. Sloth Went. Shum, Benson, illus. 2020. (ENG.). 32p. (J). 17.99 *(978-1-5476-0245-2(7)*, 900207573, Bloomsbury Children's Bks.) Bloomsbury Publishing USA.

Levy, Didier. Jojo & the Food Fight! Dieterle, Nathalie, illus. 2018. (ENG.). 32p. (J). (gr. -1-2). 16.99 *(978-1-78285-409-8(6))*; pap. 9.99 *(978-1-78285-410-4(X))* Barefoot Bks., Inc.

—Jojo & the Food Fight! 2019. (ENG.). 32p. (J). (gr. k-1). 17.96 *(978-1-64310-946-6(4))* Penworthy Co., LLC, The.

Levy, Janey. Jenny in the Jungle, 1 vol. 2006. (Neighborhood Readers Ser.). (ENG.). 8p. (gr. k-1). pap. 5.15 *(978-1-4042-5702-3(0)*, f10f1808-ba27-4c63-8c90-edb3be735942, Rosen Classroom) Rosen Publishing Group, Inc., The.

Lewis, J. Patrick. Jungle Surprises, Bk. 2. Denise, Christopher, illus. 2011. (I AM a READER!: Tugg & Teeny Ser.). (ENG.). 40p. (J). (gr. 2-3). pap. 3.99 *(978-1-58536-686-6(2)*, 202374); lib. bdg. 9.95 *(978-1-58536-515-9(7)*, 202205) Sleeping Bear Pr.

—That's What Friends Are For. Denise, Christopher, illus. 2012. (I AM a READER!: Tugg & Teeny Ser.). (ENG.). 40p. (J). (gr. 2-3). pap. 3.99 *(978-1-58536-687-3(0)*, 202376); lib. bdg. 9.95 *(978-1-58536-516-6(5)*, 202206) Sleeping Bear Pr.

Lomsen, Boy. El Bosque en Peligro. (SPA.). 141p. (J). (gr. 3-5). *(978-84-279-3451-1(3)*, NG0993) Noguer y Caralt Editores, S. A. ESP. Dist: Lectorum Pubns., Inc.

Madden, Gloria. Grandmothers Bedtime Stories. 2008. 68p. (gr. -1-7). pap. 10.49 *(978-1-4343-9201-5(5))* AuthorHouse.

Maelor, Gwawr, et al. Tân Yn y Jyngl. 2005. (WEL., Illus.). 16p. pap. *(978-1-85644-842-0(8))* CAA.

McDonnell, Flora. Splash! 2004. (Illus.). (J). 25p. *(978-1-85269-489-0(0))*; 25p. *(978-1-85269-488-3(2))*; (ENG & URD., 28p. pap. *(978-1-85269-492-0(0))*; (ENG & BEN., 28p. pap. *(978-1-85269-486-9(6))* Mantra Lingua.

McElligott, Matthew. The Lion's Share. McElligott, Matthew, illus. (ENG., Illus.). (J). (gr. k-8). 2012. 40p. pap. 8.99 *(978-0-8027-2360-4(8)*, 900078463) 2009. 32p. 17.99 *(978-0-8027-9768-1(7)*, 900051430) Bloomsbury Publishing USA. (Bloomsbury USA Childrens).

McKee, David. Elmer's Walk. McKee, David, illus. 2018. (Elmer Ser.). (ENG., Illus.). 32p. (J). (gr. -1-3). 17.99 *(978-1-5415-3554-1(5)*, 5065be78-503a-4ed9-b0c9-1c9e170daf43) Lerner Publishing Group.

Milgrim, David. Ride, Otto, Ride! Ready-To-Read Pre-Level 1. Milgrim, David, illus. 2016. (Adventures of Otto Ser.). (ENG., Illus.). 32p. (J). (gr. -1-k). pap. 4.99 *(978-1-4814-6793-3(X)*, Simon Spotlight) Simon Spotlight.

Moore, Judith. Jessica the Furry Baroo. Brown, Karen, illus. 2007. 44p. per. 14.95 *(978-1-59858-364-9(6))* Dog Ear Publishing, LLC.

Morris, Richard T. Fear the Bunny. Burris, Priscilla, illus. 2019. (ENG.). 40p. (J). (gr. -1-3). 17.99 *(978-1-4814-7800-7(1))* Simon & Schuster Children's Publishing.

Murray, Andrew. The Very Sleepy Sloth. Tickle, Jack, tr. Tickle, Jack, illus. 2003. 32p. (J). tchr. ed. 15.95 *(978-1-58925-033-8(8))* Tiger Tales.

Nille, Peggy, illus. Hidden in the Jungle: A Search & Find Book. 2018. (ENG.). 26p. (J). 12.99 *(978-1-4413-2653-9(7)*, a8e10753-1eec-46d4-9f64-c8a19eef4b3b) Peter Pauper Pr. Inc.

Okeke, Paulicap Okechukwu. Biribamba the Lonely Elephant. 2011. (Illus.). 28p. pap. 13.50 *(978-1-4634-2992-8(4))* AuthorHouse.

Omari Jr. The Jungle Save. 2009. 20p. pap. 13.99 *(978-1-4490-4205-9(8))* AuthorHouse.

Osborne, Mary Pope. Tigers at Twilight. unabr. ed. 2004. (Magic Tree House Ser.: No. 19). 72p. (J). (gr. k-3). pap. 17.00 incl. audio *(978-0-8072-0928-8(7)*, S FTR 251 SP, Listening Library) Random Hse. Audio Publishing Group.

Osborne, Mary Pope, et al. Tigres Al Anochecer. Murdocca, Sal, illus. 2008. (Casa del Arbol Ser.: 19).Tr. of Tigers at Twilight. (SPA.). (J). (gr. 2-4). pap. 8.99 *(978-1-933032-49-8(9))* Lectorum Pubns., Inc.

Paley-Phillips, Giles. Superchimp. Newson, Karl, illus. 2016. (J). *(978-1-4351-6574-8(8))* Barnes & Noble, Inc.

Parragon Staff. Lion King. 2010. (Disney Diecut Classics). (Illus.). 72p. (J). (gr. -1-1). *(978-1-4075-8936-7(9))* Parragon, Inc.

Phinn, Gervase. Who Am I? Ross, Tony, illus. 2012. (ENG.). 32p. (J). (gr. -1-3). 16.95 *(978-0-7613-8996-5(2)*, 63b6fb3b-21dd-4f17-b375-3472edbb76ab) Lerner Publishing Group.

Phumiruk, Dow. Mela & the Elephant. Chen, Ziyue, illus. 2018. (ENG.). 32p. (J). (gr. k-3). 18.99 *(978-1-58536-998-0(5)*, 204407) Sleeping Bear Pr.

PLOURDE, Weidner. Wake up Baby Bear. 2018. (Illus.). 40p. (J). (gr. -1-12). 17.95 *(978-1-60893-971-8(5))* Down East Bks.

Poitier, Anton. Flippy Floppy Jungle Animals. Touliatou, Sophia, illus. 2013. 16p. (J). 12.99 *(978-1-61067-169-9(4))* Kane Miller.

Poulin, Andrée. Monkey in the Mud, 1 vol. Eudes-Pascal, Élisabeth, illus. 2009. (Rainy Day Readers Ser.). (ENG.). 32p. (J). (gr. 1-2). 27.27 *(978-1-60754-370-1(2)*, 5131cf14-a2fd-4f18-8757-ace21e9c9915); pap. 11.55 *(978-1-60754-371-8(0)*, a3c27341-a9ae-467b-82ea-0094df091457) Rosen Publishing Group, Inc., The. (Windmill Bks.).

Pritchett, Dylan. The First Music. Banks, Erin, illus. 2006. (ENG.). 32p. (J). (gr. -1-3). 16.95 *(978-0-87483-776-6(6))* August Hse. Pubs., Inc.

Reasoner, Charles. Jungle. Devaney, Adam, illus. 2009. (Learning Tab Board Bks.). 10p. (J). (gr. -1-k). bds. 9.99 *(978-1-934650-79-0(X))* Just For Kids Pr., LLC.

—Jungle Animals. Doherty, Paula, illus. 2009. (Little Big Flap Bks.). 10p. (J). (gr. -1-k). 9.99 *(978-1-934650-22-6(6))* Just For Kids Pr., LLC.

—Jungle Babies. Devaney, Adam & Doherty, Paula, illus. 2009. (Baby Animal Board Bks.). 12p. (J). (gr. -1-k). bds. 7.99 *(978-1-934650-50-9(1))* Just For Kids Pr., LLC.

Redbank, Tennant. The Saggy Baggy Elephant. Hathi, Garva, illus. 2016. (Step into Reading Ser.). 32p. (J). (gr. -1-1). pap. 4.99 *(978-0-553-53588-4(9)*, Random Hse. Bks. for Young Readers) Random Hse. Children's Bks.

Redlich, Ben. Who Flung Dung? 2013. (ENG., Illus.). 28p. (J). (gr. -1-k). 16.95 *(978-1-62087-543-8(8)*, 620543, Sky Pony Pr.) Skyhorse Publishing Co., Inc.

Reece, William James. The Great Hippo Migration. 2007. 92p. per. 19.95 *(978-1-4241-9770-5(8))* America Star Bks.

Rigby Education Staff. The Jungle Sun. (Sails Literacy Ser.). (Illus.). 16p. (gr. 2-3). 27.00 *(978-0-7635-9941-6(7)*, 699417C99) Rigby Education.

Rippin, Sally. Billie's Wild Jungle Adventure. Coburn, Alisa, illus. 2017. (ENG.). 24p. (J). 10.99 *(978-1-61067-553-6(3))* Kane Miller.

Roddie, Shen. The Gossipy Parrot. Terry, Michael, tr. Terry, Michael, illus. 2004. 32p. (J). (gr. k-2). 20.00 *(978-0-7475-6079-1(X))* Bloomsbury Publishing Plc GBR. Dist: Independent Pubs. Group.

Rose, Gerald. Horrible Melena. (SPA.). (J). 8.95 *(978-958-04-7343-5(9))* Norma S.A. COL. Dist: Distribuidora Norma, Inc.

Sams II, Carl R. & Stoick, Jean, photos by. When Snowflakes Fall. 2009. (ENG., Illus.). 14p. bds. 7.95 *(978-0-9770108-9-9(9))* Sams, II, Carl R. Photography, Inc.

Sattler, Jennifer. Frankie the Blankie. 2016. (ENG., Illus.). 32p. (J). 16.99 *(978-1-61963-675-0(1)*, 900145316, Bloomsbury USA Childrens) Bloomsbury Publishing USA.

Simon, Kristen Koerner. Jack's Knack: Book Three of the Blue Forest Series: Book Three of the Blue Forest Series. 2010. (Illus.). 32p. (J). 12.99 *(978-1-60706-190-8(2))* Image Comics.

Squillace, Elisa, illus. Down in the Jungle. (Classic Books with Holes Big Book Ser.). (J). (gr. -1-3). 2006. 16p. spiral bd. *(978-1-84643-009-1(7))* 2005. 14p. spiral bd. *(978-1-904550-61-7(4))* Child's Play International Ltd.

Talbott, Hudson. Safari Journal. Talbott, Hudson, illus. 2003. (ENG., Illus.). 64p. (J). (gr. 3-7). 18.00 *(978-0-15-216393-8(X)*, 1200873, Clarion Bks.) HarperCollins Pubs.

Tashiro, Chisato. Chameleon's Colors. Martens, Marianne, tr. 2007. (Michael Neugebauer Books (Paperback) Ser.). (ENG., Illus.). 32p. (J). (gr. -1-3). pap. 7.95 *(978-0-7358-2111-8(9))* North-South Bks., Inc.

Tatsuyama, Sayuri. Happy Happy Clover, Vol. 4. Tatsuyama, Sayuri, illus. 2010. (Happy Happy Clover Ser.: 4). (ENG., Illus.). 192p. (J). pap. 7.99 *(978-1-4215-2735-2(9))* Viz Media.

Taylor, Thomas. The Loudest Roar. 2003. (Illus.). (J). pap. *(978-0-439-50131-6(8)*, Levine, Arthur A. Bks.) Scholastic, Inc.

Thorne, Jenny, illus. The Jungle Book. 2016. 24p. (J). (gr. -1-12). pap. 7.99 *(978-1-86147-814-6(3)*, Armadillo) Anness Publishing GBR. Dist: National Bk. Network.

Ticktock Media, Ltd. Staff. Jungle. 2009. (Animal Fun Touch & Feel Ser.). (ENG.). 10p. (J). (gr. -1-k). bds. 4.95 *(978-1-84696-828-0(3)*, TickTock Books) Octopus Publishing Group GBR. Dist: Independent Pubs. Group.

Top That Publishing Staff, ed. Jungle Numbers. Parry, Jo, illus. 2007. (Magnetic - Numbers Ser.). 10p. (J). (gr. -1). bds. *(978-1-84666-163-1(3)*, Tide Mill Pr.) Top That! Publishing PLC.

Top That! Jungle Numbers (large Version) Parry, Jo, illus. 2007. 10p. (J). (gr. -1). *(978-1-84666-552-3(3)*, Tide Mill Pr.) Top That! Publishing PLC.

Vetsch, Rita Kaye. The Many Colors of Friendship. 2009. 40p. pap. 16.50 *(978-1-60693-756-3(1)*, Eloquent Bks.) Strategic Book Publishing & Rights Agency (SBPRA).

Walter-Sereg, D. Bonnie Tracks a Jungle Animal. 2012. 24p. 24.95 *(978-1-4626-5857-2(1))* America Star Bks.

Ward, Jennifer. The Busy Tree, 0 vols. Falkenstern, Lisa, illus. 2012. (ENG.). 32p. (J). (gr. -1-2). 17.99 *(978-0-7614-5550-9(7)*, 9780761455509, Two Lions) Amazon Publishing.

Watt, Fiona. Baby's Very First Noisy Book Jungle. 2017. (Picture Bks.). (ENG.). 10p. (J). 15.99 *(978-0-7945-3986-3(6)*, Usborne) EDC Publishing.

Weston Woods Staff, creator. Fletcher & the Snowflake Christmas. 2011. 29.95 *(978-0-545-42619-0(7))* Weston Woods Studios, Inc.

Whybrow, Ian. Say Hello to the Jungle Animals! Eaves, Edward, illus. 2017. (J). *(978-1-4351-6511-3(X))* Barnes & Noble, Inc.

The Wildlife Adventures of Mugwa & Washtucna. 2008. (Illus.). 54p. (J). 19.95 *(978-0-9799493-0-2(0))* Carol Kalhagen-Tamanaha.

Willis, Jeanne. Elephants Can't Jump! Reynolds, Adrian, illus. 2015. (ENG.). 32p. (J). (gr. -1-3). 16.95 *(978-1-4677-6316-5(0)*, d46d17e7-ae4f-4e76-a66b-2f1a9fe3b95a); E-Book 27.99 *(978-1-4677-6320-2(9))* Lerner Publishing Group.

—Hippospotamus. Ross, Tony, illus. 2012. (Andersen Press Picture Bks). (ENG.). 32p. (J). (gr. -1-3). 16.95 *(978-1-4677-0316-1(8))* Lerner Publishing Group.

—El Nino Que Perdio el Ombligo. Ross, Tony, illus. (SPA.). (J). 8.95 *(978-958-04-5632-2(1))* Norma S.A. COL. Dist: Lectorum Pubns., Inc., Distribuidora Norma, Inc.

Wilson, Karma. Bear's New Friend. Chapman, Jane, illus. 2009. (Bear Bks.). (ENG.). 34p. (J). (gr. -1-2). bds. 7.99 *(978-1-4169-5438-5(4)*, Little Simon) Little Simon.

—Hilda Must Be Dancing. Watts, Suzanne, illus. 2004. (ENG.). 32p. (J). (gr. -1-3). 19.99 *(978-0-689-84788-2(2)*, McElderry, Margaret K. Bks.) McElderry, Margaret K. Bks.

—Hilda Must Be Dancing. Watts, Suzanne, illus. 2008. (ENG.). 32p. (J). (gr. -1-3). 7.99 *(978-1-4169-5083-7(4))* Simon & Schuster, Inc.

Witte, Anna. El Loro Tico Tango. Witte, Anna, illus. 2019. (SPA., Illus.). 24p. (J). (gr. -1-2). pap. 9.99 *(978-1-78285-423-4(1))* Barefoot Bks., Inc.

—The Parrot Tico Tango. Witte, Anna, illus. 2019. (ENG., Illus.). 24p. (J). (gr. -1-2). pap. 9.99 *(978-1-78285-422-7(3))* Barefoot Bks., Inc.

Woodman, Melissa. Lessons with Our Jungle Friends. 2011. 32p. pap. 24.95 *(978-1-4626-1902-3(9))* America Star Bks.

Wright, Maureen. Earth Day, Birthday!, 0 vols. Kim, Violet, illus. 2012. (ENG.). 32p. (J). (gr. -1-2). 17.99 *(978-0-7614-6109-8(4)*, 9780761461098, Two Lions) Amazon Publishing.

Wyss, Tyan. African Dream. Immelman, Sarita, illus. 2006. 48p. (J). pap. 15.95 *(978-1-58939-915-0(3))* Virtualbookworm.com Publishing, Inc.

Zadrozny, Alicia & Church, Caroline Jayne. The Wild Little Jungle: A Mix-and-Match Flap Book. 2008. (ENG.). 10p. (J). bds. 12.99 *(978-0-7944-1605-8(5))* Reader's Digest Assn., Inc., The.

Ziefert, Harriet. Monkey's Noisy Jungle. Newton, Jill, illus. 2007. bds. 7.95 *(978-1-59354-598-7(3))* Blue Apple Bks.

JUNGLES

Alderton, David. Jungle Animals Around the World. 2014. (Animals Around the World Ser.). (ENG., Illus.). 32p. (J). (gr. 2-5). 31.35 *(978-1-62588-194-6(0)*, 19259, Smart Apple Media) Black Rabbit Bks.

AZ Books Staff. Living Book of the Jungle. Gasteva, Julia, ed. 2012. (Our Amazing World Ser.). (ENG.). 12p. (J). (gr. 1-3). bds. 19.95 *(978-1-61889-024-5(7))* AZ Bks. LLC.

Borten, Helen, illus. The Jungle. 2018. (ENG.). 40p. (J). (gr. -1-4). 16.95 *(978-1-59270-230-5(9))* Enchanted Lion Bks., LLC.

Bradley, Timothy J. Terror in the Tropics, 1 vol. 2nd rev. ed. 2013. (TIME for KIDS(r): Informational Text Ser.). (ENG., Illus.). 64p. (J). (gr. 4-8). pap. 14.99 *(978-1-4333-4898-3(5))* Teacher Created Materials, Inc.

DK. Ultimate Sticker Book: Jungle: More Than 250 Reusable Stickers. 2017. (Ultimate Sticker Book Ser.). (ENG.). 32p. (J). (gr. k-2). pap. 6.99 *(978-1-4654-5694-6(5)*, DK Children) Dorling Kindersley Publishing, Inc.

Doane, Beth. From the Jungle: Stories & Original Art from Children Living in Rainforests. 2012. 40p. pap. 15.95 *(978-1-4525-6090-8(0))* Balboa Pr.

Doeden, Matt. Can You Survive the Jungle? An Interactive Survival Adventure. 2011. (You Choose: Survival Ser.). (ENG.). 112p. (J). (gr. 3-4). pap. 41.70 *(978-1-4296-7350-1(8)*, 16840, Capstone Pr.) Capstone.

Doeden, Matt & Penn, Jim. Can You Survive the Jungle? An Interactive Survival Adventure, 1 vol. 2011. (You Choose: Survival Ser.). (ENG., Illus.). 112p. (J). (gr. 3-7). lib. bdg. 32.65 *(978-1-4296-6588-9(2)*, 115711); pap. 6.95 *(978-1-4296-7349-5(4)*, 116886) Capstone. (Capstone Pr.).

Ferri, Francesca, illus. Jungle: A Soft Book & Mirror for Baby! 2016. 6p. (J). (gr. -1 — 1). 10.99 *(978-1-4380-7759-8(9))* Sourcebooks, Inc.

Jungle Fun. 2003. 32p. 12.98 *(978-1-4054-2004-4(9))* Parragon, Inc.

Levete, Sarah. Jungle Crash! 2011. (ENG.). 24p. (J). pap. *(978-0-7787-7871-4(1))*; (gr. 3-6). *(978-0-7787-7849-3(5))* Crabtree Publishing Co.

MacKenzie, Catherine. Helen Roseveare: What's in the Parcel? rev. ed. 2012. (Little Lights Ser.). (ENG.). 24p. (J). 7.99 *(978-1-84550-383-3(X)*, a968cdf5-b466-4c2a-886f-66cec838ae8d) Christian Focus Pubns. GBR. Dist: Baker & Taylor Publisher Services (BTPS).

Markovics, Joyce L. Patterns in the Jungle. 2014. (Math Blast!: Seeing Patterns All Around Ser.). (ENG.). 32p. (J). (gr. -1-3). lib. bdg. 28.50 *(978-1-62724-338-4(0))* Bearport Publishing Co., Inc.

Neal, Tony, illus. Seek & Peek Jungle: A Lift the Flap Pop-Up Book about Colors! 2018. (ENG.). 10p. (J). (gr. -1 — 1). 9.99 *(978-1-4380-5046-1(1))* Sourcebooks, Inc.

Peek Inside the Jungle. 2017. (Peek Inside BDs Ser.). (ENG.). (J). bds. 11.99 *(978-0-7945-3920-7(3)*, Usborne) EDC Publishing.

Rice, William B. Survival! Jungle, 1 vol. 2nd rev. ed. 2012. (TIME for KIDS(r): Informational Text Ser.). (ENG., Illus.). 48p. (gr. 4-5). pap. 13.99 *(978-1-4333-4820-4(9))* Teacher Created Materials, Inc.

Robinson, Fay. In the Jungle. Lopez, Paul, illus. 2004. (Treasure Tree Ser.). 32p. (J). *(978-0-7166-1604-7(1))* World Bk., Inc.

Vetere, Lori. Jungle Tribes. 2018. (J). *(978-1-4222-4092-2(4))* Mason Crest.

West, David. Ten of the Best Adventures in the Jungle. 2015. (Ten of the Best: Stories of Exploration & Adventure Ser.).

(ENG., Illus.). 24p. (J). (gr. 3-4). *(978-0-7787-1837-6(9))* Crabtree Publishing Co.

JUNGLES—FICTION

Achebe, Chinua. How the Leopard Got His Claws. GrandPre, Mary, illus. 2011. (ENG.). 32p. (J). (gr. 2-5). 16.99 *(978-0-7636-4805-3(1))* Candlewick Pr.

Adams, Pam. Tiger. 2005. (ENG., Illus.). 12p. (J). (gr. -1-k). bds. *(978-1-904550-28-0(2))* Child's Play International Ltd.

Alcott, Louisa. The Louisa Alcott Reader: A Supplementar. 2006. pap. *(978-1-4065-0590-0(0))* Dodo Pr.

Aristizabal, Nora. La Selva Maravillosa/the Wonderful Jungle. Reyes, Maria Margarita, illus. 2005. (Bilingual Collection). (SPA.). 31p. (J). *(978-958-30-1966-1(6))* Panamericana Editorial.

Ballantyne, R. M. Gorilla Hunters A Tale of the Wilds of A. 2006. pap. 36.95 *(978-1-4286-5952-0(8))* Kessinger Publishing, LLC.

Ballaz, Jesús, adapted by. The Jungle Book, 1 vol. 2007. (Illustrated Classics Ser.). (ENG., Illus.). 40p. (J). (gr. 3-5). lib. bdg. 28.67 *(978-0-8368-7663-5(6)*, af4794d9-6ebf-4715-b092-a67a286d03e8, Gareth Stevens Learning Library) Stevens, Gareth Publishing LLLP.

Barroux. Where's the Elephant? Barroux, illus. 2016. (ENG., Illus.). 32p. (J). (gr. -1-2). 14.99 *(978-0-7636-8110-4(5))* Candlewick Pr.

Bell-Jackson, Sylvia. Bree's Bubble Gum Adventures: The Pajamas from the Bahamas. 2012. 36p. pap. 13.97 *(978-1-61204-299-2(6)*, Strategic Bk. Publishing) Strategic Book Publishing & Rights Agency (SBPRA).

Bell, Michele Ashman. Rescue: A Jungle Adventure. 2006. 246p. (J). pap. *(978-1-59811-093-7(4))* Covenant Communications.

Beresford, Shane. In the Jungle. 2008. 36p. 19.95 *(978-1-4357-0351-3(0))* Lulu Pr., Inc.

Bhandari, D. Growing Wings: Parrot's Day Out. 2010. 28p. 17.99 *(978-1-4520-1102-8(8))* AuthorHouse.

Bollinger/Papp, illus. King Kong: Meet Kong & Ann. 2005. 32p. (J). lib. bdg. 13.85 *(978-1-4242-0615-5(4))* Fitzgerald Bks.

Bramucci, Stephen. The Danger Gang & the Pirates of Borneo! Chung, Arree, illus. 2017. (ENG.). 384p. (J). 16.99 *(978-1-61963-692-7(1)*, 900145716, Bloomsbury USA Childrens) Bloomsbury Publishing USA.

Broutin, Christian & Delafosse, Claude. In the Jungle. Broutin, Christian, illus. 2013. (ENG., Illus.). 36p. (J). (gr. -1-k). spiral bd. 19.99 *(978-1-85103-417-8(X))* Moonlight Publishing, Ltd. GBR. Dist: Independent Pubs. Group.

Brown, Bruce. Mwumba. O'Reilly, Sean Patrick, ed. 2011. (Illus.). 48p. (J). pap. 7.95 *(978-1-897548-03-5(6))* Arcana Studio, Inc.

Bush, John & Geraghty, Paul. The Bungle in the Jungle. (Illus.). 32p. (J). 17.95 *(978-0-09-174056-6(8))* Penguin Random Hse. GBR. Dist: Trafalgar Square Publishing.

Carter, Jani R. Long Ago in the African Jungle. 2008. 108p. pap. 10.99 *(978-1-4389-1233-2(1))* AuthorHouse.

Chapman, Bunny. Shanu the Watcher. 2013. 138p. pap. 9.99 *(978-0-9855008-4-9(0))* Champlain Avenue Bks., Inc.

Cline, Renee. Kawndra the Tiger. 2009. 28p. pap. 15.49 *(978-1-4389-6484-3(6))* AuthorHouse.

Cole, Bob. Power Reading: Classics/Jungle Book. Connor, Robin, illus. 2004. 94p. (J). (gr. 4-18). vinyl bd. 39.95 *(978-1-883186-61-6(7)*, PPCL2) National Reading Styles Institute, Inc.

—Power Reading: Comic Book/Jungle Book. Connor, Robin, illus. 2005. 62p. (J). (gr. 3-18). vinyl bd. 39.95 *(978-1-883186-74-6(9)*, PPCLC2) National Reading Styles Institute, Inc.

Condon, Bill. How to Survive in the Jungle by the Person Who Knows, 1 vol. rev. ed. 2013. (Literary Text Ser.). (ENG., Illus.). 28p. (J). (gr. 2-3). pap. 10.99 *(978-1-4333-5599-8(X))*; lib. bdg. 19.96 *(978-1-4807-1721-3(5))* Teacher Created Materials, Inc.

Costello, Judi. Gertrude & the Creature. Bouthyette, Valerie, illus. 2008. 28p. pap. 24.95 *(978-1-60672-737-9(0))* America Star Bks.

Cyrus, Kurt. Invisible Lizard. Atkins, Andy, illus. 2017. (ENG.). 32p. (J). (gr. k-2). 16.99 *(978-1-58536-378-0(2)*, 204320) Sleeping Bear Pr.

Demois, Agathe & Godeau, Vincent. The Great Journey. 2016. (ENG., Illus.). 32p. (J). (gr. k-2). 19.95 *(978-1-84976-375-2(5)*, 1662201) Tate Publishing, Ltd. GBR. Dist: Abrams, Inc.

Drake, Christina M. Milo the Monkey. 2013. 88p. *(978-1-4602-2323-9(3))* FriesenPress.

Dubuvoy, Silvia, et al. Murmullos de la Selva. Tsuda, Efrain Rodriguez, illus. 2004. (Montana Encantada Ser.). (SPA.). 60p. (J). (gr. 3-5). pap. 9.99 *(978-84-241-8660-9(5))* Everest Editora ESP. Dist: Lectorum Pubns., Inc.

Dufresne, Michèle. The Big Game: Little Dinosaur Chapter Books. 2007. (Little Dinosaur Chapter Ser.). (J). per. 7.67 *(978-1-932570-68-7(3))* Pioneer Valley Bks.

Dumortier, Marjorie, illus. Zoe & Her Zany Animals. 2006. (ENG.). 32p. (J). (gr. -1-3). 14.99 *(978-0-7145-3306-3(8))* Boyars, Marion Pubs., Ltd. GBR. Dist: Consortium Bk. Sales & Distribution.

Eldridge, VonDa. Wiggles the Worm, 1 vol. 2010. 26p. pap. 24.95 *(978-1-4489-2547-6(9))* PublishAmerica, Inc.

Elliott, David. Evangeline Mudd & the Golden-Haired Apes of the Ikkinasti Jungle. Wesson, Andrea, illus. 2004. 208p. pap. *(978-0-7445-8379-3(9))* Walker Bks., Ltd.

Evans, Michelle D. I Don't Belong in the Jungle. 2011. 20p. pap. 24.95 *(978-1-4626-1382-3(9))* America Star Bks.

Flyte, Min. Would You Dare... ? A Lift-The-flap Adventure. Hunt, Matt, illus. 2017. (ENG.). 24p. (J). (gr. -1-2). 14.99 *(978-0-7636-9619-1(6))* Candlewick Pr.

Foreman, Michael. Can't Catch Me! 2013. (Silver Tales Ser.). (ENG., Illus.). 28p. (J). (gr. -1-1). pap. *(978-1-74352-442-8(0))* Hinkler Bks. Pty, Ltd.

Fraser, Jess, illus. Jungle Jingles. 2007. (J). cd-rom 9.99 *(978-0-9795190-8-6(X))* Color & Learn.

Freedman, Claire. Aliens Love Dinopants. Cort, Ben, illus. 2016. (Underpants Bks.). (ENG.). 32p. (J). (gr. -1-2). 17.99 *(978-1-4814-6736-0(0)*, Aladdin) Simon & Schuster Children's Publishing.

Freer, Ida. Panama Girl. 2011. 116p. (gr. 4-6). 20.95 *(978-1-4620-3081-1(5))*; pap. 10.95 *(978-1-4620-3079-8(3))* iUniverse, Inc.

Gilchrist, J. Into the Land of Nede. 2010. 108p. (gr. 4-6). 20.95 *(978-1-4502-5433-5(0))*; pap. 10.95 *(978-1-4502-5432-8(2))* iUniverse, Inc.

Gollub, Matthew. Jazz Fly 2: The Jungle Pachanga. 2010. (Jazz Fly Ser.). (ENG., Illus.). 32p. (J). (gr. k-2). 18.95 *(978-1-889910-44-4(9))* Tortuga Pr.

—Jazz Fly 2: The Jungle Pachanga. Hanke, Karen, illus. 2010. (J). *(978-1-889910-45-1(7))* Tortuga Pr.

Gondek, Heather. Who's in the Jungle? Lift-the-Flap 'n' Learn. Gilvan-Cartwright, Chris, illus. 2005. (Fun with Animals Ser.). 10p. (J). 9.95 *(978-1-58117-075-7(0)*, Intervisual/Piggy Toes) Bendon, Inc.

Grimm, Jacob & Grimm, Wilhelm K. Hut in the Forest, 20 vols. Lawson, Polly, tr. Stietencron, Bettina, illus. 2007. (Grimm's Fairy Tales Ser.). (ENG.). 28p. (J). *(978-0-86315-615-1(0))* Floris Bks.

Grylls, Bear. The Jungle Challenge. McCann, Emma, illus. 2017. 117p. (J). *(978-1-61067-768-4(4))* Kane Miller.

Hapka, Catherine, pseud. One Big Blue Family. 2014. (I Can Read! Level 2 Ser.). (J). lib. bdg. 13.55 *(978-0-606-35063-1(2))* Turtleback.

—Vacation in the Wild. 2014. (I Can Read! Level 2 Ser.). (J). lib. bdg. 13.55 *(978-0-606-35064-8(0))* Turtleback.

Hapka, Cathy, pseud. Jungle Adventure. 2014. (LEGO Friends Chapter Bks.: 6). lib. bdg. 14.75 *(978-0-606-36363-1(7))* Turtleback.

Hart, Teresa. The Ant & the Lost Spider, 1 vol. 2009. 76p. pap. 19.95 *(978-1-60749-296-2(2))* America Star Bks.

Harter, Debbie. The Animal Boogie. Harter, Debbie, illus. (Illus.). 32p. pap. 6.99 *(978-1-84148-996-4(4))* Barefoot Bks., Inc.

—The Animal Boogie. 2005. (ENG., Illus.). 32p. (J). (gr. -1-2). 9.99 *(978-1-905236-22-0(0))* Barefoot Bks., Inc.

—The Animal Boogie. Harter, Debbie, illus. 2005. (ENG., Illus.). 32p. (J). (gr. -1-2). 6.99 *(978-1-905236-60-2(3))* Barefoot Bks., Inc.

—De Paseo Por la Selva. Ugalde, Raquel, tr. Harter, Debbie, illus. 2003. (SPA., Illus.). 32p. (J). pap. 6.99 *(978-1-84148-995-7(6))* Barefoot Bks., Inc.

Hayes, Celeste. Cacao & the Jaded Orb: A Sphinx & Trevi Adventure. 2011. (Illus.). 62p. (J). pap. 22.95 *(978-0-9785695-2-5(0))* Adam's Creations Publishing, LLC.

Hoppey, Tim. Jungle Scout: A Vietnam War Story, 1 vol. Espinoza, Ramon, illus. 2008. (Historical Fiction Ser.). (ENG.). 56p. (J). (gr. 3-6). pap. 6.25 *(978-1-4342-0846-0(X)*, 95207, Stone Arch Bks.) Capstone.

Illek, Nuala. The Chinese Sausage Dog, the Panicky Porcupine & Mrs.Shoo an Animal Tale of Friendship in Chin. 2009. 50p. pap. 9.99 *(978-1-60860-781-5(X)*, Eloquent Bks.) Strategic Book Publishing & Rights Agency (SBPRA).

Jenisch, Betty. Rennie. 2007. 9.00 *(978-0-8059-8947-2(1))* Dorrance Publishing Co., Inc.

Johnson, Terry Lynn. Lost! Orban, Jani, illus. 2018. (Survivor Diaries). (ENG.). 112p. (J). (gr. 1-5). 9.99 *(978-0-544-97118-9(3)*, 1662530); pap. 6.99 *(978-1-328-51907-8(4)*, 1720643) HarperCollins Pubs. (Clarion Bks.).

—Lost! 2018. (Survivor Diaries). lib. bdg. 16.00 *(978-0-606-41210-0(7))* Turtleback.

Jones, Allan Frewin. Legend of the Anaconda King. 2006. 186p. (J). pap. *(978-0-439-85670-6(1))* Scholastic, Inc.

Kadakia, Sameep. Colors of the Jungle. 2007. (ENG.). 24p. pap. 12.90 *(978-1-4343-4334-5(0))* AuthorHouse.

Kayler, Ralph. The Tea Party in the Tree Tops. 2009. 48p. pap. 19.49 *(978-1-4389-8000-3(0))* AuthorHouse.

Kehret, Peg. Secret Journey. 2008. (ENG.). 144p. (J). (gr. 3-7). pap. 8.99 *(978-1-4169-9112-0(3)*, Simon & Schuster/Paula Wiseman Bks.) Simon & Schuster/Paula Wiseman Bks.

Kendrick, Robert. Treasure Quest: Journey to the Jungle. 2004. (ENG.). 46p. 24.95 *(978-1-4137-1467-8(6))* PublishAmerica, Inc.

Kipling, Rudyard. The Jungle Book, 1 vol. Wolek, Guy, illus. 2011. (Calico Illustrated Classics Ser.: No. 4). (ENG.). 112p. (J). (gr. 2-5). 38.50 *(978-1-61641-616-4(5)*, 4047, Calico Chapter Bks.) ABDO Publishing Co.

—The Jungle Book. 2010. 318p. (gr. 3-7). pap. 30.75 *(978-1-142-79715-7(5))* Creative Media Partners, LLC.

—The Jungle Book. 2008. (Bring the Classics to Life Ser.). (ENG., Illus.). 72p. (gr. 1-12). pap., act. bk. ed. 10.95 *(978-1-55576-355-8(3)*, EDCTR-109B) EDCON Publishing Group.

—The Jungle Book. 2009. 122p. (gr. 3-7). pap. 19.99 *(978-1-4589-2084-3(4))* General Bks. LLC.

—The Jungle Book. 2013. (Vintage Children's Classics Ser.). (Illus.). 256p. (J). (gr. 4-7). pap. 10.99 *(978-0-09-957302-9(4))* Penguin Random Hse. GBR. Dist: Independent Pubs. Group.

—The Jungle Book. 2014. (Word Cloud Classics Ser.). (ENG., Illus.). 320p. pap. 14.99 *(978-1-62686-258-6(3)*, Canterbury Classics) Printers Row Publishing Group.

—The Jungle Books. 2004. (Barnes & Noble Classics Ser.). (ENG., Illus.). 432p. pap. 7.95 *(978-1-59308-109-6(X))* Barnes & Noble, Inc.

—The Jungle Books. 2013. (ENG.). 384p. (gr. 12). mass mkt. 5.95 *(978-0-451-41918-7(9)*, Signet) Penguin Publishing Group.

—Rikki-Tikki-Tavi & Toomai of the Elephants. 2008. (Unabridged Classics (in Audio) Ser.). (J). pap. 36.00 incl. audio compact disk *(978-1-58472-431-5(5)*, In Audio) Sound Room Pubs., Inc.

Kirk, Trish. I Think There's a Bear Out There. 2009. 36p. pap. 16.99 *(978-1-4389-6097-5(2))* AuthorHouse.

Landolf, Diane Wright. The Jungle Book. Rowe, John, illus. 2008. (Stepping Stone Book(TM) Ser.). (ENG.). 112p. (J). (gr. 1-4). per. 4.99 *(978-0-375-84276-4(4)*, Random Hse. Bks. for Young Readers) Random Hse. Children's Bks.

Lannen, Jon Jon. The Giraffe That Taught Me How to Laugh. 2010. 28p. pap. 14.99 *(978-1-4490-5930-9(9))* AuthorHouse.

Lawati, A. The Jungle Adventure of Chimpoo. 2011. 40p. pap. 21.99 *(978-1-4634-2921-8(5))* AuthorHouse.

LeapFrog Staff. Disney Lion King - U. K. 2003. (Illus.). spiral bd. 14.99 *(978-1-59319-006-4(9))* LeapFrog Enterprises, Inc.

Lee, Curtis Jamie. Donde van los globos? 2004. (SPA., Illus.). 28p. (J). 21.99 *(978-84-8488-056-1(7))* Serres, Ediciones, S. L. ESP. Dist: Lectorum Pubns., Inc.

Lornsen, Boy. El Bosque en Peligro. (SPA.). 141p. (J). (gr. 3-5). *(978-84-279-3451-1(3)*, NG0993) Noguer y Caralt Editores, S. A. ESP. Dist: Lectorum Pubns., Inc.

Ludy, Mark. Jujo: The Youngest Tribesman. Ludy, Mark, illus. 2007. (ENG., Illus.). 32p. (J). (gr. k-2). 16.95 *(978-0-9664276-5-3(3))* Scribble & Sons.

Lynch, Stephen D. The Travels of Kui, the African Spurred Tortoise. Richard, Keisha Luana, illus. 2007. 36p. per. 24.95 *(978-1-4137-1802-7(7))* America Star Bks.

MacCracken, Joan. Trisba & Sula: A Miskitu Folktale from Nicaragua (Una Leyenda de los Miskitos de Nicaragua) Macdonald, Isabel et al, trs. Silva, Augusto Alves da, illus. 2005. (ENG & SPA.). 16.95 *(978-0-9646018-2-6(6))* Tiffin Pr. of Maine.

Macdonald, John A. Pachunga. 2010. (ENG.). 256p. 26.95 *(978-1-4502-1823-8(7))*; pap. 16.95 *(978-1-4502-1821-4(0))* iUniverse, Inc.

MacIver, Juliette. Gwendolyn! Baynton, Terri Rose, illus. 2018. 32p. pap. 6.99 *(978-0-7333-3518-1(7))* ABC Bks. AUS. Dist: HarperCollins Pubs.

Madden, Gloria. Grandmothers Bedtime Stories. 2008. 68p. (gr. -1-7). pap. 10.49 *(978-1-4343-9201-5(5))* AuthorHouse.

Maggs, William Alan. The Jungle Adventures of Henry Littlejohn. 2012. 96p. pap. 11.52 *(978-1-4669-1252-6(9))* Trafford Publishing.

Magic Painting Jungle. 2017. (Magic Painting Bks.). (ENG.). (J). pap. 9.99 *(978-0-7945-3982-5(3)*, Usborne) EDC Publishing.

Martin, Nicole. The Werewolf. 2006. 146p. pap. 14.99 *(978-1-4120-8802-2(X))* Trafford Publishing.

Mason, Charlene. Landon's Backyard Adventures. 2012. 24p. pap. 24.95 *(978-1-4626-7470-1(4))* America Star Bks.

Mason, Christine. The Mystery of Nan Madol a Pacific Island Adventure. 2011. 166p. pap. 11.95 *(978-1-61170-025-1(6))* Robertson Publishing.

McBrayer, Cassidy. You Can, Toucan! You Can. 2008. 20p. pap. 15.95 *(978-1-4327-1132-0(6))* Outskirts Pr., Inc.

McCall Smith, Alexander. The Mystery of the Missing Lion. 2014. (Precious Ramotswe Mysteries for Young Readers Ser.: 3). (ENG., Illus.). 112p. (J). (gr. 2-5). pap. 7.99 *(978-0-8041-7327-8(3)*, Anchor) Knopf Doubleday Publishing Group.

McKee, David. Elmer's Walk. McKee, David, illus. 2018. (Elmer Ser.). (ENG., Illus.). 32p. (J). (gr. -1-3). 17.99 *(978-1-5415-3554-1(5)*, 5065be78-503a-4ed9-b0c9-1c9e170daf43) Lerner Publishing Group.

McLisky, Marie. Kancil the Mouse Deer. 2017. (ENG., Illus.). 31p. (J). pap. 13.95 *(978-1-78554-253-4(2)*, 9f5a01d4-04a9-47af-920d-b2fae74c771b) Austin Macauley Pubs. Ltd. GBR. Dist: Baker & Taylor Publisher Services (BTPS).

McNaney, Jeanne. Miracle in Sumatra: The Story of Gutsy Gus. Cochard, David, illus. 2009. (ENG.). 32p. (J). (gr. -1-3). 16.95 *(978-0-9814534-6-0(5))* Ovation Bks.

Meloy, Maile. The Apprentices. Schoenherr, Ian, illus. 2014. (Apothecary Ser.: 2). (ENG.). 432p. (J). (gr. 5). pap. 9.99 *(978-0-14-242598-5(2)*, Puffin Books) Penguin Young Readers Group.

Merberg, Julie & Bober, Suzanne. Dreaming with Rousseau. 2007. (Mini Masters Ser.: 10). (ENG., Illus.). 22p. (J). (gr. -1 — 1). bds. 6.99 *(978-0-8118-5712-3(3))* Chronicle Bks. LLC.

Millett, Peter & Morden, Richard. It's a Jungle Out There. 2008. (Rigby Focus Forward: Level N Ser.). (Illus.). 24p. (J). (gr. -1-3). pap. *(978-1-4190-3838-9(9)*, Rigby) Pearson Education Australia.

Mitchell, Melanie, illus. Deep in the Jungle. 2011. (ENG.). 6p. (J). (gr. -1-k). 14.95 *(978-1-61524-471-3(9)*, Intervisual/Piggy Toes) Bendon, Inc.

Moll, Amanda. Liam's Lost It. 2013. 24p. 15.99 *(978-0-9886409-4-8(5))* Mindstir Media.

Napoli, Donna Jo & Johnston, Shelagh. Hotel Jungle. Spengler, Kenneth, tr. Spengler, Kenneth, illus. 2004. 33p. (J). 15.95 *(978-1-59336-002-3(9))*; pap. *(978-1-59336-003-0(7))* Mondo Publishing.

Nino, Jairo Anibal. Zoro. 2003. (SPA., Illus.). 97p. (YA). (gr. -1-7). pap. *(978-958-30-0291-5(7)*, PV4489) Panamericana Editorial COL. Dist: Lectorum Pubns., Inc.

Okorafor-Mbachu, Nnedi. Zahrah the Windseeker. 2008. (ENG., Illus.). 320p. (J). (gr. 5-7). pap. 8.99 *(978-0-547-02028-0(7)*, 1031897, Clarion Bks.) HarperCollins Pubs.

Parker, Amy. Night Night, Jungle, 1 vol. Allyn, Virginia, illus. 2018. (Night Night Ser.). (ENG.). 20p. (J). bds. 9.99 *(978-0-7180-9086-9(1)*, Tommy Nelson) Nelson, Thomas Inc.

Peretti, Frank E. The Deadly Curse of Toco-Rey. Life Publishers International Staff, tr. from ENG. 2005. (RUS., Illus.). 156p. (J). *(978-0-7361-0347-3(3))* Life Pubs. International.

Phillips, Helen. Here Where the Sunbeams Are Green. 2013. (ENG.). 304p. (J). (gr. 5). 7.99 *(978-0-307-93145-0(5)*, Yearling) Random Hse. Children's Bks.

Phumiruk, Dow. Mela & the Elephant. Chen, Ziyue, illus. 2018. (ENG.). 32p. (J). (gr. k-3). 18.99 *(978-1-58536-998-0(5)*, 204407) Sleeping Bear Pr.

Pixton, Kaaren. Indestructibles: Jungle Rumble! Chew Proof · Rip Proof · Nontoxic · 100% Washable (Book for Babies, Newborn Books, Safe to Chew) 2010. (Indestructibles Ser.). (ENG., Illus.). 12p. (J). (gr. -1 — 1). pap. 5.99 *(978-0-7611-5858-5(8)*, 15858) Workman Publishing Co., Inc.

The Quest for Forgiveness. 2006. (Amazing Travels of Wannabe Ser.). (Illus.). 32p. (J). (gr. -1-3). 8.99 *(978-0-7847-1803-2(2)*, 04129) Standard Publishing.

Richards, Lucy, illus. Jumping Jungle (W/Hang Tag) 2004. (Cuddly Cuffs Ser.: No. 7). 12p. (J). tchr. ed. 5.95 *(978-1-58925-727-6(8))* Tiger Tales.

—Jumping Jungle (W/Header Card) 2004. (Cuddly Cuffs Ser.: 7). 6p. (J). tchr. ed. 5.95 *(978-1-58925-731-3(6))* Tiger Tales.

Richardson, Dick. The Oglin: A Hero's Journey Across Africa... Towards the Tomorrows. Feek, Cathy, illus. 2004. 417p. (J). 24.95 *(978-0-9759440-3-5(7))* Savanna Pr.

Robertson, Betsey. Frisky's Forest Friends: Robin Rescue. 2009. 28p. pap. 12.49 *(978-1-4389-1906-5(9))* AuthorHouse.

Robinson, Valerie. Jungle Jingles. 2010. (ENG.). 24p. pap. 15.99 *(978-1-4500-9927-1(0))* Xlibris Corp.

Rowe, John, ed. The Jungle Book. Alexander, Gregory, illus. 2003. (Chrysalis Childrens Classics Ser.). 159p. (YA). pap. *(978-1-84365-038-6(X)*, Pavilion Children's Books) Pavilion Bks.

Ruben's Jungle. 2003.Tr. of Selva de Ruben. (SPA., Illus.). 26p. bds. 16.95 *(978-0-9706953-1-4(4))* Globo Libros.

Rundell, Katherine. Into the Jungle: Stories for Mowgli. Williams, Kristjana S., illus. 2018. (ENG.). 240p. (J). (gr. 3-7). 24.99 *(978-1-5362-0527-5(3))* Candlewick Pr.

Saddleback Educational Publishing Staff, ed. River, 1 vol. unabr. ed. 2010. (Heights Ser.). (ENG.). 50p. (gr. 4-8). pap. 9.75 *(978-1-61651-281-1(4))* Saddleback Educational Publishing, Inc.

Sams, Carl R., II & Stoick, Jean. Lost in the Woods: A Photographic Fantasy. Herrick, Mark J., illus. 2005. (Connect-It Ser.). 68p. (J). (gr. -1-3). pap. 24.95 *(978-0-9749412-2-6(0))* EDCO Publishing, Inc.

San Souci, Robert D. Double-Dare to Be Scared: Another Thirteen Chilling Tales. Ouimet, David, illus. 2004. (Dare to Be Scared Ser.). (ENG.). 144p. (J). 17.95 *(978-0-8126-2716-9(4))* Cricket Bks.

San Souci, Robert D. & Burroughs, Edgar. Tarzan. McCurdy, Michael, illus. 2004. 31p. (J). (gr. k-4). reprint ed. 16.00 *(978-0-7567-7576-6(0))* DIANE Publishing Co.

Saunders, Harry M. Teenagers on an Adventure: Journey of Two Boys & a Girl. 2013. 168p. pap. 19.95 *(978-1-62709-466-5(0))* America Star Bks.

Schick, Joel, illus. The Jungle Book: A Story about Loyalty. 2006. (J). 6.99 *(978-1-59939-023-9(X))* Cornerstone Pr.

The Show: Individual Title Six-Packs. (Sails Literacy Ser.). 16p. (gr. k-18). 27.00 *(978-0-7635-4413-3(2))* Rigby Education.

Sithole, Thelma. The Little Monkey & the Crocodile. Montague, Christine, illus. 2007. 32p. per. 12.00 *(978-1-59858-204-8(6))* Dog Ear Publishing, LLC.

Slade, Nicholas. Joon the Zsun & His Magical Spoon. 2009. (Illus.). 32p. pap. 12.99 *(978-1-4389-3496-9(3))* AuthorHouse.

Smith, Roland. Cryptid Hunters. 2006. (ENG.). 352p. (J). (gr. 5-9). pap. 7.99 *(978-0-7868-5162-1(7))* Little, Brown Bks. for Young Readers.

—Mutation (Cryptid Hunters #4) 2016. (Cryptid Hunters Ser.: 4). (ENG.). 352p. (J). (gr. 3-7). pap. 7.99 *(978-0-545-08181-8(5)*, Scholastic Pr.) Scholastic, Inc.

Spann, Bill. The Agents of Little Woods. 2005. 116p. pap. 19.95 *(978-1-4137-6574-8(2))* America Star Bks.

Squillace, Elisa, illus. Down in the Jungle. (Classic Books with Holes Big Book Ser.). (J). (gr. -1-3). 2006. 16p. spiral bd. *(978-1-84643-009-1(7))* 2005. 14p. spiral bd. *(978-1-904550-61-7(4))* Child's Play International Ltd.

Stephenson, Omri. Freddie Finds Out. 2010. (ENG.). 34p. pap. 21.50 *(978-1-4457-5726-1(5))* Lulu Pr., Inc.

Stilton, Geronimo. Four Mice Deep in the Jungle (Geronimo Stilton #5), Volume 5. 2004. (Geronimo Stilton Ser.: No. 5). (ENG., Illus.). 128p. (J). (gr. 2-5). pap. 7.99 *(978-0-439-55967-6(7)*, Scholastic Paperbacks) Scholastic, Inc.

Stilton, Gerónimo. Rumble in the Jungle. 2013. (Geronimo Stilton Ser.: 53). lib. bdg. 18.40 *(978-0-606-31527-2(6))* Turtleback.

Taylor, Christine. Red Riding Hood & the Toad. 2009. (Illus.). 44p. (gr. -1 — 1). 18.49 *(978-1-4389-3483-9(1))* AuthorHouse.

Taylor, Mark. Henry Explores the Jungle. Booth, Graham, illus. 2012. (ENG.). 48p. (J). (gr. -1-3). 18.95 *(978-1-930900-56-1(2))* Purple Hse. Pr.

Tempest, Annabel, illus. Jungle Book: A BabyLit Storybook, 1 vol. 2018. (BabyLit Ser.). 28p. (J). (gr. -1-k). 12.99 *(978-1-4236-4922-9(2))* Gibbs Smith, Publisher.

Thornewell, Danielle. The Merns. 2007. (ENG.). 52p. per. 16.95 *(978-1-4241-6106-5(1))* PublishAmerica, Inc.

Thottam, Meena, adapted by. Brothers of the Jungle. 2006. (J). 3.95 *(978-0-9776917-4-6(8)*, Curcumin Bks.) Davlaw Press.

ToyBox Innovations, creator. Deep in the Jungle. abr. ed. 2006. (Disney's Read along Collection). (ENG.). (J). (gr. -1-3). pap. *(978-0-7634-2182-3(0))* Walt Disney Records.

Tub Tales: The Jungle. 2003. (Illus.). 10p. (J). 6.00 *(978-0-9713507-2-4(8)*, 843) Panline U.S.A., Inc.

Tulip, Jenny, illus. Who's Hiding in the Jungle? A Mystery Touch-and-Feel Flap Book! 2008. 10p. (gr. -1-k). bds. 6.99 *(978-1-57755-784-5(0))* Flying Frog Publishing.

Unknown. Meg in the Jungle. 2017. (Illus.). 32p. (J). (gr. 2-5). pap. 12.99 *(978-0-14-136740-8(7))* Penguin Bks., Ltd. GBR. Dist: Independent Pubs. Group.

Vetsch, Rita Kaye. The Many Colors of Friendship. 2009. 40p. pap. 16.50 *(978-1-60693-756-3(1)*, Eloquent Bks.) Strategic Book Publishing & Rights Agency (SBPRA).

Wallace, Dianne. Jungle in the Sky. 2012. (ENG.). 27p. (J). pap. 16.95 *(978-1-4327-4527-1(1))* Outskirts Pr., Inc.

Welch, Kathleen & McGillivray, Alan. Sometimes Even Elephants Forget: A Story about Alzheimer's Disease for Young Children, 1 vol. Welch, Kathleen & McGillivray, Alan, illus. 2019. (ENG., Illus.). 32p. (J). (gr. -1-3). 16.99 *(978-1-4556-2469-0(1)*, Pelican Publishing) Arcadia Publishing.

West, Robert. Attack of the Spider Bots, 1 vol. 2008. (Star-Fighters of Murphy Street Ser.: 2). (ENG., Illus.). 160p. (J). (gr. 4-7). pap. 6.99 *(978-0-310-71426-2(5))* Zonderkidz.

Whited, Melissa F. The Bear Brothers' Big Adventure, 1 vol. 2009. 23p. pap. 24.95 *(978-1-60749-258-0(X))* America Star Bks.

Wildsmith, Brian. Jungle Party, 1 vol. Wildsmith, Brian, illus. 2006. (ENG., Illus.). 32p. (J). pap. 6.95 *(978-1-59572-053-5(7))*; (gr. -1-3). 17.95 *(978-1-59572-052-8(9))* Star Bright Bks., Inc.

Willis, Tacey Lynn. Ellie, Tellie & Mellie: Best Jungle Friends Forever. 2010. 28p. pap. 12.49 *(978-1-4520-1903-1(7))* AuthorHouse.

Youngberg, Norma R. Jungle Thorn. 2010. (Illus.). 132p. reprint ed. per. 11.95 *(978-1-57258-157-9(3)*, 945-6024) TEACH Services, Inc.

Zadrozny, Alicia & Church, Caroline Jayne. The Wild Little Jungle: A Mix-and-Match Flap Book. 2008. (ENG.). 10p. (J). bds. 12.99 *(978-0-7944-1605-8(5))* Reader's Digest Assn., Inc., The.

JUNK

see Waste Products

JUPITER (PLANET)

Adamson, Thomas K. Jupiter [Scholastic]: Revised Edition. 2010. (Exploring the Galaxy Ser.). (ENG.). 24p. pap. 0.49 (978-1-4296-5810-2(X), Capstone Pr.) Capstone.

—The Secrets of Jupiter. 2015. (Planets Ser.). (ENG., Illus.). 32p. (J). (gr. 2-4). lib. bdg. 32.65 (978-1-4914-5864-8(X), 128827, Capstone Pr.) Capstone.

Alexander, richard. Exploring Jupiter. 2017. (Journey Through Our Solar System Ser.). 24p. (gr. 1-2). 49.50 (978-1-5345-2251-0(4), KidHaven Publishing) Greenhaven Publishing LLC.

Allyn, Daisy. Jupiter, 1 vol. 2010. (Our Solar System Ser.). (ENG.). 24p. (J). (gr. k-2). pap. 9.15 (978-1-4339-3822-1(7), db9522b1-3d48-452c-bb8a-f61459b15d65); (Illus.). lib. bdg. 25.27 (978-1-4339-3821-4(9), 0b145983-9100-4465-b73f-2cf3325b26d0) Stevens, Gareth Publishing LLLP.

Arnold, Quinn M. Jupiter. 2018. (Semillas Del Saber Ser.). 24p. (J). (SPA.). (gr. -1-k). (978-1-60818-948-9(1), 19582, Creative Education); (FRE., Illus.). (978-1-77092-406-2(X), 19695); (ENG., Illus.). (gr. -1-k). (978-1-60818-914-4(7), 19580, Creative Education); (ENG., Illus.). (gr. -1-k). pap. 7.99 (978-1-62832-530-0(5), 19578, Creative Paperbacks) Creative Co., The.

Bloom, J. P. Jupiter, 1 vol. 2015. (Planets Ser.). (ENG., Illus.). 24p. (J). (gr. -1-2). lib. bdg. 32.79 (978-1-62970-716-7(3), 17231, Abdo Kids) ABDO Publishing Co.

—Jupiter. 2017. (Planets Ser.). (ENG.). 24p. (J). (gr. -1-2). pap. 7.95 (978-1-4966-1281-6(7), 135013, Capstone Classroom) Capstone.

—Júpiter. 2017. (Planetas Ser.). (SPA.). 24p. (J). (gr. -1-2). pap. 7.95 (978-1-4966-1299-1(X), 135021, Capstone Classroom) Capstone.

—Jupiter (Jupiter), 1 vol. 2016. (Planetas (Planets) Ser.). (SPA., Illus.). 24p. (J). (gr. -1-2). lib. bdg. 32.79 (978-1-68080-753-0(6), 22668, Abdo Kids) ABDO Publishing Co.

Capaccio, George. Jupiter, 1 vol. 2010. (Space! Ser.). (ENG.). 64p. (gr. 5-5). lib. bdg. 35.50 (978-0-7614-4244-8(8), dd5e55e2-59d4-4cc4-8de3-4f316daa9ec8) Cavendish Square Publishing LLC.

Carson, Mary Kay. Far-Out Guide to Jupiter, 1 vol. 2010. (Far-Out Guide to the Solar System Ser.). (ENG., Illus.). 48p. (gr. 4-6). 27.93 (978-0-7660-3184-5(5), 6a16612d-06e6-4802-ac66-df8c9269eafe); pap. 11.53 (978-1-59845-186-3(3), 4b5484a6-d5b3-4d70-8e96-e53c1da4f205, Enslow Elementary) Enslow Publishing, LLC.

Chiger, Arielle & Elkin, Matthew. 20 Fun Facts about Gas Giants, 1 vol. 2014. (Fun Fact File: Space! Ser.). (ENG.). 32p. (J). (gr. 2-3). 27.93 (978-1-4824-1001-3(X), 7ae9a641-b1d0-422a-9dfe-2c66f19a7594); pap. 11.50 (978-1-4824-1002-0(8), ed9d7e5f-5dcd-478b-80bf-bb18a853525b) Stevens, Gareth Publishing LLLP.

Coates, Eileen S. Galileo, Jupiter's Moons, & the Telescope, 1 vol. 2018. (STEM Milestones: Historic Inventions & Discoveries Ser.). (ENG.). 24p. (gr. 3-3). 25.27 (978-1-5383-4357-9(6), db41cac0-ded3-470c-9ed4-ffe42e79d84a, PowerKids Pr.) Rosen Publishing Group, Inc., The.

Cunningham, Greg P. Journey to Jupiter, 1 vol. 2014. (Spotlight on Space Science Ser.). (ENG.). 32p. (J). (gr. 5-5). pap. 12.75 (978-1-4994-0370-1(4), 39e8d1d6-b91b-4627-9ee2-1627bf7d9083, PowerKids Pr.) Rosen Publishing Group, Inc., The.

Geiger, Beth. The Inside Story of Jupiter. 2006. (J). 7.80 (978-1-933798-07-3(6)) Sally Ride Science.

Glaser, Chaya. Jupiter: El Mayor de Los Planetas. 2015. (Fuera de Este Mundo Ser.). (SPA., Illus.). 24p. (J). (gr. -1-3). lib. bdg. 23.93 (978-1-62724-590-6(1)) Bearport Publishing Co., Inc.

—Jupiter: The Biggest Planet. 2015. (Out of This World Ser.). (ENG.). 24p. (J). (gr. -1-3). lib. bdg. 23.93 (978-1-62724-565-4(0)) Bearport Publishing Co., Inc.

Goldstein, Margaret J. Discover Jupiter. 2018. (Searchlight Books (tm) — Discover Planets Ser.). (ENG., Illus.). 32p. (J). (gr. 3-5). 30.65 (978-1-5415-2335-7(0), 33b5311d-1f09-4c8b-b340-e673428817c4, Lerner Pubns.) Lerner Publishing Group.

—Jupiter. 2005. (Pull Ahead Bks.). (Illus.). 32p. (gr. 2-4). lib. bdg. 22.60 (978-0-8225-4652-8(3)) Lerner Publishing Group.

Hansen, Rosanna. Jupiter. 2009. (Early Bird Astronomy Ser.). (ENG.). 48p. (gr. 2-5). lib. bdg. 26.60 (978-0-7613-4153-6(6)) Lerner Publishing Group.

Hantula, Richard & Asimov, Isaac. Júpiter (Jupiter), 1 vol. 2003. (Isaac Asimov's Biblioteca Del Universo Del Siglo XXI (Isaac Asimov's 21st Century Library of the Universe) Ser.). (SPA., Illus.). 32p. (gr. 3-5). (J). pap. 9.95 (978-0-8368-3867-1(X), 6445f9f3-ad38-48a6-9889-7c75f91d2446, Weekly Reader); lib. bdg. 28.67 (978-0-8368-3854-1(8), f7ba75eb-ea29-476f-90e2-126821ed266e, Gareth Stevens Learning Library) Stevens, Gareth Publishing LLLP.

Jefferis, David. Mighty Megaplanets: Jupiter & Saturn. 2008. (Exploring Our Solar System Ser.). (ENG., Illus.). 32p. (J). (gr. 3-7). pap. (978-0-7787-3753-7(5)) Crabtree Publishing Co.

Jupiter. 2013. (Explore Outer Space Ser.). 32p. (J). (gr. 3-6). pap. 60.00 (978-1-61533-770-5(9), PowerKids Pr.) Rosen Publishing Group, Inc., The.

Kazunas, Ariel. Jupiter. 2011. (21st Century Junior Library: Solar System Ser.). (ENG., Illus.). 24p. (gr. 2-5). lib. bdg. 29.21 (978-1-61080-086-0(9), 201082) Cherry Lake Publishing.

Murray, Julie. Jupiter. 2018. (Planets (Dash!) Ser.). (ENG., Illus.). 24p. (J). (gr. k-4). lib. bdg. 31.36 (978-1-5321-2527-0(5), 30063, Abdo Zoom-Dash) ABDO Publishing Co.

Orme, Helen & Orme, David. Let's Explore Jupiter, 1 vol. 2007. (Space Launch! Ser.). (ENG., Illus.). 24p. (gr. 2-4). lib. bdg. 25.67 (978-0-8368-7940-7(6), f96af924-c58b-4937-b72c-095161989104, Gareth Stevens Learning Library) Stevens, Gareth Publishing LLLP.

Owen, Ruth. Jupiter, 1 vol. 2013. (Explore Outer Space Ser.). (ENG.). 32p. (J). (gr. 2-3). 29.93 (978-1-61533-726-2(1), b78398d7-dad3-49f0-9711-a4f1a12f7306); pap. 11.00 (978-1-61533-769-9(5), 35fa7dfb-6e0e-4619-be6e-93e969e9d0a0) Rosen Publishing Group, Inc., The. (PowerKids Pr.).

Oxlade, Chris. Jupiter, Neptune, & Other Outer Planets, 1 vol. 2007. (Earth & Space Ser.). (ENG., Illus.). 48p. (YA). (gr. 6-6). lib. bdg. 34.47 (978-1-4042-3736-0(4), 24557517-dcfe-4798-aa18-f3a4a8c9c1d5) Rosen Publishing Group, Inc., The.

Rathburn, Betsy. Jupiter. 2019. (Space Science Ser.). (ENG., Illus.). 24p. (J). (gr. 3-7). lib. bdg. 26.95 (978-1-62617-972-1(7), Torque Bks.) Bellwether Media.

Ring, Susan. Jupiter. (J). 2013. (978-1-62127-264-9(8)) 2013. pap. (978-1-62127-273-1(7)) 2004. pap. 8.95 (978-1-59036-230-3(6)) Weigl Pubs., Inc.

Ring, Susan & Roumanis, Alexis. Jupiter. 2016. (Illus.). 24p. (J). (978-1-5105-0974-0(7)) SmartBook Media, Inc.

Roumanis, Alexis. Jupiter. 2016. (978-1-5105-2047-9(3)) SmartBook Media, Inc.

—Jupiter. 2015. (J). (978-1-4896-3284-5(0)) Weigl Pubs., Inc.

Slade, Suzanne. A Look at Jupiter. 2009. (Astronomy Now! Ser.). 24p. (gr. 2-3). 42.50 (978-1-61511-468-9(8), PowerKids Pr.) Rosen Publishing Group, Inc., The.

Sparrow, Giles. Destination Jupiter, 1 vol. 2009. (Destination Solar System Ser.). (ENG.). 32p. (J). (gr. 3-4). lib. bdg. 28.93 (978-1-4358-3444-6(5), 6346701b-3b76-4d97-94d5-37bf4f6c15d9); (Illus.). pap. 11.00 (978-1-4358-3487-3(9), d9aa450f-c5b0-4538-a0f1-fb7c5548bd8e) Rosen Publishing Group, Inc., The. (PowerKids Pr.).

Taylor-Butler, Christine. Jupiter. 2007. (Scholastic News Nonfiction Readers Ser.). (ENG., Illus.). 24p. (J). (gr. 1-2). 22.00 (978-0-531-14696-5(0)) Scholastic Library Publishing.

Wimmer, Teresa. Jupiter. 2007. (My First Look at: Planets Ser.). (Illus.). 24p. (J). (gr. -1-3). lib. bdg. 24.25 (978-1-58341-517-7(3), Creative Education) Creative Co., The.

World Book, Inc. Staff, contrib. by. Jupiter. 2006. (World Book's Solar System & Space Exploration Library). (Illus.). 63p. (J). (978-0-7166-9505-9(7)) World Bk., Inc.

—Jupiter & the Asteroids. 2010. (J). (978-0-7166-9537-0(5)) World Bk., Inc.

—Jupiter, Ceres & the Asteroids. 2nd ed. 2006. (World Book's Solar System & Space Exploration Library). (Illus.). 64p. (J). (978-0-7166-9515-8(4)) World Bk., Inc.

Young, Abby. Jupiter. (Library of Planets Ser.). 48p. (gr. 5-8). 2009. 55.90 (978-1-60853-816-4(8), Rosen Reference) 2007. (ENG.). (J). 34.47 (978-1-4042-1967-0(6), 0411773a-06f9-4320-96e5-1b46dfce93c8) Rosen Publishing Group, Inc., The.

Zobel, Derek. Jupiter. 2010. (Exploring Space Ser.). (ENG., Illus.). 24p. (J). (gr. k-3). lib. bdg. 26.95 (978-1-60014-406-6(3), Blastoff! Readers) Bellwether Media.

JURISPRUDENCE

see Law

JURISTS

see Lawyers

JURY

De Capua, Sarah. Serving on a Jury (a True Book: Civics) 2012. (True Book (Relaunch) Ser.). (ENG., Illus.). 48p. (J). (gr. 3-5). pap. 6.95 (978-0-531-26214-6(6), Children's Pr.) Scholastic Library Publishing.

—A True Book - Civics: Serving on a Jury. 2012. (ENG., Illus.). 48p. (J). lib. bdg. 29.00 (978-0-531-26042-5(9), Children's Pr.) Scholastic Library Publishing.

Furgang, Kathy. Seventh Amendment: The Right to a Jury Trial, 1 vol. 2011. (Amendments to the United States Constitution: the Bill of Rights Ser.). (ENG.). 64p. (YA). (gr. 6-6). pap. 13.95 (978-1-4488-2308-6(0), 31999344-03c2-4f15-8bcd-c588609b1010, Rosen Reference) Rosen Publishing Group, Inc., The.

—The Seventh Amendment: The Right to a Jury Trial, 1 vol. 2011. (Amendments to the United States Constitution: the Bill of Rights Ser.). (ENG., Illus.). 64p. (YA). (gr. 6-6). lib. bdg. 37.13 (978-1-4488-1262-2(3), 1e1b5cd2-1ef7-4821-83da-d2624ed21e56) Rosen Publishing Group, Inc., The.

Heing, Bridey. What Does a Juror Do?, 1 vol. 2018. (What Does a Citizen Do? Ser.). (ENG.). 48p. (gr. 5-5). 30.93 (978-0-7660-9863-3(X), a29916be-0415-41ff-81b1-b4c674cdf298) Enslow Publishing, LLC.

Manning, Jack. Serving on a Jury, 1 vol. 2014. (Our Government Ser.). (ENG.). 24p. (J). (gr. 1-3). lib. bdg. 27.99 (978-1-4914-0333-4(0), 125846) Capstone.

Morlock, Jeremy. Trial Juries & Grand Juries, 1 vol. 2019. (Court Is in Session Ser.). (ENG.). 32p. (gr. 4-5). pap. 11.00 (978-1-5383-4332-6(0), c3ec3643-fd00-4dd6-9a0b-d504d9dac87e, PowerKids Pr.) Rosen Publishing Group, Inc., The.

Murray, Hallie. The Right to a Jury Trial: The Seventh Amendment, 1 vol. 2017. (Bill of Rights Ser.). (ENG.). 48p. (gr. 5-6). lib. bdg. 29.60 (978-0-7660-8561-9(9), 97c24bff-9f77-4112-897d-72bd7c771881) Enslow Publishing, LLC.

Reyes, Sonja. What Is a Jury? Understanding Government, 1 vol. 2018. (Civics for the Real World Ser.). (ENG.). 16p. (gr. 2-3). pap. (978-1-5383-6536-6(7), 50078350-06b3-4349-8cff-5ba22a0eba8a, Rosen Classroom) Rosen Publishing Group, Inc., The.

Walker, Kaisa. The Importance of Jury Service, 1 vol. 2017. (Spotlight on Civic Action Ser.). (ENG.). 32p. (J). (gr. 4-5). 27.93 (978-1-5081-6403-6(7), ef43b9aa-8a09-40d2-a1fc-36e6e9376957, PowerKids Pr.) Rosen Publishing Group, Inc., The.

JUSTICE, ADMINISTRATION OF

see also Courts; Crime

Aldridge, Rebecca, ed. Mass Incarceration, 1 vol. 2017. (Opposing Viewpoints Ser.). (ENG.). 296p. (gr. 10-12). pap. 34.80 (978-1-5345-0043-3(X), cbdc726e-9eec-4c29-b762-0daeb825fc14); lib. bdg. 50.43 (978-1-5345-0045-7(6), 3f9817a6-6912-49fe-8b33-8c1d0909c1ff) Greenhaven Publishing LLC.

Beier, Anne. The Supreme Court & the Judicial Branch. 2009. (Primary Source Library of American Citizenship Ser.). 32p. (gr. 5-5). 47.90 (978-1-61511-230-2(8), Rosen Reference) Rosen Publishing Group, Inc., The.

Cuthbert, Megan & Siemens, Jared. Courthouse. 2016. (J). (978-1-5105-1883-4(5)) SmartBook Media, Inc.

Dudley Gold, Susan. In Re Gault: Do Minors Have the Same Rights As Adults?, 1 vol. 2008. (Supreme Court Milestones Ser.). (ENG., Illus.). 128p. (YA). (gr. 8-8). lib. bdg. 45.50 (978-0-7614-2584-7(5), d0479fd5-ac61-4693-ad71-0d03efabaa2c) Cavendish Square Publishing LLC.

Duignan, Brian & DeCarlo, Carolyn, eds. The Judicial Branch: Evaluating & Interpreting Laws, 1 vol. 2018. (Checks & Balances in the U. S. Government Ser.). (ENG.). 128p. (gr. 10-10). lib. bdg. 39.00 (978-1-5383-0167-8(9), a5909be8-8644-4ad0-a3d0-6da8c846c43b) Rosen Publishing Group, Inc., The.

Dupont, Ellen. The U. S. Justice System, Vol. 20. Gomez, Manny, ed. 2016. (Crime & Detection Ser.). (Illus.). 96p. (J). (gr. 7). 24.95 (978-1-4222-3488-4(6)) Mason Crest.

—The United States Justice System. 2004. (Crime & Detection Ser.). (Illus.). 96p. (YA). (gr. 7-18). lib. bdg. 22.95 (978-1-59084-377-2(0)) Mason Crest.

Emert, Phyllis Raybin. Attorneys General: Enforcing the Law. 2005. (In the Cabinet Ser.). (Illus.). 176p. (J). (gr. 7-18). lib. bdg. 24.95 (978-1-881508-66-3(8)) Oliver Pr., Inc.

Grinapol, Corinne. Racial Profiling & Discrimination: Your Legal Rights, 1 vol. 2015. (Know Your Rights Ser.). (ENG., Illus.). 64p. (J). (gr. 7-7). 36.47 (978-1-4777-8020-6(3), 5ceacb72-a9ca-4d3b-a623-3cccceb4ac46, Rosen Young Adult) Rosen Publishing Group, Inc., The.

Hand, Carol. Using Computer Science in High Tech Criminal Justice Careers, 1 vol. 2017. (Coding Your Passion Ser.). (ENG., Illus.). 80p. (J). (gr. 7-7). 37.47 (978-1-5081-7511-7(X), 6e321a5c-7471-4297-b448-1de8f720622a, Rosen Young Adult) Rosen Publishing Group, Inc., The.

Hanrahan, Clare, ed. Legal System, 1 vol. 2007. (Opposing Viewpoints Ser.). (ENG., Illus.). 240p. (gr. 10-12). 50.43 (978-0-7377-3757-8(3), 818ae1e3-90a2-4098-bc2c-8e1764ce3f55); pap. 34.80 (978-0-7377-3758-5(1), e76e3c01-9914-48cb-aa8c-ebd7ea95eaa2) Greenhaven Publishing LLC. (Greenhaven Publishing).

Harris, Nancy. What's the State Judicial Branch? rev. ed. 2016. (First Guide to Government Ser.). (ENG.). 32p. (J). (gr. 1-3). pap. 8.29 (978-1-4846-3691-6(0), 134103, Heinemann) Capstone.

Hile, Kevin. Trial of Juveniles As Adults. 2003. (Point/Counterpoint: Issues in Contemporary American Society Ser.). (ENG., Illus.). 112p. (gr. 9-13). 35.00 (978-0-7910-7374-2(2), P113798, Facts On File) Infobase Holdings, Inc.

Hunter, David. Unequal Justice. 2017. 80p. (J). (978-1-4222-3789-2(3)) Mason Crest.

Jacobs, Thomas A. They Broke the Law - You Be the Judge: True Cases of Teen Crime. 2003. (ENG.). 224p. (YA). (gr. 7-18). pap. 16.99 (978-1-57542-134-6(8), 824) Free Spirit Publishing Inc.

Juvenile Justice. 2nd rev. ed. 2010. (ENG., Illus.). 104p. (gr. 9-18). 35.00 (978-1-60413-508-4(5), P178897, Facts On File) Infobase Holdings, Inc.

Krueger, Naomi J. How the Judicial Branch Works. 2016. (How America Works). (ENG.). 24p. (J). (gr. 3-6). 32.79 (978-1-5038-0905-5(6), 210662) Child's World, Inc, The.

Lange, Donna. On the Edge of Disaster: Youth in the Juvenile Court System. 2003. (Youth with Special Needs Ser.). (Illus.). 127p. (YA). (gr. 7). pap. 14.95 (978-1-4222-0428-3(6)) Mason Crest.

Lansford, Tom. Justice, Policing, & the Rule of Law, Vol. 8. Lansford, Tom, ed. 2016. (Foundations of Democracy Ser.). (Illus.). 64p. (J). (gr. 7). 23.95 (978-1-4222-3630-7(7)) Mason Crest.

LeVert, Suzanne. State Courts, 1 vol. 2005. (Kaleidoscope: Government Ser.). (ENG., Illus.). 48p. (gr. 4-4). lib. bdg. 32.64 (978-0-7614-1594-7(7), bb913a26-8734-4156-930c-12985b2541c2) Cavendish Square Publishing LLC.

Libal, Autumn. The True Costs of Prisons. 2017. (Illus.). 80p. (J). (978-1-4222-3781-6(8)) Mason Crest.

Linde, Barbara M. State & County Courts, 1 vol. 2019. (Court Is in Session Ser.). (ENG.). 32p. (gr. 4-5). pap. 11.00 (978-1-5383-4328-9(2), 6c039694-0816-48b2-b7ab-c6eb39b2acc9, PowerKids Pr.) Rosen Publishing Group, Inc., The.

Mattern, Joanne. Attorney General. 2003. (America's Leaders Ser.). (Illus.). 32p. (J). 24.94 (978-1-56711-278-8(1), Blackbirch Pr., Inc.) Cengage Gale.

McMeans, Julia. Justice in Our Society, 1 vol. 2017. (Civic Values Ser.). (ENG.). 32p. (gr. 3-3). pap. 11.58 (978-1-5026-3193-0(8), 2f6afba1-2027-40ee-8e9b-506f7d8396c6) Cavendish Square Publishing LLC.

Merino, Noël, ed. Criminal Justice, 1 vol. 2012. (Opposing Viewpoints Ser.). (ENG., Illus.). 232p. (gr. 10-12). pap. 34.80 (978-0-7377-6307-2(8), 80dd24c7-abd4-4a62-a96f-75643545d884, Greenhaven Publishing) Greenhaven Publishing LLC.

—Criminal Justice, 1 vol. 2012. (Opposing Viewpoints Ser.). (ENG., Illus.). 232p. (gr. 10-12). lib. bdg. 50.43 (978-0-7377-6306-5(X), 688e0454-555a-4888-a754-61de92aa2f7f, Greenhaven Publishing) Greenhaven Publishing LLC.

My Children Publishing, prod. I am the Judge. 2008. (Illus.). 154p. (YA). pap. 19.95 (978-0-9799376-0-6(4)) My Children Publishing Inc.

Ogden, Charlie. Law & Justice. 2017. (Our Values - Level 3 Ser.). (Illus.). 32p. (J). (gr. 5-6). (978-0-7787-3721-6(7)) Crabtree Publishing Co.

Park, Peggy J. Is the Death Penalty Just? 2014. (In Controversy Ser.). (ENG., Illus.). 80p. (J). lib. bdg. (978-1-60152-714-1(4)) ReferencePoint Pr., Inc.

Schauer, Peter J. What You Need to Know about Violent Crimes, Felonies, & the Law, 1 vol. 2014. (Know Your Rights Ser.). (ENG., Illus.). 64p. (J). (gr. 6-7). 36.47 (978-1-4777-8024-4(6), 31ac1ee4-b564-4067-ab09-447d5f532e24, Rosen Reference) Rosen Publishing Group, Inc., The.

Smith-Llera, Danielle. Exploring the Judicial Branch. 2019. (Searchlight Books (tm) — Getting into Government Ser.). (ENG., Illus.). 32p. (J). (gr. 3-5). pap. 9.99 (978-1-5415-7479-3(6), 476b3988-59a5-4cee-b093-a1e355d8b611, Lerner Pubns.) Lerner Publishing Group.

Smith, Roger & McIntosh, Martha. Juveniles Growing up in Prison. 2017. (Illus.). 80p. (J). (978-1-4222-3783-0(4)) Mason Crest.

Stevenson, Bryan. Just Mercy (Adapted for Young Adults) A True Story of the Fight for Justice. 2018. 288p. (YA). (gr. 7). 18.99 (978-0-525-58003-4(4)); (ENG.). lib. bdg. 21.99 (978-0-525-58004-1(2)) Random Hse. Children's Bks. (Delacorte Pr.).

Tolli, Jenna. Federal Courts, 1 vol. 2019. (Court Is in Session Ser.). (ENG.). 32p. (gr. 4-5). pap. 11.00 (978-1-5383-4320-3(7), b6d50661-8c8d-4e0b-b7a0-6a3987d34f28, PowerKids Pr.) Rosen Publishing Group, Inc., The.

TRIALS & the COURTS. 2010. (ENG., Illus.). 128p. (gr. 6-12). 35.00 (978-1-60413-616-6(2), P179315, Facts On File) Infobase Holdings, Inc.

JUSTINIAN I, EMPEROR OF THE EAST, 483?-565

Rodgers, Kelly. Justinian I: Byzantine Emperor, 1 vol. rev. ed. 2012. (Social Studies: Informational Text Ser.). (ENG.). 32p. (gr. 4-8). pap. 11.99 (978-1-4333-5002-3(5)) Teacher Created Materials, Inc.

JUVENILE DELINQUENCY

see also Child Welfare

Barrington, Richard. The Junevile Court System: Your Legal Rights, 1 vol. 2015. (Know Your Rights Ser.). (ENG., Illus.). 64p. (J). (gr. 6-6). pap. 13.95 (978-1-4777-8621-5(X), dd34a719-e6aa-4de4-afce-615777a955e9, Rosen Young Adult) Rosen Publishing Group, Inc., The.

Becnel, Barbara, ed. Gangs & the Abuse of Power: Stanley Tookie Williams Street Peace Series, 8 bks., Vol. 1, Bk. 7. 2008. 24p. (J). 6.95 (978-0-9753584-7-4(2)) Damamli Publishing Co.

—Gangs & Violence: Stanley Tookie Williams Street Peace Series, 8 bks., Vol. 1, Bk. 3. 2008. 24p. (J). 6.95 (978-0-9753584-4-3(8)) Damamli Publishing Co.

—Gangs & Your Neighborhood: Stanley Tookie Williams Street Peace Series, 8 bks., Vol. 1, Bk. 8. 2008. 24p. (J). 6.95 (978-0-9753584-8-1(0)) Damamli Publishing Co.

Brennan, Janette. Child Convicts. 2015. (ENG., Illus.). 32p. (J). (gr. 3-7). 16.99 (978-0-7636-7326-0(9)) Candlewick Pr.

Brezina, Corona. Deadly School & Campus Violence, 1 vol. 2008. (Violence & Society Ser.). (ENG., Illus.). 64p. (YA). (gr. 6-6). lib. bdg. 37.13 (978-1-4042-1792-8(4), 2796ee01-5e1c-4616-a833-a36d1cb1df48) Rosen Publishing Group, Inc., The.

—Frequently Asked Questions about Juvenile Detention, 1 vol. 2011. (FAQ: Teen Life Ser.). (ENG.). 64p. (YA). (gr. 5-6). lib. bdg. 37.13 (978-1-4488-5560-5(8), 66dec199-eb9c-46b5-b17c-9f10970e37a1) Rosen Publishing Group, Inc., The.

Gottfried Hollander, Barbara. Conduct Disorder, 1 vol. 2013. (Teen Mental Health Ser.). (ENG.). 48p. (YA). (gr. 5-6). 34.47 (978-1-4777-1752-3(8), 767192b4-d0a4-4cd1-826a-0dfa76d4bd0f) Rosen Publishing Group, Inc., The.

Haerens, Margaret, ed. Juvenile Crime, 1 vol. 2013. (Global Viewpoints Ser.). (ENG., Illus.). 248p. (gr. 10-12). pap. 32.70 (978-0-7377-6443-7(0), 2e760ff6-40f2-4655-ad2b-d287e6913f8e); lib. bdg. 47.83 (978-0-7377-6267-9(5), 72a34ef5-1d05-4c64-bee2-590aeac28cc8) Greenhaven Publishing LLC. (Greenhaven Publishing).

Hiber, Amanda, ed. Gangs, 1 vol. 2013. (Issues That Concern You Ser.). (ENG., Illus.). 128p. (gr. 7-10). lib. bdg. 43.63 (978-0-7377-6294-5(2), b2d56476-7590-4c3f-bd90-cfd48f8bc348, Greenhaven Publishing) Greenhaven Publishing LLC.

Hile, Kevin. Trial of Juveniles As Adults. 2003. (Point/Counterpoint: Issues in Contemporary American Society Ser.). (ENG., Illus.). 112p. (gr. 9-13). 35.00 (978-0-7910-7374-2(2), P113798, Facts On File) Infobase Holdings, Inc.

Jones, Patrick. Teen Incarceration: From Cell Bars to Ankle Bracelets. 2016. (ENG., Illus.). 120p. (YA). (gr. 6-12). lib. bdg. 37.32 (978-1-4677-7572-4(X), 58d0d81c-d5b0-474f-ad5f-8de2d5a24ba5, Twenty-First Century Bks.) Lerner Publishing Group.

—Teen Incarceration: From Cell Bars to Ankle Bracelets. 2016. (ENG., Illus.). 120p. (YA). (gr. 6-12). E-Book 55.99 (978-1-5124-1138-6(8), Twenty-First Century Bks.) Lerner Publishing Group.

Juvenile Justice. 2nd rev. ed. 2010. (ENG., Illus.). 104p. (gr. 9-18). 35.00 (978-1-60413-508-4(5), P178897, Facts On File) Infobase Holdings, Inc.

Krygier, Leora. Juvenile Court: A Judge's Guide for Young Adults & Their Parents. 2008. (ENG., Illus.). 196p. (J). (gr. -1-12). 55.00 (978-0-8108-6127-5(5)) Scarecrow Pr., Inc.

Lange, Donna. On the Edge of Disaster: Youth in the Juvenile Court System. 2004. (Youth with Special Needs Ser.). (Illus.). 128p. (YA). lib. bdg. 24.95 (978-1-59084-741-1(5)) Mason Crest.

—On the Edge of Disaster: Youth in the Juvenile Court System. 2003. (Youth with Special Needs Ser.). (Illus.). 127p. (YA). (gr. 7). pap. 14.95 (978-1-4222-0428-3(6)) Mason Crest.

Langwith, Jacqueline, ed. Juvenile Crime, 1 vol. 2014. (Introducing Issues with Opposing Viewpoints Ser.). (ENG., Illus.). 120p. (gr. 7-10). lib. bdg. 43.63 (978-0-7377-6925-8(4), 248c2ff5-52f2-4f27-a272-9851b7f1c23a, Greenhaven Publishing) Greenhaven Publishing LLC.

Latchana Kenney, Karen. The Hidden Story of Gangs & Crime, 1 vol., 1. 2013. (Undercover Story Ser.). (ENG.). 48p. (J). (gr. 5-5). 34.41 (978-1-4777-2799-7(X), 9026e669-133f-4844-a582-9dc59c91a5cb, Rosen Reference) Rosen Publishing Group, Inc., The.

Leverich, Jean, ed. Juvenile Justice, 1 vol. 2009. (Issues on Trial Ser.). (ENG., Illus.). 248p. (gr. 10-12). 49.93 (978-0-7377-4178-0(3),

224d7e74-f4e0-43ee-9493-3406077e6057, Greenhaven Publishing) Greenhaven Publishing LLC.

Meyer, Terry Teague. Juvenile Detention Centers: Your Legal Rights, 1 vol. 2015. (Know Your Rights Ser.). (ENG., Illus.). 64p. (J). (gr. 6-6). 36.47 *(978-1-4777-8036-7(X),* 066fe441-40f5-4783-b58c-97d6fa96e0a3, Rosen Young Adult) Rosen Publishing Group, Inc., The.

Micklos, John, Jr. True Stories of Teen Prisoners, 1 vol. 2017. (True Teen Stories Ser.). (ENG.). 112p. (YA). (gr. 9-9). 44.50 *(978-1-5026-3160-2(1),* 7f0437b7-c9a0-4615-9e86-2d31e867d9c2); pap. 20.99 *(978-1-5026-3403-0(1),* 32b4fe58-6f10-4617-9a9d-bc6aad138951) Cavendish Square Publishing LLC.

mooney, carla. Teen Violence. 2013. (ENG.). 96p. (YA). lib. bdg. *(978-1-60152-496-6(X))* ReferencePoint Pr., Inc.

Parks, Peggy J. School Violence. 2008. (Compact Research Ser.). 104p. (YA). (gr. 7-12). lib. bdg. 43.93 *(978-1-60152-057-9(3))* ReferencePoint Pr., Inc.

Smith, Roger & McIntosh, Martha. Juveniles Growing up in Prison. 2017. (Illus.). 80p. (J). *(978-1-4222-3783-0(4))* Mason Crest.

Spencer, Betty. Life Is Fragile: One Girl's Story of the Bath School Disaster. Gallinger, Jared, illus. 2007. 68p. per. 19.95 *(978-1-60441-772-2(2))* America Star Bks.

Watson, Stephanie. Incarcerated Youth. 2016. (ENG.). 80p. (J). (gr. 5-12). lib. bdg. *(978-1-60152-982-4(1))* ReferencePoint Pr., Inc.

Wolny, Philip. Defeating Gangs in Your Neighborhood & Online, 1 vol., 1. 2015. (Effective Survival Strategies Ser.). (ENG.). 64p. (J). (gr. 6-6). 36.13 *(978-1-4994-6151-0(8),* 5a9a497b-5b83-4ace-b9a3-10430e1abdc4, Rosen Young Adult) Rosen Publishing Group, Inc., The.

JUVENILE DELINQUENCY—FICTION

Berry, Julie & Gardner, Sally Faye. The Rat Brain Fiasco. 2010. (Splurch Academy for Disruptive Boys Ser.: 1). (ENG.). 187p. (J). (gr. 4-6). 21.19 *(978-0-448-45359-0(2))* Penguin Young Readers Group.

Brouwer, Sigmund. Heavy Freight, 1 vol. 2017. (Orca Soundings Ser.). (ENG.). 168p. (YA). (gr. 8-12). pap. 9.95 *(978-1-4598-1475-2(4))* Orca Bk. Pubs. USA.

De La Peña, Matt. We Were Here. 2010. (ENG.). 368p. (YA). (gr. 8-12). lib. bdg. 26.19 *(978-0-385-90622-7(6))* Random House Publishing Group.

de la Peña, Matt. We Were Here. 2010. (ENG.). 384p. (YA). (gr. 9). pap. 11.99 *(978-0-385-73670-1(3),* Ember) Random Hse. Children's Bks.

Deen, Natasha. Sleight of Hand, 1 vol. 2015. (Orca Soundings Ser.). (ENG.). 144p. (YA). (gr. 8-12). pap. 9.95 *(978-1-4598-1120-1(8))* Orca Bk. Pubs. USA.

Ducie, Joe. Crystal Force. 2016. (ENG.). 288p. (YA). (gr. 7). pap. 9.99 *(978-1-4714-0455-9(2))* Bonnier Publishing GBR. Dist: Independent Pubs. Group.

Frye, Mark. School Shooter: In His Own Words. 2005. 194p. (J). per. 14.95 *(978-0-595-34751-3(7))* iUniverse, Inc.

Ghislain, Gary. How I Stole Johnny Depp's Alien Girlfriend. 2011. (ENG., Illus.). 208p. (YA). (gr. 7-17). 16.99 *(978-0-8118-7460-1(5))* Chronicle Bks. LLC.

Griffin, Paul. Ten Mile River. 2011. (ENG.). 208p. (YA). (gr. 7-18). 7.99 *(978-0-14-241983-0(4),* Speak) Penguin Young Readers Group.

Ius, Dawn. Overdrive. (ENG.). (YA). (gr. 9). 2017. 368p. pap. 10.99 *(978-1-4814-3945-9(6))* 2016. (Illus.). 352p. 17.99 *(978-1-4814-3944-2(8))* Simon Pulse. (Simon Pulse).

Mason, Simon. Kid Alone: a Garvie Smith Mystery: A Garvie Smith Mystery. 2017. (ENG.). 384p. (YA). (gr. 9). 18.99 *(978-1-338-03649-7(1))* Scholastic, Inc.

McClintock, Norah. Down, 1 vol. 2007. (Orca Soundings Ser.). (ENG.). 128p. (YA). (gr. 8-12). pap. 9.95 *(978-1-55143-766-8(X))* Orca Bk. Pubs. USA.

—In Too Deep, No. 8. 2013. (Robyn Hunter Mysteries Ser.: 8). (ENG.). 224p. (YA). (gr. 6-12). pap. 8.95 *(978-1-4677-0702-2(3),* 19db96f6-0e11-4371-9352-7fa4a1010d67); lib. bdg. 27.99 *(978-0-7613-8318-5(2),* acbb334b-c787-4cc4-baca-5a288444976f) Lerner Publishing Group. (Darby Creek).

McLaughlin, Lauren. The Free. 2018. (ENG.). 288p. (YA). (gr. 9). pap. 10.99 *(978-1-61695-874-9(X),* Soho Teen) Soho Pr., Inc.

Morgan, Kass. Homecoming. 2015. (100 Ser.: 3). (ENG.). 352p. (YA). (gr. 10-17). pap. 12.99 *(978-0-316-38196-3(9))* Little, Brown Bks. for Young Readers.

Myers, Walter Dean. Lockdown. (ENG.). (YA). (gr. 8). 2011. 272p. pap. 10.99 *(978-0-06-121482-0(5))* 2010. 256p. 16.99 *(978-0-06-121480-6(9))* HarperCollins Pubs. (Amistad).

Pérez, Ashley Hope. The Knife & the Butterfly. 2014. (ENG.). 216p. (YA). (gr. 9-12). pap. 9.95 *(978-1-4677-1624-6(3),* d11dcdac-0b78-4118-a992-5883e53d80b5, Carolrhoda Lab™) Lerner Publishing Group.

Sachar, Louis. Buracos. pap. 29.95 *(978-85-336-1280-8(X))* Livraria Martins Editora BRA. Dist: Distribooks, Inc.

—Holes. l.t. ed. 2017. (ENG.). 289p. 24.95 *(978-1-4328-4186-7(6))* Cengage Gale.

—Holes. 2008. (KOR., Illus.). 334p. (J). pap. *(978-89-364-5602-3(4))* Chang-jag and Bipyeong Co.

—Holes. 2018. (ENG., Illus.). 272p. (J). 21.99 *(978-0-374-31264-0(8),* 900201609, Farrar, Straus & Giroux (BYR)) Farrar, Straus & Giroux.

—Holes. 2008. (ENG.). (J). 39.99 *(978-0-7393-7103-9(7))* Findaway World, LLC.

—Holes. 2014. (CHI & ENG.). 246p. (J). (gr. 4-8). pap. *(978-7-5442-7158-5(7))* Fukuinkan Shoten.

—Holes. 2009. 9.14 *(978-0-7848-1394-2(9),* Everbind) Marco Bk. Co.

—Holes. 240p. (J). (gr. 4-6). pap. 5.99 *(978-0-8072-8073-7(9),* Listening Library) Random Hse. Audio Publishing Group.

—Holes, 4 vols. (J). 2006. 46.75 *(978-1-4193-6136-4(8))* 2004. 1.25 *(978-1-4025-6758-2(8))* Recorded Bks., Inc.

—Holes. l.t. ed. 2003. 288p. pap. 10.95 *(978-0-7862-6190-1(0))* Thorndike Pr.

—Small Steps. 2008. (Readers Circle Ser.). 257p. (gr. 5-9). 20.00 *(978-0-7569-9130-2(7))* Perfection Learning Corp.

—Small Steps. (ENG.). (YA). (gr. 7-9). 2008. (Holes Ser.: 2). 288p. pap. 10.99 *(978-0-385-73315-1(1),* Ember) 2006. 272p. lib. bdg. 26.19 *(978-0-385-90333-2(2),* Delacorte Pr.) Random Hse. Children's Bks.

—Small Steps. rev. l.t. ed. 2006. 339p. 23.95 *(978-0-7862-8297-5(5))* Thorndike Pr.

Schuh, Eileen. The Traz. 2012. (Illus.). 148p. pap. *(978-1-926997-61-2(1))* Imajin Bks.

Simonet, Andrew. Wilder. 2021. (ENG.). 320p. (YA). pap. 10.99 *(978-1-250-21159-0(X),* 900189992) Square Fish.

Spradlin, Michael P. Live & Let Shop. 2005. (Spy Goddess Ser.: Bk. 1). (ENG., Illus.). 224p. (gr. 7-18). 15.99 *(978-0-06-059407-7(1))* HarperCollins Pubs.

Strasser, Todd. Boot Camp. 2012. (ENG.). 272p. (YA). (gr. 7). pap. 12.99 *(978-1-4424-3358-8(2),* Simon & Schuster Bks. For Young Readers) Simon & Schuster Bks. For Young Readers.

—Boot Camp. 2007. (ENG.). 235p. (YA). (gr. 7-12). 21.19 *(978-1-4169-0848-7(X))* Simon & Schuster, Inc.

Tagged. 2015. 208p. (YA). (gr. 7). lib. bdg. 16.95 *(978-1-58089-583-5(2))* Charlesbridge Publishing, Inc.

Trueman, Terry. Inside Out. 128p. 2003. (J). lib. bdg. 16.89 *(978-0-06-623963-7(X))* 2004. (ENG.). (YA). (gr. 9). reprint ed. pap. 9.99 *(978-0-06-447376-7(7),* HarperTeen) HarperCollins Pubs.

Volponi, Paul. Rikers High. 2011. (ENG.). 272p. (YA). (gr. 7-18). 9.99 *(978-0-14-241778-2(5),* Speak) Penguin Young Readers Group.

Voorhees, Coert. On the Free. 2017. (ENG.). 280p. (YA). (gr. 9-12). 17.99 *(978-1-5124-2913-8(9),* 43e96ca4-2df6-49e1-b581-bfb0ae0a00f1, Carolrhoda Lab™) Lerner Publishing Group.

JUVENILE LITERATURE

see Children's Literature

K

KAFKA, FRANZ, 1883-1924

Férriz, Ramón Gónzalez. Franz Kafka -el miedo a la Vida. 2005. (SPA.). 96p. (YA). *(978-958-30-1360-7(9))* Panamericana Editorial.

KAHLO, FRIDA, 1910-1954

Alvarez, Mateo. Frida Kahlo: Famous Mexican Artist, 1 vol. 2015. (Exceptional Latinos Ser.). (ENG.). 24p. (gr. 3-4). pap. 10.35 *(978-0-7660-6714-1(9),* 74200deb-9c85-4dea-9363-dcd85c1a59f9) Enslow Publishing, LLC.

Anholt, Laurence. Frida Kahlo & the Bravest Girl in the World: Famous Artists & the Children Who Knew Them. 2016. (Anholt's Artists Books for Children Ser.). (ENG., Illus.). 32p. (J). (gr. k-3). 16.99 *(978-0-7641-6837-6(1))* Sourcebooks, Inc.

Berenger, Al. Pocket Bios: Frida Kahlo. Berenger, Al, illus. 2018. (Pocket Bios Ser.). (ENG., Illus.). 32p. (J). 14.99 *(978-1-250-16875-7(9),* 900187746) Roaring Brook Pr.

Berne, Emma Carlson. Frida Kahlo: Groundbreaking Artist, 1 vol. 2009. (Essential Lives Set 4 Ser.). (ENG., Illus.). 112p. (YA). (gr. 6-12). lib. bdg. 41.36 *(978-1-60453-701-7(9),* 6693, Essential Library) ABDO Publishing Co.

Brown, Monica. Frida Kahlo & Her Animalitos. Parra, John, illus. 2017. (ENG.). 40p. (J). (gr. -1-3). 18.95 *(978-0-7358-4269-4(8))* North-South Bks., Inc.

Colbert, David & Chambers, Mark. Frida Kahlo. 2009. (10 Days Ser.). (ENG.). 160p. (J). (gr. 3-8). pap. 6.99 *(978-1-4169-6809-2(1),* Simon & Schuster/Paula Wiseman Bks.) Simon & Schuster/Paula Wiseman Bks.

Collier Hillstrom, Laurie. Frida Kahlo: Painter, 1 vol. 2008. (Twentieth Century's Most Influential Hispanics Ser.). (ENG., Illus.). 104p. (gr. 7-10). 41.03 *(978-1-4205-0019-6(8),* a30b590c-d8db-4a58-ac9e-a9a77f8fe4a0, Lucent Pr.) Greenhaven Publishing LLC.

Devera, Czeena. Frida Kahlo. Bane, Jeff, illus. 2017. (My Early Library: My Itty-Bitty Bio Ser.). (ENG.). 24p. (J). (gr. k-1). 30.64 *(978-1-63472-815-7(7),* 209686) Cherry Lake Publishing.

Doeden, Matt. Frida Kahlo: Artist & Activist. 2020. (Gateway Biographies Ser.). (ENG., Illus.). 48p. (J). (gr. 4-8). pap. 11.99 *(978-1-5415-8888-2(6),* 4e95bb11-576b-4bed-b211-32e60ca411e8); lib. bdg. 31.99 *(978-1-5415-7745-9(0),* 2a8ec86f-831c-4113-b8a2-fb3ac0b696ba) Lerner Publishing Group. (Lerner Pubns.).

Fabiny, Sarah. Who Was Frida Kahlo? 2013. (Who Was... ? Ser.). lib. bdg. 16.00 *(978-0-606-34164-6(1))* Turtleback.

Fabiny, Sarah & Who HQ. Who Was Frida Kahlo? Hoare, Jerry, illus. 2013. (Who Was? Ser.). 112p. (J). (gr. 3-7). 6.99 *(978-0-448-47938-5(9),* Penguin Workshop) Penguin Young Readers Group.

Feldman, Thea. A Parrot in the Painting: The Story of Frida Kahlo & Bonito (Ready-To-Read Level 2) Sanson, Rachel, illus. 2018. (Tails from History Ser.). (ENG.). 32p. (J). (gr. k-2). 17.99 *(978-1-5344-2230-8(7));* pap. 4.99 *(978-1-5344-2229-2(3))* Simon Spotlight. (Simon Spotlight).

Fink, Nadia. Frida Kahlo para Niñas y Niños. Saa, Pitu, illus. 2016.Tr. of Frida Kalho for Girls & Boys. (SPA.). (gr. 2-12). pap. 12.99 *(978-0-9973280-0-4(2))* Bks. del Sur.

Frida Kahlo. 2018. (J). *(978-0-7166-2282-6(3))* World Bk., Inc.

Laidlaw, Jill A. Frida Kahlo. 2003. (Artists in Their Time Ser.). (ENG., Illus.). 48p. (J). (gr. 5-7). pap. 6.95 *(978-0-531-16642-0(2),* Watts, Franklin) Scholastic Library Publishing.

Lenero, Carmen. Frida Kahlo. Mesquita, Camila, illus. 2004. (Niñez de...Ser.). 24p. pap. 6.95 *(978-85-7416-216-4(7))* Callis Editora Ltda BRA. Dist: Independent Pubs. Group.

Medina, Mariana & Mcintosh Wooten, Sara. Frida Kahlo: Self-Portrait Artist, 1 vol. 2015. (Influential Latinos Ser.). (ENG., Illus.). 128p. (gr. 7-7). 38.93 *(978-0-7660-6997-8(4),* 07bd4b04-4536-45a2-b6f1-5574150be40a) Enslow Publishing, LLC.

Meltzer, Brad. Soy Frida Kahlo. Eliopoulos, Christopher, illus. 2023.Tr. of I Am Frida Kahlo. (SPA.). (J). (gr. k-3). pap. 14.99 ***(978-1-5433-8604-2(0))*** Vista Higher Learning, Inc.

Morales, Yuyi. Viva Frida. Morales, Yuyi & O'Meara, Tim, illus. 2014. (ENG.). 40p. (J). (gr. -1-3). 19.99 *(978-1-59643-603-9(4),* 900065746) Roaring Brook Pr.

Nardo, Don. Frida Kahlo, 1 vol. 2012. (Eye on Art Ser.). (ENG., Illus.). 104p. (gr. 7-7). lib. bdg. 41.03 *(978-1-4205-0850-5(4),* 0d29b11b-0d31-429f-894d-3e5dbb106df0, Lucent Pr.) Greenhaven Publishing LLC.

Reef, Catherine. Frida & Diego: Art, Love, Life. 2014. (ENG., Illus.). 176p. (YA). (gr. 7-12). 18.99 *(978-0-547-82184-9(0),* 1497178, Clarion Bks.) HarperCollins Pubs.

Sabbeth, Carol. Frida Kahlo & Diego Rivera: Their Lives & Ideas, 24 Activities. 2005. (For Kids Ser.: 18). (ENG., Illus.). 160p. (J). (gr. 4). pap. 17.95 *(978-1-55652-569-8(9),* 1241061) Chicago Review Pr., Inc.

Sanchez Vegara, Maria Isabel & Fan, Eng Gee. Frida Kahlo (Little People Big Dreams) 2016. (Little People, Big Dreams Ser.). (ENG., Illus.). 32p. (J). 14.99 *(978-1-84780-770-0(4),* Frances Lincoln Children's Bks.) Quarto Publishing Group UK GBR. Dist: Littlehampton Bk Services, Ltd.

Thomas, Isabel. Frida Kahlo (Little Guides to Great Lives) Madriz, Marianna, illus. 2018. (Little Guides to Great Lives Ser.). (ENG.). 64p. (J). (gr. 2-6). 11.99 *(978-1-78627-300-0(4),* King, Laurence Publishing) Orion Publishing Group, Ltd. GBR. Dist: Hachette Bk. Group.

KAIULANI, PRINCESS OF HAWAII, 1875-1899

McDonnell, Peter. The Last Princess. 2005. (Illus.). 16p. *(978-0-7367-2910-9(0))* Zaner-Bloser, Inc.

KALAHARI DESERT

Aloian, Molly. The Kalahari Desert. 2012. (ENG.). 32p. (J). lib. bdg. *(978-0-7787-0712-7(1));* (Illus.). pap. *(978-0-7787-0720-2(2))* Crabtree Publishing Co.

KAMEHAMEHA I, THE GREAT, KING OF THE HAWAIIAN ISLANDS, -1819

Crowe, Ellie. Kamehameha: The Boy Who Became a Warrior King. Robinson, Don, illus. rev. ed. 2008. (ENG.). 62p. (J). (gr. k-k). pap. *(978-1-59700-591-3(6))* Island Heritage Publishing.

KANGAROO RATS

Phillips, Dee. Kangaroo Rat's Burrow. 2015. (Illus.). 24p. (J). lib. bdg. 26.99 *(978-1-62724-310-0(0))* Bearport Publishing Co., Inc.

KANGAROOS

Austen, Amy. The Life Cycle of a Kangaroo, 1 vol. 2015. (Watch Them Grow! Ser.). (ENG., Illus.). 24p. (J). (gr. 1-1). pap. 9.25 *(978-1-4994-0672-6(X),* cd9e57d0-f327-4baa-a6a2-2acb703b981a, PowerKids Pr.) Rosen Publishing Group, Inc., The.

Borgert-Spaniol, Megan. Baby Kangaroos. 2016. (Super Cute! Ser.). (ENG., Illus.). 24p. (J). (gr. k-3). 26.95 *(978-1-62617-389-7(3),* Blastoff! Readers) Bellwether Media.

Bredeson, Carmen. Kangaroos up Close, 1 vol. 2009. (Zoom in on Animals! Ser.). (ENG., Illus.). 24p. (gr. k-2). pap. 10.95 *(978-1-59845-416-1(1),* 8bc1659d-4a84-4083-8540-68e24fb0dd30); lib. bdg. 25.60 *(978-0-7660-3079-4(2),* 3ac3f13f-6288-408e-bd82-36ff29b47982) Enslow Publishing, LLC. (Enslow Elementary).

Burke, Juliet. A Kangaroo Mob, 1 vol. 2013. (Animal Groups Ser.). (ENG., Illus.). 24p. (J). (gr. 1-2). pap. 9.15 *(978-1-4339-8200-2(5),* 29b2de7c-c4b2-4ea1-bc57-38c7cd105ca3); lib. bdg. 25.27 *(978-1-4339-8199-9(8),* c2c80671-76e0-47ad-af42-c80a358d3dc6) Stevens, Gareth Publishing LLLP.

—A Kangaroo Mob / una Manada de Canguros, 1 vol. 2013. (Animal Groups / Grupos de Animales Ser.). (ENG & SPA., Illus.). 24p. (gr. 1-2). 25.27 *(978-1-4339-8804-2(6),* 301e992c-86cc-4a72-9782-dba11407ba07) Stevens, Gareth Publishing LLLP.

Calhoun, Kelly. High-Speed Hoppers: Kangaroo. 2015. (Guess What Ser.). (ENG.). 24p. (J). (gr. k-2). pap. 12.79 *(978-1-63362-712-3(8),* 206681) Cherry Lake Publishing.

—Saltarines de Alta Velocidad (High-Speed Hoppers) Canguro (Kangaroo) 2016. (Adivina (Guess What) Ser.). (SPA., Illus.). 24p. (J). (gr. k-2). 30.64 *(978-1-63471-449-5(0),* 208859) Cherry Lake Publishing.

Clark, Willow. Tree Kangaroos, 1 vol. 2012. (Up a Tree Ser.). (ENG., Illus.). 24p. (J). (gr. 2-3). pap. 9.25 *(978-1-4488-6337-2(6),* d476aa47-d538-491f-a30b-60ec80e5bba1, PowerKids Pr.); lib. bdg. 26.27 *(978-1-4488-6189-7(6),* 38b5035e-a22d-4d56-a149-89909444a404) Rosen Publishing Group, Inc., The.

Clausen-Grace, Nicki. Kangaroos. 2018. (Wild Animal Kingdom (Continuation) Ser.). (ENG.). 32p. (gr. 2-7). 9.95 *(978-1-68072-735-7(4));* (J). (gr. 4-6). pap. 9.99 *(978-1-64466-288-5(4),* 12405); (J). (gr. 4-6). lib. bdg. *(978-1-68072-441-7(X),* 12404) Black Rabbit Bks. (Bolt).

Costain, Meredith. Kangaroo, 1 vol. Jackson-Carter, Stuart, illus. 2016. (Wild World Ser.). (ENG.). 32p. (J). (gr. 1-2). pap. 11.00 *(978-1-4994-8212-6(4),* 0e3fb7ef-2d94-46a3-9d4c-9bf948459a06, Windmill Bks.) Rosen Publishing Group, Inc., The.

Davin, Rose. Kangaroos. 2017. (Meet Desert Animals Ser.). (ENG., Illus.). 24p. (J). (gr. -1-2). lib. bdg. 27.32 *(978-1-5157-4604-1(6),* 134288, Capstone Pr.) Capstone.

De la Bédoyère, Camilla. Joey to Kangaroo. 2012. (ENG., Illus.). 24p. (gr. 1-3). pap. 7.95 *(978-1-926853-38-3(5))* Saunders Bk. Co. CAN. Dist: RiverStream Publishing.

De Luca, Daniela. Buster the Kangaroo. 2008. (It's a Wildlife, Buddy! Ser.). (ENG., Illus.). 30p. (J). (gr. -1-1). 12.95 *(978-88-89272-62-6(7))* McRae Bks. Srl ITA. Dist: Independent Pubs. Group.

Esbaum, Jill. Explore My World: Kangaroos. 2018. (Explore My World Ser.). (Illus.). 32p. (J). (gr. -1-k). pap. 4.99 *(978-1-4263-3157-2(6),* National Geographic Kids) Disney Publishing Worldwide.

Franks, Katie. Kangaroos. 2014. (Zoo's Who's Who Ser.). (Illus.). 24p. (J). (gr. k-2). pap. 49.50 *(978-1-4777-6573-9(5),* PowerKids Pr.) Rosen Publishing Group, Inc., The.

French, Jackie. How High Can a Kangaroo Hop? 2008. (ENG., Illus.). 258p. pap. *(978-0-7322-8544-9(5))* HarperCollins Pubs. Australia.

Gillespie, Katie. A Kangaroo's World. 2018. (Illus.). 24p. (J). *(978-1-4896-5668-1(5),* AV2 by Weigl) Weigl Pubs., Inc.

Gish, Melissa. Living Wild: Kangaroos. 2011. (Living Wild Ser.). (ENG.). 48p. (J). (gr. 4-7). pap. 12.00 *(978-0-89812-553-5(7),* 22208, Creative Paperbacks) Creative Co., The.

Hewett, Joan. A Kangaroo Joey Grows Up. Hewett, Richard, photos by. 2005. (Baby Animals Ser.). (Illus.). 32p. (J). (gr. k-3). lib. bdg. 21.27 *(978-1-57505-165-9(6))* Lerner Publishing Group.

Jango-Cohen, Judith. Kangaroos, 1 vol. 2007. (Animals, Animals Ser.). (ENG., Illus.). 48p. (gr. 5-5). lib. bdg. 32.64 *(978-0-7614-1869-6(5),* 5e77dd1a-4db2-4f3d-8e75-6548f5f92967) Cavendish Square Publishing LLC.

Kras, Sara Louise. Kangaroos: A 4D Book. rev. ed. 2018. (Australian Animals Ser.). (ENG., Illus.). 24p. (J). (gr. -1-2). lib. bdg. 29.32 *(978-1-9771-0000-9(7),* 138163, Capstone Pr.) Capstone.

Lawrence, Ellen. A Kangaroo's Life. 2012. (Animal Diaries: Life Cycles Ser.). 24p. (J). (gr. -1-3). lib. bdg. 26.99 *(978-1-61772-415-2(7))* Bearport Publishing Co., Inc.

Leigh, Anna. Meet a Baby Kangaroo. 2017. (Lightning Bolt Books (r) — Baby Australian Animals Ser.). (ENG., Illus.). 24p. (J). (gr. 1-3). 29.32 *(978-1-5124-3384-5(5),* 1d985e09-6abd-4483-8c7f-f4cd71f451a3, Lerner Pubns.); pap. 9.99 *(978-1-5124-5588-5(1),* a77fec06-48b6-4b77-8bbf-9d20c4799369) Lerner Publishing Group.

—Meet a Baby Wallaby. 2017. (Lightning Bolt Books (r) — Baby Australian Animals Ser.). (ENG., Illus.). 24p. (J). (gr. 1-3). 29.32 *(978-1-5124-3386-9(1),* bef73b2d-3d7a-43bc-8f37-9d5117919ad8, Lerner Pubns.); pap. 9.99 *(978-1-5124-5591-5(1),* 11157161-0098-4447-b7ab-6ebe225d3fde) Lerner Publishing Group.

Levine, Michelle. Jumping Kangaroos. 2005. (Pull Ahead Bks.). (J). 22.60 *(978-0-8225-2421-2(X),* Lerner Pubns.); (ENG., Illus.). 32p. pap. 7.99 *(978-0-8225-2440-3(6),* 6a589af4-57cd-4806-a80a-276d07da254a, First Avenue Editions) Lerner Publishing Group.

Linde, Barbara M. The Bizarre Life Cycle of a Kangaroo, 1 vol. 2012. (Strange Life Cycles Ser.). (ENG., Illus.). 24p. (J). (gr. 2-3). 25.27 *(978-1-4339-7047-4(3),* 53572866-638b-4a3c-a34e-3477c3decaef); pap. 9.15 *(978-1-4339-7048-1(1),* 66cd8e55-6706-41b2-be58-c2c137cd6291) Stevens, Gareth Publishing LLLP. (Gareth Stevens Learning Library).

Lunde, Darrin. Hello, Mama Wallaroo. Wynne, Patricia J., illus. 2013. (ENG.). 32p. (J). (gr. -1-2). pap. 6.95 *(978-1-57091-797-4(3));* lib. bdg. 15.95 *(978-1-57091-796-7(5))* Charlesbridge Publishing, Inc.

Lunis, Natalie. Red Kangaroo: The World's Largest Marsupial. 2010. (More SuperSized! Ser.). (Illus.). 24p. (J). (gr. k-3). lib. bdg. 26.99 *(978-1-936087-24-2(3))* Bearport Publishing Co., Inc.

McNeil, Niki, et al. HOCPP 1121 Kangaroos. 2006. spiral bd. 12.50 *(978-1-60308-121-4(6))* In the Hands of a Child.

McRae, Anne & Morris, Neil. Buster the Kangaroo. De Luca, Daniela, illus. 2017. 31p. (J). *(978-0-7166-3523-9(2))* World Bk., Inc.

Meachen Rau, Dana. Guess Who Hops, 1 vol. 2009. (Guess Who? Ser.). (ENG.). 32p. (gr. k-1). pap. 9.23 *(978-0-7614-3554-9(9),* b7e78011-ddc2-4cdc-b459-eaf01d782419) Cavendish Square Publishing LLC.

Meister, Cari. Do You Really Want to Meet a Kangaroo? Fabbri, Daniele, illus. 2015. (Do You Really Want to Meet ... ? Ser.). (ENG.). 24p. (J). (gr. 1-4). lib. bdg. 19.95 *(978-1-60753-734-2(6),* 15265) Amicus.

Montgomery, Sy. The Quest for the Tree Kangaroo: An Expedition to the Cloud Forest of New Guinea. Bishop, Nic, photos by. 2009. (Scientists in the Field Ser.). (ENG., Illus.). 80p. (J). (gr. 5-7). pap. 10.99 *(978-0-547-24892-9(X),* 1100904, Clarion Bks.) HarperCollins Pubs.

Moore Niver, Heather. How Kangaroos Grow Up, 1 vol. 2018. (Animals Growing Up Ser.). (ENG.). 24p. (gr. 1-2). 24.27 *(978-0-7660-9647-9(5),* 536dd635-2344-4d4a-8eab-0d0ee98a450e) Enslow Publishing, LLC.

Murray, Julie. Kangaroos. (Animal Kingdom Ser.). (ENG., Illus.). (J). 2019. 32p. (gr. 2-5). lib. bdg. 34.21 *(978-1-5321-1641-4(1),* 32393, Big Buddy Bks.) 2016. 24p. (gr. -1-2). lib. bdg. 31.36 *(978-1-68080-905-3(9),* 23285, Abdo Kids) 2011. 32p. (gr. 2-5). 34.21 *(978-1-61783-011-2(9),* 2874, Big Buddy Bks.) ABDO Publishing Co.

Nickel, Bonnie. Those Kooky Kangaroos. 2012. (Those Amazing Animals Ser.). (ENG., Illus.). 56p. (J). (gr. -1-12). 14.95 *(978-1-56164-534-3(6));* pap. 9.95 *(978-1-56164-535-0(4))* Pineapple Pr., Inc.

Phillips, Dee. Tree Kangaroo. 2013. (Science Slam: Treed-Animal Life in the Trees Ser.). 24p. (J). (gr. -1-3). lib. bdg. 26.99 *(978-1-61772-914-0(0))* Bearport Publishing Co., Inc.

Pohl, Kathleen. Kangaroos, 1 vol. 2007. (Let's Read about Animals Ser.). (ENG., Illus.). 24p. (gr. k-2). pap. 9.15 *(978-0-8368-7824-0(8),* 2af0f812-d428-460b-af50-99e9d71fe0ca); lib. bdg. 24.67 *(978-0-8368-7817-2(5),* a0831587-b98a-4e1e-9f66-c42f22f94873) Stevens, Gareth Publishing LLLP. (Weekly Reader Leveled Readers).

—Kangaroos / Canguros, 1 vol. 2007. (Let's Read about Animals / Conozcamos a Los Animales Ser.). (ENG & SPA., Illus.). 24p. (gr. k-2). (J). lib. bdg. 24.67 *(978-0-8368-8006-9(4),* bf36d60d-5cbb-4602-8d74-734485f573a1); pap. 9.15 *(978-0-8368-8013-7(7),* 16b5f9bc-8879-4bea-b903-b5c353f20ece) Stevens, Gareth Publishing LLLP. (Weekly Reader Leveled Readers).

Rebus, Anna. Kangaroos. 2006. (Amazing Animals Ser.). (Illus.). 24p. (J). (gr. 3-7). pap. 8.95 *(978-1-59036-399-7(X));* lib. bdg. 24.45 *(978-1-59036-393-5(0))* Weigl Pubs., Inc.

Reilly, Pauline. Kangaroo. Russell, Gayle, illus. (Picture Roo Bks.). 32p. (J). pap. *(978-0-86417-538-0(8),* Kangaroo Pr.) Simon & Schuster Australia.

Ricciuti, Edward R. Adivina Quién Salta / Guess Who Hops, 1 vol. 2009. (Adivina Quién / Guess Who? Ser.). (ENG & SPA.). 32p. (gr. k-2). 25.50 *(978-0-7614-2884-8(4),* 47f2430d-a043-4a1f-99b6-d7c2d13e013d) Cavendish Square Publishing LLC.

—Adivina Quién Salta (Guess Who Hops), 1 vol. 2009. (Adivina Quién (Guess Who?) Ser.). (SPA.). 32p. (gr. k-2).

25.50 *(978-0-7614-2867-1(4),* 93440931-208e-487a-b77c-dbd66468d1ba) Cavendish Square Publishing LLC.

—Guess Who Hops, 1 vol. 2006. (Guess Who? Ser.). (ENG., Illus.). 32p. (gr. k-1). 25.50 *(978-0-7614-1764-4(8),* 3afdb6f6-ba5b-4ef4-8fe3-ec30b5416d6a) Cavendish Square Publishing LLC.

Rigby Education Staff. Kangaroo. (Illus.). (J). suppl. ed. 20.00 *(978-0-7635-6461-2(3),* 764613C99) Rigby Education.

Riggs, Kate. Kangaroos. (Seedlings Ser.). (J). 2017. (ENG., Illus.). 24p. (gr. k-2). pap. 9.99 *(978-1-62832-335-1(3),* 20729, Creative Paperbacks) 2016. (ENG., Illus.). 24p. (gr. -1-k). *(978-1-60818-739-3(X),* 20731, Creative Education) 2012. 25.65 *(978-1-60818-108-7(1),* Creative Education) Creative Co., The.

Robbins, Lynette. Kangaroos. (J). 2012. 49.50 *(978-1-4488-5160-7(2),* PowerKids Pr.) 2011. (ENG.). 24p. (gr. 2-3). pap. 9.25 *(978-1-4488-5159-1(9),* 86511555-1241-4011-8d03-b0fed3fba6b2, PowerKids Pr.) 2011. (ENG.). 24p. (gr. 2-3). lib. bdg. 26.27 *(978-1-4488-5013-6(4),* 9c60f796-2849-4f72-bacd-f7282a16135a) Rosen Publishing Group, Inc., The.

Schuetz, Kari. Kangaroos. 2013. (Animal Safari Ser.). (ENG., Illus.). 24p. (J). (gr. k-3). lib. bdg. 26.95 *(978-1-60014-864-4(6),* Blastoff! Readers) Bellwether Media.

Schuh, Mari. Kangaroos. 2015. (J). lib. bdg. 25.65 *(978-1-62031-175-2(5),* Bullfrog Bks.) Jump! Inc.

Staff, Gareth Editorial Staff. Kangaroos, 1 vol. 2004. (All about Wild Animals Ser.). (ENG., Illus.). 32p. (gr. 2-4). lib. bdg. 28.67 *(978-0-8368-4119-0(0),* c8980046-0927-47ae-8a39-b2d9ce59a8a8, Gareth Stevens Learning Library) Stevens, Gareth Publishing LLLP.

Stockburger, Susan. Adventures of Sugar Pie! 2011. 20p. (gr. -1). pap. 11.00 *(978-1-4567-5356-6(8))* AuthorHouse.

Swanson, Diane. Welcome to the World of Kangaroos. 2003. (Welcome to the World Ser.: 0). (ENG., Illus.). 28p. (J). (gr. -1-2). pap. 7.95 *(978-1-55285-471-6(X),* 82acd7c3-738b-4c46-8543-d6cb2a9a1d6f) Whitecap Bks., Ltd. CAN. Dist: Firefly Bks., Ltd.

Turnbull, Stephanie. Kangaroo. 2015. (Big Beasts Ser.). (ENG., Illus.). 24p. (J). (gr. 1-4). 28.50 *(978-1-62588-166-3(5),* 17275) Black Rabbit Bks.

—Kangaroo. 2015. (ENG., Illus.). 24p. (J). pap. 8.95 *(978-1-77092-214-3(8))* RiverStream Publishing.

Twine, Alice. Kangaroos. (Baby Animals Ser.). 24p. (gr. 1-1). 2009. 42.50 *(978-1-61511-491-7(2))* 2008. (ENG., Illus.). (J). lib. bdg. 26.27 *(978-1-4042-4145-9(0),* db5508bb-b8ef-4133-993e-98780e97ca5e) Rosen Publishing Group, Inc., The. (PowerKids Pr.).

—Kangaroos/Canguros. 2009. (Baby Animals/Animales bebé Ser.). (ENG & SPA.). 24p. (gr. 1-1). 42.50 *(978-1-61511-503-7(X),* Editorial Buenas Letras) Rosen Publishing Group, Inc., The.

—Kangaroos/Canguros, 1 vol. Obregon, Jose Maria, tr. 2007. (Baby Animals / Animales Bebé Ser.). (SPA & ENG., Illus.). 24p. (J). (gr. 1-1). lib. bdg. 26.27 *(978-1-4042-7684-0(X),* 697c9662-7298-4e09-be20-050f7e95b139) Rosen Publishing Group, Inc., The.

Wilsdon, Christina. Kangaroos, 1 vol. 2010. (Amazing Animals Ser.). (ENG.). 48p. (J). (gr. 3-5). pap. 11.50 *(978-1-4339-4017-0(5),* 30a43052-981e-4ae0-bbfb-c08135d89047); lib. bdg. 30.67 *(978-1-4339-4016-3(7),* a39bdf46-4095-4aaa-824c-58447149fb1d) Stevens, Gareth Publishing LLLP. (Gareth Stevens Learning Library).

—Kangaroos. 2006. (J). *(978-1-59939-078-9(7),* Reader's Digest Young Families, Inc.) Studio Fun International.

KANGAROOS—FICTION

Aldrick, Shirley H. F. Hazel, the Hoppity Kangaroo. 2010. 28p. pap. 12.50 *(978-1-60860-743-3(7),* Strategic Bk. Publishing) Strategic Book Publishing & Rights Agency (SBPRA).

Angel, Ido. Vipo in Australia: The Koala & the Kangaroo. 2015. (AV2 Animated Storytime Ser.). (ENG.). (J). lib. bdg. 29.99 *(978-1-4896-3905-9(5),* AV2 by Weigl) Weigl Pubs., Inc.

Baker, David. The Roos, A home for Baby. 2005. 14p. 12.49 *(978-1-4116-2290-6(1))* Lulu Pr., Inc.

—The Roos, Baby's new Friend. 2006. 18p. 12.49 *(978-1-4116-9123-0(7))* Lulu Pr., Inc.

Baldree, Travis. Jumpin' Joey. 2nd ed. 2013. 28p. pap. 9.99 *(978-0-9855312-9-4(0))* Bolton Publishing LLC.

Barraza, Cindy Lou. Mexiroo Dice, ¡Qué Importa! 2013. 32p. pap. 12.99 *(978-1-890900-80-9(X))* Insight Publishing Group.

Benjamin, A. H. Baa! Moo! What Will We Do? Chapman, Jane, tr. Chapman, Jane, illus. 2003. 32p. (J). pap. 6.95 *(978-1-58925-381-0(7))* Tiger Tales.

Berg, Dick. Padunkapoo: The Hawaiian Kangaroo. Berg, Gary, ed. l.t. ed. 2005. (Illus.). 28p. (J). per. 6.99 *(978-0-9769985-1-8(3))* Grace Publishing.

Blackstone, Stella. Who Are You, Baby Kangaroo? Beaton, Clare, illus. 2005. (ENG.). 24p. (J). (gr. -1-2). bds. 6.99 *(978-1-905236-19-0(0))* Barefoot Bks., Inc.

Blyton, Enid. Mister Meddle's Muddles. (Illus.). 111p. (J). pap. 6.95 *(978-0-7475-3860-8(3))* Bloomsbury Publishing Plc GBR. Dist: Trafalgar Square Publishing.

Bornemann, Elsa. Cuentos a Salto de Canguro. 2003. (SPA., Illus.). 97p. (J). (gr. 3-5). pap. 9.95 *(978-950-511-245-6(9))* Alfaguara S.A. de Ediciones ARG. Dist: Santillana USA Publishing Co., Inc.

Bourguignon, Laurence. Heart in the Pocket. D'heur, Valérie, illus. 2008. 26p. (J). (gr. -1-3). 16.50 *(978-0-8028-5343-1(9))* Eerdmans, William B. Publishing Co.

Bright, J. E. The Fastest Pet on Earth, 1 vol. Baltazar, Art, illus. 2011. (DC Super-Pets Ser.). (ENG.). 56p. (J). (gr. 1-3). lib. bdg. 25.32 *(978-1-4048-6264-7(1),* 113677, Stone Arch Bks.) Capstone.

Bump! KinderReaders Individual Title, 6 pack. (Kinderstarters Ser.). 8p. (gr. -1-1). 21.00 *(978-0-7635-8649-2(8))* Rigby Education.

Butler, Ethel And Steven, creator. Callie the Kangie Traveling America. 2012. 32p. pap. 15.99 *(978-1-4685-6197-5(9))* AuthorHouse.

Cadet, John. The Kangaroo's Adventure. 2012. 24p. pap. 24.95 *(978-1-4560-2861-9(8))* America Star Bks.

Chichester Clark, Emma. Happy Birthday, Blue Kangaroo! (Blue Kangaroo) Chichester Clark, Emma, illus. 2020. (Blue Kangaroo Ser.). (ENG., Illus.). 32p. (J). pap. 6.99 *(978-0-00-826630-1(1),* HarperCollins Children's Bks.) HarperCollins Pubs. Ltd. GBR. Dist: HarperCollins Pubs.

—I'll Show You, Blue Kangaroo! (Blue Kangaroo) Chichester Clark, Emma, illus. 2019. (Blue Kangaroo Ser.). (ENG., Illus.). 32p. (J). pap. 6.99 *(978-0-00-826627-1(1),* HarperCollins Children's Bks.) HarperCollins Pubs. Ltd. GBR. Dist: HarperCollins Pubs.

—It Was You, Blue Kangaroo (Blue Kangaroo) Chichester Clark, Emma, illus. 2018. (Blue Kangaroo Ser.). (ENG., Illus.). 32p. pap. 6.99 *(978-0-00-826626-4(3),* HarperCollins Children's Bks.) HarperCollins Pubs. Ltd. GBR. Dist: HarperCollins Pubs.

—Merry Christmas, Blue Kangaroo! (Blue Kangaroo) Chichester Clark, Emma, illus. 2017. (Blue Kangaroo Ser.). (ENG., Illus.). 32p. 17.99 *(978-0-00-824219-0(4),* HarperCollins Children's Bks.) HarperCollins Pubs. Ltd. GBR. Dist: HarperCollins Pubs.

—What Shall We Do, Blue Kangaroo? (Blue Kangaroo) Chichester Clark, Emma, illus. 2019. (Blue Kangaroo Ser.). (ENG., Illus.). 32p. (J). pap. 6.99 *(978-0-00-826629-5(8),* HarperCollins Children's Bks.) HarperCollins Pubs. Ltd. GBR. Dist: HarperCollins Pubs.

—Where Are You, Blue Kangaroo? (Blue Kangaroo) Chichester Clark, Emma, illus. 2019. (Blue Kangaroo Ser.). (ENG., Illus.). 32p. (J). pap. 6.99 *(978-0-00-826628-8(X),* HarperCollins Children's Bks.) HarperCollins Pubs. Ltd. GBR. Dist: HarperCollins Pubs.

Collins, Diana Sue. Elfin, the Elf. 2011. 44p. pap. 24.95 *(978-1-4560-8493-6(3))* America Star Bks.

Cook, Sherry & Johnson, Terri. Kitchen Chemistry Kal, 26 vols. Kuhn, Jesse, illus. l.t. ed. 2006. (Quirkles — Exploring Phonics through Science Ser.: 11). 32p. (J). 7.99 *(978-1-933815-10-7(8),* Quirkles, The) Creative 3, LLC.

Cox, Robert & Robins, Jim. The Kangaroo Who Couldn't Hop. 2005. (Illus.). 32p. (J). (gr. -1 — 1). pap., pap. *(978-0-7344-0717-7(3),* Lothian Children's Bks.) Hachette Australia.

Crouch, Cheryl. Troo Makes a Big Splash, 1 vol. Zimmer, Kevin, illus. 2011. (I Can Read! / Rainforest Friends Ser.). (ENG.). 32p. (J). (gr. -1-2). pap. 4.99 *(978-0-310-71810-9(4))* Zonderkidz.

—Troo's Big Climb, 1 vol. Zimmer, Kevin, illus. 2011. (I Can Read! / Rainforest Friends Ser.). (ENG.). 32p. (J). (gr. -1-2). pap. 4.99 *(978-0-310-71808-6(2))* Zonderkidz.

—Troo's Secret Clubhouse, 1 vol. Zimmer, Kevin, illus. 2011. (I Can Read! / Rainforest Friends Ser.). (ENG.). 32p. (J). (gr. -1-2). pap. 4.99 *(978-0-310-71809-3(0))* Zonderkidz.

Dean, Natalia. The Dream. 2012. 30p. 24.95 *(978-1-4626-6008-7(8))* America Star Bks.

Dellolio, Kristina. Penelope's Tea Party Oh No Where's Kangaroo. 2012. 28p. pap. 24.95 *(978-1-4626-9748-9(8))* America Star Bks.

DeLuise, Dom & Carter, Derek. Pouch Potato. 2007. 33p. pap. 9.95 *(978-0-9717952-0-4(7))* Bacchus Bks.

deRubertis, Barbara. Kylie Kangaroo's Karate Kickers. Alley, R. W., illus. 2011. (Animal Antics A to Z Ser.). 32p. (J). pap. 45.32 *(978-0-7613-7657-6(7));* (ENG.). lib. bdg. 22.60 *(978-1-57565-332-7(X));* (gr. -1-3). pap. 7.95 *(978-1-57565-323-5(0),* c3134011-d19e-4bad-ae5c-2bfeafd9f34d, Kane Press) Astra Publishing Hse.

deRubertis, Barbara & DeRubertis, Barbara. Kylie Kangaroo's Karate Kickers. Alley, R. W., illus. 2012. (Animal Antics A to Z Ser.). 32p. (J). (gr. 2 — 1). cd-rom 7.95 *(978-1-57565-404-1(0))* Astra Publishing Hse.

Dubosarsky, Ursula. Brindabella. Joyner, Andrew, illus. 2019. (ENG.). 208p. (J). (gr. 3-5). pap. 13.99 *(978-1-76011-204-2(6),* A&U Children's) Allen & Unwin AUS. Dist: Independent Pubs. Group.

Duckers, John. The Amazing Adventures of the Silly Six. 2013. (Illus.). 188p. pap. *(978-1-78148-626-9(3))* Grosvenor Hse. Publishing Ltd.

Dumbleton, Mike. Digger. Cowcher, Robin, illus. 2018. (ENG.). 32p. (J). (gr. k-3). 19.99 *(978-1-76029-673-5(2))* Allen & Unwin AUS. Dist: Independent Pubs. Group.

Edwards, Pamela Duncan. McGillycuddy Could! Date not set. 32p. (J). (gr. -1-1). pap. 5.99 *(978-0-06-443688-5(8))* HarperCollins Pubs.

—McGillycuddy Could! Porter, Sue, illus. 2005. 32p. (J). (gr. -1-1). 14.99 *(978-0-06-029001-6(3))* HarperCollins Pubs.

Evans, Hilda Clark. Karbee the Kangaroo Says. 2013. (ENG.). 24p. (J). pap. 11.95 *(978-1-4787-2076-8(X))* Outskirts Pr., Inc.

ffoulkes, Joy. Kitty Kangaroo. 2010. (Illus.). 84p. pap. *(978-1-84748-685-1(1))* Athena Pr.

Finke, Margot. Kangaroo Clues. Delioglu, Mustafa, illus. 2013. 16p. pap. 9.95 *(978-1-61633-368-3(5))* Guardian Angel Publishing, Inc.

Flora, James, creator. Kangaroo for Christmas. 2011. (Illus.). 40p. (J). (gr. -1-3). 16.95 *(978-1-59270-113-1(2))* Enchanted Lion Bks., LLC.

Foust, Cindy. Kristy Kangaroo. 2008. (J). 12.94 *(978-0-9749220-6-5(4))* Alpha-kidZ.

Glover, Matt. But It's True. 2012. (Illus.). 32p. pap. 13.50 *(978-1-78035-330-2(8),* Fastprint Publishing) Upfront Publishing Ltd. GBR. Dist: Printondemand-worldwide.com.

Goodhart, Pippa. Hoppy Birthday, Jo-Jo! Birkett, Georgie, illus. 2005. (Green Bananas Ser.). (ENG.). 48p. (J). lib. bdg. *(978-0-7787-1025-7(4))* Crabtree Publishing Co.

Hamilton, Elizabeth L. Katie Kangaroo's Leap of Courage. l.t. ed. 2005. (Character Critters Ser.: No. 9). (Illus.). 32p. (J). per. 5.95 *(978-0-9754629-6-6(2),* Character-in-Action) Quiet Impact, Inc.

Hanson, Anders. Kangaroo Boxers. Nobens, C. A., illus. 2006. (Fact & Fiction Ser.). 24p. (J). pap. 48.42 *(978-1-59679-946-2(3))* ABDO Publishing Co.

Heaton, Maria. Kangaroos Say Sorry, Too, 1 vol. 2006. (Neighborhood Readers Ser.). (ENG.). 12p. (gr. 1-2). pap. 5.90 *(978-1-4042-7030-5(2),* 9ae5b2ff-1a8c-4467-bfef-5e1a4995d3d1, Rosen Classroom) Rosen Publishing Group, Inc., The.

Henderson, Milagros. Lulu the Bouncing Kangaroo. 2012. 36p. (-18). pap. 20.99 *(978-1-4772-8899-3(6))* AuthorHouse.

Johnson, Rebecca. The Kangaroos' Great Escape, 1 vol. 2005. (Animal Storybooks Ser.). (ENG., Illus.). 24p. (gr. k-2). lib. bdg. 24.67 *(978-0-8368-5971-3(5),* 76e39ccf-a9c6-4ae0-9fcc-e565899995ab, Gareth Stevens Learning Library) Stevens, Gareth Publishing LLLP.

Jones, Elwynn. Frank's Frantic Friday. 2010. 40p. pap. 16.95 *(978-1-60911-750-4(6),* Eloquent Bks.) Strategic Book Publishing & Rights Agency (SBPRA).

Joyce, Rita. Wandawillie. 2005. (J). lib. bdg. 17.95 *(978-1-59094-095-2(4))* Jawbone Publishing Corp.

Kangaroo at the Zoo IR. 2017. (Phonics Readers Ser.). (ENG.). (J). pap. 6.99 *(978-0-7945-3716-6(2),* Usborne) EDC Publishing.

Kim, HoJeong. Kanga & Anger. Kim, SookKyeong, illus. rev. ed. 2014. (MySELF Bookshelf Ser.). (ENG.). 32p. (J). (gr. k-2). pap. 11.94 *(978-1-60357-652-9(5));* lib. bdg. 25.27 *(978-1-59953-643-9(9))* Norwood Hse. Pr.

Krulik, Nancy. Never Box with a Kangaroo. 2016. (Magic Bone Ser.: 11). lib. bdg. 14.75 *(978-0-606-38842-9(7))* Turtleback.

Laconi, Kristin. Karma the Kangaroo Takes the Court. 2010. 24p. pap. 12.99 *(978-1-4490-3227-2(3))* AuthorHouse.

Langeland, Deirdre. Be Careful, Kangaroo! Ordaz, Frank, illus. 2005. (Soundprints' Read-and-Discover Ser.). (ENG.). 48p. (J). (gr. -1-1). 12.95 *(978-1-59249-146-9(4),* PS2010) Soundprints.

—Be Careful, Kangaroo!, Level 1. 2005. (ENG., Illus.). 32p. (J). (gr. -1-1). pap. 3.95 *(978-1-59249-145-2(6),* S2010) Soundprints.

—Kangaroo Island: A Story of an Australian Mallee Forest. 2005. (Soundprints' Wild Habitats Ser.). (ENG., Illus.). 32p. (J). (gr. 1-4). 8.95 *(978-1-59249-095-0(6))* Soundprints.

Lee, Brian. Bouncey the Elf & Friends - Bedtime St. 2005. (ENG., Illus.). 53p. pap. *(978-0-7552-1023-7(9))* Authors OnLine, Ltd.

Lee, Karin. Zangadoo Kangaroo & the Mysterious Boomerang. Porterfield, Scott, illus. 2012. 94p. pap. 6.99 *(978-0-9847428-2-0(4))* Zangadoo Entertainment.

Lewis, Edwina. Who Jumps? Parker, Ant, illus. 2003. (Who... Ser.). 16p. (YA). *(978-1-85602-447-1(4),* Pavilion Children's Books) Pavilion Bks.

Liora, Iimma. Flick Goes Bush. 2013. 32p. pap. 16.95 *(978-1-4525-0819-1(4),* Balboa Pr.) Author Solutions, LLC.

Maar, Paul. El Canguro Aprende a Volar (Kangaroo Learns to Fly) (SPA.). 56p. (J). (gr. 2). 7.95 *(978-958-04-1490-2(4),* 10266271) Norma S.A. COL. Dist: Distribuidora Norma, Inc.

MacKey, Garry. Joey: The Christmas Kangaroo. 2012. 24p. pap. 9.95 *(978-1-4575-1592-7(X))* Dog Ear Publishing, LLC.

Martinez Jover, Carmen. The Twin Kangaroo Treasure Hunt, a Gay Parenting Story. Martinez, Rosemary, illus. 2013. 32p. pap. *(978-607-00-6545-3(X))* Martínez Jover, María del Carmen Dorotea.

McBratney, Sam. I Love It When You Smile. Fuge, Charles, illus. 2012. (ENG.). 32p. (J). (gr. -1-3). 10.99 *(978-0-06-222133-9(7),* HarperCollins) HarperCollins Pubs.

McDonald, Dawn M. Kiki Koala Wanders Away. 2008. 28p. per. 24.95 *(978-1-4241-9924-2(7))* America Star Bks.

Morecroft, Judith. Malu Kangaroo. Bancroft, Bronwyn, illus. 2008. (ENG.). 40p. (J). (gr. k-2). pap. 13.95 *(978-1-921272-51-6(1))* Little Hare Bks. AUS. Dist: Independent Pubs. Group.

Most, Bernard. The Very Boastful Kangaroo. Most, Bernard, illus. 2003. (ENG., Illus.). 24p. (J). (gr. -1-3). pap. 4.99 *(978-0-15-204840-2(5),* 1194615, Clarion Bks.) HarperCollins Pubs.

Mueller, Kirk Jay. Harriet Can Carry It, 1 vol. Vonthron-Laver, Sarah, illus. 2014. (ENG.). 32p. (J). 16.99 *(978-1-59572-675-9(6))* Star Bright Bks., Inc.

Nancee Jean. The Boomerang Babies Club. 2012. 36p. pap. 13.95 *(978-1-4525-5243-9(6))* Balboa Pr.

Neusner, Sam. Bounce Bounce Bounce. 2012. 24p. pap. 12.56 *(978-1-4669-4558-6(3))* Trafford Publishing.

Nixon, Sidney. Chikka the Kangaroo. 2012. (Illus.). 28p. pap. 21.35 *(978-1-4772-4284-1(8))* AuthorHouse.

Numeroff, Laura. Nighty-Night, Cooper. Munsinger, Lynn, illus. 2013. (ENG.). 32p. (J). (gr. -1-3). 17.99 *(978-0-547-40205-5(8),* 1427979, Clarion Bks.) HarperCollins Pubs.

Owens, Carmen. Katy, the Cooking Kangaroo. Otis, Michelle, ed. Middleton, Taquon, illus. 2013. (J). pap. 12.95 *(978-0-9888644-5-0(2))* KP Publishing Co.

Pedley, Ethel C. Dot & the Kangaroo. 2004. reprint ed. pap. 15.95 *(978-1-4191-1659-9(2));* pap. 1.99 *(978-1-4192-1659-6(7))* Kessinger Publishing, LLC.

Phillips, Dee & Ticktock Media, Ltd. Staff. What Do Kangaroos Do? 2009. (What Do Animals Do? Ser.). (ENG.). 5p. (J). (gr. k — 1). bds. 4.95 *(978-1-84696-959-1(X),* TickTock Books) Octopus Publishing Group GBR. Dist: Independent Pubs. Group.

Price, W. Morris. A Gnu with a Shoe. 2009. 20p. pap. 10.49 *(978-1-4389-4388-6(1))* AuthorHouse.

Rebuck, Anthony. Skippy's Favourite Honey. Plagerson, Crock, illus. 2016. 42p. (J). 44.35 *(978-1-5144-4613-3(8));* (ENG.). pap. 28.22 *(978-1-5144-4612-6(X))* Xlibris Corp.

Richardson, Kiowa. The Christmas Kangaroo: Written & Illustrated by Kiowa Richardson. 2012. 16p. pap. 7.95 *(978-1-4497-4329-1(3),* WestBow Pr.) Author Solutions, LLC.

Roberson, Margaret. Maggie Poo the Kangaroo Adventures. 2008. 36p. pap. 14.95 *(978-1-4327-0674-6(8))* Outskirts Pr., Inc.

Roderick, Judith. Katie the Kangaroo & Her Five Acts of Kindness. 2011. 24p. pap. 11.50 *(978-1-4634-7457-7(1))* AuthorHouse.

Sakmar-Sullivan, Eva M. Kangaroo's Out of This World Restaurant, 1 vol. 2013. (ENG., Illus.). 32p. (J). (gr. -1-3). 14.99 *(978-0-7643-4519-7(2),* 4889) Schiffer Publishing, Ltd.

Saunders, Len. Joey the Kangaroo: An Adventure in Exercise. 2010. 32p. pap. 14.95 *(978-1-4389-3992-6(2))* AuthorHouse.

Shepherd, Sandra. Kangapoo & the Monster at Kakadu. 2012. 40p. pap. 32.70 *(978-1-4691-6123-5(0))* Xlibris Corp.

Simms, Mattie. Q. 2006. (J). pap. 2.99 *(978-0-9772077-1-8(4))* Kanlearn, Inc.

Simon, Francesca. Pablo Diablo Y la Cangura Fantasma. 2005. (Pablo Diablo Ser.). Tr. of Horrid Harry & the Kangaroo Ghost. (SPA., Illus.). (J). (gr. 2-3). pap. 8.95 *(978-84-348-9684-0(2))* SM Ediciones ESP. Dist: Iaconi, Mariuccia Bk. Imports.

Slinkard, Doreen. Wicky Wacky Farm Stories: Peppi Goes to China. 2012. 44p. pap. 14.97 *(978-1-60976-309-1(2),* Strategic Bk. Publishing) Strategic Book Publishing & Rights Agency (SBPRA).

Smith, Marvelyn A. The Kangaroo & the Crocodile. 2008. 28p. pap. 12.49 *(978-1-4343-9650-1(9))* AuthorHouse.

Stein, David Ezra. Pouch! Stein, David Ezra, illus. 2012. (ENG., Illus.). 32p. (J). (gr. -1 — 1). bds. 8.99 *(978-0-399-25738-4(1),* Nancy Paulsen Books) Penguin Young Readers Group.

Thomas, Pam. Mamarswpial. 2005. (WEL., Illus.). 128p. pap. *(978-0-86243-360-4(6))* Y Lolfa.

Tonderum, Angela. Kaycee Kangaroo Lost in Alphabet Forest: Adventures of Kaycee Kangaroo. Carlson, Christine, illus. 2008. 41p. pap. 24.95 *(978-1-60672-601-3(3))* America Star Bks.

Torres, Jos A. & Torres, Jose A. Joey Kanga Roo: Plays the Trumpet. 2009. 36p. pap. 15.99 *(978-1-4389-7434-7(5))* AuthorHouse.

Torres, Jose A. Joey Kanga Roo: First Day of School. 2009. 36p. pap. 15.99 *(978-1-4389-3964-3(7))* AuthorHouse.

van Genechten, Guido. Kangaroo Christine. van Genechten, Guido, illus. 2005. (Illus.). 24p. (J). (gr. 3-7). pap. 6.95 *(978-1-58925-396-4(5))* Tiger Tales.

Waterhouse, Raymond & Lawrie, Gabrielle. Yoppi A Bear Story. 2007. 158p. pap. 19.50 *(978-1-84753-876-5(2))* Lulu Pr., Inc.

KANSAS

Bjorklund, Ruth & Strain Trueit, Trudi. Kansas, 1 vol. 2nd rev. ed. 2009. (Celebrate the States (Second Edition) Ser.). (ENG.). 144p. (gr. 6-6). lib. bdg. 39.79 *(978-0-7614-3400-9(3),* cb603466-f653-4661-92df-ecf9e597bc69) Cavendish Square Publishing LLC.

Deinard, Jenny. How to Draw Kansas's Sights & Symbols. 2009. (Kid's Guide to Drawing America Ser.). 32p. (gr. k-k). 50.50 *(978-1-61511-065-0(8),* PowerKids Pr.) Rosen Publishing Group, Inc., The.

Drummond, Allan. Green City: How One Community Survived a Tornado & Rebuilt for a Sustainable Future. 2016. (Green Power Ser.). (ENG., Illus.). 40p. (J). 18.99 *(978-0-374-37999-5(8),* 900065068, Farrar, Straus & Giroux (BYR)) Farrar, Straus & Giroux.

Fredeen, Charles. Kansas. 2012. (J). lib. bdg. 25.26 *(978-0-7613-4533-6(7),* Lerner Pubns.) Lerner Publishing Group.

Gamble, Adam & Jasper, Mark. Good Night Kansas. Veno, Joe, illus. 2017. (Good Night Our World Ser.). 20p. (J). (— 1). bds. 9.95 *(978-1-60219-223-2(5))* Good Night Bks.

Heinrichs, Ann. Kansas. Kania, Matt, illus. 2017. (U. S. A. Travel Guides). (ENG.). 40p. (J). (gr. 2-5). lib. bdg. 38.50 *(978-1-5038-1956-6(6),* 211593) Child's World, Inc, The.

Kansas: The Sunflower State. 2014. (Illus.). 32p. (J). *(978-0-531-29166-5(9))* Bellwether Media.

Kavanagh, James & Waterford Press Staff. Sydney. Leung, Raymond, illus. 2016. (Wildlife & Nature Identification Ser.). (ENG.). 12p. 7.95 *(978-1-58355-047-2(X))* Waterford Pr., Inc.

King, David C. Kansas, 1 vol. Santoro, Christopher, illus. 2004. (It's My State! (First Edition)(r) Ser.). (ENG.). 80p. (gr. 4-4). lib. bdg. 34.07 *(978-0-7614-1688-3(9),* 21eb00a0-5ac0-489c-b671-6277e7fd64fd) Cavendish Square Publishing LLC.

Kmeck, Angela. This Is Kansas City. Hare, John, illus. 2015. (ENG.). 20p. (J). bds. 11.99 *(978-0-9962289-4-7(2))* Possum Trot Productions LLC.

Labairon, Cassandra Sharri. Kansas. 2008. (This Land Called America Ser.). 32p. (YA). (gr. 3-6). 22.95 *(978-1-58341-641-9(2))* Creative Co., The.

Marsh, Carole. The Cool Kansas Coloring Book. 2004. (Carole Marsh Kansas Bks.). (Illus.). 32p. (J). (gr. k-2). pap. 3.95 *(978-0-7933-9856-0(8))* Gallopade International.

—Kansas Current Events Projects: 30 Cool, Activities, Crafts, Experiments & More for Kids to Do to Learn about Your State! 2003. (Kansas Experience Ser.). 32p. (gr. k-5). pap. 5.95 *(978-0-635-02035-2(1),* Marsh, Carole Bks.) Gallopade International.

—Kansas Geography Projects: 30 Cool, Activities, Crafts, Experiments & More for Kids to Do to Learn about Your State! 2003. (Kansas Experience Ser.). 32p. (gr. k-5). pap. 5.95 *(978-0-635-01835-9(7),* Marsh, Carole Bks.) Gallopade International.

—Kansas Government Projects: 30 Cool, Activities, Crafts, Experiments & More for Kids to Do to Learn about Your State! 2003. (Kansas Experience Ser.). 32p. (gr. k-5). pap. 5.95 *(978-0-635-01935-6(3),* Marsh, Carole Bks.) Gallopade International.

—Kansas Jeopardy! Answers & Questions about Our State! 2004. (Carole Marsh Kansas Bks.). (Illus.). 32p. (J). (gr. 3-8). pap. 7.95 *(978-0-7933-9798-3(7))* Gallopade International.

—Kansas "Jography" A Fun Run Thru Your State! 2004. 32p. (J). (gr. 3-8). pap. 7.95 *(978-0-7933-9827-0(4))* Gallopade International.

—Kansas People Projects: 30 Cool, Activities, Crafts, Experiments & More for Kids to Do to Learn about Your State! 2003. (Kansas Experience Ser.). 32p. (gr. k-5). pap. 5.95 *(978-0-635-01985-1(X),* Marsh, Carole Bks.) Gallopade International.

—Kansas Symbols & Facts Projects: 30 Cool, Activities, Crafts, Experiments & More for Kids to Do to Learn about Your State! 2003. (Kansas Experience Ser.). 32p. (gr. k-5). pap. 5.95 *(978-0-635-01885-4(3),* Marsh, Carole Bks.) Gallopade International.

—My First Book about Kansas. 2004. (Carole Marsh Kansas Bks.). (Illus.). 32p. (J). (gr. k-4). pap. 7.95 *(978-0-7933-9885-0(1))* Gallopade International.

Meyer, Diana Lambdin. A Kid's Guide to Kansas City. 3rd ed. 2005. 184p. (J). per. 14.95 *(978-0-9763873-0-5(1))* Kansas City Guidebooks.

Murray, Julie. Kansas, 1 vol. 2006. (Buddy Book Ser.). (ENG., Illus.). 32p. (gr. 2-4). 27.07 *(978-1-59197-675-2(8),* Buddy Bks.) ABDO Publishing Co.

Nault, Jennifer. Kansas. 2011. (Guide to American States Ser.). (Illus.). 48p. (YA). (gr. 3-6). 29.99 *(978-1-61690-788-4(6))* Weigl Pubs., Inc.

—Kansas: The Sunflower State. 2016. (J). *(978-1-4896-4863-1(1))* Weigl Pubs., Inc.

Obregon, Jose Maria. Kansas, 1 vol. 2005. (Bilingual Library of the United States of America Ser.: Set 1). (ENG & SPA., Illus.). 32p. (J). (gr. 2-2). lib. bdg. 28.93

(978-1-4042-3081-1(5), c26e037e-2c28-4fe0-957e-6a4469415efe) Rosen Publishing Group, Inc., The.

Obregón, José María. Kansas. 2009. (Bilingual Library of the United States of America Ser.). (ENG & SPA.). 32p. (gr. 2-2). 47.90 *(978-1-60853-361-9(1),* Editorial Buenas Letras) Rosen Publishing Group, Inc., The.

Ryan, Pat & Hoena, Blake. Kansas. 2013. (Exploring the States Ser.). (ENG., Illus.). 32p. (J). (gr. 3-7). lib. bdg. 27.95 *(978-1-62617-015-5(0),* Blastoff! Readers) Bellwether Media.

Scillian, Devin. One Kansas Farmer: A Kansas Number Book. Bowles, Doug, illus. 2009. (America by the Numbers Ser.). (ENG.). 40p. (J). (gr. 1-3). 19.99 *(978-1-58536-182-3(8),* 202031) Sleeping Bear Pr.

—S Is for Sunflower: A Kansas Alphabet. Bowles, Doug, illus. 2004. (Discover America State by State Ser.). (ENG.). 40p. (J). (gr. 1-3). 18.99 *(978-1-58536-061-1(9),* 201962) Sleeping Bear Pr.

Taylor-Butler, Christine. Kansas. 2006. (Rookie Read-About Geography Ser.). (ENG., Illus.). 32p. (J). (gr. 1-2). lib. bdg. 20.50 *(978-0-516-24966-7(5),* Children's Pr.) Scholastic Library Publishing.

Thomas, Bill. Kansas, 1 vol. 2005. (Portraits of the States Ser.). (ENG., Illus.). 32p. (gr. 3-5). pap. 11.50 *(978-0-8368-4684-3(2),* 071cf600-3e22-4b54-bda8-a9adc6ffe0b0); lib. bdg. 28.67 *(978-0-8368-4665-2(6),* 0fd0bab2-5a6a-42e4-9f16-541be82a5b7e) Stevens, Gareth Publishing LLLP. (Gareth Stevens Learning Library).

KANSAS—FICTION

Adee, Donna & Adee, Ed. Jonathan Finds True Treasure. Rectenbaugh, Marci, illus. 2004. (Jonathan Ser.: Bk. 2). 344p. (J). per. 10.95 *(978-0-9654272-5-8(0))* Harvest Pubns.

Barnes, Derrick. We Could Be Brothers. 2010. (Illus.). 164p. (J). *(978-0-545-13574-0(5),* Scholastic Pr.) Scholastic, Inc.

Baum, L. Frank. Mago di Oz. pap. 14.95 *(978-88-451-2500-3(9))* Fabbri Editori - RCS Libri ITA. Dist: Distribooks, Inc.

Bird, Roy & Harp, Kim. Hark! I Hear a Meadowlark! Battis, Gwen, illus. 2013. 34p. 16.99 *(978-1-939054-08-1(7));* 36p. pap. 10.99 *(978-1-939054-07-4(9))* Rowe Publishing.

Boushell, Mike. Gridiron Hero. (J). pap. 9.99 *(978-0-88092-601-0(5))* Royal Fireworks Publishing Co.

Brashear, Amy. No Saints in Kansas. 2018. 336p. (YA). (gr. 9). pap. 10.99 *(978-1-61695-934-0(7),* Soho Teen) Soho Pr., Inc.

Busch, Darcy J. Lily & the Hidden Secrets, 1 vol. 2009. 164p. pap. 24.95 *(978-1-60836-498-5(4))* America Star Bks.

Cheaney, J. B. & Cheaney, Janie. The Middle of Somewhere. 2008. (ENG., Illus.). 224p. (J). (gr. 3-7). 7.99 *(978-0-440-42165-8(9),* Yearling) Random Hse. Children's Bks.

Coleman, K. R. The Recruit. 2018. (Kick! Ser.). (ENG.). 104p. (YA). (gr. 6-12). pap. 7.99 *(978-1-5415-0033-4(4),* 8714fcaf-1a32-43d7-a256-c6d64123d3d0); lib. bdg. 25.32 *(978-1-5415-0023-5(7),* 12d0d5b1-c032-4689-a2b7-81d88d28de4b) Lerner Publishing Group. (Darby Creek).

Duvall, Deborah L. Rabbit Goes to Kansas. Jacob, Murv, illus. 2007. (ENG.). 32p. (J). (gr. 1-18). 16.95 *(978-0-8263-4181-5(0),* P128171) Univ. of New Mexico Pr.

Garner, Phillip. Biff Cardova from Rooster Pool Kansas. 2010. 56p. pap. 21.99 *(978-1-4490-7664-1(5))* AuthorHouse.

Garretson, Jerri. Kansas Tall Tales: Tenth Anniversary Anthology. Garretson, Jerri & Dollar, Diane A., illus. 2008. 106p. (J). pap. 19.95 *(978-0-9659712-7-0(9))* Ravenstone Pr.

Garris, Rebekah. Whither Thou Goest, I Will Go. 2005. pap. 24.95 *(978-1-4137-8823-5(8))* PublishAmerica, Inc.

Grigsby, Cynthia. Hollow Creek: A Haunted Beginning, 01. 2006. 163p. (J). 14.95 *(978-0-9786840-0-6(1))* Grigsby, Cynthia.

Gutman, Dan. The Talent Show. 2010. (ENG.). 224p. (J). (gr. 3-7). 18.99 *(978-1-4169-9003-1(8),* Simon & Schuster Bks. For Young Readers) Simon & Schuster Bks. For Young Readers.

Hill, Janet Muirhead. Kendall & Kyleah. Leonhard, Herb, illus. 2012. (J). pap. 14.00 *(978-1-937849-05-4(8))* Raven Publishing Inc. of Montana.

—Kyleah's Tree. Leonhard, Herb, illus. 2011. (J). pap. 12.00 *(978-0-9827377-9-8(3))* Raven Publishing Inc. of Montana.

Hopkinson, Deborah. Our Kansas Home. Faricy, Patrick, illus. 2005. 64p. (J). lib. bdg. 15.00 *(978-1-59054-910-0(4))* Fitzgerald Bks.

—Our Kansas Home. Faricy, Patrick, illus. 2003. (Prairie Skies Ser.). 69p. (J). 11.65 *(978-0-7569-3448-4(6))* Perfection Learning Corp.

Jacobs, Lily. The Littlest Bunny in Kansas: An Easter Adventure. Dunn, Robert, illus. 2015. (Littlest Bunny Ser.). (ENG.). 32p. (J). (gr. -1-3). 9.99 *(978-1-4926-1090-8(9),* Hometown World) Sourcebooks, Inc.

—The Littlest Bunny in Kansas City: An Easter Adventure. Dunn, Robert, illus. 2015. (Littlest Bunny Ser.). (ENG.). 32p. (J). (gr. -1-3). 9.99 *(978-1-4926-1093-9(3),* Hometown World) Sourcebooks, Inc.

James, Eric. Santa's Sleigh Is on Its Way to Kansas: A Christmas Adventure. Dunn, Robert, illus. 2016. (Santa's Sleigh Is on Its Way Ser.). (ENG.). 32p. (J). (gr. k-2). 12.99 *(978-1-4926-4330-2(0),* 9781492643302, Hometown World) Sourcebooks, Inc.

—Santa's Sleigh Is on Its Way to Kansas City: A Christmas Adventure. Dunn, Robert, illus. 2016. (Santa's Sleigh Is on Its Way Ser.). (ENG.). 32p. (J). (gr. k-2). 12.99 *(978-1-4926-4331-9(9),* 9781492643319, Hometown World) Sourcebooks, Inc.

—The Spooky Express Kansas. Piwowarski, Marcin, illus. 2017. (Spooky Express Ser.). (ENG.). 32p. (J). (gr. k-6). 9.99 *(978-1-4926-5361-5(6),* Hometown World) Sourcebooks, Inc.

—The Spooky Express Kansas City. Piwowarski, Marcin, illus. 2017. (Spooky Express Ser.). (ENG.). 32p. (J). (gr. k-6). 9.99 *(978-1-4926-5362-2(4),* Hometown World) Sourcebooks, Inc.

—Tiny the Kansas City Easter Bunny. 2018. (Tiny the Easter Bunny Ser.). (ENG.). 40p. (J). (gr. k-3). 9.99 *(978-1-4926-5929-7(0),* Hometown World) Sourcebooks, Inc.

—Tiny the Kansas Easter Bunny. 2018. (Tiny the Easter Bunny Ser.). (ENG.). 40p. (J). (gr. k-3). 9.99 *(978-1-4926-5928-0(2),* Hometown World) Sourcebooks, Inc.

Kadohata, Cynthia. The Thing about Luck. Kuo, Julia, illus. (ENG.). (J). (gr. 5-9). 2014. 304p. pap. 8.99 *(978-1-4424-7465-9(3),* Atheneum Bks. for Young Readers) 2013. 288p. 16.99 *(978-1-4169-1882-0(5))* Simon & Schuster Children's Publishing.

—The Thing about Luck. 2014. lib. bdg. 18.40 *(978-0-606-35798-2(X))* Turtleback.

Keeley, Jenny Conner. The Hollow: A Kansas Fairytale. 2011. 154p. pap. 15.95 *(978-1-4327-6670-2(8))* Outskirts Pr., Inc.

Kelly, David A. The All-Star Joker. Meyers, Mark, illus. 2012. (Ballpark Mysteries Ser.: Bk. 5). lib. bdg. 14.75 *(978-0-606-26401-3(9))* Turtleback.

Ketchen, Susan. Made That Way. 2010. (ENG.). 160p. (J). pap. 12.95 *(978-0-88982-270-2(0))* Oolichan Bks. CAN. Dist: Univ. of Toronto Pr.

King, Judy. When Summer Comes Again. King, Judy, illus. 2013. (Illus.). 160p. (J). pap. *(978-1-884377-20-4(3))* Green Pastures Pr.

Kurtz, Jane. Anna Was Here. 2013. (ENG.). 288p. (J). (gr. 3-7). 16.99 *(978-0-06-056493-3(8),* Greenwillow Bks.) HarperCollins Pubs.

—Lemon Sand. 2011. (J). lib. bdg. 17.89 *(978-0-06-056494-0(6),* Greenwillow Bks.) HarperCollins Pubs.

Lassieur, Allison. Journey to a Promised Land: A Story of the Exodusters. Freeberg, Eric, illus. 2019. (I Am America Ser.). (ENG.). 160p. (J). (gr. 3-4). pap. 8.99 *(978-1-63163-276-1(0),* 1631632760); lib. bdg. 28.50 *(978-1-63163-275-4(2),* 1631632752) North Star Editions. (Jolly Fish Pr.).

Lester, James D. Corn Flower in Blowing Snow on the Great Plains: Third in a Fiction Series Based on the Four Seasons. 2019. (ENG., Illus.). 118p. (J). (gr. 8-12). pap. 16.95 *(978-1-63293-273-0(3))* Sunstone Pr.

Marie, Tina. Raccoon Round-Up at the Diamond R Ranch. 2012. 30p. 24.95 *(978-1-62709-237-1(4));* 32p. pap. 24.95 *(978-1-4626-7599-9(9))* America Star Bks.

McMullan, Kate. For This Land Bk. 2: Meg's Prairie Diary. 2003. (My America Ser.). (ENG., Illus.). 112p. (J). 10.95 *(978-0-439-37059-2(0),* Scholastic Pr.) Scholastic, Inc.

McPhail, J. A. Dawn of Day. Battis, Gwen, illus. 2012. 200p. pap. 10.99 *(978-0-9851196-1-4(6))* Rowe Publishing.

Meyer, Linda Ross. The Recipe Box. 2010. 73p. pap. 7.99 *(978-0-557-54210-9(3))* Lulu Pr., Inc.

Moss, Marissa. Rose's Journal: The Story of a Girl in the Great Depression. Moss, Marissa, illus. 2003. (Young American Voices Ser.). (ENG., Illus.). 56p. (J). (gr. 3-7). pap. 7.99 *(978-0-15-204605-7(4),* 1193867, Clarion Bks.) HarperCollins Pubs.

Murphy, Thomas. Island Boy. 2007. 124p. per. 19.95 *(978-1-4241-7940-4(8))* America Star Bks.

Novel Units. Little House on the Prairie Novel Units Student Packet. 2019. (Little House Ser.). (ENG.). (J). (gr. 3-6). pap. 13.99 *(978-1-56137-834-0(8),* Novel Units, Inc.) Classroom Library Co.

Osborne, Mary Pope. Twister on Tuesday. 2004. (Magic Tree House Ser.: No. 23). 70p. (J). (gr. k-3). pap. 17.00 incl. audio *(978-0-8072-9932-6(4),* Listening Library) Random Hse. Audio Publishing Group.

Penner, Evelyn. The Kid Who Ate Dog Food. Chullabrahm, T. M., illus. 2008. 32p. (J). 15.99 *(978-0-9796500-0-0(3))* Peppernut Publishing.

Peters, Julie Anne. Pretend You Love Me. 2011. (ENG.). 304p. (YA). (gr. 10-17). pap. 16.99 *(978-0-316-12741-7(8))* Little, Brown Bks. for Young Readers.

Phelan, Matt. The Storm in the Barn. 2011. (ENG., Illus.). 208p. (J). (gr. 5). pap. 15.99 *(978-0-7636-5290-6(3))* Candlewick Pr.

Powell, Anthony. Our Cat Hogan - Could He Be Part Dog? Stodden, Lindsay, illus. 2012. 24p. (J). 19.95 *(978-1-61863-358-3(9))* Bookstand Publishing.

Redgate, Riley. Seven Ways We Lie. 2017. (ENG.). 368p. (YA). (gr. 8-17). pap. 9.95 *(978-1-4197-2348-3(0),* 1132503, Amulet Bks.) Abrams, Inc.

Richardson, Steve. Billy's Mountain. Leonhard, Herb, illus. 2007. 52p. 14.95 *(978-0-9786422-0-4(1))* Impossible Dreams Publishing Co.

Richardson, Travis. Lost in Clover. 2012. 198p. pap. 9.99 *(978-1-61187-466-2(1))* Untreed Reads Publishing, LLC.

Robinson, Robin, illus. L. Frank Baum's the Wonderful Wizard of Oz. 2013. (Penguin Young Readers, Level 4 Ser.). 48p. (J). (gr. 3-4). mass mkt. 5.99 *(978-0-448-45588-4(9),* Penguin Young Readers) Penguin Young Readers Group.

Ruby, Lois. Red Menace. 2020. (ENG., Illus.). 224p. (J). (gr. 6-8). 17.99 *(978-1-5415-5749-9(2),* 85d52fc4-d672-4bce-a708-5bd9a1658221, Carolrhoda Bks.) Lerner Publishing Group.

Sargent, Daina. Kansas: Conquer Fear. Lenoir, Jane, illus. l.t. ed. 2004. (Double Trouble Ser.). 48p. (J). pap. 10.95 *(978-1-59381-125-9(X));* lib. bdg. 23.60 *(978-1-59381-124-2(1))* Ozark Publishing.

Sawyer, Kim Vogel. Katy's Debate, 1 vol., 2. 2010. (Katy Lambright Ser.: No. 2). (ENG.). 208p. (YA). (gr. 9-12). pap. 9.99 *(978-0-310-71923-6(2))* Zondervan.

—Katy's New World, 1 vol., 1. 2010. (Katy Lambright Ser.: No. 1). (ENG.). 208p. (YA). (gr. 9-12). pap. 9.99 *(978-0-310-71924-3(0))* Zondervan.

Schantz, Sarah Elizabeth. Fig. 2016. (ENG.). 352p. (YA). (gr. 9). pap. 11.99 *(978-1-4814-2359-5(2),* McElderry, Margaret K. Bks.) McElderry, Margaret K. Bks.

Scillian, Devin. Johnny Kaw: A Tall Tale. Sneed, Brad, illus. 2013. (ENG.). 32p. (J). (gr. 1-4). 15.95 *(978-1-58536-791-7(5),* 202353) Sleeping Bear Pr.

Seely, Debra. Grasslands. 2017. (ENG., Illus.). (J). (gr. 4-6). pap. 9.99 *(978-0-922820-18-4(X))* Watermark Pr., Inc.

Sully, Katherine. Night-Night Kansas. Poole, Helen, illus. 2017. (Night-Night Ser.). (ENG.). 20p. (J). (gr. -1-1). bds. 9.99 *(978-1-4926-5483-4(3),* Hometown World) Sourcebooks, Inc.

—Night-Night Kansas. Poole, Helen, illus. 2016. (Night-Night Ser.). (ENG.). 20p. (J). (gr. -1-1). bds. 9.99 *(978-1-4926-3941-1(9),* 9781492639411, Hometown World) Sourcebooks, Inc.

—Night-Night Kansas City. Poole, Helen, illus. 2017. (Night-Night Ser.). (ENG.). 20p. (J). (gr. -1-1). bds. 9.99 *(978-1-4926-5490-2(6),* Hometown World) Sourcebooks, Inc.

Sundstrom, Dainel H. The Return of Oz. 2007. pap. 10.00 *(978-0-8059-8944-1(7))* Dorrance Publishing Co., Inc.

Sutton, Laurie S. The Secret of the Flying Saucer. Neely, Scott, illus. 2015. (You Choose Stories: Scooby-Doo Ser.). (ENG.). 112p. (J). (gr. 2-6). lib. bdg. 32.65 *(978-1-4965-0478-4(X),* 128504, Stone Arch Bks.) Capstone.

Trivas, Tracy. The Wish Stealers. 2011. (ENG.). 288p. (J). (gr. 3-7). pap. 8.99 *(978-1-4169-8726-0(6),* Aladdin) Simon & Schuster Children's Publishing.

Uncle Markie. Piglette & Bobo in Kansas City. 2003. (YA). ring bd. 9.95 *(978-1-933129-08-2(5))* Studio 403.

Vanderpool, Clare. Moon over Manifest. 2012. (CHI.). 304p. (J). (gr. 3-7). pap. *(978-986-6319-46-4(6))* Marco Polo Pr. A Division of Cite Publishing Ltd.

—Moon over Manifest. l.t. ed. 2011. (ENG.). 451p. 23.99 *(978-1-4104-3780-8(9))* Thorndike Pr.

—Moon over Manifest. 2011. lib. bdg. 18.40 *(978-0-606-23875-5(1))* Turtleback.

—Moon over Manifest. 2013. (CHI.). 357p. (J). (gr. 3-7). pap. *(978-7-5414-5415-8(X))* Yunnan Juvenile and Children's Bks. Pr.

—Moon over Manifest: (Newbery Medal Winner) 2011. 384p. (J). (gr. 3-7). 8.99 *(978-0-375-85829-1(6),* Yearling) Random Hse. Children's Bks.

Volkov, Alexander. Tales of Magic Land 1. 2010. 360p. pap. 22.95 *(978-0-557-44825-8(5))* Lulu Pr., Inc.

Waggoner, Sandra. Maggie's Treasure, 4 vols., Vol. 1. 2005. (Gatlin Fields Ser.: One). (ENG.). 108p. (J). per. 9.95 *(978-0-9766823-0-1(3))* Sable Creek Pr. LLC.

—Son of an Honest Man. 2013. 136p. (J). pap. 10.95 *(978-0-9890667-2-3(X))* Sable Creek Pr. LLC.

Walter, Dan. Hello, Willie! 2007. (J). 14.95 *(978-1-932888-52-2(7))* Amplify Publishing Group.

Wentz, Lorraine. Who Has Barney. 2013. 38p. pap. 10.99 *(978-1-62697-124-0(2))* Salem Author Services.

Wilder, Laura Ingalls. Little House on the Prairie. Williams, Garth, illus. 2008. (Little House Ser.: 3). (ENG.). 352p. (J). (gr. 3-7). pap. 8.99 *(978-0-06-440002-2(6),* HarperCollins) HarperCollins Pubs.

—Little House on the Prairie: Full Color Edition. Williams, Garth, illus. 2004. (Little House Ser.: 3). (ENG.). 352p. (J). (gr. 3-7). pap. 9.99 *(978-0-06-058181-7(6),* HarperCollins) HarperCollins Pubs.

Wilson, N. D. The Chestnut King (100 Cupboards Book 3) 2011. (100 Cupboards Ser.: 3). (ENG., Illus.). 512p. (J). (gr. 3-7). 9.99 *(978-0-375-83886-6(4),* Yearling) Random Hse. Children's Bks.

—Dandelion Fire (100 Cupboards Book 2) 2009. (100 Cupboards Ser.: 2). (ENG., Illus.). 480p. (J). (gr. 3-7). 9.99 *(978-0-375-83884-2(8),* Yearling) Random Hse. Children's Bks.

—100 Cupboards, 1. 2007. (100 Cupboards Ser.: Bk. 1). (ENG., Illus.). 289p. (J). (gr. 4-6). lib. bdg. 22.44 *(978-0-375-93881-8(8))* Random House Publishing Group.

—100 Cupboards (100 Cupboards Book 1) 2008. (100 Cupboards Ser.: 1). (ENG.). 320p. (J). (gr. 3-7). 8.99 *(978-0-375-83882-8(1),* Yearling) Random Hse. Children's Bks.

KANSAS—HISTORY

Baginski, Deanna Fisher. Harvest Time at the Fisher Farms. 2011. 24p. pap. 12.79 *(978-1-4670-2643-7(3))* AuthorHouse.

Bailer, Darice. What's Great about Kansas? 2015. (Our Great States Ser.). (ENG., Illus.). 32p. (J). (gr. 2-5). 26.65 *(978-1-4677-3884-2(0),* b8e7ce95-6f83-4571-a7e2-64e3315bbc96, Lerner Pubns.) Lerner Publishing Group.

Bailey, Diane. Kansas: Past & Present, 1 vol. 2010. (United States: Past & Present Ser.). (ENG.). 48p. (YA). (gr. 5-5). pap. 12.75 *(978-1-4358-9508-9(8),* 59fd673e-f9a1-4b46-815b-4487e5371a7f); lib. bdg. 34.47 *(978-1-4358-9481-5(2),* d498cf83-98ba-43a6-b9dc-d009b40e3d16) Rosen Publishing Group, Inc., The. (Rosen Reference).

Cannarella, Deborah. America the Beautiful: Kansas (Revised Edition) 2014. (America the Beautiful, Third Ser. (Revised Edition) Ser.). (ENG., Illus.). 144p. (J). lib. bdg. 40.00 *(978-0-531-28280-9(5))* Scholastic Library Publishing.

Fleming, Thomas. The King of Prussia & a Peanut Butter Sandwich. 2009. (ENG.). 48p. (J). (gr. 2-4). pap. 6.99 *(978-1-4424-1215-6(1),* Atheneum Bks. for Young Readers) Simon & Schuster Children's Publishing.

Glaser, Jason. Kansas: The Sunflower State, 1 vol. 2010. (Our Amazing States Ser.). (ENG., Illus.). 24p. (J). (gr. 3-3). pap. 9.25 *(978-1-4358-9782-3(X),* b9d2aa4a-5dfa-4181-adbb-5fa1bc108451); lib. bdg. 26.27 *(978-1-4358-9395-5(6),* 517957d4-3fa9-4981-9e39-d40cb8c191ae) Rosen Publishing Group, Inc., The. (PowerKids Pr.).

Gregory, Josh. Kansas (a True Book: My United States) (Library Edition) 2018. (True Book (Relaunch) Ser.). (ENG., Illus.). 48p. (J). (gr. 3-5). 31.00 *(978-0-531-23560-7(2),* Children's Pr.) Scholastic Library Publishing.

Hamilton, John. Kansas, 1 vol. 2016. (United States of America Ser.). (ENG., Illus.). 48p. (J). (gr. 5-9). 34.21 *(978-1-68078-318-6(1),* 21621, Abdo & Daughters) ABDO Publishing Co.

Herschbach, Elisabeth. Lower Plains: Kansas, Nebraska, Vol. 19. 2015. (Let's Explore the States Ser.). (Illus.). 64p. (J). (gr. 5). 23.95 *(978-1-4222-3326-9(X))* Mason Crest.

Ingram, W. Scott. Kansas. 2009. (From Sea to Shining Sea, Second Ser.). (ENG.). 80p. (J). pap. 7.95 *(978-0-531-21131-1(2),* Children's Pr.) Scholastic Library Publishing.

Jerome, Kate B. Lucky to Live in Kansas. 2017. (Arcadia Kids Ser.). (ENG., Illus.). 32p. (J). 16.99 *(978-0-7385-2798-7(X))* Arcadia Publishing.

Marsh, Carole. Exploring Kansas Through Project-Based Learning. 2016. (Kansas Experience Ser.). (ENG.). (J). pap. 9.99 *(978-0-635-12340-4(1))* Gallopade International.

—I'm Reading about Kansas. 2014. (Kansas Experience Ser.). (ENG., Illus.). (J). pap., pap. 8.99 *(978-0-635-11291-0(4))* Gallopade International.

—Jeopardy. 2004. (New York Experience! Ser.). 32p. (J). (gr. 3-8). pap. 7.95 *(978-0-635-00161-0(6))* Gallopade International.

—Kansas History Projects: 30 Cool, Activities, Crafts, Experiments & More for Kids to Do to Learn about Your State! 2003. (Kansas Experience Ser.). 32p. (gr. k-5). pap. 5.95 *(978-0-635-01785-7(7),* Marsh, Carole Bks.) Gallopade International.

Mead, James R., et al. Hunting & Trading in Kansas, 1859-1875. 2015. (J). *(978-1-929731-25-1(6))* Rowfant Pr.

Miller, Jake. Brown vs. Board of Education of Topeka: Challenging School Segregation in the Supreme Court, 1 vol. 2003. (Library of the Civil Rights Movement Ser.). (ENG., Illus.). 24p. (J). (gr. 3-3). lib. bdg. 26.27 *(978-0-8239-6250-1(4),* 184de3f3-dc5b-4394-bb50-bc67c24250b5) Rosen Publishing Group, Inc., The.

Robertson, Theda Robinson. Journey to a Free Land: The Story of Nicodemus, the First All Black Town West of the Mississippi. 2006. (Illus.). (J). *(978-0-9705721-6-5(6))* Written Images, Inc.

Swanson, Angie & Parker, Bridget. Kansas. 2016. (States Ser.). (ENG., Illus.). 32p. (J). (gr. 3-6). lib. bdg. 27.99 *(978-1-5157-0403-4(3),* 132014, Capstone Pr.) Capstone.

Yasuda, Anita. Kansas: The Sunflower State. 2012. (J). *(978-1-61913-351-8(2));* pap. *(978-1-61913-352-5(0))* Weigl Pubs., Inc.

KANSAS—HISTORY—FICTION

Barnhart, Aaron. Firebrand. 2015. (ENG., Illus.). 168p. (J). 19.95 *(978-0-9669258-6-9(6))* Quindaro Pr.

Boeve, Eunice. Echoes of Kansas Past. Peterson-Shea, Julie, illus. 2012. 176p. pap. 10.99 *(978-0-9851196-9-0(1))* Rowe Publishing.

Breault, Christie Merriman. Logan West, Printer's Devil. Archembault, Matthew, illus. 2006. 142p. (J). pap. *(978-1-59336-762-6(7))* Mondo Publishing.

Brown, Irene Bennett. Before the Lark. 2011. (ENG.). 208p. (J). (gr. 4-6). pap. 18.95 *(978-0-89672-727-4(0),* P193202) Texas Tech Univ. Pr.

Helget, Nicole. Wonder at the Edge of the World. 2015. (ENG., Illus.). 384p. (J). (gr. 3-7). 17.00 *(978-0-316-24510-4(0))* Little, Brown Bks. for Young Readers.

Helwani, Najiyah Diana. Sophia's Journal: Time Warp 1857. 2008. (YA). per. *(978-0-9793577-2-5(1))* Muslim Writers Publishing.

Kimmel, E. Cody. In the Eye of the Storm. Snow, Scott, illus. 2003. (Adventures of Young Buffalo Bill Ser.). (ENG.). 144p. (J). (gr. 3-7). 15.99 *(978-0-06-029115-0(X))* HarperCollins Pubs.

Kimmel, Elizabeth Cody. In the Eye of the Storm. Snow, Scott, illus. 2003. (Adventures of Young Buffalo Bill Ser.). 144p. (J). (gr. 3-7). lib. bdg. 16.89 *(978-0-06-029116-7(8))* HarperCollins Pubs.

McClure, Wendy. Wanderville. 2014. (Wanderville Ser.: 1). (ENG.). 240p. (J). (gr. 3-7). pap. 7.99 *(978-1-59514-701-1(2),* Razorbill) Penguin Young Readers Group.

McMullan, Kate. A Fine Start Bk. 3: Meg's Prairie Diary. 2003. (My America Ser.). (ENG.). 112p. (J). 12.95 *(978-0-439-37061-5(2))* Scholastic, Inc.

McPhail, J. A. Dawn of Day. Battis, Gwen, illus. 2012. 200p. 17.99 *(978-0-9851196-2-1(4))* Rowe Publishing.

Moss, Marissa. Rose's Journal: The Story of a Girl in the Great Depression. 2004. (Young American Voice Bks.). (Illus.). (gr. 3-7). 17.00 *(978-0-7569-4230-4(6))* Perfection Learning Corp.

Ormsbee, Kathryn. The Great Unknowable End. 2019. (ENG., Illus.). 400p. (YA). (gr. 7). 19.99 *(978-1-5344-2050-2(9),* Simon & Schuster Bks. For Young Readers) Simon & Schuster Bks. For Young Readers.

Thomas, Carroll. The Town on Rambling Creek: A Matty Trescott Novel. 2004. (Illus.). ix, 185p. (J). *(978-1-57525-376-3(3))* Smith & Kraus Pubs., Inc.

Villani, Donna. The Capture of Art. 2008. 244p. pap. 14.95 *(978-1-60693-104-2(0),* Eloquent Bks.) Strategic Book Publishing & Rights Agency (SBPRA).

KANSAS CITY CHIEFS (FOOTBALL TEAM)

Burgess, Zack. Meet the Kansas City Chiefs. 2016. (Big Picture Sports Ser.). (ENG., Illus.). 24p. (J). (gr. k-3). lib. bdg. 22.60 *(978-1-59953-730-6(3))* Norwood Hse. Pr.

Caffrey, Scott. The Story of the Kansas City Chiefs. 2009. (NFL Today Ser.). 48p. (YA). (gr. 5-9). 22.95 *(978-1-58341-760-7(5))* Creative Co., The.

Cohn, Nate. Kansas City Chiefs. 2018. (Illus.). 24p. (J). *(978-1-4896-5522-6(0),* AV2 by Weigl) Weigl Pubs., Inc.

Fishman, Jon M. Patrick Mahomes. 2019. (Sports All-Stars (Lerner (tm) Sports) Ser.). (ENG., Illus.). 32p. (J). (gr. 2-5). pap. 9.99 *(978-1-5415-7847-0(3),* c531f44b-e08a-4b58-86fd-4d5c334af4b4, Lerner Pubns.) Lerner Publishing Group.

Frisch, Aaron. Kansas City Chiefs. 2011. (Super Bowl Champions Ser.). (J). (gr. 1-3). 24.25 *(978-1-60818-020-2(4))* Creative Co., The.

—Kansas City Chiefs. 2014. (Illus.). 24p. (J). *(978-1-60818-378-4(5),* Creative Education) Creative Co., The.

Frisch, Nate. The Story of the Kansas City Chiefs. 2013. (Illus.). 48p. (J). 35.65 *(978-1-60818-307-4(6),* Creative Education) Creative Co., The.

Hawkes, Brian. The History of the Kansas City Chiefs. 2004. (NFL Today Ser.). (Illus.). 32p. (YA). (gr. 5-9). 18.95 *(978-1-58341-301-2(4))* Creative Co., The.

Kortemeier, Todd. Kansas City Chiefs, 1 vol. 2016. (NFL up Close Ser.). (ENG.). 32p. (J). (gr. 3-9). lib. bdg. 32.79 *(978-1-68078-221-9(5),* 22043, SportsZone) ABDO Publishing Co.

Lajiness, Katie. Kansas City Chiefs. 2016. (NFL's Greatest Teams Set 3 Ser.). (ENG., Illus.). 32p. (J). (gr. 2-5). lib. bdg. 34.21 *(978-1-68078-536-4(2),* 23635, Big Buddy Bks.) ABDO Publishing Co.

Peters, Rob, illus. Kansas City Chiefs ABCs And 1-2-3s. 2015. (ENG.). 26p. (J). bds. 18.95 *(978-0-9961944-0-2(1))* Ascend Bks., LLC.

Stewart, Mark. The Kansas City Chiefs. rev. ed. 2012. (Team Spirit Ser.). (ENG.). 48p. (J). (gr. 3-6). lib. bdg. 29.27 *(978-1-59953-527-2(0))* Norwood Hse. Pr.

J K L

Whiting, Jim. Kansas City Chiefs. rev. ed. 2019. (NFL Today Ser.). (ENG.). 48p. (J). (gr. 4-7). pap. 12.00 (978-1-62832-708-3(1), 19043, Creative Paperbacks) Creative Co., The.

Wyner, Zach. Kansas City Chiefs. (Illus.). 32p. (J). 2015. pap. (978-1-4896-0843-7(5)) 2014. (ENG., (gr. 4-7). lib. bdg. 28.55 (978-1-4896-0842-0(7), AV2 by Weigl) Weigl Pubs., Inc.

KANSAS CITY ROYALS (BASEBALL TEAM)

Gilbert, Sara. The Story of the Kansas City Royals. 2007. (Baseball, the Great American Game Ser.). (Illus.). 48p. (YA). (gr. 4-7). lib. bdg. 32.80 (978-1-58341-490-3(8)) Creative Co., The.

LeBoutillier, Nate. The Story of the Kansas City Royals. 2011. (J). 35.65 (978-1-60818-043-1(3), Creative Education) Creative Co., The.

Sauver, Dennis St. Kansas City Royals. 2018. (MLB's Greatest Teams Ser.). (ENG., Illus.). 32p. (J). (gr. 2-5). lib. bdg. 34.21 (978-1-5321-1809-8(0), 30664, Big Buddy Bks.) ABDO Publishing Co.

Stewart, Mark. The Kansas City Royals. 2012. (Team Spirit Ser.). 48p. (J). (gr. 3-6). lib. bdg. 29.27 (978-1-59953-484-8(3)) Norwood Hse. Pr.

KARATE

see also Tae Kwon Do

Craats, Rennay. For the Love of Karate. Nault, Jennifer & Turner, Kara, eds. 2003. (For the Love of Sports Ser.). (Illus.). 24p. (J). pap. 8.95 (978-1-59036-071-2(0)) Weigl Pubs., Inc.

Di Marino, Stefano & Ghetti, Roberto. A Complete Guide to Karate, 1 vol. 2017. (Mastering Martial Arts Ser.). (ENG.). 128p. (gr. 6-6). lib. bdg. 38.93 (978-0-7660-8539-8(2), e47c14dd-f5cb-4085-a398-f7aa3a98138e) Enslow Publishing, LLC.

Drewett, Jim & Martin, Ashley. How to Improve at Karate. 2007. (How to Improve At- Ser.). (ENG., Illus.). 48p. (J). (gr. 3-9). lib. bdg. (978-0-7787-3568-7(0)) Crabtree Publishing Co.

Early Macken, JoAnn. Karate, 1 vol. 2004. (After-School Fun Ser.). (ENG., Illus.). 24p. (gr. k-2). lib. bdg. 23.67 (978-0-8368-4514-3(5), 7d34bba0-e815-4499-91fc-010139855212, Weekly Reader Leveled Readers) Stevens, Gareth Publishing LLLP.

Gifford, Clive. Karate. 2010. (Combat Sports Ser.). 32p. (J). (gr. 2-5). lib. bdg. 28.50 (978-1-59771-275-0(2)) Sea-To-Sea Pubns.

Hicks, Terry Allan. Karate, 1 vol. 2011. (Martial Arts in Action Ser.). (ENG.). 48p. (gr. 5-5). lib. bdg. 32.64 (978-0-7614-4934-8(5), 273372bb-2ee2-495b-aa60-0ed668645119) Cavendish Square Publishing LLC.

Johnson, Nathan. Karate: Winning Ways. James, Adam, ed. 2015. (Mastering Martial Arts Ser.). (Illus.). 96p. (J). (gr. 5). lib. bdg. 24.95 (978-1-4222-3238-5(7)) Mason Crest.

Kalman, Bobbie & MacAulay, Kelley. Karate in Action, 1 vol. 2005. (Sports in Action Ser.). (ENG., Illus.). 32p. (J). (gr. 2-3). pap. (978-0-7787-0361-7(4)) Crabtree Publishing Co.

Karate: A Master's Secrets of Uechi-Ryu. 2003. (Illus.). 576p. (YA). pap. 49.95 (978-0-9746989-0-8(3)) Iron Arm International.

MacAulay, Kelley & Kalman, Bobbie. Le Karaté. 2009. (Sans Limites Ser.). (FRE., Illus.). 32p. (J). (gr. 1-7). pap. 9.95 (978-2-89579-251-2(8)) Bayard Canada Livres CAN. Dist: Crabtree Publishing Co.

MacKay, Jennifer. Taekwondo, 1 vol. 2014. (Science Behind Sports Ser.). (ENG., Illus.). 112p. (gr. 7-7). lib. bdg. 41.03 (978-1-4205-0940-3(3), 7dbd7449-510b-4e4e-b8b6-466c0f938515, Lucent Pr.) Greenhaven Publishing LLC.

Mara, Wil. Karate. 2012. (J). pap. (978-0-531-20925-7(3)); lib. bdg. (978-0-531-20856-4(7)) Children's Pr., Ltd.

Martin, Ashley. How to Improve at Karate. 2007. (How to Improve At- Ser.). (ENG., Illus.). 48p. (J). (gr. 3-7). pap. (978-0-7787-3590-8(7)) Crabtree Publishing Co.

McNulty, Mark. Karate, 1 vol. 2015. (Inside Martial Arts Ser.). (ENG., Illus.). 48p. (J). (gr. 3-6). lib. bdg. 34.21 (978-1-62403-603-3(1), 17073, SportsZone) ABDO Publishing Co.

O'Brien, Andrew & O'Brien, Emma. The Little Bubishi: A History of Karate for Children. 2010. 172p. pap. 40.00 (978-1-60911-717-7(4), Eloquent Bks.) Strategic Book Publishing & Rights Agency (SBPRA).

Pawlett, Ray. The Karate Handbook. (Martial Arts Ser.). 256p. (gr. 8-8). 2009. 79.90 (978-1-61514-367-2(X)) 2008. (ENG., Illus.). (YA). lib. bdg. 47.80 (978-1-4042-1394-4(5), c5b7eafd-aed2-4984-ac45-47ab3c93a87e) Rosen Publishing Group, Inc., The.

Schuetz, Kari. Karate. 2011. (My First Sports Ser.). (ENG., Illus.). 24p. (J). (gr. 2-5). lib. bdg. 26.95 (978-1-60014-570-4(1), Blastoff! Readers) Bellwether Media.

—Karate. 2011. pap. (978-0-531-20636-2(X)) Grolier Publishing.

Wood, Alix. Karate, 1 vol. 2013. (Kid's Guide to Martial Arts Ser.). (ENG., Illus.). 32p. (J). (gr. 2-3). pap. 12.75 (978-1-4777-0350-2(0), fa3c4b91-e4af-418f-87d1-9084a8abfee3); lib. bdg. 30.27 (978-1-4777-0314-4(4), f90323b9-836a-45de-9066-0b9841112d0e) Rosen Publishing Group, Inc., The. (PowerKids Pr.).

KARATE—FICTION

Barnes, Dawn. Seven Wheels of Power. Chang, Bernard, illus. 2005. (Black Belt Club Ser.: No. 1). (ENG.). 173p. (J). (gr. 3-6). 17.44 (978-0-439-63936-1(0)) Scholastic, Inc.

Barnes, Susan. Kelly Karate: Discovers the Ice Princess. 2004. 138p. (J). (gr. 4-8). pap. 5.95 (978-0-9705777-3-3(7)) McBook Pubs., LLC.

Bidoli, Katie. Karate Adventures of Kisho, Hana, & Nobu: Karate Is for Everyone! 2006. (Illus.). 16p. (J). 10.00 (978-1-60243-029-7(2)) Keen's Martial Arts Academy.

Bowman, Rachael Ann. Sammy the Karate Squirrel. 2013. 28p. pap. 13.95 (978-1-4624-0800-9(1), Inspiring Voices) Author Solutions, LLC.

Carey, Michael. Little Kathy Likes Karate. Connors, Jackie, ed. 2003. (Illus.). 30p. (J). spiral bd. 10.95 (978-0-9743679-1-0(5)) Reiki Blessings.

Chin, Oliver. Julie Black Belt: The Kung Fu Chronicles. Chua, Charlene, illus. 2008. (Julie Black Belt Ser.). (ENG.). 36p. (J). (gr. k-1). 15.95 (978-1-59702-009-1(5)) Immedium.

deRubertis, Barbara. Kylie Kangaroo's Karate Kickers. Alley, R. W., illus. 2011. (Animal Antics A to Z Ser.). 32p. (J). pap. 45.32 (978-0-7613-7657-6(7)); (ENG.). lib. bdg. 22.60 (978-1-57565-332-7(X)); (gr. -1-3). pap. 7.95 (978-1-57565-323-5(0), c3134011-d19e-4bad-ae5c-2bfeafd9f34d, Kane Press) Astra Publishing Hse.

deRubertis, Barbara & DeRubertis, Barbara. Kylie Kangaroo's Karate Kickers. Alley, R. W., illus. 2012. (Animal Antics A to Z Ser.). 32p. (J). (gr. 2 — 1). cd-rom 7.95 (978-1-57565-404-1(0)) Astra Publishing Hse.

Hearst, Allyson. White Pajamas: A Karate Story. 2011. 68p. pap. 19.95 (978-1-4626-3871-0(6)) America Star Bks.

Knowles, Jo. Living with Jackie Chan. (ENG.). 384p. (YA). (gr. 9). 2015. pap. 8.99 (978-0-7636-7663-6(2)) 2013. 16.99 (978-0-7636-6280-6(1)) Candlewick Pr.

Lever, Jill. The Worm Who Knew Karate! Denton, Terry, illus. 2019. 32p. (J). (gr. k-3). 15.99 (978-0-14-350602-7(1), Puffin) Penguin Bks., Ltd. GBR. Dist: Independent Pubs. Group.

Maddox, Jake. Karate Countdown, 1 vol. Tiffany, Sean, illus. 2009. (Jake Maddox Sports Stories Ser.). (ENG.). 72p. (J). (gr. 3-6). lib. bdg. 25.99 (978-1-4342-1200-9(9), 95399, Stone Arch Bks.) Capstone.

Manushkin, Fran. Pedro el Ninja. Trusted Translations, Trusted, tr. Lyon, Tammie, illus. 2018. (Pedro en Español Ser.). (SPA.). 32p. (J). (gr. k-2). lib. bdg. 21.32 (978-1-5158-2510-4(8), 137568, Picture Window Bks.) Capstone.

—Pedro the Ninja. Lyon, Tammie, illus. 2017. (Pedro Ser.). (ENG.). 32p. (J). (gr. k-2). lib. bdg. 21.32 (978-1-5158-1904-2(3), 136538, Picture Window Bks.) Capstone.

Nevius, Carol. Karate Hour, 0 vols. Thomson, Bill, illus. 2012. (ENG.). 34p. (J). (gr. -1-2). pap. 9.99 (978-0-7614-5840-1(9), 9780761458401, Two Lions) Amazon Publishing.

Noppe-Brandon, Gail. Tilly Takes a Try. Farkouh, Michelle, illus. 2010. (ENG.). 36p. pap. 16.99 (978-1-4520-7662-1(6)) AuthorHouse.

Shammas, Anna. Recorder Karate. Guiza, Victor, illus. 2012. 32p. pap. 8.95 (978-0-9843869-2-5(0), Castlebridge Bks.) Big Tent Bks.

Stevens, Elizabeth. Mister D. Frongia, Daniela, illus. 2012. 24p. (J). 16.95 (978-1-60131-114-6(1)) Big Tent Bks.

Stilton, Gerónimo. The Karate Mouse. 2010. (Geronimo Stilton Ser.: 40). lib. bdg. 18.40 (978-0-606-06847-5(3)) Turtleback.

Thielbar, Melinda. The Secret Ghost: A Mystery with Distance & Measurement. Ota, Yuko Geneviev, illus. 2010. (Manga Math Mysteries Ser.: 3). (ENG.). 48p. (J). (gr. 3-5). pap. 6.99 (978-0-7613-5245-7(7), af4534ce-d5c6-48f8-a05a-62530c2a5001, Graphic Universe™) Lerner Publishing Group.

Tosten, Sharon. Troy's Amazing Universe: K for Karate. 2006. 144p. per. 13.95 (978-0-9743185-2-3(3)) Booklocker.com, Inc.

KARTS AND KARTING

Adamson, Thomas K. Karts. 2019. (Full Throttle Ser.). (ENG., Illus.). 24p. (J). (gr. 3-7). lib. bdg. 26.95 (978-1-62617-933-2(6), Epic Bks.) Bellwether Media.

Barger, Jeff. Go-Karts. 2016. (How It Works). (ENG.). 24p. (gr. 1-3). 28.50 (978-1-68191-685-9(1), 9781681916859) Rourke Educational Media.

Challen, Paul C. Kart Racing, 1 vol. 2014. (Checkered Flag Ser.). (ENG., Illus.). 32p. (J). (gr. 4-5). lib. bdg. 27.93 (978-1-4994-0163-9(9), 1f7656be-09f1-4246-ade1-d564e66319e5, PowerKids Pr.) Rosen Publishing Group, Inc., The.

David, Jack. Karts. 2008. (Cool Rides Ser.). (ENG., Illus.). 24p. (J). (gr. 3-7). lib. bdg. 26.95 (978-1-60014-149-2(8)) Bellwether Media.

Dugan, Christine. Final Lap! Go-Kart Racing, 1 vol. 2nd rev. ed. (TIME for KIDS(r): Informational Text Ser.). (ENG., 48p. (gr. 4-5). 2013. Illus.). (J). lib. bdg. 29.96 (978-1-4807-1108-2(X)) 2012. pap. 13.99 (978-1-4333-4832-7(2)) Teacher Created Materials, Inc.

Hamilton, John. Go-Kart Racing. 2014. (Action Sports Ser.). (ENG., Illus.). 32p. (J). (gr. 3-9). lib. bdg. 32.79 (978-1-62403-440-4(3), 1155, Abdo & Daughters) ABDO Publishing Co.

Icanberry, Mark, creator. Electric Lunch. 2010. (Look, Learn & Do Ser.). (Illus.). 48p. (J). 7.95 (978-1-893327-03-0(5)) Look, Learn & Do Pubns.

Randolph, Ryan P. Karts, 1 vol. 2011. (Fast Lane: Open-Wheel Racing Ser.). (ENG., Illus.). 24p. (J). (gr. 2-3). 25.27 (978-1-4339-5758-1(2), 4cdfc456-c5b9-4ee1-a210-a8397e839f59); pap. 9.15 (978-1-4339-5760-4(4), f30879f5-7a93-4266-852c-7fd7b92bd497) Stevens, Gareth Publishing LLLP. (Gareth Stevens Learning Library).

KARTS AND KARTING—FICTION

Gordon, Elizabeth. Milo on Wheels, 1 vol. 2018. (Club Ser.). (ENG.). 88p. (YA). (gr. 2-3). 24.55 (978-1-5383-8238-7(5), dd1da155-2c2f-4432-9683-4d1bc69e21fa); pap. 14.85 (978-1-5383-8237-0(7), 3469d4d8-0af3-48b2-8593-03b8bb1c9ed5) Enslow Publishing, LLC.

Maddox, Jake. Go-Kart Rush. Tiffany, Sean, illus. 2007. (Jake Maddox Sports Stories Ser.). (ENG.). 72p. (J). (gr. 3-6). pap. 5.95 (978-1-59889-415-8(3), 93562, Stone Arch Bks.) Capstone.

—Kart Crash, 1 vol. Tiffany, Sean, illus. 2008. (Jake Maddox Sports Stories Ser.). (ENG.). 72p. (J). (gr. 3-6). 25.99 (978-1-4342-0777-7(3), 95182); pap. 5.95 (978-1-4342-0873-6(7), 95234) Capstone. (Stone Arch Bks.).

Midnight Lightning, 6 vols., Pack. (Bookweb Ser.). 32p. (gr. 5-18). 34.00 (978-0-7635-3790-6(X)) Rigby Education.

Montanari, Eva. Go-Cart Number 1, 1 vol. 2004. (Go-Cart Number 1 Ser.). (ENG., Illus.). 32p. (gr. k-2). lib. bdg. 28.67 (978-0-8368-4478-8(5), b4774ea9-0b63-48d5-987b-fe550702fb11, Gareth Stevens Learning Library) Stevens, Gareth Publishing LLLP.

KEATS, JOHN, 1795-1821

Kirkpatrick, Patricia. John Keats. Delessert, Etienne, illus. 2005. (Voices in Poetry Ser.). 43p. (J). (gr. 5-9). 21.95 (978-1-58341-345-6(6), Creative Education) Creative Co., The.

KELLER, HELEN, 1880-1968

Adams, Colleen. The Courage of Helen Keller. 2009. (Reading Room Collection 2 Ser.). 24p. (gr. 3-4). 42.50 (978-1-60851-992-7(9), PowerKids Pr.) Rosen Publishing Group, Inc., The.

Auster, Michael A. They Led the Way. 2005. (Yellow Umbrella Fluent Level Ser.). (ENG.). 16p. (gr. k-1). pap. 35.70 (978-0-7368-5315-6(4), Capstone Pr.) Capstone.

Benge, Janet. Helen Keller: Facing Her Challenges - Challenging the World, 1 bk. James, Kennon, illus. 2003. (Another Great Achiever Ser.). (J). lib. bdg. 23.95 incl. audio (978-1-57537-793-3(4)) Advance Publishing, Inc.

Bodden, Valerie. Helen Keller: Educator, Activist & Author. 2016. (Essential Lives Set 10 Ser.). (ENG., Illus.). 112p. (J). (gr. 8-12). lib. bdg. 41.36 (978-1-68078-299-8(1), 21735, Essential Library) ABDO Publishing Co.

Butler, Darren J. Helen Keller: Leader Without Sight or Sound. 2012. (Illus.). 108p. (J). pap. (978-1-59421-083-9(7)) Seacoast Publishing, Inc.

Carlson-Berne, Emma. What's Your Story, Helen Keller? 2015. (Cub Reporter Meets Famous Americans Ser.). (ENG., Illus.). 32p. (J). (gr. k-3). 26.65 (978-1-4677-7968-5(7), 8c8b987f-64b0-49dc-8200-1cd19647d0c3, Lerner Pubns.) Lerner Publishing Group.

Chally, Jeanne. Helen Keller: A Triumph of Spirit. 2003. (Shutterbug Books: Social Studies). (Illus.). 16p. (J). (gr. -1-3). pap. 4.10 (978-0-7398-7648-0(1)) Steck-Vaughn.

Cline-Ransome, Lesa. Helen Keller: The World in Her Heart. Ransome, James E., illus. 2008. 32p. (J). (gr. k-4). lib. bdg. 17.89 (978-0-06-057075-0(X), Collins) HarperCollins Pubs.

Dolan, Sean J. Helen Keller. 2006. (Rookie Biographies Ser.). (ENG., Illus.). 32p. (J). (gr. 1-2). per. 4.95 (978-0-516-25481-4(2), Children's Pr.) Scholastic Library Publishing.

Edison, Erin. Helen Keller, 1 vol. 2014. (Great Women in History Ser.). (ENG., Illus.). 24p. (J). (gr. -1-2). lib. bdg. 24.65 (978-1-4765-4217-1(1), 124315, Pebble) Capstone.

Fetty, Margaret. Helen Keller: Break down the Walls! (Defining Moments: Overcoming Challenges Ser.). (Illus.). 32p. (J). (gr. 2-7). 2018. (ENG.). pap. 7.99 (978-1-59716-299-9(X)) 2006. lib. bdg. 25.27 (978-1-59716-271-5(X)) Bearport Publishing Co., Inc.

Haldy, Emma E. Helen Keller. Bane, Jeff, illus. 2016. (My Early Library: My Itty-Bitty Bio Ser.). (ENG.). 24p. (J). (gr. k-1). 30.64 (978-1-63471-020-6(7), 208160) Cherry Lake Publishing.

Helenthal, Janet. Helen Keller. 2005. (Illus.). 16p. (J). (978-0-7367-2853-9(8)) Zaner-Bloser, Inc.

Hollingsworth, Tamara. Helen Keller: A New Vision, 1 vol. 2nd rev. ed. (TIME for KIDS(r): Informational Text Ser.). (ENG., 48p. (gr. 4-5). 2013. Illus.). (J). lib. bdg. 29.96 (978-1-4807-1115-0(2)) 2012. pap. 13.99 (978-1-4333-4863-1(2)) Teacher Created Materials, Inc.

Jazynka, Kitson. National Geographic Readers: Helen Keller (Level 2) 2017. (Readers Bios Ser.). (Illus.). 32p. (J). (gr. 1-3). pap. 4.99 (978-1-4263-2669-1(6), National Geographic Kids) Disney Publishing Worldwide.

Kennon, Caroline. Helen Keller in Her Own Words. 2014. (Eyewitness to History Ser.). 32p. (J). (gr. 4-6). pap. 63.00 (978-1-4824-0812-6(0)) Stevens, Gareth Publishing LLLP.

Lawson, Barbara Spilman. Helen Keller Against All Odds. 2016. (Spring Forward Ser.). (J). (gr. 2). (978-1-4900-9472-4(5)) Benchmark Education Co.

Leavitt, Amie Jane. Helen Keller. 2007. (What's So Great About...? Ser.). (Illus.). 32p. (J). (gr. 2-4). lib. bdg. 25.70 (978-1-58415-583-6(3)) Mitchell Lane Pubs.

MacLeod, Elizabeth. Helen Keller. Krystoforski, Andrej, illus. 2007. (Kids Can Read Ser.). 32p. (J). (gr. 1-3). 14.95 (978-1-55337-999-7(3)) Kids Can Pr., Ltd. CAN. Dist: Hachette Bk. Group.

McDonald, Caryl. Who Was Helen Keller?, 1 vol. 2012. (InfoMax Readers Ser.). (ENG., Illus.). 24p. (J). (gr. 1-1). pap. 8.25 (978-1-4488-9040-8(3), 57b571bb-4ede-4433-8f93-9adfd6b3d306, Rosen Classroom) Rosen Publishing Group, Inc., The.

Meltzer, Brad. I Am Helen Keller. Eliopoulos, Christopher, illus. 2015. (Ordinary People Change the World Ser.). 40p. (J). (gr. k-4). 15.99 (978-0-525-42851-0(8), Dial Bks) Penguin Young Readers Group.

Mills, Nathan & Peck, Audrey. Helen Keller: Miracle Child, 1 vol. 2012. (Rosen Readers Ser.). (ENG., Illus.). 24p. (J). (gr. 1-2). pap. 8.25 (978-1-4488-8824-5(7), 4870d10f-4237-4f28-bc91-622475a3a847, Rosen Classroom) Rosen Publishing Group, Inc., The.

Nakamura, May. A Puppy for Helen Keller: Ready-To-Read Level 2. Sanson, Rachel, illus. 2018. (Tails from History Ser.). (ENG.). 32p. (J). (gr. k-2). 17.99 (978-1-5344-2910-9(7)); pap. 4.99 (978-1-5344-2909-3(3)) Simon Spotlight. (Simon Spotlight).

Norwich, Grace. I Am Helen Keller. Elliott, Mark, illus. 2012. (I Am Ser.: 3). (ENG.). 128p. (J). (gr. 3-5). pap. 5.99 (978-0-545-44779-9(8)) Scholastic, Inc.

O'Brien, John A. Who Was Helen Keller? Harrison, Nancy, illus. 2003. (Who Was...? Ser.). 107p. (J). (gr. 3-7). 12.65 (978-0-7569-1596-4(1)) Perfection Learning Corp.

O'Brien, John A. & Thompson, Gare. Who Was Helen Keller? Harrison, Nancy, illus. 2003. (Who Was...? Ser.). 107p. (J). (gr. 3-7). 16.00 (978-0-613-63485-4(3)) Turtleback.

Peck, Audrey. Helen Keller: Miracle Child, 1 vol. 2012. (Beginning Biographies Ser.). (ENG., Illus.). 24p. (J). (gr. 1-2). 26.27 (978-1-4488-8593-0(0), 01d48232-e725-4281-a3eb-1235e4a32875, PowerKids Pr.) Rosen Publishing Group, Inc., The.

Rappaport, Doreen. Helen's Big World: The Life of Helen Keller. Tavares, Matt, illus. 2012. (Big Words Book Ser.: 6). (ENG.). 48p. (J). (gr. 1-3). 18.99 (978-0-7868-0890-8(X)) Little, Brown Bks. for Young Readers.

Romero, Libby. DK Life Stories: Helen Keller. Ager, Charlotte, illus. 2019. (DK Life Stories Ser.). (ENG.). 128p. (J). (gr. 3-7). pap. 5.99 (978-1-4654-7474-2(9), DK Children) Dorling Kindersley Publishing, Inc.

Sabin, Francene & Mattern, Joanne. Helen Keller, Girl of Courage. Meyer, Jean, illus. 2006. 56p. (J). (978-0-439-66043-3(2)) Scholastic, Inc.

Sutcliffe, Jane. Helen Keller. 2009. (History Maker Biographies Ser.). (gr. k-2). 27.93 (978-0-7613-4223-6(0), Lerner Pubns.) Lerner Publishing Group.

—Helen Keller. Verstraete, Elaine, illus. 2003. (On My Own Biographies Ser.). 48p. (J). (gr. 1-3). 6.95 (978-0-87614-903-4(4), Carolrhoda Bks.) Lerner Publishing Group.

Thompson, Gare & Who HQ. Who Was Helen Keller? Harrison, Nancy, illus. 2003. (Who Was? Ser.). 112p. (J). (gr. 3-7). pap. 6.99 (978-0-448-43144-4(0), Penguin Workshop) Penguin Young Readers Group.

KELLER, HELEN, 1880-1968—FICTION

Miller, Sarah. Miss Spitfire: Reaching Helen Keller. (ENG.). (J). (gr. 5-7). 2010. 256p. pap. 8.99 (978-1-4424-0851-7(0)) 2007. 240p. 17.99 (978-1-4169-2542-2(2)) Simon & Schuster Children's Publishing. (Atheneum Bks. for Young Readers).

KENNEDY, EDWARD M. (EDWARD MOORE), 1932-2009

Goldsworthy, Steve. Edward Kennedy. 2010. (Remarkable People Ser.). (Illus.). 24p. (J). (gr. 4-6). pap. 11.95 (978-1-61690-170-7(5)); lib. bdg. 25.70 (978-1-61690-169-1(1)) Weigl Pubs., Inc.

Kennedy, Edward M. My Senator & Me: A Dog's-Eye View of Washington, D. C. Small, David, illus. 2011. (J). (gr. 2-5). 29.95 (978-0-545-04379-3(4)) Weston Woods Studios, Inc.

Krull, Kathleen. The Brothers Kennedy: John, Robert, Edward. Bates, Amy June, illus. 2010. (ENG.). 40p. (J). (gr. -1-3). 16.99 (978-1-4169-9158-8(1), Simon & Schuster Bks. For Young Readers) Simon & Schuster Bks. For Young Readers.

McElroy, Lisa Tucker. Ted Kennedy: A Remarkable Life in the Senate. 2009. (Gateway Biographies Ser.). (ENG., Illus.). 48p. (J). (gr. 4-8). 26.60 (978-0-7613-4457-5(8)) Lerner Publishing Group.

Ted Kennedy. 2009. (Political Profiles Ser.). 144p. (YA). (gr. 5-9). 28.95 (978-1-59935-089-9(0)) Reynolds, Morgan Inc.

KENNEDY, JOHN F. (JOHN FITZGERALD), 1917-1963

Adler, David A. A Picture Book of John F. Kennedy. Casilla, Robert, illus. 2018. (Picture Book Biography Ser.). (ENG.). 32p. (J). (gr. -1-3). 7.99 (978-0-8234-4048-1(6)) Holiday Hse., Inc.

Anderson, Catherine Corley. John F. Kennedy. 2004. (Presidential Leaders Ser.). (ENG., Illus.). 112p. (gr. 6-12). 29.27 (978-0-8225-0812-0(5), Lerner Pubns.) Lerner Publishing Group.

Barretta, Gene. Lincoln & Kennedy: A Pair to Compare. Barretta, Gene, illus. 2016. (ENG., Illus.). 40p. (J). 18.99 (978-0-8050-9945-4(X), 900127126, Holt, Henry & Co. Bks. For Young Readers) Holt, Henry & Co.

Baxter, Kathleen & McConnell, Robert L., contrib. by. Assassination & Its Aftermath: How a Photograph Reassured a Shocked Nation, 1 vol. 2013. (Captured History Ser.). (ENG., Illus.). 64p. (J). (gr. 5-9). 35.32 (978-0-7565-4692-2(3), Compass Point Bks.) Capstone.

Bodden, Valerie. The Assassination of John F. Kennedy. 2016. (Turning Points Ser.). (ENG.). 48p. (J). (gr. 4-7). pap. 12.00 (978-1-62832-342-9(6), 20802, Creative Paperbacks); (Illus.). (978-1-60818-746-1(2), 20804, Creative Education) Creative Co., The.

Brown, Jonatha A. John F. Kennedy, 1 vol. 2005. (Gente Que Hay Que Conocer (People We Should Know) Ser.). 24p. (gr. 2-4). (SPA.). pap. 9.15 (978-0-8368-4768-0(7), 451ad457-199c-4f94-a0fb-3c7df1b50798); (SPA., Illus.). lib. bdg. 24.67 (978-0-8368-4761-1(X), c348c315-d42d-45a8-b925-6d50253cb9ad); (ENG., Illus.). lib. bdg. 24.67 (978-0-8368-4747-5(4), d187ed88-dbf8-4aa8-9c08-c0def88c1eff) Stevens, Gareth Publishing LLLP. (Weekly Reader Leveled Readers).

Burgan, Michael. TV Shapes Presidential Politics in the Kennedy-Nixon Debates: 4D an Augmented Reading Experience. 2018. (Captured Television History 4D Ser.). (ENG., Illus.). 64p. (J). (gr. 5-9). pap. 8.99 (978-0-7565-5827-7(1), 138352, Compass Point Bks.) Capstone.

Corey, Shana. A Time to Act: John F. Kennedy's Big Speech. Christie, R. Gregory, illus. 2017. (ENG.). 56p. (J). (gr. 3). 18.95 (978-0-7358-4275-5(2)) North-South Bks., Inc.

Edison, Erin. John F. Kennedy, 1 vol. (Presidential Biographies Ser.). (ENG.). 24p. (J). (gr. -1-2). 2014. pap. 6.29 (978-1-4765-9632-7(8), 125428, Pebble) 2012. lib. bdg. 27.32 (978-1-4296-8738-6(X), 119531, Capstone Pr.) Capstone.

Goldsmith, Howard. John F. Kennedy & the Stormy Sea. Benoit, Renné, illus. 2006. 32p. (J). lib. bdg. 15.00 (978-1-4242-0958-3(7)) Fitzgerald Bks.

—John F. Kennedy & the Stormy Sea: Ready-To-Read Level 2. Benoit, Renne, illus. 2006. (Ready-To-Read Childhood of Famous Americans Ser.). (ENG.). 32p. (J). (gr. k-2). pap. 4.99 (978-0-689-86816-0(2), Simon Spotlight) Simon Spotlight.

Gunderson, Megan M. John F. Kennedy, 1 vol. 2016. (United States Presidents *2017 Ser.). (ENG., Illus.). 40p. (J). (gr. 2-5). lib. bdg. 35.64 (978-1-68078-105-2(7), 21827, Big Buddy Bks.) ABDO Publishing Co.

Hansen, Grace. John F. Kennedy, 1 vol. 2014. (United States President Biographies (Abdo Kids Jumbo) Ser.). (ENG.). 24p. (J). (gr. -1-2). lib. bdg. 32.79 (978-1-62970-090-8(8), 1721, Abdo Kids) ABDO Publishing Co.

Heiligman, Deborah. High Hopes (Direct Mail Edition) A Photobiography of John F. Kennedy. 2003. (Photobiographies Ser.). (ENG., Illus.). 64p. (J). (gr. 5-9). 17.95 (978-0-7922-6141-4(0)) National Geographic Society.

Hollar, Sherman, contrib. by. John F. Kennedy, 1 vol. 2012. (Pivotal Presidents: Profiles in Leadership Ser.). (ENG.). 80p. (YA). (gr. 8-8). lib. bdg. 36.47 (978-1-61530-943-6(8), 1599df6c-2c8d-4a10-a865-042c024199ca); (Illus.). 72.94 (978-1-61530-957-3(8), 7f6f0469-f9a4-415a-abc3-9184509f4c6b) Rosen Publishing Group, Inc., The.

Jones, Brenn. Learning about Public Service from the Life of John F. Kennedy Jr. 2009. (Character Building Book Ser.). 24p. (gr. 2-3). 42.50 (978-1-61511-002-5(X), PowerKids Pr.) Rosen Publishing Group, Inc., The.

The check digit for ISBN-10 appears in parentheses after the full ISBN-13

Jones, Veda Boyd. John F. Kennedy. 2006. (Rookie Biographies Ser.). (ENG., Illus.). 32p. (J). (gr. 1-2). pap. 4.95 *(978-0-516-29797-2(X)*, Children's Pr.) Scholastic Library Publishing.

Kaplan, Howard S. DK Biography: John F. Kennedy: A Photographic Story of a Life. 2004. (DK Biography Ser.). (ENG., Illus.). 128p. (J). (gr. 5-12). pap. 6.99 *(978-0-7566-0340-3(4)*, DK Children) Dorling Kindersley Publishing, Inc.

Kawa, Katie. Before John F. Kennedy Was President, 1 vol. 2017. (Before They Were President Ser.). (ENG.). 24p. (J). (gr. 2-3). pap. 9.15 *(978-1-5382-1072-7(X)*, b9174323-4f41-4e85-b4bd-5757181b3fb4) Stevens, Gareth Publishing LLLP.

Keenan, Sheila. John F. Kennedy the Brave. Ko, Chin, illus. 2017. 25p. (J). *(978-1-5182-4585-5(4))* Harper & Row Ltd.

—John F. Kennedy the Brave. Ko, Chin, illus. 2017. (I Can Read Level 2 Ser.). (ENG.). 32p. (J). (gr. -1-3). pap. 4.99 *(978-0-06-243258-2(3)*, HarperCollins) HarperCollins Pubs.

Krull, Kathleen. The Brothers Kennedy: John, Robert, Edward. Bates, Amy June, illus. 2010. (ENG.). 40p. (J). (gr. -1-3). 16.99 *(978-1-4169-9158-8(1)*, Simon & Schuster Bks. For Young Readers) Simon & Schuster Bks. For Young Readers.

Manolis, Kay & Todd, Anne. John F. Kennedy: A Life of Citizenship. 2007. (People of Character Ser.). (ENG., Illus.). 24p. (J). (gr. 2-5). lib. bdg. 26.95 *(978-1-60014-087-7(4))* Bellwether Media.

Mara, Wil. John F. Kennedy, 1 vol. 2010. (Presidents & Their Times Ser.). (ENG.). 96p. (gr. 6-6). 36.93 *(978-0-7614-3628-7(6)*, 467bf370-4420-4ea1-848f-38b72f6db0e4) Cavendish Square Publishing LLC.

Marcovitz, Hal. John F. Kennedy. 2004. (Childhood of the Presidents Ser.). (Illus.). 48p. (J). (gr. 4-18). lib. bdg. 17.95 *(978-1-59084-272-0(3))* Mason Crest.

Margaret, Amy. John F. Kennedy Library & Museum. 2009. (Presidential Libraries Ser.). 24p. (gr. 3-3). 42.50 *(978-1-60851-487-8(0)*, PowerKids Pr.) Rosen Publishing Group, Inc., The.

Marsh, Carole. John F. Kennedy. 2003. 12p. (gr. k-4). 2.95 *(978-0-635-02127-4(7))* Gallopade International.

Mcdonough, Yona Zeldis. Quien Fue John F. Kennedy? (Who Was John F. Kennedy?) 2018. (Who Was... ? Ser.). lib. bdg. 20.85 *(978-0-606-41276-6(X))* Turtleback.

McDonough, Yona Zeldis & Who HQ. Who Was John F. Kennedy? Weber, Jill, illus. 2004. (Who Was? Ser.). 112p. (J). (gr. 3-7). pap. 6.99 *(978-0-448-43743-9(0)*, Penguin Workshop) Penguin Young Readers Group.

Olson, Nathan. John F. Kennedy: American Visionary, 1 vol. Bascle, Brian, illus. 2007. (Graphic Biographies Ser.). (ENG.). 32p. (J). (gr. 3-9). per. 8.10 *(978-0-7368-7904-0(8)*, 93901) Capstone.

Rappaport, Doreen. Jack's Path of Courage: The Life of John F. Kennedy. Tavares, Matt, illus. (Big Words Book Ser.: 5). (ENG.). 48p. (J). (gr. 1-3). 2016. pap. 8.99 *(978-1-4847-4961-6(8))* 2010. 17.99 *(978-1-4231-2272-2(0))* Little, Brown Bks. for Young Readers.

Rowell, Rebecca. John F. Kennedy's Presidency. 2016. (Presidential Powerhouses Ser.). (ENG., Illus.). 104p. (YA). (gr. 6-12). E-Book 54.65 *(978-1-4677-8600-3(4)*, Lerner Pubns.) Lerner Publishing Group.

Roxburgh, Ellis. John F. Kennedy vs. Nikita Khrushchev: Cold War Adversaries, 1 vol. 2014. (History's Greatest Rivals Ser.). (ENG., Illus.). 48p. (J). (gr. 6-8). lib. bdg. 33.60 *(978-1-4824-2221-4(2)*, bfc1cb51-8eeb-416d-af93-4cb9dbc51ac4) Stevens, Gareth Publishing LLLP.

Sommer, Shelley. John F. Kennedy: His Life & Legacy. 2005. (Illus.). 160p. (J). 16.99 *(978-0-06-054135-4(0))* HarperCollins Pubs.

Sutcliffe, Jane. John F. Kennedy. (History Maker Bios Ser.). (J). 2005. (Illus.). 48p. 26.60 *(978-0-8225-1546-3(6))* 2004. pap. 8.95 *(978-0-8225-2540-0(2))* Lerner Publishing Group. (Lerner Pubns.).

Upadhyay, Ritu. John F Kennedy the Making of a Leader. 2005. 44p. (J). lib. bdg. 15.00 *(978-1-4242-0851-7(3))* Fitzgerald Bks.

Upadhyay, Ritu & Time for Kids Editors. The Making of a Leader. 2005. (Time for Kids Ser.). (ENG., Illus.). 48p. (J). (gr. 2-4). pap. 3.99 *(978-0-06-057602-8(2))* HarperCollins Pubs.

Venezia, Mike. John F. Kennedy: Thirty-Fifth President 1961-1963, 32. Venezia, Mike, illus. 2007. (Getting to Know the U. S. Presidents Ser.). (ENG., Illus.). 32p. (J). (gr. 3-6). 22.44 *(978-0-516-22639-2(8))* Scholastic Library Publishing.

Winter, Jonah. JFK. Ford, A. G., illus. 2013. (ENG.). 32p. (J). (gr. -1-3). 17.99 *(978-0-06-176807-1(3)*, Tegen, Katherine Bks) HarperCollins Pubs.

Zamora, Dulce. How to Draw the Life & Times of John Fitzgerald Kennedy. 2009. (Kid's Guide to Drawing the Presidents of the United States of America Ser.). 32p. (gr. 4-4). 50.50 *(978-1-61511-151-0(4)*, PowerKids Pr.) Rosen Publishing Group, Inc., The.

KENNEDY, JOHN F. (JOHN FITZGERALD), 1917-1963—ASSASSINATION

Benoit, Peter. The Assassination of JFK. 2013. (ENG.). 64p. (J). 30.00 *(978-0-531-28200-7(7))*; pap. 8.95 *(978-0-531-27665-5(1))* Scholastic Library Publishing.

Coates, Tim. The Shooting of John F. Kennedy 1963: The Warren Commission. 2003. (Moments of History Ser.). (Illus.). 320p. *(978-1-84381-025-4(5))* Coates, Tim.

Collins, Terry. The Assassination of John F. Kennedy: November 22 1963, 1 vol. Yishan, Li, illus. 2014. (24-Hour History Ser.). (ENG.). 48p. (J). (gr. 3-9). pap. 8.95 *(978-1-4329-9300-9(3)*, 124616, Heinemann) Capstone.

Engdahl, Sylvia, ed. The John F. Kennedy Assassination, 1 vol. 2010. (Perspectives on Modern World History Ser.). (ENG., Illus.). 208p. (gr. 10-12). 49.43 *(978-0-7377-5006-5(5)*, c5089fe4-baa8-4e35-9354-7ee5075c04b3, Greenhaven Publishing) Greenhaven Publishing LLC.

Harkins, Susan Sales & Harkins, William H. The Assassination of John F. Kennedy 1963. 2007. (Monumental Milestones Ser.). (Illus.). 48p. (YA). (gr. 4-7). lib. bdg. 29.95 *(978-1-58415-540-9(X))* Mitchell Lane Pubs.

Hibbert, Clare. A Day That Changed History: The Assassination of John F Kennedy. 2013. (Turning Points in History Ser.). 48p. (gr. 5-12). 37.10 *(978-1-59920-971-5(3))* Black Rabbit Bks.

Kallen, Stuart A. The John F. Kennedy Assassination, 1 vol. 2009. (Crime Scene Investigations Ser.). (ENG., Illus.). 112p. (gr. 7-7). lib. bdg. 42.03 *(978-1-4205-0110-0(0)*, 7b1a53c0-09dc-466b-9b36-d5ceb8ad1fd5, Lucent Pr.) Greenhaven Publishing LLC.

Kelley, Tracey. Assassination of John F. Kennedy. 2013. (Turning Points in History Ser.). 48p. (gr. 5-9). 24.95 *(978-1-59920-771-1(0))* Black Rabbit Bks.

Mishkin, Dan. Warren Commission Report: A Graphic Investigation into the Kennedy Assassination. Colon, Ernie & Drozd, Jerzy, illus. 2014. (ENG.). 160p. 29.95 *(978-1-4197-1230-2(6)*, 1074801); pap. 17.95 *(978-1-4197-1231-9(4)*, 1074803) Abrams, Inc. (Abrams ComicArts).

Moore, Shannon Baker. John F. Kennedy's Assassination Rocks America. 2018. (Events That Changed America Ser.). (ENG.). 32p. (J). (gr. 3-6). lib. bdg. 35.64 *(978-1-5038-2518-5(3)*, 212325, MOMENTUM) Child's World, Inc, The.

Otfinoski, Steven. Tragedy in Dallas: The Story of the Assassination of John F. Kennedy. 2016. (Tangled History Ser.). (ENG., Illus.). 112p. (J). (gr. 3-9). lib. bdg. 32.65 *(978-1-4914-8451-7(9)*, 130897, Capstone Pr.) Capstone.

Spencer, Lauren. The Assassination of John F. Kennedy. 2009. (Library of Political Assassinations Ser.). 64p. (gr. 5-5). 58.50 *(978-1-60853-826-3(5))* Rosen Publishing Group, Inc., The.

Stanley, Joseph. The John F. Kennedy Assassination: The Shooting That Shook America, 1 vol. 2017. (Crime Scene Investigations Ser.). (ENG.). 112p. (gr. 7-7). 42.03 *(978-1-5345-6087-1(4)*, 397f78e7-e868-44b6-8a14-7732ab298bb5, Lucent Pr.) Greenhaven Publishing LLC.

Swanson, James L. The President Has Been Shot!: the Assassination of John F. Kennedy. 2013. (ENG., Illus.). 288p. (J). (gr. 7-7). 18.99 *(978-0-545-49007-8(3)*, Scholastic Pr.) Scholastic, Inc.

KENNEDY, ROBERT F., 1925-1968

Krull, Kathleen. The Brothers Kennedy: John, Robert, Edward. Bates, Amy June, illus. 2010. (ENG.). 40p. (J). (gr. -1-3). 16.99 *(978-1-4169-9158-8(1)*, Simon & Schuster Bks. For Young Readers) Simon & Schuster Bks. For Young Readers.

KENNEDY, ROBERT F., 1925-1968—ASSASSINATION

Ching, Juliet. The Assassination of Robert F. Kennedy. 2009. (Library of Political Assassinations Ser.). 64p. (gr. 5-5). 58.50 *(978-1-60853-829-4(X))* Rosen Publishing Group, Inc., The.

KENNEDY FAMILY

Krull, Kathleen. The Brothers Kennedy: John, Robert, Edward. Bates, Amy June, illus. 2010. (ENG.). 40p. (J). (gr. -1-3). 16.99 *(978-1-4169-9158-8(1)*, Simon & Schuster Bks. For Young Readers) Simon & Schuster Bks. For Young Readers.

KENOBI, OBI-WAN (FICTITIOUS CHARACTER)—FICTION

Blackman, Haden. Star Wars: Clone Wars Adventures. Brothers, Fillbach, illus. 2011. (Star Wars Digests Ser.). (ENG.). 96p. (J). (gr. 3-8). 34.21 *(978-1-59961-905-7(9)*, 13753, Graphic Novels) Spotlight.

Blackman, Haden & Caldwell, Ben. Star Wars: Clone Wars Adventures. 2011. (Star Wars Digests Ser.). (ENG., Illus.). 96p. (J). (gr. 3-8). 34.21 *(978-1-59961-904-0(0)*, 13752, Graphic Novels) Spotlight.

Blackman, Haden & The Fillbach Brothers. Clone Wars Adventures. Brothers, Fillbach, illus. 2011. (Star Wars Digests Ser.). (ENG.). 96p. (J). (gr. 3-8). 34.21 *(978-1-59961-906-4(7)*, 13754, Graphic Novels) Spotlight.

BookSource Staff, compiled by. Obi-Wan Kenobi: Jedi Knight. 2012. (Star Wars DK Readers Level 3 Ser.). lib. bdg. 13.55 *(978-0-606-26678-9(X))* Turtleback.

Fillbach. Clone Wars Adventures, 7. Fillbach, illus. 2013. (Star Wars Digests Ser.). (ENG., Illus.). 80p. (J). (gr. 3-8). lib. bdg. 34.21 *(978-1-61479-058-7(2)*, 13761, Graphic Novels) Spotlight.

—Star Wars: Clone Wars Adventures. Fillbach, illus. 2013. (Star Wars Digests Ser.). (ENG., Illus.). 80p. (J). (gr. 3-8). lib. bdg. 34.21 *(978-1-61479-059-4(0)*, 13762, Graphic Novels) Spotlight.

Fillbach, Brothers & Blackman, Haden. Clone Wars Adventures. 2011. (Star Wars Digests Ser.). (ENG., Illus.). 96p. (J). (gr. 3-8). 34.21 *(978-1-59961-907-1(5)*, 13755, Graphic Novels) Spotlight.

Fillbach, Brothers, et al. Clone Wars Adventures. 2011. (Star Wars Digests Ser.). (ENG., Illus.). 88p. (J). (gr. 3-8). 34.21 *(978-1-59961-909-5(1)*, 13757, Graphic Novels) Spotlight.

Landers, Ace. Anakin to the Rescue. 2012. (LEGO Star Wars 8X8 Ser.). lib. bdg. 13.55 *(978-0-606-26774-8(3))* Turtleback.

Lucas Film Book Group. Trouble on Tatooine. 2017. (Star Wars: World of Reading Ser.). (J). lib. bdg. 14.75 *(978-0-606-39963-0(1))* Turtleback.

Saunders, Catherine. The Jedi & the Force. 2014. (Illus.). 144p. (J). *(978-1-4351-5416-2(9))* Dorling Kindersley Publishing, Inc.

Watson, Jude. The Desperate Mission. 2005. (Star Wars Ser.: No. 1). 168p. (J). lib. bdg. 20.00 *(978-1-4242-0774-9(6))* Fitzgerald Bks.

KENTUCKY

Allen, Nancy. Daniel Boone: Trailblazer, 1 vol. 2005. (ENG., Illus.). 32p. (J). (gr. k-3). 16.99 *(978-1-58980-212-4(8)*, Pelican Publishing) Arcadia Publishing.

Barrett, Tracy. Kentucky, 1 vol. 2nd rev. ed. 2008. (Celebrate the States (Second Edition) Ser.). (ENG.). 144p. (gr. 6-6). lib. bdg. 39.79 *(978-0-7614-2715-5(5)*, ecb4eb9a-b8c2-4c34-bbec-fa4d7c2a0d91) Cavendish Square Publishing LLC.

Brandt, Keith & Macken, JoAnn Early. Daniel Boone: Frontier Explorer. Lawn, John, illus. 2008. 55p. (J). pap. *(978-0-439-02020-6(4))* Scholastic, Inc.

Brown, Dottie. Kentucky. 2012. (J). lib. bdg. 25.26 *(978-0-7613-4534-3(5)*, Lerner Pubns.) Lerner Publishing Group.

Brown, Vanessa. Kentucky. 2009. (Bilingual Library of the United States of America Ser.). (ENG & SPA.). 32p. (gr. 2-2). 47.90 *(978-1-60853-362-6(X)*, Editorial Buenas Letras) Rosen Publishing Group, Inc., The.

—Kentucky, 1 vol. Brusca, Maria Cristina, tr. 2005. (Bilingual Library of the United States of America Ser.: Set 1). (ENG & SPA., Illus.). 32p. (J). (gr. 2-2). lib. bdg. 28.93 *(978-1-4042-3082-8(3)*, 2e0ac190-1db2-4974-a342-42cbada2d113) Rosen Publishing Group, Inc., The.

Burton, K. Melissa. Now That's Interesting Kentucky's Capitol. Asher, James, photos by. 2007. (Illus.). 40p. (J). per. 14.95 *(978-0-913383-96-4(1))* McClanahan Publishing Hse., Inc.

Davidson, Tish. East South-Central States: Kentucky & Tennessee, Vol. 19. 2015. (Let's Explore the States Ser.). (Illus.). 64p. (J). (gr. 5). 23.95 *(978-1-4222-3322-1(7))* Mason Crest.

Deinard, Jenny. How to Draw Kentucky's Sights & Symbols. 2009. (Kid's Guide to Drawing America Ser.). 32p. (gr. k-k). 50.50 *(978-1-61511-066-7(6)*, PowerKids Pr.) Rosen Publishing Group, Inc., The.

Evdokimoff, Natasha. Kentucky. 2011. (Illus.). 48p. (YA). (gr. 3-6). 29.99 *(978-1-61690-789-1(4))*; (J). *(978-1-61690-465-4(8))* Weigl Pubs., Inc.

Graham Gaines, Ann. Kentucky, 1 vol. Santoro, Christopher, illus. 2003. (It's My State! (First Edition)(r) Ser.). (ENG.). 80p. (gr. 4-4). 34.07 *(978-0-7614-1525-1(4)*, 994f03d6-b84f-49f3-bb7f-e0e0d0acd3b3) Cavendish Square Publishing LLC.

—Kentucky, 1 vol. 2nd rev. ed. 2013. (It's My State! (Second Edition)(r) Ser.). (ENG.). 80p. (gr. 4-4). pap. 18.64 *(978-1-62712-093-7(9)*, ae7eb257-2a3a-4a17-80a7-12abfb5bec52) Cavendish Square Publishing LLC.

Johnston, Marianne. Daniel Boone. 2009. (American Legends Ser.). 24p. (gr. 3-3). 42.50 *(978-1-61511-380-4(0)*, PowerKids Pr.) Rosen Publishing Group, Inc., The.

Kramer, S. A. & Who HQ. Who Was Daniel Boone? Ulrich, George, illus. 2006. (Who Was? Ser.). 112p. (J). (gr. 3-7). pap. 5.99 *(978-0-448-43902-0(6)*, Penguin Workshop) Penguin Young Readers Group.

Labairon, Cassandra Sharri. Kentucky. 2008. (This Land Called America Ser.). 32p. (YA). (gr. 3-6). 22.95 *(978-1-58341-642-6(0))* Creative Co., The.

Lantier, Pat. Kentucky, 1 vol. 2005. (Portraits of the States Ser.). (ENG., Illus.). 32p. (gr. 3-5). pap. 11.50 *(978-0-8368-4685-0(0)*, 685998be-cb54-4fe9-a3f7-eb82f1d8f97a); lib. bdg. 28.67 *(978-0-8368-4666-9(4)*, fb7267a8-d07c-4cab-a726-2a1d633e39ca) Stevens, Gareth Publishing LLLP. (Gareth Stevens Learning Library).

Marsh, Carole. The Kentucky Coloring Book. 2004. (Kentucky Experience! Ser.). (Illus.). 32p. (J). (gr. k-2). pap. 3.95 *(978-0-7933-9471-5(6))* Gallopade International.

—The Kentucky Experience Pocket Guide. 2004. (Kentucky Experience! Ser.). (Illus.). 96p. (J). (gr. 3-8). pap. 6.95 *(978-0-7933-9451-7(1))* Gallopade International.

—Kentucky Geography Projects: 30 Cool, Activities, Crafts, Experiments & More for Kids to Do to Learn about Your State! 2003. (Kentucky Experience Ser.). 32p. (gr. k-5). pap. 5.95 *(978-0-635-01836-6(5)*, Marsh, Carole Bks.) Gallopade International.

—Kentucky Government Projects #4: 30 Cool Activities, Crafts, Experiments & More for Kids to Do! 2003. (Kentucky Experience Ser.). (Illus.). 32p. (J). (gr. k-5). pap. 5.95 *(978-0-635-01936-3(1)*, Marsh, Carole Bks.) Gallopade International.

—Kentucky Jeopardy! Answers & Questions about Our State! 2004. (Kentucky Experience! Ser.). (Illus.). 32p. (J). (gr. 3-8). pap. 7.95 *(978-0-7933-9516-3(X))* Gallopade International.

—Kentucky "Jography" A Fun Run Thru Our State! 2004. (Kentucky Experience! Ser.). (Illus.). 32p. (J). (gr. 3-8). pap. 7.95 *(978-0-7933-9517-0(8))* Gallopade International.

—Kentucky People Projects: 30 Cool, Activities, Crafts, Experiments & More for Kids to Do to Learn about Your State! 2003. (Kentucky Experience Ser.). 32p. (gr. k-5). pap. 5.95 *(978-0-635-01986-8(8)*, Marsh, Carole Bks.) Gallopade International.

—Kentucky Symbols & Facts Projects: 30 Cool, Activities, Crafts, Experiments & More for Kids to Do to Learn about Your State! 2003. (Kentucky Experience Ser.). 32p. (gr. k-5). pap. 5.95 *(978-0-635-01886-1(1)*, Marsh, Carole Bks.) Gallopade International.

—My First Book about Kentucky. 2004. (Kentucky Experience! Ser.). (Illus.). 32p. (J). (gr. k-4). pap. 7.95 *(978-0-7933-9515-6(1))* Gallopade International.

Murray, Julie. Kentucky, 1 vol. 2006. (United States (BB) Ser.). (ENG.). 32p. (gr. k-4). 27.07 *(978-1-59197-676-9(6)*, Buddy Bks.) ABDO Publishing Co.

Nemerson, Roy. Daniel Boone. Marcos, Pablo, illus. 2005. (Heroes of America Ser.). 239p. (gr. 3-8). lib. bdg. 27.07 *(978-1-59679-256-2(6)*, Abdo & Daughters) ABDO Publishing Co.

Sanford, William R. & Green, Carl R. Daniel Boone: Courageous Frontiersman, 1 vol. 2013. (Courageous Heroes of the American West Ser.). (ENG., Illus.). 48p. (J). (gr. 5-7). 25.27 *(978-0-7660-4002-1(X)*, e7ed4ece-6466-4883-85c1-b36dff28492c); pap. 11.53 *(978-1-4644-0085-8(7)*, 7820d612-b137-454a-a658-ae080ae9c295) Enslow Publishing, LLC.

Santella, Andrew. America the Beautiful, Third Series: Kentucky (Revised Edition) 2014. (America the Beautiful Ser.: 3). (ENG.). 144p. (J). lib. bdg. 40.00 *(978-0-531-24885-0(2))* Scholastic Library Publishing.

Smith, Andrea P. Daniel Boone. (Illus.). 24p. (J). 2012. 63.60 *(978-1-4488-5227-7(7))* 2011. (ENG., (gr. 2-3)). pap. 11.60 *(978-1-4488-5226-0(9)*, 3e6572b2-7fbe-448b-9b30-5f364d8f9ab8) 2011. (ENG., (gr. 2-3)). lib. bdg. 28.93 *(978-1-4488-5194-2(7)*, 6fedb0e8-f5a9-4101-8329-8e6fb1c21d30) Rosen Publishing Group, Inc., The. (PowerKids Pr.).

Valzania, Kimberly. Kentucky. 2003. (Rookie Read-About Geography Ser.). (ENG., Illus.). 32p. (J). (gr. 1-2). 20.50 *(978-0-516-22697-2(5)*, Children's Pr.) Scholastic Library Publishing.

Zronik, John Paul & Zronik, John. Daniel Boone: Woodsman of Kentucky, 1 vol. 2006. (In the Footsteps of Explorers Ser.). (ENG., Illus.). 32p. (J). (gr. 4-7). pap. *(978-0-7787-2464-3(6)*, 1253442); lib. bdg. *(978-0-7787-2428-5(X)*, 1253442) Crabtree Publishing Co.

KENTUCKY—FICTION

Allen, Nancy. Amazing Grace: A Kentucky Girl with Gumption During World War II. Shapiro, Meryl R. B., illus. 2014. Orig. Title: Amazing Grace; a Kentucky Girl with Gumption During World War II. (ENG.). 160p. (gr. 4-7). 29.99 *(978-1-62619-405-2(X)*, History Pr., The) Arcadia Publishing.

Altsheler, Joseph A. The Forest Runners: A Story of the Great War Trail in Early Kentucky. (Young Trailers Ser.: Vol. 2). (J). 25.95 *(978-0-8488-1236-2(0))* Amereon Ltd.

—The Forest Runners: A Story of the Great War Trail in Early Kentucky. (Young Trailers Ser.: Vol. 2). (J). reprint ed. 2010. 386p. pap. 33.75 *(978-1-149-35494-0(1)*, BiblioLife) 2008. 248p. 24.99 *(978-0-554-34443-0(2))* Creative Media Partners, LLC.

—The Forest Runners: A Story of the Great War Trail in Early Kentucky. 2006. (Young Trailers Ser.: Vol. 2). (J). reprint ed. pap. *(978-1-4065-0810-9(1))* Dodo Pr.

—The Forest Runners: A Story of the Great War Trail in Early Kentucky. 2010. (Young Trailers Ser.: Vol. 2). (Illus.). 142p. (J). (gr. 4-7). reprint ed. pap. 19.99 *(978-1-153-70291-1(6))* General Bks. LLC.

—The Keepers of the Trail: A Story of the Great Woods. 2008. (Young Trailers Ser.: Vol. 3). 256p. (J). reprint ed. pap. *(978-1-4099-1719-9(3))* Dodo Pr.

—The Keepers of the Trail: A Story of the Great Woods. 2009. (Young Trailers Ser.: Vol. 3). 224p. (gr. 4-7). reprint ed. pap. 15.45 *(978-1-4385-1899-2(4)*, Bk. Jungle) Standard Publications, Inc.

—The Riflemen of the Ohio: A Story of Early Days along the Beautiful River. (Young Trailers Ser.: Vol. 6). (J). reprint ed. 25.95 *(978-0-8488-1239-3(5))* Amereon Ltd.

—The Riflemen of the Ohio: A Story of Early Days along the Beautiful River. 2009. (Young Trailers Ser.: Vol. 6). 312p. (J). reprint ed. pap. *(978-1-4099-2567-5(6))* Dodo Pr.

—The Riflemen of the Ohio: A Story of Early Days along the Beautiful River. 2008. (Young Trailers Ser.: Vol. 6). 192p. (J). reprint ed. pap. *(978-1-4068-2807-8(6))* Echo Library.

—The Riflemen of the Ohio: A Story of Early Days along the Beautiful River. 2010. (Young Trailers Ser.: Vol. 6). (Illus.). 180p. (J). (gr. 4-7). reprint ed. pap. 19.99 *(978-1-153-79466-4(7))* General Bks. LLC.

—The Riflemen of the Ohio: A Story of Early Days along the Beautiful River. 2012. (Young Trailers Ser.: Vol. 6). 340p. (J). (gr. 4-7). pap. *(978-3-8472-2473-0(5))* tredition Verlag.

—The Young Trailers. 2007. (Young Trailers Ser.: Vol. 1). 248p. reprint ed. per. 12.45 *(978-1-60424-031-3(8)*, Bk. Jungle) Standard Publications, Inc.

—The Young Trailers: A Story of Early Kentucky. 2006. (Young Trailers Ser.: Vol. 1). (J). 27.95 *(978-1-4218-2970-8(3))*; reprint ed. pap. 12.95 *(978-1-4218-3070-4(1))* 1st World Publishing, Inc.

—The Young Trailers: A Story of Early Kentucky. (Young Trailers Ser.: Vol. 1). (J). reprint ed. 25.95 *(978-0-89190-824-1(2))* Amereon Ltd.

—The Young Trailers: A Story of Early Kentucky. 2008. (Young Trailers Ser.: Vol. 1). 224p. (J). reprint ed. 24.99 *(978-0-554-36772-9(6))* Creative Media Partners, LLC.

—The Young Trailers: A Story of Early Kentucky. 2007. (Young Trailers Ser.: Vol. 1). 228p. (J). reprint ed. per. *(978-1-4065-6553-9(9))* Dodo Pr.

—The Young Trailers: A Story of Early Kentucky. 2007. (Young Trailers Ser.: Vol. 1). 144p. (J). reprint ed. per. *(978-1-4068-1694-5(9))* Echo Library.

—The Young Trailers: A Story of Early Kentucky. (Young Trailers Ser.: Vol. 1). (J). reprint ed. 2010. 180p. (gr. 4-7). 30.36 *(978-1-169-27791-5(8))* 2010. 180p. (gr. 4-7). pap. 18.36 *(978-1-162-71336-6(4))* 2010. 37.95 *(978-1-161-48200-3(8))* 2004. pap. 1.99 *(978-1-4192-8924-8(1))* 2004. pap. 22.95 *(978-1-4191-8924-1(7))* Kessinger Publishing, LLC.

—The Young Trailers: A Story of Early Kentucky. 2012. (Young Trailers Ser.: Vol. 1). 200p. (J). (gr. 4-7). reprint ed. pap. *(978-3-8472-3210-0(X))* tredition Verlag.

—The Young Trailers - A Story of Early Kentucky. 2008. (Young Trailers Ser.: Vol. 1). 244p. reprint ed. pap. 14.45 *(978-1-60597-191-9(X)*, Bk. Jungle) Standard Publications, Inc.

Barkley, Roger C. Johnny Grasshopper. 2006. 52p. pap. 16.95 *(978-1-4241-0221-1(9))* PublishAmerica, Inc.

Birdseye, Tom. A Tough Nut to Crack. 2006. (ENG.). 128p. (J). (gr. 3-7). 16.95 *(978-0-8234-1967-8(3))* Holiday Hse., Inc.

Bonnie, Compton-Hanson. Holly Jean & the Secret of Razorback Ridge, 5 vols., Vol. 1. 2011. (ENG.). 164p. (J). pap. 7.99 *(978-1-59317-431-6(4))* Warner Pr., Inc.

Booher, Brock. Healing Stone. 2014. 329p. (YA). pap. 15.99 *(978-1-4621-1394-1(X)*, Horizon Pubs.) Cedar Fort, Inc./CFI Distribution.

Bradbury, Jennifer. River Runs Deep. 2015. (ENG., Illus.). 336p. (J). (gr. 4-8). 17.99 *(978-1-4424-6824-5(6)*, Atheneum Bks. for Young Readers) Simon & Schuster Children's Publishing.

Brogle, Jennifer. The Adventures of Jennifer & Sherry: Summertime. 2013. 60p. pap. 25.36 *(978-1-4669-7560-6(1))* Trafford Publishing.

Bryan, Jennifer Liu & Kendle, Hazel Cole. Cole Family Christmas. Julich, Jennifer, illus. 2008. (ENG.). 74p. (J). (gr. 4-7). 17.95 *(978-0-9816265-0-5(5))* Next Chapter Pr.

Buhlig Meister, Victoria. Tell Me a Story, Please, Mi-Mi! 2009. 36p. pap. 16.99 *(978-1-4389-2430-4(5))* AuthorHouse.

Byars, Betsy. Keeper of the Doves. 2004. (Illus.). 128p. (J). (gr. 3-7). reprint ed. 7.99 *(978-0-14-240063-0(7)*, Puffin Books) Penguin Young Readers Group.

Caudill, Rebecca. Up & down the River. Merwin, Decie, illus. 2005. 143p. (J). (gr. -1-17). pap. 11.95 *(978-1-883937-81-2(7))* Bethlehem Bks.

Clarke, Nancy & Muire, Penny. Stormy Hill's Challenge. 2013. 248p. 26.00 *(978-1-62212-803-7(6)*, Strategic Bk. Publishing) Strategic Book Publishing & Rights Agency (SBPRA).

Clevenger, Lee. IncrediBoy: Be Careful What You Wish. 2004. 267p. (J). pap. 12.95 *(978-0-9764052-0-7(2))* Thomas Max Publishing.

Combs, Sarah. Breakfast Served Anytime. (ENG.). 272p. (YA). (gr. 7). 2016. pap. 7.99 *(978-0-7636-8752-6(9))* 2014. 16.99 *(978-0-7636-6791-7(9))* Candlewick Pr.

J
K
L

Crum, Shutta. My Mountain Song. 2007. (Illus.). 32p. (J). 16.00 *(978-1-4223-6590-8(5))* DIANE Publishing Co.

Dowell, Frances O'Roark. Trouble the Water. (ENG., Illus.). (J). (gr. 4-8). 2017. 304p. pap. 8.99 *(978-1-4814-2464-6(5))* 2016. 288p. 16.99 *(978-1-4814-2463-9(7))* Simon & Schuster Children's Publishing.

—Trouble the Water. 2017. lib. bdg. 18.40 *(978-0-606-40126-5(1))* Turtleback.

Duncan-Pauley, Chadney. A Bull's Paradise. 2009. (ENG.). 32p. pap. 15.60 *(978-0-557-17660-1(3))* Lulu Pr., Inc.

Durrant, Lynda. Imperfections. 2008. (ENG., Illus.). 176p. (J). (gr. 5-7). 16.00 *(978-0-547-00357-3(9),* 1029147, Clarion Bks.) HarperCollins Pubs.

Elliott, R. Kenley. Stories from a Kentucky Boy. 2012. 74p. pap. 12.95 *(978-1-4772-5429-5(3))* AuthorHouse.

Ernst, Kathleen. Midnight in Lonesome Hollow: A Kit Mystery. 2007. (American Girl Mysteries Ser.). (ENG., Illus.). 192p. (gr. 4-7). 10.95 *(978-1-59369-161-5(0),* American Girl) American Girl Publishing, Inc.

Florence, Leigh Anne. The Adoption. Asher, James, illus. 2003. (Woody: the Kentucky Wiener Ser.). 32p. (J). (gr. -1-3). per. 12.95 *(978-0-9741417-0-1(4))* HotDiggetyDog Pr.

—Welcomes a Dad, Vol. 2. Asher, James, illus. 2004. (Woody: the Kentucky Wiener Ser.). 32p. (J). (gr. -1-3). per. 12.95 *(978-0-9741417-1-8(2))* HotDiggetyDog Pr.

Fuchs-Rice, Dwayne. Shades of Ember. 2008. 456p. pap. 24.95 *(978-0-595-53315-2(9))* iUniverse, Inc.

Giurco, Diane. The Adventures of Willy & Nilly. 2008. (Illus.). 32p. pap. 14.49 *(978-1-4389-1134-2(3))* AuthorHouse.

Godby, Ron. The King of Imperial Hill. 2006. 76p. pap. 16.95 *(978-1-4241-1061-2(0))* PublishAmerica, Inc.

Hart, Alison. Gabriel's Journey, 1 vol. 2011. (Racing to Freedom Ser.: 2). 160p. (J). (gr. 3-7). pap. 4.99 *(978-1-56145-530-0(X))* Peachtree Publishing Co. Inc.

Henson, Heather. Dream of Night. 2010. (ENG.). 224p. (J). (gr. 3-7). 17.99 *(978-1-4169-4899-5(6),* Atheneum Bks. for Young Readers) Simon & Schuster Children's Publishing.

Jacobs, Lily. The Littlest Bunny in Kentucky: An Easter Adventure. Dunn, Robert, illus. 2015. (Littlest Bunny Ser.). (ENG.). 32p. (J). (gr. -1-3). 9.99 *(978-1-4926-1096-0(8),* Hometown World) Sourcebooks, Inc.

James, Eric. Santa's Sleigh Is on Its Way to Kentucky: A Christmas Adventure. Dunn, Robert, illus. 2015. (Santa's Sleigh Is on Its Way Ser.). (ENG.). 32p. (J). (gr. k-2). 12.99 *(978-1-4926-2761-6(5),* Hometown World) Sourcebooks, Inc.

—The Spooky Express Kentucky. Piwowarski, Marcin, illus. 2017. (Spooky Express Ser.). (ENG.). 32p. (J). (gr. k-6). 9.99 *(978-1-4926-5363-9(2),* Hometown World) Sourcebooks, Inc.

—Tiny the Kentucky Easter Bunny. 2018. (Tiny the Easter Bunny Ser.). (ENG.). 40p. (J). (gr. k-3). 9.99 *(978-1-4926-5930-3(4),* Hometown World) Sourcebooks, Inc.

James L. Fuller. The Lost Coal Mine to Oz. 2009. 184p. pap. 16.60 *(978-1-4269-1829-2(1))* Trafford Publishing.

Johnston, Annie Fell. The Little Colonel. 2006. (Illus.). pap. *(978-1-4065-1132-1(3))* Dodo Pr.

—The Little Colonel. 2005. reprint ed. pap. 21.95 *(978-0-7661-9402-1(7))* Kessinger Publishing, LLC.

Johnston, Annie Fellows. The Giant Scissors. Barry, Etheldred B., illus. 2005. reprint ed. pap. 22.95 *(978-1-4179-0341-2(4))* Kessinger Publishing, LLC.

—In the Desert of Waiting the Legend of Camel Back Mountain. 2005. reprint ed. pap. 15.95 *(978-1-4179-3370-9(4))* Kessinger Publishing, LLC.

—The Little Colonel's Chum: Mary Ware. 2018. (ENG., Illus.). 182p. (YA). (gr. 7-12). pap. *(978-93-5297-428-3(X))* Alpha Editions.

—The Little Colonel's Hero. 2018. (ENG., Illus.). 166p. (YA). (gr. 7-12). pap. *(978-93-5297-429-0(8))* Alpha Editions.

—The Little Colonel's Hero. 2017. (ENG., Illus.). (J). 23.95 *(978-1-374-96147-0(7));* pap. 13.95 *(978-1-374-96146-3(9))* Capital Communications, Inc.

—The Little Colonel's House Party. 2018. (ENG., Illus.). 158p. (YA). (gr. 7-12). pap. *(978-93-5297-430-6(1))* Alpha Editions.

—The Little Colonel's House Party. 2017. (ENG., Illus.). (J). 23.95 *(978-1-374-96551-5(0))* Capital Communications, Inc.

—The Little Colonel's House Party. Meynell, Louis, illus. 2007. 176p. per. *(978-1-4065-3514-3(1))* Dodo Pr.

—Mary Ware the Little Colonel's Chum. Barry, Etheldred B., illus. 2004. reprint ed. pap. 30.95 *(978-1-4179-1704-4(0))* Kessinger Publishing, LLC.

—Two Little Knights of Kentucky. 2018. (ENG., Illus.). 108p. (YA). (gr. 7-12). pap. *(978-93-5297-432-0(8))* Alpha Editions.

Knight, Mary. Saving Wonder. 2016. (ENG.). 288p. (J). (gr. 3-7). 16.99 *(978-0-545-82893-2(7),* Scholastic Pr.) Scholastic, Inc.

Lafantasie, Shilo. House of Love. 2012. 32p. pap. 24.95 *(978-1-4560-9404-1(1))* America Star Bks.

Leet, Karen. Sarah's Courage: A Kentucky Frontier Kidnapping. Schlessinger, Sarah, illus. 2014. Orig. Title: Sarah's Courage: a Kentucky Frontier Kidnapping. (ENG.). 144p. (gr. 4-7). 29.99 *(978-1-62619-477-9(7),* History Pr., The) Arcadia Publishing.

Marsh, Carole. The Mystery at the Kentucky Derby. 2009. (Real Kids, Real Places Ser.). (Illus.). 146p. (J). lib. bdg. 18.99 *(978-0-635-07002-9(2),* Marsh, Carole Mysteries) Gallopade International.

Martinez, Jessica. The Vow. 2014. (ENG., Illus.). 448p. (YA). (gr. 9). pap. 11.99 *(978-1-4424-5865-9(8),* Simon Pulse) Simon Pulse.

Meister, Victoria Buhlig. Our Playtime Friend. 2011. 28p. 13.59 *(978-1-4567-2883-0(0))* AuthorHouse.

Newhall, Mary & Campbell, Joanna. Bridal Dreams. 2005. (Thoroughbred Ser.). (Illus.). 163p. (gr. 3-7). 15.00 *(978-0-7569-5359-1(6))* Perfection Learning Corp.

—Samantha's Irish Luck. 2005. (Thoroughbred Ser.). (Illus.). 156p. (gr. 3-7). 15.00 *(978-0-7569-5350-8(2))* Perfection Learning Corp.

Paine, Ralph D. First down, Kentucky! 2011. 354p. 51.95 *(978-1-258-07497-5(4))* Literary Licensing, LLC.

Payne, C. C. Something to Sing About. 2008. (ENG.). 167p. (J). (gr. 4-7). pap. 8.50 *(978-0-8028-5344-8(7))* Eerdmans, William B. Publishing Co.

Ramage, Rosalyn Rikel. The Graveyard: N/a. 2012. 184p. (gr. 4-6). pap. 11.88 *(978-1-4669-5033-7(1))* Trafford Publishing.

Rand, Johnathan. American Chillers #27 Kentucky Komodo Dragons. 2009. 208p. (J). pap. 5.99 *(978-1-893699-90-8(0))* AudioCraft Publishing, Inc.

Ransom, Candice. The Underground Adventure of Arly Dunbar, Cave Explorer. Hammond, Ted & Carbajal, Richard Pimentel, illus. 2011. (History's Kid Heroes Set III Ser.). pap. 51.02 *(978-0-7613-7640-8(2),* Graphic Universe™) Lerner Publishing Group.

Raven, Margot Theis. Night Boat to Freedom. Lewis, E. B., illus. 2008. (ENG.). 40p. (J). (gr. 1-4). pap. 10.99 *(978-0-312-55018-9(9),* 900055951) Square Fish.

Rice, Alice Caldwell Hegan. Mrs. Wiggs of the Cabbage Patch. (Illus.). 153p. reprint ed. lib. bdg. 88.00 *(978-0-7222-4934-5(9))* Library Reprints, Inc.

Rice, Alice Hegan. Mrs. Wiggs of the Cabbage Patch. 2004. (ENG.). 168p. (gr. 17). pap. 14.95 *(978-0-8131-9074-7(6),* 978-0-8131-9074-7) Univ. Pr. of Kentucky.

Ritchie, Polly. A Pocket Full of Frogs. 2007. 124p. pap. 10.00 *(978-0-9795103-2-8(5))* Ascended Ideas.

Skinner, Constance Lindsay. Becky Landers: Frontier Warrior. 2006. (Living History Library). (ENG.). 198p. (J). (gr. 4-6). per. 12.95 *(978-1-932350-06-7(3))* Ignatius Pr.

Standish, Burt L. Frank Merriwell in Kentucky. Rudman, Jack, ed. 2003. (Frank Merriwell Ser.). 29.95 *(978-0-8373-9363-6(9));* pap. 9.95 *(978-0-8373-9063-5(X))* Merriwell, Frank Inc.

Stevens, Courtney. Dress Codes for Small Towns. (ENG.). (YA). (gr. 9). 2018. 368p. pap. 10.99 *(978-0-06-239852-9(0))* 2017. 352p. 17.99 *(978-0-06-239851-2(2))* HarperCollins Pubs. (HarperTeen).

Sully, Katherine. Night-Night Kentucky. Poole, Helen, illus. 2017. (Night-Night Ser.). (ENG.). 20p. (J). (gr. -1-1). bds. 9.99 *(978-1-4926-4776-8(4),* 9781492647768, Hometown World) Sourcebooks, Inc.

Taylor, Pearl Fleming. Snowbird Weenie, 1 vol. 2009. 59p. pap. 16.95 *(978-1-60836-745-0(2))* America Star Bks.

Thomas, Leah. Wild & Crooked. 2019. (ENG.). 448p. (YA). 18.99 *(978-1-5476-0002-1(0),* 900194772, Bloomsbury Young Adult) Bloomsbury Publishing USA.

Tyre, Lisa Lewis. Hope in the Holler. 2019. 240p. (J). (gr. 5). 8.99 *(978-0-399-54632-7(4),* Puffin Books) Penguin Young Readers Group.

—Hope in the Holler. 2020. (Penworthy Picks YA Fiction Ser.). (ENG.). 212p. (J). (gr. 4-5). 20.96 *(978-1-64697-195-4(7))* Penworthy Co., LLC, The.

Varble, Rachel McBrayer. Beth & Seth. Reynolds, Doris, illus. 2012. 208p. 44.95 *(978-1-258-25079-9(9));* pap. 29.95 *(978-1-258-25542-8(1))* Literary Licensing, LLC.

Watts, Julia. Kindred Spirits. 2008. (ENG.). 147p. (J). (gr. 3-18). pap. 8.95 *(978-0-9667359-9-4(4))* OH Industries.

—Revived Spirits. 2011. (ENG.). 170p. (J). (gr. 7). pap. 8.95 *(978-0-9831032-2-6(4),* BeanPole Bks.) OH Industries.

Wedekind, Annie. A Horse of Her Own. 2009. (ENG.). 288p. (YA). (gr. 5-9). pap. 8.99 *(978-0-312-58146-6(7),* 900062001) Square Fish.

Whitaker, Alecia. The Queen of Kentucky. 2013. (ENG.). 384p. (J). (gr. 7-17). pap. 19.99 *(978-0-316-12494-2(X),* Poppy) Little, Brown Bks. for Young Readers.

White, Herman H. Valley of the Flames. 2004. (ENG.). 96p. 19.95 *(978-1-932278-09-5(5))* Mayhaven Publishing, Inc.

Wiechman, Kathy Cannon. Empty Places. 2016. (ENG., Illus.). 240p. (J). (gr. 4-7). 17.95 *(978-1-62979-451-8(1),* Calkins Creek) Highlights Pr., c/o Highlights for Children, Inc.

Williamson, Linda. Groundhog Breakfast, Soft Petals, & a Roof That Don't Leak Too Much, 1 vol. Mollett, Irene, illus. 2009. 23p. pap. 24.95 *(978-1-60749-618-2(6))* America Star Bks.

KENTUCKY—HISTORY

Appelt, Kathi & Schmitzer, Jeanne Cannella. Down Cut Shin Creek: The Pack Horse Librarians of Kentucky. 2019. (ENG., Illus.). 58p. (J). (gr. 3-7). 19.95 *(978-1-948959-10-0(0))* Purple Hse. Pr.

Blair, Eric. Daniel Boone, 1 vol. Chambers-Goldberg, Micah, illus. 2011. (My First Classic Story Ser.). (ENG.). 32p. (J). (gr. k-3). lib. bdg. 23.32 *(978-1-4048-6578-5(0),* 114428, Picture Window Bks.) Capstone.

Brooks-Simon, Barbara. Escape to Freedom: The Underground Railroad Adventures of Callie & William. 2004. (I Am American Ser.). (Illus.). 40p. (J). (gr. 3-7). pap. 6.99 *(978-0-7922-6551-1(3),* National Geographic Kids) Disney Publishing Worldwide.

Burgan, Michael. Death at Kent State: How a Photograph Brought the Vietnam War Home to America. 2016. (Captured History Ser.). (ENG., Illus.). 64p. (J). (gr. 5-9). lib. bdg. 35.32 *(978-0-7565-5424-8(1),* 132560, Compass Point Bks.) Capstone.

Burton, K. Melissa. Kentucky's Boone: The Pioneer Spirit. Asher, James, illus. 2008. 30p. (J). (gr. 4-7). pap. 14.95 *(978-1-934898-03-1(1))* McClanahan Publishing Hse., Inc.

Cook, Colleen Ryckert. Kentucky: Past & Present, 1 vol. 2010. (United States: Past & Present Ser.). (ENG.). 48p. (YA). (gr. 5-5). pap. 12.75 *(978-1-4358-9509-6(6),* 1ac276b7-8493-4972-8245-12cae2fc2ec6); lib. bdg. 34.47 *(978-1-4358-9482-2(0),* cc774ad5-02d2-4285-aa75-53047c3925c4) Rosen Publishing Group, Inc., The. (Rosen Reference).

Dean, Arlan. The Wilderness Trail: From the Shenandoah Valley to the Ohio River. 2009. (Famous American Trails Ser.). 24p. (gr. 3-3). 42.50 *(978-1-61512-493-0(4),* PowerKids Pr.) Rosen Publishing Group, Inc., The.

Doeden, Matt. The Haunted Sanatorium: A Chilling Interactive Adventure. 2017. (You Choose: Haunted Places Ser.). (ENG., Illus.). 112p. (J). (gr. 3-7). lib. bdg. 32.65 *(978-1-5157-3651-6(2),* 133624, Capstone Pr.) Capstone.

Evdokimoff, Natasha. Kentucky: The Bluegrass State. 2016. (J). *(978-1-4896-4866-2(6))* Weigl Pubs., Inc.

Gamble, Adam, et al. Good Night Kentucky. 2014. (Good Night Our World Ser.). (ENG., Illus.). 20p. (J). (— 1). bds. 9.95 *(978-1-60219-089-4(5))* Good Night Bks.

Glaser, Jason. Kentucky: The Bluegrass State, 1 vol. 2010. (Our Amazing States Ser.). (ENG., Illus.). 24p. (J). (gr. 3-3). pap. 9.25 *(978-1-4358-9784-7(6),* 84a09010-226d-43a5-95c1-b7c72dace244); lib. bdg. 26.27 *(978-1-4358-9396-2(4),* e5357d95-80d0-41ce-9ce4-5a7d8c503273) Rosen Publishing Group, Inc., The. (PowerKids Pr.).

Graham Gaines, Ann. Kentucky, 1 vol. 2nd rev. ed. 2013. (It's My State! (Second Edition)(r) Ser.). (ENG.). 80p. (gr. 4-4). 35.93 *(978-1-60870-880-2(2),* 5fff62db-cb7f-495e-a371-5761af096876) Cavendish Square Publishing LLC.

Graham Gaines, Ann, et al. Kentucky: The Bluegrass State, 1 vol. 3rd rev. ed. 2016. (It's My State! (Third Edition)(r) Ser.). (ENG.). 80p. (gr. 4-4). 35.93 *(978-1-62713-198-8(1),* 752b4d00-e196-4b29-aa73-c444a943c981) Cavendish Square Publishing LLC.

Hamilton, John. Kentucky, 1 vol. 2016. (United States of America Ser.). (ENG., Illus.). 48p. (J). (gr. 5-9). 34.21 *(978-1-68078-319-3(X),* 21623, Abdo & Daughters) ABDO Publishing Co.

The Hatfields & the McCoys, 1 vol. 2014. (Jr. Graphic American Legends Ser.). (ENG., Illus.). 24p. (J). (gr. 2-3). lib. bdg. 28.93 *(978-1-4777-7193-8(X),* 9a03d15c-200e-4c50-bd9b-7d0e162521d8, PowerKids Pr.) Rosen Publishing Group, Inc., The.

Jerome, Kate B. Lucky to Live in Kentucky. 2017. (Arcadia Kids Ser.). (ENG., Illus.). 32p. (J). 16.99 *(978-0-7385-2797-0(1))* Arcadia Publishing.

Kennedy, Emily. Daniel Boone: & His Adventures, 1 vol. 2014. (American Legends & Folktales Ser.). (ENG., Illus.). 32p. (gr. 3-3). lib. bdg. 31.21 *(978-1-62712-280-1(X),* 4b4d32bf-716f-4e72-9cd0-7f03afc1a00b) Cavendish Square Publishing LLC.

The Kentucky Adventure Program Kit: All program components for the Kentucky Adventure, 1 vol. 2009. 129.95 *(978-1-4236-0717-5(1))* Gibbs Smith, Publisher.

Linda Bartlett & Wen Marcec. Keby the Earth-Friendly Bear. 2009. 36p. pap. 21.32 *(978-1-4415-3989-2(1))* Xlibris Corp.

Marsh, Carole. Exploring Kentucky Through Project-Based Learning. 2016. (Kentucky Experience Ser.). (ENG.). (J). pap. 9.99 *(978-0-635-12341-1(X))* Gallopade International.

—Kentucky History Projects #1: 30 Cool Activities, Crafts, Experiments & More for Kids to Do! 2003. (Kentucky Experience Ser.). (Illus.). 32p. (J). (gr. k-5). pap. 5.95 *(978-0-635-01786-4(5),* Marsh, Carole Bks.) Gallopade International.

—Let's Discover Kentucky! 2004. (J). (gr. 2-8). cd-rom 14.95 *(978-0-7933-9490-6(2))* Gallopade International.

Saddleback Educational Publishing Staff, ed. Daniel Boone, 1 vol. unabr. ed. 2007. (Graphic Biographies Ser.). (ENG., Illus.). 25p. (YA). (gr. 4-12). pap. 9.75 *(978-1-59905-219-9(9))* Saddleback Educational Publishing, Inc.

Williams, Suzanne & Williams, Suzanne M. From Sea to Shining Sea: Kentucky. 2008. (ENG.). 80p. (J). pap. 7.95 *(978-0-531-20805-2(2),* Children's Pr.) Scholastic Library Publishing.

Yasuda, Anita. Kentucky: The Bluegrass State. 2012. (J). 27.13 *(978-1-61913-353-2(9))* Weigl Pubs., Inc.

Zeiger, Jennifer. Kentucky (a True Book: My United States) (Library Edition) 2018. (True Book (Relaunch) Ser.). (ENG., Illus.). 48p. (J). (gr. 3-5). 31.00 *(978-0-531-23165-4(8),* Children's Pr.) Scholastic Library Publishing.

KENYA

Alembi, Ezekiel. Jaramogi Oginga Odinga: People's Revolutionary. 2004. (Lion Books). (Illus.). x, 78p. (J). *(978-9966-951-24-3(5))* Sasa Sema Publications Ltd.

Bankston, John. We Visit Kenya. 2012. (J). lib. bdg. 33.95 *(978-1-61228-304-3(7))* Mitchell Lane Pubs.

Bartell, Jim. Kenya. 2011. (Exploring Countries Ser.). (ENG., Illus.). 32p. (J). (gr. 3-7). lib. bdg. 27.95 *(978-1-60014-576-6(0),* Blastoff! Readers) Bellwether Media.

Barysh, Ann, et al. The Suitcase Scholar Goes to Kenya, Set. Lerner Publications, Department of Geography Staff, ed. (Suitcase Scholar Ser.). (J). (gr. 4-6). lib. bdg., tchr. ed. 66.95 *(978-0-8225-4001-4(0),* Lerner Pubns.) Lerner Publishing Group.

Bentley, Joyce. Kenya: Our Lives, Our World. 2005. 32p. 18.95 *(978-1-59389-225-8(X))* Chrysalis Education.

Burgess, Maryellen. Life in Kenya, 1 vol. 2012. (InfoMax Readers Ser.). (ENG., Illus.). 24p. (J). (gr. 1-1). pap. 8.25 *(978-1-4488-9022-4(5),* 946e1dee-ca50-4383-80e1-9929cb33ba4b, Rosen Classroom) Rosen Publishing Group, Inc., The.

Burns, Kylie. Cultural Traditions in Kenya. 2015. (Cultural Traditions in My World Ser.). (ENG., Illus.). 32p. (J). (gr. 2-3). *(978-0-7787-8063-2(5))* Crabtree Publishing Co.

Corrigan, Jim. Kenya. Rotberg, Robert I., ed. 2012. (Evolution of Africa's Major Nations Ser.). (Illus.). 80p. (J). (gr. 7). 22.95 *(978-1-4222-2180-8(6))* Mason Crest.

—Kenya. 2011. (J). pap. *(978-1-4222-2208-9(X))* Mason Crest.

Deedy, Carmen Agra. 14 Cows for America, 1 vol. Gonzalez, Thomas, illus. 36p. (J). (gr. 2-5). 2016. pap. 8.99 *(978-1-56145-961-2(5))* 2009. 17.99 *(978-1-56145-490-7(7))* Peachtree Publishing Co. Inc.

—14 Cows for America. Gonzalez, Thomas, illus. 2016. (ENG.). 36p. (J). (gr. -1-3). lib. bdg. 19.60 *(978-0-606-39065-1(0))* Turtleback.

Ellas, Josie & Pateman, Robert. Kenya, 1 vol. 3rd rev. ed. 2014. (Cultures of the World (Third Edition)(r) Ser.). (ENG., Illus.). 144p. (gr. 5-5). lib. bdg. 48.79 *(978-0-7614-8012-9(9),* f4a3ef72-4cfb-4aa7-971c-e683a84d2cff) Cavendish Square Publishing LLC.

Ferguson, Amanda. The Attack Against the U. S. Embassies in Kenya & Tanzania. 2009. (Terrorist Attacks Ser.). 64p. (gr. 5-5). 58.50 *(978-1-60853-309-1(3))* Rosen Publishing Group, Inc., The.

Fontes, Justine & Fontes, Ron. Kenya - A-Z. 2004. (A to Z Ser.). (ENG.). 40p. (J). (gr. 2-4). pap. 6.95 *(978-0-516-26813-2(9),* Children's Pr.) Scholastic Library Publishing.

Giles, Bridget. (CW) Kenya (Direct Mail Edition) 2009. (Countries of the World Ser.). (ENG., Illus.). 64p. (J). (gr. 5-9). 19.95 *(978-0-7922-7628-9(0))* National Geographic Society.

Graham, Ian. Kenya. 2003. (Country Files Ser.). 32p. (J). lib. bdg. 24.25 *(978-1-58340-238-2(1))* Black Rabbit Bks.

Gregory, Joy. Kenya. 2016. (Illus.). 32p. (J). *(978-1-4896-5417-5(8))* Weigl Pubs., Inc.

Haskins, James & Benson, Kathleen. Count Your Way Through Kenya. Leveque, Lyne, illus. 2006. (Count Your Way Ser.). 24p. (J). (gr. -1-3). lib. bdg. 19.93 *(978-1-57505-884-9(7),* Millbrook Pr.) Lerner Publishing Group.

Hibbert, Clare. Elephant Orphans, 1 vol. 2014. (Save the Animals Ser.). (ENG.). 32p. (J). (gr. 4-5). pap. 11.00 *(978-1-4777-5896-0(8),* c93578ac-294b-4ef0-b0ce-6e85ede5217d, PowerKids Pr.) Rosen Publishing Group, Inc., The.

Juarez, Christine. Kenya, 1 vol. 2014. (Countries Ser.). (ENG., Illus.). 24p. (J). (gr. -1-2). lib. bdg. 27.32 *(978-1-4765-4229-4(5),* 124341, Capstone Pr.) Capstone.

Kalman, Bobbie. Spotlight on Kenya. 2013. (ENG.). 32p. (J). *(978-0-7787-0866-7(7));* (Illus.). pap. *(978-0-7787-0870-4(5))* Crabtree Publishing Co.

Kirk, Daniel. Rhino in the House: The Story of Saving Samia. 2017. (ENG., Illus.). 40p. (J). (gr. -1-3). 17.95 *(978-1-4197-2316-2(2),* 1157201) Abrams, Inc.

Klepeis, Alicia Z. Kenya, 1 vol. 2017. (Exploring World Cultures (First Edition) Ser.). (ENG., Illus.). 32p. (gr. 3-3). pap. 12.16 *(978-1-5026-2504-5(0),* 4cdeb873-1a47-4e8c-aa5f-07f8df9501b8) Cavendish Square Publishing LLC.

Kras, Sara Louise. Kenya: A Question & Answer Book. rev. ed. 2016. (Questions & Answers: Countries Ser.). (ENG.). 32p. (J). (gr. 3-6). pap. 7.95 *(978-1-5157-5851-8(6),* 134816, Capstone Pr.) Capstone.

Levy, Janey. A Primary Source Guide to Kenya. 2009. (Countries of the World). 24p. (gr. 2-3). 42.50 *(978-1-61512-038-3(6),* PowerKids Pr.) Rosen Publishing Group, Inc., The.

Markovics, Joyce L. Kenya. 2019. (Countries We Come From Ser.). (ENG., Illus.). 32p. (J). (gr. k-3). 19.95 *(978-1-64280-196-5(8))* Bearport Publishing Co., Inc.

Marshall, David & Sayer, Geoff. Kenya. (World Focus Ser.). (Illus.). 32p. (J). (gr. 3-7). pap. 3.99 *(978-0-431-07255-5(8))* Oxfam Publishing GBR. Dist: Stylus Publishing, LLC.

McCollum, Sean. Kenya. 2008. (Country Explorers Ser.). (Illus.). 48p. (J). (gr. 2-5). lib. bdg. 27.93 *(978-0-8225-8661-6(4));* pap. 40.95 *(978-0-8225-9304-1(1))* Lerner Publishing Group.

Mills, Nathan & Cortland, Riley. I'm from Kenya, 1 vol. 2012. (Rosen Readers Ser.). (ENG., Illus.). 24p. (J). (gr. 1-1). pap. 8.25 *(978-1-4488-8803-0(4),* 4f9828dc-00c7-40a8-a776-5fd4b666b532, Rosen Classroom) Rosen Publishing Group, Inc., The.

Mis, Melody S. How to Draw Kenya's Sights & Symbols. 2009. (Kid's Guide to Drawing the Countries of the World Ser.). 48p. (gr. 4-4). 53.00 *(978-1-61511-117-6(4),* PowerKids Pr.) Rosen Publishing Group, Inc., The.

Murray, Julie. Kenya. 2017. (Explore the Countries Set 4 Ser.). (ENG., Illus.). 40p. (J). (gr. 2-5). lib. bdg. 35.64 *(978-1-5321-1049-8(9),* 25674, Big Buddy Bks.) ABDO Publishing Co.

Napoli, Donna Jo. Mama Miti: Wangari Maathai & the Trees of Kenya. Nelson, Kadir, illus. 2010. (ENG.). 40p. (J). (gr. -1-3). 19.99 *(978-1-4169-3505-6(3),* Simon & Schuster/Paula Wiseman Bks.) Simon & Schuster/Paula Wiseman Bks.

Parkes, Elle. Let's Explore Kenya. 2017. (Bumba Books (r) — Let's Explore Countries Ser.). (ENG., Illus.). 24p. (J). (gr. -1-1). 26.65 *(978-1-5124-3364-7(0),* 83672cb0-1118-44ca-830d-4dcfb3891311, Lerner Pubns.) Lerner Publishing Group.

Pateman, Robert. Kenya, 1 vol. 2nd rev. ed. 2004. (Cultures of the World (Second Edition)(r) Ser.). (ENG., Illus.). 144p. (gr. 5-5). lib. bdg. 49.79 *(978-0-7614-1701-9(X),* 71e1c208-33b2-4882-800b-b09ad4780e28) Cavendish Square Publishing LLC.

Rechner, Amy. Kenya. 2019. (Country Profiles Ser.). (ENG., Illus.). 32p. (J). (gr. 3-8). lib. bdg. 27.95 *(978-1-62617-961-5(1),* Blastoff! Discovery) Bellwether Media.

Reynolds, Jan. Only the Mountains Do Not Move: A Maasai Story of Culture & Conservation, 1 vol. 2011. (ENG., Illus.). 40p. (J). (gr. 3-6). pap. 11.95 *(978-1-60060-844-5(2),* leelowbooks); (gr. 1-6). pap. 18.95 *(978-1-60060-333-4(5))* Lee & Low Bks., Inc.

Schuh, Mari. Crayola (r) Colors of Kenya. 2020. (Crayola (r) Country Colors Ser.). (ENG., Illus.). 24p. (J). (gr. k-3). lib. bdg. 29.32 *(978-1-5415-7269-0(6),* 775c3936-fb8e-4354-ab0b-2ee262cf2b10, Lerner Pubns.) Lerner Publishing Group.

Sheen, Barbara. Foods of Kenya, 1 vol. 2010. (Taste of Culture Ser.). (ENG., Illus.). 64p. (gr. 3-6). 36.83 *(978-0-7377-4813-0(3),* 0165d76f-09aa-43d5-9733-b33c5cf1f5cd, KidHaven Publishing) Greenhaven Publishing LLC.

Taylor, Trace. Kenya. (ICP Our World Ser.). (gr. k-1). 2013. (ENG.). 16p. (J). pap. 8.00 *(978-1-61541-132-0(1))* 2010. pap. 39.62 *(978-1-61541-133-7(X))* American Reading Co.

Taylor, Trace & SáNchez, LucíA M. Kenya. 2010. pap. 39.62 *(978-1-61541-156-6(9))* American Reading Co.

Taylor, Trace & Sánchez, Lucía M. Kenya. 2015. (1Y Nuestro Mundo Ser.). (SPA.). 16p. (J). (gr. k-1). pap. 8.00 *(978-1-61541-155-9(0))* American Reading Co.

Thomson, Ruth. Living in Kenya. Hampton, David, photos by. 2006. (Living In- Ser.). (Illus.). 32p. (J). (gr. 4-7). lib. bdg. 27.10 *(978-1-59771-044-2(X))* Sea-To-Sea Pubns.

Ward, Chris. Discover Kenya. 2010. (Illus.). 32p. (J). 63.60 *(978-1-61532-298-5(1),* 1307264); (ENG.). (gr. 4-4). pap. 11.60 *(978-1-61532-297-8(3),* 6152f57d-ab4c-448b-a50c-818260305965) Rosen Publishing Group, Inc., The. (PowerKids Pr.).

KENYA—FICTION

Ahern, Carolyn L. Tino Turtle Travels to Kenya - the Great Safari. Burt Sullivan, Neallia, illus. 2009. (ENG & SWA.). 32p. (J). (gr. -1-4). 19.95 incl. audio compact disk *(978-0-9793158-3-1(2))* Tino Turtle Travels, LLC.

Allende, Isabel. Forest of the Pygmies. 2009.Tr. of Bosque de los Pigmeos. (ENG.). 320p. pap. 14.99 *(978-0-06-182510-1(7),* HarperVia) HarperCollins Pubs.

—Forest of the Pygmies. Peden, Margaret Sayers, tr. from SPA. (City of the Beasts Ser.: Bk. 3).Tr. of Bosque de los Pigmeos. 304p. (J). (gr. 5-12). 2006. (ENG.). pap. 10.99 *(978-0-06-076198-1(9))* 2005. 19.99 *(978-0-06-076196-7(2))* HarperCollins Pubs. (Rayo).

—Forest of the Pygmies. l.t. ed. 2005. (City of the Beasts Ser.: Bk. 3).Tr. of Bosque de los Pigmeos. 304p. (J). (gr. 5-18). pap. 19.99 *(978-0-06-076200-1(4),* Rayo) HarperCollins Pubs.

Anderson, Natalie C. City of Saints & Thieves. 2018. (ENG.). 432p. (YA). (gr. 7). pap. 11.99 *(978-0-399-54759-1(2)*, Speak) Penguin Young Readers Group.

Anthony, Horowitz. Crocodile Tears, 9 vols. 2010. (Alex Rider Adventure Ser.: 8). (J). 81.75 *(978-1-4407-5451-7(9))*; 1.25 *(978-1-4407-5459-3(4))*; 79.75 *(978-1-4407-5453-1(5))*; 102.75 *(978-1-4407-5456-2(X))*; 100.75 *(978-1-4407-5458-6(6))* Recorded Bks., Inc.

—Crocodile Tears. 2010. (Alex Rider Ser.: 8). lib. bdg. 19.65 *(978-0-606-23639-3(2))* Turtleback.

Arensen, Shel. The Poison Arrow Tree. 2003. (Rugendo Rhino Ser.). (Illus.). 128p. (J). pap. 5.99 *(978-0-8254-2041-2(5))* Kregel Pubns.

Barasch, Lynne. First Come the Zebra. Barasch, Lynne, illus. 2009. (ENG., Illus.). 40p. (J). (gr. 1-6). 18.95 *(978-1-60060-365-5(3))* Lee & Low Bks., Inc.

—First Come the Zebra, 1 vol. 2005. (ENG., Illus.). 40p. (J). (gr. 1-4). pap. 12.95 *(978-1-62014-029-1(2)*, leelowbooks) Lee & Low Bks., Inc.

Browne, Eileen. Handa's Hen. 2011. (ENG., Illus.). 32p. (J). (gr. -1-2). pap. 7.99 *(978-0-7636-5361-3(6))* Candlewick Pr.

—Handa's Surprise: Read & Share. Browne, Eileen, illus. 2004. (ENG & BEN., Illus.). 32p. (J). pap. *(978-1-85269-472-2(6))*; pap. *(978-1-85269-473-9(4))*; pap. *(978-1-85269-474-6(2))*; pap. *(978-1-85269-475-3(0))*; pap. *(978-1-85269-477-7(7))*; pap. *(978-1-85269-478-4(5))*; pap. *(978-1-85269-507-1(2))*; pap. *(978-1-85269-508-8(0))*; pap. *(978-1-85269-509-5(9))*; pap. *(978-1-85269-510-1(2))* Mantra Lingua.

—Handa's Surprise: Read & Share. 2004. (ENG., Illus.). 32p. (J). pap. *(978-1-85269-511-8(0))* Mantra Lingua.

—Handa's Surprise: Read & Share. Browne, Eileen, illus. 2004. (ENG & TAM., Illus.). 32p. (J). pap. *(978-1-85269-512-5(9))*; pap. *(978-1-85269-513-2(7))*; pap. *(978-1-85269-515-6(3))*; pap. *(978-1-85269-476-0(9))*; pap. *(978-1-85269-514-9(5))* Mantra Lingua.

—Handa's Surprise Big Book. Browne, Eileen, illus. 2011. (Read & Share Ser.). (ENG., Illus.). 32p. (J). (gr. -1-2). pap. 27.99 *(978-0-7636-5385-9(3))* Candlewick Pr.

Browne, Eileen & Habashi, Azza. Handa's Surprise: Read & Share. 2004. (ENG & ARA., Illus.). 32p. (J). pap. *(978-1-85269-471-5(8))* Mantra Lingua.

Bustani, Juma. Adventure in Nairobi. 2005. (Illus.). 72p. pap. *(978-9966-46-842-0(0))* Heinemann Kenya, Limited (East African Educational Publishers Ltd E.A.E.P.) KEN. Dist: Michigan State Univ. Pr.

Carlson, Martin D. Rfaud Tastes Wisdom. Oketch, Alphonce Omondi, illus. 2013. 36p. pap. 11.00 *(978-0-9848791-2-0(9))* BoCook Publishing.

Chamberlin, Richard & Chamberlin, Mary. Mama Panya's Pancakes: A Market Day in Kenya. Cairns, Julia, illus. 2005. 40p. (J). *(978-1-84148-160-9(2))* Barefoot Bks., Inc.

Cunnane, Kelly. For You Are a Kenyan Child. Juan, Ana, illus. 2006. (ENG.). 40p. (J). (gr. -1-3). 17.99 *(978-0-689-86194-9(X)*, Atheneum Bks. for Young Readers) Simon & Schuster Children's Publishing.

Franklin, Carolyn. Lion. 2014. (Animal Journals). (Illus.). 32p. (J). (gr. 1-3). 31.35 *(978-1-906370-72-5(9))* Book Hse. GBR. Dist: Black Rabbit Bks.

Grey, Chelsea Gillian. Leperit the Zebra. Denman, Michael & Huiett, William, illus. 2005. (Internet Interactive Ser.). (ENG.). 36p. (J). (gr. -1-3). 8.95 *(978-1-59249-440-8(4)*, SD6505); (gr. 2-2). 14.95 *(978-1-59249-438-5(2)*, H6505); (gr. 2-2). pap. 6.95 *(978-1-59249-439-2(0)*, S6505) Soundprints.

—Leperit the Zebra: African Wildlife Foundation. Denman, Michael L. & Huiett, William J., illus. 2005. (Meet Africa's Animals Ser.). (ENG.). 36p. (J). (gr. -1-2). 2.95 *(978-1-59249-441-5(2)*, S6555) Soundprints.

Horowitz, Anthony. Crocodile Tears. 2010. (Alex Rider Ser.: 8). (ENG.). 416p. (J). (gr. 5-18). 8.99 *(978-0-14-241719-5(X)*, Puffin Books) Penguin Young Readers Group.

Hunt, Elizabeth Singer. Secret Agent Jack Stalwart: Book 6: the Pursuit of the Ivory Poachers: Kenya. 2008. (Secret Agent Jack Stalwart Ser.: 6). (ENG., Illus.). 144p. (J). (gr. 1-4). pap. 5.99 *(978-1-60286-021-6(1))* Hachette Bk. Group.

Larkin, Jim & Rambo, Lee Elliot. Books for Oliver. Brown, Dan, illus. 2006. (J). *(978-1-59336-336-9(2))*; pap. *(978-1-59336-337-6(0))* Mondo Publishing.

Macgoye, Marjorie Oludhe. The Black Hand Gang. 2003. (Illus.). 64p. (gr. 4-7). pap. *(978-9966-46-016-5(0))* Heinemann Kenya, Limited (East African Educational Publishers Ltd E.A.E.P.) KEN. Dist: Michigan State Univ. Pr.

Malaika: Safari Adventure to Kenya. 2006. (J). 4.99 *(978-0-9765982-0-6(5))* Simba Publishing Co.

Mary and Rich Chamberlin. Las Crepes de Mama Panya: Un Relato de Kenia. Cairns, Julia, illus. 2016. (SPA.). 40p. (J). (gr. k-5). pap. 9.99 *(978-1-78285-072-4(4))* Barefoot Bks., Inc.

—Mama Panya's Pancakes. Cairns, Julia, illus. 2006. (ENG.). 40p. (J). (gr. k-5). pap. 9.99 *(978-1-905236-64-0(6))* Barefoot Bks., Inc.

Mbuthia, Waithira. My Sister's Wedding: A Story of Kenya. Karanja, Geoffrey Gacheru, illus. 2005. (Make Friends Around the World Ser.). (ENG.). 32p. (J). (gr. k-3). 19.95 *(978-1-56899-898-5(8)*, BC8006); 15.95 *(978-1-56899-896-1(1)*, B8006) Soundprints.

Milway, Katie Smith. Mimi's Village: And How Basic Health Care Transformed It. Fernandes, Eugenie, illus. 2012. (CitizenKid Ser.). (ENG.). 32p. (J). (gr. 3-7). 18.99 *(978-1-55453-722-8(3))* Kids Can Pr., Ltd. CAN. Dist: Hachette Bk. Group.

The Mystery of the Lion's Tail. 2014. (Greetings from Somewhere Ser.: 5). (ENG., Illus.). 128p. (J). (gr. -1-4). pap. 6.99 *(978-1-4814-1464-7(X)*, Little Simon) Little Simon.

Naidoo, Beverley. Burn My Heart. 2008. (ENG.). 224p. (J). (gr. 5-18). 17.99 *(978-0-06-143297-2(0)*, Quill Tree Bks.) HarperCollins Pubs.

Nyong'o, Lupita. Sulwe. Harrison, Vashti, illus. 2019. Orig. Title: Sulwe. (ENG.). 48p. (J). (gr. -1-3). 17.99 *(978-1-5344-2536-1(5)*, Simon & Schuster Bks. For Young Readers) Simon & Schuster Bks. For Young Readers.

Odhiambo, Tori. Close to Home: The African Savannah. 2012. 32p. pap. 21.99 *(978-1-4691-9510-0(0))* Xlibris Corp.

Osborne, Jill. Riley Mae & the Sole Fire Safari, 1 vol. 2014. (Faithgirlz / the Good News Shoes Ser.: 3). (ENG.). 256p. (J). pap. 7.99 *(978-0-310-74283-8(8))* Zonderkidz.

Peattie, Cindy & Benchmark Education Co. Staff. The Secret Language of Elephants. 2014. (Text Connections Ser.). (J). (gr. 5). *(978-1-4900-1367-1(9))* Benchmark Education Co.

Pedraza, M. Eugenia Rueda. Nico's Voyage. 2013. 32p. pap. *(978-1-4602-2360-4(8))* FriesenPress.

Richardson, Justin & Parnell, Peter. Christian, the Hugging Lion. Bates, Amy June, illus. 2010. (ENG.). 32p. (J). (gr. -1-3). 19.99 *(978-1-4169-8662-1(6)*, Simon & Schuster Bks. For Young Readers) Simon & Schuster Bks. For Young Readers.

Richler, Mordecai. Jacob Two-Two & the Dinosaur. Petricic, Dusan, illus. 2009. (Jacob Two-Two Ser.). (ENG.). 104p. (J). (gr. 4-7). 10.95 *(978-0-88776-926-9(8))* Tundra Bks. CAN. Dist: Random Hse., Inc.

Simwenyi, Robbinson Namasaka. The Young Detectives. 2012. 84p. pap. 17.95 *(978-1-4512-2168-8(1))* America Star Bks.

Sorrells, W. A. Nairobi Nightmare. Bancroft, Tom & Corley, Rob, illus. 2007. 144p. (J). *(978-0-9792912-1-0(6))* KidsGive, LLC.

Stegall, Kim. Mumsi Meets a Lion. Batti, Kimberly Rose, illus. 2008. (gr. -1-1). pap. 7.99 *(978-1-59166-871-8(9))* BJU Pr.

Sullivan, Dana. Kay Kay's Alphabet Safari. Sullivan, Dana, illus. 2014. (ENG., Illus.). 40p. (J). (gr. 1-4). 15.99 *(978-1-58536-905-8(5)*, 203666) Sleeping Bear Pr.

Talbott, Hudson. Safari Journal. Talbott, Hudson, illus. 2003. (ENG., Illus.). 64p. (J). (gr. 3-7). 18.00 *(978-0-15-216393-8(X)*, 1200873, Clarion Bks.) HarperCollins Pubs.

Tomaselli, Mela. The Magic Pot: Folk Tales & Legends of the Giriama of Kenya. 2004. (Illus.). 80p. *(978-9966-21-950-3(1))* Paulines Pubns., Africa.

Walters, Eric. Hope Springs. Fernandes, Eugenie, illus. 2014. 32p. (J). (gr. 1-4). 17.99 *(978-1-77049-530-2(4)*, Tundra Bks.) Tundra Bks. CAN. Dist: Penguin Random Hse. LLC.

—My Name Is Blessing. Fernandes, Eugenie, illus. 2013. 32p. (J). (gr. 1-4). 17.95 *(978-1-77049-301-8(8)*, Tundra Bks.) Tundra Bks. CAN. Dist: Penguin Random Hse. LLC.

—Today Is the Day. Fernandes, Eugenie, illus. 2015. 32p. (J). (gr. 1-4). 16.99 *(978-1-77049-648-4(3)*, Tundra Bks.) Tundra Bks. CAN. Dist: Penguin Random Hse. LLC.

—Walking Home. 2014. (ENG.). 304p. (J). (gr. 5). pap. 10.99 *(978-0-385-68157-5(7))* Doubleday Canada, Ltd. CAN. Dist: Penguin Random Hse. LLC.

Williams, Alexandra & Williams, David, illus. Fairy Nyumbani. 2005. 24p. *(978-9966-956-41-5(7))* Jacarada Designs Ltd.

Winter, Jeanette. Wangari's Trees of Peace. 2018. lib. bdg. 18.40 *(978-0-606-41005-2(8))* Turtleback.

KEPLER, JOHANNES, 1571-1630

Bortz, Fred. Johannes Kepler & the Three Laws of Planetary Motion, 1 vol. 2013. (Revolutionary Discoveries of Scientific Pioneers Ser.). (ENG.). 80p. (YA). (gr. 6-6). 38.41 *(978-1-4777-1805-6(2)*, 6cf78c48-ba6a-4c63-893e-eec434e67800) Rosen Publishing Group, Inc., The.

Harmon, Daniel E. Johannes Kepler, 1 vol. 2017. (Leaders of the Scientific Revolution Ser.). (ENG., Illus.). 112p. (J). (gr. 8-8). 38.80 *(978-1-5081-7472-1(5)*, 63e6f89d-004b-4e5d-b701-bf2a915009c6, Rosen Young Adult) Rosen Publishing Group, Inc., The.

Hasan, Heather. Kepler & the Laws of Planetary Motion. (Primary Sources of Revolutionary Scientific Discoveries & Theories Ser.). 64p. (gr. 5-5). 2009. 58.50 *(978-1-60851-845-6(0))* 2004. (ENG., Illus.). (J). lib. bdg. 37.13 *(978-1-4042-0308-2(7)*, 84a6d4f6-afd6-4ec9-bb57-167f2a91361a) Rosen Publishing Group, Inc., The.

Ruiz, Jaime Alejandro Rodriguez. Johannes Kepler -Del otro lado está Dios. 2005. (SPA.). 124p. (YA). *(978-958-30-1647-9(0))* Panamericana Editorial.

KEROSENE

see Petroleum

KETTERING, CHARLES FRANKLIN, 1876-1958

Marsh, Carole. Charles Kettering: Patent Giant. 2004. (1000 Readers Ser.). (Illus.). 14p. (J). (gr. k-4). pap. 2.95 *(978-0-635-02525-8(6))* Gallopade International.

KEY, FRANCIS SCOTT, 1779-1843

Brannon, Cecelia H. Zoom in on the National Anthem, 1 vol. 2016. (Zoom in on American Symbols Ser.). (ENG., Illus.). 24p. (gr. 2-2). pap. 10.95 *(978-0-7660-8446-9(9)*, 70dcf44c-43c7-46a5-872f-c8dd7f1a1c43) Enslow Publishing, LLC.

Craven, Tracy Leininger. Our Flag Was Still There: The Story of the Star-Spangled Banner. Farnsworth, Bill, illus. 2004. (J). *(978-0-9724287-3-6(9))* Vision Forum, Inc., The.

Crewe, Sabrina & Ingram, Scott. The Writing of the Star-Spangled Banner, 1 vol. 2004. (Events That Shaped America Ser.). (ENG., Illus.). 32p. (gr. 3-5). lib. bdg. 28.67 *(978-0-8368-3409-3(7)*, a54f622d-575c-4918-8132-a69cb08e8a37, Gareth Stevens Learning Library) Stevens, Gareth Publishing LLLP.

Damanda, Lori. The Story of the "Star-Spangled Banner", 1 vol. (American History Milestones Ser.). (ENG.). 32p. (J). (gr. 5-5). 2009. lib. bdg. 28.93 *(978-1-4358-3015-8(6)*, f2e5f903-40c2-4903-afa4-1d952dbeb193) 2008. (Illus.). pap. 10.00 *(978-1-4358-0205-6(5)*, 4f301343-44f2-47a1-9f74-353cdd17b026) Rosen Publishing Group, Inc., The. (PowerKids Pr.).

—The Story of the Star-Spangled Banner. 2009. (American History Milestones Ser.). 32p. (gr. 5-5). 47.90 *(978-1-61511-375-0(4)*, PowerKids Pr.) Rosen Publishing Group, Inc., The.

Ferry, Joseph. The Star-Spangled Banner: Story of Our National Anthem. Moreno, Barry, ed. 2014. (Patriotic Symbols of America Ser.: 20). 48p. (J). (gr. 4-18). 20.95 *(978-1-4222-3132-6(1))* Mason Crest.

Gaspar, Joe. The National Anthem, 1 vol. 2013. (PowerKids Readers: American Symbols Ser.). (ENG.). 24p. (J). (gr. k-k). 26.27 *(978-1-4777-0740-1(9)*, ff65aee1-5513-4b6a-9de3-34effc7028c1); (Illus.). pap. 9.25 *(978-1-4777-0821-7(9)*, 57794ebc-a538-4a97-b2ed-62d887a777bf) Rosen Publishing Group, Inc., The. (PowerKids Pr.).

—The National Anthem / el Himno Nacional, 1 vol. Alamn, Eduardo, ed. 2013. (PowerKids Readers: Símbolos de América / American Symbols Ser.). (ENG & SPA.). 24p. (J). (gr. k-k). 26.27 *(978-1-4777-1208-5(9)*, e37a3c7f-a2f3-44a0-86e6-47c33e70d673, PowerKids Pr.) Rosen Publishing Group, Inc., The.

Grove, Tim. Star-Spangled: The Story of a Flag, a Battle, & the American Anthem. 2020. (ENG., Illus.). 176p. (J). (gr. 5-9). 19.99 *(978-1-4197-4102-9(0)*, 1211801, Abrams Bks. for Young Readers) Abrams, Inc.

Hartland, Jessie. Our Flag Was Still There: The True Story of Mary Pickersgill & the Star-Spangled Banner. Hartland, Jessie, illus. 2019. (ENG., Illus.). 48p. (J). (gr. -1-3). 17.99 *(978-1-5344-0233-1(0)*, Simon & Schuster Bks. For Young Readers) Simon & Schuster Bks. For Young Readers.

Healy, Nick. The Star-Spangled Banner. 2003. (J). *(978-1-58417-055-6(7))*; pap. *(978-1-58417-118-8(9))* Lake Street Pubs.

Hess, Debra. The Star Spangled Banner, 1 vol. 2005. (Symbols of America Ser.). (ENG., Illus.). 40p. (gr. 3-3). lib. bdg. 32.64 *(978-0-7614-1710-1(9)*, 78ac45ea-2a1f-4af8-a561-fdddb72608b4) Cavendish Square Publishing LLC.

—The Star-Spangled Banner, 1 vol. 2008. (Symbols of America Ser.). (ENG.). 40p. (gr. 3-3). pap. 9.23 *(978-0-7614-3392-7(9)*, 80f9c4eb-419a-487b-9908-119fa761e234) Cavendish Square Publishing LLC.

Ingram, Scott. The Writing of the Star-Spangled Banner, 1 vol. 2004. (Landmark Events in American History Ser.). (ENG., Illus.). 48p. (gr. 5-8). pap. 15.05 *(978-0-8368-5418-3(7)*, e93295b0-1af5-42c3-842e-4db0ec8fced3); lib. bdg. 33.67 *(978-0-8368-5390-2(3)*, 5058ce85-66a6-4f57-9bab-0adc8a80c538) Stevens, Gareth Publishing LLLP. (Gareth Stevens Secondary Library).

Jacobson, Ryan. The Story of the Star-Spangled Banner, 1 vol. Martin, Cynthia & Beatty, Terry, illus. 2006. (Graphic History Ser.). (ENG.). 32p. (J). (gr. 3-9). 31.32 *(978-0-7368-5493-1(2)*, 90154) Capstone.

Kjelle, Marylou Morano. Francis Scott Key. 2006. (What's So Great About... ? Ser.). (Illus.). 32p. (YA). (gr. 2-4). lib. bdg. 25.70 *(978-1-58415-474-7(8))* Mitchell Lane Pubs.

Kulling, Monica. Francis Scott Key's Star-Spangled Banner. Walz, Richard, illus. 2012. (Step into Reading Ser.). (ENG.). 48p. (J). (gr. k-3). pap. 3.99 *(978-0-375-86725-5(2)*, Random Hse. Bks. for Young Readers) Random Hse. Children's Bks.

—Francis Scott Key's Star-Spangled Banner. 2012. (Step into Reading Level 3 Ser.). lib. bdg. 13.55 *(978-0-606-23857-1(3))* Turtleback.

Lambert, Nancy R. The Star-Spangled Banner. 2016. (Smithsonian Ser.). (Illus.). 48p. (J). (gr. 3-4). pap. 4.99 *(978-1-101-99607-2(2)*, Penguin Young Readers) Penguin Young Readers Group.

Lowitz, Sadyebeth & Lowitz, Anson. Mr Key's Song: The Star Spangled Banner. 2011. 58p. 36.95 *(978-1-258-10511-2(X))* Literary Licensing, LLC.

Lusted, Marcia Amidon. The Star-Spangled Banner. 2019. (Shaping the United States of America Ser.). (ENG., Illus.). 24p. (J). (gr. 1-3). pap. 7.95 *(978-1-9771-1013-8(4)*, 140956); lib. bdg. 25.99 *(978-1-9771-0844-9(X)*, 140463) Capstone. (Pebble).

Monroe, Tyler. The Star-Spangled Banner. 2013. (U. S. Symbols Ser.). (ENG.). 24p. (J). (gr. -1-2). 27.32 *(978-1-4765-3087-1(4)*, 123064); pap. 7.95 *(978-1-4765-3536-4(1)*, 123582) Capstone. (Capstone Pr.).

The National Anthem. 2013. (PowerKids Readers: American Symbols Ser.). 24p. (J). (gr. k-2). pap. 49.50 *(978-1-4777-0822-4(7)*, PowerKids Pr.) Rosen Publishing Group, Inc., The.

Nelson, Maria. The National Anthem, 1 vol. 2014. (Symbols of America Ser.). (ENG.). 24p. (J). (gr. 1-2). 24.27 *(978-1-4824-1874-3(6)*, a7320d58-b460-4703-b4bc-1febd8bd6cf2) Stevens, Gareth Publishing LLLP.

Owens, Tom. The Star-Spangled Banner: The Flag & Its Anthem. 2003. (Illus.). 48p. (J). pap. *(978-0-7891-5890-1(6))* Perfection Learning Corp.

Pearl, Norman. Our National Anthem. Skeens, Matthew, illus. 2006. (American Symbols Ser.). (ENG.). 24p. (J). (gr. 1-3). lib. bdg. 27.32 *(978-1-4048-2215-3(1)*, 92386, Picture Window Bks.) Capstone.

Pingry, Patricia A. O Little Town of Bethlehem. 2008. (ENG., Illus.). 16p. (J). bds. 12.99 *(978-0-8249-6566-2(3)*, Ideals Pubns.) Worthy Publishing.

—Story of Star Spangled Banner. 2014. (ENG., Illus.). 24p. (J). (gr. -1-1). bds. 6.99 *(978-0-8249-1930-6(0)*, Ideals Pubns.) Worthy Publishing.

Raum, Elizabeth. The Star Spangled Banner in Translation: What It Really Means. rev. ed. 2017. (Kids' Translations Ser.). (ENG., Illus.). 32p. (J). (gr. 3-6). lib. bdg. 27.99 *(978-1-5157-9134-8(3)*, 136569, Capstone Pr.) Capstone.

Rustad, Martha E. H. Can You Sing the Star-Spangled Banner ? Poling, Kyle, illus. 2014. (Cloverleaf Books (tm) — Our American Symbols Ser.). (ENG.). 24p. (J). (gr. k-2). pap. 8.99 *(978-1-4677-4469-0(7)*, a30911a1-2455-470b-aa68-eabc8745855b, Millbrook Pr.) Lerner Publishing Group.

Schwaeber, Barbie. The Star-Spangled Banner. 2006. (American Favorites Ser.). (ENG., Illus.). 32p. (J). (gr. 3-7). 9.85 *(978-1-59249-652-5(0))* Soundprints.

Troupe, Thomas Kingsley. Birth of the Star-Spangled Banner: A Fly on the Wall History. Tejido, Jomike, illus. 2018. (Fly on the Wall History Ser.). (ENG.). 32p. (J). (gr. 1-3). lib. bdg. 27.99 *(978-1-5158-1601-0(X)*, 136254, Picture Window Bks.) Capstone.

Welch, Catherine A. La Bandera de Estrellas Centelleantes; the Star-Spangled Banner. 2008. pap. 40.95 *(978-0-7613-3867-3(5))* Lerner Publishing Group.

—The Star-Spangled Banner. Warwick, Carrie, illus. 2004. (On My Own History Ser.). 48p. (J). (gr. 1-3). pap. 6.95 *(978-1-57505-697-5(6))*; (ENG.). (gr. 2-4). 25.26 *(978-1-57505-590-9(2))* Lerner Publishing Group.

Wesolowski, Harriet. The Songs We Sing: Honoring Our Country, 1 vol. 2012. (I'm an American Citizen Ser.). (ENG., Illus.). 24p. (J). (gr. 1-2). 26.27 *(978-1-4488-8581-7(7)*, d0e84b88-61f5-4cdc-a0e5-8c808b2c9380, PowerKids Pr.) Rosen Publishing Group, Inc., The.

KEY, FRANCIS SCOTT, 1779-1843—FICTION

Winstead, Amy. The Star-Spangled Banner. Dacey, Bob & Bandelin, Debra, illus. 2003. (ENG.). 32p. (J). 18.65 *(978-0-8249-5462-8(9)*, Ideals Pubns.) Worthy Publishing.

KEYS

see Locks and Keys

KHRUSHCHEV, NIKITA SERGEEVICH, 1894-1971

Roxburgh, Ellis. John F. Kennedy vs. Nikita Khrushchev: Cold War Adversaries, 1 vol. 2014. (History's Greatest Rivals Ser.). (ENG., Illus.). 48p. (J). (gr. 6-8). lib. bdg. 33.60 *(978-1-4824-2221-4(2)*, bfc1cb51-8eeb-416d-af93-4cb9dbc51ac4) Stevens, Gareth Publishing LLLP.

KIBBUTZIM—FICTION

Edwards, Michelle. Chicken Man. (ENG.). 32p. (J). 2009. pap. 10.95 *(978-1-58838-237-5(0)*, 8701) 3rd ed. 2007. (Illus.). 16.95 *(978-1-58838-223-8(0)*, 8700) NewSouth, Inc. (NewSouth Bks.).

KIDD, WILLIAM, -1701

Stefoff, Rebecca. Captain Kidd. 2015. (J). lib. bdg. *(978-1-62713-529-0(4))* 2014. (ENG.). 48p. (gr. 4-4). 33.07 *(978-1-5026-0205-3(9)*, 50a7e25c-f746-41b5-96c6-58937ec3879c) Cavendish Square Publishing LLC.

Weintraub, Aileen. Captain Kidd: 17th-Century Pirate of the Indian Ocean & African Coast. (Library of Pirates Ser.). 24p. (gr. 3-3). 2009. 42.50 *(978-1-60853-811-9(7)*, PowerKids Pr.) 2005. (ENG., Illus.). (YA). lib. bdg. 26.27 *(978-0-8239-5797-2(7)*, 9c5dfa96-1096-456b-a6f9-50a8f7c69632) Rosen Publishing Group, Inc., The.

KIDD, WILLIAM, -1701—FICTION

Stewart, Shannon. Captain Jake, 1 vol. Hodson, Ben, illus. 2008. (Orca Echoes Ser.). (ENG.). 64p. (J). (gr. 1-3). pap. 6.95 *(978-1-55143-896-2(8))* Orca Bk. Pubs. USA.

KIDNAPPING

Burns, Jan. Kidnapping, 1 vol. 2007. (Crime Scene Investigations Ser.). (ENG., Illus.). 104p. (gr. 7-7). lib. bdg. 42.03 *(978-1-59018-989-4(2)*, 78dbce14-ca2c-476c-8c17-f29c99d6c50f, Lucent Pr.) Greenhaven Publishing LLC.

Guard, Anara. What If a Stranger Approaches You?, 1 vol. Madden, Colleen, illus. 2011. (Danger Zone Ser.). (ENG.). 24p. (J). (gr. k-2). pap. 7.49 *(978-1-4048-7031-4(8)*, 116803, Picture Window Bks.) Capstone.

Mara, Wil. What Should I Do? If a Stranger Comes Near. 2011. (Community Connections: What Should I Do? Ser.). (ENG., Illus.). 24p. (gr. 2-5). lib. bdg. 29.21 *(978-1-61080-049-5(4)*, 201040) Cherry Lake Publishing.

Mcdonald, P. J. A Cry for Help No One Heard. 2011. 148p. (gr. 10-12). pap. 14.95 *(978-1-4670-7105-5(6))* AuthorHouse.

Ridenour, Melissa Harker. What Would You Do? A Kid's Guide to Staying Safe in a World of Strangers. Fehling, Leslie, illus. 2011. (J). *(978-0-938467-11-3(5))* Headline Bks., Inc.

Roensch, Greg. The Lindbergh Baby Kidnapping Trial: A Primary Source Account, 1 vol. 2003. (Great Trials of the Twentieth Century Ser.). (ENG., Illus.). 64p. (gr. 5-8). lib. bdg. 37.13 *(978-0-8239-3971-8(5)*, 16c459b2-818a-403a-8400-724858aeafa6, Rosen Reference) Rosen Publishing Group, Inc., The.

Rooney, Anne. Kidnaps. 2010. (Solve It with Science Ser.). (YA). (gr. 5-9). 34.25 *(978-1-59920-331-7(6))* Black Rabbit Bks.

Spikes, James L. Taffey Pop Kids Presents the Adventures of Lemmon Head & Mudd Duck: What to Do if Someone Tries to Grab YOU!!! Spikes, Leon, Jr., illus. 2007. 32p. (J). 14.95 *(978-0-9771438-0-1(5))* Taffey Pop Kids Publishing.

Steele, Philip. Hostage Takers. 2016. (Behind the News Ser.). (Illus.). 48p. (J). (gr. 6-9). *(978-0-7787-2587-9(1))* Crabtree Publishing Co.

Stephens, Ronald, ed. Stranger Danger. 2014. (Safety First Ser.: 11). 48p. (J). (gr. 5-18). 20.95 *(978-1-4222-3054-1(6))* Mason Crest.

Thiel, Kristin. True Stories of Teen Terrorist Hostages, 1 vol. 2017. (True Teen Stories Ser.). (ENG.). 112p. (YA). (gr. 9-9). pap. 20.99 *(978-1-5026-3405-4(8)*, 46fcbc21-6e4a-4c01-95dc-31f2ec5da466) Cavendish Square Publishing LLC.

Turner, Patrenia. My Little Golden Book About Queen Patrenialla: A Fairy-Tail About the Queen of England Patrenia Turner. Turner, Troyius, ed. 2017. (Little Golden Book Ser.). (Illus.). pap. 4.99 *(978-0-578-19815-6(0))* The Sleeping Bear Pr.

—Queen Patrenialla: A Fairy-Tail About the Queen of England Patrenia Turner. Turner, Troyius, ed. 2017. (Illus.). pap. *(978-0-578-19814-9(2))* The Sleeping Bear Pr.

Turner, Queen of England Patrenia. Queen Patrenialla - A Canadian Story Poem. Turner, Keeng of England Troyius, ed. 2015. (Illus.). pap. *(978-0-578-18000-7(6))* Royalty Patrenia Turner Publications.

KIDNAPPING—FICTION

Abbott, Tony. The Serpent's Curse. 2014. (Illus.). 496p. pap. 9.99 *(978-0-06-235159-3(1))* HarperCollins Pubs.

Adams, Carolyn Lee. Ruthless. 2015. (ENG., Illus.). 256p. (YA). (gr. 9). 17.99 *(978-1-4814-2262-8(6)*, Simon Pulse) Simon Pulse.

The adventures of officer Byrd. 2007. (J). 16.99 *(978-0-9787322-0-2(0))* Officer Byrd Publishing Co.

Alger, Horatio. Helping Himself. 2006. 180p. pap. 19.99 *(978-1-4264-0881-6(1))*; (ENG.). 168p. pap. 21.99 *(978-1-4264-0862-5(5))* Creative Media Partners, LLC.

—Helping Himself. 2006. pap. *(978-1-4065-0709-6(1))* Dodo Pr.

—Jack's Ward. 2005. 28.95 *(978-1-4218-1454-4(4))*; 260p. pap. 13.95 *(978-1-4218-1554-1(0))* 1st World Publishing, Inc. (1st World Library - Literary Society).

—Jack's Ward. 2006. pap. *(978-1-4065-0711-9(3))* Dodo Pr.

—Jack's Ward: Or, The Boy Guardian. 2006. 176p. pap. 19.99 *(978-1-4264-0882-3(X))*; (ENG.). 168p. pap. 21.99 *(978-1-4264-0863-2(3))* Creative Media Partners, LLC.

—Timothy Crump's Ward. 2005. 27.95 *(978-1-4218-1451-3(X))*; 220p. pap. 12.95 *(978-1-4218-1551-0(6))* 1st World Publishing, Inc. (1st World Library - Literary Society).

Allan, Nicholas. Android in the Attic. 2013. (ENG., Illus.). 192p. (J). (gr. 2-4). pap. 7.99 *(978-0-340-99706-2(0))* Hachette Children's Group GBR. Dist: Hachette Bk. Group.

Altebrando, Tara. The Leaving. 2016. (ENG.). 432p. (YA). 18.99 *(978-1-61963-803-7(7)*, 900149146, Bloomsbury USA Childrens) Bloomsbury Publishing USA.

Angleberger, Tom. Didi Dodo, Future Spy: Double-O Dodo (Didi Dodo, Future Spy #3) Chapman. Jared, illus. 2020. (Flytrap Files Ser.). (ENG.). 112p. (J). (gr. 1-4). 12.99 *(978-1-4197-4097-8(0)*, 1259601, Amulet Bks.) Abrams, Inc.

Anstey, Cindy. Duels & Deception. 2017. (ENG.). 368p. (YA). pap. 26.99 *(978-1-250-11909-4(X)*, 900172672) Feiwel & Friends.

Antieau, Kim. Broken Moon. 2007. (ENG.). 192p. (YA). (gr. 9-12). 16.99 *(978-1-4169-1767-0(5)*, McElderry, Margaret K. Bks.) McElderry, Margaret K. Bks.

Argyle, Michelle Davidson. The Breakaway. 2012. 320p. pap. 15.99 *(978-1-936850-61-7(3))* Rhemalda Publishing.

Awiakta, Marilou. Rising Fawn & the Fire Mystery. 2007. (ENG., Illus.). 96p. (J). (gr. 4-7). pap. 14.95 *(978-1-55591-600-8(7))* Fulcrum Publishing.

Axelsson, Carina. Paris. 2014. (Model Undercover Ser.: 1). (ENG.). 368p. (J). (gr. 4-7). pap. 10.99 *(978-1-4022-8587-5(6))* Sourcebooks, Inc.

Babbitt, Natalie. Tuck Everlasting. 2008. (J). 39.99 *(978-0-7393-7111-4(8))* Findaway World, LLC.

—Tuck Everlasting. 139p. (J). (gr. 4-6). pap. 4.95 *(978-0-8072-1385-8(3)*, Listening Library) Random Hse. Audio Publishing Group.

Bailey, Em. The Special Ones. 2018. (ENG.). 304p. (YA). (gr. 7). pap. 15.99 *(978-1-328-90106-4(8)*, 1700164, Clarion Bks.) HarperCollins Pubs.

—The Special Ones. 2018. lib. bdg. 20.85 *(978-0-606-40993-3(9))* Turtleback.

Baker, E. D. A Prince among Frogs. 2nd ed. 2015. (Tales of the Frog Princess Ser.). (ENG.). 240p. (YA). (gr. 3-6). pap. 9.99 *(978-1-61963-624-8(7)*, 900142485, Bloomsbury USA Childrens) Bloomsbury Publishing USA.

Barbieri, Kara. White Stag: A Permafrost Novel. 2019. (ENG.). 368p. (YA). pap. *(978-1-250-22619-8(8)*, Wednesday Bks.) St. Martin's Pr.

Barrett, Tracy. Marabel & the Book of Fate. 2018. (Marabel Novel Ser.). (ENG.). 304p. (J). (gr. 3-7). 16.99 *(978-0-316-43399-0(3))* Little, Brown Bks. for Young Readers.

Basil of Baker Street, 1 vol. 2016. (Your Reading Path Ser.: 1). (Illus.). 112p. (J). (gr. 4-4). pap. *(978-1-4814-6401-7(9)*, c557f760-fd35-4d9b-81b4-60e49570d332, Rosen Classroom) Rosen Publishing Group, Inc., The.

Bath, K. P. Flip Side. 2009. (YA). 16.99 *(978-0-316-03836-2(9))* Little Brown & Co.

Bauer, Deidre. Silver Mountain. 2008. 38p. pap. 8.00 *(978-0-8059-7672-4(8))* Dorrance Publishing Co., Inc.

Bayerl, Katie. A Psalm for Lost Girls. 2018. 368p. (YA). (gr. 7). pap. 10.99 *(978-0-399-54527-6(1)*, Speak) Penguin Young Readers Group.

Beck, Ricky. A Puzzled Heart. 2008. 85p. pap. 19.95 *(978-1-60441-385-4(9))* America Star Bks.

Beil, Michael D. Lantern Sam & the Blue Streak Bandits. 2015. (ENG., Illus.). 288p. (J). (gr. 3-7). pap. 7.99 *(978-0-385-75320-3(9)*, Yearling) Random Hse. Children's Bks.

Bell, Braden. The Kindling. 2012. (YA). *(978-1-4621-1027-8(4))* Cedar Fort, Inc./CFI Distribution.

Bennett, Cindy C. Rapunzel Untangled. 2013. (ENG.). 294p. (gr. 7). 16.99 *(978-1-4621-1156-5(4)*, Sweetwater Bks.) Cedar Fort, Inc./CFI Distribution.

Berenato, Dave. Medlocks: The Peractio Blackout. 2011. 284p. (gr. 10-12). 27.95 *(978-1-4620-5219-6(3))*; pap. 17.95 *(978-1-4620-5217-2(7))* iUniverse, Inc.

Biedrzycki, David. Ace Lacewing: Bug Detective. Biedrzycki, David, illus. 2008. (Ace Lacewing, Bug Detective Ser.). (Illus.). 40p. (J). (gr. k-4). pap. 8.95 *(978-1-57091-684-7(5))* Charlesbridge Publishing, Inc.

Biggs, K. E. The Dawn of Hope. 2010. 112p. pap. 10.99 *(978-1-4490-8931-3(3))* AuthorHouse.

Blabey, Aaron. Los tipos malos en el alienígena vs los tipos malos (The Bad Guys in Alien vs Bad Guys) 2018. (Bad Guys Ser.: 6). (Illus.). 137p. (J). lib. bdg. 16.00 *(978-0-606-41473-9(8))* Turtleback.

Black, Cally. In the Dark Spaces. 2017. (ENG.). 328p. (YA). (gr. 7). pap. 18.99 *(978-1-76012-864-7(3))* Hardie Grant Children?s Publishing AUS. Dist: Independent Pubs. Group.

Blackstock, Terri. Southern Storm, 1 vol. 2014. (Cape Refuge Ser.: 2). (ENG.). 400p. pap. 17.99 *(978-0-310-34280-9(5))* Zondervan.

Bladek, John. Lost in Ghostville. 2016. (Middle-Grade Novels Ser.). (ENG., Illus.). 208p. (J). (gr. 4-7). lib. bdg. 25.99 *(978-1-4965-3360-9(7)*, 132508, Stone Arch Bks.) Capstone.

Blair, Jamie. Leap of Faith. (ENG.). 240p. (YA). (gr. 9). 2014. pap. 11.99 *(978-1-4424-4716-5(8))* 2013. (Illus.). 16.99 *(978-1-4424-4713-4(3))* Simon & Schuster Bks. For Young Readers. (Simon & Schuster Bks. For Young Readers).

Bloor, Edward. Taken. 2007. (ENG.). 256p. (J). (gr. 7-12). lib. bdg. 24.94 *(978-0-375-93636-4(X))* Random House Publishing Group.

—Taken. 2009. 256p. (YA). (gr. 7). pap. 8.99 *(978-0-440-42128-3(4)*, Knopf Bks. for Young Readers) Random Hse. Children's Bks.

Boissery, Beverley. Sophie's Exile: 0. 2008. (Sophie Mallory Ser.: 3). (ENG.). 280p. (J). (gr. 5-8). pap. 12.99 *(978-1-55002-810-2(3))* Dundurn Pr. CAN. Dist: Publishers Group West (PGW).

Bosch, Pseudonymous. The Name of This Book Is Secret. 2008. (Secret Ser.: 1). (ENG.). 400p. (J). (gr. 3-7). pap. 9.99 *(978-0-316-11369-4(7))* Little, Brown Bks. for Young Readers.

—The Name of This Book Is Secret. 2009. 18.00 *(978-1-60686-518-7(8))* Perfection Learning Corp.

—The Name of This Book Is Secret. 2008. (Secret Ser.: 1). (J). lib. bdg. 19.65 *(978-1-4178-2975-0(3))* Turtleback.

Boulton, M. T. Megan Button & the Brim-Tree. 2012. 106p. pap. *(978-1-909039-06-3(3))* Legend Pr.

Bowditch, Eden Unger. The Atomic Weight of Secrets or the Arrival of the Mysterious Men in Black. 2011. (Young Inventors Guild Ser.: 1). (ENG.). 320p. (YA). 19.95 *(978-1-61088-002-2(1)*, 3affde56-4139-4a62-9c5d-612313bb8c2d) Bancroft Pr.

—The Ravens of Solemano or the Order of the Mysterious Men in Black. 2015. (Young Inventors Guild Ser.: 2). (ENG.). 464p. (YA). 22.95 *(978-1-61088-121-0(4)*, 6d91e1bf-e0c9-4398-9146-640ac1b2d392) Bancroft Pr.

Bowen, Carl. Shadow Squadron: Black Anchor, 1 vol. Tortosa, Wilson & Fuentes, Benny, illus. 2013. (Shadow Squadron Ser.). (ENG.). 112p. (J). (gr. 4-8). lib. bdg. 27.32 *(978-1-4342-4605-9(1)*, 120592, Stone Arch Bks.) Capstone.

Bowler, Tim. Storm Catchers. 2003. (ENG., Illus.). 208p. (YA). (gr. 7). 18.99 *(978-0-689-84573-4(1)*, McElderry, Margaret K. Bks.) McElderry, Margaret K. Bks.

Bradford, Chris. Bodyguard: Hijack (Book 3), Bk. 3. 2017. (Bodyguard Ser.: 3). (ENG.). 272p. (J). (gr. 5). pap. 8.99 *(978-1-5247-3701-6(1)*, Philomel Bks.) Penguin Young Readers Group.

—Bodyguard: Hostage (Book 2), Bk. 2. 2017. (Bodyguard Ser.: 2). (ENG.). 224p. (J). (gr. 5). pap. 8.99 *(978-1-5247-3699-6(6)*, Philomel Bks.) Penguin Young Readers Group.

—Bodyguard: Ransom (Book 4), Bk. 4. 2017. (Bodyguard Ser.: 4). (ENG.). 224p. (J). (gr. 5). pap. 9.99 *(978-1-5247-3703-0(8)*, Philomel Bks.) Penguin Young Readers Group.

Bramucci, Stephen. The Danger Gang & the Isle of Feral Beasts! Chung, Arree, illus. 2018. (ENG.). 352p. (J). 16.99 *(978-1-61963-694-1(8)*, 900145711, Bloomsbury Children's Bks.) Bloomsbury Publishing USA.

—The Danger Gang & the Pirates of Borneo! Chung, Arree, illus. 2017. (ENG.). 384p. (J). 16.99 *(978-1-61963-692-7(1)*, 900145716, Bloomsbury USA Childrens) Bloomsbury Publishing USA.

Brezenoff, Steve. Field Trip Mysteries: the Yellowstone Kidnapping That Wasn't. Canga, Chris & Calo, Marcos, illus. 2012. (Field Trip Mysteries Ser.). (ENG.). 88p. (J). (gr. 3-6). pap. 5.95 *(978-1-4342-4200-6(5)*, 120258); lib. bdg. 25.32 *(978-1-4342-3789-7(3)*, 117088) Capstone. (Stone Arch Bks.).

Brindley, John. The Rule of Claw. Benfold Haywood, Ian P., illus. 2009. (Exceptional Reading & Language Arts Titles for Intermediate Grades Ser.). (ENG.). 408p. (YA). (gr. 7-12). 18.95 *(978-1-58013-608-2(7))* Lerner Publishing Group.

Brook, Harry, retold by. Kidnapped. 2004. (Paperback Classics Ser.). 144p. (J). lib. bdg. 12.95 *(978-1-58086-640-8(9)*, Usborne) EDC Publishing.

Brooks, Kevin. The Bunker Diary. 2019. (ENG.). 264p. (YA). (gr. 8-12). pap. 12.99 *(978-1-5415-7760-2(4)*, f5fd38ee-2d19-4f5d-a8c6-397cc3319b05, Carolrhoda Lab™) Lerner Publishing Group.

Brooks-Scrivanich, Olivia. Fiscal Pear & Shimmer in the Call of River Whale. 2008. (ENG.). 92p. pap. 14.99 *(978-1-4196-9589-6(4))* CreateSpace Independent Publishing Platform.

Brown, Anne. The Dumari Chronicles: Year One: Year One. 2007. 376p. (YA). per. 20.95 *(978-0-595-45725-0(8))* iUniverse, Inc.

Bruchac, Joseph. The Legend of Skeleton Man: Skeleton Man & the Return of Skeleton Man. 2019. (ENG.). 288p. (J). (gr. 3-7). pap. 7.99 *(978-0-06-274768-6(1)*, HarperCollins) HarperCollins Pubs.

—Skeleton Man. 2003. (Skeleton Man Ser.: 1). (ENG., Illus.). 128p. (J). (gr. 3-8). pap. 9.99 *(978-0-06-440888-2(4)*, HarperCollins) HarperCollins Pubs.

—Skeleton Man. Comport, Sally Wern, illus. 2003. 114p. (J). (gr. 5). 12.65 *(978-0-7569-3399-9(4))* Perfection Learning Corp.

Bruzon, Louise A. The Grimstone Galleries. 2010. 192p. pap. *(978-1-907652-17-2(5))* Grosvenor Hse. Publishing Ltd.

Bryers, Paul. Kobal. 2009. 1.00 *(978-1-4074-4320-1(8))* Recorded Bks., Inc.

Buckley, Michael. Nerds 5: Attack of the Bullies. 2013. (Nerds Ser.). (ENG.). 336p. (YA). (gr. 3-7). pap. 7.95 *(978-1-4197-1046-9(X))* Abrams, Inc.

—The Problem Child. 2017. (Sisters Grimm Ser.: 3). (J). lib. bdg. 19.60 *(978-0-606-39687-5(X))* Turtleback.

—The Problem Child (the Sisters Grimm #3) 10th Anniversary Edition. Ferguson, Peter, illus. 10th ed. 2017. (Sisters Grimm Ser.). (ENG.). 288p. (J). (gr. 3-7). pap. 9.99 *(978-1-4197-2004-8(X)*, 580606, Amulet Bks.) Abrams, Inc.

Bunting, Eve. The Lambkins. Keegan, Jonathan, illus. 2005. (ENG.). 192p. (J). (gr. 5-18). 15.99 *(978-0-06-059906-5(5)*, Cotler, Joanna Books) HarperCollins Pubs.

Cameron, Ann. Colibri. 2005. (ENG.). 256p. (YA). (gr. 7). mass mkt. 7.99 *(978-0-440-42052-1(0)*, Laurel Leaf) Random Hse. Children's Bks.

Carlson, Melody. Spring Breakdown, 1 vol. 2014. (Carter House Girls Ser.: 7). (ENG.). 208p. (YA). pap. 9.99 *(978-0-310-74809-0(7))* Zondervan.

Carter, Ally. Not If I Save You First. (ENG.). 304p. (gr. 7). 2019. (J). pap. 10.99 *(978-1-338-13415-5(9))* 2018. (YA). 18.99 *(978-1-338-13414-8(0))* Scholastic, Inc. (Scholastic Pr.).

Cartwright, Ran. The Adventures of Billy Space Boy, 1 vol. 2010. 208p. pap. 24.95 *(978-1-4489-3901-5(1))* America Star Bks.

Chee, Traci. The Reader. (Reader Ser.: 1). 464p. (YA). (gr. 7). 2017. pap. 11.99 *(978-0-14-751805-7(9)*, Speak)Bk. 1. 2016. 19.99 *(978-0-399-17677-7(2)*, G.P. Putnam's Sons Books for Young Readers) Penguin Young Readers Group.

—The Reader. 2017. (Sea of Ink & Gold Ser.: 1). lib. bdg. 22.10 *(978-0-606-40001-5(X))* Turtleback.

—The Speaker. 2018. (Reader Ser.: 2). 512p. (YA). (gr. 7). pap. 10.99 *(978-0-14-751806-4(7)*, Speak) Penguin Young Readers Group.

Chiu, Harry. Enve Lopt Unfolded. 2007. 268p. per. 17.95 *(978-0-595-44707-7(4))* iUniverse, Inc.

Christopher, Lucy. Stolen. 2012. (ENG.). 320p. (YA). (gr. 9). pap. 10.99 *(978-0-545-17094-9(X)*, Chicken Hse., The) Scholastic, Inc.

—Stolen. 2012. lib. bdg. 20.85 *(978-0-606-23955-4(3))* Turtleback.

C.J. Elgert. The Elder Brothers & the Padstow Crystals. 2009. 284p. 27.95 *(978-1-4401-7678-4(7))*; pap. 17.95 *(978-1-4401-7676-0(0))* iUniverse, Inc.

Clark, Sherryl. The Littlest Pirate. Jellett, Tom, illus. 2019. (Puffin Nibbles Ser.). 80p. (J). (gr. k-2). pap. 9.99 *(978-0-14-131338-2(2)*, Puffin) Penguin Random Hse. AUS. Dist: Independent Pubs. Group.

Clarke, Cat. The Lost & the Found. 2016. (ENG.). 368p. (YA). (gr. 9). 17.99 *(978-1-101-93204-9(X)*, Crown Books For Young Readers) Random Hse. Children's Bks.

Clarke, E. J. A Fairy's Courage. (Oakwing Ser.: 2). (ENG.). 208p. (J). (gr. 2-6). 2019. pap. 7.99 *(978-1-4814-8193-9(2))* 2018. (Illus.). 16.99 *(978-1-4814-8194-6(0))* Simon & Schuster Children's Publishing. (Aladdin).

Cochrane, Mick. Fitz. 2013. (ENG.). 192p. (YA). (gr. 7). pap. 8.99 *(978-0-375-84611-3(5)*, Ember) Random Hse. Children's Bks.

Colbert, Brandy. Pointe. 2015. 352p. (YA). (gr. 9). pap. 10.99 *(978-0-14-751441-7(X)*, Speak) Penguin Young Readers Group.

Coley, Liz. Pretty Girl-13. 2013. (ENG.). 352p. (YA). (gr. 9). 17.99 *(978-0-06-212737-2(3)*, Tegen, Katherine Bks) HarperCollins Pubs.

Colfer, Eoin. Artemis Fowl, 3 vols., Set. 2010. (Artemis Fowl Ser.). (ENG.). 944p. (J). (gr. 5-17). pap. 19.99 *(978-1-4231-3681-1(0))* Disney Pr.

—Artemis Fowl. (Artemis Fowl Ser.: Bk. 1). (FRE.). pap. 34.95 *(978-2-07-054681-7(0))* Gallimard, Editions FRA. Dist: Distribooks, Inc.

—Artemis Fowl. (Artemis Fowl Ser.: Bk. 1). pap. 34.95 *(978-88-04-49788-2(2))* Mondadori ITA. Dist: Distribooks, Inc.

—Artemis Fowl. (Artemis Fowl Ser.: 1). (YA). 2007. 1.25 *(978-1-4193-6020-6(5))* 2006. 52.75 *(978-1-4193-6023-7(X))* 2006. 54.75 *(978-1-4193-6021-3(3))* 2006. 54.75 *(978-1-4193-6026-8(4))* 2006. 132.75 *(978-1-4193-6022-0(1))* 2005. 56.75 *(978-1-4193-6024-4(8))* Recorded Bks., Inc.

—Artemis Fowl. 2009. (Artemis Fowl Ser.: 1). (J). (gr. 5-8). lib. bdg. 19.65 *(978-0-613-60637-0(X))* Turtleback.

—Eoin Colfer: Artemis Fowl: the Graphic Novel. 2019. (Artemis Fowl Ser.). (ENG., Illus.). 128p. (J). (gr. 3-7). 21.99 *(978-1-368-04314-4(3)*, Disney-Hyperion) Disney Publishing Worldwide.

—EL MUNDO SUBTERRÁNEO (ARTEMIS FOWL 1) (Artemis Fowl Ser.: Bk. 1). (SPA.). 288p. pap. *(978-84-8441-115-4(X)*, MO31567) Grijalbo Mondadori, S.A.-Montena.

—The Opal Deception. 2006. (Artemis Fowl Ser.: Bk. 4). 17.10 *(978-0-7569-6828-1(3))* Disney Pr.

—The Opal Deception. (Artemis Fowl Ser.: 4). (J). 2007. 1.25 *(978-1-4193-6041-1(8))* 2006. 69.75 *(978-1-4193-6047-3(7))* 2006. 72.75 *(978-1-4193-6045-9(0))* Recorded Bks., Inc.

Collins, David Paul. Shanghaied. 2011. (ENG.). 320p. 29.95 *(978-1-4620-3184-9(6))*; pap. 19.95 *(978-1-4620-3183-2(8))* iUniverse, Inc.

Columbus, Chris & Vizzini, Ned. House of Secrets: Battle of the Beasts. Call, Greg, illus. 2014. (House of Secrets Ser.: 2). (ENG.). 480p. (J). (gr. 3-7). 17.99 *(978-0-06-219249-3(3)*, Balzer & Bray) HarperCollins Pubs.

Cooney, Caroline B. The Face on the Milk Carton. 2009. 9.14 *(978-0-7848-0397-4(8)*, Everbind) Marco Bk. Co.

—The Face on the Milk Carton. 2012. (Janie Bks.: 1). lib. bdg. 20.85 *(978-0-606-26368-9(3))* Turtleback.

—Hit the Road. rev. l.t. ed. 2007. (Thorndike Literacy Bridge Ser.). 259p. (YA). (gr. 7-12). 23.95 *(978-0-7862-9429-9(9))* Thorndike Pr.

—What Janie Found. 2012. (Face on the Milk Carton Ser.). 208p. (YA). (gr. 7). pap. 10.99 *(978-0-385-74241-2(X)*, Ember) Random Hse. Children's Bks.

—What Janie Found. 2012. (Janie Bks.: 4). lib. bdg. 20.85 *(978-0-606-26370-2(5))* Turtleback.

—Whatever Happened to Janie? 2012. (Face on the Milk Carton Ser.). 224p. (YA). (gr. 7). pap. 10.99 *(978-0-385-74239-9(8)*, Ember) Random Hse. Children's Bks.

Coppel, Chris. Far from Burden Dell. 2005. 286p. (J). (gr. 6-16). per. 4.95 *(978-0-9746481-6-3(7))* Brown Barn Bks.

Corder, Zizou. Lionboy. 2004. (ENG., Illus.). 304p. (J). (gr. 3-7). reprint ed. pap. 8.99 *(978-0-14-240226-9(5)*, Puffin Books) Penguin Young Readers Group.

—Lionboy: the Truth, 3. 2006. (ENG., Illus.). 240p. (J). (gr. 3-7). 7.99 *(978-0-14-240705-9(4)*, Puffin Books) Penguin Young Readers Group.

Côté, Denis. La Machination du Scorpion Noir. 2004. (Mon Roman Ser.). (FRE.). 160p. (J). (gr. 2). pap. *(978-2-89021-667-9(5))* Diffusion du livre Mirabel (DLM).

Cox, Judy. The Case of the Purloined Professor, 0 vols. Rayyan, Omar, illus. 2009. (Tails of Frederick & Ishbu Ser.: 0). (ENG.). 256p. (J). (gr. 5-7). 16.99 *(978-0-7614-5544-8(2)*, 9780761455448, Two Lions) Amazon Publishing.

Crutcher, Chris. Period 8. 2013. (ENG.). 288p. (YA). (gr. 9). 17.99 *(978-0-06-191480-5(0)*, Greenwillow Bks.) HarperCollins Pubs.

Dailey, Reid. Ross the Reader & the Adventure of the Pirate's Treasure. Edgerley, Ross, illus. 2009. 44p. pap. 16.95 *(978-1-59858-900-9(8))* Dog Ear Publishing, LLC.

Daneshvari, Gitty. The League of Unexceptional Children. (League of Unexceptional Children Ser.: 1). (ENG., Illus.). (J). (gr. 3-7). 2016. 256p. pap. 7.99 *(978-0-316-40568-3(X))* 2015. 240p. 17.00 *(978-0-316-40570-6(1))* Little, Brown Bks. for Young Readers.

Daniels, J. M. The Secret of the Little Dutch Doll. 2009. 68p. pap. 25.49 *(978-1-4343-9356-2(9))* AuthorHouse.

Darlison, Aleesah. Krystal's Choice. Brailsford, Jill, illus. 2017. (Unicorn Riders Ser.). (ENG.). 112p. (J). (gr. 3-5). pap. 5.95 *(978-1-4795-6554-2(7)*, 128544, Picture Window Bks.) Capstone.

—Quinn's Riddles. Brailsford, Jill, illus. 2017. (Unicorn Riders Ser.). (ENG.). 112p. (J). (gr. 3-5). pap. 5.95 *(978-1-4795-6552-8(0)*, 128542, Picture Window Bks.) Capstone.

Davies, Stephen. Outlaw. 2011. (ENG.). 304p. (YA). (gr. 7). 16.99 *(978-0-547-39017-8(3))* Houghton Mifflin Harcourt Publishing Co.

Davis, Susan Page. Feather. 2006. (Illus.). 213p. (J). 8.99 *(978-1-59166-668-4(6))* BJU Pr.

De Brunhoff, Jean. Babar & Zephir. De Brunhoff, Jean., illus. 2005. (Illus.). 38p. (J). (gr. k-4). reprint ed. 16.00 *(978-0-7567-8935-0(4))* DIANE Publishing Co.

Dematteis, J. M. Stardust Kid. Ploog, Mike, illus. 2008. (ENG.). 128p. pap. 14.99 *(978-1-934506-04-2(4))* BOOM! Studios.

DeStefano, Lauren. Wither, 9 vols. (Chemical Garden Ser.: 1). (YA). 90.75 *(978-1-4561-2060-3(3))*; 1.25 *(978-1-4561-2064-1(6))*; 256.75 *(978-1-4561-2059-7(X))*; 2011. 120.75 *(978-1-4561-2063-4(8))*; 2011. 122.75 *(978-1-4561-2061-0(1))* Recorded Bks., Inc.

—Wither. 2011. (Chemical Garden Trilogy Ser.: 1). (ENG.). 384p. (YA). (gr. 9). pap. 13.99 *(978-1-4424-0906-4(1)*, Simon & Schuster Bks. For Young Readers) Simon & Schuster Bks. For Young Readers.

Devlin, Calla. Right Where You Left Me. 2017. (ENG., Illus.). 256p. (YA). (gr. 9). 17.99 *(978-1-4814-8699-6(3)*, Atheneum Bks. for Young Readers) Simon & Schuster Children's Publishing.

Diamand, Emily. Raiders' Ransom. 2011. (Raiders' Ransom Ser.: 1). (ENG.). 368p. (J). (gr. 6-8). 22.44 *(978-0-545-14298-4(9))* Scholastic, Inc.

Dickens, Charles. Oliver Twist, 1 vol. 2009. (Foundation Classics Ser.). (ENG., Illus.). 56p. (J). (gr. 5-5). lib. bdg. 32.60 *(978-1-60754-542-2(X)*, 9899534b-2ed0-46e5-86cf-4f5e01b17974, Windmill Bks.) Rosen Publishing Group, Inc., The.

Disney Press Editors. Miles from Tomorrowland: Who Stole the Stellosphere? 2015. (World of Reading Ser.). (J). lib. bdg. 13.55 *(978-0-606-36902-2(3))* Turtleback.

Dixon, Franklin W. Bound for Danger. 2016. (Hardy Boys Adventures Ser.: 13). (ENG., Illus.). 144p. (J). (gr. 3-7). pap. 6.99 *(978-1-4814-6831-2(6)*, Aladdin) Simon & Schuster Children's Publishing.

—Bound for Danger. 2016. (Hardy Boys Adventures Ser.: 13). (ENG., Illus.). 144p. (J). (gr. 3-7). 17.99 *(978-1-4814-6832-9(4)*, Simon & Schuster/Paula Wiseman Bks.) Simon & Schuster/Paula Wiseman Bks.

—Kidnapped at the Casino. 2007. (Hardy Boys Undercover Brothers: Super Mystery Ser.: 2). (ENG., Illus.). 240p. (J). (gr. 3-7). pap. 5.99 *(978-1-4169-3923-8(7)*, Aladdin) Simon & Schuster Children's Publishing.

Dixon, Ken. Cobweb Jack & the Sacred Khunjar. 2009. 210p. pap. 28.50 *(978-1-4092-8919-7(2))* Lulu Pr., Inc.

Donbavand, Tommy. Scream Street: Terror of the Nightwatchman. 2014. (Scream Street Ser.: 9). (ENG., Illus.). 128p. (J). (gr. 3-7). pap. 5.99 *(978-0-7636-5761-1(1))* Candlewick Pr.

Draper, Sharon M. Panic. 2013. (ENG., Illus.). 272p. (YA). (gr. 9). 19.99 *(978-1-4424-0896-8(0)*, Atheneum Bks. for Young Readers) Simon & Schuster Children's Publishing.

Ducharme, Huguette. Enquete Tres Speciale. Caron, Romi, illus. 2004. (Collection des 6 Ans: Vol. 32). (FRE.). 68p. (YA). 7.95 *(978-2-922565-94-2(7))* Editions de la Paix CAN. Dist: World of Reading, Ltd.

Duff, Hilary. Devoted: An Elixir Novel. (Elixir Ser.). (ENG.). 368p. (YA). (gr. 9). 2012. pap. 9.99 *(978-1-4424-0856-2(1))* 2011. 17.99 *(978-1-4424-0855-5(3))* Simon & Schuster Bks. For Young Readers. (Simon & Schuster Bks. For Young Readers).

Duncan, Lois. The Third Eye. 2012. (ENG.). 288p. (J). (gr. 7-17). pap. 15.99 *(978-0-316-09908-0(2))* Little, Brown Bks. for Young Readers.

Dunlop, Ed. Sherlock Jones: The Missing Diamond. 2005. (Sherlock Jones Ser.). 109p. (J). (gr. 3-7). per. 8.99 *(978-1-59166-316-4(4))* BJU Pr.

Eagar, Lindsay. Race to the Bottom of the Sea. (ENG.). 432p. (J). (gr. 3-7). 2019. pap. 9.99 *(978-0-7636-9877-5(6))* 2017. 17.99 *(978-0-7636-7923-1(2))* Candlewick Pr.

Ehrenhaft, Daniel. Drawing a Blank: Or How I Tried to Solve a Mystery, End a Feud, & Land the Girl of My Dreams. Ristow, Trevor, illus. 2009. (ENG.). 352p. (J). pap. 8.99 *(978-0-06-075254-5(8)*, HarperTeen) HarperCollins Pubs.

Ehrlich, Amy. Joyride. 2008. (ENG., Illus.). 256p. (YA). (gr. 7). pap. 8.99 *(978-0-7636-2321-0(0))* Candlewick Pr.

Eisenstein, Ann. Fallen Prey, a Sean Gray Junior Special Agent Mystery. Waugh, Leslie, ed. 2013. 190p. pap. 9.99 *(978-1-935711-31-5(8))* Peak City Publishing, LLC.

Emerson, Kevin. Any Second. 2018. (ENG.). 400p. (YA). (gr. 7). 17.99 *(978-0-553-53482-5(3)*, Crown Books For Young Readers) Random Hse. Children's Bks.

Epstein, Adam Jay & Jacobson, Andrew. The Familiars. 2010. (Familiars Ser.: 1). (ENG., Illus.). 368p. (J). (gr. 3-7). 17.99 *(978-0-06-196108-3(6)*, HarperCollins) HarperCollins Pubs.

Erdrich, Louise. Chickadee. Erdrich, Louise, illus. (Birchbark House Ser.: 4). (ENG., Illus.). (J). (gr. 3-7). 2013. 224p. pap. 7.99 *(978-0-06-057792-6(4))* 2012. 208p. 16.99 *(978-0-06-057790-2(8))* HarperCollins Pubs. (HarperCollins).

Erickson, John. The Case of the Kidnapped Collie. Holmes, Gerald L., illus. 2011. (Hank the Cowdog Ser.). (ENG.). 113p. (J). (gr. 3-6). pap. 5.99 *(978-1-59188-126-1(9))* Maverick Bks., Inc.

Eustache, Harold. Shuswap Journey. 2004. (Shuswap Journey Ser.). (ENG.). 176p. pap. 15.95 *(978-1-894778-15-2(4))* Theytus Bks., Ltd. CAN. Dist: Univ. of Toronto Pr.

Evans, Richard Paul. Michael Vey 4: Hunt for Jade Dragon. 2015. (Michael Vey Ser.: 4). (ENG., Illus.). 336p. (YA). (gr. 7). pap. 12.99 *(978-1-4814-2439-4(4))* Simon & Schuster, Inc.

—Michael Vey 4: Hunt for Jade Dragon. 2014. (Michael Vey Ser.: 4). (ENG., Illus.). 336p. (YA). (gr. 7). 19.99 *(978-1-4814-2438-7(6)*, Simon Pulse/Mercury Ink) Simon Pulse/Mercury Ink.

—Michael Vey 7: The Final Spark. 2017. (Michael Vey Ser.: 7). (ENG., Illus.). 336p. (YA). (gr. 7). 19.99 *(978-1-4814-9703-9(0)*, Simon Pulse/Mercury Ink) Simon Pulse/Mercury Ink.

Evelyn Gill Hilton. Kidnapped by Pirates: Based on the true story of a fourteen year-old boy, Charles Tilton, who was kidnapped alone from an Amer. 2010. (ENG.). 124p. 21.95 *(978-1-4269-2018-9(0))*; (gr. 1-2). pap. 11.95 *(978-1-4269-2017-2(2))* Trafford Publishing.

Fagan, Cary. The Boy in the Box: Master Melville's Medicine Show. 2012. (ENG., Illus.). 288p. (J). (gr. 5-7). 16.99 *(978-0-547-75268-6(7)*, 1487593, Clarion Bks.) HarperCollins Pubs.

Farshtey, Greg. Way of the Ninja. 2012. (LEGO Ninjago Ser.). (ENG.). 32p. (J). (gr. 1-3). pap. 3.99 *(978-0-545-40113-5(5))* Scholastic, Inc.

Faunce-Brown, Michael. Slave Children. 2015. (ENG., Illus.). 140p. (J). pap. *(978-1-78222-422-8(X))* Paragon Publishing, Rothersthorpe.

Feinstein, John. Vanishing Act: Mystery at the U. S. Open (the Sports Beat, 2) 2008. (Sports Beat Ser.: 2). (ENG.). 304p.

(J). (gr. 3-7). 9.99 *(978-0-440-42125-2(X)*, Yearling) Random Hse. Children's Bks.
Feldmann, Claudia, tr. ARTEMIS FOWL. (Artemis Fowl Ser.: Bk. 1). (GER.). pap. 24.95 *(978-3-548-60320-9(3))* Ullstein-Taschenbuch-Verlag DEU. Dist: Distribooks, Inc.
Flanagan, John. The Caldera. 2018. (Brotherband Chronicles Ser.: 7). (ENG.). 384p. (J). (gr. 5). 9.99 *(978-0-14-242729-3(2)*, Puffin Books) Penguin Young Readers Group.
—The Icebound Land. 2007. (Ranger's Apprentice Ser.: Bk. 3). 260p. (J). 25.66 *(978-1-4287-4632-9(3)*, Follettbound) Follett School Solutions.
—The Icebound Land: Book Three, Bk. 3. 2008. (Ranger's Apprentice Ser.: 3). (ENG.). 304p. (J). (gr. 5-18). 9.99 *(978-0-14-241075-2(6)*, Puffin Books) Penguin Young Readers Group.
—The Sorcerer of the North. 2009. (Ranger's Apprentice Ser.: 5). lib. bdg. 19.65 *(978-0-606-02237-8(6))* Turtleback.
—The Sorcerer of the North: Book Five. 5 vols., Bk. 5. (Ranger's Apprentice Ser.: 5). (ENG.). (J). (gr. 5-18). 2009. 336p. pap. 9.99 *(978-0-14-241429-3(8)*, Puffin Books) 2008. 304p. 18.99 *(978-0-399-25032-3(8)*, Philomel Bks.) Penguin Young Readers Group.
Flannigan, Liz. Cara & the Wizard, 2 vols. Docampo, Valeria, illus. 2013. (Magic Stories Ser.). 48p. (J). (gr. 1-4). pap. 8.99 *(978-1-84686-780-4(0))* Barefoot Bks., Inc.
Fogg, K. L. Widow's Revenge: A Novel. 2007. 355p. (J). *(978-1-59811-319-8(4))* Covenant Communications.
Fox Mazer, Norma. Taking Terri Mueller. 2015. (ENG.). 224p. (J). (gr. 5). pap. 12.95 *(978-1-939601-38-4(X))* Ig Publishing, Inc.
Frances, Barbara. Lottie's Adventure: A Kidnapping Unraveled. 2007. 180p. pap. 12.95 *(978-0-615-16787-9(X))* Positive Imaging, LLC.
Fraser, Ivan. Peggy of the Cove: Secrets. 2008. (ENG.). 182p. (J). pap. 15.00 *(978-0-9736872-6-2(6)*, ec4e87eb-e8d2-4197-a60f-1136aac623d9) Nimbus Publishing, Ltd. CAN. Dist: Baker & Taylor Publisher Services (BTPS).
Frederick, Heather Vogel. Once upon a Toad. 2013. (ENG., Illus.). 288p. (J). (gr. 5-9). pap. 7.99 *(978-1-4169-8479-5(8)*, Simon & Schuster Bks. For Young Readers) Simon & Schuster Bks. For Young Readers.
—Once upon a Toad. 2012. (ENG., Illus.). 272p. (J). (gr. 5-9). 16.99 *(978-1-4169-8478-8(X))* Simon & Schuster, Inc.
Frost, Andrew David. The Magician & the Priestess. 2010. 416p. pap. 17.99 *(978-1-4490-7830-0(3))* AuthorHouse.
Frost, Helen. Hidden. 2015. (ENG.). (J). (gr. 5-9). lib. bdg. 17.60 *(978-1-62765-725-9(8))* Perfection Learning Corp.
Funke, Cornelia. Inkdeath (Inkheart Trilogy, Book 3) 2010. (Inkheart Ser.: 3).Tr. of Tintentod. (ENG.). 704p. (J). (gr. 3-8). 12.99 *(978-0-439-86629-3(4)*, Scholastic Paperbacks) Scholastic, Inc.
Furlong, C. T. Killer Strangelets. 2011. (Arctic6 Ser.). 208p. (J). pap. *(978-0-9562315-6-7(X))* Inside Pocket Publishing, Ltd.
Fussell, Sandy. Samurai Kids #4: Monkey Fist. James, Rhian Nest, illus. 2012. (Samurai Kids Ser.: 4). (ENG.). 272p. (J). (gr. 4-7). pap. 6.99 *(978-0-7636-5827-4(8))* Candlewick Pr.
Gaines, Pat. O. O. Octopus: Sheriff of Blue Ribbon Sound. 2008. (Illus.). 24p. (J). lib. bdg. *(978-0-9801376-4-4(0))*; per. *(978-0-9801376-5-1(9))* Dragonfly Publishing, Inc.
Garber, Stephanie. Caraval. l.t. ed. 2017. (Caraval Ser.). (ENG.). 510p. 24.95 *(978-1-4328-4221-5(8))* Cengage Gale.
—Caraval. (ENG.). (YA). 2018. (Caraval Ser.: 1). 448p. pap. 11.99 *(978-1-250-09526-8(3)*, 900160654) 2017. (gr. 8-12). pap. 11.99 *(978-1-250-14149-1(4))* 2017. (Caraval Ser.: 1). 416p. 18.99 *(978-1-250-09525-1(5)*, 900160653) Flatiron Bks.
—Caraval. 2018. (YA). lib. bdg. 22.10 *(978-0-606-41093-9(7))* Turtleback.
Gentry, Brad. The Hollywood Princess. 2009. 40p. pap. 20.99 *(978-1-4490-3545-7(0))* AuthorHouse.
Gibbes, Lesley. Fizz & the Handbag Dognapper. King, Stephen Michael, illus. 2017. (J). (ENG.). 80p. pap. 4.99 *(978-1-61067-615-1(7))*; 67p. *(978-1-61067-642-7(4))* Kane Miller.
Gioseffi, Anthony P. Mainframe. 2007. 144p. per. 11.95 *(978-0-595-44953-8(0))* iUniverse, Inc.
Girdner, Randall P. Mr. Ping's Almanac of the Twisted & Weird presents Boyd Mccloyd & the Perpetual Motion Machine. 2009. 473p. pap. 25.00 *(978-0-615-25755-6(0))* Acclimated Spooks, Light, & Power.
Grainger, A. J. Captive. 2016. (ENG.). 272p. (YA). (gr. 7). pap. 11.99 *(978-1-4814-2904-7(3))* Simon & Schuster Children's Publishing.
Grant, Holly. The League of Beastly Dreadfuls Book 1. (League of Beastly Dreadfuls Ser.: 1). (Illus.). (J). (gr. 3-7). 2016. 336p. 8.99 *(978-0-385-37010-3(5)*, Yearling) 2015. 320p. 16.99 *(978-0-385-37007-3(5)*, Random Hse. Bks. for Young Readers) Random Hse. Children's Bks.
Grisham, John. The Abduction. 2009. (Theodore Boone Ser.: Bk. 2). 9.68 *(978-0-7848-3783-2(X)*, Everbind) Marco Bk. Co.
—The Abduction. 2012. (Theodore Boone Ser.: 2). lib. bdg. 19.65 *(978-0-606-26079-4(X))* Turtleback.
—Theodore Boone: the Abduction, 2 vols. (Theodore Boone Ser.: 2). (ENG.). 256p. (J). (gr. 3-7). 2012. pap. 8.99 *(978-0-14-242137-6(5)*, Puffin Books) 2011. 16.99 *(978-0-525-42557-1(8)*, Dutton Books for Young Readers) Penguin Young Readers Group.
Grove, S. E. The Waning Age. 2019. 352p. (YA). (gr. 9). 18.99 *(978-0-451-47985-3(8)*, Viking Books for Young Readers) Penguin Young Readers Group.
Grover, Lorie Ann. Hold Me Tight. 2007. (ENG.). 352p. (J). (gr. 5-9). pap. 16.95 *(978-1-4169-6753-8(2)*, McElderry, Margaret K. Bks.) McElderry, Margaret K. Bks.
Haddix, Margaret Peterson. Escape from Memory. 2012. (ENG.). 272p. (YA). (gr. 7). pap. 8.99 *(978-1-4424-4602-1(1)*, Simon & Schuster Bks. For Young Readers) Simon & Schuster Bks. For Young Readers.
—Escape from Memory. 2003. (ENG., Illus.). 224p. (YA). (gr. 7). 17.99 *(978-0-689-85421-7(8))* Simon & Schuster, Inc.
—Revealed. 2015. (Missing Ser.: 7). lib. bdg. 19.65 *(978-0-606-37847-5(2))* Turtleback.
Hancocks, Helen. Penguin in Peril. Hancocks, Helen, illus. 2014. (ENG., Illus.). 32p. (J). (gr. -1-2). 18.99 *(978-0-7636-7159-4(2)*, Templar) Candlewick Pr.
Handwerk, Marina. Hey Cool, I've Never Seen a Teacher with His Head Cut off Before! 2007. 284p. per. 11.95 *(978-1-4327-0332-5(3))* Outskirts Pr., Inc.
Hardinge, Frances. Fly Trap. 2012. 592p. (J). (gr. 5). pap. 7.99 *(978-0-06-088046-0(5))* HarperCollins Pubs.
Harrison, Michelle. 13 Curses. 2012. (13 Treasures Trilogy Ser.: 2). (ENG.). 512p. (J). (gr. 5-9). pap. 23.99 *(978-0-316-04149-2(1))* Little, Brown Bks. for Young Readers.
—13 Curses. 2012. (13 Treasures Ser.: 2). (J). lib. bdg. 19.65 *(978-0-606-26160-9(5))* Turtleback.
Hartley, James. Berlina's Quest. Legge, Barbara, ed. Kelsey, Amanda, illus. 2013. 146p. (J). pap. 17.99 *(978-1-61572-948-7(8))* Damnation Bks.
Hautman, Pete. Snatched. 2007. (Bloodwater Mysteries Ser.: 1). 224p. (J). (gr. 5-7). 7.99 *(978-0-14-240795-0(X)*, Puffin Books) Penguin Young Readers Group.
Hawkins, Mia K. The Broken Guild of Twelve Pirates, 1 vol. 2009. 201p. pap. 24.95 *(978-1-61546-333-6(X))* PublishAmerica, Inc.
Henry, April. Count All Her Bones. 2018. (Girl, Stolen Ser.: 2). (ENG.). 256p. (YA). pap. 12.99 *(978-1-250-15874-1(5)*, 900156292) Square Fish.
—The Night She Disappeared. 2013. (ENG.). 256p. (YA). (gr. 7-12). pap. 10.99 *(978-1-250-01674-4(6)*, 900087088) Square Fish.
Hicks, John. Divided World. 2003. 192p. (YA). per. 6.50 *(978-0-9742829-1-6(X))* Quiet Man Publishing.
Higson, Charlie. The Young Bond Series, Book Three: Double or Die, 3. 2011. (Young Bond Ser.: Bk. 3). (ENG.). 400p. (YA). (gr. 6-8). 22.44 *(978-1-4231-1099-6(4))* Hyperion Bks. for Children.
Holland. Little Manuel, the Captive Boy. 2003. 63p. 88.00 *(978-0-7950-5545-4(5))* New Library Press LLC.
Holub, Joan & Williams, Suzanne. Zeus & the Thunderbolt of Doom. Phillips, Craig, illus. 2012. (Heroes in Training Ser.: 1). (ENG.). 112p. (J). (gr. 1-4). 18.99 *(978-1-4424-5787-4(2))*; pap. 6.99 *(978-1-4424-5263-3(3))* Simon & Schuster Children's Publishing. (Aladdin).
Hoover, Krystal Dawn. Tabby Town. 2011. 40p. pap. *(978-1-4269-7276-8(8))* Trafford Publishing (UK) Ltd.
Hopkins, Ellen. The You I've Never Known. (ENG.). (YA). (gr. 9). 2018. 624p. pap. 14.99 *(978-1-4814-4291-6(0))* 2017. (Illus.). 608p. 18.99 *(978-1-4814-4290-9(2))* McElderry, Margaret K. Bks. (McElderry, Margaret K. Bks.).
Hopkins, Howard. The Nightmare Club #3: the Willow Witch. 2008. (ENG.). 104p. pap. 9.98 *(978-0-578-00361-0(9))* Golden Perils Pr.
Houts, Michelle. Winterfrost. 2016. (ENG.). 272p. (J). (gr. 3-7). pap. 8.99 *(978-0-7636-9101-1(1))* Candlewick Pr.
Howard, Jenny. Bittersweet Voyage. 2012. 172p. pap. 12.95 *(978-1-4685-7573-6(2))* AuthorHouse.
Hubbard, Crystal. Alive & Unharmed. 2013. 164p. (J). pap. 12.95 *(978-1-60043-144-9(5))* Parker Publishing Inc.
Hulme-Cross, Benjamin. Viper Attack. 2018. (Mission Alert Ser.). (ENG., Illus.). 72p. (J). (gr. 5-8). pap. 7.99 *(978-1-5415-2635-8(X)*, 37ed1a29-87bb-4c86-8008-c787d7fb4c3f); lib. bdg. 26.65 *(978-1-5415-2582-5(5)*, 20dc948f-9702-402f-9a96-e489206343b6) Lerner Publishing Group. (Darby Creek).
Hunt, Bonnie. The Missing Chimp: A Grayson Twins Adventures, 1 vol. 2009. 100p. pap. 19.95 *(978-1-60813-481-6(4))* America Star Bks.
Hunt, Elizabeth Singer. Secret Agent Jack Stalwart: Book 5: the Secret of the Sacred Temple: Cambodia. 2008. (Secret Agent Jack Stalwart Ser.: 5). (ENG., Illus.). 128p. (J). (gr. 1-4). per. 5.99 *(978-1-60286-003-2(3)*, Da Capo Lifelong) Hachette Bks.
Hunter, C. C. In Another Life: A Novel. 2019. (ENG.). 352p. (YA). 18.99 *(978-1-250-31227-3(2)*, 900198231, Wednesday Bks.) St. Martin's Pr.
Jacques, Brian. The Sable Quean, 21 vols. 2011. (Redwall Ser.: 21). 368p. (J). (gr. 5). 8.99 *(978-0-441-01998-4(6)*, Ace) Penguin Publishing Group.
—The Sable Quean. Elliot, David, illus. 2012. (Redwall Ser.: 21). lib. bdg. 19.65 *(978-0-606-23646-1(5))* Turtleback.
Jakobsen, Lars. The Santa Fe Jail. Jakobsen, Lars, illus. 2012. (Mortensen's Escapades Ser.: 2). (Illus.). 48p. (gr. 6-12). pap. 6.95 *(978-0-8225-9421-5(8)*, Graphic Universe™) Lerner Publishing Group.
Jasper, Elizabeth. The Golden Cuckoo. 2013. 102p. (J). pap. *(978-1-78299-195-3(6))* FeedARead.com.
Jennings, Sharon. Batnapped. 2019. *(978-1-897039-30-4(1))* High Interest Publishing (HIP).
Jones, Chris. Cameron Jack & the Key to the Universe. 2010. (Illus.). 136p. pap. 10.99 *(978-1-4490-6547-8(3))* AuthorHouse.
Jones, Diana Wynne. Castle in the Air. 2008. (World of Howl Ser.: 2). (ENG.). 400p. (J). (gr. 3-7). pap. 9.99 *(978-0-06-147877-2(6)*, Greenwillow Bks.) HarperCollins Pubs.
—Castle in the Air, 7 vols. 2009. (J). 91.75 *(978-1-4361-6121-3(5))*; 94.75 *(978-1-4361-6119-0(3))*; 70.75 *(978-1-4361-6117-6(7))*; 156.75 *(978-1-4361-6116-9(9))*; 73.75 *(978-1-4361-6115-2(0))*; 1.25 *(978-1-4361-6112-1(6))* Recorded Bks., Inc.
Kay, Alan. Breaking the Rules. 2007. (Young Heroes of History Ser.: 7). 149p. (J). pap. 7.95 *(978-1-57249-389-6(5)*, White Mane Kids) White Mane Publishing Co., Inc.
Kehret, Peg. Abduction! 2006. (ENG.). 224p. (J). (gr. 5-18). 8.99 *(978-0-14-240617-5(1)*, Puffin Books) Penguin Young Readers Group.
—Abduction! 2007. 215p. (gr. 3-7). 17.00 *(978-0-7569-8282-9(0))* Perfection Learning Corp.
—Deadly Stranger. 2012. (ENG.). 176p. (J). (gr. 3-7). pap. 9.99 *(978-1-4424-6044-7(X)*, Simon & Schuster/Paula Wiseman Bks.) Simon & Schuster/Paula Wiseman Bks.
—Desert Danger. 2008. (Frightmares Ser.). (ENG.). 128p. (J). (gr. 3-7). pap. 7.99 *(978-1-4169-9111-3(5)*, Simon & Schuster/Paula Wiseman Bks.) Simon & Schuster/Paula Wiseman Bks.
—Stolen Children. 2010. (ENG.). 176p. (J). (gr. 3-7). 7.99 *(978-0-14-241513-9(8)*, Puffin Books) Penguin Young Readers Group.
Kehret, Peg & the Cat, Pete. Spy Cat. 2008. (Pete the Cat Ser.: 2). (ENG.). 192p. (J). (gr. 3-7). 5.99 *(978-0-14-241219-0(8)*, Puffin Books) Penguin Young Readers Group.
—Trapped! 2008. (Pete the Cat Ser.: 3). (ENG.). 192p. (J). (gr. 3-7). 7.99 *(978-0-14-241189-6(2)*, Puffin Books) Penguin Young Readers Group.
Kennedy, A. L. Uncle Shawn & Bill & the Almost Entirely Unplanned Adventure. Correll, Gemma, illus. 2018. (ENG.). 192p. (J). pap. 5.99 *(978-1-61067-740-0(4))* Kane Miller.
Kennedy, Leo B. Devin & the Greedy Ferret. 2013. 86p. (gr. 4-6). pap. 9.99 *(978-1-4497-8429-4(1)*, WestBow Pr.) Author Solutions, LLC.
King, Wesley. The Vindico. (YA). (gr. 7). 2013. 320p. pap. 8.99 *(978-0-14-242656-2(3)*, Speak)1. 2012. (ENG.). 304p. 24.94 *(978-0-399-25654-7(7))* Penguin Young Readers Group.
Korman, Gordon. The Rescue. 3. 2006. (Kidnapped Ser.: 3). (ENG.). 140p. (J). (gr. 4-6). 17.44 *(978-0-439-84779-7(6))* Scholastic, Inc.
Lago-Weed, Melissa. The Hairys: Don't Talk to Strangers. 2004. 33p. pap. 24.95 *(978-1-4137-3223-8(2))* PublishAmerica, Inc.
Lasky, Kathryn. The Quest of the Cubs (Bears of the Ice #1) 2018. (Bears of the Ice Ser.: 1). (ENG.). 240p. (J). (gr. 3-7). pap. 7.99 *(978-0-545-68306-7(8)*, Scholastic Pr.) Scholastic, Inc.
Law, Jerel. Spirit Fighter, 1 vol. 2012. (Son of Angels, Jonah Stone Ser.). (ENG.). 256p. (J). pap. 9.99 *(978-1-4003-1843-8(2)*, Tommy Nelson) Nelson, Thomas Inc.
Leet, Karen. Sarah's Courage: A Kentucky Frontier Kidnapping. Schlessinger, Sarah, illus. 2014. Orig. Title: Sarah's Courage: a Kentucky Frontier Kidnapping. (ENG.). 144p. (gr. 4-7). 29.99 *(978-1-62619-477-9(7)*, History Pr., The) Arcadia Publishing.
Leicht, Martin & Neal, Isla. The World Forgot. 2015. 279p. (YA). pap. *(978-1-4424-2967-3(4)*, Simon & Schuster Bks. For Young Readers) Simon & Schuster Bks. For Young Readers.
Leitich Smith, Greg. Chronal Engine. Henry, Blake, illus. 2013. (ENG.). 192p. (J). (gr. 5-7). pap. 6.99 *(978-0-544-02277-5(7)*, 1528498, Clarion Bks.) HarperCollins Pubs.
Leray, Merrill. The Kidnapping. 2009. 58p. pap. 15.99 *(978-1-4415-4380-6(5))* Xlibris Corp.
Leszczynski, Diana. Fern Verdant & the Silver Rose. 2009. (Playaway Children Ser.). (J). 59.99 *(978-1-4332-7708-5(5))* Findaway World, LLC.
Leveen, Tom. Shackled. 2015. (ENG., Illus.). 224p. (YA). (gr. 9). 17.99 *(978-1-4814-2249-9(9)*, Simon Pulse) Simon Pulse.
Lewis, Gill. Gorilla Dawn. Meyer, Susan, illus. 2018. (ENG.). 448p. (J). (gr. 4-9). pap. 8.99 *(978-1-4814-8658-3(6))* Simon & Schuster Children's Publishing.
Lewis, Micahel G. Battle for the Knotty List, 1 vol. Jaskiel, Stan, illus. 2016. (ENG.). 32p. (J). (gr. k-8). 16.99 *(978-1-4556-2133-0(1)*, Pelican Publishing) Arcadia Publishing.
Lin, Grace. When the Sea Turned to Silver. 2017. (J). lib. bdg. 20.85 *(978-0-606-40629-1(8))* Turtleback.
—When the Sea Turned to Silver (National Book Award Finalist) (ENG.). (J). (gr. 3-7). 2017. 400p. pap. 11.99 *(978-0-316-12594-9(6))* 2016. (Illus.). 384p. 18.99 *(978-0-316-12592-5(X))* Little, Brown Bks. for Young Readers.
Littke, Lael. Searching for Selene. 2003. 203p. (J). pap. 13.95 *(978-1-59038-179-3(3))* Deseret Bk. Co.
Littlewood, Kathryn. Bite-Sized Magic. McGuire, Erin, illus. 2015. (Bliss Bakery Trilogy Ser.: 3). (ENG.). 432p. (J). (gr. 3-7). pap. 7.99 *(978-0-06-208427-9(5)*, Tegen, Katherine Bks) HarperCollins Pubs.
Livingston, Lesley. The Valiant. 2018. (Valiant Ser.: 1). (ENG.). 400p. (YA). (gr. 7). pap. 9.99 *(978-0-448-49379-4(9)*, Razorbill) Penguin Young Readers Group.
Lo, Malinda. Inheritance. 2014. (ENG.). 480p. (YA). (gr. 10-17). pap. 21.99 *(978-0-316-19799-1(8))* Little, Brown Bks. for Young Readers.
Locke, Terry. Spencer Hurley & the Aliens: Book One: the Abduction, Vol. 1. Hucks, Robin, ed. Locke, Terry, illus. 2008. (Spencer Hurley & the Aliens Ser.: 1). (Illus.). 256p. (J). per. 8.99 *(978-0-9786940-1-2(5))* Dream Workshop Publishing Co., LLC, The.
Long, Angela Pulliam. Salvador the Spy in the Case of the Missing Cats. 2008. 32p. pap. 24.95 *(978-1-60672-724-9(9))* America Star Bks.
Lord, Gabrielle. Revenge. 2012. (Illus.). 193p. (J). *(978-1-61067-082-1(5))* Kane Miller.
Lovelady, W. f. The Adventures of Johnny Saturday: Back to the Drawing Board. 2012. 76p. pap. 12.95 *(978-1-4685-5286-7(4))* AuthorHouse.
Low, Dene. The Entomological Tales of Augustus T. Percival. Corace, Jen, illus. 2009. (ENG.). 208p. (J). (gr. 6-8). 18.69 *(978-0-547-15250-9(7))* Houghton Mifflin Harcourt Publishing Co.
Lynn, Jenna. Hoodnapped: Book 3. Cruz, Abigail Dela, illus. 2018. (Robyn Hood Ser.). (ENG.). 48p. (J). (gr. 3-7). lib. bdg. 34.21 *(978-1-5321-3378-7(2)*, 31179, Spellbound) Magic Wagon.
Lynne, Kimberlee, illus. The Frog & the Mouse. 2011. (First Steps in Music Ser.). (ENG.). 32p. (J). (gr. k-2). 17.95 *(978-1-57999-802-8(X))* G I A Pubns., Inc.
MacDonald, George. The Wise Woman. 2009. 128p. 23.95 *(978-1-60664-614-4(1))*; pap. 10.95 *(978-1-60664-352-5(5))* Rodgers, Alan Bks.
Marko, Cyndi. Heroes on the Side. Marko, Cyndi, illus. 2014. (Kung Pow Chicken Ser.: 4). (ENG., Illus.). 80p. (J). (gr. k-2). 15.99 *(978-0-545-61077-3(X))* Scholastic, Inc.
—Heroes on the Side. 2014. (Kung Pow Chicken Ser.: 4). lib. bdg. 14.75 *(978-0-606-36049-4(2))* Turtleback.
—Heroes on the Side: a Branches Book (Kung Pow Chicken #4) Marko, Cyndi, illus. 2014. (Kung Pow Chicken Ser.: 4). (ENG., Illus.). 80p. (J). (gr. k-2). pap. 6.99 *(978-0-545-61074-2(5))* Scholastic, Inc.
Martens, Kara. The Two Missing Kids. 2008. 80p. pap. 11.49 *(978-1-4343-8696-0(1))* AuthorHouse.
Martin, J. Marshall. The Bird. 2008. 88p. pap. 12.50 *(978-0-9801224-1-1(4))* Boys Read Bks.
Massey, David. Taken. 2014. (ENG.). 320p. (YA). E-Book *(978-0-545-66129-4(3))*; (gr. 9). 18.99 *(978-0-545-66128-7(5)*, Chicken Hse., The) Scholastic, Inc.
Mathieu, Jennifer. Afterward. 2017. (YA). lib. bdg. 20.85 *(978-0-606-40590-4(9))* Turtleback.
Mazer, Norma Fox. The Missing Girl. 2010. (ENG.). 304p. (YA). (gr. 8-12). pap. 9.99 *(978-0-06-447365-1(1)*, HarperTeen) HarperCollins Pubs.
Mbalia, Kwame. Rick Riordan Presents Tristan Strong Destroys the World (a Tristan Strong Novel, Book 2) (Tristan Strong Ser.: 2). (J). (gr. 3-7). 2021. 48p. pap. 8.99 *(978-1-368-04240-6(6))* 2020. (Illus.). 12p. 17.99 *(978-1-368-04238-3(4))* Disney Publishing Worldwide. (Riordan, Rick).
McBride, Kristina. The Bakersville Dozen. 2017. (ENG.). 320p. (J). (gr. 8-8). 17.99 *(978-1-5107-0805-1(7)*, Sky Pony Pr.) Skyhorse Publishing Co., Inc.
McCabe, James Dabney, Jr. Planting the Wilderness or, the Pioneer Boys: a Story of Frontier Life. 2007. pap. 27.95 *(978-1-4304-8187-4(0))* Kessinger Publishing, LLC.
McKay, Sharon E. War Brothers: The Graphic Novel. Bell, Jennifer A., illus. 3rd ed. 2013. (ENG.). 208p. (YA). (gr. 9-12). pap. 18.95 *(978-1-55451-488-5(6)*, 9781554514885) Annick Pr., Ltd. CAN. Dist: Publishers Group West (PGW).
McMann, Lisa. Dead to You. 2012. (ENG.). (YA). (gr. 9). 272p. pap. 11.99 *(978-1-4424-0389-5(6))*; 256p. 16.99 *(978-1-4424-0388-8(8))* Simon Pulse. (Simon Pulse).
McNeil, Natalie. Wylli Nilly's Amazing Adventures. 2011. (Illus.). 56p. pap. 20.38 *(978-1-4567-7672-5(X))* AuthorHouse.
McQuestion, Karen. Favorite, 0 vols. unabr. ed. 2011. (ENG.). 172p. (gr. 7-9). pap. 9.95 *(978-1-935597-25-4(6)*, 9781935597254, Skyscape) Amazon Publishing.
Mellon, David. Silent. 2017. (ENG.). 320p. (YA). (gr. 9-12). 17.99 *(978-1-5072-0168-8(0)*, Simon Pulse) Simon Pulse.
Merialdo, Lee K. Kidnapped. 2006. 112p. pap. 10.95 *(978-0-7414-3407-4(5))* Infinity Publishing.
Meyer, L. A. Rapture of the Deep: Being an Account of the Further Adventures of Jacky Faber, Soldier, Sailor, Mermaid, Spy. 2011. (Bloody Jack Adventures Ser.: 7). (ENG.). 464p. (YA). (gr. 9). pap. 9.99 *(978-0-547-55120-3(7)*, 1450433, Clarion Bks.) HarperCollins Pubs.
Miller, Daniel, et al. A Miller Cousin Mystery. 2010. 120p. pap. 49.00 *(978-0-557-57235-9(5))*; pap. 17.80 *(978-0-557-57118-5(9))* Lulu Pr., Inc.
Millman, Selena. More Than a Hero. 2006. 92p. (YA). per. 11.37 *(978-1-4243-2351-7(7))* Independent Publisher Services.
Miranda, Megan. The Safest Lies. 2017. (ENG.). 384p. (YA). (gr. 9). pap. 11.99 *(978-0-553-53754-3(7)*, Ember) Random Hse. Children's Bks.
Mohr, L. C. Krumbuckets. Musheno, Erica, illus. 2007. (ENG.). 144p. (J). (gr. 2-7). 13.95 *(978-0-9769417-6-7(7))* Blooming Tree Pr.
Moldavsky, Goldy. Kill the Boy Band. 2017. lib. bdg. 20.85 *(978-0-606-39701-8(9))* Turtleback.
Monaghan, Annabel. A Girl Named Digit. 2013. (ENG.). 192p. (YA). (gr. 7). pap. 8.99 *(978-0-544-02248-5(3)*, 1528483, Clarion Bks.) HarperCollins Pubs.
Moser, Elise. Lily & Taylor. 2013. (ENG.). 224p. E-Book *(978-1-55498-336-0(3))* Groundwood Bks.
—Lily & Taylor, 1 vol. 2013. (ENG.). 192p. (J). (gr. 9). 16.95 *(978-1-55498-334-6(7))* Groundwood Bks. CAN. Dist: Publishers Group West (PGW).
Mould, Chris. The Great Cheese Robbery. Mould, Chris, illus. 2018. (Pocket Pirates Ser.: 1). (ENG., Illus.). 160p. (J). (gr. 1-4). 17.99 *(978-1-4814-9115-0(6))*; pap. 6.99 *(978-1-4814-9114-3(8))* Simon & Schuster Children's Publishing. (Aladdin).
Mulazzi, Paola, et al. Disney Fairies Graphic Novel #4: Tinker Bell to the Rescue. 2010. (Disney Fairies Ser.: 4). (ENG., Illus.). 80p. (J). (gr. 1-6). 12.99 *(978-1-59707-230-4(3))* Papercutz.
Napoli, Donna Jo. Lights on the Nile. 2013. (ENG.). 288p. (J). (gr. 3-7). 6.99 *(978-0-06-166795-4(1))* HarperCollins Pubs.
—Three Days. 2003. (Illus.). 160p. (J). (gr. 5-18). pap. 5.99 *(978-0-14-250025-5(9)*, Puffin Books) Penguin Young Readers Group.
—Three Days. 2003. 151p. (J). (gr. 5-9). 13.65 *(978-0-7569-6313-2(3))* Perfection Learning Corp.
Neff, Henry H. The Hound of Rowan. 1. Neff, Henry H., illus. 2007. (Tapestry Ser.: Bk. 1). (ENG., Illus.). 432p. (J). (gr. 4-6). lib. bdg. 24.94 *(978-0-375-93894-8(X))* Random House Publishing Group.
—The Hound of Rowan: Book One of the Tapestry. 2008. (Tapestry Ser.: 1). (ENG., Illus.). 448p. (J). (gr. 3-7). 9.99 *(978-0-375-83895-8(3)*, Yearling) Random Hse. Children's Bks.
Nelson, James Gary. Dientecito y la Placa Peligros. Bumstead, Debbie, illus. 2011. 16p. pap. 9.95 *(978-1-61633-132-0(1))* Guardian Angel Publishing, Inc.
—Smileytooth & Bushwack Plaque. Bumstead, Debbie, illus. 2009. 16p. pap. 9.95 *(978-1-61633-009-5(0))* Guardian Angel Publishing, Inc.
Nielsen, Jennifer A. The Traitor's Game (the Traitor's Game, Book One), 1 vol. (Traitor's Game Ser.: 1). (ENG.). 400p. (YA). (gr. 7-7). 2019. pap. 10.99 *(978-1-338-04538-3(5))* 2018. 17.99 *(978-1-338-04537-6(7)*, Scholastic Pr.) Scholastic, Inc.
Nixon, Joan Lowery. The Kidnapping of Christina Lattimore. 2004. (ENG.). 320p. (YA). (gr. 7-12). pap. 8.99 *(978-0-15-205031-3(0)*, 1195194, Clarion Bks.) HarperCollins Pubs.
Nwaubani, Adaobi Tricia & Mazza, Viviana. Buried Beneath the Baobab Tree. 2018. (ENG.). 336p. (YA). (gr. 8). 17.99 *(978-0-06-269672-4(6)*, Tegen, Katherine Bks) HarperCollins Pubs.
Omori, Fujino. Is It Wrong to Try to Pick up Girls in a Dungeon? Familia Chronicle, Vol. 1 (light Novel) Episode Lyu. 2018. (Is It Wrong to Try to Pick up Girls in a Dungeon? Familia Chronicle (light Novel) Ser.: 1). (ENG., Illus.). 224p. (gr. 8-17). pap. 14.00 *(978-0-316-44825-3(7)*, Yen Pr.) Yen Pr. LLC.
Paquette, Jessica E. Sophie the Clown in Crinkle Town. 2013. 258p. (gr. 4-6). 26.95 *(978-1-4759-7322-8(5))*; pap. 16.95 *(978-1-4759-7321-1(7))* iUniverse, Inc.

J
K
L

Parker, Robert B. Chasing the Bear. 2009. (ENG.). 176p. (YA). (gr. 7-12). 22.44 *(978-0-399-24776-7(9))* Penguin Young Readers Group.

—Chasing the Bear: A Young Spenser Novel. 2010. (ENG.). 176p. (YA). (gr. 7-18). 8.99 *(978-0-14-241573-3(1)*, Speak) Penguin Young Readers Group.

Parrish, Emma. Lou. 2010. (ENG.). 106p. pap. 15.95 *(978-1-4452-6573-5(7))* Lulu Pr., Inc.

Patterson, James. The Dangerous Days of Daniel X. 2014. lthr. 79.00 *(978-1-62715-506-9(6))* Leatherbound Bestsellers.

—The Dangerous Days of Daniel X. (Daniel X Ser.: 1). (ENG., (J). (gr. 3-7). 2010. Illus.). 272p. pap. 8.99 *(978-0-316-11970-2(9))* 2009. 288p. mass mkt. 7.99 *(978-0-446-50913-8(2))* 2008. 304p. pap. 19.99 *(978-0-316-03025-0(2))* Little Brown & Co. (Jimmy Patterson).

—The Dangerous Days of Daniel X. 2010. (Daniel X Ser.: 1). (J). lib. bdg. 18.45 *(978-0-606-14720-0(9))* Turtleback.

—Maximum Ride Boxed Set #1. 2010. (ENG.). 1392p. (YA). (gr. 5-17). pap. 32.99 *(978-0-316-12825-4(2)*, Jimmy Patterson) Little Brown & Co.

Paulsen, Gary. Woods Runner. 2011. (ENG.). 176p. (YA). (gr. 7). pap. 9.99 *(978-0-375-85908-3(X)*, Lamb, Wendy Bks.) Random Hse. Children's Bks.

Paulson, Ingrid. Valkyrie Rising. 2012. (ENG.). 352p. (YA). (gr. 8). 17.99 *(978-0-06-202572-2(4)*, HarperTeen) HarperCollins Pubs.

Peters, Tony. Kids on a Case: The Case of the Ten Grand Kidnapping. 2008. 84p. pap. 9.95 *(978-1-60693-173-8(3)*, Eloquent Bks.) Strategic Book Publishing & Rights Agency (SBPRA).

Peterson, Megan Cooley. The Liar's Daughter. 2019. 288p. (YA). (gr. 9). 17.99 *(978-0-8234-4418-2(X))* Holiday Hse., Inc.

Phillips, Grant R. Jay Walker & the Case of the Missing Action Figure. 2004. (J). pap. 10.95 *(978-0-9749608-4-5(5))* Quiet Storm Publishing Group.

Pierce, Tamora. Mastiff: The Legend of Beka Cooper #3. 2012. (Beka Cooper Ser.: 3). (ENG.). 608p. (YA). (gr. 7-11). pap. 11.99 *(978-0-375-83818-7(X)*, Ember) Random Hse. Children's Bks.

Plum, Amy. Until the Beginning. 2016. (After the End Ser.: 2). (ENG.). 352p. (YA). (gr. 8). pap. 9.99 *(978-0-06-222564-1(2)*, HarperTeen) HarperCollins Pubs.

Plum-Ucci, Carol. The Body of Christopher Creed. 2011. 8.98 *(978-0-7848-3578-4(0)*, Everbind) Marco Bk. Co.

Polatin, Daria. Devil in Ohio. 2018. (ENG.). 336p. (YA). pap. 12.99 *(978-1-250-18077-3(5)*, 900170879) Square Fish.

Poole, Richard. Jewel & Thorn. 2007. (Book of Lowmoor Ser.: 1). (ENG., Illus.). 400p. (J). (gr. 7-12). pap. 11.95 *(978-0-689-87290-7(9))* Simon & Schuster, Ltd. GBR. Dist: Simon & Schuster, Inc.

Porter, Kevin Don. Missing. 2013. 166p. pap. 11.99 *(978-0-9857014-7-5(1))* Artists' Orchard, LLC, The.

Portes, Andrea. Liberty: The Spy Who (Kind of) Liked Me. 2017. (ENG.). 400p. (J). *(978-0-06-267332-9(7)*, HarperTeen) HarperCollins Pubs.

Pounder, Sibéal. Bad Mermaids Make Waves. Cockcroft, Jason, illus. 2018. (Bad Mermaids Ser.). (ENG.). 256p. (J). 13.99 *(978-1-68119-792-0(8)*, 900187211, Bloomsbury Children's Bks.) Bloomsbury Publishing USA.

Prasad, Sunayna. Alyssa Mccarthy's Magical Missions: Book 1. 2013. 216p. pap. *(978-1-4602-0701-7(7))* FriesenPress.

Preston, Natasha. The Cellar. 2014. 368p. (YA). (gr. 10-12). pap. 10.99 *(978-1-4926-0097-8(0)*, 9781492600978) Sourcebooks, Inc.

Prophet, John M. Body in the Salt Marsh Boatyard: A Casey Miller Mystery. 2004. 162p. (YA). pap. 13.95 *(978-0-595-30991-7(7)*, Mystery & Suspense Pr.) iUniverse, Inc.

Pullman, Philip. Der goldene Kompass. (GER.). pap. 27.95 *(978-3-453-13744-8(2))* Verlag Wilhelm Heyne DEU. Dist: Distribooks, Inc.

Pyle, Howard. The Story of Jack Ballister's Fortunes: Being the Narrative of the Adventures of a Young Gentleman of Good Family, Who Was Kidnapped in the Year 1719 & Carried to the Plantations of the Continent of Virginia, Where He Fell in with That Famous Pirate Captain Edward Teach, or Blackbeard: of His Escape from the Pirates & the Rescue of a Young Lady from Out Their Hands. unabr. ed. 2012. (Illus.). 436p. 49.99 *(978-1-4622-8858-8(8))* Repressed Publishing LLC.

Raffa, Edwina & Rigsby, Annelle. Kidnapped in Key West. (Florida Historical Fiction for Youth Ser.). (ENG.). (J). (gr. -1-12). 2012. 136p. pap. 9.95 *(978-1-56164-537-4(0))* 2008. (Illus.). 127p. 14.95 *(978-1-56164-413-1(7))* Pineapple Pr., Inc.

Ramage, Rosalyn Rikel. The Windmill. 2013. 182p. (gr. 4-6). pap. 11.66 *(978-1-4907-0909-3(6))* Trafford Publishing.

Rapp, Adam. The Children & the Wolves. 2012. (ENG., Illus.). 160p. (YA). (gr. 9). 16.99 *(978-0-7636-5337-8(3))* Candlewick Pr.

Rautenberg, Karen Rita. Lady Lucy's Gallant Knight. 2007. (ENG.). 156p. (J). (gr. 4-7). per. *(978-1-933255-22-4(6))* DNA Pr.

Regan, Dian Curtis. Space Boy & the Snow Monster. Neubecker, Robert, illus. 2017. (Space Boy Ser.). (ENG.). 32p. (J). (gr. -1-2). 17.95 *(978-1-59078-957-5(1)*, Astra Young Readers) Astra Publishing Hse.

—Space Boy & the Space Pirate. Neubecker, Robert, illus. 2016. (Space Boy Ser.). (ENG.). 40p. (J). (gr. -1-2). 16.95 *(978-1-59078-956-8(3)*, Astra Young Readers) Astra Publishing Hse.

Reiss, Kathryn. A Bundle of Trouble: A Rebecca Mystery. Giovine, Sergio, illus. 2011. (American Girl Mysteries Ser.). (ENG.). 192p. (YA). (gr. 4-6). pap. 21.19 *(978-1-59369-754-9(6))* American Girl Publishing, Inc.

Revealed. 2014. (Missing Ser.: 7). (ENG., Illus.). 448p. (J). (gr. 3-7). 19.99 *(978-1-4169-8986-8(2)*, Simon & Schuster Bks. For Young Readers) Simon & Schuster Bks. For Young Readers.

Rice, Luanne. Pretend She's Here. 2019. (ENG.). 352p. (YA). (gr. 7-7). 18.99 *(978-1-338-29850-5(X)*, Scholastic Pr.) Scholastic, Inc.

Rifkin, L. (Lauren). The Nine Lives of Romeo Crumb: Life Two. 2010. (ENG.). 277p. (J). pap. 8.95 *(978-0-9743221-4-8(8))* Stratford Road Pr., Ltd.

Rivera, Raquel. Orphan Ahwak, 1 vol. 2007. (ENG.). 144p. (J). (gr. 4-7). per. 7.95 *(978-1-55143-653-1(1))* Orca Bk. Pubs. USA.

Roberts, Willo Davis. Baby-Sitting Is a Dangerous Job. 2016. (ENG., Illus.). 224p. (J). (gr. 3-7). pap. 7.99 *(978-1-4814-3704-2(6)*, Aladdin) Simon & Schuster Children's Publishing.

—Baby-Sitting Is a Dangerous Job. 2016. (ENG., Illus.). 224p. (J). (gr. 3-7). 17.99 *(978-1-4814-3705-9(4)*, Simon & Schuster/Paula Wiseman Bks.) Simon & Schuster/Paula Wiseman Bks.

—Hostage. 2016. (ENG., Illus.). 176p. (J). (gr. 3-7). pap. 7.99 *(978-1-4814-5788-0(8)*, Aladdin) Simon & Schuster Children's Publishing.

—Hostage. 2016. (ENG., Illus.). 176p. (J). (gr. 3-7). 17.99 *(978-1-4814-5789-7(6)*, Simon & Schuster/Paula Wiseman Bks.) Simon & Schuster/Paula Wiseman Bks.

—The Kidnappers. 2016. (ENG., Illus.). 208p. (J). (gr. 3-7). pap. 7.99 *(978-1-4814-4904-5(4)*, Aladdin) Simon & Schuster Children's Publishing.

—The One Left Behind. 2007. (ENG., Illus.). 144p. (J). (gr. 3-7). pap. 8.99 *(978-0-689-85083-7(2)*, Aladdin) Simon & Schuster Children's Publishing.

—Scared Stiff. 2016. (ENG., Illus.). 256p. (J). (gr. 3-7). pap. 8.99 *(978-1-4814-4910-6(9)*, Aladdin) Simon & Schuster Children's Publishing.

Robinson, W. Heath. The Adventures of Uncle Lubin. 2013. (Dover Children's Classics Ser.). (ENG., Illus.). 128p. (J). (gr. 6-8). pap. 9.95 *(978-0-486-49821-8(2)*, 498212) Dover Pubns., Inc.

Rocha, K. E. Mission to Moon Farm. 2016. (Illus.). 209p. (J). *(978-0-545-81316-7(6)*, Scholastic Pr.) Scholastic, Inc.

Rodriguez, Angelica. Mia y Primos/Mia & Cousins: Yo grito,corro y grito / I scream, run & Scream. 2009. 24p. pap. 12.49 *(978-1-4389-7095-0(1))* AuthorHouse.

Roscoe, Charlie. The Red Prince. Cole, Tom Clohosy, illus. 2016. (ENG.). 32p. (J). (-k). 16.99 *(978-0-7636-8912-4(2)*, Templar) Candlewick Pr.

Round, J. The Catcher. 2008. (ENG.). 168p. pap. 14.95 *(978-1-4092-0372-8(7))* Lulu Pr., Inc.

Roy, Ron. Capital Mysteries #13: Trapped on the D. C. Train! Bush, Timothy, illus. 2011. (Capital Mysteries Ser.: 13). 96p. (J). (gr. 1-4). 5.99 *(978-0-375-85926-7(8)*, Random Hse. Bks. for Young Readers) Random Hse. Children's Bks.

—A to Z Mysteries Super Edition #11: Grand Canyon Grab. Gurney, John Steven, illus. 2019. (to Z Mysteries Ser.: 11). 144p. (J). (gr. 1-4). 6.99 *(978-0-525-57886-4(2)*, Random Hse. Bks. for Young Readers) Random Hse. Children's Bks.

—A to Z Mysteries Super Edition 3: White House White-Out. Gurney, John Steven, illus. 2008. (to Z Mysteries Ser.: 3). 144p. (J). (gr. 1-4). 6.99 *(978-0-375-84721-9(9)*, Random Hse. Bks. for Young Readers) Random Hse. Children's Bks.

—White House White-Out. Gurney, John, illus. 2008. (A to Z Mysteries Ser.: No. 3). 124p. (gr. 1-4). 15.00 *(978-0-7569-8799-2(7))* Perfection Learning Corp.

Rozen, R. In Trit Fun Di Farkhapte Kinder. Krishevski, E., illus. 2018. (YID.). 58p. (J). *(978-1-68091-243-2(7))* Kinder Shpiel USA, Inc.

Ruby, Laura. Bone Gap. (ENG.). 368p. (YA). (gr. 9). 2016. pap. 9.99 *(978-0-06-231762-9(8))* 2015. 17.99 *(978-0-06-231760-5(1))* HarperCollins Pubs. (Balzer & Bray).

—Bone Gap. 2016. (YA). lib. bdg. 20.85 *(978-0-606-38739-2(0))* Turtleback.

Rylander, Chris. The Legend of Greg. 2018. (Epic Series of Failures Ser.: 1). (ENG.). 352p. (J). (gr. 3-7). 16.99 *(978-1-5247-3972-0(3)*, G.P. Putnam's Sons Books for Young Readers) Penguin Young Readers Group.

Saddleback Educational Publishing Staff, ed. Ransom, 1 vol. 2013. (Heights Ser.). (ENG.). 50p. (gr. 4-8). 9.75 *(978-1-62250-047-5(4))* Saddleback Educational Publishing, Inc.

—Score, 1 vol. unabr. ed. 2011. (Heights Ser.). (ENG.). 50p. (gr. 4-8). 9.75 *(978-1-61651-624-6(0))* Saddleback Educational Publishing, Inc.

—Swamp, 1 vol. unabr. ed. 2011. (Heights Ser.). (ENG.). 50p. (gr. 4-8). 9.75 *(978-1-61651-625-3(9))* Saddleback Educational Publishing, Inc.

Sadler, Karen. Rebellion, 1 vol. 2014. (Tankborn Ser.: 3). (ENG.). 400p. (YA). (gr. 7-12). 19.95 *(978-1-60060-984-8(8)*, leelowtu) Lee & Low Bks., Inc.

Sage, Angie. TodHunter Moon, Book One: PathFinder. Zug, Mark, illus. 2014. (World of Septimus Heap Ser.: 1). (ENG.). 480p. (J). (gr. 3-7). 17.99 *(978-0-06-227245-4(4)*, Tegen, Katherine Bks) HarperCollins Pubs.

Samphire, Patrick. Secrets of the Dragon Tomb. 2017. (J). lib. bdg. 18.40 *(978-0-606-39941-8(0))* Turtleback.

Sanders, Scott Loring. Gray Baby. 2009. (ENG.). 336p. (YA). (gr. 7-18). 17.00 *(978-0-547-07661-4(4)*, 1042029, Clarion Bks.) HarperCollins Pubs.

Scarborough, Sheryl. To Right the Wrongs. 2019. (Erin Blake Ser.: 2). (ENG.). 320p. (YA). pap. 13.99 *(978-0-7653-8194-1(X)*, 900151025, Tor Teen) Doherty, Tom Assocs., LLC.

Schlitz, Laura Amy. Splendors & Glooms. (ENG.). 400p. (J). 2017. (gr. 5-9). pap. 10.99 *(978-0-7636-9449-4(5))* 2012. (Illus.). (gr. 4-7). 17.99 *(978-0-7636-5380-4(2))* Candlewick Pr.

—Splendors & Glooms. 2014. (ENG.). (J). (gr. 4-7). lib. bdg. 18.60 *(978-1-62765-443-2(7))* Perfection Learning Corp.

—Splendors & Glooms. 2014. lib. bdg. 18.40 *(978-0-606-35170-6(1))* Turtleback.

Sclafani, Terry. The Thompson Twins Cruise Adventure. 2007. 84p. per. 10.95 *(978-1-4327-1542-7(9))* Outskirts Pr., Inc.

Scott, Elizabeth. Living Dead Girl. 2009. (ENG.). 176p. (YA). (gr. 10). pap. 11.99 *(978-1-4169-6060-7(0)*, Simon Pulse) Simon Pulse.

Service, Pamela F. Alien Encounter. Gorman, Mike, illus. 2010. (Alien Agent Ser.: 4). (ENG.). 152p. (J). (gr. 4-6). 16.95 *(978-0-8225-8873-3(0)*, 07e31f3f-08b4-4f75-89d0-8685b56dd365, Darby Creek) Lerner Publishing Group.

—Alien Expedition. 2010. pap. 33.92 *(978-0-7613-6958-5(9))* Lerner Publishing Group.

—Escape from Planet Yastol. Gorman, Mike, illus. (Way-Too-Real Aliens Ser.: 1). (ENG.). 112p. (J). (gr. 4-6). 2015. E-Book 53.32 *(978-1-4677-5960-1(0)*, 9781467759601, Lerner Digital)No. 1. 2011. pap. 5.95 *(978-0-7613-7921-8(5)*, Darby Creek) Lerner Publishing Group.

—#4 Alien Encounter. Gorman, Mike, illus. 2011. (Alien Agent Ser.). 152p. (J). pap. 33.92 *(978-0-7613-7608-8(9)*, Darby Creek) Lerner Publishing Group.

Sewell, Helen & Coatsworth, Elizabeth. The White Horse. 2005. (ENG., Illus.). 169p. (J). (gr. 3-4). per. 11.95 *(978-1-883937-86-7(8))* Ignatius Pr.

Shackelford, Mary. Cinnamon's Quest. 2005. 115p. pap. 19.95 *(978-1-4137-6430-7(4))* America Star Bks.

Sheinmel, Courtney. Twinsanity. Bell, Jennifer A., illus. 2017. (Zacktastic Ser.). (ENG.). 272p. (J). (gr. 2-4). 11.99 *(978-1-58536-936-2(5)*, 204319); pap. 6.99 *(978-1-58536-937-9(3)*, 204333) Sleeping Bear Pr.

Shepard, Sara. Follow Me. 2017. (Amateurs Ser.: 2). (ENG.). 272p. (YA). (gr. 9-17). 17.99 *(978-1-4847-4228-0(1))* Little, Brown Bks. for Young Readers.

—Follow Me. 2018. (Amateurs Ser.: 2). (ENG.). 288p. (YA). (gr. 7-17). pap. 9.99 *(978-1-4847-4636-3(8))* Little, Brown Bks. for Young Readers.

—Last Seen. 2012. (Amateurs Ser.: 3). (ENG.). 304p. (YA). (gr. 7-17). 17.99 *(978-1-4847-4229-7(X))* Little, Brown Bks. for Young Readers.

Sherrard, Valerie. Eyes of a Stalker: A Shelby Belgarden Mystery. 2006. (ENG.). 180p. (YA). (gr. 6). pap. 12.99 *(978-1-55002-643-6(7))* Dundurn Pr. CAN. Dist: Publishers Group West (PGW).

Shreve, Susan. The Search for Baby Ruby. 2015. 213p. (J). pap. *(978-0-545-41784-6(8))* Scholastic, Inc.

Skrypuch, Marsha Forchuk. Stolen Girl. 2019. (ENG.). 208p. (J). (gr. 3-7). 17.99 *(978-1-338-23304-9(1)*, Scholastic Pr.) Scholastic, Inc.

Skuse, C. J. Rockoholic. 2012. (YA). *(978-0-545-44251-0(6))* Scholastic, Inc.

Skye, Lucy. The Adventure of Maisie Voyager. 2012. 240p. (J). pap. 17.95 *(978-1-84905-287-0(5)*, 694623) Kingsley, Jessica Pubs. GBR. Dist: Hachette UK Distribution.

Slade, Mark. A Week of Mushrooming Book One. 2013. 88p. pap. 8.00 *(978-1-927558-14-0(X))* Birch Tree Publishing.

Smith, Cynthia Leitich. Feral Pride. (Feral Ser.: 3). 304p. (YA). (gr. 9). 2018. pap. 7.99 *(978-1-5362-0367-7(X))* 2015. (ENG.). 17.99 *(978-0-7636-5911-0(8))* Candlewick Pr.

Smith, Dan. Boy X. 2017. 274p. (J). *(978-1-338-17150-1(X))* Scholastic, Inc.

Smith, Roland. Jack's Run. 2007. (ENG.). 256p. (J). (gr. 5-9). pap. 6.99 *(978-1-4231-0407-0(2))* Hyperion Pr.

Springer, Nancy. The Case of the Gypsy Good-Bye, 6 vols., 6. 2012. (Enola Holmes Mystery Ser.: 6). (ENG.). 176p. (J). (gr. 6-8). 18.69 *(978-0-399-25236-5(3))* Penguin Young Readers Group.

—Enola Holmes: the Case of the Left-Handed Lady: An Enola Holmes Mystery. 2008. (Enola Holmes Mystery Ser.: 2). (ENG.). 256p. (J). (gr. 3-7). 8.99 *(978-0-14-241190-2(6)*, Puffin Books) Penguin Young Readers Group.

Starobinets, Anna. Claws of Rage: A Beastly Crimes Book (#3) Bugaeva, Jane, tr. Muravski, Marie, illus. 2019. (ENG.). 208p. (gr. 2-6). 16.99 *(978-0-486-82952-4(9)*, 829529) Dover Pubns., Inc.

Staunton, Ted. Coda, 1 vol. 2014. (Seven Sequels Ser.: 5). (ENG., Illus.). 224p. (J). (gr. 4-7). pap. 10.95 *(978-1-4598-0549-1(6))* Orca Bk. Pubs. USA.

Stevens, Court. The June Boys, 1 vol. 2020. (ENG., Illus.). (YA). 384p. pap. 12.99 *(978-0-7852-2194-4(8))*; 368p. 18.99 *(978-0-7852-2190-6(5))* Nelson, Thomas Inc.

Stevenson, Robert Louis. Kidnapped. 2020. (ENG.). (J). (gr. 5). 180p. 19.95 *(978-1-64799-263-7(X))*; 178p. pap. 9.95 *(978-1-64799-262-0(1))* Bibliotech Pr.

—Kidnapped. (ENG.). (J). (gr. 5). 2020. 240p. pap. 11.95 *(978-1-714-68474-8(1))* 2019. 224p. 20.99 *(978-0-368-65626-2(8))* 2019. 224p. 23.99 *(978-0-368-65625-5(X))* 2019. 224p. pap. 7.99 *(978-0-368-65627-9(6))* Blurb, Inc.

—Kidnapped. 2018. (ENG., Illus.). 324p. (J). pap. 16.95 *(978-1-377-49570-5(1))* Creative Media Partners, LLC.

—Kidnapped. (ENG.). (J). (gr. 5). 2019. 218p. pap. 24.99 *(978-1-7077-8899-6(5))* 2019. 754p. pap. 43.99 *(978-1-6965-8428-9(0))* 2019. 310p. pap. 13.99 *(978-1-7018-8473-1(9))* 2019. 754p. pap. 43.99 *(978-1-6958-4227-4(8))* 2019. 236p. pap. 14.45 *(978-1-6927-5856-1(X))* 2019. 474p. pap. 26.99 *(978-1-6913-9137-0(9))* 2019. 216p. pap. 15.99 *(978-1-0891-4601-8(9))* 2019. 472p. pap. 26.99 *(978-1-0898-6789-0(1))* 2019. 326p. pap. 12.99 *(978-1-6896-0376-8(3))* 2019. 516p. pap. 32.99 *(978-1-0827-4762-5(9))* 2019. 472p. pap. 31.99 *(978-1-0809-0466-2(2))* 2019. 472p. pap. 32.99 *(978-1-0774-0928-6(1))* 2019. 354p. pap. 19.99 *(978-1-0726-3706-6(5))* 2019. 754p. pap. 43.99 *(978-1-0726-7197-8(2))* 2019. 474p. pap. 31.00 *(978-1-0754-0548-8(3))* 2019. 494p. pap. 26.99 *(978-1-0952-4192-9(3))* 2019. 474p. pap. 26.99 *(978-1-0971-5449-4(1))* 2019. 756p. pap. 43.99 *(978-1-0987-6220-9(7))* 2019. 228p. pap. 13.99 *(978-1-0995-5205-2(2))* 2019. 472p. pap. 26.99 *(978-1-0707-1013-6(X))* 2019. 332p. pap. 18.00 *(978-1-7988-4185-3(1))* 2019. 472p. pap. 30.99 *(978-1-0913-7211-5(X))* 2019. 490p. pap. 29.99 *(978-1-7962-8303-7(7))* 2018. 522p. pap. 31.99 *(978-1-7916-6452-7(0))* 2018. (Illus.). 222p. pap. 13.99 *(978-1-7919-1519-3(1))* Independently Published.

—Kidnapped. 2020. (ENG.). (J). (gr. 5). 190p. 19.95 *(978-1-64439-331-4(X))*; 188p. pap. 10.95 *(978-1-64439-330-7(1))* IndoEuropeanPublishing.com.

—Kidnapped. 2018. (ENG., Illus.). 190p. (J). 19.99 *(978-1-5154-2229-7(1))* Wilder Pubns., Corp.

—Kidnapped & Catriona. 2007. 480p. per. 15.00 *(978-1-84697-033-7(4))* Birlinn, Ltd. GBR. Dist: Casemate Pubs. & Bk. Distributors, LLC.

—Secuestrado. 3rd ed. (Coleccion Clasicos en Accion).Tr. of Kidnapped. (SPA., Illus.). 80p. (YA). (gr. 5-8). 15.95 *(978-84-241-5781-4(8)*, EV1487) Everest Editora ESP. Dist: Lectorum Pubns., Inc.

Stevenson, Robert Louis & Hole, W. B. Kidnapped. 2017. (ENG.). 334p. (J). (gr. 5). pap. *(978-3-7447-6112-3(6))* Creation Pubs.

Stevenson, Robert Louis & Rhead, Louis. Kidnapped. 2020. (ENG., Illus.). 224p. (J). (gr. 5). *(978-1-78943-112-4(3))*; pap. *(978-1-78943-111-7(5))* Benediction Classics.

Stewart, Dianne C. Season of the Cold Moon. 2011. (ENG.). 108p. (J). (gr. 2). pap. 8.95 *(978-0-9831032-0-2(8)*, BeanPole Bks.) OH Industries.

Stewart, E. J. The Wayfaring Dolphin. 2010. 298p. pap. 16.95 *(978-0-557-33701-9(1))* Lulu Pr., Inc.

Stilton, Thea. Thea Stilton & the Secret of the Old Castle. 2012. (Thea Stilton Ser.: 10). lib. bdg. 19.65 *(978-0-606-23930-1(8))* Turtleback.

Stokes, Jonathan W. Addison Cooke & the Treasure of the Incas. 2017. (Addison Cooke Ser.: 1). 352p. (J). (gr. 3-7). 9.99 *(978-0-14-751563-6(7)*, Puffin Books) Penguin Young Readers Group.

Stolarz, Laurie Faria. Jane Anonymous: A Novel. 2020. (ENG.). 320p. (YA). 18.99 *(978-1-250-30370-7(2)*, 900197163, Wednesday Bks.) St. Martin's Pr.

Stone, Sonja. Dark Divide: A Desert Dark Novel. 2018. (Desert Dark Novel Ser.: 2). (ENG.). 384p. (YA). (gr. 7). 18.99 *(978-0-8234-3836-5(8))* Holiday Hse., Inc.

Stork, Francisco X. Disappeared. 2017. (ENG.). 336p. (YA). (gr. 7-7). 17.99 *(978-0-545-94447-2(3)*, Scholastic Pr.) Scholastic, Inc.

Strasser, Todd. Wish You Were Dead. (ENG.). 240p. (gr. 9-12). 2010. (YA). pap. 9.99 *(978-1-60684-138-9(6)*, 83351663-102d-409d-ba04-349ec33baab2) 2009. 16.99 *(978-1-60684-007-8(X))* Lerner Publishing Group. (Carolrhoda Lab™).

Stratton, Allan. Chanda's Wars. 2011. 10.36 *(978-0-7848-3486-2(5)*, Everbind) Marco Bk. Co.

Strickler, Ashley. Once upon A Time. 2007. 212p. pap. 12.95 *(978-1-4327-0207-6(6))* Outskirts Pr., Inc.

Surrisi, C. M. The Maypop Kidnapping: A Quinnie Boyd Mystery. (Quinnie Boyd Mysteries Ser.). (ENG.). 304p. (J). (gr. 4-8). 2018. pap. 9.99 *(978-1-5415-1490-4(4)*, c6bfb82b-5feb-4601-a681-edbe24d09c92) 2016. E-Book 26.65 *(978-1-4677-9560-9(7))* Lerner Publishing Group. (Carolrhoda Bks.).

Sutton, Laurie S. The Draco. Nathan, James, illus. 2017. (Bug Team Alpha Ser.). (ENG.). 112p. (J). (gr. 3-6). lib. bdg. 26.65 *(978-1-4965-5186-3(9)*, 136189, Stone Arch Bks.) Capstone.

—Legend of the Gator Man. Neely, Scott, illus. 2016. (Scooby-Doo Comic Chapter Bks.). (ENG.). 88p. (J). (gr. 3-7). lib. bdg. 27.32 *(978-1-4965-3584-9(7)*, 132730, Stone Arch Bks.) Capstone.

Swindells, Robert. Kidnap at Denton Farm. Hartas, Leo, illus. 2021. (Outfit Ser.). (ENG.). 104p. (J). (gr. 5-8). 26.65 *(978-1-5415-7907-1(0)*, dbbab570-fdfa-415d-9ec9-153c99cd581c); pap. 7.99 *(978-1-5415-8687-1(5)*, 9859d6f1-4ba2-41bc-9c76-3f0e8585dd93) Lerner Publishing Group. (Darby Creek).

Sylvester, Kevin, illus. Neil Flambé & the Aztec Abduction. 2010. (Neil Flambé Capers Ser.: No. 2). 304p. (J). (gr. 4-7). *(978-1-55470-329-6(8))* Me to We.

Tanner, Lian. City of Lies. 2012. (ENG.). 288p. (J). (gr. 4-7). 7.99 *(978-0-375-85979-3(9)*, Yearling) Random Hse. Children's Bks.

Tate, Meredith. The Red Labyrinth. 2019. (ENG., Illus.). 352p. (YA). (gr. 9-12). pap. 14.99 *(978-1-63583-034-7(6)*, 1635830346, Flux) North Star Editions.

Telmosse, Gerard. The Curse of the Sourlands. 2008. 132p. pap. 14.51 *(978-1-4357-0169-4(0))* Lulu Pr., Inc.

Titus, Eve. Basil of Baker Street. Galdone, Paul, illus. 2016. (Great Mouse Detective Ser.: 1). (ENG.). 112p. (J). (gr. 1-4). 16.99 *(978-1-4814-6402-4(7)*, Aladdin) Simon & Schuster Children's Publishing.

Town, Vicky. Mayhem in the Museum. 2013. 74p. pap. 9.99 *(978-1-61720-974-1(0))* Wilder Pubns., Corp.

Tozier, Christopher. Olivia Brophie & the Sky Island. 2014. (ENG.). 304p. (J). (gr. -1-12). pap. 12.95 *(978-1-56164-680-7(6))* Pineapple Pr., Inc.

Trine, Greg. Invasion from Planet Dork. Montijo, Rhode, illus. 2010. (Melvin Beederman, Superhero Ser.: 8). (ENG.). 144p. (J). (gr. 2-7). pap. 11.99 *(978-0-8050-8167-1(4)*, 900040241) Square Fish.

Turner, Henry. Ask the Dark. 2016. (ENG.). 256p. (YA). (gr. 9). pap. 9.99 *(978-0-544-81353-3(7)*, 1641941, Clarion Bks.) HarperCollins Pubs.

Twain, Mark, pseud & Stead, Philip C. The Purloining of Prince Oleomargarine. Stead, Erin, illus. 160p. (J). (gr. 3-7). 2021. pap. 9.99 *(978-0-593-30382-5(2)*, Yearling) 2017. 24.99 *(978-0-553-52322-5(8)*, Doubleday Bks. for Young Readers) Random Hse. Children's Bks.

Van Tol, Alex. Gravity Check, 1 vol. 2011. (Orca Sports Ser.). (ENG.). 176p. (J). (gr. 4-7). pap. 9.95 *(978-1-55469-349-8(7))* Orca Bk. Pubs. USA.

Varley, Dax. The Crow. Proctor, Jon, illus. 2016. (Demon Slayer Ser.). (ENG.). 48p. (J). (gr. 3-7). lib. bdg. 34.21 *(978-1-62402-160-2(3)*, 21567, Spellbound) Magic Wagon.

—Graveyard Dirt. Proctor, Jon, illus. 2016. (Demon Slayer Ser.). (ENG.). 48p. (J). (gr. 3-7). lib. bdg. 34.21 *(978-1-62402-158-9(1)*, 21563, Spellbound) Magic Wagon.

—Hideout. Proctor, Jon, illus. 2016. (Demon Slayer Ser.). (ENG.). 48p. (J). (gr. 3-7). lib. bdg. 34.21 *(978-1-62402-157-2(3)*, 21561, Spellbound) Magic Wagon.

—The Locket. Proctor, Jon, illus. 2016. (Demon Slayer Ser.). (ENG.). 48p. (J). (gr. 3-7). lib. bdg. 34.21 *(978-1-62402-159-6(X)*, 21565, Spellbound) Magic Wagon.

Vaughan, M. M. Six. 2015. (ENG., Illus.). 368p. (J). (gr. 3-7). 16.99 *(978-1-4814-2069-3(0)*, McElderry, Margaret K. Bks.) McElderry, Margaret K. Bks.

Vegas, Peter. Bones of the Sun God. (Pyramid Hunters Ser.: 2). (ENG.). 416p. (J). (gr. 5-9). 2018. pap. 8.99 *(978-1-4814-4583-2(9))* 2017. (Illus.). 17.99 *(978-1-4814-4582-5(0))* Simon & Schuster Children's Publishing. (Aladdin).

Vernon, Ursula. Hamster Princess: Little Red Rodent Hood. 2018. (Hamster Princess Ser.: 6). (Illus.). 224p. (J). (gr. 3-7). 14.99 *(978-0-399-18658-5(1)*, Dial Bks) Penguin Young Readers Group.

Villeneuve, Marie-Paule & Audet, Patrice. Qui a Enleve Polka? 2004. (FRE., Illus.). 122p. (J). 8.95 *(978-2-922565-81-2(5))* Editions de la Paix CAN. Dist: World of Reading, Ltd.
Vincent, Rachel. 99 Lies. 2018. (100 Hours Ser.: 2). (ENG.). 416p. (YA). (gr. 9). 17.99 *(978-0-06-241159-4(4),* Tegen, Katherine Bks) HarperCollins Pubs.
—100 Hours. 2018. (100 Hours Ser.: 1). (ENG.). 384p. (YA). (gr. 9). pap. 9.99 *(978-0-06-241157-0(8),* Tegen, Katherine Bks) HarperCollins Pubs.
Walden, Mark. Dreadnought. (H. I. V. E. Ser.: 4). (ENG.). (J). (gr. 3-7). 2012. 320p. pap. 8.99 *(978-1-4424-1368-9(9))* 2011. 304p. 18.99 *(978-1-4424-2186-8(X))* Simon & Schuster Bks. For Young Readers. (Simon & Schuster Bks. For Young Readers).
Walsh, Laurence & Walsh, Suella. In the Middle of the Night. 2006. (J). pap. *(978-0-88092-473-3(X))* Royal Fireworks Publishing Co.
Wardale, David. Psico. 2013. 302p. (J). pap. *(978-1-78299-172-4(7))* FeedARead.com.
Webb, Holly. Rose & the Lost Princess. 2014. (Rose Ser.: 2). (ENG.). 256p. (J). (gr. 3-6). pap. 10.99 *(978-1-4022-8584-4(1))* Sourcebooks, Inc.
—Rose & the Magician's Mask. 2014. (Rose Ser.: 3). (ENG.). 224p. (J). (gr. 3-6). pap. 10.99 *(978-1-4926-0430-3(5),* 9781492604303) Sourcebooks, Inc.
Weiner, Ellis. The Templeton Twins Have an Idea: Book 1. Holmes, Jeremy, illus. 2013. (Templeton Twins Ser.). (ENG.). 240p. (J). (gr. 3-7). pap. 7.99 *(978-1-4521-2704-0(2))* Chronicle Bks. LLC.
Whitehouse, Howard. The Faceless Fiend: Being the Tale of a Criminal Mastermind, His Masked Minions & a Princess with a Butter Knife, Involving Explosives & a Certain Amount of Pushing & Shoving. Slavin, Bill, illus. 2007. (Mad Misadventures of Emmaline & Rubberbones Ser.). (ENG.). 272p. (J). (gr. 4-7). 7.95 *(978-1-55453-180-6(2))* Kids Can Pr., Ltd. CAN. Dist: Hachette Bk. Group.
—The Island of Mad Scientists: Being an Excursion to the Wilds of Scotland, Involving Many Marvels of Experimental Invention, Pirates, a Heroic Cat, a Mechanical Man & a Monkey. Slavin, Bill, illus. 2008. (Mad Misadventures of Emmaline & Rubberbones Ser.). 264p. (J). (gr. 4-7). pap. 7.95 *(978-1-55453-237-7(X))* Kids Can Pr., Ltd. CAN. Dist: Hachette Bk. Group.
Wicke, Ed. Mattie & the Highwaymen. 2012. 216p. (J). per. 9.99 *(978-0-9677652-1-1(8),* BlacknBlue Pr. UK) Blacknblue Pr.
Widavsky, Rachel. The Secret of Rover. Caparo, Antonio, illus. 2015. (ENG.). 360p. (J). (gr. 4-8). pap. 7.95 *(978-1-4197-1968-4(8),* 681103, Amulet Bks.) Abrams, Inc.
Willey, Margaret. Four Secrets. Hauser, Bill, illus. 2012. (ENG.). 288p. (YA). (gr. 7-12). 17.95 *(978-0-7613-8535-6(5),* 3c7c2fe3-b5be-4d7a-8fa8-fb970186384a, Carolrhoda Lab™) Lerner Publishing Group.
Williams, Mandi Tillotson. The Many Adventures of Mortimer Crump: Mortimer's Sweet Retreat. 2011. 28p. pap. 13.83 *(978-1-4634-2637-8(2))* AuthorHouse.
Wilson, Heather Gemmen. Lydia Barnes & the Escape from Shark Bay. 2008. 160p. (J). 9.99 *(978-0-89827-352-6(8))* Wesleyan Publishing Hse.
Wofford, Delaney. For Courage. 2010. 229p. pap. 17.98 *(978-0-557-17045-6(1))* Lulu Pr., Inc.
Wynne-Jones, Tim. The Ruinous Sweep. 400p. (YA). (gr. 9). 2019. pap. 9.99 *(978-1-5362-0879-5(5))* 2018. (ENG.). 18.99 *(978-0-7636-9745-7(1))* Candlewick Pr.
Yaccarino, Dan. Los Cuatro Vientos. (SPA.). (J). 7.95 *(978-958-04-7606-1(3))* Norma S.A. COL. Dist: Distribuidora Norma, Inc.
Young, Andrea. Finny & the Boy from Horse Mountain. 2013. (ENG.). 320p. (J). (gr. 6-6). 16.95 *(978-1-62087-682-4(5),* 620682, Sky Pony Pr.) Skyhorse Publishing Co., Inc.
Young, Moira. Blood Red Road. (Dust Lands Ser.: 1). (ENG.). (YA). (gr. 9). 2012. 480p. pap. 12.99 *(978-1-4424-2999-4(2))* 2011. (Illus.). 464p. 17.99 *(978-1-4424-2998-7(4))* McElderry, Margaret K. Bks. (McElderry, Margaret K. Bks.).
—Blood Red Road, 9 vols. 2011. (YA). 122.75 *(978-1-4618-0629-5(1));* 1.25 *(978-1-4640-2632-4(7));* 120.75 *(978-1-4618-0630-1(5));* 286.75 *(978-1-4618-0634-9(8));* 120.75 *(978-1-4618-0633-2(X))* Recorded Bks., Inc.
—Rebel Heart. 2012. (Dust Lands Ser.: 2). (ENG., Illus.). 432p. (YA). (gr. 9). 17.99 *(978-1-4424-3000-6(1),* McElderry, Margaret K. Bks.) McElderry, Margaret K. Bks.
4RV Publishing LLC Staff. Case of the Missing Coach. 2007. (Illus.). 144p. (J). per. 18.99 *(978-0-9797513-1-8(4))* 4RV Pub.

KILLING, MERCY

see Euthanasia

KINDERGARTEN

Bailey, Carrie. Simply K: A Developmental Approach to Kindergarten. 2019. (ENG.). 436p. (gr. k). pap. 44.99 *(978-1-68344-171-7(0),* Master Books) New Leaf Publishing Group.
Beck, Isabel L., et al. Trophies Kindergarten: The Party. 2003. (Trophies Ser.). (gr. k-6). 13.80 *(978-0-15-329523-2(6))* Harcourt Schl. Pubs.
Dealey, Erin. K Is for Kindergarten. Cowman, Joseph, illus. 2017. (ENG.). 32p. (J). (gr. -1-1). 16.99 *(978-1-58536-995-9(0),* 204326) Sleeping Bear Pr.
Hoffman, Joan. Kindergarten Basics. 2019. (ENG.). 64p. (J). (gr. k-k). pap., wbk. ed. 4.49 *(978-1-58947-036-1(2),* 05263dbb-7375-435c-b093-3ed5f563d050) School Zone Publishing Co.
—Kindergarten Basics. Boyer, Robin, illus. 2004. (ENG.). 32p. (J). pap. 2.99 *(978-1-58947-436-9(8))* School Zone Publishing Co.
Johnson, Anne, et al. Songbooks - Shukaiaka Shake: Songs for a Young Child's Day, 1 vol. 2011. (Songbooks Ser.). (ENG., Illus.). 64p. (J). pap. 24.95 incl. audio compact disk *(978-1-4081-4657-6(6))* HarperCollins Pubs. Ltd. GBR. Dist: Independent Pubs. Group.
Kannenberg, Stacey. Let's Get Ready for Kindergarten! rev. ed. 2006. (Let's Get Ready Ser.). (Illus.). 30p. (J). (gr. -1-1). per. 19.00 *(978-1-933476-00-1(1))* Cedar Valley Publishing.
Marx, Trish & Senisi, Ellen B. Kindergarten Day USA & China. 2010. (ENG., Illus.). 44p. (J). (gr. 4-6). 22.44 *(978-1-58089-219-3(1))* Charlesbridge Publishing, Inc.
Munamarty, Lasya. Fun Days at School. 2012. 76p. (gr. 1-2). pap. 10.95 *(978-1-4620-8347-3(1))* iUniverse, Inc.
Practice Power School Bus Book: Kindergarten. 2003. 24p. (J). spiral bd. *(978-1-930355-42-2(4))* Bright of America.
Scholastic. My First Learning Library Box Set: Scholastic Early Learners (My First), Set. 2017. (Scholastic Early Learners Ser.). (ENG.). 104p. (J). (gr. -1 — 1). 12.99 *(978-1-338-20243-4(X),* Cartwheel Bks.) Scholastic, Inc.
School Zone Interactive Staff. Kindergarten. 2006. (ENG.). (J). cd-rom 24.99 *(978-1-58947-682-0(4))* School Zone Publishing Co.
School Zone Publishing. Kindergarten. 2003. (Power Packs Ser.). (ENG., Illus.). (J). 24.99 *(978-1-58947-530-4(5))* School Zone Publishing Co.
Troupe, Thomas Kingsley. My First Day at School. Uno, Kat, illus. 2019. (School Rules Ser.). (ENG.). 24p. (J). (gr. k-2). pap. 8.95 *(978-1-5158-4062-6(X),* 140056, Picture Window Bks.) Capstone.

KINDERGARTEN—FICTION

Ali, A. E. Our Favorite Day of the Year. Bell, Raheie Jomepour, illus. 2020. (ENG.). 40p. (J). (gr. -1-3). 17.99 *(978-1-4814-8563-0(6),* Salaam Reads) Simon & Schuster Bks. For Young Readers.
Anderson, Patricia. It's Time for Kindergarten PJ & Parker. 2012. (Illus.). 26p. (J). 19.95 *(978-1-61863-379-8(1))* Bookstand Publishing.
Argueta, Jorge. Moony Luna, 1 vol. Gómez, Elizabeth, illus. 2014.Tr. of Luna, Lunita Lunera. (ENG.). 32p. (J). (gr. 2-4). pap. 11.95 *(978-0-89239-306-0(8),* leelowcbp, Children's Book Press) Lee & Low Bks., Inc.
Barnes, Derrick. The King of Kindergarten. Brantley-Newton, Vanessa, illus. 2019. 32p. (J). (-k). 17.99 *(978-1-5247-4074-0(8),* Nancy Paulsen Books) Penguin Young Readers Group.
—The Queen of Kindergarten. Brantley-Newton, Vanessa, illus. 2022. (ENG.). 32p. (J). (-k). 17.99 *(978-0-593-11142-0(7),* Nancy Paulsen Books) Penguin Young Readers Group.
Bieber, Hartmut. Busy Bear Goes to Kindergarten. 2004. (Illus.). 14p. (J). 5.99 *(978-1-59384-049-5(7))* Parklane Publishing.
Biro, Sharon. Snaggleoopus. 2008. (Illus.). 36p. pap. 24.95 *(978-1-60474-118-6(X))* America Star Bks.
Bowie, C. W. Laboriosos deditos de las Manos. Canetti, Yanitzia, tr. Willingham, Fred, illus. 2004.Tr. of Busy Fingers. 28p. (J). (gr. -1-1). 22.44 *(978-1-58089-043-4(1))* Charlesbridge Publishing, Inc.
Buzzeo, Toni. Adventure Annie Goes to Kindergarten. Wummer, Amy, illus. 2013. 32p. (J). (gr. -1-k). mass mkt. 8.99 *(978-0-14-242695-1(4),* Puffin Books) Penguin Young Readers Group.
Cardoza, Kristina. Pinky Bunny's First Day of Kindergarten. 2011. 16p. pap. 8.75 *(978-1-4634-8753-9(3))* AuthorHouse.
Carlson, Nancy. Henry's 100 Days of Kindergarten. Carlson, Nancy, illus. 2004. (ENG., Illus.). 32p. (J). (gr. -1-1). 18.69 *(978-0-670-05977-5(3),* Viking) Penguin Publishing Group.
—Henry's 100 Days of Kindergarten. 2007. 16.00 *(978-1-4177-5983-5(6))* Turtleback.
—Henry's Amazing Imagination. 2010. (ENG.). 32p. (J). (gr. k-2). 18.69 *(978-0-670-06296-6(0))* Penguin Young Readers Group.
—Henry's Show & Tell. Carlson, Nancy, illus. 2012. (Nancy Carlson Picture Bks). (Illus.). 32p. (J). (gr. k-2). 56.72 *(978-0-7613-9308-5(0),* Carolrhoda Bks.) Lerner Publishing Group.
—Look Out Kindergarten, Here I Come/Preparate, Kindergarten!Alla Voy! Carlson, Nancy, illus. 2004.Tr. of Look Out Kindergarten, Here I Come/Preparate, Kindergarten!Alla Voy! (Illus.). 32p. (J). (gr. -1-k). 17.99 *(978-0-670-03673-8(0),* Viking Books for Young Readers) Penguin Young Readers Group.
Cathcart Jr., George R. Ernie Goes to Kindergarten. 2013. 24p. pap. 24.95 *(978-1-4626-9628-4(7))* America Star Bks.
Cerullo, Claudio V. Isabella Goes to Kindergarden, 1 vol. 2010. 24p. 24.95 *(978-1-4489-2455-4(3))* PublishAmerica, Inc.
Chang, Hae-Kyung. Oh No, School! Bisaillon, Josée, illus. 2014. 32p. (J). *(978-1-4338-1333-7(5),* Magination Pr.) American Psychological Assn.
Cleary, Beverly. Ramona la Chinche. Palacios, Argentina, tr. Darling, Louis, illus. 2006. (Ramona Quimby Spanish Ser.: 2).Tr. of Ramona the Pest. (SPA.). 181p. (J). (gr. 4-7). lib. bdg. 16.00 *(978-0-613-00464-0(7))* Turtleback.
—Ramona la Chinche: Ramona the Pest (Spanish Edition), 1 vol. Rogers, Jacqueline, illus. 2006.Tr. of Ramona the Pest. (SPA.). 192p. (J). (gr. 3-7). pap. 7.99 *(978-0-688-14888-1(3),* MR2295) HarperCollins Español.
—Ramona the Pest. Rogers, Jacqueline, illus. 2020. (Ramona Ser.: 2). (ENG.). 240p. (J). (gr. 3-7). 16.99 *(978-0-688-21721-1(4));* pap. 7.99 *(978-0-380-70954-0(6))* HarperCollins Pubs. (HarperCollins).
—Ramona the Pest. (Ramona Quimby Ser.). (J). (gr. 3-5). Random House Publishing Group.
—Ramona the Pest. (Ramona Quimby Ser.). 192p. (J). (gr. 3-5). pap. 4.99 *(978-0-8072-1438-1(8),* Listening Library) Random Hse. Audio Publishing Group.
Cohen, Jeff. Eva & Sadie & the Best Classroom EVER! Allen, Elanna, illus. 2015. (ENG.). 32p. (J). (gr. -1-3). 17.99 *(978-0-06-224938-8(X),* HarperCollins) HarperCollins Pubs.
Cole, Anjennetta. Cory's Classroom Rules. 2012. 28p. pap. 15.99 *(978-1-4685-3652-2(4))* AuthorHouse.
Davis, Katie. Kindergarten Rocks! A First Day of School Book for Kids. Davis, Katie, illus. 2005. (ENG., Illus.). 32p. (J). (gr. -1-3). 17.99 *(978-0-15-204932-4(0),* 1194894, Clarion Bks.) HarperCollins Pubs.
—Kindergarten Rocks! A Kindergarten Readiness Book for Kids. Davis, Katie, illus. 2008. (ENG., Illus.). 32p. (J). (gr. -1-3). pap. 7.99 *(978-0-15-206468-6(0),* 1199319, Clarion Bks.) HarperCollins Pubs.
dePaola, Tomie. Stagestruck. 2007. (Illus.). 32p. (J). (gr. -1-3). pap. 6.99 *(978-0-14-240899-5(9),* Puffin Books) Penguin Young Readers Group.
—Stagestruck. dePaola, Tomie, illus. 2007. (Illus.). (gr. -1-3). 17.00 *(978-0-7569-8159-4(X))* Perfection Learning Corp.
Dozier, Mike. Zack & the Bean Stalk. 2009. pap. 10.00 *(978-1-61584-582-8(8))* Independent Pub.
Elliott, Laura Malone. Hunter's Best Friend at School. Munsinger, Lynn, illus. 2005. (gr. -1-2). 17.00 *(978-0-7569-5786-5(9))* Perfection Learning Corp.
Friedman, Darlene. Star of the Week: A Story of Love, Adoption, & Brownies with Sprinkles. 2009. (ENG., Illus.). 32p. (J). (gr. k-3). 17.99 *(978-0-06-114136-2(4),* HarperCollins) HarperCollins Pubs.
Ganz-Schmitt, Sue. Planet Kindergarten. Prigmore, Shane, illus. 2016. (ENG.). 36p. (J). (gr. -1-k). 7.99 *(978-1-4521-5644-6(1))* Chronicle Bks. LLC.
—Planet Kindergarten. Prigmore, Shane, illus. 2014. 37.75 *(978-1-4906-3417-3(7));* 1.25 *(978-1-4906-3415-9(0));* 39.75 *(978-1-4906-3418-0(5))* Recorded Bks., Inc.
Hall, Rosemary. The Kids Knee Garden from the Adventures with Lamb E. Boy Series. 2008. (ENG.). 30p. pap. 9.13 *(978-1-4196-8967-3(3))* CreateSpace Independent Publishing Platform.
Hapka, Catherine A., et al. How to Start Kindergarten: A Book for Kindergarteners. Palen, Debbie, illus. 2018. (Step into Reading Ser.). 32p. (J). (gr. -1-1). pap. 5.99 *(978-1-5247-1551-9(4),* Random Hse. Bks. for Young Readers) Random Hse. Children's Bks.
Hays, Anna Jane. Kindergarten Countdown: A Book for Kindergarteners. Davick, Linda, illus. 2013. 24p. (J). (gr. -1-2). 8.99 *(978-0-385-75371-5(3),* Dragonfly Bks.) Random Hse. Children's Bks.
Himle, Lisa. Hands as Warm as Toast. Langton, Bruce, illus. 2006. 32p. (J). (gr. -1-3). 17.95 *(978-1-58726-298-2(3),* Mitten Pr.) Ann Arbor Editions LLC.
Houdek, Andi. Mice in My Tummy. 2006. (J). per. 16.95 *(978-0-9771939-9-8(3),* 012) New World Publishing.
Howard, Kate, illus. On Our Way to First Grade. 2015. 32p. (J). *(978-0-545-82340-1(4))* Scholastic, Inc.
Huxman, K. D. Dragon Talk. 2007. (Illus.). 24p. (J). per. 11.99 *(978-0-9797574-9-5(5))* Dragonfly Publishing, Inc.
Huxman, Karin (K. D.). Dragon Talk. 2006. (Illus.). 24p. (J). lib. bdg. 24.95 *(978-0-9778651-7-8(7))* Dragonfly Publishing, Inc.
Kattan, Peter & Kattan, Nicola. More Kindergarten Sudoku: 4x4 Classic Sudoku Puzzles for Kids. 2008. (ENG.). 48p. pap. 7.50 *(978-0-615-18718-1(8))* Kattan, Peter I.
Klein, Adria F. Max Goes to School. Gallagher-Cole, Mernie, illus. 2007. (Read-It! Readers: the Life of Max Ser.). (ENG.). 24p. (J). (gr. -1-2). per. 3.95 *(978-1-4048-3059-2(6),* 94335, Picture Window Bks.) Capstone.
—Max Va a la Escuela, 1 vol. Lozano, Clara, tr. Gallagher-Cole, Mernie, illus. 2007. (Read-It! Readers en Español: la Vida de Max Ser.). (SPA.). 24p. (J). (gr. -1-3). per. 3.95 *(978-1-4048-3037-0(5),* 94375, Picture Window Bks.) Capstone.
Kramer, Joyce. The Gingerbread Man Goes to Kindergarten. 2012. 71p. (gr. 2-2). 24.99 *(978-1-4797-2374-4(6));* pap. 15.99 *(978-1-4797-2373-7(8))* Xlibris Corp.
Labadie, Sally Zolkosky. The Schoolhouse Mouse. 2013. 32p. pap. *(978-1-4602-3128-9(7))* FriesenPress.
Lee, Quinlan B. Kindergarten, Here We Come! Bermejo, Ana, illus. 2016. 32p. (J). *(978-0-545-94860-9(6))* Scholastic, Inc.
Lloyd, Jennifer. The Best Thing about Kindergarten. Leng, Qin, illus. 2013. (ENG.). 36p. (J). (gr. -1-1). 16.95 *(978-1-897476-82-6(5))* Simply Read Bks. CAN. Dist: Ingram Publisher Services.
Loewen, Nancy. The Last Day of Kindergarten, 0 vols. Yoshikawa, Sachiko, illus. 2012. (ENG.). 32p. (J). (gr. -1-k). 16.99 *(978-0-7614-5807-4(7),* 9780761458074, Two Lions) Amazon Publishing.
MacDowell, Maureen. Tomorrow Is the First Day of School. Hergenrother, Max, illus. 2007. 32p. (J). 15.95 *(978-0-9791463-0-5(5))* Wading River Bks., LLC.
Mackall, Dandi Daley. Natalie: School's First Day of Me, 1 vol. Blakeslee, Lys, illus. 2009. (That's Nat! Ser.: 3). (ENG.). 96p. (J). (gr. 1-4). pap. 4.99 *(978-0-310-71568-9(7))* Zonderkidz.
—Natalie & the Downside-Up Birthday, 1 vol. Blakeslee, Lys, illus. 2009. (That's Nat! Ser.: 4). (ENG.). 96p. (J). (gr. 1-4). pap. 4.99 *(978-0-310-71569-6(5))* Zonderkidz.
Marie, Lynne. Hedgehog Goes to Kindergarten. Kennedy, Anne, illus. 2011. (J). pap. *(978-0-545-29874-2(1))* Scholastic, Inc.
McCourt, Lisa. Ready for Kindergarten, Stinky Face? Moore, Cyd, illus. 2010. (Scholastic Reader: Level 1 Ser.). (ENG.). 32p. (J). (gr. -1-1). 16.19 *(978-0-545-11518-6(3))* Scholastic, Inc.
Mcghee, Alison. Countdown to Kindergarten. Bliss, Harry, illus. pap. 39.95 incl. audio *(978-1-59112-529-5(X));* pap. incl. audio compact disk *(978-1-59112-469-6(7))* Live Oak Media.
McGhee, Alison. Countdown to Kindergarten: A Kindergarten Readiness Book for Kids. Bliss, Harry, illus. 2006. (ENG.). 32p. (J). (gr. -1-3). reprint ed. pap. 8.99 *(978-0-15-205586-8(X),* 1196800, Clarion Bks.) HarperCollins Pubs.
McGinty, Alice B. Eliza's Kindergarten Pet, 0 vols. Speir, Nancy, illus. 2012. (ENG.). 32p. (J). (gr. -1-1). 15.99 *(978-0-7614-5702-2(X),* 9780761457022, Two Lions) Amazon Publishing.
McGowan, Joby. Bossy Bianc. 2011. 20p. pap. 24.95 *(978-1-4626-2908-4(3))* America Star Bks.
McGrail-Gamble, Vicki. Kindergarten Colors. 2010. 28p. 15.99 *(978-1-4520-4681-5(6))* AuthorHouse.
Minuto, Kristin. My First Day of Kindergarten. 2011. 28p. pap. 21.99 *(978-1-4568-6470-5(X))* Xlibris Corp.
The Night Before Kindergarten. 2014. (Night Before Ser.). (ENG.). 32p. (J). (gr. 7-12). 8.24 *(978-1-63245-263-4(4))* Lectorum Pubns., Inc.
Park, Barbara. Junie B. Jones Complete Kindergarten Collection: Books 1-17, 17 vols. Brunkus, Denise, illus. 2014. (Junie B. Jones Ser.). (ENG.). 96p. (gr. 1-4). 84.83 *(978-0-385-37694-5(4),* Random Hse. Bks. for Young Readers) Random Hse. Children's Bks.
—Junie B. Jones Third Boxed Set Ever! Books 9-12, 4 vols., Bks. 9-12. Brunkus, Denise, illus. 2003. (Junie B. Jones Ser.). (ENG.). (J). (gr. 1-4). 19.96 *(978-0-375-82552-1(5),* Random Hse. Bks. for Young Readers) Random Hse. Children's Bks.
Penn, Audrey. Un Beso en Mi Mano (the Kissing Hand) Harper, Ruth, illus. 2006. (ENG.). 32p. (J). (gr. -1-3). 18.99 *(978-1-933718-01-9(3))* Tanglewood Pr.
—The Kissing Hand. Harper, Ruth, illus. 2007. (ENG.). 32p. (J). (gr. -1-3). 28.95 *(978-1-933718-07-1(2))* Tanglewood Pr.
—A Kissing Hand for Chester Raccoon. Gibson, Barbara, illus. 2014. (Kissing Hand Ser.). (ENG.). 14p. (J). (gr. -1-2). bds. 8.99 *(978-1-933718-77-4(3))* Tanglewood Pr.
Penn, Audrey, et al, illus. The Kissing Hand. 2010. 23.05 *(978-0-7569-9299-6(0))* Natl Bk. Network.
Plucker, Sheri. Me, Hailey. Fargo, Todd, illus. 2005. (Turtle Books). 32p. (J). (gr. k-3). pap. 9.95 *(978-0-944727-49-2(2));* lib. bdg. 15.95 *(978-0-944727-50-8(6),* Turtle Bks.) Jason & Nordic Pubs.
Portis, Antoinette. Kindergarten Diary. Portis, Antoinette, illus. 2010. (ENG., Illus.). 32p. (J). (gr. -1-3). 12.99 *(978-0-06-145691-6(8),* HarperCollins) HarperCollins Pubs.
Rabe, Tish. On the First Day of Kindergarten. Hughes, Laura, illus. 2016. (ENG.). 32p. (J). (gr. -1-3). 10.99 *(978-0-06-234834-0(5),* HarperCollins) HarperCollins Pubs.
Rippin, Sally. Billie's Yummy Bakery Adventure. Coburn, Alisa, illus. 2017. (ENG.). 24p. (J). 10.99 *(978-1-61067-554-3(1))* Kane Miller.
Robbins, Jacqui. The New Girl ... & Me. Phelan, Matt, illus. 2006. (ENG.). 32p. (J). (gr. -1-2). 19.99 *(978-0-689-86468-1(X),* Atheneum/Richard Jackson Bks.) Simon & Schuster Children's Publishing.
Rockwell, Anne. Welcome to Kindergarten. Rockwell, Anne, illus. 2004. (ENG., Illus.). 32p. (J). (gr. -1-1). pap. 7.99 *(978-0-8027-7664-8(7),* 900032897, Bloomsbury USA Childrens) Bloomsbury Publishing USA.
Rothenberg, B. Annye. I'm Getting Ready for Kindergarten. Bright, Bonnie04, illus. 2012. 48p. (J). pap. 9.95 *(978-0-9790420-5-8(4))* Perfecting Parenting Pr.
Rowlett, Dana. Treasures from a Kindergarten Room. 2012. 50p. pap. 15.99 *(978-1-4691-9849-1(5))* Xlibris Corp.
Rutland, Mirium. Miss Pistachios Big Day. 2007. (Illus.). 48p. pap. *(978-1-58690-063-2(3))* Mould, Paul Publishing.
Schmitt, H. D. Pee Wee Pickle Goes to Kinder-Garden. Spears, Sheri, illus. 2008. 20p. pap. 24.95 *(978-1-60672-731-7(1))* America Star Bks.
Shakespeare, Nancy. Benjamin the Bear Goes to Kindergarten. Clouette, Katie, illus. 2013. (Benjamin the Bear Ser.). (ENG.). (J). (gr. -1-k). 14.95 *(978-1-62086-320-6(0))* Amplify Publishing Group.
Slate, Joseph. Miss Bindergarten Celebrates the Last Day of Kindergarten. Wolff, Ashley, illus. 2008. 40p. (J). (gr. -1-k). pap. 8.99 *(978-0-14-241060-8(8),* Puffin Books) Penguin Young Readers Group.
—Miss Bindergarten Has a Wild Day in Kindergarten. Wolff, Ashley, illus. 2006. 40p. (J). (gr. -1-k). reprint ed. pap. 8.99 *(978-0-14-240709-7(7),* Puffin Books) Penguin Young Readers Group.
—Miss Bindergarten Stays Home from Kindergarten. Wolff, Ashley, illus. 2004. 40p. (J). (gr. -1-k). reprint ed. pap. 8.99 *(978-0-14-230127-2(2),* Puffin Books) Penguin Young Readers Group.
—Miss Bindergarten Takes a Field Trip with Kindergarten. Wolff, Ashley, illus. 2004. 40p. (J). (gr. -1-k). pap. 8.99 *(978-0-14-240139-2(0),* Puffin Books) Penguin Young Readers Group.
Smith, Jane. It's the First Day of Kindergarten, Chloe Zoe! Smith, Jane, illus. 2016. (Chloe Zoe Ser.). (ENG., Illus.). 32p. (J). (gr. -1-3). 12.99 *(978-0-8075-2458-9(1),* 807524581) Whitman, Albert & Co.
St. Mark Kindergarten. Kindergarten Goes to Outer Space for the Day. 2009. 28p. pap. 12.49 *(978-1-4490-0587-0(X))* AuthorHouse.
Steinberg, D. J. Kindergarten, Here I Come! Chambers, Mark, illus. 2012. (Here I Come! Ser.). 32p. (J). (gr. -1-k). pap. 5.99 *(978-0-448-45624-9(9),* Grosset & Dunlap) Penguin Young Readers Group.
Sturges, Philemon. I Love School! Halpern, Shari, illus. 2014. 32p. pap. 7.00 *(978-1-61003-329-9(9))* Center for the Collaborative Classroom.
—I Love School! Halpern, Shari, illus. 2004. 32p. (J). (gr. -1-1). lib. bdg. 14.89 *(978-0-06-009285-6(8))* HarperCollins Pubs.
Underwood, Deborah. Super Saurus Saves Kindergarten. Young, Ned, illus. 2017. (ENG.). 40p. (J). (gr. -1-k). 16.99 *(978-1-4231-7568-1(9))* Little, Brown Bks. for Young Readers.
Urdahl, Catherine. Polka-Dot Fixes Kindergarten. Kemble, Mai S., illus. 2011. 32p. (J). (gr. -1-3). 16.95 *(978-1-57091-737-0(X));* pap. 7.95 *(978-1-57091-738-7(8))* Charlesbridge Publishing, Inc.
VanDenhoven, Godelieve. Louis in Kindergarten. 2009. 40p. pap. 14.50 *(978-1-60693-752-5(9),* Eloquent Bks.) Strategic Book Publishing & Rights Agency (SBPRA).
Vernick, Audrey. Is Your Buffalo Ready for Kindergarten? Jennewein, Daniel, illus. 2010. (ENG.). 32p. (J). (gr. -1-3). 16.99 *(978-0-06-176275-8(X),* Balzer & Bray) HarperCollins Pubs.
Wells, Rosemary. Kindergators: Miracle Melts Down. 2012. (ENG., Illus.). 40p. (J). (gr. -1-3). 14.99 *(978-0-06-192115-5(7),* Tegen, Katherine Bks) HarperCollins Pubs.
—Kindergators: Hands off, Harry! Wells, Rosemary, illus. 2011. (ENG., Illus.). 40p. (J). (gr. -1-1). 16.99 *(978-0-06-192112-4(2),* Tegen, Katherine Bks) HarperCollins Pubs.
Wing, Natasha. The Night Before Kindergarten. Durrell, Julie, illus. 2014. (Night Before Ser.). 32p. (J). (gr. -1-k). 12.99 *(978-0-448-48255-2(X),* Grosset & Dunlap) Penguin Young Readers Group.
Winget, Susan. Tucker's Four-Carrot School Day. Winget, Susan, illus. 2005. (ENG., Illus.). 40p. (J). (gr. -1-k). 12.99 *(978-0-06-054642-7(5))* HarperCollins Pubs.
Wolfgang, Jane. Art Today. 2013. (ENG., Illus.). 32p. (J). 14.95 *(978-1-56290-706-8(9))* Crystal Productions.
Yum, Hyewon. Mom, It's My First Day of Kindergarten!, 1 vol. Yum, Hyewon, illus. 2012. (ENG., Illus.). 40p. (J). (gr. -1-2). 19.99 *(978-0-374-35004-8(3),* 900077454, Farrar, Straus & Giroux (BYR)) Farrar, Straus & Giroux.

KINDNESS—FICTION

Alexander, Brooke. Little Mia's Big Heart. 2013. 72p. pap. *(978-1-4602-1670-5(9))* FriesenPress.
Allison, Teresa J. Bobble Stories: The Humbobble's Lost Hum. Allison, Charles T., illus. 2013. 48p. pap. 12.99 *(978-0-9887612-1-6(1))* Tawnsy Publishing.
Allred, Chris Ross. Sir E. Bobbo! 2004. 21p. pap. 24.95 *(978-1-4137-2785-2(9))* PublishAmerica, Inc.

JKL

Bakker, Merel. Maks & Mila on a Special Journey. Mini Pois Etc, illus. 2013. 54p. (978-2-9700865-0-5(6)) Mila Publishing, Merel Bakker.

Banta, Sandra F. Fancy the Beautiful Little Dragon: Book Number Two Little One's Series. Hecker, Vera, illus. l.t. ed. 2006. 45p. per. 11.99 (978-1-59879-157-0(5)) Lifevest Publishing, Inc.

Barnett, Brandi. Glamour. 2008. 231p. 19.95 (978-1-930709-68-3(4)) HAWK Publishing Group.

Barnhouse Ms Ncc, Natalie. Shimmy Saves the Day: A Tale about Embracing Your Differences. 2012. 28p. pap. 19.99 (978-1-4772-9933-3(5)) AuthorHouse.

Berenstain, Jan, et al. Kindness Counts, 1 vol. 2010. (Berenstain Bears/Living Lights: a Faith Story Ser.). (ENG., Illus.). 32p. (J). (gr. -1-2). pap. 4.99 (978-0-310-71257-2(2)) Zonderkidz.

Beverly-Barrier, Essie. Ouse the Mouse. Allen, Joshua, illus. 2009. 20p. pap. 12.99 (978-1-4389-4518-7(3)) AuthorHouse.

Bongiovanni, Debbie. Kindness Pays Off, 1 vol. 2010. 58p. pap. 16.95 (978-1-4489-6320-1(6)) America Star Bks.

Brightwood, Laura, illus. Little Freddie & His Whistle. Brightwood, Laura, . 2007. (J). DVD (978-1-934409-01-5(4)) 3-C Institute for Social Development.

Brosgol, Vera. The Little Guys. 2019. (ENG., Illus.). 40p. (J). 17.99 (978-1-62672-442-6(3), 900157395) Roaring Brook Pr.

Brown, Shirley B. Li Pan & the Dragon. 2016. (ENG., illus.). 36p. (J). 23.00 (978-1-4809-1251-9(4)) Dorrance Publishing Co., Inc.

Capozzi, Suzy. I Am Kind: A Positive Power Story. Unten, Eren & Unten, Eren, illus. 2017. (Rodale Kids Curious Readers/Level 2 Ser.: 2). 32p. (J). (gr. -1-1). pap. 4.99 (978-1-62336-878-4(2), 9781623368784, Rodale Kids) Random Hse. Children's Bks.

Castle, Jennifer. Together at Midnight. 2018. (ENG.). 352p. (YA). (gr. 9). 17.99 (978-0-06-225051-3(5), HarperTeen) HarperCollins Pubs.

Cerullo, Claudio V. A Thankful Day. Avila, Jesus Villicana, illus. 2008. 25p. pap. 24.95 (978-1-60672-599-3(8)) America Star Bks.

Chrisagis, Shawn & Chrisagis, Brian. Prejudice in Mandi's Garden: Seeds of Kindness. 2006. 24p. (J). pap. 2.99 (978-1-59958-009-8(8)) Journey Stone Creations, LLC.

Clark, Janice E. Roscoe Is a RAKster: You Can Be One Too. 2010. 24p. pap. 12.99 (978-1-4520-9235-5(4)) AuthorHouse.

Corderoy, Tracey. It's Only One! Neal, Tony, illus. 2020. (ENG.). 32p. (J). (gr. -1-2). 17.99 (978-1-68010-227-7(3)) Tiger Tales.

Costello, Judi. Gertrude & the Creature. Bouthyette, Valerie, illus. 2008. 28p. pap. 24.95 (978-1-60672-737-9(0)) America Star Bks.

Cowen-Fletcher, Jane. Baby Be Kind. Cowen-Fletcher, Jane, illus. 2012. (ENG., Illus.). 18p. (J). (gr. k— 1). bds. 7.99 (978-0-7636-5647-8(X)) Candlewick Pr.

Cummins, Maria S. The Lamplighter. 2011. 308p. pap. 16.99 (978-1-61203-228-3(1)) Bottom of the Hill Publishing.

Cuyler, Margery. Kindness Is Cooler, Mrs. Ruler. Yoshikawa, Sachiko, illus. 2007. (ENG.). 48p. (J). (gr. k-5). 19.99 (978-0-689-87344-7(1), Simon & Schuster Bks. For Young Readers) Simon & Schuster Bks. For Young Readers.

Dahl, Michael. Be a Star, Wonder Woman! Lozano, Omar, illus. 2017. (DC Super Heroes Ser.). (ENG.). 32p. (J). (gr. -1-2). 15.95 (978-1-62370-875-7(3), 135196, Stone Arch Bks.) Capstone.

Dharma Publishing Staff. A Wise Ape Teaches Kindness: A Story about the Power of Positive Actions. 2nd ed. 2013. (Jataka Tales Ser.). (Illus.). 36p. (J). (gr. -1-7). pap. 8.95 (978-0-89800-519-6(1)) Dharma Publishing.

Ding, Sean. Monkey Ming & the Dream Team. 2013. 34p. pap. (978-981-07-0631-9(6)) Lukano Publishing Pte, Ltd.

—Zediogram. 2013. 118p. pap. (978-981-07-5534-8(1)) Lukano Publishing Pte, Ltd.

Domogala, Sophia Z. Buzzin' with Kindness. 2012. 24p. pap. 15.99 (978-1-4797-5023-8(9)) Xlibris Corp.

Dudley, Rebecca. Hank Finds an Egg. Dudley, Rebecca, photos by. 2013. (ENG., Illus.). 40p. (J). 16.99 (978-1-4413-1158-0(0), 302680cb-33e6-46cb-8a69-8d52946a6a7b) Peter Pauper Pr. Inc.

Early, Kelly. Something for Nothing. Sherman, Shandel, illus. l.t. ed. 2007. 13p. (J). per. 8.95 (978-1-59879-100-6(1)); (gr. -1-3). 14.95 (978-1-59879-131-0(1)) Lifevest Publishing, Inc.

Easton, Tom. Pirates Can Be Kind, 1 vol., 1. 2015. (Pirate Pals Ser.). (ENG.). 32p. (J). (gr. 1-2). pap. 11.00 (978-1-5081-9145-2(X), 5cbf1da5-5682-4587-b537-6466058a22b7, Windmill Bks.) Rosen Publishing Group, Inc., The.

Edwards, M. J. Dontayan. 2008. 62p. pap. 19.95 (978-1-60610-026-4(2)) America Star Bks.

Elk, Ronit. A Surprise at Dancing Fields. 2009. 76p. pap. 10.49 (978-1-4490-2064-4(X)) AuthorHouse.

Fields, Terri. One Good Deed. Melmon, Deborah, illus. 2015. (ENG.). 24p. (J). (gr. -1-3). pap. 7.99 (978-1-4677-3479-0(9), 426fe59e-11b7-4c68-b6d5-5def82f3b7cc, Kar-Ben Publishing) Lerner Publishing Group.

Freeman, Don. Fly High, Fly Low. Freeman, Don, illus. 2007. (Illus.). 56p. (J). (gr. -1-3). 18.00 (978-0-7569-8001-6(1)) Perfection Learning Corp.

—Fly High, Fly Low (50th Anniversary Ed.) 50th anniv. ed. 2007. (Illus.). 64p. (J). (gr. -1-k). 8.99 (978-0-14-240817-9(4), Puffin Books) Penguin Young Readers Group.

Friend, R. R. Friend - Hats off to Heroes. 2005. (Down on Friendly Acres Ser.: 3). (J). lib. bdg. (978-0-9743627-5-5(1)); (Illus.). 90p. per. (978-0-9743627-2-4(7)) Sunflower Seeds Pr.

Gales, Rick. Granny Puckerlips: Keepin' it Real with Kindness & Respect. 2013. 108p. (gr. 9-12). pap. 11.95 (978-1-4908-0437-8(4), WestBow Pr.) Author Solutions, LLC.

Galvin, Laura Gates & Studio Mouse Editorial. Cinderella & Belle: Kindness Counts. Williams, Tracee, ed. 2008. (ENG., Illus.). 24p. (J). (gr. -1). 4.99 (978-1-59069-652-1(2)) Studio Mouse LLC.

Gates, Pat. The Apple Tree's Secret, 1 vol. Hosselkus, Devin, illus. 2009. 47p. pap. 24.95 (978-1-60836-637-8(5)) America Star Bks.

Gault, Linda Fulford. The Chosen Tree. 2011. 28p. pap. 12.95 (978-1-4567-1561-8(5)) AuthorHouse.

Gifford, Kathie Lee. The Gift That I Can Give, 1 vol. Seal, Julia, illus. 2018. (ENG.). 32p. (J). 17.99 (978-1-4002-0924-8(2), Tommy Nelson) Nelson, Thomas Inc.

Gillen, Lynea. Good People Everywhere. Swarner, Kristina, illus. 2012. (ENG.). 32p. (J). (gr. -1-2). 15.95 (978-0-9799289-8-7(2)) Three Pebble Pr., LLC.

Goetz, Bracha. It Only Takes a Minute. Bolton, Bill, illus. 2017. (ENG.). 22p. (J). 11.95 (978-1-945560-02-6(9)) Hachai Publishing.

Gould, M&R. What Would Jesus Do? Purity of Intention. 2008. 35p. pap. 24.95 (978-1-60672-675-4(7)) America Star Bks.

Graham, Judith A. The Didley-Doo's, 1 vol. 2009. 36p. pap. 24.95 (978-1-60836-035-2(0)) America Star Bks.

Hall, S.C. Turns of Fortune & Other Tales. 2007. (ENG.). 116p. per. (978-1-4065-1586-2(8)) Dodo Pr.

Hansen, Kate. Spike the Sewer Cat. Illustrations byVoigt, Karen S., illus. 2008. 27p. pap. 24.95 (978-1-60474-094-3(9)) America Star Bks.

Harbo, Christopher. The Flash Is Caring. Frampton, Otis, illus. 2018. (DC Super Heroes Character Education Ser.). (ENG.). 24p. (J). (gr. k-2). pap. 4.95 (978-1-62370-955-6(5), 137173, Stone Arch Bks.) Capstone.

Harkrader, Lisa. No Place Like Space (Book 5) Kindness. Warrick, Jessica, illus. 2017. (How to Be an Earthling (r) Ser.: 5). (ENG.). 64p. (J). (gr. 1-3). E-Book 34.65 (978-1-57565-851-3(8)) Astra Publishing Hse.

Harpan, Gaile. The Ballad of Calvin the Cat. Reddy, Sneha, illus. 2008. 24p. pap. 12.95 (978-0-9817572-6-1(X)) Peppertree Pr., The.

Harris, Dee. The Croaker Sack Bunny. Bohart, Lisa, illus. 2012. 24p. pap. 12.95 (978-1-61493-043-3(0)) Peppertree Pr., The.

Harris, Patrice. Grandma Asks: Were You Good at School Today? Harrison, Nicholas, illus. 2013. 26p. pap. 10.00 (978-0-9892358-5-3(8)) CLF Publishing.

Hart, Caryl. Together We Can! A Heart-Warming Ode to Friendship, Compassion, & Kindness. Pye, Ali, illus. 2019. (ENG.). 32p. (J). (gr. -1-2). 14.99 (978-1-4380-5076-8(3)) Sourcebooks, Inc.

Hayes, Sean & Icenogle, Scott. Plum. Thompson, Robin, illus. 2018. (ENG.). 48p. (J). (gr. -1-3). 17.99 (978-1-5344-0404-5(X), Simon & Schuster Bks. For Young Readers) Simon & Schuster Bks. For Young Readers.

Hendricks, Brenda K. What's Better Than That, Seren Dippity? Hendricks, Brenda K., illus. 2013. (Illus.). 32p. pap. 9.99 (978-0-9826582-4-6(9)) Two Small Fish Pubns.

Henn, Sophy. Pass It On. Henn, Sophy, illus. 2017. (ENG., Illus.). 32p. (J). (gr. -1-2). 18.99 (978-0-399-54775-1(4), Philomel Bks.) Penguin Young Readers Group.

Hill, Meggan. Nico & Lola: Kindness shared between a boy & a dog. 2009. 32p. (J). (978-0-615-23040-5(7)) Genuine Prints, LLC.

Hinkel, Patricia. Frog in My Bucket. 2012. 16p. pap. 15.99 (978-1-4772-4815-7(3)) AuthorHouse.

Hische, Jessica. Tomorrow I'll Be Kind. Hische, Jessica, illus. 2020. (ENG., Illus.). (J). (gr. -1-2). 32p. bds. 9.99 (978-1-5247-8705-9(1)); 40p. 17.99 (978-1-5247-8704-2(3)) Penguin Young Readers Group. (Penguin Workshop).

Holling, Prudence. Grace Has a Secret. 2013. 32p. pap. 16.95 (978-1-4525-7145-4(7), Balboa Pr.) Author Solutions, LLC.

Hollis, Nicole Phillips. My Neighborhood Super Kids. 2012. 44p. pap. 21.99 (978-1-4685-6169-2(3)) AuthorHouse.

Howell, Trisha Adelena. The Adventures of Melon & Turnip. Lopez, Paul, illus. 2004. 32p. 15.95 (978-1-931210-04-1(7)) Howell Canyon Pr.

Irvin, Vanessa. Jack's Perfect World. 2011. 48p. pap. 31.99 (978-1-4568-5502-4(6)) Xlibris Corp.

John, Jory. The Cool Bean. Oswald, Pete, illus. 2019. (Food Group Ser.). (ENG.). 40p. (J). (gr. -1-3). 18.99 (978-0-06-295452-7(0), HarperCollins) HarperCollins Pubs.

Jones, Julie. The Problem at Pepperpine Zoo. Jones, Julie., illus. l.t. ed. 2004. (Illus.). 24p. (J). pap. 7.95 (978-0-9745553-0-0(4)) Greenwood Street Publishing. GSP.

Jorden, Edwin W. Cookie Paws/Spreadin' the Sweetness. Waywell, Valerie J., illus. 2008. 32p. (J). 12.95 (978-0-9793483-1-0(5)) Gilded Dog Enterprises LLC.

Karol, Leslee. Sylvie the Littlest Guardian Angel: Cassie Makes a Friend. 2013. 48p. pap. 21.99 (978-1-4817-0864-7(3)) AuthorHouse.

Kaye, Christian Thomas. Rachel the Homely Rabbit: A Story about Kindness. Albright, Audrey, illus. 2011. 30p. pap. 9.95 (978-1-60844-763-3(4)) Dog Ear Publishing, LLC.

Kerascoët & Kerascoët. I Walk with Vanessa: A Picture Book Story about a Simple Act of Kindness. 2018. (Illus.). 40p. (J). (gr. -1-3). 17.99 (978-1-5247-6955-0(X)) Random Hse. Children's Bks.

Kerwin, Betsy. The Adventures of Floret the Woodland Fairy: The Adventures Begin. 2008. 44p. pap. 18.49 (978-1-4343-9426-2(3)) AuthorHouse.

Kiffel-Alcheh, Jamie. Kol Hakavod: Way to Go! Mercer, Sarah-Jayne, illus. 2019. (ENG.). 24p. (J). (gr. -1-1). 12.99 (978-1-5415-2211-4(7), b84a0d64-9428-41c8-bd4e-62d67e465030); pap. 7.99 (978-1-5415-3835-1(8), 7e7eff52-94d5-4a87-97c2-47a1b22118b3) Lerner Publishing Group. (Kar-Ben Publishing).

Kim, Cecil. Nicknames. Han, SooJin, illus. 2014. (MySELF Bookshelf Ser.). (ENG.). 32p. (J). (gr. k-2). pap. 11.94 (978-1-60357-699-4(1)); lib. bdg. 25.27 (978-1-59953-664-4(1)) Norwood Hse. Pr.

Kretzer, Joyce B. Shane & the Jackadoo: A Butcher Hollow Fantasy. 2008. 24p. pap. 11.49 (978-1-4389-1894-5(1)) AuthorHouse.

Laconi, Kristin. Karma the Kangaroo Takes the Court. 2010. 24p. pap. 12.99 (978-1-4490-3227-2(3)) AuthorHouse.

Lampson, Rosalie. Give Mom a Minute. 2009. 32p. pap. 13.99 (978-1-4490-1407-0(0)) AuthorHouse.

Lang, Andrew. The Queen & the Mouse: A Story about Friendship. Lohmann, Renate, illus. 2006. (J). (978-1-59939-081-9(7), Reader's Digest Young Families, Inc.) Studio Fun International.

Lasser, Jon & Foster-Lasser, Sage. Grow Kind. 2020. (Illus.). 32p. (J). (978-1-4338-3050-1(7), Magination Pr.) American Psychological Assn.

Logan, Laura. Little Butterfly. Logan, Laura, illus. 2016. (ENG., Illus.). 32p. (J). (gr. -1-3). 14.99 (978-0-06-228126-5(7), Balzer & Bray) HarperCollins Pubs.

Lord, Janet. Albert the Fix-It Man, 1 vol. Paschkis, Julie, illus. 2015. 32p. (J). (gr. -1-3). pap. 7.95 (978-1-56145-830-1(9)) Peachtree Publishing Co. Inc.

Love, Katie. Fruit to Live By..., 1 vol. 2009. 62p. pap. 16.95 (978-1-60836-122-9(5)) PublishAmerica, Inc.

MacDonald, George. A Rough Shaking. 2017. (ENG., Illus.). (J). pap. 16.95 (978-1-374-88365-9(4)) Capital Communications, Inc.

Madden, Michelle. The Butterfly Garden. 2008. 24p. pap. 24.95 (978-1-60813-375-8(3)) America Star Bks.

Markarian, Margie. The Princess & the Cafe on the Moat. Douglass, Chloe, illus. 2018. (ENG.). 32p. (J). (gr. k-3). 16.99 (978-1-58536-397-9(5), 204402) Sleeping Bear Pr.

Mayer, Mercer. Little Critter: Just a Teacher's Pet. Mayer, Mercer, illus. 2015. (My First I Can Read Ser.). (ENG., Illus.). 32p. (J). (gr. -1-3). pap. 4.99 (978-0-06-147819-2(9), HarperCollins) HarperCollins Pubs.

Mazzafro, Howard. No Room for George. 2011. (Illus.). 24p. (gr. -1). pap. 14.93 (978-1-4269-6782-5(9)) Trafford Publishing.

McBay, Bruce. Angels Inc, 1 vol. LaFave, Kim, illus. 2008. (ENG.). 71p. (J). (gr. 1-3). pap. 7.95 (978-1-896580-30-2(0)) Tradewind Bks. CAN. Dist: Orca Bk. Pubs. USA.

McCloud, Carol & Butzke, Caryn. Bucket Filling from a to Z: The Key to Being Happy. Zimmer, Glenn, illus. 2017. 32p. (J). (gr. -1-4). pap. 9.95 (978-0-9974864-3-8(0), Bucket Fillosophy) Cardinal Rule Pr.

McMurtrie, Kevin. The Very Thoughtful Turtle. 2013. (ENG.). 24p. (YA). pap. 13.77 (978-1-4907-0940-6(1)) Trafford Publishing.

Meadows, Daisy. Esther the Kindness Fairy. 2017. (Rainbow Magic — Friendship Fairies Ser.: 1). (Illus.). 65p. (J). lib. bdg. 14.75 (978-0-606-40175-3(X)) Turtleback.

Mello, Roger. You Can't Be Too Careful! Hahn, Daniel, tr. Mello, Roger, illus. 2017. (Illus.). 36p. (J). (gr. k-3). 18.00 (978-0-914671-64-0(2), Elsewhere Editions) Steerforth Pr.

Metallinos, Sophia. The Heavenly Place. l.t. ed. 2016. (ENG., Illus.). (J). pap. 9.99 (978-1-58169-640-0(X), Axiom Pr.) Genesis Communications, Inc.

Mims, Melanie. Neeko's Angel: A Story about Kindness. Floyd, John, Jr., illus. 2006. (Fruit of the Spirit Ser.). 24p. (J). (gr. -1-1). 6.95 (978-0-9752860-7-4(2)) OurRainbow Pr., LLC.

Mitchell, Laurence. Patty Liz & Kindness: Character Tales. 2009. 24p. pap. 12.00 (978-1-4389-5408-0(5)) AuthorHouse.

Moroney, Trace. When I'm Feeling Kind. 2018. (Feelings Ser.). (ENG., Illus.). 24p. (J). (— 1). 10.99 (978-1-76068-064-0(8)) Bonnier Publishing GBR. Dist: Independent Pubs. Group.

Murphy Payne, Lauren. We Can Get along / Podemos Llevarnos Bien: A Child's Book of Choices / un Libro de Alternativas para Ninos. Iwai, Melissa, illus. 2018. (ENG.). 48p. (J). (gr. -1-3). pap. 12.99 (978-1-63198-338-2(5), 83382) Free Spirit Publishing Inc.

Myracle, Lauren. Non-Random Acts of Kindness. Henry, Jed, illus. 2015. (Life of Ty Ser.: 2). (ENG.). 128p. (J). (gr. 1-4). 5.99 (978-0-14-242319-6(X), Puffin Books) Penguin Young Readers Group.

Nelson, Kadir. If You Plant a Seed: An Easter & Springtime Book for Kids. Nelson, Kadir, illus. 2015. (ENG., Illus.). 32p. (J). (gr. -1-3). 18.99 (978-0-06-229889-8(5), Balzer & Bray) HarperCollins Pubs.

Nevers, Merri B. Lonely Lucille. 2012. 28p. pap. 16.95 (978-1-4497-4246-1(7), WestBow Pr.) Author Solutions, LLC.

Nevins, Mary. The Adventures of Molly. 2009. 20p. pap. 14.50 (978-1-60693-919-2(X), Eloquent Bks.) Strategic Book Publishing & Rights Agency (SBPRA).

Norton Kreider, Barbara. The Surprise Party. Dimbylow, Jube, illus. 2013. 30p. pap. (978-1-921883-37-8(5), MBS Pr.) Pick-a-Woo Woo Pubs.

Osborne, Amber & Osborne, Dwight. Puffy Buffy Jones Jones Osborne Dadoot Da Do. Osborne, Amber, illus. 2006. (Illus.). (J). pap. 11.99 (978-0-9786431-0-2(0)) AAO Publishing.

Parker, Lucy. Acorn Meadow has a Secret. 2010. (ENG., Illus.). 80p. pap. (978-1-84748-600-4(2)) Athena Pr.

Percival, Tom. Goat's Coat. Pym, Christine, illus. 2018. (ENG.). 32p. (J). 16.99 (978-1-68119-901-6(7), 900191665, Bloomsbury Children's Bks.) Bloomsbury Publishing USA.

Perrault, Charles. Cinderella. Innocenti, Roberto, illus. 2013. (ENG.). 32p. (J). (gr. 2-5). pap. 7.99 (978-0-89812-828-4(5), 22040, Creative Paperbacks) Creative Co., The.

Persaud, Sandhya S. One Day. Ahmad, Maryam & Ramotar, Alexandra, illus. 2009. 12p. pap. 12.99 (978-1-4389-4437-1(3)) AuthorHouse.

Phumiruk, Dow. Mela & the Elephant. Chen, Ziyue, illus. 2018. (ENG.). 32p. (J). (gr. k-3). 18.99 (978-1-58536-998-0(5), 204407) Sleeping Bear Pr.

Polacco, Patricia. Tucky Jo & Little Heart. Polacco, Patricia, illus. 2015. (ENG., Illus.). 48p. (J). (gr. -1-3). 19.99 (978-1-4814-1584-2(0), Simon & Schuster Bks. For Young Readers) Simon & Schuster Bks. For Young Readers.

Poole, Susie. All These Things: Based on 1 Corinthians 13:4-7. 2012. (ENG., Illus.). 26p. bds. 7.99 (978-1-904637-27-1(2), 1904637272, Pupfish) Authentic Media GBR. Dist: EMI CMG Distribution.

Price, Cheryl. The Golden Aspen. 2009. 36p. pap. 15.95 (978-1-4490-2855-8(1)) AuthorHouse.

Qahhaar El-Amin, Mary M. Baby Ears: The Littlest Elephant. 2010. 37p. (J). pap. 20.95 (978-1-4327-2369-9(3)) Outskirts Pr., Inc.

The Quest for Kindness. 2006. (Amazing Travels of Wannabe Ser.). (Illus.). 32p. (J). (gr. -1-3). 8.99 (978-0-7847-1802-5(4), 04128) Standard Publishing.

Regis-Etumnu, Anusjka. Sid the Kindest Kid: Sweets ... Sweets ... Sweets! 2012. (Illus.). 32p. pap. 21.35 (978-1-4772-2283-6(9)) AuthorHouse.

Reul, Sarah Lynne. The Breaking News. Reul, Sarah Lynne, illus. 2018. (ENG., Illus.). 48p. (J). 19.99 (978-1-250-15356-2(5), 900183878) Roaring Brook Pr.

Rice, Dona Herwick & Bradley, Kathleen. Molly Pitcher, 1 vol. rev. ed. 2009. (Reader's Theater Ser.). (ENG., Illus.). 24p. (gr. 2-4). pap. 8.99 (978-1-4333-0993-9(9)) Teacher Created Materials, Inc.

Richards, Laura Elizabeth Howe. Queen Hildegarde. 2007. 92p. per. (978-1-4068-3867-1(5)) Echo Library.

Roscitt, Donna. The Birthday Train: Book 1. 2013. (ENG.). 48p. (J). 24.95 (978-1-4787-2236-6(3)) Outskirts Pr., Inc.

Rosenthal, Amy Krouse. Plant a Kiss Board Book. Reynolds, Peter H., illus. 2015. (ENG.). 36p. (J). (gr. -1 — 1). bds. 7.99 (978-0-06-241652-0(9), HarperFestival) HarperCollins Pubs.

Rosenthal, Sally. Matzo Frogs. Sheldon, David, illus. 2014. (ENG.). 32p. (J). 17.95 (978-1-58838-302-0(4), 8911, NewSouth Bks.) NewSouth, Inc.

Rubel, David. The Carpenter's Gift: A Christmas Tale about the Rockefeller Center Tree. LaMarche, Jim, illus. 2011. (ENG.). 48p. (J). (gr. k-4). 18.99 (978-0-375-86922-8(0), Random Hse. Bks. for Young Readers) Random Hse. Children's Bks.

Ryden, Linda. Henry Is Kind: A Story of Mindfulness, 1 vol. Malone, Shearry, illus. 2018. (Henry & Friends Mindfulness Ser.: 0). (ENG.). 36p. (J). (gr. k-5). 16.95 (978-0-88448-661-9(3), 884661) Tilbury Hse. Pubs.

Schieber, Barry J. An Open Heart: A Story about Moritz. 2006. (Illus.). 32p. (J). 17.00 (978-0-9721457-2-5(9)) Silent Moon Bks.

Schneider, Richard H. Why Christmas Trees Aren't Perfect. 2016. (ENG.). 32p. 14.99 (978-1-5018-2583-5(6), 15307) Abingdon Pr.

Sesame Workshop. Kindness Makes the World Go Round. 2018. (Sesame Street Scribbles Ser.: 0). (ENG.). 40p. (J). (gr. -1-3). 10.99 (978-1-4926-6056-9(6)) Sourcebooks, Inc.

Sewell, Anna. Black Beauty: And a Discussion of Kindness. Martin, Richard, illus. 2003. (Values in Action Illustrated Classics Ser.). 191p. (J). (978-1-59203-028-6(9)) Learning Challenge, Inc.

Sheinmel, Courtney. The Kindness Club: Chloe on the Bright Side. 2016. (Kindness Club Ser.). (ENG.). 224p. (J). 15.99 (978-1-68119-091-4(5), 900158417, Bloomsbury USA Childrens) Bloomsbury Publishing USA.

—The Kindness Club: Designed by Lucy. (Kindness Club Ser.). (ENG.). 224p. (J). 2018. pap. 7.99 (978-1-68119-899-6(1), 900191667, Bloomsbury Children's Bks.) 2017. 15.99 (978-1-68119-117-1(2), 900159227, Bloomsbury USA Childrens) Bloomsbury Publishing USA.

Sherwood, Lance. Grandpa Tales. 2012. 54p. pap. 14.95 (978-0-615-72525-3(2)) Spitzer, Lance.

Simon, Mary Manz. Kitty Shows Kindness. Clearwater, Linda, illus. 2006. (First Virtues for Toddlers Ser.). 20p. (J). 5.99 (978-0-7847-1408-9(8), 04036) Standard Publishing.

Simon, Tanya & Simon, Richard. Oskar & the Eight Blessings. Siegel, Mark, illus. 2015. (ENG.). 40p. (J). (gr. -1-3). 19.99 (978-1-59643-949-8(1), 900123918) Roaring Brook Pr.

Smith, Bryan. Kindness Counts: A Story for Teaching Random Acts of Kindness, Volume 1. Martin, Brian, illus. 2016. (Without Limits Ser.). (ENG.). 31p. (J). (gr. k-5). pap. 11.95 (978-1-944882-01-3(4)) Boys Town Pr.

Sparks, Favre. Agnes, the Eggless Quail. 2009. 28p. pap. 16.50 (978-1-60693-491-3(0), Strategic Bk. Publishing) Strategic Book Publishing & Rights Agency (SBPRA).

Speak, Steven. Skip & L, Guardian Angel. 2011. 20p. pap. 12.45 (978-1-4525-3643-9(0)) Get Published.

Spurgeon, C. H. Queen Victoria's Request. 2008. (Story Time Ser.). (ENG., Illus.). 24p. (J). (gr. -1-3). 7.99 (978-1-84550-325-3(2), 02bbf606-b30d-425b-85ba-7fd206cb260b) Christian Focus Pubns. GBR. Dist: Baker & Taylor Publisher Services (BTPS).

Stepp, Shirley. Pongo Penguin's Whale of a Tale. 2012. 24p. 24.95 (978-1-4626-5478-9(9)) America Star Bks.

Sterling, L. E. True North. 2018. (True Born Ser.: 2). (ENG.). 304p. (YA). pap. 9.99 (978-1-63375-915-2(6), 900185555) Entangled Publishing, LLC.

Stevens, Carla & Stevens, Chapman. Who's Knocking at the Door?, 1 vol. Chapman, Lee, illus. 2004. (ENG.). 32p. (J). 16.95 (978-0-7614-5168-6(4)) Marshall Cavendish Corp.

Stott, Apryl. Share Some Kindness, Bring Some Light. Stott, Apryl, illus. 2020. (Coco & Bear Ser.). (ENG., Illus.). 40p. (J). (gr. -1-3). 17.99 (978-1-5344-6238-0(4), Simon & Schuster Bks. For Young Readers) Simon & Schuster Bks. For Young Readers.

Stoutland, Allison. What Can I Do Today? To Make This World a Happier Place. Hofner, Cathy, illus. 2005. 32p. (J). (gr. -1-3). 16.95 (978-0-9670941-3-7(5)) Inch By Inch Pubns., LLC.

Studio Mouse, creator. Kindness Counts. rev. ed. 2008. (Learn-Aloud Bks.). (ENG., Illus.). (J). 12.99 (978-1-59069-627-9(1)) Studio Mouse LLC.

Studio Mouse Staff. Kindness Counts. rev. ed. 2004. (Kindness Counts Ser.). (ENG., Illus.). 36p. (J). (gr. -1-3). 12.99 (978-1-59069-364-3(7), 1A500) Studio Mouse LLC.

Telle, Anita. Always Time for Kindness. 2012. (ENG.). (J). pap. (978-1-4675-2560-2(X)) Independent Pub.

Tenney, Shawna J. C., illus. Brunhilda's Backwards Day. 2016. (ENG.). 32p. (J). (gr. -1-k). 16.99 (978-1-63450-691-5(X), Sky Pony Pr.) Skyhorse Publishing Co., Inc.

Theobald the Iron Hearted or Love to Ene. 2004. reprint ed. pap. 15.95 (978-1-4191-8941-8(7)) Kessinger Publishing, LLC.

Theobald the Iron Hearted or Love to Enemies. 2004. reprint ed. pap. 1.99 (978-1-4192-8941-5(1)) Kessinger Publishing, LLC.

Thong, Roseanne. Fly Free. Neilan, Eujin Kim, illus. 2010. (ENG.). 32p. (J). (gr. -1-3). 17.99 (978-1-59078-550-8(9), Astra Young Readers) Astra Publishing Hse.

Tollefson, Carol & Shelton, Kim. McTavich That Rascal Squirrel. 2015. (ENG., Illus.). 20p. pap. 12.00 (978-1-62288-101-7(X), P476290) Austin, Stephen F. State Univ. Pr.

Tolstoi, Leo. Shoemaker Martin. Watts, Bernadette, illus. 2018. (ENG.). 32p. (J). (gr. -1-3). 17.95 (978-0-7358-4304-2(X)) North-South Bks., Inc.

Van Dusen, Ross, illus. How Crocka Dog Came to Be. 2015. (J). (978-1-936744-39-8(2)) LPD Pr.

VanDenhoven, Godelieve. Louis in Kindergarten. 2009. 40p. pap. 14.50 (978-1-60693-752-5(9), Eloquent Bks.) Strategic Book Publishing & Rights Agency (SBPRA).

Vincent, Victoria. The City of Kind Words: A Story by Tory. l.t. ed. 2006. (Illus.). 56p. (J). per. 19.95 (978-0-9788950-0-6(2)) All Over Creation.

Wade, Cleo. What the Road Said. de Moyencourt, Lucie, illus. 2021. (ENG.). 40p. (J). 18.99 *(978-1-250-26949-2(0),* 900222825) Feiwel & Friends.

Wainwright, Joann M. Winston, the Polite St Bernard. Ross, Adam, illus. 2009. 28p. pap. 14.99 *(978-1-4389-2704-6(5))* AuthorHouse.

Wallace, Nancy Elizabeth. The Kindness Quilt, 0 vols. 2012. (ENG., Illus.). 48p. (J). (gr. -1-3). 16.99 *(978-0-7614-5313-0(X),* 9780761453130, Two Lions) Amazon Publishing.

Wekelo, Kerry Alison. Audrey's Journey: Playful Namaste. 2012. 16p. pap. 15.99 *(978-1-4772-7207-7(0))* AuthorHouse.

Wheeler, Christine. Bella's Marigold Cake. 2008. 20p. pap. 18.50 *(978-1-60693-100-4(8),* Eloquent Bks.) Strategic Book Publishing & Rights Agency (SBPRA).

Wildsmith, Brian. Hunter & His Dog, 1 vol. 2008. (ENG., Illus.). 32p. (J). 16.95 *(978-1-59572-123-5(1))* Star Bright Bks., Inc.

Will, R. K. Harry's Flowers. 2012. 24p. 24.95 *(978-1-4626-5967-8(5))* America Star Bks.

Williamson, Pam. Sweet & Sour Milk. 2011. 24p. pap. 12.79 *(978-1-4634-0725-4(4))* AuthorHouse.

Woodson, Jacqueline. Each Kindness. Lewis, E. B., illus. 2012. 32p. (J). (gr. k-3). 18.99 *(978-0-399-24652-4(5),* Nancy Paulsen Books) Penguin Young Readers Group.

Yamada, Shale. Rainbow Kitty Saves the Day. Riedler, Amelia, ed. 2013. (Story Lines Ser.). (ENG.). 24p. (J). (gr. -1-3). 9.95 *(978-1-935414-92-6(5))* Compendium, Inc., Publishing & Communications.

Zhang, Gracey. Lala's Words. Zhang, Gracey, illus. 2021. (ENG., Illus.). 48p. (J). (gr. -1-3). 18.99 *(978-1-338-64823-2(3),* Orchard Bks.) Scholastic, Inc.

Zietlow Miller, Pat. Be Kind. Hill, Jen, illus. (Be Kind Ser.: 1). (ENG.). (J). 2023. 22p. bds. 8.99 ***(978-1-250-89845-6(5),*** 900289718) 2018. 32p. 18.99 *(978-1-62672-321-4(4),* 900152054) Roaring Brook Pr.

KINDNESS TO ANIMALS

see Animals—Treatment

KINETICS

see Dynamics; Motion

KING, BILLIE JEAN, 1943-

Monnig, Alex. Serena Williams vs. Billie Jean King. 2017. (Versus Ser.). (ENG., Illus.). 32p. (J). (gr. 3-6). lib. bdg. 32.79 *(978-1-5321-1357-4(9),* 27655, SportsZone) ABDO Publishing Co.

Skinner, J. E. Billie Jean King vs. Bobby Riggs. 2018. (21st Century Skills Library: Sports Unite Us Ser.). (ENG., Illus.). 32p. (J). (gr. 3-6). lib. bdg. 32.07 *(978-1-5341-2962-7(6),* 211892) Cherry Lake Publishing.

Strand, Jennifer. Billie Jean King. 2016. (Trailblazing Athletes Ser.). (ENG.). 24p. (J). (gr. -1-2). 49.94 *(978-1-68079-418-2(3),* 23039, Abdo Zoom-Launch) ABDO Publishing Co.

KING, CORETTA SCOTT, 1927-2006

Gelfand, Dale Evva. Coretta Scott King. 2nd rev. ed. 2006. (Black Americans of Achievement Legacy Edition Ser.). (ENG., Illus.). 137p. (gr. 7-12). lib. bdg. 35.00 *(978-0-7910-9522-5(3),* P120094, Facts On File) Infobase Holdings, Inc.

Hally, Ashleigh. Coretta Scott King. 2012. (Illus.). 24p. (J). *(978-1-935884-78-1(6));* pap. *(978-1-935884-84-2(0))* State Standards Publishing, LLC.

Herman, Gail. Who Was Coretta Scott King? 2019. (Who HQ Ser.). (ENG.). 108p. (J). (gr. 2-3). 16.36 *(978-1-64310-859-9(X))* Penworthy Co., LLC, The.

Herman, Gail & Who HQ. Who Was Coretta Scott King? Copeland, Gregory, illus. 2017. (Who Was? Ser.). 112p. (J). (gr. 3-7). 5.99 *(978-0-451-53261-9(9),* Penguin Workshop) Penguin Young Readers Group.

Krull, Kathleen. Women Who Broke the Rules: Coretta Scott King. Freeman, Laura, illus. 2015. (Women Who Broke the Rules Ser.). (ENG.). 48p. (J). (gr. 1-4). pap. 7.99 *(978-0-8027-3827-1(3),* 900141989, Bloomsbury USA Childrens) Bloomsbury Publishing USA.

Mattern, Joanne. Coretta Scott King: Civil Rights Activist. 2009. (Women Who Shaped History Ser.). 24p. (gr. 2-3). 42.50 *(978-1-60854-816-3(3),* PowerKids Pr.) Rosen Publishing Group, Inc., The.

McPherson, Stephanie Sammartino. Biography Coretta Scott King. 2007. (Biography Ser.). (Illus.). 112p. (YA). (gr. 7-12). lib. bdg. 29.27 *(978-0-8225-7156-8(0))* Twenty First Century Bks.

Mis, Melody S. Meet Coretta Scott King, 1 vol. 2007. (Civil Rights Leaders Ser.). (ENG., Illus.). 24p. (YA). (gr. 2-3). lib. bdg. 26.27 *(978-1-4042-4211-1(2),* 6665c8c6-5932-449a-ba9d-55d71f765f26) Rosen Publishing Group, Inc., The.

Rivers, Lawrence. Coretta Scott King, Vol. 9. 2018. (Civil Rights Leaders Ser.). 144p. (J). (gr. 7). lib. bdg. 35.93 *(978-1-4222-4004-5(5))* Mason Crest.

Shange, Ntozake. Coretta Scott. Nelson, Kadir, illus. (ENG.). 32p. (J). (gr. -1-4). 2011. pap. 9.99 *(978-0-06-125366-9(9))* 2009. 17.99 *(978-0-06-125364-5(2))* HarperCollins Pubs. (Tegen, Katherine Bks).

Spiller, Sara. Coretta Scott King. Bane, Jeff, illus. 2019. (My Early Library: My Itty-Bitty Bio Ser.). (ENG.). 24p. (J). (gr. k-1). pap. 12.79 *(978-1-5341-3924-4(9),* 212525); lib. bdg. 30.64 *(978-1-5341-4268-8(1),* 212524) Cherry Lake Publishing.

Stanley, George E. Coretta Scott King: First Lady of Civil Rights. Henderson, Meryl, illus. 2008. (Childhood of Famous Americans Ser.). (ENG.). 224p. (J). (gr. 3-7). pap. 7.99 *(978-1-4169-6800-9(8),* Simon & Schuster/Paula Wiseman Bks.) Simon & Schuster/Paula Wiseman Bks.

Wallace Sharp, Anne. Coretta Scott King, 1 vol. 2008. (People in the News Ser.). (ENG., Illus.). 104p. (gr. 7-7). lib. bdg. 41.03 *(978-1-4205-0067-5(2),* 3acb37e4-8132-4b3b-8a4f-197584949e62, Lucent Pr.) Greenhaven Publishing LLC.

Waxman, Laura Hamilton. Coretta Scott King. 2008. pap. 52.95 *(978-0-8225-9387-4(4));* (ENG., Illus.). 48p. (gr. 3-6). lib. bdg. 27.93 *(978-0-8225-7168-1(4),* Lerner Pubns.) Lerner Publishing Group.

KING, MARTIN LUTHER, JR., 1929-1968

Adler, David A. A Picture Book of Martin Luther King, Jr. Casilla, Robert, illus. 2004. (Picture Book Biography Ser.). (J). (gr. -1-3). pap. 18.95 incl. audio compact disk *(978-1-59112-773-4(4))* Live Oak Media.

Albee, Sarah. Martin Luther King Jr.: A Peaceful Leader. Ko, Chin, illus. 2018. (I Can Read Level 2 Ser.). (ENG.). 32p. (J). (gr. -1-3). 16.99 *(978-0-06-243276-6(1),* HarperCollins) HarperCollins Pubs.

—Martin Luther King Jr.: a Peaceful Leader. Ko, Chin, illus. 2018. (I Can Read Level 2 Ser.). (ENG.). 32p. (J). (gr. -1-3). pap. 4.99 *(978-0-06-243275-9(3),* HarperCollins) HarperCollins Pubs.

Alexander, Florence. Dare to Be. . . Martin Luther King Jr. Whitmore, Yvette, illus. 2003. (ENG & SPA.). 17p. (J). 3.99 *(978-0-915960-65-1(6))* Ebon Research Systems Publishing, LLC.

Archer, Jules. They Had a Dream: The Struggles of Four of the Most Influential Leaders of the Civil Rights Movement, from Frederick Douglass to Marcus Garvey to Martin Luther King Jr. & Malcolm X. 2016. (Jules Archer History for Young Readers Ser.). (ENG., Illus.). 272p. (J). (gr. 6-6). 16.99 *(978-1-63450-194-1(2),* Sky Pony Pr.) Skyhorse Publishing Co., Inc.

Aretha, David. Martin Luther King Jr. & the 1963 March on Washington. 2014. (Illus.). 112p. (J). 28.95 *(978-1-59935-372-2(5))* Reynolds, Morgan Inc.

—Selma & the Voting Rights Act. 2007. (Civil Rights Movement Ser.). (Illus.). 128p. (J). (gr. 3-7). lib. bdg. 27.95 *(978-1-59935-056-1(4))* Reynolds, Morgan Inc.

Bader, Bonnie. My Little Golden Book about Martin Luther King Jr. Cornelison, Sue, illus. 2018. (Little Golden Book Ser.). 24p. (J). (gr. -1-3). 5.99 *(978-0-525-57870-3(6),* Golden Bks.) Random Hse. Children's Bks.

—Who Was Martin Luther King, Jr. ? Wolf, Elizabeth, illus. 2008. (Who Was... ? Ser.). 105p. (J). (gr. 2-5). 12.65 *(978-0-7569-8935-4(3))* Perfection Learning Corp.

Bader, Bonnie & Who HQ. Who Was Martin Luther King, Jr. ? Wolf, Elizabeth, illus. 2007. (Who Was? Ser.). 112p. (J). (gr. 3-7). pap. 5.99 *(978-0-448-44723-0(1),* Penguin Workshop) Penguin Young Readers Group.

Bailey, Gerry & Foster, Karen. Martin Luther King Jr.'s Microphone. Radford, Karen & Noyes, Leighton, illus. 2008. (Stories of Great People Ser.). (ENG.). 40p. (J). (gr. 3-8). pap. *(978-0-7787-3711-7(X));* lib. bdg. *(978-0-7787-3689-9(X))* Crabtree Publishing Co.

Ball, Jacqueline A. Martin Luther King, Jr: I Have a Dream! 2005. (Defining Moments Ser.). (Illus.). 32p. (J). (gr. 2-5). lib. bdg. 28.50 *(978-1-59716-077-3(6))* Bearport Publishing Co., Inc.

Beringer Mckissack, Lisa. Martin Luther King, Jr. , Day: Count & Celebrate!, 1 vol. 2009. (Holidays: Count & Celebrate! Ser.). (ENG., Illus.). 32p. (gr. k-2). lib. bdg. 26.60 *(978-0-7660-3105-0(5),* a9434699-c117-493d-b597-a6677a1718c5) Enslow Publishing, LLC.

Berlatsky, Noah, ed. The Assassination of Martin Luther King, Jr, 1 vol. 2011. (Perspectives on Modern World History Ser.). (ENG., Illus.). 192p. (gr. 10-12). lib. bdg. 49.43 *(978-0-7377-5259-5(9),* 01c9e106-ea69-44bd-b4d1-bbc8faa368de, Greenhaven Publishing) Greenhaven Publishing LLC.

Bodden, Valerie. The Assassination of Martin Luther King Jr. 2016. (Turning Points Ser.). (ENG., Illus.). 48p. (J). (gr. 4-7). *(978-1-60818-747-8(0),* 20807, Creative Education) Creative Co., The.

Boerst, William J. Marching in Birmingham. 2007. (Civil Rights Movement Ser.). (Illus.). 112p. (J). (gr. 3-7). lib. bdg. 27.95 *(978-1-59935-055-4(6))* Reynolds, Morgan Inc.

Bolden, Tonya. M. L. K. The Journey of a King. 2007. (ENG., Illus.). 128p. (J). (gr. 5-9). 27.95 *(978-0-8109-5476-2(1),* Abrams Bks. for Young Readers) Abrams, Inc.

Boyd, Herb. Martin Luther King, Jr. Marcos, Pablo, illus. 2005. (Heroes of America Ser.). 239p. (gr. 3-8). 27.07 *(978-1-59679-258-6(2),* Abdo & Daughters) ABDO Publishing Co.

Brown, Jonatha A. Martin Luther King, Jr, 1 vol. 2004. (Gente Que Hay Que Conocer (People We Should Know) Ser.). (SPA., Illus.). 24p. (gr. 2-4). lib. bdg. 24.67 *(978-0-8368-4583-9(8),* 28ba9144-fe49-42f7-beb8-4baac26e8e88, Weekly Reader Leveled Readers) Stevens, Gareth Publishing LLLP.

—Martin Luther King, Jr, 1 vol. 2004. (People We Should Know Ser.). (ENG., Illus.). 24p. (gr. 2-4). pap. 9.15 *(978-0-8368-4474-0(2),* 6c1cd9f0-0595-48f9-9968-594d6400259c); lib. bdg. 24.67 *(978-0-8368-4467-2(X),* 0ed64341-15ad-4bea-99d5-d4495e64245d) Stevens, Gareth Publishing LLLP. (Weekly Reader Leveled Readers).

Buckley, James, Jr. Martin Luther King Jr.: Voice for Equality! YouNeek Studios, illus. 2019. (Show Me History! Ser.). (ENG.). 96p. (J). (gr. 3-7). 12.99 *(978-1-68412-546-3(4),* Portable Pr.) Printers Row Publishing Group.

Bull, Angela. DK Readers L4: Free at Last: the Story of Martin Luther King, Jr. 2009. (DK Readers Level 4 Ser.). (ENG.). 48p. (J). (gr. 3-7). 4.99 *(978-0-7566-5615-7(X),* DK Children) Dorling Kindersley Publishing, Inc.

Bunting, Eve. The Cart That Carried Martin. Tate, Don, illus. 2018. (ENG.). 32p. (J). (gr. 1-4). 7.99 *(978-1-58089-388-6(0))* Charlesbridge Publishing, Inc.

—The Cart That Carried Martin. 2013. 32p. pap. 16.95 *(978-1-60734-601-2(X))* Charlesbridge Publishing, Inc.

—The Cart That Carried Martin. Tate, Don, illus. 2013. 32p. (J). (gr. 1-4). lib. bdg. 16.95 *(978-1-58089-387-9(2))* Charlesbridge Publishing, Inc.

Calkhoven, Laurie. DK Life Stories: Martin Luther King Jr. Ager, Charlotte, illus. 2019. (DK Life Stories Ser.). (ENG.). 128p. (J). (gr. 3-7). pap. 5.99 *(978-1-4654-7435-3(8),* DK Children) Dorling Kindersley Publishing, Inc.

Carson, Mary Kay. What Was Your Dream, Dr. King? And Other Questions About... Martin Luther King, Jr. Madsen, Jim, illus. 2013. (Good Question! Ser.). (ENG.). 32p. (J). (gr. 2). pap. 6.95 *(978-1-4027-9045-4(7))* Sterling Publishing Co., Inc.

Cella, Clara. Martin Luther King Jr. Day. 2012. (Let's Celebrate Ser.). (ENG.). 24p. (J). (gr. k-1). pap. 43.74 *(978-1-4296-9389-9(4),* 18592); (Illus.). (gr. -1-2). 27.32 *(978-1-4296-8733-1(9),* 119526); (Illus.). (gr. -1-2). pap. 7.29 *(978-1-4296-9388-2(6),* 120391) Capstone. (Capstone Pr.).

Clayton, Ed. Martin Luther King: The Peaceful Warrior. Bermudez, Donald, illus. 2017. (ENG.). 128p. (J). (gr. 3-7). 16.99 *(978-0-7636-7471-7(0))* Candlewick Pr.

Colbert, David. Martin Luther King Jr. 2008. (10 Days Ser.). (ENG.). 160p. (J). (gr. 3-8). pap. 8.99 *(978-1-4169-6805-4(9),* Aladdin) Simon & Schuster Children's Publishing.

Collins, Terry. The Assassination of Martin Luther King, Jr: April 4 1968, 1 vol. Ginevra, Dante, illus. 2014. (24-Hour History Ser.). (ENG.). 48p. (J). (gr. 3-9). pap. 8.95 *(978-1-4329-9302-3(X),* 124618); lib. bdg. 33.99 *(978-1-4329-9296-5(1),* 124613) Capstone. (Heinemann).

Conciatore Senter, Jacqueline. Martin Luther King Jr: Fulfilling a Dream, 1 vol. 2017. (Peaceful Protesters Ser.). (ENG.). 112p. (YA). (gr. 9-9). 44.50 *(978-1-5026-3116-9(4),* 732cbef2-8e3b-4d15-aa1d-97193f456ead); pap. 20.99 *(978-1-5026-3395-8(7),* 64747d2c-0d02-4da8-9bd6-f8ec9b4c6800) Cavendish Square Publishing LLC.

Conklin, Wendy. Martin Luther King Jr, 1 vol. rev. ed. 2007. (Social Studies: Informational Text Ser.). (ENG.). 32p. (J). (gr. 4-8). pap. 11.99 *(978-0-7439-0671-5(3))* Teacher Created Materials, Inc.

Cooke, Tim. Martin Luther King Jr, 1 vol. 2016. (Meet the Greats Ser.). (ENG.). 48p. (J). (gr. 5-5). pap. 15.65 *(978-1-4824-5952-4(3),* fe39fcdb-5a5e-4b1e-933c-6afdae0fd1f7) Stevens, Gareth Publishing LLLP.

Darby, Jean. Martin Luther King Jr. 2005. (Just the Facts Biographies Ser.). (ENG., Illus.). 112p. (gr. 5-12). 27.93 *(978-0-8225-2471-7(6))* Lerner Publishing Group.

Dash, Meredith. MLK Jr. Day, 1 vol. 2014. (National Holidays Ser.). (ENG.). 24p. (J). (gr. -1-2). lib. bdg. 32.79 *(978-1-62970-045-8(2),* 1534, Abdo Kids) ABDO Publishing Co.

The Day Martin Luther King Jr Died, 6 vols. (Multicultural Programs Ser.). 16p. (gr. 1-6). 31.95 *(978-0-7802-8325-1(2))* Wright Group/McGraw-Hill.

Dayton, Connor. Martin Luther King, Jr. Day, 1 vol. 2012. (American Holidays Ser.). (ENG.). 24p. (J). (gr. 1-1). pap. 9.25 *(978-1-4488-6246-7(9),* 2a03f3e5-a0c6-439c-b23f-81016f7f50b7); lib. bdg. 26.27 *(978-1-4488-6144-6(6),* 90fdb303-8cf1-4174-96d1-fa693689a810) Rosen Publishing Group, Inc., The. (PowerKids Pr.).

—Martin Luther King Jr. Day: Natalicio de Martin Luther King Jr, 1 vol. Alamán, Eduardo, tr. 2012. (American Holidays / Celebraciones en Los Estados Unidos Ser.). (SPA & ENG.). 24p. (gr. 1-1). lib. bdg. 26.27 *(978-1-4488-6710-3(X),* 4918ed17-ac0e-463f-a052-ad87f4b7608a, PowerKids Pr.) Rosen Publishing Group, Inc., The.

Dean, Sheri. Martin Luther King Jr. Day. 2010. (Our Country's Holidays Ser.). (ENG.). 24p. (J). (gr. k-2). 18.95 *(978-1-5311-8642-5(4))* Perfection Learning Corp.

—Martin Luther King Jr. Day, 1 vol. (Our Country's Holidays (Second Edition) Ser.). (ENG.). 24p. (gr. k-2). 2010. (J). pap. 9.15 *(978-1-4339-3918-1(5),* 7629ca2d-368b-4bef-8789-ef2ab28451d6) 2010. (J). lib. bdg. 25.27 *(978-1-4339-3917-4(7),* 01490952-0879-4e5e-aefb-0b5df1bd3ebc) 2005. (Illus.). lib. bdg. 24.67 *(978-0-8368-6506-6(5),* 2b38af0c-ae36-4f70-8e4b-deb7df2404ef) Stevens, Gareth Publishing LLLP.

deRubertis, Barbara. Let's Celebrate Martin Luther King, Jr. Day. Griffith, Gershom, illus. 2013. (Holidays & Heroes Ser.). (ENG.). 32p. (J). (gr. 1-4). E-Book 38.65 *(978-1-57565-639-7(6))* Astra Publishing Hse.

Fandel, Jennifer. Martin Luther King, Jr. 2005. (Genius Ser.). (Illus.). 48p. (J). (gr. 5-9). lib. bdg. 21.95 *(978-1-58341-329-6(4),* Creative Education) Creative Co., The.

Farris, Christine King. March On! The Day My Brother Martin Changed the World. Ladd, London, illus. 2011. (J). (gr. 2-7). 29.95 *(978-0-545-10689-4(3))* Weston Woods Studios, Inc.

—My Brother Martin: A Sister Remembers Growing up with the Rev. Dr. Martin Luther King Jr. Soentpiet, Chris, illus. 2003. (ENG.). 32p. (J). (gr. 1-6). 19.99 *(978-0-689-84387-7(9),* Simon & Schuster Bks. For Young Readers) Simon & Schuster Bks. For Young Readers.

—My Brother Martin: A Sister Remembers Growing up with the Rev. Dr. Martin Luther King Jr. Soentpiet, Chris, illus. 2006. (ENG.). 40p. (J). (gr. 1-6). 8.99 *(978-0-689-84388-4(7),* Aladdin) Simon & Schuster Children's Publishing.

Fishman, Jon M. Martin Luther King Jr.: Walking in the Light. 2019. (Gateway Biographies Ser.). (ENG., Illus.). 48p. (J). (gr. 4-8). 31.99 *(978-1-5415-3918-1(4),* 2135e841-305b-4c7c-99fd-f7192fb7ad43, Lerner Pubns.) Lerner Publishing Group.

Fitzgerald, Stephanie. Martin Luther King, Jr. Memorial (Rookie National Parks) (Library Edition) 2019. (Rookie National Parks Ser.). (ENG., Illus.). 32p. (J). (gr. 1-2). lib. bdg. 25.00 *(978-0-531-13321-7(4),* Children's Pr.) Scholastic Library Publishing.

Fleming. Famous Americans Series: Martin Luther King. 2003. (Illus.). 32p. (J). pap. 9.95 *(978-0-590-53545-8(5))* Scholastic, Inc.

Flowers, Arthur. I See the Promised Land: A Life of Martin Luther King, Jr., 1 vol. Chitrakar, Manu, illus. rev. ed. 2013. (ENG.). 156p. (J). (gr. 6-7). 16.95 *(978-1-55498-328-5(2))* Groundwood Bks. CAN. Dist: Publishers Group West (PGW).

Foran, Jill. Martin Luther King Jr. Day. 2004. (American Holidays Ser.). (Illus.). 24p. (J). lib. bdg. 24.45 *(978-1-59036-107-8(5));* (gr. 1-3). per. 8.95 *(978-1-59036-167-2(9))* Weigl Pubs., Inc.

—Martin Luther King, Jr. Day. 2015. (Illus.). 24p. (J). *(978-1-5105-0112-6(6))* SmartBook Media, Inc.

—Martin Luther King, Jr. Day. 2010. (American Celebrations Ser.). (Illus.). 24p. (J). (gr. 3-5). pap. 11.95 *(978-1-60596-779-0(3));* lib. bdg. 25.70 *(978-1-60596-772-1(6))* Weigl Pubs., Inc.

Frey, Wendy. Citizen Heroes. 2007. (Illus.). 68p. (J). *(978-1-4105-0888-1(9)); (978-1-4105-0887-4(0))* Building Wings LLC.

Ganeri, Anita. I Have a Dream: Martin Luther King, Jr. & the Fight for Equal Rights. 2013. (Turning Points in History Ser.). (Illus.). 48p. (gr. 5-12). 37.10 *(978-1-59920-972-2(1))* Black Rabbit Bks.

—Martin Luther King's I Have a Dream Speech. 2013. (Turning Points in History Ser.). 48p. (gr. 5-9). 24.95 *(978-1-59920-772-8(9))* Black Rabbit Bks.

Gelfand, Dale Evva. Coretta Scott King. 2nd rev. ed. 2006. (Black Americans of Achievement Legacy Edition Ser.). (ENG., Illus.). 137p. (gr. 7-12). lib. bdg. 35.00 *(978-0-7910-9522-5(3),* P120094, Facts On File) Infobase Holdings, Inc.

Gnojewski, Carol & Ponto, Joanna. Martin Luther King Jr. Day, 1 vol. 2016. (Story of Our Holidays Ser.). (ENG., Illus.). 32p. (gr. 3-3). pap. 11.52 *(978-0-7660-8340-0(3),* fd394b20-e8f0-40d9-a830-d9072dd33c2b) Enslow Publishing, LLC.

Gosman, Gillian. Martin Luther King, Jr, 1 vol. 2011. (Life Stories Ser.). (ENG., Illus.). 24p. (J). (gr. 3-3). pap. 9.25 *(978-1-4488-2755-8(8),* a3706aa2-c1e5-43da-ac0d-35bf91dc5a2d, PowerKids Pr.); lib. bdg. 26.27 *(978-1-4488-2583-7(0),* 9b332699-9ed0-4c81-9b0e-9bbd8bc2f68c, PowerKids Pr.); lib. bdg. 26.27 *(978-1-4488-3217-0(9),* 0ca0540c-f610-4d06-bc6c-aea7fa0faa89) Rosen Publishing Group, Inc., The.

Gotsch, Patrice. Martin Luther King, Jr: Changing Lives. Arreola, Gil, illus. 2006. 19p. pap. 6.30 *(978-1-55501-779-8(7))* Ballard & Tighe Pubs.

Grack, Rachel. Martin Luther King, Jr. Day. 2018. (Celebrating Holidays Ser.). (ENG., Illus.). 24p. (J). (gr. k-3). lib. bdg. 26.95 *(978-1-62617-752-9(X),* Blastoff! Readers) Bellwether Media.

Graves, Kerry A. I Have a Dream: The Story Behind Martin Luther King JR. 's Most Famous Speech. 2003. (America in Words & Song Ser.). (Illus.). 32p. (gr. 4-6). lib. bdg. 23.00 *(978-0-7910-7335-3(1),* Facts On File) Infobase Holdings, Inc.

Haldy, Emma E. Martin Luther King, Jr. Bane, Jeff, illus. 2016. (My Early Library: My Itty-Bitty Bio Ser.). (ENG.). 24p. (J). (gr. k-1). 30.64 *(978-1-63470-477-9(0),* 207639) Cherry Lake Publishing.

—Martin Luther King, Jr. SP. Bane, Jeff, illus. 2018. (My Early Library: Mi Mini Biografía (My Itty-Bitty Bio) Ser.). (SPA.). 24p. (J). (gr. k-1). lib. bdg. 30.64 *(978-1-5341-2998-6(7),* 212040) Cherry Lake Publishing.

Hally, Ashleigh. Coretta Scott King. 2012. (Illus.). 24p. (J). *(978-1-935884-78-1(6));* pap. *(978-1-935884-84-2(0))* State Standards Publishing, LLC.

Hansen, Grace. Martin Luther King, Jr. Civil Rights Leader, 1 vol. 2015. (History Maker Biographies (Abdo Kids Jumbo) Ser.). (ENG., Illus.). 24p. (J). (gr. -1-2). lib. bdg. 32.79 *(978-1-62970-704-4(X),* 17015, Abdo Kids) ABDO Publishing Co.

—Martin Luther King, Jr.: Civil Rights Leader. 2017. (History Maker Biographies Ser.). (ENG., Illus.). 24p. (J). (gr. -1-2). pap. 7.95 *(978-1-4966-1227-4(2),* 134991, Capstone Classroom) Capstone.

—Martin Luther King Jr.: Líder de Los Derechos Humanos (Martin Luther King Jr.: Civil Rights Leader) 2016. (Biografías: Personas Que Han Hecho Historia (History Maker Biographies) Ser.). (SPA., Illus.). 24p. (J). (gr. -1-2). lib. bdg. 32.79 *(978-1-68080-741-7(2),* 22644, Abdo Kids) ABDO Publishing Co.

Hayes, Amy. Celebrate Martin Luther King Jr. Day, 1 vol. 2014. (Our Holidays Ser.). (ENG., Illus.). 24p. (J). (gr. 1-1). pap. 9.23 *(978-1-5026-0229-9(6),* 8fa1396c-7f5a-4392-8b20-d8433eac9124) Cavendish Square Publishing LLC.

Hinton, KaaVonia. Martin Luther King, Jr. 2008. (What's So Great About... ? Ser.). (Illus.). 32p. (YA). (gr. 2-4). lib. bdg. 25.70 *(978-1-58415-724-3(0))* Mitchell Lane Pubs.

Jacoby, Randolph. Martin Luther King, Jr, Vol. 9. 2018. (Civil Rights Leaders Ser.). 144p. (J). (gr. 7). lib. bdg. 35.93 *(978-1-4222-4008-3(8))* Mason Crest.

Jakoubek, Robert. Martin Luther King, Jr. 2008. (Black Americans of Achievement Legacy Edition Ser.). 112p. (gr. 6-12). pap. 11.95 *(978-1-60413-328-8(7),* Checkmark Bks.) Infobase Holdings, Inc.

Jazynka, Kitson. National Geographic Readers: AfricanAmerican History Makers. 2018. (Readers Bios Ser.). (Illus.). 144p. (J). (gr. 1-3). pap. 7.99 *(978-1-4263-3201-2(7),* National Geographic Kids) Disney Publishing Worldwide.

—National Geographic Readers: Martin Luther King, Jr. 2012. (Readers Bios Ser.). 48p. (J). (gr. 1-3). pap. 4.99 *(978-1-4263-1087-4(0),* National Geographic Kids); (ENG.). lib. bdg. 14.90 *(978-1-4263-1088-1(9),* National Geographic Children's Bks.) Disney Publishing Worldwide.

Jeffrey, Gary. Martin Luther King Jr: The Life of a Civil Rights Leader. 2009. (Graphic Nonfiction Biographies Ser.). (ENG.). 48p. (YA). (gr. 4-5). 58.50 *(978-1-61513-021-4(7),* Rosen Reference) Rosen Publishing Group, Inc., The.

—Martin Luther King Jr: The Life of a Civil Rights Leader, 1 vol. Forsey, Christopher, illus. 2006. (Graphic Nonfiction Biographies Ser.). (ENG.). 48p. (gr. 4-5). pap. 14.05 *(978-1-4042-0921-3(2),* 32fa3f42-b45e-4609-a68a-a028f40af317) Rosen Publishing Group, Inc., The.

—Martin Luther King Jr: The Life of a Civil Rights Leader, 1 vol. Forsey, Chris, illus. 2006. (Graphic Nonfiction Biographies Ser.). (ENG.). 48p. (YA). (gr. 4-5). lib. bdg. 37.13 *(978-1-4042-0858-2(5),* 080b58d9-3684-4460-a4fb-15120035adcf) Rosen Publishing Group, Inc., The.

—Martin Luther King Jr. & the March on Washington, 1 vol. 2012. (Graphic History of the Civil Rights Movement Ser.). (ENG., Illus.). 24p. (J). (gr. 3-3). pap. 9.15 *(978-1-4339-7492-2(4),* 660c2669-a44f-4b1e-ac6a-83d83b4a9e32); lib. bdg. 26.60 *(978-1-4339-7491-5(6),* 9a90d534-e135-43ee-a177-faedc8341952) Stevens, Gareth Publishing LLLP.

Jones, Rob Lloyd. Martin Luther King, Jr. 2006. (Illus.). 62p. (J). pap. *(978-0-439-02299-6(1))* Scholastic, Inc.

—Martin Luther King Jr. Le Rolland, Leonard, illus. 2006. (Usborne Famous Lives Gift Bks.). 64p. (J). (gr. 2-5). 8.99 *(978-0-7945-1260-6(7),* Usborne) EDC Publishing.

Kaplan, Leslie C. Martin Luther King Jr. Day. (Library of Holidays Ser.). 24p. (gr. 2-3). 2009. 42.50

J K L

(978-1-60853-714-3(5)) 2003. (ENG., Illus.). (J). lib. bdg. 26.27 (978-0-8239-6661-5(5), dcac4c1a-588d-477b-9986-10714cfe252c) Rosen Publishing Group, Inc., The. (PowerKids Pr.).

Kelley, Kitty. Martin's Dream Day. 2017. (ENG., Illus.). 40p. (J). (gr. k). 17.99 (978-1-4814-6766-7(2)) Simon & Schuster Children's Publishing.

King Farris, Christine. My Brother Martin: A Sister Remembers Growing up with the Rev. Dr. Martin Luther King Jr. Soentpiet, Chris K., illus. 2005. 35p. (J). (gr. 4-7). 15.65 (978-0-7569-6552-5(7)) Perfection Learning Corp.

King, Martin Luther, Jr. I Have a Dream. 2007. (Illus.). 40p. (J). (gr. -1-3). 14.65 (978-0-7569-8119-8(0)) Perfection Learning Corp.

King, Martin Luther, III. My Daddy, Dr. Martin Luther King, Jr. Ford, A. G., illus. (ENG.). 32p. (J). (gr. -1-3). 2018. pap. 8.99 (978-0-06-446209-9(9)) 2013. 17.99 (978-0-06-028075-8(1)) HarperCollins Pubs. (Amistad).

Krull, Kathleen. Women Who Broke the Rules: Coretta Scott King. Freeman, Laura, illus. 2015. (Women Who Broke the Rules Ser.). (ENG.). 48p. (J). (gr. 1-4). pap. 7.99 (978-0-8027-3827-1(3), 900141989, Bloomsbury USA Childrens) Bloomsbury Publishing USA.

Kurtz, Jane. Martin's Dream: Ready-To-Read Level 1. Bates, Amy June, illus. 2008. (Ready-To-Read Ser.). (ENG.). 32p. (J). (gr. -1-1). pap. 4.99 (978-1-4169-2774-7(3), Aladdin) Simon & Schuster Children's Publishing.

Lee, Sally. Celebrate Martin Luther King Jr. Day. 2019. (U. S. Holidays Ser.). (ENG., Illus.). 24p. (J). (gr. 1-3). lib. bdg. 25.99 (978-1-9771-0277-5(8), 139273, Capstone Pr.) Capstone.

Lee, T. S. The Martin Luther King, Jr. Story: The Boy Who Broke Barriers with Faith. 2010. (J). pap. 14.95 (978-0-9819542-4-0(3)) DASANBOOKS.

Linde, Barbara M. Martin Luther King Jr, 1 vol. 2011. (Civil Rights Crusaders Ser.). (ENG., Illus.). 24p. (gr. 2-3). (J). pap. 9.15 (978-1-4339-5692-8(6), 106ff978-a7a2-4836-a474-fd596be5f106, Gareth Stevens Learning Library); (YA). lib. bdg. 25.27 (978-1-4339-5690-4(X), c7197cde-dd6b-4ff7-b300-888d349ba87f) Stevens, Gareth Publishing LLLP.

Linney, Susan. Martin Luther King, Jr: With a Discussion of Responsibility. 2004. (Values in Action Ser.). (J). (978-1-59203-069-9(6)) Learning Challenge, Inc.

Lowery, Linda. Martin Luther King Jr. Day, 2nd Edition. Mitchell, Hetty, illus. rev. ed. 2003. (On My Own Holidays Ser.). (ENG.). 56p. (J). (gr. 2-4). pap. 7.99 (978-1-57505-709-5(3), 974832be-31ad-4d58-af23-f139930cf202, First Avenue Editions) Lerner Publishing Group.

Malam, John. Martin Luther King. (Illus.). 24p. (978-0-237-51919-3(4)) Evans Brothers, Ltd.

Maloof, Torrey. Martin Luther King Jr: Destined to Lead. rev. ed. 2016. (Social Studies: Informational Text Ser.). (ENG., Illus.). 32p. (gr. 2-4). pap. 10.99 (978-1-4938-2559-2(3)) Teacher Created Materials, Inc.

—You Are There! March on Washington, August 28, 1963. 2nd rev. ed. 2017. (TIME(r): Informational Text Ser.). (ENG., Illus.). 32p. (gr. 6-8). pap. 13.99 (978-1-4938-3929-2(2)) Teacher Created Materials, Inc.

—You Are There! March on Washington, August 28 1963. 2017. (Time for Kids Nonfiction Readers Ser.). lib. bdg. 19.65 (978-0-606-40288-0(8)) Turtleback.

Manheimer, Ann S. Martin Luther King Jr: Dreaming of Equality. 2004. (Trailblazer Biographies Ser.). (ENG., Illus.). 112p. (gr. 5-9). 31.93 (978-1-57505-627-2(5), Carolrhoda Bks.) Lerner Publishing Group.

Mara, Wil. Martin Luther King Jr. 2013. (Rookie Biographies(r) Ser.). (ENG.). 32p. (J). pap. 5.95 (978-0-531-24704-4(X)); (gr. 1-2). lib. bdg. 18.69 (978-0-531-24738-9(4), Children's Pr.) Scholastic Library Publishing.

Martin Luther King Jr. (Illus.). 112p. pap. 9.95 (978-0-8225-5316-8(3)) Lerner Publishing Group.

Martin Luther King, JR. 2007. (Illus.). 33p. (J). per. 6.95 (978-0-9795887-0-9(7)) EZ Comics.

Marzollo, Jean. Happy Birthday, Martin Luther King Jr. Pinkney, J. Brian, illus. 2006. (Scholastic Bookshelf Ser.). (ENG.). 32p. (J). (gr. -1-k). per. 8.99 (978-0-439-78224-1(4), Scholastic Paperbacks) Scholastic, Inc.

Mattern, Joanne. Coretta Scott King: Civil Rights Activist. 2009. (Women Who Shaped History Ser.). 24p. (gr. 2-3). 42.50 (978-1-60854-816-3(3), PowerKids Pr.) Rosen Publishing Group, Inc., The.

—Martin Luther King, Jr. National Memorial: A Stone of Hope. 2017. (Core Content Social Studies -- Let's Celebrate America Ser.). (ENG., Illus.). 32p. (J). (gr. 2-5). pap. 8.99 (978-1-63440-237-8(5), 0cb298c1-d6e0-443a-a3c8-833b15dd797f); lib. bdg. 26.65 (978-1-63440-227-9(8), e01c5cb3-4ce1-4148-88fa-1ab88866015b) Red Chair Pr.

Mckissack, Patricia & Mckissack, Fredrick. Martin Luther King, Jr: Civil Rights Leader, 1 vol. 2013. (Famous African Americans Ser.). (ENG.). 24p. (gr. k-2). pap. 10.35 (978-1-4644-0203-6(5), dcecf1fd-85e6-4178-bf60-5fdeafbfee1e); (Illus.). 25.27 (978-0-7660-4099-1(2), 0f91c640-e3f1-427e-98d5-dc4fced0487f) Enslow Publishing, LLC. (Enslow Elementary).

McNeil, Niki, et al. HOCPP 1055 Martin Luther King Jr. 2006. spiral bd. 18.50 (978-1-60308-055-2(4)) In the Hands of a Child.

McPherson, Stephanie Sammartino. Biography Coretta Scott King. 2007. (Biography Ser.). (Illus.). 112p. (YA). (gr. 7-12). lib. bdg. 29.27 (978-0-8225-7156-8(0)) Twenty First Century Bks.

Meltzer, Brad. I Am Martin Luther King, Jr. Eliopoulos, Christopher, illus. 2016. (Ordinary People Change the World Ser.). 32p. (J). (gr. k-4). 15.99 (978-0-525-42852-7(6), Dial Bks) Penguin Young Readers Group.

Michelson, Richard. As Good As Anybody: Martin Luther King, Jr. , & Abraham Joshua Heschel's Amazing March Toward Freedom. ón, Raul, illus. 2013. (ENG.). 40p. (J). (gr. 1-4). 8.99 (978-0-385-75387-6(X), Dragonfly Bks.) Random Hse. Children's Bks.

Miller, Reagan. Martin Luther King, Jr. Day. 2009. (Celebrations in My World Ser.). (ENG., Illus.). 32p. (J). (gr. 1-3). pap. (978-0-7787-4308-8(X)); lib. bdg. (978-0-7787-4290-6(3)) Crabtree Publishing Co.

Mis, Melody S. Meet Coretta Scott King. (Civil Rights Leaders Ser.). 24p. (gr. 2-3). 2009. 42.50 (978-1-61511-851-9(9), PowerKids Pr.) 2007. (ENG., Illus.). (YA). lib. bdg. 26.27 (978-1-4042-4211-1(2), 6665c8c6-5932-449a-ba9d-55d71f765f26) Rosen Publishing Group, Inc., The.

—Meet Martin Luther King Jr. 2009. (Civil Rights Leaders Ser.). 24p. (gr. 2-3). 42.50 (978-1-61511-854-0(3), PowerKids Pr.) Rosen Publishing Group, Inc., The.

—Meet Martin Luther King Jr., 1 vol. 2007. (Civil Rights Leaders Ser.). (ENG., Illus.). 24p. (YA). (gr. 2-3). lib. bdg. 26.27 (978-1-4042-4209-8(0), a4ce3b17-20e4-45f2-82ea-b24cbcab11c3) Rosen Publishing Group, Inc., The.

Murcia, Rebecca Thatcher. The Civil Rights Movement. 2005. (Monumental Milestones Ser.). (Illus.). 48p. (YA). (gr. 4-7). lib. bdg. 29.95 (978-1-58415-401-3(2)) Mitchell Lane Pubs.

Murray, Julie. Martin Luther King Jr. Memorial. 2016. (US Landmarks Ser.). (ENG., Illus.). 24p. (J). (gr. -1-2). lib. bdg. 31.36 (978-1-68080-912-1(1), 23299, Abdo Kids) ABDO Publishing Co.

Myers, Walter Dean. I've Seen the Promised Land: The Life of Dr. Martin Luther King, Jr. Jenkins, Leonard, illus. (ENG.). 40p. (J). (gr. -1-3). 2012. pap. 7.99 (978-0-06-225002-5(7)) 2003. 17.99 (978-0-06-027703-1(3)) HarperCollins Pubs. (Amistad).

Nagelhout, Ryan. Martin Luther King Jr, 1 vol. 2015. (Heroes of Black History Ser.). (ENG.). 32p. (J). (gr. 3-4). 28.27 (978-1-4824-2906-0(3), 8eb07716-f86f-4c57-add7-37a247cd4d87) Stevens, Gareth Publishing LLLP.

Nelson, Maria. Coretta Scott King, 1 vol. 2011. (Civil Rights Crusaders Ser.). (ENG.). 24p. (gr. 2-3). (J). pap. 9.15 (978-1-4339-5680-5(2), 42e4948d-7214-4eb5-bd66-a30da15a5357, Gareth Stevens Learning Library); (YA). lib. bdg. 25.27 (978-1-4339-5678-2(0), 38c095e0-c3f3-4292-a8fb-34d6f4f1da90) Stevens, Gareth Publishing LLLP.

Nelson, Robin. Martin Luther King, Jr. Day. 2003. (First Step Nonfiction Ser.). (Illus.). 24p. (J). (gr. k-2). lib. bdg. 18.60 (978-0-8225-1282-0(3)) Lerner Publishing Group.

Nelson, Vaunda Micheaux. Dream March: Dr. Martin Luther King, Jr. , & the March on Washington. Comport, Sally Wern, illus. 2017. (Step into Reading Ser.). 48p. (J). (gr. k-3). 4.99 (978-1-101-93669-6(X), Random Hse. Bks. for Young Readers) Random Hse. Children's Bks.

Nichols, Kaitlyn. Martin Luther King. 2009. pap. 13.25 (978-1-60559-065-3(7)) Hameray Publishing Group, Inc.

Norwich, Grace. I Am Martin Luther King Jr. (I Am #4) 2012. (I Am Ser.: 4). (ENG., Illus.). 128p. (J). (gr. 3-5). pap. 5.99 (978-0-545-44780-5(1), Scholastic Paperbacks) Scholastic, Inc.

Oswald, Vanessa. Marching for Equality: The Journey from Selma to Montgomery, 1 vol. 2017. (Lucent Library of Black History Ser.). (ENG.). 104p. (J). (gr. 7-7). pap. 20.99 (978-1-5345-6296-7(6), 2e40c4b5-df77-47da-b603-1f02397c6f5a); lib. bdg. 41.03 (978-1-5345-6241-7(9), 9382b94f-df2a-4f5d-9400-d772dfccda12) Greenhaven Publishing LLC. (Lucent Pr.).

Patrick, Denise Lewis. A Lesson for Martin Luther King Jr: Ready-To-Read Level 2. Pate, Rodney S., illus. 2003. (Ready-To-Read Childhood of Famous Americans Ser.). (ENG.). 32p. (J). (gr. k-2). pap. 4.99 (978-0-689-85397-5(1), Simon Spotlight) Simon Spotlight.

Pinkney, Andrea Davis. Martin & Mahalia: His Words, Her Song. 2013. (ENG., Illus.). 40p. (J). (gr. 1-17). 18.99 (978-0-316-07013-3(0)) Little, Brown Bks. for Young Readers.

—Martin Rising: Requiem for a King. Pinkney, Brian, illus. 2018. (ENG.). 128p. (J). (gr. 4-7). 19.99 (978-0-545-70253-9(4), Scholastic Pr.) Scholastic, Inc.

Rappaport, Doreen. Martin's Big Words: The Life of Dr. Martin Luther King, Jr. (Caldecott Honor Book) Collier, Bryan, illus. rev. ed. 2007. (Big Words Book Ser.: 1). (ENG.). 40p. (J). (gr. -1-3). pap. 8.99 (978-1-4231-0635-7(0)) Little, Brown Bks. for Young Readers.

Ridley, Sarah. Martin Luther King: ...And the Fight for Equality. 2013. (History Makers Ser.). (ENG., Illus.). 24p. (J). (gr. 2-4). 25.65 (978-1-59771-389-4(9)) Sea-To-Sea Pubns.

Rivera, Sheila. Martin Luther King, Jr: A Life of Determination. 2006. (Illus.). 32p. (J). pap. 6.95 (978-0-8225-5697-8(9)) Lerner Publishing Group.

—Martin Luther King Jr: A Life of Determination. 2006. (Pull Ahead Bks.). (Illus.). 32p. (J). (gr. 3-7). lib. bdg. 22.60 (978-0-8225-3477-8(0), Lerner Pubns.) Lerner Publishing Group.

—Martin Luther King Jr: Una vida de determinación (A Life of Determination) 2006. (Libros para Avanzar-Biografías (Pull Ahead Books-Biographies Ser.). (Illus.). 32p. (J). (gr. 3-7). per. 6.95 (978-0-8225-6556-7(0), Ediciones Lerner) Lerner Publishing Group.

Robert Sheldon Stradford. Dj's First Parade. 2009. 44p. pap. 19.99 (978-1-4389-5864-4(1)) AuthorHouse.

Roop, Peter & Roop, Connie. Let's Dream, Martin Luther King, Jr.! 2004. (Scholastic Chapter Book Biography Ser.). (Illus.). 59p. (J). pap. (978-0-439-55443-5(8)) Scholastic, Inc.

Ruffin, Frances E. Martin Luther King & the March on Washington. 2014. (Penguin Young Readers, L3 Ser.). (ENG.). 48p. (J). (gr. 1-2). 8.24 (978-1-63245-254-2(5)) Lectorum Pubns., Inc.

Rustad, Martha E. H. & Leslie, Tonya. Martin Luther King, Jr: A Life of Fairness. 2007. (People of Character Ser.). (ENG., Illus.). 24p. (J). (gr. 2-5). lib. bdg. 26.95 (978-1-60014-090-7(4)) Bellwether Media.

Saddleback Educational Publishing Staff, ed. Martin Luther King Jr., 1 vol. unabr. ed. 2007. (Graphic Biographies Ser.). (ENG., Illus.). 25p. (YA). (gr. 4-12). pap. 9.75 (978-1-59905-227-4(X)) Saddleback Educational Publishing, Inc.

Schuldt, Lori Meek. Martin Luther King, Jr: With Profiles of Mohandas K. Gandhi & Nelson Mandela. 2006. (Biographical Connections Ser.). (Illus.). 112p. (J). (978-0-7166-1822-5(2)) World Bk., Inc.

Schuman, Michael A. The Life of Martin Luther King, Jr: Leader for Civil Rights, 1 vol. 2014. (Legendary African Americans Ser.). (ENG., Illus.). 96p. (gr. 6-7). 31.61 (978-0-7660-6147-7(7), 4ba0d49d-85a7-44d7-9a67-b67ab5faa5aa) Enslow Publishing, LLC.

Schuman, Michael A. & Schraff, Anne E. Martin Luther King Jr: Fighting for Civil Rights, 1 vol. 2017. (Rebels with a Cause Ser.). (ENG.). 128p. (gr. 8-8). lib. bdg. 38.93 (978-0-7660-8511-4(2), 7a340404-6627-4d60-9799-7a9b25a8b7a0) Enslow Publishing, LLC.

Schwartz, Heather E. The March on Washington: A Primary Source Exploration of the Pivotal Protest, 1 vol. 2014. (We Shall Overcome Ser.). (ENG.). 32p. (J). (gr. 3-6). lib. bdg. 27.99 (978-1-4914-0223-8(7), 125795) Capstone.

Shange, Ntozake. Coretta Scott. Nelson, Kadir, illus. (ENG.). 32p. (J). (gr. -1-4). 2011. pap. 9.99 (978-0-06-125366-9(9)) 2009. 17.99 (978-0-06-125364-5(2)) HarperCollins Pubs. (Tegen, Katherine Bks).

Spence, Kelly. Martin Luther King Jr. & Peaceful Protest, 1 vol. 2016. (Primary Sources of the Civil Rights Movement Ser.). (ENG., Illus.). 64p. (gr. 6-6). 35.93 (978-1-5026-1864-1(8), 73f31652-3792-42c7-a262-6049a98b218c) Cavendish Square Publishing LLC.

Spiller, Sara. Coretta Scott King. Bane, Jeff, illus. 2019. (My Early Library: My Itty-Bitty Bio Ser.). (ENG.). 24p. (J). (gr. k-1). pap. 12.79 (978-1-5341-3924-4(9), 212525); lib. bdg. 30.64 (978-1-5341-4268-8(1), 212524) Cherry Lake Publishing.

Staley, Erin. Martin Luther King Jr. & the Speech That Inspired the World, 1 vol. 2014. (Celebration of the Civil Rights Movement Ser.). (ENG.). 80p. (YA). (gr. 6-6). 37.47 (978-1-4777-7745-9(8), 8b6a61dd-ecba-4719-8f88-7e12ebc34fee) Rosen Publishing Group, Inc., The.

Stanmyre, Jackie F. Coretta Scott King & the Center for Nonviolent Social Change, 1 vol. 2016. (Primary Sources of the Civil Rights Movement Ser.). (ENG., Illus.). 64p. (gr. 6-6). 35.93 (978-1-5026-1876-4(1), e79c9046-d704-4932-b41f-dd5e2fdbd0ac) Cavendish Square Publishing LLC.

Swain, Gwenyth. Riding to Washington. Geister, David, illus. 2007. (Tales of Young Americans Ser.). (ENG.). 40p. (J). (gr. 1-4). 17.95 (978-1-58536-324-7(3), 202128) Sleeping Bear Pr.

Swanson, James L. Chasing King's Killer: the Hunt for Martin Luther King, Jr. 's Assassin. 2018. (ENG., Illus.). 384p. (YA). (gr. 7). 19.99 (978-0-545-72333-6(7), Scholastic Pr.) Scholastic, Inc.

Taylor-Butler, Christine. Martin Luther King, Jr. Memorial (a True Book: National Parks) (Library Edition) 2019. (True Book (Relaunch) Ser.). (ENG., Illus.). 48p. (J). (gr. 3-5). lib. bdg. 31.00 (978-0-531-12934-0(9), Children's Pr.) Scholastic Library Publishing.

Teitelbaum, Michael & Helfand, Lewis. Martin Luther King Jr.: Let Freedom Ring: Campfire Biography-Heroes Line. Banerjee, Sankha, illus. 2013. (Campfire Graphic Novels Ser.). (ENG.). 88p. (YA). (gr. 5). pap. 11.99 (978-93-80028-69-9(5), Campfire) Steerforth Pr.

Tisdale, Rachel. The March on Washington, 1 vol., 1. 2014. (We Shall Overcome Ser.). (ENG.). 32p. (J). (gr. 4-5). 28.93 (978-1-4777-6069-7(5), 98cf5a6c-ed9e-4cbb-80b9-c07644e15cd1, PowerKids Pr.) Rosen Publishing Group, Inc., The.

Trueit, Trudi Strain. Rookie Read-About Holidays: Martin Luther King Jr. Day. 2006. (Rookie Read-About Holidays Ser.). (ENG., Illus.). 32p. (J). (gr. 1-2). lib. bdg. 20.50 (978-0-531-12459-8(2)) Scholastic Library Publishing.

Vaughn, Wally G. & Davis, Mattie Campbell, eds. The Selma Campaign, 1963-1965: The Decisive Battle of the Civil Rights Movement. 2006. (ENG., Illus.). 244p. pap. 19.95 (978-0-912469-44-7(7)) Majority Pr., The.

Vietze, Andrew. The Life & Death of Martin Luther King Jr. 2017. (Spotlight on the Civil Rights Movement Ser.). (Illus.). 48p. (J). (gr. 10-15). 70.50 (978-1-5383-8038-3(2)); (ENG., (gr. 6-6). pap. 12.75 (978-1-5383-8039-0(0), 119383a8-59e0-43b8-81f6-bb0064f5f386) Rosen Publishing Group, Inc., The.

Ward, Jill. Martin Luther King, Jr: Georgia, My State Biographies. l.t. ed. 2008. (ENG., Illus.). 24p. (J). (gr. k-2). 22.60 (978-1-935077-01-5(5)); pap. 22.60 (978-1-935077-08-4(2)) State Standards Publishing, LLC.

Watkins, Angela Farris. Love Will See You Through: Martin Luther King Jr. 's Six Guiding Beliefs (as Told by His Niece) Comport, Sally Wern, illus. 2014. (ENG.). 32p. (J). (gr. 1-6). 18.99 (978-1-4169-8693-5(6), Simon & Schuster Bks. For Young Readers) Simon & Schuster Bks. For Young Readers.

—My Uncle Martin's Words for America: Martin Luther King Jr. 's Niece Tells How He Made a Difference. Velasquez, Eric, illus. 2015. (ENG.). 40p. (J). (gr. 1-4). 9.95 (978-1-4197-1836-6(3), 1004703, Abrams Bks. for Young Readers) Abrams, Inc.

Watson, Stephanie. Martin Luther King Jr. & the March on Washington, 1 vol. 2015. (Stories of the Civil Rights Movement Ser.). (ENG., Illus.). 48p. (J). (gr. 4-8). 35.64 (978-1-62403-881-5(6), 18132) ABDO Publishing Co.

Waxman, Laura Hamilton. Coretta Scott King. 2008. pap. 52.95 (978-0-8225-9387-4(4)); (ENG., Illus.). 48p. (gr. 3-6). lib. bdg. 27.93 (978-0-8225-7168-1(4), Lerner Pubns.) Lerner Publishing Group.

Weakland, Mark. When Martin Luther King Jr. Wore Roller Skates. Ballesteros, Patrick, illus. (J). 2017. 31p. (978-1-5158-0141-2(1)) 2016. (ENG.). 32p. (gr. 1-4). lib. bdg. 28.65 (978-1-4795-9685-0(X), 132341) Capstone. (Picture Window Bks.).

Weatherford, Carole Boston. Be a King: Dr. Martin Luther King Jr. 's Dream & You. Ransome, James E., illus. 2018. (ENG.). 40p. (J). 17.99 (978-0-8027-2368-0(3), 900079719, Bloomsbury USA Childrens) Bloomsbury Publishing USA.

Weston Woods Staff, creator. March on! the Day My Brother Martin Changed the World. 2011. 38.75 (978-0-545-31399-5(6)); 18.95 (978-0-545-31398-8(8)) Weston Woods Studios, Inc.

—Martin's Big Words. 2011. 38.75 (978-0-545-15256-3(9)) 2011. 18.95 (978-0-545-15251-8(8)) 2004. (J). 29.95 (978-1-55592-133-0(7)) Weston Woods Studios, Inc.

Who Was Martin Luther King, Jr? (Guided Reading Levels Ser.). 28.56 (978-0-7362-1055-3(5)) CENGAGE Learning.

Winget, Mary. Martin Luther King, Jr. 2004. (History Maker Bios Ser.). (Illus.). 48p. (J). pap. 8.95 (978-0-8225-4804-1(6), Lerner Pubns.) Lerner Publishing Group.

Wittenstein, Barry. A Place to Land: Martin Luther King Jr. & the Speech That Inspired a Nation. Pinkney, Jerry, illus. 2019. (ENG.). 48p. (J). (gr. 2-5). 18.99 (978-0-8234-4331-4(0), Neal Porter Bks) Holiday Hse., Inc.

KING PHILIP'S WAR, 1675-1676—FICTION

Smith, Mary P. Wells. The Young Puritans in King Philip's War. Bridgman, L. J., illus. 2011. 396p. 54.95 (978-1-258-05550-9(3)) Literary Licensing, LLC.

KINGFISHERS—FICTION

Burns, Dal. The Kookaburra & Other Stories. 2007. (ENG.). 76p. per. 16.95 (978-1-4241-1770-3(4)) PublishAmerica, Inc.

KINGS, QUEENS, RULERS, ETC.

see also Dictators; Prime Ministers

also names of countries with the subdivision Kings and Rulers, e.g. Great Britain—Kings and Rulers; also names of individual kings and rulers, e.g. Elizabeth I, Queen of England, 1533-1603

Abbott, Jacob. Cleopatra. 2019. (J). pap. (978-1-947644-17-5(3)) Canon Pr.

—Elizabeth I. 2019. (J). pap. (978-1-947644-18-2(1)) Canon Pr.

—Nero. 2009. 202p. (J). pap. 12.00 (978-1-59128-057-6(5)) Canon Pr.

Aldritt, Jeremy. Thomas Paine & the Power of Common Sense, 1 vol. 2015. (Spotlight on American History Ser.). (ENG., Illus.). 24p. (J). (gr. 4-6). pap. 11.00 (978-1-4994-1765-4(9), 6d93e3a5-db18-41c4-af43-5de9b1569455, PowerKids Pr.) Rosen Publishing Group, Inc., The.

Aller, Susan Bivin. Sitting Bull. 2004. (History Maker Bios Ser.). (J). pap. 6.95 (978-0-8225-2072-6(9)) Lerner Publishing Group.

—Sitting Bull. Parlin, Tim, tr. Parlin, Tim, illus. 2004. (History Maker Bios Ser.). 47p. (J). 26.60 (978-0-8225-0700-0(5), Carolrhoda Bks.) Lerner Publishing Group.

Aronin, Miriam. Merciless Monarchs & Ruthless Royalty. 2015. (ShockZone (tm) — Villains Ser.). (ENG., Illus.). 32p. (J). (gr. 5-8). E-Book 46.65 (978-1-4677-6003-4(X), 9781467760034, Lerner Digital) Lerner Publishing Group.

Bailey, Gerry & Foster, Karen. Queen Victoria's Diamond. Noyes, Leighton & Radford, Karen, illus. 2008. (Stories of Great People Ser.). (ENG.). 40p. (J). (gr. 3-6). lib. bdg. (978-0-7787-3697-4(0)); pap. (978-0-7787-3719-3(5)) Crabtree Publishing Co.

—Sitting Bull's Tomahawk. Radford, Karen & Noyes, Leighton, illus. 2008. (Stories of Great People Ser.). (ENG.). 40p. (J). (gr. 3-8). pap. (978-0-7787-3714-8(4)); lib. bdg. (978-0-7787-3692-9(X)) Crabtree Publishing Co.

Bankston, John. The Life & Times of Alexander the Great. 2004. (Biography of Ancient Civilizations Ser.). (Illus.). 48p. (J). lib. bdg. (978-1-58415-235-4(4)) Mitchell Lane Pubs.

Barnes-Murphy, Rowan. Kings & Queens of Britain. 2003. (Illus.). 40p. (YA). (978-1-84365-027-0(4), Pavilion Children's Books) Pavilion Bks.

Baum, Margaux & Forsyth, Fiona. Augustus, 1 vol. 2016. (Leaders of the Ancient World Ser.). (ENG., Illus.). 112p. (J). (gr. 6-6). 38.80 (978-1-5081-7242-0(0), 12038024-1931-4939-b82f-b3acfbb5e4b5) Rosen Publishing Group, Inc., The.

Baum, Margaux & Morgan, Julian. Constantine, 1 vol. 2016. (Leaders of the Ancient World Ser.). (ENG.). 112p. (J). (gr. 6-6). 38.80 (978-1-5081-7252-9(8), 21146d9b-688f-46d2-a2bb-3f62820d7720) Rosen Publishing Group, Inc., The.

Beaumont, Steve. How to Draw Magical Kings & Queens, 1 vol. 2007. (Drawing Fantasy Art Ser.: Vol. 2). (ENG., Illus.). 32p. (J). (gr. 4-5). lib. bdg. 30.27 (978-1-4042-3860-2(3), fa9dbb20-8b50-4999-b746-415e8efcb148) Rosen Publishing Group, Inc., The.

Behnke, Alison. The Conquests of Alexander the Great. 2007. (Pivotal Moments in History Ser.). (ENG., Illus.). 160p. (J). (gr. 9-12). lib. bdg. 38.60 (978-0-8225-5920-7(X)) Lerner Publishing Group.

Benson, Lyn. Who Were the Magi. Joshua, Benson Benson Joshua, illus. 2007. 56p. pap. 23.99 (978-0-615-13524-3(2)) Benson, Lyn.

Bhote, Themina. Charlemagne: Life & Times of an Early Medieval Emperor, 1 vol. 2004. (Leaders of the Middle Ages Ser.). (ENG., Illus.). 112p. (YA). (gr. 5-8). lib. bdg. 39.80 (978-1-4042-0161-3(0), fccead80-3af4-4c39-87f2-7b6a486b86fa) Rosen Publishing Group, Inc., The.

—Charlemagne: The Life & Times of an Early Medieval Emperor. 2009. (Leaders of the Middle Ages Ser.). 112p. (gr. 5-8). 66.50 (978-1-61513-896-8(X), Rosen Reference) Rosen Publishing Group, Inc., The.

Bodden, Valerie. Conquistadors. 2017. (X-Books: Fighters Ser.). (ENG., Illus.). 32p. (J). (gr. 3-6). (978-1-60818-812-3(4), 20369, Creative Education) Creative Co., The.

Brennan, Joseph K. What Is an Oligarchy?, 1 vol. Crabtree Publishing Staff, ed. 2012. (Forms of Government Ser.: No. 5). (ENG.). 48p. (J). pap. (978-0-7787-5327-8(1)) Crabtree Publishing Co.

Brooks, E. s. & Brooks, E. S. Historic Boys. 2013. 208p. pap. (978-3-95507-947-5(3)) DOGMA. in Europäischer Hochschulverlag GmbH & Co. KG.

Burgan, Michael. Dracula's Dark World. 2010. (HorrorScapes Ser.). (Illus.). 32p. (J). (gr. 4-7). lib. bdg. 25.27 (978-1-936087-96-9(0)) Bearport Publishing Co., Inc.

Burnett, Alan & Burnett, Allan. Mary Queen of Scots & All That. Anderson, Scoular, illus. 2016. (and All That Ser.). 112p. (gr. 4-8). pap. 7.95 (978-1-78027-388-4(6)) Birlinn, Ltd. GBR. Dist: Casemate Pubs. & Bk. Distributors, LLC.

Cachola, Jean Iwata, et al. O Kamehameha III: Kauikeaouli. 2004. (HAW & ENG., Illus.). xiv, 120p. (J). pap. (978-0-87336-047-0(8)) Kamehameha Publishing.

Caravantes, Peggy. Cleopatra: Powerful Leader or Ruthless Pharaoh? 2015. (Perspectives on History Ser.). (ENG., Illus.). 32p. (J). (gr. 3-6). lib. bdg. 27.99 *(978-1-4914-2042-3(1)*, 127520) Capstone.

Carton, Gerard. We Four Kings. 2009. (Illus.). 52p. pap. *(978-1-84748-474-1(3))* Athena Pr.

Cassidy, Tam. The White Lady Ghost, 1 vol. 2014. (Jr. Graphic Ghost Stories Ser.). (ENG.). 24p. (J). (gr. 2-3). lib. bdg. 28.93 *(978-1-4777-7125-9(5)*, b04d0732-9ca9-4870-b557-d2ea6ca034e6, PowerKids Pr.) Rosen Publishing Group, Inc., The.

Chambers, Catherine. An Emperor's Guide. Pentney, Ryan, illus. 2017. (How-To Guides for Fiendish Rulers Ser.). (ENG.). 32p. (J). (gr. 3-6). E-Book 4.99 *(978-1-5124-3621-1(6)*, 9781512436211); E-Book 42.65 *(978-1-5124-3620-4(8)*, 9781512436204) Lerner Publishing Group. (Hungry Tomato (r)).

Clark, Connie. Who in the World Was the Unready King: The Story of Ethelred. 2005. (Who in the World Ser.: 0). (ENG., Illus.). 54p. (gr. 2-18). pap. 9.50 *(978-0-9728603-7-6(1)*, 86037) Well-Trained Mind Pr.

Collier, James Lincoln. The Tecumseh You Never Knew. 2004. (You Never Knew Ser.). (ENG., Illus.). 80p. (J). 25.50 *(978-0-516-24426-6(4)*, Children's Pr.) Scholastic Library Publishing.

Connors, Kathleen. The Life of Cleopatra, 1 vol., Vol. 1. 2013. (Famous Lives Ser.). (ENG.). 24p. (J). (gr. 1-2). 25.27 *(978-1-4824-0384-8(6)*, e5b3209d-d905-48c4-b15f-aeb6393fb94f) Stevens, Gareth Publishing LLLP.

Daning, Tom. Mitologia Romana: Rómulo y Remo, 1 vol. Obregón, José María, illus. 2009. (Historietas Juveniles: Mitologías (Jr. Graphic Mythologies) Ser.). (SPA.). 24p. (J). (gr. 2-3). lib. bdg. 28.93 *(978-1-4358-8570-7(8)*, eb4c1f63-3750-40d6-87ee-d6a1fe792f51) Rosen Publishing Group, Inc., The.

—Roman Mythology: Romulus & Remus, 1 vol. 2006. (Jr. Graphic Mythologies Ser.). (ENG., Illus.). 24p. (gr. 2-3). (J). lib. bdg. 28.93 *(978-1-4042-3397-3(0)*, a6131d89-6894-4339-ba74-879c71059bd6); pap. 10.60 *(978-1-4042-2150-5(6)*, 74468897-ef96-4a12-a960-c0a85d3093f1, PowerKids Pr.) Rosen Publishing Group, Inc., The.

Daning, Tom & Obregón, José María. Mitologia Romana: Rómulo y Remo, 1 vol. 2009. (Historietas Juveniles: Mitologías (Jr. Graphic Mythologies) Ser.). (SPA., Illus.). 24p. (gr. 2-3). pap. 10.60 *(978-1-4358-3334-0(1)*, b6199b97-3861-4cbd-ba50-bfec01e62f2f) Rosen Publishing Group, Inc., The.

Davis, Kenneth C. Don't Know Much about the Kings & Queens of England. Date not set. 48p. (J). (gr. 1-4). pap. 5.99 *(978-0-06-446229-7(3))* HarperCollins Pubs.

Day, Nick. Queens of England. 2016. (Uncommon Women Ser.). (ENG., Illus.). 48p. (gr. 3-8). 27.99 *(978-1-62920-578-6(8))* Scobre Pr. Corp.

Dean, Arlan. With All My Might: Cochise & the Indian Wars. 2009. (Great Moments in American History Ser.). 32p. (gr. 3-3). 47.90 *(978-1-61513-137-2(X))* Rosen Publishing Group, Inc., The.

DeFord, Diane. Chief Sitting Bull. 2009. pap. 13.25 *(978-1-60559-070-7(3))* Hameray Publishing Group, Inc.

Dell, Pamela. Queen Noor, 1 vol. 2013. (Leading Women Ser.). (ENG.). 128p. (YA). (gr. 7-7). 42.64 *(978-0-7614-4958-4(2)*, 552592c1-3555-489d-9243-53b4e3eafb6a); pap. 20.99 *(978-1-62712-116-3(1)*, 506d66d2-3481-4700-981b-44403f2703aa) Cavendish Square Publishing LLC.

Demi. Alexander the Great, 0 vols. 2012. (ENG., Illus.). 64p. (J). (gr. 4-6). 19.99 *(978-0-7614-5700-8(3)*, 9780761457008, Two Lions) Amazon Publishing.

Demirel, Ruhi, et al. Abu Bakr As-Siddiq. 2016. (Age of Bliss Ser.). (ENG.). 82p. (J). (gr. 4-8). pap. 5.95 *(978-1-59784-371-3(7)*, Tughra Bks.) Blue Dome, Inc.

—Uthman Ibn Affan. 2016. (Age of Bliss Ser.). 72p. (J). (gr. 4-8). pap. 5.95 *(978-1-59784-373-7(3)*, Tughra Bks.) Blue Dome, Inc.

Doeden, Matt. Queen Elizabeth II: Modern Monarch. 2020. (Gateway Biographies Ser.). (ENG., Illus.). 48p. (J). (gr. 4-8). pap. 11.99 *(978-1-5415-8890-5(8)*, d27f41fe-3781-414d-b279-a28c91290d8a); lib. bdg. 31.99 *(978-1-5415-7744-2(2)*, 5b7c8ba0-1f4c-45e5-810e-b1f721b705ec) Lerner Publishing Group. (Lerner Pubns.).

Doyle, William. Napoleon Bonaparte: Emperor, 1 vol. 2016. (History Makers Ser.). (ENG., Illus.). 144p. (YA). (gr. 9-9). 47.36 *(978-1-5026-2447-5(8)*, b7639853-43b4-4b44-beae-186162b5d27f) Cavendish Square Publishing LLC.

Dyan, Penelope. A Royal Residence — A Kid's Guide to Windsor Castle. Weigand, John D., photos by. 2011. (Illus.). 40p. pap. 12.95 *(978-1-935630-65-4(2))* Bellissima Publishing, LLC.

Eastwood, Kay. Medieval Society, 1 vol. 2003. (Medieval World Ser.). (ENG., Illus.). 32p. (J). (gr. 5). pap. *(978-0-7787-1377-7(6))* Crabtree Publishing Co.

Emperor Ashoka of India: What Makes a Ruler Legitimate? (NCHS) (YA). (gr. 6-9). spiral bd., tchr.'s planning gde. ed. 11.50 *(978-0-382-44467-8(1))* Cobblestone Publishing Co.

Evento, Susan. Sitting Bull. 2005. (Rookie Biographies Ser.). (ENG., Illus.). 32p. (J). (gr. 1-2). pap. 4.95 *(978-0-516-25829-4(X)*, Children's Pr.) Scholastic Library Publishing.

Fisk Pack, Mary. Cleopatra: "Serpent of the Nile" Malone, Peter, illus. 2011. (Thinking Girl's Treasury of Dastardly Dames Ser.). (ENG.). 32p. (J). (gr. 3-8). 18.95 *(978-0-9834256-0-1(4))* Goosebottom Bks. LLC.

Forsyth, Fiona. Augustus: The First Emperor. 2009. (Ancient Leaders Ser.). 112p. (gr. 5-8). 66.50 *(978-1-61511-419-1(X)*, Rosen Reference) Rosen Publishing Group, Inc., The.

Gamblin, Rose Tooley & Hernández, Oscar. The Queen of Sheba. 2008. (SPA & ENG.). (J). *(978-0-8127-0482-2(7))* Autumn Hse. Publishing Co.

George, Enzo. The Tomb of China's First Emperor. 2017. (Crypts, Tombs, & Secret Rooms Ser.). 48p. (gr. 4-5). pap. 84.30 *(978-1-5382-0645-4(5))* Stevens, Gareth Publishing LLLP.

Gibson, Karen Bush. The Life & Times of Catherine the Great. 2005. (Biography from Ancient Civilizations Ser.). (Illus.). 48p. (J). (gr. 4-7). lib. bdg. 29.95 *(978-1-58415-347-4(4))* Mitchell Lane Pubs.

Gigliotti, Jim & Who HQ. Who Was Napoleon? Copeland, Gregory, illus. 2018. (Who Was? Ser.). 112p. (J). (gr. 3-7). 5.99 *(978-0-448-48860-8(4)*, Penguin Workshop) Penguin Young Readers Group.

Goldberg, Enid A. & Itzkowitz, Norman. Wicked History: Vlad the Impaler: The Real Count Dracula. Goldberg, Enid, illus. 2008. (Wicked History Ser.). (ENG.). 128p. (J). (gr. 8-13). 18.69 *(978-0-531-12599-1(8)*, Watts, Franklin) Scholastic Library Publishing.

Goldberg, Jan. Napoleon Bonaparte. 2004. (ZB Reads Trio Books). 87p. (gr. 5-7). pap. 5.00 *(978-0-7367-1799-1(4))* Zaner-Bloser, Inc.

Gorman, Jacqueline & Guy, John. British Kings & Queens: 1,000 Years of Intrigue, Struggle, Passion & Power. 2009. (ENG.). 128p. (J). (gr. 4-7). pap. 12.95 *(978-1-84696-987-4(5)*, TickTock Books) Octopus Publishing Group GBR. Dist: Independent Pubs. Group.

Green, Richard L. A Salute to Historic African Kings & Queens. 2011. (Empak "Black History" Publication Ser.: Vol. 6). (J). *(978-0-9616156-5-9(6))* Empak Publishing Co.

Greenblatt, Miriam. Napoleon Bonaparte & Imperial France, 1 vol. 2007. (Rulers & Their Times Ser.). (ENG., Illus.). 80p. (J). (gr. 6-6). lib. bdg. 36.93 *(978-0-7614-1837-5(7)*, e263ac46-7d98-4d74-8dd2-972dc76f7518) Cavendish Square Publishing LLC.

—Süleyman the Magnificent & the Ottoman Empire, 1 vol. 2003. (Rulers & Their Times Ser.). (ENG., Illus.). 80p. (gr. 6-6). 36.93 *(978-0-7614-1489-6(4)*, 48cdd3b8-efa7-4e6c-9607-c7284779278c) Cavendish Square Publishing LLC.

Gülen, Asiye & Duman, Clare. Umar Ibn Al-Khattab. 2016. (Age of Bliss Ser.). 72p. (J). (gr. 4-8). pap. 5.95 *(978-1-59784-372-0(5)*, Tughra Bks.) Blue Dome, Inc.

Gülen, Asiye, et al. Ali Ibn Abi Talib. 2016. (Age of Bliss Ser.). (ENG., Illus.). 69p. (J). (gr. 4-8). pap. 5.95 *(978-1-59784-374-4(1)*, Tughra Bks.) Blue Dome, Inc.

Hardyman, Robyn. What Is a Monarchy?, 1 vol., Vol. 1. 2013. (Understanding Political Systems Ser.). (ENG.). 48p. (J). (gr. 6-8). 34.61 *(978-1-4824-0314-5(5)*, a8132d02-1b4d-464e-9d95-4932d919abab); pap. 15.05 *(978-1-4824-0315-2(3)*, d772339c-0246-4a73-b8a2-5d48a826151c) Stevens, Gareth Publishing LLLP.

Harrison, Paul. History VIPs: Boudicca. 2017. (History VIPs Ser.). (ENG., Illus.). 32p. (J). (gr. 4-6). pap. 12.99 *(978-0-7502-9917-6(7)*, Wayland) Hachette Children's Group GBR. Dist: Hachette Bk. Group.

Havemeyer, Janie. Catherine de' Medici: "The Black Queen" Malone, Peter, illus. 2011. (Thinking Girl's Treasury of Dastardly Dames Ser.). (ENG.). 32p. (J). (gr. 3-8). 18.95 *(978-0-9834256-3-2(9))* Goosebottom Bks. LLC.

—Njinga the Warrior Queen. Malone, Peter, illus. 2011. (Thinking Girl's Treasury of Dastardly Dames Ser.). 32p. (J). (gr. 3-8). 18.95 *(978-0-9834256-6-3(3))* Goosebottom Bks. LLC.

Hayhurst, Chris. Sitting Bull: Sioux Chief = Toro Sentado: Jefe Sioux, 1 vol. de la Vega, Eida, tr. 2003. (Famous People in American History / Grandes Personajes en la Historia de Los Estados Unidos Ser.). (ENG & SPA., Illus.). 32p. (gr. 2-3). lib. bdg. 29.13 *(978-0-8239-4168-1(X)*, 7c2b3e50-df9d-4b60-95e9-904698643800, Editorial Buenas Letras) Rosen Publishing Group, Inc., The.

—Sitting Bull: Sioux War Chief. 2009. (Primary Sources of Famous People in American History Ser.). 32p. (gr. 2-3). 47.90 *(978-1-60851-724-4(1))* Rosen Publishing Group, Inc., The.

—Sitting Bull / Toro Sentado: Sioux War Chief / Jefe Sioux. 2009. (Famous People in American History/Grandes personajes en la historia de los Estados Unidos Ser.). (SPA.). 32p. (gr. 2-3). 47.90 *(978-1-61512-555-5(8)*, Editorial Buenas Letras) Rosen Publishing Group, Inc., The.

—Toro Sentado: Jefe Sioux, 1 vol. 2003. (Grandes Personajes en la Historia de Los Estados Unidos (Famous People in American History) Ser.). (SPA.). 32p. (gr. 3-4). pap. 10.00 *(978-0-8239-4238-1(4)*, 3bb38c5c-d5ef-4f35-9217-a163596589ee); (Illus.). lib. bdg. 29.13 *(978-0-8239-4144-5(2)*, 76f2b3f4-2601-49c2-9de3-680b1ae6835e, Editorial Buenas Letras) Rosen Publishing Group, Inc., The.

—Toro Sentado: Jefe sioux (Sitting Bull: Sioux War Chief) 2009. (Grandes personajes en la historia de los Estados Unidos (Famous People in American History) Ser.). (SPA.). 32p. (gr. 2-3). 47.90 *(978-1-61512-809-9(3)*, Editorial Buenas Letras) Rosen Publishing Group, Inc., The.

Heyer, Carol, illus. & retold by. Excalibur. Heyer, Carol, retold by. *(978-1-59093-022-9(3)*, Eager Minds Pr.) Warehousing & Fulfillment Specialists, LLC (WFS, LLC).

Hilliam, David. Eleanor of Aquitaine: The Richest Queen in Medieval Europe. (Leaders of the Middle Ages Ser.). 112p. (gr. 5-8). 2009. 66.50 *(978-1-61513-897-5(8)*, Rosen Reference) 2004. (ENG., Illus.). (J). lib. bdg. 39.80 *(978-1-4042-0162-0(9)*, 850fb274-c843-423e-8e2a-fff96d825369) Rosen Publishing Group, Inc., The.

—Richard the Lionheart & the Third Crusade: The English King Confronts Saladin in AD 1191. 2009. (Library of the Middle Ages Ser.). 64p. (gr. 5-8). 58.50 *(978-1-60853-902-4(4)*, Rosen Reference) Rosen Publishing Group, Inc., The.

—Richard the Lionhearted & the Third Crusade: The English King Confronts Saladin, AD 1191, 1 vol. 2003. (Library of the Middle Ages Ser.). (ENG., Illus.). 64p. (YA). (gr. 5-8). lib. bdg. 37.13 *(978-0-8239-4213-8(9)*, 9615dcf4-03e8-4f9c-87be-a8d4f0c6c92f, Rosen Reference) Rosen Publishing Group, Inc., The.

Hilliam, Paul. Elizabeth I: Queen of England's Golden Age. 2009. (Rulers, Scholars, & Artists of the Renaissance Ser.). 112p. (gr. 5-8). 66.50 *(978-1-60852-940-7(1)*, Rosen Reference) Rosen Publishing Group, Inc., The.

Hinds, Kathryn. The Court, 1 vol. 2005. (Life in the Renaissance Ser.). (ENG., Illus.). 80p. (gr. 6-6). lib. bdg. 36.93 *(978-0-7614-1676-0(5)*, 1232a1ca-e953-4253-8ad1-6f6dfd2df73c) Cavendish Square Publishing LLC.

Hockinson, Liz. Marie Antoinette "Madame Deficit" Malone, Peter, illus. 2011. (Thinking Girl's Treasury of Dastardly Dames Ser.). (ENG.). 32p. (J). (gr. 3-8). 18.95 *(978-0-9834256-4-9(7))* Goosebottom Bks. LLC.

Hollander, Barbara Gottfried. Elizabeth I: Queen of England, 1 vol. 2017. (Women Who Changed History Ser.). (ENG., Illus.). 48p. (J). (gr. 6-7). lib. bdg. 28.41 *(978-1-68048-643-8(8)*, 251dc564-d495-4be1-82c8-296e89b76a95, Britannica Educational Publishing) Rosen Publishing Group, Inc., The.

Hollihan, Kerrie Logan. Elizabeth I, the People's Queen: Her Life & Times, 21 Activities. 2011. (For Kids Ser.: 38). (ENG., Illus.). 144p. (J). (gr. 4-18). pap. 18.99 *(978-1-56976-349-0(6))* Chicago Review Pr., Inc.

Jeffrey, Gary. Sitting Bull: The Life of a Lakota Chief. 2009. (Graphic Nonfiction Biographies Ser.). (ENG.). 48p. (YA). (gr. 4-5). 58.50 *(978-1-61513-027-6(6)*, Rosen Reference) Rosen Publishing Group, Inc., The.

Jeffrey, Gary & Petty, Kate. Sitting Bull: The Life of a Lakota Sioux Chief, 1 vol. 2005. (Graphic Nonfiction Biographies Ser.). (ENG., Illus.). 48p. (YA). (gr. 4-6). lib. bdg. 37.13 *(978-1-4042-0247-4(1)*, 9175d2ac-487b-4e78-831d-01c6d6e70097) Rosen Publishing Group, Inc., The.

Kaplan, Arie. Dracula: The Life of Vlad the Impaler, 1 vol. 2011. (Vampires Ser.). (Illus.). 64p. (J). (ENG.). (gr. 5-5). pap. 13.95 *(978-1-4488-2232-4(7)*, 4bfcfbbb-794b-455d-a512-b24bef640664, Rosen Reference); (ENG., (gr. 5-5). lib. bdg. 37.13 *(978-1-4488-1229-5(1)*, e9db5b59-211d-4fb4-b1f8-1bc704b374c4); 77.70 *(978-1-4488-2233-1(5)*, Rosen Reference) Rosen Publishing Group, Inc., The.

Kelly, Richard, ed. 100 Facts Kings & Queens. 2017. 48p. (J). pap. 9.95 *(978-1-78209-373-2(7))* Miles Kelly Publishing, Ltd. GBR. Dist: Parkwest Pubns., Inc.

Kenney, Karen Latchana. Real-Life Kings. 2019. (Bumba Books (r) — Real-Life Royalty Ser.). (ENG., Illus.). 24p. (J). (gr. -1-1). 26.65 *(978-1-5415-5730-7(1)*, 4f9532af-9060-45da-ab24-a7113edd11da, Lerner Pubns.) Lerner Publishing Group.

—Real-Life Queens. 2019. (Bumba Books (r) — Real-Life Royalty Ser.). (ENG., Illus.). 24p. (J). (gr. -1-1). pap. 8.99 *(978-1-5415-7359-8(5)*, 9befe4ad-247a-4f8f-951a-f63f322136cd); lib. bdg. 26.65 *(978-1-5415-5731-4(X)*, f7c8b522-94a6-437f-bef5-bf76ef4b1dbc) Lerner Publishing Group. (Lerner Pubns.).

Kerrigan, Michael. The Untold History of the Roman Emperors, 1 vol. 2016. (History Exposed Ser.). (ENG.). 256p. (YA). (gr. 9-9). 56.71 *(978-1-5026-1910-5(5)*, 0bd096da-b016-47a9-8189-7e0183c037b7) Cavendish Square Publishing LLC.

Kings Curriculum Binder: Absolute Monarchs Curriculum with Audio CD. 2006. 208p. (YA). ring bd. 135.00 *(978-0-9791118-0-8(3))* History Jukebox, LLC.

Knox, Barbara. Forbidden City: China's Imperial Palace. 2006. (Castles, Palaces, & Tombs Ser.). (Illus.). 32p. (J). (gr. 2-5). lib. bdg. 25.27 *(978-1-59716-070-4(9)*, 1251394) Bearport Publishing Co., Inc.

Koh, Frederick. The 10 Mightiest Conquerors. 2008. (J). 14.99 *(978-1-55448-517-8(7))* Scholastic Library Publishing.

Kramer, Ann. World History Biographies: Eleanor of Aquitaine: The Queen Who Rode off to Battle. 2006. (National Geographic World History Biographies Ser.). (ENG., Illus.). 64p. (J). (gr. 4-7). 17.95 *(978-0-7922-5895-7(9)*, National Geographic Children's Bks.) National Geographic Society.

Leaders of the Ancient World: Set 2, 16 vols. 2017. (Leaders of the Ancient World Ser.). (ENG.). 112p. (gr. 6-6). 310.40 *(978-1-4994-6629-4(3)*, c39b9aab-d13e-4f63-bca8-e772ecf462b1, Rosen Young Adult) Rosen Publishing Group, Inc., The.

Lee, Sally. Kings & Queens, 1 vol. 2013. (Royalty Ser.). (ENG., Illus.). 24p. (J). (gr. -1-2). lib. bdg. 27.32 *(978-1-62065-123-0(8)*, 120816, Capstone Pr.) Capstone.

Loh-Hagan, Virginia. The Real Anne Boleyn. 2018. (History Uncut Ser.). (ENG., Illus.). 32p. (J). (gr. 4-8). lib. bdg. 32.07 *(978-1-5341-2949-8(9)*, 211840, 45th Parallel Press) Cherry Lake Publishing.

—The Real King Tut. 2018. (History Uncut Ser.). (ENG., Illus.). 32p. (J). (gr. 4-8). lib. bdg. 32.07 *(978-1-5341-2954-2(5)*, 211860, 45th Parallel Press) Cherry Lake Publishing.

Lowe, Ruby Hasegawa, et al. O Kamehameha IV: Alexander Liholiho. 2004. (HAW & ENG., Illus.). x, 115p. (J). pap. *(978-0-87336-054-8(0))* Kamehameha Publishing.

Lowery, Zoe & Morgan, Julian. Cleopatra, 1 vol. 2016. (Leaders of the Ancient World Ser.). (ENG.). 112p. (J). (gr. 6-6). 38.80 *(978-1-5081-7254-3(4)*, 1614daeb-6b6f-4e20-bb05-8386ddb83b69) Rosen Publishing Group, Inc., The.

—Nero, 1 vol. 2016. (Leaders of the Ancient World Ser.). (ENG.). 112p. (J). (gr. 6-6). 38.80 *(978-1-5081-7256-7(0)*, 167c953e-c1d8-49b3-986f-90c2c3e781f3) Rosen Publishing Group, Inc., The.

Lunge-Larsen, Lise. The Race of the Birkebeiners. Azarian, Mary, illus. 2007. (ENG.). 32p. (J). (gr. k — 1). 7.99 *(978-0-618-91599-6(0)*, 1014894, Clarion Bks.) HarperCollins Pubs.

Macdonald, Fiona. Top 10 Worst Wicked Rulers, 1 vol. Antram, David, illus. 2012. (Top 10 Worst Ser.). (ENG.). 32p. (J). (gr. 3-5). pap. 11.50 *(978-1-4339-6701-6(4)*, b10c209f-ba20-4de0-8dfb-f1b6d39e8d4a); lib. bdg. 29.27 *(978-1-4339-6700-9(6)*, e0f08476-c20c-456f-8150-916afb2b9eaf) Stevens, Gareth Publishing LLLP. (Gareth Stevens Learning Library).

MacLeod, Elizabeth. Royal Murder: The Deadly Intrigue of Ten Sovereigns. Lewis, Robin Baird, illus. 2008. (ENG.). 128p. (J). (gr. 5-7). pap. 14.95 *(978-1-55451-127-3(5)*, 9781554511273) Annick Pr., Ltd. CAN. Dist: Publishers Group West (PGW).

Madame M. Trauma Queens/Trauma Kings. l.t. ed. 2003. (Madame M Presents:). (Illus.). 68p. (YA). per. 15.95 *(978-0-9704159-3-6(1)*, 0970415931) Creepy Little Productions.

Marsh, Carole. King George III. 2004. 12p. (gr. k-4). 2.95 *(978-0-635-02364-3(4))* Gallopade International.

—Sitting Bull. 2003. 12p. (gr. k-4). 2.95 *(978-0-635-02378-0(4))* Gallopade International.

Marsico, Katie. Alexander the Great: Ancient King & Conqueror, 1 vol. 2009. (Essential Lives Set 3 Ser.). (ENG., Illus.). 112p. (YA). (gr. 6-12). lib. bdg. 41.36 *(978-1-60453-520-4(2)*, 6669, Essential Library) ABDO Publishing Co.

Maurer, Gretchen. Mary Tudor: "Bloody Mary" Malone, Peter, illus. 2011. (Thinking Girl's Treasury of Dastardly Dames Ser.). (ENG.). 32p. (J). (gr. 3-8). 18.95 *(978-0-9834256-2-5(0))* Goosebottom Bks. LLC.

Mayfield, Christine & Quinn, Kristine M. Hammurabi: Babylonian Ruler, 1 vol. rev. ed. 2007. (Social Studies: Informational Text Ser.). (ENG.). 32p. (gr. 4-8). pap. 11.99 *(978-0-7439-0441-4(9))* Teacher Created Materials, Inc.

McDaniel, Sarita. Duchesses, 1 vol. 2019. (Meet the Royals Ser.). (ENG.). 24p. (gr. 1-2). pap. 10.35 *(978-1-9785-1197-2(3)*, 734dccfc-82b2-4efb-8dd6-6baf546e9a67) Enslow Publishing, LLC.

—Dukes, 1 vol. 2019. (Meet the Royals Ser.). (ENG.). 24p. (gr. 1-2). pap. 10.35 *(978-1-9785-1193-4(0)*, 89cbf796-3bb6-449a-ad1a-7f7a0e817b02) Enslow Publishing, LLC.

—Kings, 1 vol. 2019. (Meet the Royals Ser.). (ENG.). 24p. (gr. 1-2). pap. 10.35 *(978-1-9785-1177-4(9)*, 87214a4c-252e-4e1e-bf08-ccac1b77aa42) Enslow Publishing, LLC.

Mehta, Sonia. Rani Lakshmibai (Junior Lives) 2018. (Junior Lives Ser.). (ENG., Illus.). 48p. (J). pap. 8.99 *(978-0-14-342825-1(X)*, Puffin) Penguin Bks. India PVT, Ltd IND. Dist: Independent Pubs. Group.

Miller, Reagan. What Is a Monarchy? Crabtree Publishing Staff, ed. 2012. (Forms of Government Ser.: No. 4). (ENG.). 48p. (J). (gr. 5-8). pap. *(978-0-7787-5325-4(5))* Crabtree Publishing Co.

Miller, Reagan & Brennan, Joseph K. What Is an Oligarchy? 2012. (Forms of Government Ser.). (ENG.). 48p. (J). (gr. 5-9). lib. bdg. *(978-0-7787-5320-9(4))* Crabtree Publishing Co.

Mills Hoffman, Megan. Napoleon Bonaparte, 1 vol. 2017. (Great Military Leaders Ser.). (ENG., Illus.). 128p. (J). (gr. 9-9). 47.36 *(978-1-5026-2782-7(5)*, 98bb5a2a-a196-42e6-8a97-29a738de85e0) Cavendish Square Publishing LLC.

Morgan, Julian. Constantine: Ruler of Christian Rome. 2009. (Ancient Leaders Ser.). 112p. (gr. 5-8). 66.50 *(978-1-61511-422-1(X)*, Rosen Reference) Rosen Publishing Group, Inc., The.

—Hadrian: Consolidating the Empire. 2009. (Ancient Leaders Ser.). 112p. (gr. 5-8). 66.50 *(978-1-61511-423-8(8)*, Rosen Reference) Rosen Publishing Group, Inc., The.

—Nero: Destroyer of Rome. 2009. (Ancient Leaders Ser.). 112p. (gr. 5-8). 66.50 *(978-1-61511-426-9(2)*, Rosen Reference) Rosen Publishing Group, Inc., The.

Nagelhout, Ryan. Ivan the Terrible: Terrifying Tyrant of Russia, 1 vol. 2016. (History's Most Murderous Villains Ser.). (ENG., Illus.). 32p. (J). (gr. 4-5). pap. 11.50 *(978-1-4824-4794-1(0)*, 92f30fa1-6cf8-4e3a-890c-b3f7655d9e04) Stevens, Gareth Publishing LLLP.

Nardo, Don. Cleopatra. 2016. (ENG.). 80p. (J). 38.60 *(978-1-60152-948-0(1))* ReferencePoint Pr., Inc.

Novel Units. Can't You Make Them Behave, King George? Novel Units Teacher Guide. 2019. (ENG.). (J). pap., tchr. ed. 12.99 *(978-1-56137-402-1(4)*, Novel Units, Inc.) Classroom Library Co.

Pfeffer, Wendy. Mysterious Spinners. Kim, Julie J., illus. 2005. 48p. (J). *(978-1-59336-315-4(X))*; pap. *(978-1-59336-316-1(8))* Mondo Publishing.

Phillips, Charles. Kings & Queens of Britain's Modern Age: From Hanover to Windsor - 1714-Today. 2009. (Illus.). 96p. pap. 14.99 *(978-1-84476-520-1(2))* Anness Publishing GBR. Dist: National Bk. Network.

Phillips, Larissa. Cochise: Apache Chief. 2009. (Primary Sources of Famous People in American History Ser.). 32p. (gr. 2-3). 47.90 *(978-1-60851-660-5(1))* Rosen Publishing Group, Inc., The.

—Cochise: Apache Chief / Cochise: Jefe Apache. 2009. (Famous People in American History/Grandes personajes en la historia de los Estados Unidos Ser.). (ENG & SPA.). 32p. (gr. 2-3). 47.90 *(978-1-61512-540-1(X)*, Editorial Buenas Letras) Rosen Publishing Group, Inc., The.

—Cochise: Jefe Apache, 1 vol. de la Vega, Eida, tr. 2003. (Grandes Personajes en la Historia de Los Estados Unidos (Famous People in American History) Ser.). (SPA., Illus.). 32p. (gr. 3-4). pap. 10.00 *(978-0-8239-4223-7(6)*, 78727065-ac30-44c5-8197-d0ca1e0721c8); (J). lib. bdg. 29.13 *(978-0-8239-4129-2(9)*, 792cb486-94fb-48f0-bcc7-1ac55441242a, Editorial Buenas Letras) Rosen Publishing Group, Inc., The.

—Cochise: Jefe apache (Cochise: Apache Chief) 2009. (Grandes personajes en la historia de los Estados Unidos (Famous People in American History) Ser.). (SPA.). 32p. (gr. 2-3). 47.90 *(978-1-61512-792-4(5)*, Editorial Buenas Letras) Rosen Publishing Group, Inc., The.

Phillips, Robin. Who in the World Was the Acrobatic Empress? The Story of Theodora. unabr. ed. 2010. (Jim Weiss Audio Collection: 0). (ENG.). 1p. 12.95 *(978-1-933339-39-9(X)*, 333939) Well-Trained Mind Pr.

Plain, Nancy. Eleanor of Aquitaine & the High Middle Ages, 1 vol. 2007. (Rulers & Their Times Ser.). (ENG., Illus.). 80p. (gr. 6-6). lib. bdg. 36.93 *(978-0-7614-1834-4(2)*, 047cd939-e7d7-4819-9889-f0ec13ebce85) Cavendish Square Publishing LLC.

Poulakidas, Georgene. Black Hawk's War. (Primary Sources of American Wars Ser.). 24p. (gr. 3-4). 2009. 42.50 *(978-1-60851-518-9(4)*, PowerKids Pr.) 2005. (ENG., Illus.). (J). lib. bdg. 26.27 *(978-1-4042-2682-1(6)*, d6920471-3f0f-48af-a064-34c9ea91155e) Rosen Publishing Group, Inc., The.

Pratt, Mary K. Elizabeth I: English Renaissance Queen, 1 vol. 2011. (Essential Lives Set 7 Ser.). (ENG., Illus.). 112p. (YA). (gr. 6-12). lib. bdg. 41.36 *(978-1-61783-003-7(8)*, 6745, Essential Library) ABDO Publishing Co.

Price-Groff, Claire. Queen Victoria & Nineteenth-Century England, 1 vol. 2003. (Rulers & Their Times Ser.). (ENG., Illus.). 80p. (gr. 6-6). 36.93 (978-0-7614-1488-9(6), a5457368-9ea7-4c07-a900-a3c624bb17f8) Cavendish Square Publishing LLC.

Reef, Catherine. Victoria: Portrait of a Queen. 2017. (ENG., Illus.). 256p. (YA). (gr. 7). 18.99 (978-0-544-71614-8(0), 1629697, Clarion Bks.) HarperCollins Pubs.

Rice, Earle. The Life & Times of Clovis. 2009. (Biography from Ancient Civilizations Ser.). (Illus.). 48p. (J). (gr. 4-8). 29.95 (978-1-58415-742-7(9)) Mitchell Lane Pubs.

—The Life & Times of Eleanor of Aquitaine. 2009. (Biography of Ancient Civilizations Ser.). (Illus.). 48p. (J). (gr. 4-8). 29.95 (978-1-58415-743-4(7)) Mitchell Lane Pubs.

Rojo, Sara, illus. Why the Sea Is Salty. 2009. (First Reading Level 4 Ser.). 48p. (J). 6.99 (978-0-7945-2308-4(0), Usborne) EDC Publishing.

Roumain, Maryse Noel. Anacaona, Ayiti's Taíno Queen/Anacaona, la Reine Taino D'Ayiti. 2012. 36p. pap. 18.41 (978-1-4669-5199-0(0)) Trafford Publishing.

Rowe, Brooke. What Kind of Royalty Are You? 2016. (Best Quiz Ever Ser.). (ENG., Illus.). 32p. (J). (gr. 4-8). 32.07 (978-1-63471-107-4(6), 208539, 45th Parallel Press) Cherry Lake Publishing.

Rucker, Jeffrey A. La historia de Toro Sentado (the Story of Sitting Bull) 2009. (Reading Room Collection: Spanish Ser.). (SPA.). 24p. (gr. 3-4). 42.50 (978-1-60854-178-2(9), Editorial Buenas Letras) Rosen Publishing Group, Inc., The.

—The Story of Sitting Bull. (Reading Room Collection 2 Ser.). 24p. (gr. 3-4). 2009. 42.50 (978-1-60851-998-9(8), PowerKids Pr.) 2003. (ENG.). 43.95 (978-0-8239-8731-3(0)) Rosen Publishing Group, Inc., The.

Rulers & Their Times, 8 vols., Group 4. Incl. Eleanor of Aquitaine & the High Middle Ages. Plain, Nancy. lib. bdg. 36.93 (978-0-7614-1834-4(2), 047cd939-e7d7-4819-9889-f0ec13ebce85); Han Wu Di & Ancient China. Greenblatt, Miriam. lib. bdg. 36.93 (978-0-7614-1835-1(0), 2a371786-147f-4cdc-9152-f3b7617d6e57); Julius Caesar & the Roman Republic. Greenblatt, Miriam. lib. bdg. 36.93 (978-0-7614-1836-8(9), f465e7fb-ce85-4174-90f8-155c5cced41c); Napoleon Bonaparte & Imperial France. Greenblatt, Miriam. (J). lib. bdg. 36.93 (978-0-7614-1837-5(7), e263ac46-7d98-4d74-8dd2-972dc76f7518); (Illus.). 80p. (gr. 6-6). (Rulers & Their Times Ser.). (ENG.). 2007. 147.72 (978-0-7614-1833-7(4), 82aed3cf-acf4-4096-9258-fd925d4d3529, Cavendish Square) Cavendish Square Publishing LLC.

Rulers, Scholars, & Artists of the Renaissance, 10 vols. 2004. (Rulers, Scholars, & Artists of the Renaissance Ser.). (ENG.). (YA). (gr. 5-8). lib. bdg. 199.00 (978-1-4042-0370-9(2), 386bc1e3-90a6-4d4c-b61c-3d8ee910a763) Rosen Publishing Group, Inc., The.

Sanford, William R. Hunkpapa Lakota Chief Sitting Bull, 1 vol. 2013. (Native American Chiefs & Warriors Ser.). (ENG., Illus.). 48p. (gr. 5-7). lib. bdg. 25.27 (978-0-7660-4097-7(6), 01439197-4907-4648-b855-91378a6c060e) Enslow Publishing, LLC.

—Seminole Chief Osceola, 1 vol. 2013. (Native American Chiefs & Warriors Ser.). (ENG., Illus.). 48p. (J). (gr. 5-7). lib. bdg. 25.27 (978-0-7660-4117-2(4), 71a840ed-b1cb-4569-abd7-17f460cdc077) Enslow Publishing, LLC.

Santillian, Beatriz & Morgan, Julian. Hadrian: Emperor of Rome, 1 vol. 2017. (Leaders of the Ancient World Ser.). (ENG., Illus.). 112p. (J). (gr. 6-6). 38.80 (978-1-5081-7484-4(9), 1ec256a1-3c9d-416c-8596-284ded145c9a, Rosen Young Adult) Rosen Publishing Group, Inc., The.

Santillian, Beatriz & Morris, Ian Macgregor. Leonidas I: Warrior King of Sparta, 1 vol. 2017. (Leaders of the Ancient World Ser.). (ENG., Illus.). 112p. (J). (gr. 6-6). 38.80 (978-1-5081-7520-9(9), ca244ba1-044d-4db5-80a2-6ae6c29c1c70, Rosen Young Adult) Rosen Publishing Group, Inc., The.

Sapet, Kerrily. Eleanor of Aquitaine: Medieval Queen. 2006. (European Queens Ser.). (Illus.). 192p. (J). (gr. 6-12). lib. bdg. 26.95 (978-1-931798-90-7(7)) Reynolds, Morgan Inc.

Saxena, Shalini. Nero: Ruthless Roman Emperor, 1 vol. 2016. (History's Most Murderous Villains Ser.). (ENG., Illus.). 32p. (J). (gr. 4-5). pap. 11.50 (978-1-4824-4799-6(1), b3b131ea-2cca-45bf-ad07-d0fb72992d7d) Stevens, Gareth Publishing LLLP.

Schanzer, Rosalyn. George vs. George: The Revolutionary War As Seen by Both Sides. 2004. (Illus.). 64p. (J). (gr. 3-7). 16.95 (978-0-7922-7349-3(4), National Geographic Children's Bks.) Disney Publishing Worldwide.

Schiel, Katy. Monarchy: A Primary Source Analysis. (Primary Sources of Political Systems Ser.). 64p. (gr. 5-8). 2009. 58.50 (978-1-60851-838-8(8)) 2004. (ENG., Illus.). (J). lib. bdg. 37.13 (978-0-8239-4520-7(0), 7d8f9a3c-cce4-4908-ba6e-cc4f195b817f) Rosen Publishing Group, Inc., The.

Seong-eun, Kim. Jumong: Founder of Goguryeo. Park, Christian J. & Park, Christian J., trs. Ji-won, Lee, illus. 2011. (ENG.). 40p. 14.00 (978-89-91913-49-3(0), 1619) Seoul Selection KOR. Dist: Univ. of Hawaii Pr.

Serrano, Francisco. The Poet King of Tezcoco: A Great Leader of Ancient Mexico, 1 vol. Serrano, Pablo, illus. 2007. (ENG.). 48p. (J). (gr. 3-6). 18.95 (978-0-88899-787-6(6)) Groundwood Bks. CAN. Dist: Publishers Group West (PGW).

Shea, John M. Vlad the Impaler: Bloodthirsty Medieval Prince, 1 vol. 2016. (History's Most Murderous Villains Ser.). (ENG., Illus.). 32p. (J). (gr. 4-5). pap. 11.50 (978-1-4824-4804-7(1), 19708463-85cf-4935-b779-21041863dee6) Stevens, Gareth Publishing LLLP.

Shecter, Vicky Alvear. Cleopatra Rules! The Amazing Life of the Original Teen Queen. 2013. (ENG., Illus.). 176p. (J). (gr. 5-9). pap. 10.99 (978-1-62091-032-0(2), Astra Young Readers) Astra Publishing Hse.

—Warrior Queens: True Stories of Six Ancient Rebels Who Slayed History. Mayer, Bill, illus. 2019. 160p. (J). (gr. 4-7). 17.99 (978-1-62979-679-6(4), Astra Young Readers) Astra Publishing Hse.

Shone, Rob. Elizabeth I: The Life of England's Renaissance Queen. 2009. (Graphic Nonfiction Biographies Ser.). (Illus.). 48p. (YA). (gr. 4-5). 58.50 (978-1-61513-016-0(0), Rosen Reference) Rosen Publishing Group, Inc., The.

Shone, Rob & Ganeri, Anita. Elizabeth I: The Life of England's Renaissance Queen, 1 vol. 2005. (Graphic Nonfiction Biographies Ser.). (ENG., Illus.). 48p. (YA). (gr. 4-6). lib. bdg. 37.13 (978-1-4042-0246-7(3), 7541c584-63d3-44a1-a308-c12e83baf2dc) Rosen Publishing Group, Inc., The.

Silate, Jennifer. Seeing the Future: The Final Vision of Sitting Bull. 2009. (Great Moments in American History Ser.). 32p. (gr. 3-3). 47.90 (978-1-61513-150-1(7)) Rosen Publishing Group, Inc., The.

Spilsbury, Richard. Geronimo, 1 vol. Faure, Florence, illus. 2013. (Hero Journals). (ENG.). 48p. (J). (gr. 4-6). pap. 9.95 (978-1-4109-5367-4(X), 123251, Raintree) Capstone.

Stathis, Roberta & Blanch, Gregory. Women Who Ruled. 2003. (Explore the Ages Ser.). (Illus.). 79p. 17.00 (978-1-55501-592-3(1)) Ballard & Tighe Pubs.

Stefoff, Rebecca. Faisal: World Leaders: Past & Present. 2008. (ENG., Illus.). 112p. pap. 22.95 (978-1-891785-10-8(9)) Fons Vitae of Kentucky, Inc.

Storrie, Paul D. Yu the Great. 2008. pap. 52.95 (978-0-8225-9464-2(1)) Lerner Publishing Group.

—Yu the Great: Conquering the Flood [a Chinese Legend]. Carruthers, Sandy, illus. 2008. (Graphic Myths & Legends Ser.). (ENG.). 48p. (J). (gr. 4-8). per. 9.99 (978-0-8225-6562-8(5), 441fddbb-130c-4d31-9e42-76aa044efd2a, Graphic Universe™) Lerner Publishing Group.

Stuckey, Rachel. Your Guide to Medieval Society. 2017. (Destination: Middle Ages Ser.). (ENG., Illus.). 32p. (J). (gr. 5-5). (978-0-7787-2991-4(5)); pap. (978-0-7787-2997-6(4)) Crabtree Publishing Co.

Sutcliffe, Jane. Chief Joseph. 2004. (History Maker Bios Ser.). (J). pap. 6.95 (978-0-8225-2068-9(0)) Lerner Publishing Group.

—Chief Joseph. Parlin, Tim, tr. Parlin, Tim, illus. 2004. (History Maker Bios Ser.). 48p. (J). (gr. 3-5). lib. bdg. 26.60 (978-0-8225-0696-6(3)) Lerner Publishing Group.

Tait, Leia. Queen Rania Al-Abdullah. 2007. (Remarkable People Ser.). (Illus.). 24p. (J). (gr. 3-7). pap. 8.95 (978-1-59036-646-2(8)); (gr. 4-7). lib. bdg. 24.45 (978-1-59036-645-5(X)) Weigl Pubs., Inc.

Taykutgul, Selcuk & Akin, Ferruh. Uthman Ibn Affan: Bearer of Two Pure Lights. 2012. 100p. (J). (gr. 8-12). pap. 8.95 (978-1-59784-267-9(2), Tughra Bks.) Blue Dome, Inc.

Thomas, Susanna. Akhenaten & Tutankhamen: The Religious Revolution. 2009. (Ancient Leaders Ser.). 112p. (gr. 5-8). 66.50 (978-1-61511-417-7(3), Rosen Reference) Rosen Publishing Group, Inc., The.

—Snefru: The Pyramid Builder. 2009. (Ancient Leaders Ser.). 112p. (gr. 5-8). 66.50 (978-1-61511-428-3(9), Rosen Reference) Rosen Publishing Group, Inc., The.

Trumbauer, Lisa. King Ludwig's Castle: Germany's Neuschwanstein. 2005. (Castles, Palaces, & Tombs Ser.). 32p. (J). lib. bdg. 28.50 (978-1-59716-002-5(4)) Bearport Publishing Co., Inc.

Turner, Patrenia. A Christmas Carol For Keeng Troyius. 2016. (Illus.). pap. (978-0-578-18261-2(0)) Royalty Patrenia Turner Publications.

—My Little Golden Book About Queen Patrenialla: A Fairy-Tail About the Queen of England Patrenia Turner. Turner, Troyius, ed. 2017. (Little Golden Book Ser.). (Illus.). pap. 4.99 (978-0-578-19815-6(0)) The Sleeping Bear Pr.

—Queen Patrenialla: A Fairy-Tail About the Queen of England Patrenia Turner. Turner, Troyius, ed. 2017. (Illus.). pap. (978-0-578-19814-9(2)) The Sleeping Bear Pr.

Turner, Queen of England Patrenia. Queen Patrenialla - A Canadian Story Poem. Turner, Keeng of England Troyius, ed. 2015. (Illus.). pap. (978-0-578-18000-7(6)) Royalty Patrenia Turner Publications.

Turner, Tracey & Lenman, Jamie. Hard As Nails Kings & Queens. 2015. (Hard As Nails in History Ser.). (ENG., Illus.). 64p. (J). (gr. 4-5). lib. bdg. (978-0-7787-1519-1(1)) Crabtree Publishing Co.

Uhl, Xina M. Cleopatra: Queen of Egypt, 1 vol. 2017. (Women Who Changed History Ser.). (ENG., Illus.). 48p. (J). (gr. 6-7). 28.41 (978-1-68048-639-1(X), a122930c-51d1-4423-9e50-440ed921805d, Britannica Educational Publishing) Rosen Publishing Group, Inc., The.

Watling, James, illus. Jehoshaphat: 2 Chronicles 20:1-30. 2005. (Little Learner Bible Story Books). 16p. (J). pap. 2.29 (978-0-7586-0945-8(0)) Concordia Publishing Hse.

Webb, Sarah Powers. Marie Antoinette: Fashionable Queen or Greedy Royal? 2015. (Perspectives on History Ser.). (ENG., Illus.). 32p. (J). (gr. 3-6). pap. 7.95 (978-1-4914-2216-8(5), 127727) Capstone.

Weston Woods Staff, creator. Can't You Make Them Behave, King George? 2004. 29.95 (978-1-55592-378-5(X)); (J). 18.95 (978-1-55592-377-8(1)); (J). 38.75 (978-1-55592-379-2(8)) Weston Woods Studios, Inc.

Whiting, Jim. The Life & Times of Augustus Caesar. 2005. (Biography from Ancient Civilizations Ser.). (Illus.). 48p. (J). (gr. -1-7). lib. bdg. 29.95 (978-1-58415-336-8(9)) Mitchell Lane Pubs.

—The Life & Times of Nero. 2005. (Biography from Ancient Civilizations Ser.). (Illus.). 48p. (J). (gr. 5-8). lib. bdg. 29.95 (978-1-58415-349-8(0)) Mitchell Lane Pubs.

Wilhelm, Doug. Alexander the Great: Master of the Ancient World. 2009. (Wicked History Ser.). (ENG.). 224p. (J). (gr. 5-9). 31.00 (978-0-531-21275-2(0)) Scholastic Library Publishing.

Woodman, Ros. The Great Celebration: A Puzzle Book about Hezekiah. rev. ed. 2008. (Puzzle Ser.). (ENG.). 24p. (J). 4.99 (978-1-84550-403-8(8), 0cbb3cd9-1b95-423d-b4b7-e1d67559359f) Christian Focus Pubns. GBR. Dist: Baker & Taylor Publisher Services (BTPS).

Yim Bridges, Shirin. Agrippina: "Atrocious & Ferocious" Malone, Peter, illus. 2011. (Thinking Girl's Treasury of Dastardly Dames Ser.). (ENG.). 32p. (J). (gr. 3-8). 18.95 (978-0-9834256-1-8(2)) Goosebottom Bks. LLC.

—Isabella of Castile. Nguyen, Albert, illus. 2010. (Thinking Girl's Treasury of Real Princesses Ser.). (ENG.). 24p. (J). (gr. 3-8). 18.95 (978-0-9845098-4-3(4)) Goosebottom Bks. LLC.

—Nur Jahan of India. Nguyen, Albert, illus. 2010. (Thinking Girl's Treasury of Real Princesses Ser.). 24p. (J). (gr. 3-8). 18.95 (978-0-9845098-5-0(2)) Goosebottom Bks. LLC.

KINGS, QUEENS, RULERS, ETC.—FICTION

Abbott, Tony. Escape from Jabar-Loo (the Secrets of Droon #30) Merrell, David, illus. 2016. (Star Wars: Jedi Academy Ser.: 30). (ENG.). 128p. (J). (gr. 3-7). E-Book 12.99 (978-0-545-41843-0(7), Scholastic Paperbacks) Scholastic, Inc.

—The Riddle of Zorfendorf Castle. Merrell, David, illus. 2005. (Secrets of Droon Ser.: No. 25). 124p. (J). lib. bdg. 15.38 (978-1-4242-0310-9(4)) Fitzgerald Bks.

Adeniyi, Bab. The Servant, the King, & the Princess. 2012. 28p. pap. 15.99 (978-1-4691-4989-9(3)) Xlibris Corp.

Adler, David A. The Secret Service Mystery. Natti, Susanna, illus. 2008. (Cam Jansen Ser.: Bk. 26). 57p. (J). (gr. 2-5). 11.65 (978-0-7569-8917-0(5)) Perfection Learning Corp.

Aguiar, Judy Lee. The Littlest Camel: And the Journey of the Three Kings. Rodriguez, Tom, illus. 2008. 176p. (J). per. (978-0-9725231-2-7(X)) Turnapaige & Reed Moore.

Alexander, Lloyd. Dream-Of-Jade: The Emperor's Cat. Burkett, D. Brent, illus. 2005. (ENG.). 48p. (J). (gr. 3-7). 17.95 (978-0-8126-2736-7(9)) Cricket Bks.

Allcock, Phil. Grumpy King Colin. Stone, Steve, illus. 2019. (Early Bird Readers — Purple (Early Bird Stories (tm)) Ser.). (ENG.). 32p. (J). (gr. k-3). 30.65 (978-1-5415-4223-5(1), adb90bc4-8b5f-4ceb-aac3-3a41598c7f63); pap. 9.99 (978-1-5415-7423-6(0), 05d87a56-81cf-4fb3-89be-30e52448326c) Lerner Publishing Group. (Lerner Pubns.).

Amery, H. & Cartwright, S. The Royal Broomstick. 2004. (First Stories Ser.). 16p. (J). lib. bdg. 12.95 (978-1-58086-572-2(0)) EDC Publishing.

Andersen, D. R. Why the Moon Changes in the Night Sky. 2005. (J). pap. (978-1-4108-4190-2(1)) Benchmark Education Co.

Andersen, Hans Christian. The Emperor's New Clothes. Yim, Gyeong-mi, illus. 2015. (World Classics Ser.). (ENG.). 32p. (J). (gr. k-4). 27.99 (978-1-925186-10-9(5), 75c94028-5d52-40d8-85fe-c11393e6dcc2); 7.99 (978-1-925186-04-8(0), f7f3027b-8239-449e-aa31-981bdabfe701) ChoiceMaker Pty. Ltd., The AUS. (Big and SMALL). Dist: Lerner Publishing Group.

—The Emperor's New Clothes. Burton, Virginia Lee, illus. (Folk Tale Classics Ser.). (ENG.). 48p. (J). (gr. -1-3). 2014. 9.99 (978-0-544-15952-5(7), 1550259) 2004. pap. 9.99 (978-0-618-34420-8(9), 480621) HarperCollins Pubs. (Clarion Bks.).

Anderson, Hans Christian. The Emperor's New Clothes. 2005. (SPA.). 12p. (J). pap. (978-958-30-1782-7(5)) Panamericana Editorial.

—The Nightingale. Oleynikov, Igor, illus. 2007.Tr. of Nattergalen. (ENG.). 40p. (J). (gr. k). lib. bdg. 16.50 (978-1-933327-31-0(6)); (gr. 1). 15.95 (978-1-933327-30-3(8)) Purple Bear Bks., Inc.

—Snezhnaya Koroleva - the Snow Queen. Pym, T., illus. 2013. 56p. (978-1-909115-60-6(6)) Planet, The.

—The Snow Queen. Tatarnikov, Pavel, illus. 2006.Tr. of ??????? ???????? (ENG.). 48p. (J). (gr. 1). 15.95 (978-1-933327-22-8(7)); lib. bdg. 16.50 (978-1-933327-23-5(5)) Purple Bear Bks., Inc.

—El Traje Nuevo del Emperador.Tr. of Emperor's New Clothes. (SPA., Illus.). 48p. (J). (gr. 3-5). (978-84-241-5527-8(0), EV0621) Everest Editora ESP. Dist: Lectorum Pubns., Inc.

—El Traje Nuevo del Emperador.Tr. of Emperor's New Clothes. (SPA.). 64p. (J). 9.50 (978-84-207-3349-4(0)) Grupo Anaya, S.A. ESP. Dist: AIMS International Bks., Inc.

Anderson, M. T., et al. Fatal Throne: the Wives of Henry VIII Tell All. 2018. 416p. (YA). (gr. 7). 18.99 (978-1-5247-1619-6(7), Schwartz & Wade Bks.) Random Hse. Children's Bks.

Anna, Jennifer. Year of the Dragon. 2nd ed. 2007. (Illus.). 56p. (J). pap. 24.99 (978-1-59092-155-5(0)) Blue Forge Pr.

Anthony, David & David, Charles. Knightscares #5: (Knightscares) 2004. (Illus.). 200p. (J). per. 5.99 (978-0-9728461-4-1(X), 1236107) Sigil Publishing.

Arnett, Mindee. Shadow & Flame. (ENG.). 496p. (YA). (gr. 9). 2020. pap. 12.99 (978-0-06-265271-3(0)) 2019. (Illus.). 17.99 (978-0-06-265269-0(9)) HarperCollins Pubs. (Balzer & Bray).

Atwater-Rhodes, Amelia. Wolfcry. 2008. (Kiesha'ra Ser.: Bk. 4). (ENG.). 208p. (YA). (gr. 9-12). pap. 7.99 (978-0-440-23886-7(2), Delacorte Pr.) Random Hse. Children's Bks.

Aumuller, Kimberly. Dragon's Hope: Tale of the Guardians. 2009. 224p. 25.95 (978-0-595-50945-4(2)); pap. 15.95 (978-0-595-52209-5(2)) iUniverse, Inc.

Avi. The Player King. 2018. (ENG.). 208p. (J). (gr. 3-7). pap. 7.99 (978-1-4814-3769-1(0)) Simon & Schuster Children's Publishing.

Azad, Nafiza. The Candle & the Flame. 2019. (ENG.). 416p. (YA). (gr. 7-7). 18.99 (978-1-338-30604-0(9), Scholastic Pr.) Scholastic, Inc.

The Bad Luck of King Fred: Individual Title Six-Packs. (Action Packs Ser.). 104p. (gr. 3-5). 44.00 (978-0-7635-8408-5(8)) Rigby Education.

Bannen, Megan. The Bird & the Blade. (ENG.). 432p. (YA). (gr. 8). 2019. pap. 9.99 (978-0-06-267416-6(1)) 2018. (Illus.). 17.99 (978-0-06-267415-9(3)) HarperCollins Pubs. (Balzer & Bray).

Barchers, Suzanne. The Tale of the Oki Islands: A Tale from Japan. Yokota, Hiromitsu, illus. 2013. (Tales of Honor Ser.). (ENG.). 32p. (J). (gr. 1-3). pap. 8.99 (978-1-937529-62-8(2), 37673377-32eb-4b42-80ea-6f0d4a809b98) Red Chair Pr.

Bardugo, Leigh. King of Scars. 2019. (Illus.). 528p. (J). (978-1-5101-0445-7(3)) ETT Imprint.

—King of Scars. 2019. (ENG., Illus.). 514p. (J). (gr. 9-13). pap. 11.99 (978-1-250-23107-9(8)) ImPrint.

—King of Scars. 2019. (King of Scars Duology Ser.: 1). (ENG., Illus.). 528p. (YA). 19.99 (978-1-250-14228-3(8), 900180180) Imprint IND. Dist: Macmillan.

—King of Scars. 2020. (King of Scars Duology Ser.: 1). (ENG., Illus.). 528p. (YA). pap. 12.99 (978-1-250-61897-9(5), 900180181) Square Fish.

Barry, Rick. Kiriath's Quest. 2008. (J). 8.99 (978-1-59166-905-0(7)) BJU Pr.

Bauer, Deidre. Silver Mountain. 2008. 38p. pap. 8.00 (978-0-8059-7672-4(8)) Dorrance Publishing Co., Inc.

Baum, L. Frank. Glinda of Oz. 2007. 108p. 22.95 (978-1-60312-591-8(4)) Aegypan.

Beaty, Noel. The Legend of Snowy the Shrew. 2007. 168p. per. (978-0-7552-0295-9(3)) Authors OnLine, Ltd.

Becker, Aaron. Return. Becker, Aaron, illus. 2016. (ENG., Illus.). 40p. (J). (gr. -1-3). 17.99 (978-0-7636-7730-5(2)) Candlewick Pr.

Beddor, Frank. ArchEnemy: The Looking Glass Wars, Book Three, 3 vols. 2010. (Looking Glass Wars Ser.: 3). (ENG.). 384p. (YA). (gr. 7-18). 10.99 (978-0-14-241689-1(4), Speak) Penguin Young Readers Group.

—The Looking Glass Wars, 1 vol. 2007. (Looking Glass Wars Ser.: 1). (ENG., Illus.). 400p. (YA). (gr. 7-18). 12.99 (978-0-14-240941-1(3), Speak) Penguin Young Readers Group.

—Seeing Redd: The Looking Glass Wars, Book Two. 2008. (Looking Glass Wars Ser.: 2). (ENG.). 400p. (YA). (gr. 7-18). 11.99 (978-0-14-241209-1(0), Speak) Penguin Young Readers Group.

Beiler, Joyce. The Kingdom of Laughter. 2012. 30p. pap. 13.95 (978-1-4497-6596-5(3), WestBow Pr.) Author Solutions, LLC.

Bell, Hilari. Crown of Earth. Willis, Drew, illus. 2010. (Shield, Sword, & Crown Ser.: 3). (ENG.). 272p. (J). (gr. 3-7). pap. 5.99 (978-1-4169-0599-8(5), Aladdin) Simon & Schuster Children's Publishing.

—Shield of Stars, No. 1. 2008. (Shield, Sword, & Crown Ser.: 1). (ENG.). 288p. (J). (gr. 3-7). pap. 13.99 (978-1-4169-0595-0(2), Simon & Schuster/Paula Wiseman Bks.) Simon & Schuster/Paula Wiseman Bks.

—Sword of Waters, No. 2. Willis, Drew, illus. 2008. (Shield, Sword, & Crown Ser.: 2). (ENG.). 368p. (J). (gr. 3-7). 16.99 (978-1-4169-0596-7(0), Simon & Schuster/Paula Wiseman Bks.) Simon & Schuster/Paula Wiseman Bks.

Bernreuter, Bob J. The Gift. 2006. (Illus.). 25p. (J). (978-1-4120-7546-6(7)) Trafford Publishing.

Besson, Luc. Arthur & the Forbidden City. Sowchek, Ellen, tr. 2006. (ENG., Illus.). 192p. (J). (gr. 3-7). pap., pap. 5.99 (978-0-06-059628-6(7), Harper Trophy) HarperCollins Pubs.

—Arthur & the Forbidden City. 2005. (ENG., Illus.). 192p. (J). 15.99 (978-0-06-059626-2(0)) HarperCollins Pubs.

Biachi, Kelvin K. Tortoise the King. 2010. 74p. pap. 21.50 (978-1-60911-875-4(8), Eloquent Bks.) Strategic Book Publishing & Rights Agency (SBPRA).

Binder, Mark. Kings, Wolves, Princesses & Lions: 28 Illustrated Stories for Young Readers. 2012. (ENG., Illus.). 122p. (J). pap. 14.99 (978-0-9824707-8-7(9)) Light Pubns.

Binus, Ari, illus. Izzy Hagbah. 2005. 37p. (J). (gr. 1-4). 16.95 (978-1-932687-38-5(6)); per. 9.95 (978-1-932687-39-2(4)) Simcha Media Group. (Devora Publishing).

Bishop, Anne. Anne Bishop's Christmas Dram: The Gift of Three. 2013. 28p. pap. 24.95 (978-1-4626-8276-8(6)) America Star Bks.

Bishop, Jennie. The Three Gifts of Christmas. McDaniels, Preston, illus. 2009. 32p. (J). (gr. 3-18). 15.99 incl. audio compact disk (978-1-59317-378-4(4)) Warner Pr., Inc.

Black, Holly. How the King of Elfhame Learned to Hate Stories. Cai, Rovina, illus. 2020. (Folk of the Air Ser.). (ENG.). 192p. (YA). (gr. 9-17). 17.99 (978-0-316-54088-9(9)) Little, Brown Bks. for Young Readers.

—The Queen of Nothing. (Folk of the Air Ser.: 3). (ENG., Illus.). (YA). (gr. 9-17). 2020. 336p. pap. 12.99 (978-0-316-31037-6(9)) 2019. 320p. 19.99 (978-0-316-31042-0(5)) Little, Brown Bks. for Young Readers.

—The Wicked King. 2022. (ENG.). (YA). 45.00 (978-1-955876-17-9(7)) LitJoy Crate.

—The Wicked King. (Folk of the Air Ser.: 2). (ENG., Illus.). (J). (gr. 9-17). 2020. 368p. pap. 12.99 (978-0-316-31032-1(8)) 2019. 336p. 19.99 (978-0-316-31035-2(2)) Little, Brown Bks. for Young Readers.

Blake, Kendare. One Dark Throne. (YA). 2019. (Three Dark Crowns Ser.: 2). (ENG.). 480p. (gr. 9). pap. 12.99 (978-0-06-238547-5(X), Quill Tree Bks.) 2017. (Three Dark Crowns Ser.: 2). (ENG., Illus.). 464p. (gr. 9). 18.99 (978-0-06-238546-8(1), Quill Tree Bks.) 2017. (Illus.). 448p. (978-0-06-279729-2(8), HarperTeen) 2017. (Illus.). 448p. (978-0-06-269730-1(7), HarperTeen) 2017. (Illus.). 448p. (978-0-06-269045-6(0), HarperTeen) 2017. (Illus.). 448p. (978-0-06-269935-0(0), HarperTeen) 2017. (Illus.). 448p. (978-0-06-274764-8(9), HarperTeen) HarperCollins Pubs.

—Three Dark Crowns. (Three Dark Crowns Ser.: 1). (ENG.). (YA). (gr. 9). 2018. 432p. pap. 15.99 (978-0-06-238544-4(5)) 2016. (Illus.). 416p. 17.99 (978-0-06-238543-7(7)) HarperCollins Pubs. (Quill Tree Bks.).

—Three Dark Crowns. 2018. (YA). lib. bdg. 22.10 (978-0-606-40404-4(X)) Turtleback.

—Two Dark Reigns. 2018. (Three Dark Crowns Ser.: 3). (ENG., Illus.). 464p. (YA). (gr. 9). 18.99 (978-0-06-268614-5(3), Quill Tree Bks.) HarperCollins Pubs.

—Two Dark Reigns: Three Dark Crowns Book 3. 2018. (ENG., Illus.). 432p. (J). (978-1-5098-7649-5(9), HarperTeen) HarperCollins Pubs.

Bland, Nick, illus. King Pig. 2013. (J). pap. (978-0-545-67013-5(6)) Scholastic, Inc.

Bogumill, Mark P. KingMaker: The Swamp Crusade, 4 vols. 2003. 310p. (YA). bds. 25.00 (978-0-9744870-0-7(7)) KingMaker Bks. LLC.

Bolton, Michael. The Secret of the Lost Kingdom. Jermann, David, illus. 2004. 36p. (J). (gr. k-4). reprint ed. (978-0-7567-7849-1(2)) DIANE Publishing Co.

—El Secreto del Reino Perdido. Jermann, David, illus. (Buenas Noches Ser.). (SPA.). (J). (gr. 3). pap. 7.16 (978-958-04-4904-1(X)) Norma S.A. COL. Dist: Lectorum Pubns., Inc.

Booth, Bradley. Esther: A Star Is Born. 2009. (J). pap. 12.99 (978-0-8163-2359-3(3)) Pacific Pr. Publishing Assn.

Bowles, David. Rise of the Halfling King, 1 vol. Bowles, Charlene, illus. 2020. (Tales of the Feathered Serpent Ser.: 1). (ENG.). 64p. (J). (gr. 4-8). pap. 14.95 (978-1-947627-37-6(6), 23353382, Cinco Puntos Press) Lee & Low Bks., Inc.

Bowles, David & Bowles, Charlene, illus. The Rise of the Halfling King. 2021. 63p. (J). *(978-1-947627-36-9(8),* Cinco Puntos Press) Lee & Low Bks., Inc.

Bowman, Crystal. Little David's Big Heart, 1 vol. Hartung, Susan Kathleen & Endersby, Frank, illus. 2010. (I Can Read! Ser.). (ENG.). 32p. (J). pap. 4.99 *(978-0-310-71708-9(6))* Zonderkidz.

Boyce, Catherine & Boyce, Peter. Tea with the Queen. Sibert, Stephanie Grace, illus. 2006. 32p. (J). per. 16.95 net. incl. audio compact disk *(978-0-9778420-0-1(2),* 10,000) Semper Studio.

Boyd, David. Hidden Message. Alward, Jeff, illus. 2007. 48p. (J). lib. bdg. 23.08 *(978-1-4242-1637-6(0))* Fitzgerald Bks.

Bracken, Beth & Fraser, Kay. Wish, 1 vol. Sawyer, Odessa, illus. 2013. (Faerieground Ser.). (ENG.). 304p. (J). (gr. 4-8). 12.95 *(978-1-62370-003-4(5),* 122309, Capstone Young Readers) Capstone.

Brandes, Nadine. Romanov. 2019. 341p. (YA). *(978-1-4041-1165-3(4))* Nelson, Thomas Inc.

Brazier, Yuvonne. Princess Jordan Saves Golden Tree. 2008. 20p. pap. 12.49 *(978-1-4389-3591-1(9))* AuthorHouse.

Brenner, Peter. King for One Day. Wyss, Manspeter, illus. 36p. (J). (gr. -1-3). 12.95 *(978-0-87592-027-6(6))* Scroll Pr., Inc.

Brightwood, Laura, illus. Debate in Sign Language. Brightwood, Laura, . 2006. (J). *(978-0-9779290-6-1(X))* 3-C Institute for Social Development.

—King's New Suit. Brightwood, Laura, . 2007. (J). DVD *(978-1-934409-05-3(7))* 3-C Institute for Social Development.

—Wise People of Helm. Brightwood, Laura, . 2006. (J). *(978-0-9779290-4-7(3))* 3-C Institute for Social Development.

Brown, Gladys. The Adventures of King Flapjack. 2005. 36p. pap. 13.95 *(978-1-4116-2694-2(X))* Lulu Pr., Inc.

Bucay, Jorge. The King & the Magician. Gusti, illus. 2014. (ENG.). 52p. (J). (gr. -1). 14.95 *(978-0-7892-1204-7(8),* 791204, Abbeville Kids) Abbeville Pr., Inc.

Buckmaster, Heath L. The Dragons of Tarnack. 2008. 142p. pap. 13.99 *(978-1-4357-4624-4(4))* Lulu Pr., Inc.

Bulla, Lynda. Freedom Rings: An American Parable. 2005. (Illus.). 32p. (J). lib. bdg. 14.99 *(978-0-9724272-3-4(6))* Katydid Publishing LLC.

Bunce, Elizabeth C. StarCrossed. 2011. (ENG.). 368p. (YA). pap. 9.99 *(978-0-545-13606-8(7),* Levine, Arthur A. Bks.) Scholastic, Inc.

Burgis, Stephanie. The Girl with the Dragon Heart. 2019. (Dragon Heart Ser.). (ENG.). 304p. (J). pap. 8.99 *(978-1-5476-0244-5(9),* 900207565, Bloomsbury Children's Bks.) Bloomsbury Publishing USA.

Burkart, Jeffrey. The Hidden Prince. 2011. (YA). 16.95 *(978-0-9825713-3-0(X))* Clifton Carriage House Pr.

Burkart, Jeffrey E., retold by. The Hidden Prince. 2003. (Illus.). 32p. (J). 9.99 incl. audio compact disk *(978-0-570-07174-7(7))* Concordia Publishing Hse.

Burks, David W. Full Circle: The Story of Outlaw-Prince Edwin, High King of England. 2007. 124p. 20.95 *(978-0-595-70485-9(9));* per. 10.95 *(978-0-595-46753-2(9))* iUniverse, Inc.

Burnett, Frances. The Land of Blue Flower. 2007. 76p. pap. 14.45 *(978-1-59462-742-2(8),* Bk. Jungle) Standard Publications, Inc.

—The Land of the Blue Flower. 2007. 76p. per. 9.45 *(978-1-59462-779-8(7),* Bk. Jungle) Standard Publications, Inc.

—The Lost Prince. (J). 25.95 *(978-0-8488-0691-0(3))* Amereon Ltd.

Burns, Dal. The Adventures of Phoo. 2006. 148p. pap. 24.95 *(978-1-4241-1773-4(9))* PublishAmerica, Inc.

Cadic, Oliver, et al. Queen Margot - The Bloody Wedding. 2007. (Queen Margot Ser.: 2). (ENG., Illus.). 48p. (J). (gr. -1-12). pap. 13.95 *(978-1-905460-19-9(8))* CineBook GBR. Dist: National Bk. Network.

Cadic, Olivier & Gheysens, Francois. Queen Margot - The Age of Innocence. Derenne, Juliette & Barroux, Sophie, illus. 2007. (Queen Margot Ser.: 1). (ENG.). 48p. (J). (gr. 4-7). per. 13.95 *(978-1-905460-10-6(4))* CineBook GBR. Dist: National Bk. Network.

Cahoon, Rebecca. The Magic Garden. 2012. (Illus.). 44p. pap. 9.99 *(978-0-9836771-3-0(1))* Mindstir Media.

Carey, Anna. Once, 2. 2013. (Eve Ser.: 2). (ENG.). 384p. (YA). (gr. 8-12). pap. 10.99 *(978-0-06-204855-4(4),* HarperCollins) HarperCollins Pubs.

—Rise. 2013. (Eve Ser.: 3). (ENG.). 336p. (YA). (gr. 8). pap. 10.99 *(978-0-06-204858-5(9),* HarperCollins) HarperCollins Pubs.

—Rise: An Eve Novel. 2013. (Illus.). 320p. (YA). pap. 9.99 *(978-0-06-226273-8(4))* HarperCollins Pubs.

Carey, Janet Lee. Dragon's Keep. 2007. 302p. (J). *(978-1-4287-3929-1(7))* Harcourt Trade Pubs.

Carpenter, Nancy, illus. Queen Victoria's Bathing Machine. 2014. (ENG.). 40p. (J). (gr. k-3). 18.99 *(978-1-4169-2753-2(0),* Simon & Schuster/Paula Wiseman Bks.) Simon & Schuster/Paula Wiseman Bks.

Carson, Rae. The Crown of Embers. 2019. (Girl of Fire & Thorns Ser.: 2). (ENG.). 432p. (YA). (gr. 8). pap. 10.99 *(978-0-06-202653-8(4),* Greenwillow Bks.) HarperCollins Pubs.

—The Girl of Fire & Thorns. (Girl of Fire & Thorns Ser.: 1). (ENG.). (YA). (gr. 8). 2019. 448p. pap. 11.99 *(978-0-06-202650-7(X))* 2011. 432p. 17.99 *(978-0-06-202648-4(8))* HarperCollins Pubs. (Greenwillow Bks.).

Carter, Grant Matthew. The Disaster Caster. Morling, Donovan, illus. 2012. 38p. pap. 16.00 *(978-1-4349-8432-6(X),* RoseDog Bks.) Dorrance Publishing Co., Inc.

Carter, Todd. A Monarch Universe Package Set: Children's Picture Book. 2007. (Illus.). 34p. (J). pap. 32.95 incl. cd-rom *(978-0-9800222-3-0(1))* UPfirst.com Bks.

Casey, Dawn. The Great Race: The Story of the Chinese Zodiac. Wilson, Anne, illus. 2006. (ENG.). 32p. (J). (gr. -1-3). 16.99 *(978-1-905236-77-0(8))* Barefoot Bks., Inc.

Castillo, Darryl. The Great Green Bird King. 2008. (ENG.). 24p. per. 15.99 *(978-1-4257-9383-8(5))* Xlibris Corp.

Castor, H. M. VIII. 2013. (ENG., Illus.). 432p. (YA). (gr. 7). 17.99 *(978-1-4424-7418-5(1),* Simon & Schuster Bks. For Young Readers) Simon & Schuster Bks. For Young Readers.

Cavendish, Grace. The Grace Mysteries: Assassin & Betrayal. 2011. (Grace Mysteries Ser.). (ENG.). 384p. (J). (gr. 3-7). pap. 6.99 *(978-0-385-74005-0(0),* Delacorte Bks. for Young Readers);1. (gr. 6-8). lib. bdg. 21.19 *(978-0-385-90821-4(0),* Delacorte Pr.) Random Hse. Children's Bks.

Chainani, Soman. A Crystal of Time. Bruno, Iacopo, illus. 2019. 624p. (J). *(978-0-06-290697-7(6)); (978-0-06-288641-5(X)); (978-0-06-289559-2(1)); (978-0-06-290764-6(6))* Harper & Row Ltd.

—A Crystal of Time. 2019. (School for Good & Evil Ser.: 5). (ENG., Illus.). 640p. (J). (gr. 3-7). pap. 10.50 *(978-0-06-288575-3(8),* HarperCollins) HarperCollins Pubs. Ltd. GBR. Dist: HarperCollins Pubs.

Charbonneau, Joelle. Dividing Eden. (YA). 2018. (ENG.). 432p. (gr. 8). pap. 9.99 *(978-0-06-245385-3(8))* 2017. 318p. *(978-0-06-274088-5(1))* HarperCollins Pubs. (HarperTeen).

Cherubini. Pinocchio in Africa. 2004. reprint ed. pap. 15.95 *(978-1-4191-4166-9(X));* pap. 1.99 *(978-1-4192-4166-6(4))* Kessinger Publishing, LLC.

Chester, Laura. Hiding Glory. Lippincott, Gary A., illus. 2007. (ENG.). 160p. (J). (gr. 3-7). 18.95 *(978-1-59543-616-0(2))* Willow Creek Pr., Inc.

Chima, Cinda Williams. The Crimson Crown. 2013. (Seven Realms Novel Ser.: 4). (ENG.). 624p. (YA). (gr. 7-17). pap. 11.99 *(978-1-4231-5214-9(X))* Little, Brown Bks. for Young Readers.

Church, Alfred J. Three Greek Children. 2008. (Illus.). 160p. pap. 9.95 *(978-1-59915-081-9(6))* Yesterday's Classics.

Clinton, J. Noel. The Prince of Warwood & the King's Key. 2005. (YA). per. 9.99 *(978-0-9773115-1-4(1))* C2 (C squared) Publishing.

Coe, Mary E. The Prince of Betherland. 2008. 117p. 24.95 *(978-0-557-03112-2(5))* Lulu Pr., Inc.

—The Prince of Betherland a Wonderful World of Fantasy. 2009. 112p. pap. 9.95 *(978-0-557-09297-0(3))* Lulu Pr., Inc.

Cole, Nikki. Princess Hope. 2012. 40p. pap. 14.95 *(978-1-886528-39-0(X))* ASA Publishing Corp.

Colfer, Chris. Adventures from the Land of Stories: Queen Red Riding Hood's Guide to Royalty. 2017. (Land of Stories Ser.). (ENG.). 128p. (J). (gr. 3-7). 13.99 *(978-0-316-38336-3(8))* Little, Brown Bks. for Young Readers.

—Queen Red Riding Hood's Guide to Royalty. Dorman, Brandon, illus. 2015. 118p. (J). *(978-0-316-38339-4(2))* Little Brown & Co.

—Trollbella Throws a Party: A Tale from the Land of Stories. Dorman, Brandon, illus. 2017. (Land of Stories Ser.). (ENG.). 32p. (J). (gr. -1-3). 17.99 *(978-0-316-38340-0(6))* Little, Brown Bks. for Young Readers.

Colum, Padraic & Pogány, Willy. The Adventures of Odysseus & the Tale of Troy. 2008. 280p. per. 27.95 *(978-0-548-81877-0(0))* Kessinger Publishing, LLC.

Comrie, Margaret S. The Heroes of Castle Bretten. 2003. (Illus.). 229p. (J). *(978-1-894666-65-7(8))* Inheritance Pubns.

Conners, Beatrice. The VeryVery Enchanted Kingdom, 1 vol. 2010. 48p. pap. 16.95 *(978-1-4512-9112-4(4))* PublishAmerica, Inc.

Coonan, Candace N. Where Shadows Linger: Tales from Fadreama: Book 2. 2012. 304p. (gr. 2-4). pap. 18.30 *(978-1-4669-3541-9(3))* Trafford Publishing.

Cooney, Caroline B. Enter Three Witches: A Story of Macbeth. l.t. ed. 2007. (Thorndike Literacy Bridge Young Adult Ser.). 343p. (YA). (gr. 8-12). 22.95 *(978-0-7862-9889-1(8))* Thorndike Pr.

Cooney, Caroline B. & Shakespeare, William. Enter Three Witches: A Story of Macbeth. 2007. 281p. (YA). pap. *(978-0-545-01972-9(9))* Scholastic, Inc.

Cordero, Silvia Jaeger & Cordero, Silvia Jaegar. El Huevo Azul. Sunset Producciones & Producciones, Sunset, illus. rev. ed. 2005. (Castillo de la Lectura Verde Ser.). (SPA & ENG.). 136p. (J). (gr. -1-7). pap. 7.95 *(978-970-20-0127-0(7))* Castillo, Ediciones, S. A. de C. V. MEX. Dist: Macmillan.

Corvino, Lucy, illus. Classic Starts(r): Arabian Nights. 2008. (Classic Starts(r) Ser.). (ENG.). 160p. (J). (gr. 2-4). 7.99 *(978-1-4027-4573-7(7))* Sterling Publishing Co., Inc.

Cotes, Everard. The Story of Sonny Sahib. 2004. reprint ed. pap. 1.99 *(978-1-4192-8402-1(9));* pap. 15.95 *(978-1-4191-8402-4(4))* Kessinger Publishing, LLC.

Courtney, Kateri. Welby & the Knobby King. 2003. pap. 14.95 *(978-0-9743588-0-2(0))* Castlegate Pr.

Creech, Sharon. The Castle Corona. Diaz, David, illus. (J). 2013. (ENG.). 352p. (gr. 3-7). pap. 7.99 *(978-0-06-206395-3(2,* HarperCollins) 2007. 336p. (gr. 4-7). lib. bdg. 19.89 *(978-0-06-084622-0(4),* Cotler, Joanna Books) HarperCollins Pubs.

Crichton, Julie. The King & the Queen & the Jelly Bean. Swaim, illus. l.t. ed. 2005. (SPA.). 24p. (J). bds. 7.95 *(978-0-9761990-0-7(9))* Bean Bk. Publishing.

—El rey y la reina y el frijolito de Goma. Swaim, Ramon, illus. l.t. ed. 2005. 24p. (J). bds. 7.95 *(978-0-9761990-1-4(7))* Bean Bk. Publishing.

Cronin, Doreen. Bloom. Small, David, illus. 2016. (ENG.). 40p. (J). (gr. -1-3). 17.99 *(978-1-4424-0620-9(8))* Simon & Schuster Children's Publishing.

Cronshaw, Joseph. Podge & Dodge. 2009. 32p. pap. 13.50 *(978-1-60693-868-3(1),* Strategic Bk. Publishing) Strategic Book Publishing & Rights Agency (SBPRA).

Cross, Frances. The Mystery of the Green Elephant. 2007. (Blobber Ser.). (ENG.). 84p. (J). per. *(978-1-84167-559-6(8))* Ransom Publishing Ltd.

Crowl, Janice. Kili & the Singing Snails. Orme, Harinani, illus. 2011. (J). 16.95 *(978-1-58178-104-5(0))* Bishop Museum Pr.

Dadey, Debbie. The Crook & the Crown. Avakyan, Tatevik, illus. 2015. (Mermaid Tales Ser.: 13). (ENG.). 128p. (J). (gr. 1-4). pap. 6.99 *(978-1-4814-4075-2(6),* Aladdin) Simon & Schuster Children's Publishing.

Darden, Amy. Yesterday Once Again: Guenevere's Quest. 2003. (J). pap. 11.00 *(978-0-8059-9238-0(3),* RoseDog Bks.) Dorrance Publishing Co., Inc.

Dargaw, Kate. Who Came First. Oleynikov, Igor, illus. 2008. 32p. 15.95 *(978-1-933327-45-7(6))* Purple Bear Bks., Inc.

Day George, Jessica. Wednesdays in the Tower. 2013. (Tuesdays at the Castle Ser.). (ENG.). 240p. (J). (gr. 3-6). E-Book 6.39 *(978-1-61963-051-2(6),* Bloomsbury USA Childrens) Bloomsbury Publishing USA.

De Boer, Joan. THE SULTAN AND THE MICE. 2007. (ENG., Illus.). 36p. (J). 18.95 *(978-84-96788-84-8(9))* OQO, Editora ESP. Dist: Baker & Taylor Bks.

De Haan, Linda & Nijland, Stern. King & King. De Haan, Linda & Nijland, Stern, illus. 2003. (ENG., Illus.). 32p. (J). (gr. k-3). 17.99 *(978-1-58246-061-1(2),* Tricycle Pr.) Random Hse. Children's Bks.

de la Cruz, Melissa. The Ring & the Crown (Extended Edition): the Ring & the Crown, Book 1. 2017. (ENG.). 480p. (J). (gr. 9-12). pap. 10.99 *(978-1-4847-9925-3(9),* Disney-Hyperion) Disney Publishing Worldwide.

de la Ramée, Louise & Ouida. Bimbi. 2007. 152p. per. 13.95 *(978-1-60312-344-0(X));* 24.95 *(978-1-60312-682-3(1))* Aegypan.

Dennis, Peter, illus. The Adventures of King Arthur. 2003. (Young Reading Ser.). 64p. (J). (gr. k-7). pap. 5.99 *(978-0-7945-0447-2(7),* Usborne) EDC Publishing.

—The Adventures of King Arthur. 2003. (Usborne Young Reading: Series Two Ser.). 64p. (J). (gr. k-7). 8.99 *(978-0-7945-1871-4(0),* Usborne) EDC Publishing.

dePaola, Tomie. In a Small Kingdom. Salati, Doug, illus. 2016. (J). *(978-0-8234-3551-7(2))* Holiday Hse., Inc.

—In a Small Kingdom. Salati, Doug, illus. 2018. (ENG.). 48p. (J). (gr. -1-3). 17.99 *(978-1-4814-9800-5(2),* Simon & Schuster Bks. For Young Readers) Simon & Schuster Bks. For Young Readers.

Derting, Kimberly. The Essence: A Pledge Novel. 2013. (Pledge Trilogy Ser.). (ENG., Illus.). (YA). (gr. 9). 368p. pap. 9.99 *(978-1-4424-4560-4(2));* 352p. 16.99 *(978-1-4424-4559-8(9))* McElderry, Margaret K. Bks. (McElderry, Margaret K. Bks.).

—The Pledge. (Pledge Trilogy Ser.). (ENG., Illus.). (YA). (gr. 9). 2012. 352p. pap. 12.99 *(978-1-4424-2202-5(5))* 2011. 336p. 16.99 *(978-1-4424-2201-8(7))* McElderry, Margaret K. Bks. (McElderry, Margaret K. Bks.).

Dharma Publishing Staff. The King Who Understood Animals: A Story about Using Knowledge Wisely. 2nd ed. 2013. (Jataka Tales Ser.). (Illus.). 36p. (gr. -1-7). pap. 8.95 *(978-0-89800-520-2(5))* Dharma Publishing.

—Three Wise Birds: A Story about Wisdom & Leadership. 3rd ed. 2013. (Jataka Tales Ser.). (Illus.). 36p. (gr. -1-7). pap. 8.95 *(978-0-89800-521-9(3))* Dharma Publishing.

DiMarco, Carol & Bowman, Sharon. The Tale of Two Kingdoms. 2009. (ENG.). 88p. (J). pap. 10.99 *(978-1-59092-170-8(4))* Blue Forge Pr.

Dines, Carol. The Queen's Soprano. 2007. (ENG., Illus.). 336p. (YA). (gr. 9). pap. 18.95 *(978-0-15-206102-9(9))* Houghton Mifflin Harcourt Publishing Co.

Dixon, Heather. Entwined. 2012. (ENG.). 480p. (YA). (gr. 8). pap. 10.99 *(978-0-06-200104-7(3),* Greenwillow Bks.) HarperCollins Pubs.

—Illusionarium. 2015. (ENG.). 368p. (YA). (gr. 8). 17.99 *(978-0-06-200105-4(1),* Greenwillow Bks.) HarperCollins Pubs.

Do, Kim-Thu, tr. from ENG. Tang Monk Disciples Monkey King: English/Vietnamese. Ma, Wenhai, illus. 2005. (Adventures of Monkey King Ser.: No. 3). (ENG & VIE.). 32p. (J). 16.95 *(978-1-57227-087-9(X))* Pan Asia Pubns. (USA), Inc.

Dokey, Cameron. The Storyteller's Daughter: A Retelling of "the Arabian Nights" 2007. (Once upon a Time Ser.). (ENG., Illus.). 240p. (YA). (gr. 9). mass mkt. 8.99 *(978-1-4169-3776-0(5),* Simon Pulse) Simon Pulse.

Donaldson, Julia. The Cook & the King. Roberts, David, illus. 2019. (ENG.). 32p. (J). (gr. -1-2). 16.99 *(978-1-4197-3757-2(0),* 1281801) Abrams, Inc.

—Zog & the Flying Doctors. Scheffler, Axel, illus. 2017. (ENG.). 32p. (J). (gr. -1-3). 17.99 *(978-1-338-13417-9(5),* Levine, Arthur A. Bks.) Scholastic, Inc.

Dorfman, Ariel. The Rabbits' Rebellion. Riddell, Chris, illus. 2020. (ENG.). 64p. (J). (gr. 2). 13.95 *(978-1-60980-937-9(8),* Triangle Square) Seven Stories Pr.

Dougherty, John. Stinkbomb & Ketchup-Face & the Badness of Badgers. Ricks, Sam, illus. 2018. (Stinkbomb & Ketchup-Face Ser.: 1). (ENG.). 160p. (J). (gr. 3-7). 7.99 *(978-1-101-99663-8(3),* Puffin Books) Penguin Young Readers Group.

Doyle, Malachy. King Donal's Secret. Watson, Richard, illus. 2005. (ENG.). 24p. (J). lib. bdg. 23.65 *(978-1-59646-740-8(1))* Dingles & Co.

Duffy, Carol Ann. The Princess's Blankets. Hyde, Catherine, illus. 2009. (ENG.). 40p. (J). (gr. k-3). 18.99 *(978-0-7636-4547-2(8),* Templar) Candlewick Pr.

—Queen Munch & Queen Nibble. Monks, Lydia, illus. 2008. (ENG.). 64p. (J). (gr. -1-3). *(978-1-59692-238-9(9))* MacAdam/Cage Publishing, Inc.

Dunn, Carolyn. A Pie Went By. Date not set. 32p. (J). (gr. -1-1). pap. 4.99 *(978-0-06-443649-6(7))* HarperCollins Pubs.

Durkee, Noura. The King, the Prince & the Naughty Sheep. Durkee, Noura, illus. 2007. (ENG., Illus.). 24p. (J). (gr. k-5). 16.00 *(978-1-879402-58-4(0))* Tahrike Tarsile Quran, Inc.

Dutta, Arup Kumar. The Boy Who Became King. Arya, Viki, illus. 2004. 122p. (J). *(978-81-291-0405-2(9))* Rupa & Co.

Edgson, Alison, illus. The Emperor's New Clothes. 2007. (Flip-Up Fairy Tales Ser.). 24p. (J). (gr. -1-2). *(978-1-84643-093-0(3))* Child's Play International Ltd.

Edwards, R. Katie King's Journal. 2004. 376p. (YA). 31.95 *(978-0-595-66890-8(9))* iUniverse, Inc.

Elerya. One Step Higher: Piano Paradise Book II, 1 vol. 2009. 79p. pap. 16.95 *(978-1-60749-477-5(9))* PublishAmerica, Inc.

Ella, Sara. Unbreakable, 1 vol. 2018. (Unblemished Trilogy Ser.: 3). (ENG.). 384p. (YA). 16.99 *(978-0-7180-8105-8(6))* Nelson, Thomas Inc.

Elliott, David. Bull. 2019. (ENG.). 224p. (YA). (gr. 9). pap. 9.99 *(978-1-328-59633-8(8),* 1731318, Clarion Bks.) HarperCollins Pubs.

Ellis, Sarah. The Queen's Feet, 1 vol. Petricic, Dusan, illus. 2008. (ENG.). 32p. (J). (gr. -1-1). 6.95 *(978-0-88995-414-4(3),* 3f9107d4-8cc8-4556-b35b-8f583a40f68d) Trifolium Bks., Inc. CAN. Dist: Firefly Bks., Ltd.

Essama, Molly Jane. The Prince & the Three Ugly Hags. 2010. 28p. pap. 16.95 *(978-1-4490-5587-5(7))* AuthorHouse.

Eyre, David. Breaking the Blood. Kalahele, Imaikalani, illus. 2008. 40p. 14.95 *(978-0-87336-162-0(8))* Kamehameha Publishing.

Fairchild, Simone. Queen Bee's Midnight Caper, 3 vols. Key, Pamela Marie, illus. 2006. 33p. (J). (gr. -1-3). per. 17.95 *(978-0-9771971-4-9(X))* W & B Pubs.

Fantaskey, Beth. Jessica Rules the Dark Side. 2012. (ENG.). 320p. (YA). (gr. 9). 16.99 *(978-0-547-39309-4(1),* 1426896, Clarion Bks.) HarperCollins Pubs.

Farah, Barbara. Parabola O Jednom Mostu: Parable of the Bridge. 2005. (CRO., Illus.). 36p. pap. 15.00 *(978-0-9769346-0-8(4))* Farah, Barbara.

Farooqi, Imran A. The Spell of the Witch-Queen. 2006. (Illus.). 60p. pap. *(978-1-84401-816-1(4))* Athena Pr.

Farrow, G. e. & Farrow, G. E. The Wallypug in London. 2011. 106p. 23.95 *(978-1-4638-9696-6(4))* Rodgers, Alan Bks.

Fast, David R. Doctor Dave's Dragon Tales. Ciesinska, Izabela, illus. 2007. 160p. (J). per. 13.95 *(978-0-9793944-8-5(1))* Digi-Tall Media.

Ferguson, M. J. The Mirror in the Box: A Children's Story & a Parable. 2013. 66p. (gr. 4-6). pap. 9.99 *(978-1-4497-7804-0(6),* WestBow Pr.) Author Solutions, LLC.

Ferguson, Sarah. Tea for Ruby. Glasser, Robin Preiss, illus. 2008. (ENG.). 40p. (J). (gr. -1-3). 19.99 *(978-1-4169-5419-4(8),* Simon & Schuster/Paula Wiseman Bks.) Simon & Schuster/Paula Wiseman Bks.

—Tea for Ruby. Glasser, Robin Preiss, illus. 2012. (ENG.). 40p. (J). (gr. -1-3). pap. 8.99 *(978-1-4169-5420-0(1),* Simon & Schuster/Paula Wiseman Bks.) Simon & Schuster/Paula Wiseman Bks.

Ferris, Jean. Once upon a Marigold. 2004. 275p. (gr. 5). 17.00 *(978-0-7569-3613-6(6))* Perfection Learning Corp.

—Twice upon a Marigold. 2009. (ENG., Illus.). 304p. (J). (gr. 3-7). pap. 6.99 *(978-0-15-206692-5(6),* 1099004, Clarion Bks.) HarperCollins Pubs.

Feuti, Norm. The King of Kazoo: a Graphic Novel. 2016. (ENG., Illus.). 208p. (J). (gr. 3-5). 22.99 *(978-0-545-77088-0(2),* Graphix) Scholastic, Inc.

Field, Brett. Screno Magic Medieval Collision. 2007. 52p. per. 10.00 *(978-1-4257-4700-8(0))* Xlibris Corp.

Fine, Sarah. The Cursed Queen. 2017. (Impostor Queen Ser.: 2). (ENG., Illus.). 432p. (YA). (gr. 7). 19.99 *(978-1-4814-4193-3(0),* McElderry, Margaret K. Bks.) McElderry, Margaret K. Bks.

—The Impostor Queen. (Impostor Queen Ser.: 1). (ENG., Illus.). (YA). (gr. 7). 2017. 448p. pap. 13.99 *(978-1-4814-4191-9(4))* 2016. 432p. 18.99 *(978-1-4814-4190-2(6))* McElderry, Margaret K. Bks. (McElderry, Margaret K. Bks.).

—The True Queen. 2018. (Impostor Queen Ser.: 3). (ENG., Illus.). 384p. (YA). (gr. 7). 19.99 *(978-1-4814-9060-3(5),* McElderry, Margaret K. Bks.) McElderry, Margaret K. Bks.

Finn, Perdita, adapted by. Meet Crystal Winter. 2016. (Illus.). 31p. (J). *(978-1-5182-2557-4(8))* Little Brown & Co.

Fischer, Lavanya Regunathan. One Tree, One King & the Open Road. 2015. 212p. 14.99 *(978-93-5177-028-2(1),* HarperCollins) HarperCollins Pubs.

Fisscher, Tiny. RUBY & the LION. 2008. (ENG.). 48p. (J). (gr. 1-7). 11.95 *(978-1-60136-014-4(2))* Audio Holdings, LLC.

Flanagan, John. The Emperor of Nihon-Ja. 2012. (Ranger's Apprentice Ser.: 10). lib. bdg. 19.65 *(978-0-606-23641-6(4))* Turtleback.

—The Emperor of Nihon-Ja: Book Ten, 10 vols., Bk. 10. (Ranger's Apprentice Ser.: 10). (ENG.). (J). (gr. 5-18). 2012. 464p. 9.99 *(978-0-14-241859-8(5),* Puffin Books) 2011. (Illus.). 448p. 18.99 *(978-0-399-25500-7(1),* Philomel Bks.) Penguin Young Readers Group.

—The Kings of Clonmel: Book Eight, Bk. 8. 2011. (Ranger's Apprentice Ser.: 8). (ENG., Illus.). 400p. (J). (gr. 5-18). 9.99 *(978-0-14-241857-4(9),* Puffin Books) Penguin Young Readers Group.

Fletcher, Susan. Flight of the Dragon Kyn. 2010. (Dragon Chronicles Ser.). (ENG.). 240p. (J). (gr. 3-7). pap. 12.99 *(978-1-4169-9713-9(X),* Atheneum Bks. for Young Readers) Simon & Schuster Children's Publishing.

Fontes, Ron. Sunjata: Warrior King of Mali: A West African Legend. Carruthers, Sandy, illus. 2008. (Graphic Myths & Legends Ser.). 48p. (J). (gr. 3-7). lib. bdg. 26.60 *(978-0-8225-6758-5(X),* Graphic Universe™) Lerner Publishing Group.

French, Jackie. Ophelia: Queen of Denmark. 2021. 288p. 8.99 *(978-0-7322-9852-4(0),* HarperCollins) HarperCollins Pubs.

Friesner, Esther. Sphinx's Princess. 2010. (Princesses of Myth Ser.). (ENG.). 400p. (YA). (gr. 7). pap. 9.99 *(978-0-375-85655-6(2),* Random Hse. Bks. for Young Readers) Random Hse. Children's Bks.

—Sphinx's Queen. 2011. (Princesses of Myth Ser.). (ENG., Illus.). 368p. (YA). (gr. 7). pap. 9.99 *(978-0-375-85658-7(7),* Ember) Random Hse. Children's Bks.

Fujimoto, Yoshie. The Ninjas & Goblins. 2008. pap. 13.00 *(978-0-8059-8638-9(3))* Dorrance Publishing Co., Inc.

Furgang, Kathy. A Throne for the King: Set Of 6. 2010. (Early Connections Ser.). (J). 37.00 net. *(978-1-4108-1372-5(X))* Benchmark Education Co.

—A Throne for the King & un trono para el Rey: 6 English, 6 Spanish Adaptations. 2011. (ENG & SPA.). (J). 75.00 net. *(978-1-4108-5657-9(7))* Benchmark Education Co.

Fussell, Sandy. Samurai Kids #2: Owl Ninja. James, Rhian Nest, illus. 2011. (Samurai Kids Ser.: 2). (ENG.). 272p. (J). (gr. 4-7). 15.99 *(978-0-7636-5003-2(X))* Candlewick Pr.

Gallego Garcia, Laura & Bellm, Dan. The Legend of the Wandering King. 2005. (J). *(978-0-439-58557-6(0),* Levine, Arthur A. Bks.) Scholastic, Inc.

Galloway, Priscilla. Aleta y la Reina: Una Historia de la Antigua Grecia.Tr. of Aleta & the Queen: A Tale of Ancient Greece. (SPA.). (YA). (gr. 5-8). pap. *(978-968-6582-27-7(4))* Samara, Ediciones, S. A. de C. V.

Geddes, Meia. The Little Queen. Alexander, Lindsey, ed. Miller, Sara Zieve, illus. 2017. (ENG.). 107p. (J). pap. 8.00 *(978-1-945366-66-6(4))* Poetose Pr.

George, Jessica Day. Dragon Flight. 2009. (Dragon Slippers Ser.). (ENG.). 288p. (J). (gr. 5-8). pap. 9.99 *(978-1-59990-359-0(8),* 900058935, Bloomsbury USA Childrens) Bloomsbury Publishing USA.

—Dragon Spear. 2010. (Dragon Slippers Ser.). (ENG.). 272p. (YA). (gr. 5-8). pap. 8.99 *(978-1-59990-516-7(7),* 900068448, Bloomsbury USA Childrens) Bloomsbury Publishing USA.

—Wednesdays in the Tower. 2017. (Tuesdays at the Castle Ser.). (ENG.). 256p. (J). pap. 8.99 *(978-1-68119-219-2(5),*

900164104, Bloomsbury USA Childrens) Bloomsbury Publishing USA.

Gerhardt, Barbara. I Am of Scram. 2007. (Illus.). pap. 12.95 *(978-1-934246-15-3(8))* Peppertree Pr., The.

Gerhardt, Paul L. The Diversity King. 2007. 35p. 19.50 *(978-0-615-16208-9(8))* Gerhardt, Paul L.

Gilman, Phoebe. The Balloon Tree. 2004. (J). (gr. k-3). spiral bd. *(978-0-616-01650-3(6))* Canadian National Institute for the Blind/Institut National Canadien pour les Aveugles.

Glynn, Connie. The Rosewood Chronicles #1: Undercover Princess. (Rosewood Chronicles Ser.: 1). (ENG.). (J). (gr. 3-7). 2019. 464p. pap. 9.99 *(978-0-06-284782-9(1))* 2018. 448p. 16.99 *(978-0-06-284780-5(5))* HarperCollins Pubs. (HarperCollins).

Glynn, W. Celebrando a Diario con el Rey.Tr. of Daily with the King. (SPA.). 10.99 *(978-958-9269-28-2(1)*, 490190) Editorial Unilit.

Gogonya, Carol. The African Mermaid & Other Stories. 2011. 40p. pap. 32.70 *(978-1-4568-5416-4(X))* Xlibris Corp.

Going, K. L. The Liberation of Gabriel King. 2005. (ENG.). 151p. (J). (gr. 6-8). 21.19 *(978-0-399-23991-5(X))* Penguin Young Readers Group.

Goldblatt, Mark. Finding the Worm (Twerp Sequel) 2016. (Twerp Ser.: 2). 368p. (J). (gr. 4-7). 7.99 *(978-0-385-39111-5(0)*, Yearling) Random Hse. Children's Bks.

Gooderham, Chris. More Wicked Rhymes. 2008. 68p. pap. 13.95 *(978-1-4092-1663-6(2))* Lulu Pr., Inc.

Goodlett, Ellen. Rule. 2019. (Rule Ser.: 1). (ENG.). 400p. (YA). (gr. 9-17). pap. 10.99 *(978-0-316-51529-0(9))* Little, Brown Bks. for Young Readers.

Goodrum, Smith. The Marble War: The game of chess as told to Steven. 2011. 28p. pap. 14.95 *(978-1-4567-5690-1(7))* AuthorHouse.

Gordon, Mike, illus. The Emperor's New Clothes. 2006. 24p. (J). (gr. -1-3). 9.99 *(978-0-7945-1350-4(6)*, Usborne) EDC Publishing.

Goss, Leon. King for a Day. Nichols, Chris, illus. 2005. (J). pap. *(978-1-933156-09-5(0))*; per. 16.99 *(978-1-933156-01-9(5))* GSVQ Publishing. (VisionQuest Kids).

Graham, Baxter. Old King Stinky Toes. Martin, James R., illus. 2005. 32p. (J). 15.95 *(978-0-9764791-0-9(9))* Drumstick Media.

Grandoit, Jean. In the Quest for Inshalla: Simbies of the Caribbean at the World Under. 2010. 68p. pap. 25.49 *(978-1-4520-3900-8(3))* AuthorHouse.

Green, Rich. Pearlsus. 2007. 140p. per. 10.95 *(978-0-595-45166-1(7))* iUniverse, Inc.

Grindley, Sally. Queen Ella's Feet. Aguilar, Sandra, illus. 2011. (My Phonics Readers: Level 3 Ser.). 24p. (J). (gr. -1-1). 24.25 *(978-1-84898-513-1(4))* Sea-To-Sea Pubns.

Gruffudd, Elena & Owen, Carys Eurwen. Clustiau March. 2005. (WEL., Illus.). 36p. pap. *(978-0-86381-329-0(1))* Gwasg Carreg Gwalch.

Guridi. The King of Nothing. Endor, Saul, tr. 2018. (Illus.). 32p. (J). (gr. -1-3). 16.95 *(978-1-68137-290-7(8)*, NYR Children's Collection) New York Review of Bks., Inc., The.

Haack, Daniel. Prince & Knight. Lewis, Stevie, illus. 2018. (ENG.). 40p. (J). (gr. -1-3). 17.99 *(978-1-4998-0552-9(7))* Little Bee Books Inc.

Haack, Daniel & Galupo, Isabel. Maiden & Princess. Human, Becca, illus. 2019. (ENG.). 40p. (J). (gr. -1-3). 17.99 *(978-1-4998-0776-9(7))* Little Bee Books Inc.

Haddix, Margaret Peterson. Risked. 2013. (Missing Ser.: 6). (ENG., Illus.). 320p. (J). (gr. 3-7). 18.99 *(978-1-4169-8984-4(6)*, Simon & Schuster Bks. For Young Readers) Simon & Schuster Bks. For Young Readers.

—Sent. (Missing Ser.: 2). (YA). 2011. 82.75 *(978-1-4407-2678-1(7))* 2009. 1.25 *(978-1-4407-2679-8(5))* 2009. 218.75 *(978-1-4407-2670-5(1))* 2009. 98.75 *(978-1-4407-2675-0(2))* Recorded Bks., Inc.

—Sent. (Missing Ser.: 2). (ENG.). (J). (gr. 3-7). 2010. 336p. pap. 8.99 *(978-1-4169-5423-1(6))* 2009. 320p. 16.99 *(978-1-4169-5422-4(8))* Simon & Schuster Bks. For Young Readers. (Simon & Schuster Bks. For Young Readers).

—Sent. abr. ed. 2009. *(978-1-4424-0767-1(0))* Simon & Schuster Children's Publishing.

—Sent. l.t. ed. 2010. (Missing Ser.: Bk. 2). (ENG.). 345p. 23.99 *(978-1-4104-3245-2(9))* Thorndike Pr.

—Sent. 2010. (Missing Ser.: 2). lib. bdg. 18.40 *(978-0-606-14699-9(7))* Turtleback.

Hale, Shannon. Palace of Stone. 2015. (Princess Academy Ser.: 2). (YA). lib. bdg. 18.40 *(978-0-606-36439-3(0))* Turtleback.

—Princess Academy: Palace of Stone. (Princess Academy Ser.: 2). (ENG.). (gr. 5-8). 2015. 352p. (J). pap. 8.99 *(978-1-61963-257-8(8)*, 900131475) 2012. 336p. (YA). 17.99 *(978-1-59990-873-1(5)*, 900082614) Bloomsbury Publishing USA. (Bloomsbury USA Childrens).

—Princess Academy: the Forgotten Sisters. (Princess Academy Ser.: 3). (ENG.). 2016. 352p. (J). pap. 9.99 *(978-1-61963-933-1(5)*, 900152540) 2015. 336p. (YA). (gr. 5-8). 18.99 *(978-1-61963-485-5(6)*, 900138574) Bloomsbury Publishing USA. (Bloomsbury USA Childrens).

Hancock, R. C. An Uncommon Blue. 2014. (Illus.). xi, 275p. (YA). pap. 16.99 *(978-1-4621-1488-7(1))* Cedar Fort, Inc./CFI Distribution.

Hand, Cynthia, et al. My Lady Jane. (Lady Janies Ser.). (ENG.). 512p. (YA). (gr. 8). 2017. pap. 11.99 *(978-0-06-239176-6(3))* 2016. 18.99 *(978-0-06-239174-2(7))* HarperCollins Pubs. (HarperTeen).

Harrison, Christy Gremore. Once upon A Monday. 2010. 40p. pap. 16.99 *(978-1-4490-5854-8(X))* AuthorHouse.

Harrison, Mette Ivie. The Princess & the Hound. (YA). 2008. (ENG.). 432p. (gr. 8). pap. 8.99 *(978-0-06-113189-9(X)*, HarperTeen) 2007. 410p. (gr. 7-18). lib. bdg. 18.89 *(978-0-06-113188-2(1)*, Eos) HarperCollins Pubs.

Harte, Bret. The Queen of the Pirate Isle. Kate Greenaway, illus. 2010. 56p. pap. 3.49 *(978-1-60386-381-0(8)*, Watchmaker Publishing) Wexford College Pr.

Harvey, Damian. A Gift for the King. Remphry, Martin, illus. 2005. (Reading Corner Ser.). 24p. (J). (gr. k-3). lib. bdg. 22.80 *(978-1-59771-013-8(X))* Sea-To-Sea Pubns.

Hatton, Fredrick D. Dusty & a Gift for a King, 1 vol. 2009. 23p. pap. 24.95 *(978-1-61546-094-6(2))* America Star Bks.

Hausman, Gerald & Hausman, Loretta. Farewell, Josephine: The Romance of Josephine & Napoleon. 2013. 248p. pap. 13.95 *(978-1-61720-381-7(5))* Wilder Pubns., Corp.

Hawkins, Mia K. The Broken Guild of Twelve Pirates, 1 vol. 2009. 201p. pap. 24.95 *(978-1-61546-333-6(X))* PublishAmerica, Inc.

Hayes, Sean & Icenogle, Scott. Plum. Thompson, Robin, illus. 2018. (ENG.). 48p. (J). (gr. -1-3). 17.99 *(978-1-5344-0404-5(X)*, Simon & Schuster Bks. For Young Readers) Simon & Schuster Bks. For Young Readers.

HB Staff. The King Who Loved to Dance. 97th ed. 2003. (Signatures Ser.). (gr. 1-18). pap. 16.50 *(978-0-15-308161-3(9))* Harcourt Schl. Pubs.

Headrick, Tammy Hill. That Famous Bird, Sir Thornton the Third. 2009. 24p. pap. 12.00 *(978-1-4269-0550-6(5))* Trafford Publishing.

Healey, Bruce. The Delightfully Dreadful Tale of King Drod, 1 vol. 2009. 48p. pap. 16.95 *(978-1-61582-545-5(2))* America Star Bks.

Heap, Bridgette. The Pursuit of Pizan, 1 vol. Chodagiri, Shanthi, illus. 2009. 35p. pap. 24.95 *(978-1-61546-994-9(X))* America Star Bks.

Hendrickson, Kevis. The Legend of Witch Bane. 2008. 348p. per. 11.95 *(978-1-4327-1298-3(5))* Outskirts Pr., Inc.

Hendry, Frances. Quest for a Queen: The Lark. 2006. (Illus.). 251p. pap. *(978-1-905665-04-4(0))* Pollinger In Print.

Henty, George. At Agincourt: A Tale of the White Hoods of Paris. 2011. 332p. pap. 19.95 *(978-1-61179-111-2(1))* Fireship Pr.

—A March on London: A Story of Wat Tyler's Insurrection. 2004. reprint ed. pap. 1.99 *(978-1-4192-0224-7(3))*; pap. 27.95 *(978-1-4191-0224-0(9))* Kessinger Publishing, LLC.

Herbert, Bethany Zohner. The Perfect Fool. 2015. 279p. (YA). pap. 17.99 *(978-1-4621-1620-1(5))* Cedar Fort, Inc./CFI Distribution.

Hewins, Shirley, illus. Rainy Brown & the Seven Midgets. l.t. ed. 2006. (J). (gr. k-3). pap. 11.95 *(978-1-884242-24-3(3)*, RB1STED); 44p. lib. bdg. 19.95 *(978-1-884242-25-0(1)*, RB1STED) Multicultural Pubns.

Hockerman, Dennis, illus. The Little Seed: A Tale about Integrity. 2006. (J). *(978-1-59939-094-9(9)*, Reader's Digest Young Families, Inc.) Studio Fun International.

Hodge, Rosamund. Crimson Bound. 2016. (ENG.). 464p. (YA). (gr. 8). pap. 9.99 *(978-0-06-222477-4(8)*, Balzer & Bray) HarperCollins Pubs.

Hollier, Jo. Roary O'Rourke Challenge of the Trolls, Bk. 3. 2004. pap. 9.95 *(978-1-59374-115-0(4))* Whiskey Creek Pr., LLC.

—Roary O'Rourke the Princess & Dooley Do, Bk. 2. 2004. (J). pap. 9.95 *(978-1-59374-091-7(3))* Whiskey Creek Pr., LLC.

—Roary O'Rourke Victorious Duo, Bk. 4. 2004. (J). pap. 9.95 *(978-1-59374-117-4(0))* Whiskey Creek Pr., LLC.

Holman, Nedra. Beautiful Queen. Velitchenko, Olga, illus. 2008. 40p. (J). *(978-1-4363-5461-5(7))* Xlibris Corp.

Homberg, Ruth. Across the Sea (Disney Frozen) RH Disney, illus. 2016. (Step into Reading Ser.). (ENG.). 24p. (J). (gr. -1-1). 5.99 *(978-0-7364-3398-3(8)*, RH/Disney) Random Hse. Children's Bks.

Hong, Chen Jiang. The Tiger Prince. Waters, Alyson, tr. 2018. (ENG., Illus.). 40p. (J). (gr. -1-3). 18.95 *(978-1-68137-294-5(0)*, NYR Children's Collection) New York Review of Bks., Inc., The.

Hoobler, Dorothy & Hoobler, Thomas. The Sword That Cut the Burning Grass. 2006. 211p. (gr. 5-9). 17.00 *(978-0-7569-6907-3(7))* Perfection Learning Corp.

Hood, Douglas. The Stone Hat. Simonton, Tom, illus. 2005. (ENG.). 16p. (J). 5.75 *(978-1-57274-754-8(4)*, 2784, Bks. for Young Learners) Owen, Richard C. Pubs., Inc.

Hosford, Kate. How the Queen Found the Perfect Cup of Tea. Swiatkowska, Gabi, illus. 2017. (ENG.). 40p. (J). (gr. k-3). 18.99 *(978-1-4677-3904-7(9)*, 7c02bedb-b44a-40c9-aa37-01918276516a); E-Book 29.32 *(978-1-4677-9563-0(1))*; E-Book 29.32 *(978-1-5124-3272-5(5)*, 9781512432725); E-Book 9.99 *(978-1-5124-3273-2(3)*, 9781512432732) Lerner Publishing Group. (Carolrhoda Bks.).

Howard, Annabelle. Hammurabi's Law & Order. 2005. (J). pap. *(978-1-4108-4233-6(9))* Benchmark Education Co.

Howell, Gill. Snow King. Cann, Helen, illus. 2005. (ENG.). 24p. (J). lib. bdg. 23.65 *(978-1-59646-742-2(8))* Dingles & Co.

Jae, Ava. Into the Black. 2017. (Beyond the Red Trilogy Ser.: 2). (ENG., Illus.). 372p. (YA). (gr. 7-13). 17.99 *(978-1-5107-2236-1(X)*, Sky Pony Pr.) Skyhorse Publishing Co., Inc.

James, Dalton. The Sneakiest Pirates. 2008. 20p. pap. 10.95 *(978-1-4327-2477-1(0))* Outskirts Pr., Inc.

James, Ian. Why the Sky Is Far Away: A Tale from Nigeria. 2006. (J). pap. *(978-1-4108-6172-6(4))* Benchmark Education Co.

Janer, Montserrat. El Rey Listo y el Rey Fuerte. (SPA.). (J). pap. *(978-84-236-3342-5(X))* Edebé ESP. Dist: Lectorum Pubns., Inc.

Jay, Stacey. Of Beast & Beauty. 2014. (ENG.). 400p. (YA). (gr. 9). pap. 9.99 *(978-0-385-74321-1(1)*, Ember) Random Hse. Children's Bks.

Jesus, Opal De. The Golden Apple Kingdom, 1 vol. 2009. 48p. pap. 16.95 *(978-1-60749-414-0(0))* America Star Bks.

Jinks, Catherine. Pagan in Exile: Book Two of the Pagan Chronicles. 2005. (Pagan Chronicles Ser.: 2). (ENG., Illus.). 336p. (YA). (gr. 7-18). reprint ed. pap. 6.99 *(978-0-7636-2691-4(0))* Candlewick Pr.

Johnson, Alaya Dawn. The Summer Prince, 1 vol. 2014. (ENG.). 304p. (YA). (gr. 9). pap. 12.99 *(978-0-545-41780-8(5)*, Levine, Arthur A. Bks.) Scholastic, Inc.

Johnston, E. K. A Thousand Nights. 2015. (ENG.). 336p. (J). (gr. 9-17). 18.99 *(978-1-4847-2227-5(2))* Hyperion Bks. for Children.

Jones, Katy Huth. Treachery & Truth: A Story of Sinners, Servants, & Saints. 2016. 163p. (YA). pap. *(978-0-8198-7535-8(X))* Pauline Bks. & Media.

Jones, Marcia & Dadey, Debbie. The Other Side of Magic, 2. 2009. (Keyholders Ser.: 2). (ENG.). 144p. (J). (gr. 4-7). 17.44 *(978-0-7653-5983-4(9)*, 9780765359834) Doherty, Tom Assocs., LLC.

Joslin. Minstrel's Tale. (J). pap. 8.95 *(978-0-7459-3966-7(X)*, Lion Books) Lion Hudson PLC GBR. Dist: Trafalgar Square Publishing.

Journey to see the King. 2006. (J). *(978-0-9791168-0-3(5))* Lighthouse Bk. Publishing.

Jovanovic, Katarina. The King Has Goat Ears, 1 vol. Béha, Philippe, illus. 2008. (ENG.). 32p. (J). (gr. -1-k). 16.95 *(978-1-896580-22-7(X))* Tradewind Bks. CAN. Dist: Orca Bk. Pubs. USA.

Judybee. Queen Amina of Zari: Queens of Africa Book 1. LittlePinkPebble, illus. 2011. 28p. pap. *(978-1-908218-43-8(6))* MX Publishing, Ltd.

—Queen Esther: Queens of Africa Book 4. LittlePinkPebble, illus. 2011. 28p. pap. *(978-1-908218-52-0(5))* MX Publishing, Ltd.

—Queen Idi: Queens of Africa Book 5. LittlePinkPebble, illus. 2011. 24p. pap. *(978-1-908218-55-1(X))* MX Publishing, Ltd.

—Queen Maked: Queens of Africa Book 2. LittlePinkPebble, illus. 2011. 28p. pap. *(978-1-908218-46-9(0))* MX Publishing, Ltd.

—Queen Moremi: Queens of Africa Book 3. LittlePinkPebble, illus. 2011. 28p. pap. *(978-1-908218-49-0(5))* MX Publishing, Ltd.

Karandeev, Oleg. Dmitri II: The Kind Storyteller Book Two of Five. Ciesinska, Izabela, illus. 2007. 76p. (YA). per. 15.95 *(978-0-9793944-3-0(0))* Digi-Tall Media.

Kato, Etsuo. The King Who Saved the Dove. Yasui, Koji, illus. 2014. (J). 8.95 *(978-1-935523-68-0(6))* World Tribune Pr.

Kats, Jewel. Prince Preemie: A Tale of a Tiny Puppy Who Arrives Early. Lenart, Claudia, illus. 2016. 28p. (J). pap. *(978-1-61599-306-2(1))* Loving Healing Pr., Inc.

Keegan, Shannon. Legend of the Sea Fairies. 2006. (Illus.). (J). per. 14.99 *(978-0-9773433-0-0(8))* Bixie Gate Publishing.

Keep, Richard & Lowery, Linda. The Chocolate Tree: [a Mayan Folktale]. Porter, Janice Lee, illus. 2009. (On My Own Folklore Ser.). (ENG.). 48p. (J). (gr. 2-4). pap. 8.99 *(978-1-58013-851-2(9)*, e84a6f14-bd58-4f3c-9870-b92636c6c1b6, First Avenue Editions) Lerner Publishing Group.

Kent, Jaden. Ella & Owen 6: Dragon Spies! Bodnaruk, Iryna, illus. 2017. (Ella & Owen Ser.: 6). (ENG.). 112p. (J). (gr. k-3). 16.99 *(978-1-4998-0476-8(8))*; pap. 5.99 *(978-1-4998-0475-1(X))* Little Bee Books Inc.

Khan, Joshua. Dream Magic. 2018. (Shadow Magic Novel Ser.). (ENG.). 352p. (J). (gr. 3-7). pap. 6.99 *(978-1-4847-3798-9(9))* Hyperion Bks. for Children.

Kilgore, Lee. Widga's Quest, 1 vol. 2009. 48p. pap. 16.95 *(978-1-4489-2517-9(7))* America Star Bks.

Kimmel, Eric A. Joha Makes a Wish: A Middle Eastern Tale, 0 vols. Rayyan, Omar, illus. 2013. (ENG.). 40p. (J). (gr. -1-3). pap. 7.99 *(978-1-4778-1687-5(9)*, 9781477816875, Two Lions) Amazon Publishing.

Kincaid, S. J. The Empress. (Diabolic Ser.: 2). (ENG.). 384p. (YA). (gr. 9). 2018. pap. 13.99 *(978-1-5344-0993-4(9))* 2017. (Illus.). 17.99 *(978-1-5344-0992-7(0))* Simon & Schuster Bks. For Young Readers. (Simon & Schuster Bks. For Young Readers).

Kindl, Patrice. Goose Chase. 2010. (ENG.). 240p. (J). (gr. 5-7). pap. 7.99 *(978-0-547-33164-5(9)*, 1417430, Clarion Bks.) HarperCollins Pubs.

King of the Mountain. Date not set. 5.95 *(978-0-89868-357-8(2))*; lib. bdg. 10.95 *(978-0-89868-356-1(4))* ARO Publishing Co.

King Robert the First. 2004. per. 26.00 *(978-0-8059-9391-2(6))* Dorrance Publishing Co., Inc.

The King's Ring: KinderReaders Individual Title Six-Packs. (Kinderstarters Ser.). 8p. (gr. -1-1). 21.00 *(978-0-7635-8656-0(0))* Rigby Education.

Kingsley, Kaza. The Secret of Ashona. Ng, James, illus. 2012. (Erec Rex Ser.: 5). (ENG.). 528p. (J). (gr. 5-9). 16.99 *(978-1-4169-7992-0(1)*, Simon & Schuster Bks. For Young Readers) Simon & Schuster Bks. For Young Readers.

Klimo, Kate. Dog Diaries #12: Susan. Jessell, Tim, illus. 2018. (Dog Diaries: 12). 160p. (J). (gr. 2-5). pap. 7.99 *(978-1-5247-1964-7(1)*, Random Hse. Bks. for Young Readers) Random Hse. Children's Bks.

—Susan. 2018. (Dog Diaries: 12). lib. bdg. 18.40 *(978-0-606-40925-4(4))* Turtleback.

Korczak, Janusz. King Matt the First. Lourie, Richard, tr. 2004. (ENG.). 344p. (J). pap. 23.99 *(978-1-56512-442-4(1)*, 72442) Algonquin Bks. of Chapel Hill.

Kraljic, Helena & Skerl, Peter. Cleopatra. 2017. (SPA.). 32p. (J). (gr. 1-4). 16.95 *(978-84-9145-008-5(4))* Ediciones Obelisco ESP. Dist: Spanish Pubs., LLC.

Kulkarni, Suresh. The Wise King & Other Stories. 2011. 44p. pap. 21.99 *(978-1-4535-0463-5(X))* Xlibris Corp.

Kwarta, Darlene. Walking with King Tut. 2008. 48p. pap. 9.95 *(978-1-60693-040-3(0)*, Eloquent Bks.) Strategic Book Publishing & Rights Agency (SBPRA).

LaFevers, Robin. Courting Darkness. 2019. (Courting Darkness Duology Ser.). (ENG., Illus.). 512p. (YA). (gr. 9). 17.99 *(978-0-544-99119-4(2)*, 1666582, Clarion Bks.) HarperCollins Pubs.

Laky, Esther. Just Fairy Tales. 2010. 95p. pap. 11.80 *(978-0-557-01926-7(5))* Lulu Pr., Inc.

Lamplighter Staff. True Princess. 2004. pap. 14.00 *(978-1-58474-051-3(5))* Cornerstone Family Ministries/Lamplighter Publishing.

The Land of the Blue Flower. 2006. 76p. pap. 7.45 *(978-1-59462-377-6(5)*, 413, Bk. Jungle) Standard Publications, Inc.

Lang, Andrew. The Queen & the Mouse: A Story about Friendship. Lohmann, Renate, illus. 2006. (J). *(978-1-59939-081-9(7)*, Reader's Digest Young Families, Inc.) Studio Fun International.

Larson, Sara B. Bright Burns the Night. 2018. (ENG., Illus.). 320p. (YA). (gr. 7-7). 17.99 *(978-1-338-06878-8(4)*, Scholastic Pr.) Scholastic, Inc.

Lasky, Kathryn. The Golden Tree. 2007. (Guardians of Ga'Hoole Ser.: 12). (Illus.). 192p. lib. bdg. 17.20 *(978-1-4177-8260-4(9))* Turtleback.

Lawson, Barbara. Huff the Magicless Dragon, 1 vol. Swope, Brenda, illus. 2009. 35p. pap. 24.95 *(978-1-61546-419-7(0))* PublishAmerica, Inc.

Lee, Honest & Gilbert, Matthew J. The Rude & Ridiculous Royals of Classroom 13. 2018. (Classroom 13 Ser.: 6). (ENG., Illus.). 128p. (J). (gr. 1-5). pap. 5.99 *(978-0-316-43786-8(7))* Little, Brown Bks. for Young Readers.

Legrand, Claire. Kingsbane: The Empirium Trilogy Book 2. (Empirium Trilogy Ser.: 2). (YA). (gr. 8-12). 2020. 624p. pap. 12.99 *(978-1-7282-0696-7(0))* 2019. (ENG., Illus.). 608p. 18.99 *(978-1-4926-5665-4(8))* Sourcebooks, Inc.

Lendler, Ian. An Undone Fairy Tale. Martin, Whitney, illus. 2005. (ENG.). 32p. (J). (gr. 1-5). 19.99 *(978-0-689-86677-7(1)*, Simon & Schuster Bks. For Young Readers) Simon & Schuster Bks. For Young Readers.

Leonard, M. G. Revenge of the Beetle Queen (Beetle Trilogy, Book 2) 2018. (Beetle Boy Ser.). (ENG.). 304p. (J). (gr. 3-7). 16.99 *(978-0-545-85348-4(6)*, Chicken Hse., The) Scholastic, Inc.

Lesler, Rebecca. The Magic Stone: Return of Two Kings. 2008. 73p. pap. 19.95 *(978-1-60610-101-8(3))* America Star Bks.

Levine, Gail Carson. A Tale of Two Castles. Call, Greg, illus. (ENG.). (J). (gr. 3-7). 2012. 352p. pap. 7.99 *(978-0-06-122967-1(9))* 2011. 336p. 16.99 *(978-0-06-122965-7(2))* HarperCollins Pubs. (HarperCollins).

Lewis, Jill. Don't Read This Book! Allwright, Deborah, illus. 2010. (ENG.). 32p. (J). (gr. -1-2). 15.95 *(978-1-58925-094-9(X))* Tiger Tales.

Liddiment, Carol, illus. The Wooden Sword: A Jewish Folktale from Afghanistan. 2012. (ENG.). 32p. (J). (gr. -1-3). 16.99 *(978-0-8075-9201-4(3)*, 807592013) Whitman, Albert & Co.

Lindgren, Astrid. Mio, My Son. Wikland, Ilon, illus. 2003.Tr. of Mio, Min Mio. 179p. (J). 17.95 *(978-1-930900-23-3(6))* Purple Hse. Pr.

Liv‡n, Paco. THE THING THAT HURTS MOST IN THE WORLD. 2007. (ENG., Illus.). 36p. (J). 17.95 *(978-84-96788-89-3(X))* OQO, Editora ESP. Dist: Baker & Taylor Bks.

Lou, Cindy, illus. & text. The King of Ing Wants to Sing. Lou, Cindy, text. 2008. (J). 12.00 *(978-1-935332-00-8(7))* Kite Tales Publishing.

Low, Vicki. First Emperor. Mayhew, Sara E., illus. 2007. 48p. (J). lib. bdg. 23.08 *(978-1-4242-1626-0(5))* Fitzgerald Bks.

Luberto, Bradley. Clide & Druce: A Repulsive Tale of Trolls & Tax Money. 2006. (ENG.). 48p. per. 16.95 *(978-1-4241-5012-0(4))* PublishAmerica, Inc.

Lucado, Max. The Song of the King (Redesign) Gillies, Chuck, illus. 2014. (ENG.). 32p. (J). 17.99 *(978-1-4335-4290-9(0))* Crossway.

Lucier, Makiia. Isle of Blood & Stone. (Tower of Winds Ser.). (ENG.). (YA). (gr. 7). 2019. 416p. pap. 9.99 *(978-1-328-60429-3(2)*, 1731502) 2018. 400p. 17.99 *(978-0-544-96857-8(3)*, 1662274) HarperCollins Pubs. (Clarion Bks.).

Lucio, Mick. Kings for a Day: A Western. 2012. 24p. 24.95 *(978-1-4626-5422-2(3))* America Star Bks.

Lynes, William. Pirates, Scoundrels, & Kings. 2013. 450p. (gr. 10-12). 33.95 *(978-1-4759-6562-9(1))*; pap. 23.95 *(978-1-4759-6561-2(3))* iUniverse, Inc.

Ma, Wenhai, illus. Tang Monk Disciples Monkey King. 2005. (Adventures of Monkey King Ser.: No. 3). 32p. (J). 16.95 *(978-1-57227-084-8(5))* Pan Asia Pubns. (USA), Inc.

—Tang Monk Disciples Monkey King: English/Chinese. 2005. (Adventures of Monkey King Ser.: No. 3). (ENG & CHI.). 32p. (J). 16.95 *(978-1-57227-086-2(1))* Pan Asia Pubns. (USA), Inc.

Maas, Sarah J. Crown of Midnight. 2014. (Throne of Glass Ser.: 2). (YA). lib. bdg. 22.10 *(978-0-606-36441-6(2))* Turtleback.

—Empire of Storms. 2017. (Throne of Glass Ser.: 5). (YA). lib. bdg. 22.10 *(978-0-606-40598-0(4))* Turtleback.

MacDonald, George. Light Princess. l.t. ed. 2006. pap. *(978-1-84702-350-6(9))* Echo Library.

—The Light Princess & Other Fairy Stories. 2007. 102p. pap. 18.99 *(978-1-4346-1408-7(5))* Creative Media Partners, LLC.

MacHado, Ana Maria. Un Buen Coro. (Torre de Papel Ser.). (SPA., Illus.). (J). 7.95 *(978-958-04-4525-8(7)*, NR30643) Norma S.A. COL. Dist: Lectorum Pubns., Inc., Distribuidora Norma, Inc.

—Del Otro Lado Hay Secretos. (SPA.). pap. 11.95 *(978-950-07-2221-6(6))* Editorial Sudamericana S.A. ARG. Dist: Distribooks, Inc.

Maddern, Eric. The King with Horse's Ears. Hess, Paul, illus. 2003. (ENG.). 36p. (J). *(978-0-7112-1957-1(5))* ReiseArt Buchhandlung GmbH.

The Magic King. 2003. (J). *(978-1-4120-3345-9(4))* Black Dot Pubns.

Magness, Vicki. Victor the Victorious: And the Tale of Two Cities. 2012. 40p. pap. 21.99 *(978-1-4797-1955-6(2))* Xlibris Corp.

Major, Roberta Olsen. The Ice Cream Crone. 2007. (Royal Pains Ser.: 5). (YA). pap. 11.95 *(978-1-59705-801-8(7))* Wings ePress, Inc.

—The 24-Karat King. 2008. (Royal Pains Ser.: 7). (ENG.). (YA). pap. 11.95 *(978-1-59705-671-7(5))* Wings ePress, Inc.

Marchetta, Melina. Quintana of Charyn: The Lumatere Chronicles. (Lumatere Chronicles Ser.: 3). (ENG.). 528p. (YA). (gr. 9). 2014. pap. 10.99 *(978-0-7636-6930-0(X))* 2013. 18.99 *(978-0-7636-5835-9(9))* Candlewick Pr.

Marciano, Johnny & Chenoweth, Emily. Klawde: Evil Alien Warlord Cat #1. Mommaerts, Robb, illus. 2019. (Klawde: Evil Alien Warlord Cat Ser.: 1). 224p. (J). (gr. 3-7). 14.99 *(978-1-5247-8720-2(5)*, Penguin Workshop) Penguin Young Readers Group.

Marr, Melissa. Fragile Eternity, 3. 2010. (Wicked Lovely Ser.: 3). (ENG.). 448p. (YA). (gr. 8-12). pap. 8.99 *(978-0-06-121473-8(6)*, HarperCollins) HarperCollins Pubs.

—Fragile Eternity, 9 vols. 2009. (Wicked Lovely Ser.: 3). (YA). 265.75 *(978-1-4407-3037-5(7))*; 112.75 *(978-1-4407-3036-8(9))*; 1.25 *(978-1-4407-3044-3(X))*; 110.75 *(978-1-4407-3038-2(5))*; 132.75 *(978-1-4407-3040-5(7))*; 130.75 *(978-1-4407-3042-9(3))* Recorded Bks., Inc.

—Ink Exchange. (Wicked Lovely Ser.: 2). (ENG.). (YA). (gr. 8). 2009. 352p. pap. 10.99 *(978-0-06-121470-7(1))* 2008. 336p. 17.99 *(978-0-06-121468-4(X))* HarperCollins Pubs. (HarperCollins).

—Wicked Lovely, 1. 2008. (Wicked Lovely Ser.: 1). (ENG.). 352p. (YA). (gr. 8-12). pap. 9.99 *(978-0-06-121467-7(1)*, HarperCollins) HarperCollins Pubs.

Märtha Louise, Princess. Why Kings & Queens Don't Wear Crowns (with CD) Sevig-Fajardo, Mari Elise, tr. from NOR. Nyhus, Svein, illus. 2006. Orig. Title: Fvorfor de kongelige ikke har krone på Hodet. 32p. (J). 19.95 incl. audio compact disk (978-1-57534-038-8(0), CSC 100C) Skandisk, Inc.

Martin, J. P. Uncle. Blake, Quentin, illus. 2017. (Uncle Ser.). (ENG.). 176p. (J). (gr. 4-7). pap. 9.99 (978-1-68137-185-6(5), NYRB Kids) New York Review of Bks., Inc., The.

—Uncle Cleans Up. Blake, Quentin, illus. 2008. (Uncle Ser.). (ENG.). 184p. (J). (gr. 4-7). 17.95 (978-1-59017-276-6(0), NYR Children's Collection) New York Review of Bks., Inc., The.

Martin, Rafe. The Shark God. Shannon, David, illus. 2007. (Scholastic Bookshelf Ser.). (ENG.). 32p. (J). (gr. k-2). 18.69 (978-0-590-39570-0(X)) Scholastic, Inc.

Martin, Sara Hines. Shakin' up the Kingdom: Princess Lucinda Becomes the Queen. 2012. 66p. pap. 27.95 (978-1-4497-4922-4(4), WestBow Pr.) Author Solutions, LLC.

Martinez, Rene. The Journey of the Golden Sword. 2011. (ENG.). 64p. pap. 15.99 (978-1-4535-9187-1(7)) Xlibris Corp.

Masters, Elaine. The Royal Waker-Upper. Leung, Andrew, illus. 2003. (ENG.). 39p. (J). (978-0-89610-992-6(5)) Island Heritage Publishing.

Mastromonaco, Pina. King Bartholomew & the Jesters Riddle. Martin, David Lozell, illus. 2005. 32p. (J). (gr. -1-7). 15.95 (978-0-9744307-1-3(4)) Merry Lane Pr.

Matthew, Annie. Legacy & the Queen. 2019. (Legacy & the Queen Ser.: 1). 208p. (J). (gr. 4-12). 16.99 (978-1-949520-03-3(X)) Granity Studios.

Matthews, Rodney, illus. Tales of King Arthur. rev. ed. 2007. (Usborne Classics Retold Ser.). 139p. (J). (gr. 4-7). per. 4.99 (978-0-7945-1483-9(9), Usborne) EDC Publishing.

Mayo, Frank, illus. King Midas & the Golden Touch: A Tale about Greed. 2006. (J). 6.99 (978-1-59939-022-2(1)) Cornerstone Pr.

McCarthy, Cory & Capetta, A. R. Once & Future. (ENG.). (YA). (gr. 9-17). 2020. 384p. pap. 10.99 (978-0-316-44926-7(1)) 2019. 368p. 18.99 (978-0-316-44927-4(X)) Little Brown & Co. (Jimmy Patterson).

McCaughrean, Geraldine. Casting the Gods Adrift: A Tale of Ancient Egypt. Ludlow, Patricia D., illus. 2003. (ENG.). 112p. (J). (gr. 4-7). 15.95 (978-0-8126-2684-1(2)) Cricket Bks.

—Stories from Shakespeare. 2017. (ENG.). 176p. (J). (gr. 4-6). pap. 7.99 (978-1-5101-0145-6(4), Orion Children's Bks.) Hachette Children's Group GBR. Dist: Hachette Bk. Group.

McCloskey, Larry. Murder Fit for a King. 2007. (ENG.). 168p. (J). (gr. 6). pap. 11.99 (978-1-55002-669-6(0)) Dundurn Pr. CAN. Dist: Publishers Group West (PGW).

McCullough, L. E. We Three Kings: A Christmas Story. Maxwell, Cassandre, illus. 2006. 24p. (J). 7.95 (978-0-88271-010-5(9)) Regina Pr., Malhame & Co.

McGee, Katharine. American Royals II: Majesty. (American Royals Ser.: 2). (ENG.). (YA). (gr. 9). 2022. 400p. pap. 12.99 (978-1-9848-3024-1(4), Ember) 2020. 384p. 18.99 (978-1-9848-3021-0(X), Random Hse. Bks. for Young Readers) Random Hse. Children's Bks.

—American Royals III: Rivals. 2022. (American Royals Ser.: 3). (ENG.). 400p. (YA). (gr. 9). 19.99 (978-0-593-42970-9(2)); lib. bdg. 22.99 (978-0-593-42971-6(0)) Random Hse. Children's Bks. (Random Hse. Bks. for Young Readers).

McGriff, Shawna A. Princess Pink: Princess Pink Saves the Girls of Lahappyville. 2010. 44p. pap. 18.49 (978-1-4520-3936-7(4)) AuthorHouse.

McKibben, Marion A. Pearl the Rodeo Queen. 2006. 24p. (J). per. 12.00 (978-1-59971-711-1(5)) Aardvark Global Publishing.

McKillip, Patricia A. The Changeling Sea. 2003. (ENG., Illus.). 144p. (YA). (gr. 7-7). 5.99 (978-0-14-131262-0(9), Firebird) Penguin Young Readers Group.

McPhate, Paul J. The Puggle King. 2008. 52p. pap. 16.95 (978-1-60703-709-5(2)) America Star Bks.

McRoberts, Eddison. Sneaking Treats. Gadra, Jessica, illus. 2013. 48p. pap. 9.95 (978-1-62137-298-1(7)) Virtualbookworm.com Publishing, Inc.

Mead, Richelle. Vampire Academy. 2007. (Vampire Academy Ser.: 1). 336p. (YA). (gr. 7-18). 11.99 (978-1-59514-174-3(X), Razorbill) Penguin Young Readers Group.

Meadows, Daisy. Alicia the Snow Queen Fairy. 2017. (Illus.). 159p. (J). (978-1-5182-2779-0(1)) Scholastic, Inc.

Meconis, Dylan. Queen of the Sea. Meconis, Dylan, illus. (ENG., Illus.). 400p. (J). (gr. 5-9). 2020. pap. 14.99 (978-1-5362-1517-5(1)) 2019. 24.99 (978-1-5362-0498-8(6)) Candlewick Pr.

Menge, Dawn. Queen Vernita's Visitors. Switzer, Bobbi, illus. 2008. 36p. pap. 19.95 (978-1-59800-714-5(9)) Outskirts Pr., Inc.

Meredith, Susan Markowitz. The Royal Zookeeper. 2011. (Early Connections Ser.). (J). (978-1-61672-678-2(4)) Benchmark Education Co.

Meyer, Carolyn. Cleopatra Confesses. (ENG.). 304p. (YA). (gr. 7). 2012. pap. 12.99 (978-1-4169-8728-4(2)) 2011. 16.99 (978-1-4169-8727-7(4)) Simon & Schuster/Paula Wiseman Bks. (Simon & Schuster/Paula Wiseman Bks.).

—Doomed Queen Anne: A Young Royals Book. 2004. (Young Royals Ser.: 3). (ENG., Illus.). 240p. (YA). (gr. 7-12). pap. 11.99 (978-0-15-205086-3(8), 1063332, Clarion Bks.) HarperCollins Pubs.

—Patience, Princess Catherine: A Young Royals Book. 2009. (Young Royals Ser.: 4). (ENG., Illus.). 208p. (YA). (gr. 7-12). pap. 13.95 (978-0-15-205447-2(2), 1063331, Clarion Bks.) HarperCollins Pubs.

—Victoria Rebels. (ENG., Illus.). 272p. (YA). (gr. 7). 2014. pap. 9.99 (978-1-4169-8730-7(4)) 2013. 16.99 (978-1-4169-8729-1(0)) Simon & Schuster/Paula Wiseman Bks. (Simon & Schuster/Paula Wiseman Bks.).

—The Wild Queen: The Days & Nights of Mary, Queen of Scots. 2013. (Young Royals Ser.). (ENG.). 432p. (YA). (gr. 7). pap. 8.99 (978-0-544-02219-5(X), 1528477, Clarion Bks.) HarperCollins Pubs.

Meyer, Marissa. Cress. 2014. (YA). (Lunar Chronicles Ser.: 3). (ENG.). 560p. (gr. 7-12). 24.99 (978-0-312-64297-6(0), 900078310); 552p. (978-1-250-05632-0(2)) Feiwel & Friends.

—Fairest: Levana's Story. 2016. (Lunar Chronicles Ser.: 0). (YA). lib. bdg. 20.85 (978-0-606-38438-4(3)) Turtleback.

—Fairest: The Lunar Chronicles: Levana's Story. 2015. (YA). 222p. (978-1-250-06959-7(9)); (ENG.). 272p. (gr. 7-12). 19.99 (978-1-250-06055-6(9), 900141423) Feiwel & Friends.

—Winter. 2015. (Lunar Chronicles Ser.: 4). (ENG.). 832p. (YA). (gr. 7-12). 28.99 (978-0-312-64298-3(9), 900078311) Feiwel & Friends.

—Winter. 2018. (Lunar Chronicles Ser.: 4). (YA). lib. bdg. 24.50 (978-0-606-40586-7(0)) Turtleback.

Michaelides, M. Rainbow Angel. 2012. 120p. (gr. 4-6). 20.95 (978-1-4759-6249-9(5)); pap. 10.95 (978-1-4759-6248-2(7)) iUniverse, Inc.

Miller, Linsey. Mask of Shadows. 2018. (Mask of Shadows Ser.: 1). lib. bdg. 22.10 (978-0-606-41234-6(4)) Turtleback.

—Ruin of Stars. 2019. (Mask of Shadows Ser.: 2). 416p. (YA). (gr. 8-12). pap. 12.99 (978-1-4926-7879-3(1)) Sourcebooks, Inc.

Miller, Sarah. The Lost Crown. (ENG., Illus.). 448p. (YA). (gr. 7). 2012. pap. 12.99 (978-1-4169-8341-5(4)) 2011. 17.99 (978-1-4169-8340-8(6)) Simon & Schuster Children's Publishing. (Atheneum Bks. for Young Readers).

Miller, Victoria, illus. Dora & the Unicorn King. 2011. (Dora the Explorer Ser.). (ENG.). 24p. (J). pap. 3.99 (978-1-4424-1312-2(3), Simon Spotlight/Nickelodeon) Simon Spotlight/Nickelodeon.

Millman, Selena. The Prince & Me. 2006. 146p. (YA). per. 11.20 (978-1-4243-2353-1(3)) Independent Publisher Services.

Mini Cuentos: Rey de los Sapos, Sapatillas Rojas.Tr. of Mini Fairy Tales: King & His Shoes. (SPA.). (J). (gr. k-4). 4.98 (978-970-607-619-9(0)) Larousse, Ediciones, S. A. de C. V. MEX. Dist: Continental Bk. Co., Inc.

Miyares, Daniel. Bring Me a Rock! Miyares, Daniel, illus. 2016. (ENG., Illus.). 40p. (J). (gr. -1-3). 18.99 (978-1-4814-4602-0(9), Simon & Schuster Bks. For Young Readers) Simon & Schuster Bks. For Young Readers.

Moore, Inga. Captain Cat. Moore, Inga, illus. 2013. (ENG., Illus.). 48p. (J). (gr. -1-2). 15.99 (978-0-7636-6151-9(1)) Candlewick Pr.

Moore, Raina. A Charming Princess. 2005. (Charming Classics). 256p. (J). pap. 6.99 (978-0-06-059604-0(X), HarperFestival) HarperCollins Pubs.

Morgan-Cole, Trudy J. Esther: Courage to Stand. 2010. 144p. (J). pap. 12.99 (978-0-8280-2430-3(8)) Review & Herald Publishing Assn.

Mrozek, Elizabeth. The Fifth Chair. Mrozek, Elizabeth, illus. 2013. (Illus.). 38p. 19.95 (978-1-935766-80-3(5)) Windy City Pubs.

Muhammad, Shahid. The Adventures of the Math Doctor: Book One: King Jafiz & the Evil Farmer Nimra. 2007. (J). per. 7.95 (978-1-59872-778-4(8)) Instant Pub.

mulholland, robin. Bolivia & the sunshine King. 2008. (ENG.). 147p. pap. 14.98 (978-0-557-01401-9(8)) Lulu Pr., Inc.

Munson, Kyle Lloyd. The King They Call Dumm. 2008. 32p. per. 24.95 (978-1-60441-215-4(1)) America Star Bks.

Murdock, Catherine Gilbert. Princess Ben. 2009. (ENG.). 352p. (YA). (gr. 7). pap. 9.99 (978-0-547-22325-4(0), 1061789, Clarion Bks.) HarperCollins Pubs.

Muthu, Antony M. Athim. 2008. 48p. pap. 19.49 (978-1-4389-3074-9(7)) AuthorHouse.

Nadler, Ben. The White Snake: A TOON Graphic. 2019. (Illus.). (J). (gr. 3-7). 64p. 16.99 (978-1-943145-37-9(7)); 60p. pap. 11.99 (978-1-943145-38-6(5)) Astra Publishing Hse. (Toon Books).

Nance, Andrew Jordan. The Barefoot King: A Story about Feeling Frustrated. Holden, Olivia, illus. 2020. 32p. (J). (gr. -1-3). 16.95 (978-1-61180-748-6(4), Bala Kids) Shambhala Pubns., Inc.

Nelson, Brett Alan. The Magical Forest. Ueda, Kumiko, illus. 2020. (ENG.). 42p. (J). (gr. k-4). 19.95 (978-0-9655078-7-5(4)) Windsong Publishing Co.

Neuschwander, Cindy. Sir Cumference & All the King's Tens. Geehan, Wayne, illus. 2009. (Sir Cumference Ser.). 32p. (J). (gr. 3-7). 16.95 (978-1-57091-727-1(2)) Charlesbridge Publishing, Inc.

—Sir Cumference & the off-The-Charts Dessert. Geehan, Wayne, illus. 2013. (Sir Cumference Ser.). 32p. (J). (gr. 3-7). pap. 7.99 (978-1-57091-199-6(1)) Charlesbridge Publishing, Inc.

—Sir Cumference & the off-The-Charts Dessert. 2013. (Sir Cumference Ser.). lib. bdg. 18.40 (978-0-606-34743-3(7)) Turtleback.

Ngan, Natasha. Girls of Paper & Fire. (YA). 2019. (ENG.). 416p. (gr. 10-17). pap. 12.99 (978-0-316-56135-8(5)) 2018. 385p. (978-0-316-45220-5(3)) 2018. (ENG.). 400p. (gr. 10-17). 19.99 (978-0-316-56136-5(3)) 2018. 385p. (978-0-316-45352-3(8)) 2018. 385p. (978-0-316-53040-8(9)) Little Brown & Co. (Jimmy Patterson).

—Girls of Paper & Fire. 2019. (ENG.). 416p. lib. bdg. 21.80 (978-1-6636-2724-7(X)) Perfection Learning Corp.

Nielsen, Jennifer A. The Runaway King. 2014. (Ascendance Trilogy Ser.: 2). lib. bdg. 18.40 (978-0-606-35663-3(0)) Turtleback.

—The Runaway King (the Ascendance Series, Book 2), 1 vol. 2014. (Ascendance Ser.: 2). (ENG.). 352p. (YA). (gr. 3-7). pap. 8.99 (978-0-545-28416-5(3), Scholastic Paperbacks) Scholastic, Inc.

—The Shadow Throne (the Ascendance Series, Book 3) (Ascendance Ser.: 3). (ENG.). 336p. (gr. 3-7). 2015. (YA). pap. 8.99 (978-0-545-28418-9(X), Scholastic Paperbacks) 2014. (J). 18.99 (978-0-545-28417-2(1), Scholastic Pr.) Scholastic, Inc.

Nobisso, Josephine. El Peso de Una Misa: Un Relato de fe. Szegedi, Katalin, illus. 2003. Orig. Title: The Weight of a Mass a Tale of Faith. (SPA.). 32p. (J). (gr. k-2). pap. 9.95 (978-0-940112-17-9(5)) Gingerbread Hse.

—El Peso de Una Misa: Un Relato de Fe. Szegedi, Katalin, illus. 2003. Orig. Title: The Weight of a Mass a Tale of Faith. (SPA.). 32p. (J). (gr. k-2). 17.95 (978-0-940112-15-5(9)) Gingerbread Hse.

—Take It to the Queen. 2009. 32p. 17.95 (978-0-8146-3288-8(2), Liturgical Pr. Bks.) Liturgical Pr.

—Take It to the Queen: A Tale of Hope. Szegedi, Katalin, illus. 2008. (Theological Virtues Trilogy Ser.). 32p. (J). (gr. k-2). (ENG.). 17.95 (978-0-940112-19-3(1)); pap. 9.95 (978-0-940112-21-6(3)) Gingerbread Hse.

La Noche en Que Casi Vimos a los Reyes Magos. (SPA.). (J). (978-0-9710860-9-8(5)) Libros, Encouraging Cultural Literacy.

North, Laura. The Princess & the Frozen Peas. Dreidemy, Joelle, illus. 2014. (Tadpoles: Fairytale Twists Ser.). (ENG.). 32p. (J). (gr. 1-2). (978-0-7787-0446-1(7)); pap. (978-0-7787-0481-2(5)) Crabtree Publishing Co.

Nussbaum, Ben & Studio Mouse Editorial. Snow White: A New Beginning. 2008. (ENG., Illus.). 36p. (J). (gr. -1). 7.99 (978-1-59069-437-4(6)) Studio Mouse LLC.

O'Callaghan, G. Slave Prince. 2007. 172p. per. (978-1-84693-031-7(6)) Best Global Publishing Ltd.

Ofori-Mankata. Dede Akai. 2012. 48p. pap. 21.88 (978-1-4669-1569-5(2)) Trafford Publishing.

Oh, Ellen. Warrior. 2015. (Prophecy Ser.: 2). (ENG.). 352p. (YA). (gr. 8). pap. 9.99 (978-0-06-209113-0(1), HarperTeen) HarperCollins Pubs.

Old King Cole: 6 Small Books. (gr. k-2). 23.00 (978-0-7635-8493-1(2)) Rigby Education.

Olsen, Kent L. Tales of Kalindia. 2004. 356p. (YA). 30.95 (978-0-595-65998-2(5)); pap. 20.95 (978-0-595-29426-8(X)) iUniverse, Inc.

Oppel, Kenneth. The King's Taster. Fancher, Lou & Johnson, Steve, illus. 2009. (ENG.). 32p. (J). (gr. -1-1). 17.99 (978-0-06-075372-6(2), HarperCollins) HarperCollins Pubs.

Ortiz, Zirzeria. The Queen in Me & My Bumblebee. 2008. 48p. pap. 24.95 (978-1-60441-045-7(0)) America Star Bks.

Osterbach, Batya Kirshenbaum. Pini the Pitcher: A Story for Hanukkah. Eisby, Lizzy, illus. 2005. 32p. (J). (gr. 1-4). 16.95 (978-1-932687-50-7(5), Devora Publishing) Simcha Media Group.

Otis, James. Calvert of Maryland: A Story of Lord Baltimore's Colony. 2007. 140p. per. 9.95 (978-0-9790876-6-0(X)) Living Bks. Pr.

Ovani, Germano, illus. The Monkey King. 2007. (Young Reading Series 1 Gift Bks). 47p. (J). (gr. -1-3). 8.99 (978-0-7945-1593-5(2), Usborne) EDC Publishing.

Owen, Margaret. The Merciful Crow. 2019. (Merciful Crow Ser.: 1). (ENG., Illus.). 384p. (YA). 18.99 (978-1-250-19192-2(0), 900192893, Holt, Henry & Co. Bks. For Young Readers) Holt, Henry & Co.

—The Merciful Crow. 2020. (Merciful Crow Ser.: 1). (ENG.). 400p. (YA). pap. 10.99 (978-1-250-25094-0(3), 900192894) Square Fish.

Packard, Mary. I Am King! Gore, Leonid, illus. 2003. (My First Reader Ser.). (ENG.). 32p. (J). 18.50 (978-0-516-22927-0(3), Children's Pr.) Scholastic Library Publishing.

Paige, Danielle. Stealing Snow. (Stealing Snow Ser.). (ENG.). 384p. (YA). 2018. pap. 10.99 (978-1-68119-546-9(1), 900177244, Bloomsbury Young Adult) 2016. (gr. 9-12). 18.99 (978-1-68119-076-1(1), 900158388, Bloomsbury USA Childrens) Bloomsbury Publishing USA.

—Stealing Snow (Spanish Edition) Angulo Fernández, María, tr. 2017. (SPA.). 386p. (J). (gr. 9). 18.95 (978-84-16700-68-4(0)) Penguin Random House Grupo Editorial ESP. Dist: Penguin Random Hse. LLC.

—Yellow Brick War. 2016. (Dorothy Must Die Ser.: 3). (ENG.). 288p. (YA). (gr. 9-12). 18.99 (978-0-06-228073-2(2), HarperCollins) HarperCollins Pubs.

Parragon Staff. Lion King. 2010. (Disney Diecut Classics). (Illus.). 72p. (J). (gr. -1-1). (978-1-4075-8936-7(9)) Parragon, Inc.

Paulsen, Gary & Roberts, Esyllt Nest. Plygu Amser. 2005. (WEL.). 80p. pap. (978-0-86381-683-3(5)) Gwasg Carreg Gwalch.

Pearl, Alexa. Tales of Sasha 7: the Royal Island. Sordo, Paco, illus. 2018. (Tales of Sasha Ser.: 7). (ENG.). 112p. (J). (gr. k-3). 16.99 (978-1-4998-0603-8(5)); pap. 5.99 (978-1-4998-0602-1(7)) Little Bee Books Inc.

Percival, J. M., ed. Romanian Fairy Tales. 2008. 160p. 25.95 (978-1-60664-929-9(9)); pap. 14.95 (978-1-60664-049-4(6)) Aegypan.

Peterson, Mark. The Tater Tot King. 2011. 16p. 12.68 (978-1-4269-5395-8(X)) Trafford Publishing.

Philpot, Graham, illus. The Emperor & the Nightingale. 2007. (First Reading Level 4 Ser.). 48p. (J). (gr. -1-3). 8.99 (978-0-7945-1614-7(9), Usborne) EDC Publishing.

Pierce, Tamora. Mastiff: The Legend of Beka Cooper #3. 2012. (Beka Cooper Ser.: 3). (ENG.). 608p. (YA). (gr. 7-11). pap. 11.99 (978-0-375-83818-7(X), Ember) Random Hse. Children's Bks.

—Trickster's Queen. 2005. (Daughter of the Lioness Ser.: Bk. 2). (Illus.). 467p. (gr. 7-12). 20.00 (978-0-7569-5482-6(7)) Perfection Learning Corp.

Pilegard, Virginia Walton. The Warlord's Messengers, 1 vol. Debon, Nicolas, illus. 2005. (Warlord's Ser.). (ENG.). 32p. (J). (gr. k-3). 16.99 (978-1-58980-271-1(3), Pelican Publishing) Arcadia Publishing.

Pittar, Gill. Milly, Molly & What Was That? (book W/dolls) 2006. 28p. pap. (978-1-86972-105-3(5)) Milly Molly Bks.

Plumides, Damon. The Adventures of Caterwaul the Cat: Feline Pie. 2011. (ENG., Illus.). 226p. (J). (gr. 4-7). pap. 17.95 (978-1-937084-19-6(1)) Boutique of Quality Books Publishing Co., Inc.

Pounder, Sibéal. Bad Mermaids Make Waves. Cockcroft, Jason, illus. 2018. (Bad Mermaids Ser.). (ENG.). 256p. (J). 13.99 (978-1-68119-792-0(8), 900187211, Bloomsbury Children's Bks.) Bloomsbury Publishing USA.

Princess Protection Program Staff. The Palace of Mystery, No. 4. 2010. (Princess Protection Program Ser.). 144p. pap. 4.99 (978-1-4231-2727-7(7)) Disney Pr.

Pugliano-Martin, Carol. The Very Mean King: Set Of 6. 2010. (Early Connections Ser.). (J). pap. 37.00 net. (978-1-4108-1365-7(7)) Benchmark Education Co.

—The Very Mean King & el rey Malo: 6 English, 6 Spanish Adaptations. 2011. (ENG & SPA.). (J). 75.00 net. (978-1-4108-5648-7(8)) Benchmark Education Co.

The Quest for Seven Castles. 2006. (J). per. 7.99 (978-0-9785523-1-2(8)) Cross & Crown Publishing.

Quinn, Jordan. Let the Games Begin! McPhillips, Robert, illus. 2015. (Kingdom of Wrenly Ser.: 7). (ENG.). 128p. (J). (gr. k-4). pap. 6.99 (978-1-4814-2379-3(7), Little Simon) Little Simon.

—The Lost Stone. McPhillips, Robert, illus. 2014. (Kingdom of Wrenly Ser.: 1). (ENG.). 128p. (J). (gr. k-4). pap. 6.99 (978-1-4424-9690-3(8), Little Simon) Little Simon.

—The Lost Stone. 2014. (Kingdom of Wrenly Ser.: 1). lib. bdg. 16.00 (978-0-606-35443-1(3)) Turtleback.

—The Scarlet Dragon. McPhillips, Robert, illus. 2014. (Kingdom of Wrenly Ser.: 2). (ENG.). 128p. (J). (gr. k-4). pap. 6.99 (978-1-4424-9693-4(2), Little Simon) Little Simon.

—The Scarlet Dragon. 2014. (Kingdom of Wrenly Ser.: 2). lib. bdg. 16.00 (978-0-606-35444-8(1)) Turtleback.

—Sea Monster! McPhillips, Robert, illus. 2014. (Kingdom of Wrenly Ser.: 3). (ENG.). 128p. (J). (gr. k-4). pap. 6.99 (978-1-4814-0072-5(X), Little Simon) Little Simon.

—The Secret World of Mermaids. McPhillips, Robert, illus. 2015. (Kingdom of Wrenly Ser.: 8). (ENG.). 128p. (J). (gr. k-4). pap. 6.99 (978-1-4814-3122-4(6), Little Simon) Little Simon.

Ramirez, Gamaliel, illus. The Night We Almost Saw the Three Kings. 32p. (J). (gr. 1-18). 16.00 (978-0-9710860-8-1(7)) Libros, Encouraging Cultural Literacy.

Redwine, C. J. The Shadow Queen. 2016. (Ravenspire Ser.: 1). (ENG.). (YA). (gr. 8). 416p. pap. 10.99 (978-0-06-236025-0(6)); (Illus.). 400p. 17.99 (978-0-06-236024-3(8)) HarperCollins Pubs. (Balzer & Bray).

—The Shadow Queen. 2016. (Ravenspire Ser.: 1). (YA). lib. bdg. 20.85 (978-0-606-39615-8(2)) Turtleback.

Reese, Jacob. Copperweight. 2008. 231p. pap. 24.95 (978-1-60813-240-9(4)) America Star Bks.

Reuker, Heidi. Queen of the Rats. 2007. 56p. per. 16.95 (978-1-4137-9801-2(2)) America Star Bks.

Rey, H. A. Curious George What Do You See? (CGTV Board Book) 2009. (Curious George Ser.). (ENG., Illus.). 10p. (J). (gr. -1 — 1). bds. 6.99 (978-0-547-18263-6(5), 1056020, Clarion Bks.) HarperCollins Pubs.

Rice, Morgan. A Grant of Arms. 2013. 238p. pap. 14.99 (978-1-939416-61-2(2)) Morgan Rice Bks.

—A Land of Fire. 2014. 196p. 26.99 (978-1-939416-87-2(6)) Morgan Rice Bks.

—A Land of Fire (Book #12 in the Sorcerer's Ring) 2014. 196p. (YA). pap. 15.99 (978-1-939416-86-5(8), Morgan Rice) Morgan Rice Bks.

—Night of the Bold (Kings & Sorcerers — Book 6) 2016. (ENG., Illus.). 162p. (J). pap. 12.99 (978-1-63291-497-2(2), Morgan Rice) Morgan Rice Bks.

—A Reign of Steel (Book #11 in the Sorcerer's Ring) 2014. 216p. (YA). pap. 15.99 (978-1-939416-76-6(0), Morgan Rice) Morgan Rice Bks.

—A Rite of Swords. 2013. 266p. 25.99 (978-1-939416-58-2(2)); pap. 14.99 (978-1-939416-57-5(4)) Morgan Rice Bks.

—A Vow of Glory. 2013. (Sorcerer's Ring Ser.: Bk. 5). 274p. pap. 13.99 (978-1-939416-28-5(0)) Morgan Rice Bks.

Richey, Denise. The Handwriting on the Wall. 2012. 28p. pap. 19.99 (978-1-4772-6606-9(2)) AuthorHouse.

—The King's Bad Dream. 2009. 32p. pap. 12.99 (978-1-4490-1303-5(1)) AuthorHouse.

Riddle, Sharon Kay & Sanders, Nancy/Ida. The King's Silverware. Lowe, Frank Allen, illus. 2007. 32p. (J). pap. 15.00 (978-0-9761583-5-6(3)) Olive Leaf Pubns.

Rifkin, L. (Lauren). The Nine Lives of Romeo Crumb: Life Two. 2010. (ENG.). 277p. (J). pap. 8.95 (978-0-9743221-4-8(8)) Stratford Road Pr., Ltd.

Rigby Education Staff. Queen of Hearts. (gr. k-2). 21.00 (978-0-7635-2406-7(9)) Rigby Education.

Riley, Lehman C. Meeting Dr. Martin Luther King. 2004. (Adventures of Papa Lemon's Little Wanderers Ser.: Bk. 1). 35p. (978-0-9760523-0-2(X)) Matter of Africa America Time.

Rinaldi, Ann. Nine Days a Queen. 2006. (ENG.). 240p. (J). (gr. 8-12). pap. 8.99 (978-0-06-054925-1(4), HarperCollins) HarperCollins Pubs.

Rinehart, J. D. Crown of Three. (Crown of Three Ser.: 1). (ENG., (J). (gr. 4-8). 2016. Illus.). 432p. pap. 8.99 (978-1-4814-2444-8(0)) 2015. 416p. 17.99 (978-1-4814-2443-1(2)) Simon & Schuster Children's Publishing. (Aladdin).

—The Lost Realm. (Crown of Three Ser.: 2). (ENG., Illus.). (J). (gr. 4-8). 2017. 512p. pap. 9.99 (978-1-4814-2447-9(5)) 2016. 496p. 17.99 (978-1-4814-2446-2(7)) Simon & Schuster Children's Publishing. (Aladdin).

Risso, Eduardo. Mysteries of the Red Moon, Vol. 3. 2006. (SPA.). 48p. pap. 16.95 (978-1-59497-163-1(3)) Public Square Bks.

Risso, Eduardo & Trillo, Carlos. Los Misterios de la Luna Roja Vol. 2: El Ataque del Circo. 2006. (SPA., Illus.). 72p. (J). (gr. 1). per. 16.95 (978-1-59497-162-4(5)) Public Square Bks.

Roberts, Daniel. The Dragon, the Princess & the Peanut Butter Sandwiches. 2009. 36p. pap. 16.99 (978-1-4389-8277-9(1)) AuthorHouse.

Roehl, Tessa. Tiana's Best Surprise. 2018. (Disney Princess Beginnings Ser.). lib. bdg. 17.20 (978-0-606-40954-4(8)) Turtleback.

Ross, Joel. Beast & Crown. 2017. (ENG.). 384p. (J). (gr. 3-7). 16.99 (978-0-06-248459-8(1), HarperCollins) HarperCollins Pubs.

Ross, Rebecca. The Queen's Resistance. (ENG.). 2020. (Queen's Rising Ser.: 2). 496p. (YA). (gr. 9). pap. 11.99 (978-0-06-247139-0(2)) 2019. (Queen's Rising Ser.: 2). (Illus.). 480p. (YA). (gr. 9). 17.99 (978-0-06-247138-3(4))Book 2. 2018. (Illus.). 480p. (J). (978-0-00-824601-3(7)) HarperCollins Pubs. (HarperTeen).

Ross, Tony. I Want a Sister! Ross, Tony, illus. 2013. (ENG., Illus.). 32p. (J). (gr. -1-3). 16.95 (978-1-4677-2047-2(X)) Andersen Pr. GBR. Dist: Lerner Publishing Group.

—I Want My Dad! Ross, Tony, illus. 2018. (Little Princess Ser.). (ENG., Illus.). 32p. (J). (gr. -1-3). 17.99 (978-1-5415-1453-9(X), 6c777235-f7e2-4b44-b636-3cfe645539db) Lerner Publishing Group.

Rovetch, L. Bob & Whitman, Emily. Sir Henry, the Polite Knight. Barnard, Bryn, illus. 2006. (J). (978-1-58987-204-2(5)) Kindermusik International.

Rowe, W. W. The Wizard's Wayward Wand. 2010. (ENG.). 99p. (J). (gr. 3-7). pap. 12.95 (978-0-9843754-0-0(6)) Sanctuary Publishing, Inc.

Rowley, Melissa. The Falcon Shield. 2009. (J). 6.99 (978-1-60641-103-2(9)) Deseret Bk. Co.

Rowley, M'lin. The Silver Coat. 2009. (Knights of Right Ser.: Bk. 2). 71p. (J). (gr. 1-5). pap. 6.99 (978-1-60641-104-9(7), Shadow Mountain) Shadow Mountain Publishing.

Rowling, J. K. The Ickabog, 1 vol. 2020. (ENG.). 304p. (J). (gr. 3-3). 26.99 *(978-1-338-73287-0(0))* Scholastic, Inc.

Roy, Jennifer. Cordially Uninvited. 2012. (ENG., Illus.). 256p. (J). (gr. 3-7). 15.99 *(978-1-4424-3920-7(3))* Simon & Schuster, Inc.

A Royal Tea. 2014. (Mermaid Tales Ser.: 9). (ENG., Illus.). 112p. (J). (gr. 1-4). pap. 6.99 *(978-1-4814-0254-5(4),* Aladdin) Simon & Schuster Children's Publishing.

Royde-Smith, N. G. Una and the Red Cross Knight & Other T. 2006. (Illus.). pap. 28.95 *(978-1-4254-8407-1(7))* Kessinger Publishing, LLC.

Rudden, Dave. The Endless King. 2018. (J). *(978-0-553-52305-8(8))* Random Hse., Inc.

Rutkoski, Marie. The Jewel of the Kalderash: The Kronos Chronicles: Book III. 2013. (Kronos Chronicles Ser.: 3). (ENG.). 336p. (J). (gr. 5-9). pap. 18.99 *(978-1-250-01025-4(X),* 900084763) Square Fish.

Ryan, Brittney. The Legend of Holly Claus. Long, Laurel, illus. 2004. (Julie Andrews Collection). 544p. (J). (gr. 4-18). 16.99 *(978-0-06-058511-2(0))*; lib. bdg. 17.89 *(978-0-06-058514-3(5))* HarperCollins Pubs. (Julie Andrews Collection).

Sadi. The Careless King & Other Stories. 2005. (Illus.). 64p. (J). *(978-969-542-068-3(0))* Children Pubns.

Salimena, Kathleen Elizabeth. The Royal Yacht. 2008. (Illus.). 24p. (J). (gr. 11-18). 15.95 *(978-0-9798624-0-3(X))* Royal Imprint Pr., Inc.

Salisbury, Melinda. The Sin Eater's Daughter (Unabridged Edition), 1 vol. unabr. ed. 2015. (ENG.). 2p. (J). (gr. 9). audio compact disk 39.99 *(978-0-545-83830-6(4))* Scholastic, Inc.

Sanders, Roy E. Land of Pink. Patzelt, Kasie, illus. 2007. (Not So Far Ago Ser.). 37p. (J). (gr. -1-3). 19.99 *(978-1-59879-327-7(6))* Lifevest Publishing, Inc.

Sanderson, Jeanette. Robin Hood Shoots for the Queen: A Legend from England. 2006. (J). pap. *(978-1-4108-7167-1(3))* Benchmark Education Co.

Santillo, LuAnn. Dip & Sip. Santillo, LuAnn, ed. 2003. (Half-Pint Kids Readers Ser.). (Illus.). 7p. (J). (gr. -1-1). pap. 1.00 *(978-1-59256-051-6(2))* Half-Pint Kids, Inc.

—The King. Santillo, LuAnn, ed. 2003. (Half-Pint Kids Readers Ser.). (Illus.). 7p. (J). (gr. -1-1). pap. 1.00 *(978-1-59256-050-9(4))* Half-Pint Kids, Inc.

Santore, Charles, illus. William the Curious. Knight of the Water Lilies. 2012. (J). *(978-1-60464-034-2(0))* Appleseed Pr. Bk. Pub. LLC.

Sargent, Dave & Sargent, Pat. Whiskers: (Roan) Pride & Peace, 30 vols., Vol. 59. Lenoir, Jane, illus. 2003. (Saddle up Ser.: Vol. 59). 42p. (J). pap. 10.95 *(978-1-56763-806-6(6))* Ozark Publishing.

Saunders, Kate. The Little Secret. Carman, William, illus. 2012. (ENG.). 240p. (J). (gr. 3-6). pap. 11.99 *(978-0-312-67427-4(9),* 900072842) Square Fish.

Scam, Busta. The Kingdom of Nome. 2006. (Illus.). 44p. pap. 12.95 *(978-1-59663-516-6(9),* Castle Keep Pr.) Rock, James A. & Co. Pubs.

Schlitt, Jayme & Schlitt, Ron. Rags, Riches & the Robe. 2010. 32p. 17.25 *(978-1-4269-4666-0(X))* Trafford Publishing.

Schmidt, Andy. This Is Black Panther. 2018. (Marvel World of Reading Level 1 Ser.). (J). lib. bdg. 14.75 *(978-0-606-40716-8(2))* Turtleback.

Scholte, Astrid. Four Dead Queens. (ENG.). (YA). (gr. 7). 2020. 464p. pap. 12.99 *(978-0-525-51394-0(9),* Penguin Books) 2019. 432p. 17.99 *(978-0-525-51392-6(2),* G.P. Putnam's Sons Books for Young Readers) Penguin Young Readers Group.

Scieszka, Jon. Los Caballeros de la Mesa de la Cocina. Smith, Lane, illus. (SPA.). (J). (gr. 5-8). 7.95 *(978-958-04-3400-9(X),* NR4516) Norma S.A. COL. Dist: Lectorum Pubns., Inc., Distribuidora Norma, Inc.

Scotton, Rob. Splat the Cat: on with the Show. Scotton, Rob, illus. 2013. (Splat the Cat Ser.). (ENG., Illus.). 24p. (J). (gr. -1-3). pap. 3.99 *(978-0-06-209010-2(0),* HarperFestival) HarperCollins Pubs.

Sebastian, Laura. Ash Princess. 2018. (Illus.). 437p. (YA). *(978-0-525-57826-0(9),* Delacorte Pr) Random House Publishing Group.

—Ash Princess. (Ash Princess Ser.: 1). (ENG.). (YA). (gr. 7). 2019. 464p. pap. 11.99 *(978-1-5247-6709-9(3),* Ember) 2018. (Illus.). 448p. 18.99 *(978-1-5247-6706-8(9),* Delacorte Pr.) 2018. (Illus.). 448p. lib. bdg. 21.99 *(978-1-5247-6707-5(7),* Delacorte Pr.) Random Hse. Children's Bks.

—Ember Queen. 2020. (Ash Princess Ser.: 3). (ENG., Illus.). 480p. (YA). (gr. 7). 18.99 *(978-1-5247-6714-3(X))*; lib. bdg. 21.99 *(978-1-5247-6715-0(8))* Random Hse. Children's Bks. (Delacorte Pr.).

—Lady Smoke. 2020. (Ash Princess Ser.: 2). (ENG.). 528p. (YA). (gr. 7). pap. 11.99 *(978-1-5247-6713-6(1),* Ember) Random Hse. Children's Bks.

Seiss, Ellie & Random House Staff. Dora & the Unicorn King. 2013. (Dora the Explorer Step into Reading Ser.). (Illus.). 24p. lib. bdg. 13.55 *(978-0-606-32415-1(1))* Turtleback.

Sewell, Helen & Coatsworth, Elizabeth. The White Horse. 2005. (ENG., Illus.). 169p. (J). (gr. 3-4). per. 11.95 *(978-1-883937-86-7(8))* Ignatius Pr.

Shahegh, Mahvash. The Green Musician. Ewart, Claire, illus. 2015. 36p. (J). (gr. k-3). 16.95 *(978-1-937786-42-7(0),* Wisdom Tales) World Wisdom, Inc.

Shakespeare, William. Macbeth, 1 vol. Ferran, Daniel, illus. 2011. (Shakespeare Graphics Ser.). (ENG.). 88p. (J). (gr. 5-9). pap. 7.15 *(978-1-4342-3447-6(9),* 116468); lib. bdg. 28.65 *(978-1-4342-2506-1(2),* 113327) Capstone. (Stone Arch Bks.).

—Macbeth: The Graphic Novel, 1 vol. 2010. (Classic Graphic Novel Collection). (ENG., Illus.). 144p. (J). (gr. 7-10). 41.03 *(978-1-4205-0373-9(1),* 8beacdff-6ff3-4c8d-8b26-7888a357344f, Lucent Pr.) Greenhaven Publishing LLC.

—Manga Shakespeare: Hamlet. Vieceli, Emma, illus. 2007. (ENG.). 204p. (J). (gr. 2-8). pap. 14.99 *(978-0-8109-9324-2(4))* Abrams, Inc.

Sharp, Laura. The Key Prince. 2012. 24p. pap. 24.95 *(978-1-4626-8959-0(0))* America Star Bks.

Sharplin, Emory. Scrap. 2013. 352p. (J). pap. 14.95 *(978-1-938416-35-4(X))* River Grove Bks.

Sheldon, Dyan. The Moon Dragons. Blythe, Gary, illus. 2015. (ENG.). 32p. (J). (gr. -1-3). 16.95 *(978-1-4677-6314-1(4),* f7d8fcba-4623-4aea-9eac-d9ec51f6cc1c); E-Book 27.99 *(978-1-4677-6318-9(7))* Lerner Publishing Group.

Shulevitz, Uri. One Monday Morning. Shulevitz, Uri, illus. 2003. (ENG., Illus.). 48p. (J). (gr. -1-1). reprint ed. pap. 9.99 *(978-0-374-45648-1(8),* 900021257) Square Fish.

—One Monday Morning. 2003. (J). (gr. -1-2). lib. bdg. 18.40 *(978-0-613-71877-6(1))* Turtleback.

Shurtliff, Liesl. Grump: the (Fairly) True Tale of Snow White & the Seven Dwarves. 2019. (ENG.). 336p. (J). (gr. 3-7). 8.99 *(978-1-5247-1704-9(5),* Yearling) Random Hse. Children's Bks.

Siegel, Pete. Light Switch to Heaven. 2012. (ENG.). 46p. (J). pap. 22.95 *(978-1-4327-8818-6(3))*; pap. 15.95 *(978-1-4327-8817-9(5))* Outskirts Pr., Inc.

Signor Sr., S. Ernest. The Book of Esther. 2013. 28p. pap. 13.99 *(978-1-4525-7313-7(1))* Balboa Pr.

Simonson, Louise. Snow White & the Seven Robots: A Graphic Novel. Sanchez, Jimena S., illus. 2015. (Far Out Fairy Tales Ser.). (ENG.). 40p. (J). (gr. 3-6). lib. bdg. 25.32 *(978-1-4342-9648-1(2),* 126939, Stone Arch Bks.) Capstone.

Sims, Lesley. Snow Queen. 2005. 24p. (J). 9.95 *(978-0-7945-1160-9(0),* Usborne) EDC Publishing.

Skidmore, Lauren. What Is Lost. 2015. 217p. (YA). pap. 16.99 *(978-1-4621-1621-8(3))* Cedar Fort, Inc./CFI Distribution.

Sklyar, Igor. King & the Star. 2005. (Illus.). 50p. pap. *(978-1-84401-048-6(1))* Athena Pr.

Skye, Evelyn. The Crown's Game. 2017. (Crown's Game Ser.: 1). (ENG.). 432p. (YA). (gr. 8). pap. 9.99 *(978-0-06-242259-0(6),* Balzer & Bray) HarperCollins Pubs.

—The Crown's Game. 2017. (Crown's Game Ser.: bk.1). (ENG.). (YA). lib. bdg. 20.85 *(978-0-606-39645-5(4))* Turtleback.

Sloane, Richard. Back to the Dark Ages! 2013. 138p. (gr. 4-6). 22.95 *(978-1-4669-7401-2(X))*; pap. 12.95 *(978-1-4669-7399-2(4))* Trafford Publishing.

Smedman, Lisa. Sacrifice of the Widow. 2007. (Lady Penitent Ser.: Bk. 1). 311p. *(978-1-4287-1497-7(9))* Wizards of the Coast.

Smith, Peggy. The Kingdom of Nod: A Sweet Tale about an Unlucky Young Queen, & the Men Who Try to Win Her Hand, for the Barton Reading & Spelling System. 2003. (J). pap. 7.95 *(978-0-9744343-6-0(1),* SA-401) Bright Solutions for Dyslexia, LLC.

Snell, Gordon. The King of Quizzical Island. McKee, David, illus. 2009. (ENG.). 40p. (J). (gr. -1-3). 16.99 *(978-0-7636-3857-3(9))* Candlewick Pr.

Snelson, Brian & Sellars, Rodney. Shaturanga: The Story of Onus. 2003. 244p. pap. 16.95 *(978-0-595-29569-2(X))* iUniverse, Inc.

Sommer, Carl. The Great Royal Race. Westbrook, Dick, illus. 2014. (J). pap. *(978-1-57537-952-4(X))* Advance Publishing, Inc.

—The Great Royal Race. 2003. (Another Sommer-Time Story Ser.). (Illus.). 48p. (J). (gr. k-4). lib. bdg. 23.95 incl. audio *(978-1-57537-758-2(6))* Advance Publishing, Inc.

—The Great Royal Race. Westbrook, Dick, illus. 2003. (Another Sommer-Time Story Ser.). 48p. (J). (gr. k-4). lib. bdg. 23.95 incl. audio compact disk *(978-1-57537-708-7(X))* Advance Publishing, Inc.

—The Great Royal Race. 2003. (Another Sommer-Time Story Ser.). (Illus.). 48p. (J). (gr. 1-4). 16.95 incl. audio *(978-1-57537-557-1(5))* Advance Publishing, Inc.

—The Great Royal Race. Westbrook, Dick, illus. 2003. (Another Sommer-Time Story Ser.). 48p. (J). (gr. 1-4). 16.95 incl. audio compact disk *(978-1-57537-508-3(7))* Advance Publishing, Inc.

—The Great Royal Race(La Gran Carrera Real) Westbrook, Dick, illus. 2009. (Another Sommer-Time Story Bilingual Ser.). (SPA & ENG.). 48p. (J). lib. bdg. 16.95 *(978-1-57537-152-8(9))* Advance Publishing, Inc.

—The Race. Budwine, Greg, illus. 2009. (Quest for Success Ser.). (ENG.). 56p. (YA). lib. bdg. 12.95 *(978-1-57537-256-3(8))* Advance Publishing, Inc.

—The Race(La Carrera) Budwine, Greg, illus. 2009. (Quest for Success Bilingual Ser.). (SPA & ENG.). 104p. (YA). lib. bdg. 14.95 *(978-1-57537-230-3(4))* Advance Publishing, Inc.

—The Racing Fools. Budwine, Greg, illus. 2009. (Quest for Success Ser.). (ENG.). 56p. (YA). pap. 4.95 *(978-1-57537-281-5(9))* Advance Publishing, Inc.

Sorensen, Launa. The King's First Journey, Bk. 1. 2007. 280p. (YA). pap. 15.99 *(978-1-59092-572-0(6))* Blue Forge Pr.

Souhami, Jessica. Rama & the de Mon King: An Ancient Tale from India. 2006. (Illus.). 30p. (J). (gr. k-4). reprint ed. 15.00 *(978-0-7567-9813-0(2))* DIANE Publishing Co.

Spinale, Wendy. Ozland (the Everland Trilogy, Book 3) 2018. (Everland Ser.: 3). (ENG.). 288p. (YA). (gr. 7-7). 17.99 *(978-0-545-95322-1(7),* Scholastic Pr.) Scholastic, Inc.

Spring, Manda. Emerald & the Withered Willow. 2007. 148p. pap. 18.00 *(978-1-4303-1353-3(6))* Lulu Pr., Inc.

Spurgeon, C. H. Queen Victoria's Request. 2008. (Story Time Ser.). (ENG., Illus.). 24p. (J). (gr. -1-3). 7.99 *(978-1-84550-325-3(2),* 02bbf606-b30d-425b-85ba-7fd206cb260b) Christian Focus Pubns. GBR. Dist: Baker & Taylor Publisher Services (BTPS).

Squatrito, J. Michael, Jr. The Talisman of Unification: The Overlords. 2007. (ENG., Illus.). 424p. (YA). per. 22.95 *(978-0-595-47343-4(1))* iUniverse, Inc.

Stanek, Robert, pseud. The Elf Queen & the King III. 2007. 232p. (YA). pap. 15.00 *(978-1-57545-086-5(0))* RP Media.

—The Elf Queen & the King IV. 2008. 238p. (YA). pap. 15.00 *(978-1-57545-087-2(9))* RP Media.

Stanley, Diane. Bella at Midnight. Ibatoulline, Bagram, illus. 2007. (ENG.). 304p. (J). (gr. 3-7). pap. 7.99 *(978-0-06-077575-9(0),* HarperCollins) HarperCollins Pubs.

—The Cup & the Crown. 2013. (Silver Bowl Ser.: 2). (ENG.). 368p. (J). (gr. 3-7). pap. 6.99 *(978-0-06-196323-0(2),* HarperCollins) HarperCollins Pubs.

—The Princess of Cortova. 2013. 311p. (J). lib. bdg. *(978-0-06-204731-1(0))* HarperCollins Pubs.

—The Silver Bowl. (Silver Bowl Ser.: 1). (ENG.). (J). (gr. 5). 2012. 336p. pap. 6.99 *(978-0-06-157546-4(1))* 2011. 320p. 16.99 *(978-0-06-157543-3(7))* HarperCollins Pubs. (HarperCollins).

Staska, H. M. How George Became King. 2012. 40p. pap. 32.70 *(978-1-4771-1475-9(0))* Xlibris Corp.

Steel, Flora. The Adventures of Akbar. 2007. 116p. per. 9.95 *(978-1-60312-207-8(9))* Aegypan.

Stein, Evaleen. Our Little Crusader Cousin of Long Ago. Meister, Charles E., illus. 2007. 136p. per. 8.95 *(978-1-59915-243-1(6))* Yesterday's Classics.

—Our Little Frankish Cousin of Long Ago. Landau, Helena Von & Meister, Charles, illus. 2007. 92p. per. 8.95 *(978-1-59915-244-8(4))* Yesterday's Classics.

Stephaan, Kynza. Empress Kynza of Skroltz: You Are Special. 2012. 24p. pap. 17.99 *(978-1-4772-7239-8(9))* AuthorHouse.

Stevens, Dan. The Magic of the Brass Ring. 2009. 84p. pap. 19.95 *(978-1-4489-7759-8(2))* America Star Bks.

Stevenson, Steve. The King of Scotland's Sword. 2013. (Agatha Girl of Mystery Ser.: 3). lib. bdg. 16.00 *(978-0-606-31688-0(4))* Turtleback.

Stewart, Dianne C. Longitude - Zero Degrees. 2009. (ENG.). 200p. pap. 8.95 *(978-0-9667359-4-9(3),* BeanPole Bks.) OH Industries.

Summerill, Erin. Ever the Brave. (Clash of Kingdoms Novel Ser.: bk.2). (ENG., Illus.). (YA). (gr. 7). 2018. 480p. pap. 9.99 *(978-1-328-49795-6(X),* 1717847) 2017. 464p. 17.99 *(978-0-544-66446-3(9),* 1625025) HarperCollins Pubs. (Clarion Bks.).

—Once a King. 2018. (Clash of Kingdoms Novel Ser.). (ENG., Illus.). 464p. (YA). (gr. 7). 17.99 *(978-1-328-94997-4(4),* 1705582, Clarion Bks.) HarperCollins Pubs.

Surget, Alain & Yeardley, Glynne. Cleopatra Must Be Saved! Parme, Fabrice, illus. 2014. 95p. (J). *(978-1-4351-5329-5(4))* Barnes & Noble, Inc.

Sutcliff, Rosemary. The Mark of the Horse Lord. 2015. (Rediscovered Classics Ser.: 21). (ENG.). 296p. (YA). (gr. 7). pap. 12.95 *(978-1-61373-154-3(X))* Chicago Review Pr., Inc.

Sutherland, Tui T. The Hidden Kingdom (Wings of Fire #3), 1 vol. 2013. (Wings of Fire Ser.: 3). (ENG., Illus.). 336p. (J). (gr. 4-7). 17.99 *(978-0-545-34920-8(6),* Scholastic Pr.) Scholastic, Inc.

The Sword, the Ring, & the Parchment. 2006. (J). per. 7.99 *(978-0-9785523-0-5(X))* Cross & Crown Publishing.

Sypolt, Carl W. Adventures of David the Honeybee. 2003. 51p. pap. 9.95 *(978-0-7414-1526-4(7))* Infinity Publishing.

Tappan, Eva March. In the Days of Queen Victori. 2009. 160p. pap. 9.95 *(978-1-60459-620-5(1))* Wilder Pubns., Corp.

Thomas, Jane Resh. The Counterfeit Princess. 2005. (J). (ENG.). 208p. (gr. 5-7). 15.00 *(978-0-395-93870-6(8),* 112679); 197p. *(978-0-618-93780-6(3))* HarperCollins Pubs. (Clarion Bks.).

Thomas, Rhiannon. A Wicked Thing. 2015. (ENG.). 352p. (YA). (gr. 9). 17.99 *(978-0-06-230353-0(8),* HarperTeen) HarperCollins Pubs.

Thomas, Sherry. The Immortal Heights. 2015. (Elemental Trilogy Ser.: 3). (ENG.). 448p. (YA). (gr. 9). 17.99 *(978-0-06-220735-7(0),* Balzer & Bray) HarperCollins Pubs.

Thompson, James A., Jr. The Amarna Experiment. 2003. 128p. (YA). 21.95 *(978-0-595-65753-7(2))*; pap. 11.95 *(978-0-595-28296-8(2))* iUniverse, Inc.

Thompson, Nina C. The Puzzle King. 2009. 56p. pap. 9.95 *(978-1-60860-149-3(8),* Eloquent Bks.) Strategic Book Publishing & Rights Agency (SBPRA).

Thurber, James. The Tiger Who Would Be King. Yoon, JooHee, illus. 2015. 40p. (J). (gr. k-4). 18.95 *(978-1-59270-182-7(5))* Enchanted Lion Bks., LLC.

Tillworth, Mary. King for a Day! (PAW Patrol) Jackson, Mike, illus. 2016. (Step into Reading Ser.). (ENG.). 24p. (J). (gr. -1-1). 4.99 *(978-1-101-93684-9(3),* Random Hse. Bks. for Young Readers) Random Hse. Children's Bks.

Timms, E. H. Ring of Nine. 2010. 156p. pap. 16.95 *(978-1-4452-4512-6(4))* Lulu Pr., Inc.

Tomlin, Chris. Good Good Father, 1 vol. 2016. (ENG., Illus.). 32p. (J). 17.99 *(978-0-7180-8695-4(3),* Tommy Nelson) Nelson, Thomas Inc.

Tort, Pep & Josep, Tort. El Rey Ignacio. Duran, Teresa., illus. 2006. (Montana Encantada Ser.). (SPA.). 47p. (J). per. *(978-84-241-8558-9(7))* Everest Editora.

Townsend, S. P. The Star of Persia. 2007. 120p. 33.50 *(978-1-84799-236-9(6))* Lulu Pr., Inc.

Turk, Cheri. The Stone Between Kings. Turk, Cheri, illus. 2012. (Illus.). 36p. pap. 12.99 *(978-0-9860024-0-3(2))* Specialty Greetings.

Turner, Megan Whalen. A Conspiracy of Kings. (Queen's Thief Ser.: 4). (ENG.). (YA). (gr. 8). 2017. 368p. pap. 10.99 *(978-0-06-264299-8(5))* 2011. 352p. pap. 7.99 *(978-0-06-187095-8(1))* 2010. 336p. 17.99 *(978-0-06-187093-4(5))* HarperCollins Pubs. (Greenwillow Bks.).

—A Conspiracy of Kings, 6 vols. 2010. (Queen's Thief Ser.: BK.4). (YA). (ENG.). 73.75 *(978-1-4498-4570-4(3))*; (ENG.). 230.75 *(978-1-4498-4569-8(X))*; 1.25 *(978-1-4498-4574-2(6))*; 88.75 *(978-1-4498-4573-5(8))*;No. 4. (ENG.). 90.75 *(978-1-4498-4571-1(1))* Recorded Bks., Inc.

—The King of Attolia. (Queen's Thief Ser.: 3). (ENG.). (YA). (gr. 8). 2017. 432p. pap. 10.99 *(978-0-06-264298-1(7))* 2007. 432p. pap. 7.99 *(978-0-06-083579-8(6))* 2006. 400p. 17.99 *(978-0-06-083577-4(X))* HarperCollins Pubs. (Greenwillow Bks.).

—The King of Attolia. 2007. (Queen's Thief Ser.: BK.3). 387p. (YA). 18.00 *(978-0-7569-8106-8(9))* Perfection Learning Corp.

—The King of Attolia. (YA). 2008. (Queen's Thief Ser.: BK.3). (ENG.). 84.49 *(978-1-4281-8027-7(3))* 2007. (Attolia Ser.: 3). 119.75 *(978-1-4281-1722-8(9))* 2007. (Queen's Thief Ser.: BK.3). (ENG.). 92.75 *(978-1-4281-1716-7(4))* 2006. (Queen's Thief Ser.: BK.3). (ENG.). 90.75 *(978-1-4281-1718-1(0))* 2006. (Queen's Thief Ser.: BK.3). (ENG.). 122.75 *(978-1-4281-1720-4(2))* 2006. (Queen's Thief Ser.: BK.3). (ENG.). 251.75 *(978-1-4281-1717-4(2))* 2006. (Queen's Thief Ser.: BK.3). 281.75 *(978-1-4281-1721-1(0))* 2006. (Queen's Thief Ser.: BK.3). (ENG.). 1.25 *(978-1-4281-1713-6(X))* Recorded Bks., Inc.

—The Queen of Attolia. (Queen's Thief Ser.: 2). (ENG.). (YA). (gr. 8). 2017. 416p. pap. 12.99 *(978-0-06-264297-4(9))* 2006. 368p. pap. 6.99 *(978-0-06-084182-9(6))* HarperCollins Pubs. (Greenwillow Bks.).

—The Queen of Attolia, 8 vols. (Attolia Ser.: 2). (J). 2013. 188.75 *(978-1-4281-5237-3(7))* 2009. 73.75 *(978-1-4361-6574-7(1))* 2008. 104.75 *(978-1-4281-5236-6(9))* 2008. 75.75 *(978-1-4281-5234-2(2))* 2007. 78.75 *(978-1-4281-5232-8(6))* 2007. 101.75 *(978-1-4281-5238-0(5))* 2007. 162.75 *(978-1-4281-5233-5(4))* 2007. 1.25 *(978-1-4281-5229-8(6))* Recorded Bks., Inc.

—The Queen of Attolia. 2017. (Queen's Thief Ser.: BK.2). (ENG.). (YA). lib. bdg. 20.85 *(978-0-606-40331-3(0))* Turtleback.

—Thick As Thieves. (Queen's Thief Ser.: 5). (ENG.). (YA). (gr. 8). 2018. 384p. pap. 11.99 *(978-0-06-256826-7(4))* 2017. 352p. 17.99 *(978-0-06-256824-3(8))* HarperCollins Pubs. (Greenwillow Bks.).

Turner, Patrenia. Barbie In The Queen Patrenialla Fairy - Tale. Turner, Keeng Troyius, ed. 2014. (Illus.). 31p. pap. *(978-0-578-14812-0(9))* Patrenialla Turner, Queen .

Twain, Mark, pseud & Stead, Philip C. The Purloining of Prince Oleomargarine. Stead, Erin, illus. 160p. (J). (gr. 3-7). 2021. pap. 9.99 *(978-0-593-30382-5(2),* Yearling) 2017. 24.99 *(978-0-553-52322-5(8),* Doubleday Bks. for Young Readers) Random Hse. Children's Bks.

Twist, Clint. Cleopatra: Queen of Egypt. Andrew, Ian, illus. 2012. (Historical Notebooks Ser.). (ENG.). 30p. (J). (gr. 3-7). 19.99 *(978-0-7636-6095-6(7),* Templar) Candlewick Pr.

Valentino, Serena. Fairest of All: A Villains Graphic Novel. 2017. (Villains Ser.: 1). (ENG.). 272p. (YA). (gr. 7-12). pap. 10.99 *(978-1-368-01146-4(2),* Disney Press Books) Disney Publishing Worldwide.

Van Dusen, Chris. King Hugo's Huge Ego. 2011. (ENG., Illus.). 40p. (J). (gr. -1-2). 18.99 *(978-0-7636-5004-9(8))* Candlewick Pr.

Verplancke, Klaas. The King's Golden Beard. 2021. (Illus.). 48p. (J). (gr. -1-3). 18.99 *(978-1-6626-5039-0(6),* Minedition) Penguin Young Readers Group.

Vines, Audrey. Miranda. 2010. 28p. 15.99 *(978-1-4520-1105-9(2))* AuthorHouse.

Vision, David. Who's That Crying! Alcantara, Ignacio, illus. 2009. 64p. 17.00 *(978-0-9659538-1-8(5))* Von Curtis Publishing.

Voigt, Cynthia. The Tale of Elske. 2015. (Tales of the Kingdom Ser.: 4). (ENG., Illus.). 368p. (YA). (gr. 7). 19.99 *(978-1-4814-2189-8(1),* Atheneum Bks. for Young Readers) Simon & Schuster Children's Publishing.

Volpe, Theresa. The King's Mapmaker. 2006. (Early Explorers Ser.). (J). pap. *(978-1-4108-6129-0(5))* Benchmark Education Co.

Wade, Kerry. A Page Turns Twelve & Comes of Age. 2006. 9.00 *(978-0-8059-9169-7(7))* Dorrance Publishing Co., Inc.

Wadham, Tim. The Queen of France. Denton, Kady MacDonald, illus. 2011. (ENG.). 32p. (J). (gr. -1-3). 16.99 *(978-0-7636-4102-3(2))* Candlewick Pr.

Wakefield, Beth. The Cleaner. 2010. 151p. pap. 14.50 *(978-1-4457-6809-0(7))* Lulu Pr., Inc.

Wallace, Karen & Chapman, Neil. Arthur the King. 2009. (Hopscotch Adventures Ser.). (Illus.). 31p. (J). (gr. 1). lib. bdg. 25.65 *(978-1-59771-173-9(X))* Sea-To-Sea Pubns.

Walsleben, Edda Brigitte. The Little Bee Who Would Be Queen. 2012. 224p. 45.00 *(978-1-937911-33-1(0))*; pap. 33.00 *(978-1-937911-32-4(2))* Heavenly Realm Publishing.

Warner, Larry. Chocolate Island, 1 vol. 2010. 42p. pap. 24.95 *(978-1-4489-7372-9(4))* PublishAmerica, Inc.

Warner, Sally. EllRay Jakes the Recess King! 2015. (EllRay Jakes Ser.: 8). lib. bdg. 16.00 *(978-0-606-36777-6(2))* Turtleback.

Wasserman, Mira. Too Much of a Good Thing. Carolan, Christine, illus. 2003. 32p. (J). (gr. -1-3). pap. 6.95 *(978-1-58013-066-0(6))*; (ENG.). 15.95 *(978-1-58013-082-0(8))* Lerner Publishing Group. (Kar-Ben Publishing).

Webb, Beth. Fleabag Trilogy. 2005. 640p. (J). pap. 14.00 *(978-0-7459-4977-2(0),* Lion Books) Lion Hudson PLC GBR. Dist: Trafalgar Square Publishing.

Weinbrecht, William. Stories for Amand. 2009. 48p. pap. 15.50 *(978-1-60693-150-9(4),* Eloquent Bks.) Strategic Book Publishing & Rights Agency (SBPRA).

Weiss, Ellen. Babar: Four Stories to Read & Share. Gibert, Jean Claude & Gray, J. M. L., illus. 2006. (J). 9.99 *(978-0-8109-9308-2(2),* Abrams Bks. for Young Readers) Abrams, Inc.

Welch, Julie. Happy Hearts, 1 vol. 2009. 52p. pap. 16.95 *(978-1-4489-1971-0(1))* America Star Bks.

Wend, Arran. The King & the Fire Chanter. 2007. (ENG., Illus.). 373p. (J). 15.95 *(978-0-9793284-0-4(3),* 9780979328404) Antiquity Publishing.

West, Hannah. Palace of Silver: A Nissera Novel. 2020. (Nissera Chronicles Ser.: 3). (Illus.). 464p. (YA). (gr. 7). 18.99 *(978-0-8234-4443-4(0))* Holiday Hse., Inc.

What Is Hidden. 2014. 281p. (YA). pap. 16.99 *(978-1-4621-1429-0(6))* Cedar Fort, Inc./CFI Distribution.

Wheeler, Jeff. The Hollow Crown. 2017. (Kingfountain Ser.: 4). (ENG., Illus.). 302p. pap. 14.95 *(978-1-5039-4396-4(8),* 9781503943964, 47North) Amazon Publishing.

Wilde, Oscar. The House of Pomegranates. 2005. (ENG.). 81p. pap. *(978-1-4065-0242-8(1))* Dodo Pr.

Wilkins, James Francis. The Queen & Mr Brown: Meet the Rats. (Queen & Mr Brown Ser.). (ENG., Illus.). 48p. (J). (gr. k-2). 2019. pap. 12.99 *(978-0-565-09446-1(7))* 2017. 17.99 *(978-0-565-09438-6(6))* Natural History Museum Pubns. GBR. Dist: Independent Pubs. Group.

Williams, Brenda. The Real Princess. Fatus, Sophie, illus. 2008. (ENG.). 40p. (J). (gr. -1-3). 16.99 *(978-1-905236-88-6(3))* Barefoot Bks., Inc.

Williams, Brenda & Barefoot Books Staff. Una Princesa Real: Un Cuento Matemagico. Fatus, Sophie, illus. 2014. 40p. (J). (gr. k-4). pap. 8.99 *(978-1-78285-078-6(3))* Barefoot Bks., Inc.

Williams, Rozanne Lanczak. Fairy Tale Mail. Allen, Joy, illus. (Learn to Write Ser.). 16p. (J). 2007. pap. 8.99 *(978-1-59198-359-0(2))* 2006. pap. 3.49 *(978-1-59198-301-9(0),* 6195) Creative Teaching Pr., Inc.

Willsea, Heidi. The Heath of the Graves. 2009. (ENG.). 371p. pap. 31.50 *(978-1-4092-2226-2(8))* Lulu Pr., Inc.

Wilson, N. D. The Chestnut King (100 Cupboards Book 3) 2011. (100 Cupboards Ser.: 3). (ENG., Illus.). 512p. (J). (gr. 3-7). 9.99 *(978-0-375-83886-6(4),* Yearling) Random Hse. Children's Bks.

Wolfe, Robert Hewitt. The Goblin Crown: Billy Smith & the Goblins, Book 1. 2016. (Billy Smith & the Goblins Ser.: 1).

(ENG.). 336p. (J). 31.95 *(978-1-68162-613-0(6))*; pap. 16.95 *(978-1-68162-612-3(8))* Turner Publishing Co.

Wolfe, Sean Fay. The Elementia Chronicles #2: the New Order: An Unofficial Minecraft-Fan Adventure. 2015. (Elementia Chronicles Ser.: 2). (ENG.). 496p. (J). (gr. 3-7). pap. 9.99 *(978-0-06-241634-6(0)*, HarperCollins) HarperCollins Pubs.

Wood, Audrey. King Bidgood's in the Bathtub. Wood, Don, illus. 2010. (ENG.). 32p. (J). (gr. -1-3). pap. 7.99 *(978-0-15-205435-9(9)*, 1196356, Clarion Bks.) HarperCollins Pubs.

Woodford, Pamela. King Giggle. 2013. (Brighter Little Minds Ser.). (ENG., Illus.). 18p. (J). 10.95 *(978-1-871305-80-7(2))* Orpen Pr. IRL. Dist: Dufour Editions, Inc.

Wrede, Patricia C. Calling on Dragons. unabr. ed. 2004. (Enchanted Forest Chronicles: Bk. 3). 244p. (J). (gr. 6-18). pap. 38.00 incl. audio *(978-0-8072-0792-5(6)*, LYA 347 SP, Listening Library) Random Hse. Audio Publishing Group.

—Talking to Dragons. unabr. ed. 2004. (Enchanted Forest Chronicles: Bk. 4). 255p. (J). (gr. 6-18). pap. 38.00 incl. audio *(978-0-8072-0983-7(X)*, S YA 385 SP, Listening Library) Random Hse. Audio Publishing Group.

Wyss, Tyan. The Solitaire Prince. 2006. 168p. (YA). per. 12.95 *(978-1-58939-906-8(4))* Virtualbookworm.com Publishing, Inc.

Yerushalmi, Miriam. Gedalia the Goldfish Who Wanted Be Just Like the King. Weinberg, Devorah, illus. 2007. 26p. (J). (gr. -1-3). 16.50 *(978-0-911643-36-7(2))* Aura Printing, Inc.

Yolen, Jane. Sword of the Rightful King: A Novel of King Arthur. 2004. (ENG., Illus.). 384p. (YA). (gr. 7-12). reprint ed. pap. 7.99 *(978-0-15-202533-5(2)*, 1193075, Clarion Bks.) HarperCollins Pubs.

Yonge, Charlotte M. The Little Duke. 2005. 26.95 *(978-1-4218-0318-0(6))*; 164p. pap. 11.95 *(978-1-4218-0418-7(2))* 1st World Publishing, Inc. (1st World Library - Literary Society).

—The Little Duke. 2004. reprint ed. pap. 1.99 *(978-1-4179-9908-8(X))*; pap. 15.95 *(978-1-4179-9958-3(6))* Kessinger Publishing, LLC.

—The Little Duke. 2008. 112p. pap. 9.05 *(978-1-60459-557-4(4))* Wilder Pubns., Corp.

Young, Judy. Hu Wan & the Sleeping Dragon. Solano, Jordi, illus. 2017. (ENG.). 32p. (J). (gr. 1-4). 16.99 *(978-1-58536-977-5(2)*, 204324) Sleeping Bear Pr.

KINGS AND RULERS

see Kings, Queens, Rulers, etc.

KINGS CANYON NATIONAL PARK (CALIF.)

Nicholas, Jeff D. Sequoia & Kings Canyon. 2004. (Illus.). per. 4.95 *(978-1-58071-054-1(9)*, Wish You Were Here) Sierra Pr.

KINGSLEY, MARY HENRIETTA, 1862-1900

Cooke, Tim. Explore with Mary Kingsley. 2017. (Travel with the Great Explorers Ser.). (Illus.). 32p. (J). (gr. 4-5). *(978-0-7787-3920-3(1))*; pap. *(978-0-7787-3926-5(0))* Crabtree Publishing Co.

KINKAJOU

Lynette, Rachel. Kinkajous. 2013. (Jungle Babies of the Amazon Rain Forest Ser.). 24p. (J). (gr. -1-3). lib. bdg. 25.65 *(978-1-61772-752-8(0))* Bearport Publishing Co., Inc.

KINKAJOU—FICTION

Kimmelman, Leslie. Bat & Sloth Lost & Found (Bat & Sloth: Time to Read, Level 2) Braun, Seb, illus. 2020. (Time to Read Ser.). (ENG.). 32p. (J). (gr. k-2). 12.99 *(978-0-8075-0586-1(2)*, 807505862) Whitman, Albert & Co.

Parente, Peter. Peeper the Kinkajou. Lt. ed. 2004. (Peeper & Friends Ser.). (Illus.). 28p. (J). 15.95 *(978-0-9745052-0-6(X)*, Peeper & Friends) Tree Of Life Publishing.

KIPLING, RUDYARD, 1865-1936—FICTION

Kipling, Rudyard. Rudyard Kipling's Just So Comics: Tales of the World's Wildest Beasts. Rodriguez, Pedro, illus. 2013. (Graphic Spin Ser.). (ENG.). 144p. (J). (gr. 3-6). pap., pap., pap. 12.95 *(978-1-4342-4880-0(1)*, 121868, Stone Arch Bks.) Capstone.

Spillebeen, Geert. Kipling's Choice. 2007. (ENG.). 160p. (YA). (gr. 7-9). pap. 12.95 *(978-0-618-80035-3(2)*, 496440, Clarion Bks.) HarperCollins Pubs.

—Kipling's Choice. Edelstein, Terese, tr. 2007. 147p. (YA). (gr. 7-9). 15.65 *(978-0-7569-8061-0(5))* Perfection Learning Corp.

KIPPER (FICTITIOUS CHARACTER: INKPEN)—FICTION

Inkpen, Mick. Hide Me, Kipper. 2016. (Kipper Ser.). (ENG., Illus.). 32p. (J). (gr. -1-k). 7.99 *(978-1-4449-2977-5(1))* Hachette Children's Group GBR. Dist: Hachette Bk. Group.

—Kipper. (ENG & FRE., Illus.). 32p. (J). *(978-1-85430-330-1(9)*, 93450); *(978-1-85430-333-2(3)*, 93451) Little Tiger Pr. Group.

—Kipper's Toybox. (Illus.). 25p. (J). (CHI, ENG, URD, VIE & FRE.). *(978-1-85430-350-9(3)*, 93452); (ENG, FRE, URD, VIE & CHI., *(978-1-85430-351-6(1)*, 93453) Little Tiger Pr. Group.

KISSINGER, HENRY, 1923-

Wagner, Heather Lehr. Henry Kissinger. 2006. (ENG., Illus.). 111p. (gr. 9-12). lib. bdg. 30.00 *(978-0-7910-9222-4(4)*, P114558, Facts On File) Infobase Holdings, Inc.

KITCHEN GARDENS

see Vegetable Gardening

KITCHEN UTENSILS

see Household Equipment and Supplies

KITCHENS

Bloom, Chrissa. In the Kitchen with Solids, Liquids, & Gases, 1 vol. 2008. (Real Life Readers Ser.). (ENG.). 12p. (gr. 1-2). pap. 5.90 *(978-1-4042-7897-4(4)*, e43da252-1047-465c-b8ff-11988b838565, Rosen Classroom) Rosen Publishing Group, Inc., The.

La Cocina: Individual Title Two-Packs. (Chiquilibros Ser.). (SPA.). (gr. -1-1). 12.00 *(978-0-7635-8560-0(2))* Rigby Education.

Connors, Kathleen. We Play Kitchen!, 1 vol. 2018. (Ways to Play Ser.). (ENG.). 24p. (gr. k-k). 24.27 *(978-1-5382-2881-4(5)*, cae721c7-7b67-41e9-ab6e-af1d5615aa79) Stevens, Gareth Publishing LLLP.

In the Kitchen, 6 Packs. (Bookweb Ser.). 32p. (gr. 3-18). 34.00 *(978-0-7635-3951-1(1))* Rigby Education.

In the Kitchen. 2005. (J). *(978-1-59564-720-7(1))* Steps To Literacy, LLC.

Miller, Connie Colwell. Chef Cuisinier. Baroncelli, Silvia, illus. 2016. (Plus Tard, Je Serai... Ser.). (FRE.). 24p. (J). (gr. 1-4). *(978-1-77092-353-9(5)*, 17616) Amicus.

KITES

Amado, Elisa. Un Barrilete / Barrilete, 1 vol. Hairs, Joya, photos by. 2012.Tr. of Para el Dia de los Muertos. (ENG & SPA., Illus.). 32p. (J). (gr. k-4). pap. 9.95 *(978-1-55498-112-0(3))* Groundwood Bks. CAN. Dist: Publishers Group West (PGW).

Avett, Harper. Go Fly a Kite! Reason with Shapes & Their Attributes, 1 vol. 2014. (Rosen Math Readers Ser.). (ENG., Illus.). 24p. (J). (gr. 3-3). pap. 8.25 *(978-1-4777-4881-7(4)*, 004fdc4a-3d91-422d-9cb6-38d30bb743b4, Rosen Classroom) Rosen Publishing Group, Inc., The.

Benchmark Education Co., LLC. Play, Play, Play All Day Big Book. 2014. (Shared Reading Foundations Ser.). (J). (gr. -1). *(978-1-4509-9434-7(2))* Benchmark Education Co.

Dinmont, Kerry. Abby Flies a Kite: A Book about Wind. 2017. (My Day Readers Ser.). (ENG.). 24p. (J). (gr. -1-2). lib. bdg. 32.79 *(978-1-5038-2014-2(9)*, 211861) Child's World, Inc, The.

Hosking, Wayne. Asian Kites: Asian Arts & Crafts for Creative Kids. 2017. (Asian Arts & Crafts for Creative Kids Ser.). (ENG., Illus.). 64p. (J). 9.95 *(978-0-8048-4869-5(6))* Tuttle Publishing.

Kites. (Early Intervention Levels Ser.). 21.30 *(978-0-7362-0368-5(0))* CENGAGE Learning.

Lafette, Jordan. Kites: Shapes in the Air: Reason with Shapes & Their Attributes, 1 vol. 2014. (InfoMax Math Readers Ser.). (ENG.). 24p. (J). (gr. 3-3). pap. 8.25 *(978-1-4777-4582-3(3)*, e296efa3-8d3c-43fa-83a1-cae4da4cd6e2, Rosen Classroom) Rosen Publishing Group, Inc., The.

Make a Kite: Individual Title Six-Packs. (Story Steps Ser.). (gr. k-2). 29.00 *(978-0-7635-9588-3(8))* Rigby Education.

Mini Kites. 2004. (Formula Fun Ser.). (Illus.). 48p. (J). *(978-1-84229-580-9(2))* Top That! Publishing PLC.

Nagle, Jeanne. Kite Surfing & Kite Skiing, 1 vol. 2015. (Sports to the Extreme Ser.). (ENG., Illus.). 48p. (J). (gr. 5-6). 33.47 *(978-1-4994-3561-0(4)*, 98769588-9b0e-4595-a052-bfe49bc7fbaa, Rosen Central) Rosen Publishing Group, Inc., The.

Ostrovsky, Alexsandr. Paper Kite. Ostrovsky, Alexsandr, illus. (Childrens Ser.). (Illus.). (Orig.). (J). pap. 14.95 *(978-0-934393-18-8(4))* Rector Pr., Ltd.

Packard, Mary. The Kite. Huang, Benrei, illus. 2003. (My First Reader Ser.). (ENG.). 32p. (J). 18.50 *(978-0-516-22930-0(3)*, Children's Pr.) Scholastic Library Publishing.

Torrijos, Eduardo & Garcia, Gretel. Papalotes: Tecnicas de Armado y Vuelo. Torrijos, Eduardo, illus. 2004. (SPA., Illus.). 157p. (J). pap. *(978-970-643-734-1(7))* Selector, S.A. de C.V. MEX. Dist: Spanish Pubs., LLC.

Wardle, Sue & Porter, Eleanor H. Kites Funstation. 2014. (ENG.). 251p. 17.50 *(978-1-872700-40-3(3))* Award Pubns. Ltd. GBR. Dist: Parkwest Pubns., Inc.

KITES—FICTION

Ayer, Jacqueline, creator. Nu Dang & His Kite. 2017. (Illus.). 40p. (J). (gr. -1-3). 16.95 *(978-1-59270-231-2(7))* Enchanted Lion Bks., LLC.

Baumgart, Klaus. Laura's Secret. Waite, Judy, tr. from GER. 2003. (Illus.). 32p. (J). (gr. -1-2). tchr. ed. 16.95 *(978-1-58925-031-4(1))* Tiger Tales.

Berenstain, Stan & Berenstain, Jan. Berenstain Bears: We Like Kites. 2004. (Step into Reading Ser.). (Illus.). 32p. (J). (gr. -1-1). pap. 4.99 *(978-0-679-89231-1(1)*, Random Hse. Bks. for Young Readers) Random Hse. Children's Bks.

—We Like Kites. 2004. (Step into Reading - Level 1 Ser.). (gr. -1-2). lib. bdg. 13.55 *(978-0-613-87779-4(9))* Turtleback.

Bickel, Karla. The Kite Who Was Afraid to Fly. Bickel, Karla, illus. Lt. ed. 2004. (Illus.). 16p. (J). (gr. -1-6). pap. 5.00 *(978-1-891452-08-6(8)*, 6) Heart Arbor Bks.

Blanco, Alberto. Angel's Kite (La estrella de Angel), 1 vol. Bellm, Dan, tr. Morales, Rodolfo, illus. 2014. (ENG.). 32p. (J). (gr. 1-5). pap. 11.95 *(978-0-89239-156-1(1)*, leelowcbp) Lee & Low Bks., Inc.

—La Estrella de Angel. 2004.Tr. of Angel's Kite. (ENG & SPA., Illus.). (J). (gr. k-3). spiral bd. *(978-0-616-14604-0(3))* Canadian National Institute for the Blind/Institut National Canadien pour les Aveugles.

Bliss, Emily. Unicorn Princesses 5: Breeze's Blast. Hanson, Sydney, illus. 2018. (Unicorn Princesses Ser.: 5). (ENG.). 128p. (J). 16.99 *(978-1-68119-650-3(6)*, 900179833); pap. 5.99 *(978-1-68119-649-7(2)*, 900179849) Bloomsbury Publishing USA. (Bloomsbury USA Childrens).

Bloser, Cheryl. Little Mouse & the Muddy Feet. 2012. 28p. pap. 9.99 *(978-0-9836771-1-6(5))* Mindstir Media.

Brown, Adam. The Adventures of Wormie Wormington Book Two: Wormie & the Kite. Smart, Andy, illus. 2013. 48p. pap. *(978-0-9919196-2-8(9))* Beckon Creative.

Burchard, Patti. Cows Really Do Fly Kites: Patti Burchard. 2012. 24p. pap. 15.00 *(978-1-4685-7627-6(5))* AuthorHouse.

Clark, Katherine. Seagull Sam. Huntington, Amy, illus. 2007. (ENG.). 32p. (J). (gr. -1-3). 15.95 *(978-0-89272-715-5(2))* Down East Bks.

Compestine, Ying Chang. The Story of Kites: Amazing Chinese Inventions. Xuan, YongSheng, illus. 2016. (Amazing Chinese Inventions Ser.). 40p. (J). (gr. -1-3). 15.95 *(978-1-59702-122-7(9))* Immedium.

Deubreau, Sharon. Heather & Avery & the Magic Kite. Pileggi, Steve, illus. Lt. ed. 2006. 23p. (J). per. 11.99 *(978-1-59879-143-3(5))* Lifevest Publishing, Inc.

Dunham, Wendy. A Windy Spring Day: God Gives Us Friends When We're Afraid. 2018. (Tales of Buttercup Grove Ser.). (ENG., Illus.). 64p. (J). (gr. -1-2). 12.99 *(978-0-7369-7200-0(5)*, 6972000) Harvest Hse. Pubs.

Engelman, Beth. The Kite Race. 2007. 7p. 10.95 *(978-1-58117-593-6(0)*, Intervisual/Piggy Toes) Bendon, Inc.

Fenske, Jonathan. Love is in the Air. Fenske, Jonathan, illus. 2012. (Penguin Young Readers, Level 2 Ser.). (Illus.). 32p. (J). (gr. 1-2). mass mkt. 5.99 *(978-0-448-49647-4(X)*, Penguin Young Readers) Penguin Young Readers Group.

Flor Ada, Alma. The Kite. (Stories the Year 'Round Ser.). (Illus.). 16p. (J). (gr. k-3). pap. 8.95 *(978-1-58105-206-0(5))* Santillana USA Publishing Co., Inc.

Fox, Paula. La Cometa Rota.Tr. of Eagle Kite. (SPA., Illus.). 120p. (YA). (gr. 5-8). *(978-84-279-3213-5(8)*, NG7615) Noguer y Caralt Editores, S. A. ESP. Dist: Lectorum Pubns., Inc.

Greensall, Maxine. Keith the Kite. 2009. (Illus.). 16p. pap. 8.49 *(978-1-4389-5768-5(8))* AuthorHouse.

Hall, Bruce Edward. Henry & the Kite Dragon. Low, William, illus. 2004. 40p. (J). (gr. 1-4). 18.99 *(978-0-399-23727-0(5)*, Philomel Bks.) Penguin Young Readers Group.

Harvey, Alex. Olivia & the Kite Party. Spaziante, Patrick, illus. 2012. (Olivia Ready-To-Read Level 1 Ser.). lib. bdg. 13.55 *(978-0-606-26360-3(8))* Turtleback.

Highway, Tomson. Dragonfly Kites: Kiweeginapiseek. 2004. (Illus.). (J). (gr. k-3). spiral bd. *(978-0-616-14619-4(1))* Canadian National Institute for the Blind/Institut National Canadien pour les Aveugles.

Hillenbrand, Will. Kite Day: A Bear & Mole Story. (Bear & Mole Ser.: 2). (ENG., Illus.). 32p. (J). (-k). 2013. pap. 7.99 *(978-0-8234-2758-1(7))* 2012. 17.99 *(978-0-8234-1603-5(8))* Holiday Hse., Inc.

Hillert, Margaret. Dear Dragon Flies a Kite. Jack Pullan, illus. 2015. (Beginning-To-Read Ser.). (ENG.). 32p. (J). (gr. k-2). pap. 13.26 *(978-1-60357-709-0(2))* Norwood Hse. Pr.

—Dear Dragon Flies a Kite. Pullan, Jack, illus. 2014. (BeginningtoRead Ser.). (ENG.). 32p. (J). (gr. k-2). lib. bdg. 22.60 *(978-1-59953-674-3(9))* Norwood Hse. Pr.

—Funny Ride. 2016. (Beginning-To-Read Ser.). (ENG., Illus.). 32p. (J). (gr. k-2). pap. 13.26 *(978-1-60357-978-0(8))* Norwood Hse. Pr.

—The Funny Ride. Selivanova, Elena, illus. 2016. (BeginningtoRead Ser.). (ENG.). 32p. (J). (gr. k-2). 22.60 *(978-1-59953-816-7(4))* Norwood Hse. Pr.

Holub, Joan. Mini Myths: Be Careful, Icarus! Patricelli, Leslie, illus. 2015. (ENG.). 22p. (J). (gr. -1 — 1). bds. 6.95 *(978-1-4197-1677-5(8)*, 1110510) Abrams, Inc.

Hong, Chen Jian. La Leyenda De la Cometa. (SPA.). 32p. *(978-84-95150-39-4(5))*; *(978-84-95150-29-5(8))* Corimbo, Editorial S.L.

Jeffers, Oliver. Stuck. Jeffers, Oliver, illus. 2011. (ENG., Illus.). 32p. (J). (gr. -1-2). 19.99 *(978-0-399-25737-7(3)*, Philomel Bks.) Penguin Young Readers Group.

Jiang, Ji-Li. Red Kite, Blue Kite. Ruth, Greg, illus. 2013. (ENG.). 32p. (J). (gr. 1-3). 18.99 *(978-1-4231-2753-6(6))* Hyperion Pr.

Kann, Victoria. Pinkalicious: Cherry Blossom. Kann, Victoria, illus. 2015. (I Can Read Level 1 Ser.). (ENG., Illus.). 32p. (J). (gr. -1-3). 16.99 *(978-0-06-224593-9(7)*, HarperCollins) HarperCollins Pubs.

—Pinkalicious: Cherry Blossom: A Springtime Book for Kids. Kann, Victoria, illus. 2015. (I Can Read Level 1 Ser.). (ENG., Illus.). 32p. (J). (gr. -1-3). pap. 5.99 *(978-0-06-224594-6(5)*, HarperCollins) HarperCollins Pubs.

Khan, Rukhsana. King for a Day, 1 vol. Krömer, Christiane, illus. (ENG.). 32p. (J). 2019. (gr. 1-5). pap. 10.95 *(978-1-64379-056-5(0)*, leelowbooks) 2014. 17.95 *(978-1-60060-659-5(8))* Lee & Low Bks., Inc.

Klepeis, Alicia & Ventura, Gabriela Baeza. Francisco's Kites. Undercuffler, Gary, illus. 2015. (SPA & ENG.). (J). 17.95 *(978-1-55885-804-6(0)*, Piñata Books) Arte Publico Pr.

Kohake, Beverly. The Red Dragon Kite. 2007. (ENG., Illus.). 48p. pap. 9.95 *(978-1-4357-1568-4(3))* Lulu Pr., Inc.

Kuhn, Douglas Wolcik. Uncle Kyle's Magic Kite. Kuhn, Douglas Wolcik, illus. 2012. (Illus.). 28p. pap. 24.95 *(978-1-4626-9699-4(6))* America Star Bks.

Lebost, Diana. Mr. Kite & the Perilous Flight: Izzy & Daisy. Ersoz, Sahin, illus. 2013. 88p. pap. 18.95 *(978-0-9912023-5-5(X))* Pep & Olie Publishing.

L'Heureux, Christine. Caillou, Ma Maman. braille ed. 2004. (FRE., Illus.). (J). (gr. 1). spiral bd. *(978-0-616-03083-7(5))* Canadian National Institute for the Blind/Institut National Canadien pour les Aveugles.

—Caillou, Mon Papa. braille ed. 2004. (FRE., Illus.). (J). (gr. 1). bds. *(978-0-616-03084-4(3))* Canadian National Institute for the Blind/Institut National Canadien pour les Aveugles.

Lin, Grace. Kite Flying. 2004. (Illus.). 32p. (J). (gr. -1-2). pap. 8.99 *(978-0-553-11254-2(6)*, Dragonfly Bks.) Random Hse. Children's Bks.

Lindsay, Maud. Mother Stories. 2005. 25.95 *(978-1-4218-1492-6(7))*; 120p. pap. 10.95 *(978-1-4218-1592-3(3))* 1st World Publishing, Inc. (1st World Library - Literary Society).

Little Blue Kite & Friends Activity Book. 2005. (YA). per. *(978-1-59872-122-5(4))* Instant Pub.

Little Boo Kite. 2005. (J). per. 9.25 *(978-1-59872-032-7(5))* Instant Pub.

Lorenzi, Natalie Dias. Flying the Dragon. 240p. (J). (gr. 4-7). 2014. (ENG.). pap. 8.95 *(978-1-58089-435-7(6))* 2012. 16.95 *(978-1-58089-434-0(8))* Charlesbridge Publishing, Inc.

Maunder, Brian. Polly's Little Kite. Maunder, Brian, illus. 2014. (ENG., Illus.). 44p. (J). (gr. -1-3). pap. 11.95 *(978-1-56548-528-0(9))* New City Press of the Focolare.

Mayer, Mercer. Little Critter: Just a Kite. Mayer, Mercer, illus. 2014. (My First I Can Read Ser.). (ENG., Illus.). 32p. (J). (gr. -1-3). 16.99 *(978-0-06-207197-2(1))*; pap. 4.99 *(978-0-06-147814-7(8))* HarperCollins Pubs. (HarperCollins).

—Little Critter: Just a Kite 6c Clip Strip. 2014. (ENG.). 100p. (J). 23.94 *(978-0-06-230135-2(7))* HarperCollins Pubs.

—Shibumi & the Kitemaker, 1 vol. 2003. (ENG., Illus.). 32p. (J). (gr. -1-3). pap. 5.95 *(978-0-7614-5145-7(5))* Marshall Cavendish Corp.

McCaughrean, Geraldine. The Kite Rider. 2003. (ENG., Illus.). 320p. (YA). (gr. 8-18). pap. 15.99 *(978-0-06-441091-5(9)*, HarperTeen) HarperCollins Pubs.

McCune, Susan. Anisa's Kite, 1 vol., 1. 2015. (Rosen REAL Readers: STEM & STEAM Collection). (ENG.). 12p. (J). (gr. k-1). pap. 6.33 *(978-1-5081-1536-6(2)*, 0e7568aa-80d4-4f81-ba6f-c52407b2ca07, Rosen Classroom) Rosen Publishing Group, Inc., The.

McLaurin, Corey F. Larry, Lisa & the Missing Kite, 1 vol. Dixon, Corey, illus. 2009. 20p. pap. 24.95 *(978-1-61546-590-3(1))* America Star Bks.

Moore, Sharon. The Runaway Kite, 1 vol. 2006. (Neighborhood Readers Ser.). (ENG.). 8p. (gr. k-1). pap. 5.15 *(978-1-4042-6714-5(X)*, 6113cc37-5e03-412c-8ec9-7b9f6bf00abb, Rosen Classroom) Rosen Publishing Group, Inc., The.

My Kite: KinderConcepts Individual Title Six-Packs. (Kinderstarters Ser.). 8p. (gr. -1-1). 21.00 *(978-0-7635-8715-4(X))* Rigby Education.

Nicholls, Maureen. Sylvester. 2008. 120p. pap. *(978-1-84923-016-2(1))* YouWriteOn.

O'Keefe, Lauren. Raindrop Flies a Kite. 2012. 16p. pap. 12.68 *(978-1-4669-7000-7(6))* Trafford Publishing.

Okereke, Laurence. Barry & the Gombeys. 2007. (ENG., Illus.). 20p. (J). *(978-0-9795739-2-7(0))* Dion's Pubn.

Park, Linda Sue. The Kite Fighters. 2010. (ENG., Illus.). 144p. (J). (gr. 3-7). pap. 8.99 *(978-0-547-32863-8(X)*, 1416976, Clarion Bks.) HarperCollins Pubs.

Pilegard, Virginia Walton. The Warlord's Kites, 1 vol. Debon, Nicolas, illus. 2004. (Warlord's Ser.). (ENG.). 32p. (J). (gr. k-3). 16.99 *(978-1-58980-180-6(6)*, Pelican Publishing) Arcadia Publishing.

Pohl, William L. The Amazing Flight of Daisy: A Runaway Kite Circles the World on the Back of the Wind. 2006. 72p. 20.00 *(978-1-4257-0666-1(5))* Xlibris Corp.

Random House. The Runaway Kite. 2018. (Thomas & Friends Step into Reading Ser.). lib. bdg. 14.75 *(978-0-606-40931-5(9))* Turtleback.

Reinheimer, Melinda T. Little Blue Kite Makes A Friend: Another Adventure of the Little Blue Kite. 2005. 24p. (J). per. 9.95 *(978-1-59196-908-2(5))* Instant Pub.

Rey, H. A. Curious George & the Kite. 2007. (Curious George TV Ser.). (ENG., Illus.). 24p. (J). (gr. -1-3). 4.99 *(978-0-618-72396-6(X)*, 419819, Clarion Bks.) HarperCollins Pubs.

—Curious George Flies a Kite. 2004. (J). (gr. k-3). spiral bd. *(978-0-616-01770-8(7))*; spiral bd. *(978-0-616-01771-5(5))* Canadian National Institute for the Blind/Institut National Canadien pour les Aveugles.

Roller, Pat Kellogg. Pink Hat's Adventure with Kites. Salazar, Riana, illus. Roller, John, photos by. 2009. 36p. pap. 10.95 *(978-1-59858-957-3(1))* Dog Ear Publishing, LLC.

Schories, Pat, illus. Biscuit Flies a Kite. 2017. 29p. (J). *(978-0-605-96911-7(6))* Harper & Row Ltd.

Sheard, Jean. A Chinese Fantasy - Cave in a Casket. (ENG.). 128p. 2007. 34.95 *(978-1-84753-349-4(3))* 2006. (Illus.). pap. *(978-1-84753-249-7(7))* Lulu Pr., Inc.

Spalding, Andrea. The Most Beautiful Kite in the World, 1 vol. 2005. (ENG., Illus.). 32p. (J). (gr. k-2). pap. 8.95 *(978-1-55041-805-7(X)*, 62e6e225-52d8-427f-9ad8-62b8184e8f61) Fitzhenry & Whiteside, Ltd. CAN. Dist: Firefly Bks., Ltd.

Spurr, Elizabeth. In the Wind, 1 vol. Oliphant, Manelle, illus. 2016. (In the Weather Ser.). 22p. (J). (gr. -1 — 1). bds. 6.99 *(978-1-56145-854-7(6))* Peachtree Publishing Co. Inc.

Thiessen, Andrea G. Little Kite & the Big Wind. 2013. 24p. *(978-1-4602-1850-1(7))*; pap. *(978-1-4602-0803-8(X))* FriesenPress.

Top That! Playtime Shapes (large Version) Parry, Jo, illus. 2007. 10p. (J). (gr. -1). *(978-1-84666-555-4(8)*, Tide Mill Pr.) Top That! Publishing PLC.

Watson, Myrtle. Kite Flying in the Village: A Guyanese Girl's Story. 2011. 20p. 10.03 *(978-1-4520-8632-3(X))* AuthorHouse.

Wilcox, Michael. Colors Around Us. Barber, Julia, illus. 2004. 32p. (J). per. 19.95 *(978-1-931780-32-2(3))* School of Color Publishing.

Yolen, Jane. The Emperor & the Kite. Young, Ed, illus. 2015. 32p. pap. 7.00 *(978-1-61003-535-4(6))* Center for the Collaborative Classroom.

KKK

see Ku Klux Klan (1915-)

KLONDIKE RIVER VALLEY (YUKON)—GOLD DISCOVERIES

Berton, Pierre. The Golden Trail: The Story of the Klondike Rush, 1 vol. 2005. (ENG., Illus.). 144p. pap. *(978-1-894856-04-1(X))* Fitzhenry & Whiteside, Ltd.

—The Great Klondike Gold Rush: An Omnibus. 2007. (History for Young Canadians Ser.). (ENG., Illus.). 300p. (gr. k). per. 17.95 *(978-1-897252-05-5(6)*, b2042157-7769-4dc1-9d04-6515a44b9ab1) Fifth Hse. Pubs. CAN. Dist: Firefly Bks., Ltd.

KLONDIKE RIVER VALLEY (YUKON)—GOLD DISCOVERIES—FICTION

Duncan, Sandy Frances. Gold Rush Orphan. 2005. (ENG., Illus.). 280p. (J). pap. 10.95 *(978-1-55380-012-5(5))* Ronsdale Pr. CAN. Dist: Literary Pr. Group of Canada.

Piotrowski, Robert. Gold Rush. Alward, Jeff, illus. 2007. 48p. (J). lib. bdg. 23.08 *(978-1-4242-1628-4(1))* Fitzgerald Bks.

KNIGHTHOOD

see Knights and Knighthood

KNIGHTS AND KNIGHTHOOD

see also Heraldry

Arnold, Tedd. Castles. 2017. (Fly Guy Presents Ser.). lib. bdg. 13.55 *(978-0-606-39716-2(7))* Turtleback.

Barter, James. A Medieval Knight. 2005. (Working Life Ser.). (ENG., Illus.). 112p. (YA). (gr. 7-10). lib. bdg. 29.95 *(978-1-59018-580-3(3)*, Lucent Bks.) Cengage Gale.

Baum, Margaux & Hopkins, Andrea. Jousts, Tournaments, & War Training, 1 vol. 2016. (Life in the Middle Ages Ser.). (ENG., Illus.). 64p. (J). (gr. 5-5). 36.13 *(978-1-4994-6474-0(6)*, ec601171-e572-426b-b6dc-05dcff48d913) Rosen Publishing Group, Inc., The.

Bergin, Mark. Knights & Castles, 1 vol. 2011. (It's Fun to Draw Ser.). (ENG., Illus.). 32p. (J). (gr. 2-2). lib. bdg. 31.27 *(978-1-61533-352-3(5)*, 5f046ba9-b6a4-430d-87e3-16cd5b71845f, Windmill Bks.) Rosen Publishing Group, Inc., The.

Bodden, Valerie. Gladiators. 2017. (X-Books: Fighters Ser.). (ENG., Illus.). 32p. (J). (gr. 3-6). *(978-1-60818-813-0(2)*, 20372, Creative Education) Creative Co., The.

Butterfield, Moira. Knight. 2009. (Medieval Lives Ser.). (J). 32.80 *(978-1-59920-168-9(2))* Black Rabbit Bks.

Chambers, Catherine. Why Why Why... Did Knights Wear Heavy Armor? 2010. (Why Why Why Ser.). (Illus.). 32p. (J). (gr. 1-3). lib. bdg. 18.95 *(978-1-4222-1575-3(X))* Mason Crest.

Claybourne, Anna. Knight Survival Guide. 2011. (ENG.). 24p. (J). pap. *(978-0-7787-7877-6(0))*; (gr. 3-6). *(978-0-7787-7855-4(X))* Crabtree Publishing Co.

J
K
L

Coggins, Jack. The Illustrated Book of Knights. 2006. (Dover Children's Classics Ser.). (ENG., Illus.). 112p. (J). (gr. 3-8). per. 16.95 (978-0-486-45134-3(8), 451348) Dover Pubns., Inc.

Cutler, U. Waldo. Stories of King Arthur & His Knights. 2011. 160p. 24.95 (978-1-4638-9661-4(1)) Rodgers, Alan Bks.

Dargie, Richard. Knights & Castles, 1 vol. 2007. (Age of Castles Ser.). (ENG., Illus.). 48p. (J). (gr. 4-5). lib. bdg. 32.93 (978-1-4042-4295-1(3), 1bbfa69a-1d88-4905-b64b-62eda493f3df, PowerKids Pr.) Rosen Publishing Group, Inc., The.

Dixon, Philip. Knights & Castles. 2007. (Insiders Ser.). (ENG., Illus.). 64p. (J). (gr. 3-7). 17.99 (978-1-4169-3864-4(8), Simon & Schuster Bks. For Young Readers) Simon & Schuster Bks. For Young Readers.

Eastwood, Kay. The Life of a Knight, 1 vol. 2003. (Medieval World Ser.). (ENG., Illus.). 32p. (J). (gr. 5). pap. (978-0-7787-1374-6(1)) Crabtree Publishing Co.

English Heritage Staff. My Life as a Knight. 2005. (Illus.). 32p. pap. 19.95 (978-1-85074-985-1(X)) Historic England Publishing GBR. Dist: Casemate Academic.

Firth, Rachel. Knights. (Discovering History Ser.). 48p. 2009. (YA). (gr. 3-18). 8.99 (978-0-7945-2388-6(9), Usborne) 2004. (SPA & ENG., Illus.). (J). pap. 8.95 (978-0-7945-0385-7(3), Usborne) 2004. (SPA., Illus.). (J). lib. bdg. 16.95 (978-1-58086-509-8(7)) EDC Publishing.

—Knights & Armor. Gaudenzi, Giacinto & Montgomery, Lee, illus. 2006. 95p. (J). (gr. 4-7). 17.99 (978-0-7945-1279-8(8), Usborne) EDC Publishing.

Foran, Racquel. Knights. 2013. (Great Warriors Ser.). (ENG., Illus.). 48p. (J). (gr. 4-8). pap. 18.50 (978-1-61783-774-6(1), 10806) ABDO Publishing Co.

Gilbert, Henry. King Arthur's Knights: The Tales Retold for Boys & Girls. 2004. reprint ed. pap. 1.99 (978-1-4192-2865-0(X)); pap. 27.95 (978-1-4191-2865-3(5)) Kessinger Publishing, LLC.

Gravett, Christopher. Eyewitness Knight: Explore the Lives of Medieval Mounted Warriors — From the Battlefield to the Banqu. 2015. (DK Eyewitness Ser.). (ENG., Illus.). 72p. (J). (gr. 3-7). pap. 9.99 (978-1-4654-3572-9(7), DK Children) Dorling Kindersley Publishing, Inc.

—Real Knights: Over 20 True Stories of Battle & Adventure, 1 vol. James, John, illus. 2009. (Real Adventurers Ser.). (ENG.). 48p. (J). (gr. 3-3). 25.50 (978-1-59270-034-9(9), 03f95177-8176-4480-be61-74b0cacf8f72, Cavendish Square) Cavendish Square Publishing LLC.

Hanel, Rachael. Life as a Knight: An Interactive History Adventure. 2010. (You Choose: Warriors Ser.). (ENG.). 112p. (gr. 3-4). pap. 41.70 (978-1-4296-5098-4(2), Capstone Pr.) Capstone.

Hanel, Rachel. Knights. 2007. (Fearsome Fighters Ser.). (Illus.). 48p. (J). (gr. 3-6). lib. bdg. 31.35 (978-1-58341-536-8(X)) Creative Co., The.

Hare, Christopher. Bayard the Good Knight Without Fear & Without Reproach. 2004. reprint ed. pap. 1.99 (978-1-4192-0906-2(X)) Kessinger Publishing, LLC.

Hartson, Tamara. Castles & Knights, 1 vol. 2019. (Super Explorers Ser.). (ENG., Illus.). 64p. (J). pap. 6.99 (978-1-926700-98-4(8), 3ece1447-c74b-4987-b954-428830e9150b) Blue Bike Bks. CAN. Dist: Lone Pine Publishing USA.

Hindley, J. Knights & Castles. rev. ed. 2004. (Time Traveler Ser.). (Illus.). 32p. (J). pap. 6.95 (978-0-7945-0335-2(7)) EDC Publishing.

Hindley, Judy. Knights & Castles. Wheatley, Abigail, ed. Goffe, Toni, illus. 2006. (Time Traveler Ser.). 32p. (J). (gr. 3). lib. bdg. 14.95 (978-1-58086-554-8(2)) EDC Publishing.

Hoena, Blake. Medieval Knights: Europe's Fearsome Armored Soldiers. Orban, Jaños, illus. 2019. (Graphic History: Warriors Ser.). (ENG.). 32p. (J). (gr. 3-9). pap. 7.95 (978-1-5435-5928-6(X), 139906); lib. bdg. 33.32 (978-1-5435-5501-1(2), 139374) Capstone.

Hopkins, Andrea. A Day in the Life of a Knight. 2009. (Day in the Life Ser.). 32p. (gr. 4-5). 47.90 (978-1-61511-004-9(6), PowerKids Pr.) Rosen Publishing Group, Inc., The.

—A Day in the Life of a Knight, 1 vol. Firenze, Inklink, illus. 2007. (Day in the Life Ser.: Vol. 4). (ENG.). 32p. (J). (gr. 4-5). lib. bdg. 28.93 (978-1-4042-3851-0(4), 2b49ead3-7b3f-41ec-b2d1-e5f2fbf07660) Rosen Publishing Group, Inc., The.

Hubbard, Ben. Gladiators, 1 vol. 2016. (Conquerors & Combatants Ser.). (ENG.). 224p. (YA). (gr. 9-9). lib. bdg. 56.71 (978-1-5026-2457-4(5), 4e64a503-772d-447b-aa71-b30978e0908c) Cavendish Square Publishing LLC.

Jeffrey, Gary. Knights. Spender, Nick, illus. 2014. (Graphic Medieval History Ser.). (ENG.). 48p. (J). (gr. 5-5). (978-0-7787-0398-3(3)); pap. (978-0-7787-0404-1(1)) Crabtree Publishing Co.

Knights & Warriors. 2009. (FACT ATLAS Ser.). 72p. (J). pap. 13.99 (978-0-8437-0859-2(X)) Hammond World Atlas Corp.

Lacey, Minna & Davidson, Susanna. Gladiators. Cerisier, Emmanuel, illus. 2006. (Usborne Young Reading Ser.). 64p. (J). (gr. 3-7). 8.99 (978-0-7945-1268-2(2), Usborne) EDC Publishing.

Lassieur, Allison. Medieval Knight Science: Armor, Weapons, & Siege Warfare. 2016. (Warrior Science Ser.). (ENG., Illus.). 32p. (J). (gr. 3-9). 28.65 (978-1-4914-8130-1(7), 130621, Capstone Pr.) Capstone.

Limke, Jeff. El Rey Arturo: La Espada Excalibur Desenvainada; King Arthur: Excalibur Unsheathed. 2008. pap. 52.95 (978-0-8225-9636-3(9)) Lerner Publishing Group.

Loh-Hagan, Virginia. Samurai vs. Knights. 2019. (Battle Royale: Lethal Warriors Ser.). (ENG., Illus.). 32p. (J). (gr. 4-8). lib. bdg. 32.07 (978-1-5341-4766-9(7), 213514, 45th Parallel Press) Cherry Lake Publishing.

—Samurais vs. Knights. 2019. (Battle Royale: Lethal Warriors Ser.). (ENG., Illus.). 32p. (J). (gr. 4-8). pap. 14.21 (978-1-5341-5052-2(8), 213515, 45th Parallel Press) Cherry Lake Publishing.

Macdonald, Fiona. Do You Want to Be a Medieval Knight? 2015. (Do You Want to Be... Ser.). (Illus.). 32p. (gr. 3-6). 28.50 (978-1-909645-35-6(4)) Book Hse. GBR. Dist: Black Rabbit Bks.

MacDonald, Fiona. Knights & Castles. 2009. (History Explorers Ser.). (ENG.). 24p. (J). (gr. k-2). pap. 5.95 (978-1-84696-215-8(3), TickTock Books) Octopus Publishing Group GBR. Dist: Independent Pubs. Group.

Macdonald, Fiona. Knights, Castles, & Warfare in the Middle Ages, 1 vol. 2005. (World Almanac(r) Library of the Middle Ages Ser.). (ENG., Illus.). 48p. (gr. 5-8). pap. 15.05 (978-0-8368-5904-1(9), 8bfc5058-6c7c-4392-8caf-ad75e92215cb); lib. bdg. 33.67 (978-0-8368-5895-2(6), 058d95bb-6e8e-46b3-95fd-f94a3829197d) Stevens, Gareth Publishing LLLP. (Gareth Stevens Secondary Library).

—The Medieval Chronicles: Vikings, Knights, & Castles. Antram, David, illus. 2013. 92p. (J). (978-1-4351-5067-6(8)) Barnes & Noble, Inc.

Mason, Paul. Want to Be a Knight? 2011. (ENG.). 24p. (J). pap. (978-0-7787-7867-7(3)); (gr. 3-6). (978-0-7787-7845-5(2)) Crabtree Publishing Co.

Mayer, Cassie. Knights & Castles. 2012. (Illus.). 64p. (J). pap. 12.99 (978-1-62267-007-9(8)) Bright Connections Media.

McLeese, Don. Knights. 2009. 32p. pap. 7.99 (978-0-8249-1447-9(3), Ideals Pubns.) Worthy Publishing.

Media, Cont. Knights & Castles. 2008. (ENG., Illus.). 48p. (YA). 12.99 (978-1-931703-24-6(8)) Crosby Advanced Medical Systems Inc.

Murrell, Deborah. Knights & Armor, 1 vol. 2008. (Medieval Warfare Ser.). (ENG.). 32p. (gr. 3-3). (J). lib. bdg. 28.67 (978-0-8368-9210-9(0), 70d52ad7-e696-42e3-a36b-adcd12a89f22, Gareth Stevens Secondary Library); pap. 11.50 (978-0-8368-9337-3(9), 4cf7c546-a668-4647-9ac4-ca8964c9e443) Stevens, Gareth Publishing LLLP.

Murrell, Deborah Jane & Dennis, Peter. Knight. 2012. (ENG., Illus.). 32p. (gr. 3-5). pap. 8.95 (978-1-926853-54-3(7)) Saunders Bk. Co. CAN. Dist: RiverStream Publishing.

Nishida, Masaki. Drawing Manga Medieval Castles & Knights, 1 vol. 2007. (How to Draw Manga Ser.: Vol. 4). (ENG., Illus.). 24p. (J). (gr. 3-3). lib. bdg. 28.93 (978-1-4042-3849-7(2), 86560970-7456-4bfa-8e37-b7f28ac38c76) Rosen Publishing Group, Inc., The.

O'Brian, Pliny. Knights: Warriors of the Middle Ages. 2015. (J). lib. bdg. (978-1-62713-407-1(7)) 2014. (ENG., Illus.). 48p. (gr. 4-4). 33.07 (978-1-5026-0120-9(6), 5367d25b-50fd-4353-8b6a-f566cf53e240) Cavendish Square Publishing LLC.

O'Brien, Cynthia. Your Guide to Knights & the Age of Chivalry. 2017. (Destination: Middle Ages Ser.). (ENG., Illus.). 32p. (J). (gr. 5-5). (978-0-7787-2992-1(3)); pap. (978-0-7787-2998-3(2)) Crabtree Publishing Co.

Park, Louise & Love, Timothy. The Medieval Knights, 1 vol. 2010. (Ancient & Medieval People Ser.). (ENG.). 32p. (gr. 5-5). 31.21 (978-0-7614-4444-2(0), 5b728dea-b765-41c5-bf85-20110653fc5a) Cavendish Square Publishing LLC.

Pratt, Leonie. Knights & Castles Things to Make & Do. Thompson, Josephine Et Al, illus. 2006. 32p. (J). pap. 6.99 (978-0-7945-1355-9(7), Usborne) EDC Publishing.

Pyle, Howard. The Story of the Champions of the Round Table. (ENG.). (J). 2018. 354p. 46.95 (978-0-343-80058-1(6)) 2018. 354p. pap. 29.95 (978-0-343-80057-4(8)) 2017. (Illus.). pap. 17.95 (978-1-375-49020-7(6)) 2015. (Illus.). 356p. 27.95 (978-1-296-63329-5(2)) 2015. (Illus.). 356p. 27.95 (978-1-298-65508-0(0)) Creative Media Partners, LLC.

—The Story of the Champions of the Round Table. 2004. reprint ed. pap. 28.95 (978-1-4191-8405-5(9)); pap. 1.99 (978-1-4192-8405-2(3)) Kessinger Publishing, LLC.

Riggs, Kate. Knights. 2011. (Great Warriors Ser.). (Illus.). 24p. (J). (gr. k-2). 16.95 (978-1-60818-001-1(8), Creative Education) Creative Co., The.

Shirley, Rebekah Joy. I Want to Be a Knight, 1 vol. 2011. (Let's Play Dress Up Ser.). (ENG., Illus.). 24p. (J). (gr. 2-3). pap. 11.60 (978-1-61533-392-9(4), f28889e0-cb1c-459e-9508-749f32ff1ec7, Windmill Bks.) Rosen Publishing Group, Inc., The.

Stiefel, Chana. Sweaty Suits of Armor: Could You Survive Being a Knight?, 1 vol. 2012. (Ye Yucky Middle Ages Ser.). (ENG., Illus.). 48p. (gr. 5-7). pap. 11.53 (978-1-59845-376-8(9), 2451bd9d-f80d-496c-a053-8691f17fd749); lib. bdg. 27.93 (978-0-7660-3784-7(3), 270e1703-3c3a-43fe-aecb-ac276caf6bca) Enslow Publishing, LLC.

Storey, Rita. Knights & Castles. 2013. (Have Fun with Arts & Crafts Ser.). 32p. (gr. 4-7). 31.35 (978-1-59920-899-2(7)) Black Rabbit Bks.

Taylor, Barbara. The Amazing History of Castles & Knights. 2016. (Illus.). 64p. (J). (gr. -1-12). 12.99 (978-1-86147-717-0(1), Armadillo) Anness Publishing GBR. Dist: National Bk. Network.

Terp, Gail. Knights. 2019. (History's Warriors Ser.). (ENG., Illus.). 32p. (J). (gr. 4-6). pap. 9.99 (978-1-64466-041-6(5), 12753); lib. bdg. (978-1-68072-850-7(4), 12752) Black Rabbit Bks. (Bolt).

Walker, Jane. Knights & Castles. 2013. (Illus.). 48p. (J). (978-1-4351-5093-5(7)) Barnes & Noble, Inc.

—Knights & Castles. 2015. (100 Facts Ser.). (Illus.). (J). (978-1-78209-374-9(5)) Miles Kelly Publishing, Ltd.

—100 Things You Should Know about Knights & Castles. 2008. (Illus.). 64p. (978-1-84236-002-6(7)) Miles Kelly Publishing, Ltd.

Watson, Danielle. The Castle in Medieval Europe, 1 vol. 2016. (Life in Medieval Europe Ser.). (ENG., Illus.). 80p. (gr. 6-6). 37.36 (978-1-5026-1878-8(8), 2ca93be3-fb06-4b0b-b36d-b3f30eb06bb4) Cavendish Square Publishing LLC.

Weatherly, Myra. William Marshal: Medieval England's Greatest Knight. 2004. (British Heroes Ser.). (Illus.). 112p. (YA). (gr. 6-12). 23.95 (978-1-883846-48-0(X), First Biographies) Reynolds, Morgan Inc.

West, David. Lots of Things You Want to Know about Knights. 2015. (Lots of Things You Want to Know About Ser.). (ENG., Illus.). 24p. (J). 28.50 (978-1-62588-091-8(X), 19302, Smart Apple Media) Black Rabbit Bks.

Williams, Colleen Madonna Flood. My Adventure with Knights. 2009. (ENG.). 44p. (J). 8.99 (978-1-59092-456-3(8)) Blue Forge Pr.

Woog, Adam. A Medieval Knight. 2003. (Daily Life Ser.). (ENG., Illus.). 48p. (J). (gr. 4-6). pap. 27.00 (978-0-7377-0992-6(8), Kidhaven) Cengage Gale.

World Book, Inc. Staff, contrib. by. The Age of Knights & Castles. 2011. (J). (978-0-7166-1787-7(0)) World Bk., Inc.

KNIGHTS AND KNIGHTHOOD—FICTION

Agee, Jon. The Wall in the Middle of the Book. Agee, Jon, illus. 2018. (ENG., Illus.). 48p. (J). (gr. -1-3). 18.99 (978-0-525-55545-2(5), Dial Bks) Penguin Young Readers Group.

Amery, H. & Cartwright, S. The Tournament. 2004. (First Stories Ser.). 16p. (J). pap. 4.95 (978-0-7945-0520-2(1)); lib. bdg. 12.95 (978-1-58086-571-5(2)) EDC Publishing.

Andrews, Julie & Hamilton, Emma Walton. Dragon. 2004. (Julie Andrews Collection). 192p. (J). (gr. 4-18). 16.99 (978-0-06-057119-1(5), Julie Andrews Collection) HarperCollins Pubs.

Anthony, David & David, Charles. Knightscares #4: (Knightscares) 2004. (Illus.). 208p. (J). per. 5.99 (978-0-9728461-3-4(1)) Sigil Publishing.

Banerjee, Anjali. The Silver Spell. Fiegenshuh, Emily, illus. 2005. (Knights of the Silver Dragon Ser.: Bk. 8). 174p. (J). (978-1-4156-1645-1(0), Mirrorstone) Wizards of the Coast.

Banks, Steven. Lost in Time. The Artifact Group, illus. 2006. 22p. (J). lib. bdg. 15.00 (978-1-4242-0977-4(3)) Fitzgerald Bks.

Barandela, Jeremy. United We Stand. 2007. 376p. per. 20.95 (978-1-4327-1495-6(3)) Outskirts Pr., Inc.

Barnes, Charles. Knight Light. 2006. 48p. pap. 16.95 (978-1-4241-3831-9(0)) PublishAmerica, Inc.

Beekman, Kelley Lee. Sir Eli & the Halloween Dragon: The Legend of the Toasted Marshmallow. 2006. 55p. pap. 16.95 (978-1-4241-4047-3(1)) PublishAmerica, Inc.

Bell, Hilari. The Goblin Gate. (ENG.). (YA). (gr. 8). 2011. 400p. pap. 8.99 (978-0-06-165104-5(4)) 2010. 384p. 16.99 (978-0-06-165102-1(8)) HarperCollins Pubs. (HarperTeen).

—The Goblin Wood. 2004. (Illus.). 371p. (J). (gr. 5-9). 14.65 (978-0-7569-3253-4(X)) Perfection Learning Corp.

—The Last Knight. 2007. (Knight & Rogue Ser.: 1). (ENG.). 368p. (YA). (gr. 8-12). 16.99 (978-0-06-082503-4(0), HarperTeen) HarperCollins Pubs.

—Player's Ruse. 2010. (Knight & Rogue Ser.: 3). (ENG.). 384p. (YA). (gr. 8-10). 17.99 (978-0-06-082509-6(X), HarperTeen) HarperCollins Pubs.

—Rogue's Home. 2008. (Knight & Rogue Ser.: 2). (ENG.). 432p. (YA). (gr. 8-18). 17.99 (978-0-06-082506-5(5), HarperTeen) HarperCollins Pubs.

Bellairs, John. The Secret of the Underground Room (A Johnny Dixon Mystery: Book Eight) 2011. 96p. pap. 14.95 (978-1-61756-352-2(8)) Open Road Integrated Media, Inc.

Bess, Alex Marie. The Scrapper. 2011. 188p. (J). pap. 13.95 (978-1-936184-85-9(0)) Kidpub Pr.

Bishop, Jennie. The Squire & the Scroll: A Tale of the Rewards of a Pure Heart. McDaniels, Preston, illus. 2009. (ENG.). 32p. (J). 15.99 (978-1-59317-382-1(2)) Warner Pr., Inc.

Black, Chuck. Lady Carliss & the Waters of Moorue. 2010. (Knights of Arrethtrae Ser.: 4). (ENG.). 208p. (YA). (gr. 5-7). pap. 9.99 (978-1-60142-127-2(3), Multnomah Bks.) Crown Publishing Group, The.

—Sir Bentley & Holbrook Court. 2009. (Knights of Arrethtrae Ser.: 2). (ENG., Illus.). 208p. (YA). (gr. 5-7). pap. 9.99 (978-1-60142-125-8(7), Multnomah Bks.) Crown Publishing Group, The.

—Sir Dalton & the Shadow Heart. 2009. (Knights of Arrethtrae Ser.: 3). (ENG., Illus.). 176p. (YA). (gr. 7-9). pap. 9.99 (978-1-60142-126-5(5), Multnomah Bks.) Crown Publishing Group, The.

—Sir Quinlan & the Swords of Valor. 2010. (Knights of Arrethtrae Ser.: 5). (ENG., Illus.). 208p. (YA). (gr. 4-7). pap. 9.99 (978-1-60142-128-9(1), Multnomah Bks.) Crown Publishing Group, The.

—Sir Rowan & the Camerian Conquest. 2010. (Knights of Arrethtrae Ser.: 6). (ENG., Illus.). 192p. (J). (gr. 4-7). pap. 9.99 (978-1-60142-129-6(X), Multnomah Bks.) Crown Publishing Group, The.

Black, Kat. A Templar's Apprentice. 2009. (Book of Tormod Ser.: 1). (ENG.). 288p. (J). (gr. 7-18). 17.99 (978-0-545-05654-0(3)) Scholastic, Inc.

—Templar's Apprentice, 1. 2010. (Book of Tormod Ser.: 1). (ENG.). 288p. (J). (gr. 7-12). 24.94 (978-0-545-23411-5(5)) Scholastic, Inc.

—The Book of Tormod: A Templar's Gifts. 2011. (Book of Tormod Ser.: 2). (ENG.). 272p. (YA). (gr. 7-7). 17.99 (978-0-545-05675-5(6), Scholastic Pr.) Scholastic, Inc.

Bolger, Kevin. Sir Fartsalot Hunts the Booger. Gilpin, Stephen, illus. 2009. (ENG.). 224p. (J). (gr. 4-6). 18.69 (978-1-59514-176-7(6), Razorbill) Penguin Young Readers Group.

Bowler, Michael J. Children of the Knight [Library Edition]. 2013. 344p. pap. 17.99 (978-1-62380-925-6(8), Harmony Ink Pr.) Dreamspinner Pr.

Brinker, Spencer. A Knight in a Fight. 2019. (Read & Rhyme Level 3 Ser.). (ENG., Illus.). 16p. (J). (gr. -1-1). 24.21 (978-1-64280-558-1(0)) Bearport Publishing Co., Inc.

Los Caballeros del Rey Arturo. (SPA., Illus.). (YA). 14.95 (978-84-7281-107-2(7), AF1107) Auriga, Ediciones S.A. ESP. Dist: Continental Bk. Co., Inc.

Callahan, Lauren & Callahan, Michael T. Hello, Knightro! Williams, Tim, illus. 2013. (ENG.). (J). (gr. 4-7). 14.95 (978-1-62086-169-1(0)) Amplify Publishing Group.

Cervantes, Miguel De & Brook, Henry. Don Quixote: From the Story by Miguel de Cervantes Saavedra. 2005. (Illus.). 144p. (J). pap. 4.95 (978-0-7945-0955-2(X), Usborne) EDC Publishing.

Collins, Tim. The Long-Lost Secret Diary of the World's Worst Knight. Horne, Sarah, illus. 2018. (Long-Lost Secret Diary Ser.). (ENG.). 216p. (J). (gr. 4-5). lib. bdg. 28.50 (978-1-63163-136-8(5), 1631631365, Jolly Fish Pr.) North Star Editions.

—World's Worst Knight. Horne, Sarah, illus. 2017. (Long-Lost Secret Diary Ser.). (ENG.). 216p. (J). (gr. 4-5). pap. 9.99 (978-1-63163-137-5(3), 1631631373, Jolly Fish Pr.) North Star Editions.

Comrie, Margaret S. The Heroes of Castle Bretten. 2003. (Illus.). 229p. (J). (978-1-894666-65-7(8)) Inheritance Pubns.

Coutinho, Lucy M. The Rangers of Andor: The Beginning. 2011. 278p. pap. 27.95 (978-1-4626-1014-3(5)) America Star Bks.

Cremer, Andrea. Rift. 2013. (Nightshade Novels Ser.). (ENG.). 464p. (YA). (gr. 8-12). 26.19 (978-0-399-25613-4(X)) Penguin Young Readers Group.

Crum, Shutta. Thomas & the Dragon Queen. Wildish, Lee, illus. 2013. (ENG.). 272p. (J). (gr. 4-6). 21.19 (978-0-375-85703-4(6)) Random House Publishing Group.

Davey, Owen. Night Knight. Davey, Owen, illus. 2012. (ENG., Illus.). 32p. (J). (gr. k-k). 15.99 (978-0-7636-5838-0(3), Templar) Candlewick Pr.

Davies, Katie. Knights Sticker Dressing. 2010. 24p. (J). 8.99 (978-0-7945-2891-1(0)) EDC Publishing.

Davis, Toby K. The Ever Part of Always: Keely Tucker's First Adventure. 2012. 208p. (gr. 4-6). 24.95 (978-1-4697-4592-3(5)); pap. 14.95 (978-1-4697-4591-6(7)) iUniverse, Inc.

Davis, Tony. Brand New Page, 2. Rogers, Gregory, illus. 2012. (Roland Wright Ser.). (ENG.). 144p. (J). (gr. 1-4). lib. bdg. 18.69 (978-0-385-90707-1(9), Yearling) Random Hse. Children's Bks.

—Roland Wright: at the Joust. Rogers, Gregory, illus. 2011. (Roland Wright Ser.: 3). (ENG.). 144p. (J). (gr. 1-4). 6.99 (978-0-375-87328-7(7), Yearling) Random Hse. Children's Bks.

—Roland Wright: Future Knight. Rogers, Gregory, illus. 2010. (Roland Wright Ser.: 1). (ENG.). 160p. (J). (gr. 1-4). 6.99 (978-0-385-73801-9(3), Yearling) Random Hse. Children's Bks.

de Bonneval, Gwen. William & the Lost Spirit. Bonhomme, Matthieu, illus. 2013. (ENG.). 160p. (YA). (gr. 8-12). lib. bdg. 30.65 (978-0-7613-8567-7(3), 38866c96-abfc-4e7f-9449-c6a5f12f8f1a, Graphic Universe™) Lerner Publishing Group.

Dean, James, illus. Sir Pete the Brave. 2016. 32p. (J). (978-1-5182-0881-2(9)) Harper & Row Ltd.

Denise, Christopher. Knight Owl (Caldecott Honor Book) 2022. (ENG., Illus.). 48p. (J). (gr. -1-3). 17.99 (978-0-316-31062-8(X)) Little, Brown Bks. for Young Readers.

DiTerlizzi, Tony. Kenny & the Dragon. 2008. (Playaway Children Ser.). (J). (gr. 3-7). 39.99 (978-1-60640-958-9(1)) Findaway World, LLC.

—Kenny & the Dragon. DiTerlizzi, Tony, illus. 2012. (Kenny & the Dragon Ser.). (ENG., Illus.). 176p. (J). (gr. 3-7). pap. 8.99 (978-1-4424-3651-0(4), Simon & Schuster Bks. For Young Readers) Simon & Schuster Bks. For Young Readers.

—Kenny & the Dragon. DiTerlizzi, Tony, illus. 2008. (Illus.). 160p. (J). (gr. 3-7). 15.99 Simon & Schuster Children's Publishing.

—Kenny & the Dragon. DiTerlizzi, Tony, illus. 2008. (Kenny & the Dragon Ser.). (ENG., Illus.). 160p. (J). (gr. 3-7). 17.99 (978-1-4169-3977-1(6)) Simon & Schuster, Inc.

Docherty, Helen. The Storybook Knight. Docherty, Thomas, illus. 2016. (ENG.). 32p. (J). (gr. k-4). 17.99 (978-1-4926-3814-8(5), 9781492638148, Sourcebooks Jabberwocky) Sourcebooks, Inc.

Doeden, Matt. Beauty & the Beast: An Interactive Fairy Tale Adventure. Miramon, Sabrina, illus. 2018. (You Choose: Fractured Fairy Tales Ser.). (ENG.). 112p. (J). (gr. 3-7). lib. bdg. 32.65 (978-1-5435-3007-0(9), 138604, Capstone Pr.) Capstone.

Donaldson, Julia. A Gold Star for Zog. Scheffler, Axel, illus. 2012. (ENG.). 32p. (J). (gr. -1-3). 18.99 (978-0-545-41724-2(4), Levine, Arthur A. Bks.) Scholastic, Inc.

Donnell, Annie Hamil. Three Young Knights. 2004. reprint ed. pap. 15.95 (978-1-4191-8994-4(8)) Kessinger Publishing, LLC.

Donnell, Annie Hamilton. Three Young Knights. 2004. reprint ed. pap. 1.99 (978-1-4192-8994-1(2)) Kessinger Publishing, LLC.

Dorling Kindersley Publishing Staff & Murray, Helen. Stop the Stone Monsters! 2017. (DK Reader Level 1 Ser.). lib. bdg. 13.55 (978-0-606-39896-1(1)) Turtleback.

Dormer, Frank W. The Sword in the Stove. Dormer, Frank W., illus. 2016. (ENG., Illus.). 40p. (J). (gr. -1-3). 17.99 (978-1-4814-3167-5(6)) Simon & Schuster, Inc.

Downey, Glen. Gladiators. 2007. (Illus.). 48p. (J). lib. bdg. 23.08 (978-1-4242-1627-7(3)) Fitzgerald Bks.

Dragt, Tonke. The Letter for the King (winter Edition) 2018. (ENG., Illus.). 512p. (J). (gr. 3-7). pap. 15.95 (978-1-78269-081-8(6), Pushkin Children's Bks.) Steerforth Pr.

Dube, Pierrette. How to Become a Perfect Knight in Five Days, 1 vol. Hamel, Caroline, illus. 2009. (Rainy Day Readers Ser.). (ENG.). 32p. (J). (gr. 1-2). 27.27 (978-1-60754-373-2(7), 02996f15-da64-44dc-b3db-f83cf3e00c75); pap. 11.55 (978-1-60754-374-9(5), 34ae855b-b6ea-454c-a54d-360988528e6f) Rosen Publishing Group, Inc., The. (Windmill Bks.).

Ebers, Georg. The Greylock. 2004. reprint ed. pap. 15.95 (978-1-4191-6506-1(2)); pap. 1.99 (978-1-4192-6506-8(7)) Kessinger Publishing, LLC.

Ezirim, E. C. Jet Black & the Ebony Knights. 2010. 40p. 16.99 (978-1-4520-7567-9(0)) AuthorHouse.

Fafoutakis, Anne. Enchanted Talisman & Other Stories for Children of All Ages. 2004. 132p. pap. 13.50 (978-1-84426-296-0(0)) Upfront Publishing Ltd. GBR. Dist: Printondemand-worldwide.com.

Finnegan, Delphine. The Big Birthday Surprise! Hall, Susan, illus. 2017. 24p. (J). (978-1-5182-5213-6(3)) Random Hse., Inc.

—The Big Birthday Surprise! (Nella the Princess Knight) Hall, Susan, illus. 2017. (Step into Reading Ser.). (ENG.). 24p. (J). (gr. -1-1). pap. 4.99 (978-1-5247-1688-2(X), Random Hse. Bks. for Young Readers) Random Hse. Children's Bks.

Flanagan, John. The Icebound Land. 2007. (Ranger's Apprentice Ser.: Bk. 3). 260p. (J). 25.66 (978-1-4287-4632-9(3), Follettbound) Follett School Solutions.

—The Icebound Land: Book Three, Bk. 3. 2008. (Ranger's Apprentice Ser.: 3). (ENG.). 304p. (J). (gr. 5-18). 9.99 (978-0-14-241075-2(6), Puffin Books) Penguin Young Readers Group.

Flinders, Benjamin. Excalibur: Traveling Trunk Adventure 3. 2011. (Traveling Trunk Adventure Ser.). (ENG.). 162p. (J). (gr. 2-4). 9.95 *(978-0-9843955-6-9(3))* Flinders Pr.

French, Jackie. My Dad the Dragon. King, Stephen Michael, illus. 2018. (Wacky Families Ser.: 03). (ENG.). 128p. 5.99 *(978-0-207-19950-9(7),* HarperCollins) HarperCollins Pubs.

Funke, Cornelia. Ghost Knight. 2013.Tr. of Geisterritter. (ENG., Illus.). 352p. (J). (gr. 3-7). pap. 18.99 *(978-0-316-05616-8(2))* Little, Brown Bks. for Young Readers.

Gabán, Jesús. El libro de Don Quijote para niños: Nueva edición) 2016. (SPA., Illus.). 112p. (J). (gr. 4-7). 20.95 *(978-84-16075-98-0(0),* B De Blook) Penguin Random House Grupo Editorial ESP. Dist: Penguin Random Hse. LLC.

Gashler, Stephen. The Bent Sword. 2010. (YA). pap. 15.99 *(978-1-59955-401-3(1))* Cedar Fort, Inc./CFI Distribution.

Gibbs, Stuart. Once upon a Tim. Curtis, Stacy, illus. 2022. (J). *(978-1-5344-9926-3(1));* (Once upon a Tim Ser.: 1). (ENG.). 160p. (gr. 2-5). 12.99 *(978-1-5344-9925-6(3))* Simon & Schuster Bks. For Young Readers. (Simon & Schuster Bks. For Young Readers).

Gilbert, Henry. King Arthur's Knights: The Tales Re-Told for Boys & Girls. 2017. (ENG., Illus.). (J). (gr. -1-12). 26.95 *(978-1-374-86860-1(4));* (gr. 3). pap. 16.95 *(978-1-374-86859-5(0))* Capital Communications, Inc.

—King Arthur's Knights: The Tales Retold for Boys & Girls. 2016. (ENG., Illus.). (J). (gr. 3). 28.95 *(978-1-358-28787-9(2))* Creative Media Partners, LLC.

Gilman, Laura Anne. The Camelot Spell. 2006. (Grail Quest Ser.: No. 1). 291p. (J). (gr. 5-9). 10.99 *(978-0-06-077279-6(4))* HarperCollins Pubs.

Graham, Denise R. Curse of the Lost Grove. 2005. (Knights of the Silver Dragon Ser.: Bk. 10). (Illus.). 177p. (J). *(978-1-4156-3841-5(1),* Mirrorstone) Wizards of the Coast.

Grahame, Kenneth. The Reluctant Dragon (Illustrated Edition) 2015. (ENG., Illus.). 42p. pap. *(978-1-5154-0330-2(0),* Illustrated Bks.) Jorge Pinto Bks.

Grant, K. M. Blaze of Silver, 3. 2008. (De Granville Trilogy Ser.). (ENG.). 261p. (YA). (gr. 6-8). 22.44 *(978-0-8027-9625-7(7),* 9780802796257) Walker & Co.

—Blood Red Horse. 2006. (DeGranville Trilogy Ser.: 1). (ENG.). 320p. (YA). (gr. 5-9). pap. 10.99 *(978-0-8027-7734-8(1),* 900039395, Bloomsbury USA Childrens) Bloomsbury Publishing USA.

Haack, Daniel. Prince & Knight. Lewis, Stevie, illus. 2018. (ENG.). 40p. (J). (gr. -1-3). 17.99 *(978-1-4998-0552-9(7))* Little Bee Books Inc.

Haberdasher, Violet. Knightley Academy. 2011. (ENG.). 512p. (J). (gr. 3-7). pap. 5.99 *(978-1-4169-9144-1(1),* Aladdin) Simon & Schuster Children's Publishing.

—Knightley Academy. 2010. (ENG.). 480p. (J). (gr. 3-7). 16.99 *(978-1-4169-9143-4(3),* Simon & Schuster/Paula Wiseman Bks.) Simon & Schuster/Paula Wiseman Bks.

—The Secret Prince: A Knightley Academy Book. (ENG.). 512p. (J). (gr. 3-7). 2012. pap. 7.99 *(978-1-4169-9146-5(8))* 2011. 16.99 *(978-1-4169-9145-8(X))* Simon & Schuster/Paula Wiseman Bks. (Simon & Schuster/Paula Wiseman Bks.).

Hall, Frank. The Prince Who Did Not Want to be King. 2011. 132p. 28.95 *(978-1-4497-1440-6(4));* (J). pap. 11.95 *(978-1-4497-1438-3(2))* Author Solutions, LLC. (WestBow Pr.).

Harvey, Damian & Remphry, Martin. Robin & the Friar. 2009. (Hopscotch Adventures Ser.). (Illus.). 31p. (J). (gr. 1). lib. bdg. 25.65 *(978-1-59771-177-7(2))* Sea-To-Sea Pubns.

Hedlund, Jody. A Daring Sacrifice, 1 vol. 2016. (ENG.). 224p. (YA). pap. 12.99 *(978-0-310-74937-0(9))* Zondervan.

—An Uncertain Choice, 1 vol. 2015. (ENG.). 256p. (YA). pap. 12.99 *(978-0-310-74919-6(0))* Zondervan.

Hemingway, Mike. The Legend of Vysallimore. 2010. 72p. pap. 28.00 *(978-1-4520-5648-7(X))* AuthorHouse.

Hensley, Judith Victoria. Sir Thomas the Eggslayer. 2008. 156p. pap. 14.95 *(978-0-9795103-8-0(4))* Ascended Ideas.

Henty, George. At Agincourt: A Tale of the White Hoods of Paris. 2011. 332p. pap. 19.95 *(978-1-61179-111-2(1))* Fireship Pr.

Hightman, Jason. The Saint of Dragons. 2004. 304p. (J). (gr. 7-18). (ENG.). 16.99 *(978-0-06-054011-1(7));* lib. bdg. 17.89 *(978-0-06-054012-8(5))* HarperCollins Pubs.

Hill, Kevin Kelvin. The Red Baron, the Knight of Many Talents. 2009. 40p. pap. 20.99 *(978-1-4490-0642-6(6))* AuthorHouse.

HIT Entertainment Staff. Meet Mike! 2013. (Mike the Knight Ser.). (ENG.). 24p. (J). (gr. -1-1). 16.19 *(978-1-4424-7429-1(7),* Simon Spotlight) Simon & Schuster Children's Publishing.

Hoena, Blake. The Not-So-Helpless Princess. Cunyat, Pol, illus. 2016. (Thud & Blunder Ser.). (ENG.). 56p. (J). (gr. 1-3). lib. bdg. 23.99 *(978-1-4965-3218-3(X),* 132413, Stone Arch Bks.) Capstone.

Hoffman, Mary. Women of Camelot: Queens & Enchantresses at the Court of King Arthur. Balit, Christina, illus. 2006. 69p. (YA). (gr. 5-9). 20.00 *(978-1-4223-5260-1(9))* DIANE Publishing Co.

Holub, Joan. The Knights Before Christmas. Magoon, Scott, illus. 2015. (ENG.). 32p. (J). (gr. k-3). 16.99 *(978-0-8050-9932-4(8),* 900126311, Holt, Henry & Co. Bks. For Young Readers) Holt, Henry & Co.

Howard, Cheryl L. Mikhael the Mighty: Be True to Who You Are & You Can Never Go Wrong. 2009. 52p. pap. 18.50 *(978-1-60860-760-0(7),* Strategic Bk. Publishing) Strategic Book Publishing & Rights Agency (SBPRA).

Hulme-Cross, Benjamin. The Knight's Enemies. Rinaldi, Angelo, illus. 2015. (Warrior Heroes Ser.). (ENG.). 160p. (J). (gr. 6-6). *(978-0-7787-1765-2(8))* Crabtree Publishing Co.

Jenkins, Amanda & Reeves, Tara McClary. The Knight & the Firefly: A Boy, a Bug, & a Lesson in Bravery. Fernandez, Daniel, illus. 2017. (Firefly Chronicles Ser.). (ENG.). 32p. (J). (gr. -1-3). pap. 3.99 *(978-1-4627-4519-7(9),* 005793882, B&H Kids) B&H Publishing Group.

Kimmelman, Leslie. The Eight Knights of Hanukkah. Bernstein, Galia, illus. 2020. 48p. (J). (gr. -1-3). 17.99 *(978-0-8234-3958-4(5))* Holiday Hse., Inc.

Kingsbury, Karen. The Brave Young Knight, 1 vol. Grimard, Gabrielle, illus. 2011. (ENG.). 40p. (J). (gr. -1-2). 15.99 *(978-0-310-71645-7(4))* Zonderkidz.

—The Princess & the Three Knights, 1 vol. Grimard, Gabrielle, illus. 2009. (ENG.). 40p. (J). (gr. -1-2). 15.99 *(978-0-310-71641-9(1))* Zonderkidz.

Kirkman, Robert. Marvel Knights 2099. 2005. (Marvel Heroes Ser.). (Illus.). 120p. (YA). pap. 13.99 *(978-0-7851-1613-4(3))* Marvel Worldwide, Inc.

Knights. (Awesome Adventures Ser.). 16p. (J). *(978-2-7643-0120-3(0))* Phidal Publishing, Inc./Editions Phidal, Inc.

Koller, Jackie French & Köller. Horace the Horrible: A Knight Meets His Match, 1 vol. Urbanovic, Jackie, illus. 2003. (ENG.). 32p. (J). 16.95 *(978-0-7614-5150-1(1))* Marshall Cavendish Corp.

Kraegel, Kenneth. King Arthur's Very Great Grandson. Kraegel, Kenneth, illus. 2012. (ENG., Illus.). 40p. (J). (gr. k-3). 16.99 *(978-0-7636-5311-8(X))* Candlewick Pr.

Ladybird. The Red Knight. 2016. (Ladybird Readers Ser.). (Illus.). 64p. (J). (gr. 2-4). pap. 9.99 *(978-0-241-25384-7(5))* Penguin Bks., Ltd. GBR. Dist: Independent Pubs. Group.

Lang, Andrew. The Red Romance Book; Tales of Knights. 2006. 396p. per. *(978-1-84664-477-1(1),* Obscure Pr.) Read Bks.

Lang, Andrew & Ford, H. J. The Tale of the Cid: And Other Stories of Knights & Chivalry. Ford, H. J., illus. 2007. (Dover Children's Classics Ser.). (ENG., Illus.). 208p. (J). (gr. 4-7). per. 9.95 *(978-0-486-45470-2(3),* 454703) Dover Pubns., Inc.

Leung, Julie. Mice of the Round Table #1: a Tail of Camelot. Carr, Lindsey, illus. 2016. (Mice of the Round Table Ser.: 1). (ENG.). 304p. (J). (gr. 3-7). 16.99 *(978-0-06-240399-5(0),* HarperCollins) HarperCollins Pubs.

Limke, Jeff. King Arthur: Excalibur Unsheathed [an English Legend]. Yeates, Thomas, illus. 2007. (Graphic Myths & Legends Ser.). (ENG.). 48p. (J). (gr. 4-8). per. 9.99 *(978-0-8225-6483-6(1),* 85571467-04bb-430e-96a6-246adebaa4c9, Graphic Universe™) Lerner Publishing Group.

—El Rey Arturo: La Espada Excalibur Desenvainada: Una Leyenda Inglesa. Translations.com Staff, tr. from ENG. Yeates, Thomas, illus. 2007. (Mitos y leyendas en viñetas (Graphic Myths & Legends) Ser.).Tr. of King Arthur - Excalibur Unsheathed [An English Legend. (SPA.). 48p. (J). (gr. 4-8). per. 8.95 *(978-0-8225-7968-7(5))* Lerner Publishing Group.

Lochran, Steven. The Riders of Thunder Realm, Volume 1. 2018. (Paladero Ser.: 1). (ENG.). 320p. (J). (gr. 5-7). pap. 9.99 *(978-1-76012-470-0(2))* Hardie Grant Children?s Publishing AUS. Dist: Independent Pubs. Group.

Lowenstein, Sallie, illus. Sir Kyle & Lady Madeline. Lowenstein, Sallie, . 2007. 32p. (J). 18.95 *(978-0-9658486-6-4(3))* Lion Stone Bks.

Lucado, Max. The Song of the King (Redesign) Gillies, Chuck, illus. 2014. (ENG.). 32p. (J). 17.99 *(978-1-4335-4290-9(0))* Crossway.

Macgregor, Kinley, pseud & Furth, Robin. Knight of Darkness. 2010. (Lords of Avalon Ser.: Bk. 2). (Illus.). 144p. pap. 14.99 *(978-0-7851-2769-7(0))* Marvel Worldwide, Inc.

March, Julia. Meet the Knights. 2016. (DK Reader Level 2 Ser.). lib. bdg. 13.55 *(978-0-606-38227-4(5))* Turtleback.

—Monster Battles. 2016. (Illus.). 63p. (J). *(978-1-5182-1852-1(0))* Dorling Kindersley Publishing, Inc.

Marcotte, Jennifer. The Nightly Knight. 2009. 28p. pap. 14.99 *(978-1-4490-1943-3(9))* AuthorHouse.

Marks, Alan, illus. The Stories of Knights. 2004. (Young Reading Series One Ser.). 48p. (J). (gr. 2-18). pap. 5.95 *(978-0-7945-0755-8(7),* Usborne) EDC Publishing.

Martin, George R. R. & Avery, Ben. The Sworn Sword: The Graphic Novel, 0 vols. Miller, Mike S., illus. 2014. (Game of Thrones Ser.: 2). (ENG.). 184p. pap. 14.95 *(978-1-4778-4929-3(7),* 9781477849293, Jet City Comics) Amazon Publishing.

Matthews, John. The Barefoot Book of Knights. Manna, Giovanni, illus. 2009. (ENG.). 80p. (J). 19.99 *(978-1-84686-307-3(4))* Barefoot Bks., Inc.

—Knights. Manna, Giovanni, illus. 2014. (Barefoot Bks.). 79p. (J). (gr. 3-6). 15.99 *(978-1-78285-165-3(8))* Barefoot Bks., Inc.

Matthews, John & Matthe, John. Arthur of Albion. Tatarnikau, Pavel, illus. 2008. 96p. (J). (gr. 3-6). 24.99 *(978-1-84686-049-2(0))* Barefoot Bks., Inc.

Mayer, Mercer. The Bravest Knight. 2007. (Illus.). 32p. (J). (gr. -1-3). 17.99 *(978-0-8037-3206-3(6),* Dial Bks) Penguin Young Readers Group.

Mayhew, James. The Knight Who Took All Day. 2018. (ENG., Illus.). 32p. (J). (gr. k-2). pap. 13.99 *(978-1-912050-45-1(5))* Graffeg Limited GBR. Dist: Independent Pubs. Group.

McCarthy, Cory & Capetta, A. R. Once & Future. (ENG.). (YA). (gr. 9-17). 2020. 384p. pap. 10.99 *(978-0-316-44926-7(1))* 2019. 368p. 18.99 *(978-0-316-44927-4(X))* Little Brown & Co. (Jimmy Patterson).

McKee, David. Mr. Benn: Red Knight. 2011. (ENG., Illus.). 48p. (J). (gr. -1-3). 14.50 *(978-1-85437-990-0(9))* Tate Publishing, Ltd. GBR. Dist: Abrams, Inc.

McMullan, Kate. Knight for a Day #5, 5. Basso, Bill, illus. 2003. (Dragon Slayers' Academy Ser.: 5). (ENG.). 112p. (J). (gr. 2-5). 5.99 *(978-0-448-43277-9(3),* Grosset & Dunlap) Penguin Young Readers Group.

—Sir Lancelot, Where Are You? #6, 6. Basso, Bill, illus. 2003. (Dragon Slayers' Academy Ser.: 6). (ENG.). 112p. (J). (gr. 2-5). 5.99 *(978-0-448-43278-6(1),* Grosset & Dunlap) Penguin Young Readers Group.

Memling, Carl. The Sword in the Stone (Disney) RH Disney, illus. 2015. (Little Golden Book Ser.). (ENG.). 24p. (J). (-k). 5.99 *(978-0-7364-3374-7(0),* Golden/Disney) Random Hse. Children's Bks.

Milbourne, Anna. Stories of Knights & Castles. Doherty, Gillian, ed. Marks, Alan, illus. 2007. (Stories for Young Children Ser.). 96p. (J). 16.99 *(978-0-7945-1466-2(9),* Usborne) EDC Publishing.

Miles, Colin. Naughty Nicky & the Good Ship Oggy. Miles, Gail, illus. 2013. 24p. pap. *(978-1-909202-16-0(9))* Little Acorns Publishing.

Mohler, Marie. The Knight & His Armored Heart. 2008. (ENG.). 40p. pap. 18.95 *(978-1-4357-4572-8(8))* Lulu Pr., Inc.

Moore, Shawn. Sam & the Tale of the Dragon Prints. Baker, David, illus. 2011. 28p. pap. 24.95 *(978-1-4560-7724-2(4))* America Star Bks.

Morris, Gerald. The Adventures of Sir Balin the Ill-Fated. Renier, Aaron, illus. 2013. (Knights' Tales Ser.: 4). (ENG.). 112p. (J). (gr. 1-4). pap. 6.99 *(978-0-544-10488-4(9),* 1540796, Clarion Bks.) HarperCollins Pubs.

—The Adventures of Sir Gawain the True, 3. Renier, Aaron, illus. 2013. (Knights' Tales Ser.: 3). (ENG.). 128p. (J). (gr. 2-4). 21.19 *(978-0-547-41855-1(8))* Houghton Mifflin Harcourt Publishing Co.

—The Adventures of Sir Givret the Short. Renier, Aaron, illus. 2009. (Knights' Tales Ser.: 2). (ENG.). 112p. (J). (gr. 1-4). pap. 8.95 *(978-0-547-24818-9(0),* 1100708, Clarion Bks.) HarperCollins Pubs.

—The Ballad of Sir Dinadan. 2008. (Squire's Tales Ser.: 5). (ENG.). 256p. (J). (gr. 5-7). pap. 15.95 *(978-0-547-01473-9(2),* 1031086, Clarion Bks.) HarperCollins Pubs.

—The Legend of the King. 2010. (Squire's Tales Ser.: 10). (ENG.). 304p. (YA). (gr. 5-7). 16.99 *(978-0-547-14420-7(2),* 1050377, Clarion Bks.) HarperCollins Pubs.

—The Lioness & Her Knight. 2008. (Squire's Tales Ser.: 7). (ENG.). 352p. (J). (gr. 5-7). pap. 19.99 *(978-0-547-01485-2(6),* 1031103, Clarion Bks.) HarperCollins Pubs.

—The Princess, the Crone, & the Dung-Cart Knight. 2008. (Squire's Tales Ser.: 6). (ENG.). 320p. (J). (gr. 5-7). pap. 7.99 *(978-0-547-01480-7(5),* 1031094, Clarion Bks.) HarperCollins Pubs.

—The Quest of the Fair Unknown. 2008. (Squire's Tales Ser.: 8). (ENG.). 272p. (J). (gr. 5-7). pap. 15.99 *(978-0-547-01484-5(8),* 1031100, Clarion Bks.) HarperCollins Pubs.

—The Squire's Tale. 2008. (Squire's Tales Ser.: 1). (ENG.). 224p. (J). (gr. 5-7). pap. 7.99 *(978-0-618-73743-7(X),* 410325, Clarion Bks.) HarperCollins Pubs.

Mortensen, Erik. Sir Cook, the Knight? Harrison, Laura, illus. 2008. *(978-0-9782026-5-1(1))* Crackjaw Publishing.

Moss, Barbara E. The Adventures of Sir Goblin, the Feline Knight. Houx, Emily Marie Cornell du, illus. 2009. 336p. pap. 15.95 *(978-1-882190-03-4(3))* Solon Ctr. for Research & Publishing.

Moxilada, J. L. Jonty Jones Takes Guard. 2005. 242p. pap. 16.88 *(978-1-4116-4126-6(4))* Lulu Pr., Inc.

Murray, Helen. Stop the Stone Monsters! 2017. (Illus.). 24p. (J). *(978-1-5182-3635-8(9))* Dorling Kindersley Publishing, Inc.

Muschla, Gary Robert. Crusader. 2006. (YA). pap. *(978-0-88092-491-7(8))* Royal Fireworks Publishing Co.

—The Sword & the Cross. 2009. (YA). lib. bdg. *(978-0-88092-471-9(3))* Royal Fireworks Publishing Co.

Nunes, Rachel Ann. The Secret of the King. Ward, Jay Bryant, illus. 2005. 32p. (J). (gr. -1-3). 17.95 *(978-1-59038-241-7(2),* Shadow Mountain) Shadow Mountain Publishing.

Oceanak, Karla. Kerfuffle: An Aldo Zelnick Comic Novel. Spanjer, Kendra, illus. 2016. (Aldo Zelnick Comic Novel Ser.: 11). (ENG.). 160p. (J). (gr. 1-8). pap. 8.95 *(978-1-934649-75-6(9))* Bailiwick Pr.

Oladokun, Alexander. Acrux Manor: The Prodigal's Curse (Hardcover) 2013. (ENG.). 204p. 28.50 *(978-1-300-68651-4(0))* Lulu Pr., Inc.

Osborn, Kelly. The Green Knight. 2006. 64p. pap. 19.95 *(978-1-4241-1741-3(0))* America Star Bks.

Osborne, Mary Pope. El Caballero Del Alba. 2004. (Casa del Arbol Ser.: 2). (SPA.). (J). pap. 6.99 *(978-1-930332-50-8(5))* Lectorum Pubns., Inc.

—The Knight at Dawn. unabr. ed. 2004. (Magic Tree House Ser.: No. 2). 66p. (J). (gr. k-3). pap. 17.00 incl. audio *(978-0-8072-0331-6(9),* Listening Library) Random Hse. Audio Publishing Group.

Peirce, Lincoln. Max & the Midknights. 2019. (Max & the Midknights Ser.: 1). (Illus.). 288p. (J). (gr. 3-7). 13.99 *(978-1-101-93108-0(6),* Crown Books For Young Readers) Random Hse. Children's Bks.

—Max & the Midknights: Battle of the Bodkins. 2020. (Max & the Midknights Ser.: 2). (ENG., Illus.). 272p. (J). (gr. 3-7). 13.99 *(978-0-593-12590-8(8));* E-Book *(978-0-593-12592-2(4))* Random Hse. Children's Bks. (Crown Books For Young Readers).

—Max & the Midknights: the Tower of Time. 2022. (Illus.). 262p. (J). *(978-0-593-37792-5(3))* Bantam Doubleday Dell Large Print Group, Inc.

—Max & the Midknights: the Tower of Time. 2022. (Max & the Midknights Ser.: 3). (Illus.). 272p. (J). (gr. 3-7). 13.99 *(978-0-593-37789-5(3),* Crown Books For Young Readers) Random Hse. Children's Bks.

Perkins, John. Perceval: King Arthur's Knight of the Holy Grail, 1 vol. Spirin, Gennady, illus. 2007. (ENG.). 40p. (J). (gr. 3-7). 16.99 *(978-0-7614-5339-0(3))* Marshall Cavendish Corp.

Phelan, Matt. Knights vs. Dinosaurs. Phelan, Matt, illus. (ENG., Illus.). (J). (gr. 3-7). 2019. 176p. pap. 7.99 *(978-0-06-268624-4(0))* 2018. 160p. 16.99 *(978-0-06-268623-7(2))* HarperCollins Pubs. (Greenwillow Bks.).

—Knights vs. Monsters. Phelan, Matt, illus. 2019. (ENG., Illus.). 176p. (J). (gr. 3-7). 16.99 *(978-0-06-268626-8(7),* Greenwillow Bks.) HarperCollins Pubs.

Pierce, Tamora. Alanna: The First Adventure, 1. Heyer, illus. 2011. (Song of the Lioness Ser.: Bk. 1). (ENG.). 240p. (J). (gr. 7-12). 26.19 *(978-0-689-85323-4(8))* Simon & Schuster, Inc.

—In the Hand of the Goddess. (Song of the Lioness Ser.: 2). (ENG., Illus.). (YA). (gr. 7). 2014. 288p. 21.99 *(978-1-4814-3960-2(X))* 2011. 256p. pap. 12.99 *(978-1-4424-2764-8(7))* Simon & Schuster Children's Publishing. (Atheneum Bks. for Young Readers).

—Lioness Rampant. 2011. (Song of the Lioness Ser.: 4). (ENG., Illus.). 368p. (YA). (gr. 7). pap. 12.99 *(978-1-4424-2766-2(3),* Atheneum Bks. for Young Readers) Simon & Schuster Children's Publishing.

—The Woman Who Rides Like a Man. (Song of the Lioness Ser.: 3). (ENG., Illus.). (YA). (gr. 7). 2014. 288p. 22.99 *(978-1-4814-3962-6(6))* 2011. 272p. pap. 12.99 *(978-1-4424-2765-5(5))* Simon & Schuster Children's Publishing. (Atheneum Bks. for Young Readers).

Pontacoloni, Edward. The Adventures of Firstyr the Younger Knight Errata of Cort: Bed Time Stories for First Year Lawyers. 2008. (ENG.). 36p. per. 15.99 *(978-1-4257-6527-9(0))* Xlibris Corp.

Pyle, Ernie Howard. Men of Iron. 2005. 272p. 28.95 *(978-1-4218-0617-4(7),* 1st World Library - Literary Society) 1st World Publishing, Inc.

Pyle, Howard. Men of Iron. (ENG.). (J). 2019. 366p. (gr. 3-7). 27.95 *(978-0-530-75856-5(3),* Wentworth Pr.) 2019. 366p. (gr. 3-7). pap. 17.95 *(978-0-530-75855-8(5),* Wentworth Pr.) 2018. (Illus.). 368p. pap. 17.95 *(978-1-376-43690-7(6))* 2018. (Illus.). 394p. pap. 17.95 *(978-1-378-60148-8(3))* Creative Media Partners, LLC.

—Men of Iron. (ENG.). (J). (gr. 3-7). 2019. 384p. pap. 16.99 *(978-1-6989-2230-0(2))* 2019. 384p. pap. 15.99 *(978-1-7016-2605-8(5))* 2019. 384p. pap. 22.99 *(978-1-6898-0524-7(2))* 2019. 420p. pap. 29.99 *(978-1-6932-0510-1(6))* 2019. 318p. pap. 21.99 *(978-1-0865-6092-3(2))* 2019. 280p. pap. 16.99 *(978-1-0896-7342-2(6))* 2019. 666p. pap. 41.99 *(978-1-0816-8933-9(1))* 2019. 204p. pap. 16.99 *(978-1-0803-8632-1(7))* 2019. 666p. pap. 37.99 *(978-1-0828-3193-5(X))* 2019. 420p. pap. 21.99 *(978-1-0774-2791-4(3))* 2019. 418p. pap. 26.99 *(978-1-0779-9401-0(X))* 2019. 666p. pap. 37.99 *(978-1-0728-7603-8(5))* 2019. 318p. pap. 17.99 *(978-1-0730-0672-4(7))* 2019. 418p. pap. 26.99 *(978-1-0753-6850-9(2))* 2019. 666p. pap. 37.99 *(978-1-0772-0476-8(0))* 2019. 382p. pap. 22.99 *(978-1-0711-0725-6(9))* 2019. 280p. pap. 16.99 *(978-1-0968-7665-6(5))* 2019. 204p. pap. 15.99 *(978-1-0706-0834-1(3))* 2019. 420p. pap. 24.99 *(978-1-0996-9490-5(6))* 2019. 670p. pap. 38.99 *(978-1-0986-2296-1(0))* 2019. 382p. pap. 22.99 *(978-1-0931-1736-3(2))* 2019. 384p. pap. 22.99 *(978-1-0933-5985-5(4))* 2019. 420p. pap. 24.99 *(978-1-0955-3299-7(5))* 2019. 418p. pap. 25.99 *(978-1-0912-0742-4(9))* 2019. 384p. pap. 24.99 *(978-1-0905-0124-0(2))* 2019. 420p. pap. 24.99 *(978-1-7969-0412-3(0))* 2018. 384p. pap. 23.99 *(978-1-7917-2949-3(5))* 2018. (Illus.). 222p. pap. 8.99 *(978-1-7903-0534-6(9))* Independently Published.

—The Men of Iron. 2019. (ENG.). 310p. (J). (gr. 3-7). pap. *(978-0-359-78679-4(0))* Lulu Pr., Inc.

—Men of Iron. unabr. ed. 2003. (Dover Children's Classics Ser.). (ENG.). 192p. (J). (gr. 3-8). pap. 10.95 *(978-0-486-42841-3(9),* 428419) Dover Pubns., Inc.

—The Story of King Arthur & His Knights. 2006. (ENG., Illus.). 416p. (gr. 12-18). 6.95 *(978-0-451-53024-0(1),* Signet) Penguin Publishing Group.

—The Story of Sir Lancelot & His Companions. 2004. reprint ed. pap. 27.95 *(978-1-4179-5609-8(7))* Kessinger Publishing, LLC.

Quinn, Jordan. Let the Games Begin! McPhillips, Robert, illus. 2015. (Kingdom of Wrenly Ser.: 7). (ENG.). 128p. (J). (gr. k-4). pap. 6.99 *(978-1-4814-2379-3(7),* Little Simon) Little Simon.

—The Sorcerer's Shadow. McPhillips, Robert, illus. 2017. (Kingdom of Wrenly Ser.: 12). (ENG.). 128p. (J). (gr. k-4). 17.99 *(978-1-5344-0000-9(1));* pap. 6.99 *(978-1-4814-9999-6(8))* Little Simon. (Little Simon).

—The Thirteenth Knight. McPhillips, Robert, illus. 2018. (Kingdom of Wrenly Ser.: 13). (ENG.). 128p. (J). (gr. k-4). 17.99 *(978-1-5344-1275-0(1));* pap. 6.99 *(978-1-5344-1274-3(3))* Little Simon. (Little Simon).

Ransom, Candice. Key to the Griffon's Lair. Fiegenshuh, Emily, illus. 2005. (Knights of the Silver Dragon Ser.: Bk. 9). 182p. (J). *(978-1-4156-3032-7(1),* Mirrorstone) Wizards of the Coast.

Read, Leon. George the Knight. 2011. (Tadpoles Ser.: No. 32). (ENG., Illus.). 24p. (J). (gr. k-3). pap. *(978-0-7787-0589-5(7))* Crabtree Publishing Co.

Reed, Janet. Brave Dave & the Dragons. Fraser, Kara-Anne, illus. 2009. 12p. (J). *(978-0-545-16142-8(8))* Scholastic, Inc.

REID, D. H. Fantasies & Dreams. 2008. 208p. pap. 18.95 *(978-0-557-01592-4(8))* Lulu Pr., Inc.

Remsburg, Rebecca. Night, Night, Knight, 1 vol. 2009. 19p. pap. 24.95 *(978-1-60836-942-3(0))* America Star Bks.

Rice, Morgan. A Grant of Arms. 2013. 238p. pap. 14.99 *(978-1-939416-61-2(2))* Morgan Rice Bks.

—A Land of Fire. 2014. 196p. 26.99 *(978-1-939416-87-2(6))* Morgan Rice Bks.

—A Land of Fire (Book #12 in the Sorcerer's Ring) 2014. 196p. (YA). pap. 15.99 *(978-1-939416-86-5(8),* Morgan Rice) Morgan Rice Bks.

—Night of the Bold (Kings & Sorcerers — Book 6) 2016. (ENG., Illus.). 126p. (J). pap. 12.99 *(978-1-63291-497-2(2),* Morgan Rice) Morgan Rice Bks.

—A Quest of Heroes. 2012. (Sorcerer's Ring Ser.: Bk. 1). (ENG.). 348p. (YA). 22.99 *(978-1-939416-21-6(3));* pap. 10.99 *(978-1-939416-20-9(5))* Morgan Rice Bks.

—A Reign of Steel (Book #11 in the Sorcerer's Ring) 2014. 216p. (YA). pap. 15.99 *(978-1-939416-76-6(0),* Morgan Rice) Morgan Rice Bks.

—A Rite of Swords. 2013. 266p. 25.99 *(978-1-939416-58-2(2));* pap. 14.99 *(978-1-939416-57-5(4))* Morgan Rice Bks.

—A Rule of Queens (Book #13 in the Sorcerer's Ring) 2014. 238p. (YA). pap. 15.99 *(978-1-939416-92-6(2),* Morgan Rice) Morgan Rice Bks.

—A Vow of Glory. 2013. (Sorcerer's Ring Ser.: Bk. 5). 274p. pap. 13.99 *(978-1-939416-28-5(0))* Morgan Rice Bks.

Richards, C. E., illus. King Arthur. 2010. (Classic Fiction Ser.). 72p. 4.75 *(978-1-4342-2603-7(4),* Stone Arch Bks.) Capstone.

Roche, Art. The Knights of Boo'Gar. 2017. (ENG., Illus.). 176p. (J). pap. 9.99 *(978-1-4494-7987-9(1))* Andrews McMeel Publishing.

Rovetch, L. Bob & Whitman, Emily. Sir Henry, the Polite Knight. Barnard, Bryn, illus. 2006. (J). *(978-1-58987-204-2(5))* Kindermusik International.

Rowley, Melissa. The Falcon Shield. 2009. (J). 6.99 *(978-1-60641-103-2(9))* Deseret Bk. Co.

Rowley, M'lin. Knights of Right, BK 4: The Fiery Gloves. 2010. 80p. (J). pap. 6.99 *(978-1-60641-241-1(8),* Shadow Mountain) Shadow Mountain Publishing.

—The Silver Coat. 2009. (Knights of Right Ser.: Bk. 2). 71p. (J). (gr. 1-5). pap. 6.99 *(978-1-60641-104-9(7),* Shadow Mountain) Shadow Mountain Publishing.

Rowleym'Lin. Knights of Right, BK 3: The Warrior's Guard. 2010. 80p. (J). pap. 6.99 (978-1-60641-240-4(X), Shadow Mountain) Shadow Mountain Publishing.

Royde-Smith, N. G. Una and the Red Cross Knight & Other T. 2006. (Illus.). pap. 28.95 (978-1-4254-8407-1(7)) Kessinger Publishing, LLC.

Rudden, Dave. The Endless King. 2018. (J). (978-0-553-52305-8(8)) Random Hse., Inc.

—The Forever Court (Knights of the Borrowed Dark, Book 2) 2017. (Knights of the Borrowed Dark Ser.: 2). (ENG.). 432p. (J). (gr. 5). 16.99 (978-0-553-52301-0(5), Random Hse. Bks. for Young Readers) Random Hse. Children's Bks.

Santore, Charles. William the Curious: Knight of the Water Lilies: the Classic Edition. 2014. (Charles Santore Children's Classics Ser.). (ENG., Illus.). 44p. (J). (gr. -1). 16.95 (978-1-60433-474-6(6)) Cider Mill Pr. Bk. Pubs., LLC.

Schurch, Maylan. The Sword of Denis Anwyck. 2009. (J). pap. 10.99 (978-0-8280-2425-9(1)) Review & Herald Publishing Assn.

Scieszka, Jon. Knights of the Kitchen Table. (Time Warp Trio Ser.: No. 1). 55p. (J). (gr. 2-4). pap. 3.99 (978-0-8072-1301-8(2), Listening Library) Random Hse. Audio Publishing Group.

Scott, Walter. Ivanhoe. 2017. (ENG., Illus.). (J). pap. 21.95 (978-1-374-90171-1(7)) Capital Communications, Inc.

Scott, Walter, ed. Ivanhoe. (SPA., Illus.). 176p. (YA). 14.95 (978-84-7281-096-9(8), AF1096) Auriga, Ediciones S.A. ESP. Dist: Continental Bk. Co., Inc.

—Ivanhoe. 2008. (Bring the Classics to Life Ser.). (Illus.). 72p. (gr. 5-12). pap., act. bk. ed. 10.95 (978-1-55576-099-1(6), EDN506B) EDCON Publishing Group.

Shapiro D., Brian. Plaquetooth. 2008. 28p. pap. 13.99 (978-1-4343-8913-8(8)) AuthorHouse.

Simon, Elizabeth. Tyler Adams & the Adventures of Bravura: the First Quest. 2009. (ENG.). 49p. pap. 19.95 (978-0-557-06290-4(X)) Lulu Pr., Inc.

Sleiman, Dina L. Chivalrous. 2015. (Valiant Hearts Ser.: 2). (ENG.). 360p. (YA). pap. 16.00 (978-0-7642-1313-7(X)) Bethany Hse. Pubs.

—Courageous. 2016. (Valiant Hearts Ser.: 3). (ENG.). 362p. (YA). pap. 16.00 (978-0-7642-1314-4(8)) Bethany Hse. Pubs.

Sperring, Mark. Princess Scallywag & the Brave, Brave Knight. Powell, Claire, illus. 2019. (ENG.). 32p. (J). pap. 6.99 (978-0-00-832597-8(9), HarperCollins Children's Bks.) HarperCollins Pubs. Ltd. GBR. Dist: HarperCollins Pubs.

Spinner, Stephanie. Damosel: In Which the Lady of the Lake Renders a Frank & Often Startling Account of Her Wondrous Life & Times. 2010. (ENG.). 208p. (YA). (gr. 7-12). lib. bdg. 24.94 (978-0-375-93634-0(3)) Random House Publishing Group.

Spradlin, Michael. Keeper of the Grail: Book 1, Bk. 1. 2009. (Youngest Templar Ser.: 1). (ENG.). 272p. (J). (gr. 5-6). 7.99 (978-0-14-241461-3(1), Puffin Books) Penguin Young Readers Group.

—Orphan of Destiny, 3 vols. 2011. (Youngest Templar Ser.: 3). (ENG.). 272p. (J). (gr. 5-18). 7.99 (978-0-14-241959-5(1), Puffin Books) Penguin Young Readers Group.

—Trail of Fate: Book 2, 2 vols., Bk. 2. 2010. (Youngest Templar Ser.: 2). (ENG.). 256p. (J). (gr. 5-7). 7.99 (978-0-14-241707-2(6), Puffin Books) Penguin Young Readers Group.

Spradlin, Michael P. Orphan of Destiny. 2012. (Youngest Templar Ser.: 3). (ENG., Illus.). 256p. (J). (gr. 6-8). 22.44 (978-0-399-24765-1(3)) Penguin Young Readers Group.

Stanley, Diane. Bella at Midnight. Ibatoulline, Bagram, illus. 2007. (ENG.). 304p. (J). (gr. 3-7). pap. 7.99 (978-0-06-077575-9(0), HarperCollins) HarperCollins Pubs.

Sterer, Gideon. The Night Knights. Godbey, Cory, illus. 2018. (ENG.). 40p. (J). (gr. -1-3). 17.99 (978-1-4197-2846-4(6), 1117801, Abrams Bks. for Young Readers) Abrams, Inc.

Stewart, Paul & Riddell, Chris. Dragon's Hoard. Riddell, Chris, illus. 2014. (Knight's Story Ser.: 3). (ENG., Illus.). 144p. (J). (gr. 2-6). pap. 13.99 (978-1-4814-2890-3(X), Atheneum Bks. for Young Readers) Simon & Schuster Children's Publishing.

—Edge Chronicles: the Winter Knights. 2010. (Edge Chronicles Ser.: 5). (ENG.). 400p. (J). (gr. 3-7). 8.99 (978-0-385-73612-1(6), Yearling) Random Hse. Children's Bks.

—Joust of Honor. Riddell, Chris, illus. 2014. (Knight's Story Ser.: 2). (ENG., Illus.). 144p. (J). (gr. 2-6). pap. 13.99 (978-1-4814-2889-7(6), Atheneum Bks. for Young Readers) Simon & Schuster Children's Publishing.

—Lake of Skulls. Riddell, Chris, illus. 2014. (Knight's Story Ser.: 1). (ENG., Illus.). 144p. (J). (gr. 2-6). pap. 13.99 (978-1-4814-2888-0(8), Atheneum Bks. for Young Readers) Simon & Schuster Children's Publishing.

Stine, R. L. Fright Knight & the Ooze: Twice Terrifying Tales. 2010. (R. L. Stine's Ghosts of Fear Street Ser.). (ENG.). 240p. (J). (gr. 3-7). pap. 7.99 (978-1-4169-9135-9(2), Aladdin) Simon & Schuster Children's Publishing.

Streit, Jakob. Three Knight Tales, 1 vol. Kuettel, Nina, tr. 2013. (ENG.). 76p. pap. 12.00 (978-1-936367-24-5(6)) Waldorf Publications.

Sweet, Susan D., et al. Jacqueline & the Beanstalk: A Tale of Facing Giant Fears. 2017. (ENG., Illus.). 32p. (J). 15.95 (978-1-4338-2682-5(8), Magination Pr.) American Psychological Assn.

Taylor, Dereen. The Knight's First Tournament. Kavanagh, Peter, illus. 2012. 12p. (J). (gr. 1-6). 16.99 (978-1-84322-760-1(6)) Anness Publishing GBR. Dist: National Bk. Network.

Thomas, Shelley Moore. Get Well, Good Knight. Plecas, Jennifer, illus. 2004. (Penguin Young Readers, Level 3 Ser.). 48p. (J). (gr. 1-3). 4.99 (978-0-14-240050-0(5), Penguin Young Readers) Penguin Young Readers Group.

—Get Well, Good Knight. Plecas, Jennifer, illus. 2004. (Easy-to-Read Ser.). 44p. (gr. k-3). 14.00 (978-0-7569-2923-7(7)) Perfection Learning Corp.

—Get Well, Good Knight. 2004. (Penguin Young Readers: Level 3 Ser.). 13.55 (978-0-613-97291-8(0)) Turtleback.

—Happy Birthday, Good Knight. 2014. (Penguin Young Readers: Level 3 Ser.). lib. bdg. 13.55 (978-0-606-35728-9(9)) Turtleback.

Timmers, Leo. Where Is the Dragon? Timmers, Leo, illus. 2021. (ENG., Illus.). 40p. (J). (gr. -1-k). 17.99 (978-1-77657-311-0(0), 215d4b6d-94aa-45a1-8654-7e5e7dc59b89) Gecko Pr. NZL. Dist: Lerner Publishing Group.

Tompert, Ann. The Errant Knight. Keith, Doug, illus. 2003. 32p. 15.95 (978-0-9701907-6-5(X)) Illumination Arts Publishing Co., Inc.

Tulien, Sean. The Not-So-Deadly Dragon. Cunyat, Pol, illus. 2016. (Thud & Blunder Ser.). (ENG.). 56p. (J). (gr. 1-3). lib. bdg. 23.99 (978-1-4965-3220-6(1), 132415, Stone Arch Bks.) Capstone.

—The Not-So-Evil Wizard. Cunyat, Pol, illus. 2016. (Thud & Blunder Ser.). (ENG.). 56p. (J). (gr. 1-3). lib. bdg. 23.99 (978-1-4965-3221-3(X), 132416, Stone Arch Bks.) Capstone.

Twain, Mark, pseud. A Connecticut Yankee in King Arthur's Court. 2008. (Bring the Classics to Life Ser.). (ENG., Illus.). 72p. (gr. 3-12). pap., act. bk. ed. 10.95 (978-1-55576-357-2(X), EDCTR-309B) EDCON Publishing Group.

Van Genechten, Guido. Knight Ricky. 2010. (Ricky Ser.). (ENG., Illus.). 30p. (J). (gr. -1-k). 16.95 (978-1-60537-059-0(2)) Clavis Publishing.

Vande Velde, Vivian. The Book of Mordred. 2007. (ENG.). 352p. (YA). (gr. 7-12). pap. 8.99 (978-0-618-80916-5(3), 497456, Clarion Bks.) HarperCollins Pubs.

Ventura, Marne. The Worry Warriors, 4 vols. Trinidad, Leo, illus. 2016. (Worry Warriors Ser.). (ENG.). 96p. (J). (gr. 2-4). 106.60 (978-1-4965-3665-5(7), 25145, Stone Arch Bks.) Capstone.

Vernon, Ursula. Dragonbreath #10: Knight-Napped! 2015. (Dragonbreath Ser.: 10). (Illus.). 208p. (J). (gr. 3-7). 14.99 (978-0-8037-3849-2(8), Dial Bks) Penguin Young Readers Group.

Wallace, Karen & Chapman, Neil. The Round Table. 2009. (Hopscotch Adventures Ser.). (Illus.). 31p. (J). (gr. 1). lib. bdg. 25.65 (978-1-59771-175-3(6)) Sea-To-Sea Pubns.

—Sir Lancelot & the Ice Castle. 2009. (Hopscotch Adventures Ser.). (Illus.). 31p. (J). (gr. 1). lib. bdg. 25.65 (978-1-59771-174-6(8)) Sea-To-Sea Pubns.

Webster, Sheryl. Space Knights & Ice Dragons (Reading Ladder Level 2) Watson, Richard, illus. 2017. (Reading Ladder Level 2 Ser.). (ENG.). 48p. (gr. k-2). pap. 7.99 (978-1-4052-7822-5(6), Reading Ladder) Farshore GBR. Dist: Independent Pubs. Group, HarperCollins Pubs.

Weyn, Suzanne. The Night Dance: A Retelling of "the Twelve Dancing Princesses" 2008. (Once upon a Time Ser.). (ENG., Illus.). 224p. (YA). (gr. 7). mass mkt. 8.99 (978-1-4169-6132-1(1), Simon Pulse) Simon Pulse.

Wheeler, Jeff. The Hollow Crown. 2017. (Kingfountain Ser.: 4). (ENG., Illus.). 302p. pap. 14.95 (978-1-5039-4396-4(8), 9781503943964, 47North) Amazon Publishing.

Wheeler, Lisa. Boogie Knights. Siegel, Mark, illus. 2008. (ENG.). 40p. (J). (gr. -1-3). 16.99 (978-0-689-87639-4(4), Atheneum/Richard Jackson Bks.) Simon & Schuster Children's Publishing.

KNIGHTS OF THE ROUND TABLE

see Arthur, King

KNITTING

Blanchette, Peg & Thibault, Terri. 12 Easy Knitting Projects. Martin-Jourdenals, Norma Jean, illus. 2008. (ENG.). 64p. (J). (gr. 3-7). 12.95 (978-0-8249-6784-0(4), Ideals Pubns.) Worthy Publishing.

Blaxland, Wendy. Sweaters, 1 vol. 2010. (How Are They Made? Ser.). (ENG., Illus.). 32p. (J). (gr. 4-4). lib. bdg. 21.27 (978-0-7614-4756-6(3), 77807708-6bb9-41b4-892f-6620e65770e9) Cavendish Square Publishing LLC.

Dyer, Janice. Get into Knitting. 2016. (Get-Into-It Guides). (ENG.). 32p. (J). (gr. 3-6). (978-0-7787-2641-8(X)) Crabtree Publishing Co.

Easy-To-Make Spool Knit Animals: Simple & Charming Projects to Make with Spool Knitting! 2013. (Craft Box Kids Ser.). (ENG., Illus.). 48p. (J). (978-1-77132-025-2(7)) SpiceBox Products Ltd.

Eckman, Edie. I Can Knit. 2012. (I Can Ser.). (ENG., Illus.). 32p. (J). (gr. 4-7). pap. 7.95 (978-1-59217-440-9(X), Annie's) Annie's Publishing, LLC.

Editors of Klutz. Finger Knitting. 2015. (ENG.). 56p. (J). (gr. 3-7). 21.99 (978-0-545-85845-8(3)) Klutz.

Falick, Melanie. Kids Knitting: Projects for Kids of All Ages. Nicholas, Kristin, illus. Hartlove, Chris, photos by. 2003. (ENG.). 128p. (J). pap. 18.99 (978-1-57965-241-8(7), 85241) Artisan.

Fryer, Jane Eayre. The Mary Frances Knitting & Crocheting Book 100th Anniversary Edition: A Childrens Story-Instruction Book with Doll Clothes Patterns for 18-Inch Dolls. 2011. (ENG., Illus.). 208p. pap. 21.95 (978-1-937564-05-6(3), Classic Bookwrights) Lindaloo Enterprises.

Gildersleeve, Mary C. Great Yarns for the Close-Knit Family: Over Two Dozen Original Hand-Knit Designs Inspired by One Dozen Family Read-alouds. 2008. 157p. pap. 14.99 (978-0-9798469-4-6(3)) Hillside Education.

Hayes, Amy. Turning Wool into Sweaters, 1 vol. 2015. (Step-By-Step Transformations Ser.). (ENG., Illus.). 24p. (gr. 1-1). 25.93 (978-1-5026-0455-2(8), d73b70f9-3d34-4ca3-92fc-ea5b2caafb48) Cavendish Square Publishing LLC.

Johnson, Anne Akers. Knitting: Learn to Knit Six Great Projects. 2004. (Illus.). 96p. (J). 24.95 (978-1-57054-861-1(7)) Klutz.

Kallmeyer-Mehlhorn, Margarete. The Wondrous Ball of Yarn: A Facsimile of the Previously Unpublished Manuscript. 2008.Tr. of Wunderknaul. (ENG & GER., Illus.). 40p. 41.00 (978-0-9745168-2-0(1)) Cotsen Occasional Pr.

Knitting: Learn to Knit Six Great Projects. 2013. 96p. (J). (gr. 5). 24.99 (978-0-545-56167-9(1)) Klutz.

Kuskowski, Alex. Cool Knitting for Kids: A Fun & Creative Introduction to Fiber Art. 2014. (Cool Fiber Art Ser.). (ENG.). 32p. (J). (gr. 3-6). lib. bdg. 34.21 (978-1-62403-308-7(3), 1278, Checkerboard Library) ABDO Publishing Co.

McClure, Kelly. Knitting Projects You'll Purl Over. 2018. (Crafty Creations Ser.). (ENG., Illus.). 48p. (J). (gr. 4-8). lib. bdg. 31.99 (978-1-5157-7446-4(5), 135795, Capstone Pr.) Capstone.

Nelson, Robin. From Sheep to Sweater. 2003. (Start to Finish Ser.). (Illus.). 24p. (J). 18.60 (978-0-8225-0716-1(1), Lerner Pubns.) Lerner Publishing Group.

Rau, Dana Meachen. Learning to Knit. 2012. (How-To Library). (ENG.). 32p. (gr. 3-6). pap. 14.21 (978-1-61080-651-0(4), 202261); (Illus.). 32.07 (978-1-61080-477-6(5), 202087) Cherry Lake Publishing.

Steege, Gwen W. & Hansen, Robin. Knit Mittens/Knit Hats. (ENG., Illus.). 119.60 (978-1-58017-901-0(0), 67901) Storey Publishing, LLC.

Switzer, Chris. Projects for Alpaca & Llama. 2004. 16.00 (978-0-9642663-2-2(6)) Switzer Land Enterprises.

Thalacker, Karen & Dwyer, Mindy. Knitting with Gigi: Includes Step-By-Step Instructions & 8 Patterns. 2007. (Illus.). 32p. (J). pap. (978-1-56477-799-7(5)) Martingale & Co.

Thalcker, Karen. Knitting with Gigi. Dwyer, Mindy, illus. 2007. (ENG.). 32p. 24.95 (978-1-56477-816-1(9)) Martingale & Co.

Tronci, Nicoletta. Teach Me to Knit: Super Simple for Kids & Other Beginners! 2016. (Illus.). 64p. (J). pap. (978-1-4647-4325-2(8), 1400919) Leisure Arts, Inc.

Warwick, Ellen. Fully Woolly. Lum, Bernice, illus. 2007. (Planet Girl Ser.). 80p. (J). (gr. 5-9). 12.95 (978-1-55337-798-6(2)) Kids Can Pr., Ltd. CAN. Dist: Hachette Bk. Group.

Watt, Fiona. How to Knit. Baggott, Stella, illus. Allman, Howard, photos by. 2007. (Art Ideas Ser.). 64p. (J). (gr. 4-7). pap. 14.99 (978-0-7945-1577-5(0), Usborne) EDC Publishing.

KNOTS AND SPLICES

Adkins, Jan. Line: Tying It up, Tying It Down. 2004. (ENG., Illus.). 48p. (J). (gr. 3-7). 12.95 (978-0-937822-83-8(3)) WoodenBoat Pubns.

Chen, D. M. & Sun, Michelle. Tie a Wish with Bracelets: Easy & Fun Chinese Knotting. 2012. (ENG., Illus.). 71p. (J). (gr. 4). pap. 10.95 (978-1-937489-01-4(9)) StoryRobin Co.

Editors of Klutz. The Klutz Book of Knots. 2017. (ENG.). 22p. (J). (gr. 3-7). 14.99 (978-1-338-10642-8(2)) Scholastic, Inc.

Graham, Oakley. I Can Tie My Own Shoelaces. Green, Barry, illus. 2014. (I Can Bks.). (ENG.). 12p. (J). (gr. -1). spiral bd. 10.99 (978-1-78244-824-2(1)) Top That! Publishing PLC GBR. Dist: Independent Pubs. Group.

Groves. Knots & Knocks, Bk. 16. Date not set. (Illus.). 32p. (J). pap. 129.15 (978-0-582-18059-8(7)) Addison-Wesley Longman, Ltd. GBR. Dist: Trans-Atlantic Pubns., Inc.

Mooney, Carla. Get All Tied Up: Tying Knots. 2010. (Creative Adventure Guides). 48p. (J). (gr. 3-6). lib. bdg. 26.60 (978-1-59953-384-1(7)) Norwood Hse. Pr.

Rau, Dana Meachen. Making Knot Projects. Petelinsek, Kathleen, illus. 2016. (How-To Library). (ENG.). 32p. (J). (gr. 3-6). 32.07 (978-1-63471-420-4(2), 208459) Cherry Lake Publishing.

Sadler, Judy Ann & Sadler, Judy. Knotting: Make Your Own Basketball Nets, Guitar Straps, Sports Bags & More. Gagnon, Cileste & Gagnon, Celeste, illus. 2006. (Kids Can Do It Ser.). 40p. (J). (gr. 3-7). 6.95 (978-1-55337-834-1(2)) Kids Can Pr., Ltd. CAN. Dist: Hachette Bk. Group.

Smith, A. G. Celtic Knotwork Stained Glass Colouring Book. 2006. (Dover Design Coloring Bks.). (ENG., Illus.). 32p. (gr. 3-8). 7.99 (978-0-486-44816-9(9), 448169) Dover Pubns., Inc.

Wilson, Patrick. Ropes & Knots for Survival. Carney, John, ed. 2014. (Extreme Survival in the Military Ser.: 12). 64p. (J). (gr. 7-18). lib. bdg. 23.95 (978-1-4222-3083-1(X)) Mason Crest.

KNOWLEDGE, SOCIOLOGY OF

The Big Book of Knowledge. 2003. 384p. (J). 9.98 (978-0-7525-8436-2(7)) Parragon, Inc.

KNOWLEDGE, THEORY OF

Here are entered works that treat the origin, nature, methods and limits of human knowledge.

see also Belief and Doubt; Intellect; Perception; Senses and Sensation

Baxter, Nicola. Kaleidoscope Book: My First Book of Learning. Elliott, Rebecca, illus. 2013. (ENG.). 16p. (J). (gr. -1-12). bds. 16.99 (978-1-84322-930-8(7), Armadillo) Anness Publishing GBR. Dist: National Bk. Network.

Brown Bear Books. Cognitive Development. 2011. (Psychology Ser.). (ENG.). 112p. (J). (gr. 9-12). lib. bdg. 42.80 (978-1-936333-17-2(1), 16775) Brown Bear Bks.

—Intellectual Development. 2011. (Psychology Ser.). (ENG., Illus.). 112p. (J). (gr. 9-12). lib. bdg. 42.80 (978-1-936333-18-9(X), 16776) Brown Bear Bks.

Carlson, Dale. The Teen Brain Book: Who & What Are You? Teasdale, Nancy, ed. Nicklaus, Carol, illus. 2004. (ENG.). 230p. (gr. 7-12). pap. 14.95 (978-1-884158-29-2(3)) Bick Publishing Hse.

Cooke, Tim. Knowledge & Education, 1 vol. 2017. (What's the Big Idea? a History of the Ideas That Shape Our World Ser.). (ENG.). 48p. (gr. 6-6). lib. bdg. 33.07 (978-1-5026-2818-3(X), 0a3a3953-a45a-40b7-9d1c-00b414d3334f) Cavendish Square Publishing LLC.

De Medeiros, Michael. Common Sense. 2009. (World of Wonder Ser.). (Illus.). 24p. (J). (gr. 2-4). pap. 8.95 (978-1-60596-063-0(2)); lib. bdg. 24.45 (978-1-60596-062-3(4)) Weigl Pubs., Inc.

DK. Knowledge Encyclopedia (Updated & Enlarged Edition) The World As You've Never Seen It Before. 2013. (DK Knowledge Encyclopedias Ser.). (ENG.). 360p. (J). (gr. 4-7). 29.99 (978-1-4654-1417-5(7), DK Children) Dorling Kindersley Publishing, Inc.

Hansen, Sharon A. The Executive Functioning Workbook for Teens: Help for Unprepared, Late, & Scattered Teens. 2013. (ENG.). 144p. (YA). (gr. 6-12). pap. 18.95 (978-1-60882-656-8(2), 26568) New Harbinger Pubns.

Higgins, Melissa. We All Have Different Abilities, 1 vol. 2012. (Celebrating Differences Ser.). (ENG.). 24p. (J). (gr. -1-2). 27.32 (978-1-4296-7575-8(6), 117172); (J). (gr. -1-2). pap. 7.29 (978-1-4296-7888-9(7), 118220); (gr. k-1). pap. 41.70 (978-1-4296-8321-0(X), Capstone Pr.) Capstone.

Lo Bosco, Maryellen. David Hume & a Treatise of Human Nature. 2016. (J). lib. bdg. (978-1-68048-547-9(4)) Windmill Bks.

Orr, Tamra B. Tracking an Epidemic. 2014. (Explorer Library: Science Explorer Ser.). (ENG., Illus.). 32p. (J). (gr. 4-8). 32.07 (978-1-62431-776-7(6), 203300) Cherry Lake Publishing.

Porchetta, Renato L. Universal Methodology: UNIVERSAL SCIENTIFIC PROGRAMMING CONTROL-HUMAN INTELLIGENCE AMPLIFICATION MANAGEMENT-SCIENCE of the COMPOSITION of the SIGNIFICANCE,SEMANTICS-SCIENCE of MANAGEMENT-the Mosaic Thinking, 2 vols, Vol.1. 2nd ed. 2007. (ENG., Illus.). 490p. lib. bdg. 100.00 (978-0-9769931-0-0(4)) Ce Code Efficiency, Inc.

Reade, Clara. La Intuicin: El Sexto Sentido / Intuition: the Sixth Sense, 1 vol., 1. De La Vega, Eida, ed. 2014. (Tus Cinco Sentidos y Tu Sexto Sentido / Your Five Senses & Your Sixth Sense Ser.). (SPA & ENG.). 24p. (J). (gr. 1-2). 26.27 (978-1-4777-3280-9(2), c6a75677-ee38-4dac-b924-52b37a95f121, PowerKids Pr.) Rosen Publishing Group, Inc., The.

Schwartz, Heather. Outside the Box: New Ideas! (Level 2) 2017. (TIME for KIDS(r): Informational Text Ser.). (ENG., Illus.). 28p. (J). (gr. 2-3). pap. 10.99 (978-1-4258-4966-5(0)) Teacher Created Materials, Inc.

KNOX, HENRY, 1750-1806

Strum, Richard. Henry Knox: Washington's Artilleryman. 2006. (Forgotten Heroes of the American Revolution Ser.). (Illus.). 88p. (J). (gr. 5-11). lib. bdg. 23.95 (978-1-59556-013-1(0)) OTTN Publishing.

Strum, Richard M. Henry Knox: Washington's Artilleryman. 2006. (J). pap. (978-1-59556-018-6(1)) OTTN Publishing.

KOALA

Barwood, Lee. Klassic Koalas: Ancient Aboriginal Tales in New Retellings, BW Edition. 2007. (ENG., Illus.). 24p. (J). pap. 14.99 (978-0-9764698-6-5(3)) Koala Jo Publishing.

Besel, Jen. Koala Joeys. 2020. (Baby Animals Ser.). 24p. (J). (gr. k-3). pap. 8.99 (978-1-64466-096-6(2), 14379, Bolt Jr.) Black Rabbit Bks.

Bodden, Valerie. Amazing Animals - Koalas. 2009. (Amazing Animals Ser.). 24p. (J). (gr. 1-5). 24.25 (978-1-58341-715-7(X), Creative Education) Creative Co., The.

—Koalas. 2015. (J). (978-1-62832-257-6(8), Creative Paperbacks) Creative Co., The.

Borgert-Spaniol, Megan. Baby Koalas. 2015. (Super Cute! Ser.). (ENG., Illus.). 24p. (J). (gr. k-3). lib. bdg. 26.95 (978-1-62617-219-7(6), Blastoff! Readers) Bellwether Media.

Boyer, Crispin. So Cute! Koalas. 2019. (Cool/Cute Ser.). (Illus.). 32p. (J). (gr. -1-k). 6.99 (978-1-4263-3527-3(X), National Geographic Kids) Disney Publishing Worldwide.

Caswell, Deanna. Baby Koalas. 2018. (Adorable Animals Ser.). (ENG.). 32p. (J). (gr. 4-6). pap. 9.99 (978-1-64466-244-1(2), 12231); lib. bdg. (978-1-68072-397-7(9), 12230) Black Rabbit Bks. (Bolt).

Clark, Willow. Koalas, 1 vol. 2012. (Up a Tree Ser.). (ENG., Illus.). 24p. (J). (gr. 2-3). pap. 9.25 (978-1-4488-6329-7(5), 1a2a1702-3eb5-4776-9fc9-6af144c40732, PowerKids Pr.); lib. bdg. 26.27 (978-1-4488-6185-9(3), 31162793-c06e-494c-bc5b-5cab982f38d3) Rosen Publishing Group, Inc., The.

Eckart, Edana. Koala. 2005. (Welcome Bks.). (ENG., Illus.). 24p. (J). (gr. -1-2). pap. 4.95 (978-0-516-25164-6(3), Children's Pr.) Scholastic Library Publishing.

Fishman, Jon M. Meet a Baby Koala. 2017. (Lightning Bolt Books (r) — Baby Australian Animals Ser.). (ENG., Illus.). 24p. (J). (gr. 1-3). 29.32 (978-1-5124-3383-8(7), 36fe5f32-786e-4d74-9021-ab950fcb74c3, Lerner Pubns.); pap. 9.99 (978-1-5124-5589-2(X), f7217d3f-bf2d-45f3-b6d7-d094f258a2e3) Lerner Publishing Group.

Gregory, Josh. Koalas. 2016. (Nature's Children Ser.). (ENG., Illus.). 48p. (J). pap. 6.95 (978-0-531-22518-9(6), Children's Pr.) Scholastic Library Publishing.

Hanel, Rachael. Koalas. 2009. (Living Wild Ser.). (ENG., Illus.). 48p. (J). (gr. 5-8). 22.95 (978-1-58341-655-6(2), 22185, Creative Education) Creative Co., The.

Hendrix, Emilia. Koalas & Joeys, 1 vol. 2015. (Animal Family Ser.). (ENG., Illus.). 24p. (J). (gr. k-k). pap. 9.15 (978-1-4824-3779-9(1), 2487e765-aa2e-4200-83e1-8b3bbeb357cb) Stevens, Gareth Publishing LLLP.

Hewett, Richard, illus. & photos by. A Koala Joey Grows Up. Hewett, Richard, photos by. Hewett, Joan, photos by. 2004. (Baby Animals Ser.). 32p. (J). (gr. k-3). lib. bdg. 21.27 (978-1-57505-198-7(2)) Lerner Publishing Group.

Hoff, Mary King. Koalas. 2005. (Wild World of Animals (Creative Education) Ser.). (Illus.). 32p. (J). (gr. 2-5). lib. bdg. 18.95 (978-1-58341-351-7(0), Creative Education) Creative Co., The.

Jacobs, Liza. Koalas. 2003. (Wild Wild World Ser.). (Illus.). 24p. (J). 23.70 (978-1-4103-0049-2(8), Blackbirch Pr., Inc.) Cengage Gale.

Kalman, Bobbie, et al. Les Koalas. 2005. (Petit Monde Vivant Ser.). (FRE., Illus.). 32p. (J). pap. 9.95 (978-2-89579-033-4(7)) Bayard Canada Livres CAN. Dist: Crabtree Publishing Co.

Kawa, Katie. Baby Koalas, 1 vol. 2011. (Cute & Cuddly: Baby Animals Ser.). (Illus.). 24p. (gr. k-k). (ENG.). (J). pap. 9.15 (978-1-4339-5528-0(8), 291cf0f7-34c9-4f8b-a340-c6ff0db4aed2); (ENG., (J). lib. bdg. 25.27 (978-1-4339-5526-6(1), b58a4f41-144e-4b22-a1a7-327151090b87); 69.20 (978-1-4339-6892-1(4)) Stevens, Gareth Publishing LLLP.

Kissock, Heather. Heather Kissock. 2015. (Illus.). 24p. (J). (978-1-4896-4113-7(0)) Weigl Pubs., Inc.

Kras, Sara Louise. Koalas: A 4D Book. rev. ed. 2018. (Australian Animals Ser.). (ENG., Illus.). 24p. (J). (gr. -1-2). lib. bdg. 29.32 (978-1-9771-0001-6(5), 138162, Capstone Pr.) Capstone.

Lang, Aubrey. Baby Koala, 1 vol. Lynch, Wayne, photos by. 2004. (Nature Babies Ser.). (ENG., Illus.). 36p. (J). (gr. k-3). pap. 7.95 (978-1-55041-876-7(9), 3e37bc07-9542-45f5-8080-97b857e8fd1b) Clockwise Pr. CAN. Dist: Firefly Bks., Ltd.

—Baby Koala, 1 vol. Lynch, Wayne, photos by. 2004. (Nature Babies Ser.). (ENG., Illus.). 36p. (J). (gr. k-3). 16.95 (978-1-55041-874-3(2), a83dd177-69b3-4099-a42f-df21d922e7e7) Trifolium Bks., Inc. CAN. Dist: Firefly Bks., Ltd.

Marsh, Laura. National Geographic Readers: Koalas. 2014. (Readers Ser.). (ENG., Illus.). 32p. (J). (gr. -1-k). lib. bdg. 13.90 (978-1-4263-1467-4(1), National Geographic Kids) Disney Publishing Worldwide.

Marsico, Katie. Koala Bears. 2012. (21st Century Basic Skills Library: Baby Zoo Animals Ser.). (ENG.). 24p. (gr. k-3). pap. 12.79 (978-1-61080-631-2(X), 202241); (Illus.). 26.35 (978-1-61080-457-8(0), 202067) Cherry Lake Publishing.

Murray, Julie. Koala Joeys. 2017. (Baby Animals (Abdo Kids Junior) Ser.). (ENG., Illus.). 24p. (J). (gr. -1-2). lib. bdg. 31.36 (978-1-5321-0004-8(3), 25094, Abdo Kids) ABDO Publishing Co.

Murray, Laura K. Koala. (Grow with Me Ser.). (ENG.). 32p. (J). (gr. 3-6). 2016. pap. 12.00 (978-1-62832-163-0(6), 20871, Creative Paperbacks) 2015. (Illus.). (978-1-60818-562-7(1), 20870, Creative Education) Creative Co., The.

Otfinoski, Steven. Koalas, 1 vol. 2008. (Animals, Animals Ser.). (ENG., Illus.). 48p. (gr. 5-5). lib. bdg. 32.64 (978-0-7614-2526-7(8), f2862947-8782-4985-9466-381eb3b5fe41) Cavendish Square Publishing LLC.

Owen, Ruth. Koalas, 1 vol., 1. 2013. (Dr. Bob's Amazing World of Animals Ser.). (ENG.). 32p. (J). (gr. 2-3). 31.27 (978-1-4777-9024-3(1), 80b0ab6f-a8c4-4cc8-bd9f-3689a54a0fec, Windmill Bks.) Rosen Publishing Group, Inc., The.

Phillips, Dee. Koala. 2013. (Science Slam: Treed-Animal Life in the Trees Ser.). 24p. (J). (gr. -1-3). lib. bdg. 26.99 (978-1-61772-916-4(7)) Bearport Publishing Co., Inc.

Pohl, Kathleen. Koalas / Koalas, 1 vol. 2007. (Let's Read about Animals / Conozcamos a Los Animales Ser.). (SPA & ENG., Illus.). 24p. (gr. k-2). lib. bdg. 24.67 (978-0-8368-8007-6(2), 23530ae2-45bd-4582-a3e6-1da380b83f02, Weekly Reader Leveled Readers) Stevens, Gareth Publishing LLLP.

Riggs, Kate. Seedlings: Koalas. 2015. (Seedlings Ser.). 24p. (J). (gr. -1-1). pap. 8.99 (978-1-62832-044-2(3), 21417, Creative Paperbacks) Creative Co., The.

Riggs, Kate & Aaron Frisch, Aaron. Koalas. 2014. (Seedlings Ser.). (ENG.). 24p. (J). (gr. -1-k). (978-1-60818-455-2(2), 21416, Creative Education) Creative Co., The.

Riley, Joelle. Koalas. 2005. (Early Bird Nature Bks.). (ENG., Illus.). 48p. (gr. 2-5). lib. bdg. 26.60 (978-0-8225-2870-8(3), Lerner Pubns.) Lerner Publishing Group.

Rose, Deborah Lee & Kelly, Susan. Jimmy the Joey: The True Story of an Amazing Koala Rescue. 2013. (Baby Animal Tales Ser.). (Illus.). 32p. (J). (gr. -1-k). 16.95 (978-1-4263-1371-4(3), National Geographic Kids) Disney Publishing Worldwide.

Saxby, Claire. Koala. Vivas, Julie, illus. 2019. (Read & Wonder Ser.). (ENG.). 32p. (J). (gr. -1-3). 7.99 (978-1-5362-0896-2(5)) Candlewick Pr.

Schuetz, Kari. Koalas. 2011. (Animal Safari Ser.). (ENG., Illus.). 24p. (J). (gr. k-3). lib. bdg. 26.95 (978-1-60014-607-7(4), Blastoff! Readers) Bellwether Media.

Szymanski, Jennifer. National Geographic Readers: Climb, Koala! 2017. (Readers Ser.). (Illus.). 24p. (J). (gr. -1-k). pap. 4.99 (978-1-4263-2784-1(6)); (ENG., lib. bdg. 14.90 (978-1-4263-2785-8(4)) Disney Publishing Worldwide. (National Geographic Kids).

KOALA—FICTION

Angel, Ido. Vipo in Australia: The Koala & the Kangaroo. 2015. (AV2 Animated Storytime Ser.). (ENG.). (J). lib. bdg. 29.99 (978-1-4896-3905-9(5), AV2 by Weigl) Weigl Pubs., Inc.

Azman, Hacer. The Adventures of Kyle. 2011. (ENG.). 96p. (J). (gr. k-1). 14.95 (978-1-59784-231-0(1), Tughra Bks.) Blue Dome, Inc.

Bettinger, John & Kina. Koa Becomes a Friend. 2012. 32p. (-18). pap. 13.95 (978-1-4497-6153-0(4), WestBow Pr.) Author Solutions, LLC.

Blabey, Aaron. Don't Call Me Bear! Blabey, Aaron, illus. 2019. (ENG., Illus.). 32p. (J). (gr. -1-k). 14.99 (978-1-338-36002-8(7), Scholastic Pr.) Scholastic, Inc.

Book Buddy: Koala with Story Book. Orig. Title: Child's Play. (Illus.). 10p. (J). (gr. -1-4). reprint ed. (978-1-881469-43-8(3)) Safari, Ltd.

Bright, Rachel. The Koala Who Could. Field, Jim, illus. 2017. (ENG.). 32p. (J). (gr. -1-k). 18.99 (978-1-338-13908-2(8), Scholastic Pr.) Scholastic, Inc.

Brown, Gina Bates. Zen & Bodhi's Snowy Day. Hinder, Sarah Jane, illus. 2014. (ENG.). 24p. (J). 15.95 (978-1-61429-165-7(9)) Wisdom Pubns.

Chronicle Books. Baby Koala: Finger Puppet Book. Huang, Yu-Hsuan, illus. 2018. (Baby Animal Finger Puppets Ser.: 10). (ENG.). 12p. (J). (gr. -1 — 1). bds. 7.99 (978-1-4521-6374-1(X)) Chronicle Bks. LLC.

Craig, Bobby & Manifold, Delwyn. The Learning Adventures of Spot. 2011. 28p. pap. 24.95 (978-1-4560-3110-7(4)) America Star Bks.

Dennard, Deborah. Koala Country: A Story of an Australian Eucalyptus Forest. 2005. (Soundprints' Wild Habitats Ser.). (ENG., Illus.). 32p. (J). (gr. 1-4). 8.95 (978-1-59249-106-3(5), SC7018) Soundprints.

Dennis, Jen. Snoozy Sam. 2013. 42p. pap. (978-1-922204-78-3(1)) Vivid Publishing.

deRubertis, Barbara. Kylie Kangaroo's Karate Kickers. Alley, R. W., illus. 2011. (Animal Antics A to Z Ser.). 32p. (J). pap. 45.32 (978-0-7613-7657-6(7)); (ENG.). lib. bdg. 22.60 (978-1-57565-332-7(X)); (gr. -1-3). pap. 7.95 (978-1-57565-323-5(0), c3134011-d19e-4bad-ae5c-2bfeafd9f34d, Kane Press) Astra Publishing Hse.

deRubertis, Barbara & DeRubertis, Barbara. Kylie Kangaroo's Karate Kickers. Alley, R. W., illus. 2012. (Animal Antics A to Z Ser.). 32p. (J). (gr. 2 — 1). cd-rom 7.95 (978-1-57565-404-1(0)) Astra Publishing Hse.

Earl, David G. Koala Koala, I'm Not a Bear, I'm a Koala. Gentry, T. Kyle, illus. 2009. 32p. pap. 12.95 (978-1-936051-22-9(2)) Peppertree Pr., The.

Galvin, Laura. Baby Koala & Mommy. 2008. (Smithsonian Baby Animals Ser.). (ENG., Illus.). 16p. (gr. -1-k). 13.95 (978-1-59249-791-1(8)) Soundprints.

Galvin, Laura Gates. Baby Koala & Mommy. 2007. (Baby Animals Ser.). (ENG., Illus.). 16p. (gr. -1-k). 6.95 (978-1-59249-744-7(6)) Soundprints.

Gehl, Laura. Koala Challah. Mola, Maria, illus. 2017. (ENG.). 24p. (J). (gr. -1-1). 17.99 (978-1-5124-2087-6(5), 7d5ffbf3-fe90-45a2-a1fb-59032b3a9cd4); pap. 7.99 (978-1-5124-2088-3(3), 26c316b4-e7ec-4d95-9055-b608e472f570) Lerner Publishing Group. (Kar-Ben Publishing).

Griffiths, Andy. Killer Koalas from Outer Space & Lots of Other Very Bad Stuff That Will Make Your Brain Explode! Denton, Terry, illus. 2012. (ENG.). 192p. (J). (gr. 3-7). pap. 8.99 (978-1-250-01017-9(9), 900084754) Square Fish.

Hamilton, Martha & Weiss, Mitch. Why Koala Has a Stumpy Tail. Wrenn, Tom, illus. 2007. (Story Cove Ser.). (ENG.). 24p. (J). (gr. -1-3). pap. 4.95 (978-0-87483-879-4(7)) August Hse. Pubs., Inc.

Kylie's Concert: Evaluation Guide. 2006. (J). (978-1-55942-413-4(3)) Witcher Productions.

Kylie's Song: Evaluation Guide. 2006. (J). (978-1-55942-414-1(1)) Witcher Productions.

Lang, Valerie E. Jet's Day: A Whisker Team Story. 2011. 32p. pap. 13.00 (978-1-61204-178-0(7), Strategic Bk. Publishing) Strategic Book Publishing & Rights Agency (SBPRA).

Larson, Angela. Harry Hiccers: Friends of A Feether. 2012. pap. (978-1-4507-7996-8(4)) Independent Pub.

Law, Felicia. Kimberly the Koala: A Tale of Independence, 1 vol. Danson, Lesley, illus. 2010. (Animal Fair Values Ser.). (ENG.). 32p. (J). (gr. 2-2). pap. 11.55 (978-1-60754-909-3(3), cfc08d6e-6671-4d78-b1c8-6b6c65e4a58d); lib. bdg. 27.27 (978-1-60754-902-4(6), 97439e9a-18c3-41f8-b3c4-63f83053636a) Rosen Publishing Group, Inc., The. (Windmill Bks.).

McGee, Warner, illus. Run, Run, Koala! 2010. (Go Diego Go! Ser.). (ENG.). 24p. (J). (gr. -1-1). 16.19 (978-1-4169-9937-9(X)) Simon & Schuster, Inc.

Morris, J. E. Fish Are Not Afraid of Doctors. Morris, J. E., illus. 2019. (Maud the Koala Ser.). (ENG., Illus.). 32p. (J). (gr. k-2). 5.99 (978-0-593-09596-6(0), Penguin Workshop) Penguin Young Readers Group.

Quintana, Josephine F. Tiwi the Lost Baby Koala. 2008. (ENG., Illus.). 30p. (J). pap. 16.95 (978-1-60594-035-9(6), Llumina Kids) Aeon Publishing Inc.

Sakmar-Sullivan, Eva M. Kangaroo's Out of This World Restaurant, 1 vol. 2013. (ENG., Illus.). 32p. (J). (gr. -1-3). 14.99 (978-0-7643-4519-7(2), 4889) Schiffer Publishing, Ltd.

Smith, Clara Batton. Elliott & Anastaci. Smith, Clara Batton, illus. 2012. (Illus.). 16p. pap. 9.95 (978-1-61633-233-4(6)) Guardian Angel Publishing, Inc.

Storti, Jill. Keiko the Koala. 2011. 24p. (gr. -1 — 1). pap. 12.95 (978-1-4567-3110-6(6)) AuthorHouse.

Tabernik, John. Ricky the Picky Koala. Wise, Catlin, illus. 2005. (J). 14.95 (978-0-9773936-0-2(7)) Little Munchkin Bks.

Thompson, Michael. Los Otros Osos/ the Other Bears (Spanish Edition) (Spanish & English Edition) 2013. (ENG., Illus.). 40p. (J). 16.99 (978-1-59572-644-5(6)) Star Bright Bks., Inc.

—The Other Bears: English, 1 vol. Thompson, Michael, illus. 2013.Tr. of Os Outros Ursos. (ENG., Illus.). 32p. (J). 16.99 (978-1-59572-638-4(1)); pap. 6.99 (978-1-59572-639-1(X)) Star Bright Bks., Inc.

—The Other Bears: Spanish, 1 vol. Thompson, Michael, illus. 2013. (SPA., Illus.). 32p. (J). pap. 6.99 (978-1-59572-664-3(0)) Star Bright Bks., Inc.

Wall, Dorothy. The Complete Adventures of Blinky Bill. 2011. (Illus.). 442p. (978-1-84902-571-3(1)) Benediction Classics.

Williams, E. D. Tupamonku Takes on Australia. Wood, R. F., illus. 2006. (ENG.). 68p. per. 29.99 (978-1-4259-6553-2(9)) AuthorHouse.

Witt, Gerri Ann, et al. My Little One: A Mother's Lullaby. Sargent, Shannon Marie, illus. 2008. (J). (978-0-87839-299-5(8)) North Star Pr. of St. Cloud.

KOBAYASHI, ISSA, 1763-1827

Gollub, Matthew. Cool Melons - Turn to Frogs! The Life & Poems of Issa. 2004. (Illus.). (J). (gr. k-3). spiral bd. (978-0-616-03095-0(9)) Canadian National Institute for the Blind/Institut National Canadien pour les Aveugles.

KOCH, ROBERT, 1843-1910

Tracy, Kathleen. Robert Koch & the Study of Anthrax. 2004. (Uncharted, Unexplored, & Unexplained Ser.). (Illus.). 48p. (J). (gr. 4-8). lib. bdg. 29.95 (978-1-58415-261-3(3)) Mitchell Lane Pubs.

KOREA

Behnke, Alison. Kim Jong Il's North Korea. 2007. (Dictatorships Ser.). (ENG., Illus.). 160p. (gr. 9-12). lib. bdg. 38.60 (978-0-8225-7282-4(6), Twenty-First Century Bks.) Lerner Publishing Group.

—North Korea in Pictures. 2nd ed. 2005. (Visual Geography Ser.). (Illus.). 80p. (YA). (gr. 7-12). 27.93 (978-0-8225-1908-9(9)) Lerner Publishing Group.

Bowler, Ann Martin. All about Korea: Stories, Songs, Crafts & More. Barg, Soosoonam, illus. 2011. (ENG.). 64p. (J). (gr. k-4). 16.95 (978-0-8048-4012-5(1)) Tuttle Publishing.

De Capua, Sarah. Korea, 1 vol. 2006. (Discovering Cultures Ser.). (ENG., Illus.). 48p. (gr. 3-4). 31.21 (978-0-7614-1794-1(X), 6b00ac5c-f0f8-404c-a6c3-0a7c19caf907) Cavendish Square Publishing LLC.

Dubois, Jill. Korea, 1 vol. 2nd rev. ed. 2006. (Cultures of the World (Second Edition)(r) Ser.). (ENG., Illus.). 144p. (gr. 5-5). 49.79 (978-0-7614-1786-6(9), 3f194182-3313-4717-8742-e25c07b3e52a) Cavendish Square Publishing LLC.

Gifford, Clive. North Korea, 1 vol. 2010. (Global Hotspots Ser.). (ENG.). 32p. (gr. 5-5). lib. bdg. 21.27 (978-0-7614-4761-0(X), 6dde05dd-9036-4ba7-8076-7ab5c0d23d17) Cavendish Square Publishing LLC.

Han, Suzanne C. Let's Color Korea-Traditional Lifestyles. 2006. (ENG., Illus.). 24p. (J). (gr. k-3). pap. 12.50 (978-0-930878-94-8(9)) Hollym International Corp.

Hart, Joyce. Kim Jong Il: Leader of North Korea. 2009. (Newsmakers Ser.). 112p. (gr. 9-10). 63.90 (978-1-60851-133-4(2)) Rosen Publishing Group, Inc., The.

Hill, Valerie. Korea. 2004. (Ask about Asia Ser.). (Illus.). 48p. (J). (gr. 4-18). lib. bdg. 19.95 (978-1-59084-206-5(5)) Mason Crest.

Ingram, Scott. Korean Americans, 1 vol. 2006. (World Almanac(r) Library of American Immigration Ser.). (ENG., Illus.). 48p. (gr. 5-8). pap. 15.05 (978-0-8368-7328-3(9), 949799b3-5bae-4eff-a35c-320c545fcf59); lib. bdg. 33.67 (978-0-8368-7315-3(7), 7cecba9a-484f-44d3-9be6-b91d8d57c354) Stevens, Gareth Publishing LLLP. (Gareth Stevens Secondary Library).

Italia, Bob. South Korea. 2003. (Countries Set 4 Ser.). 40p. (gr. k-6). 27.07 (978-1-57765-846-7(9), Checkerboard Library) ABDO Publishing Co.

Jones, B. J. Let's Color Korea - Everyday Life in Traditional. 2005. (ENG., Illus.). 26p. (J). (gr. k-3). pap. 12.50 (978-0-930878-98-6(1)) Hollym International Corp.

Kjelle, Marylou Morano. Korea. 2009. (J). (978-1-58415-790-8(9)) Mitchell Lane Pubs.

—Meet Our New Student from Korea. 2008. (Meet Our New Student Ser.). (Illus.). 48p. (YA). (gr. 2-5). lib. bdg. 29.95 (978-1-58415-649-9(X)) Mitchell Lane Pubs.

Kwek, Karen & Masse, Johanna. Welcome to South Korea, 1 vol. 2011. (Welcome to My Country Ser.). (ENG., Illus.). 48p. (J). (gr. 3-3). 31.21 (978-1-60870-159-9(X), 911f6d63-521e-464d-bf3a-00b18c342957) Cavendish Square Publishing LLC.

Martin, Jennifer C. The Korean Americans. 2003. (Immigrants in America Ser.). (ENG., Illus.). 112p. (J). (gr. 4-7). lib. bdg. 30.85 (978-1-59018-079-2(8), Lucent Bks.) Cengage Gale.

Matray, James I. Korea Divided: The 38th Parallel & the Demilitarized Zone. 2004. (Arbitrary Borders Ser.). (ENG., Illus.). 120p. (gr. 9-13). 35.00 (978-0-7910-7829-7(9), P114002, Facts On File) Infobase Holdings, Inc.

Mis, Melody S. How to Draw South Korea's Sights & Symbols. 2009. (Kid's Guide to Drawing the Countries of the World Ser.). 48p. (gr. 4-4). 53.00 (978-1-61511-126-8(3), PowerKids Pr.) Rosen Publishing Group, Inc., The.

Nahm, Andrew C. & Jones, B. J. I Love Korea! Lee, Gi-eun, ed. 2nd ed. 2004. (ENG., Illus.). 86p. (J). (gr. k-5). 29.50 (978-0-930878-87-0(6)) Hollym International Corp.

Orr, Tamra. Korean Heritage. 2018. (21st Century Junior Library: Celebrating Diversity in My Classroom Ser.). (ENG., Illus.). 24p. (J). (gr. 2-4). pap. 12.79 (978-1-5341-0839-4(4), 210720); lib. bdg. 30.64 (978-1-5341-0740-3(1), 210719) Cherry Lake Publishing.

Park, Frances and Ginger. My Freedom Trip: A Child's Escape from North Korea. 2010. (ENG., Illus.). 32p. (gr. k-2). 29.94 (978-1-56397-468-7(1)) Highlights Pr., c/o Highlights for Children, Inc.

Piddock, Charles. North Korea, 1 vol. 2006. (Nations in the News Ser.). (ENG., Illus.). 48p. (gr. 5-8). pap. 15.05 (978-0-8368-6716-9(5), 7dda41bd-5c86-4a60-8258-621a6364cad8); lib. bdg. 33.67 (978-0-8368-6709-1(2), e1fbfb8b-3744-428e-bd80-0e7ee04c5128) Stevens, Gareth Publishing LLLP. (Gareth Stevens Secondary Library).

Pugliano-Martin, Carol. Discover Seoul. 2006. (J). pap. (978-1-4108-6424-6(3)) Benchmark Education Co.

—Seoul, Korea. 2006. (J). pap. (978-1-4108-6421-5(9)) Benchmark Education Co.

Roberts, Russell. Kim Jong Un: Supreme Leader of North Korea. 2018. (World Leaders Ser.). (ENG., Illus.). 48p. (J). (gr. 5-6). pap. 11.95 (978-1-63517-619-3(0), 1635176190); lib. bdg. 34.21 (978-1-63517-547-9(X), 163517547X) North Star Editions. (Focus Readers).

Salter, Christopher L. North Korea. 2nd rev. ed. 2007. (Modern World Nations Ser.). (ENG., Illus.). 125p. (gr. 7-12). lib. bdg. 35.00 (978-0-7910-9513-3(4), P129249, Facts On File) Infobase Holdings, Inc.

Senker, Cath. North & South Korea, 1 vol. 2012. (Our World Divided Ser.). (ENG., Illus.). 48p. (J). (gr. 5-5). 34.47 (978-1-4488-6029-6(6), 21190743-7e7a-405d-bd0d-5fa41bdc95f9, Rosen Reference) Rosen Publishing Group, Inc., The.

Shalant, Phyllis. Look What We've Brought You from Korea: Crafts, Games, Recipes, Stories & Other Cultural Activities from Korean-Americans. Park, Soyoo H., illus. (J). (gr. 2-18). pap. 7.95 (978-0-382-24994-5(1)) Silver, Burdett & Ginn, Inc.

Sheen, Barbara. Foods of Korea, 1 vol. 2010. (Taste of Culture Ser.). (ENG.). 64p. (gr. 3-6). 36.83 (978-0-7377-5115-4(0), 9be6a541-c8a6-485f-a3ad-3a732b7ecf45, KidHaven Publishing) Greenhaven Publishing LLC.

Stevens, Cara J. Bts: Rise of Bangtan. 2018. (ENG., Illus.). 96p. (J). (gr. 3-7). pap. 8.99 (978-0-06-288648-4(7), HarperCollins) HarperCollins Pubs.

Stickler, John. Land of Morning Calm: Korean Culture Then & Now, 1 vol. Han, Soma, illus. 2014. (ENG.). 32p. (J). (gr. 3-6). 16.95 (978-1-885008-22-0(8), leelowshens, Shen's Bks.) Lee & Low Bks., Inc.

Stickler, John & Han, Soma. Land of Morning Calm: Korean Culture Then & Now, 1 vol. 2014. (ENG., Illus.). 32p. (J). (gr. 3-6). pap. 8.95 (978-1-885008-47-3(3), leelowshens, Shen's Bks.) Lee & Low Bks., Inc.

Suyenaga, Ruth. Korean Children's Day. Kyong-Nan, Nani, illus. 2004. 23p. (J). (gr. 4-8). reprint ed. pap. 15.00 (978-0-7567-7068-6(8)) DIANE Publishing Co.

Suyenaga, Ruth, et al. Korean Children's Day. Kyong-Nan, Nani, illus. 2005. (Multicultural Celebrations Ser.). 32p. (J). 4.95 (978-1-59373-011-6(X)) Bunker Hill Publishing, Inc.

Walters, Tara. North Korea. 2008. (True Bks.). (ENG.). 48p. (J). pap. 6.95 (978-0-531-20728-4(5)); (Illus.). (gr. 3-7). 29.00 (978-0-531-16854-7(9)) Scholastic Library Publishing. (Children's Pr.).

—South Korea. 2008. (True Bks.). (ENG.). 48p. (J). pap. 6.95 (978-0-531-20729-1(3), Children's Pr.) Scholastic Library Publishing.

Weber, Valerie J. I Come from South Korea, 1 vol. 2006. (This Is My Story Ser.). (ENG., Illus.). 24p. (gr. 2-4). lib. bdg. 24.67 (978-0-8368-7237-8(1), 639a1b20-a602-44db-960b-a99720757f5a, Weekly Reader Leveled Readers) Stevens, Gareth Publishing LLLP.

Weber, Valerie J. & Weber, Valerie J. I Come from South Korea, 1 vol. 2006. (This Is My Story Ser.). (ENG., Illus.). 24p. (gr. 2-4). pap. 9.15 (978-0-8368-7244-6(4), 4d5e8a06-bf89-487e-ba44-32eaeb2f1df6, Weekly Reader Leveled Readers) Stevens, Gareth Publishing LLLP.

KOREA—FICTION

Alexander, Carol. When My Name Was Keoko. Friedland, Joyce & Kessler, Rikki, eds. 2008. (Novel-Ties Ser.). 29p. pap. 16.95 (978-0-7675-1520-7(X)) Learning Links Inc.

Bohmer, Kara Dale. Walking Sarah: First Day Out. 2013. 32p. (978-1-4602-0076-6(4)); pap. (978-1-4602-0077-3(2)) FriesenPress.

Cha, Hanna. Tiny Feet Between the Mountains. Cha, Hanna, illus. 2019. (ENG., Illus.). 40p. (J). (gr. -1-3). 17.99 (978-1-5344-2992-5(1), Simon & Schuster Bks. For Young Readers) Simon & Schuster Bks. For Young Readers.

Cho, Tina. Rice from Heaven: The Secret Mission to Feed North Koreans. Jin Song, Keum, illus. 2018. (ENG.). 40p. (J). (gr. -1-3). 17.99 (978-1-4998-0682-3(5)) Little Bee Books Inc.

Clamp Staff, contrib. by. Legend of Chun Hyang, Vol. 1. 2004. (Illus.). 192p. (gr. 2-5). pap. 9.99 (978-1-59182-763-4(9), Tokyopop Adult) TOKYOPOP, Inc.

Farley, Christina. Gilded, 0 vols. 2014. (Gilded Ser.: 1). (ENG.). 352p. (YA). (gr. 7-12). pap. 9.99 (978-1-4778-1097-2(8), 9781477810972, Skyscape) Amazon Publishing.

Groot, De. Black Moon. Spear, Luke, tr. Rodrigue, illus. 2007. (Clifton Ser.: 4). 48p. (J). (gr. 4-7). pap. 9.99 (978-1-905460-30-4(9)) CineBook GBR. Dist: National Bk. Network.

Jolley, Dan. Pigling: A Cinderella Story [a Korean Tale]. Timmons, Anne, illus. 2009. (Graphic Myths & Legends Ser.). (ENG.). 48p. (J). (gr. 4-8). pap. 9.99 (978-1-58013-825-3(X), a5e6c85f-65b6-4717-b067-ede393b1a551, Graphic Universe™) Lerner Publishing Group.

Kim, Sagwa. B, Book, & Me. Jeong, Sunhee, tr. 2020. (ENG.). 160p. (YA). pap. 16.95 (978-1-931883-96-2(3)) Two Lines Pr.

Lee, Marie Myung-Ok. Somebody's Daughter: A Novel. 2006. 280p. per. 21.00 (978-0-8070-8389-5(5), Beacon Pr.) Beacon Pr.

Lee, Uk-Bae. When Spring Comes to the DMZ. Lee, Uk-Bae, illus. 2019. (Illus.). 40p. (J). (gr. -1-3). 17.95 (978-0-87486-972-9(2)) Plough Publishing Hse.

Made in Korea: Six-Pack. (Greetings Ser.: Vol. 3). (gr. 3-5). 31.00 (978-0-7635-1824-0(7)) Rigby Education.

Moon, Young-Sook. Across the Tumen: A North Korean Kkotjebi Boy's Quest. 2014.Tr. of 꽃제비 영대: 죽음을 넘어 희망을 찾아간 소년. (ENG.). 128p. pap. 16.99 (978-1-62412-009-1(1), 2715) Seoul Selection KOR. Dist: Univ. of Hawaii Pr.

Mounts, Samia. Frunk the Skunk. Matricardi, Luca, illus. 2008. (ENG.). 150p. (J). (gr. 4-6). pap. 9.95 (978-0-9798841-0-8(1)) 4N Publishing LLC.

Novel Units. A Single Shard Novel Units Student Packet. 2019. (ENG.). (J). (gr. 5-6). pap., stu. ed. 13.99 (978-1-58130-771-9(3), Novel Units, Inc.) Classroom Library Co.

—Year of Impossible Goodbyes Novel Units Student Packet. 2019. (ENG.). (J). (gr. 5-6). pap., stu. ed. 13.99 (978-1-58130-799-3(3), Novel Units, Inc.) Classroom Library Co.

O'Brien, Anne Sibley. In the Shadow of the Sun. 2017. (ENG., Illus.). 336p. (YA). (gr. 3-7). 17.99 (978-0-545-90574-9(5), Levine, Arthur A. Bks.) Scholastic, Inc.

Park, Linda Sue. Archer's Quest. 2018. (ENG., Illus.). 176p. (J). (gr. 5-7). pap. 7.99 (978-1-328-89575-2(0), 1699653, Clarion Bks.) HarperCollins Pubs.

—Bee-Bim Bop! Lee, Ho Baek, illus. 2005. (ENG.). 32p. (J). (gr. -1-3). 17.99 (978-0-618-26511-4(2), 111270, Clarion Bks.) HarperCollins Pubs.

—The Firekeeper's Son. Downing, Julie, illus. 2009. (ENG.). 40p. (J). (gr. -1-3). pap. 8.99 (978-0-547-23769-5(3), 1083886, Clarion Bks.) HarperCollins Pubs.

—The Kite Fighters. 2010. (ENG., Illus.). 144p. (J). (gr. 3-7). pap. 8.99 (978-0-547-32863-8(X), 1416976, Clarion Bks.) HarperCollins Pubs.

—Seesaw Girl. Tseng, Mou-Sien & Tseng, Jean, illus. 2009. (ENG.). 96p. (J). (gr. 3-7). pap. 8.99 (978-0-547-24888-2(1), 1100900, Clarion Bks.) HarperCollins Pubs.

—A Single Shard. 2011. 9.00 (978-0-7848-3611-8(6), Everbind) Marco Bk. Co.

—A Single Shard. unabr. ed. 2004. (Middle Grade Cassette Librariestm Ser.). (J). (gr. 5-9). pap. 36.00 incl. audio (978-0-8072-1760-3(3), S YA 349 SP, Listening Library) Random Hse. Audio Publishing Group.

—A Single Shard. 2011. (gr. 5-8). lib. bdg. 18.40 (978-0-613-57327-6(7)) Turtleback.

—A Single Shard: A Newbery Award Winner. 2011. (ENG.). 176p. (J). (gr. 5-7). pap. 10.99 (978-0-547-53426-8(4), 1447661, Clarion Bks.) HarperCollins Pubs.

—When My Name Was Keoko. 2004. 199p. (J). (gr. 5). 14.65 (978-0-7569-2928-2(8)) Perfection Learning Corp.

—When My Name Was Keoko. 2012. lib. bdg. 18.40 (978-0-606-24716-0(5)) Turtleback.

Park, So Hee, creator. Goong, Vol. 13: The Royal Palace, Vol. 13. 2013. (Goong Ser.: 13). (ENG., Illus.). 384p. (J). (gr. 8-17). pap. 25.00 (978-0-7595-3157-4(9)) Yen Pr. LLC.

—Goong, Vol. 14: The Royal Palace. 2014. (Goong Ser.: 14). (ENG., Illus.). 368p. (J). (gr. 8-17). pap. 25.00 (978-0-7595-3158-1(7)) Yen Pr. LLC.

Patel, Sonia. Bloody Seoul, 1 vol. 2019. (ENG.). 224p. (YA). (gr. 8-12). 17.95 (978-1-947627-20-8(1), 23353382, Cinco Puntos Press) Lee & Low Bks., Inc.

RIGBY. The Moneybag: a Tale from Korea: Third Grade Big Books. 2003. (Rigby on Our Way to English Ser.). (ENG.). 24p. (gr. 3-3). pap. 50.70 (978-0-7578-4214-6(3)) Rigby Education.

Samson, Lucretia. Hungry Tiger & Clever Rabbit: A Tale from Korea, 1 vol. Bijloo, Adrian, illus. 2016. (ENG.). 24p. (J). pap. 9.95 (978-1-927244-58-6(7)) Clean Slate Pr. Ltd. NZL. Dist: Flying Start Bks.

—Hungry Tiger & Clever Rabbit (Big Book Edition) A Tale from Korea. Bijloo, Adrian, illus. 2016. 24p. (J). pap. (978-1-927244-68-5(4)) Flying Start Bks.

Schoettler, Joan. Good Fortune in a Wrapping Cloth. Lanan, Jessica, illus. 2011. (ENG.). 32p. (J). (gr. k-3). 17.95 (978-1-885008-40-4(6), leelowshens, Shen's Bks.) Lee & Low Bks., Inc.

Sherman, M. Zachary. Damage Control, 1 vol. Cage, Josef, illus. 2012. (Bloodlines Ser.). (ENG.). 88p. (J). (gr. 4-8). lib. bdg. 27.32 (978-1-4342-3765-1(6), 117026, Stone Arch Bks.) Capstone.

Stickler, John C. & Han, Soma. Maya & the Turtle: A Korean Fairy Tale. Han, Soma, illus. 2012. (ENG., Illus.). 32p. (J). (gr. -1-3). 14.95 (978-0-8048-4277-8(9)) Tuttle Publishing.

Watkins, Yoko Kawashima. So Far from the Bamboo Grove. 2008. (ENG., Illus.). 192p. (J). (gr. 3-7). reprint ed. pap. 9.99 (978-0-688-13115-9(8), HarperCollins) HarperCollins Pubs.

KOREA (NORTH)

Allen, John. Living in North Korea. 2018. (ENG.). 80p. (YA). (gr. 6-12). 39.93 (978-1-68282-475-7(6)) ReferencePoint Pr., Inc.

Berlatsky, Noah, ed. North & South Korea, 1 vol. 2013. (Opposing Viewpoints Ser.). (ENG.). 216p. (gr. 10-12). pap. 34.80 (978-0-7377-6964-7(5), d17e5569-d642-4525-a872-0a010e8d80ef); lib. bdg. 50.43

(978-0-7377-6963-0(7), 36ee8d4f-5a9b-4d8a-a39c-cb73f649c794) Greenhaven Publishing LLC. (Greenhaven Publishing).

Fishman, Jon M. Kim Jong Un: Secretive North Korean Leader. 2019. (Gateway Biographies Ser.). (ENG., Illus.). 48p. (J). (gr. 4-8). lib. bdg. 31.99 (978-1-5415-3919-8(2), babb14b8-f2cc-410f-a982-82ab6b24772e, Lerner Pubns.) Lerner Publishing Group.

Hulick, Kathryn. North Korea Today. 2017. (Special Reports Set 3 Ser.). (ENG., Illus.). 112p. (J). (gr. 6-12). lib. bdg. 41.36 (978-1-5321-1334-5(X), 27542, Essential Library) ABDO Publishing Co.

Murray, Julie. North Korea, 1 vol. 2015. (Explore the Countries Ser.). (ENG., Illus.). 40p. (J). (gr. 2-5). 35.64 (978-1-68078-069-7(7), 19176, Big Buddy Bks.) ABDO Publishing Co.

Raben, Molly. Explore North Korea: 12 Key Facts. 2019. (Country Profiles Ser.). (ENG., Illus.). 32p. (J). (gr. 3-6). 9.95 (978-1-63235-614-7(7), 13963); lib. bdg. 32.80 (978-1-63235-559-1(0), 13954) Bookstaves, LLC. (12-Story Library).

Rice Jr., Earle. The Evolution of Government & Politics in North & South Korea. 2014. (Illus.). 47p. (J). (gr. 4-8). 29.95 (978-1-61228-588-7(0)) Mitchell Lane Pubs.

Wyborny, Sheila. Kim Jong Il, 1 vol. 2009. (People in the News Ser.). (ENG., Illus.). 104p. (gr. 7-7). lib. bdg. 41.03 (978-1-4205-0091-2(0), bce6fd4e-5a78-42b1-8c19-1ce498c0d927, Lucent Pr.) Greenhaven Publishing LLC.

KOREA (SOUTH)

Berlatsky, Noah, ed. North & South Korea, 1 vol. 2013. (Opposing Viewpoints Ser.). (ENG.). 216p. (gr. 10-12). pap. 34.80 (978-0-7377-6964-7(5), d17e5569-d642-4525-a872-0a010e8d80ef); lib. bdg. 50.43 (978-0-7377-6963-0(7), 36ee8d4f-5a9b-4d8a-a39c-cb73f649c794) Greenhaven Publishing LLC. (Greenhaven Publishing).

Blevins, Wiley. South Korea (Follow Me Around) (Library Edition) 2018. (Follow Me Around... Ser.). (ENG., Illus.). 32p. (J). (gr. 3-4). 27.00 (978-0-531-12922-7(5), Children's Pr.) Scholastic Library Publishing.

Brown, Jennifer. South Korea. 2019. (Illus.). 96p. (J). (978-1-4222-4263-6(3)) Mason Crest.

Dalrymple, Lisa. Cultural Traditions in South Korea. 2016. (ENG., Illus.). 32p. (J). lib. bdg. (978-0-7787-8088-5(0)) Crabtree Publishing Co.

Daniels-Cowart, Catrina. South Korea. 2019. (Asian Countries Today Ser.). (Illus.). 96p. (J). (gr. 12). lib. bdg. 34.60 (978-1-4222-4267-4(6)) Mason Crest.

DuBois, Jill & Nevins, Debbie. South Korea. 2015. (J). lib. bdg. (978-1-62713-369-2(0)) Cavendish Square Publishing LLC.

Dubois, Jill & Nevins, Debbie. South Korea, 1 vol. 3rd rev. ed. 2014. (Cultures of the World (Third Edition)(r) Ser.). (ENG.). 144p. (gr. 5-5). 48.79 (978-1-5026-0079-0(X), 2dcaab06-8c8f-4bf1-b9b6-b70d17dfa778) Cavendish Square Publishing LLC.

Foran, Racquel. South Korea, 1 vol. 2013. (Countries of the World Set 2 Ser.). (ENG.). 144p. (YA). (gr. 6-12). lib. bdg. 42.79 (978-1-61783-636-7(2), 4896, Essential Library) ABDO Publishing Co.

Hye-sook, Lee. Suro: The First King of Gaya. Park, Christian J., tr. Dong-sung, Kim, illus. 2011. (ENG.). 44p. 14.00 (978-89-91913-48-6(2), 2040) Seoul Selection KOR. Dist: Univ. of Hawaii Pr.

Kallen, Stuart A. K-Pop: Korea's Musical Explosion. 2014. (ENG., Illus.). 64p. (YA). (gr. 6-12). lib. bdg. 33.32 (978-1-4677-2042-7(9), e792689b-ac3e-4e00-99f3-ac7e6feeb14a, Twenty-First Century Bks.) Lerner Publishing Group.

Kalman, Bobbie. Spotlight on South Korea, 1 vol. 2013. (ENG., Illus.). 32p. (J). pap. (978-0-7787-0868-1(3)) Crabtree Publishing Co.

Murray, Julie. South Korea, 1 vol. 2015. (Explore the Countries Ser.). (ENG., Illus.). 40p. (J). (gr. 2-5). 35.64 (978-1-68078-070-3(0), 19178, Big Buddy Bks.) ABDO Publishing Co.

Perkins, Chloe. Living in ... South Korea: Ready-To-Read Level 2. Woolley, Tom, illus. 2017. (Living In... Ser.). (ENG.). 32p. (J). (gr. k-2). 17.99 (978-1-5344-0143-3(1)); pap. 4.99 (978-1-5344-0142-6(3)) Simon Spotlight. (Simon Spotlight).

Rice Jr., Earle. The Evolution of Government & Politics in North & South Korea. 2014. (Illus.). 47p. (J). (gr. 4-8). 29.95 (978-1-61228-588-7(0)) Mitchell Lane Pubs.

Rudolph, Jessica. South Korea. 2015. (Countries We Come From Ser.). (ENG., Illus.). 32p. (J). (gr. k-3). lib. bdg. 28.50 (978-1-62724-854-9(4)) Bearport Publishing Co., Inc.

Senker, Cath. Samsung: The Business Behind the Technology. 2016. (Big Brands Ser.). (ENG., Illus.). 32p. (J). (gr. 4-6). 26.65 (978-1-5124-0591-0(4), 8d66e1c7-0185-45eb-826d-8428526910c2, Lerner Pubns.) Lerner Publishing Group.

Sheafer, Silvia Anne. Roh Moo Hyun. 2008. (Modern World Leaders Ser.). (ENG., Illus.). 136p. (gr. 7-12). 30.00 (978-0-7910-9760-1(9), P159141, Facts On File) Infobase Holdings, Inc.

Sullivan, Laura L. South Korea, 1 vol. 2018. (Exploring World Cultures (First Edition) Ser.). (ENG.). 32p. (gr. 3-3). 31.64 (978-1-5026-3814-4(2), 49956cc5-a3d4-4171-a1ec-fcd4dd2172f3) Cavendish Square Publishing LLC.

Wiseman, Blaine. South Korea. 2018. (J). (978-1-5105-3568-8(3)) SmartBook Media, Inc.

Yasuda, Anita. South Korea. 2014. (J). (978-1-4896-3066-7(X)) Weigl Pubs., Inc.

Zobel, Derek. South Korea. 2011. (Exploring Countries Ser.). (ENG., Illus.). 32p. (J). (gr. 3-7). lib. bdg. 27.95 (978-1-60014-624-4(4), Blastoff! Readers) Bellwether Media.

KOREA (SOUTH)—FICTION

Cho, Kat. Wicked Fox. 2019. 448p. (YA). (gr. 7). 18.99 (978-1-9848-1234-6(3), G.P. Putnam's Sons Books for Young Readers) Penguin Young Readers Group.

Oh, Axie. Rebel Seoul, 1 vol. Hue, Sebastien, illus. 2017. (Rebel Seoul Ser.). (ENG.). 400p. (YA). (gr. 6-12). 21.95 (978-1-62014-299-8(6), leelowtu, Tu Bks.) Lee & Low Bks., Inc.

KOREAN AMERICANS

Bryan, Nichol. Korean Americans, 1 vol. 2004. (One Nation Set 2 Ser.). (ENG.). 32p. (gr. k-6). 27.07 (978-1-59197-530-4(1), Checkerboard Library) ABDO Publishing Co.

Ingram, Scott. Korean Americans, 1 vol. 2006. (World Almanac(r) Library of American Immigration Ser.). (ENG., Illus.). 48p. (gr. 5-8). pap. 15.05 (978-0-8368-7328-3(9), 949799b3-5bae-4eff-a35c-320c545fcf59); lib. bdg. 33.67 (978-0-8368-7315-3(7), 7cecba9a-484f-44d3-9be6-b91d8d57c354) Stevens, Gareth Publishing LLLP. (Gareth Stevens Secondary Library).

Martin, Jennifer C. The Korean Americans. 2003. (Immigrants in America Ser.). (ENG., Illus.). 112p. (J). (gr. 4-7). lib. bdg. 30.85 (978-1-59018-079-2(8), Lucent Bks.) Cengage Gale.

Moreno, Barry. The Korean Americans. (Major American Immigration Ser.). (YA). 2010. (Illus.). 64p. (gr. 9-12). 22.95 (978-1-4222-0612-6(2)) 2007. pap. 9.95 (978-1-4222-0679-9(3)) Mason Crest.

Noonan, Sheila Smith. Korean Immigration. 2005. (Changing Face of North America Ser.). (Illus.). 112p. (YA). lib. bdg. 24.95 (978-1-59084-693-3(1)) Mason Crest.

Snyder, Gail. Korean Americans. (Successful Americans Ser.). 64p. (YA). 2009. (gr. 9-12). 22.95 (978-1-4222-0518-1(5)) 2007. (gr. 7-18). pap. 9.95 (978-1-4222-0864-9(8)) Mason Crest.

Taus-Bolstad, Stacy. Koreans in America. 2005. (In America Ser.). (ENG., Illus.). 80p. (gr. 5-8). lib. bdg. 27.93 (978-0-8225-4874-4(7), Lerner Pubns.) Lerner Publishing Group.

Thomas, William David. Korean Americans, 1 vol. 2010. (New Americans Ser.). (ENG.). 80p. (gr. 5-5). 38.36 (978-0-7614-4306-3(1), ad720f6d-7d20-484b-8775-6914bd396756) Cavendish Square Publishing LLC.

Weber, Valerie J. I Come from South Korea, 1 vol. 2006. (This Is My Story Ser.). (ENG., Illus.). 24p. (gr. 2-4). lib. bdg. 24.67 (978-0-8368-7237-8(1), 639a1b20-a602-44db-960b-a99720757f5a, Weekly Reader Leveled Readers) Stevens, Gareth Publishing LLLP.

Weber, Valerie J. & Weber, Valerie J. I Come from South Korea, 1 vol. 2006. (This Is My Story Ser.). (ENG., Illus.). 24p. (gr. 2-4). pap. 9.15 (978-0-8368-7244-6(4), 4d5e8a06-bf89-487e-ba44-32eaeb2f1df6, Weekly Reader Leveled Readers) Stevens, Gareth Publishing LLLP.

KOREAN AMERICANS—FICTION

An, Na. Wait for Me. 2017. (ENG., Illus.). (YA). (gr. 7). 192p. 19.99 (978-1-4814-4242-8(2)); 208p. pap. 10.99 (978-1-4814-4243-5(0)) Simon & Schuster Children's Publishing. (Atheneum/Caitlyn Dlouhy Books).

Bahk, Jane. Juna's Jar. Hoshino, Felicia, illus. 2015. (ENG.). 32p. (J). 17.95 (978-1-60060-853-7(1), 9781600000000) Lee & Low Bks., Inc.

Bonin, Liane. Pretty on the Outside: Fame Unlimited. 2007. 288p. (YA). pap. 9.99 (978-0-451-22122-3(2), NAL) Penguin Publishing Group.

Brandon, Anthony G. Moving Day. Yee, Wong Herbert, illus. 2005. (ENG.). 32p. (J). (gr. -1-3). pap. 4.99 (978-0-15-205652-0(1), 1196995, Clarion Bks.) HarperCollins Pubs.

Cho, John. Troublemaker. (ENG.). 224p. (J). (gr. 3-7). 2023. pap. 7.99 (978-0-7595-5446-7(3)) 2022. 16.99 (978-0-7595-5447-4(1)) Little, Brown Bks. for Young Readers.

Farley, Christina. Gilded, 0 vols. 2014. (Gilded Ser.: 1). (ENG.). 352p. (YA). (gr. 7-12). pap. 9.99 (978-1-4778-1097-2(8), 9781477810972, Skyscape) Amazon Publishing.

The Fold. 2017. (ENG., Illus.). (YA). (gr. 7). 256p. 19.99 (978-1-4814-4239-8(2)); 272p. pap. 12.99 (978-1-4814-4240-4(6)) Simon & Schuster Children's Publishing. (Atheneum/Caitlyn Dlouhy Books).

Goo, Maurene. Since You Asked... 2013. (YA). 262p. pap. (978-0-545-44822-2(0)); (ENG.). 272p. (gr. 7). 17.99 (978-0-545-44821-5(2)) Scholastic, Inc. (Scholastic Pr.).

—Somewhere Only We Know. 2019. (ENG.). 336p. (YA). 17.99 (978-0-374-31057-8(2), 900193167, Farrar, Straus & Giroux (BYR)) Farrar, Straus & Giroux.

—Somewhere Only We Know. 2020. (ENG.). 336p. (YA). pap. 10.99 (978-1-250-25078-0(1), 900193168) Square Fish.

—The Way You Make Me Feel. 2018. (ENG.). 336p. (J). pap. (978-0-374-31195-7(1)) Farrar, Straus & Giroux.

—The Way You Make Me Feel. 2019. (ENG.). 352p. (YA). pap. 9.99 (978-1-250-30880-1(1), 900158638) Square Fish.

Han, Jenny. Clara Lee & the Apple Pie Dream. 2014. (ENG.). 160p. (J). (gr. 3-7). pap. 10.99 (978-0-316-07037-9(8)) Little, Brown Bks. for Young Readers.

Jung, Mike. Unidentified Suburban Object. 2019. (Penworthy Picks Middle School Ser.). (ENG.). 265p. (J). (gr. 4-5). 17.96 (978-1-64310-936-7(7)) Penworthy Co., LLC, The.

—Unidentified Suburban Object. 2017. (ENG.). 272p. (J). (gr. 3-7). pap. 7.99 (978-0-545-78227-2(9)) Scholastic, Inc.

Keller, Tae. When You Trap a Tiger. 2020. 304p. (J). (978-0-593-17534-7(4)) Random Hse., Inc.

—When You Trap a Tiger: (Newbery Medal Winner) (J). (gr. 3-7). 2023. 320p. pap. 8.99 (978-1-5247-1573-1(5), Yearling) 2020. (ENG.). 304p. 17.99 (978-1-5247-1570-0(0), Random Hse. Bks. for Young Readers) 2020. (ENG.). 304p. lib. bdg. 19.99 (978-1-5247-1571-7(9), Random Hse. Bks. for Young Readers) Random Hse. Children's Bks.

Kent, Rose. Kimchi & Calamari. 2010. (ENG.). 240p. (J). (gr. 3-7). pap. 6.99 (978-0-06-083771-6(3), HarperCollins) HarperCollins Pubs.

Kim, Aram. Let's Go to Taekwondo! A Story about Persistence, Bravery, & Breaking Boards. 2020. (Yoomi, Friends, & Family Ser.). (Illus.). 40p. (J). (gr. -1-2). 17.99 (978-0-8234-4360-4(4)) Holiday Hse., Inc.

—No Kimchi for Me! 2017. (Yoomi, Friends, & Family Ser.). (ENG., Illus.). 40p. (J). (gr. -1-2). 18.99 (978-0-8234-3762-7(0)) Holiday Hse., Inc.

Kim, Patti. I'm Ok. 2018. (ENG., Illus.). 288p. (J). (gr. 5). 16.99 (978-1-5344-1929-2(2), Atheneum Bks. for Young Readers) Simon & Schuster Children's Publishing.

Kline, Suzy. Horrible Harry & the Dragon War. Remkiewicz, Frank, illus. 2003. (Horrible Harry Ser.: 14). 64p. (J). (gr. 2-4). 4.99 (978-0-14-250166-5(2), Puffin Books) Penguin Young Readers Group.

—Horrible Harry & the Dragon War. 2003. (Horrible Harry Ser.: 14). lib. bdg. 14.75 (978-0-613-92539-6(4)) Turtleback.

Making Heaven (Koreans) 76p. (YA). (gr. 6-12). pap. 9.95 (978-0-8224-3801-4(1)) Globe Fearon Educational Publishing.

Na, An. A Step from Heaven. 2011. (ENG.). 160p. (YA). (gr. 7-11). 22.44 (978-0-14-250027-9(5)) Penguin Young Readers Group.

Oh, Jina, reader. A Step from Heaven. 2004. 160p. (J). (gr. 6-18). pap. 36.00 incl. audio (978-0-8072-2287-4(9), Listening Library) Random Hse. Audio Publishing Group.

Park, Linda Sue. Project Mulberry. 2022. (ENG.). 272p. (J). (gr. 3-7). pap. 7.99 (978-0-544-93521-1(7), 1658126, Clarion Bks.) HarperCollins Pubs.

—Project Mulberry. 2007. 225p. (gr. 4-7). 17.00 (978-0-7569-7921-8(8)) Perfection Learning Corp.

Recorvits, Helen. My Name Is Yoon. Swiatkowska, Gabi, illus. 2003. (ENG.). 32p. (J). (gr. -1-3). 18.99 (978-0-374-35114-4(7), 900020207, Farrar, Straus & Giroux (BYR)) Farrar, Straus & Giroux.

—My Name Is Yoon. Swiatkowska, Gabi, illus. 2014. (ENG.). 32p. (J). (gr. -1-3). 8.99 (978-1-250-05711-2(6), 900139124) Square Fish.

Shin, Sun Yung. Cooper's Lesson. Cogan, Kim & Paek, Min, trs. from ENG. Cogan, Kim, illus. 2004. (ENG & KOR.). 32p. (J). 16.95 (978-0-89239-193-6(6)) Lee & Low Bks., Inc.

—Cooper's Lesson, 1 vol. 2015. (ENG., Illus.). 32p. (J). (gr. 1-5). pap. 11.95 (978-0-89239-361-9(0), leelowcbp, Children's Book Press) Lee & Low Bks., Inc.

Son, John. Finding My Hat (First Person Fiction) 2005. (First Person Fiction Ser.). (ENG.). 192p. (J). (gr. 7). reprint ed. pap. 6.99 (978-0-439-43539-0(0), Scholastic Paperbacks) Scholastic, Inc.

A Step from Heaven. 2016. (ENG., Illus.). 160p. (YA). (gr. 7). 19.99 (978-1-4814-4235-0(X)); pap. 10.99 (978-1-4814-4236-7(8)) Simon & Schuster Children's Publishing. (Atheneum/Caitlyn Dlouhy Books).

Sullivan, Maureen. Cabbages & Queens. Ferrando, Carol, illus. 2010. 57p. (J). pap. (978-0-9820381-3-0(5)) MoJo InkWorks.

Wait for Me. 2007. 169p. (gr. 4-7). 18.00 (978-0-7569-7959-1(5)) Perfection Learning Corp.

Williams, Laura E. Slant. 2008. (ENG.). 160p. (J). (gr. 2-8). pap. 6.95 (978-1-57131-682-0(5)) Milkweed Editions.

Yangsook, Choi. The Name Jar. 2014. (ENG.). 40p. (J). (gr. k-2). 11.24 (978-1-63245-313-6(4)) Lectorum Pubns., Inc.

Yoo, David. The Detention Club. 2012. (ENG.). 304p. (J). (gr. 5). pap. 6.99 (978-0-06-178380-7(3), Balzer & Bray) HarperCollins Pubs.

Yoo, Paula. Good Enough. 2012. (ENG.). 336p. (YA). (gr. 8). pap. 7.99 (978-0-06-079090-5(3), HarperTeen) HarperCollins Pubs.

Yoon, David. Frankly in Love. (ENG.). (YA). (gr. 9). 2020. 448p. pap. 12.99 (978-1-9848-1222-3(X), Penguin Books) 2019. 432p. 18.99 (978-1-9848-1220-9(3), G.P. Putnam's Sons Books for Young Readers) Penguin Young Readers Group.

Yoon, Nicola. The Sun Is Also a Star. (ENG.). 384p. (YA). (gr. 7). 2019. pap. 12.99 (978-0-553-49671-0(9), Ember) 2016. 19.99 (978-0-553-49668-0(9), Delacorte Pr.) Random Hse. Children's Bks.

—The Sun Is Also a Star Movie Tie-In Edition. 2019. (ENG.). 384p. (YA). (gr. 7). pap. 12.99 (978-1-9848-4939-7(5), Ember) Random Hse. Children's Bks.

KOREAN LANGUAGE

Animals Habitats, 1 vol., 1. 2015. (Our Wonderful World Ser.). 8p. (J). (gr. 2-4). pap. 9.35 (978-1-5081-1239-6(8), c94f7dae-c8ff-48f9-aefe-b26697b83bd8, Rosen Classroom) Rosen Publishing Group, Inc., The.

Burke, David. GOLDILOCKS (Korean to English - Level 2) Learn ENGLISH Through Fairy Tales. 2007. (KOR & ENG.). (J). per. 14.95 incl. audio compact disk (978-1-891888-10-6(2)) Slangman Publishing.

In Our Words. Korean Letter Story. 2012.Tr. of 한글나라 이야기. (KOR., Illus.). 66p. (J). 29.99 (978-1-938040-00-9(7)) In Our Words Inc.

Karapetian, Marjam. Bilingual Content Dictionary: English to Korean. 2004. (KOR & ENG.). 4.95 (978-0-9764829-7-0(5)); 4.95 (978-0-9764829-6-3(7)); 13.95 (978-0-9767958-0-3(9)); 9.95 (978-0-9764829-8-7(3)); 15.95 (978-0-9767958-1-0(7)) WizdomInc.

—Bilingual Content Dictionary: English to Korean: Social Studies - American History Through 1776. 2004. (KOR & ENG.). 14.95 (978-0-9764829-9-4(1)) WizdomInc.

Kudela, Katy R. My First Book of Korean Words. Translations.com Staff, tr. 2011. (Bilingual Picture Dictionaries Ser.). (MUL.). 32p. (gr. 1-2). pap. 47.70 (978-1-4296-6166-9(6), Capstone Pr.) Capstone.

Lee, Sungun, et al, creators. Korean Language I: Easy to Learn, 5 vols. 2nd ed. 2004. 152p. (C). pap. 15.00 (978-0-9762990-1-1(1)) Korean Culture Research, Inc.

Mahoney, Judy. Teach Me Everyday Korean V. 1, Vol 1. 2008. (ENG., Illus.). 32p. (J). (gr. -1). 19.95 (978-1-59972-110-1(4)) Teach Me Tapes, Inc.

Milet Publishing Staff. Animals, 1 vol. 2011. (My First Bilingual Book Ser.). (ENG., Illus.). 24p. (J). (gr. k — 1). bds. 8.99 (978-1-84059-615-1(5)) Milet Publishing.

—Bilingual Visual Dictionary CD-ROM (English-Korean) 2011. (Milet Multimedia Ser.). (ENG & KOR., Illus.). 1p. (J). (gr. k-2). cd-rom 19.95 (978-1-84059-587-1(6)) Milet Publishing.

—Colors - My First Bilingual Book, 1 vol. 2011. (My First Bilingual Book Ser.). (ENG.). 24p. (J). (gr. k — 1). bds. 8.99 (978-1-84059-601-4(5)) Milet Publishing.

—My Bilingual Book-Hearing, 1 vol. 2014. (My Bilingual Book Ser.). (ENG., Illus.). 24p. (J). (gr. -1-k). 9.95 (978-1-84059-779-0(8)) Milet Publishing.

—My Bilingual Book-Sight, 1 vol. 2014. (My Bilingual Book Ser.). (ENG., Illus.). 24p. (J). (gr. -1-k). 9.95 (978-1-84059-795-0(X)) Milet Publishing.

—My Bilingual Book-Smell, 1 vol. 2014. (My Bilingual Book Ser.). (ENG., Illus.). 24p. (J). (gr. -1-k). 9.95 (978-1-84059-811-7(5)) Milet Publishing.

—My Bilingual Book-Taste (English-Korean), 1 vol. 2014. (My Bilingual Book Ser.). (ENG., Illus.). 24p. (J). (gr. -1-k). 9.95 (978-1-84059-827-8(1)) Milet Publishing.

—My Bilingual Book-Touch, 1 vol. 2014. (My Bilingual Book Ser.). (ENG., Illus.). 24p. (J). (gr. -1-k). 9.95 (978-1-84059-843-8(3)) Milet Publishing.

—My First Bilingual Book - Fruit, 60 vols. 2011. (My First Bilingual Book Ser.). (ENG., Illus.). 24p. (J). (gr. k — 1). bds. 8.99 (978-1-84059-631-1(7)) Milet Publishing.

—My First Bilingual Book - Home, 1 vol. 2011. (My First Bilingual Book Ser.). (ENG., Illus.). 24p. (J). (gr. k — 1). bds. 8.99 (978-1-84059-647-2(3)) Milet Publishing.

—My First Bilingual Book-Jobs (English-Korean), 1 vol. 2012. (My First Bilingual Book Ser.). (ENG., Illus.). 24p. (J). (gr. k — 1). bds. 7.99 (978-1-84059-707-3(0)) Milet Publishing.

—My First Bilingual Book-Music (English-Korean), 1 vol. 2012. (My First Bilingual Book Ser.). (ENG., Illus.). 24p. (J). (gr. k — 1). bds. 7.99 (978-1-84059-723-3(2)) Milet Publishing.

—My First Bilingual Book-Opposites (English-Korean), 1 vol. 2012. (My First Bilingual Book Ser.). (ENG., Illus.). 24p. (J). (gr. k — 1). bds. 8.99 (978-1-84059-739-4(9)) Milet Publishing.

—My First Bilingual Book-Sports (English-Korean), 1 vol. 2012. (My First Bilingual Book Ser.). (ENG., Illus.). 24p. (J). (gr. k — 1). bds. 7.99 (978-1-84059-755-4(0)) Milet Publishing.

—My First Bilingual Book-Vegetables, 1 vol. 2011. (My First Bilingual Book Ser.). (ENG., Illus.). 24p. (J). (gr. k — 1). bds. 7.99 (978-1-84059-663-2(5)) Milet Publishing.

Park, Kyubyong & Amen, Henry J. My First Book of Korean Words: An ABC Rhyming Book of Korean Language & Culture. Padron, Aya, illus. 2017. (My First Words Ser.). 32p. (J). (gr. -1-3). 10.95 (978-0-8048-4940-1(4)) Tuttle Publishing.

Pihl, Marshall R. Korean Word Book. 2004. (KOR., Illus.). 112p. pap. 14.95 (978-1-57306-197-1(2)) Bess Pr., Inc.

The Rosetta Stone Language Library: Korean Level 1. 2005. (J). (gr. 1-18). cd-rom 209.00 (978-1-883972-78-3(7)) Rosetta Stone Ltd.

Turhan, Sedat. New Bilingual Visual Dictionary (English-Korean), 1 vol. 2017. (New Bilingual Visual Dictionary Ser.). (ENG., Illus.). 148p. (J). (gr. k-2). 19.95 (978-1-78508-888-9(2)) Milet Publishing.

KOREAN WAR, 1950-1953

Blohm, Craig E. Cause & Effect: The Korean War. 2017. (ENG.). 80p. (YA). (gr. 5-12). (978-1-68282-164-0(1)) ReferencePoint Pr., Inc.

Boehme, Gerry. The Partition of the Korean Peninsula, 1 vol. 2018. (Redrawing the Map Ser.). (ENG.). 112p. (YA). (gr. 9-9). lib. bdg. 45.93 (978-1-5026-3577-8(1), 60f6e97b-b4d5-4f64-9ac3-309786b65770) Cavendish Square Publishing LLC.

Burgan, Michael. The Korean War: An Interactive Modern History Adventure, 1 vol. 2014. (You Choose: Modern History Ser.). (ENG., Illus.). 112p. (J). (gr. 3-7). lib. bdg. 32.65 (978-1-4914-0355-6(1), 125861, Capstone Pr.) Capstone.

Doak, Robin. The Korean War, 1 vol. 2006. (Wars That Changed American History Ser.). (ENG., Illus.). 48p. (gr. 5-8). pap. 15.05 (978-0-8368-7303-0(3), cd7e3187-4263-4a66-aea3-e30c5fe21f09, Gareth Stevens Secondary Library) Stevens, Gareth Publishing LLLP.

Feldman, Ruth Tenzer. The Korean War. 2004. (Chronicle of America's Wars Ser.). (Illus.). 96p. (J). (gr. 5-12). 27.93 (978-0-8225-4716-7(3)) Lerner Publishing Group.

George, Enzo. The Korean War: Showdown with China, 1 vol. 2014. (Voices of War Ser.). (ENG.). 48p. (gr. 4-4). lib. bdg. 33.07 (978-1-62712-870-4(0), 91966662-713b-4f29-b0cc-c127baa7989f) Cavendish Square Publishing LLC.

Grant, R. G. The Korean War, 1 vol. 2004. (Atlas of Conflicts Ser.). (ENG., Illus.). 64p. (gr. 6-8). pap. 15.05 (978-0-8368-5673-6(2), dc811cb9-fdf6-4481-98b8-7f1823453e1e); lib. bdg. 36.67 (978-0-8368-5666-8(X), a1cf6718-485e-4142-bde5-c0d8244d528e) Stevens, Gareth Publishing LLLP. (Gareth Stevens Secondary Library).

Higgins, Melissa. Sgt. Reckless - The War Horse: Korean War Hero. Iglesias, Álvaro, illus. 2014. (Animal Heroes Ser.). (ENG.). 32p. (J). (gr. k-2). 29.32 (978-1-4795-5462-1(6), 126111, Picture Window Bks.) Capstone.

Hosch, William L. Korean War & the Vietnam War: People, Politics, & Power, 1 vol. 2010. (America at War Ser.). (ENG., Illus.). 232p. (J). (gr. 10-10). lib. bdg. 52.59 (978-1-61530-011-2(2), ac3dd829-b1e0-46de-a740-8d1cb2c3f3af) Rosen Publishing Group, Inc., The.

—The Korean War & the Vietnam War: People, Politics, & Power, 4 vols. 2010. (America at War Ser.). (ENG.). 232p. (YA). (gr. 10-10). 105.18 (978-1-61530-088-4(0), 204dd3bd-432d-4c01-92e3-a9020fbb76cd) Rosen Publishing Group, Inc., The.

Jeffrey, Gary & Riley, Terry, illus. The Korean War. 2013. (ENG.). 48p. (J). (978-0-7787-1234-3(6)); pap. (978-0-7787-1238-1(9)) Crabtree Publishing Co.

MacCarald, Clara. The Battle of Inchon: Turning Point of the Korean War. 2017. (Major Battles in US History Ser.). (ENG., Illus.). 32p. (J). (gr. 3-5). lib. bdg. 31.35 (978-1-63517-019-1(2), 1635170192, Focus Readers) North Star Editions.

Makos, Adam. Devotion (Adapted for Young Adults) An Epic Story of Heroism & Friendship. 2022. (Illus.). 368p. (YA). (gr. 7). 18.99 (978-0-593-48145-5(3)); (ENG., lib. bdg. 21.99 (978-0-593-48146-2(1)) Random Hse. Children's Bks. (Delacorte Pr.).

—Devotion (Young Readers Edition) An Epic Story of Heroism & Friendship. 2022. (ENG.). 368p. (YA). (gr. 7). pap. 12.99 (978-0-593-48148-6(8), Ember) Random Hse. Children's Bks.

Malkasian, Carter. The Korean War, 1 vol. 2008. (Essential Histories: War & Conflict in Modern Times Ser.). (ENG., Illus.). 96p. (YA). (gr. 10-10). lib. bdg. 38.47 (978-1-4042-1834-5(3), 5db45bbf-3e65-40c9-8e60-f54806e8b5d1) Rosen Publishing Group, Inc., The.

McCormick, Patricia. Sergeant Reckless: The True Story of the Little Horse Who Became a Hero. Bruno, Iacopo, illus. 2017. (ENG.). 40p. (J). (gr. 1-5). 17.99 (978-0-06-229259-9(5), Balzer & Bray) HarperCollins Pubs.

Miller, Derek. Minority Soldiers Fighting in the Korean War, 1 vol. 2017. (Fighting for Their Country: Minorities at War Ser.). (ENG.). 112p. (YA). (gr. 8-8). 44.50 (978-1-5026-2665-3(9),

4c864aac-c5d2-42be-9702-de415ff53155) Cavendish Square Publishing LLC.

Moore, Shannon Baker. Korean War, 1 vol. 2013. (Essential Library of American Wars Ser.). (ENG.). 112p. (YA). (gr. 6-12). lib. bdg. 41.36 *(978-1-61783-878-1(0),* 6605, Essential Library) ABDO Publishing Co.

Perritano, John. Korean War. (America at War Ser.). 32p. (J). 2011. (ENG.). (gr. 4-6). 24.94 *(978-0-531-24910-9(7))* 2010. 27.00 *(978-0-531-23207-1(7))* Scholastic Library Publishing. (Watts, Franklin).

Rice, Earle. Overview of the Korean War. 2008. (Monumental Milestones Ser.). (Illus.). 48p. (J). (gr. 4-7). lib. bdg. 29.95 *(978-1-58415-695-6(3))* Mitchell Lane Pubs.

Seth, Shaun. Key Figures of the Korean War, 1 vol. 2015. (Biographies of War Ser.). (ENG., Illus.). 112p. (J). (gr. 7-8). 35.47 *(978-1-68048-060-3(X),* 9ab2143d-ac83-4efd-bbd4-2a860ef7d388, Britannica Educational Publishing) Rosen Publishing Group, Inc., The.

Seth, Shaun, ed. Key Figures of the Korean War, 4 vols. 2015. (Biographies of War Ser.). (ENG.). 112p. (YA). (gr. 7-8). 70.94 *(978-1-68048-061-0(8),* 51acfa5f-9de5-4786-8b30-1c0ff001af45, Britannica Educational Publishing) Rosen Publishing Group, Inc., The.

Small, Cathleen. Strategic Inventions of the Korean War, 1 vol. 2016. (Tech in the Trenches Ser.). (ENG., Illus.). 112p. (YA). (gr. 9-9). 44.50 *(978-1-5026-2345-4(5),* 12a6e201-fa7a-481d-b720-d560c44d31ed) Cavendish Square Publishing LLC.

Streissguth, Thomas. The Korean War. 2017. (J). *(978-1-5105-3508-4(X))* SmartBook Media, Inc.

Ziff, John. The Korean War, Vol. 11. Musteen, Jason R., ed. 2015. (Major U. S. Historical Wars Ser.). (Illus.). 64p. (J). (gr. 7). lib. bdg. 23.95 *(978-1-4222-3356-6(1))* Mason Crest.

KOREAN WAR, 1950-1953—FICTION

Sherman, M. Zachary. Blood Brotherhood, 1 vol. Casas, Fritz, illus. 2011. (Bloodlines Ser.). (ENG.). 88p. (J). (gr. 4-8). pap. 6.95 *(978-1-4342-3098-0(8),* 114738, Stone Arch Bks.) Capstone.

—Damage Control, 1 vol. Cage, Josef, illus. 2012. (Bloodlines Ser.). (ENG.). 88p. (J). (gr. 4-8). lib. bdg. 27.32 *(978-1-4342-3765-1(6),* 117026, Stone Arch Bks.) Capstone.

Williams, Annie Morris. Marianne's Secret Cousins. Oldham, Cindi, illus. 2005. (Family History Adventures for Young Readers Ser.: 2). 240p. (J). per. 10.00 *(978-0-9645272-8-7(6))* Field Stone Pubs.

KOREANS—UNITED STATES

Thomas, William David. Korean Americans, 1 vol. 2010. (New Americans Ser.). (ENG.). 80p. (gr. 5-5). 38.36 *(978-0-7614-4306-3(1),* ad720f6d-7d20-484b-8775-6914bd396756) Cavendish Square Publishing LLC.

Yoo, Paula. Sixteen Years in Sixteen Seconds: The Sammy Lee Story, 1 vol. Lee, Dom, illus. 2010. (ENG.). 32p. (J). (gr. 3-6). 24.94 *(978-1-58430-247-6(X))* Lee & Low Bks., Inc.

KOREANS—UNITED STATES—FICTION

Choi, Yangsook. The Name Jar. 2003. (gr. k-3). lib. bdg. 18.40 *(978-0-613-82979-3(4))* Turtleback.

de la Cruz, Melissa. 29 Dates. 2018. (ENG.). 400p. (YA). 18.99 *(978-1-335-54154-3(3))* Harlequin Enterprises ULC CAN. Dist: HarperCollins Pubs.

—29 Dates. 2020. (ENG.). 384p. (YA). pap. 10.99 *(978-1-335-99471-4(8))* Harlequin Enterprises ULC CAN. Dist: HarperCollins Pubs.

Oh, Ellen. Finding Junie Kim. 2021. (ENG.). 368p. (J). (gr. 3-7). 16.99 *(978-0-06-298798-3(4),* HarperCollins) HarperCollins Pubs.

KOUFAX, SANDY, 1935-

Doeden, Matt. Sandy Koufax. 2007. (YA). pap. 9.95 *(978-0-8225-6692-2(3))* 2006. (Illus.). 106p. (J). (gr. 3-7). lib. bdg. 27.93 *(978-0-8225-5961-0(7),* Twenty-First Century Bks.) Lerner Publishing Group.

Giordano, Geraldine. Sandy Koufax. 2009. (Baseball Hall of Famers Ser.). 112p. (gr. 5-8). 63.90 *(978-1-61511-516-7(1),* Rosen Reference) Rosen Publishing Group, Inc., The.

Winter, Jonah. You Never Heard of Sandy Koufax?! Carrilho, Andre, illus. 2016. 40p. (J). (gr. -1-3). 8.99 *(978-0-553-49842-4(8),* Dragonfly Bks.) Random Hse. Children's Bks.

KU KLUX KLAN (1915-)

Bartoletti, Susan Campbell. They Called Themselves the K. K. K: The Birth of an American Terrorist Group. (ENG., Illus.). 176p. (YA). (gr. 7). 2014. pap. 14.99 *(978-0-544-22582-4(1),* 1563371) 2010. 19.00 *(978-0-618-44033-7(X),* 581244) HarperCollins Pubs. (Clarion Bks.).

—They Called Themselves the K. K. K. The Birth of an American Terrorist Group. 2014. lib. bdg. 24.50 *(978-0-606-35334-2(8))* Turtleback.

Bowers, Rick. Superman Versus the Ku Klux Klan: The True Story of How the Iconic Superhero Battled the Men of Hate. 2012. (Illus.). 160p. pap. *(978-0-545-43745-5(8))* Scholastic, Inc.

Brimner, Larry Dane. Birmingham Sunday. 2010. (ENG., Illus.). 48p. (J). (gr. 7-12). 18.99 *(978-1-59078-613-0(0),* Calkins Creek) Highlights Pr., c/o Highlights for Children, Inc.

KU KLUX KLAN (1915-)—FICTION

Crawford, Ann Fears. Keechee: The Witch of the Woods. 2005. (J). *(978-1-931823-21-0(9))* Halcyon Pr.

Hesse, Karen. Witness. 2004. 168p. (J). (gr. 5-9). pap. 29.00 incl. audio *(978-0-8072-2094-8(9),* Listening Library) Random Hse. Audio Publishing Group.

—Witness (Scholastic Gold) (ENG.). (J). (gr. 4-7). 2019. 192p. pap. 7.99 *(978-1-338-35967-1(3))* 2003. (Illus.). 176p. pap. 7.99 *(978-0-439-27200-1(9),* Scholastic Paperbacks) Scholastic, Inc.

McMullan, Margaret. When I Crossed No-Bob. 2008. (ENG.). 224p. (J). (gr. 6-8). 22.44 *(978-0-618-71715-6(3))* Houghton Mifflin Harcourt Publishing Co.

Rucker, Rhonda. Welcome to Bombingham, 1 vol. 2019. (ENG., Illus.). 272p. (J). (gr. 6-12). 14.95 *(978-1-4556-2492-8(6),* Pelican Publishing) Arcadia Publishing.

Stanley, George E. Night Fires. 2009. (ENG.). 192p. (J). (gr. 3-7). 15.99 *(978-1-4169-7559-5(4),* Aladdin) Simon & Schuster Children's Publishing.

—Night Fires. 2011. (ENG.). 192p. (J). (gr. 3-7). pap. 6.99 *(978-1-4169-1250-7(9),* Simon & Schuster/Paula Wiseman Bks.) Simon & Schuster/Paula Wiseman Bks.

Vander Zee, Ruth. Mississippi Morning. Cooper, Floyd, illus. 2004. 32p. (J). 16.00 *(978-0-8028-5211-3(4))* Eerdmans, William B. Publishing Co.

KUBLAI KHAN, 1216-1294

Krull, Kathleen. Kubla Khan: The Emperor of Everything. Byrd, Robert, illus. 2010. 48p. (J). (gr. 3-7). 18.99 *(978-0-670-01114-8(2),* Viking Books for Young Readers) Penguin Young Readers Group.

KUBLAI KHAN, 1216-1294—FICTION

Jones Yang, Dori. Daughter of Xanadu. 2012. (ENG.). 352p. (YA). (gr. 7). pap. 9.99 *(978-0-385-73924-5(9),* Ember) Random Hse. Children's Bks.

McCaughrean, Geraldine. The Kite Rider. 2003. (ENG., Illus.). 320p. (YA). (gr. 8-18). pap. 15.99 *(978-0-06-441091-5(9),* HarperTeen) HarperCollins Pubs.

Scieszka, Jon. Marco? Polo! McCauley, Adam, illus. 2008. (Time Warp Trio Ser.: No. 16). 90p. (J). (gr. 4-6). 12.65 *(978-0-7569-8923-1(X))* Perfection Learning Corp.

—Marco? Polo! #16, No. 16. McCauley, Adam, illus. 2008. (Time Warp Trio Ser.: 16). 96p. (J). (gr. 2-4). 5.99 *(978-0-14-241177-3(9),* Puffin Books) Penguin Young Readers Group.

KUNG FU

Casarella, Antonello & Ghetti, Roberto. A Complete Guide to Kung Fu, 1 vol. 2017. (Mastering Martial Arts Ser.). (ENG.). 128p. (gr. 6-6). lib. bdg. 38.93 *(978-0-7660-8541-1(4),* dee6a27c-d268-4147-b3d5-afdae502dfd7) Enslow Publishing, LLC.

Colligan, Douglas. Kung Fu, 1 vol. 2011. (Martial Arts in Action Ser.). (ENG.). 48p. (gr. 5-5). lib. bdg. 32.64 *(978-0-7614-4937-9(X),* 5a73aa7e-5af6-48cd-a034-cda721deec23) Cavendish Square Publishing LLC.

Eng, Paul. Kungfu for Kids. Tok, Stephanie, illus. 2016. (Martial Arts for Kids Ser.). (ENG.). 48p. (J). (gr. k-3). 8.95 *(978-0-8048-4740-7(1))* Tuttle Publishing.

Howell, Brian. Kung Fu, 1 vol. 2015. (Inside Martial Arts Ser.). (ENG., Illus.). 48p. (J). (gr. 3-6). lib. bdg. 34.21 *(978-1-62403-604-0(X),* 17075, SportsZone) ABDO Publishing Co.

Johnson, Nathan. Kung Fu: Winning Ways. James, Adam, ed. 2015. (Mastering Martial Arts Ser.). (Illus.). 96p. (J). (gr. 5). lib. bdg. 24.95 *(978-1-4222-3240-8(9))* Mason Crest.

Smith, Tony. Shaolin Monks. 2012. (History's Greatest Warriors Ser.). (ENG., Illus.). 24p. (J). (gr. 3-7). lib. bdg. 26.95 *(978-1-60014-748-7(8),* Torque Bks.) Bellwether Media.

Wood, Alix. Kung Fu, 1 vol. 2013. (Kid's Guide to Martial Arts Ser.). (ENG., Illus.). 32p. (J). (gr. 2-3). pap. 12.75 *(978-1-4777-0360-1(8),* 4075b612-8d6b-480b-b97c-58a556efe2dc); lib. bdg. 30.27 *(978-1-4777-0319-9(5),* 3f0a0c3e-7d02-4227-96a8-6693fbbe1876) Rosen Publishing Group, Inc., The. (PowerKids Pr.).

KUWAIT

DiPiazza, Francesca Davis. Kuwait in Pictures. 2nd ed. 2007. (Visual Geography Series, Second Ser.). (ENG., Illus.). 80p. (gr. 5-12). lib. bdg. 31.93 *(978-0-8225-6589-5(7))* Lerner Publishing Group.

Marcovitz, Hal. Kuwait. 2010. (Major Muslim Nations Ser.). 112p. (YA). (gr. 5-18). lib. bdg. 25.95 *(978-1-4222-1386-5(2))* Mason Crest.

O'Shea, Maria & Spilling, Michael. Kuwait, 1 vol. 2nd rev. ed. 2010. (Cultures of the World (Second Edition)(r) Ser.). (ENG.). 144p. (gr. 5-5). 49.79 *(978-0-7614-4479-4(3),* 780c4e26-861a-4001-9796-377f9615f754) Cavendish Square Publishing LLC.

Ray, Kurt. A Historical Atlas of Kuwait. (Historical Atlases of South Asia, Central Asia, & the Middle East Ser.). 64p. (gr. 6-6). 2009. 61.20 *(978-1-61513-323-9(2))* 2003. (ENG., Illus.). lib. bdg. 37.13 *(978-0-8239-3981-7(2),* 843b5c28-1c1d-44ca-93ff-576bf656c840) Rosen Publishing Group, Inc., The.

Tracy, Kathleen. We Visit Kuwait. 2011. (Your Land & My Land Ser.). (Illus.). 64p. (J). (gr. 4-7). lib. bdg. 33.95 *(978-1-58415-958-2(8))* Mitchell Lane Pubs.

KWANZAA

Aloian, Molly. Kwanzaa. 2008. (Celebrations in My World Ser.). (ENG., Illus.). 32p. (J). (gr. k-3). pap. *(978-0-7787-4302-6(0))* Crabtree Publishing Co.

Benn, Lisa. Leroy's Kwanza Lesson. 2009. pap. 16.95 *(978-1-61623-891-9(7))* Independent Pub.

Beringer Mckissack, Lisa. Kwanzaa: Count & Celebrate!, 1 vol. 2009. (Holidays: Count & Celebrate! Ser.). (ENG., Illus.). 32p. (gr. k-2). lib. bdg. 26.60 *(978-0-7660-3102-9(0),* 2b7e9975-862d-48e0-8c60-2a9cad1d91a9) Enslow Publishing, LLC.

Bullard, Lisa. Kevin's Kwanzaa. Basaluzzo, Constanza, illus. 2012. (Cloverleaf Books (tm) — Fall & Winter Holidays Ser.). (ENG.). 24p. (J). (gr. k-2). 8.99 *(978-0-7613-8588-2(6),* ffbe2c22-12c2-4de4-888b-64583b9f13d8, Millbrook Pr.) Lerner Publishing Group.

—My Family Celebrates Kwanzaa. Basaluzzo, Constanza, illus. 2018. (Holiday Time (Early Bird Stories (tm)) Ser.). (ENG.). 24p. (J). (gr. k-2). 29.32 *(978-1-5415-2011-0(4),* 63aa084e-6e2c-4b89-bd7f-de31db99a559, Lerner Pubns.) Lerner Publishing Group.

Cain, Marie Mowery. Celebrate Kwanzaa. 2013. (Big Books, Red Ser.). (ENG & SPA., Illus.). 16p. pap. 33.00 *(978-1-59246-223-0(5))* Big Books, by George!

Corwin, Judith Hoffman. Kwanzaa Crafts: A Holiday Craft Book. 2004. (Illus.). 48p. (J). (gr. k-4). reprint ed. pap. 6.00 *(978-0-7567-7711-1(9))* DIANE Publishing Co.

Felix, Rebecca. We Celebrate Kwanzaa in Winter. 2014. (21st Century Basic Skills Library: Let's Look at Winter Ser.). (ENG., Illus.). 24p. (J). (gr. k-3). 26.35 *(978-1-63137-611-5(X),* 205227) Cherry Lake Publishing.

Heller, Daryl. Kwanzaa. (My Library of Holidays Ser.). 24p. (gr. 1-1). 2009. 37.50 *(978-1-61514-696-3(2))* 2003. (ENG., Illus.). (J). lib. bdg. 22.27 *(978-1-4042-2528-2(5),* 1ea1e743-7c91-467d-9945-ee896b4ac0dd) Rosen Publishing Group, Inc., The. (PowerKids Pr.).

—Kwanzaa, 1 vol. Gonzalez, Tomas, tr. 2003. (My Library of Holidays / Mi Biblioteca de Celebraciones Ser.). (ENG & SPA., Illus.). 24p. (J). (gr. 1-1). lib. bdg. 22.27 *(978-1-4042-7528-7(2),* f646cff2-bfc2-4c02-bdc6-363bc491c552, PowerKids Pr.) Rosen Publishing Group, Inc., The.

—Kwanzaa / Kwanzaa. 2009. (My Library of Holidays / Mi biblioteca de celebraciones Ser.). (ENG & SPA.). 24p. (gr. 1-1). 37.50 *(978-1-61514-702-1(0),* Editorial Buenas Letras) Rosen Publishing Group, Inc., The.

Hull, Bunny. Happy, Happy Kwanzaa: Kwanzaa for the World. Saint-James, Synthia, illus. 2003. 24p. (J). (gr. k-5). pap. 16.95 incl. audio compact disk *(978-0-9721478-1-1(0),* KCC/HHKCD810, Kid's Creative Classics) BrassHeart Music.

Johnson, Dolores. The Children's Book of Kwanzaa: A Guide to Celebrating the Holiday. 2007. (Illus.). 159p. (J). pap. 7.00 *(978-1-4223-6600-4(6))* DIANE Publishing Co.

Kwanzaa, 6 vols. (Multicultural Programs Ser.). 16p. (gr. 1-3). 24.95 *(978-0-7802-9208-6(1))* Wright Group/McGraw-Hill.

Linde, Barbara. Celebrating Kwanzaa, 1 vol. 2019. (History of Our Holidays Ser.). (ENG.). 24p. (gr. 1-2). pap. 9.15 *(978-1-5382-3878-3(0),* 43ff72ba-17b4-4ac9-a08a-de37dae32bee) Stevens, Gareth Publishing LLLP.

Marsh, Carole. Kwanzaa: Activities, Crafts, Recipes & More! 2003. 32p. (J). (gr. 1-6). pap. 6.95 *(978-0-635-02173-1(0))* Gallopade International.

McGee, Randel. Paper Crafts for Kwanzaa, 1 vol. 2008. (Paper Craft Fun for Holidays Ser.). (ENG., Illus.). 48p. (gr. 3-3). pap. 11.53 *(978-1-4644-0327-9(9),* 108c01b4-c48c-4cbd-986f-c906d52dc354); lib. bdg. 27.93 *(978-0-7660-2949-1(2),* 07ba43cf-802d-4ae2-9f3a-6b91f4d277b2) Enslow Publishing, LLC. (Enslow Elementary).

Murray, Julie. Kwanzaa. 2018. (Holidays (Abdo Kids Junior) Ser.). (ENG., Illus.). 24p. (J). (gr. -1-2). lib. bdg. 31.36 *(978-1-5321-8173-3(6),* 29819, Abdo Kids) ABDO Publishing Co.

Pettiford, Rebecca. Kwanzaa. 2014. (Illus.). 24p. (J). lib. bdg. 25.65 *(978-1-62031-131-8(3),* Bullfrog Bks.) Jump! Inc.

Ponto, Joanna & Gnojewski, Carol. Kwanzaa, 1 vol. 2016. (Story of Our Holidays Ser.). (ENG., Illus.). 32p. (gr. 3-3). pap. 11.52 *(978-0-7660-7621-1(0),* 207cb298-6b4d-4c8e-9c15-1ba82b2cb8c8) Enslow Publishing, LLC.

Raabe, Emily. A Kwanzaa Holiday Cookbook. 2009. (Festive Foods for the Holidays Ser.). 24p. (gr. 3-3). 42.50 *(978-1-61512-596-8(5),* PowerKids Pr.) Rosen Publishing Group, Inc., The.

Ross, Kathy. All New Crafts for Kwanzaa. Holm, Sharon Lane, illus. 2006. (All New Holiday Crafts for Kids Ser.). 48p. (J). (gr. -1-3). per. 7.95 *(978-0-8225-3435-8(5),* First Avenue Editions) Lerner Publishing Group.

Schuh, Mari. Kwanzaa. 2020. (Spot Holidays Ser.). (ENG.). 16p. (J). (gr. -1-1). pap. 9.99 *(978-1-68152-533-4(X),* 10732) Amicus.

Strain Trueit, Trudi. Kwanzaa, 1 vol. 2011. (Holiday Fun Ser.). (ENG.). 24p. (gr. k-1). 25.50 *(978-0-7614-4887-7(X),* 156d7797-413f-4406-b9b3-88a4ec710a40) Cavendish Square Publishing LLC.

Zocchi, Judy. On Kwanzaa. Wallis, Rebecca, illus. 2006. (Global Adventures I Ser.). (J). pap. 10.95 *(978-1-59646-200-7(0));* 32p. lib. bdg. 21.65 *(978-1-891997-49-5(1));* 32p. per. 10.95 *(978-1-59646-201-4(9))* Dingles & Co.

—On Kwanzaa/la Kwanzaa. Wallis, Rebecca, illus. 2006. (Global Adventures I Ser.).Tr. of Kwanzaa. (ENG & SPA.). 32p. (J). pap. 10.95 *(978-1-59646-202-1(7));* lib. bdg. 21.65 *(978-1-891997-50-1(5));* per. 10.95 *(978-1-59646-203-8(5))* Dingles & Co.

KWANZAA—FICTION

Amaker, Anthony D. Makeba's New Adventure. 2009. (ENG.). 26p. pap. 15.99 *(978-1-4415-1438-7(4))* Xlibris Corp.

Burden-Patmon, Denise. Imani's Gift at Kwanzaa. (J). 48.95 *(978-0-8136-2248-4(4))* Modern Curriculum Pr.

Flor Ada, Alma. Celebrate Kwanzaa with Boots & Her Kittens. Docampo, Valeria, illus. 2007. (Cuentos para Celebrar / Stories to Celebrate Ser.). 30p. (gr. k-6). per. 11.95 *(978-1-59820-135-2(2))* Santillana USA Publishing Co., Inc.

Katz, Karen. My First Kwanzaa. Katz, Karen, illus. 2014. (My First Holiday Ser.). (ENG., Illus.). 32p. (J). (gr. -1-k). 8.99 *(978-1-250-05046-5(4),* 900134033) Square Fish.

Meachen Rau, Dana. Holiday Time. 2004. (Compass Point Early Reader Ser.). (J). 18.60 *(978-0-7565-0571-4(2),* Compass Point Bks.) Capstone.

Shea, Therese. The Kwanzaa Surprise, 1 vol. 2006. (Neighborhood Readers Ser.). (ENG.). 12p. (gr. k-1). pap. 5.90 *(978-1-4042-6746-6(8),* 047873d1-d052-4768-9c46-c71bdae65c19, Rosen Classroom) Rosen Publishing Group, Inc., The.

Washington, Donna L. Li'l Rabbit's Kwanzaa: A Kwanzaa Holiday Book for Kids. Evans, Shane W., illus. 2010. (ENG.). 32p. (J). (gr. -1-2). 13.99 *(978-0-06-072816-8(7),* Tegen, Katherine Bks) HarperCollins Pubs.

L

LABOR

Here are entered works on the collective human activities involved in the production and distribution of goods and services. Works on the physical or mental exertion of individuals to produce or accomplish something are entered under Work.

see also Child Labor; Migrant Labor; Working Class

Acks, Alex. Key Labor Laws, 1 vol. 2019. (Laws That Changed History Ser.). (ENG.). 80p. (gr. 7-7). pap. 18.65 *(978-1-5026-5529-5(2),* 24508bf9-a952-403a-83d9-8d65c9c04223); lib. bdg. 37.36 *(978-1-5026-5530-1(6),* f0a453a6-d771-430e-b402-2b4cf66f4557) Cavendish Square Publishing LLC.

—Key Labor Laws. 2019. (J). pap. *(978-1-9785-1440-9(9))* Enslow Publishing, LLC.

Arnold, Quinn M. Construction Workers. 2017. (Seedlings Ser.). (ENG., Illus.). 24p. (J). (gr. -1-k). pap. 9.99 *(978-1-62832-486-0(4),* 20349, Creative Paperbacks) Creative Co., The.

Barber, Nicola. Ancient Roman Jobs, 1 vol. 2010. (Ancient Communities: Roman Life Ser.). (ENG., Illus.). 32p. (J). (gr. 4-4). pap. 11.60 *(978-1-61532-317-3(1),* ef772b05-c222-4fcc-9411-cc42272ebd3d); lib. bdg. 30.27 *(978-1-61532-307-4(4),* d0ccd0fd-8bd5-4d66-b590-b7da4e773aef) Rosen Publishing Group, Inc., The. (PowerKids Pr.).

Boothroyd, Jennifer. From Assembly Lines to Home Offices: How Work Has Changed. 2011. (Comparing Past & Present Ser.). pap. 7.95 *(978-0-7613-7842-6(1));* pap. 45.32 *(978-0-7613-8389-5(1));* (ENG., Illus.). 32p. lib. bdg. 26.60 *(978-0-7613-6748-2(9))* Lerner Publishing Group.

Bowman, Chris. Construction Workers. 2018. (Community Helpers Ser.). (ENG., Illus.). 24p. (J). (gr. k-3). lib. bdg. 26.95 *(978-1-62617-743-7(0),* Blastoff! Readers) Bellwether Media.

Bozek, Rachel, ed. Automation of Labor, 1 vol. 2019. (Opposing Viewpoints Ser.). (ENG.). 200p. (gr. 10-12). pap. 34.80 *(978-1-5345-0507-0(5),* 4f2ed896-9ebc-47fd-b565-4ee5e25cbcac) Greenhaven Publishing LLC.

Budd, Anitra, et al. Disgusting Jobs in History: The down & Dirty Details. 2018. (Disgusting Jobs in History Ser.). (ENG.). 32p. (J). (gr. 3-6). 119.96 *(978-1-5435-0378-4(0),* 27633, Capstone Pr.) Capstone.

Early Macken, JoAnn. Sanitation Workers, 1 vol. 2010. (People in My Community (Second Edition) Ser.). (ENG.). 24p. (J). (gr. k-2). pap. 9.15 *(978-1-4339-3810-8(3),* 3900cc00-7f18-4d20-9731-a2fcd3d69a89); lib. bdg. 25.27 *(978-1-4339-3809-2(X),* 5ee91a61-212b-4918-81a2-ebea9dee3c73) Stevens, Gareth Publishing LLLP.

Farrell, Mary Cronk. Fannie Never Flinched: One Woman's Courage in the Struggle for American Labor Union Rights. 2016. (ENG., Illus.). 56p. (J). (gr. 5-9). 19.95 *(978-1-4197-1884-7(3),* 1083701, Abrams Bks. for Young Readers) Abrams, Inc.

Hatton, Fran. Learning about Earning, 1 vol. 2014. (First-Glance Finance Ser.). (ENG.). 48p. (gr. 4-4). 33.07 *(978-1-5026-0094-3(3),* 6e6ca5b6-ab8f-472c-8e71-e3de69e898f0) Cavendish Square Publishing LLC.

Horn, Geoffrey M. Construction Worker, 1 vol. 2008. (Cool Careers: Helping Careers Ser.). (ENG.). 32p. (gr. 3-3). pap. 11.50 *(978-0-8368-9325-0(5),* f7fab0cd-319b-4cc8-bd5e-05c710a77198); (YA). lib. bdg. 28.67 *(978-0-8368-9192-8(9),* 8108f670-2997-47d7-baf1-023263089434) Stevens, Gareth Publishing LLLP.

Hurt, Avery Elizabeth, ed. Labor Unions & Workers' Rights, 1 vol. 2019. (Opposing Viewpoints Ser.). (ENG.). 176p. (gr. 10-12). pap. 34.80 *(978-1-5345-0594-0(6),* 901cfa08-31bc-4288-9e9a-515a3762e1b3) Greenhaven Publishing LLC.

Kalman, Bobbie. Ayudantes de Mi Comunidad. 2010. (SPA.). 24p. (J). pap. *(978-0-7787-8589-7(0));* lib. bdg. *(978-0-7787-8563-7(7))* Crabtree Publishing Co.

Kitts, W. L. Great Jobs in the Skilled Trades. 2019. (Great Jobs Ser.). (ENG.). 80p. (YA). (gr. 6-12). *(978-1-68282-525-9(6))* ReferencePoint Pr., Inc.

Less, Emma. Construction Workers. 2018. (Real-Life Superheroes Ser.). (ENG.). 16p. (J). (gr. k-2). pap. 7.99 *(978-1-68152-273-9(X),* 14912) Amicus.

Mahoney, Emily. What Do Construction Workers Do All Day?, 1 vol. 2020. (What Do They Do? Ser.). (ENG.). 24p. (gr. 1-2). pap. 9.15 *(978-1-5382-5683-1(5),* 5b30e00d-4a46-435c-b340-a1695830c5c4) Stevens, Gareth Publishing LLLP.

Mara, Wil. The Silversmith, 1 vol. 2011. (Colonial People Ser.). (ENG.). 48p. (gr. 4-4). 34.07 *(978-0-7614-4804-4(7),* b281651d-0b8b-491e-94d1-f1b43f638296) Cavendish Square Publishing LLC.

McGill, Jordan. Edificios. 2012. (SPA.). (J). *(978-1-61913-208-5(7))* Weigl Pubs., Inc.

—Medios de Transporte. 2012. (SPA.). (J). *(978-1-61913-213-9(3))* Weigl Pubs., Inc.

Meachen Rau, Dana. Los Constructores / Builders, 1 vol. 2009. (Instrumentos de Trabajo / Tools We Use Ser.). (ENG & SPA., Illus.). 32p. (gr. k-2). lib. bdg. 25.50 *(978-0-7614-2821-3(6),* 574410b8-03bc-47a1-9082-2210698ec54a) Cavendish Square Publishing LLC.

Omoth, Tyler. Oil Rig Workers in Action. 2017. (Dangerous Jobs in Action Ser.). (ENG.). 32p. (J). (gr. 3-6). lib. bdg. 35.64 *(978-1-5038-1631-2(1),* 211147) Child's World, Inc, The.

Paige, Joy. Cool Careers Without College for People Who Love to Build Things. 2009. (Cool Careers Without College Ser.). 144p. (gr. 6-6). 66.50 *(978-1-61511-970-7(1))* Rosen Publishing Group, Inc., The.

Pearce, Q. L. Given Kachepa: Advocate for Human Trafficking Victims, 1 vol. 2007. (Young Heroes Ser.). (ENG., Illus.). 48p. (gr. 4-8). lib. bdg. 37.33 *(978-0-7377-3668-7(2),* dfb81306-01be-4abb-b38b-3ab790d1a238, KidHaven Publishing) Greenhaven Publishing LLC.

Polansky, Marisa. Today I'm a Construction Worker. Lee, Maxine, illus. 2018. (Today I'm A... Ser.). (ENG.). 14p. (J). bds. 8.99 *(978-0-374-30441-6(6),* 900159319, Farrar, Straus & Giroux (BYR)) Farrar, Straus & Giroux.

Roza, Greg. Why People Work, 1 vol. 2008. (Real Life Readers Ser.). (ENG.). 16p. (gr. 2-3). pap. 7.05 *(978-1-4358-0045-8(1),* 6b4445ff-4ddb-469a-9b4c-ce1f7d0a134, Rosen Classroom) Rosen Publishing Group, Inc., The.

Tafolla, Carmen & Teneyuca, Sharyll. That's Not Fair! / No Es Justo! Emma Tenayuca's Struggle for Justice/la Lucha de Emma Tenayuca Por la Justicia. 2008. (ENG & SPA., Illus.). 40p. (J). (gr. k-2). 22.95 *(978-0-916727-33-8(5),* P459884) Wings Pr.

Tol, Alex Van & National Geographic Learning Staff. Dolores Huerta: Voice for the Working Poor. 2010. (ENG., Illus.). 112p. (J). pap. *(978-0-7787-2545-9(6))* Crabtree Publishing Co.

JKL

Waldendorf, Kurt. Hooray for Construction Workers! 2016. (Bumba Books (r) — Hooray for Community Helpers! Ser.). (ENG., Illus.). 24p. (J). (gr. -1-1). 26.65 *(978-1-5124-1441-7(7),* 3dde1865-8e45-4e50-b7c4-3b7638bee866, Lerner Pubns.) Lerner Publishing Group.

—¡Que Vivan Los Obreros de Construcción! (Hooray for Construction Workers!) 2017. (Bumba Books (r) en Español — ¡Que Vivan Los Ayudantes Comunitarios! (Hooray for Community Helpers!) Ser.). (SPA., Illus.). 24p. (J). (gr. -1-1). pap. 8.99 *(978-1-5124-5385-0(4),* cb3c1726-4689-4441-9d55-39453258adf7); lib. bdg. 26.65 *(978-1-5124-4136-9(8),* de28242f-421b-490d-93aa-b0400479c58e) Lerner Publishing Group. (Ediciones Lerner).

Whelan, Gloria. Waiting for the Owl's Call. Milelli, Pascal, illus. 2009. (Tales of the World Ser.). (ENG.). 32p. (J). (gr. 1-4). 19.99 *(978-1-58536-418-3(5),* 202153) Sleeping Bear Pr.

LABOR—FICTION

Creech, Sharon. Ruby Holler. 2004. (Joanna Cotler Bks.). 310p. (gr. 3-7). 17.00 *(978-0-7569-1940-5(1))* Perfection Learning Corp.

Evans, Nate. Bang! Boom! Roar! a Busy Crew of Dinosaurs. 2012. (ENG., Illus.). 40p. (J). (gr. -1-2). 15.99 *(978-0-06-087960-0(2),* HarperCollins) HarperCollins Pubs.

Evans, Nate & Brown, Stephanie Gwyn. Dinosaur ABC. Santoro, Christopher, illus. 2011. (J). lib. bdg. 16.89 *(978-0-06-087962-4(9))* HarperCollins Pubs.

Francesco, D'Adamo. Iqbal. 2014. (ENG.). 128p. (J). (gr. 3-7). 11.24 *(978-1-63245-261-0(8))* Lectorum Pubns., Inc.

Haddix, Margaret Peterson. Uprising. 2007. (ENG.). 352p. (YA). (gr. 7-18). 19.99 *(978-1-4169-1171-5(5),* Simon & Schuster Bks. For Young Readers) Simon & Schuster Bks. For Young Readers.

Hargreaves, Adam. Mr. Adventure. 2016. (Mr. Men & Little Miss Ser.). (ENG., Illus.). 32p. (J). (gr. -1-2). pap. 4.99 *(978-0-451-53415-6(8),* Grosset & Dunlap) Penguin Young Readers Group.

Kipling, Rudyard. The Bridge Builders. 2005. pap. *(978-1-4065-0310-4(X))* Dodo Pr.

Malaspina, Ann. Yasmin's Hammer. Chayka, Doug, illus. 2010. (ENG.). 40p. (J). (gr. k-6). 18.95 *(978-1-60060-359-4(9))* Lee & Low Bks., Inc.

Mello, Roger. Charcoal Boys. Hahn, Daniel, tr. Mello, Roger, illus. 2019. (ENG., Illus.). 46p. (J). (gr. k-3). 20.00 *(978-1-939810-19-9(1),* Elsewhere Editions) Steerforth Pr.

Paterson, Katherine. Bread & Roses, Too. 2006. (ENG.). 288p. (J). (gr. 4-6). 22.44 *(978-0-618-65479-6(3),* Clarion Bks.) HarperCollins Pubs.

Pugliano-Martin, Carol. John Henry: An American Tall Tale. 2006. (J). pap. *(978-1-4108-6170-2(8))* Benchmark Education Co.

Renner, Jodie, et al. Childhood Regained: Canadian Schools Edition. 2016. (ENG., Illus.). (J). pap. *(978-0-9937004-7-7(0))* Cobalt Bks.

Ryan, Pam Muñoz. Esperanza Rising. Lt. ed. 2019. (ENG.). 260p. (J). (gr. 6-10). pap. 12.99 *(978-1-4328-6388-3(6),* Large Print Pr.) Thorndike Pr.

Salkey, Andrew. Riot, 1 vol. 2011. (Caribbean Modern Classics Ser.). (ENG., Illus.). 176p. (J). (gr. 7). pap. 14.95 *(978-1-84523-181-1(3))* Peepal Tree Pr., Ltd. GBR. Dist: Independent Pubs. Group.

Sheth, Kashmira. Boys Without Names. 2011. (ENG.). 320p. (J). (gr. 4-7). pap. 9.99 *(978-0-06-185762-1(9),* Balzer & Bray) HarperCollins Pubs.

Sinclair, Upton, et al. The Jungle. (Classics Illustrated Ser.). (Illus.). 52p. (YA). pap. 4.95 *(978-1-57209-025-5(1))* Classics International Entertainment, Inc.

Stokes, Jordan & Belinkie, Matt. Gilded Delirium. 2007. (YA). pap. *(978-1-4114-9670-5(1),* Spark Publishing Group) Sterling Publishing Co., Inc.

Sullivan, Paul. Breaker at Dawn. 2010. (J). pap. *(978-0-88092-705-5(4))* Royal Fireworks Publishing Co.

LABOR—UNITED STATES

Brill, Marlene Targ. Annie Shapiro & the Clothing Workers' Strike. Akib, Jamel, illus. 2010. (History Speaks: Picture Books Plus Reader's Theater Ser.). (ENG.). 48p. (gr. 2-4). pap. 9.95 *(978-0-7613-6132-9(4))* Lerner Publishing Group.

Broyles, Janell. The Triangle Shirtwaist Factory Fire Of 1911. 2009. (Tragic Fires Throughout History Ser.). 48p. (gr. 5-8). 53.00 *(978-1-60854-584-1(9),* Rosen Reference) Rosen Publishing Group, Inc., The.

Casil, Amy Sterling. The Department of Labor. (This Is Your Government Ser.). 64p. 2009. (gr. 5-6). 58.50 *(978-1-60854-374-8(9),* Rosen Reference) 2005. (ENG., Illus.). (J). (gr. 4-6). lib. bdg. 37.13 *(978-1-4042-0210-8(2),* 61c352ef-04f8-434f-bb98-46ed77407c41) 2005. (ENG., Illus.). (gr. 4-6). per. 12.95 *(978-1-4042-0663-2(9),* b0f547f1-6fdc-4da4-86c0-b1df61398173) Rosen Publishing Group, Inc., The.

Crewe, Sabrina & Schaefer, Adam. The Triangle Shirtwaist Factory Fire, 1 vol. 2004. (Events That Shaped America Ser.). (ENG., Illus.). 32p. (gr. 3-5). lib. bdg. 28.67 *(978-0-8368-3402-4(X),* aefb702f-ab39-4955-b21f-908dd17b92d9, Gareth Stevens Learning Library) Stevens, Gareth Publishing LLLP.

Dudley Gold, Susan. Taft-Hartley Act, 1 vol. 2012. (Landmark Legislation Ser.). (ENG., Illus.). 128p. (YA). (gr. 8-8). 42.64 *(978-1-60870-488-0(2),* 5a3468b1-170e-4b8f-a5ab-5658f0e92704) Cavendish Square Publishing LLC.

Greene, Jacqueline Dembar. The Triangle Shirtwaist Factory Fire. 2007. (Code Red Ser.). (Illus.). 32p. (YA). (gr. 2-5). lib. bdg. 28.50 *(978-1-59716-359-0(7))* Bearport Publishing Co., Inc.

Gunderson, Jessica. The Triangle Shirtwaist Factory Fire. Miller, Phil & Barnett III, Charles, illus. 2006. (Disasters in History Ser.). (ENG.). 32p. (J). (gr. 3-9). per. 8.10 *(978-0-7368-6878-5(X),* 91581); pap. 48.60 *(978-0-7368-6999-7(9),* 5667) Capstone. (Capstone Pr.).

Heinrichs, Ann. The Shoemaker, 1 vol. 2011. (Colonial People Ser.). (ENG.). 48p. (gr. 4-4). 34.07 *(978-0-7614-4798-6(9),* fed9550a-1bb6-4923-be20-62feec6eac51) Cavendish Square Publishing LLC.

Hernández, José M. & Dario, Zárate Figueroa. From Farmworker to Astronaut / de Campesino a Astronauta: My Path to the Stars / Mi Viaje a Las Estrellas. 2019. (ENG & SPA.). 128p. (J). (gr. 4-7). pap. 10.95 *(978-1-55885-868-8(7),* Piñata Books) Arte Publico Pr.

Miklowitz, Gloria. Cesar Chavez. 2009. pap. 13.25 *(978-1-60559-056-1(8))* Hameray Publishing Group, Inc.

Peters, Jennifer. Inside the Department of Labor, 1 vol. 2018. (Understanding the Executive Branch Ser.). (ENG.). 48p. (gr. 5-5). 29.60 *(978-0-7660-9696-1(6),* 709e2d00-87e4-4abf-b0c7-86b2e1355650) Enslow Publishing, LLC.

Santos, Rita, ed. Critical Perspectives on Labor Unions, 1 vol. 2019. (Analyzing the Issues Ser.). (ENG.). 232p. (gr. 8-8). 50.93 *(978-1-9785-0330-4(X),* f6611246-5dc5-40b7-9708-b632fe6d47be) Enslow Publishing, LLC.

Shea, Therese & Shea, Therese M. Inside the Labor Movement. 2018. (Eyewitness to History Ser.). (ENG.). 32p. (J). (gr. 4-7). 21.30 *(978-1-5311-8907-5(5))* Perfection Learning Corp.

Shea, Therese M. Inside the Labor Movement, 1 vol. 2017. (Eyewitness to History Ser.). (ENG.). 32p. (J). (gr. 4-5). pap. 11.50 *(978-1-5382-1161-8(0),* ca740460-66c5-4d5e-870f-318142c38ed1) Stevens, Gareth Publishing LLLP.

Summers, Jacque. Disgusting Jobs in Modern America: The down & Dirty Details. 2018. (Disgusting Jobs in History Ser.). (ENG., Illus.). 32p. (J). (gr. 3-6). lib. bdg. 27.99 *(978-1-5435-0366-1(7),* 137199, Capstone Pr.) Capstone.

Thompson, E. L. Cesar Chavez, with Profiles of Terence V. Powderly & Dolores Huerta. 2006. (Biographical Connections Ser.). (Illus.). 112p. (J). *(978-0-7166-1827-0(3))* World Bk., Inc.

Warren, Sarah. Dolores Huerta: A Hero to Migrant Workers, 0 vols. Casilla, Robert, illus. 2012. (ENG.). 32p. (J). (gr. 1-4). 17.99 *(978-0-7614-6107-4(8),* 9780761461074, Two Lions) Amazon Publishing.

Winter, Jonah. Mother Jones & Her Army of Mill Children. Carpenter, Nancy, illus. 2020. (ENG.). 40p. (J). (gr. -1-3). 20.99 *(978-0-449-81292-1(8),* Schwartz & Wade Bks.) Random Hse. Children's Bks.

LABOR AND LABORING CLASSES

see Labor; Working Class

LABOR DAY

Dash, Meredith. Labor Day, 1 vol. 2014. (National Holidays Ser.). (ENG., Illus.). 24p. (J). (gr. -1-2). lib. bdg. 32.79 *(978-1-62970-044-1(4),* 1533, Abdo Kids) ABDO Publishing Co.

Dayton, Connor. Labor Day, 1 vol. 2012. (American Holidays Ser.). (ENG.). 24p. (J). (gr. 1-1). pap. 9.25 *(978-1-4488-6252-8(3),* f6f360a3-5636-445b-a6c9-f7340f5d223e); lib. bdg. 26.27 *(978-1-4488-6147-7(0),* 77b48d0f-ffee-4082-920c-eec039d8c933) Rosen Publishing Group, Inc., The. (PowerKids Pr.).

—Labor Day: Día Del Trabajo, 1 vol. Alamán, Eduardo, tr. 2012. (American Holidays / Celebraciones en Los Estados Unidos Ser.). (ENG & SPA.). 24p. (gr. 1-1). lib. bdg. 26.27 *(978-1-4488-6713-4(4),* a35e8a0a-33c9-4c43-92bf-694e65155eea, PowerKids Pr.) Rosen Publishing Group, Inc., The.

Felice, Frank. Why Do We Celebrate Labor Day?, 1 vol. 2018. (Celebrating U. S. Holidays Ser.). (ENG.). 24p. (J). (gr. 1-1). 25.27 *(978-1-5081-6647-4(1),* c337c68d-ab5e-4ced-99bb-a00b9e46ffd0, PowerKids Pr.) Rosen Publishing Group, Inc., The.

Grack, Rachel. Labor Day. 2018. (Celebrating Holidays Ser.). (ENG., Illus.). 24p. (J). (gr. k-3). lib. bdg. 26.95 *(978-1-62617-789-5(9),* Blastoff! Readers) Bellwether Media.

Hamilton, Lynn. Labor Day. (American Celebrations Ser.). (Illus.). 24p. (J). 2010. (gr. 3-5). pap. 11.95 *(978-1-60596-777-6(7))* 2010. (gr. 3-5). lib. bdg. 25.70 *(978-1-60596-770-7(X))* 2004. (gr. -1-3). per. 8.95 *(978-1-59036-166-5(0))* 2004. lib. bdg. 24.45 *(978-1-59036-129-0(6))* Weigl Pubs., Inc.

McNeil, Niki, et al. Labor Day. 2007. (In the Hands of a Child: Project Pack Continent Study Ser.). (Illus.). 75p. spiral bd. 19.00 *(978-1-60308-104-7(6))* In the Hands of a Child.

Morrison, Jessica. Labour Day. 2010. (Illus.). 24p. *(978-1-55388-619-8(4));* pap. *(978-1-55388-620-4(8))* Weigl Educational Pubs. Ltd.

Nelson, Robin. Labor Day. 2009. (First Step Nonfiction - American Holidays Ser.). (J). (gr. k-2). 19.93 *(978-0-7613-4933-4(2))* Lerner Publishing Group.

Shava, Ryder. Labor Day, 1 vol., 1. 2015. (Rosen REAL Readers: Social Studies Nonfiction / Fiction: Myself, My Community, My World Ser.). (ENG.). 12p. (J). (gr. k-1). pap. 6.33 *(978-1-5081-1728-5(4),* e5516127-2ee4-415d-87c4-b90527987b3c, Rosen Classroom) Rosen Publishing Group, Inc., The.

Walker, Robert. Labor Day. 2010. (Celebrations in My World Ser.). (ENG., Illus.). 32p. (J) (gr. k-3). pap. *(978-0-7787-4936-3(3));* lib. bdg. *(978-0-7787-4929-5(0))* Crabtree Publishing Co.

LABOR (OBSTETRICS)

see Childbirth

LABOR ORGANIZATIONS

see Guilds; Labor Unions

LABOR REPRESENTATION IN REGULATION OF INDUSTRY

see Management—Employee Participation

LABOR UNIONS

Bridegam, Martha. Unions & Labor Laws. 2009. (Point/Counterpoint: Issues in Contemporary American Society Ser.). (ENG., Illus.). 128p. (gr. 9-18). 35.00 *(978-1-60413-511-4(5),* P174391, Facts On File) Infobase Holdings, Inc.

Brown, Jonatha A. César Chávez, 1 vol. (Gente Que Hay Que Conocer (People We Should Know) Ser.). 2005. (SPA.). 24p. (gr. 2-4). pap. 9.15 *(978-0-8368-4766-6(0),* b98ea793-6731-49c5-adf5-131db8ecbb55, Weekly Reader Leveled Readers) 2005. (SPA., Illus.). 24p. (gr. 2-4). lib. bdg. 24.67 *(978-0-8368-4759-8(8),* 47c9aecc-dbd0-4961-9b94-8813dc904c2a, Weekly Reader Leveled Readers) 2005. (ENG., Illus.). 24p. (gr. 2-4). lib. bdg. 24.67 *(978-0-8368-4745-1(8),* b08a0da5-bcb9-4d07-916b-08fbc9b54ab5, Weekly Reader Leveled Readers) 2004. (ENG., Illus.). 48p. (gr. 5-8). lib. bdg. 33.67 *(978-0-8368-5097-0(1),* 90a1df70-6160-4ee6-9805-349b20666679, Gareth Stevens Secondary Library) Stevens, Gareth Publishing LLLP.

Cesar Chavez, Lider Laboral. 2003. pap. 48.95 *(978-0-8136-9205-0(9))* Modern Curriculum Pr.

Collins, David R. Cesar Chavez. 2005. (Just the Facts Biographies Ser.). (Illus.). 112p. (J). (gr. 6-12). 27.93 *(978-0-8225-2248-5(9))* Lerner Publishing Group.

Ebon Research Systems Staff. Dare to Be... A Hero Vol. 3: Cesar Chavez. Lt. ed. 2003.Tr. of Atrevete Ser... Un Heroe Cesar Chavez. (ENG & SPA., Illus.). 16p. (J). 3.99 *(978-0-9648313-6-0(8))* Ebon Research Systems Publishing, LLC.

Farrell, Mary Cronk. Fannie Never Flinched: One Woman's Courage in the Struggle for American Labor Union Rights. 2016. (ENG., Illus.). 56p. (J). (gr. 5-9). 19.95 *(978-1-4197-1884-7(3),* 1083701, Abrams Bks. for Young Readers) Abrams, Inc.

Finkelstein, Norman H. Union Made: Labor Leader Samuel Gompers & His Fight for Workers' Rights. 2019. (Illus.). 112p. (J). (gr. 5-12). 17.95 *(978-1-62979-638-3(7),* Calkins Creek) Highlights Pr., c/o Highlights for Children, Inc.

Frey, Wendy. Citizen Heroes. 2007. (Illus.). 68p. (J). *(978-1-4105-0887-4(0)); (978-1-4105-0888-1(9))* Building Wings LLC.

Gay, Kathlyn. César Chávez: Fighting for Migrant Farmworkers, 1 vol. 2017. (Rebels with a Cause Ser.). (ENG.). 128p. (gr. 8-8). lib. bdg. 38.93 *(978-0-7660-8951-8(7),* e2b2d68f-f299-4b3b-b1d2-aee8b9baba8e) Enslow Publishing, LLC.

—Mother Jones. 2006. (American Workers Ser.). (Illus.). 144p. (J). (gr. 3-7). lib. bdg. 28.95 *(978-1-59935-016-5(5))* Reynolds, Morgan Inc.

Hurt, Avery Elizabeth, ed. Labor Unions & Workers' Rights, 1 vol. 2019. (Opposing Viewpoints Ser.). (ENG.). 176p. (gr. 10-12). pap. 34.80 *(978-1-5345-0594-0(6),* 901cfa08-31bc-4288-9e9a-515a3762e1b3) Greenhaven Publishing LLC.

Krull, Kathleen. Cosechando Esperanza: La Historia de César Chávez (Harvesting Hope Spanish Edition) Ada, Alma Flor & Campoy, F. Isabel, trs. Morales, Yuyi, illus. 2004. (SPA.). 48p. (J). (gr. -1-3). pap. 7.99 *(978-0-15-205169-3(4),* 1195591, Clarion Bks.) HarperCollins Pubs.

—Harvesting Hope: The Story of Cesar Chavez. Morales, Yuyi, illus. 2003. (ENG.). 48p. (J). (gr. -1-3). 17.99 *(978-0-15-201437-7(3),* 1189864, Clarion Bks.) HarperCollins Pubs.

Magoon, Kekla. Cesar Chavez: Crusader for Labor Rights, 1 vol. 2010. (Essential Lives Set 5 Ser.). (ENG., Illus.). 112p. (YA). (gr. 6-12). lib. bdg. 41.36 *(978-1-61613-512-6(3),* 6707, Essential Library) ABDO Publishing Co.

Miklowitz, Gloria. Cesar Chavez. 2009. pap. 13.25 *(978-1-60559-056-1(8))* Hameray Publishing Group, Inc.

Miklowitz, Gloria D. César Chávez. 2004. (ENG., Illus.). 29p. (J). (gr. 2-5). pap. 5.97 net. *(978-0-7685-1215-1(8),* Dominie Elementary) Savvas Learning Co.

Miller, Calvin Craig. A. Philip Randolph & the African American Labor Movement. 2005. (Civil Rights Leaders Ser.). (Illus.). 160p. (YA). (gr. 6-12). 26.95 *(978-1-931798-50-1(8))* Reynolds, Morgan Inc.

Miller, Connie Colwell. Mother Jones: Labor Leader, 1 vol. Erwin, Steve & Barnett, Charles, III, illus. 2006. (Graphic Biographies Ser.). (ENG.). 32p. (J). (gr. 3-9). per. 8.10 *(978-0-7368-9662-7(7),* 93447, Capstone Pr.) Capstone.

Ruby, Lois. Strike! Mother Jones & the Colorado Coal Field War. 2012. (Illus.). 224p. (J). pap. 8.95 *(978-0-86541-141-8(7))* Filter Pr., LLC.

Seidman, David. Cesar Chavez: Labor Leader. 2004. (Great Life Stories Ser.). (ENG., Illus.). 128p. (J). 30.50 *(978-0-531-12319-5(7),* Watts, Franklin) Scholastic Library Publishing.

Shea, Therese & Shea, Therese M. Inside the Labor Movement. 2018. (Eyewitness to History Ser.). (ENG.). 32p. (J). (gr. 4-7). 21.30 *(978-1-5311-8907-5(5))* Perfection Learning Corp.

Shea, Therese M. Inside the Labor Movement, 1 vol. 2017. (Eyewitness to History Ser.). (ENG.). 32p. (J). (gr. 4-5). pap. 11.50 *(978-1-5382-1161-8(0),* ca740460-66c5-4d5e-870f-318142c38ed1) Stevens, Gareth Publishing LLLP.

Skurzynski, Gloria. Sweat & Blood: A History of U. S. Labor Unions. 2008. (People's History Ser.). (ENG.). 112p. (gr. 5-12). lib. bdg. 33.26 *(978-0-8225-7594-8(9))* Lerner Publishing Group.

Soto, Gary. Cesar Chavez: A Hero for Everyone. Lohstoeter, Lori, illus. 2003. (Milestone Ser.). (ENG.). 80p. (J). (gr. 2-5). pap. 6.99 *(978-0-689-85922-9(8),* Simon & Schuster/Paula Wiseman Bks.) Simon & Schuster/Paula Wiseman Bks.

Tol, Alex Van & National Geographic Learning Staff. Dolores Huerta: Voice for the Working Poor. 2010. (ENG., Illus.). 112p. (J). pap. *(978-0-7787-2545-9(6))* Crabtree Publishing Co.

Van Tol, Alex. Dolores Huerta: Voice for the Working Poor. 2010. (Crabtree Groundbreaker Biographies Ser.). (ENG., Illus.). 112p. (J). (gr. 5-8). lib. bdg. *(978-0-7787-2536-7(7))* Crabtree Publishing Co.

Wadsworth, Ginger. Cesar Chavez. Schroeder, Mark, illus. 2005. (Yo Solo - Biografías (on My Own - Biographies) Ser.). (SPA.). 48p. (J). (gr. 2-4). per. 6.95 *(978-0-8225-3125-8(9))* Lerner Publishing Group.

—Cesar Chavez. 2005. (On My Own Biography Ser.). (Illus.). 48p. (J). 25.26 *(978-1-57505-652-4(6),* Carolrhoda Bks.) Lerner Publishing Group.

—Cesar Chavez. Schroder, Mark, illus. 2005. (On My Own Biography Ser.). (ENG.). 48p. (J). (gr. 2-4). pap. 7.99 *(978-1-57505-826-9(X),* 3096e92a-3c32-4501-b3d1-51b70163fef7, First Avenue Editions) Lerner Publishing Group.

—César Chávez. Schroeder, Mark, illus. 2005. (Yo Solo: Biografías (on My Own Biographies) Ser.). (SPA.). 48p. (J). (gr. 2-4). lib. bdg. 25.32 *(978-0-8225-3124-1(0),* 76116012-0cf6-4ba4-9705-0a63dc62bf1c, Ediciones Lerner) Lerner Publishing Group.

Wagner, Viqi, ed. Labor Unions, 1 vol. 2007. (Opposing Viewpoints Ser.). (ENG., Illus.). 240p. (gr. 10-12). lib. bdg. 50.43 *(978-0-7377-3822-3(7),* c398f0a8-36fd-4c71-bcd2-23ca17e6abbe, Greenhaven Publishing) Greenhaven Publishing LLC.

Warren, Sarah. Dolores Huerta: A Hero to Migrant Workers, 0 vols. Casilla, Robert, illus. 2012. (ENG.). 32p. (J). (gr. 1-4). 17.99 *(978-0-7614-6107-4(8),* 9780761461074, Two Lions) Amazon Publishing.

Wheeler, Jill C. Cesar Chavez. 2003. (Breaking Barriers Ser.). 64p. (gr. 3-8). 27.07 *(978-1-57765-905-1(8),* Abdo & Daughters) ABDO Publishing Co.

LABORATORY ANIMALS

Cagno, Stefano. Lou, Buc & All the Others. 2012. 178p. pap. 7.99 *(978-1-61667-441-0(5))* Raider Publishing International.

Dunn, Joeming & Dunn, Ben. Albert II: The 1st Monkey in Space, 1 vol. 2011. (Famous Firsts: Animals Making History Ser.). (ENG., Illus.). 32p. (J). (gr. 3-8). 32.79 *(978-1-61641-637-9(8),* 7204, Graphic Planet - Fiction) Magic Wagon.

Lawrence, Riley. Should Animal Testing Be Banned?, 1 vol. 2018. (Points of View Ser.). (ENG.). 24p. (gr. 3-3). 26.23 *(978-1-5345-2791-1(5),* 58ae6dd9-600a-435b-9ca8-1ebe5e603e60, KidHaven Publishing) Greenhaven Publishing LLC.

Lubka, S. Ruth. Pupniks: The Story of Two Space Dogs, 1 vol. 2003. (ENG., Illus.). 32p. (J). (gr. k-3). 16.95 *(978-0-7614-5137-2(4))* Marshall Cavendish Corp.

Rowser, A. L. Ethical Beauty Products, 1 vol. 2019. (Ethical Living Ser.). (ENG., Illus.). 64p. (J). (gr. 6-6). pap. 13.95 *(978-1-5081-8085-2(7),* d789ad5a-5a26-4b7d-8edc-9ff060543e38) Rosen Publishing Group, Inc., The.

Terp, Gail. Animal Testing. 2018. (Illus.). 48p. (J). *(978-1-4896-9625-0(3),* AV2 by Weigl) Weigl Pubs., Inc.

Watson, Stephanie. Animal Testing: Issues & Ethics. 2009. (Science & Society Ser.). 64p. (gr. 5-6). 58.50 *(978-1-60853-006-9(X))* Rosen Publishing Group, Inc., The.

LABORERS

see Labor

LABOURE, CATHERINE, SAINT, 1806-1876

Trouvé, Marianne Lorraine. Saint Catherine Labouré: And Our Lady of the Miraculous Medal. 2011. (ENG., Illus.). 119p. (J). pap. 7.95 *(978-0-8198-7224-1(5))* Pauline Bks. & Media.

Windle, Margaret. St Catherine Laboure. 2007. (Illus.). 53p. (J). 11.99 *(978-0-9798889-2-2(1))* Growing with the Saints, Inc.

LADYBIRDS

see Ladybugs

LADYBUGS

Allen, Judy. Are You a Ladybug? Humphries, Tudor, illus. 2003. (Backyard Bks.). (ENG.). 31p. (J). (gr. k-3). pap. 7.99 *(978-0-7534-5603-3(6),* 900052551, Kingfisher) Roaring Brook Pr.

Anderson, Jo Marie. If I Were a Ladybug, 1 vol. 2017. (I'm a Bug! Ser.). (ENG.). 24p. (gr. 1-1). 25.27 *(978-1-5081-5723-6(5),* a98d8538-607a-41c4-969d-9cdb3b043280, PowerKids Pr.) Rosen Publishing Group, Inc., The.

Appleby, Alex. I See a Ladybug, 1 vol. 2013. (In My Backyard Ser.). (ENG., Illus.). 24p. (J). (gr. k-k). 25.27 *(978-1-4339-8555-3(1),* 6568ad10-d5dd-4475-a3fa-a5d95bbbde7f); pap. 9.15 *(978-1-4339-8556-0(X),* 24974f82-d988-4882-a3ec-89051dd57a7b) Stevens, Gareth Publishing LLLP.

—I See a Ladybug / Puedo Ver una Mariquita, 1 vol. 2013. (In My Backyard / en Mi Jardín Ser.). (SPA & ENG., Illus.). 24p. (J). (gr. k-k). lib. bdg. 25.27 *(978-1-4339-8798-4(8),* e6a795ff-53b3-4b2c-bfba-3414bbeefd42) Stevens, Gareth Publishing LLLP.

Arrhenius, Ingela P., illus. Where's the Ladybug? 2017. (Where's The Ser.). (ENG.). 10p. (J). (— 1). bds. 9.99 *(978-0-7636-9335-0(9))* Candlewick Pr.

Ashley, Susan. Incredible Ladybugs, 1 vol. 2011. (Incredible World of Insects Ser.). (ENG., Illus.). 24p. (J). (gr. 1-2). pap. 9.15 *(978-1-4339-4592-2(4),* 3f426065-a258-4476-a365-56ccc728e943); lib. bdg. 25.27 *(978-1-4339-4591-5(6),* ae87f04d-9b97-435e-8a01-7718df156a49) Stevens, Gareth Publishing LLLP.

—Ladybugs, 1 vol. 2004. (Let's Read about Insects Ser.). (ENG., Illus.). 24p. (gr. k-2). pap. 9.15 *(978-0-8368-4062-9(3),* 4ed8b084-3b0a-4696-b8d0-0cd2b1f8d689); lib. bdg. 24.67 *(978-0-8368-4055-1(0),* 91a7974f-2dd3-499b-a59e-4e3d6b7ae26f) Stevens, Gareth Publishing LLLP. (Weekly Reader Leveled Readers).

Berger, Melvin & Berger, Gilda. De Larva a Mariquita: Grub to Ladybug. 2006. (ENG & SPA., Illus.). (J). pap. *(978-0-439-87985-9(X))* Scholastic, Inc.

—Ladybugs. 2011. (Illus.). 16p. (J). pap. *(978-0-545-24444-2(7))* Scholastic, Inc.

Black, Nessa. Ladybugs. (Spot Creepy Crawlies Ser.). (ENG.). 16p. (J). (gr. -1-2). 2018. pap. 9.99 *(978-1-68152-228-9(4),* 14759) 2017. 17.95 *(978-1-68151-109-2(6),* 14640) Amicus.

Carr, Aaron. Ladybugs. (World Languages Ser.). (J). (gr. k-2). 2017. (ENG.). 24p. lib. bdg. 35.70 *(978-1-4896-6560-7(9),* AV2 by Weigl) 2014. *(978-1-4896-3208-1(5))* Weigl Pubs., Inc.

Cleland, Joann. Ladybug, Ladybug, What Are You Doing? 2008. (My First Science Discovery Library). (Illus.). 24p. (J). (gr. k-2). lib. bdg. 21.35 *(978-1-60472-537-7(0))* Rourke Educational Media.

Coughlan, Cheryl. Ladybugs. rev. ed. 2016. (Insects Ser.). (ENG.). 24p. (J). (gr. -1-2). pap. 5.95 *(978-1-5157-4227-2(X),* 133990) Capstone.

Enslow, Brian. Counting Ladybugs 1-2-3, 1 vol. 2011. (All about Counting Bugs 1-2-3 Ser.). (ENG., Illus.). 24p. (gr. -1-1). pap. 10.35 *(978-1-59845-251-8(7),* fd7cfa8e-13d7-4849-a5db-7a327dfebe70); lib. bdg. 25.27 *(978-0-7660-3922-3(6),* 7d666f47-516a-487c-8d91-abd605c160bb) Enslow Publishing, LLC. (Enslow Publishing).

Frisch, Aaron. Ladybugs. 2014. (Seedlings Ser.). (ENG.). 24p. (J). (gr. -1-k). *(978-1-60818-459-0(5),* 21420, Creative Education) Creative Co., The.

—Seedlings: Ladybugs. 2015. (ENG.). 24p. (J). (gr. -1-1). pap. 10.99 *(978-1-62832-045-9(1),* 21421, Creative Paperbacks) Creative Co., The.

Gallagher, Debbie & Gallagher, Brendan. Ladybugs, 1 vol. 2012. (Mighty Minibeasts Ser.). (ENG.). 32p. (gr. 3-3). 31.21 *(978-1-60870-546-7(3),* cf803198-2ba9-4b9d-843d-6e4c109fb6f5) Cavendish Square Publishing LLC.

Gibbons, Gail. Ladybugs. 2013. (ENG., Illus.). 32p. (J). (gr. -1-3). pap. 8.99 *(978-0-8234-2760-4(9))* Holiday Hse., Inc.

Godkin, Celia. What about Ladybugs? (Sierra Club Books (Sierra)) 2015. (ENG., Illus.). 40p. (J). (gr. -1-3). pap. 7.95 *(978-0-87156-921-9(3),* 7c323d30-37de-4474-b653-ed16060c1451) Fitzhenry & Whiteside, Ltd. CAN. Dist: Firefly Bks., Ltd.

Hall, Margaret. Ladybugs [Scholastic]. 2010. (Bugs, Bugs, Bugs! Ser.). 24p. pap. 0.52 *(978-1-4296-5053-3(2),* Capstone Pr.) Capstone.

Ho, Cammie. Ladybug Ladybug. 2016. (Life Cycle Bks.). (ENG., Illus.). 29p. (J). (gr. k-2). pap. 7.99 *(978-1-943241-02-6(3))* Phonic Monic.

Huliska-Beith, Laura, illus. Cinco Pequeñas Mariquitas. 2005.Tr. of Five Little Ladybugs. (SPA & ENG.). 12p. (J). 4.95 *(978-1-58117-333-8(4),* Intervisual/Piggy Toes) Bendon, Inc.

Humphries, Tudor & Allen, Judy. Are You a Ladybug? 2003. (Backyard Bks.). (J). (gr. -1-2). lib. bdg. 17.20 *(978-0-613-90173-4(8))* Turtleback.

Ladybug. 2003. (J). 36.95 *(978-0-8136-9269-2(5));* 38.95 *(978-0-8136-4166-9(7))* Modern Curriculum Pr.

Ladybugs: Red, Fiery, & Bright. 2007. 32p. (J). (gr. k-4). pap. 6.95 *(978-0-8225-6989-3(2),* First Avenue Editions) Lerner Publishing Group.

Leaf, Christina. Ladybugs. 2017. (Insects up Close Ser.). (ENG., Illus.). 24p. (J). (gr. k-3). lib. bdg. 26.95 *(978-1-62617-667-6(1),* Blastoff! Discovery) Bellwether Media.

Lewellyn, Claire. Starting Life Ladybug. Mendez, Simon, illus. 2004. (Starting Life Ser.). (ENG.). 24p. (J). (gr. k-3). 16.95 *(978-1-55971-892-9(7))* Cooper Square Publishing Llc.

Marsico, Katie. Cómo Crece una Mariquita. 2008. (Scholastic News Nonfiction Readers en Espanol Ser.). 24p. (J). pap. 6.95 *(978-0-531-20644-7(0))* Scholastic Library Publishing.

—A Ladybug Larva Grows Up. 2007. (Scholastic News Nonfiction Readers Ser.). (ENG., Illus.). 24p. (J). (gr. 1-2). pap. 6.95 *(978-0-531-18697-8(0))* Scholastic Library Publishing.

Mattern, Joanne. It's a Good Thing There Are Ladybugs. 2014. (Rookie Read-About(r) Science — It's a Good Thing... Ser.). (ENG., Illus.). 32p. (J). lib. bdg. *(978-0-531-22358-1(2))* Scholastic Library Publishing.

—It's a Good Thing There Are Ladybugs (Rookie Read-About Science: It's a Good Thing...) 2014. (Rookie Read-About Science Ser.). (ENG., Illus.). 32p. (J). (gr. 1-2). pap. 5.95 *(978-0-531-22830-2(4),* Children's Pr.) Scholastic Library Publishing.

McLaughlin, Kari Massie. My Adventure with Ladybugs. 2009. (ENG.). 44p. (J). 8.99 *(978-1-59092-457-0(6))* Blue Forge Pr.

Meachen Rau, Dana. Crawl, Ladybug, Crawl!, 1 vol. 2008. (Go, Critter, Go! Ser.). (ENG., Illus.). 24p. (gr. k-1). lib. bdg. 25.50 *(978-0-7614-2652-3(3),* 56ffedff-cccb-4544-b5ed-cfd1471a7b7f, Cavendish Square) Cavendish Square Publishing LLC.

—¡Trepa Mariquita, Trepa! / Crawl, Ladybug, Crawl!, 1 vol. 2009. (¡Vamos, Insecto, Vamos! / Go, Critter, Go! Ser.). (ENG & SPA., Illus.). 24p. (gr. k-1). lib. bdg. 25.50 *(978-0-7614-2817-6(8),* 0faf6d74-003f-457b-b630-c74df4602a17) Cavendish Square Publishing LLC.

—¡Trepa Mariquita, Trepa! (Crawl, Ladybug, Crawl!), 1 vol. 2009. (¡Vamos, Insecto, Vamos! (Go, Critter, Go!) Ser.). (SPA., Illus.). 24p. (gr. k-1). lib. bdg. 25.50 *(978-0-7614-2793-3(7),* aed0f722-5347-4d1a-bd52-6950b075e216) Cavendish Square Publishing LLC.

O'Brien, Joan. Lucky Ladybug Stickers. 2004. (Dover Little Activity Books Stickers Ser.). (ENG., Illus.). 4p. (J). (gr. k-3). pap. 2.50 *(978-0-486-43008-9(1),* 430081) Dover Pubns., Inc.

Owings, Lisa. From Egg to Ladybug. 2016. (Start to Finish, Second Ser.). (ENG., Illus.). 24p. (J). (gr. k-3). 23.99 *(978-1-5124-0910-9(3),* b14d4bf8-9d63-4e95-95d6-5b5b0359a4d9, Lerner Pubns.) Lerner Publishing Group.

Posada, Mia. Ladybugs: Red, Fiery & Bright. 2005. (Picture Bks.). (Illus.). 32p. (gr. k-2). 15.95 *(978-0-87614-334-6(6))* Lerner Publishing Group.

Reher, Matt. Ladybug Babies. 2015. (2G Bugs Ser.). (ENG., Illus.). 36p. (J). pap. 8.00 *(978-1-63437-089-9(9))* American Reading Co.

Riggs, Kate. Ladybug. (Grow with Me Ser.). (ENG.). 32p. (J). (gr. 3-6). 2013. pap. 12.00 *(978-0-89812-770-6(X),* 21981, Creative Paperbacks) 2012. 19.95 *(978-1-60818-217-6(7),* 21975, Creative Education) Creative Co., The.

Ross, Michael Elsohn. Ladybugology. Erickson, Darren, illus. Grogan, Brian, photos by. 2005. (Backyard Buddies Ser.). 48p. (gr. 3-6). 19.93 *(978-1-57505-435-3(3))* Lerner Publishing Group.

Rustad, Martha E. H. Ladybugs. 2007. (World of Insects Ser.). (ENG., Illus.). 24p. (J). (gr. k-3). lib. bdg. 26.95 *(978-1-60014-077-8(7))* Bellwether Media.

Santos, Penelope. I See a Ladybug, 1 vol. 2015. (Rosen REAL Readers: STEM & STEAM Collection). (ENG.). 8p. (gr. k-1). pap. 5.46 *(978-1-4994-9664-2(8),* eec6fa6a-67ea-43db-99ef-394d7df8fb62, Rosen Classroom) Rosen Publishing Group, Inc., The.

Schuh, Mari. Ladybugs. 2013. (ENG., Illus.). 24p. (J). lib. bdg. 25.65 *(978-1-62031-055-7(4))* Jump! Inc.

Sexton, Colleen. The Life Cycle of a Ladybug. 2010. (Life Cycles Ser.). (ENG., Illus.). 24p. (J). (gr. k-3). lib. bdg. 26.95 *(978-1-60014-309-0(1),* Blastoff! Readers) Bellwether Media.

Shea, Therese. Ladybugs up Close, 1 vol. 2019. (Bugs up Close! Ser.). (ENG.). 24p. (gr. 1-2). pap. 9.25 *(978-1-7253-0798-8(7),* 9b4cf5c3-c8c5-4ce5-9f95-65b77347632b, PowerKids Pr.) Rosen Publishing Group, Inc., The.

Slade, Suzanne. Ladybugs. (Under the Microscope: Backyard Bugs Ser.). 24p. (gr. 2-3). 2009. 42.50 *(978-1-60854-616-9(0),* PowerKids Pr.) 2007. (ENG., Illus.). (J). lib. bdg. 26.27 *(978-1-4042-3818-3(2),* d3c83fed-2b93-4001-b6a1-ed5d6587e96a) Rosen Publishing Group, Inc., The.

Small World Creations. Ladybug's Pond: Bathtime Fun with Rattly Rings & a Friendly Bug Pal. Haines, Emma, illus. 2018. (ENG.). 8p. (J). (gr. -1 — 1). 6.99 *(978-1-4380-7906-6(0))* Sourcebooks, Inc.

Smith, Molly. Helpful Ladybugs. (No Backbone! Insects Ser.). (Illus.). 24p. (J). (gr. k-3). 2016. (ENG.). pap. 7.99 *(978-1-944998-47-9(0))* 2008. lib. bdg. 26.99 *(978-1-59716-584-6(0))* Bearport Publishing Co., Inc.

Smith, Sian. Ladybugs, 1 vol. 2012. (Creepy Critters Ser.). (ENG., Illus.). 24p. (J). (gr. -1-k). pap. 9.95 *(978-1-4109-4822-9(6),* 119459, Raintree) Capstone.

Stewart, Melissa. Zoom in on Ladybugs, 1 vol. 2014. (Zoom in on Insects! Ser.). (ENG.). 24p. (gr. k-2). 25.60 *(978-0-7660-4215-5(4),* 6cbcbd3b-c0d2-4206-b7b6-d4ab506ff22c); pap. 10.95 *(978-1-4644-0373-6(2),* b5604e78-675e-4fbc-b627-f09050635aa4, Enslow Elementary) Enslow Publishing, LLC.

Thomson, Ruth. The Life Cycle of a Ladybug, 1 vol. 2009. (Learning about Life Cycles Ser.). (ENG., Illus.). 24p. (J). (gr. 2-2). pap. 9.25 *(978-1-4358-2865-8(2),* 923e914b-8f6e-4230-8e8a-e8b4bce7b957, PowerKids Pr.) Rosen Publishing Group, Inc., The.

Tracqui, Valérie. Face-to-Face with the Ladybug: Little Garden Monster. Lorne, Patrick, photos by. 2004. (Face-to-Face Ser.). (Illus.). 28p. (J). (gr. -1-2). 9.95 *(978-1-57091-453-9(2))* Charlesbridge Publishing, Inc.

LADYBUGS—FICTION

Adams, Gary. The Ladybug Story. 2012. 76p. pap. 28.99 *(978-1-4772-5627-5(X))* AuthorHouse.

Adams, Wayne. Laci the Ladybug. Kern, Shelly, illus. 2012. 16p. pap. 24.95 *(978-1-4626-7615-6(4))* America Star Bks.

Anna, Jennifer. The Best Thing: An Almost True Story of Ladybugs & Sisters. 2007. (Illus.). 64p. (Orig.). (J). pap. 14.99 *(978-1-59092-154-8(2))* Blue Forge Pr.

Arpaci, Halis. Eric & Derrick. 2011. (ENG.). 160p. (J). (gr. 3-7). 11.95 *(978-1-59784-232-7(X),* Tughra Bks.) Blue Dome, Inc.

Basha, Irena Canaj. The Birthday Party, It Was Saturday... 2013. 16p. pap. 24.95 *(978-1-62709-182-4(3))* America Star Bks.

Blankenship, Paula. We Both Read-Lulu's Wild Party. Reinhart, Larry, illus. 2009. (We Both Read Ser.). 44p. (J). 9.95 *(978-1-60115-231-2(0));* pap. 5.99 *(978-1-60115-232-9(9))* Treasure Bay, Inc.

Boazu, Elena & Balestrieri, Mauro. Lila's Quest. 2007. 48p. per. 13.95 *(978-1-4327-0985-3(2))* Outskirts Pr., Inc.

Brahney, Jenny. Spotty, 1 vol. 2010. 30p. pap. 24.95 *(978-1-4489-8497-8(1))* PublishAmerica, Inc.

Branford, Anna. Violet Mackerel's Natural Habitat. Allen, Elanna, illus. 2013. (Violet Mackerel Ser.). (ENG.). 112p. (J). (gr. 1-5). 15.99 *(978-1-4424-3594-0(1));* pap. 6.99 *(978-1-4424-3595-7(X))* Simon & Schuster Children's Publishing.

Bull, Ginger Lee. Ginger Lady Bug's Adventures "Morro Bay by the Sea" 2005. (ENG.). 30p. pap. 13.99 *(978-1-59926-503-2(6))* Xlibris Corp.

Carle, Eric. Hugs & Kisses for the Grouchy Ladybug. Carle, Eric, illus. 2018. (ENG., Illus.). 32p. (J). (gr. -1-3). 9.99 *(978-0-06-283568-0(8),* HarperCollins) HarperCollins Pubs.

Chapman, Mary Beth & Chapman, Steven Curtis. Shaoey & Dot: A Trip to Dr. Betterbee. 2005. 20p. (J). 6.99 *(978-1-4003-0568-1(3))* Nelson, Thomas Inc.

—Shaoey & Dot: Thunder & Lightning Bugs. 2005. 20p. (J). 6.99 *(978-1-4003-0570-4(5))* Nelson, Thomas Inc.

Coccia, Mina. Mother Nature & Mz Bee. 2012. 36p. pap. 14.95 *(978-1-4575-0709-0(9))* Dog Ear Publishing, LLC.

Cross, Jenny. Sadie the Ladybug. Bohart, Lisa, illus. 2009. 44p. pap. 14.95 *(978-1-936051-39-7(7))* Peppertree Pr., The.

Cuartas, Jennifer M. The Adventures of Delilah Doodle: Mealy Bug Stew. 2012. 24p. pap. 24.95 *(978-1-4626-8147-1(6))* America Star Bks.

Cummings, Troy. The Eensy Weensy Spider Freaks Out! Big-Time! 2015. lib. bdg. 18.40 *(978-0-606-37713-3(1))* Turtleback.

Cummins, Judi, creator. It's Raining Acorns & Ladybugs. 2005. (Illus.). 28p. (J). per. *(978-0-9760377-4-3(2))* Cummins, Judi.

Cunningham, Karen. I See a Bug, 1 vol. 2010. 16p. pap. 24.95 *(978-1-4489-4181-0(4))* PublishAmerica, Inc.

Cureton-Heifner, Donna Lynn. The Adventures of Itsy & Willy Wabbit: In Search of Lillian the Ladybug. 2012. 16p. pap. 24.95 *(978-1-4626-8547-9(1))* America Star Bks.

Davis, Jacky. Ladybug Girl Ready for Snow. Soman, David, illus. 2014. (Ladybug Girl Ser.). 14p. (J). (gr. -1 — 1). bds. 7.99 *(978-0-8037-4137-9(5),* Dial Bks) Penguin Young Readers Group.

—Ladybug Girl Says Good Night. Soman, David, illus. 2014. (Ladybug Girl Ser.). 12p. (J). (gr. -1 — 1). bds. 7.99 *(978-0-8037-3893-5(5),* Dial Bks) Penguin Young Readers Group.

Deal, Sarah E. The Spotless Ladybug. 2008. 31p. pap. 24.95 *(978-1-60672-964-9(0))* America Star Bks.

Devant, Jourdan. The Little Ladybug. 2006. (Illus.). 15p. (J). per. 10.99 *(978-1-59879-219-5(9))* Lifevest Publishing, Inc.

DK. Counting with a Ladybug. 2018. (Learn with a Ladybug Ser.). (ENG., Illus.). 12p. (J). (-k). bds. 10.99 *(978-1-4654-6390-6(9),* DK Children) Dorling Kindersley Publishing, Inc.

Eisele, Barbara. Miss Thistle & Friends. 2009. 48p. pap. 12.99 *(978-1-4490-2007-1(0))* AuthorHouse.

Finn, Isobel. The Very Lazy Ladybug. Tickle, Jack, illus. 2005. 16p. (J). bds. 6.95 *(978-1-58925-758-0(8))* Tiger Tales.

Finn, Isobel & Tickle, Jack. The Very Lazy Ladybug. 2003. (Illus.). (J). 16p. tchr. ed. 15.95 *(978-1-58925-714-6(6));* 32p. pap. 6.95 *(978-1-58925-379-7(5))* Tiger Tales.

Fisher, Meaghan. I Love Ladybugs! Mathieu, Middy, illus. 2012. 16p. pap. 6.99 *(978-1-938768-00-2(0))* Gypsy Pubns.

Florie, Christine. Rookie Ready to Learn en Español: la Mariquita Lara. Dalby, Danny Brooks, illus. 2011. (Rookie Ready to Learn Español Ser.). Orig. Title: Rookie Ready to Learn: Lara Ladybug. (SPA.). 32p. (J). pap. 5.95 *(978-0-531-26783-7(0),* Children's Pr.) Scholastic Library Publishing.

Florie, Christine & Dalby, Danny Brooks. La Mariquita Lara. Dalby, Danny Brooks, illus. 2011. (Rookie Ready to Learn Español Ser.). (SPA., Illus.). 32p. (J). lib. bdg. 23.00 *(978-0-531-26115-6(8),* Children's Pr.) Scholastic Library Publishing.

Fox, Mem. Yoo-Hoo, Ladybug! Ljungkvist, Laura, illus. 2013. (ENG.). 32p. (J). (gr. -1-3). 19.99 *(978-1-4424-3400-4(7))* Simon & Schuster Children's Publishing.

Frances, Janie. Krissy the Littlest Ladybug. 2013. 32p. pap. 8.95 *(978-0-9837403-9-1(9))* JGracia Publishing.

French, Vivian. Ladybird Ladybird. Young, Selina, illus. 2003. (ENG.). 32p. pap. *(978-1-84255-284-1(8),* Orion Children's Bks.) Hachette Children's Group.

Gaydos, Stellisa. Lulu the Lucky Ladybug. 2011. 20p. 11.00 *(978-1-4567-3826-6(7))* AuthorHouse.

Gerth, Melanie. Five Little Ladybugs with Hand Puppet. Beith, Laura Huliska, illus. 2009. (ENG.). 12p. 12.95 *(978-1-58117-889-0(1),* Intervisual/Piggy Toes) Bendon, Inc.

—Ten Little Ladybugs. Huliska-Beith, Laura, illus. 2007. (ENG.). 22p. (J). (gr. -1-3). bds. 15.95 *(978-1-58117-578-3(7),* Intervisual/Piggy Toes) Bendon, Inc.

Golden Books. The Little Grumpy Cat That Wouldn't (Grumpy Cat) Laberis, Steph, illus. 2016. (Little Golden Book Ser.). 24p. (J). (gr. -1-1). 5.99 *(978-0-399-55354-7(1),* Golden Bks.) Random Hse. Children's Bks.

Gopinath, Karin Ursula. Friends in the Garden. Sutanto, Tommy, illus. 2008. 34p. (J). per. 19.95 *(978-0-9800637-0-7(1))* Lotus Art Works Inc.

Greban, Quentin. Mommy, I Love You. Greban, Quentin, illus. 2005. (Illus.). 32p. (J). 15.95 *(978-0-689-03922-5(0),* Milk & Cookies) ibooks, Inc.

Hooray for Boys & Girls! 2006. (J). 15.95 *(978-0-9776837-0-3(2))* West Woods Pr.

Jaramillo, J.C. Best Buggies, 1 vol. 2010. 16p. pap. 24.95 *(978-1-4489-4928-1(9))* PublishAmerica, Inc.

Kayaalp, Suzan. Inch Worm Inch Worm. Merrifield, Monarca, illus. 2013. 20p. pap. 12.95 *(978-1-62838-072-9(1))* Page Publishing Inc.

Keene, Carolyn. Cupcake Chaos. 34. Pamintuan, Macky, illus. 2013. (Nancy Drew & the Clue Crew Ser.: 34). (ENG.). 96p. (J). (gr. 1-4). pap. 5.99 *(978-1-4424-5351-7(6),* Aladdin) Simon & Schuster Children's Publishing.

Ladybird. Anansi Helps a Friend: Ladybird Readers Level 1. 2016. (Ladybird Readers Ser.). (Illus.). 48p. (J). pap. 9.99 *(978-0-241-25409-7(4))* Penguin Bks., Ltd. GBR. Dist: Independent Pubs. Group.

Ladybug, Ladybug: Individual Title Six-Pack. (Story Steps Ser.). (gr. k-2). 23.00 *(978-0-7635-9802-0(X))* Rigby Education.

Lenny's Lost Spots. 2005. (J). per. 8.95 *(978-1-59566-131-9(X))* QEB Publishing Inc.

Lotorto-Soroka, Mary. Who Needs Spots Anyways? 2009. 24p. pap. 12.99 *(978-1-4490-3947-9(2))* AuthorHouse.

Lurie, Craig. Butterflies, Ladybugs, & Bumble Bees & the wonderful world this could Be .... 2011. 36p. (gr. -1). pap. 14.95 *(978-1-4567-6300-8(8))* AuthorHouse.

Marranzino, Sami. The Littlest Ladybug. Currey, Andrew K., illus. 2012. 32p. pap. 24.95 *(978-1-4626-7781-8(9))* America Star Bks.

Martin, Anne E. There's A Ladybug in My House. Martin, Anne E., illus. l.t. ed. 2006. (Illus.). 45p. (J). per. 12.99 *(978-1-59879-165-5(6))* Lifevest Publishing, Inc.

McCabe, Lauren A. How Many Spots Have I Got? Foulke, Nancy, illus. 2005. (J). 16.00 *(978-1-893516-02-1(4))* Our Child Pr.

Miller, Amanda K. Lily's Grand Adventures. 2011. 36p. pap. 24.95 *(978-1-4626-2493-5(6))* America Star Bks.

Moore, Roland D. Bugging in the City. 2011. 80p. pap. 32.26 *(978-1-4567-4130-3(6))* AuthorHouse.

Morrow, John. Lilly Lightbug. 2017. (ENG., Illus.). 32p. (J). (gr. -1-6). 19.95 *(978-0-9790832-0-4(6),* Three Ring Circus Publishing Hse., Inc.) 405 Pubns.

Newton-Kowalsky, Jacqueline. Itsy Bitsy Stories for Itsy Bitsy Tigers. 2012. 32p. pap. *(978-1-77097-138-7(6))* FriesenPress.

Nielander, Amy. The Ladybug Race. Nielander, Amy, illus. 2015. (ENG., Illus.). 40p. (J). 19.95 *(978-0-7649-7187-7(5),* POMEGRANATE KIDS) Pomegranate Communications, Inc.

Pantelides, Sherry. It's Blue Like You! A Story about Loyalty. Perez, Debi, illus. 2007. 32p. (J). 12.99 *(978-0-9771076-1-2(2))* Lacey Productions.

—It's Red Like Me! A Story about the Blood of Jesus. Perez, Debi, illus. 2007. (J). lib. bdg. 12.99 *(978-0-9771076-0-5(4))* Lacey Productions.

—Make A Choice to Rejoice! A Story about Being Cheerful. Perez, Debi, illus. 2007. 32p. (J). 12.99 *(978-0-9771076-2-9(0))* Lacey Productions.

Parrott, Darcie. Ladybug's Walk. 2007. (ENG.). 32p. (J). (gr. -1-k). 10.95 *(978-0-9772692-8-0(0))* Birch Island.

Perry, Tally. Saving Sunny Stream, a Wormie Wormald Adventure. 2009. 60p. pap. 22.00 *(978-1-60860-296-4(6),* Eloquent Bks.) Strategic Book Publishing & Rights Agency (SBPRA).

Peterson, Mary. Snail Has Lunch. Peterson, Mary, illus. 2016. (Pix Ser.). (ENG., Illus.). 64p. (J). (gr. 1-4). 12.99 *(978-1-4814-5302-8(5),* Aladdin) Simon & Schuster Children's Publishing.

Pova, Rosie. Ladybug & Caterpillar: The Way to Friendship. 2008. 16p. pap. 24.95 *(978-1-60474-950-2(4))* America Star Bks.

Puzzi, Jessica. Rosy & Simon's Front Yard Adventure, 1 vol. 2010. 18p. pap. 24.95 *(978-1-4489-2601-5(7))* PublishAmerica, Inc.

Quanty, Donna. Dottie's New Look. 2008. 28p. pap. 24.95 *(978-1-60474-211-4(9))* America Star Bks.

Rist, Stephen. Ladybirds Don't Like Scrambled Eggs. 2010. (Illus.). 36p. 15.49 *(978-1-4490-6614-7(3))* AuthorHouse.

Rooks, Jo. Layla's Luck. 2020. (Illus.). 32p. (J). *(978-1-4338-3238-3(0),* Magination Pr.) American Psychological Assn.

Satterfield, April. Leah Bug & Her Flying Friends. Guthrie, Lewis, illus. 2011. 20p. pap. 24.95 *(978-1-4560-8422-6(4))* America Star Bks.

Seward, Toni Gibson. Kloey & the Ladybug. 2013. 24p. pap. *(978-1-4602-3066-4(3))* FriesenPress.

Simee. Giggles Feel Good, 1 vol. 2010. 18p. pap. 24.95 *(978-1-4489-4878-9(9))* PublishAmerica, Inc.

Small, Lily. Bella the Bunny: Fairy Animals of Misty Wood. 2015. (Fairy Animals of Misty Wood Ser.: 2). (ENG., Illus.). 144p. (J). (gr. k-3). pap. 6.99 *(978-1-62779-142-7(6),* 900137175, Holt, Henry & Co. Bks. For Young Readers) Holt, Henry & Co.

Soler, Michael. The Ladybug & Me. Eisenberg, Serge, illus. 2007. 24p. (J). per. 8.99 *(978-0-9795469-0-7(7))* Soler, Michael.

Stanek, Robert, pseud. The Bugville Critters So Many Lessons to Learn. 2009. (Illus.). 68p. (J). pap. 18.95 *(978-1-57545-237-1(5),* Reagent Pr. Bks. for Young Readers) RP Media.

—Have a Backyard Picnic. 2009. (Bugville Critters Ser.: No. 14). (ENG., Illus.). 52p. (J). 14.95 *(978-1-57545-210-4(3),* Reagent Pr. Bks. for Young Readers) RP Media.

—Have a Bad Day. 2009. (Bugville Critters Ser.: No. 11). (ENG., Illus.). 52p. (J). 14.95 *(978-1-57545-207-4(3),* Reagent Pr. Bks. for Young Readers) RP Media.

—Have a Surprise Party. 2009. (Bugville Critters Ser.: No. 13). (ENG., Illus.). 52p. (J). 14.95 *(978-1-57545-209-8(X),* Reagent Pr. Bks. for Young Readers) RP Media.

—Have Trouble at School. 2009. (Illus.). 24p. pap. 9.99 *(978-1-57545-212-8(X));* 52p. (J). pap. 14.95 *(978-1-57545-204-3(9))* RP Media. (Reagent Pr. Bks. for Young Readers).

—Stay after School. 2009. (Bugville Critters Ser.: No. 10). (ENG., Illus.). 52p. (J). 14.95 *(978-1-57545-206-7(5),* Reagent Pr. Bks. for Young Readers) RP Media.

—Visit City Hall. 2009. (Bugville Critters Ser.: No. 12). (ENG., Illus.). 52p. (J). 14.95 *(978-1-57545-208-1(1),* Reagent Pr. Bks. for Young Readers) RP Media.

Thomas, Jan. Can You Make a Scary Face? Thomas, Jan, illus. 2009. (ENG., Illus.). 40p. (J). (gr. -1-3). 16.99 *(978-1-4169-8581-5(6),* Beach Lane Bks.) Beach Lane Bks.

Tickle, Jack. Look Out, Ladybug! Tickle, Jack, illus. 2013. (ENG., Illus.). 32p. (J). (gr. -1-2). 12.95 *(978-1-58925-128-1(8))* Tiger Tales.

Treviño, Hilda L. Ladybugs on a Mission. 2013. 70p. (gr. 4-6). pap. 8.95 *(978-1-4759-7762-2(X))* iUniverse, Inc.

Turner-Rahman, Gregory. Ellabug. 2009. 40p. pap. 12.95 *(978-1-935290-09-4(6))* Diversion Pr.

Walshaw, Sam. Lulu Ladybug. 2012. (Illus.). (J). *(978-1-4351-3863-6(5))* Barnes & Noble, Inc.

Watt, Fiona. Busy Bug Book. Mantle, Ben, illus. 2011. (Pull-Back Books Ser.). 10p. (J). ring bd. 24.99 *(978-0-7945-2941-3(0),* Usborne) EDC Publishing.

Woodson, Vera. Lady Bug, Beetle Boy, & Friends: Bullies Be Gone! 2013. (ENG., Illus.). (J). 14.95 *(978-1-62086-049-6(X))* Amplify Publishing Group.

Younger, Mary. You're Not A Ladybird You've Got No Spots. 2011. (Illus.). 24p. 14.09 *(978-1-4567-7082-2(9))* AuthorHouse.

Yurksaitis, Anne. Genevieve the Singing Ladybug. Yurksaitis, Stephanie, illus. 2013. 28p. pap. 24.95 *(978-1-63000-927-4(X))* America Star Bks.

Zoehfeld, Kathleen Weidner & Smithsonian Institution Staff. Ladybug at Orchard Avenue (Mariquite en la avenida Orchard) 2008. (MUL.). 16p. 14.95 *(978-1-59249-844-4(2))* Soundprints.

LAFAYETTE, MARIE JOSEPH PAUL YVES ROCH GILBERT DU MOTIER, MARQUIS DE, 1757-1834

Bishop, Claire Huchet. Lafayette: French-American Hero. Brevannes, Maurice, illus. 2011. 82p. 37.95 *(978-1-258-03539-6(1))* Literary Licensing, LLC.

Castrovilla, Selene. Revolutionary Friends: General George Washington & the Marquis de Lafayette. Kozjan, Drazen, illus. 2013. (ENG.). 40p. (J). (gr. 2-5). 16.99 *(978-1-59078-880-6(X),* Calkins Creek) Highlights Pr., c/o Highlights for Children, Inc.

Collins, Kathleen. El Marques de Lafayette: Heroe Frances de la Guerra de Independencia, 1 vol. 2003. (Grandes Personajes en la Historia de Los Estados Unidos (Famous People in American History) Ser.). (SPA.). 32p. (gr. 3-4). pap. 10.00 *(978-0-8239-4233-6(3),* 611571c8-b964-4b87-9954-e1eb2363af67, Rosen Classroom) Rosen Publishing Group, Inc., The.

—Marquis de Lafayette: French Hero of the American Revolution. (Primary Sources of Famous People in American History Ser.). 32p. 2009. (gr. 2-3). 47.90 *(978-1-60851-703-9(9))* 2003. (ENG., Illus.). (gr. 3-4). pap. 10.00 *(978-0-8239-4187-2(6),* 76f1c1b2-baea-4384-bb95-dfa273dcbe8f) 2003. (ENG & SPA., Illus.). (gr. 2-3). lib. bdg. 29.13 *(978-0-8239-4163-6(9),* 22b96b9a-22f4-4124-a502-dda13c946bf7, Editorial Buenas Letras) 2003. (ENG., Illus.). (gr. 3-4). lib. bdg. 29.13 *(978-0-8239-4115-5(9),* cfd9a7dc-c003-4a32-8751-4ccf0644f249, Rosen Reference) Rosen Publishing Group, Inc., The.

—Marquis de Lafayette / el Marques de Lafayette: French Hero of the American Revolution / Héroe francés de la Revolución Estadounidense. 2009. (Famous People in American History/Grandes personajes en la historia de los Estados Unidos Ser.). (ENG & SPA.). 32p. (gr. 2-3). 47.90 *(978-1-61512-550-0(7),* Editorial Buenas Letras) Rosen Publishing Group, Inc., The.

Corporate Contributor Staff & Colozza Cocca, Lisa. Marquis de Lafayette: Fighting for America's Freedom. 2012. (ENG.). 48p. (J). *(978-0-7787-0802-5(0));* pap. *(978-0-7787-0813-1(6))* Crabtree Publishing Co.

Dugan, Christine. Marquis de Lafayette & the French (Alexander Hamilton) rev. ed. 2017. (Social Studies: Informational Text Ser.). (ENG., Illus.). 32p. (gr. 4-8). pap. 11.99 *(978-1-4258-6353-1(1))* Teacher Created Materials, Inc.

Hale, Nathan. Lafayette! (Nathan Hale's Hazardous Tales #8) A Revolutionary War Tale. 2018. (Nathan Hale's Hazardous Tales Ser.). (ENG., Illus.). 128p. (J). (gr. 3-7). 14.99 *(978-1-4197-3148-8(3),* 1128201, Amulet Bks.) Abrams, Inc.

Jensen, Dorothea. A Buss from Lafayette. 2016. (ENG.). 266p. (YA). (gr. 7-12). pap. 16.95 *(978-1-939371-90-4(2))* Boutique of Quality Books Publishing Co., Inc.

Randolph, Joanne. The Call of Liberty: Marquis de Lafayette & the American Revolution. (Great Moments in American History Ser.). 32p. (gr. 3-3). 2009. 47.90 *(978-1-61513-152-5(3))* 2003. (ENG., Illus.). (YA). lib. bdg. 29.13 *(978-0-8239-4368-5(2),*

J K L

ae5f27e2-ceda-436e-8b56-08866465528a) Rosen Publishing Group, Inc., The.

LAFITTE, JEAN, 1782-1854—FICTION

Webber, Jake. Lafitte's Black Box: Boit Noir. 2009. 228p. 32.95 *(978-1-60594-361-9(4))*; pap. 14.95 *(978-1-60594-360-2(6))* Aeon Publishing Inc. (Llumina Pr.).

LA GUARDIA, FIORELLO H. (FIORELLO HENRY), 1882-1947

Leoni, Cristiana. New York in the 1930s with la Guardia, 1 vol. Cappon, Manuela, illus. 2009. (Come See My City Ser.). (ENG.). 48p. (gr. 4-4). 31.21 *(978-0-7614-4336-0(3),* 8018822b-c09d-4855-b1fe-9641b91bec49) Cavendish Square Publishing LLC.

LAKE MICHIGAN

see Michigan, Lake

LAKES

Allman, Barbara. Lakes & Rivers, 1 vol. 2019. (Investigate Earth Science Ser.). (ENG.). 24p. (gr. 2-2). pap. 10.95 *(978-1-9785-0868-2(9),* 83b5dbc1-2ea3-426c-89a8-2a2f617c4718) Enslow Publishing, LLC.

Amstutz, Lisa J. Bringing Back Our Freshwater Lakes. 2017. (Conservation Success Stories Ser.). (ENG., Illus.). 112p. (J). (gr. 6-12). lib. bdg. 41.36 *(978-1-5321-1314-7(5),* 27522, Essential Library) ABDO Publishing Co.

AZ Books Staff. Frog's Pond. Potapenko, Olga, ed. 2012. (Talking Plush Animals Ser.). (ENG.). 10p. (J). (gr. -1-k). bds. 10.95 *(978-1-61889-113-6(8))* AZ Bks. LLC.

Barnes, J. Lou. 101 Facts about Lakes, 1 vol. 2003. (101 Facts about Our World Ser.). (ENG., Illus.). 32p. (gr. 2-4). lib. bdg. 28.67 *(978-0-8368-3707-0(X),* 9225c187-a3cb-4b60-bc96-6e5efda3814c, Gareth Stevens Learning Library) Stevens, Gareth Publishing LLLP.

Berne, Emma Carlson. Lakes, 1 vol. 2008. (Geography Zone: Landforms Ser.). (ENG., Illus.). 24p. (J). (gr. 2-3). lib. bdg. 26.27 *(978-1-4042-4208-1(2),* 6ce355d0-0176-4412-8e54-9a6204a5bf4e) Rosen Publishing Group, Inc., The.

Best, Arthur. Lakes, 1 vol. 2017. (Our World of Water Ser.). (ENG.). 24p. (gr. 1-1). pap. 9.22 *(978-1-5026-3090-2(7),* b84d621b-3ff3-40d5-9bd1-c42fb40e38ec) Cavendish Square Publishing LLC.

Best, B. J. How Are Lakes Formed?, 1 vol. 2017. (Nature's Formations Ser.). (ENG., Illus.). 24p. (gr. 1-1). pap. 9.22 *(978-1-5026-2549-6(0),* 1ba25d5b-59b4-449a-938a-aaddf40bc8ba) Cavendish Square Publishing LLC.

Byerly, Robbie. At the Lake. rev. ed. 2010. (1-3Y in My World Ser.). (ENG., Illus.). 16p. (J). (gr. k-1). pap. 9.60 *(978-1-61541-411-6(8))* American Reading Co.

Carlson Berne, Emma. Lakes. 2009. (Geography Zone: Landforms Ser.). 24p. (gr. 2-3). 42.50 *(978-1-61512-711-5(9),* PowerKids Pr.) Rosen Publishing Group, Inc., The.

Casado, Dami & Casado, Alicia. Los Rios y Lagos. 2005. (Yo Te Hablare De... Ser.). (SPA., Illus.). 14p. (J). per., bds. 8.99 *(978-84-272-7387-0(8))* Molino, Editorial ESP. Dist: Santillana USA Publishing Co., Inc.

Declus, Jennifer. What Might I Find on a Pond. Kalasea, illus. 2004. (J). *(978-0-9743690-2-0(0))* Britt Allcroft Productions.

Dorling Kindersley Publishing Staff. Rivers & Lakes. 2003. (DK Eye Wonder Ser.). (ENG., Illus.). 48p. (J). (gr. 3-6). lib. bdg. 22.44 *(978-0-7894-9047-6(1))* Dorling Kindersley Publishing, Inc.

Early Macken, JoAnn. Lagos (Lakes), 1 vol. 2005. (¿Conoces la Tierra? Geografía Del Mundo (Where on Earth? World Geography) Ser.). (SPA., Illus.). 24p. (gr. 2-4). pap. 9.15 *(978-0-8368-6550-9(2),* 903a5805-4391-4815-b285-fa978520afdf); lib. bdg. 24.67 *(978-0-8368-6543-1(X),* ae1367f1-6bc7-43f5-97ff-f946e1d523f2) Stevens, Gareth Publishing LLLP. (Weekly Reader Leveled Readers).

—Lakes, 1 vol. 2005. (Water Habitats Ser.). (ENG., Illus.). 24p. (gr. k-2). pap. 9.15 *(978-0-8368-4891-5(3),* f1ecdc70-25bf-410f-993e-65138d770e2c); (gr. k-2). lib. bdg. 24.67 *(978-0-8368-4884-7(5),* f085dd3d-3e66-4581-bc65-b4c6270fb1d2); (gr. 2-4). pap. 9.15 *(978-0-8368-6401-4(8),* 5d588adc-caf6-4053-8dfd-438822c559af); (gr. 2-4). lib. bdg. 24.67 *(978-0-8368-6394-9(1),* 30b296e5-37bd-4de1-9468-c98a619ef731) Stevens, Gareth Publishing LLLP. (Weekly Reader Leveled Readers).

—Lakes / Lagos, 1 vol. 2005. (Water Habitats / Hábitats Acuáticos Ser.). (SPA & ENG., Illus.). 24p. (gr. k-2). pap. 9.15 *(978-0-8368-6036-8(5),* 5ef872b3-fc2c-4930-88b1-d51a1dabc366); lib. bdg. 24.67 *(978-0-8368-6029-0(2),* 7b23925b-98ae-49a0-9fea-e525d0e7af7b) Stevens, Gareth Publishing LLLP. (Weekly Reader Leveled Readers).

Frisch, Aaron. Lakes. 2008. (Our World Ser.). (Illus.). 24p. (J). (gr. -1-3). lib. bdg. 24.25 *(978-1-58341-571-9(8),* Creative Education) Creative Co., The.

Gamble, Adam. Good Night Lake. Stevenson, Harvey, illus. 2008. (Good Night Our World Ser.). (ENG.). 28p. (J). (gr. k — 1). bds. 9.95 *(978-1-60219-028-3(3))* Good Night Bks.

Gingold, Janet. My Adventure on a Lake: Advanced My Adventure. 2009. (ENG.). 72p. (J). pap. 9.99 *(978-1-59092-442-6(8))* Blue Forge Pr.

Gleisner, Jenna Lee. A Lake in Winter. 2018. (Welcoming the Seasons Ser.). (ENG.). 24p. (J). (gr. -1-2). lib. bdg. 32.79 *(978-1-5038-2385-3(7),* 212228) Child's World, Inc, The.

Gray, Leon. Rivers & Lakes. 2015. (Amazing Biomes Ser.). (ENG., Illus.). 32p. (J). (gr. 3-6). 31.35 *(978-1-78121-244-8(9),* 16392) Brown Bear Bks.

Green, Emily K. Lakes. 2006. (Learning about the Earth Ser.). (ENG., Illus.). 24p. (J). (gr. k-3). lib. bdg. 26.95 *(978-1-60014-037-2(8))* Bellwether Media.

—Lakes. 2011. (Blastoff! Readers Ser.). 24p. (J). pap. 5.95 *(978-0-531-26030-2(5),* Children's Pr.) Scholastic Library Publishing.

Haney, Johannah. Lakes & Ponds! With 25 Science Projects for Kids. Casteel, Tom, illus. 2018. (Explore Your World Ser.). 96p. (J). (gr. 3-4). 19.95 *(978-1-61930-699-8(9),* 00a6d3cb-2790-4c28-a74e-827594171c12) Nomad Pr.

Head, Honor. Poisoned Rivers & Lakes, 1 vol. 2018. (Totally Toxic Ser.). (ENG.). 48p. (gr. 4-5). pap. 15.05 *(978-1-5382-3500-3(5),* ab036dd4-0190-431c-a938-f8e84f087c3f) Stevens, Gareth Publishing LLLP.

Hibbert, Adam. Life in a Pond, 1 vol. 2010. (Nature in Focus Ser.). (ENG., Illus.). 32p. (gr. 3-4). (J). pap. 11.50 *(978-1-4339-3412-4(4),* 727af3be-5f8e-4bd1-945e-64b170a6d66e, Gareth Stevens Learning Library); (YA). lib. bdg. 28.67 *(978-1-4339-3411-7(6),* ec8318cf-d92b-4a90-9337-e14c2778c78a) Stevens, Gareth Publishing LLLP.

Johnson, Rebecca L. A Journey into a Lake. Saroff, Phyllis V., illus. 2004. (Biomes of North America Ser.). (J). pap. 6.95 *(978-0-8225-2043-6(5))*; 48p. (gr. 3-6). lib. bdg. 23.93 *(978-1-57505-594-7(5))* Lerner Publishing Group.

Klepeis, Alicia Z. 24 Hours in a Lake, 1 vol. 2017. (Day in an Ecosystem Ser.). (ENG., Illus.). 48p. (J). (gr. 4-4). 33.07 *(978-1-5026-2480-2(X),* 7ec0079e-9a36-4779-ae73-00f276eda52b) Cavendish Square Publishing LLC.

Kochanoff, Peggy. Be a Pond Detective: Solving the Mysteries of Lakes, Swamps, & Pools, 1 vol. 2016. (Be a Nature Detective Ser.). (ENG., Illus.). 40p. (J). (gr. 1-3). pap. 14.95 *(978-1-77108-394-2(8),* ecb27076-3f28-4591-a8a1-b58d0c43027e) Nimbus Publishing, Ltd. CAN. Dist: Baker & Taylor Publisher Services (BTPS).

Lowrie, Paul. Hooray for Minnesota Lakes. 2008. 19.95 *(978-0-9755801-8-9(3))* Questmarc Publishing.

Lynch, Seth. There's a Lake in My Backyard!, 1 vol. 2016. (Backyard Biomes Ser.). (ENG.). 24p. (J). (gr. 1-2). pap. 9.15 *(978-1-4824-5563-2(3),* 9a2b0f47-b979-4bad-8b1e-796950bbca41) Stevens, Gareth Publishing LLLP.

Minden, Cecilia. The World Around Us: Lakes. 2010. (21st Century Basic Skills Library: the World Around Us Ser.). (ENG., Illus.). 24p. (gr. k-3). lib. bdg. 26.35 *(978-1-60279-859-5(1),* 200584) Cherry Lake Publishing.

Nadeau, Isaac. Water in Rivers & Lakes. 2009. (Water Cycle Ser.). 24p. (gr. 4-4). 42.50 *(978-1-60854-271-0(8),* PowerKids Pr.) Rosen Publishing Group, Inc., The.

National Geographic Learning. Reading Expeditions (Social Studies: the Land Around Us): Rivers & Lakes. 2007. (Rise & Shine Ser.). (ENG., Illus.). 32p. (J). pap. 18.95 *(978-0-7922-4561-2(X))* CENGAGE Learning.

Nemeth, Jason D. Rivers, Lakes, & Oceans, 1 vol. 2012. (Our Changing Earth Ser.). (ENG.). 24p. (J). (gr. 2-3). pap. 9.25 *(978-1-4488-6300-6(7),* ce8cfc52-b506-4397-90b6-e5ca09c737b4, PowerKids Pr.); lib. bdg. 26.27 *(978-1-4488-6171-2(3),* 3cd615a4-4e19-4b57-bc6c-a637bda1fb22) Rosen Publishing Group, Inc., The.

Ostopowich, Melanie. Oceans, Lakes, & Rivers. 2015. (Illus.). 24p. (J). *(978-1-5105-0052-5(9))* SmartBook Media, Inc.

—Oceans, Lakes, & Rivers. 2010. (Water Science Ser.). (Illus.). 24p. (gr. 3-5). (J). pap. 11.95 *(978-1-61690-007-6(5))*; (YA). lib. bdg. 25.70 *(978-1-61690-001-4(6))* Weigl Pubs., Inc.

—Oceans, Rivers, & Lakes. 2005. (Science Matters Ser.). (Illus.). 24p. (J). (gr. 3-7). lib. bdg. 24.45 *(978-1-59036-304-1(3))* Weigl Pubs., Inc.

Rice, William & Franklin, Yvonne. Ponds, 1 vol. rev. ed. 2009. (Science: Informational Text Ser.). (ENG.). 32p. (gr. 2-4). pap. 11.99 *(978-1-4333-0318-0(3))* Teacher Created Materials, Inc.

Rivers Lakes & Oceans. 2009. (ENG.). 112p. (gr. 5-9). 35.00 *(978-0-7910-9797-7(8),* P159148, Facts On File) Infobase Holdings, Inc.

Silverman, Buffy. Let's Visit the Lake. 2016. (Lightning Bolt Books (r) — Biome Explorers Ser.). (ENG., Illus.). 32p. (J). (gr. 1-3). lib. bdg. 29.32 *(978-1-5124-1193-5(0),* 597c362f-121b-4e84-b235-0bbf9252939e, Lerner Pubns.) Lerner Publishing Group.

Smith, Ben. How Are Oceans & Lakes Alike? 2012. (Level F Ser.). (ENG., Illus.). 16p. (J). (gr. k-2). pap. 7.95 *(978-1-927136-55-3(5),* 19408) RiverStream Publishing.

Spilsbury, Richard & Spilsbury, Louise. At Home in Rivers & Lakes, 1 vol., 1. 2015. (Home in the Biome Ser.). (ENG.). 32p. (J). (gr. 3-4). pap. 11.00 *(978-1-5081-4556-1(3),* c2296a8c-1aa9-4507-960a-a484d71a29b1, PowerKids Pr.) Rosen Publishing Group, Inc., The.

Taylor, Trace, et al. En el Lago. 2011. (2Y Lugares Adonde Voy Ser.).Tr. of At the Lake. (SPA.). 16p. (J). (gr. k-2). pap. 9.60 *(978-1-61541-413-0(4))* American Reading Co.

Zollman, Pam. Lake Tahoe. 2006. (Rookie Read-About Geography Ser.). (ENG., Illus.). 32p. (J). (gr. 1-2). lib. bdg. 20.50 *(978-0-516-25036-6(1),* Children's Pr.) Scholastic Library Publishing.

LAMBS

see Sheep

LAMPS—FICTION

Diroma, Joseph. Pinuccio. Jones. Bob, illus. 2009. 24p. pap. 14.99 *(978-1-60844-036-8(2))* Dog Ear Publishing, LLC.

Ghazwah, Sura, illus. Aladdin & His Magic Lamp: One Thousand & One Nights. 2016. (ENG.). 64p. pap. 7.95 *(978-1-911091-00-4(X))* Real Reads Ltd. GBR. Dist: Casemate Pubs. & Bk. Distributors, LLC.

Heine, Theresa & Barefoot Books Staff. Chandra's Magic Light. Gueyfier, Judith, illus. 2013. (J). 16.99 *(978-1-84686-493-3(3))* Barefoot Bks., Inc.

LANCASTER COUNTY (PA.)—FICTION

Brenneman, Lynette Leaman, photos by. Susanna's Surprise: A Day at the Hans Herr House. 2012. (Illus.). 32p. (J). *(978-0-9859737-0-4(6))* Brenneman, Lynette.

LAND

see Land Use

LAND, RECLAMATION OF

see Reclamation of Land

LAND SURVEYING

see Surveying

LAND USE

Here are entered general works which cover such topics as types of land, the utilization, distribution and development of land and the economic factors which affect the value of land. Works which treat only of ownership of land are entered under Real Estate.

see also Agriculture; Farms; Feudalism; Reclamation of Land

Arnold, Quinn M. La Terre. 2018. (Graines de Savoir Ser.). (FRE., Illus.). 24p. (J). *(978-1-77092-405-5(1),* 19694) Creative Co., The.

Banting, Erinn. England - The Land, 1 vol. 2012. (ENG.). 32p. (J). pap. *(978-0-7787-9832-3(1))* Crabtree Publishing Co.

Crabtree Publishing Company Staff & Greil, Marlene. United States: The Land. 2012. (ENG.). 32p. (J). *(978-0-7787-9835-4(6))*; pap. *(978-0-7787-9838-5(0))* Crabtree Publishing Co.

Gagne, Tammy. Life on Reservations. 2013. (ENG.). 48p. (J). (gr. 4-8). lib. bdg. 29.95 *(978-1-61228-444-6(2))* Mitchell Lane Pubs.

Greene, Carol. I Love Our Land, 1 vol. 2012. (I Love Our Earth Ser.). (ENG., Illus.). 24p. (gr. 3-3). 25.27 *(978-0-7660-4040-3(2),* 9dbc07ee-6c2a-4795-a287-114896501c2e, Enslow Elementary) Enslow Publishing, LLC.

Gregory, Helen. Changing the Land, 1 vol. 2011. (Wonder Readers Early Level Ser.). (ENG.). 16p. (gr. -1-1). (J). pap. 6.25 *(978-1-4296-7800-1(3),* 117972); pap. 35.94 *(978-1-4296-8076-9(8))* Capstone. (Capstone Pr.).

Holt, Rinehart and Winston Staff. Environmental Science Chptr. 14: Land. 4th ed. Date not set. pap. 11.20 *(978-0-03-068074-8(3))* Holt McDougal.

Hyde, Natalie. Population Patterns: What Factors Determine the Location & Growth of Human Settlements?, 1 vol. 2010. (Investigating Human Migration & Settlement Ser.). (ENG., Illus.). 48p. (J). (gr. 5-8). *(978-0-7787-5182-3(1))*; pap. *(978-0-7787-5197-7(X))* Crabtree Publishing Co.

Linde, Barbara M. Urban Sprawl, 1 vol., Vol. 1. 2013. (Habitat Havoc Ser.). (ENG.). 32p. (J). (gr. 3-4). 29.27 *(978-1-4339-9866-9(1),* 794743b1-55f6-4a65-a30b-fd6d16a5613f); pap. 11.50 *(978-1-4339-9868-3(8),* 1aa41a06-1445-45ec-ba9e-91a73adfa2af) Stevens, Gareth Publishing LLLP.

MacLeod, Elizabeth. Secrets Underground: North America's Buried Past. 2014. (ENG., Illus.). 96p. (YA). (gr. 5-12). pap. 14.95 *(978-1-55451-630-8(7),* 9781554516308) Annick Pr., Ltd. CAN. Dist: Publishers Group West (PGW).

—Secrets Underground: North America's Buried Past. Martchenko, Michael, illus. 2014. (ENG.). 96p. (YA). (gr. 5-12). 24.95 *(978-1-55451-631-5(5),* 9781554516315) Annick Pr., Ltd. CAN. Dist: Publishers Group West (PGW).

Morgan, Sally. Changing Planet: What is the Environmental Impact of Human Migration & Settlement?, 1 vol. 2010. (Investigating Human Migration & Settlement Ser.). (ENG., Illus.). 48p. (J). (gr. 5-8). *(978-0-7787-5179-3(1))*; pap. *(978-0-7787-5194-6(5))* Crabtree Publishing Co.

Peters, Katie. Rural Places. 2021. (My Community (Pull Ahead Readers — Nonfiction) Ser.). (ENG., Illus.). 16p. (J). (gr. -1-1). 27.99 *(978-1-5415-9013-7(9),* 8db937dc-e8de-475d-bfba-ca9d125ad9e7, Lerner Pubns.) Lerner Publishing Group.

Price, Jane. Underworld: Exploring the Secret World Beneath Your Feet, 0 vols. Hancock, James Gulliver, illus. 2014. (ENG.). 96p. (J). (gr. 3-7). 18.95 *(978-1-894786-89-8(0))* Kids Can Pr., Ltd. CAN. Dist: Hachette Bk. Group.

Rae, Rowena. Land Use. 2018. (J). *(978-1-5105-2177-3(1))* SmartBook Media, Inc.

Rice, Dona Herweck. Land, 1 vol. 2nd rev. ed. 2011. (TIME for KIDS(r): Informational Text Ser.). (ENG.). 12p. (gr. k-1). 7.99 *(978-1-4333-3574-7(3))* Teacher Created Materials, Inc.

—Terreno. 2nd rev. ed. 2011. (TIME for KIDS(r): Informational Text Ser.). (SPA.). 12p. (gr. k-1). 7.99 *(978-1-4333-4413-8(0))* Teacher Created Materials, Inc.

Roza, G. On Flat Land: Learning the FL Sound. 2009. (PowerPhonics Ser.). 24p. (gr. 1-1). 39.90 *(978-1-60851-463-2(3),* PowerKids Pr.) Rosen Publishing Group, Inc., The.

Stefoff, Rebecca. Managing Land Use, 1 vol. 2012. (Environment at Risk Ser.). (ENG., Illus.). 112p. (YA). (gr. 7-7). 42.64 *(978-1-60870-478-1(5),* 2e49a77b-5b5d-4886-9314-2b0c9b31ef91) Cavendish Square Publishing LLC.

Weber, Valerie & Redlin, Janice L. Land Use. 2017. (J). *(978-1-5105-2201-5(8))* SmartBook Media, Inc.

Ylvisake, Anne. Land & Water: World Rivers. (Fact Finders Ser.). (Illus.). (J). (gr. 3-4). lib. bdg. 90.40 *(978-0-7368-2559-7(2))* Capstone.

LANDFORMS

see also Sand Dunes; Wetlands

Anderson, Sheila. Landforms: Classroom Set. 2008. pap. 34.95 *(978-0-8225-9941-8(4))* Lerner Publishing Group.

—Landforms: Complete Set. 2008. pap. 208.95 *(978-0-8225-9269-3(X))* Lerner Publishing Group.

—Plains. 2008. pap. 34.95 *(978-0-8225-9938-8(4))* 2015. (ENG., Illus.). 24p. (J). E-Book 35.99 *(978-1-5124-1044-0(6),* Lerner Pubns.) Lerner Publishing Group.

—Plateaus. 2008. pap. 34.95 *(978-0-8225-9939-5(2))* 2015. (ENG., Illus.). 24p. (J). E-Book 35.99 *(978-1-5124-1045-7(4),* Lerner Pubns.) Lerner Publishing Group.

—Valleys. 2008. pap. 34.95 *(978-0-8225-9940-1(6))* 2015. (ENG., Illus.). 24p. (J). E-Book 35.99 *(978-1-5124-1046-4(2),* Lerner Pubns.) Lerner Publishing Group.

Benchmark Education Company, LLC Staff, compiled by. Landforms. 2006. spiral bd. 610.00 *(978-1-4108-6793-3(5))* Benchmark Education Co.

Benoit, Peter. Tundra. 2011. (True Bk Ser.). 48p. (J). (ENG.). pap. 6.95 *(978-0-531-28102-4(7))*; (gr. 3-5). 29.00 *(978-0-531-20553-2(3))* Scholastic Library Publishing. (Children's Pr.).

Berne, Emma Carlson. Hills, 1 vol. 2008. (Geography Zone: Landforms Ser.). (ENG., Illus.). 24p. (J). (gr. 2-3). lib. bdg. 26.27 *(978-1-4042-4207-4(4),* 96479659-a509-482c-8a00-6670a72e59fc) Rosen Publishing Group, Inc., The.

—Plains, 1 vol. 2008. (Geography Zone: Landforms Ser.). (ENG., Illus.). 24p. (J). (gr. 2-3). lib. bdg. 26.27 *(978-1-4042-4204-3(X),* c7318280-eb8e-48e0-bb7f-c1ebdf9b73e9) Rosen Publishing Group, Inc., The.

Bow, James. Tundras Inside Out. 2014. (Ecosystems Inside Out Ser.). (ENG., Illus.). 32p. (J). (gr. 4-5). *(978-0-7787-0639-7(7))* Crabtree Publishing Co.

Capelle, Jenna. Plains. 2018. (Landforms Ser.). (ENG., Illus.). 32p. (J). (gr. 2-3). pap. 9.95 *(978-1-63517-996-5(3),* 1635179963); lib. bdg. 31.35 *(978-1-63517-895-1(9),* 1635178959) North Star Editions. (Focus Readers).

Carlson Berne, Emma. Plains. 2009. (Geography Zone: Landforms Ser.). 24p. (gr. 2-3). 42.50 *(978-1-61512-712-2(7),* PowerKids Pr.) Rosen Publishing Group, Inc., The.

Carlson-Berne, Emma. Valleys, 1 vol. 2008. (Geography Zone: Landforms Ser.). (ENG., Illus.). 24p. (J). (gr. 2-3). lib. bdg. 26.27 *(978-1-4042-4203-6(1),* b26db264-0245-4472-8330-3984a5155a63) Rosen Publishing Group, Inc., The.

Carlson Berne, Emma. Valleys. 2009. (Geography Zone: Landforms Ser.). 24p. (gr. 2-3). 42.50 *(978-1-61512-713-9(5),* PowerKids Pr.) Rosen Publishing Group, Inc., The.

Casil, Amy Sterling. The Creation of Canyons. 2009. (Illus.). 64p. (J). 77.70 *(978-1-4358-5591-5(4))*; (ENG., (YA). (gr. 5-6). pap. 13.95 *(978-1-4358-5590-8(6),* 54550f3b-2ceb-427c-ba58-b50ada161cdd); (ENG., (YA). (gr. 5-6). lib. bdg. 37.13 *(978-1-4358-5296-9(6),* baa80286-378b-42f0-9956-82b3732fbe28) Rosen Publishing Group, Inc., The.

Ciocchi, Catherine & Morrison, Cathy. Esta Tierra, Es Tu País. Morrison, Cathy, illus. 2015.Tr. of This Land Is Your Land. (SPA., Illus.). 32p. (J). (gr. 2-3). pap. 11.95 *(978-1-62855-575-2(0),* b1156dab-dbdd-4156-9707-e005531fa7d9) Arbordale Publishing.

—This Land Is Your Land, 1 vol. 2015. (ENG., Illus.). 32p. (J). (gr. 1-4). 17.95 *(978-1-62855-557-8(2))* Arbordale Publishing.

Craats, Rennay. Natural Landmarks. 2004. (American Symbols Ser.). (Illus.). 24p. (J). (gr. 4-7). per. 8.95 *(978-1-59036-177-1(6))*; (gr. 1-3). lib. bdg. 24.45 *(978-1-59036-133-7(4))* Weigl Pubs., Inc.

Early Macken, JoAnn. Plains, 1 vol. 2005. (Where on Earth? World Geography Ser.). (ENG., Illus.). 24p. (gr. 2-4). pap. 9.15 *(978-0-8368-6403-8(4),* f12586e0-e251-457f-bb2d-d8c41bc2a8a4, Weekly Reader Leveled Readers) Stevens, Gareth Publishing LLLP.

Emminizer, Theresa. Water & Rock: How the Grand Canyon Formed, 1 vol. 2019. (Earth's History Through Rocks Ser.). (ENG.). 32p. (gr. 4-5). 27.93 *(978-1-7253-0166-5(0),* 5f3e9413-0e9c-40bf-9e59-fd2a359424f7, PowerKids Pr.) Rosen Publishing Group, Inc., The.

Faust, Daniel R. Layers of Stone: How Earth's Biggest Caves Formed, 1 vol. 2019. (Earth's History Through Rocks Ser.). (ENG.). 32p. (gr. 4-5). pap. 11.00 *(978-1-7253-0152-8(0),* 38b92f23-8ff5-49ea-b4d1-40ae5b7bb00d, PowerKids Pr.) Rosen Publishing Group, Inc., The.

Frankston, Evan. Mountains & Valleys: What's the Difference? 2013. (InfoMax Readers Ser.). (ENG.). 24p. (J). (gr. 3-4). pap. 49.50 *(978-1-4777-2464-4(8))*; (Illus.). pap. 8.25 *(978-1-4777-2463-7(X),* 9bbb2a78-2025-4a94-a20f-298a43e9ef05) Rosen Publishing Group, Inc., The. (Rosen Classroom).

Gagne, Tammy. Tundra Ecosystems, 1 vol. 2015. (Ecosystems of the World Ser.). (ENG., Illus.). 48p. (J). (gr. 4-8). 35.64 *(978-1-62403-857-0(3),* 18084) ABDO Publishing Co.

Graham, Amy. What Are the 7 Wonders of the Natural World?, 1 vol. 2013. (What Are the Seven Wonders of the World? Ser.). (ENG.). 48p. (gr. 4-6). 27.93 *(978-0-7660-4153-0(0),* af6a964e-2dd9-4996-b6ec-350ba4d998dd); pap. 11.53 *(978-1-4644-0232-6(9),* 33939e7a-ef2d-4ea9-a044-7ce3d21da59b) Enslow Publishing, LLC.

Granger, Ronald. Exploring Earth's Surface, 1 vol. 2012. (Exploring Earth & Space Ser.). (ENG., Illus.). 24p. (J). (gr. 1-2). 26.27 *(978-1-4488-8570-1(1),* 7750f35b-17fe-4187-9c30-7924e5d198fc, PowerKids Pr.) Rosen Publishing Group, Inc., The.

Green, Jen. Life on the Tundra, 1 vol. 2010. (Nature in Focus Ser.). (ENG., Illus.). 32p. (gr. 3-4). (J). pap. 11.50 *(978-1-4339-3418-6(3),* 316b91e5-94f2-477d-99cd-d72a9837ecf9, Gareth Stevens Learning Library); (YA). lib. bdg. 28.67 *(978-1-4339-3417-9(5),* 1df7e4ca-d7b7-434d-b63e-9e15834d579f) Stevens, Gareth Publishing LLLP.

Hale, Christy. Water Land: Land & Water Forms Around the World. Hale, Christy, illus. 2018. (ENG., Illus.). 32p. (J). 21.99 *(978-1-250-15244-2(5),* 900183618) Roaring Brook Pr.

Hansen, Grace. Tundra Biome, 1 vol. 2016. (Biomes Ser.). (ENG., Illus.). 24p. (J). (gr. -1-2). lib. bdg. 32.79 *(978-1-68080-505-5(3),* 21290, Abdo Kids) ABDO Publishing Co.

Heos, Bridget. The Creation of Peninsulas. 2009. (J). 77.70 *(978-1-4358-5601-1(5))*; (ENG.). 64p. (YA). (gr. 5-6). pap. 13.95 *(978-1-4358-5600-4(7),* c426fd0e-6cb8-4906-8be7-e2978b9221d8); (ENG., Illus.). 64p. (YA). (gr. 5-6). lib. bdg. 37.13 *(978-1-4358-5301-0(6),* 2ce9e816-6617-4483-848b-2f42f7eb5bae) Rosen Publishing Group, Inc., The.

How Water Got to the Plains: Individual Title Six-Packs. (gr. k-1). 23.00 *(978-0-7635-8843-4(1))* Rigby Education.

Hutchison, Patricia. Valleys. 2018. (Landforms Ser.). (ENG., Illus.). 32p. (J). (gr. 2-3). pap. 9.95 *(978-1-63517-998-9(X),* 163517998X); lib. bdg. 31.35 *(978-1-63517-897-5(5),* 1635178975) North Star Editions. (Focus Readers).

Hutmacher, Kimberly M. The World Was Once Covered by Giant Mushrooms & Other Cool Earth Facts. 2019. (Mind-Blowing Science Facts Ser.). (ENG., Illus.). 32p. (J). (gr. 4-6). lib. bdg. 28.65 *(978-1-5435-5768-8(6),* 139724) Capstone.

Kalman, Bobbie. Earth's Coasts. 2008. (Looking at Earth Ser.). (ENG., Illus.). 32p. (J). (gr. 1-4). pap. *(978-0-7787-3216-7(9))* Crabtree Publishing Co.

—I Can Write a Book about Landforms. 2012. (ENG.). 32p. (J). *(978-0-7787-7992-6(0))*; pap. *(978-0-7787-8001-4(5))* Crabtree Publishing Co.
—Introducción a los Accidentes Geográficos. 2009. (SPA.). 32p. (J). *(978-0-7787-8242-1(5))*; pap. *(978-0-7787-8259-9(X))* Crabtree Publishing Co.
—What Are Natural Structures? 2008. (Looking at Nature Ser.). (ENG., Illus.). 24p. (J). (gr. -1-2). pap. *(978-0-7787-3343-0(2))*; lib. bdg. *(978-0-7787-3323-2(8))* Crabtree Publishing Co.
Kalman, Bobbie & MacAulay, Kelley. Introducing Landforms. 2008. (Looking at Earth Ser.). (ENG., Illus.). 32p. (J). (gr. 3-7). pap. *(978-0-7787-3213-6(4))* Crabtree Publishing Co.
Leavitt, Amie Jane. The Science Behind Wonders of Earth: Cave Crystals, Balancing Rocks, & Snow Donuts. 2016. (Science Behind Natural Phenomena Ser.). (ENG., Illus.). 32p. (J). (gr. 3-9). lib. bdg. 28.65 *(978-1-5157-0773-8(3)*, 132115, Capstone Pr.) Capstone.
LernerClassroom Editors, ed. Landforms. 2008. pap. 7.95 *(978-0-8225-9221-1(5))* Lerner Publishing Group.
The Library of Landforms, 10 vols. 2005. (Library of Landforms Ser.). (ENG., Illus.). (J). (gr. 3-4). 131.35 *(978-1-4042-3293-8(1)*, 3d47cc18-8482-4541-ac8a-6074768f4ddc) Rosen Publishing Group, Inc., The.
Lindeen, Mary. Landforms. 2017. (Beginning-To-Read Ser.). (ENG.). 32p. (J). (gr. k-2). pap. 13.26 *(978-1-68404-093-3(0))*; (Illus.). 22.60 *(978-1-59953-874-7(1))* Norwood Hse. Pr.
Looye, Juliette, text. I Live near a Canyon. 2004. (Illus.). 16p. (J). pap. *(978-0-7367-1937-7(7))* Zaner-Bloser, Inc.
Maloof, Torrey. Weathering & Erosion, 1 vol. rev. ed. 2014. (Science: Informational Text Ser.). (ENG.). 32p. (gr. 2-3). pap. 10.99 *(978-1-4807-4611-4(8))* Teacher Created Materials, Inc.
McClish, Bruce. New World Continents & Land Bridges: North & South America. rev. ed. 2016. (Continents Ser.). (ENG.). 32p. (J). (gr. 4-6). pap. 8.99 *(978-1-4846-3639-8(2)*, 134035, Heinemann) Capstone.
Meachen Rau, Dana. Land, 1 vol. 2009. (Earth Matters Ser.). (ENG.). 32p. (gr. 1-2). lib. bdg. 25.50 *(978-0-7614-3043-8(1)*, 36cf1a21-dca9-464d-afc8-08f3bdb3e081) Cavendish Square Publishing LLC.
Michele, Tracey. Earth's Land & Water. 2011. (Learn-Abouts Ser.). (Illus.). 16p. (J). pap. 7.95 *(978-1-59920-593-9(9))* Black Rabbit Bks.
Mills, Nathan & Granger, Ronald. Exploring Earth's Surface, 1 vol. 2012. (Rosen Readers Ser.). (ENG., Illus.). 24p. (J). (gr. 1-2). pap. 8.25 *(978-1-4488-8839-9(5)*, c8af5650-765b-489b-b69b-817707040ebb, Rosen Classroom) Rosen Publishing Group, Inc., The.
Mis, Melody S. Exploring Canyons. 2009. (Geography Zone: Landforms Ser.). 24p. (gr. 2-3). 42.50 *(978-1-61512-692-7(9))*; (ENG., Illus.). (J). pap. 9.25 *(978-1-4358-3114-8(4)*, 9f39dda8-9801-4629-8ebb-664ae9800f83) Rosen Publishing Group, Inc., The. (PowerKids Pr.)
—Exploring Peninsulas. 2009. (Geography Zone: Landforms Ser.). 24p. (gr. 2-3). 42.50 *(978-1-61512-707-8(0))*; (ENG., Illus.). (J). lib. bdg. 26.27 *(978-1-4358-2711-0(2)*, 31edd90f-0d3b-4266-978e-1ae694ac176a) Rosen Publishing Group, Inc., The. (PowerKids Pr.)
Nadeau, Isaac. Peninsulas. 2009. (Library of Landforms Ser.). 24p. (gr. 3-4). 42.50 *(978-1-60853-728-0(5)*, PowerKids Pr.) Rosen Publishing Group, Inc., The.
—Water in Rivers & Lakes. 2009. (Water Cycle Ser.). 24p. (gr. 4-4). 42.50 *(978-1-60854-271-0(8)*, PowerKids Pr.) Rosen Publishing Group, Inc., The.
Nagel, Rob. UXL Encyclopedia of Landforms & Other Geologic Features, 3 vols. 2003. (Illus.). xxviii, 314p. (J). *(978-0-7876-7670-4(5))*; *(978-0-7876-7671-1(3))*; *(978-0-7876-7672-8(1))* Cengage Gale. (UXL).
National Geographic Learning. Language, Literacy & Vocabulary - Reading Expeditions (Earth Science): Earth's Changing Land. 2007. (Avenues Ser.). (ENG., Illus.). 36p. (J). pap. 20.95 *(978-0-7922-5427-0(9))* CENGAGE Learning.
Nelson, Robin. Land. 2005. (First Step Nonfiction — Geography Ser.). (ENG., Illus.). 8p. (J). (gr. k-2). pap. 5.99 *(978-0-8225-5392-2(9)*, a359b25e-5ddc-4b02-923f-ff680157934f) Lerner Publishing Group.
Rand McNally. Map It! Jr Landforms Boardbook. 2018. (ENG., Illus.). (J). bds. *(978-0-528-02089-6(7))* Rand McNally Canada.
Rau, Dana Meachen. A True Book: U. S. Landforms. 2012. (True Book Ser.). (ENG., Illus.). 48p. (J). lib. bdg. 29.00 *(978-0-531-24854-6(2)*, Children's Pr.) Scholastic Library Publishing.
Rice, William B. Landforms, 1 vol. rev. ed. 2014. (Science: Informational Text Ser.). (ENG.). 32p. (gr. 2-3). pap. 10.99 *(978-1-4807-4608-4(8))* Teacher Created Materials, Inc.
Roza, G. On Flat Land: Learning the FL Sound. 2009. (PowerPhonics Ser.). 24p. (gr. 1-1). 39.90 *(978-1-60851-463-2(3)*, PowerKids Pr.) Rosen Publishing Group, Inc., The.
Science stories foss spanish landforms ea Cr05. 2005. (J). *(978-1-59242-597-6(6))* Delta Education, LLC.
Sexton, Colleen. Tundra. 2008. (Learning about the Earth Ser.). (ENG., Illus.). 24p. (J). (gr. k-3). lib. bdg. 26.95 *(978-1-60014-229-1(X))* Bellwether Media.
Sohn, Emily & Harter, Adam. Landforms. 2019. (iScience Ser.). (ENG., Illus.). 48p. (J). (gr. 5-6). 23.94 *(978-1-68450-950-8(5))* Norwood Hse. Pr.
Somervill, Barbara A. Plains & Plateaus. 2009. (21st Century Skills Library: Real World Math Ser.). (ENG.). 32p. (gr. 4-8). lib. bdg. 32.07 *(978-1-60279-493-1(6)*, 200318) Cherry Lake Publishing.
Spilsbury, Louise. What Is a Landform?, 1 vol., 1. 2013. (Let's Find Out! Earth Science Ser.). (ENG.). 32p. (gr. 2-3). 27.04 *(978-1-62275-256-0(2)*, bc160494-1015-4335-9d8a-04b07a5ba3dd) Rosen Publishing Group, Inc., The.
Spilsbury, Louise & Spilsbury, Richard. Tundra Biomes. 2018. (Earth's Natural Biomes Ser.). (Illus.). 32p. (J). (gr. 4-4). *(978-0-7787-3997-5(X))* Crabtree Publishing Co.
Spilsbury, Louise & Spilsbury, Richard, contrib. by. TUNDRA BIOMES. 2018. (Earth's Natural Biomes Ser.). (Illus.). 32p. (J). (gr. 4-4). pap. *(978-0-7787-4182-4(6))* Crabtree Publishing Co.
Spilsbury, Richard & Spilsbury, Louise. Landforms, 1 vol. 2018. (Flowchart Smart Ser.). (ENG.). 48p. (gr. 4-5). pap. 15.05 *(978-1-5382-3485-3(8)*, d15abb67-8dc8-40f0-a0d9-7cad49144805) Stevens, Gareth Publishing LLLP.
Sweeney, Alyse. Canyons. 2010. (Natural Wonders Ser.). (ENG.). 24p. (gr. k-1). pap. 41.70 *(978-1-4296-5593-4(3)*, Capstone Pr.) Capstone.
Taylor, Barbara. Understanding Landforms. 2007. (Geography Skills/Watts Ser.). (Illus.). 46p. (J). (gr. 4-7). lib. bdg. 32.80 *(978-1-59920-049-1(X))* Black Rabbit Bks.
Terp, Gail. Amazing Canyons Around the World. 2019. (Passport to Nature Ser.). (ENG., Illus.). 32p. (J). (gr. 4-6). lib. bdg. 28.65 *(978-1-5435-5778-7(3)*, 139734) Capstone.
Van Gorp, Lynn. Investigating Landforms, 1 vol. rev. ed. 2007. (Science: Informational Text Ser.). (ENG., Illus.). 32p. (gr. 4-6). pap. 12.99 *(978-0-7439-0557-2(1))* Teacher Created Materials, Inc.
Warhol, Tom. Tundra, 1 vol. 2007. (Earth's Biomes Ser.). (ENG., Illus.). 80p. (gr. 6-6). lib. bdg. 36.93 *(978-0-7614-2193-1(9)*, f2e3a69a-84e0-4ff0-817b-dff2e2956dc5) Cavendish Square Publishing LLC.
Wilder, Nellie. On Land, 1 vol. rev. ed. 2014. (Science: Informational Text Ser.). (ENG., Illus.). 24p. (gr. k-1). pap. 9.99 *(978-1-4807-4532-2(4))* Teacher Created Materials, Inc.
Woods, Michael & Woods, Mary B. Seven Natural Wonders of Africa. 2009. (Seven Wonders Ser.). (ENG., Illus.). 80p. (gr. 5-8). lib. bdg. 33.26 *(978-0-8225-9071-2(9))* Lerner Publishing Group.
—Seven Natural Wonders of Asia & the Middle East. 2009. (Seven Wonders Ser.). (ENG., Illus.). 80p. (gr. 5-8). 33.26 *(978-0-8225-9073-6(5))* Lerner Publishing Group.
—Seven Natural Wonders of Australia & Oceania. 2009. (Seven Wonders Ser.). (ENG., Illus.). 80p. (gr. 5-8). 33.26 *(978-0-8225-9074-3(3))* Lerner Publishing Group.
—Seven Natural Wonders of Central & South America. 2009. (Seven Wonders Ser.). (Illus.). 80p. (YA). (gr. 5-9). lib. bdg. 33.26 *(978-0-8225-9070-5(0))* Twenty First Century Bks.
—Seven Natural Wonders of the Arctic, Antarctica, & the Oceans. 2009. (Seven Wonders Ser.). (ENG., Illus.). 80p. (gr. 5-8). 33.26 *(978-0-8225-9075-0(1))* Lerner Publishing Group.
World Book, Inc. Staff, contrib. by. Carved by Time. 2017. (Illus.). 40p. (J). *(978-0-7166-3365-5(5))* World Bk.-Childcraft International.
—Enchanted Landscapes. 2017. (Illus.). 40p. (J). *(978-0-7166-3366-2(3))* World Bk., Inc.

LANDMARKS, PRESERVATION OF

see Natural Monuments

LANDSCAPE ARCHITECTURE

see also Cemeteries; Landscape Gardening

Conklin, Wendy. On the Job: Landscape Architects: Perimeter (Grade 3) 2017. (Mathematics in the Real World Ser.). (ENG., Illus.). 32p. (J). (gr. 3-4). pap. 11.99 *(978-1-4807-5809-4(4))* Teacher Created Materials, Inc.
Dunlap, Julie & Olmsted, Frederick Law. Parks for the People: The Life of Frederick Law Olmsted. 2011. (ENG., Illus.). 112p. (J). (gr. 4-7). pap. 12.95 *(978-1-55591-470-7(5))* Fulcrum Publishing.
Kjelle, Marylou Morano. A Kid's Guide to Landscape Design. 2008. (Gardening for Kids Ser.). (Illus.). 48p. (YA). (gr. 1-4). lib. bdg. 29.95 *(978-1-58415-637-6(6))* Mitchell Lane Pubs.
Lewis, Anna M. Women of Steel & Stone: 22 Inspirational Architects, Engineers, & Landscape Designers. 2014. (Women of Action Ser.: 6). (ENG., Illus.). 272p. (YA). (gr. 7). 19.95 *(978-1-61374-508-3(7))* Chicago Review Pr., Inc.
Mason, Helen. Landscape Designer. 2014. (Creative Careers Ser.). 48p. (J). (gr. 4-8). pap. 84.30 *(978-1-4824-1301-4(9))* Stevens, Gareth Publishing LLLP.
Wishinsky, Frieda. The Man Who Made Parks: The Story of Parkbuilder Frederick Law Olmsted. Zhang, Song Nan, illus. 2009. 32p. (J). (gr. k-4). pap. 10.95 *(978-0-88776-902-3(0)*, Tundra Bks.) Tundra Bks. CAN. Dist: Penguin Random Hse. LLC.

LANDSCAPE GARDENING

see also Landscape Architecture; Shrubs; Trees

Avery, Sebastian. A Landscaper's Tools, 1 vol. 2015. (Community Helpers & Their Tools Ser.). (ENG.). 24p. (J). (gr. 2-3). 25.27 *(978-1-4994-0899-7(4)*, 7873fc42-f838-4a5a-a2ec-5acf36fc8478, PowerKids Pr.) Rosen Publishing Group, Inc., The.
Buchanan, Heather. Logan's Landscaping: Foundations for Multiplication. 2014. (Rosen Math Readers Ser.). (ENG.). 24p. (J). (gr. 2-3). pap. 49.50 *(978-1-4777-4649-3(8))*; (Illus.). 25.27 *(978-1-4777-6400-8(3)*, fbd7baea-735f-4aee-b5ce-860ec124fe49); (Illus.). pap. 8.25 *(978-1-4777-4648-6(X)*, ef95f9b4-70c0-47ee-b046-18dd14723b4f) Rosen Publishing Group, Inc., The. (Rosen Classroom).
Gerber, Larry. Careers in Landscaping & Gardening, 1 vol. 2013. (Essential Careers Ser.). (ENG.). 80p. (YA). (gr. 6-6). lib. bdg. 37.47 *(978-1-4488-9477-2(8)*, d18f08f2-1f78-45c8-aee1-ee726b1ae07d) Rosen Publishing Group, Inc., The.

LANDSCAPE PAINTING

Bodden, Valerie. Landscapes. 2013. (Brushes with Greatness Ser.). (ENG.). 48p. (J). (gr. 5-9). pap. 12.00 *(978-0-89812-764-5(5)*, 21945, Creative Paperbacks) Creative Co., The.
Freedman, Jeri. Land Formation: The Shifting, Moving, Changing Earth: The Creation of Mountains. 2009. (J). 77.70 *(978-1-4358-5599-1(X))* Rosen Publishing Group, Inc., The.
Thomson, Leo. Sense of Place: Landscapes. 2005. (Artventures Ser.). (Illus.). 32p. (YA). (gr. 3-6). lib. bdg. 27.10 *(978-1-58340-622-9(0)*, 1247320) Black Rabbit Bks.
Yaeger, Bert D. The Hudson River School: American Landscape Artists, Vol. 8. 2018. (American Artists Ser.). 80p. (J). (gr. 7). 33.27 *(978-1-4222-4157-8(2))* Mason Crest.

LANGUAGE AND LANGUAGES

Here are entered general works on the history, philosophy, origin, etc. of language. Comparative studies of languages are entered under Philology, Comparative.

see also Grammar; Phonetics; Rhetoric; Semantics; Speech; Voice; Writing

also names of languages or groups of cognate languages, e.g. English Language; etc.; also classes of people with the subdivision Language, e.g. Children—Language; etc.

Abondolo, Daniel. Colloquial Finnish: The Complete Course for Beginners. 2nd rev. ed. 2011. (Colloquial Ser.). (ENG & FIN., Illus.). 368p. pap. 43.95 *(978-0-415-49966-8(6)*, 0415499666) Routledge.
Abondolo, Daniel Mario. Colloquial Finnish Mp3. 2nd ed. 2011. (ENG., Illus.). xiii, 354p. cd-rom 44.95 *(978-0-415-49967-5(4))* Routledge.
Aigner-Clark, Julie. La Guardería de Idiomas (The Guarderia Language) 2004. (Baby Einstein Ser.). (SPA., Illus.). 16p. (J). bds. *(978-970-718-153-3(2)*, Silver Dolphin en Español) Advanced Marketing, S. de R. L. de C. V.
Amery, Heather, et al. First Hundred Words in Maori. 2008. (MAO., Illus.). 40p. pap. 14.00 *(978-1-86969-304-6(3))* Huia Pubs. NZL. Dist: Univ. of Hawaii Pr.
Athans, Sandra K. & Parente, Robin W. Tips & Tricks for Determining Point of View & Purpose, 1 vol. 2014. (Common Core Readiness Guide to Reading Ser.). (ENG.). 64p. (J). (gr. 6-6). 36.13 *(978-1-4777-7555-4(2)*, d947b5da-ca60-4d30-8084-35038bdf3a8f, Rosen Reference) Rosen Publishing Group, Inc., The.
Bancroft, Bronwyn. Possum & Wattle: My Big Book of Australian Words. Bancroft, Bronwyn, illus. 2010. (ENG., Illus.). 48p. (J). (gr. -1-1). pap. 12.99 *(978-1-921541-67-4(9))* Little Hare Bks. AUS. Dist: Independent Pubs. Group.
Bardakjian, K. D. & Thompson, Robert W. Western Armenian, 8 cass., Set. (ARM.). 319p. (YA). (gr. 10-12). pap. 185.00 incl. audio *(978-0-88432-444-7(3)*, AFAR15) Pavilion Pubs.
Barfell, Judith A. Learn & Sign Funtime: Sign with God's Angels. 2005. (Beginnings Ser.). (J). per. 14.95 *(978-0-9753717-0-1(3))* Learn & Sign Funtime Bks.
Batot, Yvonne & Gose, Senora. Flip Flop French: Ages 3-5: Level 1. 2007. (Illus.). 84p. (J). spiral bd. 25.00 *(978-1-60402-967-3(6))* Flip n Flop Learning, LLC.
Beard, Adrian. Language Change. 2004. (Intertext Ser.). (ENG., Illus.). 128p. (C). 105.00 *(978-0-415-32055-9(0)*, RU26854); per. 35.95 *(978-0-415-32056-6(9)*, RU26855) Routledge.
Benati, R., et al. Meine Freunde und ich. Sammelmappe für Kinder. Mit Audio-CD: Zum Sammeln der Übungsblätter. 2005. (GER.). pap. 10.95 *(978-3-468-49503-8(X))* Langenscheidt Publishing Group.
Bilingual Picture Dictionary [Capstone Sole Source]. 2010. (Bilingual Picture Dictionaries Ser.). 32p. lib. bdg. 155.94 *(978-1-4296-5847-8(9)*, Capstone Pr.) Capstone.
Bluedorn, Johannah. Little Bitty Baby Learns Greek. Bluedorn, Johannah, illus. 2006. (GRE & ENG., Illus.). 30p. (J). bds. *(978-1-933228-06-8(7))* Trivium Pursuit.
Bowers, Linda, et al. No Glamour Language & Reasoning. 2003. (J). per. 41.95 *(978-0-7606-0500-4(9))* LinguiSystems, Inc.
Boyles, Peggy Palo & Prentice Hall Dictionary Editors. Realidades Vol. 2: Level 2, 2 vols. l.t. ed. 2003. (ENG.). 508p. (YA). (gr. 9-9). 254.00 *(978-0-13-035951-3(3))* Savvas Learning Co.
Boyles, Peggy Palo & Prentice Hall Direct Education Staff. Realidades: Level B, 2 vols. l.t. ed. 2003. (SPA & ENG.). 416p. (YA). (gr. 7-7). 208.00 *(978-0-13-035967-4(X)*, Prentice Hall) Savvas Learning Co.
Boyles, Peggy Palo & Prentice Hall Directories Staff. Realidades: Level 1, 2 vols. l.t. ed. 2003. (ENG.). 564p. (YA). (gr. 8-9). stu. ed. 282.00 *(978-0-13-101687-3(3)*, Prentice Hall) Savvas Learning Co.
—Realidades: Level A. l.t. ed. 2003. (SPA & ENG.). 322p. (YA). (gr. 7-7). stu. ed. 161.00 *(978-0-13-035966-7(1)*, Prentice Hall) Savvas Learning Co.
Boyles, Peggy Palo, et al. Realidades, Level 3, 2 vols. l.t. ed. 2003. (SPA & ENG.). 614p. (YA). (gr. 10-10). 307.00 *(978-0-13-035968-1(8)*, Prentice Hall) Savvas Learning Co.
Bridge to Communication Level C: Class Set. (Illus.). (J). (gr. 2-5). 275.00 *(978-1-56014-777-0(6))* Santillana USA Publishing Co., Inc.
Bridge to Communication Level C: Student Language Book. (J). (gr. 2-5). 9.50 *(978-1-56014-752-7(0))*; (YA). (gr. 6-8). 9.50 *(978-1-56014-755-8(5))* Santillana USA Publishing Co., Inc.
Bridge to Communication Level A: Student Language Book. (J). (gr. 2-5). 9.50 *(978-1-56014-750-3(4))*; (YA). (gr. 6-8). 9.50 *(978-1-56014-753-4(9))* Santillana USA Publishing Co., Inc.
Bridge to Communication Level B: Student Language Book. (J). (gr. 2-5). 9.50 *(978-1-56014-751-0(2))*; (YA). (gr. 6-8). 9.50 *(978-1-56014-754-1(7))* Santillana USA Publishing Co., Inc.
Bullard, Lisa. My Language, Your Language. Becker, Paula J., illus. 2015. (Cloverleaf Books (tm) — Alike & Different Ser.). (ENG.). 24p. (J). (gr. k-2). pap. 8.99 *(978-1-4677-6034-8(X)*, 53caddf6-31fd-4de9-9423-7a372a4c742e); lib. bdg. 25.32 *(978-1-4677-4906-0(0)*, 5a47036a-a109-4136-b17a-70054880655f) Lerner Publishing Group. (Millbrook Pr.).
Burke, David. GOLDILOCKS (Japanese to English - Level 2) Learn ENGLISH Through Fairy Tales. 2007. (JPN & ENG.). (J). per. 14.95 incl. audio compact disk *(978-1-891888-04-5(8))* Slangman Publishing.
Burke, John & Burke, Fatti. Focloiropedia: A Journey Through the Irish Language from Aran to Zu. 2018. (ENG., Illus.). 96p. 45.00 *(978-0-7171-7554-3(5))* Gill Bks. IRL. Dist: Casemate Pubs. & Bk. Distributors, LLC.
Burrill, Richard L. Somewhere Behind the Eyes: Language Treasures Aha! Date not set. (Illus.). 85p. (J). (gr. 4-12). 15.95 *(978-1-878464-16-3(7))* Anthro Co., The.
Carole Marsh. Ah,So! Japanese for Kids. 2004. (Little Linguist Ser.). 32p. (gr. 2-6). pap. 5.95 *(978-0-635-02434-3(9))* Gallopade International.
—It Really Is Greek to Me! Greek for Kids. 2004. (Little Linguist Ser.). 32p. (gr. 2-6). pap. 5.95 *(978-0-635-02432-9(2))* Gallopade International.
—Say What When You Sneeze? German for Kids. 2004. (Little Linguist Ser.). 32p. (gr. 2-6). pap. 5.95 *(978-0-635-02431-2(4))* Gallopade International.
Caswell, Deanna. Making Secret Codes & Messages. 24p. (J). 2019. (Illus.). pap. *(978-1-68072-742-5(7))* 2018. (ENG.). (gr. 1-3). pap. 8.99 *(978-1-64466-295-3(7)*, 12475, Hi Jinx) Black Rabbit Bks.
Cleary, Brian P. Breezier, Cheesier, Newest, & Bluest: What Are Comparatives & Superlatives? Gable, Brian, illus. 2013. (Words Are CATegorical (r) Ser.). (ENG.). 32p. (J). (gr. 2-5). lib. bdg. 16.95 *(978-0-7613-5362-1(3)*, 0d77201c-0fca-4a55-898e-77411ac9c6e0, Millbrook Pr.) Lerner Publishing Group.
DeCesare, Ruth. Songs for the German Class. (GER.). (J). 9.95 *(978-0-8442-2262-2(3)*, National Textbook Co.) McGraw-Hill/Contemporary.
Dennis, Angela, et al. Dah Dzāhge Esigits: We Write Our Language, 1 vol. Morin, Peter et al, illus. 2017. (ATH & ENG.). 112p. (J). (gr. -1-k). pap. 19.95 *(978-1-926886-49-7(6))* Theytus Bks., Ltd. CAN. Dist: Orca Bk. Pubs. USA.
Dual Language Add-On Package. 2003. 170.50 *(978-0-673-57714-6(7))* Celebration Pr.
Dual Language Classroom Library. 2003. 769.50 *(978-0-673-77836-9(3))* Celebration Pr.
Elwell, Maggie. My Mom, the Coconut MacHine. 2009. 24p. pap. 12.00 *(978-1-4389-2674-2(X))* AuthorHouse.
Epps, S. Emmanuel & Robateau, Lisa. Bubble Brain: Story Time Rhymes That Build the Mind. 2013. 34p. pap. 12.95 *(978-0-9911410-0-5(8))* Addi-Boo Bks.
Erdogan, Fatih. Ece Ve Efe Ile Türkçe, 1 vol. Hambleton, Laura, illus. 2007. (Abby & Zak Ser.). (ENG.). 48p. (J). (gr. k-2). pap. 16.95 *(978-1-84059-493-5(4))* Milet Publishing.
Fatus, Sophie & Couëlle, Jennifer. My Big Barefoot Book of French & English Words. 2016. (FRE & ENG., Illus.). (J). pap. *(978-1-78285-303-9(0))* Barefoot Bks., Inc.
Fatus, Sophie & Paris, Mertxe. My Big Barefoot Book of Spanish & English Words. 2016. (SPA & ENG.). (J). pap. *(978-1-78285-275-9(1))* Barefoot Bks., Inc.
Fremdwoerterbuch. (Duden-Schuelerduden Ser.). (GER.). 480p. (YA). 27.95 *(978-3-411-05143-4(4))* Bibliographisches Institut & F. A. Brockhaus AG DEU. Dist: International Bk. Import Service, Inc.
Froman, Craig. Passport to the World: Your a to Z Guided Language Tour. 2010. (ENG.). 64p. (YA). (gr. 4-6). lib. bdg. 15.99 *(978-0-89051-595-2(6)*, Master Books) New Leaf Publishing Group.
Gasmen, Imelda Fines. Tuttle Tagalog for Kids Flash Cards Kit: [Includes 64 Flash Cards, Audio CD, Wall Chart & Learning Guide]. 2008. (Tuttle Flash Cards Ser.). (ENG., Illus.). 1p. (J). (gr. 1-8). 19.95 *(978-0-8048-3957-0(3))* Tuttle Publishing.
Gigarjian, Ani & Avedikian, Linda. My Second Book of Armenian Words. 2nd ed. 2006. (J). 18.00 *(978-0-9717799-1-4(0))* Gigarjian, Ani & Linda Avedikian.
Gilbert, Keith & Schuh, Leesa. TEENAGERS: Your Essential Guide to the Weird World of... Adults 2nd Edition. 2007. (ENG.). 180p. pap. 15.95 *(978-1-4452-4859-2(X))* Lulu Pr., Inc.
Giulieri, Anne. Oral Language-Book a: Speaking & Listening in the Classroom. 2012. (Engage Literacy Ser.). (ENG.). 28p. (J). (gr. k-2). 75.00 *(978-1-4296-9558-9(7)*, 195226, Capstone Pr.) Capstone.
—Oral Language-Book B: Speaking & Listening in the Classroom. 2012. (Engage Literacy Ser.). (ENG.). 28p. (J). (gr. k-2). 75.00 *(978-1-4296-9559-6(5)*, 195227, Capstone Pr.) Capstone.
Greeley, August. Writing in Ancient Egypt. 2009. (Writing in the Ancient World Ser.). 24p. (gr. 3-3). 42.50 *(978-1-60854-905-4(4)*, PowerKids Pr.) Rosen Publishing Group, Inc., The.
—Writing in Ancient India. 2009. (Writing in the Ancient World Ser.). 24p. (gr. 3-3). 42.50 *(978-1-60854-906-1(2)*, PowerKids Pr.) Rosen Publishing Group, Inc., The.
—Writing in Ancient Mesopotamia. 2009. (Writing in the Ancient World Ser.). 24p. (gr. 3-3). 42.50 *(978-1-60854-907-8(0)*, PowerKids Pr.) Rosen Publishing Group, Inc., The.
—Writing in Ancient Phoenicia. 2009. (Writing in the Ancient World Ser.). 24p. (gr. 3-3). 42.50 *(978-1-60854-908-5(9)*, PowerKids Pr.) Rosen Publishing Group, Inc., The.
Gu, Licheng & Hambleton, Laura. Chinese with Lulu & Maomao, 1 vol. 2008. (Abby & Zak Ser.). (ENG., Illus.). 48p. (J). (gr. k-2). pap. 16.95 *(978-1-84059-514-7(0))* Milet Publishing.
Hanson, Tracie. New World Baby - the Collection. 2007. (ENG, FRE, SPA, ITA & GER., Illus.). 28p. (J). 48.00 *(978-0-9799185-4-4(5))* Hanson, Tracie.
Haskins, James & Benson, Kathleen. Count Your Way Through Afghanistan. Moore, Megan, illus. 2006. (Count Your Way Ser.). 40p. (J). (gr. -1-3). lib. bdg. 19.93 *(978-1-57505-880-1(4)*, Millbrook Pr.) Lerner Publishing Group.
—Count Your Way Through Egypt. Rama, Sue, illus. 2006. (Count Your Way Ser.). 24p. (J). (gr. -1-3). lib. bdg. 19.93 *(978-1-57505-882-5(0)*, Millbrook Pr.) Lerner Publishing Group.
—Count Your Way Through Iran. Zaman, Farida, illus. 2006. (Count Your Way Ser.). 40p. (J). (gr. -1-3). lib. bdg. 19.93 *(978-1-57505-881-8(2)*, Millbrook Pr.) Lerner Publishing Group.
—Count Your Way Through Kenya. Leveque, Lyne, illus. 2006. (Count Your Way Ser.). 24p. (J). (gr. -1-3). lib. bdg. 19.93 *(978-1-57505-884-9(7)*, Millbrook Pr.) Lerner Publishing Group.
Haskins, Jim & Benson, Kathleen. Count Your Way Through South Africa. Neibert, Alissa, illus. 2006. (Count Your Way Ser.). (ENG.). 24p. (gr. 2-5). lib. bdg. 19.93 *(978-1-57505-883-2(9)*, Millbrook Pr.) Lerner Publishing Group.
—Count Your Way Through Zimbabwe. Park, Janie Jaehyun, illus. 2006. (Count Your Way Ser.). (ENG.). 24p. (gr. 2-5). lib. bdg. 19.93 *(978-1-57505-885-6(5)*, Millbrook Pr.) Lerner Publishing Group.

Hindi Level One: The Rosetta Stone Language Library. 2005. (J). (gr. 1-18). cd-rom 209.00 *(978-1-58022-043-9(6))* Rosetta Stone Ltd.

Hippocrene Books Staff. Children's Illustrated Czech Dictionary: English-Czech/Czech-English. 2003. (Hippocrene Children's Illustrated Foreign Language Dictionaries Ser.). (ENG., Illus.). 96p. pap. 11.95 *(978-0-7818-0987-0(8))* Hippocrene Bks., Inc.

Hippocrene Books Staff, ed. Bengali Children's Picture Dictionary: English-Bengali/Bengali-English. 2006. (ENG.). 114p. 14.95 *(978-0-7818-1128-6(7))* Hippocrene Bks., Inc.

Hobson, Mark, tr. Language Helper German: Helpin you speak more German. 2007. (GER & ENG., Illus.). 195p. (J). pap. 22.95 *(978-0-9789152-0-9(8))* Chou Chou Pr.

Holt, Rinehart and Winston Staff. Elements of Language: Developing Language Skills. 4th ed. Date not set. (Elements of Language Ser.). (YA). (gr. 10). pap. 17.20 *(978-0-03-070063-7(9))*; (YA). (gr. 11). pap. 17.20 *(978-0-03-070064-4(7))*; (YA). (gr. 12). pap. 17.20 *(978-0-03-070066-8(3))*; (J). (gr. 6). pap. 17.20 *(978-0-03-070058-3(2))*; (YA). (gr. 7). pap. 17.20 *(978-0-03-070059-0(0))*; (YA). (gr. 8). pap. 17.20 *(978-0-03-070061-3(2))*; (YA). (gr. 9). pap. 17.20 *(978-0-03-070062-0(0))* Holt McDougal.

—Elements of Language: Developing Language Skills Answer Key. 4th ed. Date not set. (J). (gr. 6). pap. 12.80 *(978-0-03-070067-5(1))*; (YA). (gr. 7). pap. 12.80 *(978-0-03-070068-2(X))*; (YA). (gr. 8). pap. 12.80 *(978-0-03-070069-9(8))* Holt McDougal.

Jennings, Brien J. Fact, Fiction, & Opinions: The Differences Between Ads, Blogs, News Reports, & Other Media. 2018. (All about Media Ser.). (ENG., Illus.). 24p. (J). (gr. 1-3). lib. bdg. 27.99 *(978-1-5435-0222-0(9)*, 137140, Capstone Pr.) Capstone.

Khare, Pratibha & Bekooy Khare, Catherine. Hindi Primer, Pt. 1. 2nd ed. 2004. (HIN & ENG.). 172p. spiral bd. *(978-0-9663831-3-3(3))* Mukund Pubns.

Kiraz, George. The Syriac Alphabet for Children. 2004. (ENG.). (J). 52p. 25.00 *(978-1-59333-113-9(4))*; 54p. pap. 15.00 *(978-1-59333-112-2(6))* Gorgias Pr., LLC.

Kumar, Monica & Kumar, Manisha. Diwali: A Festival of Lights & Fun. Sona & Jacob, illus. 2006.Tr. of Diwali: Khushiyon Ka Tyohaar. (ENG & HIN.). 32p. (J). 11.00 *(978-0-9773645-7-2(7))* MeeraMasi, Inc.

Lanza, Janet R., et al. Artic to Go. 2004. (J). per. 35.95 *(978-0-7606-0540-0(8))* LinguiSystems, Inc.

Learn Bangla 2004. 2004. (J). cd-rom 29.95 *(978-0-9748503-8-2(1))* Griha.

Level One - Workbook 2005. 2007. (J). pap. *(978-0-932416-14-8(4))* Papaloizos Pubns., Inc.

LoGiudice, Carolyn & McConnell, Nancy. Room 28 a Social Language Program. 2004. (YA). per. 25.95 *(978-0-7606-0530-1(0))* LinguiSystems, Inc.

Losada, Basilio. Isabel la Catolica. (SPA., Illus.). 192p. (YA). 11.95 *(978-84-7281-122-5(0)*, AF1122) Auriga, Ediciones S.A. ESP. Dist: Continental Bk. Co., Inc.

Marsh, Carole. It Really Is Greek to Me! Greek for Kids. Beard, Chad, ed. 2004. (Little Linguist Ser.). (Illus.). 32p. (J). (gr. 2-9). 29.95 *(978-0-635-02440-4(3))* Gallopade International.

—Say What When You Sneeze?! German for Kids. Beard, Chad, ed. 2004. (Little Linguist Ser.). (Illus.). 31p. 29.95 *(978-0-635-02439-8(X))* Gallopade International.

Mcgraw, Caroline. Litsemamba! Litsemba! 2009. pap. 15.00 *(978-1-61584-004-5(4))* Independent Pub.

Metropolitan Museum of Art & Roehrig, Catharine. Fun with Hieroglyphs. 2008. (ENG.). 48p. (J). (gr. 4-7). 34.99 *(978-1-4169-6114-7(3)*, Simon & Schuster Bks. For Young Readers) Simon & Schuster Bks. For Young Readers.

Milet Publishing Staff. Milet Interactive for Kids - Turkish for English Speakers. 2012. (Milet Interactive for Kids Ser.). (ENG., Illus.). 1p. (J). (gr. k-2). cd-rom 24.95 *(978-1-84059-679-3(1))* Milet Publishing.

—My Bilingual Book - Sight, 1 vol. 2014. (My Bilingual Book Ser.). (ENG., Illus.). 24p. (J). (gr. -1-k). 9.95 *(978-1-84059-801-8(8))* Milet Publishing.

—My Bilingual Book-Hearing, 1 vol. 2014. (My Bilingual Book Ser.). (ENG., Illus.). 24p. (J). (gr. -1-k). 9.95 *(978-1-84059-785-1(2))* Milet Publishing.

—My Bilingual Book-Hearing (English-Bengali), 1 vol. 2014. (My Bilingual Book Ser.). (ENG & BEN., Illus.). 24p. (J). (gr. -1-k). 9.95 *(978-1-84059-773-8(9))* Milet Publishing.

—My Bilingual Book-Hearing (English-Farsi), 1 vol. 2014. (My Bilingual Book Ser.). (ENG., Illus.). 24p. (J). (gr. -1-k). 9.95 *(978-1-84059-775-2(5))* Milet Publishing.

—My Bilingual Book-Hearing (English-Somali), 1 vol. 2014. (My Bilingual Book Ser.). (ENG., Illus.). 24p. (J). (gr. -1-k). 9.95 *(978-1-84059-783-7(6))* Milet Publishing.

—My Bilingual Book-Hearing (English-Urdu), 1 vol. 2014. (My Bilingual Book Ser.). (ENG., Illus.). 24p. (J). (gr. -1-k). 9.95 *(978-1-84059-786-8(0))* Milet Publishing.

—My Bilingual Book-Sight (English-Bengali), 1 vol. 2014. (My Bilingual Book Ser.). (ENG & BEN., Illus.). 24p. (J). (gr. -1-k). 9.95 *(978-1-84059-789-9(5))* Milet Publishing.

—My Bilingual Book-Sight (English-Farsi), 1 vol. 2014. (My Bilingual Book Ser.). (ENG., Illus.). 24p. (J). (gr. -1-k). 9.95 *(978-1-84059-791-2(7))* Milet Publishing.

—My Bilingual Book-Sight (English-Somali), 1 vol. 2014. (My Bilingual Book Ser.). (ENG., Illus.). 24p. (J). (gr. -1-k). 9.95 *(978-1-84059-799-8(2))* Milet Publishing.

—My Bilingual Book-Sight (English-Urdu), 1 vol. 2014. (My Bilingual Book Ser.). (ENG., Illus.). 24p. (J). (gr. -1-k). 9.95 *(978-1-84059-802-5(6))* Milet Publishing.

—My Bilingual Book-Smell (English-Bengali), 1 vol. 2014. (My Bilingual Book Ser.). (ENG & BEN., Illus.). 24p. (J). (gr. -1-k). 9.95 *(978-1-84059-805-6(0))* Milet Publishing.

—My Bilingual Book-Smell (English-Farsi), 1 vol. 2014. (My Bilingual Book Ser.). (ENG., Illus.). 24p. (J). (gr. -1-k). 9.95 *(978-1-84059-807-0(7))* Milet Publishing.

—My Bilingual Book-Smell (English-Turkish), 1 vol. 2014. (My Bilingual Book Ser.). (ENG., Illus.). 24p. (J). (gr. -1-k). 9.95 *(978-1-84059-817-9(4))* Milet Publishing.

—My Bilingual Book-Smell (English-Urdu), 1 vol. 2014. (My Bilingual Book Ser.). (ENG., Illus.). 24p. (J). (gr. -1-k). 9.95 *(978-1-84059-818-6(2))* Milet Publishing.

—My Bilingual Book-Taste (English-Bengali), 1 vol. 2014. (My Bilingual Book Ser.). (ENG & BEN., Illus.). 24p. (J). (gr. -1-k). 9.95 *(978-1-84059-821-6(2))* Milet Publishing.

—My Bilingual Book-Taste (English-Farsi), 1 vol. 2014. (My Bilingual Book Ser.). (ENG., Illus.). 24p. (J). (gr. -1-k). 9.95 *(978-1-84059-823-0(9))* Milet Publishing.

—My Bilingual Book-Taste (English-Somali), 1 vol. 2014. (My Bilingual Book Ser.). (ENG., Illus.). 24p. (J). (gr. -1-k). 9.95 *(978-1-84059-831-5(X))* Milet Publishing.

—My Bilingual Book-Taste (English-Turkish), 1 vol. 2014. (My Bilingual Book Ser.). (ENG., Illus.). 24p. (J). (gr. -1-k). 9.95 *(978-1-84059-833-9(6))* Milet Publishing.

—My Bilingual Book-Taste (English-Urdu), 1 vol. 2014. (My Bilingual Book Ser.). (ENG., Illus.). 24p. (J). (gr. -1-k). 9.95 *(978-1-84059-834-6(4))* Milet Publishing.

—My Bilingual Book-Taste (English-Vietnamese), 1 vol. 2014. (My Bilingual Book Ser.). (ENG., Illus.). 24p. (J). (gr. -1-k). 9.95 *(978-1-84059-835-3(2))* Milet Publishing.

—My Bilingual Book-Touch (English-Bengali), 1 vol. 2014. (My Bilingual Book Ser.). (ENG & BEN., Illus.). 24p. (J). (gr. -1-k). 9.95 *(978-1-84059-837-7(9))* Milet Publishing.

—My Bilingual Book-Touch (English-Farsi), 1 vol. 2014. (My Bilingual Book Ser.). (ENG., Illus.). 24p. (J). (gr. -1-k). 9.95 *(978-1-84059-839-1(5))* Milet Publishing.

—My Bilingual Book-Touch (English-Somali), 1 vol. 2014. (My Bilingual Book Ser.). (ENG., Illus.). 24p. (J). (gr. -1-k). 9.95 *(978-1-84059-847-6(6))* Milet Publishing.

—My Bilingual Book-Touch (English-Turkish), 1 vol. 2014. (My Bilingual Book Ser.). (ENG., Illus.). 24p. (J). (gr. -1-k). 9.95 *(978-1-84059-849-0(2))* Milet Publishing.

—My Bilingual Book-Touch (English-Urdu), 1 vol. 2014. (My Bilingual Book Ser.). (ENG., Illus.). 24p. (J). (gr. -1-k). 9.95 *(978-1-84059-850-6(6))* Milet Publishing.

Ministry of Education Staff, creator. Te Kete Kupu: 300 Essential Words in Maori. 2007. (Illus.). 43p. (J). (gr. 4-7). pap. 9.00 *(978-1-86969-174-5(1))* Univ. of Hawaii Pr.

Morris, Paul. 101 Language Activities. 2004. (J). per. 35.95 *(978-0-7606-0532-5(7))* LinguiSystems, Inc.

Moshi Moshi. 2004. (Yoroshiku Ser.: Stages 1 and 2). (JPN., Illus.). (gr. k-12). 152p. pap., tchr. ed. 32.95 *(978-1-86366-143-0(3))*; 148p. pap., stu. ed. 39.95 *(978-1-86366-146-1(8))* Education Services Australia Ltd. AUS. Dist: Cheng & Tsui Co.

Mullin, René. Aibitir. 2013. (ENG., Illus.). 40p. (J). pap. 7.95 *(978-0-85640-917-2(0))* Blackstaff Pr., Ltd. GBR. Dist: Casemate Pubs. & Bk. Distributors, LLC.

National Curriculum Development Centre Staff. Luo. 2004. Bk. 1. pap., pupil's gde. ed. *(978-0-521-78936-3(2))*Bk. 2. pap., pupil's gde. ed. *(978-0-521-78937-0(0))*Bk. 3. pap., pupil's gde. ed. *(978-0-521-78938-7(9))*Bk. 4. pap., pupil's gde. ed. *(978-0-521-78939-4(7))* Cambridge Univ. Pr.

National Indonesian Curriculum Project Staff. Suara Siswa: Indonesian Language, Stages 1-2. 2004. (IND.). 242p. pap., tchr. ed., ldr.'s hndbk. ed. 39.95 *(978-1-86366-125-6(5))* Education Services Australia Ltd. AUS. Dist: Cheng & Tsui Co.

National Japanese Curriculum Project Staff. Pera Pera. 2004. (Yoroshiku Ser.: Stages 3 and 4). (JPN.). 224p. (gr. k-12). pap., stu. ed. 45.95 *(978-1-86366-147-8(6))* Education Services Australia Ltd. AUS. Dist: Cheng & Tsui Co.

Nordstrom, Ursula. The Secret Language. 167p. (J). (gr. 3-5). pap. 4.95 *(978-0-8072-1425-1(6)*, Listening Library) Random Hse. Audio Publishing Group.

Nunn, Daniel. Colors in German: Die Farben, 1 vol. 2012. (World Languages - Colors Ser.). (GER.). 24p. (gr. 1-3). (J). lib. bdg. 25.32 *(978-1-4329-6653-9(7)*, 119266); pap. 6.29 *(978-1-4329-6660-7(X)*, 119272) Capstone. (Heinemann).

—World Languages - Families. 2013. (World Languages - Families Ser.). (MUL.). 24p. (J). (gr. 1-3). 101.28 *(978-1-4329-7178-6(6)*, 19071, Heinemann) Capstone.

Omary, Rachel, illus. Animals in Pashto. I.t. ed. 2003. 4p. (J). spiral bd. 10.95 *(978-0-9740535-5-4(4))* Knight Publishing.

Palazzo-Craig, Janet. Language Development Variety Text, 1 vol. 2003. (BrainBuilders Ser.). (ENG.). 48p. (gr. k-4). pap. 5.25 *(978-1-4042-8567-5(9)*, be1b94ee-3c86-47cc-9dc1-965b420c18f4); pap. 5.25 *(978-1-4042-8562-0(8)*, 8b99e9cf-5e7c-449e-80c3-5a d7a60f6cf4) Rosen Publishing Group, Inc., The.

Papaloizos, Theodore C. Workbook for Learning Greek. 2003. (GRE & ENG.). 76p. (YA). pap. *(978-0-932416-32-2(2))* Papaloizos Pubns., Inc.

Pera Pera. 2004. (Yoroshiku Ser.: Stages 3 and 4). (JPN.). 136p. (gr. k-12). pap., tchr. ed., ldr.'s hndbk. ed. 45.95 *(978-1-86366-141-6(7))* Education Services Australia Ltd. AUS. Dist: Cheng & Tsui Co.

Peterson, Hiromi & Omizo, Naomi. Adventures in Japanese Level 1, 4 vols. Muronaka, Michael & Kaylor, Emiko, illus. 2nd ed. 2005. pap., stu. ed., wbk. ed. 24.95 *(978-0-88727-450-3(1))* Cheng & Tsui Co.

Phillips, Lori. Yapese Alphabet. 2006. (Island Alphabet Books). (Illus.). 52p. (J). (gr. -1-k). 4.95 *(978-1-57306-260-2(X))* Bess Pr., Inc.

Prior, Jennifer. Map Skills Grade 3. 2003. (Practice Makes Perfect Ser.). (ENG., Illus.). 48p. (gr. 3). pap. 5.99 *(978-0-7439-3728-3(7))* Teacher Created Resources, Inc.

El Recuerdo Egipcio. (SPA., Illus.). 70p. (YA). (gr. 7-9). pap. *(978-88-8148-446-1(3))* EMC/Paradigm Publishing.

Rembisz, Linda. Count with Balloons. Liebeck, Lisa, illus. 2009. 28p. pap. 12.49 *(978-1-4490-1989-1(7))* AuthorHouse.

Ristuccia, Christine. The Entire World of Attributes. 2003. (J). 29.99 *(978-0-9723457-7-4(9))* Say It Right.

Ristuccia, Christine & Ristuccia, James. The Entire World of S & Z Screening Kit. 2003. (Illus.). 20p. (J). pap. 9.99 *(978-0-9723457-6-7(0))* Say It Right.

Robertson, James. Katie's a Tae Z: An Alphabet for Wee Folk. Sutherland, Karen, illus. 2014. 20p. (J). (-k). bds. 12.99 *(978-1-84502-754-4(X))* Black and White Publishing Ltd. GBR. Dist: Independent Pubs. Group.

Romero, Victor Eclar. Learn Filipino: Book One, Book One. Francisco, Manny, illus. 2004. 384p. per. 29.95 *(978-1-932956-41-2(7))* Magsimba Pr.

Romulo, Liana. My First Book of Tagalog Words: An ABC Rhyming Book of Filipino Language & Culture. Laurel, Jaime, illus. 2018. (My First Words Ser.). 32p. (J). (gr. -1-3). 10.99 *(978-0-8048-5014-8(3))* Tuttle Publishing.

The Rosetta Stone Language Library: Dutch Level 2. 2005. (J). (gr. 1-18). cd-rom 239.00 *(978-1-58022-046-0(0))* Rosetta Stone Ltd.

The Rosetta Stone Language Library: Thai Level 1. 2005. (J). (gr. 1-18). cd-rom 209.00 *(978-1-883972-75-2(2))* Rosetta Stone Ltd.

Ruffenach, Jessie, ed. Baby Learns to Count. Thomas, Peter, tr. Blacksheep, Beverly, illus. I.t. ed. 2003. (NAV & ENG.). 16p. (J). (gr. -1-12). 7.95 *(978-1-893354-47-0(4))* Salina Bookshelf Inc.

Savage, Leah, et al. POW Wow: Niimiwin Everyone Dance. 2009. (J). *(978-0-9820870-6-0(3))* IGI Pr.

Schmitt, Conrad J. & Glencoe McGraw-Hill Staff. Invitation to Languages: Exploratory Program. 2006. (Invitation to Languages Ser.). (ENG., Illus.). 298p. (gr. 6-8). stu. ed. 60.96 *(978-0-07-874249-1(8)*, 0078742498) McGraw-Hill Higher Education.

Shah, Sapna Jaiswal. Sapna Aunty's Hindi Book of Colors: Rang. 2004. (HIN.). (J). 8.00 *(978-0-9741686-0-9(2))* 3N Media Group.

Sona & Jacob, illus. Varnamala Geet. 2006. (HIN & ENG.). 3p. (J). 12.00 *(978-0-9773645-6-5(9))* MeeraMasi, Inc.

Takarai, Saori. Manga Moods: 40 Faces + 80 Phrases. 2010. (ENG., Illus.). 96p. (YA). 9.99 *(978-4-921205-13-3(2)*, 4855a4b5-5258-4e54-9d0d-fa606f8c8d48) Japanime Co., Ltd. JPN. Dist: Diamond Comic Distributors, Inc.

Thompson, Richard & Thompson, Ofa. Ko 'Eku Tohi 'oe Fanga Manu. Slutz, Stephani, illus. I.t. ed. 2004. (TON.). 16p. (J). (gr. -1-18). 5.00 *(978-0-9678979-2-9(0))* Friendly Isles Pr.

Treadwell, Harriette Taylor & Free, Margaret. A Furst Readin Book in Ulster Scot. 2011. (Illus.). 124p. pap. *(978-1-904808-68-8(9))* Evertype.

Trim, John & Kohl, Katrin M. Deutsch Direkt! Textbook. (J). (gr. 9-12). 16.95 *(978-0-8219-0225-7(3)*, 45290) EMC/Paradigm Publishing.

Turhan, Sedat. New Bilingual Visual Dictionary (English-Bengali), 1 vol. 2nd ed. 2017. (New Bilingual Visual Dictionary Ser.). (ENG., Illus.). 148p. (J). (gr. k-2). 19.95 *(978-1-78508-882-7(3))* Milet Publishing.

—New Bilingual Visual Dictionary (English-Farsi), 16 vols. 2nd ed. 2017. (New Bilingual Visual Dictionary Ser.). (ENG., Illus.). 148p. (J). (gr. k-2). 24.95 *(978-1-78508-884-1(X))* Milet Publishing.

Turhan, Sedat & Hagin, Sally. Milet Flashwords. 2005. (Milet Flashwords Ser.). (ENG., Illus.). 60p. (J). (gr. 4-7). 8.95 *(978-1-84059-410-2(1))*; 8.95 *(978-1-84059-418-8(7))* Milet Publishing.

Verdick, Elizabeth. Words Are Not for Hurting. Heinlen, Marieka, illus. 2004. (Best Behavior(r) Paperback Ser.). (ENG.). 40p. (J). (gr. k-3). pap. 11.99 *(978-1-57542-156-8(9)*, 854) Free Spirit Publishing Inc.

Wilson, P. R. Readle the Reading Beetle: The Journey to Love Read Land. 2007. 26p. pap. 8.95 *(978-0-7414-4318-2(X))* Infinity Publishing.

Workbook - My First Book. 2007. (J). pap. 20.00 *(978-0-932416-13-1(6))* Papaloizos Pubns., Inc.

LANGUAGE AND LANGUAGES—VOCATIONAL GUIDANCE

Miller, Anne Meeker. Baby Sing & Sign: A Play-filled Language Development Program for Hearing Infants & Toddlers. 2004. (J). spiral bd. 14.95 *(978-0-9749924-0-2(2))* Love Language Pubns.

LANGUAGE ARTS

see Communication; English Language; Reading; Speech

LAOS

Doeden, Matt. Laos in Pictures. 2007. (Visual Geography Series, Second Ser.). (ENG., Illus.). 80p. (gr. 5-12). 31.93 *(978-0-8225-6590-1(0))* Lerner Publishing Group.

Markovics, Adam. Laos. 2018. (Countries We Come From Ser.). (ENG., Illus.). 32p. (J). (gr. k-3). 19.95 *(978-1-68402-692-0(X))* Bearport Publishing Co., Inc.

Oachs, Emily Rose. Laos. 2016. (Exploring Countries Ser.). (ENG., Illus.). 32p. (J). (gr. 3-7). 27.95 *(978-1-62617-404-7(0)*, Blastoff! Readers) Bellwether Media.

LAOS—HISTORY

Mansfield, Stephen & Koh, Magdalene. Laos, 1 vol. 2nd rev. ed. 2009. (Cultures of the World (Second Edition)(r) Ser.). (ENG.). 144p. (gr. 5-5). lib. bdg. 49.79 *(978-0-7614-3035-3(0)*, 7e5f592e-37cb-483f-9fe6-4f8c96bafe37) Cavendish Square Publishing LLC.

Mansfield, Stephen, et al. Laos, 1 vol. 2017. (Cultures of the World (Third Edition)(r) Ser.). (ENG.). 144p. (gr. 5-5). lib. bdg. 48.79 *(978-1-5026-3233-3(0)*, 4f0875d8-1eaa-4321-90ff-efbe9d08cfbb) Cavendish Square Publishing LLC.

LAPLAND

Alatalo, Jaakko. Iina-Marja's Day: From Dawn to Dusk in Lapland. 2011. (Child's Day Ser.). (ENG., Illus.). 32p. (J). (gr. k-3). pap. 8.95 *(978-1-84507-993-2(0)*, White Lion Publishing) Quarto Publishing Group UK GBR. Dist: Hachette Bk. Group.

LAPLAND—FICTION

d'Aulaire, Ingri & d'Aulaire, Edgar Parin. Children of the Northlights. 2012. (Illus.). 40p. 16.95 *(978-0-8166-7923-2(1))* Univ. of Minnesota Pr.

Penny, Anne. Scraper. 2006. (Illus.). 56p. pap. *(978-1-84401-921-2(7))* Athena Pr.

LARGE TYPE BOOKS

Aardvark, D. The Congraduation Fish. Aardvark, D., illus. I.t. ed. 2005. (Illus.). 48p. (J). per. 12.95 *(978-0-9755567-1-9(1))* Aardvark's Weedpatch Pr.

—Merry Kissmoose. Aardvark, D., illus. I.t. ed. 2005. (Illus.). 48p. (J). per. 12.95 *(978-0-9755567-2-6(X))* Aardvark's Weedpatch Pr.

—Punkin's upside down Day. I.t. ed. 2004. (Illus.). 40p. (J). per. 10.95 *(978-0-9755567-0-2(3))* Aardvark's Weedpatch Pr.

The Adventures of Chip Green the Forestry Kid I.t. ed. 2005. (Illus.). 34p. (J). per. *(978-0-9729753-8-4(1))* Really Big Coloring Bks., Inc.

The Adventures of Little Nina: Nina's First Trip. I.t. ed. 2005. (Illus.). 40p. (J). 16.95 *(978-0-9769662-0-3(4))* Strategies Publishing Co.

The Adventures of Marc John Jefferies: The Missing Princess. I.t. ed. 2004. (Illus.). 110p. (YA). per. *(978-0-9747218-3-5(2)*, 100, Young Women Programming) Harper Kids Hse.

The Adventures of Pinocchio. I.t. ed. 2004. (Large Print Ser.). 229p. 25.00 *(978-1-58287-732-7(7))* North Bks.

The Adventures of the Original Pumpkin Patch Pals. I.t. ed. 2005. (Illus.). 32p. (J). 15.00 *(978-0-9770960-1-5(7))* 3 Pals Media, LLC.

Ahmad, Iftikhar. World Cultures: A Global Mosaic, 8 vols. I.t. ed. 2004. 2467p. (YA). (gr. 6-9). 1236.00 *(978-0-13-036895-9(4)*, A-L00012-00) Prentice Hall Pr.

Albert, Toni Diana. Saving the Rain Forest with Cammie & Cooper. Bowles, Carol, illus. I.t. ed. 2003. 32p. (J). pap. 7.95 *(978-1-929432-02-8(X)*, 800-353-2791) Trickle Creek Bks.

Albright, Thomas B. Universal English: Second Language for All. unabr. I.t. ed. 2003. (Languages: Universal English for All). (ENM.). 128p. pap. 7.00 *(978-1-888264-17-3(9))* Twenty-First Century Co., The.

Alex, N. L. Smile All the While. I.t. ed. 2005. (Illus.). 16p. (J). 4.99 *(978-0-9766080-0-4(6))* Joe Girl Ink.

Alexander, Florence & Alexander, Stanley. Come with Me & See... African People. I.t. ed. 2003. (ENG & SPA., Illus.). 13p. (J). 3.99 *(978-0-9648313-8-4(4))* Ebon Research Systems Publishing, LLC.

—Come with Me & See... Birds of the World. I.t. ed. 2003. (Illus.). 32p. (J). 7.99 net. *(978-0-915960-95-8(8))* Ebon Research Systems Publishing, LLC.

—Come with Me & See... Children of the World. I.t. ed. 2003. (ENG & SPA., Illus.). 32p. (J). 9.99 *(978-0-9648313-9-1(2))* Ebon Research Systems Publishing, LLC.

—Jesus Child Is Born: Dare to Be Great. I.t. ed. 2003. (Illus.). 32p. (YA). 7.99 net. *(978-0-915960-85-9(0))* Ebon Research Systems Publishing, LLC.

Alexander, Geoff. Toothbugs! Carole, Isaacs, illus. I.t. ed. 2005. 12p. (J). bds. 12.95 *(978-0-9760944-0-1(1))* Alexander-Marcus Publishing.

Alexander, Ian. Do You See a Dozen?, Vol. 2. I.t. ed. 2005. (Sadlier Phonics Reading Program). (Illus.). 8p. (gr. -1-1). 23.00 net. *(978-0-8215-7347-1(0))* Sadlier, William H. Inc.

Alexie, Sherman. The Absolutely True Diary of a Part-Time Indian. I.t. ed. 2008. (Thorndike Literacy Bridge Ser.). (ENG., Illus.). 301p. (YA). (gr. 7-12). 23.95 *(978-1-4104-0499-2(4))* Thorndike Pr.

Allen, Toi Lynn. Game Day/Test Day: Who's Keeping Score? I.t. ed. 2004. (Illus.). (YA). pap. 14.95 *(978-0-9753787-0-0(8))* Allen, Toi Operations.

Allende, Isabel. Forest of the Pygmies. I.t. ed. 2005. (City of the Beasts Ser.: Bk. 3).Tr. of Bosque de los Pigmeos. 304p. (J). (gr. 5-18). pap. 19.99 *(978-0-06-076200-1(4)*, Rayo) HarperCollins Pubs.

Allgood, Jean. Come Follow Me Bk. 1: Understanding One's Worth: Color Orange. Smith, Sandra, illus. I.t. ed. 2004. 23p. (J). 14.95 *(978-0-9741627-3-7(6))* PricePoint+Publications.

Alston, E. B. The Last Voyage of the Dan-D. Garrett, Toni, illus. I.t. ed. 2003. 47p. (J). per. 8.00 *(978-0-9747735-0-6(6))* Righter Publishing Co., Inc.

Altsheler, Joseph A. The Scouts of Stonewall: The Story of the Great Valley Campaign. I.t. ed. 2007. (Civil War Ser.: Vol. 3). (ENG.). 240p. (J). reprint ed. pap. 22.99 *(978-1-4264-1531-9(1))* Creative Media Partners, LLC.

—The Sword of Antietam: A Story of the Nation's Crisis. I.t. ed. 2006. (Civil War Ser.: Vol. 4). 262p. (J). reprint ed. pap. 23.99 *(978-1-4264-2714-5(X))* Creative Media Partners, LLC.

Anderson, Hans Christian, tr. Andersen's Fairy Tales. I.t. ed. 2004. (Large Print Ser.). 266p. 25.00 *(978-1-58287-629-0(0))* North Bks.

Andreu Iglesias, Cesar & Hernández, Juan A. A Mal Tiempo, Buena Cara: El Humor en el Periodismo Puertorriqueno. I.t. ed. 2003. (SPA., Illus.). 48p. pap. *(978-0-9743102-0-6(4))* Casa de Periodistas Editorial.

Andrews-McKinney, Joyce. Jentle & Jewel Fix Things Andrews-McKinney, Joyce, illus. I.t. ed. 2006. (Illus.). 17p. (J). pap. 8.00 *(978-0-9728975-4-9(2))* JA-M Pubs., LLC.

Appleby, Ellen. Les Trois Barbichu, Big Bk. I.t. ed. (FRE.). (J). ring bd. 29.99 *(978-0-590-71769-4(3))* Scholastic, Inc.

Aresty, Reecy. Getting into College & Paying for It: Solutions for High School & College Families Guaranteed to Cut the Cost! I.t. ed. 2003.Tr. of Sueno Americano: Como Ingresar a la Universidad Y Pagar Los Mas Bajos Costos! (SPA., Illus.). 258p. (YA). per. 27.95 *(978-0-9760251-1-5(6))* College Assistance, Inc.

Asner, Anne-Marie. Kvetchy Boy. Asner, Anne-Marie, illus. I.t. ed. 2006. (ENG., Illus.). 32p. (J). per. 6.95 *(978-0-9753629-3-8(3))* Matzah Ball Bks.

—Noshy Boy. Asner, Anne-Marie, illus. I.t. ed. 2004. (ENG., Illus.). 32p. (J). (gr. -1-3). per. 6.95 *(978-0-9753629-1-4(7))* Matzah Ball Bks.

—Shmutzy Girl. Asner, Anne-Marie, illus. I.t. ed. 2004. (ENG., Illus.). 32p. (J). (gr. -1-3). per. 6.95 *(978-0-9753629-0-7(9))* Matzah Ball Bks.

Auxier, Bryan. Where Have All the Unicorns Gone? Daniels, Regina, illus. I.t. ed. 2003. 16p. (J). 7.95 *(978-0-9719144-1-4(9))* Where? Pr., Inc.

Ayers, Linda. Tiger Goes Collecting. Hunt, Jane, illus. I.t. ed. 2004. 55p. (J). per. 7.95 *(978-0-9760505-2-0(8))* Blue Thistle Pr.

Azzopardi, Jeannie. Maricio & the Magic Suitcase. I.t. ed. 2004. (Illus.). 93p. (J). per. 14.00 incl. cd-rom *(978-0-9744391-3-6(4)*, MAR-BKCD-1st, Once Upon A Time in a Classroom) Interactive Media Publishing.

Babineaux, Jim. Cody Cottontail Makes a Wise Choice! Babineaux, Jim, illus. I.t. ed. 2005. (Illus.). 18p. (J). *(978-0-9769769-0-5(0))* ALCAPS, LLC.

Baldwin, Christy. Remembering Wilma. Barnes, Sarah, illus. I.t. ed. 2005. 22p. (J). per. 9.95 *(978-0-9765072-0-8(X))* Tribute Bks.

Barr, Mabel. Hamster Huey & the Gooey Kablooie: The Renowned Hero's Most Famous Adventure. I.t. ed. 2004. (Illus.). 8p. (J). 6.95 *(978-0-9749090-0-4(9)*, 214) Hamster Huey Pr.

Barrie, James Matthew. Peter Pan. I.t. ed. 2003. (Perennial Bestsellers Ser.). (ENG.). 248p. (J). 29.95 *(978-0-7862-5263-3(4))* Thorndike Pr.

Baum, L. Frank. Dorothy & the Wizard of Oz. I.t. ed. 2004. (Large Print Ser.). lib. bdg. 25.00 *(978-1-58287-769-3(6))* North Bks.

—The Enchanted Island of Yew. I.t. ed. 2005. 228p. pap. *(978-1-84637-102-8(3))* Echo Library.

—The Enchanted Island of Yew. I.t. ed. 2004. (Large Print Ser.). 207p. 25.00 *(978-1-58287-737-2(8))* North Bks.

—Glinda of Oz. I.t. ed. 2004. (Large Print Ser.). 210p. 25.00 *(978-1-58287-740-2(8))* North Bks.

—The Lost Princess of Oz. l.t. ed. 2004. (Large Print Ser.). 241p. 25.00 *(978-1-58287-739-6(4))* North Bks.
—The Magic of Oz. l.t. ed. 2004. (Large Print Ser.). lib. bdg. 25.00 *(978-1-58287-775-4(0))* North Bks.
—The Marvelous Land of Oz. l.t. ed. 2004. (Large Print Ser.). lib. bdg. 25.00 *(978-1-58287-768-6(8))* North Bks.
—Ozma of Oz. l.t. ed. 2004. (Large Print Ser.). 210p. 25.00 *(978-1-58287-736-5(X))* North Bks.
—The Patchwork Girl of OZ. l.t. ed. 2004. (Large Print Ser.). lib. bdg. 25.00 *(978-1-58287-771-6(8))* North Bks.
—Rinkitink in Oz. l.t. ed. 2004. (Large Print Ser.). lib. bdg. 25.00 *(978-1-58287-774-7(2))* North Bks.
—The Road to Oz. l.t. ed. 2004. (Large Print Ser.). lib. bdg. 25.00 *(978-1-58287-770-9(X))* North Bks.
—The Scarecrow of Oz. l.t. ed. 2004. (Large Print Ser.). lib. bdg. 25.00 *(978-1-58287-773-0(4))* North Bks.
—Sky Island. l.t. ed. 2004. (Large Print Ser.). lib. bdg. 25.00 *(978-1-58287-792-1(0))* North Bks.
—The Tin Woodman of Oz. l.t. ed. 2005. 256p. pap. *(978-1-84637-112-7(0))* Echo Library.
—The Tin Woodman of Oz. l.t. ed. 2004. (Large Print Ser.). 230p. 25.00 *(978-1-58287-741-9(6))* North Bks.
Beck, Randy. Teen Quest. l.t. ed. 2004. 80p. (YA). per. 12.95 *(978-1-59196-535-0(7))* Instant Pub.
Beckler, Bruce. My Daddy Is A Deputy Sheriff. Finney, Simone, illus. l.t. ed. 2004. 14p. (J). per. 5.59 *(978-0-9745210-4-6(3))* Myers Publishing Co.
—My Daddy Is A Fire Fighter: My Daddy Is A Fireman. Peek, Jeannette, illus. l.t. ed. 2004. 16p. (J). 5.59 *(978-0-9745210-8-4(6))* Myers Publishing Co.
—My Daddy is a Police Officer: My Daddy Wears a Star. Finney, Simone, illus. l.t. ed. 2004. 14p. (J). per. 5.59 *(978-0-9745210-3-9(5))* Myers Publishing Co.
—My Daddy Is A Police Officer: Wears A Badge, 8 bks. Finney, Simone, illus. l.t. ed. 2004. 14p. (J). per. 5.59 *(978-0-9745210-2-2(7))* Myers Publishing Co.
—My Mommy Is A Deputy Sheriff. Finney, Simone, illus. l.t. ed. 2004. 14p. (J). 5.59 *(978-0-9745210-7-7(8))* Myers Publishing Co.
—My Mommy Is A Nurse. Peek, Jeannette, illus. l.t. ed. 2004. 20p. (J). 5.59 *(978-0-9745210-9-1(4))* Myers Publishing Co.
—My Mommy Is A Police Officer: My Mommy Wears A Badge. Finney, Simone, illus. l.t. ed. 2004. 14p. (J). per. 5.59 *(978-0-9745210-5-3(1))* Myers Publishing Co.
—My Mommy Is A Police Officer: My Mommy Wears A Star. Finney, Simone, illus. l.t. ed. 2004. 14p. (J). 5.59 *(978-0-9745210-6-0(X))* Myers Publishing Co.
—The Secret Tunnels of Spring Mountain. l.t. ed. 2004. (Illus.). 220p. (J). per. 13.99 *(978-0-9745210-0-8(0))* Myers Publishing Co.
—The Secrets of the Green Mansion. l.t. ed. 2004. (Illus.). 240p. (J). per. 13.99 *(978-0-9745210-1-5(9))* Myers Publishing Co.
Becoming a Girl of Faith: According to God's Word. l.t. ed. 2004. 90p. (YA). 12.95 *(978-0-9764304-2-1(8))* Girls of Faith.
Beeson, Lea Ann. A Leopard Is More Than His Spots. Popovich, Richard E., ed. Rockfield, Darryl, illus. l.t. ed. 2005. 51p. (J). lib. bdg. 19.95 *(978-0-9604876-1-5(1))* REP Pubs.
Beken, Robert A. Tijuana River Estuary & Border Field State Park: Land of diversity, land of Hope. l.t. ed. 2004. (Illus.). 260p. spiral bd. 34.95 *(978-0-9761726-0-4(7))* Tritium Pr.
Bell, N. Wayne. Childrens' Economics: A Book on Money & Finance. l.t. ed. 2004. (Illus.). 32p. (J). per. *(978-0-9729753-5-3(7))* Really Big Coloring Bks., Inc.
—The Really Big Book of Zoo Animals. l.t. ed. 2004. (Illus.). 32p. (J). per. *(978-0-9729753-6-0(5))* Really Big Coloring Bks., Inc.
Bell, Nasherrall, creator. Child Safety at Home, School & Play l.t. ed. 2004. (Illus.). 32p. (J). pap. *(978-0-9729753-3-9(0))* Really Big Coloring Bks., Inc.
Benevenia, Rose. Dolly & Babe. Benevenia, Rose, illus. l.t. ed. 2004. (Illus.). 9p. (J). (gr. k-2). pap. 9.00 *(978-0-9729044-0-7(9))* Cabbage Patch Pr.
Berg, Dick. Padunkapoo: The Hawaiian Kangaroo. Berg, Gary, ed. l.t. ed. 2005. (Illus.). 28p. (J). per. 6.99 *(978-0-9769985-1-8(3))* Grace Publishing.
Berggren, Jeff. Chicken Cherries. Hansen, Tammy A., ed. Berggren, Jeff, illus. l.t. ed. 2005. (Illus.). 32p. (J). per. 14.95 *(978-0-9755033-0-0(8))* Deep Dish Design.
Bernal, Mitchell. Skelanimals: Dead Animals Need Love Too Bernal, Mitchell, illus. l.t. ed. 2005. (Illus.). 22p. (J). per. 12.95 *(978-0-9766621-0-5(8),* 818 554-8965) Worn Pants.
Bernstein, Susan H. N. E. Pominonous Epstein & Change. l.t. ed. 2003. (E. Pominonous Epstein Ser.: No. 3). (Illus.). 20p. (Orig.). (J). (gr. k-3). pap. 8.95 *(978-0-9706596-2-0(8))* Bernstein, Susan.
Bersson, Robert & Shoup, Dolores. Stripes & Stars. Bersson, Robert & Trobaugh, Scott, illus. l.t. ed. 2003. 40p. (J). (gr. 1-4). per. 16.95 *(978-0-9740585-0-4(5))* Legacy Group Productions, LLC.
Bickel, Karla. The Animals' Debate. Bickel, Karla, illus. l.t. ed. 2004. (Illus.). 16p. (J). (gr. -1-6). pap. 5.00 *(978-1-891452-16-1(9),* 10) Heart Arbor Bks.
—Easter Lights. Bickel, Karla, illus. l.t. ed. 2004. (Illus.). 16p. (J). (gr. -1-6). pap. 5.00 *(978-1-891452-14-7(2),* 7) Heart Arbor Bks.
—Fishnet Valentine. Bickel, Karla, illus. l.t. ed. 2004. (Illus.). 16p. (J). (gr. -1-5). pap. 5.00 *(978-1-891452-13-0(4),* 4) Heart Arbor Bks.
—Handmade Necklace. Bickel, Karla, illus. l.t. ed. 2004. (Illus.). 16p. (J). (gr. -1-6). pap. 5.00 *(978-1-891452-11-6(8),* 1) Heart Arbor Bks.
—Heart Petals on the Hearth: A Collection of Children's Stories. Bickel, Karla, illus. 2004. (Illus.). 64p. (J). (gr. -1-6). 20.00 *(978-1-891452-00-0(2))* Heart Arbor Bks.
—The Kite Who Was Afraid to Fly. Bickel, Karla, illus. l.t. ed. 2004. (Illus.). 16p. (J). (gr. -1-6). pap. 5.00 *(978-1-891452-08-6(8),* 6) Heart Arbor Bks.
—Lilac Rose: A Flower's Lifetime. Bickel, Karla, illus. l.t. ed. 2004. (Illus.). 16p. (J). (gr. -1-6). pap. 5.00 *(978-1-891452-10-9(X),* 8) Heart Arbor Bks.
—The Reading Machine. Bickel, Karla, illus. l.t. ed. 2004. (Illus.). 16p. (J). (gr. -1-6). pap. 5.00 *(978-1-891452-15-4(0),* 9) Heart Arbor Bks.
—Surprise Christmas Birthday Party. Bickel, Karla, illus. l.t. ed. 2004. (Illus.). 16p. (J). (gr. -1-6). pap. 5.00 *(978-1-891452-12-3(6),* 3) Heart Arbor Bks.
—Teacher's Remarkable Secret. Bickel, Karla, illus. l.t. ed. 2004. (Illus.). 16p. (J). (gr. -1-6). pap. 5.00 *(978-1-891452-09-3(6),* 2) Heart Arbor Bks.
Billiot, Wendy Wilson. Before the Saltwater Came. l.t. ed. 2005. (Illus.). 32p. (J). 19.95 *(978-0-9762592-0-6(6))* Billiot, Wendy Wilson.
Birdsall, Jeanne. The Penderwicks: A Summer Tale of Four Sisters, Two Rabbits & a Very Interesting Boy. l.t. ed. 2006. (Penderwick Ser.). 304p. (J). (gr. 3-7). 23.95 *(978-0-7862-8897-7(3))* Thorndike Pr.
Blackburn, C. Edward. The Stories of Christmas: As Told by a Little Lamb. Bishop, Megan, illus. l.t. ed. 2005. 24p. (J). 9.95 *(978-0-9727440-3-4(7))* Redline Bks.
Bock, Suzanne, illus. Meet the Angels l.t. ed. 2004. 10p. (J). bds. 12.99 *(978-0-9758709-4-5(7),* 13401) Journey Stone Creations, LLC.
Bolme, Edward Sarah. Baby Bible Board Books Collection No. 1: Stories of Jesus, 4 vols. Gillette, Tim, illus. l.t. ed. 2003. 20p. (J). bds. 23.99 *(978-0-9725546-4-0(5))* CREST Pubns.
—Jesus Feeds the People. Gillette, Tim, illus. l.t. ed. 2003. 20p. (J). bds. 6.99 *(978-0-9725546-0-2(2))* CREST Pubns.
—Jesus Heals a Little Girl. Gillette, Tim, illus. l.t. ed. 2003. 20p. (J). bds. 6.99 *(978-0-9725546-1-9(0))* CREST Pubns.
—Jesus Helps a Blind Man. Gillette, Tim, illus. l.t. ed. 2003. 20p. (J). bds. 6.99 *(978-0-9725546-2-6(9))* CREST Pubns.
—Jesus Stops a Storm. Gillette, Tim, illus. l.t. ed. 2003. 20p. (J). bds. 6.99 *(978-0-9725546-3-3(7))* CREST Pubns.
Boone, Melvin, Jr. JD Mc Doil What's up with Oil. l.t. ed. 2003. (Illus.). 32p. (J). 19.95 *(978-0-9741750-0-3(5))* Never Stop Reading Never Stop Learning.
Boritzer, Etan. What Is Right? Sale, Graham, illus. l.t. ed. 2005. (What Is? Ser.). 40p. (J). (gr. k-5). pap. 6.95 *(978-0-9762743-0-8(2)); (978-0-9762743-1-5(0))* Lane, Veronica Bks.
Boye, B. D. Easy As 1, 2, 3. Boye, B. D., illus. l.t. ed. 2005. (Illus.). 22p. (J). per. 4.99 *(978-0-9768078-0-3(7))* Innerchild Publishing, Inc.
—The Look Book. Boye, B. D., illus. l.t. ed. 2004. (Illus.). 20p. (J). per. 4.99 *(978-0-9768078-1-0(5),* 100001) Innerchild Publishing, Inc.
—Our New Home. Boye, B. D., illus. l.t. ed. 2005. (Illus.). 18p. (J). per. 4.99 *(978-0-9768078-2-7(3))* Innerchild Publishing, Inc.
Boyles, Peggy Palo & Prentice Hall Dictionary Editors. Realidades Vol. 2: Level 2, 2 vols. l.t. ed. 2003. (ENG.). 508p. (YA). (gr. 9-9). 254.00 *(978-0-13-035951-3(3))* Savvas Learning Co.
Boyles, Peggy Palo & Prentice Hall Direct Education Staff. Realidades: Level B, 2 vols. l.t. ed. 2003. (SPA & ENG.). 416p. (YA). (gr. 7-7). 208.00 *(978-0-13-035967-4(X),* Prentice Hall) Savvas Learning Co.
Boyles, Peggy Palo & Prentice Hall Directories Staff. Realidades: Level 1, 2 vols. l.t. ed. 2003. (ENG.). 564p. (YA). (gr. 8-9). stu. ed. 282.00 *(978-0-13-101687-3(3),* Prentice Hall) Savvas Learning Co.
—Realidades: Level A. l.t. ed. 2003. (SPA & ENG.). 322p. (YA). (gr. 7-7). stu. ed. 161.00 *(978-0-13-035966-7(1),* Prentice Hall) Savvas Learning Co.
Boyles, Peggy Palo, et al. Realidades, Level 3, 2 vols. l.t. ed. 2003. (SPA & ENG.). 614p. (YA). (gr. 10-10). 307.00 *(978-0-13-035968-1(8),* Prentice Hall) Savvas Learning Co.
Boyne, John. The Boy in the Striped Pajamas. rev. l.t. ed. 2007. (Thorndike Literacy Bridge Ser.). (ENG.). 247p. (YA). (gr. 7-12). 23.95 *(978-0-7862-9425-1(6))* Thorndike Pr.
Brady, Bill. A Charm for Jo. Brady, Laurie, illus. l.t. ed. 2005. (Turtle Books). 32p. (J). (gr. 2-5). lib. bdg. 15.95 *(978-0-944727-48-5(4))* Jason & Nordic Pubs.
Brady, Karen. God Is Great: A Collection of 13 Story Book Poems, 1. l.t. ed. 2004. (Illus.). 20p. (J). 12.50 *(978-0-9754169-0-7(1))* Bradybooks.biz.
Breems, Beau A. La Gran Historia: The Illustrated Gospel from Creation to Resurrection Breems, Beau A., illus. l.t. ed. 2005.Tr. of His Story. (SPA., Illus.). 50p. (J). 19.95 *(978-0-9768680-1-9(6),* 1000); per. 14.95 *(978-0-9768680-3-3(2),* 3000) Burning Bush Creation.
—His Story: The Illustrated Gospel from Creation to Resurrection. Breems, Beau A., illus. l.t. ed. 2005.Tr. of Gran Historia. (Illus.). 50p. (J). 19.95 *(978-0-9768680-0-2(8),* 0-9768680-0-8) Burning Bush Creation.
Brez, Lisa. Hickerdoodle Gets Lost. l.t. ed. 2003. (Illus.). 32p. (J). per. 6.99 *(978-0-9743758-4-7(5))* Red Engine Pr.
—Hickerdoodle Gets the Hiccups. l.t. ed. 2003. (Illus.). 32p. (J). per. 6.99 *(978-0-9743758-3-0(7))* Red Engine Pr.
—Hickerdoodle Meets a Chigger. l.t. ed. 2004. (Illus.). 40p. (J). per. 6.99 *(978-0-9743758-5-4(3))* Red Engine Pr.
Brown, Jane. Who Has Four Feet? l.t. ed. 2005. (Sadlier Phonics Reading Program: Vol. 1). (Illus.). 8p. (gr. -1-1). 23.00 net. *(978-0-8215-7340-2(3))* Sadlier, William H. Inc.
Brown, Mark. Tommy Books: Faith, 10 vols. Mekis, Pete, illus. l.t. ed. 2005. 24p. (J). 12.99 *(978-0-9762690-0-7(7))* Tommy Bks. Pubng.
—Tommy Books: Kings, 10 vols. Mekis, Pete, illus. l.t. ed. 2005. 24p. (J). 12.99 *(978-0-9762690-4-5(X))* Tommy Bks. Pubng.
—Tommy Books Vol. 4: Praise, 10 vols. Mekis, Pete, illus. l.t. ed. 2005. 20p. (J). 12.99 *(978-0-9762690-3-8(1))* Tommy Bks. Pubng.
Bryant, Louella. Two Tracks in the Snow. Fargo, Todd, illus. l.t. ed. 2004. (Turtle Bks.). 32p. (J). lib. bdg. 15.95 *(978-0-944727-46-1(8),* Turtle Bks.) Jason & Nordic Pubs.
Brzycki, M. L. & Krueger, S. L. It Came from the Freezer ... or Was it the Drapes? l.t. ed. 2004. (Illus.). 110p. (YA). per. 13.00 *(978-0-9747581-0-7(8))* StrangeDays Publishing.
Bucki, Jo Dee & O'Malley, John. Maya Visits a Hospital: Love Is the Best Medicine, 110 vols. Hicks, Mindy, ed. Matthews, Ashley, illus. l.t. ed. 2007. 32p. (J). per. 4.95 *(978-0-9769069-0-2(2))* Strategic Visions Inc.
Buckler, Carol. Feathered Tales from the Barnyard. l.t. ed. 2004. (J). per. 5.95 *(978-1-932496-20-8(3))* Penman Publishing, Inc.
Bucky Badger A Children's Story: Becky Gets a Brother, 4 vols. l.t. ed. 2005. (Illus.). (J). 9.99 *(978-0-9765510-0-3(4))* Badgerland Bks. LLC.
Burchett, Loni R. Bear & Katie in a Day at Nestlenook Farm. l.t. ed. 2004. (ENG., Illus.). 76p. (J). per. 11.95 *(978-0-9742815-1-3(4))* Black Lab Publishing LLC.
—Bear & Katie in a Day with Friends, Vol. 3. l.t. ed. 2005. (Illus.). 68p. (J). per. 11.95 *(978-0-9742815-2-0(2),* bk003) Black Lab Publishing LLC.
—Bear & Katie in the Great Searsport Caper. l.t. ed. 2004. (Illus.). 81p. (J). per. 12.95 *(978-0-9742815-0-6(6))* Black Lab Publishing LLC.
Burnett, Frances. A Little Princess: Being the whole story of Sara Crewe now told for T. l.t. ed. 2007. (ENG.). 210p. per. 22.99 *(978-1-4346-7029-8(5))* Creative Media Partners, LLC.
—A Little Princess: The Story of Sara Crewe. l.t. ed. 2005. 376p. pap. *(978-1-84637-117-2(1))* Echo Library.
—A Little Princess: The Story of Sara Crewe. l.t. ed. 2005. (Large Print Ser.). lib. bdg. 26.00 *(978-1-58287-814-0(5))* North Bks.
—A Little Princess: The Story of Sara Crewe. l.t. ed. 2003. 342p. pap. 10.95 *(978-0-7862-6247-2(8))* Thorndike Pr.
Bumford, Sheila. The Incredible Journey. (J). (gr. 6-8). 18.95 *(978-0-88411-099-6(0))* Amereon Ltd.
Busic, Valerie. Jason's First Day. OI Foundation, ed. Meyers, Jeff, illus. l.t. ed. 2004. 48p. per. 8.50 *(978-0-9642189-4-9(1))* Osteogenesis Imperfecta Foundation.
Byars, Betsy. Trouble River. l.t. ed. 2004. (Beeler Mystery Ser.). 28.95 *(978-1-58118-120-3(5))* LRS.
Campbell, Ellen Langas. Will Stephanie Get the Story?, 3 bks., No. 1. 2004. (Girls Know How Ser.: #1 - Journalism). (ENG., Illus.). 112p. (J). pap. 4.95 *(978-0-9743604-0-9(6),* GIRLS KNOW HOW) NouSoma Communications, Inc.
Candy, Wolf. The Tree, the House & the Hurricane. l.t. ed. 2005. (Illus.). 24p. (J). 7.00 *(978-0-9762292-3-0(4))* New Global Publishing.
Carmine, Mary & Baynton, Martin. Daniel et Ses Dinosaures. l.t. ed.Tr. of Daniel et Ses Dinosaures. (FRE., Illus.). (J). bds. 29.99 *(978-0-590-74124-8(1))* Scholastic, Inc.
Casey, Bert. Acoustic Guitar Book 2 Deluxe Edition: Book/DVD/CD, vol. 2. l.t. ed. 2003. (Watch & Learn Ser.: 2). (ENG., Illus.). 80p. pap. 15.95 incl. audio compact disk *(978-1-893907-43-0(0),* 256-535) Watch & Learn, Inc.
Cast, P. C. & Cast, Kristin. Marked. l.t. ed. 2008. (House of Night Ser.: No. 1). (ENG.). 442p. (YA). 23.95 *(978-1-4104-1021-4(8))* Thorndike Pr.
—Untamed. l.t. ed. 2009. (House of Night Ser.: Bk. 4). (ENG.). 510p. (YA). 23.95 *(978-1-4104-1965-1(7))* Thorndike Pr.
Cast, P. C. & Kristin. Chosen. l.t. ed. 2009. (House of Night Ser.: Bk. 3). (ENG.). 406p. (YA). 23.95 *(978-1-4104-1608-7(9))* Thorndike Pr.
Causton, Linda. Lester's Rainy Lake Pony. l.t. ed. 2004. (Illus.). 32p. (J). 12.00 *(978-1-930374-09-6(7))* DeForest Pr.
Chabon, Michael. Summerland. l.t. ed. 2003. 615p. (J). 25.95 *(978-0-7862-5143-8(3))* Thorndike Pr.
Chamberlain, Lyn. Quonby & the Tree Den. Weltner, Dave, illus. l.t. ed. 2004. 12p. (J). 7.95 *(978-0-9706654-8-5(2))* Sprite Pr.
Ching, Jerry Yu & Onghai, Mike. The Greatest King. Ching, Jerry Yu, illus. 2nd l.t. ed. 2003. (Illus.). 52p. *(978-0-9743215-0-9(8))* WebCartoons, LLC.
Christian, Reinar Carl, Sr. Nate: The New Bus on the Block! l.t. ed. 2005. (Illus.). 41p. (J). 16.99 *(978-0-9769866-0-7(4))* Meritage Publishing.
The Christmas Chair l.t. ed. 2004. (Illus.). 27p. (J). 12.95 *(978-0-9763633-1-6(3))* Williams, Thomas.
Cintron, Carlos Juan, Sr., ed. Mis Primeros Pasos: Red de Niños. deluxe l.t. ed. 2005. (SPA., Illus.). 85p. (J). 12.00 *(978-0-9765828-5-4(6))* Editorial Vida Abundante.
Cioffi, Dom, illus. Digby & the Lake Monster. l.t. ed. 2006. 36p. (J). per. *(978-0-9745931-0-4(9))* Vermont Bookworks.
Claire, Elizabeth. Help Your Buddy Learn English, Bk. 1. Nichols, Dave, illus. l.t. ed. 2003. 64p. 15.00 *(978-0-937630-04-4(7))* Eardley Pubns.
Clements, Andrew. No Talking. Elliott, Mark, illus. l.t. ed. 2007. (Literacy Bridge Middle Reader Ser.). 155p. (J). (gr. 3-7). 23.95 *(978-1-4104-0294-3(0))* Thorndike Pr.
Clyde, Addie M. Sophie the Sofa. l.t. ed. 2004. 40p. (J). per. *(978-1-59196-744-6(9))* Instant Pub.
Cofer, Amadeus. Friendship Rules: How to Make & Keep Friends, 1. l.t. ed. 2004. (Illus.). 36p. (J). 14.00 *(978-1-932957-00-6(6))* Legacy Pubs.
—Mystery of the Golden Pearls: A Halloween Adventure in Clarkesville, 1. l.t. ed. 2004. (Illus.). 36p. (J). 14.00 *(978-1-932957-02-0(2))* Legacy Pubs.
Cohen, Judith Love. You Can Be A Chemist. Katz, David A., illus. l.t. ed. 2005. Orig. Title: You Can Be A Woman Chemist. 40p. (J). per. 7.00 *(978-1-880599-71-6(6))* Cascade Pass, Inc.
—You Can Be A Woman Chemist. Katz, David A., illus. l.t. ed. 2005. 40p. (J). 13.95 *(978-1-880599-72-3(4))* Cascade Pass, Inc.
—You Can Be A Woman Video Game Producer. l.t. ed. 2005. (Illus.). 72p. (J). 17.95 *(978-1-880599-74-7(0))*; pap. 12.95 *(978-1-880599-73-0(2))* Cascade Pass, Inc.
Cohen, Sonia. Gigi. l.t. ed. 2005. (Illus.). 34p. (J). 14.95 *(978-0-615-12926-6(9))* Gigi Enterprises.
Collins, Suzanne. The Hunger Games. l.t. ed. 2009. (Hunger Games Trilogy: Bk. 1). (ENG.). 485p. (YA). 23.95 *(978-1-4104-1986-6(X))* Thorndike Pr.
—Mockingjay. l.t. ed. 2010. (Hunger Games Trilogy: Bk. 3). (ENG.). 503p. (YA). 23.99 *(978-1-4104-2841-7(9))* Thorndike Pr.
Condie, Ally. Matched. l.t. ed. 2011. (Matched Trilogy: Bk. 1). (ENG.). 449p. 23.99 *(978-1-4104-3954-3(2))* Thorndike Pr.
Conquistadore, H. Omni Presents the Universe. West, Jeremy, illus. l.t. ed. 2003. 51p. per. 8.99 *(978-1-932338-14-0(4))* Lifevest Publishing, Inc.
Coolidge, Susan. What Katy Did. l.t. ed. 2007. (ENG.). 160p. pap. 21.99 *(978-1-4346-5944-6(5))* Creative Media Partners, LLC.
Cope-Robinson, Lyn. Cat Tails. Cope-Robinson, Lyn, illus. l.t. ed. 2003. (Illus.). 32p. (J). lib. bdg. *(978-1-887774-14-7(9),* Wynden) Canmore Pr.
Counce, Paula. A Journey Remembered. l.t. ed. 2004. (Illus.). 135p. (J). 19.95 *(978-0-9762776-0-6(3))* Counce, Paula.
A Cow Had a Wish. l.t. ed. Date not set. (Illus.). 32p. (J). (gr. 1-6). *(978-0-9653327-1-2(3))* BF Publishing.
Crawford, Ann Fears. Rosa: A German Woman on the Texas Frontier. Fain, Cheryl, illus. l.t. ed. 2003. 60p. (J). (gr. 3-8). 16.95 *(978-1-931823-09-8(X))* Halcyon Pr.
Crichton, Julie. The King & the Queen & the Jelly Bean. Swaim, illus. l.t. ed. 2005. (SPA.). 24p. (J). bds. 7.95 *(978-0-9761990-0-7(9))* Bean Bk. Publishing.
—El rey y la reina y el frijolito de Goma. Swaim, Ramon, illus. l.t. ed. 2005. 24p. (J). bds. 7.95 *(978-0-9761990-1-4(7))* Bean Bk. Publishing.
Crosby, Vernon H. The Adventures of Scurry Little: Lost in my Dream. l.t. ed. 2004. 40p. (J). per. 10.95 *(978-1-59196-819-1(4))* Instant Pub.
Cross, Linda B. Lines from Linda. l.t. ed. 2003. 104p. (YA). per. 7.00 *(978-0-9748591-2-5(5),* MSP) Yetto Publishing Co.
Cruzan, Patricia & Solly, Gloria, illus. Molly's Mischievous Dog. l.t. ed. 2004. 121p. (J). per. *(978-0-9653543-3-2(4))* Clear Creek Pubs.
Curry, Casey. I Remember You Today: An Interactive Picturebook for Children Dealing with the Loss of a Sibling or Parent. 2003. (Illus.). 24p. (J). wbk. ed. *(978-1-884878-15-2(6))* Annapolis Publishing Co.
Curtiss, A. B. The Little Chapel That Stood Golino, Mirto, illus. l.t. ed. 2005. (ENG.). 36p. (J). (gr. -1-3). 18.95 *(978-0-932529-77-0(1))* Oldcastle Publishing.
Damon - Beyond the Glory. l.t. ed. 2003. (Illus.). 152p. per. 14.95 *(978-0-9724033-2-0(9))* Backroads Pr.
Das, Christina. Coo Coo Duckling. l.t. ed. 2005. (Illus.). 32p. (J). 15.95 *(978-0-9763082-4-9(X),* A JuneOne Production) JuneOne Publishing Hub.
—Munchy Mouse. l.t. ed. 2005. (Illus.). 32p. (J). 15.95 *(978-0-9763082-0-1(7),* A JuneOne Production) JuneOne Publishing Hub.
—Oomph-Pa-Pa at the Circus. l.t. ed. 2005. (Illus.). 32p. (J). 15.95 *(978-0-9763082-2-5(3),* A JuneOne Production) JuneOne Publishing Hub.
—The Red Spotted Balloon. l.t. ed. 2005. (Illus.). 32p. (J). 15.95 *(978-0-9763082-3-2(1),* A JuneOne Production) JuneOne Publishing Hub.
—Swinging under the Stars. l.t. ed. 2005. (Illus.). 32p. (J). 15.95 *(978-0-9763082-1-8(5),* A JuneOne Production) JuneOne Publishing Hub.
Davis, Adda Leah. Caleb's Song. l.t. ed. 2003. (Illus.). 56p. (J). *(978-0-9747904-0-4(0))* Golden Harvest Publishing Co.
Davis, Darren & Davis, Darren G. ABC's for Superheroes. l.t. ed. 2006. (Atlas Ser.). (ENG., Illus.). 12p. (J). (gr. -1-12). 5.99 *(978-1-59559-110-4(9))* Bluewater Productions, Inc.
De Saint-Exupéry, Antoine. The Little Prince. l.t. ed. 2005.Tr. of Petit Prince. (ENG.). 168p. (J). (gr. 5-8). pap. 15.99 *(978-0-7862-7539-7(1))* Cengage Gale.
de Trevino, Elizabeth Borton. I, Juan de Pareja. l.t. ed. 2005. 244p. 20.95 *(978-0-7862-7666-0(5))* Thorndike Pr.
Demers, David & Demers, Lee Ann. My Grandpa Loves Trains: A Storybook for Preschoolers. Demers, David, photos by. l.t. ed. 2005. (Illus.). 76p. (J). per. 19.95 *(978-0-922993-23-9(8))* Marquette Bks.
Denny, Joe. Triune: Jimmy's Escape. 2005. 80p. (J). pap. *(978-0-9772240-0-5(7))* JD Entertainment.
DeSantis, Debi. A Bunch of Giggles & Hugs. l.t. ed. 2005. (Illus.). 26p. (J). 12.95 *(978-0-9770043-0-0(9))* New Global Publishing.
DeVos, Janie. Path Winds Home. Marsh, Nancy, illus. l.t. ed. 2005. 32p. 16.95 *(978-0-9743758-0-9(2))* Red Engine Pr.
Diaz, T. Richard. Little Growler, Big Heart. l.t. ed. 2003. (Illus.). 12p. (J). lib. bdg. 11.95 *(978-1-932338-21-8(7))* Lifevest Publishing, Inc.
Dicamillo, Kate. The Tale of Despereaux: Being the Story of a Mouse, a Princess, Some Soup & a Spool of Thread. Ering, Timothy Basil, illus. l.t. ed. 2004. (Thorndike Literacy Bridge Ser.). (ENG.). 247p. (J). pap. 11.95 *(978-1-4104-1527-1(9))* Thorndike Pr.
Dicicco, Joe. Planet Baseball, Japanese Edition, Volume 1: Making the Play, Vol. 1. Jimenez, Ruben D., tr. Dicicco, Joe, illus. l.t. ed. 2009. (JPN & ENG., Illus.). 14p. (J). (gr. -1-3). 7.95 *(978-1-929528-03-5(5))* Punta Gorda Pr.
Dickens, Charles. The Cricket on the Hearth. l.t. ed. 2005. (ENG.). 112p. pap. 17.95 *(978-1-59688-048-1(1),* 1-59688-048-1) Large Print Bk. Co., The.
Dickman, Jean M. Santa in Space. l.t. ed. 2003. (Illus.). 32p. (J). per. 9.95 *(978-0-9743718-0-1(7))* Tintagel Publications.
DiSunno, Rebecca, et al. Jeremy Goes to Camp Good Grief. l.t. ed. 2004. (Illus.). 48p. (J). per. 14.95 *(978-0-9754932-0-5(5))* East End Hospice, Inc.
Dolphin Halloween & Elsie's Scrapbook. l.t. ed. 2004. (Illus.). 32p. (J). mass mkt. 4.99 *(978-0-9760868-0-2(8))* Pluegl Bks.
Doolin, Jimmy. The Day the Circus Came to My Backyard. l.t. ed. 2003. 39p. lib. bdg. *(978-0-9710432-4-4(8))* Children's Literacy Pubns.
Dozier, Kim. The Ear-Less Kingdom. Dozier, Ashlyn McCauley, illus. l.t. ed. 2003. (ENG.). 24p. (J). 7.50 *(978-0-9745839-1-4(X),* Fun to Read Bks. with Royally Good Morals) MKADesigns.
—The Forgetful Princess. Dozier, Ashlyn McCauley, illus. 2nd l.t. ed. 2003. (ENG.). 24p. (J). 10.00 *(978-0-9745839-0-7(1),* Fun to Read Bks. with Royally Good Morals) MKADesigns.
—Where's Dwight Dragon. Dozier, Ashlyn McCauley, illus. l.t. ed. 2004. (ENG.). 32p. (J). 10.00 *(978-0-9745839-2-1(8),* Fun to Read Bks. with Royally Good Morals) MKADesigns.
Duchene-Marshall, Michele A. Charley Finds A Family. Marshall, Alan David, ed. Ousley, Clayton Gerard, photos by. l.t. ed. 2004. Orig. Title: Charley finds a Home. (Illus.). 20p. (J). spiral bd. 10.00 *(978-0-9761675-2-5(2))* Storybook Acres.
—Shirley's Red Satin Shoes. Marshall, Alan David, ed. Ousley, Clayton Gerard, photos by. l.t. ed. 2003. (Illus.). 17p. (J). spiral bd. 10.00 *(978-0-9761675-1-8(4))* Storybook Acres.
Dunbar, Paula J. Ruby's Rainbow: A Story of Acadia National Park. l.t. ed. 2005. (Illus.). 32p. (J). *(978-1-931207-59-1(3))* Dilligaf Publishing.
Eagle, Golden. It's Good to Laugh at Yourself (Coyote Medicine. l.t. ed. 2004. (Illus.). 22p. (J). per. 12.99 *(978-1-932338-36-2(5))* Lifevest Publishing, Inc.
—It's Good to Shed Your Skin (Snake Medicine) l.t. ed. 2004. (Illus.). 20p. (J). per. 12.99 *(978-1-932338-38-6(1))* Lifevest Publishing, Inc.
—It's Okay to Cry (Frog Medicine) l.t. ed. 2004. (Illus.). 16p. (J). per. 12.99 *(978-1-932338-37-9(3))* Lifevest Publishing, Inc.

J
K
L

—The Owl Who Lives in My House. l.t. ed. 2003. (Illus.). 24p. (J). per. 12.99 *(978-1-932338-34-8(9))* Lifevest Publishing, Inc.

Ebon Research Systems Staff. Dare to Be: Roberto Clemente. l.t. ed. 2003.Tr. of Atrevete a Ser un Heroe. . . Roberto Clemente. (ENG & SPA., Illus.). 22p. 3.99 *(978-0-9648313-5-3(X))* Ebon Research Systems Publishing, LLC.

—Dare to Be Vol. 2: Lessons in the Life of Esperanza. l.t. ed. 2003.Tr. of Atrevete a Ser... Un Heroe. (ENG & SPA., Illus.). 16p. (J). 3.99 *(978-0-9648313-4-6(1))* Ebon Research Systems Publishing, LLC.

—Dare to Be... A Hero Vol. 3: Cesar Chavez. l.t. ed. 2003.Tr. of Atrevete a Ser... Un Heroe Cesar Chavez. (ENG & SPA., Illus.). 16p. (J). 3.99 *(978-0-9648313-6-0(8))* Ebon Research Systems Publishing, LLC.

Eckdahl, Judith & Eckdahl, Kathryn. A Collection of Street Games. O'Regan, Lucy, ed. Miranda, Pedro, illus. 2005. 42p. pupil's gde. ed. 13.95 *(978-0-9767200-0-3(0))* Lesen Pub.

Ehlin, Gina. Emma & Friends: Emma's Airport Adventure. Ayzenberg, Nina, illus. l.t. ed. 2005. 32p. (J). per. 10.99 *(978-1-59879-014-6(5))* Lifevest Publishing, Inc.

—Emma's Airport Adventure. Ayesenberg, Nina, illus. l.t. ed. 2005. (Emma & Friends Ser.). 34p. (J). 15.99 *(978-1-59879-015-3(3))* Lifevest Publishing, Inc.

Eifrig, Kate. I'll Be a Pirate: World of Discovery II. Graves, Dennis, illus. l.t. ed. 2006. (SPA & ENG.). 12p. (gr. k-2). pap. 7.95 *(978-1-57874-053-6(3)*, Kaeden Bks.) Kaeden Corp.

Ellis, Marvie. Tacos Anyone? Bk. 2: An Autism Story Book. l.t. ed. 2005.Tr. of Alguien quiere Tacos? (SPA., Illus.). 32p. (J). per. 16.95 *(978-1-933319-01-8(1))* Speech Kids Texas Pr.

Epstein, Brad M. Arizona State University 101: My First Text-Board-Book. l.t. ed. 2003. (101 — My First Text-Board Books). (Illus.). 20p. (J). bds. *(978-0-9727702-3-1(2)*, 101 Bk.) Michaelson Entertainment.

—Auburn University 101: My First Text-Board-Book. l.t. ed. 2003. (My First Text Board Bks.). (Illus.). 20p. (J). bds. *(978-0-9727702-7-9(5))* Michaelson Entertainment.

—Clemson University 101: My First Text-Board-Book. l.t. ed. 2004. (101 — My First Text-Board Books). (ENG., Illus.). 20p. (J). bds. *(978-1-932530-06-3(1)*, 101 Bk.) Michaelson Entertainment.

—Columbia University 101: My First Text-Board-Book. l.t. ed. 2005. (101 — My First Text-Board Books). (Illus.). 20p. (J). bds. *(978-0-9727702-1-7(6))* Michaelson Entertainment.

—Cornell University 101: My First Text-Board-Book. l.t. ed. 2004. (101 — My First Text-Board Books). (Illus.). 20p. (J). bds. *(978-1-932530-00-1(2))* Michaelson Entertainment.

—Dartmouth College 101. l.t. ed. 2003. (My First Text Board Bks.). (Illus.). 20p. (J). bds. *(978-0-9727702-5-5(9))* Michaelson Entertainment.

—Louisiana State University 101: My First Text-Board-Book. l.t. ed. 2004. (My First Text Board Bks.). (Illus.). 20p. (J). bds. *(978-1-932530-09-4(6))* Michaelson Entertainment.

—Penn State University 101: My First Text-Board-Book. l.t. ed. 2004. (101 — My First Text-Board Books). (Illus.). 20p. (J). bds. *(978-1-932530-04-9(5)*, 101 Bk.) Michaelson Entertainment.

—Purdue University 101: My First Text-Board-Book. l.t. ed. 2004. (101 — My First Text-Board Books). (ENG., Illus.). 20p. (J). bds. *(978-1-932530-11-7(8)*, 101 Bk.) Michaelson Entertainment.

—UCLA 101: My First Text-Board-Book. l.t. ed. 2004. (My First Text Board Bks.). (Illus.). 20p. (J). bds. *(978-1-932530-15-5(0)*, 101 Bk.) Michaelson Entertainment.

—University of Florida 101: My First Text-Board-Book. l.t. ed. 2004. (101 — My First Text-Board Books). (Illus.). 20p. (J). bds. *(978-1-932530-21-6(5)*, 101 Bk.) Michaelson Entertainment.

—University of Georgia 101: My First Text-Board-Book. l.t. ed. 2004. (101 — My First Text-Board Books). (ENG., Illus.). 20p. (J). bds. *(978-1-932530-08-7(8)*, 101 Bk.) Michaelson Entertainment.

—University of Illinois 101: My First Text-Board-Book. l.t. ed. 2004. (101 — My First Text-Board Books). (ENG., Illus.). 20p. (J). bds. *(978-1-932530-17-9(7)*, 101 Bk.) Michaelson Entertainment.

—Usc 101: My First Text-Board-Book. l.t. ed. 2004. (101 — My First Text-Board Books). (ENG., Illus.). 20p. (J). bds. *(978-0-9727702-0-0(8)*, 101 Bk.) Michaelson Entertainment.

Evans, Mary. Cats! Cats! Cats!, 2. Kovalcik, Terry, illus. l.t. ed. 2005. (Sadlier Phonics Reading Program). 8p. (gr. -1-1). 23.00 net. *(978-0-8215-7348-8(9))* Sadlier, William H. Inc.

—Good Pets, Vol. 3. l.t. ed. 2005. (Sadlier Phonics Reading Program). (Illus.). 8p. (gr. -1-1). 23.00 net. *(978-0-8215-7350-1(0))* Sadlier, William H. Inc.

Fabris, Judith. Money...Cool! Brolin, Carol, illus. l.t. ed. 2003. 155p. (YA). pap. 9.95 *(978-1-893335-12-7(7))* Archipelago Pr.

Fabulas de Siempre. l.t. ed.Tr. of Traditional Fables. (SPA.). (J). 3.98 *(978-84-7630-901-8(5))* Selector, S.A. de C.V. MEX. Dist: Spanish Pubs., LLC.

Falkner, J. Meade. Moonfleet. l.t. ed. 2004. (Large Print Ser.). 370p. 26.00 *(978-1-58287-658-0(4))* North Bks.

Farrow, Stephanie, ed. Blue Wolf & Friends Storybook, 1 Vol., Units 1-4. l.t. ed. 2004. (Illus.). 93p. *(978-0-9758759-2-6(2))* Progressive Language, Inc.

Faye, Joanne & Whaley, Stacey Lynn. Conversations with Kids Ages 3 to 6. l.t. ed. 2004. (Illus.). 24p. (J). 9.95 *(978-0-9747375-0-8(X))* Joanne Faye Pr.

Fetzer, Erin & Sonday, Arlene. SS1 Readers L6a-10c. l.t. ed. 2004. (ENG., Illus.). 12p. (J). 59.99 *(978-1-891602-14-6(4))* Winsor Learning, Inc.

Fey, Sid & Vitello, Kathy. The Being Game: For the Love of Your Life. l.t. ed. 2004. (Illus.). 66p. per. 14.95 *(978-0-9753530-5-9(5))* Fey, Sid Designs, Inc.

Feyh, Janelle. Does God Have a Remote Control? Feyh, Alexa & Deghand, Tim, illus. l.t. ed. 2003. 66p. (J). per. 11.95 *(978-1-932344-26-4(8))* Thornton Publishing, Inc.

A Fifty Year Affair: Living with Light Planes. l.t. ed. 2004. (Illus.). 208p. (YA). pap. 18.95 *(978-0-9745564-0-3(2))* Julson, D. K.

Fisher, Phyllis Mae Richardson, illus. Chrissy: #1 in the 1989 Family Friends Paper Doll Set. l.t. ed. 2004. (ENG.). 24p. (J). 10.00 *(978-0-9745615-5-4(X))* PJs Corner Gift Shoppe.

Foce, Natalia, tr. from ENG. Jesus el Milagroso. Anderson, Jeff, illus. l.t. ed. 2009. Orig. Title: Jesus the Miracle Worker. (SPA & ENG.). 24p. (J). 3.49 *(978-1-932789-28-7(6))* Editorial Sendas Antiguas, LLC.

—Jesus Maestro. Anderson, Jeff, illus. l.t. ed. 2009. Orig. Title: Jesus the Teacher. (SPA & ENG.). 24p. (J). 3.49 *(978-1-932789-26-3(X))* Editorial Sendas Antiguas, LLC.

—Jesus Narrador. Anderson, Jeff, illus. l.t. ed. 2009. Orig. Title: Jesus the Storyteller. (SPA & ENG.). 24p. (J). 3.49 *(978-1-932789-25-6(1))* Editorial Sendas Antiguas, LLC.

—Jesus Niño. Anderson, Jeff, illus. l.t. ed. 2009. Orig. Title: Jesus the Child. (SPA & ENG.). 24p. (J). 3.49 *(978-1-932789-24-9(3))* Editorial Sendas Antiguas, LLC.

—Jesus Salvador. Anderson, Jeff, illus. l.t. ed. 2009. Orig. Title: Jesus the Saviour. (SPA & ENG.). 24p. (J). 3.49 *(978-1-932789-29-4(4))* Editorial Sendas Antiguas, LLC.

—Jesus Sanador. Anderson, Jeff, illus. l.t. ed. 2009. Orig. Title: Jesus the Healer. (SPA & ENG.). 24p. (J). 3.49 *(978-1-932789-27-0(8))* Editorial Sendas Antiguas, LLC.

Fontanez, Edwin. On This Beautiful Island. Fontanez, Edwin, illus. l.t. ed. 2004. (Illus.). 32p. (J). 18.95 *(978-0-9640868-6-9(7)*, 1241077) Exit Studio.

Forbes, Esther Hoskins. Johnny Tremain Set: Illustrated American Classics, 2 vols., l.t. ed. (J). reprint ed. *(978-0-89064-029-6(7))* National Assn. for Visually Handicapped.

Foster, Kathryn Joy. Always Room for One More. l.t. ed. 2004. (Illus.). 12p. (J). spiral bd. 13.00 *(978-0-9728779-6-1(7)*, TBK-21007) Read All Over Publishing.

Frazier, Janet. The Case of the Theme Park Cry. l.t. ed. 2004. 90p. (J). per. *(978-1-59196-737-8(6))* Instant Pub.

Frontiera, Deborah K. Eric & the Enchanted Leaf: The First Adventure Scott, Korey, illus. 2nd l.t. ed. 2004. 32p. (J). pap. 16.95 *(978-0-9753410-0-1(6))* Jade Enterprises.

—Eric & the Enchanted Leaf / Eric y la Hoja Encantada: A Visit with Canis Lupis / una Visita con Canis Lupis. Santillan-Cruz, Silvia R., tr. Scott, Korey, illus. 2nd l.t. ed. 2005. (SPA & ENG.). 32p. (J). lib. bdg. 16.95 *(978-0-9663629-8-5(5))* By Grace Enterprises.

Furbush, Helen. Lying Awake. McCroskey, Christine, illus. l.t. ed. 2004. 32p. (J). (gr. 1-6). 15.95 *(978-0-9741787-0-7(5)*, 1239134) Harbor Island Bks.

Fussell, Bonnie. More Than a Stove. Sadler, Dale, illus. l.t. ed. 2004. 32p. (J). pap. 7.99 *(978-0-615-12702-6(9))* Blackberry Pubs.

Gardiner, John Reynolds. Stone Fox. Sewall, Marcia, illus. 25th anniv. ed. 2005. (ENG.). 96p. (J). (gr. 2-6). 16.99 *(978-0-690-03983-2(2)*, HarperCollins) HarperCollins Pubs.

Garrick, Lainie. Losing Papou: One Child's Journey Towards Understanding & Accepting Death. Mandarino, Gene, illus. l.t. ed. 2003. 32p. (J). *(978-0-9765725-0-3(8))* printONDEMANDpublisher.com.

George, Jean Craighead. Julie of the Wolves. l.t. ed. 2004. (Beeler Mystery Ser.). 32.95 *(978-1-58118-121-0(3))* LRS.

Gibbs, Dreene. Am I Pretty, Momma? 2nd l.t. ed. 2004. (Illus.). 32p. (J). bds. 12.95 *(978-0-9741406-1-2(9)*, 0138) Cranberry Quill Publishing Co.

Giunta, Brian. The Seven Presidents. Chapin, Patrick O., illus. l.t. ed. 2003. 24p. (J). 8.95 *(978-1-58597-172-5(3))* Leathers Publishing.

Golden Eagle Productions Staff. Grandmother Moon & Sammy the Loon, 36 vols. l.t. ed. 2003. (Illus.). 24p. per. 12.99 *(978-1-932338-24-9(1))* Lifevest Publishing, Inc.

Goldish, Meish. How Many Are Here? Meyerhoff, Jill, illus. l.t. ed. 2005. (Sadlier Phonics Reading Program). 8p. (gr. -1-1). 23.00 net. *(978-0-8215-7344-0(6))* Sadlier, William H. Inc.

—Nice Vine, Quite Fine, Vol. 2. Sargent, Claudia Karabaic, illus. l.t. ed. 2005. (Little Books & Big Books: Vol. 7). 8p. (gr. k-2). 23.00 net. *(978-0-8215-7516-1(3))* Sadlier, William H. Inc.

—Zack Can Fix It!, Vol. 4. Scruton, Clive, illus. l.t. ed. 2005. (Sadlier Phonics Reading Program). 8p. (gr. -1-1). 23.00 net. *(978-0-8215-7359-4(4))* Sadlier, William H. Inc.

Gonzalez, David J. There Are No Space Aliens! 12 Biblical Points Disproving Space Aliens. l.t. ed. 2003. 48p. 9.95 *(978-0-9741561-0-1(8))* Gonzalez, David J. Ministries.

Goodwin, Carol. Does This Belong Here? A Twiggyleaf Adventure. McDaniel, Thomas, illus. l.t. ed. 2003. 32p. (J). 14.95 *(978-0-9741072-1-9(2))* CornerWind Media, L.L.C.

—The Great Acorn: A Twiggyleaf Adventure. McDaniel, Thomas, illus. l.t. ed. 2004. 32p. (J). 14.95 *(978-0-9741072-2-6(0))* CornerWind Media, L.L.C.

—Tippy Needs A Home: A Twiggyleaf Adventure. McDaniel, Thomas, illus. l.t. ed. 2003. 32p. (J). per. 14.95 *(978-0-09-741072-2(1))* CornerWind Media, L.L.C.

—What's the Hurry, Furry? A Twiggyleaf Adventure. McDaniel, Thomas, illus. l.t. ed. 2003. 32p. (J). 14.95 *(978-0-9741072-0-2(4))* CornerWind Media, L.L.C.

Gorgas, Paula Blais. Little Lost Leprechaun. Taylor, Chet, illus. l.t. ed. 2005. 20p. (J). 17.99 *(978-0-9755888-4-0(2))* Dragonfly Publishing, Inc.

Gould, Carol. My Native American School. Drzewiecki, Paul, illus. l.t. ed. 2003. (ENG.). 16p. (gr. k-2). pap. 7.95 *(978-1-879835-77-1(0)*, Kaeden Bks.) Kaeden Corp.

Grandma Janet Mary. Grandma's Treasure Chest. Pennington, Craig, illus. l.t. ed. 2005. (Grandma Janet Mary Ser.). 50p. (J). 16.95 *(978-0-9742732-3-5(6))* My Grandma & Me Pubs.

Graziani, Maria. The Adventures of Valeria Veterinarian: Las Aventuras de Valeria Veterinaria, 1. Elejalde, Eliana, illus. l.t. ed. 2004. (SPA.). 23p. (J). 7.00 *(978-0-9762361-0-8(9))* Ed. Acespanish S.A.C.- Lima, Peru.

—A Black Cat on Halloween: Un Gato Negro en Dia de Brujas. Elejalde, Eliana, illus. l.t. ed. 2004. (SPA.). 23p. (J). 7.00 *(978-0-9762361-1-5(7))* Ed. Acespanish S.A.C.- Lima, Peru.

Greendyk, William, tr. from ENG. Las Doce Historias de la Tía Margarita. l.t. ed. 2004. Orig. Title: Aunt Margaret's Twelve Stories. (SPA.). 84p. (J). pap. 3.99 *(978-1-932789-00-3(6)*, X001N) Editorial Sendas Antiguas, LLC.

—Los DOS Osos. l.t. ed. 2004. (SPA.). 152p. (J). pap. 5.99 *(978-1-932789-02-7(2)*, R009N) Editorial Sendas Antiguas, LLC.

—La Hierba Mala. l.t. ed. 2004.Tr. of Hierba Mala. (SPA.). 156p. (J). pap. 5.99 *(978-1-932789-01-0(4)*, X002N) Editorial Sendas Antiguas, LLC.

—El Hijo de la Viuda. l.t. ed. 2004. Orig. Title: The Widow's Son. (SPA., Illus.). 92p. (J). pap. *(978-1-932789-11-9(1))* Editorial Sendas Antiguas, LLC.

—Los Niños de la Biblia. l.t. ed. 2004. (SPA.). 94p. (J). pap. 3.99 *(978-1-932789-03-4(0)*, X003N) Editorial Sendas Antiguas, LLC.

—Primeras Impresiones de Dios. l.t. ed. 2004.Tr. of Primeras Impresiones de Dios. (SPA.). 94p. (J). pap. 3.99 *(978-1-932789-04-1(9)*, W001N) Editorial Sendas Antiguas, LLC.

Gremila, Elaine Demetri. Seasons of the Heart. l.t. ed. 2003. (Illus.). 140p. per. 11.95 *(978-1-932338-16-4(0))* Lifevest Publishing, Inc.

Grimm, Jacob & Grimm, Wilhelm K. Grimm's Fairy Tales. l.t. ed. 2004. (Large Print Ser.). 477p. 26.00 *(978-1-58287-627-6(4))* North Bks.

Hairston, Angelica. Did Noah Have Whales on the Ark? Ferguson, Tamara, illus. l.t. ed. 2004. 44p. (J). *(978-0-9716136-1-4(3))* Broadcast Quality Productions, Inc.

Hall / Waltz. Mortimer Jones: The Bubble Gum Nerd, 1. l.t. ed. 2003. (Illus.). 32p. 19.95 *(978-0-9741774-2-7(3))* D. W. Publishing.

Hall, Nancy R. My Grandparents Live in an RV Hall, Nancy R., illus. l.t. ed. 2005. (Illus.). 32p. (J). 16.95 *(978-0-9761759-0-2(8))* Jasnans Publishing Co.

Halse Anderson, Laurie. Chains. l.t. ed. 2009. (ENG.). 390p. (YA). 23.95 *(978-1-4104-1425-0(6))* Thorndike Pr.

Hamilton, Elizabeth L. Katie Kangaroo's Leap of Courage. l.t. ed. 2005. (Character Critters Ser.: No. 9). (Illus.). 32p. (J). per. 5.95 *(978-0-9754629-6-6(2)*, Character-in-Action) Quiet Impact, Inc.

—Ricky Raccoon's Trustworthiness Tree. l.t. ed. 2005. (Character Critters Ser.: No. 11). (Illus.). 32p. (J). per. 5.95 *(978-0-9754629-8-0(9)*, Character-in-Action) Quiet Impact, Inc.

Hamilton, Patricia Birdsong & Scripts Publishing Staff. What's Up: William Explains Ataxia to His New Friends. l.t. ed. 2005. (Ataxia: A Lifestyle Change). 44p. 18.95 *(978-1-889826-90-5(1))* Scripts Publishing.

Hamilton, Virginia. M. C. Higgins, the Great. 2006. 271p. (gr. 8-12). 18.00 *(978-0-7569-6809-0(7))* Perfection Learning Corp.

—M. C. Higgins, the Great. 2006. (ENG., Illus.). 288p. (J). (gr. 3-7). pap. 7.99 *(978-1-4169-1407-5(2)*, Aladdin) Simon & Schuster Children's Publishing.

Hampton, Randall. A Christmas Kiss. l.t. ed. 2005. (Illus.). 48p. (J). per. 16.95 *(978-1-59879-048-1(X))* Lifevest Publishing, Inc.

Handford, S. A. Aesop's Fables. Winter, Nilo, illus. l.t. ed. Date not set. (J). (gr. 1-12). lib. bdg. 22.95 *(978-0-88411-991-3(2))* Amereon Ltd.

Hanna, James Milton, Sr. Once upon a Time in the South. l.t. ed. 2004. (Illus.). 235p. per. 12.95 *(978-1-930052-15-4(4))* Cherokee Bks.

Hanson, Paige & Hanson, Jon. Harry Spotter: The Incontinent Puppy Sellers, Amy, illus. l.t. ed. 2005. 44p. (J). per. 20.00 *(978-0-9721146-1-5(0))* Monroe Educational Media.

Harbo, Gary. The Northern Woods Adventure: Early Reader. Harbo, Gary, illus. l.t. ed. 2004. (If You Want to Succeed, You Need to Read! Ser.: 6). (ENG., Illus.). 33p. (J). 10.95 *(978-1-884149-16-0(2))* Kutie Kari Bks., Inc.

Harkes, Willy. Little Dutch Girl in World War II. Blair, Jocelyn, illus. l.t. ed. 2004. 22p. (J). pap. 13.95 *(978-0-9741627-1-3(X))* PricePoint+Publications.

Harper, Stephan J. The Black Sheep Beach, Mary FitzGerald, illus. l.t. ed. 2005. 32p. (J). lib. bdg. 16.95 *(978-0-9741800-1-4(7))* Inspire Press, Inc.

Haworth, Margaret. Jarry, Garry Palas: Cat Tail Stories. Haworth, Margaret, photos by. l.t. ed. 2003. (Books That Help Ser.: Vol. 3). (Illus.). 34p. (J). (gr. 1-6). pap. 9.95 *(978-0-9740313-5-4(6))* Haworth, Margaret.

Hawthorne, Nathanial. A Wonder Book & Tanglewood Tales. l.t. ed. 2004. (Large Print Ser.). 563p. 26.00 *(978-1-58287-673-3(8))* North Bks.

Hazelton, Jack W. Charlie Duck. Hazelton, Jack W., illus. l.t. ed. 2003. (Illus.). 24p. (J). 12.95 *(978-1-928907-54-1(7))* Jack's Bookshelf, Inc.

Hein, Connie L. Toliver in Time; for a Journey West: History in a Nutshell. Theobald, Denise, illus. l.t. ed. 2005. 28p. (J). lib. bdg. 17.95 *(978-0-9740855-6-2(1))*; per. 9.95 *(978-0-9740855-7-9(X))* Still Water Publishing.

Heller, Andrew. No Bones about It. Rene, Perez, illus. l.t. ed. 2003. 12p. (J). 7.99 *(978-0-9722038-5-2(0))* Mr Do It All, Inc.

Heller, Ruth. Nous Ne Sommes Pas Nes/Oeuf! l.t. ed. (FRE., Illus.). (J). bds. 29.99 *(978-0-590-73029-7(0))* Scholastic, Inc.

Henderson, Tim. Butterflies & Magic Dreams. Hansen, Melissa, illus. l.t. ed. 2003. 28p. (J). *(978-0-9728691-0-2(7))* Logan Bks.

Henny, Rose. Teddy Finds His Way: A Teddy Tale. Henny, Rose, illus. l.t. ed. 2005. (Illus.). 22p. (J). per. 17.95 *(978-0-9705458-7-9(8))* Royalty Bks. International, Inc.

Hensley, Sarah M. Caillou Visits the Circus. Storch, Ellen N., illus. l.t. ed. 2005. (HRL Board Book Ser.). (J). (gr. -1-k). pap. 10.95 *(978-1-57332-309-3(8)*, HighReach Learning, Incorporated) Carson-Dellosa Publishing, LLC.

Herron, Carolivia, photos by & told to. Little Georgia & the Apples: A Retelling of Aunt Georgia's First Catalpa Tale Herron, Carolivia, told to. l.t. ed. 2004. (Illus.). 33p. (J). 10.00 *(978-0-9760222-0-6(6)*, Catalpa01) Epicenter Literary Software.

Heyman, Carly. My Extra Special Brother: How to Love, Understand, & Celebrate Your Sibling with Special Needs. Conley, Stephanie, illus. l.t. ed. 2003. 112p. pap. 12.95 *(978-0-9727865-0-8(3)*, 1003894) Fragile X Assn. of Georgia.

Hill, Grace Livingston. Cloudy Jewel. (J). reprint ed. lib. bdg. 24.95 *(978-0-89190-037-5(3)*, Rivercity Pr.) Amereon Ltd.

Hiris, Monica. Just Like Dad. Drzewiecki, Paul, illus. l.t. ed. 2003. (ENG.). 8p. (gr. k-1). pap. 7.95 *(978-1-879835-76-4(2)*, Kaeden Bks.) Kaeden Corp.

—Sleepy Polar Bear. Harston, Jerry, illus. l.t. ed. 2006. (ENG.). 24p. (gr. k-2). pap. 8.95 *(978-1-57874-072-7(X)*, Kaeden Bks.) Kaeden Corp.

Hoban, Russell. A Bargain for Frances. Hoban, Lillian, illus. l.t. ed. 2003. (I Can Read Level 2 Ser.). (ENG.). 64p. (J). (gr. k-3). pap. 4.99 *(978-0-06-444001-1(X)*, HarperCollins) HarperCollins Pubs.

Hock, Dan. The Birthday Bash 2 vols. An Iggy & Igor Mystery (#2) Hock, Dan, illus. l.t. ed. 2004. (Illus.). 51p. (J). per. 4.99 *(978-0-9754046-1-4(X))* Anticipation Pr.

Hoenecke, Karen. Little Mouse. Gedeon, Gloria, illus. l.t. ed. 2005. (ENG.). 12p. (gr. k-2). pap. 7.95 *(978-1-57874-023-9(1)*, Kaeden Bks.) Kaeden Corp.

—Snake Hunts for Lunch. Drzewiecki, Paul, illus. l.t. ed. 2005. (ENG.). 12p. (gr. k-2). pap. 7.95 *(978-1-57874-006-2(1)*, Kaeden Bks.) Kaeden Corp.

Hollaway, David. Quigley Mccormick: And the Curse of the Polka Dotted Pig, 3 vols. l.t. ed. 2005. (Illus.). 156p. (J). (gr. -1-3). per. 15.95 *(978-1-933211-54-1(7))* Quackenworth Publishing.

Holofcener, Mark. Evan's Earthly Adventure. l.t. ed. 2003. (Illus.). 202p. (YA). mass mkt. 11.00 *(978-0-9718626-1-6(3))* Holofcener, Mark.

Hood, Karen Jean Matsko. Washington State: Activity & Coloring Book. l.t. ed. 2014. (Educational Activity & Coloring Book Ser.). (J). 19.95 *(978-1-930948-56-3(5))* Whispering Pine Pr. International, Inc.

Hooker, Karen. Camping. Biddle, Bruce, illus. l.t. ed. 2003. (ENG.). 16p. (gr. k-1). pap. 7.95 *(978-1-879835-32-0(0)*, Kaeden Bks.) Kaeden Corp.

Hooker, Lou. The Year of the Fire. l.t. ed. 2004. (Illus.). 102p. (J). pap. 8.95 *(978-0-9755106-0-5(6))* Hooker, Lou.

Horowitz, Alena Netia. The Tlyltetflym Tree. Horowitz, Alena Netia & De La Fuente, Mary, illus. l.t. ed. 2003. 64p. (J). per. 12.95 *(978-0-923550-42-4(9))* Tetrahedron Publishing LLC.

Hortten, Jacqueline Faye. Pu Beach. l.t. ed. 2004. (Illus.). 27p. (J). pap. 14.95 *(978-0-9728393-0-3(5))* Children's Bookshoppe Stop, The.

House, Darrell. Miller the Green Caterpillar. Argoff, Patti, illus. l.t. ed. 2005. 32p. 16.95 *(978-0-9663276-9-4(1))* Red Engine Pr.

Howard-Parham, Pam. Caillou Finds Colors. Gillen, Lisa P., illus. l.t. ed. 2005. (HRL Board Book Ser.). (J). (gr. -1-k). bds. 10.95 *(978-1-57332-313-0(6)*, HighReach Learning, Incorporated) Carson-Dellosa Publishing, LLC.

—This Is Farmer Greg. Coates, Jennifer, illus. l.t. ed. 2005. (HRL Board Book Ser.). (gr. -1-k). pap. 10.95 *(978-1-57332-305-5(5)*, HighReach Learning, Incorporated) Carson-Dellosa Publishing, LLC.

Hugh Granville Tilley North Carolina House of Representatives 1887 And 1889, 1 book. l.t. ed. 2007. (ENG., Illus.). 50p. lib. bdg. 36.99 *(978-0-9722724-3-8(7))* Blackfoot Burkino Cherokee Publishing.

Hunter, Erin. The Quest Begins. l.t. ed. 2008. (Seekers Ser.: No. 1). 372p. (J). pap. 16.99 *(978-0-06-170951-7(4))* HarperCollins Pubs.

Hunter, Julius K. Absurd Alphabedtime Stories. Bauman, Todd, illus. 2nd rev. l.t. ed. 2004. 32p. (J). 16.95 *(978-0-9761422-0-1(1))* J.K.H. Enterprises.

The Incarnation of Christ: Immanuel l.t. ed. 2004. (CHI., Illus.). 52p. (J). *(978-0-9752775-0-8(2)*, 0-9752775-0-2) Unitrust Design.

Jackson, Vicky, illus. Poepal's Purpose. l.t. ed. 2005. 20p. (J). 7.95 *(978-0-9718741-0-7(7))* Tawa Productions.

Jacques, Brian. Triss. l.t. ed. 2004. (Redwall Ser.). 596p. (J). 23.95 *(978-0-7862-6207-6(9))* Thorndike Pr.

Jarrell, Pamela R. Caillou's Musical Band. Gray, Stacy A., illus. l.t. ed. 2005. (HRL Board Book Ser.). (J). (gr. -1-k). 10.95 *(978-1-57332-311-6(X)*, HighReach Learning, Incorporated) Carson-Dellosa Publishing, LLC.

Jauregui, Patricia. Sentimientos. Jauregui, Reginald, ed. Pineda, Jesus, illus. l.t. ed. 2004. (SPA.). 39p. (YA). pap. 19.95 *(978-1-931481-41-0(5))* LiArt-Literature & Art.

Jax, T. L. Fraidy-Frieda's Light Show. Jax, T. L., illus. l.t. ed. 2004. (Illus.). 30p. (J). 9.95 *(978-0-9743890-2-8(1))* Flaxenfluff Pr., LLC.

Johnson, Nevlynn L., Sr. Faith, Courage & Wisdom: A Journey to Manhood. 3rd rev. l.t. ed. 2003. Orig. Title: Finding My Way: a Journey to Manhood. 240p. per. 14.95 *(978-0-9741413-0-5(5))* Lone Cypress Pubs.

Johnson, Sandi & Fefie, Flora. Zemo to the Rescue: Dorp 7 Rock Band. l.t. ed. 2003. (Illus.). 15p. (J). (gr. k-5). spiral bd. 4.99 *(978-1-929063-25-3(3)*, 327) Moons & Stars Publishing For Children.

Jones, David C. One Person to Another: Smoking, Chewing Tobacco & Young Peopole. l.t. ed. 2003. 20p. (YA). 4.00 *(978-1-878400-17-8(7))* Dolphin Publishing.

Jones, Julie. The Problem at Pepperpine Zoo. Jones, Julie., illus. l.t. ed. 2004. (Illus.). 24p. (J). pap. 7.95 *(978-0-9745553-0-0(4))* Greenwood Street Publishing. GSP.

Jougla, Frederic. Tricked on Halloween: Rina & Jax's Stories. Jougla, Karina, illus. l.t. ed. 2004. 36p. (J). bds. 14.99 *(978-0-9754287-0-2(5))* Imagery Pr.

Kassandra, ed. V antologia nuevo Milenio: Narración (Cuentos) y Poesía. Ramírez, Antonio & Morrissey, Kay, photos by. l.t. ed. 2004. (SPA., Illus.). 100p. (YA). pap. 12.00 *(978-1-931481-86-1(5))* LiArt-Literature & Art.

Keaster, Diane W. Darby - the Cow Dog, 9 vols. Page, Debbie et al, illus. l.t. ed. 2005. (ZC Horses: 9). (ENG.). 68p. (J). per. 7.95 *(978-0-9721496-8-6(6))* ZC Horses Series of Children's Bks.

—Goldie - the Wise, 25 vols. Page, Debbie, illus. l.t. ed. 2004. (ZC Horses: 7). (ENG.). 87p. (J). per. 7.95 *(978-0-9721496-6-2(X))* ZC Horses Series of Children's Bks.

—Leroy - the Stallion, 25 vols. Page, Debbie, illus. l.t. ed. 2003. (ZC Horses: 6). (ENG.). 79p. (J). per. 7.95 *(978-0-9721496-5-5(1))* ZC Horses Series of Children's Bks.

Keller, Rebecca W. Real Science-4-Kids Chemistry Level I Student Textbook. l.t. ed. 2005. (Real Science-4-Kids Ser.). (ENG., Illus.). 64p. (gr. 3-6). 32.95 *(978-0-9749149-0-9(8))* Gravitas Pubns., Inc.

Ketchum, Ron, illus. Rochestrivia: 2,000 Amazing questions & answers all about Rochester NY, it's people & surrounding Towns. l.t. ed. 2005. 250p. per. 19.95 *(978-0-930249-01-4(1))* LL Cameron Group, LLC.

Keyes, Eric, 3rd, et al. The Light in the Dark, 1. Marie, Paula Braxton, illus. l.t. ed. 2004. (ENG.). 40p. (J). pap. 14.99 *(978-0-9722795-5-0(5))*, Highest Good Pubns.) GEM Bk. Club.

Kitze, Carrie A. We See the Moon. Jinshan Painting Academy, illus. l.t. ed. 2003. 32p. (J). (gr. -1-3). 16.95 *(978-0-9726244-0-4(6))* EMK Pr.

Knapp, Susan. Bells Goes to the Fair. Whitehurst, John et al, illus. l.t. ed. 2003. 40p. (J). (gr. -1-3). 12.95 *(978-1-888223-34-7(0))* McMillen Publishing.

Krinard, Susan. Dark of the Moon. l.t. ed. 2008. 475p. (J). 23.95 *(978-1-4104-0956-0(2))* Thorndike Pr.

Kurz, Ron. The Inner Music Experience. l.t. ed. 2003. 124p. (YA). 75.00 *(978-0-939829-07-1(X)*, Item#3) Kurz, Ron.

Lang, Andrew, ed. The Lilac Fairy Book. l.t. ed. 2004. (Large Print Ser.). lib. bdg. 26.00 *(978-1-58287-778-5(5))* North Bks.

—The Pink Fairy Book. l.t. ed. 2004. (Large Print Ser.). lib. bdg. 26.00 *(978-1-58287-781-5(5))* North Bks.

Larson, Eric. How Did Carpet Get in This House? Burns, William G., ed. l.t. ed. 2003. (Illus.). 62p. (YA). (gr. 4-7). pap. *(978-0-9673696-2-4(2))* Caliber Pubns.

Lawrence, Ava. A Button for a Crown. Ford, Christina, illus. l.t. ed. 2003. 84p. (J). 14.95 *(978-0-9651048-4-5(2))* Papillon Publishing.

Layne, Carmela C. I See Many Colors Around My House: Los Colores que Veo Por Mi Casa. Layne, Carmela C., ed. Arevalo, Jose Daniel, illus. l.t. ed. 2005. (SPA.). 24p. (J). (gr. -1-3). pap. 6.95 *(978-0-9769538-0-7(3))* Pannycake Pubn.

Layos, Alexandra. An Almost True Horse Tale. Bauer, Dana, illus. l.t. ed. 2003. 20p. (J). (gr. 1-5). pap. 8.95 *(978-0-9655501-3-0(3))* Saddle & Bridle, Inc.

LeGrand, Hank, 3rd. Paddle Tail. Merrison, Stacy, illus. l.t. ed. 2004. 63p. (J). per. 7.95 *(978-1-59466-020-7(4)*, Growing Years) Port Town Publishing.

Levine, Gail Carson. Ella Enchanted. 2008. (J). 39.99 *(978-0-7393-7107-7(X))* Findaway World, LLC.

—Ever. 2011. (ENG.). 272p. (J). (gr. 3-7). pap. 7.99 *(978-0-06-122964-0(4)*, HarperCollins) HarperCollins Pubs.

Li, Deborah, illus. Tricia & the Blue Cap. l.t. ed. 2003. 28p. (J). 7.95 net. *(978-0-9706654-5-4(8))* Sprite Pr.

Likins, Kim. Charlie's Perfect Day. Magalinska, Ingrid, illus. l.t. ed. 2003. 32p. (J). bds. *(978-0-9729987-0-3(5))* Island Friends LLC.

Looper, Grace W. Molasses Making Time. l.t. ed. 2004. 152p. (YA). pap. 8.95 *(978-0-9747685-5-7(3))* Bella Rosa Bks.

Loper, Kathleen. Angelina Katrina: Bugs in My Backyard. Waltz, Dan, illus. l.t. ed. 2004. 24p. (J). 17.95 *(978-0-9741774-4-1(X))* D. W. Publishing.

—Angelina Katrina: Builds Troy Snowman. Waltz, Dan, illus. l.t. ed. 2004. 36p. (J). 17.95 *(978-0-9741774-5-8(8))* D. W. Publishing.

Louthain, J. A. Ame the Elephant: Terrorized by Evil Mice. Eberbach, Andrea, illus. 2nd l.t. ed. 2003. 48p. (J). 12.97 *(978-0-9679416-2-2(8)*, 0-9679416-2-8) Alexie Bks.

Lowes, Tom, illus. Casey's Four Holiday Celebrations. l.t. ed. 2003. 38p. (J). 16.95 *(978-0-9722099-9-1(9)*, C4HC) Caseys World Bks.

Lu, Marie. Champion: A Legend Novel. 2014. (Legend Ser.: 3). (ENG.). 416p. (YA). (gr. 7). pap. 12.99 *(978-0-14-751228-4(X)*, Speak) Penguin Young Readers Group.

Lucado, Max. The Handi-Size Giant Print Bible. l.t. ed. 2013. (ENG.). 1776p. (gr. 12). 2.99 *(978-0-529-10169-3(6)*, HG50BL); 2.99 *(978-0-529-10170-9(X)*, HG50BL-I) HarperChristian Resources.

Lyford, Cabot. Arthur the Moose. Lyford, Cabot, illus. l.t. ed. 2004. (Illus.). 32p. (J). lib. bdg. *(978-0-9748145-0-6(4))* Castlebay, Inc.

Mabie, Hamilton Wright. Heroes Every Child Should Know. l.t. ed. 2006. (ENG.). 258p. pap. 23.99 *(978-1-4264-1445-9(5))* Creative Media Partners, LLC.

MacCoon, Nancy. Backyard Wonders. Watkins, Courtney, illus. l.t. ed. 2003. 38p. (J). pap. 14.95 *(978-0-9742495-0-6(5))* Vibatorium LLC.

Mackenzie, Carin. David el Luchador Valiente Foce, Natalia, tr. Apps, Fred, illus. l.t. ed. 2004. (Biblewise Ser.). (SPA.). 32p. (J). pap. 4.50 *(978-1-932789-18-8(9)*, bd04170e-10f9-4622-9342-cefa1ae482f9, CF4Kids) Christian Focus Pubns. GBR. Dist: Baker & Taylor Publisher Services (BTPS).

Mackenzie, Carine. Daniel, el Príncipe que Oraba Foce, Natalia, tr. Apps, Fred, illus. l.t. ed. 2004. (Biblewise Ser.). (SPA.). 32p. (J). pap. 4.50 *(978-1-932789-19-5(7)*, 1434af2d-43fa-41db-bc9e-13acdb88436d, CF4Kids) Christian Focus Pubns. GBR. Dist: Baker & Taylor Publisher Services (BTPS).

—La Historia de Pablo — Viajes de Aventura, 1. Foce, Natalia, tr. Apps, Fred, illus. l.t. ed. 2004. (Biblewise Ser.). Orig. Title: Journeys of Adventure — the Story of Paul. (SPA.). 32p. (J). pap. 4.50 *(978-1-932789-23-2(5)*, efac6dff-4e7f-4558-9d9d-e2637b85f563, CF4Kids) Christian Focus Pubns. GBR. Dist: Baker & Taylor Publisher Services (BTPS).

—Jose el Sonador de Dios Foce, Natalia, tr. Apps, Fred, illus. l.t. ed. 2004. (Biblewise Ser.). (SPA.). 32p. (J). pap. 4.50 *(978-1-932789-16-4(2)*, 45545360-0975-4e2b-93f4-605e93caf8c0, CF4Kids) Christian Focus Pubns. GBR. Dist: Baker & Taylor Publisher Services (BTPS).

—El Nacimiento de Jesús: El Niño Prometido, 1. Foce, Natalia, tr. Apps, Fred, illus. l.t. ed. 2004. (Biblewise Ser.). Orig. Title: The Birth of Jesus — the Promised Child. (SPA.). 32p. (J). pap. 4.50 *(978-1-932789-20-1(0)*, f4652f8c-e9f5-4524-a9d9-78b84dc0b3bb, CF4Kids) Christian Focus Pubns. GBR. Dist: Baker & Taylor Publisher Services (BTPS).

—El Plan de Rescate: La Historia de Noe, 1. Foce, Natalia, tr. Apps, Fred, illus. l.t. ed. 2004. (Biblewise Ser.). Orig. Title: The Rescue Plan. (SPA.). 32p. (J). pap. 4.50 *(978-1-932789-15-7(4)*, 4c0355ad-bd8f-4f33-abfe-1edc64f1ecef, CF4Kids) Christian Focus Pubns. GBR. Dist: Baker & Taylor Publisher Services (BTPS).

—La Resurrección: Jesús Está Vivo, 1. Foce, Natalia, tr. Apps, Fred, illus. l.t. ed. 2004. (Biblewise Ser.). Orig. Title: The Resurrection — Jesus Is Alive. (SPA.). 32p. (J). pap. 4.50 *(978-1-932789-21-8(9)*, dc3ffeed-60b5-4a2d-b0e4-8f6331fa9528, CF4Kids) Christian Focus Pubns. GBR. Dist: Baker & Taylor Publisher Services (BTPS).

—Samuel, el Niño que Escuchaba. Foce, Natalia, tr. Apps, Fred, illus. l.t. ed. 2004. (Biblewise Ser.). (SPA.). 32p. (J). pap. 4.50 *(978-1-932789-17-1(0)*, f2437bbe-4496-4d7f-b872-9ab2be341cfc, CF4Kids) Christian Focus Pubns. GBR. Dist: Baker & Taylor Publisher Services (BTPS).

—Saúl — el Milagro en el Camino, 1. Foce, Natalia, tr. Apps, Fred, illus. l.t. ed. 2004. (Biblewise Ser.). Orig. Title: Saul — the Miracle on the Road. (SPA.). 32p. (J). pap. 4.50 *(978-1-932789-22-5(7)*, 989958f2-14a9-4571-8fbf-bbc02893e8b7, CF4Kids) Christian Focus Pubns. GBR. Dist: Baker & Taylor Publisher Services (BTPS).

Madame M. Trauma Queens/Trauma Kings. l.t. ed. 2003. (Madame M Presents:). (Illus.). 68p. (YA). per. 15.95 *(978-0-9704159-3-6(1)*, 0970415931) Creepy Little Productions.

Mader, Jan. My Brother Wants to Be Like Me. Palmer, Kate Salley, illus. l.t. ed. 2005. (ENG.). 16p. (gr. k-2). pap. 7.95 *(978-1-879835-27-6(4)*, Kaeden Bks.) Kaeden Corp.

Madison, Ron. Ned Learns to Say No: A Lesson about Drugs. Covolo, David, illus. l.t. ed. 2003. (Health & Safety Ser.). 24p. pap. 4.95 *(978-1-887206-23-5(X))* Ned's Head Productions.

Magi, Aria. The Lulilites: And the Star of Seven Rays. l.t. ed. 2005. (Illus.). 34p. (J). (gr. -1-3). 19.95 *(978-0-9759631-0-4(4))* Lulilite Productions.

Magnus, Kellie. Little Lion Goes to School. Robinson, Michael, illus. l.t. ed. 2003. 16p. (J). 9.99 *(978-0-9744211-0-0(3))* Media Magic New York.

Mandala Publishing, Mandala. Jagannatha. l.t. ed. 2007. (ENG., Illus.). 32p. (J). 6.95 *(978-0-945475-29-3(2)*, 1203) Mandala Publishing.

Mandracchia, Charles, creator. A Wacky Wonder World. l.t. ed. 2005. (Illus.). 24p. (J). 13.95 *(978-0-9721957-1-3(8))* Mandracchia, Charles.

Mankamyer, Laura. The Adventures of the Stonycreek Gang. Mankamyer, Laura, illus. l.t. ed. 2003. (Illus.). 84p. (J). 12.99 *(978-0-9728431-4-0(0))* Mankamyer, Laura.

Marek, Catherine. Sara's 1st Haircut Mitchell, Hazel, illus. l.t. ed. 2007. (ENG.). 32p. (J). (gr. -1-3). per. *(978-0-9748251-3-7(1))* Zoe Life Christian Communications.

Marjorie, as told by. A Flower Unfolds: Inspirational Teachings in Verse from Kwan Yin, Bodhisattva of Mercy & Compassion. l.t. ed. 2003. (Illus.). 52p. 12.95 *(978-0-9745712-0-1(2))* Sun Sprite Publishing.

Markarian, Marianne. The Pesky Bird Wasielewski, Margaret M., illus. l.t. ed. 2005. 32p. (J). 16.00 *(978-0-9767377-0-4(1))* Pomegranate Publishing.

Marrero, Rafelito. Amar sin decir Nada. 1000th l.t. ed. 2003. 137p. per. 14.95 net. *(978-0-9747569-0-5(3))* Marrero, Rafael.

Marrs, Christie, creator. The Perfect Gift: I B Hoofinit's Horse Tales. l.t. ed. 2004. (Illus.). 57p. (J). mass mkt. 5.99 *(978-1-928890-19-5(9))* I. B. Hoofinit Co.

Martin, Oscar, Jr., creator. Birth of Jesus l.t. ed. 2003. (Illus.). 25p. (J). E-Book 19.95 incl. cd-rom *(978-0-9748416-4-9(1))* Build Your Story.

—Civil Rights Leaders. l.t. ed. 2004. (Illus.). 25p. (J). E-Book 19.95 incl. cd-rom *(978-0-9748416-9-4(2))* Build Your Story.

—The Creation Story l.t. ed. 2003. (Illus.). 25p. (J). E-Book 19.95 incl. cd-rom *(978-0-9748416-0-1(9))* Build Your Story.

—David & Goliath l.t. ed. 2003. (Illus.). 25p. (J). E-Book 19.95 incl. cd-rom *(978-0-9748416-3-2(3))* Build Your Story.

—Doctors l.t. ed. 2003. (Illus.). 25p. (J). E-Book 19.95 incl. cd-rom *(978-0-9748416-5-6(X))* Build Your Story.

—Famous Women l.t. ed. 2003. (Illus.). 25p. (J). E-Book 19.95 incl. cd-rom *(978-0-9748416-8-7(4))* Build Your Story.

—History of Music l.t. ed. 2003. (Illus.). 25p. (J). E-Book 19.95 incl. cd-rom *(978-0-9748416-7-0(6))* Build Your Story.

—Noah l.t. ed. 2003. (Illus.). 25p. (J). E-Book 19.95 incl. cd-rom *(978-0-9748416-1-8(7))* Build Your Story.

—Sports Legends l.t. ed. 2003. (Illus.). 25p. (J). E-Book 19.95 incl. cd-rom *(978-0-9748416-6-3(8))* Build Your Story.

—The Story of Moses l.t. ed. 2003. (Illus.). 25p. (J). E-Book 19.95 incl. cd-rom *(978-0-9748416-2-5(5))* Build Your Story.

Martin, Tyler. I Have a Question, Vol. 4. Williams, Toby, illus. l.t. ed. 2005. (Sadlier Phonics Reading Program). 8p. (gr. -1-1). 23.00 net. *(978-0-8215-7356-3(X))* Sadlier, William H. Inc.

Martinucci, Suzanne. At Space Camp, Vol. 2. l.t. ed. 2005. (Little Books & Big Bks.: Vol. 6). (Illus.). 8p. (gr. k-2). 23.00 net. *(978-0-8215-7515-4(5))* Sadlier, William H. Inc.

Matson, Laurie. Jaz-O & 'G' in Key West. Matson, Laurie, illus. l.t. ed. 2003. (Illus.). (J). 4.95 *(978-0-9673704-5-3(0))* Seastory Pr.

McCloskey, Robert. Homer Price. l.t. ed. (J). (gr. 4-6). reprint ed. 10.00 *(978-0-89064-072-2(6))* National Assn. for Visually Handicapped.

McGovern, Sheila. The Entire World of S & Z Book of Stories: 58 Targeted S & Z Pure Stories to Remediate Frontal & Lateral Lisps. l.t. ed. 2003. (Illus.). 148p. per. 34.99 *(978-0-9723457-5-0(2))* Say It Right.

McHaney, Eric & McHaney, Mandy. Rich the Itch. Smith, Jordyn, illus. l.t. ed. 2005. 20p. (J). *(978-0-9769086-0-9(3))* RTI Publishing, LLC.

McKee, Ruby. The Land of Phonicia: An Enchanted Tale to Learn Phonics. Allen, Timothy, illus. l.t. ed. 2003. 52p. (J). per. 39.95 *(978-0-9744944-0-1(2))* Jewel Publishing.

Mears, Richard Chase. Saint Nick & the Space Nicks. Westerfield, William Stephen, illus. l.t. ed. 2004. 32p. (J). 16.95 *(978-0-9754056-0-4(8))* Tuxedo Blue, LLC.

Mecham, Janeal A. Christmas Gifts. Mecham, Janeal A., illus. l.t. unabr. ed. 2003. (Illus.). 32p. (J). (gr. k-3). 12.95 *(978-1-932280-16-6(2)*, 80162) Granite Publishing & Distribution.

Messinger, Robert M. & Messinger, Laura M. Why Me? Why Did I Have to Get Diabetes? l.t. ed. 2004. (Illus.). 64p. 12.95 *(978-1-893237-02-5(8))* Little Mai Pr.

Meyer, Kay L. The Adventures of Billie & Annie — Baby Bison. Kirchoff, Arthur, illus. l.t. ed. 2004. 32p. (J). 6.00 *(978-0-9744536-0-6(9)*, 9780974453606) Meyer, Tjaden.

Meyers, Susan A. Callie & the Stepmother. Gauss, Rose, illus. l.t. ed. 2005. (ENG.). 64p. (J). (gr. -1-3). pap. 6.95 *(978-0-9718348-0-4(6))* Blooming Tree Pr.

Michaels, David. Bye-Bye, Katy, Vol. 3. Platt, Pierre, illus. l.t. ed. 2005. (Sadlier Phonics Reading Program). 8p. (gr. -1-1). 23.00 net. *(978-0-8215-7354-9(3))* Sadlier, William H. Inc.

Michels, Dia L. Look What I See! Where Can I Be? With My Animal Friends. Bowles, Michael J. N., photos by. l.t. ed. 2005. (Look What I See! Where Can I Be? Ser.: 3). (Illus.). 32p. (J). (gr. -1-12). 9.95 *(978-1-930775-07-7(5))* Platypus Media, L.L.C.

Mike. Lemon Drop Rain: Poems & Drawings by Mr. Mike. Mike, illus. l.t. ed. 2003. (ENG., Illus.). 180p. (J). pap. 14.95 *(978-0-9658365-6-2(8))* Beetle Bug Bks.

—New Pet. Mike, illus. l.t. ed. 2005. (ENG., Illus.). 32p. (J). lib. bdg. 14.95 *(978-0-9658365-8-6(4))* Beetle Bug Bks.

Milano, Jacque. Stay-at-Home Hank: The Little Hummingbird That Couldn't Fly. Milano, Jacque, illus. l.t. ed. 2003. (Illus.). 30p. (J). 9.95 *(978-0-9728432-0-1(5))* Milano, Jacque & Assocs.

Miller, Kyle Linda. Dillo - A Baby Armadillo's Adventure on Sanibel Island. Eddy, Randon T., illus. l.t. ed. 2005. (ENG.). 64p. (J). 16.95 *(978-0-9769332-0-5(9))* Jungle Hse. Pubns.

Miller, Roger Carlton. The Ant & the Grasshopper l.t. ed. 2003. Orig. Title: Same. (Illus.). 14p. *(978-0-9712104-2-4(X))* Texas Woman's Univ. Pr.

Miranda, Anne. The Best Place. l.t. ed. 2005. (Little Books & Big Bks.: Vol. 5). (Illus.). 8p. (gr. k-2). 23.00 net. *(978-0-8215-7514-7(7))* Sadlier, William H. Inc.

—Looking at Lizards, Vol. 2. l.t. ed. 2005. (Sadlier Phonics Reading Program). (Illus.). 8p. (gr. -1-1). 23.00 net. *(978-0-8215-7346-4(2))* Sadlier, William H. Inc.

—Peach Tree Street, Vol. 2. Lodge, Katherine, illus. l.t. ed. 2005. (Little Books & Big Bks.: Vol. 10). 8p. (gr. k-2). 23.00 net. *(978-0-8215-7519-2(8))* Sadlier, William H. Inc.

—Weather Wise, Vol. 3. l.t. ed. 2005. (Sadlier Phonics Reading Program). (Illus.). 8p. (gr. -1-1). 23.00 net. *(978-0-8215-7351-8(9))* Sadlier, William H. Inc.

Modica, Cathy & Van Eyck, Laura. Niik & Bling: The Friendship Begins. Modica, Cathy, photos by. l.t. ed. 2005. (Illus.). 40p. (J). 19.95 *(978-0-9762466-0-2(0))* Wholesome Puppy Tales.

Moeckel, Christine. Dick the Duck. Moeckel, Christine, illus. l.t. ed. 2004. (Illus.). 31p. (J). spiral bd. 9.98 *(978-0-9720350-2-6(8))* Duckpond Publishing, Inc.

Moller, Jonathan R. Bath Time: Picture Book. l.t. ed. 2003. (Illus.). 71p. pap. 19.95 *(978-0-9740169-0-0(X))* Lemonflavor Productions.

Montgomery, L. M. Anne of Green Gables. l.t. ed. 2006. pap. *(978-1-4068-3174-0(3))* Echo Library.

—Anne of the Island. l.t. ed. 2006. (ENG.). pap. *(978-1-4068-3175-7(1))* Echo Library.

—Anne of the Island. l.t. ed. 2004. 396p. 26.00 *(978-1-58287-640-5(1))* North Bks.

Moore, Jim. The All Animal Band. Hall, Norris, illus. l.t. ed. 2004. 36p. (J). 16.00 *(978-0-9752619-0-3(8))* Animal Band Productions, Inc., The.

Mracek, Ann. Friendship Flies the Sun: The Ancient Egyptian Legend of Scarab Beetle. l.t. ed. 2005. (DAN., Illus.). 32p. (J). per. 15.99 *(978-0-9766488-0-2(6))* Mracek, Ann.

Mucha Aydlott, Julie A. My Favorite Time of Year. Mucha-Sullivan, Kalie A. & Mucha-Sullivan, Emily V., illus. l.t. ed. 2004. 22p. (J). 5.95 *(978-0-9746093-2-4(3))* JA Pubns., Ltd.

Mullican, Judy. My Toys. Bicking, Judith, illus. l.t. ed. 2005. (HRL Board Book Ser.). (J). (gr. -1-k). pap. 10.95 *(978-1-57332-307-9(1)*, HighReach Learning, Incorporated) Carson-Dellosa Publishing, LLC.

Mullican, Judy & Crowell, Knox. Caillou Finds Shapes. Gillen, Lisa P., illus. l.t. ed. 2005. (HRL Board Book Ser.). (J). (gr. -1-k). bds. 10.95 *(978-1-57332-312-3(8)*, HighReach Learning, Incorporated) Carson-Dellosa Publishing, LLC.

Mumaugh, Lene. Touch of Christmas. Skrbic, Melissa, illus. l.t. ed. 2003. 28p. per. 9.95 *(978-1-932344-19-6(5))* Thornton Publishing, Inc.

Murdock, Kita Helmetag & Helmetag, Patricia. Cecily Cicada 2004th l.t. ed. 2004. (Illus.). 28p. (J). pap. 9.95 *(978-0-615-12548-0(4))* Possum Products.

The Mysteries of Shapeville. l.t. ed. 2005. (Illus.). 48p. (J). 18.95 *(978-0-9747509-1-0(3))* Del Gatto, Maria.

Nadimi, Suzan. The Hungry Cat Downie, Christopher, illus. l.t. ed. 2005. (PER.). 32p. 5.95 net. *(978-0-9764947-0-6(1))* Nur Pubns.

Naji, Jamilla. Musical Storyland: A Sing-A-Long Book with Musical Disc. l.t. ed. 2004. (Illus.). 32p. (J). per. 19.99 *(978-0-9745568-0-2(7))* Worlds In Ink Publishing, Inc.

Nelson, Holly. Ig's Apples. l.t. ed. 2003. (Illus.). 15p. (J). per. 9.99 *(978-1-932338-17-1(9))* Lifevest Publishing, Inc.

Nesbit, E. Five Children & It. l.t. ed. 2005. 296p. pap. *(978-1-84637-200-1(3))* Echo Library.

Nettrour, Nelani. Banshees Bk. 2: Dragon Lands. Nettrour, Heather, illus. l.t. ed. 2003. 114p. (J). pap. 11.95 *(978-1-932657-03-6(7))* Third Millennium Pubns.

—The Dragonlands Bk. 3: The Village. l.t. ed. 2004. (Illus.). 148p. (J). pap. 19.95 *(978-1-932657-12-8(6))* Third Millennium Pubns.

—Jodi & the Seasons. Nettrour, Heather, illus. l.t. ed. 2004. 88p. pap. 11.95 *(978-1-932657-16-6(9))* Third Millennium Pubns.

—Jodi's Bugs. Nettrour, Heather, illus. l.t. ed. 2003. 66p. (J). pap. 11.95 *(978-1-932657-04-3(5))* Third Millennium Pubns.

New Mexico School for the Deaf Staff, 2nd Grade. Too Many Hands??? l.t. ed. 2004. (Illus.). 32p. (J). 16.95 *(978-1-929115-10-5(5))* Azro Pr., Inc.

Nicholas, Melissa. Pumpkin Days, Vol. 3. l.t. ed. 2005. (Sadlier Phonics Reading Program). (Illus.). 8p. (gr. -1-1). 23.00 net. *(978-0-8215-7352-5(7))* Sadlier, William H. Inc.

—Stop by a Pond. Gram, Patrick, illus. l.t. ed. 2005. (Little Books & Big Bks.: Vol. 3). 8p. (gr. k-2). 23.00 net. *(978-0-8215-7512-3(0))* Sadlier, William H. Inc.

—Who Is My Mom? Cassels, Jean, illus. l.t. ed. 2005. (Sadlier Phonics Reading Program). 8p. (gr. -1-1). 23.00 net. *(978-0-8215-7341-9(1))* Sadlier, William H. Inc.

Nickles, Clay & Ayres, Ella. Ali's Treasure. l.t. ed. 2005. (Illus.). 38p. (J). per. 16.95 *(978-1-59879-006-1(4))* Lifevest Publishing, Inc.

Norman, Dayle. Tre's Surprise the Move. l.t. ed. 2005. 35p. (J). per. 8.00 *(978-1-59196-896-2(8))* Instant Pub.

O'Dell, Scott. Island of the Blue Dolphins. l.t. ed. 2005. (ENG.). 223p. pap. 10.95 *(978-0-7862-7254-9(6)*, Large Print Pr.) Thorndike Pr.

O'Donnell, Sallie. Animals, Vegetables & Minerals from A to Z. Plumley, Alea, illus. l.t. ed. 2005. 60p. pap. 9.95 *(978-0-9764982-5-4(1))* Legacy Publishing Services, Inc.

Olivares, Katie Lydon. ABC Book of Shadows. l.t. ed. 2005. (Illus.). 30p. (J). bds. 9.99 *(978-0-9768573-0-3(8))* Itty Bitty Witch Works.

Olivia, Cynthia. In January & June, Vol. 4. l.t. ed. 2005. (Sadlier Phonics Reading Program: Vol. 16). (Illus.). 8p. (gr. -1-1). 23.00 net. *(978-0-8215-7355-6(1))* Sadlier, William H. Inc.

Olker, Constance. The Punctuation Pals Go Snow Skiing. l.t. ed. 2005. (Illus.). (J). per. 17.95 *(978-0-9761289-7-7(7))* Nightengale Pr.

—The Punctuation Pals Go to the Baseball Park. l.t. ed. 2005. (Illus.). 22p. (J). per. 17.95 *(978-0-9761289-8-4(5))* Nightengale Pr.

—The Punctuation Pals Go to the Beach. l.t. ed. 2005. (Illus.). 22p. (J). per. 17.95 *(978-0-9761289-5-3(0))* Nightengale Pr.

—The Punctuation Pals Go to the Moon. l.t. ed. 2005. (Illus.). (J). per. 19.95 *(978-0-9761289-6-0(9))* Nightengale Pr.

—The Punctuation Pals Meet at School. l.t. ed. 2005. (Illus.). 18p. (J). per. 16.95 *(978-0-9761289-4-6(2))* Nightengale Pr.

Omary, Rachel, illus. Animals in Dari. l.t. ed. 2003. 4p. (J). spiral bd. 10.95 *(978-0-9740535-3-0(8))* Knight Publishing.

—Animals in Farsi. l.t. ed. 2003. 4p. (J). spiral bd. 10.95 *(978-0-9740535-4-7(6))* Knight Publishing.

—Animals in Pashto. l.t. ed. 2003. 4p. (J). spiral bd. 10.95 *(978-0-9740535-5-4(4))* Knight Publishing.

—Shapes & Colors in Farsi. l.t. ed. 2004. 5p. (J). spiral bd. 14.95 *(978-0-9740535-6-1(2))* Knight Publishing.

—Shapes & Colors in Pashto. l.t. ed. 2004. 5p. (J). spiral bd. 14.95 *(978-0-9740535-8-5(9))* Knight Publishing.

The Origin of Chinese, 1. l.t. ed. 2004. (CHI., Illus.). 60p. (J). *(978-0-9752775-1-5(0)*, 0-9752775-1-0) Unitrust Design.

Owens, Katherine. Tree Seasons Ball, 1 bk. l.t. ed. 2004. (Illus.). 40p. (J). per. 19.99 *(978-0-9760419-0-0(1)*, TREESEASONSBALL) ThatsMyLife Co.

Ozaki, Yei Theodora, ed. Japanese Fairy Tales. l.t. ed. 2004. (Large Print Ser.). 335p. 26.00 *(978-1-58287-750-1(5))* North Bks.

Palmer, Catherine. Fatal Harvest. l.t. ed. 2004. (Matthew 25 Ser.). 496p. (YA). 28.95 *(978-0-7862-6259-5(1))* Thorndike Pr.

Palmer, Edward G. Book of Edward Christian Mythology, 4 vols., Set. l.t. ed. 2005. (Illus.). 1306p. per. 123.80 *(978-0-9768833-4-0(1)*, 0976883341) JVED Publishing.

—Book of Edward Christian Mythology: Itching Christian Ears, 4 vols., Vol. 3. l.t. ed. 2005. (Illus.). 616p. per. 39.95 *(978-0-9768833-2-6(5)*, 0976883325) JVED Publishing.

—Book of Edward Christian Mythology Vol. II: God Does Not Change, 4 vols. l.t. ed. 2005. (Illus.). 356p. per. 27.95 *(978-0-9768833-1-9(7)*, 0976883317) JVED Publishing.

—Book of Edward Christian Mythology Vol. IV: Appendixes Reference, 4 vols. l.t. ed. 2005. (Illus.). 208p. per. 27.95 *(978-0-9768833-3-3(3)*, 0976883333) JVED Publishing.

Parente, Peter. Boomer to the Rescue. Ivanov, Aleksey, illus. l.t. ed. 2005. 28p. 15.95 *(978-0-9745052-3-7(4)*, Peeper & Friends) Tree Of Life Publishing.

—Peeper the Kinkajou. l.t. ed. 2004. (Peeper & Friends Ser.). (Illus.). 28p. (J). 15.95 *(978-0-9745052-0-6(X)*, Peeper & Friends) Tree Of Life Publishing.

Parker, Sandy. What Day is Today? Hofher, Cathy, illus. l.t. ed. 2003. 24p. (gr. k-1). 13.95 *(978-0-9643462-3-9(0)*, 10, Just Think Bks.) Canary Connect Pubns.

Paschal, Janey Loree Fisher, ed. Melly: #2 in the 1989 Family Friends Paper Doll Set, 3 nos., no. 2. Fisher, Phyllis Mae Richardson, illus. l.t. ed. 2004. (ENG.). 24p. (J). act. bk. ed. 10.00 *(978-0-9745615-6-1(8))* PJs Corner Gift Shoppe.

Patterson, James. The Dangerous Days of Daniel X. l.t. ed. 2008. (Daniel X Ser.: 1). (ENG.). 304p. (J). (gr. 3-7). pap. 19.99 *(978-0-316-03025-0(2)*, Jimmy Patterson) Little Brown & Co.

—Max: A Maximum Ride Novel. l.t. ed. 2009. (Maximum Ride Ser.: 5). (ENG.). 416p. (YA). (gr. 5-17). 38.99 *(978-0-316-03759-4(1)*, Jimmy Patterson) Little Brown & Co.

—Saving the World & Other Extreme Sports. l.t. ed. 2007. (Maximum Ride Ser.: No. 3). 489p. (J). (gr. 3-7). 23.95 *(978-0-7862-9887-7(1))* Thorndike Pr.

Paul, Kate. The Best Ride, Vol. 2. l.t. ed. 2005. (Sadlier Phonics Reading Program). (Illus.). 8p. (gr. -1-1). 23.00 net. *(978-0-8215-7345-7(4))* Sadlier, William H. Inc.

Paulsen, Gary. Foxman. l.t. ed. 2004. (YA). (gr. 6-12). 27.95 *(978-1-58118-112-8(4))* LRS.

Paulson, Michael W. The Baker Street Bunch No. 1: A Double Mystery Book. l.t. ed. 2004. (Illus.). 154p. (J). per. *(978-0-9754241-0-0(6))* MiMar Publishing.

—The Baker Street Bunch & the Missing Pig Mystery. l.t. ed. 2004. (Illus.). 90p. (J). per. 3.95 *(978-0-9754241-1-7(4))* MiMar Publishing.

Peck, Richard. The Teacher's Funeral. 2006. (ENG.). 224p. (J). (gr. 3-7). reprint ed. 8.99 *(978-0-14-240507-9(8)*, Puffin Books) Penguin Young Readers Group.

Perkins, Lynne Rae. Criss Cross: A Newbery Award Winner. 2007. (ENG., Illus.). 368p. (J). (gr. 5-9). pap. 9.99 *(978-0-06-009274-0(2)*, Greenwillow Bks.) HarperCollins Pubs.

Persinger, Eric. Plaid the Platypus. l.t. ed. 2004. (Illus.). 25p. (J). per. 8.99 *(978-1-932338-54-6(3))* Lifevest Publishing, Inc.

Peters, Kathryn. A Pet for Elizabeth Rose. Peters, Kathryn, illus. l.t. ed. 2005. (Illus.). 42p. (J). 8.99 *(978-0-9752647-9-9(6))* Proton Arts.

Phillips, Rachelle. Dinkey the Donkey. Randolph, Carolyn, illus. l.t. ed. 2004. 24p. (J). 7.50 *(978-0-9748591-5-6(X)*, MSP) Yetto Publishing Co.

Pintozzi, Nick. Bentley & the Great Fire. Pintozzi, Nick et al, illus. l.t. ed. 2004. 120p. per. 17.95 *(978-0-9749465-1-1(6))* BentDaiSha.

Pipkin, Evelyn Ruth. The Pretty Little Red Bird. l.t. ed. 2004. 19p. (J). (gr. 1-3). 7.95 *(978-0-9755789-0-2(1))* Two Seed Planters Inc.

Pohrte, Kathysue, et al. In the Land of Liviaann. Pohrte, Kathysue, ed. Pohrte, Olivia & Pohrte, Juliann, illus. l.t. ed. 2003. 36p. (J). pap. 17.95 *(978-0-9722296-0-9(4)*, 872493) Pohrte, Dorey Publishing, Inc.

Portman, Michelle Eva. Compost, by Gosh! An Adventure with Vermicomposting. Portman, Michelle Eva, illus. l.t. ed. 2003. (ENG., Illus.). 42p. (J). 16.95 *(978-0-942256-16-1(6)*, Falcon Guides) Globe Pequot Pr., The.

Poussin, Nichol. Still Spins the Spider of Rennes-le-Chateau. l.t. ed. 2004. Tr. of L'arraignee tisse sa toile a Rennes-le-Chateaua. (Illus.). 347p. pap. *(978-0-9541527-1-0(9)*, http/www.keysofantiquity.com) DEK Publishing.

Priest, Saira, photos by & des. If We Were... Priest, Saira, des. l.t. ed. 2003. (Illus.). 20p. 12.95 *(978-0-9726628-7-1(1))* Niche Publishing & Marketing.

Princess Aurora: A Special Day in Her Life. l.t. ed. 2005. (Illus.). 32p. (J). 5.95 *(978-0-9766640-0-0(3)*, 212-279-3492) Attitudes in Dressing, Inc.

Pritchard, Herman S. The Nautical Road: A Straight Forward Approach to Learning the Navigation Rules. Helwig, Teresa L., ed. Sink, Cynthia, illus. 2nd rev. l.t. ed. 2004. 176p. (YA). 29.95 *(978-0-9716479-3-0(3))* Selby Dean Ventures, Inc.

Progressive Langauge Staff, prod. Bluw Wolf & Friends, Units 1-4. l.t. ed. 2004. (Illus.). 53p. act. bk. ed. *(978-0-9758759-3-3(0))* Progressive Language, Inc.

Purcell, John M. American City Flags Vols. 9&10: 146 Flags from Akron to Yonkers. Kaye, Edward B., ed. l.t. ed. 2004. (Illus.). 400p. per. 35.00 *(978-0-9747728-0-6(1)*, 48) North American Vexillological Assoc. (NAVA).

Pyle, Howard. The Merry Adventures of Robin Hood. l.t. ed. 2004. (Large Print Ser.). 518p. 26.00 *(978-1-58287-684-9(3))* North Bks.

Rainville, Doris I., creator. The Girl Who Never Let Her Mother Brush Her Hair. l.t. ed. 2003. (Illus.). 24p. (J). per. 7.95 *(978-0-9744879-0-8(2))* Magical Creations.

—The Power of Love. l.t. ed. 2003. (Illus.). 24p. (J). per. 7.95 *(978-0-9744879-1-5(0))* Magical Creations.

Ramona Quimby, Age 8. 2005. (J). *(978-1-59564-976-8(X))* Steps To Literacy, LLC.

Ratway, Michael J. & Ratway, Virginia K. Fractured Femur Fable. l.t. ed. 2003. (Illus.). 24p. (J). spiral bd. 10.00 *(978-0-9724698-1-4(8))* Ratway, Michael.

Really Big Coloring Books Staff. ABC 123 Learn My Letters & Numbers. l.t. ed. 2003. Orig. Title: 123-ABC Learn My Letters & Numbers. (Illus.). 321p. (J). *(978-0-9729753-1-5(4))* Really Big Coloring Bks., Inc.

Redding, David Asbury. He Never Spoke Without a Parable: His Kingdom, Your Antagonist, It's up to You, 3 bks, 5 vols. l.t. ed. 2003. pap. 16.00 *(978-0-9671701-3-8(3)*, 0-9671701-3-3) Redding Stenner, Marion.

Renaud, Andrea. Sammy the Surfing Pelican Meets Steve the Surf Guru. l.t. ed. 2003. (Illus.). 32p. (J). per. *(978-0-9717041-3-8(9))* A Happy Friend, Inc.

Richmond, Marianne. Grand-o-grams: Postcards to Keep in Touch with Your Grandkids All-Year-Round. l.t. ed. 2004. (Marianne Richmond Ser.: 0). (Illus.). 44p. 9.95 *(978-0-9753528-7-8(3)*, Sourcebooks Jabberwocky) Sourcebooks, Inc.

—Love-U-Grams: Postcards, Notes & Coupons to Connect with Your Kids. l.t. ed. 2005. (ENG., Illus.). 44p. (J). pap. 9.95 *(978-0-9753528-9-2(X)*, Marianne Richmond Studios, Inc.) Sourcebooks, Inc.

Riker, Richard K. Scary Days Daze. l.t. ed. 2005. (Illus.). 224p. (J). 15.95 *(978-0-9760416-1-0(8)*, 3,000) Family Christian Ctr.

Riley, John B. Benjamin Franklin: A Photo Biography. l.t. ed. 2004. (First Biographies Ser.). (Illus.). 24p. (YA). (gr. 5-18). 16.95 *(978-1-883846-64-0(1)*, First Biographies) Reynolds, Morgan Inc.

—George Washington Carver: A Photo Biography. l.t. ed. 2004. (First Biographies Ser.). (Illus.). 24p. (YA). (gr. 5-18). 16.95 *(978-1-883846-62-6(5)*, First Biographies) Reynolds, Morgan Inc.

—Jane Addams: A Photo Biography. l.t. ed. 2004. (First Biographies Ser.). (Illus.). 24p. (J). (gr. 5-18). 16.95 *(978-1-883846-61-9(7)*, First Biographies) Reynolds, Morgan Inc.

—John Paul Jones: A Photo Biography. l.t. ed. 2004. (First Biographies Ser.). (Illus.). 24p. (YA). (gr. 5-18). 16.95 *(978-1-883846-63-3(3)*, First Biographies) Reynolds, Morgan Inc.

Riordan, Rick. The Battle of the Labyrinth. l.t. ed. 2008. (Percy Jackson & the Olympians Ser.: Bk. 4). (ENG.). 462p. (J). (gr. 4-7). 23.95 *(978-1-4104-1018-4(8))* Thorndike Pr.

—Percy Jackson & the Lightning Thief. rev. l.t. ed. 2006. (Percy Jackson & the Olympians Ser.: 1). (ENG.). 483p. (gr. 5-18). 22.99 *(978-0-7862-8225-8(8))* Thorndike Pr.

—Percy Jackson & the Olympians. l.t. ed. 2009. (Percy Jackson & the Olympians Ser.: 5). (ENG.). 485p. (J). 22.99 *(978-1-4104-1678-0(X))* Cengage Gale.

—The Red Pyramid. l.t. ed. 2010. (Kane Chronicles: Bk. 1). (ENG.). 671p. 23.95 *(978-1-4104-2536-2(3))* Thorndike Pr.

—The Son of Neptune. l.t. ed. 2011. (Heroes of Olympus Ser.: Bk. 2). (ENG.). 616p. 23.99 *(978-1-4104-4122-5(9))* Thorndike Pr.

—The Throne of Fire. l.t. ed. 2011. (Kane Chronicles: Bk. 2). (ENG.). 589p. 23.99 *(978-1-4104-3607-8(1))* Thorndike Pr.

Ristuccia, Christine & Ristuccia, James. The Entire World of S & Z Instructional Workbook: A Comprehensive Approach to Remediate Frontal & Lateral Lisps. l.t. ed. 2003. (Illus.). 208p. (J). per. 34.99 *(978-0-9723457-4-3(4))* Say It Right.

Robinson, Kelley. The Magic of Lo: Book 1, lo Trilogy. l.t. ed. 2004. (Illus.). 160p. (YA). per. 9.95 *(978-0-9745865-0-2(1)*, SarahRose Children's Bks.) SarahRose Publishing.

Rock, Maria. MiMi's Garden, It's a Kid Thing! A Guide for Beginning Gardeners. l.t. ed. 2003. (Illus.). 45p. (J). 12.95 *(978-0-9726979-0-3(X))* Rock Ink.

Rose, John N. Direct Approach: Maya 5. l.t. ed. 2003. (Illus.). 302p. per. 49.95 *(978-0-9742948-0-3(2)*, DA-Ma5) Platinum Rose Publishing.

Rothman, Cynthia Anne. Funny Bugs. Lester, Mike, illus. l.t. ed. 2005. (Little Books & Big Bks.: Vol. 4). 8p. (gr. k-2). 23.00 net. *(978-0-8215-7513-0(9))* Sadlier, William H. Inc.

—I Love to Read, 3. l.t. ed. 2005. (Sadlier Phonics Reading Program). (Illus.). 8p. (gr. -1-1). 23.00 net. *(978-0-8215-7353-2(5))* Sadlier, William H. Inc.

—A Party for Nine. l.t. ed. 2005. (Sadlier Phonics Reading Program). (Illus.). 8p. (gr. -1-1). 23.00 net. *(978-0-8215-7349-5(7))* Sadlier, William H. Inc.

—Violets & Vegetables, Vol. 4. l.t. ed. 2005. (Sadlier Phonics Reading Program). (Illus.). 8p. (gr. -1-1). 23.00 net. *(978-0-8215-7357-0(8))* Sadlier, William H. Inc.

—What Does Sam Sell? Alley, R. W., illus. l.t. ed. 2005. (Sadlier Phonics Reading Program). 8p. (gr. -1-1). 23.00 net. *(978-0-8215-7342-6(X))* Sadlier, William H. Inc.

—Yes, You Can, Vol. 4. l.t. ed. 2005. (Sadlier Phonics Reading Program). (Illus.). 8p. (gr. -1-1). 23.00 net. *(978-0-8215-7358-7(6))* Sadlier, William H. Inc.

Rowling, J. K. Harry Potter & the Chamber of Secrets. l.t. ed. 2003. (Harry Potter Ser.: Year 2). (ENG.). 466p. pap. 13.95 *(978-1-59413-001-4(9))* Thorndike Pr.

—Harry Potter & the Deathly Hallows. l.t. ed. 2009. (ENG.). 970p. pap. 14.95 *(978-1-59413-355-8(7)*, Large Print Pr.) 2007. (Harry Potter Ser.: Year 7). (Illus.). 969p. (J). (gr. 4-7). 34.95 *(978-0-7862-9665-1(8))* Thorndike Pr.

—Harry Potter & the Half-Blood Prince. l.t. ed. 2005. (Harry Potter Ser.: Year 6). (Illus.). 831p. (J). (gr. 4-8). 29.95 *(978-0-7862-7745-2(9)*, Large Print Pr.) Thorndike Pr.

—Harry Potter & the Order of the Phoenix. l.t. ed. 2003. (Harry Potter Ser.: Year 5). 1093p. 29.95 *(978-0-7862-5778-2(4)*, Large Print Pr.) Thorndike Pr.

—Harry Potter & the Order of the Phoenix. GrandPré, Mary, illus. l.t. ed. 2003. (Thorndike Young Adult Ser.). (ENG.). 1232p. (J). (gr. 4-7). per. 14.95 *(978-1-59413-112-7(0)*, Large Print Pr.) Thorndike Pr.

Royster, D. A. Adoption Is... l.t. ed. 2005. (Illus.). 30p. (J). bds. 15.99 *(978-0-9761538-0-1(7))* Unspeakable Joy Pr.

Sabol, Elizabeth, illus. Day Is Done: A Lullaby l.t. ed. 2004. 26p. (J). pap. incl. audio compact disk *(978-0-9747382-0-8(4))* LeDor Publishing.

Sanders, Stephanie. Q. T. Pie Meets Smart E. Pauling, Galen T., illus. l.t. ed. 2003. (Q.T. Pie Ser.). (ENG.). 36p. (J). (gr. k-2). mass mkt. 4.99 *(978-0-9670875-4-2(6)*, 313-533-7383) SanPaul Group, LLC, The.

Sargent, Daina. Alaska: Be Brave, 4 vols. Lenoir, Jane, illus. l.t. ed. 2004. (Double Trouble Ser.: 4). 48p. (J). pap. 10.95 *(978-1-59381-121-1(7))*; lib. bdg. 23.60 *(978-1-59381-120-4(9))* Ozark Publishing.

—Arkansas: Dream Big. Lenoir, Jane, illus. l.t. ed. 2004. (Double Trouble Ser.). 48p. (J). pap. 10.95 *(978-1-59381-123-5(3))*; lib. bdg. *(978-1-59381-122-8(5))* Ozark Publishing.

—Colors & the Number 10, 11 vols. Lenoir, Jane, illus. l.t. ed. 2004. (Learn to Read Ser.). 24p. (J). lib. bdg. 20.95 *(978-1-59381-048-1(2))* Ozark Publishing.

—Colors & the Number 2, 11 vols. Lenoir, Jane, illus. l.t. ed. 2004. (Learn to Read Ser.). 24p. (J). lib. bdg. 20.95 *(978-1-59381-032-0(6))* Ozark Publishing.

—Colors & the Number 6, 11 vols. Lenoir, Jane, illus. l.t. ed. 2004. (Learn to Read Ser.). 24p. (J). lib. bdg. 20.95 *(978-1-59381-040-5(7))* Ozark Publishing.

—Colors & the Number 7, 11 vols. Lenoir, Jane, illus. l.t. ed. 2004. (Learn to Read Ser.). 24p. (J). lib. bdg. 20.95 *(978-1-59381-042-9(3))* Ozark Publishing.

—Colors & the Number 8, 11 vols. Lenoir, Jane, illus. l.t. ed. 2004. (Learn to Read Ser.). 24p. (J). lib. bdg. 20.95 *(978-1-59381-044-3(X))* Ozark Publishing.

—Colors & the Number 9, 11 vols. Lenoir, Jane, illus. l.t. ed. 2004. (Learn to Read Ser.). 24p. (J). lib. bdg. 20.95 *(978-1-59381-046-7(6))* Ozark Publishing.

—Introduction to Colors & Numbers, 11 vols. Lenoir, Jane, illus. l.t. ed. 2004. (Learn to Read Ser.: 11). 24p. (J). lib. bdg. 20.95 *(978-1-59381-050-4(4))* Ozark Publishing.

—Introduction to Colors & Numbers/Introduccion a los Colores Numeros, 11 vols. Lenoir, Jane, illus. l.t. ed. 2005. (Learn to Read Ser.: 11). (SPA & ENG.). 24p. (J). pap. 10.95 *(978-1-59381-149-5(7))* Ozark Publishing.

—Kansas: Conquer Fear. Lenoir, Jane, illus. l.t. ed. 2004. (Double Trouble Ser.). 48p. (J). pap. 10.95 *(978-1-59381-125-9(X))*; lib. bdg. 23.60 *(978-1-59381-124-2(1))* Ozark Publishing.

—Missouri: Teamwork. Lenoir, Jane, illus. l.t. ed. 2004. (Double Trouble Ser.). 48p. (J). pap. 10.95 *(978-1-59381-127-3(6))*; lib. bdg. 23.60 *(978-1-59381-126-6(8))* Ozark Publishing.

Sargent, Dave & Sargent, Pat. The Colorado Blizzard: Be Determined, 10 vols., Vol. 8. Lenoir, Jane, illus. l.t. ed. 2004. (Colorado Cowboys Ser.: 8). 32p. (J). (gr. 3-8). lib. bdg. 23.60 *(978-1-59381-026-9(1))* Ozark Publishing.

Sargent, Dave, et al. Berry Picking Time Vol. 3: (Apache) Be Brave, 20 vols. Lenoir, Jane, illus. l.t. ed. 2003. (Story Keeper Ser.: 3). 42p. (J). Vol. 3. lib. bdg. 23.60 *(978-1-56763-907-0(0)*, 1228136)vol. 3. pap. 6.95 *(978-1-56763-908-7(9)*, 1228136) Ozark Publishing.

—The Bundle Keeper: (Pawnee) Be Responsible, 20 vols., Vol. 18. Lenoir, Jane, illus. l.t. ed. 2004. (Story Keeper Ser.: 18). 48p. (J). pap. 10.95 *(978-1-56763-938-4(0))* Ozark Publishing.

—Counting Coup Vol. 4: (Cheyenee) Be Proud, 20 vols. Lenoir, Jane, illus. l.t. ed. 2003. (Story Keeper Ser.). 42p. (J). lib. bdg. 23.60 *(978-1-56763-909-4(7))* Ozark Publishing.

—Fields of Golden Corn Vol. 6: (Navajo) Be Energetic, 20 vols. Lenoir, Jane, illus. l.t. ed. 2003. (Story Keeper Ser.: 6). 42p. (J). lib. bdg. 23.60 *(978-1-56763-913-1(5))* Ozark Publishing.

—A Hole in the Sun: (Choctaw) Be Independent, 20, Vol. 1. Lenoir, Jane, illus. l.t. ed. 2003. (Story Keeper Ser.: 1). 42p. (J). pap. 6.95 *(978-1-56763-904-9(6))* Ozark Publishing.

—Keeping Ghosts Away Vol. 8: (Creek) Be Respectful, 20 vols. Lenoir, Jane, illus. l.t. ed. 2003. (Story Keeper Ser.: Vol. 8). 42p. (J). pap. 10.95 *(978-1-56763-918-6(6)*, 1228135) Ozark Publishing.

—Knocking the Rice Vol. 9: (Chippewa) Be Powerful, 20 vols. Lenoir, Jane, illus. l.t. ed. 2003. (Story Keeper Ser.: 9). 42p. (J). pap. 10.95 *(978-1-56763-920-9(8))*; lib. bdg. 23.60 *(978-1-56763-919-3(4))* Ozark Publishing.

—Ladder at the Door Vol. 10: (Hopi) Be Curious, 20 vols. Lenoir, Jane, illus. l.t. ed. 2004. (Story Keeper Ser.: 10). 48p. (J). pap. 10.95 *(978-1-56763-922-3(4))*; lib. bdg. 23.60 *(978-1-56763-921-6(6))* Ozark Publishing.

—Land of the Sun Vol. 11: (Ute) Respect Elders, 20 vols., Vol. 11. Lenoir, Jane, illus. l.t. ed. 2004. (Story Keeper Ser.: 11). 48p. (J). lib. bdg. 23.60 *(978-1-56763-923-0(2))*; pap. 10.95 *(978-1-56763-924-7(0))* Ozark Publishing.

—Little One Vol. 12: (Cherokee) Be Inventive, 20 vols. Lenoir, Jane, illus. l.t. ed. 2003. (Story Keeper Ser.: Vol. 12). 42p. (J). pap. 10.95 *(978-1-56763-926-1(7))* Ozark Publishing.

—On the Banks of the Wallowa River: (Nez Perce) Use Your Talent, 20 vols., Vol. 13. Lenoir, Jane, illus. l.t. ed. 2004. (Story Keeper Ser.: 13). 48p. (J). pap. 10.95 *(978-1-56763-928-5(3))*; lib. bdg. 23.60 *(978-1-56763-927-8(5))* Ozark Publishing.

—Rays of the Sun Vol. 15: (shoshone) Learn Lessons, 20 vols. Lenoir, Jane, illus. l.t. ed. 2004. (Story Keeper Ser.: 15). 48p. (J). pap. 10.95 *(978-1-56763-932-2(1))* Ozark Publishing.

—Rays of the Sun Vol. 15: (Shoshone) Learn Lessons, 20 vols. Lenoir, Jane, illus. l.t. ed. 2004. (Story Keeper Ser.: 15). 48p. (J). lib. bdg. 23.60 *(978-1-56763-931-5(3))* Ozark Publishing.

—A Strand of Wampum Vol. 2: Be Honest, 20 vols. Lenoir, Sue, illus. l.t. ed. 2003. (Story Keeper Ser.: 2). 42p. (J). pap. 10.95 *(978-1-56763-906-3(2))* Ozark Publishing.

—Summer Milky Way: (Blackfeet) Be Compassionate, 20 vols., Vol. 16. Lenoir, Jane, illus. l.t. ed. 2004. (Story Keeper Ser.). 48p. (J). lib. bdg. 23.60 *(978-1-56763-933-9(X))*; pap. 10.95 *(978-1-56763-934-6(8))* Ozark Publishing.

—Tattoos of Honor Vol. 17: (Osage) Be Gentle & Giving, 20 vols. Lenoir, Jane, illus. l.t. ed. 2004. (Story Keeper Ser.: Vol. 17). 42p. (J). pap. 10.95 *(978-1-56763-936-0(4))*; lib. bdg. 23.60 *(978-1-56763-935-3(6))* Ozark Publishing.

—Truth, Power & Freedom Vol. 19: (Sioux) Show Respect, 20 vols., Vol. 19. Lenoir, Jane, illus. l.t. ed. 2004. (Story Keeper Ser.: 19). 42p. (J). pap. 10.95 *(978-1-56763-940-7(2))* Ozark Publishing.

—Valley Oaks Acorns Vol. 20: (Maidu) Be Helpful, 20 vols. Lenoir, Jane, illus. l.t. ed. 2004. (Story Keeper Ser.: 20). 48p. (J). pap. 10.95 *(978-1-56763-942-1(9))* Ozark Publishing.

Sargent, Pat L. The Cheetah, 6 vols., Vol. 6. Lenoir, Jane, illus. l.t. ed. 2004. (Barney the Bear Killer Ser.: No. 6). 146p. (YA). pap. 10.95 *(978-1-56763-974-2(7))* Ozark Publishing.

Scalzo, Linda V. Carazona's Coloring Book. l.t. ed. 2004. (Illus.). 8p. (J). 2.99 *(978-0-9753724-3-2(2))* Carazona Creations LLC.

—El circo llega al Pueblo: Version de Lectura Temprana. Torres, Marcela H., tr. Spalinski, Amanda, illus. l.t. ed. 2005. (SPA.). 24p. per. 9.99 *(978-0-9753724-2-5(4))* Carazona Creations LLC.

—The Circus Is coming to Town: Early Reader Version. Spalinski, Amanda, illus. l.t. ed. 2005. 24p. (J). per. 9.99 *(978-0-9753724-1-8(6))* Carazona Creations LLC.

—The Circus Is Coming to Town: Full-Length Version. l.t. ed. 2004. (Illus.). 32p. (J). 9.99 *(978-0-9753724-0-1(8))* Carazona Creations LLC.

Scheber, George. Earl Joins the Circus. Spicer, Bridgett, illus. l.t. ed. 2005. (Adventures of Earl the Squirrel Ser.). 32p. (J). (gr. -1-3). 12.95 *(978-1-878847-01-0(5))* Make Me A Story Pr.

—Earl the Squirrel. Spicer, Bridgett, illus. l.t. ed. 2005. (Adventures of Earl the Squirrel Ser.). 32p. (J). (gr. -1-2). 12.95 *(978-1-878847-00-3(7))* Make Me A Story Pr.

Schneider, Stephen A. Color My Chess World. l.t. ed. 2004. (Illus.). 48p. (J). act. bk. ed. 19.50 incl. audio compact disk *(978-0-9729456-9-1(5))* Championship Chess.

Schuepbach, Lynnette. Froggy Hollow. Schuepbach, Lynnette, illus. l.t. ed. 2004. (Illus.). 32p. (J). pap. 7.00 net. *(978-0-9759613-0-8(6))* Creative Sources.

—Shhhh!!! Schuepbach, Lynnette, illus. l.t. ed. 2004. (ENG., Illus.). 32p. (J). pap. 12.95 *(978-0-9759613-1-5(4))* Creative Sources.

Schumacher, Stef. Amazing Blue Animals, Vol. 2. l.t. ed. 2005. (Little Books & Big Bks.: Vol. 9). (Illus.). 8p. (gr. k-2). 23.00 net. *(978-0-8215-7518-5(X))* Sadlier, William H. Inc.

Schwiebert, Pat & DeKlyen, Chuck. Tear Soup: A Recipe for Healing after Loss. Bills, Taylor, illus. 2nd rev. l.t. ed. 2004. (ENG.). 56p. (gr. -1-12). reprint ed. 19.95 *(978-0-9615197-6-6(2)*, 798) Grief Watch.

Scott, Michael. The Sorceress. 2010. (Secrets of the Immortal Nicholas Flamel Ser.: 3). (ENG.). 512p. (YA). (gr. 7-18). pap. 11.99 *(978-0-385-73530-8(8)*, Ember) Random Hse. Children's Bks.

Seagreaves, Kelly E. The Best Pet. Zoller, Jayson D., illus. l.t. ed. 2004. 29p. (J). per. 8.99 *(978-1-932338-53-9(5))* Lifevest Publishing, Inc.

Sewell, Anna. Black Beauty, 2 vols., Set. l.t. ed. (YA). (gr. 8-18). reprint ed. 10.00 *(978-0-89064-017-3(3))* National Assn. for Visually Handicapped.

—Black Beauty. l.t. ed. 2004. (Large Print Ser.). 268p. 25.00 *(978-1-58287-619-1(3))* North Bks.

Shaffert, Charles. Googus, the Toothless Alligator. Stringer, Margaret, illus. l.t. ed. 2003. 30p. (J). per. 7.95 *(978-1-932338-27-0(6))* Lifevest Publishing, Inc.

Shams, K. The Piggle. Spears, Ashley E., illus. l.t. ed. 2004. 20p. (J). 9.99 *(978-0-9728872-9-8(6))* Trent's Prints.

Shaw, Mary. Brady Brady & the Puck on the Pond, 11 vols. Temple, Chuck, illus. l.t. ed. 2005. 32p. (J). per. *(978-1-897169-07-0(8))* Brady Brady, Inc.

Shemin, Craig. Families Are Forever McCoy, John, illus. l.t. ed. 2003. 34p. 9.95 *(978-0-9728666-0-6(4)*, 1) As Simple As That Publishing.

Simpson, Matt, creator. Happy Heart: English Book 1. l.t. ed. 2003. (Illus.). 44p. (J). per. *(978-0-9727660-0-5(6))* Bks. by Matt.

Singer, Isaac Bashevis. Short Friday & Other Stories. l.t. ed. (YA). (gr. 10-12). reprint ed. 10.00 *(978-0-89064-057-9(2))* National Assn. for Visually Handicapped.

Sinke, Grandma Janet Mary. Grandma's Christmas Tree. Pennington, Craig, illus. l.t. ed. 2004. (Grandma Janet Mary Ser.). 50p. (J). *(978-0-9742732-1-1(X))* My Grandma & Me Pubs.

Slamp, Kathy. Little House in the Arctic: An Adventure Story. l.t. ed. 2004. Orig. Title: Our Little House in the Arctic. (Illus.). 228p. pap. 17.95 *(978-0-9713345-3-3(6))* Vessel Ministries.

Smith, Dianne M. Cyanne Rose & Sherbet Are Best Friends. l.t. ed. 2004. 22p. (YA). per. *(978-1-59196-678-4(7))* Instant Pub.

—Happy Birthday to You! l.t. ed. 2004. 24p. per. *(978-1-59196-679-1(5))* Instant Pub.

—I Don't Want To! l.t. ed. 2004. (YA). per. *(978-1-59196-683-8(3))* Instant Pub.

Solice, Deborah. The Eye of the Undead: The Hidden Channel: an Adventure Series in Time. l.t. ed. 2005. (ENG., Illus.). 100p. (J). per. 7.59 *(978-1-933300-01-6(9))* Wandering Sage Pubns., LLC.

Spellman, Rhonda J., as told by. When I Was a Little Boy, by Jesus: Written for Children, Illustrated by Children: Experience the Life Jesus Lived When Jesus Was a Little Boy. l.t. ed. 2003. (Illus.). 32p. (J). per. 19.95 *(978-0-9741009-0-6(0))* Creative Cranium Concept, The.

Spinelle, Nancy Louise. Moose's Loose Tooth. Gedeon, Gloria, illus. l.t. ed. 2005. (ENG.). 16p. (gr. k-2). pap. 7.95 *(978-1-57874-032-1(0)*, Kaeden Bks.) Kaeden Corp.

Sportelli-Rehak, Angela. Moving Again Mom! Hinlicky, Gregg, illus. 2004. (Uncle Sam's Kids Ser.: Bk. 2). 40p. (J). (gr. -1-7). pap. 7.95 *(978-0-9714515-0-6(8))* Abidenme Bks.

Sprecher, John. Eric & the Angrry Frog, Vol. 2. Forrest, James, illus. l.t. ed. Date not set. (Special Kids "Special Message" Book Ser.). 32p. (J). (gr. k-4). pap. 10.00 *(978-1-892186-01-0(2))* Anythings Possible, Inc.

—Tori & Cassandra & the Pelican in Peril. Forrest, James, illus. l.t. ed. Date not set. (Special Kids "Special Message" Book Ser.: Vol. 3). 32p. (J). (gr. k-4). pap. 10.00 *(978-1-892186-02-7(0))* Anythings Possible, Inc.

—Zoe & the Very Unmerry Bear. Forrest, James, illus. l.t. ed. Date not set. (Special Kids "Special Message" Book Ser.). 32p. (J). (gr. k-4). pap. 10.00 *(978-1-892186-03-4(9)*, SKPB4) Anythings Possible, Inc.

Spyri, Johanna. Heidi. l.t. ed. 2004. (Large Print Ser.). 433p. 26.00 *(978-1-58287-666-5(5))* North Bks.

Squires, Mary L. Margaret Who Dared to Dream. l.t. ed. 2003. (Illus.). 45p. 12.95 *(978-0-9631547-3-6(7))* Popular Truth, Inc.

Staheli, Bee, ed. The Owl Who Couldn't Say Whoo. Clish, Lori, illus. l.t. ed. (J). (gr. k-5). pap. 7.95 *(978-1-928632-50-4(5))* Writers Marketplace:Consulting, Critiquing & Publishing.

Stanley, Charles F. The Spirit-Filled Life: Discover the Joy of Surrendering to the Holy Spirit. l.t. ed. 2014. (ENG.). 304p. (gr. 12). E-Book 8.90 *(978-0-529-10168-6(8)*, 9780529101686) Nelson, Thomas Inc.

StarKidz: I Am Who I Am. l.t. ed. 2003. (Illus.). 28p. (J). 16.95 *(978-0-9743964-1-5(9))* Roseann Miller & Linda Stephens-Hooe.

Steele, James M. Sadie Listens: An Inward Journey. l.t. ed. 2003. (Inward Journey Ser.: Vol. 1). (Illus.). iv, 48p. 17.95 *(978-0-9716811-3-2(9))* Steele Studios.

Stephenson, Nancy. The Three Little Kittens. Faris, Eva, illus. l.t. ed. 2003. 30p. (J). per. 7.99 *(978-1-932338-13-3(6))* Lifevest Publishing, Inc.

Stokes, N. L. Mystery of the Missing Teacup. l.t. ed. 2003. (Illus.). 48p. per. 19.95 *(978-0-9729411-1-2(8))* Stylewriter Pubns.

Storie Tree Inc, Staff. A Pocket Pearl of Light: Twinkle & Shinmet Come Home. l.t. ed. 2003. (Illus.). 27p. pap. 6.00 *(978-0-9679014-9-7(9))* Storie Tree, Inc., The.

Stormer, Kate. Casey's Unexpected Friend. Lowes, Tom, illus. l.t. ed. 2003. 38p. (J). 16.95 *(978-0-9722099-7-7(2)*, CUF) Caseys World Bks.

Stoutland, Allison. Take a Deep Breath: Little Lessons from Flowers for a Happier World. Hofher, Cathy, illus. l.t. ed. 2003. 32p. 14.95 *(978-0-9670941-2-0(7))* Inch By Inch Pubns., LLC.

Stuart, Matt. Who Can Run Fast? l.t. ed. 2005. (Little Books & Big Bks.: Vol. 1). (Illus.). 8p. (gr. k-2). 23.00 net. *(978-0-8215-7510-9(4))* Sadlier, William H. Inc.

Stuck in the MUD. l.t. ed. 2004. (Illus.). 20p. (J). cd-rom 19.95 *(978-0-9759370-0-6(6))* Brown&Matthews.

Sundance/Newbridge LLC Staff. Birds, Birds, Birds. 2004. (Reading PowerWorks Ser.). (gr. 1-3). 37.50 *(978-0-7608-9783-6(2))* Sundance/Newbridge Educational Publishing.

Sundberg, Peggy. Isabelle Lives a Dream. Wiles, Pat, illus. l.t. ed. 2003. (ENG.). 32p. (J). pap. 16.95 *(978-0-9721057-1-2(9))* Cowgirl Peg Enterprises.

Sutryn, Barbara M. Heartstrings: A Biography of Wilmos Csehy. l.t. ed. 2004. (Illus.). 160p. (YA). 21.00 *(978-1-892135-33-9(7))* Lamp Post Publishing, Inc.

Tanner, Dawn Leasman. A Kitty Named Indra/Una Gata Llamada Indra. Leasman, Nancy Packard, illus. l.t. ed. 2003. (SPA & ENG.). 36p. (J). per. 6.95 *(978-0-9741725-0-7(2))* Leatherwood Publishing.

Tarazona, Oscar, illus. Volando con Alas Propias. l.t. ed. 2004. (SPA.). 116p. (YA). pap. 12.00 *(978-1-931481-88-5(1))* LiArt-Literature & Art.

Tarver, Monroe S. Little Light Shine Bright. Tarver, Monroe S., illus. l.t. ed. 2004. (Illus.). 32p. (J). 6.99 *(978-0-9743568-4-6(0))* Tarver, Monroe.

Tarver, S., 1st. Imaga & the Magic Pearls 2nd l.t. ed. 2003. (Illus.). 20p. (J). 6.99 *(978-0-9743568-0-8(8))* Tarver, Monroe.

Tate, Suzanne. Sandy Seal: A Tale of Sea Dogs. Melvin, James, illus. l.t. ed. 2004. (Suzanne Tate's Nature Ser.: No. 27). 28p. (J). pap. 4.95 *(978-1-878405-49-4(7))* Nags Head Art, Inc.

Taylor, Beth. Tina's Toys. l.t. ed. 2005. (Sadlier Phonics Reading Program). (Illus.). 8p. (gr. -1-1). 23.00 net. *(978-0-8215-7343-3(8))* Sadlier, William H. Inc.

Taylor, Chet. Last, but Not Least. Taylor, Chet, illus. l.t. ed. 2004. (Illus.). 20p. (J). lib. bdg. 22.99 *(978-0-9755888-1-9(8))* Dragonfly Publishing, Inc.

Tennyson, Patrick & Bickford, Nicole. Tarantula Tracks: Rosie's Wild Adventure. l.t. ed. 2004. (Illus.). 32p. (J). 2.95 *(978-0-9729000-1-0(2))* Butterfly Pavilion.

The Concerned Group, prod. See Baby Jesus. l.t. ed. 2012. (Illus.). 8p. (gr. 5). pap. 3.99 *(978-1-58938-004-2(5))* Concerned Communications.

Thistle, Louise. Dramatizando la Gallinita Roja: Un Cuento para Contar y Actuar. Packer, Emily, illus. l.t. ed. 2003.Tr. of Dramatizing the Little Red Hen. (SPA.). 32p. (J). (gr. k-2). pap. 10.00 *(978-0-9644186-4-6(9))* Literature Dramatization Pr.

—Dramatizing the Little Red Hen. Landes, William-Alan, ed. Packer, Emily, illus. l.t. ed. 2003. 32p. (J). (gr. k-2). pap. 10.00 *(978-0-9644186-5-3(7))* Literature Dramatization Pr.

Thomas, Dina M. & Thomas, Andy, eds. The Artful Journey: The Artwork of Andy Thomas. Thomas, Tria M., photos by. l.t. ed. 2003. (Illus.). 122p. 50.00 *(978-0-9742285-0-1(8))* Maze Creek Studio.

Thryce, Marc & Robinson, Tim. Look at the Pictures. l.t. ed. 2005. (Little Books & Big Bks.: Vol. 2). (Illus.). 8p. (gr. k-2). 23.00 net. *(978-0-8215-7511-6(2))* Sadlier, William H. Inc.

Tillman, Nancy. On the Night You Were Born, 1. l.t. ed. 2005. (Illus.). 32p. (J). 17.95 *(978-0-9765761-0-5(4))* Darling Pr. LLC.

Tinkler, David. Revenge of the Dinner Ladies. l.t. ed. 2005. (J). pap. *(978-0-7540-7804-3(3)*, CLP 185) AudioGo.

Toews, Rita Y. The Bully: A Discussion & Activity Story. Ljungberg, Jon, illus. l.t. ed. 2004. (ENG.). 40p. (J). *(978-0-9736224-0-9(7))* Birds Hill Publishing.

Toledo, Leila J. Little Peter & Sela. Davis, Chad L., illus. l.t. ed. 2004. 17p. (J). pap. 8.95 *(978-0-9753118-0-6(8))* Bimini Bks.

Tommy Books: Fear, 10 vols. l.t. ed. 2005. (Illus.). 24p. (J). 12.99 *(978-0-9762690-5-2(8))* Tommy Bks. Pubng.

Tommy Books: Forgiveness, 10 vols. l.t. ed. 2005. (Illus.). 24p. (J). 12.99 *(978-0-9762690-6-9(6))* Tommy Bks. Pubng.

Tommy Books: Grace & Mercy, 10 Vols. l.t. ed. 2005. (Illus.). 24p. (J). 12.99 *(978-0-9762690-8-3(2))* Tommy Bks. Pubng.

Tommy Books: Thank You, 10 vols. l.t. ed. 2005. (Illus.). 24p. (J). 12.99 *(978-0-9762690-9-0(0))* Tommy Bks. Pubng.
Tommy Books: Who Am I, 10 vols. l.t. ed. 2005. (Illus.). 24p. (J). 12.99 *(978-0-9762690-7-6(4))* Tommy Bks. Pubng.
Tompkins, Robyn Lee. Miss Molly's Adventure in the Park: Another Great Adventure Brought to You by Miss Molly & Her Dog Reyburn, 10 vols. Carson, Shawn K., illus. l.t. ed. 2005. (ENG.). 60p. (J). per. *(978-0-9741647-6-2(3))* NRG Pubns.
Torgerson, Scotty Delray. Jacob Goes to the Moon. 2nd l.t. ed. 2005. (Illus.). 32p. (J). 10.00 *(978-0-9767116-0-5(5))* Torgerson Meadows Publishing.
Torrel, Wendy. GUARDIAN of DREAMS (1st Edition) Klingbeil, Kendall, illus. l.t. ed. 2004. 32p. (J). 14.95 *(978-0-9746890-0-5(9))*; pap. 10.95 *(978-0-9746890-1-2(7))* White Tulip Publishing.
Trogdon, Wendell. Who Killed Hoosier Hysteria? Sport Survives amid Fading Fervor. l.t. ed. 2004. (Illus.). 168p. (YA). pap. *(978-0-9724033-3-7(7))* Backroads Pr.
Turman, Evelyn. J. B. 's Christmas Presents. Turman, Adam, illus. l.t. ed. 2004. 28p. (J). 15.95 *(978-0-9753042-0-4(8))* Turman, E.
Turner, Barbara. A Day in San Francisco, Vol. 1. l.t. ed. 2003. (Illus.). 32p. (J). per. 14.95 *(978-0-9747019-0-5(4))* Turner, Barbara.
Ulmer, Louise. The Bible That Wouldn't Burn: How the Tyndale English Version of the Bible Came About. 2nd l.t. ed. 2003. (Illus.). 32p. 4.95 *(978-0-941367-01-1(0))* Peach Blossom Pubns.
VanDerTuuk-Perkins, Jennifer E. Life with Gabriel. VanDerTuuk-Perkins, Jennifer E. & Perkins, Rodney R., illus. l.t. ed. 2004. 22p. (J). per. 9.95 *(978-0-9749862-0-3(8))* Theragogy.com.
Vogel, Rob & Azarov, Max. Garry the Groundhog. l.t. ed. 2005. (Illus.). 10p. (J). spiral bd. 19.95 incl. DVD *(978-0-9768455-0-8(4),* N/A) Vogel, Robert.
Voigt, Cynthia. A Solitary Blue. l.t. ed. 2005. (Tillerman Cycle Ser.: Bk. 3). 359p. (J). pap. 10.95 *(978-0-7862-7912-8(5))* Thorndike Pr.
Vonthron, Satanta C. Caillov Visits the Farmer's Market. Meier, Kerry L., illus. l.t. ed. 2005. (HRL Board Book Ser.). (J). (gr. -1-k). pap. 10.95 *(978-1-57332-310-9(1),* HighReach Learning, Incorporated) Carson-Dellosa Publishing, LLC.
—Down at the Shore. Storch, Ellen N., illus. l.t. ed. 2005. (HRL Board Book Ser.). (J). (gr. -1-k). pap. 10.95 *(978-1-57332-306-2(3),* HighReach Learning, Incorporated) Carson-Dellosa Publishing, LLC.
Vorndran, Judith Clay. Mr. Bear Lives There. l.t. ed. 2005. (Illus.). 11p. (J). pap. 7.98 *(978-0-9772439-0-7(7))* Vorndran, Judith Clay.
Vroom, Angela. Airplane Letters to God. l.t. ed. 2004. (Illus.). 24p. (J). pap. 8.50 *(978-0-9762935-0-7(1))* Perkins Crawford.
Wade, Linda R. Condoleezza Rice. 2004. (Illus.). 32p. (J). lib. bdg. 25.70 *(978-1-58415-332-0(6))* Mitchell Lane Pubs.
Wagner, Jeff. My Day... at the Zoo. Alvarado, Paulo, illus. 2004. 20p. (J). bds. *(978-0-9754515-0-2(2))* Wagner Entertainment.
Walling, Sandy Seeley. A Day at the Beach: A Seaside Counting Book from One to Ten. Walling, Sandy Seeley, illus. 2003. (Illus.). 28p. (J). 6.95 *(978-0-9741940-0-4(X))* Abernathy Hse. Publishing.
Walling, Sandy Seeley, illus. & text. ABC's at the Zoo! The Fun Way to Teach Your Child the Relationship between Upper Case & Lower Case Letters Walling, Sandy Seeley, text. l.t. ed. 2004. 36p. (J). per. 7.95 *(978-0-9741940-1-1(8))* Abernathy Hse. Publishing.
Waltz, Dan. Kornstalkers: Corn Maze Massacre. Waltz, Dan, illus. l.t. ed. 2005. (Chilled to the Bone! Ser.: No. 1). (Illus.). 120p. (J). per. 6.99 *(978-0-9741774-3-4(1))* D. W. Publishing.
Waltz, Dan Hall. Freckles the Frog: A Read-a-Long/Sing-a-Long Story Book. Waltz, Dan Hall, illus. l.t. ed. 2003. (Illus.). 24p. (J). 19.95 *(978-0-9741774-0-3(7))* D. W. Publishing.
Watkins, Albert. The Brothers Three. l.t. ed. 2004. (Illus.). 48p. (J). pap. 22.95 *(978-0-9629124-4-3(1))* Floppinfish Publishing Co., Ltd.
Watkins, Patricia. Boyd-Friend: His Yippie-Skippie Journey to a Forever Home. Watkins, Christopher, illus. l.t. ed. 2004. 44p. 10.95 *(978-0-9753397-0-1(2))* Frayed Pages Publishing.
Watson, Don. The Legend of Red Leaf. Robbins, Ashley, illus. l.t. ed. 2005. 125p. (J). pap. 9.95 *(978-0-9714358-6-5(3))* Longhorn Creek Pr.
Watson, Regal. The Ant That Can't, 1. l.t. ed. 2005. (Illus.). 50p. (J). per. 10.95 *(978-0-9763686-0-1(9))* Rapha Publishing.
Watson, W. Hamp, Jr. Frederick Wilson Still Speaks - Big Words for Our Time. Watson, W. Hamp, Jr., ed. l.t. ed. 2004. (J). per. 12.95 *(978-0-9746976-0-4(5))* Cambridge Way Publishing.
Weddington, Carole. D+Anger I'm Mad! Anger Management Teen Style. l.t. ed. 2003. (YA). 28.00 *(978-0-9638007-7-0(9))* J M Pubns.
Weeks, Timothy A. The Wise Mullet of Cook Bayou l.t. ed. 2004. (Illus.). 48p. (J). per. *(978-0-9713573-8-9(2))* Thomas Expressions, LLC.
Westerfeld, Scott. Leviathan. l.t. ed. 2010. (Leviathan Trilogy: Bk. 1). (ENG.). 525p. 23.95 *(978-1-4104-2572-0(X))* Thorndike Pr.
White, Russ. Cat Got Your Tongue? A Book of Idioms. Cornelison, Reuel, illus. l.t. ed. 2004. 44p. (J). per. *(978-0-9742885-0-5(0),* 00) White, Russ.
White, T. H. The Sword in the Stone. l.t. ed. 2003. (Children's Large Print Ser.). 35.95 *(978-1-58118-110-4(8))* LRS.
Whitedove, Michelle. My Invisible Friends. Poynter, Linda, illus. l.t. ed. 2005. 30p. (gr. -1-3). spiral bd. 18.95 *(978-0-9714908-4-0(8))* Whitedove Pr.
Wilde, Oscar. The Happy Prince & Other Tales. l.t. ed. 2006. 92p. pap. *(978-1-84637-306-0(9))* Echo Library.
Wilder, Laura Ingalls. These Happy Golden Years. l.t. ed. (J). (gr. 3-6). 35.95 *(978-1-58118-102-9(7))* LRS.
Williams, Deborah. Little Rabbit Is Sad. Gedeon, Gloria, illus. l.t. ed. 2005. (ENG.). 12p. (Orig.). (gr. k-1). pap. 7.95 *(978-1-879835-99-3(1),* Kaeden Bks.) Kaeden Corp.
—Nickels & Pennies. Gedeon, Gloria, illus. l.t. ed. 2005. (ENG.). 12p. (gr. k-1). pap. 7.95 *(978-1-879835-87-0(8),* Kaeden Bks.) Kaeden Corp.
Williams, Heather L. & Muench-Williams, Heather. Caillov Learns about Space. Storch, Ellen N., illus. l.t. ed. 2005. (HRL Board Book Ser.). (J). (gr. -1-k). bds. 10.95 *(978-1-57332-308-6(X),* HighReach Learning, Incorporated) Carson-Dellosa Publishing, LLC.
Williams, Thomas. The Christmas Chair. l.t. ed. 2004. (Illus.). 27p. (J). audio compact disk 22.95 *(978-0-9763633-0-9(5))* Williams, Thomas.
Wilson, Rebekah. Grandmother's Hope Chest: Lucie's Snowflakes. l.t. ed. 2004. (Illus.). 80p. (J). 15.00 *(978-1-59565-003-0(2))* Hope Chest Legacy, Inc.
—Grandmother's Hope Chest: The Running Rooster. l.t. ed. 2004. (Illus.). 52p. (J). 15.00 *(978-1-59565-002-3(4))* Hope Chest Legacy, Inc.
Winter, Max. Did You Know?, Vol. 2. Rechin, Kevin, illus. l.t. ed. 2005. (Little Books & Big Bks.: Vol. 8). 8p. (gr. k-2). 23.00 net. *(978-0-8215-7517-8(1))* Sadlier, William H. Inc.
Wong, Benedict Norbert. Lo & Behold. Wong, Benedict Norbert, illus. l.t. ed. 2003. (Illus.). 38p. (gr. 1-18). 16.95 *(978-0-9728192-0-6(7),* LOBE) Taiji Arts Publishing.
—Lo & Behold: Good Enough to Eat. Wong, Benedict Norbert, illus. l.t. ed. 2003. (Illus.). 40p. (J). (gr. 1-12). 16.95 *(978-0-9728192-1-3(5),* 1002LB) Taiji Arts Publishing.
Wood, Debra. William Warrior Bear. Blake, Joshua Aaron, illus. l.t. ed. 2005. 30p. (J). per. 12.95 *(978-1-59879-001-6(3))* Lifevest Publishing, Inc.
Wooding, Sharon. Mark Twain in Nevada, a History Coloring Book for Children. l.t. ed. 2003. (Illus.). 25p. (J). (SPA.). pap. 5.95 *(978-0-9727757-1-7(4))*; pap. 5.95 *(978-0-9727757-0-0(6))* Susy & Livy Pubns.
Wright, Mary H. Grandma Spoils Me. Megenhardt, Bill, illus. l.t. ed. 2005. 32p. (J). lib. bdg. 16.95 *(978-0-9645493-4-0(4))* Bluebonnets, Boots & Bks. Pr.
Yamada, Debbie Leung. Striking It Rich: Treasures from Gold Mountain. Tang, You-shan, illus. l.t. ed. 2004. 128p. (J). (gr. 4-8). pap. 13.95 *(978-1-879965-21-8(6))* Polychrome Publishing Corp.
Young, Patricia A. The Holy Monks of Mt. Athos. Young, Patricia A., illus. l.t. ed. 2005. (Illus.). 28p. (J). 20.00 *(978-0-913026-24-3(7))*; 10.00 *(978-0-913026-49-6(2))* St. Nectarios Pr.
Young Scribes Staff. Unlock the Secrets of Exeter: The Young Scribes of Exeter, NH. l.t. ed. 2004. (Illus.). 172p. (J). pap. 15.00 *(978-0-9744803-9-8(8))* PublishingWorks.
Zabrosky, Joseph. Herbie Hanson, 1 vol., 4 bks. l.t. ed. 2005. (Illus.). 32p. (J). per. *(978-0-9768831-0-4(4))* Elohim Bks.
—Rudy Cazootie, 3 vols., 4 bks. l.t. ed. 2005. (Illus.). 32p. (J). per. *(978-0-9768831-2-8(0))* Elohim Bks.
—Sunny & Hunny, 2 vols., 4 bks. l.t. ed. 2005. (Illus.). 32p. (J). per. *(978-0-9768831-1-1(2))* Elohim Bks.
Zabrosky, Joseph & Jacobs, Nathaniel. The Christmas Tree, 4 vols., 4bks. l.t. ed. 2005. (Illus.). 32p. (J). per. *(978-0-9768831-3-5(9))* Elohim Bks.
Zoller, Jayson D. The Laziest Duck. l.t. ed. 2004. (Illus.). 13p. (J). per. 7.99 *(978-1-932338-52-2(7))* Lifevest Publishing, Inc.

LAS VEGAS (NEV.)

Davis, Alan S. The Fun Seeker's Las Vegas: The Ultimate Guide to One of the World's Hottest Cities. 2nd rev. ed. 2006. (Illus.). 224p. pap. 19.95 *(978-0-9759022-1-9(0))* Davis, A. S. Media Group.
Erlic, Lily. Las Vegas. 2020. (J). *(978-1-7911-1582-1(9),* AV2 by Weigl) Weigl Pubs., Inc.

LA SALLE, ROBERT CAVELIER, SIEUR DE, 1643-1687

Aretha, David. La Salle: French Explorer of the Mississippi, 1 vol. 2009. (Great Explorers of the World Ser.). (ENG., Illus.). 112p. (gr. 6-7). lib. bdg. 35.93 *(978-1-59845-098-9(0),* 2b91d3c2-fd41-4889-a6f1-505cb03714e4) Enslow Publishing, LLC.
Crompton, Samuel Willard. Robert de la Salle. 2009. (Great Explorers Ser.). (ENG., Illus.). 112p. (gr. 6-12). 30.00 *(978-1-60413-419-3(4),* P173417, Facts On File) Infobase Holdings, Inc.
Donaldson-Forbes, Jeff. La Salle. 2009. (Primary Source Library of Famous Explorers Ser.). 24p. (gr. 4-4). 42.50 *(978-1-60854-129-4(0),* PowerKids Pr.) Rosen Publishing Group, Inc., The.
Hazleton, Amie. Sieur de la Salle: An Explorer of the Great West. 2017. (World Explorers Ser.). (ENG., Illus.). 32p. (J). (gr. 3-6). lib. bdg. 27.99 *(978-1-5157-4206-7(7),* 133973, Capstone Pr.) Capstone.
Herr, Melody. Exploring the New World: An Interactive History Adventure. rev. ed. 2016. (You Choose: History Ser.). (ENG., Illus.). 112p. (J). (gr. 3-7). pap. 6.95 *(978-1-5157-4258-6(X),* 134012, Capstone Pr.) Capstone.
Kuligowski, Stephanie. La Salle: Early Texas Explorer, 1 vol. rev. ed. 2012. (Social Studies: Informational Text Ser.). (ENG.). 32p. (gr. 3-5). pap. 11.99 *(978-1-4333-5043-6(2))* Teacher Created Materials, Inc.
Mitchell, Mark. Raising la Belle. Mitchell, Mark, illus. (Professor Wigglestix & the Weather Ser.). (Illus.). 112p. 10.95 *(978-1-57168-703-6(3))* Eakin Pr.
Owens, Lisa L. A Journey with Sieur de la Salle. 2017. (Primary Source Explorers Ser.). (ENG., Illus.). 40p. (J). (gr. 3-5). 30.65 *(978-1-5124-0775-4(5),* 6ffa2a44-c9c5-4023-aa81-e9e9b293546f, Lerner Pubns.) Lerner Publishing Group.
Payment, Simone. La Salle: Claiming the Mississippi River for France. (Library of Explorers & Exploration Ser.). 112p. (gr. 5-8). 2009. 66.50 *(978-1-60853-610-8(6))* 2003. (ENG., Illus.). lib. bdg. 39.80 *(978-0-8239-3628-1(7),* fe0169b6-c923-4a81-8e33-bf4e8db3a854) Rosen Publishing Group, Inc., The. (Rosen Reference).
Zronik, John Paul. Sieur de la Salle: New World Adventurer. 2005. (In the Footsteps of Explorers Ser.). (ENG., Illus.). 32p. (J). (gr. 4-5). pap. *(978-0-7787-2449-0(2))* Crabtree Publishing Co.

LASERS

Amazing Lasers: Fourth Grade Guided Comprehension Level K. (On Our Way to English Ser.). (gr. 4-18). 34.50 *(978-0-7578-7148-1(8))* Rigby Education.
Duhig, Holly. Tractor Beams, 1 vol. 2017. (Science Fiction to Science Fact Ser.). (ENG.). 32p. (J). (gr. 4-5). pap. 11.50 *(978-1-5382-1489-3(X),* 496c8e06-4bb5-4140-bcf7-7314b9823d7d); lib. bdg. 28.27 *(978-1-5382-1390-2(7),* 23b6365a-729d-4eb1-96d6-33d825076439) Stevens, Gareth Publishing LLLP.
Gregory, Daniel. Solid State Lasers for the Laser Enthusiast - Pulse Edition, 1. American LaserTechnic. ed. 2003. (Illus.). 352p. (YA). per. 89.99 *(978-0-9741805-0-2(5))* American LaserTechnic.
Kamberg, Mary-Lane. Fab Lab Creating with Laser Cutters & Engravers, 1 vol. 2016. (Getting Creative with Fab Lab Ser.). (ENG.). 64p. (J). (gr. 6-6). 36.13 *(978-1-4994-6504-4(1),* 82340bb9-b692-4376-bd3f-32ab1f60a110) Rosen Publishing Group, Inc., The.
Labrecque, Ellen. Patricia Bath & Laser Surgery. 2017. (21st Century Junior Library: Women Innovators Ser.). (ENG., Illus.). 24p. (J). (gr. 2-5). lib. bdg. 29.21 *(978-1-63472-180-6(2),* 209292) Cherry Lake Publishing.
Laser-Sailing Starships: Meet NASA Inventor Philip Lubin & His Team's. 2017. (J). *(978-0-7166-6159-7(4))* World Bk., Inc.
National Geographic Learning. Reading Expeditions (Science: Everyday Science): Science at the Grocery. 2007. (ENG., Illus.). 24p. (J). pap. 15.95 *(978-0-7922-4567-4(9))* CENGAGE Learning.
Sill, Lisa. Stem: Lasers: Measuring Length (Grade 2) 2018. (Mathematics in the Real World Ser.). (ENG., Illus.). 32p. (J). (gr. 2-3). pap. 10.99 *(978-1-4258-5753-0(1))* Teacher Created Materials, Inc.
Sill, Lisa M. CTIM - Láseres: Medición de la Longitud. rev. ed. 2018. (Mathematics in the Real World Ser.). (SPA., Illus.). 32p. (J). (gr. 2-3). pap. 10.99 *(978-1-4258-2870-7(1))* Teacher Created Materials, Inc.
Wyckoff, Edwin Brit. Laser Man: Theodore H. Maiman & His Brilliant Invention, 1 vol. 2008. (Genius at Work! Great Inventor Biographies Ser.). (ENG., Illus.). 32p. (gr. 3-3). lib. bdg. 25.60 *(978-0-7660-2848-7(8),* 2a2ba42f-9b68-4fc0-b905-acf0c322a5fe, Enslow Elementary) Enslow Publishing, LLC.
—The Man Who Invented the Laser: The Genius of Theodore H. Maiman, 1 vol. 2013. (Genius Inventors & Their Great Ideas Ser.). (ENG.). 48p. (gr. 3-3). pap. 11.53 *(978-1-4644-0208-1(6),* d3f32df7-a703-4e06-bfc3-45b4864f0bc1); (Illus.). 27.93 *(978-0-7660-4138-7(7),* 101a9735-0fa2-47eb-928c-e7705772b974) Enslow Publishing, LLC. (Enslow Elementary).

LATCHKEY CHILDREN—FICTION

Brenda Seabrooke. Jerry on the Line. 2010. 132p. pap. 10.95 *(978-1-4401-8766-7(5))* iUniverse, Inc.
Horowitz, Jeanine. Latch Key Kid. 2006. 75p. (YA). lib. bdg. 12.99 *(978-1-934190-10-4(1))* Ocean Front Bk. Publishing, Inc.
Mantell, Paul & Christopher, Matt. Mountain Bike Mania. l.t. ed. 2007. (New Matt Christopher Sports Library). 160p. (J). (gr. 4-6). lib. bdg. 26.60 *(978-1-59953-108-3(9))* Norwood Hse. Pr.
Ocean Front Books. Coloring Book. l.t. ed. 2006. (Illus.). (J). lib. bdg. *(978-1-934190-02-9(0))* Ocean Front Bk. Publishing, Inc.
Salvatierra, Dante. Latchkey Kids & the Fight for A Free F. 2006. (ENG.). 236p. pap. 13.95 *(978-1-4303-0969-7(5))* Lulu Pr., Inc.
—The Latchkey Kids & the Trip Through T. 2005. (ENG.). 234p. pap. 12.99 *(978-1-4116-3814-3(X))* Lulu Pr., Inc.
Sizer, Ralph Robuck. Rashad & Rameen. 2011. 26p. pap. 16.95 *(978-1-4560-6459-4(2))* America Star Bks.

LATIMER, LEWIS HOWARD, 1848-1928

Marsico, Katie. Lewis Howard Latimer. Bane, Jeff, illus. 2018. (My Early Library: My Itty-Bitty Bio Ser.). (ENG.). 24p. (J). (gr. k-1). lib. bdg. 30.64 *(978-1-5341-2880-4(8),* 211564) Cherry Lake Publishing.

LATIN AMERICA

see also South America

Ancona, George. Mis Fiestas: My Celebrations. 2005. (Somos Latinos (We Are Latinos) Ser.).Tr. of My Celebrations. (SPA., Illus.). 32p. (J). (gr. 1-3). lib. bdg. 21.00 *(978-0-516-25290-2(9))* Scholastic Library Publishing.
Brimson, Samuel. Volume 3: Ecuador-Honduras, 1 vol., Vol. 3. 2003. (Nations of the World Ser.: Vol. 3). (ENG., Illus.). 64p. (gr. 5-8). lib. bdg. 33.67 *(978-0-8368-5487-9(X),* 32bfd28e-555e-4895-98f0-9913e42fa014, Gareth Stevens Secondary Library) Stevens, Gareth Publishing LLLP.
DePietro, Frank. Latino American Cuisine. 2012. (Illus.). 64p. (J). pap. *(978-1-4222-2337-6(X))* Mason Crest.
—Latino American Cuisine. Limón, José E., ed. 2012. (Hispanic Americans: Major Minority Ser.). (Illus.). 64p. (J). (gr. 4). 22.95 *(978-1-4222-2320-8(5))* Mason Crest.
Goring, Ruth. Dias Festivos y Celebraciones. Palacios, Argentina, tr. Date not set. (Vida Latina Ser.). (SPA., Illus.). 48p. (J). (gr. 4-8). lib. bdg. 18.95 *(978-0-86625-564-6(8))* Rourke Educational Media.
Rodriguez, Patty & Stein, Ariana. Life of/la Vida de Celia, 1 vol. Reyes, Citlali, illus. 2018. (SPA.). 22p. (J). (gr. -1-k). bds. 9.99 *(978-0-9861099-5-9(9))* Little Libros, LLC.
Schon, Isabel. The Best of Latino Heritage, 1996-2002: A Guide to the Best Juvenile Books about Latino People. 2003. (ENG., Illus.). 272p. 87.00 *(978-0-8108-4669-2(1))* Scarecrow Pr., Inc.
Thatcher Murcia, Rebecca. What It's Like to Be Shakira. de la Vega, Eida, tr. from SPA. 2010. (What It's Like to Be/Que se Siente al Ser Ser.). (ENG & SPA., Illus.). 32p. (J). (gr. -1-2). lib. bdg. 25.70 *(978-1-58415-851-6(4))* Mitchell Lane Pubs.
Thomas, Isabel. Latin Dance. 2011. (On the Radar: Dance Ser.). (ENG., Illus.). 32p. (gr. 4-8). lib. bdg. 26.60 *(978-0-7613-7762-7(X))* Lerner Publishing Group.
Walker, Kathryn. See How Cats Grow, 1 vol. 2009. (See How They Grow Ser.). (ENG., Illus.). 24p. (J). (gr. 2-2). pap. 9.25 *(978-1-4358-2875-9(5),* b0d9bdeb-ed74-44cf-b652-a1b5f37d9897, PowerKids Pr.) Rosen Publishing Group, Inc., The.
Williams, Zella. Llamas & Other Latin American Camels: Llamas y Otros Camélidos de Latinoamérica, 1 vol. 2009. (Animals of Latin America / Animales de Latinoamérica Ser.). (SPA & ENG.). 24p. (gr. 2-2). pap. 8.25 *(978-1-4358-3388-3(0),* f0b64cd8-7eea-4f2c-b56d-4abf08d8c0c6, PowerKids Pr.) Rosen Publishing Group, Inc., The.
Zaragoza, Gonzalo. America Latina: Epoca Colonial. (Biblioteca Iberoamericana Ser.). (SPA.). 96p. (YA). 16.50 *(978-84-7525-445-6(4),* ANY454) Grupo Anaya, S.A. ESP. Dist: Continental Bk. Co., Inc.

LATIN AMERICA—BIOGRAPHY

Brown, Monica. My Name Is Celia (Me Llamo Celia) The Life of Celia Cruz (La Vida de Celia Cruz) López, Rafael, illus. 2015. (ENG, MUL & SPA.). 32p. (J). (gr. k-3). pap. 7.95 *(978-1-58979-998-1(4))* Jaffe Book Solutions.
Chambers, Veronica. Celia Cruz, Queen of Salsa. Maren, Julie, illus. 2008. (J). (gr. -1-3). 28.95 incl. audio compact disk *(978-1-4301-0284-7(5))*; 25.95 incl. audio *(978-1-4301-0281-6(0))*; pap. 16.95 incl. audio *(978-1-4301-0280-9(2))* Live Oak Media.
—Celia Cruz, Queen of Salsa. Maren, Julie, illus. 2007. (gr. 2-5). 17.00 *(978-0-7569-8153-2(0))* Perfection Learning Corp.
Crompton, Samuel Willard. Che Guevara: the Making of a Revolutionary, 1 vol. 2009. (Life Portraits Ser.). (ENG., Illus.). 112p. (J). (gr. 6-8). lib. bdg. 38.67 *(978-1-4339-0053-2(X),* 5d738a89-ba5a-4280-a185-bd7be733cc43) Stevens, Gareth Publishing LLLP.
Krohn, Katherine. Biography Shakira. 2007. (Biography Ser.). (Illus.). 112p. (J). (gr. -1). lib. bdg. 30.60 *(978-0-8225-7159-5(5),* Twenty-First Century Bks.) Lerner Publishing Group.
Murcia, Rebecca Thatcher. Shakira. 2007. (Blue Banner Biography Ser.). (Illus.). 32p. (YA). (gr. 4-7). lib. bdg. 25.70 *(978-1-58415-609-3(0))* Mitchell Lane Pubs.
Smith-Llera, Danielle. Che Guevara's Face: How a Cuban Photographer's Image Became a Cultural Icon. 2016. (Captured World History Ser.). (ENG., Illus.). 64p. (J). (gr. 5-9). lib. bdg. 35.32 *(978-0-7565-5440-8(3),* 132575, Compass Point Bks.) Capstone.
Uschan, Michael V. Che Guevara: Revolutionary, 1 vol. 2006. (Twentieth Century's Most Influential Hispanics Ser.). (ENG., Illus.). 104p. (gr. 7-10). lib. bdg. 37.73 *(978-1-59018-970-2(1),* aa4b39ad-f981-4547-8b3d-6ade2bc40cb7, Lucent Pr.) Greenhaven Publishing LLC.
Williams, Zella. Shakira: Star Singer, 1 vol. 2010. (Hispanic Headliners Ser.). (ENG.). 24p. (J). (gr. 2-3). pap. 9.25 *(978-1-4488-1480-0(4),* ddc78bf0-e43e-4a50-8ffb-288391671e1b); lib. bdg. 26.27 *(978-1-4488-1457-2(X),* fb1a05d7-e0b5-4a93-ad2a-cdd3c7b85e39) Rosen Publishing Group, Inc., The. (PowerKids Pr.).
—Shakira: Star Singer - Estrella de la Canción, 1 vol. 2010. (Hispanic Headliners / Hispanos en Las Noticias Ser.). (SPA & ENG.). 24p. (J). (gr. 2-3). lib. bdg. 26.27 *(978-1-4488-0714-7(X),* 03c78672-66a9-4ec6-95ec-308d75bcbb7c) Rosen Publishing Group, Inc., The.

LATIN AMERICA—FICTION

Baez, Josefina. Comrade, Bliss Ain't Playing: Un Cuento de la Republica Dominicana. Cortes, Paulina, illus. 2008. (Marisol Ser.: Vol. 1). (ENG.). 100p. (Orig.). (gr. k-3). pap. 12.95 *(978-1-882161-01-0(7))* I.Om.Be Pr.
Byers, Arlene. Rainbows for Rosa. Halverson, Randal, illus. 2016. (ENG.). 172p. 9.50 *(978-0-7399-2521-8(0))* Rod & Staff Pubs., Inc.
Delacre, Lulu. Salsa Stories. Delacre, Lulu, illus. 2012. (ENG., Illus.). 112p. (J). (gr. 2-5). pap. 6.99 *(978-0-545-43098-2(4),* Scholastic Pr.) Scholastic, Inc.
—Us, in Progress: Short Stories about Young Latinos. Delacre, Lulu, illus. (ENG., Illus.). 256p. (J). (gr. 3-7). 2019. pap. 9.99 *(978-0-06-239215-2(8))* 2017. 18.99 *(978-0-06-239214-5(X))* HarperCollins Pubs. (HarperCollins).
Iturralde, Edna. Verde Fue Mi Selva. Arroba, Doris et al, eds. Cornejo, Eulalia, illus. 2008. (Alfaguara Infantil Ser.).Tr. of My Forest Was Green. 152p. (J). (gr. 5-8). pap. *(978-9978-07-097-0(4))* Ediciones Alfaguara.
Joseph, Lynn. The Color of My Words. 2019. (ENG.). 160p. (J). (gr. 3-7). pap. 9.99 *(978-0-06-447204-3(3),* HarperCollins) HarperCollins Pubs.
LeapFrog Staff. Disney Princess Stories - Latin America. 2003. (Illus.). (J). spiral bd. 14.99 *(978-1-59319-001-9(8))* LeapFrog Enterprises, Inc.
Martinez, Rueben. Once upon a Time/Habia una Vez: Traditional Latin American Tales/Cuentos Tradicionales Latinoamericanos (Bilingual English-Spanish) ón, Raúl, illus. 2010. (ENG.). 96p. (J). (gr. -1-3). 19.99 *(978-0-06-146895-7(9))* HarperCollins Español.
Porras, Javier Fernando, illus. Historias de Amores y Desvarios en America. 2004. (Literatura Juvenil (Panamericana Editorial) Ser.). (SPA.). 179p. (J). (gr. -1-7). pap. *(978-958-30-0569-5(X),* PV4378) Centro de Informacion y Desarrollo de la Comunicacion y la Literatura MEX. Dist: Lectorum Pubns., Inc.
Skarmeta, Antonio. The Composition, 1 vol. Ruano, Alfonso, illus. 2003. (ENG.). 36p. (J). (gr. 3-3). pap. 8.95 *(978-0-88899-550-6(4))* Groundwood Bks. CAN. Dist: Publishers Group West (PGW).

LATIN AMERICA—HISTORY

Coletti, Sharon. Everything You Need to Teach Latin America. 2005. (YA). ring bd. 149.95 *(978-1-933558-03-5(2))* InspirEd Educators.
Crompton, Samuel Willard. Che Guevara: the Making of a Revolutionary, 1 vol. 2009. (Life Portraits Ser.). (ENG., Illus.). 112p. (J). (gr. 6-8). lib. bdg. 38.67 *(978-1-4339-0053-2(X),* 5d738a89-ba5a-4280-a185-bd7be733cc43) Stevens, Gareth Publishing LLLP.
DePietro, Frank. Spain Arrives in the Americas. Limón, José E., ed. 2012. (Hispanic Americans: Major Minority Ser.). 64p. (J). (gr. 4). 22.95 *(978-1-4222-2330-7(2))* Mason Crest.
Exploring Latin America. 2017. (Exploring Latin America Ser.). 48p. (gr. 10-12). pap. 56.20 *(978-1-5081-0526-8(X))*; (ENG.). (gr. 6-7). 113.64 *(978-1-5081-0524-4(3),* 23a7b8d5-020e-4768-9e33-94d45710720c) Rosen Publishing Group, Inc., The. (Britannica Educational Publishing).
Gerdes, Louise I., ed. Latin America, 1 vol. 2009. (Opposing Viewpoints Ser.). (ENG., Illus.). 264p. (gr. 10-12). pap. 34.80 *(978-0-7377-4373-9(5),*

J K L

63bb4310-ee94-4179-95a0-258e07cb861f); lib. bdg. 50.43 *(978-0-7377-4374-6(3),* 7b1e2910-e093-4713-950a-59bb27c69c31) Greenhaven Publishing LLC. (Greenhaven Publishing).

Hirsch, E. D., Jr., ed. Independence for Latin America, Level 6. tchr. ed. 9.95 *(978-0-7690-5090-4(5));* stu. ed. 49.95 *(978-0-7690-2855-2(1))* Pearson Learning.

Kallen, Stuart A. The History of Latin Music, 1 vol. 2013. (Music Library). (ENG., Illus.). 128p. (gr. 7-10). lib. bdg. 41.03 *(978-1-4205-0947-2(0),* d4693430-b0e5-4412-9286-bcbeb05dde14, Lucent Pr.) Greenhaven Publishing LLC.

Miller, Calvin Craig. Che Guevara: In Search of Revolution. 2006. (World Leaders Ser.). (Illus.). 192p. (J). (gr. 6-12). lib. bdg. 26.95 *(978-1-931798-93-8(1))* Reynolds, Morgan Inc.

Mooney, Carla. The Economy of Latin America. 2017. (Exploring Latin America Ser.). (Illus.). 48p. (J). (gr. 10-12). 84.30 *(978-1-68048-678-0(0),* Britannica Educational Publishing) Rosen Publishing Group, Inc., The.

Nichols, Susan. The History of Latin America, 1 vol. 2017. (Exploring Latin America Ser.). (ENG., Illus.). 48p. (J). (gr. 6-7). pap. 15.05 *(978-1-68048-681-0(0),* e98a2fbc-3107-479c-82c5-7fc684204190, Britannica Educational Publishing) Rosen Publishing Group, Inc., The.

—The People & Culture of Latin America, 1 vol. 2017. (Exploring Latin America Ser.). (ENG., Illus.). 48p. (J). (gr. 6-7). pap. 15.05 *(978-1-68048-689-6(6),* 31403e5f-d6c5-442f-b23e-2c49dbd78f4b, Britannica Educational Publishing) Rosen Publishing Group, Inc., The.

Pearce, Q. L. La Llorona: The Crying Woman, 1 vol. 2009. (Mysterious Encounters Ser.). (ENG., Illus.). 48p. (gr. 4-8). 30.63 *(978-0-7377-4571-9(1),* 37429b5b-c7c7-4c2f-b204-9791d1b9ea5e, KidHaven Publishing) Greenhaven Publishing LLC.

Putumayo Kids Staff, creator. Latin America Sticker Coll. 2011. (J). pap. 11.95 *(978-1-58759-285-0(1))* Putumayo World Music & Crafts.

Rice, Earle, Jr. A Brief Political & Geographic History of Latin America: Where Are... Gran Colombia, la Plata, & Dutch Guiana. 2007. (Places in Time Ser.). (Illus.). 112p. (J). (gr. 5-9). lib. bdg. 37.10 *(978-1-58415-626-0(0),* 1270683) Mitchell Lane Pubs.

Salinas, Eva. Lo Inventaron los Latinoamericanos: Innovaciones Asombrosas. Galouchko, Annouchka, illus. 2012. (ENG.). 48p. (J). (gr. 3-7). 21.95 *(978-1-55451-379-6(0),* 9781554513796) Annick Pr., Ltd. CAN. Dist: Publishers Group West (PGW).

—Latin Americans Thought of It: Amazing Innovations. 2012. (We Thought of It Ser.). (ENG., Illus.). 48p. (J). (gr. 4-6). 21.95 *(978-1-55451-377-2(4),* 9781554513772) Annick Pr., Ltd. CAN. Dist: Publishers Group West (PGW).

Sebastian, Emily. The Colonial & Postcolonial Experience in Latin America & the Caribbean, 1 vol. 2016. (Colonial & Postcolonial Experience Ser.). (ENG., Illus.). 256p. (J). (gr. 10-10). 55.59 *(978-1-5081-0439-1(5),* 6083d7af-3889-4012-9b3a-9c8057fca86a) Rosen Publishing Group, Inc., The.

Shea, Therese. The Land & Climate of Latin America, 1 vol. 2017. (Exploring Latin America Ser.). (ENG.). 48p. (J). (gr. 6-7). pap. 15.05 *(978-1-68048-685-8(3),* dba71570-3007-4b47-b8c8-ac27d9a4d9db, Britannica Educational Publishing) Rosen Publishing Group, Inc., The.

Williams, Zella. Coqui Frogs & Other Latin American Frogs, 1 vol. 2009. (Animals of Latin America / Animales de Latinoamérica Ser.). (SPA & ENG., Illus.). 24p. (gr. 2-2). pap. 8.25 *(978-1-4358-3382-1(1),* 80e0fdee-6844-4f8d-b2b3-405b29b28117, PowerKids Pr.) Rosen Publishing Group, Inc., The.

—Coqui Frogs & Other Latin American Frogs/Coquies y Otras Ranas de Latinoamerica, 1 vol. 2009. (Animals of Latin America / Animales de Latinoamérica Ser.). (SPA & ENG., Illus.). 24p. (J). (gr. 2-2). lib. bdg. 26.27 *(978-1-4042-8148-6(7),* 5d549894-f59a-480e-bb2d-caff8316df38, PowerKids Pr.) Rosen Publishing Group, Inc., The.

LATIN AMERICA—POLITICS AND GOVERNMENT

Day, Meredith, ed. Revolution & Independence in Latin America, 4 vols. 2015. (Age of Revolution Ser.). (ENG.). 184p. (YA). (gr. 9-10). 75.64 *(978-1-68048-030-6(8),* 95ba83e6-e26d-4147-b17f-650f4f8fc6dc, Britannica Educational Publishing) Rosen Publishing Group, Inc., The.

Dunn, John M. Life in Castro's Cuba. 2004. (Way People Live Ser.). (ENG., Illus.). 112p. (J). (gr. 7-10). 30.85 *(978-1-59018-464-6(5))* Cengage Gale.

LATIN AMERICA—SOCIAL CONDITIONS

Arkham, Thomas. Latino Americans & Their Jobs. 2013. (Illus.). 64p. (J). pap. *(978-1-4222-2340-6(X))* Mason Crest.

—Latino Americans & Their Jobs. Limón, José E., ed. 2012. (Hispanic Americans: Major Minority Ser.). (Illus.). 64p. (J). (gr. 4). 22.95 *(978-1-4222-2323-9(X))* Mason Crest.

Duhig, Holly. Cultural Contributions from Latin America: Tortillas, Color TV, & More, 1 vol. 2018. (Great Cultures, Great Ideas Ser.). (ENG.). 32p. (gr. 3-4). 27.93 *(978-1-5383-3829-2(7),* 805fe5fd-6106-4ee2-aa8e-d4a400003dff, PowerKids Pr.) Rosen Publishing Group, Inc., The.

Dunn, John M. Life in Castro's Cuba. 2004. (Way People Live Ser.). (ENG., Illus.). 112p. (J). (gr. 7-10). 30.85 *(978-1-59018-464-6(5))* Cengage Gale.

Hollihan, Kerrie Logan. Christmas Traditions in Latin America: Tradiciones Navidenas en Latinoamérica, 1 vol. Sanz, Ma Pilar, tr. 2010. (Latin American Celebrations & Festivals / Celebraciones y Festivales en Latinoamérica Ser.). (SPA & ENG., Illus.). 24p. (J). (gr. 2-3). lib. bdg. 26.27 *(978-1-4358-9365-8(4),* 70682eba-de22-4b95-b754-9c7926c4a4ec) Rosen Publishing Group, Inc., The.

Hulick, Kathryn. The South American Family Table, Vol. 11. 2018. (Connecting Cultures Through Family & Food Ser.). (Illus.). 64p. (J). (gr. 7). 31.93 *(978-1-4222-4051-9(7))* Mason Crest.

Nichols, Susan. The People & Culture of Latin America, 1 vol. 2017. (Exploring Latin America Ser.). (ENG., Illus.). 48p. (J). (gr. 6-7). 28.41 *(978-1-68048-691-9(8),* 4cc6cb41-df1e-41e6-a227-074f24f9aab9, Britannica Educational Publishing) Rosen Publishing Group, Inc., The.

Worth, Richard. The 1950s To 1960s, 1 vol. 2010. (Hispanic America Ser.). (ENG.). 80p. (gr. 5-5). 36.93 *(978-0-7614-4177-9(8),* be97564a-71ed-4280-b913-1ef20a16eaaa) Cavendish Square Publishing LLC.

LATIN AMERICAN LITERATURE—HISTORY AND CRITICISM

Bloom, Harold, ed. Gabriel Garcia Marrquez's Love in the Time of Cholera. 2005. (Modern Critical Interpretations Ser.). (ENG., Illus.). 144p. (gr. 9-13). 45.00 *(978-0-7910-8120-4(6),* P114130, Facts On File) Infobase Holdings, Inc.

LATIN AMERICANS

Here are entered works on citizens of Latin American countries. Works on citizens of Latin American countries in the United States are entered under Latin Americans—United States. Works on United States citizens of Latin American descent are entered under Hispanic Americans.

Engle, Margarita. Bravo! Poems about Amazing Hispanics. Lopez, Rafael, illus. 2017. (ENG.). 48p. (J). 19.99 *(978-0-8050-9876-1(3),* 900122994, Holt, Henry & Co. Bks. For Young Readers) Holt, Henry & Co.

LATIN AMERICANS—FICTION

Cuentos, Mitos y Leyendas para Ninos de America Latina (Stories, Myths & Legends for Latin American Children) (SPA., Illus.). 72p. (J). 9.95 *(978-958-04-0957-1(9),* NOR9609) Norma S.A. COL. Dist: Distribuidora Norma, Inc.

Kyle, Tracey. Pepe & the Parade: A Celebration of Hispanic Heritage. Ortega, Mirelle, illus. 2019. (ENG.). 32p. (J). (gr. -1-3). 16.99 *(978-1-4998-0666-3(3))* Little Bee Books Inc.

North, Julian. State of Order. 2017. (ENG.). 344p. (YA). pap. *(978-0-9992658-0-2(6))* Plebeian Media.

Quintero, Isabel. My Papi Has a Motorcycle. Peña, Zeke, illus. 2019. (ENG.). 40p. (J). (gr. -1-3). 18.99 *(978-0-525-55341-0(X),* Kokila) Penguin Young Readers Group.

Robleda, Margarita. Paco: A Latino Boy in the U.S. 2004. (Paco & María Ser.). (SPA.). 36p. (gr. 3-5). pap. 13.95 *(978-1-59437-560-6(7),* Alfaguara) Santillana USA Publishing Co., Inc.

LATIN AMERICANS—UNITED STATES

Ada, Alma Flor & Campoy, F. Isabel. Yes! We Are Latinos: Poems & Prose about the Latino Experience. Diaz, David, illus. 2016. 96p. (J). (gr. 5). pap. 9.95 *(978-1-58089-549-1(2))* Charlesbridge Publishing, Inc.

Winter, Jonah. Beisbol!: Pioneros y Leyendas Del Beisbol Latino (Spanish Edition), 1 vol. 2017. (SPA., Illus.). 32p. (J). (gr. 1-6). pap. 10.95 *(978-1-58430-036-6(1),* leelowbooks) Lee & Low Bks., Inc.

Worth, Richard. The 1970s to The 1980s, 1 vol. 2010. (Hispanic America Ser.). (ENG.). 80p. (gr. 5-5). 36.93 *(978-0-7614-4178-6(6),* 96cd516d-96be-4c76-9718-5b4584d99fae) Cavendish Square Publishing LLC.

LATIN LANGUAGE

Baddorf, Robert A. & Perrin, Christopher. Latin for Children, Primer a Activity Book! 2005. (Latin for Childred Ser.). (ENG.). 163p. (J). (gr. -1-3). pap., act. bk. ed. 16.95 *(978-1-60051-005-2(1))* Classical Academic Pr.

Bolchazy, Marie Carducci. Quis Me Amat?/Who Loves Me? 2003. (I Am Reading Latin Ser.). (ENG., Illus.). 64p. (J). (gr. k-3). pap. 10.00 *(978-0-86516-541-0(6))* Bolchazy-Carducci Pubs.

Carole Marsh. Of All the Gaul! Latin for Kids. 2004. (Little Linguist Ser.). 32p. (gr. 2-6). pap. 5.95 *(978-0-635-02429-9(2))* Gallopade International.

Griffith, Timothy. Orbis Naturalis. 2012. (Illus.). (J). *(978-1-59128-116-0(4))* Canon Pr.

Latin Grammar Student Workbook. 2003. stu. ed., ring bd., wbk. ed. *(978-1-931680-42-4(6))* Teaching Point, Inc.

Lowe, Leigh. Prima Latina Student Book: Introduction to Christian Latin. 2nd ed. 2003. (Classical Trivium Core Ser.). 128p. (J). per. 14.00 *(978-1-930953-51-2(8),* 002) Memoria Pr.

Lundquist, Joegil K. & Lundquist, Jeanne L. English from the Roots up, Volume II: Help for Reading, Writing, Spelling & S. A. T. Scores. 2011. (English from the Roots Up Ser.). (ENG., Illus.). 107p. (J). (gr. -1-3). 44.95 *(978-1-885942-30-2(3))* Cune Pr., LLC.

—English from the Roots up Volume II: Help for Reading, Writing, Spelling, & S. A. T. Scores, vols. 2, II. 2003. (Illus.). 125p. 29.95 net. *(978-1-885942-31-9(1))* Cune Pr., LLC.

Marsh, Carole. Of All the Gaul! Latin for Kids. Beard, Chad, ed. 2004. (Little Linguist Ser.). (Illus.). 32p. 29.95 *(978-0-635-02437-4(3))* Gallopade International.

Minkova, Milena & Tunberg, Terence O. Lingua Latina Perennis: An Introductory Course to the Language of the Ages. 2008. (ENG.). tchr. ed. 99.00 *(978-0-86516-562-5(9))* Bolchazy-Carducci Pubs.

Osburn, LeaAnn. Latin Verbs Rock! Exercise Book. 2007. spiral bd. 18.00 *(978-0-9760046-6-0(6))* L & L Enterprises.

The Rosetta Stone Language Library: Latin Level 1. 2005. (J). (gr. 1-18). cd-rom 209.00 *(978-1-58022-026-2(6))* Rosetta Stone Ltd.

Sheikh-Miller, Jonathan. Latin Words Sticker Book. Cartwright, Stephen, illus. 2006. (Latin Words Sticker Book Ser.). 16p. (J). (gr. 1). pap. 8.99 *(978-0-7945-1145-6(7),* Usborne) EDC Publishing.

LATIN LANGUAGE—READERS

Baddorf, Robert & Perrin, Christopher. Latin for Children. Baddorf, Robert, illus. 2006. (Latin for Childred Ser.). (ENG., Illus.). 162p. (J). (gr. 4-7). pap., act. bk. ed. 16.95 *(978-1-60051-017-5(5))* Classical Academic Pr.

—Latin for Children, Primer B Activity Book! Baddorf, Robert, illus. 2005. (Latin for Childred Ser.). (ENG., Illus.). 196p. (J). (gr. 4-7). pap., act. bk. ed. 16.95 *(978-1-60051-011-3(6))* Classical Academic Pr.

Bolchazy, Marie Carducci. Quo Colore Est?/What Color Is It? 2003. (I Am Reading Latin Ser.). (ENG., Illus.). 64p. (J). (gr. k-3). pap. 10.00 *(978-0-86516-539-7(4))* Bolchazy-Carducci Pubs.

Larsen, Aaron & Perrin, Christopher. Latin for Children, Primer B. 2004. (Latin for Childred Ser.). (ENG., Illus.). 286p. (J). (gr. -1-12). pap. 24.95 *(978-1-60051-006-9(X))* Classical Academic Pr.

—Latin for Children, Primer B Answer Key. 2004. (Latin for Childred Ser.). (ENG.). 144p. (J). (gr. 4-7). pap. 14.95 *(978-1-60051-007-6(8))* Classical Academic Pr.

—Latin for Children, Primer C. 2005. (Latin for Childred Ser.). (ENG., Illus.). 310p. (J). (gr. 4-7). pap. 24.95 *(978-1-60051-012-0(4))* Classical Academic Pr.

—Latin for Children, Primer C Answer Key. 2005. (Latin for Childred Ser.). (ENG.). 142p. (J). (gr. 4-7). pap. 14.95 *(978-1-60051-013-7(2))* Classical Academic Pr.

MacLaren, Dorothy H. Esopus Hodie, Aesop Today, Vol. 1. (ENG & LAT.). 64p. (YA). (gr. 9-12). 9.75 *(978-0-939507-06-1(4),* B20) American Classical League, The.

Moore, Karen. Latin for Children: A History Reader. 2005. (Latin for Childred Ser.). (ENG., Illus.). 56p. (J). (gr. 4-7). pap. 9.95 *(978-1-60051-004-5(3))* Classical Academic Pr.

Moore, Karen & Davis, Erin. Latin for Children, Primer B History Reader. 2005. (Latin for Childred Ser.). (ENG., Illus.). 154p. (J). (gr. 4-7). pap. 12.95 *(978-1-60051-010-6(8))* Classical Academic Pr.

—Latin for Children, Primer C History Reader: Libellus de Historia. 2005. (Latin for Childred Ser.). (ENG., Illus.). 188p. (J). (gr. 4-7). pap. 16.95 *(978-1-60051-016-8(7))* Classical Academic Pr.

Robinson, Lorna. Telling Tales in Latin: A New Latin Course & Storybook for Children. 2013. (ENG., Illus.). 112p. (J). (gr. 4-7). pap. 15.95 *(978-0-285-64179-2(4))* Souvenir Pr. Ltd. GBR. Dist: Consortium Bk. Sales & Distribution.

Rose, Williams. Octavus Octopus. James, Estes, illus. 2008. (ENG.). 20p. (J). pap. 10.00 *(978-0-86516-698-1(6))* Bolchazy-Carducci Pubs.

—Rena Rhinoceros. James, Estes, illus. 2008. (ENG.). 20p. (J). pap. 10.00 *(978-0-86516-699-8(4))* Bolchazy-Carducci Pubs.

—Taurus Rex. James, Estes, illus. 2008. (ENG.). 20p. (J). pap. 10.00 *(978-0-86516-700-1(1))* Bolchazy-Carducci Pubs.

—Ursus et Porcus. James, Estes, illus. 2008. (ENG.). 20p. (J). pap. 10.00 *(978-0-86516-701-8(X))* Bolchazy-Carducci Pubs.

Williams, Rose. The Young Romans. 2007. (ENG.). pap. 23.00 *(978-0-86516-670-7(6))* Bolchazy-Carducci Pubs.

LATIN LITERATURE

Kerrigan, Michael. Romans, 1 vol. 2011. (Ancients in Their Own Words Ser.). (ENG., Illus.). 64p. (gr. 6-6). 35.50 *(978-1-60870-067-7(4),* 7b54880f-f286-4ed0-909a-1a46e3c457dd) Cavendish Square Publishing LLC.

LATTER-DAY SAINTS

see Mormons and Mormonism

LATVIA

Aizpuriete, Amanda. Latvia. Hartgers, Katarina, tr. Bultje, Jan Willem, photos by. 2006. (Looking at Europe Ser.). (Illus.). 48p. (YA). (gr. 5-8). 22.95 *(978-1-881508-37-3(4))* Oliver Pr., Inc.

Barlas, Robert & Wong, Winnie. Latvia, 1 vol. 2nd rev. ed. 2010. (Cultures of the World (Second Edition)(r) Ser.). (ENG.). 144p. (gr. 5-5). 49.79 *(978-0-7614-4857-0(8),* df9ced52-45f7-46a1-96f2-92bae5fb7f93) Cavendish Square Publishing LLC.

Docalavich, Heather & Indovino, Shaina Carmel. Latvia. 2012. (J). *(978-1-4222-2249-2(7));* pap. *(978-1-4222-2280-5(2))* Mason Crest.

LAVOISIER, ANTOINE LAURENT, 1743-1794

Van Gorp, Lynn. Antoine Lavoisier: Founder of Modern Chemistry, 1 vol. rev. ed. 2007. (Science: Informational Text Ser.). (ENG.). 32p. (gr. 3-6). pap. 12.99 *(978-0-7439-0582-4(2))* Teacher Created Materials, Inc.

Yount, Lisa. Antoine Lavoisier: Founder of Modern Chemistry, 1 vol. rev. ed. 2009. (Great Minds of Science Ser.). (ENG., Illus.). 128p. (gr. 5-6). lib. bdg. 35.93 *(978-0-7660-3011-4(3),* 7534c8ac-e848-4b49-be71-31df072564e6) Enslow Publishing, LLC.

—Antoine Lavoisier: Genius of Modern Chemistry, 1 vol. 2014. (Genius Scientists & Their Genius Ideas Ser.). (ENG.). 96p. (gr. 5-5). 29.60 *(978-0-7660-6520-8(0),* fc4c76c5-872d-4ba2-809e-c075eb5d2feb); pap. 13.88 *(978-0-7660-6521-5(9),* 6df074a3-0f43-443c-a7ae-9642c28db1aa) Enslow Publishing, LLC.

LAW

see also Courts; Judges; Jury; Lawyers; Police

also special branches of law, e.g. International Law; For laws on special subjects see names of subjects with the subdivision Laws and Regulations, e.g. Automobiles—Laws and Regulations

Acks, Alex. Key Social Safety Laws. 2019. (J). pap. *(978-1-9785-1443-0(3))* Enslow Publishing, LLC.

Arbetman, Lee P., et al. Street Law: A Course in Practical Law. 7th ed. 2004. (Ntc: Street Law Ser.). (ENG., Illus.). 684p. (gr. 9-12). stu. ed. 121.44 *(978-0-07-860019-7(7),* 0078600197) McGraw-Hill Higher Education.

Bailey, Rachel A. The Triangle Shirtwaist Factory Fire: A History Perspectives Book. 2014. (Perspectives Library). (ENG., Illus.). 32p. (J). (gr. 4-8). 32.07 *(978-1-63137-620-7(9),* 205263) Cherry Lake Publishing.

Beel, Rory. The Second Informant. 2005. 65p. pap. 16.95 *(978-1-4137-8359-9(7))* PublishAmerica, Inc.

Boocock, Charles & Yu, Jennifer. The 10 Most Memorable Court Cases. 2008. 14.99 *(978-1-55448-548-2(7))* Scholastic Library Publishing.

Bowers, Matt. Understanding How Laws Are Made. 2019. (Sequence American Government Ser.). (ENG.). 32p. (J). (gr. 2-5). lib. bdg. *(978-1-68151-672-1(1),* 10804) Amicus.

Brignall, Richard. Real Justice: a Police Mr. Big Sting Goes Wrong: The Story of Kyle Unger, 1 vol. 2015. (Lorimer Real Justice Ser.). (ENG., Illus.). 136p. (YA). (gr. 9-12). pap. 12.95 *(978-1-4594-0862-3(4),* 3444302a-f2fb-42e7-9ab1-824251b03735) James Lorimer & Co. Ltd., Pubs. CAN. Dist: Lerner Publishing Group.

Byers, Ann. Massachusetts Body of Liberties, 1 vol. 2018. (America's Most Important Documents: Inquiry into Historical Sources Ser.). (ENG.). 64p. (gr. 6-6). lib. bdg. 37.36 *(978-1-5026-3613-3(1),* ff55a05c-256f-492b-a265-0c54b6489c05) Cavendish Square Publishing LLC.

Cane, Ella. The U. S. House of Representatives, 1 vol. 2014. (Our Government Ser.). (ENG., Illus.). 24p. (J). (gr. 1-3). lib. bdg. 27.99 *(978-1-4765-4201-0(5),* 124305) Capstone.

—The U. S. Senate, 1 vol. 2014. (Our Government Ser.). (ENG., Illus.). 24p. (J). (gr. 1-3). lib. bdg. 27.99 *(978-1-4765-4202-7(3),* 124306) Capstone.

Cavell-Clarke, Steffi. Respecting Rules & Laws. 2018. (Our Values - Level 2 Ser.). 24p. (J). (gr. 2-3). *(978-0-7787-5427-5(8))* Crabtree Publishing Co.

Dosen, Anthony, et al. Investigating Legal Studies for Queensland. 2013. (ENG.). pap. *(978-1-107-65346-7(0))* Cambridge Univ. Pr.

—Legal Studies for Queensland Bundle, 1 vol. 2013. (ENG.). pap., E-Book *(978-1-107-67198-0(1))* Cambridge Univ. Pr.

Engdahl, Sylvia, ed. Driving, 1 vol. 2014. (Teen Rights & Freedoms Ser.). (ENG., Illus.). 120p. (gr. 10-12). lib. bdg. 43.63 *(978-0-7377-6997-5(1),* d3bf3e1f-6f28-4edb-8b90-cacede71cb0e, Greenhaven Publishing) Greenhaven Publishing LLC.

Fontichiaro, Kristin & Rodgers, Emily Puckett. Shared Creations: Making Use of Creative Commons. 2013. (Explorer Library: Information Explorer Ser.). (ENG., Illus.). 32p. (gr. 4-8). 32.07 *(978-1-62431-020-1(6),* 202531) Cherry Lake Publishing.

Fridell, Ron. Miranda Law, 1 vol. 2007. (Supreme Court Milestones Ser.). (ENG., Illus.). 128p. (YA). (gr. 8-8). lib. bdg. 45.50 *(978-0-7614-1942-6(X),* 258d9e51-b77e-458d-b524-19f6a57488ff) Cavendish Square Publishing LLC.

Gagne, Tammy. Immigration in the United States. 2013. (My Guide to U.S. Citizenship Ser.). (ENG.). 48p. (J). (gr. 4-6). lib. bdg. 29.95 *(978-1-61228-446-0(9))* Mitchell Lane Pubs.

Glencoe McGraw-Hill Staff. Street Law, StudentWorks CD-ROM. 8th ed. 2009. (Ntc: Street Law Ser.). (ENG.). (gr. 9-12). cd-rom 131.56 *(978-0-07-889521-0(9),* 0078895219) McGraw-Hill Education.

Goldman, Arnold J. Study Guide: Used with ... Goldman-Business Law: Principles & Practices. 6th ed. 2003. (YA). pap., stu. ed. 34.76 *(978-0-618-30295-6(6),* 319043) CENGAGE Learning.

Hall, Kevin. Montesquieu & the Spirit of Laws. 2016. (J). lib. bdg. *(978-1-68048-546-2(6))* Rosen Publishing Group, Inc., The.

Hernández, Carlos. It's the Law!, 1 vol. 2012. (InfoMax Readers Ser.). (ENG., Illus.). 24p. (J). (gr. 1-1). pap. 8.25 *(978-1-4488-9073-6(X),* a0ddd50b-65ea-4a28-98bd-69e9693b0c33, Rosen Classroom) Rosen Publishing Group, Inc., The.

Higgins, Melissa. Night Dad Went to Jail: What to Expect When Someone You Love Goes to Jail. Kirwan, Wednesday, illus. 2013. (Life's Challenges Ser.). (ENG.). 24p. (J). (gr. 2-3). 8.99 *(978-1-4795-2142-5(6),* 123847, Picture Window Bks.) Capstone.

Hollander, Barbara Gottfried. Marriage Rights & Gay Rights: Interpreting the Constitution, 1 vol. 2014. (Understanding the United States Constitution Ser.). (ENG., Illus.). 112p. (J). (gr. 7-7). 38.80 *(978-1-4777-7514-1(5),* 5e882933-2bd2-415a-a480-3d5a39cd6d4f) Rosen Publishing Group, Inc., The.

Hurt, Avery Elizabeth. Key Environmental Laws, 1 vol. 2019. (Laws That Changed History Ser.). (ENG.). 80p. (gr. 7-7). pap. 18.65 *(978-1-5026-5523-3(3),* e02df3f4-f59b-4faa-8a5b-b72edf42774f); lib. bdg. 37.36 *(978-1-5026-5524-0(1),* 63b2efec-c2c3-41c9-bda8-1b0c7927c81f) Cavendish Square Publishing LLC.

—Key Environmental Laws. 2019. (J). pap. *(978-1-9785-1434-8(4))* Enslow Publishing, LLC.

Know Your Rights: Set 2, 12 vols. 2015. (Know Your Rights Ser.). (ENG.). 64p. (J). (gr. 7-7). lib. bdg. 218.82 *(978-1-4994-6191-6(7),* c944e90a-64e1-4f66-9791-d387d27d9849, Rosen Young Adult) Rosen Publishing Group, Inc., The.

Kowalski, Kathiann M. Judges & Courts: A Look at the Judicial Branch. 2012. (Searchlight Books How Does Government Work Ser.). (ENG., Illus.). 40p. (gr. 3-5). pap. 51.01 *(978-0-7613-9233-0(5));* (J). pap. 9.99 *(978-0-7613-8562-2(2),* 66009f4b-a4c1-4553-9516-d52896dd7403) Lerner Publishing Group.

Laine, Carolee. Content Ownership & Copyright, 1 vol. 2016. (Essential Library of the Information Age Ser.). (ENG., Illus.). 112p. (J). (gr. 8-12). lib. bdg. 41.36 *(978-1-68078-284-4(3),* 21723, Essential Library) ABDO Publishing Co.

Landmark Supreme Court Cases, 35 bks., Set. (Illus.). (YA). (gr. 6-12). lib. bdg. 733.25 *(978-0-89490-572-8(4))* Enslow Publishing, LLC.

Law Enforcement & Intelligence Gathering, 8 vols. 2016. (Law Enforcement & Intelligence Gathering Ser.). (ENG.). 00104p. (YA). (gr. 8-8). 151.28 *(978-1-5081-0293-9(7),* 4fb38f41-48cc-4bd9-91c9-816e9a0bd225, Britannica Educational Publishing) Rosen Publishing Group, Inc., The.

Leavitt, Amie Jane. United States Immigration Services. 2013. (My Guide to U.S. Citizenship Ser.). (ENG.). 48p. (J). (gr. 4-6). lib. bdg. 29.95 *(978-1-61228-447-7(7))* Mitchell Lane Pubs.

LeVert, Suzanne. How States Make Laws, 1 vol. 2005. (Kaleidoscope: Government Ser.). (ENG., Illus.). 48p. (gr. 4-4). lib. bdg. 32.64 *(978-0-7614-1595-4(5),* 0f73330b-051f-4516-95bc-6a5214d7f6ff) Cavendish Square Publishing LLC.

—State Courts, 1 vol. 2005. (Kaleidoscope: Government Ser.). (ENG., Illus.). 48p. (gr. 4-4). lib. bdg. 32.64 *(978-0-7614-1594-7(7),* bb913a26-8734-4156-930c-12985b2541c2) Cavendish Square Publishing LLC.

Lindeen, Carol K. Who Makes Our Laws?, 6 vols., Set. 2004. (Phonics Readers Books 37-72 Ser.). (ENG.). 8p. (gr. k-1). pap. 35.70 *(978-0-7368-4073-6(7))* Capstone.

Lindner, Anna E., ed. Whistleblowers, 1 vol. 2019. (Current Controversies Ser.). (ENG.). 200p. (gr. 10-12). pap. 33.00 *(978-1-5345-0531-5(8),* 67d2491f-9695-4ef5-88eb-c25ea768782e) Greenhaven Publishing LLC.

Lüsted, Marcia Amidon. What You Need to Know about Your Status As an Immigrant under the Law, 1 vol. 2015. (Know Your Rights Ser.). (ENG., Illus.). 64p. (J). (gr. 7-7). 36.47

(978-1-4777-8102-9(1), 4b5d5d30-96a2-4347-b3a6-6bd9add399fc, Rosen Young Adult) Rosen Publishing Group, Inc., The.

Luthringer, Chelsea. So What Is Justice Anyway? 2009. (Student's Guide to American Civics Ser.). 48p. (gr. 5-8). 53.00 (978-1-61511-239-5(1), Rosen Reference) Rosen Publishing Group, Inc., The.

Marshall, Derek. What Is a Law?, 1 vol. 2008. (Real Life Readers Ser.). (ENG.). 16p. (gr. 2-3). pap. 7.05 (978-1-4358-0097-7(4), a82b5726-1d93-4740-90da-5fcde585fcf3, Rosen Classroom) Rosen Publishing Group, Inc., The.

Maybury, Richard J. Uncle Eric Talks about Personal, Career, & Financial Security. Williams, Jane A. & Daniels, Kathryn, eds. 2nd ed. 2004. ("Uncle Eric" Bk.: 1). (ENG., Illus.). 187p. pap. 14.95 (978-0-942617-38-2(X)) Bluestocking Pr.

McGraw Hill. Street Law: a Course in Practical Law, Student Workbook. (Ntc: Street Law Ser.). (ENG., (gr. 9-12). 7th ed. 2004. Illus.). 112p. per., wbk. ed. 6.36 (978-0-07-861208-4(X), 007861208X) 8th ed. 2009. 144p. pap., stu. ed., wbk. ed. 13.52 (978-0-07-889518-0(9), 0078895189) McGraw-Hill Education.

Merino, Noël, ed. Emancipation, 1 vol. 2014. (Teen Rights & Freedoms Ser.). (ENG., Illus.). 152p. (gr. 10-12). lib. bdg. 43.63 (978-0-7377-6999-9(8), 9582398a-302d-495a-9116-ad93053f1a2d, Greenhaven Publishing) Greenhaven Publishing LLC.

Meyer, Susan. Understanding Digital Piracy, 1 vol. 2013. (Digital & Information Literacy Ser.). (ENG.). 48p. (J). (gr. 5-5). 33.47 (978-1-4488-9514-4(6), d5f736d2-c772-424f-9628-ff5479f75b88) Rosen Publishing Group, Inc., The.

Mills, Nathan & Ripley, Ellen. What Are Rules & Laws?, 1 vol. 2012. (Rosen Readers Ser.). (ENG., Illus.). 24p. (J). (gr. 1-2). pap. 8.25 (978-1-4488-8860-3(3), 2990ef1f-a668-4fc1-826e-e40a55cd581b, Rosen Classroom) Rosen Publishing Group, Inc., The.

Mooney, Carla. Online Privacy & Business. 2014. (Privacy in the Online World). (ENG., Illus.). 80p. (J). lib. bdg. (978-1-60152-724-0(1)) ReferencePoint Pr., Inc.

Morlock, Rachael. A Jury of Your Peers: A Look at the Sixth & Seventh Amendments, 1 vol. 2018. (Our Bill of Rights Ser.). (ENG.). 32p. (gr. 5-5). pap. 11.00 (978-1-5383-4304-3(5), 210dddbd-1351-46b1-91cb-579ec469e60d, PowerKids Pr.) Rosen Publishing Group, Inc., The.

Ogden, Charlie. Law & Justice. 2017. (Our Values - Level 3 Ser.). (Illus.). 32p. (J). (gr. 5-6). (978-0-7787-3721-6(7)) Crabtree Publishing Co.

Ohnaka, Kathryn. Do Immigrants Have the Right to Come to the United States?, 1 vol. 2019. (Ask the Constitution Ser.). (ENG.). 48p. (gr. 5-5). 29.60 (978-1-9785-0711-1(9), 1570a032-8e61-46a6-8f56-485a3b2e7d82) Enslow Publishing, LLC.

Payno, Manuel. Los Bandidos de Rio Frio. Camacho, Ricardo, illus. 2003. (SPA.). 91p. (J). pap. (978-970-643-638-2(3)) Selector, S.A. de C.V. MEX. Dist: Spanish Pubs., LLC.

Pegis, Jessica. Why Do We Need Rules & Laws? 2016. (Citizenship in Action Ser.). (ENG., Illus.). 24p. (J). (gr. 1-3). (978-0-7787-2598-5(7)) Crabtree Publishing Co.

—Why Do We Need Rules & Laws? 2016. (Citizenship in Action Ser.). (ENG.). 24p. (J). (gr. 1-3). 18.75 (978-1-5311-8584-8(3)) Perfection Learning Corp.

Peppas, Lynn. Workers' Rights. 2016. (Uncovering the Past: Analyzing Primary Sources Ser.). (ENG.). 48p. (J). (gr. 5-9). (978-0-7787-2861-0(7)) Crabtree Publishing Co.

Porterfield, Jason. File Sharing: Rights & Risks, 1 vol. 2014. (Digital & Information Literacy Ser.). (ENG., Illus.). 48p. (J). (gr. 6-6). pap. 12.75 (978-1-4777-7641-4(9), 79f8a16d-c80c-4bf3-8be1-a3166990989d, Rosen Reference) Rosen Publishing Group, Inc., The.

Rabbat, Suzy. Citing Sources: Learning to Use the Copyright Page. 2013. (Explorer Junior Library: Information Explorer Junior Ser.). (ENG.). 24p. (gr. 1-4). pap. 12.79 (978-1-62431-047-8(8), 202545); (Illus.). 32.07 (978-1-62431-023-2(0), 202543) Cherry Lake Publishing.

Reid, David. The Honorable Fido Lincoln, Judge Teaches Property Law. 2014. (ENG.). 15.99 (978-1-4951-0555-5(5)) Independent Pub.

Rodgers, Emily Puckett & Fontichiaro, Kristin. Creative Commons. 2013. (Explorer Library: Information Explorer Ser.). (ENG.). 32p. (J). (gr. 4-8). pap. 14.21 (978-1-62431-044-7(3), 202533) Cherry Lake Publishing.

Schauer, Peter J. What You Need to Know about Violent Crimes, Felonies, & the Law, 1 vol. 2014. (Know Your Rights Ser.). (ENG., Illus.). 64p. (J). (gr. 6-7). 36.47 (978-1-4777-8024-4(6), 31ac1ee4-b564-4067-ab09-447d5f532e24, Rosen Reference) Rosen Publishing Group, Inc., The.

Schulz, Elizabeth. Respect for Rules & Laws, 1 vol. 2017. (Civic Values Ser.). (ENG.). 32p. (gr. 3-3). pap. 11.58 (978-1-5026-3204-3(7), ae765bb5-d285-4c53-8f28-2a376e35efb1) Cavendish Square Publishing LLC.

Shea, Therese. What Are Community Rules & Laws?, 1 vol. 2017. (Let's Find Out! Communities Ser.). (ENG., Illus.). 32p. (J). (gr. 2-3). pap. 13.90 (978-1-68048-721-3(3), 256aa4ea-b4ef-4db4-9380-6f71797663b3, Britannica Educational Publishing) Rosen Publishing Group, Inc., The.

Trembinski, Donna. Medieval Law & Punishment, 1 vol. 2005. (Medieval World Ser.). (ENG., Illus.). 32p. (J). (gr. 5-9). pap. (978-0-7787-1392-0(X)); lib. bdg. (978-0-7787-1360-9(1)) Crabtree Publishing Co.

Turner, Joshua. The Purpose of Rules & Laws, 1 vol. 2018. (Civic Virtue: Let's Work Together Ser.). (ENG.). 24p. (J). (gr. 3-3). 25.27 (978-1-5081-6694-8(3), 09d4f0cf-b91f-4efd-9aa9-a768ace41e43); pap. 9.25 (978-1-5081-6696-2(X), 035b999f-da81-4030-aa94-1dbda071a60a) Rosen Publishing Group, Inc., The. (PowerKids Pr.).

Wallace, L. Jean & Cypert, Christopher F. What Every Teen Should Know about Texas Law. 2018. (ENG.). 254p. (gr. 9-14). pap. 19.95 (978-1-4773-1563-7(2)) Univ. of Texas Pr.

Zarate, Gustavo Azgad. Youth Law: A Practical Guide to Legal Issues That Affect Young Adults. 2nd ed. 2005. (YA). per. 25.00 (978-0-9763167-9-4(X)) Living Ministry, Inc.

LAW, CONSTITUTIONAL

see Constitutional Law

LAW, INTERNATIONAL

see International Law

LAW—UNITED STATES

Axelrod-Contrada, Joan. Reno V. Aclu: Internet Censorship, 1 vol. 2007. (Supreme Court Milestones Ser.). (ENG., Illus.). 128p. (YA). (gr. 8-8). lib. bdg. 45.50 (978-0-7614-2144-3(0), b8cb54ba-eff9-4bc1-a337-1ce93d2d0e3b) Cavendish Square Publishing LLC.

Beier, Anne. The Supreme Court & the Judicial Branch, 1 vol. 2003. (Primary Source Library of American Citizenship Ser.). (ENG., Illus.). 32p. (gr. 5-5). lib. bdg. 29.13 (978-0-8239-4478-1(6), 8d29fc15-bd1e-40ae-bd8e-3adeb26adac8, Rosen Reference) Rosen Publishing Group, Inc., The.

bjornlund, lydia. Marijuana. 2011. (Compact Research Ser.). 96p. (YA). (gr. 7-12). lib. bdg. 43.93 (978-1-60152-160-6(X)) ReferencePoint Pr., Inc.

Bodden, Valerie. Environmental Law. 2010. (Earth Issues Ser.). (Illus.). 48p. (YA). (gr. 5-18). 23.95 (978-1-58341-981-6(0), Creative Education) Creative Co., The.

Bright-Moore, Susan & Bedesky, Baron. How Is a Law Passed? 2008. (Your Guide to Government Ser.). (ENG., Illus.). 32p. (J). (gr. k-5). pap. (978-0-7787-4331-6(4)) Crabtree Publishing Co.

Byers, Ann. Immigration: Interpreting the Constitution, 1 vol. 2014. (Understanding the United States Constitution Ser.). (ENG.). 112p. (YA). (gr. 7-7). 38.80 (978-1-4777-7512-7(9), 9923eb4a-70b3-4cfc-8322-494d957b3bb7) Rosen Publishing Group, Inc., The.

Castle, Caroline. For Every Child: The UN Convention on the Rights of the Child in Words & Pictures. 2004. (J). (gr. k-3). spiral bd. (978-0-616-14618-7(3)); spiral bd. (978-0-616-14617-0(5)) Canadian National Institute for the Blind/Institut National Canadien pour les Aveugles.

Cefrey, Holly. The Interstate Commerce ACT: The Government Takes Control of Trade Between the States, 1 vol. 2003. (Primary Sources of America's Industrial Society in the 19th Century Ser.). (ENG., Illus.). 32p. (gr. 4-5). pap. 10.00 (978-0-8239-4282-4(1), a1ecf6c8-d134-4916-8d9c-1fdef4e6451c) Rosen Publishing Group, Inc., The.

—The Sherman Antitrust Act: Getting Big Business under Control, 1 vol. 2003. (America's Industrial Society in the 19th Century Ser.). (ENG., Illus.). 32p. (gr. 4-5). lib. bdg. 29.13 (978-0-8239-4032-5(2), e7d9287f-5305-439c-be32-9f917074a5c8, Rosen Reference) Rosen Publishing Group, Inc., The.

Donovan, Sandy. Making Laws: A Look at How a Bill Becomes a Law. 2004. (How Government Works Ser.). (Illus.). 56p. (J). (gr. 4-8). lib. bdg. 25.26 (978-0-8225-1346-9(3)) Lerner Publishing Group.

Duignan, Brian & DeCarlo, Carolyn, eds. The Judicial Branch: Evaluating & Interpreting Laws, 1 vol. 2018. (Checks & Balances in the U. S. Government Ser.). (ENG.). 128p. (gr. 10-10). lib. bdg. 39.00 (978-1-5383-0167-8(9), a5909be8-8644-4ad0-a3d0-6da8c846c43b) Rosen Publishing Group, Inc., The.

Egan, Tracie. How a Bill Becomes a Law. (Primary Source Library of American Citizenship Ser.). 32p. (gr. 5-5). 2009. 47.90 (978-1-61511-219-7(7)) 2003. (ENG., Illus.). lib. bdg. 29.13 (978-0-8239-4471-2(9), 70c063f9-adca-438a-9685-e0e96dd533c8) Rosen Publishing Group, Inc., The. (Rosen Reference).

Engdahl, Sylvia, ed. Medical Rights, 1 vol. 2008. (Issues on Trial Ser.). (ENG., Illus.). 216p. (gr. 10-12). 49.93 (978-0-7377-4179-7(1), f02a9bda-62cb-452b-b2de-a82caedd68f1, Greenhaven Publishing) Greenhaven Publishing LLC.

Freedman, Jeri. Intellectual Property, 1 vol. 2008. (Cyber Citizenship & Cyber Safety Ser.). (ENG., Illus.). 48p. (YA). (gr. 5-5). lib. bdg. 34.47 (978-1-4042-1348-7(1), 168ef94f-406e-4837-8109-4332842600f7) Rosen Publishing Group, Inc., The.

Friedman, Lauri S., ed. The Patriot Act, 1 vol. 2009. (Introducing Issues with Opposing Viewpoints Ser.). (ENG., Illus.). 144p. (gr. 7-10). 43.63 (978-0-7377-4172-8(4), eba1c48d-81ab-476a-b78e-a32a241126cd, Greenhaven Publishing) Greenhaven Publishing LLC.

Gale Research Inc. Unlocking Current Issues: 5 Volume Set, 5 vols. 2018. (Unlocking Current Issues Ser.). (ENG., Illus.). xxv, 207p. 232.00 (978-1-4103-8091-3(2)) Cengage Gale.

Gitlin, Martin, ed. Transgender Rights, 1 vol. 2017. (Issues That Concern You Ser.). (ENG.). 112p. (YA). (gr. 7-10). pap. 29.30 (978-1-5345-0283-3(1), 070381e3-7129-4974-a3f3-e5de23e20491) Greenhaven Publishing LLC.

Gold, Susan Dudley. Saluting the Flag: West Virginia State Board of Education V. Barnette. 2012. (J). 42.79 (978-1-60870-911-3(6)) Marshall Cavendish Corp.

Gordon, Sherri Mabry. Downloading Copyrighted Stuff from the Internet: Stealing or Fair Use?, 1 vol. 2005. (Issues in Focus Today Ser.). (ENG., Illus.). 104p. (gr. 6-7). lib. bdg. 35.93 (978-0-7660-2164-8(5), 10985f0c-c9d9-497d-a903-860b824189d1) Enslow Publishing, LLC.

Gorman, Jacqueline Laks. Why Do We Have Laws? 2008. (Know Your Government Ser.). (ENG.). 24p. (J). (gr. 1-3). 18.95 (978-1-5311-8600-5(9)) Perfection Learning Corp.

Gunderson, Jessica. The Triangle Shirtwaist Factory Fire. Miller, Phil & Barnett III, Charles, illus. 2006. (Disasters in History Ser.). (ENG.). 32p. (J). (gr. 3-9). per. 8.10 (978-0-7368-6878-5(X), 91581, Capstone Pr.) Capstone.

Hanrahan, Clare, ed. Legal System, 1 vol. 2007. (Opposing Viewpoints Ser.). (ENG., Illus.). 240p. (gr. 10-12). 50.43 (978-0-7377-3757-8(3), 818ae1e3-90a2-4098-bc2c-8e1764ce3f55); pap. 34.80 (978-0-7377-3758-5(1), e76e3c01-9914-48cb-aa8c-ebd7ea95eaa2) Greenhaven Publishing LLC. (Greenhaven Publishing).

Haugen, David M. Criminal Justice. 2008. (Opposing Viewpoints Ser.). (ENG., Illus.). 240p. (YA). (gr. 10-12). 29.45 (978-0-7377-4199-5(6), LML02109-243131); lib. bdg. 42.95 (978-0-7377-4198-8(8), LML02109-243098) Cengage Gale. (Greenhaven Pr., Inc.).

Howell, Sara. Immigrants' Rights, Citizens' Rights. 2014. (American Mosaic: Immigration Today Ser.). 24p. (J). (gr. 3-6). pap. 49.50 (978-1-4777-6647-7(2), PowerKids Pr.) Rosen Publishing Group, Inc., The.

—Los Derechos de Los Inmigrantes, Los Derechos de Los Ciudadanos, 1 vol. 2014. (Mosaico Americano: la Inmigración Hoy en día (the American Mosaic: Immigration Today) Ser.). (SPA., Illus.). 24p. (J). (gr. 2-3). lib. bdg. 25.27 (978-1-4777-6819-8(X), 17a43118-2698-4e14-a621-18a99be21637, PowerKids Pr.) Rosen Publishing Group, Inc., The.

Hubbard, Ben. My Digital Rights & Rules. Vaisberg, Diego, illus. 2019. (Digital Citizens Ser.). (ENG.). 32p. (J). (gr. 2-5). 27.99 (978-1-5415-3881-8(1), d99cfe58-3a93-4e25-82ee-796876e676f9, Lerner Pubns.) Lerner Publishing Group.

Jacobs, Thomas A. & Jacobs, Natalie. Every Vote Matters: The Power of Your Voice, from Student Elections to the Supreme Court. Jacobs, Natalie, illus. 2016. (Teens & the Law Ser.). (ENG.). 224p. (YA). (gr. 8-12). pap. 16.99 (978-1-63198-069-5(6)) Free Spirit Publishing Inc.

—Every Vote Matters: The Power of Your Voice, from Student Elections to the Supreme Court. 2016. lib. bdg. 28.15 (978-0-606-37931-1(2)) Turtleback.

Kishel, Ann-Marie. Rules & Laws. 2007. (First Step Nonfiction Ser.). (Illus.). 23p. (J). (gr. 3-7). lib. bdg. 18.60 (978-0-8225-6396-9(7), Lerner Pubns.) Lerner Publishing Group.

Krull, Kathleen. No Truth Without Ruth: The Life of Ruth Bader Ginsburg. Zhang, Nancy, illus. 2018. (ENG.). 48p. (J). (gr. -1-3). 17.99 (978-0-06-256011-7(5), Quill Tree Bks.) HarperCollins Pubs.

Laks Gorman, Jacqueline. ¿Por Qué Tenemos Leyes? (Why Do We Have Laws?), 1 vol. 2008. (Conoce Tu Gobierno (Know Your Government) Ser.). (SPA., Illus.). 24p. (gr. 2-4). pap. 9.15 (978-0-8368-8858-4(8), 785fa080-e113-44e4-bfac-a93e360945ed); lib. bdg. 24.67 (978-0-8368-8853-9(7), 77e8cec0-47e5-44c2-98f2-4c89d8f0c76f) Stevens, Gareth Publishing LLLP. (Weekly Reader Leveled Readers).

—Why Do We Have Laws?, 1 vol. 2008. (Know Your Government Ser.). (ENG., Illus.). 24p. (gr. 2-4). pap. 9.15 (978-0-8368-8848-5(0), 94aaf7d7-864f-496d-8f2f-92155655c709, Weekly Reader Leveled Readers) Stevens, Gareth Publishing LLLP.

Law: Career Launcher. 2010. (Ferguson Career Launcher Ser.). (ENG.). 160p. (gr. 9-18). pap. 14.95 (978-0-8160-7992-6(7), P174246, Checkmark Bks.) Infobase Holdings, Inc.

Libal, Joyce. A House Between Homes: Youth in the Foster Care System. 2003. (Youth with Special Needs Ser.). (Illus.). 127p. (YA). pap. 14.95 (978-1-4222-0419-1(7)) Mason Crest.

The Library of American Laws & Legal Principles, 12 vols. 2005. (Library of American Laws & Legal Principles Ser.). (ENG., Illus.). (YA). (gr. 5-8). 206.82 (978-1-4042-0621-2(3), c0149337-acc4-447f-8911-cd11574b97ef, Rosen Reference) Rosen Publishing Group, Inc., The.

Marsh, Carole. Georgia Law: Make It, Don't Break It! (HC) Make It, Don't Break It! (HC) 2004. 28p. 29.95 (978-0-635-02687-3(2)) Gallopade International.

—Georgia Law: Make It, Don't Break It! (PB) Make It, Don't Break It! (PB) 2004. 28p. pap. 5.95 (978-0-635-02686-6(4)) Gallopade International.

Marzilli, Alan, ed. Point/Counterpoint: Issues in Contemporary American Society. (Illus.). (gr. 9-13). lib. bdg. 519.00 (978-0-7910-8468-7(X), Facts On File) Infobase Holdings, Inc.

Micklos, John Joseph, Jr. Descubre Tus Derechos Legales. 2020. (Guía para Jóvenes Sobre el Gobierno Ser.).Tr. of Understanding Your Legal Rights. (SPA., Illus.). 32p. (J). (gr. 3-6). lib. bdg. 27.99 (978-1-4966-5723-7(3), 142064) Capstone.

Micklos Jr., John. Understanding Your Legal Rights. 2018. (Kids' Guide to Government Ser.). (ENG., Illus.). 32p. (J). (gr. 3-6). lib. bdg. 27.99 (978-1-5435-0317-3(9), 137183, Capstone Pr.) Capstone.

Miller, Jake. Brown vs. Board of Education of Topeka: Challenging School Segregation in the Supreme Court, 1 vol. 2003. (Library of the Civil Rights Movement Ser.). (ENG., Illus.). 24p. (J). (gr. 3-3). lib. bdg. 26.27 (978-0-8239-6250-1(4), 184de3f3-dc5b-4394-bb50-bc67c24250b5) Rosen Publishing Group, Inc., The.

Morgan, J. Tom. Ignorance Is No Defense: A Teenager's Guide to Georgia Law. 2007. (Illus.). 212p. (YA). pap. 15.00 (978-0-9796625-1-5(6)) GDG Publishing.

New, David W. The Ten Commandments for Beginners. 2004. 60p. (YA). per. 4.95 (978-0-9721333-4-0(8)) Pocket Pubn., A.

Noble, William. Presidential Power on Trial: From Watergate to All the President's Men, 1 vol. 2009. (Famous Court Cases That Became Movies Ser.). (ENG., Illus.). 128p. (gr. 6-7). lib. bdg. 35.93 (978-0-7660-3058-9(X), ccd06e6e-8d4e-4e9b-bf78-58d3af9a0a5a) Enslow Publishing, LLC.

Orr, Tamra. Careers in the Courts, 1 vol. 2009. (Careers in Criminal Justice Ser.). (ENG., Illus.). 112p. (J). (gr. 7-7). lib. bdg. 39.80 (978-1-4358-5265-5(6), 7aa5ac21-4c18-4432-b5dd-fd679d4b8fc7) Rosen Publishing Group, Inc., The.

Riley, Gail Blasser. And Justice for All. 2003. (Illus.). 60p. (J). 11.60 net. (978-0-7398-5175-3(6)) Steck-Vaughn.

Ripley, Ellen. What Are Rules & Laws?, 1 vol. 2012. (I'm an American Citizen Ser.). (ENG., Illus.). 24p. (J). (gr. 1-2). 26.27 (978-1-4488-8585-5(X), e5335958-bf3b-4f42-bdba-46a6e1058f8b, PowerKids Pr.) Rosen Publishing Group, Inc., The.

Rodger, Ellen. What Is the Judicial Branch? 2013. (ENG.). 32p. (J). (978-0-7787-0880-3(2)); pap. (978-0-7787-0906-0(X)) Crabtree Publishing Co.

Roland, James. Ruth Bader Ginsburg: Iconic Supreme Court Justice. 2016. (Gateway Biographies Ser.). (ENG., Illus.). 48p. (J). (gr. 4-8). E-Book 47.99 (978-1-5124-0597-2(3), Lerner Pubns.) Lerner Publishing Group.

Santos, Rita. What Does a Petitioner Do?, 1 vol. 2018. (What Does a Citizen Do? Ser.). (ENG.). 48p. (gr. 5-5). 30.93 (978-0-7660-9869-5(9), 38ddccb1-48c0-4e8a-8c3a-c82558d74d45) Enslow Publishing, LLC.

Santos, Rita, ed. Critical Perspectives on Whistleblowers & Leakers, 1 vol. 2018. (Analyzing the Issues Ser.). (ENG.). 232p. (gr. 8-8). 50.93 (978-0-7660-9860-2(5), 676e9bea-4ff2-4c8f-8080-f66eb2495f65) Enslow Publishing, LLC.

Smith-Llera, Danielle. Exploring the Judicial Branch. 2019. (Searchlight Books (tm) — Getting into Government Ser.). (ENG., Illus.). 32p. (J). (gr. 3-5). pap. 9.99 (978-1-5415-7479-3(6), 476b3988-59a5-4cee-b093-a1e355d8b611, Lerner Pubns.) Lerner Publishing Group.

Sommers, Michael A. A Timeline of the Supreme Court, 1 vol. 2004. (Timelines of American History Ser.). (ENG., Illus.). 32p. (gr. 4-4). lib. bdg. 29.13 (978-0-8239-4541-2(3), de6a6a6c-6ee8-4a0c-aa97-19e64a51d5ff, Rosen Reference) Rosen Publishing Group, Inc., The.

Suen, Anastasia. The U. S. Supreme Court, 1 vol. Skeens, Matthew, illus. 2008. (American Symbols Ser.). (ENG.). 24p. (J). (gr. 1-3). 27.32 (978-1-4048-4707-1(3), 95118, Picture Window Bks.) Capstone.

Supreme Court Milestones - Group 5, 10 vols., Set. Incl. Plessy V. Ferguson: Separate but Unequal. Axelrod-Contrada, Joan. lib. bdg. 45.50 (978-0-7614-2951-7(4), a3e6613e-d3f8-4e02-8703-fc09a859b6ce); Roberts V. Jaycees: Women's Rights. Dudley Gold, Susan. lib. bdg. 45.50 (978-0-7614-2952-4(2), 04f9ffbc-33ce-4da1-a392-41abaff897a0); U. S. V. Eichman: Flag Burning & Free Speech. Fridell, Ron. lib. bdg. 45.50 (978-0-7614-2953-1(0), 7f038b36-3bb1-4f21-a39a-5bf77dfbfc17); U. S. V. Nixon: The Limits of Presidential Privilege. Stefoff, Rebecca. lib. bdg. 45.50 (978-0-7614-2955-5(7), 4db6aa1a-1655-4841-87db-dd1d01e53f02); Worcester V. Georgia: American Indian Rights. Dudley Gold, Susan. lib. bdg. 45.50 (978-0-7614-2956-2(5), 6c168d5f-1554-4a47-b5c9-55ffb19b2600); 128p. (YA). (gr. 8-8). (Supreme Court Milestones Ser.). (ENG.). 2009. Set lib. bdg. 227.50 (978-0-7614-2949-4(2), 1e58a2e6-2c2b-45a6-9776-aeb6675e200c, Cavendish Square) Cavendish Square Publishing LLC.

Swann, Kristina. US Law - Student Text. 2005. (Illus.). 48p. (YA). 11.95 (978-1-58804-397-9(5)) P C I Education.

Taylor, Chad. The United States Has Rules & Laws, 1 vol. 2016. (Rosen REAL Readers: Social Studies Nonfiction / Fiction: Myself, My Community, My World Ser.). (ENG.). 12p. (gr. k-1). pap. 6.33 (978-1-5081-2329-3(2), 148ac74a-8b2f-4ae8-815f-b55586fa587e, Rosen Classroom) Rosen Publishing Group, Inc., The.

Troisi-Paton, Kimberly, ed. The Right to Due Process, 1 vol. 2005. (Bill of Rights Ser.). (ENG.). 144p. (gr. 10-12). lib. bdg. 44.83 (978-0-7377-1941-3(9), ac78a5f2-f1f0-4cae-85b8-8821bf7530ce, Greenhaven Publishing) Greenhaven Publishing LLC.

Walker, Ida. William Blackstone & Commentaries upon the Laws of England. 2016. (J). lib. bdg. (978-1-68048-552-3(0)) Rosen Publishing Group, Inc., The.

Wallace Sharp, Anne & Taylor, Robert. The Right to Die, 1 vol. 2009. (Hot Topics Ser.). (ENG., Illus.). 120p. (gr. 7-7). lib. bdg. 41.03 (978-1-59018-834-7(9), ea904de4-5fdd-40f7-8e38-23e70214c014, Lucent Pr.) Greenhaven Publishing LLC.

Whelan, Elaine P., narrated by. My Mom's Making History: The Story of Computer Software, Copyrights & Creativity, 1. 2nd ed. 2003. 80p. (J). per. 12.99 (978-0-9726871-0-2(6)) Mainstreet Systems & Software Inc.

Wilberforce, Bertram. Why We Need Laws. (Explore Citizenship Ser.). 24p. (gr. 3-3). 2009. 42.50 (978-1-61512-342-1(3), PowerKids Pr.) 2009. (ENG.). (J). lib. bdg. 26.27 (978-1-4358-2977-0(8), 028c220e-b28d-4d44-b752-8bb8c10a50f7, PowerKids Pr.) 2008. (ENG.). pap. 8.25 (978-1-4358-0135-6(0), cad51bfd-ae25-4fd5-bce4-34f78339943d, Rosen Classroom) Rosen Publishing Group, Inc., The.

Worth, Richard. Sherman Antitrust Act, 1 vol. 2012. (Landmark Legislation Ser.). (ENG., Illus.). 128p. (YA). (gr. 8-8). 42.64 (978-1-60870-487-3(4), 66ba3781-fb7c-446d-9881-adcb08bd092d) Cavendish Square Publishing LLC.

Wroble, Lisa A. The Right to Counsel: From Gideon V. Wainwright to Gideon's Trumpet, 1 vol. 2009. (Famous Court Cases That Became Movies Ser.). (ENG., Illus.). 104p. (gr. 6-7). lib. bdg. 35.93 (978-0-7660-3057-2(1), 54eadea1-20f9-4133-ad4c-186d5574f8dc) Enslow Publishing, LLC.

LAW—VOCATIONAL GUIDANCE

Ferguson. Law. 3rd rev. ed. 2009. (Ferguson's Careers in Focus Ser.). (ENG.). 208p. (gr. 6-12). 32.95 (978-0-8160-7299-6(X), P166653, Ferguson Publishing Company) Infobase Holdings, Inc.

Furgang, Kathy. Getting a Job in the Legal Profession, 1 vol. 2016. (Job Basics: Getting the Job You Need Ser.). (ENG., Illus.). 80p. (J). (gr. 8-8). 38.41 (978-1-4777-8562-1(0), 74ecfcff-80c7-48f9-9df1-c63837ae08d0) Rosen Publishing Group, Inc., The.

Harvey, Janet. Working As a Legal Advocate, 1 vol. 2018. (Careers in Your Community Ser.). (ENG., Illus.). 80p. (YA). (gr. 7-7). 37.47 (978-1-4994-6727-7(3), 19e81323-3cda-4eff-a5ea-acbb6783beea) Rosen Publishing Group, Inc., The.

Hayhurst, Chris. Jobs in Environmental Law. 2010. (Green Careers Ser.). 80p. (YA). (gr. 7-12). E-Book 61.20 (978-1-4488-0133-6(8)) Rosen Publishing Group, Inc., The.

Law: Career Launcher. 2010. (Ferguson Career Launcher Ser.). (ENG.). 160p. (gr. 9-18). pap. 14.95 (978-0-8160-7992-6(7), P174246, Checkmark Bks.) Infobase Holdings, Inc.

Mooney, Carla. Careers in the Legal Profession. 2018. (ENG.). 80p. (YA). (gr. 5-12). (978-1-68282-313-2(X)) ReferencePoint Pr., Inc.

Orr, Tamra. Careers in the Courts, 1 vol. 2009. (Careers in Criminal Justice Ser.). (ENG., Illus.). 112p. (J). (gr. 7-7). lib. bdg. 39.80 (978-1-4358-5265-5(6), 7aa5ac21-4c18-4432-b5dd-fd679d4b8fc7) Rosen Publishing Group, Inc., The.

LAW ENFORCEMENT
see also Police
Aleo, Cyndy, ed. Critical Perspectives on Effective Policing & Police Brutality, 1 vol. 2017. (Analyzing the Issues Ser.). (ENG.). 232p. (gr. 8-8). 50.93 *(978-0-7660-9170-2(8),* 56057bdf-634b-41c0-9481-99ea263b0300) Enslow Publishing, LLC.
Behnke, Alison Marie. Racial Profiling: Everyday Inequality. 2017. (ENG., Illus.). 160p. (YA). (gr. 6-12). 35.99 *(978-1-5124-0268-1(0),* 9dc52845-fa56-4bc3-afd5-958a6b6775aa); E-Book 54.65 *(978-1-5124-2851-3(5));* E-Book 9.99 *(978-1-5124-3920-5(7),* 9781512439205); E-Book 54.65 *(978-1-5124-3921-2(5),* 9781512439212) Lerner Publishing Group. (Twenty-First Century Bks.).
Chrismer, Melanie. Lone Star Legacy: The Texas Rangers Then & Now, 1 vol. 2016. (ENG., Illus.). 144p. (J). (gr. 4-7). pap. 10.95 *(978-1-4556-2104-0(8),* Pelican Publishing) Arcadia Publishing.
Clapper, Kathryn N., et al. FBI Agents. 2018. (U. S. Federal Agents Ser.). (ENG., Illus.). 32p. (J). (gr. 3-9). lib. bdg. 27.32 *(978-1-5435-0141-4(9),* 137078, Capstone Pr.) Capstone.
—U. S. Marshals. 2018. (U. S. Federal Agents Ser.). (ENG., Illus.). 32p. (J). (gr. 3-9). lib. bdg. 27.32 *(978-1-5435-0140-7(0),* 137077, Capstone Pr.) Capstone.
Eggleton, Jill. The Eye of the Law. 2007. (Connectors Ser.). (gr. 2-5). pap. *(978-1-877453-14-4(5))* Global Education Systems Ltd.
Emert, Phyllis Raybin. Attorneys General: Enforcing the Law. 2005. (In the Cabinet Ser.). (Illus.). 176p. (J). (gr. 7-18). lib. bdg. 24.95 *(978-1-881508-66-3(8))* Oliver Pr., Inc.
Extreme Law Enforcement, 12 vols. 2013. (Extreme Law Enforcement Ser.). (ENG.). 112p. (YA). (gr. 7-7). 238.62 *(978-1-4777-1720-2(X),* 6c7112c5-b94f-4227-9ba9-cada235b2f0b) Rosen Publishing Group, Inc., The.
Hahn, Kathy L., ed. Racial Profiling, 1 vol. 2010. (At Issue Ser.). (ENG.). 96p. (gr. 10-12). 41.03 *(978-0-7377-5093-5(6),* 58059a89-26f8-4991-9eed-ee8e3b522ed6); pap. 28.80 *(978-0-7377-5094-2(4),* 660dd690-e70b-41c8-bc34-299772a80c06) Greenhaven Publishing LLC. (Greenhaven Publishing).
Hand, Carol. Using Computer Science in High Tech Criminal Justice Careers, 1 vol. 2017. (Coding Your Passion Ser.). (ENG., Illus.). 80p. (J). (gr. 7-7). 37.47 *(978-1-5081-7511-7(X),* 6e321a5c-7471-4297-b448-1de8f720622a, Rosen Young Adult) Rosen Publishing Group, Inc., The.
Kamberg, Mary-Lane. Getting a Job in Law Enforcement, Security, & Corrections, 1 vol. 2013. (Job Basics: Getting the Job You Need Ser.). (ENG.). 80p. (YA). (gr. 8-8). 38.41 *(978-1-4488-9605-9(3),* 041d2734-ea1d-4cde-b641-fe4af6b54775) Rosen Publishing Group, Inc., The.
La Bella, Laura. Drones & Law Enforcement, 1 vol. 2016. (Inside the World of Drones Ser.). (ENG., Illus.). 64p. (J). (gr. 7-7). 36.13 *(978-1-5081-7343-4(5),* 13e3ca74-0dbc-460d-8f05-aec736704be1, Rosen Young Adult) Rosen Publishing Group, Inc., The.
Lansford, Tom. Justice, Policing, & the Rule of Law, Vol. 8. Lansford, Tom, ed. 2016. (Foundations of Democracy Ser.). (Illus.). 64p. (J). (gr. 7). 23.95 *(978-1-4222-3630-7(7))* Mason Crest.
Lewis, Daniel. Public Safety & Law, Vol. 10. 2018. (Careers in Demand for High School Graduates Ser.). 112p. (J). (gr. 7). 34.60 *(978-1-4222-4141-7(6))* Mason Crest.
Lindeen, Mary. Law Enforcement Robots. 2017. (Cutting-Edge Robotics (Alternator Books (r)) Ser.). (ENG., Illus.). 32p. (J). (gr. 3-6). 29.32 *(978-1-5124-4011-9(6),* 16cec008-1069-4a09-b7b3-15aef65d0e86, Lerner Pubns.) Lerner Publishing Group.
Mara, Wil. FBI Special Agent. 2015. (21st Century Skills Library: Cool STEAM Careers Ser.). (ENG., Illus.). 32p. (J). (gr. 4-7). pap. 14.21 *(978-1-63362-648-5(2),* 1391909) Cherry Lake Publishing.
Meyer, Jared. Homeland Security Officers. 2009. (Extreme Careers Ser.). 64p. (gr. 5-5). 58.50 *(978-1-61512-398-8(9),* Rosen Reference) Rosen Publishing Group, Inc., The.
Murley, Leon. Working the Case: Law Enforcement, Police Work, & Police Organizations, 1 vol. 2016. (Law Enforcement & Intelligence Gathering Ser.). (ENG., Illus.). 96p. (J). (gr. 8-8). lib. bdg. 37.82 *(978-1-5081-0380-6(1),* 1addad64-fe5b-47a1-8942-6d3b5ed23bdc, Britannica Educational Publishing) Rosen Publishing Group, Inc., The.
Newcomb, Tim. FBI Agent, Vol. 12. 2015. (On a Mission Ser.). 48p. (J). (gr. 5). 20.95 *(978-1-4222-3394-8(4))* Mason Crest.
Savage, Jeff. Quick-Draw Gunfighters: True Tales of the Wild West, 1 vol. 2012. (True Tales of the Wild West Ser.). (ENG., Illus.). 48p. (gr. 5-7). pap. 11.53 *(978-1-4644-0029-2(6),* aac891de-4be3-4d12-acc9-87ad5075d450) Enslow Publishing, LLC.
Woog, Adam. Careers in State, County, & City Police Forces, 1 vol. 2014. (Law & Order Jobs Ser.). (ENG., Illus.). 96p. (gr. 6-6). 42.63 *(978-1-62712-425-6(X),* 45f3ce27-625b-479a-879e-4babb914c919) Cavendish Square Publishing LLC.
—Careers in the ATF, 1 vol. 2014. (Law & Order Jobs Ser.). (ENG.). 96p. (gr. 6-6). 42.63 *(978-1-62712-428-7(4),* b4feb2f6-4a96-435b-985d-89ab20138f96) Cavendish Square Publishing LLC.
—Careers in the ATF. 2012. (J). 34.21 *(978-1-60870-956-4(6))* Marshall Cavendish Corp.
—Careers in the Secret Service, 1 vol. 2014. (Law & Order Jobs Ser.). (ENG.). 112p. (gr. 6-6). 42.63 *(978-1-62712-434-8(9),* b731810a-5b8e-4283-89fc-94e8a69ff4de) Cavendish Square Publishing LLC.
Wyatt Earp. 2010. (ENG., Illus.). 112p. (gr. 6-12). 35.00 *(978-1-60413-597-8(2),* P179311, Facts On File) Infobase Holdings, Inc.

LAW ENFORCEMENT—VOCATIONAL GUIDANCE
Ferguson, creator. Law Enforcement. 2008. (Discovering Careers for Your Future Ser.). (ENG.). 92p. (gr. 4-9). 21.95 *(978-0-8160-7293-4(0),* P179096, Ferguson Publishing Company) Infobase Holdings, Inc.
Harmon, Daniel E. Working As a Law Enforcement Officer in Your Community, 1 vol. 2015. (Careers in Your Community Ser.). (ENG., Illus.). 80p. (J). (gr. 7-8). 37.47 *(978-1-4994-6115-2(1),* 9d3b3cbf-9eaf-465d-b807-9ddd762c9e6c, Rosen Young Adult) Rosen Publishing Group, Inc., The.
Larson, Kirsten W. Federal Air Marshals. 2016. (Protecting Our People Ser.). (ENG., Illus.). 32p. (J). (gr. 2-5). lib. bdg. 20.95 *(978-1-60753-984-1(5),* 15775) Amicus.
Meyer, Jared. Homeland Security Officers, 1 vol. 2007. (Extreme Careers Ser.). (ENG., Illus.). 64p. (J). (gr. 5-5). lib. bdg. 37.13 *(978-1-4042-0945-9(X),* 03f95474-3eae-4225-b097-7fb2f15f714d) Rosen Publishing Group, Inc., The.
Porterfield, Jason. Careers in Undercover Gang Investigation, 1 vol. 2013. (Extreme Law Enforcement Ser.). (ENG.). 112p. (YA). (gr. 7-7). 39.77 *(978-1-4777-1712-7(9),* e9e32884-da60-4d50-9e6b-c583ee983807) Rosen Publishing Group, Inc., The.
Roby, Cynthia A. A Career As an Atf Agent, 1 vol. 2015. (Federal Forces: Careers As Federal Agents Ser.). (ENG.). 32p. (J). (gr. 4-5). pap. 11.00 *(978-1-4994-1053-2(0),* 85768e30-9762-4f13-8048-193c5f85780d, PowerKids Pr.) Rosen Publishing Group, Inc., The.
Rogers, Kate. Air Marshals, 1 vol., 1. 2015. (Careers for Heroes Ser.). (ENG., Illus.). 24p. (J). (gr. 3-4). pap. 9.25 *(978-1-5081-4387-1(0),* 39ac8020-8f6f-4a41-a63a-d1e5c0599095, PowerKids Pr.) Rosen Publishing Group, Inc., The.
Sanna, Ellyn. Homeland Security Officer. Riggs, Ernestine G. & Gholar, Cheryl, eds. 2013. (Careers with Character Ser.: 18). 96p. (J). (gr. 7-18). 22.95 *(978-1-4222-2757-2(X))* Mason Crest.
Suen, Anastasia. Careers with Swat Teams, 1 vol. 2013. (Extreme Law Enforcement Ser.). (ENG., Illus.). 112p. (J). (gr. 7-7). 39.77 *(978-1-4777-1708-0(0),* 802afed7-68bb-403d-a035-4bd24e0413dc) Rosen Publishing Group, Inc., The.
Thomas, William David. How to Become an FBI Agent. 2009. (FBI Story Ser.). 64p. (J). (gr. 4-7). lib. bdg. 22.95 *(978-1-4222-0571-6(1))* Mason Crest.
Uschan, Michael V. Careers in Law Enforcement. 2017. (ENG., Illus.). 80p. (J). (gr. 5-12). *(978-1-68282-106-0(4))* ReferencePoint Pr., Inc.
Watson, Stephanie. A Career as a Police Officer, 1 vol. 2010. (Essential Careers Ser.). (ENG.). 80p. (YA). (gr. 6-6). lib. bdg. 37.47 *(978-1-4358-9469-3(3),* b7a8281b-d194-4a9e-93b1-8b74823c0e47) Rosen Publishing Group, Inc., The.
Woog, Adam. Careers in the Secret Service. 2013. (J). 34.21 *(978-1-60870-960-1(4))* Marshall Cavendish Corp.

LAW OF NATIONS
see International Law

LAWN TENNIS
see Tennis

LAWRENCE, T. E. (THOMAS EDWARD), 1888-1935
Jeffrey, Gary. Lawrence of Arabia & the Middle East & Africa. 2013. (ENG., Illus.). 48p. (J). *(978-0-7787-0912-1(4));* pap. *(978-0-7787-0918-3(3))* Crabtree Publishing Co.

LAWS
see Law

LAWYERS
see also Judges; Law—Vocational Guidance
Aaron, Lance. Thurgood Marshall, Vol. 9. 2018. (Civil Rights Leaders Ser.). 144p. (J). (gr. 7). lib. bdg. 35.93 *(978-1-4222-4013-7(4))* Mason Crest.
Adams, Ashely. Standing in the Attorney General's Shoes, 1 vol. 2017. (My Government Ser.). (ENG.). 32p. (gr. 3-3). 30.21 *(978-1-5026-3360-6(4),* fb6470e3-3b5a-433e-a1d3-826a091ab416) Cavendish Square Publishing LLC.
Brezina, Corona. Amal & George Clooney, 1 vol. 2019. (Power Couples Ser.). (ENG., Illus.). 112p. (J). (gr. 7-7). pap. 18.65 *(978-1-5081-8875-9(0),* 0cf25556-ad79-4a52-991c-5d56f8c2fa4e) Rosen Publishing Group, Inc., The.
Calkhoven, Laurie. Ruth Bader Ginsburg: Ready-To-Read Level 3. Vukovic, Elizabet, illus. 2019. (You Should Meet Ser.). (ENG.). 48p. (J). (gr. 1-1). 17.99 *(978-1-5344-4858-2(6));* pap. 4.99 *(978-1-5344-4857-5(8))* Simon Spotlight. (Simon Spotlight).
Carey Rohan, Rebecca. Thurgood Marshall: The First African-American Supreme Court Justice, 1 vol. 2016. (Great American Thinkers Ser.). (ENG.). 128p. (J). (gr. 9-9). 47.36 *(978-1-5026-1932-7(6),* 756c9265-9225-4c4f-8b5b-6445c19afc2c) Cavendish Square Publishing LLC.
Cooper, Ann Goode & Bowlin, William Harrison. Lawyer Will: The Story of an Appalachian Lawyer. Jessee, Diana, illus. 2004. 36p. (J). 12.95 *(978-1-887905-90-9(1))* Parkway Pubs., Inc.
Dudley Gold, Susan. Engle V. Vitale, 1 vol. 2007. (Supreme Court Milestones Ser.). (ENG., Illus.). 128p. (YA). (gr. 8-8). lib. bdg. 45.50 *(978-0-7614-1940-2(3),* f3b29fa8-3ae5-49e1-bd54-f04e88e5c823) Cavendish Square Publishing LLC.
Edwards, Roberta. Michelle Obama: Primera Dama y Primera Mama. Call, Ken, illus. 2010. (SPA.). 48p. (gr. 3-5). pap. 9.99 *(978-1-60396-946-8(2))* Santillana USA Publishing Co., Inc.
Emert, Phyllis Raybin. Attorneys General: Enforcing the Law. 2005. (In the Cabinet Ser.). (Illus.). 176p. (J). (gr. 7-18). lib. bdg. 24.95 *(978-1-881508-66-3(8))* Oliver Pr., Inc.
Hannigan, Kate. A Lady Has the Floor: Belva Lockwood Speaks Out for Women's Rights. Jay, Alison, illus. 2018. 32p. (J). (gr. 2-5). 17.95 *(978-1-62979-453-2(8),* Calkins Creek) Highlights Pr., c/o Highlights for Children, Inc.
Harris, Nancy. What's the State Judicial Branch? rev. ed. 2016. (First Guide to Government Ser.). (ENG.). 32p. (J). (gr. 1-3). pap. 8.29 *(978-1-4846-3691-6(0),* 134103, Heinemann) Capstone.
Horn, Geoffrey M. Thurgood Marshall, 1 vol. 2004. (Trailblazers of the Modern World Ser.). (ENG., Illus.). 48p. (gr. 5-8). pap. 15.05 *(978-0-8368-5258-5(3),* 0eaf0b52-0726-4be3-b1fa-870937b22719); lib. bdg. 33.67 *(978-0-8368-5098-7(X),* 243d2da1-a59e-4bd5-a401-db59905c50c5) Stevens, Gareth Publishing LLLP. (Gareth Stevens Secondary Library).
Leaf, Christina. Michelle Obama: Health Advocate. 2019. (Women Leading the Way Ser.). (ENG., Illus.). 24p. (J). (gr. k-3). lib. bdg. 26.95 *(978-1-62617-942-4(5),* Blastoff! Readers) Bellwether Media.
—Michelle Obama: Health Advocate. 2019. (Women Leading the Way Ser.). (ENG., Illus.). 24p. (J). (gr. k-3). pap. 7.99 *(978-1-61891-502-3(9),* 12153, Blastoff! Readers) Bellwether Media.
Lucas, Eileen. Mahatma Gandhi: Fighting for Indian Independence, 1 vol. 2017. (Rebels with a Cause Ser.). (ENG.). 128p. (gr. 8-8). lib. bdg. 38.93 *(978-0-7660-8513-8(9),* 7939188e-3ec5-4be9-bb21-fc0384bf8c3d) Enslow Publishing, LLC.
Machajewski, Sarah. Michelle Obama, 1 vol. 2016. (Superwomen Role Models Ser.). (ENG., Illus.). 32p. (J). (gr. 3-4). 27.93 *(978-1-5081-4812-8(0),* 8d67cc38-9de9-4c10-90bc-efee1f99a1f6, PowerKids Pr.) Rosen Publishing Group, Inc., The.
Mara, Wil. Thurgood Marshall: Champion for Civil Rights. 2004. (Great Life Stories Ser.). (ENG., Illus.). 128p. (J). 30.50 *(978-0-531-12058-3(9),* Watts, Franklin) Scholastic Library Publishing.
Marcovitz, Hal. Michelle. 2007. (Obamas Ser.). 64p. (YA). (gr. 3-6). pap. 9.95 *(978-1-4222-1485-5(0));* (gr. 4-7). lib. bdg. 19.95 *(978-1-4222-1478-7(8))* Mason Crest.
Mattern, Joanne. What's So Great about Michelle Obama. 2009. (What's So Great About...? Ser.). 32p. (J). (gr. 2-4). lib. bdg. 25.70 *(978-1-58415-833-2(6))* Mitchell Lane Pubs.
Michelle Obama. 2009. (Political Profiles Ser.). 112p. (YA). (gr. 5-9). lib. bdg. 28.95 *(978-1-59935-090-5(4))* Reynolds, Morgan Inc.
Nault, Jennifer. Michelle Obama. 2009. (Remarkable People Ser.). (Illus.). 24p. (J). (gr. 4-6). pap. 8.95 *(978-1-60596-666-3(5));* lib. bdg. 24.45 *(978-1-60596-665-6(7))* Weigl Pubs., Inc.
Norgren, Jill. Belva Lockwood: The Woman Who Would Be President. 2007. (ENG., Illus.). 311p. 89.00 *(978-0-8147-5834-2(7),* 8431, NYU Pr.) New York Univ. Pr.
Obama, Michelle. Becoming: Adapted for Young Readers. 2021. (ENG., Illus.). 432p. (J). (gr. 5). 18.99 *(978-0-593-30374-0(1));* lib. bdg. 21.99 *(978-0-593-30375-7(X))* Random Hse. Children's Bks. (Delacorte Bks. for Young Readers).
Oliver, Alison. Be Bold, Baby: Michelle Obama. Oliver, Alison, illus. 2018. (Be Bold, Baby Ser.). (ENG., Illus.). 20p. (J). (— 1). bds. 9.99 *(978-1-328-51989-4(9),* 1720769, Clarion Bks.) HarperCollins Pubs.
Sarantou, Katlin. Reshma Saujani. Bane, Jeff, illus. 2019. (My Early Library: My Itty-Bitty Bio Ser.). (ENG.). 24p. (J). (gr. k-1). pap. 12.79 *(978-1-5341-4985-4(6),* 213247); lib. bdg. 30.64 *(978-1-5341-4699-0(7),* 213246) Cherry Lake Publishing.
Schwartz, Heather E. Michelle Obama: Political Icon. 2020. (Boss Lady Bios (Alternator Books (r)) Ser.). (ENG., Illus.). 32p. (J). (gr. 3-6). 30.65 *(978-1-5415-9707-5(9),* 4af4e01e-075b-4761-8eac-25b4a12854ed, Lerner Pubns.) Lerner Publishing Group.
Stevenson, Bryan. Just Mercy (Adapted for Young Adults) A True Story of the Fight for Justice. 2018. 288p. (YA). (gr. 7). 18.99 *(978-0-525-58003-4(4));* (ENG.). lib. bdg. 21.99 *(978-0-525-58004-1(2))* Random Hse. Children's Bks. (Delacorte Pr.).
Stoltman, Joan. Hillary Clinton, 1 vol. 2017. (Little Biographies of Big People Ser.). (ENG.). 24p. (J). (gr. 1-2). pap. 9.15 *(978-1-5382-0927-1(6),* 45d15419-e1ba-485e-aecd-492bac53ea80) Stevens, Gareth Publishing LLLP.
—Hillary Clinton, 1 vol. Garcia, Ana Maria, tr. 2017. (Pequeñas Biografías de Grandes Personajes (Little Biographies of Big People) Ser.). (SPA.). 24p. (J). (gr. 1-2). pap. 9.15 *(978-1-5382-1558-6(6),* 223ef883-505a-47a7-9806-85242aebbfaf); lib. bdg. 24.27 *(978-1-5382-1531-9(4),* c288e1b0-b83a-4715-865d-2d96d21028a1) Stevens, Gareth Publishing LLLP.
Wagner, Heather Lehr. Benjamin Hooks. 2003. (African American Leaders Ser.). (ENG., Illus.). 112p. (gr. 6-12). 30.00 *(978-0-7910-7685-9(7),* P113974, Facts On File) Infobase Holdings, Inc.
Wheeler, Jill C. Thurgood Marshall. 2003. (Breaking Barriers Ser.). 64p. (gr. 3-8). lib. bdg. 27.07 *(978-1-57765-907-5(4),* Abdo & Daughters) ABDO Publishing Co.

LAWYERS—FICTION
Bauer, Joan. Backwater. 2005. 185p. 18.00 *(978-0-7569-5779-7(6))* Perfection Learning Corp.
Clifford, Ross. The Shiddakovich Adventure. 2008. (ENG.). 122p. pap. 12.88 *(978-1-4092-3520-0(3))* Lulu Pr., Inc.
Grisham, John. The Abduction. 2009. (Theodore Boone Ser.: Bk. 2). 9.68 *(978-0-7848-3783-2(X),* Everbind) Marco Bk. Co.
—The Abduction. 2012. (Theodore Boone Ser.: 2). lib. bdg. 19.65 *(978-0-606-26079-4(X))* Turtleback.
—The Accused. 2013. (Theodore Boone Ser.: 3). lib. bdg. 18.40 *(978-0-606-31696-5(5))* Turtleback.
—The Fugitive. 2016. (Theodore Boone Ser.: 5). 272p. lib. bdg. 18.40 *(978-0-606-38847-4(8))* Turtleback.
—Kid Lawyer. l.t. ed. 2010. (Theodore Boone Ser.: Bk. 1). (ENG.). 278p. (J). 24.99 *(978-1-4104-3050-2(2))* Thorndike Pr.
—Kid Lawyer. 2011. (Theodore Boone Ser.: 1). lib. bdg. 19.65 *(978-0-606-23071-1(8))* Turtleback.
—Theodore Boone: Kid Lawyer. 2014. lthr. 79.00 *(978-1-62715-259-4(8))* Leatherbound Bestsellers.
—Theodore Boone: Kid Lawyer. 2011. 18.00 *(978-1-60686-999-4(X))* Perfection Learning Corp.
—Theodore Boone: Kid Lawyer. 2011. (Theodore Boone Ser.: 1). (ENG.). 288p. (J). (gr. 3-7). 8.99 *(978-0-14-241722-5(X),* Puffin Books) Penguin Young Readers Group.
—Theodore Boone: the Abduction, 2 vols. (Theodore Boone Ser.: 2). (ENG.). 256p. (J). (gr. 3-7). 2012. pap. 8.99 *(978-0-14-242137-6(5),* Puffin Books) 2011. 16.99 *(978-0-525-42557-1(8),* Dutton Books for Young Readers) Penguin Young Readers Group.
—Theodore Boone: the Accused. 2013. (Theodore Boone Ser.: 3). (ENG.). 304p. (J). (gr. 3-7). pap. 8.99 *(978-0-14-242613-5(X),* Puffin Books) Penguin Young Readers Group.
—Theodore Boone: the Activist. (Theodore Boone Ser.: 4). (ENG.). (J). (gr. 3-7). 2014. 320p. pap. 8.99 *(978-0-14-242309-7(2),* Puffin Books) 2013. 304p. 17.99 *(978-0-525-42577-9(2),* Dutton Books for Young Readers) Penguin Young Readers Group.
—Theodore Boone: the Fugitive. 2015. (Theodore Boone Ser.: 5). (ENG.). 256p. (J). (gr. 3-7). 17.99 *(978-0-525-42638-7(8),* Dutton Books for Young Readers) Penguin Young Readers Group.
—Theodore Boone: the Scandal. 2016. (Theodore Boone Ser.: 6). (ENG.). 224p. (J). (gr. 3-7). 17.99 *(978-0-525-42639-4(6),* Dutton Books for Young Readers) Penguin Young Readers Group.
Henry, O. & Escott, John. Oxford Bookworms Playscripts: One Thousand Dollars & Other Plays: Level 2: 700-Word Vocabulary. 2nd ed. 2008. (ENG., Illus.). 64p. 11.00 *(978-0-19-423520-4(3))* Oxford Univ. Pr., Inc.
Pontacoloni, Edward. The Adventures of Firstyr the Younger Knight Errata of Cort: Bed Time Stories for First Year Lawyers. 2008. (ENG.). 36p. per. 15.99 *(978-1-4257-6527-9(0))* Xlibris Corp.
RealBuzz Studios Staff. Hits & Misses, No. 3. 2007. 128p. (YA). pap. 4.97 *(978-1-59789-571-2(7),* Barbour Bks.) Barbour Publishing, Inc.
Segal, Howard. My Daddy the Lawyer: Mommy-Daddy Books. 2009. 16p. pap. 9.49 *(978-1-4343-0883-2(9))* AuthorHouse.
Tricarico, Mark. Zoe Pope: Unlicensed Lawyer. 2007. 80p. per. 8.95 *(978-0-595-46943-7(4))* iUniverse, Inc.

LAYOUT AND TYPOGRAPHY
see Printing

LEADERSHIP
Addington, Judith. A-Z Leader Alphabook. 2012. (ENG.). (J). spiral bd. 14.95 *(978-1-4675-3105-4(7))* Independent Pub.
—Building Blocks for Leaders. 2012. (ENG.). (J). spiral bd. 19.95 *(978-1-4675-3106-1(5))* Independent Pub.
Army JROTC: Leadership Education & Training, Cadet Reference. 2nd ed. 2003. (Illus.). vi, 56p. (J). *(978-0-536-74189-9(1),* Dept. of the Army) United States Government Printing Office.
Asgedom, Mawi. Win the Inner Battle: The Ultimate Teen Leadership Journal. Berger, Dave, ed. 2003. 96p. (YA). spiral bd. 14.00 *(978-0-9743901-8-5(6))* Mawi, Inc.
Auster, Michael A. They Led the Way. 2005. (Yellow Umbrella Fluent Level Ser.). (ENG.). 16p. (gr. k-1). pap. 35.70 *(978-0-7368-5315-6(4),* Capstone Pr.) Capstone.
Ball, Heather. Great Women Leaders, 1 vol. 2004. (Women's Hall of Fame Ser.: 4). (ENG., Illus.). 100p. (J). (gr. 4-8). pap. 10.95 *(978-1-896764-81-8(9))* Second Story Pr. CAN. Dist: Orca Bk. Pubs. USA.
Be a Community Leader. 2014. (Be a Community Leader Ser.). 32p. (J). (gr. 4-6). pap. 60.00 *(978-1-4777-7215-7(4),* PowerKids Pr.) Rosen Publishing Group, Inc., The.
Boyd, Bentley. George Washington Leads the Way. 2011. (Mount Vernon Comix Ser.). (Illus.). 24p. (J). (gr. 3-9). pap. 6.95 *(978-1-933122-44-1(7))* Chester Comix, LLC.
Capstone Classroom & Stead, Tony. If I Were in Charge... 2017. (What's the Point? Reading & Writing Expository Text Ser.). (ENG., Illus.). 32p. (J). (gr. 5-5). pap. 7.95 *(978-1-4966-0733-1(3),* 132368, Capstone Classroom) Capstone.
Chapman, Kelly. Princess with a Purpose. Lyon, Tammie, illus. ldr.'s ed. 2009. pap. 12.99 *(978-0-7369-2743-7(3))* Harvest Hse. Pubs.
Chatlien, Ruth Hull. Modern American Indian Chiefs. 2009. (Sharing the American Dream Ser.). (Illus.). 64p. (YA). (gr. 7-12). 22.95 *(978-1-4222-0592-1(4))* Mason Crest.
Drayton, Bill, frwd. Be a Changemaker: How to Start Something That Matters. 2014. (ENG., Illus.). 240p. (YA). (gr. 7). 19.99 *(978-1-58270-465-4(1));* pap. 15.99 *(978-1-58270-464-7(3))* Simon Pulse/Beyond Words.
Duignan, Brian, ed. The Britannica Guide to the World's Most Influential People (Print/Ebook Combo Set) Print/Ebook Combo Set, 64 vols. Incl. 100 Most Influential Philosophers of All Time. (ENG.). 368p. (YA). (gr. 10-10). 2010. 113.18 *(978-1-61530-072-3(4),* 247aac42-c737-4e0d-8e4a-b7306f082367); (Britannica Guide to the World's Most Influential People Ser.). (ENG.). 336-384p. 2010. 905.44 *(978-1-61530-165-2(8),* ea8db089-fd00-4db0-8986-b9239413f7c8) Rosen Publishing Group, Inc., The.
Durrie, Karen. Diversión. 2012. (SPA.). (J). 27.13 *(978-1-61913-209-2(5))* Weigl Pubs., Inc.
Freedman, Jeri. Being a Leader: Organizing & Inspiring a Group, 1 vol. 2011. (Communicating with Confidence Ser.). (ENG., Illus.). 80p. (YA). (gr. 7-7). pap. 15.15 *(978-1-4488-5631-2(0),* 2de5da8e-2bcd-4e5a-96c4-bf4535c2a929); lib. bdg. 38.47 *(978-1-4488-5521-6(7),* 81ea258b-21b1-41dd-9655-21af485b7999) Rosen Publishing Group, Inc., The.
—Step-By-Step Guide to Becoming a Leader at School & on the Job, 1 vol. 2014. (Winning at Work Readiness Ser.). (ENG.). 64p. (YA). (gr. 6-6). 36.13 *(978-1-4777-7778-7(4),* f7d8d0f0-660c-4a97-b8c4-ba820efa755f) Rosen Publishing Group, Inc., The.
Furstinger, Nancy. Women & Leadership, 1 vol. 2012. (Young Woman's Guide to Contemporary Issues Ser.). (ENG., Illus.). 112p. (YA). (gr. 8-9). lib. bdg. 39.80 *(978-1-4488-8402-5(0),* 54a004f4-ae4b-49b1-9c48-d0eb4f2eb510) Rosen Publishing Group, Inc., The.
Ganeri, Anita. The Top Ten Leaders That Changed the World. 2009. (J). 60.00 *(978-1-4358-9166-1(X),* PowerKids Pr.); (ENG., Illus.). 32p. (J). (gr. 4-5). pap. 11.00 *(978-1-4358-9165-4(1),* 3b811668-8509-412a-9644-35bfef082751, PowerKids Pr.); (ENG., Illus.). 32p. (YA). (gr. 4-5). 30.27 *(978-1-4358-9164-7(3),* 2ce1f0bb-e00f-44c3-8ff3-31056aced95f) Rosen Publishing Group, Inc., The.
Gerety, Ed. Combinations: Opening the Door to Student Leadership. 2003. 160p. (YA). per. 14.95 *(978-0-9725938-3-0(7))* Whaleback Publishing.
Goddu, Krystyna Poray. George Washington's Presidency. 2016. (Presidential Powerhouses Ser.). (ENG., Illus.). 104p. (YA). (gr. 6-12). 35.99 *(978-1-4677-7924-1(5),*

5ef17340-8503-4d31-9be2-86617a0a3921); E-Book 54.65 *(978-1-4677-8598-3(9))* Lerner Publishing Group. (Lerner Pubns.).

Great Military Leaders, 16 vols. 2017. (Great Military Leaders Ser.). (ENG.). 128p. (gr. 9-9). lib. bdg. 378.88 *(978-1-5026-2686-8(1),* a5fae9b3-a623-466e-afa0-d9ae4500cf93, Cavendish Square) Cavendish Square Publishing LLC.

Gwartney, Becky, et al. Lead On: Destination Reality. 2003. (YA). pap. 14.99 *(978-0-89265-968-5(8))* Randall Hse. Pubns.

Harcourt School Publishers Staff. Leaders for Peace. 3rd ed. 2003. (Horizons Ser.). (Illus.). (J). (gr. 3). pap. 5.50 *(978-0-15-333278-4(6))* Harcourt Schl. Pubs.

Harris, Laurie Lanzen. Biography for Beginners: African-American Leaders. 2007. (J). lib. bdg. 30.00 *(978-1-931360-35-7(9))* Favorable Impressions.

Harris, Laurie Lanzen, ed. Biography for Beginners Vol. 2: African-American Leaders. 2008. 316p. (YA). (gr. 5-10). lib. bdg. 30.00 *(978-1-931360-36-4(7))* Favorable Impressions.

Hemingway, Al. Chuck Norris. 2007. (Sharing the American Dream Ser.). 64p. (YA). (gr. 7-18). pap. 9.95 *(978-1-4222-0758-1(7))* Mason Crest.

Hollar, Sherman, contrib. by. George Washington, 1 vol. 2012. (Pivotal Presidents: Profiles in Leadership Ser.). (ENG., Illus.). 80p. (gr. 8-8). (J). lib. bdg. 36.47 *(978-1-61530-939-9(X),* 5406dae3-454b-476c-bd1c-9cfe62bfa85b); (YA). 72.94 *(978-1-61530-956-6(X),* 6d4e4612-5ccc-4364-9d13-da5d6b06182c) Rosen Publishing Group, Inc., The.

Killcoyne, Hope Lourie & Wolny, Philip, eds. The 100 Most Influential Religious Leaders of All Time, 1 vol., 1. 2016. (Britannica Guide to the World's Most Influential People Ser.). (ENG., Illus.). 376p. (J). (gr. 10-10). 56.59 *(978-1-68048-277-5(7),* ffaeb020-ef9f-478e-b780-c1095058d60a, Britannica Educational Publishing) Rosen Publishing Group, Inc., The.

Kishel, Ann-Marie. Our Leaders. 2007. (First Step Nonfiction - Government Ser.). (ENG., Illus.). 24p. (gr. k-2). lib. bdg. 23.93 *(978-0-8225-6395-2(9),* Lerner Pubns.) Lerner Publishing Group.

Laks Gorman, Jacqueline. ¿Quiénes Gobiernan Nuestro País? (Who Leads Our Country?), 1 vol. 2008. (Conoce Tu Gobierno (Know Your Government) Ser.). (SPA.). 24p. (gr. 2-4). pap. 9.15 *(978-0-8368-8856-0(1),* b4060846-c7a1-4172-82df-81a71c4141ca); (Illus.). lib. bdg. 24.67 *(978-0-8368-8851-5(0),* d8616f2c-6b52-4373-93f8-e10b92427a89) Stevens, Gareth Publishing LLLP. (Weekly Reader Leveled Readers).

—Who Leads Our Country?, 1 vol. 2008. (Know Your Government Ser.). (ENG.). 24p. (gr. 2-4). pap. 9.15 *(978-0-8368-8846-1(4),* e85f725a-b64a-4121-b207-b9126d5bb638); (Illus.). lib. bdg. 24.67 *(978-0-8368-8841-6(3),* 232ad48e-f3c0-41de-bf43-9a723b1aa950) Stevens, Gareth Publishing LLLP. (Weekly Reader Leveled Readers).

Landau, Jennifer, ed. Teens Talk about Leadership & Activism. 2017. (Teen Voices: Real Teens Discuss Real Problems Ser.). (Illus.). 64p. (J). (gr. 12-17). 77.70 *(978-1-5081-7635-0(3))* Rosen Publishing Group, Inc., The.

Leaders of the Middle Ages, 8 vols., Set. 2004. (Leaders of the Middle Ages Ser.). (ENG.). (J). (gr. 5-8). 159.20 *(978-1-4042-0345-7(1),* 31cd7da8-a2f2-42e9-a5bc-bdee8bbbbb0a) Rosen Publishing Group, Inc., The.

Lee, George L. Worldwide Interesting People: 162 History Makers of African Descent, 1 vol. alt. ed. 2012. (ENG., Illus.). 144p. pap. 19.99 *(978-0-7864-6768-6(1),* 5db30b06-2ea6-4191-b975-47d4abeb4110) McFarland & Co., Inc. Pubs.

Lewers, Rob & Murphy, Ed. The Hidden Hurt: How to Beat Bullying in Schools. 96p. pap. *(978-1-876367-66-4(0))* Wizard Bks.

Lindeen, Mary. Leading the Way. (Wonder Readers Fluent Level Ser.). (ENG.). (gr. -1-2). 2011. 16p. pap. 35.94 *(978-1-4296-8099-8(7))* 2017. 20p. (J). pap. 6.25 *(978-1-5435-0539-9(2),* 137355) Capstone. (Capstone Pr.).

Linder, Nani Aki. All about Me Look at Me I'm a Star: Children's Workbook. 2003. 121p. pap. 97.00 *(978-0-7414-1677-3(8))* Infinity Publishing.

Loh-Hagan, Virginia. Girl Bosses. 2019. (History's Yearbook Ser.). (ENG., Illus.). 32p. (J). (gr. 4-8). pap. 14.21 *(978-1-5341-5078-2(1),* 213619); lib. bdg. 32.07 *(978-1-5341-4792-8(6),* 213618) Cherry Lake Publishing. (45th Parallel Press).

Making a Difference. 2014. (Making a Difference: Leaders Who Are Changing the World Ser.). 48p. (YA). (gr. 5-8). pap. 84.30 *(978-1-62275-765-7(3))* Rosen Publishing Group, Inc., The.

Making a Difference: Leaders Who Are Changing the World, 24 vols. 2014. (Making a Difference: Leaders Who Are Changing the World Ser.). (ENG.). 48p. (YA). (gr. 5-5). 340.92 *(978-1-62275-754-1(8),* d7900435-d71c-46fa-87bc-9c1a7429c0cf) Rosen Publishing Group, Inc., The.

Mayer, Cassie. Being a Leader, 1 vol. Beech, Mark, illus. 2007. (Citizenship Ser.). (ENG.). 24p. (J). (gr. -1-1). pap. 6.29 *(978-1-4034-9494-8(0),* 96162, Heinemann) Capstone.

—Ser un Líder, 1 vol. 2007. (Civismo Ser.). (SPA., Illus.). 24p. (J). (gr. -1-1). pap. 6.29 *(978-1-4329-0408-1(6),* 97253, Heinemann) Capstone.

McCabe, Matthew. 12 Business Leaders Who Changed the World. 2016. (Change Makers Ser.). (ENG., Illus.). 32p. (J). (gr. 3-6). 32.80 *(978-1-63235-145-6(5),* 11935, 12-Story Library) Bookstaves, LLC.

Miller, Amanda. What Does the President Do? 2009. (Scholastic News Nonfiction Readers Ser.). (Illus.). 24p. (J). (gr. 1-2). 22.00 *(978-0-531-21088-8(X))* Scholastic Library Publishing.

Mr. Blue. From Underdog to Wonderdog: Top Ten Tricks to Lead Your Pack. 2012. (ENG., Illus.). 52p. (J). (gr. 1-5). pap. 14.95 *(978-1-936354-26-9(8),* Tremendous Leadership) Tremendous Life Bks.

Myers, Jeff. Secrets of Everyday Leaders Student Text: Create Positive Change & Inspire Extraordinary Results. 2006. 112p. stu. ed., per. 17.99 *(978-0-8054-6886-1(2))* B&H Publishing Group.

—Secrets of Great Communicators Student Text: Simple, Powerful Strategies for Reaching the Heart of Your Audience, Student Textbook. 2006. 158p. stu. ed., per. 17.99 *(978-0-8054-6880-9(3))* B&H Publishing Group.

—Secrets of World Changers Student Text: How to Achieve Lasting Influence as a Leader. 2006. 75p. pap., stu. ed. 12.99 *(978-0-8054-6883-0(8))* B&H Publishing Group.

Nelson, Robin. Being a Leader. 2003. (First Step Nonfiction — Citizenship Ser.). (Illus.). 24p. (J). (gr. k-2). (ENG.). pap. 6.99 *(978-0-8225-1324-7(2),* bb68e7b6-0df1-4f00-9673-5ca7ddf19558); lib. bdg. 18.60 *(978-0-8225-1287-5(4))* Lerner Publishing Group.

Photo-Illustrated Biographies. 2010. (Photo-Illustrated Biographies Ser.). (ENG.). 24p. (gr. 2-3). pap. 662.40 *(978-1-4296-5209-4(8),* Capstone Pr.) Capstone.

Rotberg, Robert I. Governance & Leadership in Africa. Rotberg, Robert I. & Ojakorotu, Victor, eds. 2013. (Africa: Progress & Problems Ser.: 13). (Illus.). 112p. (J). (gr. 7-18). 24.95 *(978-1-4222-2940-8(8))* Mason Crest.

Schuh, Mari. How to Be King of Pride Rock: Confidence with Simba. 2019. (Disney Great Character Guides). (ENG., Illus.). 32p. (J). (gr. 1-4). pap. 8.99 *(978-1-5415-4604-2(0),* Lerner Pubns.) Lerner Publishing Group.

Schuh, Mari C. How to Be a Snow Queen: Leadership with Elsa. 2019. (Disney Great Character Guides). (ENG., Illus.). 32p. (J). (gr. 1-4). 27.99 *(978-1-5415-3899-3(4),* Lerner Pubns.) Lerner Publishing Group.

—How to Be King of Pride Rock: Leadership with Simba. 2019. (Disney Great Character Guides). (ENG., Illus.). 32p. (J). (gr. 1-4). 27.99 *(978-1-5415-3904-4(4),* Lerner Pubns.) Lerner Publishing Group.

Shames, Stephen. Transforming Lives: Turning Uganda's Forgotten Children into Leaders. Shames, Stephen, photos by. 2009. (Illus.). 40p. (YA). pap. 12.95 *(978-1-59572-213-3(0))* Star Bright Bks., Inc.

Shofner, Melissa Raé. How Can I Be a Leader? Taking Civic Action, 1 vol. 2018. (Civics for the Real World Ser.). (ENG.). 8p. (gr. k-1). pap. *(978-1-5383-6388-1(7),* 0f37475f-0320-4fa9-ba89-8c1f9a3a5198, Rosen Classroom) Rosen Publishing Group, Inc., The.

—I Am a Leader: Taking Civic Action, 1 vol. 2018. (Civics for the Real World Ser.). (ENG.). 8p. (gr. k-1). pap. *(978-1-5383-6385-0(2),* cfc61338-9983-43ca-8c87-2808e84ae26a, Rosen Classroom) Rosen Publishing Group, Inc., The.

Strack, Jay. Leadership Rocks: Becoming a Student of Influence, 1 vol. 2006. (Student Leadership University Study Guide Ser.). (ENG.). 144p. (YA). pap. 9.99 *(978-1-4185-0593-6(5))* HarperChristian Resources.

Strack, Jay E. Life: How to Get There from Here, 1 vol. 2006. (Student Leadership University Study Guide Ser.). (ENG.). 144p. (YA). pap. 9.99 *(978-1-4185-0599-8(4))* HarperChristian Resources.

Thomas, Wendy Russell & Ruchman, Laura. Bliss Live It! Bliss Give It! Starmer, Anika & Wertz, Michael, illus. 2010. 60p. (YA). *(978-0-88441-754-5(9))* Girl Scouts of the USA.

Thompson, Laurie Ann. Be a Changemaker: How to Start Something That Matters. 2014. (ENG., Illus.). (YA). (gr. 7). lib. bdg. 24.60 *(978-1-68065-004-4(1))* Perfection Learning Corp.

Tibbs, Janet. Being A Leader, 8 vols., Vol. 7. 2004. (Illus.). (J). per. *(978-1-932062-33-5(5))* Idea Magic Bks.

Turner, Joshua. How to Make Decisions As a Group, 1 vol. 2018. (Civic Virtue: Let's Work Together Ser.). (ENG.). 24p. (gr. 3-3). 25.27 *(978-1-5081-6683-2(8),* fdcb68eb-7d6f-487c-815e-a32239a22313, PowerKids Pr.) Rosen Publishing Group, Inc., The.

Wambach, Abby. Wolfpack (Young Readers Edition) 2020. (ENG., Illus.). 112p. (J). 16.99 *(978-1-250-76686-1(9),* 900232554) Roaring Brook Pr.

Witt, Marcos. Liderazgo Al Extremo, 1 vol. 2004. (ENG.). 112p. pap. 11.99 *(978-0-88113-762-0(6))* Grupo Nelson.

Wolny, Philip, ed. The 100 Most Influential Religious Leaders of All Time, 4 vols. 2016. (Britannica Guide to the World's Most Influential People Ser.). (ENG.). 376p. (gr. 10-10). 113.18 *(978-1-68048-240-9(8),* e73a2b13-1bff-4961-8423-cbe35e11cdd3, Britannica Educational Publishing) Rosen Publishing Group, Inc., The.

Wooster, Patricia. So, You Want to Be a Leader? An Awesome Guide to Becoming a Head Honcho. 2016. (Be What You Want Ser.). (ENG., Illus.). 192p. (J). (gr. 3-7). pap. 11.99 *(978-1-58270-547-7(X))* Aladdin/Beyond Words.

WorldVenture Guide for Leaders of Grades 1-6. 2003. pap. 8.99 *(978-1-56309-634-1(X))* Woman's Missionary Union.

LEAKEY, L. S. B. (LOUIS SEYMOUR BAZETT), 1903-1972

Timmons, Angie. The Leakeys: The Family That Traced Human Origins to Africa. 2019. (J). pap. *(978-1-9785-1464-5(6))* Enslow Publishing, LLC.

LEARNING, ART OF

see Study Skills

LEARNING AND SCHOLARSHIP

see also Culture; Education; Humanism; Research

Cornell, Kari A. Classroom up Close. 2016. (Illus.). 24p. (J). *(978-0-87659-704-0(5))* Gryphon Hse., Inc.

Howell, Dusti & Howell, Deanne, prods. Dr. Wiley Makes Sense. 2005. (YA). pap. 249.95 incl. cd-rom *(978-0-9677328-9-3(1))* SolidA, Inc.

Perry, William G., Jr. Learn to Love to Learn. Date not set. 300p. (YA). (gr. 8-12). pap. *(978-1-887946-01-8(2))* Learning Net, The.

Reed, Avery. Who Were the Brothers Grimm? O'brien, John, illus. 2015. (Who Was-? Chapters Ser.). (ENG.). 112p. (J). (gr. 3-6). 18.69 *(978-1-4844-6177-8(0),* Penguin Workshop) Penguin Young Readers Group.

Scott, John, text. How to Financially Fund Your College Education. 2004. (YA). 30.00 *(978-1-879498-83-9(9))* SportAmerica.

Silva, Patricia & Pauli, Erika. Modern Times, 1 vol. Baldanzi, Alessandro, illus. 2009. (Reading & Writing Ser.). (ENG.). 32p. (gr. 4-4). 31.21 *(978-0-7614-4322-3(3),* 7dbe8905-aa51-4531-b174-ecbd61167701) Cavendish Square Publishing LLC.

LEARNING DISABILITIES

Allen, William H., creator. TEH Learns to Read: (13 Volume Set), 13 Volume Set. 2004. (Illus.). 40p. (J). 399.95 *(978-0-9745938-0-7(X))* LD Coach, LLC.

Borus, Audrey. Coping with a Learning Disability, 1 vol. 2019. (Coping Ser.). (ENG.). 112p. (J). (gr. 7-7). pap. 19.24 *(978-1-5081-8733-2(9),* 86c1f5f7-98d8-4443-af46-2a3b4220c30e) Rosen Publishing Group, Inc., The.

Bow, James. Life with a Learning Disorder. 2018. (Everyday Heroes Ser.). (ENG.). 24p. (J). (gr. 3-6). lib. bdg. 32.79 *(978-1-5038-2515-4(9),* 212332, MOMENTUM) Child's World, Inc, The.

Brinkerhoff, Shirley. Learning Disabilities. Albers, Lisa et al, eds. 2014. (Living with a Special Need Ser.: 16). 128p. (J). (gr. 7-18). 25.95 *(978-1-4222-3040-4(6))* Mason Crest.

—Why Can't I Learn Like Everyone Else? Youth with Learning Disabilities. (Youth with Special Needs Ser.). (Illus.). (YA). 2004. 128p. 24.95 *(978-1-59084-730-5(X))* 2003. 127p. (gr. 7). pap. 14.95 *(978-1-4222-0432-0(4))* Mason Crest.

Cooper, Barbara & Widdows, Nancy. The Social Success Workbook for Teens: Skill-Building Activities for Teens with Nonverbal Learning Disorder, Asperger's Disorder, & Other Social-Skill Problems. 2008. (ENG., Illus.). 144p. (YA). (gr. 6-12). pap. 18.95 *(978-1-57224-614-0(6),* 6140, Instant Help Books) New Harbinger Pubns.

Doering Tourville, Amanda. My Friend Has Dyslexia, 1 vol. Sorra, Kristin, illus. 2010. (Friends with Disabilities Ser.). (ENG.). 24p. (J). (gr. k-3). lib. bdg. 26.65 *(978-1-4048-5752-0(4),* 102489, Picture Window Bks.) Capstone.

Edwards, Nicola. My Friend Has Dyslexia. 2004. (J). lib. bdg. 27.10 *(978-1-59389-167-1(9))* Chrysalis Education.

—My Friend Has Dyspraxia. 2004. (J). lib. bdg. 27.10 *(978-1-59389-168-8(7))* Chrysalis Education.

Flath, Camden, told to. Kids with Special Needs: IDEA (Individuals with Disabilities Education Act), 11 vols., Set. Incl. Finding My Voice: Kids with Speech Impairment. Stewart, Sheila. pap. 7.95 *(978-1-4222-1925-6(9));* Hidden Child: Kids with Autism. Stewart, Sheila. pap. 7.95 *(978-1-4222-1927-0(5));* I Can Do It! Kids with Physical Challenges. Stewart, Sheila. pap. 7.95 *(978-1-4222-1926-3(7));* Listening with Your Eyes: Kids Who Are Deaf & Hard of Hearing. Stewart, Sheila. pap. 7.95 *(978-1-4222-1920-1(8));* My Name Is Not Slow: Kids with Intellectual Disabilities. Stewart, Sheila. pap. 7.95 *(978-1-4222-1921-8(6));* Sick All the Time: Kids with Chronic Illness. Chastain, Zachary. pap. 7.95 *(978-1-4222-1922-5(4));* Something's Wrong! Kids with Emotional Disturbance. Stewart, Sheila. pap. 7.95 *(978-1-4222-1923-2(2));* Speed Racer: Kids with Attention-Deficit/Hyperactivity Disorder. Stewart, Sheila. pap. 7.95 *(978-1-4222-1924-9(0));* What's Wrong with My Brain? Kids with Brain Injury. Stewart, Sheila. pap. 7.95 *(978-1-4222-1928-7(3));* Why Can't I Learn Like Everyone Else? Kids with Learning Disabilities. Stewart, Sheila. pap. 7.95 *(978-1-4222-1929-4(1));* 48p. (YA). (gr. 5-18). 2009. 2011. Set pap. 87.45 *(978-1-4222-1918-8(6))* Mason Crest.

Gillard, Arthur, ed. Learning Disabilities, 1 vol. 2011. (Issues That Concern You Ser.). (ENG., Illus.). 136p. (gr. 7-10). 43.63 *(978-0-7377-5695-1(0),* 0060a9e5-b847-456b-953c-d9677b964c73, Greenhaven Publishing) Greenhaven Publishing LLC.

Gillen-Connell, Linda. Dumb Bunny. 2005. 67p. (J). (gr. 4-6). pap. 16.95 *(978-1-4137-8454-1(2))* PublishAmerica, Inc.

Gunton, Sharon, ed. Learning Disabilities, 1 vol. 2007. (Social Issues Firsthand Ser.). (ENG., Illus.). 128p. (gr. 10-12). lib. bdg. 39.93 *(978-0-7377-3840-7(5),* e97c9bc1-2c18-4056-90cd-e3045821836e, Greenhaven Publishing) Greenhaven Publishing LLC.

Landau, Jennifer, ed. Teens Talk about Learning Disabilities & Differences. 2017. (Teen Voices: Real Teens Discuss Real Problems Ser.). (Illus.). 64p. (J). (gr. 12-17). 77.70 *(978-1-5081-7636-7(1))* Rosen Publishing Group, Inc., The.

Libal, Autumn. My Name Isn't Slow: Youth with Mental Retardation. 2004. (Youth with Special Needs Ser.). (Illus.). 128p. (YA). 24.95 *(978-1-59084-731-2(8))* Mason Crest.

McMurchie, Susan. Understanding My Learning Differences. 2003. 148p. (gr. 4-5). spiral bd. 29.00 incl. audio compact disk *(978-1-57861-497-4(X),* IEP Resources) Attainment Co., Inc.

Miles, Brenda S. & Patterson, Colleen A. How I Learn: A Kid's Guide to Learning Disability. Heinrichs, Jane, illus. 2014. 32p. (J). *(978-1-4338-1660-4(1));* (ENG.). pap. *(978-1-4338-1661-1(X))* American Psychological Assn.

Nelson, Sheila & Livingston, Phyllis. Youth Who Are Gifted: Integrating Talents & Intelligence. 2007. (Helping Youth with Mental, Physical, & Social Challenges Ser.). (Illus.). 128p. (YA). pap. 14.95 *(978-1-4222-0435-1(9))* Mason Crest.

Packiam Alloway, Tracy Packiam. How Can I Remember All That? Simple Stuff to Improve Your Working Memory. O'Connell, David, illus. 2019. 64p. 17.95 *(978-1-78592-633-4(0),* 697019) Kingsley, Jessica Pubs. GBR. Dist: Hachette UK Distribution.

Paquette, Penny Hutchins & Tuttle, Cheryl Gerson. Learning Disabilities: The Ultimate Teen Guide. rev. ed. 2006. (It Happened to Me Ser.: 1). (ENG., Illus.). 312p. per. 25.00 *(978-0-8108-5643-1(3))* Scarecrow Pr., Inc.

Parks, Peggy J. Learning Disabilities. 2009. (Compact Research Ser.). 96p. (YA). (gr. 7-12). lib. bdg. 43.93 *(978-1-60152-077-7(8))* ReferencePoint Pr., Inc.

Rea, Amy C. Living with Learning Disabilities. 2018. (Living with Disorders & Disabilities Ser.). (ENG.). 80p. (YA). (gr. 6-12). 39.93 *(978-1-68282-481-8(0))* ReferencePoint Pr., Inc.

Stanton, Lidia. Tricky Punctuation in Cartoons. 2020. (Illus.). 272p. 18.95 *(978-1-78775-402-7(2),* 743651) Kingsley, Jessica Pubs. GBR. Dist: Hachette UK Distribution.

Stern, Judith M. & Ben-Ami, Uzi. Many Ways to Learn: A Kid's Guide to LD. Chesworth, Michael & Pearce, Carl, illus. 2nd rev. ed. 2010. 112p. (J). (gr. 3-8). 14.95 *(978-1-4338-0739-8(4));* pap. 9.95 *(978-1-4338-0740-4(8))* American Psychological Assn. (Magination Pr.).

Stewart, Sheila. Why Can't I Learn Like Everyone Else? Kids with Learning Disabilities. 2009. (Kids with Special Needs Ser.). 48p. (YA). (gr. 5-18). pap. 7.95 *(978-1-4222-1929-4(1))* Mason Crest.

Stewart, Sheila & Flath, Camden. Why Can't I Learn Like Everyone Else? Kids with Learning Disabilities. 2010. (Kids with Special Needs Ser.). 48p. (YA). (gr. 5-18). lib. bdg. 19.95 *(978-1-4222-1726-9(4))* Mason Crest.

LEARNING DISABILITIES—FICTION

Asher, Diana Harmon. Sidetracked. (ENG.). (J). (gr. 3-7). 2018. 256p. pap. 8.99 *(978-1-4197-3139-6(4),* 1153303) 2017. 240p. 16.99 *(978-1-4197-2601-9(3),* 1153301) Abrams, Inc. (Amulet Bks.).

Butler, Dori Hillestad. Alexandra Hopewell, Labor Coach. 2005. 136p. (J). (gr. 3-6). 15.99 *(978-0-8075-0242-6(1))* Whitman, Albert & Co.

Delacre, Lulu. Jay & Ben, 1 vol. 2013. (ENG., Illus.). 18p. (J). (gr. k-13). bds. 20.00 *(978-1-60060-460-7(9),* d05c1df9-9c2d-4abf-a276-0b1ebf5efee9) Lee & Low Bks., Inc.

Ellis, Mark. Words. 2006. (ENG., Illus.). 40p. 19.95 *(978-0-88982-227-6(1))* Oolichan Bks. CAN. Dist: Univ. of Toronto Pr.

Flake, Sharon G. Pinned. 2014. (ENG.). 240p. (YA). (gr. 9-9). pap. 10.99 *(978-0-545-05733-2(7),* Scholastic Pr.) Scholastic, Inc.

Gehret, Jeanne. The Don't-Give-Up Kid: And Learning Disabilities. LaDuca, Michael, illus. 4th ed. 2009. (Coping Ser.). (ENG.). 32p. (J). (gr. 1-3). 17.95 *(978-0-9821982-0-9(5))* Verbal Images Pr.

Gramp's Magic Gift. 2011. 98p. 24.99 *(978-1-4628-2980-4(5));* pap. 15.99 *(978-1-4628-2979-8(1))* Xlibris Corp.

Hansen, Joyce. Yellow Bird & Me. 2005. (ENG.). 160p. (J). (gr. 5-7). pap. 7.99 *(978-0-618-61116-4(9),* 100446, Clarion Bks.) HarperCollins Pubs.

Holland, Nikki Richardson. Meet Lanceamus Jones: A Special Kid with Special Needs. 2011. 24p. (J). pap. 12.95 *(978-1-4520-7649-2(9))* AuthorHouse.

Janover, Caroline D. Josh: A Boy with Dyslexia. 2004. 108p. (J). pap. 9.95 *(978-0-595-31381-5(7),* Backinprint.com) iUniverse, Inc.

McClintock, Norah. Watch Me, 1 vol. 2008. (Orca Currents Ser.). (ENG.). 128p. (J). (gr. 4-7). pap. 9.95 *(978-1-55469-039-8(0))* Orca Bk. Pubs. USA.

Morrison, Laurie. Up for Air. 2019. (ENG., Illus.). 288p. (YA). (gr. 5-9). 16.99 *(978-1-4197-3366-6(4),* 1215601, Amulet Bks.) Abrams, Inc.

Nichol, Tim. Stephen Harris in Trouble: A Dyspraxic Drama in Several Clumsy Acts. 2003. 144p. (J). pap. 21.95 *(978-1-84310-134-5(3),* 695197) Kingsley, Jessica Pubs. GBR. Dist: Hachette UK Distribution.

Polacco, Patricia. The Art of Miss Chew. Polacco, Patricia, illus. 2012. (Illus.). 40p. (J). (gr. k-3). 18.99 *(978-0-399-25703-2(9),* G.P. Putnam's Sons Books for Young Readers) Penguin Young Readers Group.

Ramos, NoNieqa. The Disturbed Girl's Dictionary. 2019. (ENG.). 344p. (YA). (gr. 9-12). pap. 9.99 *(978-1-5415-7761-9(2),* d73da4a1-3776-49ed-af48-f2cce9e8d6b6, Carolrhoda Lab™) Lerner Publishing Group.

Schmatz, Pat. Bluefish. 2013. (ENG.). 240p. (YA). (gr. 7). pap. 9.99 *(978-0-7636-6341-4(7))* Candlewick Pr.

Vision, David & Vision, Mutiya Sahar. If Only I Could! Alcantara, Ignacio, illus. 2009. 32p. 17.00 *(978-0-9659538-8-7(2))* Von Curtis Publishing.

Walters, Eric. Special Edward, 1 vol. 2009. (Orca Currents Ser.). (ENG.). 136p. (J). (gr. 4-7). pap. 9.95 *(978-1-55469-092-3(7))* Orca Bk. Pubs. USA.

Whitlow, Crystal K. Charles Gordon Willingham. Fisher, Bonnie & Wolski, Bobbi, illus. 2006. per. *(978-0-9777361-0-2(5))* Day3 Productions, Inc.

Winkler, Henry & Oliver, Lin. Barfing in the Backseat: How I Survived My Family Road Trip. Watson, Jesse Joshua, illus. 2007. (Hank Zipzer Ser.: No. 12). 152p. (gr. 4-7). 15.00 *(978-0-7569-8162-4(X))* Perfection Learning Corp.

—Bookmarks Are People Too! 2014. (Here's Hank Ser.: 1). lib. bdg. 16.00 *(978-0-606-34142-4(0))* Turtleback.

—Bookmarks Are People Too! #1, No. 1. Garrett, Scott, illus. 2014. (Here's Hank Ser.: 1). (ENG.). 128p. (J). (gr. 1-3). 6.99 *(978-0-448-47997-2(4),* Penguin Workshop) Penguin Young Readers Group.

—A Brand-New Me! #17. 2010. (Hank Zipzer Ser.: 17). (ENG., Illus.). 160p. (J). (gr. 3-7). pap. 6.99 *(978-0-448-45210-4(3),* Grosset & Dunlap) Penguin Young Readers Group.

—The Curtain Went up, My Pants Fell Down #11. 2007. (Hank Zipzer Ser.: 11). (ENG., Illus.). 160p. (J). (gr. 3-7). pap. 6.99 *(978-0-448-44267-9(1),* Grosset & Dunlap) Penguin Young Readers Group.

—Fake Snakes & Weird Wizards #4. Garrett, Scott, illus. 2015. (Here's Hank Ser.: 4). (ENG.). 128p. (J). (gr. 1-3). 6.99 *(978-0-448-48252-1(5),* Penguin Workshop) Penguin Young Readers Group.

—Holy Enchilada! #6. 2004. (Hank Zipzer Ser.: 6). (ENG., Illus.). 160p. (J). (gr. 3-7). pap. 6.99 *(978-0-448-43353-0(2),* Grosset & Dunlap) Penguin Young Readers Group.

—How to Hug an Elephant #6. Garrett, Scott, illus. 2015. (Here's Hank Ser.: 6). 128p. (J). (gr. 1-3). bds. 6.99 *(978-0-448-48656-7(3),* Grosset & Dunlap) Penguin Young Readers Group.

—The Life of Me (Enter at Your Own Risk) 2008. (Hank Zipzer Ser.: No. 14). (Illus.). 186p. (gr. 3-7). 16.00 *(978-0-7569-8819-7(5))* Perfection Learning Corp.

—My Dog's a Scaredy-Cat #10: A Halloween Tail, 10 vols. 2006. (Hank Zipzer Ser.: 10). (ENG., Illus.). 160p. (J). (gr. 3-7). pap. 6.99 *(978-0-448-43878-8(X),* Grosset & Dunlap) Penguin Young Readers Group.

—Niagara Falls, or Does It? 2004. (Hank Zipzer Ser.: No. 1). 128p. (J). (gr. 2-6). pap. 29.00 incl. audio *(978-1-4000-9006-8(7),* Listening Library) Random Hse. Audio Publishing Group.

—Niagara Falls, or Does It? #1. 2004. (Hank Zipzer Ser.: 1). (ENG., Illus.). 144p. (J). (gr. 3-7). pap. 7.99 *(978-0-448-43162-8(9),* Grosset & Dunlap) Penguin Young Readers Group.

—Summer School! What Genius Thought That Up? 2006. (Hank Zipzer Ser.: No. 8). (Illus.). 157p. (J). (gr. 3-9). lib. bdg. 24.21 *(978-1-59961-107-5(4))* Spotlight.

—The Zippity Zinger #4: The Zippity Zinger the Mostly True Confessions of the World's Best Underachiever, 4 vols. 2004. (Hank Zipzer Ser.: 4). (ENG., Illus.). 160p. (J). (gr. 3-7).

J
K
L

mass mkt. 6.99 *(978-0-448-43193-2(9)*, Grosset & Dunlap) Penguin Young Readers Group.
Zemach, Kaethe. Ms. McCaw Learns to Draw. 2006. (J). *(978-0-439-82915-1(1)*, Levine, Arthur A. Bks.) Scholastic, Inc.

LEATHERWORK

Eastman, Linda Sue. Leathercraft. 2008. (ENG., Illus.). 120p. (gr. 4-7). pap. 14.95 *(978-1-56523-370-6(0)*, 3706) Fox Chapel Publishing Co., Inc.

LEAVES

Bishop, Celeste. ¿Por Qué Las Plantas Tienen Hojas? / Why Do Plants Have Leaves?, 1 vol., 1. 2015. (Partes de la Planta / Plant Parts Ser.). (ENG & SPA., Illus.). 24p. (J). (gr. 1-1). 25.27 *(978-1-5081-4741-1(8)*, a12a4e4d-a1d7-483f-a194-c3fb3f6a6eb2, PowerKids Pr.) Rosen Publishing Group, Inc., The.
—Why Do Plants Have Leaves?, 1 vol., 1. 2015. (Plant Parts Ser.). (ENG., Illus.). 24p. (J). (gr. 1-1). pap. 9.25 *(978-1-5081-4221-8(1)*, d8e271da-fa58-4094-8fbe-b450ee7b9af7, PowerKids Pr.) Rosen Publishing Group, Inc., The.
Blackaby, Susan. Catching Sunlight: A Book about Leaves, 1 vol. Delage, Charlene, illus. 2003. (Growing Things Ser.). (ENG.). 24p. (J). (gr. -1-2). per. 8.95 *(978-1-4048-0387-9(4)*, 92513, Picture Window Bks.) Capstone.
Bodach, Vijaya K. Leaves [Scholastic]. 2010. (Plant Parts Ser.). 24p. pap. 0.52 *(978-1-4296-5058-8(3)*, Capstone Pr.) Capstone.
Bodach, Vijaya Khisty. Leaves. rev. ed. 2016. (Plant Parts Ser.). (ENG.). 24p. (J). (gr. -1-2). pap. 7.29 *(978-1-5157-4244-9(X)*, 134003, Capstone Pr.) Capstone.
Brennan, Linda Crotta. Leaves Change Color. 2014. (Tell Me Why Library). (ENG., Illus.). 24p. (J). (gr. 2-5). 29.21 *(978-1-63188-008-7(X)*, 205439) Cherry Lake Publishing.
Bulion, Leslie. Leaf Litter Critters, 1 vol. Meganck, Robert, illus. 2018. 48p. (J). (gr. 3-7). 14.95 *(978-1-56145-950-6(X))* Peachtree Publishing Co. Inc.
Bullard, Lisa. Leaves Fall Down: Learning about Autumn Leaves, 1 vol. Takvorian, Nadine, illus. 2010. (Autumn Ser.). (ENG.). 24p. (J). (gr. -1-3). pap. 8.95 *(978-1-4048-6390-3(7)*, 114141, Picture Window Bks.) Capstone.
Charman, Andrew. I Wonder Why Leaves Change Color: And Other Questions about Plants. 2012. (I Wonder Why Ser.). (ENG., Illus.). (J). (gr. k-3). pap. 6.99 *(978-0-7534-6697-1(X)*, 900076411, Kingfisher) Roaring Brook Pr.
Edwards, Nicola. Leaves, 1 vol. 2007. (See How Plants Grow Ser.). (ENG., Illus.). 24p. (J). (gr. 2-2). lib. bdg. 26.27 *(978-1-4042-3703-2(8)*, b08468de-4b11-416b-b7f8-e3bd0f9cb602, PowerKids Pr.) Rosen Publishing Group, Inc., The.
Felix, Rebecca. What Happens to Leaves in Fall? 2013. (21st Century Basic Skills Library: Let's Look at Fall Ser.). (ENG.). 24p. (gr. k-3). pap. 12.79 *(978-1-61080-934-4(3)*, 202617); (Illus.). 26.35 *(978-1-61080-909-2(2)*, 202615); (Illus.). E-Book 43.50 *(978-1-61080-984-9(X)*, 202618) Cherry Lake Publishing.
Figorito, Christine. How Leaves Change Color. 2009. (Reading Room Collection 2 Ser.). 24p. (gr. 3-4). 42.50 *(978-1-60851-971-2(6)*, PowerKids Pr.) Rosen Publishing Group, Inc., The.
Gerber, Carole. Leaf Jumpers. Evans, Leslie, illus. (J). 2017. 28p. (— 1). bds. 7.99 *(978-1-58089-782-2(7))* 2006. (ENG.). 32p. (gr. -1-2). per. 7.95 *(978-1-57091-498-0(2))* Charlesbridge Publishing, Inc.
Glaser, Rebecca. Leaves. 2012. (ENG., Illus.). 24p. (J). lib. bdg. 25.65 *(978-1-62031-025-0(2))* Jump! Inc.
Granger, Ronald. Know Your Leaves, 1 vol. 2013. (InfoMax Readers Ser.). (ENG.). 24p. (J). (gr. 2-2). pap. 8.25 *(978-1-4777-2422-4(2)*, abb0a585-a41b-4ec0-a6aa-04d12ab6e04b); pap. 49.50 *(978-1-4777-2425-5(7))* Rosen Publishing Group, Inc., The. (Rosen Classroom).
Harvey, Calvin. Let's Look at Leaves, 1 vol. 2016. (We Love Spring! Ser.). (ENG., Illus.). 24p. (J). (gr. k-k). pap. 9.15 *(978-1-4824-5493-2(9)*, acb18b7d-a6dc-4acf-a482-153cdaffb463) Stevens, Gareth Publishing LLLP.
Hicks, Terry Allan. Why Do Leaves Change Color?, 1 vol. 2011. (Tell Me Why, Tell Me How Ser.). (ENG.). 32p. (gr. 3-3). 32.64 *(978-0-7614-4827-3(6)*, 4e35c465-589b-4bc8-b546-8dc4ff33cda3) Cavendish Square Publishing LLC.
Jason Fulford, Tamara Shopsin. A Pile of Leaves: Published in Collaboration with the Whitney Museum of American Art. 2018. (ENG., Illus.). 24p. (gr. -1 — 1). bds. 18.95 *(978-0-7148-7720-4(4))* Phaidon Pr., Inc.
Kirkman, Marissa. Leaves. 2019. (Plant Parts Ser.). (ENG., Illus.). 24p. (J). (gr. -1-2). pap. 6.95 *(978-1-9771-1022-0(3)*, 141098, Pebble) Capstone.
Lake, Darlene A. Leaf Collecting & Preserving Made Easy. 2nd ed. 2003. (Illus.). 49p. (J). 12.00 *(978-0-9747654-0-2(6)*, Egap Gifa Bks.) Leafcollecting.com Publishing Co.
Lara, Enrique & Garcia, Luis. Leaves. 2004. (Illus.). (J). *(978-81-89020-07-1(2))* Katha.
Lawrence, Carol. Leaves. Zito, Francesco, illus. 2018. (Baby Explorer Ser.). (ENG.). 24p. (J). (gr. -1 — 1). bds. 6.99 *(978-0-8075-0516-8(1)*, 807505161) Whitman, Albert & Co.
Leaves. 2006. 10.95 *(978-1-933427-72-0(8))* teNeues Publishing Co.
Linden, Joanne. Fiddleheads to Fir Trees: Leaves in All Seasons, 1 vol. Laurie, Caple, illus. 2013. (ENG.). 32p. (J). 12.00 *(978-0-87842-606-5(X))* Mountain Pr. Publishing Co., Inc.
MacAulay, Kelley. What Are Leaves? 2013. (ENG., Illus.). 24p. (J). *(978-0-7787-1287-9(7))*; pap. *(978-0-7787-0017-3(8))* Crabtree Publishing Co.
Mack, Steve. Rookie Preschool: My First Rookie Reader: the Leaves Fall All Around. 2009. (Rookie Preschool Ser.). (ENG.). 24p. (J). (gr. -1). 23.00 *(978-0-531-24402-9(4))* Scholastic Library Publishing.
Maestro, Betsy. Why Do Leaves Change Color? Krupinski, Loretta, illus. 2015. (Let's-Read-And-Find-Out Science 2 Ser.). (ENG.). 32p. (J). (gr. -1-3). pap. 7.99 *(978-0-06-238201-6(2)*, HarperCollins) HarperCollins Pubs.
—Why Do Leaves Change Color? 2015. (Let's-Read-And-Find-Out Science: Stage 2 Ser.). (J). lib. bdg. 17.20 *(978-0-606-37893-2(6))* Turtleback.
Morgan, Sally. Under a Leaf in Forests & Jungles. 2006. (Hidden Habitats Ser.). (J). *(978-1-59389-284-5(5))* Chrysalis Education.
Owen, Ruth. Science & Craft Projects with Trees & Leaves, 1 vol. 2013. (Get Crafty Outdoors Ser.). (ENG., Illus.). 32p. (J). (gr. 2-3). 30.27 *(978-1-4777-0248-2(2)*, 4ec901d9-4d27-4a64-8507-e1ed446eed8f); pap. 12.75 *(978-1-4777-0259-8(8)*, be0f4e5a-740f-4a00-8387-bffd8afc2443) Rosen Publishing Group, Inc., The. (PowerKids Pr.).
—What Do Roots, Stems, Leaves, & Flowers Do?, 1 vol. 2014. (World of Plants Ser.). (ENG.). 32p. (J). (gr. 2-3). lib. bdg. 27.93 *(978-1-4777-7137-2(9)*, 73734378-9cc3-4b7c-a6fc-63aba6a08bcd, PowerKids Pr.) Rosen Publishing Group, Inc., The.
Pearson Learning Staff, creator. Trees & Leaves. 2004. (ENG.). (J). (gr. k-k). pap. 7.56 *(978-0-7652-5136-7(1)*, Celebration Pr.) Savvas Learning Co.
Peters, Katie. Fall Leaves. 2019. (Seasons All Around Me (Pull Ahead Readers — Nonfiction) Ser.). (ENG., Illus.). 16p. (J). (gr. -1-1). pap. 8.99 *(978-1-5415-7344-4(7)*, 1c615723-68ef-49a3-ad49-d229a2b0b1dd, Lerner Pubns.) Lerner Publishing Group.
Posada, Mia. Summer Green to Autumn Gold: Uncovering Leaves' Hidden Colors. Posada, Mia, illus. 2019. (ENG., Illus.). 32p. (J). (gr. k-4). 19.99 *(978-1-5415-2899-4(9)*, 17e87e93-903c-45d0-b291-39270d6751b1, Millbrook Pr.) Lerner Publishing Group.
Pressberg, Dava. How Leaves Work, 1 vol. 2013. (Rosen Readers Ser.). (ENG.). 24p. (J). (gr. 2-2). pap. 8.25 *(978-1-4777-2272-5(6)*, 19bef24d-9607-4e5a-abb1-92a8366b33c5); pap. 49.50 *(978-1-4777-2273-2(4))* Rosen Publishing Group, Inc., The. (Rosen Classroom).
Ren&apos, et al. Investigating Why Leaves Change Their Color, 1 vol. 2008. (Science Detectives Ser.). (ENG., Illus.). 24p. (J). (gr. 2-3). lib. bdg. 26.27 *(978-1-4042-4485-6(9)*, e80643c4-8e1e-4888-8b38-bd2f9c5b745c) Rosen Publishing Group, Inc., The.
René, Ellen. Investigating Why Leaves Change Their Color. 2009. (Science Detectives Ser.). 24p. (gr. 2-3). 42.50 *(978-1-60853-017-5(5)*, PowerKids Pr.) Rosen Publishing Group, Inc., The.
Roesser, Marie. Why Do Leaves Change Colors?, 1 vol. 2020. (Everyday Mysteries Ser.). (ENG.). 24p. (J). (gr. 1-2). pap. 9.15 *(978-1-5382-5651-0(7)*, 935d9d5b-7a3c-4c88-99b1-cf621568b486) Stevens, Gareth Publishing LLLP.
Roza, G. Lots of Leaves: Learning the L Sound. 2009. (PowerPhonics Ser.). 24p. (gr. 1-1). 39.90 *(978-1-60851-457-1(9)*, PowerKids Pr.) Rosen Publishing Group, Inc., The.
Rustad, Martha E. H. Diversión con Las Hojas de Otoño (Fall Leaves Fun) Enright, Amanda, illus. 2019. (Diversión en Otoño (Fall Fun) (Early Bird Stories (tm) en Español) Ser.). (SPA.). 24p. (J). (gr. k-2). 29.32 *(978-1-5415-4082-8(4)*, 403d05ba-cb5c-4885-9716-4e8d2a344d9f, Ediciones Lerner) Lerner Publishing Group.
—Fall Leaves: Colorful & Crunchy. Enright, Amanda, illus. 2011. (Fall's Here! Ser.). pap. 39.62 *(978-0-7613-8646-9(7))*; (ENG.). 24p. (J). pap. 8.99 *(978-0-7613-8505-9(3)*, f59ac8b7-f544-443b-a803-37bc7a2e7b00) Lerner Publishing Group. (Millbrook Pr.).
—Fall Leaves Fun. Enright, Amanda, illus. 2018. (Fall Fun (Early Bird Stories (tm)) Ser.). (ENG.). 24p. (J). (gr. k-2). pap. 9.99 *(978-1-5415-2720-1(8)*, c659dbe0-7852-496f-a2ed-4f5682f0485e) Lerner Publishing Group.
—Las Hojas en Otoño/Leaves in Fall. 2009. (Todo Acerca Del Otoño/All about Fall Ser.).Tr. of Leaves in Fall. (MUL.). 24p. (J). (gr. -1-2). 29.32 *(978-1-4296-3260-7(7)*, 95644) Capstone.
—Leaves in Fall, 1 vol. 2007. (All about Fall Ser.). (ENG., Illus.). 24p. (J). (gr. -1-2). 29.32 *(978-1-4296-0024-8(1)*, 94168, Capstone Pr.) Capstone.
Schnell, Lisa K. Leaves Fall. 2018. (I Know Ser.). (ENG., Illus.). 16p. (gr. -1-2). pap. 9.95 *(978-1-64156-225-6(0)*, 9781641562256) Rourke Educational Media.
Schuh, Mari. Leaves in Fall. 2013. (ENG., Illus.). 24p. (J). lib. bdg. 25.65 *(978-1-62031-059-5(7))* Jump! Inc.
Shapiro, Sara. What Do You See? A Book about the Seasons. 2009. (Illus.). 16p. (J). pap. *(978-0-545-16154-1(1))* Scholastic, Inc.
Sheffield, S. When Leaves Turn: Learning the UR Sound. 2009. (PowerPhonics Ser.). 24p. (gr. 1-1). 39.90 *(978-1-60851-480-9(3)*, PowerKids Pr.) Rosen Publishing Group, Inc., The.
Snow, Virginia B. Fall Walk, 1 vol. (ENG.). 32p. (J). 2019. (gr. -1-3). 8.99 *(978-1-4236-5391-2(2))* 2013. (Illus.). 16.99 *(978-1-4236-3261-0(3))* Gibbs Smith, Publisher.
Sterling, Kristin. Exploring Leaves. 2011. (First Step Nonfiction / Let's Look at Plants Ser.). pap. 33.92 *(978-0-7613-8615-5(7))*; lib. bdg. 21.27 *(978-0-7613-5780-3(7))* Lerner Publishing Group.
Stone, Lynn. Leaves. 2007. (Plant Parts Ser.). (Illus.). 24p. (J). (gr. 2-4). per. 7.95 *(978-1-60044-693-1(0))* Rourke Educational Media.
Throp, Claire. All about Leaves. rev. ed. 2016. (All about Plants Ser.). (ENG.). 24p. (J). (gr. -1-1). pap. 5.99 *(978-1-4846-3847-7(6)*, 134788, Heinemann) Capstone.

LEBANON

Abirached, Zeina. I Remember Beirut. Abirached, Zeina, illus. 2014. (ENG., Illus.). 96p. (YA). (gr. 8-12). pap. 11.99 *(978-1-4677-4458-4(1)*, 69b3f232-512a-4c66-8514-4517324523a0, Graphic Universe™) Lerner Publishing Group.
Boutros, Jill, et al. Lebanon A to Z: A Middle Eastern Mosaic. Sabbagh, Tatiana, illus. 2006. (ENG.). 40p. (J). (gr. -1-3). 25.00 *(978-0-9744803-4-3(7))* PublishingWorks.
Etheredge, Laura. Syria, Lebanon, & Jordan, 1 vol. 2011. (Middle East: Region in Transition Ser.). (ENG., Illus.). 248p. (YA). (gr. 10-10). lib. bdg. 43.59 *(978-1-61530-329-8(4)*, b19482da-7bc4-4f09-9f95-b00cd6590743) Rosen Publishing Group, Inc., The.
McDaniel, Jan. Lebanon. 2010. (Major Muslim Nations Ser.). 128p. (YA). (gr. 5-18). lib. bdg. 25.95 *(978-1-4222-1387-2(0))* Mason Crest.
Mcdaniel, Jan. Lebanon, Vol. 13. 2015. (Major Nations of the Modern Middle East Ser.). (Illus.). 128p. (J). (gr. 7). lib. bdg. 25.95 *(978-1-4222-3446-4(0))* Mason Crest.
Owings, Lisa. Lebanon. 2015. (Exploring Countries Ser.). (ENG., Illus.). 32p. (J). (gr. 3-7). lib. bdg. 27.95 *(978-1-62617-176-3(9)*, Blastoff! Readers) Bellwether Media.
Perdew, Laura. Understanding Lebanon Today. 2014. (Illus.). 63p. (J). (gr. 3-6). 33.95 *(978-1-61228-653-2(4))* Mitchell Lane Pubs.
Rice Jr., Earle. Hezbollah. 2017. lib. bdg. 29.95 *(978-1-68020-053-9(4))* Mitchell Lane Pubs.
Sheehan, Sean & Latif, Zawiah Abdul. Lebanon, 1 vol. 2nd rev. ed. 2008. (Cultures of the World (Second Edition)(r) Ser.). (ENG.). 144p. (gr. 5-5). lib. bdg. 49.79 *(978-0-7614-2081-1(9)*, 89e7847e-f81c-4ddc-b8f6-f094bc9bf0c7) Cavendish Square Publishing LLC.
Sheehan, Sean, et al. Lebanon, 1 vol. 2017. (Cultures of the World (Third Edition)(r) Ser.). (ENG., Illus.). 144p. (gr. 5-5). 48.79 *(978-1-5026-2612-7(8)*, e88769c8-afa6-43a6-84a0-2f63f8ef8e28) Cavendish Square Publishing LLC.
Skahill, Carolyn. A Historical Atlas of Lebanon, 1 vol. 2003. (Historical Atlases of South Asia, Central Asia, & the Middle East Ser.). (ENG., Illus.). 64p. (gr. 6-6). lib. bdg. 37.13 *(978-0-8239-3982-4(0)*, eec4a157-4bc0-40ca-8c9a-7a4d95af5f7d) Rosen Publishing Group, Inc., The.
Skahill, Carolyn M. A Historical Atlas of Lebanon. 2009. (Historical Atlases of South Asia, Central Asia, & the Middle East Ser.). 64p. (gr. 6-6). 61.20 *(978-1-61513-325-3(9))* Rosen Publishing Group, Inc., The.
Willis, Terri. Lebanon. 2005. (Enchantment of the World Ser.). (ENG., Illus.). 144p. (YA). (gr. 5-9). 39.00 *(978-0-516-23685-8(7))* Scholastic Library Publishing.

LEBANON—FICTION

Laird, Elizabeth. Oranges in No Man's Land. 2008. (ENG., Illus.). 128p. (J). (gr. 2-5). pap. 14.95 *(978-1-931859-56-1(6))* Haymarket Bks.
Marston, Elsa. The Olive Tree. Ewart, Claire, illus. 2014. 32p. (J). (gr. -1-2). 16.95 *(978-1-937786-29-8(3)*, Wisdom Tales) World Wisdom, Inc.
St. John, Patricia. Nothing Else Matters. 2003. 176p. 6.49 *(978-0-85421-972-8(2))* Scripture Union GBR. Dist: Gabriel Resources.

LEE, HENRY, 1756-1818

Bodie, Idella. Light-Horse Harry. 2004. (Illus.). 86p. (J). pap. 6.95 *(978-0-87844-172-3(7))* Sandlapper Publishing Co., Inc.

LEE, ROBERT E. (ROBERT EDWARD), 1807-1870

Anderson, Paul Christopher. Robert E. Lee: Legendary Commander of the Confederacy. 2009. (Library of American Lives & Times Ser.). 112p. (gr. 5-5). 69.20 *(978-1-60853-501-9(0))* Rosen Publishing Group, Inc., The.
Archer, Jules. A House Divided: The Lives of Ulysses S. Grant & Robert E. Lee. rev. ed. 2015. (Jules Archer History for Young Readers Ser.). (ENG., Illus.). 176p. (J). (gr. 6-6). 16.99 *(978-1-63220-604-6(8)*, Sky Pony Pr.) Skyhorse Publishing Co., Inc.
Bader, Bonnie. Who Was Robert E. Lee? 2014. (Who Was... ? Ser.). lib. bdg. 16.00 *(978-0-606-35693-0(2))* Turtleback.
Bader, Bonnie & Who HQ. Who Was Robert E. Lee? O'Brien, John, illus. 2014. (Who Was? Ser.). 112p. (J). (gr. 3-7). 5.99 *(978-0-448-47909-5(5)*, Penguin Workshop) Penguin Young Readers Group.
Benoit, Peter. The Surrender at Appomattox. 2012. (Cornerstones of Freedom, Third Ser.). (ENG.). 64p. (J). (gr. 4-6). lib. bdg. 24.94 *(978-0-531-25041-9(5))* Scholastic Library Publishing.
Conklin, Wendy. Robert E. Lee, 1 vol. rev. ed. 2005. (Social Studies: Informational Text Ser.). (ENG.). 24p. (gr. 4-8). pap. 10.99 *(978-0-7439-8918-3(X))* Teacher Created Materials, Inc.
Gaines, Alison. Robert E. Lee: Commander of the Confederate Army, 1 vol. 2018. (Hero or Villain? Claims & Counterclaims Ser.). (ENG.). 112p. (YA). (gr. 8-8). lib. bdg. 45.93 *(978-1-5026-3529-7(1)*, 51372946-9a07-4231-b080-f8ec6d117800) Cavendish Square Publishing LLC.
Hale, Sarah Elder, ed. Robert E. Lee: Duty & Honor. 2005. (ENG., Illus.). 48p. (J). (gr. 3-9). 17.95 *(978-0-8126-7905-2(9))* Cobblestone Pr.
Kantor, MacKinlay. Lee & Grant at Appomattox. 2015. (ENG.). 144p. pap. 9.95 *(978-0-9904604-0-4(1))* Flying Point Pr.
Kerby, Mona. Robert E. Lee: Commander of the Confederate Army, 1 vol. 2014. (Legendary American Biographies Ser.). (ENG.). 96p. (gr. 6-6). 29.60 *(978-0-7660-6490-4(5)*, 83de6c2e-704b-4a17-aa56-59de926c7052); pap. 13.88 *(978-0-7660-6491-1(3)*, adf03c17-1d10-4dc3-9477-564459c43713) Enslow Publishing, LLC.
Marrin, Albert. Virginia's General: Robert E. Lee & the Civil War. 2003. (Illus.). 201p. (YA). pap. 14.95 *(978-1-893103-14-6(5))* Beautiful Feet Bks.
McNeese, Tim. Robert E. Lee. 2009. (Leaders of the Civil War Era Ser.). (ENG., Illus.). 152p. (gr. 6-12). lib. bdg. 35.00 *(978-1-60413-304-2(X)*, P162088, Facts On File) Infobase Holdings, Inc.
Pingry, Patricia A. Meet Robert E. Lee. Johnson, Meredith, illus. 2004. (J). 9.95 *(978-0-8249-5465-9(3)*, Ideals Pubns.) Worthy Publishing.
Ransom, Candice. Robert E. Lee. 2006. (History Maker Bios Ser.). (Illus.). 48p. (J). (gr. 3-7). lib. bdg. 26.60 *(978-0-8225-2437-3(6)*, Lerner Pubns.) Lerner Publishing Group.
—Willie Mclean & the Civil War Surrender. Reeves, Jeni, illus. 2004. (On My Own History Ser.). (ENG.). 48p. (J). (gr. 2-4). pap. 8.99 *(978-1-57505-698-2(4)*, 89edad43-6a3a-40ef-aa5e-51fc2307aa25, First Avenue Editions) Lerner Publishing Group.
Rice, Earle, Jr. Robert E. Lee: First Soldier of the Confederacy. 2005. (Civil War Leaders Ser.). (Illus.). 176p. (J). (gr. 6-12). 28.95 *(978-1-931798-47-1(8))* Reynolds, Morgan Inc.
Robertson, James I., Jr. Robert E. Lee: Virginian Soldier, American Citizen. 2005. (ENG., Illus.). 176p. (YA). (gr. 7-12). 29.99 *(978-0-689-85731-7(4)*, Atheneum Bks. for Young Readers) Simon & Schuster Children's Publishing.

LEE, ROBERT E. (ROBERT EDWARD), 1807-1870—FICTION

Altsheler, Joseph A. The Shades of the Wilderness: A Story of Lee's Great Stand. 2006. (Civil War Ser.: Vol. 7). 308p. (J). reprint ed. 29.95 *(978-1-4218-2336-2(5))*; pap. 14.95 *(978-1-4218-2436-9(1))* 1st World Publishing, Inc. (1st World Library - Literary Society).
—The Shades of the Wilderness: A Story of Lee's Great Stand. (Civil War Ser.: Vol. 7). 312p. (J). reprint ed. lib. bdg. 25.95 *(978-0-88411-940-1(8))* Amereon Ltd.
—The Shades of the Wilderness: A Story of Lee's Great Stand. 2008. (Civil War Ser.: Vol. 7). 280p. (J). reprint ed. 25.99 *(978-0-554-33603-9(0))* Creative Media Partners, LLC.
—The Shades of the Wilderness: A Story of Lee's Great Stand. 2006. (Civil War Ser.: Vol. 7). (J). reprint ed. pap. *(978-1-4065-0822-2(5))* Dodo Pr.
—The Shades of the Wilderness: A Story of Lee's Great Stand. 2007. (Civil War Ser.: Vol. 7). 180p. (J). reprint ed. per. *(978-1-4068-1686-0(8))* Echo Library.
—The Shades of the Wilderness: A Story of Lee's Great Stand. 2010. (Civil War Ser.: Vol. 7). (Illus.). 162p. (J). (gr. 4-7). reprint ed. pap. 19.99 *(978-1-153-72059-5(0))* General Bks. LLC.
—The Shades of the Wilderness: A Story of Lee's Great Stand. (Civil War Ser.: Vol. 7). (J). reprint ed. 2011. (gr. 4-7). *(978-1-164-50265-4(4))* 2010. 324p. (gr. 4-7). pap. 24.76 *(978-1-163-19558-1(8))* 2008. 324p. 45.95 *(978-1-4366-8424-8(2))* 2007. 324p. per. 30.95 *(978-1-4325-9861-7(9))* Kessinger Publishing, LLC.
—The Shades of the Wilderness: A Story of Lee's Great Stand. 2007. (Civil War Ser.: Vol. 7). 308p. reprint ed. per. 16.45 *(978-1-60424-029-0(6)*, Bk. Jungle) Standard Publications, Inc.
—The Shades of the Wilderness: A Story of Lee's Great Stand. 2011. (Civil War Ser.: Vol. 7). 280p. (J). reprint ed. pap. *(978-3-8424-4396-9(X))* tredition Verlag.
—The Tree of Appomattox: A Story of the Civil War's Close. 2006. (Civil War Ser.: Vol. 8). 324p. (J). reprint ed. 29.95 *(978-1-4218-2338-6(1))*; pap. 14.95 *(978-1-4218-2438-3(8))* 1st World Publishing, Inc. (1st World Library - Literary Society).
—The Tree of Appomattox: A Story of the Civil War's Close. 2007. (Civil War Ser.: Vol. 8). (ENG.). 266p. (J). reprint ed. pap. 21.99 *(978-1-4346-1190-1(6))* Creative Media Partners, LLC.
—The Tree of Appomattox: A Story of the Civil War's Close. 2006. (Civil War Ser.: Vol. 8). (J). reprint ed. pap. *(978-1-4065-0828-4(4))* Dodo Pr.
—The Tree of Appomattox: A Story of the Civil War's Close. 2007. (Civil War Ser.: Vol. 8). 192p. (J). reprint ed. per. *(978-1-4068-1693-8(0))* Echo Library.
—The Tree of Appomattox: A Story of the Civil War's Close. 2010. (Civil War Ser.: Vol. 8). (Illus.). 174p. (J). (gr. 4-7). reprint ed. pap. 19.99 *(978-1-153-72402-9(2))* General Bks. LLC.
—The Tree of Appomattox: A Story of the Civil War's Close. Wrenn, Charles L., illus. (Civil War Ser.: Vol. 8). 332p. (J). (gr. 4-7). reprint ed. 2011. 45.95 *(978-1-169-88135-8(1))* 2010. 36.76 *(978-1-163-21361-2(6))* 2010. pap. 24.76 *(978-1-162-78752-7(X))* Kessinger Publishing, LLC.
—The Tree of Appomattox: A Story of the Civil War's Close. 2005. (Civil War Ser.: Vol. 8). (J). reprint ed. pap. 30.95 *(978-1-4179-2071-6(8))* Kessinger Publishing, LLC.
—The Tree of Appomattox: A Story of the Civil War's Close. Wrenn, Charles L., illus. 2005. (Civil War Ser.: Vol. 8). 332p. (J). reprint ed. 45.95 *(978-1-4326-1333-4(2))* Kessinger Publishing, LLC.
—The Tree of Appomattox: A Story of the Civil War's Close. 2011. (Civil War Ser.: Vol. 8). 294p. (J). (gr. 4-7). reprint ed. pap. *(978-3-8424-8485-6(2))* tredition Verlag.

LEEUWENHOEK, ANTONI VAN, 1632-1723

Alexander, Lori. All in a Drop: How Antony Van Leeuwenhoek Discovered an Invisible World. Mildenberger, Vivien, illus. 2019. (ENG.). 96p. (J). (gr. 3-7). 17.99 *(978-1-328-88420-6(1)*, 1698170, Clarion Bks.) HarperCollins Pubs.
Yount, Lisa. Antoni Van Leeuwenhoek: First to See Microscopic Life, 1 vol. rev. ed. 2009. (Great Minds of Science Ser.). (ENG., Illus.). 128p. (gr. 5-6). lib. bdg. 35.93 *(978-0-7660-3012-1(1)*, dac680c1-ca1a-41f8-af72-aaeff98dce53) Enslow Publishing, LLC.
—Antoni Van Leeuwenhoek: Genius Discoverer of Microscopic Life, 1 vol. 2014. (Genius Scientists & Their Genius Ideas Ser.). (ENG.). 96p. (gr. 5-5). 29.60 *(978-0-7660-6525-3(1)*, e5734917-5b05-43e7-9909-c0835f58d414); pap. 13.88 *(978-0-7660-6526-0(X)*, db072058-a2a3-416c-a7e1-619e9409190f) Enslow Publishing, LLC.

LEFT (POLITICAL SCIENCE)

see Right and Left (Political Science)

LEFT- AND RIGHT-HANDEDNESS—FICTION

Barrett, Judith & Barrett, Ron. The Marshmallow Incident. Barrett, Ron, illus. 2009. (Illus.). (J). pap. *(978-0-545-04654-1(8)*, Scholastic Pr.) Scholastic, Inc.
Ritter, John H. Choosing up Sides. 2004. 166p. (gr. 5-9). 16.00 *(978-0-7569-4094-2(X))* Perfection Learning Corp.

LEG

Brown, Jonatha A. Animal Feet & Legs, 1 vol. 2006. (Why Animals Look Different Ser.). (ENG., Illus.). 24p. (J). (gr. 2-4). lib. bdg. 24.67 *(978-0-8368-6860-9(9)*, e90cad37-e6b8-4230-a52f-695384ed46b1, Weekly Reader Leveled Readers) Stevens, Gareth Publishing LLLP.
—Las Patas y Los Pies de Los Animales (Animal Feet & Legs), 1 vol. 2006. (En Qué Se Diferencian Los Animales (Why Animals Look Different) Ser.).Tr. of Animal Feet & Legs. (SPA., Illus.). 24p. (J). (gr. 2-4). lib. bdg. 24.67 *(978-0-8368-7414-3(5)*, 2fcfcb7d-f339-4301-b61f-61115aaf459a, Weekly Reader Leveled Readers) Stevens, Gareth Publishing LLLP.

Douglas, Lloyd G. My Legs & Feet. 2004. (Welcome Bks.). (ENG.). 24p. (J). (gr. -1-2). pap. 4.95 *(978-0-516-22130-4(2),* Children's Pr.) Scholastic Library Publishing.

Gill, Monica & Viegas, Jennifer. The Lower Limbs in 3D, 1 vol. 2015. (Human Body In 3D Ser.). (ENG., Illus.). 64p. (J). (gr. 5-6). 36.13 *(978-1-4994-3601-3(7),* aafedb99-1efe-43dd-a053-600011582850, Rosen Central) Rosen Publishing Group, Inc., The.

Holland, Mary. Animal Legs, 1 vol. 2016. (Animal Adaptations Ser.). (ENG., Illus.). 32p. (J). (gr. k-3). 17.95 *(978-1-62855-843-2(1))* Arbordale Publishing.

—Patas de Los Animales, 1 vol. 2016. (SPA., Illus.). 32p. (J). (gr. 4-5). pap. 11.95 *(978-1-62855-845-6(8),* 53a970d3-a283-409c-b29b-b07150534bbd) Arbordale Publishing.

Schaefer, Lola M. Some Kids Wear Leg Braces: A 4D Book. 2018. (Understanding Differences Ser.). (ENG., Illus.). 24p. (J). (gr. -1-2). lib. bdg. 29.32 *(978-1-5435-0999-1(1),* 137672, Capstone Pr.) Capstone.

—Some Kids Wear Leg Braces: Revised Edition. rev. ed. 2008. (Understanding Differences Ser.). (ENG., Illus.). 24p. (J). (gr. -1-2). pap. 6.29 *(978-1-4296-1777-2(2),* 94825) Capstone.

LEGAL HOLIDAYS

see Holidays

LEGAL PROFESSION

see Lawyers

LEGAL TENDER

see Paper Money

LEGENDS

see also Fables; Fairy Tales; Folklore; Mythology

Abdo, Kenny. Dr. Jekyll & Mr. Hyde. 2018. (Hollywood Monsters Ser.). (ENG., Illus.). 24p. (J). (gr. 2-8). lib. bdg. 31.36 *(978-1-5321-2316-0(7),* 28399, Abdo Zoom-Fly) ABDO Publishing Co.

—Dracula. 2018. (Hollywood Monsters Ser.). (ENG., Illus.). 24p. (J). (gr. 2-8). lib. bdg. 31.36 *(978-1-5321-2317-7(5),* 28401, Abdo Zoom-Fly) ABDO Publishing Co.

Adil, Hajjah Amina & Sperling, Karima. My Little Lore of Light: A Child's Version of Lore of Light. 2005. (Illus.). x, 193p. (J). 22.00 *(978-1-930409-35-4(4))* Islamic Supreme Council of America.

Au, May Parker. Princess Huilua & Kamapuaa. 2007.Tr. of Ke Kamalii Wahine o Huilua a me Kamapuaa. (ENG & HAW.). (J). lib. bdg. *(978-0-9773495-4-8(3))* Na Kamalei Koolauloa Early Education Program.

Bassington, Cyril. Legends, 1 vol. 2019. (Cultures Connect Us! Ser.). (ENG.). 24p. (gr. 1-2). pap. 9.15 *(978-1-5382-3842-4(X),* 16a21c72-7ff8-4cdb-93be-0728b502ba20) Stevens, Gareth Publishing LLLP.

Belinda, Gallagher. Myths & Legends. Kelly, Richard, ed. 2017. (Illus.). 5120p. (J). pap. 23.95 *(978-1-78617-126-9(0))* Miles Kelly Publishing, Ltd. GBR. Dist: Parkwest Pubns., Inc.

Benge, Janet & Benge, Geoffrey Francis. Heroes of History - Books 1-5 Gift Set, 5 vols. 2006. (ENG.). per. 59.95 *(978-1-883002-89-3(3))* Emerald Bks.

Biggs, Fiona & Potter, Tony, eds. Pocket Irish Legends. Dixey, Kay, illus. 2014. (ENG.). 256p. (J). 10.00 *(978-0-7171-5899-7(3))* Gill Bks. IRL. Dist: Casemate Pubs. & Bk. Distributors, LLC.

Bingham, Jane. Classical Myth: A Treasury of Greek & Roman Legends, Art, & History. 2007. (Myth Ser.). (Illus.). 96p. (J). (gr. 4-7). pap. 7.99 *(978-0-7858-2350-6(6))* Book Sales, Inc.

—Classical Myth: a Treasury of Greek & Roman Legends, Art, & History: A Treasury of Greek & Roman Legends, Art, & History. 2007. (ENG., Illus.). 96p. (C). (gr. 6-18). lib. bdg. 165.00 *(978-0-7656-8104-1(8),* Y181755) Routledge.

Blackwood, Gary L. Unsolved History, 8 vols., Set. Incl. Debatable Deaths. lib. bdg. 36.93 *(978-0-7614-1888-7(1),* 1f7dd58d-6113-41d0-8ec5-9b9f1b3d02d7); Enigmatic Events. lib. bdg. 36.93 *(978-0-7614-1889-4(X),* caf3ca7f-1709-4b5d-ba15-64069a3585e5); Legends or Lies? lib. bdg. 36.93 *(978-0-7614-1891-7(1),* 369003c7-9062-499b-a51f-2690f0a4e600); Perplexing People. lib. bdg. 36.93 *(978-0-7614-1890-0(3),* 1a2fbb41-d52d-4f7a-81c3-a8d3d1b7bfb4); (Illus.). 80p. (gr. 6-6). (Unsolved History Ser.). (ENG.). 2007. 147.72 *(978-0-7614-1892-4(X),* c728de03-d76d-40b2-b2b7-f4cdced83eea, Cavendish Square) Cavendish Square Publishing LLC.

Blackwood, Gary L. & Siburt, Ruth. Legends or Lies?, 1 vol. 2010. (History's Mysteries Ser.). (ENG.). 32p. (gr. 3-3). 31.21 *(978-0-7614-4359-9(2),* 758c1f57-b9d3-45ba-a68a-7dad885448c2) Cavendish Square Publishing LLC.

Bosco, Don. Island of Legends. 2016. (ENG., Illus.). 96p. (J). pap. 16.95 *(978-981-4751-36-0(7))* Marshall Cavendish International (Asia) Private Ltd. SGP. Dist: Independent Pubs. Group.

Braun, Eric & Bowman, James Cloyd. Pecos Bill Tames a Colossal Cyclone, 1 vol. Weber, Lisa K., illus. 2014. (American Folk Legends Ser.). (ENG.). 32p. (J). (gr. k-2). lib. bdg. 27.99 *(978-1-4795-5429-4(4),* 126077, Picture Window Bks.) Capstone.

Brinkerhoff, Shirley. Contemporary Folklore. 2004. (North American Folklore Ser.). (Illus.). 112p. (J). (gr. 7-18). lib. bdg. 22.95 *(978-1-59084-331-4(2))* Mason Crest.

Briswalter, Maren, illus. The Pied Piper of Hamelin, 40 vols. 2014. Orig. Title: Rattenfänger Von Hameln. 32p. (J). 17.95 *(978-1-78250-035-3(9))* Floris Bks. GBR. Dist: Consortium Bk. Sales & Distribution.

Burtinshaw, Julie. Romantic Ghost Stories, 1 vol., Vol. 1. Wangler, Chris, ed. rev. ed. 2003. (Ghost Stories Ser.: 41). (ENG., Illus.). 224p. (gr. 4). pap. 12.95 *(978-1-894877-28-2(4),* be123977-5a4e-4674-b5a9-5154889e2599, Ghost Hse. Bks.) Lone Pine Publishing USA.

Carroll, Yvonne. A Child's Treasury of Irish Stories & Poems. Waters, Fiona, ed. 2004. (ENG., Illus.). 194p. (J). 32.95 *(978-0-7171-3795-4(3))* Gill Bks. IRL. Dist: Casemate Pubs. & Bk. Distributors, LLC.

Ceceri, Kathy. World Myths & Legends: 25 Projects You Can Build Yourself. Braley, Shawn, illus. 2010. (Build It Yourself Ser.). (ENG.). 128p. (J). (gr. 3-7). pap. 15.95 *(978-1-934670-43-9(X),* e1cb6f9c-402f-4a59-9a63-a7866d4431af) Nomad Pr.

Clay, Kathryn & Vonne, Mira. Top 10 Urban Legends, 1 vol. 2012. (Top 10 Unexplained Ser.). (ENG.). 32p. (J). (gr. 3-9). 27.32 *(978-1-4296-7638-0(8),* 117235, Capstone Pr.) Capstone.

Confederated Salish and Kootenai Tribes. Bull Trout's Gift: By the Confederated Salish & Kootenai Tribes. 2011. (ENG., Illus.). 70p. 21.95 *(978-0-8032-3491-8(0))* Univ. of Nebraska Pr.

Daning, Tom. Chinese Mythology: The\Four Dragons, 1 vol. 2006. (Jr. Graphic Mythologies Ser.). (ENG., Illus.). 24p. (gr. 2-3). pap. 10.60 *(978-1-4042-2153-6(0),* 3f24e985-65e7-4288-b252-95b87a6a0347, PowerKids Pr.) Rosen Publishing Group, Inc., The.

Dias, Christina & Abreu, Aline. O Misterio Da Bola Castanho-Avermelhada. 2010. (POR.). (J). 12.00 *(978-1-58432-665-6(4))* Educa Vision Inc.

Dragonslayers, 12 vols. 2014. (Heroes & Legends Ser.). (ENG.). 80p. (YA). (gr. 8-8). lib. bdg. 232.80 *(978-1-4777-8171-5(4),* 0f2dd92e-0ae2-4315-bcf5-9eba0394dbb8, Rosen Young Adult) Rosen Publishing Group, Inc., The.

Encyclopaedia Britannica, Inc. Staff, compiled by. Legends, Myths & Folktales. 2003. (Illus.). 64p. 14.95 *(978-1-59339-037-2(8))* Encyclopaedia Britannica, Inc.

Famous Legends. 2015. (Famous Legends Ser.). (ENG.). 32p. (J). (gr. 2-3). pap., pap., pap. 378.00 *(978-1-4824-3462-0(8))*; pap., pap., pap. 63.00 *(978-1-4824-3463-7(6))*; lib. bdg. 161.58 *(978-1-4824-2545-1(9),* a2a6b6b6-aa4c-4158-8f4a-f9633f623ea6) Stevens, Gareth Publishing LLLP.

Famous Legends: Set 2. 2017. (Famous Legends Ser.). 32p. (gr. 2-3). pap. 63.00 *(978-1-5382-0481-8(9))*; (ENG.). lib. bdg. 161.58 *(978-1-5382-0466-5(5),* 7817fbb8-d76d-4e66-a4d7-a721b6ab5cd1) Stevens, Gareth Publishing LLLP.

Ganeri, Anita & West, David. Heroes of Myths & Legends. (J). 2012. 70.50 *(978-1-4488-5239-0(0))* 2011. (ENG.). 32p. (gr. 4-5). pap. 12.75 *(978-1-4488-5238-3(2),* cdba53ca-c148-4701-9727-a32941d59fda) 2011. (ENG.). 32p. (gr. 4-5). lib. bdg. 30.27 *(978-1-4488-5200-0(5),* 2968ef38-1b94-4695-9632-13f01b2978ea) Rosen Publishing Group, Inc., The. (PowerKids Pr.).

Guillain, Charlotte. Writing & Staging Myths & Legends. 2016. (Writing & Staging Plays Ser.). (ENG., Illus.). 48p. (J). (gr. 4-6). lib. bdg. 35.99 *(978-1-4846-2772-3(5),* 131331, Heinemann) Capstone.

Haberstroh, Marilyn & Panik, Sharon. A Quetzalcóatl Tale of Corn. Castle, Lynn, illus. 2014. (Quetzalcóatl Tales Ser.). (ENG.). 48p. (J). (gr. k-5). pap. 9.95 *(978-1-60732-345-7(1))* Univ. Pr. of Colorado.

Herdling, Glenn. African Mythology: Anansi. 2009. (Jr. Graphic Mythologies Ser.). (ENG.). 24p. (J). (gr. 2-3). 47.90 *(978-1-61513-855-5(2),* PowerKids Pr.) Rosen Publishing Group, Inc., The.

Heroes & Legends: Set 2, 10 vols. 2015. (Heroes & Legends Ser.). (ENG.). 88p. (YA). (gr. 8-8). lib. bdg. 194.00 *(978-1-4994-6193-0(3),* 1d2e7071-e78c-4b85-a068-6f0f106a420b, Rosen Young Adult) Rosen Publishing Group, Inc., The.

Jacq, Christian. Cuentos y Leyendas de la Epoca de Las Pirámides. Corral, Mercedes, tr. from FRE. 6th ed. 2003. (Fables & Legends Ser.). (SPA., Illus.). 144p. (J). 9.95 *(978-84-239-8893-8(7))* Espasa Calpe, S.A. ESP. Dist: Planeta Publishing Corp.

Kaslik, Ibi. Tales from the Tundra: A Collection of Inuit Stories, 1 vol. Brennan, Anthony, illus. 2018. (ENG.). 58p. (J). (gr. 1-3). pap. 11.95 *(978-1-77227-184-3(5))* Inhabit Media Inc. CAN. Dist: Consortium Bk. Sales & Distribution.

Kenney, Karen Latchana. Spine-Tingling Urban Legends. 2017. (Searchlight Books (tm) — Fear Fest Ser.). (ENG., Illus.). 32p. (J). (gr. 3-5). pap. 9.99 *(978-1-5124-5607-3(1),* 0ae6c3b2-7de1-49f4-a941-ed62f81098e6) Lerner Publishing Group.

Lassieur, Allison. Is the Loch Ness Monster Real? 2015. (Unexplained: What's the Evidence? Ser.). (ENG., Illus.). 32p. (J). (gr. 2-5). lib. bdg. 19.95 *(978-1-60753-805-9(9),* 15315) Amicus.

Lawrence, Sandra. Myths & Legends. Trithart, Emma, illus. 2017. (ENG.). 64p. (J). *(978-1-84857-596-7(3),* 360 Degrees) Tiger Tales.

Light, Kate. Mermaid Legends, 1 vol. 2017. (Famous Legends Ser.). (ENG.). 32p. (J). (gr. 2-3). pap. 11.50 *(978-1-5382-0244-9(1),* 7efe3f38-6a72-4ee9-b3ec-30931dbf98b7) Stevens, Gareth Publishing LLLP.

Lynette, Rachel. Urban Legends, 1 vol. 2008. (Mysterious Encounters Ser.). (ENG., Illus.). 48p. (gr. 4-8). lib. bdg. 35.23 *(978-0-7377-4049-3(3),* 0e878326-93b2-40c9-b3b6-297f68ab653b, KidHaven Publishing) Greenhaven Publishing LLC.

Mabie, Hamilton Wright. Legends That Every Child Should Know. 2004. reprint ed. pap. 22.95 *(978-1-4191-2963-6(5))*; pap. 1.99 *(978-1-4192-2963-3(X))* Kessinger Publishing, LLC.

—Legends That Every Child Should Know: A Selection of the Great Legends of All Times for Young People. 2007. (ENG.). 216p. pap. 20.99 *(978-1-4264-4960-4(7))* Creative Media Partners, LLC.

Massey, Eithne. Irish Legends: Newgrange, Tara & the Boyne Valley. Jackson, Lisa, illus. 2016. (ENG.). 64p. (J). 20.00 *(978-1-84717-683-7(6))* O'Brien Pr., Ltd., The IRL. Dist: Casemate Pubs. & Bk. Distributors, LLC.

McCullum, Kenya. 12 Creepy Urban Legends. 2017. (Scary & Spooky Ser.). (ENG., Illus.). 32p. (J). (gr. 3-6). 32.80 *(978-1-63235-292-7(3),* 11776, 12-Story Library) Bookstaves, LLC.

McGinnis, Mark W. The Show-Off Monkey & Other Taoist Tales. 2017. (Illus.). 80p. (J). (gr. k-4). 19.95 *(978-1-61180-347-1(0))* Shambhala Pubns., Inc.

Miller, Reagan & Stone, Janet. How to Tell a Legend. Crabtree Publishing Staff, ed. 2011. (Text Styles Ser.: No. 3). (ENG.). 32p. (J). (gr. 3-6). pap. *(978-0-7787-1637-2(6))* Crabtree Publishing Co.

—How to Tell a Legend. 2011. (Text Styles Ser.). (ENG.). 32p. (J). (gr. 3-6). lib. bdg. *(978-0-7787-1632-7(5))* Crabtree Publishing Co.

Montgomery, R. A. Journey under the Sea. Sundaravej, Sittisan, illus. 2006. (ENG.). 144p. (J). (gr. 4-8). per. 7.99 *(978-1-933390-02-4(6),* CHCL02) Chooseco LLC.

—Journey under the Sea. 2006. (Choose Your Own Adventure Ser.: 2). 17.20 *(978-1-4177-6410-5(4))* Turtleback.

Morley, Jacqueline & Salariya, David. World of Myths & Legends. Franklin, Carolyn, illus. 2013. (Mythology Ser.). 64p. (gr. 3-6). 41.35 *(978-1-908973-93-1(5))* Book Hse. GBR. Dist: Black Rabbit Bks.

Morpurgo, Michael. Beowulf. Foreman, Michael, illus. 2015. (ENG.). 160p. (J). (gr. 3-7). pap. 8.99 *(978-0-7636-7297-3(1))* Candlewick Pr.

Mythology & Legends Around the World, 16 vols. 2017. (Mythology & Legends Around the World Ser.). (ENG., Illus.). (J). (gr. 4-4). lib. bdg. 287.44 *(978-1-5026-3301-9(9),* e8534701-26e6-4f7b-b4a4-e66bad702d55) Cavendish Square Publishing LLC.

Myths from Around the World, 12 vols., Set. Incl. Ancient Greek Myths. Green, Jen. lib. bdg. 33.67 *(978-1-4339-3524-4(4),* 1e4d0cc8-74d9-4741-92c0-0a40cb90d7f0); Ancient Roman Myths. Innes, Brian. lib. bdg. 33.67 *(978-1-4339-3527-5(9),* 9e91eb08-9824-4bf8-8578-aa4f1cfe7fcc); Chinese & Japanese Myths. Green, Jen. lib. bdg. 33.67 *(978-1-4339-3533-6(3),* 9261b862-cb91-4c9d-afd7-6f52540c9af0); Mesoamerican Myths. Dalal, Anita. lib. bdg. 33.67 *(978-1-4339-3539-8(2),* f5b2a7b1-80b5-4db5-b7d3-be0d6cea955c); Native American Myths. Dalal, Anita. lib. bdg. 33.67 *(978-1-4339-3530-5(9),* c0083934-7d65-40ea-906a-efb36ec8341e); West African Myths. Giles, Bridget. lib. bdg. 33.67 *(978-1-4339-3536-7(8),* 91a104ec-ce3a-47ef-89ff-616a00cc969a); (YA). (gr. 6-8). (Myths from Around the World Ser.). (ENG.). 48p. 2010. Set lib. bdg. 202.02 *(978-1-4339-3591-6(0),* 0a0fd9da-79cd-4c9f-a7b6-03e462572fbd, Gareth Stevens Secondary Library) Stevens, Gareth Publishing LLLP.

Nardo, Don. American Mythology, 1 vol. 2013. (Mythology & Culture Worldwide Ser.). (ENG., Illus.). 104p. (gr. 7-10). lib. bdg. 41.03 *(978-1-4205-0904-5(7),* 0a2cfedc-9d6f-444d-82c5-b525a942bd8b, Lucent Pr.) Greenhaven Publishing LLC.

Oliveira, Jô de. Kuarup, a Festa DOS Mortos: Lendas DOS Povos Indigenas Do Xingu. 2010. (POR.). (J). 12.00 *(978-1-58432-661-8(1))* Educa Vision Inc.

Owings, Lisa. What Are Legends, Folktales, & Other Classic Stories? 2014. (Name That Text Type! Ser.). (ENG., Illus.). 32p. (J). (gr. 2-4). lib. bdg. 26.65 *(978-1-4677-4061-6(6),* 03d1952f-f40d-43af-bc27-aeca116e125c, Lerner Pubns.) Lerner Publishing Group.

Pearce, Q. L. La Llorona: The Crying Woman, 1 vol. 2009. (Mysterious Encounters Ser.). (ENG., Illus.). 48p. (gr. 4-8). 30.63 *(978-0-7377-4571-9(1),* 37429b5b-c7c7-4c2f-b204-9791d1b9ea5e, KidHaven Publishing) Greenhaven Publishing LLC.

Pearson, Maggie. Magic & Misery: Traditional Tales from Around the World. Greenwood, Francesca, illus. 2016. (World of Stories Ser.). (ENG.). 176p. (J). (gr. 2-6). 26.65 *(978-1-5124-1319-9(4),* f025840c-e5d7-4247-8039-9cc41aace5d4, Darby Creek) Lerner Publishing Group.

Randall, Ronne. Children's Stories from Myths & Legends: Classic Tales from Around the World. Howells, Graham, illus. 2017. 128p. (J). (gr. 3-12). 16.99 *(978-1-86147-852-8(6),* Armadillo) Anness Publishing GBR. Dist: National Bk. Network.

Reed, Natasha. Mythical Creatures: Sticker Book. Kincaid, Angela, illus. 2005. (Stickertastic Ser.). 24p. (J). (gr. -1-7). pap. *(978-1-84510-119-0(7))* Top That! Publishing PLC.

Sanna, Ellyn. Folk Tales & Legends. 2004. (North American Folklore Ser.). (Illus.). 112p. (J). (gr. 7-18). lib. bdg. 22.95 *(978-1-59084-346-8(0))* Mason Crest.

Schulte, Mary. The Dover Demon, 1 vol. 2009. (Mysterious Encounters Ser.). (ENG., Illus.). 48p. (gr. 4-8). 35.23 *(978-0-7377-4570-2(3),* 662c62b6-291d-489d-861b-7a8c091f651f, KidHaven Publishing) Greenhaven Publishing LLC.

Shea, Therese M. Fables, Myths, & Legends, 1 vol. 2018. (Let's Learn about Literature Ser.). (ENG.). 24p. (gr. 1-2). pap. 10.35 *(978-0-7660-9595-3(9),* 58fadc45-4efe-420c-82e7-1a011310bf6b) Enslow Publishing, LLC.

Steele, Philip. Incredible Quests: Epic Journeys in Myth & Legend. Climpson, Sue, illus. 2006. 48p. (J). (gr. 3-7). pap. 11.99 *(978-1-84476-247-7(5))* Anness Publishing GBR. Dist: National Bk. Network.

Tappan, Eva March. The Children's Hour, Volume 4. Stories of Legendary Heroes. 2013. 514p. pap. 33.45 *(978-1-4733-1070-4(9))* Borah Pr.

Tonatiuh, Duncan. The Princess & the Warrior: A Tale of Two Volcanoes. 2016. (ENG., Illus.). 40p. (J). (gr. 1-4). 18.99 *(978-1-4197-2130-4(5),* 1103401, Abrams Bks. for Young Readers) Abrams, Inc.

Vickers, Roy Henry & Budd, Robert. Cloudwalker. Vickers, Roy Henry, illus. 2014. (Northwest Coast Legends Ser.). (ENG., Illus.). 40p. (J). *(978-1-55017-619-3(6),* 26d4340d-fed4-4857-a474-a36bef9fe4fb) Harbour Publishing Co., Ltd.

—Orca Chief. Vickers, Roy Henry, illus. 2015. (Northwest Coast Legends Ser.). (ENG., Illus.). 40p. (J). *(978-1-55017-693-3(5),* 478b05e9-a80e-4572-86d0-b3f65284b124) Harbour Publishing Co., Ltd.

—Peace Dancer. Vickers, Roy Henry, illus. 2016. (Northwest Coast Legends Ser.). (ENG., Illus.). 40p. (J). *(978-1-55017-739-8(7),* e9a2f57b-6a2c-4a39-86d2-398cf6d3398b) Harbour Publishing Co., Ltd.

—Raven Brings the Light. Vickers, Roy Henry, illus. 2013. (Northwest Coast Legends Ser.). (ENG., Illus.). 40p. (J). *(978-1-55017-593-6(9),* 22f5280d-9482-4421-830b-80cd31d6658c) Harbour Publishing Co., Ltd.

Wildwood, Gretchen. Ancient Mesopotamian Civilization, 1 vol. Cantucci, Alessandro & Morandi, Andrea, illus. 2009. (Ancient Civilizations & Their Myths & Legends Ser.). (ENG.). 48p. (YA). (gr. 6-6). lib. bdg. 34.47 *(978-1-4042-8037-3(5),* d4c1502f-6782-45a0-9920-2a2811f55808) Rosen Publishing Group, Inc., The.

Wilkinson, Philip. Chinese Myth: A Treasury of Legends, Art, & History. 2007. (Myth Ser.). (Illus.). 96p. (J). (gr. 4-7). pap. 7.99 *(978-0-7858-2348-3(4),* Chartwell) Book Sales, Inc.

Williams, Rose. The Labors of Aeneas: What a Pain It Was to Found the Roman Race. 2003. (ENG., Illus.). (YA). pap. 18.00 *(978-0-86516-556-4(4))* Bolchazy-Carducci Pubs.

World Book, Inc. Staff, contrib. by. Tales Through Time: A Supplement to Childcraft-The How & Why Library. 2009. (Illus.). 204p. (J). *(978-0-7166-0622-2(4))* World Bk., Inc.

Yasuda, Anita. The 12 Most Amazing American Myths & Legends. 2015. (Amazing America Ser.). (ENG., Illus.). 32p. (J). (gr. 3-6). 32.80 *(978-1-63235-010-7(6),* 11549); pap. 9.95 *(978-1-63235-070-1(X),* 11555) Bookstaves, LLC. (12-Story Library).

LEGENDS—AFRICA

Randolph, Joanne, ed. The Myths & Legends of Ancient Egypt & Africa, 1 vol. 2017. (Mythology & Legends Around the World Ser.). (ENG.). 64p. (gr. 4-4). pap. 13.93 *(978-1-5026-3445-0(7),* f92e3081-c15c-4af9-a6a3-75e1bb6b1c5d); lib. bdg. 35.93 *(978-1-5026-3277-7(2),* f7fa4bfc-01d6-4c16-9924-313ae939a233) Cavendish Square Publishing LLC.

World Book, Inc. Staff, contrib. by. Myths & Legends of Africa. 2015. (Illus.). 64p. (J). *(978-0-7166-2631-2(4))* World Bk., Inc.

LEGENDS—AUSTRALIA

Marshall, James Vance. Stories from the Billabong. Firebrace, Francis, illus. 2010. (ENG.). 64p. (J). (gr. k-3). pap. 9.99 *(978-1-84780-124-1(2),* Frances Lincoln Children's Bks.) Quarto Publishing Group UK GBR. Dist: Hachette Bk. Group.

LEGENDS, CELTIC

see Celts—Folklore; Legends—Ireland

LEGENDS—CHINA

Casey, Dawn. The Great Race: The Story of the Chinese Zodiac. Wilson, Anne, illus. 2006. (ENG.). 32p. (J). (gr. -1-3). 16.99 *(978-1-905236-77-0(8))* Barefoot Bks., Inc.

Daning, Tom. Chinese Mythology: The Four Dragons. 2009. (Jr. Graphic Mythologies Ser.). (ENG.). 24p. (J). (gr. 2-3). 47.90 *(978-1-61513-858-6(7),* PowerKids Pr.) Rosen Publishing Group, Inc., The.

—Mitología China: Los Cuatro Dragones, 1 vol. 2009. (Historietas Juveniles: Mitologías (Jr. Graphic Mythologies) Ser.). (SPA., Illus.). 24p. (gr. 2-3). pap. 10.60 *(978-1-4358-3326-5(0),* 6d7cffcd-d246-4f3a-b346-cd7d5c1c3776) Rosen Publishing Group, Inc., The.

Wilkinson, Philip. Chinese Myth: a Treasury of Legends, Art, & History: A Treasury of Legends, Art, & History. 2007. (ENG., Illus.). 96p. (C). (gr. 6-18). lib. bdg. 180.00 *(978-0-7656-8103-4(X),* Y181705) Routledge.

LEGENDS—EGYPT

Kramer, Ann. Egyptian Myth: A Treasury of Legends, Art, & History. 2007. (Myth Ser.). (Illus.). 96p. (J). (gr. 4-7). pap. 7.99 *(978-0-7858-2347-6(6),* Chartwell) Book Sales, Inc.

—Egyptian Myth: a Treasury of Legends, Art, & History: A Treasury of Legends, Art, & History. 2007. (ENG., Illus.). 96p. (C). (gr. 6-18). lib. bdg. 180.00 *(978-0-7656-8105-8(6),* Y182128) Routledge.

Macdonald, Fiona. Egyptian Myths & Legends. 2013. (All about Myths Ser.). (ENG.). 48p. (J). (gr. 4-7). pap. 56.50 *(978-1-4109-4982-0(6),* 18998, Raintree) Capstone.

Randolph, Joanne, ed. The Myths & Legends of Ancient Egypt & Africa, 1 vol. 2017. (Mythology & Legends Around the World Ser.). (ENG.). 64p. (gr. 4-4). pap. 13.93 *(978-1-5026-3445-0(7),* f92e3081-c15c-4af9-a6a3-75e1bb6b1c5d); lib. bdg. 35.93 *(978-1-5026-3277-7(2),* f7fa4bfc-01d6-4c16-9924-313ae939a233) Cavendish Square Publishing LLC.

World Book, Inc. Staff, contrib. by. Myths & Legends of Ancient Egypt. 2015. (Illus.). 64p. (J). *(978-0-7166-2633-6(0))* World Bk., Inc.

LEGENDS—GERMANY

Bindrim, Hans-Wolfgang. Wilhelm Hauffs «Die Errettung Fatmes»: Textanalyse und Interpretation- ein Beitrag Zum Kreativen Umgang Mit Dem Volksmaerchen in Einem Kunstmaerchen. 2012. (Europaeische Hochschulschriften / European University Studies / Publications Universitaires Européennes Ser.: 2028). (GER.). 130p. pap. 44.75 *(978-3-631-63429-5(3),* 263429) Lang, Peter GmbH, Internationaler Verlag der Wissenschaften DEU. Dist: Lang, Peter AG International Academic Publishers.

LEGENDS—HAWAII

Holokai, Ben W., Jr. Myths & Legends of Hawai'i Coloring Book. 2004. (Illus.). 32p. 5.95 *(978-1-57306-212-1(X))* Bess Pr., Inc.

Kaopio, Matthew. Hawaiian Family Legends. 2003. (Illus.). 55p. (J). *(978-1-56647-623-2(2))* Mutual Publishing LLC.

LEGENDS—INDIA

Adhikary, Qiron. Feminist Folktales from India. 2003. (Illus.). 97p. (YA). per. 9.95 *(978-0-9714127-3-6(1))* Masalai Pr.

Besant, Annie W. Legends & Tales Lotus Leaves for the Y. 2006. pap. 19.95 *(978-1-4286-2494-8(5))* Kessinger Publishing, LLC.

Husain, Shahrukh. Indian Myths. Willey, Bee, illus. 2007. (Stories from Ancient Civilisations Ser.). 32p. (J). pap. 10.99 *(978-0-237-53376-2(6))* Evans Brothers, Ltd. GBR. Dist: Independent Pubs. Group.

Novesky, Amy. Elephant Prince: The Story of Ganesh. 2004. (ENG., Illus.). 32p. 16.95 *(978-1-886069-16-9(6),* BK2304HB) Insight Editions.

Novesky, Amy & Wedman, Belgin K. The Elephant Prince: The Story of Ganesh. 2005. (Illus.). 32p. (J). 16.95 *(978-1-932771-16-9(6))* Mandala Publishing.

LEGENDS, INDIAN

see Indians of Mexico—Folklore; Indians of North America—Folklore; Indians of South America—Folklore

LEGENDS—IRELAND

Carroll, Yvonne. Great Irish Legends for Children. Lawrie, Robin, illus. 2005. (ENG.). 64p. (J). pap. 20.95 incl. audio compact disk (978-0-7171-3872-2(0)) M.H. Gill & Co. U. C. IRL. Dist: Dufour Editions, Inc.

Milligan, Bryce. Brigid's Cloak: An Ancient Irish Story. Cann, Helen, illus. 2004. 32p. (J). (gr. k-18). 16.00 (978-0-8028-5224-3(6)) Eerdmans, William B. Publishing Co.

LEGENDS—JAPAN

Boutland, Craig. Gashadokuro the Giant Skeleton & Other Legendary Creatures of Japan, 1 vol. 2018. (Cryptozoologist's Guide to Curious Creatures Ser.). (ENG.). 32p. (gr. 4-5). lib. bdg. 28.27 (978-1-5382-2714-5(2), 3ab7138a-4dc7-4e97-ad50-7058e2e26684) Stevens, Gareth Publishing LLLP.

LEGENDS, JEWISH

see Jewish Legends

LEGENDS—SCANDINAVIA

Rayner, Olivia, illus. World Book Myths & Legends Series, 8 vols., Vol. 8. 2007. (World Book Myths & Legends Ser.). 64p. (gr. 4-8). 239.00 (978-0-7166-2613-8(6), 31020) World Bk., Inc.

LEGENDS—SPAIN

Leyendas Espanolas. (SPA., Illus.). (YA). 11.95 (978-84-7281-212-3(X), AF0099) Auriga, Ediciones S.A. ESP. Dist: Continental Bk. Co., Inc.

LEGENDS—UNITED STATES

Asfar, Dan. Ghost Stories of the Old West, 1 vol., Vol. 1. Kubish, Shelagh, ed. rev. ed. 2003. (Ghost Stories Ser.: 28). (ENG., Illus.). 216p. (gr. 4). pap. 12.95 (978-1-894877-17-6(9), 355d39a7-c37d-4d5a-a626-7b521018354f, Ghost Hse. Bks.) Lone Pine Publishing USA.

Cocca, Lisa Colozza. Sleepy Hollow, 1 vol. 2014. (Jr. Graphic Ghost Stories Ser.). (ENG., Illus.). 24p. (J) (gr. 2-3). lib. bdg. 28.93 (978-1-4777-7084-9(4), 425cad7e-d571-4a0f-bd43-c625ea70ee21, PowerKids Pr.) Rosen Publishing Group, Inc., The.

Delano, Marfe Ferguson & Delano, Marfe. American Heroes (Direct Mail Edition) 2005. (ENG., Illus.). 240p. (J). (gr. 5-9). 24.95 (978-0-7922-7208-3(0)) National Geographic Society.

Dwyer, Mindy. Coyote in Love: The Story of Crater Lake. 2014. (ENG., Illus.). 32p. (J). (gr. -1-3). pap. 10.99 (978-0-88240-997-9(2), 9780882409979, West Winds Pr.) West Margin Pr.

Ferrell, David L. Pecos Bill, 1 vol. 2014. (Jr. Graphic American Legends Ser.). (ENG., Illus.). 24p. (J). (gr. 2-3). lib. bdg. 28.93 (978-1-4777-7189-1(1), 2f066cf9-5bda-427c-bba9-7b0c76977b73, PowerKids Pr.) Rosen Publishing Group, Inc., The.

Ferut, Michael. Winchester Mystery House. 2014. (Scariest Places on Earth Ser.). (ENG., Illus.). 24p. (J). (gr. 3-7). lib. bdg. 26.95 (978-1-60014-998-6(7), Torque Bks.) Bellwether Media.

Jameson, W. C. Buried Treasures of California. Hall, Wendell E., illus. 2006. (Buried Treasure Ser.). (ENG.). 175p. (Orig.). (J). (gr. 4-17). pap. 14.95 (978-0-87483-406-2(6)) August Hse. Pubs., Inc.

Jopp, Kelsey. Tammy Duckworth. 2020. (Groundbreaking Women in Politics Ser.). (ENG., Illus.). 48p. (J). (gr. 5-6). pap. 11.95 (978-1-64493-166-0(4), 1644931664); lib. bdg. 34.21 (978-1-64493-087-8(0), 1644930870) North Star Editions. (Focus Readers).

Joseph, Frank. Legends & Lore of Ancient America, 1 vol., 1. 2013. (Discovering Ancient America Ser.). (ENG.). 296p. (YA). (gr. 8-8). lib. bdg. 42.41 (978-1-4777-2807-9(4), af5814bf-1e3b-4d01-8f69-d4d39c3d2d54) Rosen Publishing Group, Inc., The.

Jr. Graphic American Legends: Set 2, 12 vols. 2014. (Jr. Graphic American Legends Ser.). (ENG.). 24p. (J). (gr. 2-3). 173.58 (978-1-4777-7096-2(8), 27a292e2-291e-4541-82b6-24fe272c0152, PowerKids Pr.) Rosen Publishing Group, Inc., The.

Jr. Graphic American Legends: Sets 1-2. 2014. (Jr. Graphic American Legends Ser.). 24p. (J). (gr. 3-6). pap. 127.20 (978-1-4777-7262-1(6), PowerKids Pr.) Rosen Publishing Group, Inc., The.

Mackall, Dandi Daley. The Legend of Ohio. LaFever, Gregory, illus. 2005. (Myths, Legends, Fairy & Folktales Ser.). (ENG.). 40p. (J). (gr. 2-5). 17.95 (978-1-58536-244-8(1), 202067) Sleeping Bear Pr.

Meister, Cari. Davy Crockett & the Great Mississippi Snag, 1 vol. George, Peter, illus. 2014. (American Folk Legends Ser.). (ENG.). 32p. (J). (gr. k-2). lib. bdg. 27.99 (978-1-4795-5431-7(6), 126079, Picture Window Bks.) Capstone.

Montileaux, Donald F. Tatanka & Other Legends of the Lakota People. 2019. (DAK & ENG., Illus.). (J). (978-1-941813-22-5(4)) South Dakota Historical Society Pr.

Mott, A. S. Ghost Stories of America: Volume II, 1 vol., Vol. 2. Kubish, Shelagh, ed. rev. ed. 2003. (Ghost Stories Ser.: 23). (ENG., Illus.). 248p. (gr. 4). pap. 12.95 (978-1-894877-31-2(4), ac8b422a-917b-4007-abdf-c5aff7878759, Ghost Hse. Bks.) Lone Pine Publishing USA.

Petruccio, Steven James. American Legends & Tall Tales. 2011. (Dover Classic Stories Coloring Book Ser.). (ENG., Illus.). 32p. (J). (gr. 3-6). pap. 3.99 (978-0-486-47786-2(X), 47786X) Dover Pubns., Inc.

Smitten, Susan. Ghost Stories of New England, 1 vol., Vol. 1. Wangler, Chris, ed. rev. ed. 2003. (Ghost Stories Ser.: 26). (ENG., Illus.). 224p. (gr. 4). pap. 12.95 (978-1-894877-12-1(8), 89b5979a-4b32-4017-8308-e3a446cc10a3, Ghost Hse. Bks.) Lone Pine Publishing USA.

LEGENDS—WALES

Eastwood, Richard. Seven Welsh Folk Tales. 2006. (ENG., Illus.). 96p. (J). pap. 7.50 (978-1-84323-598-9(6)) Gomer Pr. GBR. Dist: Casemate Pubs. & Bk. Distributors, LLC.

LEGERDEMAIN

see Magic

LEGISLATORS

Benge, Janet & Benge, Geoff. Heroes of History - William Wilberforce: Take up the Fight. 2015. (ENG.). 218p. (YA). pap. 11.99 (978-1-62486-057-7(5)) Emerald Bks.

Blashfield, Jean F. Hillary Clinton, 1 vol. 2011. (Leading Women Ser.). (ENG.). 96p. (YA). (gr. 7-7). 42.64 (978-0-7614-4954-6(X), e653b8cd-2fce-4ce2-be4a-065c33d4a87f) Cavendish Square Publishing LLC.

Brignall, Richard. Big Train: The Legendary Ironman of Sport, Lionel Conacher, 1 vol. 2009. (Lorimer Recordbooks Ser.). (ENG., Illus.). 168p. (YA). (gr. 6-12). 16.95 (978-1-55277-451-9(1), 451); 9.95 (978-1-55277-450-2(3), 450) James Lorimer & Co. Ltd., Pubs. CAN. Dist: Formac Lorimer Bks. Ltd.

Brill, Marlene Targ. Barack Obama (Revised Edition) 2009. pap. 52.95 (978-0-7613-5031-6(4)) Lerner Publishing Group.

David, Alex. Examining Give Me Liberty or Give Me Death by Patrick Henry, 1 vol. 2020. (American Debates & Speeches Ser.). (ENG.). 64p. (gr. 7-7). pap. 16.24 (978-1-9785-1506-2(5), 9aed1dc4-4f63-4774-9704-68285b1b5a46) Enslow Publishing, LLC.

Doeden, Matt. Michele Bachmann: Tea Party Champion. 2011. (Gateway Biographies Ser.). (YA). (gr. 4-7). lib. bdg. 26.60 (978-0-7613-9074-9(X)) Lerner Publishing Group.

Furgang, Kathy. The Declaration of Independence & Richard Henry Lee of Virginia. 2009. (Framers of the Declaration of Independence Ser.). 24p. (gr. 3-3). 42.50 (978-1-61512-630-9(9), PowerKids Pr.) Rosen Publishing Group, Inc., The.

—The Declaration of Independence & Roger Sherman of Connecticut. 2009. (Framers of the Declaration of Independence Ser.). 24p. (gr. 3-3). 42.50 (978-1-61512-632-3(5), PowerKids Pr.) Rosen Publishing Group, Inc., The.

Furstinger, Nancy. Davy Crockett. 2018. (Illus.). 24p. (J). pap. (978-1-4896-9548-2(6), AV2 by Weigl) Weigl Pubs., Inc.

Gay, Oonagh & Leopold, Patricia, eds. Conduct Unbecoming? The Regulation of Parliamentary Behaviour. Gay, Oonagh & Leopold, Patricia, trs. 2004. vi, 378p. 39.95 (978-1-84275-055-1(0)) Politico's Publishing Ltd. GBR. Dist: Consortium Bk. Sales & Distribution.

Haldy, Emma E. Davy Crockett. Bane, Jeff, illus. 2017. (My Early Library: My Itty-Bitty Bio Ser.). (ENG.). 24p. (J). (gr. k-1). lib. bdg. 30.64 (978-1-63472-151-6(9), 209176) Cherry Lake Publishing.

Halfmann, Janet. Seven Miles to Freedom: The Robert Smalls Story, 1 vol. Smith, Duane, illus. 2008. (ENG.). 40p. (J). (gr. 1-6). pap. 12.95 (978-1-60060-986-2(4), leelowbooks) Lee & Low Bks., Inc.

Haskins, Jim & Benson, Kathleen. John Lewis in the Lead: A Story of the Civil Rights Movement, 1 vol. Andrews, Benny, illus. 2006. (ENG.). 40p. (J). (gr. 3-8). pap. 12.95 (978-1-60060-849-0(3), leelowbooks) Lee & Low Bks., Inc.

Immell, Myra, ed. The Mccarthy Era, 1 vol. 2011. (Perspectives on Modern World History Ser.). (ENG.). 184p. (gr. 10-12). lib. bdg. 49.43 (978-0-7377-5260-1(2), 9f2a225c-bbae-4f14-8e0c-b4f9b0d5cbd1, Greenhaven Publishing) Greenhaven Publishing LLC.

Kaiser, Emma. Alexandria Ocasio-Cortez. 2020. (Groundbreaking Women in Politics Ser.). (ENG., Illus.). 48p. (J). (gr. 5-6). pap. 11.95 (978-1-64493-168-4(0)); lib. bdg. 34.21 (978-1-64493-089-2(7), 1644930897) North Star Editions. (Focus Readers).

Leigh, Anna. Alexandria Ocasio-Cortez: Political Headliner. 2020. (Gateway Biographies Ser.). (ENG., Illus.). 48p. (J). (gr. 4-8). pap. 11.99 (978-1-5415-8887-5(8), 4c9370a0-46fb-4703-a708-f4b25f51427b); lib. bdg. 31.99 (978-1-5415-7747-3(7), 9d524870-e3ff-4ed2-81fb-53c71f64c3bd) Lerner Publishing Group. (Lerner Pubns.).

Marcovitz, Hal. Nancy Pelosi: Politician. 2009. (Women of Achievement Ser.). (ENG., Illus.). 160p. (gr. 6-12). 35.00 (978-1-60413-075-1(X), P161420, Facts On File) Infobase Holdings, Inc.

McElroy, Lisa Tucker. Ted Kennedy: A Remarkable Life in the Senate. 2009. (Gateway Biographies Ser.). (ENG., Illus.). 48p. (J). (gr. 4-8). 26.60 (978-0-7613-4457-5(8)) Lerner Publishing Group.

Moriarty, J. T. Davy Crockett: Defensor de la Frontera, 1 vol. 2003. (Grandes Personajes en la Historia de Los Estados Unidos (Famous People in American History) Ser.). (SPA.). 32p. (gr. 3-4). pap. 10.00 (978-0-8239-4226-8(0), d788d920-5fb2-4495-ad81-34d87f3a6a4c, Rosen Classroom) Rosen Publishing Group, Inc., The.

Nagelhout, Ryan. Standing in a Senator's Shoes, 1 vol. 2015. (My Government Ser.). (ENG.). 32p. (gr. 4-4). pap. 11.58 (978-1-5026-0472-9(8), 574090e3-f63e-42c0-9613-59ed9de6ad6d) Cavendish Square Publishing LLC.

Raatma, Lucia. Shirley Chisholm, 1 vol. 2011. (Leading Women Ser.). (ENG., Illus.). 96p. (J). (gr. 7-7). 42.64 (978-0-7614-4953-9(1), 76e44034-3809-4585-b09c-6019d0e95e1c) Cavendish Square Publishing LLC.

Really Big Coloring Books. Ted Cruz to the Future - Comic Coloring Activity Book. 2013. (ENG., Illus.). 24p. (J). (978-1-61953-095-9(3)) Really Big Coloring Bks., Inc.

Rose, Simon. House of Representatives. 2016. (Illus.). 32p. (J). (978-1-5105-2245-9(X)) SmartBook Media, Inc.

Santos, Rita. Mike Pence: U. S. Vice President, 1 vol. 2018. (Junior Biographies Ser.). (ENG.). 24p. (gr. 3-4). 24.27 (978-1-9785-0207-9(9), c3213dc1-c30b-41f3-aac6-8ac82032347b) Enslow Publishing, LLC.

Sapet, Kerrily. John Lewis. 2009. (Political Profiles Ser.). 100p. (YA). (gr. 5-9). 28.95 (978-1-59935-130-8(7)) Reynolds, Morgan Inc.

Silate, Jennifer. The Calhoun-Randolph Debate on the Eve of the War of 1812: A Primary Source Investigation, 1 vol. 2004. (Great Historic Debates & Speeches Ser.). (ENG., Illus.). 64p. (YA). (gr. 5-8). lib. bdg. 37.13 (978-1-4042-0150-7(5), b416568f-5db1-4b00-bf4b-5f8362e684ce) Rosen Publishing Group, Inc., The.

—The Calhoun-Randolph Debate on the Eve of the War Of 1812: A Primary Source Investigation. 2009. (Great Historic Debates & Speeches Ser.). 64p. (gr. 5-8). 58.50 (978-1-61513-124-2(8)) Rosen Publishing Group, Inc., The.

Summers, Portia. Hillary Clinton: Politician & Activist, 1 vol. 2017. (Junior Biographies Ser.). (ENG.). 24p. (gr. 3-4). lib. bdg. 24.27 (978-0-7660-8670-8(4), 59cfec20-341d-41a9-96cc-64292ade5e0c) Enslow Publishing, LLC.

Susienka, Kristen. Kamala Harris. 2019. (African American Leaders of Courage Ser.). (ENG.). 24p. (gr. 1-2). 49.50 (978-1-7253-1107-7(0)); 25.27 (978-1-7253-1108-4(9), 4e2109a4-d349-47c8-a8b5-44023ed065f5); pap. 9.25 (978-1-7253-1106-0(2), ee39cad4-ad14-4571-a791-f352a4c007b4) Rosen Publishing Group, Inc., The. (PowerKids Pr.).

Turner, Carolyn. Sam Houston. 2010. pap. 9.95 (978-1-61690-066-3(0)); 24p. (J). (gr. 2-4). lib. bdg. 25.70 (978-1-61690-065-6(2)) Weigl Pubs., Inc.

Young, Jeff C. Joe Biden. 2009. (Political Profiles Ser.). (Illus.). 100p. (J). (gr. 5-9). 28.95 (978-1-59935-131-5(5)) Reynolds, Morgan Inc.

LEGISLATORS—UNITED STATES

see also United States—Congress

Allen, Charles F. David Crockett: Scout, Small Boy, Pilgrim, Mountaineer, Soldier, Bear-Hunter, & Congressman, Defender of the Alamo. (Illus.). 308p. reprint ed. lib. bdg. 98.00 (978-0-7222-4856-0(3)) Library Reprints, Inc.

Asim, Jabari. Preaching to the Chickens: The Story of Young John Lewis. Lewis, E. B., illus. 2016. 32p. (J). (gr. k-3). 17.99 (978-0-399-16856-7(7), Nancy Paulsen Books) Penguin Young Readers Group.

Barack Obama. 2007. (Political Profiles Ser.). (Illus.). 128p. (YA). (gr. 5-9). lib. bdg. 27.95 (978-1-59935-045-5(9)) Reynolds, Morgan Inc.

Barbara Jordan. 2004. 12p. (gr. k-4). 2.95 (978-0-635-02616-3(3)) Gallopade International.

Barton, Chris. The Amazing Age of John Roy Lynch. Tate, Don, illus. 2015. (ENG.). 50p. (J). 17.00 (978-0-8028-5379-0(X), Eerdmans Bks For Young Readers) Eerdmans, William B. Publishing Co.

—What Do You Do with a Voice Like That? The Story of Extraordinary Congresswoman Barbara Jordan. Holmes, Ekua, illus. 2018. (ENG.). 48p. (J). (gr. -1-3). 18.99 (978-1-4814-6561-8(9), Beach Lane Bks.) Beach Lane Bks.

Bodden, Valerie. Hillary Clinton: Historic Leader. 2009. (Essential Lives Set 4 Ser.). (ENG., Illus.). 112p. (YA). (gr. 6-12). lib. bdg. 41.36 (978-1-60453-699-7(3), 6689, Essential Library) ABDO Publishing Co.

Boehme, Gerry. John Lewis & Desegregation, 1 vol. 2016. (Primary Sources of the Civil Rights Movement Ser.). (ENG., Illus.). 64p. (gr. 6-6). 35.93 (978-1-5026-1868-9(0), dbee6433-90ac-49d9-ba9d-b207631cbf14) Cavendish Square Publishing LLC.

Bourcier, Cammy S. Barack Obama. 2009. (Sharing the American Dream Ser.). (Illus.). 64p. (J). (gr. 7-12). 22.95 (978-1-4222-0574-7(6)) Mason Crest.

Brager, Bruce L. John Kerry: Senator from Massachusetts. 2005. (Twentieth Century Leaders Ser.). (Illus.). 128p. (J). (gr. 6-12). lib. bdg. 23.95 (978-1-931798-64-8(8)) Reynolds, Morgan Inc.

Brill, Marlene Targ. Barack Obama: Working to Make a Difference. 2006. (J). pap. 6.95 (978-0-8225-6056-2(9), First Avenue Editions); (Illus.). 48p. 23.93 (978-0-8225-3417-4(7)) Lerner Publishing Group.

Buckley, James, Jr. Bill Bradley. 2009. (Basketball Hall of Famers Ser.). 112p. (gr. 5-8). 63.90 (978-1-61511-529-7(3), Rosen Reference) Rosen Publishing Group, Inc., The.

Cane, Ella. The U. S. House of Representatives, 1 vol. 2014. (Our Government Ser.). (ENG., Illus.). 24p. (J). (gr. 1-3). lib. bdg. 27.99 (978-1-4765-4201-0(5), 124305) Capstone.

—The U. S. Senate, 1 vol. 2014. (Our Government Ser.). (ENG., Illus.). 24p. (J). (gr. 1-3). lib. bdg. 27.99 (978-1-4765-4202-7(3), 124306) Capstone.

Caravantes, Peggy. American in Texas: The Story of Sam Houston. 2004. (Notable Americans Ser.). (Illus.). 144p. (YA). (gr. 6-12). 23.95 (978-1-931798-19-8(2)) Reynolds, Morgan Inc.

Cefrey, Holly. Congress, 1 vol. 2003. (Primary Source Library of American Citizenship Ser.). (ENG., Illus.). 32p. (YA). (gr. 5-5). lib. bdg. 29.13 (978-0-8239-4470-5(0), d875e169-eb95-4947-abb2-c260ce266c91) Rosen Publishing Group, Inc., The.

Cham, Stephanie. Patsy Mink. 2018. (Great Asian Americans Ser.). (ENG., Illus.). 24p. (J). (gr. -1-2). lib. bdg. 27.32 (978-1-5157-9954-2(9), 136952, Capstone Pr.) Capstone.

—Tammy Duckworth. 2018. (Great Asian Americans Ser.). (ENG., Illus.). 24p. (J). (gr. -1-2). lib. bdg. 27.32 (978-1-5157-9955-9(7), 136953, Capstone Pr.) Capstone.

Chambers, Veronica. Shirley Chisholm Is a Verb. Baker, Rachelle, illus. 2020. 40p. (J). (gr. -1-3). 18.99 (978-0-8037-3089-2(6), Dial Bks) Penguin Young Readers Group.

Coddington, Andrew. Davy Crockett: Frontiersman, 1 vol. Lapegüe, Matías, illus. 2016. (American Legends & Folktales Ser.). (ENG.). 32p. (gr. 3-3). 30.21 (978-1-5026-2193-1(2), 9b7823f4-3a30-481b-a7ce-fac9d0a1a2a1) Cavendish Square Publishing LLC.

Cohen, Sheila & Terman Cohen, Sheila. Gaylord Nelson: Champion for Our Earth. 2010. (Badger Biographies Ser.). (ENG., Illus.). 120p. (J). pap. 12.95 (978-0-87020-443-2(2)) Wisconsin Historical Society.

Collard, Sneed B., III. David Crockett: Fearless Frontiersman, 1 vol. 2007. (American Heroes Ser.). (ENG., Illus.). 48p. (gr. 3-3). lib. bdg. 32.64 (978-0-7614-2160-3(2), 2038e960-fec3-45e4-bd5d-bcb5eb5fba37) Cavendish Square Publishing LLC.

—John Glenn: Hooked on Flying, 1 vol. 2009. (American Heroes Ser.). (ENG., Illus.). 48p. (gr. 3-3). lib. bdg. 32.64 (978-0-7614-3066-7(0), 0802b8b4-5c46-44f3-bfaf-f60b33b36ace) Cavendish Square Publishing LLC.

Collier Hillstrom, Laurie. Al Gore, 1 vol. 2008. (People in the News Ser.). (ENG., Illus.). 112p. (gr. 7-7). lib. bdg. 41.03 (978-1-4205-0086-8(4), 0b1655b8-69b1-4fa8-b474-e619552cd947, Lucent Pr.) Greenhaven Publishing LLC.

Coy, Cissie. Dennis Chávez: The First Hispanic US Senator / Dennis Chávez: el Primer Senador Hispano de Los Estados Unidos. 2017. (SPA & ENG., Illus.). 64p. (J). (gr. 4-8). pap. 9.95 (978-1-55885-852-7(0), Piñata Books) Arte Publico Pr.

Crawford, Ann Fears. Barbara Jordan: Breaking the Barriers. 2003. (Illus.). 90p. (J). (gr. 7-9). lib. bdg. 19.95 (978-1-931823-11-1(1)) Halcyon Pr., Ltd.

Davis, William Michael. Barack Obama: The Politics of Hope. 2007. (Illus.). 168p. (J). (gr. 10-18). lib. bdg. 25.95 (978-1-59556-024-7(6), 1291988); (gr. 8-18). pap. 16.99 (978-1-59556-032-2(7), 1291988) OTTN Publishing.

De Medeiros, James. Al Gore. 2008. (Remarkable People Ser.). (Illus.). 24p. (J). (gr. 4-6). pap. 8.95 (978-1-59036-993-7(9)); lib. bdg. 24.45 (978-1-59036-992-0(0)) Weigl Pubs., Inc.

De Medeiros, Michael. Barack Obama. (J). 2013. (978-1-62127-388-2(1)) 2008. (Illus.). 24p. (gr. 4-6). pap. 8.95 (978-1-59036-989-0(0)) 2008. (Illus.). 24p. (gr. 4-6). lib. bdg. 24.45 (978-1-59036-988-3(2)) Weigl Pubs., Inc.

Doak, Robin S. Hillary Clinton. 2013. (True Book: Biographies Ser.). (ENG., Illus.). 48p. (J). (gr. 3-5). lib. bdg. 21.19 (978-0-531-21906-5(2), Children's Pr.); pap. 6.95 (978-0-531-23877-6(6)) Scholastic Library Publishing.

Doeden, Matt. John Lewis: Courage in Action. 2018. (Gateway Biographies Ser.). (ENG., Illus.). 48p. (J). (gr. 4-8). 31.99 (978-1-5415-1238-2(3), c3bd6e6c-7a71-4a92-a1fb-b9894d102410, Lerner Pubns.) Lerner Publishing Group.

Driscoll, Laura. Hillary Clinton: An American Journey. Wood, Judith V., illus. 2008. (ENG.). 48p. (J). (gr. 3-6). 16.19 (978-0-448-44787-2(8)) Penguin Young Readers Group.

Egan, Tracie. How a Bill Becomes a Law, 1 vol. 2003. (Primary Source Library of American Citizenship Ser.). (ENG., Illus.). 32p. (gr. 5-5). lib. bdg. 29.13 (978-0-8239-4471-2(9), 70c063f9-adca-438a-9685-e0e96dd533c8, Rosen Reference) Rosen Publishing Group, Inc., The.

Epstein, Brad M. Barack Obama 101. l.t. ed. 2009. (My First Presidential Board Book Ser.). (Illus.). 28p. (J). (gr. -1-1). bds. (978-1-60730-044-1(3), 101 Bk.) Michaelson Entertainment.

Epstein, Dwayne. Hillary Clinton, 1 vol. 2009. (People in the News Ser.). (ENG., Illus.). 128p. (gr. 7-7). 41.03 (978-1-4205-0268-8(9), d39b223e-42d3-45d4-a896-84157b4a51bf, Lucent Pr.) Greenhaven Publishing LLC.

—Nancy Pelosi, 1 vol. 2008. (People in the News Ser.). (ENG., Illus.). 104p. (gr. 7-7). lib. bdg. 41.03 (978-1-4205-0057-8(0), 9eb2b367-5ac1-4f36-b140-7b3dc00bd1b1, Lucent Pr.) Greenhaven Publishing LLC.

Falk, Laine. Meet President Barack Obama. 2009. (Scholastic News Nonfiction Readers Ser.). (ENG., Illus.). 24p. (J). (gr. k-3). 21.19 (978-0-531-23403-7(7), Children's Pr.) Scholastic Library Publishing.

—Meet President John McCain. 2009. (J). (978-0-531-23650-5(1)) Children's Pr., Ltd.

Feinstein, Stephen. Barack Obama, 1 vol. 2008. (African-American Heroes Ser.). (ENG., Illus.). 24p. (gr. k-2). lib. bdg. 25.27 (978-0-7660-2893-7(3), 69df780e-533b-4c3f-82e5-c16548d680f1, Enslow Elementary) Enslow Publishing, LLC.

Finley, Toiya Kristen. Russell Simmons. 2007. (Sharing the American Dream Ser.). 64p. (YA). (gr. 7-18). pap. 9.95 (978-1-4222-0762-8(5)) Mason Crest.

Flynn, Jean. Henry B. Gonzalez: Rebel with a Cause. 2003. (Illus.). v, 140p. (J). 16.95 (978-1-57168-780-7(7), Eakin Pr.) Eakin Pr.

Freedman, Jeri. Elizabeth Warren: Democratic Senator from Massachusetts, 1 vol. 2017. (Leading Women Ser.). (ENG., Illus.). 112p. (YA). (gr. 7-7). 41.64 (978-1-5026-2699-8(3), fd6cd751-fce0-41ed-92f6-f460528a8cbf) Cavendish Square Publishing LLC.

—Hillary Rodham Clinton: Profile of a Leading Democrat. 2009. (Career Profiles Ser.). 112p. (gr. 9-10). 63.90 (978-1-61511-794-9(6)) Rosen Publishing Group, Inc., The.

Gabriel, Dani. John Mccain: Get to Know the Brave POW & Senator. 2019. (People You Should Know Ser.). (ENG., Illus.). 32p. (J). (gr. 3-6). pap. 7.95 (978-1-5435-7466-1(1), 140906); lib. bdg. 27.99 (978-1-5435-7184-4(0), 140435) Capstone.

Giblin, James Cross. The Rise & Fall of Senator Joe Mccarthy. 2009. (ENG., Illus.). 304p. (YA). (gr. 7-18). 22.00 (978-0-618-61058-7(8), 100444, Clarion Bks.) HarperCollins Pubs.

Gibson, Karen Bush. The Historic Fight for the 2008 Democratic Presidential Nomination: The Obama View. 2009. (Monumental Milestones Ser.). (Illus.). 48p. (YA). (gr. 4-7). lib. bdg. 29.95 (978-1-58415-732-8(1)) Mitchell Lane Pubs.

Goldsworthy, Kaite. Gabrielle Giffords. 2012. (J). (978-1-61913-535-2(3)); pap. (978-1-61913-590-1(6)) Weigl Pubs., Inc.

Goldsworthy, Steve. Edward Kennedy. 2010. (Remarkable People Ser.). (Illus.). 24p. (J). (gr. 4-6). pap. 11.95 (978-1-61690-170-7(5)); lib. bdg. 25.70 (978-1-61690-169-1(1)) Weigl Pubs., Inc.

Gormley, Beatrice. John Mccain: An American Hero. 2018. (ENG.). 224p. (J). (gr. 3-7). 17.99 (978-1-5344-4386-0(X)); (Illus.). pap. 7.99 (978-1-5344-4385-3(1)) Simon & Schuster Children's Publishing. (Aladdin).

Grimes, Nikki. Barack Obama: Son of Promise, Child of Hope. Collier, Bryan, illus. (ENG.). 48p. (J). (gr. k-3). 2012. 9.99 (978-1-4424-4092-0(9)) 2008. pap. 19.99 (978-1-4169-7144-3(0)) Simon & Schuster Bks. For Young Readers. (Simon & Schuster Bks. For Young Readers).

—Kamala Harris: Rooted in Justice. Freeman, Laura, illus. 2020. (ENG.). 40p. (J). (gr. -1-3). 17.99 (978-1-5344-6267-0(8), Atheneum Bks. for Young Readers) Simon & Schuster Children's Publishing.

Guernsey, JoAnn B. Hillary Rodham Clinton. 2005. (Biography Ser.). (Illus.). 112p. (J). (gr. 6-18). pap. 7.95 (978-0-8225-9613-4(X)) Lerner Publishing Group.

Guernsey, Joann Bren. Hillary Rodham Clinton. 2005. (Biography Ser.). (Illus.). 112p. (J). (gr. 3-7). lib. bdg. 29.27 (978-0-8225-2372-7(8), Lerner Pubns.) Lerner Publishing Group.

Haldy, Emma E. Davy Crockett SP. Bane, Jeff, illus. 2018. (My Early Library: Mi Mini Biografía (My Itty-Bitty Bio) Ser.). (SPA.). 24p. (J). (gr. k-1). lib. bdg. 30.64 *(978-1-5341-2995-5(2)*, 212028) Cherry Lake Publishing.

Halfmann, Janet. Seven Miles to Freedom: The Robert Smalls Story. Smith, Duane, illus. 2008. 40p. (J). (gr. 1-6). 17.95 *(978-1-60060-232-0(0))* Lee & Low Bks., Inc.

Harmon, Daniel E. Al Gore & Global Warming. 2009. (Celebrity Activists Ser.). 112p. (gr. 8-8). 66.50 *(978-1-61511-826-7(8))* Rosen Publishing Group, Inc., The.

Harness, Cheryl. Hillary Clinton: American Woman of the World. 2016. (Real-Life Story Ser.). (ENG., Illus.). 192p. (J). (gr. 3-7). 17.99 *(978-1-4814-6057-6(9)*, Aladdin) Simon & Schuster Children's Publishing.

Harris, Kamala. Los Superhéroes Están en Todas Partes. Roe, Mechal Renee, illus. 2019. (SPA.). 40p. (J). (gr. -1-2). 17.99 *(978-0-593-11332-5(2)*, Philomel Bks.) Penguin Young Readers Group.

—The Truths We Hold: An American Journey (Young Readers Edition) (ENG., Illus.). 304p. (gr. 7). 2020. (J). pap. 10.99 *(978-0-593-11317-2(9)*, Penguin Books) 2019. (YA). 17.99 *(978-1-9848-3706-6(0)*, Philomel Bks.) Penguin Young Readers Group.

Haskins, Jim & Benson, Kathleen. John Lewis in the Lead: A Story of the Civil Rights Movement, 1 vol. Andrews, Benny, illus. 2006. (ENG.). 40p. (J). (gr. 2-7). 17.95 *(978-1-58430-250-6(X))* Lee & Low Bks., Inc.

—The Story of Civil Rights Hero John Lewis, 1 vol. Boyd, Aaron, illus. 2019. (Story Of Ser.). (ENG.). 64p. (J). (gr. 4-8). pap. 10.95 *(978-1-62014-854-9(4)*, leelowbooks) Lee & Low Bks., Inc.

Herman, Gail. Who Was Davy Crockett? 2013. (Who Was... ? Ser.). lib. bdg. 16.00 *(978-0-606-32133-4(0))* Turtleback.

Herman, Gail & Who HQ. Who Was Davy Crockett? Squier, Robert, illus. 2013. (Who Was? Ser.). (ENG.). 112p. (J). (gr. 3-7). 5.99 *(978-0-448-46704-7(6)*, Penguin Workshop) Penguin Young Readers Group.

Hiram Bingham & the Dream of Gold. 2014. (ENG.). 192p. (J). (gr. 3-7). pap. 13.95 *(978-1-59077-350-5(0))* Evans, M. & Co., Inc.

Hoe, Susan. Rosa Parks. 2007. (Sharing the American Dream Ser.). 64p. (YA). (gr. 7-18). pap. 9.95 *(978-1-4222-0760-4(9))* Mason Crest.

Horn, Geoffrey M. John Mccain, 1 vol. 2009. (People We Should Know (Second Series) Ser.). (ENG., Illus.). 32p. (J). (gr. 3-5). pap. 11.50 *(978-1-4339-0160-7(9)*, fbdf5273-8ceb-4a6e-93dd-e54d3db41f8f); lib. bdg. 33.67 *(978-1-4339-0020-4(3)*, 9a51add1-6bb7-4cac-bcd4-e17aafea87d6) Stevens, Gareth Publishing LLLP. (Gareth Stevens Learning Library).

—Nancy Pelosi, 1 vol. 2009. (People We Should Know (Second Series) Ser.). (ENG.). 32p. (J). (gr. 3-5). pap. 11.50 *(978-1-4339-0162-1(5)*, cc982ed7-636a-43f2-8bf3-727da0c3c27f); lib. bdg. 33.67 *(978-1-4339-0021-1(1)*, 89210acd-7b88-4f6a-a1f2-f17328b75db2) Stevens, Gareth Publishing LLLP. (Gareth Stevens Learning Library).

Hurt, Avery Elizabeth, ed. Gender Diversity in Government, 1 vol. 2019. (Global Viewpoints Ser.). (ENG.). 200p. (gr. 10-12). 47.83 *(978-1-5345-0557-5(1)*, 66827825-8b20-438b-a00a-2fe38a76ce73) Greenhaven Publishing LLC.

Iorio, Nicole. Joe Biden, 1 vol. 2009. (People We Should Know (Second Series) Ser.). (ENG.). 48p. (J). (gr. 3-5). pap. 11.50 *(978-1-4339-2148-3(0)*, 8df0f9b1-ac05-4d34-89b8-7c5ed05ff358); lib. bdg. 33.67 *(978-1-4339-1949-7(4)*, 3e91239f-da97-4d2b-b7a2-40f7ce2dd22c) Stevens, Gareth Publishing LLLP. (Gareth Stevens Learning Library).

Jackson, Garnet N. Shirley Chisholm, Congresswoman. 2012. (ENG., Illus.). (J). (gr. 1-4). pap. 7.47 net. *(978-0-8136-5247-4(2)*, Modern Curriculum Pr.) Savvas Learning Co.

Jakubiak, David J. What Does a Congressional Representative Do? 2010. (How Our Government Works Ser.). 24p. (J). (gr. 3-6). lib. bdg., E-Book 42.50 *(978-1-4488-0033-9(1))* Rosen Publishing Group, Inc., The.

—What Does a Senator Do? 2010. (How Our Government Works Ser.). 24p. (J). (gr. 3-6). lib. bdg., E-Book 42.50 *(978-1-4488-0029-2(3))*; (ENG., Illus.). pap. 9.25 *(978-1-4358-9816-5(8)*, f8b66662-3a5d-4737-a336-fbdfc51c4804, PowerKids Pr.); (ENG., Illus.). lib. bdg. 26.27 *(978-1-4358-9360-3(3)*, 72d2509e-ccb7-41e4-aee2-aeabeb327ae7, PowerKids Pr.) Rosen Publishing Group, Inc., The.

Jarnow, Jesse. Davy Crockett: Defensor de la frontera (Davy Crockett: Frontier Hero) 2009. (Grandes personajes en la historia de los Estados Unidos (Famous People in American History) Ser.). (SPA.). 32p. (gr. 2-3). 47.90 *(978-1-61512-797-9(6)*, Editorial Buenas Letras) Rosen Publishing Group, Inc., The.

—Davy Crockett: Frontier Hero / Defensor de la Frontera. 2009. (Famous People in American History/Grandes personajes en la historia de los Estados Unidos Ser.). (ENG & SPA.). 32p. (gr. 2-3). 47.90 *(978-1-61512-543-2(4)*, Editorial Buenas Letras) Rosen Publishing Group, Inc., The.

—Patrick Henry's Liberty or Death Speech: A Primary Source Investigation. (Great Historic Debates & Speeches Ser.). 64p. (gr. 5-8). 2009. 58.50 *(978-1-61513-120-4(5))* 2004. (ENG., Illus.). (J). lib. bdg. 37.13 *(978-1-4042-0152-1(1)*, 33578fa0-39bc-431d-85a9-66a4ee0c1715) Rosen Publishing Group, Inc., The.

Johnston, Marianne. Davy Crockett. 2009. (American Legends Ser.). 24p. (gr. 3-3). 42.50 *(978-1-61511-381-1(9)*, PowerKids Pr.) Rosen Publishing Group, Inc., The.

Jones-Radgowski, Jehan. John Lewis: Get to Know the Statesman Who Marched for Civil Rights. 2019. (People You Should Know Ser.). (ENG., Illus.). 32p. (J). (gr. 3-6). pap. 7.95 *(978-1-5435-5924-8(7)*, 139902, Capstone Pr.) Capstone.

Jopp, Kelsey. Kamala Harris. 2020. (Groundbreaking Women in Politics Ser.). (ENG., Illus.). 48p. (J). (gr. 5-6). pap. 11.95 *(978-1-64493-167-7(2)*, 1644931672); lib. bdg. 34.21 *(978-1-64493-088-5(9)*, 1644930889) North Star Editions. (Focus Readers).

Kann, Bob. Belle & Bob la Follette: Partners in Politics. 2008. (Badger Biographies Ser.). (ENG., Illus.). 144p. (J). (gr. 3-7). pap. 12.95 *(978-0-87020-407-4(6))* Wisconsin Historical Society.

Kawa, Katie. Alexandria Ocasio-Cortez: Making a Difference in Politics, 1 vol. 2020. (People Who Make a Difference Ser.). (ENG.). 24p. (J). (gr. 3-3). pap. 9.25 *(978-1-5345-3468-1(7)*, ad2e3bae-0197-4318-ac69-caeccb29798b, KidHaven Publishing) Greenhaven Publishing LLC.

Kennedy, Edward M. My Senator & Me: A Dog's-Eye View of Washington, D. C. Small, David, illus. 2011. (J). (gr. 2-5). 29.95 *(978-0-545-04379-3(4))* Weston Woods Studios, Inc.

Kiely Miller, Barbara. Sam Houston, 1 vol. 2007. (Great Americans Ser.). 24p. (gr. 2-4). (ENG.). pap. 9.15 *(978-0-8368-8323-7(3)*, 181dab52-3918-43bb-b2a9-666f98196091); (SPA.). pap. 9.15 *(978-0-8368-8336-7(5)*, c6ff82ce-7527-4a48-acc7-8db99cbe62ff); (ENG.). lib. bdg. 24.67 *(978-0-8368-8316-9(0)*, c0d85d45-374f-44a0-82b7-fe4611ee39a8); (SPA., Illus.). lib. bdg. 24.67 *(978-0-8368-8329-9(2)*, 468581b2-c389-4f19-87a2-91fb6d86c83c) Stevens, Gareth Publishing LLLP. (Weekly Reader Leveled Readers).

Klein, Adria F. Barack Obama. 2009. pap. 13.25 *(978-1-60559-055-4(X))* Hameray Publishing Group, Inc.

Krull, Kathleen. The Brothers Kennedy: John, Robert, Edward. Bates, Amy June, illus. 2010. (ENG.). 40p. (J). (gr. -1-3). 16.99 *(978-1-4169-9158-8(1)*, Simon & Schuster Bks. For Young Readers) Simon & Schuster Bks. For Young Readers.

—Fly High, John Glenn: The Story of an American Hero. Quarello, Maurizio A. C., illus. 2020. (ENG.). 48p. (J). (gr. -1-3). 18.99 *(978-0-06-274714-3(2)*, HarperCollins) HarperCollins Pubs.

Kupperberg, Paul. John Glenn, 1 vol. 2003. (Library of Astronaut Biographies Ser.). (ENG., Illus.). 112p. (J). (gr. 5-8). lib. bdg. 39.80 *(978-0-8239-4460-6(3)*, 5c6c20ec-1cf4-4796-88d3-ca865db23e40, Rosen Reference) Rosen Publishing Group, Inc., The.

Laks Gorman, Jacqueline. Member of Congress, 1 vol. 2009. (Know Your Government Ser.). (ENG.). 24p. (J). (gr. 3-3). pap. 9.15 *(978-1-4339-0122-5(6)*, a8f5d767-0414-4dd2-ae32-18152928b16e); lib. bdg. 24.67 *(978-1-4339-0094-5(7)*, 2ff26ad8-8cbd-4683-b732-3009679d7942) Stevens, Gareth Publishing LLLP. (Weekly Reader Leveled Readers).

—Miembro Del Congreso (Member of Congress), 1 vol. 2009. (Conoce Tu Gobierno (Know Your Government) Ser.). (SPA.). 24p. (gr. 3-3). (J). lib. bdg. 24.67 *(978-1-4339-0101-0(3)*, 1d70021d-068b-4a0e-afde-55dfa720a3a0); pap. 9.15 *(978-1-4339-0129-4(3)*, a8fedf7b-e2a4-4a2e-bb40-d1ff20ddbc96) Stevens, Gareth Publishing LLLP. (Weekly Reader Leveled Readers).

Lawson, Lela. A Career As a Senator: Understanding Government, 1 vol. 2018. (Civics for the Real World Ser.). (ENG.). 16p. (gr. 2-3). pap. *(978-1-5383-6515-1(4)*, d537219a-8fb2-4388-a2a4-8405f739e37a, Rosen Classroom) Rosen Publishing Group, Inc., The.

Leavitt, Amie Jane. Nancy Pelosi. 2007. (Blue Banner Biography Ser.). (Illus.). 32p. (YA). (gr. 4-7). lib. bdg. 25.70 *(978-1-58415-613-0(9))* Mitchell Lane Pubs.

Leigh, Anna. Nancy Pelosi: Political Powerhouse. 2020. (Gateway Biographies Ser.). (ENG., Illus.). 48p. (J). (gr. 4-8). pap. 11.99 *(978-1-5415-8889-9(4)*, 71ecdbfb-6ecb-45d4-817d-86bb18fb8795); lib. bdg. 31.99 *(978-1-5415-7746-6(9)*, 3d6a23df-da43-4277-ab99-14602397f693) Lerner Publishing Group. (Lerner Pubns.).

Levy, Janey. Shirley Chisholm, 1 vol. 2020. (Heroes of Black History Ser.). (ENG.). 32p. (gr. 3-4). pap. 11.50 *(978-1-5382-5798-2(X)*, 414f5e2f-acf0-470d-aa1b-7d2d9baeaccd) Stevens, Gareth Publishing LLLP.

Mapua, Jeff. Hillary Clinton, 1 vol. 2014. (Britannica Beginner Bios Ser.). (ENG., Illus.). 32p. (J). (gr. 2-3). 26.06 *(978-1-62275-689-6(4)*, c6a1ac5c-edfc-4d9f-8b71-fe87854a49f1, Britannica Educational Publishing) Rosen Publishing Group, Inc., The.

Marcovitz, Hal. Barack. 2007. (Obamas Ser.). (Illus.). 64p. (YA). (gr. 3-6). pap. 9.95 *(978-1-4222-1484-8(2))*; (gr. 4-7). lib. bdg. 19.95 *(978-1-4222-1477-0(X))* Mason Crest.

—Michelle. 2007. (Obamas Ser.). 64p. (YA). (gr. 3-6). pap. 9.95 *(978-1-4222-1485-5(0))*; (gr. 4-7). lib. bdg. 19.95 *(978-1-4222-1478-7(8))* Mason Crest.

Marie Ford, Jeanne. Ilhan Omar. 2020. (Groundbreaking Women in Politics Ser.). (ENG., Illus.). 48p. (J). (gr. 5-6). pap. 11.95 *(978-1-64493-169-1(9)*, 1644931699); lib. bdg. 34.21 *(978-1-64493-090-8(0)*, 1644930900) North Star Editions. (Focus Readers).

Marsh, Carole. Ben Nighthorse Campbell. 2003. 12p. (gr. k-4). 2.95 *(978-0-635-02383-4(0))* Gallopade International.

—Carol Moseley Braun. 2003. 12p. (gr. k-4). 2.95 *(978-0-635-02384-1(9))* Gallopade International.

Marsico, Katie. Irma Rangel. Bane, Jeff, illus. 2018. (My Early Library: My Itty-Bitty Bio Ser.). (ENG.). 24p. (J). (gr. k-1). lib. bdg. 30.64 *(978-1-5341-2889-7(1)*, 211600) Cherry Lake Publishing.

McAuliffe, Bill. The U. S. House of Representatives. 2016. (By the People Ser.). (ENG., Illus.). 48p. (J). (gr. 4-7). pap. 12.00 *(978-1-62832-271-2(3)*, 20573, Creative Paperbacks) Creative Co., The.

—The U.S. House of Representatives. 2016. (By the People Ser.). (ENG., Illus.). 48p. (J). (gr. 4-7). 39.95 *(978-1-60818-675-4(X)*, 20575, Creative Education) Creative Co., The.

—The U.S. Senate. 2016. (By the People Ser.). (ENG., Illus.). 48p. (J). (gr. 4-7). 39.95 *(978-1-60818-677-8(6)*, 20581, Creative Education) Creative Co., The.

McDonnell, Julia. Before Barack Obama Was President, 1 vol. 2018. (Before They Were President Ser.). (ENG.). 24p. (gr. 2-3). 24.27 *(978-1-5382-2909-5(9)*, 4cbd92b9-440c-41b5-8bd3-7af73085d418) Stevens, Gareth Publishing LLLP.

McElroy, Lisa Tucker. Nancy Pelosi. 2008. pap. 52.95 *(978-0-8225-9477-2(3))* Lerner Publishing Group.

—Nancy Pelosi: First Woman Speaker of the House. 2007. (Gateway Biographies Ser.). (ENG., Illus.). 48p. (J). (gr. 4-8). lib. bdg. 26.60 *(978-0-8225-8685-2(1)*, Lerner Pubns.) Lerner Publishing Group.

McGowan, Joseph. Al Gore, 1 vol. 2009. (People We Should Know (Second Series) Ser.). (ENG.). 48p. (J). (gr. 3-5). pap. 11.50 *(978-1-4339-2146-9(4)*, d085d240-5610-4f6c-a156-448650d8b212); lib. bdg. 33.67 *(978-1-4339-1947-3(8)*, 30467b93-158a-4097-996b-f59ce266e739) Stevens, Gareth Publishing LLLP. (Gareth Stevens Learning Library).

Modifica, Lisa. A Timeline of Congress. (Timelines of American History Ser.). 32p. (gr. 4-4). 2009. 47.90 *(978-1-60854-380-9(3))* 2004. (ENG., Illus.). lib. bdg. 29.13 *(978-0-8239-4534-4(0)*, 4740c1bb-7f39-4535-9926-368abf823701) Rosen Publishing Group, Inc., The. (Rosen Reference).

Moriarty, J. T. Davy Crockett: Frontier Hero. 2009. (Primary Sources of Famous People in American History Ser.). 32p. (gr. 2-3). 47.90 *(978-1-60851-670-4(9))* Rosen Publishing Group, Inc., The.

—Davy Crockett: Frontier Hero = Defensor de la Frontera, 1 vol. 2003. (Famous People in American History / Grandes Personajes en la Historia de Los Estados Unidos Ser.). (ENG & SPA., Illus.). 32p. (J). (gr. 2-3). lib. bdg. 29.13 *(978-0-8239-4156-8(6)*, 053f4de4-9a56-4d3b-81e2-66f81220ca56) Rosen Publishing Group, Inc., The.

Morlock, Rachael. Barack Obama: A Life of Leadership, 1 vol. annot. ed. 2019. (People in the News Ser.). (ENG.). 104p. (gr. 7-7). pap. 20.99 *(978-1-5345-6840-2(9)*, 1dbae1b7-6a06-489e-8227-e56a3ac990bb); lib. bdg. 41.03 *(978-1-5345-6841-9(7)*, ca00a648-b9d2-4f3f-ae82-795d317aa70f) Greenhaven Publishing LLC. (Lucent Pr.).

Morretta, Alison. John Lewis: Civil Rights Champion & Congressman, 1 vol. 2019. (African American Trailblazers Ser.). (ENG.). 128p. (gr. 9-9). pap. 22.16 *(978-1-5026-4548-7(3)*, eec318ac-b171-4d0d-a4cc-1624eff3acc4) Cavendish Square Publishing LLC.

Nelson, Maria. Becoming a House Representative, 1 vol. 2015. (Who's Your Candidate? Choosing Government Leaders Ser.). (ENG., Illus.). 32p. (J). (gr. 3-4). pap. 11.50 *(978-1-4824-4035-5(0)*, 1ddbf9ea-45e1-4e16-897c-b7f50c2c6eb6) Stevens, Gareth Publishing LLLP.

—Becoming a Senator, 1 vol. 2015. (Who's Your Candidate? Choosing Government Leaders Ser.). (ENG., Illus.). 32p. (J). (gr. 3-4). pap. 11.50 *(978-1-4824-4043-0(1)*, 5e429fa5-efe3-4d4a-b6a5-0fd6f14b972f) Stevens, Gareth Publishing LLLP.

Nichols, Kaitlyn. Davey Crockett. 2009. pap. 13.25 *(978-1-60559-057-8(6))* Hameray Publishing Group, Inc.

Peppas, Lynn. Why Sam Houston Matters to Texas, 1 vol. 2013. (Texas Perspectives Ser.). (ENG., Illus.). 32p. (J). (gr. 4-4). lib. bdg. 28.93 *(978-1-4777-0912-2(6)*, 60e60101-a7ab-4741-8c21-e08fda6394f0) Rosen Publishing Group, Inc., The.

Raatma, Lucia. Barbara Jordan, 1 vol. 2013. (Leading Women Ser.). (ENG.). 96p. (YA). (gr. 7-7). 42.64 *(978-0-7614-4956-0(6)*, bbcd5f27-0fcc-47f5-88e7-57e8052fa895); pap. 20.99 *(978-1-62712-114-9(5)*, c1f7fc2d-5916-43ad-b6a4-acdad06e7612) Cavendish Square Publishing LLC.

Radomski, Kassandra Kathleen. So You Want to Be a U. S. Representative. 2019. (Being in Government Ser.). (ENG., Illus.). 32p. (J). (gr. 3-6). pap. 7.95 *(978-1-5435-7528-6(5)*, 141058); lib. bdg. 27.99 *(978-1-5435-7196-7(4)*, 140441) Capstone.

—So You Want to Be a U. S. Senator. 2019. (Being in Government Ser.). (ENG., Illus.). 32p. (J). (gr. 3-6). pap. 7.95 *(978-1-5435-7529-3(3)*, 141060); lib. bdg. 27.99 *(978-1-5435-7195-0(6)*, 140440) Capstone.

Rice, Liz. Bill Richardson. (Sharing the American Dream Ser.). (Illus.). 64p. (J). (gr. 7-12). 2009. 22.95 *(978-1-4222-0589-1(4))* 2007. pap. 9.95 *(978-1-4222-0761-1(7))* Mason Crest.

Riddolls, Tom & Wearing, Judy. Hillary Clinton. 2009. (Remarkable People Ser.). (Illus.). 24p. (J). (gr. 4-6). pap. 8.95 *(978-1-60596-621-2(5))*; lib. bdg. 24.45 *(978-1-60596-620-5(7))* Weigl Pubs., Inc.

Robinson, Tom. Barack Obama: 44th U. S. President, 1 vol. 2009. (Essential Lives Set 3 Ser.). (ENG., Illus.). 112p. (YA). (gr. 6-12). lib. bdg. 41.36 *(978-1-60453-527-3(X)*, 6683, Essential Library) ABDO Publishing Co.

Rose, Simon. The House of Representatives. 2014. (J). *(978-1-4896-1938-9(0))* Weigl Pubs., Inc.

Saddleback Educational Publishing Staff, ed. Davy Crockett, 1 vol. unabr. ed. 2007. (Graphic Biographies Ser.). (ENG., Illus.). 25p. (YA). (gr. 4-12). pap. 9.75 *(978-1-59905-220-5(2))* Saddleback Educational Publishing, Inc.

Sales, Amanda. Mike Pence: Vice President of the United States, 1 vol. 2018. (Influential Lives Ser.). (ENG.). 128p. (J). (gr. 7-7). 40.27 *(978-1-9785-0343-4(1)*, c918029a-a9fb-4d28-b202-6de6d25fab1e) Enslow Publishing, LLC.

Sanford, William R. & Green, Carl R. Davy Crockett: Courageous Hero of the Alamo, 1 vol. 2013. (Courageous Heroes of the American West Ser.). (ENG., Illus.). 48p. (J). (gr. 5-7). 25.27 *(978-0-7660-4005-2(4)*, 6a5cf7d7-f8de-4af4-b900-46401c5edaf1); pap. 11.53 *(978-1-4644-0086-5(5)*, 5b090086-0a64-4b32-80db-f849a4ed5b0f) Enslow Publishing, LLC.

—Sam Houston: Courageous Texas Hero, 1 vol. 2013. (Courageous Heroes of the American West Ser.). (ENG., Illus.). 48p. (J). (gr. 5-7). pap. 11.53 *(978-1-4644-0092-6(X)*, 82c855d2-5888-4c8e-acf5-64777f78ae2a); lib. bdg. 25.27 *(978-0-7660-4009-0(7)*, 49b9d718-c81f-4cc1-81fd-c8181672b4fc) Enslow Publishing, LLC.

Sapet, Kerrily. Al Gore. 2007. (Political Profiles Ser.). (Illus.). 112p. (YA). (gr. 5-9). lib. bdg. 27.95 *(978-1-59935-070-7(X))* Reynolds, Morgan Inc.

Sarantou, Katlin. Tammy Duckworth. Bane, Jeff, illus. 2019. (My Early Library: My Itty-Bitty Bio Ser.). (ENG.). 24p. (J). (gr. k-1). pap. 12.79 *(978-1-5341-4990-8(2)*, 213267); lib. bdg. 30.64 *(978-1-5341-4704-1(7)*, 213266) Cherry Lake Publishing.

Schuh, Mari C. The U. S. House of Representatives, 1 vol. 2012. (U. S. Government Ser.). (ENG.). 24p. (J). (gr. -1-2). lib. bdg. 27.32 *(978-1-4296-7565-9(9)*, 117163, Capstone Pr.) Capstone.

Schuman, Michael A. Barack Obama: We Are One People, 1 vol. rev. ed. 2008. (African-American Biography Library). (ENG., Illus.). 160p. (gr. 6-7). lib. bdg. 35.93 *(978-0-7660-3649-9(9)*, 38ae7d97-e2eb-4050-b3ef-e12048222213) Enslow Publishing, LLC.

Schwartz, Heather E. John Mccain: The Courage of Conviction. 2018. (Gateway Biographies Ser.). (ENG., Illus.). 48p. (J). (gr. 4-8). lib. bdg. 31.99 *(978-1-5415-3839-9(0)*, 1189939d-de06-4a0c-a070-19dbd43e5cbf, Lerner Pubns.) Lerner Publishing Group.

Shea, Therese M. Meet the House of Representatives, 1 vol. 2012. (Guide to Your Government Ser.). (ENG., Illus.). 32p. (J). (gr. 4-5). 29.27 *(978-1-4339-7252-2(2)*, d03b9a91-3b2c-4ed3-bb24-823328c6b05c); pap. 11.50 *(978-1-4339-7253-9(0)*, 49fe7bfa-8b45-4768-8785-a19832acaedd) Stevens, Gareth Publishing LLLP. (Gareth Stevens Learning Library).

Shichtman, Sandra H. Nancy Pelosi. 2008. (Political Profiles Ser.). (Illus.). 112p. (YA). (gr. 5-9). lib. bdg. 27.95 *(978-1-59935-049-3(1))* Reynolds, Morgan Inc.

Silate, Jennifer. The Calhoun-Randolph Debate on the Eve of the War of 1812: A Primary Source Investigation, 1 vol. 2004. (Great Historic Debates & Speeches Ser.). (ENG., Illus.). 64p. (YA). (gr. 5-8). lib. bdg. 37.13 *(978-1-4042-0150-7(5)*, b416568f-5db1-4b00-bf4b-5f8362e684ce) Rosen Publishing Group, Inc., The.

Smith, Andrea P. Davy Crockett. (Illus.). 24p. (J). 2012. 63.60 *(978-1-4488-5223-9(4))* 2011. (ENG., (gr. 2-3). pap. 11.60 *(978-1-4488-5222-2(6)*, f86cea71-ff29-4c80-9b17-a3d7ed457f3a) 2011. (ENG., (gr. 2-3). lib. bdg. 28.93 *(978-1-4488-5192-8(0)*, bedb43e6-ebca-415a-b6a2-fe06de680194) Rosen Publishing Group, Inc., The. (PowerKids Pr.).

Smith-Llera, Danielle. Exploring the Legislative Branch. 2019. (Searchlight Books (tm) — Getting into Government Ser.). (ENG., Illus.). 32p. (J). (gr. 3-5). pap. 9.99 *(978-1-5415-7480-9(X)*, d78367e6-108e-4ae3-bdff-9b3c215366d6); lib. bdg. 30.65 *(978-1-5415-5587-7(2)*, dc731c7d-8730-4f90-b41c-74a22b4f7cf1) Lerner Publishing Group. (Lerner Pubns.).

Spath, Carolyn E. W. Standing in the Shoes of a Member of the House of Representatives, 1 vol. 2015. (My Government Ser.). (ENG., Illus.). 32p. (gr. 4-4). lib. bdg. 30.21 *(978-1-5026-0470-5(1)*, b6a485c0-11da-449a-acab-a9e7d39cb20c) Cavendish Square Publishing LLC.

Stanley, George Edward. Davy Crockett: Frontier Legend. 2008. (Sterling Biographies Ser.). (ENG., Illus.). 123p. (J). (gr. 6-8). 18.69 *(978-1-4027-6057-0(4))* Sterling Publishing Co., Inc.

Stefoff, Rebecca. Al Gore: Fighting for a Greener Planet. rev. ed. 2008. (Gateway Biographies Ser.). (ENG.). 48p. (gr. 4-8). 26.60 *(978-1-57505-948-8(7))* Lerner Publishing Group.

Stoltman, Joan. Hillary Clinton, 1 vol. 2017. (Little Biographies of Big People Ser.). (ENG.). 24p. (J). (gr. 1-2). pap. 9.15 *(978-1-5382-0927-1(6)*, 45d15419-e1ba-485e-aecd-492bac53ea80) Stevens, Gareth Publishing LLLP.

—Hillary Clinton, 1 vol. Garcia, Ana Maria, tr. 2017. (Pequeñas Biografías de Grandes Personajes (Little Biographies of Big People) Ser.). (SPA.). 24p. (J). (gr. 1-2). pap. 9.15 *(978-1-5382-1558-6(6)*, 223ef883-505a-47a7-9806-85242aebbfaf); lib. bdg. 24.27 *(978-1-5382-1531-9(4)*, c288e1b0-b83a-4715-865d-2d96d21028a1) Stevens, Gareth Publishing LLLP.

Ted Kennedy. 2009. (Political Profiles Ser.). 144p. (YA). (gr. 5-9). 28.95 *(978-1-59935-089-9(0))* Reynolds, Morgan Inc.

Thomas, Garen. Yes We Can: A Biography of President Barack Obama. 2nd rev. ed. 2008. (ENG., Illus.). 256p. (J). (gr. 3-6). 12.99 *(978-0-312-58639-3(6)*, 900062157) Feiwel & Friends.

Topinka, Joseph Baar. Just Judy: A Citizen & Leader for Illinois. 2017. (ENG.). (J). pap. 16.95 *(978-0-9983282-2-5(7))* Hilton Publishing Co.

Tracy, Kathleen. The Historic Fight for the 2008 Democratic Presidential Nomination: The Clinton View. 2009. (Monumental Milestones Ser.). (Illus.). 48p. (YA). (gr. 4-7). lib. bdg. 29.95 *(978-1-58415-731-1(3))* Mitchell Lane Pubs.

—The McCarthy Era. 2008. (Monumental Milestones Ser.). (Illus.). 48p. (YA). (gr. 4-7). lib. bdg. 29.95 *(978-1-58415-694-9(5))* Mitchell Lane Pubs.

Tukan, Jaytoe Anthony, Sr. United States Senators from North Carolina 1954 - 2008. 2003. per. 12.95 *(978-0-9665909-5-1(3))* Kalawantis Publishing Services, Inc.

Uschan, Michael V. Joe Biden, 1 vol. 2010. (People in the News Ser.). (ENG., Illus.). 104p. (J). (gr. 7-7). 41.03 *(978-1-4205-0260-2(3)*, 13a915de-0998-448b-a8be-f4c4cdd76705, Lucent Pr.) Greenhaven Publishing LLC.

Uschan, Michael V. & Devaney, Sherri. Barack Obama, 1 vol. 2009. (People in the News Ser.). (ENG.). 104p. (gr. 7-7). lib. bdg. 41.03 *(978-1-4205-0206-0(9)*, 0f599642-cdf7-4910-bdbf-993a8537a06a, Lucent Pr.) Greenhaven Publishing LLC.

Wagner, Heather Lehr. Barack Obama. 2008. (Black Americans of Achievement Legacy Edition Ser.). 104p. (gr. 6-12). pap. 11.95 *(978-1-60413-324-0(4)*, Checkmark Bks.) Infobase Holdings, Inc.

Warren, Andrea. Enemy Child: The Story of Norman Mineta, a Boy Imprisoned in a Japanese American Internment Camp During World War II. 2019. (Illus.). 224p. (J). (gr. 5). 22.99 *(978-0-8234-4151-8(2)*, Margaret Ferguson Books) Holiday Hse., Inc.

Watson, Marilyn Myrick. Barry Goldwater: State Greats Arizona. 2007. (Acacia Biographies Ser.). (Illus.). 28p. (J).

J K L

(gr. 4-7). per. 6.95 *(978-0-9790826-0-3(9))* Acacia Publishing, Inc.

—Bary Goldwater: State Greats Arizona. 2007. (Acacia Biographies Ser.). (Illus.). 28p. (J). (gr. 3-7). lib. bdg. 16.95 *(978-0-9788283-4-9(8))* Acacia Publishing, Inc.

Welch, Catherine A. Patrick Henry. 2006. (History Maker Bios Ser.). (Illus.). 48p. (J). (gr. 3-6). lib. bdg. 26.60 *(978-0-8225-5941-2(2)*, Lerner Pubns.) Lerner Publishing Group.

Wells, Catherine. Hillary Clinton. 2007. (Political Profiles Ser.). (Illus.). 112p. (YA). (gr. 5-9). lib. bdg. 27.95 *(978-1-59935-047-9(5))* Reynolds, Morgan Inc.

—John McCain. 2008. (Political Profiles Ser.). (Illus.). 112p. (YA). (gr. 5-9). lib. bdg. 27.95 *(978-1-59935-046-2(7))* Reynolds, Morgan Inc.

Wheeler, Jill C. Hillary Rodham Clinton. 2003. (Breaking Barriers Ser.). 64p. (gr. 3-8). lib. bdg. 27.07 *(978-1-57765-741-5(1)*, Abdo & Daughters) ABDO Publishing Co.

Winders, Richard Bruce. Davy Crockett: The Legend of the Wild Frontier. 2009. (Library of American Lives & Times Ser.). 112p. (gr. 5-5). 69.20 *(978-1-60853-476-0(6))* Rosen Publishing Group, Inc., The.

Winget, Mary Mueller. Gerald R. Ford. 2007. (Presidential Leaders Ser.). (Illus.). 112p. (J). (gr. 3-7). lib. bdg. 29.27 *(978-0-8225-1509-8(1)*, Twenty-First Century Bks.) Lerner Publishing Group.

Winter, Jonah. Barack. Ford, A. G., illus. 2010. (ENG.). 32p. (J). (gr. -1-2). pap. 8.99 *(978-0-06-170396-6(6)*, Tegen, Katherine Bks) HarperCollins Pubs.

Wood, Susan. Elizabeth Warren: Nevertheless, She Persisted. Green, Sarah, illus. 2018. (ENG.). 48p. (J). (gr. 1-4). 18.99 *(978-1-4197-3162-4(9)*, 1210001, Abrams Bks. for Young Readers) Abrams, Inc.

Woodward, Mac. Sam Houston: For Texas & the Union. 2009. (Library of American Lives & Times Ser.). 112p. (gr. 5-5). 69.20 *(978-1-60853-504-0(5))* Rosen Publishing Group, Inc., The.

LEGUMES

Here are entered works on those plants belonging to the family Leguminosae, the pods or seeds of which are edible for man or domestic animals, e.g. peas, beans, lentils, etc. treated collectively.

Cleary, Brian P. & Goneau, Martin. Black Beans & Lamb, Poached Eggs & Ham: What Is in the Meat & Beans Group? 2011. (Food Is CATegorical Ser.). pap. 45.32 *(978-0-7613-8349-9(2)*, Millbrook Pr.) Lerner Publishing Group.

Dilkes, D. H. Beans, Nuts, & Oils, 1 vol. 2011. (All about Good Foods We Eat Ser.). (ENG., Illus.). 24p. (gr. -1-1). pap. 10.35 *(978-1-59845-256-3(8)*, 1333a1ab-74ba-4448-97ee-77cbdc5f82ca, Enslow Publishing) Enslow Publishing, LLC.

Dunn, Mary R. A Bean's Life Cycle. 2017. (Explore Life Cycles Ser.). (ENG., Illus.). 24p. (J). (gr. -1-2). lib. bdg. 27.32 *(978-1-5157-7051-0(6)*, 135481, Capstone Pr.) Capstone.

Mattern, Joanne. Growing a Beanstalk for Jack. 2020. (Fairy Tale Science Ser.). (ENG., Illus.). 32p. (J). (gr. 2-3). pap. 9.95 *(978-1-64493-106-6(0)*, 1644931060); lib. bdg. 31.35 *(978-1-64493-027-4(7)*, 1644930277) North Star Editions. (Focus Readers).

Mitchell, Melanie S. Beans. 2005. (First Step Nonfiction Ser.). (Illus.). 24p. (gr. k-2). lib. bdg. 17.27 *(978-0-8225-4608-5(6))* Lerner Publishing Group.

Murray, Laura K. Bean. 2016. (Grow with Me Ser.). (ENG.). 32p. (J). (gr. 3-6). pap. 9.99 *(978-1-62832-161-6(X)*, 20865, Creative Paperbacks) Creative Co., The.

Peters, Katie. Let's Look at Beans. 2020. (Plant Life Cycles (Pull Ahead Readers — Nonfiction) Ser.). (ENG., Illus.). 16p. (J). (gr. -1-1). 27.99 *(978-1-5415-9024-3(4)*, fc461fad-9448-4dc4-b1a6-16c1491291fb, Lerner Pubns.) Lerner Publishing Group.

Royston, Angela. A Bean's Life. 2011. (ENG., Illus.). 24p. (J). pap. *(978-0-7787-7862-2(2))*; (gr. 3-6). *(978-0-7787-7840-0(1))* Crabtree Publishing Co.

Schwartz, David M. Bean. Kuhn, Dwight, photos by. (Life Cycles Ser.). (Illus.). 16p. (J). (gr. 1-3). pap. 2.99 *(978-1-57471-580-4(1)*, 3060) Creative Teaching Pr., Inc.

Shea, Therese. Watch Peas Grow. 2011. (Watch Plants Grow! Ser.). 24p. (gr. k-2). 69.20 *(978-1-4339-6157-1(1))* Stevens, Gareth Publishing LLLP.

Singer, Jane E. Soybeans. 2013. (Feeding the World Ser.: 8). (Illus.). 48p. (J). (gr. 4-18). 19.95 *(978-1-4222-2748-0(0))* Mason Crest.

LEIA, PRINCESS (FICTITIOUS CHARACTER)—FICTION

Barlow, Jeremy & Soriano, Carlo. Star Wars Adventures: Princess Leia & the Royal Ransom. 2011. (Star Wars Digests Ser.). (ENG., Illus.). 80p. (J). (gr. 3-8). 34.21 *(978-1-59961-902-6(4)*, 13750, Graphic Novels) Spotlight.

Charretier, Elsa & Jody Houser. Star Wars: Forces of Destiny. 2018. (Illus.). (J). lib. bdg. 24.50 *(978-0-606-41292-6(1))* Turtleback.

Landers, Ace. Empire Strikes Out. 2013. (LEGO Star Wars Chapter Bks.). lib. bdg. 14.75 *(978-0-606-31554-8(3))* Turtleback.

Wang, Jack & Wang, Holman. Star Wars Epic Yarns: Return of the Jedi. 2015. (ENG., Illus.). 24p. (J). (gr. -1 — 1). 9.95 *(978-1-4521-3500-7(2))* Chronicle Bks. LLC.

LEIF ERICSON, -APPROXIMATELY 1020

see Leiv Eiriksson, -approximately 1020

LEIGH-MALLORY, GEORGE HERBERT, 1886-1924

see Mallory, George, 1886-1924

LEISURE

see also Hobbies; Recreation

Barker, Geoff. Sports & Leisure Careers. 2010. (In the Workplace Ser.). 48p. (J). 35.65 *(978-1-60753-094-7(5))* Amicus Learning.

Barker, Geoff & Savery, Annabel. Sports & Leisure Careers. 2011. (Been There! Ser.). 32p. (gr. 3-6). lib. bdg. 31.35 *(978-1-59920-474-1(6))* Black Rabbit Bks.

Diwrnod i'r Brenin: Chwaraeon, Hamdden a Thwristiaeth Er 1900. 2005. *(978-1-902346-01-4(7))* Addysg Y Cyfryngau Cymru.

Emlyn, Non ap. Hamddena. 2005. (WEL., Illus.). 20p. pap. *(978-1-86085-603-7(9))* ICA Video.

—Hamddena: Llawlyfr i Athrawon. 2005. (WEL.). 28p. pap. *(978-1-86085-604-4(7))* ICA Video.

—Hamddena - Llyfr 1 Lefel 3/4. 2005. (WEL., Illus.). 20p. pap. *(978-1-86085-600-6(4))* ICA Video.

—Hamddena - Llyfr 3 Lefel 5/6. 2005. (WEL., Illus.). 20p. pap. *(978-1-86085-602-0(0))* ICA Video.

Jupo, Frank. Time to Spare: The Story of Man's Leisure Hours. 2011. 66p. 36.95 *(978-1-258-07710-5(8))* Literary Licensing, LLC.

Knapman, Timothy. Leisure & Entertainment since 1900: Band 13/Topaz (Collins Big Cat) 2016. (Collins Big Cat Ser.). (ENG.). 32p. (J). (gr. 2-3). pap. 10.99 *(978-0-00-816382-2(0))* HarperCollins Pubs. Ltd. GBR. Dist: Independent Pubs. Group.

Nardo, Don. Arts, Leisure, & Sport in Ancient Egypt. 2005. (Lucent Library of Historical Eras Ser.). (ENG., Illus.). 112p. (YA). (gr. 7-12). lib. bdg. 33.45 *(978-1-59018-706-7(7))* Cengage Gale.

Whittaker, Helen. How Toys Slide. 2012. (Toys & Forces Ser.). 32p. (gr. 1-4). lib. bdg. 28.50 *(978-1-59920-466-6(5))* Black Rabbit Bks.

Whittaker, Helen & Lewis, Helen. Leisure: Information & Projects to Reduce Your Environmental Footprint, 1 vol. MacInnes, Cat, illus. 2012. (Living Green Ser.). (ENG.). 32p. (gr. 4-4). 31.21 *(978-1-60870-575-7(7)*, 7aead22f-e713-4722-9c7a-e4d6f129c7c0) Cavendish Square Publishing LLC.

LEIV EIRIKSSON, -APPROXIMATELY 1020

Defries, Cheryl L. Leif Eriksson: Viking Explorer of the New World, 1 vol. 2009. (Great Explorers of the World Ser.). (ENG., Illus.). 112p. (gr. 6-7). lib. bdg. 35.93 *(978-1-59845-126-9(X)*, f7aabf72-a3ae-4c0d-a7a8-53f0a6f5ea26) Enslow Publishing, LLC.

Hyde, Natalie. Explore with Leif Eriksson. 2014. (Travel with the Great Explorers Ser.). (ENG., Illus.). 32p. (J). (gr. 4-5). *(978-0-7787-1427-9(6))* Crabtree Publishing Co.

Knudsen, Shannon. Leif Eriksson. Oldroyd, Mark, illus. 2005. (On My Own Biography Ser.). (ENG.). 48p. (gr. 2-4). (J). pap. 7.99 *(978-1-57505-828-3(6)*, 33194921-1e69-48b6-9e3e-3c60df1b5a8b, First Avenue Editions); lib. bdg. 25.26 *(978-1-57505-649-4(6)*, Carolrhoda Bks.) Lerner Publishing Group.

LEMMINGS

Pettiford, Rebecca. Collared Lemmings. 2019. (Animals of the Arctic Ser.). (ENG., Illus.). 24p. (J). (gr. k-3). lib. bdg. 26.95 *(978-1-62617-936-3(0)*, Blastoff! Readers) Bellwether Media.

Phillips, Dee. Collared Lemming. 2015. (Arctic Animals: Life Outside the Igloo Ser.). (ENG.). 24p. (J). (gr. -1-3). lib. bdg. 26.99 *(978-1-62724-528-9(6))* Bearport Publishing Co., Inc.

Slade, Suzanne. What If There Were No Lemmings? A Book about the Tundra Ecosystem, 1 vol. Schwartz, Carol, illus. 2010. (Food Chain Reactions Ser.). (ENG.). 24p. (J). (gr. 2-4). pap. 9.95 *(978-1-4048-6396-5(6)*, 114147); lib. bdg. 27.32 *(978-1-4048-6021-6(5)*, 102985) Capstone. (Picture Window Bks.).

LEMMINGS—FICTION

Dyckman, Ame. Read the Book, Lemmings! OHora, Zachariah, illus. 2017. (ENG.). 40p. (J). (gr. -1-3). 17.99 *(978-0-316-34348-0(X))* Little, Brown Bks. for Young Readers.

LEMON

Royston, Angela. Experiments with a Lemon. 2016. (One-Stop Science Ser.). 32p. (gr. 2-5). 31.35 *(978-1-62588-140-3(1)*, Smart Apple Media) Black Rabbit Bks.

LEMURS

Arnold, Quinn M. Slow Lorises. 2019. (Creatures of the Night Ser.). (ENG.). 24p. (J). (gr. 1-4). *(978-1-64026-120-4(6)*, 18949, Creative Education); pap. 8.99 *(978-1-62832-683-3(2)*, 18950, Creative Paperbacks) Creative Co., The.

Aronin, Miriam. Aye-Aye: An Evil Omen. 2016. (Uncommon Animals Ser.). (ENG., Illus.). 32p. (J). (gr. 2-7). pap. 7.99 *(978-1-944998-60-8(8))* Bearport Publishing Co., Inc.

Baicker, Karen. Lemurs. 2007. (J). *(978-1-59939-132-8(5)*, Reader's Digest Young Families, Inc.) Studio Fun International.

Bluemel Oldfield, Dawn. Aye-Aye. 2018. (Even Weirder & Cuter Ser.). (ENG.). 24p. (J). (gr. -1-3). 17.95 *(978-1-68402-468-1(4))* Bearport Publishing Co., Inc.

Buckingham, Suzanne. Meet the Ring-Tailed Lemur. 2009. (Scales & Tails Ser.). 24p. (gr. 2-3). 42.50 *(978-1-60852-985-8(1)*, PowerKids Pr.) Rosen Publishing Group, Inc., The.

Carr, Aaron. Lemur. 2014. (J). *(978-1-4896-2633-2(6))* Weigl Pubs., Inc.

Costain, Meredith. Lemur, 1 vol. Jackson-Carter, Stuart, illus. 2016. (Wild World Ser.). (ENG.). 32p. (J). (gr. 1-2). pap. 11.00 *(978-1-4994-8215-7(9)*, 8d965c22-aa9d-4dc7-bf9d-4dcdd1dbf2f8, Windmill Bks.) Rosen Publishing Group, Inc., The.

Delaney, Kate, et al. Lemurs, 1 vol. 2009. (Amazing Animals Ser.). (ENG.). 48p. (J). (gr. 3-5). pap. 11.50 *(978-1-4339-2124-7(3)*, c8f0dd80-297f-45a3-858f-4292f57c4eac, Gareth Stevens Learning Library); lib. bdg. 30.67 *(978-0-8368-9120-1(1)*, b44f75f3-b354-4f8c-b96e-05be8a8e5c67) Stevens, Gareth Publishing LLLP.

Gish, Melissa. Lemurs. 2017. (Living Wild Ser.). (ENG., Illus.). 48p. (J). (gr. 4-7). *(978-1-60818-830-7(2)*, 20195, Creative Education) Creative Co., The.

—Living Wild: Lemurs. 2017. (Living Wild Ser.). (ENG., Illus.). 48p. (J). (gr. 5-7). pap. 12.00 *(978-1-62832-433-4(3)*, 20196, Creative Paperbacks) Creative Co., The.

Gregory, Josh. Lemurs. 2016. (Nature's Children Ser.). (ENG., Illus.). 48p. (J). pap. 6.95 *(978-0-531-21937-9(2)*, Children's Pr.) Scholastic Library Publishing.

Jolly, Alison. Ny Aiay Ako: Ako the Aye-Aye. Rasamimanana, Hantanirina, tr. Ross, Deborah, illus. 2005. (MLA & ENG.). (J). 20.00 *(978-0-9766009-0-9(0))* Lemur Conservation Foundation.

Kalman, Bobbie. Baby Lemurs. 2010. (Fun to Learn about Baby Animals Ser.). (ENG.). 24p. (J). (gr. k-3). *(978-0-7787-4893-9(6))*; pap. *(978-0-7787-4898-4(7))* Crabtree Publishing Co.

Marino, Angie. Lemurs! Greene's 29 after school art students, K., illus. 2013. 46p. pap. 11.99 *(978-0-9892732-0-6(2))* Illustrate to Educate.

Markovics, Joyce. My Tail Is Long & Striped (Lemur) 2014. (Zoo Clues Ser.). 24p. (J). (gr. -1-3). lib. bdg. 26.99 *(978-1-62724-107-6(8))* Bearport Publishing Co., Inc.

Markovics, Joyce L. Mi Cola Es Larga y Rayada. 2015. (Pistas de Animales Ser.). (SPA.). 24p. (J). (gr. -1-3). lib. bdg. 26.99 *(978-1-62724-586-9(3))* Bearport Publishing Co., Inc.

Owen, Ruth. Ring-Tailed Lemurs, 1 vol., 1. 2013. (Dr. Bob's Amazing World of Animals Ser.). (ENG.). 32p. (J). (gr. 2-3). 31.27 *(978-1-4777-9040-3(3)*, 8d4b0b23-da93-4eb1-a7a4-3bf25e248f17, Windmill Bks.) Rosen Publishing Group, Inc., The.

Owings, Lisa. Aye-Aye. 2014. (Extremely Weird Animals Ser.). (ENG., Illus.). 24p. (J). (gr. 3-8). lib. bdg. 27.95 *(978-1-62617-073-5(8)*, Pilot Bks.) Bellwether Media.

Phillips, Dee. Flying Lemur. 2013. (Science Slam: Treed-Animal Life in the Trees Ser.). 24p. (J). (gr. -1-3). lib. bdg. 26.99 *(978-1-61772-911-9(6))* Bearport Publishing Co., Inc.

Riley, Joelle. Ring-Tailed Lemurs. 2009. (Early Bird Nature Bks.). (ENG.). 48p. (gr. 2-5). 26.60 *(978-0-8225-9434-5(X)*, Lerner Pubns.) Lerner Publishing Group.

Schuetz, Kari. Lemurs. 2013. (Animal Safari Ser.). (ENG., Illus.). 24p. (J). (gr. k-3). lib. bdg. 26.95 *(978-1-60014-865-1(4)*, Blastoff! Readers) Bellwether Media.

Storm, Marysa. Ring-Tailed Lemurs. 2020. (Awesome Animal Lives Ser.). (ENG.). 24p. (J). (gr. k-3). pap. 8.99 *(978-1-64466-104-8(7)*, 14411, Bolt Jr.) Black Rabbit Bks.

Terp, Gail. Ring-Tailed Lemurs. 2017. (Wild Animal Kingdom Ser.). (ENG., (J). (gr. 4-7). Illus.). 31p. pap. 9.95 *(978-1-68072-488-2(6))*; 32p. pap. 9.99 *(978-1-64466-225-0(6)*, 11503); (Illus.). 32p. lib. bdg. *(978-1-68072-190-4(9)*, 10565) Black Rabbit Bks. (Bolt).

Thomas, K. Clyde the Long Fingered Lemur. 2013. (ENG.). (J). pap. 9.99 *(978-1-4675-2874-0(9))* Independent Pub.

LEMURS—FICTION

Colfer, Eoin. The Time Paradox. 2009. (Artemis Fowl Ser.: 6). (J). lib. bdg. 19.65 *(978-0-606-10579-8(4))* Turtleback.

Cousins, Lucy. Jazzy in the Jungle. Cousins, Lucy, illus. 2013. (ENG., Illus.). 32p. (J). (-k). 17.99 *(978-0-7636-6806-8(0))* Candlewick Pr.

Dennard, Deborah. Lemur Landing: A Story of a Madagascan Dry Tropical Forest. Kest, Kristin, illus. 2005. (Wild Habitats Ser.). (ENG.). 32p. (J). (gr. 1-4). 19.95 *(978-1-56899-980-7(1))* Soundprints.

Dennard, Deborah & Kest, Kristin. Lemur Landing: A Story of a Madagascan Dry Tropical Forest. 2005. (Wild Habitats Ser.). (ENG., Illus.). 32p. (J). (gr. 1-4). pap. 6.95 *(978-1-56899-979-1(8)*, S7019) Soundprints.

Dicmas, Courtney. Lemur Dreamer. Dicmas, Courtney, illus. 2018. (Illus.). (J). 12.99 *(978-1-61067-767-7(6))* Kane Miller.

Morrison Walton, Jeannie. The Little Lemur, a Fable of Pride. 2009. 32p. pap. 12.99 *(978-1-4389-8090-4(6))* AuthorHouse.

Preston-Gannon, Frann. How to Lose a Lemur. 2016. (ENG., Illus.). 30p. (J). (gr. -1 — 1). bds. 6.95 *(978-1-4549-2095-3(5))* Sterling Publishing Co., Inc.

LENIN, VLADIMIR ILICH, 1870-1924

Goldstein, Margaret J. V. I. Lenin. 2007. (Biography Ser.). (Illus.). 112p. (J). (gr. 3-7). lib. bdg. 29.27 *(978-0-8225-5977-1(3)*, Twenty-First Century Bks.) Lerner Publishing Group.

Joihnson, Robert, compiled by. Lenin, Stalin & Communist Russia: The Myth & Reality of Communism. 2003. (Studymates Ser.). (Illus.). 132p. (C). pap. 27.50 *(978-1-84285-039-8(3))* GLMP Ltd. GBR. Dist: Chicago Distribution Ctr.

Schmermund, Elizabeth & Edwards, Judith. Vladimir Lenin & the Russian Revolution, 1 vol. 2015. (People & Events That Changed the World Ser.). (ENG., Illus.). 128p. (gr. 7-8). 38.93 *(978-0-7660-7414-9(5)*, d258c502-f6ad-49b2-a0ec-49c69ee3ba93) Enslow Publishing, LLC.

LENSES

Allman, Toney. From Octopus Eyes to Powerful Lenses, 1 vol. 2006. (Imitating Nature Ser.). (ENG., Illus.). 32p. (gr. 3-6). lib. bdg. 28.88 *(978-0-7377-3631-1(3)*, 13af9fff-1269-4817-bcb6-15cb16cb2077, KidHaven Publishing) Greenhaven Publishing LLC.

I Spy! Individual Title Six-Packs. (Bookweb Ser.). 32p. (gr. 3-18). 34.00 *(978-0-7635-3948-1(1))* Rigby Education.

Roberts, Abigail B. Using Lenses, 1 vol. 2017. (Super Science Tools Ser.). (ENG.). 24p. (J). (gr. 1-2). pap. 9.15 *(978-1-4824-6389-7(X)*, 06ccbcb4-5d77-4834-bb28-a783df8cfefc) Stevens, Gareth Publishing LLLP.

Sévigny, Eric, illus. The Jungle Explorer. 2010. (Clubhouse Ser.). (ENG.). 24p. (J). (gr. -1-1). pap. 3.99 *(978-2-89450-724-7(0))* Caillouet, Gerry.

Williams, Brian. The Science of a Pair of Glasses, 1 vol. 2009. (Science Of... Ser.). (ENG., Illus.). 32p. (YA). (gr. 4-5). lib. bdg. 28.67 *(978-1-4339-0044-0(0)*, 31f40d75-9525-4c30-8af8-0b5b56cd1ff5) Stevens, Gareth Publishing LLLP.

LEONARDO, DA VINCI, 1452-1519

Agrimbau, Diego & Aballay, Diego. Leonardo Da Vinci. Trusted Translations, Trusted, tr. 2017. (Graphic Lives Ser.). (ENG., Illus.). 80p. (J). (gr. 3-9). lib. bdg. 32.65 *(978-1-5157-9163-8(7)*, 136605, Capstone Pr.) Capstone.

Anderson, Maxine. Amazing Leonardo Da Vinci Inventions: You Can Build Yourself. 2006. (Build It Yourself Ser.). (Illus.). 128p. (J). (gr. 3-7). pap. 15.95 *(978-0-9749344-2-6(9)*, 18fa9126-fd2c-4938-afe1-1738ffa9ce49) Nomad Pr.

Bailey, Gerry & Foster, Karen. Leonardo's Pallete. Radford, Karen & Noyes, Leighton, illus. 2008. (Stories of Great People Ser.). (ENG.). 40p. (J). (gr. 3-8). lib. bdg. *(978-0-7787-3687-5(3))* Crabtree Publishing Co.

Brasch, Nicholas. Leonardo Da Vinci, 1 vol. 2013. (Discovery Education: Discoveries & Inventions Ser.). (ENG.). 32p. (J). (gr. 4-5). 28.93 *(978-1-4777-1330-3(1)*, ea95200d-a82b-4e89-b3c2-9514b425abf7, PowerKids Pr.) Rosen Publishing Group, Inc., The.

—Leonardo Da Vinci: The Greatest Inventor. 2013. (Discovery Education: Discoveries & Inventions Ser.). 32p. (J). (gr. 3-6). pap. 60.00 *(978-1-4777-1503-1(7)*, PowerKids Pr.) Rosen Publishing Group, Inc., The.

Brasch, Nicolas. Leonardo Da Vinci: The Greatest Inventor, 1 vol. 2013. (Discovery Education: Discoveries & Inventions Ser.). (ENG., Illus.). 32p. (J). (gr. 4-5). pap. 11.00 *(978-1-4777-1502-4(9)*, 3020c0f3-c19e-4c49-91d5-84e39db0f080, PowerKids Pr.) Rosen Publishing Group, Inc., The.

Byrd, Robert. Leonardo, the Beautiful Dreamer. Byrd, Robert, illus. 2003. (Illus.). 48p. (J). (gr. 2-5). 17.99 *(978-0-525-47033-5(6)*, Dutton Books for Young Readers) Penguin Young Readers Group.

Cashin, John. Leonardo Da Vinci, Vol. 11. 2018. (Scientists & Their Discoveries Ser.). (Illus.). 96p. (J). (gr. 7). lib. bdg. 34.60 *(978-1-4222-4032-8(0))* Mason Crest.

Ciovacco, Justine. Leonardo Da Vinci, 1 vol. 2014. (Britannica Beginner Bios Ser.). (ENG., Illus.). 32p. (J). (gr. 2-3). 26.06 *(978-1-62275-677-3(0)*, 0c6a37f7-5c23-4479-9483-d8fa300ed764, Britannica Educational Publishing) Rosen Publishing Group, Inc., The.

Conklin, Wendy. 16th Century Superstar: Da Vinci. 2nd rev. ed. 2017. (TIME(r): Informational Text Ser.). (ENG., Illus.). 32p. (gr. 6-8). pap. 13.99 *(978-1-4938-3630-7(7))* Teacher Created Materials, Inc.

—16th Century Superstar: Da Vinci. 2017. (Time for Kids Nonfiction Readers Ser.). lib. bdg. 19.65 *(978-0-606-40291-0(8))* Turtleback.

Dickins, Rosie & Ball, Karen. Leonardo Da Vinci. Unzner, Christa, illus. 2007. (Famous Lives Gift Bks). 63p. (J). (gr. 4-7). 8.99 *(978-0-7945-1594-2(0)*, Usborne) EDC Publishing.

Edwards, Roberta. Who Was Leonardo da Vinci? Kelley, True, illus. 2005. (Who Was... ? Ser.). 106p. (J). (gr. 2-6). 12.65 *(978-0-7569-6971-4(9))* Perfection Learning Corp.

Gruener, Nina. Jackie & Mona Lisa: How the First Lady of the United States Shared the First Lady of Art with a Nation. Smith, Heidi, illus. 2019. (J). *(978-1-338-16233-2(0)*, Orchard Bks.) Scholastic, Inc.

Hall, M. C. Leonardo Da Vinci, 1 vol. 2007. (Essential Lives Set 1 Ser.). (ENG., Illus.). 112p. (YA). (gr. 6-12). lib. bdg. 41.36 *(978-1-59928-844-4(3)*, 6641, Essential Library) ABDO Publishing Co.

Harris, Godfrey & Brockwell, Maurice Walter. The Life & Contributions of Leonardo Da Vinci. 2006. (ENG., Illus.). 58p. (J). pap. *(978-0-935047-60-8(3))* Americas Group, The.

Hawcock, David. Leonardo Da Vinci: Incredible Machines. 2019. (Dover Science for Kids Ser.). (ENG., Illus.). 24p. 24.95 *(978-0-486-83236-4(8)*, 832368) Dover Pubns., Inc.

January, Brendan. Leonardo Da Vinci: Renaissance Painter. 2013. (People of Importance Ser.: 21). (Illus.). 32p. (J). (gr. 4-18). 19.95 *(978-1-4222-2848-7(7))* Mason Crest.

Kalz, Jill. The Mona Lisa. 2004. (What in the World? Ser.). (Illus.). 48p. 19.95 *(978-1-58341-272-5(7)*, Creative Education) Creative Co., The.

Kennon, Caroline. Leonardo Da Vinci in His Own Words, 1 vol. 2015. (Eyewitness to History Ser.). (ENG.). 32p. (J). (gr. 4-5). pap. 11.50 *(978-1-4824-4074-4(1)*, d1c607ef-02d8-4160-a02b-5560c7538834) Stevens, Gareth Publishing LLLP.

Koestler-Grack, Rachel A. Leonardo Da Vinci: Renaissance Man. 2005. (Makers of the Middle Ages & Renaissance Ser.). (ENG., Illus.). 152p. (gr. 5-8). lib. bdg. 32.95 *(978-0-7910-8626-1(7)*, P114342, Facts On File) Infobase Holdings, Inc.

Krull, Kathleen. Leonardo Da Vinci. Kulikov, Boris, illus. 2005. (Giants of Science Ser.). (ENG.). 124p. (J). (gr. 5-9). 18.69 *(978-0-670-05920-1(X)*, Viking) Penguin Publishing Group.

—Leonardo Da Vinci. Kulikov, Boris, illus. 2008. (Giants of Science Ser.). 128p. (J). (gr. 3-7). 7.99 *(978-0-14-240821-6(2)*, Puffin Books) Penguin Young Readers Group.

Kuligowski, Stephanie. Leonardo Da Vinci: Renaissance Artist & Inventor, 1 vol. rev. ed. 2012. (Social Studies: Informational Text Ser.). (ENG.). 32p. (gr. 4-8). pap. 11.99 *(978-1-4333-5008-5(4))* Teacher Created Materials, Inc.

Lebscky, Ibi. Leonardo. Cardoni, Paolo, illus. (Coleccion Seran Famosos).Tr. of Little Leonardo de Vinci. (SPA.). 28p. (J). (gr. 2-4). 10.36 *(978-84-233-1399-0(9))* Ediciones Destino ESP. Dist: Lectorum Pubns., Inc.

Leidtke, Amy. Leonardo's Art Workshop: Invent, Create, & Make STEAM Projects Like a Genius. 2018. (Leonardo's Workshop Ser.). (ENG., Illus.). 144p. (J). (gr. 5-8). pap. 22.99 *(978-1-63159-522-6(9)*, 303402, Rockport Publishers) Quarto Publishing Group USA.

Leonardo & Harris, Godfrey. Leonardo's "Quotebook" Thoughts by & about Leonardo Da Vinci. 2006. (ENG.). 104p. (J). pap. *(978-0-935047-57-8(3))* Americas Group, The.

Leoni, Maria Teresa Zanobini. Leonardo Da Vinci. 2005. (Great Artists Ser.). (Illus.). 40p. (J). (gr. 5). per. 7.95 *(978-1-59270-048-6(9))* Enchanted Lion Bks., LLC.

Malam, John. Leonardo Da Vinci: El Genio Que Definio el Renacimiento. P. López, Wendy, tr. from ENG. 2007. (Altea Biografías Ser.).Tr. of Leonardo da Vinci. (SPA., Illus.). 64p. (J). (gr. -1-3). 17.99 *(978-84-372-2467-1(5))* Altea, Ediciones, S.A. - Grupo Santillana ESP. Dist: Santillana USA Publishing Co., Inc.

Meltzer, Brad. I Am Leonardo Da Vinci. Eliopoulos, Christopher, illus. 2020. (Ordinary People Change the World Ser.). 40p. (J). (gr. k-4). 16.99 *(978-0-525-55588-9(9)*, Dial Bks) Penguin Young Readers Group.

Nardo, Don. Leonardo Da Vinci, 1 vol. 2012. (Eye on Art Ser.). (ENG., Illus.). 112p. (gr. 7-7). lib. bdg. 41.03 *(978-1-4205-0735-5(4)*, 7ed900e8-2ba4-4c61-9cac-bf63b1dd0656, Lucent Pr.) Greenhaven Publishing LLC.

Nichols, Catherine. Leonardo Da Vinci, 1 vol. 2005. (Primary Source Library of Famous Artists Ser.). (ENG., Illus.). 32p. (J). (gr. 3-4). lib. bdg. 27.60 *(978-1-4042-2762-0(8)*, 75695994-479b-4ca3-a08b-bef4d09cabba, PowerKids Pr.) Rosen Publishing Group, Inc., The.

—Leonardo da Vinci. 2009. (Primary Source Library of Famous Artists Ser.). 32p. (gr. 3-4). 42.50 *(978-1-60854-101-0(0)*, PowerKids Pr.) Rosen Publishing Group, Inc., The.

Novelli, Luca. Leonardo Da Vinci & the Pen That Drew the Future. 2017. (Flashes of Genius Ser.). (ENG., Illus.). 112p.

(J). (gr. 3). pap. 9.99 *(978-1-61373-869-6(2))* Chicago Review Pr., Inc.

Olinger, Heidi. Leonardo's Science Workshop: Invent, Create, & Make STEAM Projects Like a Genius. 2019. (Leonardo's Workshop Ser.). (ENG., Illus.). 144p. (J). (gr. 5-8). pap. 22.99 *(978-1-63159-524-0(5)*, 304041, Rockport Publishers) Quarto Publishing Group USA.

Orr, Tamra B. Leonardo Da Vinci: Renaissance Genius, 1 vol. 2018. (Eye on Art Ser.). (ENG.). 104p. (gr. 7-7). pap. 20.99 *(978-1-5345-6531-9(0)*, ace4da44-5913-43f9-8194-1dcabd94c49c, Lucent Pr.) Greenhaven Publishing LLC.

Osborne, Mary Pope & Boyce, Natalie Pope. Leonardo Da Vinci: A Nonfiction Companion to Magic Tree House Merlin Mission #10: Monday with a Mad Genius. Murdocca, Sal, illus. 2009. (Magic Tree House (R) Fact Tracker Ser.: 19). 128p. (J). (gr. 2-5). 6.99 *(978-0-375-84665-6(4)*, Random Hse. Bks. for Young Readers) Random Hse. Children's Bks.

—Leonardo Da Vinci: A Nonfiction Companion to Monday with a Mad Genius. 2009. (Magic Tree House Fact Tracker Ser.: 19). lib. bdg. 16.00 *(978-0-606-01834-0(4))* Turtleback.

Phillips, Cynthia & Priwer, Shana. 101 Things You Didn't Know about Da Vinci: Inventions, Intrigue, & Unfinished Works. 2018. (101 Things Ser.). (ENG., Illus.). 256p. pap. 14.99 *(978-1-5072-0659-1(3))* Adams Media Corp.

Phillips, John. World History Biographies: Leonardo Da Vinci: The Genius Who Defined the Renaissance. 2008. (National Geographic World History Biographies Ser.). (Illus.). 64p. (J). (gr. 3-7). pap. 7.99 *(978-1-4263-0248-0(7)*, National Geographic Kids) Disney Publishing Worldwide.

Raynham, Alex. Leonardo Da Vinci. 3rd ed. 2013. (Illus.). 64p. pap. 11.00 *(978-0-19-423670-6(6))* Oxford Univ. Pr., Inc.

Rinaldo, Denise. Leonardo Da Vinci: With a Discussion of Imagination. 2003. (Values in Action Ser.). (J). *(978-1-59203-066-8(1))* Learning Challenge, Inc.

Rockett, Paul. Leonardo Da Vinci, 1 vol., 1. 2015. (Inspiring Artists Ser.). (ENG.). 48p. (J). (gr. 7-7). 33.47 *(978-1-5081-7054-9(1)*, 7a67d0ef-0d9c-4029-9c65-6e68eac634ea, Rosen Young Adult) Rosen Publishing Group, Inc., The.

Romeo, Francesca. Leonardo Da Vinci. 2008. (Art Masters Ser.). 64p. (YA). (gr. 6-18). lib. bdg. 24.95 net. *(978-1-934545-00-3(7))* Oliver Pr., Inc.

Rossi, Renzo. In Renaissance Florence with Leonardo, 1 vol. 2009. (Come See My City Ser.). (ENG., Illus.). 48p. (gr. 4-4). lib. bdg. 31.21 *(978-0-7614-4329-2(0)*, cc58e45d-3aa0-44a8-8fb1-fe5c4d3ee51c) Cavendish Square Publishing LLC.

Stanley, George E. Leonardo Da Vinci: Young Artist, Writer, & Inventor. 2005. (Childhood of World Figures Ser.). (ENG.). 176p. (J). (gr. 3-7). pap. 6.99 *(978-1-4169-0570-7(7)*, Simon & Schuster/Paula Wiseman Bks.) Simon & Schuster/Paula Wiseman Bks.

Strom, Laura Layton. Shockwave: Leonardo Da Vinci. 2007. (Shockwave: Life Stories Ser.). (ENG., Illus.). 36p. (J). (gr. 3-5). 25.00 *(978-0-531-17771-6(8)*, Children's Pr.) Scholastic Library Publishing.

Thomas, Isabel. Little Guides to Great Lives: Leonardo Da Vinci. Spitzer, Katja, illus. 2018. (Little Guides to Great Lives Ser.). (ENG.). 64p. (J). (gr. 2-6). 11.99 *(978-1-78627-188-4(5)*, King, Laurence Publishing) Orion Publishing Group, Ltd. GBR. Dist: Hachette Bk. Group.

Tracy, Kathleen. Leonardo Da Vinci. 2008. (Art Profiles for Kids Ser.). (Illus.). 48p. (YA). (gr. 4-7). lib. bdg. 29.95 *(978-1-58415-711-3(9))* Mitchell Lane Pubs.

Venezia, Mike. Leonardo Da Vinci (Revised Edition) (Getting to Know the World's Greatest Artists) Venezia, Mike, illus. rev. ed. 2015. (Getting to Know the World's Greatest Artists Ser.). (ENG., Illus.). 40p. (J). (gr. 3-4). pap. 7.95 *(978-0-531-21289-9(0)*, Children's Pr.) Scholastic Library Publishing.

Vinci, Leonardo Da & Benchmark Education Co. Staff. The Da Vinci Notebooks. 2014. (Text Connections Ser.). (J). (gr. 5). *(978-1-4900-1370-1(9))* Benchmark Education Co.

Williams, Colleen Madonna Flood. My Adventure with Leonardo da Vinci. 2009. (ENG.). 44p. (J). 8.99 *(978-1-59092-458-7(4))* Blue Forge Pr.

Wood, Alix. Leonardo Da Vinci, 1 vol. 2013. (Artists Through the Ages Ser.). (ENG., Illus.). 32p. (J). (gr. 2-3). pap. 11.00 *(978-1-61533-629-6(X)*, 00ee068c-79c2-43cb-a1c3-64c5b82f9993); lib. bdg. 29.93 *(978-1-61533-621-0(4)*, 4dfe0b66-1936-4431-ac2f-9a3f52312cac) Rosen Publishing Group, Inc., The. (Windmill Bks.).

Zaczek, Iain. Leonardo Da Vinci, 1 vol. 2014. (Great Artists Ser.). (ENG.). 32p. (J). (gr. 4-4). pap. 11.50 *(978-1-4824-1214-7(4)*, 2455baf2-62e8-450a-b795-db93428fb787) Stevens, Gareth Publishing LLLP.

Zanobini Leoni, Maria Teresa. Leonardo Da Vinci. 2003. (Great Artists Ser.). (Illus.). 40p. (J). 15.95 *(978-1-59270-007-3(1))* Enchanted Lion Bks., LLC.

LEONARDO, DA VINCI, 1452-1519—FICTION

Duey, Kathleen. Leonardo. Epstein, Eugene, illus. 2009. (Time Soldiers Ser.). (ENG.). (J). (gr. k-2). 95p. 9.95 *(978-1-929945-89-4(2))*;Bk. 8. 48p. 15.95 *(978-1-929945-88-7(4))* Big Guy Bks., Inc.

Elliott, L. M. Da Vinci's Tiger. 2017. (ENG.). 320p. (YA). (gr. 8). pap. 9.99 *(978-0-06-074426-7(X)*, Tegen, Katherine Bks) HarperCollins Pubs.

Elliott, Laura Malone. Da Vinci's Tiger. 2015. (ENG.). 304p. (YA). (gr. 8). 17.99 *(978-0-06-074424-3(3)*, Tegen, Katherine Bks) HarperCollins Pubs.

Friedlander, Mark P., Jr. Innovators in Action! Leonardo Da Vinci Gets a Do-Over. Sakprayoonpong, Worachet Boon, illus. 2014. (Innovators in Action Ser.: 1). 208p. (J). (gr. 5-9). pap. 12.95 *(978-0-9678020-6-0(7))* Science, Naturally!

Grey, Christopher. Leonardo's Shadow: Or, My Astonishing Life As Leonardo Da Vinci's Servant. 2008. (ENG.). 400p. (YA). (gr. 7). pap. 13.99 *(978-1-4169-0544-8(8)*, Atheneum Bks. for Young Readers) Simon & Schuster Children's Publishing.

Kelley, J. Patrick. The Stolen Smile. Kelley, Gary, illus. 2nd ed. 2015. (ENG.). 40p. (J). (gr. 2-4). 16.99 *(978-1-56846-281-3(6)*, 21102, Creative Editions) Creative Co., The.

Konigsburg, E. L. The Second Mrs. Giaconda. 3rd ed. (J). pap. 4.95 *(978-0-13-800061-5(1))* Prentice Hall (Schl. Div.).

Mayhew, James. Katie: Katie & the Mona Lisa. 2016. (Katie Ser.). (ENG., Illus.). 32p. (J). (gr. -1-k). pap. 10.99 *(978-1-4083-3194-1(2)*, Orchard Bks.) Hachette Children's Group GBR. Dist: Hachette Bk. Group.

McCarthy, Meghan. Steal Back the Mona Lisa! McCarthy, Meghan, illus. 2006. (ENG., Illus.). 40p. (J). (gr. -1-3). 16.00 *(978-0-15-205368-0(9)*, 1196166, Clarion Bks.) HarperCollins Pubs.

Napoli, Donna Jo. The Smile. 2009. 272p. (YA). (gr. 7-18). 7.99 *(978-0-14-241492-7(1)*, Speak) Penguin Young Readers Group.

Osborne, Mary Pope. Monday with a Mad Genius. Murdocca, Sal, illus. 2009. (Magic Tree House (R) Merlin Mission Ser.: 10). 144p. (J). (gr. 2-5). 5.99 *(978-0-375-83730-2(2)*, Random Hse. Bks. for Young Readers) Random Hse. Children's Bks.

—Monday with a Mad Genius. 2009. (Magic Tree House Merlin Missions Ser.: 10). lib. bdg. 16.00 *(978-0-606-01777-0(1))* Turtleback.

Osborne, Mary Pope, et al. Un Lunes con un Genio Loco. Murdocca, Sal, illus. 2018. (SPA.). 132p. (J). (gr. 2-4). pap. 6.99 *(978-1-63245-681-6(8))* Lectorum Pubns., Inc.

Pryor, Michael. Leo Da Vinci vs the Ice-Cream Domination League. Faber, Jules, illus. 2015. (Leo Da Vinci Ser.). 192p. (J). (gr. 4-7). 8.99 *(978-0-85798-837-9(9))* Random Hse. Australia AUS. Dist: Independent Pubs. Group.

Scieszka, Jon. Da Wild, Da Crazy, Da Vinci. McCauley, Adam, illus. 2006. (Time Warp Trio Ser.: No. 14). 72p. (gr. 4-7). 15.00 *(978-0-7569-6677-5(9))* Perfection Learning Corp.

—Da Wild, Da Crazy, Da Vinci #14, No. 14. McCauley, Adam, illus. 2006. (Time Warp Trio Ser.: 14). 96p. (J). (gr. 2-4). 5.99 *(978-0-14-240465-2(9)*, Puffin Books) Penguin Young Readers Group.

Wurge, B. B. The Last Notebook of Leonardo. 2010. (LeapKids Ser.). (ENG., Illus.). 154p. (J). (gr. 1-7). pap. 9.95 *(978-1-935248-14-9(6))* Leapfrog Pr.

LEOPARD

Anderson, Justin. Snow Leopard: Ghost of the Mountains. Benson, Patrick, illus. 2019. (ENG.). 32p. (J). (gr. k-3). 16.99 *(978-1-5362-0540-4(0))* Candlewick Pr.

Archer, Claire. Leopards, 1 vol. 2014. (Big Cats Ser.). (ENG.). 24p. (J). (gr. -1-2). lib. bdg. 32.79 *(978-1-62970-003-8(7)*, 1226, Abdo Kids) ABDO Publishing Co.

Bodden, Valerie. Snow Leopards. 2018. (Amazing Animals Ser.). (ENG., Illus.). 24p. (J). (gr. 1-3). pap. 9.99 *(978-1-62832-500-3(3)*, 23064, Creative Paperbacks) Creative Co., The.

Borgert-Spaniol, Megan. Leopards. 2012. (Animal Safari Ser.). (ENG., Illus.). 24p. (J). (gr. k-3). lib. bdg. 26.95 *(978-1-60014-769-2(0)*, Blastoff! Readers) Bellwether Media.

—Snow Leopards. 2014. (Animal Safari Ser.). (ENG.). 24p. (J). (gr. k-3). lib. bdg. 26.95 *(978-1-60014-968-9(5)*, Blastoff! Readers) Bellwether Media.

Bowman, Donna H. Big Cats. Wald, Christina, illus. 2008. (ENG.). 24p. (J). (gr. 3-18). 19.95 *(978-1-58117-781-7(X)*, Intervisual/Piggy Toes) Bendon, Inc.

Carr, Aaron. Snow Leopard. 2014. (J). *(978-1-4896-2641-7(7))* Weigl Pubs., Inc.

Chang, Kirsten. Cheetah or Leopard? 2019. (Spotting Differences Ser.). (ENG., Illus.). 24p. (J). (gr. k-3). lib. bdg. 26.95 *(978-1-64487-033-4(9)*, Blastoff! Readers) Bellwether Media.

Dibble, Traci. Leopards. 2011. (Predator Animals Ser.). 16p. pap. 39.62 *(978-1-61541-372-0(3))*; (ENG.). (J). pap. 9.60 *(978-1-61541-371-3(5))* American Reading Co.

Dibble, Traci & Sánchez, Lucia M. Leopardos: Leopards. 2011. (1-3A Animales Ser.). (SPA.). 16p. (J). (gr. k-2). pap. 9.60 *(978-1-61541-373-7(1))* American Reading Co.

Dibble, Traci & Sanchez, Lucia M. Leopardos (Leopards) 2011. (Animales depredadores Ser.). (SPA.). 16p. pap. 39.62 *(978-1-61541-374-4(X))* American Reading Co.

Ellis, Carol. Leopards, 1 vol. 2010. (Endangered! Ser.). (ENG.). 48p. (gr. 3-3). lib. bdg. 32.64 *(978-0-7614-4052-9(6)*, 314cdb75-6c1a-459f-834a-3d11951a8230) Cavendish Square Publishing LLC.

Esbaum, Jill. Explore My World Snow Leopards. 2014. (Explore My World Ser.). (Illus.). 32p. (J). (gr. -1-k). pap. 4.99 *(978-1-4263-1703-3(4)*, National Geographic Kids) Disney Publishing Worldwide.

Gish, Melissa. Leopards. 2010. (Living Wild Ser.). (ENG.). 48p. (J). (gr. 5-8). pap. 12.00 *(978-0-89812-555-9(3)*, 22211, Creative Paperbacks) Creative Co., The.

—Living Wild - Leopards. 2010. (Living Wild Ser.). 46p. (YA). (gr. 5-18). 23.95 *(978-1-58341-972-4(1)*, Creative Education) Creative Co., The.

—Snow Leopards. (Living Wild Ser.). (ENG., Illus.). 48p. (J). (gr. 4-7). 2017. pap. 12.00 *(978-1-62832-306-1(X)*, 20630, Creative Paperbacks) 2016. *(978-1-60818-710-2(1)*, 20632, Creative Education) Creative Co., The.

Goldsworthy, Steve. Leopards. 2014. (J). *(978-1-4896-0922-9(9))* Weigl Pubs., Inc.

Green, Jen. Leopards. 2009. (Illus.). 52p. (J). *(978-0-7172-8027-8(6))* Grolier, Ltd.

—Snow Leopards: Band 11 Lime/Band 12 Copper (Collins Big Cat Progress) 2014. (Collins Big Cat Progress Ser.). (ENG., Illus.). 32p. (J). (gr. 2-3). pap. 10.99 *(978-0-00-751932-3(X))* HarperCollins Pubs. Ltd. GBR. Dist: Independent Pubs. Group.

Greenberg, Daniel A. Leopards, 1 vol. 2003. (Animals, Animals Ser.). (ENG., Illus.). 48p. (gr. 5-5). 32.64 *(978-0-7614-1448-3(7)*, 1dea7855-6813-4643-9d70-5f3d903a9571) Cavendish Square Publishing LLC.

Group/McGraw-Hill, Wright. Leopard Level: Adventure Journal Set. (Wildcats Ser.). (gr. 2-8). 31.95 *(978-0-322-05792-0(2))* Wright Group/McGraw-Hill.

—Leopard Level: Wildcats Leopard Complete Kit. (Wildcats Ser.). (gr. 2-8). 599.95 *(978-0-322-06485-0(6))* Wright Group/McGraw-Hill.

Herrington, Lisa M. Cheetahs & Leopards. 2015. (Rookie Read-About Science: What's the Difference? Ser.). (ENG., Illus.). 32p. (J). lib. bdg. 25.00 *(978-0-531-21481-7(8)*, Children's Pr.) Scholastic Library Publishing.

Kalman, Bobbie & Dyer, Hadley. Les Léopards. 2010. (Petit Monde Vivant Ser.). (FRE., Illus.). 32p. (J). pap. 9.95 *(978-2-89579-316-8(6))* Bayard Canada Livres CAN. Dist: Crabtree Publishing Co.

Landau, Elaine. Snow Leopards: Hunters of the Snow & Ice, 1 vol. 2010. (Animals of the Snow & Ice Ser.). (ENG., Illus.). 32p. (gr. 3-3). 26.60 *(978-0-7660-3463-1(1)*, 43124556-ac3a-4cb5-a9cf-001326db73a1) Enslow Publishing, LLC.

MacDonald, Lisa. Raising Clouded Leopards (Grade 3) rev. ed. 2018. (Smithsonian: Informational Text Ser.). (ENG., Illus.). 32p. (J). (gr. 3-4). pap. 11.99 *(978-1-4938-6676-2(1))* Teacher Created Materials, Inc.

Macheske, Felicia. Frosty Felines: Snow Leopard. 2017. (Guess What Ser.). (ENG., Illus.). 24p. (J). (gr. k-2). lib. bdg. 30.64 *(978-1-63472-174-5(8)*, 209268) Cherry Lake Publishing.

Macy, Carolyn. The Great Leopard Hunt. 2017. (ENG., Illus.). (J). 29.99 *(978-0-9989127-0-7(0))*; pap. 19.99 *(978-0-9988838-9-2(1))* Macy, Carolyn.

Maimone, Sofia. Snow Leopards in Danger, 1 vol. 2013. (Animals at Risk Ser.). 24p. (J). (gr. 2-3). (ENG.). pap. 9.15 *(978-1-4339-9175-2(6)*, c7654946-538a-4555-b5df-bf7aa7bd1007); pap. 48.90 *(978-1-4339-9176-9(4))*; (ENG., Illus.). lib. bdg. 25.27 *(978-1-4339-9174-5(8)*, a5649cc0-b528-4c80-befa-8b588d6bae87) Stevens, Gareth Publishing LLLP.

Markle, Sandra. The Great Leopard Rescue: Saving the Amur Leopards. 2016. (Sandra Markle's Science Discoveries Ser.). (ENG., Illus.). 48p. (J). (gr. 4-6). E-Book 47.99 *(978-1-4677-9755-9(3)*, Millbrook Pr.) Lerner Publishing Group.

—Snow School. Marks, Alan, illus. 2013. 32p. (J). (gr. -1-3). lib. bdg. 16.95 *(978-1-58089-410-4(0))* Charlesbridge Publishing, Inc.

Montgomery, Sy. Saving the Ghost of the Mountain: An Expedition among Snow Leopards in Mongolia. Bishop, Nic, photos by. (Scientists in the Field Ser.). (ENG., Illus.). 80p. (J). (gr. 5-7). 2012. pap. 10.99 *(978-0-547-72734-9(8)*, 1483153) 2009. 18.00 *(978-0-618-91645-0(8)*, 1014922) HarperCollins Pubs. (Clarion Bks.).

Newman, Aline Alexander. National Geographic Kids Chapters: Lucky Leopards! And More True Stories of Amazing Animal Rescues! 2014. (NGK Chapters Ser.). (Illus.). 112p. (J). (gr. 3-7). pap. 5.99 *(978-1-4263-1457-5(4)*, National Geographic Kids) Disney Publishing Worldwide.

Nuzzolo, Deborah. Leopards. 2010. (African Animals Ser.). (ENG.). 24p. (gr. k-1). pap. 41.70 *(978-1-4296-5081-6(8)*, Capstone Pr.) Capstone.

Prebeg, Rick. Night Cat. Prebeg, Rick, photos by. 2005. (Illus.). (J). *(978-1-933248-15-8(7))* World Quest Learning.

Raatma, Lucia. Nature's Children: Snow Leopards. 2013. (ENG.). 48p. (J). pap. 6.95 *(978-0-531-25160-7(8))* Scholastic Library Publishing.

—Snow Leopards. 2013. (ENG.). 48p. (J). 28.00 *(978-0-531-23362-7(6))* Scholastic Library Publishing.

Riggs, Kate. Amazing Animals: Leopards. 2012. (Amazing Animals Ser.). (ENG., Illus.). 24p. (J). (gr. 1-3). pap. 9.99 *(978-0-89812-695-2(9)*, 22095, Creative Paperbacks) Creative Co., The.

—Leopards. 2012. (Amazing Animals Ser.). (ENG., Illus.). 24p. (J). (gr. 1-4). 25.65 *(978-1-60818-110-0(3)*, 22090, Creative Education) Creative Co., The.

Rudolph, Jessica. Mi Pelambre Es Gruesa y Moteada. 2015. (Pistas de Animales Ser.). (SPA.). 24p. (J). (gr. -1-3). lib. bdg. 26.99 *(978-1-62724-581-4(2))* Bearport Publishing Co., Inc.

—My Fur Is Thick & Spotted (Snow Leopard) 2014. (Zoo Clues Ser.). 24p. (J). (gr. -1-3). lib. bdg. 26.99 *(978-1-62724-113-7(2))* Bearport Publishing Co., Inc.

Ryndak, Rob. Leopard or Jaguar?, 1 vol. 2015. (Animal Look-Alikes Ser.). (ENG., Illus.). 24p. (J). (gr. 1-2). pap. 9.15 *(978-1-4824-2720-2(6)*, 3c4a7be3-29bd-4c5c-ae24-8282504aba90) Stevens, Gareth Publishing LLLP.

Shaffer, Lindsay. Snow Leopards. 2019. (Animals of the Mountains Ser.). (ENG., Illus.). 24p. (J). (gr. k-3). lib. bdg. 26.95 *(978-1-64487-017-4(7)*, Blastoff! Readers) Bellwether Media.

Shores, Erika L. Snow Leopards, 1 vol. 2010. (Wildcats Ser.). (ENG.). 24p. (J). (gr. -1-2). lib. bdg. 27.32 *(978-1-4296-4483-9(4)*, 102955, Capstone Pr.) Capstone.

Silverman, Buffy. Can You Tell a Cheetah from a Leopard? 2011. (Animal Look-Alikes Ser.). pap. 45.32 *(978-0-7613-8384-0(0))*; (ENG., Illus.). 32p. (J). (gr. 1-3). pap. 9.99 *(978-0-7613-7847-1(2)*, 6012f227-d35d-4669-abbe-a48ed40df624) Lerner Publishing Group.

Simpson, Phillip. Life Cycle of a Leopard: A Sequence & Order Text, 1 vol. 2014. (Text Structures Ser.). (ENG.). 32p. (J). (gr. 1-3). pap. 7.99 *(978-1-4846-0416-8(4)*, 126584, Heinemann) Capstone.

Sommer, Nathan. Gorilla vs. Leopard. 2020. (Animal Battles Ser.). (ENG.). 24p. (J). (gr. 3-7). lib. bdg. 26.95 *(978-1-64487-156-0(4)*, Torque Bks.) Bellwether Media.

Terp, Gail. Is It a Cheetah or a Leopard? 2019. (Can You Tell the Difference? Ser.). (ENG.). 24p. (J). (gr. 2-4). pap. 9.99 *(978-1-64466-053-9(9)*, 12905); (Illus.). (gr. 4-6). lib. bdg. *(978-1-68072-898-9(9)*, 12904) Black Rabbit Bks. (Hi Jinx).

Vogel, Elizabeth. Leopards. 2009. (Big Cats (Powerkids Readers) Ser.). 24p. (gr. 1-1). 37.50 *(978-1-61511-569-3(2)*, PowerKids Pr.) Rosen Publishing Group, Inc., The.

Von Zumbusch, Amelie. Leopards: Silent Stalkers, 1 vol. 2007. (Dangerous Cats Ser.). (ENG., Illus.). 24p. (J). (gr. 2-3). lib. bdg. 26.27 *(978-1-4042-3633-2(3)*, f3cd00fa-ab59-420e-9a20-032fae390f05, PowerKids Pr.) Rosen Publishing Group, Inc., The.

von Zumbusch, Amelie. Leopards: Silent Stalkers. 2009. (Dangerous Cats Ser.). 24p. (gr. 2-3). 42.50 *(978-1-61512-128-1(5)*, PowerKids Pr.) Rosen Publishing Group, Inc., The.

Walden, Katherine. Leopards of the African Plains. 2009. (Safari Animals Ser.). 24p. (gr. 1-1). 42.50 *(978-1-60852-953-7(3))*; (ENG.). (J). lib. bdg. 26.27 *(978-1-4358-2690-8(6)*, 8860206d-bf28-41f2-bed5-b190b2e715ac); (ENG., Illus.). (J). pap. 9.25 *(978-1-4358-3064-6(4)*, b994f215-7810-4412-be2a-5e76df9ef646) Rosen Publishing Group, Inc., The. (PowerKids Pr.).

Zane, Dory. How to Track a Leopard, 1 vol., 1. 2013. (Scatalog: a Kid's Field Guide to Animal Poop Ser.). (ENG.). 24p. (J). (gr. 2-3). 27.27 *(978-1-61533-885-6(3)*, b9d9f82c-04f4-4684-bf73-1147621d3f34, Windmill Bks.) Rosen Publishing Group, Inc., The.

LEOPARD—FICTION

Achebe, Chinua. How the Leopard Got His Claws. GrandPre, Mary, illus. 2011. (ENG.). 32p. (J). (gr. 2-5). 16.99 *(978-0-7636-4805-3(1))* Candlewick Pr.

Anderson, Airlie, illus. A Very Spotty Flap Book. 2004. 10p. (J). bds. 5.95 *(978-1-58925-703-0(0))* Tiger Tales.

Basu, Anjana. Leopard in the Laboratory. 2016. (ENG., Illus.). 194p. pap. *(978-81-7993-370-1(9))* Energy and Resources Institute, The IND. Dist: Motilal (UK) Bks. of India.

Beeson, Lea Ann. A Leopard Is More Than His Spots. Popovich, Richard E., ed. Rockfield, Darryl, illus. I.t. ed. 2005. 51p. (J). lib. bdg. 19.95 *(978-0-9604876-1-5(1))* REP Pubs.

Castleton, Chaffee. Runty's Adventure: A Story of Love. Queen, Dana, illus. 2010. (ENG.). 97p. (J). pap. 17.95 *(978-0-578-06109-2(0))* Castleton, Julia J.

Dickins, Rosie. How the Leopard Got His Spots. 2018. (Picture Bks.). (ENG.). 24p. (J). 9.99 *(978-0-7945-4201-6(8)*, Usborne) EDC Publishing.

Emerson, Joan. Meet the Beanie Boos (Beanie Boos) 2018. (Beanie Boos Ser.). (ENG.). 24p. (J). (gr. -1-3). pap. 4.99 *(978-1-338-25621-5(1))* Scholastic, Inc.

Fox, Mem. Two Little Monkeys. Barton, Jill, illus. 2012. (ENG.). 32p. (J). (gr. -1-3). 16.99 *(978-1-4169-8687-4(1)*, Beach Lane Bks.) Beach Lane Bks.

Frampton, David. The Whole Night Through. Frampton, David, illus. Date not set. (Illus.). 32p. (J). (gr. -1-1). pap. 5.99 *(978-0-06-443652-6(7))* HarperCollins Pubs.

—The Whole Night Through: A Lullaby. Frampton, David, illus. 2004. (Illus.). 30p. (J). (gr. k-4). reprint ed. *(978-0-7567-7723-4(2))* DIANE Publishing Co.

Fraser, Kayo. Listen to Your Spirit: A Novel. 2019. (ENG., Illus.). 180p. (J). pap. *(978-1-937849-53-5(8))* Raven Publishing Inc. of Montana.

Froggatt, Sarah H. E. Leopard Spots: How the Clouded Leopard Got Her Spots. 2012. 32p. pap. 32.70 *(978-1-4771-3891-5(9))* Xlibris Corp.

Harper, Kathryn. Leopard & His Spots Red Band. Mosedale, Julian, illus. 2016. (Cambridge Reading Adventures Ser.). (ENG.). 16p. pap. 7.95 *(978-1-316-50308-9(9))* Cambridge Univ. Pr.

Jaco, Paul. The Leopards of Sh'ong. 2010. 260p. pap. *(978-0-7981-4930-3(2))* NB Pubs. Ltd.

Kipling, Rudyard. How the Leopard Got His Spots: The Graphic Novel, 1 vol. Rodriguez, Pedro, illus. 2012. (Graphic Spin Ser.). (ENG.). 40p. (J). (gr. 3-6). pap. 5.95 *(978-1-4342-3881-8(4)*, 118062); lib. bdg. 23.99 *(978-1-4342-3223-6(9)*, 116195) Capstone. (Stone Arch Bks.).

Knutson, Barbara. Sungura & Leopard: A Swahili Trickster Tale. Knutson, Barbara, illus. 2007. (Illus.). 26p. (J). (gr. -1-3). per. 6.95 *(978-0-8225-6801-8(2)*, First Avenue Editions) Lerner Publishing Group.

Landau, Orna. Leopardpox! Hoffmann, Omer, illus. 2015. (ENG.). 40p. (J). (gr. -1-3). 16.99 *(978-0-544-29001-3(1)*, 1572456, Clarion Bks.) HarperCollins Pubs.

Lodge, Ali, illus. The Leopard & the Sky God. 2007. (Usborne First Reading: Level 3 Ser.). 48p. (J). (gr. -1-3). 8.99 *(978-0-7945-1838-7(9)*, Usborne) EDC Publishing.

McGowan, Steve. The Adventures of Keke & the Golden Coconut. 2012. 48p. pap. 21.92 *(978-1-4251-4407-4(1))* Trafford Publishing.

McMaster, Alex. Giant George & Little Leo. 2012. 24p. pap. 14.95 *(978-1-4669-5080-1(3))* Trafford Publishing.

Nussbaum, Ben. Loli the Leopard. Wenzel, Gregory, illus. (ENG.). (J). (gr. -1-2). 2006. 32p. 9.95 *(978-1-59249-516-0(8)*, PS6556) 2006. 36p. 8.95 *(978-1-59249-514-6(1)*, SD6506) 2005. 36p. 14.95 *(978-1-59249-512-2(5)*, H6506) 2005. 36p. pap. 6.95 *(978-1-59249-513-9(3)*, S6506) Soundprints.

Nussbaum, Ben & Wenzell, Gregory. Loli Leopard. 2005. (ENG., Illus.). 36p. (J). (gr. -1-2). 2.95 *(978-1-59249-515-3(X)*, S6556) Soundprints.

Parker, Vic, compiled by. How the Leopard Got His Spots & Other Silly Stories, 1 vol. 2015. (Silly Stories Ser.). (ENG.). 40p. (J). (gr. 2-3). pap. 15.05 *(978-1-4824-4191-8(8)*, 5d212f9c-2fa8-496a-bbd2-f971bc984fb2) Stevens, Gareth Publishing LLLP.

Petkovic, Milisava. Snowy: A Leopard of the High Mountains. Xuan, Xuan Loc, illus. 2018. (ENG.). 38p. (J). 14.99 *(978-1-64124-015-4(6)*, 0154) Fox Chapel Publishing Co., Inc.

Sargent, Pat. The Black Panther, 6 vols., Vol. 2. Lenoir, Jane, illus. 2003. (Barney the Bear Killer Ser.: Vol. 2). 137p. (J). pap. 10.95 *(978-1-56763-966-7(6))* Ozark Publishing.

St. John, Lauren. The Last Leopard. 2010. (ENG.). 224p. (J). (gr. 3-7). 6.99 *(978-0-14-241515-3(4)*, Puffin Books) Penguin Young Readers Group.

Uncool!, 6 Packs. (Bookweb Ser.). 32p. (gr. 6-18). 34.00 *(978-0-7578-0901-9(4))* Rigby Education.

White, Paul. Jungle Doctor Spots a Leopard. rev. ed. 2008. (Flamingo Fiction 9-13s Ser.). (ENG., Illus.). 176p. (J). (gr. 5-7). per. 8.99 *(978-1-84550-301-7(5)*, 19e1be96-5b42-4620-a898-bc67dd924342) Christian Focus Pubns. GBR. Dist: Baker & Taylor Publisher Services (BTPS).

LEOPARDS

see Leopard

LEPIDOPTERA

see Butterflies; Moths

LEPROSY

Benge, Janet & Benge, Geoff. Paul Brand: Helping Hands. 2011. (ENG.). (YA). pap. 11.99 *(978-1-57658-536-8(0))* YWAM Publishing.

Donnelly, Karen. Leprosy (Hansen's Disease) 2009. (Epidemics Ser.). 64p. (gr. 5-5). 58.50 *(978-1-61512-290-5(7))* Rosen Publishing Group, Inc., The.

Leech, Bonnie Coulter. Prisms, 1 vol. 2006. (Exploring Shapes Ser.: Vol. 3). (ENG., Illus.). 24p. (J). (gr. 2-3). lib. bdg. 26.27 *(978-1-4042-3498-7(5)*,

98c912f6-b3ef-4a44-b319-99db4687fae4) Rosen Publishing Group, Inc., The.

LEPROSY—FICTION

Durango, Julia. The Walls of Cartagena. Pohrt, Tom, illus. 2008. (ENG.). 160p. (J). (gr. 3-7). 19.99 *(978-1-4169-4102-6(9))*, Simon & Schuster Bks. For Young Readers) Simon & Schuster Bks. For Young Readers.

Ellis, Deborah. No Ordinary Day, 1 vol. 2011. (ENG.). (J). 144p. (gr. 3-7). 16.95 *(978-1-55498-134-2(4))*; 160p. (gr. 4-7). pap. 9.95 *(978-1-55498-108-3(5))* Groundwood Bks. CAN. Dist: Publishers Group West (PGW).

—No Ordinary Day. 2013. 164p. pap. *(978-1-4596-6451-7(5))* ReadHowYouWant.com, Ltd.

Hargrave, Kiran Millwood. The Island at the End of Everything. 2018. (ENG.). 256p. (J). (gr. 5). lib. bdg. 19.99 *(978-0-553-53533-4(1))*, Knopf Bks. for Young Readers) Random Hse. Children's Bks.

LETTER WRITING

see also Commercial Correspondence

Ashley, Susan. I Can Write a Letter, 1 vol. 2004. (I Can Do It! Ser.). (ENG., Illus.). 24p. (J). (gr. k-2). pap. 9.15 *(978-0-8368-4335-4(5))*, e112be37-7cb8-478a-8b1e-8697de6740f2); lib. bdg. 23.67 *(978-0-8368-4328-6(2))*, dd5d8e9b-62c6-452b-bfe4-9ccab6ed0680) Stevens, Gareth Publishing LLLP. (Weekly Reader Leveled Readers).

Fields, Jan. You Can Write Great Letters & E-Mails. 2012. (You Can Write Ser.). (ENG.). 24p. (J). (gr. 1-2). pap. 41.70 *(978-1-4296-8385-2(6))*; (J). pap. 7.29 *(978-1-4296-7963-3(8))*, 118296); (J). lib. bdg. 25.99 *(978-1-4296-7613-7(2))*, 117210) Capstone. (Capstone Pr.).

Leleu, Sinead & Greck-Ismair, Michaela. German Pen Pals Made Easy: A Fun Way to Write German & Make a New Friend. 2010. (Illus.). 57p. pap. *(978-0-85747-144-4(9))* Brilliant Pubns.

Loewen, Nancy. Sincerely Yours: Writing Your Own Letter, 1 vol. Lyles, Christopher, illus. 2009. (Writer's Toolbox Ser.). (ENG.). 32p. (J). (gr. 2-4). pap. 8.95 *(978-1-4048-5339-3(1))*, 95561, Picture Window Bks.) Capstone.

Lynette, Rachel. Leah & Leshawn Build a Letter. Cox, Steve, illus. 2012. (Writing Builders Ser.). 32p. (J). (gr. 2-4). pap. 11.94 *(978-1-60357-390-0(9))*; lib. bdg. 25.27 *(978-1-59953-510-4(6))* Norwood Hse. Pr.

Minden, Cecilia. Writing a Letter. Herring, Carol, illus. 2019. (Write It Right Ser.). (ENG.). 24p. (J). (gr. 1-4). pap. 12.79 *(978-1-5341-5001-0(3))*, 213311); lib. bdg. 30.64 *(978-1-5341-4715-7(2))*, 213310) Cherry Lake Publishing.

—Writing a Thank-You Letter. Herring, Carol, illus. 2019. (Write It Right Ser.). (ENG.). 24p. (J). (gr. 1-4). pap. 12.79 *(978-1-5341-5006-5(4))*, 213331); lib. bdg. 30.64 *(978-1-5341-4720-1(9))*, 213330) Cherry Lake Publishing.

Minden, Cecilia & Roth, Kate. How to Write a Thank-You Letter. 2012. (Explorer Junior Library: Language Arts Explorer Junior Ser.). (ENG.). 24p. (J). (gr. 1-4). pap. 12.79 *(978-1-61080-663-3(8))*, 202273); (Illus.). 29.21 *(978-1-61080-489-9(9))*, 202099) Cherry Lake Publishing.

—How to Write an E-Mail. 2011. (Explorer Junior Library: How to Write Ser.). (ENG., Illus.). 24p. (gr. 1-4). lib. bdg. 29.21 *(978-1-60279-993-6(8))*, 200986) Cherry Lake Publishing.

Practice Power Bilingual Practice Book: Cursive Letters. 2003. (Illus.). 16p. (J). (gr. k-2). spiral bd. *(978-1-930355-46-0(7))* Bright of America.

Practice Power Bilingual Practice Book: Manuscript Letters. 2003. (Illus.). 16p. (J). (gr. -1-1). spiral bd. *(978-1-930355-45-3(9))* Bright of America.

Proudfit, Benjamin. Writing Letters, 1 vol. 2014. (Write Right! Ser.). (ENG.). 24p. (J). (gr. 2-3). 25.27 *(978-1-4824-1132-4(6))*, bcd19f4a-d9b5-4acc-9793-2f74d7406977) Stevens, Gareth Publishing LLLP.

Publications International Ltd. Staff, creator. Dora the Explorer Learn to Write. 2007. (Play-A-Sound Bks.). (Illus.). (J). (gr. -1-3). 19.98 *(978-1-4127-6659-3(1))* Publications International, Ltd.

Santos, Rita. How to Write Great Letters. 2019. (J). pap. *(978-1-9785-1395-2(X))* Enslow Publishing, LLC.

Summers, Jean. The Kids' Guide to Writing Great Thank-You Notes. 2010. (Illus.). 48p. (J). 9.95 *(978-1-59411-125-9(1))* Writers' Collective, The.

Top That Publishing Staff, ed. Fairy Princess Letter Writing. 2004. (Letter Writing Kits Ser.). (Illus.). 24p. (J). pap. *(978-1-84229-874-9(7))* Top That! Publishing PLC.

—Magical Horses Letter Writing. 2004. (Letter Writing Kits Ser.). (Illus.). 24p. (J). pap. *(978-1-84510-015-5(8))* Top That! Publishing PLC.

—Princess Letter Writing. 2005. (Illus.). 24p. pap. *(978-1-84510-762-8(4))* Top That! Publishing PLC.

LETTER WRITING—FICTION

Atwood, Megan. Molly Discovers Magic (Then Wants to un-Discover It) Fleming, Lucy, illus. 2016. (Dear Molly, Dear Olive Ser.). (ENG.). 96p. (J). (gr. 1-3). lib. bdg. 21.99 *(978-1-4795-8694-3(3))*, 130930, Picture Window Bks.) Capstone.

—Olive Finds Treasure (of the Most Precious Kind) Fleming, Lucy, illus. (Dear Molly, Dear Olive Ser.). (ENG.). 96p. (J). (gr. 1-3). 2017. pap. 5.95 *(978-1-62370-615-9(7))*, 130932, Capstone Young Readers) 2016. lib. bdg. 21.99 *(978-1-4795-8693-6(5))*, 130929, Picture Window Bks.) Capstone.

Borden, Louise. Across the Blue Pacific: A World War II Story. Parker, Robert Andrew, illus. 2015. (ENG.). 48p. (J). (gr. -1-3). 7.99 *(978-0-544-55552-5(X))*, 1610459, Clarion Bks.) HarperCollins Pubs.

Croteau, Marie-Danielle. Fred & the Mysterious Letter. St-Aubin, Bruno, illus. 2005. 61p. (J). lib. bdg. 12.00 *(978-1-4242-1199-9(9))* Fitzgerald Bks.

Danziger, Paula & Martin, Ann M. P. S. Longer Letter Later. (Tara Starr & Elizabeth Ser.). 240p. (J). (gr. 3-5). pap. 4.99 *(978-0-8072-1537-1(6))*, Listening Library) Random Hse. Audio Publishing Group.

Hesse, Karen. Letters from Rifka. 2009. 9.00 *(978-0-7848-2599-0(8))*, Everbind) Marco Bk. Co.

—Letters from Rifka. 2008. (ENG.). 148p. 17.00 *(978-1-60686-224-7(3))* Perfection Learning Corp.

—Letters from Rifka. 2009. (ENG.). 176p. (J). (gr. 4-6). pap. 7.99 *(978-0-312-53561-2(9))*, 900054737) Square Fish.

Ives, David. Scrib. 2005. 208p. (J). (gr. 5-18). lib. bdg. 17.89 *(978-0-06-059842-6(5))* HarperCollins Pubs.

Iwasa, Megumi. Yours Sincerely, Giraffe. Takabatake, Jun, illus. 2017. (ENG.). 104p. (J). (gr. k-3). 16.99 *(978-1-927271-88-9(6))*, 4f529eba-51e5-4e27-8bb3-91fa7b989948) Gecko Pr. NZL. Dist: Lerner Publishing Group.

Kaufman Orloff, Karen. I Wanna New Room. Catrow, David, illus. 2010. 32p. (J). (gr. k-3). 18.99 *(978-0-399-25405-5(6))*, G.P. Putnam's Sons Books for Young Readers) Penguin Young Readers Group.

Manushkin, Fran. Sincerely, Katie: Writing a Letter with Katie Woo, 1 vol. Lyon, Tammie, illus. 2013. (Katie Woo: Star Writer Ser.). (ENG.). 32p. (J). (gr. k-2). pap. 6.95 *(978-1-4795-1921-7(9))*, 123628); lib. bdg. 21.32 *(978-1-4048-8126-6(3))*, 121933) Capstone. (Picture Window Bks.).

Nichol, Barbara. Beethoven Vive Arriba. 2003.Tr. of Beethoven Lives Upstairs. (SPA., Illus.). 48p. (J). (gr. 3-5). 10.95 *(978-1-56014-619-3(2))*, SAN619) Santillana USA Publishing Co., Inc.

Parenteau, Shirley. Ship of Dolls. 2017. (Friendship Dolls Ser.). (ENG.). 272p. (J). (gr. 3-7). pap. 7.99 *(978-0-7636-9779-2(6))* Candlewick Pr.

Sis, Peter. Ice Cream Summer. Sis, Peter, illus. 2015. (ENG., Illus.). 40p. (J). (gr. -1-3). 18.99 *(978-0-545-73161-4(5))*, Scholastic Pr.) Scholastic, Inc.

LETTERING

Bukiet, Suzanne. Scripts of the World. 2nd ed. (Illus.). 91p. (YA). reprint ed. 19.95 *(978-0-9656274-1-2(1))* Another Language Pr.

Editors of Klutz. Lettering in Crazy, Cool, Quirky Style: In Crazy Cool Quirky Style. Editors of Klutz, ed. 2006. (ENG., Illus.). 56p. (J). (gr. 3-7). 18.95 *(978-1-57054-428-6(X))* Klutz.

—Neon Chalk Lettering. 2016. (ENG.). 76p. (J). (gr. 3-7). 18.99 *(978-1-338-03754-8(4))* Scholastic, Inc.

Mappin, J. Lettering Book - O/P. 2004. (ENG., Illus.). 12p. (J). *(978-1-74124-129-7(4))* Five Mile Australia.

Santo, Nicole Miyuki. The Kids' Book of Hand Lettering: 20 Lessons & Projects to Decorate Your World. 2018. (ENG., Illus.). 192p. (J). (gr. 4-17). pap. 12.99 *(978-0-7624-6339-8(2))*, Running Pr. Kids) Running Pr.

Top That Publishing Staff, ed. Create Your Own Lettering. 2005. (Illus.). 48p. *(978-1-84510-304-0(1))* Top That! Publishing PLC.

Warnaar, Dawn Nicole. Adventures in Lettering: 40 Exercises to Improve Your Lettering Skills. 2016. (ENG.). 128p. (J). (gr. 3-7). pap. 16.95 *(978-1-63322-173-4(3))*, Walter Foster Jr) Quarto Publishing Group USA.

LETTERS

Amazing Grace: Letters Alone My Journey. 2004. 160p. pap. 14.95 net. *(978-0-9747983-0-1(4))* Lewis-Thornton, Rae.

Enea, Paul J. Letters to My Granddaughter. 2007. 64p. per. 9.95 *(978-0-595-43781-8(8))* iUniverse, Inc.

Jakobsen, Kathy. My New York. Jakobsen, Kathy, illus. anniv. rev. ed. 2005. (Illus.). 54p. (J). (gr. k-4). 19.00 *(978-0-7567-8588-8(X))* DIANE Publishing Co.

—My New York. anniv. ed. 2003. (ENG., Illus.). 48p. (J). (gr. -1-3). 20.99 *(978-0-316-92711-6(2))* Little, Brown Bks. for Young Readers.

McPherson, Stephanie Sammartino. My Dear Husband: Important Letters of Abigail Adams, 1 vol. 2003. (Great Moments in American History Ser.). (ENG., Illus.). 32p. (gr. 3-3). lib. bdg. 29.13 *(978-0-8239-4323-4(2))*, 7378e0e7-c711-4f03-8d06-57a544602911, Rosen Reference) Rosen Publishing Group, Inc., The.

Murray, Julie. Mail Carriers, 1 vol. 2015. (My Community: Jobs Ser.). (ENG., Illus.). 24p. (J). (gr. -1-2). 31.36 *(978-1-62970-915-4(8))*, 18288, Abdo Kids) ABDO Publishing Co.

Prehistoric World - Group 2, 8 vols. 2005. (Letters from the Battlefront Ser.). (ENG., Illus.). 96p. (gr. 6-6). lib. bdg. 147.72 *(978-0-7614-1658-6(7))*, 9bb6a0b4-1978-4378-a20f-1d7f8d477a1b, Cavendish Square) Cavendish Square Publishing LLC.

Reed, Gregory J. Dear Mrs. Parks: a Dialogue with Today's Youth, 1 vol. 2013. (ENG., Illus.). 111p. (J). (gr. 1-5). reprint ed. per. 16.95 *(978-1-880000-61-8(X))*, leelowbooks) Lee & Low Bks., Inc.

Spence, Kelly & Burns, Kylie. Be a Diary Detective. 2017. (Be a Document Detective Ser.). (ENG., Illus.). 24p. (J). (gr. 2-2). *(978-0-7787-3053-8(0))* Crabtree Publishing Co.

Stokes, Betty Southard. Postcards from George, 1763-1781: George Rogers Clark Writes Home to Virginia from the Kentucky Wilderness. Cable, Annette, illus. 2010. (J). *(978-1-935497-12-7(X))* Butler Bks.

Zourelias, Diana. Laugh Out Loud Letters for Boys: The Easy Way to Create Fast & Funny Notes! 2011. (Dover Children's Activity Bks.). (ENG., Illus.). 48p. (J). (gr. 2-5). pap. 5.99 *(978-0-486-47788-6(6))* Dover Pubns., Inc.

—Laugh Out Loud Letters for Girls! The Easy Way to Create Fast & Funny Notes! 2011. (Dover Children's Activity Bks.). (ENG., Illus.). 48p. (J). (gr. 2-5). pap. 5.99 *(978-0-486-47787-9(8))* Dover Pubns., Inc.

LETTERS—FICTION

Ada, Alma Flor & Zubizarreta, Gabriel M. Con Cariño, Amalia (Love, Amalia) 2013. (SPA., Illus.). 160p. (J). (gr. 3-7). pap. 7.99 *(978-1-4424-2406-7(0))* Simon & Schuster Children's Publishing.

—Love, Amalia. (ENG., Illus.). (J). (gr. 3-7). 2013. 160p. pap. 7.99 *(978-1-4424-2403-6(6))* 2012. 144p. 18.99 *(978-1-4424-2402-9(8))* Simon & Schuster Children's Publishing. (Atheneum Bks. for Young Readers).

Alexander, Kwame & Rand Hess, Mary. Swing, 1 vol. 2019. (ENG.). 448p. (YA). (gr. 8). pap. 14.99 *(978-0-310-76194-5(8))*, Clarion Bks.) HarperCollins Pubs.

—Swing ITPE SC, 1 vol. 2018. (ENG., Illus.). 448p. (YA). (gr. 8). pap. 10.99 *(978-0-310-76193-8(X))*, Clarion Bks.) HarperCollins Pubs.

Alger Jr. Horatio Staff. Andy Grants Pluck. rev. ed. 2006. 312p. 29.95 *(978-1-4218-1762-0(4))*; pap. 14.95 *(978-1-4218-1862-7(0))* 1st World Publishing, Inc. (1st World Library - Literary Society).

Amodeo, Darlene. Samantha & the Soldier: A Letter of Love. 2012. 40p. pap. 20.99 *(978-1-4772-9263-1(2))* AuthorHouse.

Andracki, Zenon. Dear Ashley: A Middle Grade Novel. 2006. (ENG.). 84p. per. 19.95 *(978-1-4241-6168-3(1))* America Star Bks.

Anholt, Laurence & Coplestone, Jim. Seven for a Secret. 2006. (ENG., Illus.). 32p. (J). pap. *(978-1-84507-590-3(0))*, White Lion Publishing) Quarto Publishing Group UK.

Armstrong, Bill. Letters from Ozo, 1. 2005. (Illus.). 190p. (J). per. *(978-0-9771676-0-9(7))* Rubicon Bks.

Arno, Ronni. Dear Poppy. 2016. (Mix Ser.). (ENG., Illus.). 256p. (J). (gr. 4-8). pap. 7.99 *(978-1-4814-3759-2(3))*, Aladdin) Simon & Schuster Children's Publishing.

—Dear Poppy. 2016. (Mix Ser.). (ENG., Illus.). 256p. (J). (gr. 4-8). 17.99 *(978-1-4814-3760-8(7))*, Simon & Schuster/Paula Wiseman Bks.) Simon & Schuster/Paula Wiseman Bks.

Ashman, Linda. The Twelve Days of Christmas in Colorado. Beacon, Dawn, illus. 2018. (Twelve Days of Christmas in America Ser.). (ENG.). 22p. (J). (-k). bds. 7.95 *(978-1-4549-2927-7(8))* Sterling Publishing Co., Inc.

Asquith, Ros. Letters from an Alien Schoolboy. (ENG., Illus.). 192p. (J). (gr. 1-5). 2015. pap. 9.95 *(978-1-62914-614-0(5))* 2013. 12.95 *(978-1-62087-536-0(5))*, 620536) Skyhorse Publishing Co., Inc. (Sky Pony Pr.).

Baratz-Logsted, Lauren. I Love You, Michael Collins. 2019. (Penworthy Picks Middle School Ser.). (ENG.). 230p. (J). (gr. 4-5). 19.49 *(978-1-64310-918-3(9))* Penworthy Co., LLC, The.

—I Love You, Michael Collins. 2018. (ENG.). 240p. (J). pap. 8.99 *(978-1-250-15845-1(1))*, 900158161) Square Fish.

—I Love You, Michael Collins. 2018. (J). lib. bdg. 18.40 *(978-0-606-41098-4(8))* Turtleback.

Battista, Brianna. I Want to Be a Postman, 1 vol. 2018. (What Do I Want to Be? Ser.). (ENG.). 24p. (J). (gr. 1-1). 25.27 *(978-1-5383-2999-3(9))*, 16791dc8-e0b0-414e-bcf9-4be4488a8e7f); pap. 9.25 *(978-1-5383-3001-2(6))*, 5e405ebc-2ec7-4fd7-aec2-f729d0fbb634) Rosen Publishing Group, Inc., The. (PowerKids Pr.).

Behar, Ruth. Letters from Cuba. 2020. (ENG., Illus.). 272p. (J). (gr. 5). 17.99 *(978-0-525-51647-7(6))*, Nancy Paulsen Books) Penguin Young Readers Group.

Bellisario, Gina. The Twelve Days of Christmas in Illinois. Ebbeler, Jeffrey, illus. 2018. (Twelve Days of Christmas in America Ser.). 22p. (J). (-k). bds. 7.95 *(978-1-4549-2928-4(6))* Sterling Publishing Co., Inc.

Bennett, Evelyn & Benson, Jenny, creators. Life Letters: Kid's Stuff. 2003. (J). 19.95 *(978-0-9746022-2-6(1))* Life Letters Publishing.

Beverly, Cleary. Dear Mr. Henshaw. 2014. (Cleary Reissue Ser.). (ENG.). 160p. (J). (gr. 7-12). 10.24 *(978-1-63245-195-8(6))* Lectorum Pubns., Inc.

Blackaby, Susan. The Twelve Days of Christmas in Oregon. Conahan, Carolyn Digby, illus. (Twelve Days of Christmas in America Ser.). (ENG.). (J). (-k). 2018. 22p. bds. 7.95 *(978-1-4549-2997-0(9))* 2014. 40p. 12.95 *(978-1-4549-0891-3(2))* Sterling Publishing Co., Inc.

Bliss, Bryan. We'll Fly Away. (ENG.). 416p. (YA). (gr. 9). 2019. pap. 10.99 *(978-0-06-249428-3(7))* 2018. 18.99 *(978-0-06-249427-6(9))* HarperCollins Pubs. (Greenwillow Bks.).

Blos, Joan W. Letters from the Corrugated Castle: A Novel of Gold Rush California, 1850-1852. 2008. (ENG.). 320p. (J). (gr. 5-9). pap. 5.99 *(978-0-689-87078-1(7))*, Atheneum Bks. for Young Readers) Simon & Schuster Children's Publishing.

Bond, Michael. Love from Paddington. Fortnum, Peggy & Alley, R. W., illus. 2016. (Paddington Ser.). (ENG.). 144p. (J). (gr. 3-7). pap. 5.99 *(978-0-06-242526-3(9))*, HarperCollins) HarperCollins Pubs.

Boyd, Lizi. I Wrote You a Note: (Children's Friendship Books, Animal Books for Kids, Rhyming Books for Kids) 2017. (ENG., Illus.). 36p. (J). 16.99 *(978-1-4521-5957-7(2))* Chronicle Bks. LLC.

Bryant, Annie. Letters from the Heart. 2004. (Beacon Street Girls Ser.: No. 3). 224p. (J). 7.99 *(978-0-9746587-8-0(2))*, Beacon Street Girls) B*tween Productions, Inc.

Butler, Dori Hillestad. Dear Beast. Atteberry, Kevan, illus. 2020. (Dear Beast Ser.: 1). 80p. (J). (gr. 1-4). 15.99 *(978-0-8234-4492-2(9))* Holiday Hse., Inc.

Callaghan, Cindy. Lost in Ireland. 2016. (Mix Ser.). (ENG., Illus.). 224p. (J). (gr. 4-8). pap. 7.99 *(978-1-4814-6206-8(7))*, Aladdin) Simon & Schuster Children's Publishing.

—Lucky Me. 2014. (Mix Ser.). (ENG., Illus.). 224p. (J). (gr. 4-8). pap. 6.99 *(978-1-4424-8950-9(2))*, Aladdin) Simon & Schuster Children's Publishing.

Candy, T. M. & Fisher, W. A. Dear Mister Mayor. 2010. 126p. pap. 15.54 *(978-0-557-09733-3(9))* Lulu Pr., Inc.

Carroll, Emma. In Darkling Wood. 2018. (ENG.). 256p. (J). (gr. 5). 6.99 *(978-0-399-55604-3(4))*, Yearling) Random Hse. Children's Bks.

Chbosky, Stephen & Perez-Sauquillo, Vanesa. Las Ventajas de Ser Invisible. 2013. (SPA.). 272p. (YA). (gr. 7). pap. 15.99 *(978-1-4767-3245-9(0))*, MTV Bks.) MTV Books.

Clark, Anthony. Little Wolf's Book of Badness. 2008. (Oberon Modern Plays Ser.). (ENG.). 96p. (J). pap. 14.95 *(978-1-84002-823-2(8))*, 900241395) Oberon Bks., Ltd. GBR. Dist: Macmillan.

Clements, Andrew. Extra Credit. Elliott, Mark, illus. (ENG.). (J). (gr. 3-7). 2011. 224p. pap. 7.99 *(978-1-4169-4931-2(3))* 2009. 192p. 18.99 *(978-1-4169-4929-9(1))* Simon & Schuster Children's Publishing. (Atheneum Bks. for Young Readers).

Coffelt, Soraya Diase. It's Not about You Mr. Santa Claus: A Love Letter about the True Meaning of Christmas. 2014. (Love Letters Book Ser.). (ENG., Illus.). 34p. pap. 8.99 *(978-1-63047-261-0(1))* Morgan James Publishing.

Cole, Barbara H. Anna & Natalie, 1 vol. Himler, Ronald, illus. (ENG.). 32p. (J). 2010. pap. 6.95 *(978-1-59572-211-9(4))* 2007. 16.95 *(978-1-59572-105-1(3))* Star Bright Bks., Inc.

Cook, Danielle, ills. Letters from Pyggles, 1. 2003. 24p. 9.00 *(978-0-9729914-0-7(9))* Oden, Rachel.

Coyle, Carmela LaVigna. Thank You, Aunt Tallulah! MacPherson, Bruce, illus. 2006. (ENG.). 32p. (J). (gr. -1-3). 15.95 *(978-0-87358-891-1(6))* Cooper Square Publishing Llc.

Creedle, Laura. The Love Letters of Abelard & Lily. (ENG.). 352p. (YA). (gr. 7). 2019. pap. 10.99 *(978-1-328-60366-1(0))*, 1732073) 2017. 17.99 *(978-0-544-93205-0(6))*, 1658576) HarperCollins Pubs. (Clarion Bks.).

Cummings, Troy. Can I Be Your Dog? (Illus.). 40p. (J). (gr. -1-2). 2022. pap. 8.99 *(978-0-593-38006-2(1))*, Dragonfly Bks.) 2018. 17.99 *(978-0-399-55452-0(1))*, Random Hse. Bks. for Young Readers) 2018. (ENG., lib. bdg. 19.99 *(978-0-399-55453-7(X))*, Random Hse. Bks. for Young Readers) Random Hse. Children's Bks.

Cumyn, Alan. Dear Sylvia, 1 vol. 2008. (ENG.). 184p. (J). (gr. 3-6). pap. 8.95 *(978-0-88899-848-4(1))* Groundwood Bks. CAN. Dist: Publishers Group West (PGW).

Danneberg, Julie. First Year Letters. Love, Judy, illus. 2014. 32p. pap. 7.00 *(978-1-61003-320-6(5))* Center for the Collaborative Classroom.

Dashner, James. The Journal of Curious Letters. Beus, Bryan, illus. 2008. (13th Reality Ser.: Bk. 1). 434p. (J). (gr. 4-7). 17.95 *(978-1-59038-831-0(3))*, Shadow Mountain) Shadow Mountain Publishing.

—The Journal of Curious Letters. Beus, Bryan, illus. 2009. (13th Reality Ser.: 1). (ENG.). 528p. (J). (gr. 3-7). pap. 9.99 *(978-1-4169-9152-6(2))*, Aladdin) Simon & Schuster Children's Publishing.

Daywalt, Drew. The Crayon Box: the Day the Crayons Quit Slipcased Edition, 2 vols. Jeffers, Oliver, illus. 2016. (ENG.). 88p. (J). (gr. -1-2). 40.00 *(978-0-399-54892-5(0))*, Philomel Bks.) Penguin Young Readers Group.

—The Day the Crayons Quit. 2014. (CHI.). 32p. (J). *(978-7-5448-3406-3(9))* Jieli Publishing Hse.

—The Day the Crayons Quit. Jeffers, Oliver, illus. 2013. (ENG.). 40p. (J). (gr. -1-2). 17.99 *(978-0-399-25537-3(0))*, Philomel Bks.) Penguin Young Readers Group.

Donovan, Jane Monroe. Small, Medium & Large. Donovan, Jane Monroe, illus. 2010. (ENG., Illus.). 32p. (J). (gr. 1-4). 15.95 *(978-1-58536-447-3(9))*, 202172) Sleeping Bear Pr.

Doughtie, Patrick & Doughtie, Heather. Letters to God, 1 vol. Lyon, Tammie, illus. 2016. (Letters to God Ser.). (ENG.). 32p. (J). 16.99 *(978-0-310-75395-7(3))* Zonderkidz.

Dowell, Frances O'Roark. Anybody Shining. (ENG., Illus.). (J). (gr. 5-7). 2015. 256p. pap. 8.99 *(978-1-4424-3293-2(4))* 2014. 240p. 16.99 *(978-1-4424-3292-5(6))* Simon & Schuster Children's Publishing. (Atheneum Bks. for Young Readers).

Fishbone, Greg. The Penguins of Doom. 2007. (From the Desk of Septina Nash Ser.). (ENG., Illus.). 182p. (J). (gr. 2-7). 13.95 *(978-1-933831-03-9(0))* Blooming Tree Pr.

Frank, Hillary. I Can't Tell You. 2004. (ENG.). 208p. (YA). (gr. 7). pap. 12.99 *(978-0-618-49491-0(X))*, 485873, Clarion Bks.) HarperCollins Pubs.

—I Can't Tell You. 2004. 208p. (YA). (gr. 7). 16.00 *(978-0-618-41202-0(6))* Houghton Mifflin Harcourt Trade & Reference Pubs.

Gil, Lydia. Letters from Heaven. 2014.Tr. of Cartas Del Cielo. (ENG & SPA.). 128p. (J). pap. 9.95 *(978-1-55885-798-8(2))*, Piñata Books) Arte Publico Pr.

Goss, Matt. Bear Crimbo. 2010. (ENG., Illus.). 72p. (J). 17.95 *(978-0-9815381-3-6(4))* Hilton Publishing Co.

Grant, Joyce. Gabby, 1 vol. Dolby, Jan, illus. 2012. (ENG.). 32p. (J). (gr. -1-1). 18.95 *(978-1-55455-250-4(8))*, b9c8a04a-d7fe-47c8-92ce-bef39565a596) Fitzhenry & Whiteside, Ltd. CAN. Dist: Firefly Bks., Ltd.

Gray, Dianne. Holding up the Earth. 2006. (ENG.). 210p. (J). (gr. 5-7). pap. 12.95 *(978-0-618-73747-5(2))*, 486718, Clarion Bks.) HarperCollins Pubs.

Grindley, Sally. Bravo, Max! Ross, Tony, illus. 2007. (ENG.). 160p. (J). (gr. 1-4). pap. 8.99 *(978-1-4169-3645-9(9))*, Simon & Schuster/Paula Wiseman Bks.) Simon & Schuster/Paula Wiseman Bks.

—Dear Max. Ross, Tony, illus. 2006. (ENG.). 144p. (J). (gr. 2-4). 17.44 *(978-1-4169-0392-5(5))* Simon & Schuster, Inc.

—Dear Max. Ross, Tony, illus. 2007. (ENG.). 144p. (J). (gr. 1-4). pap. 7.99 *(978-1-4169-3443-1(X))*, Simon & Schuster/Paula Wiseman Bks.) Simon & Schuster/Paula Wiseman Bks.

Haber, Melissa Glenn. Dear Anjali. 2010. (ENG.). 288p. (J). (gr. 4-8). 16.99 *(978-1-4169-9599-9(4))*, Simon & Schuster/Paula Wiseman Bks.) Simon & Schuster/Paula Wiseman Bks.

—Your Best Friend, Meredith. 2011. (ENG.). 288p. (J). (gr. 4-8). pap. 6.99 *(978-1-4169-9600-2(1))*, Aladdin) Simon & Schuster Children's Publishing.

Harley, Bill. Dear Santa: The Letters of James B. Dobbins. Alley, R. W., illus. 2005. 32p. (J). (ENG.). 15.99 *(978-0-06-623778-7(5))*; lib. bdg. 16.89 *(978-0-06-623779-4(3))* HarperCollins Pubs.

Harper, Suzanne. The Juliet Club. (YA). 2010. (ENG.). 416p. (gr. 8). pap. 9.99 *(978-0-06-136693-2(5))*, Greenwillow Bks.) 2008. 402p. (gr. 7-18). lib. bdg. 18.89 *(978-0-06-136692-5(7))*, HarperTeen) HarperCollins Pubs.

Harris, Christine. The Silver Path. (Illus.). (J). (ENG & VIE.). 26p. *(978-1-85430-327-1(9))*, 93381); (CHI & ENG., 32p. *(978-1-85430-323-3(6))*, 93425) Little Tiger Pr. Group.

Hedstrom-Page, Deborah. From Log Cabin to White House with Abraham Lincoln. Martinez, Sergio, illus. 2007. (My American Journey Ser.). 82p. (J). (gr. 3-9). 9.99 *(978-0-8054-3269-5(8))* B&H Publishing Group.

Helene Bridge, Chris. Red Envelopes: Sobres Rojos. 2018. (ENG., Illus.). 32p. (J). 19.95 *(978-1-942945-65-9(5))*, a81528e3-b1fe-457c-a1d0-3c4bafb6b8d7) Night Heron Media.

Helmore, Jim & Wall, Karen. Letterbox Lil. (ENG., Illus.). 32p. (J). (gr. -1-1). 10.99 *(978-0-19-279201-3(6))* Oxford Univ. Pr., Inc.

Hensley, Sarah M. Caillou's Trip to the Harbor. Gillen, Lisa P., illus. l.t. ed. 2004. (HRL Board Book Ser.). (J). (gr. -1-1). pap. 10.95 *(978-1-57332-290-4(3))*, HighReach Learning, Incorporated) Carson-Dellosa Publishing, LLC.

—Helping Farmer Joe. Crowell, Knox, illus. l.t. ed. 2004. (HRL Little Book Ser.). (J). (gr. -1). pap. 10.95 *(978-1-57332-296-6(2))*; pap. 10.95 *(978-1-57332-295-9(4))* Carson-Dellosa Publishing, LLC. (HighReach Learning, Incorporated).

Hest, Amy. Letters to Leo. Denos, Julia, illus. 2012. (ENG.). 160p. (J). (gr. 3-7). 14.99 *(978-0-7636-3695-1(9))* Candlewick Pr.

—Letters to Leo. Denos, Julia, illus. 2014. (ENG.). 160p. (J). (gr. 3-7). pap. 8.99 *(978-0-7636-7165-5(7))* Candlewick Pr.

Holland, Marci. The Birth Day Letter. 2005. 116p. 23.99 *(978-1-4208-2920-4(3))* AuthorHouse.

—The Birth Day Letter: An Alzheimer's Story. 2005. 116p. pap. 14.95 *(978-1-4208-2921-1(1))* AuthorHouse.

Holmes, Sara Lewis. Letters from Rapunzel. 2007. 184p. (J). (gr. 3-7). lib. bdg. 16.89 *(978-0-06-078074-6(6))* HarperCollins Pubs.

Hopkinson, Deborah. A Letter to My Teacher: A Teacher Appreciation Gift. Carpenter, Nancy, illus. 2017. 40p. (J). (gr. -1-3). 18.99 *(978-0-375-86845-0(3)*, Schwartz & Wade Bks.) Random Hse. Children's Bks.

House, Silas & Vaswani, Neela. Same Sun Here. Schenker, Hilary, illus. 2013. (ENG.). 304p. (J). (gr. 4-7). pap. 8.99 *(978-0-7636-6451-0(0))* Candlewick Pr.

Howard-Parham, Pam. Caillou Waits for Dinner. Crowell, Knox, illus. l.t. ed. 2004. (HRL Board Book Ser.). (J). (gr. -1-1). pap. 10.95 *(978-1-57332-289-8(X)*, HighReach Learning, Incorporated) Carson-Dellosa Publishing, LLC.

—The Dinosaur Surprise. Neveu, Fred, illus. l.t. ed. 2004. (HRL Big Book Ser.). (J). (gr. -1-1). pap. 10.95 *(978-1-57332-293-5(8))*; pap. 10.95 *(978-1-57332-294-2(6))* Carson-Dellosa Publishing, LLC. (HighReach Learning, Incorporated).

—Loving Our Country. Teeple, Jackie, illus. l.t. ed. 2004. (HRL Little Book Ser.). (J). (gr. -1-1). pap. 10.95 *(978-1-57332-302-4(0))*; pap. 10.95 *(978-1-57332-301-7(2))* Carson-Dellosa Publishing, LLC. (HighReach Learning, Incorporated).

Isern, Susanna. The Lonely Mailman. 2018. lib. bdg. 20.80 *(978-0-606-41236-0(0))* Turtleback.

Iwasa, Megumi. Dear Professor Whale. Takabatake, Jun, illus. 2018. (ENG.). 104p. (J). (gr. k-3). 16.99 *(978-1-77657-206-9(8)*, 99e443a3-c963-40f9-861a-c55409bd2ce8) Gecko Pr. NZL. Dist: Lerner Publishing Group.

—Yours Sincerely, Giraffe. Takabatake, Jun, illus. 2017. (Gecko Press Titles Ser.). (ENG.). 104p. (gr. k-3). 9.99 *(978-1-77657-114-7(2))* Gecko Pr. NZL. Dist: Lerner Publishing Group.

Izakson, Meron H. & Raday, Leanne. The Essential List: A Letter to the Teacher. 2017. (ENG., Illus.). 59p. (J). pap. *(978-965-229-919-2(7))* Gefen Publishing Hse., Ltd.

James, Helen Foster. With Love, Grandma. Brown, Petra, illus. 2018. (ENG.). 32p. (J). (gr. k-2). 15.99 *(978-1-58536-942-3(X)*, 204330) Sleeping Bear Pr.

Jarrell, Pamela R. Flitter, Flutter Butterfly. Middleton, Mikell, illus. l.t. ed. 2005. (HRL Board Book Ser.). 12p. (J). (gr. -1-1). pap. 10.95 *(978-1-57332-286-7(5)*, HighReach Learning, Incorporated) Carson-Dellosa Publishing, LLC.

Johnson, Maureen. The Last Little Blue Envelope. (13 Little Blue Envelopes Ser.: 2). (ENG., 288p. (YA). (gr. 8). 2016. Illus.). pap. 10.99 *(978-0-06-243912-3(X))* 2012. pap. 9.99 *(978-0-06-197681-0(4))* HarperCollins Pubs. (HarperTeen).

—13 Little Blue Envelopes. (13 Little Blue Envelopes Ser.: 1). (ENG., Illus.). (YA). (gr. 8-18). 2005. 336p. 17.99 *(978-0-06-054141-5(5))* 2010. 368p. reprint ed. pap. 9.99 *(978-0-06-054143-9(1))* HarperCollins Pubs. (HarperTeen).

—13 Little Blue Envelopes. 2007. 317p. 20.00 *(978-0-7569-7830-3(0))* Perfection Learning Corp.

Jones, Patrick. Outburst. 2014. (Alternative Ser.). (ENG.). 104p. (YA). (gr. 6-12). pap. 7.95 *(978-1-4677-4484-3(0)*, 19373d2e-a571-4166-b228-9cdb9f563141, Darby Creek) Lerner Publishing Group.

Jules, Jacqueline. Las Cartas Especiales de la Abuela. Smith, Kim, illus. 2018. (Sofia Martinez en Español Ser.). (SPA.). 32p. (J). (gr. k-2). lib. bdg. 21.32 *(978-1-5158-2444-2(6)*, 137547, Picture Window Bks.) Capstone.

Kaufman Orloff, Karen. I Wanna Go Home. Catrow, David, illus. 2014. 32p. (J). (gr. k-3). 18.99 *(978-0-399-25407-9(2)*, G.P. Putnam's Sons Books for Young Readers) Penguin Young Readers Group.

—I Wanna Iguana. Catrow, David, illus. 2004. 32p. (J). (gr. -1-3). 18.99 *(978-0-399-23717-1(8)*, G.P. Putnam's Sons Books for Young Readers) Penguin Young Readers Group.

Kemmerer, Brigid. Letters to the Lost. 2017. (ENG.). 400p. (YA). 18.99 *(978-1-68119-008-2(7)*, 900154802, Bloomsbury USA Childrens) Bloomsbury Publishing USA.

Kephart, Beth. Undercover. 2009. (ENG.). 304p. (YA). (gr. 8). pap. 8.99 *(978-0-06-123895-6(3)*, HarperTeen) HarperCollins Pubs.

Kieper, Rienhold Richard. Ten Letters for Our Children. 2004. 26p. (J). pap. 10.00 *(978-0-9719284-1-1(X))* Blue Thunder One, Inc.

Kirsch, Vincent. From Archie to Zack. 2020. (ENG., Illus.). 40p. (J). (gr. -1-3). 17.99 *(978-1-4197-4367-2(8)*, 1685701, Abrams Bks. for Young Readers) Abrams, Inc.

Klise, Kate. Dying to Meet You. Klise, M. Sarah, illus. 2010. (43 Old Cemetery Road Ser.: Bk. 1). (ENG.). 160p. (J). (gr. 3-7). pap. 6.99 *(978-0-547-39848-8(4)*, 1427649, Clarion Bks.) HarperCollins Pubs.

—Greetings from the Graveyard. Klise, M. Sarah, illus. 2015. (43 Old Cemetery Road Ser.). (ENG.). 160p. (J). (gr. 3-7). pap. 7.99 *(978-0-544-54010-1(7)*, 1608837, Clarion Bks.) HarperCollins Pubs.

—Hollywood, Dead Ahead. Klise, M. Sarah, illus. 2014. (43 Old Cemetery Road Ser.: 5). (ENG.). 144p. (J). (gr. 3-7). pap. 7.99 *(978-0-544-33661-2(5)*, 1584183, Clarion Bks.) HarperCollins Pubs.

—The Loch Ness Punster. Klise, M. Sarah, illus. 2016. (43 Old Cemetery Road Ser.: 7). (ENG.). 144p. (J). (gr. 3-7). pap. 7.99 *(978-0-544-81085-3(6)*, 1641667, Clarion Bks.) HarperCollins Pubs.

—The Phantom of the Post Office. Klise, M. Sarah, illus. 2013. (43 Old Cemetery Road Ser.: 4). (ENG.). 160p. (J). (gr. 3-7). pap. 7.99 *(978-0-544-02281-2(5)*, 1528502, Clarion Bks.) HarperCollins Pubs.

—The Phantom of the Post Office. 2013. (43 Old Cemetery Road Ser.: 4). lib. bdg. 17.20 *(978-0-606-31668-2(X))* Turtleback.

—Till Death Do Us Bark. 2012. (43 Old Cemetery Road Ser.: 3). lib. bdg. 17.20 *(978-0-606-26543-0(0))* Turtleback.

Klise, Kate & Klise, Kate. Regarding the Bees: A Lesson, in Letters, on Honey, Dating, & Other Sticky Subjects. Klise, M. Sarah, illus. 2009. (Regarding The ... Ser.: Bk. 5). (ENG.). 144p. (J). (gr. 3-7). pap. 6.99 *(978-0-15-206668-0(3)*, 1099002, Clarion Bks.) HarperCollins Pubs.

Klise, Kate & Klise, M. Sarah. Regarding the Trees: A Splintered Saga Rooted in Secrets. Klise, Kate & Klise, M. Sarah, illus. 2007. (Regarding The ... Ser.: Bk. 3). (ENG., Illus.). 160p. (J). (gr. 3-7). pap. 7.99 *(978-0-15-206090-9(1)*, 1198293, Clarion Bks.) HarperCollins Pubs.

Knaus, Patricia. Letters from Space. The Mousekins Staff, illus. 2004. 112p. (J). (gr. 3-4). pap. 8.50 *(978-0-9758742-0-2(9)*, 10704) KnausWorks.

LaFleur, Suzanne. Love, Aubrey. 2011. (ENG.). 272p. (J). (gr. 3-7). pap. 7.99 *(978-0-375-85159-9(3)*, Yearling) Random Hse. Children's Bks.

Lake, Nick. Whisper to Me. 2016. (ENG.). 544p. (YA). 17.99 *(978-1-61963-456-5(2)*, 900137473, Bloomsbury USA Childrens) Bloomsbury Publishing USA.

LeSourd, Nancy. Adventures in Jamestown, 1 vol. 2008. (Liberty Letters Ser.). (ENG., Illus.). 240p. (J). pap. 7.99 *(978-0-310-71392-0(7))* Zonderkidz.

—Attack at Pearl Harbor, 1 vol. 2008. (Liberty Letters Ser.). (ENG.). 224p. (J). pap. 7.99 *(978-0-310-71389-0(7))* Zonderkidz.

—Escape on the Underground Railroad, 1 vol. 2008. (Liberty Letters Ser.). (ENG.). 224p. (J). pap. 7.99 *(978-0-310-71391-3(9))* Zonderkidz.

—Secrets of Civil War Spies, 1 vol. 2008. (Liberty Letters Ser.). (ENG.). 224p. (J). pap. 7.99 *(978-0-310-71390-6(0))* Zonderkidz.

Lewis, Norma. Dear Santa, I Know It Looks Bad, but It Wasn't My Fault. Beckman, Olivia, illus. 2018. (ENG.). 40p. (J). 16.99 *(978-1-4413-2421-4(6)*, af65c62f-41d5-4fa2-adec-cc94bc70dba9) Peter Pauper Pr. Inc.

Low, A. J. Sherlock Sam & the Sinister Letters in Bras Basah. 2016. (Sherlock Sam Ser.: Vol. 3). (ENG., Illus.). 127p. (J). (gr. 2-6). 26.99 *(978-1-4494-8614-3(2))* Andrews McMeel Publishing.

Luthardt, Kevin. Larabee, 1 vol. 2009. (Illus.). 32p. (J). (gr. -1-k). pap. 7.95 *(978-1-56145-482-2(6))* Peachtree Publishing Co. Inc.

Lyons, Mary E. Letters from a Slave Boy: The Story of Joseph Jacobs. 2009. (ENG.). 208p. (YA). (gr. 7). mass mkt. 7.99 *(978-0-689-87868-8(0)*, Simon Pulse) Simon Pulse.

—Letters from a Slave Girl: The Story of Harriet Jacobs. 2008. (Illus.). 175p. (gr. 7-12). 16.00 *(978-0-7569-8474-8(2))* Perfection Learning Corp.

—Letters from a Slave Girl: The Story of Harriet Jacobs. 2007. (ENG., Illus.). 192p. (YA). (gr. 7). mass mkt. 7.99 *(978-1-4169-3637-4(8)*, Simon Pulse) Simon Pulse.

Malcolm, Jahnna N. The Write Stuff. 2011. (Love Letters Ser.). (ENG.). 192p. (YA). (gr. 7). pap. 9.99 *(978-1-4424-3100-3(8)*, Simon Pulse) Simon Pulse.

Mansbach, Adam & Zweibel, Alan. Benjamin Franklin: You've Got Mail. 2017. (Benjamin Franklin Ser.: 2). (ENG.). 224p. (J). (gr. 5-9). 12.99 *(978-1-4847-1305-1(2))* Hyperion Bks. for Children.

Mcdonald, Megan. Stink & the Incredible Super-Galactic Jawbreaker. Reynolds, Peter H., illus. 2010. (Stink Ser.: No. 2). (ENG.). 128p. (J). (gr. 1-5). 31.36 *(978-1-59961-684-1(X)*, 13831, Chapter Bks.) Spotlight.

—Stink & the Incredible Super-Galactic Jawbreaker. 2013. (Stink Ser.: 2). lib. bdg. 14.75 *(978-0-606-31588-3(8))* Turtleback.

McDonald, Megan. Stink & the Incredible Super-Galactic Jawbreaker, Bk. 2. Reynolds, Peter H., illus. 2013. (Stink Ser.: 2). (ENG.). 128p. (J). (gr. 1-4). 14.99 *(978-0-7636-6389-6(1))* Candlewick Pr.

McElroy, Lisa Tucker. Love, Lizzie: Letters to a Military Mom. Paterson, Diane, illus. 2009. (ENG.). 32p. (J). (gr. -1-3). pap. 7.99 *(978-0-8075-4778-6(6)*, 807547786) Whitman, Albert & Co.

McGhee, Alison. Dear Sister. Bluhm, Joe, illus. 2019. (ENG.). 192p. (J). (gr. 5). pap. 7.99 *(978-1-4814-5143-7(X)*, Atheneum Bks. for Young Readers) Simon & Schuster Children's Publishing.

Menon, Sandhya. From Twinkle, with Love. 2018. (ENG., Illus.). 336p. (YA). (gr. 7). 18.99 *(978-1-4814-9540-0(2)*, Simon Pulse) Simon Pulse.

Morris, Jennifer E. Please Write Back! 2010. (Scholastic Reader Level 1 Ser.). lib. bdg. 13.55 *(978-0-606-06822-2(8))* Turtleback.

Morrissey, Bridget. When the Light Went Out. 2019. (ENG.). 320p. (YA). (gr. 8-12). pap. 12.99 *(978-1-4926-7098-8(7))* Sourcebooks, Inc.

Mullican, Judy. May We Go to the Zoo? Gray, Stacy A., illus. l.t. ed. 2004. (HRL Little Book Ser.). (J). (gr. -1-1). pap. 10.95 *(978-1-57332-304-8(7))*; pap. 10.95 *(978-1-57332-303-1(9))* Carson-Dellosa Publishing, LLC. (HighReach Learning, Incorporated).

—Pretend. Meler, Kerry L., illus. l.t. ed. 2005. (HRL Board Book Ser.). 10p. (J). (gr. -1-1). pap. 10.95 *(978-1-57332-283-6(0)*, HighReach Learning, Incorporated) Carson-Dellosa Publishing, LLC.

Nagus, Kari. Congratulations Q & U. 2010. (ENG.). 18p. pap. 8.49 *(978-1-4520-5153-6(4))* AuthorHouse.

Noel, Alyson. Forever Summer. 2011. (ENG.). 464p. (YA). (gr. 8-12). pap. 29.99 *(978-0-312-60439-4(4)*, 900076464, St. Martin's Griffin) St. Martin's Pr.

Nolen, Jerdine & Kelliher, Brian. Plantzilla. Catrow, David, illus. 2005. (ENG.). 32p. (J). (gr. -1-3). reprint ed. pap. 7.99 *(978-0-15-205392-5(1)*, 1196232, Clarion Bks.) HarperCollins Pubs.

O'Kelley, Jeff. Sharing Our Stories. 2006. (Early Explorers Ser.). (J). pap. *(978-1-4108-6127-6(9))* Benchmark Education Co.

Ouchley, Amy Griffin. Swamper: Letters from a Louisiana Swamp Rabbit. 2013. (ENG., Illus.). 72p. (gr. 4-7). 22.50 *(978-0-8071-5074-0(6)*, 1763) Louisiana State Univ. Pr.

Oxley, Jennifer & Aronson, Billy. Peg + Cat: the Big Dog Problem: a Level 2 Reader. 2017. (Peg + Cat Ser.). (ENG.). 48p. (J). (gr. k-3). 14.99 *(978-0-7636-9787-7(7))*; pap. 4.99 *(978-0-7636-9790-7(7))* Candlewick Pr. (Candlewick Entertainment).

Parham, Pam H. When I Take a Bath. Gillen, Lisa P., illus. l.t. ed. 2005. (HRL Board Book Ser.). 12p. (J). (gr. -1-1). pap. 10.95 *(978-1-57332-284-3(9)*, HighReach Learning, Incorporated) Carson-Dellosa Publishing, LLC.

PeachMoon Publishing. The Lizard in the Mailbox. 2007. (J). pap. 9.95 *(978-0-9795831-0-0(1))* PeachMoon Publishing.

Pennypacker, Sara. Clementine's Letter. Frazee, Marla, illus. 2009. (Clementine Ser.: 3). (ENG.). 160p. (J). (gr. 1-5). pap. 5.99 *(978-0-7868-3885-1(X))* Little, Brown Bks. for Young Readers.

Pichard, Alexandra. Pen Pals. Pichard, Alexandra, illus. 2017. (ENG., Illus.). 48p. (J). (gr. -1-2). 17.99 *(978-1-4814-7247-0(X)*, Simon & Schuster/Paula Wiseman Bks.) Simon & Schuster/Paula Wiseman Bks.

Pitcher, Annabel. Yours Truly. 2014. (ENG., Illus.). 288p. (YA). (gr. 7-17). pap. 9.99 *(978-0-316-24678-1(6))* Little, Brown Bks. for Young Readers.

PS, I Love You, Gramps: Individual Title, 6 packs. (Action Packs Ser.). 120p. (gr. 3-5). 44.00 *(978-0-7635-8389-7(8))* Rigby Education.

Rader, Laura. The Twelve Days of Christmas in California. 2017. (Twelve Days of Christmas in America Ser.). (ENG., Illus.). 22p. (J). (-k). bds. 7.95 *(978-1-4549-2792-1(5))* Sterling Publishing Co., Inc.

—The Twelve Days of Christmas in California. Rader, Laura, illus. 2009. (Twelve Days of Christmas in America Ser.). (ENG., Illus.). 40p. (J). (gr. k-3). 12.95 *(978-1-4027-6247-5(X))* Sterling Publishing Co., Inc.

Radzinski, Kandy. What Cats Want for Christmas. Radzinski, Kandy, illus. rev. ed. 2007. (ENG., Illus.). 32p. (J). (gr. 1-4). 16.95 *(978-1-58536-340-7(5)*, 202130) Sleeping Bear Pr.

Rakusin, Sudie. Dear Calla Roo... Love, Savannah Blue No. 2: A Letter about Getting Sick & Feeling Better. Rakusin, Sudie, illus. 2003. (Illus.). 32p. (J). (gr. -1-4). 16.95 *(978-0-9664805-3-5(8))* Winged Willow Pr.

Ransom, Candice. The Twelve Days of Christmas in Washington, D. C. Hollander, Sarah, illus. 2018. (Twelve Days of Christmas in America Ser.). (ENG.). 22p. (J). (-k). bds. 7.95 *(978-1-4549-2966-6(9))* Sterling Publishing Co., Inc.

Rapp, Adam. Punkzilla. 2009. (ENG., Illus.). 256p. (YA). (gr. 9). 16.99 *(978-0-7636-3031-7(4))* Candlewick Pr.

Rex, Adam. Xo, Ox: A Love Story. Campbell, Scott, illus. 2017. (ENG.). 40p. (J). 17.99 *(978-1-62672-288-0(9)*, 900149172) Roaring Brook Pr.

Rissman, Angelica. Julius & the Lost Letter to Santa. 2003. (J). 7.99 *(978-1-59384-019-8(5))* Parklane Publishing.

Rosenberg, Amye. A Surprise in the Mail! Salanitro, Robert, illus. 2009. (Discovery Ser.). (ENG.). 12p. (J). 7.99 *(978-1-60436-018-9(6))* Educational Publishing LLC.

Ryan, Pam Muñoz. Tony Baloney: Pen Pal. Fotheringham, Ed, illus. 2014. 39p. (J). pap. *(978-0-545-69227-4(X)*, Scholastic Pr.) Scholastic, Inc.

Salonen, Roxane Beauclair. The Twelve Days of Christmas in North Dakota. Golden, Jessica, illus. 2017. (Twelve Days of Christmas in America Ser.). (ENG.). 40p. (J). (gr. k). 12.95 *(978-1-4549-2008-3(4))* Sterling Publishing Co., Inc.

Scholastic, Inc. Staff. Dear Mrs. Larue. 2005. (ENG.). (J). pap. 550.00 *(978-0-439-70787-9(0)*, Sidekicks TM) Scholastic, Inc.

Sedgwick, Chantele. Love, Lucas. 2015. (Love, Lucas Novel Ser.: 1). (ENG.). 280p. (J). (gr. 6-6). 16.99 *(978-1-63220-417-2(7)*, Sky Pony Pr.) Skyhorse Publishing Co., Inc.

Sís, Peter. Ice Cream Summer. Sís, Peter, illus. 2015. (ENG., Illus.). 40p. (J). (gr. -1-3). 18.99 *(978-0-545-73161-4(5)*, Scholastic Pr.) Scholastic, Inc.

Smith, Yeardley. I, Lorelei. 2009. 352p. (J). (gr. 3-7). lib. bdg. 17.89 *(978-0-06-149345-4(7)*, Geringer, Laura Book) HarperCollins Pubs.

Snicket, Lemony, pseud. The Beatrice Letters. 2006. (Series of Unfortunate Events Ser.). (ENG., Illus.). 72p. (J). (gr. 5-7). 22.99 *(978-0-06-058658-4(3)*, HarperCollins) HarperCollins Pubs.

Spain, Susan Rosson. The Twelve Days of Christmas in Georgia. Dulemba, Elizabeth O., illus. 2018. (Twelve Days of Christmas in America Ser.). (ENG.). 22p. (J). (-k). bds. 7.95 *(978-1-4549-2995-6(2))* Sterling Publishing Co., Inc.

Spinelli, Jerry. Love, Stargirl. 2009. (Stargirl Ser.: 2). (ENG.). 288p. (YA). (gr. 7). pap. 9.99 *(978-0-375-85644-0(7)*, Ember) Random Hse. Children's Bks.

Stead, Judy, illus. The Twelve Days of Christmas in North Carolina. 2017. (Twelve Days of Christmas in America Ser.). (ENG.). 22p. (J). (-k). bds. 7.95 *(978-1-4549-2285-8(0))* Sterling Publishing Co., Inc.

Stewart, Jennifer J. The Twelve Days of Christmas in Arizona. Avril, Lynne, illus. 2018. (Twelve Days of Christmas in America Ser.). (ENG.). 22p. (J). (-k). bds. 7.95 *(978-1-4549-2994-9(4))* Sterling Publishing Co., Inc.

Stewart, Sarah. The Gardener. Small, David, illus. 2003. (J). (gr. -1-2). 28.95 incl. audio compact disk *(978-1-59112-531-0(6))*; 28.95 incl. audio compact disk *(978-1-59112-531-0(6))* Live Oak Media.

—The Gardener. Small, David, illus. 2007. (ENG.). 40p. (J). (gr. -1-2). per. 8.99 *(978-0-312-36749-7(X)*, 900042354) Square Fish.

—The Quiet Place, 1 vol. Small, David, illus. 2012. (ENG.). 44p. (J). (gr. k-4). 19.99 *(978-0-374-32565-7(0)*, 900065971, Farrar, Straus & Giroux (BYR)) Farrar, Straus & Giroux.

Stone, Nic. Dear Martin. (ENG.). (gr. 9). 2018. 240p. (YA). pap. 10.99 *(978-1-101-93952-9(4)*, Ember) 2017. 224p. (YA). 18.99 *(978-1-101-93949-9(4)*, Crown Books For Young Readers)1. 2018. 240p. 28.69 *(978-1-5364-4655-5(6)*, Ember) Random Hse. Children's Bks.

—Dear Martin. 2018. lib. bdg. 20.85 *(978-0-606-41555-2(6))* Turtleback.

Tennant Iain Staff. Alby's Letters to Henry: Written from Isle of Mull. Smith, William, illus. 2007. (ENG.). 176p. (J). pap. 15.99 *(978-1-903071-14-4(3))* Bene Factum Publishing, Ltd. GBR. Dist: Independent Pubs. Group.

Tolkien, J. R. R. & Tolkien, Baillie. Letters from Father Christmas. 2004. (ENG., Illus.). 128p. pap. 25.00 *(978-0-618-51265-2(9)*, 689483, William Morrow Paperbacks) HarperCollins Pubs.

Vonthron, Satanta C. Caillou's Dinosaur Day. Neveu, Fred, illus. l.t. ed. 2004. (HRL Board Book Ser.). (J). (gr. -1-1). pap. 10.95 *(978-1-57332-288-1(1)*, HighReach Learning, Incorporated) Carson-Dellosa Publishing, LLC.

Wallace, Bill. Pick of the Litter. 2006. (ENG.). 176p. (J). (gr. 3-7). pap. 5.99 *(978-1-4169-2511-8(2)*, Aladdin) Simon & Schuster Children's Publishing.

Warwick, Ellen. The Twelve Days of Christmas in Canada. Smith, Kimberly, illus. 2015. (Twelve Days of Christmas in America Ser.). (ENG.). 40p. (J). (gr. k). 12.95 *(978-1-4549-1431-0(9))* Sterling Publishing Co., Inc.

Wells, Sheila Rae. Waiting for a Letter. 2004. 37p. (J). pap. 7.97 *(978-1-4116-0908-2(5))* Lulu Pr., Inc.

Whitman, Sylvia. The Milk of Birds. (ENG., Illus.). 384p. (YA). (gr. 9). 2014. pap. 12.99 *(978-1-4424-4683-0(8))* 2013. 16.99 *(978-1-4424-4682-3(X)*, Atheneum Bks. for Young Readers) Simon & Schuster Children's Publishing.

Whybrow, Ian. Little Wolf, Terror of the Shivery Sea. Ross, Tony, illus. 2004. (Little Wolf Adventures Ser.). (ENG.). 144p. (J). (gr. 3-6). 14.95 *(978-1-57505-629-6(1))* Lerner Publishing Group.

—Little Wolf's Diary of Daring Deeds. Ross, Tony, illus. (Middle Grade Fiction Ser.). 132p. (gr. 3-6). 2005. 14.95 *(978-1-57505-411-7(6))* 2003. (J). pap. 6.95 *(978-0-87614-536-4(5)*, Carolrhoda Bks.) Lerner Publishing Group.

—Lobito Aprende a Ser Malo. Azaola, Miguel, tr. from ENG. Ross, Tony, illus. 2007. (Ediciones Lerner Single Titles Ser.). (SPA.). 136p. (J). (gr. 3-6). per. 6.95 *(978-0-8225-8644-9(4)*, Ediciones Lerner) Lerner Publishing Group.

Wilkerson, Dana. Mustang Macy. 2017. (ENG.). 122p. (J). (gr. 2-5). pap. 7.99 *(978-1-948148-00-9(5))* Dana Wilkerson, LLC.

Williams, Heather L. Caillou's Castle. Meler, Kerry L., illus. l.t. ed. 2005. (HRL Board Book Ser.). (J). (gr. -1-1). pap. 10.95 *(978-1-57332-291-1(1)*, HighReach Learning, Incorporated) Carson-Dellosa Publishing, LLC.

Winthrop, Elizabeth. Franklin Delano Roosevelt: Letters from a Mill Town Girl. Winthrop, Elizabeth, illus. unabr. ed. 2003. (Illus.). (J). (gr. 4-7). 25.95 incl. audio *(978-1-59112-213-5(9))* Live Oak Media.

Wittlinger, Ellen. Heart on My Sleeve. 2006. (ENG., Illus.). 240p. (YA). (gr. 7). reprint ed. pap. 10.99 *(978-0-689-84999-2(0)*, Simon & Schuster Bks. For Young Readers) Simon & Schuster Bks. For Young Readers.

Wood, Francis Eusene. The Christmas Letter. Wood, Christine & Marken, Jon, eds. McDermott, Robert, illus. Wood, Christine, photos by. 2007. pap. 9.95 *(978-0-9746372-6-6(2))* Tip-Of-The-Moon Publishing Co.

Woodson, Jacqueline. Peace, Locomotion. (ENG.). (J). 2010. 176p. (gr. 5-18). 8.99 *(978-0-14-241512-2(X)*, Puffin Books) 2009. 144p. (gr. 4-6). 22.44 *(978-0-399-24655-5(X))* Penguin Young Readers Group.

Wrede, Patricia C. & Stevermer, Caroline. The Mislaid Magician or Ten Years After: Being the Private Correspondence Between Two Prominent FamiliesRegarding a Scandal Touching the Highest Levels of Government & TheSecurity of the Realm. 2009. (ENG., Illus.). 336p. (YA). (gr. 7). pap. 18.95 *(978-0-15-206209-5(2)*, 1099016, Clarion Bks.) HarperCollins Pubs.

Zweibel, Alan. Our Tree Named Steve. Catrow, David, illus. 2007. 32p. (J). (gr. -1-k). pap. 8.99 *(978-0-14-240743-1(7)*, Puffin Books) Penguin Young Readers Group.

—Our Tree Named Steve. 2007. 16.00 *(978-1-4177-6974-2(2))* Turtleback.

LETTERS OF CREDIT

see Credit

LETTERS OF THE ALPHABET

see Alphabet

LEUKEMIA

Apel, Melanie Ann. Coping with Leukemia. 2009. (Coping Ser.). 192p. (gr. 7-12). 63.90 *(978-1-61512-001-7(7))* Rosen Publishing Group, Inc., The.

Brent, Mary & Caitlin, Knutsson. Chemo to the Rescue: A Children's Book about Leukemia. 2008. 48p. pap. 17.49 *(978-1-4343-9720-1(3))* AuthorHouse.

Chilman-Blair, Kim, et al. Medikidz Explain Leukaemia: What's up with Richard? 2009. (ENG., Illus.). 32p. (J). pap. *(978-1-906935-05-4(X))* Medikidz Ltd.

Coerr, Eleanor. Sadako & the Thousand Paper Cranes (Puffin Modern Classics) Himler, Ronald, illus. 2004. (Puffin Modern Classics Ser.). (ENG.). 80p. (J). (gr. 3-7). pap. 7.99 *(978-0-14-240113-2(7)*, Puffin Books) Penguin Young Readers Group.

Harmon, Daniel E. Leukemia, 1 vol. 2011. (Cancer & Modern Science Ser.). (ENG.). 64p. (gr. 5-5). lib. bdg. 37.13 *(978-1-4488-1311-7(5)*, d39e299d-f3e3-48b1-93f8-14511ac49390) Rosen Publishing Group, Inc., The.

Klosterman, Lorrie. Leukemia, 1 vol. 2007. (Health Alert Ser.). (ENG., Illus.). 64p. (gr. 4-4). lib. bdg. 35.50 *(978-0-7614-1916-7(0)*, a40b0dfc-28e0-4168-af9f-95cf9621114d) Cavendish Square Publishing LLC.

Mack, Lorna B. Lorna's Whale. 2011. 56p. pap. 26.12 *(978-1-4634-1610-2(5))* AuthorHouse.

Novel Units. Sadako & the Thousand Paper Cranes Novel Units Student Packet. 2019. (ENG.). (J). (gr. k-6). pap. 13.99 *(978-1-56137-631-5(0)*, Novel Units, Inc.) Classroom Library Co.

—Sadako & the Thousand Paper Cranes Novel Units Teacher Guide. 2019. (ENG.). (J). pap. 12.99 *(978-1-56137-178-5(5)*, Novel Units, Inc.) Classroom Library Co.

Parks, Peggy J. Leukemia. 2010. (Compact Research Ser.). (YA). (gr. 7-12). 43.93 *(978-1-60152-099-9(9))* ReferencePoint Pr., Inc.

Wilmoth Lerner, Adrienne, ed. Leukemia, 1 vol. 2009. (Perspectives on Diseases & Disorders Ser.). (ENG., Illus.). 160p. (gr. 10-12). lib. bdg. 45.93 *(978-0-7377-4247-3(X)*, d4928b96-9b41-4e4e-8e6a-d2119cbb5434, Greenhaven Publishing) Greenhaven Publishing LLC.

LEUKEMIA—FICTION

Andrews, Jesse. Me & Earl & the Dying Girl. 2015. (CHI.). 320p. (YA). (gr. 9-17). pap. *(978-986-344-282-0(8))* Rye Field Publishing, Co.

—Me & Earl & the Dying Girl. 2015. lib. bdg. 20.80 *(978-0-606-37113-1(3))* Turtleback.

—Me & Earl & the Dying Girl (Revised Edition) rev. ed. 2015. (ENG.). 320p. (YA). (gr. 9-17). pap. 11.99 *(978-1-4197-1960-8(2)*, 1003806) Abrams, Inc.

Bryant, Cathy. The Doctor Said I Have Leukemi. Bunker, Thomas, illus. 2012. 24p. pap. 24.95 *(978-1-4560-6929-2(2))* America Star Bks.

Dee, Barbara. Halfway Normal. 2017. (ENG., Illus.). 256p. (J). (gr. 4-8). 16.99 *(978-1-4814-7851-9(6)*, Aladdin) Simon & Schuster Children's Publishing.

Devlin, Calla. Tell Me Something Real. 2016. (ENG., Illus.). 304p. (YA). (gr. 9). 17.99 *(978-1-4814-6115-3(X)*, Atheneum

Bks. for Young Readers) Simon & Schuster Children's Publishing.

Gilman, David. Monkey & Me. 2014. (ENG.). 240p. (J). (gr. 4-7). pap. 11.99 *(978-1-84877-335-6(8))* Bonnier Publishing GBR. Dist: Independent Pubs. Group.

Johnston, Carol Shaw. Lily & Sophie: Sisters & Best Friends. 2010. (ENG.). 65p. pap. 26.99 *(978-0-557-35894-6(9))* Lulu Pr., Inc.

Murphy, Julie. Side Effects May Vary. 2014. (ENG.). 336p. (YA). (gr. 9). 17.99 *(978-0-06-224535-9(X)*, Balzer & Bray) HarperCollins Pubs.

Nicholls, Sally. Ways to Live Forever. 2011. (ENG.). 224p. (J). (gr. 6-8). 21.19 *(978-0-545-06949-6(1)*, Levine, Arthur A. Bks.) Scholastic, Inc.

Nicklas, Rita. The B-Liminator & I Fight Cancer. 2009. (ENG.). 40p. pap. 18.50 *(978-0-557-04764-2(1))* Lulu Pr., Inc.

Novak, Ali. The Heartbreakers. 2015. (Heartbreak Chronicles Ser.: 1). 336p. (YA). (gr. 6-12). pap. 12.99 *(978-1-4926-1256-8(1)*, 9781492612568) Sourcebooks, Inc.

O'Brien, Frances. Sheer Bliss: Confessions of a (Reluctant) Celebrity Spawn. 2006. (ENG.). 144p. *(978-1-905886-32-6(2))* Troubador Publishing Ltd.

Rushford, Patricia H. Secrets of Ghost Island. 2007. (J). *(978-88-02-46255-4(0))* Moody Pubs.

Stimkorb, Patricia. All about Me! Regular Version. 2005. (Illus.). 12p. (J). bds. 12.99 *(978-0-9758709-8-3(X)*, A.W.A. Gang) Journey Stone Creations, LLC.

Tucker, Seletha Marie Head. A Hat for Melinda: Fighting Leukemia Together. Lee, Anais, illus. 2013. *(978-1-62086-164-6(X))* Amplify Publishing Group.

Willner, Judy. How My Sun Got Its Smile: The Story of Deana Vega. 2010. 48p. pap. 20.99 *(978-1-4520-7720-8(7))* AuthorHouse.

Wilson, Robert. Pippy: The Miracle of A Dream. 2011. 136p. 21.95 *(978-1-4620-6634-6(8))*; pap. 11.95 *(978-1-4620-6633-9(X))* iUniverse, Inc.

LEVANT

see Middle East

LEWIS, C. S. (CLIVE STAPLES), 1898-1963

Bacher, Lindsay. Biblical Allusions, 1 vol. 2015. (Essential Literary Themes Ser.). (ENG., Illus.). 112p. (YA). (gr. 6-12). 41.36 *(978-1-62403-802-0(6)*, 17802, Essential Library) ABDO Publishing Co.

Bell, James Stuart, et al. Inside the Lion the Witch & Wardrobe. 2005. (ENG., Illus.). 240p. (YA). (gr. 8-13). pap. 19.99 *(978-0-312-34744-4(8)*, 900031213, St. Martin's Griffin) St. Martin's Pr.

Benge, Janet & Benge, Geoff. Christian Heroes - Then & Now - C. S. Lewis: Master Storyteller. 2007. (Christian Heroes Ser.). (ENG.). 192p. (YA). (gr. 3-7). pap. 11.99 *(978-1-57658-385-2(6))* YWAM Publishing.

C. S. Lewis: Twentieth Century Pilgrim. 2011. (World Writers Ser.). 128p. (gr. 7-9). lib. bdg. 28.95 *(978-1-59935-112-4(9))* Reynolds, Morgan Inc.

Coren, Michael. C. S. Lewis: The Man Who Created Narnia. 2006. (ENG., Illus.). 139p. per. 14.95 *(978-1-58617-109-4(7))* Ignatius Pr.

Edwards, Anfrew & Edwards, Fleur. Footsteps of the past: C S Lewis: The story of one of the world's most famous authors who sold over a hundred million Books. 2007. (Footsteps of the Past Ser.). 32p. pap. 6.00 *(978-1-84625-091-0(9))* DayOne Pubns. GBR. Dist: Send The Light Distribution LLC.

Gillespie, Natalie. Believing in Narnia: A Kid's Guide to Unlocking the Secret Symbols of Faith in C. S. Lewis' the Chronicles of Narnia, 1 vol. 2008. (ENG., Illus.). 192p. (J). (gr. 2-6). pap. 12.99 *(978-1-4003-1282-5(5)*, Tommy Nelson) Nelson, Thomas Inc.

Gormley, Beatrice. C. S. Lewis: The Man Behind Narnia. 2nd ed. 2005. (ENG., Illus.). 192p. (gr. 8-12). per. 14.00 *(978-0-8028-5301-1(3)*, Eerdmans Bks For Young Readers) Eerdmans, William B. Publishing Co.

Lappi, Megan. C. S. Lewis. 2005. (My Favorite Writer Ser.). (Illus.). 32p. (J). (gr. 5-7). lib. bdg. 26.00 *(978-1-59036-285-3(3))* Weigl Pubs., Inc.

LEWIS, JOHN LLEWELLYN, 1880-1969

Haskins, Jim & Benson, Kathleen. John Lewis in the Lead: A Story of the Civil Rights Movement, 1 vol. Andrews, Benny, illus. 2006. (ENG.). 40p. (J). (gr. 3-8). pap. 12.95 *(978-1-60060-849-0(3)*, leelowbooks) Lee & Low Bks., Inc.

LEWIS, MERIWETHER, 1774-1809

Bodden, Valerie. Through the American West. 2011. (Great Expeditions Ser.). (ENG., Illus.). 48p. (J). (gr. 5-8). 35.65 *(978-1-60818-065-3(4)*, 22151, Creative Education) Creative Co., The.

Fox, Michael D. & Fox, Suzanne G. Meriwether Lewis & William Clark: The Corps of Discovery & the Exploration of the American Frontier, 1 vol. 2004. (Library of American Lives & Times Ser.). (ENG., Illus.). 112p. (J). (gr. 5-5). lib. bdg. 38.27 *(978-1-4042-2650-0(8)*, 96e27260-6d09-4b7f-888a-42a5dd16e882) Rosen Publishing Group, Inc., The.

Fox, Suzanne G. Meriwether Lewis & William Clark: The Corp of Discovery & the Exploration of the American Frontier. 2009. (Library of American Lives & Times Ser.). 112p. (gr. 5-5). 69.20 *(978-1-60853-493-7(6))* Rosen Publishing Group, Inc., The.

Fruge, William. Lewis & Clark: A Journey West, 1 vol. 2008. (Real Life Readers Ser.). (ENG.). 24p. (gr. 3-4). pap. 8.25 *(978-1-4358-0040-3(0)*, 5ed12ac1-6749-4846-bd9a-bf3568d6f159, Rosen Classroom) Rosen Publishing Group, Inc., The.

Ganeri, Anita. On Expedition with Lewis & Clark. 2010. (ENG.). 32p. (J). (gr. 3-5). *(978-0-7787-9896-5(8))*; (Crabtree Connections Ser.: No. 2). pap. *(978-0-7787-9917-7(4))* Crabtree Publishing Co.

Gondosch, Linda. Where Did Sacagawea Join the Corps of Discovery? And Other Questions about the Lewis & Clark Expedition. 2011. (Six Questions of American History Ser.). (ENG.). 48p. (gr. 4-6). pap. 56.72 *(978-0-7613-7644-6(5))*; (Illus.). (J). pap. 11.99 *(978-0-7613-7131-1(1)*, 061f662a-a998-4abe-ac16-604cd15f7710); (Illus.). (J). lib. bdg. 30.65 *(978-0-7613-5226-6(0)*, fd798483-1f32-4a50-af83-88af79191609, Lerner Pubns.) Lerner Publishing Group.

Jeffrey, Gary. The Explorations of Lewis & Clark, 1 vol. Riley, Terry, illus. 2012. (Graphic History of the American West Ser.). (ENG.). 24p. (J). (gr. 3-3). pap. 9.15 *(978-1-4339-6737-5(5)*, a5e61c12-ec79-4b33-bc2b-54274e669486, Gareth Stevens Learning Library); lib. bdg. 26.60 *(978-1-4339-6735-1(9)*, 7760c7a6-c4c3-430a-a866-f81c5327488b) Stevens, Gareth Publishing LLLP.

Keller, Susanna. The True Story of Lewis & Clark, 1 vol. 2013. (What Really Happened? Ser.). (ENG., Illus.). 24p. (J). (gr. 2-3). pap. 9.25 *(978-1-4488-9846-6(3)*, e0a93e44-5e16-4d0a-8805-6b38d2ae6877); lib. bdg. 26.27 *(978-1-4488-9694-3(0)*, 45b0e550-b940-425e-969e-33f6e3bf16f) Rosen Publishing Group, Inc., The. (PowerKids Pr.).

Lawrence, Blythe. The Lewis & Clark Expedition. 2018. (Expansion of Our Nation Ser.). (ENG., Illus.). 32p. (J). (gr. 3-5). pap. 9.95 *(978-1-63517-983-5(1)*, 1635179831, Focus Readers) North Star Editions.

—The Lewis & Clark Expedition. 2018. (Illus.). 32p. (J). *(978-1-4896-9870-4(1)*, AV2 by Weigl) Weigl Pubs., Inc.

Levy, Janey. Lewis & Clark in Their Own Words, 1 vol., Vol. 1. 2014. (Eyewitness to History Ser.). (ENG.). 32p. (J). (gr. 4-5). 29.27 *(978-1-4339-9929-1(3)*, f6377acd-b9ac-4838-8b85-72be01888a2b); pap. 11.50 *(978-1-4339-9930-7(7)*, a1e4799d-12bc-438c-9624-9fddec8edc01) Stevens, Gareth Publishing LLLP.

Lynette, Rachel. Meriwether Lewis & William Clark, 1 vol. 2013. (Pioneer Spirit: the Westward Expansion Ser.). 24p. (J). (ENG.). (gr. 2-3). 26.27 *(978-1-4777-0783-8(2)*, c3379d73-e58a-46ba-a505-004b5518497d); (gr. 3-6). pap. 49.50 *(978-1-4777-0900-9(2))*; (ENG., Illus.). (gr. 2-3). pap. 9.25 *(978-1-4777-0899-6(5)*, a7e102b5-f175-4b5e-9fee-d0fde36daf27) Rosen Publishing Group, Inc., The. (PowerKids Pr.).

Marsh, Carole. Meriwether Lewis & William Clark: Explorers of the Uncharted West: Explorers of the Uncharted West. 2003. 12p. (gr. k-4). 2.95 *(978-0-635-02133-5(1))* Gallopade International.

Meloche, Renee Taft. Heroes of History for Young Readers - Meriwether Lewis: Journey Aross America. Pollard, Brian, illus. 2006. (Heroes of History Ser.). (ENG.). 32p. (J). (gr. -1-3). 8.99 *(978-1-932096-27-9(2))* Emerald Bks.

Morley, Jacqueline. You Wouldn't Want to Explore with Lewis & Clark! An Epic Journey You'd Rather Not Make. Bergin, Mark, illus. 2013. (You Wouldn't Want to... Ser.). (ENG.). 32p. (J). 29.00 *(978-0-531-25942-9(0)*, Watts, Franklin) Scholastic Library Publishing.

—You Wouldn't Want to Explore with Lewis & Clark! An Epic Journey You'd Rather Not Make. 2013. (You Wouldn't Want To Ser.). lib. bdg. 20.80 *(978-0-606-31633-0(7))* Turtleback.

Morlock, Rachael. Lewis & Clark Explore the Louisiana Territory, 1 vol. 2018. (Real-Life Scientific Adventures Ser.). (ENG.). 32p. (gr. 4-5). 29.27 *(978-1-5081-6850-8(4)*, 7235896b-7bfb-4480-91b5-538c4973a4fc, PowerKids Pr.) Rosen Publishing Group, Inc., The.

Mulhall, Jill K. Lewis & Clark. rev. ed. 2017. (Social Studies: Informational Text Ser.). (ENG., Illus.). 32p. (gr. 4-8). pap. 11.99 *(978-1-4938-3886-8(5))* Teacher Created Materials, Inc.

Orr, Tamra. The Lewis & Clark Expedition: A Primary Source History of the Journey of the Corps of Discovery. (Primary Sources in American History Ser.). 64p. (gr. 5-8). 2009. 58.50 *(978-1-60851-498-4(6))* 2004. (ENG., Illus.). lib. bdg. 37.13 *(978-0-8239-4005-9(5)*, 1c22f8d5-a1e3-4eae-9fd0-d91c04328a1a, Rosen Reference) Rosen Publishing Group, Inc., The.

Perritano, John. True Books: the Lewis & Clark Expedition. 2010. (True Book Ser.). (ENG., Illus.). 48p. (J). (gr. 2-5). 29.00 *(978-0-531-20582-2(7))* Scholastic Library Publishing.

Ransom, Candice. Lewis & Clark. 2003. (History Maker Bios Ser.). (Illus.). 48p. (J). (gr. 2-4). 26.60 *(978-0-8225-0394-1(8)*, Lerner Pubns.) Lerner Publishing Group.

Robinson, Kate. Lewis & Clark: Exploring the American West, 1 vol. 2009. (Great Explorers of the World Ser.). (ENG., Illus.). 112p. (gr. 6-7). 35.93 *(978-1-59845-124-5(3)*, 5a91466e-b841-429e-a58d-e2b90c9c3a72) Enslow Publishing, LLC.

Rodger, Ellen. Lewis & Clark: Opening the American West, 1 vol. 2005. (In the Footsteps of Explorers Ser.). (ENG., Illus.). 32p. (J). (gr. -1-9). pap. *(978-0-7787-2446-9(8))*; lib. bdg. *(978-0-7787-2410-0(7))* Crabtree Publishing Co.

Sapp, Richard. Lewis & Clark on Their Journey to the Pacific, 1 vol. 2005. (In the Footsteps of American Heroes Ser.). (ENG., Illus.). 64p. (gr. 5-8). lib. bdg. 36.67 *(978-0-8368-6429-8(8)*, b5fc7f92-3c47-4d52-af0b-18c81c16af7d, Gareth Stevens Secondary Library) Stevens, Gareth Publishing LLLP.

Schanzer, Rosalyn. How We Crossed the West: The Adventures of Lewis & Clark. 2012. (ENG.). 48p. (J). (gr. 3-7). lib. bdg. 27.00 *(978-1-4263-1328-8(4)*, National Geographic Children's Bks.) Disney Publishing Worldwide.

Smalley, Carol Parenzan. Lewis & Clark. 2008. (What's So Great About... ? Ser.). (Illus.). 32p. (YA). (gr. 2-4). lib. bdg. 25.70 *(978-1-58415-725-0(9))* Mitchell Lane Pubs.

St. George, Judith. What Was the Lewis & Clark Expedition? 2014. (What Was... Ser.). lib. bdg. 16.00 *(978-0-606-36185-9(5))* Turtleback.

St. George, Judith & Who HQ. What Was the Lewis & Clark Expedition? Foley, Tim, illus. 2014. (What Was? Ser.). 112p. (J). (gr. 3-7). pap. 5.99 *(978-0-448-47901-9(X)*, Penguin Workshop) Penguin Young Readers Group.

Strand, Jennifer. Lewis & Clark. 2016. (Pioneering Explorers Ser.). (ENG.). 24p. (J). (gr. -1-2). 49.94 *(978-1-68079-411-3(6)*, 23032, Abdo Zoom-Launch) ABDO Publishing Co.

Stuckey, Rachel. Explore with Lewis & Clark. 2014. (Travel with the Great Explorers Ser.). (ENG., Illus.). 32p. (J). (gr. 4-5). *(978-0-7787-1247-3(8))*; pap. *(978-0-7787-1259-6(1))* Crabtree Publishing Co.

Swanson, Jennifer. Lewis & Clark, 1 vol. 2016. (Spotlight on Explorers & Colonization Ser.). (ENG., Illus.). 48p. (J). (gr. 6-6). pap. 12.75 *(978-1-5081-7237-6(4)*, 9b0ecfa8-404b-406a-b9d5-b6b3587fe196) Rosen Publishing Group, Inc., The.

LEWIS AND CLARK EXPEDITION (1804-1806)

Blashfield, Jean F. The Amazing Lewis & Clark Expedition. 2017. (Landmarks in U. S. History Ser.). (ENG., Illus.). 32p. (J). (gr. 3-6). lib. bdg. 27.99 *(978-1-5157-7120-3(2)*, 135519, Capstone Pr.) Capstone.

Bloom Fradin, Judith & Brindell Fradin, Dennis. The Lewis & Clark Expedition, 1 vol. 2008. (Turning Points in U. S. History Ser.). (ENG., Illus.). 48p. (gr. 4-4). lib. bdg. 34.07 *(978-0-7614-2044-6(4)*, 7f2d646f-467e-4a5c-ab42-787f757e9373) Cavendish Square Publishing LLC.

Blumberg, Rhoda. York's Adventures with Lewis & Clark: An African-American's Part in the Great Expedition. 2004. (ENG., Illus.). 96p. (J). (gr. 3-18). 17.99 *(978-0-06-009111-8(8))* HarperCollins Pubs.

Bodden, Valerie. Through the American West. 2011. (Great Expeditions Ser.). (ENG., Illus.). 48p. (J). (gr. 5-8). 35.65 *(978-1-60818-065-3(4)*, 22151, Creative Education) Creative Co., The.

Buffalohead, Julie, illus. Sacagawea. 2005. (Libros Ilustrados (Picture Bks.)). (SPA & ENG.). 40p. (J). (gr. 3-6). 16.95 *(978-0-8225-3191-3(7)*, Ediciones Lerner) Lerner Publishing Group.

Byers, Ann. Sacagawea, 1 vol. 2020. (Inside Guide: Famous Native Americans Ser.). (ENG.). 32p. (gr. 4-5). pap. 11.58 *(978-1-5026-5064-1(9)*, 1a6f2658-afa0-4e6b-8867-726a692bb62f) Cavendish Square Publishing LLC.

Clifton, Chuck & Clifton, Joyce. A Daily Walk with Lewis & Clark - 1804. 2003. 308p. (J). spiral bd. 14.95 *(978-0-9669760-3-8(7))* Maple Canyon Co.

—A Daily Walk with Lewis & Clark - 1805. 2003. 390p. (J). spiral bd. 14.95 *(978-0-9669760-4-5(5))* Maple Canyon Co.

—A Daily Walk with Lewis & Clark - 1806. 2003. 292p. (J). spiral bd. 14.95 *(978-0-9669760-5-2(3))* Maple Canyon Co.

Collard, Sneed B., III. Sacagawea: Brave Shoshone Girl, 1 vol. 2007. (American Heroes Ser.). (ENG., Illus.). 48p. (gr. 3-3). lib. bdg. 32.64 *(978-0-7614-2166-5(1)*, 8319f4a1-5531-4f32-9e8b-4de0fdedd320) Cavendish Square Publishing LLC.

Collins, Kathleen. On the Trail with Lewis & Clark: Learning to Use Line Graphs. 2004. (Math Big Bookstm Ser.). (ENG.). 16p. (gr. 2-3). 37.95 *(978-0-8239-7639-3(4))* Rosen Publishing Group, Inc., The.

Conant, Susan Sens. Lewis & Clark's Journey of Discovery: A Guide for Young Explorers. Lynn, Rick, illus. 2004. 48p. (J). pap. *(978-0-9725584-1-9(1))* Little Blue Pr.

Crosby, Michael T. Sacagawea: Lewis & Clark's Pathfinder. 2007. 144p. (J). (gr. 6-18). 25.95 *(978-1-59556-026-1(2))* OTTN Publishing.

Davis, Hasan. The Journey of York: The Unsung Hero of the Lewis & Clark Expedition. Harris, Alleanna, illus. (ENG.). 40p. (J). (gr. 3-4). 2021. pap. 7.95 *(978-1-5435-1286-1(0)*, 137749) 2019. lib. bdg. 17.95 *(978-1-5435-1282-3(8)*, 137748) Capstone. (Capstone Editions).

Ditchfield, Christin. The Lewis & Clark Expedition. 2006. (True Bks.). (ENG., Illus.). 48p. (J). (gr. 3-7). pap. 6.95 *(978-0-516-25222-3(4)*, Children's Pr.) Scholastic Library Publishing.

Domnauer, Teresa. The Lewis & Clark Expedition (Cornerstones of Freedom: Third Series) 2012. (Cornerstones of Freedom. Third Ser.). (ENG., Illus.). 64p. (J). (gr. 4-6). pap. 8.95 *(978-0-531-28159-8(0)*, Children's Pr.) Scholastic Library Publishing.

Edwards, Judith. The Journey of Lewis & Clark in United States History, 1 vol. 2014. (In United States History Ser.). (ENG., Illus.). 96p. (gr. 5-6). 31.61 *(978-0-7660-6058-6(6)*, 892fda6b-0126-4fa2-ae2f-26993dcaf615) Enslow Publishing, LLC.

Fifer, Barbara. Going along with Lewis & Clark. 2004. (Illus.). 48p. (YA). (gr. 7-18). pap. 12.95 *(978-1-56037-151-9(X))* Farcountry Pr.

Fox, Michael D. & Fox, Suzanne G. Meriwether Lewis & William Clark: The Corps of Discovery & the Exploration of the American Frontier, 1 vol. 2004. (Library of American Lives & Times Ser.). (ENG., Illus.). 112p. (J). (gr. 5-5). lib. bdg. 38.27 *(978-1-4042-2650-0(8)*, 96e27260-6d09-4b7f-888a-42a5dd16e882) Rosen Publishing Group, Inc., The.

Fox, Suzanne G. Meriwether Lewis & William Clark: The Corp of Discovery & the Exploration of the American Frontier. 2009. (Library of American Lives & Times Ser.). 112p. (gr. 5-5). 69.20 *(978-1-60853-493-7(6))* Rosen Publishing Group, Inc., The.

Franklin, Virgil. The Story of Sacagawea. 2009. (Reading Room Collection 2 Ser.). 24p. (gr. 3-4). 42.50 *(978-1-60851-997-2(X)*, PowerKids Pr.) Rosen Publishing Group, Inc., The.

Frazier, Neta. Path to the Pacific: The Story of Sacagawea. 2017. (Great Leaders & Events Ser.). (ENG.). (J). (gr. 4-8). lib. bdg. 35.99 *(978-1-942875-44-4(4))* Quarto Publishing Group USA.

Fruge, William. Lewis & Clark: A Journey West, 1 vol. 2008. (Real Life Readers Ser.). (ENG.). 24p. (gr. 3-4). pap. 8.25 *(978-1-4358-0040-3(0)*, 5ed12ac1-6749-4846-bd9a-bf3568d6f159, Rosen Classroom) Rosen Publishing Group, Inc., The.

Ganeri, Anita. On Expedition with Lewis & Clark. 2010. (ENG.). 32p. (J). (gr. 3-5). *(978-0-7787-9896-5(8))*; (Crabtree Connections Ser.: No. 2). pap. *(978-0-7787-9917-7(4))* Crabtree Publishing Co.

Gingrich, Callista. From Sea to Shining Sea. Arciero, Susan, illus. 2014. (Ellis the Elephant Ser.: 4). (ENG.). 40p. (J). (gr. -1-3). 14.99 *(978-1-62157-253-4(6)*, Regnery Kids) Regnery Publishing.

Gondosch, Linda. Where Did Sacagawea Join the Corps of Discovery? And Other Questions about the Lewis & Clark Expedition. 2011. (Six Questions of American History Ser.). (ENG.). 48p. (gr. 4-6). pap. 56.72 *(978-0-7613-7644-6(5))*; (Illus.). (J). pap. 11.99 *(978-0-7613-7131-1(1)*, 061f662a-a998-4abe-ac16-604cd15f7710); (Illus.). (J). lib. bdg. 30.65 *(978-0-7613-5226-6(0)*, fd798483-1f32-4a50-af83-88af79191609, Lerner Pubns.) Lerner Publishing Group.

Griffiths, Katie. Sacagawea: Shoshone Guide, Interpreter, & Leading Member of the Corps of Discovery, 1 vol. 2017. (Fearless Female Soldiers, Explorers, & Aviators Ser.). (ENG., Illus.). 128p. (YA). (gr. 9-9). 47.36 *(978-1-5026-2747-6(7)*, 43f581b4-a050-4edd-9ddf-cd88d992402f) Cavendish Square Publishing LLC.

Group/McGraw-Hill, Wright. Lewis & Clark: Mapping the West, 6 vols. (Book2WebTM Ser.). (gr. 4-8). 36.50 *(978-0-322-04460-9(X))* Wright Group/McGraw-Hill.

Gunderson, Jessica. Sacagawea: Journey into the West, 1 vol. Martin, Cynthia & Schulz, Barbara, illus. 2006. (Graphic Biographies Ser.). (ENG.). 32p. (J). (gr. 3-9). per. 8.10 *(978-0-7368-9663-4(5)*, 93450) Capstone.

Gunderson, Jessica Sarah. Your Life As a Private on the Lewis & Clark Expedition, 1 vol. Madden, Colleen, illus. 2012. (Way It Was Ser.). (ENG.). 32p. (J). (gr. 2-5). pap. 8.95 *(978-1-4048-7746-7(0)*, 120459, Picture Window Bks.) Capstone.

Haldy, Emma E. Sacagawea. Bane, Jeff, illus. 2016. (My Early Library: My Itty-Bitty Bio Ser.). (ENG.). 24p. (J). (gr. k-1). 30.64 *(978-1-63470-482-3(7)*, 207659) Cherry Lake Publishing.

—Sacagawea SP. Bane, Jeff, illus. 2018. (My Early Library: Mi Mini Biografía (My Itty-Bitty Bio) Ser.). (SPA.). 24p. (J). (gr. k-1). lib. bdg. 30.64 *(978-1-5341-3000-5(4)*, 212048) Cherry Lake Publishing.

Isserman, Maurice. Across America: The Lewis & Clark Expedition. 2nd rev. ed. 2009. (Discovery & Exploration Ser.). (ENG., Illus.). 128p. (gr. 5-8). 35.00 *(978-1-60413-192-5(6)*, P174273, Facts On File) Infobase Holdings, Inc.

Johmann, Carol A. The Lewis & Clark Expedition: Join the Corps of Discovery to Explore Uncharted Territory. 2008. (ENG., Illus.). 112p. (J). (gr. 4-6). pap. 14.25 *(978-1-885593-73-3(2)*, Ideals Pubns.) Worthy Publishing.

Keller, Susanna. The True Story of Lewis & Clark, 1 vol. 2013. (What Really Happened? Ser.). (ENG., Illus.). 24p. (J). (gr. 2-3). pap. 9.25 *(978-1-4488-9846-6(3)*, e0a93e44-5e16-4d0a-8805-6b38d2ae6877); lib. bdg. 26.27 *(978-1-4488-9694-3(0)*, 45b0e550-b940-425e-969e-33f6e3bf16f) Rosen Publishing Group, Inc., The. (PowerKids Pr.).

Kimmel, Elizabeth Cody. As Far as the Eye Can Reach: Lewis & Clark's Westward Quest. 2005. (Illus.). 119p. (YA). (gr. 4-8). reprint ed. 5.00 *(978-0-7567-9660-0(1))* DIANE Publishing Co.

King, Margaret. The Legacy & Legend of Sacagawea. rev. ed. 2017. (Social Studies: Informational Text Ser.). (ENG., Illus.). 32p. (gr. 4-8). pap. 11.99 *(978-1-4938-3793-9(1))* Teacher Created Materials, Inc.

Klepeis, Alicia Z. Lewis & Clark & Exploring the Louisiana Purchase, 1 vol. 2017. (Primary Sources of Westward Expansion Ser.). (ENG., Illus.). 64p. (gr. 6-6). 35.93 *(978-1-5026-2639-4(X)*, 4c1afc12-b4ad-4ebd-a36d-64694b2924f9) Cavendish Square Publishing LLC.

Labrecque, Ellen. What's Your Story, Sacagawea? 2015. (Cub Reporter Meets Famous Americans Ser.). (ENG., Illus.). 32p. (J). (gr. k-3). 26.65 *(978-1-4677-7966-1(0)*, 3f1f6a96-7cc7-42cf-9a5d-c74c0bbe7a47, Lerner Pubns.) Lerner Publishing Group.

Lawrence, Blythe. The Lewis & Clark Expedition. 2018. (Expansion of Our Nation Ser.). (ENG., Illus.). 32p. (J). (gr. 3-5). pap. 9.95 *(978-1-63517-983-5(1)*, 1635179831); lib. bdg. 31.35 *(978-1-63517-882-1(7)*, 1635178827) North Star Editions. (Focus Readers).

—The Lewis & Clark Expedition. 2018. (Illus.). 32p. (J). *(978-1-4896-9870-4(1)*, AV2 by Weigl) Weigl Pubs., Inc.

Levy, Janey. Lewis & Clark in Their Own Words, 1 vol., Vol. 1. 2014. (Eyewitness to History Ser.). (ENG.). 32p. (J). (gr. 4-5). pap. 11.50 *(978-1-4339-9930-7(7)*, a1e4799d-12bc-438c-9624-9fddec8edc01) Stevens, Gareth Publishing LLLP.

Lewis & Clark Hands on Art And. 2004. (J). pap. 14.95 *(978-0-9715970-5-1(7))* Visual Manna.

Lynette, Rachel. Meriwether Lewis & William Clark, 1 vol. 2013. (Pioneer Spirit: the Westward Expansion Ser.). 24p. (J). (ENG.). (gr. 2-3). 26.27 *(978-1-4777-0783-8(2)*, c3379d73-e58a-46ba-a505-004b5518497d); (gr. 3-6). pap. 49.50 *(978-1-4777-0900-9(2))*; (ENG., Illus.). (gr. 2-3). pap. 9.25 *(978-1-4777-0899-6(5)*, a7e102b5-f175-4b5e-9fee-d0fde36daf27) Rosen Publishing Group, Inc., The. (PowerKids Pr.).

Marsh, Carole. Lewis & Clark Go on a Hike. 2003. 32p. (J). (gr. 3-8). pap. 5.95 *(978-0-635-02122-9(6))* Gallopade International.

Maynard, Charles W. Fort Clatsop. 2009. (Famous Forts Throughout American History Ser.). 24p. (gr. 3-4). 42.50 *(978-1-61512-515-9(9)*, PowerKids Pr.) Rosen Publishing Group, Inc., The.

McAneney, Caitie. The Life of Sacagawea, 1 vol. 2016. (Native American Biographies Ser.). (ENG., Illus.). 32p. (J). (gr. 4-5). 27.93 *(978-1-5081-4819-7(8)*, 81bd3657-d037-4879-a46c-de5150deaa6f, PowerKids Pr.) Rosen Publishing Group, Inc., The.

Meinke, Amanda & Stegmann, Lisa. Lewis & Clark Famous Faces. Adams Marks, Elizabeth, illus. 2003. 2p. (J). pap. 2.99 *(978-1-56472-289-8(9))* Edupress, Inc.

Meltzer, Brad. I Am Sacagawea. Eliopoulos, Christopher, illus. (Ordinary People Change the World Ser.). 40p. (J). (gr. k-4). 2023. pap. 9.99 *(978-0-593-61918-6(8)*, Rocky Pond Bks.) 2017. 15.99 *(978-0-525-42853-4(4)*, Dial Bks) Penguin Young Readers Group.

Micklos, John, Jr. Discovering the West: The Expedition of Lewis & Clark, 1 vol. 2014. (Adventures on the American Frontier Ser.). (ENG., Illus.). 32p. (J). (gr. 3-6). 27.99 *(978-1-4914-0185-9(0)*, 125779) Capstone.

Moran, Margaret. Lewis & Clark: Set Of 6. 2011. (Navigators Ser.). (J). pap. 48.00 net. *(978-1-4108-0432-7(1))* Benchmark Education Co.

—Lewis & Clark & Lewis y Clark: 6 English, 6 Spanish Adaptations. 2011. (ENG & SPA.). (J). 97.00 net. *(978-1-4108-5712-5(3))* Benchmark Education Co.

Morley, Jacqueline. The Story of Lewis & Clark. David Antram, illus. 2017. (Explorers Ser.). 32p. (gr. 3-6). 31.35 *(978-1-910706-89-3(2))* Book Hse. GBR. Dist: Black Rabbit Bks.

—You Wouldn't Want to Explore with Lewis & Clark! An Epic Journey You'd Rather Not Make. Bergin, Mark, illus. 2013. (You Wouldn't Want to... Ser.). (ENG.). 32p. (J). 29.00

(978-0-531-25942-9(0), Watts, Franklin) Scholastic Library Publishing.

Morlock, Rachael. Lewis & Clark Explore the Louisiana Territory, 1 vol. 2018. (Real-Life Scientific Adventures Ser.). (ENG.). 32p. (gr. 4-5). 29.27 (978-1-5081-6850-8(4), 7235896b-7bfb-4480-91b5-538c4973a4fc, PowerKids Pr.) Rosen Publishing Group, Inc., The.

Mulhall, Jill K. Lewis & Clark. rev. ed. (Social Studies: Informational Text Ser.). (ENG., (gr. 4-8). 2017. Illus.). 32p. pap. 11.99 (978-1-4938-3886-8(5)) 2005. 24p. (J). pap. 10.99 (978-0-7439-8906-0(6)) Teacher Created Materials, Inc.

Nelson, Maria. The Life of Sacagawea, 1 vol. 2012. (Famous Lives Ser.). (ENG., Illus.). 24p. (J). (gr. 1-2). pap. 9.15 (978-1-4339-6359-9(0), 7d54f17b-b6a2-43d9-b239-7dc9a194049c); lib. bdg. 25.27 (978-1-4339-6357-5(4), 017bd324-2a9a-4cd4-b51c-3b2ba2208e5f) Stevens, Gareth Publishing LLLP.

On the Trail of Lewis & Clark Poster Map. 2004. (J). (978-0-9759433-1-1(6)) Maps For Kids Inc.

On the Trail of Lewis & Clark Timeline/Fact Poster. 2004. (J). (978-0-9759433-2-8(4)) Maps For Kids Inc.

Orr, Tamra. The Lewis & Clark Expedition: A Primary Source History of the Journey of the Corps of Discovery. (Primary Sources in American History Ser.). 64p. (gr. 5-8). 2009. 58.50 (978-1-60851-498-4(6)) 2004. (ENG., Illus.). lib. bdg. 37.13 (978-0-8239-4005-9(5), 1c22f8d5-a1e3-4eae-9fd0-d91c04328a1a, Rosen Reference) Rosen Publishing Group, Inc., The.

Perritano, John. True Books: the Lewis & Clark Expedition. 2010. (True Book Ser.). (ENG., Illus.). 48p. (J). (gr. 2-5). 29.00 (978-0-531-20582-2(7)) Scholastic Library Publishing.

Pringle, Laurence. Dog of Discovery: A Newfoundland's Adventures with Lewis & Clark. 2004. (ENG., Illus.). 152p. (J). (gr. 4-7). pap. 10.95 (978-1-59078-267-5(4), Calkins Creek) Highlights Pr., c/o Highlights for Children, Inc.

Raabe, Emily. Thomas Jefferson & the Louisiana Purchase. 2009. (Westward Ho! Ser.). 24p. (gr. 2-3). 42.50 (978-1-60854-763-0(9), PowerKids Pr.) Rosen Publishing Group, Inc., The.

Ransom, Candice. Lewis & Clark. 2003. (History Maker Bios Ser.). (Illus.). 48p. (J). (gr. 2-4). 26.60 (978-0-8225-0394-1(8), Lerner Pubns.) Lerner Publishing Group.

Rausch, Monica. Sacagawea, 1 vol. 2007. (Grandes Personajes (Great Americans) Ser.). 24p. (gr. 2-4). (SPA.). pap. 9.15 (978-0-8368-7991-9(0), 867793cb-be46-4835-b2e0-95234bf0f2f2, Weekly Reader Leveled Readers); (ENG., Illus.). pap. 9.15 (978-0-8368-7692-5(X), fca24c8a-5c3c-4f07-9459-871423b2e8e0, Weekly Reader Leveled Readers); (SPA., Illus.). lib. bdg. 24.67 (978-0-8368-7984-1(8), f0398bb5-29a9-4689-829b-5a3f299c15cc); (ENG., Illus.). lib. bdg. 24.67 (978-0-8368-7685-7(7), a6b3bcda-7778-4816-8efa-d05bb06d6d16, Weekly Reader Leveled Readers) Stevens, Gareth Publishing LLLP.

Redmond, Shirley Raye. Lewis & Clark: A Prairie Dog for the President. Manders, John, illus. 2003. (Step into Reading Ser.). 48p. 14.00 (978-0-7569-1697-8(6)) Perfection Learning Corp.

—Lewis & Clark: A Prairie Dog for the President. Manders, John, illus. 2003. (Step into Reading Ser.: No. 3). 48p. (J). (gr. k-3). pap. 5.99 (978-0-375-81120-3(6), Random Hse. Bks. for Young Readers) Random Hse. Children's Bks.

Robinson, Kate. Lewis & Clark: Exploring the American West, 1 vol. 2009. (Great Explorers of the World Ser.). (ENG., Illus.). 112p. (gr. 6-7). 35.93 (978-1-59845-124-5(3), 5a91466e-b841-429e-a58d-e2b90c9c3a72) Enslow Publishing, LLC.

Rodger, Ellen. Lewis & Clark: Opening the American West, 1 vol. 2005. (In the Footsteps of Explorers Ser.). (ENG., Illus.). 32p. (J). (gr. -1-9). pap. (978-0-7787-2446-9(8)); lib. bdg. (978-0-7787-2410-0(7)) Crabtree Publishing Co.

Ruffing, Faith Elizabeth. Lewis & Clark Bicentenial Corps of Discovery Journal & Record Book. 2003. (Illus.). 162p. spiral bd. 29.95 (978-0-9763970-0-7(5)) Lewis & Clark Bicentennial Corps of Discovery Arch.

Sanford, William R. & Green, Carl R. Sacagawea: Courageous American Indian Guide, 1 vol. 2013. (Courageous Heroes of the American West Ser.). (ENG., Illus.). 48p. (J). (gr. 5-7). 25.27 (978-0-7660-4006-9(2), 3f6b8c1b-2727-4911-bb11-7579059ee616) Enslow Publishing, LLC.

Sapp, Richard. Lewis & Clark on Their Journey to the Pacific, 1 vol. 2005. (In the Footsteps of American Heroes Ser.). (ENG., Illus.). 64p. (gr. 5-8). lib. bdg. 36.67 (978-0-8368-6429-8(8), b5fc7f92-3c47-4d52-af0b-18d81c16af7d, Gareth Stevens Secondary Library) Stevens, Gareth Publishing LLLP.

Shea, Therese M. The Louisiana Purchase & the Lewis & Clark Expedition, 1 vol. 2017. (Westward Expansion: America's Push to the Pacific Ser.). (ENG., Illus.). 48p. (J). (gr. 6-7). pap. 15.05 (978-1-68048-790-9(6), e3a8ec93-25d6-4e7e-82ab-fe30c88fb8d1, Britannica Educational Publishing) Rosen Publishing Group, Inc., The.

Sheely, Tiffany, illus. Captain William Clark's Great Montana Adventure. 2003. 32p. (J). mass mkt. 3.95 (978-0-9711667-0-7(6)) Outlook Publishing, Inc.

Smalley, Carol Parenzan. Lewis & Clark. 2008. (What's So Great About... ? Ser.). (Illus.). 32p. (YA). (gr. 2-4). lib. bdg. 25.70 (978-1-58415-725-0(9)) Mitchell Lane Pubs.

Smith, Jeff. William Clark: Explorer & Diplomat. 2016. (ENG., Illus.). 48p. (J). pap. 27.00 (978-1-61248-178-4(7)) Truman State Univ. Pr.

St. George, Judith. Sacagawea. 2006. pap. 8.75 (978-0-15-365175-5(X)) Harcourt Schl. Pubs.

—What Was the Lewis & Clark Expedition? 2014. (What Was... Ser.). lib. bdg. 16.00 (978-0-606-36185-9(5)) Turtleback.

St. George, Judith & Who HQ. What Was the Lewis & Clark Expedition? Foley, Tim, illus. 2014. (What Was? Ser.). 112p. (J). (gr. 3-7). pap. 5.99 (978-0-448-47901-9(X), Penguin Workshop) Penguin Young Readers Group.

Stuckey, Rachel. Explore with Lewis & Clark. 2014. (Travel with the Great Explorers Ser.). (ENG., Illus.). 32p. (J). (gr. 4-5). (978-0-7787-1247-3(8)); pap. (978-0-7787-1259-6(1)) Crabtree Publishing Co.

Sullivan, Laura. Life As an Explorer with Lewis & Clark, 1 vol. 2015. (Life As... Ser.). (ENG., Illus.). 32p. (gr. 3-3). pap. 11.58 (978-1-5026-1078-2(7), a7c1a42e-2fae-40ab-84e6-53fd8a16109c) Cavendish Square Publishing LLC.

Sutcliffe, Jane. Sacagawea. 2009. (History Maker Biographies Ser.). (ENG.). 48p. (gr. 3-6). 27.93 (978-0-7613-4222-9(2), Lerner Pubns.) Lerner Publishing Group.

Swanson, Jennifer. Lewis & Clark, 1 vol. 2016. (Spotlight on Explorers & Colonization Ser.). (ENG., Illus.). 48p. (J). (gr. 6-6). pap. 12.75 (978-1-5081-7237-6(4), 9b0ecfa8-404b-406a-b9d5-b6b3587fe196) Rosen Publishing Group, Inc., The.

Uhl, Xina M. & Orr, Tamra. A Primary Source Investigation of the Lewis & Clark Expedition, 1 vol. 2018. (Uncovering American History Ser.). (ENG.). 64p. (gr. 6-6). pap. 13.95 (978-1-5081-8417-1(8), 4cb70725-cfb4-460d-b296-f9aecd66051d, Rosen Reference) Rosen Publishing Group, Inc., The.

Yomtov, Nel. Lewis & Clark Map the American West. 2015. (Extraordinary Explorers Ser.). (ENG., Illus.). 24p. (J). (gr. 3-8). lib. bdg. 29.95 (978-1-62617-293-7(5), Black Sheep) Bellwether Media.

LEWIS AND CLARK EXPEDITION (1804-1806)—FICTION

Bohner, Charles H. Bold Journey: West with Lewis & Clark. 2004. (ENG.). 192p. (J). (gr. 5-7). pap. 7.99 (978-0-618-43718-4(5), 495901, Clarion Bks.) HarperCollins Pubs.

Bruchac, Joseph. Sacajawea. 2008. (ENG., Illus.). 208p. (YA). (gr. 7). pap. 7.99 (978-0-15-206455-6(9), 1199286, Clarion Bks.) HarperCollins Pubs.

—Sacajawea: The Story of Bird Woman & the Lewis & Clark Expedition. 2003. (Illus.). 199p. (J). (gr. 4-7). 12.65 (978-0-7569-0732-7(2)) Perfection Learning Corp.

Eubank, Patricia Reeder. Seaman's Journal. 2010. (ENG.). 40p. (J). (gr. -1-3). pap. 9.99 (978-0-8249-5619-6(2), Ideals Pubns.) Worthy Publishing.

Karwoski, Gail Langer. SeaMan: The Dog Who Explored the West with Lewis & Clark, 1 vol. Watling, James, illus. 2003. 192p. (J). (gr. 3-7). 16.95 (978-1-56145-276-7(9), Q20194); pap. 9.99 (978-1-56145-190-6(8), Q20194) Peachtree Publishing Co. Inc.

Munves, James. We Were There with Lewis & Clark. 2006. 128p. (J). pap. 13.95 (978-0-9779000-0-8(2)) American Home-School Publishing, LLC.

Napoli, Donna Jo. The Crossing. Madsen, Jim, illus. 2011. (ENG.). 40p. (J). (gr. -1-3). 19.99 (978-1-4169-9474-9(2), Atheneum Bks. for Young Readers) Simon & Schuster Children's Publishing.

Oczkus, Lori. Close Reading with Paired Texts, Level 5. rev. ed. 2015. (Close Reading with Paired Texts). (ENG., Illus.). 128p. (gr. 5-5). pap. 19.99 (978-1-4258-1361-1(5)) Shell Educational Publishing.

O'Dell, Scott. Streams to the River, River to the Sea. 2008. (ENG., Illus.). 208p. (J). (gr. 5-7). pap. 7.99 (978-0-547-05316-5(9), 1036244, Clarion Bks.) HarperCollins Pubs.

Olsen, Lauri. Pacific Bound: The Adventures of Lewis & Clark. Toonz Animation, ed. 2005. (Illus.). 44p. (J). 18.95 (978-0-9742502-5-0(2)) Gossamer Bks., LLC.

—Pacific Bound: The Adventures of Lewis & Clark. 2004. (Illus.). 46p. (J). per. 15.95 (978-0-9742502-4-3(4)) Gossamer Bks., LLC.

Rice, Dona Herwick & Bradley, Kathleen. Lewis & Clark, 1 vol. rev. ed. 2009. (Reader's Theater Ser.). (ENG., Illus.). 32p. (gr. 4-8). pap. 11.99 (978-1-4333-0540-5(2)) Teacher Created Materials, Inc.

Sargent, Dave & Sargent, Pat. Mack: (Medicine Hat Paint) Be a Leader, 30 vols., Vol. 39. Lenoir, Jane, illus. 2003. (Saddle up Ser.: Vol. 39). 42p. (J). pap. 10.95 (978-1-56763-700-7(0)) Ozark Publishing.

Smith, Roland. The Captain's Dog: My Journey with the Lewis & Clark Tribe. 2008. (Great Episodes Ser.). (ENG., Illus.). 304p. (J). (gr. 5-7). pap. 8.99 (978-0-15-202696-7(7), 1193556, Clarion Bks.) HarperCollins Pubs.

Wolf, Allan. New Found Land: Lewis & Clark's Voyage of Discovery. 2007. (ENG., Illus.). 512p. (YA). (gr. 7-9). per. 19.99 (978-0-7636-3288-5(0)) Candlewick Pr.

LEXINGTON, BATTLE OF, LEXINGTON, MASS., 1775

Crewe, Sabrina & Uschan, Michael V. Lexington & Concord, 1 vol. 2004. (Events That Shaped America Ser.). (ENG., Illus.). 32p. (J). (gr. 3-5). lib. bdg. 28.67 (978-0-8368-3398-0(8), 30937a1f-fc4b-47f4-8c23-50802b4fda0b, Gareth Stevens Learning Library) Stevens, Gareth Publishing LLLP.

—Lexington y Concord (Lexington & Concord), 1 vol. 2006. (Hitos de la Historia de Estados Unidos (Landmark Events in American History) Ser.). (SPA.). 48p. (gr. 5-8). pap. 12.70 (978-0-8368-7474-7(9), 3536b44a-9886-4b37-ad50-e920a01e7313, Gareth Stevens Learning Library); (Illus.). lib. bdg. 29.67 (978-0-8368-7467-9(6), 9d2cce53-79e4-4662-9949-23c93427626c, Gareth Stevens Secondary Library) Stevens, Gareth Publishing LLLP.

Fradin, Dennis Brindell. Let It Begin Here! Lexington & Concord: First Battles of the American Revolution. Day, Larry, illus. 2009. (ENG.). 40p. (J). (gr. 2-4). pap. 9.99 (978-0-8027-9711-7(3), 900049550, Bloomsbury USA Childrens) Bloomsbury Publishing USA.

Harasymiw, Mark. Team Time Machine Leads the Way at Lexington & Concord, 1 vol. 2019. (Team Time Machine: American Revolution Ser.). (ENG.). 32p. (J). (gr. 2-3). pap. 11.50 (978-1-5382-4686-3(4), 9fcbe405-b76a-488b-9ea4-bff1f9cebdc2) Stevens, Gareth Publishing LLLP.

Haugen, Brenda. The Split History of the Battles of Lexington & Concord: A Perspectives Flip Book. 2018. (Perspectives Flip Books: Famous Battles Ser.). (ENG., Illus.). 64p. (J). (gr. 5-9). lib. bdg. 34.65 (978-0-7565-5692-1(9), 137037, Compass Point Bks.) Capstone.

Kallio, Jamie. 12 Questions about Paul Revere's Ride. 2017. (Examining Primary Sources Ser.). (ENG., Illus.). 32p. (J). (gr. 3-6). 32.80 (978-1-63235-286-6(9), 11755); pap. 9.95 (978-1-63235-336-8(9), 11763) Bookstaves, LLC. (12-Story Library).

Mara, Wil. The Battles of Lexington & Concord: Start of the American Revolution. 2017. (Major Battles in US History Ser.). (ENG., Illus.). 32p. (J). (gr. 3-5). lib. bdg. 31.35 (978-1-63517-023-8(0), 1635170230, Focus Readers) North Star Editions.

Samuels, Charlie. The Battles of Lexington & Concord, 1 vol., Vol. 1. 2013. (Turning Points in U. S. Military History Ser.). (ENG.). 48p. (J). (gr. 5-6). 34.61 (978-1-4824-0417-3(6), adabfd2e-80d2-4597-bc08-8e34ea17bb1c) Stevens, Gareth Publishing LLLP.

Uschan, Michael V. Lexington & Concord, 1 vol. 2003. (Landmark Events in American History Ser.). (ENG., Illus.). 48p. (gr. 5-8). pap. 15.05 (978-0-8368-5407-7(1), d10b398e-21b3-430b-8266-1825f5179b5d); lib. bdg. 33.67 (978-0-8368-5379-7(2), 0daf71ea-32e5-4ef1-97b4-f03ad1b845b4) Stevens, Gareth Publishing LLLP. (Gareth Stevens Secondary Library).

Von Zumbusch, Amelie. The True Story of the Battle of Lexington & Concord, 1 vol. 2008. (What Really Happened? Ser.). (ENG., Illus.). 24p. (YA). (gr. 2-3). lib. bdg. 26.27 (978-1-4042-4480-1(8), 8b6f76cd-3217-4d31-b183-3e675c3d528c) Rosen Publishing Group, Inc., The.

von Zumbusch, Amelie. The True Story of the Battle of Lexington & Concord. 2009. (What Really Happened? Ser.). 24p. (gr. 2-3). 42.50 (978-1-60854-767-8(1), PowerKids Pr.) Rosen Publishing Group, Inc., The.

Waldman, Scott P. The Battle of Lexington & Concord. 2009. (Atlas of Famous Battles of the American Revolution Ser.). 24p. (gr. 3-3). 42.50 (978-1-60853-328-2(X), PowerKids Pr.) Rosen Publishing Group, Inc., The.

Whitelaw, Nancy. The Shot Heard Round the World: The Battles of Lexington & Concord. 2004. (First Battles Ser.). (Illus.). 112p. (J). (gr. 6-12). 23.95 (978-1-883846-75-6(7), First Biographies) Reynolds, Morgan Inc.

Whitwell, Stephen. The Battles of Lexington & Concord: First Shots of the American Revolution, 1 vol. 2015. (Spotlight on American History Ser.). (ENG., Illus.). 24p. (J). (gr. 4-6). pap. 11.00 (978-1-4994-1719-7(5), 0f011c73-4696-4197-bf4f-ccf9e7ba5121, PowerKids Pr.) Rosen Publishing Group, Inc., The.

LEYTE GULF, BATTLE OF, PHILIPPINES, 1944

Kevin, McDonald. Tin Can Sailors Save the Day. 2015. (Illus.). 86p. (J). pap. 10.95 (978-1-55571-786-5(1), Paloma Bks.) L & R Publishing, LLC.

LIBERIA

Baughan, Brian. Liberia. 2012. (Illus.). 87p. (J). pap. (978-1-4222-2226-3(8)) Mason Crest.

—Liberia. Rotberg, Robert I., ed. (Evolution of Africa's Major Nations Ser.). (Illus.). 2012. 88p. (J). (gr. 7). 22.95 (978-1-4222-2198-3(9)) 2009. 87p. (YA). (gr. 3-7). lib. bdg. 21.95 (978-1-4222-0088-9(4)) Mason Crest.

Hicks, Kyra E. Martha Ann's Quilt for Queen Victoria. Födi, Lee Edward, illus. 2012. 32p. (J). pap. 12.95 (978-0-9824796-8-1(9)) Black Threads Pr.

Levy, Patricia & Spilling, Michael. Liberia, 1 vol. 2nd rev. ed. 2009. (Cultures of the World (Second Edition)(r) Ser.). (ENG.). 144p. (gr. 5-5). lib. bdg. 49.79 (978-0-7614-3414-6(3), be6c812e-e49f-4e9c-b79d-5ab9d65b3dec) Cavendish Square Publishing LLC.

Levy, Patricia, et al. Liberia, 1 vol. 2018. (Cultures of the World (Third Edition)(r) Ser.). (ENG.). 144p. (gr. 5-5). 48.79 (978-1-5026-3626-3(3), de6b452f-f9b8-4418-ba9f-649f39e4f35a) Cavendish Square Publishing LLC.

Ng, Yumi. Welcome to Liberia, 1 vol. 2004. (Welcome to My Country Ser.). (ENG., Illus.). 48p. (gr. 2-4). lib. bdg. 29.67 (978-0-8368-2566-4(7), 2e2d085e-7ce0-4d8f-bb5b-4c1be30c9fea) Stevens, Gareth Publishing LLLP.

Rozario, Paul A. Liberia, 1 vol. 2003. (Countries of the World Ser.). (ENG., Illus.). 96p. (gr. 6-8). lib. bdg. 33.67 (978-0-8368-2366-0(4), 4b60a05a-5be5-498c-b013-dfd23ebb5f75) Stevens, Gareth Publishing LLLP.

Seigerman, David. Tamba Hali. 2017. (Real Sports Content Network Presents Ser.). (ENG., Illus.). 144p. (J). (gr. 3-7). 17.99 (978-1-4814-8220-2(3), Aladdin) Simon & Schuster Children's Publishing.

Streissguth, Tom. Liberia in Pictures. 2006. (Visual Geography Series, Second Ser.). (ENG., Illus.). 80p. (gr. 5-12). lib. bdg. 31.93 (978-0-8225-2465-6(1)) Lerner Publishing Group.

LIBERIA—FICTION

Allen, C. William. The African Interior Mission. Lee, Xiongpao, illus. 2006. 232p. (J). pap. 20.00 (978-0-9653308-5-5(0)) Africana Homestead Legacy Pubs., Inc.

de Graaf, Anne. Son of a Gun. 2013. (ENG., Illus.). 125p. (J). (gr. 6-8). pap. 22.44 (978-0-8028-5406-3(0)) Eerdmans, William B. Publishing Co.

Gibney, Shannon. Dream Country. 2019. (ENG., Illus.). 368p. (YA). (gr. 9). pap. 10.99 (978-0-7352-3168-9(0), Penguin Books) Penguin Young Readers Group.

Toh, Irene. Kumi the Bear. Hagan, Stacy, illus. 2008. (ENG.). 24p. pap. 12.75 (978-1-4389-1368-1(0)) AuthorHouse.

Watkins, Samuel R. Ant-Bee Kingdom. 2011. 12p. (gr. -1). pap. 12.68 (978-1-4269-5272-2(4)) Trafford Publishing.

—Precious Palm Tree. 2011. 32p. (gr. -1). pap. 17.25 (978-1-4269-5267-8(8)) Trafford Publishing.

Wilson, Heather Gemmen. Lydia Barnes & the Blood Diamond Treasure. 2007. (Global Warning Ser.). 159p. (J). (gr. 3-7). per. 7.99 (978-0-89827-350-2(1)) Wesleyan Publishing Hse.

LIBERTY

see also Anarchism; Assembly, Right of; Civil Rights; Equality; Freedom of Religion

Amnesty International. Dreams of Freedom. 2015. (ENG., Illus.). 48p. (J). (gr. 1-4). 19.99 (978-1-84780-453-2(5), 312305, Frances Lincoln Children's Bks.) Quarto Publishing Group UK GBR. Dist: Hachette UK Distribution.

Aronson, Marc & Budhos, Marina. Sugar Changed the World: A Story of Magic, Spice, Slavery, Freedom, & Science. 2010. (ENG., Illus.). 176p. (YA). (gr. 7-18). 21.99 (978-0-618-57492-6(1), 100422, Clarion Bks.) HarperCollins Pubs.

Beveridge, Amy. Let's Thank God for Freedom. 2006. 24p. (J). bds. 6.99 (978-0-7847-1505-5(X), 04384) Standard Publishing.

Bradley, Catherine. Freedom of Movement. 2005. (What Do We Mean by Human Rights? Ser.). (Illus.). 46p. (YA). (gr. 5-9). lib. bdg. 29.95 (978-1-932889-64-2(7)) Sea-To-Sea Pubns.

Collins, Terry. Liberty, 1 vol. Bascle, Brian, illus. 2009. (Cartoon Nation Ser.). (ENG.). 32p. (J). (gr. 3-9). lib. bdg. 31.32 (978-1-4296-2340-7(3), 95068, Capstone Pr.) Capstone.

Golden, Nancy. The British Are Coming! The Midnight Ride of Paul Revere. 2009. (Great Moments in American History Ser.). 32p. (gr. 3-3). 47.90 (978-1-61513-136-5(1)) Rosen Publishing Group, Inc., The.

Hanson, Anders. Land of the Free: The Kids' Book of Freedom, 1 vol. 2014. (What We Stand For Ser.). (ENG.). 24p. (J). (gr. k-4). lib. bdg. 32.79 (978-1-62403-295-0(8), 1730, Super SandCastle) ABDO Publishing Co.

Hess, Karl. Capitalism for Kids: Growing up to Be Your Own Boss. Williams, Jane A. & Daniels, Kathryn, eds. rev. ed. 2006. (ENG.). 196p. (YA). pap. 14.95 (978-0-942617-35-1(5)) Bluestocking Pr.

King, Wilma. Children of the Emancipation. 2005. (Picture the American Past Ser.). (Illus.). 48p. (J). (gr. 2-5). 22.60 (978-1-57505-396-7(9)) Lerner Publishing Group.

Kukathas, Uma, ed. Personal Liberty, 1 vol. 2009. (Issues on Trial Ser.). (ENG.). 216p. (gr. 10-12). 49.93 (978-0-7377-4343-2(3), f6777168-59d4-4af1-a4ba-15f001cc4175, Greenhaven Publishing) Greenhaven Publishing LLC.

Lewison, Wendy Cheyette. L Is for Liberty. Hines, Laura Freeman, illus. 2003. 24p. (J). (gr. -1-3). mass mkt. 5.99 (978-0-448-43228-1(5), Grosset & Dunlap) Penguin Young Readers Group.

Lord, Jonathan. John Locke & the Second Treatise of Civil Government. 2016. (J). lib. bdg. (978-1-68048-548-6(2)) Rosen Publishing Group, Inc., The.

Nelson, Kadir. Nelson Mandela. Nelson, Kadir, illus. 2019. (ENG., Illus.). 40p. (J). (gr. -1-3). pap. 9.99 (978-0-06-178377-7(3), Tegen, Katherine Bks) HarperCollins Pubs.

—Nelson Mandela. 2014. (SPA.). (J). (gr. 2-4). 21.99 (978-84-261-4069-2(6)) Juventud, Editorial ESP. Dist: Lectorum Pubns., Inc.

Ogden, Charlie. Human Rights & Liberty. 2017. (Our Values - Level 3 Ser.). (Illus.). 32p. (J). (gr. 5-6). (978-0-7787-3267-9(3)) Crabtree Publishing Co.

Parker, Regina F. Let Freedom Ring. 2004. pap. 14.95 (978-0-9754131-0-4(4)) Kids Donate, Inc.

Rees, Peter. Shockwave: Liberty. 2007. (Shockwave: the Human Experience Ser.). (ENG., Illus.). 36p. (J). (gr. 3-5). 25.00 (978-0-531-17760-0(2), Children's Pr.) Scholastic Library Publishing.

Riddell, Chris, illus. My Little Book of Big Freedoms. 2017. (ENG.). 40p. (J). (gr. -1-3). 9.99 (978-1-5247-8634-2(9), Penguin Workshop) Penguin Young Readers Group.

Rondeau, Amanda & Scheunemann, Pam. Freedom. 2003. (United We Stand Ser.). (Illus.). 24p. (J). (gr. k-3). lib. bdg. 24.21 (978-1-57765-878-8(7), SandCastle) ABDO Publishing Co.

Shamir, Ruby. What's the Big Deal about Freedom. Faulkner, Matt, illus. 2017. (What's the Big Deal About Ser.: 2). 32p. (J). (gr. -1-3). 17.99 (978-0-399-54728-7(2), Philomel Bks.) Penguin Young Readers Group.

Silate, Jennifer. Betsy Ross: Creadora de la bandera estadounidense (Betsy Ross: Creator of the American Flag) 2009. (Grandes personajes en la historia de los Estados Unidos (Famous People in American History) Ser.). (SPA.). 32p. (gr. 2-3). 47.90 (978-1-61512-791-7(7), Editorial Buenas Letras) Rosen Publishing Group, Inc., The.

—Betsy Ross: Creator of the American Flag. 2009. (Primary Sources of Famous People in American History Ser.). 32p. (gr. 2-3). 47.90 (978-1-60851-657-5(1)) Rosen Publishing Group, Inc., The.

—Betsy Ross: Creator of the American Flag / Creadora de la bandera Estadounidense. 2009. (Famous People in American History/Grandes personajes en la historia de los Estados Unidos Ser.). (ENG & SPA.). 32p. (gr. 2-3). 47.90 (978-1-61512-539-5(6), Editorial Buenas Letras) Rosen Publishing Group, Inc., The.

To Be Free. 2003. (Illus.). pap. 5.60 (978-0-7398-7507-0(8)) Steck-Vaughn.

Turner, Joshua. What Is Individual Freedom?, 1 vol. 2019. (Principles of Democracy Ser.). (ENG.). 24p. (gr. 3-3). pap. 9.25 (978-1-5383-4276-3(6), be88d449-52ab-4878-826a-e52c985c25c0, PowerKids Pr.) Rosen Publishing Group, Inc., The.

York, Marion. Happy to Be Me. 2009. (ENG., Illus.). 26p. (J). pap. 15.95 (978-0-9773738-9-5(4)) Bryson Taylor Publishing.

LIBERTY BELL

Ashley, Susan. The Liberty Bell, 1 vol. 2004. (Places in American History Ser.). (ENG., Illus.). 24p. (YA). (gr. 2-4). lib. bdg. 24.67 (978-0-8368-4141-1(7), e704d18f-590d-4eb1-9031-afc9d9257503, Weekly Reader Leveled Readers) Stevens, Gareth Publishing LLLP.

Chang, Kirsten. The Liberty Bell. 2018. (Symbols of American Freedom Ser.). (ENG., Illus.). 24p. (J). (gr. k-3). pap. 7.99 (978-1-61891-470-5(7), 12123); lib. bdg. 26.95 (978-1-62617-884-7(4)) Bellwether Media. (Blastoff! Readers).

Douglas, Lloyd G. The Liberty Bell. 2003. (Welcome Bks.). (Illus.). 24p. (J). 19.00 (978-0-516-25852-2(4), Children's Pr.) Scholastic Library Publishing.

—Welcome Books: Liberty Bell. 2003. (Welcome Bks.). (ENG., Illus.). 24p. (J). (gr. -1-2). pap. 4.95 (978-0-516-27875-9(4), Children's Pr.) Scholastic Library Publishing.

Eldridge, Alison & Eldridge, Stephen. The Liberty Bell: An American Symbol, 1 vol. 2012. (All about American Symbols Ser.). (ENG.). 24p. (gr. -1-1). 25.27 (978-0-7660-4059-5(3), 0d12a906-9890-419d-a9e6-66d158e6537c); (Illus.). pap. 10.35 (978-1-4644-0048-3(2), 90f95d86-6452-436a-b463-7afe4a85ec6b) Enslow Publishing, LLC. (Enslow Publishing).

Figley, Marty Rhodes. Salvar a la Campana de la Libertad. Lepp, Kevin, illus. 2005. (Yo Solo - Historia (on My Own - History) Ser.). (SPA.). 48p. (J). (gr. 3-7). lib. bdg. 25.26

(978-0-8225-3094-7(5), Ediciones Lerner) Lerner Publishing Group.

—Salvar a la Campana de la Libertad; Saving the Liberty Bell. 2008. pap. 40.95 *(978-0-7613-3933-5(7))* Lerner Publishing Group.

—Saving the Liberty Bell. Lepp, Kevin, illus. 2004. (On My Own History Ser.). (ENG.). 48p. (J). (gr. 2-4). pap. 8.99 *(978-1-57505-696-8(8)*, 910d2276-4910-411d-bd61-133c42e06133, First Avenue Editions) Lerner Publishing Group.

Firestone, Mary. The Liberty Bell, 1 vol. Skeens, Matthew, illus. 2007. (American Symbols Ser.). (ENG.). 24p. (J). (gr. 1-3). 9.95 *(978-1-4048-3467-5(2)*, 93813, Picture Window Bks.) Capstone.

Francis, Jo. Visit the Liberty Bell, 1 vol. 2012. (Landmarks of Liberty Ser.). (ENG.). 24p. (J). (gr. 2-3). pap. 9.15 *(978-1-4339-6394-0(9)*, dbe2768e-01d9-4c9e-a42c-12097075ff58, Gareth Stevens Learning Library); lib. bdg. 25.27 *(978-1-4339-6392-6(2)*, 750ed45a-9d3a-43a9-a855-60dd38323110) Stevens, Gareth Publishing LLLP.

Gaspar, Joe. The Liberty Bell, 1 vol. 2013. (PowerKids Readers: American Symbols Ser.). 24p. (J). (gr. k-k). (ENG.). 26.27 *(978-1-4777-0739-5(5)*, f34396f7-151d-4c01-9837-dafc44ff2fe2); pap. 49.50 *(978-1-4777-0820-0(0))*; (ENG., Illus.). pap. 9.25 *(978-1-4777-0819-4(7)*, 94a113a2-e374-41fb-bf75-ef52d011bb65) Rosen Publishing Group, Inc., The. (PowerKids Pr.).

—The Liberty Bell / la Campana de la Libertad, 1 vol. Alamn, Eduardo, ed. 2013. (PowerKids Readers: Símbolos de América / American Symbols Ser.). (ENG & SPA.). 24p. (J). (gr. k-k). 26.27 *(978-1-4777-1207-8(0)*, cfea2c87-c6b4-46d8-a39b-fac86550b150, PowerKids Pr.) Rosen Publishing Group, Inc., The.

Healy, Nick. The Liberty Bell. 2003. (J). pap. *(978-1-58417-119-5(7))*; lib. bdg. *(978-1-58417-057-0(3))* Lake Street Pubs.

Hess, Debra. The Liberty Bell, 1 vol. (Symbols of America Ser.). (ENG.). 40p. (gr. 3-3). 2008. pap. 9.23 *(978-0-7614-3391-0(0)*, af9316c8-f6a9-47dc-8f4b-2dafafd22aad) 2005. (Illus.). lib. bdg. 32.64 *(978-0-7614-1713-2(3)*, 3eb2ff5b-c14e-4bcd-8489-cd93bec4f034) Cavendish Square Publishing LLC.

Hicks, Terry Allan. Symbols of America Group 2, 12 vols., Set. Incl. Bald Eagle. lib. bdg. 32.64 *(978-0-7614-2133-7(5)*, 4cc77ac4-353f-4135-8229-fee1fad1bf3b); Capitol. lib. bdg. 32.64 *(978-0-7614-2132-0(7)*, 983498dc-4064-4d9b-a5fd-9541490d6e2c); Declaration of Independence. lib. bdg. 32.64 *(978-0-7614-2135-1(1)*, b672c79b-ebcf-460a-bf6f-c79934c3be91); Ellis Island. lib. bdg. 32.64 *(978-0-7614-2134-4(3)*, eadd5cdd-45bd-4dab-99b1-a60a5a76c2ba); Pledge of Allegiance. lib. bdg. 32.64 *(978-0-7614-2136-8(X)*, 4f80c1f0-d3ea-4dd5-b747-5d88842745a5); Uncle Sam. lib. bdg. 32.64 *(978-0-7614-2137-5(8)*, e6f9da10-1cd5-4edb-8cd5-0e9e233d21ec); (Illus.). 40p. (gr. 3-3). (Symbols of America Ser.). (ENG.). 2007. Set lib. bdg. 195.84 *(978-0-7614-2130-6(0)*, b2a0354a-8705-48f9-b041-df7983c1050e, Cavendish Square) Cavendish Square Publishing LLC.

Hopper, Whitney. I Visit the Liberty Bell, 1 vol. 2016. (Symbols of Our Country Ser.). (ENG., Illus.). 24p. (J). (gr. 1-1). pap. 9.25 *(978-1-4994-2732-5(8)*, 5a1749f2-87a7-406b-a79b-61fa716fbca5, PowerKids Pr.) Rosen Publishing Group, Inc., The.

James, Lincoln. Making History: The Liberty Bell, 1 vol. 2005. (Content-Area Literacy Collections). (ENG.). 24p. (gr. 3-4). pap. 8.85 *(978-1-4042-5587-6(7)*, 9da605d6-4ef8-4d56-9135-f7e98974d5be) Rosen Publishing Group, Inc., The.

Jango-Cohen, Judith. The Liberty Bell. 2003. (Pull Ahead Books — American Symbols Ser.). (ENG., Illus.). 32p. (J). (gr. k-3). pap. 7.99 *(978-0-8225-3754-0(0)*, 10dda843-6754-45da-b70b-a61749669699, First Avenue Editions) Lerner Publishing Group.

Kopp, Megan. La Campana de la Libertad. 2014. (SPA., Illus.). 24p. (J). *(978-1-62127-619-7(8))* Weigl Pubs., Inc.

—Liberty Bell with Code. 2012. (AV2 American Icons Ser.). (ENG., Illus.). 24p. (J). pap. 12.95 *(978-1-61913-301-3(6))*; lib. bdg. 27.13 *(978-1-61913-078-4(5))* Weigl Pubs., Inc. (AV2 by Weigl).

Mattern, Joanne. The Liberty Bell: History's Silent Witness. 2017. (Core Content Social Studies — Let's Celebrate America Ser.). (ENG., Illus.). 32p. (J). (gr. 2-5). pap. 8.99 *(978-1-63440-235-4(9)*, 28ed5c3f-ee1c-4654-af96-f22535bc1256); lib. bdg. 26.65 *(978-1-63440-225-5(1)*, 0b005936-2891-4184-8159-c5ba8f4d5d28) Red Chair Pr.

McDonald, Megan. Saving the Liberty Bell. 2005. (ENG., Illus.). 32p. (J). (gr. k-3). 19.99 *(978-0-689-85167-4(7)*, Atheneum/Richard Jackson Bks.) Simon & Schuster Children's Publishing.

Meredith, Susan Markowitz. The Liberty Bell. 2016. (Spring Forward Ser.). (J). (gr. 1). *(978-1-4900-2233-8(3))* Benchmark Education Co.

Murray, Julie. Liberty Bell. 2019. (US Symbols (AK) Ser.). (ENG., Illus.). 24p. (J). (gr. -1-2). lib. bdg. 31.36 *(978-1-5321-8536-6(7)*, 31410, Abdo Kids) ABDO Publishing Co.

Nelson, Maria. The Liberty Bell, 1 vol. 2014. (Symbols of America Ser.). (ENG.). 24p. (J). (gr. 1-2). 24.27 *(978-1-4824-1870-5(3)*, a979d57a-63b9-408e-abff-f80f2742c4b0) Stevens, Gareth Publishing LLLP.

Orr, Tamra B. The Liberty Bell: Introducing Primary Sources. 2016. (Introducing Primary Sources Ser.). (ENG., Illus.). 32p. (J). (gr. -1-2). lib. bdg. 28.65 *(978-1-4914-8224-7(9)*, 130686, Capstone Pr.) Capstone.

Rustad, Martha E. H. Can We Ring the Liberty Bell? Poling, Kyle, illus. 2014. (Cloverleaf Books (tm) — Our American Symbols Ser.). (ENG.). 24p. (J). (gr. k-2). pap. 8.99 *(978-1-4677-4467-6(0)*, b17becb7-9a69-4951-8e08-465b29f5a72b, Millbrook Pr.) Lerner Publishing Group.

Shea, Therese M. Zoom in on the Liberty Bell, 1 vol. 2016. (Zoom in on American Symbols Ser.). (ENG.). 24p. (gr. 2-2). pap. 10.95 *(978-0-7660-8454-4(X)*, 29bcffc1-53ab-4b6a-b299-3c7b55c42b82) Enslow Publishing, LLC.

Silate, Jennifer. The Liberty Bell. (Primary Sources of American Symbols Ser.). 24p. (gr. 3-3). 2009. 42.50 *(978-1-60851-509-7(5)*, PowerKids Pr.) 2005. (ENG., Illus.). (J). lib. bdg. 26.27 *(978-1-4042-2687-6(7)*, 63263e67-6bed-4b81-8eda-1c3a62718d92) Rosen Publishing Group, Inc., The.

LIBERTY OF SPEECH

see Freedom of Speech

LIBRARIANS

Alarcon, Roben. Librarians Then & Now, 1 vol. rev. ed. 2006. (Social Studies: Informational Text Ser.). (ENG.). 32p. (gr. 2-3). pap. 11.99 *(978-0-7439-9376-0(4))* Teacher Created Materials, Inc.

Ames, Michelle. Librarians in Our Community, 1 vol. 2009. (On the Job Ser.). (ENG., Illus.). 24p. (J). (gr. 1-1). pap. 9.25 *(978-1-4358-2458-4(X)*, a836bbff-bc4b-42be-8e6c-5d12281bf9cf); lib. bdg. 26.27 *(978-1-4042-8072-4(3)*, 969eedb1-cc4f-4497-867b-19654afc4c30) Rosen Publishing Group, Inc., The. (PowerKids Pr.).

Ardely, Anthony. I Can Be a Librarian, 1 vol. 2018. (I Can Be Anything! Ser.). (ENG.). 24p. (J). (gr. k-k). pap. 9.15 *(978-1-5382-1762-7(7)*, 43f0898c-2ac7-4259-a500-428508b5dc37); lib. bdg. 24.27 *(978-1-5382-1760-3(0)*, a1543c70-01cc-4740-96f6-6c5f08aef03f) Stevens, Gareth Publishing LLLP.

Austen, Mary. Librarians on the Job, 1 vol. 2016. (Jobs in Our Community Ser.). (ENG.). 24p. (J). (gr. 1-1). pap. 9.25 *(978-1-5345-2145-2(3)*, c3641dd4-3e1a-48b5-9e3f-1a3fa10d48ba, KidHaven Publishing) Greenhaven Publishing LLC.

—Que Hacen Los Bibliotecarios? / What Do Librarians Do?, 1 vol. 2015. (Ayudantes de la Comunidad / Helping the Community Ser.). (ENG & SPA.). 24p. (J). (gr. 1-1). 25.27 *(978-1-4994-0647-4(9)*, 77fa87b2-1dc6-4c49-9081-4d2355627194, PowerKids Pr.) Rosen Publishing Group, Inc., The.

—What Do Librarians Do?, 1 vol. 2015. (Helping the Community Ser.). (ENG., Illus.). 24p. (J). (gr. 1-1). pap. 9.25 *(978-1-4994-0640-5(1)*, acd64180-abfc-457d-b2ff-9ad5d4ad1dc5, PowerKids Pr.) Rosen Publishing Group, Inc., The.

Bell, Samantha. Librarian. Bane, Jeff, illus. 2017. (My Early Library: My Friendly Neighborhood Ser.). (ENG.). 24p. (J). (gr. k-1). lib. bdg. 30.64 *(978-1-63472-833-1(5)*, 209758) Cherry Lake Publishing.

Bellisario, Gina. Let's Meet a Librarian. Myer, Ed, illus. 2013. (Cloverleaf Books (tm) — Community Helpers Ser.). (ENG.). 24p. (J). (gr. k-2). pap. 8.99 *(978-1-4677-0803-6(8)*, 33e76a30-935a-4ae5-ab54-853ff4e082c7, Millbrook Pr.) Lerner Publishing Group.

—Librarians in My Community. Myer, Ed, illus. 2018. (Meet a Community Helper (Early Bird Stories (tm)) Ser.). (ENG.). 24p. (J). (gr. k-2). pap. 9.99 *(978-1-5415-2708-9(9)*, 2f2c6f9a-e719-464b-b790-96d3e6a4f9d9); lib. bdg. 29.32 *(978-1-5415-2021-9(1)*, 971cf00d-8d6a-48eb-9938-ddf4d9744895, Lerner Pubns.) Lerner Publishing Group.

Carr, Aaron. The Library. 24p. 2014. (Illus.). (J). *(978-1-62127-346-2(6))* 2013. pap. 12.95 *(978-1-62127-351-6(2))* Weigl Pubs., Inc.

Conrad, Vicki. Just Like Beverly: A Biography of Beverly Cleary. Hohn, David, illus. 2019. (Growing to Greatness Ser.). 48p. (J). (gr. k-4). 18.99 *(978-1-63217-222-8(4)*, Little Bigfoot) Sasquatch Bks.

Crabtree, Marc. Meet My Neighbor, the Librarian. 2012. (ENG., Illus.). 24p. (J). *(978-0-7787-4559-4(7))*; pap. *(978-0-7787-4564-8(3))* Crabtree Publishing Co.

Davenport, Jefferson. Let's Help the Librarian!, 1 vol. 2013. (InfoMax Math Readers Ser.). (ENG.). 24p. (J). (gr. 1-1). pap. 8.25 *(978-1-4777-2121-6(5)*, 7b6b555a-dfad-49aa-a65d-16d075c02a3a, Rosen Classroom) Rosen Publishing Group, Inc., The.

—Let's Help the Librarian! Subtract Within 20. 2013. (InfoMax Math Readers Ser.). (ENG.). 24p. (J). (gr. 1-2). pap. 49.50 *(978-1-4777-2122-3(3)*, Rosen Classroom) Rosen Publishing Group, Inc., The.

Denise, Anika Aldamuy. Planting Stories: the Life of Librarian & Storyteller Pura Belpré. Escobar, Paola, illus. 2019. (ENG.). 40p. (J). (gr. -1-3). 18.99 *(978-0-06-274868-3(8)*, HarperCollins) HarperCollins Pubs.

Gaertner, Meg. Librarians. 2018. (Community Workers Ser.). (ENG., Illus.). 24p. (J). (gr. 1-1). pap. 8.95 *(978-1-63517-807-4(X)*, 163517807X) North Star Editions.

—Librarians. 2018. (Community Workers Ser.). (ENG., Illus.). 24p. (J). (gr. k-3). lib. bdg. 31.36 *(978-1-5321-6012-7(7)*, 28656, Pop! Cody Koala) Pop!

Garrett, Winston. What Does a Library Media Specialist Do?, 1 vol. 2014. (Jobs in My School Ser.). (ENG.). 24p. (J). (gr. 1-2). lib. bdg. 25.27 *(978-1-4777-6546-3(8)*, a1850f21-7494-41d5-a298-ecf37cbf9af0, PowerKids Pr.) Rosen Publishing Group, Inc., The.

—What Does a Library Media Specialist Do? (¿Qué Hace el Especialista de Medios de la Biblioteca Escolar?), 1 vol. de la Vega, Eida, ed. 2014. (Oficios en Mi Escuela / Jobs in My School Ser.). (SPA & ENG.). 24p. (J). (gr. 1-2). lib. bdg. 25.27 *(978-1-4777-6796-2(7)*, 9bf473f5-57bd-4a6a-9303-c0b42f4d9292, PowerKids Pr.) Rosen Publishing Group, Inc., The.

Glenn, Sharlee. Library on Wheels: Mary Lemist Titcomb & America's First Bookmobile. 2018. (ENG., Illus.). 56p. (J). (gr. 3-7). 18.99 *(978-1-4197-2875-4(X)*, 1127801, Abrams Bks. for Young Readers) Abrams, Inc.

Hoena, Blake A. The Library: A 4D Book. rev. ed. 2018. (Visit To... Ser.). (ENG., Illus.). 24p. (J). (gr. -1-2). lib. bdg. 29.32 *(978-1-5435-0830-7(8)*, 137593, Capstone Pr.) Capstone.

Honders, Christine. Why Should I Listen to My Librarian?, 1 vol. 2019. (Listening to Leaders Ser.). (ENG.). 24p. (gr. 2-2). pap. 9.25 *(978-1-5383-4164-3(6)*, a37d62de-162b-4bae-9594-950c2ef53a4e, PowerKids Pr.) Rosen Publishing Group, Inc., The.

Jango-Cohen, Judith. Librarians. 2005. (Pull Ahead Bks.). (Illus.). 32p. (J). lib. bdg. 22.60 *(978-0-8225-1691-0(8))* Lerner Publishing Group.

Jeffries, Joyce. Meet the Librarian, 1 vol. 2013. (People Around Town Ser.). (Illus.). 24p. (J). (gr. k-k). (ENG.). pap. 9.15 *(978-1-4339-9373-2(2)*, 8852d567-fcb6-4615-8a5a-982e5bb20616); (ENG., lib. bdg. 25.27 *(978-1-4339-9372-5(4)*, f8130ad8-22f0-4836-8c28-4f9a3a024bac); pap. 48.90 *(978-1-4339-9374-9(0))* Stevens, Gareth Publishing LLLP.

—Meet the Librarian / Conoce a Los Bibliotecarios, 1 vol. 2013. (People Around Town / Gente de Mi Ciudad Ser.). (SPA & ENG.). 24p. (J). (gr. k-k). 25.27 *(978-1-4339-9468-5(2)*, b586ef7b-36fa-460f-b551-409e8ce5c50e) Stevens, Gareth Publishing LLLP.

Kawa, Katie. A Day with a Librarian. 2020. (J). *(978-1-5026-5325-3(7))* Cavendish Square Publishing LLC.

—My First Trip to the Library / Mi Primera Visita a la Biblioteca, 1 vol. Livingston, Jessica, illus. 2012. (My First Adventures / Mis Primeras Aventuras Ser.). (ENG & SPA.). 24p. (J). (gr. k-k). lib. bdg. 25.27 *(978-1-4339-6631-6(X)*, e582c9ff-1eb7-45b0-9a70-490bf195c1fe) Stevens, Gareth Publishing LLLP.

Kenan, Tessa. Hooray for Librarians! 2017. (Bumba Books (r) — Hooray for Community Helpers! Ser.). (ENG., Illus.). 24p. (J). (gr. -1-1). pap. 8.99 *(978-1-5124-5553-3(9)*, 14a36803-53e4-4b5c-986c-89fc6e123074); lib. bdg. 26.65 *(978-1-5124-3353-1(5)*, 5e97c1ef-5821-4a14-811d-8cfc1e5e82be, Lerner Pubns.) Lerner Publishing Group.

Laks Gorman, Jacqueline. Librarians, 1 vol. 2010. (People in My Community (Second Edition) Ser.). (ENG., Illus.). 24p. (gr. k-2). pap. 9.15 *(978-1-4339-3342-4(X)*, adbc6c35-689b-4232-8a6b-41706b67d7b6) Stevens, Gareth Publishing LLLP.

—Librarians / Bibliotecarios, 1 vol. 2010. (People in My Community / Mi Comunidad Ser.). (SPA & ENG., Illus.). 24p. (gr. k-2). pap. 9.15 *(978-1-4339-3760-6(3)*, fd6b829c-d7b8-4ad7-8816-1751339176f2) Stevens, Gareth Publishing LLLP.

Leone, Laura. Choosing a Career in Information Science. 2009. (World of Work Ser.). 64p. (gr. 5-5). 58.50 *(978-1-60854-332-8(3))* Rosen Publishing Group, Inc., The.

Less, Emma. Librarians. 2018. (Real-Life Superheroes Ser.). (ENG.). 16p. (J). (gr. k-2). pap. 7.99 *(978-1-68152-278-4(0)*, 14917) Amicus.

Liebman, Dan. I Want to Be a Librarian. 2003. (I Want to Be Ser.). (ENG., Illus.). 24p. (J). (gr. -1-2). pap. 3.99 *(978-1-55297-689-0(0)*, 1d2e9ee0-48c3-44bb-8d54-086b9292a7ce) Firefly Bks., Ltd.

Liebman, Dan & Liebman, Dan. I Want to Be a Librarian. 2003. (I Want to Be Ser.). (ENG., Illus.). 24p. (J). (gr. -1-2). 16.19 *(978-1-55297-691-3(2)*, 188f5ba8-cbdd-499e-9d3a-a6411a2cb016) Firefly Bks., Ltd.

—Quiero Ser Bibliotecario. 2003. (Quiero Ser). (SPA., Illus.). 24p. (J). (gr. -1-2). pap. 5.99 *(978-1-55297-726-2(9)*, bfe6feab-99d6-454c-ad00-d9095dd1650c) Firefly Bks., Ltd.

Marsico, Katie. Working at the Airport. 2009. (21st Century Junior Library: Careers Ser.). (ENG., Illus.). 24p. (gr. 2-5). lib. bdg. 29.21 *(978-1-60279-510-5(X)*, 200279) Cherry Lake Publishing.

—Working at the Library. 2009. (21st Century Junior Library: Careers Ser.). (ENG., Illus.). 24p. (gr. 2-5). lib. bdg. 29.21 *(978-1-60279-511-2(8)*, 200278) Cherry Lake Publishing.

Meachen Rau, Dana. Librarian. 2007. (J). *(978-0-7614-2621-9(3))* Marshall Cavendish.

—Librarians, 1 vol. 2008. (Tools We Use Ser.). (ENG.). 32p. (gr. k-1). pap. 9.23 *(978-0-7614-3293-7(0)*, 19d858e0-780e-435d-99f2-a9e4c0cdab49); (Illus.). lib. bdg. 25.50 *(978-0-7614-2662-2(0)*, a4e0706d-b945-4dfa-ad07-2954c1de9545) Cavendish Square Publishing LLC.

—Los Bibliotecarios / Librarians, 1 vol. 2009. (Instrumentos de Trabajo / Tools We Use Ser.). (ENG & SPA., Illus.). 32p. (gr. k-2). lib. bdg. 25.50 *(978-0-7614-2826-8(7)*, cd825d78-3b7b-4138-b590-dc7d17ac3e61) Cavendish Square Publishing LLC.

—Los Bibliotecarios (Librarians), 1 vol. 2009. (Instrumentos de Trabajo (Tools We Use) Ser.). (SPA., Illus.). 32p. (gr. k-2). lib. bdg. 25.50 *(978-0-7614-2802-2(X)*, a80f21fc-20bb-43bc-a89b-fcb114712bda) Cavendish Square Publishing LLC.

Meister, Cari. Librarians. 2014. (ENG., Illus.). 24p. (J). lib. bdg. 25.65 *(978-1-62031-076-2(7))* Jump! Inc.

Miller, Connie Colwell. I'll Be a Librarian. Baroncelli, Silvia, illus. 2018. (When I Grow Up Ser.). (ENG.). 24p. (J). (gr. 1-4). pap. 8.99 *(978-1-68152-317-0(5)*, 15058); lib. bdg. *(978-1-68151-397-3(8)*, 15052) Amicus.

Moening, Kate. Librarians. 2018. (Community Helpers Ser.). (ENG., Illus.). 24p. (J). (gr. k-3). lib. bdg. 26.95 *(978-1-62617-899-1(2)*, Blastoff! Readers) Bellwether Media.

Monroe, Judy. A Day in the Life of a Librarian, 1 vol. 2004. (Community Helpers at Work Ser.). (ENG., Illus.). 24p. (J). (gr. 1-3). 25.99 *(978-0-7368-2630-3(0)*, 89748, Capstone Pr.) Capstone.

Murray, Julie. Librarians, 1 vol. 2015. (My Community: Jobs Ser.). (ENG.). 24p. (J). (gr. -1-2). 31.36 *(978-1-62970-914-7(X)*, 18286, Abdo Kids) ABDO Publishing Co.

O'Brian, Virginia. A Librarian's Job, 1 vol. 2014. (Community Workers Ser.). (ENG.). 24p. (gr. 1-1). 25.93 *(978-1-62712-357-0(1)*, 4160a960-623d-45a9-89cb-9f610591abd3) Cavendish Square Publishing LLC.

Oliver-Miles, Zelda. Amelia Gayle Gorgas: First Woman of Position. 2005. (Alabama Roots Biography Ser.). (Illus.). 100p. (J). pap. *(978-1-59421-017-4(9))* Seacoast Publishing, Inc.

Ready, Dee. Librarians Help. 2013. (Our Community Helpers Ser.). (ENG.). 24p. (J). (gr. k-1). pap. 37.74 *(978-1-62065-848-2(8)*, 19420, Pebble) Capstone.

Ready, Dee & Ready, Dee. Librarians Help, 1 vol. 2013. (Our Community Helpers Ser.). (ENG.). 24p. (J). (gr. -1-2). pap. 6.29 *(978-1-62065-847-5(X)*, 121788); lib. bdg. 24.65 *(978-1-62065-084-4(3)*, 120784) Capstone. (Pebble).

Roza, Greg. My First Trip to the Library, 1 vol. 2019. (My First Trip Ser.). (ENG.). 24p. (gr. 1-1). 25.27 *(978-1-5383-4435-4(1)*, cfb42f80-0830-4a90-968d-2117f071e2ce, PowerKids Pr.) Rosen Publishing Group, Inc., The.

Shepherd, Jodie. A Day with Librarians. 2012. (Rookie Read-About Community Ser.). (ENG.). 32p. (J). pap. 5.95 *(978-0-531-29252-5(5))*; lib. bdg. 23.00 *(978-0-531-28952-5(4))* Scholastic Library Publishing.

Siemens, Jared. Librarians. 2016. (J). *(978-1-5105-2107-0(0))* SmartBook Media, Inc.

—Librarians. 2015. 24p. (J). *(978-1-4896-3649-2(8))* Weigl Pubs., Inc.

Stamaty, Mark Alan. Alia's Mission: Saving the Books of Iraq. 2010. 32p. (J). (gr. k-3). pap. 7.99 *(978-0-375-85763-8(X)*, Dragonfly Bks.) Random Hse. Children's Bks.

—Muhimat Al Sayyda Alia: Inkaz Kuttub Al Iraq. 2005.Tr. of Alia's Mission - Saving the Books of Iraq. 32p. pap. 12.00 *(978-977-6171-01-5(X)*, 706-001) Al-Balsam Pubng. Hse. EGY. Dist: Baker & Taylor Publisher Services (BTPS).

Vasquez, Lidia. Damaged Friends: Sad but True Stories about Damaged Books. 2010. (ENG.). 26p. pap. 13.99 *(978-1-4520-1548-4(1))* AuthorHouse.

Vogel, Elizabeth. Meet the Librarian. 2009. (My School Ser.). 24p. (gr. 1-2). 37.50 *(978-1-61514-706-9(3)*, PowerKids Pr.) Rosen Publishing Group, Inc., The.

Waxman, Laura Hamilton. Librarian Tools. 2019. (Bumba Books (r) — Community Helpers Tools of the Trade Ser.). (ENG., Illus.). 24p. (J). (gr. -1-1). 26.65 *(978-1-5415-5561-7(9)*, 5dc78b18-e36e-4016-b84a-3cbe1c48e8dc); pap. 8.99 *(978-1-5415-7352-9(8)*, 89ed298c-17cf-456f-9b6c-94c7ca5b2ad0) Lerner Publishing Group. (Lerner Pubns.).

Winter, Jeanette. Biblioburro: A True Story from Colombia. Winter, Jeanette, illus. 2010. (ENG., Illus.). 32p. (J). (gr. 1-4). 18.99 *(978-1-4169-9778-8(4)*, Beach Lane Bks.) Beach Lane Bks.

—The Librarian of Basra: A True Story from Iraq. 2019. (ENG., Illus.). 32p. (J). (gr. -1-3). pap. 8.99 *(978-0-358-14183-9(4)*, 1755716, Clarion Bks.) HarperCollins Pubs.

—The Librarian of Basra: A True Story from Iraq. Winter, Jeanette, illus. 2005. (ENG., Illus.). 32p. (J). (gr. -1-3). 17.99 *(978-0-15-205445-8(6)*, 1196387, Clarion Bks.) HarperCollins Pubs.

LIBRARIANS—FICTION

Aris, Mary. Bartholomew. 2010. 86p. pap. 36.95 *(978-1-4457-8958-3(2))*; pap. 36.50 *(978-1-4457-5351-5(0))* Lulu Pr., Inc.

Asher, Sandy. Chicken Story Time. Fearing, Mark, illus. 2016. (ENG.). 40p. (J). (-k). 18.99 *(978-0-8037-3944-4(3)*, Dial Bks) Penguin Young Readers Group.

Barnett, Mac. Brixton Brothers Mysterious Case of Cases: The Case of the Case of Mistaken Identity; the Ghostwriter Secret; It Happened on a Train; Danger Goes Berserk. Rex, Adam & Myers, Matt, illus. 2013. (Brixton Brothers Ser.). (ENG.). 1024p. (J). (gr. 3-7). pap. 33.99 *(978-1-4424-9818-1(8)*, Simon & Schuster Bks. For Young Readers) Simon & Schuster Bks. For Young Readers.

—The Case of the Case of Mistaken Identity. Rex, Adam, illus. (Brixton Brothers Ser.: 1). (ENG.). (J). (gr. 3-7). 2010. 208p. pap. 7.99 *(978-1-4169-7816-9(X))* 2009. 192p. 15.99 *(978-1-4169-7815-2(1))* Simon & Schuster Bks. For Young Readers. (Simon & Schuster Bks. For Young Readers).

Bellisario, Gina. Queen of the Spelling Bee. Von Innerebner, Jessika, illus. 2016. (Ellie Ultra Ser.). (ENG.). 128p. (J). (gr. 1-3). lib. bdg. 25.99 *(978-1-4965-3141-4(8)*, 132195, Stone Arch Bks.) Capstone.

Berg, Brook. What Marion Taught Willis. Alberg, Nathan, illus. 2005. (J). 16.95 *(978-1-932146-31-8(8)*, 1242215) Highsmith Inc.

Bernheimer, Kate. The Lonely Book. Sheban, Chris, illus. 2012. 40p. (J). (gr. -1-3). 17.99 *(978-0-375-86226-7(9)*, Schwartz & Wade Bks.) Random Hse. Children's Bks.

Bottner, Barbara. Miss Brooks Loves Books (and I Don't) 2016. (CHI.). 32p. (J). (gr. k-3). *(978-7-5552-3723-5(7))* Qingdao Publishing Hse.

—Miss Brooks Loves Books (and I Don't) Emberley, Michael, illus. 2018. (ENG.). 32p. (J). (gr. -1-2). 8.99 *(978-1-9848-5210-6(8)*, Dragonfly Bks.) Random Hse. Children's Bks.

Brouwer, Sigmund. Justine Mckeen, Pooper Scooper, 1 vol. Whamond, Dave, illus. 2012. (Orca Echoes Ser.). (ENG.). 64p. (J). (gr. 1-3). pap. 6.95 *(978-1-55469-931-5(2))* Orca Bk. Pubs. USA.

Buzzeo, Toni. Fire up with Reading! Yoshikawa, Sachiko, illus. 2007. 32p. 17.95 *(978-1-60213-019-7(1)*, Upstart Bks.) Highsmith Inc.

—The Great Dewey Hunt. Yoshikawa, Sachiko, illus. 2009. (Mrs. Skorupski Story Ser.). (J). 36p. (gr. -1-3). 17.95 *(978-1-60213-041-8(8))*; *(978-1-60213-029-6(9))* Highsmith Inc. (Upstart Bks.).

—The Library Doors. Westcott, Nadine Bernard, illus. 2008. (J). (gr. -1-3). 17.95 *(978-1-60213-037-1(X)*, Upstart Bks.) Highsmith Inc.

—Our Librarian Won't Tell Us Anything! Yoshikawa, Sachiko, illus. 2006. 32p. (J). (gr. -1-k). lib. bdg. 17.95 *(978-1-932146-73-8(3)*, Upstart Bks.) Highsmith Inc.

Casale, Karen. Never Let a Ghost Borrow Your Library Book: Book Care Guidelines from the Library Secret Service. Rebora, Cecilia, illus. 2012. 32p. (J). 17.75 *(978-1-60213-061-6(2)*, Upstart Bks.) Highsmith Inc.

Colfer, Eoin. The Legend of Spud Murphy. McCoy, Glenn, illus. 2005. (Eoin Colfer's Legend Of... Ser.). 95p. (gr. 2-6). 16.00 *(978-0-7569-6514-3(4))* Perfection Learning Corp.

Curious George Librarian for a Day (Reader Level 1) 2012. (Curious George Ser.). (ENG., Illus.). 24p. (J). (gr. -1-3). pap. 4.99 *(978-0-547-85281-2(9)*, 1501410, Clarion Bks.) HarperCollins Pubs.

Dahl, Michael. Attack of the Paper Bats: 10th Anniversary Edition. Blanco, Martin, illus. 10th ed. 2017. (Library of Doom Ser.). (ENG.). 48p. (J). (gr. 4-8). pap. 6.25 *(978-1-4965-5537-3(6)*, 136561); lib. bdg. 23.99 *(978-1-4965-5531-1(7)*, 136555) Capstone. (Stone Arch Bks.).

—The Beast Beneath the Stairs: 10th Anniversary Edition. Moffett, Patricia, illus. 10th ed. 2017. (Library of Doom Ser.).

(ENG.). 48p. (J). (gr. 4-8). pap. 6.25 *(978-1-4965-5536-6(8),* 136560); lib. bdg. 23.99 *(978-1-4965-5530-4(9),* 136554) Capstone. (Stone Arch Bks.).
—The Book That Dripped Blood: 10th Anniversary Edition. Kendall, Bradford, illus. 10th ed. 2017. (Library of Doom Ser.). (ENG.). 48p. (J). (gr. 4-8). pap. 6.25 *(978-1-4965-5535-9(X),* 136559); lib. bdg. 23.99 *(978-1-4965-5529-8(5),* 136553) Capstone. (Stone Arch Bks.).
—Cave of the Bookworms, 1 vol. Kendall, Bradford, illus. 2008. (Library of Doom Ser.). (ENG.). 40p. (J). (gr. 4-8). pap. 6.25 *(978-1-4342-0549-0(5),* 94467, Stone Arch Bks.) Capstone.
—The Creeping Bookends, 1 vol. Kendall, Bradford, illus. 2008. (Library of Doom Ser.). (ENG.). 40p. (J). (gr. 4-8). pap. 6.25 *(978-1-4342-0546-9(0),* 94464, Stone Arch Bks.) Capstone.
—La Cueva de Los Gusanos. Aparicio Publishing LLC, Aparicio Publishing, tr. Kendall, Bradford, illus. 2020. (Biblioteca Maldita Ser.).Tr. of Cave of the Bookworms. (SPA.). 40p. (J). (gr. 4-8). pap. 6.95 *(978-1-4965-9309-2(X),* 142321); lib. bdg. 24.65 *(978-1-4965-9170-8(4),* 142083) Capstone. (Stone Arch Bks.).
—Dictionary of 1,000 Rooms, 1 vol. Kendall, Bradford, illus. 2011. (Return to the Library of Doom Ser.). (ENG.). 72p. (J). (gr. 4-8). lib. bdg. 23.99 *(978-1-4342-3229-8(8),* 116201, Stone Arch Bks.) Capstone.
—Don't Open It! 2016. (ENG., Illus.). 40p. (J). pap. *(978-1-4747-1054-1(9),* Stone Arch Bks.) Capstone.
—Escape de la Prisión de Papel. Aparicio Publishing LLC, Aparicio Publishing, tr. Kendall, Bradford, illus. 2020. (Biblioteca Maldita Ser.).Tr. of Escape from the Pop-Up Prison. (SPA.). 40p. (J). (gr. 4-8). pap. 6.95 *(978-1-4965-9310-8(3),* 142322); lib. bdg. 24.65 *(978-1-4965-9171-5(2),* 142084) Capstone. (Stone Arch Bks.).
—Escape from the Pop-Up Prison. Kendall, Bradford, illus. 2008. (Library of Doom Ser.). (ENG.). 40p. (J). (gr. 4-8). pap. 6.25 *(978-1-4342-0550-6(9),* 94468, Stone Arch Bks.) Capstone.
—The Eye in the Graveyard: 10th Anniversary Edition. Molinari, Fernando, illus. 10th ed. 2017. (Library of Doom Ser.). (ENG.). 48p. (J). (gr. 4-8). pap. 6.25 *(978-1-4965-5534-2(1),* 136558); lib. bdg. 23.99 *(978-1-4965-5528-1(7),* 136552) Capstone. (Stone Arch Bks.).
—The Golden Book of Death, 1 vol. Souleiman, Serg, illus. 2008. (Library of Doom Ser.). (ENG.). 40p. (J). (gr. 4-8). per. 6.25 *(978-1-4342-0547-6(9),* 94465, Stone Arch Bks.) Capstone.
—Killer App, 1 vol. Kendall, Bradford, illus. 2011. (Return to the Library of Doom Ser.). (ENG.). 72p. (J). (gr. 4-8). lib. bdg. 23.99 *(978-1-4342-3231-1(X),* 116203, Stone Arch Bks.) Capstone.
—The Last Word. 2016. (ENG., Illus.). 40p. (J). pap. *(978-1-4747-1055-8(7),* Stone Arch Bks.) Capstone.
—El Libro Dorado de la Muerte. Aparicio Publishing LLC, Aparicio Publishing, tr. Souleiman, Serg, illus. 2020. (Biblioteca Maldita Ser.).Tr. of Golden Book of Death. (SPA.). 40p. (J). (gr. 4-8). pap. 6.95 *(978-1-4965-9308-5(1),* 142320); lib. bdg. 24.65 *(978-1-4965-9169-2(0),* 142082) Capstone. (Stone Arch Bks.).
—Los Sujetalibros Horripilantes. Aparicio Publishing LLC, Aparicio Publishing, tr. Kendall, Bradford, illus. 2020. (Biblioteca Maldita Ser.).Tr. of Creeping Bookends. (SPA.). 40p. (J). (gr. 4-8). pap. 6.95 *(978-1-4965-9307-8(3),* 142319); lib. bdg. 24.65 *(978-1-4965-9168-5(2),* 142081) Capstone. (Stone Arch Bks.).
—The Lost Page. Evergreen, Nelson, illus. 2015. (Library of Doom: the Final Chapters Ser.). (ENG.). 40p. (J). (gr. 4-8). 23.99 *(978-1-4342-9679-5(2),* 126988, Stone Arch Bks.) Capstone.
—Night of the Scrawler. 2016. (ENG., Illus.). 40p. (J). pap. *(978-1-4747-1056-5(5),* Stone Arch Bks.) Capstone.
—Poison Pages: 10th Anniversary Edition. Blanco, Martin, illus. 10th ed. 2017. (Library of Doom Ser.). (ENG.). 48p. (J). (gr. 4-8). lib. bdg. 23.99 *(978-1-4965-5527-4(9),* 136551, Stone Arch Bks.) Capstone.
—The Smashing Scroll: 10th Anniversary Edition. 10th ed. 2017. (Library of Doom Ser.). (ENG., Illus.). 48p. (J). (gr. 4-8). pap. 6.25 *(978-1-4965-5532-8(5),* 136556, Stone Arch Bks.) Capstone.
—The Spine Tingler. Evergreen, Nelson, illus. 2015. (Library of Doom: the Final Chapters Ser.). (ENG.). 40p. (J). (gr. 4-8). 23.99 *(978-1-4342-9680-1(6),* 126987, Stone Arch Bks.) Capstone.
—Thesaurus Rex. 2016. (ENG., Illus.). 40p. (J). pap. *(978-1-4747-1057-2(3),* Stone Arch Bks.) Capstone.
—Tome Raider. Evergreen, Nelson, illus. 2015. (Library of Doom: the Final Chapters Ser.). (ENG.). 40p. (J). (gr. 4-8). 23.99 *(978-1-4342-9677-1(6),* 126985, Stone Arch Bks.) Capstone.
—The Twister Trap, 1 vol. Kendall, Bradford, illus. 2008. (Library of Doom Ser.). (ENG.). 40p. (J). (gr. 4-8). pap. 6.25 *(978-1-4342-0548-3(7),* 94466, Stone Arch Bks.) Capstone.
—The Word Eater, 1 vol. Kendall, Bradford, illus. 2008. (Library of Doom Ser.). (ENG.). 40p. (J). (gr. 4-8). lib. bdg. 23.99 *(978-1-4342-0491-2(X),* 94439); per. 6.25 *(978-1-4342-0551-3(7),* 94469) Capstone. (Stone Arch Bks.).
Dailey, Reid. The Legend of Ross the Reader: A Story of How a Smart Cowboy Saved the Prairie One Book at a Time. Edgerley, Ross, illus. 2007. 32p. pap. 15.95 *(978-1-59858-483-7(9))* Dog Ear Publishing, LLC.
—Ross the Reader & the Adventure of the Pirate's Treasure. Edgerley, Ross, illus. 2009. 44p. pap. 16.95 *(978-1-59858-900-9(8))* Dog Ear Publishing, LLC.
Darden, Amy. Yesterday Once Again: Guenevere's Quest. 2003. (J). pap. 11.00 *(978-0-8059-9238-0(3),* RoseDog Bks.) Dorrance Publishing Co., Inc.
Deedy, Carmen Agra. The Library Dragon, 1 vol. White, Michael P., illus. 2012. (ENG.). 32p. (J). (gr. 1-4). 16.95 *(978-1-56145-091-6(X),* Q06826) Peachtree Publishing Co. Inc.
—Return of the Library Dragon, 1 vol. White, Michael P., illus. 2012. (ENG.). 32p. (J). (gr. -1-3). 16.95 *(978-1-56145-621-5(7))* Peachtree Publishing Co. Inc.
Donald, Alison. The New Libearian. Willmore, Alex, illus. 2018. (ENG.). 32p. (J). (gr. -1-3). 16.99 *(978-0-544-97365-7(8),* 1663219, Clarion Bks.) HarperCollins Pubs.
Foxe, Steve. Mr. Kazarian, Alien Librarian. Boller, Gary, illus. 2019. (Mr. Kazarian, Alien Librarian Ser.). (ENG.). 64p. (J). (gr. 3-5). 21.99 *(978-1-4965-8366-6(3),* 140650, Stone Arch Bks.) Capstone.
French, Vivian. The Cherry Pie Princess. Kissi, Marta, illus. 2018. (ENG.). 176p. (J). pap. 5.99 *(978-1-61067-733-2(1))* Kane Miller.
Garland, Michael. Miss Smith & the Haunted Library. 2012. 32p. (J). (gr. -1-2). 7.99 *(978-0-14-242122-2(7),* Puffin Books) Penguin Young Readers Group.
Gómez Cerda, Alfredo. Barro de Medellín/ Mud of Medellín. Lopez, Xan, illus. 2010. (SPA.). 146p. (YA). (gr. 5-8). *(978-84-263-6849-2(2))* Vives, Luis Editorial (Edelvives).
González, Lucía. The Storyteller's Candle: La Velita de Los Cuentos, 1 vol. Delacre, Lulu, illus. 2013. (ENG.). 32p. (J). (gr. 1-6). pap. 11.95 *(978-0-89239-237-7(1),* leelowcbp, Children's Book Press) Lee & Low Bks., Inc.
Gonzalez, Lucia M. & Delacre, Lulu. The Storyteller's Candle. 2008.Tr. of La Velita de los Cuentos. (SPA & ENG., Illus.). 32p. (J). (gr. k-4). 16.95 *(978-0-89239-222-3(3))* Lee & Low Bks., Inc.
Haight, Jessica & Robinson, Stephanie. Fairday Morrow & the Talking Library. 2017. (ENG., Illus.). 228p. (J). (gr. 3-6). pap. 9.99 *(978-0-9993449-1-0(9));* (Fairday Morrow Ser.: Vol. 2). 24.99 *(978-0-9993449-0-3(0))* Pronoun, Inc.
Henson, Heather. That Book Woman. Small, David, illus. 2008. (ENG.). 40p. (J). (gr. -1-3). 17.99 *(978-1-4169-0812-8(9),* Atheneum Bks. for Young Readers) Simon & Schuster Children's Publishing.
—That Book Woman. Small, David, illus. 2011. (J). (gr. 2-4). 29.95 *(978-0-545-23715-4(7))* Weston Woods Studios, Inc.
Hopkins, Jackie Mims. Goldie Socks & the Three Libearians. Manders, John, illus. 2007. (J). *(978-1-932146-68-4(7),* Upstart Bks.) Highsmith Inc.
Hubbell, Patricia. Check It Out! Reading, Finding, Helping: Reading, Finding, Helping, 0 vols. Speir, Nancy, illus. 2012. (ENG.). 32p. (J). (gr. -1-3). 16.99 *(978-0-7614-5803-6(4),* 9780761458036, Two Lions) Amazon Publishing.
Jenkins, Emily. The Little Bit Scary People. Boiger, Alexandra, illus. 2008. (ENG.). 32p. (J). (gr. -1-1). 16.99 *(978-1-4231-0075-1(1))* Hyperion Pr.
Knudsen, Michelle. Evil Librarian. 2014. (ENG.). 352p. (YA). (gr. 9). 16.99 *(978-0-7636-6038-3(8))* Candlewick Pr.
Luper, Eric. The Wizard's War (Key Hunters #4) 2017. (Key Hunters Ser.: 4). (ENG., Illus.). 128p. (J). (gr. 2-5). pap. 5.99 *(978-0-545-82213-8(0),* Scholastic Paperbacks) Scholastic, Inc.
McQuinn, Anna. Lola at the Library. Beardshaw, Rosalind, illus. 2006. (Lola Reads Ser.: 1). (ENG.). 32p. (J). (gr. -1 — 1). 16.99 *(978-1-58089-113-4(6));* 7.99 *(978-1-58089-142-4(X))* Charlesbridge Publishing, Inc.
Miller, Nathan. The Official Librarian: Bessy's Back! 2009. 124p. pap. 12.49 *(978-1-4490-2391-1(6))* AuthorHouse.
Moon, Sarah. Sparrow. 2019. (ENG.). 272p. (YA). (gr. 7-7). pap. 10.99 *(978-1-338-31286-7(3),* Levine, Arthur A. Bks.) Scholastic, Inc.
Morris, Carla. The Boy Who Was Raised by Librarians. Sneed, Brad, illus. 32p. (J). (gr. -1-3). 2019. pap. 7.95 *(978-1-68263-123-2(0))* 2007. (ENG.). 16.95 *(978-1-56145-391-7(9))* Peachtree Publishing Co. Inc.
North, Pearl. Libyrinth. 2010. (Libyrinth Ser.: 1). (ENG.). 336p. (YA). (gr. 7-18). 26.19 *(978-0-7653-2096-4(7))* Doherty, Tom Assocs., LLC.
Osborne, Mary Pope. Magic Tree House Books 17-20 Boxed Set: The Mystery of the Enchanted Dog, 4 vols., Bks. 17-20. Murdocca, Sal, illus. 2009. (Magic Tree House (R) Ser.). 96p. (J). (gr. 1-4). 27.96 *(978-0-375-85811-6(3),* Random Hse. Bks. for Young Readers) Random Hse. Children's Bks.
Peck, Richard. Here Lies the Librarian. 2006. (ENG.). 160p. (J). (gr. 6-8). 21.19 *(978-0-8037-3080-9(2),* Dial) Penguin Publishing Group.
—Here Lies the Librarian. 2007. (ENG.). 160p. (J). (gr. 5-18). 8.99 *(978-0-14-240908-4(1),* Puffin Books) Penguin Young Readers Group.
—Here Lies the Librarian. 2007. 145p. (J). (gr. 4-7). 14.65 *(978-0-7569-8193-8(X))* Perfection Learning Corp.
—Here Lies the Librarian. rev. l.t. ed. 2007. (Thorndike Literacy Bridge Ser.). (ENG.). 173p. (J). (gr. 5-9). 23.95 *(978-0-7862-9183-0(4))* Thorndike Pr.
Rey, H. A. & Rey, Margret. Librarian for a Day. 2012. (Curious George TV Tie-In Early Reader Ser.). lib. bdg. 13.55 *(978-0-606-26602-4(X))* Turtleback.
Ruurs, Margriet & Gooderham, Andrew. Ms. Bee's magical bookcase. 2004. (Illus.). 32p. (J). pap. 8.95 *(978-1-894601-10-8(6))* Chestnut Publishing Group CAN. Dist: Hushion Hse. Publishing, Ltd.
Sager Weinstein, Jacob. Lyric Mckerrigan, Secret Librarian. Brosgol, Vera, illus. 2018. (ENG.). 48p. (J). (gr. -1-3). 17.99 *(978-0-544-80122-6(9),* 1640248, Clarion Bks.) HarperCollins Pubs.
Sanderson, Brandon. Alcatraz Versus the Evil Librarians, 6 vols. 2011. (Alcatraz Ser.: 1). (J). 88.75 *(978-1-4618-0832-9(4));* 90.75 *(978-1-4618-0830-5(8));* 245.75 *(978-1-4618-0831-2(6));* 245.75 *(978-1-4618-0828-2(6));* 88.75 *(978-1-4618-0829-9(4));* 1.25 *(978-1-4640-1982-1(7))* Recorded Bks., Inc.
—Alcatraz Versus the Scrivener's Bones. 2009. (Alcatraz Ser.: 2). (ENG.). 336p. (J). (gr. 4-6). 21.19 *(978-0-439-92554-9(1))* Scholastic, Inc.
—Alcatraz vs. the Evil Librarians. Lazo, Hayley, illus. (Alcatraz Versus the Evil Librarians Ser.: 1). (ENG.). 320p. (J). 2022. pap. 9.99 *(978-0-7653-7895-8(7),* 900141062) 2016. 18.99 *(978-0-7653-7894-1(9),* 900141060) Doherty, Tom Assocs., LLC. (Starscape).
—The Knights of Crystallia: Alcatraz vs. the Evil Librarians. 2016. (Alcatraz Versus the Evil Librarians Ser.: 3). (ENG., Illus.). 320p. (J). 23.99 *(978-0-7653-7898-9(1),* 900141065, Starscape) Doherty, Tom Assocs., LLC.
—The Scrivener's Bones: Alcatraz vs. the Evil Librarians. Lazo, Hayley, illus. 2016. (Alcatraz Versus the Evil Librarians Ser.: 2). (ENG.). 368p. (J). 18.99 *(978-0-7653-7896-5(5),* 900141063, Starscape) Doherty, Tom Assocs., LLC.
—The Shattered Lens: Alcatraz vs. the Evil Librarians. 2016. (Alcatraz Versus the Evil Librarians Ser.: 4). (ENG., Illus.). 336p. (J). 23.99 *(978-0-7653-7900-9(7),* 900141067, Starscape) Doherty, Tom Assocs., LLC.
Shields, Gillian. Library Lily. Chessa, Francesca, illus. 2011. (ENG.). 26p. (YA). 16.00 *(978-0-8028-5401-8(X))* Eerdmans, William B. Publishing Co.
Sneed, Brad. The Boy Who Was Raised by Librarians. Sneed, Brad, illus. 2008. (Illus.). (J). (gr. k-3). 27.95 incl. audio *(978-0-8045-6965-1(7))* Spoken Arts, Inc.
Taylor, Laini. Strange the Dreamer. LitJoy Crate et al, illus. 2021. (YA). 59.99 *(978-1-7350633-7-9(1))* LitJoy Crate.
—Strange the Dreamer. 2017. 536p. (YA). *(978-0-316-43120-0(6))* Little Brown & Co.
—Strange the Dreamer. (Strange the Dreamer Ser.: 1). (ENG.). (YA). (gr. 9-17). 2018. 560p. pap. 14.99 *(978-0-316-34167-7(3))* 2017. 544p. 22.99 *(978-0-316-34168-4(1))* Little, Brown Bks. for Young Readers.
—Strange the Dreamer. 2018. (J). lib. bdg. 24.50 *(978-0-606-40987-2(4))* Turtleback.
Thaler, Mike. The Librarian from the Black Lagoon. Lee, Jared, illus. unabr. ed. 2007. (J). (gr. k-2). pap. 14.95 incl. audio *(978-0-439-02773-1(X))* Scholastic, Inc.
—The Librarian from the Black Lagoon, 1 vol. Lee, Jared, illus. 2011. (Black Lagoon Ser.: No. 1). (ENG.). 32p. (J). (gr. k-4). lib. bdg. 31.36 *(978-1-59961-795-4(1),* 3621, Picture Bk.) Spotlight.
Time, Nicholas O. Stay a Spell. 2016. (In Due Time Ser.: 2). lib. bdg. 17.20 *(978-0-606-38986-0(5))* Turtleback.
Varnes, Allison. Property of the Rebel Librarian. 2019. (Illus.). 288p. (J). (gr. 3-7). 7.99 *(978-1-5247-7150-8(3),* Yearling) Random Hse. Children's Bks.
Weatherford, Carole Boston. The Library Ghost. White, Lee, illus. 2008. 22p. (J). (gr. -1-3). 17.95 *(978-1-60213-017-3(5),* Upstart Bks.) Highsmith Inc.
Young, Karen Romano. A Girl, a Raccoon, & the Midnight Moon: (Juvenile Fiction, Mystery, Young Reader Detective Story, Light Fantasy for Kids) Bagley, Jessixa, illus. 2020. (ENG.). 392p. (J). (gr. 5-9). 16.99 *(978-1-4521-6952-1(7))* Chronicle Bks. LLC.

LIBRARIANSHIP

see Library Science

LIBRARIES

see also School Libraries

Ames, Michelle. Librarians in Our Community, 1 vol. 2009. (On the Job Ser.). (ENG., Illus.). 24p. (J). (gr. 1-1). pap. 9.25 *(978-1-4358-2458-4(X),* a836bbff-bc4b-42be-8e6c-5d12281bf9cf); lib. bdg. 26.27 *(978-1-4042-8072-4(3),* 969eedb1-cc4f-4497-867b-19654afc4c30) Rosen Publishing Group, Inc., The. (PowerKids Pr.).
Amidon Lusted, Marcia, ed. Banned Books, 1 vol. 2017. (At Issue Ser.). (ENG.). 88p. (J). (gr. 10-12). pap. 28.80 *(978-1-5345-0071-6(5),* bd4b3bc0-536b-40e2-8ac5-f2c3af05f8ba); lib. bdg. 41.03 *(978-1-5345-0075-4(8),* 671c1187-1a68-4b28-8989-a67cfa76391a) Greenhaven Publishing LLC.
Anderson, Sheila. Library. 2008. pap. 22.95 *(978-0-8225-9372-0(6));* (ENG., Illus.). 8p. (J). pap. 5.99 *(978-0-8225-8839-9(0),* 81ba5622-fe85-4e55-b3ad-e295afe8ae31) Lerner Publishing Group.
Ardely, Anthony. I Can Be a Librarian, 1 vol. 2018. (I Can Be Anything! Ser.). (ENG.). 24p. (J). (gr. k-k). pap. 9.15 *(978-1-5382-1762-7(7),* 43f0898c-2ac7-4259-a500-428508b5dc37) Stevens, Gareth Publishing LLLP.
Austen, Mary. Librarians on the Job, 1 vol. 2016. (Jobs in Our Community Ser.). (ENG.). 24p. (J). (gr. 1-1). pap. 9.25 *(978-1-5345-2145-2(3),* c3641dd4-3e1a-48b5-9e3f-1a3fa10d48ba, KidHaven Publishing) Greenhaven Publishing LLC.
Balice, Mary Lee, ed. Information Science, 1 vol., 1. 2016. (Study of Science Ser.). (ENG.). 144p. (J). (gr. 8-8). 37.82 *(978-1-68048-232-4(7),* b7e67877-0370-47f4-bad4-55f9a4c123e3, Britannica Educational Publishing) Rosen Publishing Group, Inc., The.
Bell, Samantha. Librarian. Bane, Jeff, illus. 2017. (My Early Library: My Friendly Neighborhood Ser.). (ENG.). 24p. (J). (gr. k-1). lib. bdg. 30.64 *(978-1-63472-833-1(5),* 209758) Cherry Lake Publishing.
Bellamy, Adam. This Is My Library, 1 vol. 2016. (All about My World Ser.). (ENG., Illus.). 24p. (J). (gr. k-1). pap. 10.35 *(978-0-7660-8089-8(7),* d50255c2-0ba1-4aa4-a793-ba6464350f05) Enslow Publishing, LLC.
Bily, Cynthia A., ed. Banned Books, 1 vol. 2012. (Introducing Issues with Opposing Viewpoints Ser.). (ENG., Illus.). 128p. (J). (gr. 7-10). lib. bdg. 43.63 *(978-0-7377-5671-5(3),* d6de35ea-b0d8-4c96-8f58-c7470102a9f1, Greenhaven Publishing) Greenhaven Publishing LLC.
Bishop, Celeste. Craft Time at the Library, 1 vol. 2016. (Places in My Community Ser.). (ENG.). 24p. (J). (gr. 1-1). 25.27 *(978-1-4994-3012-7(4),* 36748258-ef69-4a0e-bbad-45c87a51cfc4); pap. 9.25 *(978-1-4994-2775-2(1),* 33125f2d-39bc-4485-ac02-ac25044541b2) Rosen Publishing Group, Inc., The. (PowerKids Pr.).
Bloom, Paul. Rules in the Library, 1 vol. 2015. (School Rules Ser.). (ENG., Illus.). 24p. (J). (gr. k-k). pap. 9.15 *(978-1-4824-2649-6(8),* 5fcb3154-6d07-46f7-b5f0-1ee1bf881241) Stevens, Gareth Publishing LLLP.
Bodden, Valerie. Navigating the Library. 2012. (Research for Writing Ser.). (ENG.). 48p. (J). (gr. 4-7). 23.95 *(978-1-60818-206-0(1),* 21954, Creative Education) Creative Co., The.
Brinker, Spencer. At the Library. 2019. (I Spy Ser.). (ENG., Illus.). 16p. (J). (gr. -1-1). 6.99 *(978-1-64280-395-2(2))* Bearport Publishing Co., Inc.
Buzzeo, Toni. Inside the Books: Readers & Libraries Around the World. Daly, Jude, illus. 2012. 32p. (J). 17.95 *(978-1-60213-058-6(2),* Upstart Bks.) Highsmith Inc.
Carr, Aaron. The Library. 24p. 2014. (Illus.). (J). *(978-1-62127-346-2(6))* 2013. pap. 12.95 *(978-1-62127-351-6(2))* Weigl Pubs., Inc.
Clark, Rosalyn. A Visit to the Library. 2017. (Bumba Books (r) — Places We Go Ser.). (ENG., Illus.). 24p. (J). (gr. -1-1). pap. 8.99 *(978-1-5124-5562-5(8),* c82e29d1-5a78-4713-8d57-94983db7153c) Lerner Publishing Group.
Colby, Jennifer. Library. 2016. (21st Century Junior Library: Explore a Workplace Ser.). (ENG., Illus.). 24p. (J). (gr. 2-5). 29.21 *(978-1-63471-075-6(4),* 208379) Cherry Lake Publishing.
Coldwell, Lamar. The Library in My Town, 1 vol. 2016. (Rosen REAL Readers: Social Studies Nonfiction / Fiction: Myself, My Community, My World Ser.). (ENG.). 8p. (gr. k-1). pap. 5.46 *(978-1-5081-2260-9(1),* 7341340e-9aa8-4759-89d6-8bfdd4b82974, Rosen Classroom) Rosen Publishing Group, Inc., The.
Dinmont, Kerry. Libraries Past & Present. 2018. (Bumba Books (r) — Past & Present Ser.). (ENG., Illus.). 24p. (J). (gr. -1-1). pap. 8.99 *(978-1-5415-2689-1(9),* 736148f0-62d0-4c4c-ae9d-8f10812c7ac4); lib. bdg. 26.65 *(978-1-5415-0330-4(9),* cef2ea3c-e0a3-40d7-a5b2-e1a8328c0f06, Lerner Pubns.) Lerner Publishing Group.
Dixon, Dale. Helping at the Library: Step by Step, 1 vol. 2017. (Computer Science for the Real World Ser.). (ENG.). 12p. (gr. 1-2). pap. *(978-1-5383-5144-4(7),* a32c0f67-52fa-46a5-a274-0883418f07ee, Rosen Classroom) Rosen Publishing Group, Inc., The.
Farmer, Bonnie. Abc Letters in the Library. l.t. ed. 2012. 60p. (J). pap. *(978-1-4596-3446-6(2))* ReadHowYouWant.com, Ltd.
Finn, Carrie. Manners in the Library. Lensch, Chris, illus. (Way to Be!: Manners Ser.). 24p. (gr. -1-2). 2009. pap. 0.63 *(978-1-4048-5994-4(2))* 2007. (ENG.). (J). per. 7.95 *(978-1-4048-3557-3(1),* 93927) Capstone. (Picture Window Bks.).
Flanagan, Alice K. Discovering Today's Library, 1 vol. 2006. (Discovering Today's Library). (ENG., Illus.). 64p. (gr. 3-5). lib. bdg. 32.67 *(978-0-8368-7426-6(9),* 35cb21a3-612b-453d-9da2-d62ff2707663, Gareth Stevens Learning Library) Stevens, Gareth Publishing LLLP.
Getting to Know the Library, Bk. A. (J). (gr. 1-2). suppl. ed. *(978-0-590-06374-6(X))* Scholastic, Inc.
Glenn, Sharlee. Library on Wheels: Mary Lemist Titcomb & America's First Bookmobile. 2018. (ENG., Illus.). 56p. (J). (gr. 3-7). 18.99 *(978-1-4197-2875-4(X),* 1127801, Abrams Bks. for Young Readers) Abrams, Inc.
Goldman, Phyllis, ed. Monkeyshines on the Library: For Your Information. 2003. (Illus.). 112p. (YA). per. 32.95 *(978-1-888325-28-7(3))* Allosaurus Pubs.
Graham Gaines, Ann. Master the Library & Media Center, 1 vol. 2009. (Ace It! Information Literacy Ser.). (ENG., Illus.). 48p. (gr. 3-3). lib. bdg. 27.93 *(978-0-7660-3393-1(7),* 37a32d0f-af8e-4981-abbc-47f5b448a02a) Enslow Publishing, LLC.
Green, Lyric & Graham Gaines, Ann. Future Ready Library & Media Center Mastery, 1 vol. 2017. (Future Ready Project Skills Ser.). (ENG.). 48p. (gr. 3-4). pap. 12.70 *(978-0-7660-8777-4(8),* 95a62506-35cc-490a-ac13-2421632e54cb); lib. bdg. 29.60 *(978-0-7660-8657-9(7),* b4de4f08-d801-4e4f-b929-81d10476eaf7) Enslow Publishing, LLC.
Hamilton, John. Libraries & Reference Materials, 1 vol. 2005. (Straight to the Source Ser.). (ENG.). 32p. (gr. k-6). 27.07 *(978-1-59197-545-8(X),* Checkerboard Library) ABDO Publishing Co.
Harasymiw, Therese. How Do I Use a Library?, 1 vol. 2014. (Research Tools You Can Use Ser.). (ENG.). 32p. (J). (gr. 2-3). 26.06 *(978-1-62275-379-6(8),* 2e912f4f-8e91-4b3f-adab-a9dbae4b884a) Rosen Publishing Group, Inc., The.
Hicks, Dwayne. Rules at the Library, 1 vol. 2019. (Rules at School Ser.). (ENG.). 24p. (J). (gr. 1-1). 25.27 *(978-1-5383-4436-1(X),* 23d6c261-5cb5-46be-906e-ceb19f07f746, PowerKids Pr.) Rosen Publishing Group, Inc., The.
Hill, Oriah. My Day at the Library. 2012. (ENG.). 24p. pap. 15.99 *(978-1-4772-7954-0(7))* AuthorHouse.
Hoena, Blake A. The Library: A 4D Book. rev. ed. 2018. (Visit To... Ser.). (ENG., Illus.). 24p. (J). (gr. -1-2). lib. bdg. 29.32 *(978-1-5435-0830-7(8),* 137593, Capstone Pr.) Capstone.
Honders, Christine. Why Should I Listen to My Librarian?, 1 vol. 2019. (Listening to Leaders Ser.). (ENG.). 24p. (gr. 2-2). pap. 9.25 *(978-1-5383-4164-3(6),* a37d62de-162b-4bae-9594-950c2ef53a4e, PowerKids Pr.) Rosen Publishing Group, Inc., The.
Jango-Cohen, Judith. Librarians. 2005. (Pull Ahead Bks.). (Illus.). 32p. (J). lib. bdg. 22.60 *(978-0-8225-1691-0(8))* Lerner Publishing Group.
Kawa, Katie. A Day with a Librarian. 2020. (J). *(978-1-5026-5325-3(7))* Cavendish Square Publishing LLC.
—My First Trip to the Library, 1 vol. Livingston, Jessica, illus. 2012. (My First Adventures Ser.). (ENG.). 24p. (J). (gr. k-k). pap. 9.15 *(978-1-4339-6251-6(9),* e66ad206-da7d-4bd0-abd3-585ea65ad668); lib. bdg. 25.27 *(978-1-4339-6249-3(7),* 95668e5d-9334-4a17-8293-1476c1033f70) Stevens, Gareth Publishing LLLP.
—My First Trip to the Library / Mi Primera Visita a la Biblioteca, 1 vol. Livingston, Jessica, illus. 2012. (My First Adventures / Mis Primeras Aventuras Ser.). (ENG & SPA.). 24p. (J). (gr. k-k). lib. bdg. 25.27 *(978-1-4339-6631-6(X),* e582c9ff-1eb7-45b0-9a70-490bf195c1fe) Stevens, Gareth Publishing LLLP.
Kenan, Tessa. Hooray for Librarians! 2017. (Bumba Books (r) — Hooray for Community Helpers! Ser.). (ENG., Illus.). 24p. (J). (gr. -1-1). pap. 8.99 *(978-1-5124-5553-3(9),* 14a36803-53e4-4b5c-986c-89fc6e123074); lib. bdg. 26.65 *(978-1-5124-3353-1(5),* 5e97c1ef-5821-4a14-811d-8cfc1e5e82be, Lerner Pubns.) Lerner Publishing Group.
Keogh, Josie. A Trip to the Library, 1 vol. 2012. (PowerKids Readers: My Community Ser.). (ENG., Illus.). 24p. (J). (gr. k-k). pap. 9.25 *(978-1-4488-7481-5(5),* 9da0abed-c4ed-4c4e-86bb-d44dddd7050c); lib. bdg. 26.27 *(978-1-4488-7402-6(5),*

JKL

fbc2cc6c-1ec1-4261-afaf-c8ad0a381d41) Rosen Publishing Group, Inc., The. (PowerKids Pr.).

—A Trip to the Library: De Visita en la Biblioteca. 1 vol. 2012. (PowerKids Readers: Mi Comunidad / My Community Ser.). (SPA & ENG., Illus.). 24p. (gr. k-k). lib. bdg. 26.27 (978-1-4488-7833-8(0), ee151b27-09ba-46f8-adee-aefcd7060625, PowerKids Pr.) Rosen Publishing Group, Inc., The.

King, M. G. Librarian on the Roof: A True Story. Gilpin, Stephen, illus. 2012. (J). (978-1-61913-147-7(1)) Weigl Pubs., Inc.

Kreisman, Rachelle. Places We Go: A Kids' Guide to Community Sites. Haggerty, Tim, illus. 2015. (Start Smart (tm) — Community Ser.). (ENG.). 32p. (J). (gr. 1-3). E-Book 39.99 (978-1-937529-36-9(3)) Red Chair Pr.

Laks Gorman, Jacqueline. Librarians, 1 vol. 2010. (People in My Community (Second Edition) Ser.). (ENG., Illus.). 24p. (gr. k-2). 25.27 (978-1-4339-3341-7(1), 6f201e6b-f920-49e2-8cc8-7fc7651d9f01); pap. 9.15 (978-1-4339-3342-4(X), adbc6c35-689b-4232-8a6b-41706b67d7b6) Stevens, Gareth Publishing LLLP.

—Librarians / Bibliotecarios, 1 vol. 2010. (People in My Community / Mi Comunidad Ser.). (SPA & ENG., Illus.). 24p. (gr. k-2). pap. 9.15 (978-1-4339-3760-6(3), fd6b829c-d7b8-4ad7-8816-1751339176f2) Stevens, Gareth Publishing LLLP.

—The Library, 1 vol. 2004. (I Like to Visit Ser.). (ENG., Illus.). 24p. (gr. k-2). pap. 9.15 (978-0-8368-4459-7(9), d11da05c-89b2-4a68-afb9-0409fa163906); lib. bdg. 24.67 (978-0-8368-4452-8(1), 94e7298c-90fd-41e8-a483-83cb56b8a293) Stevens, Gareth Publishing LLLP. (Weekly Reader Leveled Readers).

—The Library / la Biblioteca, 1 vol. 2004. (I Like to Visit / Me Gusta Visitar Ser.). (ENG & SPA.). 24p. (gr. k-2). pap. 9.15 (978-0-8368-4603-4(6), ff21d657-6a57-42a8-b542-62d64967caae); (Illus.). (J). lib. bdg. 24.67 (978-0-8368-4596-9(X), 0a9c9e8f-8687-4656-9353-fb628b8e49be) Stevens, Gareth Publishing LLLP. (Weekly Reader Leveled Readers).

Leggett Abouraya, Karen. Hands Around the Library: Protecting Egypt's Treasured Books. Roth, Susan L., illus. 2012. 40p. (J). (gr. -1-k). 17.99 (978-0-8037-3747-1(5), Dial Bks) Penguin Young Readers Group.

Leone, Laura. Choosing a Career in Information Science. 2009. (World of Work Ser.). 64p. (gr. 5-5). 58.50 (978-1-60854-332-8(3)) Rosen Publishing Group, Inc., The.

Less, Emma. Librarians. 2018. (Real-Life Superheroes Ser.). (ENG.). 16p. (J). (gr. k-2). pap. 7.99 (978-1-68152-278-4(0), 14917) Amicus.

Libeary Skills. 125p. (gr. k-3). 11.99 (978-0-513-02043-6(8), TSD20438) Denison, T. S. & Co., Inc.

Lindeen, Mary. A Visit to the Library. 2015. (Beginning-To-Read Ser.). (ENG.). 32p. (J). (gr. k-2). pap. 13.26 (978-1-60357-751-9(3)); (Illus.). lib. bdg. 22.60 (978-1-59953-691-0(9)) Norwood Hse. Pr.

Malam, John. Library: From Ancient Scrolls to the Worldwide Web: A Building Works Book. Malam, John, illus. 2006. (Illus.). 32p. (J). (gr. 4-18). reprint ed. 17.00 (978-1-4223-5173-4(4)) DIANE Publishing Co.

Manning, Mick. Books! Books! Books! Explore the Amazing Collection of the British Library. Granström, Brita, illus. 2017. (ENG.). 48p. (J). (gr. 3-7). 17.99 (978-0-7636-9757-0(5)) Candlewick Pr.

Marsico, Katie. Working at the Airport. 2009. (21st Century Junior Library: Careers Ser.). (ENG., Illus.). 24p. (gr. 2-5). lib. bdg. 29.21 (978-1-60279-510-5(X), 200279) Cherry Lake Publishing.

—Working at the Library. 2009. (21st Century Junior Library: Careers Ser.). (ENG., Illus.). 24p. (gr. 2-5). lib. bdg. 29.21 (978-1-60279-511-2(8), 200278) Cherry Lake Publishing.

Martin, Isabel. A Library Field Trip. 2015. (Let's Take a Field Trip Ser.). (ENG., Illus.). 24p. (J). (gr. -1-2). pap. 6.95 (978-1-4914-2315-8(3), 127773) Capstone.

Meachen Rau, Dana. Librarian. 2007. (J). (978-0-7614-2621-9(3)) Marshall Cavendish.

—Librarians, 1 vol. 2008. (Tools We Use Ser.). (ENG.). 32p. (gr. k-1). pap. 9.23 (978-0-7614-3293-7(0), 19d858e0-780e-435d-99f2-a9e4c0cdab49); (Illus.). lib. bdg. 25.50 (978-0-7614-2662-2(0), a4e0706d-b945-4dfa-ad07-2954c1de9545) Cavendish Square Publishing LLC.

—Los Bibliotecarios / Librarians, 1 vol. 2009. (Instrumentos de Trabajo / Tools We Use Ser.). (ENG & SPA., Illus.). 32p. (gr. k-2). lib. bdg. 25.50 (978-0-7614-2826-8(7), cd825d78-3b7b-4138-b590-dc7d17ac3e61) Cavendish Square Publishing LLC.

—Los Bibliotecarios (Librarians), 1 vol. 2009. (Instrumentos de Trabajo (Tools We Use) Ser.). (SPA., Illus.). 32p. (gr. k-2). lib. bdg. 25.50 (978-0-7614-2802-2(X), a80f21fc-20bb-43bc-a89b-fcb114712bda) Cavendish Square Publishing LLC.

Meister, Cari. La Biblioteca Pública. 2016. (Los Primeros Viajes Escolares (First Field Trips)).Tr. of Public Library. (SPA., Illus.). 24p. (J). (gr. k-2). lib. bdg. 25.65 (978-1-62031-327-5(8), Bullfrog Bks.) Jump! Inc.

—Librarians. 2014. (ENG., Illus.). 24p. (J). lib. bdg. 25.65 (978-1-62031-076-2(7)) Jump! Inc.

—Public Library. Fretland VanVoorst, Jenny, ed. 2016. (First Field Trips). (Illus.). 24p. (J). (gr. k-2). lib. bdg. 25.65 (978-1-62031-296-4(4), Bullfrog Bks.) Jump! Inc.

Miller, Connie Colwell. You Can Control Your Voice: Loud or Quiet? Assanelli, Victoria, illus. 2017. (Making Good Choices Ser.). (ENG.). 24p. (J). (gr. 1-4). lib. bdg. 20.95 (978-1-68151-167-2(3), 14655) Amicus.

—You Can Control Your Voice: Loud or Quiet? 2018. (Making Good Choices Ser.). (ENG., Illus.). 24p. (J). (gr. k-3). pap. 10.99 (978-1-68152-236-4(5), 14774) Amicus.

Mortensen, Lori. Manners Matter in the Library. Hunt, Lisa, illus. (First Graphics: Manners Matter Ser.). (ENG.). 24p. (gr. 1-2). 2011. pap. 35.70 (978-1-4296-6393-9(6)) 2010. (J). lib. bdg. 24.65 (978-1-4296-5330-5(2), 113758) Capstone.

Murray, Julie. The Library, 1 vol. 2016. (My Community: Places Ser.). (ENG., Illus.). 24p. (J). (gr. -1-2). lib. bdg. 31.36 (978-1-68080-537-6(1), 21354, Abdo Kids) ABDO Publishing Co.

My First Library. Date not set. (Illus.). (J). bds. 7.98 (978-0-7525-8724-0(2)) Parragon, Inc.

The Need to Know Library. 2017. (Need to Know Library). 64p. (gr. 12-11). pap. 77.70 (978-1-4994-6642-3(0), Rosen Young Adult) Rosen Publishing Group, Inc., The.

The Need to Know Library: Set 3, 14 vols. 2018. (Need to Know Library). (ENG.). 64p. (gr. 6-6). lib. bdg. 252.91 (978-1-5081-7922-1(0), e55bd094-c66c-49de-a0ff-676288ceedbb) Rosen Publishing Group, Inc., The.

Nugent, Samantha. Local Library Volunteer. 2016. (Illus.). 32p. (J). (978-1-4896-5857-9(2), AV2 by Weigl) Weigl Pubs., Inc.

O'Brian, Virginia. A Librarian's Job, 1 vol. 2014. (Community Workers Ser.). (ENG.). 24p. (gr. 1-1). 25.93 (978-1-62712-357-0(1), 4160a960-623d-45a9-89cb-9f610591abd3) Cavendish Square Publishing LLC.

Owings, Lisa. Learn about Authors & Illustrators. 2013. (Library Smarts Ser.). (ENG., Illus.). 24p. (J). (gr. -1-2). lib. bdg. 23.99 (978-1-4677-1502-7(6), 6111d072-b960-4d70-b67a-cc393c073560, Lerner Pubns.) Lerner Publishing Group.

Paul, Miranda. Little Libraries, Big Heroes. Parra, John, illus. 2019. (ENG.). 40p. (J). (gr. -1-3). 17.99 (978-0-544-80027-4(3), 1640324, Clarion Bks.) HarperCollins Pubs.

Prieto, Anita C. B Is for Bookworm: A Library Alphabet. Graef, Renee, illus. 2007. (J). (gr. k-7). 16.10 (978-0-7569-6657-7(4)) Perfection Learning Corp.

—B Is for Bookworm: A Library Alphabet. Graef, Renée, illus. 2007. (ENG.). 40p. (J). (gr. 1-4). per. 7.95 (978-1-58536-326-1(X), 202290) Sleeping Bear Pr.

Ready, Dee. Librarians Help. 2013. (Our Community Helpers Ser.). (ENG.). 24p. (J). (gr. k-1). pap. 37.74 (978-1-62065-848-2(8), 19420, Pebble) Capstone.

Ready, Dee & Ready, Dee. Librarians Help, 1 vol. 2013. (Our Community Helpers Ser.). (ENG.). 24p. (J). (gr. -1-2). pap. 6.29 (978-1-62065-847-5(X), 121788); lib. bdg. 24.65 (978-1-62065-084-4(3), 120784) Capstone. (Pebble).

Rosenstock, Barb. Thomas Jefferson Builds a Library. O'Brien, John, illus. 2013. (ENG.). 32p. (J). (gr. 2-5). 17.99 (978-1-59078-932-2(6), Calkins Creek) Highlights Pr., c/o Highlights for Children, Inc.

Roza, Greg. My First Trip to the Library, 1 vol. 2019. (My First Trip Ser.). (ENG.). 24p. (gr. 1-1). 25.27 (978-1-5383-4435-4(1), cfb42f80-0830-4a90-968d-2117f071e2ce, PowerKids Pr.) Rosen Publishing Group, Inc., The.

Rudolph, Jessica. Spooky Libraries. 2016. (Tiptoe into Scary Places Ser.). (ENG.). 24p. (J). (gr. k-3). 26.99 (978-1-68402-049-2(2)) Bearport Publishing Co., Inc.

Ruurs, Margriet. My Librarian Is a Camel: How Books Are Brought to Children Around the World. 2005. (ENG., Illus.). 32p. (J). (gr. 2-5). 17.99 (978-1-59078-093-0(0), Astra Young Readers) Astra Publishing Hse.

Scholastic, Inc. Staff. Let's Go to the Library. 2012. (Rookie Toddler Ser.). (ENG., Illus.). 12p. (J). bds. 6.95 (978-0-531-20853-3(2), Children's Pr.) Scholastic Library Publishing.

Shepherd, Jodie. A Day with Librarians. 2012. (Rookie Read-About Community Ser.). (ENG.). 32p. (J). pap. 5.95 (978-0-531-29252-5(5)); lib. bdg. 23.00 (978-0-531-28952-5(4)) Scholastic Library Publishing.

Siemens, Jared. Librarians. 2016. (J). (978-1-5105-2107-0(0)) SmartBook Media, Inc.

—Librarians. 2015. 24p. (J). (978-1-4896-3649-2(8)) Weigl Pubs., Inc.

Stamaty, Mark Alan. Alia's Mission: Saving the Books of Iraq. 2010. 32p. (J). (gr. k-3). pap. 7.99 (978-0-375-85763-8(X), Dragonfly Bks.) Random Hse. Children's Bks.

—Muhimat Al Sayyda Alia: Inkaz Kuttub Al Iraq. 2005.Tr. of Alia's Mission - Saving the Books of Iraq. 32p. pap. 12.00 (978-977-6171-01-5(X), 706-001) Al-Balsam Pubng. Hse. EGY. Dist: Baker & Taylor Publisher Services (BTPS).

Taylor, Troy. Creepy Libraries. (Scary Places Ser.). (ENG.). 32p. (J). (gr. 4-8). 2017. 7.99 (978-1-68402-604-3(0)) 2015. lib. bdg. 28.50 (978-1-62724-862-4(5)) Bearport Publishing Co., Inc.

Terrazzini, Daniela Jaglenka, concept. My Miniature Library: 30 Tiny Books to Make, Read & Treasure. 2017. (ENG., Illus.). 54p. (J). (gr. 2-6). 19.99 (978-1-78627-026-9(9), King, Laurence Publishing) Orion Publishing Group, Ltd. GBR. Dist: Hachette Bk. Group.

The Need to Know Library: Set 1, 12 vols. 2017. (Need to Know Library). (ENG.). 64p. (gr. 5-6). 216.78 (978-1-4994-6640-9(4), 90d67e77-6ec2-4f60-9290-97a10351131a, Rosen Young Adult) Rosen Publishing Group, Inc., The.

Vogel, Elizabeth. Meet the Librarian. 2009. (My School Ser.). 24p. (gr. 1-2). 37.50 (978-1-61514-706-9(3), PowerKids Pr.) Rosen Publishing Group, Inc., The.

Vogel, Jennifer. A Library Story: Building a New Central Library. 2006. (Exceptional Social Studies Titles for Intermediate Grades). (ENG., Illus.). 64p. (gr. 4-6). lib. bdg. 26.60 (978-0-8225-5916-0(1), Millbrook Pr.) Lerner Publishing Group.

Weatherford, Carole Boston. Schomburg: The Man Who Built a Library. 2017. (J). 31.99 (978-1-5200-8717-7(9)); 31.99 (978-1-5200-8716-0(0)) Dreamscape Media, LLC.

—Schomburg: the Man Who Built a Library. Velasquez, Eric, illus. 2017. (ENG.). 48p. (J). (gr. 4-7). 18.99 (978-0-7636-8046-6(X)) Candlewick Pr.

Winter, Jeanette. The Librarian of Basra: A True Story from Iraq. 2019. (ENG., Illus.). 32p. (J). (gr. -1-3). pap. 8.99 (978-0-358-14183-9(4), 1755716, Clarion Bks.) HarperCollins Pubs.

—The Librarian of Basra: A True Story from Iraq. Winter, Jeanette, illus. 2005. (ENG., Illus.). 32p. (J). (gr. -1-3). 17.99 (978-0-15-205445-8(6), 1196387, Clarion Bks.) HarperCollins Pubs.

Wohlrabe, Sarah C. A Visit to the Library. Thompson, Jeffrey, illus. 2011. (First Graphics: My Community Ser.). (ENG.). 24p. (gr. 1-2). pap. 35.70 (978-1-4296-6404-2(5)) Capstone.

—A Visit to the Library, 1 vol. Thompson, Jeffrey, illus. 2010. (First Graphics: My Community Ser.). (ENG.). 24p. (J). (gr. 1-3). lib. bdg. 24.65 (978-1-4296-5371-8(X), 113801) Capstone.

LIBRARIES, CHILDREN'S

see Children's Libraries; School Libraries

LIBRARIES—FICTION

Alexander, William. A Festival of Ghosts. Murphy, Kelly, illus. 2018. (ENG.). 272p. (J). (gr. 3-7). 17.99 (978-1-4814-6918-0(5), McElderry, Margaret K. Bks.) McElderry, Margaret K. Bks.

—A Properly Unhaunted Place. Murphy, Kelly, illus. 2017. (ENG.). 192p. (J). (gr. 3-7). 16.99 (978-1-4814-6915-9(0), McElderry, Margaret K. Bks.) McElderry, Margaret K. Bks.

—A Properly Unhaunted Place. 2019. (Penworthy Picks Middle School Ser.). (ENG.). 182p. (J). (gr. 4-5). 18.96 (978-1-64310-942-8(1)) Penworthy Co., LLC, The.

Bedford, David. Birdy & Bou. Stanley, Mandy, illus. 2018. (J). (978-1-4351-6727-8(9)) Barnes & Noble, Inc.

Beiko, S. M. The Lake & the Library. l.t. ed. 2013. 542p. pap. (978-1-4596-6871-3(5)) ReadHowYouWant.com, Ltd.

Beinstein, Phoebe & Silverhardt, Lauryn. Dora's Little Library. 2009. (Dora the Explorer Ser.). (ENG.). 70p. (J). 6.99 (978-1-4169-8029-2(6), Simon Spotlight/Nickelodeon) Simon Spotlight/Nickelodeon.

Bertram, Debbie & Bloom, Susan. The Best Book to Read. Garland, Michael, illus. 2011. 32p. (J). (gr. -1-2). pap. 7.99 (978-0-375-87300-3(7), Dragonfly Bks.) Random Hse. Children's Bks.

Bliss, Emily. Unicorn Princesses 7: Firefly's Glow. Hanson, Sydney, illus. 2018. (Unicorn Princesses Ser.: 7). (ENG.). 128p. (J). 16.99 (978-1-68119-927-6(0), 900192376); pap. 5.99 (978-1-68119-926-9(2), 900192401) Bloomsbury Publishing USA. (Bloomsbury Children's Bks.).

Blue, Rose & Naden, Corinne. Ron's Big Mission. Tate, Don, illus. 2009. 32p. (J). (gr. 1-3). 18.99 (978-0-525-47849-2(3), Dutton Books for Young Readers) Penguin Young Readers Group.

Brennan-Nelson, Denise & Bucci, Marco. Good Night, Library. 2019. (ENG., Illus.). 32p. (J). (gr. -1-2). 16.99 (978-1-58536-406-0(1), 204658) Sleeping Bear Pr.

Brezenoff, Steve. The Library Shelves: An Interactive Mystery Adventure. Calo, Marcos, illus. 2019. (You Choose Stories: Field Trip Mysteries Ser.). (ENG.). 112p. (J). (gr. 3-7). lib. bdg. 32.65 (978-1-4965-4860-3(4), 135459, Stone Arch Bks.) Capstone.

Brown, Marc. D W 's Library Card. 2003. (Arthur's Little Sister, DW Ser.: 7). (J). (gr. -1-2). lib. bdg. 17.20 (978-0-613-71812-7(7)) Turtleback.

Brown, Marc & Sarfatti, Esther. D. W. y el Carne de Biblioteca. 2004.Tr. of D.W.'s Library Card. (ENG & SPA., Illus.). (J). pap. 6.95 (978-1-930332-47-8(5)) Lectorum Pubns., Inc.

Brown, Monica. Waiting for the Biblioburro. Parra, John, illus. 2011. (ENG.). 32p. (J). (gr. k-3). 18.99 (978-1-58246-353-7(0), Tricycle Pr.) Random Hse. Children's Bks.

Browne, Anthony. Willy's Stories. Browne, Anthony, illus. 2015. (ENG., Illus.). 32p. (J). (gr. k-3). 16.99 (978-0-7636-7761-9(2)) Candlewick Pr.

Butler, Dori H. The Hide-And-Seek Ghost. 2016. (Haunted Library: 8). lib. bdg. 14.75 (978-0-606-38838-2(9)) Turtleback.

Butler, Dori Hillestad. The Case of the Library Monster. Tugeau, Jeremy, illus. 2012. (Buddy Files Ser.: 5). (J). lib. bdg. 16.00 (978-0-606-23839-7(5)) Turtleback.

—The Haunted Library. 2014. (Haunted Library: 1). lib. bdg. 14.75 (978-0-606-35702-9(5)) Turtleback.

—The Haunted Library #1. Damant, Aurore, illus. 2014. (Haunted Library: 1). 128p. (J). (gr. 1-3). 6.99 (978-0-448-46242-4(7), Grosset & Dunlap) Penguin Young Readers Group.

—The Hide-And-Seek Ghost #8. Damant, Aurore, illus. 2016. (Haunted Library: 8). 128p. (J). (gr. 1-3). 6.99 (978-0-448-48942-1(2), Grosset & Dunlap) Penguin Young Readers Group.

—The Secret Room #5. Damant, Aurore, illus. 2015. (Haunted Library: 5). 128p. (J). (gr. 1-3). bds. 6.99 (978-0-448-48332-0(7), Grosset & Dunlap) Penguin Young Readers Group.

—The Underground Ghosts. 2017. (Haunted Library). (Illus.). 191p. (J). lib. bdg. 18.40 (978-0-606-40111-1(3)) Turtleback.

—The Underground Ghosts #10: A Super Special. Damant, Aurore, illus. 2017. (Haunted Library: 10). 192p. (J). (gr. 1-3). 7.99 (978-0-515-15711-6(2), Grosset & Dunlap) Penguin Young Readers Group.

Buzbee, Lewis. Steinbeck's Ghost. 2010. (ENG.). 368p. (J). (gr. 4-6). pap. 19.99 (978-0-312-60211-6(1), 900064224) Square Fish.

Buzzeo, Toni. Fire up with Reading! Yoshikawa, Sachiko, illus. 2007. 32p. 17.95 (978-1-60213-019-7(1), Upstart Bks.) Highsmith Inc.

—The Great Dewey Hunt. Yoshikawa, Sachiko, illus. 2009. (Mrs. Skorupski Story Ser.). (J). 36p. (gr. -1-3). 17.95 (978-1-60213-041-8(8)); (978-1-60213-029-6(9)) Highsmith Inc. (Upstart Bks.).

—The Library Doors. Westcott, Nadine Bernard, illus. 2008. (J). (gr. -1-3). 17.95 (978-1-60213-037-1(X)); (978-1-60213-027-2(2)) Highsmith Inc. (Upstart Bks.).

—No T. Rex in the Library. Yoshikawa, Sachiko, illus. 2010. (ENG.). 32p. (J). (gr. -1-3). 19.99 (978-1-4169-3927-6(X), McElderry, Margaret K. Bks.) McElderry, Margaret K. Bks.

—Our Librarian Won't Tell Us Anything! Yoshikawa, Sachiko, illus. 2006. 32p. (J). (gr. -1-k). lib. bdg. 17.95 (978-1-932146-73-8(3), Upstart Bks.) Highsmith Inc.

—Penelope Popper, Book Doctor. Christy, Jana, illus. 2011. 32p. (J). 17.95 (978-1-60213-054-8(X), Upstart Bks.) Highsmith Inc.

Caine, Rachel, pseud. Ash & Quill. 2018. (Great Library: 3). (ENG.). 368p. (YA). (gr. 9). pap. 9.99 (978-0-451-47315-8(9), Berkley) Penguin Publishing Group.

—Paper & Fire. 2017. (Great Library: 2). (ENG.). 400p. (YA). (gr. 9). pap. 12.00 (978-0-451-47314-1(0), Berkley) Penguin Publishing Group.

—Paper & Fire. 2017. (Great Library: 2). lib. bdg. 20.85 (978-0-606-40361-0(2)) Turtleback.

Candlewick Press Staff. Peppa Pig & the Library Visit. 2017. (Peppa Pig Ser.). (ENG., Illus.). 32p. (J). (gr. -1-2). 12.99 (978-0-7636-9788-4(5), Candlewick Entertainment) Candlewick Pr.

Capucilli, Alyssa Satin. Biscuit Loves the Library. Schories, Pat, illus. 2014. (My First I Can Read Ser.). (ENG.). 32p. (J). (gr. -1-3). 16.99 (978-0-06-193507-7(7)); pap. 4.99 (978-0-06-193506-0(9)) HarperCollins Pubs. (HarperCollins).

Carle, Eric. My Very First Library: My Very First Book of Colors, My Very First Book of Shapes, My Very First Book of Numbers, My Very First Books of Words, 4 vols. 2006. (ENG., Illus.). 72p. (J). (gr. -1 — 1). 27.99 (978-0-399-24666-1(5)) Penguin Young Readers Group.

Carnavas, Peter. The Children Who Loved Books. 2013. (ENG., Illus.). 32p. (J). 11.99 (978-1-61067-145-3(7)) Kane Miller.

Casale, Karen. Never Let a Ghost Borrow Your Library Book: Book Care Guidelines from the Library Secret Service. Rebora, Cecilia, illus. 2012. 32p. (J). 17.75 (978-1-60213-061-6(2), Upstart Bks.) Highsmith Inc.

Chapman, Susan Margaret. Too Much Noise in the Library. Carter, Abby, illus. 2010. 32p. (J). (gr. 1-4). 17.95 (978-1-60213-026-5(4), Upstart Bks.) Highsmith Inc.

Child, Lauren. Charlie & Lola: but Excuse Me That Is My Book. 2006. (Charlie & Lola Ser.). (ENG., Illus.). 32p. (J). (gr. -1-3). 17.99 (978-0-8037-3096-0(9), Dial Bks) Penguin Young Readers Group.

Clifford, Eth. Help! I'm a Prisoner in the Library. 2004. (Jo-Beth & Mary Rose Mystery Ser.). (ENG., Illus.). 112p. (J). (gr. 3-7). pap. 7.99 (978-0-618-49482-8(0), 483926, Clarion Bks.) HarperCollins Pubs.

Cockroft, Kimberly. Reading Beauty, 1 vol. Corpus, Mary, illus. 2018. (ENG.). 32p. (J). (gr. -1-3). 16.99 (978-1-4556-2359-4(8), Pelican Publishing) Arcadia Publishing.

Coelho, Joseph. Luna Loves Library Day. Lumbers, Fiona, illus. 2018. (ENG.). 32p. (J). 12.99 (978-1-61067-675-5(0)) Kane Miller.

Colfer, Eoin. The Legend of Spud Murphy. McCoy, Glenn, illus. 2005. (Eoin Colfer's Legend Of... Ser.). 95p. (gr. 2-6). 16.00 (978-0-7569-6514-3(4)) Perfection Learning Corp.

Colin, Thompson. How to Live Forever. 2008. 32p. 16.99 (978-0-681-49757-3(2), State Street Pr.) Borders Pr.

Conn, Marla. At the Library with Dear Dragon, 10 vols. David Schimmell, illus. 2019. (Dear Dragon Developing Readers Ser.). (ENG.). 24p. (J). (gr. k-k). pap. 11.94 (978-1-68404-315-6(8)) Norwood Hse. Pr.

Cousins, Lucy. Maisy Goes to the Library. 2009. (Maisy First Experiences Ser.). lib. bdg. 17.20 (978-0-606-06687-7(X)) Turtleback.

—Maisy Goes to the Library: A Maisy First Experience Book. Cousins, Lucy, illus. 2009. (Maisy Ser.). (ENG., Illus.). 32p. (J). (gr. k-k). pap. 6.99 (978-0-7636-4371-3(8)) Candlewick Pr.

Cummings, Pat. Trace. 2019. (ENG., Illus.). 320p. (J). (gr. 3-7). 16.99 (978-0-06-269884-1(2), HarperCollins) HarperCollins Pubs.

Cummings, Troy. Boa Constructor: a Branches Book (the Binder of Doom #2) Cummings, Troy, illus. 2019. (Binder of Doom Ser.: 2). (ENG., Illus.). 96p. (J). (gr. 1-3). pap. 5.99 (978-1-338-31469-4(6)) Scholastic, Inc.

—Boa Constructor: a Branches Book (the Binder of Doom #2) (Library Edition) Cummings, Troy, illus. 2019. (Binder of Doom Ser.: 2). (ENG., Illus.). 96p. (J). (gr. 1-3). 24.99 (978-1-338-31470-0(X)) Scholastic, Inc.

—Brute-Cake: a Branches Book (the Binder of Doom #1) Cummings, Troy, illus. 2019. (Binder of Doom Ser.: 1). (ENG., Illus.). 96p. (J). (gr. 1-3). pap. 5.99 (978-1-338-31466-3(1)) Scholastic, Inc.

Curious George Visits the Library. 2013. (Curious George Ser.). (ENG., Illus.). 24p. (J). (gr. -1-3). pap. 4.99 (978-0-544-11450-0(7), 1541812, Clarion Bks.) HarperCollins Pubs.

Dahl, Michael. Dictionary of 1,000 Rooms, 1 vol. Kendall, Bradford, illus. 2011. (Return to the Library of Doom Ser.). (ENG.). 72p. (J). (gr. 4-8). lib. bdg. 23.99 (978-1-4342-3229-8(8), 116201, Stone Arch Bks.) Capstone.

—Don't Open It! 2016. (ENG., Illus.). 40p. (J). pap. (978-1-4747-1054-1(9), Stone Arch Bks.) Capstone.

—The Last Word. 2016. (ENG., Illus.). 40p. (J). pap. (978-1-4747-1055-8(7), Stone Arch Bks.) Capstone.

—The Lost Page. Evergreen, Nelson, illus. 2015. (Library of Doom: the Final Chapters Ser.). (ENG.). 40p. (J). (gr. 4-8). 23.99 (978-1-4342-9679-5(2), 126988, Stone Arch Bks.) Capstone.

—Night of the Scrawler. 2016. (ENG., Illus.). 40p. (J). pap. (978-1-4747-1056-5(5), Stone Arch Bks.) Capstone.

—The Spine Tingler. Evergreen, Nelson, illus. 2015. (Library of Doom: the Final Chapters Ser.). (ENG.). 40p. (J). (gr. 4-8). 23.99 (978-1-4342-9680-1(6), 126987, Stone Arch Bks.) Capstone.

—Thesaurus Rex. 2016. (ENG., Illus.). 40p. (J). pap. (978-1-4747-1057-2(3), Stone Arch Bks.) Capstone.

—Tome Raider. Evergreen, Nelson, illus. 2015. (Library of Doom: the Final Chapters Ser.). (ENG.). 40p. (J). (gr. 4-8). 23.99 (978-1-4342-9677-1(6), 126985, Stone Arch Bks.) Capstone.

—Zombie in the Library, 1 vol. Kendall, Bradford, illus. 2010. (Return to the Library of Doom Ser.). (ENG.). 72p. (J). (gr. 4-8). lib. bdg. 23.99 (978-1-4342-2145-2(8), 102875, Stone Arch Bks.) Capstone.

de Las Casas, Dianne. There's a Dragon in the Library, 1 vol. Gentry, Marita, illus. 2011. (ENG.). 32p. (J). (gr. k-3). 16.99 (978-1-58980-844-7(4), Pelican Publishing) Arcadia Publishing.

De Smet, Marian. Anna's Tight Squeeze. Meijer, Marja, illus. 2003. Orig. Title: Op Slot. 32p. (J). pap. 5.95 (978-1-58925-378-0(7)) Tiger Tales.

Deedy, Carmen Agra. The Library Dragon, 1 vol. White, Michael P., illus. 2012. (ENG.). 32p. (J). (gr. 1-4). 16.95 (978-1-56145-091-6(X), Q06826) Peachtree Publishing Co. Inc.

—Return of the Library Dragon, 1 vol. White, Michael P., illus. 2012. (ENG.). 32p. (J). (gr. -1-3). 16.95 (978-1-56145-621-5(7)) Peachtree Publishing Co. Inc.

Dewdney, Anna. Llama Llama's Little Library, 4 vols. 2013. (Llama Llama Ser.). (ENG., Illus.). 56p. (J). (— 1). bds. 27.96 (978-0-670-01648-8(9), Viking Books for Young Readers) Penguin Young Readers Group.

Donald, Alison. The New Libearian. Willmore, Alex, illus. 2018. (ENG.). 32p. (J). (gr. -1-3). 16.99 (978-0-544-97365-7(8), 1663219, Clarion Bks.) HarperCollins Pubs.

Downey, Lisa & Fox, Kathleen. The Pirates of Plagiarism. Downey, Lisa, illus. 2010. (Illus.). 32p. (J). (gr. 1-4). lib. bdg. 17.95 *(978-1-60213-053-1(1),* Upstart Bks.) Highsmith Inc.

Eland, Lindsay. A Summer of Sundays. 2013. (ENG.). 336p. (J). (gr. 3-7). 16.99 *(978-1-60684-030-6(4),* Carolrhoda Bks.) Lerner Publishing Group.

Enderle, Dotti. The Library Gingerbread Man. Madden, Colleen M., illus. 2010. 32p. (J). (gr. -1). 17.95 *(978-1-60213-048-7(5),* Upstart Bks.) Highsmith Inc.

Forte, Lauren. Olivia Goes to the Library. 2013. (Olivia Ready-To-Read Level 1 Ser.). lib. bdg. 13.55 *(978-0-606-35186-7(8))* Turtleback.

Funk, Josh. Lost in the Library: A Story of Patience & Fortitude. Lewis, Stevie, illus. 2018. (New York Public Library Book Ser.). (ENG.). 40p. (J). 18.99 *(978-1-250-15501-6(0),* 900184517, Holt, Henry & Co. Bks. For Young Readers) Holt, Henry & Co.

Garland, Michael. Miss Smith & the Haunted Library. 2012. 32p. (J). (gr. -1-2). 7.99 *(978-0-14-242122-2(7),* Puffin Books) Penguin Young Readers Group.

Garton, Sam. Otter: I Love Books! Garton, Sam, illus. 2019. (My First I Can Read Ser.). (ENG., Illus.). 32p. (J). (gr. -1-3). 17.99 *(978-0-06-284508-5(X),* Balzer & Bray) HarperCollins Pubs.

Gassman, Julie. Do Not Bring Your Dragon to the Library. Elkerton, Andy, illus. (ENG.). 32p. (J). (gr. -1-2). 2018. pap. 7.95 *(978-1-5158-3897-5(8),* 139671, Picture Window Bks.) 2016. 14.95 *(978-1-62370-651-7(3),* 131438, Capstone Young Readers) 2016. lib. bdg. 21.32 *(978-1-4795-9175-6(0),* 131437, Picture Window Bks.) Capstone.

Gómez Cerdá, Alfredo. El Monstruo y la Bibliotecaria. 4th ed. (SPA., Illus.). 62p. (J). (gr. 3-5). *(978-84-279-3456-6(4),* NG1580) Noguer y Caralt Editores, S. A. ESP. Dist: Lectorum Pubns., Inc.

González, Lucía. The Storyteller's Candle: La Velita de Los Cuentos, 1 vol. Delacre, Lulu, illus. 2013. (ENG.). 32p. (J). (gr. 1-6). pap. 11.95 *(978-0-89239-237-7(1),* leelowcbp, Children's Book Press) Lee & Low Bks., Inc.

Grabenstein, Chris. Escape from Mr. Lemoncello's Library. (Mr. Lemoncello's Library: 1). (ENG.). (J). (gr. 3-7). 2014. 336p. 8.99 *(978-0-307-93147-4(1),* Yearling) 2013. 304p. 18.99 *(978-0-375-87089-7(X),* Random Hse. Bks. for Young Readers) Random Hse. Children's Bks.

—Escape from Mr. Lemoncello's Library. 2014. lib. bdg. 18.40 *(978-0-606-37114-8(1))* Turtleback.

—Mr. Lemoncello's All-Star Breakout Game. 2019. (Mr. Lemoncello's Library: 4). (ENG., Illus.). 288p. (J). (gr. 3-7). 16.99 *(978-0-525-64644-0(2),* Random Hse. Bks. for Young Readers) Random Hse. Children's Bks.

—Mr. Lemoncello's Great Library Race. 2018. (Mr. Lemoncello's Library: 3). (ENG.). 320p. (J). (gr. 3-7). 7.99 *(978-0-553-53609-6(5),* Yearling) Random Hse. Children's Bks.

—Mr. Lemoncello's Library Olympics. 2017. (Mr. Lemoncello's Library: 2). (ENG., Illus.). 320p. (J). (gr. 3-7). 8.99 *(978-0-553-51042-3(8),* Yearling) Random Hse. Children's Bks.

—Mr. Lemoncello's Library Olympics. 2017. lib. bdg. 18.40 *(978-0-606-39875-6(9))* Turtleback.

Grambling, Lois G. Can I Bring Woolly to the Library, Ms. Reeder? Love, Judy, illus. 2012. (Prehistoric Pets Ser.: 2). 32p. (J). (gr. k-3). pap. 7.95 *(978-1-58089-282-7(5));* lib. bdg. 16.95 *(978-1-58089-281-0(7))* Charlesbridge Publishing, Inc.

Grau, Sheila & Sutphin, Joe. Gorilla Tactics: Dr. Critchlore's School for Minions #2. 2017. (Dr. Critchlore's School for Minions Ser.). (ENG., Illus.). 312p. (J). (gr. 3-7). pap. 7.95 *(978-1-4197-2645-3(5),* 1132103, Amulet Bks.) Abrams, Inc.

Greene, Rhonda Gowler. No Pirates Allowed! Said Library Lou. Ajhar, Brian, illus. 2013. (ENG.). 40p. (J). (gr. 1-3). 15.95 *(978-1-58536-796-2(6),* 202364) Sleeping Bear Pr.

Gutman, Dan. Rappy Goes to the Library. Bowers, Tim, illus. 2017. (I Can Read Level 2 Ser.). (ENG.). 32p. (J). (gr. -1-3). pap. 4.99 *(978-0-06-225265-4(8),* HarperCollins) HarperCollins Pubs.

Hanif, Cristina. Logan & the Magic Tree. Stenton, Murray, illus. 2019. (J). *(978-1-61599-422-9(X))* Loving Healing Pr., Inc.

Hanson, Jean. The 5,000 Friends of Veronica Veetch. Parry, Laurie, illus. 2017. (ENG.). 32p. (J). 17.95 *(978-1-934649-27-5(9))* Bailiwick Pr.

Harper, Charise Mericle. A Big Surprise for Little Card. Raff, Anna, illus. 2016. (ENG.). 40p. (J). (gr. -1-3). 16.99 *(978-0-7636-7485-4(0))* Candlewick Pr.

Harris, Wendy. Daniel Visits the Library. 2015. (Daniel Tiger's Neighborhood Ready-To-Read Ser.). lib. bdg. 13.55 *(978-0-606-37875-8(8))* Turtleback.

Harrison, Paul. Noisy Books, 1 vol. Florin, Fabiano, illus. 2009. (Get Ready Readers Ser.). (ENG.). 32p. (J). (gr. k-k). lib. bdg. 27.27 *(978-1-60754-258-2(7),* 1735ba23-2ce1-444c-80e1-234ea7574c53, Windmill Bks.) Rosen Publishing Group, Inc., The.

Hillert, Margaret. Dear Dragon Goes to the Library. Schimmell, David, illus. 2008. (BeginningtoRead Ser.). 32p. (J). (gr. k-2). lib. bdg. 22.60 *(978-1-59953-160-1(7))* Norwood Hse. Pr.

—Dear Dragon Goes to the Library (Querido Dragon Va a la Biblioteca) Del Risco, Eida, tr. from ENG. Schimmell, David, illus. 2010. (BeginningtoRead Ser.). (SPA & ENG.). 32p. (J). (gr. k-2). lib. bdg. 22.60 *(978-1-59953-361-2(8))* Norwood Hse. Pr.

—Querido Dragón Va a la Biblioteca/Dear Dragon Goes to the Library. del Risco, Eida, tr. Schimmell, David, illus. 2010. (BeginningtoRead Ser.). 32p. (J). (-2). pap. 11.94 *(978-1-60357-549-2(9))* Norwood Hse. Pr.

Hoffman, Mary. Special Powers. (ENG.). 200p. pap. *(978-0-340-62670-2(4))* Hodder & Stoughton.

Hopkins, Jackie Mims. Picture Book & Library Lessons. Thornburgh, Rebecca, illus. 2004. 32p. (gr. -1-2). 16.95 *(978-1-932146-27-1(X),* K67-39703, Upstart Bks.) Highsmith Inc.

—The Shelf Elf. Thornburgh, Rebecca McKillip, illus. 2004. (J). (gr. k-3). 17.95 *(978-1-932146-16-5(4),* 1237659) Highsmith Inc.

—The Shelf Elf Helps Out. Thornburgh, Rebecca McKillip, illus. 2006. (J). *(978-1-932146-45-5(8),* Upstart Bks.) Highsmith Inc.

Hopkins, Lee Bennett. Jumping off Library Shelves. Manning, Jane, illus. 2015. (ENG.). 32p. (J). (gr. k-4). 17.95 *(978-1-59078-924-7(5),* 1396014, Wordsong) Highlights Pr., c/o Highlights for Children, Inc.

Jennings, Sharon, et al. Franklin's Library Book. Gagnon, Céleste, illus. 2005. 32p. (J). *(978-0-439-82297-8(1))* Scholastic, Inc.

Johnson, Angela. Lottie Paris & the Best Place. Fischer, Scott M., illus. 2013. (ENG.). 32p. (J). (gr. k-4). 19.99 *(978-0-689-87378-2(6),* Simon & Schuster Bks. For Young Readers) Simon & Schuster Bks. For Young Readers.

Joyce, William. The Fantastic Flying Books of Mr. Morris Lessmore. 2006. *(978-0-06-050838-8(8))* HarperCollins Canada, Ltd.

—The Fantastic Flying Books of Mr. Morris Lessmore. Joyce, William & Bluhm, Joe, illus. 2012. (ENG.). 56p. (J). (gr. -1-3). 19.99 *(978-1-4424-5702-7(3),* Atheneum Bks. for Young Readers) Simon & Schuster Children's Publishing.

Just Mrs. Goose. 2004. (Illus.). 152p. 12.95 *(978-0-9746457-0-4(2))* Green Mansion Pr. LLC.

K-2 Inclusive Fiction: Classroom Library. 2018. (ENG.). (J). (gr. k-2). pap. 473.18 *(978-1-4965-8211-9(X),* Stone Arch Bks.) Capstone.

Kerrin, Jessica Scott. The Spotted Dog Last Seen, 1 vol. 2013. (ENG.). 208p. (J). (gr. 4-6). 14.95 *(978-1-55498-387-2(8))* Groundwood Bks. CAN. Dist: Publishers Group West (PGW).

Kirk, Daniel. Library Mouse, No. 1. 2007. (ENG., Illus.). 32p. (J). (gr. 1-4). 18.99 *(978-0-8109-9346-4(5),* 5735, Abrams Bks. for Young Readers) Abrams, Inc.

—Library Mouse: A World to Explore. 2010. (ENG., Illus.). 30p. (J). (gr. 1-4). 18.99 *(978-0-8109-8968-9(9),* 647401, Abrams Bks. for Young Readers) Abrams, Inc.

—Library Mouse: Home Sweet Home. 2013. (ENG., Illus.). 40p. (J). (gr. k-4). 18.99 *(978-1-4197-0544-1(X),* 1007601, Abrams Bks. for Young Readers) Abrams, Inc.

—Library Mouse #2: a Friend's Tale Bk. 2. 2009. (ENG., Illus.). 32p. (J). (gr. 1-4). 18.99 *(978-0-8109-8927-6(1),* 647301, Abrams Bks. for Young Readers) Abrams, Inc.

Klein, Adria F. Max Goes to the Library. Gallagher-Cole, Mernie, illus. 2007. (Read-It! Readers: the Life of Max Ser.). (ENG.). 24p. (J). (gr. -1-2). per. 3.95 *(978-1-4048-3062-2(6),* 94338, Picture Window Bks.) Capstone.

—Max Va a la Biblioteca, 1 vol. Lozano, Clara, tr. Gallagher-Cole, Mernie, illus. 2007. (Read-It! Readers en Español: la Vida de Max Ser.). (SPA.). 24p. (J). (gr. -1-3). per. 3.95 *(978-1-4048-3036-3(7),* 94374, Picture Window Bks.) Capstone.

—Tia Tape Measure, 1 vol. Rowland, Andrew, illus. 2011. (Tool School Ser.). (ENG.). 32p. (J). (gr. 1-2). pap. 6.25 *(978-1-4342-3388-2(X),* 116395); lib. bdg. 22.65 *(978-1-4342-3046-1(5),* 114624) Capstone. (Stone Arch Bks.).

Klimo, Kate. The Dragon in the Library. 3. Shroades, John, illus. 2011. (Dragon Keepers Ser.: No. 3). (ENG.). 224p. (J). (gr. 4-6). lib. bdg. 21.19 *(978-0-375-95591-4(7),* Yearling) Random Hse. Children's Bks.

—Dragon Keepers #3: the Dragon in the Library. Shroades, John, illus. 2011. (Dragon Keepers Ser.: 3). 240p. (J). (gr. 3-7). 7.99 *(978-0-375-85592-4(0),* Yearling) Random Hse. Children's Bks.

Knudsen, Michelle. Library Lion. Hawkes, Kevin, illus. (ENG.). 48p. (J). (gr. -1-3). 2009. pap. 7.99 *(978-0-7636-3784-2(X))* 2006. 18.99 *(978-0-7636-2262-6(1))* Candlewick Pr.

—Library Lion. 2009. lib. bdg. 17.20 *(978-0-606-06666-2(7))* Turtleback.

Kohara, Kazuno. The Midnight Library. Kohara, Kazuno, illus. 2014. (ENG., Illus.). 32p. (J). (gr. -1-1). 18.99 *(978-1-59643-985-6(8),* 900128314) Roaring Brook Pr.

Kuphal, Shirley M. Flavor's Wild Wish. 2008. 36p. pap. 21.99 *(978-1-4363-0656-0(6))* Xlibris Corp.

Lasky, Kathryn. Spiders on the Case, Bk. 2. Gilpin, Stephen, illus. 2011. (ENG.). 176p. (J). (gr. 2-5). 15.99 *(978-0-545-11682-4(1),* Scholastic Pr.) Scholastic, Inc.

Leiloglou, Carolyn. Library's Most Wanted. Pogue, Sarah, illus. 2020. (ENG.). 32p. (gr. -1-3). 16.99 *(978-1-4556-2517-8(5),* Pelican Publishing) Arcadia Publishing.

Lies, Brian. Bats at the Library. (Bat Book Ser.). (ENG., Illus.). 32p. (J). (gr. -1-3). 2014. pap. 9.99 *(978-0-544-33920-0(7),* 1584491) 2008. 18.99 *(978-0-618-99923-1(X),* 1027891) HarperCollins Pubs. (Clarion Bks.).

Luper, Eric. Battle of the Bots. 2018. (Key Hunters Ser.: 7). (ENG., Illus.). 128p. (J). (gr. 2-5). pap. 4.99 *(978-1-338-21233-4(8),* Scholastic Paperbacks) Scholastic, Inc.

—The Haunted Howl. Weber, Lisa K., illus. 2016. (Key Hunters Ser.: 3). (ENG.). 128p. (J). (gr. 2-5). pap. 4.99 *(978-0-545-82211-4(4),* Scholastic Paperbacks) Scholastic, Inc.

—The Mysterious Moonstone (Key Hunters #1) 2016. (Key Hunters Ser.: 1). (ENG., Illus.). 128p. (J). (gr. 2-5). pap. 5.99 *(978-0-545-82204-6(1))* Scholastic, Inc.

—The Risky Rescue (Key Hunters #6) 2017. (Key Hunters Ser.: 6). (ENG., Illus.). 128p. (J). (gr. 2-5). pap. 5.99 *(978-1-338-21229-7(X),* Scholastic Paperbacks) Scholastic, Inc.

—The Spy's Secret (Key Hunters #2) 2016. (Key Hunters Ser.: 2). (ENG.). 128p. (J). (gr. 2-5). pap. 5.99 *(978-0-545-82206-0(8))* Scholastic, Inc.

—The Wizard's War (Key Hunters #4) 2017. (Key Hunters Ser.: 4). (ENG., Illus.). 128p. (J). (gr. 2-5). pap. 5.99 *(978-0-545-82213-8(0),* Scholastic Paperbacks) Scholastic, Inc.

Lynellen Sullivan & Bryan Castle. Poppers to the Rescue: Book 1 of the Popcorn Series. 2010. 72p. pap. 8.95 *(978-1-4401-9764-2(4))* iUniverse, Inc.

MacHale, D. J. Black Moon Rising (the Library Book 2) (Library: 2). 304p. (J). (gr. 3-7). 2018. pap. 7.99 *(978-1-101-93260-5(0),* Yearling) 2017. 16.99 *(978-1-101-93257-5(0),* Random Hse. Bks. for Young Readers) Random Hse. Children's Bks.

—Curse of the Boggin (the Library Book 1) 2016. (Library: 1). 256p. (J). (gr. 3-7). 16.99 *(978-1-101-93253-7(8),* Random Hse. Bks. for Young Readers) Random Hse. Children's Bks.

—Oracle of Doom (the Library Book 3) 2018. (Library: 3). 304p. (J). (gr. 3-7). 16.99 *(978-1-101-93261-2(9),* Random Hse. Bks. for Young Readers) Random Hse. Children's Bks.

—Surrender the Key (the Library Book 1) 2017. (Library: 1). 272p. (J). (gr. 3-7). 7.99 *(978-1-101-93256-8(2),* Yearling) Random Hse. Children's Bks.

Malaspina, Ann. Finding Lincoln. Bootman, Colin, illus. 2009. (ENG.). 32p. (J). (gr. -1-3). 16.99 *(978-0-8075-2435-0(2),* 807524352) Whitman, Albert & Co.

Maloney, Peter & Zekauskas, Felicia. Late for the Library: Just Schoolin' Around Series. 2004. (Just Schoolin' Around Ser.). (Illus.). (J). *(978-0-439-55361-2(X))* Scholastic, Inc.

McDonald, Megan. When the Library Lights Go Out. Tillotson, Katherine, illus. 2009. (ENG.). 40p. (J). (gr. -1-1). 9.99 *(978-1-4169-8028-5(8),* Atheneum Bks. for Young Readers) Simon & Schuster Children's Publishing.

McQuinn, Anna. Lola at the Library. Beardshaw, Rosalind, illus. 2007. 22p. (gr. -1). 16.95 *(978-0-7569-7931-7(5))* Perfection Learning Corp.

Meister, Cari. Shark in the Library!, 1 vol. Simard, Rémy, illus. (My First Graphic Novel Ser.). (ENG.). 32p. (J). (gr. k-2). 2011. pap. 6.25 *(978-1-4342-3104-8(6),* 114744) 2010. 24.65 *(978-1-4342-2058-5(3),* 102802) Capstone. (Stone Arch Bks.).

Miedoso, Andres. The Scary Library Shusher. Rivas, Victor, illus. 2018. (Desmond Cole Ghost Patrol Ser.: 5). (ENG.). 128p. (J). (gr. k-4). 17.99 *(978-1-5344-2692-4(2));* pap. 6.99 *(978-1-5344-2691-7(4))* Little Simon. (Little Simon).

Miller, Amanda. The Library's Secret: A Hidden Adventure. 2010. 88p. pap. 10.49 *(978-1-4520-7012-4(1))* AuthorHouse.

Miller, Pat. We're Going on a Book Hunt. Bernard Westcott, Nadine, illus. 2008. (J). (gr. -1). 17.95 *(978-1-60213-034-0(5),* Upstart Bks.) Highsmith Inc.

Miller, William. Richard Wright y el Carne de Biblioteca / Richard Wright & the Library Card (Spanish Edition) 2003. (ENG., Illus.). 1p. (J). 16.95 *(978-1-58430-180-6(5))* Lee & Low Bks., Inc.

Mitchell, Malcolm. The Magician's Hat. Lew-Vriethoff, Joanne, illus. 2018. (ENG.). 32p. (J). (gr. -1-3). 18.99 *(978-1-338-11454-6(9))* Scholastic, Inc.

Montoya, Martha, creator. No, no a la Biblioteca! Take-Home. 2005. (Los Kitos Ser.). (SPA.). (YA). (gr. 1-3). 15.00 *(978-0-8215-8812-3(5))* Sadlier, William H. Inc.

Mora, Pat. Tomas & the Library Lady. Colón, Raúl, illus. 2007. (gr. k-3). 18.00 *(978-0-7569-7935-5(8))* Perfection Learning Corp.

—Tomas y la Senora de la Biblioteca. 2004. (SPA., Illus.). (J). (gr. k-3). spiral bd. *(978-0-616-03092-9(4))* Canadian National Institute for the Blind/Institut National Canadien pour les Aveugles.

Morris, Carla. The Boy Who Was Raised by Librarians. Sneed, Brad, illus. 32p. (J). (gr. -1-3). 2019. pap. 7.95 *(978-1-68263-123-2(0))* 2007. (ENG.). 16.95 *(978-1-56145-391-7(9))* Peachtree Publishing Co. Inc.

Morrison, Toni & Morrison, Slade. Please, Louise. Strickland, Shadra, illus. 2014. (ENG.). 32p. (J). (gr. -1-3). 19.99 *(978-1-4169-8338-5(4),* Simon & Schuster Bks. For Young Readers) Simon & Schuster Bks. For Young Readers.

Morton, Carlene. The Library Pages. Docampo, Valeria, illus. 2010. 32p. (J). (gr. k-4). 17.95 *(978-1-60213-045-6(0),* Upstart Bks.) Highsmith Inc.

Nickerson, Sara. How to Disappear Completely & Never Be Found. Comport, Sally Wern, illus. 2003. (ENG.). 288p. (J). (gr. 5-18). pap. 5.99 *(978-0-06-441027-4(7))* HarperCollins Pubs.

Numeroff, Laura. Beatrice Doesn't Want To. Munsinger, Lynn, illus. 2008. (ENG.). 32p. (J). (gr. -1-2). pap. 7.99 *(978-0-7636-3843-6(9))* Candlewick Pr.

OHora, Zachariah. The Not So Quiet Library. 2016. (Illus.). 40p. (J). (-k). 17.99 *(978-0-8037-4140-9(5),* Dial Bks) Penguin Young Readers Group.

Papp, Lisa. Madeline Finn & the Library Dog, 1 vol. 2016. (ENG., Illus.). 32p. (J). (gr. -1-3). 17.95 *(978-1-56145-910-0(0))* Peachtree Publishing Co. Inc.

Paratore, Coleen Murtagh. The Cupid Chronicles. 2008. (Wedding Planner's Daughter Ser.). (ENG.). 224p. (J). (gr. 4-8). pap. 6.99 *(978-1-4169-5484-2(8),* Aladdin) Simon & Schuster Children's Publishing.

Parish, Herman. Amelia Bedelia, Bookworm. Sweat, Lynn, illus. (I Can Read Level 2 Ser.). (ENG.). 64p. (J). (gr. k-3). 2005. pap. 4.99 *(978-0-06-051892-9(8))* 2003. 17.99 *(978-0-06-051890-5(1))* HarperCollins Pubs. (Greenwillow Bks.).

—Amelia Bedelia, Bookworm. Sweat, Lynn, illus. 2005. (I Can Read Bks.). 63p. (gr. -1-3). 14.00 *(978-0-7569-5766-7(4))* Perfection Learning Corp.

—Amelia Bedelia's Backpack Bundle. Sweat, Lynn, illus. 2012. 192p. (J). *(978-1-4351-4392-0(2),* Greenwillow Bks.) HarperCollins Pubs.

—Amelia Bedelia's First Library Card. Avril, Lynne, illus. 2013. (Amelia Bedelia Ser.). (ENG.). 32p. (J). (gr. -1-3). 17.99 *(978-0-06-209512-1(9),* Greenwillow Bks.) HarperCollins Pubs.

Parsley, Elise. If You Ever Want to Bring a Circus to the Library, Don't! 2017. (Magnolia Says DON'T! Ser.: 3). (ENG., Illus.). 40p. (J). (gr. -1-3). 18.99 *(978-0-316-37651-7(2))* Little, Brown Bks. for Young Readers.

Paull, Lorenz. The Fox in the Library. Schärer, Kathrin & Schärer, Kathrin, illus. 2015. (ENG.). 32p. (J). (gr. -1-2). pap. 7.95 *(978-0-7358-4213-7(2))* North-South Bks., Inc.

—The Fox in the Library. Schärer, Kathrin, illus. 2013. (ENG.). 32p. (J). (gr. -1-3). 17.95 *(978-0-7358-4150-5(0))* North-South Bks., Inc.

Pearson, Mary E. I Can Do It All. Shelley, Jeff, illus. 2011. (Rookie Ready to Learn - I Can! Ser.). 32p. (J). (gr. -1-k). lib. bdg. 23.00 *(978-0-531-26429-4(7),* Children's Pr.) Scholastic Library Publishing.

—Rookie Ready to Learn en Español: Puedo Hacer de Todo. Shelly, Jeff, illus. 2011. (Rookie Ready to Learn Español Ser.). Orig. Title: Rookie Ready to Learn: I Can Do It All. (SPA.). 40p. (J). pap. 5.95 *(978-0-531-26787-5(3),* Children's Pr.) Scholastic Library Publishing.

Pearson, Mary E. & Shelly, Jeff. Puedo Hacer de Todo. Shelly, Jeff, illus. 2011. (Rookie Ready to Learn Español Ser.).Tr. of I Can Do It All. (SPA., Illus.). 40p. (J). lib. bdg. 23.00 *(978-0-531-26119-4(0),* Children's Pr.) Scholastic Library Publishing.

Phillips, Dee. Fright at the Freemont Library. 2016. (Cold Whispers II Ser.). (ENG., Illus.). 32p. (J). (gr. 2-6). 28.50 *(978-1-944102-36-4(1))* Bearport Publishing Co., Inc.

Ponti, James. Trapped! 2018. (Framed! Ser.: 3). (ENG., Illus.). 384p. (J). (gr. 3-7). 19.99 *(978-1-5344-0891-3(6),* Aladdin) Simon & Schuster Children's Publishing.

Rey, H. A. Curious George Visits the Library/Jorge el Curioso Va a la Biblioteca: Bilingual English-Spanish. 2011. (Curious George Ser.). (ENG., Illus.). 24p. (J). (gr. -1-3). pap. 4.99 *(978-0-547-55075-6(8),* 1450249, Clarion Bks.) HarperCollins Pubs.

Rey, H. A. & Rey, Margret. Librarian for a Day. 2012. (Curious George TV Tie-In Early Reader Ser.). lib. bdg. 13.55 *(978-0-606-26602-4(X))* Turtleback.

RH Disney, illus. Doc Mcstuffins Little Golden Book Library (Disney Junior: Doc Mcstuffins) As Big As a Whale; Snowman Surprise; Bubble-Rific!; Boomer Gets His Bounce Back; a Knight in Sticky Armor, 5 vols. 2015. (Little Golden Book Ser.). (ENG.). 120p. (J). (-k). 29.95 *(978-0-7364-3407-2(0),* Golden/Disney) Random Hse. Children's Bks.

Richards, Natalie D. What You Hide. 2018. (ENG.). 384p. (YA). (gr. 8-12). pap. 10.99 *(978-1-4926-5718-7(2))* Sourcebooks, Inc.

Robins, Eleanor. Library Book Mystery, 1 vol. unabr. ed. 2011. (Carter High Mysteries Ser.). (ENG.). 48p. (YA). (gr. 9-12). 9.75 *(978-1-61651-564-5(3))* Saddleback Educational Publishing, Inc.

Rockwell, Anne. Library Day. Rockwell, Lizzy, illus. 2016. (My First Experience Book Ser.). (ENG.). 32p. (J). (gr. -1-3). 16.99 *(978-1-4814-2731-9(8),* Aladdin) Simon & Schuster Children's Publishing.

—Library Day. 2017. lib. bdg. 18.40 *(978-0-606-39759-9(0))* Turtleback.

Rogerson, Margaret. Sorcery of Thorns. 2019. (ENG., Illus.). 464p. (YA). (gr. 9). 19.99 *(978-1-4814-9761-9(8),* McElderry, Margaret K. Bks.) McElderry, Margaret K. Bks.

Rylant, Cynthia. Mr. Putter & Tabby Turn the Page. Howard, Arthur, illus. 2015. (Mr. Putter & Tabby Ser.). (ENG.). 40p. (J). (gr. 1-4). pap. 5.99 *(978-0-544-58232-3(2),* 1613542, Clarion Bks.) HarperCollins Pubs.

—Mr. Putter & Tabby Turn the Page. 2015. (Mr. Putter & Tabby Ser.). lib. bdg. 16.00 *(978-0-606-37453-8(1))* Turtleback.

Sanderson, Brandon. Alcatraz Versus the Scrivener's Bones. 2009. (Alcatraz Ser.: 2). (ENG.). 336p. (J). (gr. 4-6). 21.19 *(978-0-439-92554-9(1))* Scholastic, Inc.

Santos, Gloria. Good Manners at the Library, 1 vol. 2017. (Manners Matter Ser.). (ENG.). 24p. (J). (gr. 1-1). 25.27 *(978-1-5081-5728-1(6),* de535bed-0895-4d4d-819d-7227ca94ceb1, PowerKids Pr.) Rosen Publishing Group, Inc., The.

Sazaklis, John. Recess Is Ruined. Robinson, Lee, illus. 2016. (Billy Burger, Model Citizen Ser.). (ENG.). 96p. (J). (gr. 2-4). lib. bdg. 22.65 *(978-1-4965-2588-8(4),* 130717, Stone Arch Bks.) Capstone.

Schwab, Victoria. The Archived. 2014. (Archived Ser.). (ENG., Illus.). 352p. (J). (gr. 7-12). pap. 10.99 *(978-1-4231-7108-9(X))* Little, Brown Bks. for Young Readers.

Shea, Bob. Dinosaur vs. the Library. Shea, Bob, illus. 2011. (Dinosaur vs. Book Ser.: 3). (ENG., Illus.). 40p. (J). (gr. -1-3). 17.99 *(978-1-4231-3338-4(2))* Hyperion Pr.

Shulman, Polly. The Grimm Legacy. 2011. (ENG.). (J). 352p. (gr. 5-18). 8.99 *(978-0-14-241904-5(4),* Puffin Books);1. (Illus.). 336p. (gr. 6-8). 24.94 *(978-0-399-25096-5(4))* Penguin Young Readers Group.

Sierra, Judy. Mind Your Manners, B. B. Wolf. 2012. lib. bdg. 18.40 *(978-0-606-26784-7(0))* Turtleback.

—Wild about Books. Brown, Marc, illus. 2004. (ENG.). 40p. (J). (gr. -1-2). 18.99 *(978-0-375-82538-5(X),* Knopf Bks. for Young Readers) Random Hse. Children's Bks.

Silvestro, Annie. Bunny's Book Club. Mai-Wyss, Tatjana, illus. 2017. 40p. (J). (gr. -1-2). 17.99 *(978-0-553-53758-1(X),* Doubleday Bks. for Young Readers) Random Hse. Children's Bks.

Slater, David Michael. The Boy & the Book: [a Wordless Story]. Kolar, Bob, illus. 2015. 32p. (J). (-k). lib. bdg. 16.95 *(978-1-58089-562-0(X))* Charlesbridge Publishing, Inc.

Sneed, Brad. The Boy Who Was Raised by Librarians. Sneed, Brad, illus. 2008. (Illus.). (J). (gr. k-3). 27.95 incl. audio *(978-0-8045-6965-1(7))* Spoken Arts, Inc.

Stanek, Robert, pseud. Bugville Critters Visit the Library. 2011. (Illus.). 28p. pap. 4.99 *(978-1-57545-259-3(6),* Reagent Pr. Bks. for Young Readers) RP Media.

—Visit the Library. 2010. 28p. pap. 8.99 *(978-1-57545-176-3(X),* Reagent Pr. Bks. for Young Readers) RP Media.

Stoop, Naoko. Red Knit Cap Girl & the Reading Tree. 2014. (ENG., Illus.). 40p. (J). (gr. -1-3). 17.99 *(978-0-316-22886-2(9))* Little, Brown Bks. for Young Readers.

Style Guide, illus. PJ Masks Save the Library! Ready-To-Read Level 1. 2016. (PJ Masks Ser.). (ENG.). 32p. (J). (gr. -1-1). pap. 3.99 *(978-1-4814-8892-1(9),* Simon Spotlight) Simon Spotlight.

Swanson Sateren, Shelley. Max & Zoe at the Library, 1 vol. Sullivan, Mary, illus. 2013. (Max & Zoe Ser.). (ENG.). 32p. (J). (gr. k-2). pap. 5.19 *(978-1-4048-8058-0(5),* 121734, Picture Window Bks.) Capstone.

Tacang, Brian. Bully-Be-Gone: The Misadventures of Millicent Madding #1. 2006. (Illus.). 216p. (J). (gr. 3-7). 17.89 *(978-0-06-073912-6(6))* HarperCollins Pubs.

Tan, Amy Rebecca. A Kind of Paradise. 2019. (ENG.). 304p. (J). (gr. 3-7). 16.99 *(978-0-06-279541-0(4),* HarperCollins) HarperCollins Pubs.

Terry, Sonya. L Is for Library. Wong, Nicole, illus. 2006. 32p. (J). (gr. -1-3). lib. bdg. 16.95 *(978-1-932146-44-8(X),* Upstart Bks.) Highsmith Inc.

Thielbar, Melinda. The Book Bandit: A Mystery with Geometry. Chow, Candice & Lee, Jennifer A., illus. 2011. (Manga Math Mysteries Ser.: 7). (ENG.). 48p. (J). (gr. 3-5). pap. 7.99 *(978-0-7613-8136-5(8),* e0e0aea2-a276-4124-9f9e-f3e70f31022c, Graphic Universe™) Lerner Publishing Group.

—#7 the Book Bandit: A Mystery with Geometry. Lee, Jenn Manley & Chow, Candice, illus. 2011. (Manga Math

JKL

Mysteries Set II Ser.). pap. 39.62 *(978-1-7613-8364-2(6),* Graphic Universe™) Lerner Publishing Group.
Time, Nicholas O. Going, Going, Gone. 2016. (In Due Time Ser.: 1). (ENG., Illus.). 160p. (J). (gr. 3-7). pap. 6.99 *(978-1-4814-6729-2(8),* Simon Spotlight) Simon Spotlight.
—Going, Going, Gone. 2016. (In Due Time Ser.: 1). lib. bdg. 17.20 *(978-0-606-38985-3(7))* Turtleback.
Troupe, Thomas Kingsley. The Final Frankenstein. Bonet, Xavier, illus. 2019. (Michael Dahl Presents: Midnight Library 4D Ser.). (ENG.). 80p. (J). (gr. 4-6). lib. bdg. 25.99 *(978-1-4965-7896-9(1),* 139611, Stone Arch Bks.) Capstone.
—The Gulliver Giant. Bonet, Xavier, illus. 2019. (Michael Dahl Presents: Midnight Library 4D Ser.). (ENG.). 80p. (J). (gr. 4-6). lib. bdg. 25.99 *(978-1-4965-7894-5(5),* 139609, Stone Arch Bks.) Capstone.
—The Minotaur Maze. Bonet, Xavier, illus. 2019. (Michael Dahl Presents: Midnight Library 4D Ser.). (ENG.). 80p. (J). (gr. 4-6). lib. bdg. 25.99 *(978-1-4965-7895-2(3),* 139610, Stone Arch Bks.) Capstone.
Tubb, Kristin O'Donnell. The Story Collector: A New York Public Library Book. Bruno, Iacopo, illus. 2018. (Story Collector Ser.: 1). (ENG.). 256p. (J). 16.99 *(978-1-250-14380-8(2),* 900180568, Holt, Henry & Co. Bks. For Young Readers) Holt, Henry & Co.
Twohy, Mike. Poindexter Makes a Friend. Twohy, Mike, illus. 2011. (ENG., Illus.). 32p. (J). (gr. -1-3). 15.99 *(978-1-4424-0965-1(7),* Simon & Schuster/Paula Wiseman Bks.) Simon & Schuster/Paula Wiseman Bks.
Varnes, Allison. Property of the Rebel Librarian. 2019. (Illus.). 288p. (J). (gr. 3-7). 7.99 *(978-1-5247-7150-8(3),* Yearling) Random Hse. Children's Bks.
Vaughan, Grace. Annie & the Magic Book. 2012. 30p. pap. 19.99 *(978-1-4772-5498-1(6))* AuthorHouse.
Weatherford, Carole Boston. The Library Ghost. White, Lee, illus. 2008. 22p. (J). (gr. -1-3). 17.95 *(978-1-60213-017-3(5),* Upstart Bks.) Highsmith Inc.
Weston Woods Staff, creator. Wild about Books. 2011. 29.95 *(978-0-439-80485-1(X))* Weston Woods Studios, Inc.
Wexler, Django. The Fall of the Readers: The Forbidden Library: Volume 4. 2017. (Forbidden Library: 4). 368p. (J). (gr. 5). 17.99 *(978-0-399-53920-6(4),* Kathy Dawson Books) Penguin Young Readers Group.
—The Forbidden Library. 2015. (Forbidden Library: 1). (ENG., Illus.). 400p. (J). (gr. 5). 8.99 *(978-0-14-242681-4(4),* Puffin Books) Penguin Young Readers Group.
—The Palace of Glass: The Forbidden Library: Volume 3. 2016. (Forbidden Library: 3). (ENG., Illus.). 368p. (J). (gr. 5). 16.99 *(978-0-8037-3978-9(8),* Kathy Dawson Books) Penguin Young Readers Group.
Williams, Zachary. Lions at the Library?, 1 vol. 2006. (Neighborhood Readers Ser.). (ENG.). 12p. (gr. 1-2). pap. 5.90 *(978-1-4042-6863-0(4),* 1a815c85-15cd-4245-b8ba-ba6a36b2df1e, Rosen Classroom) Rosen Publishing Group, Inc., The.
Willis, Jeanne. Delilah D. at the Library. Reeve, Rosie, illus. 2007. (ENG.). 32p. (J). (gr. -1-3). 16.00 *(978-0-618-78195-9(1),* 100544, Clarion Bks.) HarperCollins Pubs.
Willson, Sarah. La Mochila de Dora. Roper, Robert, illus. 2003. (Dora the Explorer Ser.).Tr. of Dora's Backpack. (SPA.). 24p. (J). pap. 3.99 *(978-0-689-86306-6(3),* Libros Para Ninos) Libros Para Ninos.
Yoo, Tae-Eun. The Little Red Fish. 2007. (Illus.). (J). *(978-1-4287-3601-6(8),* Dial) Penguin Publishing Group.
Young, Karen Romano. A Girl, a Raccoon, & the Midnight Moon: (Juvenile Fiction, Mystery, Young Reader Detective Story, Light Fantasy for Kids) Bagley, Jessixa, illus. 2020. (ENG.). 392p. (J). (gr. 5-9). 16.99 *(978-1-4521-6952-1(7))* Chronicle Bks. LLC.

LIBRARIES—POETRY

Lewis, J. Patrick. Please Bury Me in the Library. Stone, Kyle M., illus. 2005. (ENG.). 32p. (J). (gr. -1-3). 17.99 *(978-0-15-216387-7(5),* 1200853, Clarion Bks.) HarperCollins Pubs.

LIBRARIES, SCHOOL

see School Libraries

LIBRARY ORIENTATION

Here are entered works dealing with the instruction of readers in library use..

Buzzeo, Toni. R Is for Research. Wong, Nicole, illus. 2008. 17.95 *(978-1-60213-032-6(9),* Upstart Bks.) Highsmith Inc.
Harper, Leslie. Cómo Mantenerse Informado. 2014. (Sé un líder de la Comunidad (Be a Community Leader) Ser.). (SPA.). 32p. (J). (gr. 4-6). pap. 60.00 *(978-1-4777-6923-2(4),* PowerKids Pr.) Rosen Publishing Group, Inc., The.
—Cómo Mantenerse Informados, 1 vol. 2014. (Sé un líder de la Comunidad (Be a Community Leader) Ser.). (SPA.). 32p. (J). (gr. 5-5). lib. bdg. 27.93 *(978-1-4777-6921-8(8),* 829dbc4b-55b0-4ea3-a1f3-e1095203f601, PowerKids Pr.) Rosen Publishing Group, Inc., The.
—How to Stay Informed, 1 vol. 2014. (Be a Community Leader Ser.). (ENG.). 32p. (J). (gr. 5-5). lib. bdg. 27.93 *(978-1-4777-6701-6(0),* 4a2c32a5-e6f5-4ed4-b05f-5f02918f88db, PowerKids Pr.) Rosen Publishing Group, Inc., The.

LIBRARY SCIENCE

Here are entered general works on the organization and administration of libraries. Works about services offered by libraries to patrons are entered under Library Service.

Bodden, Valerie. Doing Primary Research. 2012. (Research for Writing Ser.). (ENG.). 48p. (J). (gr. 4-7). 23.95 *(978-1-60818-204-6(5),* 21952, Creative Education) Creative Co., The.
—Navigating the Library. 2012. (Research for Writing Ser.). (ENG.). 48p. (J). (gr. 4-7). 23.95 *(978-1-60818-206-0(1),* 21954, Creative Education) Creative Co., The.
Colby, Jennifer. Library. 2016. (21st Century Junior Library: Explore a Workplace Ser.). (ENG., Illus.). 24p. (J). (gr. 2-5). 29.21 *(978-1-63471-075-6(4),* 208379) Cherry Lake Publishing.
Crabtree, Marc. Meet My Neighbor, the Librarian. 2012. (ENG., Illus.). 24p. (J). *(978-0-7787-4559-4(7));* pap. *(978-0-7787-4564-8(3))* Crabtree Publishing Co.
Gerber, Larry. The Distortion of Facts in the Digital Age, 1 vol. 2012. (Digital & Information Literacy Ser.). (ENG., Illus.). 48p. (YA). (gr. 6-6). 33.47 *(978-1-4488-8357-8(1),* 277f2634-5014-4225-9fe2-01ead6459e2a); pap. 12.75 *(978-1-4488-8368-4(7),* e5d5507e-d10b-42a8-9453-32c99c56992a) Rosen Publishing Group, Inc., The. (Rosen Reference).
Graham Gaines, Ann. Master the Library & Media Center, 1 vol. 2009. (Ace It! Information Literacy Ser.). (ENG., Illus.). 48p. (gr. 3-3). lib. bdg. 27.93 *(978-0-7660-3393-1(7),* 37a32d0f-af8e-4981-abbc-47f5b448a02a) Enslow Publishing, LLC.
Jango-Cohen, Judith. Librarians. 2005. (Pull Ahead Bks.). (Illus.). 32p. (J). lib. bdg. 22.60 *(978-0-8225-1691-0(8))* Lerner Publishing Group.
Miller, Connie Colwell. I'll Be a Librarian. Baroncelli, Silvia, illus. 2018. (When I Grow Up Ser.). (ENG.). 24p. (J). (gr. 1-4). pap. 8.99 *(978-1-68152-317-0(5),* 15058); lib. bdg. *(978-1-68151-397-3(8),* 15052) Amicus.

LIBRARY SCIENCE—VOCATIONAL GUIDANCE

Ferguson, creator. Library & Information Science. 2008. (Discovering Careers for Your Future Ser.). (ENG.). 91p. (gr. 4-9). 21.95 *(978-0-8160-7282-8(5),* P179086, Ferguson Publishing Company) Infobase Holdings, Inc.
Leone, Laura. Choosing a Career in Information Science. 2009. (World of Work Ser.). 64p. (gr. 5-5). 58.50 *(978-1-60854-332-8(3))* Rosen Publishing Group, Inc., The.

LIBYA

DiPiazza, Francesca Davis. Libya in Pictures. 2005. (Visual Geography Series, Second Ser.). (Illus.). 80p. (YA). (gr. 7-12). lib. bdg. 27.93 *(978-0-8225-2549-3(6))* Lerner Publishing Group.
Harmon, Daniel E. Libya. 2010. (Major Muslim Nations Ser.). 119p. (YA). (gr. 5-18). lib. bdg. 25.95 *(978-1-4222-1388-9(9))* Mason Crest.
Hasday, Judy L. Libya. Rotberg, Robert I., ed. 2012. (Evolution of Africa's Major Nations Ser.). (Illus.). 80p. (J). (gr. 7). 22.95 *(978-1-4222-2181-5(4))* Mason Crest.
—Libya. 2011. (J). pap. *(978-1-4222-2209-6(8))* Mason Crest.
—Libya. Rotberg, Robert I., ed. 2009. (Africa Ser.). (Illus.). 79p. (YA). (gr. 3-7). lib. bdg. 21.95 *(978-1-4222-0083-4(3))* Mason Crest.
Hunter, Nick. Hoping for Peace in Libya, 1 vol. 2012. (Peace Pen Pals Ser.). (ENG., Illus.). 48p. (J). (gr. 6-6). 34.60 *(978-1-4339-7735-0(4),* 04d7ac94-f6af-4ab8-8759-8de77ed3b297); pap. 15.05 *(978-1-4339-7736-7(2),* 0e47f492-c52d-4bbd-9e4f-665b23b3b9a0) Stevens, Gareth Publishing LLLP.
Malcolm, Peter. Libya, 1 vol. 2nd rev. ed. 2004. (Cultures of the World (Second Edition)(r) Ser.). (ENG., Illus.). 144p. (gr. 5-5). lib. bdg. 49.79 *(978-0-7614-1702-6(8),* 4fe48a71-5342-444e-b4cf-825c37fe2416) Cavendish Square Publishing LLC.
Malcolm, Peter, et al. Libya, 1 vol. 3rd rev. ed. (Cultures of the World (Third Edition)(r) Ser.). (ENG., 144p. (gr. 5-5). 2015. Illus.). lib. bdg. 48.79 *(978-1-5026-0798-0(0),* 9ad202e1-3060-4ff9-b5d5-faf6bca03b8d) 2012. lib. bdg. 48.79 *(978-1-60870-992-2(2),* 97086ff3-cba2-40a6-83af-8c2585f3075b) Cavendish Square Publishing LLC.
O'Neal, Claire. We Visit Libya. 2012. (J). lib. bdg. 33.95 *(978-1-61228-310-4(1))* Mitchell Lane Pubs.
Rozario, Paul A. Libya, 1 vol. 2004. (Countries of the World Ser.). (ENG., Illus.). 96p. (gr. 6-8). lib. bdg. 33.67 *(978-0-8368-3111-5(X),* 769956a1-5590-4550-90de-785c68c0fb55) Stevens, Gareth Publishing LLLP.
Sullivan, Kimberly L. Muammar Al-Qaddafi's Libya. 2008. (Dictatorships Ser.). (Illus.). 144p. (J). (gr. 7-12). lib. bdg. 38.60 *(978-0-8225-8666-1(5))* Twenty First Century Bks.
Willis, Terri. Libya. 2008. (Enchantment of the World Ser.). (ENG., Illus.). 144p. (J). (gr. 5-9). 40.00 *(978-0-531-12480-2(0))* Scholastic Library Publishing.

LIBYA—FICTION

Stolz, Joelle. The Shadows of Ghadames. 2006. (ENG.). 128p. (J). (gr. 3-7). 5.99 *(978-0-440-41949-5(2),* Yearling) Random Hse. Children's Bks.

LIFE

House, Behrman. The Time of Our Lives. 2003. (ENG., Illus.). 1p. (J). pap. 14.95 *(978-0-87441-718-0(X),* aef8a532-afc2-470d-bf5b-3cee3581f857) Behrman Hse., Inc.
Kansil, J. Q. Conversations with Opa: Sharing Wisdom about the Universe & Lesser Things. 2011. 168p. pap. 18.00 *(978-1-61614-497-5(1))* Prometheus Bks., Pubs.
Morrison, Matthew. Big Questions: Incredible Adventures in Thinking. 2011. (ENG., Illus.). 204p. (J). (gr. 4-8). pap. 7.95 *(978-1-84046-670-6(7))* Icon Bks., Ltd. GBR. Dist: Publishers Group West (PGW).
Mortensen, Lori. Cycle of Life. 2016. (Spring Forward Ser.). (J). (gr. 2). *(978-1-4900-9474-8(1))* Benchmark Education Co.
Pearce, Q. L. Reincarnation, 1 vol. 2009. (Mysterious Encounters Ser.). (ENG., Illus.). 48p. (gr. 4-8). lib. bdg. 35.23 *(978-0-7377-4412-5(X),* 5ba01ecb-2b6f-4a29-bec2-bbc430ed0739, KidHaven Publishing) Greenhaven Publishing LLC.
Prentice-Hall Staff. Parade of Life: Animals. 2nd ed. (J). pap., act. bk. ed. *(978-0-13-400458-7(2))* Prentice Hall (Schl. Div.).
Steck-Vaughn Staff. Life on the Tallest Tree. 2003. pap. 4.10 *(978-0-7398-7636-7(8))* Steck-Vaughn.

LIFE (BIOLOGY)

see also Biology; Genetics; Old Age; Reproduction

Aleo, Karen. Living Things Need Air. 2019. (What Living Things Need Ser.). (ENG., Illus.). 24p. (J). (gr. -1-2). pap. 6.95 *(978-1-9771-1034-3(7),* 141110); lib. bdg. 24.65 *(978-1-9771-0884-5(9),* 140492) Capstone. (Pebble).
—Living Things Need Food. 2019. (What Living Things Need Ser.). (ENG., Illus.). 24p. (J). (gr. -1-2). pap. 6.95 *(978-1-9771-1035-0(5),* 141111); lib. bdg. 24.65 *(978-1-9771-0885-2(7),* 140493) Capstone. (Pebble).
—Living Things Need Light. 2019. (What Living Things Need Ser.). (ENG., Illus.). 24p. (J). (gr. -1-2). pap. 6.95 *(978-1-9771-1036-7(3),* 141112); lib. bdg. 24.65 *(978-1-9771-0886-9(5),* 140494) Capstone. (Pebble).
—Living Things Need Shelter. 2019. (What Living Things Need Ser.). (ENG., Illus.). 24p. (J). (gr. -1-2). pap. 6.95 *(978-1-9771-1037-4(1),* 141113); lib. bdg. 24.65 *(978-1-9771-0919-4(5),* 140520) Capstone. (Pebble).
—Living Things Need Water. 2019. (What Living Things Need Ser.). (ENG., Illus.). 24p. (J). (gr. -1-2). pap. 6.95 *(978-1-9771-1038-1(X),* 141114); lib. bdg. 24.65 *(978-1-9771-0887-6(3),* 140495) Capstone. (Pebble).
Anderson, Judith. Once There Was a Seed. Gordon, Mike, illus. 2010. (Nature's Miracles Ser.). (ENG.). 32p. (J). (gr. k-3). 18.69 *(978-0-7641-4493-6(6),* B.E.S. Publishing) Peterson's.
Anderson, Michael. A Closer Look at Living Things, 1 vol. 2011. (Introduction to Biology Ser.). (ENG.). 88p. (J). (gr. 8-8). lib. bdg. 35.29 *(978-1-61530-533-9(5),* 5b0b6012-0c29-45cd-bb9b-04e6487ab52f) Rosen Publishing Group, Inc., The.
Answers to Evolution Wall Chart. 2004. *(978-1-890947-87-3(3))* Rose Publishing.
Arbuthnott, Gill. Your Guide to Life on Earth. Mones, Marc, illus. 2016. (ENG.). 64p. (J). lib. bdg. *(978-0-7787-2243-4(0))* Crabtree Publishing Co.
Austen, Elizabeth. Living!, 1 vol. rev. ed. 2014. (Science: Informational Text Ser.). (ENG., Illus.). 24p. (gr. -1-1). pap. 9.99 *(978-1-4807-4520-9(0))* Teacher Created Materials, Inc.
—What Do Living Things Need?, 1 vol. rev. ed. 2014. (Science: Informational Text Ser.). (ENG., Illus.). 24p. (gr. -1-1). lib. bdg. 22.96 *(978-1-4938-1133-5(9));* pap. 9.99 *(978-1-4807-4523-0(5))* Teacher Created Materials, Inc.
Banqueri, Eduardo. Life on Earth. 2005. (Our Planet Ser.). (Illus.). 32p. (gr. 4-6). lib. bdg. 28.00 *(978-0-7910-9010-7(8),* Chelsea Clubhse.) Infobase Holdings, Inc.
Benchmark Education Company, LLC Staff, compiled by. Life Science. 2006. spiral bd. 475.00 *(978-1-4108-6943-2(1))* 2006. spiral bd. 75.00 *(978-1-4108-6928-9(8))* 2006. spiral bd. 215.00 *(978-1-4108-6926-5(1))* 2006. spiral bd. 255.00 *(978-1-4108-6947-0(4))* 2005. spiral bd. 360.00 *(978-1-4108-3852-0(8))* 2005. spiral bd. 165.00 *(978-1-4108-3853-7(6))* 2005. spiral bd. 260.00 *(978-1-4108-3860-5(9))* 2005. spiral bd. 145.00 *(978-1-4108-3861-2(7))* 2005. spiral bd. 75.00 *(978-1-4108-3867-4(6))* 2005. spiral bd. 50.00 *(978-1-4108-3868-1(4))* 2005. spiral bd. 75.00 *(978-1-4108-3875-9(7))* 2005. spiral bd. 35.00 *(978-1-4108-3876-6(5))* 2005. spiral bd. 680.00 *(978-1-4108-4514-6(1))* 2005. spiral bd. 950.00 *(978-1-4108-5433-9(7))* 2005. spiral bd. 395.00 *(978-1-4108-5434-6(5))* 2005. spiral bd. 550.00 *(978-1-4108-5846-7(4))* 2005. spiral bd. 295.00 *(978-1-4108-5847-4(2))* 2005. spiral bd. 305.00 *(978-1-4108-3831-5(5))* 2005. spiral bd. 320.00 *(978-1-4108-3830-8(7))* Benchmark Education Co.
Braun, Eric. Gertrude & Reginald the Monsters Talk about Living & Nonliving, 1 vol. Bernardini, Cristian, illus. 2012. (In the Science Lab Ser.). (ENG.). 24p. (J). (gr. k-3). pap. 9.95 *(978-1-4048-7237-0(X),* 118176, Picture Window Bks.) Capstone.
Callery, Sean. Life Cycles: Rainforest. 2018. (Lifecycles Ser.). (ENG.). 32p. (J). pap. 7.99 *(978-0-7534-7382-5(8),* 9780753473825, Kingfisher) Roaring Brook Pr.
Claybourne, Anna. Life Processes, 1 vol. 2012. (Web of Life Ser.). (ENG.). 48p. (J). (gr. 6-10). pap. 9.49 *(978-1-4109-4430-6(1),* 117494, Raintree) Capstone.
—What Do You Know about Life Cycles?, 1 vol. 2017. (Test Your Science Skills Ser.). (ENG.). 32p. (J). (gr. 5-5). pap. 12.75 *(978-1-5383-2308-3(7),* e5c8549a-e9d3-44e5-b023-432d7dfb44de); lib. bdg. 29.27 *(978-1-5081-6264-3(6),* 29c49848-a468-4fae-a747-b109eeef34ca) Rosen Publishing Group, Inc., The. (PowerKids Pr.).
Dartnell, Lewis. Astrobiology: Exploring Life in the Universe, 1 vol. 2011. (Contemporary Issues Ser.). (ENG., Illus.). 166p. (YA). (gr. 9-9). lib. bdg. 42.47 *(978-1-4488-1862-4(1),* 653e8d65-11c4-410c-a9b3-f1bd73a572f3) Rosen Publishing Group, Inc., The.
De la Bédoyère, Camilla. Encyclopedia of Life. Kelly, Richard, ed. 2017. (ENG., Illus.). 512p. (J). 39.95 *(978-1-78617-020-0(5))* Miles Kelly Publishing, Ltd. GBR. Dist: Parkwest Pubns., Inc.
Dickmann, Nancy. Life Cycles, 1 vol. 2015. (Earth Figured Out Ser.). (ENG., Illus.). 32p. (gr. 4-4). pap. 11.58 *(978-1-5026-0862-8(6),* ae46c382-d34b-497c-b4e9-dfeeae154bdb) Cavendish Square Publishing LLC.
Drake, Jane & Love, Ann. Alien Invaders: Species That Threaten Our World. Thurman, Mark, illus. 2013. 56p. (J). (gr. 4-7). pap. 8.95 *(978-1-77049-512-8(6),* Tundra Bks.) Tundra Bks. CAN. Dist: Penguin Random Hse. LLC.
Eggleton, Jill. The Right to Survive. 2007. (Connectors Ser.). (gr. 2-5). pap. *(978-1-877453-16-8(1))* Global Education Systems Ltd.
Evans, David & Williams, Claudette. Living Things. (Let's Explore Science Ser.). (Illus.). (J). 12.95 *(978-0-590-74945-9(5))* Scholastic, Inc.
Hartman, Eve & Meshbesher, Wendy. What Is the Threat of Invasive Species?, 1 vol. 2012. (Sci-Hi: Science Issues Ser.). (ENG., Illus.). 48p. (gr. 6-10). (J). lib. bdg. 35.99 *(978-1-4109-4465-8(4),* 117648); pap. 9.95 *(978-1-4109-4472-6(7),* 117654) Capstone. (Raintree).
Holland, Gini. Alive & Not Alive, 1 vol. 2007. (I Know Opposites Ser.). (ENG.). 16p. (gr. k-2). pap. 6.30 *(978-0-8368-8298-8(9),* 5a57531a-9989-46bb-988d-172ddc36df83); lib. bdg. 21.67 *(978-0-8368-8293-3(8),* c21adca9-87f4-4870-8dfe-3912dbf78aa2) Stevens, Gareth Publishing LLLP. (Weekly Reader Leveled Readers).
—Alive & Not Alive / Vivo y No Vivo, 1 vol. 2007. (I Know Opposites / Conceptos Contrarios Ser.). (SPA & ENG., Illus.). 16p. (gr. k-2). pap. 6.30 *(978-0-8368-8308-4(X),* c2e80e72-8498-4d2e-a788-c8d25a7094cd); lib. bdg. 21.67 *(978-0-8368-8303-9(9),* 1def279f-722c-4e9a-bc9a-0e458e5edf24) Stevens, Gareth Publishing LLLP. (Weekly Reader Leveled Readers).
Holt, Rinehart and Winston Staff. Holt Science & Technology. 4th ed. 2004. (Holt Science & Technology Ser.). (ENG., Illus.). 880p. (gr. 6-6). 96.80 *(978-0-03-073164-8(X))* Houghton Mifflin Harcourt Publishing Co.
How Life Science Works, 12 vols. 2017. (How Life Science Works). 24p. (ENG.). (gr. 3-3). 151.62 *(978-1-5081-5582-9(8),* b08166eb-4933-41b8-9194-45a8647e955f); (gr. 7-8). pap. 49.50 *(978-1-5081-5583-6(6))* Rosen Publishing Group, Inc., The. (PowerKids Pr.).
Hunter, Rebecca. Living Organisms. 2010. (21st Century Science Ser.). (ENG.). 112p. (YA). (gr. 9-12). 42.80 *(978-1-933834-74-0(9),* 16385) Brown Bear Bks.
Jackson, Tom. Life & Death: Why We Are Here & Where We Go, 1 vol. 2017. (Big Questions Ser.). (ENG.). 200p. (YA). (gr. 9-9). lib. bdg. 49.50 *(978-1-5026-2810-7(4),* 5eb630d5-8788-41f7-bbad-4809b963509b) Cavendish Square Publishing LLC.
Kalman, Bobbie. ¿Esto Es un Ser Vivo? 2008. (SPA.). 24p. (J). pap. *(978-0-7787-8689-4(7))* Crabtree Publishing Co.
—I Am a Living Thing. 2007. (Introducing Living Things Ser.). (ENG., Illus.). 24p. (J). (gr. k-4). lib. bdg. *(978-0-7787-3229-7(0));* (gr. 1-4). pap. *(978-0-7787-3253-2(3))* Crabtree Publishing Co.
—Is It a Living Thing? 2007. (Introducing Living Things Ser.). (ENG., Illus.). 24p. (J). (gr. 1-4). pap. *(978-0-7787-3254-9(1))* Crabtree Publishing Co.
—Living Things Need Water, 1 vol. 2007. (Introducing Living Things Ser.). (ENG., Illus.). 24p. (J). (gr. 1-4). pap. *(978-0-7787-3256-3(8))* Crabtree Publishing Co.
—What Is a Bat, 32 bks. Incl. How Do Animals Move? Walker, Niki. (gr. 2-3). 1999. lib. bdg. *(978-0-86505-981-8(0));* What Are Wetlands? (gr. 3-6). 2003. lib. bdg. 24.94 *(978-0-86505-993-1(4));* What Is a Bear? Crossingham, John. (gr. 2-3). 2000. lib. bdg. *(978-0-86505-983-2(7));* What Is a Cat? Bishop, Amanda. (gr. 2-3). 2002. lib. bdg. *(978-0-86505-990-0(X));* What Is a Dog? Sotzek, Hannelore. (gr. 2-3). 1999. lib. bdg. *(978-0-86505-979-5(9));* What Is a Forest? Smithyman, Kathryn. (gr. 2-3). 2002. lib. bdg. *(978-0-86505-992-4(6));* What Is a Horse? Levigne, Heather. (gr. 2-3). 2000. lib. bdg. *(978-0-86505-984-9(5));* What Is an Arthropod? (gr. 2-3). 2002. lib. bdg. *(978-0-86505-991-7(8));* What Is an Elephant? Crossingham, John. (gr. 2-3). 2001. lib. bdg. *(978-0-86505-989-4(6));* (J). (ENG., Illus.). 32p. *(978-0-86505-996-2(9));* Set pap. *(978-0-86505-974-0(8))* Crabtree Publishing Co.
—What Kind of Living Thing Is It? 2010. (Introducing Living Things Ser.). (ENG.). 24p. (J). (gr. 1-4). pap. *(978-0-7787-3259-4(2));* lib. bdg. *(978-0-7787-3235-8(5))* Crabtree Publishing Co.
Kalman, Bobbie & Sjonger, Rebecca. Animal Life Cycles: Growing & Changing. 2008. (ENG.). 32p. (J). *(978-0-7787-7723-6(5))* Crabtree Publishing Co.
—Metamorphosis: Changing Bodies. 2008. (ENG.). 32p. (J). *(978-0-7787-7714-4(6))* Crabtree Publishing Co.
Kim, Sue. How Does a Seed Grow? A Book with Foldout Pages. 2010. (ENG., Illus.). 14p. (J). (gr. -1-1). bds. 9.99 *(978-1-4169-9435-0(1),* Little Simon) Little Simon.
Kurtz, Kevin. Living Things & Nonliving Things: A Compare & Contrast Book, 1 vol. 2017. (Compare & Contrast Book Ser.). (ENG., Illus.). 32p. (J). (gr. k-3). 11.95 *(978-1-62855-986-6(1))* Arbordale Publishing.
Kurtz, Kevin, et al. Seres Vivos y No Vivos: Un Libro de Comparación y Contraste. 2017. (SPA., Illus.). (J). pap. 11.95 *(978-1-62855-987-3(X))* Arbordale Publishing.
Lindeen, Mary. What Animals Need. 2018. (BeginningtoRead Ser.). (ENG.). 32p. (J). (gr. -1-2). lib. bdg. 22.60 *(978-1-59953-899-0(7));* (gr. k-2). pap. 13.26 *(978-1-68404-146-6(5))* Norwood Hse. Pr.
—What Plants Need. 2018. (BeginningtoRead Ser.). (ENG.). 32p. (J). (gr. -1-2). lib. bdg. 22.60 *(978-1-59953-898-3(9));* (gr. k-2). pap. 13.26 *(978-1-68404-145-9(7))* Norwood Hse. Pr.
Lomberg, Michelle. Animal Cells. 2016. (Illus.). 32p. (J). *(978-1-5105-1184-2(9))* SmartBook Media, Inc.
Marcolla, Bernardo. Me & You & the Universe. Marcolla, Bernardo, illus. 2020. (ENG., Illus.). 36p. (J). (gr. k-3). 16.99 *(978-1-63198-522-5(1),* 85225) Free Spirit Publishing Inc.
Mason, Helen. Weird Nature. 2013. (ENG.). 32p. (J). *(978-0-7787-1127-8(7));* pap. *(978-0-7787-1131-5(5))* Crabtree Publishing Co.
Meachen Rau, Dana. Las Plantas / Plants, 1 vol. 2010. (Los Ciclos de la Naturaleza / Nature's Cycles Ser.). (ENG & SPA.). 32p. (gr. 1-2). lib. bdg. 25.50 *(978-0-7614-4790-0(3),* af024ce9-decb-486a-9611-df4e150437dc) Cavendish Square Publishing LLC.
—Life, 1 vol. 2009. (Earth Matters Ser.). (ENG.). 32p. (gr. 1-2). pap. 9.23 *(978-0-7614-3570-9(0),* 6a17e03b-d31f-43b9-86c3-b4e3001d6f72); lib. bdg. 25.50 *(978-0-7614-3044-5(X),* 503e5fcb-1f54-410a-b810-519e51c64b68, Cavendish Square) Cavendish Square Publishing LLC.
—La Vida / Life, 1 vol. 2010. (Nuestro Planeta Es Importante / Earth Matters Ser.). (ENG & SPA.). 32p. (gr. 1-2). lib. bdg. 25.50 *(978-0-7614-3491-7(7),* 74579308-ab57-49bc-a996-5a57120bddc2) Cavendish Square Publishing LLC.
—La Vida (Life), 1 vol. 2010. (Nuestro Planeta Es Importante (Earth Matters) Ser.). (SPA.). 32p. (gr. 1-2). lib. bdg. 25.50 *(978-0-7614-3467-2(4),* 3cb125dc-5d03-44af-9330-f8842820a88c) Cavendish Square Publishing LLC.
Parker, Steve. Complete Guides Our World. 2012. (ENG.). 144p. (J). *(978-1-4351-4406-4(6))* Barnes & Noble, Inc.
Rice, David L. Lifetimes. Maydak, Michael S., illus. 2015. 32p. pap. 9.00 *(978-1-61003-549-1(6))* Center for the Collaborative Classroom.
Richards, Jon & Simkins, Ed. Life on Earth, 1 vol. 2017. (Infographics: How It Works). (ENG.). 32p. (J). (gr. 4-5). pap. 11.50 *(978-1-5382-1348-3(6),* 92664f88-9f01-4e00-8765-437b10178f37); lib. bdg. 28.27 *(978-1-5382-1350-6(8),* d26dce53-fe9f-4f5b-86a4-b5bec252b40c) Stevens, Gareth Publishing LLLP.
Rissman, Rebecca. Is It Living or Nonliving? 2013. (Is It Living or Nonliving? Ser.). (ENG.). 24p. (J). (gr. k-2). pap., pap., pap. 41.70 *(978-1-4109-5393-3(9),* 19936, Raintree) Capstone.
—Living & Nonliving in the Desert, 1 vol. 2013. (Is It Living or Nonliving? Ser.). (ENG.). 24p. (J). (gr. k-2). pap. 6.95 *(978-1-4109-5387-2(4),* 123327, Raintree) Capstone.

—Living & Nonliving in the Grasslands, 1 vol. 2013. (Is It Living or Nonliving? Ser.). (ENG.). 24p. (J). (gr. k-2). pap. 6.95 *(978-1-4109-5391-9(2),* 123331, Raintree) Capstone.
—Living & Nonliving in the Mountains, 1 vol. 2013. (Is It Living or Nonliving? Ser.). (ENG.). 24p. (J). (gr. k-2). pap. 6.95 *(978-1-4109-5392-6(0),* 123332, Raintree) Capstone.
—Living & Nonliving in the Polar Regions, 1 vol. 2013. (Is It Living or Nonliving? Ser.). (ENG.). 24p. (J). (gr. k-2). pap. 6.95 *(978-1-4109-5390-2(4),* 123330, Raintree) Capstone.
—Living & Nonliving in the Rain Forest, 1 vol. 2013. (Is It Living or Nonliving? Ser.). (ENG.). 24p. (J). (gr. k-2). 25.99 *(978-1-4109-5382-7(3),* 123311); pap. 6.95 *(978-1-4109-5389-6(0),* 123329) Capstone. (Raintree).
Rivera, Andrea. Living & Nonliving. 2017. (Science Concepts Ser.). (ENG., Illus.). 24p. (J). (gr. -1-2). lib. bdg. 31.36 *(978-1-5321-2053-4(2),* 25356, Abdo Zoom-Launch) ABDO Publishing Co.
Rivera, Sheila. I Know It Is Living. 2006. (First Step Nonfiction — Living or Nonliving Ser.). (ENG., Illus.). 8p. (J). (gr. k-2). pap. 5.99 *(978-0-8225-5687-9(1),* f51f5ac8-2937-4f88-a78d-4cc53016dc64) Lerner Publishing Group.
—I Know It Is Nonliving. 2006. (First Step Nonfiction — Living or Nonliving Ser.). (ENG., Illus.). 8p. (J). (gr. k-2). pap. 5.99 *(978-0-8225-5685-5(5),* 75fa5313-814f-4f73-b8a0-1d4911de9df3) Lerner Publishing Group.
—Is It Living or Nonliving? 2006. (First Step Nonfiction — Living or Nonliving Ser.). (ENG., Illus.). 8p. (J). (gr. k-2). pap. 5.99 *(978-0-8225-5686-2(3),* b65d5cbb-711e-4e7d-97e3-45539c10b74b) Lerner Publishing Group.
Ross, Michael. Life Cycles. Moore, Gustav, illus. 2003. 32p. (J). (gr. 2-5). pap. 7.95 *(978-0-7613-1975-7(1),* First Avenue Editions) Lerner Publishing Group.
Royston, Angela. Life Cycles, 1 vol. 2013. (Life Science Stories Ser.). (ENG., Illus.). 32p. (J). (gr. 3-4). pap. 11.50 *(978-1-4339-8712-0(0),* f41a6392-6d96-4caa-9ff7-32ff2dc53009); lib. bdg. 29.27 *(978-1-4339-8711-3(2),* be442267-0c66-4947-9ee1-fa60a37fa646) Stevens, Gareth Publishing LLLP.
—Looking at Life Cycles: How Do Plants & Animals Change?, 1 vol. 2008. (Looking at Science: How Things Change Ser.). (ENG., Illus.). 32p. (gr. k-2). lib. bdg. 26.60 *(978-0-7660-3091-6(1),* 2e10e189-42c6-46cf-a571-bb63a3e72b0e, Enslow Elementary) Enslow Publishing, LLC.
Salas, Laura Purdie. Are You Living? A Song about Living & Nonliving Things, 1 vol. Garofoli, Viviana, illus. 2009. (Science Songs Ser.). (ENG.). 24p. (J). (gr. 1-3). lib. bdg. 27.32 *(978-1-4048-5302-7(2),* 95538, Picture Window Bks.) Capstone.
Schutten, Jan Paul. The Mystery of Life: How Nothing Became Everything. Watkinson, Laura, tr. Rieder, Floor, illus. 2015. (ENG.). 240p. (YA). (gr. 5-9). 15.99 *(978-1-58270-525-5(9),* Simon & Schuster/Paula Wiseman Bks.) Simon & Schuster/Paula Wiseman Bks.
The Science of Life. 2016. (Illus.). 48p. (J). *(978-1-4222-3514-0(9))* Mason Crest.
Science Stories Foss Spanish Structures of Life EA CR05. 2005. (J). *(978-1-59242-589-1(5))* Delta Education, LLC.
Siemens, Jared & Willis, John. Organisms. 2017. (Illus.). 24p. (J). *(978-1-5105-1044-9(3))* SmartBook Media, Inc.
Silverstein, Alvin & Silverstein, Virginia. Metamorphosis: Nature's Magical Transformations. unabr. ed. 2013. (Dover Science for Kids Ser.). (ENG., Illus.). 80p. (J). (gr. 3-8). pap. 5.95 *(978-0-486-42396-8(4),* 423964) Dover Pubns., Inc.
Somervill, Barbara A. Animal Cells & Life Processes, 1 vol. 2010. (Investigating Cells Ser.). (ENG., Illus.). 48p. (J). (gr. 3-6). 35.99 *(978-1-4329-3877-2(0),* 112793, Heinemann) Capstone.
Spilsbury, Louise. What Are Living & Nonliving Things?, 1 vol., 1. 2013. (Let's Find Out! Life Science Ser.). (ENG.). 32p. (gr. 2-3). 27.04 *(978-1-62275-226-3(0),* 9eb616c5-46be-4601-9c27-fe9eccb3204c) Rosen Publishing Group, Inc., The.
—What Is a Life Cycle?, 1 vol., 1. 2013. (Let's Find Out! Life Science Ser.). (ENG.). 32p. (gr. 2-3). 27.04 *(978-1-62275-231-7(7),* aba51756-172c-49f0-9f02-fae4cd0b1718) Rosen Publishing Group, Inc., The.
Stoyles, Pennie & Pentland, Peter. Life on Earth, 1 vol. 2012. (Energy in Action Ser.). (ENG., Illus.). 32p. (gr. 6-6). 31.21 *(978-1-60870-565-8(X),* 483376c2-a125-428b-9295-e1cdfe523740) Cavendish Square Publishing LLC.
Sundance/Newbridge LLC Staff. Animals & Their Babies. 2007. (Early Science Ser.). (gr. k-3). 18.95 *(978-1-4007-6215-6(4));* pap. 6.10 *(978-1-4007-6211-8(1))* Sundance/Newbridge Educational Publishing.
—Is It Alive? 2007. (Early Science Ser.). (gr. k-3). 18.95 *(978-1-4007-6152-4(2));* pap. 6.10 *(978-1-4007-6148-7(4))* Sundance/Newbridge Educational Publishing.
—What Is a Cycle? 2007. (Early Science Ser.). (gr. k-3). 18.95 *(978-1-4007-6242-2(1));* pap. 6.10 *(978-1-4007-6238-5(3))* Sundance/Newbridge Educational Publishing.
Thomson, Ruth. Let's Look at Life Cycles, 8 vols., Set. Incl. Bee's Life Cycle. lib. bdg. 26.27 *(978-1-61532-216-9(7),* 2d3ad0c5-cc6a-489d-a58c-d2188976f212); Chicken's Life Cycle. lib. bdg. 26.27 *(978-1-61532-217-6(5),* 2cb8f167-5490-4ac8-b33f-cfb97596eb0a); Frog's Life Cycle. lib. bdg. 26.27 *(978-1-61532-218-3(3),* e583a576-f674-41e2-8e35-697dddd02579); Sunflower's Life Cycle. lib. bdg. 26.27 *(978-1-61532-219-0(1),* 5cc10af6-f27e-4ba8-9539-c722ce95c5fb); (J). (gr. 2-2). (Let's Look at Life Cycles Ser.). (ENG., Illus.). 24p. 2010. Set lib. bdg. 105.08 *(978-1-4488-0281-4(4),* a862be36-7f8b-4358-b238-710e7865d94d, PowerKids Pr.) Rosen Publishing Group, Inc., The.
Thornhill, Jan. I Am Josephine: (and I Am a Living Thing) Lee, Jacqui, illus. 2019. (ENG.). 32p. (J). (gr. k-2). pap. 9.95 *(978-1-77147-353-8(3))* Owlkids Bks. Inc. CAN. Dist: Publishers Group West (PGW).
Vogt, Gregory. The Biosphere: Realm of Life. 2007. (Earth's Spheres Ser.). (ENG., Illus.). 80p. (gr. 6-8). lib. bdg. 29.27 *(978-0-7613-2840-7(8))* Lerner Publishing Group.
Weber, Rebecca. El Ciclo de Tu Vida/the Cycle of Your Life, 1 vol. 2011. (Salud y Tu Cuerpo/Health & Your Body Ser.). (MUL.). 24p. (J). (gr. -1-2). 27.32 *(978-1-4296-6894-1(6),* 116508) Capstone.
World Book, Inc. Staff. The Circulatory System. 2014. 32p. *(978-0-7166-1841-6(9))* World Bk., Inc.

LIFE, CHRISTIAN
see Christian Life

LIFE, FUTURE
see Future Life

LIFE—ORIGIN
Darwin, Charles. The Riverbank. Negrin, Fabian, illus. 2010. (ENG.). 32p. (J). (gr. 1-3). 17.95 *(978-1-56846-207-3(7),* 22068, Creative Editions) Creative Co., The.
Dupont, Clemence. A Brief History of Life on Earth. 2019. (ENG., Illus.). 76p. (J). (gr. 1-4). 24.95 *(978-3-7913-7373-7(0))* Prestel Verlag GmbH & Co KG. DEU. Dist: Penguin Random Hse. LLC.
Morgan, Jennifer. From Lava to Life: The Universe Tells Our Earth Story. Andersen, Dana Lynne, illus. 48p. (J). 2012. (gr. 2-5). 16.95 *(978-1-58469-043-6(7))* 2003. (gr. 3-8). pap. 9.99 *(978-1-58469-042-9(9))* Sourcebooks, Inc. (Dawn Pubns.).
Whitt, Stephen. The Turtle & the Universe. Hernandez, Stephanie, illus. 2008. 86p. (J). (gr. 3-7). pap. 14.99 *(978-1-59102-626-6(1))* Prometheus Bks., Pubs.

LIFE, SPIRITUAL
see Spiritual Life

LIFE AFTER DEATH
see Future Life

LIFE ON OTHER PLANETS
see also Interstellar Communication
Ames, Lee J. & Estrada, Ric. Draw 50 Aliens: The Step-By-Step Way to Draw UFOs, Galaxy Ghouls, Milky Way Marauders, & Other Extraterrestrial Creatures. 2013. (Draw 50 Ser.). (ENG., Illus.). 64p. pap. 9.99 *(978-0-8230-8616-0(X),* Watson-Guptill) Potter/Ten Speed/Harmony/Rodale.
Berkowitz, Jacob. Out of This World: The Amazing Search for an Alien Earth. 2009. (Illus.). 40p. (J). (gr. 3-7). 16.95 *(978-1-55453-197-4(7))* Kids Can Pr., Ltd. CAN. Dist: Hachette Bk. Group.
Bishop, Nic. Is There Anyone Out There?: Band 10/White (Collins Big Cat) Bishop, Nic, photos by. 2005. (Collins Big Cat Ser.). (ENG., Illus.). 352p. (J). (gr. 2-3). pap. 10.99 *(978-0-00-718635-8(5))* HarperCollins Pubs. Ltd. GBR. Dist: Independent Pubs. Group.
Bortz, Fred. Astrobiology. 2008. pap. 52.95 *(978-0-8225-9326-3(2))* 2007. (ENG., Illus.). 48p. (gr. 4-8). lib. bdg. 27.93 *(978-0-8225-6771-4(7),* Lerner Pubns.) Lerner Publishing Group.
Cohen, Sheldon & Drawing Staff. How to Draw & Save Your Planet from Alien Invasion! 2011. (Dover How to Draw Ser.). (ENG.). 72p. (J). (gr. 3-5). pap. 4.99 *(978-0-486-47833-3(5),* 478335) Dover Pubns., Inc.
Culp, Jennifer. How We Find Other Earths: Technology & Strategies to Detect Planets Similar to Ours, 1 vol., 1. 2015. (Search for Other Earths Ser.). (ENG., Illus.). 112p. (J). (gr. 7-7). 38.80 *(978-1-4994-6292-0(1),* 420a1f57-be56-415d-81f2-9f198fab51ac, Rosen Young Adult) Rosen Publishing Group, Inc., The.
Dartnell, Lewis. Astrobiology: Exploring Life in the Universe, 1 vol. 2011. (Contemporary Issues Ser.). (ENG., Illus.). 166p. (YA). (gr. 9-9). lib. bdg. 42.47 *(978-1-4488-1862-4(1),* 653e8d65-11c4-410c-a9b3-f1bd73a572f3) Rosen Publishing Group, Inc., The.
Donald, Rhonda Lucas. Life on Other Planets. 2004. (Watts Library). (ENG.). 64p. (J). (gr. 5-7). pap. 8.95 *(978-0-531-16374-0(1),* Watts, Franklin) Scholastic Library Publishing.
Firestone, Mary. SETI Scientist. 2005. (Weird Careers in Science Ser.). (ENG., Illus.). 88p. (gr. 5-8). lib. bdg. 25.00 *(978-0-7910-8701-5(8),* P114396, Facts On File) Infobase Holdings, Inc.
Gale, Ryan. The Search for Alien Life. 2019. (Aliens Ser.). (ENG., Illus.). 32p. (J). (gr. 4-6). 30.65 *(978-1-5435-7108-0(5),* 140400) Capstone.
Gonzalez, David J. There Are No Space Aliens! 12 Biblical Points Disproving Space Aliens. l.t. ed. 2003. 48p. 9.95 *(978-0-9741561-0-1(8))* Gonzalez, David J. Ministries.
Hand, Carol. Is There Life Out There? The Likelihood of Alien Life & What It Would Look Like, 1 vol., 1. 2015. (Search for Other Earths Ser.). (ENG., Illus.). 112p. (J). (gr. 7-7). 38.80 *(978-1-4994-6294-4(8),* accb05cb-b4fc-43b6-9fd4-dff3ddfb8939, Rosen Young Adult) Rosen Publishing Group, Inc., The.
Hantula, Richard & Asimov, Isaac. Is There Life in Outer Space?, 1 vol. 2004. (Isaac Asimov's 21st Century Library of the Universe: Fact & Fantasy Ser.). (ENG., Illus.). 32p. (gr. 3-5). lib. bdg. 28.67 *(978-0-8368-3950-0(1),* 1853261a-58ea-4fc4-aa2b-0f7b2f7b76f2) Stevens, Gareth Publishing LLLP.
Herbst, Judith. Aliens. 2004. (Unexplained Ser.). (Illus.). 48p. (J). pap. 8.95 *(978-0-8225-2402-1(3),* Lerner Pubns.); (ENG., (gr. 5-12). lib. bdg. 26.60 *(978-0-8225-0960-8(1))* Lerner Publishing Group.
Jackson, Tom. Are We Alone in the Universe? Theories about Intelligent Life on Other Planets, 1 vol. 2018. (Beyond the Theory: Science of the Future Ser.). (ENG.). 48p. (gr. 5-6). lib. bdg. 33.60 *(978-1-5382-2673-5(1),* 299ad556-a2a5-4f44-b065-d2508950da44) Stevens, Gareth Publishing LLLP.
Jedicke, Peter. Seti: The Search for Alien Intelligence. 2003. (Hot Science Ser.). (Illus.). 48p. (J). (gr. 6). lib. bdg. 28.50 *(978-1-58340-369-3(8))* Black Rabbit Bks.
Kallen, Stuart K. The Search for Extraterrestrial Life. 2011. (Extraterrestrial Life Ser.). (Illus.). 80p. (YA). (gr. 7-12). lib. bdg. 43.93 *(978-1-60152-171-2(5))* ReferencePoint Pr., Inc.
Kelly, Dave & Coddington, Andrew. Aliens, UFOs, & Unexplained Encounters, 1 vol. 2017. (Paranormal Investigations Ser.). (ENG.). 64p. (gr. 6-8). 35.93 *(978-1-5026-2845-9(7),* 19ee3e24-8ead-49da-b2aa-b93608779b37) Cavendish Square Publishing LLC.
Kenney, Karen Latchana. Breakthroughs in the Search for Extraterrestrial Life. 2019. (Space Exploration (Alternator Books (r)) Ser.). (ENG., Illus.). 32p. (J). (gr. 3-6). 29.32 *(978-1-5415-3872-6(2),* be10ae37-ef0f-4396-8317-c713fbd7bc41, Lerner Pubns.) Lerner Publishing Group.
Kent, Lindsay. DK Readers L4: Star Wars: Ultimate Duels: Find Out about the Deadliest Battles! 2011. (DK Readers Level 4 Ser.). (ENG.). 48p. (J). (gr. 3-7). 4.99 *(978-0-7566-8263-7(0),* DK Children) Dorling Kindersley Publishing, Inc.
Kocienda, Genevieve. Aliens: Is Anybody Out There? Low Intermediate Book with Online Access, 1 vol. 2014. (ENG., Illus.). 24p. (J). pap., E-Book, E-Book 9.50 *(978-1-107-66000-7(9))* Cambridge Univ. Pr.
Kortemeier, Todd. Searching for Alien Life. 2017. (Science Frontiers Ser.). (ENG., Illus.). 32p. (J). (gr. 3-6). 32.80 *(978-1-63235-380-1(6),* 11874, 12-Story Library) Bookstaves, LLC.
Kruesi, Liz. Finding Earthlike Planets. 2018. (Illus.). 48p. (J). pap. *(978-1-4896-9823-0(X),* AV2 by Weigl) Weigl Pubs., Inc.
La Bella, Laura. The Goldilocks Zone: Conditions Necessary for Extraterrestrial Life, 1 vol., 1. 2015. (Search for Other Earths Ser.). (ENG., Illus.). 112p. (J). (gr. 7-7). 38.80 *(978-1-4994-6298-2(0),* c9973932-942a-47f7-bbe6-8aede45759f5, Rosen Young Adult) Rosen Publishing Group, Inc., The.
Langley, Andrew. Planet Hunting: Racking up Data & Looking for Life. 2019. (Future Space Ser.). (ENG., Illus.). 32p. (J). (gr. 3-9). pap. 7.95 *(978-1-5435-7516-3(1),* 141047); lib. bdg. 28.65 *(978-1-5435-7270-4(7),* 140601) Capstone.
McEvoy, Paul. The Alien Files. 2003. (Real Deal Ser.). (Illus.). 32p. (J). pap. *(978-0-7608-6691-7(0))* Sundance/Newbridge Educational Publishing.
Meachen Rau, Dana. Aliens, 1 vol. 2011. (For Real? Ser.). (ENG.). 24p. (gr. 3-3). 25.50 *(978-0-7614-4861-7(6),* a60bbfc4-5d94-4026-adbc-690229028b78) Cavendish Square Publishing LLC.
Murray, Laura K. Aliens. 2017. (Are They Real? Ser.). (ENG., Illus.). 24p. (J). (gr. 1-4). pap. 8.99 *(978-1-62832-367-2(1),* 20051, Creative Paperbacks); *(978-1-60818-759-1(4),* 20053, Creative Education) Creative Co., The.
Netzley, Patricia D. Alien Encounters. 2011. (Extraterrestrial Life Ser.). 80p. (YA). (gr. 7-12). lib. bdg. 43.93 *(978-1-60152-169-9(3))* ReferencePoint Pr., Inc.
O'Brien, Cynthia. Searching for Extraterrestrials. 2019. (Mission: Space Science Ser.). (Illus.). 48p. (J). (gr. 5-5). *(978-0-7787-5394-0(8));* pap. *(978-0-7787-5405-3(7))* Crabtree Publishing Co.
O'Brien, Patrick. You Are the First Kid on Mars. O'Brien, Patrick, illus. 2009. (Illus.). 32p. (J). (gr. k-3). 17.99 *(978-0-399-24634-0(7),* G.P. Putnam's Sons Books for Young Readers) Penguin Young Readers Group.
Orme, Helen. Life in Space. Mongiovi, Jorge, illus. 2008. (Trailblazers Ser.). (ENG.). 36p. pap. *(978-1-84167-690-6(X))* Ransom Publishing Ltd.
Pipe, Jim. Aliens, 1 vol. 2013. (Twilight Realm Ser.). (ENG., Illus.). 32p. (J). (gr. 4-5). 29.27 *(978-1-4339-8747-2(3),* d60aec07-ad3f-48ac-ad00-ba20bb9d9143); pap. 11.50 *(978-1-4339-8748-9(1),* 430bf51e-7e87-4a1d-a68d-9c7526c95396) Stevens, Gareth Publishing LLLP. (Gareth Stevens Learning Library).
Porterfield, Jason. Aliens at Home: Studying Extreme Environment Species to Learn about Extraterrestrial Life, 1 vol., 1. 2015. (Search for Other Earths Ser.). (ENG.). 112p. (J). (gr. 7-7). 38.80 *(978-1-4994-6297-5(2),* 2e78f9a2-256d-4451-b304-9195350925fc, Rosen Young Adult) Rosen Publishing Group, Inc., The.
Portman, Michael. Is There Life on Mars?, 1 vol. 2013. (Space Mysteries Ser.). (ENG., Illus.). 32p. (J). (gr. 2-3). 29.27 *(978-1-4339-8272-9(2),* e5c1ea31-d67a-4dd0-a633-ad634732257e); pap. 11.50 *(978-1-4339-8273-6(0),* a4e69fe5-ed91-4867-84dc-426bca60476b) Stevens, Gareth Publishing LLLP. (Gareth Stevens Learning Library).
Roleff, Tamara L., ed. Alien Abductions. 2003. (Illus.). 160p. (J). lib. bdg. 32.45 *(978-0-7377-1589-7(8),* Greenhaven Pr., Inc.) Cengage Gale.
Scott, Elaine. Mars & the Search for Life. 2008. (ENG., Illus.). 64p. (J). (gr. 5-7). 17.00 *(978-0-618-76695-6(2),* 100538, Clarion Bks.) HarperCollins Pubs.
Storm, Marysa. Aliens. 2020. (Little Bit Spooky Ser.). (ENG.). 24p. (J). (gr. k-3). lib. bdg. *(978-1-62310-174-9(3),* 14442, Bolt Jr.) Black Rabbit Bks.
Summers, Portia & Meachen Rau, Dana. Are Aliens Real?, 1 vol. 2016. (I Want to Know Ser.). (ENG.). 32p. (gr. 3-3). pap. 11.52 *(978-0-7660-8228-1(8),* c871c5d7-33e6-41ac-8b25-ac74293265bd) Enslow Publishing, LLC.
Surviving Alien Contact & Warfare. 2016. (Surviving Alien Contact & Warfare Ser.). 00048p. (J). (gr. 10-10). pap. 35.25 *(978-1-4994-6565-5(3),* Rosen Young Adult) Rosen Publishing Group, Inc., The.
Thomas, Rachael L. Ancient Aliens: Did Historic Contact Happen? 2018. (Science Fact or Science Fiction? Ser.). (ENG., Illus.). 32p. (J). (gr. 3-6). lib. bdg. 32.79 *(978-1-5321-1537-0(7),* 28928, Checkerboard Library) ABDO Publishing Co.
Turner, Pamela S. Life on Earth - & Beyond: An Astrobiologist's Quest. 2008. (Illus.). 112p. (J). (gr. 4-7). 19.95 *(978-1-58089-133-2(0))* Charlesbridge Publishing, Inc.

LIFE ON OTHER PLANETS—FICTION
Agee, Jon. Life on Mars. 2017. (ENG., Illus.). 32p. (J). (gr. -1-3). 18.99 *(978-0-399-53852-0(6),* Dial Bks) Penguin Young Readers Group.
Appleton, Victor. Tom Swift & the Visitor from Planet X. 2006. pap. *(978-1-4068-0728-8(1))* Echo Library.
Arnett, Mindee. Avalon. 2014. (Avalon Ser.: 1). (ENG.). 432p. (YA). (gr. 8). 17.99 *(978-0-06-223559-6(1),* Balzer & Bray) HarperCollins Pubs.
—Polaris. 2015. (Avalon Ser.: 2). (ENG.). 432p. (YA). (gr. 8). 17.99 *(978-0-06-223562-6(1),* Balzer & Bray) HarperCollins Pubs.
Artifact Group, The. The Trash Planet. 2009. (Backyardigans Ser.: 12). (ENG.). 24p. (J). pap. 3.99 *(978-1-4169-6868-9(7),* Simon Spotlight/Nickelodeon) Simon Spotlight/Nickelodeon.
Barrett, Judith. Cloudy with a Chance of Meatballs 3: Planet of the Pies. Mones, Isidre, illus. 2013. (ENG.). 32p. (J). (gr. -1-3). 18.99 *(978-1-4424-9027-7(6),* Atheneum Bks. for Young Readers) Simon & Schuster Children's Publishing.
Blackman, Haden. Star Wars: Clone Wars Adventures. Brothers, Fillbach, illus. 2011. (Star Wars Digests Ser.). (ENG.). 96p. (J). (gr. 3-8). 34.21 *(978-1-59961-905-7(9),* 13753, Graphic Novels) Spotlight.
Blackman, Haden & Caldwell, Ben. Star Wars: Clone Wars Adventures. 2011. (Star Wars Digests Ser.). (ENG., Illus.). 96p. (J). (gr. 3-8). 34.21 *(978-1-59961-904-0(0),* 13752, Graphic Novels) Spotlight.
Blackman, Haden & The Fillbach Brothers. Clone Wars Adventures. Brothers, Fillbach, illus. 2011. (Star Wars Digests Ser.). (ENG.). 96p. (J). (gr. 3-8). 34.21 *(978-1-59961-906-4(7),* 13754, Graphic Novels) Spotlight.
Brackett, Leigh & Coppel, Jr., Alfred. Planet Stories - Summer 1949. 2008. 128p. (YA). pap. 14.95 *(978-1-59798-181-1(8))* Adventure Hse.
Bradley, James. The Silent Invasion: the Change Trilogy 1. 2017. (Change Trilogy Ser.: 1). (ENG.). 300p. (YA). (gr. 7). 7.95 *(978-1-74354-989-6(X),* Pan) Pan Macmillan Australia Pty, Ltd. AUS. Dist: Independent Pubs. Group.
Brezenoff, Steve. A Hole in the Dome. Calle Velez, Juan, illus. 2019. (Michael Dahl Presents: Screams in Space 4D Ser.). (ENG.). 112p. (J). (gr. 3-5). lib. bdg. 27.32 *(978-1-4965-7903-4(8),* 139613, Stone Arch Bks.) Capstone.
Caine, Rachel, pseud & Aguirre, Ann. Honor Bound. (Honors Ser.: 2). (ENG.). (YA). (gr. 8). 2020. 496p. pap. 12.99 *(978-0-06-257103-8(6))* 2019. (Illus.). 480p. 17.99 *(978-0-06-257102-1(8))* HarperCollins Pubs. (Tegen, Katherine Bks).
Calero, Dennis. You're Not the Captain of Me! 2011. (ENG.). 272p. (J). (gr. 4-7). pap. 9.95 *(978-1-59687-375-9(2))* IBks., Inc.
Capetta, Amy Rose. Entangled. 2013. (ENG.). 336p. (YA). (gr. 9). 17.99 *(978-0-544-08744-6(5),* 1538242, Clarion Bks.) HarperCollins Pubs.
Carbone, Courtney. Star Wars: the Phantom Menace (Star Wars) Martinez, Heather, illus. 2015. (Little Golden Book Ser.). (ENG.). 24p. (J). (-k). 4.99 *(978-0-7364-3542-0(5),* Golden Bks.) Random Hse. Children's Bks.
Cerasi, Chris. Star Wars Adventures: Chewbacca & the Slavers of the Shadowlands. Meyer, Jennifer L., illus. 2013. (Star Wars Digests Ser.). (ENG.). 80p. (J). (gr. 3-8). lib. bdg. 34.21 *(978-1-61479-057-0(4),* 13760, Graphic Novels) Spotlight.
Cerberus Jones. The Ancient Starship. 2017. (ENG.). 160p. (J). pap. 5.99 *(978-1-61067-501-7(0))* Kane Miller.
—The Midnight Mercenary: The Gateway. 2017. (ENG., Illus.). 160p. (J). pap. 5.99 *(978-1-61067-500-0(2))* Kane Miller.
Chatten, Vicky. Bonding. 2004. 173p. pap. 24.95 *(978-1-4137-5348-6(5))* America Star Bks.
Coe, Catherine. Collins Big Cat Phonics for Letters & Sounds - Mog & Mim: Band 01B/Pink B, Bd. 1B. Brown, Judy, illus. 2018. (Collins Big Cat Phonics Ser.). (ENG.). 16p. (J). (gr. -1-k). pap. 6.99 *(978-0-00-825139-0(8))* HarperCollins Pubs. Ltd. GBR. Dist: Independent Pubs. Group.
Cole, Olivia A. An Anatomy of Beasts. 2019. (ENG.). 432p. (YA). (gr. 8). 17.99 *(978-0-06-264424-4(6),* Tegen, Katherine Bks) HarperCollins Pubs.
—A Conspiracy of Stars. (ENG.). (YA). (gr. 8). 2019. 448p. pap. 9.99 *(978-0-06-264422-0(X))* 2018. 432p. 17.99 *(978-0-06-264421-3(1))* HarperCollins Pubs. (Tegen, Katherine Bks).
Collins, A. L. Redworld: Year One. Tikulin, Tomislav, illus. 2018. (Redworld Ser.). (ENG.). 320p. (J). (gr. 3-8). pap., pap., pap. 8.95 *(978-1-62370-986-0(5),* 137317, Capstone Young Readers) Capstone.
Delhohne, Jean-Philippe. Visit to Another Planet. 2004. (Illus.). 31p. (J). (gr. k-4). reprint ed. *(978-0-7567-7768-5(2))* DIANE Publishing Co.
Denofsky, Howard. Sillyishis, Beanie & the Hobblebobs. 2012. 32p. 24.95 *(978-1-4626-6211-1(0))* America Star Bks.
Disney Book Group Staff & Michaels, Kay. Star Wars Rebels. 2014. (Star Wars: World of Reading Ser.). (J). lib. bdg. 13.55 *(978-0-606-35282-6(1))* Turtleback.
Dorling Kindersley Publishing Staff. Attack of the Clones. 2013. (LEGO Star Wars DK Reader Ser.). lib. bdg. 13.55 *(978-0-606-32111-2(X))* Turtleback.
Duffett-Smith, James. A Curious Robot on Mars! Straker, Bethany, illus. 2013. (ENG.). 32p. (J). (gr. -1-k). 14.95 *(978-1-62087-994-8(8),* 620994, Sky Pony Pr.) Skyhorse Publishing Co., Inc.
Echeverria-Bis, Olivia. The EGGbees. Echeverria Gyorkos, Charmaine, illus. 2009. (ENG & SPA.). 32p. (J). (gr. -1-3). 16.95 *(978-1-55885-529-8(7),* Piñata Books) Arte Publico Pr.
Edge, Christopher. The Jamie Drake Equation. (ENG.). (J). (gr. 4-7). 2019. 208p. 6.99 *(978-1-5247-1364-5(3),* Yearling) 2018. 192p. 16.99 *(978-1-5247-1361-4(9),* Delacorte Bks. for Young Readers) Random Hse. Children's Bks.
Elizabeth, Lauren. Far from Forgotten. 2013. 112p. pap. 10.00 *(978-1-4575-2316-8(7))* Dog Ear Publishing, LLC.
—Looks of an Angel. 2012. 148p. (-18). pap. 12.00 *(978-1-4575-1445-6(1))* Dog Ear Publishing, LLC.
Emerson, Kevin. The Shores Beyond Time. (Chronicle of the Dark Star Ser.: 3). (ENG.). 512p. (J). (gr. 3-7). 2020. pap. 8.99 *(978-0-06-230678-4(2))* 2019. 16.99 *(978-0-06-230677-7(4))* HarperCollins Pubs. (Walden Pond Pr.).
Fentiman, David. New Adventures. 2015. (Illus.). 47p. (J). *(978-1-4806-9626-6(9))* Dorling Kindersley Publishing, Inc.
Fillbach. Clone Wars Adventures, 7. Fillbach, illus. 2013. (Star Wars Digests Ser.). (ENG., Illus.). 80p. (J). (gr. 3-8). lib. bdg. 34.21 *(978-1-61479-058-7(2),* 13761, Graphic Novels) Spotlight.
—Star Wars: Clone Wars Adventures. Fillbach, illus. 2013. (Star Wars Digests Ser.). (ENG., Illus.). 80p. (J). (gr. 3-8). lib. bdg. 34.21 *(978-1-61479-059-4(0),* 13762, Graphic Novels) Spotlight.
Fillbach, Brothers & Blackman, Haden. Clone Wars Adventures. 2011. (Star Wars Digests Ser.). (ENG., Illus.). 96p. (J). (gr. 3-8). 34.21 *(978-1-59961-907-1(5),* 13755, Graphic Novels) Spotlight.
Fillbach, Brothers, et al. Clone Wars Adventures. 2011. (Star Wars Digests Ser.). (ENG., Illus.). 88p. (J). (gr. 3-8). 34.21 *(978-1-59961-909-5(1),* 13757, Graphic Novels) Spotlight.
Gentry, Stephen. Journey to the Stars & Back. 2005. 52p. (J). pap. 16.49 *(978-1-4116-5985-8(6))* Lulu Pr., Inc.

J
K
L

Gillen, Kieron. Shadows & Secrets: Volume 1. Larroca, Salvador & Delgado, Edgar, illus. 2016. (Star Wars: Darth Vader Set 2 Ser.). (ENG.). 24p. (J). (gr. 6-12). lib. bdg. 31.36 *(978-1-61479-547-6(9))*, 24381, Graphic Novels) Spotlight.

—Shadows & Secrets: Volume 2. Larroca, Salvador & Delgado, Edgar, illus. 2016. (Star Wars: Darth Vader Set 2 Ser.). (ENG.). 24p. (J). (gr. 6-12). lib. bdg. 31.36 *(978-1-61479-548-3(7))*, 24382, Graphic Novels) Spotlight.

—Shadows & Secrets: Volume 3. Larroca, Salvador & Delgado, Edgar, illus. 2016. (Star Wars: Darth Vader Set 2 Ser.). (ENG.). 24p. (J). (gr. 6-12). lib. bdg. 31.36 *(978-1-61479-549-0(5))*, 24383, Graphic Novels) Spotlight.

—Shadows & Secrets: Volume 4. Larroca, Salvador & Delgado, Edgar, illus. 2016. (Star Wars: Darth Vader Set 2 Ser.). (ENG.). 24p. (J). (gr. 6-12). lib. bdg. 31.36 *(978-1-61479-550-6(9))*, 24384, Graphic Novels) Spotlight.

—Shadows & Secrets: Volume 5. Larroca, Salvador & Delgado, Edgar, illus. 2016. (Star Wars: Darth Vader Set 2 Ser.). (ENG.). 24p. (J). (gr. 6-12). lib. bdg. 31.36 *(978-1-61479-551-3(7))*, 24385, Graphic Novels) Spotlight.

—Shadows & Secrets: Volume 6. Larroca, Salvador & Delgado, Edgar, illus. 2016. (Star Wars: Darth Vader Set 2 Ser.). (ENG.). 24p. (J). (gr. 6-12). lib. bdg. 31.36 *(978-1-61479-552-0(5))*, 24386, Graphic Novels) Spotlight.

Golden Books. Star Wars: Attack of the Clones (Star Wars) Beavers, Ethen, illus. 2015. (Little Golden Book Ser.). (ENG.). 24p. (J). (-k). 4.99 *(978-0-7364-3546-8(8))*, Golden Bks.) Random Hse. Children's Bks.

—Star Wars: the Force Awakens (Star Wars) Meurer, Caleb, illus. 2016. (Little Golden Book Ser.). (ENG.). 24p. (J). (-k). 5.99 *(978-0-7364-3491-1(7))*, Golden Bks.) Random Hse. Children's Bks.

Golden Books, illus. The Star Wars Little Golden Book Library (Star Wars) The Phantom Menace; Attack of the Clones; Revenge of the Sith; a New Hope; the Empire Strikes Back; Return of the Jedi, 6 vols. 2015. (Little Golden Book Ser.). (ENG.). 144p. (J). (-k). 29.94 *(978-0-7364-3470-6(4))*, Golden Bks.) Random Hse. Children's Bks.

Grahame, Howard. The Wishing Book 2 - Return to Mars. 2009. 102p. (J). pap. *(978-1-905809-80-6(8))* Pneuma Springs Publishing.

Grange, Emma. Lego Star Wars: The Return of the Jedi. 2014. (LEGO Star Wars DK Reader Ser.). lib. bdg. 13.55 *(978-0-606-35735-7(1))* Turtleback.

Hatke, Ben. Zita the Spacegirl. 2011. (Zita the Spacegirl Ser.: 1). (ENG., Illus.). 192p. (J). (gr. 3-7). 21.99 *(978-1-59643-695-4(6))*, 900073109); pap. 14.99 *(978-1-59643-446-2(5))*, 900054803) Roaring Brook Pr. (First Second Bks.).

—Zita the Spacegirl. 2011. (Zita the Spacegirl Ser.: 1). (J). lib. bdg. 24.50 *(978-0-606-21623-4(5))* Turtleback.

Hayes, Vicki C. Home Planet, 1 vol. 2015. (Red Rhino Ser.). (ENG.). 72p. (J). (gr. 4-7). mass mkt. 9.95 *(978-1-62250-966-9(8))* Saddleback Educational Publishing, Inc.

Heddle, Jennifer & Roux, Stéphane. Star Wars Rebels: Sabine's Art Attack, 1 vol. 2015. (World of Reading Level 1 Ser.). (ENG., Illus.). 32p. (J). (gr. -1-3). lib. bdg. 31.36 *(978-1-61479-365-6(4))*, 18200) Spotlight.

Hirschfeld, Robert. Martians Are People, Too. 2011. (Navigators Ser.). (J). pap. *(978-1-61672-969-1(4))* Benchmark Education Co.

Howard, Grahame. The Wishing Book 3 - Extermination. 2010. 170p. (J). pap. *(978-1-905809-90-5(5))* Pneuma Springs Publishing.

Jeapes, Ben. His Majesty's Starship. 2013. 348p. pap. *(978-1-909016-18-7(7))* Monico.

Johnston, E. K. Star Wars: Ahsoka. 2017. (ENG.). 384p. (J). (gr. 7-12). pap. 10.99 *(978-1-4847-8231-6(3))*, Disney Lucasfilm Press) Disney Publishing Worldwide.

Jones, Cerberus. The Lost Home World. 2017. (Illus.). 136p. (J). *(978-1-61067-694-6(7))* Kane Miller.

—The Lost Home World: The Gateway. 2018. (ENG., Illus.). 144p. (J). pap. 5.99 *(978-1-61067-660-1(2))* Kane Miller.

—The Midnight Mercenary. 2016. (Illus.). 146p. (J). *(978-1-61067-573-4(8))* Kane Miller.

Kaufman, Amie & Spooner, Meagan. Unearthed. 2018. (Unearthed Ser.: 1). (ENG.). 352p. (YA). (gr. 9-17). pap. 9.99 *(978-1-4847-9983-3(6))* Hyperion Bks. for Children.

Kogge, Michael. Battle to the End, 1 vol. 2015. (Star Wars Rebels Ser.). (ENG., Illus.). 144p. (J). (gr. 2-6). lib. bdg. 31.36 *(978-1-61479-440-0(5))*, 19509, Chapter Bks.) Spotlight.

—Ezra's Duel with Danger, 3. 2015. (Star Wars Rebels: Chapter Bks.). (ENG., Illus.). 128p. (J). (gr. 2-4). 18.69 *(978-1-4844-5079-6(5))* Disney Pr.

—Rise of the Rebels, 1 vol. 2015. (Star Wars Rebels Ser.). (ENG., Illus.). 128p. (J). (gr. 2-6). lib. bdg. 31.36 *(978-1-61479-443-1(X))*, 19512, Chapter Bks.) Spotlight.

—Rise of the Rebels. 2014. (Star Wars Rebels Chapter Bks.). (J). lib. bdg. 16.00 *(978-0-606-35281-9(3))* Turtleback.

Krosoczka, Jarrett J. The Principal Strikes Back. 2018. (Illus.). 176p. (J). *(978-1-76066-157-1(0))* Scholastic, Inc.

Krosoczka, Jarrett J., illus. The Force Oversleeps. 2017. 172p. (J). *(978-1-338-20871-9(3))* Scholastic, Inc.

Landers, Ace. Anakin to the Rescue. 2012. (LEGO Star Wars 8X8 Ser.). lib. bdg. 13.55 *(978-0-606-26774-8(3))* Turtleback.

Lavoie, Rejean. Des Legumes Pour Frank Einstein. Begin, Jean-Guy, illus. 2004. (Des 9 Ans. Ser.: Vol. 44). (FRE.). 120p. (J). 8.95 *(978-2-89599-006-2(9))* Editions de la Paix CAN. Dist: World of Reading, Ltd.

Levine, Caroline Anne. Jay Grows an Alien. 2007. 73p. (J). (gr. 5-13). pap. 13.95 *(978-1-931282-29-1(3))* Autism Asperger Publishing Co.

Locke, Thomas, pseud. Renegades. 2017. (Recruits Ser.). (ENG.). 288p. pap. 16.00 *(978-0-8007-2790-1(8))* Revell.

Lucasfilm Press, Lucasfilm. 5-Minute Star Wars Stories Strike Back. 2017. (Illus.). 20p. (J). (gr. 1-3). 12.99 *(978-1-368-00351-3(6))*, Disney Lucasfilm Press) Disney Publishing Worldwide.

Manchee, William. Tarizon the Liberator: Tarizon Trilogy Vol 1. 2008. 340p. (YA). (gr. 7-18). lib. bdg. 24.00 *(978-1-929976-48-5(8))*, TOP) Top Pubns., Ltd.

McCliggott, Timothy M. A Report on Quibnoida. McCliggott, Timothy M., illus. 2007. (Illus.). 52p. (YA). pap. 17.00 *(978-0-8059-7289-4(7))* Dorrance Publishing Co., Inc.

McDougall, Sophia. Mars Evacuees. (ENG.). (J). (gr. 3-7). 2016. 432p. pap. 7.99 *(978-0-06-229400-5(8))* 2015. 416p. 16.99 *(978-0-06-229399-2(0))* HarperCollins Pubs. (HarperCollins).

Metzger, Joanna. The Space Program. Elizalde, Marcelo, illus. 2006. 142p. (J). *(978-1-59336-695-7(7))* Mondo Publishing.

Mordenga, Michael P. Spirit Box. 2007. 280p. per. 17.95 *(978-0-595-43785-6(0))* iUniverse, Inc.

My Teacher Glows in the Dark. 2014. (My Teacher Bks.: 3). (ENG., Illus.). 192p. (J). (gr. 3-7). 17.99 *(978-1-4814-0432-7(6))*, Simon & Schuster/Paula Wiseman Bks.) Simon & Schuster/Paula Wiseman Bks.

North, Phoebe. Starbreak. 2014. (Starglass Sequence Ser.). (ENG., Illus.). 432p. (YA). (gr. 7). 17.99 *(978-1-4424-5956-4(5))*, Simon & Schuster Bks. For Young Readers) Simon & Schuster Bks. For Young Readers.

O'Malley, Kevin & O'Brien, Patrick. Captain Raptor & the Perilous Planet. O'Brien, Patrick, illus. 2018. (Captain Raptor Ser.: 3). (Illus.). 32p. (J). (gr. -1-3). lib. bdg. 17.99 *(978-1-58089-809-6(2))* Charlesbridge Publishing, Inc.

Patterson, James. Not So Normal Norbert. Aly, Hatem, illus. 2018. (ENG.). 368p. (J). (gr. 3-9). 13.99 *(978-0-316-46541-0(0))*, Jimmy Patterson) Little Brown & Co.

Pavlou, Stel. Daniel Coldstar #2: the Betrayer. 2019. (Daniel Coldstar Ser.: 2). (ENG.). 304p. (J). (gr. 3-7). 16.99 *(978-0-06-212609-2(1))*, HarperCollins) HarperCollins Pubs.

Peterson, Alyson. The Exiled Prince. 2017. (ENG.). (YA). (gr. 8-12). pap. 17.99 *(978-1-4621-2035-2(0))*, Sweetwater Bks.) Cedar Fort, Inc./CFI Distribution.

Pike, Christopher, pseud. Aliens in the Sky. 2014. (Spooksville Ser.: 4). (ENG., Illus.). 128p. (J). (gr. 3-7). pap. 7.99 *(978-1-4814-1058-8(X))*, Aladdin) Simon & Schuster Children's Publishing.

Piper, Henry Beam. Little Fuzzy. l.t. ed. 2007. (ENG.). 188p. per. 21.99 *(978-1-4346-2952-4(X))* Creative Media Partners, LLC.

Pittman, Eddie. Red's Planet. 2016. (Red's Planet Ser.: 1). (J). lib. bdg. 20.80 *(978-0-606-38203-8(8))* Turtleback.

Pringle, Eric. Big George & the Winter King. Paine, Colin, illus. 2004. 208p. (J). pap. 12.99 *(978-0-7475-6341-9(1))* Bloomsbury Publishing Plc GBR. Dist: Independent Pubs. Group.

Reintgen, Scott. Nyxia Unleashed. (Nyxia Triad Ser.: 2). (ENG.). (YA). (gr. 7). 2019. 416p. pap. 10.99 *(978-0-399-55686-9(9))*, Ember) 2018. 400p. 17.99 *(978-0-399-55683-8(4))*, Crown Books For Young Readers) Random Hse. Children's Bks.

—Nyxia Uprising. 2019. (Nyxia Triad Ser.: 3). (ENG.). 368p. (YA). (gr. 7). 17.99 *(978-0-399-55687-6(7))*, Crown Books For Young Readers) Random Hse. Children's Bks.

Richards, Barnaby. Blip! TOON Level 1. 2016. (Illus.). 40p. (J). (gr. -1-1). 12.95 *(978-1-935179-98-6(5))*, TOON Books) Astra Publishing Hse.

Robinson, R. M. Death by Paradox. 2014. (Illus.). 320p. 29.95 *(978-1-934934-14-2(9))* Firefall Editions.

Rossignol, Manon Éléonor & Lecor, Tex. Isory Poutch et le Sortilege de Cacouna. 2004. (FRE., Illus.). 398p. (J). *(978-2-9807852-1-4(0))*, Spotlight Poets) Editions le Poutchoman.

Schaefer, Elizabeth. The Force Awakens: Episode VII. White, Dave, illus. 2016. (LEGO Star Wars 8X8 Ser.). (ENG.). 24p. (J). (gr. -1-3). 13.55 *(978-0-606-39117-7(7))* Turtleback.

Scholastic Editors & Fry, Jason. Darth Vader. 2017. (Backstories Ser.: Vol. 6). (ENG., Illus.). 128p. (J). (gr. 3-7). 16.00 *(978-0-606-39145-0(2))* Turtleback.

Scieszka, Jon. AstroNuts Mission One: the Plant Planet. Weinberg, Steven, illus. 2019. (AstroNuts Ser.). (ENG.). 220p. (J). (gr. 3-7). 14.99 *(978-1-4521-7119-7(X))* Chronicle Bks. LLC.

—Baloney (Henry P.) Smith, Lane, illus. 2005. (gr. -1-3). 17.00 *(978-0-7569-5494-9(0))* Perfection Learning Corp.

Smith, Geof. Star Wars: a New Hope (Star Wars) Meurer, Caleb, illus. 2015. (Little Golden Book Ser.). (ENG.). 24p. (J). (-k). 5.99 *(978-0-7364-3538-3(7))*, Golden Bks.) Random Hse. Children's Bks.

—Star Wars: Revenge of the Sith (Star Wars) Spaziante, Patrick, illus. 2015. (Little Golden Book Ser.). (ENG.). 24p. (J). (-k). 4.99 *(978-0-7364-3540-6(9))*, Golden Bks.) Random Hse. Children's Bks.

—Star Wars: the Empire Strikes Back (Star Wars) Kennett, Chris, illus. 2015. (Little Golden Book Ser.). (ENG.). 24p. (J). (-k). 4.99 *(978-0-7364-3544-4(1))*, Golden Bks.) Random Hse. Children's Bks.

Snyder, Maria V. Navigating the Stars. 2018. (ENG.). 444p. (YA). (gr. 18-18). pap. 17.95 *(978-1-946381-01-9(2))* Snyder, Maria V.

Stadler, Alexander. Trash Crisis on Earth (Julian Rodriguez #1), 1 vol., No. 1. Stadler, Alexander, illus. 2009. (ENG.). 128p. (J). (gr. 2-5). pap. 5.99 *(978-0-439-91970-8(3))* Scholastic, Inc.

Star Wars Digests, 4 vols. 2013. (Star Wars Digests Ser.: 4). (ENG.). 80p. (J). (gr. 3-8). lib. bdg. 125.44 *(978-1-61479-055-6(8))*, 13758, Graphic Novels) Spotlight.

Stock, Lisa. Battle for Naboo. 2012. (Star Wars DK Readers Level 3 Ser.). lib. bdg. 13.55 *(978-0-606-26564-5(3))* Turtleback.

Sullivan, Tom. Out There. Sullivan, Tom, illus. 2019. (ENG., Illus.). 32p. (J). (gr. -1-3). 17.99 *(978-0-06-285449-0(6))*, Balzer & Bray) HarperCollins Pubs.

Trine, Greg. Willy Maykit in Space. Burks, James, illus. (ENG.). 208p. (J). (gr. 3-7). 2016. pap. 7.99 *(978-0-544-66848-5(0))*, 1625468) 2015. 14.99 *(978-0-544-31351-4(8))*, 1581676) HarperCollins Pubs. (Clarion Bks.).

Victor, Pamela. Baj & the Word Launcher: Space Age Asperger Adventures in Communication. 2006. (Illus.). 112p. (J). (gr. 4-7). per. 21.95 *(978-1-84310-830-6(5))*, 695732) Kingsley, Jessica Pubs. GBR. Dist: Hachette UK Distribution.

Walsh, Jill Paton. The Green Book. Bloom, Lloyd, illus. 2012. (ENG.). 80p. (J). (gr. 4-6). pap. 7.99 *(978-0-312-64122-1(2))*, 900077762) Square Fish.

Watson, Jude. Death on Naboo. 2006. (Star Wars Ser.: No. 4). 135p. (J). lib. bdg. 13.00 *(978-1-4242-0777-0(0))* Fitzgerald Bks.

—The Desperate Mission. 2005. (Star Wars Ser.: No. 1). 168p. (J). lib. bdg. 20.00 *(978-1-4242-0774-9(9))* Fitzgerald Bks.

—Underworld. 2005. (Star Wars Ser.: No. 3). 137p. (J). lib. bdg. 20.00 *(978-1-4242-0776-3(2))* Fitzgerald Bks.

Waugh, Sylvia. Carrera Espacial. (SPA.). (YA). 8.95 *(978-958-04-6028-2(0))* Norma S.A. COL. Dist: Distribuidora Norma, Inc.

Wells, H. G. The War of the Worlds. 2008. 256p. (J). (gr. 3-7). 29.95 *(978-1-4344-6610-5(8))*; pap. 14.95 *(978-1-4344-6609-9(4))* Wildside Pr., LLC.

White, Ruth. You'll Like It Here (Everybody Does) 2012. 272p. (J). (gr. 4-7). 7.99 *(978-0-375-86596-1(9))*, Yearling) Random Hse. Children's Bks.

Williams, Suzanne. Human or Alien? Carter, Abby, illus. 2004. (Marvelous Mind of Matthew Mcghee Age 8 Ser.). 57p. (J). (gr. 1-4). 11.65 *(978-0-7569-5529-8(7))* Perfection Learning Corp.

Willis, Jeanne. Dr Xargle's Book of Earth Relations. Ross, Tony, illus. (ENG.). 32p. (J). pap. 9.99 *(978-1-84270-307-6(2))* Andersen Pr. GBR. Dist: Trafalgar Square Publishing.

—Dr Xargle's Book of Earth Tiggers. Ross, Tony, illus. 2012. (ENG.). 28p. (J). (gr. -1-k). pap. 11.99 *(978-1-84939-297-6(8))* Andersen Pr. GBR. Dist: Independent Pubs. Group.

—Dr Xargle's Book of Earthlets. Ross, Tony, illus. 2012. (ENG.). 28p. (J). (gr. -1-k). pap. 12.99 *(978-1-84939-292-1(7))* Andersen Pr. GBR. Dist: Independent Pubs. Group.

Wilson, Eva Adriana. My Power Ball. 2013. 48p. pap. 17.45 *(978-1-4525-7676-3(9))*, Balboa Pr.) Author Solutions, LLC.

Windham, Ryder. Ezra's Gamble. 2014. (Star Wars Rebels Chapter Bks.). 154p. (J). lib. bdg. 17.20 *(978-0-606-35283-3(X))* Turtleback.

—Ezra's Gamble: An Original Novel. 2014. 154p. (J). *(978-1-4242-6296-0(8))* Disney Publishing Worldwide.

—The Wrath of Darth Maul. 2012. 216p. (J). *(978-0-545-43367-9(3))* Scholastic, Inc.

LIFE SKILLS

Here are entered works that discuss a combination of the skills needed by an individual to exist in modern society, including skills related to education, employment, finance, health, housing, psychology, etc.

see also Conduct of Life

Adler, Mia Sharon. Essential Proteen, Student Journal: A Life Skills Program for Helping Teens Succeed. 2006. (ENG.). 48p. pap. 14.99 *(978-0-87822-582-8(X))*, P466760) Research Pr.

Barlow, C. E. Scary Man. Tharp, Lauren R., illus. 2009. 44p. pap. 18.99 *(978-1-4269-1060-9(6))* Trafford Publishing.

Bernstein, Ben. Stressed Out! for Teens: How to Be Calm, Confident & Focused. 2014. (ENG., Illus.). 270p. (gr. 8-12). pap. 18.95 *(978-1-939629-38-8(1))*, 552938) Familius LLC.

Berry, Joy. Get over it! Set, 6 vols. 2005. (Winning Skills Ser.). (ENG., Illus.). 1p. (J). pap. 19.95 *(978-1-57687-292-5(0))*, PowerHouse Kids) powerHse. Bks.

Berry, Joy, contrib. by. Go for it! Set. 2005. (Winning skills series, go for It! Ser.). (ENG., Illus.). 48p. (J). pap. 19.95 *(978-1-57687-294-9(7))*, PowerHouse Kids) powerHse. Bks.

Borgenicht, David, et al. The Worst-Case Scenario Survival Handbook: Middle School. 2009. (Worst Case Scenario Ser.). (ENG., Illus.). 128p. (J). (gr. 6-8). pap. 10.99 *(978-0-8118-6864-8(8))* Chronicle Bks. LLC.

Boyd, Ervin D., Sr. Help for the Hurting: Getting Beyond This Veil of Tears! 2003. (Illus.). 200p. (YA). spiral bd. 22.00 *(978-0-9744024-0-6(0))* Anointed Word Pubns.

Brown, Cherie. Love Doesn't Hurt: Life Lessons for Young Women. 2003. (YA). *(978-0-9743676-0-6(5))* Avant-garde Bks.

Building a Culture of Life Leader's Manual. 2nd ed. 2004. (YA). per. 19.95 *(978-0-9764572-0-6(2))* Together, Inc.

Building a Culture of Life Study Guide. 2004. (YA). per. 17.95 *(978-0-9764572-1-3(0))* Together, Inc.

Carle, Gilda. Teen Talk with Dr. Gilda: A Girl's Guide to Dating. 2003. (ENG.). 304p. pap. 19.99 *(978-0-06-095871-8(5))*, William Morrow Paperbacks) HarperCollins Pubs.

Castaldo, Nancy & Mortimer, J. R. This or That? 3: Even More Wacky Choices to Reveal the Hidden You. 2015. (Illus.). 176p. (J). (gr. 3-7). pap. 12.99 *(978-1-4263-1881-8(2))*, National Geographic Kids) Disney Publishing Worldwide.

Champion, Neil. Finding Food & Water. 2010. (Survive Alive Ser.). (ENG.). 32p. (J). (gr. 3-7). lib. bdg. 28.50 *(978-1-60753-037-4(6))*, 17220) Amicus.

—Fire & Cooking. 2010. (Survive Alive Ser.). (ENG.). 32p. (J). (gr. 3-7). lib. bdg. 28.50 *(978-1-60753-039-8(2))*, 17222) Amicus.

—In an Emergency. 2010. (Survive Alive Ser.). (ENG.). 32p. (J). (gr. 3-7). lib. bdg. 28.50 *(978-1-60753-040-4(6))*, 17224) Amicus.

—Tools & Crafts. 2010. (Survive Alive Ser.). (ENG.). 32p. (J). (gr. 3-7). lib. bdg. 28.50 *(978-1-60753-042-8(2))*, 17226) Amicus.

Champion, Neil & Ganeri, Anita. Tools & Crafts. 2011. (How the World Makes Music Ser.). 32p. (gr. 4-7). lib. bdg. 31.35 *(978-1-59920-481-9(9))* Black Rabbit Bks.

Chronicle Books Staff. 101 Things to Do While You Wait. (J). 15.95 *(978-0-8118-3922-8(2))* Chronicle Bks. LLC.

Colby, Jennifer. Stories of Persistence. 2018. (21st Century Skills Library: Social Emotional Library). (ENG.). 32p. (J). (gr. 4-7). pap. 14.21 *(978-1-5341-0840-0(8))*, 210724); (Illus.). lib. bdg. 32.07 *(978-1-5341-0741-0(X))*, 210723) Cherry Lake Publishing.

Cope, Andy, et al. Diary of a Brilliant Kid: Top Secret Guide to Awesomeness. 2018. (ENG., Illus.). 224p. pap. 18.00 *(978-0-85708-786-7(X))*, Capstone) Wiley, John & Sons, Inc.

Coping. 2005. 192p. (gr. 7-12). lib. bdg. 1735.65 *(978-0-8239-3906-0(5))* Rosen Publishing Group, Inc., The.

Coping: Working Against the Odds, 8 bks. Incl. Coping When a Brother or Sister Is Autistic. Rosenberg, Marsha Sarah. lib. bdg. 39.80 *(978-0-8239-3194-1(3))*, aaa6e778-cfee-4406-81b9-09b364657388); Coping When Someone in Your Family Has Cancer. Rocha, Toni L. lib. bdg. 39.80 *(978-0-8239-3195-8(1))*, 6f6047b4-46d5-4eca-a459-d3bed3aa53da); Coping with Dangers on the Internet. Rothman, Kevin F. lib. bdg. 39.80 *(978-0-8239-3201-6(X))*, 3851f9ab-9d13-4134-8c8d-06fc67f9acf5); Coping with Leukemia. Apel, Melanie Ann. lib. bdg. 39.80 *(978-0-8239-3200-9(1))*, 75c4b077-7144-4d08-8fda-d344cdca2abe); Coping with Lyme Disease. Donnelly, Karen J. lib. bdg. 39.80 *(978-0-8239-3199-6(4))*, e30b57c0-c6f4-4ef6-ab46-b91f5f99327e); Coping with Vision Disorders. Stanley, Debbie. lib. bdg. 39.80 *(978-0-8239-3198-9(6))*, 6f23000d-afee-4280-9602-82bf279b2c18); 128p. (YA). (gr. 7-12). 2000. (Illus.). Set lib. bdg. 202.00 *(978-0-8239-9206-5(3))* Rosen Publishing Group, Inc., The.

Crow, Gary & Crow, Marissa. The Yes Bank. 2003. (Illus.). 73p. (J). pap. 9.95 *(978-0-9718758-7-6(1))* Koenisha Pubns.

Currie-McGhee, Leanne. Living on Your Own. 2019. (Teen Life Skills Ser.). (ENG.). 64p. (J). (gr. 6-12). 41.27 *(978-1-68282-747-5(X))* ReferencePoint Pr., Inc.

Dewey D's Life Skills Curriculum. (J). ring bd. 95.00 *(978-1-56230-706-6(1))* Syndistar, Inc.

Do You Have What It Takes. 2007. (YA). per. 35.00 *(978-0-9661256-9-6(X))* Youth Communication - New York Center.

Earl, C. F. & Vanderhoof, Gabrielle. Army Rangers. 2010. (Special Forces Ser.). (Illus.). 64p. (YA). (gr. 7-18). lib. bdg. 22.95 *(978-1-4222-1838-9(4))* Mason Crest.

Earnhardt, Crystal. Race to Victory Lane. 2003. 75p. per. 2.49 *(978-0-8280-1775-6(1))* Review & Herald Publishing Assn.

Eirienne, Arielle. The You Behind the Mascara: A Growing-up Guide for Teenage Girls. 2009. 41p. pap. 14.64 *(978-0-557-09624-4(3))* Lulu Pr., Inc.

Endres, Hollie J. The Letter Dd Set: Things I Can Do, 6 vols. 2004. (Letter Bks.). (ENG.). 8p. (gr. k-1). pap. 29.70 *(978-0-7368-4103-0(2))* Capstone.

Everly, Nita. Early Social Behavior Books Can You Be a Helper? 2007. (J). spiral bd. 11.95 *(978-0-7606-0741-1(9))* LinguiSystems, Inc.

Falk, Emily. 78 Things they Didn't Teach You in School: But You Do Need to Know. 2004. (Illus.). 123p. (YA). pap. 10.95 *(978-1-58786-016-4(3))*, Rabbit's Foot Pr.) Blue Mountain Arts Inc.

Fear Not My Child, I Am Here: Emerging from the Spiral of Fear the Practical Mystic's Guide for Embracing Your Heart's Desire. 2003rd ed. 2003. 240p. per. 15.95 *(978-0-9742213-0-4(9))* Community Works!

Fey, Sid & Vitello, Kathy. The Being Game: For the Love of Your Life. l.t. ed. 2004. (Illus.). 66p. per. 14.95 *(978-0-9753530-5-9(5))* Fey, Sid Designs, Inc.

Foster, John. Llinynnau. 2005. (WEL., Illus.). 78p. pap. *(978-1-85644-327-2(2))* CAA.

Foster, John & Stewart, Peter. Llinynnau. Isaac, Colin, tr. 2005. (WEL., Illus.). 71p. pap. *(978-1-85644-328-9(0))* CAA.

Francesconi, Gino. Life Skills Biographies (Set), 12 vols. 2007. (21st Century Skills Library: Life Skills Biographies Ser.). (ENG.). 48p. (gr. 4-8). 419.16 *(978-1-60279-110-7(4))*, 200037) Cherry Lake Publishing.

Ganeri, Anita. Stringed Instruments. 2011. (How the World Makes Music Ser.). (ENG.). 32p. (J). (gr. 4-7). lib. bdg. 31.35 *(978-1-59920-480-2(0))*, 19296, Smart Apple Media) Black Rabbit Bks.

—Wind Instruments. 2011. (How the World Makes Music Ser.). (ENG.). 32p. (J). (gr. 4-7). lib. bdg. 31.35 *(978-1-59920-482-6(7))*, 19298, Smart Apple Media) Black Rabbit Bks.

Glasser, Debbie, et al. New Kid, New Scene: A Guide to Moving & Switching Schools. 2011. (Illus.). 112p. (J). 14.95 *(978-1-4338-1039-8(5))*, Magination Pr.) American Psychological Assn.

Gomez Seitz, M. Stella. The Master Cookie-Maker: A True Life Story for Children. 2003. 133p. (J). pap. 13.95 *(978-0-595-26314-1(3))*, Writers Club Pr.) iUniverse, Inc.

Grossman, Laurie & Ms Moses's Fourth Grade Class. Breath Friends Forever: A Mindfulness Story for Kids by Kids. 2018. (ENG., Illus.). 40p. (J). (gr. -1-2). 16.95 *(978-1-68403-168-9(0))*, 41689, Instant Help Books) New Harbinger Pubns.

Hansen, Mark & Ferber, Kevin S. Success 101 for Teens: Dollars & Sense for a Winning Financial Life. 2012. (ENG.). 176p. pap. 12.95 *(978-1-55778-901-3(0))*, 5e304a18-9516-4718-a318-b52a07c05a38) Paragon Hse. Pubs.

Harrington, Paul. The Secret to Teen Power. 2010. (JPN., Illus.). 254p. (YA). *(978-4-04-791630-2(7))* Fukuinkan Shoten.

—The Secret to Teen Power. 2009. (ENG., Illus.). 192p. (YA). (gr. 7-18). 19.99 *(978-1-4169-9498-5(X))* Simon Pulse/Beyond Words.

Hawran, Mary. How to Be A Recycling Hero. 2004. (Illus.). 64p. 7.95 *(978-0-9753758-0-8(6))* Stourbridge Distributors, Inc.

Hollis, Randy. Meet Sneazle, 1. Rahn, Jess, illus. 2004. 20p. (J). 6.95 *(978-0-9758815-0-7(7))* SNZ Publishing.

Holt, Rinehart and Winston Staff. A Lifetime of Health: Life Skills. 4th ed. Date not set. pap., wbk. ed. 11.20 *(978-0-03-068117-2(0))* Holt McDougal.

Johnson, Leona. Strengthening Family & Self: Teaching Package Teacher's Annotated Edition. annot. ed. 845p. (gr. 9-12). tchr. ed. 69.00 *(978-1-59070-123-2(2))* Goodheart-Willcox Pub.

—Strengthening Family & Self: Teaching Package Teacher's Resource Guide. 424p. (gr. 9-12). tchr. ed. 64.00 *(978-1-59070-125-6(9))* Goodheart-Willcox Pub.

—Strengthening Family & Self: Teaching Package Teacher's Resource Portfolio. 460p. (gr. 9-12). tchr. ed. 136.00 *(978-1-59070-126-3(7))* Goodheart-Willcox Pub.

Jones, Steven. Journey to Excellence: An Introduction to E4. 2003. 75p. (YA). per. 19.99 *(978-0-9729798-0-1(8))* Keytochange Publishing, Inc.

King, Emily. Mrs. Twiggenbotham Goes to a Party. 2003. (Illus.). 32p. (J). 12.99 *(978-0-8254-3065-7(8))* Kregel Pubns.

Machen Pritchard, M. Ann. Phil the Pill & Friends: Making Positive Choices. Machen Pritchard, M. Ann, illus. 2005. (Illus.). 75p. (J). per. 11.99 *(978-0-9772210-0-4(8))*, Phil the Pill & Friends) MAMP Creations.

Mack, Cassandra. Cool, Confident & Strong: 52 Power Moves for Girls. 2007. 100p. per. 11.95 *(978-0-595-47560-5(4))*, Authors Choice Pr.) iUniverse, Inc.

Magness, Valerie. A Special Book about Me! 2004. 40p. spiral bd. 10.00 *(978-1-4116-2500-6(5))* Lulu Pr., Inc.

Mahoney, Ellen Voelckers. Coping: A Specialized Title for Everyone, 6 bks. Rosen, Roger, ed. Incl. Coping: Now You've Got Your Period. rev. ed. (Illus.). 192p. (YA). (gr. 7-12). 1993. lib. bdg. 38.10 *(978-0-8239-1662-7(6))*,

The check digit for ISBN-10 appears in parentheses after the full ISBN-13

COPERI); (Illus.). Set lib. bdg. 151.50 *(978-0-8239-9303-1(5))* Rosen Publishing Group, Inc., The.

Mathias, Adeline. How a Young Brave Survived. Hamilton, Penny, ed. 2009. (ENG., Illus.). 30p. (J). pap. 5.95 *(978-1-934594-04-9(0))* Salish Kootenia College Pr.

McDougal, Anna. We Make Cookies: Working at the Same Time, 1 vol. 2017. (Computer Science for the Real World Ser.). (ENG.). 8p. (gr. k-1). pap. *(978-1-5383-5099-7(8),* 3016d89e-b8df-4ca4-a67a-f862810c38be, Rosen Classroom) Rosen Publishing Group, Inc., The.

McGraw, Jay. Jay Mcgraw's Life Strategies for Dealing with Bullies. Björkman, Steve, illus. 2008. (ENG.). 192p. (J). (gr. 4-8). 17.99 *(978-1-4169-7473-4(3),* Aladdin) Simon & Schuster Children's Publishing.

McTavish, Sandra. Life Skills: 225 Ready-To-Use Health Activities for Success & Well-Being (Grades 6-12) 2003. (ENG., Illus.). 288p. pap. 32.95 *(978-0-7879-6959-2(1),* Jossey-Bass) Wiley, John & Sons, Inc.

Michael O'Mara Books UK Staff. The Gift for Boys. 2010. (ENG., Illus.). 64p. (J). (gr. 1-7). 4.95 *(978-1-84317-423-3(5))* O'Mara, Michael Bks., Ltd. GBR. Dist: Independent Pubs. Group.

Moss, Marissa. Amelia's Bully Survival Guide. Moss, Marissa, illus. 2012. (Amelia Ser.). (ENG., Illus.). 40p. (J). (gr. 2-5). pap. 6.99 *(978-1-4169-1288-0(6),* Simon & Schuster/Paula Wiseman Bks.) Simon & Schuster/Paula Wiseman Bks.

Mulcahy, Lisa, et al. Bye Bye Boredom! The Girl's Life Big Book of Fun. 2003. (Illus.). 124p. (J). *(978-0-439-44976-2(6))* Scholastic, Inc.

Nagle, Jeanne. Great Lifelong Learning Skills. 2009. (Work Readiness Ser.). 64p. (gr. 6-6). 58.50 *(978-1-60854-825-5(2))* Rosen Publishing Group, Inc., The.

Nagle, Jeanne M. Great Lifelong Learning Skills, 1 vol. 2008. (Work Readiness Ser.). (ENG., Illus.). 64p. (YA). (gr. 6-6). lib. bdg. 37.13 *(978-1-4042-1424-8(0),* 177e38f6-1fe1-4d52-ae61-03fa7988d1f3) Rosen Publishing Group, Inc., The.

Naish, Sarah & Jefferies, Rosie. William Wobbly & the Mysterious Holey Jumper: A Story about Fear & Coping. Evans, Megan, illus. 2017. (Therapeutic Parenting Bks.). (ENG.). 32p. (C). pap. 17.95 *(978-1-78592-281-7(5),* 696520) Kingsley, Jessica Pubs. GBR. Dist: Hachette UK Distribution.

National Crime Prevention Council (U.S.) Staff, contrib. by. McGruff & Scruff(r)'s Stories & Activities for Children of Promise. 2004. (Illus.). 24p. (J). *(978-1-59686-001-8(4))* National Crime Prevention Council.

The Need to Know Library: Learning to Deal with Problems Facing Every Teen, 9 bks. Incl. Everything You Need to Know about Cancer. Massari, Francesca. lib. bdg. 37.13 *(978-0-8239-3164-4(1),* 75344c2a-67d1-4bc9-bc49-b136e2b93fbe); Everything You Need to Know about Drug Abuse. 5th rev. ed. Herscovitch, Arthur. lib. bdg. 37.13 *(978-0-8239-3036-4(X),* 5cb1a7af-33aa-42d7-92c3-ba6430a0d1ff); Everything You Need to Know about Looking & Feeling Your Best: A Guide for Girls. Sommers, Annie Leah. lib. bdg. 37.13 *(978-0-8239-3079-1(3),* fb4cccb5-b69b-4ed6-a162-086f24870d38); Everything You Need to Know about Looking & Feeling Your Best: A Guide for Guys. Sommers, Michael A. lib. bdg. 37.13 *(978-0-8239-3080-7(7),* fa9dcede-4a7e-46d4-a2a0-2b1f26f55b10); Everything You Need to Know about Public Speaking. rev. ed. Blumstein, Rachel. lib. bdg. 37.13 *(978-0-8239-3087-6(4),* 115011c5-ec15-43d3-84cc-3acfff4fea8c); Everything You Need to Know about Weapons in School & at Home. 2nd rev. ed. Schleifer, Jay. lib. bdg. 37.13 *(978-0-8239-3315-0(6),* 0eb89e44-160e-4985-afcc-59f884c66dfa); 64p. (YA). (gr. 5-5). 1999. (Illus.). Set lib. bdg. 227.25 *(978-0-8239-9283-6(7))* Rosen Publishing Group, Inc., The.

The Need to Know Library: Overcoming Life's Obstacles, 8 bks. Incl. Everything You Need to Know about Bias Incidents. 2nd rev. ed. Osborn, Kevin. (gr. 7-12). 1997. lib. bdg. 31.95 *(978-0-8239-2600-8(1),* NTBIIN); Everything You Need to Know about Incest. rev. ed. Spies, Karen Bornemann. (gr. 4-6). 1997. lib. bdg. 27.95 *(978-0-8239-2607-7(9),* NTINCE); Everything You Need to Know about Your Parent's Divorce. rev. ed. Johnson, Linda Carlson. (gr. 7-12). 1998. lib. bdg. 35.45 *(978-0-8239-2876-7(4),* NTPDIV); Everything You Need to Know When a Parent Is Out of Work. rev. ed. St. Pierre, Stephanie. (gr. 7-12). 1997. lib. bdg. 31.95 *(978-0-8239-2608-4(7),* NTPAOU); 64p. (YA). (Illus.). Set lib. bdg. 202.00 *(978-0-8239-9441-0(4))* Rosen Publishing Group, Inc., The.

Neusom, Sherman. Big Fat Hunka Cheese's Quest Restored Svelte. 2003. (J). per. 799.00 *(978-0-9742811-6-2(6))* Professional Publishing Hse. LLC.

Nip It in the Bud. 2003. (Humble Heart Ser.). (J). spiral bd. *(978-0-9746148-3-0(1))* Common Courtesy.

Nunes, Bill. 284 Things a Bright Midwest Boy Should Know How to Do. 2010. 344p. pap. 19.95 *(978-0-9787994-7-2(X))* Nunes, H. William.

Olsen, Mary-Kate & Olsen, Ashley. The Ultimate Guide to Mary-Kate & Ashley. 2004. (Illus.). 93p. *(978-0-00-718136-0(1))* HarperCollins Pubs. Australia.

Outram, Richard. The Adventures of Exokid & the Teachings of Money. Kapatos, Elizabeth, illus. 2009. 36p. pap. 12.95 *(978-1-59858-898-9(2))* Dog Ear Publishing, LLC.

Pofahl, Jane. Everyday Life: Middle Ages. (Time Traveler Ser.). (Illus.). 32p. (gr. 3-6). 6.99 *(978-0-513-02194-5(9),* TSD21949) Denison, T. S. & Co., Inc.

Random House Australia, Random House. Love You, Me. 2016. (ENG., Illus.). 96p. (YA). (gr. 8). 9.99 *(978-0-85798-585-9(X))* Random Hse. Australia AUS. Dist: Independent Pubs. Group.

Robinson, Matthew. Making Smart Choices about Relationships, 1 vol. 2008. (Making Smart Choices Ser.). (ENG., Illus.). 48p. (YA). (gr. 5-5). lib. bdg. 34.47 *(978-1-4042-1390-6(2),* a4826c2f-a6cc-4fe2-aeec-8f5965ce9ff3) Rosen Publishing Group, Inc., The.

Rush, Ryan. Home on Time: Life Management by the Book. 2003. 192p. per. 10.99 *(978-0-9728899-0-2(6))* 21st Century Pr.

Salas, Laura Purdie. Taking the Plunge: A Teen's Guide to Independence. 2004. (ENG., Illus.). 127p. pap. 12.95 *(978-1-58760-012-8(9),* P544307, Child & Family Pr.) Child Welfare League of America, Inc.

Saul, "Aunt" Laya. You Don't Have to Learn Everything the Hard Way: What I Wish Someone Had Told Me. 2004. 214p. (YA). per. 14.95 net. *(978-0-9723229-4-2(9))* Kadima Pr.

Scholastic News Nonfiction Readers: Kids Like Me (Global Awareness), 5 vols., Set. Incl. This Is the Way We Dress. Behrens, Janice. lib. bdg. 21.19 *(978-0-531-21338-4(2));* This Is the Way We Eat Our Food. Falk, Laine. lib. bdg. 21.19 *(978-0-531-21339-1(0));* This Is the Way We Go to School. Falk, Laine. lib. bdg. 21.19 *(978-0-531-21341-4(2),* Children's Pr.); This Is the Way We Help at Home. Miller, Amanda. lib. bdg. 21.19 *(978-0-531-21340-7(4));* This Is the Way We Play. Miller, Amanda. lib. bdg. 21.19 *(978-0-531-21342-1(0));* 24p. (J). (gr. k-3). 2009. Set lib. bdg. 110.00 *(978-0-531-21035-2(9),* Children's Pr.) Scholastic Library Publishing.

Shapiro, Lawrence E. Let's Be Friends: A Workbook to Help Kids Learn Social Skills & Make Great Friends. 2008. (ENG., Illus.). 144p. (J). (gr. k-5). pap. 19.95 *(978-1-57224-610-2(3),* 6102, Instant Help Books) New Harbinger Pubns.

Stewart, Jan. STARS: Knowing Yourself. 2004. (STARS Life Skills Program Ser.: 4). (ENG., Illus.). 32p. (J). pap. 9.95 *(978-0-89793-311-7(7),* Hunter Hse.) Turner Publishing Co.

Storeby, Jordan. A Boy's Book of Daily Thoughts: For Ages 8 To 12. 2004. 374p. (J). pap. 12.95 *(978-0-929636-20-7(1))* Syren Bk. Co.

Sullivan, James Kevin, illus. What Went Right Today? Journal: WWRT Journal. 2007. 72p. (J). spiral bd. 12.95 *(978-0-9766990-1-9(X))* Buz-Land Presentations, Inc.

Swain, Claudia. What's a Girl to Do? 2004. 128p. pap. 6.99 *(978-1-56309-440-8(1),* New Hope Pubs.) Iron Stream Media.

Tapper, Alice Paul. Raise Your Hand. Kissi, Marta, illus. 2019. 32p. (J). (gr. -1-3). 17.99 *(978-1-5247-9120-9(2),* Penguin Workshop) Penguin Young Readers Group.

Taylor, Sally. On My Own: The Ultimate How-to Guide for Young Adults. 2nd ed. 2004. (Illus.). 640p. (YA). (gr. 11-12). reprint ed. per. 34.95 incl. cd-rom *(978-0-9711500-0-3(1))* Silly Goose Productions, LLC.

UFlipp. You & Your Military Hero: Building Positive Thinking Skills During Your Hero's Deployment. 2009. 72p. (J). pap. 19.95 *(978-1-59298-268-4(9))* Beaver's Pond Pr., Inc.

Understanding Catechesis. 2004. (Effective Dre Ser.). pap. *(978-0-8294-1054-9(6))* Loyola Pr.

Vargas, Daraciela, adapted by. Refranero Popular de Puerto Rico. 2003. lib. bdg. 10.99 *(978-0-9702021-5-4(6))* Conexion Educativa.

Veillette, Sally M. Coming to Your Senses: Soaring with Your Soul. 2005. (ENG., Illus.). 251p. pap. 19.95 *(978-0-9741854-1-5(8),* 9780974185415) Pop the Cork Publishing.

Wallace, Mary & Wallace, Jessica. American Popular Piano - Christmas: Level 3. Smith, Scott McBride, ed. Dávila, Claudia, illus. 2009. (ENG.). 20p. (gr. 4-8). pap. 6.25 *(978-1-897379-47-9(1),* 00220309) Novus Via Music Group Inc. CAN. Dist: Leonard, Hal Corp.

Webster, Jeanne. If You Could Be Anything What Would You Be? A Teen's Guide to Mapping Out the Future. Nelson, Dianne, ed. 2004. (Illus.). 137p. (J). (gr. 5-18). pap. 19.95 *(978-0-9749199-0-4(X))* Dupuis North Publishing.

Weierbach, Jane & Phillips-Hershey, Elizabeth. Mind over Basketball: Coach Yourself to Handle Stress. Beyl, Charles, illus. 2007. (Coach Yourself to Handle Stress Ser.). 48p. (J). (gr. 3-7). 14.95 *(978-1-4338-0135-8(3),* 4418006); per. 9.95 *(978-1-4338-0136-5(1),* 4418007) American Psychological Assn. (Magination Pr.).

White, Kelly. The Girls' Life Guide to Being the Best You! Parett, Lisa, illus. 2003. 124p. (J). *(978-0-439-44978-6(2))* Scholastic, Inc.

Whitfield, Kate. The Empowered Gal's 9 Life Lessons: Keys, Tips, Strategies, Advice & Everything You Need to Know to be a Confident, Successful, in Control Gal. 2008. 236p. pap. 18.95 *(978-0-595-47829-3(8))* iUniverse, Inc.

Whitney, Brooks. How to Survive Almost Anything. 2004. (Illus.). 80p. (J). pap. *(978-0-439-57900-1(7))* Scholastic, Inc.

Williams, Anna Graf, et al. The Family Guide to the American Workplace. Williams, Anna Graf, ed. 2003. (Illus.). 272p. per. 31.00 *(978-0-9705790-4-1(7),* 866/332-5905) Learnovation, LLC.

Wolny, Philip. Hurricane: True Stories of Survival. 2009. (Survivor Stories Ser.). 48p. (gr. 5-5). 53.00 *(978-1-60853-254-4(2),* Rosen Reference) Rosen Publishing Group, Inc., The.

Zellmann, Anton Josef. I Read Minds: And So Do You! l.t. ed. 2005. (Illus.). 264p. 35.00 *(978-0-9763325-0-3(7))* Zellmann Publishing, LLC.

LIFE SUPPORT SYSTEMS (SPACE ENVIRONMENT)

see also Astronauts—Clothing; Project Apollo (U.S.)

Baker, David. Living in Space. 2008. (Exploring Space Ser.). (Illus.). 32p. (J). (gr. 4-6). lib. bdg. 26.00 *(978-1-59036-769-8(3))* Weigl Pubs., Inc.

Baker, David & Kissock, Heather. Living in Space. 2008. (Exploring Space Ser.). (Illus.). 32p. (J). (gr. 4-6). pap. 9.95 *(978-1-59036-770-4(7))* Weigl Pubs., Inc.

Bredeson, Carmen. Living on a Space Shuttle. 2003. (Rookie Read-About Science: Space Science Ser.). (ENG., Illus.). 32p. (J). (gr. 1-2). 17.44 *(978-0-516-22528-9(6),* Children's Pr.) Scholastic Library Publishing.

Clay, Kathryn. Living in Space. 2017. (Little Astronauts Ser.). (ENG., Illus.). 32p. (J). (gr. -1-2). lib. bdg. 28.65 *(978-1-5157-3657-8(1),* 133642, Capstone Pr.) Capstone.

—Spacewalks. 2017. (Little Astronauts Ser.). (ENG., Illus.). 32p. (J). (gr. -1-2). lib. bdg. 28.65 *(978-1-5157-3658-5(X),* 133643, Capstone Pr.) Capstone.

Hayden, Kate. Astronaut: Living in Space. 2013. (DK Reader Level 2 Ser.). (gr. k-3). lib. bdg. 13.55 *(978-0-613-24252-3(1))* Turtleback.

—DK Readers L2: Astronaut: Living in Space. 2013. (DK Readers Level 2 Ser.). (ENG.). 32p. (J). (gr. 1-4). pap. 4.99 *(978-1-4654-0241-7(1),* DK Children) Dorling Kindersley Publishing, Inc.

Klepeis, Alicia Z. Space Survival: Keeping People Alive in Space. 2019. (Future Space Ser.). (ENG., Illus.). 32p. (J). (gr. 3-9). pap. 7.95 *(978-1-5435-7521-7(8),* 141052); lib. bdg. 28.65 *(978-1-5435-7265-0(0),* 140596) Capstone.

Littlejohn, Randy. Life in Outer Space. (Life in Extreme Environments Ser.). 64p. (gr. 5-8). 2009. 53.00 *(978-1-61514-269-9(X))* 2003. (ENG., Illus.). lib. bdg. 37.13 *(978-0-8239-3989-3(8),* e1a48f16-b307-4fad-a22f-dde0324840fa) Rosen Publishing Group, Inc., The. (Rosen Reference).

Wishinsky, Frieda. Could We Live on the Moon? 2004. (ENG., Illus.). 24p. (J). (gr. 2-2). pap. 10.92 *(978-0-7652-5178-7(7),* Celebration Pr.) Savvas Learning Co.

LIFESAVING

Gordon, Nick. Coast Guard Rescue Swimmer. 2012. (Dangerous Jobs Ser.). (ENG., Illus.). 24p. (J). (gr. 3-7). lib. bdg. 26.95 *(978-1-60014-778-4(X),* Torque Bks.) Bellwether Media.

La Bella, Laura. Search & Rescue Swimmers, 1 vol. 2008. (Extreme Careers Ser.). (ENG., Illus.). 64p. (YA). (gr. 5-5). lib. bdg. 37.13 *(978-1-4042-1786-7(X),* a630f377-e969-4dc6-9f5e-797f8f893314) Rosen Publishing Group, Inc., The.

—Search-and-rescue Swimmers. 2009. (Extreme Careers Ser.). 64p. (gr. 5-5). 58.50 *(978-1-61512-405-3(5),* Rosen Reference) Rosen Publishing Group, Inc., The.

Lewis, Mark L. Fire Rescues. 2019. (Rescues in Focus Ser.). (ENG., Illus.). 32p. (J). (gr. 2-3). pap. 9.95 *(978-1-64185-841-0(9),* 1641858419, Focus Readers) North Star Editions.

Perish, Patrick. Survive a Fire. 2017. (Survival Zone Ser.). (ENG., Illus.). 24p. (J). (gr. 3-7). lib. bdg. 26.95 *(978-1-62617-581-5(0),* Torque Bks.) Bellwether Media.

Roza, Greg. Frequently Asked Questions about Emergency Lifesaving Techniques, 1 vol. 2009. (FAQ: Teen Life Ser.). (ENG., Illus.). 64p. (J). (gr. 5-6). lib. bdg. 37.13 *(978-1-4358-5327-0(X),* 80b355a5-1adf-44a8-8585-d2b71d941913) Rosen Publishing Group, Inc., The.

Staniford, Linda. Rescue at Sea Around the World. 2016. (To the Rescue! Ser.). (ENG., Illus.). 24p. (J). (gr. k-2). lib. bdg. 25.99 *(978-1-4846-2753-2(9),* 131310, Heinemann) Capstone.

Weintraub, Aileen. First Response by Sea. 2007. (High Interest Books: Natural Disasters Ser.). (ENG., Illus.). 48p. (J). (gr. 7-9). lib. bdg. 18.69 *(978-0-531-12434-5(7))* Scholastic Library Publishing.

Zullo, Allan. The Rescuers: Kids Who Risked Everything to Save Others. 2006. 135p. pap. *(978-0-439-85483-2(0))* Scholastic, Inc.

LIFTS

see Elevators; Hoisting Machinery

LIGHT

see also Color; Lasers; Optics; Radiation; Radioactivity; X-Rays

Aboff, Marcie. Light the Way. 2016. (Spring Forward Ser.). (J). (gr. 1). *(978-1-4900-9388-8(5))* Benchmark Education Co.

Adams, Alison. Light. 2011. (Early Connections Ser.). (J). *(978-1-61672-525-9(7))* Benchmark Education Co.

Adler, David A. Light Waves. Raff, Anna, illus. 2018. 32p. (J). (gr. 1-4). 17.99 *(978-0-8234-3682-8(9))* Holiday Hse., Inc.

Aleo, Karen. Living Things Need Light. 2019. (What Living Things Need Ser.). (ENG., Illus.). 24p. (J). (gr. -1-2). pap. 6.95 *(978-1-9771-1036-7(3),* 141112); lib. bdg. 24.65 *(978-1-9771-0886-9(5),* 140494) Capstone. (Pebble).

Amson-Bradshaw, Georgia. Light, 1 vol. 2017. (Science in a Flash Ser.). (ENG.). 32p. (J). (gr. 5-5). pap. 11.50 *(978-1-5382-1481-7(4),* b1c42990-585e-4ec4-81e5-75c461a8286b); lib. bdg. 28.27 *(978-1-5382-1398-8(2),* 18f80fdd-03b0-4d94-a633-04b02137271c) Stevens, Gareth Publishing LLLP.

Anderson, Michael, ed. Light, 1 vol. 2012. (Introduction to Physics Ser.). (ENG., Illus.). 80p. (gr. 8-8). (J). 35.29 *(978-1-61530-840-8(7),* 6a4751e0-8353-430d-a282-f61c9d2d1b0a); (YA). 70.58 *(978-1-61530-847-7(4),* 43f1d219-b7d6-4938-a67b-f0050b72d6aa) Rosen Publishing Group, Inc., The.

Ballard, Carol. Exploring Light, 1 vol. 2007. (How Does Science Work? Ser.). (ENG., Illus.). 32p. (J). (gr. 2-3). lib. bdg. 30.27 *(978-1-4042-4280-7(5),* 488a3c5d-bc17-4775-a235-2525ff10182c) Rosen Publishing Group, Inc., The.

Bang, Molly. My Light: How Sunlight Becomes Electricity. Bang, Molly, illus. 2004. (ENG., Illus.). 40p. (J). (gr. -1-3). 18.99 *(978-0-439-48961-4(X),* Blue Sky Pr., The) Scholastic, Inc.

Bell, Samantha. Color & Wavelengths. Bane, Jeff, illus. 2018. (Mi Mini Biografía (My Itty-Bitty Bio): My Early Library). (ENG.). 24p. (J). (gr. k-1). pap. 12.79 *(978-1-5341-0826-4(2),* 210668); lib. bdg. 30.64 *(978-1-5341-0727-4(4),* 210667) Cherry Lake Publishing.

Benchmark Education Co., LLC Staff & Furgang, Kathy. The Light Around Us: Big Book Edition. 2015. (Content Connections Ser.). (J). (gr. 1). *(978-1-4900-0478-5(5))* Benchmark Education Co.

Benchmark Education Company, LLC Staff, compiled by. Light & Sound: Theme Set. 2006. (J). 215.00 *(978-1-4108-7121-3(5))* Benchmark Education Co.

Bernhardt, Carolyn. Light. 2018. (Science Starters Ser.). (ENG., Illus.). 24p. (J). (gr. k-3). pap. 7.99 *(978-1-61891-464-4(2),* 12117); lib. bdg. 26.95 *(978-1-62617-808-3(9))* Bellwether Media. (Blastoff! Readers).

Best, Arthur. Reflectiveness of Light, 1 vol. 2018. (Properties of Matter Ser.). (ENG.). 24p. (J). (gr. 1-1). pap. 9.22 *(978-1-5026-4240-0(9),* ab4dfe13-523e-45b0-8471-bb2f2c06d651) Cavendish Square Publishing LLC.

Bodach, Vijaya Khisty. Reflection. 2008. (Discovering & Exploring Science Ser.). (Illus.). 16p. (J). (gr. -1-3). lib. bdg. 12.95 *(978-0-7569-8428-1(9))* Perfection Learning Corp.

Boothroyd, Jennifer. The Energy We See: A Look at Light. 2011. (Lightning Bolt Books Exploring Physical Science Ser.). 32p. pap. 45.32 *(978-0-7613-7648-4(8));* (ENG., Illus.). (J). (gr. 1-3). pap. 9.99 *(978-0-7613-7104-5(4),* 707326af-0cc4-415f-b043-92e660f32f9c); (ENG., Illus.). (J). (gr. 1-3). lib. bdg. 29.32 *(978-0-7613-6092-6(1),* 5b8b1bc9-149a-45c5-b604-ece0fb90db87, Lerner Pubns.) Lerner Publishing Group.

—Sending Messages with Light & Sound. 2014. (First Step Nonfiction — Light & Sound Ser.). (ENG., Illus.). 24p. (J). (gr. k-2). pap. 6.99 *(978-1-4677-4504-8(9),* 7d501c9a-3689-405d-b5b6-437bbb351e1a) Lerner Publishing Group.

Bortz, Alfred B. The Photon, 1 vol. 2003. (Library of Subatomic Particles Ser.). (ENG., Illus.). 64p. (gr. 6-6). lib. bdg. 37.13 *(978-0-8239-4531-3(6),* 161c055e-d902-45e0-a2a0-44689ebb6393) Rosen Publishing Group, Inc., The.

Bortz, Fred. The Photon. 2009. (Library of Subatomic Particles Ser.). 64p. (gr. 6-6). 58.50 *(978-1-60853-883-6(4))* Rosen Publishing Group, Inc., The.

Boulter, Carol & Wadsworth, Pamela. Golau. 2005. (WEL., Illus.). 24p. pap. *(978-1-85596-231-6(4))* Dref Wen.

—Rhagor Am Olau. 2005. (WEL., Illus.). 24p. pap. *(978-1-85596-232-3(2))* Dref Wen.

Brasch, Nicolas. Tricks of Sound & Light. 2010. (Science Behind Ser.). 32p. lib. bdg. 28.50 *(978-1-59920-564-9(5))* Black Rabbit Bks.

—Why Do Shadows Change? Level 5 Factbook. 2010. (Cambridge Young Readers Ser.). (ENG., Illus.). 24p. pap. 7.16 *(978-0-521-13731-7(4))* Cambridge Univ. Pr.

—Why Do Shadows Lengthen?, 1 vol. 2010. (Solving Science Mysteries Ser.). (ENG., Illus.). 24p. (gr. 4-5). (J). pap. 9.25 *(978-1-61531-913-8(1),* 1567c549-a675-4d53-b750-6824f69e7aa2, PowerKids Pr.); (YA). lib. bdg. 26.27 *(978-1-61531-891-9(7),* 82df3909-363c-42ec-9e66-87d93386a3b0) Rosen Publishing Group, Inc., The.

—Why Do Shadows Lengthen? All about Light. 2010. (Illus.). 24p. (J). 49.50 *(978-1-61531-914-5(X),* PowerKids Pr.) Rosen Publishing Group, Inc., The.

Braun, Eric. Curious Pearl Investigates Light: 4D an Augmented Reality Science Experience. Dehennin, Stephanie, illus. 2017. (Curious Pearl, Science Girl 4D Ser.). (ENG.). 24p. (J). (gr. k-2). lib. bdg. 25.99 *(978-1-5158-1345-3(2),* 135147, Picture Window Bks.) Capstone.

Brent, Lynnette R. I've Discovered Light!, 1 vol. 2009. (Eureka! Ser.). (ENG.). 32p. (gr. 4-4). lib. bdg. 31.21 *(978-0-7614-3198-5(5),* 159c8b89-5cfa-4fca-abb7-ca1d20001e30) Cavendish Square Publishing LLC.

Brown Bear Books. Light & Sound. 2011. (Introducing Physics Ser.). (ENG.). 64p. (J). (gr. 8-11). lib. bdg. 39.95 *(978-1-936333-06-6(6),* 16503) Brown Bear Bks.

Building Blocks of Science: Light Teacher's Guide. 2007. (Illus.). ring bd. *(978-0-89278-339-7(7))* Carolina Biological Supply Co.

Caes, Charles J. Discovering the Speed of Light, 1 vol. 2011. (Scientist's Guide to Physics Ser.). (ENG., Illus.). 112p. (YA). (gr. 7-7). lib. bdg. 39.80 *(978-1-4488-4699-3(4),* 1b8657cc-8041-42be-8f09-06206583a90f) Rosen Publishing Group, Inc., The.

—How Do We Know the Speed of Light? 2009. (Great Scientific Questions & the Scientists Who Answered Them Ser.). 112p. (gr. 7-12). 63.90 *(978-1-61513-207-2(4))* Rosen Publishing Group, Inc., The.

Carlson Berne, Emma. Bright! Light Energy, 1 vol. 2013. (Energy Everywhere Ser.). (ENG., Illus.). 24p. (J). (gr. 2-3). 26.27 *(978-1-4488-9649-3(5),* 4dc02626-11ec-49fe-8e10-5b007b4b44a2); pap. 9.25 *(978-1-4488-9756-8(4),* c28bd8fe-2455-42ee-b762-2431265d5ca1) Rosen Publishing Group, Inc., The. (PowerKids Pr.).

Cavell-Clarke, Steffi. Light. (First Science Ser.). (J). (gr. 1-1). 2017. pap. 49.50 *(978-1-5345-2073-8(2))* 2016. (ENG.). 24p. pap. 9.25 *(978-1-5345-2072-1(4),* 953cad73-c1d3-4c1f-89a4-71c663a6cfa2) 2016. (ENG.). 24p. lib. bdg. 26.23 *(978-1-5345-2074-5(0),* 620a22cc-01df-43b7-aada-34699b60074b) Greenhaven Publishing LLC. (KidHaven Publishing).

Chesborough, E. D. What Is Light Energy?, 1 vol. 2017. (Let's Find Out! Forms of Energy Ser.). (ENG., Illus.). 32p. (J). (gr. 2-3). pap. 13.90 *(978-1-68048-705-3(1),* 50055992-9401-4dac-bc4a-b3f5b4622e0c, Britannica Educational Publishing) Rosen Publishing Group, Inc., The.

Clark, John O. E. The Basics of Light, 1 vol. 2014. (Core Concepts Ser.). (ENG., Illus.). 96p. (YA). (gr. 7-7). lib. bdg. 39.77 *(978-1-4777-7762-6(8),* 541206be-7acd-4b6a-bf0e-22a78895e136) Rosen Publishing Group, Inc., The.

Clark, Michael. Ludicrous Light, 1 vol. 2017. (Strange Science & Explosive Experiments Ser.). (ENG.). 32p. (J). (gr. 4-5). 29.27 *(978-1-5383-2270-3(6),* 707ecc47-17ca-4673-a102-3bdf8196f097); pap. 12.75 *(978-1-5383-2366-3(4),* 3a173671-9fd2-4c89-8692-d388a53be0c5) Rosen Publishing Group, Inc., The. (PowerKids Pr.).

Claybourne, Anna. Glaring Light & Other Eye-Burning Rays. 2013. (ENG., Illus.). 32p. (J). *(978-0-7787-0945-9(0));* pap. *(978-0-7787-0955-8(8))* Crabtree Publishing Co.

—Secrets of Light, 1 vol. 2011. (Science Secrets Ser.). (ENG.). 32p. (gr. 4-4). 31.21 *(978-1-60870-139-1(5),* 305cb365-9fa4-49db-8592-a4d4be0396cb) Cavendish Square Publishing LLC.

Coan, Sharon. Light Makes a Rainbow, 1 vol. rev. ed. 2014. (Science: Informational Text Ser.). (ENG., Illus.). 24p. (gr. 1-2). pap. 9.99 *(978-1-4807-4566-7(9))* Teacher Created Materials, Inc.

Colson, Mary. The Science of Light, 1 vol. 2015. (Flowchart Smart Ser.). (ENG.). 48p. (J). (gr. 4-5). pap. 15.05 *(978-1-4824-4143-7(8),* bc050e36-fd5e-4b5c-b98b-05629aa22fd5) Stevens, Gareth Publishing LLLP.

Connors, Kathleen. Light & Color, 1 vol. 2018. (Look at Physical Science Ser.). (ENG.). 32p. (gr. 2-2). 28.27 *(978-1-5382-2151-8(9),* 40e58afd-6ac6-4ff2-8909-aa19240051d3) Stevens, Gareth Publishing LLLP.

Crane, Cody. Light (Rookie Read-About Science: Physical Science) (Library Edition) 2019. (Rookie Read-About Science Ser.). (ENG., Illus.). 32p. (J). (gr. 1-2). lib. bdg. 25.00

J K L

(978-0-531-13408-5(3), Children's Pr.) Scholastic Library Publishing.

Deeds, Christopher. Light & Color: What We See. 2013. (InfoMax Readers Ser.). (ENG.). 24p. (J). (gr. 3-4). pap. 49.50 (978-1-4777-2638-9(1)); (Illus.). pap. 8.25 (978-1-4777-2637-2(3), 70970738-e231-4b1b-9fd8-d4d580e4ad32) Rosen Publishing Group, Inc., The. (Rosen Classroom).

Delta Education. Sci Res Bk Foss Grade 1 Next Gen Ea. 2015. (Illus.). 244p. (J). lib. bdg. (978-1-62571-445-9(9)) Delta Education, LLC.

Dicker, Katie. Light, 1 vol. 2010. (Sherlock Bones Looks at Physical Science Ser.). (ENG.). 32p. (YA). (gr. 5-5). lib. bdg. 29.93 (978-1-61533-212-0(X), a4b0a2cd-7c2a-4793-bc6a-2256718d5ea9, Windmill Bks.) Rosen Publishing Group, Inc., The.

Dodd, Emily. Light: Band 17/Diamond (Collins Big Cat) 2016. (Collins Big Cat Ser.). (ENG.). 56p. (J). (gr. 5-6). pap. 9.95 (978-0-00-816399-0(5)) HarperCollins Pubs. Ltd. GBR. Dist: Independent Pubs. Group.

Dunne, Abbie. Light. 2016. (Physical Science Ser.). (ENG., Illus.). 24p. (J). (gr. -1-2). lib. bdg. 27.32 (978-1-5157-0937-4(X), 132236, Capstone Pr.) Capstone.

Ferrie, Chris. Optical Physics for Babies. 2017. (J). (978-1-4926-5606-7(2)); (Baby University Ser.: 0). (Illus.). 24p. (gr. -1-k). bds. 9.99 (978-1-4926-5621-0(6)) Sourcebooks, Inc.

Fields, B. H. & Bortz, Fred. Understanding Photons, 1 vol. 2015. (Exploring the Subatomic World Ser.). (ENG., Illus.). 64p. (YA). (gr. 8-8). lib. bdg. 35.93 (978-1-5026-0544-3(9), ddfa05f4-cdad-4c8b-9be7-9f541a9750ef) Cavendish Square Publishing LLC.

Fink, Charles. Light Show: Reflection & Absorption. 2009. (Amazing Science Ser.). 24p. (gr. 3-3). 42.50 (978-1-61511-329-3(0), PowerKids Pr.) Rosen Publishing Group, Inc., The.

Fliess, Sue. Flash & Gleam: Light in Our World. Le, Khoa, illus. 2020. (ENG.). 32p. (J). (gr. k-2). lib. bdg. 19.99 (978-1-5415-5770-3(0), 37b7c8e0-3bfd-45cd-908a-b94dfe0a3f87, Millbrook Pr.) Lerner Publishing Group.

Flynn, Claire E. Why Plants Need Light, 1 vol. 2008. (Real Life Readers Ser.). (ENG.). 12p. (gr. 1-2). pap. 5.90 (978-1-4042-7919-3(9), b9c64519-425c-4205-b25a-5ce49f2a4f78, Rosen Classroom) Rosen Publishing Group, Inc., The.

Frenkel, Karen A. Light & Sound Technology: Text Pairs. 2008. (Bridges/Navigators Ser.). (J). (gr. 4). 94.00 (978-1-4108-8386-5(8)) Benchmark Education Co.

—Looking at Light: Set Of 6. 2011. (Navigators Ser.). (J). pap. 48.00 net. (978-1-4108-6226-6(7)) Benchmark Education Co.

—Looking at Light: Text Pairs. 2008. (Bridges/Navigators Ser.). (J). (gr. 4). 89.00 (978-1-4108-8388-9(4)) Benchmark Education Co.

Friesen, Helen Lepp. Uses of Light. 2011. (J). (gr. 4-6). pap. 12.95 (978-1-61690-841-6(6), AV2 by Weigl); (Illus.). 24p. (gr. 3-6). 27.13 (978-1-61690-837-9(8)) Weigl Pubs., Inc.

Gardner, Robert. Experiments with Light, 1 vol. 2017. (Science Whiz Experiments Ser.). (ENG.). 128p. (gr. 5-5). 38.93 (978-0-7660-8680-7(1), 5011bd3b-e954-4473-a6ed-c6af4ffc5708) Enslow Publishing, LLC.

Gardner, Robert & Conklin, Joshua. A Kid's Book of Experiments with Color, 1 vol. 2015. (Surprising Science Experiments Ser.). (ENG., Illus.). 48p. (gr. 4-4). lib. bdg. 29.60 (978-0-7660-7201-5(0), fa5bcd03-a12a-4a47-a5bd-0e64f4d7faac) Enslow Publishing, LLC.

—A Kid's Book of Experiments with Light, 1 vol. 2015. (Surprising Science Experiments Ser.). (ENG., Illus.). 48p. (gr. 4-4). 29.60 (978-0-7660-7205-3(3), 415607dd-2f50-4b02-999e-94bc995993f7) Enslow Publishing, LLC.

Garstecki, Julia & Derkovitz, Stephanie. Make Your Own LED Flashlight. 2020. (J). pap. (978-1-62310-127-5(1), Bolt) Black Rabbit Bks.

Gilles, Renae & Rylands, Warren. Northern Lights. 2019. (Illus.). 24p. (J). (978-1-4896-8011-2(X), AV2 by Weigl) Weigl Pubs., Inc.

Gish, Melissa. Light. 2005. (My First Look at Science Ser.). (Illus.). 24p. (J). (gr. k-3). lib. bdg. 15.95 (978-1-58341-373-9(1), Creative Education) Creative Co., The.

Gorman, John. Light: An Investigation, 1 vol. 2007. (Science Investigations Ser.). (ENG., Illus.). 32p. (YA). (gr. 4-5). lib. bdg. 30.27 (978-1-4042-4286-9(4), aa8f0dcc-aebb-4e8f-8a9e-5f947862ca18) Rosen Publishing Group, Inc., The.

Gray, Leon. Light, 1 vol. 2013. (Physical Science Ser.). 48p. (J). (gr. 4-5). (ENG.). pap. 15.05 (978-1-4339-9513-2(1), 452e7aed-502d-429a-8810-ecc612cf47c9); pap. 84.30 (978-1-4339-9514-9(X)); (ENG., Illus.). lib. bdg. 34.61 (978-1-4339-9512-5(3), 2a599467-2cdf-4a19-ac13-31e68e53d971) Stevens, Gareth Publishing LLLP.

Group/McGraw-Hill, Wright. Set 2: La Luz, 6 vols., Vol. 2. (First Explorers. Primeros Exploradores Nonfiction Sets Ser.). (SPA.). (gr. 1-2). 34.95 (978-0-7699-1485-5(3)) Shortland Pubns. (U. S. A.) Inc.

Hamilton, Gina L. Light. 2016. (J). (978-1-5105-2239-8(5)) SmartBook Media, Inc.

—Light. 2008. (Science Q & A Ser.). (Illus.). 48p. (YA). (gr. 5-8). pap. 10.95 (978-1-59036-947-0(5)); lib. bdg. 29.05 (978-1-59036-946-3(7)) Weigl Pubs., Inc.

—Light Q & A. 2013. (J). (978-1-62127-415-5(2)); pap. (978-1-62127-421-6(7)) Weigl Pubs., Inc.

Hansen, Grace. Light. 2018. (Beginning Science Ser.). (ENG., Illus.). 24p. (J). (gr. -1-2). lib. bdg. 32.79 (978-1-5321-0809-9(5), 28179, Abdo Kids) ABDO Publishing Co.

Hartman, Eve & Meshbesher, Wendy. Light & Sound. rev. ed. 2016. (Sci-Hi: Physical Science Ser.). (ENG.). 48p. (J). (gr. 6-10). pap. 8.99 (978-1-4109-8536-1(9), 134122, Raintree) Capstone.

Herold, Vickey. Discover Light. 2006. (J). pap. (978-1-4108-6491-8(X)) Benchmark Education Co.

—Light & Color. 2006. (J). pap. (978-1-4108-6488-8(X)) Benchmark Education Co.

Hewitt, Sally. Amazing Light. 2007. (Amazing Science Ser.). (ENG.). 32p. (J). pap. (978-0-7787-3626-4(1)) Crabtree Publishing Co.

Higgins, Melissa. Light. 2019. (Little Physicist Ser.). (ENG., Illus.). 32p. (J). (gr. 1-3). pap. 6.95 (978-1-9771-1064-0(9), 141138); lib. bdg. 28.65 (978-1-9771-0961-3(6), 140552) Capstone. (Pebble).

Holt, Rinehart and Winston Staff. Holt Science & Technology Chapter 22: Physical Science: The Nature of Light. 5th ed. 2004. (Illus.). pap. 12.86 (978-0-03-030439-2(3)) Holt McDougal.

—Holt Science & Technology Chapter 23: Physical Science: Light & Our World. 5th ed. 2004. (Illus.). pap. 12.86 (978-0-03-030441-5(5)) Holt McDougal.

Hotchkins, Dewayne. Darkness & Light, 1 vol. 2016. (Rosen REAL Readers: STEM & STEAM Collection). (ENG.). 8p. (gr. k-1). pap. 5.46 (978-1-5081-2407-8(8), b37cdf43-815e-453f-93d1-fa24e5473843, Rosen Classroom) Rosen Publishing Group, Inc., The.

Hutchison, Patricia. Focus on Light. 2017. (Hands-On STEM Ser.). (ENG., Illus.). 32p. (J). (gr. 2-3). pap. 9.95 (978-1-63517-349-9(3), 1635173493); lib. bdg. 31.35 (978-1-63517-284-3(5), 1635172845) North Star Editions. (Focus Readers).

Hyde, Natalie. Glow-In-the-Dark Creatures, 1 vol. 2014. (ENG., Illus.). 32p. (J). (gr. 1-2). 19.95 (978-1-55455-330-3(X), 213f23a7-6893-422a-adf8-97fec34c8c10) Trifolium Bks., Inc. CAN. Dist: Firefly Bks., Ltd.

James, Emily. The Simple Science of Light. 2017. (Simply Science Ser.). (ENG., Illus.). 32p. (J). (gr. -1-2). lib. bdg. 27.99 (978-1-5157-7082-4(6), 135506, Capstone Pr.) Capstone.

Jankowski, Connie. All about Light & Sound, 1 vol. rev. ed. 2007. (Science: Informational Text Ser.). (ENG.). 32p. (J). (gr. 3-6). pap. 12.99 (978-0-7439-0579-4(2)) Teacher Created Materials, Inc.

—Pioneers of Light & Sound, 1 vol. rev. ed. 2007. (Science: Informational Text Ser.). (ENG.). 32p. (gr. 3-6). pap. 12.99 (978-0-7439-0580-0(6)) Teacher Created Materials, Inc.

Jennings, Terry. Light & Dark. 2009. (Science Alive Ser.). (ENG., Illus.). 32p. (J). (gr. 4-7). pap. (978-1-897563-56-4(6)) Saunders Bk. Co.

Jennings, Terry J. Light & Dark. 2009. (J). 28.50 (978-1-59920-270-9(0)) Black Rabbit Bks.

Johnson, Robin. The Science of Light Waves. 2017. (Catch a Wave Ser.). (Illus.). 32p. (J). (gr. 4-4). (978-0-7787-2944-0(3)) Crabtree Publishing Co.

—What Are Light Waves? 2014. (Light & Sound Waves Close-Up Ser.). (ENG., Illus.). 24p. (J). (gr. 1-2). (978-0-7787-0519-2(6)) Crabtree Publishing Co.

—What Are Shadows & Reflections? 2014. (Light & Sound Waves Close-Up Ser.). (ENG., Illus.). 24p. (J). (gr. 1-2). (978-0-7787-0521-5(8)) Crabtree Publishing Co.

Kelly, Lynne. Simple Concepts in Physics: Sound & Light. (Illus.). 88p. (J). (gr. 5-6). pap. (978-1-875739-69-1(6)) Wizard Bks.

Kenney, Karen Latchana. The Science of Color: Investigating Light. 2015. (Science in Action Ser.). (ENG., Illus.). 32p. (J). (gr. 3-6). 32.79 (978-1-62403-960-7(X), 19417, Checkerboard Library) ABDO Publishing Co.

Keranen, Rachel. The Big Bang Theory & Light Spectra, 1 vol. 2016. (Space Systems Ser.). (ENG., Illus.). 112p. (J). (gr. 8-8). lib. bdg. 44.50 (978-1-5026-2295-2(5), a65f561b-ae97-4098-8171-fb224d9c8181) Cavendish Square Publishing LLC.

Kittinger, Jo S. Light (a True Book: Physical Science) (Library Edition) 2019. (True Book (Relaunch) Ser.). (ENG., Illus.). 48p. (J). (gr. 3-5). lib. bdg. 31.00 (978-0-531-13140-4(8), Children's Pr.) Scholastic Library Publishing.

Kleiner, Mariela. Meet Einstein. Garofoli, Viviana, illus. 2011. 28p. (J). (gr. -1-1). lib. bdg. (978-0-615-31579-9(8)) Meet Bks., LLC.

Koontz, Robin. Light in the Real World. 2013. (Science in the Real World Ser.). (ENG., Illus.). 48p. (J). (gr. 4-8). pap. 18.50 (978-1-61783-791-3(1), 14615) ABDO Publishing Co.

Kopp, Megan. Light Works. 2011. (J). 27.13 (978-1-61690-385-5(6)); (J). (gr. 4-6). pap. 12.95 (978-1-61690-839-3(4), AV2 by Weigl); (Illus.). 24p. (YA). (gr. 3-6). 27.13 (978-1-61690-835-5(1)) Weigl Pubs., Inc.

Lang, Sheri. Let's Measure Daylight: Organizing Data, 1 vol. 2017. (Computer Kids: Powered by Computational Thinking Ser.). (ENG.). 24p. (J). (gr. 4-5). 25.27 (978-1-5383-2406-6(7), 8dd2301d-3165-45f6-b943-41d8c629d15d, PowerKids Pr.); pap. (978-1-5081-3764-1(1), f32c7c0a-4bfa-4c31-a3af-8fa0b019a8b4, Rosen Classroom) Rosen Publishing Group, Inc., The.

Lawrence, Ellen. Light. 2014. (Science Slam: FUN-Damentals Ser.). 24p. (J). (gr. -1-3). lib. bdg. 26.99 (978-1-62724-093-2(4)) Bearport Publishing Co., Inc.

Light. (Jump Ser.). (Illus.). 32p. (J). (gr. 2-7). pap. (978-1-882210-28-2(X)) Action Publishing, Inc.

Light. 2009. 67p. pap. 18.00 (978-0-9841252-1-0(3)) Poet's Passage Pr., The.

LIGHT & SOUND. 2010. (ENG., Illus.). 128p. (gr. 6-12). 35.00 (978-1-60413-344-8(9), P179270, Facts On File) Infobase Holdings, Inc.

Lindeen, Mary. Light. 2017. (Beginning-To-Read Ser.). (ENG.). 32p. (J). (gr. k-2). pap. 13.26 (978-1-68404-100-8(7)); (Illus.). 22.60 (978-1-59953-881-5(4)) Norwood Hse. Pr.

Lowery, Lawrence F. Dark As a Shadow. 2014. (I Wonder Why Ser.). (ENG., Illus.). 36p. (gr. k-3). pap. 11.95 (978-1-941316-06-1(9), P241370) National Science Teachers Assn.

Mader, Jan. How Does Light Move?, 1 vol. 2018. (How Does It Move? Forces & Motion Ser.). (ENG.). 32p. (gr. 3-3). 30.21 (978-1-5026-3779-6(0), 99f686a1-0295-4473-b47c-739b44cb55cc) Cavendish Square Publishing LLC.

Madgwick, Wendy. First Science Library: Light & Dark. 2014. (ENG., Illus.). 32p. (J). (gr. k-2). 8.99 (978-1-86147-355-4(9), Armadillo) Anness Publishing GBR. Dist: National Bk. Network.

Mahaney, Ian F. Light. (Energy in Action Ser.). 24p. (gr. 3-3). 2009. 42.50 (978-1-61512-259-2(1), PowerKids Pr.) 2007. (ENG., Illus.). (YA). lib. bdg. 26.27 (978-1-4042-3476-5(4), 6f958087-0feb-4b4d-865d-94bbf08a35e0) 2006. (ENG.). pap. 7.05 (978-1-4042-2185-7(9), 8285358c-ac3f-4cc4-8e3d-478e7179ec1c, PowerKids Pr.) Rosen Publishing Group, Inc., The.

Mattern, Joanne. The Sun & Animals. 2019. (Power of the Sun Ser.). (ENG.). 32p. (gr. 3-3). 63.48 (978-1-5026-4663-7(3)) Cavendish Square Publishing LLC.

Matthews, John R. The Light Bulb. 2005. (Inventions That Shaped the World Ser.). (Illus.). 80p. (J). (gr. 5-8). 17.60 (978-0-7569-6858-8(5)) Perfection Learning Corp.

Maurer, Daniel D. Do You Really Want to Walk in the Dark? A Book about Light. Alberini, Teresa, illus. 2016. (Adventures in Science Ser.). (ENG.). 24p. (J). (gr. 1-4). lib. bdg. 20.95 (978-1-60753-960-5(8), 15632) Amicus.

Monroe, Tilda. What Do You Know about Light?, 1 vol. 2010. (20 Questions: Physical Science Ser.). (ENG.). 24p. (J). (gr. 2-3). pap. 9.25 (978-1-4488-1250-9(X), e0113836-f8f0-4eaa-9b5e-54fc6ed8c570, PowerKids Pr.); lib. bdg. 26.27 (978-1-4488-0672-0(0), 7dc66f7d-c46c-481d-bdd7-07406766fb99) Rosen Publishing Group, Inc., The.

Moon, Walt K. Let's Explore Light. 2018. (Bumba Books (r) — a First Look at Physical Science Ser.). (ENG., Illus.). 24p. (J). (gr. -1-1). 26.65 (978-1-5124-8270-6(6), 136f1721-36e0-4e38-b599-1c0d08e3027d, Lerner Pubns.) Lerner Publishing Group.

Murray, Julie. Light & Dark. 2018. (Opposites Ser.). (ENG., Illus.). 24p. (J). (gr. -1-2). lib. bdg. 31.36 (978-1-5321-8181-8(7), 29835, Abdo Kids) ABDO Publishing Co.

National Geographic Learning. Language, Literacy & Vocabulary - Reading Expeditions (Physical Science): Looking at Light. 2007. (Avenues Ser.). (ENG., Illus.). 36p. (J). pap. 20.95 (978-0-7922-5438-6(4)) CENGAGE Learning.

—Reading Expeditions (Science: on Assignment): Peering into Darkness. 2007. (ENG., Illus.). 32p. (J). pap. 18.95 (978-0-7922-8451-2(8)) CENGAGE Learning.

—Reading Expeditions (Science: Physical Science): the Magic of Light & Sound. 2006. (Nonfiction Reading & Writing Workshops Ser.). (ENG., Illus.). 32p. (J). pap. 18.95 (978-0-7922-8886-2(6)) CENGAGE Learning.

Nunn, Daniel. Light, 1 vol. 2012. (Why Living Things Need Ser.). (ENG.). 24p. (gr. -1-1). pap. 6.29 (978-1-4329-5922-7(0), 117624, Heinemann) Capstone.

—Light & Dark, 1 vol. 2012. (Light All Around Us Ser.). (ENG.). 24p. (gr. -1-1). pap. 6.29 (978-1-4329-6627-0(8), 119253, Heinemann) Capstone.

O'Dell, Kathryn. The Science of Light Low Intermediate Book with Online Access, 1 vol. 2014. (ENG., Illus.). 28p. (J). pap., E-Book, E-Book 9.50 (978-1-107-68198-9(7)) Cambridge Univ. Pr.

Peterson, Megan Cooley. Scooby-Doo! a Science of Light Mystery: The Angry Alien. Brizuela, Dario, illus. 2017. (Scooby-Doo Solves It with S. T. E. M. Ser.). (ENG.). 32p. (J). (gr. 3-6). pap. 7.95 (978-1-5157-3704-9(7), 133673, Capstone Pr.) Capstone.

Pfeffer, Wendy. Light Is All Around Us. Meisel, Paul, illus. 2015. (Let's-Read-And-Find-Out Science 2 Ser.). (ENG.). 40p. (J). (gr. -1-3). pap. 6.99 (978-0-06-238190-3(3), HarperCollins) HarperCollins Pubs.

Prentice-Hall Staff. Sound & Light. 2nd ed. (J). stu. ed. 7.97 (978-0-13-400565-2(1)); pap., act. bk. ed. (978-0-13-400581-2(3)) Prentice Hall (Schl. Div.).

Pronnette, Veronica H. The Ancestors Anansi & the Light: A Delightful African Proverb Retold about How Light was Created by a Spider. 2009. 32p. pap. 14.49 (978-1-4343-5430-3(X)) AuthorHouse.

Rajczak Nelson, Kristen. Rainbows, 1 vol. 2012. (Nature's Light Show Ser.). (ENG., Illus.). 24p. (J). (gr. 2-3). pap. 9.15 (978-1-4339-7032-0(5), 5163d1c2-ca97-4b9f-a70a-f30739698ca0); lib. bdg. 25.27 (978-1-4339-7031-3(7), 6af4df4a-cd24-4078-b2f1-bc3c5dbf63cd) Stevens, Gareth Publishing LLLP.

Randolph, Joane. Light in My World. 2009. (My World of Science Ser.). 24p. (gr. 2-2). 37.50 (978-1-61514-725-0(X), PowerKids Pr.) Rosen Publishing Group, Inc., The.

Randolph, Joanne. Light in My World, 1 vol. (Journeys Ser.). (ENG.). 24p. (gr. k-2). 2006. pap. 7.05 (978-1-4042-8420-3(6), 9f628779-7532-472b-abd2-a7ba5288a87e, Rosen Classroom) 2005. (Illus.). (J). lib. bdg. 22.27 (978-1-4042-3286-0(9), 17155b7b-8a4e-46f5-ac7e-66609ddd4737, PowerKids Pr.) Rosen Publishing Group, Inc., The.

—Light in My World: La Luz en Mi Mundo, 1 vol. 2005. (My World of Science / la Ciencia en Mi Mundo Ser.). (ENG & SPA.). 24p. (J). (gr. 2-2). 22.27 (978-1-4042-3317-1(2), 6eeff538-4b3f-48c7-bfff-c9aaf2433d96) Rosen Publishing Group, Inc., The.

—Light in My World/la luz en mi Mundo. 2009. (My World of Science/la ciencia en mi mundo Ser.). (ENG & SPA.). 48p. (gr. 2-2). 37.50 (978-1-61514-737-3(3), Editorial Buenas Letras) Rosen Publishing Group, Inc., The.

Rea, Thelma. I Wonder Why the Sky Is Blue. 2009. (Reading Room Collection 2 Ser.). 24p. (gr. 3-4). 42.50 (978-1-60851-973-6(2), PowerKids Pr.) Rosen Publishing Group, Inc., The.

Rector, Rebecca Kraft. Color. 2019. (Let's Learn about Matter Ser.). (ENG.). 24p. (gr. 1-2). 56.10 (978-1-9785-0906-1(5)) Enslow Publishing, LLC.

Richards, Jon. Light & Sight. 2009. (Science Factory Ser.). 32p. (gr. 4-5). 50.50 (978-1-60853-022-9(1), PowerKids Pr.) Rosen Publishing Group, Inc., The.

Riley, Peter. Light, 1 vol. 2016. (Moving up with Science Ser.). (ENG.). 32p. (J). (gr. 3-4). pap. 11.00 (978-1-4994-3145-2(7), 9a5f3cc4-c4fd-40ea-ae67-44531723f4ce, PowerKids Pr.) Rosen Publishing Group, Inc., The.

—Light & Seeing. 2007. (Essential Science/Watts Ser.). (Illus.). 32p. (J). (gr. 4-7). lib. bdg. 28.50 (978-1-59920-028-6(7)) Black Rabbit Bks.

Rivera, Andrea. Light. 2017. (Science Concepts Ser.). (ENG., Illus.). 24p. (J). (gr. -1-2). lib. bdg. 31.36 (978-1-5321-2052-7(4), 25354, Abdo Zoom-Launch) ABDO Publishing Co.

Roberts, Abigail B. Using Lenses, 1 vol. 2017. (Super Science Tools Ser.). (ENG.). 24p. (J). (gr. 1-2). pap. 9.15 (978-1-4824-6389-7(X), 06ccbcb4-5d77-4834-bb28-a783df8cfefc) Stevens, Gareth Publishing LLLP.

Rogers, K. Light, Sound & Electricity. 2004. (Library of Science Ser.). 64p. (J). lib. bdg. 17.95 (978-1-58086-376-6(0)) EDC Publishing.

Rose, Simon. Sources of Light. 2011. (J). (978-1-61690-386-2(4)); (J). (gr. 4-6). pap. 12.95 (978-1-61690-840-9(8), AV2 by Weigl); (Illus.). 24p. (YA). (gr. 3-6). 27.13 (978-1-61690-836-2(X)) Weigl Pubs., Inc.

—What Is Light? 2011. (J). (gr. 4-6). pap. 12.95 (978-1-61690-842-3(4), AV2 by Weigl); (Illus.). 24p. (YA). (gr. 3-6). 27.13 (978-1-61690-838-6(6)) Weigl Pubs., Inc.

Royston, Angela. Light & Dark, 1 vol. 2011. (Science Corner Ser.). (ENG., Illus.). 24p. (J). (gr. 2-2). lib. bdg. 26.27 (978-1-4488-5258-1(7), 6770ef8e-d5ef-4169-8405-7c3a87b7831e) Rosen Publishing Group, Inc., The.

Rubio, Elizabeth. Understanding & Using Visible Light, 1 vol. 2021. (Electromagnetic Spectrum Ser.). (ENG.). 64p. (J). (gr. 7-7). pap. 16.24 (978-1-9785-1497-3(2), f669fc00-d56b-4347-8e0d-0f71649eab55) Enslow Publishing, LLC.

Ruchlis, Hyman. The Wonder of Light: A Picture Story of How & Why We See. Hirsh, Alice, illus. 2011. 160p. 41.95 (978-1-258-09816-2(4)) Literary Licensing, LLC.

Schuh, Mari. Crayola (r) la Ciencia Del Color (Crayola (r) Science of Color) 2019. (Crayola (r) Colorología (tm) (Crayola (r) Colorology (tm)) Ser.). (SPA., Illus.). 32p. (J). (gr. -1-3). pap. 7.99 (978-1-5415-4534-2(6), defbe99e-29b3-4c7b-ae43-f698da3a2a31, Ediciones Lerner) Lerner Publishing Group.

—Crayola (r) Science of Color. 2018. (Crayola (r) Colorology (tm) Ser.). (ENG., Illus.). 32p. (J). (gr. -1-3). 29.32 (978-1-5124-6691-1(3), 9dbd0048-40e9-49f1-96f6-fe6b2d03f3fd, Lerner Pubns.) Lerner Publishing Group.

—How Are Shadows & Reflections Made? 2019. (Let's Look at Light Ser.). (ENG., Illus.). 24p. (J). (gr. -1-2). pap. 6.95 (978-1-9771-1041-1(X), 141117, Pebble) Capstone.

—Is It Light or Dark? 2019. (Let's Look at Light Ser.). (ENG., Illus.). 24p. (J). (gr. -1-2). 29.32 (978-1-9771-0893-7(8), 140500, Pebble) Capstone.

—Light. 2007. (First Science Ser.). (ENG., Illus.). 24p. (J). (gr. 2-5). lib. bdg. 26.95 (978-1-60014-097-6(1)) Bellwether Media.

—Where Does Light Come From? 2019. (Let's Look at Light Ser.). (ENG., Illus.). 24p. (J). (gr. -1-2). pap. 6.95 (978-1-9771-1042-8(8), 141118, Pebble) Capstone.

—Why Is Light Important? 2019. (Let's Look at Light Ser.). (ENG., Illus.). 24p. (J). (gr. -1-2). 29.32 (978-1-9771-0896-8(2), 140503, Pebble) Capstone.

Shaffer, Jody Jensen. Vampires & Light, 6 vols. Flocco, Gervasio, illus. 2013. (Monster Science Ser.). (ENG.). 32p. (J). (gr. 3-4). pap. 48.60 (978-1-62065-821-5(6), 19402); pap. 8.10 (978-1-62065-820-8(8), 121776); lib. bdg. 31.32 (978-1-4296-9928-0(0), 120638) Capstone. (Capstone Pr.).

Silverman, Buffy. Let's Investigate Light. 2012. (My Science Library). (ENG., Illus.). 24p. (gr. 4-5). pap. 8.95 (978-1-61810-241-6(9), 9781618102416) Rourke Educational Media.

—Me & My Shadow: A Book about Light. 2011. (My Science Library). (ENG., Illus.). 24p. (gr. 1-2). pap. 9.95 (978-1-61741-943-0(5), 9781617419430) Rourke Educational Media.

Sohn, Emily. The Illuminating World of Light with Max Axiom, Super Scientist, 1 vol. Derington, Nick, illus. 2008. (Graphic Science Ser.). (ENG.). 32p. (J). (gr. 3-9). pap. 8.10 (978-1-4296-1768-0(3), 94815) Capstone.

Spilsbury, Richard & Spilsbury, Louise. The Cave of Shadows. 2015. (Science Adventures Ser.). (ENG., Illus.). 32p. (J). (gr. 3-7). 31.35 (978-1-62588-147-2(9)) Black Rabbit Bks.

—What Is Light? Exploring Science with Hands-On Activities, 1 vol. 2007. (In Touch with Basic Science Ser.). (ENG., Illus.). 32p. (gr. 3-3). lib. bdg. 26.60 (978-0-7660-3097-8(0), 9482faf9-028c-468b-9d70-cacec94c16fb, Enslow Elementary) Enslow Publishing, LLC.

Sundance/Newbridge LLC Staff. Light. 2007. (Early Science Ser.). (gr. k-3). 18.95 (978-1-4007-6314-6(2)); pap. 6.10 (978-1-4007-6310-8(X)) Sundance/Newbridge Educational Publishing.

Taylor, Kim. Light. (Illus.). 32p. (YA). (gr. 3-18). lib. bdg. 27.10 (978-1-931983-75-4(5)) Chrysalis Education.

Top That Publishing Staff, ed. Light Science. 2004. (Top That! Labs Ser.). (Illus.). 24p. (J). (978-1-84510-153-4(7)) Top That! Publishing PLC.

Torrence, Jack. Light Show: Reflection & Absorption, 1 vol. (Amazing Science Ser.). (ENG.). 24p. (gr. 3-3). 2009. (J). lib. bdg. 26.27 (978-1-4358-2974-9(3), 6b3dd7ff-2d8a-438a-87a8-c6695025c252, PowerKids Pr.) 2008. pap. 8.25 (978-1-4358-0096-0(6), a2dafbf8-b955-4129-acd3-e7c864fbcc88, Rosen Classroom) Rosen Publishing Group, Inc., The.

Trumbauer, Lisa. All about Light (Rookie Read-About Science: Physical Science: Previous Editions) 2004. (Rookie Read-About Science Ser.). (ENG.). 32p. (J). (gr. 1-2). pap. 4.95 (978-0-516-25842-3(7), Children's Pr.) Scholastic Library Publishing.

Twist, Clint. Light & Sound. 2010. (Science Everywhere! Ser.). 24p. 24.25 (978-1-84898-297-0(6)) Black Rabbit Bks.

—Light & Sound: The Best Start in Science. 2013. (Little Science Stars Ser.). (ENG.). 24p. (J). (gr. k-3). 18.69 (978-1-84696-191-5(2), TickTock Books) Octopus Publishing Group GBR. Dist: Children's Plus, Inc.

Upgrade kit dsm-3 Color&light. (J). 2004. (978-1-59242-527-3(5)) 2003. (978-1-59242-410-8(4)) Delta Education, LLC.

Wadsworth, Pamela. Golwg Gyntaf Ar Olau. 2005. (WEL., Illus.). 24p. pap. (978-1-85596-249-1(7)) Dref Wen.

Walker, Sally M. Investigating Light. 2011. (Searchlight Books (tm) — How Does Energy Work? Ser.). (ENG., Illus.). (gr. 3-5). 40p. (J). pap. 9.99 (978-0-7613-7873-0(1), 4e1eea73-0b1a-498c-8b83-98c112c041f4); pap. 51.01 (978-0-7613-8407-6(3)) Lerner Publishing Group.

—Light. 2006. (Illus.). 48p. (J). pap. 8.95 *(978-0-8225-2842-5(8))* Lerner Publishing Group.

—Light. King, Andy, photos by. 2005. (Early Bird Energy Ser.). (ENG., Illus.). 48p. (gr. 2-5). lib. bdg. 26.60 *(978-0-8225-2925-5(4)*, Lerner Pubns.) Lerner Publishing Group.

—La Luz. Translations.com Staff, tr. from ENG. King, Andy, photos by. 2007. (Libros de Energía para madrugadores (Early Bird Energy) Ser.). (SPA., Illus.). 48p. (J). (gr. 2-5). lib. bdg. 26.60 *(978-0-8225-7719-5(4))* Lerner Publishing Group.

—La Luz; Light. 2008. pap. 52.95 *(978-0-8225-9869-5(8))* Lerner Publishing Group.

Way, Steve & Bailey, Gerry. Light & Color, 1 vol. 2008. (Simply Science Ser.). (ENG., Illus.). 32p. (YA). (gr. 3-5). lib. bdg. 28.67 *(978-0-8368-9229-1(1)*, a0065aac-ef79-4132-b45c-125c8202d1c7) Stevens, Gareth Publishing LLLP.

Weakland, Mark. What Is Light? 2019. (Science Basics Ser.). (ENG., Illus.). 24p. (J). (gr. 1-3). pap. 7.95 *(978-1-9771-0509-7(2)*, 139898, Capstone Pr.) Capstone.

Whitfield, David. Northern Lights. 2006. (Science Matters Ser.). (Illus.). 24p. (J). (gr. 3-7). lib. bdg. 24.45 *(978-1-59036-413-0(9))*; pap. 8.95 *(978-1-59036-419-2(8))* Weigl Pubs., Inc.

Whiting, Jim. Light. (Mysteries of the Universe Ser.). (ENG., Illus.). 48p. (J). (gr. 5-9). 2013. pap. 12.00 *(978-0-89812-915-1(X)*, 21929, Creative Paperbacks) 2012. 23.95 *(978-1-60818-190-2(1)*, 21922, Creative Education) Creative Co., The.

Wick, Walter. A Ray of Light. Wick, Walter, illus. 2019. (ENG., Illus.). 40p. (J). (gr. 1-3). 19.99 *(978-0-439-16587-7(3)*, Scholastic Pr.) Scholastic, Inc.

Winterberg, Jenna. Light & Its Effects. 2015. (Science: Informational Text Ser.). (ENG., Illus.). 32p. (J). (gr. 3-5). pap. 11.99 *(978-1-4807-4685-5(1))* Teacher Created Materials, Inc.

Woodford, Chris. Light: Investigating Visible & Invisible Electromagnetic Radiation, 1 vol. 2012. (Scientific Pathways Ser.). (ENG., Illus.). 48p. (J). (gr. 5-5). lib. bdg. 34.47 *(978-1-4488-7202-2(2)*, 2ba1389a-a391-4d9f-b53a-6647d2c6e83d, Rosen Reference) Rosen Publishing Group, Inc., The.

—Light & Radiation. 2004. (Routes of Science Ser.). (Illus.). 40p. (J). (gr. 4-7). 24.95 *(978-1-4103-0297-7(0)*, Blackbirch Pr., Inc.) Cengage Gale.

World Book, Inc. Staff, contrib. by. Light. 2011. (J). *(978-0-7166-1426-5(X))* World Bk., Inc.

Wyatt, Katherine. The Science of Light & Color, 1 vol. 2013. (Rosen Readers Ser.). (ENG.). 24p. (J). (gr. 3-3). pap. 8.25 *(978-1-4777-2575-7(X)*, ed88b046-7807-492f-8117-7d518e27053a); pap. 49.50 *(978-1-4777-2576-4(8))* Rosen Publishing Group, Inc., The. (Rosen Classroom).

Yasuda, Anita. Explore Light & Optics! With 25 Great Projects. Stone, Bryan, illus. 2016. (Explore Your World Ser.). (ENG.). 96p. (J). (gr. 1-5). 19.95 *(978-1-61930-376-8(0)*, 249eee93-cd95-4566-a2bd-cbe9681cb26b); pap. 14.95 *(978-1-61930-380-5(9)*, 43f6238f-1c00-4c39-b7ec-01737b816ac2) Nomad Pr.

LIGHT—EXPERIMENTS

Boothroyd, Jennifer. Playing with Light & Shadows. 2014. (First Step Nonfiction — Light & Sound Ser.). (ENG., Illus.). 24p. (J). (gr. k-2). pap. 6.99 *(978-1-4677-4503-1(0)*, 071b5ea1-3d71-4aea-999d-b65c550ed5c3) Lerner Publishing Group.

Canavan, Thomas. Super Experiments with Light & Sound. Linley, Adam, illus. 2017. (Mind-Blowing Science Experiments Ser.). 32p. (gr. 4-5). pap. 63.00 *(978-1-5382-0733-8(8))* Stevens, Gareth Publishing LLLP.

Claybourne, Anna. Light & Dark. 2012. (ENG., Illus.). 24p. (gr. k-4). pap. 7.95 *(978-1-926853-57-4(1))* Saunders Bk. Co. CAN. Dist: RiverStream Publishing.

—Recreate Discoveries about Light. 2018. (Recreate Scientific Discoveries Ser.). (Illus.). 32p. (J). (gr. 4-5). *(978-0-7787-5052-9(3))* Crabtree Publishing Co.

Cook, Trevor. Experiments with Light & Sound, 1 vol. 2009. (Science Lab Ser.). (ENG.). 32p. (J). (gr. 4-4). lib. bdg. 30.27 *(978-1-4358-2808-7(9)*, b61bea01-717d-45c1-b683-2575f99682f9); (Illus.). pap. 11.00 *(978-1-4358-3221-3(3)*, cad2d49f-cf1b-4498-a90d-b9ac44faa841) Rosen Publishing Group, Inc., The. (PowerKids Pr.).

Edom, H. Science Activities, Vol. 1. 2010. (Science Activities Ser.). 72p. (J). 13.99 *(978-0-7945-2752-5(3)*, Usborne) EDC Publishing.

Gardner, Robert. Easy Genius Science Projects with Light: Great Experiments & Ideas, 1 vol. 2008. (Easy Genius Science Projects Ser.). (ENG., Illus.). 128p. (gr. 5-6). lib. bdg. 35.93 *(978-0-7660-2926-2(3)*, 536e0326-ced6-4dbb-9ac3-95cf79547ba6) Enslow Publishing, LLC.

—Light, Sound, & Waves Science Fair Projects, Using the Scientific Method, 1 vol. 2010. (Physics Science Projects Using the Scientific Method Ser.). (ENG., Illus.). 160p. (gr. 5-6). 38.60 *(978-0-7660-3416-7(X)*, a9e26572-5a3f-47d1-bd08-f3116b6e00ac) Enslow Publishing, LLC.

Gardner, Robert & Conklin, Joshua. A Kid's Book of Experiments with Light, 1 vol. 2015. (Surprising Science Experiments Ser.). (ENG.). 48p. (gr. 4-4). pap. 12.70 *(978-0-7660-7203-9(7)*, a89bbe49-c054-4332-9967-36b12e086a73) Enslow Publishing, LLC.

Jackson, Tom. Experiments with Light & Color, 1 vol. 2010. (Cool Science Ser.). (ENG., Illus.). 32p. (J). (gr. 4-5). pap. 11.50 *(978-1-4339-3454-4(X)*, ae1e39cc-058a-41f7-9f7b-fd2a25aa0fef); lib. bdg. 30.67 *(978-1-4339-3453-7(1)*, 371ab775-e76c-46eb-9e22-c01ad4211ac3) Stevens, Gareth Publishing LLLP. (Gareth Stevens Learning Library).

Jacobson, Ryan. Light & Vision. 2016. (J). *(978-1-4896-5283-6(3))* Weigl Pubs., Inc.

Kessler, Colleen. A Project Guide to Light & Optics. 2011. (Physical Science Projects for Kids Ser.). (Illus.). 48p. (J). (gr. 3-6). lib. bdg. 29.95 *(978-1-58415-969-8(3)*, 1327831) Mitchell Lane Pubs.

Meiani, Antonella. Light. 2003. (Experimenting with Science Ser.). (Illus.). 40p. (J). (gr. 4-8). lib. bdg. 23.93 *(978-0-8225-0084-1(1))* Lerner Publishing Group.

Merrill, Amy French. Everyday Physical Science Experiments with Light, 1 vol. 2005. (Content-Area Literacy Collections). (ENG.). 24p. (gr. 3-4). pap. 8.85 *(978-1-4042-5679-8(2)*, 0470f6a5-c2b4-451a-90f6-00627ebbb844) Rosen Publishing Group, Inc., The.

—Everyday Physical Science Experiments with Light & Sound. 2009. (Science Surprises Ser.). 24p. (gr. 3-3). 42.50 *(978-1-60853-061-8(2)*, PowerKids Pr.) Rosen Publishing Group, Inc., The.

Oxlade, Chris. Experiments with Sound & Light, 1 vol. 2014. (Excellent Science Experiments Ser.). (ENG., Illus.). 32p. (J). (gr. 4-5). lib. bdg. 29.27 *(978-1-4777-5965-3(4)*, 8ceee608-5c78-425e-82f9-1b8d9e130ea2, PowerKids Pr.) Rosen Publishing Group, Inc., The.

—Super Science Light & Sound Experiments: 10 Amazing Experiments with Step-By-Step Photographs. 2016. (ENG., Illus.). (J). pap. *(978-1-78209-421-0(0))* Miles Kelly Publishing, Ltd.

Rau, Dana Meachen. Light. 2009. (Explorer Library: Science Explorer Ser.). (ENG., Illus.). 32p. (gr. 4-8). lib. bdg. 32.07 *(978-1-60279-531-0(2)*, 200285) Cherry Lake Publishing.

Richards, Jon. Light & Sight, 1 vol. Moores, Ian & Thompson, Ian, illus. 2007. (Science Factory Ser.). (ENG.). 32p. (YA). (gr. 4-5). lib. bdg. 30.27 *(978-1-4042-3904-3(9)*, b65db607-440b-4923-b761-626b8d517a7e) Rosen Publishing Group, Inc., The.

Riley, Peter D. Light. 2011. (Real Scientist Investigates Ser.). (Illus.). 32p. (J). (gr. 3-5). lib. bdg. 28.50 *(978-1-59771-281-1(7))* Sea-To-Sea Pubns.

Rowe, Brooke. Making a Rainbow. Bane, Jeff, illus. 2017. (My Early Library: My Science Fun Ser.). (ENG.). 24p. (J). (gr. k-1). lib. bdg. 30.64 *(978-1-63472-819-5(X)*, 209702) Cherry Lake Publishing.

Royston, Angela. Experiments with a Flashlight. 2016. (One-Stop Science Ser.). 32p. (gr. 2-5). 31.35 *(978-1-62588-141-0(X)*, Smart Apple Media) Black Rabbit Bks.

Schneider, Christa. Light It! Creations That Glow, Shine, & Blink. 2017. (Cool Makerspace Gadgets & Gizmos Ser.). (ENG.). 32p. (J). (gr. 3-6). lib. bdg. 34.21 *(978-1-5321-1253-9(X)*, 27584, Checkerboard Library) ABDO Publishing Co.

Spilsbury, Richard. Investigating Light. 2018. (Investigating Science Challenges Ser.). (ENG., Illus.). 32p. (J). (gr. 4-4). *(978-0-7787-4207-4(5))*; pap. *(978-0-7787-4294-4(6))* Crabtree Publishing Co.

Thomas, Isabel. Experiments with Light. 2015. (Read & Experiment Ser.). (ENG., Illus.). 32p. (J). (gr. 2-4). 33.32 *(978-1-4109-6837-1(5)*, 128047, Raintree) Capstone.

Walker, Richard. Light & Sound, 1 vol. 2005. (Real World Science Ser.). (ENG., Illus.). 32p. (gr. 3-5). lib. bdg. 28.67 *(978-0-8368-6306-2(2)*, 9809b3f3-dd5e-495a-8481-dce1ae4538e1, Gareth Stevens Learning Library) Stevens, Gareth Publishing LLLP.

LIGHT AMPLIFICATION BY STIMULATED EMISSION OF RADIATION

see Lasers

LIGHT AND SHADE

see Shadows

LIGHT SHIPS

see Lightships

LIGHTHOUSES

see also Lightships

Batchelor, John. Lighthouses of the World. 2004. (Dover World History Coloring Bks.). (ENG., Illus.). 32p. (J). (gr. 3-8). pap. 4.99 *(978-0-486-43685-2(3)*, 436853) Dover Pubns., Inc.

Bissonette, Aimee. Miss Colfax's Light. Ewen, Eileen Ryan, illus. 2016. (ENG.). 32p. (J). (gr. 1-4). 16.99 *(978-1-58536-955-3(1)*, 204029) Sleeping Bear Pr.

Clifford, Mary Louise & Clifford, J. Candace. Mind the Light, Katie: The History of Thirty-Three Female Lighthouse Keepers. 2006. (Illus.). iv, 136p. (J). per. 12.95 *(978-0-9636412-7-4(1))* Cypress Communications.

The Colors of the Lighthouse: A Children's History of Absecon Lighthouse. 2006. (J). 8.95 *(978-0-9779988-0-7(0))* Absecon Lighthouse.

De Wire, Elinor. Florida Lighthouses for Kids. 2004. (ENG., Illus.). 64p. (J). (gr. -1-12). pap. 12.95 *(978-1-56164-323-3(8))* Pineapple Pr., Inc.

Glupker, Dianne & Delsi, Dawna. Great Lights of Michigan. Delsi, Dawna, illus. 2005. (Illus.). (J). per. 9.95 *(978-0-9769846-0-3(1)*, 318924) Harambee Pr.

Holden, Pam. About Lighthouses, 1 vol. 2015. (ENG., Illus.). 16p. (-1). pap. *(978-1-77654-077-8(8)*, Red Rocket Readers) Flying Start Bks.

House, Katherine L. Lighthouses for Kids: History, Science, & Lore with 21 Activities. 2008. (For Kids Ser.: 26). (ENG., Illus.). 128p. (J). (gr. 4-7). pap. 16.99 *(978-1-55652-720-3(9))* Chicago Review Pr., Inc.

Keep the Lights Burning. 9.95 *(978-1-59112-293-7(7))* Live Oak Media.

Krebs, Laurie. A Day in the Life of a Colonial Lighthouse Keeper. (Library of Living & Working in Colonial Times Ser.). 24p. (gr. 3-3). 2009. 42.50 *(978-1-60853-733-4(1)*, PowerKids Pr.) 2003. (ENG., Illus.). (J). lib. bdg. 26.27 *(978-0-8239-6226-6(1)*, 41475366-8539-435f-8390-3e2e08bc9bcf) Rosen Publishing Group, Inc., The.

Orr, Tamra B. How Did They Build That? Lighthouse. 2011. (Community Connections: How Did They Build That? Ser.). (ENG., Illus.). 24p. (gr. 2-5). lib. bdg. 29.21 *(978-1-61080-114-0(8)*, 201122) Cherry Lake Publishing.

A Pocketful of Passage. 2007. (Great Lakes Books Ser.). (ENG., Illus.). 96p. (gr. 3-7). cd-rom 12.95 *(978-0-8143-3341-9(9)*, P120523) Wayne State Univ. Pr.

PRESS, Celebration. Lighthouses: Beacons of the Past. 2003. (ENG.). (J). (gr. 2-5). pap., stu. ed. 34.95 *(978-0-673-62841-1(8)*, Celebration Pr.) Savvas Learning Co.

Roop, Connie & Roop, Peter. Keep the Lights Burning, Abbie. Hanson, Peter E., illus. 2016. (On My Own History Ser.). (ENG.). 40p. (J). (gr. 2-4). 38.65 *(978-1-5124-1862-0(5)*, Millbrook Pr.) Lerner Publishing Group.

Ruth, Angie. My Adventure at a Lighthouse. 2006. 44p. (J). 8.99 *(978-1-59092-316-0(2))* Blue Forge Pr.

Shardlow, Alice L. Crossing Completed: How the People of Eastham Saved Nauset Light. Sabin, Shirley C., photos by. 2006. (ENG.). 38p. pap. 15.99 *(978-1-4257-1638-7(5))* Xlibris Corp.

Silcox, Diane. A Light to Keep. Moates, Carol Meetze, illus. 2013. 30p. pap. 14.95 *(978-1-938101-36-6(7))* Indigo Sea Pr., LLC.

Weintraub, Aileen. Alcatraz Island Light: The West Coast's First Lighthouse. 2009. (Great Lighthouses of North America Ser.). 24p. (gr. 3-3). 42.50 *(978-1-61513-127-3(2)*, PowerKids Pr.) Rosen Publishing Group, Inc., The.

—Boston Light: The First Lighthouse in North America. 2009. (Great Lighthouses of North America Ser.). 24p. (gr. 3-3). 42.50 *(978-1-61513-128-0(0)*, PowerKids Pr.) Rosen Publishing Group, Inc., The.

—Cape Disappointment Light: The First Lighthouse in the Pacific Northwest. 2009. (Great Lighthouses of North America Ser.). 24p. (gr. 3-3). 42.50 *(978-1-61513-129-7(9)*, PowerKids Pr.) Rosen Publishing Group, Inc., The.

—Cape Hatteras Light: The Tallest Lighthouse in the United States. 2009. (Great Lighthouses of North America Ser.). 24p. (gr. 3-3). 42.50 *(978-1-61513-130-3(2)*, PowerKids Pr.) Rosen Publishing Group, Inc., The.

—Navesink Twin Lights: The First U. S. Lighthouse to Use a Fresnel Lens. 2009. (Great Lighthouses of North America Ser.). 24p. (gr. 3-3). 42.50 *(978-1-61513-131-0(0)*, PowerKids Pr.) Rosen Publishing Group, Inc., The.

—Point Pinos Light: The West Coast's Oldest Continuously Active Lighthouse. 2009. (Great Lighthouses of North America Ser.). 24p. (gr. 3-3). 42.50 *(978-1-61513-132-7(9)*, PowerKids Pr.) Rosen Publishing Group, Inc., The.

Wilbur, Helen L. B Is for Beacon: A Great Lakes Lighthouse Alphabet. Graef, Renée, illus. 2016. (ENG.). 32p. (J). (gr. 1-4). 18.99 *(978-1-58536-916-4(0)*, 204025) Sleeping Bear Pr.

Zepke, Terrance. Lighthouses of the Carolinas for Kids. 2009. (Carolinas for Kids Ser.). (ENG., Illus.). 64p. (J). (gr. -1-12). pap. 12.95 *(978-1-56164-429-2(3))* Pineapple Pr., Inc.

LIGHTHOUSES—FICTION

Acton, Vanessa. Skeleton Tower. 2016. (Atlas of Cursed Places Ser.). (ENG.). 104p. (YA). (gr. 6-12). lib. bdg. 26.65 *(978-1-5124-1322-9(4)*, 9ce51df2-0ee1-48f4-b48f-412a486a94d2, Darby Creek) Lerner Publishing Group.

Armitage, Ronda & Armitage, Donald. Lighthouse Keeper's Lunch. Date not set. (ENG., Illus.). 32p. (J). pap. *(978-0-05-004387-5(0))* Addison-Wesley Longman, Inc.

Blackall, Sophie. Hello Lighthouse (Caldecott Medal Winner) 2018. (ENG., Illus.). 48p. (J). (gr. -1-3). 18.99 *(978-0-316-36238-2(7))* Little, Brown Bks. for Young Readers.

Brown, Ruth. Gracie, the Lighthouse Cat. Brown, Ruth, illus. 2011. (Andersen Press Picture Bks). (ENG., Illus.). 32p. (J). (gr. -1-3). 16.95 *(978-0-7613-7454-1(X))* Lerner Publishing Group.

Bunting, Eve. Ghost Cat. Barry, Kevin M., illus. 2017. (ENG.). 32p. (J). (gr. k-2). 16.99 *(978-1-58536-993-5(4)*, 204323) Sleeping Bear Pr.

Butler, Gloria. Lighthouse Lindy. 2008. 16.95 *(978-0-9790469-6-4(3))* Arbor Bks.

Castro-Bran, Rose. The Adventures of Port Herman Lighthouse. 2008. 32p. pap. 14.95 *(978-1-4343-6547-7(6))* AuthorHouse.

Chakravorty, Amita. Rupadil's Lighthouse. 2011. 48p. pap. 19.67 *(978-1-4520-1904-8(5))* AuthorHouse.

Chase, Diana. The Light House Kids. 2003. (Illus.). 256p. (J). pap. 13.50 *(978-1-86368-346-3(1))* Fremantle Pr. AUS. Dist: Independent Pubs. Group.

Clark, Joyce. Katie. 2006. 196p. 27.43 *(978-1-4122-0067-7(9))* Trafford Publishing.

Coons, Susan. The Lighthouse Mouse. 2006. 19.99 *(978-0-9721410-1-7(4))* Vinland Pr.

Copeland, Cynthia L. Elin's Island. 2003. (Single Titles Ser.: up). (ENG.). 144p. (YA). (gr. 6-12). lib. bdg. 22.60 *(978-0-7613-2522-2(0)*, Millbrook Pr.) Lerner Publishing Group.

Cotter, Charis. The Painting. 2017. (Illus.). 288p. (J). (gr. 4-7). 16.99 *(978-1-101-91887-6(X)*, Tundra Bks.) Tundra Bks. CAN. Dist: Penguin Random Hse. LLC.

Crew, Gary. The Cat on the Island. Warden, Gillian, illus. 2008. 32p. *(978-0-207-20070-0(X))* HarperCollins Pubs. Australia.

Dilley, Ray. Brian's Lighthouse. 2013. 40p. pap. 19.99 *(978-1-4772-6663-2(1))* AuthorHouse.

Doyle, Patrick H. T. Edgar Font's Hunt for a House to Haunt: Adventure One: the Castle Tower Lighthouse. 2006. (Illus.). 213p. (J). (gr. -1). per. 6.99 *(978-0-9786132-0-4(1))* Armadillo Bks.

Dunn, Joeming & Warner, Gertrude Chandler. The Lighthouse Mystery, 1 vol., Bk. 14. Dunn, Ben, illus. 2011. (Boxcar Children Graphic Novels Ser.). (ENG.). 32p. (J). (gr. 2-8). 32.79 *(978-1-61641-122-0(8)*, 3684, Graphic Planet - Fiction) Magic Wagon.

Farren, Rick. Eliza's Wish. 2007. 154p. (J). per. 14.95 *(978-0-9794863-8-8(6))* Summerland Publishing.

—The Secret of the Lighthouse. 2004. (J). per. 12.95 *(978-0-9748087-3-4(3))* Journey Pubns., LLC.

—The Secret of the Lighthouse. 2007. 127p. (J). (gr. 1-7). per. 12.95 *(978-0-9794863-7-1(8))* Summerland Publishing.

Fletcher, Susan. Walk Across the Sea. 2003. (ENG., Illus.). 224p. (J). (gr. 4-8). pap. 11.95 *(978-0-689-85707-2(1)*, Atheneum Bks. for Young Readers) Simon & Schuster Children's Publishing.

Gutzschhahn, Uwe-Michael. The Lighthouse under the Clouds. Docherty, Thomas, illus. 2008. (ENG.). 32p. (J). (gr. -1-k). 19.00 *(978-1-906367-03-9(5))* National Maritime Museum GBR. Dist: Independent Pubs. Group.

Herman, Gail. Scooby-Doo in the Lighthouse Mystery, 1 vol. 2015. (Scooby-Doo! Ser.). (ENG., Illus.). 32p. (J). (gr. k-4). lib. bdg. 31.36 *(978-1-61479-410-3(3)*, 19449, Picture Bk.) Spotlight.

Hernandez, Ruben. Elisa Escuchaba el Canto de Las Ballenas. Corichi, Yadhira, illus. rev. ed. 2003. (Castillo de la Lectura Blanca Ser.). (SPA & ENG.). 48p. (J). (gr. 1-3). pap. 6.95 *(978-970-20-0141-6(2))* Castillo, Ediciones, S. A. de C. V. MEX. Dist: Macmillan.

Janis, Tim. Shine Like a Lighhouse. Steve, Lavigne, illus. 2nd ed. 2007. (J). 12.95 *(978-0-9773335-1-6(5))* Janis, Tim Ensemble, Inc.

Jansson, Tove. Moominpappa at Sea. Hart, Kingsley, tr. Jansson, Tove, illus. 2010. (Moomins Ser.: 7). (ENG., Illus.). 240p. (J). (gr. 4-7). pap. 8.99 *(978-0-312-60892-7(6)*, 900065186) Square Fish.

Kinkade, Thomas. Katherine's Story. 2004. (Girls of Lighthouse Lane Ser.). 176p. (J). (gr. 5-18). 13.89 *(978-0-06-054342-6(6))* HarperCollins Pubs.

Kinkade, Thomas & Tamar, Erika. Rose's Story. 2004. (Girls of Lighthouse Lane Ser.: No. 2). (Illus.). 192p. (J). (gr. 5-18). 12.99 *(978-0-06-054344-0(2))* HarperCollins Pubs.

Levy, Dana Alison. The Family Fletcher Takes Rock Island. 2017. (Family Fletcher Ser.: 2). (ENG.). 272p. (J). (gr. 4-7). 7.99 *(978-0-553-52133-7(0)*, Yearling) Random Hse. Children's Bks.

Licameli, Doris. Rowing to the Rescue: The Story of Ida Lewis, Famous Lighthouse Heroine. 2007. (ENG.). 80p. pap. 13.95 *(978-1-84728-668-0(2))* Lulu Pr., Inc.

Love, Pamela. Lighthouse Seeds. Warner, Linda, illus. 2004. (ENG.). 32p. (J). (gr. k-2). 15.95 *(978-0-89272-541-0(9))* Down East Bks.

Marsh, Carole. The Mystery on the Great Lakes. 2010. (Real Kids, Real Places Ser.). (Illus.). 158p. (J). 18.99 *(978-0-635-07449-2(4)*, Marsh, Carole Mysteries) Gallopade International.

Martin, Carol. The Lighthouse. 2011. 16p. 7.95 *(978-1-4497-0962-4(1)*, WestBow Pr.) Author Solutions, LLC.

Mason, Jane B. & Stephens, Sarah Hines. Bella Baxter & the Lighthouse Mystery. Shelley, John, illus. 2006. (Bella Baxter Ser.: 3). (ENG.). 80p. (J). (gr. 1-4). pap. 6.99 *(978-0-689-86282-3(2)*, Simon & Schuster/Paula Wiseman Bks.) Simon & Schuster/Paula Wiseman Bks.

McKinty, Adrian. The Lighthouse Land. 2006. (ENG., Illus.). 200p. (YA). (gr. 6-10). 16.95 *(978-0-8109-5480-9(X))* Abrams, Inc.

Messer, Celeste M. The Ghost of Piper's Landing. Hoeffner, Deb, illus. 2004. 82-92p. 4.95 *(978-0-9702171-7-2(X))* AshleyAlan Enterprises.

Panagopoulos, Janie Lynn. A Castle at the Straits. Evans, Laura, illus. 2003. 48p. (J). (gr. 1-6). *(978-0-911872-83-5(3))* Mackinac State Historic Parks.

Parsons, Carol. Mystery at Eagle Harbor Lighthouse. 2006. (J). pap. 11.95 *(978-1-59705-985-5(4))* Wings ePress, Inc.

Patterson, Nancy. May the Magnificent Lighthouse. Patterson, Nancy, illus. 2012. (Illus.). 24p. 18.95 *(978-0-615-61021-4(8))* Bayberry Cottage Gallery.

Pike, Christopher, pseud. The Howling Ghost. 2014. (Spooksville Ser.: 2). (ENG., Illus.). 128p. (J). (gr. 3-7). pap. 7.99 *(978-1-4814-1052-6(0)*, Aladdin) Simon & Schuster Children's Publishing.

Preus, Margi. Storm's Coming! Geister, David, illus. 2016. (ENG.). 32p. (J). 16.95 *(978-1-68134-018-0(6))* Minnesota Historical Society Pr.

Roy, James. Ichabod Hart & the Lighthouse Mystery. 2003. (Steampunk Ser.). (Illus.). 392p. pap. *(978-0-7022-3364-7(1))* Univ. of Queensland Pr.

Rylant, Cynthia. The Bear. McDaniels, Preston, illus. (Lighthouse Family Ser.: 8). (ENG.). 48p. (J). (gr. 1-5). 2019. pap. 5.99 *(978-1-4814-6029-3(3))* 2018. 17.99 *(978-1-4814-6028-6(5))* Beach Lane Bks. (Beach Lane Bks.).

—The Eagle. McDaniels, Preston, illus. 2004. (Lighthouse Family Ser.: 3). (ENG.). 64p. (J). (gr. 1-5). 17.99 *(978-0-689-86243-4(1)*, Simon & Schuster Bks. For Young Readers) Simon & Schuster Bks. For Young Readers.

—The Octopus. McDaniels, Preston, illus. 2005. (Lighthouse Family Ser.: 5). (ENG.). 64p. (J). (gr. 1-5). 17.99 *(978-0-689-86246-5(6)*, Simon & Schuster Bks. For Young Readers) Simon & Schuster Bks. For Young Readers.

—The Otter. McDaniels, Preston, illus. 2016. (Lighthouse Family Ser.: 6). (ENG.). 48p. (J). (gr. 1-5). 17.99 *(978-1-4814-6045-3(5)*, Beach Lane Bks.) Beach Lane Bks.

—The Sea Lion. McDaniels, Preston, illus. (Lighthouse Family Ser.: 7). (ENG.). 48p. (J). (gr. 1-5). 2018. pap. 5.99 *(978-1-4814-6026-2(9))* 2017. 17.99 *(978-1-4814-6025-5(0))* Beach Lane Bks. (Beach Lane Bks.).

—The Turtle. McDaniels, Preston, illus. 2006. (Lighthouse Family Ser.). 47p. (J). (gr. -1-3). 11.65 *(978-0-7569-6611-9(6))* Perfection Learning Corp.

—The Turtle. McDaniels, Preston, illus. 2005. (Lighthouse Family Ser.: 4). (ENG.). 48p. (J). (gr. 1-5). 17.99 *(978-0-689-86244-1(X)*, Simon & Schuster Bks. For Young Readers) Simon & Schuster Bks. For Young Readers.

Schaap, Annet. Of Salt & Shore. Watkinson, Laura, tr. from DUT. 2020. (ENG., Illus.). 352p. (J). (gr. 5). 16.99 *(978-1-62354-230-6(8))* Charlesbridge Publishing, Inc.

Schneider, Richard H. The Lighthouse Boy: A Story about Courage. Petrov, Anton, illus. 2007. (ENG.). 32p. (J). (gr. -1-3). pap. 8.99 *(978-0-8249-5557-1(9)*, Ideals Pubns.) Worthy Publishing.

Smith, Lauren E. Ashley Enright Investigations. 2006. 48p. pap. 16.95 *(978-1-4241-2963-8(X))* America Star Bks.

Smith, Ruth. Buddy Bear: Visits Michigan Lighthouses. 2010. 28p. pap. 13.99 *(978-1-4490-8363-2(3))* AuthorHouse.

Smucker, Anna Egan. To Keep the South Manitou Light. (Great Lakes Books Ser.). (ENG., Illus.). 2006. 130p. (gr. 3-7). per. 14.95 *(978-0-8143-3236-8(6)*, P120417) 2004. 140p. 23.95 *(978-0-8143-3235-1(8)*, P029609) Wayne State Univ. Pr.

Snowman, Sally R. Sammy the Boston Lighthouse Dog. 2005. (J). (gr. 3-5). 15.00 *(978-0-9674666-2-0(8))* Snowman Learning Center, The.

Stainton, Sue. The Lighthouse Cat. Mortimer, Anne, illus. 2004. (ENG.). 32p. (J). (gr. -1-2). 17.99 *(978-0-06-009604-5(7)*, Tegen, Katherine Bks) HarperCollins Pubs.

Stevenson, Charles. The Adventures of the Glo-Worm Family. 2012. (ENG., Illus.). 34p. pap. 9.99 *(978-1-78035-338-8(3)*, Fastprint Publishing) Upfront Publishing Ltd. GBR. Dist: Printondemand-worldwide.com.

Stonehouse, Frederick. My Summer at the Lighthouse: A Boy's Journal. 2003. (Illus.). 32p. (J). (gr. 3-9). *(978-1-892384-18-8(3))* Avery Color Studios, Inc.

Swift, Hildegarde H. The Little Red Lighthouse & the Great Gray Bridge: Restored Edition. Ward, Lynd, illus. 2003. (ENG.). 64p. (J). (gr. -1-3). pap. 9.99 *(978-0-15-204573-9(2),* 1193768, Clarion Bks.) HarperCollins Pubs.

Thiele, Colin. The Hammerhead Light. (Illus.). 196p. pap. *(978-0-7344-0401-5(8),* Lothian Children's Bks.) Hachette Australia.

Valentine, Sally. The Ghost of the Charlotte Lighthouse. 2006. (ENG.). (J). pap. *(978-1-59531-013-2(4))* North Country Bks., Inc.

VanRiper, Justin & VanRiper, Gary. The Lost Lighthouse. Gary, Glenn, illus. 2003. (Adirondack Kids Ser.: Vol. 3). 82p. (J). (gr. 2-7). pap. 9.95 *(978-0-9707044-2-9(9),* ADK3) Adirondack Kids Pr.

Veissid, Jacqueline. Caspian Finds a Friend: (Picture Book about Friendship for Kids, Bear Book for Children) Brown, Merrilees, illus. 2019. (ENG.). 36p. (J). (gr. k-3). 17.99 *(978-1-4521-3780-3(3))* Chronicle Bks. LLC.

Walton, O. F. Saved at Sea A Lighthouse Story. 2004. reprint ed. pap. 1.99 *(978-1-4192-4623-4(2));* pap. 15.95 *(978-1-4191-4623-7(8))* Kessinger Publishing, LLC.

Weston Woods Staff, creator. Little Red Lighthouse & the Great Gray Bridge. 2011. 18.95 *(978-0-439-72750-1(2));* 29.95 *(978-0-439-73487-5(8));* 38.75 *(978-0-439-72751-8(0))* Weston Woods Studios, Inc.

Woodruff, Elvira. Fearless. 2011. (ENG.). 240p. (YA). (gr. 4-7). pap. 6.99 *(978-0-439-67704-2(1),* Scholastic Pr.) Scholastic, Inc.

LIGHTING

see also Candles

Bailer, Darice. Why Does It Thunder & Lightning?, 1 vol. 2011. (Tell Me Why, Tell Me How Ser.). (ENG.). 32p. (gr. 3-3). 32.64 *(978-0-7614-4825-9(X),* cb67043a-050a-40c9-9906-aa8cdfb227e7) Cavendish Square Publishing LLC.

Cox Cannons, Helen. Thunder & Lightning, 1 vol. 2014. (Weather Wise Ser.). (ENG., Illus.). 24p. (J). (gr. -1-1). 25.32 *(978-1-4846-0548-6(9),* 126643, Heinemann) Capstone.

Edison, Erin. Lightning. 2011. (Weather Basics Ser.). (ENG.). 24p. (J). (gr. k-1). pap. 43.74 *(978-1-4296-7085-2(1),* 16678, Capstone Pr.) Capstone.

Herriges, Ann. Lightning. 2006. (Weather Ser.). (ENG., Illus.). 24p. (J). (gr. k-3). lib. bdg. 26.95 *(978-1-60014-025-9(4))* Bellwether Media.

Hughes, Mónica. Lights: Band 03/Yellow (Collins Big Cat) 2006. (Collins Big Cat Ser.). (ENG., Illus.). 136p. (J). (gr. 1-1). pap. 7.99 *(978-0-00-718680-8(0))* HarperCollins Pubs. Ltd. GBR. Dist: Independent Pubs. Group.

Johanson, Paula. Lightning & Thunder, 1 vol. 2018. (Nature's Mysteries Ser.). (ENG.). 32p. (gr. 2-3). pap. 13.90 *(978-1-5081-0651-7(7),* e3f46e0d-fd22-4519-8fc7-5aa5aa23bb0a, Britannica Educational Publishing) Rosen Publishing Group, Inc., The.

Kallio, Jamie. 12 Things to Know about Wild Weather. 2015. (Today's News Ser.). (ENG., Illus.). 32p. (J). (gr. 3-6). 32.80 *(978-1-63235-035-0(1),* 11613, 12-Story Library) Bookstaves, LLC.

Mullins, Lisa. Inventing the Electric Light. 2007. (Breakthrough Inventions Ser.). (ENG., Illus.). 32p. (J). (gr. 3-7). lib. bdg. *(978-0-7787-2818-4(8));* pap. *(978-0-7787-2840-5(4))* Crabtree Publishing Co.

Rice, Dona & Otterman, Joseph. Seeing More Stars. rev. ed. 2019. (Smithsonian: Informational Text Ser.). (ENG., Illus.). 24p. (J). (gr. 1-2). pap. 8.99 *(978-1-4938-6660-1(5))* Teacher Created Materials, Inc.

Roland, James. How LEDs Work. 2016. (Connect with Electricity Ser.). (ENG., Illus.). 40p. (J). (gr. 4-6). 30.65 *(978-1-5124-0780-8(1),* eceef61e-673e-4590-9d3b-fd15d36e1ec5, Lerner Pubns.) Lerner Publishing Group.

Scirri, Kaitlin. The Science of Controlling Electricity & Weather, 1 vol. 2018. (Science of Superpowers Ser.). (ENG.). 48p. (J). (gr. 4-4). 33.07 *(978-1-5026-3796-3(0),* b66bd2b4-672a-4355-b63a-80fef333e8a5) Cavendish Square Publishing LLC.

Tolhurst, Marilyn. Lights & Candles. Date not set. (Sense of History Ser.). (Illus.). 24p. pap. 27.69 *(978-0-582-04026-7(4))* Addison-Wesley Longman, Ltd. GBR. Dist: Trans-Atlantic Pubns., Inc.

Winchell, Mike. The Electric War: Edison, Tesla, Westinghouse, & the Race to Light the World. 2019. (ENG., Illus.). 272p. (YA). 19.99 *(978-1-250-12016-8(0),* 900172928, Holt, Henry & Co. Bks. For Young Readers) Holt, Henry & Co.

LIGHTNING

Bendick, Jeanne. Lightning. 2012. 62p. 36.95 *(978-1-258-22925-2(0));* pap. 21.95 *(978-1-258-24664-8(3))* Literary Licensing, LLC.

Fleisher, Paul. Lightning, Hurricanes, & Blizzards: The Science of Storms. 2010. (Weatherwise Ser.). (ENG., Illus.). 48p. (J). (gr. 4-8). lib. bdg. 29.27 *(978-0-8225-7536-8(1))* Lerner Publishing Group.

French, Cathy. Snap, Crackle, & Flow & Chasquea, cruje y Fluye: 6 English, 6 Spanish Adaptations. 2011. (ENG & SPA.). (J). 97.00 net. *(978-1-4108-5697-5(6))* Benchmark Education Co.

Galiano, Dean. Thunderstorms & Lightning. (Weather Watcher's Library). 48p. (gr. 5-8). 2009. 53.00 *(978-1-60854-275-8(0))* 2003. (Illus.). (YA). lib. bdg. 23.95 *(978-0-8239-3093-7(9),* WETHLI) Rosen Publishing Group, Inc., The. (Rosen Reference).

Hamilton, John. Lightning, 1 vol. 2006. (Nature's Fury Ser.). (ENG., Illus.). 32p. (gr. 3-8). 27.07 *(978-1-59679-332-3(5),* Abdo & Daughters) ABDO Publishing Co.

Hansen, Grace. Thunder & Lightning, 1 vol. 2015. (Weather Ser.). (ENG., Illus.). 24p. (J). (gr. -1-2). 32.79 *(978-1-62970-934-5(4),* 18326, Abdo Kids) ABDO Publishing Co.

Herriges, Ann. Lightning. 2011. (Blastoff! Readers Ser.). 24p. (J). pap. 5.95 *(978-0-531-27621-1(X),* Children's Pr.) Scholastic Library Publishing.

Hidalgo, Maria. Lightning. 2006. (My First Look at Weather Ser.). (Illus.). 24p. (J). (gr. -1-3). lib. bdg. 15.95 *(978-1-58341-450-7(9),* Creative Education) Creative Co., The.

Lawrence, Ellen. What Is Lightning? 2015. (Weather Wise Ser.). (ENG., Illus.). 24p. (J). (gr. -1-3). lib. bdg. 26.99 *(978-1-62724-863-1(3))* Bearport Publishing Co., Inc.

McGraw Hill, creator. Lightning. 2008. (MS Literature Booksource Ser.). (ENG., Illus.). 32p. (gr. 6-8). 25.20 *(978-0-06-088435-2(5),* 0060884355) McGraw-Hill Education.

Nagelhout, Ryan. When Lightning Strikes, 1 vol. 2015. (Eye on the Sky Ser.). (ENG., Illus.). 32p. (J). (gr. 3-4). pap. 11.50 *(978-1-4824-2892-6(X),* 6f64c966-c9ba-4508-9d00-df3088de6de5) Stevens, Gareth Publishing LLLP.

Person, Stephen. Struck by Lightning! 2010. (Disaster Survivors Ser.). (Illus.). 32p. (YA). (gr. 4-7). lib. bdg. 28.50 *(978-1-936087-47-1(2))* Bearport Publishing Co., Inc.

Peters, Katie. When Lightning Strikes. 2019. (Let's Look at Weather (Pull Ahead Readers — Nonfiction) Ser.). (ENG., Illus.). 16p. (J). (gr. -1-1). pap. 8.99 *(978-1-5415-7327-7(7),* f0063607-a21d-4ade-8e41-9123d0e769f4); lib. bdg. 27.99 *(978-1-5415-5838-0(3),* afc0e8c4-1b1e-4116-ad32-854636a556de) Lerner Publishing Group. (Lerner Pubns.).

Rajczak Nelson, Kristen. Lightning, 1 vol. 2012. (Nature's Light Show Ser.). (ENG., Illus.). 24p. (J). (gr. 2-3). pap. 9.15 *(978-1-4339-7024-5(4),* e89b5527-8424-4d8e-b3b5-3c861337d98e); lib. bdg. 25.27 *(978-1-4339-7023-8(6),* b0219960-b9f7-4a3f-b99d-737b2e40b1b6) Stevens, Gareth Publishing LLLP.

Riley, Gail Blasser. Cornerstones of Freedom: Benjamin Franklin & Electricity. 2004. (Cornerstones of Freedom Ser.). (ENG., Illus.). 48p. (J). (gr. 4-7). 26.00 *(978-0-516-24240-8(7))* Scholastic Library Publishing.

Roesser, Marie. What Makes Lightning & Thunder?, 1 vol. 2020. (Everyday Mysteries Ser.). (ENG.). 24p. (J). (gr. 1-2). pap. 9.15 *(978-1-5382-5647-3(9),* 916e3b66-0f31-4513-8dd6-fa0b33af3154) Stevens, Gareth Publishing LLLP.

Roland, James. How LEDs Work. 2016. (Connect with Electricity Ser.). (ENG., Illus.). 40p. (J). (gr. 4-6). E-Book 46.65 *(978-1-5124-1009-9(8),* Lerner Pubns.) Lerner Publishing Group.

LIGHTSHIPS

Floca, Brian. Lightship. Floca, Brian, illus. 2007. (ENG., Illus.). 48p. (J). (gr. -1-3). 19.99 *(978-1-4169-2436-4(1),* Atheneum/Richard Jackson Bks.) Simon & Schuster Children's Publishing.

—Lightship. 2007. (J). (gr. k-3). 29.95 incl. audio compact disk *(978-0-8045-4185-5(X));* 27.95 incl. audio *(978-0-8045-6962-0(2))* Spoken Arts, Inc.

LIMERICKS

see also Nonsense Verses

Bodden, Valerie. Limericks. 2009. (Poetry Basics Ser.). (ENG., Illus.). 32p. (J). (gr. 5-8). 19.95 *(978-1-58341-777-5(X),* 22277, Creative Education) Creative Co., The.

Bumbalough, Jerry. Purple pup girls are grape Jelly. Bennett, Harry, Jr., illus. 2007. 16p. (J). 8.95 *(978-0-9797960-0-5(8))* Thirsty Sponge Publishing Co.

Cleary, Brian P. Something Sure Smells Around Here: Limericks. Rowland, Andy, illus. 2015. (Poetry Adventures Ser.). (ENG.). 32p. (J). (gr. 2-5). pap. 8.99 *(978-1-4677-6035-5(8),* 571acf70-9c4e-4741-ac1b-b6cad985868b, Millbrook Pr.) Lerner Publishing Group.

Early Macken, JoAnn. Read, Recite, & Write Limericks. 2014. (Poet's Workshop Ser.). (ENG., Illus.). 32p. (J). (gr. 4-4). *(978-0-7787-0409-6(2))* Crabtree Publishing Co.

Foster, John, ed. Loopy Limericks. 2011. (ENG., Illus.). 96p. (gr. k-4). pap. 5.99 *(978-0-00-711181-7(9),* HarperCollins Children's Bks.) HarperCollins Pubs. Ltd. GBR. Dist: HarperCollins Pubs.

Hubbell, Patricia. Boo! Halloween Poems & Limericks, 1 vol. Spackman, Jeff, illus. 2005. (ENG.). 32p. (YA). pap. 5.95 *(978-0-7614-5151-8(X))* Marshall Cavendish Corp.

LIMITATION OF ARMAMENT

see Disarmament

LIN, MAYA YING, 1959-

Harvey, Jeanne Walker. Maya Lin: Artist-Architect of Light & Lines. Phumiruk, Dow, illus. 2017. (ENG.). 32p. (J). 19.99 *(978-1-250-11249-1(4),* 900170467, Holt, Henry & Co. Bks. For Young Readers) Holt, Henry & Co.

Spiller, Sara. Maya Lin. Bane, Jeff, illus. 2019. (My Early Library: My Itty-Bitty Bio Ser.). (ENG.). 24p. (J). (gr. k-1). pap. 12.79 *(978-1-5341-3926-8(5),* 212533); lib. bdg. 30.64 *(978-1-5341-4270-1(3),* 212532) Cherry Lake Publishing.

LINCOLN, ABRAHAM, 1809-1865

Abnett, Dan. Abraham Lincoln & the Civil War. (Jr. Graphic Biographies Ser.). (ENG.). 24p. (gr. 2-3). 2009. (J). 47.90 *(978-1-61513-807-4(2),* PowerKids Pr.) 2006. (Illus.). (J). lib. bdg. 28.93 *(978-1-4042-3392-8(X),* 92e3c8e5-f3e2-4a55-954a-8ef3b235e069) 2006. (Illus.). pap. 10.60 *(978-1-4042-2145-1(X),* 0586a643-99bf-4e0d-bd7a-2e7c219dab67, PowerKids Pr.) Rosen Publishing Group, Inc., The.

—Abraham Lincoln y la Guerra Civil, 1 vol. 2009. (Historietas Juveniles: Biografías (Jr. Graphic Biographies) Ser.). (SPA., Illus.). 24p. (gr. 2-3). (J). 28.93 *(978-1-4358-8561-5(9),* 7466c29f-c43f-4229-a2b0-ce29cbcf5047); pap. 10.60 *(978-1-4358-3316-6(3),* 6881a164-d615-429e-aaaf-9ff20b30d04e) Rosen Publishing Group, Inc., The.

—Jr. Graphic Biographies, 10 vols., Set. Incl. Abraham Lincoln & the Civil War. lib. bdg. 28.93 *(978-1-4042-3392-8(X),* 92e3c8e5-f3e2-4a55-954a-8ef3b235e069); Christopher Columbus & the Voyage Of 1492. lib. bdg. 28.93 *(978-1-4042-3390-4(3),* d84bba85-3b79-4445-a67f-e180efd44190); George Washington & the American Revolution. lib. bdg. 28.93 *(978-1-4042-3395-9(4),* f5ebb962-806c-4e30-beef-2ed75efa306a); Harriet Tubman & the Underground Railroad. lib. bdg. 28.93 *(978-1-4042-3393-5(8),* faf3f8b3-291f-45bf-a467-b7772adb82ea); Hernan Cortes & the Fall of the Aztec Empire. lib. bdg. 28.93 *(978-1-4042-3391-1(1),* 8dd7d5ac-b879-43a8-962f-3015d0941234); Sitting Bull & the Battle of the Little Bighorn. lib. bdg. 28.93 *(978-1-4042-3394-2(6),* f0e34536-71fb-4966-826f-56f539643bb7); (Illus.). (J). (gr. 2-3). 2006. (Jr. Graphic Biographies Ser.). (ENG.). 24p. 2006. Set lib. bdg. 144.65 *(978-1-4042-3550-2(7),* 2bee43b0-dccd-408a-8002-bc515651b66b) Rosen Publishing Group, Inc., The.

Abraham Lincoln: A Life of Respect. 2006. (J). pap. 6.95 *(978-0-8225-5700-5(2))* Lerner Publishing Group.

Abraham Lincoln & Slavery. 95p. (YA). (gr. 8-12). pap. 14.50 *(978-0-382-40942-4(6));* spiral bd., tchr.'s planning gde. ed. 13.00 *(978-0-382-40941-7(8))* Cobblestone Publishing Co.

Abraham Lincoln's Shining Star: The Inspiring Story of Abraham Lincoln & Nebraska. 2010. (Illus.). 64p. 18.95 *(978-0-615-34265-8(5))* America's Great Stories.

Alexander, Carol. The Big Squeal: A True Story about a Homeless Pig's Search for Life, Liberty & the Pursuit of Happiness. 2013. (ENG., Illus.). 32p. (J). pap. 16.00 *(978-1-61009-112-1(4),* Acorn) Oak Tree Publishing.

—The Big Squeal: A True Story about a Homeless Pig's Search for Life, Liberty & the Pursuit of Happiness. Kalpart Designs, illus. 2012. (ENG.). 24p. (J). 24.00 *(978-1-61009-036-0(5),* Acorn) Oak Tree Publishing.

Allen, Roger MacBride & Allen, Thomas B. Mr. Lincoln's High-Tech War: How the North Used the Telegraph, Railroads, Surveillance Balloons, Ironclads, High-Powered Weapons, & More to Win the Civil War. 2009. (Illus.). 144p. (J). (gr. 5-9). 18.95 *(978-1-4263-0379-1(3),* National Geographic Kids) Disney Publishing Worldwide.

Aloian, Molly. Emancipation. 2013. (ENG., Illus.). 48p. (J). *(978-0-7787-1100-1(5));* pap. *(978-0-7787-1120-9(X))* Crabtree Publishing Co.

Andersen, Ron L. Ingenious Abe: Stories from the Life of Abraham Lincoln. 2016. (ENG.). (J). pap. 8.99 *(978-1-4621-1789-5(9))* Cedar Fort, Inc./CFI Distribution.

Anderson, Michael, contrib. by. Abraham Lincoln, 1 vol. 2012. (Pivotal Presidents: Profiles in Leadership Ser.). (ENG., Illus.). 80p. (gr. 8-8). (J). lib. bdg. 36.47 *(978-1-61530-942-9(X),* 3e79c9e2-6cf7-49e1-8a7e-6f531fd252d5); (YA). 72.94 *(978-1-61530-953-5(5),* fe64ec48-46cf-4b6d-afb3-c461b9174bea) Rosen Publishing Group, Inc., The.

Andronik, Catherine M. & Kenney, Karen Latchana. Abraham Lincoln's Presidency. 2016. (Presidential Powerhouses Ser.). (ENG., Illus.). 104p. (YA). (gr. 6-12). 35.99 *(978-1-4677-7925-8(3),* 9e967ebf-e20b-4c3c-82d8-9a5d2ae0b0db); E-Book 54.65 *(978-1-4677-8547-1(4))* Lerner Publishing Group. (Lerner Pubns.).

Armentrout, David & Armentrout, Patricia. The Emancipation Proclamation. 2005. (Documents that Shaped the Nation Ser.). (Illus.). 48p. (J). (gr. 4-6). 20.95 *(978-1-59515-233-6(4))* Rourke Educational Media.

Aronson, Billy. Abraham Lincoln, 1 vol. 2009. (Presidents & Their Times Ser.). (ENG.). 96p. (gr. 6-6). lib. bdg. 36.93 *(978-0-7614-2839-8(9),* a404bef1-3923-404a-bd06-75978e2cbebe) Cavendish Square Publishing LLC.

Bader, Bonnie. My Little Golden Book about Abraham Lincoln. Garofoli, Viviana, illus. 2016. (Little Golden Book Ser.). 24p. (J). (gr. -1-3). 5.99 *(978-1-101-93971-0(0),* Golden Bks.) Random Hse. Children's Bks.

Baldwin, James. Four Great Americans. 2006. pap. *(978-1-4065-0509-2(9))* Dodo Pr.

—Four Great Americans: Washington Franklin Webster Lincoln; a Book for Young Americans. 2017. (ENG., Illus.). (J). (gr. 3-7). 23.95 *(978-1-374-89694-9(2));* pap. 13.95 *(978-1-374-89693-2(4))* Capital Communications, Inc.

—Four Great Americans: Washington, Franklin, Webster, Lincoln. a Book for Young Americans. 2017. (ENG., Illus.). (J). (gr. 3-7). pap. *(978-0-649-58735-3(9))* Trieste Publishing Pty Ltd.

Barretta, Gene. Lincoln & Kennedy: A Pair to Compare. Barretta, Gene, illus. 2016. (ENG., Illus.). 40p. (J). 18.99 *(978-0-8050-9945-4(X),* 900127126, Holt, Henry & Co. Bks. For Young Readers) Holt, Henry & Co.

Bauer, Marion Dane. Abraham Lincoln (My First Biography) Dubois, Liz Goulet, illus. 2012. (My First Biography Ser.). (ENG.). 32p. (J). (gr. -1-k). pap. 3.99 *(978-0-545-34294-0(5))* Scholastic, Inc.

Benoit, Peter. Abraham Lincoln. (Cornerstones of Freedom, Third Ser.). (J). 2012. (ENG.). 64p. (gr. 4-6). lib. bdg. 24.94 *(978-0-531-25025-9(3))* 2011. (Illus.). 48p. pap. 6.95 *(978-0-531-26621-2(4))* Scholastic Library Publishing. (Children's Pr.).

Berenger, Al. Pocket Bios: Abraham Lincoln. Berenger, Al, illus. 2018. (Pocket Bios Ser.). (ENG., Illus.). 32p. (J). 14.99 *(978-1-250-16611-1(X),* 900187188) Roaring Brook Pr.

Bertsch, Michael L. Leaning Forward. rev. ed. 2010. (ENG.). 277p. (C). 125.99 *(978-0-7575-8105-2(6),* P695129) Kendall Hunt Publishing Co.

Best, B. J. Abraham Lincoln, the Emancipation Proclamation, & the 13th Amendment, 1 vol. 2015. (Primary Sources of the Abolitionist Movement Ser.). (ENG., Illus.). 64p. (gr. 6-6). lib. bdg. 35.93 *(978-1-5026-0530-6(9),* 5c51cbc4-3e82-49b1-ae18-5508c4cc5f81) Cavendish Square Publishing LLC.

Bolden, Tonya. Emancipation Proclamation: Lincoln & the Dawn of Liberty. 2013. (ENG., Illus.). 128p. (J). (gr. 5-9). 24.95 *(978-1-4197-0390-4(0),* 672401, Abrams Bks. for Young Readers) Abrams, Inc.

Bowers, John. The Life of Abraham Lincoln. 2006. (ENG.). 68p. per. 16.95 *(978-1-4286-2279-1(9))* Kessinger Publishing, LLC.

Brandt, Keith & Macken, JoAnn Early. Abraham Lincoln: Road to the White House. Lawn, John, illus. 2007. 53p. (J). *(978-0-439-88005-3(X))* Scholastic, Inc.

Brindell Fradin, Dennis. The Emancipation Proclamation, 1 vol. 2008. (Turning Points in U. S. History Ser.). (ENG., Illus.). 48p. (J). (gr. 4-4). lib. bdg. 34.07 *(978-0-7614-2038-5(X),* e0c254de-5d25-4baf-bfe6-f3f40a5f3650) Cavendish Square Publishing LLC.

Burleigh, Robert. Abraham Lincoln Comes Home. Minor, Wendell, illus. 2009. (J). (gr. 3-5). 27.95 incl. audio *(978-0-8045-6977-4(0))* Spoken Arts, Inc.

—O Captain, My Captain: Walt Whitman, Abraham Lincoln, & the Civil War. Hundley, Sterling, illus. 2019. (ENG.). 64p. (J). (gr. 5-17). 19.99 *(978-1-4197-3358-1(3),* 1120101, Abrams Bks. for Young Readers) Abrams, Inc.

Byers, Ann. The Emancipation Proclamation, 1 vol. 2018. (America's Most Important Documents: Inquiry into Historical Sources Ser.). (ENG.). 64p. (J). (gr. 6-6). lib. bdg. 37.36 *(978-1-5026-3598-3(4),* 7f22fdda-24b7-47c9-8648-ab69c99a32a1) Cavendish Square Publishing LLC.

Colbert, David. Abraham Lincoln. 2009. (10 Days Ser.). (ENG.). 160p. (J). (gr. 3-9). pap. 8.99 *(978-1-4169-6807-8(5),* Aladdin) Simon & Schuster Children's Publishing.

Collard, Sneed B., III. Abraham Lincoln: A Courageous Leader, 1 vol. 2007. (American Heroes Ser.). (ENG., Illus.). 48p. (gr. 3-3). lib. bdg. 32.64 *(978-0-7614-2162-7(9),* a82c585e-4cbb-4af2-9285-a34c366a5da6) Cavendish Square Publishing LLC.

Cunningham, Kevin. The Emancipation Proclamation. 2020. (Civil War Ser.). (ENG., Illus.). 48p. (J). (gr. 5-6). pap. 11.95 *(978-1-64493-159-2(1),* 1644931591); lib. bdg. 34.21 *(978-1-64493-080-9(3),* 1644930803) North Star Editions. (Focus Readers).

D'Aulaire, Ingri & D'Aulaire, Edgar Parin. Abraham Lincoln. 2008. (Illus.). *(978-1-893103-27-6(7));* pap. *(978-1-893103-26-9(9))* Beautiful Feet Bks.

D'Aulaire, Ingri & D'Aulaire, Edgar Parin, illus. Abraham Lincoln. 75th ed. 2015. (J). *(978-1-893103-60-3(9))* Beautiful Feet Bks.

Davis, Kenneth C. Don't Know Much about Abraham Lincoln, Vol. 4. Shepperson, Rob, illus. 2003. (Don't Know Much About Ser.). 144p. (J). (gr. 3-7). pap. 4.99 *(978-0-06-442127-0(9))* HarperCollins Pubs.

—Don't Know Much about Abraham Lincoln Abraham Lincoln, Vol. 4. Shepperson, Rob, illus. 2004. (Don't Know Much About Ser.). 144p. (J). (gr. 2-5). 15.89 *(978-0-06-028820-4(5))* HarperCollins Pubs.

Dayton, Connor. Presidents' Day, 1 vol. 2012. (American Holidays Ser.). (ENG., Illus.). 24p. (J). (gr. 1-1). pap. 9.25 *(978-1-4488-6242-9(6),* 2561629b-cfaa-442a-80cd-8c3650d2d59c); lib. bdg. 26.27 *(978-1-4488-6142-2(X),* 82401d5e-c56c-405b-9b30-4fdbd5f9a52d) Rosen Publishing Group, Inc., The. (PowerKids Pr.).

Dean, Sheri. Presidents' Day, 1 vol. (Our Country's Holidays (First Edition) Ser.). (ENG., Illus.). 24p. (gr. k-2). 2006. pap. 9.15 *(978-0-8368-6515-8(4),* a373ec74-336e-49ac-9c56-6c78673d92b5, Weekly Reader Leveled Readers) 2005. lib. bdg. 24.67 *(978-0-8368-6508-0(1),* d6994cbb-bbd2-4f33-9fb2-913147a5eba5) Stevens, Gareth Publishing LLLP.

Demers, Roxanna. The Rusty Bucket Kids, A Behind the Scenes Look at the Rusty Bucket Kids, Lincoln, Journey To 16. Eason, D. M, illus. 2010. (ENG.). 82p. (J). pap. 19.99 *(978-1-935711-04-9(0))* Peak City Publishing, LLC.

Demi. President Lincoln: From Log Cabin to White House. 2016. (Illus.). 32p. (J). (gr. k-3). 16.95 *(978-1-937786-50-2(1),* Wisdom Tales) World Wisdom, Inc.

Diemer, Lauren & Cuthbert, Megan. Abraham Lincoln. 2014. (Illus.). 24p. (J). *(978-1-62127-308-0(3))* Weigl Pubs., Inc.

Dodson Wade, Mary. Presidents' Day, 1 vol. 2016. (Story of Our Holidays Ser.). (ENG., Illus.). 32p. (gr. 3-3). pap. 11.52 *(978-0-7660-8345-5(4),* 062ea253-ce24-487f-a0a8-1def4836fc84) Enslow Publishing, LLC.

Dover Publications Inc. Staff, ed. Abraham Lincoln, Kit. 2008. (ENG.). 96p. (J). (gr. 1). 19.99 *(978-0-486-46720-7(1))* Dover Pubns., Inc.

Dussling, Jennifer. Long, Tall Lincoln. Ko, Chin, illus. 2017. (I Can Read Level 2 Ser.). (ENG.). 32p. (J). (gr. -1-3). pap. 4.99 *(978-0-06-243255-1(9),* HarperCollins) HarperCollins Pubs.

Dyan, Penelope. Abraham Lincoln Was Here! a Kid's Guide to Washington D C. Weigand, John D., photos by. 2009. (Illus.). 44p. pap. 11.95 *(978-1-935118-82-4(X))* Bellissima Publishing, LLC.

Edison, Erin. Abraham Lincoln, 1 vol. (Presidential Biographies Ser.). (ENG.). 24p. (J). (gr. -1-2). 2014. pap. 6.29 *(978-1-4765-9629-7(8),* 125425, Pebble) 2012. (Illus.). lib. bdg. 27.32 *(978-1-4296-8735-5(5),* 119528, Capstone Pr.) Capstone.

—The Lincoln Memorial: A 4D Book. 2018. (National Landmarks Ser.). (ENG., Illus.). 24p. (J). (gr. 1-3). lib. bdg. 27.99 *(978-1-5435-3130-5(X),* 138735, Capstone Pr.) Capstone.

The Emancipation Proclamation & the End of Slavery in America, 1 vol. 2014. (Celebration of the Civil Rights Movement Ser.). (ENG., Illus.). 80p. (J). (gr. 6-6). 37.47 *(978-1-4777-7749-7(0),* 20d82c0d-2d59-4140-9fc1-adf790e79e4c) Rosen Publishing Group, Inc., The.

Engle, Margarita. Dancing Hands: How Teresa Carreño Played the Piano for President Lincoln. López, Rafael & López, Rafael, illus. 2019. (ENG.). 40p. (J). (gr. -1-3). 18.99 *(978-1-4814-8740-5(X))* Simon & Schuster Children's Publishing.

Erin, Audrey. Visit the Lincoln Memorial, 1 vol. 2012. (Landmarks of Liberty Ser.). (ENG.). 24p. (J). (gr. 2-3). pap. 9.15 *(978-1-4339-6398-8(1),* 536b5fd4-2ef4-446d-9fe7-8a550bca52ba, Gareth Stevens Learning Library); lib. bdg. 25.27 *(978-1-4339-6396-4(5),* 06471bd3-8fe6-41fd-99fa-85978d55e4c0) Stevens, Gareth Publishing LLLP.

Figley, Marty Rhodes. President Lincoln, Willie Kettles, & the Telegraph Machine. 2010. pap. 56.72 *(978-0-7613-6929-5(5))* Lerner Publishing Group.

Fontes, Justine & Fontes, Ron. DK Readers L3: Abraham Lincoln: Lawyer, Leader, Legend. 2009. (DK Readers Level 3 Ser.). (ENG.). 48p. (J). (gr. 2-4). 4.99 *(978-0-7566-5689-8(3),* DK Children) Dorling Kindersley Publishing, Inc.

Ford, Carin T. The Emancipation Proclamation, Lincoln, & Slavery Through Primary Sources, 1 vol. 2013. (Civil War Through Primary Sources Ser.). (ENG.). 48p. (gr. 4-6). pap. 11.53 *(978-1-4644-0187-9(X),*

39a9f8dc-63ab-4b9b-94df-bb3af9d021ae); (Illus.). (J). lib. bdg. 27.93 *(978-0-7660-4129-5(8),* b2263e7e-8ce7-4531-a353-b06b36d2fe69) Enslow Publishing, LLC.

Gilpin, Caroline Crosson. National Geographic Readers: Abraham Lincoln. 2012. (Readers Bios Ser.). 32p. (J). (gr. 1-3). pap. 4.99 *(978-1-4263-1085-0(4),* National Geographic Kids); (ENG.). lib. bdg. 14.90 *(978-1-4263-1086-7(2),* National Geographic Children's Bks.) Disney Publishing Worldwide.

Giovanni, Nikki. Lincoln & Douglass: An American Friendship. Collier, Bryan, illus. 2013. (ENG.). 40p. (J). (gr. 2-6). 10.99 *(978-1-250-01869-4(2),* 900087706) Square Fish.

—Lincoln & Douglass: An American Friendship. Collier, Bryan, illus. 2011. (J). (gr. -1-3). 29.95 *(978-0-545-13457-6(9))* Weston Woods Studios, Inc.

Gosman, Gillian. Abraham Lincoln, 1 vol. 2011. (Life Stories Ser.). (Illus.). 24p. (J). (gr. 3-3). (ENG.). pap. 9.25 *(978-1-4488-2753-4(1),* c38f1529-a0ed-443e-bf35-44e20428e06e, PowerKids Pr.); (SPA & ENG., lib. bdg. 26.27 *(978-1-4488-3216-3(0),* 9ff069b3-954b-4d8d-8616-3464ce80badb); (ENG., lib. bdg. 26.27 *(978-1-4488-2582-0(2),* 07f83246-a876-470e-b803-905a492eb466, PowerKids Pr.) Rosen Publishing Group, Inc., The.

Gregory, Josh. Abraham Lincoln: The 16th President. 2015. (First Look at America's Presidents Ser.). (ENG.). 24p. (J). (gr. -1-3). lib. bdg. 26.99 *(978-1-62724-554-8(5))* Bearport Publishing Co., Inc.

Group/McGraw-Hill, Wright. Abraham Lincoln: The Civil War President, 6 vols. (Book2WebTM Ser.). (gr. 4-8). 36.50 *(978-0-322-04462-3(6))* Wright Group/McGraw-Hill.

Gunderson, Jessica. The Election Of 1860: A Nation Divides on the Eve of War. 2016. (Presidential Politics Ser.). (ENG.). 48p. (J). pap. 54.70 *(978-1-4914-8737-2(2),* 24425); (Illus.). (gr. 3-6). lib. bdg. 29.99 *(978-1-4914-8240-7(0),* 130711) Capstone.

Haldy, Emma E. Abraham Lincoln. Bane, Jeff, illus. 2016. (My Early Library: My Itty-Bitty Bio Ser.). (ENG.). 24p. (J). (gr. k-1). 30.64 *(978-1-63470-476-2(2),* 207635) Cherry Lake Publishing.

—Abraham Lincoln SP. Bane, Jeff, illus. 2018. (My Early Library: Mi Mini Biografía (My Itty-Bitty Bio) Ser.). (SPA.). 24p. (J). (gr. k-1). lib. bdg. 30.64 *(978-1-5341-2993-1(6),* 212020) Cherry Lake Publishing.

Hall, Brianna. Freedom from Slavery: Causes & Effects of the Emancipation Proclamation, 1 vol. 2014. (Cause & Effect Ser.). (ENG., Illus.). 32p. (J). (gr. 3-6). lib. bdg. 27.99 *(978-1-4765-3930-0(8),* 123928) Capstone.

Hally, Ashleigh. Abraham Lincoln. 2012. (Illus.). 24p. (J). *(978-1-935884-41-5(7));* pap. *(978-1-935884-50-7(6))* State Standards Publishing, LLC.

Hamilton, Lynn. Presidents' Day. 2015. (Illus.). 24p. (J). *(978-1-5105-0116-4(9))* SmartBook Media, Inc.

—Presidents' Day. (American Celebrations Ser.). (Illus.). 24p. (J). 2010. (gr. 3-5). pap. 11.95 *(978-1-60596-931-2(1))* 2010. (gr. 3-5). lib. bdg. 18.99 *(978-1-60596-773-8(4))* 2004. (gr. 1-3). lib. bdg. 24.45 *(978-1-59036-108-5(3))* 2004. (gr. 1-3). per. 8.95 *(978-1-59036-169-6(5))* Weigl Pubs., Inc.

Harness, Cheryl. Abe Lincoln Goes to Washington: 1837-1865. 2nd ed. 2008. (Illus.). 48p. (J). (gr. 3-7). pap. 7.95 *(978-1-4263-0436-1(6),* National Geographic Children's Bks.) Disney Publishing Worldwide.

—Young Abe Lincoln: The Frontier Days: 1809-1837. 2nd ed. 2008. (Illus.). 32p. (J). (gr. 3-7). pap. 7.95 *(978-1-4263-0437-8(4),* National Geographic Children's Bks.) Disney Publishing Worldwide.

Helweg, Laura. How Abraham Lincoln Fought the Civil War, 1 vol. 2017. (Presidents at War Ser.). (ENG.). 128p. (gr. 8-8). lib. bdg. 38.93 *(978-0-7660-8525-1(2),* 32e10f4d-cea7-4f45-af17-c9cffae4f869) Enslow Publishing, LLC.

Herbert, Janis. Abraham Lincoln for Kids: His Life & Times with 21 Activities. 2007. (For Kids Ser.: 23). (ENG., Illus.). 160p. (J). (gr. 4-7). pap. 18.99 *(978-1-55652-656-5(3))* Chicago Review Pr., Inc.

Herda, D. J. Slavery & Citizenship: The Dred Scott Case, 1 vol. 2016. (U. S. Supreme Court Landmark Cases Ser.). (ENG., Illus.). 128p. (J). (gr. 7-7). 38.93 *(978-0-7660-8426-1(4),* ffcb8d36-7c36-4d76-8da3-8ca5072dc032) Enslow Publishing, LLC.

Holzer, Harold. Lincoln: How Abraham Lincoln Ended Slavery in America: a Companion Book for Young Readers to the Steven Spielberg Film. 2013. (ENG., Illus.). 240p. pap. 7.99 *(978-0-06-226511-1(3),* Newmarket for It Bks.) HarperCollins Pubs.

—Lincoln: How Abraham Lincoln Ended Slavery in America: A Companion Book for Young Readers to the Steven Spielberg Film. 2012. (ENG., Illus.). 240p. 16.99 *(978-0-06-226509-8(1),* Newmarket for It Bks.) HarperCollins Pubs.

Jeffery, Gary & Petty, Kate. Abraham Lincoln: The Life of America's Sixteenth President, 1 vol. Lacey, Mike, illus. 2005. (Graphic Nonfiction Biographies Ser.). (ENG.). 48p. (gr. 4-6). pap. 14.05 *(978-1-4042-5164-9(2),* 131931e3-eb5d-4490-ad08-e2e48485fa8d) Rosen Publishing Group, Inc., The.

Jeffrey, Gary. Abraham Lincoln: The Life of America's Sixteenth President. 2009. (Graphic Nonfiction Biographies Ser.). (ENG.). 48p. (YA). (gr. 4-5). 58.50 *(978-1-61513-011-5(X),* Rosen Reference) Rosen Publishing Group, Inc., The.

Kalman, Maira. Looking at Lincoln. Kalman, Maira, illus. (ENG., Illus.). (J). (gr. k-3). 2017. 48p. pap. 8.99 *(978-0-14-751798-2(2),* Puffin Books) 2012. 32p. 17.99 *(978-0-399-24039-3(X),* Nancy Paulsen Books) Penguin Young Readers Group.

Kanefield, Teri. Abraham Lincoln: The Making of America #3. (Making of America Ser.). (ENG.). (J). (gr. 5-9). 2019. 256p. pap. 7.99 *(978-1-4197-3625-4(6),* 1198003) 2018. (Illus.). 240p. 16.99 *(978-1-4197-3159-4(9),* 1198001, Abrams Bks. for Young Readers) Abrams, Inc.

Keating, Frank. Abraham. Wimmer, Mike, illus. 2017. (Mount Rushmore Presidential Ser.). (ENG.). 32p. (J). (gr. 1-4). 17.99 *(978-1-4424-9319-3(4),* Simon & Schuster/Paula Wiseman Bks.) Simon & Schuster/Paula Wiseman Bks.

Kenison, Misti. Where's Your Hat, Abe Lincoln? 2017. (Young Historians Ser.: 0). (Illus.). 28p. (J). (gr. -1-k). bds. 9.99 *(978-1-4926-5250-2(4))* Sourcebooks, Inc.

Kirkman, Marissa. The Life & Times of Abraham Lincoln & the U. S. Civil War. 2016. (Life & Times Ser.). (ENG., Illus.). 24p. (J). (gr. 1-3). lib. bdg. 27.99 *(978-1-5157-2474-2(3),* 132846, Capstone Pr.) Capstone.

Klimo, Kate. Dog Diaries #13: Fido. Jessell, Tim, illus. 2018. (Dog Diaries: 13). (ENG.). 160p. (J). (gr. 2-5). pap. 7.99 *(978-1-5247-1967-8(6),* Random Hse. Bks. for Young Readers) Random Hse. Children's Bks.

Knudsen, Shannon. When Were the First Slaves Set Free During the Civil War? And Other Questions about the Emancipation Proclamation. 2010. (Six Questions of American History Ser.). (ENG.). (gr. 4-6). pap. 56.72 *(978-0-7613-6948-6(1));* (Illus.). 48p. (J). pap. 11.99 *(978-0-7613-6121-3(9),* 439921d9-9f33-4651-8e71-fe9a4cd4c225); (Illus.). 48p. (J). lib. bdg. 30.65 *(978-1-58013-670-9(2),* 5021e694-5f71-402d-8d11-6438e13df8bb, Lerner Pubns.) Lerner Publishing Group.

Koutras Bozonelis, Helen. 200 Years with Abraham Lincoln: One Man's Life & Legacy, 1 vol. 2008. (Prime (Middle/Senior) Ser.). (ENG., Illus.). 64p. (gr. 5-6). lib. bdg. 31.93 *(978-0-7660-3266-8(3),* 89afca66-0494-4089-b103-803fdf0a9798) Enslow Publishing, LLC.

Krisher, Trudy. An Affectionate Farewell: the Story of Old Abe & Old Bob. Dodson, Bert, illus. 2015. (ENG.). 32p. (J). (gr. 6-2). 17.95 *(978-1-59373-155-7(8))* Bunker Hill Publishing, Inc.

Krull, Kathleen & Brewer, Paul. Lincoln Tells a Joke: How Laughter Saved the President (and the Country) Innerst, Stacy, illus. 2010. (ENG.). 40p. (J). (gr. 1-4). 17.99 *(978-0-15-206639-0(X),* 1199695, Clarion Bks.) HarperCollins Pubs.

Landau, Elaine. The Emancipation Proclamation: Would You Do What Lincoln Did?, 1 vol. 2008. (What Would You Do? Ser.). (ENG., Illus.). 48p. (gr. 3-3). (J). lib. bdg. 27.93 *(978-0-7660-2899-9(2),* 39c1ee83-f4bc-4608-8499-383b6829d109); pap. 11.53 *(978-1-59845-194-8(4),* ecefcba4-d07c-4bb8-83db-4ac89f6f1c78) Enslow Publishing, LLC. (Enslow Elementary).

—Lincoln's Emancipation Proclamation: Would You Sign the Great Document?, 1 vol. 2014. (What Would You Do? Ser.). (ENG.). 48p. (gr. 3-4). (J). 27.93 *(978-0-7660-6290-0(2),* 37f0154d-481d-46d8-bc19-2898c06edb7a); pap. 11.53 *(978-0-7660-6291-7(0),* a46b69f5-a3d3-442c-86d5-136b35468973, Enslow Elementary) Enslow Publishing, LLC.

Lee, T. S. The Lincoln Story: The Boy Who Embraced a Nation. 4th ed. 2010. (Great Heroes Ser.). 184p. (J). pap. 14.95 *(978-0-9819542-3-3(5))* DASANBOOKS.

Lynch, Seth. The Emancipation Proclamation, 1 vol. 2018. (Look at U. S. History Ser.). (ENG.). 32p. (J). (gr. 2-2). 28.27 *(978-1-5382-2119-8(5),* 6585d053-970a-4d85-9432-f4efcb166780) Stevens, Gareth Publishing LLLP.

Magoon, Kekla. Abraham Lincoln, 1 vol. 2007. (Essential Lives Set 1 Ser.). (ENG., Illus.). 112p. (gr. 6-12). lib. bdg. 41.36 *(978-1-59928-839-0(7),* 6631, Essential Library) ABDO Publishing Co.

Maloof, Torrey. Abraham Lincoln: Addressing a Nation. rev. ed. 2017. (Social Studies: Informational Text Ser.). (ENG., Illus.). 32p. (gr. 4-8). pap. 11.99 *(978-1-4938-3805-9(9))* Teacher Created Materials, Inc.

Manolis, Kay & Leslie, Tonya. Abraham Lincoln: A Life of Honesty. 2007. (People of Character Ser.). (ENG., Illus.). 24p. (J). (gr. 2-5). lib. bdg. 26.95 *(978-1-60014-091-4(2))* Bellwether Media.

Mara, Wil. Abraham Lincoln. 2014. (Rookie Biographies(r) Ser.). (ENG.). 32p. (J). lib. bdg. 23.00 *(978-0-531-21058-1(8))* Scholastic Library Publishing.

Margaret, Amy. Presidents' Day. 2009. (Library of Holidays Ser.). 24p. (gr. 2-3). 42.50 *(978-1-60853-716-7(1),* PowerKids Pr.) Rosen Publishing Group, Inc., The.

Meltzer, Brad. I Am Abraham Lincoln. Eliopoulos, Christopher, illus. 2014. (Ordinary People Change the World Ser.). 40p. (J). (gr. k-4). 15.99 *(978-0-8037-4083-9(2),* Dial Bks) Penguin Young Readers Group.

Meltzer, Brad. Soy Abraham Lincoln. Eliopoulos, Christopher, illus. 2023.Tr. of I Am Abraham Lincoln. (SPA.). (J). (gr. k-3). pap. 14.99 ***(978-1-5433-8602-8(4))*** Vista Higher Learning, Inc.

Meltzer, Milton. Lincoln in His Own Words. Alcorn, Stephen, illus. 2018. (ENG.). 240p. (YA). (gr. 7). pap. 12.99 *(978-1-328-89574-5(2),* 1699521, Clarion Bks.) HarperCollins Pubs.

Metzger, Steve & Kronheimer, Ann. Lincoln & Grace: Why Abraham Lincoln Grew a Beard: Why Abraham Lincoln Grew a Beard. 2013. (ENG.). 40p. (J). (gr. 2-5). pap. 6.99 *(978-0-545-48432-9(4))* Scholastic, Inc.

Moody, D. L. President Lincoln Listened. 2006. (Story Time Ser.). (ENG., Illus.). 24p. (J). (gr. -1-4). 7.99 *(978-1-84550-115-0(2),* 65bf2af5-67d8-43d6-be1d-dff7a798cd6e) Christian Focus Pubns. GBR. Dist: Baker & Taylor Publisher Services (BTPS).

Morlock, Theresa. Before Abraham Lincoln Was President, 1 vol. 2017. (Before They Were President Ser.). (ENG.). 24p. (J). (gr. 2-3). pap. 9.15 *(978-1-5382-1056-7(8),* 8cbab250-9a8d-4368-9727-89120df16c3b) Stevens, Gareth Publishing LLLP.

Nagelhout, Ryan. Emancipation Proclamation, 1 vol. 2016. (Documents of American Democracy Ser.). (ENG., Illus.). 32p. (J). (gr. 5-5). pap. 11.00 *(978-1-4994-2081-4(1),* 515d919a-4b81-4a74-9fc0-c271ac727e37, PowerKids Pr.) Rosen Publishing Group, Inc., The.

Nathan, Adele Gutman. Lincoln's Americ. 2011. 92p. 38.95 *(978-1-258-10382-8(6))* Literary Licensing, LLC.

Nelson, Maria. The Life of Abraham Lincoln, 1 vol. 2012. (Famous Lives Ser.). (ENG., Illus.). 24p. (J). (gr. 1-2). pap. 9.15 *(978-1-4339-6343-8(4),* 35b633d2-3bab-4aff-b2f9-48b3fbaf0130); lib. bdg. 25.27 *(978-1-4339-6341-4(8),* 2e73a321-4531-40ed-b3a9-a2ce545666ac) Stevens, Gareth Publishing LLLP.

—The Life of Abraham Lincoln / la Vida de Abraham Lincoln, 1 vol. 2012. (Famous Lives / Vidas Extraordinarias Ser.). (ENG & SPA., Illus.). 24p. (J). (gr. 1-2). 25.27 *(978-1-4339-6651-4(4),* f9d4d72c-d9cb-4703-8cc6-fafb97e5a16e) Stevens, Gareth Publishing LLLP.

Nicolay, Helen. The Boys' Life of Abraham Lincoln. 2007. 136p. per. *(978-1-4065-4046-8(3))* Dodo Pr.

—The Boys Life of Abraham Lincoln. 2005. 26.95 *(978-1-4218-0834-5(X))* 2004. 192p. pap. 11.95 *(978-1-59540-434-3(1))* 2004. 192p. per. 15.95 *(978-1-59540-991-1(2))* 1st World Publishing, Inc. (1st World Library - Literary Society).

Oney, Yannick. Abe Lincoln: President for the People. 2005. (World Discovery History Readers Ser.). (Illus.). 32p. (J). pap. *(978-0-439-66556-8(6))* Scholastic, Inc.

Osborne, Mary Pope. Abe Lincoln at Last! Murdocca, Sal, illus. 2013. (Magic Tree House (R) Merlin Mission Ser.: 19). 144p. (J). (gr. 2-5). 6.99 *(978-0-375-86797-2(X),* Random Hse. Bks. for Young Readers) Random Hse. Children's Bks.

Osborne, Mary Pope & Boyce, Natalie Pope. Abraham Lincoln: A Nonfiction Companion to Magic Tree House Merlin Mission #19: Abe Lincoln at Last. Murdocca, Sal, illus. 2011. (Magic Tree House (R) Fact Tracker Ser.: 25). 128p. (J). (gr. 2-5). 6.99 *(978-0-375-87024-8(5),* Random Hse. Bks. for Young Readers) Random Hse. Children's Bks.

Pace, Betty. Abraham Lincoln. Walker, Bobbie H., illus. 2008. 32p. pap. 12.99 *(978-1-4343-7969-6(8))* AuthorHouse.

Parker, Christi E. Abraham Lincoln, 1 vol. rev. ed. 2005. (Social Studies: Informational Text Ser.). (ENG.). 24p. (gr. 4-8). pap. 10.99 *(978-0-7439-8916-9(3))* Teacher Created Materials, Inc.

Pascal, Janet B. & Who HQ. Who Was Abraham Lincoln? O'Brien, John, illus. 2008. (Who Was? Ser.). 112p. (J). (gr. 3-7). pap. 5.99 *(978-0-448-44886-2(6),* Penguin Workshop) Penguin Young Readers Group.

Patrick, Bethanne Kelly. Abraham Lincoln. 2004. (Childhoods of the Presidents Ser.). (Illus.). 48p. (J). (gr. 4-18). lib. bdg. 17.95 *(978-1-59084-275-1(8))* Mason Crest.

Petty, Kate. Abraham Lincoln: The Life of America's Sixteenth President, 1 vol. 2005. (Graphic Nonfiction Biographies Ser.). (ENG., Illus.). 48p. (YA). (gr. 4-6). lib. bdg. 37.13 *(978-1-4042-0237-5(4),* 54d2fdab-786d-46f7-b0aa-86fcc4d88aac) Rosen Publishing Group, Inc., The.

Phillips, Ellen Blue. Abraham Lincoln: From Pioneer to President. 2007. (Sterling Biographies Ser.). (ENG., Illus.). 124p. (J). (gr. 6-8). 18.69 *(978-1-4027-4745-8(4))* Sterling Publishing Co., Inc.

Porterfield, Jason. The Lincoln-Douglas Senatorial Debates of 1858: A Primary Source Investigation, 1 vol. 2004. (Great Historic Debates & Speeches Ser.). (ENG., Illus.). 64p. (YA). (gr. 5-8). lib. bdg. 37.13 *(978-1-4042-0153-8(X),* 4e73e7f0-7984-4000-b09f-46efd13e52ab) Rosen Publishing Group, Inc., The.

—The Lincoln-Douglas Senatorial Debates Of 1858: A Primary Source Investigation. 2009. (Great Historic Debates & Speeches Ser.). 64p. (gr. 5-8). 58.50 *(978-1-61513-126-6(4))* Rosen Publishing Group, Inc., The.

Prentzas, G. S. The Emancipation Proclamation. 2011. (Cornerstones of Freedom, Third Ser.). (Illus.). 64p. (J). (ENG.). pap. 8.95 *(978-0-531-26557-4(9));* lib. bdg. 30.00 *(978-0-531-25032-7(6))* Scholastic Library Publishing. (Children's Pr.).

Press, David P. Abraham Lincoln: The Great Emancipator. 2013. (ENG., Illus.). 64p. (J). *(978-0-7787-1061-5(0));* pap. *(978-0-7787-1064-6(5))* Crabtree Publishing Co.

Randolph, Joanne, ed. Mr. Lincoln, 1 vol. 2018. (Civil War & Reconstruction: Rebellion & Rebuilding Ser.). (ENG.). 32p. (gr. 4-5). 27.93 *(978-1-5383-4093-6(3),* 14df60c2-99ff-4d63-b23a-bf306f950ba2, PowerKids Pr.) Rosen Publishing Group, Inc., The.

Rappaport, Doreen. Abe's Honest Words. Nelson, Kadir, illus. 2009. (J). (gr. 2-4). 27.95 incl. audio *(978-0-8045-6984-2(3))* Spoken Arts, Inc.

—Abe's Honest Words: The Life of Abraham Lincoln. Nelson, Kadir, illus. (Big Words Book Ser.: 5). (ENG.). 48p. (J). (gr. -1-3). 2016. pap. 8.99 *(978-1-4847-4958-6(8))* 2008. 16.99 *(978-1-4231-0408-7(0))* Little, Brown Bks. for Young Readers.

Raum, Elizabeth. Abraham Lincoln, 1 vol. Oxford Designers and Illustrators, illus. 2012. (American Biographies Ser.). (ENG.). 48p. (gr. 4-6). pap. 9.95 *(978-1-4329-6464-1(X),* 119063); (J). lib. bdg. 35.32 *(978-1-4329-6453-5(4),* 119052) Capstone. (Heinemann).

Rivera, Sheila. Abraham Lincoln: Una Vida de Respeto. 2006. (Libros para Avanzar Ser.). (ENG & SPA., Illus.). 32p. (J). (gr. 3-7). lib. bdg. 22.60 *(978-0-8225-6236-8(7))* Lerner Publishing Group.

—Abraham Lincoln: Una vida de respeto (A Life of Respect) 2006. (Libros para Avanzar-Biografías (Pull Ahead Books-Biographies Ser.). (Illus.). 32p. (J). (gr. 3-7). per. 6.95 *(978-0-8225-6559-8(5),* Ediciones Lerner) Lerner Publishing Group.

RJF Publishing Staff & Hankins, Chelsey. The Lincoln Memorial. 2009. (Symbols of American Freedom Ser.). 48p. (gr. 4-6). 30.00 *(978-1-60413-518-3(2),* Chelsea Clubhse.) Infobase Holdings, Inc.

Roberts, Jeremy. Abraham Lincoln. 2004. (Presidential Leaders Ser.). (Illus.). 112p. (J). (gr. 6-12). lib. bdg. 29.27 *(978-0-8225-0817-5(6))* Lerner Publishing Group.

Roxburgh, Ellis. Abraham Lincoln vs. Jefferson Davis: Presidents of a Divided Nation, 1 vol. 2015. (History's Greatest Rivals Ser.). (ENG., Illus.). 48p. (J). (gr. 6-8). pap. 15.05 *(978-1-4824-4219-9(1),* b135bb93-4357-466b-a1e4-3a9fd5bddc79) Stevens, Gareth Publishing LLLP.

Ruffin, Frances E. The Lincoln Memorial, 1 vol. 2005. (Places in American History Ser.). (ENG., Illus.). 24p. (gr. 2-4). pap. 9.15 *(978-0-8368-6418-2(2),* 6077f5f0-4f2d-49bc-ae23-0d36382a36a4); lib. bdg. 24.67 *(978-0-8368-6411-3(5),* 61b9d970-2d0f-42ee-948b-8a392a052d9d) Stevens, Gareth Publishing LLLP. (Weekly Reader Leveled Readers).

Rumsch, BreAnn. Abraham Lincoln, 1 vol. 2016. (United States Presidents *2017 Ser.). (ENG., Illus.). 40p. (J). (gr. 2-5). 35.64 *(978-1-68078-106-9(5),* 21829, Big Buddy Bks.) ABDO Publishing Co.

Rustad, Martha E. H. What Is Inside the Lincoln Memorial? Poling, Kyle, illus. 2014. (Cloverleaf Books (tm) — Our American Symbols Ser.). (ENG.). 24p. (J). (gr. k-2). pap. 8.99 *(978-1-4677-4468-3(9),* 69730893-3fa4-4300-abfe-b2b4217f7202, Millbrook Pr.) Lerner Publishing Group.

Saddleback Educational Publishing Staff, ed. Abraham Lincoln, 1 vol. unabr. ed. 2007. (Graphic Biographies Ser.). (ENG., Illus.). 25p. (YA). (gr. 4-12). per. 9.75 *(978-1-59905-211-3(3))* Saddleback Educational Publishing, Inc.

Sandburg, Carl. Abe Lincoln Grows Up. 2009. (ENG., Illus.). 224p. (YA). (gr. 7-18). reprint ed. pap. 7.99 *(978-0-15-602615-4(5),* 1063351, Clarion Bks.) HarperCollins Pubs.

Schmidt, Roderic. How to Draw the Life & Times of Abraham Lincoln. (Kid's Guide to Drawing the Presidents of the United States of America Ser.). 32p. (gr. 4-4). 2009. 50.50 *(978-1-61511-130-5(1),* PowerKids Pr.) 2005. (ENG.). (YA). 30.27 *(978-1-4042-2993-8(0),* e616c85a-5859-425f-a597-fb99df3a7e08) Rosen Publishing Group, Inc., The.

Schott, Jane A. Abraham Lincoln. 2003. (History Maker Biographies Ser.). (ENG., Illus.). 48p. (gr. 3-6). pap. 8.95 *(978-0-8225-0381-1(6),* Lerner Pubns.) Lerner Publishing Group.

Schroeder, Alan. Abe Lincoln: His Wit & Wisdom from A to Z. O'brien, John, illus. 2015. (ENG.). 32p. (J). (gr. 1-4). 17.95 *(978-0-8234-2420-7(0))* Holiday Hse., Inc.

—Abe Lincoln: His Wit & Wisdom from A-Z. O'Brien, John, illus. 2016. (ENG.). 32p. (J). (gr. 1-4). 7.99 *(978-0-8234-3575-3(X))* Holiday Hse., Inc.

Sheinkin, Steve. Lincoln's Grave Robbers (Scholastic Focus) 2013. (ENG.). 224p. (J). (gr. 5-8). 16.99 *(978-0-545-40572-0(6),* Scholastic Pr.) Scholastic, Inc.

Smith, Adam I. P. Abraham Lincoln: President, 1 vol. 2016. (History Makers Ser.). (ENG., Illus.). 144p. (J). (gr. 9-9). 47.36 *(978-1-5026-1912-9(1),* a00797b5-af27-4994-925c-24cf2ac38b7d) Cavendish Square Publishing LLC.

Stewart, Whitney. Mr. Lincoln's Gift: A Civil War Story. Dunham Akiyama, Laine, illus. 2008. 32p. (J). 19.95 *(978-0-9754917-4-4(1))* Friends of Hildene, Inc.

Stock, Catherine. Vinnie & Abraham. unabr. ed. 2008. (J). (gr. 2-5). 27.95 incl. audio *(978-0-8045-6967-5(3));* 29.95 incl. audio compact disk *(978-0-8045-4190-9(6))* Spoken Arts, Inc.

Strand, Jennifer. Abraham Lincoln. 2016. (Legendary Leaders Ser.). (ENG.). 24p. (J). (gr. -1-2). 49.94 *(978-1-68079-402-1(7),* 23023, Abdo Zoom-Launch) ABDO Publishing Co.

Swanson, Shari. Honey, the Dog Who Saved Abe Lincoln. Groenink, Chuck, illus. 2020. (ENG.). 40p. (J). (gr. -1-3). 18.99 *(978-0-06-269900-8(8),* Tegen, Katherine Bks) HarperCollins Pubs.

Tarbell, Ida. M. Boy Scouts' Life of Lincoln. 2005. pap. 27.95 *(978-1-885529-53-4(8))* Stevens Publishing.

Thomson, Sarah L. What Lincoln Said. Ransome, James E., illus. 2009. 32p. (J). (gr. k-3). lib. bdg. 18.89 *(978-0-06-084820-0(0))* HarperCollins Pubs.

Tiwari, Saral. Abraham Lincoln: The Civil War President. Turner, Ginger, illus. 2004. 48p. (J). pap. 17.95 *(978-0-9742502-1-2(X))* Gossamer Bks., LLC.

Tiwari, Saral, illus. Abraham Lincoln: The Civil War President 2004. 48p. (J). 15.95 *(978-0-9742502-0-5(1))* Gossamer Bks., LLC.

Trumbauer, Lisa. Abraham Lincoln & the Civil War. rev. ed. 2016. (Life in the Time Of Ser.). (ENG.). 32p. (J). (gr. 1-3). pap. 8.29 *(978-1-4846-3822-4(0),* 134722, Heinemann) Capstone.

Turner, Ann. Abe Lincoln Remembers. Minor, Wendell, illus. 2003. (ENG.). 32p. (J). (gr. 1-4). pap. 8.99 *(978-0-06-051107-4(9),* HarperCollins) HarperCollins Pubs.

Uglow, Loyd. Abraham Lincoln: Will You Ever Give Up?, 1bk. James, Kennon, illus. 2003. (Another Great Achiever Ser.). (J). lib. bdg. 23.95 incl. audio *(978-1-57537-790-2(X));* (ENG.). 48p. (YA). lib. bdg. 23.95 incl. audio compact disk *(978-1-57537-740-7(3))* Advance Publishing, Inc.

Vescia, Monique. The Emancipation Proclamation, 1 vol. 2016. (Let's Find Out! Primary Sources Ser.). (ENG., Illus.). 32p. (J). (gr. 2-3). lib. bdg. 26.06 *(978-1-5081-0405-6(0),* bf2c8f3c-c00f-498d-9c78-61f20b774f67) Rosen Publishing Group, Inc., The.

Vierow, Wendy. The 1864 Presidential Election: A War-Weary Nation Reelects President Abraham Lincoln. (Headlines from History Ser.). 24p. (gr. 3-3). 2009. 42.50 *(978-1-61513-239-3(2),* PowerKids Pr.) 2004. (ENG., Illus.). (J). lib. bdg. 26.27 *(978-0-8239-6224-2(5),* 102e5709-9d05-4831-ae6d-ef5ba17ce89f) Rosen Publishing Group, Inc., The.

Wearing, Judy. Abraham Lincoln. 2010. (My Life Ser.). 24p. (J). (gr. 2-4). lib. bdg. 25.70 *(978-1-61690-056-4(3))* Weigl Pubs., Inc.

—Abraham Lincoln: My Life. 2010. pap. 9.95 *(978-1-61690-057-1(1))* Weigl Pubs., Inc.

Winters, Kay. Abe Lincoln: Abe Lincoln. Carpenter, Nancy, illus. 2003. (ENG.). 40p. (J). (gr. k-3). 19.99 *(978-0-689-82554-5(4),* Simon & Schuster Bks. For Young Readers) Simon & Schuster Bks. For Young Readers.

—Abe Lincoln: The Boy Who Loved Books. Carpenter, Nancy, illus. 2004. 38p. (J). (gr. -1-3). reprint ed. 17.00 *(978-0-7567-7969-6(3))* DIANE Publishing Co.

—Abe Lincoln: The Boy Who Loved Books. Carpenter, Nancy, illus. 2006. (ENG.). 40p. (J). (gr. k-3). reprint ed. 8.99 *(978-1-4169-1268-2(1),* Aladdin) Simon & Schuster Children's Publishing.

LINCOLN, ABRAHAM, 1809-1865—ANECDOTES

Hansen, Grace. Abraham Lincoln, 1 vol. 2014. (United States President Biographies (Abdo Kids Jumbo) Ser.). (ENG.). 24p. (J). (gr. -1-2). lib. bdg. 32.79 *(978-1-62970-085-4(1),* 1716, Abdo Kids) ABDO Publishing Co.

LINCOLN, ABRAHAM, 1809-1865—ASSASSINATION

Brindell Fradin, Dennis. The Assassination of Abraham Lincoln, 1 vol. 2007. (Turning Points in U. S. History Ser.). (ENG., Illus.). 48p. (gr. 4-4). lib. bdg. 34.07 (978-0-7614-2123-8(8), 12dd41a1-36d5-4e0e-a468-d45f3b974e88) Cavendish Square Publishing LLC.

Denenberg, Barry. Lincoln Shot: A President's Life Remembered. Bing, Christopher, illus. 2011. (ENG.). 96p. (J). (gr. 5-9). pap. 14.99 (978-0-312-60442-4(4), 900076473) Square Fish.

Gunderson, Jessica. President Lincoln's Killer & the America He Left Behind: The Assassin, the Crime, & Its Lasting Blow to Freedom & Equality. 2018. (Assassins' America Ser.). (ENG., Illus.). 64p. (J). (gr. 4-9). lib. bdg. 30.65 (978-0-7565-5716-4(X), 137215, Compass Point Bks.) Capstone.

—The Wound Is Mortal: The Story of the Assassination of Abraham Lincoln. 2015. (Tangled History Ser.). (ENG., Illus.). 112p. (J). (gr. 3-9). pap. 6.95 (978-1-4914-7080-0(1), 129462, Capstone Pr.) Capstone.

Gunderson, Jessica & Tougas, Joseph. Assassins' America: Four Killers, Four Murdered Presidents, & the Country They Left Behind. 2018. (ENG.). 208p. (J). (gr. 4-9). pap., pap., pap. 9.95 (978-1-62370-981-5(4), 137226, Capstone Young Readers) Capstone.

Jones, Rebecca C. Mystery of Mary Surratt: The Plot to Kill President Lincoln, 1 vol. 2009. (ENG., Illus.). 96p. (gr. 3-6). pap. 9.95 (978-0-87033-560-0(X), 3679, Cornell Maritime Pr./Tidewater Pubs.) Schiffer Publishing, Ltd.

Langston-George, Rebecca. The Booth Brothers: Drama, Fame, & the Death of President Lincoln. 2017. (Encounter: Narrative Nonfiction Stories Ser.). (ENG., Illus.). 112p. (J). (gr. 3-7). lib. bdg. 31.32 (978-1-5157-7338-2(8), 135667, Capstone Pr.) Capstone.

Marinelli, Debra A. The Assassination of Abraham Lincoln. 2009. (Library of Political Assassinations Ser.). 64p. (gr. 5-5). 58.50 (978-1-60853-824-9(9)) Rosen Publishing Group, Inc., The.

Olson, Kay Melchisedech. The Assassination of Abraham Lincoln, 1 vol. Lohse, Otha Zackariah Edward, illus. 2005. (Graphic History Ser.). (ENG.). 32p. (J). (gr. 3-9). per. 8.10 (978-0-7368-5241-8(7), 86987, Capstone Pr.) Capstone.

O'Reilly, Bill & Zimmerman, Dwight Jon. Lincoln's Last Days. 2014. (J). lib. bdg. 24.50 (978-0-606-35526-1(X)) Turtleback.

—Lincoln's Last Days: The Shocking Assassination That Changed America Forever. 2014. (ENG., Illus.). 352p. (J). (gr. 5). pap. 14.99 (978-1-250-04429-7(4), 900128322) Square Fish.

Swanson, James L. Chasing Lincoln's Killer: the Search for John Wilkes Booth. 2009. (ENG., Illus.). 208p. (J). (gr. 7-18). 17.99 (978-0-439-90354-7(8), Scholastic Pr.) Scholastic, Inc.

LINCOLN, ABRAHAM, 1809-1865—ASSASSINATION—FICTION

Blackwood, Gary L. Second Sight. 2007. (Illus.). 279p. (J). (gr. 5-9). 14.65 (978-0-7569-8132-7(8)) Perfection Learning Corp.

Rinaldi, Ann. An Acquaintance with Darkness. 2005. (Great Episodes Ser.). (ENG.). 384p. (YA). (gr. 7-8). pap. 9.99 (978-0-15-205387-1(5), 1196220, Clarion Bks.) HarperCollins Pubs.

—An Acquaintance with Darkness. 2005. (Great Episodes Ser.). 374p. (gr. 7-12). 18.00 (978-0-7569-5040-8(6)) Perfection Learning Corp.

LINCOLN, ABRAHAM, 1809-1865—FICTION

Biros, Florence W. Love & Loyalty: The Traits That Made Lincoln Great. 2005. (Illus.). 320p. pap. 14.95 (978-0-936369-92-1(2)) Son-Rise Pubns. & Distribution Co.

Blackwood, Gary. Second Sight. 2007. (ENG.). 288p. (J). (gr. 5-18). 8.99 (978-0-14-240747-9(X), Puffin Books) Penguin Young Readers Group.

Brandeis, Gayle. My Life with the Lincolns. 2010. (ENG.). 256p. (J). (gr. 5-9). 35.99 (978-0-8050-9013-0(4), 900059042, Holt, Henry & Co. Bks. For Young Readers) Holt, Henry & Co.

Brewer, Caroline. Kara & Friends Meet Abraham Lincoln. 2004. (Illus.). 40p. (J). 17.95 (978-0-9717790-4-4(X)) Unchained Spirit Enterprises.

Cavanah, Frances. Abe Lincoln Gets His Chance. 2007. 72p. per. (978-1-4068-4447-4(0)) Echo Library.

Hedstrom-Page, Deborah. From Log Cabin to White House with Abraham Lincoln. Martinez, Sergio, illus. 2007. (My American Journey Ser.). 82p. (J). (gr. 3-9). 9.99 (978-0-8054-3269-5(8)) B&H Publishing Group.

Hicks, Clifford B. Alvin Fernald's Incredible Buried Treasure. Bradfield, Roger, illus. 2009. (J). 17.95 (978-1-930900-43-1(0)) Purple Hse. Pr.

Hopkinson, Deborah. Abe Lincoln Crosses a Creek: A Tall, Thin Tale (Introducing His Forgotten Frontier Friend) Hendrix, John, illus. 2016. 40p. (J). (gr. -1-3). 7.99 (978-1-5247-0158-1(0), Dragonfly Bks.) Random Hse. Children's Bks.

Jackson, Ellen. Abe Lincoln Loved Animals. Ettlinger, Doris, illus. 2013. (AV2 Fiction Readalong Ser.: Vol. 56). (ENG.). 32p. (J). 34.28 (978-1-62127-864-1(6), AV2 by Weigl) Weigl Pubs., Inc.

Jakubowski, Michele. The Professor's Discovery. Pinelli, Amerigo, illus. 2016. (Sleuths of Somerville Ser.). (ENG.). 144p. (J). (gr. 4-6). lib. bdg. 25.99 (978-1-4965-3177-3(9), 132216, Stone Arch Bks.) Capstone.

—The Professor's Discovery. Pinelli, Amerigo, illus. 2017. (Sleuths of Somerville Ser.). (ENG.). 144p. (J). (gr. 4-6). pap. 6.95 (978-1-4965-3181-0(7), Stone Arch Bks.) Capstone.

Lyons, Kelly Starling. Hope's Gift. Tate, Don, illus. 2012. 32p. (J). (gr. 1-3). 17.99 (978-0-399-16001-1(9), G.P. Putnam's Sons Books for Young Readers) Penguin Young Readers Group.

Malaspina, Ann. Finding Lincoln. Bootman, Colin, illus. 2009. (ENG.). 32p. (J). (gr. -1-3). 16.99 (978-0-8075-2435-0(2), 807524352) Whitman, Albert & Co.

Mazer, Harry. My Brother Abe: Sally Lincoln's Story. 2009. (ENG.). 208p. (J). (gr. 3-7). pap. 5.99 (978-1-4169-3894-1(X), Simon & Schuster Bks. For Young Readers) Simon & Schuster Bks. For Young Readers.

—My Brother Abe: Sally Lincoln's Story. 2009. (ENG.). 208p. (J). (gr. 3-7). 15.99 (978-1-4169-3884-2(2)) Simon & Schuster, Inc.

Myers, Anna. Assassin. 2007. (ENG.). 224p. (YA). (gr. 7). per. 10.99 (978-0-8027-9643-1(5), 900044367, Bloomsbury USA Childrens) Bloomsbury Publishing USA.

—Assassin. 2011. (ENG.). 192p. (YA). (gr. 4-6). 22.44 (978-0-8027-8989-1(7), 9780802789891) 2005. (J). (978-978-080-278-3(9)) Walker & Co.

Osborne, Mary Pope. Abe Lincoln at Last! 2013. (Magic Tree House Merlin Missions Ser.: 19). lib. bdg. 16.00 (978-0-606-35563-6(4)) Turtleback.

Perry, Fred. Time Lincoln, Vol. 1. 2011. (ENG.). 122p. (YA). pap., pap. 19.95 (978-0-9831823-7-5(X), cd022291-ebe4-480a-87a0-41bd78130b2d) Antarctic Pr., Inc.

Polacco, Patricia. Just in Time Abraham Lincoln. 2012. 29.95 (978-0-8045-4240-1(6)) Spoken Arts, Inc.

Rack, Charlene. The Adventures of Delaware Bear & Young Abraham Lincoln. 2011. 24p. (gr. -1). pap. 12.79 (978-1-4567-5619-2(2)) AuthorHouse.

Schmidt, Bryan Thomas. Abraham Lincoln Dinosaur Hunter. 2013. 80p. pap. 5.99 (978-1-61941-054-1(0)) Delabarre Publishing.

Sheinkin, Steve. Abraham Lincoln, Pro Wrestler. Swaab, Neil, illus. 2019. (Time Twisters Ser.). (ENG.). 176p. (J). pap. 8.99 (978-1-250-20787-6(8), 900201775) Roaring Brook Pr.

—Lincoln's Grave Robbers (Scholastic Focus) 2018. (ENG.). 224p. (J). (gr. 4-7). pap. 9.99 (978-1-338-29013-4(4)) Scholastic, Inc.

Strasser, Todd. Abe Lincoln for Class President. 2010. 144p. pap. 10.95 (978-1-4502-1244-1(1)) iUniverse, Inc.

Strickland, James R. Lincoln's Lost Papers. 2008. 131p. (J). pap. 11.95 (978-0-7414-4601-5(4)) Infinity Publishing.

Sullivan, Michael John & Petrone, Susan. The Sockkids Meet Lincoln. 2013. 42p. pap. 10.99 (978-0-9727077-7-0(8)) Scribe Publishing.

Sun Edit and Book Design, ed. Abraham Lincoln & the Forest of Little Pigeon Creek. 2007. (Illus.). 56p. (J). 19.95 (978-0-9798739-0-4(8)) AmeriTales Entertainment, LLC.

Tarbell, Ida. M. Father Abraham. Campbell, Blendon, illus. 2004. reprint ed. pap. 15.95 (978-1-4179-0070-1(9)) Kessinger Publishing, LLC.

Wells, Rosemary. Lincoln & His Boys. Lynch, P. J., illus. (ENG.). 96p. (J). (gr. 3-7). 2015. pap. 9.99 (978-0-7636-8069-5(9)) 2008. 16.99 (978-0-7636-3723-1(8)) Candlewick Pr.

LINCOLN, ABRAHAM, 1809-1865—GETTYSBURG ADDRESS

Armentrout, David & Armentrout, Patricia. The Gettysburg Address. 2004. (ENG.). 48p. (gr. 4-6). pap. 10.95 (978-1-59515-333-3(0)) Rourke Educational Media.

Armentrout, David, et al. The Gettysburg Address. 2005. (Documents that Shaped the Nation Ser.). (Illus.). 48p. (gr. 4-6). 20.95 (978-1-59515-232-9(6)) Rourke Educational Media.

Armstrong, Jennifer. A Three-Minute Speech: Lincoln's Remarks at Gettysburg. Lorenz, Albert, illus. 2003. (Milestone Ser.). (ENG.). 96p. (J). pap. 4.99 (978-0-689-85622-8(9), Simon & Schuster/Paula Wiseman Bks.) Simon & Schuster/Paula Wiseman Bks.

—The True Story Behind Lincoln's Gettysburg Address. Lorenz, Albert, illus. 2013. (ENG.). 96p. (J). (gr. 2-5). 15.99 (978-1-4424-9388-9(7)); pap. 5.99 (978-1-4424-9387-2(9)) Simon & Schuster/Paula Wiseman Bks. (Simon & Schuster/Paula Wiseman Bks.).

Butzer, C. M. The Gettysburg. Butzer, C. M., illus. 2009. (ENG., Illus.). 80p. (YA). (gr. 4-9). pap. 9.99 (978-0-06-156175-7(4)) HarperCollins Pubs.

—Gettysburg: The Graphic Novel. Butzer, C. M., illus. 2008. (ENG., Illus.). 80p. (J). (gr. 5-9). 16.99 (978-0-06-156176-4(2), HarperAlley) HarperCollins Pubs.

Ford, Carin T. The Battle of Gettysburg & Lincoln's Gettysburg Address, 1 vol. 2004. (Civil War Library). (ENG., Illus.). 48p. (gr. 3-3). lib. bdg. 27.93 (978-0-7660-2253-9(6), a6bd528d-8814-4bf0-92d6-163b2d6e27dc) Enslow Publishing, LLC.

—Lincoln's Gettysburg Address & the Battle of Gettysburg Through Primary Sources, 1 vol. 2013. (Civil War Through Primary Sources Ser.). (ENG.). 48p. (gr. 4-6). lib. bdg. 27.93 (978-0-7660-4126-4(3), 9da9ea5b-2b66-4e0d-aa21-1a75f57167a9) Enslow Publishing, LLC.

Gregory, Josh. The Gettysburg Address. 2013. (ENG.). 64p. (J). pap. 8.95 (978-0-531-27669-3(4)) Scholastic Library Publishing.

Kenison, Misti. Where's Your Hat, Abe Lincoln? 2017. (Young Historians Ser.: 0). (Illus.). 28p. (J). (gr. -1-k). bds. 9.99 (978-1-4926-5250-2(4)) Sourcebooks, Inc.

Leavitt, Amie Jane, et al. Kids' Translations. rev. ed. 2017. (Kids' Translations Ser.). (ENG.). 32p. (J). (gr. 3-6). 149.95 (978-1-5157-9144-7(0), 27305, Capstone Pr.) Capstone.

Miller, Mirella S. 12 Questions about the Gettysburg Address. 2017. (Examining Primary Sources Ser.). (ENG., Illus.). 32p. (J). (gr. 3-6). 32.80 (978-1-63235-284-2(2), 11753, 12-Story Library) Bookstaves, LLC.

Olson, Kay Melchisedech. The Gettysburg Address in Translation: What It Really Means. rev. ed. 2017. (Kids' Translations Ser.). (ENG., Illus.). 32p. (J). (gr. 3-6). lib. bdg. 27.99 (978-1-5157-9136-2(X), 136570, Capstone Pr.) Capstone.

Olson, Steve. Lincoln's Gettysburg Address: A Primary Source Investigation, 1 vol. 2004. (Great Historic Debates & Speeches Ser.). (ENG.). 64p. (YA). (gr. 5-8). pap. 13.95 (978-1-4358-3275-6(2), 0f4bd463-1b63-4906-8041-7269a5e59f9a) Rosen Publishing Group, Inc., The.

Olson, Steven P. Lincoln's Gettysburg Address: A Primary Source Investigation. 2009. (Great Historic Debates & Speeches Ser.). 64p. (gr. 5-8). 58.50 (978-1-61513-115-0(9)) Rosen Publishing Group, Inc., The.

Pingry, Patricia A. The Story of Gettysburg. Britt, Stephanie, illus. 2003. (ENG.). 26p. (J). (gr. -1-k). bds. 7.69 (978-0-8249-6503-7(5), Ideals Pubns.) Worthy Publishing.

Sjonger, Rebecca. Abraham Lincoln: The Gettysburg Address. 2019. (Deconstructing Powerful Speeches Ser.). 48p. (J). (gr. 6-6). pap. (978-0-7787-5253-0(4)) Crabtree Publishing Co.

Tanaka, Shelley. Gettysburg: The Legendary Battle & the Address That Inspired a Nation. Craig, David, illus. 2003. (Day That Changed America Ser.). (ENG.). 48p. 16.99 (978-0-7868-1922-5(7)) Hyperion Pr.

LINCOLN, ABRAHAM, 1809-1865—MONUMENTS

Carr, Aaron. Lincoln Memorial. 2013. (J). (978-1-62127-202-1(8)); pap. (978-1-62127-206-9(0)) Weigl Pubs., Inc.

Chang, Kirsten. The Lincoln Memorial. 2019. (Symbols of American Freedom Ser.). (ENG., Illus.). 24p. (J). (gr. k-3). pap. 7.99 (978-1-61891-493-4(6), 12143, Blastoff! Readers) Bellwether Media.

Kissock, Heather. Lincoln Memorial. 2017. (Illus.). 24p. (J). (978-1-5105-0602-2(0)) SmartBook Media, Inc.

Linde, Barbara M. The Lincoln Memorial, 1 vol. 2018. (Symbols of America Ser.). (ENG.). 24p. (gr. 1-2). 24.27 (978-1-5382-2899-9(8), ec4147a1-3f4f-4d4e-a904-02d3f9a65154) Stevens, Gareth Publishing LLLP.

Marcovitz, Hal. Lincoln Memorial: Shrine to an American Hero. Moreno, Barry, ed. 2014. (Patriotic Symbols of America Ser.: 20). (Illus.). 48p. (J). (gr. 4-18). 20.95 (978-1-4222-3127-2(5)) Mason Crest.

Nelson, Kristin L. The Lincoln Memorial. (Lightning Bolt Bks.). 2010. (Illus.). 32p. (J). (gr. k-2). lib. bdg. 25.26 (978-0-7613-6018-6(2), Lerner Pubns.) 2010. (ENG., Illus.). 32p. (J). (gr. 1-3). pap. 9.99 (978-0-7613-6051-3(4), b20768c5-10c3-4d4c-9038-f47fd5e8bb0c) 2010. pap. 45.32 (978-0-7613-6992-9(9)) 2003. (ENG., Illus.). 32p. (J). (gr. k-3). pap. 7.99 (978-0-8225-3761-8(3), 384a595f-45c2-4185-bd52-7127ca59c4d5, First Avenue Editions) Lerner Publishing Group.

RJF Publishing Staff & Hankins, Chelsey. The Lincoln Memorial. 2009. (Symbols of American Freedom Ser.). 48p. (gr. 4-6). 30.00 (978-1-60413-518-3(2), Chelsea Clubhse.) Infobase Holdings, Inc.

LINCOLN, MARY TODD, 1818-1882

Hull, Mary E. Mary Todd Lincoln: Civil War's First Lady, 1 vol. 2014. (Legendary American Biographies Ser.). (ENG.). 96p. (gr. 6-6). 29.60 (978-0-7660-6480-5(8), 2334efaa-2847-413e-92a3-b06892d78510); pap. 13.88 (978-0-7660-6481-2(6), 77e849a6-625a-4e25-a5bb-d16442ad7740) Enslow Publishing, LLC.

Jones, Lynda. Mrs. Lincoln's Dressmaker: The Unlikely Friendship of Elizabeth Keckley & Mary Todd Lincoln. 2009. (Illus.). 80p. (J). (gr. 5-9). 18.95 (978-1-4263-0377-7(7), National Geographic Kids) Disney Publishing Worldwide.

Krull, Kathleen. Mary Todd Lincoln: I'm Usually the Smartest Person in the Room. Baddeley, Elizabeth, illus. 2015. (Women Who Broke the Rules Ser.). (ENG.). 48p. (J). (gr. 1-4). pap. 6.99 (978-0-8027-3825-7(7), 9780802738257, Bloomsbury USA Childrens) Bloomsbury Publishing USA.

Larkin, Tanya. What Was Cooking in Mary Todd Lincoln's White House? 2009. (Cooking Throughout American History Ser.). 24p. (gr. 3-3). 42.50 (978-1-61511-954-7(X), PowerKids Pr.) Rosen Publishing Group, Inc., The.

Strand, Jennifer. Mary Todd Lincoln. 2018. (First Ladies (Launch!) Ser.). (ENG., Illus.). 24p. (J). (gr. -1-2). lib. bdg. 31.36 (978-1-5321-2285-9(3), 28337, Abdo Zoom-Launch) ABDO Publishing Co.

LINCOLN, MARY TODD, 1818-1882—FICTION

Rinaldi, Ann. An Unlikely Friendship: A Novel of Mary Todd Lincoln & Elizabeth Keckley. 2008. (Great Episodes Ser.). (ENG., Illus.). 256p. (J). (gr. 5-7). pap. 7.99 (978-0-15-206398-6(6), 1199153, Clarion Bks.) HarperCollins Pubs.

LINCOLN MEMORIAL (WASHINGTON, D.C.)

Carr, Aaron. Lincoln Memorial. 2013. (J). (978-1-62127-202-1(8)); pap. (978-1-62127-206-9(0)) Weigl Pubs., Inc.

Chang, Kirsten. The Lincoln Memorial. 2019. (Symbols of American Freedom Ser.). (ENG., Illus.). 24p. (J). (gr. k-3). pap. 7.99 (978-1-61891-493-4(6), 12143, Blastoff! Readers) Bellwether Media.

Edison, Erin. The Lincoln Memorial: A 4D Book. 2018. (National Landmarks Ser.). (ENG., Illus.). 24p. (J). (gr. 1-3). lib. bdg. 27.99 (978-1-5435-3130-5(X), 138735, Capstone Pr.) Capstone.

Erin, Audrey. Visit the Lincoln Memorial, 1 vol. 2012. (Landmarks of Liberty Ser.). (ENG.). 24p. (J). (gr. 2-3). pap. 9.15 (978-1-4339-6398-8(1), 536b5fd4-2ef4-446d-9fe7-8a550bca52ba, Gareth Stevens Learning Library); lib. bdg. 25.27 (978-1-4339-6396-4(5), 06471bd3-8fe6-41fd-99fa-85978d55e4c0) Stevens, Gareth Publishing LLLP.

Hopkinson, Deborah. Sweet Land of Liberty, 1 vol. Jenkins, Leonard, illus. 2019. 32p. (J). (gr. 1-4). pap. 7.95 (978-1-68263-124-9(9)) Peachtree Publishing Co. Inc.

Linde, Barbara M. The Lincoln Memorial, 1 vol. 2018. (Symbols of America Ser.). (ENG.). 24p. (gr. 1-2). 24.27 (978-1-5382-2899-9(8), ec4147a1-3f4f-4d4e-a904-02d3f9a65154) Stevens, Gareth Publishing LLLP.

Marcovitz, Hal. Lincoln Memorial: Shrine to an American Hero. Moreno, Barry, ed. 2014. (Patriotic Symbols of America Ser.: 20). (Illus.). 48p. (J). (gr. 4-18). 20.95 (978-1-4222-3127-2(5)) Mason Crest.

Murray, Julie. Lincoln Memorial. 2016. (US Landmarks Ser.). (ENG., Illus.). 24p. (J). (gr. -1-2). lib. bdg. 31.36 (978-1-68080-911-4(3), 23297, Abdo Kids) ABDO Publishing Co.

Nelson, Kristin L. The Lincoln Memorial. (Lightning Bolt Bks.). 2010. (Illus.). 32p. (J). (gr. k-2). lib. bdg. 25.26 (978-0-7613-6018-6(2), Lerner Pubns.) 2010. (ENG., Illus.). 32p. (J). (gr. 1-3). pap. 9.99 (978-0-7613-6051-3(4), b20768c5-10c3-4d4c-9038-f47fd5e8bb0c) 2010. pap. 45.32 (978-0-7613-6992-9(9)) 2003. (ENG., Illus.). 32p. (J). (gr. k-3). pap. 7.99 (978-0-8225-3761-8(3), 384a595f-45c2-4185-bd52-7127ca59c4d5, First Avenue Editions) Lerner Publishing Group.

—El Monumento a Lincoln. 2005. (Libros para Avanzar (Pull Ahead Bks.)). (SPA., Illus.). 32p. (J). (gr. k-3). per. 5.95 (978-0-8225-3143-2(7), Ediciones Lerner) Lerner Publishing Group.

Rustad, Martha E. H. What Is Inside the Lincoln Memorial? Poling, Kyle, illus. 2014. (Cloverleaf Books (tm) — Our American Symbols Ser.). (ENG.). 24p. (J). (gr. k-2). pap. 8.99 (978-1-4677-4468-3(9), 69730893-3fa4-4300-abfe-b2b4217f7202, Millbrook Pr.) Lerner Publishing Group.

LINDBERGH, CHARLES A. (CHARLES AUGUSTUS), 1902-1974

Fleming, Candace. The Rise & Fall of Charles Lindbergh. 2020. (Illus.). 384p. (YA). (gr. 7). 18.99 (978-0-525-64654-9(X)); (ENG., 21.99 (978-0-525-64655-6(8)) Random Hse. Children's Bks. (Schwartz & Wade Bks.).

Lindbergh, Charles A., Jr. The Spirit of St Louis. 2003. 562p. pap. 29.00 (978-0-7581-3991-7(8)) Textbook Pubs.

Marsh, Carole. Charles Lindbergh. 2003. 12p. (gr. k-4). 2.95 (978-0-635-02130-4(7)) Gallopade International.

Rowell, Rebecca. Charles Lindbergh: Groundbreaking Aviator, 1 vol. 2010. (Essential Lives Set 5 Ser.). (ENG.). 112p. (YA). (gr. 6-12). lib. bdg. 41.36 (978-1-61613-516-4(6), 6715, Essential Library) ABDO Publishing Co.

Saddleback Educational Publishing Staff, ed. Charles Lindbergh, 1 vol. unabr. ed. 2007. (Graphic Biographies Ser.). (ENG., Illus.). 25p. (YA). (gr. 4-12). pap. 9.75 (978-1-59905-218-2(0)) Saddleback Educational Publishing, Inc.

Webber, Diane. Celebrity's Son Snatched: Can Handwriting Help Nab the Perp? 2011. (J). pap. (978-0-545-32810-4(1)) Scholastic, Inc.

LINE-ENGRAVING

see Engraving

LINGUISTICS

see Language and Languages

LINNAEUS, CAROLUS, 1707-1778

see Linne, Carl Von, 1707-1778

LINNE, CARL VON, 1707-1778

Anderson, Margaret J. Carl Linnaeus: Father of Classification, 1 vol. 2009. (Great Minds of Science Ser.). (ENG., Illus.). 128p. (gr. 5-6). lib. bdg. 35.93 (978-0-7660-3009-1(1), b4a47fe9-85d9-4947-b0ad-cdbcc62f40db) Enslow Publishing, LLC.

—Carl Linnaeus: Genius of Classification, 1 vol. 2014. (Genius Scientists & Their Genius Ideas Ser.). (ENG.). 96p. (gr. 5-5). pap. 13.88 (978-0-7660-6541-3(3), f46de9af-6872-45da-aa5e-e0751b90bbce) Enslow Publishing, LLC.

Magnuson Beil, Karen. What Linnaeus Saw: A Scientist's Quest to Name Every Living Thing. 2019. (ENG., Illus.). 256p. (J). (gr. 5-12). 21.95 (978-1-324-00468-4(1), 340468, Norton Young Readers) Norton, W. W. & Co., Inc.

National Geographic Learning. Reading Expeditions (Science: Life Science): Classification Clues. 2007. (Nonfiction Reading & Writing Workshops Ser.). (ENG., Illus.). 32p. (J). pap. 18.95 (978-0-7922-4576-6(8)) CENGAGE Learning.

LION

Albee, Sarah. Lions. 2006. (J). 7.99 (978-1-59939-035-2(3)) Cornerstone Pr.

—Lions, 1 vol. 2009. (Amazing Animals Ser.). (ENG.). 48p. (gr. 3-5). (J). pap. 11.50 (978-1-4339-2125-4(1), 747d4e51-26e0-45c0-b260-b32ecfe9a4f9, Gareth Stevens Learning Library); (YA). lib. bdg. 30.67 (978-0-8368-9121-8(X), cc2074d1-41d8-4bce-a99c-1540b7036953) Stevens, Gareth Publishing LLLP.

Archer, Claire. Leones, 1 vol. 2014. (Grandes Felinos (Big Cats) Ser.). (SPA.). 24p. (J). (gr. k-2). lib. bdg. 32.79 (978-1-62970-298-8(6), 8996, Abdo Kids) ABDO Publishing Co.

—Lions, 1 vol. 2014. (Big Cats Ser.). (ENG., Illus.). 24p. (J). (gr. -1-2). lib. bdg. 32.79 (978-1-62970-004-5(5), 1227, Abdo Kids) ABDO Publishing Co.

Barnes, J. Lou. 101 Facts about Lions, 1 vol. 2004. (101 Facts about Predators Ser.). (ENG., Illus.). 32p. (gr. 2-4). lib. bdg. 28.67 (978-0-8368-4037-7(2), cdefef19-93c0-4c84-be96-ba65396713c1, Gareth Stevens Learning Library) Stevens, Gareth Publishing LLLP.

Bergeron, Alain M., et al. Les Lions. 2011. (FRE., Illus.). 64p. (J). pap. 8.95 (978-2-89435-510-7(6)) Quintin Pubs./Editions Michel Quintin CAN. Dist: Crabtree Publishing Co.

Best, Arthur. A Lion's Den, 1 vol. 2018. (Animal Homes Ser.). (ENG.). 24p. (J). (gr. 1-1). 27.36 (978-1-5026-3662-1(X), 8d44694d-0b8e-4e31-b5dd-35124d12cf4e) Cavendish Square Publishing LLC.

Big Cats, 1 vol. 2014. (Animal Q & A Ser.). (ENG., Illus.). 24p. (J). (gr. 2-2). lib. bdg. 26.27 (978-1-4777-9182-0(5), ef15a050-1d4a-480e-be87-af3038b278d1, Windmill Bks.) Rosen Publishing Group, Inc., The.

Blewett, Ashlee Brown. National Geographic Kids Mission: Lion Rescue: All about Lions & How to Save Them. 2014. (Illus.). 128p. (J). (gr. 5-9). pap. 12.99 (978-1-4263-1492-6(2), National Geographic Kids) Disney Publishing Worldwide.

Bodden, Valerie. Amazing Animals - Lions. 2010. (Amazing Animals Ser.). 24p. (J). (gr. -1-3). 16.95 (978-1-58341-807-9(5), Creative Education) Creative Co., The.

Books Are Fun 8 Title Animal Lives Set: Lions. 2006. (J). (978-1-59566-311-5(8)) QEB Publishing Inc.

Bowman, Donna H. Big Cats. Wald, Christina, illus. 2008. (ENG.). 24p. (J). (gr. 3-18). 19.95 (978-1-58117-781-7(X), Intervisual/Piggy Toes) Bendon, Inc.

Bredeson, Carmen. Lions up Close, 1 vol. 2008. (Zoom in on Animals! Ser.). (ENG., Illus.). 24p. (gr. k-2). pap. 10.95 (978-1-59845-417-8(X), 571b8f17-1929-49bb-93d8-b39a2e435104); lib. bdg. 25.60 (978-0-7660-3080-0(6), c48919d6-5f6c-40b1-9ed9-c236deba121b) Enslow Publishing, LLC. (Enslow Elementary).

Brown Bear Books. Lions. 2012. (Animal Families Ser.). (ENG., Illus.). 32p. (J). (gr. 3-6). 31.35 (978-1-78121-004-8(7), 16427) Brown Bear Bks.

Browne, Philippa-Alys. "Lion roars" (African Animals ABC) (Illus.). 14.99 (978-1-84148-752-6(X)) Barefoot Bks., Inc.

Buller, Laura. DK Readers Level 2: the Lion's Tale. 2019. (DK Readers Level 2 Ser.). (ENG., Illus.). 48p. (J). (gr. k-2). pap. 3.99 (978-1-4654-7913-6(9), DK Children) Dorling Kindersley Publishing, Inc.

Calhoun, Kelly. Ferocidad Felina (Fiercely Feline) León (Lion) 2016. (Adivina (Guess What) Ser.). (SPA., Illus.). 24p. (J).

(gr. k-2). 30.64 (978-1-63471-448-8(2), 208855) Cherry Lake Publishing.

—Fiercely Feline: Lion. 2015. (Guess What Ser.). (ENG., Illus.). 24p. (J). (gr. k-2). pap. 12.79 (978-1-63362-713-0(6), 206673) Cherry Lake Publishing.

Chronicle Books, et al. Little Lion: Finger Puppet Book. 2009. (Little Finger Puppet Board Bks.). (ENG., Illus.). 12p. (J). (gr. -1 — 1). 7.99 (978-0-8118-6788-7(9)) Chronicle Bks. LLC.

Clark, Willow. Lions: Life in the Pride, 1 vol. 2011. (Animal Families Ser.). (ENG.). 24p. (J). (gr. 1-1). pap. 9.25 (978-1-4488-2612-4(8), 8acfca2e-8ae7-4f79-af69-66199993d4f1); (Illus.). lib. bdg. 26.27 (978-1-4488-2513-4(X), 2d2c8936-a5ee-415e-8a1f-24bc90dfb4fc) Rosen Publishing Group, Inc., The. (PowerKids Pr.).

Cline, Gina. Lions. Rupp, Kristina, illus. 2015. (1G Predator Animals Ser.). (ENG.). 24p. (J). pap. 9.60 (978-1-61406-320-9(6)) American Reading Co.

Cline, Gina & Sánchez, Lucía M. La Manada de Leones. 2010. (2V Animales Depredadores Ser.). (SPA., Illus.). 32p. (J). pap. 8.00 (978-1-61541-502-1(5)) American Reading Co.

Daly, Ruth. Lions. 2014. (J). pap. (978-1-4896-0927-4(X)) Weigl Pubs., Inc.

Dineen, Jacqueline. Lions. (Amazing Animals Ser.). (Illus.). 24p. (J). 2009. (gr. 2-4). pap. 8.95 (978-1-60596-151-4(5)) 2009. (gr. 2-4). lib. bdg. 24.45 (978-1-60596-150-7(7)) 2003. lib. bdg. 21.35 (978-1-58340-230-6(6)) Weigl Pubs., Inc.

Durrie, Karen. I Am a Lion. 2012. (J). (978-1-61913-228-3(1)); 27.13 (978-1-61913-227-6(3)) Weigl Pubs., Inc.

—León. 2013. (SPA.). (J). (978-1-62127-571-8(X)) Weigl Pubs., Inc.

Eszterhas, Suzi. Eye on the Wild: Lion. 2012. (Eye on the Wild Ser.: 3). (Illus.). 32p. (J). (978-1-84780-310-8(5), White Lion Publishing) Quarto Publishing Group UK.

Franks, Katie. Lions, 1 vol. 2014. (Zoo's Who's Who Ser.). (ENG., Illus.). 24p. (J). (gr. 1-2). 25.27 (978-1-4777-6475-6(5), 914772d6-403b-42d1-b74b-31fda4861ec8, PowerKids Pr.) Rosen Publishing Group, Inc., The.

Frisch, Aaron. Lions. 2006. (Wild World of Animals Ser.). (Illus.). 31p. (J). 18.95 (978-1-58341-433-0(9), Creative Education) Creative Co., The.

Gagne, Tammy. Lions: Built for the Hunt. 2016. (Predator Profiles Ser.). (ENG., Illus.). 24p. (J). (gr. 1-3). lib. bdg. 27.99 (978-1-4914-8260-5(5), 130748, Capstone Pr.) Capstone.

Gardner, Robert. How Hot Is Hot? Science Projects with Temperature, 1 vol. 2014. (Hot Science Experiments Ser.). (ENG.). 48p. (gr. 3-4). E-Book 26.93 (978-0-7660-6609-0(6), e836d299-7fe9-40ce-bafd-789cdb29acbd) Enslow Publishing, LLC.

Gish, Ashley. Sea Lions. 2019. (X-Books: Marine Mammals Ser.). (ENG.). 32p. (J). (gr. 3-6). (978-1-64026-191-4(5), 19220, Creative Education) Creative Co., The.

Gish, Melissa. Lions. 2017. (X-Books: Predators Ser.). (ENG., Illus.). 32p. (J). (gr. 3-6). (978-1-60818-819-2(1), 20390, Creative Education) Creative Co., The.

—X-Books: Lions. 2017. (X-Bks.). (ENG., Illus.). 32p. (J). (gr. 3-7). pap. 9.99 (978-1-62832-422-8(8), 20391, Creative Paperbacks) Creative Co., The.

Glaser, Rebecca. Lions Roar. 2016. (ENG., Illus.). 16p. (J). (gr. -1 — 1). bds. 7.99 (978-1-68152-071-1(0), 15817) Amicus.

Group/McGraw-Hill, Wright. Lion Level: Adventure Journal Set. (Wildcats Ser.). (gr. 2-8). 31.95 (978-0-322-05789-0(2)) Wright Group/McGraw-Hill.

—Lion Level: Wildcats Lion Complete Kit. (Wildcats Ser.). (gr. 2-8). 599.95 (978-0-322-06482-9(1)) Wright Group/McGraw-Hill.

Guillain, Charlotte. Mighty Lions, 1 vol. 2013. (Walk on the Wild Side Ser.). (ENG.). 32p. (J). (gr. 3-5). pap. 8.95 (978-1-4109-5222-6(3), 122554, Raintree) Capstone.

Hanel, Rachael. Lions. 2009. (Living Wild Ser.). (ENG., Illus.). 48p. (J). (gr. 5-8). 22.95 (978-1-58341-656-3(0), 22188, Creative Education) Creative Co., The.

Humphrey, Natalie K. Lions & Cubs, 1 vol. 2020. (Animal Family Ser.). (ENG.). 24p. (gr. k-k). pap. 9.15 (978-1-5382-5578-0(2), d1f5cdb7-b54b-4ae3-8133-ea366f85057a) Stevens, Gareth Publishing LLLP.

Idzikowski, Lisa. How Lions Grow Up, 1 vol. 2018. (Animals Growing Up Ser.). (ENG.). 24p. (gr. 1-2). 24.27 (978-0-7660-9651-6(3), 1f731381-a52d-496d-b802-1b0a788a164c) Enslow Publishing, LLC.

Ipcizade, Catherine. Lions. 2010. (African Animals Ser.). (ENG.). 24p. (gr. k-1). pap. 41.70 (978-1-4296-5082-3(6), Capstone Pr.) Capstone.

—Lions [Scholastic]. 2010. (African Animals Ser.). 24p. pap. 0.49 (978-1-4296-5782-2(0), Capstone Pr.) Capstone.

Joubert, Beverly & Joubert, Dereck. Face to Face with Lions. 2010. (Face to Face with Animals Ser.). (Illus.). 32p. (J). (gr. 3-7). pap. 6.95 (978-1-4263-0627-3(X), National Geographic Kids) Disney Publishing Worldwide.

Kalman, Bobbie. The Life Cycle of A Lion. 2007. (ENG.). 32p. (J). (978-0-7787-7703-8(0)) Crabtree Publishing Co.

Kalman, Bobbie & Bishop, Amanda. El Ciclo de Vida Del León. 2005. (Serie Ciclos de Vida Ser.). (SPA., Illus.). 32p. (J). lib. bdg. (978-0-7787-8664-1(1)); (gr. 1-4). pap. (978-0-7787-8710-5(9)) Crabtree Publishing Co.

Keller, Susanna. Meet the Lion, 1 vol. 2010. (At the Zoo Ser.). (ENG.). 24p. (J). (gr. 1-1). pap. 9.25 (978-1-4358-9730-4(7), f8cb50f4-0510-4349-bb62-74de836ebc13); (Illus.). lib. bdg. 26.27 (978-1-4358-9309-2(3), c42ff47d-26ba-4d04-a66a-c1052ecb1822) Rosen Publishing Group, Inc., The. (PowerKids Pr.).

Kelley, K. C. Baby Lions. 2018. (Spot Baby Animals Ser.). (ENG.). 16p. (J). (gr. -1-2). pap. 7.99 (978-1-68152-254-8(3), 14846) Amicus.

Keppeler, Jill. Lions, 1 vol. 2019. (Killers of the Animal Kingdom Ser.). (ENG.). 24p. (gr. 3-3). pap. 9.25 (978-1-7253-0613-4(1), 1f31b745-001e-4436-ba90-de2607f8243d, PowerKids Pr.) Rosen Publishing Group, Inc., The.

Kjelle, Marylou Morano. Lion Paperback. 2013. (Great Predators Ser.). (ENG., Illus.). 48p. (J). (gr. 4-8). pap. 18.50 (978-1-62403-015-4(7), 10791) ABDO Publishing Co.

Klepeis, Alicia Z. Lions on the Hunt. 2017. (Searchlight Books (tm) — Predators Ser.). (ENG., Illus.). 32p. (J). (gr. 3-5). 30.65 (978-1-5124-3395-1(0), 01585504-76b7-4471-a276-d9ab2c058689, Lerner Pubns.); pap. 9.99 (978-1-5124-5610-3(1), 4c3e0947-6ecf-4c34-801d-cc944761195c) Lerner Publishing Group.

Klukow, Mary Ellen. Lions. 2019. (Spot African Animals Ser.). (ENG.). 16p. (J). (gr. -1-2). lib. bdg. (978-1-68151-642-4(X), 10774) Amicus.

—Los Leones. 2019. (Animales Africanos Ser.). (SPA.). 16p. (J). (gr. -1-2). (978-1-68151-881-7(3), 10826) Amicus.

Kopp, Megan. Gallinas/Megan Kopp. 2014. (SPA., Illus.). 24p. (J). (978-1-62127-861-0(1)) Weigl Pubs., Inc.

Kortuem, Amy. A Pride of Lions. 2019. (Animal Groups Ser.). (ENG., Illus.). 24p. (J). (gr. -1-2). pap. 6.95 (978-1-9771-1047-3(9), 141123); lib. bdg. 27.32 (978-1-9771-0951-4(9), 140549) Capstone. (Pebble).

Koster, Amy Sky. Explore My World: Lions. 2018. (Explore My World Ser.). (Illus.). 32p. (J). (gr. -1-k). pap. 4.99 (978-1-4263-2988-3(1), National Geographic Kids) Disney Publishing Worldwide.

Lang, Aubrey. Baby Lion, 1 vol. Lynch, Wayne, photos by. 2003. (Nature Babies Ser.). (ENG., Illus.). 36p. (J). (gr. k-3). 16.95 (978-1-55041-711-1(8), 6939a2bd-5c85-4f6a-931a-60fdce269afa) Clockwise Pr. CAN. Dist: Firefly Bks., Ltd.

—Baby Lion, 1 vol. Lynch, Wayne, photos by. 2004. (Nature Babies Ser.). (ENG., Illus.). 36p. (J). (gr. k-3). pap. 7.95 (978-1-55041-713-5(4), 03fd9412-88ff-4daa-a980-0bcfbbec8132) Fitzhenry & Whiteside, Ltd. CAN. Dist: Firefly Bks., Ltd.

Latta, Jan. Lisa the Lion, 1 vol. 2007. (Wild Animal Families Ser.). (ENG., Illus.). 24p. (gr. 2-4). pap. 9.15 (978-0-8368-7777-9(2), 91421e28-cd8a-4874-a8a1-9b6b2435720d); lib. bdg. 26.67 (978-0-8368-7770-0(5), e46b2e57-d713-44b0-a653-197ff4ae6d01) Stevens, Gareth Publishing LLLP. (Gareth Stevens Learning Library).

Leaf, Christina. Baby Lions. 2014. (Super Cute! Ser.). (ENG., Illus.). 24p. (J). (gr. k-3). lib. bdg. 26.95 (978-1-60014-974-0(X), Blastoff! Readers) Bellwether Media.

Los Leones (Lions) 2006. (J). pap. 7.95 (978-0-8225-6628-1(1), Ediciones Lerner) Lerner Publishing Group.

Levy, Janey. Lion vs. Komodo Dragon, 1 vol. 2018. (Bizarre Beast Battles Ser.). (ENG.). 24p. (J). (gr. 2-3). 24.27 (978-1-5382-1931-7(X), a5d2ad7f-b657-4370-8dec-5b913c6e5aa2) Stevens, Gareth Publishing LLLP.

Lindeen, Mary. Lions. 2013. (ENG., Illus.). 24p. (J). lib. bdg. 25.65 (978-1-62031-064-9(3)) Jump! Inc.

Lion: Killer King of the Plains. 2013. (Top of the Food Chain Ser.). 32p. (J). (gr. k-5). pap. 60.00 (978-1-61533-798-9(9), PowerKids Pr.) Rosen Publishing Group, Inc., The.

Lions, 6 bks. 2005. (Animal Predators Ser.). (Illus.). 40p. (J). (gr. 3-6). pap. 46.95 (978-0-8225-5491-2(7)) Lerner Publishing Group.

Markle, Sandra. I Wish I Was a Lion. 2017. (Illus.). 31p. (J). (978-1-5182-5201-3(X)) Harper & Row Ltd.

—Los Leones. 2006. (Animales Depredadores (Animal Predators) Ser.). (SPA., Illus.). 39p. (J). (gr. 3-7). lib. bdg. 25.26 (978-0-8225-6491-1(2), Ediciones Lerner) Lerner Publishing Group.

—Lions. 2005. (Animal Predators Ser.). (Illus.). 40p. (J). (gr. 4-6). pap. 7.95 (978-1-57505-744-6(1)); (gr. 3-6). lib. bdg. 25.26 (978-1-57505-727-9(1)) Lerner Publishing Group.

—Los Leones; Lions. 2008. pap. 46.95 (978-0-8225-7089-9(0)) Lerner Publishing Group.

—Ranger Rick: I Wish I Was a Lion. 2017. (I Can Read Level 1 Ser.). (ENG., Illus.). 32p. (J). (gr. -1-3). pap. 4.99 (978-0-06-243206-3(0), HarperCollins) HarperCollins Pubs.

—Ranger Rick: I Wish I Was a Lion. 2017. (I Can Read Level 1 Ser.). (ENG., Illus.). 32p. (J). (gr. -1-3). 16.99 (978-0-06-243205-6(2), HarperCollins) HarperCollins Pubs.

Marsh, Laura. National Geographic Readers: Lions. 2015. (Readers Ser.). (Illus.). 32p. (J). (gr. -1-k). pap. 4.99 (978-1-4263-1939-6(8)); (ENG., lib. bdg. 14.90 (978-1-4263-1940-2(1)) Disney Publishing Worldwide. (National Geographic Kids).

McCune, Jamie. Lion Cub Roars: Baby Animals. 2010. (ENG., Illus.). 16p. (J). (978-1-60727-203-8(2)) Soundprints.

Meachen Rau, Dana. El león en la Hierba (the Lion in the Grass), 1 vol. 2008. (Naturaleza (Nature) Ser.). (SPA., Illus.). 24p. (gr. k-1). lib. bdg. 25.50 (978-0-7614-2411-6(3), b79d62c2-de66-4e40-b6cc-ecbc40eb10c1) Cavendish Square Publishing LLC.

Meinking, Mary. Lion vs. Gazelle, 1 vol. 2011. (Predator vs. Prey Ser.). (ENG., Illus.). 32p. (J). (gr. 2-4). pap. 8.29 (978-1-4109-3943-2(X), 113910, Raintree) Capstone.

—Lions. 2017. (Animals of Africa Ser.). (ENG., Illus.). 32p. (J). (gr. 2-3). pap. 9.95 (978-1-63517-331-4(0), 1635173310); lib. bdg. 31.35 (978-1-63517-266-9(7), 1635172667) North Star Editions. (Focus Readers).

—Predator vs. Prey, 8 vols., Set. Incl. Lion vs. Gazelle. (ENG., Illus.). 32p. (J). (gr. 2-4). 2011. pap. 8.29 (978-1-4109-3943-2(X), 113910, Raintree); (Predator vs. Prey Ser.). (ENG.). 32p. 2011. pap., pap., pap. 66.32 o.p. (978-1-4109-3951-7(0), 15346, Raintree) Capstone.

Meister, Cari. Do You Really Want to Meet a Lion? Fabbri, Daniele, illus. 2015. (Do You Really Want to Meet ... ? Ser.). (ENG.). 24p. (J). (gr. 1-4). lib. bdg. 19.95 (978-1-60753-735-9(4), 15266) Amicus.

Moldovo, Eustacia. Baby Lions at the Zoo, 1 vol. 2015. (All about Baby Zoo Animals Ser.). (ENG., Illus.). 24p. (gr. -1-1). pap. 10.35 (978-0-7660-7085-1(9), 70694cd4-a76e-49e8-95e8-e0b2b8473381) Enslow Publishing, LLC.

Morgan, Paul & Drewett, Jim. Toughest Test. 2005. (ENG., Illus.). 254p. 25.00 (978-1-905326-04-4(1)) Penguin Publishing Group.

Murray, Julie. Lion Pride. 2018. (Animal Groups (Abdo Kids Junior) Ser.). (ENG., Illus.). 24p. (J). (gr. -1-2). lib. bdg. 31.36 (978-1-5321-0781-8(1), 28123, Abdo Kids) ABDO Publishing Co.

—Lions. 2019. (Animal Kingdom Ser.). (ENG.). 32p. (J). (gr. 2-5). lib. bdg. 34.21 (978-1-5321-1643-8(8), 32397, Big Buddy Bks.) ABDO Publishing Co.

Neuman, Susan B. National Geographic Readers: Go Cub! 2014. (Readers Ser.). 24p. (J). (gr. -1-k). pap. 4.99 (978-1-4263-1512-1(0), National Geographic Kids) Disney Publishing Worldwide.

—NGR Go Cub! (Special Sales UK Edition) 2014. (Readers Ser.). (ENG., Illus.). 24p. (J). (gr. -1-k). pap. 4.99 (978-1-4263-1794-1(8)) National Geographic Society.

Orme, Helen. Lions in Danger. 2006. (Wildlife Survival Ser.). (Illus.). 32p. (YA). (gr. 2-5). lib. bdg. 28.50 (978-1-59716-262-3(0)) Bearport Publishing Co., Inc.

Owen, Ruth. Lion Cubs. 2011. (Wild Baby Animals Ser.). 24p. (J). (gr. k-3). lib. bdg. 25.65 (978-1-61772-159-5(X)); lib. bdg., E-Book 39.93 (978-1-61772-240-0(5)) Bearport Publishing Co., Inc.

—Lions, 1 vol. 2012. (Dr. Bob's Amazing World of Animals Ser.). (ENG., Illus.). 32p. (J). (gr. 2-3). pap. 12.75 (978-1-61533-554-1(4), 53d60aaa-6dda-4c04-86b4-a5f6490ded35); lib. bdg. 31.27 (978-1-61533-547-3(1), a033d4a6-b778-43df-bfc1-39e9bfd2c1d9) Rosen Publishing Group, Inc., The. (Windmill Bks.).

Owings, Lisa. The African Lion. 2012. (Nature's Deadliest Ser.). (ENG., Illus.). 24p. (J). (gr. 3-8). lib. bdg. 27.95 (978-1-60014-740-1(2), Pilot Bks.) Bellwether Media.

—The African Lion. 2012. (ENG., Illus.). 24p. 23.00 (978-0-531-20879-3(6), Children's Pr.) Scholastic Library Publishing.

Pallotta, Jerry. Lion vs. Tiger (Who Would Win?) Bolster, Rob, illus. 2015. (Who Would Win? Ser.). (ENG.). 32p. (J). (gr. 1-3). pap. 3.99 (978-0-545-17571-5(2)) Scholastic, Inc.

Patterson, John Henry. The Man-Eaters of Tsavo. 2011. 148p. pap. 7.49 (978-1-61382-001-8(1)); (ENG., Illus.). (J). 13.99 (978-1-61382-860-1(8)) Simon & Brown.

—The Man-Eaters of Tsavo. 2018. (ENG., Illus.). 152p. (J). 14.99 (978-1-5154-3297-5(1)) Wilder Pubns., Corp.

Pelusey, Michael & Pelusey, Jane. Lions & Tigers, 1 vol. 2009. (Zoo Animals Ser.). (ENG.). 32p. (gr. 2-2). lib. bdg. 21.27 (978-0-7614-3151-0(9), 0b10e42f-c952-460e-8738-7ecf87a74c11) Cavendish Square Publishing LLC.

Prebeg, Rick. Looking for Lions. Prebeg, Rick, photos by. 2005. (Illus.). (J). (978-1-933248-12-7(2)) World Quest Learning.

Quinton, Sasha. Yay-Hooray: A Phonics Reader. 2009. (Illus.). pap. (978-1-936199-07-5(6)) Book Shop, Ltd., The.

Reade, Clara. Lions, 1 vol. 2012. (PowerKids Readers: Safari Animals Ser.). (ENG., Illus.). 24p. (J). (gr. k-k). pap. 9.25 (978-1-4488-7470-5(X), 4fc543fc-c425-460f-85c1-d928d0ee29c2); lib. bdg. 26.27 (978-1-4488-7391-3(6), 09dee7ce-7c39-4fa1-b1a1-bb6d5741f106) Rosen Publishing Group, Inc., The. (PowerKids Pr.).

Rebman, Nick. Lions. 2018. (Animals Ser.). (ENG., Illus.). 16p. (J). (gr. k-1). pap. 7.95 (978-1-63517-952-1(1), 1635179521); lib. bdg. 25.64 (978-1-63517-851-7(7), 1635178517) North Star Editions. (Focus Readers).

Ricciuti, Edward R. Adivina Quién Ruge / Guess Who Roars, 1 vol. 2008. (Adivina Quién / Guess Who? Ser.). (ENG & SPA., Illus.). 32p. (gr. k-2). lib. bdg. 25.50 (978-0-7614-2466-6(0), 6acbb7d0-dcef-4684-889d-59d69543e750) Cavendish Square Publishing LLC.

—Adivina Quién Ruge (Guess Who Roars), 1 vol. 2008. (Adivina Quién (Guess Who?) Ser.). (SPA., Illus.). 32p. (gr. k-2). lib. bdg. 25.50 (978-0-7614-2386-7(9), 8d0eb239-8216-4594-adf9-72ead2dabacf) Cavendish Square Publishing LLC.

—Guess Who Roars, 1 vol. (Guess Who? Ser.). (ENG.). 32p. (gr. k-1). 2008. pap. 9.23 (978-0-7614-3322-4(8), 0e2ef7cb-e88f-43ad-86da-bbfc94cf3cd3) 2005. (Illus.). lib. bdg. 25.50 (978-0-7614-1556-5(4), c9327ca1-f0c2-4756-ba28-9f7ce7ed0c3d) Cavendish Square Publishing LLC.

Riggs, Kate. Lions. 2012. (Seedlings Ser.). (ENG., Illus.). 24p. (J). (gr. -1-k). 15.95 (978-1-60818-277-0(0), 21995, Creative Education) Creative Co., The.

—Seedlings: Lions. 2013. (Seedlings Ser.). (ENG.). 24p. (J). (gr. -1-k). pap. 8.99 (978-0-89812-784-3(X), 22001, Creative Paperbacks) Creative Co., The.

Riley, Joelle. African Lions. 2009. pap. 40.95 (978-0-8225-9316-4(5)) 2007. (ENG., Illus.). 32p. (J). per. 7.99 (978-0-8225-6707-3(5), 1c7c58d6-be26-420b-93d1-90fde97e94b5, First Avenue Editions) Lerner Publishing Group.

Ringstad, Arnold. Leopards. 2014. (Wild Cats Ser.). (ENG., Illus.). 24p. (J). (gr. 1-4). 27.10 (978-1-60753-602-4(1), 16065) Amicus.

—Lions. 2014. (Wild Cats Ser.). (ENG.). 24p. (J). (gr. 1-4). 27.10 (978-1-60753-603-1(X), 16066) Amicus.

Ritchey, Kate. Lion, Tiger, & Bear. 2015. (Penguin Young Readers, Level 4 Ser.). (ENG., Illus.). 48p. (J). (gr. 3-4). pap. 4.99 (978-0-448-48336-8(X), Penguin Young Readers) Penguin Young Readers Group.

Roome, Hugh. Lions. 2019. (J). lib. bdg. (978-0-531-12717-9(6), Children's Pr.) Scholastic Library Publishing.

Schafer, Susan & Meredith, Susan. Lions, 1 vol. 2010. (Animals Ser.). (ENG.). 24p. (gr. 3-3). 26.93 (978-0-7614-4344-5(4), f79612ba-4a63-46db-9a3f-91adbe307213) Cavendish Square Publishing LLC.

Schuh, Mari. How to Be King of Pride Rock: Confidence with Simba. 2019. (Disney Great Character Guides). (ENG., Illus.). 32p. (J). (gr. 1-4). pap. 8.99 (978-1-5415-4604-2(0), Lerner Pubns.) Lerner Publishing Group.

Schuh, Mari C. How to Be King of Pride Rock: Leadership with Simba. 2019. (Disney Great Character Guides). (ENG., Illus.). 32p. (J). (gr. 1-4). 27.99 (978-1-5415-3904-4(4), Lerner Pubns.) Lerner Publishing Group.

Scott, Jonathan & Scott, Angela. Scarface: the Real Lion King Gold Band. 2016. (Cambridge Reading Adventures Ser.). (ENG., Illus.). 24p. pap. 8.80 (978-1-107-56047-5(0)) Cambridge Univ. Pr.

Server, Lee. Lions, Vol. 12. 2018. (Animals in the Wild Ser.). (Illus.). 72p. (J). (gr. 7). 33.27 (978-1-4222-4171-4(8)) Mason Crest.

—Lions - Pb: A Portrait of the Animal World. 2013. (Portrait of the Animal World Ser.). (Illus.). 72p. pap. 9.95 (978-1-59764-331-3(9)) New Line Bks.

Shea, Mary Molly. Lions, 1 vol. 2010. (Animals That Live in the Grasslands Ser.). (ENG.). 24p. (J). (gr. 1-1). pap. 9.15 (978-1-4339-3873-3(1), 035cd3ae-cc1d-487e-82d9-fb47ea75bdcd); lib. bdg. 25.27 (978-1-4339-3872-6(3), e384b9ea-dd29-4492-bca2-e0b661963324) Stevens, Gareth Publishing LLLP.

Shea, Therese M. Lions, 1 vol. 2012. (Killer Cats Ser.). (ENG., Illus.). 24p. (J). (gr. 2-3). pap. 9.15 (978-1-4339-7008-5(2), 53761f48-e560-4ae9-94e9-5a14e5d6ba73); lib. bdg. 25.27 (978-1-4339-7007-8(4), 6d9bf34a-4183-4c3c-93f6-61ef861de016) Stevens, Gareth Publishing LLLP.

Simpson, Phillip. Lion Habitats under Threat: A Cause & Effect Text, 1 vol. 2014. (Text Structures Ser.). (ENG., Illus.). 32p. (J). (gr. 1-3). pap. 7.99 (978-1-4846-0417-5(2), 126585, Heinemann) Capstone.

Sommer, Nathan. Lion vs. Hyena Clan. 2020. (Animal Battles Ser.). (ENG.). 24p. (J). (gr. 3-7). lib. bdg. 26.95 (978-1-64487-159-1(9), Torque Bks.) Bellwether Media.

Spilsbury, Louise. Lion, 1 vol. 2013. (Top of the Food Chain Ser.). (ENG.). 32p. (J). (gr. 2-3). pap. 11.00 (978-1-61533-797-2(0), e6d2f399-047c-4316-974c-ae895728a070, PowerKids Pr.) Rosen Publishing Group, Inc., The.

Statts, Leo. Lions. 2016. (Savanna Animals Ser.). (ENG.). 24p. (J). (gr. -1-2). 49.94 (978-1-68079-370-3(5), 22991, Abdo Zoom-Launch) ABDO Publishing Co.

Stefoff, Rebecca. Lions, 1 vol. 2007. (Animal Ways Ser.). (ENG., Illus.). 112p. (gr. 6-6). lib. bdg. 38.36 (978-0-7614-1746-0(X), ba5233f9-b2a1-4f21-88f7-369232b3f665) Cavendish Square Publishing LLC.

Storm, Marysa. Lions. 2020. (Awesome Animal Lives Ser.). (ENG.). 24p. (J). (gr. k-3). lib. bdg. (978-1-62310-150-3(6), 14394, Bolt Jr.) Black Rabbit Bks.

Taylor, Trace. African Lions. 2011. (ARC Press / Power 50 - Predators Ser.). pap. 45.32 (978-1-61541-030-9(9)) American Reading Co.

—Lions of Africa. Taylor, Trace, illus. 2015. (1-3Y Wild Animals Ser.). (ENG., Illus.). 24p. (J). (gr. k-2). pap. 8.00 (978-1-59301-654-8(9)) American Reading Co.

Taylor, Trace & SáNchez, LucíA M. Leones Africanos (African Lions) 2011. (ARC Press / el poder de 50 - Animales depredadores (Power 50 - Predators) Ser.). (SPA.). pap. 45.32 (978-1-61541-287-7(5)) American Reading Co.

Terp, Gail. Lions. 2017. (Wild Animal Kingdom Ser.). (ENG.). (J). (gr. 4-7). pap. 9.95 (978-1-68072-487-5(8)); 32p. pap. 9.99 (978-1-64466-224-3(8), 11501); (Illus.). 32p. lib. bdg. (978-1-68072-191-1(7), 10563) Black Rabbit Bks. (Bolt).

Turnbull, Stephanie. Lion. 2015. (Big Beasts Ser.). (ENG., Illus.). 24p. (J). (gr. 1-4). 28.50 (978-1-62588-167-0(3), 17279) Black Rabbit Bks.

—Lion. 2015. (ENG., Illus.). 24p. (J). pap. 8.95 (978-1-77092-216-7(4)) RiverStream Publishing.

Vogel, Elizabeth. Lions. 2009. (Big Cats (Powerkids Readers) Ser.). 24p. (gr. 1-1). 37.50 (978-1-61511-570-9(6), PowerKids Pr.) Rosen Publishing Group, Inc., The.

Von Zumbusch, Amelie. Lions, 1 vol. 2007. (Safari Animals Ser.). (ENG., Illus.). 24p. (J). (gr. 1-1). lib. bdg. 26.27 (978-1-4042-3612-7(0), ad95ed25-da22-4f35-9488-87a43c0313d4, PowerKids Pr.) Rosen Publishing Group, Inc., The.

von Zumbusch, Amelie. Lions. 2009. (Safari Animals Ser.). 24p. (gr. 1-1). 42.50 (978-1-60852-956-8(8), PowerKids Pr.) Rosen Publishing Group, Inc., The.

Von Zumbusch, Amelie. Lions: King of the Beasts, 1 vol. 2007. (Dangerous Cats Ser.). (ENG., Illus.). 24p. (J). (gr. 2-3). lib. bdg. 26.27 (978-1-4042-3631-8(7), 10a5c776-e1fc-4245-b6cc-9b87d2226141) Rosen Publishing Group, Inc., The.

von Zumbusch, Amelie. Lions: King of the Beasts. 2009. (Dangerous Cats Ser.). 24p. (gr. 2-3). 42.50 (978-1-61512-129-8(3), PowerKids Pr.) Rosen Publishing Group, Inc., The.

Von Zumbusch, Amelie. Lions/Leones, 1 vol. 2006. (Safari Animals / Animales de Safari Ser.: Vol. 1). (ENG & SPA., Illus.). 24p. (J). (gr. 1-1). lib. bdg. 26.27 (978-1-4042-7608-6(4), 0d8df005-8404-4931-bd53-6d9b156b26c2) Rosen Publishing Group, Inc., The.

von Zumbusch, Amelie. Lions/Leones. 2009. (Safari Animals/Animales de safari Ser.). (ENG & SPA.). 24p. (gr. 1-1). 42.50 (978-1-60852-978-0(9), Editorial Buenas Letras) Rosen Publishing Group, Inc., The.

Zane, Dory. How to Track a Lion, 1 vol., 1. 2014. (Scatalog: a Kid's Field Guide to Animal Poop Ser.). (ENG.). 24p. (J). (gr. 2-3). 27.27 (978-1-61533-884-9(5), 95fc89bf-a4db-414b-ba31-75affe2e573d, Windmill Bks.) Rosen Publishing Group, Inc., The.

Zeiger, Jennifer. Lions. 2012. (Nature's Children Ser.). (ENG., Illus.). 48p. (J). (gr. 3-5). lib. bdg. 28.00 (978-0-531-20903-5(2), Children's Pr.) Scholastic Library Publishing.

—Lions - Nature's Children. 2012. (Nature's Children Ser.). (ENG., Illus.). 48p. (J). pap. 6.95 (978-0-531-21078-9(2), Children's Pr.) Scholastic Library Publishing.

Zobel, Derek. Lions. 2011. (Animal Safari Ser.). (ENG., Illus.). 24p. (J). (gr. k-3). lib. bdg. 26.95 (978-1-60014-608-4(2), Blastoff! Readers) Bellwether Media.

Zorzi, Gina & Cline, Gina. The Lion Pride. Dibble, Traci, illus. 2010. (2G Predator Animals Ser.). (ENG.). 32p. (J). (gr. k-2). pap. 8.00 (978-1-61541-500-7(9)) American Reading Co.

Zorzi, Gina & Dibble, Traci. The Lion Pride. 2011. (ARC Press / Power 100 - Predator Animals Ser.). pap. 45.32 (978-1-61541-501-4(7)) American Reading Co.

Zubek, Adeline. Counting Lions, 1 vol. 2011. (Animal Math Ser.). (ENG.). 24p. (J). (gr. 1-2). pap. 9.15 (978-1-4339-5664-5(0), ecb51ec8-bf7a-4316-8654-5375181668e2); lib. bdg. 25.27 (978-1-4339-5662-1(4),

3f3ba38e-394e-432b-943d-ae4b85c8d5be) Stevens, Gareth Publishing LLLP.

LION—FICTION

Abercrombie, Barbara. The Show-And-Tell Lion. Avril, Lynne, illus. 2006. (ENG.). 32p. (J). (gr. -1-2). 19.99 *(978-0-689-86408-7(6)*, McElderry, Margaret K. Bks.) McElderry, Margaret K. Bks.

Adams, Alison. Androcles & the Lion: Classic Tales Series. Greenhead, Bill, illus. 2011. (Classic Tales Ser.). (J). *(978-1-936258-60-4(9))* Benchmark Education Co.

Aesop. The Lion & the Mouse. 2007. (ENG., Illus.). 32p. (J). (gr. -1-1). pap. 9.95 *(978-0-7358-2129-3(1))* North-South Bks., Inc.

Aesop, Aesop. The Lion & the Mouse. 2016. (ENG.). 79.82 *(978-1-367-86708-6(8))* Blurb, Inc.

—The Lion & the Mouse, 1 vol. 2017. (Let's Learn Aesop's Fables Ser.). (ENG.). 24p. (gr. 2-2). 26.27 *(978-1-4994-8369-7(4)*, 671d2cb3-f561-416e-b63d-842bf50098cd); pap. 9.25 *(978-1-4994-8374-1(0)*, a893e800-3002-4315-81fc-fa50b67aca2f) Rosen Publishing Group, Inc., The. (Windmill Bks.).

Agee, Jon. Lion Lessons. 2016. (Illus.). 32p. (J). (gr. -1-3). 18.99 *(978-0-8037-3908-6(7)*, Dial Bks) Penguin Young Readers Group.

Ahmed, Shamim. Man & the Cub. 2022. (ENG.). 125p. (YA). pap. 4.67 *(978-1-4116-1196-2(9))* Lulu Pr., Inc.

Aina, Olaiya E. Ijapa, the Lion, & the Boar. 2010. 20p. 13.80 *(978-1-4269-3183-3(2))* Trafford Publishing.

Andreae, Giles. Leo, the Lovable Lion. 2004. (Illus.). *(978-0-439-65567-5(6))* Scholastic, Inc.

Award, Anna & Aesop, Aesop. The Donkey & the Lapdog with the Lion & the Mouse. Biro, Val, illus. 2014. (ENG.). 24p. (J). pap. 6.95 *(978-1-84135-953-3(X))* Award Pubns. Ltd. GBR. Dist: Parkwest Pubns., Inc.

Award, Anna, et al. The Farmer & His Sons & The Donkey in the Lion's Skin. 2014. (ENG.). 24p. (J). pap. 6.95 *(978-1-84135-960-1(2))* Award Pubns. Ltd. GBR. Dist: Parkwest Pubns., Inc.

—The Hare & the Tortoise & The Sick Lion. 2014. (ENG.). 24p. (J). pap. 6.95 *(978-1-84135-954-0(8))* Award Pubns. Ltd. GBR. Dist: Parkwest Pubns., Inc.

Axtell, David. We're Going on a Lion Hunt. Axtell, David, illus. 2007. (ENG., Illus.). 32p. (J). (gr. -1-1). 10.99 *(978-0-8050-8219-7(0)*, 900041018) Square Fish.

AZ Books, creator. Baby Lion Searches for His Dad. 2012. (Plush Baby Ser.). (ENG., Illus.). 10p. (J). (gr. -1 — 1). 11.95 *(978-1-61889-217-1(7))* AZ Bks. LLC.

AZ Books Staff. Who Is the Lion Looking For? Shestakova, Anna, ed. 2012. (Who Is There Ser.). (ENG.). 10p. (J). (-k). bds. 11.95 *(978-1-61889-041-2(7))* AZ Bks. LLC.

Barkow, Henriette. Buri & the Maroow. Finlay, Lizzie, illus. 2004. (ENG & FRE.). 24p. (J). pap. *(978-1-85269-583-5(8))* Mantra Lingua.

Baron, Lindamichelle. The Lion & the Man: A Fable. Huggins, Carl, illus. 2009. 72p. pap. 15.95 *(978-0-940938-25-0(1))* Harlin Jacque Pubns.

Barreto, Sandra Maciel. No Fundo Do Fundo Do Mar. Rodrigues, Felipe Lima, illus. 2014. (POR.). 59p. (J). *(978-85-420-0460-1(4))* Expressao Grafica e Editora Ltda.

Baum, Roger S. The Oz Odyssey. Seitzinger, Victoria, illus. 2006. 176p. (J). 19.95 *(978-1-57072-299-8(4))* Overmountain Pr.

Behling, Steve, adapted by. Bunga the Wise. 2016. (Illus.). 32p. (J). *(978-1-4806-9875-8(X))* Disney Publishing Worldwide.

Bender, Chris. The Lion & the Lamb. 2011. 24p. 14.93 *(978-1-4269-5732-1(7))* Trafford Publishing.

Berry, Ron. Can You Roar Like a Lion? Sharp, Chris, illus. 2009. (ENG.). 14p. bds. 10.99 *(978-0-8249-1433-2(3)*, Ideals Pubns.) Worthy Publishing.

Bewley, Elizabeth. The Moon Followed Me Home. Furukawa, Masumi, illus. 2007. (ENG.). 6p. (J). (gr. -1-3). 12.95 *(978-1-58117-598-1(1)*, Intervisual/Piggy Toes) Bendon, Inc.

Binder, Mark. Kings, Wolves, Princesses & Lions: 28 Illustrated Stories for Young Readers. 2012. (ENG., Illus.). 122p. (J). pap. 14.99 *(978-0-9824707-8-7(9))* Light Pubns.

Blair, Eric. The Donkey in the Lion's Skin: A Retelling of Aesop's Fable, 1 vol. Silverman, Dianne, illus. 2013. (My First Classic Story Ser.). (ENG.). 24p. (J). (gr. k-3). pap. 7.10 *(978-1-4795-1855-5(7)*, 123445, Picture Window Bks.) Capstone.

Brennan-Nelson, Denise. Leopold the Lion. Barshaw, Ruth McNally, illus. 2015. (ENG.). 32p. (J). (gr. 1-3). 16.99 *(978-1-58536-828-0(8)*, 203951) Sleeping Bear Pr.

Brett, Jan. Honey... Honey... Lion! Brett, Jan, illus. 2005. (Illus.). 32p. (J). (gr. -1-3). 18.99 *(978-0-399-24463-6(8)*, G.P. Putnam's Sons Books for Young Readers) Penguin Young Readers Group.

Brightwood, Laura, illus. Lion & Mousie. Brightwood, Laura, . 2007. (J). DVD *(978-1-934409-00-8(6))* 3-C Institute for Social Development.

Brooke, Susan Rich, adapted by. The Lion King. 2003. (Illus.). (J). *(978-0-7853-9380-1(3))* Publications International, Ltd.

Brown, J. A. Lion's Mane. Knight, Paula, illus. 2003. (Funny Faces Ser.). 10p. (J). 3.95 *(978-1-58925-718-4(9))* Tiger Tales.

Brown, Ruth & Brown, Ken. Lion in the Long Grass. 2013. (Silver Tales Ser.). (ENG., Illus.). (J). (gr. -1-2). pap. *(978-1-74352-445-9(5))* Hinkler Bks. Pty, Ltd.

Browne, Anthony. The Little Bear Book. Browne, Anthony, illus. 2014. (ENG., Illus.). 24p. (J). (gr. -1-2). 15.99 *(978-0-7636-7007-8(3))* Candlewick Pr.

Buitrago, Jairo. Walk with Me, 1 vol. Amado, Elisa, tr. Yockteng, Rafael, illus. 2017. (ENG.). 32p. (J). (gr. -1-1). 18.95 *(978-1-55498-857-0(8))* Groundwood Bks. CAN. Dist: Publishers Group West (PGW).

Buller, Ginny. Happy Misunderstanding: How Folly Gets his Name. Chettle, Julie, illus. 2012. (ENG.). 29p. (J). pap. 16.95 *(978-1-4327-8234-4(7))* Outskirts Pr., Inc.

Burkert, Rand. Mouse & Lion. Burkert, Nancy Ekholm, illus. 2011. (ENG.). 32p. (J). (gr. -1-3). 18.99 *(978-0-545-10147-9(6)*, Di Capua, Michael) Scholastic, Inc.

Busch, Miriam. Lion, Lion. Day, Larry, illus. 2014. (ENG.). 32p. (J). (gr. -1-3). 17.99 *(978-0-06-227104-4(0)*, Balzer & Bray) HarperCollins Pubs.

Bushar, Carol. Robby the Lion Doesn't Eat Meat. 2006. 30p. 12.96 *(978-1-4116-9113-1(X))* Lulu Pr., Inc.

Byrne, Lex. Ever Met the Hooferjackal? 2009. 32p. pap. 14.95 *(978-1-4490-4630-9(4))* AuthorHouse.

Cebollero, Julie. The Lion That Roared. 2012. (ENG.). 61p. pap. 9.95 *(978-1-4327-8067-8(0))* Outskirts Pr., Inc.

Chalekian, Bobbie. The Legend of the Lamb & the Lion. 2011. 32p. (gr. 2-4). pap. 14.99 *(978-1-4567-2713-0(3))* AuthorHouse.

Chidebelu-Eze / Dove Publishing, Chibueze Obi. The Lion That Finally Roared: Inspirational Story of Purpose & Destiny. Newborne, David / F., illus. 2008. 80p. (J). 17.99 *(978-0-9766578-5-9(6))*; pap. 11.99 *(978-0-9766578-6-6(4))* Dove Publishing, Inc.

Clarke, Jane. How to Tuck in Your Sleepy Lion. Birkett, Georgie, illus. 2017. 16p. (J). bds. 8.99 *(978-1-61067-496-0(0))* Kane Miller.

Cook, Gina J. Just a Little Lion: A Little Cheetah Learns the Truth about Little Lions As We Learn the Truth about Little Lies. 2012. 38p. pap. 13.95 *(978-1-4497-6352-7(9)*, WestBow Pr.) Author Solutions, LLC.

Corder, Zizou. Lionboy. 2004. (ENG., Illus.). 304p. (J). (gr. 3-7). reprint ed. pap. 8.99 *(978-0-14-240226-9(5)*, Puffin Books) Penguin Young Readers Group.

—Lionboy: the Truth, 3. 2006. (ENG., illus.). 240p. (J). (gr. 3-7). 7.99 *(978-0-14-240705-9(4)*, Puffin Books) Penguin Young Readers Group.

Coxe, Molly. Lion Spies a Tiger. 2019. (Bright Owl Bks.). (Illus.). 40p. (J). (gr. -1-2). 17.99 *(978-1-63592-106-9(6)*, b5245a88-10d5-484f-9634-8c6491357b00, Kane Press) Astra Publishing Hse.

Crowley, Jennifer Brasington. Lyndsay & Lainey Lion: E Is for Dragon. 2012. (ENG.). (J). pap. *(978-1-4675-5417-6(0))* Independent Pub.

—Lyndsay & Lainey Lion: F Is for Dragon. 2012. (ENG.). (J). pap. *(978-1-4675-5418-3(9))* Independent Pub.

Crowley, Jennifer Brasington, ed. Lyndsay & Lainey Lion: D Is for Dragon. 2012. (ENG.). (J). pap. *(978-1-4675-5416-9(2))* Independent Pub.

Curry, Kenneth. Mandu & Minka. 2007. (Illus.). 22p. (J). 10.95 *(978-0-9798364-7-3(6))* Curry Brothers Publishing Group.

Danby, Aaron. Jazzmin's Jamboree. Martin, M. J., illus. 2005. 40p. 13.95 *(978-0-9730583-3-8(1))* Lion & Mouse Tales, Inc. CAN. Dist: Hushion Hse. Publishing, Ltd.

Dean, Walter. How Leo the Lion Learned to Roar. 2013. 44p. pap. 12.95 *(978-0-9844342-6-8(7))* C&K Publishing Co.

—How Leo the Lion Learned to Roar Student/ Teacher Workbook. 2013. 54p. pap. 14.95 *(978-0-9844342-5-1(9))* C&K Publishing Co.

Debesay, Samson. Cubby, the Lionsheep: Son, you are a lion, live like One! 2011. (Illus.). 24p. pap. 14.89 *(978-1-4567-7899-6(4))* AuthorHouse.

Del Riego, Erica. The Heart of Life. 2010. 36p. pap. 17.75 *(978-1-4389-7572-6(4))* AuthorHouse.

Depken, Kristen L. Tawny Scrawny Lion. DiCicco, Sue, illus. 2016. (Step into Reading Ser.). 32p. (J). (gr. -1-1). pap. 4.99 *(978-1-101-93424-1(7)*, Random Hse. Bks. for Young Readers) Random Hse. Children's Bks.

Dharma Publishing Staff. The Power of a Promise: A Story about the Power of Keeping Promises. 2010. 36p. (gr. -1-7). pap. 8.95 *(978-0-89800-603-2(1))* Dharma Publishing.

—The Rabbit Who Overcame Fear: A Story about Wise Action. 2nd ed. 2013. (Jataka Tales Ser.). (Illus.). 36p. (gr. -1-7). pap. 8.95 *(978-0-89800-492-2(6))* Dharma Publishing.

—The Value of Friends: A Story about Helping Friends in Need. 2nd ed. 2015. (Jataka Tales Ser.). (Illus.). 36p. (gr. -1-7). pap. 8.95 *(978-0-89800-493-9(4))* Dharma Publishing.

Dirks, Adam. Unstoppable Me, 1 vol. Guile, Gill, illus. 2018. (ENG.). 26p. (J). bds. 9.99 *(978-0-310-76497-7(1))* Zonderkidz.

Disney Classic Story Collection: 3 Movie Storybooks. 2017. *(978-1-368-00723-8(6))* Disney Publishing Worldwide.

Disney Editors. Disney the Lion King Movie Comic. 2016. (ENG.). 64p. (J). (gr. 4-7). 18.40 *(978-0-606-39084-2(7))* Turtleback.

Disney Enterprises Inc. Staff, creator. Disney Caritas Felices: Simba. 2007. (Illus.). 8p. (J). (gr. -1). *(978-970-718-392-6(6)*, Silver Dolphin en Español) Advanced Marketing, S. de R. L. de C. V.

Disney Storybook Artists Staff, et al, illus. Disney's the Lion King. 2007. (Play-A-Sound Ser.). 16p. (J). (gr. -1-3). 16.98 *(978-1-4127-8776-5(9))* Publications International, Ltd.

Dony, John. Leah's Lions. 2nd ed. 2012. (ENG.). 62p. (J). 15.99 *(978-0-9854076-6-7(2))* Dewberry Pr.

Douglas, Babette. The Lyon Bear. Johnson, John, illus. 2006. (Kiss a Me Teacher Creature Stories Ser.). (J). (gr. -1-3). 9.99 *(978-1-890343-18-7(8))* Kiss A Me Productions, Inc.

Dubuc, Marianne, creator. The Lion & the Bird. 2014. (ENG., Illus.). 64p. (J). (gr. -1). 17.95 *(978-1-59270-151-3(5))* Enchanted Lion Bks., LLC.

Duey, Kathleen. Leo: A Baby Lion's Story. Gurin, Lara, illus. 2008. (My Animal Family Ser.). 32p. (J). (gr. -1-3). 12.99 *(978-0-8249-1817-0(7)*, Ideals Pubns.) Worthy Publishing.

—Leo the Lion - Book & Dvd. Gurin, Laura, illus. 2007. 32p. 14.99 *(978-0-8249-6724-6(0)*, Ideals Pubns.) Worthy Publishing.

—Nanuq: A Baby Polar Bear's Story. Gurin, Lara, illus. 2008. (ENG.). 32p. (J). (gr. -1-3). 12.99 *(978-0-8249-1818-7(5)*, Ideals Pubns.) Worthy Publishing.

Dunbar, Polly. A Lion Is a Lion. Dunbar, Polly, illus. 2018. (ENG., Illus.). 40p. (J). (gr. -1-2). 15.99 *(978-0-7636-9731-0(1))* Candlewick Pr.

—A Lion Is a Lion. 2018. (Illus.). 40p. (J). *(978-1-4063-7153-6(X))* Candlewick Pr.

Dyckman, Ame. Roary the Lion Roars Too Loud. Griffiths, Alex G., illus. 2018. (Wee Beasties Ser.). (ENG.). 22p. (J). (gr. -1-k). bds. 8.99 *(978-1-5344-1078-7(3)*, Little Simon) Little Simon.

Dynamo. Googly Eyes: Leo Lion's Noisy Roar! 2014. (ENG., Illus.). 12p. (J). (gr. -1-2). bds. 6.99 *(978-1-84322-906-3(4)*, Armadillo) Anness Publishing GBR. Dist: National Bk. Network.

Eastman, Brock & Eastman, Kinley. Daddy's Favorite Sound: What's Better Than a Woosh or a Giggle? 2019. (ENG., Illus.). 32p. (J). (gr. -1-3). 16.99 *(978-0-7369-7474-5(1)*, 6974745) Harvest Hse. Pubs.

Easton, Marilyn. Eris to the Rescue. 2013. (LEGO Legends of Chima: Comic Reader Ser.: 3). lib. bdg. 13.55 *(978-0-606-32398-7(8))* Turtleback.

Ebwelleson, Nelson. The Helpless King. 2012. 24p. pap. 17.99 *(978-1-4772-8262-5(9))* AuthorHouse.

Edwards, Pamela Duncan. Roar! A Noisy Counting Book. Cole, Henry, illus. Date not set. 32p. (J). (gr. -1-2). pap. 5.99 *(978-0-06-443572-7(5))* HarperCollins Pubs.

Emberley, Rebecca. The Lion & the Mice. Emberley, Ed, illus. 2012. (I Like to Read Ser.). (ENG.). 24p. (J). (gr. -1-3). pap. 7.99 *(978-0-8234-2641-6(6))* Holiday Hse., Inc.

Evans, Robert J. Dorothy's Mystical Adventures in Oz. 2004. reprint ed. pap. 1.99 *(978-1-4192-1658-9(9))* Kessinger Publishing, LLC.

Everett, George W. G. W. Frog & the Circus Lion. 2010. 32p. 16.95 *(978-1-4497-0443-8(3)*, WestBow Pr.) Author Solutions, LLC.

Fagan, Cary. The Hollow under the Tree, 1 vol. 2018. (ENG.). 128p. (J). (gr. 3-6). 14.95 *(978-1-55498-999-7(X))* Groundwood Bks. CAN. Dist: Publishers Group West (PGW).

Farshtey, Greg. Beware of the Wolves. 2013. (LEGO Legends of Chima Chapter Bks.: 2). lib. bdg. 14.75 *(978-0-606-32014-6(8))* Turtleback.

Fatio, Louise. The Happy Lion. Duvoisin, Roger, illus. 2015. 32p. (J). (gr. -1-2). 8.99 *(978-0-553-50850-5(4)*, Dragonfly Bks.) Random Hse. Children's Bks.

Fisher, Barbara. Nobody's Lion. Huismann, Duane, illus. 2004. (J). per. 16.95 *(978-1-59571-049-9(3))* Word Association Pubs.

Fisscher, Tiny. RUBY & the LION. 2008. (ENG.). 48p. (J). (gr. 1-7). 11.95 *(978-1-60136-014-4(2))* Audio Holdings, LLC.

Foley, Greg. Willoughby & the Lion. 2009. (ENG., Illus.). 40p. (J). (gr. -1-2). 17.99 *(978-0-06-154750-8(6))* HarperCollins Pubs.

Foust, Cindy. Louis Lion. 2008. (J). 12.94 *(978-0-9749220-7-2(2))* Alpha-kidZ.

Franciosa, John F. Little Johnny Lion. 2009. 24p. pap. 11.99 *(978-1-4389-8810-8(9))* AuthorHouse.

Franklin, Carolyn. Lion. 2014. (Animal Journals). (Illus.). 32p. (J). (gr. 1-3). 31.35 *(978-1-906370-72-5(9))* Book Hse. GBR. Dist: Black Rabbit Bks.

Fuerst, Jeff. The Lion & the Rabbit: A Fable from India. 2006. (J). pap. *(978-1-4108-7156-5(8))* Benchmark Education Co.

Funk, Josh. Lost in the Library: A Story of Patience & Fortitude. Lewis, Stevie, illus. 2018. (New York Public Library Book Ser.). (ENG.). 40p. (J). 18.99 *(978-1-250-15501-6(0)*, 900184517, Holt, Henry & Co. Bks. For Young Readers) Holt, Henry & Co.

Fusek Peters, Andrew. Rabbit Cooks up a Cunning Plan. Robert, Bruno, illus. 2007. (Traditional Tales with a Twist Ser.). 32p. (J). (gr. 2-2). pap. *(978-1-84643-097-8(6))* Child's Play International Ltd.

Galvin, Laura Gates. Norman the Lion. Leeper, Christopher, illus. 2005. (African Wildlife Foundation Ser.). (ENG.). 36p. (J). (gr. -1-2). 2.95 *(978-1-59249-191-9(X)*, S6553) Soundprints.

—Norman the Lion. Leeper, Christopher J., tr. Leeper, Christopher J., illus. 2005. (African Wildlife Foundation Ser.). (ENG.). 36p. (J). (gr. -1-2). 14.95 *(978-1-59249-189-6(8)*, H6503); pap. 6.95 *(978-1-59249-190-2(1)*, S6503) Soundprints.

—Norman the Lion. Leeper, Christopher, illus. 2004. (ENG.). 36p. (J). (gr. -1-2). 9.95 *(978-1-59249-192-6(8)*, PS6553); 8.95 *(978-1-59249-208-4(8)*, SD6503) Soundprints.

Gerovasiliou, Oreanthy. Yuri the Lion: Three Stories. 2010. (Illus.). 48p. pap. 13.00 *(978-1-60888-069-0(9))* Nimble Bks. LLC.

Godley, Christina. Lion at the Gateway. 2010. 36p. pap. 16.99 *(978-1-4520-4508-5(9))* AuthorHouse.

Gold, Gina. Unlikely Friends. 2018. (World of Reading Ser.). (ENG.). 32p. (J). (gr. -1-1). 9.00 *(978-1-64310-409-6(8))* Penworthy Co., LLC, The.

Grant, Carrie and David. Lion's Speedy Sauce: Jump up & Join In. Busby, Allie, illus. 2013. 32p. (J). pap. 7.99 *(978-1-61067-180-4(5))* Kane Miller.

Graves, Sue. Lion Is Worried, 1 vol. Dunton, Trevor, illus. 2016. (Behavior Matters Ser.). (ENG.). 32p. (J). (gr. 2-3). lib. bdg. 28.93 *(978-1-4994-8084-9(9)*, 58f7caaf-621c-465c-ab00-d43eba50160a, Windmill Bks.) Rosen Publishing Group, Inc., The.

Green, George & Brooke, Amy/ J. George Green's, the Lion Who Couldn't Roar. 2008. (Illus.). (J). per. 16.99 *(978-1-933156-14-9(7)*, Visikid Bks.) GSVQ Publishing.

Gregory, Steven. The Lion's Drum: A Retelling of an African Folk Tale. Obata, Claudia, illus. 2007. 32p. (J). 13.95 *(978-0-615-15540-1(5))* Words & Music.

Griffiths, Allen & Godinez, Mary. Rusty Finds a Home: A Christmas Miracle. Ulrich, Kelly, illus. 2012. 32p. pap. *(978-1-4602-0937-0(0))* FriesenPress.

Harper, Benjamin. The Lion & the Mouse & the Invaders from Zurg: A Graphic Novel. Rodriguez, Pedro, illus. 2017. (Far Out Fables Ser.). (ENG.). 40p. (J). (gr. 3-6). pap. 4.95 *(978-1-4965-5426-0(4)*, 136359); lib. bdg. 25.32 *(978-1-4965-5422-2(1)*, 136355) Capstone. (Stone Arch Bks.).

Harrison, Paula. The Moonlight Mystery. 2013. (Rescue Princesses Ser.: 3). lib. bdg. 14.75 *(978-0-606-31988-1(3))* Turtleback.

Hasan, K. A. Rufus' Big Scare. Primmasone, Bruce, illus. 2011. 48p. pap. 24.95 *(978-1-4626-0660-3(1))* America Star Bks.

Hill, Susanna Leonard. When Your Lion Needs a Bath. Wiseman, Daniel, illus. 2017. (When Your... Ser.). (ENG.). 26p. (J). (gr. -1 — 1). bds. 7.99 *(978-1-4814-9502-8(X)*, Little Simon) Little Simon.

Hockerman, Dennis, illus. The Lion & the Mouse: A Tale about Being Helpful. 2006. (J). 6.99 *(978-1-59939-007-9(8))* Cornerstone Pr.

Howland, Leila. Nantucket Summer (Nantucket Blue & Nantucket Red Bind-Up) 2017. (Nantucket Blue Ser.). (ENG.). 608p. (J). (gr. 9-17). pap. 11.99 *(978-1-368-00212-7(9))* Hyperion Bks. for Children.

Hunter, Erin. Bravelands #1: Broken Pride. Richardson, Owen, illus. 2018. (Bravelands Ser.: 1). (ENG.). 352p. (J). (gr. 3-7). pap. 7.99 *(978-0-06-264204-2(9)*, HarperCollins) HarperCollins Pubs.

—Bravelands #2: Code of Honor. 2018. (Bravelands Ser.: 2). (ENG.). 400p. (J). (gr. 3-7). pap. 7.99 *(978-0-06-264208-0(1)*, HarperCollins) HarperCollins Pubs.

—Bravelands #3: Blood & Bone. (Bravelands Ser.: 3). (ENG.). (J). (gr. 3-7). 2019. 320p. pap. 9.99 *(978-0-06-264212-7(X))* 2018. (Illus.). 304p. 16.99 *(978-0-06-264210-3(3))* 2018. (Illus.). 304p. lib. bdg. 17.89 *(978-0-06-264211-0(1))* HarperCollins Pubs. (HarperCollins).

—Bravelands #4: Shifting Shadows. (Bravelands Ser.: 4). (ENG.). (J). (gr. 3-7). 2020. 352p. pap. 9.99 *(978-0-06-264216-5(2))* 2019. (Illus.). 336p. 16.99 *(978-0-06-264214-1(6))* 2019. (Illus.). 336p. lib. bdg. 17.89 *(978-0-06-264215-8(4))* HarperCollins Pubs. (HarperCollins).

Huusmann, Thomas-Bo & Fables, Aesops. The Lion & the Mouse. 2013. 26p. pap. *(978-87-995724-4-1(3))* Huusmann, Thomas-Bo.

Ingram, Doreen. My Sanctuary: A Place I Call Home - Keepers of the Wild. Josh Green, illus. 2013. 54p. pap. 17.50 *(978-1-62516-273-1(1)*, Strategic Bk. Publishing) Strategic Book Publishing & Rights Agency (SBPRA).

Ismail, Yasmeen. Specs for Rex. 2015. (ENG., Illus.). 32p. (J). (gr. -1-3). 16.99 *(978-1-61963-710-8(3)*, 900146307, Bloomsbury USA Childrens) Bloomsbury Publishing USA.

Jackson, Kathryn. Tawney Scrawny Lion. Tenggren, Gustaf, illus. deluxe ed. Date not set. (J). (gr. -1-2). reprint ed. *(978-1-929566-61-7(1))* Cronies.

—Tawny Scrawny Lion: Classic Edition. Tenggren, Gustaf, illus. Date not set. 23p. (J). (gr. -1-1). reprint ed. *(978-1-929566-55-6(7))* Cronies.

James, Laura. Safari Pug. Ceulemans, Eglantine, illus. 2018. (Adventures of Pug Ser.). (ENG.). 112p. (J). 16.99 *(978-1-68119-884-2(3)*, 900191401); pap. 6.99 *(978-1-68119-883-5(5)*, 900191400) Bloomsbury Publishing USA. (Bloomsbury Children's Bks.).

—Safari Pug. 2018. (Adventures of Pug Ser.: 3). (J). lib. bdg. 17.20 *(978-0-606-41083-0(X))* Turtleback.

Jarman, Julia. Lovely Old Lion. Varley, Susan, illus. 2015. (ENG.). 32p. (J). (gr. -1-3). 17.99 *(978-1-4677-9310-0(8)*, 12677906-782b-42f6-b94e-9d731d0f6d29); E-Book 27.99 *(978-1-4677-9543-2(7)*, 9781467795432) Lerner Publishing Group.

Jenkins, Amanda. The Lion & the Mouse Shoot Hoops. 2006. (J). pap. *(978-1-4108-7173-2(8))* Benchmark Education Co.

Johnson, Sandi. The Peaceful Lion. Johnson, Britt, ed. Kraft, Lauri, illus. l.t. ed. 2014. (ENG.). 28p. (J). (gr. k-5). pap. 12.99 *(978-1-929063-95-6(4)*, 325) Moons & Stars Publishing For Children.

Judith Anne Moody. Golden Eye & the Killer Cat. 2009. 248p. pap. 19.49 *(978-1-4251-7684-6(4))* Trafford Publishing.

Kasza, Keiko. The Mightiest. 2003. (Illus.). 32p. (J). (gr. -1-k). pap. 6.99 *(978-0-14-250185-6(9)*, Puffin Books) Penguin Young Readers Group.

Kellogg, Elijah. Lion Ben of Elm Island. 2005. pap. 27.95 *(978-1-4179-9427-4(4))* Kessinger Publishing, LLC.

Kerr, Valerie. The Adventures of Selwyn & Robert: Saving Whako the White Lion. 2013. 40p. pap. 16.46 *(978-1-4669-9252-8(2))* Trafford Publishing.

Kilimo, R. The, Donkey Who Wanted to Be a Lion. 2004. (Illus.). 16p. pap. *(978-9966-25-169-5(3))* Heinemann Kenya, Limited (East African Educational Publishers Ltd E.A.E.P.) KEN. Dist: Michigan State Univ. Pr.

King, Trey. The Legend Begins. 2013. (LEGO Legends of Chima: Comic Reader Ser.: 1). lib. bdg. 13.55 *(978-0-606-32012-2(1))* Turtleback.

Kinney, Kendall. Tiger Tails. 2004. 68p. (J). per. 10.95 *(978-1-932196-21-4(8))* WordWright.biz, Inc.

Kitzing, Constanze V. Are You Sleeping? Kitzing, Constanze V., illus. (ENG., Illus.). 32p. (J). (gr. -1-k). 2019. pap. 6.99 *(978-1-78285-402-9(9))* 2018. 9.99 *(978-1-78285-395-4(2))* Barefoot Bks., Inc.

—Can't Catch Me! Kitzing, Constanze V., illus. 2019. (ENG., Illus.). 32p. (J). (gr. -1 — 1). pap. *(978-1-78285-403-6(7))* Barefoot Bks., Ltd.

—I'm the Best! Kitzing, Constanze V., illus. 2018. (ENG., Illus.). 32p. (J). (gr. -1-k). 9.99 *(978-1-78285-394-7(4))* Barefoot Bks., Inc.

Kleyn, Diana & Beeke, Joel R. How God Used a Snowdrift. rev. ed. 2013. (Building on the Rock Ser.). (ENG., Illus.). 176p. (J). pap. 8.99 *(978-1-85792-817-4(2)*, cba4a9ca-6757-4eaf-8b54-b1a1926a786f, CF4Kids) Christian Focus Pubns. GBR. Dist: Baker & Taylor Publisher Services (BTPS).

Knudsen, Michelle. Library Lion. Hawkes, Kevin, illus. (ENG.). 48p. (J). (gr. -1-3). 2009. pap. 7.99 *(978-0-7636-3784-2(X))* 2006. 18.99 *(978-0-7636-2262-6(1))* Candlewick Pr.

—Library Lion. 2009. lib. bdg. 17.20 *(978-0-606-06666-2(7))* Turtleback.

Koffsky, Ann. Shabbat Shalom, Hey! Koffsky, Ann, illus. 2015. (ENG., Illus.). 24p. (J). (gr. -1-k). lib. bdg. 9.99 *(978-1-4677-4917-6(6)*, d719be77-c753-4940-809e-dd42198c6358); E-Book 23.99 *(978-1-4677-6208-3(3))* Lerner Publishing Group. (Kar-Ben Publishing).

Kompelien, Tracy. Lion Manes. Nobens, C. A., illus. 2006. (Fact & Fiction Ser.). 24p. (J). pap. 48.42 *(978-1-59679-950-9(1))* ABDO Publishing Co.

Korman, Justine. The Lion King (Disney the Lion King) Williams, Don & Russell, H. R., illus. 2003. (Little Golden Book Ser.). (ENG.). 24p. (J). (gr. -1-2). 5.99 *(978-0-7364-2095-2(9)*, Golden/Disney) Random Hse. Children's Bks.

Lamb, Jim. Ryan the Lion Finds His Roar. Schallmo, Carolyn, illus. 2011. 32p. 22.95 *(978-1-60844-880-7(0))*; pap. 12.95 *(978-1-60844-879-1(7))* Dog Ear Publishing, LLC.

Latimer, Alex. Lion vs. Rabbit, 1 vol. 2017. (ENG., Illus.). 32p. (J). (gr. -1-3). pap. 7.95 *(978-1-56145-898-1(8))* Peachtree Publishing Co. Inc.

Law, Felicia. Limpopo the Lion: A Tale of Laziness & Lethargy, 1 vol. Messina, Lilli, illus. 2009. (Animal Fair Values Ser.). (ENG.). 32p. (J). (gr. 2-2). pap. 11.55 *(978-1-60754-808-9(9)*, d1903f80-3c78-4770-9a62-d63b8bbb7a33); lib. bdg. 27.27 *(978-1-60754-804-1(6)*, 5bbbc020-d15b-4a7e-8b61-201f65278e1c) Rosen Publishing Group, Inc., The. (Windmill Bks.).

LeapFrog Staff. Disney Lion King - U. K. 2003. (Illus.). spiral bd. 14.99 *(978-1-59319-006-4(9))* LeapFrog Enterprises, Inc.

Lewis, C. S. The Lion, the Witch & the Wardrobe. 2008. (Chronicles of Narnia Ser.: 2). (J). 18.40 *(978-0-613-94066-5(0))* Turtleback.

The Lion & the Hare: [an East African Folktale]. 2009. (On My Own Folklore Ser.). (gr. 3-5). pap. 6.95 *(978-1-58013-849-9(7),* First Avenue Editions) Lerner Publishing Group.

Lion Country. 2003. (J). per. *(978-1-884907-39-5(3));* per. *(978-1-884907-38-8(5))* Paradise Pr., Inc.

Lion King: Far from the Pridelands. (Read-Along Ser.). (J). 7.99 incl. audio *(978-1-55723-673-9(9))* Walt Disney Records.

Lion's Mane. Date not set. (Touch & Feel Ser.). (J). 4.98 *(978-0-7525-9569-6(5))* Parragon, Inc.

The Little Lion. (Early Intervention Levels Ser.). 21.30 *(978-0-7362-0367-8(2))* CENGAGE Learning.

Lochmandy, Sandy. Kids & Critters on an Adventure. 2009. 36p. pap. 14.95 *(978-1-60860-387-9(3),* Eloquent Bks.) Strategic Book Publishing & Rights Agency (SBPRA).

Loesch, Joe. Lions, Lions Everywhere: The Story of Daniel as told by God's Animals. Hutchinson, Cheryl, ed. Cox, Brain T., illus. 2004. (Bible Stories for Kids Ser.). 56p. (J). bds. 16.95 incl. audio compact disk *(978-1-932332-24-7(3))* Toy Box Productions.

Loewen, Nancy. The Lion & the Mouse, Narrated by the Timid but Truthful Mouse. Bernardini, Cristian, illus. 2018. (Other Side of the Fable Ser.). (ENG.). 24p. (J). (gr. -1-3). lib. bdg. 27.99 *(978-1-5158-2866-2(2),* 138404, Picture Window Bks.) Capstone.

Mahy, Margaret. A Lion in the Meadow. Williams, Jenny, illus. 2017. 57p. pap. *(978-1-897136-78-2(1),* 73-W6781) Hachette New Zealand.

Manning, L. L. Fuzz. 2010. (ENG.). 26p. pap. 15.99 *(978-1-4500-5755-4(1))* Xlibris Corp.

Martin, Janelle. Lexis, the Hiccupping Lion. 2013. 12p. pap. 7.95 *(978-1-4908-0545-0(1),* WestBow Pr.) Author Solutions, LLC.

Marwood, Diane. The Lion & the Mouse. 2012. (ENG., Illus.). 24p. (J). *(978-0-7787-7893-6(2));* pap. *(978-0-7787-7905-6(X))* Crabtree Publishing Co.

Mason, Charlene. Landon's Backyard Adventures. 2012. 24p. pap. 24.95 *(978-1-4626-7470-1(4))* America Star Bks.

Mason, Jane B. Wonder Woman: Attack of the Cheetah, 1 vol. Schoening, Dan, illus. 2010. (Wonder Woman Ser.). (ENG.). 56p. (J). (gr. 3-6). pap. 4.95 *(978-1-4342-2254-1(3),* 103117, Stone Arch Bks.) Capstone.

Matteren, Joanne. The Old Lion & the Fox. 2005. (J). pap. *(978-1-4108-4206-0(1))* Benchmark Education Co.

McBrayer, Cassidy. You Can, Toucan! You Can. 2008. 20p. pap. 15.95 *(978-1-4327-1132-0(6))* Outskirts Pr., Inc.

McCall Smith, Alexander. The Mystery of the Missing Lion. 2014. (Precious Ramotswe Mysteries for Young Readers Ser.: 3). (ENG., Illus.). 112p. (J). (gr. 2-5). pap. 7.99 *(978-0-8041-7327-8(3),* Anchor) Knopf Doubleday Publishing Group.

McElligott, Matthew. The Lion's Share. McElligott, Matthew, illus. (ENG., Illus.). (J). (gr. k-8). 2012. 40p. pap. 8.99 *(978-0-8027-2360-4(8),* 900078463) 2009. 32p. 17.99 *(978-0-8027-9768-1(7),* 900051430) Bloomsbury Publishing USA. (Bloomsbury USA Childrens).

McGonagle, Joanne L. The Tiniest Tiger. 2008. (ENG.). 52p. pap. 15.00 *(978-1-4196-8467-8(1))* CreateSpace Independent Publishing Platform.

McKayhan, Norma J. The Mighty King & the Small Creature. 2012. 24p. pap. 12.55 *(978-1-4669-1463-6(7))* Trafford Publishing.

McKendry, Sam. Are You Ticklish? Mitchell, Melanie, illus. 2006. (ENG.). 12p. (J). (gr. -1-18). bds. 10.95 *(978-1-58117-376-5(8),* Intervisual/Piggy Toes) Bendon, Inc.

—Are You Ticklish? Mitchell, Melanie, illus. 2008. (ENG.). 12p. (J). bds. 5.95 *(978-1-58117-706-0(2),* Intervisual/Piggy Toes) Bendon, Inc.

McKenzie, Larry. Leonardo the Lopsided Lion. 2012. 28p. pap. 16.09 *(978-1-4669-5979-8(7))* Trafford Publishing.

McOmber, Rachel B., ed. McOmber Phonics Storybooks: Chatsworth. rev. ed. (Illus.). (J). *(978-0-944991-74-9(2))* Swift Learning Resources.

McPhail, David. Pig Pig Meets the Lion. McPhail, David, illus. 2012. (Illus.). pap. 15.95 *(978-1-60734-080-5(1));* (ENG., 32p. (J). (gr. -1-3). 15.95 *(978-1-58089-358-9(9))* Charlesbridge Publishing, Inc.

Meachen Rau, Dana. The Lion in the Grass, 1 vol. 2007. (Nature Ser.). (ENG., Illus.). 24p. (gr. k-1). lib. bdg. 25.50 *(978-0-7614-2305-8(2),* 3c5c407e-f318-4ed2-adf0-b6453fdf0922) Cavendish Square Publishing LLC.

Mehlhaff, Christine. Don't Talk to Strangers. Ember, Kathi, illus. 2007. (J). *(978-0-545-00103-8(X))* Scholastic, Inc.

Mejuto Rial, Eva. RUN PUMPKIN, RUN. 2007. (ENG., Illus.). 36p. (J). 17.95 *(978-84-96788-88-6(1))* OQO, Editora ESP. Dist: Baker & Taylor Bks.

Merlo, Maria. El Leon Ruge. Keeter, Susan, illus. 2012. (SPA.). 16p. (J). pap. 54.70 *(978-0-663-62198-9(4))* Silver, Burdett & Ginn, Inc.

Messimer, Wanda Fay. Tiny Teacup & Pot Belly Pig Go to Africa to Meet the 'Great Lion' 2013. 24p. pap. 24.95 *(978-1-4626-8736-7(9))* America Star Bks.

Michaels, Andie. ACHOO! ACHOO! I've Got the Flu. (ENG.). (J). 2021. pap. 14.95 *(978-1-7330663-2-7(2))* 2019. 32p. 19.95 *(978-1-7330663-0-3(6))* Mulberry Street Publishing.

Millett, Peter & Wallace-Mitchell, Jane. Lions! 2008. (Rigby Focus Forward: Level G Ser.). (Illus.). 24p. (J). (gr. 4-7). pap. *(978-1-4190-3717-7(X),* Rigby) Pearson Education Australia.

Modern Publishing Staff. ABCs! 2007. (Disney Bath Time Bubble Bks.). (Illus.). (J). (gr. -1-k). 4.99 *(978-0-7666-2551-8(6))* Modern Publishing.

Moran, Colette. Disney the Lion King: Look & Find: Look & Find. Jaime Diaz Studios, illus. 2019. (ENG.). 24p. (J). 10.99 *(978-0-7853-9532-4(6),* 4707, PI Kids) Phoenix International Publications, Inc.

Mullins, Rebecca. Tristan, 1 vol. 2009. 23p. pap. 24.95 *(978-1-60672-257-2(3))* America Star Bks.

Munsch, Robert. Roar! Martchenko, Michael, illus. 2019. (ENG.). 32p. (J). pap. 7.99 *(978-0-545-98020-3(8))* Scholastic Canada, Ltd. CAN. Dist: Publishers Group West (PGW).

Myers, Don. My Life with Roger. 2009. (Illus.). 49p. (J). pap. 12.95 *(978-1-4327-3873-0(9))* Outskirts Pr., Inc.

The Mystery of the Lion's Tail. 2014. (Greetings from Somewhere Ser.: 5). (ENG., Illus.). 128p. (J). (gr. -1-4). pap. 6.99 *(978-1-4814-1464-7(X),* Little Simon) Little Simon.

Nayer, Judy. Androcles & the Lion: An Aesop's Fable. 2006. (J). pap. *(978-1-4108-6165-8(1))* Benchmark Education Co.

O'Donnell, Shannon. The Lion's Son. 2012. 42p. 24.95 *(978-1-4626-5013-2(9))* America Star Bks.

Osborn School Students. Paw-Sing for Positive Daily Affirmations: Lion Pride. Rosa, M. Nina & Perrien, Vicki, eds. 2003. (J). pap. 16.99 *(978-0-9740267-0-1(0))* Mz. Rosa Notions.

Osborne, Mary Pope. Lions at Lunchtime. unabr. ed. 2004. (Magic Tree House Ser.: No. 11). 70p. (J). (gr. k-3). pap. 17.00 incl. audio *(978-0-8072-0536-5(2),* Listening Library) Random Hse. Audio Publishing Group.

Otukile, Mpho. The Lion's Deceit. Dow, S. B., illus. 2011. (ENG.). 32p. (J). pap. *(978-0-9867460-0-0(2))* Village Life Bks.

Papineau, Lucie. Leonardo le Lionceau. 2004. (FRE., Illus.). (J). (gr. k-3). spiral bd. *(978-0-616-07264-6(3))* Canadian National Institute for the Blind/Institut National Canadien pour les Aveugles.

Parker, Emma & Aesop, Aesop. The Lion & the Mouse. 2010. (Illus.). pap. *(978-1-877547-45-4(X))* First Edition Ltd.

Parragon Staff. Lion King. 2010. (Disney Diecut Classics). (Illus.). 72p. (J). (gr. -1-1). *(978-1-4075-8936-7(9))* Parragon, Inc.

Paulus, Kristin Harkison. There's a Lion on the Dance Floor. 2010. (Illus.). 28p. pap. 12.98 *(978-1-4490-2692-9(3))* AuthorHouse.

Pierce, Tamora. Lioness Rampant. unabr. ed. 2004. (Song of the Lioness Ser.: Bk. 4). 308p. (J). (gr. 6-18). pap. 38.00 incl. audio *(978-0-8072-0985-1(6),* S YA 388 SP, Listening Library) Random Hse. Audio Publishing Group.

Pistinier, Caroline. ThÃ(c)o et le Lion. 2010. (FRE.). 32p. pap. 17.95 *(978-1-4457-7871-6(8))* Lulu Pr., Inc.

pistinier, caroline. Théo & the Lion. 2010. 32p. pap. 17.95 *(978-1-4457-8804-3(7))* Lulu Pr., Inc.

Pogo the Clown. A Brave Little Lion: Harley's Great Adventures. Miller, Richard D., illus. 2005. (J). 12.95 *(978-0-9755253-5-7(2))* Chiliric Pubns.

Powell, Daniel M. King Grrr-egory & the Angel. 2010. 26p. 13.99 *(978-0-557-53182-0(9))* Lulu Pr., Inc.

Powell, Richard. Leo Lion. Rhodes, Katie, illus. 2004. (Fuzzy Friends Ser.). 10p. (J). 7.95 *(978-1-58925-719-1(7))* Tiger Tales.

Price, Olivia. Bible Stories: A Touch & Feel Book. Mitchell, Melanie, illus. 2008. (ENG.). 12p. (J). (gr. -1). 12.95 *(978-1-58117-802-9(6),* Intervisual/Piggy Toes) Bendon, Inc.

Proimos III, James, Jr. Apocalypse Meow Meow. Proimos III, James, Jr., illus. 2015. (ENG., Illus.). 224p. (J). (gr. 3-6). 15.99 *(978-1-61963-472-5(4),* 900137802, Bloomsbury USA Childrens) Bloomsbury Publishing USA.

Publications International Ltd. Staff, ed. Disney Lion King - We Can Share. 2011. 12p. (J). bds. *(978-1-4508-1383-9(6))* Publications International, Ltd.

Pugliano-Martin, Carol. Little Lion. 2011. (Early Connections Ser.). (J). *(978-1-61672-585-3(0))* Benchmark Education Co.

—Little Lion: Set Of 6. 2011. (Early Connections Ser.). (J). pap. 37.00 net. *(978-1-4108-1092-2(5))* Benchmark Education Co.

Remey, Grace Anne. Lion's Pride: A Tail of Deployment. Remey, Grace Anne, illus. 2012. (ENG., Illus.). 38p. pap. 12.95 *(978-0-9855445-0-8(3))* Remey, Lisa.

Rempel, Jennifer, illus. Lavi the Lion Finds His Pride. 2005. (J). 15.95 *(978-0-9744715-2-5(6),* Towers Maguire Publishing) Local History Co., The.

Rice, Dona Herwick. The Lion & the Mouse, 1 vol. rev. ed. 2008. (Reader's Theater Ser.). (ENG.). 24p. (gr. 1-3). pap. 8.99 *(978-1-4333-0293-0(4))* Teacher Created Materials, Inc.

Richardson, Justin & Parnell, Peter. Christian, the Hugging Lion. Bates, Amy June, illus. 2010. (ENG.). 32p. (J). (gr. -1-3). 19.99 *(978-1-4169-8662-1(6),* Simon & Schuster Bks. For Young Readers) Simon & Schuster Bks. For Young Readers.

Robaard, Jedda. The Little Lion Who Lost Her Roar. 2014. (Illus.). 9p. (J). *(978-1-4351-5391-2(X))* Barnes & Noble, Inc.

Robertson, Rachel. When You Just Have to Roar! Prentice, Priscilla, illus. 2015. (ENG.). 32p. (J). (gr. -1-k). 17.95 *(978-1-60554-362-8(4))* Redleaf Pr.

Rogers, Terry, illus. Androcles & the Lion: A Roman Legend. 2003. (Dominie Collection of Myths & Legends). (SPA.). 20p. (J). lib. bdg. *(978-0-7685-2419-2(9))* Dominie Pr., Inc.

—Androcles & the Lion: A Roman Legend. 2004. (SPA & ENG.). 20p. (J). (gr. 3-3). pap. 6.47 net. *(978-0-7685-2122-1(X),* Dominie Elementary) Savvas Learning Co.

Rose, Gerald. Horrible Melena. (SPA.). (J). 8.95 *(978-958-04-7343-5(9))* Norma S.A. COL. Dist: Distribuidora Norma, Inc.

Safari Press Staff, ed. Book Buddy - Lion with Story Book. (Illus.). 10p. (J). (gr. -1-3). pap. *(978-1-881469-84-1(0))* Safari, Ltd.

Sendak, Maurice. Pierre Board Book: A Cautionary Tale in Five Chapters & a Prologue. Sendak, Maurice, illus. 2017. (ENG., Illus.). 38p. (J). (gr. -1-3). bds. 7.95 *(978-0-06-266810-3(2),* HarperCollins) HarperCollins Pubs.

Senior, Patricia. Mischief on Mumpit Mountain. 2009. 36p. pap. 14.75 *(978-1-60693-661-0(1),* Eloquent Bks.) Strategic Book Publishing & Rights Agency (SBPRA).

Shaw, Rebecca. Elisha's Great Mission. 2010. 32p. pap. 11.95 *(978-1-935268-43-7(0))* Halo Publishing International.

Silverstein, Shel. Lafcadio, el Leon Que Disparo Al Cazador. Rioja, Alberto Jimenez, tr. from ENG. 2011.Tr. of Lafcadio, the Lion Who Shot Back. (SPA., Illus.). 112p. (J). (gr. 2-3). 16.99 *(978-1-933032-74-0(X))* Lectorum Pubns., Inc.

—Lafcadio, the Lion Who Shot Back. Silverstein, Shel, illus. 2013. (ENG., Illus.). 112p. (J). (gr. -1-3). 17.99 *(978-0-06-025675-3(3),* HarperCollins) HarperCollins Pubs.

—Lafcadio, the Lion Who Shot Back. 2009. (CHI., Illus.). (J). *(978-7-5442-4521-0(7))* Nanhai Publishing Co.

Simon, Mary Manz. Lion Can Share. Harris, Phyllis & Clearwater, Linda, illus. 2006. (First Virtuestm for Toddlers Ser.). 20p. (J). 5.99 *(978-0-7847-1576-5(9),* 04070) Standard Publishing.

Sleepytime Lion. 2005. (J). *(978-0-9767179-5-9(6))* ABC Development, Inc.

Smalley, Roger, adapted by. The Big-Hearted Monkey & the Lion. 2005. (J). *(978-1-933248-02-8(5))* World Quest Learning.

Smith, Alex T. Little Red & the Very Hungry Lion. Smith, Alex T., illus. 2016. (ENG., Illus.). 32p. (J). (gr. -1-k). 18.99 *(978-0-545-91438-3(8),* Scholastic Pr.) Scholastic, Inc.

Smith, Carrie. The Lion & the Rabbit: Classic Tales Edition. Greenhead, Bill, illus. 2011. (Classic Tales Ser.). (J). *(978-1-936258-65-9(X))* Benchmark Education Co.

Soffe, Caroline Dawn. The Burrows of Trother. 2011. 60p. pap. 19.95 *(978-1-4560-5202-7(0))* America Star Bks.

Sommer, Carl. I Am a Lion! Budwine, Greg, illus. 2014. (J). *(978-1-57537-403-1(X))* Advance Publishing, Inc.

—I Am a Lion! 2003. (Another Sommer-Time Story Ser.). (Illus.). 48p. (J). (gr. k-4). lib. bdg. 23.95 incl. audio *(978-1-57537-759-9(4))* Advance Publishing, Inc.

—I Am a Lion! Budwine, Greg, illus. 2003. (Another Sommer-Time Story Ser.). (ENG.). 48p. (J). (gr. k-4). lib. bdg. 23.95 incl. audio compact disk *(978-1-57537-709-4(8))* Advance Publishing, Inc.

—I Am a Lion! 2003. (Another Sommer-Time Story Ser.). (Illus.). 48p. (J). (gr. 1-4). 16.95 incl. audio *(978-1-57537-558-8(3))* Advance Publishing, Inc.

—I Am a Lion! Budwine, Greg, illus. 2003. (Another Sommer-Time Story Ser.). (ENG.). 48p. (J). (gr. 1-4). 16.95 incl. audio compact disk *(978-1-57537-509-0(5))* Advance Publishing, Inc.

—I Am a Lion!(Yo Soy un León!) Budwine, Greg, illus. 2009. (Another Sommer-Time Story Bilingual Ser.). (SPA & ENG.). 48p. (J). lib. bdg. 16.95 *(978-1-57537-153-5(7))* Advance Publishing, Inc.

—The Lion & the Mouse. Mercado, Jorge, illus. 2014. (Sommer-Time Story Classics Ser.). (ENG.). 32p. (J). (gr. k-4). 16.95 *(978-1-57537-082-8(4))* Advance Publishing, Inc.

—The Roar. Budwine, Greg, illus. 2009. (Quest for Success Ser.). (ENG.). 56p. (YA). pap. 4.95 *(978-1-57537-284-6(3));* lib. bdg. 12.95 *(978-1-57537-259-4(2))* Advance Publishing, Inc.

—The Roar(El Rugido) Budwine, Greg, illus. 2009. (Quest for Success Bilingual Ser.). (SPA & ENG.). 96p. (YA). lib. bdg. 14.95 *(978-1-57537-233-4(9))* Advance Publishing, Inc.

Spreng, Robert C. The Tahoe Tiger & the Lahontan Lion. 2008. 38p. pap. 14.50 *(978-0-557-02370-7(X))* Lulu Pr., Inc.

Stanbro, Heather. The Lion Without A Roar. 2011. 28p. pap. 12.95 *(978-1-4567-2768-0(0))* AuthorHouse.

Stegall, Kim. Mumsi Meets a Lion. Batti, Kimberly Rose, illus. 2008. (gr. -1-1). pap. 7.99 *(978-1-59166-871-8(9))* BJU Pr.

Stein, Kristen. The Vegetarian Lion. 2006. 36p. (J). pap. 13.28 *(978-1-4116-6459-3(0))* Lulu Pr., Inc.

Stratten, Lou. Hello, I'm Sir Frettrick! Let's Say Hello to Our New Friends! Bennett, Judy, ed. Denaro, Sal, illus. 2006. (J). (gr. -1-2). pap. 6.95 incl. audio compact disk *(978-0-9747173-1-9(2))* Stratten, Lou.

Suritsch, Gina. Magical Tales from India: The Secret of the White Elephant & Mukti the Lion Finds Himself. 2013. 44p. pap. 22.99 *(978-1-4828-1435-4(8))* Partridge Pub.

Templar Books. I Thought I Saw a Lion! Nichols, Lydia, illus. 2018. (I Thought I Saw Ser.). (ENG.). 10p. (J). (— 1). bds. 8.99 *(978-0-7636-9946-8(2),* Templar) Candlewick Pr.

Thomasson, Daniel E. The Lion & the Egg. 2012. 56p. pap. 24.20 *(978-1-4669-1303-5(7))* Trafford Publishing.

Tolstoy, Leo. The Lion & the Puppy: And Other Stories for Children. Riordan, James, tr. Sievert, Claus, illus. 2012. (ENG.). 76p. (J). (gr. 4-7). 16.95 *(978-1-61608-484-4(7),* 608484, Sky Pony Pr.) Skyhorse Publishing Co., Inc.

Trent, Sandy Chase. Tommy's Amazing Journey: The Cat that Could Fly. 2011. 16p. pap. 24.95 *(978-1-4626-2363-1(8))* America Star Bks.

Vollmer, Cheryl. A Hungry Lion in My Tummy. Dimitriadis, Nick, illus. 2009. 24p. pap. 9.99 *(978-0-9825255-9-3(1))* Epigraph Bks.

Walsh, Sheila. Will, God's Mighty Warrior, 1 vol., 1. Johnson, Meredith, illus. 2006. (Will, God's Mighty Warrior Ser.: 1). (ENG.). 32p. (J). (gr. -1-3). 14.99 *(978-1-4003-0805-7(4),* Tommy Nelson) Nelson, Thomas Inc.

Watt, F. & Wells, R. That's Not My Lion. 2004. (Touchy-Feely Board Bks.). (SPA.). 10p. (J). 7.99 *(978-0-7945-0047-4(1),* Usborne) EDC Publishing.

Weaver, Amy Garrett. Zoe the Zebra. Schneider, Robin, illus. 2009. 33p. pap. 24.95 *(978-1-60749-552-9(X))* PublishAmerica, Inc.

Weidensee, Ralph. The Cry'N Lion. 2010. 28p. pap. 21.99 *(978-1-4415-7923-2(0))* Xlibris Corp.

Weigl Publishers, creator. The Lion & the Mouse: Can Little Friends Be Great Friends? 2013. (AV2 Animated Storytime Ser.: Vol. 15). (ENG., Illus.). 32p. (J). (gr. -1-3). lib. bdg. 29.99 *(978-1-62127-919-8(7),* AV2 by Weigl) Weigl Pubs., Inc.

Weiss, Ellen. Simba's Moon. Cuddy, Robin, illus. Date not set. (ENG.). 32p. (J). (gr. -1-2). 12.99 *(978-0-7868-3267-5(3))* Disney Pr.

White, Mark. The Lion & the Mouse: A Retelling of Aesop's Fable, 1 vol. Rojo Pérez, Sara, illus. 2011. (My First Classic Story Ser.). (ENG.). 24p. (J). (gr. k-3). pap. 7.10 *(978-1-4048-7365-0(1),* 118580, Picture Window Bks.) Capstone.

White, Paul. Jungle Doctor Meets a Lion. 2011. (Flamingo Fiction 9-13s Ser.). (ENG., Illus.). 176p. (J). 8.99 *(978-1-84550-392-5(9),* 0590f404-45d7-4593-b5b3-7e20994a2ae9) Christian Focus Pubns. GBR. Dist: Baker & Taylor Publisher Services (BTPS).

White, Robb. The Lion's Paw. Ray, Ralph, illus. 2008. 243p. (J). (gr. 4-7). 29.95 *(978-0-9820932-0-7(9))* A. W. Ink, Inc.

Whitney, Elliott. The Blind Lion of the Congo. 2011. 128p. pap. 9.99 *(978-1-61203-066-1(1))* Bottom of the Hill Publishing.

William H. Sadlier Staff. The Lion & the Mouse, Vol. 2. 2005. (Fluent Library). (gr. 1-3). 29.34 *(978-0-8215-8968-7(7))* Sadlier, William H. Inc.

Williams, Zachary. Lions at the Library?, 1 vol. 2006. (Neighborhood Readers Ser.). (ENG.). 12p. (gr. 1-2). pap. 5.90 *(978-1-4042-6863-0(4),* 1a815c85-15cd-4245-b8ba-ba6a36b2df1e, Rosen Classroom) Rosen Publishing Group, Inc., The.

Wilson, Gerrard. Alice on Top of the World. 2009. 159p. pap. 17.50 *(978-0-9561553-0-6(8))* Wilson, Gerrard IRL. Dist: Lulu Pr., Inc.

Wise Brown, Margaret & Sebring Lowrey, Janette. The Poky Little Puppy & Friends: the Nine Classic Little Golden Books. 2017. (Illus.). 224p. (J). (-k). 12.99 *(978-1-5247-6683-2(6),* Golden Bks.) Random Hse. Children's Bks.

Wolf, Gita. The Very Hungry Lion: A Folktale. Roy, Indrapramit, illus. 2006. (ENG.). 24p. 20.95 *(978-81-86211-02-1(0))* Tara Publishing IND. Dist: Consortium Bk. Sales & Distribution.

World of Lions. 2003. (J). per. *(978-1-884907-55-5(5))* Paradise Pr., Inc.

LION—HABITS AND BEHAVIOR

Jackson, Tom. Inside the Mind of a Fierce Lion, 1 vol. 2012. (Animal Instincts Ser.). (ENG.). 32p. (J). (gr. 3-3). pap. 11.00 *(978-1-4488-7074-5(7),* e2febb93-9d64-4044-a38f-c9805a8cc7ba); lib. bdg. 28.93 *(978-1-4488-7032-5(1),* 59d1310b-451e-4584-90e8-b19d37f3b2a0) Rosen Publishing Group, Inc., The. (PowerKids Pr.).

Spilsbury, Richard & Spilsbury, Louise. Lion Prides, 1 vol. 2013. (Animal Armies Ser.). (ENG., Illus.). 32p. (J). (gr. 2-3). pap. 11.00 *(978-1-4777-0334-2(9),* 68616110-b856-4556-9263-c98fa4c0d373); lib. bdg. 28.93 *(978-1-4777-0306-9(3),* b8354066-af31-422e-b9fd-0987d5771ba5) Rosen Publishing Group, Inc., The. (PowerKids Pr.).

LIONS

see Lion

LIQUID FUEL

see Gasoline; Petroleum As Fuel

LIQUIDS

Adamson, Heather & Adamson, Thomas K. How Do You Measure Liquids? 2010. (Measure It! Ser.). (ENG.). 32p. (J). (gr. 1-2). pap. 49.60 *(978-1-4296-6458-5(4),* 16213, Capstone Pr.) Capstone.

Adamson, Thomas K. & Adamson, Heather. ¿Cómo Mides los Líquidos? 2011. (Mídelo/Measure It Ser.).Tr. of How Do You Measure Liquids? (MUL.). 32p. (J). (gr. -1-2). 27.99 *(978-1-4296-6890-3(3),* 116505, Capstone Pr.) Capstone.

—How Do You Measure Liquids?, 1 vol. 2010. (Measure It! Ser.). (ENG.). 32p. (J). (gr. -1-2). pap. 8.10 *(978-1-4296-6331-1(6),* 115532) Capstone.

Bentley, Joyce. Wet. 2006. (Things Around Us Ser.). (J). *(978-1-59389-279-1(9))* Chrysalis Education.

Bloom, Chrissa. In the Kitchen with Solids, Liquids, & Gases, 1 vol. 2008. (Real Life Readers Ser.). (ENG.). 12p. (gr. 1-2). pap. 5.90 *(978-1-4042-7897-4(4),* e43da252-1047-465c-b8ff-11988b838565, Rosen Classroom) Rosen Publishing Group, Inc., The.

Boothroyd, Jennifer. What Floats? What Sinks? 2010. pap. 45.32 *(978-0-7613-6933-2(3))* Lerner Publishing Group.

—What Floats? What Sinks? A Look at Density. 2010. (Lightning Bolt Books (r) — Exploring Physical Science Ser.). (ENG., Illus.). 32p. (J). (gr. 1-3). pap. 9.99 *(978-0-7613-6055-1(7),* 27e7b6bc-dbf0-4608-b876-b5185f62578d) Lerner Publishing Group.

—What Is a Liquid? 2007. (First Step Nonfiction — States of Matter Ser.). (ENG., Illus.). 24p. (J). (gr. k-2). pap. 6.99 *(978-0-8225-6817-9(9),* cd12103f-719e-4123-8f8a-3e9a207947e0) Lerner Publishing Group.

Brannon, Barbara. Discover Liquids. 2005. (J). pap. *(978-1-4108-5118-5(4))* Benchmark Education Co.

Braun, Eric. Joe-Joe the Wizard Brews up Solids, Liquids, & Gases, 1 vol. Boyden, Robin, illus. 2012. (In the Science Lab Ser.). (ENG.). 24p. (J). (gr. k-3). pap. 9.95 *(978-1-4048-7238-7(8),* 118177, Picture Window Bks.) Capstone.

Cardenas, Ernesto A. Liquid or Solid? 2009. 23.95 *(978-1-60698-041-5(6));* pap. 4.95 *(978-1-60698-039-2(4))* Milo Educational Bks. & Resources.

Clark, Jennifer. The Wizard's Workshop. 2018. (ENG.). (J). pap. 13.99 *(978-1-4621-2167-0(5))* Cedar Fort, Inc./CFI Distribution.

Doudna, Kelly. Let's Be Kids & Measure Liquids!, 1 vol. 2007. (Science Made Simple Ser.). (Illus.). 24p. (J). (gr. k-3). lib. bdg. 24.21 *(978-1-59928-610-5(6),* SandCastle) ABDO Publishing Co.

Kjelle, Marylou Morano. The Properties of Liquids. (Library of Physical Science Ser.). 24p. (gr. 4-4). 2009. 42.50 *(978-1-60853-791-4(9),* PowerKids Pr.) 2006. (ENG., Illus.). (YA). lib. bdg. 26.27 *(978-1-4042-3422-2(5),* 1a8479c1-c0a1-401c-bc1e-d71386b6f4df) 2006. (ENG., Illus.). pap. 7.05 *(978-1-4042-2169-7(7),* dbae3dcd-a6a2-4e23-b120-c621bda98618, PowerKids Pr.) Rosen Publishing Group, Inc., The.

Lawrence, Ellen. Liquids & Solids. 2014. (Science Slam: FUN-Damentals Ser.). (ENG., Illus.). 24p. (J). (gr. -1-3). lib. bdg. 26.99 *(978-1-62724-311-7(9))* Bearport Publishing Co., Inc.

Merrill, Amy French. Everyday Physical Science Experiments with Liquids. 2009. (Science Surprises Ser.). 24p. (gr. 3-3). 42.50 *(978-1-60853-062-5(0),* PowerKids Pr.) Rosen Publishing Group, Inc., The.

Mezzanotte, Jim. Líquidos (Liquids), 1 vol. 2006. (Estados de la Materia (States of Matter) Ser.). (SPA.). 24p. (gr. 2-4). pap. 9.15 *(978-0-8368-7409-9(9),* 44c04bf9-2159-4285-b12f-99afb46535be); (Illus.). lib. bdg. 24.67 *(978-0-8368-7404-4(8),* 2170d9f5-212f-4d94-a0a6-564522078c1a) Stevens, Gareth Publishing LLLP. (Weekly Reader Leveled Readers).

—Liquids, 1 vol. 2006. (States of Matter Ser.). (ENG.). 24p. (gr. 2-4). pap. 9.15 *(978-0-8368-6804-3(8),* 05623b67-6488-4c6f-a049-deb21ad42760); (Illus.). lib. bdg. 24.67 *(978-0-8368-6799-2(8),* 4e11d179-92e0-4709-bce5-13a431252fdc) Stevens, Gareth Publishing LLLP. (Weekly Reader Leveled Readers).

Montgomery, Anne. Solid or Liquid?, 1 vol. rev. ed. 2014. (Science: Informational Text Ser.). (ENG., Illus.). 24p. (J). (gr. k-1). pap. 9.99 *(978-1-4807-4527-8(8))* Teacher Created Materials, Inc.

Mullins, Matt. Junior Scientists: Experiment with Liquids. 2010. (Explorer Junior Library: Science Explorer Junior Ser.). (ENG., Illus.). 32p. (gr. 3-6). lib. bdg. 32.07 *(978-1-60279-846-5(X),* 200558) Cherry Lake Publishing.

Nelson, Robin. Freezing & Melting. 2003. (First Step Nonfiction — Water Ser.). (Illus.). 24p. (J). (gr. k-2). (ENG.). pap. 6.99

J
K
L

(978-0-8225-4591-0(8), 45fa9ba6-a3d8-49c4-bf5e-0360baaa3084); lib. bdg. 18.60 *(978-0-8225-4590-3(X))* Lerner Publishing Group.

Parker, Janice. The Science of Liquids & Solids. 2003. (Living Science Ser.). (Illus.). 32p. (J). (gr. 1-3). pap. 9.95 *(978-1-930954-11-3(5))* Weigl Pubs., Inc.

Peppas, Lynn. What Is a Liquid? 2012. (ENG.). 24p. (J). *(978-0-7787-0770-7(9))*; (Illus.). (gr. 2-3). pap. *(978-0-7787-0777-6(6))* Crabtree Publishing Co.

Randolph, Joanne. Liquids in My World. (My World of Science Ser.). 24p. 2009. (gr. 2-2). 37.50 *(978-1-61514-726-7(8),* PowerKids Pr.) 2006. (ENG.). (gr. k-2). pap. 7.05 *(978-1-4042-8421-0(4),* ddd6e1c1-8a00-4d79-a718-ea05f688754d, Rosen Classroom) 2005. (ENG., Illus.). (J). (gr. k-2). lib. bdg. 22.27 *(978-1-4042-3285-3(0),* 8a401747-0f5d-476c-a91e-f2a2fe9c080a, PowerKids Pr.) Rosen Publishing Group, Inc., The.

—Liquids in My World/Los líquidos en mi Mundo. 2009. (My World of Science/la ciencia en mi mundo Ser.). (ENG & SPA.). 48p. (gr. 2-2). 37.50 *(978-1-61514-738-0(1),* Editorial Buenas Letras) Rosen Publishing Group, Inc., The.

Rodriguez, Cindy. Liquidos. 2013. (SPA.). (J). *(978-1-62127-603-6(1))* Weigl Pubs., Inc.

—Liquids, with Code. 2012. (What Is Matter? Ser.). (ENG., Illus.). 24p. (J). (gr. -1-3). pap. 12.95 *(978-1-61913-605-2(8),* AV2 by Weigl) Weigl Pubs., Inc.

—Liquids with Code. 2012. (What Is Matter? Ser.). (ENG., Illus.). 24p. (J). (gr. -1-3). lib. bdg. 27.13 *(978-1-61913-603-8(1),* AV2 by Weigl) Weigl Pubs., Inc.

Rodriguez, Cindy & Siemens, Jared. Liquid. 2016. (J). *(978-1-4896-5746-6(0))* Weigl Pubs., Inc.

—Liquids. 2017. (Illus.). 24p. (J). *(978-1-5105-0907-8(0))* SmartBook Media, Inc.

Royston, Angela. Experiments with a Lemon. 2016. (One-Stop Science Ser.). 32p. (gr. 2-5). 31.35 *(978-1-62588-140-3(1),* Smart Apple Media) Black Rabbit Bks.

—Experiments with Water. 2016. (One-Stop Science Ser.). 32p. (gr. 2-5). 31.35 *(978-1-62588-142-7(8),* Smart Apple Media) Black Rabbit Bks.

Rustad, Martha E. H. Measuring Volume. 2019. (Measuring Masters Ser.). (ENG., Illus.). 24p. (J). (gr. -1-2). lib. bdg. 27.32 *(978-1-9771-0368-0(5),* 139342, Capstone Pr.) Capstone.

Shores, Lori. How to Make a Liquid Rainbow: A 4D Book. rev. ed. 2018. (Hands-On Science Fun Ser.). (ENG., Illus.). 24p. (J). (gr. -1-2). pap. 6.95 *(978-1-5435-0952-6(5),* 137659); lib. bdg. 29.32 *(978-1-5435-0946-5(0),* 137653) Capstone. (Capstone Pr.).

Sjonger, Rebecca. Changing Matter in My Makerspace. 2018. (Matter & Materials in My Makerspace Ser.). 32p. (J). (gr. 2-3). *(978-0-7787-4606-5(2))* Crabtree Publishing Co.

Spilsbury, Louise & Spilsbury, Richard. Solids, Liquids, & Gases. 1 vol. 2013. (Essential Physical Science Ser.). (ENG., Illus.). 48p. (J). (gr. 4-6). pap. 9.95 *(978-1-4329-8160-0(9),* 123400, Heinemann) Capstone.

Sullivan, Erin Ash. Liquids & Gases: Set Of 6. 2010. (Navigators Ser.). (J). pap. 44.00 net. *(978-1-4108-5071-3(4))* Benchmark Education Co.

—Liquids & Gases: Text Pairs. 2008. (Bridges/Navigators Ser.). (J). (gr. 3). 89.00 *(978-1-4108-8366-7(3))* Benchmark Education Co.

Weakland, Mark. The Solid Truth about Matter. Lum, Bernice, illus. 2012. (LOL Physical Science Ser.). (ENG.). 32p. (J). (gr. 3-4). pap. 49.60 *(978-1-4296-9303-5(7),* 18534, Capstone Pr.) Capstone.

Wood, Ira. Water, Ice, & Steam. 2006. (Rosen Real Readers Big Bookstm Ser.). (ENG., Illus.). 12p. (gr. 1-2). 33.50 *(978-1-4042-6215-7(6))* Rosen Publishing Group, Inc., The.

Zoehfeld, Kathleen Weidner. What Is the World Made Of? All about Solids, Liquids, & Gases. Meisel, Paul, illus. 2015. (Let's-Read-And-Find-Out Science 2 Ser.). (ENG.). 32p. (J). (gr. -1-3). pap. 6.99 *(978-0-06-238195-8(4),* HarperCollins) HarperCollins Pubs.

LISTER, JOSEPH, BARON, 1827-1912

Bankston, John. Joseph Lister & the Story of Antiseptics. 2004. (Uncharted, Unexplored, & Unexplained Ser.). (Illus.). 48p. (J). (gr. 4-8). lib. bdg. 29.95 *(978-1-58415-262-0(1))* Mitchell Lane Pubs.

LISZT, FRANZ, 1811-1886

Whiting, Jim. The Life & Times of Franz Liszt. 2004. (Masters of Music Ser.). (Illus.). 48p. (gr. 4-8). lib. bdg. 20.95 *(978-1-58415-280-4(X))* Mitchell Lane Pubs.

LITERACY

Conciatore Senter, Jacqueline. Navigating Filter Bubbles. 1 vol. 2018. (News Literacy Ser.). (ENG.). 64p. (gr. 5-5). pap. 16.28 *(978-1-5026-4131-1(3),* bbb6ee85-d90c-44c5-b6fa-1da3da63d5ac) Cavendish Square Publishing LLC.

Corso, Phil. Conspiracy Theories & Fake News. 1 vol. 2018. (Young Citizen's Guide to News Literacy Ser.). (ENG.). 32p. (gr. 4-5). 27.93 *(978-1-5383-4498-9(X),* c2bfdd9b-0252-4cab-999b-9d7c86d8692a, PowerKids Pr.) Rosen Publishing Group, Inc., The.

Dias, Marley. Marley Dias Gets It Done: & So Can You! 2018. (ENG., Illus.). 208p. (J). (gr. 5-5). pap. 14.99 *(978-1-338-13689-0(5),* Scholastic Pr.) Scholastic, Inc.

Digital & Information Literacy: Set 10, 14 vols. 2016. (Digital & Information Literacy Ser.). (ENG.). 00048p. (J). (gr. 6-6). 234.29 *(978-1-5081-7367-0(2),* 4265cb5a-5271-4729-8eec-7b36cb276c60, Rosen Central) Rosen Publishing Group, Inc., The.

Digital & Information Literacy: Set 11, 12 vols. 2017. (Digital & Information Literacy Ser.). (ENG.). (J). (gr. 6-6). lib. bdg. 200.82 *(978-1-4994-3960-1(1),* 9fe95e8e-29a7-4117-8c53-69a6a53e1586, Rosen Reference) Rosen Publishing Group, Inc., The.

Digital & Information Literacy: Set 8. 2016. (Digital & Information Literacy Ser.). 00048p. (J). (gr. 6-6). pap. 82.25 *(978-1-5081-7381-6(8),* Rosen Central) Rosen Publishing Group, Inc., The.

DK. 1000 Useful Words: Build Vocabulary & Literacy Skills. 2018. (Vocabulary Builders Ser.). (ENG., Illus.). 64p. (J). (gr. -1-2). 14.99 *(978-1-4654-7084-3(0),* DK Children) Dorling Kindersley Publishing, Inc.

Essential Literary Themes, 8 vols. 2015. (Essential Literary Themes Ser.: Vol. 8). (ENG.). 112p. (YA). (gr. 6-12). 330.88 *(978-1-62403-800-6(X),* 17798, Essential Library) ABDO Publishing Co.

Feldman, Jean & Karapetkova, Holly. ABC 123. unabr. ed. 2010. (ENG.). 16p. (gr. -1-k). 12.99 *(978-1-61741-589-0(8))* Rourke Educational Media.

Jennings, Brien J. Fact, Fiction, & Opinions: The Differences Between Ads, Blogs, News Reports, & Other Media. 2018. (All about Media Ser.). (ENG., Illus.). 24p. (J). (gr. 1-3). pap. 7.95 *(978-1-5435-0226-8(1),* 137144, Capstone Pr.) Capstone.

Nations, Susan & Alonso, Mellissa. Primary Literacy Responses: Core Tasks for Readers & Writers. 2014. (Maupin House Ser.). (ENG.). 224p. pap. 29.95 *(978-1-62521-520-8(7))* Capstone.

Paxen Learning Staff. Career Pathways Doc Lit: Document Literacy. 2011. (Illus.). 218p. (YA). pap. 49.95 *(978-1-934350-38-6(9))* Paxen Publishing LLC.

Rice, Dona Herweck. Money Matters: A Classroom Economy: Adding & Subtracting Decimals (Grade 5) rev. ed. 2018. (Mathematics in the Real World Ser.). (ENG., Illus.). 32p. (J). (gr. 4-8). pap. 11.99 *(978-1-4258-5820-9(1))* Teacher Created Materials, Inc.

richmond, keli. Literacy Speaks 2. 2008. (J). pap. 197.00 *(978-0-9799245-5-2(3))* Northern Speech Services.

Skidmore, Sharon, et al. Balanced Literacy Grade 5. 2008. per. 34.00 *(978-1-879097-34-6(6))* Kagan Publishing.

LITERACY—FICTION

Breault, Christie Merriman. Logan West, Printer's Devil. Archambault, Matthew, illus. 2006. 142p. (J). pap. *(978-1-59336-762-6(7))* Mondo Publishing.

Crossley-Holland, Kevin. Crossing to Paradise. 2008. (Illus.). 339p. (J). pap. *(978-0-545-05868-1(6),* Levine, Arthur A. Bks.) Scholastic, Inc.

Dean, Carolee. Take Me There. 2010. (ENG.). 336p. (YA). (gr. 9-18). pap. 8.99 *(978-1-4169-8950-9(1),* Simon Pulse) Simon Pulse.

Green, Tim. The Big Game. (ENG.). (J). (gr. 3-7). 2019. 336p. pap. 9.99 *(978-0-06-248561-8(X))* 2018. 320p. 16.99 *(978-0-06-248504-5(0))* HarperCollins Pubs. (HarperCollins).

Haseley, Dennis. A Story for Bear. LaMarche, Jim, illus. 2018. (ENG.). 32p. (J). (gr. -1-3). pap. 7.99 *(978-1-328-74048-9(X),* 1677013, Clarion Bks.) HarperCollins Pubs.

Hest, Amy. Mr. George Baker. Muth, Jon J., illus. 2007. (ENG.). 32p. (J). (gr. k-3). 7.99 *(978-0-7636-3308-0(9))* Candlewick Pr.

—Mr. George Baker. 2007. lib. bdg. 17.20 *(978-1-4177-9067-8(9))* Turtleback.

Jacobson, Jennifer Richard. This Is MY Room! (No Tigers Allowed) Neonakis, Alexandria, illus. 2019. (ENG.). 48p. (J). (gr. -1-3). 17.99 *(978-1-5344-0211-9(X),* Simon & Schuster Bks. For Young Readers) Simon & Schuster Bks. For Young Readers.

Kinsey-Warnock, Natalie. Lumber Camp Library. Bernardin, James, illus. 2003. (ENG.). 96p. (J). (gr. 2-5). pap. 4.99 *(978-0-06-444292-3(6),* HarperCollins) HarperCollins Pubs.

McKissack, Patricia C. A Picture of Freedom (Dear America) 2011. (Dear America Ser.). (ENG.). 240p. (J). (gr. 3-9). 14.99 *(978-0-545-24253-0(3),* Scholastic Pr.) Scholastic, Inc.

O'Donnell, Liam. Media Meltdown: A Graphic Guide Adventure. 1 vol. Deas, Mike, illus. 2009. (Graphic Guides: 4). (ENG.). 64p. (J). (gr. 4-7). pap. 9.95 *(978-1-55469-065-7(X))* Orca Bk. Pubs. USA.

Paterson, Katherine. My Brigadista Year. 2017. (ENG.). 160p. (J). (gr. 5-9). 15.99 *(978-0-7636-9508-8(4))* Candlewick Pr.

—My Brigadista Year. Lt. ed. 2018. (ENG.). 324p. (J). lib. bdg. 22.99 *(978-1-4328-4930-6(1))* Cengage Gale.

Paul, Ann Whitford. Word Builder. Cyrus, Kurt, illus. 2009. (ENG.). 32p. (J). (gr. k-2). 19.99 *(978-1-4169-3981-8(4),* Simon & Schuster Bks. For Young Readers) Simon & Schuster Bks. For Young Readers.

Reedy, Trent. Words in the Dust. 2013. (ENG.). 272p. (J). (gr. 5-9). pap. 8.99 *(978-0-545-26126-5(0),* Levine, Arthur A. Bks.) Scholastic, Inc.

Schmatz, Pat. Bluefish. 2011. (ENG., Illus.). 240p. (YA). (gr. 7). 15.99 *(978-0-7636-5334-7(9))* Candlewick Pr.

Schurch, Maylan. The Sword of Denis Anwyck. 2009. (J). pap. 10.99 *(978-0-8280-2425-9(1))* Review & Herald Publishing Assn.

Stanley, Diane. Raising Sweetness. 4 bks. Karas, G. Brian, illus. 2004. (J). pap. 39.95 incl. audio compact disk *(978-1-59112-524-2(3))* Live Oak Media.

—Raising Sweetness. 2003. (Illus.). (J). 28.95 incl. audio compact disk *(978-1-59112-516-7(2))*; 25.95 incl. audio *(978-1-59112-266-1(X))* Live Oak Media.

—Raising Sweetness, 4 bks. Stanley, Diane, illus. 2003. (Illus.). (J). pap. 37.95 incl. audio *(978-1-59112-267-8(8))* Live Oak Media.

Stolz, Joelle. The Shadows of Ghadames. 2006. (ENG.). 128p. (J). (gr. 3-7). 5.99 *(978-0-440-41949-5(2),* Yearling) Random Hse. Children's Bks.

LITERARY CHARACTERS

see Characters and Characteristics in Literature

LITERARY CRITICISM

see Criticism; Literature—History and Criticism

LITERARY STYLE

see Style, Literary

LITERATURE—BIOGRAPHY

see Authors

LITERATURE—CRITICISM

see Literature—History and Criticism

LITERATURE—EVALUATION

see Books and Reading; Criticism; Literature—History and Criticism

LITERATURE—HISTORY AND CRITICISM

see also Authors; Criticism

Beers. Elements of Literature. 5th ed. 2003. (Elements of Literature Ser.). (Illus.). 78.60 *(978-0-03-068373-2(4))*; tchr. ed. 134.46 *(978-0-03-068382-4(3))* Holt McDougal.

Bloom, Harold. One Hundred Years of Solitude. annot. ed. 2006. (Bloom's Guides). (ENG.). 80p. (gr. 9-12). 30.00 *(978-0-7910-8578-3(3),* P114309, Facts On File) Infobase Holdings, Inc.

Bloom, Harold, ed. Bloom's Literary Places. (gr. 9-13). (Illus.). pap. 41.85 *(978-0-7910-8391-8(8))*; (Illus.). lib. bdg. 95.85 *(978-0-7910-7835-8(3))*; 2005. 150p. (C). 240.00 *(978-0-7910-8719-0(0))* Infobase Holdings, Inc. (Facts On File).

—Bloom's Modern Critical Views. (Illus.). (gr. 9-13). lib. bdg. 189.75 *(978-0-7910-8487-8(6),* Facts On File) Infobase Holdings, Inc.

—Bloom's Period Studies. (Illus.). (gr. 9-13). lib. bdg. 379.50 *(978-0-7910-7893-8(0),* Facts On File) Infobase Holdings, Inc.

—Modern Critical Views 2003, 10 vols., Set. Incl. E. L. Doctorow. 200p. (gr. 8-18). 2001. 45.00 *(978-0-7910-6451-1(4),* P113483, Facts On File); Set lib. bdg. 227.70 *(978-0-7910-7194-6(4),* 021846S, Facts On File) Infobase Holdings, Inc.

Bosco, Maryellen Lo. Fall from Grace. 1 vol. 2015. (Essential Literary Themes Ser.). (ENG., Illus.). 112p. (YA). (gr. 6-12). 41.36 *(978-1-62403-804-4(2),* 17806, Essential Library) ABDO Publishing Co.

Factor, Judith, ed. Pearl Workbook for 6th Grade: Mosdos Press Literature Series. 2003. (gr. 6-18). pap. 16.00 *(978-0-9671009-8-2(4))* Mosdos Pr.

Faulkner, Nicholas, ed. 101 Authors. 1 vol. 2016. (People You Should Know Ser.). (ENG.). 184p. (J). (gr. 8-8). lib. bdg. 38.84 *(978-1-68048-506-6(7),* 2d2cc59e-4816-4146-806b-a75c987c2d67) Rosen Publishing Group, Inc., The.

Fernández de Moratín, Leandro. El Sí de la Ninas. annot. ed. (SPA., Illus.). 176p. (J). 15.95 *(978-84-207-2634-2(6),* ANY008) Grupo Anaya, S.A. ESP. Dist: Continental Bk. Co., Inc.

Fuentes, Carlos. The Death of Artemio Cruz. Bloom, Harold, ed. 2006. (Modern Critical Interpretations Ser.). (ENG.). 150p. (gr. 9). lib. bdg. 45.00 *(978-0-7910-8587-5(2),* P114315, Facts On File) Infobase Holdings, Inc.

Guillain, Charlotte. Looking at Literature: What Are Novels, Graphic Novels, Short Stories, & Poems? 2015. (Connect with Text Ser.). (ENG., Illus.). 112p. (J). (gr. 2-4). pap., pap., pap. 11.95 *(978-1-4109-6831-9(6),* 128012, Raintree) Capstone.

Hacht, Anne Marie. Literary Themes for Students, 2 vols., Vol. 12. 2006. (Literary Themes for Students Ser.). (ENG., Illus.). 1200p. 285.00 *(978-1-4144-0271-0(6))* Cengage Gale.

Harper, Amelia. Literary Lessons from The Lord of the Rings. Howe, John, illus. 2004. 622p. (YA). (gr. 7-12). stu. ed., spiral bd. 50.00 *(978-0-9754934-1-0(8),* Literary Lessons) HomeScholar Bks.

Herron, Paul, ed. & contrib. by. A Cafe in Space: The Anais Nin Literary Journal, 8 vols., Vol. 2. Herron, Paul, contrib. by. 2004. (Illus.). 160p. pap. 15.00 *(978-0-9652364-9-2(8))* Sky Blue Pr.

Holt, Rinehart and Winston Staff. Elements of Literature: Family Involvement Activities. 5th ed. 2003. (SPA & ENG., Illus.). pap. 38.80 *(978-0-03-073853-1(9))* Holt McDougal.

—Elements of Literature: Holt Adapted Reader Answer Key. 5th ed. 2003. pap. 23.20 *(978-0-03-035911-8(2))*; pap. 23.20 *(978-0-03-035909-5(0))* Holt McDougal.

—Elements of Literature: Holt Reader. 5th ed. 2003. (Elements of Literature Ser.). (ENG., Illus.). 424p. (gr. 9-9). pap. 17.15 *(978-0-03-068393-0(9))* Houghton Mifflin Harcourt Publishing Co.

—Elements of Literature: Holt Reader: Interactive Worktext - Georgia Edition. 3rd ed. 2003. (gr. 6). pap. 11.00 *(978-0-03-070197-9(X))*; (gr. 7). pap. 11.00 *(978-0-03-070198-6(8))*; (gr. 8). pap. 11.00 *(978-0-03-070199-3(6))* Holt McDougal.

—Elements of Literature: Holt Reader: Interactive Worktext - Mississippi Edition. 3rd ed. 2003. (YA). (gr. 10). pap. 11.00 *(978-0-03-071196-1(7))*; (J). (gr. 6). pap. 11.00 *(978-0-03-071191-6(6))*; (gr. 7). pap. 11.00 *(978-0-03-071192-3(4))*; (gr. 8). pap. 11.00 *(978-0-03-071193-0(2))* Holt McDougal.

—Elements of Literature: Mississippi Edition. 3rd annot. ed. 2003. (gr. 6). tchr. ed. 121.60 *(978-0-03-071797-0(3))* Holt McDougal.

—Elements of Literature 2005 - The Holt Reader. 5th ed. 2003. (Elements of Literature Ser.). (ENG., Illus.). 400p. (gr. 11-11). pap. 17.15 *(978-0-03-068396-1(3))* Houghton Mifflin Harcourt Publishing Co.

—Holt Reader. 5th ed. 2003. (Elements of Literature Ser.). (ENG., Illus.). 392p. (gr. 12-12). pap. 17.15 *(978-0-03-068397-8(1))*; 384p. (gr. 7-7). pap. 17.15 *(978-0-03-068391-6(2))* Houghton Mifflin Harcourt Publishing Co.

—The Holt Reader. 5th ed. 2003. (Elements of Literature Ser.). (ENG., Illus.). 368p. (gr. 8-8). pap. 17.15 *(978-0-03-068392-3(0))* Houghton Mifflin Harcourt Publishing Co.

—Reader Fourth Course. 4th ed. 2003. (Elements of Literature Ser.). (ENG., Illus.). 408p. (gr. 10-10). pap. 17.15 *(978-0-03-068394-7(7))* Houghton Mifflin Harcourt Publishing Co.

Kafer, Kathy & Benchmark Education Co. Staff. Opinions about Difficult Times Portrayed in Literature. 2014. (Text Connections Ser.). (J). (gr. 5). *(978-1-4900-1388-6(1))* Benchmark Education Co.

Lit Crit Guides: Set 3, 12 vols. 2016. (Lit Crit Guides). (ENG.). 176p. (J). (gr. 6-6). lib. bdg. 249.60 *(978-0-7660-8397-4(7),* 3d93396b-35af-45f0-8f74-50b414f3665e) Enslow Publishing, LLC.

Lit Crit Guides: Set 4, 12 vols. 2017. (Lit Crit Guides). (ENG.). 160p. (gr. 8-8). lib. bdg. 249.60 *(978-0-7660-8572-5(4),* c58b09c5-93ef-4424-a193-1c803eeb994b) Enslow Publishing, LLC.

Magill, Frank N., ed. Masterplots II: Juvenile & Young Adult Literature Series Supplement, 3 vols., 3 vols. 2009. (Masterplots Ser.). (ENG.). 1536p. (C). (gr. 8-18). lib. bdg., suppl. ed. 289.00 *(978-0-89356-916-7(X),* P165081) Salem Pr., Inc.

Mason, Antony. Literature. 2004. (Culture Encyclopedia Ser.). (Illus.). 40p. (YA). (gr. 5-18). lib. bdg. 19.95 *(978-1-59084-478-6(5))* Mason Crest.

Mirande, Jaqueline. Arturo y los Caballeros de la Tabla Redonda. 2003. (Advanced Reading Ser.). (SPA., Illus.). 134p. (J). 11.95 *(978-84-239-7072-8(8))* Espasa Calpe, S.A. ESP. Dist: Planeta Publishing Corp.

Moore Niver, Heather. Nonfiction. 1 vol. 2018. (Let's Learn about Literature Ser.). (ENG.). 24p. (gr. 1-2). 24.27 *(978-0-7660-9602-8(5),* a32bce08-a107-46ef-829f-10197eab355c) Enslow Publishing, LLC.

Nagle, Jeanne, ed. Great Authors of Classic Literature. 1 vol. 2013. (Essential Authors for Children & Teens Ser.). (ENG.). 200p. (YA). (gr. 8-8). 48.59 *(978-1-62275-084-9(5),* 78331980-9a92-4b31-94b8-fdc5da6b2d85) Rosen Publishing Group, Inc., The.

—Great Authors of Nonfiction. 1 vol. 2013. (Essential Authors for Children & Teens Ser.). (ENG.). 184p. (YA). (gr. 8-8). 48.59 *(978-1-62275-092-4(6),* 21c1c6df-8f9e-4b40-91ed-93af8397ca16) Rosen Publishing Group, Inc., The.

—Great Poets & Playwrights. 1 vol. 2013. (Essential Authors for Children & Teens Ser.). (ENG.). 200p. (YA). (gr. 8-8). 48.59 *(978-1-62275-088-7(8),* 88a5a7c5-e144-4575-bf85-bcd3ed08f773) Rosen Publishing Group, Inc., The.

Nardo, Don. Art & Literature in Ancient Mesopotamia. 1 vol. 2008. (Lucent Library of Historical Eras Ser.). (ENG., Illus.). 104p. (gr. 7-10). lib. bdg. 39.08 *(978-1-4205-0099-8(6),* 79705d54-1d7a-4312-be12-369e9510187f, Lucent Pr.) Greenhaven Publishing LLC.

Novel Units. Anne of Green Gables Novel Units Teacher Guide. 2019. (Avonlea Ser.: No. 1). (ENG.). (YA). (gr. 5-8). pap. 12.99 *(978-1-56137-341-3(9),* Novel Units, Inc.) Classroom Library Co.

—Banner in the Sky Novel Units Teacher Guide. 2019. (ENG.). (J). pap. 12.99 *(978-1-56137-481-6(4),* Novel Units, Inc.) Classroom Library Co.

—The Bean Trees Novel Units Student Packet. 2019. (ENG.). (YA). pap. 13.99 *(978-1-56137-891-3(7),* NU8917SP, Novel Units, Inc.) Classroom Library Co.

—Bunnicula Novel Units Student Packet. 2019. (ENG.). (J). pap., stu. ed. 13.99 *(978-1-56137-712-1(0),* Novel Units, Inc.) Classroom Library Co.

—Call It Courage Novel Units Student Packet. 2019. (ENG.). (YA). pap. 13.99 *(978-1-56137-492-2(X),* Novel Units, Inc.) Classroom Library Co.

—Call It Courage Novel Units Teacher Guide. 2019. (ENG.). (YA). pap. 12.99 *(978-1-56137-245-4(5),* Novel Units, Inc.) Classroom Library Co.

—Charlotte's Web Novel Units Student Packet. 2019. (ENG.). (J). pap. 13.99 *(978-1-56137-630-8(2),* NU6302SP, Novel Units, Inc.) Classroom Library Co.

—Frankenstein Novel Units Student Packet. 2019. (ENG.). (YA). pap. 13.99 *(978-1-56137-751-0(1),* Novel Units, Inc.) Classroom Library Co.

—Freckle Juice Novel Units Student Packet. 2019. (ENG.). (J). pap. 13.99 *(978-1-56137-822-7(4),* Novel Units, Inc.) Classroom Library Co.

—Freckle Juice Novel Units Teacher Guide. 2019. (ENG.). (J). pap. 12.99 *(978-1-56137-008-5(8),* Novel Units, Inc.) Classroom Library Co.

—Great Expectations Novel Units Student Packet. 2019. (ENG.). (YA). pap. 13.99 *(978-1-56137-515-8(2),* NU5152SP, Novel Units, Inc.) Classroom Library Co.

—Hiroshima Novel Units Teacher Guide. 2019. (ENG.). (YA). (gr. 7-12). pap. 12.99 *(978-1-56137-136-5(X),* BK8279, Novel Units, Inc.) Classroom Library Co.

—Lord of the Flies Novel Units Student Packet. 2019. (ENG.). (YA). pap. 13.99 *(978-1-56137-384-0(2),* NU3842SP, Novel Units, Inc.) Classroom Library Co.

—Night Novel Units Student Packet. 2019. (ENG.). (YA). pap. 13.99 *(978-1-56137-805-0(4),* NU8054SP, Novel Units, Inc.) Classroom Library Co.

—The Old Man & the Sea Novel Units Student Packet. 2019. (ENG.). (YA). pap. 13.99 *(978-1-56137-404-5(0),* NU4040SP, Novel Units, Inc.) Classroom Library Co.

—Skinnybones Novel Units Student Packet. 2019. (ENG.). (J). pap. 13.99 *(978-1-58130-605-7(9),* Novel Units, Inc.) Classroom Library Co.

—Skinnybones Novel Units Teacher Guide. 2019. (ENG.). (J). pap. 12.99 *(978-1-58130-604-0(0),* Novel Units, Inc.) Classroom Library Co.

—Sylvester & the Magic Pebble Novel Units Teacher Guide. 2019. (ENG.). (J). pap. 12.99 *(978-1-56137-019-1(3),* Novel Units, Inc.) Classroom Library Co.

—A Tale of Two Cities Novel Units Student Packet. 2019. (ENG.). (YA). pap. 13.99 *(978-1-56137-433-5(4),* NU4334SP, Novel Units, Inc.) Classroom Library Co.

—The Taming of the Shrew Novel Units Teacher Guide. 2019. (ENG.). (YA). pap. 12.99 *(978-1-56137-768-8(6),* Novel Units, Inc.) Classroom Library Co.

—Things Fall Apart Novel Units Student Packet. 2019. (ENG.). (YA). pap. 13.99 *(978-1-56137-813-5(5),* NU8135SP, Novel Units, Inc.) Classroom Library Co.

Peacock, Scott. Beacham's Guide to Literature for Young Adults, Vol. 16. 2003. (Beacham's Literature for Young Adults Ser.). (ENG.). 608p. 183.00 *(978-0-7876-5836-6(7),* UXL) Cengage Gale.

Persky, Stan. The Short Version: An ABC Book. 2005. (ENG., Illus.). 352p. per. 21.00 *(978-1-55420-016-0(4))* New Star Bks., Ltd. CAN. Dist: SPD-Small Pr. Distribution.

Remarque, Erich Maria. All Quiet on the Western Front. Bloom, Harold, ed. annot. ed. 2008. (Bloom's Guides). 128p. (C). (gr. 9-18). 30.00 *(978-0-7910-9830-1(3),* Facts On File) Infobase Holdings, Inc.

Responding to Literature. 912p. (YA). (gr. 8). 52.95 *(978-0-8219-1364-2(6),* 35456) EMC/Paradigm Publishing.

Schoenberg, Thomas J. & Trudeau, Lawrence J., eds. Twentieth-Century Literary Criticism, Volume 199, Vol. 199. annot. ed. 2008. (Twentieth-Century Literary Criticism Ser.: 199). (ENG.). 544p. 483.00 *(978-0-7876-9974-1(8))* Cengage Gale.

Smith, Kiley. Young Adult Literature: Dystopian Worlds (Grade 6) 2nd rev. ed. 2016. (TIME(r): Informational Text Ser.). (ENG., Illus.). 48p. (J). (gr. 5-8). pap. 13.99 *(978-1-4938-3599-7(8))* Teacher Created Materials, Inc.

Spartz, Emerson & Schoen, Ben. Mugglenet.com's Harry Potter Should Have Died: Controversial Views from the #1 Fan Site. 2009. (ENG.). 180p. (J). (gr. 3). pap. 14.95 *(978-1-56975-711-6(9))* Ulysses Pr.

Stobaugh, James. World Literature Student. 2005. (Broadman & Holman Literature Ser.). 272p. stu. ed. 24.99 *(978-0-8054-5892-3(1))* B&H Publishing Group.

Story Studio Vol. 2: Transmitting Stories Across the Curriculum. 2005. spiral bd. 39.95 *(978-1-56820-173-3(7))* Story Time Stories That Rhyme.

Williams, Heidi, ed. Plagiarism, 1 vol. 2008. (Issues That Concern You Ser.). (ENG., Illus.). 104p. (gr. 7-10). 38.58 *(978-0-7377-4072-1(8),* 8fc21df7-ba2a-4ad4-807a-e73def26afd4, Greenhaven Publishing) Greenhaven Publishing LLC.

Wills, Adele. Texts Through History. 2004. (Routledge a Level English Guides). (ENG., Illus.). 94p. (C). 105.00 *(978-0-415-31909-6(9),* RU26769); per. 29.95 *(978-0-415-31910-2(2),* RU26770) Routledge.

Zebrowski, Debra. World Literature Student Activity Book. Matthews, Douglas L., ed. 2003. (Illus.). stu. ed., per., wbk. ed. *(978-1-931680-53-0(1),* Expert Systems for Teachers) Teaching Point, Inc.

LITERATURE—PHILOSOPHY

Williams, Heidi, ed. Plagiarism, 1 vol. 2008. (Issues That Concern You Ser.). (ENG., Illus.). 104p. (gr. 7-10). 38.58 *(978-0-7377-4072-1(8),* 8fc21df7-ba2a-4ad4-807a-e73def26afd4, Greenhaven Publishing) Greenhaven Publishing LLC.

LITERATURE—STORIES, PLOTS, ETC.

Beck, Isabel L., et al. Julian's Glorious Summer. 2003. (Trophies Ser.). (gr. 3-18). 50.40 *(978-0-15-319277-7(1))* Harcourt Schl. Pubs.

Bodden, Valerie. Classic Literature. 2016. (Essential Literary Genres Ser.). (ENG., Illus.). 112p. (J). (gr. 6-12). lib. bdg. 41.36 *(978-1-68078-377-3(7),* 23519, Essential Library) ABDO Publishing Co.

Carlson-Berne, Emma. What Are Graphic Novels? 2014. (Name That Text Type! Ser.). (ENG., Illus.). 32p. (J). (gr. 2-4). lib. bdg. 26.65 *(978-1-4677-3666-4(X),* b6df2171-adb6-43df-b92f-85d9819fa46a, Lerner Pubns.) Lerner Publishing Group.

Holt, Rinehart and Winston Staff. Elemental Literature - Elements of Literature. 5th ed. 2003. (Elements of Literature Ser.). (ENG., Illus.). 160p. (gr. 6-6). pap. 17.15 *(978-0-03-035709-1(8))* Houghton Mifflin Harcourt Publishing Co.

—Elements of Literature: Adapted Reader. 5th ed. 2003. (Elements of Literature Ser.). (ENG., Illus.). 168p. (gr. 10-10). pap. 17.15 *(978-0-03-035458-8(7))* Houghton Mifflin Harcourt Publishing Co.

—Elements of Literature: Holt Adapted Reader. 5th ed. 2004. (Elements of Literature Ser.). (ENG.). 184p. (gr. 7-7). pap. 17.15 *(978-0-03-035711-4(X))* Houghton Mifflin Harcourt Publishing Co.

—Elements of Literature - Adapted Reader. 5th ed. 2003. (Elements of Literature Ser.). (ENG., Illus.). 184p. (gr. 12-12). pap. 17.15 *(978-0-03-035461-8(7))* Houghton Mifflin Harcourt Publishing Co.

—Elements of Literature - Holt Adapted Reader. 5th ed. 2003. (Elements of Literature Ser.). (ENG., Illus.). 208p. (gr. 11-11). pap. 17.15 *(978-0-03-035459-5(5))*; (gr. 9-9). pap. 17.15 *(978-0-03-035454-0(4))* Houghton Mifflin Harcourt Publishing Co.

—Holt Adapted Reader. (Elements of Literature Ser.). (ENG.). 3rd ed. 2003. 216p. (gr. 9-9). pap. 15.60 *(978-0-03-067866-0(8))* 3rd ed. 2003. 224p. (gr. 12-12). pap. 15.60 *(978-0-03-067869-1(2))* 5th ed. 2004. (Illus.). 224p. (gr. 8-8). pap. 17.15 *(978-0-03-035712-1(8))* Houghton Mifflin Harcourt Publishing Co.

—Holt Adapted Reader 2003 - Elemental Literature. 3rd ed. 2003. (Elements of Literature Ser.). (ENG.). 176p. (gr. 10-10). pap. 15.60 *(978-0-03-067867-7(6))* Houghton Mifflin Harcourt Publishing Co.

Jaffe, Charlotte & Roberts, Barbara. A Day No Pigs Would Die: L-I-T Guide. Date not set. (J). (gr. 4-10). pap. 8.95 *(978-1-56644-005-9(X),* 005-XAP) Educational Impressions.

Loewen, Nancy. No Kidding, Mermaids Are a Joke! The Story of the Little Mermaid As Told by the Prince. Tayal, Amit, illus. 2013. (Other Side of the Story Ser.). (ENG.). 24p. (J). (gr. -1-3). 27.99 *(978-1-4048-8303-1(7),* 122386); 9.95 *(978-1-4795-1947-7(2),* 123648) Capstone. (Picture Window Bks.).

Novel Units. Killing Mr. Griffin Novel Units Student Packet. 2019. (ENG.). (YA). pap. 13.99 *(978-1-56137-343-7(5),* NU3435SP, Novel Units, Inc.) Classroom Library Co.

LITERATURE AS A PROFESSION

see Authors; Authorship; Journalism; Journalists

LITHUANIA

Bultje, Jan Willem. Lithuania. Hoving, Wilma, tr. 2006. (Looking at Europe Ser.). 48p. (YA). (gr. 5-8). 22.95 *(978-1-881508-43-4(9))* Oliver Pr., Inc.

Docalavich, Heather & Indovino, Shaina Carmel. Lithuania. 2012. (J). *(978-1-4222-2250-8(0))*; pap. *(978-1-4222-2281-2(0))* Mason Crest.

Kagda, Sakina. Lithuania, 1 vol. 2017. (Cultures of the World (Third Edition)(r) Ser.). (ENG.). 144p. (gr. 5-5). 48.79 *(978-1-5026-2739-1(6),* beac36ab-33f6-473e-91f0-3e69c3f8caa8) Cavendish Square Publishing LLC.

Kagda, Sakina & Latif, Zawiah Abdul. Lithuania, 1 vol. 2nd rev. ed. 2008. (Cultures of the World (Second Edition)(r) Ser.). (ENG.). 144p. (gr. 5-5). lib. bdg. 49.79 *(978-0-7614-2087-3(8),* ec57c5ad-1d37-488f-bd72-5635fecc4be3) Cavendish Square Publishing LLC.

LITTERING

see Refuse and Refuse Disposal

LITTLE, MALCOLM, 1925-1965

see X, Malcolm, 1925-1965

LITTLE, STUART (FICTITIOUS CHARACTER)—FICTION

Rubin, Bruce Joel & Michaels, Julie. Stuart Little 2 Vol. 2: El Libro de la Película. 2003. (SPA., Illus.). 60p. (J). (gr. 3-5). 14.95 *(978-84-204-6503-6(8))* Santillana USA Publishing Co., Inc.

White, E. B. Le Avventure di Stuart Little. Tr. of Stuart Little. (ITA.). pap. 17.95 *(978-88-451-2736-6(2))* Fabbri Editori - RCS Libri ITA. Dist: Distribooks, Inc.

—Stuart Little. Date not set. 141p. 18.95 *(978-0-8488-2602-4(7))* Amereon Ltd.

—Stuart Little. 2008. (J). 34.99 *(978-0-7393-7101-5(0))* Findaway World, LLC.

—Stuart Little. Williams, Garth, illus. 60th anniv. ed. 2005. (ENG.). 144p. (J). (gr. 3-7). 18.99 *(978-0-06-026395-9(4),* HarperCollins) HarperCollins Pubs.

—Stuart Little. 131p. (J). pap. 5.95 *(978-0-8072-8333-2(9))*; 2004. (gr. 3-7). pap. 29.00 incl. audio *(978-0-8072-8332-5(0),* YA165SP) Random Hse. Audio Publishing Group. (Listening Library).

—Stuart Little 75th Anniversary Edition. Williams, Garth, illus. 60th anniv. ed. 2020. (ENG.). 144p. (J). (gr. 3-7). pap. 9.99 *(978-0-06-440056-5(5),* HarperCollins) HarperCollins Pubs.

—Stuart Little: Full Color Edition. Williams, Garth & Wells, Rosemary, illus. 60th anniv. ed. 2005. (ENG.). 144p. (J). (gr. 3-7). pap. 9.99 *(978-0-06-441092-2(7),* HarperCollins) HarperCollins Pubs.

White, E. B. & White, E. Stuart Little. 2005. (J). (gr. 3-6). lib. bdg. 17.20 *(978-0-8085-3806-6(3))* Turtleback.

LITTLE BEAR (FICTITIOUS CHARACTER: MINARIK)—FICTION

Little Bear. 2003. (Goodnight Mr. Moon Ser.). (Illus.). (J). bds. 2.98 *(978-0-7525-4740-4(2))* Parragon, Inc.

Minarik, Else Holmelund. Los Amigos de Osito. Benavides, Rosa, tr. Sendak, Maurice, illus. 2nd ed. (Infantil Alfaguara Ser.: 32).Tr. of Little Bear's Friends. (SPA.). 64p. (J). 7.95 *(978-84-204-3049-2(8))* Santillana USA Publishing Co., Inc.

—Un Beso para Osito. Benavides, Rosa, tr. Sendak, Maurice, illus. 2003. (Infantil Alfaguara Ser.: 31).Tr. of Kiss for Little Bear. (SPA.). 36p. (J). (gr. k-3). 11.95 *(978-84-204-3050-8(1),* AF1633) Ediciones Alfaguara ESP. Dist: Lectorum Pubns., Inc., Santillana USA Publishing Co., Inc.

—Un Beso para Osito. Sendak, Maurice, tr. Sendak, Maurice, illus.Tr. of Kiss for Little Bear. (SPA.). 34p. (J). (gr. k-3). pap. 8.95 *(978-84-204-4827-5(3))* Santillana USA Publishing Co., Inc.

—Little Bear. Sendak, Maurice, illus. 2003. (I Can Read Level 1 Ser.). (ENG.). 64p. (J). (gr. k-3). pap. 4.95 *(978-0-06-444004-2(4),* HarperCollins) HarperCollins Pubs.

—Little Bear. 2003. (Little Bear: I Can Read! Ser.). (J). (gr. k-3). lib. bdg. 13.55 *(978-0-8085-2618-6(9))* Turtleback.

—Little Bear's Visit. Sendak, Maurice, illus. (J). pap. 12.95 incl. audio Weston Woods Studios, Inc.

—Osito. Aguilar, Joaquina, tr. Sendak, Maurice, illus. 2003. (Infantil Alfaguara Ser.: 25).Tr. of Little Bear. (SPA.). 60p. (J). (gr. k-3). pap. 8.95 *(978-84-204-3044-7(7),* AF1346) Santillana USA Publishing Co., Inc.

—Papa Oso Vuelve a Casa. Benavides, Rosa, tr. Sendak, Maurice, illus. 2nd ed. 2003. (Infantil Alfaguara Ser.: 29).Tr. of Father Bear Comes Home. (SPA.). 63p. (J). (gr. -1-3). pap. *(978-84-204-3048-5(X),* AF1359) Ediciones Alfaguara ESP. Dist: Santillana USA Publishing Co., Inc.

—La Visita de Osito. Puncel, María, tr. Sendak, Maurice, illus. 2006. (Osito / Little Bear Ser.).Tr. of Little Bear's Visit. (SPA.). 64p. (gr. k-3). pap. 8.95 *(978-968-19-0623-8(3),* AF1060) Santillana USA Publishing Co., Inc.

Weston Woods Staff, creator. A Kiss for Little Bear. 2011. 29.95 *(978-0-439-73481-3(9))*; 18.95 *(978-0-439-72735-8(9))*; 38.75 *(978-0-439-72739-6(1))* Weston Woods Studios, Inc.

LITTLE BEAR (FICTITIOUS CHARACTER: WADDELL)—FICTION

Waddell, Martin. Can't You Sleep, Little Bear? (CHI & ENG., Illus.). 32p. (J). *(978-1-85430-315-8(5),* 93445) Little Tiger Pr. Group.

—Let's Go Home, Little Bear. 2004. (Illus.). (J). (gr. k-3). spiral bd. *(978-0-616-01804-0(5))*; spiral bd. *(978-0-616-01805-7(3))* Canadian National Institute for the Blind/Institut National Canadien pour les Aveugles.

—You & Me, Little Bear. 2004. (Illus.). (J). (gr. -1-2). spiral bd. *(978-0-616-01803-3(7))*; spiral bd. *(978-0-616-01802-6(9))* Canadian National Institute for the Blind/Institut National Canadien pour les Aveugles.

LITTLE BIGHORN, BATTLE OF THE, MONT., 1876

Abnett, Dan. Sitting Bull & the Battle of the Little Bighorn. (Jr. Graphic Biographies Ser.). (ENG.). 24p. (gr. 2-3). 2009. (J). 47.90 *(978-1-61513-822-7(6),* PowerKids Pr.) 2006. (Illus.). (J). lib. bdg. 28.93 *(978-1-4042-3394-2(6),* f0e34536-71fb-4966-826f-56f539643bb7) 2006. (Illus.). pap. 10.60 *(978-1-4042-2147-5(6),* a9929d73-f261-48e9-ae0a-ace8c3e521bc, PowerKids Pr.) Rosen Publishing Group, Inc., The.

—Toro Sentado y la Batalla de Little Bighorn, 1 vol. 2009. (Historietas Juveniles: Biografías (Jr. Graphic Biographies) Ser.). (SPA., Illus.). 24p. (gr. 2-3). (J). 28.93 *(978-1-4358-8562-2(7),* 2879172c-3b85-4fcd-aa7a-41f6781a356c); pap. 10.60 *(978-1-4358-3318-0(X),* 643c8a66-07a0-409b-938a-c5a86c6e7064) Rosen Publishing Group, Inc., The.

Aller, Susan Bivin. Sitting Bull. 2004. (History Maker Bios Ser.). (J). pap. 6.95 *(978-0-8225-2072-6(9))* Lerner Publishing Group.

—Sitting Bull. Parlin, Tim, tr. Parlin, Tim, illus. 2004. (History Maker Bios Ser.). 47p. (J). 26.60 *(978-0-8225-0700-0(5),* Carolrhoda Bks.) Lerner Publishing Group.

Anderson, Paul C. George Armstrong Custer: The Indian Wars & the Battle of the Little Bighorn. 2009. (Library of American Lives & Times Ser.). 112p. (gr. 5-5). 69.20 *(978-1-60853-483-8(9))* Rosen Publishing Group, Inc., The.

Brindell Fradin, Dennis. Custer's Last Stand, 1 vol. 2007. (Turning Points in U. S. History Ser.). (ENG., Illus.). 48p. (gr. 4-4). lib. bdg. 34.07 *(978-0-7614-2124-5(6),* 2df4829d-0a02-4a0d-aafb-98abc97067cb) Cavendish Square Publishing LLC.

Collard, Sneed B., III. Sitting Bull, 1 vol. 2010. (American Heroes Ser.). (ENG.). 48p. (gr. 3-3). 32.64 *(978-0-7614-4059-8(3),* d331b804-8748-40a1-a55d-cc9e79408f93) Cavendish Square Publishing LLC.

DeFord, Diane. Chief Sitting Bull. 2009. pap. 13.25 *(978-1-60559-070-7(3))* Hameray Publishing Group, Inc.

Dolan, Edward F., Jr. & Dolan, Edward F. The Battle of Little Bighorn, 1 vol. 2003. (Kaleidoscope: American History Ser.). (ENG., Illus.). 48p. (gr. 4-4). 32.64 *(978-0-7614-1457-5(6),* 416428f1-22f4-4ef5-a4be-32ded00b4de7) Cavendish Square Publishing LLC.

Duffield, Katy. The Battle of Little Bighorn: Legendary Battle of the Great Sioux War. 2017. (Major Battles in US History Ser.). (ENG., Illus.). 32p. (J). (gr. 3-5). pap. 9.95 *(978-1-63517-076-4(1),* 1635170761, Focus Readers) North Star Editions.

Dunn, Joeming W. Custer's Last Stand, 1 vol. Smith, Tim, illus. 2008. (Graphic History Ser.). (ENG.). 32p. (J). (gr. 3-8). 32.79 *(978-1-60270-181-6(4),* 9054, Graphic Planet - Fiction) Magic Wagon.

Evento, Susan. Sitting Bull. 2005. (Rookie Biographies Ser.). (ENG., Illus.). 32p. (J). (gr. 1-2). pap. 4.95 *(978-0-516-25829-4(X),* Children's Pr.) Scholastic Library Publishing.

Goble, Paul. Custer's Last Battle: Red Hawk's Account of the Battle of the Little Bighorn. 2013. (Illus.). 44p. (J). (gr. 2-4). 16.95 *(978-1-937786-11-3(0),* Wisdom Tales) World Wisdom, Inc.

Griffin, Brett. Sitting Bull: Native American Leader, 1 vol. 2017. (History Makers Ser.). (ENG.). 144p. (J). (gr. 9-9). 47.36 *(978-1-5026-3293-7(4),* f98882c3-7827-4232-82fd-1edf10bf0c2a) Cavendish Square Publishing LLC.

Higgins, Nadia. Last Stand: Causes & Effects of the Battle of the Little Bighorn. 2015. (Cause & Effect: American Indian History Ser.). (ENG., Illus.). 32p. (J). (gr. 3-6). pap. 7.95 *(978-1-4914-2208-3(4),* 127719, Capstone Pr.) Capstone.

January, Brendan. Little Bighorn: June 25 1876, 1 vol. 2006. (American Battlefields Ser.). (ENG., Illus.). 32p. (J). (gr. 4-4). 26.93 *(978-1-59270-028-8(4),* f744c89c-3076-40a9-a5ee-0637a6cce4a3, Cavendish Square) Cavendish Square Publishing LLC.

Jeffrey, Gary. The Battle of the Little Bighorn, 1 vol. Spender, Nick, illus. 2012. (Graphic History of the American West Ser.). (ENG.). 24p. (J). (gr. 3-3). pap. 9.15 *(978-1-4339-6733-7(2),* 6c0e527d-6499-4952-8385-0e1c8aa19d0b, Gareth Stevens Learning Library); lib. bdg. 26.60 *(978-1-4339-6731-3(6),* 0040bc55-5cf5-469d-a2a4-3a30abc6de6b) Stevens, Gareth Publishing LLLP.

—Sitting Bull: The Life of a Lakota Chief. 2009. (Graphic Nonfiction Biographies Ser.). (ENG.). 48p. (YA). (gr. 4-5). 58.50 *(978-1-61513-027-6(6),* Rosen Reference) Rosen Publishing Group, Inc., The.

Jeffrey, Gary & Petty, Kate. Sitting Bull: The Life of a Lakota Sioux Chief, 1 vol. 2005. (Graphic Nonfiction Biographies Ser.). (ENG., Illus.). 48p. (YA). (gr. 4-6). lib. bdg. 37.13 *(978-1-4042-0247-4(1),* 9175d2ac-487b-4e78-831d-01c6d6e70097) Rosen Publishing Group, Inc., The.

Josephson, Judith P. Who Was Sitting Bull? And Other Questions about the Battle of Little Bighorn. 2011. (Six Questions of American History Ser.). (ENG.). 48p. (gr. 4-6). pap. 56.72 *(978-0-7613-7645-3(3))* Lerner Publishing Group.

King, Zelda & Levy, Janey. The Battle of the Little Bighorn: Both Sides of the Story, 1 vol. 2008. (Real Life Readers Ser.). (ENG.). 32p. (gr. 5-6). pap. 10.00 *(978-1-4358-0197-4(0),* a35740e8-dc5b-4be1-848f-ce41232e0457, Rosen Classroom) Rosen Publishing Group, Inc., The.

Link, Theodore. George Armstrong Custer: General de la caballería Estadounidense, 1 vol. 2003. (Grandes Personajes en la Historia de Los Estados Unidos (Famous People in American History) Ser.). (SPA.). 32p. (gr. 3-4). pap. 10.00 *(978-0-8239-4228-2(7),* a3d5578c-4708-4b0e-aa8f-8828084500a9, Rosen Classroom) Rosen Publishing Group, Inc., The.

—George Armstrong Custer: General de la caballería estadounidense (George Armstrong Custer: General of the U. S. Cavalry) 2009. (Grandes personajes en la historia de los Estados Unidos (Famous People in American History) Ser.). (SPA.). 32p. (gr. 2-3). 47.90 *(978-1-61512-799-3(2),* Editorial Buenas Letras) Rosen Publishing Group, Inc., The.

—George Armstrong Custer: General of the U. S. Cavalry. (Primary Sources of Famous People in American History Ser.).Tr. of George Armstrong Custer: General de la Caballería Estadounidense. 32p. (gr. 2-3). 2009. 47.90 *(978-1-60851-680-3(6))* 2003. (ENG & SPA., Illus.). lib. bdg. 29.13 *(978-0-8239-4158-2(2),* e97ac072-83b4-46f2-a0fc-b11714411c70, Editorial Buenas Letras) Rosen Publishing Group, Inc., The.

—George Armstrong Custer: General of the U. S. Cavalry / General de la caballería Estadounidense. 2009. (Famous People in American History/Grandes personajes en la historia de los Estados Unidos Ser.). (ENG & SPA.). 32p. (gr. 2-3). 47.90 *(978-1-61512-545-6(0),* Editorial Buenas Letras) Rosen Publishing Group, Inc., The.

Mapua, Jeff. Sitting Bull, 1 vol., 1. 2015. (Britannica Beginner Bios Ser.). (ENG., Illus.). 32p. (J). (gr. 2-3). pap. 13.90 *(978-1-5081-0062-1(4),* 126be1f2-b54a-447b-9f5f-6fd2ef0dbddc, Britannica Educational Publishing) Rosen Publishing Group, Inc., The.

Rice, Earle. The Life & Times of the Brothers Custer: Galloping to Glory. 2008. (Profiles in American History Ser.). (Illus.). 48p. (J). (gr. 4-8). lib. bdg. 29.95 *(978-1-58415-665-9(1))* Mitchell Lane Pubs.

Roxburgh, Ellis. Sitting Bull vs. George Armstrong Custer: The Battle of the Little Bighorn, 1 vol. 2015. (History's Greatest Rivals Ser.). (ENG., Illus.). 48p. (J). (gr. 6-8). pap. 15.05 *(978-1-4824-4235-9(3),* aa50f84d-c548-4b07-b750-1ecf1f5453f1) Stevens, Gareth Publishing LLLP.

Sanford, William R. Hunkpapa Lakota Chief Sitting Bull, 1 vol. 2013. (Native American Chiefs & Warriors Ser.). (ENG., Illus.). 48p. (gr. 5-7). lib. bdg. 25.27 *(978-0-7660-4097-7(6),* 01439197-4907-4648-b855-91378a6c060e) Enslow Publishing, LLC.

—Oglala Sioux Chief Crazy Horse, 1 vol. 2013. (Native American Chiefs & Warriors Ser.). (ENG.). 48p. (gr. 5-7). pap. 11.53 *(978-1-4644-0261-6(2),* cdc54fb0-41e7-4d79-a371-fd02399b293b); (Illus.). (J). 25.27 *(978-0-7660-4094-6(1),* d3a6da54-3177-4a47-a968-3fd06fe2d3ba) Enslow Publishing, LLC.

Silate, Jennifer. The Last Stand: The Final Military Campaign of General George Armstrong Custer. (Great Moments in American History Ser.). 32p. (gr. 3-3). 2009. 47.90 *(978-1-61513-154-9(X))* 2003. (ENG., Illus.). lib. bdg. 29.13 *(978-0-8239-4353-1(4),* 73b38920-9b6e-4001-8329-eb9cc2cc9410, Rosen Reference) Rosen Publishing Group, Inc., The.

Sitting Bull. 2010. (ENG., Illus.). 128p. (gr. 6-12). 35.00 *(978-1-60413-527-5(1),* P179303, Facts On File) Infobase Holdings, Inc.

Snelson, Bob. Riding into Glory: An Introduction to the Battle of the Little Bighorn. 2004. (Illus.). 170p. (YA). per. 12.00 *(978-0-9723935-4-6(4))* Snelsonbks.com.

Theunissen, Steve. The Battle of the Little Bighorn. 2004. (History of the Old West Ser.). (Illus.). 64p. (YA). (gr. 5-18). lib. bdg. 19.95 *(978-1-59084-065-8(8))* Mason Crest.

Walker, Paul. Remember Little Bighorn (Direct Mail Edition) Indians, Soldiers, & Scouts Tell Their Stories. 2006. (ENG., Illus.). 64p. (J). (gr. 5-9). 17.95 *(978-0-7922-5521-5(6))* National Geographic Society.

Walker, Paul Robert. Remember Little Bighorn: Indians, Soldiers, & Scouts Tell Their Stories. 2015. (Illus.). 64p. (J). (gr. 5-9). pap. 7.99 *(978-1-4263-2246-4(1),* National Geographic Kids) Disney Publishing Worldwide.

Warren Ferrell, Nancy. The Battle of the Little Bighorn in United States History, 1 vol. 2014. (In United States History Ser.). (ENG., Illus.). 96p. (gr. 5-6). (J). pap. 13.88 *(978-0-7660-6098-2(5),* 4f649879-a7f2-4b9b-947a-1fd0b040dbd3); 31.61 *(978-0-7660-6097-5(7),* 6fef2d59-8f01-42df-9197-2595cee69eab) Enslow Publishing, LLC.

LITTLE LEAGUE BASEBALL—FICTION

Day, Karen. No Cream Puffs. 2008. (ENG.). 224p. (J). (gr. 6-8). lib. bdg. 21.19 *(978-0-375-93775-0(7),* Lamb, Wendy Bks.) Random Hse. Children's Bks.

Dixon, Franklin. The Missing Playbook. David, Matt, illus. 2016. (Hardy Boys Clue Book Ser.: 2). (ENG.). 96p. (J). (gr. 1-4). 16.99 *(978-1-4814-5178-9(2),* Aladdin) Simon & Schuster Children's Publishing.

Green, Tim. Best of the Best. 2011. (Baseball Great Ser.: 3). (ENG.). 272p. (J). (gr. 3-7). 16.99 *(978-0-06-168622-1(0),* HarperCollins) HarperCollins Pubs.

—Best of the Best: A Baseball Great Novel. 2011. (Playaway Children Ser.). (J). (gr. 5-8). 64.99 *(978-1-61707-137-9(4))* Findaway World, LLC.

—Best of the Best: A Baseball Great Novel. 2012. (Baseball Great Ser.: 3). (ENG.). 288p. (J). (gr. 3-7). pap. 9.99 *(978-0-06-168624-5(7),* HarperCollins) HarperCollins Pubs.

—Best of the Best: A Baseball Great Novel. 2012. (Baseball Great Ser.: 3). (J). lib. bdg. 17.20 *(978-0-606-23590-7(6))* Turtleback.

Lupica, Mike. Heat. 2007. (ENG.). 256p. (J). (gr. 5-18). 8.99 *(978-0-14-240757-8(7),* Puffin Books) Penguin Young Readers Group.

—Heat. 2007. 220p. (gr. 5-9). 18.00 *(978-0-7569-8131-0(X))* Perfection Learning Corp.

—Heat. 2007. 18.40 *(978-1-4177-7264-3(6))* Turtleback.

Preller, James. Six Innings. 2010. (ENG.). 176p. (YA). (gr. 4-6). pap. 16.99 *(978-0-312-60240-6(5),* 900064240) Square Fish.

Tellier, Derek. Anderson's Heat. 2016. (What's Your Dream? Ser.). (ENG., Illus.). 96p. (J). (gr. 4-6). lib. bdg. 25.99 *(978-1-4965-3441-5(7),* 132559, Stone Arch Bks.) Capstone.

LIVERPOOL (ENGLAND)—FICTION

Boyce, Frank Cottrell. The Unforgotten Coat. 2011. (ENG., Illus.). 112p. (J). (gr. 3-7). 16.99 *(978-0-7636-5729-1(8))* Candlewick Pr.

—The Unforgotten Coat. 2011. (Playaway Children Ser.). (ENG.). (J). (gr. 4-7). 39.99 *(978-1-4558-4539-2(6))* Findaway World, LLC.

Hughes, Shirley. Whistling in the Dark. 2017. (ENG., Illus.). 240p. (J). (gr. 5). 16.99 *(978-0-7636-9072-4(4))* Candlewick Pr.

Kristen, Judith. Once upon a Time in Liverpool. Cash, Eric, illus. 2012. 40p. pap. 15.95 *(978-0-9849505-2-2(4))* Aquinas & Krone Publishing, LLC.

Naughton, Bill. Pony Boy. 2012. (ENG.). 256p. (YA). pap. *(978-1-4482-0327-7(9),* 144335, Bloomsbury Reader) Bloomsbury Publishing Plc.

LIVESTOCK

see also Cattle; Cows; Dairying; Domestic Animals; Donkeys; Horses; Mules; Sheep; Veterinary Medicine

Alkire, Jessie. Farm Animal Rights. 2017. (Animal Rights Ser.). (ENG., Illus.). 32p. (J). (gr. 3-6). lib. bdg. 32.79 *(978-1-5321-1259-1(9),* 27576, Checkerboard Library) ABDO Publishing Co.

Barghoorn, Linda. Temple Grandin: Pioneer for Animal Rights & Autism Awareness. 2016. (Remarkable Lives Revealed Ser.). (ENG., Illus.). 32p. (J). (gr. 2-5). *(978-0-7787-2688-3(6))* Crabtree Publishing Co.

Barker, C. Penny. The Farm. 2004. 56p. spiral bd. 25.00 *(978-1-4116-2501-3(3))* Lulu Pr., Inc.

Bauman, Amy. Farm Animal Sounds. 2010. 12p. (J). (gr. -1). 9.95 *(978-1-60747-708-2(4),* Pickwick Pr.) Phoenix Bks., Inc.

Becker, John E. Frenemies for Life: Cheetahs & Anatolian Shepherd Dogs. 2010. 56p. (YA). (gr. 5-8). pap. 8.95 *(978-0-9841554-1-5(4))*; lib. bdg. 18.95 *(978-0-9841554-0-8(6))* Columbus Zoo & Aquarium, The.

Bergin, Mark. Farm Animals, 1 vol. 2012. (It's Fun to Draw Ser.). (ENG., Illus.). 32p. (J). (gr. 2-2). lib. bdg. 31.27 *(978-1-61533-599-2(4),* 757e0f54-3c5e-4401-a1ca-fe30c5cade81, Windmill Bks.) Rosen Publishing Group, Inc., The.

Bodden, Valerie. Caring for Horses. 2013. (Horsing Around (Creative Education) Ser.). (ENG., Illus.). 24p. (J). (gr. -1-3). 25.65 *(978-1-60818-470-5(6),* Creative Education) Creative Co., The.

Citro, Asia. Pigeon Math. Watson, Richard, illus. 2019. (ENG.). 40p. (J). (gr. k-5). 16.99 *(978-1-943147-62-5(0),* b0b01c77-c2cc-438d-bb9a-f16d4f6aa9eb) Innovation Pr., The.

Devera, Czeena. At the Farm. 2019. (I Can See Ser.). (ENG.). 16p. (J). (gr. -1-2). pap. 11.36 *(978-1-5341-3915-2(X),* 212495, Cherry Blossom Press) Cherry Lake Publishing.

JKL

Galvin, Laura Gates. First Look at Farm Animals. Fulcher, Roz, illus. 2009. (ENG.). 16p. bds. 6.95 (978-1-59249-999-1(6)) Soundprints.

Glaser, Rebecca. Cows Moo. 2016. (Illus.). 14p. (J). (gr. -1 — 1). bds. 7.99 (978-1-68152-125-1(3), 15811) Amicus.

—Horses Neigh. 2016. (Amicus Ink Board Bks.). (ENG., Illus.). 14p. (J). (gr. -1-k). bds. 7.99 (978-1-68152-126-8(1), 15816) Amicus.

Grimm, Sandra. Baby Farm Animals. Sodré, Julie, illus. 2012. (ENG.). 20p. (J). (gr. -1-1). 12.95 (978-1-61608-654-1(8), 608654, Sky Pony Pr.) Skyhorse Publishing Co., Inc.

Holden, Pam. Farm Friends, 1 vol. Hawley, Kelvin, illus. 2009. (Red Rocket Readers Ser.). (ENG.). 16p. (gr. -1-1). pap. (978-1-877363-14-6(6), Red Rocket Readers) Flying Start Bks.

James, Diane. En la Granja. 2004. (Descubre los Animales Ser.).Tr. of On the Farm. (SPA., Illus.). 24p. (J). (gr. -1-2). 9.95 (978-1-58728-489-2(8), Two-Can Publishing) T&N Children's Publishing.

Kallen, Stuart A., ed. Is Factory Farming Harming America?, 1 vol. 2006. (At Issue Ser.). (ENG., Illus.). 152p. (gr. 10-12). pap. 28.80 (978-0-7377-3438-6(8), 36b6f302-17fc-452b-855b-e4c5c8ff501e); lib. bdg. 41.03 (978-0-7377-3437-9(X), bc2ce1c9-7d37-4736-af8e-e69b4bfaadd9) Greenhaven Publishing LLC. (Greenhaven Publishing).

Kalman, Bobbie. Farm Animals. 2011. (ENG.) 16p. (J). pap. (978-0-7787-9577-3(2)); lib. bdg. (978-0-7787-9552-0(7)) Crabtree Publishing Co.

Kavanaugh, Missy & Gurman, Sarah, texts. Farm Animals. 2009. (Illus.). (J). (978-1-4351-1779-2(4)) Barnes & Noble, Inc.

Kawa, Katie. My First Trip to the Farm, 1 vol. 2012. (My First Adventures Ser.). (Illus.). 24p. (gr. k-k). (ENG.). (J). pap. 9.15 (978-1-4339-7313-0(8), 584706cf-2c28-4ca2-9d6b-828af72aeafc); (ENG., (J). lib. bdg. 25.27 (978-1-4339-7312-3(X), c34de820-6944-4901-b2af-ae0fa4c6edb4); 69.20 (978-1-4339-8050-3(9)) Stevens, Gareth Publishing LLLP.

—My First Trip to the Farm /Mi Primera Visita a una Granja, 1 vol. 2012. (My First Adventures / Mis Primeras Aventuras Ser.). (SPA & ENG., Illus.). 24p. (J). (gr. k-k). lib. bdg. 25.27 (978-1-4339-7378-9(2), 83f48c09-2d3a-4445-ba2f-404bbb27a969) Stevens, Gareth Publishing LLLP.

Keppeler, Jill & Keppeler, Sam. The Unofficial Guide to Raising Animals in Minecraft, 1 vol. 2018. (STEM Projects in Minecraft(r) Ser.). (ENG.). 24p. (gr. 3-3). pap. 9.25 (978-1-5383-4252-7(9), ea0b46f4-d883-401d-8f09-33dad3353540, PowerKids Pr.) Rosen Publishing Group, Inc., The.

Lindeen, Mary. A Visit to the Farm. 2018. (BeginningtoRead Ser.). (ENG.). 32p. (J). (gr. -1-2). lib. bdg. 22.60 (978-1-59953-910-2(1)); (Illus.). (gr. k-2). pap. 13.26 (978-1-68404-166-4(X)) Norwood Hse. Pr.

Little & Large Sticker Activity on the Farm. 2008. 24p. pap. (978-1-84810-060-2(4)) Miles Kelly Publishing, Ltd.

Loh-Hagan, Virginia. Temple Grandin & Livestock Management. 2018. (21st Century Junior Library: Women Innovators Ser.). (ENG., Illus.). 24p. (J). (gr. 2-5). lib. bdg. 29.21 (978-1-5341-2914-6(6), 211700) Cherry Lake Publishing.

Maher, Jack. Animal Instincts. 2011. (J). pap. (978-0-531-22560-8(7)) Scholastic, Inc.

Mattern, Joanne. National Geographic Readers: Farm Animals (Level 1 Coreader) 2017. (Readers Ser.). (Illus.). 48p. (J). (gr. -1-k). pap. 4.99 (978-1-4263-2687-5(4), National Geographic Kids) Disney Publishing Worldwide.

Mickelson, Trina. Free-Range Farming. 2016. (Growing Green Ser.). (ENG., Illus.). 64p. (J). (gr. 6-8). E-Book 51.99 (978-1-4677-9710-8(3), Lerner Pubns.) Lerner Publishing Group.

Miles, Lisa. Origami Farm Animals, 1 vol. 2013. (Amazing Origami Ser.). 32p. (J). (gr. 2-3). (ENG.). pap. 11.50 (978-1-4339-9653-5(7), 6f1a15f2-5302-478c-8a11-48fd5eee1c2a); pap. 63.00 (978-1-4339-9654-2(5)); (ENG., Illus.). lib. bdg. 29.27 (978-1-4339-9652-8(9), 795168cf-27ac-47b6-b2c4-c0b9a4d2e0a7) Stevens, Gareth Publishing LLLP.

My First Picture Book of Farm Animals. 2012. (ENG., Illus.). 24p. (J). 6.50 (978-1-84135-554-2(2)) Award Pubns. Ltd. GBR. Dist: Parkwest Pubns., Inc.

National Geographic Learning. Windows on Literacy Step up (Science: Animals Around Us): Taking Care of Farm Animals. 2007. (ENG., Illus.). 12p. (J). pap. 11.95 (978-0-7922-8482-6(8)) CENGAGE Learning.

Paiva, Johannah Gilman, ed. Farm Find. Gardiner, Lisa M., illus. 2013. 20p. (J). (gr. -1-1). 8.99 (978-1-77093-688-1(2)) Flowerpot Children's Pr. Inc. CAN. Dist: Cardinal Pubs. Group.

Peterson, Cris. Amazing Grazing. 2003. (ENG., Illus.). 32p. (gr. 3-6). 26.19 (978-1-56397-942-2(X)) Highlights Pr., c/o Highlights for Children, Inc.

Regan, Lisa. Farm Animals, 1 vol. Thompson, Kim, illus. 2010. (I Love Animals Ser.). (ENG.). 24p. (J). (gr. 2-2). pap. 9.15 (978-1-61533-233-5(2), 8a08c595-835b-4d0d-8eab-e3879ae0d7bb); lib. bdg. 27.27 (978-1-61533-227-4(8), 293ed7d2-216a-4fae-b44b-6e22a62346f3) Rosen Publishing Group, Inc., The. (Windmill Bks.).

Reitmann, Kathleen. Cattle. 2019. (J). (978-1-7911-1636-1(1), AV2 by Weigl) Weigl Pubs., Inc.

Roza, Greg. My First Trip to a Farm, 1 vol. 2019. (My First Trip Ser.). (ENG.). 24p. (gr. 1-1). 25.27 (978-1-5383-4433-0(5), 21f0a8fa-81b6-4380-8822-84f934ea0513, PowerKids Pr.) Rosen Publishing Group, Inc., The.

Sanford, William R. & Green, Carl R. Richard King: Courageous Texas Cattleman, 1 vol. 2013. (Courageous Heroes of the American West Ser.). (ENG., Illus.). 48p. (J). (gr. 5-7). pap. 11.53 (978-1-4644-0088-9(1), 96233e19-4fed-4d10-bc24-7ca0d56b1d0e) Enslow Publishing, LLC.

Suen, Anastasia. Foals. 2019. (Spot Baby Farm Animals Ser.). (ENG.). 16p. (J). (gr. -1-2). lib. bdg. (978-1-68151-531-1(8), 14492) Amicus.

Tatchell, Judy. On the Farm. Smith, Alastair, illus. 2004. (Lift-the-Flap Learners Ser.). (ENG.). 1p. (J). (gr. 1-18). pap. 8.95 (978-0-7460-2775-2(3)) EDC Publishing.

Tate, Nikki. Down to Earth: How Kids Help Feed the World, 1 vol. 2013. (Orca Footprints Ser.: 1). (ENG., Illus.). 48p. (J). (gr. 4-7). 19.95 (978-1-4598-0423-4(6)) Orca Bk. Pubs. USA.

Walters, Eric. Bedtime 123, 1 vol. Bisaillon, Josée, illus. 2017. (ENG.). 26p. (J). (gr. -1 — 1). bds. 10.95 (978-1-4598-1073-0(2)) Orca Bk. Pubs. USA.

Watt, Fiona & Wells, Rachel. Anifeiliaid y Fferm. 2005. (WEL., Illus.). 10p. (978-1-84512-000-9(0)) Cymdeithas Lyfrau Ceredigion.

West, David. Farm Animals. 2013. (Nora the Naturalist's Animals Ser.). 24p. (gr. k-3). 28.50 (978-1-62588-000-0(6)) Black Rabbit Bks.

Woodland, Faith. Turkeys. 2019. (J). (978-1-7911-1644-6(2), AV2 by Weigl) Weigl Pubs., Inc.

Worek, Michael & Worek, Michael. What's on My Farm? 2013. (ENG., Illus.). 160p. (J). (gr. -1-k). 9.95 (978-1-77085-236-5(0), 44609577-5f10-4c2b-90b5-7ee063b9b4f2) Firefly Bks., Ltd.

LIVING FOSSILS

see also names of specific fossils, e.g Platypus

Hemstock, Annie Wendt. Living Fossils, 1 vol. 2015. (Living Fossils Ser.). (ENG.). 24p. (J). 49.50 (978-1-4994-0320-6(8), PowerKids Pr.) Rosen Publishing Group, Inc., The.

Living Fossils, 12 vols. 2014. (Living Fossils Ser.). (ENG.). 24p. (J). (gr. 2-3). lib. bdg. 151.62 (978-1-4777-5736-9(8), 0e480959-435e-4102-9d15-bdc95bb6edba, PowerKids Pr.) Rosen Publishing Group, Inc., The.

Rajczak, Kristen. Jellyfish, 1 vol. 2014. (Living Fossils Ser.). (ENG., Illus.). 24p. (J). (gr. 2-3). pap. 9.25 (978-1-4777-5827-4(5), 9a1b2fa0-2eab-4151-ad7c-6e4f3005a1ea, PowerKids Pr.) Rosen Publishing Group, Inc., The.

Ridley, Kimberly. Extreme Survivors: Animals That Time Forgot (How Nature Works), 1 vol. 2017. (How Nature Works: 0). (ENG., Illus.). 48p. (J). (gr. 2-7). 17.95 (978-0-88448-500-1(5), 884500) Tilbury Hse. Pubs.

Shofner, Melissa Raé. Crocodiles Lived with the Dinosaurs!, 1 vol. 2016. (Living with the Dinosaurs Ser.). (ENG., Illus.). 24p. (J). (gr. 2-3). pap. 9.15 (978-1-4824-5645-5(1), 09c9eddc-17c7-472a-881d-a227c9b1bc66) Stevens, Gareth Publishing LLLP.

LIVINGSTONE, DAVID, 1813-1873

Bodden, Valerie. To the Heart of Africa. 2011. (Great Expeditions Ser.). (ENG.). 48p. (J). (gr. 5-8). pap. 12.00 (978-0-89812-664-8(9), 22158, Creative Paperbacks); (Illus.). 35.65 (978-1-60818-066-0(2), 22152, Creative Education) Creative Co., The.

Mattews, Basil. Livingstone: The Pathfinder. 2003. (ENG.). 112p. (YA). pap. 9.95 (978-0-923309-86-2(1)) Hartland Pubns.

O'Brien, Cynthia. Explore with Stanley & Livingstone. 2016. (Travel with the Great Explorers Ser.). (ENG., Illus.). 32p. (J). (gr. 3-6). (978-0-7787-2848-1(X)) Crabtree Publishing Co.

Otfinoski, Steven. David Livingstone: Deep in the Heart of Africa, 1 vol. 2007. (Great Explorations Ser.). (ENG., Illus.). 80p. (gr. 6-6). lib. bdg. 36.93 (978-0-7614-2226-6(9), 7a28dbce-109c-476e-99fa-e3fac1da0bdd) Cavendish Square Publishing LLC.

LIZARDS

Allman, Toney. From Lizard Saliva to Diabetes Drugs, 1 vol. 2006. (Imitating Nature Ser.). (ENG., Illus.). 32p. (gr. 3-6). lib. bdg. 28.88 (978-0-7377-3487-4(6), cd3a993b-acc1-474b-ab14-abcb5af50765, KidHaven Publishing) Greenhaven Publishing LLC.

Ang, Karen. Collared Lizard. 2015. (Desert Animals Searchin' for Shade Ser.). (ENG.). 24p. (J). (gr. -1-3). lib. bdg. 26.99 (978-1-62724-537-1(5)) Bearport Publishing Co., Inc.

Arnosky, Jim. All about Lizards: Y Jim Arnosky. 2004. (J). 15.95 (978-0-590-48145-8(2)) Scholastic, Inc.

Aronson, Virginia & Szejko, Allyn. Iguana Invasion! Exotic Pets Gone Wild in Florida. 2010. (ENG.). 69p. (J). (gr. -1-12). 16.95 (978-1-56164-468-1(4)) Pineapple Pr., Inc.

Bach, Rachel. Geckos. (Spot Backyard Animals Ser.). (ENG., Illus.). 16p. (J). (gr. -1-2). 2018. pap. 7.99 (978-1-68152-217-3(9), 14748) 2017. 17.95 (978-1-68151-092-7(8), 14629) Amicus.

—El Geco (Geckos) 2017. (Spot Backyard Animals Ser.). (ENG & SPA., Illus.). 16p. (J). (gr. k-3). 17.95 (978-1-68151-272-3(6), Amicus Readers) Amicus Learning.

Baer, T. H. Itty Bitty Geckos, 1 vol., Vol. 1. 2013. (Itty Bitty Animals Ser.). (ENG., Illus.). 24p. (J). (gr. k-k). 25.27 (978-1-4339-9878-2(5), 75a0645f-4844-4063-baaf-0d4d95bada6c); pap. 9.15 (978-1-4339-9880-5(7), 5b71df9f-2d38-411d-8fa9-ed4e9b86eba3) Stevens, Gareth Publishing LLLP.

—Lagartijas Pequeñitas / Itty Bitty Geckos, 1 vol., Vol. 1. 2013. (Animales Pequeñitos / Itty Bitty Animals Ser.). (SPA & ENG.). 24p. (J). (gr. k-2). 25.27 (978-1-4339-9905-5(6), 2457b193-8a22-4de7-9a18-391474788deb) Stevens, Gareth Publishing LLLP.

Beer, Amy-Jane. Lizards. 2008. (Nature's Children Ser.). (Illus.). 52p. (J). (978-0-7172-6238-0(3)) Grolier, Ltd.

Belknap, Jodi P. & Montgomery, Tamara. Kraken Ka The Komodo Dragon. Dodd, Joseph D., illus. 2007. 32p. pap. 19.95 incl. audio compact disk (978-0-9723420-7-0(9)) Belknap Publishing & Design.

Bergeron, Alain M. & Quintin, Michel. Do You Know Komodo Dragons?, 1 vol. Sampar, illus. 2014. (Do You Know? Ser.). (ENG.). 64p. (J). (gr. 2-4). pap. 9.95 (978-1-55455-339-6(3), 982446e2-275e-4c5f-aace-918ed03b73f7) Trifolium Bks., Inc. CAN. Dist: Firefly Bks., Ltd.

Bernhardt, Carolyn. Gila Monster: Venomous Desert Dweller. 2016. (Real Monsters Ser.). (ENG., Illus.). 32p. (J). (gr. 3-6). lib. bdg. 32.79 (978-1-68078-420-6(X), 23699, Checkerboard Library) ABDO Publishing Co.

Betances, Roberto. Lizard Blood, 1 vol. 2014. (Nature's Grossest Ser.). (ENG., Illus.). 24p. (J). (gr. 1-2). 24.27 (978-1-4824-1843-9(6), 9d029716-a939-4c45-aea8-c1e743484d54) Stevens, Gareth Publishing LLLP.

Bjorklund, Ruth. Komodo Dragons. 2012. (Nature's Children Ser.). (ENG., Illus.). 48p. (J). (gr. 3-5). pap. 6.95 (978-0-531-21077-2(4)); lib. bdg. 28.00 (978-0-531-20902-8(4)) Scholastic Library Publishing. (Children's Pr.).

—Lizards, 1 vol. 2009. (Great Pets Ser.). (ENG.). 48p. (gr. 3-3). lib. bdg. 32.64 (978-0-7614-2997-5(2), 58f52f39-1129-4c55-90b7-5d18bc7db540) Cavendish Square Publishing LLC.

Bodden, Valerie. Amazing Animals: Iguanas. 2017. (Amazing Animals Ser.). (ENG., Illus.). 24p. (J). (gr. 1-3). pap. 10.99 (978-1-62832-362-7(0), 20036, Creative Paperbacks) Creative Co., The.

—Amazing Animals: Komodo Dragons. 2013. (Amazing Animals Ser.). (ENG.). 24p. (J). (gr. 1-3). pap. 9.99 (978-0-89812-789-8(0), 21727, Creative Paperbacks) Creative Co., The.

—Iguanas. 2017. (Amazing Animals Ser.). (ENG., Illus.). 24p. (J). (gr. 1-4). (978-1-60818-754-6(3), 20038, Creative Education) Creative Co., The.

—Komodo Dragons. 2013. (Amazing Animals Ser.). (ENG., Illus.). 24p. (J). (gr. 1-4). 25.65 (978-1-60818-087-5(5), 21726, Creative Education) Creative Co., The.

Borgert-Spaniol, Megan. Komodo Dragons. 2014. (Animal Safari Ser.). (ENG.). 24p. (J). (gr. k-3). lib. bdg. 26.95 (978-1-60014-967-2(7), Blastoff! Readers) Bellwether Media.

Bowman, Chris. Iguanas. 2015. (Illus.). 24p. (J). (978-0-531-20514-3(2)); (ENG., 26.95 (978-1-62617-164-0(5), Blastoff! Readers) Bellwether Media.

Bradshaw, Felicity. The Great Lizard Trek. MacDonald, Norma, illus. 2018. 32p. (J). (gr. 1-6). 19.95 (978-1-4863-0882-8(1)) CSIRO Publishing AUS. Dist: Stylus Publishing, LLC.

Buckingham, Suzanne. Meet the Iguana, 1 vol. 2008. (Scales & Tails Ser.). (ENG., Illus.). 24p. (J). (gr. 2-3). lib. bdg. 26.27 (978-1-4042-4499-3(9), b5e6e7cc-0fb1-4841-acaa-0caafbf15dcd, PowerKids Pr.) Rosen Publishing Group, Inc., The.

Carr, Aaron. Iguana. 2014. (Illus.). 24p. (J). (978-1-62127-295-3(8)) Weigl Pubs., Inc.

Chancellor, Deborah. Lizards. 2009. (Extreme Pets Ser.). (Illus.). 32p. (YA). (gr. 4-7). 28.50 (978-1-59920-239-6(5)) Black Rabbit Bks.

Cheshire, Gerard. Lizards - Scary Creatures. 2008. (Scary Creatures Ser.). (ENG., Illus.). 32p. (J). (gr. 2-4). 27.00 (978-0-531-20448-1(0), Children's Pr.) Scholastic Library Publishing.

Clarke, Ginjer L. Giant Lizards. Rothman, Michael, illus. 2005. (Penguin Young Readers, Level 3 Ser.). 48p. (J). (gr. 1-3). mass mkt. 4.99 (978-0-448-43120-8(3), Penguin Young Readers) Penguin Young Readers Group.

Coates, Jennifer. Lizards. (J). 2009. (Illus.). 112p. 14.95 (978-1-932904-39-0(5)) 2008. (978-1-932904-31-4(X)) Eldorado Ink.

Collard, Sneed B. Sneed B. Collard III's Most Fun Book Ever about Lizards. 2012. (ENG., Illus.). 48p. (J). (gr. 4-7). 22.44 (978-1-58089-324-4(4)) Charlesbridge Publishing, Inc.

Collard, Sneed B., III. Sneed B. Collard III's Most Fun Book Ever about Lizards. 2012. (ENG., Illus.). 48p. (J). (gr. 4-7). pap. 8.99 (978-1-58089-325-1(2)) Charlesbridge Publishing, Inc.

Connors, Kathleen. Geckos, 1 vol. 2013. (Really Wild Reptiles Ser.). (ENG., Illus.). 24p. (J). (gr. 2-3). pap. 9.15 (978-1-4339-8365-8(6), baaf378c-ebb9-482d-a3d3-ab2023fcccd5); lib. bdg. 25.27 (978-1-4339-8364-1(8), 20e1c6b1-c5d6-4a15-9df0-ade24193d918) Stevens, Gareth Publishing LLLP.

—Gila Monsters, 1 vol. 2013. (Really Wild Reptiles Ser.). (ENG., Illus.). 24p. (J). (gr. 2-3). pap. 9.15 (978-1-4339-8370-2(2), 33267391-8b01-48f6-9226-4cab4652b393); lib. bdg. 25.27 (978-1-4339-8369-6(9), ae871ce1-3af4-41d3-b3d0-d54f2839ecfa) Stevens, Gareth Publishing LLLP.

—Iguanas, 1 vol. 2013. (Really Wild Reptiles Ser.). (ENG., Illus.). 24p. (J). (gr. 2-3). pap. 9.15 (978-1-4339-8375-7(3), 7538ecfa-9f8d-4de6-a8a9-594f925b4cea); lib. bdg. 25.27 (978-1-4339-8374-0(5), 8e6c757d-63ee-49a7-aca1-250be29341e4) Stevens, Gareth Publishing LLLP.

—Komodo Dragons, 1 vol. 2013. (Really Wild Reptiles Ser.). (ENG., Illus.). 24p. (gr. 2-3). 25.27 (978-1-4339-8379-5(6), 149d95b6-4f21-462b-8ba8-17821284abaf); pap. 9.15 (978-1-4339-8380-1(X), d9237971-4997-4c21-af57-cccb4b2a16c5) Stevens, Gareth Publishing LLLP. (Gareth Stevens Learning Library).

Craats, Rennay. Gecko. 2009. (My Pet Ser.). (Illus.). 32p. (J). (gr. 3-5). pap. 9.95 (978-1-60596-099-9(3)); lib. bdg. 26.00 (978-1-60596-098-2(5)) Weigl Pubs., Inc.

Craats, Rennay & Gillespie, Katie. Gecko. 2015. (J). (978-1-4896-2958-6(0)) Weigl Pubs., Inc.

Davin, Rose. Lizards. 2017. (Meet Desert Animals Ser.). (ENG., Illus.). 24p. (J). (gr. -1-2). lib. bdg. 27.32 (978-1-5157-4599-0(6), 134283, Capstone Pr.) Capstone.

De la Bédoyère, Camilla. The Wild Life of Lizards, 1 vol. 2014. (Wild Side Ser.). (ENG.). 24p. (J). (gr. 2-2). lib. bdg. 26.27 (978-1-4777-5494-8(6), 5b78b146-cdc7-4d50-9ff2-c064f887f312, Windmill Bks.) Rosen Publishing Group, Inc., The.

Dennard, Deborah. Lizards. Dewey, Jennifer Owings, illus. 2003. (Our Wild World Ser.). (ENG.). 48p. (J). (gr. 2-5). 10.95 (978-1-55971-858-5(7)); pap. 8.95 (978-1-55971-857-8(9)) Cooper Square Publishing Llc.

Early Macken, JoAnn. Gila Monsters, 1 vol. (Animals That Live in the Desert (First Edition) Ser.). (ENG., 24p. (gr. 1-1). 2005. Illus.). pap. 9.15 (978-0-8368-4834-2(9), df704c6f-4765-4d03-9f13-4fe8e5d34829) 2nd rev. ed. 2009. (J). pap. 9.15 (978-1-4339-2449-1(8), 5ad4996f-c820-4e49-a5a8-53cddf9302e8) 2nd rev. ed. 2009. (J). lib. bdg. 25.27 (978-1-4339-1951-0(6), b6e3bc3c-cbdd-4cc7-ae1e-52f4f9b803ae) Stevens, Gareth Publishing LLLP. (Weekly Reader Leveled Readers).

—Gila Monsters / Monstruos de Gila, 1 vol. 2nd rev. ed. 2009. (Animals That Live in the Desert / Animales Del Desierto (Second Edition) Ser.). (ENG & SPA.). 24p. (J). (gr. 1-1). pap. 9.15 (978-1-4339-2457-6(9), 136108a7-350f-45bf-bbd7-579ce3d72436, Weekly Reader Leveled Readers); lib. bdg. 25.27 (978-1-4339-2062-2(X), 752deb7a-10ef-4257-9d50-d18e6a223726) Stevens, Gareth Publishing LLLP.

Eidenbuller, Bernd & Reisinger, Manfred. Beaded Lizards & Gila Monsters: Captive Care & Husbandry. 2011. (Illus.). 157p. 79.50 (978-3-89973-498-0(X)) Edition Chimaira DEU. Dist: Serpent's Tale Natural History Bk. Distributors, Inc.

Everything Changes: Individual Title Six-Packs. (Discovery World Ser.). 16p. (gr. 1-2). 28.00 (978-0-7635-8461-0(4)) Rigby Education.

Flynn, James. From Egg to Lizard. 2003. (Grow up! Ser.). (J). (978-1-58417-173-7(1)); pap. (978-1-58417-179-9(0)) Lake Street Pubs.

Gagne, Tammy. Geckos, 1 vol. 2014. (Amazing Reptiles Ser.). (ENG.). 48p. (J). (gr. 4-8). lib. bdg. 35.64 (978-1-62403-372-8(5), 1189) ABDO Publishing Co.

Garcia, Alonso. How Do Chameleons Change Color? 2017. (How Life Science Works). (Illus.). 24p. (J). (gr. 7-8). 49.50 (978-1-5081-5631-4(X), PowerKids Pr.) Rosen Publishing Group, Inc., The.

Gates, Margo. No Bugs Here. Crowther, Jeff, illus. 2019. (Let's Look at Animal Habitats (Pull Ahead Readers — Fiction) Ser.). (ENG.). 16p. (J). (gr. -1-1). pap. 8.99 (978-1-5415-7307-9(2), 40e28938-5b6a-4ebe-841c-3bf223c53ba9, Lerner Pubns.) Lerner Publishing Group.

Gish, Ashley. Geckos. 2019. (X-Books: Reptiles Ser.). (ENG.). 32p. (J). (gr. 3-5). pap. 9.99 (978-1-62832-669-7(7), 18876, Creative Paperbacks); (978-1-64026-081-8(1), 18875) Creative Co., The.

—Iguanas. 2019. (X-Books: Reptiles Ser.). (ENG.). 32p. (J). (gr. 3-5). pap. 9.99 (978-1-62832-670-3(0), 18880, Creative Paperbacks); (978-1-64026-082-5(X), 18879) Creative Co., The.

Gish, Melissa. Geckos. 2014. (Living Wild Ser.). (ENG.). 48p. (J). (gr. 4-7). (978-1-60818-417-0(X), 21376, Creative Education) Creative Co., The.

—Iguanas. (Living Wild Ser.). (ENG.). 48p. (J). 2016. (gr. 5-9). pap. 12.00 (978-1-62832-168-5(7), 20887, Creative Paperbacks) 2015. (Illus.). (gr. 4-7). (978-1-60818-567-2(2), 20886, Creative Education) Creative Co., The.

—Living Wild: Geckos. 2015. (Living Wild Ser.). (ENG.). 48p. (J). (gr. 5-8). pap. 12.00 (978-1-62832-003-9(6), 21377, Creative Paperbacks) Creative Co., The.

Goldish, Meish. Deadly Lizard Bite! 2018. (Envenomators Ser.). (ENG., Illus.). 24p. (J). (gr. 2-7). 19.45 (978-1-68402-657-9(1)) Bearport Publishing Co., Inc.

Greenberg, Daniel A. Lizards, 1 vol. 2005. (Animal Ways Ser.). (ENG., Illus.). 112p. (gr. 6-6). lib. bdg. 38.36 (978-0-7614-1580-0(7), 6b024131-fecf-447b-9916-071909239875) Cavendish Square Publishing LLC.

Gregory, Helen. All about Snakes & Lizards, 1 vol. 2011. (Wonder Readers Fluent Level Ser.). (ENG.). 16p. (gr. -1-1). (J). pap. 6.25 (978-1-4296-7796-7(1), 117968); pap. 35.94 (978-1-4296-8068-4(7)) Capstone. (Capstone Pr.).

Hamilton, S. L. Lizards. 2010. (Xtreme Predators Ser.). (ENG.). 32p. (J). (gr. 3-9). 32.79 (978-1-60453-992-9(5), 15728, Abdo & Daughters) ABDO Publishing Co.

Hansen, Grace. Iguanas, 1 vol. 2014. (Reptiles (Abdo Kids) Ser.). (ENG.). 24p. (J). (gr. -1-2). lib. bdg. 32.79 (978-1-62970-059-5(2), 1612, Abdo Kids) ABDO Publishing Co.

Harris, Terrell. Lizards, 1 vol. 2010. (Slimy, Scaly, Deadly Reptiles & Amphibians Ser.). (ENG., Illus.). 32p. (J). (gr. 3-4). pap. 11.50 (978-1-4339-3427-8(2), bd76092e-3d6b-4218-95bb-fefa7b75145c); lib. bdg. 28.67 (978-1-4339-3426-1(4), 58428da1-1f67-4761-9ea9-3544e596a54b) Stevens, Gareth Publishing LLLP. (Gareth Stevens Learning Library).

Harvey, Jillian L. Komodo Dragon: Toxic Lizard Titan. 2016. (Real Monsters Ser.). (ENG., Illus.). 32p. (J). (gr. 3-6). lib. bdg. 32.79 (978-1-68078-421-3(8), 23701, Checkerboard Library) ABDO Publishing Co.

Heos, Bridget. Do You Really Want a Lizard? Longhi, Katya, illus. 2015. (Do You Really Want a Pet? Ser.). (ENG.). 24p. (J). (gr. 1-4). lib. bdg. 19.95 (978-1-60753-750-2(8), 15280) Amicus.

Houran, Lori Haskins. Bloody Horned Lizards. 2018. (Gross-Out Defenses Ser.). (ENG.). 24p. (J). (gr. k-3). 7.99 (978-1-64280-076-0(7)) Bearport Publishing Co., Inc.

Huber, Raymond. Gecko. Lovelock, Brian, illus. 2019. (ENG.). 32p. (J). (gr. k-4). 16.99 (978-0-7636-9885-0(7)) Candlewick Pr.

Hudd, Emily. Lungless Salamanders. 2019. (Unique Animal Adaptations Ser.). (ENG., Illus.). 32p. (J). (gr. 4-6). pap. 7.95 (978-1-5435-7508-8(0), 141038) Capstone.

—Texas Horned Lizards. 2019. (Unique Animal Adaptations Ser.). (ENG., Illus.). 32p. (J). (gr. 4-6). 28.65 (978-1-5435-7165-3(4), 140431) Capstone.

Jacobs, Pat. Lizard Pals. 2018. (Pet Pals Ser.). (Illus.). 32p. (J). (gr. 3-3). pap. (978-0-7787-5733-7(1)) Crabtree Publishing Co.

Kalman, Bobbie. Les Dragons de Komodo. 2010. (Petit Monde Vivant Ser.). (FRE., Illus.). 32p. (J). pap. 9.95 (978-2-89579-315-1(8)) Bayard Canada Livres CAN. Dist: Crabtree Publishing Co.

—Endangered Komodo Dragons, 1 vol. 2004. (Earth's Endangered Animals Ser.). (ENG., Illus.). 32p. (J). pap. (978-0-7787-1903-8(0)); lib. bdg. (978-0-7787-1857-4(3)) Crabtree Publishing Co.

Kenney, Karen Latchana. Axolotls. 2017. (Weird & Unusual Animals Ser.). (ENG., Illus.). 24p. (J). (gr. 1-4). 20.95 (978-1-68151-154-2(1), 14697) Amicus.

Kingsley, Imogen. Geckos. 2019. (Lizards in the Wild Ser.). (ENG.). 24p. (J). (gr. 1-4). lib. bdg. (978-1-68151-556-4(3), 14517) Amicus.

—Green Iguanas. 2019. (Lizards in the Wild Ser.). (ENG.). 24p. (J). (gr. 1-4). lib. bdg. (978-1-68151-558-8(X), 14519) Amicus.

Lizards. (Eyes on Nature Ser.). 32p. (J). (gr. 1). pap. (978-1-882210-60-2(3)) Action Publishing, Inc.

Lizards: Level N, 6 vols. (Wonder Worldtm Ser.). 48p. 34.95 (978-0-7802-4583-9(0)) Wright Group/McGraw-Hill.

Lunis, Natalie. Black Spiny-Tailed Iguana: Lizard Lightning! 2010. (Blink of an Eye: Superfast Animals Ser.). (Illus.). 24p. (J). (gr. k-3). lib. bdg. 26.99 (978-1-936087-91-4(X), 1314839) Bearport Publishing Co., Inc.

—Green Iguanas. 2009. (Peculiar Pets Ser.). (Illus.). 24p. (YA). (gr. 2-5). lib. bdg. 26.99 *(978-1-59716-863-2(7))* Bearport Publishing Co., Inc.

—Komodo Dragon. 2018. (SuperSized! Ser.). (ENG.). 24p. (J). (gr. k-3). 7.99 *(978-1-64280-086-9(4))* Bearport Publishing Co., Inc.

—Komodo Dragon: The World's Biggest Lizard. 2007. (SuperSized! Ser.). (Illus.). 24p. (J). (gr. k-3). lib. bdg. 26.99 *(978-1-59716-392-7(9)*, 1265937) Bearport Publishing Co., Inc.

Macheske, Felicia. Smiling & Spotted: Gecko. 2017. (Guess What Ser.). (ENG., Illus.). 24p. (J). (gr. k-2). lib. bdg. 30.64 *(978-1-63472-852-2(1)*, 209834) Cherry Lake Publishing.

Magellan, Marta. Those Lively Lizards. Weaver, Steve, illus. 2008. (Those Amazing Animals Ser.). (ENG.). 58p. (J). (gr. -1-12). pap. 9.95 *(978-1-56164-427-8(7))* Pineapple Pr., Inc.

Maimone, Max Q. Hunting with Komodo Dragons, 1 vol., Vol. 1. 2014. (Animal Attack! Ser.). (ENG.). 32p. (J). (gr. 2-3). 25.27 *(978-1-4824-0497-5(4)*, 5f394436-3ebc-481d-a9c1-6b1878abb7c9) Stevens, Gareth Publishing LLLP.

Mara, Wil. Bearded Dragons. 2017. (Real-Life Dragons Ser.). (ENG., Illus.). 32p. (J). (gr. 3-9). pap. 7.95 *(978-1-5157-5074-1(4)*, 134619, Capstone Pr.) Capstone.

—Flying Dragons. 2017. (Real-Life Dragons Ser.). (ENG., Illus.). 32p. (J). (gr. 3-9). lib. bdg. 28.65 *(978-1-5157-5071-0(X)*, 134616, Capstone Pr.) Capstone.

Marsh, Laura. National Geographic Readers: Lizards. 2012. (Readers Ser.). (ENG., Illus.). 32p. (J). (gr. 1-3). lib. bdg. 15.99 *(978-1-4263-0923-6(6)*, National Geographic Kids) Disney Publishing Worldwide.

Marsico, Katie. Geckos. 2013. (ENG.). 48p. (J). 28.00 *(978-0-531-23357-3(X))* Scholastic Library Publishing.

—A Komodo Dragon Hatchling Grows Up. 2007. (Scholastic News Nonfiction Readers: Life Cycles Ser.). (ENG., Illus.). 24p. (J). (gr. k-3). 18.69 *(978-0-531-17477-7(8)*, Children's Pr.) Scholastic Library Publishing.

McFee, Shane. Deadly Lizards. (Poison! Ser.). 24p. (gr. 2-3). 2009. 42.50 *(978-1-60851-322-2(X)*, PowerKids Pr.) 2007. (ENG., Illus.). (YA). lib. bdg. 26.27 *(978-1-4042-3796-4(8)*, df94255f-b698-409d-9fc7-4ed761d64991) Rosen Publishing Group, Inc., The.

Meister, Cari. Horned Lizards. 2015. (Illus.). 24p. (J). lib. bdg. *(978-1-62031-196-7(8)*, Bullfrog Bks.) Jump! Inc.

—Komodo Dragons. 2015. (Illus.). 24p. (J). lib. bdg. *(978-1-62031-197-4(6)*, Bullfrog Bks.) Jump! Inc.

Miller, Jake. The Bearded Dragon. 2009. (Lizard Library). 24p. (gr. 3-3). 42.50 *(978-1-60854-009-9(X)*, PowerKids Pr.) Rosen Publishing Group, Inc., The.

—The Gila Monster. 2009. (Lizard Library). 24p. (gr. 3-3). 42.50 *(978-1-60854-013-6(8)*, PowerKids Pr.) Rosen Publishing Group, Inc., The.

—The Green Iguana. 2009. (Lizard Library). 24p. (gr. 3-3). 42.50 *(978-1-60854-016-7(2)*, PowerKids Pr.) Rosen Publishing Group, Inc., The.

—The Komodo Dragon. 2009. (Lizard Library). 24p. (gr. 3-3). 42.50 *(978-1-60854-019-8(7)*, PowerKids Pr.) Rosen Publishing Group, Inc., The.

—The Leopard Gecko. 2009. (Lizard Library). 24p. (gr. 3-3). 42.50 *(978-1-60854-020-4(0)*, PowerKids Pr.) Rosen Publishing Group, Inc., The.

Morey, Allan. Frilled Lizards. (Weird & Unusual Animals Ser.). (ENG., Illus.). 24p. (J). (gr. 1-4). 2018. pap. 8.99 *(978-1-68152-188-6(1)*, 16100) 2017. 20.95 *(978-1-68151-157-3(6)*, 14700) Amicus.

Morgan, Sally. Lizards & Snakes. 2012. (Pets Plus Ser.). 32p. (gr. 3-6). lib. bdg. 31.35 *(978-1-59920-704-9(4))* Black Rabbit Bks.

Murray, Julie. Iguanas. 2019. (Animal Kingdom Ser.). (ENG.). 32p. (J). (gr. 2-5). lib. bdg. 34.21 *(978-1-5321-1639-1(X)*, 32389, Big Buddy Bks.) ABDO Publishing Co.

—Lizards. (Pet Care Ser.). (ENG., Illus.). 24p. (J). 2018. (gr. k-4). lib. bdg. 31.36 *(978-1-5321-2524-9(0)*, 30057, Abdo Zoom-Dash) 2016. (gr. -1-2). lib. bdg. 31.36 *(978-1-68080-532-1(0)*, 21344, Abdo Kids) ABDO Publishing Co.

O'Donnell, Kerri. Komodo Dragons, 1 vol. 2006. (Ugly Animals Ser.). (ENG., Illus.). 24p. (J). (gr. 2-3). lib. bdg. 26.27 *(978-1-4042-3530-4(2)*, c001a036-a451-49d6-a831-e48041e28a55) Rosen Publishing Group, Inc., The.

Olson, Amy. What's Bugging Camo the Chameleon. 2009. 32p. pap. 13.00 *(978-1-60860-258-2(3)*, Strategic Bk. Publishing) Strategic Book Publishing & Rights Agency (SBPRA).

Pallotta, Jerry. Komodo Dragon vs. King Cobra (Who Would Win?) Bolster, Rob, illus. 2016. (Who Would Win? Ser.). (ENG.). 32p. (J). (gr. 1-3). pap. 3.99 *(978-0-545-30171-8(8))* Scholastic, Inc.

Perish, Patrick. Collared Lizards. 2019. (Animals of the Desert Ser.). (ENG., Illus.). 24p. (J). (gr. k-3). lib. bdg. 26.95 *(978-1-62617-921-9(2)*, Blastoff! Readers) Bellwether Media.

Phillips, Dee. Gila Monster's Burrow. 2015. (Illus.). 24p. (J). lib. bdg. 26.99 *(978-1-62724-309-4(7))* Bearport Publishing Co., Inc.

PRESS, Celebration. Looking at Lizards. 2003. (ENG.). (J). (gr. 2-5). pap., stu. ed. 34.95 *(978-0-673-62835-0(3)*, Celebration Pr.) Savvas Learning Co.

Ralph Lewis, Brenda. Lizards, 1 vol. 2005. (Nature's Monsters: Reptiles & Amphibians Ser.). (ENG., Illus.). 32p. (gr. 3-5). lib. bdg. 28.67 *(978-0-8368-6173-0(6)*, c2578d47-66c0-42d2-8826-296db53ea097, Gareth Stevens Learning Library) Stevens, Gareth Publishing LLLP.

Randolph, Joanne. My Friend the Iguana, 1 vol. 2010. (Curious Pet Pals Ser.). (ENG., Illus.). 24p. (J). (gr. 2-3). pap. 9.15 *(978-1-60754-985-7(9)*, 086916bb-5cc5-41c9-98e8-7ecaf2799ffd); lib. bdg. 27.27 *(978-1-60754-977-2(8)*, d32a21b2-3448-47c4-92a6-6840433fb1ec) Rosen Publishing Group, Inc., The. (Windmill Bks.).

Raum, Elizabeth. Geckos. 2014. (Lizards Ser.). (ENG., Illus.). 32p. (J). (gr. 2-5). lib. bdg. 28.50 *(978-1-60753-485-3(1)*, 15988) Amicus.

—Green Iguanas. 2014. (Lizards Ser.). (ENG., Illus.). 32p. (J). (gr. 2-5). lib. bdg. 28.50 *(978-1-60753-487-7(8)*, 15990) Amicus.

Reid, Siuna Ann. Reptiles Are Cool- Understanding My Lizard. Lodge, Vivienne E., ed. 2013. (Illus.). 70p. pap. *(978-0-9576568-3-3(1))* Siuna A Reid.

Riggs, Kate. Geckos. (Seedlings Ser.). (ENG., 24p. (J). 2017. Illus.). (gr. -1-k). *(978-1-60818-868-0(X)*, 20339) 2015. (gr. 1-4). *(978-1-60818-489-7(7)*, 21144) Creative Co., The. (Creative Education).

—Seedlings: Geckos. 2017. (Seedlings Ser.). (ENG., Illus.). 24p. (J). (gr. -1-1). pap. 9.99 *(978-1-62832-483-9(X)*, 20340, Creative Paperbacks) Creative Co., The.

Rudolph, Jessica. Gecko. 2016. (Weird but Cute Ser.). (ENG., Illus.). 24p. (J). (gr. -1-3). 26.99 *(978-1-62724-849-5(8))* Bearport Publishing Co., Inc.

—MIS Garras Son Largas y Curvas. 2015. (Pistas de Animales Ser.). (SPA., Illus.). 24p. (J). (gr. -1-3). lib. bdg. 26.99 *(978-1-62724-578-4(2))* Bearport Publishing Co., Inc.

—My Claws Are Large & Curved (Komodo Dragon) 2014. (Zoo Clues Ser.). 24p. (J). (gr. -1-3). lib. bdg. 26.99 *(978-1-62724-114-4(0))* Bearport Publishing Co., Inc.

Schuh, Mari. Iguanas. 2014. (Illus.). 24p. (J). lib. bdg. 25.65 *(978-1-62031-110-3(0)*, Bullfrog Bks.) Jump! Inc.

Sherman, Jill. Komodo Dragons. 2017. (Real-Life Dragons Ser.). (ENG., Illus.). 32p. (J). (gr. 3-9). lib. bdg. 28.65 *(978-1-5157-5069-7(8)*, 134614, Capstone Pr.) Capstone.

Siemens, Jared. Iguana. 2017. (Illus.). 24p. (J). *(978-1-5105-0572-8(5))* SmartBook Media, Inc.

Silverman, Buffy. Can You Tell a Gecko from a Salamander? 2012. (Animal Look-Alikes Ser.). 32p. (gr. k-2). pap. 45.32 *(978-0-7613-9255-2(6))* Lerner Publishing Group.

Silverstein, Alvin, et al. Iguanas: Cool Pets!, 1 vol. 2011. (Far-Out & Unusual Pets Ser.). (ENG., Illus.). 48p. (gr. 3-3). lib. bdg. 27.93 *(978-0-7660-3686-4(3)*, 36f65c1b-d0dd-466a-8241-649647111d73) Enslow Publishing, LLC.

Simon, Elizabeth. Iguana. 2010. pap. 9.95 *(978-1-61690-077-9(6))*; 32p. (J). (gr. 3-5). lib. bdg. 27.13 *(978-1-61690-076-2(8))* Weigl Pubs., Inc.

Sovak, Jan. Lizards. 2006. (Dover Animal Coloring Bks.). (ENG., Illus.). 32p. (J). (gr. 1-5). 3.99 *(978-0-486-44820-6(7)*, 448207) Dover Pubns., Inc.

Spalding, Maddie. Komodo Dragons. 2019. (Unique Animal Adaptations Ser.). (ENG., Illus.). 32p. (J). (gr. 4-6). 28.65 *(978-1-5435-7153-0(0)*, 140420) Capstone.

Statts, Leo. Iguanas. 2016. (Desert Animals Ser.). (ENG.). 24p. (J). (gr. -1-2). 49.94 *(978-1-68079-349-9(7)*, 22970, Abdo Zoom-Launch) ABDO Publishing Co.

—Komodo Dragons. 2016. (Desert Animals Ser.). (ENG.). 24p. (J). (gr. -1-2). 49.94 *(978-1-68079-350-5(0)*, 22971, Abdo Zoom-Launch) ABDO Publishing Co.

Stewart, Melissa. How Do Chameleons Change Color?, 1 vol. 2009. (Tell Me Why, Tell Me How Ser.). (ENG., Illus.). 32p. (gr. 3-3). lib. bdg. 32.64 *(978-0-7614-2922-7(0)*, ac7986ed-a380-4a53-9e57-bf9225d7f8be) Cavendish Square Publishing LLC.

—Salamander or Lizard? How Do You Know?, 1 vol. 2011. (Which Animal Is Which? Ser.). (ENG., Illus.). 24p. (gr. k-2). pap. 10.35 *(978-1-59845-238-9(X)*, 433dd8df-6264-45e3-8ad7-a4885ef25e17, Enslow Elementary); lib. bdg. 25.27 *(978-0-7660-3679-6(0)*, 16dd0931-7ec3-4af2-9f62-3463f9be59b8) Enslow Publishing, LLC.

Storad, Conrad J. Gila Monsters. 2008. (Early Bird Nature Books Ser.). (Illus.). 48p. (J). (gr. 3-7). lib. bdg. 26.60 *(978-0-8225-7888-8(3)*, Lerner Pubns.) Lerner Publishing Group.

Szymanski, Jennifer. National Geographic Kids Readers: Real Dragons (L1/Coreader) 2018. (Readers Ser.). (Illus.). 48p. (J). (gr. -1-k). pap. 4.99 *(978-1-4263-3046-9(4)*, National Geographic Kids) Disney Publishing Worldwide.

Thatcher, Henry. Komodo Dragons & Geckos, 1 vol., 1. 2014. (Big Animals, Small Animals Ser.). (ENG.). 32p. (J). (gr. 2-3). 28.93 *(978-1-4777-6106-9(3)*, ac7cd2b2-ac9b-4c28-96a1-84dd40ee3d86, PowerKids Pr.) Rosen Publishing Group, Inc., The.

Tobler, Elise. Geckos Walk on Walls!, 1 vol. 2020. (Reptiles Rock! Ser.). (ENG.). 32p. (J). (gr. 2-3). pap. 11.53 *(978-1-9785-1816-2(1)*, 4a01cdd8-e75b-4d3c-988b-25528e12c63b) Enslow Publishing, LLC.

—Iguanas Have an Extra Eye!, 1 vol. 2020. (Reptiles Rock! Ser.). (ENG.). 32p. (gr. 2-3). pap. 11.53 *(978-1-9785-1824-7(2)*, 6007679f-6af0-4ef1-a5d2-8658231c753f) Enslow Publishing, LLC.

—Komodo Dragons Are the Largest Lizards!, 1 vol. 2020. (Reptiles Rock! Ser.). (ENG.). 32p. (gr. 2-3). pap. 11.53 *(978-1-9785-1828-5(5)*, 41d3e0a5-7444-4512-97dd-c2e9730defe7) Enslow Publishing, LLC.

Trueit, Trudi Strain. Lizards. 2003. (True Bks.). (ENG.). 48p. (gr. 3-5). pap. 6.95 *(978-0-516-29351-6(6)*, Children's Pr.) Scholastic Library Publishing.

Truscott, Julia. Your Safari: In Search of the Real Komodo Dragon. White, Daniel, photos by. 2005. (Illus.). 48p. (J). 11.95 *(978-1-59594-014-8(6)*, Wingspan Pr.) WingSpan Publishing.

Turnbull, Stephanie. Komodo Dragon. 2015. (Big Beasts Ser.). (ENG., Illus.). 24p. (J). (gr. 1-4). 28.50 *(978-1-62588-200-4(9)*, 17277) Black Rabbit Bks.

World Book, Inc. Staff, contrib. by. Green Anoles & Other Pet Lizards. 2009. (J). *(978-0-7166-1368-8(9))* World Bk., Inc.

—Iguanas & Other Lizards. 2005. (World Book's Animals of the World Ser.). (Illus.). 64p. (J). *(978-0-7166-1268-1(2))* World Bk., Inc.

Zappa, Marcia. Thorny Devils, 1 vol. 2015. (World's Weirdest Animals Ser.). (ENG., Illus.). 32p. (J). (gr. 2-5). 34.21 *(978-1-62403-779-5(8)*, 17860, Big Buddy Bks.) ABDO Publishing Co.

LIZARDS—FICTION

Abbott, Tony. The Hidden Stairs & the Magic Carpet. Jessell, Tim, illus. 2004. (Secrets of Droon Ser.: No. 1). 80p. (gr. 2-5). 15.00 *(978-0-7569-3939-7(9))* Perfection Learning Corp.

Abrams, Penny. The Calabash Tales. Mikki, illus. 2011. 66p. 28.00 *(978-1-4349-1169-8(1))* Dorrance Publishing Co., Inc.

Ailes, Mark Cusco. The Snow Dargles: Book Two: the Chronicles of Weekland. 2010. 244p. pap. 16.95 *(978-1-4327-5223-1(5))* Outskirts Pr., Inc.

Becker, Bonny. Holbrook: A Lizard's Tale. Carter, Abby, illus. 2006. (ENG.). 160p. (J). (gr. 3-7). 15.00 *(978-0-618-71458-2(8)*, 100503, Clarion Bks.) HarperCollins Pubs.

Bennett, Steven. The Adventures of Super Dad: Colossal Encounters (Book #1) 2005. 98p. pap. 10.49 *(978-1-4116-5947-6(3))* Lulu Pr., Inc.

Bentley, Dawn. Icky Sticky Chameleon. Mack, Jeff, illus. 2005. 18p. (J). 9.95 *(978-1-58117-086-3(6)*, Intervisual/Piggy Toes) Bendon, Inc.

Berglund, Andrea Lloyd. A Good Little Horse: Thunder's Morning Stroll. 2009. 36p. (J). pap. 19.95 *(978-1-4327-3822-8(4))* Outskirts Pr., Inc.

Bernstein, Galia. Leyla. 2019. (ENG., Illus.). 32p. (J). (gr. -1-3). 16.99 *(978-1-4197-3543-1(8)*, 1268901, Abrams Bks. for Young Readers) Abrams, Inc.

Blackshaw, Win. David's Dinosaur. 2008. (ENG.). 105p. pap. 17.55 *(978-1-4092-3704-4(4))* Lulu Pr., Inc.

Bowler, Ann Martin. Gecko's Complaint: A Balinese Folktale (Bilingual Edition - English & Indonesian Text) Sukanada, I. Gusti Made, illus. 2009. (ENG.). 32p. (J). (gr. k-3). 14.95 *(978-0-7946-0484-4(6))* Tuttle Publishing.

Brian, Janeen. The Adventures of Kingii the Frilled Lizard, 1 vol. rev. ed. 2013. (Literary Text Ser.). (ENG., Illus.). 28p. (J). (gr. 2-3). pap. 10.99 *(978-1-4333-5607-0(4))*; lib. bdg. 19.96 *(978-1-4807-1729-9(0))* Teacher Created Materials, Inc.

Brodhead, Kimberly Renee. The Seedling: The Osarian Tales. 2008. 232p. pap. 24.95 *(978-1-60703-814-6(5))* America Star Bks.

Brodnax, Stephan. Dillwyn & the Purple Picnic Pack, 1 vol. 2009. 19p. pap. 24.95 *(978-1-4241-9593-0(4))* America Star Bks.

Bush, Don. Magic Smith the Chameleon. 62p. (J). (gr. 3). 6.50 *(978-0-943978-02-4(5))* Rolling Hills Pr.

Carter, Aubrey Smith. The Enchanted Lizard: La Lagartijita Mágica. Nelson, Esther Whitt, ed. Branton, Molly, illus. 2006. (ENG & SPA.). 96p. (J). 18.95 *(978-1-893271-38-8(2)*, Maverick Bks.) Trinity Univ. Pr.

Chen, E. C. Bad Alphabet. 2013. 62p. 15.99 *(978-0-9891510-0-9(X))* Zebra Ginkgo.

Conroe, Lindy. Rockafella Jones & the Hidden Treasure. Riette, Susanne, illus. 2011. 108p. (J). pap. 10.95 *(978-1-935199-00-7(5))* Blue Mustang Pr.

Cook, Sherry & Johnson, Terri. Inquisitive Inman, 26 vols. Kuhn, Jesse, illus. I.t. ed. 2006. (Quirkles — Exploring Phonics through Science Ser.: 9). 32p. (J). 7.99 *(978-1-933815-08-4(6)*, Quirkles, The) Creative 3, LLC.

Cowley, Joy. Friends: Snake & Lizard. 2011. (Gecko Press Titles Ser.). (ENG., Illus.). 144p. 16.95 *(978-1-877579-01-1(7))* Gecko Pr. NZL. Dist: Lerner Publishing Group.

Crane, Elizabeth J. Armando: The Case of the Missing Tail. 2011. 36p. pap. 15.95 *(978-1-4490-8257-4(2))* AuthorHouse.

Crow, Melinda Melton. Little Lizard's Big Party. Rowland, Andrew & Rowland, Andrew, illus. 2010. (Little Lizards Ser.). (ENG.). 32p. (J). (gr. -1-1). pap. 6.25 *(978-1-4342-2791-1(X)*, 114058, Stone Arch Bks.) Capstone.

—Little Lizard's Family Fun. Rowland, Andrew, illus. 2010. (Little Lizards Ser.). (ENG.). 32p. (J). (gr. -1-1). pap. 6.25 *(978-1-4342-2790-4(1)*, 114057, Stone Arch Bks.) Capstone.

—Little Lizard's First Day. Rowland, Andrew & Rowland, Andrew, illus. 2010. (Little Lizards Ser.). (ENG.). 32p. (J). (gr. -1-1). pap. 6.25 *(978-1-4342-2789-8(8)*, 114056); lib. bdg. 22.65 *(978-1-4342-2005-9(2)*, 102769) Capstone. (Stone Arch Bks.).

—Little Lizard's New Baby, 1 vol. Rowland, Andrew, illus. 2011. (Little Lizards Ser.). (ENG.). 32p. (J). (gr. -1-1). pap. 6.25 *(978-1-4342-3047-8(3)*, 114647, Stone Arch Bks.) Capstone.

—Little Lizard's New Bike. Rowland, Andrew & Rowland, Andrew, illus. 2010. (Little Lizards Ser.). (ENG.). 32p. (J). (gr. -1-1). pap. 6.25 *(978-1-4342-2792-8(8)*, 114059); lib. bdg. 22.65 *(978-1-4342-2008-0(7)*, 102772) Capstone. (Stone Arch Bks.).

—Little Lizard's New Friend, 1 vol. Rowland, Andrew, illus. 2011. (Little Lizards Ser.). (ENG.). 32p. (J). (gr. -1-1). pap. 6.25 *(978-1-4342-3048-5(1)*, 114648, Stone Arch Bks.) Capstone.

—Little Lizard's New Pet, 1 vol. Rowland, Andrew, illus. 2011. (Little Lizards Ser.). (ENG.). 32p. (J). (gr. -1-1). pap. 6.25 *(978-1-4342-3049-2(X)*, 114649, Stone Arch Bks.) Capstone.

Crowe, Ellie. Go to Sleep, Hide & Seek. Wu, Julie, illus. 2009. 10p. (J). bds. 11.95 *(978-1-59700-759-7(5))* Island Heritage Publishing.

Culici, Tonia. Kiku Gecko & Rainbow Girl. 2012. 44p. pap. 20.45 *(978-1-4525-0584-8(5))* Balboa Pr.

Cyr, Lynne G. Drako's ABC Adventures as an Iguana. 2006. (Illus.). 37p. (J). spiral bd. 21.95 *(978-0-9774543-0-3(4))* Cyr Design Publishing.

Cyrus, Kurt. Invisible Lizard. Atkins, Andy, illus. 2017. (ENG.). 32p. (J). (gr. k-2). 16.99 *(978-1-58536-378-0(2)*, 204320) Sleeping Bear Pr.

De Serres, Michelle. The Gecko Ball. 2011. (Illus.). 28p. pap. *(978-1-905553-78-5(1))* BookPublishingWorld.

Denise, Susan Denise. The Little Lazy Lizard. 2008. 16p. pap. 24.95 *(978-1-60474-502-3(9))* America Star Bks.

DeNucci, Sharon. Grammie & the Gecko. DeNucci, Corinne, illus. 2008. (ENG.). 38p. pap. 16.99 *(978-1-4389-1790-0(2))* AuthorHouse.

Derenge, Garett. The Adventures of Iggy the Iguana. 2013. (ENG.). 30p. (J). pap. 13.95 *(978-1-4787-1290-9(2))* Outskirts Pr., Inc.

DeSica, Melissa. Gecko & Mosquito. 2007. (Illus.). 32p. (J). 14.95 *(978-0-9790647-6-0(7))* Watermark Publishing, LLC.

DiLorenzo, Barbara. Quincy: The Chameleon Who Couldn't Blend In. 2018. (ENG., Illus.). 40p. (J). (gr. -1-3). 17.99 *(978-1-4998-0542-0(X))* Little Bee Books Inc.

Donaldson, Julia. Superworm. Scheffler, Axel, illus. 2014. (ENG.). 32p. (J). (gr. -1-3). 16.99 *(978-0-545-59176-8(7)*, Levine, Arthur A. Bks.) Scholastic, Inc.

Las Dos Iguanas.Tr. of Two Iguanas. (SPA.). (J). 9.95 *(978-968-6044-78-2(7))* Corunda, Ediciones, S.A. de C.V. MEX. Dist: AIMS International Bks., Inc.

Eagle, Golden. Father Sun & Luis the Lizard. I.t. ed. 2005. (Illus.). 22p. (J). per. 12.99 *(978-1-59879-026-9(9))* Lifevest Publishing, Inc.

Emanuel, Effie Ann. Charles Chameleon. 2007. 32p. per. 24.95 *(978-1-4241-8621-1(8))* America Star Bks.

Escott, Maria. Green Anole Meets Brown Anole, a Love Story. Wigal, Mike, illus. 2010. 28p. pap. 12.95 *(978-1-936051-82-3(6))* Peppertree Pr., The.

Fontenot, Mary Alice & Fontenot Landry, Julie. Clovis Crawfish & the Twin Sister, 1 vol. Butler, Julie Dupre & Buckner, Julie Dupre, illus. 2007. (Clovis Crawfish Ser.). (ENG.). 32p. (J). (gr. k-3). 16.99 *(978-1-58980-467-8(8)*, Pelican Publishing) Arcadia Publishing.

Giancamilli, Vanessa. Gecko Gathering. Kest, Kristin, illus. 2005. (Soundprints' Amazing Animal Adventures! Ser.). (ENG.). 32p. (J). (gr. -1-3). 19.95 *(978-1-59249-321-0(1)*, BC7107) Soundprints.

Goodyear-Brown, Paris. Gabby the Gecko. 2003. per. *(978-1-932203-54-7(0))* Sundog, Ltd.

Grace, Phillip. The Lizard of Cupcake Lake. 2006. (J). pap. 15.95 *(978-0-9601454-3-0(5)*, 06-2129LIZ) Stelucan Pr.

Gravett, Emily. Blue Chameleon. Gravett, Emily, illus. 2011. (ENG., Illus.). 32p. (J). (gr. -1-1). 16.99 *(978-1-4424-1958-2(X)*, Simon & Schuster Bks. For Young Readers) Simon & Schuster Bks. For Young Readers.

Greene, Stephanie. Owen Foote, Mighty Scientist. Smith, Catharine Bowman, illus. 2004. (ENG.). 96p. (J). (gr. 1-4). tchr. ed. 15.00 *(978-0-618-43016-1(4)*, 100349, Clarion Bks.) HarperCollins Pubs.

Hale, Bruce. The Adventures of Space Gecko. (Illus.). (J). 8.95 *(978-0-9621280-2-8(3))* Words & Pictures Publishing, Inc.

—Dial M for Mongoose: A Chet Gecko Mystery. 2010. (Chet Gecko Ser.: 15). (ENG., Illus.). 128p. (J). (gr. 3-7). pap. 6.99 *(978-0-547-48079-4(2)*, 1439406, Clarion Bks.) HarperCollins Pubs.

—Murder, My Tweet. 2005. (Chet Gecko Mystery Ser.). (Illus.). 117p. (gr. 3-7). 16.00 *(978-0-7569-5248-8(4))* Perfection Learning Corp.

—This Gum for Hire: A Chet Gecko Mystery. Hale, Bruce, illus. 2003. (Chet Gecko Ser.: 6). (ENG., Illus.). 144p. (J). (gr. 3-7). pap. 6.99 *(978-0-15-202497-0(2)*, 1192976, Clarion Bks.) HarperCollins Pubs.

—Trouble Is My Beeswax. 2004. (Chet Gecko Mystery Ser.). (Illus.). 111p. (gr. 3-7). 16.00 *(978-0-7569-3488-0(5))* Perfection Learning Corp.

Halfmann, Janet. Little Skink's Tail, 1 vol. Allen Klein, Laurie, illus. 2007. (ENG.). 32p. (J). (gr. -1-3). 15.95 *(978-0-9768823-8-1(8))* Arbordale Publishing.

Haneberg, Janet. Alamander, the Orange Salamander. 2005. (ENG.). 36p. (J). pap. 14.99 *(978-1-4116-6678-8(X))* Lulu Pr., Inc.

Haselhuhn, Hugo & Cowdell, Luke. Lucas Lightfoot & the Fire Crystal. 2016. (ENG., Illus.). 180p. (J). pap. 12.95 *(978-1-63047-783-7(4))* Morgan James Publishing.

Hilton, Marcel. The Magical Web. 2007. 38p. 19.50 *(978-1-4303-2678-6(6))* Lulu Pr., Inc.

Irwin, Bindi & Kunz, Chris. Camouflage. 2011. (Bindi's Wildlife Adventures Ser.: 4). (ENG.). 112p. (J). (gr. 3-6). pap. 6.99 *(978-1-4022-5523-6(3)*, Sourcebooks Jabberwocky) Sourcebooks, Inc.

James, Shilah & James, Michael. Little Land Adventures - Little Iguan. Castles, Heather, illus. 2010. 24p. pap. *(978-1-926635-34-7(5))* Adlibbed, Ltd.

Johnson, Rebecca. Gorgeous Geckos, 1 vol. 2017. (Reptile Adventures Ser.). (ENG.). 24p. (J). (gr. 1-2). 26.27 *(978-1-5081-9359-3(2)*, 935f2f9b-2655-4428-9eae-a038af5da6ba); pap. 9.25 *(978-1-5081-9363-0(0)*, e24f6b3e-4349-40c9-ac73-bb7d44bc0a94) Rosen Publishing Group, Inc., The. (Windmill Bks.).

Johnson, Regan. Hold on to Your Tail: Letters from Camp Lizard. Johnson, Regan, illus. 2008. (Letters From Camp Lizard Ser.). (ENG., Illus.). 112p. (J). (gr. 1-5). pap. 7.95 *(978-1-933831-04-6(9))* Blooming Tree Pr.

Johnston, Cindy. Zip, Burp & Hula. 2006. (Illus.). 32p. (J). per. 10.95 *(978-0-9787930-5-0(6))* Virtual Word Publishing.

Joyner, Andrew. Boris Gets a Lizard. 2013. (Boris Ser.: 2). lib. bdg. 14.75 *(978-0-606-31975-1(1))* Turtleback.

—Boris Gets a Lizard: a Branches Book (Boris #2) 2013. (Boris Ser.: 2). (ENG., Illus.). 80p. (J). (gr. k-2). pap. 5.99 *(978-0-545-48447-3(2))* Scholastic, Inc.

Julie, Aunt. State Symbols of Texas - Paddleduck #8. 2012. (ENG.). 50p. pap. 5.95 *(978-1-105-91163-7(2))* Lulu Pr., Inc.

Karre, Nancy. On Herman's Pond. 2005. 8.00 *(978-1-933281-00-1(6)*, 2267) Battle Creek Area Mathematics & Science Ctr.

Kelly Allen, Nancy. Dear Komodo Dragon, 1 vol. Allen Klein, Laurie, illus. 2018. (ENG.). 32p. (J). (gr. k-3). 17.95 *(978-1-60718-449-2(4)*, 9781607184492); pap. 11.95 *(978-1-60718-460-7(5)*, 9781607184607) Arbordale Publishing.

—Querido Dragón Komodo: Spanish, 1 vol. Allen Klein, Laurie, illus. 2018. (SPA.). 32p. (J). (gr. 2-3). pap. 11.95 *(978-1-60718-465-2(6)*, c3a8c076-f067-4d3f-9213-fee4f486b3ca) Arbordale Publishing.

Kiker, Jean. Jumping Lizard Tales. 2005. pap. 12.95 *(978-1-932196-51-1(X))* WordWright.biz, Inc.

Knight, Diedre. Beanie's Backyard. 2012. 28p. pap. 12.95 *(978-1-62141-812-2(X))* Booklocker.com, Inc.

Koontz, Robin. The Three Billy Goats & Gruff. Koontz, Robin, illus. 2011. (Little Birdie Readers Ser.). (ENG., Illus.). 24p. (gr. 2-3). pap. 9.95 *(978-1-61236-030-0(0)*, 9781612360300) Rourke Educational Media.

Koontz, Robin Michal. The Three Billy Goats & Gruff. 2011. (ENG., Illus.). (J). (gr. 2-3). pap. 7.95 *(978-1-63430-982-0(0))* Rourke Educational Media.

Lambert, George J. 8 Boys & 8 Beasts, 1 vol. Lambert, Celeste, illus. 2010. 24p. 24.95 *(978-1-4489-5901-3(2))* PublishAmerica, Inc.

Lemke, Donald & Lemke, Donald B. Lucha Lizards: Chameleon Cage Match! Eliopoulos, Chris, illus. 2013. (Lucha Lizards Ser.). (ENG.). 48p. (J). (gr. 3-5). pap. 5.95 *(978-1-4342-3874-0(1)*, 118055); lib. bdg. 23.99 *(978-1-4342-3285-4(9)*, 116244) Capstone. (Stone Arch Bks.).

Lingenfelser, Lynda L. The Adventures of Lizah Lizard: The Laughing, Lovable Lizard. 2006. (ENG.). 50p. (J). per. *(978-0-615-13290-7(1))* Lingenfelser, Lynda L.

J
K
L

—Lizah Lizard: Koco's Tale. 2007. (ENG.). 50p. pap. *(978-0-615-14072-8(6))* Lingenfelser, Lynda L.

Lionni, Leo. Su Propio Color (a Color of His Own, Spanish-English Bilingual Edition) Lionni, Leo, illus. 2016. (Illus.). 30p. (J). (gr. -1-k). bds. 8.99 *(978-0-553-53873-1(X),* Knopf Bks. for Young Readers) Random Hse. Children's Bks.

Little, Celeste. Scales. Motz, Mike, illus. 2012. 24p. (J). 12.95 *(978-1-60131-116-0(8))* Big Tent Bks.

Little, Jean. Emma's Strange Pet. 2004. (I Can Read Level 3 Ser.). (ENG., Illus.). 64p. (J). (gr. k-3). pap. 4.99 *(978-0-06-444259-6(4),* HarperCollins) HarperCollins Pubs.

—Emma's Strange Pet. Plecas, Jennifer, illus. 2003. (I Can Read Bks.). 64p. (J). (gr. k-3). 15.99 *(978-0-06-028350-6(5))* HarperCollins Pubs.

Mabry, Sheri. The Kid & the Chameleon Sleepover (the Kid & the Chameleon: Time to Read, Level 3) Stone, Joanie, illus. 2019. (Time to Read Ser.). (ENG.). 48p. (J). (gr. k-2). 12.99 *(978-0-8075-4180-7(X),* 080754180X) Whitman, Albert & Co.

—The Kid & the Chameleon (the Kid & the Chameleon: Time to Read, Level 3) Stone, Joanie, illus. 2019. (Time to Read Ser.). (ENG.). 48p. (J). (gr. k-2). 12.99 *(978-0-8075-4179-1(6),* 807541796) Whitman, Albert & Co.

Mendenhall, Gaylee. My Teacher Is Bald! 2011. 28p. pap. 14.99 *(978-1-4634-5032-8(X))* AuthorHouse.

Milani, Joan. The Secret Society of the Palos Verdes Lizards. Schartup, Adam, illus. 2013. (ENG.). (J). 14.95 *(978-1-62086-346-6(4))* Amplify Publishing Group.

Moon, Alice. Lucky's Special Thanksgiving. 2007. (Illus.). (J). pap. 9.95 *(978-0-9795831-2-4(8))* PeachMoon Publishing.

Morin, Tara. There's an Iguana in My Bed. 2013. 28p. pap. 15.99 *(978-1-4817-1191-3(1))* AuthorHouse.

Murakami, Jon & BeachHouse Publishing. Geckos Surf. 2007. (ENG.). 16p. (J). (gr. -1-5). bds. 7.95 *(978-1-933067-22-3(5))* Beachhouse Publishing, LLC.

—Geckos up Geckos Down. 2010. (ENG.). 20p. (J). (gr. -1-1). bds. 7.95 *(978-1-933067-31-5(4))* Beachhouse Publishing, LLC.

My Special Place: Individual Title Six-Packs. (gr. -1-2). 23.00 *(978-0-7635-8811-3(3))* Rigby Education.

Nelson, Connie. The Lizard's Secret Door. Waller, Joyce, illus. 2014. 32p. (J). 19.95 *(978-1-59298-933-1(0))* Beaver's Pond Pr., Inc.

Noth, Paul. How to Properly Dispose of Planet Earth. 2019. (ENG., Illus.). 192p. (J). 13.99 *(978-1-68119-659-6(X),* 900179851, Bloomsbury Children's Bks.) Bloomsbury Publishing USA.

Oneto, Maria Teresa. Liliana, la Iguan. 2012. 52p. pap. 25.00 *(978-1-4389-8241-0(0))* AuthorHouse.

Orozco, Maria. Lizards on 41st Street. 2011. 28p. pap. 13.59 *(978-1-4567-2412-2(6))* AuthorHouse.

Osborn, D. W. Why Can't I Ribbit?, 1 vol. 2009. 48p. pap. 16.95 *(978-1-61582-641-4(6))* America Star Bks.

Paquette, Heather. Kammy the Chameleon Goes to School. Paquette Jr., Edward D., illus. 2012. 24p. pap. 24.95 *(978-1-62709-765-9(1))* America Star Bks.

Parker, Ty. The Golden Lizards. 2011. 20p. pap. 12.95 *(978-1-4670-2820-2(7))* AuthorHouse.

Patton, Jack. The Butterfly Rebellion. 2016. (Battle Bugs Ser.: 9). (ENG., Illus.). 128p. (J). (gr. 2-5). pap. 4.99 *(978-0-545-94515-8(1),* Scholastic Paperbacks) Scholastic, Inc.

—The Lizard War. Bean, Brett, illus. 2015. 123p. (J). *(978-0-545-81265-8(8))* Scholastic, Inc.

PeachMoon Publishing. The Adventures of Lucky the Lizard Las aventuras del lagarto Lucky. 2008. (ENG & SPA., Illus.). 100p. (J). pap. 19.95 *(978-0-9795831-4-8(4))* PeachMoon Publishing.

—The Lizard in the Mailbox. 2007. (J). pap. 9.95 *(978-0-9795831-0-0(1))* PeachMoon Publishing.

—Lucky Goes to School. 2007. (J). pap. 9.95 *(978-0-9795831-1-7(X))* PeachMoon Publishing.

Perlman, Janet. The Delicious Bug. Perlman, Janet, illus. 2009. (Illus.). 32p. (J). (gr. -1-2). 16.95 *(978-1-55337-996-6(9))* Kids Can Pr., Ltd. CAN. Dist: Hachette Bk. Group.

Phinn, Gervase. Who Am I? Ross, Tony, illus. 2012. (ENG.). 32p. (J). (gr. -1-3). 16.95 *(978-0-7613-8996-5(2),* 63b6fb3b-21dd-4f17-b375-3472edbb76ab) Lerner Publishing Group.

Pickering, Jill. A Lizard Got into the Paint Pots. Wright, Petrina, illus. 2003. (ENG.). 220p. (J). (gr. -1-3). 14.95 *(978-0-333-98858-9(2))* Macmillan Caribbean GBR. Dist: Interlink Publishing Group, Inc.

Pinkwater, Daniel M. Lizard Music. Pinkwater, Daniel M., illus. 2017. (Illus.). 160p. (J). (gr. 4-7). pap. 11.99 *(978-1-68137-184-9(7),* NYRB Kids) New York Review of Bks., Inc., The.

Price, Allison W. A. The Dragons & the Words of Knowledge. 2009. 112p. pap. 14.98 *(978-0-557-05766-5(3))* Lulu Pr., Inc.

Quantz, Daniel, et al. Face-to-Face with the Lizard! 2006. (Spider-Man Ser.: No. 1). (ENG., Illus.). 24p. (J). (gr. 2-6). 31.36 *(978-1-59961-014-6(0),* 13609, Marvel Age) Spotlight.

Ramirez, Iz. Bob the Lizard, 1 vol. Swope, Brenda, illus. 2009. 26p. pap. 24.95 *(978-1-60749-232-0(6))* America Star Bks.

Richler, Mordecai. Jacob Two-Two & the Dinosaur. Petricic, Dusan, illus. 2009. (Jacob Two-Two Ser.). (ENG.). 104p. (J). (gr. 4-7). 10.95 *(978-0-88776-926-9(8))* Tundra Bks. CAN. Dist: Random Hse., Inc.

Rife, Mary Lou "Dink" & Backman, Kathleen. Spring Is in the Air with Graeagle Bear. 2010. (ENG.). 38p. pap. 21.99 *(978-1-4500-4025-9(X))* Xlibris Corp.

Roberts, Sarah E. Lunch with Sam & Max. 2012. 20p. pap. 17.99 *(978-1-4772-9053-8(2))* AuthorHouse.

Robertson, Elysia Hill. Dottie Goes to School. Robertson, Elysia Hill, illus. 2005. (Illus.). 30p. (J). per. 6.95 *(978-0-9764444-8-0(8))* E. J. Publishing.

Russell, Allyson. The Lizard Who Wanted to Be a Mouse. Bubp, Jennifer, illus. 2009. 28p. pap. 12.95 *(978-1-59858-938-2(5))* Dog Ear Publishing, LLC.

Sands, Maria. Sanjee & Her Delightful Hats. 2008. 20p. pap. 24.95 *(978-1-60563-700-6(9))* America Star Bks.

Santillo, LuAnn. Liz. Santillo, LuAnn, ed. 2003. (Half-Pint Kids Readers Ser.). (Illus.). 7p. (J). (gr. -1-1). pap. 1.00 *(978-1-59256-083-7(0))* Half-Pint Kids, Inc.

Saramago, José. The Lizard. Caistor, Nick & Caistor, Lucia, trs. Borges, J, illus. 2019. (ENG.). 24p. (J). (gr. 1-4). 17.95 *(978-1-60980-933-1(5),* Triangle Square) Seven Stories Pr.

Shamberger, Lindsey. I, I, I for Iguan. 2012. 44p. pap. 24.95 *(978-1-4626-7536-4(0))* America Star Bks.

Skelton, K. Magic from the Wishing Well. 2009. 28p. pap. 12.49 *(978-1-4389-8747-7(1))* AuthorHouse.

Smith, Rosemary. Lizard Tales: Lizzie Walks on the Wild Side. 2010. 28p. pap. 12.50 *(978-1-60911-082-6(X),* Strategic Bk. Publishing) Strategic Book Publishing & Rights Agency (SBPRA).

—Lizzie Goes to Tea. 2013. 32p. pap. 12.50 *(978-1-62212-338-4(7),* Strategic Bk. Publishing) Strategic Book Publishing & Rights Agency (SBPRA).

—Woody Gets Dunked. 2011. 28p. pap. 12.50 *(978-1-60976-628-3(8),* Eloquent Bks.) Strategic Book Publishing & Rights Agency (SBPRA).

Sparkes, Ali. Chameleon Chaos, No. 10. Collins, Ross, illus. 2014. (S. W. I. T. C. H. Ser.: 10). (ENG.). 112p. (J). (gr. 2-5). lib. bdg. 27.99 *(978-1-4677-2113-4(1),* 8c574e9c-1868-42a1-83d2-b86d8afe583a, Darby Creek) Lerner Publishing Group.

—Gecko Gladiator, No. 12. Collins, Ross, illus. 2014. (S. W. I. T. C. H. Ser.: 12). (ENG.). 104p. (J). (gr. 2-5). lib. bdg. 27.99 *(978-1-4677-2115-8(8),* cc532572-06e9-4568-a918-8e1b276481a3, Darby Creek) Lerner Publishing Group.

—Lizard Loopy, Bk. 9. Collins, Ross, illus. 2014. (S. W. I. T. C. H. Ser.: 9). (ENG.). 104p. (J). (gr. 2-5). lib. bdg. 27.99 *(978-1-4677-2112-7(3),* b130a932-7a79-4525-84ae-ef15db1971ce, Darby Creek) Lerner Publishing Group.

Staake, Bob. Can You See Me? 2019. (Beginner Books(R) Ser.). (ENG., Illus.). 40p. (J). (gr. -1-2). lib. bdg. 12.99 *(978-0-375-97197-6(1),* Random Hse. Bks. for Young Readers) Random Hse. Children's Bks.

Stine, R. L. The Lizard of Oz. 2016. 135p. (J). *(978-1-338-10392-2(X))* Scholastic, Inc.

Stockman, Hollie. Leon the Lizard. 2010. (ENG.). 36p. pap. 19.95 *(978-0-557-57889-4(2))* Lulu Pr., Inc.

Storad, Conrad J. Lizards for Lunch: A Roadrunner's Tale. 2009. (Sonoran Desert Tails Ser.). (Illus.). 32p. (J). (gr. k-4). 6.95 *(978-1-891795-00-8(7))* RGU Group, The.

Strunk, Peter, illus. & creator. Two Inch Hero: The Adventures of Lorenzo Lizard. Strunk, Peter, creator. 2006. (J). 17.95 *(978-0-9785961-0-1(2))* Smile Time Publishing.

TenNapel, Doug. The Battle for Amphibopolis: a Graphic Novel (Nnewts #3), Vol. 3. 2017. (Nnewts Ser.: 3). (ENG., Illus.). 224p. (J). (gr. 3-7). pap. 12.99 *(978-0-545-67670-0(3),* Graphix) Scholastic, Inc.

Trooboff, Rhoda. A Book for Elie. Radjou, Anna Nazaretz, illus. 2008. (ENG.). 31p. pap. 15.00 *(978-0-9773536-1-3(3))* Tenley Circle Pr.

Van Draanen, Wendelin. The Gecko & Sticky: Sinister Substitute. Gilpin, Stephen, illus. 2011. (Gecko & Sticky Ser.: 3). (ENG.). 224p. (J). (gr. 3-7). 7.99 *(978-0-440-42244-0(2),* Yearling) Random Hse. Children's Bks.

—The Gecko & Sticky: the Greatest Power. Gilpin, Stephen, illus. 2011. (Gecko & Sticky Ser.: 2). (ENG.). 208p. (J). (gr. 3-7). 7.99 *(978-0-440-42243-3(4),* Yearling) Random Hse. Children's Bks.

—The Gecko & Sticky: the Power Potion. Gilpin, Stephen, illus. 2011. (Gecko & Sticky Ser.: 4). (ENG.). 240p. (J). (gr. 3-7). 7.99 *(978-0-440-42245-7(0),* Yearling) Random Hse. Children's Bks.

Vernon, Ursula. Curse of the Were-Wiener. 2014. (Dragonbreath Ser.: 3). lib. bdg. 17.20 *(978-0-606-35710-4(6))* Turtleback.

—Dragonbreath #3: Curse of the Were-Wiener. 3rd ed. (Dragonbreath Ser.: 3). 208p. (J). (gr. 3-7). 2014. pap. 8.99 *(978-0-14-751321-2(9),* Puffin Books) 2010. (ENG.). 14.99 *(978-0-8037-3469-2(7),* Dial Bks) Penguin Young Readers Group.

—Dragonbreath #7: When Fairies Go Bad, No. 7. 7th ed. 2012. (Dragonbreath Ser.: 7). (Illus.). 208p. (J). (gr. 3-7). 14.99 *(978-0-8037-3678-8(9),* Dial Bks) Penguin Young Readers Group.

Villata, Diane A. Louie the Lizard. 2010. 28p. 12.50 *(978-1-4389-6923-7(6))* AuthorHouse.

Wagstaff, Janiel. Stella & Class: Information Experts. 2015. (ENG.). pap. 7.95 *(978-1-63133-024-7(1))* Staff Development for Educators.

Wiebe, Trina. Lizards Don't Wear Lip Gloss. Sarrazin, Marisol, illus. 2004. (Abby & Tess Pet-Sitters Ser.). 91p. 15.95 *(978-0-7569-3425-5(7))* Perfection Learning Corp.

Wiesner, David. Art & Max. 2011. (JPN.). 40p. (J). (gr. k-3). *(978-4-7764-0448-4(6))* BL Publishing Co., Ltd.

—Art & Max. 2011. (CHI.). 40p. (J). (gr. k-3). *(978-986-189-233-7(8))* Grimm Cultural Ent., Co., Ltd.

—Art & Max. 2010. (ENG., Illus.). 40p. (J). (gr. -1-3). 17.99 *(978-0-618-75663-6(9),* 100534, Clarion Bks.) HarperCollins Pubs.

—Art & Max. 2012. (CHI.). 37p. (J). *(978-7-5434-9586-9(4))* Hebei Jiaoyu Chubanshe.

Williamson, Rose. Look at Me! Look at Me! Marts, Doreen, illus. 2014. (ENG.). 32p. (J). (gr. -1-k). 16.95 *(978-1-62914-617-1(X),* Sky Pony Pr.) Skyhorse Publishing Co., Inc.

Wilson, A. c. & Wilson, A. C. Ambersil - the Legacy of Mr Harrison. 2011. 496p. pap. *(978-1-908105-45-5(3))* Grosvenor Hse. Publishing Ltd.

Winter, Barbara. Chameleon Capers. 2004. (Amazing Dictionary Ser.). (Illus.). 64p. pap. *(978-0-921156-97-0(9))* Plumleaf Press.

Yates, Gene, illus. The Chameleon Colors Book. 2006. (J). *(978-1-58865-361-1(7))* Kidsbooks, LLC.

Zinsser, Kam. Turbo Fires Up! 2012. (ENG.). 28p. (J). 16.95 *(978-1-4787-1756-0(4))* Outskirts Pr., Inc.

LLAMAS

Aspen-Baxter, Linda & Kissock, Heather. Llamas. 2012. (SPA.). (J). *(978-1-61913-189-7(7))* Weigl Pubs., Inc.

Dellaccio, Tanya. Raising Llamas, 1 vol. 2019. (Unusual Farm Animals Ser.). (ENG.). 24p. (J). (gr. 2-3). pap. 9.25 *(978-1-7253-0902-9(5),* 7c82338a-f449-4421-a635-a7c4a089fce2, PowerKids Pr.) Rosen Publishing Group, Inc., The.

Garcia, Alonso. Alpacas, 1 vol. 2017. (Wild & Woolly Ser.). (ENG.). 24p. (J). (gr. 3-3). 25.27 *(978-1-5383-2523-0(3),* 3eee6935-e631-4cc0-8f08-b6770e47309e, PowerKids Pr.) Rosen Publishing Group, Inc., The.

Gish, Melissa. Living Wild: Llamas. 2017. (Living Wild Ser.). (ENG., Illus.). 48p. (J). (gr. 5-7). pap. 12.00 *(978-1-62832-434-1(1),* 20199, Creative Paperbacks) Creative Co., The.

—Llamas. 2017. (Living Wild Ser.). (ENG., Illus.). 48p. (J). (gr. 4-7). *(978-1-60818-831-4(0),* 20198, Creative Education) Creative Co., The.

Hudak, Heather C. Llamas. 2006. (Farm Animals Ser.). (Illus.). 24p. (J). (gr. 3-7). lib. bdg. 24.45 *(978-1-59036-427-7(9),* 1266407); per. 8.95 *(978-1-59036-434-5(1),* 1266407) Weigl Pubs., Inc.

Kissock, Heather & Aspen-Baxter, Linda. Llamas. 2011. (Illus.). 24p. (J). 27.13 *(978-1-61690-930-7(7))* Weigl Pubs., Inc.

Leaf, Christina. Llama or Alpaca? 2019. (Spotting Differences Ser.). (ENG., Illus.). 24p. (J). (gr. k-3). lib. bdg. 26.95 *(978-1-64487-034-1(7),* Blastoff! Readers) Bellwether Media.

MacDhui, Lori. Llamas, 1 vol. 2017. (Wild & Woolly Ser.). (ENG.). 24p. (J). (gr. 3-3). 25.27 *(978-1-5383-2531-5(4),* 2cf94686-e8c1-4671-be65-78819fefae25, PowerKids Pr.) Rosen Publishing Group, Inc., The.

Marsico, Katie. Farm Animals: Llama. 2011. (21st Century Junior Library: Farm Animals Ser.). (ENG., Illus.). 24p. (J). (gr. 2-4). lib. bdg. 29.21 *(978-1-60279-977-6(6),* 1321598) Cherry Lake Publishing.

Myers, Maya. National Geographic Readers: Llamas (L1) 2020. (Readers Ser.). (Illus.). 32p. (J). (gr. -1-k). pap. 4.99 *(978-1-4263-3725-3(6),* National Geographic Kids) Disney Publishing Worldwide.

Orr, Tamra. Alpaca or Llama. 2019. (21st Century Junior Library: Which Is Which? Ser.). (ENG., Illus.). 24p. (J). (gr. 2-5). pap. 12.79 *(978-1-5341-5019-5(6),* 213383); lib. bdg. 30.64 *(978-1-5341-4733-1(0),* 213382) Cherry Lake Publishing.

Scott, Ellen. Glitter Llama Stickers. 2018. (Dover Little Activity Books Stickers Ser.). (ENG.). 4p. (J). (gr. 1-4). pap. 1.99 *(978-0-486-82913-5(8),* 829138) Dover Pubns., Inc.

Williams, Zella. Llamas & Other Latin American Camels: Llamas y Otros Camélidos de Latinoamérica, 1 vol. 2009. (Animals of Latin America / Animales de Latinoamérica Ser.). (SPA & ENG.). 24p. (J). (gr. 2-2). pap. 8.25 *(978-1-4358-3388-3(0),* f0b64cd8-7eea-4f2c-b56d-4abf08d8c0c6, PowerKids Pr.) Rosen Publishing Group, Inc., The.

LLAMAS—FICTION

Abrams, Kelsey. Llama Drama: A Grace Story. Tejido, Jomike, illus. 2019. (Second Chance Ranch Set 2 Ser.). (ENG.). 120p. (J). (gr. 3-4). pap. 7.99 *(978-1-63163-264-8(7),* 1631632647); lib. bdg. 27.13 *(978-1-63163-263-1(9),* 1631632639) North Star Editions. (Jolly Fish Pr.).

Bishop, Sara. Luis the Llam. 2011. 16p. pap. 24.95 *(978-1-4560-7281-0(1))* America Star Bks.

Cangilla-McAdam, Claudia. Maria's Mysterious Mission. Crum, Anna-Maria, illus. 2007. 32p. (J). (gr. 3-7). 12.95 *(978-1-56579-588-4(1))* Fielder, John Publishing.

Chiappini, Lydia. A Llama's Tale: Freesia's Little Llama Farm. 2003. (Illus.). 64p. pap. 10.00 *(978-0-9669355-9-2(4))* Chiappini, Lydia.

Conroy, Christine. Mama Wants a Llam. 2012. 16p. pap. 15.99 *(978-1-4772-1605-7(7))* AuthorHouse.

deRubertis, Barbara. Lana Llama's Little Lamb. Alley, R. W., illus. 2011. (Animal Antics A to Z Ser.). 32p. (J). pap. 45.32 *(978-0-7613-7658-3(5));* (ENG.). lib. bdg. 22.60 *(978-1-57565-333-4(8))* Astra Publishing Hse.

deRubertis, Barbara & DeRubertis, Barbara. Lana Llama's Little Lamb. Alley, R. W., illus. 2012. (Animal Antics A to Z Ser.). 32p. (J). (gr. 2 — 1). cd-rom 7.95 *(978-1-57565-405-8(9))* Astra Publishing Hse.

Dewdney, Anna. Llama Llama & the Bully Goat. 2013. (Llama Llama Ser.). (Illus.). 40p. (J). (gr. -1-k). 18.99 *(978-0-670-01395-1(1),* Viking Books for Young Readers) Penguin Young Readers Group.

—Llama Llama & the Lucky Pajamas. 2018. (Illus.). 24p. (J). lib. bdg. 14.75 *(978-0-606-40898-1(3))* Turtleback.

—Llama Llama Birthday Party! Dewdney, Anna, illus. 2013. (Llama Llama Ser.). (Illus.). 16p. (J). (gr. -1-k). 7.99 *(978-0-448-45880-9(2),* Grosset & Dunlap) Penguin Young Readers Group.

—Llama Llama Easter Egg. 2015. (Llama Llama Ser.). (Illus.). 14p. (J). (— 1). bds. 7.99 *(978-0-451-46982-3(8),* Viking Books for Young Readers) Penguin Young Readers Group.

—Llama Llama Gives Thanks. 2017. (Llama Llama Ser.). (Illus.). 14p. (J). (— 1). bds. 7.99 *(978-1-101-99715-4(X),* Viking Books for Young Readers) Penguin Young Readers Group.

—Llama Llama Gram & Grandpa. (Llama Llama Ser.). (Illus.). (J). (— 1). 2020. (ENG.). 36p. bds. 9.99 *(978-0-593-11775-0(1))* 2015. 40p. bds. 18.99 *(978-0-670-01396-8(X))* Penguin Young Readers Group. (Viking Books for Young Readers).

—Llama Llama Holiday Drama. (Llama Llama Ser.). (Illus.). (J). 2018. 36p. (— 1). bds. 14.99 *(978-1-9848-3558-1(0))* 2017. 36p. (— 1). bds. 9.99 *(978-0-425-29181-8(2))* 2010. 40p. (gr. -1-k). 18.99 *(978-0-670-01161-2(4))* Penguin Young Readers Group. (Viking Books for Young Readers).

—Llama Llama Home with Mama. 2011. (Llama Llama Ser.). (ENG., Illus.). 40p. (J). (gr. -1-k). 18.99 *(978-0-670-01232-9(7),* Viking Books for Young Readers) Penguin Young Readers Group.

—Llama Llama Hoppity-Hop. 2012. (Llama Llama Ser.). (Illus.). 14p. (J). (gr. -1 — 1). bds. 7.99 *(978-0-670-01329-6(3),* Viking Books for Young Readers) Penguin Young Readers Group.

—Llama Llama I Love You. 2014. (Llama Llama Ser.). (Illus.). 14p. (J). (gr. -1 — 1). bds. 6.99 *(978-0-451-46981-6(X),* Viking Books for Young Readers) Penguin Young Readers Group.

—Llama Llama Learns to Swim. 2018. (Llama Llama 8X8 Ser.). lib. bdg. 14.75 *(978-0-606-41334-3(0))* Turtleback.

—Llama Llama Loses a Tooth. 2018. (Penguin Young Readers Level 2 Ser.). (Illus.). 32p. (J). lib. bdg. 13.55 *(978-0-606-40882-0(7))* Turtleback.

—Llama Llama Loves Camping. 2018. (Llama Llama 8X8 Ser.). (Illus.). 24p. (J). lib. bdg. 14.75 *(978-0-606-41335-0(9))* Turtleback.

—Llama Llama Mad at Mama. Dewdney, Anna, illus. 2007. (Llama Llama Ser.). (ENG., Illus.). 40p. (J). (gr. -1-k). 18.99 *(978-0-670-06240-9(5),* Viking Books for Young Readers) Penguin Young Readers Group.

—Llama Llama Mad at Mama. 2009. (Illus.). (J). *(978-0-545-15933-3(4))* Scholastic, Inc.

—Llama Llama Misses Mama. (Llama Llama Ser.). (Illus.). (J). 2019. (ENG.). 36p. (— 1). bds. 9.99 *(978-0-593-11671-5(2))* 2009. 40p. (gr. -1-k). 18.99 *(978-0-670-06198-3(0))* Penguin Young Readers Group. (Viking Books for Young Readers).

—Llama Llama Nighty-Night. 2012. (Llama Llama Ser.). (ENG., Illus.). 14p. (J). (— 1). bds. 6.99 *(978-0-670-01327-2(7),* Viking Books for Young Readers) Penguin Young Readers Group.

—Llama Llama Red Pajama. Dewdney, Anna, illus. (Llama Llama Ser.). (ENG., Illus.). (J). 2018. 34p. (-k). bds. 15.99 *(978-0-451-48063-7(5))* 2005. 40p. (gr. -1-k). 18.99 *(978-0-670-05983-6(8))* Penguin Young Readers Group. (Viking Books for Young Readers).

—Llama Llama Red Pajama. *(978-0-439-90665-4(2));* 2006. lp *(978-0-439-90679-1(2))* Scholastic, Inc.

—Llama Llama Red Pajama: Gift Edition. Dewdney, Anna, illus. 2014. (Llama Llama Ser.). (ENG., Illus.). 40p. (J). (gr. -1-k). 26.99 *(978-0-451-46990-8(9),* Viking Books for Young Readers) Penguin Young Readers Group.

—Llama Llama Time to Share. 2012. (Llama Llama Ser.). (ENG., Illus.). 40p. (J). (gr. -1-k). 18.99 *(978-0-670-01233-6(5),* Viking Books for Young Readers) Penguin Young Readers Group.

—Llama Llama Trick or Treat. Dewdney, Anna, illus. 2014. (Llama Llama Ser.). (ENG., Illus.). 14p. (J). (— 1). bds. 6.99 *(978-0-451-46978-6(X),* Viking Books for Young Readers) Penguin Young Readers Group.

—Llama Llama Wakey-Wake. 2012. (Llama Llama Ser.). (Illus.). 14p. (J). (— 1). bds. 7.99 *(978-0-670-01326-5(9),* Viking Books for Young Readers) Penguin Young Readers Group.

—Llama Llama Yum Yum Yum! A Scratch-And-Sniff Book. 2016. (Llama Llama Ser.). (Illus.). 14p. (J). (— 1). bds. 12.99 *(978-0-448-49638-2(0),* Grosset & Dunlap) Penguin Young Readers Group.

—Llama Llama Zippity-Zoom. 2012. (Llama Llama Ser.). 14p. (J). (gr. -1 — 1). bds. 7.99 *(978-0-670-01328-9(5),* Viking Books for Young Readers) Penguin Young Readers Group.

—Love from Llama Llama. Dewdney, Anna, illus. 2022. (Llama Llama Ser.). 32p. (J). (gr. k-3). 9.99 *(978-0-593-52174-8(9),* Grosset & Dunlap) Penguin Young Readers Group.

Dewdney, Anna, creator. Llama Llama & the Lucky Pajamas. 2018. (Llama Llama Ser.). (Illus.). 24p. (J). (gr. -1-2). pap. 5.99 *(978-1-5247-8501-7(6),* Penguin Young Readers Licenses) Penguin Young Readers Group.

—Llama Llama Learns to Swim. 2018. (Llama Llama Ser.). (Illus.). 24p. (J). (gr. -1-1). pap. 5.99 *(978-1-5247-8719-6(1),* Penguin Young Readers Licenses) Penguin Young Readers Group.

—Llama Llama Loves Camping. 2018. (Llama Llama Ser.). (Illus.). 24p. (J). (gr. -1-1). pap. 4.99 *(978-1-5247-8718-9(3),* Penguin Young Readers Licenses) Penguin Young Readers Group.

Dewdney, Anna & Duncan, Reed. Llama Llama Loves to Read. Morrow, J. T., illus. 2018. (Llama Llama Ser.). 40p. (J). (-k). 18.99 *(978-0-670-01397-5(8),* Viking Books for Young Readers) Penguin Young Readers Group.

—Llama Llama Meets the Babysitter. Morrow, J. T., illus. 2021. (Llama Llama Ser.). 40p. (J). (-k). 18.99 *(978-0-593-35033-1(2),* Viking Books for Young Readers) Penguin Young Readers Group.

—Llama Llama Mess Mess Mess. 2019. (Llama Llama Ser.). (Illus.). 40p. (J). (-k). 18.99 *(978-0-670-01644-0(6),* Viking Books for Young Readers) Penguin Young Readers Group.

Fraggolosch, Audrey. Land of the Wild Llama: A Story of the Patagonian Andes. 2005. (Soundprints' Wild Habitats Ser.). (ENG., Illus.). 32p. (J). (gr. 1-4). 8.95 *(978-1-59249-110-0(3),* SC7022) Soundprints.

Gilbert, Leah. A Couch for Llama. 2018. (Illus.). 40p. (J). (gr. -1). 16.95 *(978-1-4549-2511-8(6))* Sterling Publishing Co., Inc.

Guarino, Deborah. Is Your Mama a Llama? Kellogg, Steven, illus. (ENG.). (J). (gr. -1-3). 2006. 18.95 *(978-0-439-87594-3(3))* 2004. 32p. pap. 7.99 *(978-0-439-59842-2(7),* Scholastic Paperbacks) 2006. pap. 10.99 incl. audio compact disk *(978-0-439-87588-2(9))* Scholastic, Inc.

Guarino, Deborah & Kellogg, Steven. Ta Maman Est-Elle un Lama? (FRE., Illus.). (J). pap. 7.99 *(978-0-590-74555-0(7))* Scholastic, Inc.

Hernandez, Elaine. Welcome to Humming Meadow Ranch. Hernandez, Stacy, illus. 2005. 28p. (J). lib. bdg. 16.95 *(978-0-9766431-0-4(3))* Humming Meadow Ranch.

Huy, Barbara. Llamas Need Pajamas. 2012. 36p. pap. 15.49 *(978-1-4669-5752-7(2))* Trafford Publishing.

Kerr, Mike. Crafty Llama. Liwska, Renata, illus. 2018. (ENG.). 32p. (J). 16.99 *(978-1-68119-121-8(0),* 900159672, Bloomsbury Children's Bks.) Bloomsbury Publishing USA.

Lakeshore Learning Materials Staff. Is Your Mama a Llama? Big Book Theme Packet. 2008. (J). pap. 44.50 *(978-1-60666-043-0(8))* Lakeshore Learning Materials.

Moran, Paul & Forizs, Gergely. Where's the Llama? An Around-The-World Adventure. 2019. (ENG.). 48p. (J). pap. 9.99 *(978-1-4494-9729-3(2))* Andrews McMeel Publishing.

Palacios, Argentina. El Secreto de la Llama - The Llama's Secret: Una Leyenda Peruana. 97th ed. 2003. (Leyendas del Mundo Ser.). (SPA., Illus.). 32p. (gr. 2-5). pap. 12.90 *(978-0-8167-3072-8(5))* Harcourt Schl. Pubs.

Punter, Russell. Llamas in Pajamas. 2015. (Phonics Readers (no Flaps) Ser.). (ENG.). 24p. (J). pap. 6.99 *(978-0-7945-2739-6(6),* Usborne) EDC Publishing.

Stutzman, Jonathan. Llama Destroys the World. Fox, Heather, illus. 2019. (Llama Book Ser.: 1). (ENG.). 40p. (J). 18.99 *(978-1-250-30317-2(6),* 900197052, Holt, Henry & Co. Bks. For Young Readers) Holt, Henry & Co.

—Llama Unleashes the Alpacalypse. Fox, Heather, illus. 2020. (Llama Book Ser.: 2). (ENG.). 40p. (J). 18.99

(978-1-250-22285-5(0), 900208101, Holt, Henry & Co. Bks. For Young Readers) Holt, Henry & Co.

LOAN FUNDS, STUDENT
see Student Loans

LOCKHART, SALLY (FICTITIOUS CHARACTER)—FICTION
Pullman, Philip. The Ruby in the Smoke. 2009. 9.84 (978-0-7848-2919-6(5), Everbind) Marco Bk. Co.
—The Ruby in the Smoke. 2008. (Sally Lockhart Mystery Ser.: Bk. 1). (ENG.). 230p. (YA). (gr. 7-18). 22.44 (978-0-394-98826-9(4)) Random House Publishing Group.
—The Ruby in the Smoke. 2003. (Sally Lockhart Ser.: Bk. 1). (Illus.). (YA). pap. 9.95 (978-0-375-82545-3(2), Knopf Bks. for Young Readers) Random Hse. Children's Bks.
—The Ruby in the Smoke: a Sally Lockhart Mystery. 2008. (Sally Lockhart Ser.: Bk. 1). (ENG.). 256p. (YA). (gr. 7). pap. 10.99 (978-0-375-84516-1(X), Ember) Random Hse. Children's Bks.
—Sally y el Tigre en el Pozo. 2003. (SPA.). 512p. (YA). 16.95 (978-84-95618-49-8(4), Umbriel) Ediciones Urano S. A. ESP. Dist: Spanish Pubs., LLC.
—Sally y la Sombra del Norte. 2003.Tr. of Shadow in the North. (SPA., Illus.). 352p. (YA). 14.95 (978-84-95618-43-6(5), Umbriel) Ediciones Urano S. A. ESP. Dist: Spanish Pubs., LLC.
—The Shadow in the North. 2003. (Sally Lockhart Ser.: Bk. 2). (Illus.). (J). pap. 9.95 (978-0-375-82546-0(0), Knopf Bks. for Young Readers) Random Hse. Children's Bks.
—The Tiger in the Well. 2003. (Sally Lockhart Ser.: Bk. 3). (Illus.). (J). pap. 9.95 (978-0-375-82547-7(9)) Random Hse. Children's Bks.

LOBBYING
see also Political Corruption
Bozek, Rachel, ed. The Political Elite & Special Interests, 1 vol. 2017. (Current Controversies Ser.). (ENG.). 136p. (gr. 10-12). pap. 33.00 (978-1-5345-0105-8(3), 322e9023-4d0e-4cb9-8243-1ddfa7001125); lib. bdg. 48.03 (978-1-5345-0106-5(1), 21fc5139-b0b1-47cd-8511-a1fd8d40ca35) Greenhaven Publishing LLC.
Donovan, Sandy. Special Interests: From Lobbyists to Campaign Funding. 2015. (Inside Elections Ser.). (ENG., Illus.). 64p. (J). (gr. 6-8). 26.65 (978-1-4677-7912-8(1), ca52d649-9381-485e-be5e-d2c23740c977, Lerner Pubns.) Lerner Publishing Group.
Herschbach, Elisabeth. Lobbyists & Special Interest Groups. 2016. (Illus.). 64p. (J). (978-1-61900-090-2(3)) Eldorado Ink.
Horn, Geoffrey M. Political Parties, Interest Groups, & the Media, 1 vol. 2003. (World Almanac(r) Library of American Government Ser.). (ENG., Illus.). 48p. (gr. 5-8). pap. 15.05 (978-0-8368-5483-1(7), 97efc7c4-510b-4e32-8f0f-c646243b1f7f, Gareth Stevens Secondary Library) Stevens, Gareth Publishing LLLP.

LOBSTER FISHERIES
Volovar, Vivian. Lobster Lady. 2007. (Illus.). 32p. (J). pap. 14.95 (978-0-9773725-8-4(8)) Flat Hammock Pr.

LOBSTER FISHERIES—FICTION
Baldwin, Robert F. The Fish House Door. Sheckels, Astrid, illus. 2010. (ENG.). 36p. (J). 16.95 (978-1-934031-30-8(5), 4e2fdddb-0133-414a-8d2f-864fa8aeaa26) Islandport Pr., Inc.
Hayes, Karel. The Amazing Journey of Lucky the Lobster Buoy. 2009. (ENG.). 32p. (J). (gr. -1-3). 16.95 (978-0-89272-791-9(8)) Down East Bks.

LOBSTERS
Adamson, Heather. Lobsters. 2017. (Ocean Life up Close Ser.). (ENG., Illus.). 24p. (J). (gr. k-3). lib. bdg. 26.95 (978-1-62617-642-3(6), Blastoff! Readers) Bellwether Media.
Believe It Or Not!, Ripleys, compiled by. Ripley's Believe It or Not! Lobsters Are Red: But Sometimes They're Not! 2018. (Little Bks.: 4). (ENG., Illus.). 20p. (J). bds. 6.99 (978-1-60991-210-9(1)) Ripley Entertainment, Inc.
Hirschmann, Kris. Lobsters. 2004. (Creatures of the Sea Ser.). (ENG., Illus.). 48p. (J). (gr. 4-7). 29.15 (978-0-7377-2343-4(2)) Cengage Gale.
Jordan, Apple. Guess Who Snaps, 1 vol. 2009. (Guess Who? Ser.). (ENG.). 32p. (gr. k-1). pap. 9.23 (978-0-7614-3557-0(3), 2c7d1ac0-7b03-4c74-807f-72412a55d7c9) Cavendish Square Publishing LLC.
Magby, Meryl. Lobsters, 1 vol. 2012. (Under the Sea Ser.). (ENG., Illus.). 24p. (J). (gr. 2-3). pap. 9.25 (978-1-4488-7475-0(0), 5f883854-793b-4f3d-8982-8c8afbac065a); lib. bdg. 26.27 (978-1-4488-7396-8(7), 9b667866-d459-4eeb-b190-ea42b1881746) Rosen Publishing Group, Inc., The. (PowerKids Pr.).
Marsico, Katie. A Baby Lobster Grows Up. 2007. (Scholastic News Nonfiction Readers Ser.). (ENG., Illus.). 24p. (J). (gr. 1-2). pap. 6.95 (978-0-531-18694-7(6)) Scholastic Library Publishing.
Meister, Cari. Lobsters. 2014. (Illus.). 24p. (J). lib. bdg. 25.65 (978-1-62031-099-1(6), Bullfrog Bks.) Jump! Inc.
Pallotta, Jerry. Going Lobstering. Bolster, Rob, illus. 2008. (ENG.). 20p. (J). (gr. -1-3). bds. 7.95 (978-1-57091-623-6(3)) Charlesbridge Publishing, Inc.
—Lobster vs. Crab (Who Would Win?) Bolster, Rob, illus. 2020. (Who Would Win? Ser.: 13). (ENG.). 32p. (J). (gr. 1-4). pap. 4.99 (978-0-545-68121-6(9)) Scholastic, Inc.
Ricciuti, Edward R. Adivina Quién Tritura / Guess Who Snaps, 1 vol. 2009. (Adivina Quién / Guess Who? Ser.). (ENG & SPA.). 32p. (gr. k-2). 25.50 (978-0-7614-2886-2(0), 45f6aac4-4b78-4d68-bf77-b9111b04cbf0) Cavendish Square Publishing LLC.
—Adivina Quién Tritura (Guess Who Snaps), 1 vol. 2009. (Adivina Quién (Guess Who?) Ser.). (SPA.). 32p. (gr. k-2). 25.50 (978-0-7614-2870-1(4), f7d7e793-429e-492f-b585-b1e8d4f84e06) Cavendish Square Publishing LLC.
—Guess Who Snaps, 1 vol. 2006. (Guess Who? Ser.). (ENG., Illus.). 32p. (gr. k-1). lib. bdg. 25.50 (978-0-7614-1765-1(6), 9681f3d5-986a-4597-a8aa-4adbe7ac4a04) Cavendish Square Publishing LLC.
Rustad, Martha E. H. Lobsters. 2007. (Oceans Alive Ser.). (ENG., Illus.). 24p. (J). (gr. k-3). lib. bdg. 26.95 (978-1-60014-082-2(3)) Bellwether Media.
Shaffer, Lindsay. Spiny Lobsters. 2020. (Animals of the Coral Reef Ser.). (ENG., Illus.). 24p. (J). (gr. k-3). lib. bdg. 26.95 (978-1-64487-135-5(1), Blastoff! Readers) Bellwether Media.
Siemens, Jared. I am a Lobster. 2016. (Illus.). 24p. (J). (978-1-4896-5381-9(3)) Weigl Pubs., Inc.
Soundprints Staff, ed. Oceanic Collection III: Beluga Whale, Harp Seal, Walrus & Lobster Books, 4 micro bks. (Smithsonian Oceanic Collection). (Illus.). 128p. (J). (gr. -1-2). 18.95 (978-1-56899-633-2(0)) Soundprints.
Stone, Tanya Lee. Lobsters. 2003. (Wild Wild World Ser.). 24p. (YA). 24.94 (978-1-56711-816-2(X), Blackbirch Pr., Inc.) Cengage Gale.
World Book, Inc. Staff, contrib. by. Lobsters & Other Crustaceans. 2005. (World Book's Animals of the World Ser.). (Illus.). 64p. (J). (978-0-7166-1270-4(4)) World Bk., Inc.

LOBSTERS—FICTION
Aldrich, Sandra D. Lenny Lobster Saves the Day. 2012. 38p. 19.95 (978-1-4626-9817-2(4)) America Star Bks.
Bailey, Catherine. Lucy Loves Sherman. Walters, Meg, illus. 2017. (ENG.). 32p. (J). (gr. -1-k). 16.99 (978-1-63450-705-9(3), Sky Pony Pr.) Skyhorse Publishing Co., Inc.
Chiarello, Robin Taylor. The Blue Lobster's Holiday! Bohart, Lisa, illus. 2012. 40p. pap. 16.95 (978-1-61493-053-2(8)) Peppertree Pr., The.
Ginn, Jennifer. Lobsters on the Loose, 1 vol. (ENG., Illus.). 48p. (J). (gr. -1-3). 2019. pap. 9.99 (978-0-7643-5702-2(6), 16395) 2011. 16.99 (978-0-7643-3826-7(9), 4274, Schiffer Publishing Ltd) Schiffer Publishing, Ltd.
Gist, Richard. Ayshus on the Inside. 2013. 104p. (978-1-4602-1899-0(X)); pap. (978-1-4602-1900-3(7)) FriesenPress.
Hatch, Richard W. The Curious Lobster. Wakeman, Marion Freeman, illus. 2018. 400p. (J). (gr. 2-5). 14.99 (978-1-68137-288-4(6), NYRB Kids) New York Review of Bks., Inc., The.
Hollenbeck, Kathleen M. Lobster's Secret. Weiman, Jon, illus. 2011. (Smithsonian Oceanic Collection Ser.). (ENG.). 32p. (J). (gr. -1-3). 19.95 (978-1-60727-653-1(4)); 8.95 (978-1-60727-654-8(2)) Soundprints.
Lordon, Claire. Lorenzo, the Pizza-Loving Lobster. 2016. (ENG., Illus.). 32p. (J). (gr. -1-3). 16.99 (978-1-4998-0228-3(5)) Little Bee Books Inc.
Meister, Cari. The Grumpy Lobster, 1 vol. Harpster, Steve, illus. 2012. (Ocean Tales Ser.). (ENG.). 32p. (J). (gr. 2-3). pap. 6.25 (978-1-4342-4230-3(7), 120288); lib. bdg. 22.65 (978-1-4342-4025-5(8), 118410) Capstone. (Stone Arch Bks.).
Reilly, Antoinette. Mr. Lobster & the Mermaid. 2011. 24p. pap. 14.93 (978-1-4269-5683-6(5)) Trafford Publishing.
Schwarz, Viviane. Shark & Lobster's Amazing Undersea Adventure. Stewart, Joel, illus. 2006. 34p. (J). (978-1-4156-8140-4(6)) Candlewick Pr.
Taylor-Chiarello, Robin. The Blue Lobster. Bohart, Lisa, illus. 2011. 36p. pap. 15.95 (978-1-936343-84-3(3)) Peppertree Pr., The.

LOCAL GOVERNMENT
see also Cities and Towns; Public Administration
Benchmark Education Company. Local & State Government (Teacher Guide) 2005. (978-1-4108-4639-6(3)) Benchmark Education Co.
Benchmark Education Company, LLC Staff, compiled by. Social Studies Theme: GOVT & Citizenship. 2005. spiral bd. 115.00 (978-1-4108-5331-8(4)) Benchmark Education Co.
Brannon, Barbara. Discover Local & State Government. 2005. (J). pap. (978-1-4108-5145-1(1)) Benchmark Education Co.
Fowler, Leona. Our Local Government: Breaking down the Problem, 1 vol. 2017. (Computer Kids: Powered by Computational Thinking Ser.). (ENG.). 24p. (J). (gr. 3-4). 25.27 (978-1-5383-2423-3(7), cc18a408-3cb2-4a4c-8240-2a5031bfd224, PowerKids Pr.); pap. (978-1-5081-3793-1(5), 098f2cb5-2aa5-44cc-acd9-8bd43aa35fc8, Rosen Classroom) Rosen Publishing Group, Inc., The.
Johnson, Etta. Local & State Government. 2005. (J). pap. (978-1-4108-4591-7(5)) Benchmark Education Co.
Machajewski, Sarah. What Are State & Local Government?, 1 vol. 2015. (Let's Find Out! Government Ser.). (ENG., Illus.). 32p. (J). (gr. 2-3). 26.06 (978-1-62275-986-6(9), 52c5d263-c673-4f05-b5af-a24cb9564dbb, Britannica Educational Publishing) Rosen Publishing Group, Inc., The.
Mara, Wil. Local Action. 2016. (21st Century Skills Library: a Citizen's Guide Ser.). (ENG., Illus.). 32p. (J). (gr. 4-7). 32.07 (978-1-63471-070-1(3), 208359) Cherry Lake Publishing.
McAuliffe, Bill. State & Local Government. 2016. (By the People Ser.). (ENG., Illus.). 48p. (J). (gr. 4-7). 39.95 (978-1-60818-674-7(1), 20569, Creative Education); pap. 12.00 (978-1-62832-270-5(5), 20567, Creative Paperbacks) Creative Co., The.
Miller, Jake. Who's Who in an Urban Community, 1 vol. 2004. (Communities at Work Ser.). (ENG., Illus.). 24p. (J). (gr. 2-3). lib. bdg. 26.27 (978-1-4042-2790-3(3), dbaef7ab-851e-490f-bcc7-eff7e1776d93, PowerKids Pr.) Rosen Publishing Group, Inc., The.
O'Nan, Denny. My Local Government, 1 vol. 2013. (Rosen Readers Ser.). (ENG.). 24p. (J). (gr. 3-3). pap. 8.25 (978-1-4777-2572-6(5), 54501fdf-d758-4501-a7c2-4432a396b5ee); pap. 49.50 (978-1-4777-2573-3(3)) Rosen Publishing Group, Inc., The. (Rosen Classroom).
Townsend, Chris. What Does an Officeholder Do?, 1 vol. 2018. (What Does a Citizen Do? Ser.). (ENG.). 48p. (gr. 5-5). 30.93 (978-0-7660-9881-7(8), a410a0f6-47e6-4eac-a1a4-b603bd73cc52) Enslow Publishing, LLC.
Wiles, Jon. Landon's Local Government. 2013. (InfoMax Readers Ser.). (ENG.). 24p. (J). (gr. 3-4). pap. 49.50 (978-1-4777-2635-8(7)); (Illus.). pap. 8.25 (978-1-4777-2634-1(9), 5a53d863-e9ba-40be-b5b0-91519b0e4b49) Rosen Publishing Group, Inc., The. (Rosen Classroom).

LOCH NESS (SCOTLAND)
see Ness, Loch (Scotland)

LOCH NESS MONSTER
see also Ness, Loch (Scotland)
Besel, Jen. The Loch Ness Monster. 2020. (Little Bit Spooky Ser.). (ENG.). 24p. (J). (gr. k-3). lib. bdg. (978-1-62310-179-4(4), 14462, Bolt Jr.) Black Rabbit Bks.
Bougie, Matt. Bigfoot, the Loch Ness Monster, & Unexplained Creatures, 1 vol. 2017. (Paranormal Investigations Ser.). (ENG.). 64p. (gr. 6-6). 35.93 (978-1-5026-2847-3(3), 8fb126eb-8bed-4c21-9eef-726c0160d73a) Cavendish Square Publishing LLC.
Brassey, Richard. Nessie the Loch Ness Monster. 2010. (ENG., Illus.). 24p. (gr. k-2). pap. 9.99 (978-1-4440-0056-6(X), Orion Children's Bks.) Hachette Children's Group GBR. Dist: Hachette Bk. Group.
Case, Nikki & Delrio, Martin. Searching for the Loch Ness Monster. 2011. (J). 77.70 (978-1-4488-4780-8(X)); (ENG.). 64p. (gr. 5-5). pap. 13.95 (978-1-4488-4772-3(9), 9995c1a8-0dd8-490f-a9e7-975c4841d210); (ENG.). 64p. (gr. 5-5). lib. bdg. 37.13 (978-1-4488-4763-1(X), 081d472b-1a54-4531-b7a4-3325156b8c73) Rosen Publishing Group, Inc., The.
DeMolay, Jack. The Loch Ness Monster: Scotland's Mystery Beast. (Jr. Graphic Mysteries Ser.). (ENG.). 24p. (gr. 2-3). 2009. (J). 47.90 (978-1-61513-849-4(8), PowerKids Pr.) 2006. (Illus.). (J). lib. bdg. 28.93 (978-1-4042-3406-2(3), f4db3b74-b5c7-4df7-a2c1-5aaea83e2e19) 2006. (Illus.). pap. 10.60 (978-1-4042-2159-8(X), 51d47b64-b8d1-46f8-9004-464735d5ca26) Rosen Publishing Group, Inc., The.
—Monstruo del Lago Ness: Una Misteriosa Bestia en Escocia, 1 vol. Obregón, José María, tr. 2008. (Historietas Juveniles: Misterios (Jr. Graphic Mysteries) Ser.). (SPA., Illus.). 24p. (J). (gr. 2-3). lib. bdg. 28.93 (978-1-4358-2538-3(1), 0acbe34f-f8a7-4b77-850e-be14bb727b8b) Rosen Publishing Group, Inc., The.
Flaherty, Alice Weaver. Luck of the Loch Ness Monster: A Tale of Picky Eating. Magoon, Scott, illus. 2007. (ENG.). 40p. (J). (gr. 3-7). 16.00 (978-0-618-55644-1(3), 585613, Clarion Bks.) HarperCollins Pubs.
Gish, Ashley. Loch Ness Monster. 2019. (X-Books: Mythical Creatures Ser.). (ENG.). 32p. (J). (gr. 3-6). (978-1-64026-196-9(6), 19240, Creative Education) Creative Co., The.
Hoffman, Mary Ann. Loch Ness Monster, 1 vol. 2005. (Content-Area Literacy Collections). (ENG.). 24p. (gr. 3-4). pap. 8.85 (978-1-4042-5673-6(3), 529c2a21-2725-4dd8-972f-30fb0e96506b) Rosen Publishing Group, Inc., The.
Jeffrey, Gary. The Loch Ness Monster & Other Lake Mysteries, 1 vol. Moulder, Bob, illus. 2006. (Graphic Mysteries Ser.). (ENG.). 48p. (gr. 5-5). pap. 14.05 (978-1-4042-0807-0(0), e9dfae01-0926-47b0-aadb-267d322c92f9) Rosen Publishing Group, Inc., The.
—The Loch Ness Monster & Other Lake Mysteries, 1 vol. Spender, Nik & Moulder, Bob, illus. 2006. (Graphic Mysteries Ser.). (ENG.). 48p. (YA). (gr. 5-5). lib. bdg. 37.13 (978-1-4042-0796-7(1), b7d2b5e2-c797-408b-b36c-70cfdb447689) Rosen Publishing Group, Inc., The.
—Loch Ness Monster & Other Lake Mysteries. 2009. (Graphic Mysteries Ser.). (ENG.). 48p. (YA). (gr. 5-5). 58.50 (978-1-61512-967-6(7), Rosen Reference) Rosen Publishing Group, Inc., The.
Kallen, Stuart A. The Loch Ness Monster. 2008. (Mysterious & Unknown Ser.). (YA). (gr. 7-12). 43.93 (978-1-60152-059-3(X)) ReferencePoint Pr., Inc.
Karst, Ken. Loch Ness Monster. 2014. (Enduring Mysteries Ser.). (ENG.). 48p. (J). (gr. 5-8). pap. 12.00 (978-1-62832-074-9(5), 21332, Creative Paperbacks); (Illus.). (978-1-60818-403-3(X), 21331, Creative Education) Creative Co., The.
Lassieur, Allison. Is the Loch Ness Monster Real? 2015. (Unexplained: What's the Evidence? Ser.). (ENG., Illus.). 32p. (J). (gr. 2-5). lib. bdg. 19.95 (978-1-60753-805-9(9), 15315) Amicus.
McClellan, Ray. The Loch Ness Monster. 2014. (Unexplained Mysteries Ser.). (ENG., Illus.). 24p. (J). (gr. 3-7). lib. bdg. 26.95 (978-1-62617-106-0(8), Epic Bks.) Bellwether Media.
Murray, Laura K. Loch Ness Monster. 2017. (Are They Real? Ser.). (ENG., Illus.). 24p. (J). (gr. 1-4). pap. 8.99 (978-1-62832-372-6(8), 20066, Creative Paperbacks); (978-1-60818-764-5(0), 20068, Creative Education) Creative Co., The.
Nagle, Frances. The Loch Ness Monster, 1 vol. 2016. (Monsters! Ser.). (ENG., Illus.). 32p. (J). (gr. 1-2). pap. 11.50 (978-1-4824-4863-4(7), 7f58ea00-a432-401d-9719-0d31304df99f) Stevens, Gareth Publishing LLLP.
Oachs, Emily Rose. The Loch Ness Monster. 2018. (Investigating the Unexplained Ser.). (ENG., Illus.). 32p. (J). (gr. 3-8). lib. bdg. 27.95 (978-1-62617-855-7(0), Blastoff! Discovery) Bellwether Media.
Parks, Peggy J. The Loch Ness Monster, 1 vol. 2006. (Mysterious Encounters Ser.). (ENG., Illus.). 48p. (gr. 4-8). lib. bdg. 30.38 (978-0-7377-3519-2(8), c88095ff-be8d-435d-a1ce-9f2099d31a4b, KidHaven Publishing) Greenhaven Publishing LLC.
Peabody, Erin. The Loch Ness Monster. Rivas, Victor, illus. 2017. (Behind the Legend Ser.: 1). (ENG.). 128p. (J). (gr. 2-5). pap. 9.99 (978-1-4998-0423-2(7)) Little Bee Books Inc.
Ransom, Candice. Mysterious Loch Ness Monster. 2020. (Lightning Bolt Books (r) — Spooked! Ser.). (ENG., Illus.). 24p. (J). (gr. 1-3). 29.32 (978-1-5415-9692-4(7), be215e3f-5701-4e8b-82c2-2048174b96a8, Lerner Pubns.) Lerner Publishing Group.
Rivkin, Jennifer. Searching for the Loch Ness Monster, 1 vol. 2014. (Mysterious Monsters Ser.). (ENG., Illus.). 32p. (J). (gr. 4-5). lib. bdg. 27.93 (978-1-4777-7101-3(8), b48709ad-27be-48a6-89ba-1fe805e3f8e3, PowerKids Pr.) Rosen Publishing Group, Inc., The.
Roberts, Steven. The Loch Ness Monster!, 1 vol. 2012. (Jr. Graphic Monster Stories Ser.). (ENG., Illus.). 24p. (J). (gr. 2-3). 28.93 (978-1-4488-7904-5(3), 4d312037-03f8-487e-9f58-bca3283bc9f6); pap. 11.60 (978-1-4488-8004-1(1), 1788ba57-c8d6-4f64-97cf-926d47b75d4f) Rosen Publishing Group, Inc., The. (PowerKids Pr.).
Schach, David. The Loch Ness Monster. 2010. (Unexplained Ser.). (ENG., Illus.). 24p. (J). (gr. 3-7). lib. bdg. 26.95 (978-1-60014-502-5(7), Torque Bks.) Bellwether Media.
Sievert, Terri. The Unsolved Mystery of the Loch Ness Monster, 1 vol. 2013. (Unexplained Mysteries Ser.). (ENG.). 24p. (J). (gr. 1-3). lib. bdg. 27.99 (978-1-62065-133-9(5), 120825, Capstone Pr.) Capstone.
Troupe, Thomas Kingsley. The Legend of the Loch Ness Monster, 1 vol. Ice, D. C., illus. 2011. (Legend Has It Ser.). (ENG.). 32p. (J). (gr. 2-4). lib. bdg. 27.99 (978-1-4048-6659-1(0), 114934, Picture Window Bks.) Capstone.
Uhl, Xina M. Loch Ness Monster. 2017. (Strange but True Ser.). (ENG.). 32p. (gr. 2-7). 9.95 (978-1-68072-480-6(0)); (J). (gr. 4-6). pap. 9.99 (978-1-64466-217-5(5), 11488); (Illus.). (J). (gr. 4-6). lib. bdg. (978-1-68072-183-6(6), 10550) Black Rabbit Bks. (Bolt).
Vale, Jenna. Tracking the Loch Ness Monster, 1 vol. 2018. (Paranormal Seekers Ser.). (ENG.). 64p. (J). (gr. 5-8). pap. 13.95 (978-1-5081-8573-4(5), 7c9ce101-b9df-4ccf-853a-b272fb0e7c9a) Rosen Publishing Group, Inc., The.

LOCKS AND KEYS
Cruz-Martinez, George. The Wonder of Keys for Kids. Sturgeon, Brad, illus. 2006. 43p. (J). (978-1-55452-013-8(4)) Essence Publishing.

LOCKWOOD, BELVA ANN, 1830-1917
Bardhan-Quallen, Sudipta. Ballots for Belva: The True Story of a Woman's Race for the Presidency. Martin, Courtney A., illus. 2015. (ENG.). 32p. (J). (gr. k-2). pap. 12.99 (978-1-4197-1627-0(1), 650103) Abrams, Inc.
Hannigan, Kate. A Lady Has the Floor: Belva Lockwood Speaks Out for Women's Rights. Jay, Alison, illus. 2018. 32p. (J). (gr. 2-5). 17.95 (978-1-62979-453-2(8), Calkins Creek) Highlights Pr., c/o Highlights for Children, Inc.
Norgren, Jill. Belva Lockwood: The Woman Who Would Be President. 2007. (ENG., Illus.). 311p. 89.00 (978-0-8147-5834-2(7), 8431, NYU Pr.) New York Univ. Pr.

LOCOMOTION
see Aeronautics; Automobiles; Boats and Boating; Flight; Navigation; Transportation; Walking

LOCOMOTIVES
Bone, Emily & King, Colin. See Inside Trains. 2013. (Usborne Flap Book Ser.). (ENG., Illus.). 16p. (J). 13.99 (978-0-7945-3377-9(9), Usborne) EDC Publishing.
Farrington, Karen & Constable, Nick. Build Your Own Steam Locomotive: A Complete, Easy-to-Assemble Model. Osborne, Graham, illus. 2004. 34p. (J). (gr. 4-8). reprint ed. pap. 17.00 (978-0-7567-8261-0(9)) DIANE Publishing Co.
Floca, Brian. Locomotive. Floca, Brian, illus. 2013. (ENG., Illus.). 64p. (J). (gr. -1-5). 19.99 (978-1-4169-9415-2(7), Atheneum/Richard Jackson Bks.) Simon & Schuster Children's Publishing.
Hannon, Robert A. J. L. Cowen's Postwar Lionel Trains: O-Gauge Reference Manual II, Motorized Units, Rolling Stock & Accessories. 2003. (Illus.). 160p. per. 29.95 (978-0-9710225-2-2(6), 0-9710225-2-6) CrowsNest Publishing.
Hurst, Vera J. 21st-Century Trains, 1 vol. 2018. (Feats of 21st-Century Engineering Ser.). (ENG.). 48p. (gr. 4-4). 29.60 (978-0-7660-9709-4(9), 6a14947c-2d63-441d-986f-eb98b7a0c84f) Enslow Publishing, LLC.
Mattern, Joanne. The Birth of the Locomotive (1780-1820) 2012. (Illus.). 47p. (J). (gr. 4-8). lib. bdg. 29.95 (978-1-61228-286-2(5)) Mitchell Lane Pubs.
Nelson, Jo. The Railway Revolution: Band 16/Sapphire (Collins Big Cat) 2016. (Collins Big Cat Ser.). (ENG.). 56p. (J). (gr. 4-5). pap. 12.99 (978-0-00-816395-2(2)) HarperCollins Pubs. Ltd. GBR. Dist: Independent Pubs. Group.
Piper, Watty & Hart, Charlie. You Can! Words of Wisdom from the Little Engine That Could. Howarth, Jill, illus. 2018. (Little Engine That Could Ser.). 80p. (J). (gr. 5-12). 12.99 (978-1-5247-8468-3(0), Grosset & Dunlap) Penguin Young Readers Group.
Ryan, Phillip. Passenger Trains, 1 vol. 2010. (All Aboard! Ser.). (ENG.). 24p. (J). (gr. 1-2). pap. 9.25 (978-1-4488-1215-8(1), 24bc9909-10a5-4e2f-89e7-a032a0971ea2); lib. bdg. 26.27 (978-1-4488-0637-9(2), 83bc4aea-6eb2-4e11-8b90-71083e69c7b7) Rosen Publishing Group, Inc., The. (PowerKids Pr.).
—Steam-Powered Trains, 1 vol. 2010. (All Aboard! Ser.). (ENG.). 24p. (J). (gr. 1-2). pap. 9.25 (978-1-4488-1221-9(6), 2b876c6a-dfb5-4a51-9113-1b4fd29190dc); lib. bdg. 26.27 (978-1-4488-0640-9(2), 11b05c4f-7b64-4e3d-8b93-fbc1a15bebc0) Rosen Publishing Group, Inc., The. (PowerKids Pr.).
Trombello, William. Trains & Tow Boats. Tangen, Nick, illus. 2013. 34p. pap. (978-0-9842998-1-2(5)) Roxby Media Ltd.
Turnbull, S. Trains. 2004. (Discovery Program Ser.). (SPA., Illus.). 48p. (J). (gr. 3-18). lib. bdg. 16.95 (978-1-58086-410-7(4)) EDC Publishing.
Veitch, Catherine. Big Machines Ride Rails!, 1 vol. 2014. (Big Machines Ser.). (ENG.). 24p. (J). (gr. -1-1). 25.99 (978-1-4846-0589-9(6), 126691, Heinemann) Capstone.

LOCOMOTIVES—FICTION
Amery, Heather. The Old Steam Train Kid Kit. Cartwright, Stephen, illus. rev. ed. 2007. (Kid Kits Ser.). (J). 16p. 13.99 (978-1-60130-038-6(7)); 14p. pap. 13.99 (978-1-60130-003-4(4)) EDC Publishing. (Usborne).
Awdry, W. Secret of the Green Engine. 2012. (Thomas & Friends Step into Reading Ser.). lib. bdg. 13.55 (978-0-606-26804-2(9)) Turtleback.
—A Valentine for Percy. 2015. (Thomas & Friends Step into Reading Ser.). (Illus.). 24p. lib. bdg. 14.75 (978-0-606-38471-1(5)) Turtleback.
—A Valentine for Percy. Courtney, Richard, illus. 2015. 24p. (J). (978-1-4806-9757-7(5)) Random Hse., Inc.
Burton, Virginia Lee. Choo Choo. 2017. (ENG., Illus.). 48p. (J). (gr. -1-3). 17.99 (978-0-544-74984-9(7), 1633380, Clarion Bks.) HarperCollins Pubs.
Fleming, Denise. Go, Shapes, Go! Fleming, Denise, illus. 2014. (ENG., Illus.). 40p. (J). (gr. -1-3). 18.99 (978-1-4424-8240-1(0), Beach Lane Bks.) Beach Lane Bks.

JKL

Grossman, Lev. The Silver Arrow. (ENG.). (J). (gr. 3-7). 2021. 272p. pap. 8.99 *(978-0-316-53954-8(6))* 2020. (Illus.). 272p. 16.99 *(978-0-316-53953-1(8))* 2020. (Illus.). 288p. 32.99 *(978-0-316-54170-1(2))* Little, Brown Bks. for Young Readers.

—The Silver Arrow. 2022. (Penworthy Picks YA Fiction Ser.). (ENG., Illus.). 259p. (J). (gr. 4-5). 19.46 *(978-1-68505-117-4(0))* Penworthy Co., LLC, The.

Klein, Adria F. Big Train. Cameron, Craig, illus. 2013. (Train Time Ser.). (ENG.). 32p. (J). (gr. -1-1). pap. 5.95 *(978-1-4342-4886-2(0)*, 121886, Stone Arch Bks.) Capstone.

—Big Train Takes a Trip. Cameron, Craig, illus. 2013. (Train Time Ser.). (ENG.). 32p. (gr. -1-1). pap. 35.70 *(978-1-4342-6300-1(2)*, 20273, Stone Arch Bks.) Capstone.

—Big Train Takes a Trip, 1 vol. Cameron, Craig, illus. 2013. (Train Time Ser.). (ENG.). 32p. (J). (gr. -1-1). pap. 5.95 *(978-1-4342-6194-6(8)*, 123488, Stone Arch Bks.) Capstone.

—City Train in Trouble. 2013. (Train Time Ser.). (ENG., Illus.). 32p. (J). (gr. -1-1). pap. 35.70 *(978-1-4342-6302-5(9)*, 20276, Stone Arch Bks.) Capstone.

—City Train in Trouble, 1 vol. Cameron, Craig, illus. 2013. (Train Time Ser.). (ENG.). 32p. (J). (gr. -1-1). pap. 5.95 *(978-1-4342-6196-0(4)*, 123490, Stone Arch Bks.) Capstone.

Lippman, Peter. Mini Express. (J). 119.40 *(978-0-7611-2876-2(X)*, 22876) Workman Publishing Co., Inc.

—Mini Wheels: the Mini-Express 8-Copy Counter Display. (ENG.). (J). bds. 79.60 *(978-0-7611-2883-0(2)*, 22883) Workman Publishing Co., Inc.

Little, Stephen R. The Mighty Locomotive. Duckworth, Jeffry, illus. 2012. (ENG.). 40p. pap. 20.99 *(978-1-4772-5936-8(8))* AuthorHouse.

McKinnon, Bob. Three Little Engines. Fancher, Lou & Johnson, Steve, illus. 2021. (Little Engine That Could Ser.). 48p. (J). (gr. -1-2). 18.99 *(978-1-5247-9335-7(3)*, Grosset & Dunlap) Penguin Young Readers Group.

Mitton, Tony. Terrific Trains. 2017. (Amazing Machines Ser.). (ENG.). 20p. (J). bds. 6.99 *(978-0-7534-7372-6(0)*, 900178406, Kingfisher) Roaring Brook Pr.

Mysak, Mary. Little Train! Stickley, Kelly, illus. 2004. 16p. (J). 7.50 *(978-0-9762274-0-3(1))* Helping Hands Children's Bks.

Opie, David, illus. Monkey & the Engineer. 2007. 24p. (J). 14.95 *(978-0-9793972-6-4(X))* JD Publishing.

Piper, Watty. The Little Engine That Could: Loren Long Edition. Long, Loren, illus. 2005. (Little Engine That Could Ser.). 48p. (J). (gr. -1-2). 18.99 *(978-0-399-24467-4(0)*, Philomel Bks.) Penguin Young Readers Group.

Publications International Ltd. Staff. Chuggington Little Lift & Listen. 2011. 12p. (J). bds. 10.98 *(978-1-4508-0504-9(3))* Phoenix International Publications, Inc.

Publications International Ltd. Staff, ed. Cars. 2007. (J). 9.98 *(978-1-4127-6514-5(5))* Phoenix International Publications, Inc.

—Chuggington Little Music Note Sound: Traintastic Tunes. 2011. 12p. (J). (gr. k-3). bds. 10.99 *(978-1-4508-1141-5(8)*, dd98fbb4-eb4f-47f8-80b4-3d7a907afc5f) Phoenix International Publications, Inc.

Random House. Five Tank Engine Tales (Thomas & Friends) Courtney, Richard, illus. 2015. (Step into Reading Ser.). (ENG.). 160p. (J). (gr. -1-1). pap. 8.99 *(978-0-385-38496-4(3)*, Random Hse. Bks. for Young Readers) Random Hse. Children's Bks.

Riley, Lehman C. Meeting Dr. Martin Luther King. 2004. (Adventures of Papa Lemon's Little Wanderers Ser.: Bk. 1). 35p. *(978-0-9760523-0-2(X))* Matter of Africa America Time.

Sabo, J. Train Wrecker. 2011. 28p. pap. 24.95 *(978-1-4626-4379-0(5))* America Star Bks.

Shaskan, Stephen. Big Choo. 2018. (ENG., Illus.). 40p. (J). (gr. -1-k). 16.99 *(978-0-545-70857-9(5)*, Scholastic Pr.) Scholastic, Inc.

Wise Brown, Margaret & Sebring Lowrey, Janette. The Poky Little Puppy & Friends: the Nine Classic Little Golden Books. 2017. (Illus.). 224p. (J). (-k). 12.99 *(978-1-5247-6683-2(6)*, Golden Bks.) Random Hse. Children's Bks.

Wondriska, William. Puff. 2015. (ENG., Illus.). 32p. (J). (gr. k-4). 16.95 *(978-0-7893-2911-0(5))* Universe Publishing.

LOCUSTS

Abraham, Anika. Grasshoppers, 1 vol. 2018. (Creepy Crawlers Ser.). (ENG.). 24p. (gr. 1-1). pap. 9.22 *(978-1-5026-4188-5(7)*, 4e51a0c4-659e-44a0-a10f-a6266fba0192) Cavendish Square Publishing LLC.

Alessi, Jolene. Zombie Grasshoppers, 1 vol. 2015. (Zombie Animals: Parasites Take Control! Ser.). (ENG.). 24p. (J). (gr. 2-3). 24.27 *(978-1-4824-2846-9(6)*, 53944d23-4348-4010-bdb8-9cf1de940b47) Stevens, Gareth Publishing LLLP.

Allen, Judy. Are You a Grasshopper? Humphries, Tudor, illus. 2004. (Backyard Bks.). (ENG.). 32p. (J). (gr. k-3). pap. 7.99 *(978-0-7534-5806-8(3)*, 900052582, Kingfisher) Roaring Brook Pr.

Amstutz, Lisa J. Grasshoppers. 2017. (Little Critters Ser.). (ENG., Illus.). 24p. (J). (gr. -1-2). lib. bdg. 22.65 *(978-1-5157-7824-0(X)*, 135976, Capstone Pr.) Capstone.

Ashley, Susan. Grasshoppers, 1 vol. 2004. (Let's Read about Insects Ser.). (ENG., Illus.). 24p. (gr. k-2). pap. 9.15 *(978-0-8368-4061-2(5)*, b7c92a1b-0bee-4fc8-97ea-4bfd2f69038c); lib. bdg. 24.67 *(978-0-8368-4054-4(2)*, 22b238ef-e10f-4249-97c4-1be4c6c27e80) Stevens, Gareth Publishing LLLP. (Weekly Reader Leveled Readers).

—Incredible Grasshoppers, 1 vol. 2011. (Incredible World of Insects Ser.). (ENG., Illus.). 24p. (J). (gr. 1-2). pap. 9.15 *(978-1-4339-4588-5(6)*, 990d3bcc-1121-4d3d-99b5-37633d9bbbad); lib. bdg. 25.27 *(978-1-4339-4587-8(8)*, 1dd16cd6-e5f9-42f7-9a3f-81e8ff05370d) Stevens, Gareth Publishing LLLP.

Berger, Melvin & Berger, Gilda. Grasshoppers. 2011. (Illus.). 16p. (J). pap. *(978-0-545-24445-9(5))* Scholastic, Inc.

Bodden, Valerie. Creepy Creatures: Grasshoppers. 2014. (Creepy Creatures Ser.). (ENG.). 24p. (J). (gr. 1-3). pap. 7.99 *(978-0-89812-935-9(4)*, 21493, Creative Paperbacks) Creative Co., The.

—Grasshoppers. (Creepy Creatures Ser.). (Illus.). 24p. (J). 2014. (ENG.). (gr. 1-4). *(978-1-60818-356-2(4)*, 21492) 2007. (gr. -1-3). lib. bdg. 24.25 *(978-1-58341-544-3(0))* Creative Co., The. (Creative Education).

Bronson, Wilfrid S., illus. The Grasshopper Book. 2009. 136p. (J). pap. 22.95 *(978-0-86534-690-1(9))* Sunstone Pr.

Goldish, Meish. Leaping Grasshoppers. 2008. (No Backbone! Ser.). (Illus.). 24p. (J). (gr. k-3). lib. bdg. 26.99 *(978-1-59716-586-0(7))* Bearport Publishing Co., Inc.

Gray, Susan H. Grasshopper. 2015. (21st Century Junior Library: Creepy Crawly Critters Ser.). (ENG., Illus.). 24p. (J). (gr. k-3). 29.21 *(978-1-63362-590-7(7)*, 206544) Cherry Lake Publishing.

Green, Emily K. Grasshoppers. 2006. (World of Insects Ser.). (ENG., Illus.). 24p. (J). (gr. k-3). lib. bdg. 26.95 *(978-1-60014-014-3(9))* Bellwether Media.

Hall, Margaret. Grasshoppers [Scholastic]. 2010. (Bugs, Bugs, Bugs! Ser.). 24p. pap. 0.52 *(978-1-4296-5052-6(4)*, Capstone Pr.) Capstone.

Halpert, Laine C. If I Were a Grasshopper, 1 vol. 2017. (I'm a Bug! Ser.). (ENG.). 24p. (gr. 1-1). 25.27 *(978-1-5081-5722-9(7)*, 0a89ca11-998a-4dc2-87ed-9f03c62a9732, PowerKids Pr.) Rosen Publishing Group, Inc., The.

Hansen, Grace. Becoming a Grasshopper, 1 vol. 2016. (Changing Animals Ser.). (ENG., Illus.). 24p. (J). (gr. -1-2). lib. bdg. 32.79 *(978-1-68080-510-9(X)*, 21300, Abdo Kids) ABDO Publishing Co.

Hudak, Heather C. Grasshoppers. 2008. (World of Wonder Ser.). (Illus.). 24p. (J). (gr. k-3). pap. 6.95 *(978-1-59036-871-8(1))*; lib. bdg. 24.45 *(978-1-59036-870-1(3))* Weigl Pubs., Inc.

Kravetz, Jonathan. Locusts. (Gross Bugs Ser.). 24p. (gr. 3-4). 2009. 42.50 *(978-1-61513-228-7(7))* 2005. (ENG., Illus.). (J). lib. bdg. 26.27 *(978-1-4042-3042-2(4)*, ffb7192c-a4ed-4cb1-9193-f65ad61be782) Rosen Publishing Group, Inc., The. (PowerKids Pr.).

Lunis, Natalie. Giant Weta: The World's Biggest Grasshopper. 2013. (Even More SuperSized! Ser.). (Illus.). 24p. (J). (gr. k-3). lib. bdg. 26.99 *(978-1-61772-731-3(8))* Bearport Publishing Co., Inc.

Markle, Sandra. Locusts. 2008. pap. 52.95 *(978-1-58013-282-4(0))* Lerner Publishing Group.

—Locusts: Insects on the Move. 2008. (Insect World Ser.). (ENG., Illus.). 48p. (gr. 4-8). lib. bdg. 27.93 *(978-0-8225-7298-5(2)*, Lerner Pubns.) Lerner Publishing Group.

Marwood, Diane. The Ant & the Grasshopper. 2012. (ENG., Illus.). 24p. (J). *(978-0-7787-7889-9(4))*; pap. *(978-0-7787-7901-8(7))* Crabtree Publishing Co.

McAneney, Caitie. Locusts, 1 vol. 2014. (Animals of Mass Destruction Ser.). (ENG.). 24p. (J). (gr. 2-3). 26.93 *(978-1-4824-1051-8(6)*, 0e0bf0d7-6081-4e5f-9383-9de97cbe435d); pap. 11.50 *(978-1-4824-1052-5(4)*, 41bbe35f-cbb1-482f-afa3-72b550f58193) Stevens, Gareth Publishing LLLP.

Morlock, Rachael. Grasshoppers up Close, 1 vol. 2019. (Bugs up Close! Ser.). (ENG.). 24p. (gr. 1-2). pap. 9.25 *(978-1-7253-0790-2(1)*, 1ade14e6-ae47-4b1b-8cc4-b0f2b7492d0c, PowerKids Pr.) Rosen Publishing Group, Inc., The.

Morris, Neil & Morris, Ting. Grasshopper. 2003. (Illus.). 32p. (J). lib. bdg. 27.10 *(978-1-58340-381-5(7))* Black Rabbit Bks.

Murray, Julie. Grasshoppers. 2019. (Animal Kingdom Ser.). (ENG.). 32p. (J). (gr. 2-5). lib. bdg. 34.21 *(978-1-5321-1633-9(0)*, 32377, Big Buddy Bks.) ABDO Publishing Co.

Nelson, Robin. Grasshoppers. 2009. pap. 34.95 *(978-0-7613-4107-9(2))* Lerner Publishing Group.

Perish, Patrick. Grasshoppers. 2017. (Insects up Close Ser.). (ENG., Illus.). 24p. (J). (gr. k-3). lib. bdg. 26.95 *(978-1-62617-665-2(5)*, Blastoff! Readers) Bellwether Media.

Peterson, Megan Cooley. Grand Grasshoppers: A 4D Book. 2019. (Little Entomologist 4D Ser.). (ENG., Illus.). 32p. (J). (gr. -1-2). pap. 6.95 *(978-1-9771-0572-1(6)*, 139985) Capstone.

Reher, Matt. Grasshoppers on the Go. 2015. (1G Bugs Ser.). (ENG., Illus.). 28p. (J). pap. 8.00 *(978-1-63437-091-2(0))* American Reading Co.

—Grasshoppers Sing. 2016. (1B Bugs Ser.). (ENG., Illus.). 28p. (J). pap. 9.60 *(978-1-63437-550-4(5))* American Reading Co.

Robbins, Lynette. Grasshoppers. (J). 2012. 49.50 *(978-1-4488-5164-5(5)*, PowerKids Pr.) 2011. (ENG.). 24p. (gr. 2-3). pap. 9.25 *(978-1-4488-5163-8(7)*, c23cb242-c4be-4adf-8669-bc4455b258cb, PowerKids Pr.) 2011. (ENG.). 24p. (gr. 2-3). lib. bdg. 26.27 *(978-1-4488-5015-0(0)*, b350ba2f-9709-494d-8ec2-c29b0291e635) Rosen Publishing Group, Inc., The.

Schuh, Mari. Grasshoppers. 2015. (J). lib. bdg. 25.65 *(978-1-62031-162-2(3)*, Bullfrog Bks.) Jump! Inc.

Shusterman, Danielle. Grasshoppers & Crickets. 2017. (1G Bugs Ser.). (ENG., Illus.). 28p. (J). pap. 9.60 *(978-1-63437-111-7(9))* American Reading Co.

Siemens, Jared. Grasshoppers. 2017. (Illus.). 24p. (J). *(978-1-5105-0638-1(1))* SmartBook Media, Inc.

Silverman, Buffy. Can You Tell a Cricket from a Grasshopper? 2012. (Animal Look-Alikes Ser.). 32p. (gr. k-2). pap. 45.32 *(978-0-7613-9254-5(8))*; (ENG., Illus.). (J). (gr. 1-3). pap. 9.99 *(978-0-7613-8553-0(3)*, 41e88686-8ad2-400c-986f-eff7457b4bcf) Lerner Publishing Group.

Slade, Suzanne. Grasshoppers. (Under the Microscope: Backyard Bugs Ser.). 24p. (gr. 2-3). 2009. 42.50 *(978-1-60854-615-2(2)*, PowerKids Pr.) 2007. (ENG., Illus.). (J). lib. bdg. 26.27 *(978-1-4042-3820-6(4)*, bea5ebb8-a27f-4975-a118-da33c21cfcdf) Rosen Publishing Group, Inc., The.

Smith, Sian. Grasshoppers, 1 vol. 2012. (Creepy Critters Ser.). (ENG., Illus.). 24p. (J). (gr. -1-k). pap. 9.95 *(978-1-4109-4821-2(8)*, 119458, Raintree) Capstone.

Squire, Ann O. Crickets & Grasshoppers. 2004. (True Bks.). (ENG.). 48p. (J). (gr. 3-5). pap. 6.95 *(978-0-516-29357-8(5)*, Children's Pr.) Scholastic Library Publishing.

Statts, Leo. Grasshoppers. 2017. (Backyard Animals (Launch!) Ser.). (ENG., Illus.). 24p. (J). (gr. -1-2). lib. bdg. 31.36 *(978-1-5321-2005-3(2)*, 25274, Abdo Zoom-Launch) ABDO Publishing Co.

Stewart, Melissa. Zoom in on Grasshoppers, 1 vol. 2014. (Zoom in on Insects! Ser.). (ENG.). 24p. (gr. k-2). 25.60 *(978-0-7660-4214-8(6)*, e0afa3d4-2403-4fc8-8777-d5a6801d596e); pap. 10.95 *(978-1-4644-0371-2(6)*, df04ab5d-d1a5-4943-b3a2-74c5062e7472, Enslow Elementary) Enslow Publishing, LLC.

Strain Trueit, Trudi. Grasshoppers, 1 vol. (Backyard Safari Ser.). (ENG.). 2013. 32p. (gr. 3-3). pap. 11.58 *(978-1-62712-029-6(7)*, 3f998167-0b8e-458c-8c16-6db5ad7446bf) 2013. 32p. (gr. 3-3). lib. bdg. 31.21 *(978-1-60870-246-6(4)*, 78269e1b-eb4e-4984-976d-e8559fc1c081) 2010. 24p. (gr. k-1). 25.50 *(978-0-7614-3964-6(1)*, db374ce0-cc2f-4ad0-b4bd-32596eca186a) Cavendish Square Publishing LLC.

LOCUSTS—FICTION

Aesop, Aesop. The Ant & the Grasshopper. 2012. (J). 29.99 *(978-1-61913-106-4(4))* Weigl Pubs., Inc.

—The Grasshopper & the Ant: A Tale about Planning. Hockerman, Dennis, illus. 2006. (J). *(978-1-59939-082-6(5)*, Reader's Digest Young Families, Inc.) Studio Fun International.

Aldrick, Shirley H. F. Gordon, the Great Gobbley Grasshopper. 2011. 32p. pap. 13.00 *(978-1-60976-643-6(1)*, Strategic Bk. Publishing) Strategic Book Publishing & Rights Agency (SBPRA).

Bailer, Darice, et al. El Saltamontes y Las Hormigas. Bassa, illus. 2007. (SPA & ENG.). 28p. (J). *(978-0-545-02965-0(1))* Scholastic, Inc.

Barkley, Roger C. Johnny Grasshopper. 2006. 52p. pap. 16.95 *(978-1-4241-0221-1(9))* PublishAmerica, Inc.

Basha, Irena Canaj. The Birthday Party, It Was Saturday... 2013. 16p. pap. 24.95 *(978-1-62709-182-4(3))* America Star Bks.

Berry, Jacqueline. Teeny Tiny Topper, the Grasshopper. 2007. 20p. per. 24.95 *(978-1-4241-8338-8(3))* America Star Bks.

Binkley, Carolyn. The Errand: And Stinkbugs & Grasshoppers Green. 2012. 24p. pap. 15.99 *(978-1-4691-6096-2(X))* Xlibris Corp.

Castle, Regina F. Henry Hopper. 2011. 20p. pap. 24.95 *(978-1-4560-6563-8(7))* America Star Bks.

Christianson, Leslie Rose. Malinda Matters: And Priscilla the Praying Mantis. 2010. 36p. pap. 15.49 *(978-1-4490-6914-8(2))* AuthorHouse.

Collier, Wayne Evans. Grumpy the Grasshopper. Goodman, Larry, illus. 2012. 20p. pap. 24.95 *(978-1-4626-6844-1(5))* America Star Bks.

Eyckerman, Merel, illus. The Ant & the Grasshopper. 2013. (Usborne First Reading: Level 1 Ser.). (ENG.). 32p. (J). (gr. -1-3). 6.99 *(978-0-7945-2257-5(2)*, Usborne) EDC Publishing.

Fleischman, Sid. La Maravillosa Granja de McBroom. Blake, Quentin, illus. 13th ed. 2003.Tr. of McBroom's Wonderful One-Acre Farm. (SPA.). 96p. (J). (gr. 3-5). 7.95 *(978-84-204-4885-5(0))* Ediciones Alfaguara ESP. Dist: Santillana USA Publishing Co., Inc.

Grant, Judyann Ackerman. Chicken Said, Cluck! An Easter & Springtime Book for Kids. Truesdell, Sue, illus. 2010. (My First I Can Read Ser.). (ENG.). 32p. (J). (gr. -1-3). pap. 4.99 *(978-0-06-444276-3(4)*, HarperCollins) HarperCollins Pubs.

Gray, Luli. Ant & Grasshopper. Ferri, Giuliano, illus. 2011. (ENG.). 32p. (J). (gr. -1-2). 18.99 *(978-1-4169-5140-7(7)*, McElderry, Margaret K. Bks.) McElderry, Margaret K. Bks.

Hewitt, Hazel & Gillett, Chrissy. A Locust Ate My Daddy's Underwears. 2008. 24p. pap. 13.95 *(978-1-84799-261-1(7))* Lulu Pr., Inc.

Johnston, Kathy. Get That Grasshopper! 2012. 24p. pap. 12.56 *(978-1-4669-3743-7(2))* Trafford Publishing.

Lee, WonKyeong. The Chirping Band. Jang, EunJoo, illus. 2014. (MySELF Bookshelf Ser.). (ENG.). 32p. (J). (gr. k-2). lib. bdg. 25.27 *(978-1-59953-663-7(3))* Norwood Hse. Pr.

Loewen, Nancy. The Ants & the Grasshopper, Narrated by the Fanciful but Truthful Grasshopper. Arbat, Carles, illus. 2018. (Other Side of the Fable Ser.). (ENG.). 24p. (J). (gr. -1-3). lib. bdg. 27.99 *(978-1-5158-2868-6(9)*, 138406, Picture Window Bks.) Capstone.

Mihalko, Ross, et al. Ant & the Grasshopper (Musical) 2012. (ENG.). (J). pap. 8.95 *(978-0-573-70112-2(1)*, French, Samuel , Inc.) Concord Theatricals.

Pinkney, Jerry. The Grasshopper & the Ants. 2015. (ENG., Illus.). 40p. (J). (gr. -1-3). 18.99 *(978-0-316-40081-7(5))* Little, Brown Bks. for Young Readers.

Rice, Dona Herwick & Housel, Debra. The Grasshopper & the Ants, 1 vol. rev. ed. 2008. (Reader's Theater Ser.). (ENG., Illus.). 24p. (gr. 1-3). pap. 8.99 *(978-1-4333-0292-3(6))* Teacher Created Materials, Inc.

Salusso, S. T. Billy the Roly Poly Bug. 2012. 24p. pap. 13.00 *(978-1-4269-6134-2(0))* Trafford Publishing.

Smith, Andrew. Grasshopper Jungle. 2015. lib. bdg. 22.10 *(978-0-606-36795-0(0))* Turtleback.

Smith, Michael & Oliva, Octavio. Grasshopper Buddy. Oliva, Octavio, illus. 2012. (SPA & ENG., Illus.). (J). *(978-0-9856237-0-8(5))* East West Discovery Pr.

Sommer, Carl. The Ant & the Grasshopper. Noé, Ignacio, illus. 2016. (ENG.). 32p. (J). (gr. k-4). lib. bdg. 16.95 *(978-1-57537-925-8(2)*, Another Sommer-Time Story) Advance Publishing, Inc.

Stamps, Paula. Learning Makes Friends Fun, 1 vol. 2010. 22p. 24.95 *(978-1-4512-8765-3(8))* PublishAmerica, Inc.

Stone, Forrest. The Ant & Grasshopper Show. 2006. (J). pap. *(978-1-4108-6183-2(X))* Benchmark Education Co.

Zuggo, Violeta & Zuggo, Jutka. Story Time for Kids with Nlp by the English Sisters: The Little Grasshopper & the Big Ball of Dung. Kecskés, Anna, illus. 2013. 24p. pap. *(978-1-78092-493-9(3))* MX Publishing, Ltd.

LOG CABINS

Meachen Rau, Dana. Bookworms: The Inside Story, 12 vols., Set. Incl. Castle. lib. bdg. 25.50 *(978-0-7614-2272-3(2)*, adab9f74-2818-438e-ba0f-67058d410319); Igloo. lib. bdg. 25.50 *(978-0-7614-2273-0(0)*, b4264f9e-e40b-4791-87cc-23c1251e18a5); Log Cabin. lib. bdg. 25.50 *(978-0-7614-2274-7(9)*, 0eb1f358-eb38-4d47-8e2b-9fc2cb65a564); Pyramid. lib. bdg. 25.50 *(978-0-7614-2275-4(7)*, 10863ddc-9eee-46aa-abac-fc1eac1dec26); Skyscraper. lib. bdg. 25.50 *(978-0-7614-2276-1(5)*, 21c7e684-e08a-4a1d-ba8f-a7294f9995c3); Tepee. lib. bdg. 25.50 *(978-0-7614-2277-8(3)*, 36db5006-1580-4f2f-8b71-a10cc6b6c655); (Illus.). 32p. (gr. k-1). (Inside Story Ser.). (ENG.). 2007. Set lib. bdg. 153.00 *(978-0-7614-2271-6(4)*, 26d3d7dd-7d58-4920-aa34-ec2e62335409, Cavendish Square) Cavendish Square Publishing LLC.

—Log Cabin, 1 vol. (Inside Story Ser.). (ENG.). 32p. (gr. k-1). 2008. pap. 9.23 *(978-0-7614-3300-2(7)*, 668da582-e0ef-416d-8fc1-aa2350e88fbe) 2007. (Illus.). lib. bdg. 25.50 *(978-0-7614-2274-7(9)*, 0eb1f358-eb38-4d47-8e2b-9fc2cb65a564) Cavendish Square Publishing LLC.

Rae, Thelma. Pioneer Families. 2009. (Reading Room Collection 1 Ser.). 16p. (gr. 2-3). 37.50 *(978-1-60851-948-4(1)*, PowerKids Pr.) Rosen Publishing Group, Inc., The.

Skinner, Tina. Log & Timber Frame Homes, 1 vol. 2003. (ENG., Illus.). 224p. (gr. 10-13). 44.95 *(978-0-7643-1754-5(7)*, 1841) Schiffer Publishing, Ltd.

LOGGING

see Lumber and Lumbering

LOGIC

see also Knowledge, Theory of; Probabilities; Reasoning; Thought and Thinking

Berry, Joy. Saying No. 2019. (ENG., Illus.). 34p. (J). (gr. -1-3). pap. 8.99 *(978-0-7396-0354-3(X))* Inspired Studios Inc.

Boardworks Learning Centers: Figure It Out. 2006. (J). bds. *(978-0-9755252-4-1(7))* Evergreen Pr. of Brainerd, LLC.

Brainy Baby Vertical Right/Left Tab Book. 2005. (Brainy Baby Ser.). *(978-1-59394-450-6(0))* Bendon, Inc.

Harris, Patricia. Understanding Coding Using Boolean Logic, 1 vol. 2016. (Spotlight on Kids Can Code Ser.). (ENG.). 24p. (J). (gr. 4-5). pap. 12.75 *(978-1-4994-2806-3(5)*, ecf9e894-d7b2-460d-b816-5722a815fb03, PowerKids Pr.) Rosen Publishing Group, Inc., The.

—Understanding Coding Using Conditionals. 2017. (J). *(978-1-4994-2814-8(6)*, PowerKids Pr.) Rosen Publishing Group, Inc., The.

Hillman, Emilee. Train Your Brain with Parallel Computing & If/Then Activities, 1 vol. Regan, Dana, illus. 2019. (Think Like a Programmer Ser.). (ENG.). 32p. (gr. 4-4). pap. 11.58 *(978-1-5026-4818-1(0)*, f1146c33-1d61-4433-9b30-a72466591dfe) Cavendish Square Publishing LLC.

Kofman, Victoria. Guni-Pi Academy, Math & Logic: Hands-On Textbook for 4 - 7 Year Olds. 2006. spiral bd. *(978-0-9777171-0-1(0))* VK Publishing, Inc.

—Guni-Pi Academy, Math & Logic: Hands-on Textbook for 4 - 7 Year Olds - Non-Laminated. 2006. spiral bd. *(978-0-9777171-2-5(7))* VK Publishing, Inc.

Kreeft, Peter. Socratic Logic: A Logic Text Using Socratic Method, Platonic Questions, & Aristotelian Principles. 2004. (Illus.). x, 397p. (YA). 40.00 *(978-1-890318-89-5(2))* St. Augustine's Pr., Inc.

Krieger, Emily. Myths Busted! 3: Just When You Thought You Knew What You Knew. 2015. (Myths Busted Ser.: 3). (Illus.). 208p. (J). (gr. 3-7). pap. 7.99 *(978-1-4263-1883-2(9)*, National Geographic Kids) Disney Publishing Worldwide.

—National Geographic Kids Myths: Busted! 2013. (Myths Busted Ser.). (Illus.). 208p. (J). (gr. 3-7). pap. 7.95 *(978-1-4263-1102-4(8)*, National Geographic Kids) Disney Publishing Worldwide.

—National Geographic Kids Myths Busted! Just When You Thought You Knew What You Knew..., 1. 2013. (Myths Busted Ser.). (ENG., Illus.). 208p. (J). (gr. 3-7). lib. bdg. 16.90 *(978-1-4263-1103-1(6)*, National Geographic Children's Bks.) Disney Publishing Worldwide.

Nance, James B. Intermediate Logic - Student (2nd Edition) 2nd ed. 2006. (ENG.). 209p. pap. 27.00 *(978-1-59128-035-4(4))* Canon Pr.

Nance, James B. & Wilson, Douglas J. Introductory Logic - Student (4th Edition) 4th ed. 2006. (ENG.). 250p. pap. 29.00 *(978-1-59128-033-0(8))* Canon Pr.

O'Connell, Susan, et al. Introduction to Reasoning & Proof, Grades 3-5. 2007. (ENG., Illus.). 160p. (C). (gr. 3-5). pap. 41.25 *(978-0-325-01033-5(1)*, E01033) Heinemann.

Pederson, Bridget. I Can Predict, I Wont Be Tricked!, 1 vol. 2007. (Science Made Simple Ser.). (Illus.). 24p. (J). (gr. k-3). lib. bdg. 24.21 *(978-1-59928-582-5(7)*, SandCastle) ABDO Publishing Co.

Schulz, Charles. The Peanuts Guide to the Seasons: A Jumbo Activity Book. Bennett, Elizabeth, illus. 2003. (Peanuts Club with Charlie Brown & Friends Ser.). 144p. (J). *(978-0-439-46826-8(4))* Scholastic, Inc.

Schulz, Charles & Bennett, Elizabeth. The Peanuts Guide to Sports: A Jumbo Activity Book. 2003. (Peanuts Club with Charlie Brown & Friends Ser.). (Illus.). 144p. (J). *(978-0-439-46824-4(8))* Scholastic, Inc.

Somervill, Barbara A. Does This Make Sense? Constructing Explanations. 2009. (Think Like a Scientist Ser.). 24p. (gr. 2-3). 42.50 *(978-1-60854-356-4(0)*, PowerKids Pr.) Rosen Publishing Group, Inc., The.

—What's the Big Idea? Forming Hypotheses, 1 vol. 2006. (Think Like a Scientist Ser.). (ENG.). 24p. (gr. 2-3). pap. 8.25 *(978-1-4358-2686-1(8)*, 2368c1ff-7cfd-4776-9d98-7182111a4c31, Rosen Classroom) Rosen Publishing Group, Inc., The.

LONDON, JACK, 1876-1916

Bankston, John. Jack London. 2004. (Classic Storytellers Ser.). (Illus.). 48p. (J). (gr. 4-8). lib. bdg. 29.95 *(978-1-58415-263-7(X))* Mitchell Lane Pubs.

Buckwalter, Stephanie. Reading & Interpreting the Works of Jack London, 1 vol. 2017. (Lit Crit Guides). (ENG.). 160p. (gr. 8-8). lib. bdg. 41.60 *(978-0-7660-8491-9(4)*, 6089a0e0-7edc-40ba-b805-cbde1d2c6866) Enslow Publishing, LLC.

—A Student's Guide to Jack London, 1 vol. 2008. (Understanding Literature Ser.). (ENG., Illus.). 160p. (gr. 9-10). lib. bdg. 30.93 *(978-0-7660-2707-7(4)*, 597ecd38-9662-4506-b256-7aac5a43a989) Enslow Publishing, LLC.

Streissguth, Thomas. Jack London. 2005. (Biography Ser.). (Illus.). 112p. (gr. 6-12). lib. bdg. 27.93 *(978-0-8225-4987-1(5))* Lerner Publishing Group.

LONDON (ENGLAND)

Adams, Jennifer. My Little Cities: London: (Travel Books for Toddlers, City Board Books) Pizzoli, Greg, illus. 2017. (My Little Cities Ser.). (ENG.). 22p. (J). (gr. -1-k). bds. 9.99 *(978-1-4521-5387-2(6))* Chronicle Bks. LLC.

Evanson, Ashley. London: A Book of Opposites. Evanson, Ashley, illus. 2015. (Hello, World Ser.). (Illus.). 16p. (J). (— 1). bds. 7.99 *(978-0-448-48916-2(3))*, Penguin Workshop) Penguin Young Readers Group.

Jones, Becky & Lewis, Clare. The Bumper Book of London: Everything You Need to Know about London & More... 2015. (ENG., Illus.). 280p. pap. 19.99 *(978-0-7112-3736-0(0))*, White Lion Publishing) Quarto Publishing Group UK GBR. Dist: Littlehampton Bk Services, Ltd.

Marthaler, Jon. Arsenal FC. 2017. (Europe's Best Soccer Clubs Ser.). (ENG., Illus.). 48p. (J). (gr. 3-6). lib. bdg. 34.21 *(978-1-5321-1130-3(4))*, 25836, SportsZone) ABDO Publishing Co.

Mitchell, Arnold. Arnold's Dream. 2008. (ENG.). 32p. pap. 14.95 *(978-1-4092-4776-0(7))* Lulu Pr., Inc.

Rice, Dona Herweck. Art & Culture. 2018. (Mathematics in the Real World Ser.). (ENG., Illus.). 24p. (J). (gr. 1-2). pap. 9.99 *(978-1-4258-5694-6(2))* Teacher Created Materials, Inc.

Riley, Gail Blasser. Tower of London: England's Ghostly Castle. 2006. (Castles, Palaces, & Tombs Ser.). (Illus.). 32p. (YA). (gr. 2-5). lib. bdg. 28.50 *(978-1-59716-249-4(3))* Bearport Publishing Co., Inc.

Sasek, Miroslav. This Is London. 2004. (This is ... Ser.). (ENG., Illus.). 64p. (J). (gr. 2-12). 17.95 *(978-0-7893-1062-0(7))* Universe Publishing.

Stacey, Gill. London, 1 vol. 2003. (Great Cities of the World Ser.). (ENG., Illus.). 48p. (gr. 5-8). lib. bdg. 33.67 *(978-0-8368-5022-2(X))*, e3d5fbbd-f00a-435e-a66b-e2e97aac478c, Gareth Stevens Secondary Library) Stevens, Gareth Publishing LLLP.

LONDON (ENGLAND)—FICTION

Abbott, Jacob. Rollo in London. 2008. 124p. 23.95 *(978-1-60664-942-8(6))*; pap. 10.95 *(978-1-60312-492-8(6))* Aegypan.

Ahern, Carolyn L. Tino Turtle Travels to London, England. Burt Sullivan, Neallia, illus. (J). 2007. 36p. 17.95 incl. audio compact disk *(978-0-9793158-0-0(8))* 2008. (ENG.). 32p. 19.95 incl. audio compact disk *(978-0-9816297-0-4(9))* Tino Turtle Travels, LLC.

Andrews, Julie. Little Bo: The Story of Bonnie Boadicea. No. 2. 2011. (Illus.). (J). lib. bdg. 18.89 *(978-0-06-008912-2(1))* HarperCollins Pubs.

Angel, Ido. Vipo in London: The Ravens of the London Tower. 2015. (AV2 Animated Storytime Ser.). (ENG.). (J). lib. bdg. 29.99 *(978-1-4896-3911-0(X))*, AV2 by Weigl) Weigl Pubs., Inc.

Anne-Marie-Mugwe. Cobjay's Summer Holiday & How to Catch a Squirrel. 2013. (Illus.). 36p. pap. 22.88 *(978-1-4817-8223-4(1))* AuthorHouse.

Anstey, Cindy. Duels & Deception. 2017. (ENG.). 368p. (YA). pap. 26.99 *(978-1-250-11909-4(X))*, 900172672) Feiwel & Friends.

Anthony, Horowitz. The Devil & His Boy. 2007. (ENG.). 192p. (YA). (gr. 6-8). 18.69 *(978-0-399-23432-3(2))* Penguin Young Readers Group.

—Scorpia Rising, 9 vols. (J). 2012. 256.75 *(978-1-4561-3362-7(4))* 2012. 90.75 *(978-1-4561-3363-4(2))* 2012. 1.25 *(978-1-4640-0577-0(X))* 2011. 122.75 *(978-1-4561-3365-8(9))* 2011. 120.75 *(978-1-4561-3367-2(5))* Recorded Bks., Inc.

—Scorpia Rising. 2012. (Alex Rider Ser.: 9). lib. bdg. 19.65 *(978-0-606-23638-6(4))* Turtleback.

Atwarie, Rossi. The Adventures of Fox Brown. Bachan, Krystal Ann, illus. 2011. 62p. pap. 19.00 *(978-1-60911-845-7(6))*, Eloquent Bks.) Strategic Book Publishing & Rights Agency (SBPRA).

Avi. The Traitors' Gate. Raude, Karina, illus. 2010. (ENG.). 368p. (J). (gr. 5-8). pap. 8.99 *(978-0-689-85336-4(X))*, Atheneum Bks. for Young Readers) Simon & Schuster Children's Publishing.

Axelsson, Carina. Model Undercover: London. 2016. (Model Undercover Ser.: 3). (ENG.). 368p. (J). (gr. 5-8). pap. 6.99 *(978-1-4926-2088-4(2))* Sourcebooks, Inc.

Bachmann, Stefan. The Whatnot. 2014. (Peculiar Ser.: 2). (ENG.). 432p. (J). (gr. 3-7). pap. 8.99 *(978-0-06-219522-7(0))*, Greenwillow Bks.) HarperCollins Pubs.

Banks, Piper. Geek Abroad, 2 vols. 2008. (Geek High Ser.: 2). (ENG.). 256p. (YA). (gr. 9-18). 9.99 *(978-0-451-22393-7(4))*, Berkley) Penguin Publishing Group.

—Revenge of the Geek. 2010. (Geek High Ser.: 4). (ENG.). 256p. (gr. 12-18). 9.99 *(978-0-451-23134-5(1))*, Berkley) Penguin Publishing Group.

Bardes, Cynthia. Pansy in London: The Mystery of the Missing Pup, vol. 5. Best, Virginia, illus. 2017. (Pansy the Poodle Mystery Ser.: 5th book in the series). (ENG.). 32p. (J). (gr. -1-2). 21.95 *(978-0-692-82604-1(1))* Octobre Pr.

Barradell, Isabel. Even More Tales from the Toyshop. 2008. 380p. pap. 29.95 *(978-1-60474-508-5(8))* America Star Bks.

Barrett, Tracy. The Case That Time Forgot. 3. 2011. (Sherlock Files Ser.: 3). (ENG., Illus.). 176p. (J). (gr. 4-6). pap. 10.99 *(978-0-312-56358-5(2))*, 900074759) Square Fish.

—The Missing Heir. 2012. (Sherlock Files Ser.: 4). (J). lib. bdg. 19.65 *(978-0-606-26131-9(1))* Turtleback.

Barrie, J. M. Peter Pan: Peter & Wendy & Peter Pan in Kensington Gardens. 2004. (Illus.). 272p. (gr. 12-18). 12.00 *(978-0-14-243793-3(X))*, Penguin Classics) Penguin Publishing Group.

Barrie, James Matthew. Peter Pan. (SPA.). 191p. 15.95 *(978-84-206-3689-4(4))* Alianza Editorial, S. A. ESP. Dist: Distribooks, Inc.

—Peter Pan in Kensington Gardens. 2006. pap. *(978-1-4065-0950-2(7))* Dodo Pr.

Barrie, James Matthew & Edens, Cooper. Peter Pan. (SPA.). 174p. 26.95 *(978-84-666-0760-5(9))* Ediciones B ESP. Dist: Spanish Pubs., LLC.

Barry, Dave. Peter & the Sword of Mercy. 4. 2011. (Peter & the Starcatchers Ser.: Bk. 4). (ENG., Illus.). 528p. (J). (gr. 5-9). pap. 9.99 *(978-1-4231-3070-3(7))*, Disney-Hyperion) Disney Publishing Worldwide.

Barter, Catherine. Troublemakers. 2018. (ENG.). 360p. (YA). (gr. 7-12). 17.99 *(978-1-5124-7549-4(1))*, 6501f552-14c0-47e0-aa58-d3647a7e0d10, Carolrhoda Lab™) Lerner Publishing Group.

Beecroft, Susan. Teddy Goes to Buckingham Palace. 2013. (ENG., Illus.). 24p. pap. 9.50 *(978-1-78035-606-8(4))*, Fastprint Publishing) Upfront Publishing Ltd. GBR. Dist: Printondemand-worldwide.com.

Bennett, Sophia. The Look. 2013. (ENG.). 336p. (YA). (gr. 7). 17.99 *(978-0-545-46438-3(2))*; (J). *(978-0-545-46439-0(0))* Scholastic, Inc. (Chicken Hse., The).

Berk, Sheryl & Berk, Carrie. Royal Icing: The Cupcake Club. 2014. (Cupcake Club Ser.: 6). 144p. (J). (gr. 3-7). pap. 12.99 *(978-1-4022-8333-8(4))* Sourcebooks, Inc.

Bessey, Siân Ann. You Came for Me. 2013. (ENG.). 240p. pap. 14.99 *(978-1-60861-221-5(X))* Covenant Communications, Inc.

Best, Rosie. Skulk. 2013. (ENG.). 400p. (J). (gr. 11). pap. 9.99 *(978-1-908844-70-5(1))*, Strange Chemistry) Watkins Media Limited GBR. Dist: Penguin Random Hse. LLC.

Blacker, Terence. The Angel Factory. 2012. (ENG., Illus.). 224p. (J). (gr. 5-9). pap. 10.99 *(978-0-689-86413-1(2))*, Simon & Schuster/Paula Wiseman Bks.) Simon & Schuster/Paula Wiseman Bks.

Blyton, Enid. The Secret of the Lost Necklace: 3 Great Adventure Stories. Biro, Val, illus. 2013. (ENG.). 272p. (J). 16.50 *(978-1-84135-587-0(9))* Award Pubns. Ltd. GBR. Dist: Parkwest Pubns., Inc.

Bond, Michael. Paddington & the Christmas Surprise: A Christmas Holiday Book for Kids. Alley, R. W., illus. 2015. (Paddington Ser.). (ENG.). 32p. (J). (gr. -1-3). 17.99 *(978-0-06-231842-8(X))*, HarperCollins) HarperCollins Pubs.

—Paddington Takes the Air. Fortnum, Peggy, illus. 2018. (Paddington Ser.). (ENG.). 176p. (J). (gr. 3-7). 9.99 *(978-0-06-231238-9(3))*, HarperCollins) HarperCollins Pubs.

—Paddington Takes the Air. Fortnum, Peggy, illus. 2019. (Paddington Ser.). (ENG.). 176p. (J). (gr. 3-7). pap. 6.99 *(978-0-06-243315-2(6))*, HarperCollins) HarperCollins Pubs.

—Paddington's Day Off. 2017. (Paddington — I Can Read Ser.). (J). lib. bdg. 13.55 *(978-0-606-39636-3(5))* Turtleback.

Botha, Ingrid. Chikin & Scrub. 2011. 108p. pap. 10.50 *(978-1-60976-295-7(9))*, Strategic Bk. Publishing) Strategic Book Publishing & Rights Agency (SBPRA).

Bradbury, Jennifer. Wrapped. 2011. (ENG., Illus.). 320p. (YA). (gr. 7-18). 16.99 *(978-1-4169-9007-9(0))*, Atheneum Bks. for Young Readers) Simon & Schuster Children's Publishing.

Braddock, Pauline. The long way Home. 2010. 156p. pap. 9.17 *(978-1-4452-9248-9(3))* Lulu Pr., Inc.

Bradman, Tom and Tony. Short Histories: the Baker's Boy & the Great Fire of London. 2018. (Short Histories Ser.). (ENG., Illus.). 32p. (J). (gr. 1-3). pap. 7.99 *(978-1-5263-0347-9(7))*, Wayland) Hachette Children's Group GBR. Dist: Hachette Bk. Group.

Branson, Eve. Sarky Puddleboat. Lowe, Wes, illus. 2011. (ENG.). 44p. (J). 14.99 *(978-1-4520-9754-1(2))*, dda4f9f2-b41f-400a-ad7d-1886b4446dd6) AuthorHouse.

Brown, Jeff. Flat Stanley's Worldwide Adventures #14: on a Mission for Her Majesty. Pamintuan, Macky, illus. 2017. (Flat Stanley's Worldwide Adventures Ser.: 14). (ENG.). 128p. (J). (gr. 1-5). 15.99 *(978-0-06-236607-8(6))*; pap. 4.99 *(978-0-06-236606-1(8))* HarperCollins Pubs. (HarperCollins).

Brundige, Patricia. Traveling with Aunt Patty: Aunt Patty Visits London. Wright, Cindy, ed. Hanlon, Leslie, illus. Date not set. (J). (gr. 1-4). 12.95 *(978-0-9659668-0-1(1))* Aunt Patty's Travels-London.

Buckley-Archer, Linda. The Time Quake. 3. 2009. (Gideon Trilogy Ser.: 3). (ENG.). 464p. (J). (gr. 5-9). 17.99 *(978-1-4169-1529-4(X))* Simon & Schuster, Inc.

—The Time Thief. 2008. (Gideon Trilogy Ser.: 2). (ENG.). 512p. (J). (gr. 5-9). pap. 9.99 *(978-1-4169-1528-7(1))*, Simon & Schuster Bks. For Young Readers) Simon & Schuster Bks. For Young Readers.

Bulla, Clyde Robert. A Lion to Guard Us. Chessare, Michele, illus. 2018. (ENG.). 128p. (J). (gr. 3-7). pap. 9.99 *(978-0-06-440333-7(5))*, HarperCollins) HarperCollins Pubs.

Bunzl, Peter. Cogheart. 2019. (Cogheart Adventures Ser.). (ENG.). 368p. (J). (gr. 3-7). pap. 12.99 *(978-1-63163-287-7(6))*, 1631632876, Jolly Fish Pr.) North Star Editions.

—Moonlocket. 2019. (Cogheart Adventures Ser.). (ENG.). 384p. (J). (gr. 3-7). pap. 12.99 *(978-1-63163-375-1(9))*, 1631633759, Jolly Fish Pr.) North Star Editions.

Burnett, Frances. A Little Princess. 2008. 156p. 25.95 *(978-1-60664-768-4(7))*; pap. 13.95 *(978-1-60664-141-5(7))* Aegypan.

—A Little Princess. 2008. 212p. (gr. 2-4). 27.99 *(978-0-554-29155-0(X))* Creative Media Partners, LLC.

—A Little Princess. Aldous, Kate, illus. 2005. 62p. (J). (gr. 4-7). 8.95 *(978-0-7945-1123-4(6))*, Usborne) EDC Publishing.

—A Little Princess. 2012. 212p. pap. 8.99 *(978-1-60796-454-4(6))* Meirovich, Igal.

—A Little Princess. 2011. (ENG., Illus.). (J). 15.99 *(978-1-61382-603-4(6))* Simon & Brown.

—A Little Princess. 188p. 2009. pap. 13.95 *(978-1-4385-0876-4(X))* 2008. pap. 13.45 *(978-1-4385-0194-9(3))* Standard Publications, Inc. (Bk. Jungle).

—A Little Princess. Engelbreit, Mary, illus. 2007. (Mary Engelbreit's Classic Library). (ENG.). 304p. (J). (gr. 3-7). 9.99 *(978-0-06-008137-9(6))*, HarperFestival) HarperCollins Pubs.

—A Little Princess. 2012. (Children's Classics Ser.). (ENG.). 186p. pap. 19.99 *(978-1-909438-52-1(9))*, Sovereign) Bollinger, Max GBR. Dist: Lightning Source UK, Ltd.

—A Little Princess: Being the whole story of Sara Crewe now told for T. 2007. 196p. per. 19.99 *(978-1-4346-7028-1(7))*; (ENG.). 210p. per. 22.99 *(978-1-4346-7029-8(5))* Creative Media Partners, LLC.

—A Little Princess: The Story of Sara Crewe. (J). 16.95 *(978-0-8488-1253-9(0))* Amereon Ltd.

—A Little Princess: The Story of Sara Crewe. Warren, Eliza, ed. Marcos, Pablo, illus. 2006. 239p. (YA). reprint ed. 10.00 *(978-0-7567-9835-2(3))* DIANE Publishing Co.

—A Little Princess: The Story of Sara Crewe. 2005. 112p. per. 4.95 *(978-1-4209-2529-6(6))* Digireads.com Publishing.

—A Little Princess: The Story of Sara Crewe. 2006. pap. *(978-1-4065-0559-7(5))* Dodo Pr.

—A Little Princess: The Story of Sara Crewe. l.t. ed. 2005. 376p. pap. *(978-1-84637-117-2(1))* Echo Library.

—A Little Princess: The Story of Sara Crewe. 2004. reprint ed. pap. 1.99 *(978-1-4192-0213-1(8))*; pap. 22.95 *(978-1-4191-0213-4(3))* Kessinger Publishing, LLC.

—A Little Princess: The Story of Sara Crewe. 2006. 204p. (YA). 19.95 *(978-1-934169-20-9(X))*; pap. 7.95 *(978-1-934169-21-6(8))* Norilana Bks.

—A Little Princess: The Story of Sara Crewe. 2005. (Twelve-Point Ser.). lib. bdg. 25.00 *(978-1-58287-320-6(8))*; lib. bdg. 26.00 *(978-1-58287-814-0(5))* North Bks.

—A Little Princess: The Story of Sara Crewe. Rust, Graham, illus. (J). pap. 22.95 *(978-0-590-24079-6(X))* Scholastic, Inc.

—A Little Princess: The Story of Sara Crewe. l.t. ed. 2003. 342p. pap. 10.95 *(978-0-7862-6247-2(8))* Thorndike Pr.

—A Little Princess: With a Discussion of Generosity. Gribbon, Sean & Jael, trs. Gribbon, Sean & Jael, illus. 2003. (Values in Action Illustrated Classics Ser.). (J). *(978-1-59203-050-7(5))* Learning Challenge, Inc.

—Petite Princess. pap. 19.95 *(978-2-07-051994-1(5))* Gallimard, Editions FRA. Dist: Distribooks, Inc.

—Sara Crewe. l.t. ed. 2006. 92p. pap. *(978-1-84637-263-6(1))* Echo Library.

—Sara Crewe. 2009. 68p. pap. 7.95 *(978-1-60664-388-4(6))* Rodgers, Alan Bks.

—Sara Crewe or What Happened at Miss Minc. 2005. pap. 20.95 *(978-0-7661-9708-4(5))* Kessinger Publishing, LLC.

—Sara Crewe or What Happened at Miss Minchin's. 2006. (ENG.). 88p. per. 8.95 *(978-1-59462-359-2(7))*, 395, Bk. Jungle) Standard Publications, Inc.

—Sara Crewe, or What Happened at Miss Minchin's. 2007. 48p. per. *(978-1-4068-4489-4(6))* Echo Library.

Burnett, Frances Hodgson. Classic Starts(r): a Little Princess. Corvino, Lucy, illus. 2005. (Classic Starts(r) Ser.). 160p. (J). (gr. 2-4). 6.95 *(978-1-4027-1275-3(8))* Sterling Publishing Co., Inc.

—A Little Princess. Rust, Graham, illus. 2019. (ENG.). 192p. (J). (gr. 4-7). reprint ed. 18.95 *(978-0-87923-784-4(8))* Godine, David R. Pub.

—A Little Princess. 2012. (ENG., Illus.). 280p. *(978-1-905716-04-3(4))*, Collector's Library, The) Pan Macmillan.

—A Little Princess. (Puffin Classics Ser.). (Illus.). (J). (gr. 5-7). 2012. 310p. 16.99 *(978-0-14-134171-2(8))* 2008. (ENG.). 320p. 8.99 *(978-0-14-132112-7(1))* Penguin Young Readers Group. (Puffin Books).

Burt, Marissa. The 12 Dares of Christa. 2017. (ENG.). 304p. (J). (gr. 3-7). 16.99 *(978-0-06-241618-6(9))*, Tegen, Katherine Bks) HarperCollins Pubs.

Button, Timothy D. Matthew Mcsilly. 2012. 32p. pap. 17.95 *(978-1-4772-0817-5(8))* AuthorHouse.

Byrne, Michael. Lottery Boy. 2016. (ENG.). 304p. (YA). (gr. 7). 16.99 *(978-0-7636-7996-5(8))* Candlewick Pr.

Callaghan, Cindy. Lost in London. 2013. (Mix Ser.). (ENG., Illus.). 240p. (J). (gr. 4-8). pap. 7.99 *(978-1-4424-6653-1(7))*, Aladdin) Simon & Schuster Children's Publishing.

Calloway, Cassidy. Secrets of a First Daughter. 2010. (ENG.). 208p. (YA). (gr. 8-18). pap. 8.99 *(978-0-06-172442-8(4))*, HarperTeen) HarperCollins Pubs.

Carlson, Melody. Spotlight, 1 vol. 2014. (On the Runway Ser.: 4). (ENG.). 224p. (YA). pap. 9.99 *(978-0-310-74821-2(6))* Zondervan.

Carmichael, Heather. Ellie Finds a New Home. McFarland, Shea, illus. 2008. (ENG.). 36p. pap. 16.99 *(978-1-4389-2976-7(5))* AuthorHouse.

Carter, Ally. Only the Good Spy Young. 10th anniv. ed. 2016. (Gallagher Girls Ser.: 4). (ENG.). 288p. (YA). (gr. 7-17). pap. 9.99 *(978-1-4847-8506-5(1))* Little, Brown Bks. for Young Readers.

—Only the Good Spy Young. 2016. (Gallagher Girls Ser.: 4). (J). lib. bdg. 20.85 *(978-0-606-38298-4(4))* Turtleback.

Catlow, Nikalas & Wesson, Tim. Mega Mash-Up: Ancient Egyptians vs. Pirates in a Haunted Museum. Catlow, Nikalas, illus. 2012. (Mega Mash-Up Ser.: 4). (ENG., Illus.). 96p. (J). (gr. 2-5). pap. 6.99 *(978-0-7636-5901-1(0))* Candlewick Pr.

Chadda, Sarwat. The City of Death. 2013. (J). pap. *(978-0-545-38519-0(9))* Scholastic, Inc.

Cheshire, Simon. The Frankenstein Inheritance. 2012. 204p. pap. *(978-0-9565049-7-5(3))* Cheshire, Simon.

Child, Lauren. Ruby Redfort Blink & You Die. Child, Lauren, illus. (Ruby Redfort Ser.: 6). (ENG., Illus.). 544p. (J). (gr. 5-9). 2019. pap. 8.99 *(978-1-5362-0863-4(9))* 2018. 18.99 *(978-0-7636-5472-6(8))* Candlewick Pr.

Chitty, Joan E. Charlie Macaffee: Search for the Genie's Body. 2005. 267p. pap. 27.95 *(978-1-4241-0007-1(0))* PublishAmerica, Inc.

Christen, Dennis H. Lundon's Bridge & the Three Keys. 2005. (YA). lib. bdg., act. bk. ed. 24.95 *(978-0-9718151-3-1(5))* 2006. (ENG.). (J). per. 12.95 *(978-0-9718151-2-4(7))* C-It Entertainment Group, LLC.

C.J. Elgert. The Elder Brothers & the Padstow Crystals. 2009. 284p. 27.95 *(978-1-4401-7678-4(7))*; pap. 17.95 *(978-1-4401-7676-0(0))* iUniverse, Inc.

Clare, Cassandra. Clockwork Prince. 2013. (Infernal Devices Graphic Novel Ser.: 2). lib. bdg. 24.55 *(978-0-606-32258-4(2))* Turtleback.

—The Infernal Devices: Clockwork Angel; Clockwork Prince; Clockwork Princess. 2013. (Infernal Devices Ser.: Bks. 1-3). (ENG.). 1520p. (YA). (gr. 9). 74.99 *(978-1-4424-8372-9(5))*, McElderry, Margaret K. Bks.) McElderry, Margaret K. Bks.

Clarke, E. J. A Fairy's Courage. (Oakwing Ser.: 2). (ENG.). 208p. (J). (gr. 2-6). 2019. pap. 7.99 *(978-1-4814-8193-9(2))* 2018. (Illus.). 16.99 *(978-1-4814-8194-6(0))* Simon & Schuster Children's Publishing. (Aladdin).

—Oakwing: A Fairy's Tale. 2017. (Oakwing Ser.: 1). (ENG., Illus.). 192p. (J). (gr. 2-6). 16.99 *(978-1-4814-8191-5(6))*, Aladdin) Simon & Schuster Children's Publishing.

—Oakwing: A Fairy's Tale. 2018. (Oakwing Ser.: 1). (ENG.). 208p. (J). (gr. 2-6). pap. 6.99 *(978-1-4814-8190-8(8))*, Simon & Schuster/Paula Wiseman Bks.) Simon & Schuster/Paula Wiseman Bks.

Clary, Julian. The Bolds. Roberts, David, illus. 2017. (Bolds Ser.). (ENG.). 288p. (J). (gr. 3-6). pap. 9.99 *(978-1-5124-8174-7(2))*, 0d6da9d3-74f5-4236-ac56-c272446de989, Carolrhoda Bks.) Lerner Publishing Group.

—The Bolds to the Rescue. Roberts, David, illus. 2018. (Bolds Ser.). (ENG.). 288p. (J). (gr. 3-6). pap. 8.99 *(978-1-5415-3844-3(7))*, 84dd1818-8bf6-488d-ab25-ac1e93eaf993, Carolrhoda Bks.) Lerner Publishing Group.

Cockcroft, Jason. Counter Clockwise. 2009. 208p. (J). lib. bdg. 16.89 *(978-0-06-125555-7(6))*, Tegen, Katherine Bks) HarperCollins Pubs.

The Complete Gideon Trilogy (Boxed Set) The Time Travelers; the Time Thief; the Time Quake. 2014. (Gideon Trilogy Ser.). (ENG., Illus.). 1424p. (J). (gr. 5-9). pap. 29.99 *(978-1-4814-2613-8(3))*, Simon & Schuster Bks. For Young Readers) Simon & Schuster Bks. For Young Readers.

Conan Doyle, Arthur. #09 Sherlock Holmes & the Adventure of the Six Napoleons. Rohrbach, Sophie & Morrow, Jt, illus. 2011. (On the Case with Holmes & Watson Set II Ser.). pap. 39.62 *(978-0-7613-7611-8(9))*, Graphic Universe™) Lerner Publishing Group.

Cook, Eileen. You Owe Me a Murder. 2019. (ENG.). 368p. (YA). (gr. 9). 17.99 *(978-1-328-51902-3(3))*, 1720627, Clarion Bks.) HarperCollins Pubs.

Cook, Jacqueline. The Little Bear Who Worried Too Much: Suzie Bear Goes to London. 2011. 34p. (gr. 1-4). pap. 13.50 *(978-1-60976-875-1(2))*, Eloquent Bks.) Strategic Book Publishing & Rights Agency (SBPRA).

Cooney, Caroline B. The Terrorist. 2012. (ENG.). 144p. (YA). (gr. 7-12). pap. 6.99 *(978-1-4532-7467-5(7))* Open Road Integrated Media, Inc.

Coppel, Chris. Far from Burden Dell. 2005. 286p. (J). (gr. 6-16). per. 4.95 *(978-0-9746481-6-3(7))* Brown Barn Bks.

Craig, Joe. Jimmy Coates: Assassin? 2005. 224p. (J). (gr. 5-18). 15.99 *(978-0-06-077263-5(8))* HarperCollins Pubs.

—Jimmy Coates: Assassin? 2006. 218p. (J). (gr. 5-9). per. 5.99 *(978-0-06-077265-9(4))*, Harper Trophy) HarperCollins Pubs.

Dalmatian Press Staff, adapted by. Oliver Twist. Date not set. (C). pap. *(978-0-7593-9612-8(4))*, Cengage Learning) CENGAGE Learning.

Daniels, Darla. The Magic Ring: Summer Vacation in London. 2012. 30p. 16.95 *(978-1-4626-6252-4(8))* America Star Bks.

Danziger, Paula. Thames Doesn't Rhyme with James. (Remember Me to Harold Square Ser.: No. 2). 153p. (J). pap. 3.99 *(978-0-8072-1473-2(6))*, Listening Library) Random Hse. Audio Publishing Group.

—You Can't Eat Your Chicken Pox, Amber Brown. Ross, Tony, illus. 2006. (Amber Brown Ser.: 2). (ENG.). 128p. (J). (gr. 2-5). 6.99 *(978-0-14-240629-8(5))*, Puffin Books) Penguin Young Readers Group.

—You Can't Eat Your Chicken Pox, Amber Brown. Ross, Tony, illus. 2006. (Amber Brown Ser.: No. 2). 100p. (gr. 2-5). 15.00 *(978-0-7569-6756-7(2))* Perfection Learning Corp.

—You Can't Eat Your Chicken Pox, Amber Brown. (Amber Brown Ser.: No. 2). 101p. (J). (gr. 3-6). pap. 3.50 *(978-0-8072-1290-5(3))*, Listening Library) Random Hse. Audio Publishing Group.

Davis, Penny. Annabel's Yearnings. 2012. 274p. pap. *(978-1-78003-309-9(5))* Pen Pr. Pubs., Ltd.

Dawnay, Gabby. London Calls. Barrow, Alex, illus. 2015. (ENG.). 40p. (J). (gr. -1-2). 13.95 *(978-0-84976-230-4(9))*, 1669201) Tate Publishing, Ltd. GBR. Dist: Hachette Bk. Group.

Deekster, Deek. Ozzie Rozzie. 2005. 41p. (YA). pap. 7.85 *(978-1-4116-6420-3(5))* Lulu Pr., Inc.

Dickens, Charles. Classic Starts(r): Oliver Twist: Retold from the Charles Dickens Original. Andreasen, Dan, illus. 2006. (Classic Starts(r) Ser.). 160p. (J). (gr. 2-4). 7.99 *(978-1-4027-2665-1(1))* Sterling Publishing Co., Inc.

—Great Expectations: The Graphic Novel, 1 vol. 2010. (Classic Graphic Novel Collection). (ENG.). 160p. (gr. 7-10). 41.03 *(978-1-4205-0372-2(3))*, c93617a4-5093-4c70-be39-d2ee1429dc17, Lucent Pr.) Greenhaven Publishing LLC.

—Level 6: Oliver Twist. 2nd ed. 2008. (Pearson English Graded Readers Ser.). (ENG.). 136p. pap. 15.99 *(978-1-4058-6525-8(3))*, Pearson ELT) Pearson Education.

—Oliver Twist. abr. ed. Date not set. (Nelson Readers Ser.). (J). pap. *(978-0-17-557020-1(5))* Addison-Wesley Longman, Inc.

—Oliver Twist. Ablett, Barry, illus. 2007. (Young Reading Series 3 Gift Bks.). 63p. (J). (gr. 3). 8.99 *(978-0-7945-1459-4(6))*, Usborne) EDC Publishing.

—Oliver Twist. 2008. (Bring the Classics to Life Ser.). (ENG., Illus.). 72p. (gr. 3-12). pap., act. bk. ed. 10.95 *(978-1-55576-325-1(1))*, EDCTR-308B) EDCON Publishing Group.

—Oliver Twist. abr. ed. (J). 9.95 *(978-1-56156-372-2(2))* Kidsbooks, LLC.

—Oliver Twist. 2008. (Puffin Classics Ser.). 416p. (J). (gr. 5-7). 8.99 *(978-0-14-132243-8(8))*, Puffin Books) Penguin Young Readers Group.

—Oliver Twist. 2006. 516p. (gr. 3-3). per. *(978-1-4067-9405-2(8))*, Hesperides Pr.) Read Bks.

—Oliver Twist, 1 vol. Donnelly, Karen, illus. 2009. (Real Reads Ser.). (ENG.). 64p. (YA). (gr. 5-5). pap. 14.55 *(978-1-60754-153-0(X))*, 86478a93-d43b-486b-9cbe-5c249a8a89cd, Windmill Bks.) Rosen Publishing Group, Inc., The.

—Oliver Twist. annot. ed. 2007. (Enriched Classics Ser.). (ENG.). 672p. (gr. 3). mass mkt. 5.95 *(978-1-4165-3475-4(X))* Simon & Schuster.

—Oliver Twist. Morgan, Richard & Fennell, Tracy, illus. 2008. 48p. (J). (gr. 4-7). pap. 10.00 *(978-1-4190-5075-6(3))* Steck-Vaughn.

—Oliver Twist. McKowen, Scott, illus. 2008. (Union Square Kids Unabridged Classics Ser.). 464p. (J). 14.95 *(978-1-4027-5425-8(6))* Sterling Publishing Co., Inc.

—Oliver Twist, 3 cass.; set. 2004. (Masterpiece Theatre Ser.). (gr. 7-18). tchr. ed. 59.95 incl. VHS *(978-1-57807-576-8(9))*, WG1062) WGBH Boston Video.

—Oliver Twist: With a Discussion of Honesty. 2003. (Values in Action Illustrated Classics Ser.). (J). *(978-1-59203-051-4(3))* Learning Challenge, Inc.

—Oxford Bookworms Library: Oliver Twist: Level 6: 2,500 Word Vocabulary. 2007. (Oxford Bookworms Ser.). (ENG.,

Illus.). 120p. pap. 11.00 *(978-0-19-423763-5(X))* Oxford Univ. Pr., Inc.

Doan, Lisa. The Alarming Career of Sir Richard Blackstone. 2017. (ENG.). 192p. (J). (gr. 2-7). 15.99 *(978-1-5107-1122-8(8)*, Sky Pony Pr.) Skyhorse Publishing Co., Inc.

Dolenz, Ami. Harold & Agatha: The Mysterious Jewel. 2013. 176p. *(978-1-4602-0520-4(0))*; pap. *(978-1-4602-0420-7(4))* FriesenPress.

Dolsingh, Kanisha. Once upon a Time: In London Town with Minnie Drew. 2011. 28p. pap. 16.99 *(978-1-4567-5731-1(8))* AuthorHouse.

Don, Lari. Mind Blind, 20 vols. 2014. 336p. (YA). 9.95 *(978-1-78250-053-7(7)*, Kelpies) Floris Bks. GBR. Dist: Consortium Bk. Sales & Distribution.

Dowd, Siobhan. The London Eye Mystery. 2009. (ENG.). 336p. (J). (gr. 3-7). 8.99 *(978-0-385-75184-1(2)*, Yearling) Random Hse. Children's Bks.

—The London Eye Mystery. 2009. (London Eye Mystery Ser.: 1). lib. bdg. 18.40 *(978-0-606-14413-1(7))* Turtleback.

Downey, Glen. Rebel Prince. Okum, David, illus. 2007. 48p. (J). lib. bdg. 23.08 *(978-1-4242-1642-0(7))* Fitzgerald Bks.

Durrant, S. E. Little Bits of Sky. Harnett, Katie, illus. 2017. (ENG.). 208p. (J). (gr. 3-7). 16.95 *(978-0-8234-3839-6(2))* Holiday Hse., Inc.

Eade, Oliver. The Terminus. 2013. 264p. pap. *(978-1-909411-26-5(4))* Mauve Square Publishing.

Edge, Christopher. Twelve Minutes to Midnight. 2014. (Penelope Tredwell Mysteries Ser.: 1). (ENG.). 256p. (J). (gr. 3-7). 16.99 *(978-0-8075-8133-9(X)*, 080758133X) Whitman, Albert & Co.

Egan, Tim. Dodsworth in London. Egan, Tim, illus. 2010. (Dodsworth Book Ser.). (ENG., Illus.). 48p. (J). (gr. 1-4). pap. 4.99 *(978-0-547-41440-9(4)*, 1429469, Clarion Bks.) HarperCollins Pubs.

Elgert, C. J. The Elder Brothers & the Padstow Crystals. 2013. 208p. *(978-1-4602-1788-7(8))*; pap. *(978-1-4602-1789-4(6))* FriesenPress.

Emerson, Kevin. Finding Abbey Road. 2017. 256p. (J). pap. 9.99 *(978-0-06-213402-8(7))* 2016. (Exile Ser.: 3). (ENG.). 240p. (YA). (gr. 9). 17.99 *(978-0-06-213401-1(9))* HarperCollins Pubs. (Tegen, Katherine Bks).

Eschberger, Beverly. The Elephants Visit London: An Elephant Family Adventure. Gower, Jim, illus. I.t. ed. 2007. (Elephant Family Adventure Ser.: 1). (ENG.). 96p. (J). (-1). per. 3.99 *(978-1-932926-30-9(5))* Artemesia Publishing, LLC.

Farrow, G. & Farrow, George. The Mysterious Shin Shira. 2007. 116p. per. 10.95 *(978-1-60312-225-2(7))* Aegypan.

Farrow, G. e. & Farrow, G. E. The Wallypug in London. 2011. 106p. 23.95 *(978-1-4638-9696-6(4))*; pap. 9.95 *(978-1-60664-480-5(7))* Rodgers, Alan Bks.

Feinstein, John. Rush for the Gold: Mystery at the Olympics (the Sports Beat, 6) 2013. (Sports Beat Ser.: 6). 320p. (J). (gr. 5). pap. 10.99 *(978-0-375-87168-9(3)*, Yearling) Random Hse. Children's Bks.

Fenn, G. Manville. Brownsmith's Boy. 2008. 260p. 29.95 *(978-1-60664-780-6(6))* Aegypan.

Foster, Darlene. Amanda in England: The Missing Novel. 2012. (Amanda Travels Adventure Ser.: 3). (ENG.). 118p. (J). (gr. 2-1). pap. 12.99 *(978-1-926760-77-3(8))* Central Avenue Publishing CAN. Dist: Independent Pubs. Group.

Foster, Kim. Game of Secrets. 2018. (ENG.). 368p. (YA). (gr. 7-7). 17.99 *(978-1-5107-1644-5(0)*, Sky Pony Pr.) Skyhorse Publishing Co., Inc.

Foster, Matthew. The Gateway. 2010. 172p. pap. 16.95 *(978-1-4461-5024-5(0))* Lulu Pr., Inc.

Fougasse, J. Smith. Fougasse, illus. 2015. (ENG., Illus.). 152p. (J). (gr. 5). 25.00 *(978-0-7636-7763-3(9))* Candlewick Pr.

Frank, Hannah. If I Had Three Wishes. 2008. 56p. pap. 23.99 *(978-1-4343-7529-2(3))* AuthorHouse.

—The Train to Baker Street. 2008. 44p. pap. 19.49 *(978-1-4389-1026-0(6))* AuthorHouse.

Freeman, Hilary. The Boy from France. 2012. 192p. (YA). (gr. 8). pap. 11.99 *(978-1-84812-301-4(9))* Bonnier Publishing GBR. Dist: Independent Pubs. Group.

Gardner, Sally. I, Coriander. 2007. (Illus.). 280p. (J). (gr. 5-9). 14.65 *(978-0-7569-8130-3(1))* Perfection Learning Corp.

Gier, Kerstin. Sapphire Blue, 2. Bell, Anthea, tr. 2013. (Ruby Red Trilogy Ser.: 2). (ENG.). 384p. (YA). (gr. 6-8). pap. 11.99 *(978-1-250-03416-8(7)*, 900120588) Square Fish.

Gillanders, Ann. Fairy Fleur & Doug the Dragonfly's Adventures in London: Ann Gillanders. 2012. (Illus.). 36p. pap. 22.88 *(978-1-4772-4358-9(5))* AuthorHouse.

Gillott, C. M. Nelson 'n' Deck & Friends: How the Adventures Began. 2010. (Illus.). 48p. pap. 17.49 *(978-1-4490-9593-2(3))* AuthorHouse.

Gleason, Colleen. The Chess Queen Enigma: A Stoker & Holmes Novel. 2015. (Stoker & Holmes Ser.: 3). (ENG.). 360p. (YA). (gr. 7-12). 17.99 *(978-1-4521-4317-0(X))* Chronicle Bks. LLC.

—The Spiritglass Charade: A Stoker & Holmes Novel. 2015. (Stoker & Holmes Ser.: 2). (ENG., Illus.). 368p. (YA). (gr. 7-12). pap. 9.99 *(978-1-4521-2885-6(5))* Chronicle Bks. LLC.

Goldman, Stanley M. The Doorway to Forever: September 2nd, 1666, the First Day of Forever. 2008. (ENG.). 186p. (J). (gr. 7). pap. 9.95 *(978-1-933255-46-0(3))* DNA Pr.

Gordon, Roderick. Closer. (Tunnels Ser.: 4). (J). 1.25 *(978-1-4498-2165-4(0))*; 296.75 *(978-1-4498-2158-6(8))*; 121.75 *(978-1-4498-2159-3(6))*; 2011. 132.75 *(978-1-4498-2163-0(4))*; 2011. 134.75 *(978-1-4498-2161-6(8))* Recorded Bks., Inc.

—Deeper, 15 vols. 2009. (J). 128.75 *(978-1-4361-3717-1(9))*; 134.75 *(978-1-4361-3721-8(7))*; 126.75 *(978-1-4361-3719-5(5))*; 132.75 *(978-1-4361-3723-2(3))*; 301.75 *(978-1-4361-3718-8(7))*; 1.25 *(978-1-4361-3714-0(4))* Recorded Bks., Inc.

Gordon, Roderick & Williams, Brian. Tunnels (Tunnels #1) Williams, Brian, illus. 2009. (Tunnels Ser.: 1). (ENG.). 496p. (J). (gr. 3-7). pap. 9.99 *(978-0-545-07881-8(4)*, Scholastic Paperbacks) Scholastic, Inc.

Gordon, Roderick & Williams, Brian James. Terminal. 2013. (J). *(978-0-545-47963-9(0))* Scholastic, Inc.

Gourlay, Candy. Tall Story. 2012. (ENG.). 304p. (J). (gr. 5). 8.99 *(978-0-385-75233-6(4)*, Yearling) Random Hse. Children's Bks.

Grant, Natalie. A London Art Chase, 1 vol. 2016. (Faithgirlz / Glimmer Girls Ser.). (ENG., Illus.). 208p. (J). pap. 8.99 *(978-0-310-75265-3(5))* Zonderkidz.

Greenhill, Ms Jane. Jolly Olde Teenage Alien. 2013. 258p. pap. *(978-0-9918766-2-4(8))* Greenhill, Jane.

Griffiths, Robert. Adventures of Clive. 2005. 45p. (J). pap. 10.01 *(978-1-4116-5332-0(7))*; 89p. pap. 8.81 *(978-1-4116-5191-3(X))* Lulu Pr., Inc.

Guillain, Adam. Bella Balistica & the Izta Warriors, 1 vol. 2012. (Bella Balistica Ser.). (ENG., Illus.). 192p. (J). (gr. 4-7). pap. 9.95 *(978-1-84059-771-4(2))* Milet Publishing.

Hampton, Sue. Pomp & Circumstances. 2012. (ENG.). 100p. (YA). pap. *(978-1-78228-181-8(9))* Pneuma Springs Publishing.

Hannibal, James R. The Lost Property Office. 2016. (Section 13 Ser.: 1). (ENG., Illus.). 400p. (J). (gr. 3-7). 18.99 *(978-1-4814-6709-4(3)*, Simon & Schuster Bks. For Young Readers) Simon & Schuster Bks. For Young Readers.

Harris, Brooke. London Bridge. Boyer, Lyn, illus. 2010. (Rising Readers Ser.). (J). 3.49 *(978-1-60719-702-7(2))* Newmark Learning LLC.

Haslett, Katherine A. The Day Amy Met the Prime Minister & Mrs. Blair. 2007. (Illus.). 32p. (J). pap. 8.00 *(978-0-8059-7353-2(2))* Dorrance Publishing Co., Inc.

Hendry, Frances. Quest for a Queen: The Jackdaw. 2006. pap. *(978-1-905665-05-1(9))* Pollinger In Print.

Henty, George. When London Burned: A Story of Restoration Times & the Great Fire. I.t. ed. 2005. 724p. pap. *(978-1-84637-212-4(7))* Echo Library.

Higgins, Jim. The Enchanted Nursery: Heather & Hamish, Fun in Florida, Reggie Rabbit at the Seaside, Percy Penguin's Friends. 2009. (Illus.). 36p. pap. 15.49 *(978-1-4389-9904-3(6))* AuthorHouse.

Higson, Charlie. The Dead. rev. ed. 2014. (Enemy Novel Ser.: 2). (ENG., Illus.). 512p. (YA). (gr. 9-17). pap. 10.99 *(978-1-4847-2145-2(4))* Hyperion Bks. for Children.

—The End. (Enemy Novel Ser.: 7). (ENG.). 512p. (YA). (gr. 9-17). 2017. pap. 10.99 *(978-1-4847-3291-5(X))* 2016. 17.99 *(978-1-4847-1695-3(7))* Hyperion Bks. for Children.

—The Enemy. rev. ed. 2014. (Enemy Novel Ser.: 1). (ENG., Illus.). 448p. (YA). (gr. 9-17). pap. 11.99 *(978-1-4847-2146-9(2))* Hyperion Bks. for Children.

—The Fallen. 2015. (Enemy Novel Ser.: 5). (ENG.). 560p. (YA). (gr. 9-17). pap. 9.99 *(978-1-4231-6636-8(1))* Hyperion Bks. for Children.

—The Fear. rev. ed. 2014. (Enemy Novel Ser.: 3). (ENG.). 496p. (YA). (gr. 9-17). pap. 9.99 *(978-1-4847-2144-5(6))* Hyperion Bks. for Children.

—The Hunted. (Enemy Novel Ser.: 6). (ENG.). (YA). (gr. 9-17). 2016. 480p. pap. 9.99 *(978-1-4231-6637-5(X))* 2015. 464p. 17.99 *(978-1-4231-6567-5(5))* Hyperion Bks. for Children.

Hildebrand, Jens. Team 002: The Abduction of the Queen. Garcia, Juan F., illus. 2013. 224p. pap. *(978-3-929892-46-8(4))* Hildebrand, Jutta Warped Tomato Publishing.

Hillan, Pamela & Dyan, Penelope. The Jewels of the Crown. Weigand, John, photos by. 2013. (Illus.). 128p. pap. 8.95 *(978-1-61477-111-1(1))* Bellissima Publishing, LLC.

Hobbs, Leigh. Mr Badger & the Big Surprise. I.t. ed. 2012. 120p. (J). pap. *(978-1-4596-3343-8(1))* ReadHowYouWant.com, Ltd.

—Mr Badger & the Missing Ape. I.t. ed. 2012. 120p. (J). pap. *(978-1-4596-3344-5(X))* ReadHowYouWant.com, Ltd.

Horowitz, Anthony. Scorpia. 2006. (Alex Rider Ser.: 5). (ENG.). 416p. (J). (gr. 5-18). pap. 8.99 *(978-0-14-240578-9(7)*, Puffin Books) Penguin Young Readers Group.

—Scorpia Rising. 2012. (Alex Rider Ser.: 9). (ENG.). 432p. (J). (gr. 5-18). 9.99 *(978-0-14-241985-4(0)*, Puffin Books) Penguin Young Readers Group.

Hughes, Shirley. Ruby in the Ruins. Hughes, Shirley, illus. 2018. (ENG., Illus.). 32p. (J). (gr. k-4). 15.99 *(978-0-7636-9237-7(9))* Candlewick Pr.

Hunt, Elizabeth Singer. Secret Agent Jack Stalwart: Book 4: the Caper of the Crown Jewels: England, Bk. 4. 2008. (Secret Agent Jack Stalwart Ser.: 4). (ENG., Illus.). 144p. (J). (gr. 1-4). per. 5.99 *(978-1-60286-013-1(0))* Hachette Bk. Group.

Hutton, Sam. Countdown (Special Agents, Book 3), Book 3. 2011. (Special Agents Ser.: 3). (ENG.). 224p. pap. 9.99 *(978-0-00-714843-1(7)*, HarperCollins Children's Bks.) HarperCollins Pubs. Ltd. GBR. Dist: HarperCollins Pubs.

—Deep End (Special Agents) 2010. (Special Agents Ser.). (ENG.). 240p. (gr. 5-7). pap. 9.99 *(978-0-00-714842-4(9)*, HarperCollins Children's Bks.) HarperCollins Pubs. Ltd. GBR. Dist: HarperCollins Pubs.

—Meltdown (Special Agents, Book 6), Book 6. 2005. (Special Agents Ser.: 6). (ENG., Illus.). 224p. pap. 9.99 *(978-0-00-714847-9(X)*, HarperCollins Children's Bks.) HarperCollins Pubs. Ltd. GBR. Dist: HarperCollins Pubs.

Imbernón, Maite & Dickens, Charles. Oliver Twist. 2003. (Timeless Classics Ser.). (SPA., Illus.). 92p. (J). pap. 10.95 *(978-84-204-5750-5(7))* Santillana USA Publishing Co., Inc.

James, Mayhew. Carlota visita londres. 2004. (SPA., Illus.). 36p. 16.99 *(978-84-8488-089-9(3))* Serres, Ediciones, S. L. ESP. Dist: Lectorum Pubns., Inc.

Jarman, Julia. Time-Travelling Cat & the Great Victorian Stink. 2011. (Time-Travelling Cat Ser.: 6). (ENG.). 160p. (J). (gr. 4-7). pap. 12.99 *(978-1-84939-019-4(3))* Andersen Pr. GBR. Dist: Independent Pubs. Group.

—The Time-Travelling Cat & the Great Victorian Stink. 2018. (Time-Travelling Cat Ser.). (ENG.). 160p. (J). (gr. 4-6). pap. 9.99 *(978-1-78344-618-6(8))* Andersen Pr. GBR. Dist: Independent Pubs. Group.

Jinks, Catherine. The Last Bogler. 2017. (How to Catch a Bogle Ser.: 3). (ENG.). 336p. (J). (gr. 5-7). pap. 7.99 *(978-0-544-81309-0(X)*, 1641901, Clarion Bks.) HarperCollins Pubs.

Johnson, Gillian. Thora & the Green Sea-Unicorn. Johnson, Gillian, illus. 2005. (Illus.). 272p. *(978-0-207-20016-8(5))* HarperCollins Pubs. Australia.

Johnson, Maureen. The Madness Underneath: Book 2. 2013. (Shades of London Ser.: 2). (ENG.). 304p. (YA). (gr. 7). pap. 10.99 *(978-0-14-242754-5(3)*, Speak) Penguin Young Readers Group.

—The Name of the Star. 2012. (Shades of London Ser.: 1). (ENG.). 400p. (YA). (gr. 7). pap. 12.99 *(978-0-14-242205-2(3)*, Speak) Penguin Young Readers Group.

Kassel, Roger de. Mr P & the Silver Red Bag. 2013. (ENG., Illus.). 12p. pap. 7.00 *(978-1-78035-536-8(X)*, Fastprint Publishing) Upfront Publishing Ltd. GBR. Dist: Printondemand-worldwide.com.

—Mr P & the Sticky Gum. 2013. (ENG., Illus.). 12p. pap. 7.00 *(978-1-78035-537-5(8)*, Fastprint Publishing) Upfront Publishing Ltd. GBR. Dist: Printondemand-worldwide.com.

Kelley, Ann. Inchworm. 2009. (Gussie Ser.). (ENG.). 224p. (YA). (gr. 7-12). pap. 12.95 *(978-1-906307-62-2(8))* Luath Pr. Ltd. GBR. Dist: Ingram Publisher Services.

Kennedy, Cam, illus. Dr Jekyll & Mr Hyde: RL Stevenson's Strange Case. 2008. (ENG.). 48p. (YA). (gr. 7). pap. 11.95 *(978-0-88776-882-8(2)*, Tundra Bks.) Tundra Bks. CAN. Dist: Penguin Random Hse. LLC.

Kennedy, Cecilia. Whatever Life You Wear, 1 vol. 2014. (ENG.). 312p. (J). (gr. 4-6). pap. 12.95 *(978-0-88995-514-1(X)*, cf6659d4-cf0e-420f-acf4-f0de42cafa02) Trifolium Bks., Inc. CAN. Dist: Firefly Bks., Ltd.

Kingsley, Kate. Everything but the Truth. 2010. (Young, Loaded, & Fabulous Ser.: 2). (ENG.). 304p. (YA). (gr. 9-18). pap. 9.99 *(978-1-4169-9400-8(9)*, Simon Pulse) Simon Pulse.

—Pretty on the Outside. 2010. (Young, Loaded, & Fabulous Ser.: 1). (ENG.). 320p. (YA). (gr. 9-18). pap. 9.99 *(978-1-4169-9399-5(1)*, Simon Pulse) Simon Pulse.

Knight, Chris. Karen Bighead: The Story of a Little Girl with a Big Head. 2011. (Illus.). 24p. 12.12 *(978-1-4520-7730-7(4))* AuthorHouse.

Krulik, Nancy. Be Careful What You Sniff For. 2013. (Magic Bone Ser.: 1). lib. bdg. 16.00 *(978-0-606-31680-4(9))* Turtleback.

—Be Careful What You Sniff For #1, No. 1. Braun, Sebastien, illus. 2013. (Magic Bone Ser.: 1). 128p. (J). (gr. 1-3). pap. 6.99 *(978-0-448-46399-5(7)*, Grosset & Dunlap) Penguin Young Readers Group.

Lasky, Kathryn. Double Trouble Squared: A Starbuck Twins Mystery, Book One. 2008. (ENG., Illus.). 240p. (J). (gr. 3-7). pap. 14.99 *(978-0-15-205878-4(8)*, 1197650, Clarion Bks.) HarperCollins Pubs.

Levine, Phyllis. At the Skylight with Matilda. 2007. (ENG.). 160p. per. 12.95 *(978-1-60047-089-9(0))* Wasteland Pr.

—Matilda. 2007. (ENG.). 108p. per. 12.95 *(978-1-60047-079-0(3))* Wasteland Pr.

London, Jack. The Faith of Men. 2019. (ENG.). 98p. (J). pap. 13.02 *(978-0-368-29103-6(0))* Blurb, Inc.

—The Faith of Men. 2018. (ENG., Illus.). (J). 160p. pap. 12.90 *(978-1-7903-4591-5(X))*; 108p. pap. 5.99 *(978-1-7241-6661-6(1))* Independently Published.

—Faith of Men. 2006. 116p. per. 9.95 *(978-1-59818-074-9(6))* Aegypan.

Low, Dene. The Entomological Tales of Augustus T. Percival. Corace, Jen, illus. 2009. (ENG.). 208p. (J). (gr. 6-8). 18.69 *(978-0-547-15250-9(7))* Houghton Mifflin Harcourt Publishing Co.

Macauley, Jo. Treason. 2014. (J). pap. *(978-1-4342-7944-6(8)*, Stone Arch Bks.); (ENG., Illus.). 224p. (gr. 4-7). pap. 8.95 *(978-1-62370-052-2(3)*, 124409, Capstone Young Readers) Capstone.

MacDonald, George. The Elect Lady. 2008. 148p. 24.95 *(978-1-60664-792-9(X))* Aegypan.

Madonna. The English Roses: Goodbye, Grace. 2018. (ENG., Illus.). 144p. (J). (gr. -1-k). 14.95 *(978-0-935112-70-2(7))* Callaway Editions, Inc.

Malam, John, retold by. Oliver Twist. 2014. (Graphic Classics Ser.). (Illus.). 48p. (gr. 3-6). 37.10 *(978-1-908973-89-4(7))* Book Hse. GBR. Dist: Black Rabbit Bks.

Malloy, Chris. Wizard Academies - A Special Kind of Talent. 2007. (ENG.). 142p. pap. 19.95 *(978-0-615-18505-7(3))* Wizard Academies, LLC.

Mark, Jan. Eyes Wide Open. 2003. (ENG., Illus.). 105p. *(978-0-7136-7648-8(5)*, A&C Black) Bloomsbury Publishing Plc.

Marks, Alan, illus. A Christmas Carol. 2013. (ENG.). 24p. (J). 18.99 *(978-0-7945-2910-9(0)*, Usborne) EDC Publishing.

Marsh, Carole. The Mystery at Big Ben, 1. 2006. (Carole Marsh Mysteries: Around the World in 80 Mysteries Ser.). (ENG., Illus.). 129p. (J). (gr. 4-6). 18.69 *(978-0-635-03469-4(7))* Gallopade International.

Mayhew, James. Katie: Katie's London Christmas. 2016. (Katie Ser.). (ENG., Illus.). 32p. (J). (gr. -1-k). pap. 10.99 *(978-1-4083-2642-8(6)*, Orchard Bks.) Hachette Children's Group GBR. Dist: Hachette Bk. Group.

McDonald, Abby. Sophomore Switch. 2010. (ENG., Illus.). 304p. (YA). (gr. 9). pap. 8.99 *(978-0-7636-4774-2(8))* Candlewick Pr.

McKenzie, Sophie. Every Second Counts. 2016. 405p. (YA). pap. *(978-1-4814-3927-5(8))* Simon & Schuster Children's Publishing.

—In a Split Second. 2015. (ENG., Illus.). 368p. (YA). (gr. 7). 17.99 *(978-1-4814-1394-7(5))* Simon & Schuster Children's Publishing.

McKnight, Gillian. To Catch a Prince. 2010. (ENG.). 240p. (YA). (gr. 7). pap. 11.99 *(978-1-4424-2718-1(3)*, Simon Pulse) Simon Pulse.

Mechling, Lauren & Moser, Laura. Foreign Exposure: The Social Climber Abroad. 2007. (ENG.). 320p. (YA). (gr. 7-18). pap. 18.95 *(978-0-618-66379-8(7)*, 441918, Clarion Bks.) HarperCollins Pubs.

Meloy, Maile. The Apothecary. 2013. (Apothecary Ser.: 1). (ENG.). 384p. (J). (gr. 5). pap. 9.99 *(978-0-14-242206-9(1)*, Puffin Books) Penguin Young Readers Group.

—The Apothecary. I.t. ed. 2012. (ENG.). 435p. (J). (gr. 4-7). 23.99 *(978-1-4104-4504-9(6))* Thorndike Pr.

Millar, Martin. Lonely Werewolf Girl. 2008. (ENG.). 560p. per. 16.95 *(978-0-9796636-6-6(0)*, Soft Skull Pr.) Counterpoint Pr.

Molloy, Mary. The Search for Monty. 2005. (ENG.). 100p. (J). pap. 9.60 *(978-1-4116-4505-9(7))* Lulu Pr., Inc.

Montana, Hannah. Live from London. 2010. (Hannah Montana on Tour Ser.: No. 4). 80p. (gr. 2-5). pap. 3.99 *(978-1-4231-1815-2(4))* Disney Pr.

Montefiore, Santa & Montefiore, Simon Sebag. The Royal Rabbits of London. Hindley, Kate, illus. 2018. (Royal Rabbits Ser.: 1). (ENG.). 208p. (J). (gr. 3-7). 16.99 *(978-1-4814-9860-9(6)*, Aladdin) Simon & Schuster Children's Publishing.

—The Royal Rabbits of London. Hindley, Kate, illus. 2019. (Royal Rabbits Ser.: 1). (ENG.). 224p. (J). (gr. 3-7). pap. 7.99 *(978-1-4814-9861-6(4)*, Aladdin) Simon & Schuster Children's Publishing.

Morgan, Gloria. The Ducking Stool. 2013. (Illus.). 298p. pap. 24.99 *(978-1-78035-684-6(6)*, Fastprint Publishing) Upfront Publishing Ltd. GBR. Dist: Printondemand-worldwide.com.

Morrill, Lauren. Meant to Be. 2014. (ENG.). 304p. (YA). (gr. 7). pap. 9.99 *(978-0-385-74178-1(2)*, Ember) Random Hse. Children's Bks.

Mudaly, Jessica. Cats Can Be So Cattish! 2013. 116p. pap. 10.95 *(978-1-62212-084-0(1)*, Strategic Bk. Publishing) Strategic Book Publishing & Rights Agency (SBPRA).

Mumford, Martha. The Royal Baby's Big Red Bus Tour of London. Grey, Ada, illus. 2016. (ENG.). 32p. (J). *(978-1-4088-6896-6(2)*, 282146, Bloomsbury Children's Bks.) Bloomsbury Publishing Plc.

Nadin, Joanna. Paradise. 2012. (ENG., Illus.). 272p. (YA). (gr. 9). 16.99 *(978-0-7636-5713-0(1))* Candlewick Pr.

Naidoo, Beverley. The Other Side of Truth. 2008. 252p. (gr. 5-9). 17.00 *(978-0-7569-8941-5(8))* Perfection Learning Corp.

Nesbit, E. Harding's Luck. 2006. 164p. (gr. 4-7). per. 13.95 *(978-1-59818-878-3(X))* Aegypan.

Newsome, Richard. The Billionaire's Curse. Duddle, Jonny, illus. 2011. (ENG.). 384p. (J). (gr. 3-7). pap. 8.99 *(978-0-06-194491-8(2)*, Waldon Pond Pr.) HarperCollins Pubs.

Odom, Mel. His Legacy Avenged. 2013. (Hunter's League Ser.: 4). (ENG.). 256p. (YA). (gr. 7). pap. 16.99 *(978-1-4814-0157-9(2)*, Simon Pulse) Simon Pulse.

Oldfield, Matt & Oldfield, Tom. Klinsmann. 2018. (Football Heroes - International Editions Ser.). (ENG.). 176p. (gr. 4-7). pap. 9.99 *(978-1-78606-922-1(9))* Blake, John Publishing, Ltd. GBR. Dist: Independent Pubs. Group.

Oliver & Company. (Read-Along Ser.). (J). 7.99 incl. audio *(978-1-55723-024-9(2))* Walt Disney Records.

Oliver, Helen. Ellen's First Swim. 2009. 32p. pap. 16.49 *(978-1-4389-9828-2(7))* AuthorHouse.

Osborne, Mary Pope. A Ghost Tale for Christmas Time. 2012. (Magic Tree House Merlin Missions Ser.: 16). lib. bdg. 16.00 *(978-0-606-26808-0(1))* Turtleback.

Paling, Chris. The Adventures of Rumble, Tumble, & Titch: Uncertain Times. 2010. 62p. pap. 9.99 *(978-1-60911-263-9(6)*, Eloquent Bks.) Strategic Book Publishing & Rights Agency (SBPRA).

Patterson, James & Tebbetts, Chris. Middle School: from Hero to Zero. Park, Laura, illus. 2018. (Middle School Ser.: 10). (ENG.). 288p. (J). (gr. 3-7). 13.99 *(978-0-316-34690-0(X)*, Jimmy Patterson) Little Brown & Co.

Patterson, James & Tebbetts, Christopher. From Hero to Zero. Park, Laura, illus. 2017. 268p. (J). pap. *(978-0-316-35756-2(1))* Little Brown & Co.

Patterson, José. No Buts, Becky! 2013. (ENG., Illus.). 160p. pap. *(978-1-78088-438-7(9))* Troubador Publishing Ltd.

Peacock, Shane. Eye of the Crow: The Boy Sherlock Holmes, His First Case. 2007. (Boy Sherlock Holmes Ser.: 1). 264p. (YA). (gr. 7-9). 19.95 *(978-0-88776-850-7(4)*, Tundra Bks.) Tundra Bks. CAN. Dist: Penguin Random Hse. LLC.

—Vanishing Girl: The Boy Sherlock Holmes, His Third Case. 2010. (Boy Sherlock Holmes Ser.: 3). (Illus.). 336p. (YA). (gr. 7-9). pap. 11.99 *(978-1-77049-234-9(8)*, Tundra Bks.) Tundra Bks. CAN. Dist: Penguin Random Hse. LLC.

Penn, Audrey. Blackbeard & the Gift of Silence. 2009. (ENG.). 350p. (J). (gr. 2-7). pap. 8.95 *(978-1-933718-32-3(3))* Tanglewood Pr.

Petty, Heather W. Final Fall. (Lock & Mori Ser.). (ENG.). 208p. (YA). (gr. 9). 2018. pap. 11.99 *(978-1-4814-2310-6(X))* 2017. (Illus.). 18.99 *(978-1-4814-2309-0(6))* Simon & Schuster Bks. For Young Readers. (Simon & Schuster Bks. For Young Readers).

—Lock & Mori. 2016. (Lock & Mori Ser.). (ENG.). 272p. (YA). (gr. 9). pap. 10.99 *(978-1-4814-2304-5(5))* Simon & Schuster, Inc.

Phillips, Dee. Terror in the Underground Tunnel. 2016. (Cold Whispers II Ser.). (ENG., Illus.). 32p. (J). (gr. 2-6). 28.50 *(978-1-944102-37-1(X))* Bearport Publishing Co., Inc.

Plenge, Pete. Elephants Can't Hide Forever. 2012. 238p. pap. *(978-1-909039-88-9(8))* Legend Pr.

Podwitch. 2014. (ENG.). 304p. pap. *(978-1-78306-380-2(7))* Troubador Publishing Ltd.

Poulsen, David A. The Book of Vampire. 4th rev. ed. 2007. (Salt & Pepper Chronicles). (ENG., Illus.). 160p. (J). (gr. 4-7). 6.95 *(978-1-55263-805-7(7))* Leaf Storm Pr.

Powell, Laura. Witch Fire. 2013. (ENG.). 336p. (YA). (gr. 7). 17.99 *(978-1-61963-006-2(0)*, 900098189, Bloomsbury USA Childrens) Bloomsbury Publishing USA.

Power, Barry. The First Ice Pigeon of London. 2009. 80p. pap. 10.49 *(978-1-4490-3070-4(X))* AuthorHouse.

Price, Robin. Threadneedle 01. McGrory, Paul, illus. 2016. (ENG.). 32p. (J). pap. *(978-1-906132-86-6(0))* Mogzilla.

Priestley, Chris. Death & the Arrow: A Gripping Tale of Murder & Revenge. 2007. (Tom Marlowe Ser.). (ENG., Illus.). 240p. (YA). (gr. 7). per. 12.95 *(978-0-552-55475-6(8))* Transworld Publishers Ltd. GBR. Dist: Independent Pubs. Group.

Prince, Maggie. The House on Hound Hill. 2003. (ENG.). 256p. (J). (gr. 5-7). pap. 15.95 *(978-0-618-33124-6(7)*, 493932, Clarion Bks.) HarperCollins Pubs.

Pullman, Philip. The Shadow in the North. 2006. (Sally Lockhart Ser.: Bk. 2). 23.75 *(978-0-8446-7289-2(0))* Smith, Peter Pub., Inc.

—The Shadow in the North: a Sally Lockhart Mystery. 2008. (Sally Lockhart Ser.: Bk. 2). (ENG.). 384p. (J). (gr. 7). pap. 14.99 *(978-0-375-84515-4(1)*, Ember) Random Hse. Children's Bks.

—Spring-Heeled Jack. Mostyn, D., illus. 2004. (ENG.). 112p. (J). (gr. 3-7). per. 6.99 *(978-0-440-41881-8(X)*, Yearling) Random Hse. Children's Bks.

—The Tiger in the Well: a Sally Lockhart Mystery. 2008. (Sally Lockhart Ser.: Bk. 3). (ENG.). 432p. (YA). (gr. 7). pap. 9.99 *(978-0-375-84517-8(8)*, Ember) Random Hse. Children's Bks.

Punter, Russell. Kitty Kat, Kitty Kat Where Have You Been - London. 2018. (Picture Bks.). (ENG.). 24p. (J). 9.99 *(978-0-7945-3970-2(X)*, Usborne) EDC Publishing.

Raye, Marianna & Raye, Daniel. Olis & the Big Outside. 2011. (Illus.). 32p. pap. 14.09 *(978-1-4567-7157-7(4))* AuthorHouse.

Reeve, Philip. A Darkling Plain, 4. 2012. (Predator Cities Ser.: 4). (ENG.). 544p. (J). (gr. 7-12). 24.94 *(978-0-545-22214-3(1))* Scholastic, Inc.

—Fever Crumb (the Fever Crumb Trilogy, Book 1), Bk. 1. 2011. (Fever Crumb Ser.: 1). (ENG.). 336p. (YA). (gr. 7-7). pap. 12.99 *(978-0-545-22215-0(X))* Scholastic, Inc.

Restivo, Andrea E. Arabella & the Perilous Pantheon. 2010. 28p. pap. 12.99 *(978-1-60693-790-7(1)*, Strategic Bk. Publishing) Strategic Book Publishing & Rights Agency (SBPRA).

Richardson, Justin & Parnell, Peter. Christian, the Hugging Lion. Bates, Amy June, illus. 2010. (ENG.). 32p. (J). (gr. -1-3). 19.99 *(978-1-4169-8662-1(6)*, Simon & Schuster Bks. For Young Readers) Simon & Schuster Bks. For Young Readers.

Rickett, Sally. Minky the Shoebox Monkey - a Little Monkey with a Long Way to Go. 2010. 54p. pap. 17.95 *(978-1-60860-625-2(2)*, Strategic Bk. Publishing) Strategic Book Publishing & Rights Agency (SBPRA).

Riggs, Ransom. Hollow City. Riggs, Ransom, illus. 2015. (Miss Peregrine's Peculiar Children Ser.: 2). (Illus.). lib. bdg. 22.10 *(978-0-606-36394-5(7))* Turtleback.

—Hollow City: The Second Novel of Miss Peregrine's Peculiar Children. 2015. (Miss Peregrine's Peculiar Children Ser.: 2). (Illus.). 416p. (YA). (gr. 9). pap. 14.99 *(978-1-59474-735-9(0))* Quirk Bks.

—Hollow City: The Second Novel of Miss Peregrine's Peculiar Children. Riggs, Ransom, illus. 2014. (Miss Peregrine's Peculiar Children Ser.: 2). (Illus.). 352p. (YA). (gr. 9). 18.99 *(978-1-59474-612-3(5))* Quirk Bks.

—Hollow City: the Graphic Novel: The Second Novel of Miss Peregrine's Peculiar Children. 2016. (Miss Peregrine's Peculiar Children: the Graphic Novel Ser.: 2). (ENG., Illus.). 272p. (YA). (gr. 8-17). 20.00 *(978-0-316-30679-9(7))* Yen Pr. LLC.

—Library of Souls. 2017. (Miss Peregrine's Peculiar Children Ser.: 3). (ENG.). (YA). (gr. 9). lib. bdg. 23.30 *(978-0-606-39808-4(2))* Turtleback.

—Library of Souls: The Third Novel of Miss Peregrine's Peculiar Children. 2015. (Miss Peregrine's Peculiar Children Ser.: 3). (Illus.). 400p. (YA). (gr. 9). 18.99 *(978-1-59474-758-8(X))* Quirk Bks.

Ripley's Believe It Or Not! Ripley's Bureau of Investigation 5: Wings of Fear. 2010. (Rbi Ser.: 5). (ENG.). 128p. (J). pap. 4.99 *(978-1-893951-56-3(1))* Ripley Entertainment, Inc.

Rix, Megan. The Great Fire Dogs, Bk. 8. 2016. (Illus.). 240p. (J). (gr. 4-6). pap. 11.99 *(978-0-14-136526-8(9)*, Puffin) Penguin Bks., Ltd. GBR. Dist: Independent Pubs. Group.

Roy, Ron. The Castle Crime. 2014. (to Z Mysteries Ser.: 32). lib. bdg. 16.00 *(978-0-606-35190-4(6))* Turtleback.

Rushby, Allison. The Turnkey of Highgate Cemetery. 2018. (ENG.). 256p. (J). (gr. 3-7). 15.99 *(978-0-7636-9685-6(4))* Candlewick Pr.

Sager Weinstein, Jacob & Sager Weinstein, Jacob. Hyacinth & the Stone Thief. 2018. (Hyacinth Ser.: 2). (ENG.). 320p. (J). (gr. 3-7). 16.99 *(978-0-399-55321-9(5)*, Random Hse. Bks. for Young Readers) Random Hse. Children's Bks.

Saunders, Kate. The Whizz Pop Chocolate Shop. 2014. (ENG.). 304p. (J). (gr. 5). 7.99 *(978-0-385-74302-0(5)*, Yearling) Random Hse. Children's Bks.

Schemery, Beau. The 7th of London. 2016. (ENG., Illus.). (J). 32.99 *(978-1-63477-960-9(6)*, Harmony Ink Pr.) Dreamspinner Pr.

Schroeder, Lisa. Sealed with a Secret. 2016. (ENG.). 224p. (J). (gr. 3-7). 16.99 *(978-0-545-90734-7(9)*, Scholastic Pr.) Scholastic, Inc.

Scott, Michael. The Necromancer. 2011. (Secrets of the Immortal Nicholas Flamel Ser.: 4). (ENG.). 416p. (YA). (gr. 7). pap. 11.99 *(978-0-385-73532-2(4)*, Ember) Random Hse. Children's Bks.

—The Necromancer. l.t. ed. 2010. (Secrets of the Immortal Nicholas Flamel Ser.). (ENG.). 690p. pap. 23.99 *(978-1-4104-2851-6(6))* Thorndike Pr.

Shan, Darren, pseud. The Zom-B Chronicles. 2014. (Zom-B Ser.). (ENG.). 560p. (YA). (gr. 7-17). pap. 13.00 *(978-0-316-28489-9(0))* Little, Brown Bks. for Young Readers.

Sharp, Cathy. The Boy with the Latch Key (Halfpenny Orphans, Book 4) 2018. (Halfpenny Orphans Ser.: 4). (ENG.). 416p. 12.99 *(978-0-00-827672-0(2)*, HarperCollins) HarperCollins Pubs.

Sheldon, Dyan. I Conquer Britain. 2007. (ENG., Illus.). 208p. (YA). (gr. 7). 15.99 *(978-0-7636-3300-4(3))* Candlewick Pr.

Shepherd, Megan. Her Dark Curiosity. 2014. (Madman's Daughter Ser.: 2). (ENG.). 432p. (YA). (gr. 8). 17.99 *(978-0-06-212805-8(1)*, Balzer & Bray) HarperCollins Pubs.

—Midnight Beauties. 2019. (Grim Lovelies Ser.). (ENG.). 448p. (YA). (gr. 9). 17.99 *(978-1-328-81190-5(5)*, 1688554, Clarion Bks.) HarperCollins Pubs.

Shevah, Emma. Dream on, Amber. Crawford-White, Helen, illus. 2016. (ENG.). 288p. (J). (gr. 3-7). pap. 11.99 *(978-1-4926-3592-5(8)*, 9781492635925) Sourcebooks, Inc.

Shin, Ami. Mice in the City: London. 2018. (Mice in the City Ser.: 0). (Illus.). 32p. (J). (gr. k-5). 19.95 *(978-0-500-65129-2(9)*, 565129) Thames & Hudson.

Shin, Ami & Harris, Jamie. Mice in the City: Around the World. 2018. (Mice in the City Ser.: 0). (Illus.). 40p. (J). (gr. k-3). 19.95 *(978-0-500-65152-0(3)*, 565152) Thames & Hudson.

Siggins, Gerard. Rugby Flyer: Haunting History, Thrilling Tries. 2016. (Rugby Spirit Ser.: 4). (ENG.). 176p. (J). 14.00 *(978-1-84717-819-0(7))* O'Brien Pr., Ltd., The IRL. Dist: Casemate Pubs. & Bk. Distributors, LLC.

Siobhan, Dowd. The London Eye Mystery. 2014. (ENG.). 336p. (J). (gr. 3-7). 12.24 *(978-1-63245-320-4(7))* Lectorum Pubns., Inc.

Skelton, Matthew. The Story of Cirrus Flux. 2012. (ENG., Illus.). 304p. (J). (gr. 4-6). lib. bdg. 21.19 *(978-0-385-90398-1(7))* Random House Publishing Group.

Smith, Charles. Out at First. 2010. 111p. pap. 11.95 *(978-0-557-60419-7(2))* Lulu Pr., Inc.

Smith, Jennifer E. The Statistical Probability of Love at First Sight. 2013. (ENG.). 272p. (YA). (gr. 7-17). pap. 11.99 *(978-0-316-12239-9(4)*, Poppy) Little, Brown Bks. for Young Readers.

Spinale, Wendy. Everland (the Everland Trilogy, Book 1) (Everland Trilogy Ser.: 1). (ENG.). (YA). (gr. 7-7). 2017. 336p. pap. 10.99 *(978-1-338-09553-1(6)*, Scholastic Paperbacks) 2016. 320p. 17.99 *(978-0-545-83694-4(8)*, Scholastic Pr.) Scholastic, Inc.

Stevenson, Robert Louis. Classic Starts(r): the Strange Case of Dr. Jekyll & Mr. Hyde: Retold from the Robert Louis Stevenson Original. Akib, Jamel, illus. 2006. (Classic Starts(r) Ser.). 160p. (J). (gr. 2-4). 6.95 *(978-1-4027-2667-5(8)*, 1252057) Sterling Publishing Co., Inc.

—Dr. Jekyll & Mr. Hyde. 2008. (Bring the Classics to Life Ser.). (ENG., Illus.). 72p. (gr. 4-12). pap., act. bk. ed. 10.95 *(978-0-931334-50-4(0)*, EDCTR-402B) EDCON Publishing Group.

—Dr. Jekyll & Mr Hyde Graphic Novel. 2010. (Illustrated Classics Ser.). (ENG., Illus.). 64p. (YA). (gr. 4-12). per. 11.95 *(978-1-56254-894-0(8))* Saddleback Educational Publishing, Inc.

—The Strange Case of Dr. Jekyll & Mr. Hyde. (Classics Illustrated Ser.). (Illus.). 52p. (YA). pap. 4.95 *(978-1-57209-008-8(1))* Classics International Entertainment, Inc.

—The Strange Case of Dr. Jekyll & Mr. Hyde. Andrews, Gary, illus. 2008. (Fast Track Classics Ser.). (ENG.). 48p. pap. 10.00 *(978-1-4190-5082-4(6))* Steck-Vaughn.

—The Strange Case of Dr Jekyll & Mr Hyde (Quality Library Classics) 2008. (YA). pap. 14.95 *(978-1-57545-703-1(2))* RP Media.

Stevenson, Robert Louis & Venable, Alan. The Strange Case of Dr. Jekyll & Mr. Hyde. 2005. (Classic Literature Ser.). 108p. pap. 9.95 *(978-1-4105-0119-6(1))*; pap., E-Book 69.00 incl. audio compact disk *(978-1-4105-0117-2(5))* Building Wings LLC.

Stewart, Dianne C. Longitude - Zero Degrees. 2009. (ENG.). 200p. pap. 8.95 *(978-0-9667359-4-9(3)*, BeanPole Bks.) OH Industries.

Stine, R. L. A Night in Terror Tower. 2009. (Goosebumps Ser.: 11). lib. bdg. 17.20 *(978-0-606-00240-0(5))* Turtleback.

—A Night in Terror Tower (Classic Goosebumps #12) 2009. (Classic Goosebumps Ser.: 12). (ENG.). 160p. (J). (gr. 3-7). 7.99 *(978-0-545-15887-9(7)*, Scholastic Paperbacks) Scholastic, Inc.

Stoker, Bram. Dracula. Schuler, Susan, tr. Ruiz, Alfonso, illus. 2010. (Classic Fiction Ser.). 72p. pap. 0.90 *(978-1-4342-2985-4(8)*, Stone Arch Bks.) Capstone.

—Drácula: Novela Gráfica. Schuler, Susan, tr. Ruiz, Jose, illus. 2010. (Classic Fiction Ser.). (SPA.). 72p. (J). (gr. 5-9). pap. 7.15 *(978-1-4342-2277-0(2)*, 103140, Stone Arch Bks.) Capstone.

Stretton, Hesba. Jessica's First Prayer. 2004. reprint ed. pap. 1.99 *(978-1-4192-2751-6(3))*; pap. 15.95 *(978-1-4191-2751-9(9))* Kessinger Publishing, LLC.

Stroud, Jonathan. The Golem's Eye, Bk. 2. 2nd rev. ed. 2006. (Bartimaeus Novel Ser.: 2). (ENG.). 592p. (J). (gr. 5-9). reprint ed. per. 8.99 *(978-0-7868-3654-3(7))* Little, Brown Bks. for Young Readers.

—Lockwood & Co.: the Creeping Shadow. 2016. (Lockwood & Co Ser.: 4). (ENG., Illus.). 464p. (J). (gr. 5-9). 16.99 *(978-1-4847-0967-2(5))* Little, Brown Bks. for Young Readers.

—Lockwood & Co.: the Empty Grave. 2017. (Lockwood & Co Ser.: 5). (ENG., Illus.). 448p. (J). (gr. 5-9). 16.99 *(978-1-4847-7872-2(3))* Little, Brown Bks. for Young Readers.

—Lockwood & Co.: the Hollow Boy. (Lockwood & Co Ser.: 3). (ENG.). (J). (gr. 5-9). 2016. 416p. pap. 8.99 *(978-1-4847-1189-7(0))* 2015. 400p. 37.99 *(978-1-4847-0968-9(3))* Little, Brown Bks. for Young Readers.

—Lockwood & Co.: the Screaming Staircase. 2013. (Lockwood & Co Ser.: 1). (ENG.). 400p. (J). (gr. 5-9). 16.99 *(978-1-4231-6491-3(1))* Hyperion Pr.

—Lockwood & Co.: the Screaming Staircase. 2014. (Lockwood & Co Ser.: 1). (ENG., Illus.). 416p. (J). (gr. 5-9). pap. 9.99 *(978-1-4231-8692-2(3))* Little, Brown Bks. for Young Readers.

—Lockwood & Co.: the Whispering Skull. (Lockwood & Co Ser.: 2). (ENG.). (J). (gr. 5-9). 2015. 464p. pap. 9.99 *(978-1-4231-9462-0(4))* 2014. 448p. 17.99 *(978-1-4231-6492-0(X))* Little, Brown Bks. for Young Readers.

Sutter, Marcus. Soldier Dogs #1: Air Raid Search & Rescue. Kinsella, Pat, illus. 2018. (Soldier Dogs Ser.: 1). (ENG.). 224p. (J). (gr. 3-7). pap. 7.99 *(978-0-06-284403-3(2)*, HarperFestival) HarperCollins Pubs.

A Tale of Two Cities. abr. ed. (ARA., Illus.). 48p. (J). 12.00 *(978-0-86685-627-0(7))* International Bk. Ctr., Inc.

Theobald, John Owen. A Kingdom Falls. 2018. (Ravenmaster Trilogy Ser.: 3). (ENG., Illus.). (gr. 7). 320p. (J). 9.99 *(978-1-78497-444-2(7)*, 667192, Zephyr); 368p. (YA). 22.95 *(978-1-78497-442-8(0))* Head of Zeus GBR. Dist: Bloomsbury Publishing Plc, Independent Pubs. Group.

Thompson, Lisa. The Goldfish Boy. 2018. (ENG.). 320p. (J). (gr. 3-7). pap. 7.99 *(978-1-338-05393-7(0))* Scholastic, Inc.

Travers, P. L. Mary Poppins: the Illustrated Gift Edition. Sardà, Júlia, illus. 2018. (Mary Poppins Ser.). (ENG.). 248p. (J). (gr. 5-7). 24.99 *(978-1-328-49884-7(0)*, 1717674, Clarion Bks.) HarperCollins Pubs.

Trevayne, Emma. The Accidental Afterlife of Thomas Marsden. 2016. (ENG.). 272p. (J). (gr. 3-7). pap. 8.99 *(978-1-4424-9884-6(6)*, Simon & Schuster Bks. For Young Readers) Simon & Schuster Bks. For Young Readers.

Turnbull, Ann. Josie under Fire. 2009. (Historical House Ser.). 176p. (YA). (gr. 5-18). pap. 5.99 *(978-0-7945-2335-0(8)*, Usborne) EDC Publishing.

—Mary Ann & Miss Mozart. 2009. (Historical House Ser.). 166p. (YA). (gr. 5-18). pap. 5.99 *(978-0-7945-2332-9(3)*, Usborne) EDC Publishing.

Twain, Mark, pseud. The Prince & the Pauper. 2006. (Aladdin Classics Ser.). (ENG.). 352p. (J). pap. 8.99 *(978-1-4169-2805-8(7)*, Aladdin) Simon & Schuster Children's Publishing.

Twain, Mark, pseud & Clemens, Samuel L. The Prince & the Pauper. 2013. (Works of Mark Twain). 425p. reprint ed. lthr. 79.00 *(978-0-7812-1120-8(4))* Reprint Services Corp.

Uman, Jennifer & Vidali, Valerio. Jemmy Button. Uman, Jennifer & Vidali, Valerio, illus. 2013. (ENG., Illus.). 48p. (J). (gr. 5-9). 16.99 *(978-0-7636-6487-9(1)*, Templar) Candlewick Pr.

Valentine, Jenny. Broken Soup. 2009. 216p. (YA). 17.89 *(978-0-06-085072-2(8)*, HarperTeen) HarperCollins Pubs.

Walden, Mark. Earthfall. 2013. (Earthfall Trilogy Ser.: 1). (ENG., Illus.). 272p. (J). (gr. 3-7). 16.99 *(978-1-4424-9415-2(8)*, Simon & Schuster Bks. For Young Readers) Simon & Schuster Bks. For Young Readers.

—Redemption. 2018. (Earthfall Trilogy Ser.: 3). (ENG., Illus.). 304p. (J). (gr. 3-7). 17.99 *(978-1-4424-9421-3(2)*, Simon & Schuster Bks. For Young Readers) Simon & Schuster Bks. For Young Readers.

Walker, Peter Lancaster. Space Travelers Land at Buckingham Palace. Dixit, Rama, illus. 2007. 275p. (J). 19.95 *(978-1-934138-12-0(6))* Bouncing Ball Bks., Inc.

Watson, Sally. Linnet. 2004. (YA). pap. 12.95 *(978-1-59511-002-2(X)*, 800-691-7779) Image Cascade Publishing.

Webb, Catherine. The Extraordinary & Unusual Adventures of Horatio Lyle. 2006. (ENG.). 320p. (gr. 8). 9.95 *(978-1-904233-61-9(9)*, Atom Books) Little, Brown Book Group Ltd. GBR. Dist: Hachette Bk. Group.

Weinstein, Jacob Sager. Hyacinth & the Destiny Stones. 2018. 316p. (J). pap. *(978-0-399-55322-6(3))* Random Hse., Inc.

—Hyacinth & the Secrets Beneath. 2018. (Hyacinth Ser.: 1). lib. bdg. 18.40 *(978-0-606-40938-4(6))* Turtleback.

Weir, Arabella. The Rise & Rise of Tabitha Baird. 2014. (Tabitha Baird Ser.). (ENG., Illus.). 224p. (YA). (gr. 7). pap. 13.95 *(978-1-84812-419-6(8))* Bonnier Publishing GBR. Dist: Independent Pubs. Group.

Whelan, Gloria. Farewell to the Island. 2004. 200p. (J). (gr. 4-7). per. 7.95 *(978-1-882376-92-6(7))* Thunder Bay Pr.

White, Ellen Emerson. Voyage on the Great Titanic. 2010. (Dear America Ser.). (ENG., Illus.). 208p. (J). (gr. 3-9). 12.99 *(978-0-545-23834-2(X)*, Scholastic Pr.) Scholastic, Inc.

Whyman, Matt. Goldstrike: A Thriller. 2010. (ENG.). 272p. (YA). (gr. 7-18). 16.99 *(978-1-4169-9510-4(2)*, Atheneum Bks. for Young Readers) Simon & Schuster Children's Publishing.

Whytock, Cherry. My Scrumptious Scottish Dumplings: The Life of Angelica Cookson Potts. Whytock, Cherry, illus. 2006. (ENG., Illus.). 192p. (YA). mass mkt. 5.99 *(978-0-689-86552-7(X)*, Simon Pulse) Simon Pulse.

Wicke, Ed. Akayzia Adams & the Masterdragon's Secret. 2003. 280p. (J). per. 9.99 *(978-0-9677652-3-5(4)*, BlacknBlue Pr. UK) Blacknblue Pr.

Wilkins, James Francis. The Queen & Mr Brown: Meet the Rats. (Queen & Mr Brown Ser.). (ENG., Illus.). 48p. (J). (gr. k-2). 2019. pap. 12.99 *(978-0-565-09446-1(7))* 2017. 17.99 *(978-0-565-09438-6(6))* Natural History Museum Pubns. GBR. Dist: Independent Pubs. Group.

Wilkins, Rose. So Super-Starry. 2004. (ENG.). 256p. (J). pap. *(978-0-330-42086-0(0)*, Macmillan Children's Bks.) Pan Macmillan.

The Windsor Caper. 2013. (Illus.). 258p. pap. *(978-0-9576554-0-9(1))* Good, Martin.

Wood, Maryrose. The Hidden Gallery. Klassen, Jon, illus. 2011. (Incorrigible Children of Ashton Place Ser.: Bk. 2). (J). (gr. 3-7). 16.89 *(978-0-06-179114-7(8))* HarperCollins Pubs.

—The Incorrigible Children of Ashton Place: Book II: the Hidden Gallery. Klassen, Jon, illus. 2015. (Incorrigible Children of Ashton Place Ser.: 2). (ENG.). 336p. (J). (gr. 3-7). pap. 7.99 *(978-0-06-236694-8(7)*, Balzer & Bray) HarperCollins Pubs.

—The Incorrigible Children of Ashton Place: Book III: The Unseen Guest. Klassen, Jon, illus. 2015. (Incorrigible Children of Ashton Place Ser.: 3). (ENG.). 352p. (J). (gr. 3-7). pap. 6.99 *(978-0-06-236695-5(5)*, Balzer & Bray) HarperCollins Pubs.

Wood, Maryrose & Klassen, Jon. The Hidden Gallery. 2011. (Incorrigible Children of Ashton Place Ser.: 2). (ENG., Illus.). 320p. (J). (gr. 3-7). 17.99 *(978-0-06-179112-3(1)*, Balzer & Bray) HarperCollins Pubs.

Woodfine, Katherine. The Mystery of the Clockwork Sparrow. 2017. (Illus.). 320p. (J). pap. 6.99 *(978-1-61067-437-9(5))* Kane Miller.

—The Mystery of the Painted Dragon. 2017. (Illus.). 332p. (J). *(978-1-61067-695-3(5))* Kane Miller.

Woodruff, Elvira. The Ravenmaster's Secret. 2005. (Escape from the Tower of London Ser.). (Illus.). 225p. (gr. 3-7). 16.00 *(978-0-7569-4791-0(X))* Perfection Learning Corp.

Wyre, Yvonne. The Adventures of Cuthbert the Coal Lorry. 2005. 160p. pap. *(978-1-84401-500-9(9))* Athena Pr.

LONDON (ENGLAND)—HISTORY

Alagna, Magdalena. The Great Fire of London of 1666, 1 vol. 2003. (Tragic Fires Throughout History Ser.). (ENG., Illus.). 48p. (gr. 5-8). lib. bdg. 34.47 *(978-0-8239-4485-9(9)*, 3feb1e78-1639-4b54-aa0a-117ec70c461b, Rosen Reference) Rosen Publishing Group, Inc., The.

—The Great Fire of London Of 1666. 2009. (Tragic Fires Throughout History Ser.). 48p. (gr. 5-8). 53.00 *(978-1-60854-583-4(0)*, Rosen Reference) Rosen Publishing Group, Inc., The.

Ayo's Awesome Adventures in London: City on the Thames. 2018. (J). *(978-0-7166-3641-0(7))* World Bk., Inc.

Bailey, Ellen. The London Activity Book: With Palaces, Puzzles & Pictures to Colour. Pinder, Andrew & Mosedale, Julian, illus. 2013. (ENG.). 64p. (J). (gr. 2-4). pap. 8.99 *(978-1-78055-095-4(2))* O'Mara, Michael Bks., Ltd. GBR. Dist: Independent Pubs. Group.

Ball, Jacqueline A. Windsor Castle: England's Royal Fortress. 2005. (Castles, Palaces, & Tombs Ser.). (Illus.). 32p. (J). lib. bdg. 28.50 *(978-1-59716-005-6(9))* Bearport Publishing Co., Inc.

Bloom, Harold, ed. London. 2005. (Bloom's Literary Places Ser.). (ENG., Illus.). 150p. (gr. 9-13). 40.00 *(978-0-7910-7841-9(8)*, P114013, Facts On File) Infobase Holdings, Inc.

Brook, Henry. True Stories of the Blitz. McNee, Ian, illus. 2006. (True Adventure Stories Ser.). 160p. (J). (gr. 4-7). per. 4.99 *(978-0-7945-1245-3(3)*, Usborne) EDC Publishing.

Clements, Gillian. Tudor Theatre. 2009. (Building History Ser.). (Illus.). 32p. (J). (gr. 3-5). 27.10 *(978-1-59771-147-0(0))* Sea-To-Sea Pubns.

Conley, Kate. Engineering the London Underground. 2017. (Building by Design Set 2 Ser.). (ENG., Illus.). 48p. (J). (gr. 4-8). lib. bdg. 35.64 *(978-1-5321-1374-1(9)*, 27672) ABDO Publishing Co.

Dickins, Rosie. London Sticker Book. Clarke, Phillip, ed. Lumley, Stef, photos by. 2006. (Usborne Sticker Bks.). (Illus.). 15p. (J). (gr. 2-5). pap. 8.99 *(978-0-7945-1284-2(4)*, Usborne) EDC Publishing.

Doder, Joshua. Time Traveler's Guide to Shakespeare's London. 2004. (Timetraveler's Guides). (ENG., Illus.). 96p. (J). pap. 8.99 *(978-1-904153-10-8(0))* Watling St., Ltd. GBR. Dist: Independent Pubs. Group.

—The Timetraveller's Guide to Saxon & Viking London. 2004. (Timetraveller's Guides). (ENG., Illus.). 96p. (J). (gr. 3-7). per. 8.99 *(978-1-904153-07-8(0))* Watling St., Ltd. GBR. Dist: Independent Pubs. Group.

Dyan, Penelope. Where Is London Bridge? a Kid's Guide to London. Weigand, John D., photos by. 2009. (Illus.). 44p. pap. 11.95 *(978-1-935118-80-0(3))* Bellissima Publishing, LLC.

Elborough, Travis. Highwayman, Outlaws & Bandits of London. 2004. (... , of London Ser.). (ENG., Illus.). 96p. pap. 8.99 *(978-1-904153-13-9(5))* Watling St., Ltd. GBR. Dist: Trafalgar Square Publishing.

—Rebels, Traitors & Turncoats of London. 2004. (Of London Ser.). (ENG., Illus.). 96p. (J). pap. 8.99 *(978-1-904153-15-3(1))* Tempus ESP. Dist: Independent Pubs. Group.

Goldsworthy, Kaite. St. Paul's Cathedral. 2014. (J). *(978-1-4896-1154-3(1))* Weigl Pubs., Inc.

Goodrich, Olivia. Timetraveler's Guide to Roman London. 2004. (Timetraveler's Guides). (ENG., Illus.). 96p. (J). pap. 7.95 *(978-1-904153-06-1(2))* Watling St., Ltd. GBR. Dist: Independent Pubs. Group.

Howell, Izzi. Why Do We Remember?: Guy Fawkes & the Gunpowder Plot. 2019. (Why Do We Remember? Ser.). (ENG., Illus.). 32p. (J). (gr. 1-3). pap. 11.99 *(978-1-4451-4852-6(8)*, Franklin Watts) Hachette Children's Group GBR. Dist: Hachette Bk. Group.

Jocelyn, Marthe. A Home for Foundlings: A Lord Museum Book. 2005. (Lord Museum Ser.). (Illus.). 120p. (J). (gr. 5-12). pap. 16.95 *(978-0-88776-709-8(5)*, Tundra Bks.) Tundra Bks. CAN. Dist: Penguin Random Hse. LLC.

Johnson, Anne & Townsend, Sef. London Folk Tales for Children. Evans, Belinda, illus. 2019. (ENG.). 192p. (J). (gr. 2-6). pap. 16.99 *(978-0-7509-8689-2(1))* History Pr. Ltd.,The GBR. Dist: Independent Pubs. Group.

Kidney, Christine. Medieval London. 2004. (Timetraveller's Guide Ser.). (ENG., Illus.). 96p. (J). (gr. 4-7). pap. 8.99 *(978-1-904153-08-5(9))* Watling St., Ltd. GBR. Dist: Independent Pubs. Group.

Lonely Planet. Lonely Planet Londres, 1 vol. 2012. (Lonely Planet Kids Ser.). (SPA., Illus.). 96p. (J). pap. 14.99 *(978-84-08-10913-6(8)*, 103551) Lonely Planet Pubns.

Machajewski, Sarah. El Gran Incendio de Londres (the Great Fire of London), 1 vol. Sarfatti, Esther, tr. 2015. (Desastres (Doomed) Ser.). (SPA., Illus.). 32p. (J). (gr. 4-5). lib. bdg. 28.27 *(978-1-4824-3265-7(X)*, 01eaf93c-4464-4e56-a901-1f392ca28d60) Stevens, Gareth Publishing LLLP.

—The Great Fire of London, 1 vol. 2015. (Doomed! Ser.). (ENG., Illus.). 32p. (J). (gr. 4-5). pap. 11.50 *(978-1-4824-2932-9(2)*, 6b8268ca-593f-4875-beaa-4723c3ade0e2) Stevens, Gareth Publishing LLLP.

Manning, Paul. The Thames. (River Adventures Ser.). 2014. (J). lib. bdg. 31.35 *(978-1-59920-918-0(7))* 2013. 48p. (gr. 5-11). lib. bdg. 37.10 *(978-1-59920-924-1(1))* Black Rabbit Bks.

—Thames River. 2015. (River Adventures Ser.). (Illus.). 32p. (gr. 4-7). 31.35 *(978-1-62588-588-3(1))* Black Rabbit Bks.

Mansfield, Andy. Lonely Planet Kids Pop-Up London 1. Mansfield, Andy, illus. 2016. (Lonely Planet Kids Ser.). (ENG., Illus.). 8p. (J). (gr. -1-k). 9.99 *(978-1-76034-339-2(0)*, 5339) Lonely Planet Global Ltd. IRL. Dist: Hachette Bk. Group.

Mason Crest. London, Vol. 8. 2016. (Major World Cities Ser.: Vol. 8). (ENG., Illus.). 48p. (J). (gr. 5-8). 20.95 *(978-1-4222-3541-6(6))* Mason Crest.

Meyers, Haily & Meyers, Kevin. All Aboard! London: A Travel Primer, 1 vol. 2016. (Lucy Darling Ser.). (Illus.). 22p. (J). (— 1). bds. 9.99 *(978-1-4236-4242-8(2))* Gibbs Smith, Publisher.

Narayan, Natasha. Black Death & Other Putrid Plagues of London. 2004. (... , of London Ser.). (Illus.). 96p. 8.99 *(978-1-904153-01-6(1))* Watling St., Ltd. GBR. Dist: Independent Pubs. Group.

—Spies, Secret Agents & Spooks of London. 2004. (Of London Ser.). (ENG., Illus.). 96p. (J). pap. 8.99 *(978-1-904153-14-6(3))* Tempus ESP. Dist: Independent Pubs. Group.

—Time Traveler's Guide to Victorian London. 2004. (Timetraveler's Guides). (ENG., Illus.). 96p. (J). pap. 8.99 *(978-1-904153-11-5(9))* Watling St., Ltd. GBR. Dist: Independent Pubs. Group.

—Tudor London. 2004. (Timetraveller's Guides). (ENG., Illus.). 96p. (J). pap. 8.99 *(978-1-904153-09-2(7))* Watling St., Ltd. GBR. Dist: Independent Pubs. Group.

—Witches, Wizards & Warlocks of London. 2004. (Of London Ser.). (ENG., Illus.). 96p. (J). pap. 8.99 *(978-1-904153-12-2(7))* Watling St., Ltd. GBR. Dist: Independent Pubs. Group.

Nelson, Drew. Haunted! the Tower of London. 2013. (History's Most Haunted Ser.). 32p. (J). (gr. 3-6). pap. 63.00 *(978-1-4339-9265-0(5))*; (ENG., Illus.). 29.27 *(978-1-4339-9263-6(9)*, 3ced6df9-0dcf-4682-a924-3512158bd930); (ENG., Illus.). pap. 11.50 *(978-1-4339-9264-3(7)*, b56257db-e379-4918-98c0-5a10998df1f1) Stevens, Gareth Publishing LLLP.

Nieto Ferreira, Rute & Alessandra, Amandine. The Big Letter Hunt: London: An Architectural a to Z Around the City. 2016. (ENG., Illus.). 64p. pap. 14.95 *(978-1-84994-366-6(4)*, Batsford) Pavilion Bks. GBR. Dist: Penguin Random Hse. LLC.

Pascal, Janet B. & Who HQ. Where Is the Tower of London? Malan, David, illus. 2018. (Where Is? Ser.). 112p. (J). (gr. 3-7). 7.99 *(978-1-5247-8606-9(3))*; lib. bdg. 15.99 *(978-1-5247-8608-3(X))* Penguin Young Readers Group. (Penguin Workshop).

Platt, Richard. London's Great Stink & Joseph Bazalgette: Band 09/Gold, Bd. 9. 2018. (Collins Big Cat Ser.). (ENG.). 24p. (J). pap. 7.99 *(978-0-00-823037-1(4))* HarperCollins Pubs. Ltd. GBR. Dist: Independent Pubs. Group.

Rice, Dona Herweck. You Are There! London 1666. 2nd rev. ed. 2017. (TIME(r): Informational Text Ser.). (ENG., Illus.). 32p. (gr. 6-8). pap. 13.99 *(978-1-4938-3616-1(1))* Teacher Created Materials, Inc.

—You Are There! London 1666. 2017. (Time for Kids Nonfiction Readers Ser.). lib. bdg. 19.65 *(978-0-606-40263-7(2))* Turtleback.

RollasonJane. London Level 2 Elementary. 2014. (Cambridge Experience Readers Ser.). (ENG., Illus.). 64p. pap. 14.75 *(978-1-107-61521-2(6))* Cambridge Univ. Pr.

Rossi, Renzo. & Bredeson, Carmen. In Nineteenth-Century London with Dickens, 1 vol. Baldanzi, Alessandro, illus. 2009. (Come See My City Ser.). (ENG.). 48p. (gr. 4-4). lib. bdg. 31.21 *(978-0-7614-4333-9(9),* 675b1948-1fe4-43a2-81a3-4fe56609c96e) Cavendish Square Publishing LLC.

Rudolph, Jessica. London. 2017. (Citified! Ser.). (ENG., Illus.). 24p. (J). (gr. k-3). lib. bdg. 17.95 *(978-1-68402-232-8(0))* Bearport Publishing Co., Inc.

Smith, Helen. Pirates, Swashbucklers & Buccaneers of London. 2004. (... of London Ser.). (ENG., Illus.). 96p. pap. 8.99 *(978-1-904153-17-7(8))* Watling St., Ltd. GBR. Dist: Trafalgar Square Publishing.

Warren, Andrea. Charles Dickens & the Street Children of London. 2017. (ENG., Illus.). 160p. (YA). (gr. 7). pap. 9.99 *(978-0-544-93260-9(9),* 1657974, Clarion Bks.) HarperCollins Pubs.

LONDON (ENGLAND)—HISTORY—FICTION

Adler, Irene. The Mystery of the Scarlet Rose. McGuinness, Nanette, tr. Bruno, Iacopo, illus. 2015. (Sherlock, Lupin, & Me Ser.). (ENG.). 256p. (J). (gr. 4-8). lib. bdg. 26.65 *(978-1-4342-6524-1(2),* 124281, Stone Arch Bks.) Capstone.

Bailey, Kristin. Legacy of the Clockwork Key. 2013. (Secret Order Ser.: 1). (ENG.). 416p. (YA). (gr. 9). 17.99 *(978-1-4424-4026-5(0),* Simon Pulse) Simon Pulse.

—Rise of the Arcane Fire. 2014. (Secret Order Ser.: 2). (ENG., Illus.). 464p. (YA). (gr. 9). 17.99 *(978-1-4424-6802-3(5),* Simon Pulse) Simon Pulse.

—Shadow of the War Machine. 2015. (Secret Order Ser.: 3). (ENG., Illus.). 448p. (YA). (gr. 9). 17.99 *(978-1-4424-6805-4(X),* Simon Pulse) Simon Pulse.

Bloor, Edward. London Calling. 2008. (Illus.). 304p. (YA). (gr. 7-9). per. 8.99 *(978-0-375-84363-1(9),* Ember) Random Hse. Children's Bks.

Bowling, Nicholas. Witch Born. 2018. (ENG., Illus.). 320p. (YA). (gr. 7-7). 18.99 *(978-1-338-27753-1(7),* Chicken Hse., The) Scholastic, Inc.

Clare, Cassandra. Clockwork Angel. (Infernal Devices Ser.: 1). (ENG., Illus.). (YA). (gr. 9). 2015. 544p. pap. 14.99 *(978-1-4814-5602-9(4))* 2010. 496p. 24.99 *(978-1-4169-7586-1(1))* McElderry, Margaret K. Bks. (McElderry, Margaret K. Bks.).

—Clockwork Angel. 2013. (CHI & ENG.). 240p. (YA). (gr. 8-17). pap. *(978-986-6000-84-3(2))* Spring International Pubs.

—Clockwork Angel. 2015. (Infernal Devices Ser.: Bk. 1). 544p. (YA). lib. bdg. 25.75 *(978-0-606-37737-9(9))* 2012. (Infernal Devices Graphic Novel Ser.: 1). lib. bdg. 24.55 *(978-0-606-32257-7(4))* Turtleback.

—Clockwork Prince. (Infernal Devices Ser.: 2). (YA). 2015. (ENG., Illus.). 560p. (gr. 9). pap. 14.99 *(978-1-4814-5601-2(6))* 2011. (ENG., Illus.). 528p. (gr. 9-18). 24.99 *(978-1-4169-7588-5(8))* 2011. 502p. *(978-1-4424-5174-2(2))* McElderry, Margaret K. Bks. (McElderry, Margaret K. Bks.).

—Clockwork Prince. 2015. (Infernal Devices Ser.: Bk. 2). 560p. (YA). lib. bdg. 25.75 *(978-0-606-37895-6(2))* Turtleback.

—Clockwork Princess. 2013. (YA). (Infernal Devices Ser.: 3). (ENG., Illus.). 592p. (gr. 9). 24.99 *(978-1-4169-7590-8(X));* 570p. *(978-1-4424-8541-9(8))* McElderry, Margaret K. Bks. (McElderry, Margaret K. Bks.).

—The Infernal Devices: Clockwork Angel. 2012. (Infernal Devices Ser.: 1). (ENG.). 240p. (gr. 8-17). pap. 13.00 *(978-0-316-20098-1(0),* Yen Pr.) Yen Pr. LLC.

Crilley, Paul. The Osiris Curse: A Tweed & Nightingale Adventure. 2013. (Tweed & Nightingale Adventures Ser.). (ENG.). 287p. (YA). (gr. 7). 17.99 *(978-1-61614-857-7(8),* Pyr) Start Publishing LLC.

Dalton, Annie. Fogging over (Mel Beeby, Agent Angel, Book 5), Book 5. 2010. (Mel Beeby, Agent Angel Ser.: 5). (ENG.). 160p. (gr. 4-7). pap. 7.99 *(978-0-00-720475-5(2),* HarperCollins Children's Bks.) HarperCollins Pubs. Ltd. GBR. Dist: HarperCollins Pubs.

Dickens, Charles. Oliver Twist. 2014. (Graphic Classics Ser.). (Illus.). 48p. (gr. 2-7). pap. 8.95 *(978-1-905087-97-6(7))* Book Hse. GBR. Dist: Black Rabbit Bks.

—Oliver Twist. 2013. 274p. pap. 14.99 *(978-1-4837-0319-0(3))* Bottom of the Hill Publishing.

—Oliver Twist. Belli, Alfredo, illus. 2008. (Green Apple Step Two Ser.). (ENG.). 96p. (J). (gr. 5). pap. incl. audio compact disk *(978-88-530-0580-9(7))* Cideb.

—Oliver Twist. 2013. (Vintage Children's Classics Ser.). (Illus.). 736p. (J). (gr. 4-7). pap. 12.99 *(978-0-09-958263-2(5))* Penguin Random Hse. GBR. Dist: Independent Pubs. Group.

—A Tale of Two Cities: A Classic Retelling. 2006. (Classic Retelling Ser.). (Illus.). 240p. (YA). (gr. 8-12). *(978-0-618-03150-4(2),* 2-00144) Holt McDougal.

Dickens, Charles & Hawksley, L. Dickens. A Tale of Two Cities. 2004. (Paperback Classics Ser.). 144p. (J). pap. 4.95 *(978-0-7945-0390-1(X));* lib. bdg. 12.95 *(978-1-58086-515-9(1))* EDC Publishing.

Doyle, Marissa. Bewitching Season. 2009. (ENG.). 368p. (YA). (gr. 9-12). 24.94 *(978-0-312-59695-8(2),* 9780312596958) Square Fish.

Funaro, Gregory. Alistair Grim's Odditorium. 2015. (J). lib. bdg. 18.40 *(978-0-606-37399-9(3))* Turtleback.

Gardner, Sally. I, Coriander. 2007. (ENG., Illus.). 288p. (J). (gr. 5-18). 7.99 *(978-0-14-240763-9(1),* Puffin Books) Penguin Young Readers Group.

Garfield, Leon. Smith: the Story of a Pickpocket. 2013. (ENG.). 216p. (J). (gr. 4-7). 15.95 *(978-1-59017-675-7(8),* NYR Children's Collection) New York Review of Bks., Inc., The.

Gier, Kerstin. Ruby Red. Bell, Anthea, tr. 2012. (Ruby Red Trilogy Ser.: 1). (ENG.). 352p. (YA). (gr. 7-12). pap. 11.99 *(978-0-312-55151-3(7),* 900074429) Square Fish.

Gleason, Colleen. The Chess Queen Enigma: A Stoker & Holmes Novel. 2016. (ENG.). 360p. (YA). (gr. 7-12). pap. 9.99 *(978-1-4521-5649-1(2))* Chronicle Bks. LLC.

—The Spiritglass Charade: A Stoker & Holmes Novel. 2014. (Stoker & Holmes Ser.: 2). (ENG., Illus.). 360p. (YA). (gr. 7-12). 17.99 *(978-1-4521-1071-4(9))* Chronicle Bks. LLC.

Golding, Julia. The Diamond of Drury Lane, 1. 2009. (Cat Royal Adventure Ser.: 1). (ENG., Illus.). 424p. (J). (gr. 6-8). 22.44 *(978-0-312-56123-9(7),* 900058857) Square Fish.

Hayner, Linda K. Ellanor's Exchange. 2005. 195p. (YA). 8.99 *(978-1-59166-462-8(4))* BJU Pr.

Hearn, Julie. Ivy. 2008. (ENG.). 368p. (YA). (gr. 7-18). 17.99 *(978-1-4169-2506-4(6),* Atheneum Bks. for Young Readers) Simon & Schuster Children's Publishing.

Hendry, Frances. Quest for a Queen: The Jackdaw. 2006. pap. *(978-1-905665-05-1(9))* Pollinger In Print.

Henty, George. A March on London: A Story of Wat Tyler's Insurrection. 2003. (YA). pap. *(978-1-887159-93-7(2))* Preston-Speed Pubns.

James, Brian. Dangerous Skies. 2016. (ENG., Illus.). 186p. (J). (gr. 5-7). pap. 9.99 *(978-1-910461-27-3(X))* Claret Pr. GBR. Dist: Lightning Source UK, Ltd.

Jinks, Catherine. A Plague of Bogles. 2015. (How to Catch a Bogle Ser.: 2). (ENG.). 336p. (J). (gr. 5-7). pap. 6.99 *(978-0-544-54067-5(0),* 1608871); (Illus.). 16.99 *(978-0-544-08747-7(X),* 1538140) HarperCollins Pubs. (Clarion Bks.).

Larwood, Kieran. Freaks. 2013. (J). *(978-0-545-47425-2(6),* Chicken Hse., The) Scholastic, Inc.

Lawrence, Iain. The Convicts. 2006. 15.10 *(978-0-7569-6901-1(8))* Random House Children's Books GBR. Dist: Perfection Learning Corp.

Lee, Y. S. The Agency: a Spy in the House. 2016. (Agency Ser.: 1). (ENG.). 352p. (YA). (gr. 7). pap. 9.99 *(978-0-7636-8748-9(0))* Candlewick Pr.

—The Agency: the Body at the Tower. 2016. (Agency Ser.: 2). (ENG.). 352p. (YA). (gr. 7). pap. 9.99 *(978-0-7636-8750-2(2))* Candlewick Pr.

Macauley, Jo. Treason, 1 vol. 2014. (Secrets & Spies Ser.). (ENG.). 224p. (J). (gr. 4-7). 26.65 *(978-1-4342-7946-0(4),* 124693, Stone Arch Bks.) Capstone.

MacLean, Sarah. The Season. 2010. (ENG.). 352p. (J). (gr. 7). 8.99 *(978-0-545-04887-3(7),* Orchard Bks.) Scholastic, Inc.

Maniscalco, Kerri. Stalking Jack the Ripper. 2018. (Stalking Jack the Ripper Ser.: 1). (ENG.). 416p. (YA). (gr. 10-17). mass mkt. 8.99 *(978-1-5387-6118-2(1))* Grand Central Publishing.

—Stalking Jack the Ripper. (Stalking Jack the Ripper Ser.: 1). (ENG.). (YA). (gr. 10-17). 2017. Illus.). 352p. pap. 12.99 *(978-0-316-27351-0(1))* 2016. (Illus.). 336p. 19.99 *(978-0-316-27349-7(X))* 2016. 464p. 39.99 *(978-0-316-46428-4(7))* Little Brown & Co. (Jimmy Patterson).

Meyer, L. A. The Mark of the Golden Dragon: Being an Account of the Further Adventures of Jacky Faber, Jewel of the East, Vexation of the West. 2013. (Bloody Jack Adventures Ser.: 9). (ENG.). 400p. (YA). (gr. 9). pap. 9.99 *(978-0-544-00328-6(4),* 1526370, Clarion Bks.) HarperCollins Pubs.

—The Mark of the Golden Dragon: Being an Account of the Further Adventures of Jacky Faber, Jewel of the East, Vexation of the West, & Pearl of the South China Sea. 2011. (Bloody Jack Adventures Ser.: 9). (ENG.). 384p. (YA). (gr. 9). 16.99 *(978-0-547-51764-3(5),* 1444890, Clarion Bks.) HarperCollins Pubs.

Morpurgo, Michael. Kaspar the Titanic Cat. Foreman, Michael, illus. 2012. (ENG.). 208p. (J). (gr. 3-7). 16.99 *(978-0-06-200618-9(5),* Balzer & Bray) HarperCollins Pubs.

Moss, Marissa. Bombs over London. 2014. (Mira's Diary Ser.). (ENG., Illus.). 190p. (J). (gr. 2-8). 12.99 *(978-1-939547-12-5(1),* 5ad055a5-1363-4f46-accf-d31871e40e1f) Creston Bks.

Munch, Donna. Dark Tales of the Tower. 2005. (J). pap. 9.95 *(978-1-932196-71-9(4))* WordWright.biz, Inc.

Myers, Walter Dean. Juba! A Novel. (ENG., Illus.). 208p. (YA). (gr. 8). 2016. pap. 10.99 *(978-0-06-211273-6(2),* Quill Tree Bks.) 2015. 17.99 *(978-0-06-211271-2(6),* Amistad) HarperCollins Pubs.

Nix, Garth. Newt's Emerald. 2015. (ENG.). 304p. (YA). (gr. 8-12). 18.99 *(978-0-06-236004-5(3),* Tegen, Katherine Bks) HarperCollins Pubs.

Orczy, Emmuska. The Old Man in the Corner. 2008. (J). 8.99 *(978-1-59166-952-4(9))* BJU Pr.

Orme, David. Blitz. 2004. (Shades Ser.). (ENG.). 54p. (J). pap. *(978-0-237-52624-5(7))* Evans Brothers, Ltd.

—Blitz. 2007. (Sharp Shades Ser.). (ENG., Illus.). 64p. (J). (gr. 6-8). pap. 8.99 *(978-0-237-53444-8(4))* Evans Brothers, Ltd. GBR. Dist: Independent Pubs. Group.

Pratchett, Terry. Dodger. (ENG.). 368p. (YA). (gr. 8). 2013. pap. 10.99 *(978-0-06-200951-7(6))* 2012. 17.99 *(978-0-06-200949-4(4))* HarperCollins Pubs. (Clarion Bks.).

Pullman, Philip. The Ruby in the Smoke. 2009. 9.84 *(978-0-7848-2919-6(5),* Everbind) Marco Bk. Co.

—The Ruby in the Smoke. 2008. (Sally Lockhart Mystery Ser.: Bk. 1). (ENG.). 230p. (YA). (gr. 7-18). 22.44 *(978-0-394-98826-9(4))* Random House Publishing Group.

—The Ruby in the Smoke. 2003. (Sally Lockhart Ser.: Bk. 1). (Illus.). (YA). pap. 9.95 *(978-0-375-82545-3(2),* Knopf Bks. for Young Readers) Random Hse. Children's Bks.

—The Ruby in the Smoke: a Sally Lockhart Mystery. 2008. (Sally Lockhart Ser.: Bk. 1). (ENG.). 256p. (YA). (gr. 7). pap. 10.99 *(978-0-375-84516-1(X),* Ember) Random Hse. Children's Bks.

—Two Crafty Criminals! And How They Were Captured by the Daring Detectives of the New Cut Gang. 2013. (ENG.). 288p. (J). (gr. 3-7). 7.99 *(978-0-307-93035-4(1),* Yearling) Random Hse. Children's Bks.

Rattle, Alison. V for Violet. 2016. (ENG.). 304p. (YA). (gr. 7). 13.99 *(978-1-4714-0381-1(5))* Bonnier Publishing GBR. Dist: Independent Pubs. Group.

Richards, Justin. Rewind Assassin. 2007. (Time Runners Ser.: 2). (ENG.). 208p. (J). (gr. 4-7). pap. 8.99 *(978-1-4169-2643-6(7))* Simon & Schuster, Ltd. GBR. Dist: Simon & Schuster, Inc.

Sands, Kevin. The Blackthorn Key. (Blackthorn Key Ser.: 1). (ENG., Illus.). (J). (gr. 5-9). 2016. 400p. pap. 8.99 *(978-1-4814-4652-5(5))* 2015. 384p. 19.99 *(978-1-4814-4651-8(7))* Simon & Schuster Children's Publishing. (Aladdin).

—The Blackthorn Key. 2016. lib. bdg. 18.40 *(978-0-606-38966-2(0))* Turtleback.

Schlitz, Laura Amy. Splendors & Glooms. (ENG.). 400p. (J). 2017. (gr. 5-9). pap. 10.99 *(978-0-7636-9449-4(5))* 2012. (Illus.). (gr. 4-7). 17.99 *(978-0-7636-5380-4(2))* Candlewick Pr.

—Splendors & Glooms. 2014. (ENG.). (J). (gr. 4-7). lib. bdg. 18.60 *(978-1-62765-443-2(7))* Perfection Learning Corp.

—Splendors & Glooms. 2014. lib. bdg. 18.40 *(978-0-606-35170-6(1))* Turtleback.

Selznick, Brian. The Marvels. 2016. (CHI.). (J). *(978-986-479-039-5(0))* Commonwealth Publishing Co., Ltd.

—The Marvels. Selznick, Brian, illus. 2015. (ENG., Illus.). 672p. (J). (gr. 5-7). 32.99 *(978-0-545-44868-0(9),* Scholastic Pr.) Scholastic, Inc.

Slade, Arthur G. The Hunchback Assignments, 1. 2010. (Hunchback Assignments Ser.). (ENG.). 288p. (YA). (gr. 7-12). lib. bdg. 24.94 *(978-0-385-90694-4(3))* Random House Publishing Group.

Small Acts of Amazing Courage. 2013. (ENG., Illus.). 240p. (J). (gr. 4-7). pap. 8.99 *(978-1-4424-9495-4(6),* Simon & Schuster/Paula Wiseman Bks.) Simon & Schuster/Paula Wiseman Bks.

Springer, Nancy. The Case of the Bizarre Bouquets, 3. 2008. (Enola Holmes Mystery Ser.: 3). (ENG.). 176p. (J). (gr. 6-8). 21.19 *(978-0-399-24518-3(9))* Penguin Young Readers Group.

—Enola Holmes: the Case of the Bizarre Bouquets. 2009. (Enola Holmes Mystery Ser.: 3). (ENG.). 192p. (J). (gr. 3-7). pap. 8.99 *(978-0-14-241390-6(9),* Puffin Books) Penguin Young Readers Group.

—Enola Holmes: the Case of the Left-Handed Lady: An Enola Holmes Mystery. 2008. (Enola Holmes Mystery Ser.: 2). (ENG.). 256p. (J). (gr. 3-7). 8.99 *(978-0-14-241190-2(6),* Puffin Books) Penguin Young Readers Group.

—Enola Holmes: the Case of the Missing Marquess. 2007. (Enola Holmes Mystery Ser.: 1). (ENG.). 240p. (J). (gr. 3-7). 7.99 *(978-0-14-240933-6(2),* Puffin Books) Penguin Young Readers Group.

Stewart, Paul & Riddell, Chris. Barnaby Grimes: Phantom of Blood Alley. 2013. (Barnaby Grimes Ser.: 4). (ENG.). 208p. (J). (gr. 3-7). 6.99 *(978-0-385-73700-5(9),* Yearling) Random Hse. Children's Bks.

Stretton, Hesba. Lost Gip. 2003. (Golden Inheritance Ser.: Vol. 7). (Illus.). 121p. (J). *(978-0-921100-93-5(0))* Inheritance Pubns.

Updale, Eleanor. Montmorency's Revenge. 2007. 289p. (J). 25.66 *(978-1-4287-3312-1(4),* Follettbound) Follett School Solutions.

Webb, Holly. The Case of the Feathered Mask: The Mysteries of Maisie Hitchins, Book 4. Lindsay, Marion, illus. 2017. (Mysteries of Maisie Hitchins Ser.: 4). (ENG.). 176p. (J). (gr. 3-7). pap. 5.99 *(978-0-544-94884-6(X),* 1660308, Clarion Bks.) HarperCollins Pubs.

—The Case of the Vanishing Emerald: The Mysteries of Maisie Hitchins Book 2. Lindsay, Marion, illus. 2016. (Mysteries of Maisie Hitchins Ser.: 2). (ENG.). 176p. (J). (gr. 3-7). pap. 6.99 *(978-0-544-66851-5(0),* 1625474, Clarion Bks.) HarperCollins Pubs.

Wilde, Oscar. The Picture of Dorian Gray, 1 vol. Fisher, Eric Scott, illus. 2011. (Calico Illustrated Classics Ser.: No. 4). (ENG.). 112p. (J). (gr. 2-5). 38.50 *(978-1-61641-618-8(1),* 4051, Calico Chapter Bks.) ABDO Publishing Co.

LONDON (ENGLAND)—TOWER OF LONDON

see Tower of London (London, England)

LONELINESS

Apel, Melanie Ann. Let's Talk about Feeling Lonely. 2009. (Let's Talk Library). 24p. (gr. 2-3). 42.50 *(978-1-60853-442-5(1),* PowerKids Pr.) Rosen Publishing Group, Inc., The.

Hill, Z. B. Loneliness. Croft, Cindy, ed. 2014. (Causes & Effects of Emotions Ser.: 13). 64p. (J). (gr. 7-18). 23.95 *(978-1-4222-3075-6(9))* Mason Crest.

Marcovitz, Hal. A Lonely Guy's Guide: How to Deal, 1 vol. 2014. (Guy's Guide Ser.). (ENG.). 64p. (gr. 5-7). 19.61 *(978-1-62293-025-8(8),* 8fa25b3e-2319-4f3a-b4ac-b0243aab57bb) Enslow Publishing, LLC.

Marcovitz, Hal & Snyder, Gail. A Guys' Guide to Loneliness; a Girls' Guide to Loneliness, 1 vol. 2009. (Flip-It-Over Guides to Teen Emotions Ser.). (ENG., Illus.). 128p. (gr. 5-6). lib. bdg. 35.93 *(978-0-7660-2856-2(9),* 9b69ea49-b89c-48b9-8ffe-514db75dd67a) Enslow Publishing, LLC.

Snyder, Gail. Lonely Girl? Girls Dealing with Feelings, 1 vol. 2014. (Girls Dealing with Feelings Ser.). (ENG.). 64p. (gr. 5-6). 19.61 *(978-1-62293-055-5(X),* 5f30e113-65fb-41f5-8b1d-b12aa15e40ad) Enslow Publishing, LLC.

LONELINESS—FICTION

Ackerman, Peter. The Lonely Phone Booth. Dalton, Max, illus. 2010. (ENG.). 32p. (J). (gr. k-2). 16.95 *(978-1-56792-414-5(X))* Godine, David R. Pub.

—The Lonely Typewriter. Dalton, Max, illus. 2014. (ENG.). 32p. (J). 16.95 *(978-1-56792-518-0(9))* Godine, David R. Pub.

Adler, Denise. Thank You for Looking for Me. 2010. 20p. 12.99 *(978-1-4520-2438-7(3))* AuthorHouse.

Ahlberg, Allan. The Pencil. Ingman, Bruce, illus. 2012. (ENG.). 48p. (J). (gr. -1-3). pap. 7.99 *(978-0-7636-6088-8(4))* Candlewick Pr.

—The Pencil. Ingman, Bruce, illus. 2012. lib. bdg. 17.20 *(978-0-606-26942-1(8))* Turtleback.

Andrews, Andy. Henry Hodges Needs a Friend, 1 vol. 2015. (ENG., Illus.). 32p. (J). 14.99 *(978-0-529-11576-8(X),* Tommy Nelson) Nelson, Thomas Inc.

Bauer, Marion Dane. Little Dog, Lost. Bell, Jennifer A., illus. 2013. (ENG.). 208p. (J). (gr. 3-7). pap. 7.99 *(978-1-4424-3424-0(4),* Atheneum Bks. for Young Readers) Simon & Schuster Children's Publishing.

Bernheimer, Kate. The Lonely Book. Sheban, Chris, illus. 2012. 40p. (J). (gr. -1-3). 17.99 *(978-0-375-86226-7(9),* Schwartz & Wade Bks.) Random Hse. Children's Bks.

Bondestam, Linda, illus. My Little Small. 2018. (ENG.). 52p. (J). (gr. -1-3). 15.95 *(978-1-59270-209-1(0))* Enchanted Lion Bks., LLC.

Brandes, Wendy L. MJ's Camp Crisis. Lorenzet, Eleonora, illus. 2016. (Summer Camp Ser.). (ENG.). 96p. (J). (gr. 4-6). lib. bdg. 25.32 *(978-1-4965-2598-7(1),* 130727, Stone Arch Bks.) Capstone.

Brett, Jan. Gingerbread Friends. Brett, Jan, illus. (Illus.). 32p. (J). 2017. (-k). bds. 8.99 *(978-1-5247-3942-3(1))* 2008. (gr. -1-k). 19.99 *(978-0-399-25161-0(8))* Penguin Young Readers Group. (G.P. Putnam's Sons Books for Young Readers).

Brun-Cosme, Nadine. Big Wolf & Little Wolf: The Little Leaf That Wouldn't Fall. Tallec, Olivier, illus. 2009. 32p. (J). (gr. -1-2). 16.95 *(978-1-59270-088-2(8));* 16.95 *(978-1-59270-084-4(5))* Enchanted Lion Bks., LLC.

Bruno, Linette Arthurton. Three's No Crowd: Two's Company. 2011. 33p. (J). pap. 15.95 *(978-1-4327-7125-6(6))* Outskirts Pr., Inc.

Bucher, Charlotte. Cecil Learns to Smile. 2010. 26p. (J). pap. 19.95 *(978-1-4327-4992-7(7))* Outskirts Pr., Inc.

Campbell, K. G. A Small Zombie Problem. 2019. (Zombie Problems Ser.: 1). (Illus.). 240p. (J). (gr. 3-7). 16.99 *(978-0-553-53955-4(8),* Knopf Bks. for Young Readers) Random Hse. Children's Bks.

Chan, Janette Shipston. The Tiny Tiger. 2010. 24p. (J). 13.50 *(978-1-4520-4106-3(7))* AuthorHouse.

Chartrand, Lili. The Fabulous World of Mr. Fred, 1 vol. Grimard, Gabrielle, illus. 2014. (ENG.). 32p. (J). (gr. k-2). pap. 10.95 *(978-1-55455-346-4(6),* 1ea9249a-ec28-4ad4-801a-7bc30d64bcc1) Trifolium Bks., Inc. CAN. Dist: Firefly Bks., Ltd.

Chisolm, Melinda. Remembering to Breathe. Cross, Jo Ellen, illus. 2009. 31p. pap. 24.95 *(978-1-60703-914-3(1))* America Star Bks.

Clough, Lisa. On the Hill. 2004. (ENG., Illus.). 32p. (J). (gr. -1-3). tchr. ed. 15.00 *(978-0-618-40741-5(3),* 588689, Clarion Bks.) HarperCollins Pubs.

Collier, Kristen. Joy the Jellyfish. 2007. (Illus.). (J). per. *(978-0-9797574-7-1(9)); (978-0-9797574-6-4(0))* Dragonfly Publishing, Inc.

Conner, Wendy Simpson. Princess of the Moon. (Illus.). (J). 16.95 *(978-1-889599-20-5(4))* Interstellar Publishing Co.

Corchin, D. J. I Feel... Different. 2020. (I Feel... Ser.). (Illus.). 56p. (J). (gr. -1-3). 14.99 *(978-1-7282-1970-7(1))* Sourcebooks, Inc.

Cuevas, Michelle. The Town of Turtle. Chien, Cátia, illus. 2018. (ENG.). 40p. (J). (gr. -1-3). 17.99 *(978-0-544-74982-5(0),* 1633373, Clarion Bks.) HarperCollins Pubs.

Cuthand, Beth. Sikihpsis. Cuthand, Stan, tr. Longman, Mary, illus. ed. 2007. (Little Duck Ser.). (ENG.). 28p. 17.00 *(978-1-894778-44-2(8))* Theytus Bks., Ltd. CAN. Dist: Univ. of Toronto Pr.

Damm, Antje. The Visitor. Damm, Antje, illus. 2018. (ENG., Illus.). 32p. (J). (gr. -1-k). 17.99 *(978-1-77657-188-8(6),* 23d7c46f-4a88-4af5-9c86-de0f4d43faa1) Gecko Pr. NZL. Dist: Lerner Publishing Group.

Davies, Benji. The Storm Whale. Davies, Benji, illus. 2014. (ENG., Illus.). 32p. (J). (gr. -1-3). 18.99 *(978-0-8050-9967-6(0),* 900128170, Holt, Henry & Co. Bks. For Young Readers) Holt, Henry & Co.

DeFelice, Cynthia. Signal. 2011. (ENG.). 176p. (J). (gr. 5-8). pap. 16.99 *(978-0-312-61776-9(3),* 900076913) Square Fish.

Dicamillo, Kate. Good Rosie! Bliss, Harry, illus. 2018. 40p. (J). *(978-1-4063-8357-7(0))* Candlewick Pr.

DiCamillo, Kate. Good Rosie! Bliss, Harry, illus. 2018. (ENG.). 32p. (J). (gr. k-3). 17.99 *(978-0-7636-8979-7(3))* Candlewick Pr.

Elliott, Miriam Isabel. Solita & the Purple Moon: Solita y la Luna Morada. 2007. (ENG.). 24p. per. 11.49 *(978-1-4343-4932-3(2))* AuthorHouse.

Everson, Chance. Beginnings Vol. 2: Tales of the Mandrasaurs, Volume the Second. Geary, Steve, illus. 2004. cd-rom 9.95 *(978-0-9760303-1-7(4))* R.A.R.E. TALES.

Fagan, Cary. A Cage Went in Search of a Bird, 1 vol. Erfanian, Banafsheh, illus. 2017. (ENG.). 32p. (J). (gr. k-2). 18.95 *(978-1-55498-861-7(6))* Groundwood Bks. CAN. Dist: Publishers Group West (PGW).

Floyd, Lucy. A Place for Nicholas. McPhail, David, illus. 2005. (Green Light Readers Level 2 Ser.). 18p. (gr. k-2). 13.95 *(978-0-7569-5243-3(3))* Perfection Learning Corp.

Fogg, K. L. Serpent Tide. 2006. 16.95 *(978-1-59156-861-2(7))* Covenant Communications, Inc.

Foreman, Jack. Say Hello. Foreman, Michael, illus. 2012. (ENG.). 40p. (J). (gr. -1-2). pap. 8.99 *(978-0-7636-6087-1(6))* Candlewick Pr.

Foreman, Jack & Foreman, Michael. Say Hello. 2015. 40p. pap. 7.00 *(978-1-61003-409-8(0))* Center for the Collaborative Classroom.

Foreman, Michael. El Lorito Pelon. Diego, Rapi & Flores, Martha, illus. 2008. (SPA.). 30p. (J). (gr. 1-3). 15.99 *(978-1-930332-56-0(4))* Lectorum Pubns., Inc.

Frazee, Marla. Little Brown. Frazee, Marla, illus. 2018. (ENG., Illus.). 40p. (J). (gr. -1-3). 17.99 *(978-1-4814-2522-3(6),* Beach Lane Bks.) Beach Lane Bks.

Galliez, Roxane Marie. Farewell Sadness. Lhomme, Sandrine, illus. 2010. 24p. (J). 9.99 *(978-0-8416-7139-3(7))* Hammond World Atlas Corp.

Gehl, Laura. My Pillow Keeps Moving. Weyant, Christopher, illus. 2018. 40p. (J). (gr. -1-3). 17.99 *(978-0-425-28824-5(2),* Viking Books for Young Readers) Penguin Young Readers Group.

A Gift for Roo. 2013. (Illus.). 24p. pap. 10.95 *(978-1-61633-441-3(X))* Guardian Angel Publishing, Inc.

Gil, Carmen. Un Fantasma con Asma. Webster, Sarah, illus. 2004. (Libros para Sonar Ser.). (SPA.). 40p. (J). 15.99 *(978-84-8464-186-5(4))* Kalandraka Editora, S.L. ESP. Dist: Lectorum Pubns., Inc.

Gonzalez, Rigoberto & González, Rigoberto. Soledad Sigh-Sighs, 1 vol. Ibarra, Rosa, illus. 2014.Tr. of Soledad Suspiros. (ENG.). 32p. (J). (gr. 2-4). pap. 12.95

(978-0-89239-309-1(2), leelowcbp, Children's Book Press) Lee & Low Bks., Inc.

Green, Andi. The Lonely Little Monster. 2007. (WorryWoo Monsters Ser.). (Illus.). 68p. (J). 14.99 *(978-0-9792860-0-1(X))* Monsters in My Head, LLC, The.

Hannigan, Katherine. Emmaline & the Bunny. Hannigan, Katherine, illus. 2009. (ENG., Illus.). 112p. (J). (gr. 2-7). 16.99 *(978-0-06-162654-8(6)*, Greenwillow Bks.) HarperCollins Pubs.

Harnett, Katie, illus. Archie Snufflekins Oliver Valentine Cupcake Tiberius Cat. 2016. (ENG.). 32p. (J). (gr. -1-k). 16.95 *(978-1-909263-37-6(0))* Flying Eye Bks. GBR. Dist: Penguin Random Hse. LLC.

Harris, Isobel. Little Boy Brown. Francois, Andre, illus. 2013. 48p. (J). (gr. -1-3). 15.95 *(978-1-59270-135-3(3))* Enchanted Lion Bks., LLC.

Harris, Odis Clinton. Wee Willie & the Lonely Pine. 2008. 23p. pap. 24.95 *(978-1-60563-741-9(6))* America Star Bks.

Hart, Caryl. The Princess & the Christmas Rescue. Warburton, Sarah, illus. 2017. (ENG.). 32p. (J). (gr. -1-2). 16.99 *(978-0-7636-9632-0(3))* Candlewick Pr.

Hartnett, Sonya. What the Birds See. 2007. (ENG., Illus.). 208p. (YA). (gr. 9). pap. 7.99 *(978-0-7636-3680-7(0))* Candlewick Pr.

Hayes, Sean & Icenogle, Scott. Plum. Thompson, Robin, illus. 2018. (ENG.). 48p. (J). (gr. -1-3). 17.99 *(978-1-5344-0404-5(X)*, Simon & Schuster Bks. For Young Readers) Simon & Schuster Bks. For Young Readers.

Henkes, Kevin. All Alone. Henkes, Kevin, illus. 2003. (ENG., Illus.). 40p. (J). (gr. -1-3). 16.99 *(978-0-06-054115-6(6)*, Greenwillow Bks.) HarperCollins Pubs.

Jean, Penny. Holding Grace. 2008. 28p. pap. 24.95 *(978-1-60441-692-3(0))* America Star Bks.

Johnston, Tony. The Cat with Seven Names. Davenier, Christine, illus. 2013. 40p. (J). (gr. k-3). 16.95 *(978-1-58089-381-7(3))* Charlesbridge Publishing, Inc.

Jones, Guy. The Ice Garden. 2019. (ENG.). 272p. (J). (gr. 3-7). 17.99 *(978-1-338-28533-8(5)*, Chicken Hse., The) Scholastic, Inc.

Judd, Christopher M. Bearable Moments. 2005. (Illus.). (J). 16.95 *(978-0-9766666-1-5(8))* Arcadian Hse.

Judge, Chris. The Lonely Beast. Judge, Chris, illus. 2011. (ENG., Illus.). 32p. (J). (gr. -1-3). 16.95 *(978-0-7613-8097-9(3)*, cf2839e0-7a8a-4af6-aa66-b9f0cacf9654) Lerner Publishing Group.

Kadono, Eiko. Grandpa's Soup. Ichikawa, Satomi, illus. 2009. (ENG.). 40p. (J). (gr. -1-3). pap. 9.00 *(978-0-8028-5347-9(1)*, Eerdmans Bks For Young Readers) Eerdmans, William B. Publishing Co.

Kear, Nicole C. The Fix-It Friends: Three's a Crowd. Dockray, Tracy, illus. 2018. (Fix-It Friends Ser.: 6). (ENG.). 176p. (J). pap. 8.99 *(978-1-250-08674-7(4)*, 900157587) Imprint IND. Dist: Macmillan.

Kim, Sang-Keun. Little Mole's Wish. 2019. (Illus.). 40p. (J). (gr. -1-2). 17.99 *(978-0-525-58134-5(0)*, Schwartz & Wade Bks.) Random Hse. Children's Bks.

LaCour, Nina. We Are Okay. (ENG.). (YA). (gr. 9). 2019. 256p. pap. 11.99 *(978-0-14-242293-9(2)*, Penguin Books) 2017. 240p. 17.99 *(978-0-525-42589-2(6)*, Dutton Books for Young Readers) Penguin Young Readers Group.

Lael, Anita. The Little Brick House. Gresham, Delia, illus. 2012. 30p. 24.95 *(978-1-4626-5972-2(1))* America Star Bks.

Lamar, Gail Renfroe. Moon of the Wishing Night. Mask, Cynthia, illus. 2004. 32p. (J). 17.95 *(978-1-57966-047-5(9)*, River City Kids) River City Publishing.

LaReau, Kara. Ugly Fish. Magoon, Scott, illus. 2006. (ENG.). 40p. (J). (gr. -1-3). 17.99 *(978-0-15-205082-5(5)*, 1195349, Clarion Bks.) HarperCollins Pubs.

Lescuyer, Moira. Little Life Reminders. 2010. 16p. 7.95 *(978-1-4525-0037-9(1))* Get Published.

Levithan, David. Someday. 2018. 394p. (YA). *(978-0-525-70816-2(2))* Knopf, Alfred A. Inc.

—Someday. (ENG.). 400p. (YA). (gr. 7). 2019. pap. 11.99 *(978-0-399-55308-0(8)*, Ember) 2018. 18.99 *(978-0-399-55305-9(3)*, Knopf Bks. for Young Readers) Random Hse. Children's Bks.

Linden, Dianne. Peacekeepers. 82p. (J). stu. ed. 9.95 *(978-1-55050-297-8(2))* Coteau Bks. CAN. Dist: Fitzhenry & Whiteside, Ltd.

Lindström, Eva. Everyone Walks Away. Lindström, Eva, illus. 2019. (ENG., Illus.). 32p. (J). (gr. k-2). 17.99 *(978-1-77657-186-4(X)*, 2297efca-3426-496b-917e-8d8dc5186867) Gecko Pr. NZL. Dist: Lerner Publishing Group.

MacLachlan, Patricia & Charest, Emily MacLachlan. Little Robot Alone. Phelan, Matt, illus. 2018. (ENG.). 40p. (J). (gr. -1-3). 17.99 *(978-0-544-44280-1(6)*, 1597246, Clarion Bks.) HarperCollins Pubs.

Marie, Carissa. The Lonely Puppy. 2011. 20p. 12.95 *(978-1-4490-8264-2(5))* AuthorHouse.

Markel, Michelle. Hanukkah Hamster. Ceolin, André, illus. 2018. (ENG.). 32p. (J). (gr. k-2). 16.99 *(978-1-58536-399-5(5)*, 204583) Sleeping Bear Pr.

Martin, Ann M. Everything for a Dog. 2011. (ENG.). 240p. (J). (gr. 4-7). pap. 8.99 *(978-0-312-67484-7(8)*, 900072897) Square Fish.

Mercado, Ariano. Soccer Shoes from Americ. 2011. 36p. pap. *(978-1-4269-8962-9(8))* Trafford Publishing (UK) Ltd.

Montijo, Rhode. Cloud Boy/Nino Nube. Mlawer, Teresa, tr. from ENG. 2006. (SPA & ENG., Illus.). 24p. (J). (gr. -1-3). 12.99 *(978-1-933032-06-1(5))* Lectorum Pubns., Inc.

Moroney, Trace. When I'm Feeling Lonely. 2019. (Feelings Ser.). (ENG.). 24p. (J). (— 1). 8.99 *(978-1-76068-065-7(6))* Bonnier Publishing GBR. Dist: Independent Pubs. Group.

Moskowitz, Hannah. Teeth. 2013. (ENG.). 288p. (YA). (gr. 9-12). 17.99 *(978-1-4424-6532-9(8)*, Simon Pulse) Simon Pulse.

Mullarkey, Lisa. Kianna. Franco, Paula, illus. (Chicas Poni (Pony Girls) Ser.).Tr. of Kianna. 112p. (J). 2016. (SPA.). (gr. 1-4). lib. bdg. 38.50 *(978-1-61479-624-4(6)*, 25058) 2015. (ENG.). (gr. 2-5). 38.50 *(978-1-62402-130-5(1)*, 19381) ABDO Publishing Co. (Calico Chapter Bks.).

Murphy, Sally. Pearl Verses the World. Potter, Heather, illus. 2011. (ENG.). 80p. (J). (gr. 3-7). 14.99 *(978-0-7636-4821-3(3))* Candlewick Pr.

Nesselrode, Sandra. Princess Kelsie & Her Special Gifts. 2008. 28p. pap. 19.95 *(978-1-4327-1708-7(1))* Outskirts Pr., Inc.

Ouimet, David. I Go Quiet. 2020. (ENG., Illus.). 48p. (J). (gr. 1-4). 18.95 *(978-1-324-00443-1(6)*, 340443, Norton Young Readers) Norton, W. W. & Co., Inc.

Parpan, Justin, illus. Gwango's Lonesome Trail. 2006. 32p. (J). (gr. -1-3). 15.95 *(978-1-60108-004-2(2))* Red Cygnet Pr.

Perry, Sarah. Clara's Road. 2005. 64p. (J). per. *(978-1-55306-945-4(5)*, Epic Pr.) Essence Publishing.

Peterson, John C. Adam Has No Brothers. 2009. 20p. pap. 10.99 *(978-1-4490-3207-4(9))* AuthorHouse.

Pilkey, Dav. A Friend for Dragon: an Acorn Book (Dragon #1). Pilkey, Dav, illus. 2019. (Dragon Ser.: 1). (ENG., Illus.). 64p. (J). (gr. k-2). pap. 4.99 *(978-1-338-34105-8(7))* Scholastic, Inc.

Pugliano Martin, Carol. Lonely Pluto. 2005. (J). pap. *(978-1-4108-4194-0(4))* Benchmark Education Co.

Rex, Adam. Nothing Rhymes with Orange: (Cute Children's Books, Preschool Rhyming Books, Children's Humor Books, Books about Friendship) 2017. (ENG., Illus.). 48p. (J). (gr. k-3). 16.99 *(978-1-4521-5443-5(0))* Chronicle Bks. LLC.

Rice, Clay. The Lonely Shadow. 2013. (ENG., Illus.). 64p. (gr. k-3). 19.95 *(978-1-938301-08-7(0)*, 559108) Familius LLC.

Rundell, Katherine. One Christmas Wish. Sutton, Emily, illus. 2018. (ENG.). 64p. (J). (gr. k-4). 18.99 *(978-1-4814-9161-7(X)*, Simon & Schuster Bks. For Young Readers) Simon & Schuster Bks. For Young Readers.

Ryan, Rob. The Invisible Kingdom. 2016. (Invisible Kingdom Trilogy Ser.). (ENG., Illus.). 64p. (J). 19.95 *(978-1-56656-077-1(2)*, Crocodile Bks.) Interlink Publishing Group, Inc.

Saltzberg, Barney. Dog & Rabbit. Saltzberg, Barney, illus. 2019. (Illus.). 48p. (J). (gr. -1-2). lib. bdg. 14.99 *(978-1-62354-107-1(7))* Charlesbridge Publishing, Inc.

Samarasinghe, Sara. Dalaina. 2007. 352p. pap. 18.95 *(978-0-9798997-2-0(9))* iTeenBooks Inc.

Schraff, Anne. Just Another Name for Lonely. 2008. (Passages 2000 Ser.). 107p. (J). lib. bdg. 13.95 *(978-0-7569-8402-1(5))* Perfection Learning Corp.

Sedoti, Chelsea. Hundred Lies of Lizzie Lovett. 2017. (ENG.). 400p. (YA). (gr. 8-12). 17.99 *(978-1-4926-3608-3(8)*, 9781492636083) Sourcebooks, Inc.

Siers, Sophie. The Gift Horse. 2017. (Illus.). 31p. (J). pap. *(978-0-473-40855-8(4))* Millwood Press.

Staake, Bob. Bluebird. Staake, Bob, illus. 2013. (Illus.). 40p. (J). (gr. -1-3). 17.99 *(978-0-375-87037-8(7)*, Schwartz & Wade Bks.) Random Hse. Children's Bks.

Strange, Jason. To Wake the Dead, 1 vol. Parks, Phil, illus. 2011. (Jason Strange Ser.). (ENG.). 72p. (J). (gr. 3-6). (J). 25.32 *(978-1-4342-2963-2(7)*, 114196); pap. 6.25 *(978-1-4342-3094-2(5)*, 114734) Capstone. (Stone Arch Bks.).

Stren, Patti. Hug Me. Date not set. (Illus.). 40p. (J). pap. 5.99 *(978-0-06-443754-7(X))* HarperCollins Pubs.

Syrstad, Suzi. Timmy the Tiny Troubled Turtle, 1 vol. Maki, Tab, illus. 2009. 13p. pap. 24.95 *(978-1-61546-455-5(7))* PublishAmerica, Inc.

Taylor, Theodore. The Boy Who Could Fly Without a Motor. 2004. (ENG., Illus.). 168p. (J). (gr. 3-7). pap. 11.95 *(978-0-15-204767-2(0)*, 1194383, Clarion Bks.) HarperCollins Pubs.

Teckentrup, Britta. Grumpy Cat. 2013. (ENG., Illus.). 26p. (J). (— 1). bds. 6.95 *(978-1-907967-48-1(6))* Boxer Bks., Ltd. GBR. Dist: Sterling Publishing Co., Inc.

Ttofa, Juliette. The Girl Who Collected Her Own Echo: A Story about Friendship. 2017. (Nurturing Emotional Resilience Storybooks Ser.). (ENG., Illus.). 28p. pap. 15.95 *(978-1-138-30889-3(7)*, Y367703) Routledge.

Turnbull, Victoria. Pandora. 2017. (ENG., Illus.). 32p. (J). (gr. -1-3). 17.99 *(978-0-544-94733-7(9)*, 1659597, Clarion Bks.) HarperCollins Pubs.

Ungureanu, Dan. Nara & the Island. Ungureanu, Dan, illus. 2016. (ENG., Illus.). 32p. (J). (gr. -1-3). 17.99 *(978-1-5124-1793-7(9)*, b39e93f5-4ba7-49eb-b096-f924885ca367) Lerner Publishing Group.

Veissid, Jacqueline. Caspian Finds a Friend: (Picture Book about Friendship for Kids, Bear Book for Children) Brown, Merrilees, illus. 2019. (ENG.). 36p. (J). (gr. k-3). 17.99 *(978-1-4521-3780-3(3))* Chronicle Bks. LLC.

Wall, Laura. Goose. Wall, Laura, illus. 2015. (ENG., Illus.). 48p. (J). (gr. -1-3). 12.99 *(978-0-06-232435-1(7)*, HarperCollins) HarperCollins Pubs.

Ward, Joyce Claudine. Nanny the Goat. 2008. 22p. pap. 24.95 *(978-1-4241-9139-0(4))* America Star Bks.

Webster, Frank V. The Boys of Bellwood School. 2004. reprint ed. pap. 1.99 *(978-1-4192-5509-0(6))*; pap. 20.95 *(978-1-4191-5509-3(1))* Kessinger Publishing, LLC.

Weston Woods Staff, creator. The Story about Ping. 2011. 29.95 *(978-0-439-73519-3(X))*; 38.75 *(978-0-439-72894-2(0))*; 18.95 *(978-0-439-72893-5(2))* Weston Woods Studios, Inc.

Whisler, Barbara. Shag Finds a Home. Jackson, Kay, illus. 2008. 24p. pap. 24.95 *(978-1-60703-730-9(0))* America Star Bks.

White, Amanda. Sand Sister. Morales, Yuyi, illus. 2004. (ENG.). 32p. (J). 16.99 *(978-1-84148-617-8(5))* Barefoot Bks., Inc.

Wilkins, Remy. Strays. 2017. (J). *(978-1-947644-00-7(9))* Canon Pr.

Woods, Matilda. The Boy, the Bird & the Coffin Maker. Allepuz, Anuska, illus. 2019. (ENG.). 208p. (J). (gr. 3-7). 7.99 *(978-0-525-51523-4(2)*, Puffin Books) Penguin Young Readers Group.

LONG ISLAND (N.Y.)—FICTION

Blount, Patty. The Way It Hurts. 2017. (ENG., Illus.). 400p. (YA). (gr. 8-12). pap. 10.99 *(978-1-4926-3278-8(3))* Sourcebooks, Inc.

Blume, Judy. Then Again, Maybe I Won't. (J). 125p. pap. 3.99 *(978-0-8072-1445-9(0))*; 2004. 164p. (gr. 5-9). pap. 29.00 incl. audio *(978-0-8072-0796-3(9)*, LYA 354 SP) Random Hse. Audio Publishing Group. (Listening Library).

Calonita, Jen. Reality Check. 2011. (ENG.). 288p. (YA). (gr. 7-17). pap. 15.99 *(978-0-316-04553-7(5)*, Poppy) Little, Brown Bks. for Young Readers.

Corbett, Sue. 12 Again. 2007. 240p. (J). (gr. 5-18). 6.99 *(978-0-14-240729-5(1)*, Puffin Books) Penguin Young Readers Group.

Couloumbis, Audrey. Not Exactly a Love Story. 2014. (ENG.). 288p. (YA). (gr. 7). pap. 9.99 *(978-0-375-86606-7(X)*, Ember) Random Hse. Children's Bks.

Edwards, Melvin Neal. Sticks & Stones. 2013. 114p. (gr. 2-4). 19.88 *(978-1-4669-8482-0(1))*; pap. 9.88 *(978-1-4669-8480-6(5))* Trafford Publishing.

Falk, Elizabeth Sullivan. Freedom's Fire. Wang, Qi Z., illus. 2004. (J). *(978-1-59336-321-5(4))*; pap. *(978-1-59336-322-2(2))* Mondo Publishing.

George, McKelle. Speak Easy, Speak Love. 2017. (ENG.). 432p. (YA). (gr. 8). 17.99 *(978-0-06-256092-6(1)*, Greenwillow Bks.) HarperCollins Pubs.

Hest, Amy. The Summer We Found the Baby. 2020. (ENG., Illus.). 192p. (J). (gr. 5). 16.99 *(978-0-7636-6007-9(8))* Candlewick Pr.

Jacobellis, Michelle. Dachshund Tales: Adventures on the Great South Bay. 2012. 60p. pap. 17.95 *(978-1-62709-104-6(1))* America Star Bks.

Korman, Gordon. Zoobreak. 2009. 230p. (J). *(978-0-545-20027-1(X)*, Scholastic Pr.) Scholastic, Inc.

—Zoobreak (Swindle #2) 2010. (Swindle Ser.: 2). (ENG.). 240p. (J). (gr. 4-7). pap. 8.99 *(978-0-545-12500-0(6)*, Scholastic Paperbacks) Scholastic, Inc.

Krapp, JoAnn Vergona. Trouble Times Three. Blair, June H., illus. 2015. 64p. (J). (gr. 3-5). pap. 12.95 *(978-0-9722576-4-0(0))* JoAnn Vergona Krapp & Gene Zaner.

Kristina Learns about Fishing. 2007. (J). *(978-0-9792728-0-6(7))* Tracepaper Bks. Inc.

Lane, Nathan & Elliott, Devlin. Naughty Mabel. Krall, Dan, illus. 2015. (Naughty Mabel Ser.). (ENG.). 48p. (J). (gr. -1-3). 19.99 *(978-1-4814-3022-7(X)*, Simon & Schuster Bks. For Young Readers) Simon & Schuster Bks. For Young Readers.

Miller, Meredith. Little Wrecks. 2018. (ENG.). 384p. (YA). (gr. 9). pap. 9.99 *(978-0-06-247426-1(X)*, HarperCollins) HarperCollins Pubs.

Murray, Caryn Eve. Philomena's Homecoming: The (mostly) true story of a New York prairie dog's search for a Family. 2010. 48p. pap. 8.95 *(978-1-4502-2769-8(4))* iUniverse, Inc.

Patterson, James & Grabenstein, Chris. I Even Funnier: A Middle School Story. Park, Laura, illus. (I Funny Ser.: 2). (ENG.). 368p. (J). (gr. 3-7). 2017. pap. 8.99 *(978-0-316-20695-2(4))* 2013. 13.99 *(978-0-316-20697-6(0))* Little Brown & Co. (Jimmy Patterson).

—I Totally Funniest: A Middle School Story. Park, Laura, illus. 2015. (I Funny Ser.: 3). (ENG.). 336p. (J). (gr. 3-7). 13.99 *(978-0-316-40593-5(0)*, Jimmy Patterson) Little Brown & Co.

Preller, James. Bystander. 2011. (ENG.). 256p. (YA). (gr. 5-9). pap. 8.99 *(978-0-312-54796-7(X)*, 900074323) Square Fish.

Schmidt, Gary D. The Wednesday Wars. 2008. *(978-0-545-10562-0(5))* Scholastic, Inc.

—The Wednesday Wars. 2009. lib. bdg. 18.40 *(978-0-606-10573-6(5))* Turtleback.

—The Wednesday Wars: A Newbery Honor Award Winner. (ENG.). (J). (gr. 5-7). 2009. 288p. pap. 9.99 *(978-0-547-23760-2(X)*, 1083872) 2007. 272p. 18.99 *(978-0-618-72483-3(4)*, 100515) HarperCollins Pubs. (Clarion Bks.).

Shoemaker, E. W. Mother Nature & the Tales of North Fork. 2009. 220p. pap. 18.75 *(978-1-4389-8604-3(1))* AuthorHouse.

Thimble Islands Storybook. 2005. (J). *(978-1-59872-094-5(5))* Instant Pub.

Worthington, Heather Hill. Miles of Smiles: The Story of Roxey, the Long Island Rail Road Dog. Farnsworth, Bill, illus. 2010. (J). *(978-0-9792918-4-5(4))*; pap. *(978-0-9792918-8-3(7))* Blue Marlin Pubns.

LONG ISLAND (N.Y.)—HISTORY

Castrovilla, Selene. By the Sword. Farnsworth, Bill, illus. 2007. (ENG.). 40p. (J). (gr. 1-4). 17.95 *(978-1-59078-427-3(8)*, Calkins Creek) Highlights Pr., c/o Highlights for Children, Inc.

Shodell, Elly, ed. Particles of the Past: Sandmining on Long Island, 1870s-1980s. 2nd ed. (Illus.). 43p. (YA). (gr. 9-12). reprint ed. pap. 8.95 *(978-0-9615059-0-5(7))* Port Washington Public Library.

LONG ISLAND, BATTLE OF, NEW YORK, N.Y., 1776

Castrovilla, Selene. By the Sword. Farnsworth, Bill, illus. 2007. (ENG.). 40p. (J). (gr. 1-4). 17.95 *(978-1-59078-427-3(8)*, Calkins Creek) Highlights Pr., c/o Highlights for Children, Inc.

LONGEVITY

see Old Age

LONGFELLOW, HENRY WADSWORTH, 1807-1882

Cody, Sherwin. Four American Poets. 2009. 198p. pap. 14.14 *(978-0-217-47860-1(3))* General Bks. LLC.

Kallio, Jamie. 12 Questions about Paul Revere's Ride. 2017. (Examining Primary Sources Ser.). (ENG., Illus.). 32p. (J). (gr. 3-6). 32.80 *(978-1-63235-286-6(9)*, 11755); pap. 9.95 *(978-1-63235-336-8(9)*, 11763) Bookstaves, LLC. (12-Story Library).

Lantos, Jeff. Why Longfellow Lied: The Truth about Paul Revere's Midnight Ride. 2021. (Illus.). 160p. (J). (gr. 3-7). lib. bdg. 18.99 *(978-1-58089-933-8(1))* Charlesbridge Publishing, Inc.

LONGSTOCKING, PIPPI (FICTITIOUS CHARACTER)—FICTION

Lindgren, Astrid. Pippa Mediaslargas. (Pippi Longstocking Ser.).Tr. of Pippi Longstocking. (SPA.). (J). (gr. 3-5). pap. 9.95 *(978-84-261-2304-6(X)*, JV304X) Juventud, Editorial ESP. Dist: Continental Bk. Co., Inc.

—Pippi Goes on Board. (Pippi Longstocking Ser.). 140p. (J). (gr. 3-5). pap. 3.99 *(978-0-8072-1401-5(9)*, Listening Library) Random Hse. Audio Publishing Group.

—Pippi in the South Seas. (Pippi Longstocking Ser.). 125p. (J). (gr. 3-5). pap. 3.99 *(978-0-8072-1392-6(6)*, Listening Library) Random Hse. Audio Publishing Group.

—Pippi Longstocking. 2013. (Puffin Chalk Ser.). (ENG.). 160p. (J). (gr. 3-7). pap. 7.99 *(978-0-14-242752-1(7)*, Puffin Books) Penguin Young Readers Group.

—Pippi Longstocking. (Pippi Longstocking Ser.). 160p. (J). (gr. 3-5). pap. 4.99 *(978-0-8072-1431-2(0)*, Listening Library) Random Hse. Audio Publishing Group.

—Pippi Longstocking (Puffin Modern Classics) 2005. (Puffin Modern Classics Ser.). (ENG., Illus.). 160p. (J). (gr. 3-7). pap. 7.99 *(978-0-14-240249-8(4)*, Puffin Books) Penguin Young Readers Group.

LOOKING GLASSES

see Mirrors

LOONS

Burke, Zoe. Owls & Loons. Inuit artists and printmakers of Kinngait Studios, illus. 2016. 24p. (J). bds. 10.95 *(978-0-7649-7542-4(0)*, POMEGRANATE KIDS) Pomegranate Communications, Inc.

Hodgkins, Fran. Little Loon. Hayes, Karel, illus. 2015. 32p. (J). (gr. -1-3). 16.95 *(978-1-60893-372-3(5))* Down East Bks.

Kalz, Jill. Loons. 2003. (Birds Ser.). (Illus.). 24p. (J). lib. bdg. 21.35 *(978-1-58340-133-0(4))* Black Rabbit Bks.

Love, Donna. Loons: Diving Birds of the North, Vol. 1. Turley, Joyce Mihran, tr. Turley, Joyce Mihran, illus. rev. ed. 64p. (J). (gr. 4). pap. 12.00 *(978-0-87842-482-5(2)*, 340) Mountain Pr. Publishing Co., Inc.

Ring, Elizabeth. Loon at Northwood Lake. Oughton, Taylor, illus. 2005. (Smith Sonian's Backyard Ser.). 32p. (J). (gr. -1-3). (ENG.). 6.95 *(978-1-59249-482-8(X)*, S5017); pap. 8.95 incl. audio *(978-1-59249-491-0(9)*, SC5013) Soundprints.

Vande Griek, Susan. Loon, 2 vols. Reczuch, Karen, illus. 2019. 48p. (J). (gr. k-2). 14.99 *(978-1-77306-236-5(0))* Groundwood Bks. CAN. Dist: Publishers Group West (PGW).

Woodward, John. Loons. 2008. (Nature's Children Ser.). (Illus.). 52p. (J). *(978-0-7172-6258-8(8))* Grolier, Ltd.

LOONS—FICTION

Banks, Kate. Dillon Dillon. 2005. 149p. (gr. 3-7). 18.00 *(978-0-7569-5767-4(2))* Perfection Learning Corp.

Bollendorf, Robert F. & Makely, William. Flight of the Loon: One Family's Battle with Recovery. Donlon, Eleanor, ed. 2007. 105p. 8.95 *(978-1-932514-15-5(5))* College of DuPage Pr.

Fuller, Sandy Fergus. Moon Loon. 2010. (Illus.). 32p. (J). (gr. k-17). 15.95 *(978-1-58979-453-5(2))* Taylor Trade Publishing.

Fuller, Sandy Ferguson. Moon Loon. 2010. (J). 7.95 *(978-1-58979-454-2(0))*; (Illus.). 32p. pap. 7.95 *(978-1-58979-455-9(9))* Taylor Trade Publishing.

Holmes, Katherine L. The Wide Awake Loons. 2013. 188p. pap. 9.95 *(978-1-938083-18-1(0))* Black Forge.

Lloyd, Jennifer & Wakelin, Kirsti Anne. Looking for Loons. 2007. (ENG., Illus.). 32p. (J). (gr. -1-3). 16.95 *(978-1-894965-54-5(X))* Simply Read Bks. CAN. Dist: Ingram Publisher Services.

Lowe, Tom. Louie the Loon & the Moon. Leadlove, Ben, illus. 2011. 28p. pap. 11.00 *(978-1-61170-030-5(2))* Robertson Publishing.

Trottier, Maxine. Loon Rock. Sylliboy, Helen, tr. Christmas, Dozay, illus. (ENG.). 22p. (J). (gr. k-2). pap. *(978-0-920336-84-7(1))* Cape Breton Univ. Pr.

LORD'S DAY

see Sabbath

LORD'S PRAYER

Bus, Sabrina. Our Father. 2nd ed. 2006. (ENG., Illus.). 12p. (J). (gr. -1). bds. 8.00 *(978-0-8028-5313-4(7)*, Eerdmans Bks For Young Readers) Eerdmans, William B. Publishing Co.

David C. Cook Publishing Company Staff. The Lord's Prayer. 2008. (Pencil Fun Bks). 16p. (J). pap. 9.90 *(978-0-7814-4901-4(4))* Cook, David C.

Ladwig, Tim. The Lord's Prayer. 2004. (ENG., Illus.). 32p. pap. 8.50 *(978-0-8028-5238-0(6))* Eerdmans, William B. Publishing Co.

Ladwig, Tim, illus. The Lord's Prayer. 2004. 32p. (J). (gr. -1-3). 17.00 *(978-0-8028-5180-2(0))* Eerdmans, William B. Publishing Co.

Lloyd-Jones, Sally & Jago. Loved: The Lord's Prayer, 1 vol. 2018. (Jesus Storybook Bible Ser.). (ENG., Illus.). 20p. (J). bds. 10.99 *(978-0-310-75761-0(4))* Zonderkidz.

M. A. Benjamin. When I Pray: The Lord's Prayer. 2009. (ENG.). 24p. pap. 9.99 *(978-1-4389-6317-4(3))* AuthorHouse.

Oberthür, Rainer. Our Father. Nascimbeni, Barbara, illus. 2016. (ENG.). 58p. (J). 16.00 *(978-0-8028-5468-1(0)*, Eerdmans Bks For Young Readers) Eerdmans, William B. Publishing Co.

Stella, Gloria & Price, Hannah. The Lord's Prayer for Kids. Shoaf, Eva, illus. 2020. (ENG.). 16p. (gr. -1-3). bds. 14.99 *(978-1-7339305-1-2(5))* Edifi Publishing LLC.

Walker, Joni. Follow & Do Books: The Lord's Prayer. Walker, Joni, illus. 2004. (Follow & Do Ser.). (Illus.). 32p. (J). 7.49 *(978-0-7586-0678-5(8))* Concordia Publishing Hse.

Warner Press, creator. Learning the Lord's Prayer: Coloring & Activity Book. 2008. (J). (gr. -1-3). pap. 11.34 *(978-1-59317-323-4(7))* Warner Pr., Inc.

LOS ANGELES (CALIF.)

Andrade, Mary J. Uarhiri sapirhatiecheri Jukambekua: La velacion de los Angelitos. Murguia, Jose J., illus. Andrade, Mary J., photos by. 2005. Orig. Title: The Vigil of the Little Angels. 40p. (J). (gr. 3-6). pap. 9.95 *(978-0-9665876-8-5(5))* La Oferta Publishing Co.

Barber, Nicola. Los Angeles. 2007. (Global Cities Ser.). (ENG., Illus.). 64p. (gr. 5-8). lib. bdg. 30.00 *(978-0-7910-8847-0(2)*, P114459, Facts On File) Infobase Holdings, Inc.

Cohen, Judith L. & Friend, Robyn. Los Angeles' Water Future. Katz, David A., illus. 2015. 40p. (J). pap. 7.00 *(978-1-935999-11-9(7))* Cascade Pass, Inc.

Crewe, Sabrina. Los Angeles, 1 vol. 2004. (Great Cities of the World Ser.). (ENG., Illus.). 48p. (gr. 5-8). lib. bdg. 33.67 *(978-0-8368-5029-1(7)*, d8e11102-4eca-4f27-8471-19ff87f9482, Gareth Stevens Secondary Library) Stevens, Gareth Publishing LLLP.

Epstein, Brad M. Los Angeles 101: My First City-Board-book. I.t. ed. 2009. (Illus.). 24p. (J). *(978-1-60730-002-1(8)*, 101 Bk.) Michaelson Entertainment.

Erlic, Lily. Los Angeles. 2017. (Illus.). 24p. (J). *(978-1-4896-7303-9(2)*, AV2 by Weigl) Weigl Pubs., Inc.

Flatt, Lizann. Life in a Suburban City. 2010. (Learn about Urban Life Ser.). (ENG., Illus.). 32p. (J). (gr. 3-6). lib. bdg. *(978-0-7787-7394-8(9))*; (gr. 4-9). pap. *(978-0-7787-7404-4(X))* Crabtree Publishing Co.

Friend, Robyn C. & Cohen, Judith Love. A Cleaner Port; A Brighter Future: The Greening of the Port of Los Angeles.

JKL

Katz, David Arthur, illus. 2011. 46p. (J). 13.95 *(978-1-935999-01-0(X))*; pap. 7.00 *(978-1-935999-00-3(1))* Cascade Pass, Inc.
Grabowski, John F. Alton Brown. 2012. (J). *(978-1-61900-007-0(5))* Eldorado Ink.
Kelley, K. C. Los Angeles Lakers. 2019. (Insider's Guide to Pro Basketball Ser.). (ENG.). 32p. (J). (gr. 1-4). lib. bdg. 35.64 *(978-1-5038-2462-1(4)*, 212269) Child's World, Inc, The.
MacMillan, Dianne M. Los Angeles Area Missions. 2007. (Exploring California Missions Ser.). (Illus.). 64p. (J). lib. bdg. 27.93 *(978-0-8225-0898-4(2)*, Lerner Pubns.) Lerner Publishing Group.
Markovics, Joyce L. Los Angeles. 2017. (Citified! Ser.). (ENG., Illus.). 24p. (J). (gr. k-3). 17.95 *(978-1-68402-231-1(2))* Bearport Publishing Co., Inc.
Ogintz, Eileen. Los Angeles County - Kid's Guide. 2013. (Kid's Guides Ser.). (ENG., Illus.). 160p. (J). (gr. 4-6). pap. 12.95 *(978-0-7627-9218-4(3))* Globe Pequot Pr., The.
Parhad, Elisa. Los Angeles Is ... Vidal, Alexander, illus. 2018. (ENG.). 24p. (J). (gr. -1 — 1). bds. 12.95 *(978-1-944903-23-7(2)*, 1313310, Cameron Kids) Cameron + Co.
Polsky, Cheryl. Libby & Her Friends Explore Los Angeles, Californi. 2012. 28p. pap. 17.99 *(978-1-4772-2125-9(5))* AuthorHouse.
Skewes, John & Mullin, Michael. Larry Gets Lost in Los Angeles. Skewes, John, illus. 2009. (Larry Gets Lost Ser.). (ENG., Illus.). 32p. (J). (gr. -1-2). 17.99 *(978-1-57061-568-9(3)*, Little Bigfoot) Sasquatch Bks.
When Los Angeles Was Very Young 1849-1866. 2005. (YA). *(978-1-59872-140-9(2))* Instant Pub.
Zimmerman, Bill. City Doodles: Los Angeles. 1 vol. 2013. (ENG., Illus.). 240p. (J). pap. 9.99 *(978-1-4236-3470-6(5))* Gibbs Smith, Publisher.

LOS ANGELES (CALIF.)—FICTION

Anderson, Dwayne. Partially Human. 2006. (YA). per. 12.00 *(978-0-9788612-0-9(5))* Capri Publishing.
Anderson, Laurie Halse. Acting Out. 14 vols. 2012. (Vet Volunteers Ser.: 14). (ENG.). 144p. (J). (gr. 3-7). pap. 7.99 *(978-0-14-241676-1(2)*, Puffin Books) Penguin Young Readers Group.
Arcos, Carrie. There Will Come a Time. 2014. (ENG., Illus.). 320p. (YA). (gr. 9). 17.99 *(978-1-4424-9585-2(5)*, Simon Pulse) Simon Pulse.
Arnold, Elana K. Infandous. 2015. (ENG.). 200p. (YA). (gr. 8-12). 18.99 *(978-1-4677-3849-1(2)*, 5f116506-df41-46d9-aaec-833557c7c676, Carolrhoda Lab™) Lerner Publishing Group.
Barrett, Michellene. Englisha & David's Adventurous Vacation. 2009. 86p. (gr. 3-3). pap. 9.95 *(978-1-4401-2319-1(5))* iUniverse, Inc.
Barrows, Annie. Nothing. 2018. (ENG.). 240p. (YA). (gr. 9). pap. 9.99 *(978-0-06-266824-0(2)*, Greenwillow Bks.) HarperCollins Pubs.
Bell, Taryn. In the Spotlight. 2010. (ENG.). 256p. pap. 8.99 *(978-0-545-21444-5(0))* Scholastic, Inc.
Bencastro, Mario. A Promise to Keep. Giersbach-Rascon, Susan, tr. from SPA. 2005. 134p. (J). (gr. 3-7). pap. 9.95 *(978-1-55885-457-4(6)*, Piñata Books) Arte Publico Pr.
Block, Francesca Lia. Dangerous Angels: Five Weetzie Bat Books. 2010. (Weetzie Bat Ser.). (ENG.). 496p. (YA). (gr. 9). pap. 9.99 *(978-0-06-200740-7(8)*, HarperTeen) HarperCollins Pubs.
—Wasteland. 2003. (Illus.). 160p. (YA). 16.89 *(978-0-06-028645-3(8)*, Cotler, Joanna Books) HarperCollins Pubs.
—Weetzie Bat. 2004. (Weetzie Bat Ser.: 1). (ENG.). 128p. (YA). (gr. 9). pap. 11.99 *(978-0-06-073625-5(9)*, HarperTeen) HarperCollins Pubs.
Bowler, Michael J. Children of the Knight. 2016. (ENG., Illus.). (J). 29.99 *(978-1-63477-952-4(5))* 2013. 344p. pap. 17.99 *(978-1-62380-655-2(0))* Dreamspinner Pr. (Harmony Ink Pr.).
Brian, Kate, pseud. The Princess & the Pauper. 2004. 266p. (J). (gr. 5-9). 14.65 *(978-0-7569-3531-3(8))* Perfection Learning Corp.
—The Princess & the Pauper. 2004. (ENG., Illus.). 272p. (YA). reprint ed. mass mkt. 6.99 *(978-0-689-87042-2(6)*, Simon Pulse) Simon Pulse.
Brightwood, Laura, illus. Growing up in East L. A. Brightwood, Laura. . 2006. (J). *(978-0-9779290-8-5(6))* 3-C Institute for Social Development.
Buxbaum, Julie. Tell Me Three Things. 2017. (ENG.). 352p. (YA). (gr. 7). pap. 11.99 *(978-0-553-53567-9(6)*, Ember) Random Hse. Children's Bks.
Byng, Georgia. Molly Moon Stops the World. (Illus.). (J). 2004. 384p. 16.99 *(978-0-06-051410-5(8))* 2005. (Molly Moon Ser.: 2). (ENG.). 416p. (gr. 3-7). reprint ed. pap. 7.99 *(978-0-06-051415-0(9)*, HarperCollins) HarperCollins Pubs.
Calonita, Jen. There's No Place Like Home. 2011. (Secrets of My Hollywood Life Ser.: 6). (ENG.). 400p. (YA). (gr. 7-17). pap. 19.99 *(978-0-316-04555-1(1)*, Poppy) Little, Brown Bks. for Young Readers.
Castellucci, Cecil. Beige. (ENG., Illus.). 320p. (YA). (gr. 9). 2009. pap. 8.99 *(978-0-7636-4232-7(0))* 2007. 16.99 *(978-0-7636-3066-9(7))* Candlewick Pr.
—Boy Proof. 4 vols. 2005. (YA). 62.75 *(978-1-4193-5131-0(1))* Recorded Bks., Inc.
—Don't Cosplay with My Heart. 2018. (ENG.). 288p. (YA). (gr. 7). 17.99 *(978-1-338-12549-8(4)*, Scholastic Pr.) Scholastic, Inc.
—The Queen of Cool. 2007. (ENG., Illus.). 176p. (YA). (gr. 9-18). pap. 7.99 *(978-0-7636-3413-1(1))* Candlewick Pr.
Chapman, Brenda. Trail of Secrets: A Jennifer Bannon Mystery. 2009. (Jennifer Bannon Mystery Ser.: 4). (ENG.). 144p. (YA). (gr. 7-18). pap. 9.95 *(978-1-894917-76-6(6)*, Napoleon & Co.) Dundurn Pr. CAN. Dist: Publishers Group West (PGW).
Cheng, Jack. See You in the Cosmos. 2018. lib. bdg. 19.65 *(978-0-606-41314-5(6))* Turtleback.
Cho, John. Troublemaker. (ENG.). 224p. (J). (gr. 3-7). 2023. pap. 7.99 *(978-0-7595-5446-7(3))* 2022. 16.99 *(978-0-7595-5447-4(1))* Little, Brown Bks. for Young Readers.
Clare, Cassandra. The Dark Artifices, the Complete Collection: Lady Midnight; Lord of Shadows; Queen of Air & Darkness. 2019. (Dark Artifices Ser.). (ENG., Illus.). 2288p. (YA). (gr. 9). 74.99 *(978-1-5344-4954-1(X)*, McElderry, Margaret K. Bks.) McElderry, Margaret K. Bks.
—Lady Midnight. 2016. (Dark Artifices Ser.: 1). (ENG., Illus.). 688p. (YA). (gr. 9-12). 24.99 *(978-1-4424-6835-1(1)*, McElderry, Margaret K. Bks.) McElderry, Margaret K. Bks.
—Lady Midnight. 2017. lib. bdg. 26.95 *(978-0-606-40535-5(6))* Turtleback.
—Lord of Shadows. (YA). 2018. (Dark Artifices Ser.: 2). (ENG., Illus.). 752p. (gr. 9). pap. 14.99 *(978-1-4424-6841-2(6))* 2017. (Dark Artifices Ser.: 2). (ENG., Illus.). 720p. (gr. 9). 24.99 *(978-1-4424-6840-5(8))* 2017. 699p. *(978-1-5344-0617-9(4))* McElderry, Margaret K. Bks. (McElderry, Margaret K. Bks.).
—Queen of Air & Darkness. 2018. (Dark Artifices Ser.: 3). (ENG., Illus.). 912p. (YA). (gr. 9). 24.99 *(978-1-4424-6843-6(2))*; E-Book *(978-1-4424-6845-0(9))* McElderry, Margaret K. Bks. (McElderry, Margaret K. Bks.).
Cocks, Heather & Morgan, Jessica. Messy. 2013. (ENG.). 368p. (YA). (gr. 7-17). pap. 18.99 *(978-0-316-09828-1(0)*, Poppy) Little, Brown Bks. for Young Readers.
—Spoiled. 2012. (ENG.). 384p. (YA). (gr. 10-17). pap. 19.99 *(978-0-316-09827-4(2)*, Poppy) Little, Brown Bks. for Young Readers.
Cohn, Diana. ¡Sí, Se Puede!. 1 vol. Delgado, Francisco, illus. 2009.Tr. of Yes, We Can! (ENG.). 32p. (J). (gr. k-4). pap. 11.95 *(978-0-938317-89-0(X)*, 23353382, Cinco Puntos Press) Lee & Low Bks., Inc.
Coleman, Rowan. Ruby Parker: Shooting Star. 2011. (ENG.). 256p. (gr. 6-9). pap. 9.99 *(978-0-00-725812-3(7)*, HarperCollins Children's Bks.) HarperCollins Pubs. Ltd. GBR. Dist: HarperCollins Pubs.
Conrad, Lauren. The Fame Game. 2012. (YA). (Fame Game Ser.: 1). (ENG.). 336p. (gr. 9). pap. 10.99 *(978-0-06-207519-2(5)*, HarperCollins); 313p. 12.99 *(978-0-06-209271-7(5))* HarperCollins Pubs.
—Infamous. 2013. 277p. (J). 12.00 *(978-0-06-224756-8(5))* HarperCollins Pubs.
—L. A. Candy. (L. A. Candy Ser.: 1). (ENG.). (YA). (gr. 9-18). 2010. 352p. pap. 9.99 *(978-0-06-176759-3(X))* 2009. 336p. 17.99 *(978-0-06-176758-6(1))* HarperCollins Pubs. (HarperCollins).
—Sugar & Spice. (L. A. Candy Ser.: 3). (ENG.). 288p. (YA). (gr. 9). 2011. pap. 9.99 *(978-0-06-176763-0(8))* 2010. 17.99 *(978-0-06-176762-3(X))* HarperCollins Pubs. (HarperCollins).
—Sweet Little Lies. 2010. (L. A. Candy Ser.: 2). (YA). (ENG.). 336p. (gr. 9). pap. 9.99 *(978-0-06-176761-6(1)*, HarperCollins); 309p. 9.99 *(978-0-06-198572-0(4))* HarperCollins Pubs.
Currier, Katrina Saltonstall. Kai's Journey to Gold Mountain: An Angel Island Story. 2004. 40p. 16.95 *(978-0-9667352-7-7(7))*; (Illus.). 44p. (J). pap. 10.95 *(978-0-9667352-4-6(2))* Angel Island Assoc.
Cushman, Karen. The Loud Silence of Francine Green. 2019. (ENG.). 240p. (J). (gr. 5-7). pap. 9.99 *(978-1-328-49799-4(2)*, 1717855, Clarion Bks.) HarperCollins Pubs.
—The Loud Silence of Francine Green. 2008. (ENG.). 240p. (YA). (gr. 6-8). 21.19 *(978-0-375-84117-0(2))* Random House Publishing Group.
Daswani, Kavita. Lovetorn. 2012. (ENG.). 256p. (YA). (gr. 8). 17.99 *(978-0-06-167311-5(0)*, HarperTeen) HarperCollins Pubs.
De la Cruz, Melissa. Angels on Sunset Boulevard. 2008. (Angels on Sunset Boulevard Ser.: Bk. 1). (ENG.). 240p. (YA). (gr. 9-18). pap. 8.99 *(978-1-4169-3991-7(1)*, Simon & Schuster Bks. For Young Readers) Simon & Schuster Bks. For Young Readers.
de la Peña, Matt. Ball Don't Lie. 2007. (ENG.). 304p. (YA). (gr. 9-12). pap. 12.99 *(978-0-385-73425-7(5)*, Ember) Random Hse. Children's Bks.
Del Rio, Adam. Teo in Palo Verde/Teo en Palo Verde. Ill, Noel, illus. 2008. (ENG & SPA.). 32p. (J). (gr. k-3). pap. 8.95 *(978-1-60448-001-6(7))* Lectura Bks.
Divine, L. The Fight. 2008. (Drama High Ser.: Vol. 1). 202p. (gr. 8-12). 19.95 *(978-0-7569-8830-2(6))* Perfection Learning Corp.
—Hustlin' 2009. (Drama High Ser.: 7). lib. bdg. 26.95 *(978-0-606-00156-4(5))* Turtleback.
Dixon, Franklin. Top Ten Ways to Die. 2006. 169p. (J). lib. bdg. 16.92 *(978-1-4242-0390-1(2))* Fitzgerald Bks.
Dumas Lachtman, Ofelia. Looking for la Unica. 2004. (ENG & SPA., Illus.). 190p. (J). pap. 9.95 *(978-1-55885-412-3(6)*, Piñata Books) Arte Publico Pr.
Engle, Margarita. Jazz Owls: A Novel of the Zoot Suit Riots. Gutierrez, Rudy, illus. 2018. (ENG.). 192p. (YA). (gr. 7). 17.99 *(978-1-5344-0943-9(2))* Simon & Schuster Children's Publishing.
Fleischman, Paul. Breakout. 2003. (ENG.). 160p. (J). 15.95 *(978-0-8126-2696-4(6))* Cricket Bks.
—Breakout. 2005. (ENG.). 144p. (YA). (gr. 7). reprint ed. pap. 6.99 *(978-0-689-87189-4(9)*, Simon Pulse) Simon Pulse.
Fowler, Elle & Fowler, Blair. Beneath the Glitter. 2013. (Sophia & Ava London Ser.: 1). (ENG.). 288p. (YA). (gr. 7). pap. 18.99 *(978-1-250-01715-4(7)*, 900081688, St. Martin's Griffin) St. Martin's Pr.
—Where Beauty Lies: A Beneath the Glitter Novel. 2014. (Sophia & Ava London Ser.: 2). (ENG.). 272p. (YA). (gr. 7). pap. 22.99 *(978-1-250-01714-7(9)*, 900081691, St. Martin's Griffin) St. Martin's Pr.
Francis, Pauline, retold by. The Mark of Zorro. 2010. (Essential Classics - Adventure Ser.). (Illus.). 48p. pap. *(978-0-237-54093-7(2))* Evans Brothers, Ltd.
Gamble, Adam. Good Night Los Angeles. Kelly, Cooper, illus. 2007. (Good Night Our World Ser.). (ENG.). 20p. (J). (gr. k — 1). bds. 9.95 *(978-1-60219-009-2(7))* Good Night Bks.
Garfinkle, D. L. Stuck in the 70's. 2007. 182p. (YA). *(978-1-4287-4661-9(7))* Penguin Publishing Group.
Golden, Christopher. Runaways. 2018. *(978-1-368-00135-9(1)*, Marvel Pr.) Disney Publishing Worldwide.
Green, D. L. Being a Punch Line Is No Joke: A 4D Book. Rosa, Leandra La, illus. 2018. (Funny Girl Ser.). (ENG.). 112p. (J). (gr. 3-5). lib. bdg. 26.65 *(978-1-4965-6469-6(3)*, 138378, Stone Arch Bks.) Capstone.
—Good Deeds & Other Laughing Matters: A 4D Book. Rosa, Leandra La, illus. 2018. (Funny Girl Ser.). (ENG.). 112p. (J). (gr. 3-5). lib. bdg. 26.65 *(978-1-4965-6470-2(7)*, 138379, Stone Arch Bks.) Capstone.
—Making Friends & Horsing Around: A 4D Book. Rosa, Leandra La, illus. 2018. (Funny Girl Ser.). (ENG.). 112p. (J). (gr. 3-5). lib. bdg. 26.65 *(978-1-4965-6467-2(7)*, 138376, Stone Arch Bks.) Capstone.
—Something Smells Funny at the Talent Show: A 4D Book. Rosa, Leandra La, illus. 2018. (Funny Girl Ser.). (ENG.). 112p. (J). (gr. 3-5). pap. 7.95 *(978-1-4965-6472-6(3)*, 138381, Stone Arch Bks.) Capstone.
Green, Tim. Pinch Hit. (ENG.). (J). (gr. 3-7). 2013. 336p. pap. 9.99 *(978-0-06-201247-0(9))* 2012. 320p. 16.99 *(978-0-06-201246-3(0))* HarperCollins Pubs. (HarperCollins).
Hammonds Reed, Christina. The Black Kids. (ENG.). (YA). (gr. 9). 2022. 400p. pap. 12.99 *(978-1-5344-6273-1(2))* 2020. (Illus.). 368p. 19.99 *(978-1-5344-6272-4(4))* Simon & Schuster Bks. For Young Readers. (Simon & Schuster Bks. For Young Readers).
Haugaard, Kay. No Place. 2nd ed. 2007. (ENG., Illus.). 140p. (J). (gr. 2-8). per. 6.95 *(978-1-57131-675-2(2))* Milkweed Editions.
Hennessey, M. G. The Echo Park Castaways. 2019. (ENG.). 208p. (J). (gr. 3-7). 16.99 *(978-0-06-242769-4(5)*, HarperCollins) HarperCollins Pubs.
Howland, Leila. Hello, Sunshine. 2018. (ENG.). 368p. (YA). (gr. 9-17). pap. 9.99 *(978-1-4847-2850-5(5))* Hyperion Bks. for Children.
Jacobs, Lily. The Littlest Bunny in Los Angeles: An Easter Adventure. Dunn, Robert, illus. 2015. (Littlest Bunny Ser.). (ENG.). 32p. (J). (gr. -1-3). 9.99 *(978-1-4926-1102-8(6)*, Hometown World) Sourcebooks, Inc.
James, Eric. Santa's Sleigh Is on Its Way to Los Angeles: A Christmas Adventure. Dunn, Robert, illus. 2016. (Santa's Sleigh Is on Its Way Ser.). (ENG.). 32p. (J). (gr. k-2). 12.99 *(978-1-4926-4333-3(5)*, 9781492643333, Hometown World) Sourcebooks, Inc.
—The Spooky Express Los Angeles. Piwowarski, Marcin, illus. 2017. (Spooky Express Ser.). (ENG.). 32p. (J). (gr. k-6). 9.99 *(978-1-4926-5366-0(7)*, Hometown World) Sourcebooks, Inc.
—Tiny the Los Angeles Easter Bunny. 2018. (Tiny the Easter Bunny Ser.). (ENG.). 40p. (J). (gr. k-3). 9.99 *(978-1-4926-5932-7(0)*, Hometown World) Sourcebooks, Inc.
Johnston, Tony. Any Small Goodness: a Novel of the Barrio. ón, Raúl, illus. 2003. (ENG.). 128p. (J). (gr. 2-5). pap. 6.99 *(978-0-439-23384-2(4))* Scholastic, Inc.
Kaplan, Isabel. Hancock Park. 2010. (ENG.). 272p. (YA). (gr. 9). pap. 8.99 *(978-0-06-137370-1(2)*, HarperTeen) HarperCollins Pubs.
Kelly, David A. Ballpark Mysteries #3: the L. A. Dodger. Meyers, Mark, illus. 2011. (Ballpark Mysteries Ser.: 3). (ENG.). 112p. (J). (gr. 1-4). 6.99 *(978-0-375-86885-6(2)*, Random Hse. Bks. for Young Readers) Random Hse. Children's Bks.
Klingele, Lindsey. The Broken World. (ENG.). (YA). (gr. 8). 2018. 448p. pap. 9.99 *(978-0-06-238037-1(0))* 2017. 432p. 17.99 *(978-0-06-238036-4(2))* HarperCollins Pubs. (HarperTeen).
Kogler, Jennifer Anne. Ruby Tuesday. 2005. (ENG.). 320p. (J). (gr. 7-18). 15.99 *(978-0-06-073956-0(8))* HarperCollins Pubs.
LaZebnik, Claire. Epic Fail. 2011. (ENG.). 304p. (YA). (gr. 8-18). pap. 9.99 *(978-0-06-192126-1(2)*, HarperTeen) HarperCollins Pubs.
Leray, Merrill. The Kidnapping. 2009. 58p. pap. 15.99 *(978-1-4415-4380-6(5))* Xlibris Corp.
Lisbon, Zara. Fake Plastic Girl. 2020. (ENG.). 304p. (YA). pap. 10.99 *(978-1-250-23371-4(2)*, 900184880) Square Fish.
Lopresti, Kirsten. Bright Coin Moon: A Novel. 2014. (ENG.). 272p. (J). (gr. 6-6). 16.95 *(978-1-62914-751-2(6)*, Sky Pony Pr.) Skyhorse Publishing Co., Inc.
Markel, Michelle. Dream Town. Reese, Rick, illus. 2006. (J). 15.95 *(978-1-59714-022-5(8))* Heyday.
Matas, Carol. Rosie in Los Angeles: Action! 2004. (ENG., Illus.). 128p. (J). (gr. 4-7). pap. 9.95 *(978-0-689-85716-4(0)*, Simon & Schuster/Paula Wiseman Bks.) Simon & Schuster/Paula Wiseman Bks.
McCoy, Mary. I, Claudia. 2018. (ENG.). 424p. (YA). (gr. 8-12). 18.99 *(978-1-5124-4846-7(X)*, b20fa032-6e7b-4832-b19e-6ba725ea062f, Carolrhoda Lab™) Lerner Publishing Group.
Miklowitz, Gloria D. The Enemy Has a Face. 2004. (ENG.). 143p. (YA). pap. 8.00 *(978-0-8028-5261-8(0))* Eerdmans, William B. Publishing Co.
Mitchell, Saundra. The Elementals. 2014. (ENG.). 304p. (YA). (gr. 7). pap. 16.99 *(978-0-544-30239-6(7)*, 1578442, Clarion Bks.) HarperCollins Pubs.
Noel, Alyson. Infamous. 2018. (ENG.). 432p. (YA). (Beautiful Idols Ser.: 3). (gr. 9). 17.99 *(978-0-06-232458-0(6))*; *(978-0-06-279645-5(3))* HarperCollins Pubs. (Tegen, Katherine Bks).
—Unrivaled. 2017. (Beautiful Idols Ser.: 1). (ENG.). 448p. (YA). (gr. 9). pap. 9.99 *(978-0-06-232453-5(5)*, Tegen, Katherine Bks) HarperCollins Pubs.
Oliver, Lin. Secret of the Super-Small Superstar. Gilpin, Stephen, illus. 2010. (Who Shrunk Daniel Funk? Ser.: 4). (ENG.). 160p. (J). (gr. 3-7). 14.99 *(978-1-4169-0963-7(X)*, Simon & Schuster Bks. For Young Readers) Simon & Schuster Bks. For Young Readers.
Paige, D. M. Size 0. 2013. (Opportunity Ser.). (ENG.). 120p. (YA). (gr. 6-12). pap. 7.95 *(978-1-4677-1497-6(6)*, 188ba29c-766a-4d6e-bc31-397dcd589ebe); lib. bdg. 27.99 *(978-1-4677-1372-6(4)*, 3965d843-cd43-4ac0-b97f-208bace4842e) Lerner Publishing Group. (Darby Creek).
Palund, Linda. The Little Black Dress. 2016. (ENG., Illus.). (J). 24.99 *(978-1-63477-970-8(3)*, Harmony Ink Pr.) Dreamspinner Pr.
Pinkwater, Daniel M. The Neddiad: How Neddie Took the Train, Went to Hollywood, & SavedCivilization. 2009. (ENG., Illus.). 320p. (J). (gr. 5-7). pap. 8.99 *(978-0-547-13367-6(7)*, 1048766, Clarion Bks.) HarperCollins Pubs.
—The Yggyssey: How Iggy Wondered What Happened to All the Ghosts, Found Out Where They Went, & Went There. Brown, Calef, illus. 2009. (ENG.). 256p. (J). (gr. 4-6). 18.69 *(978-0-618-59445-0(0))* Houghton Mifflin Harcourt Publishing Co.
Powell, Marie & Norton, Jeff. Keeping the Beat. 2017. (ENG.). 368p. (YA). (gr. 8-17). 17.95 *(978-1-77138-730-9(0))* Kids Can Pr., Ltd. CAN. Dist: Hachette Bk. Group.
Rabin, Staton. Black Powder. 2005. (ENG.). 256p. (YA). (gr. 7-9). 16.95 *(978-0-689-86876-4(6)*, McElderry, Margaret K. Bks.) McElderry, Margaret K. Bks.
Resnicoff, Stan. The BIG Parade: Los Angeles. 2012. (ENG.). (J). pap. *(978-1-4675-1540-5(X))* Independent Pub.
Rice, M. L. Who I Am. 2011. (ENG.). 264p. (J). (gr. 7). pap. 13.95 *(978-1-60282-231-3(X))* Bold Strokes Bks.
Richards, Linda L. Death Was in the Blood. 2013. (ENG.). 332p. 25.95 *(978-1-4328-2716-8(2)*, Five Star Trade) Cengage Gale.
Rigby, Robert. Goal! The Dream Begins. 2006. (ENG., Illus.). 240p. (YA). (gr. 7-9). pap. 7.99 *(978-0-15-205798-5(6)*, 1197425, Clarion Bks.) HarperCollins Pubs.
Roberts, Tina. Dream Watchman: Quest for the Missing Talisman Book I. 2011. 244p. pap. 15.95 *(978-1-60976-636-8(9)*, Eloquent Bks.) Strategic Book Publishing & Rights Agency (SBPRA).
Ryan, Jessica. The Mystery of Arroyo Seco. Stone, David, illus. 2011. 186p. 42.95 *(978-1-258-08470-7(8))* Literary Licensing, LLC.
Salin-Pascual, Rafael. El espectro del seÑor Amok. 2008. 151p. pap. 20.49 *(978-1-4357-4508-7(6))* Lulu Pr., Inc.
Schraff, Anne. Leap of Faith. 1 vol. unabr. ed. 2011. (Urban Underground Ser.). (ENG.). 201p. (YA). (gr. 9-12). pap. 11.95 *(978-1-61651-588-1(0))* Saddleback Educational Publishing, Inc.
—The Lost. 1 vol. unabr. ed. 2011. (Urban Underground Ser.). (ENG.). 198p. (YA). (gr. 9-12). pap. 11.95 *(978-1-61651-585-0(6))* Saddleback Educational Publishing, Inc.
—The Unforgiven. 1 vol. unabr. ed. 2011. (Urban Underground Ser.). (ENG.). 198p. (YA). (gr. 9-12). pap. 11.95 *(978-1-61651-586-7(4))* Saddleback Educational Publishing, Inc.
—The Water's Edge. unabr. ed. 2011. (Urban Underground Ser.). (ENG.). 197p. (YA). (gr. 9-12). pap. 11.95 *(978-1-61651-589-8(9))* Saddleback Educational Publishing, Inc.
Schraff, Anne E. Deliverance. 1 vol. unabr. ed. 2011. (Urban Underground Ser.). (ENG.). 198p. (YA). (gr. 9-12). pap. 11.95 *(978-1-61651-587-4(2))* Saddleback Educational Publishing, Inc.
—Second Chances. 2013. (Urban Underground — Harriet Tubman High School Ser.). (YA). lib. bdg. 20.80 *(978-0-606-31584-5(5))* Turtleback.
Scieszka, Jon. Kat's Mystery Gift: Ready-To-Read Level 1. Shannon, David et al, illus. 2013. (Jon Scieszka's Trucktown Ser.). (ENG.). 24p. (J). (gr. -1-1). 17.99 *(978-1-4814-1459-3(3)*, Simon Spotlight) Simon Spotlight.
Shreve, Susan. The Search for Baby Ruby. 2015. 213p. (J). pap. *(978-0-545-41784-6(8))* Scholastic, Inc.
Smith Jr., Charles R. Chameleon. 2010. (ENG., Illus.). 384p. (YA). (gr. 7). pap. 7.99 *(978-0-7636-4660-8(1))* Candlewick Pr.
Somtow, S. P. The Wizard's Apprentice. 2018. (ENG., Illus.). 144p. (YA). (gr. 7). pap. 13.00 *(978-1-940999-28-9(6))*; pap. 13.00 *(978-1-940999-27-2(8))* Diplodocus Pr.
Sones, Sonya. One of Those Hideous Books Where the Mother Dies. (ENG.). (YA). (gr. 7). 2013. Illus.). 288p. pap. 12.99 *(978-1-4424-9383-4(6))* 2005. 272p. reprint ed. pap. 7.99 *(978-1-4169-0788-6(2))* Simon & Schuster Bks. For Young Readers. (Simon & Schuster Bks. For Young Readers).
Soto, Gary. Chato & the Party Animals. Guevara, Susan, illus. (Chato Ser.). 25.95 incl. audio *(978-1-59112-460-3(3))*; 28.95 incl. audio compact disk *(978-1-59112-920-2(6))*; pap. 39.95 incl. audio compact disk *(978-1-59112-921-9(4))*; pap. 37.95 incl. audio *(978-1-59112-461-0(1))* Live Oak Media.
—Chato & the Party Animals. Guevara, Susan, illus. 2004. 32p. (J). (gr. -1-3). reprint ed. pap. 8.99 *(978-0-14-240032-6(7)*, Puffin Books) Penguin Young Readers Group.
—Chato & the Party Animals. Guevara, Susan, illus. 2004. (Chato Ser.). (gr. -1-3). 17.00 *(978-0-7569-2921-3(0))* Perfection Learning Corp.
—Chato y Los Amigos Pachangueros. Guevara, Susan, illus. 2004. 32p. (J). (gr. -1-3). reprint ed. pap. 8.99 *(978-0-14-240033-3(5)*, Puffin Books) Penguin Young Readers Group.
—Chato's Kitchen. Guevara, Susan, illus. 2003. (Chato Ser.). (J). (gr. -1-2). pap. 39.95 *(978-1-59112-527-3(8))* Live Oak Media.
Spieller, Lauren. She's the Worst. 2020. (ENG.). 288p. (YA). (gr. 9). pap. 12.99 *(978-1-5344-3659-6(6)*, Simon & Schuster Bks. For Young Readers) Simon & Schuster Bks. For Young Readers.
Stampler, Ann Redisch. Afterparty. 2013. (ENG., Illus.). 416p. (YA). (gr. 9). 17.99 *(978-1-4424-2324-4(2)*, Simon Pulse) Simon Pulse.
—Where It Began. 2013. (ENG.). 384p. (YA). (gr. 7-12). 26.19 *(978-1-4424-2321-3(8))*; (gr. 9). pap. 9.99 *(978-1-4424-2322-0(6))* Simon Pulse. (Simon Pulse).
Sully, Katherine. Night-Night Los Angeles. Poole, Helen, illus. 2017. (Night-Night Ser.). (ENG.). 20p. (J). (gr. -1-1). bds. 9.99 *(978-1-4926-5491-9(4)*, Hometown World) Sourcebooks, Inc.
Tashjian, Janet. My Life As a Gamer. Tashjian, Jake, illus. 2018. (My Life Ser.: 5). (ENG.). 288p. (J). pap. 8.99 *(978-1-250-14368-6(3)*, 900180543) Square Fish.
—My Life As a Joke. Tashjian, Jake, illus. 2014. (My Life Ser.: 4). (ENG.). 272p. (J). (gr. 4-7). 15.99 *(978-0-8050-9850-1(X)*, 900122324, Holt, Henry & Co. Bks. For Young Readers) Holt, Henry & Co.
—My Life As a Meme. Tashjian, Jake, illus. 2019. (My Life Ser.: 8). (ENG.). 256p. (J). 13.99 *(978-1-250-19657-6(4)*, 900194128, Holt, Henry & Co. Bks. For Young Readers) Holt, Henry & Co.
—My Life As a Stuntboy. Tashjian, Jake, illus. 2015. (My Life Ser.: 2). (ENG.). 288p. (J). (gr. 4-7). pap. 8.99 *(978-1-250-01038-4(1)*, 900084784) Square Fish.
Thomas, Jacquelin. Split Ends. 2010. (ENG.). 231p. pap. 17.99 *(978-1-4165-9879-4(0))* Pocket Books.

Toon, Paige. The Accidental Life of Jessie Jefferson. 2016. (Jessie Jefferson Novels Ser.: 1). (ENG.). 336p. (J). pap. 9.99 *(978-1-4711-4582-7(4)*, Simon & Schuster Children's) Simon & Schuster, Ltd. GBR. Dist: Simon & Schuster, Inc.
Trine, Greg. Attack of the Valley Girls, 6. Montijo, Rhode, illus. 6th ed. 2008. (Melvin Beederman, Superhero Ser.: 6). (ENG.). 137p. (J). (gr. 2-4). 22.44 *(978-0-8050-8160-2(7)*, Holt, Henry & Co.) Holt, Henry & Co.
—Attack of the Valley Girls (6) Montijo, Rhode, illus. 6th ed. 2008. (Melvin Beederman, Superhero Ser.: 6). (ENG.). 144p. (J). (gr. 2-5). pap. 9.99 *(978-0-8050-8161-9(5)*, 900040235) Square Fish.
—The Brotherhood of the Traveling Underpants. 2009. (Melvin Beederman Superhero Ser.: 7). (J). lib. bdg. 19.65 *(978-0-606-01751-0(8))* Turtleback.
—The Curse of the Bologna Sandwich. Montijo, Rhode, illus. 2006. (Melvin Beederman, Superhero Ser.: 1). (ENG.). 144p. (J). (gr. 2-5). pap. 8.99 *(978-0-8050-7836-7(3)*, 900030183) Square Fish.
—Fake Cape Caper, The (5) Montijo, Rhode, illus. 5th rev. ed. 2007. (Melvin Beederman, Superhero Ser.: 5). (ENG.). 144p. (J). (gr. 2-5). pap. 9.99 *(978-0-8050-8159-6(3)*, 900040230) Square Fish.
—The Grateful Fred. Montijo, Rhode, illus. 3rd rev. ed. 2006. (Melvin Beederman, Superhero Ser.: 3). (ENG.). 144p. (J). (gr. 2-5). pap. 9.99 *(978-0-8050-7922-7(X)*, 900031581) Square Fish.
—Invasion from Planet Dork. Montijo, Rhode, illus. 2010. (Melvin Beederman, Superhero Ser.: 8). (ENG.). 144p. (J). (gr. 2-7). pap. 11.99 *(978-0-8050-8167-1(4)*, 900040241) Square Fish.
—Melvin Beederman Superhero 4. Montijo, Rhode, illus. 4th rev. ed. 2007. (Melvin Beederman, Superhero Ser.: 4). (ENG.). 144p. (J). (gr. 2-5). pap. 9.99 *(978-0-8050-7924-1(6)*, 900031584) Square Fish.
Uss, Christina. The Colossus of Roads. 2020. 208p. (J). (gr. 4-7). 17.99 *(978-0-8234-4450-2(3)*, Margaret Ferguson Books) Holiday Hse., Inc.
Valdes-Rodriguez, Alisa. Haters, 8 vols. (YA). 2008. 198.75 *(978-1-4281-2205-5(2))* 2007. 105.75 *(978-1-4281-2204-8(4))* 2007. 79.75 *(978-1-4281-2200-0(1))* 2006. 76.75 *(978-1-4281-2202-4(8))* 2006. 102.75 *(978-1-4281-2206-2(0))* 2006. 172.75 *(978-1-4281-2201-7(X))* 2006. 1.25 *(978-1-4281-2197-3(8))* Recorded Bks., Inc.
Waid, Mark. City of Incredibles, Vol. 2. Takara, Marcio, illus. 2010. (Incredibles Ser.). (ENG.). 112p. (J). 24.99 *(978-1-60886-529-1(0))* BOOM! Studios.
Wells, Dan. Active Memory. 2018. (Mirador Ser.: 3). (ENG.). 400p. (YA). (gr. 8). 17.99 *(978-0-06-234793-0(4)*, Balzer & Bray) HarperCollins Pubs.
—Bluescreen. 2017. 456p. (YA). (gr. 9-12). pap. 17.99 *(978-987-747-261-5(9))* V&R Editoras.
West, Kasie. Fame, Fate, & the First Kiss. 2019. (ENG.). (YA). (gr. 8). 400p. pap. 11.99 *(978-0-06-285100-0(4))*; 384p. 17.99 *(978-0-06-267579-8(6))* HarperCollins Pubs. (HarperTeen).
Weston Woods Staff, creator. Chato & the Party Animals. 2011. 38.75 *(978-0-439-84581-6(5))* 2011. 18.95 *(978-0-439-73984-9(5))* 2004. 29.95 *(978-1-55592-703-5(3))* Weston Woods Studios, Inc.
—Chato's Kitchen. 2004. (J). 38.75 *(978-1-55592-388-4(7))*; 18.95 *(978-1-55592-386-0(0))* Weston Woods Studios, Inc.
Woods, Brenda. Emako Blue. 2005. 128p. (YA). (gr. 7-18). 7.99 *(978-0-14-240418-8(7)*, Speak) Penguin Young Readers Group.
—Emako Blue. 2005. 124p. (gr. 7). 16.00 *(978-0-7569-5495-6(9))* Perfection Learning Corp.
Yee, Lisa. Absolutely Maybe. 2009. (ENG.). 288p. (J). (gr. 7-7). 16.99 *(978-0-439-83844-3(4)*, Levine, Arthur A. Bks.) Scholastic, Inc.

LOS ANGELES (CALIF.)—RACE RELATIONS

Gerdes, Louise I., ed. The 1992 Los Angeles Riots, 1 vol. 2014. (Perspectives on Modern World History Ser.). (ENG., Illus.). 200p. (gr. 10-12). lib. bdg. 49.43 *(978-0-7377-7008-7(2)*, a74606ef-1de6-48db-b4a3-295274e02a0d, Greenhaven Publishing) Greenhaven Publishing LLC.

LOS ANGELES ANGELS OF ANAHEIM (BASEBALL TEAM)

Bach, Greg. Mike Trout. 2020. (J). *(978-1-4222-4440-1(7))* Mason Crest.
Gilbert, Sara. Los Angeles Angels of Anaheim. 2013. (World Series Champions Ser.). (ENG., Illus.). 24p. (J). (gr. 1-4). 25.65 *(978-1-60818-265-7(7)*, 21839, Creative Education) Creative Co., The.
—The Story of the Los Angeles Angels of Anaheim. (Illus.). 48p. 2011. (J). 35.65 *(978-1-60818-044-8(1)*, Creative Education) 2007. (YA). (gr. 4-7). lib. bdg. 32.80 *(978-1-58341-477-4(0))* Creative Co., The.
Sandler, Michael. Randy Johnson & the Arizona Diamondbacks: 2001 World Series. 2008. (World Series Superstars). (Illus.). 24p. (J). (gr. 1-4). lib. bdg. 26.99 *(978-1-59716-638-6(3))* Bearport Publishing Co., Inc.
—Troy Glaus & the Anaheim Angels: 2002 World Series. 2008. (World Series Superstars). (Illus.). 24p. (J). (gr. 1-4). lib. bdg. 26.99 *(978-1-59716-640-9(5))* Bearport Publishing Co., Inc.
Stewart, Mark. The Los Angeles Angels of Anaheim. 2012. (Team Spirit Ser.). 48p. (J). (gr. 3-6). lib. bdg. 29.27 *(978-1-59953-485-5(1))* Norwood Hse. Pr.
Wilson, Bernie. Los Angeles Angels, 1 vol. 2015. (Inside MLB Ser.). (ENG., Illus.). 48p. (J). (gr. 3-6). lib. bdg. 34.21 *(978-1-62403-473-2(X)*, 17109, SportsZone) ABDO Publishing Co.

LOS ANGELES DODGERS (BASEBALL TEAM)

Frisch, Aaron. Los Angeles Dodgers. 2009. (World Series Champions Ser.). (Illus.). 23p. (J). (gr. 2-3). 24.25 *(978-1-58341-689-1(7)*, Creative Education) Creative Co., The.
Garcia, Tom & Naga, Karun. Daddy's Heroes: Gibby's Homer: the 1988 World Series. Donnelly, Jenifer, illus. 2007. (1988 World Ser.). 32p. (J). (gr. -1-3). pap. 9.95 *(978-0-9792111-0-2(7))* Daddy's Heroes, Inc.
Gilbert, Sara. Los Angeles Dodgers. 2013. (World Series Champions Ser.). (ENG.). 24p. (J). (gr. 1-4). pap. 7.99 *(978-0-89812-817-8(X)*, 21843, Creative Paperbacks); (Illus.). 25.65 *(978-1-60818-266-4(5)*, 21842, Creative Education) Creative Co., The.
Gitlin, Marty. Los Angeles Dodgers, 1 vol. 2015. (Inside MLB Ser.). (ENG., Illus.). 48p. (J). (gr. 3-6). lib. bdg. 34.21 *(978-1-62403-474-9(8)*, 17111, SportsZone) ABDO Publishing Co.
Hammer, Max. Superstars of the Los Angeles Dodgers. 2014. (Pro Sports Superstars - MLB Ser.). (ENG.). 24p. (J). (gr. 1-4). lib. bdg. 27.10 *(978-1-60753-593-5(9)*, 16009) Amicus.
Kennedy, Mike & Stewart, Mark. Meet the Dodgers. 2010. (Smart about Sports Ser.). 24p. (J). (gr. k-3). lib. bdg. 22.60 *(978-1-59953-371-1(5))* Norwood Hse. Pr.
Lajiness, Katie. Los Angeles Dodgers. 2018. (MLB's Greatest Teams Ser.). (ENG., Illus.). 32p. (J). (gr. 2-5). lib. bdg. 34.21 *(978-1-5321-1517-2(2)*, 28870, Big Buddy Bks.) ABDO Publishing Co.
LeBoutillier, Nate. The Story of the Los Angeles Dodgers. 2011. (Illus.). 48p. (J). 35.65 *(978-1-60818-045-5(X)*, Creative Education) Creative Co., The.
Nichols, John. The Story of the Los Angeles Dodgers. 2007. (Baseball, the Great American Game Ser.). (Illus.). 48p. (YA). (gr. 4-7). lib. bdg. 32.80 *(978-1-58341-491-0(6))* Creative Co., The.
Stewart, Mark. The Los Angeles Dodgers. 2012. (Team Spirit Ser.). 48p. (J). (gr. 3-6). lib. bdg. 29.27 *(978-1-59953-486-2(X))* Norwood Hse. Pr.
Winter, Jonah. You Never Heard of Sandy Koufax?! Carrilho, Andre, illus. 2016. 40p. (J). (gr. -1-3). 8.99 *(978-0-553-49842-4(8)*, Dragonfly Bks.) Random Hse. Children's Bks.

LOUIS XIV, KING OF FRANCE, 1638-1715

Mason, Anthony. Versailles, 1 vol. 2004. (Places in History Ser.). (ENG., Illus.). 48p. (gr. 5-8). lib. bdg. 33.67 *(978-0-8368-5815-0(8)*, a9cb173a-1363-442e-b942-0f91eb84c1a1, World Almanac Library) Stevens, Gareth Publishing LLLP.
Rossi, Renzo. In the Sun King's Paris with Molière, 1 vol. 2009. (Come See My City Ser.). (ENG., Illus.). 48p. (gr. 4-4). lib. bdg. 31.21 *(978-0-7614-4332-2(0)*, e70ca7d2-2035-48ae-8f7f-8e5a1e648d94) Cavendish Square Publishing LLC.
Steinberg, D. J. King Louie's Shoes. Neubecker, Robert, illus. 2017. (ENG.). 48p. (J). (gr. -1-3). 17.99 *(978-1-4814-2657-2(5)*, Beach Lane Bks.) Beach Lane Bks.
Tagliaferro, Linda. Palace of Versailles. 2018. (Castles, Palaces Tombs Ser.). (ENG.). 32p. (J). (gr. 2-7). 7.99 *(978-1-64280-065-4(1))* Bearport Publishing Co., Inc.
—Palace of Versailles: France's Royal Jewel. 2005. (Castles, Palaces, & Tombs Ser.). 32p. (J). lib. bdg. 28.50 *(978-1-59716-003-2(2))* Bearport Publishing Co., Inc.

LOUISIANA

Bernard, Shane K. Les Cadiens et Leurs Ancêtres Acadiens: L'histoire Racontée Aux Jeunes. Hillard, Faustine, tr. 2013. (FRE., Illus.). 112p. (gr. 7-12). 20.00 *(978-1-61703-779-5(6)*, 4763) Univ. Pr. of Mississippi.
Bjorklund, Ruth. Louisiana, 1 vol. Santoro, Christopher, illus. 2005. (It's My State! (First Edition)(r) Ser.). (ENG.). 80p. (gr. 4-4). lib. bdg. 34.07 *(978-0-7614-1863-4(6)*, 793379b3-5746-4c17-a57a-166a1cb8cbd4) Cavendish Square Publishing LLC.
Bjorklund, Ruth & Steinitz, Andy. Louisiana, 1 vol. 3rd rev. ed. 2014. (It's My State! (Third Edition)(r) Ser.). (ENG.). 80p. (gr. 4-4). lib. bdg. 35.93 *(978-1-62712-740-0(2)*, 931839c6-1b01-4b20-8d28-b955088bfbf0) Cavendish Square Publishing LLC.
Bridges, Ruby. Ruby Bridges Goes to School: My True Story. 2009. (Scholastic Reader, Level 2 Ser.). (ENG., Illus.). 32p. (J). (gr. -1-3). pap. 3.99 *(978-0-545-10855-3(1))* Scholastic, Inc.
Brown, Vanessa. Louisiana. 2009. (Bilingual Library of the United States of America Ser.). (ENG & SPA.). 32p. (gr. 2-2). 47.90 *(978-1-60853-363-3(8)*, Editorial Buenas Letras) Rosen Publishing Group, Inc., The.
—Louisiana/Luisiana, 1 vol. 2005. (Bilingual Library of the United States of America Ser.: Set 1). (ENG & SPA., Illus.). 32p. (J). (gr. 2-2). lib. bdg. 28.93 *(978-1-4042-3083-5(1)*, 9f736d71-92a3-42b4-ac17-fc596be7df5b) Rosen Publishing Group, Inc., The.
Deinard, Jenny. How to Draw Louisiana's Sights & Symbols. 2009. (Kid's Guide to Drawing America Ser.). 32p. (gr. k-k). 50.50 *(978-1-61511-067-4(4)*, PowerKids Pr.) Rosen Publishing Group, Inc., The.
Downing, Johnette. Louisiana, the Jewel of the Deep South, 1 vol. Marshall, Julia, illus. 2015. (ENG.). 32p. (J). (gr. k-3). 16.99 *(978-1-4556-2096-8(3)*, Pelican Publishing) Arcadia Publishing.
Heinrichs, Ann. Louisiana. Kania, Matt, illus. 2017. (U. S. A. Travel Guides). (ENG.). 40p. (J). (gr. 2-5). lib. bdg. 38.50 *(978-1-5038-1958-0(2)*, 211595) Child's World, Inc, The.
Hyde, Judith Jensen. Rookie Read-About Geography: Louisiana. 2007. (Rookie Read-About Geography Ser.). (ENG., Illus.). 32p. (J). (gr. 1-2). 20.50 *(978-0-516-21848-9(4)*, Children's Pr.) Scholastic Library Publishing.
Johnstone, Robb. Louisiana. 2011. (Guide to American States Ser.). (Illus.). 48p. (YA). (gr. 3-6). 29.99 *(978-1-61690-790-7(8))*; (J). *(978-1-61690-466-1(6))* Weigl Pubs., Inc.
Kadair, Deborah. I Spy in the Louisiana Sky, 1 vol. Kadair, Deborah, illus. 2011. (I Spy Ser.). (ENG., Illus.). 32p. (J). (gr. k-3). 16.99 *(978-1-58980-885-0(1)*, Pelican Publishing) Arcadia Publishing.
Koontz, Robin. What Was Hurricane Katrina? 2015. (What Was... Ser.). lib. bdg. 16.00 *(978-0-606-36762-2(4))* Turtleback.
LaDoux, Rita. Louisiana. 2012. (J). lib. bdg. 25.26 *(978-0-7613-4535-0(3)*, Lerner Pubns.) Lerner Publishing Group.
LaDoux, Rita C. Louisiana. 2nd rev. exp. ed. 2003. (Hello U. S. A. Ser.). (Illus.). 84p. (J). (gr. 3-6). pap. 6.95 *(978-0-8225-4145-5(9))* Lerner Publishing Group.
Lantier, Pat. Louisiana, 1 vol. 2005. (Portraits of the States Ser.). (ENG., Illus.). 32p. (gr. 3-5). pap. 11.50 *(978-0-8368-4686-7(X)*, ed5939e8-4c34-483f-87d3-b664ab63a7d9); lib. bdg. 28.67 *(978-0-8368-4667-6(2)*, 87ca374f-5dcf-4fab-93a6-efb764f28dd7) Stevens, Gareth Publishing LLLP. (Gareth Stevens Learning Library).
LeVert, Suzanne. Louisiana, 1 vol. 2nd rev. ed. 2006. (Celebrate the States (Second Edition) Ser.). (ENG., Illus.). 144p. (gr. 6-6). lib. bdg. 39.79 *(978-0-7614-2021-7(5)*, 87ff5682-b86c-4192-bee3-63f4aadfa781) Cavendish Square Publishing LLC.
Marsh, Carole. The Louisiana Coloring Book. 2004. (Louisiana Experience! Ser.). (Illus.). 32p. (J). (gr. k-2). pap. 3.95 *(978-0-7933-9551-4(8))* Gallopade International.
—Louisiana Current Events Projects: 30 Cool, Activities, Crafts, Experiments & More for Kids to Do to Learn about Your State! 2003. (Louisiana Experience Ser.). 32p. (gr. k-8). pap. 5.95 *(978-0-635-02037-6(8)*, Marsh, Carole Bks.) Gallopade International.
—The Louisiana Experience Pocket Guide. 2004. (Louisiana Experience! Ser.). (Illus.). 96p. (J). (gr. 3-8). pap. 6.95 *(978-0-7933-9546-0(1))* Gallopade International.
—Louisiana Geography Projects: 30 Cool, Activities, Crafts, Experiments & More for Kids to Do to Learn about Your State! 2003. (Louisiana Experience Ser.). 32p. (gr. k-5). pap. 5.95 *(978-0-635-01837-3(3)*, Marsh, Carole Bks.) Gallopade International.
—Louisiana Government Projects: 30 Cool, Activities, Crafts, Experiments & More for Kids to Do to Learn about Your State! 2003. (Louisiana Experience Ser.). 32p. (gr. k-5). pap. 5.95 *(978-0-635-01937-0(X)*, Marsh, Carole Bks.) Gallopade International.
—Louisiana Jeopardy. 2004. (Louisiana Experience! Ser.). (Illus.). 32p. (J). (gr. 3-8). pap. 7.95 *(978-0-7933-9548-4(8))* Gallopade International.
—Louisiana Jography. 2004. (Louisiana Experience! Ser.). (Illus.). 32p. (J). (gr. 3-8). pap. 7.95 *(978-0-7933-9549-1(6))* Gallopade International.
—Louisiana People Projects: 30 Cool, Activities, Crafts, Experiments & More for Kids to Do to Learn about Your State! 2003. (Louisiana Experience Ser.). 32p. (gr. k-5). pap. 5.95 *(978-0-635-01987-5(6)*, Marsh, Carole Bks.) Gallopade International.
—Louisiana Symbols & Facts Projects: 30 Cool, Activities, Crafts, Experiments & More for Kids to Do to Learn about Your State! 2003. (Louisiana Experience Ser.). 32p. (gr. k-5). pap. 5.95 *(978-0-635-01887-8(X)*, Marsh, Carole Bks.) Gallopade International.
—Louisiana's Big Activity Book. 2004. (Louisiana Experience! Ser.). (Illus.). 96p. (J). (gr. 2-6). pap. 9.95 *(978-0-7933-9550-7(X))* Gallopade International.
—My First Book about Louisiana. 2004. (Louisiana Experience! Ser.). (Illus.). 32p. (J). (gr. k-4). pap. 7.95 *(978-0-7933-9547-7(X))* Gallopade International.
Miller, Derek, et al. Louisiana: The Pelican State, 1 vol. 2018. (It's My State! (Fourth Edition)(r) Ser.). (ENG.). 80p. (gr. 4-4). pap. 18.64 *(978-1-5026-4444-2(4)*, 329fe6d5-93b0-4ca4-b196-e8e7b0541005) Cavendish Square Publishing LLC.
Murray, Julie. Louisiana, 1 vol. 2006. (United States Ser.). (ENG., Illus.). 32p. (gr. 2-4). 27.07 *(978-1-59197-677-6(4)*, Buddy Bks.) ABDO Publishing Co.
O'Neill, Elizabeth. Alfred Visits Louisiana. 2007. 24p. (J). pap. 12.00 *(978-0-9790240-8-5(0))* Funny Bone Bks.
Prieto, Anita C. P Is for Pelican: A Louisiana Alphabet. Knorr, Laura, illus. 2004. (Discover America State by State Ser.). (ENG.). 40p. (J). (gr. 1-3). 18.99 *(978-1-58536-137-3(2)*, 201998) Sleeping Bear Pr.
Shofner, Shawndra. Louisiana. 2008. (This Land Called America Ser.). (Illus.). 32p. (YA). (gr. 3-6). 22.95 *(978-1-58341-643-3(9))* Creative Co., The.
Zeiger, Jennifer. Louisiana (a True Book: My United States) 2017. (True Book (Relaunch) Ser.). (ENG., Illus.). 48p. (J). (gr. 3-5). pap. 7.95 *(978-0-531-23287-3(5)*, Children's Pr.) Scholastic Library Publishing.

LOUISIANA—FICTION

Albritton, Stacy Demoran. The Diary of Marie Landry, Acadian Exile, 1 vol. Haynes, Joyce, illus. 2012. (ENG.). 160p. (J). (gr. 3-7). pap. 14.95 *(978-1-58980-865-2(7)*, Pelican Publishing) Arcadia Publishing.
Backus, Nancy. A Bayou Home: The Adventure of Swampmaster Bejeaux, 1 vol. Backus, Nancy, illus. 2019. (ENG., Illus.). 108p. (gr. 3-7). 19.99 *(978-0-578-17393-1(X)*, Pelican Publishing) Arcadia Publishing.
Ball, Marcia. Christmas Fais Do-Do. 2006. (Illus.). 36p. (J). per. 14.95 *(978-1-58939-972-3(2))* Virtualbookworm.com Publishing, Inc.
Boutte, Brock. Gris-Gris & the Cypress Tree: Louisiana. 2012. (ENG.). (J). pap. 17.95 *(978-1-4675-4497-9(3))* Independent Pub.
Bradley, John Ed. Call Me by My Name. (ENG.). (YA). (gr. 7). 2015. 288p. pap. 12.99 *(978-1-4424-9794-8(7))* 2014. (Illus.). 272p. 17.99 *(978-1-4424-9793-1(9)*, Atheneum Bks. for Young Readers) Simon & Schuster Children's Publishing.
Callender, Kacen. King & the Dragonflies. 2020. (ENG.). 272p. (J). pap. *(978-0-7023-0281-7(3)*, Scholastic Pr.) Scholastic, Inc.
Connelly, Neil. Into the Hurricane. 2017. (ENG.). 240p. (YA). (gr. 9). 17.99 *(978-0-545-85381-1(8)*, Levine, Arthur A. Bks.) Scholastic, Inc.
Crochet, Pat. Randolph Saves Christmas, 1 vol. Gramelspacher, Sarah, illus. 2018. (ENG.). 32p. (J). (gr. -1-3). 16.99 *(978-1-4556-2269-6(9)*, Pelican Publishing) Arcadia Publishing.
Doucet, Sharon Arms. Fiddle Fever. 2007. (ENG.). 176p. (J). (gr. 5-7). pap. 12.95 *(978-0-618-77682-5(6)*, 100543, Clarion Bks.) HarperCollins Pubs.
Downing, Johnette. Down in Louisiana, 1 vol. Kadair, Deborah Ousley, illus. 2007. (ENG.). 32p. (J). (gr. k-3). 16.99 *(978-1-58980-451-7(1)*, Pelican Publishing) Arcadia Publishing.
—Mademoiselle Grands Doigts: A Cajun New Year's Eve Tale, 1 vol. Stanley, Heather, illus. 2018. (ENG.). 32p. (gr. -1-3). 16.99 *(978-1-4556-2393-8(8)*, Pelican Publishing) Arcadia Publishing.
—Today Is Monday in Louisiana, 1 vol. Kadair, Deborah, illus. 2006. (ENG.). 32p. (J). (gr. k-k). 17.99 *(978-1-58980-406-7(6)*, Pelican Publishing) Arcadia Publishing.
Duey, Kathleen & Bale, Karen A. Swamp: Louisiana 1851. 2016. (Survivors Ser.). (ENG., Illus.). 160p. (J). (gr. 3-7). pap. 6.99 *(978-1-4814-2783-8(0)*, Aladdin) Simon & Schuster Children's Publishing.
Dunham, Terri Hoover. The Legend of Papa Noel: A Cajun Christmas Story. Knorr, Laura, illus. 2006. (Myths, Legends, Fairy & Folktales Ser.). (ENG.). 32p. (J). (gr. 2-5). 18.99 *(978-1-58536-256-1(5)*, 202072) Sleeping Bear Pr.
Elston, Ashley. The Lying Woods. (ENG.). 336p. (YA). (gr. 9-12). 2019. pap. 9.99 *(978-1-368-01591-2(3))* 2018. 17.99 *(978-1-368-01478-6(X))* Hyperion Bks. for Children.
—The Rules for Breaking. 2014. (Rules Ser.). (ENG.). 320p. (J). (gr. 7-12). 16.99 *(978-1-4231-6898-0(4))* Hyperion Bks. for Children.
—The Rules for Disappearing. 2014. (Rules Ser.). (ENG.). 336p. (J). (gr. 7-12). pap. 8.99 *(978-1-4231-6926-0(3))* Hyperion Bks. for Children.
Fontenot, Mary Alice. Clovis Crawfish & Bertile's Bon Voyage, 1 vol. Blazek, Scott R., illus. 2008. (Clovis Crawfish Ser.). (ENG.). 32p. (J). (gr. k-3). 16.99 *(978-1-58980-541-5(0)*, Pelican Publishing) Arcadia Publishing.
—Clovis Crawfish & His Friends, 1 vol. Graves, Keith, illus. 2009. (Clovis Crawfish Ser.). (ENG.). 32p. (J). (gr. k-3). 16.99 *(978-1-58980-762-4(6)*, Pelican Publishing) Arcadia Publishing.
—Clovis Crawfish & Michelle Mantis, 1 vol. Blazek, Scott R., illus. 2008. (Clovis Crawfish Ser.). (ENG.). 32p. (J). (gr. k-3). 16.99 *(978-1-58980-540-8(2)*, Pelican Publishing) Arcadia Publishing.
—Clovis Crawfish & Petit Papillon, 1 vol. Graves, Keith, illus. 2009. (Clovis Crawfish Ser.). (ENG.). 32p. (J). (gr. k-3). 16.99 *(978-1-58980-772-3(3)*, Pelican Publishing) Arcadia Publishing.
—Clovis Crawfish & Silvie Sulphur, 1 vol. Buckner, Julie Dupre, illus. 2004. (Clovis Crawfish Ser.). (ENG.). 32p. (J). (gr. k-3). 16.99 *(978-1-56554-864-0(7)*, Pelican Publishing) Arcadia Publishing.
Fontenot, Mary Alice & Fontenot Landry, Julie. Clovis Crawfish & the Twin Sister, 1 vol. Butler, Julie Dupre & Buckner, Julie Dupre, illus. 2007. (Clovis Crawfish Ser.). (ENG.). 32p. (J). (gr. k-3). 16.99 *(978-1-58980-467-8(8)*, Pelican Publishing) Arcadia Publishing.
Gaines, Ernest J. The Autobiography of Miss Jane Pittman: And Related Readings. 2006. (McDougal Littell Literature Connections Ser.). (ENG.). 384p. (gr. 6-8). 16.90 *(978-0-395-86993-2(5)*, 2-70829) Great Source Education Group, Inc.
Gourley, Barbara. The Legacy of Tip: The Catahoula. 2012. 40p. pap. 20.95 *(978-1-4772-6337-2(3))* AuthorHouse.
Hébert-Collins, Sheila. Jean-Paul Hébert Was There/Jean-Paul Hébert Etait Là, 1 vol. Bergeron, John W., illus. 2004. (ENG.). 32p. (J). (gr. k-3). 16.99 *(978-1-56554-928-9(7)*, Pelican Publishing) Arcadia Publishing.
Heflin, Ronald. Caddo Lake. 2011. 156p. pap. 24.95 *(978-1-4626-0093-9(X))* America Star Bks.
Holt, Kimberly Willis. Dear Hank Williams. 2016. (J). lib. bdg. 18.40 *(978-0-606-38551-0(7))* Turtleback.
—My Louisiana Sky. 208p. (gr. 5-18). (YA). 4.99 *(978-0-8072-8291-5(X))*; 2004. (J). pap. 36.00 incl. audio *(978-0-8072-8290-8(1)*, YA152SP) Random Hse. Audio Publishing Group. (Listening Library).
—Part of Me: Stories of a Louisiana Family. 2009. (ENG.). 240p. (J). (gr. 6-8). pap. 14.99 *(978-0-312-58145-9(9)*, 900061999) Square Fish.
—Part of Me: Stories of a Louisiana Family. rev. l.t. ed. 2007. (Thorndike Literacy Bridge Ser.). 223p. (J). (gr. 3-7). 23.95 *(978-0-7862-9184-7(2))* Thorndike Pr.
—Piper Reed, Rodeo Star. Davenier, Christine, illus. 2012. (Piper Reed Ser.: 5). (ENG.). 176p. (J). (gr. 3-6). pap. 9.99 *(978-1-250-00409-3(8)*, 900080156) Square Fish.
Jacobs, Lily. The Littlest Bunny in Louisiana: An Easter Adventure. Dunn, Robert, illus. 2015. (Littlest Bunny Ser.). (ENG.). 32p. (J). (gr. -1-3). 9.99 *(978-1-4926-1105-9(0)*, Hometown World) Sourcebooks, Inc.
James, Eric. Santa's Sleigh Is on Its Way to Louisiana: A Christmas Adventure. Dunn, Robert, illus. 2015. (Santa's Sleigh Is on Its Way Ser.). (ENG.). 32p. (J). (gr. k-2). 12.99 *(978-1-4926-2762-3(3)*, Hometown World) Sourcebooks, Inc.
—The Spooky Express Louisiana. Piwowarski, Marcin, illus. 2017. (Spooky Express Ser.). (ENG.). 32p. (J). (gr. k-6). 9.99 *(978-1-4926-5364-6(0)*, Hometown World) Sourcebooks, Inc.
—Tiny the Louisiana Easter Bunny. 2018. (Tiny the Easter Bunny Ser.). (ENG.). 40p. (J). (gr. k-3). 9.99 *(978-1-4926-5933-4(9)*, Hometown World) Sourcebooks, Inc.
Johnson, Temeka & Phillips, Quency. Decisions, Decisions, Decisions. 2010. 32p. 19.99 *(978-1-4520-5758-3(3))* AuthorHouse.
Jones, V. C. Anna Banana Goes to Louisiana. 2010. 16p. 8.49 *(978-1-4490-8390-8(0))* AuthorHouse.
Karwoski, Gail Langer. When Hurricane Katrina Hit Home. Marshall, Julia, illus. 2013. Orig. Title: When Hurricane Katrina Hit Home. (ENG.). 192p. (gr. 4-7). 29.99 *(978-1-62619-083-2(6)*, History Pr., The) Arcadia Publishing.
Kelly, Erin Entrada. The Land of Forgotten Girls. 2017. (ENG.). 320p. (J). (gr. 3-7). pap. 9.99 *(978-0-06-223865-8(5)*, Greenwillow Bks.) HarperCollins Pubs.
Kingsley Troupe, Thomas. Swamp of Lost Souls. Ivy, Maggie, illus. 2019. (Haunted States of America Set 2 Ser.). (ENG.). 136p. (J). (gr. 3-4). pap. 7.99 *(978-1-63163-356-0(2)*, 1631633562); lib. bdg. 27.13 *(978-1-63163-355-3(4)*, 1631633554) North Star Editions. (Jolly Fish Pr.).
LaFaye, A. Nissa's Place. 2010. (ENG.). 256p. (J). (gr. 2-8). pap. 8.00 *(978-1-57131-697-4(3))* Milkweed Editions.
—The Year of the Sawdust Man. 2008. (ENG.). 224p. (J). (gr. 2-8). pap. 6.95 *(978-1-57131-679-0(5))* Milkweed Editions.
Lamana, Julie T. Three Little Bayou Fishermen. 2010. 28p. (J). pap. 17.95 *(978-1-4327-2056-8(2))* Outskirts Pr., Inc.
Lane, Alison Hoffman. Uncle Amel & the Awful, Angry Alligator. 2009. (Uncle Amel Ser.). (Illus.). 32p. (J). 15.95 *(978-1-58980-645-0(X)*, Pelican Publishing) Arcadia Publishing.
Little, Kimberley Griffiths. Circle of Secrets. 2011. 326p. (J). *(978-0-545-38523-7(7)*, Scholastic Pr.) Scholastic, Inc.
Lovett, Darrell F. Darrell's Lake Franklin. 2007. 13.00 *(978-0-8059-8807-9(6))* Dorrance Publishing Co., Inc.

J K L

Luvd, U. R. Camp Gumbo. 2007. 113p. pap. 7.52 *(978-1-4303-1322-9(6))* Lulu Pr., Inc.

Magaro, Dan. The Adventures of Fred & Daisymae. 2010. 48p. pap. 10.99 *(978-1-60957-407-9(9))* Salem Author Services.

Mason, Dianne. Danny's Ghost. 2007. 156p. pap. 9.39 *(978-1-4116-4937-8(0))* Lulu Pr., Inc.

Mayeux, Gertie. Jesse the Oil Patch Kid. 2012. 36p. pap. 20.99 *(978-1-4772-3691-8(0))* AuthorHouse.

Mc Daniel, Jessica & Morgan, Amanda. Goodnight Tigers. 2010. 32p. (J). 17.95 *(978-1-4507-0621-6(5))* Independent Pub.

Messner, Kate. Hurricane Katrina Rescue (Ranger in Time #8) McMorris, Kelley, illus. 2018. (Ranger in Time Ser.: 8). (ENG.). 160p. (J). (gr. 2-5). pap. 5.99 *(978-1-338-13395-0(0)*, Scholastic Pr.) Scholastic, Inc.

Mock, Chara. The Cajun Nutcracker, 1 vol. Cassels, Jean, illus. 2011. (ENG.). 32p. (J). (gr. k-3). 16.99 *(978-1-58980-978-9(5)*, Pelican Publishing) Arcadia Publishing.

Morgan, Connie. Hercules on the Bayou, 1 vol. Leonhard, Herb, illus. 2016. (ENG.). 32p. (J). (gr. k-3). 16.99 *(978-1-4556-2185-9(4)*, Pelican Publishing) Arcadia Publishing.

Morrow, Dj. The Good Ol' Boys. 2012. 28p. pap. 24.95 *(978-1-4626-9533-1(7))* America Star Bks.

Moses, Jennifer Anne. The Art of Dumpster Diving. 2020. (YA). (ENG.). 26.99 *(978-1-68442-463-4(1))*; 224p. pap. 14.99 *(978-1-68442-462-7(3))* Turner Publishing Co.

Napoli, Donna Jo. Alligator Bayou. 288p. (YA). (gr. 7). 2010. pap. 8.99 *(978-0-553-49417-4(1))* 2009. (ENG.). lib. bdg. 24.94 *(978-0-385-90891-7(1))* Random Hse. Children's Bks. (Lamb, Wendy Bks.).

Pellerin, Mona. Peetie & the Marsh Aliens, 1 vol. 2010. 58p. pap. 16.95 *(978-1-4489-7017-9(2))* America Star Bks.

Poole-Carter, Rosemary. Juliette Ascending. 2007. (YA). pap. 14.00 *(978-1-929976-41-6(0)*, TOP) Top Pubns., Ltd.

Preble, Laura. Lica's Angel. 2003. 142p. (YA). 21.95 *(978-0-595-74914-0(3))*; pap. 11.95 *(978-0-595-28253-1(9))* iUniverse, Inc.

Price, Kathy Z. Mardi Gras Almost Didn't Come This Year. Williams, Carl Joe, illus. 2022. (ENG.). 48p. (J). (gr. -1-3). 17.99 *(978-1-5344-4425-6(4)*, Atheneum Bks. for Young Readers) Simon & Schuster Children's Publishing.

Quinn, Spencer, pseud. Bow Wow: a Bowser & Birdie Novel. 2018. (ENG.). 304p. (J). (gr. 3-7). pap. 8.99 *(978-1-338-09136-6(0)*, Scholastic Pr.) Scholastic, Inc.

—Woof. 2016. lib. bdg. 18.40 *(978-0-606-39011-8(1))* Turtleback.

—Woof: a Bowser & Birdie Novel. 2016. (ENG.). 304p. (J). (gr. 3-7). pap. 7.99 *(978-0-545-64332-0(5))* Scholastic, Inc.

Rhodes, Jewell Parker. Bayou Magic. 2016. (ENG.). 272p. (J). (gr. 3-7). pap. 7.99 *(978-0-316-22485-7(5))* Little, Brown Bks. for Young Readers.

—Sugar. 2014. (ENG., Illus.). 288p. (J). (gr. 3-7). pap. 8.99 *(978-0-316-04306-9(0))* Little, Brown Bks. for Young Readers.

Robertson, Missy & Robertson, Mia. Allie's Bayou Rescue, 1 vol. 2018. (Faithgirlz / Princess in Camo Ser.: 1). (ENG., Illus.). 192p. (J). pap. 8.99 *(978-0-310-76247-8(2))* Zonderkidz.

San Souci, Robert D. Six Foolish Fishermen, 1 vol. Kennedy, Doug, illus. 2011. (ENG.). 32p. (J). (gr. k-3). 16.99 *(978-1-4556-1473-8(4)*, Pelican Publishing) Arcadia Publishing.

Savage, J. Scott. Case File 13: Zombie Kid. Holgate, Doug, illus. 2013. (Case File 13 Ser.: 1). (ENG.). 304p. (J). (gr. 3-7). pap. 7.99 *(978-0-06-213327-4(6)*, HarperCollins) HarperCollins Pubs.

Schmitt, Nannette Toups. Remember Last Island. Gorman, Carolyn Portier, ed. Schmitt, Nannette Toups & Endres, Sharlene Duggan, illus. 2003. 206p. (YA). pap. 19.95 *(978-0-9740901-0-8(7)*, 11-May) Orage Publishing.

Simon, Margaret. Blessen. 2012. 120p. (J). pap. 15.00 *(978-0-9848915-2-8(8))* Border Pr.

Smallman, Steve. Santa Is Coming to Louisiana. Dunn, Robert, illus. 2nd ed. 2019. (Santa Is Coming... Ser.). (ENG.). 40p. (J). (gr. -1-3). 12.99 *(978-1-7282-0067-5(9)*, Hometown World) Sourcebooks, Inc.

Smith, Rosemary. Lizard Tales: Lizzie Walks on the Wild Side. 2010. 28p. pap. 12.50 *(978-1-60911-082-6(X)*, Strategic Bk. Publishing) Strategic Book Publishing & Rights Agency (SBPRA).

Snyder, Sandy. There's Only One I in Charlie. Ferrenburg, Susie, illus. 2011. 48p. pap. 24.95 *(978-1-4626-4086-7(9))* America Star Bks.

Sullivan, Kiki. The Dolls. 2014. (Dolls Ser.: 1). (ENG.). 384p. (YA). (gr. 8). pap. 9.99 *(978-0-06-228148-7(8)*, Balzer & Bray) HarperCollins Pubs.

Sully, Katherine. Night-Night Louisiana. Poole, Helen, illus. 2017. (Night-Night Ser.). (ENG.). 20p. (J). (gr. -1-1). bds. 9.99 *(978-1-4926-5471-1(X)*, Hometown World) Sourcebooks, Inc.

Thomas, Julie M. Poncho's Rescue: A Baby Bull & a Big Flood. 2018. (ENG., Illus.). 48p. (J). (gr. k-3). pap. 19.95 *(978-0-8071-6939-1(0)*, 7512) Louisiana State Univ. Pr.

Thomas, Wes. Down the Crawfish Hole, 1 vol. Thomas, Wes, illus. 2004. (Cajun Tall Tales Ser.). (ENG., Illus.). 32p. (J). (gr. k-3). 16.99 *(978-1-58980-163-9(6)*, Pelican Publishing) Arcadia Publishing.

Top Secret Tiaras. 2009. (Princess Protection Program Ser.: No. 3). (ENG.). 144p. (gr. 3-7). pap. 4.99 *(978-1-4231-2392-7(1))* Disney Pr.

Watts, Jane & Nobel, DeAnna. The Adventures of Alligator Tater. 2007. 64p. per. 10.95 *(978-1-4327-0228-1(9))* Outskirts Pr., Inc.

Williams, Arthur Roy. Bouki's Honey Vol. 1: The Creole (and Cajun) Folktales of Bouki & Lapin: Volume 1. Foote, L., illus. 2008. (ENG.). 30p. pap. 20.99 *(978-1-4343-0467-4(1))* AuthorHouse.

LOUISIANA—HISTORY

Bailey, Tom. Jean Baptiste le Moyne, Sieur de Bienville: Father of Mobile. 2012. (Illus.). 112p. (J). *(978-1-59421-082-2(9)*, Blackbirch Pr., Inc.) Seacoast Publishing, Inc.

Bjorklund, Ruth & Steinitz, Andy. Louisiana, 1 vol. 2nd rev. ed. 2011. (It's My State! (Second Edition)(r) Ser.). (ENG.). 80p. (gr. 4-4). lib. bdg. 34.07 *(978-1-60870-051-6(8)*, a756c5c7-d344-4cbd-8312-f2cdb2e92728) Cavendish Square Publishing LLC.

Bridges, Ruby. Through My Eyes: Ruby Bridges. Lundell, Margo, ed. Lundell, Margo, illus. 2018. (Follow Me Around... Ser.). (ENG.). 64p. (J). (gr. 3-4). E-Book 27.00 *(978-0-545-70803-6(6))* Scholastic, Inc.

Coleman, Miriam. Louisiana: The Pelican State, 1 vol. 2010. (Our Amazing States Ser.). (ENG.). 24p. (J). (gr. 3-3). pap. 9.25 *(978-1-4488-0740-6(9)*, c922fb45-a332-4e59-8f02-972d4168a0d8); lib. bdg. 26.27 *(978-1-4488-0654-6(2)*, cb3c305a-3b7f-479d-8933-64f747a6bea1) Rosen Publishing Group, Inc., The. (PowerKids Pr.).

Downing, Johnette. Today Is Monday in Louisiana, 1 vol. Thomas, Deborah, illus. 2016. (ENG.). 8p. (J). bds. 10.95 *(978-1-4556-2306-8(7)*, Pelican Publishing) Arcadia Publishing.

Eakin, Sue, et al. Louisiana: The Land & Its People, 1 vol. Culbertson, James Forrest, illus. 5th ed. 2006. (ENG.). 560p. 35.00 *(978-1-58980-303-9(5)*, Pelican Publishing) Arcadia Publishing.

Faucheux, Guy N. & Faucheux, Wallace P. Cajun Comiques Historic Louisiana: An Illustrated History for Kids of All Ages. 2004. (Illus.). 56p. (YA). lib. bdg. 16.95 *(978-0-9718433-1-8(7))* St. Roux Pr.

Freedman, Jeri. Louisiana: Past & Present, 1 vol. 2010. (United States: Past & Present Ser.). (ENG.). 48p. (YA). (gr. 5-5). pap. 12.75 *(978-1-4358-9510-2(X)*, 41c28fe3-86bb-4c7c-919d-72f57ad16a3f); lib. bdg. 34.47 *(978-1-4358-9483-9(9)*, e2528a2c-cc1a-4819-b4bb-45122d3dbdee) Rosen Publishing Group, Inc., The. (Rosen Reference).

Gagliardi, Sue. Hurricane Katrina. 2019. (21st Century Disasters Ser.). (ENG., Illus.). 32p. (J). (gr. 2-3). pap. 9.95 *(978-1-64185-809-0(5)*, 1641858095); lib. bdg. 31.35 *(978-1-64185-740-6(4)*, 1641857404) North Star Editions. (Focus Readers).

Hamilton, John. Louisiana, 1 vol. 2016. (United States of America Ser.). (ENG., Illus.). 48p. (J). (gr. 5-9). 34.21 *(978-1-68078-320-9(3)*, 21325, Abdo & Daughters) ABDO Publishing Co.

Jerome, Kate B. Lucky to Live in Louisiana. 2017. (Arcadia Kids Ser.). (ENG., Illus.). 32p. (J). 16.99 *(978-0-7385-2792-5(0))* Arcadia Publishing.

Johnstone, Robb. Louisiana: The Pelican State. 2016. (J). *(978-1-4896-4869-3(0))* Weigl Pubs., Inc.

Knudsen, Anders. Antoine de la Mothe Cadillac: French Settlements at Detroit & Louisiana. 2006. (In the Footsteps of Explorers Ser.). (ENG., Illus.). 32p. (J). (gr. 3-9). lib. bdg. *(978-0-7787-2429-2(8))*; (gr. 4-7). pap. *(978-0-7787-2465-0(4))* Crabtree Publishing Co.

Koestler-Grack, Rachel A. Daily Life in a Southern Trading Town: New Orleans. 2003. (J). *(978-1-58417-013-6(1))*; pap. *(978-1-58417-076-1(X))* Lake Street Pubs.

Kurtz, Jane. Celebrating Louisiana: 50 States to Celebrate. Canga, C. B., illus. 2016. (ENG.). 40p. (J). (gr. 1-4). pap. 4.99 *(978-0-544-51827-8(6)*, 1606225, Clarion Bks.) HarperCollins Pubs.

Lassieur, Allison. America the Beautiful, Third Series: Louisiana (Revised Edition) 2014. (America the Beautiful Ser.: 3). (ENG.). 144p. (J). lib. bdg. 40.00 *(978-0-531-24886-7(0)*, Children's Pr.) Scholastic Library Publishing.

Macaulay, Ellen. Louisiana. 2009. (From Sea to Shining Sea, Second Ser.). (ENG.). 80p. (J). pap. 7.95 *(978-0-531-21132-8(0)*, Children's Pr.) Scholastic Library Publishing.

Marsh, Carole. Exploring Louisiana Through Project-Based Learning. 2016. (Louisiana Experience Ser.). (ENG.). (J). pap. 9.99 *(978-0-635-12342-8(8))* Gallopade International.

—Let's Discover Louisiana! 2004. (J). (gr. 2-8). cd-rom 14.95 *(978-0-7933-9553-8(4))* Gallopade International.

—Louisiana History Projects: 30 Cool, Activities, Crafts, Experiments & More for Kids to Do to Learn about Your State! 2003. (Louisiana Experience Ser.). 32p. (gr. k-5). pap. 5.95 *(978-0-635-01787-1(3)*, Marsh, Carole Bks.) Gallopade International.

McGee, Randel. Paper Crafts for Mardi Gras, 1 vol. 2012. (Paper Craft Fun for Holidays Ser.). (ENG., Illus.). 48p. (gr. 3-3). lib. bdg. 27.93 *(978-0-7660-3724-3(X)*, 30ab99c7-5c11-4645-9399-96e3f6459c85) Enslow Publishing, LLC.

Miller, Derek, et al. Louisiana: The Pelican State, 1 vol. 2018. (It's My State! (Fourth Edition)(r) Ser.). (ENG.). 80p. (gr. 4-4). 35.93 *(978-1-5026-2627-1(6)*, 2c73a35a-fb87-41e7-aca9-b1bfa1ace9f0) Cavendish Square Publishing LLC.

Omoth, Tyler. The Story of the New Orleans Hornets. 2010. (NBA — A History of Hoops Ser.). 48p. (YA). (gr. 5-18). 23.95 *(978-1-58341-954-0(3)*, Creative Education) Creative Co., The.

Prieto, Anita C. Little Louisiana. Knorr, Laura, illus. 2011. (Little State Ser.). (ENG.). 20p. (J). (gr. -1-1). bds. 9.95 *(978-1-58536-184-7(4)*, 202241) Sleeping Bear Pr.

Richard, Zachary, ed. The History of the Acadians of Louisiana. 2013. (ENG.). pap. 24.95 *(978-1-935754-29-9(7))* Univ. of Louisiana at Lafayette Pr.

Vierow, Wendy. The Capture of New Orleans: Union Fleet Takes Control of the Lower Mississippi. 2009. (Headlines from History Ser.). 24p. (gr. 3-3). 42.50 *(978-1-61513-245-4(7)*, PowerKids Pr.) Rosen Publishing Group, Inc., The.

Yasuda, Anita. Louisiana. 2018. (Illus.). 24p. (J). *(978-1-4896-7437-1(3)*, AV2 by Weigl) Weigl Pubs., Inc.

—Louisiana: The Pelican State. 2012. (J). *(978-1-61913-355-6(5))*; pap. *(978-1-61913-356-3(3))* Weigl Pubs., Inc.

Ziff, John. Gulf States: Alabama, Louisiana, Mississippi, Vol. 19. 2015. (Let's Explore the States Ser.). (Illus.). 64p. (J). (gr. 5). 23.95 *(978-1-4222-3324-5(3))* Mason Crest.

LOUISIANA PURCHASE

Alagna, Magdalena. The Louisiana Purchase: Expanding America's Boundaries. (Life in the New American Nation Ser.). 32p. (gr. 4-4). 2009. 47.90 *(978-1-61514-284-2(3))* 2003. (ENG., Illus.). pap. 10.00 *(978-0-8239-4257-2(0)*, c5183072-cc67-405e-bf11-a625833488a5) 2003. (ENG., Illus.). lib. bdg. 29.13 *(978-0-8239-4039-4(X)*, 4b93a5ff-bd6e-4be7-8df2-a3030c1ca7c1, Rosen Reference) Rosen Publishing Group, Inc., The.

Brindell Fradin, Dennis. The Louisiana Purchase, 1 vol. 2010. (Turning Points in U. S. History Ser.). (ENG.). 48p. (gr. 4-4). 34.07 *(978-0-7614-4257-8(X)*, 53cdb14d-b8e2-418d-8921-ceb098a75c1e) Cavendish Square Publishing LLC.

Burgan, Michael. The Louisiana Purchase. rev. ed. 2016. (Making a New Nation Ser.). (ENG., Illus.). 48p. (J). (gr. 3-5). pap. 8.99 *(978-1-4846-3596-4(5)*, 133674, Heinemann) Capstone.

Harasymiw, Therese. The Louisiana Purchase. 2009. (American History Milestones Ser.). 32p. (gr. 5-5). 47.90 *(978-1-61511-374-3(6)*, PowerKids Pr.) Rosen Publishing Group, Inc., The.

Landau, Elaine. Jefferson's Louisiana Purchase: Would You Make the Deal of the Century?, 1 vol. 2014. (What Would You Do? Ser.). (ENG.). 48p. (gr. 3-4). 27.93 *(978-0-7660-6305-1(4)*, 4a599c69-5c92-4682-95d0-9a93f9891693); pap. 11.53 *(978-0-7660-6306-8(2)*, 0c240e39-3a16-4732-bbd2-78d7c4c61d18, Enslow Elementary) Enslow Publishing, LLC.

—The Louisiana Purchase: Would You Close the Deal?, 1 vol. 2008. (What Would You Do? Ser.). (ENG., Illus.). 48p. (gr. 3-3). pap. 11.53 *(978-1-59845-196-2(0)*, ba81a5a3-263e-4e3c-99e1-1f0721932655); lib. bdg. 27.93 *(978-0-7660-2902-6(6)*, ab076af9-e6df-4809-afdd-7ab429047f40) Enslow Publishing, LLC. (Enslow Elementary).

Lawrence, Blythe. The Louisiana Purchase. 2018. (Expansion of Our Nation Ser.). (ENG., Illus.). 32p. (J). (gr. 3-5). pap. 9.95 *(978-1-63517-984-2(X)*, 163517984X); lib. bdg. 31.35 *(978-1-63517-883-8(5)*, 1635178835) North Star Editions. (Focus Readers).

—The Louisiana Purchase. 2018. (Illus.). 32p. (J). *(978-1-4896-9874-2(4)*, AV2 by Weigl) Weigl Pubs., Inc.

Lynch, Seth. The Louisiana Purchase, 1 vol. 2018. (Look at U. S. History Ser.). (ENG.). 32p. (gr. 2-2). 28.27 *(978-1-5382-2131-0(4)*, 6a875d97-be5b-480b-a71b-9c467ad9da6c) Stevens, Gareth Publishing LLLP.

Marsh, Carole. Louisiana Purchase. 2003. 12p. (gr. k-4). 2.95 *(978-0-635-02132-8(3))* Gallopade International.

—What a Deal! The Louisiana Purchase. 2003. 32p. (J). (gr. 3-8). pap. 5.95 *(978-0-635-02123-6(4))* Gallopade International.

McNeese, Tim. The Louisiana Purchase: Growth of a Nation. 2008. (Milestones in American History Ser.). (ENG., Illus.). 144p. (gr. 7-12). 35.00 *(978-1-60413-052-2(0)*, P159426, Facts On File) Infobase Holdings, Inc.

Nelson, Sheila. Thomas Jefferson's America: The Louisiana Purchase (1800-1811) 2006. (How America Became America Ser.). (Illus.). 96p. (YA). lib. bdg. 22.95 *(978-1-59084-904-0(3))* Mason Crest.

Prince, Jennifer S. The Life & Times of Asheville's Thomas Wolfe. 2016. (True Tales for Young Readers Ser.). (ENG., Illus.). 116p. (YA). pap. 17.00 *(978-0-86526-484-7(8)*, 01OSPS) Univ. of North Carolina Pr.

Raabe, Emily. Thomas Jefferson & the Louisiana Purchase. 2009. (Westward Ho! Ser.). 24p. (gr. 2-3). 42.50 *(978-1-60854-763-0(9)*, PowerKids Pr.) Rosen Publishing Group, Inc., The.

Raum, Elizabeth. Expanding a Nation: Causes & Effects of the Louisiana Purchase, 1 vol. 2013. (Cause & Effect Ser.). (ENG.). 32p. (J). (gr. 3-6). 27.99 *(978-1-4765-0236-6(6)*, 122290); pap. 8.95 *(978-1-4765-3402-2(0)*, 123533) Capstone.

Roop, Peter & Roop, Connie. Louisiana Purchase. Comport, Sally Wern, illus. 2004. 84p. (J). lib. bdg. 15.00 *(978-1-4242-0908-8(0))* Fitzgerald Bks.

Sharp, Constance. Thomas Jefferson & the Growing United States (1800-1811) 2012. (J). pap. *(978-1-4222-2414-4(7))* Mason Crest.

—Thomas Jefferson & the Growing United States (1800-1811) Rakove, Jack N., ed. 2012. (How America Became America Ser.). 48p. (J). (gr. 3-4). 19.95 *(978-1-4222-2400-7(7))* Mason Crest.

Shea, Therese. The Louisiana Purchase, 1 vol. 2009. (American History Milestones Ser.). (ENG.). 32p. (J). (gr. 5-5). lib. bdg. 28.93 *(978-1-4358-3017-2(2)*, fc003e5c-3c18-4737-abf6-aef7cdd047af, PowerKids Pr.) Rosen Publishing Group, Inc., The.

Shea, Therese & Roza, Greg. The Louisiana Purchase, 1 vol. 2008. (Real Life Readers Ser.). (ENG., Illus.). 32p. (J). (gr. 5-6). pap. 10.00 *(978-1-4358-0209-4(8)*, f2fa402b-f1f1-44b6-8116-91aa685ca3eb, PowerKids Pr.) Rosen Publishing Group, Inc., The.

Shea, Therese M. The Louisiana Purchase & the Lewis & Clark Expedition. 2017. (Westward Expansion: America's Push to the Pacific Ser.). (Illus.). 48p. (J). (gr. 10-14). 84.30 *(978-1-5383-0013-8(3))*; (ENG., (gr. 6-7). pap. 15.05 *(978-1-68048-790-9(6)*, e3a8ec93-25d6-4e7e-82ab-fe30c88fb8d1) Rosen Publishing Group, Inc., The. (Britannica Educational Publishing).

Steele, Christy. The Louisiana Purchase, 1 vol. 2004. (America's Westward Expansion Ser.). (ENG., Illus.). 48p. (gr. 5-8). lib. bdg. 33.67 *(978-0-8368-5789-4(5)*, e395a0db-595b-4d4f-bbf9-56f204e72c90, Gareth Stevens Secondary Library) Stevens, Gareth Publishing LLLP.

Yasuda, Anita. 12 Incredible Facts about the Louisiana Purchase. 2016. (Turning Points in US History Ser.). (ENG., Illus.). 32p. (J). (gr. 3-6). 32.80 *(978-1-63235-131-9(5)*, 12003, 12-Story Library) Bookstaves, LLC.

LOVE, NAT, 1854-1921

Cefrey, Holly. From Slave to Cowboy: The Nat Love Story. (Great Moments in American History Ser.). 32p. (gr. 3-3). 2009. 47.90 *(978-1-61513-142-6(6))* 2003. (ENG., Illus.). (J). lib. bdg. 29.13 *(978-0-8239-4375-3(5)*, bfad0e14-630c-455c-a03c-1dbbaa3305e2, Rosen Reference) Rosen Publishing Group, Inc., The.

Katirgis, Jane & Penn, Sarah. Meet Nat Love: Cowboy & Former Slave. 2019. (Introducing Famous Americans Ser.). (ENG.). 32p. (gr. 3-4). 63.18 *(978-1-9785-1139-2(6))* Enslow Publishing, LLC.

Nat Love. 2010. (ENG., Illus.). 104p. (gr. 6-12). 35.00 *(978-1-60413-599-2(9)*, P179313, Facts On File) Infobase Holdings, Inc.

Penn, Sarah. Nat Love: African American Cowboy. (Primary Sources of Famous People in American History Ser.). 32p. 2009. (gr. 2-3). 47.90 *(978-1-60851-706-0(3))* 2003. (ENG., Illus.). (J). (gr. 3-4). pap. 10.00 *(978-0-8239-4188-9(4)*, 6be498a9-1f80-45ca-847a-fd10fdb2527e) 2003. (ENG., Illus.). (J). (gr. 3-4). lib. bdg. 29.13 *(978-0-8239-4116-2(7)*, d002c57f-e32f-47ee-a27c-8b7d13c4c2af, Rosen Reference) 2003. (ENG & SPA., Illus.). (gr. 2-3). lib. bdg. 29.13 *(978-0-8239-4164-3(7)*, ca6a554a-d200-470f-b144-dd8d90d95de9, Editorial Buenas Letras) Rosen Publishing Group, Inc., The.

—Nat Love: African American Cowboy / Vaquero Afroamericano. 2009. (Famous People in American History/Grandes personajes en la historia de los Estados Unidos Ser.). (ENG & SPA.). 32p. (gr. 2-3). 47.90 *(978-1-61512-551-7(5)*, Editorial Buenas Letras) Rosen Publishing Group, Inc., The.

—Nat Love: Vaquero Afroamericano, 1 vol. 2003. (Grandes Personajes en la Historia de Los Estados Unidos (Famous People in American History) Ser.). (SPA., Illus.). 32p. (J). (gr. 3-4). pap. 10.00 *(978-0-8239-4234-3(1)*, 97b78651-a0c4-4862-8de1-6901458d5d5f, Rosen Classroom); lib. bdg. 29.13 *(978-0-8239-4140-7(X)*, f0861b6d-5834-4975-8113-e48582c5b447, Editorial Buenas Letras) Rosen Publishing Group, Inc., The.

—Nat Love: Vaquero afroamericano (Nat Love: African American Cowboy) 2009. (Grandes personajes en la historia de los Estados Unidos (Famous People in American History) Ser.). (SPA.). 32p. (gr. 2-3). 47.90 *(978-1-61512-804-4(2)*, Editorial Buenas Letras) Rosen Publishing Group, Inc., The.

Underwood, Deborah. Nat Love. 2008. pap. 52.95 *(978-0-8225-9395-9(5))*; (ENG., Illus.). 48p. (J). (gr. 3-6). lib. bdg. 27.93 *(978-0-8225-7171-1(4)*, Lerner Pubns.) Lerner Publishing Group.

LOVE

see also Dating (Social Customs); Friendship; Marriage

Accord Publishing, Accord. Where Does Love Come From? Kirkova, Milena, illus. 2012. (ENG.). 18p. (J). bds. 5.99 *(978-1-4494-2884-6(3))* Andrews McMeel Publishing.

Ashour, Monica. Every Body Is a Gift: God Made Us to Love. Kaminski, Karol, illus. 2015. (J). 12.95 *(978-0-8198-2376-2(7))* Pauline Bks. & Media.

Bergren, Lisa Tawn. Mama Kisses, Papa Hugs. Zolotic, Aleksander, illus. 2020. (ENG.). 40p. (J). (gr. -1-2). 11.99 *(978-0-525-65409-4(7)*, WaterBrook Pr.) Crown Publishing Group, The.

Bloomsbury USA. Carry & Play: I Love You. 2015. (ENG., Illus.). 10p. (J). (gr. -1-1). bds. 6.99 *(978-1-61963-802-0(9)*, 900148901, Bloomsbury Activity Bks.) Bloomsbury Publishing USA.

Books, Applewood. Love (Pictorial America) Vintage Images of America's Living Past. Lantos, James, ed. 2010. (Pictorial America Ser.). (ENG.). 56p. (J). pap. 9.95 *(978-1-60889-008-8(2))* Applewood Bks.

Chidvilasananda. Good Night, Sweet Dreams, I Love You! 2004. (Illus.). (J). *(978-1-930939-01-1(9))* SYDA Foundation.

Chipman-Sullivan, Lois. What Does Love Mean, God? 2013. 36p. pap. 10.50 *(978-1-61286-141-8(5))* Avid Readers Publishing Group.

Clark, Chap P. Next Time I Fall in Love: How to Handle Sex, Intimacy, & Feelings in Dating Relationships. 2004. (ENG.). 144p. pap. 23.00 *(978-1-59244-684-1(1)*, Wipf and Stock) Wipf & Stock Pubs.

Dean, James & Dean, Kimberly. Pete the Cat's Groovy Guide to Love. Dean, James, illus. 2015. (Pete the Cat Ser.). (ENG., Illus.). 48p. (J). (gr. -1-3). 12.99 *(978-0-06-243061-8(0)*, HarperCollins) HarperCollins Pubs.

Devadasan, Rashmi Ruth. Kumari Loves a Monster. Kumariyin Ratcaca Katalan. Shyam, illus. 2010. (TAM & ENG.). 52p. pap. 17.95 *(978-93-80636-01-6(6))* Blaft Pubns.

Eastham, Chad. The Truth about Breaking Up, Making Up, & Moving On, 1 vol. 2013. (ENG.). 240p. (YA). pap. 14.99 *(978-1-4003-2115-5(8)*, Tommy Nelson) Nelson, Thomas Inc.

Feldman, Rachel S. The Little Tree. 2010. 32p. pap. 14.99 *(978-1-4520-0033-6(6))* AuthorHouse.

Foldvary-Anderson, Carol. Hearts & Roses Stained Glass Coloring Book. 2009. (Dover Romance Coloring Bks.). (ENG., Illus.). 32p. (gr. 3-8). pap. 6.99 *(978-0-486-47023-8(7)*, 470237) Dover Pubns., Inc.

Garlick, Kim. Thank You. 2012. 20p. pap. 17.99 *(978-1-4772-0485-6(7))* AuthorHouse.

Gozansky, Shana. My Art Book of Love. 2018. (ENG., Illus.). 48p. (gr. -1 — 1). bds. 18.95 *(978-0-7148-7718-1(2))* Phaidon Pr., Inc.

Greene, Kathy B. How I Love You!, 1 vol. 2009. 19p. pap. 24.95 *(978-1-60749-681-6(X))* America Star Bks.

Groenendyk, Doretta. Love You More Than Anything, 1 vol. 2017. (ENG., Illus.). 32p. (J). (gr. -1-k). 19.95 *(978-1-927502-93-8(4)*, 0d131819-71b6-4f62-9a73-ea52f3e706a8) Acorn Pr., The CAN. Dist: Baker & Taylor Publisher Services (BTPS).

Gynux. Jesus Loves Me, 1 vol. 2017. (Sing-Along Book Ser.). (ENG., Illus.). 20p. (J). bds. 8.99 *(978-0-310-75894-5(7))* Zonderkidz.

Hamilton, Alice. Loving Hands of Grandma: A True Story. 2012. 24p. pap. 24.95 *(978-1-4626-7432-9(1))* PublishAmerica, Inc.

Hammonds, Theresa D. God's Invisible Fruit of Love. 2013. 24p. pap. 15.00 *(978-0-9824550-5-0(4))* Kingdom Kaught Publishing LLC.

Harper, Suzanne. The 10 Most Tragic Romances. 2008. (J). 14.99 *(978-1-55448-546-8(0))* Scholastic Library Publishing.

Hawkins Harris, Jennifer. Love: The Book of Love for Kids. Gray Mayo, Jo Ann, illus. 2003. 20p. (J). per. 7.00 *(978-0-9705458-2-4(7))* Royalty Bks. International, Inc.

Hinds, Sandra A. I Love You Every. 2012. 32p. pap. 19.99 *(978-1-4567-2418-4(5))* AuthorHouse.

I Love You Because You're. 2004. (J). pap. 6.99 *(978-0-439-57711-3(X))* Scholastic, Inc.

Kavanaugh, Dorothy. Feeling Unloved? Girls Dealing with Feelings, 1 vol. 2014. (Girls Dealing with Feelings Ser.). (ENG.). 64p. (gr. 5-6). 19.61 *(978-1-62293-050-0(9)*,

50662006-67a2-45f3-aa65-5d91ac51334e) Enslow Publishing, LLC.

Kim Ko, Yon-Ju. Na Ui Ch'ot Chendo Suop. 2017. (KOR., Illus.). 201p. (YA). *(978-89-364-5227-8(4))* Chang-jag and Bipyeong Co.

Learn As You Grow. God Loves You So Much... Reuben, Borgen & Jenny, Lindley, photos by. 2010. (ENG., Illus.). 24p. (J). 12.95 *(978-0-9824652-3-3(8))* Learn As You Grow, L.L.C.

LeJeune, Shonda. Love Is... 2003. (Illus.). 30p. (gr. -1-3). pap. 11.50 *(978-0-87516-690-2(3))*; (gr. 2-18). 14.50 *(978-0-87516-691-9(1))* DeVorss & Co.

L'Heureux, Christine. Caillou: I Love You. Brignaud, Pierre, illus. 2012. (Hand in Hand Ser.). (ENG.). 24p. (J). (gr. -1-k). 5.99 *(978-2-89450-860-2(3))* Caillouet, Gerry.

L'heureux, Christine. Caillou Loves His Mommy. Brignaud, Pierre, illus. 2018. (Caillou's Essentials Ser.). (ENG.). 24p. (J). (gr. -1-k). bds. 7.99 *(978-2-89718-441-4(8))* Caillouet, Gerry.

Lilley, Matt. Why We Love: The Science of Affection. 2019. (Decoding the Mind Ser.). (ENG., Illus.). 64p. (J). (gr. 5-9). pap. 8.95 *(978-0-7565-6223-6(6)*, 140924); lib. bdg. 37.32 *(978-0-7565-6178-9(7)*, 140661) Capstone. (Compass Point Bks.).

Logan, John. An Unloved Guy's Guide: How to Deal, 1 vol. 2014. (Guy's Guide Ser.). (ENG.). 64p. (gr. 5-7). 19.61 *(978-1-62293-020-3(7)*, b2053143-63a8-40fe-a5e7-79b9444d9d64) Enslow Publishing, LLC.

Marsh, Carole. Someone I Love Went off to War. 2003. 24p. (gr. 1-8). pap. 5.95 *(978-0-635-02092-5(0))* Gallopade International.

Mayo, Jeanne. Uncensored: Dating, Friendship, & Sex. 2007. (Illus.). 237p. (YA). (gr. 7-12). per. 14.99 *(978-1-57794-821-6(1))* Harrison House Pubs.

McDowell, JOsh & Stewart, Ed. Struggling with Finding True Love. 2008. (Project 17:17 Ser.). (ENG.). 64p. (J). pap. 4.99 *(978-1-84550-356-7(2)*, 46c03857-b7ce-4aae-923b-c4d6c10233e1) Christian Focus Pubns. GBR. Dist: Baker & Taylor Publisher Services (BTPS).

McKnight, Scot & McKnight Barringer, Laura. Sharing God's Love: The Jesus Creed for Children. Hill, David, illus. 2014. (ENG.). 32p. (J). (gr. -1-5). pap. 15.99 *(978-1-61261-581-3(3)*, 5813) Paraclete Pr., Inc.

Miles, Lisa & Chown, Xanna Eve. How to Survive Having a Crush. 2013. (Girl Talk Ser.). 48p. (J). (gr. 5-8). pap. 70.50 *(978-1-4777-0727-2(1)*, Rosen Reference); (ENG., Illus.). pap. 12.75 *(978-1-4777-0720-3(4)*, 07eacdbd-796c-4684-bea6-141aee2ede6c, Rosen Reference); (ENG., Illus.). lib. bdg. 34.41 *(978-1-4777-0706-7(9)*, 5385159a-b8df-4c3f-908d-6ed5b03e51a3, Rosen Classroom) Rosen Publishing Group, Inc., The.

Milet Publishing. My First Bilingual Book-Love (English-Russian), 1 vol. 2018. (My First Bilingual Book Ser.). (ENG & RUS., Illus.). 24p. (J). (— 1). bds. 8.99 *(978-1-78508-902-2(1))* Milet Publishing.

Miller, Eileen Rudisill. True Love Stained Glass Coloring Book. 2011. (Dover Romance Coloring Bks.). (ENG., Illus.). 32p. (gr. 3-8). pap. 6.99 *(978-0-486-47835-7(1)*, 478351) Dover Pubns., Inc.

óMeta, CéSar. Blue Dragonflies. 2011. 64p. (gr. 4-6). pap. 9.99 *(978-1-4634-4690-1(X))* AuthorHouse.

Pears, Alison. Gus & Oliver-A Family Tale. 2012. 30p. pap. 13.99 *(978-1-4525-5472-3(2))* Balboa Pr.

Poelman, Heidi. I Can Love Like Jesus. 2017. (ENG., Illus.). (J). (gr. -1-2). 14.99 *(978-1-4621-1940-0(9))* Cedar Fort, Inc./CFI Distribution.

Poulin, Andreé. The Magic Clothesline. Arbona, Marion, illus. 2012. 32p. (J). pap. 9.95 *(978-1-4338-1195-1(2)*, Magination Pr.) American Psychological Assn.

Richardson, Joy K. A Helping Hand Series: I Love You. 2009. 16p. pap. 10.49 *(978-1-4389-9432-1(X))* AuthorHouse.

Rotner, Shelley. What's Love? 2013. (Shelley Rotner's World Ser.). (ENG.). 32p. (gr. 1-2). pap. 47.70 *(978-1-62065-757-7(0)*, Capstone Pr.) Capstone.

Rubow, Carol. God Loves You. 2010. (Illus.). 32p. (J). (gr. -1). 12.99 *(978-0-7586-1855-9(7))* Concordia Publishing Hse.

Sheriff, Marcia. God's Great Big Love. 2013. (ENG.). 24p. pap. 12.45 *(978-1-4497-9288-6(X)*, WestBow Pr.) Author Solutions, LLC.

Shumway, Lindsey. I Chose You. 2005. (Illus.). 31p. (J). 15.99 *(978-1-55517-861-1(8))* Cedar Fort, Inc./CFI Distribution.

Smith, Lori Joy. I Love You Like ... 2018. (ENG., Illus.). 32p. (J). (gr. -1-3). 16.95 *(978-1-77147-157-2(3))* Owlkids Bks. Inc. CAN. Dist: Publishers Group West (PGW).

Solomon, Iris L. & Solomon, Ron. Friendz Pakz: Love. 2003. (YA). (gr. 3-18). 4.99 *(978-1-930680-07-4(4)*, SSP-08LV) Swingset Pr., LLC.

Spencer, Lauren. Everything You Need to Know about Falling in Love. 2009. (Need to Know Library). 64p. (gr. 5-5). 58.50 *(978-1-60854-067-9(7))* Rosen Publishing Group, Inc., The.

Stewart, Elizabeth. An Angel Named Love. 2005. 17.00 *(978-0-8059-9815-3(2))* Dorrance Publishing Co., Inc.

The True Love Waits Youth Bible. 2004. (Illus.). 1294p. pap. 19.99 *(978-1-55819-621-6(8))* B&H Publishing Group.

Watanabe, Kaori. I Love You (My First Taggies Book) Watanabe, Kaori, illus. 2004. (My First Taggies Book Ser.). (ENG., Illus.). 8p. (J). (gr. -1 — 1). 12.99 *(978-0-439-64947-6(1)*, Cartwheel Bks.) Scholastic, Inc.

Weber, Penny & McCloud, Carol. Will You Fill My Bucket? Daily Acts of Love Around the World. Wells, Karen, illus. 2012. 32p. (J). (-4). pap. 9.95 *(978-1-933916-97-2(4))* Cardinal Rule Pr.

Welch, Ariel & Welch, Ashley. Waiting. 2003. 122p. (YA). pap. 13.95 *(978-0-595-27087-3(5))* iUniverse, Inc.

What Is... Love. (Illus.). 16p. (J). pap. 1.50 *(978-0-87162-827-5(9)*, E6019) Warner Pr., Inc.

Wilcox, Christine. Understanding Family & Personal Relationships. 2017. (Understanding Psychology Ser.). (ENG.). 80p. (YA). (gr. 5-12). *(978-1-68282-273-9(7))* ReferencePoint Pr., Inc.

Yonezu, Yusuke. We Love Each Other: An Interactive Book Full of Animals & Hugs. Yonezu, Yusuke, illus. 2013. (World of Yonezu Ser.). (Illus.). 28p. (J). (— 1). bds. 9.95 *(978-988-8240-56-2(0)*, Minedition) Penguin Young Readers Group.

LOVE—FICTION

Abbaszadeh, Paul. One Love: A True Love Story. 2003. 466p. (YA). pap. 28.95 *(978-0-595-28878-6(2))* iUniverse, Inc.

Abbott, Hailey. Boy Crazy. 2009. (ENG.). 240p. (YA). (gr. 9). pap. 8.99 *(978-0-06-125385-0(5)*, HarperTeen) HarperCollins Pubs.

Accord Publishing, Accord. Where Does Love Come From? Kirkova, Milena, illus. 2011. (ENG.). 18p. (J). 9.99 *(978-1-4494-0839-8(7))* Andrews McMeel Publishing.

Acocella, Nunzio. Nunu & His Best Friend. 2012. 32p. pap. 17.25 *(978-1-4669-1143-7(3))* Trafford Publishing.

Adams, Diane. Love Is: (Illustrated Story Book about Caring for Others, Book about Love for Parents & Children, Rhyming Picture Book) Keane, Claire, illus. 2017. (ENG.). 32p. (J). (gr. -1-k). 15.99 *(978-1-4521-3997-5(0))* Chronicle Bks. LLC.

Adams, Kevin. A Stegosaurus Named Sam. Adams, Kevin & Price, Michael, illus. 2004. (J). per. 12.50 *(978-0-9740683-4-3(9))* Authors & Artists Publishers of New York, Inc.

Adams, Kylie. Bling Addiction: Fast Girls, Hot Boys Series. 2006. (Fast Girls, Hot Boys Ser.: 2). (ENG.). 240p. (YA). (gr. 10-13). pap. 15.99 *(978-1-4165-2041-2(4)*, MTV Bks.) MTV Books.

Adams, L. Happy Memories: A Continuing Family Saga for Young Adults. 2003. 516p. pap. 26.95 *(978-0-595-29210-3(0))* iUniverse, Inc.

Adams, Michelle Medlock. How Much Does God Love You? Keiser, Paige, illus. 2019. (ENG.). 22p. (J). (gr. -1-1). bds. 6.99 *(978-0-8249-1689-3(1)*, Worthy Kids/Ideals) Worthy Publishing.

Adkins, Jan. A Storm Without Rain. 2004. (ENG., Illus.). 179p. (YA). (gr. 7). 14.95 *(978-0-937822-80-7(9))* WoodenBoat Pubns.

Adler, Dahlia. Just Visiting. 2015. (ENG.). 348p. (YA). (gr. 18-18). pap. 9.95 *(978-1-63392-053-8(4)*, 1396710, Spencer Hill Contemporary) Spencer Hill Pr.

Adornetto, Alexandra. Heaven. 2013. (Halo Trilogy Ser.: 3). (ENG.). 448p. (YA). (gr. 7-12). pap. 17.99 *(978-1-250-02941-6(4)*, 900118575) Square Fish.

Agresti, Aimee. Illuminate: A Gilded Wings Novel, Book One. 2013. (ENG.). 544p. (YA). (gr. 7). pap. 28.99 *(978-0-544-02222-5(X)*, 1528480, Clarion Bks.) HarperCollins Pubs.

—Infatuate: A Gilded Wings Novel, Book Two. 2013. (ENG.). 416p. (YA). (gr. 7). 17.99 *(978-0-547-62615-4(0)*, 1466666, Clarion Bks.) HarperCollins Pubs.

Aguirre, Ann. Vanguard: A Razorland Companion Novel. 2018. (Razorland Trilogy Ser.: 4). (ENG.). 368p. (YA). pap. 15.99 *(978-1-250-15867-3(2)*, 900185525) Square Fish.

Ahdieh, Renée. The Rose & the Dagger. (Wrath & the Dawn Ser.: 2). (ENG., Illus.). (YA). (gr. 7). 2017. 448p. pap. 12.99 *(978-0-14-751386-1(3)*, Penguin Books) 2016. 432p. 18.99 *(978-0-399-17162-8(2)*, G.P. Putnam's Sons Books for Young Readers) Penguin Young Readers Group.

—The Rose & the Dagger. 2017. (Wrath & the Dawn Ser.: 2). lib. bdg. 22.10 *(978-0-606-40106-7(7))* Turtleback.

—The Wrath & the Dawn. (Wrath & the Dawn Ser.: 1). (ENG.). (YA). (gr. 7). 2016. 432p. pap. 11.99 *(978-0-14-751385-4(5)*, Penguin Books) 2015. (Illus.). 416p. 18.99 *(978-0-399-17161-1(4)*, G.P. Putnam's Sons Books for Young Readers) Penguin Young Readers Group.

—The Wrath & the Dawn. 2016. lib. bdg. 22.10 *(978-0-606-38849-8(4))* Turtleback.

Ahmed, Naval. Blue Moon on Bandideau. 2008. 252p. pap. 15.50 *(978-1-4357-5458-4(1))* Lulu Pr., Inc.

Aker, Don. The Fifth Rule. 2014. (ENG.). 256p. (YA). (gr. 8). pap. 8.99 *(978-0-06-231348-5(7)*, HarperCollins) HarperCollins Pubs.

Alberts, Katharine O. Boo on the Loose. 2006. (J). 14.00 *(978-0-8059-7071-5(1))* Dorrance Publishing Co., Inc.

Alexander, Kwame. He Said, She Said. 2013. 330p. (YA). lib. bdg. *(978-0-06-211897-4(8))* Harper & Row Ltd.

—He Said, She Said. (ENG.). 336p. (YA). (gr. 9). 2014. pap. 10.99 *(978-0-06-211898-1(6))* 2013. 17.99 *(978-0-06-211896-7(X))* HarperCollins Pubs. (Amistad).

Alford, Douglas J. & Alford, Pakaket. How Do Hedgehogs Hug? Anderson, Jane A., illus. 2013. 58p. pap. 11.99 *(978-1-62495-071-1(X))* Manufacturing Application Konsulting Engineering (MAKE)in.

Allison, Catherine. Dear Daddy, I Love You. McNicholas, Shelagh, illus. 2014. (ENG.). (J). (gr. -1-3). *(978-1-74363-284-0(3))* Hinkler Bks. Pty, Ltd.

Alphen, Nick Van. One Day. 2012. 20p. pap. 24.95 *(978-1-4626-5524-3(6))* America Star Bks.

Alward, Amy. Royal Tour. 2017. (Potion Diaries). (ENG., Illus.). 432p. (YA). (gr. 7). pap. 11.99 *(978-1-4814-4382-1(8)*, Simon & Schuster Bks. For Young Readers) Simon & Schuster Bks. For Young Readers.

Ananda, Linda. Rainbow Childrenr-Magical Moving Stories: Stories with Movement, Dance, Yoga, & Song. 2012. 152p. pap. 47.95 *(978-1-4525-5475-4(7))* Balboa Pr.

Anderson, Jennifer. King of the Lake. 2013. 144p. (YA). pap. 10.99 *(978-1-62237-217-1(4))* Turquoise Morning Pr.

Anderson, Jodi Lynn. Tiger Lily. (ENG.). (YA). (gr. 8). 2019. 320p. pap. 11.99 *(978-0-06-288336-0(4))* 2013. 304p. pap. 9.99 *(978-0-06-200326-3(7))* 2012. 304p. 17.99 *(978-0-06-200325-6(9))* HarperCollins Pubs. (HarperCollins).

Anderson, Maree. Freaks in the City, Bk.2. 2015. (ENG., Illus.). 290p. pap. *(978-0-9941160-2-4(0))* Anderson, Maree.

Andreae, Giles. Heaven Is Having You. Cabban, Vanessa, illus. 2007. (Padded Board Bks.). 18p. (J). (gr. -1-1). bds. 7.95 *(978-1-58925-820-4(7))* Tiger Tales.

—Keep Love in Your Heart, Little One. Vulliamy, Clara, illus. 2007. 32p. (J). (gr. -1-3). 15.95 *(978-1-58925-066-6(4))* Tiger Tales.

—Love Is a Handful of Honey. Cabban, Vanessa, illus. 2004. 32p. (J). (gr. -1-k). 5.95 *(978-1-58925-353-7(1))* Tiger Tales.

Anne, Margo. Lily Rose. 2008. 194p. pap. 24.95 *(978-1-60703-847-4(1))* America Star Bks.

Anonuevo, Rechelle. The Moonlight Serenade. 2003. 140p. (YA). pap. 11.95 *(978-0-595-30627-5(6))* iUniverse, Inc.

Anstey, Cindy. Duels & Deception. 2017. (ENG.). 368p. (YA). pap. 26.99 *(978-1-250-11909-4(X)*, 900172672) Feiwel & Friends.

—Suitors & Sabotage. 2019. (ENG.). 352p. (YA). pap. 25.99 *(978-1-250-29473-9(8)*, 900195086) Square Fish.

Appelt, Kathi. Oh My Baby, Little One. Dyer, Jane, illus. 2006. (ENG.). 32p. (J). (gr. -1 — 1). pap. 5.99 *(978-0-15-206031-2(6)*, 1198114, Clarion Bks.) HarperCollins Pubs.

Applegate, Katherine. Beach Blondes: June Dreams, July's Promise, August Magic. 2008. (Summer Ser.: 1). (ENG.). 736p. (YA). (gr. 9). pap. 9.99 *(978-1-4169-6133-8(X)*, Simon Pulse) Simon Pulse.

—Spring Break. 2010. (Summer Ser.). (ENG., Illus.). 240p. (YA). (gr. 9-18). pap. 8.99 *(978-1-4169-9094-9(1)*, Simon Pulse) Simon Pulse.

—Sun-Kissed Christmas. 2010. (Summer Ser.). (ENG.). 208p. (YA). (gr. 9-18). pap. 8.99 *(978-1-4169-9397-1(5)*, Simon Pulse) Simon Pulse.

—Tan Lines: Sand, Surf, & Secrets; Rays, Romance, & Rivalry; Beaches, Boys, & Betrayal. 2008. (Summer Ser.: 2). (ENG.). 544p. (YA). (gr. 9). pap. 9.99 *(978-1-4169-6134-5(8)*, Simon Pulse) Simon Pulse.

Applegate, Katherine & Grant, Michael. The Islanders: Volume 2 Vol. 2: Nina Won't Tell & Ben's in Love. 2015. (Islanders Ser.: 2). (ENG.). 464p. (YA). (gr. 8). pap. 9.99 *(978-0-06-234078-8(6)*, HarperTeen) HarperCollins Pubs.

Arbuthnott, Gill. Beneath, 30 vols. 2014. 288p. (YA). 9.95 *(978-1-78250-052-0(9)*, Kelpies) Floris Bks. GBR. Dist: Consortium Bk. Sales & Distribution.

Arguello, Tito. A Dog in Love. 2005. 114p. (J). pap. 8.95 *(978-1-4116-2287-6(1))* Lulu Pr., Inc.

Armentrout, Jennifer L. The Darkest Star. 2019. (Origin Ser.: 1). (ENG.). 384p. (YA). pap. 11.99 *(978-1-250-17571-7(2)*, 900189438, Tor Teen) Doherty, Tom Assocs., LLC.

—Lux: Opposition: Special Collector's Edition. collector's ed. 2014. (Lux Novel Ser.: 5). (ENG.). 500p. (YA). 19.99 *(978-1-62266-733-8(6)*, 900146176) Entangled Publishing, LLC.

—Opposition. 2013. (Lux Ser.: Bk. 5). (ENG.). (J). pap. 9.99 *(978-1-62266-026-1(9)*, Entangled Teen) Entangled Publishing, LLC.

—Origin. 2013. (ENG.). (Lux Ser.: Bk. 4). (J). pap. 9.99 *(978-1-62061-280-4(1))*; (Lux Novel Ser.: 4). 400p. (YA). (gr. 7-12). pap. 10.99 *(978-1-62266-075-9(7)*, 900128407) Entangled Publishing, LLC.

—Stone Cold Touch. 2019. (Dark Elements Ser.: 2). (ENG.). 480p. (YA). pap. 15.99 *(978-1-335-00920-3(5))* Harlequin Enterprises ULC CAN. Dist: HarperCollins Pubs.

—White Hot Kiss. 2019. (Dark Elements Ser.: 1). (ENG.). 400p. (YA). pap. 10.99 *(978-1-335-00919-7(1))* Harlequin Enterprises ULC CAN. Dist: HarperCollins Pubs.

Armstrong-Ellis, Carey F. I Love You More Than Moldy Ham. 2015. (ENG., Illus.). 32p. (J). (gr. -1-3). 14.95 *(978-1-4197-1646-1(8)*, 1102101, Abrams Bks. for Young Readers) Abrams, Inc.

Arnold, David. Kids of Appetite. 2017. (ENG.). 368p. (YA). (gr. 9). pap. 10.99 *(978-0-14-751366-3(9)*, Speak) Penguin Young Readers Group.

—Kids of Appetite. 2017. lib. bdg. 22.10 *(978-0-606-40491-4(0))* Turtleback.

Arzave, Jose. Rabbit the Shepherd. 2013. 24p. pap. 10.99 *(978-1-62509-572-5(4))* Salem Author Services.

Asher, Jay. What Light. 2017. (ENG.). 272p. (YA). (gr. 7). pap. 10.99 *(978-0-448-49364-0(0)*, Razorbill) Penguin Young Readers Group.

—What Light. 2017. lib. bdg. 22.10 *(978-0-606-40488-4(0))* Turtleback.

Ashton, Brodi. Diplomatic Immunity. 2016. (ENG.). 368p. (YA). (gr. 8). 17.99 *(978-0-06-236856-0(7)*, Balzer & Bray) HarperCollins Pubs.

—Everbound. 2013. (Everneath Ser.: 2). (ENG.). 384p. (YA). (gr. 8). pap. 9.99 *(978-0-06-207117-0(3)*, Balzer & Bray) HarperCollins Pubs.

—Everneath. 2012. (Everneath Ser.: 1). (ENG.). 400p. (YA). (gr. 9). pap. 9.99 *(978-0-06-207114-9(9)*, Balzer & Bray) HarperCollins Pubs.

Atwood, D. E. If We Shadows. 2016. (ENG., Illus.). (J). 24.99 *(978-1-63533-033-5(5)*, Harmony Ink Pr.) Dreamspinner Pr.

Audho, Gaitree. Moral Stories for Kids. 2011. (ENG.). 32p. pap. 12.77 *(978-1-4634-4709-0(4))* AuthorHouse.

Aulbach, Kathy. Flower Sprouts: Let's have a Fest! 2009. 29p. 15.95 *(978-0-615-21683-6(8))* Flower Sprouts.

Austen, Jane. Pride & Prejudice. Kronheimer, Ann, illus. 2013. (Jane Austen Ser.). (ENG.). 64p. pap. 7.95 *(978-1-906230-06-7(4))* Real Reads Ltd. GBR. Dist: Casemate Pubs. & Bk. Distributors, LLC.

Authords, D. K. Being Alone. 2013. 120p. pap. 19.95 *(978-1-63000-114-8(7))* America Star Bks.

Avery, Lara. The Memory Book. (ENG.). (YA). 2017. 384p. (gr. 9-17). pap. 10.99 *(978-0-316-28376-2(2))* 2016. 368p. (gr. 10-17). 17.99 *(978-0-316-28374-8(6))* Little, Brown Bks. for Young Readers. (Poppy).

—The Memory Book. 2017. (YA). lib. bdg. 20.85 *(978-0-606-39907-4(0))* Turtleback.

—A Million Miles Away. 2016. (ENG.). 336p. (YA). (gr. 10-17). pap. 17.99 *(978-0-316-28372-4(X)*, Poppy) Little, Brown Bks. for Young Readers.

Babbitt, Natalie. The Eyes of the Amaryllis. 2007. (ENG.). 144p. (J). (gr. 5-8). per. 9.99 *(978-0-312-37008-4(3)*, 900044345) Square Fish.

Babcock, Nabila. To You That Give. 2012. 24p. pap. 24.95 *(978-1-4626-5215-0(8))* PublishAmerica, Inc.

Bacon, S. N. & Cunningham, Susan. Crow Flight. 2018. (ENG.). 352p. (YA). pap. 12.99 *(978-1-948705-16-5(8))* Amberjack Publishing Co.

Bader, Arlys Elaine. The Adventures of Garth & Cloey. 2008. 40p. pap. 16.99 *(978-1-4389-2472-4(0))* AuthorHouse.

Bailey, J. Leigh. Do-Gooder. (ENG., Illus.). (YA). 2017. 25.99 *(978-1-64080-360-2(2))* 2016. 24.99 *(978-1-63533-003-8(3))* Dreamspinner Pr. (Harmony Ink Pr.).

Bailey, Kristin. Legacy of the Clockwork Key. (Secret Order Ser.: 1). (ENG., (YA). (gr. 9). 2014. Illus.). 432p. pap. 9.99 *(978-1-4424-4027-2(9))* 2013. 416p. 17.99 *(978-1-4424-4026-5(0))* Simon Pulse. (Simon Pulse).

—Shadow of the War Machine. 2015. (Secret Order Ser.: 3). (ENG., Illus.). 448p. (YA). (gr. 9). 17.99 *(978-1-4424-6805-4(X)*, Simon Pulse) Simon Pulse.

Baker, Chandler. Alive. 2015. (ENG.). 368p. (J). (gr. 7-12). 17.99 *(978-1-4847-0683-1(8))* Hyperion Pr.

—Alive. 2017. (YA). lib. bdg. 20.85 *(978-0-606-39171-9(1))* Turtleback.

Baker, Jason. People Are People. 2012. (ENG.). 80p. pap. 28.00 *(978-1-105-72519-7(7))* Lulu Pr., Inc.

Baker, Jennifer. Sworn to Silence. 2014. (ENG., Illus.). 192p. (YA). (gr. 7). pap. 13.99 *(978-1-4814-2877-4(2)*, Simon Pulse) Simon Pulse.

Baker, Liza. Grandma Loves You Because You're You. McPhail, David, illus. 2018. (ENG.). 20p. (J). (gr. -1 — 1). bds. 8.99 *(978-1-338-27143-0(1)*, Cartwheel Bks.) Scholastic, Inc.

—I Love You Because You're You. McPhail, David, illus. 2008. (ENG.). 24p. (J). (gr. -1-k). bds. 8.99 *(978-0-545-02931-5(7)*, Cartwheel Bks.) Scholastic, Inc.

Baker, Roe. What's Wrong with Gretel Goann. 2010. 24p. pap. 11.50 *(978-1-60976-050-2(6)*, Eloquent Bks.) Strategic Book Publishing & Rights Agency (SBPRA).

Baldwin, James. The Story of Roland. 2013. pap. 31.93 *(978-1-4400-6789-1(9))* Forgotten Bks.

Baldwin, Kathleen. Refuge for Masterminds: A Stranje House Novel. 2018. (Stranje House Ser.: 3). (ENG.). 352p. (YA). pap. 18.99 *(978-0-7653-7605-3(9)*, 900133106, Tor Teen) Doherty, Tom Assocs., LLC.

Balog, Cyn. Sleepless. 2010. (ENG.). 240p. (YA). (gr. 7-12). 22.44 *(978-0-385-73848-4(X))* Random House Publishing Group.

Bandeira, Isabel. Bookishly Ever After: Ever after Book One. 2016. (Ever After Ser.: 1). (ENG.). 371p. (YA). (gr. 7-12). pap. 9.95 *(978-1-63392-058-3(5)*, Spencer Hill Contemporary) Spencer Hill Pr.

Banks, Anna. Of Poseidon. 2013. (Syrena Legacy Ser.: 1). (ENG.). 384p. (YA). (gr. 8-12). pap. 15.99 *(978-1-250-02736-8(5)*, 900098308) Square Fish.

—Of Triton. 2014. (Syrena Legacy Ser.: 2). (ENG., Illus.). 304p. (YA). (gr. 8-12). pap. 12.99 *(978-1-250-04431-0(6)*, 900128325) Square Fish.

Banks, Nancy. Shamoni & Noemi. 2013. 32p. pap. 24.95 *(978-1-4626-9627-7(9))* America Star Bks.

Barakiva, Michael. Hold My Hand. 2019. (ENG.). 288p. (YA). 17.99 *(978-0-374-30486-7(6)*, 900160975, Farrar, Straus & Giroux (BYR)) Farrar, Straus & Giroux.

Barcelona, Adrian. Little Derek's Dilemm. 2011. 28p. pap. 24.95 *(978-1-4560-7931-4(X))* America Star Bks.

Barchers, Suzanne. The Tale of the Oki Islands: A Tale from Japan. Yokota, Hiromitsu, illus. 2013. (Tales of Honor Ser.). (ENG.). 32p. (J). (gr. 1-3). pap. 8.99 *(978-1-937529-62-8(2)*, 37673377-32eb-4b42-80ea-6f0d4a809b98) Red Chair Pr.

Bardugo, Leigh. Ruin & Rising. 2014. (Shadow & Bone Trilogy Ser.: 3). (ENG., Illus.). 432p. (YA). (gr. 7-12). 19.99 *(978-0-8050-9461-9(X)*, 900078589, Holt, Henry & Co. Bks. For Young Readers) Holt, Henry & Co.

Barkley, Brad & Hepler, Heather. Dream Factory. 2009. 272p. (YA). (gr. 7-18). 8.99 *(978-0-14-241298-5(8)*, Speak) Penguin Young Readers Group.

Barnard, Sara. A Quiet Kind of Thunder. (ENG.). (YA). (gr. 9). 2019. 416p. pap. 12.99 *(978-1-5344-0242-3(X))* 2018. 400p. 19.99 *(978-1-5344-0241-6(1))* Simon Pulse. (Simon Pulse).

Barnes, Jennifer Lynn. Nobody. 2014. (ENG.). 400p. (YA). (gr. 7-12). pap. 14.99 *(978-1-60684-508-0(X)*, 929b4dd8-ff43-47e1-b0c4-5807b46bfe3c, Carolrhoda Lab™) Lerner Publishing Group.

Barnes, Vivi. Paper or Plastic. 2015. (Entangled Teen Ser.). (ENG.). 352p. (YA). pap. 9.99 *(978-1-62266-521-1(X)*, 9781622665211) Entangled Publishing, LLC.

Barnholdt, Lauren. Right of Way. (ENG., Illus.). (YA). (gr. 9). 2014. 336p. pap. 9.99 *(978-1-4424-5128-5(9))* 2013. 320p. 16.99 *(978-1-4424-5127-8(0))* Simon Pulse. (Simon Pulse).

—Through to You. 2014. (ENG., Illus.). 288p. (YA). (gr. 9). 17.99 *(978-1-4424-3463-9(5)*, Simon Pulse) Simon Pulse.

—Two-Way Street. 2007. (ENG.). 304p. (YA). (gr. 9-18). pap. 10.99 *(978-1-4169-1318-4(1)*, Simon Pulse) Simon Pulse.

Baron, Michael & Aronica, Lou. A Winter Discovery. 2011. 60p. pap. 4.99 *(978-1-61188-027-4(0))* Story Plant, The.

Barrett, John F. The Stories of Jake. 2008. 64p. pap. 31.99 *(978-1-4363-2010-8(0))* Xlibris Corp.

Bashford, Taryn. The Harper Effect. 2018. (ENG.). 408p. (YA). (gr. 8-8). 17.99 *(978-1-5107-2665-9(9)*, Sky Pony Pr.) Skyhorse Publishing Co., Inc.

Baskin, Nora Raleigh. Subway Love. 2014. (ENG.). 224p. (YA). (gr. 9). 16.99 *(978-0-7636-6845-7(1))* Candlewick Pr.

Bass, Alexis. Love & Other Theories. 2014. (ENG.). 384p. (YA). (gr. 9). 17.99 *(978-0-06-227532-5(1)*, HarperTeen) HarperCollins Pubs.

Batchelor, Rhonda. She Loves You. 2008. (ENG.). 136p. (YA). (gr. 7-8). pap. 11.99 *(978-1-55002-789-1(1))* Dundurn Pr. CAN. Dist: Publishers Group West (PGW).

Bateson, Catherine. Lisette's Paris Notebook. 2018. (ENG., Illus.). 304p. (YA). (gr. 8-12). pap. 15.99 *(978-1-76029-363-5(6))* Allen & Unwin AUS. Dist: Independent Pubs. Group.

Bauer, Joan. Thwonk. 2005. 224p. (YA). (gr. 7-7). pap. 7.99 *(978-0-14-240429-4(2)*, Speak) Penguin Young Readers Group.

—Thwonk. 2005. 215p. (gr. 7-12). 18.00 *(978-0-7569-5782-7(6))* Perfection Learning Corp.

Beach, Rex. Heart of the Sunset. 2004. reprint ed. pap. 1.99 *(978-1-4192-2303-7(8))* Kessinger Publishing, LLC.

Beach, Rex E. Heart of the Sunset. 2004. reprint ed. pap. 33.95 *(978-1-4179-3787-5(4))* Kessinger Publishing, LLC.

Beard, Sarah. Beyond the Rising Tide. 2016. 298p. (YA). pap. 18.99 *(978-1-4621-1874-8(7))* Cedar Fort, Inc./CFI Distribution.

Beaty, Erin. The Traitor's Kiss. 2018. (Traitor's Trilogy Ser.: 1). (ENG.). 368p. (YA). pap. 12.99 *(978-1-250-15884-0(2)*, 900172348) Square Fish.

Beckford, Avril. I Love You 65 Bulldozers. 2009. 36p. pap. 15.49 *(978-1-4389-4048-9(3))* AuthorHouse.

Bedford, David. Mole's Babies. Beardshaw, Rosalind, illus. 2012. (ENG.). 32p. (J). *(978-1-58925-108-3(3))*; pap. *(978-1-58925-435-0(X))* Tiger Tales.

—Mole's in Love. Beardshaw, Rosalind, illus. 2009. 32p. (J). (gr. -1-1). (ENG.). 21.19 *(978-1-58925-084-0(2))*; pap. 6.95 *(978-1-58925-417-6(1))* Tiger Tales.

Bedford, L. B. Carefully Everywhere Descending. 2016. (ENG., Illus.). (YA). 24.99 *(978-1-63477-946-3(0)*, Harmony Ink Pr.) Dreamspinner Pr.

JKL

Bedrick, Claudia, tr. Jerome by Heart. 2018. (ENG., Illus.). 32p. (J). 16.95 *(978-1-59270-250-3(3))* Enchanted Lion Bks., LLC.

Beer, Sophie. Love Makes a Family. 2018. (ENG., Illus.). 26p. (J). (— 1). bds. 11.99 *(978-0-525-55422-6(X)*, Dial Bks) Penguin Young Readers Group.

Behl, Colin. Noüm. 2007. 108p. per. 16.95 *(978-1-4241-4518-8(X))* PublishAmerica, Inc.

Bell, Anthea. Frog in Love. Velthuijs, Max, illus. 2015. (J). *(978-1-4351-5750-7(8))* Barnes & Noble, Inc.

Bell, Cheryl. Boy Jesus. 2011. 24p. pap. 10.95 *(978-1-4497-1636-3(9)*, WestBow Pr.) Author Solutions, LLC.

Bell, Ellis. Wuthering Heights. 2017. (ENG., Illus.). (YA). (gr. 13-16). pap. 18.11 *(978-1-375-81205-4(X))*; pap. 15.95 *(978-1-375-74786-8(X))*; pap. 24.95 *(978-1-375-53651-6(6))* Creative Media Partners, LLC.

Bell, Liz. Mohawk, Fro or Crew, It Is up to You. 2011. 24p. pap. 24.95 *(978-1-4626-3196-4(7))* America Star Bks.

Belonie, Shannon. Oliver Andrew Ostrich: My Full Name. 2008. 12p. pap. 8.74 *(978-1-4343-5849-3(6))* AuthorHouse.

Bennett-Boltinghouse, Jo Ann. Yolandababy: A Pooch Finds Her Purpose! an Adventure in Self-Esteem. Julich, Jenniffer, illus. 2007. (YolandaBaby Ser.). 28p. (J). (gr. -1-3). 16.00 *(978-0-9785151-0-2(2))* Ginger Pr., The.

Bennett, Jenn. Alex, Approximately. 2018. (ENG.). 416p. (YA). (gr. 9). pap. 12.99 *(978-1-4814-7878-6(8)*, Simon Pulse) Simon Pulse.

—Serious Moonlight. 2019. (ENG., Illus.). 432p. (YA). (gr. 9). 19.99 *(978-1-5344-2514-9(4)*, Simon Pulse) Simon Pulse.

—Starry Eyes. 2019. (ENG., Illus.). 448p. (YA). (gr. 9). pap. 12.99 *(978-1-4814-7881-6(8)*, Simon Pulse) Simon Pulse.

Berenstain, Mike. The Berenstain Bears Love One Another. 2016. (Berenstain Bears Ser.). (ENG., Illus.). 20p. (J). bds. 7.99 *(978-0-8249-1983-2(1)*, Ideals Pubns.) Worthy Publishing.

Berger, Carin. All of Us. Berger, Carin, illus. 2018. (ENG., Illus.). 40p. (J). (gr. -1-3). 17.99 *(978-0-06-269413-3(8)*, Greenwillow Bks.) HarperCollins Pubs.

Bergren, Lisa Tawn. God Gave Us Love. Bryant, Laura J., illus. 2011. (God Gave Us Ser.). (ENG.). 22p. (J). (gr. k — 1). bds. 6.99 *(978-0-307-73027-5(1)*, WaterBrook Pr.) Crown Publishing Group, The.

—God Gave Us Love. 2009. (God Gave Us Ser.). (ENG., Illus.). 40p. (gr. -1-2). 10.99 *(978-1-4000-7447-1(9)*, WaterBrook Pr.) Crown Publishing Group, The.

Bernard, Romily. Never Apart. 2017. (ENG.). 400p. (J). 17.99 *(978-1-63375-822-3(2)*, 9781633758223) Entangled Publishing, LLC.

Berne, Emma Carlson. Never Let You Go. 2012. (ENG.). 256p. (YA). (gr. 9). pap. 9.99 *(978-1-4424-4017-3(1)*, Simon Pulse) Simon Pulse.

Bernet, Marti L. Remember... I Love You! 2010. 28p. 13.54 *(978-1-4269-4695-0(3))* Trafford Publishing.

Berry, Carolyn. Buster Tells It All: Stories from Pony Creek Ranch. Cash, Eric, illus. 2011. (ENG.). 24p. (J). 16.99 *(978-1-61254-011-5(2))* Brown Books Publishing Group.

Berry, Julie. All the Truth That's in Me. 2014. (ENG.). 304p. (YA). (gr. 7). pap. 9.99 *(978-0-14-242730-9(6)*, Speak) Penguin Young Readers Group.

Bevis, Kaitlin. The Iron Queen. 2015. (ENG., Illus.). 192p. (YA). (gr. 7-12). pap. 14.95 *(978-1-61194-636-9(0)*, ImaJinn Bks.) BelleBks., Inc.

Bickel, Karla. Heart Petals on the Hearth: A Collection of Children's Stories. Bickel, Karla, illus. 2004. (Illus.). 64p. (J). (gr. -1-6). 20.00 *(978-1-891452-00-0(2))* Heart Arbor Bks.

—Heart Petals on the Hearth: A Collection of Children's Stories. 2004. (Illus.). 64p. (J). (gr. -1-6). pap. 16.00 *(978-1-891452-01-7(0))* Heart Arbor Bks.

—Heart Petals on the Hearth II: A Collection of Children's Stories. 2004. (Illus.). 80p. (J). (gr. -1-6). 25.00 *(978-1-891452-04-8(5))*; pap. 20.00 *(978-1-891452-05-5(3))* Heart Arbor Bks.

Binks. The Girl with Chipmunk Hands. Begonia, Ruby, illus. 2013. 24p. (J). 15.95 *(978-1-935448-20-4(X))* Lost Coast Pr.

Biren, Sara. The Last Thing You Said. (ENG.). (YA). (gr. 9-17). 2019. 336p. pap. 9.99 *(978-1-4197-3375-8(3)*, 1138903) 2017. 320p. 17.95 *(978-1-4197-2304-9(9)*, 1138901) Abrams, Inc. (Amulet Bks.).

Bishop, Jennie. The Garden Wall: A Story of Love Based on I Corinthians 13. Stoddard, Jeff, illus. 2006. (ENG.). 32p. (J). (gr. 2-7). 12.99 *(978-1-59317-168-1(4))* Warner Pr., Inc.

Black, Cary & Schott, Gretchen Victoria. French Quarter Tori & the Red Owl. Travis, Caroline, illus. 2012. 38p. pap. 14.95 *(978-0-9754279-7-2(0))*; pap. 12.95 *(978-0-9754279-8-9(9))* Red Owl Pubns.

Black, Holly. Black Heart. (Curse Workers Ser.: 3). (ENG.). (YA). (gr. 9). 2013. 320p. pap. 12.99 *(978-1-4424-0347-5(0))*3. 2012. 304p. 19.99 *(978-1-4424-0346-8(2))* McElderry, Margaret K. Bks. (McElderry, Margaret K. Bks.).

—The Coldest Girl in Coldtown. 2013. 419p. (YA). *(978-0-316-27755-6(X))* Little Brown & Co.

—The Coldest Girl in Coldtown. 2014. (Coldest Girl in Coldtown Ser.). (ENG.). 448p. (YA). (gr. 10-17). pap. 12.99 *(978-0-316-21309-7(8))* Little, Brown Bks. for Young Readers.

—The Darkest Part of the Forest. 2019. (ENG.). 368p. (YA). (gr. 9-17). pap. 12.99 *(978-0-316-53521-9(0))* Little, Brown Bks. for Young Readers.

—The Darkest Part of the Forest. 2016. (YA). lib. bdg. 22.10 *(978-0-606-37533-7(3))* Turtleback.

Black Ice. 2014. (ENG., Illus.). 400p. (YA). (gr. 9). 19.99 *(978-1-4424-7426-0(2)*, Simon & Schuster Bks. For Young Readers) Simon & Schuster Bks. For Young Readers.

Blackman, Malorie. Black & White. 2007. (ENG.). 512p. (YA). (gr. 9-12). pap. 13.99 *(978-1-4169-0017-7(9)*, Simon & Schuster Bks. For Young Readers) Simon & Schuster Bks. For Young Readers.

—Naughts & Crosses. 2005. (ENG., Illus.). 400p. (YA). (gr. 9-18). 21.99 *(978-1-4169-0016-0(0)*, Simon & Schuster Bks. For Young Readers) Simon & Schuster Bks. For Young Readers.

Blake, Ashley Herring. Suffer Love. 2017. (ENG.). 352p. (YA). (gr. 9). pap. 9.99 *(978-0-544-93689-8(2)*, 1658698, Clarion Bks.) HarperCollins Pubs.

—Suffer Love. 2017. (ENG.). (YA). (gr. 9). lib. bdg. 20.85 *(978-0-606-39817-6(1))* Turtleback.

Blakeslee, S. E. Once upon a Blue Moon: The Chronicles of the Blue Moon. Blakeslee, S. E., illus. 2007. (ENG., Illus.). 32p. (J). 17.95 *(978-0-9789031-0-7(2))* Blaumond Pr.

Blankman, Anne. Prisoner of Night & Fog. (ENG.). (YA). (gr. 8). 2015. 432p. pap. 10.99 *(978-0-06-227882-1(7))* 2014. 416p. 17.99 *(978-0-06-227881-4(9)*, HarperCollins Pubs. (Balzer & Bray).

Blaskovic, Eva A. Beyond the Precipice. 2013. 406p. (YA). pap. *(978-0-9881638-1-2(0))* Ashby-BP Publishing.

Bleed Like Me. 2014. (ENG., Illus.). 288p. (YA). (gr. 11). 17.99 *(978-1-4424-9890-7(0)*, Simon Pulse) Simon Pulse.

Bliss, Bryan. Meet Me Here. 2016. (ENG.). 272p. (YA). (gr. 9). 17.99 *(978-0-06-227538-7(0)*, Greenwillow Bks.) HarperCollins Pubs.

Block, Francesca Lia. Psyche in a Dress. 2008. (ENG.). 128p. (YA). (gr. 9). pap. 8.99 *(978-0-06-076376-3(0)*, HarperTeen) HarperCollins Pubs.

Blount, Patty. Nothing Left to Burn. 2015. (ENG.). 368p. (YA). (gr. 8-12). pap. 9.99 *(978-1-4926-1329-9(0)*, 9781492613299) Sourcebooks, Inc.

—Some Boys. 2014. (ENG.). 352p. (YA). (gr. 7-12). pap. 10.99 *(978-1-4022-9856-1(0)*, 9781402298561) Sourcebooks, Inc.

Blume, Judy. Forever. 2007. (ENG.). 208p. (gr. 8-12). pap. *(978-1-4169-5391-3(4))* Gallery Pr., The.

Blumenthal, Deborah. The Lifeguard. (ENG.). 288p. (YA). (gr. 8-12). 2013. 9.99 *(978-0-8075-4536-2(8)*, 807545368) 2012. 16.99 *(978-0-8075-4535-5(X)*, 080754535X) Whitman, Albert & Co.

Bochynek, Halina. A Beagle's Tale. 2008. 152p. pap. 14.99 *(978-1-4389-1960-7(3))* AuthorHouse.

Bold, Emily. Breath of Yesterday. 0 vols. Bell, Katja, tr. 2014. (Curse Ser.: 2). (ENG.). 376p. (YA). (gr. 9-12). pap. 9.99 *(978-1-4778-4714-5(6)*, 9781477847145, Skyscape) Amazon Publishing.

Bolden, Tonya. Crossing Ebenezer Creek. (ENG.). 240p. (YA). 2018. pap. 10.99 *(978-1-63119-699-2(9)*, 900182277, Bloomsbury Young Adult) 2017. 17.99 *(978-1-59990-319-4(9)*, 900054246, Bloomsbury USA Childrens) Bloomsbury Publishing USA.

—Crossing Ebenezer Creek. 2018. (YA). lib. bdg. 22.10 *(978-0-606-41078-6(3))* Turtleback.

Bonaste, Sophie. The Sacrifices We Make [Library Edition]. 2014. 190p. pap. 14.99 *(978-1-62798-187-3(X)*, Harmony Ink Pr.) Dreamspinner Pr.

Bonnell, Kris. We Love Pets. 2007. (J). pap. 5.95 *(978-1-933727-56-1(X))* Reading Reading Bks., LLC.

Boock, Paula. Dare Truth or Promise. 2009. (ENG.). 176p. (YA). (gr. 9). pap. 10.99 *(978-0-547-07617-1(7)*, 1042007, Clarion Bks.) HarperCollins Pubs.

Boone, Martina. Illusion. 2016. (Heirs of Watson Island Ser.). (ENG., Illus.). 480p. (YA). (gr. 9). 17.99 *(978-1-4814-1128-8(4)*, Simon Pulse) Simon Pulse.

Boorman, Kate A. Darkthaw: A Winterkill Novel. 2015. (Winterkill Ser.). (ENG.). 336p. (YA). (gr. 7-17). 17.95 *(978-1-4197-1663-8(8)*, 1106301, Amulet Bks.) Abrams, Inc.

—Heartfire: A Winterkill Novel. 2016. (Winterkill Ser.: 3). (ENG.). 336p. (YA). (gr. 7-17). 17.95 *(978-1-4197-2124-3(0)*, 1106401, Amulet Bks.) Abrams, Inc.

Boucher, Sarah E. Becoming Beauty: A Retelling of Beauty & the Beast. 2014. 249p. (YA). pap. 15.99 *(978-1-4621-1455-9(5))* Cedar Fort, Inc./CFI Distribution.

Bourgeois, Paulette. Un Nouvel Ami pour Benjamin. 2004.Tr. of Franklin's New Friend. (FRE., Illus.). (J). (gr. -1-2). spiral bd. *(978-0-616-01828-6(2))* Canadian National Institute for the Blind/Institut National Canadien pour les Aveugles.

Bower, Gary. Mommy Love. Bower, Jan, illus. 2012. (Little Lovable Board Bks.). (ENG.). 16p. (J). bds. 8.50 *(978-0-9845236-0-3(X))* Storybook Meadow Publishing.

The Boy I Love. 2014. (ENG., Illus.). 288p. (YA). (gr. 7). 17.99 *(978-1-4424-8056-8(4)*, Atheneum Bks. for Young Readers) Simon & Schuster Children's Publishing.

Boyd, Lizi. I Love Daddy: Super Sturdy Picture Books. Boyd, Lizi, illus. 2004. (Super Sturdy Picture Bks.). (ENG., Illus.). 24p. (J). (gr. -1 — 1). 8.99 *(978-0-7636-2217-6(6))* Candlewick Pr.

Boyle, Amanda N. The Dream. 2007. 59p. per. 8.95 *(978-1-59824-506-6(6))* E-BookTime LLC.

Bracken, Alexandra. In the Afterlight. 2015. (Darkest Minds Ser.: 3). (YA). lib. bdg. 20.85 *(978-0-606-37505-4(8))* Turtleback.

—In the Afterlight (Bonus Content)-A Darkest Minds Novel, Book 3. 2018. (Darkest Minds Novel Ser.: 3). (ENG.). 624p. (YA). (gr. 7-12). pap. 10.99 *(978-1-368-02247-7(2)*, Disney-Hyperion) Disney Publishing Worldwide.

—Passenger-Passenger, Series Book 2. 2016. (Passenger Ser.: 2). (ENG.). 512p. (YA). (gr. 9-12). pap. 9.99 *(978-1-4847-3279-3(0)*, Disney-Hyperion) Disney Publishing Worldwide.

Bradbury, Jennifer. Wrapped. 2011. (ENG., Illus.). 320p. (YA). (gr. 7-18). 16.99 *(978-1-4169-9007-9(0)*, Atheneum Bks. for Young Readers) Simon & Schuster Children's Publishing.

Bradley, Carolyn. A Gingerbread Heart: Love... a Boy & a Gingerbread Boy with a Gingerbread Heart. 2012. (ENG.). 32p. pap. 21.99 *(978-1-4771-5730-5(1))* Xlibris Corp.

Bradley, Jeanette. Love, Mama. Bradley, Jeanette, illus. 2019. (ENG., Illus.). 28p. (J). bds. 7.99 *(978-1-250-24035-4(2)*, 900211506) Roaring Brook Pr.

Brant, Wendy. Zenn Diagram. 2018. (ENG.). 328p. (YA). (gr. 9-12). pap. 10.99 *(978-1-5253-0026-4(1))* Kids Can Pr., Ltd. CAN. Dist: Hachette Bk. Group.

Brashares, Ann. The Here & Now. 2015. lib. bdg. 22.10 *(978-0-606-37649-5(6))* Turtleback.

Brassill, Amber M. My Greatest Mistake, 1 vol. 2010. 236p. pap. 24.95 *(978-1-4489-9143-3(9))* America Star Bks.

Braswell, Liz. The Nine Lives of Chloe King: The Fallen; the Stolen; the Chosen. 2011. (Nine Lives of Chloe King Ser.). (ENG.). 784p. (YA). (gr. 9). pap. 14.99 *(978-1-4424-3570-4(4)*, Simon Pulse) Simon Pulse.

—The Nine Lives of Chloe King: The Fallen; the Stolen; the Chosen. 2011. lib. bdg. 25.75 *(978-0-606-23293-7(1))* Turtleback.

Brents, Alan. Sheldon the Sheep. 2011. 24p. pap. 12.79 *(978-1-4634-8728-7(2))* AuthorHouse.

Brewer, Nancy B. Princess Bertha & the Goose. 2011. 32p. pap. 24.95 *(978-1-4560-7868-3(2))* America Star Bks.

Brewer, Zac. Madness. 2017. (ENG.). 304p. (YA). (gr. 9). 17.99 *(978-0-06-245785-1(3)*, HarperTeen) HarperCollins Pubs.

Brewis, Alan. Boris Returns A Hero! 2008. 72p. pap. 12.50 *(978-1-4357-4377-9(6))* Lulu Pr., Inc.

Brewster, Bobby. Layla the Ridgeless Rhodesian Ridgeback. 2011. 36p. (J). pap. 27.95 *(978-0-615-37153-5(1))* Brewster, Robert.

Brian, Kate, pseud. Ex-Mas. 2009. (ENG., Illus.). 224p. (YA). (gr. 9-18). pap. 9.99 *(978-1-4169-9151-9(4)*, Simon & Schuster Bks. For Young Readers) Simon & Schuster Bks. For Young Readers.

Briceno, Carole. Turtle's Journey, 1 vol. White, Tina Jorgenson, illus. 2009. 28p. pap. 24.95 *(978-1-60813-934-7(4))* America Star Bks.

Bright, Rachel. Love Monster. 2014. (Love Monster Ser.). (ENG., Illus.). 32p. (J). (gr. -1 — 1). bds. 8.99 *(978-0-374-30186-6(7)*, 900141200, Farrar, Straus & Giroux (BYR)) Farrar, Straus & Giroux.

Brin, Susannah. A Summer Romance. 2003. (Illus.). 60p. (J). 3.95 *(978-1-58659-140-3(1))* Artesian Pr.

Bronte, Emily. Wuthering Heights. Burns, John M., illus. 2011. (ENG.). 160p. lib. bdg. 24.95 *(978-1-907127-80-9(1))* Classical Comics GBR. Dist: Publishers Group West (PGW).

—Wuthering Heights. 2018. (Faber Young Adult Classics Ser.). (ENG.). 448p. (gr. 13-16). pap. 8.95 *(978-0-571-33711-8(2))* Faber & Faber, Inc.

Brooks, Kevin. Naked '76. 2016. (ENG.). 424p. (YA). (gr. 9-12). E-Book 29.32 *(978-1-5124-0445-6(4)*, Carolrhoda Lab™) Lerner Publishing Group.

Brown, Jaye Robin. No Place to Fall. 2016. (ENG.). 384p. (YA). (gr. 9). pap. 9.99 *(978-0-06-227096-2(6)*, HarperTeen) HarperCollins Pubs.

Brown, Jennifer. Thousand Words. 2014. (ENG.). 304p. (YA). (gr. 10-17). pap. 16.99 *(978-0-316-20970-0(8))* Little, Brown Bks. for Young Readers.

Brown, Marc. Who's in Love with Arthur?, Vol. 10. unabr. ed. 2004. (Arthur Chapter Bks.: Bk. 10). (Illus.). 57p. (J). (gr. 2-4). pap. 17.00 incl. audio *(978-0-8072-0407-8(2)*, Listening Library) Random Hse. Audio Publishing Group.

Brown, Tara. White Girl Problems. 2013. 266p. pap. *(978-1-927866-06-1(5))* Brown, Tara Publishing.

Brown, Teri. Born of Deception. 2014. (Born of Illusion Ser.: 2). (ENG.). 336p. (YA). (gr. 8). 17.99 *(978-0-06-218757-4(0)*, Balzer & Bray) HarperCollins Pubs.

Bruna, Dick. Miffy Says, I Love You! 2004. (Illus.). 12p. bds. 5.99 *(978-1-59226-187-1(6))* Big Tent Entertainment, Inc.

Brunner, Kym. Wanted - Dead or in Love. 2014. (ENG.). 288p. (YA). 17.99 *(978-1-4405-7057-5(4)*, Simon Pulse) Simon Pulse.

Bryan, Barbara. Starfish, Seashells, Coral & Gems. 2010. 47p. (J). pap. 27.95 *(978-1-4327-6265-0(6))*; pap. 21.95 *(978-1-4327-6009-0(2))* Outskirts Pr., Inc.

Bryant Sr., Lydia. I Love Lydia, 1 vol. 2009. 20p. pap. 24.95 *(978-1-60703-488-9(3))* America Star Bks.

Buckley, Michael. Undertow. (Undertow Trilogy Ser.). (ENG.). (YA). (gr. 7). 2016. 400p. pap. 10.99 *(978-0-544-81319-9(7)*, 1641921) 2015. 384p. 18.99 *(978-0-544-34825-7(7)*, 1585834) HarperCollins Pubs. (Clarion Bks.).

Buehlen, M. G. The Fifty-Seven Lives of Alex Wayfare. 2015. (ENG., Illus.). 324p. (YA). pap. 15.99 *(978-1-62681-872-9(X)*, Diversion Bks.) Diversion Publishing Corp.

Buggs, Matthews. Beach Party. 2006. (J). 10.00 *(978-0-9790515-3-1(3))* Pinkston, Anastasia.

Bunting, Eve. The Voyage of the Sea Wolf. 2012. (Eve Bunting's Pirate Ser.). (ENG.). 192p. (J). (gr. 7-11). pap. 8.95 *(978-1-58536-790-0(7)*, 202335); lib. bdg. 15.95 *(978-1-58536-789-4(3)*, 202334) Sleeping Bear Pr.

—You Were Loved Before You Were Born. Barbour, Karen, illus. 2008. (J). pap. *(978-0-439-04062-4(0)*, Blue Sky Pr., The) Scholastic, Inc.

Burkhart, Jessica. Wild Hearts. 2015. (If Only... Ser.). (ENG.). 368p. (YA). (gr. 7). 17.99 *(978-1-61963-258-5(6)*, 9781619632585, Bloomsbury USA Childrens) Bloomsbury Publishing USA.

Burnham, Niki. Scary Beautiful. 2006. (Romantic Comedies Ser.). (ENG.). 272p. (YA). (gr. 9-12). mass mkt. 6.99 *(978-0-689-87619-6(X)*, Simon Pulse) Simon Pulse.

—Spin Control. 2011. (Romantic Comedies Ser.). (ENG.). 256p. (YA). (gr. 9). pap. 12.99 *(978-1-4424-3112-6(1)*, Simon Pulse) Simon Pulse.

Burnham, Niki & Saidens, Amy. Royally Jacked. 2003. (Romantic Comedies Ser.). (ENG.). 208p. (YA). mass mkt. 6.99 *(978-0-689-86668-5(2)*, Simon Pulse) Simon Pulse.

Burns, Laura J. & Metz, Melinda. Sacrifice. 2011. (ENG.). 272p. (YA). (gr. 9). 17.99 *(978-1-4424-3900-9(9)*, Simon & Schuster Bks. For Young Readers) Simon & Schuster Bks. For Young Readers.

Burstein, Lisa. MIA & the Bad Boy. 2015. (ENG., Illus.). 220p. (J). pap. 14.99 *(978-1-943336-18-0(0))* Entangled Publishing, LLC.

Burton, Hallie. Tapestry. (ENG., 2016. Illus.). (J). 27.99 *(978-1-63533-078-6(5))* 2013. 276p. (YA). pap. 16.99 *(978-1-62380-355-1(1))* Dreamspinner Pr. (Harmony Ink Pr.).

—Tapestry [Library Edition]. 2013. 276p. pap. 16.99 *(978-1-62380-926-3(6)*, Harmony Ink Pr.) Dreamspinner Pr.

Burton, Sharon Ann. When I Grow Up. 2013. 28p. (J). 24.95 *(978-1-4575-1802-7(3))* Dog Ear Publishing, LLC.

The Butterpop Cafe. 2004. 26p. *(978-1-887654-08-1(9))* Premium Pr. America.

Butterworth, MyLinda. The Monster Run. Day, Linda S., ed. Mercer, Matthew, illus. l.t. ed. 2004. 32p. (J). (gr. -1-3). 14.95 *(978-1-890905-23-1(2)*, Day to Day Bks.) Day to Day Enterprises.

Buxbaum, Julie. What to Say Next. (ENG.). (YA). (gr. 7). 2018. 320p. pap. 9.99 *(978-0-553-53571-6(4)*, Ember) 2017. 304p. 18.99 *(978-0-553-53568-6(4)*, Delacorte Pr.) Random Hse. Children's Bks.

Byars, Betsy. A Blossom Promise. (Blossom Family Ser.: Bk. 4). 145p. (J). (gr. 4-6). pap. 4.50 *(978-0-8072-1444-2(2)*, Listening Library) Random Hse. Audio Publishing Group.

Byler, Linda. Little Amish Matchmaker: A Christmas Romance. 2012. (ENG.). 187p. 14.95 *(978-1-56148-776-9(7)*, Good Bks.) Skyhorse Publishing Co., Inc.

—When Strawberries Bloom: A Novel Based on True Experiences from an Amish Writer! 2010. (ENG.). 297p. pap. 13.99 *(978-1-56148-699-1(X)*, Good Bks.) Skyhorse Publishing Co., Inc.

Cabot, Meg. The Princess Diaries, Volume III: Princess in Love, Vol. 3. 2008. (Princess Diaries: 3). (ENG.). 256p. (YA). (gr. 8-12). pap. 10.99 *(978-0-06-147995-3(0)*, HarperTeen) HarperCollins Pubs.

—Princess in Love. 2004. (Princess Diaries: Vol. 3). 288p. (J). (gr. 7-18). pap. 38.00 incl. audio *(978-0-8072-2284-3(4)*, Listening Library) Random Hse. Audio Publishing Group.

Cahill, Katina. I Love You This Much. 2005. (Illus.). 24p. (J). 13.50 *(978-1-4120-4388-5(3))* Trafford Publishing.

Cain, Karen L. Squirrel's Curl. 2011. 24p. 13.00 *(978-1-4567-1466-6(X))* AuthorHouse.

Caletti, Deb. Essential Maps for the Lost. 2016. (ENG., Illus.). 336p. (YA). (gr. 9). 17.99 *(978-1-4814-1516-3(6)*, Simon Pulse) Simon Pulse.

—Honey, Baby, Sweetheart. 2008. (ENG.). 336p. (YA). (gr. 7-12). pap. 9.99 *(978-1-4169-5783-6(9)*, Simon Pulse) Simon Pulse.

—The Last Forever. 2014. (ENG., Illus.). 336p. (YA). (gr. 7-7). 17.99 *(978-1-4424-5000-4(2)*, Simon Pulse) Simon Pulse.

—The Last Forever. 2016. lib. bdg. 22.10 *(978-0-606-38271-7(2))* Turtleback.

—Love Is All You Need: Wild Roses; the Nature of Jade. 2013. (ENG.). 608p. (YA). (gr. 7-7). pap. 11.99 *(978-1-4424-6636-4(7)*, Simon Pulse) Simon Pulse.

—The Queen of Everything. 2008. (ENG.). 352p. (YA). (gr. 7-12). pap. 11.99 *(978-1-4169-5781-2(2)*, Simon Pulse) Simon Pulse.

—The Story of Us. 2012. (ENG.). 400p. (YA). (gr. 7-12). 16.99 *(978-1-4424-2346-6(3)*, Simon Pulse) Simon Pulse.

—Wild Roses. 2008. (ENG.). 320p. (YA). (gr. 7-12). pap. 8.99 *(978-1-4169-5782-9(0)*, Simon Pulse) Simon Pulse.

Campbell, Wanda Gail. Little Buckets Full of Big Love. 2008. (Illus.). 48p. pap. 19.49 *(978-1-4389-0688-1(9))* AuthorHouse.

Capetta, A. R. Echo after Echo. 2017. (ENG.). 432p. (YA). (gr. 9). 17.99 *(978-0-7636-9164-6(X))* Candlewick Pr.

Capucilli, Alyssa Satin. Blanket of Love. Boynton-Hughes, Brooke, illus. 2017. (New Books for Newborns Ser.). (ENG.). 16p. (J). (gr. -1 — 1). bds. 7.99 *(978-1-4814-8972-0(0)*, Little Simon) Little Simon.

—Panda Kisses. Widdowson, Kay, illus. 2008. (Step into Reading: Step 1 Ser.). (ENG.). 32p. (J). (gr. -1-1). lib. bdg. 16.19 *(978-0-375-94562-5(8))* Random House Publishing Group.

—Panda Kisses. Widdowson, Kay, illus. 2008. (Step into Reading Ser.). 32p. (J). (gr. -1-1). pap. 5.99 *(978-0-375-84562-8(3)*, Random Hse. Bks. for Young Readers) Random Hse. Children's Bks.

Caraballo, Samuel. Estas Manos: Manitas de Mi Familia. Costello, Shawn, illus. 2014.Tr. of These Hands: My Family's Hands. (ENG & SPA.). (J). 17.95 *(978-1-55885-795-7(8)*, Piñata Books) Arte Publico Pr.

Cardi, Annie. The Chance You Won't Return. 2014. (ENG.). 352p. (YA). (gr. 7). 16.99 *(978-0-7636-6292-9(5))* Candlewick Pr.

Carey, Anna. Once. 2. 2013. (Eve Ser.: 2). (ENG.). 384p. (YA). (gr. 8-12). pap. 10.99 *(978-0-06-204855-4(4)*, HarperCollins) HarperCollins Pubs.

—Rise. 2013. (Eve Ser.: 3). (ENG.). 336p. (YA). (gr. 8). pap. 10.99 *(978-0-06-204858-5(9)*, HarperCollins) HarperCollins Pubs.

—Rise: An Eve Novel. 2013. (Illus.). 320p. (YA). pap. 9.99 *(978-0-06-226273-8(4))* HarperCollins Pubs.

Carle, Eric. Love from the Very Hungry Caterpillar. 2015. (World of Eric Carle Ser.). (ENG., Illus.). 32p. (J). (-k). 9.99 *(978-0-448-48932-2(5))* Penguin Young Readers Group.

Carrière, Francine. Comme un Conte d'Enfant et le Clochard de New Perry. 2012. 94p. pap. *(978-1-55483-933-9(5))* Insomniac Pr.

Carson, Diana Pastora. All the Muchos in the World: A Special Story about Love. Pruitt, Ginny, illus. 2006. 32p. (J). pap. 8.95 *(978-0-8198-0779-3(6))* Pauline Bks. & Media.

Carson, Rae. The Crown of Embers. 2019. (Girl of Fire & Thorns Ser.: 2). (ENG.). 432p. (YA). (gr. 8). pap. 10.99 *(978-0-06-202653-8(4)*, Greenwillow Bks.) HarperCollins Pubs.

Cart, Michael, ed. Love & Sex. 2003. (ENG.). 240p. (YA). (gr. 8). pap. 13.95 *(978-0-689-85668-6(7)*, Simon Pulse) Simon Pulse.

Cart, Michael, et al. How Beautiful the Ordinary: Twelve Stories of Identity. 2009. (ENG.). 368p. (YA). (gr. 9-18). 17.99 *(978-0-06-115498-0(9)*, HarperTeen) HarperCollins Pubs.

Carter, Aimée & Carter, Aimée. Pawn. 2013. (Blackcoat Rebellion Ser.: 1). (ENG.). 352p. (YA). 17.99 *(978-0-373-21055-8(8)*, Harlequin Teen) Harlequin Enterprises ULC CAN. Dist: HarperCollins Pubs.

Cash, John Carter. Daddy Loves His Little Girl. Burckhardt, Marc, illus. 2010. (ENG.). 32p. (J). (gr. -1-3). 16.99 *(978-1-4169-7482-6(2)*, Little Simon Inspirations) Little Simon Inspirations.

Cass, Kiera. The Elite. (Selection Ser.: 2). (ENG.). (YA). (gr. 8). 2014. 352p. pap. 12.99 *(978-0-06-205997-0(1))* 2013. 336p. 19.99 *(978-0-06-205996-3(3))* HarperCollins Pubs. (HarperTeen).

—The Elite. 2014. (Selection Ser.: 2). (YA). lib. bdg. 20.85 *(978-0-606-35489-9(1))* Turtleback.

—La Elite / the Elite, Vol. 1. 2013. (SelecciÓn / the Selection Ser.: 2). (SPA.). 224p. (YA). (gr. 8-12). pap. 20.95 *(978-84-9918-613-9(0))* Penguin Random House Grupo Editorial ESP. Dist: Penguin Random Hse. LLC.

—La Elite/ the Elite, Vol. 2. 2017. (SelecciÓn / the Selection Ser.: 2). (SPA.). 224p. (J). (gr. 8-12). pap. 12.95 *(978-84-16240-61-6(2))* Penguin Random House Grupo Editorial ESP. Dist: Penguin Random Hse. LLC.

—Happily Ever After. 2015. (ENG., Illus.). 416p. (YA). *(978-0-00-814366-4(8))* HarperCollins Pubs.

—Happily Ever after: Companion to the Selection Series. 2015. (Selection Novella Ser.). (ENG., Illus.). 416p. (YA). (gr. 8). 18.99 *(978-0-06-241408-3(9)*, HarperTeen) HarperCollins Pubs.

—The One. (Selection Ser.: 3). (ENG.). (YA). (gr. 8). 2015. 368p. pap. 12.99 *(978-0-06-206000-6(7))* 2014. 336p. 19.99 *(978-0-06-205999-4(8))* HarperCollins Pubs. (HarperTeen).

—The Selection. (Selection Ser.: 1). (ENG.). (YA). (gr. 8). 2013. 352p. pap. 12.99 *(978-0-06-205994-9(7))* 2012. 336p. 19.99 *(978-0-06-205993-2(9))* HarperCollins Pubs. (HarperTeen).
—The Selection, Book 1. (ENG.). 336p. pap. *(978-0-00-746669-6(2),* HarperCollins Children's Bks.) HarperCollins Pubs. Ltd.
—The Selection. 2013. (Selection Ser.: 1). (YA). lib. bdg. 20.85 *(978-0-606-35488-2(3))* Turtleback.
—The Selection. 2013. (Selection Ser.: Vol. 1). (CHI & ENG.). 288p. (YA). (gr. 8). pap. *(978-986-133-471-4(8))* Yuan Shen Pr. Co., Ltd.
—The Selection Stories: the Prince & the Guard. 2014. (Selection Novella Ser.). (ENG.). 240p. (YA). (gr. 8). pap. 15.99 *(978-0-06-231832-9(2),* HarperTeen) HarperCollins Pubs.
—The Siren. (YA). 2017. (ENG.). 352p. (gr. 8). pap. 14.99 *(978-0-06-239200-8(X),* HarperTeen) 2016. 327p. pap. *(978-0-06-244954-2(0))* 2016. (ENG.). 336p. (gr. 8-12). 18.99 *(978-0-06-239199-5(2),* HarperTeen) HarperCollins Pubs.
—The Siren. 2017. (YA). lib. bdg. 20.85 *(978-0-606-40073-2(7))* Turtleback.
—The Siren. 2009. 276p. pap. 16.95 *(978-1-4401-5423-2(6))* iUniverse, Inc.
Castle, Jennifer. The Beginning of After. 2013. (ENG.). 448p. (YA). (gr. 8). pap. 9.99 *(978-0-06-198580-5(5),* HarperTeen) HarperCollins Pubs.
Castroman, Nicole. Blackhearts. 2016. (ENG., Illus.). 384p. (YA). (gr. 9). 17.99 *(978-1-4814-3269-6(9),* Simon Pulse) Simon Pulse.
Castrovilla, Selene. The Girl Next Door. 2010. 240p. (YA). (gr. 9-12). 16.95 *(978-1-934813-15-7(X))* Westside Bks.
Cauvin, Raoul. Cedric 1 - High-Risk Class. Laudec, Calvinaoul, illus. 2008. (Cedric Ser.: 1). 48p. pap. 11.95 *(978-1-905460-68-7(6))* CineBook GBR. Dist: National Bk. Network.
Cavallaro, Brittany. A Study in Charlotte. (Charlotte Holmes Novel Ser.: 1). (ENG.). (YA). (gr. 8). 2017. 352p. pap. 11.99 *(978-0-06-239891-8(1))* 2016. 336p. 17.99 *(978-0-06-239890-1(3))* HarperCollins Pubs. (Tegen, Katherine Bks).
Cebollero, Julie. The Lion That Roared. 2012. (ENG.). 61p. pap. 9.95 *(978-1-4327-8067-8(0))* Outskirts Pr., Inc.
Cefalo, Andrea. The Fairytale Keeper: Avenging the Queen. 2012. (ENG., Illus.). 274p. pap. 11.99 *(978-0-9851678-1-3(5))* Scarlet Primrose Pr.
Centeio, Tara Jaye. Mommy Loves Her Baby. Date not set. 32p. (J). (gr. -1-1). pap. 5.99 *(978-0-06-443715-8(9))* HarperCollins Pubs.
Cestari, Crystal. The Best Kind of Magic. 2018. (Windy City Magic Ser.: 1). (ENG.). 352p. (J). (gr. 7-17). pap. 9.99 *(978-1-4847-7570-7(8))* Hyperion Bks. for Children.
—The Fairest Kind of Love. 2019. (Windy City Magic Ser.: 3). (ENG.). 320p. (YA). (gr. 7-17). 17.99 *(978-1-368-03884-3(0))* Hyperion Bks. for Children.
—The Sweetest Kind of Fate. 2018. (Windy City Magic Ser.: 2). (ENG.). 320p. (YA). (gr. 7-12). pap. 9.99 *(978-1-4847-7569-1(4))* Hyperion Bks. for Children.
Chabot, Jason. Beyond: Broken Sky Chronicles, Book 3. 2017. (Broken Sky Chronicles Ser.: 3). (ENG.). 432p. (YA). 35.99 *(978-1-68162-608-6(X));* pap. 19.99 *(978-1-68162-607-9(1))* Turner Publishing Co.
Chaffin, Dawn Marie. My Love. 2010. 20p. 11.99 *(978-1-4520-0031-2(X))* AuthorHouse.
Chandler, Elizabeth. The Back Door of Midnight. 2004. (Dark Secrets Ser.: 5). (ENG.). 224p. (YA). mass mkt. 5.99 *(978-0-689-86642-5(9),* Simon Pulse) Simon Pulse.
—Everafter. (Kissed by an Angel Ser.). (ENG., 272p. (YA). (gr. 9). 2014. Illus.). pap. 11.99 *(978-1-4424-0919-4(3))* 2013. 16.99 *(978-1-4424-0918-7(5))* Simon Pulse. (Simon Pulse).
—Evercrossed. (Kissed by an Angel Ser.). (ENG.). (YA). (gr. 7). 2012. 304p. pap. 9.99 *(978-1-4424-0915-6(0))*2. 2011. 288p. 16.99 *(978-1-4424-0914-9(2))* Simon Pulse. (Simon Pulse).
—Everlasting. (Kissed by an Angel Ser.). (ENG.). (YA). (gr. 7). 2013. 336p. pap. 11.99 *(978-1-4424-0917-0(7))* 2012. 320p. 16.99 *(978-1-4424-0921-7(5))* Simon Pulse. (Simon Pulse).
—Love at First Click. 2009. (ENG.). 192p. (YA). (gr. 8-18). pap. 8.99 *(978-0-06-114311-3(1),* HarperTeen) HarperCollins Pubs.
Chapman, Elsie, et al. Hungry Hearts: 13 Tales of Food & Love. Chapman, Elsie & Richmond, Caroline Tung, eds. 2019. (ENG., Illus.). 368p. (YA). (gr. 7). 19.99 *(978-1-5344-2185-1(8),* Simon Pulse) Simon Pulse.
Charbonneau, Joelle. Graduation Day. 2015. (Testing Ser.: 3). (ENG.). 304p. (YA). (gr. 7). pap. 15.99 *(978-0-544-54120-7(0),* 1608879, Clarion Bks.) HarperCollins Pubs.
—Independent Study. 2015. (Testing Ser.: 2). lib. bdg. 20.85 *(978-0-606-36832-2(9))* Turtleback.
—Independent Study: The Testing, Book 2. (Testing Ser.: 2). (ENG.). (YA). (gr. 7). 2015. 336p. pap. 15.99 *(978-0-544-43945-0(7),* 1596844) 2014. 320p. 17.99 *(978-0-547-95920-7(6),* 1520240) HarperCollins Pubs. (Clarion Bks.).
Chastain, Emma. Confessions of a High School Disaster. 2017. (Chloe Snow's Diary Ser.). (ENG., Illus.). 352p. (YA). (gr. 7). 18.99 *(978-1-4814-8875-4(9),* Simon Pulse) Simon Pulse.
—Confessions of a High School Disaster: Freshman Year. 2018. (ENG.). 368p. (YA). (gr. 7). pap. 11.99 *(978-1-4814-8876-1(7),* Simon Pulse) Simon Pulse.
Chee, Traci. The Storyteller. 2019. (Reader Ser.: 3). 544p. (YA). (gr. 7). pap. 10.99 *(978-0-14-751807-1(5),* Penguin Books) Penguin Young Readers Group.
Chen, Justina. Return to Me. (ENG.). (YA). (gr. 7-17). 2014. 368p. pap. 19.99 *(978-0-316-10258-2(X))* 2013. 352p. 17.99 *(978-0-316-10255-1(5))* Little, Brown Bks. for Young Readers.
Cherrington, Sharnett Felicia. Bitter Sweet. 2005. (YA). per. 12.95 *(978-1-933570-70-9(9))* Aardvark Global Publishing.
Chichester Clark, Emma. Love Is My Favorite Thing. Chichester Clark, Emma, illus. 2015. (ENG., Illus.). 32p. (J). (gr. -1-k). 17.99 *(978-0-399-17503-9(2),* Nancy Paulsen Books) Penguin Young Readers Group.
Childress, Story. Momma, What's Love?, 1 vol. 2010. 28p. 24.95 *(978-1-61546-067-0(5))* PublishAmerica, Inc.
Childs, Tera Lynn. Falling for the Girl Next Door. 2016. (ENG., Illus.). (YA). pap. 16.99 *(978-1-68281-330-0(4))* Entangled Publishing, LLC.
Chris, Jerry. Beau, the Story of a Horse. 2003. 317p. (J). pap. 9.99 *(978-0-88092-482-5(9))* Royal Fireworks Publishing Co.
Church, Caroline Jayne. I Love You. Church, Caroline Jayne, illus. 2012. (ENG., Illus.). 6p. (J). (— 1). 12.99 *(978-0-545-46140-5(5),* Cartwheel Bks.) Scholastic, Inc.
Churchill, Vicky & Fuge, Charles. Butterfly Kiss. (ENG., Illus.). 28p. (J). pap. *(978-0-340-68614-0(6))* Hodder & Stoughton.
Ciocca, Gina. Last Year's Mistake. 2015. (ENG., Illus.). 320p. (YA). (gr. 9). 17.99 *(978-1-4814-3223-8(0),* Simon Pulse) Simon Pulse.
Clare, Cassandra & Chu, Wesley. The Red Scrolls of Magic. 2020. (Eldest Curses Ser.: 1). (ENG.). 384p. (YA). (gr. 9). pap. 14.99 *(978-1-4814-9509-7(7),* McElderry, Margaret K. Bks.) McElderry, Margaret K. Bks.
—The Red Scrolls of Magic. 2019. (Eldest Curses Ser.: 1). (ENG., Illus.). 368p. (YA). (gr. 9). 24.99 *(978-1-4814-9508-0(9),* SAGA Press) Simon & Schuster Bks. For Young Readers.
Clark, K. M. Beautiful Disaster. 2013. 106p. 24.99 *(978-1-4797-6506-5(6));* pap. 15.99 *(978-1-4797-6505-8(8))* Xlibris Corp.
Clark, M. H. T. L. C. 2015. 36p. 16.95 *(978-1-938298-42-4(X))* Compendium, Inc., Publishing & Communications.
Clark, Marshunna & Jones, Patrick. Duty or Desire. 2016. (Unbarred Ser.). (ENG.). 112p. (YA). (gr. 6-12). pap. 7.99 *(978-1-5124-0089-2(0),* 7e7f910c-b924-41c6-8a5b-472ea3801b0f); E-Book 42.65 *(978-1-5124-0090-8(4))* Lerner Publishing Group. (Darby Creek).
Claypoole, Joann. The Gardener's Helpers. 2015. (ENG.). 106p. (J). pap. 14.95 *(978-1-63047-532-1(7))* Morgan James Publishing.
Cleary, Beverly. The Luckiest Girl. 2007. (ENG., Illus.). 272p. (J). (gr. 5-18). pap. 6.99 *(978-0-380-72806-0(0),* HarperCollins) HarperCollins Pubs.
Clemont, Lynn C. The Angel Children. 2011. 28p. pap. 13.59 *(978-1-4567-6610-8(4))* AuthorHouse.
Clifford, Leah. A Touch Morbid. 2012. (Touch Mortal Trilogy Ser.: 2). (ENG.). 304p. (YA). (gr. 9). 16.99 *(978-0-06-200502-1(2),* Greenwillow Bks.) HarperCollins Pubs.
Clipston, Amy. Miles from Nowhere, 1 vol. 2015. (ENG.). 288p. (YA). pap. 9.99 *(978-0-310-73670-7(6))* Zondervan.
Coe, Mary E. The Prince of Betherland a Wonderful World of Fantasy. 2009. 112p. pap. 9.95 *(978-0-557-09297-0(3))* Lulu Pr., Inc.
Cohn, Rachel & Levithan, David. Nick & Norah's Infinite Playlist. 2009. 10.54 *(978-0-7848-2769-7(9),* Everbind) Marco Bk. Co.
—Nick & Norah's Infinite Playlist. 2007. 183p. (gr. 9-12). 19.00 *(978-0-7569-7949-2(8))* Perfection Learning Corp.
—Nick & Norah's Infinite Playlist. 2007. (ENG.). 208p. (YA). (gr. 9-12). pap. 9.99 *(978-0-375-83533-9(4),* Ember) Random Hse. Children's Bks.
—The Twelve Days of Dash & Lily. (Dash & Lily Ser.: 2). (ENG.). (YA). (gr. 7). 2017. 240p. pap. 10.99 *(978-0-399-55383-7(5),* Ember) 2016. (Illus.). 224p. 17.99 *(978-0-399-55380-6(0),* Knopf Bks. for Young Readers) Random Hse. Children's Bks.
Coker, Lauren. The Phantom's Lullaby: A Novel. 2008. 332p. pap. 19.95 *(978-0-595-47695-4(3))* iUniverse, Inc.
Colasanti, Susane. City Love. 2016. (City Love Ser.: 1). (ENG.). 352p. (YA). (gr. 9). pap. 9.99 *(978-0-06-230770-5(3),* Tegen, Katherine Bks) HarperCollins Pubs.
—Take Me There. 2008. (ENG.). 290p. (YA). (gr. 8-12). 22.44 *(978-0-670-06333-8(9),* Viking) Penguin Publishing Group.
Cole, Cathy. The New Girl. 2015. 210p. (YA). *(978-0-545-87876-0(4))* Scholastic, Inc.
Cole, Gwen. Ride On. 2018. (ENG.). 280p. (YA). (gr. 6-12). 16.99 *(978-1-5107-2993-3(3),* Sky Pony Pr.) Skyhorse Publishing Co., Inc.
Coley, Patrick. The Chronicles of Maxwell & His Runaways. 2012. 134p. 29.99 *(978-1-4797-0759-1(7));* pap. 19.99 *(978-1-4797-0758-4(9))* Xlibris Corp.
Collie, Brenda Faye. College Freshman 101. 2014. (ENG.). 282p. pap. 9.99 *(978-0-9840220-2-1(3),* 3c08c3a2-c1e2-4334-9d61-f48276aebfd9) Daylight Bks.
Collins, Amanda. Bff!!! or Not??? 2007. 168p. per. 20.99 *(978-1-4257-3370-4(0))* Xlibris Corp.
Collins, Amanda E. Bff!!! or Not??? 2007. 168p. 30.99 *(978-1-4257-3371-1(9))* Xlibris Corp.
Collins, Michael. Anu & the Blue. 2009. 166p. pap. 16.68 *(978-0-557-20316-1(3))* Lulu Pr., Inc.
Collins, Orlagh. No Filter. 2018. (ENG.). 368p. (YA). 17.99 *(978-1-68119-724-1(3),* 900182394, Bloomsbury USA Childrens) Bloomsbury Publishing USA.
Collins, Renee. Remember Me Always. 2017. (ENG.). 320p. (YA). (gr. 8-12). pap. 10.99 *(978-1-4926-4760-7(8))* Sourcebooks, Inc.
Collins, Tim. Notes from a Totally Lame Vampire: Because the Undead Have Feelings Too! Pinder, Andrew, illus. 2010. (ENG.). 336p. (J). (gr. 5-9). 12.99 *(978-1-4424-1183-8(X),* Aladdin) Simon & Schuster Children's Publishing.
—Prince of Dorkness: More Notes from a Totally Lame Vampire. Pinder, Andrew, illus. 2011. (ENG.). 336p. (J). (gr. 5-9). 12.99 *(978-1-4424-3388-5(4),* Aladdin) Simon & Schuster Children's Publishing.
Complete Nothing. 2014. (True Love Ser.: 2). (ENG., Illus.). 336p. (YA). (gr. 7). pap. 9.99 *(978-1-4424-7720-9(2),* Simon & Schuster Bks. For Young Readers) Simon & Schuster Bks. For Young Readers.
Connor, Leslie. The Things You Kiss Goodbye. 2014. (ENG.). 368p. (YA). (gr. 9). 17.99 *(978-0-06-089091-9(6),* Tegen, Katherine Bks) HarperCollins Pubs.
Constantine, Robin. The Promise of Amazing. 2015. (ENG.). 400p. (YA). (gr. 9). pap. 9.99 *(978-0-06-227949-1(1),* Balzer & Bray) HarperCollins Pubs.
Conway, Celeste. Unlovely. 2015. (ENG.). 254p. (YA). 17.99 *(978-1-4405-8279-0(3),* Simon Pulse) Simon Pulse.
Cook, Eileen. Remember. 2015. (ENG., Illus.). 320p. (YA). (gr. 9). 17.99 *(978-1-4814-1696-2(0),* Simon Pulse) Simon Pulse.
—What Would Emma Do? 2008. (ENG.). 320p. (YA). (gr. 9-10). pap. 8.99 *(978-1-4169-7432-1(6),* Simon Pulse) Simon Pulse.
Cook, Kristi. Eternal. (ENG., Illus.). (YA). (gr. 9). 2014. 432p. pap. 9.99 *(978-1-4424-8531-0(0))* 2013. 416p. 16.99 *(978-1-4424-8532-7(9))* Simon Pulse. (Simon Pulse).
—Magnolia. 2014. (ENG., Illus.). 336p. (YA). (gr. 9). 17.99 *(978-1-4424-8535-8(3));* pap. 10.99 *(978-1-4424-8534-1(5))* Simon Pulse. (Simon Pulse).
Cooper, Blayne. Blind Side of the Moon. 2016. (ENG.). 240p. (J). (gr. 7). pap. 16.95 *(978-1-59493-531-2(9))* Bella Bks., Inc.
Cooper, Jennifer. Guardian Angel. 2009. 155p. pap. 12.87 *(978-0-557-09330-4(9))* Lulu Pr., Inc.
Cooper, Mimi. Me Versus Cooties. 2006. 17p. 9.99 *(978-1-4116-8256-6(4))* Lulu Pr., Inc.
Cormier, Robert. Tenderness. 2004. (ENG.). 240p. (YA). (gr. 9). per. 8.99 *(978-0-385-73133-1(7),* Ember) Random Hse. Children's Bks.
Cornwell, Betsy. The Forest Queen. (ENG.). (YA). (gr. 7). 2020. 320p. pap. 9.99 *(978-0-358-13361-2(0),* 1749855) 2018. 304p. 17.99 *(978-0-544-88819-7(7),* 1653253) HarperCollins Pubs. (Clarion Bks.).
—Tides. 2014. (ENG.). 304p. (YA). (gr. 7). pap. 8.99 *(978-0-544-30296-9(6),* 1578441, Clarion Bks.) HarperCollins Pubs.
Corp, Carey. Destined for Doon, 1 vol. 2015. (Doon Novel Ser.: 2). (ENG.). 368p. (YA). pap. 12.99 *(978-0-310-74240-1(4))* Blink.
Corthron, Kara Lee. The Truth of Right Now. 2017. (ENG., Illus.). 288p. (YA). (gr. 9). 17.99 *(978-1-4814-5947-1(3),* Simon Pulse) Simon Pulse.
Cotton, Rachel. Nowhere Else but Here. 2018. (ENG.). 256p. (YA). (gr. 7). pap. 14.99 *(978-1-78530-163-6(2))* Black and White Publishing Ltd. GBR. Dist: Independent Pubs. Group.
Cotugno, Katie. Fireworks. 2018. (ENG.). 352p. (YA). (gr. 8). 2020. pap. 10.99 *(978-0-06-296393-2(7))* 2018. pap. 9.99 *(978-0-06-241828-9(9))* HarperCollins Pubs. (Balzer & Bray).
—How to Love. (ENG.). 416p. (YA). (gr. 9). 2020. pap. 10.99 *(978-0-06-296394-9(5))* 2015. pap. 9.99 *(978-0-06-221636-6(8))* HarperCollins Pubs. (Balzer & Bray).
—Top Ten. 2019. (ENG.). 384p. (YA). (gr. 8). pap. 9.99 *(978-0-06-241831-9(9),* Balzer & Bray) HarperCollins Pubs.
Coulthurst, Audrey. Of Fire & Stars. Saia, Jordan, illus. (Of Fire & Stars Ser.: 1). (ENG.). (YA). (gr. 8). 2018. 416p. pap. 10.99 *(978-0-06-243326-8(1))* 2016. 400p. 17.99 *(978-0-06-243325-1(3))* HarperCollins Pubs. (Balzer & Bray).
Covington, Jean. Nanny Planted Love. 2005. (J). lib. bdg. 19.95 *(978-0-9754728-9-7(5))* Big Ransom Studio.
Cozzo, Karole. The Truth about Happily Ever After. 2017. (ENG.). 320p. (YA). 34.99 *(978-1-250-12797-6(1),* 900175613) Feiwel & Friends.
—The Truth about Happily Ever After. 2018. (ENG.). 336p. (YA). pap. 14.99 *(978-1-250-15894-9(X),* 900185540) Square Fish.
Craig-Kendall, Ruth. Bobby Pew, That's Who. 2008. 22p. pap. 24.95 *(978-1-60672-095-0(3))* America Star Bks.
Cranford, Elizabeth A. I Love You Out Loud Daddy: I Love You Out Loud Children's Book Collection-Book #2. 2007. (ENG.). 34p. per. 15.99 *(978-1-4257-8896-4(3))* Xlibris Corp.
—I Love You Out Loud Mommy: I Love You Out Loud Children's Book Collection-Book #1. 2007. (ENG.). 36p. per. 15.99 *(978-1-4257-6723-5(0))* Xlibris Corp.
Craver, Marcella Marino. Joey Daring, Caring, & Curious. Lew-Vriethoff, Joanne, illus. 2014. 32p. (J). pap. *(978-1-4338-1653-6(9),* Magination Pr.) American Psychological Assn.
—Joey Daring Caring & Curious: How a Mischief Maker Uncovers Unconditional Love. Lew-Vriethoff, Joanne, illus. 2014. 32p. (J). *(978-1-4338-1652-9(0),* Magination Pr.) American Psychological Assn.
Creedle, Laura. The Love Letters of Abelard & Lily. (ENG.). 352p. (YA). (gr. 7). 2019. pap. 10.99 *(978-1-328-60366-1(0),* 1732073) 2017. 17.99 *(978-0-544-93205-0(6),* 1658576) HarperCollins Pubs. (Clarion Bks.).
Creel, Ann Howard. Call Me the Canyon: A Love Story. 2006. 211p. (J). per. 8.95 *(978-0-9768126-4-7(9))* Brown Barn Bks.
Cremer, Andrea. Bloodrose. 2012. (Nightshade Ser.: 3). lib. bdg. 22.10 *(978-0-606-26635-2(5))* Turtleback.
—Snakeroot. 2014. (Nightshade Ser.: 4). (ENG.). 352p. (YA). (gr. 9). pap. 10.99 *(978-0-14-750860-7(6),* Speak) Penguin Young Readers Group.
Crilley, Mark. Miki Falls: Autumn. Crilley, Mark, illus. 2007. (Miki Falls Ser.: 3). (ENG., Illus.). 176p. (J). (gr. 8-12). pap. 9.99 *(978-0-06-084618-3(6),* HarperCollins) HarperCollins Pubs.
Cross, Julie. Vortex: A Tempest Novel. 2013. (Tempest Trilogy Ser.: 2). (ENG.). 384p. (YA). (gr. 9-12). pap. 14.99 *(978-1-250-04478-5(2),* 900127471, St. Martin's Griffin) St. Martin's Pr.
Cross, Julie & Perini, Mark. Halfway Perfect. 2015. 384p. (YA). (gr. 8-12). pap. 9.99 *(978-1-4022-9719-9(X),* 9781402297199) Sourcebooks, Inc.
—You Before Anyone Else. 2016. 400p. (YA). (gr. 8-12). pap. 10.99 *(978-1-4926-0492-1(5),* 9781492604921) Sourcebooks, Inc.
Cross, Kady. Sisters of Blood & Spirit. 2016. (Sisters of Blood & Spirit Ser.: 1). (ENG.). 272p. (YA). pap. 9.99 *(978-0-373-21188-3(0),* Harlequin Teen) Harlequin Enterprises ULC CAN. Dist: HarperCollins Pubs.
—Sisters of Salt & Iron. 2016. (Sisters of Blood & Spirit Ser.: 2). (ENG.). 352p. (YA). 18.99 *(978-0-373-21176-0(7),* Harlequin Teen) Harlequin Enterprises ULC CAN. Dist: HarperCollins Pubs.
Cross, Mimi. Before Goodbye, 0 vols. 2016. (ENG.). 399p. (YA). (gr. 8-12). pap. 9.99 *(978-1-5039-4972-0(9),* 9781503949720, Skyscape) Amazon Publishing.
Croteau, Marie-Danielle. Fred & the Mysterious Letter, 1 vol. Cummins, Sarah, tr. St-Aubin, Bruno, illus. 2005. (Formac First Novels Ser.). (ENG.). 64p. (J). (gr. 2-5). 4.95 *(978-0-88780-688-9(0),* 688) Formac Publishing Co., Ltd. CAN. Dist: Formac Lorimer Bks. Ltd.
Crowley, Kieran Mark. Colm & the Lazarus Key. 2009. (ENG., Illus.). 224p. (J). pap. 14.95 *(978-1-85635-646-6(9))* Mercier Pr., Ltd., The IRL. Dist: Dufour Editions, Inc.
Crown Peak Publishing. Just Be You. Crown Peak Publishing, illus. 2008. (ENG., Illus.). 40p. (J). 19.95 *(978-0-9645663-5-4(4))* Crown Peak Publishing.
Crozier, Lorna. More Than Balloons, 1 vol. Miller, Rachelle Anne, illus. 2017. (ENG.). 26p. (J). (gr. -1 — 1). bds. 9.95 *(978-1-4598-1028-0(7))* Orca Bk. Pubs. USA.
Crystal, Billy. I Already Know I Love You. Sayles, Elizabeth, illus. 2004. 40p. (J). (ENG.). 16.99 *(978-0-06-059391-9(1));* lib. bdg. 17.89 *(978-0-06-059392-6(X))* HarperCollins Pubs.
Cuasay, Alison Taimanglo. Tasi & Matina: The Story of the First Clown Fish. 2010. 28p. pap. 12.99 *(978-1-4520-6672-1(8))* AuthorHouse.
Cuchna, Reid. Out of Love, 1 vol. 2009. 327p. pap. 29.95 *(978-1-60836-345-2(7))* America Star Bks.
Cumyn, Alan. Dear Sylvia, 1 vol. 2008. (ENG.). 184p. (J). (gr. 3-6). pap. 8.95 *(978-0-88899-848-4(1))* Groundwood Bks. CAN. Dist: Publishers Group West (PGW).
Cunningham, P. E. Slayer for Hire. 2013. 204p. pap. *(978-1-77130-285-2(2))* Evernight Publishing.
Cupidity. 2014. (Romantic Comedies Ser.). (ENG., Illus.). 288p. (YA). (gr. 9). pap. 13.99 *(978-1-4814-2746-3(6),* Simon Pulse) Simon Pulse.
Curry, Cicero. The Tickle Man. Ledbetter, John'el, illus. 2013. 44p. 24.95 *(978-1-63004-279-0(X))* America Star Bks.
Curtis, Jamie Lee. Tell Me Again about the Night I Was Born. 2004. (Illus.). (J). (gr. k-3). spiral bd. *(978-0-616-01623-7(9))* Canadian National Institute for the Blind/Institut National Canadien pour les Aveugles.
—Tell Me Again about the Night I Was Born. 2004. (Illus.). (J). (gr. k-3). spiral bd. *(978-0-616-01624-4(7))* Canadian National Institute for the Blind/Institut National Canadien pour les Aveugles.
Curtis, Marci Lyn. The Leading Edge of Now. 2018. (ENG.). 336p. (YA). (gr. 9-12). pap. 10.99 *(978-1-5253-0139-1(X))* Kids Can Pr., Ltd. CAN. Dist: Hachette Bk. Group.
Cypess, Leah. Death Sworn. 2015. (ENG.). 368p. (YA). (gr. 8). pap. 9.99 *(978-0-06-222122-3(1),* Greenwillow Bks.) HarperCollins Pubs.
Dahl, Regina. Love Is Not Selfish. 2013. (ENG.). 30p. pap. 13.95 *(978-1-4497-9289-3(8),* WestBow Pr.) Author Solutions, LLC.
Daines, Julie. Unraveled: A Tale of True Love. 2014. 192p. (J). pap. 14.99 *(978-1-62108-627-7(5))* Covenant Communications, Inc.
Dalton, Michelle. Pulled Under. 2014. (Sixteenth Summer Ser.). (ENG., Illus.). 288p. (YA). (gr. 7). pap. 9.99 *(978-1-4814-0700-7(7),* Simon Pulse) Simon Pulse.
—Swept Away. 2015. (Sixteenth Summer Ser.). (ENG., Illus.). 320p. (YA). (gr. 7). pap. 10.99 *(978-1-4814-3608-3(2),* Simon Pulse) Simon Pulse.
Daly, Maureen. Seventeenth Summer. 2010. (ENG.). 384p. (YA). (gr. 7). pap. 10.99 *(978-1-4169-9463-3(7),* Simon Pulse) Simon Pulse.
Daniel, Kashya. I Got the Terrible Twos Blues. 2010. 44p. 16.99 *(978-1-4490-9286-3(1))* AuthorHouse.
Dannenbring, McKinsey. A Lemon Without the Sour. 2009. 32p. pap. 14.49 *(978-1-4389-2367-3(8))* AuthorHouse.
Darling, Angela. Isabella's Spring Break Crush. 2014. (Crush Ser.: 6). (ENG., Illus.). 160p. (J). (gr. 3-7). pap. 5.99 *(978-1-4814-0493-8(8),* Simon Spotlight) Simon Spotlight.
—Lauren's Beach Crush. 2013. (Crush Ser.: 1). (ENG., Illus.). 176p. (J). (gr. 3-7). 15.99 *(978-1-4424-8038-4(6));* pap. 5.99 *(978-1-4424-8036-0(X))* Simon Spotlight. (Simon Spotlight).
—Lindsay's Surprise Crush. 2013. (Crush Ser.: 3). (ENG., Illus.). 144p. (J). (gr. 3-7). 15.99 *(978-1-4424-8045-2(9),* Simon Spotlight) Simon Spotlight.
—Maddie's Camp Crush. 2013. (Crush Ser.: 2). (ENG.). 160p. (J). (gr. 3-7). pap. 5.99 *(978-1-4424-8334-7(2));* (Illus.). 15.99 *(978-1-4424-8335-4(0))* Simon Spotlight. (Simon Spotlight).
—Rachel's Valentine Crush. 2013. (Crush Ser.: 5). (ENG., Illus.). 160p. (J). (gr. 3-7). 15.99 *(978-1-4424-8641-6(4));* pap. 5.99 *(978-1-4424-8640-9(6))* Simon Spotlight. (Simon Spotlight).
Darling, Tellulah. My Date from Hell. 2013. (Blooming Goddess Trilogy: 2). (ENG.). 388p. (YA). pap. *(978-0-9880540-6-6(X))* Te Da Media.
—My Life from Hell. 2014. (Blooming Goddess Trilogy: 3). (ENG.). 414p. (YA). pap. *(978-0-9880540-9-7(4))* Te Da Media.
Darwin, Florence Henrietta. The Lovers' Tasks. 2004. reprint ed. pap. 1.99 *(978-1-4192-7098-7(2))* Kessinger Publishing, LLC.
Daswani, Kavita. Lovetorn. 2012. (ENG.). 256p. (YA). (gr. 8). 17.99 *(978-0-06-167311-5(0),* HarperTeen) HarperCollins Pubs.
Davidowitz, Stacy. Camp Rolling Hills: Book Two: Crossing Over, Bk. 2. 2016. (Camp Rolling Hills Ser.: 2). (ENG., Illus.). 240p. (J). (gr. 3-7). pap. 8.95 *(978-1-4197-1880-9(0),* 1109903) Abrams, Inc.
Davies, Jacqueline. The Candy Smash. 2022. (Lemonade War Ser.: 4). (ENG., Illus.). 240p. (J). (gr. 3-7). pap. 9.99 *(978-0-544-22500-8(7),* 1563385, Clarion Bks.) HarperCollins Pubs.
Davis, Gene. Dromedarius & Camela. 2006. lib. bdg. 18.95 *(978-1-59094-115-7(2))* Jawbone Publishing Corp.
Davis, Jacky. Ladybug Girl & Her Papa. Soman, David, illus. 2017. (Ladybug Girl Ser.). 14p. (J). (— 1). bds. 6.99 *(978-0-8037-4035-8(2),* Dial Bks) Penguin Young Readers Group.
—Ladybug Girl Loves... Soman, David, illus. 2010. (Ladybug Girl Ser.). 12p. (J). (gr. -1 — 1). bds. 6.99 *(978-0-448-45374-3(6),* Grosset & Dunlap) Penguin Young Readers Group.
Davis, Lisa Selin. Lost Stars. 2017. (ENG.). 288p. (YA). (gr. 9). pap. 9.99 *(978-1-328-78731-6(1),* 1684477, Clarion Bks.) HarperCollins Pubs.
Dawn, Nyrae. Searching for Beautiful. 2014. (Entangled Teen Ser.). (ENG.). 304p. (YA). (gr. 7-12). pap. 9.99 *(978-1-62266-148-0(6),* 900129933) Entangled Publishing, LLC.
Daywalt, Drew. Love from the Crayons. Jeffers, Oliver, illus. 2019. (ENG.). 32p. (J). (gr. k-3). 9.99 *(978-1-5247-9268-8(3),* Penguin Workshop) Penguin Young Readers Group.
de Angeli, Marguerite. Elin's Amerika. 3rd ed. 2007. (Illus.). 98p. (J). pap. 15.99 *(978-0-9800761-0-3(2))* American Swedish Historical Museum.
de Gramont, Nina. Meet Me at the River. 2014. (ENG., Illus.). 384p. (YA). (gr. 9). pap. 11.99 *(978-1-4169-8016-2(4),* Atheneum Bks. for Young Readers) Simon & Schuster Children's Publishing.

J K L

de Jesus Paolicelli, Marisa. There's a Coqui in My Shoe! 2007. (Illus.). 66p. (J). 21.99 *(978-0-9797641-0-3(6))* Caribbean Experience Con Amor, LLC, A.

de la Cruz, Melissa. Alex & Eliza. (Alex & Eliza Trilogy Ser.: 1). (ENG.). (YA). (gr. 7). 2020. 400p. pap. 11.99 *(978-1-5247-3964-5(2),* Penguin Books) 2017. 368p. 18.99 *(978-1-5247-3962-1(6),* G.P. Putnam's Sons Books for Young Readers) Penguin Young Readers Group.

De la Cruz, Melissa. Alex & Eliza: A Love Story. Lt. ed. 2017. (ENG.). 444p. 22.99 *(978-1-4328-4051-8(7))* Cengage Gale.

—The Au Pairs. 2004. (Au Pairs Ser.: 1). (ENG.). 304p. (YA). 14.95 *(978-0-689-87066-8(3),* Simon & Schuster Bks. For Young Readers) Simon & Schuster Bks. For Young Readers.

de la Cruz, Melissa, et al. Snow in Love. 2018. (ENG.). 272p. (YA). (gr. 7). pap. 9.99 *(978-1-338-31018-4(6))* Scholastic, Inc.

de la Peña, Matt. Amor. Long, Loren, illus. 2018. Orig. Title: Love. 40p. (J). (gr. -1-3). 17.99 *(978-0-525-51880-8(0),* G.P. Putnam's Sons Books for Young Readers) Penguin Young Readers Group.

—Love. Long, Loren, illus. 2018. 40p. (J). (gr. -1-3). 17.99 *(978-1-5247-4091-7(8),* G.P. Putnam's Sons Books for Young Readers) Penguin Young Readers Group.

De Sena, Joseph. The Love Bug & the Light of Love. 2007. 64p. per. 19.95 *(978-1-4327-0748-8(X))* Outskirts Pr., Inc.

Delacre, Lulu. ¿Hasta dónde Me Amas? Delacre, Lulu, illus. 2014. (SPA., Illus.). 32p. (J). (gr. -1-6). pap. 12.95 *(978-1-62014-208-0(2),* leelowbooks) Lee & Low Bks., Inc.

Dellaira, Ava. Love Letters to the Dead. 2015. (YA). lib. bdg. 20.85 *(978-0-606-37590-0(2))* Turtleback.

DeLuca, Laura. Destiny. 2011. (ENG.). 276p. (YA). pap. 12.95 *(978-0-9826747-2-7(4))* Free Focus Publishing.

Demetrios, Heather. Bad Romance. 2018. (ENG.). 384p. (YA). pap. 16.99 *(978-1-250-15877-2(X),* 900159573) Square Fish.

Derting, Kimberly. Desires of the Dead. 2012. (Body Finder Ser.: 2). (ENG.). 384p. (YA). (gr. 9). pap. 8.99 *(978-0-06-177986-2(5),* HarperCollins) HarperCollins Pubs.

—The Last Echo: A Body Finder Novel, 3. 2013. (Body Finder Ser.: 3). (ENG.). 384p. (YA). (gr. 9-12). pap. 10.99 *(978-0-06-208220-6(5),* HarperCollins) HarperCollins Pubs.

Descoteaux, Chad. Once upon A Crime Syndicate: A mafia fairy Tale. 2006. 151p. pap. 24.95 *(978-1-4241-0893-0(4))* PublishAmerica, Inc.

Despain, Bree. The Eternity Key. 2015. (Into the Dark Ser.). (ENG.). 368p. (YA). (gr. 7-12). 18.99 *(978-1-60684-467-0(9),* f2df1f02-5404-4294-9108-285867af6c12); E-Book 29.32 *(978-1-5124-0179-0(X))* Lerner Publishing Group. (Carolrhoda Lab™).

—The Immortal Throne. 2016. (Into the Dark Ser.: 3). (ENG.). 344p. (YA). (gr. 7-12). 18.99 *(978-1-5124-0583-5(3),* 5f021e9e-aee4-4c3d-8519-1d2047ef1597, Carolrhoda Lab™) Lerner Publishing Group.

—The Lost Saint, 2. 2012. (Dark Divine Ser.). (ENG.). 416p. (gr. 7-12). 26.19 *(978-1-60684-058-0(4),* 9781606840580) Farshore GBR. Dist: Children's Plus, Inc.

—The Shadow Prince. (Into the Dark Ser.: Bk. 1). (ENG.). 496p. (YA). (gr. 7-12). 2015. pap. 9.99 *(978-1-60684-567-7(5),* af40ef41-9789-4250-8f17-2560460d2edc) 2014. 18.99 *(978-1-60684-247-8(1),* 5511e0e1-6e32-400a-aaae-d7ec6209d1a6) Lerner Publishing Group. (Carolrhoda Lab™).

Desrochers, Lisa. Original Sin. 2011. (Personal Demons Ser.: 2). (ENG.). 400p. (YA). (gr. 9-18). pap. 19.99 *(978-0-7653-2809-0(7),* 900070223, Tor Teen) Doherty, Tom Assocs., LLC.

Desrosiers, Sylvie. Qui Veut Entrer dans la Legende? Sylvestre, Daniel, illus. 2003. (Roman Jeunesse Ser.). (FRE.). 96p. (YA). (gr. 4-7). pap. *(978-2-89021-269-5(6))* Diffusion du livre Mirabel (DLM).

Dessen, Sarah. Once & for All. (ENG.). (YA). (gr. 7). 2018. 384p. pap. 11.99 *(978-0-425-29035-4(2),* Speak) 2017. 368p. 19.99 *(978-0-425-29033-0(6),* Viking Books for Young Readers) Penguin Young Readers Group.

Destiny, A. & Hapka, Catherine. Virtually in Love. 2015. (Flirt Ser.). (ENG., Illus.). 240p. (YA). (gr. 7). pap. 9.99 *(978-1-4814-2118-8(2),* Simon Pulse) Simon Pulse.

Destiny, A. & Kahler, A. R. Love Is in the Air. 2015. 221p. (YA). *(978-1-4814-2377-9(0),* Simon Pulse) Simon Pulse.

Destiny, A. & Lenhard, Elizabeth. Our Song. 2015. 225p. (YA). *(978-1-4424-8407-8(1),* Simon Pulse) Simon Pulse.

Deutsch, Stacia & Cohon, Rhody. In the Stars. 2012. (Romantic Comedies Ser.). (ENG.). 304p. (YA). (gr. 9). pap. 14.99 *(978-1-4424-8293-7(1),* Simon Pulse) Simon Pulse.

Dewdney, Anna. Llama Llama I Love You. 2014. (Llama Llama Ser.). (Illus.). 14p. (J). (gr. -1 — 1). bds. 6.99 *(978-0-451-46981-6(X),* Viking Books for Young Readers) Penguin Young Readers Group.

—Love from Llama Llama. Dewdney, Anna, illus. 2022. (Llama Llama Ser.). 32p. (J). (gr. k-3). 9.99 *(978-0-593-52174-8(9),* Grosset & Dunlap) Penguin Young Readers Group.

DeYoung, Andrew. On the Day You Were Baptized. Schmidt, Anita, illus. 2019. 32p. (J). (gr. -1 — 1). 17.99 *(978-1-5064-5552-5(2),* Beaming Books) 1517 Media.

Diamond, Laura. Endure. 2013. 268p. pap. 11.99 *(978-1-940223-45-2(8))* Etopia Pr.

Dicamillo, Kate. The Miraculous Journey of Edward Tulane. 2012. 22.00 *(978-1-61383-813-6(1))* Perfection Learning Corp.

—The Miraculous Journey of Edward Tulane. 2015. lib. bdg. 17.20 *(978-0-606-37892-5(8))* Turtleback.

DiCamillo, Kate. The Miraculous Journey of Edward Tulane. Ibatoulline, Bagram, illus. (ENG.). (J). 2015. 240p. (gr. 2-5). pap. 8.99 *(978-0-7636-8090-9(7))* 2009. 228p. (gr. 2-5). pap. 14.99 *(978-0-7636-4783-4(7))* 2006. 228p. (gr. 1-4). 19.99 *(978-0-7636-2589-4(2))* Candlewick Pr.

Dicamillo, Kate. The Miraculous Journey of Edward Tulane. Ibatoulline, Bagram, illus. 2009. 198p. (gr. 8-12). 23.30 *(978-1-4178-0763-5(6))* Turtleback.

Dickerson, Melanie. The Golden Braid, 1 vol. 2015. (ENG.). 320p. (YA). 16.99 *(978-0-7180-2626-4(8))* Nelson, Thomas Inc.

—The Huntress of Thornbeck Forest, 1 vol. 2015. (Medieval Fairy Tale Ser.: 1). (ENG.). 320p. pap. 15.99 *(978-0-7180-2624-0(1))* Nelson, Thomas Inc.

—The Noble Servant, 1 vol. 2017. (Medieval Fairy Tale Ser.: 3). (ENG.). 336p. (YA). 14.99 *(978-0-7180-2660-8(8))* Nelson, Thomas Inc.

—The Orphan's Wish, 1 vol. 2018. (ENG.). 352p. (YA). 16.99 *(978-0-7180-7483-8(1))* Nelson, Thomas Inc.

Did You Know That I Love You? 2014. (ENG., Illus.). 32p. (J). (gr. -1-3). 17.99 *(978-0-06-229744-0(9),* HarperCollins) HarperCollins Pubs.

Diesen, Deborah. Kiss, Kiss, Pout-Pout Fish. Hanna, Dan, illus. 2015. (Pout-Pout Fish Mini Adventure Ser.: 6). (ENG.). 14p. (J). (gr. -1 — 1). bds. 6.99 *(978-0-374-30190-3(5),* 900141730, Farrar, Straus & Giroux (BYR)) Farrar, Straus & Giroux.

Dietrich, Cale. The Love Interest. 2018. (ENG.). 384p. (YA). pap. 11.99 *(978-1-250-15864-2(8),* 900164748) Square Fish.

Diggs, Taye. I Love You More Than ... Evans, Shane W., illus. 2018. (ENG.). 32p. (J). 18.99 *(978-1-250-13534-6(6),* 900178264) Feiwel & Friends.

Dillon, Diane & Dillon, Leo, illus. Love & the Rocking Chair. 2019. (ENG.). 40p. (J). (gr. -1-k). 18.99 *(978-1-338-33265-0(1),* Blue Sky Pr., The) Scholastic, Inc.

Dillon, Elena. Crushing. 2013. 368p. (YA). pap. 13.99 *(978-0-9886353-4-0(8))* Dillon, Elena.

Disney. A Mother's Love. 2012. (Disney Princess Step into Reading Ser.). lib. bdg. 13.55 *(978-0-606-26392-4(6))* Turtleback.

Disney Books. The Little Mermaid ReadAlong Storybook & CD. 2013. (Read-Along Storybook & CD Ser.). (ENG., Illus.). 32p. (J). (gr. -1-k). pap. 6.99 *(978-1-4231-6889-8(5),* Disney Press Books) Disney Publishing Worldwide.

DK. I Love You Little One. 2018. (ENG.). 18p. (J). (— 1). bds. 12.99 *(978-1-4654-8016-3(1),* DK Children) Dorling Kindersley Publishing, Inc.

Dodd, Emma. Love. Dodd, Emma, illus. (Emma Dodd's Love You Bks.). (ENG., Illus.). (J). (— 1). 2018. 22p. bds. 9.99 *(978-0-7636-9941-3(1))* 2016. 24p. 14.99 *(978-0-7636-8941-4(6))* Candlewick Pr.

Dokey, Cameron. Beauty Sleep: A Retelling of "Sleeping Beauty" 2006. (Once upon a Time Ser.). (ENG.). 208p. (YA). (gr. 9-12). mass mkt. 8.99 *(978-1-4169-4014-2(6),* Simon Pulse) Simon Pulse.

—Before Midnight: A Retelling Of "Cinderella" 2007. (Once upon a Time Ser.). (ENG.). 208p. (YA). (gr. 7-12). mass mkt. 8.99 *(978-1-4169-3471-4(5),* Simon Pulse) Simon Pulse.

—Belle: A Retelling of " Beauty & the Beast" 2008. (Once upon a Time Ser.). (ENG.). 224p. (YA). (gr. 7-18). mass mkt. 8.99 *(978-1-4169-6131-4(3),* Simon Pulse) Simon Pulse.

Doktorski, Jennifer Salvato. How My Summer Went up in Flames. 2013. (ENG.). 320p. (YA). (gr. 9). 17.99 *(978-1-4424-5940-3(9));* pap. 10.99 *(978-1-4424-5939-7(5))* Simon Pulse. (Simon Pulse).

Donaldson, Jennifer. Lies You Never Told Me. 2019. 336p. (YA). (gr. 9). pap. 9.99 *(978-1-59514-853-7(1),* Razorbill) Penguin Young Readers Group.

Donne, Alexa. Brightly Burning. (ENG.). (YA). (gr. 7). 2020. 416p. pap. 9.99 *(978-1-328-60433-5(1),* 1732068) 2018. 400p. 17.99 *(978-1-328-94893-9(5),* 1705605) HarperCollins Pubs. (Clarion Bks.).

—The Stars We Steal. 2020. (ENG.). 400p. (YA). (gr. 7). 17.99 *(978-1-328-94894-6(3),* 1705521, HarperTeen) HarperCollins Pubs.

Donovan, Rebecca. Reason to Breathe, 0 vols. 2013. (Breathing Ser.: 1). (ENG.). 466p. (YA). (gr. 7-12). pap. 9.99 *(978-1-4778-1714-8(X),* 9781477817148, Skyscape) Amazon Publishing.

Dopirak, Kate. You're My Boo. Withrow, Lesley Breen, illus. 2016. (ENG.). 40p. (J). (gr. -1-3). 17.99 *(978-1-4424-4160-6(7),* Beach Lane Bks.) Beach Lane Bks.

Doty, Mariel. A Different Kind of Princess: Pictures of You. 2010. 260p. 26.50 *(978-1-60911-318-6(7),* Eloquent Bks.) Strategic Book Publishing & Rights Agency (SBPRA).

Doughty, Rebecca. Before You. Doughty, Rebecca, illus. 2016. (ENG., Illus.). 32p. (J). (gr. -1-3). 14.99 *(978-0-544-46317-2(X),* 1600264, Clarion Bks.) HarperCollins Pubs.

Douglas, Babette. Kiss a Me: A Little Whale Watching. Rockwell, Barry, illus. 2006. (Kiss a Me Teacher Creature Stories Ser.). (J). (gr. 3-7). 9.99 *(978-1-890343-08-8(0))* Kiss A Me Productions, Inc.

Douglas, Helen. Chasing Stars. 2016. (ENG.). 352p. (YA). 17.99 *(978-1-61963-410-7(4),* 900135715, Bloomsbury USA Childrens) Bloomsbury Publishing USA.

Douglas, L. B. Looking for Moemoe: Love Is never far Away. 2010. 24p. pap. 12.99 *(978-1-4490-2768-1(7))* AuthorHouse.

Douglas, Ryke Leigh. Molly the Trolley & Bud. 2008. 24p. pap. 11.95 *(978-1-4327-2207-4(7))* Outskirts Pr., Inc.

Doxey, Heidi. The Jane Journals at Pemberley Prep: Liam Darcy, I Loathe You. 2015. 215p. (YA). pap. 14.99 *(978-1-4621-1682-9(5))* Cedar Fort, Inc./CFI Distribution.

Drake, Brenda. Cursing Fate. 2016. (ENG., Illus.). (YA). pap. 15.99 *(978-1-68281-357-7(6))* Entangled Publishing, LLC.

—Touching Fate. 2015. (ENG., Illus.). 236p. (YA). (gr. 7). pap. 15.99 *(978-1-943892-68-6(7))* Entangled Publishing, LLC.

Du Jardin, Rosamond. A Man for Marcy. 2003. (YA). pap. 12.95 *(978-1-930009-76-9(3),* 800-691-7779) Image Cascade Publishing.

Duble, Kathleen Benner. Madame Tussaud's Apprentice: An Untold Story of Love in the French Revolution. 2014. (ENG.). 224p. (YA). 17.99 *(978-1-4405-8116-8(9),* Simon Pulse) Simon Pulse.

Duffy, Jacqueline Ann. Dillon the Dog Finds His Family. 2008. 24p. pap. 24.95 *(978-1-60563-331-2(3))* America Star Bks.

Dugan, Jennifer. Hot Dog Girl. 2019. 320p. (J). (gr. 7). 17.99 *(978-0-525-51625-5(5),* G.P. Putnam's Sons Books for Young Readers) Penguin Young Readers Group.

DuJardin, Rosamond. Boy Trouble. 2003. (YA). pap. 12.95 *(978-1-930009-70-7(4),* 800-691-7779) Image Cascade Publishing.

—The Real Thing. 2003. (YA). pap. 12.95 *(978-1-930009-71-4(2),* 800-691-7779) Image Cascade Publishing.

—Someone to Count On. 2003. (YA). pap. 12.95 *(978-1-930009-78-3(X),* 800-691-7779) Image Cascade Publishing.

Duksta, Laura. I Love You More. Keesler, Karen, illus. (J). 2013. 24p. (gr. -1-k). bds. 8.99 *(978-1-4022-9250-7(3))* 2009. 24p. bds. 6.99 *(978-1-4022-2460-7(5))* 2007. 34p. (gr. k-2). 17.99 *(978-1-4022-1126-3(0))* Sourcebooks, Inc. (Sourcebooks Jabberwocky).

—Te Quiero Más. Keesler, Karen, illus. 2013. 24p. (J). bds. 7.99 *(978-1-4022-8177-8(3),* Sourcebooks Jabberwocky) Sourcebooks, Inc.

Dumas, Alexandre. & Dumas, Alexandre., eds. La Dama de las Camelias. (SPA.). (J). 9.00 *(978-958-04-7139-4(8))* Norma S.A. COL. Dist: Distribuidora Norma, Inc.

Duncan, Lois. Debutante Hill. 2013. (ENG., Illus.). 232p. (gr. 6). pap. 12.95 *(978-1-939601-00-1(2))* lg Publishing, Inc.

Dunlap, Shannon. Izzy + Tristan. 2019. (ENG.). 336p. (YA). (gr. 9-17). 17.99 *(978-0-316-41538-5(3),* Poppy) Little, Brown Bks. for Young Readers.

Dunne, Amy. Secret Lies. 2013. (ENG.). 288p. (gr. 7). pap. 11.95 *(978-1-60282-970-1(5))* Bold Strokes Bks.

Durango, Julia & Terrones, Tyler. Here, There, Everywhere. 2017. (ENG.). 304p. (YA). (gr. 8). 17.99 *(978-0-06-231403-1(3),* HarperTeen) HarperCollins Pubs.

Dyan, Penelope. Bunny Love! a Book about Home & Bunnies. Dyan, Penelope, illus. 2013. (Illus.). 34p. pap. 11.95 *(978-1-61477-084-8(0))* Bellissima Publishing, LLC.

—Mikey & Me & the Valentines — -the Continuing Story of a Girl & Her Dog. Dyan, Penelope, illus. 2010. (Illus.). 50p. pap. 14.95 *(978-1-935118-96-1(X))* Bellissima Publishing, LLC.

—My Valentines. 2011. 34p. pap. 11.95 *(978-1-935630-52-4(0))* Bellissima Publishing, LLC.

—Some Bunny Loves You! 2013. 34p. pap. 11.95 *(978-1-61477-068-8(9))* Bellissima Publishing, LLC.

—The Warrior Mouse of Forest Hollow. Quinn, Courtney, illus. 2008. 108p. 17.95 *(978-1-935118-00-8(5))* Bellissima Publishing, LLC.

Dyer, Hadley. Here So Far Away. 2018. (ENG.). 368p. (YA). (gr. 9). 17.99 *(978-0-06-247317-2(4),* HarperTeen) HarperCollins Pubs.

Eade, Oliver. The Terminus. 2013. 264p. pap. *(978-1-909411-26-5(4))* Mauve Square Publishing.

Earhardt, Ainsley. I'm So Glad You Were Born: Celebrating Who You Are. Barnes, Kim, illus. 2022. (ENG.). 32p. (J). 18.99 *(978-0-310-77702-1(X))* Zonderkidz.

—Take Heart, My Child: A Mother's Dream. Kim, Jaime, illus. 2018. (ENG.). 34p. (J). (gr. -1-k). bds. 8.99 *(978-1-5344-2631-3(0),* Little Simon) Little Simon.

—Take Heart, My Child: A Mother's Dream. Kim, Jaime, illus. 2016. (ENG.). 32p. (J). (gr. -1-3). 18.99 *(978-1-4814-6622-6(4),* Aladdin) Simon & Schuster Children's Publishing.

Earnhardt, Heather L. The Wandering Goose: A Modern Fable of How Love Goes. Clements, Frida, illus. 2013. 64p. (J). 15.95 *(978-1-57061-881-9(X))* Sasquatch Bks.

Eastman, Brock & Eastman, Kinley. Daddy's Favorite Sound: What's Better Than a Woosh or a Giggle? 2019. (ENG., Illus.). 32p. (J). (gr. -1-3). 16.99 *(978-0-7369-7474-5(1),* 6974745) Harvest Hse. Pubs.

Ebner, Abra. Ladybird, Ladybird. 2011. 172p. (J). 16.99 *(978-0-9829505-4-8(3))* Crimson Oak Publishing LLC.

Echols, Jennifer. Most Likely to Succeed. 2015. (Superlatives Ser.). (ENG., Illus.). 352p. (YA). (gr. 9). 17.99 *(978-1-4424-7452-9(1),* Simon Pulse) Simon Pulse.

Edwards, Jean Pearce. Little Jean's War. 2008. (Illus.). 208p. pap. 14.49 *(978-1-4343-9133-9(7))* AuthorHouse.

Edwards, Jo. Go Figure. 2007. (ENG.). 288p. (YA). (gr. 9-12). pap. 13.99 *(978-1-4169-2492-0(2),* Simon Pulse) Simon Pulse.

—Love Undercover. 2006. (Romantic Comedies Ser.). (ENG.). 288p. (YA). (gr. 9-12). mass mkt. 6.99 *(978-1-4169-2465-4(5),* Simon Pulse) Simon Pulse.

Ehlert, Lois. Heart to Heart. Ehlert, Lois, illus. 2017. (ENG., Illus.). 72p. (J). (gr. -1-3). 9.99 *(978-1-4814-8087-1(1),* Beach Lane Bks.) Beach Lane Bks.

Elisabeth, Megan. A Star's Journey from Twinkle to Shine. 2012. 28p. pap. 24.95 *(978-1-62709-789-5(9))* America Star Bks.

Elkeles, Simone. Wild Cards. 2013. 352p. (YA). pap. *(978-0-8027-3738-0(2))* Walker & Co.

Ella, Sara. Coral, 1 vol. 2019. (ENG.). 384p. (YA). 18.99 *(978-0-7852-2445-7(9))* Nelson, Thomas Inc.

—Unbreakable, 1 vol. 2018. (Unblemished Trilogy Ser.: 3). (ENG.). 384p. (YA). 16.99 *(978-0-7180-8105-8(6))* Nelson, Thomas Inc.

Ellen, Tom & Ivison, Lucy. A Totally Awkward Love Story. 2018. (ENG.). 336p. (YA). (gr. 9). pap. 9.99 *(978-0-553-53735-2(0),* Ember) Random Hse. Children's Bks.

Elliott, Jenny. Save Me. 2015. (ENG.). 336p. (YA). (gr. 7-12). pap. 10.99 *(978-1-250-06147-8(4),* 900141885) Feiwel & Friends.

Elston, Ashley. The Rules for Breaking. 2014. (Rules Ser.). (ENG.). 320p. (J). (gr. 7-12). 16.99 *(978-1-4231-6898-0(4))* Hyperion Bks. for Children.

Emerson, Kevin. Encore to an Empty Room. 2016. (Exile Ser.: 2). (ENG.). 336p. (YA). (gr. 9). pap. 9.99 *(978-0-06-213399-1(3),* Tegen, Katherine Bks) HarperCollins Pubs.

—Finding Abbey Road. 2017. 256p. (J). pap. 9.99 *(978-0-06-213402-8(7))* 2016. (Exile Ser.: 3). (ENG.). 240p. (YA). (gr. 9). 17.99 *(978-0-06-213401-1(9))* HarperCollins Pubs. (Tegen, Katherine Bks).

Emery, Anne. Dinny Gordon Senior. 2004. (J). per. 9.95 *(978-1-59511-000-8(3))* Image Cascade Publishing.

Engelbreit, Mary. Baby Booky: Honey Bunny. Engelbreit, Mary, illus. 2004. (ENG., Illus.). 14p. (J). (gr. -1-18). 6.99 *(978-0-06-008135-5(X),* HarperFestival) HarperCollins Pubs.

Engle, Dawn D. Ella's Golden Hearts. 2009. 40p. pap. 14.75 *(978-1-60860-218-6(4),* Strategic Bk. Publishing) Strategic Book Publishing & Rights Agency (SBPRA).

Erickson, Timothy Ronald. Death's Whisper Recoil, 2. Erickson, Timothy Ronald, illus. 2003. (Illus.). (YA). pap. 14.95 *(978-1-59492-001-1(X))* Erickson, Tim.

Emshaw, Shea. The Wicked Deep. (ENG.). (YA). (gr. 9). 2019. 336p. pap. 12.99 *(978-1-4814-9735-0(9))* 2018. (Illus.). 320p. 19.99 *(978-1-4814-9734-3(0))* Simon Pulse. (Simon Pulse).

Escalante, Travis. The Story of Rocks & Balloons. 2013. 28p. 16.99 *(978-0-9897168-5-7(6))* Mindstir Media.

Escott, Maria. Green Anole Meets Brown Anole, a Love Story. Wigal, Mike, illus. 2010. 28p. pap. 12.95 *(978-1-936051-82-3(6))* Peppertree Pr., The.

Eshed, Tina. The Adventures of Bunzy: The Beginning. 2009. 60p. pap. 24.49 *(978-1-4389-2673-5(1))* AuthorHouse.

Estelle, Carrie. Molly Loves Her Sister. 2011. 20p. pap. 11.00 *(978-1-4567-6425-8(X))* AuthorHouse.

Esther Cravens Schwalger. Not Too Close. Eve Cravens Nawahine, illus. 2009. 16p. pap. 8.49 *(978-1-4389-6987-9(2))* AuthorHouse.

Ethington, Rebecca. Through Glass Omni 1: Omnibus Books 1-3. 2013. 324p. (YA). pap. 13.59 *(978-0-9884837-6-7(9))* Imdalind Pr.

Evangelista, Kate. The Boyfriend Bracket. 2018. (ENG.). 240p. (J). 27.99 *(978-1-250-18538-9(6),* 900191356) Feiwel & Friends.

—The Boyfriend Bracket. 2019. (ENG.). 256p. (YA). pap. 16.99 *(978-1-250-30917-4(4),* 900191357) Square Fish.

—No Love Allowed. 2016. (Dodge Cove Trilogy Ser.: 1). (ENG.). 256p. (YA). pap. 15.99 *(978-1-250-07390-7(1),* 900150895) Feiwel & Friends.

Evans, Edie. I Love You, Mommy! Demmer, Melanie, illus. 2019. (Little Golden Book Ser.). 16p. (J). (-k). 4.99 *(978-1-9848-5257-1(4),* Golden Bks.) Random Hse. Children's Bks.

Evans, Janelle. Consequences: Rory's Choice. 2017. (ENG., Illus.). 340p. (J). (gr. 6-18). pap. 17.99 *(978-1-941271-27-8(8),* Ink & Quill Pubs.) Mystic Pubs., Inc.

—Thorns of Revenge: Rory's Choice. 2018. (ENG., Illus.). 322p. (J). (gr. 6-18). pap. 17.99 *(978-1-941271-28-5(6),* Ink & Quill Pubs.) Mystic Pubs., Inc.

Evans, Loralee. The King's Heir. 2006. 287p. (YA). (gr. 8-12). per. 18.99 *(978-1-55517-865-9(0),* Bonneville Bks.) Cedar Fort, Inc./CFI Distribution.

Evans, Mari. Trusting Love. 2014. (ENG., Illus.). 200p. (YA). pap. 14.99 *(978-1-62798-955-8(2))* Dreamspinner Pr.

Everett, Sarah. Everyone We've Been. 2016. (Illus.). 400p. (YA). (gr. 7). 17.99 *(978-0-553-53844-1(6),* Knopf Bks. for Young Readers) Random Hse. Children's Bks.

Ewing, Amy. The Jewel. (Lone City Trilogy Ser.: 1). (ENG.). (YA). (gr. 9). 2015. 400p. pap. 10.99 *(978-0-06-223578-7(8))* 2014. 368p. 17.99 *(978-0-06-223579-4(6))* HarperCollins Pubs. (HarperTeen).

Fairfield, J. S. Cunning Foe: Faulkil. 2009. 88p. pap. 19.95 *(978-1-61546-603-0(7))* America Star Bks.

Falkoff, Michelle. Pushing Perfect. 2018. (ENG.). 368p. (YA). (gr. 8). pap. 9.99 *(978-0-06-231054-5(2),* HarperCollins) HarperCollins Pubs.

Fallon, Leigh. Carrier of the Mark. 2011. (Carrier of the Mark Ser.: 1). (ENG.). 352p. (YA). (gr. 8). pap. 8.99 *(978-0-06-202787-0(5),* HarperTeen) HarperCollins Pubs.

—Shadow of the Mark. 2013. (Carrier of the Mark Ser.: 2). (ENG.). 320p. (YA). (gr. 8). pap. 9.99 *(978-0-06-212800-3(0),* HarperTeen) HarperCollins Pubs.

Falter, Laury. Birthright. 2013. (Residue Ser.: bk.2). 310p. pap. 12.99 *(978-0-9855110-1-2(X))* William & William Publishing.

Farizan, Sara. If You Could Be Mine: A Novel. 2014. (ENG.). 272p. (YA). (gr. 9-12). pap. 9.95 *(978-1-61620-455-6(9),* 73455) Algonquin Young Readers.

Farrant, Natasha. What We Did for Love: Resistance, Heartbreak, Betrayal, 1 vol. 2014. (Scarlet Voyage Ser.). (ENG.). 208p. (gr. 6-7). 39.93 *(978-1-62324-028-8(X),* d31625c5-9ff5-4d47-8330-f4de9d508ec8); (Illus.). (YA). pap. 13.88 *(978-1-62324-029-5(8),* 10e6a221-1c2f-4eae-8d7f-a72204b5de2f) Enslow Publishing, LLC.

Farrington, Susan. What I Love about You. Farrington, Susan, illus. 2016. (ENG., Illus.). 32p. (J). (gr. -1-3). 17.99 *(978-0-06-239353-1(7),* Balzer & Bray) HarperCollins Pubs.

Feener, Chani Lynn. Amid Stars & Darkness. 2018. (Xenith Trilogy Ser.: 1). (ENG.). 384p. (YA). pap. 14.99 *(978-1-250-15895-6(8),* 900185541) Square Fish.

Feinstein, John. The DH (the Triple Threat, 3) 2017. (Triple Threat Ser.: 3). 304p. (J). (gr. 5). 8.99 *(978-0-553-53585-3(4),* Yearling) Random Hse. Children's Bks.

Ferrer, Caridad. When the Stars Go Blue: A Novel. 2010. (ENG.). 336p. (YA). (gr. 9-18). pap. 22.99 *(978-0-312-65004-9(3),* 900069171, St. Martin's Griffin) St. Martin's Pr.

Ferreri, Della Ross. Precious Baby. Dong, Monique, illus. 2019. 20p. (J). (gr. -1 — 1). 7.99 *(978-1-5064-4773-5(2),* Beaming Books) 1517 Media.

Fine, Sarah. Of Dreams & Rust. 2016. (ENG.). 304p. (YA). (gr. 9). pap. 11.99 *(978-1-4424-8362-0(8),* McElderry, Margaret K. Bks.) McElderry, Margaret K. Bks.

—Of Metal & Wishes. 2015. (ENG., Illus.). 352p. (YA). (gr. 9). pap. 11.99 *(978-1-4424-8359-0(8),* McElderry, Margaret K. Bks.) McElderry, Margaret K. Bks.

Fiori, Natalie. Lobsters in Seacliff. 2009. 52p. pap. 20.99 *(978-1-4490-1811-5(4))* AuthorHouse.

Firestone, Carrie. The Loose Ends List. 2016. (ENG.). 352p. (YA). (gr. 9-17). 17.99 *(978-0-316-38282-3(5))* Little, Brown Bks. for Young Readers.

Fitzpatrick, Becca. The Complete Hush, Hush Saga (Boxed Set) Hush, Hush; Crescendo; Silence; Finale. 2012. (Hush, Hush Saga Ser.: Bks. 1-4). (ENG.). 1744p. (YA). (gr. 9). 87.99 *(978-1-4424-7372-0(X),* Simon & Schuster Bks. For Young Readers) Simon & Schuster Bks. For Young Readers.

—Silence. (Hush, Hush Saga Ser.: Bk. 3). (ENG.). (YA). (gr. 9). 2013. 464p. pap. 13.99 *(978-1-4424-2665-8(9))* 2011. 448p. 21.99 *(978-1-4424-2664-1(0))* Simon & Schuster Bks. For Young Readers. (Simon & Schuster Bks. For Young Readers).

Fitzpatrick, Heather. Chuck: The Chicken That Thought He Was a Duck. 2012. 24p. pap. 17.99 *(978-1-4772-6012-8(9))* AuthorHouse.

Fitzpatrick, Huntley. What I Thought Was True. 2015. (ENG.). 448p. (YA). (gr. 9). pap. 10.99 *(978-0-14-242395-0(5),* Speak) Penguin Young Readers Group.

Fleet, Katherine. The Secret to Letting Go. 2016. (ENG., Illus.). 334p. (J). pap. 14.99 *(978-1-68281-070-5(4))* Entangled Publishing, LLC.

Fleming, Meg. I Heart You. Wright, Sarah Jane, illus. 2016. (ENG.). 40p. (J). (gr. -1-3). 17.99 *(978-1-4424-8895-3(6),* Beach Lane Bks.) Beach Lane Bks.

—I Heart You. Wright, Sarah Jane, illus. 2019. (Classic Board Bks.). (ENG.). 36p. (J). (gr. -1-3). bds. 8.99 *(978-1-5344-5130-8(7),* Little Simon) Little Simon.

Fleming, Theresa. Going Home with Jesus, 1 vol. Fleming, Yvonne B., illus. 2009. 22p. pap. 24.95 *(978-1-60813-703-9(1))* America Star Bks.

Fletcher, Erin. All Laced Up. 2016. (ENG., Illus.). (YA). (gr. 7). pap. 15.99 *(978-1-68281-316-4(9))* Entangled Publishing, LLC.

Foard, Judith P. Senior Year. 2013. 416p. pap. 16.95 *(978-1-4759-6552-0(4));* (gr. 10-12). 26.95 *(978-1-4759-6554-4(0))* iUniverse, Inc.

Fogliano, Julie. Just in Case You Want to Fly. Robinson, Christian, illus. 2019. (ENG.). 40p. (J). (gr. -1-2). 18.99 *(978-0-8234-4344-4(2),* Neal Porter Bks) Holiday Hse., Inc.

Fontaine, Nadine. More Than Anything in the World. 2008. 16p. per. 24.95 *(978-1-4241-9870-2(4))* America Star Bks.

Ford, Michael Thomas. Love & Other Curses. 2019. (ENG., Illus.). 352p. (YA). (gr. 9). 17.99 *(978-0-06-279120-7(6),* HarperTeen) HarperCollins Pubs.

Foreman, Michael. I Love You, Too! Foreman, Michael, illus. 2014. (ENG., Illus.). 32p. (J). (gr. -1-3). 16.95 *(978-1-4677-3451-6(9),* 63378a35-11be-4a7c-9c75-6054f13f3783) Lerner Publishing Group.

Forester, MaMa Eagle. Young Eagle, Pretty Flower. Spears, Ashley E., illus. 2004. 16p. (J). 7.95 *(978-0-9762389-4-2(2))* Trent's Prints.

Forian, Rosemary Talucci. My Own Angel. 2011. 28p. pap. 21.50 *(978-1-4583-3731-3(6))* Lulu Pr., Inc.

Forman, Gayle. Just One Day. 2013. (ENG.). 416p. (YA). (gr. 9). pap. 10.99 *(978-0-14-242295-3(9),* Speak) Penguin Young Readers Group.

—Just One Day. 2013. lib. bdg. 22.10 *(978-0-606-34405-0(5))* Turtleback.

—Just One Year. 2014. (ENG.). 352p. (YA). (gr. 9). pap. 10.99 *(978-0-14-242296-0(7),* Speak) Penguin Young Readers Group.

—Just One Year. 2014. lib. bdg. 22.10 *(978-0-606-36190-3(1))* Turtleback.

Foster, Jackie. Land of Anear, 1 vol. 2010. 27p. pap. 24.95 *(978-1-61546-634-4(7))* America Star Bks.

Foster, Jennifer L. The Puppy with the White Paw. 2011. 28p. pap. 12.99 *(978-1-4567-3912-6(3))* AuthorHouse.

Fox, Jeannine. Feeding Penny Pig. 2009. 32p. (J). 14.95 *(978-0-9841589-1-1(X))* Mimi's Funhouse, LLC.

Fox, Peter. April. 2004. 192p. (YA). per. *(978-0-9734848-2-3(9))* Coscom Entertainment.

Fraiberg, Jordanna. Our Song. 2014. (YA). pap. *(978-1-59514-625-0(3),* Razorbill) Penguin Publishing Group.

Frame, Andrew Graham. Ein Stein: The Chipmunk Who Succeeds by Brain Power. 2011. 52p. pap. 19.50 *(978-1-61204-416-3(6),* Strategic Bk. Publishing) Strategic Book Publishing & Rights Agency (SBPRA).

Francis, Lilian. The Supper Dance. 2009. (Illus.). 56p. pap. *(978-1-84748-531-1(6))* Athena Pr.

Frederick, Heather Vogel. Wish You Were Eyre. 2012. (Mother-Daughter Book Club Ser.). (ENG.). 464p. (J). (gr. 4-9). 16.99 *(978-1-4424-3064-8(8),* Simon & Schuster Bks. For Young Readers) Simon & Schuster Bks. For Young Readers.

Fredericks, Mariah. Love. Watkins, Liselotte, illus. 2007. (In the Cards Ser.: No. 1). (ENG.). 288p. (YA). (gr. 4-8). pap. 5.99 *(978-0-689-87655-4(6),* Simon & Schuster/Paula Wiseman Bks.) Simon & Schuster/Paula Wiseman Bks.

Freedman, Claire. I Love You, Baby! Abbot, Judi, illus. 2017. (ENG.). 32p. (J). (gr. -1-3). 17.99 *(978-1-4814-9904-0(1),* Simon & Schuster/Paula Wiseman Bks.) Simon & Schuster/Paula Wiseman Bks.

Freeman, Shannon. Listed. 2014. (Port City High Ser.: 6). (YA). lib. bdg. 20.80 *(978-0-606-36618-2(0))* Turtleback.

—A Port in Pieces. 2014. (Port City High Ser.: 8). (YA). lib. bdg. 20.80 *(978-0-606-36620-5(2))* Turtleback.

French, Vivian. Pig in Love. Archbold, Tim, illus. 2005. 32p. (J). lib. bdg. 9.00 *(978-1-4242-0889-0(0))* Fitzgerald Bks.

Friedman, Aimee. A Novel Idea. 2006. (Romantic Comedies Ser.). (ENG., Illus.). 256p. (YA). (gr. 9-12). mass mkt. 7.99 *(978-1-4169-0785-5(8),* Simon Pulse) Simon Pulse.

Friedman, Laurie. Love, Ruby Valentine. Avril, Lynne, illus. 2006. (Ruby Valentine Ser.). (ENG.). 32p. (J). (gr. k-3). lib. bdg. 16.95 *(978-1-57505-899-3(5),* 76ef85c3-9ebb-43e3-afc4-3afa1ae7878d, Carolrhoda Bks.) Lerner Publishing Group.

Friesen, Jonathan. Both of Me, 1 vol. 2016. (ENG.). 256p. (YA). pap. 9.99 *(978-0-310-73187-0(9))* Blink.

Frost, Melissa. The Dating Tutor. 2013. 98p. pap. *(978-1-77130-562-4(2))* Evernight Publishing.

Fuchs, A. P. Magic Man. 2005. 50p. per. *(978-0-9734848-7-8(X))* Coscom Entertainment.

Furman, A. I. Everygirl's Romance Stories. Furman, A. L., ed. 2011. 224p. 44.95 *(978-1-258-07094-6(4))* Literary Licensing, LLC.

Gaertner, Connie. Wake-Up Calls. 2013. 154p. (gr. 10-12). pap. 12.95 *(978-1-4759-6646-6(6))* iUniverse, Inc.

Gagnon, Jilly. #famous. 2017. (ENG.). 384p. (YA). (gr. 8). 17.99 *(978-0-06-243003-8(3),* Tegen, Katherine Bks) HarperCollins Pubs.

Galliez, Roxane Marie. Give Me Moon. Delanssay, Cathy, illus. 2009. 44p. (J). (gr. -1-3). 14.99 *(978-0-8416-7138-6(9))* Hammond World Atlas Corp.

Garcia, Kami. The Lovely Reckless. 2017. (ENG.). 400p. (YA). pap. 16.99 *(978-1-250-12968-0(0),* 900176106) Square Fish.

Garcia, Kami & Stohl, Margaret. Beautiful Chaos. 2012. (Beautiful Creatures Ser.: 3). (ENG.). 528p. (YA). (gr. 7-17). pap. 16.99 *(978-0-316-12351-8(X))* Little, Brown Bks. for Young Readers.

—Beautiful Creatures. 2010. (Beautiful Creatures Ser.: 1). (ENG.). 592p. (YA). (gr. 7-17). pap. 16.99 *(978-0-316-07703-3(8))* Little, Brown Bks. for Young Readers.

Garcia, Kami & Stohl, Margaret. Beautiful Creatures. 2010. (Beautiful Creatures Ser.: 1). (YA). lib. bdg. 23.30 *(978-0-606-26699-4(2))* Turtleback.

Garcia, Kami & Stohl, Margaret. The Beautiful Creatures Complete Paperback Collection. 2013. (Beautiful Creatures Ser.: Bks. 1-4). (ENG.). 2272p. (YA). (gr. 7-17). pap. 64.00 *(978-0-316-25090-0(2))* Little, Brown Bks. for Young Readers.

Garcia, Kami & Stohl, Margaret. Beautiful Darkness. 2010. (Beautiful Creatures Ser.: Bk. 2). (YA). 59.99 *(978-1-60941-036-0(X))* Findaway World, LLC.

—Beautiful Darkness. 2010. (Beautiful Creatures Ser.: Bk. 2). 512p. pap. 17.99 *(978-0-316-09861-8(2))* Little, Brown Bks. for Young Readers.

Garcia, Kami & Stohl, Margaret. Beautiful Darkness. 2011. (Beautiful Creatures Ser.: 2). (ENG.). 528p. (YA). (gr. 7-17). pap. 15.99 *(978-0-316-07704-0(6))* Little, Brown Bks. for Young Readers.

Garcia, Kami & Stohl, Margaret. Beautiful Darkness. 2011. (Beautiful Creatures Ser.: 2). (YA). lib. bdg. 24.50 *(978-0-606-26700-7(X))* Turtleback.

—Beautiful Redemption. 2012. (Beautiful Creatures Ser.: Bk. 4). (ENG.). 576p. (YA). (gr. 7-17). pap. 9.99 *(978-0-316-22519-9(3))* Little, Brown Bks. for Young Readers.

Garcia, Kami & Stohl, Margaret. Beautiful Redemption. 2013. (Beautiful Creatures Ser.: 4). (ENG.). 496p. (YA). (gr. 7-17). pap. 15.99 *(978-0-316-12356-3(0))* Little, Brown Bks. for Young Readers.

Garcia, Kami & Stohl, Margaret. Beautiful Redemption. 2013. (Beautiful Creatures Ser.: 4). (YA). lib. bdg. 24.50 *(978-0-606-32282-9(5))* Turtleback.

—Dangerous Creatures. 2014. 327p. (YA). *(978-0-316-37626-6(4))* Little, Brown Bks. for Young Readers.

Garcia, Kami & Stohl, Margaret. Dangerous Creatures. 2015. (ENG.). 400p. (J). (gr. 7-17). pap. 19.99 *(978-0-316-37032-5(0))* Little, Brown Bks. for Young Readers.

Garcia, Mary. Play with Me: Togetherness Time for Your Preschooler & You. (J). 2007. 16.95 *(978-0-9790931-2-8(0))* 2006. 16.95 *(978-0-9790931-0-4(4))* SMARTseeds Co., LLC, The.

—Play with Me: Togetherness Time for Your Preschooler & You: St. Valentine's Day. 2007. (J). *(978-0-9790931-1-1(2))* SMARTseeds Co., LLC, The.

Garcia, Mia. Even If the Sky Falls. 2016. (ENG.). 304p. (YA). (gr. 9). 17.99 *(978-0-06-241180-8(2),* Tegen, Katherine Bks) HarperCollins Pubs.

Gardner, Sheldon. The Converso Legacy. 2005. 264p. (J). 18.95 *(978-1-932687-18-7(1),* Devora Publishing) Simcha Media Group.

Garner, Paula. Phantom Limbs. 2018. (ENG.). 368p. (YA). (gr. 9). pap. 8.99 *(978-0-7636-9800-3(8))* Candlewick Pr.

Garza, Amy Ammons. Sterlen: And a Mosaic of Mountain Women. Ammons, David F. & Ammons, Sherilyn, eds. Cain, Doreyl Ammons, illus. 2005. 308p. (YA). per. 16.00 *(978-0-9753023-2-3(9),* Catch the Spirit of Appalachia) Ammons Communications, Ltd.

Garza, Jenny. Beautiful. 2007. 56p. per. 8.95 *(978-0-595-46756-3(3))* iUniverse, Inc.

Gaskins, Terry & Treigle, Jimmy. The Very Big Storm: Created by Terry Gaskins Inspired by Jimmy Treigle. 2009. 28p. pap. 13.99 *(978-1-4389-4220-9(6))* AuthorHouse.

Gates, Pat. The Apple Tree's Secret, 1 vol. Hosselkus, Devin, illus. 2009. 47p. pap. 24.95 *(978-1-60836-637-8(5))* America Star Bks.

Gaylord, Laurel Porter. I Love My Mommy Because... Wolff, Ashley, illus. 2004. 22p. (J). (gr. -1 — 1). bds. 7.99 *(978-0-525-47247-6(9),* Dutton Books for Young Readers) Penguin Young Readers Group.

Gazdag, Adam. The Non Born Heir. 2010. (ENG.). 313p. pap. 19.27 *(978-0-557-17709-7(X))* Lulu Pr., Inc.

Gebhart, Ryan. Of Jenny & the Aliens. 2017. 368p. (J). (gr. 11). 17.99 *(978-0-7636-8845-5(2))* Candlewick Pr.

—Of Jenny & the Aliens. Lt. ed. 2019. (ENG.). 380p. pap. 15.99 *(978-1-4328-6442-2(4))* Cengage Gale.

Geise, Brenda & Merkle, Blair Geise. Love Spot. 2008. 28p. pap. 12.99 *(978-1-4389-1102-1(5))* AuthorHouse.

George E. Keely, Jr. The Happy Day Fable. 2010. 20p. pap. 10.00 *(978-1-4269-0064-8(3))* Trafford Publishing.

George, Michele. The Rainbow of Love. 2004. (J). 5.00 *(978-0-9672049-1-8(7))* Grace & Mercy Publishing.

Geragotelis, Brittany. What the Spell. (Life's a Witch Ser.). (ENG., Illus.). (YA). (gr. 9). 2014. 352p. pap. 9.99 *(978-1-4424-6707-1(X))* 2013. 336p. 16.99 *(978-1-4424-6815-3(7))* Simon & Schuster Bks. For Young Readers. (Simon & Schuster Bks. For Young Readers).

Geras, Adèle. The Tower Room. 2005. (ENG.). 204p. (YA). (gr. 7-12). pap. 12.95 *(978-0-15-205537-0(1))* Houghton Mifflin Harcourt Publishing Co.

Gessner, Kati. What Do You See When You Look at Me. 2012. 32p. pap. 19.99 *(978-1-4772-2106-8(9))* AuthorHouse.

Gibbs, Gretchen. The Book of Maggie Bradstreet. 2012. (Bradstreet Chronicles). (ENG.). 183p. (YA). pap. 9.99 *(978-0-9852948-0-9(X))* Glenmere Pr.

Gibby, Bayne. You Mean the World to Me. Walker, David, illus. 2013. (ENG.). 24p. (J). (gr. -1-k). bds. 8.99 *(978-0-545-40570-6(X),* Cartwheel Bks.) Scholastic, Inc.

Giles, Jeff. The Brink of Darkness. 2018. (Edge of Everything Ser.). (ENG.). 352p. (YA). 18.99 *(978-1-61963-755-9(3),* 900147530, Bloomsbury Young Adult) Bloomsbury Publishing USA.

—The Edge of Everything. 2018. (YA). lib. bdg. 22.10 *(978-0-606-41079-3(1))* Turtleback.

Gillmor, Don. Yuck, a Love Story. Gay, Marie-Louise, illus. 2004. (J). (gr. k-3). spiral bd. *(978-0-616-07238-7(4));* spiral bd. *(978-0-616-08494-6(3))* Canadian National Institute for the Blind/Institut National Canadien pour les Aveugles.

Gilmore, Jennifer. We Were Never Here. (ENG.). (YA). (gr. 9). 2018. 336p. pap. 9.99 *(978-0-06-239361-6(8))* 2016. 320p. 17.99 *(978-0-06-239360-9(X))* HarperCollins Pubs. (HarperTeen).

Glaser, Mechthild. The Book Jumper. 2018. (ENG.). 400p. (YA). pap. 12.99 *(978-1-250-14423-2(X),* 900180625) Square Fish.

Gleason, Colleen. The Spiritglass Charade: A Stoker & Holmes Novel. (Stoker & Holmes Ser.: 2). (ENG., Illus.). (YA). (gr. 7-12). 2015. 368p. pap. 9.99 *(978-1-4521-2885-6(5))* 2014. 360p. 17.99 *(978-1-4521-1071-4(9))* Chronicle Bks. LLC.

Glines, Abbi. After the Game. (Field Party Ser.). (ENG., Illus.). (YA). (gr. 9). 2018. 368p. pap. 12.99 *(978-1-4814-3892-6(1))* 2017. 352p. 18.99 *(978-1-4814-3893-3(X))* Simon Pulse. (Simon Pulse).

—After the Game: A Field Party Novel. 2017. (YA). *(978-1-5344-0168-6(7),* Simon Pulse) Simon Pulse.

—Bad for You. 2015. (Sea Breeze Ser.). (ENG., Illus.). 320p. (YA). (gr. 11). pap. 12.99 *(978-1-4814-2074-7(7),* Simon Pulse) Simon Pulse.

—Because of Low. 2013. (Sea Breeze Ser.). (ENG., Illus.). 320p. (YA). (gr. 11). 17.99 *(978-1-4424-8864-9(6));* pap. 12.99 *(978-1-4424-8863-2(8))* Simon Pulse. (Simon Pulse).

—Hold on Tight. 2015. (Sea Breeze Ser.). (ENG., Illus.). 288p. (YA). (gr. 11). pap. 12.99 *(978-1-4814-2081-5(X),* Simon Pulse) Simon Pulse.

—Just for Now. 2013. (Sea Breeze Ser.). (ENG., Illus.). 336p. (J). (gr. 11). 17.99 *(978-1-4424-8861-8(1));* pap. 9.99 *(978-1-4424-8860-1(3))* Simon Pulse. (Simon Pulse).

—Losing the Field. 2018. (Field Party Ser.). (ENG., Illus.). 336p. (YA). (gr. 9). 19.99 *(978-1-5344-0389-5(2),* Simon Pulse) Simon Pulse.

—Misbehaving. 2014. (Sea Breeze Ser.). (ENG., Illus.). 352p. (YA). (gr. 11). 17.99 *(978-1-4814-0674-1(4));* pap. 12.99 *(978-1-4814-0673-4(6))* Simon Pulse. (Simon Pulse).

—The Sea Breeze Collection (Boxed Set) Breathe; Because of Low; While It Lasts; Just for Now. 2013. (Sea Breeze Ser.). (ENG., Illus.). 1312p. (YA). (gr. 11-11). pap. 39.99 *(978-1-4424-9608-8(8),* Simon Pulse) Simon Pulse.

—Under the Lights. 2016. (Field Party Ser.: 2). (ENG., Illus.). 336p. (YA). (gr. 9). 18.99 *(978-1-4814-3889-6(1),* Simon Pulse) Simon Pulse.

—Until Friday Night. 2015. (Field Party Ser.: Bk. 1). (ENG.). 336p. (YA). pap. *(978-1-4711-2502-7(5),* Simon Pulse) Simon Pulse.

—While It Lasts. 2013. (Sea Breeze Ser.). (ENG., Illus.). 304p. (YA). (gr. 11). 18.99 *(978-1-4424-8867-0(0));* pap. 10.99 *(978-1-4424-8866-3(2))* Simon Pulse. (Simon Pulse).

Gliori, Debi. No Matter What Board Book. Gliori, Debi, illus. 2008. (ENG., Illus.). 24p. (J). (gr. -1 — 1). bds. 8.99 *(978-0-15-206343-6(9),* 1198999, Clarion Bks.) HarperCollins Pubs.

—No Matter What Lap Board Book. Gliori, Debi, illus. 2012. (ENG., Illus.). 24p. (J). (gr. -1 — 1). bds. 12.99 *(978-0-547-71905-4(1),* 1481812, Clarion Bks.) HarperCollins Pubs.

Globe-Fearon Staff, ed. Jane Eyre, Grades 5-12. pap., tchr. ed. 4.95 *(978-0-8359-0109-3(2))* Globe Fearon Educational Publishing.

Godbersen, Anna. The Lucky Ones. 2013. (Bright Young Things Ser.: 3). (ENG.). 400p. (YA). (gr. 9). pap. 10.99 *(978-0-06-196271-4(6),* HarperCollins) HarperCollins Pubs.

—The Luxe. (ENG.). (YA). (gr. 9). 2018. (Luxe Ser.: 1). 480p. pap. 9.99 *(978-0-06-285216-8(7),* HarperTeen) 2008. (Luxe Ser.: 1). 464p. pap. 9.99 *(978-0-06-134568-5(7))* 2007. (Luxe Ser.: No. 1). 448p. 17.99 *(978-0-06-134566-1(0),* HarperTeen) HarperCollins Pubs.

—Rumors. (Luxe Ser.: 2). (ENG.). (YA). (gr. 9). 2018. 464p. pap. 9.99 *(978-0-06-285217-5(5),* HarperTeen) 2009. 448p. pap. 9.99 *(978-0-06-134571-5(7))* HarperCollins Pubs.

—Splendor. (Luxe Ser.: 4). (ENG.). (YA). (gr. 9). 2018. 432p. pap. 9.99 *(978-0-06-285219-9(1),* HarperTeen) 2010. 416p. pap. 9.99 *(978-0-06-162633-3(3))* HarperCollins Pubs.

Gold, Willa. Stella & Tulip: A Home for Us. 2010. (ENG.). 36p. (J). (gr. -1-3). 17.99 *(978-0-930773-95-3(0))* Black Heron Pr.

Goldstein, Meredith. Chemistry Lessons. 2018. (ENG.). 256p. (YA). (gr. 7). 17.99 *(978-1-328-76464-5(8),* 1681106, Clarion Bks.) HarperCollins Pubs.

Goo, Maurene. I Believe in a Thing Called Love. 2018. (ENG.). 352p. (YA). pap. 9.99 *(978-1-250-15841-3(9),* 900158635) Square Fish.

Goobie, Beth. Ni un Día Más, 1 vol. 2009. (Spanish Soundings Ser.). Orig. Title: Kicked Out. (SPA.). 112p. (YA). (gr. 8-12). pap. 9.95 *(978-1-55469-137-1(0))* Orca Bk. Pubs. USA.

Goode, Laura. Sister Mischief. 2013. (ENG.). 384p. (YA). (gr. 9). pap. 8.99 *(978-0-7636-6456-5(1))* Candlewick Pr.

Goode, Molly. Mama Loves. McCue, Lisa, illus. 2015. (Step into Reading Ser.). 32p. (J). (gr. -1-1). 4.99 *(978-0-553-53896-0(9),* Random Hse. Bks. for Young Readers) Random Hse. Children's Bks.

Gormally, Eleanor. The Little One Asks. 2013. (ENG.). 32p. (J). pap. 12.95 *(978-1-84730-407-0(9))* Veritas Pubns. IRL. Dist: Casemate Pubs. & Bk. Distributors, LLC.

Gorman, Dl. Pudgy Wudgy: Pudgy Wudgy Meets a Friend. 2008. 32p. pap. 12.99 *(978-1-4389-2151-8(9))* AuthorHouse.

Gottesfeld, Jeff. Crush. 2014. (Campus Confessions Ser.: 4). (YA). lib. bdg. 20.80 *(978-0-606-34001-4(7))* Turtleback.

Gould, Sasha. Cross My Heart. 2013. (ENG.). 272p. (YA). (gr. 8-12). lib. bdg. 24.94 *(978-0-375-99007-6(0),* Delacorte Pr.) Random Hse. Children's Bks.

Grace, N. B. Rev It Up! 9th ed. 2010. (Wizards of Waverly Place Ser.: No. 9). 128p. (J). (gr. 3-7). pap. 4.99 *(978-1-4231-2676-8(9))* Disney Pr.

Grady, Joi. I Like You & I Love You. 2012. 36p. pap. 20.99 *(978-1-4670-3953-6(5))* AuthorHouse.

Graham, D. R. Put It Out There (Britannia Beach, Book 1), Book 1. 2016. (Britannia Beach Ser.: 1). (ENG.). 212p. (YA). pap. 9.99 *(978-0-00-814519-4(9),* One More Chapter) HarperCollins Pubs. Ltd. GBR. Dist: HarperCollins Pubs.

Granson, Steven. Zando. 2009. 124p. pap. 10.95 *(978-1-4401-5658-8(1))* iUniverse, Inc.

Grant, Jennifer. Maybe I Can Love My Neighbor Too. Schipper, Benjamin, illus. 2019. 32p. (J). (gr. k-3). 16.99 *(978-1-5064-5201-2(9),* Beaming Books) 1517 Media.

Grant, Vicki. 36 Questions That Changed My Mind about You. 2017. (ENG., Illus.). 288p. (YA). (gr. 8-17). 17.99 *(978-0-7624-6318-3(X),* Running Pr. Kids) Running Pr.

Gray, Claudia. Afterlife. 2012. (Evernight Ser.: 4). (ENG.). 384p. (YA). (gr. 8). pap. 10.99 *(978-0-06-128451-9(3),* HarperTeen) HarperCollins Pubs.

—Balthazar. 2013. (Evernight Ser.: 5). (ENG.). 400p. (YA). (gr. 8). pap. 11.99 *(978-0-06-196119-9(1),* HarperTeen) HarperCollins Pubs.

—Evernight. 2009. (Evernight Ser.: 1). (ENG.). 352p. (YA). (gr. 8). pap. 8.99 *(978-0-06-128444-1(0),* HarperTeen) HarperCollins Pubs.

—Fateful. 2012. (ENG.). 352p. (YA). (gr. 9). pap. 9.99 *(978-0-06-200621-9(5),* HarperTeen) HarperCollins Pubs.

—Hourglass. 2011. (Evernight Ser.: 3). (ENG.). 368p. (YA). (gr. 8). pap. 10.99 *(978-0-06-128448-9(3),* HarperTeen) HarperCollins Pubs.

—A Million Worlds with You. 2016. 419p. (YA). *(978-0-06-257364-3(0),* HarperTeen) HarperCollins Pubs.

—Sorceress. 2016. (Spellcaster Ser.: 3). (ENG.). 368p. (YA). (gr. 8). pap. 9.99 *(978-0-06-196125-0(6),* HarperTeen) HarperCollins Pubs.

—Spellcaster. 2014. (Spellcaster Ser.: 1). (ENG., Illus.). 416p. (YA). (gr. 8). pap. 9.99 *(978-0-06-196121-2(3),* HarperTeen) HarperCollins Pubs.

—Ten Thousand Skies above You. (Firebird Ser.: 2). (ENG.). (YA). (gr. 9). 2016. 448p. pap. 11.99 *(978-0-06-227900-2(9))* 2015. 432p. 17.99 *(978-0-06-227899-9(1))* HarperCollins Pubs. (HarperTeen).

Gray, Lucinda. The Gilded Cage. 2017. (ENG., Illus.). 256p. (YA). pap. 12.99 *(978-1-62779-182-3(5),* 900139883) Square Fish.

Gray, Mila. Run Away with Me. (ENG.). 368p. (YA). (gr. 11). 2018. pap. 12.99 *(978-1-4814-9097-9(4))* 2017. (Illus.). 17.99 *(978-1-4814-9096-2(6))* Simon Pulse. (Simon Pulse).

—Stay with Me. 2017. (ENG.). 384p. (YA). (gr. 11). pap. 12.99 *(978-1-4814-8848-8(1),* Simon Pulse) Simon Pulse.

Gray Smith, Monique. You Hold Me Up, 1 vol. Daniel, Danielle, illus. 2017. (ENG.). 32p. (J). (gr. -1-k). 19.95 *(978-1-4598-1447-9(9))* Orca Bk. Pubs. USA.

Green, John. The Fault in Our Stars. 2013. (ENG & JPN.). 337p. (YA). (gr. 9-12). pap. *(978-4-00-116405-3(1))* Iwanami Shoten.

—The Fault in Our Stars. 2013. (CHI & ENG.). 304p. (YA). (gr. 9-12). pap. *(978-7-5448-3122-2(1))* Jieli Publishing Hse.

—The Fault in Our Stars. 2013. (ENG.). 352p. pap. *(978-0-14-134565-9(9))* Penguin Bks., Ltd.

—The Fault in Our Stars. 2014. (ENG.). 352p. (YA). (gr. 9). pap. 14.99 *(978-0-14-242417-9(X),* Penguin Books) 2012. *(978-0-525-42641-7(8))* 2012. (ENG., Illus.). 324p. (YA). (gr. 9-18). 19.99 *(978-0-525-47881-2(7),* Dutton Books for Young Readers) 2014. (ENG.). 352p. (YA). (gr. 9). reprint ed. pap. 12.99 *(978-0-14-751373-1(1),* Speak) Penguin Young Readers Group.

—The Fault in Our Stars. 2014. (ENG.). (YA). (gr. 9). lib. bdg. 23.60 *(978-1-62765-362-6(7))* Perfection Learning Corp.

—The Fault in Our Stars. Lt. ed. 2012. (ENG.). 364p. (J). (gr. 8-12). 23.99 *(978-1-4104-5001-2(5))* Thorndike Pr.

—The Fault in Our Stars. 2014. lib. bdg. 24.50 *(978-0-606-35633-6(9))* Turtleback.

—Penguin Minis: the Fault in Our Stars. 2018. (ENG.). 576p. (YA). (gr. 9). pap. 12.00 *(978-0-525-55574-2(9),* Dutton Books for Young Readers) Penguin Young Readers Group.

Green, Ken. Love in a Dustbin. (ENG.). 136p. pap. *(978-0-340-58860-4(8))* Hodder & Stoughton.

Greene, Bette. Morning Is a Long Time Coming. Lt. ed. 2004. (Beeler Mystery Ser.). 35.95 *(978-1-58118-122-7(1))* LRS.

—Philip Hall Likes Me, I Reckon Maybe. Lt. ed. 2003. (Children's Large Print Ser.). (J). 28.95 *(978-1-58118-107-4(8))* LRS.

Greenland, Shannon. Shadow of a Girl. 2016. (ENG., Illus.). (YA). (gr. 7). pap. 15.99 *(978-1-68281-303-4(7))* Entangled Publishing, LLC.

Gregory, Philippa. Fools' Gold. van Deelen, Fred, illus. 2014. (Order of Darkness Ser.: 3). (ENG.). 384p. (YA). (gr. 9). 19.99 *(978-1-4424-7690-5(7),* Simon Pulse) Simon Pulse.

Griffin, Adele. Loud Awake & Lost. 2015. (ENG.). 304p. (YA). (gr. 7). pap. 10.99 *(978-0-385-75275-6(X),* Ember) Random Hse. Children's Bks.

Grime, L. L. Do You Love Me? 2006. (ENG.). 48p. pap. 22.95 *(978-1-4357-1364-2(8))* Lulu Pr., Inc.

Grimm, Brothers. The Frog Prince. Schroeder, Binette, illus. 2013. (ENG.). 32p. (J). (gr. -1-3). 17.95 *(978-0-7358-4140-6(3))* North-South Bks., Inc.

Grogan, John. Marley Looks for Love. Cowdrey, Richard, illus. 2010. (Marley Ser.). (ENG.). 16p. (J). (gr. -1-1). 6.99 *(978-0-06-185590-0(1),* HarperFestival) HarperCollins Pubs.

—Marley's Big Adventure. 2009. (Marley: I Can Read! Ser.). (J). lib. bdg. 13.55 *(978-0-606-06942-7(9))* Turtleback.

Grosso, Salvatore. The Butterfly & the Dinosaur: A true story of fiction inspired by a Beautiful Butterfly. 2010. 32p. pap. 16.99 *(978-1-4490-6603-1(8))* AuthorHouse.

Groth, Darren & Groth, Simon. Infinite Blue, 1 vol. 2018. (ENG.). 192p. (YA). (gr. 8-12). pap. 14.95 *(978-1-4598-1513-1(0))* Orca Bk. Pubs. USA.

Grover, Lorie Ann. Hit, 1 vol. 2015. (ENG.). 224p. (YA). pap. 8.99 *(978-0-310-72938-9(6))* Blink.

Grover Swank, Denise. One Paris Summer, 1 vol. 2016. (ENG.). 352p. (YA). pap. 14.99 *(978-0-310-75516-6(6))* Blink.

Guertin, Chantel. The Rule of Thirds. 2013. (Pippa Greene Novel Ser.: 1). (ENG., Illus.). 220p. (J). (gr. 7-11). pap. 9.95 *(978-1-77041-159-3(3),* c71b80f6-6029-4991-a7f7-a1048e7fd8cd) ECW Pr. CAN. Dist: Baker & Taylor Publisher Services (BTPS).

Gupta, Jennifer. Love Shapes. 2009. 16p. pap. 8.49 *(978-1-4343-9184-1(1))* AuthorHouse.

Gutman, Dan. My Weird School #20: Mr. Louie Is Screwy! Paillot, Jim, illus. 2007. (My Weird School Ser.: 20). (ENG.). 112p. (J). (gr. 1-5). pap. 5.99 *(978-0-06-123479-8(6),* HarperCollins) HarperCollins Pubs.

Haack, Daniel & Galupo, Isabel. Maiden & Princess. Human, Becca, illus. 2019. (ENG.). 40p. (J). (gr. -1-3). 17.99 *(978-1-4998-0776-9(7))* Little Bee Books Inc.

Habel, Lia. Dearly, Departed: a Zombie Novel. 2012. (Gone with the Respiration Ser.: 1). (ENG.). 496p. (YA). (gr. 8-12). pap. 10.99 *(978-0-345-52332-7(6),* Del Rey) Random Hse. Worlds.

Haber, Karen. Crossing Infinity. 2011. (ENG.). 239p. (J). (gr. -1-12). pap. 9.95 *(978-1-59687-411-4(2))* iBks., Inc.

JKL

Half a World Away. 2014. (ENG., Illus.). 240p. (J). (gr. 5-9). 17.99 *(978-1-4424-1275-0(5)*, Atheneum Bks. for Young Readers) Simon & Schuster Children's Publishing.

Hall, Angela Marie. Priscilla Pennybrook: Hello World, I Have Arrived!, 1 vol. 2009. 55p. pap. 16.95 *(978-1-61582-899-9(0))* America Star Bks.

Hall, Sandy. A Little Something Different: Fourteen Viewpoints, One Love Story. 2014. (ENG.). 272p. (YA). (gr. 7-12). pap. 10.99 *(978-1-250-06145-4(8)*, 900141883) Feiwel & Friends.

Hall, S.C. Turns of Fortune & Other Tales. 2007. (ENG.). 116p. per. *(978-1-4065-1586-2(8))* Dodo Pr.

Hall, Traci. Wiccan Cool. 2010. (Rhiannon Godfrey Ser.). (ENG.). 264p. pap. 15.00 *(978-1-60504-611-2(6))* Samhain Publishing, LTD.

Hallinan, P. K. Grandma Loves You. 2008. (ENG., Illus.). 26p. (J). (gr. -1-k). bds. 7.99 *(978-0-8249-6728-4(3)*, Ideals Pubns.) Worthy Publishing.

—How Do I Love You? (J). 24p. pap. 5.95 *(978-0-8249-5360-7(6)*, Ideals Pubns.); 2018. (ENG., Illus.). 22p. (gr. -1-k). bds. 7.99 *(978-0-8249-1682-4(4))*; 2005. (ENG., Illus.). 24p. 7.95 *(978-0-8249-5359-1(2)*, Ideals Pubns.) Worthy Publishing.

Hamilton, Alwyn. Rebel of the Sands. 2017. (Rebel of the Sands Ser.: 1). (ENG.). 336p. (YA). (gr. 7). pap. 10.99 *(978-0-14-751797-5(4)*, Speak) Penguin Young Readers Group.

Hammerle, Julie. Any Boy but You. 2017. (ENG., Illus.). (YA). pap. 14.99 *(978-1-68281-424-6(6))* Entangled Publishing, LLC.

Han, Jenny. Always & Forever, Lara Jean. (To All the Boys I've Loved Before Ser.: 3). (ENG., Illus.). 336p. (YA). (gr. 7). 2018. pap. 10.99 *(978-1-4814-3049-4(1))* 2017. 17.99 *(978-1-4814-3048-7(3))* Simon & Schuster Bks. For Young Readers. (Simon & Schuster Bks. For Young Readers).

—P. S. I Still Love You. (To All the Boys I've Loved Before Ser.: 2). (ENG., 352p. (YA). (gr. 7). 2015. Illus.). 19.99 *(978-1-4424-2673-3(X))* 2015. (Illus.). E-Book *(978-1-4424-2675-7(6))* 2019. pap. 10.99 *(978-1-5344-6926-6(5))* Simon & Schuster Bks. For Young Readers. (Simon & Schuster Bks. For Young Readers).

—P. S. I Still Love You. 2017. (To All the Boys I've Loved Before Ser.: 2). (ENG.). 352p. (YA). (gr. 7). pap. 10.99 *(978-1-4424-2674-0(8))* Simon & Schuster Children's Publishing.

—P.S. I Still Love You. 2018. (CHI.). (YA). (gr. 7). pap. *(978-957-10-7723-9(2))* Sharp Point Publishing Co., Ltd.

—P.S. I Still Love You. 2015. (ENG.). (YA). (gr. 7). pap. 10.99 *(978-1-4814-4471-2(9))* Simon & Schuster.

—To All the Boys I've Loved Before. (To All the Boys I've Loved Before Ser.: 1). (ENG., (YA). (gr. 7-10). 2016. Illus.). 384p. pap. 12.99 *(978-1-4424-2671-9(3))* 2014. (Illus.). 368p. 19.99 *(978-1-4424-2670-2(5))* 2018. 384p. pap. 12.99 *(978-1-5344-3837-8(8))* Simon & Schuster Bks. For Young Readers. (Simon & Schuster Bks. For Young Readers).

—To All the Boys I've Loved Before. 2016. lib. bdg. 22.10 *(978-0-606-38270-0(4))* Turtleback.

—The to All the Boys I've Loved Before Collection (Boxed Set) To All the Boys I've Loved Before; P. S. I Still Love You; Always & Forever, Lara Jean. 2017. (To All the Boys I've Loved Before Ser.). (ENG., Illus.). 1056p. (YA). (gr. 7). 53.99 *(978-1-4814-9536-3(4)*, Simon & Schuster Bks. For Young Readers) Simon & Schuster Bks. For Young Readers.

—We'll Always Have Summer. 2011. (YA). 1.25 *(978-1-4640-1977-7(0))* Recorded Bks., Inc.

—We'll Always Have Summer. (Summer I Turned Pretty Ser.). (ENG., Illus.). (YA). (gr. 7). 2012. 320p. pap. 11.99 *(978-1-4169-9559-3(5))* 2011. 304p. 19.99 *(978-1-4169-9558-6(7))* Simon & Schuster Bks. For Young Readers. (Simon & Schuster Bks. For Young Readers).

Hannah, Martha. The Ghost of Hampton Court. Dowell, Larry, illus. 2006. 32p. (J). 17.95 *(978-0-9779808-0-2(4))* CicadaSun.

Hannon, Rose. Finding Agate: An Epic Story of a Poodle's Heart & His Will to Survive. 2010. 268p. pap. 16.99 *(978-1-4490-8986-3(0))* AuthorHouse.

Hansen, Lynne. The Change: Heritage of Horror Series. 2004. (Heritage of Horror Ser.: 2). 108p. (YA). pap. 9.00 *(978-0-7599-4491-6(1))* Hard Shell Word Factory.

Hantz, Sara. Falling for the Wrong Guy. 2015. (ENG., Illus.). 170p. (YA). (gr. 7). pap. 12.99 *(978-1-943892-67-9(9))* Entangled Publishing, LLC.

—There's Something about Nik. 2017. (ENG., Illus.). (YA). pap. 12.99 *(978-1-68281-425-3(4))* Entangled Publishing, LLC.

Hapka, Catherine, pseud. Love on Cue. 2009. (Romantic Comedies Ser.). (ENG.). 288p. (YA). (gr. 7-18). mass mkt. 6.99 *(978-1-4169-6857-3(1)*, Simon Pulse) Simon Pulse.

—Something Borrowed. 2008. (Romantic Comedies Ser.). (ENG.). 272p. (YA). (gr. 7-18). mass mkt. 6.99 *(978-1-4169-5441-5(4)*, Simon Pulse) Simon Pulse.

Hardegree, Maureen. Hainted Love. 2011. 184p. pap. 12.95 *(978-1-61194-014-5(1)*, Bell Bridge Bks.) BelleBks., Inc.

Hargrove, Jason. Looking Good, Cody Greer. 2006. 188p. pap. 24.95 *(978-1-4241-4013-8(7))* PublishAmerica, Inc.

Harker, Jillian. I Love You, Daddy. Parragon Books, ed. 2018. (ENG., Illus.). 32p. (J). (gr. -1-1). 6.99 *(978-1-68052-426-0(7)*, 2000250, Parragon Books) Cottage Door Pr.

Harrington, Hannah. Speechless. 2012. (ENG.). 288p. (YA). pap. 9.99 *(978-0-373-21052-7(3)*, Harlequin Teen) Harlequin Enterprises ULC CAN. Dist: HarperCollins Pubs.

Harris, Patrick. Where the Day Takes You volume One. 2010. 172p. pap. 10.00 *(978-0-557-04401-6(4))* Lulu Pr., Inc.

Harris, Rachel. A Tale of Two Centuries. 2017. (ENG., Illus.). (YA). pap. 14.99 *(978-1-68281-442-0(4))* Entangled Publishing, LLC.

Hart, Jeff. Undead with Benefits. 2014. (Eat, Brains, Love Ser.: 2). (ENG.). 416p. (YA). (gr. 8). pap. 9.99 *(978-0-06-220036-5(4)*, HarperTeen) HarperCollins Pubs.

Harvey, Sarah N. Shattered, 1 vol. 2011. (Orca Soundings Ser.). (ENG.). 128p. (YA). (gr. 8-12). pap. 9.95 *(978-1-55469-845-5(6))*; lib. bdg. 16.95 *(978-1-55469-846-2(4))* Orca Bk. Pubs. USA.

Harward, Barnaby, ed. Romeo & Juliet: Interfact Shakespeare. 2006. 144p. (YA). (gr. 6-10). reprint ed. pap. 25.00 *(978-1-4223-5004-1(5))* DIANE Publishing Co.

Hasan, Jamal I. A Journey to Remember. 2007. 64p. per. 8.95 *(978-0-595-43375-9(8))* iUniverse, Inc.

Hauman, Carrie. Zoe the Magic Love Dog. 2003. (Illus.). 32p. (J). 16.00 *(978-0-9746333-8-1(0))* Alma Pr.

Hawthorne, Rachel. Dark Guardian: Moonlight. 2009. (ENG.). 272p. (YA). (gr. 9-18). pap. 8.99 *(978-0-06-170955-5(7)*, HarperTeen) HarperCollins Pubs.

—Island Girls & Boys. 2005. (ENG.). 336p. (YA). (gr. 9). pap. 8.99 *(978-0-06-075546-1(6)*, HarperTeen) HarperCollins Pubs.

—One Perfect Summer: Labor of Love & Thrill Ride. 2015. (ENG.). 544p. (YA). (gr. 9). pap. 9.99 *(978-0-06-232134-3(X)*, HarperTeen) HarperCollins Pubs.

Hayes, Angela. The Mop Heads, 1 vol. Polly Jr., Jimmy Wayne, illus. 2009. 14p. pap. 24.95 *(978-1-61546-006-9(3))* America Star Bks.

Hayes, Gwen. Dreaming Awake. 2012. (Falling under Novel Ser.). (ENG.). 336p. (YA). (gr. 7-18). 9.99 *(978-0-451-23554-1(1)*, Berkley) Penguin Publishing Group.

Headley, Maria Dahvana. Aerie. 2016. (Magonia Ser.: 2). (ENG.). 320p. (YA). (gr. 8). 17.99 *(978-0-06-232055-1(6)*, HarperCollins) HarperCollins Pubs.

—Magonia. 2016. (Magonia Ser.: 1). (ENG.). 336p. (YA). (gr. 8). pap. 10.99 *(978-0-06-232053-7(X)*, HarperCollins) HarperCollins Pubs.

Heasley, Gwendolyn. Don't Call Me Baby. 2014. (ENG.). 304p. (YA). (gr. 8). pap. 9.99 *(978-0-06-220852-1(7)*, HarperTeen) HarperCollins Pubs.

Hecker, Anna. When the Beat Drops. 2018. (ENG.). 312p. (YA). (gr. 9-12). 17.99 *(978-1-5107-3333-6(7)*, Sky Pony Pr.) Skyhorse Publishing Co., Inc.

Heckman, Ashley. The Last Three Words. 2013. 104p. pap. *(978-1-77130-651-5(3))* Evernight Publishing.

Hedlund, Jody. A Daring Sacrifice, 1 vol. 2016. (ENG.). 224p. (YA). pap. 12.99 *(978-0-310-74937-0(9))* Zondervan.

—An Uncertain Choice, 1 vol. 2015. (ENG.). 256p. (YA). pap. 12.99 *(978-0-310-74919-6(0))* Zondervan.

Heitritter, Laura. I Love You Just Because. Villim, Jim, illus. Date not set. 16p. (Orig.). (J). (gr. -1-18). pap. 6.95 *(978-1-885964-01-4(3))* P2 Educational Services, Inc.

Helean, April K. Love Can Build a Bridge. 2012. 24p. pap. 15.99 *(978-1-4691-5621-7(0))* Xlibris Corp.

Helene Bridge, Chris. Red Envelopes: Sobres Rojos. 2018. (ENG., Illus.). 32p. (J). 19.95 *(978-1-942945-65-9(5)*, a81528e3-b1fe-457c-a1d0-3c4bafb6b8d7) Night Heron Media.

Helgeson, Kat. Say No to the Bro. 2017. (ENG., Illus.). 272p. (YA). (gr. 9). 17.99 *(978-1-4814-7193-0(7)*, Simon & Schuster Bks. For Young Readers) Simon & Schuster Bks. For Young Readers.

Hemphill, Stephanie. Hideous Love: The Story of the Girl Who Wrote Frankenstein. 2013. (ENG.). 320p. (YA). (gr. 8). 18.99 *(978-0-06-185331-9(3)*, Balzer & Bray) HarperCollins Pubs.

Henry, April. Count All Her Bones. 2018. (Girl, Stolen Ser.: 2). (ENG.). 256p. (YA). pap. 12.99 *(978-1-250-15874-1(5)*, 900156292) Square Fish.

Henry in Love. 2009. (ENG., Illus.). 48p. (J). (gr. -1-1). 16.99 *(978-0-06-114288-8(3)*, Balzer & Bray) HarperCollins Pubs.

Henry, Sherrie. Last of the Summer Tomatoes. (ENG., (YA). 2016. Illus.). (gr. 8-12). 24.99 *(978-1-63533-039-7(4))* 2013. (Young Love's Journey Ser.: 1). 246p. pap. 14.99 *(978-1-62380-959-1(2))* Dreamspinner Pr. (Harmony Ink Pr.).

—Last of the Summer Tomatoes [Library Edition]. 2013. 246p. pap. 14.99 *(978-1-62380-931-7(2)*, Harmony Ink Pr.) Dreamspinner Pr.

Hepworth, Amelia. I Love You to the Moon & Back. Warnes, Tim, illus. 2017. (ENG.). 24p. (J). (gr. -1-k). bds. 9.99 *(978-1-68010-522-3(1))* Tiger Tales.

Herbstritt, Rj. God Loves You More Than Rainbows & Butterflies! Herbstritt, T. J., illus. 2011. 40p. pap. 24.95 *(978-1-4560-6735-9(4))* America Star Bks.

Hermstad, Melanie. Bird, I Love You. Date not set. *(978-0-517-58561-0(8))* Random Hse. Value Publishing.

Heroux, Matthew & Kirwan, Wednesday. Owl Love You. 2018. (ENG., Illus.). 32p. (J). (gr. -1-3). 16.95 *(978-1-944903-35-0(6)*, 1320501, Cameron Kids) Cameron + Co.

Herrick, Ann. The Perfect Guy. 2005. 120p. (YA). pap. 9.95 *(978-0-7599-3522-8(X))* Hard Shell Word Factory.

—Summer Replacement. 2004. (ENG.). 100p. (YA). per. 9.00 *(978-0-7599-4168-7(8))* Hard Shell Word Factory.

Hesik, Annameekee. Driving Lessons: A You Know Who Girls Novel. 2014. (You Know Who Girls Ser.: 2). (ENG.). 264p. (J). pap. 11.95 *(978-1-62639-228-1(5))* Bold Strokes Bks.

Hickman, Kirt. Purple. Olson, Julie, illus. 2012. 32p. pap. 15.99 *(978-0-9796330-8-9(7))* Quillrunner Publishing LLC.

Hicks, Constance. Florabelle Bunny & the Sparrow. 2011. 24p. pap. 12.99 *(978-1-4490-9969-5(6))* AuthorHouse.

Higgins, Carter. This Is Not a Valentine: (Valentines Day Gift for Kids, Children's Holiday Books) Cummins, Lucy Ruth, illus. 2017. (ENG.). 48p. (J). (gr. k-3). 14.99 *(978-1-4521-5374-2(4))* Chronicle Bks. LLC.

Higgins, Wendy. Sweet Evil. 2012. (Sweet Evil Ser.: 1). (ENG.). 464p. (YA). (gr. 8). pap. 11.99 *(978-0-06-208561-0(1)*, HarperTeen) HarperCollins Pubs.

—Sweet Peril. 2013. (Sweet Evil Ser.: 2). (ENG.). 384p. (YA). (gr. 8). pap. 10.99 *(978-0-06-226594-4(6)*, HarperTeen) HarperCollins Pubs.

—Sweet Reckoning. 2014. (Sweet Evil Ser.: 3). (ENG.). 400p. (YA). (gr. 8). pap. 9.99 *(978-0-06-226597-5(0)*, HarperTeen) HarperCollins Pubs.

—Sweet Temptation. 2015. (Sweet Evil Ser.: 4). (ENG.). 512p. (YA). (gr. 8). pap. 15.99 *(978-0-06-238142-2(3)*, HarperTeen) HarperCollins Pubs.

Higginson, Sheila Sweeny. You're Getting a Baby Brother! Williams, Sam, illus. 2012. (ENG.). 24p. (J). (gr. -1-k). bds. 8.99 *(978-1-4424-2021-2(9)*, Little Simon) Little Simon.

—You're Getting a Baby Sister! Williams, Sam, illus. 2012. (ENG.). 24p. (J). (gr. -1-k). bds. 8.99 *(978-1-4424-2050-2(2)*, Little Simon) Little Simon.

Highley, Kendra C. The Bad Boy Bargain. 2016. (ENG., Illus.). (YA). pap. 16.99 *(978-1-68281-335-5(5))* Entangled Publishing, LLC.

—Finding Perfect. 2015. (ENG., Illus.). 248p. (J). pap. 15.99 *(978-1-943892-43-3(1))* Entangled Publishing, LLC.

Hightman, J. P. Spirit. 2008. 224p. (gr. 7-18). (ENG.). (J). 16.99 *(978-0-06-085063-0(9))*; (YA). lib. bdg. 17.89 *(978-0-06-085064-7(7))* HarperCollins Pubs. (HarperTeen).

Hilb, Jessie. The Calculus of Change. 2018. (ENG.). 336p. (YA). (gr. 9). 17.99 *(978-0-544-95333-8(9)*, 1660557, Clarion Bks.) HarperCollins Pubs.

Hilburn, Dora. Between. 2015. 247p. (YA). pap. *(978-1-56825-175-2(0))* Rainbow Bks., Inc.

Hildebrand, Jens & Ridge, Sally. Cyberstalker. 2013. 242p. pap. *(978-3-929892-45-1(6))* Hildebrand, Jutta Warped Tomato Publishing.

Hill, Carolyn Swan. A Summer to Remember. 2013. 256p. (YA). (gr. 10-12). pap. 17.99 *(978-1-4624-0543-5(6)*, Inspiring Voices) Author Solutions, LLC.

Hill, Genita. My Very Special Brother. McCall, William L., illus. 2007. 40p. per. 24.95 *(978-1-4241-8852-9(0))* America Star Bks.

Hillhouse, Joanne C. Musical Youth. Aaron, Glenroy, illus. 2014. (ENG.). 275p. (J). pap. 9.99 *(978-0-9899305-1-2(3))* CaribbeanReads.

Hinds, Gareth. Romeo & Juliet. Hinds, Gareth, illus. 2013. (ENG., Illus.). 144p. (YA). (gr. 7). pap. 15.99 *(978-0-7636-6807-5(9))* Candlewick Pr.

—Romeo & Juliet (Graphic Adaptation) 2013. lib. bdg. 24.50 *(978-0-606-32096-6(9))* Turtleback.

Hocking, Amanda. Ascend: A Trylle Novel. 2012. (Trylle Novel Ser.: 3). (ENG.). 336p. (YA). (gr. 7). pap. 13.99 *(978-1-250-00633-2(3)*, 900081191, St. Martin's Griffin) St. Martin's Pr.

—Elegy. 2014. (Watersong Novel Ser.: 4). (ENG.). 560p. (YA). (gr. 7). pap. 19.99 *(978-1-250-00809-1(3)*, 900083409, St. Martin's Griffin) St. Martin's Pr.

—Switched, 1. 2012. (Trylle Novel Ser.: 1). (ENG.). 336p. (YA). (gr. 9-12). pap. 13.99 *(978-1-250-00631-8(7)*, 900081189, St. Martin's Griffin) St. Martin's Pr.

—Tidal. 2014. (Watersong Novel Ser.: 3). (ENG.). 352p. (YA). (gr. 7). pap. 25.99 *(978-1-250-00566-3(3)*, 900080970, St. Martin's Griffin) St. Martin's Pr.

—Torn. 2012. (Trylle Novel Ser.: 2). (ENG.). 336p. (YA). (gr. 7-12). pap. 20.00 *(978-1-250-00632-5(5)*, 900081190, St. Martin's Griffin) St. Martin's Pr.

—Torn. Lt. ed. 2012. (Trylle Trilogy: Bk. 2). (ENG.). 450p. (J). (gr. 7-12). 23.99 *(978-1-4104-5013-5(9))* Thorndike Pr.

—Wake. 2013. (Watersong Novel Ser.: 1). (ENG.). 320p. (YA). (gr. 7). pap. 23.99 *(978-1-250-00564-9(7)*, 900080965, St. Martin's Griffin) St. Martin's Pr.

Hodge, Rosamund. Crimson Bound. 2016. (ENG.). 464p. (YA). (gr. 8). pap. 9.99 *(978-0-06-222477-4(8)*, Balzer & Bray) HarperCollins Pubs.

Hodkin, Michelle. The Evolution of Mara Dyer. (Mara Dyer Trilogy Ser.: 2). (ENG., Illus.). (YA). (gr. 9). 2013. 560p. pap. 14.99 *(978-1-4424-2180-6(0))* 2012. 544p. 19.99 *(978-1-4424-2179-0(7))* Simon & Schuster Bks. For Young Readers. (Simon & Schuster Bks. For Young Readers).

—The Retribution of Mara Dyer. 2014. (Mara Dyer Trilogy Ser.: 3). (ENG., Illus.). 480p. (YA). (gr. 9). 18.99 *(978-1-4424-8423-8(3)*, Simon & Schuster Bks. For Young Readers) Simon & Schuster Bks. For Young Readers.

Holder, Ramona V. Paco & Lexus Are Good Friends: Paco y Lexus son Buen Amigos. 2009. 24p. pap. 12.99 *(978-1-4389-5778-4(5))* AuthorHouse.

Hollyer, Belinda & Brontë, Charlotte. Jane Eyre. 2003. (ENG., Illus.). 48p. *(978-0-7502-3668-3(X)*, Wayland) Hachette Children's Group.

Holm, Jennifer L. Wilderness Days. unabr. ed. 2004. (Boston Jane Ser.: No. 2). 288p. (J). (gr. 5-9). pap. 38.00 incl. audio *(978-0-8072-0787-1(X)*, S YA 307 SP, Listening Library) Random Hse. Audio Publishing Group.

Holub, Joan & Williams, Suzanne. Aphrodite the Beauty. (Goddess Girls Ser.: 3). (ENG.). 176p. (J). (gr. 3-7). 2013. 17.99 *(978-1-4424-5751-5(1))* 2010. pap. 7.99 *(978-1-4169-8273-9(6))* Simon & Schuster Children's Publishing. (Aladdin).

Homberg, Ruth. The Little Mermaid. 2013. (Disney Princess Step into Reading Ser.). lib. bdg. 13.55 *(978-0-606-32202-7(7))* Turtleback.

Hoole, Elissa Janine. The Memory Jar. 2016. (ENG.). 336p. (YA). (gr. 9-12). pap. 11.99 *(978-0-7387-4731-6(9)*, 0738747319, Flux) North Star Editions.

Hoover, P. J. Solstice. 2013. (ENG.). 384p. (YA). (gr. 8). 34.99 *(978-0-7653-3469-5(0)*, 900096814, Tor Teen) Doherty, Tom Assocs., LLC.

Hopkins, Cathy. Love Lottery. 2012. (Truth or Dare Ser.). (ENG.). 208p. (YA). (gr. 7). pap. 11.99 *(978-1-4424-7176-4(X)*, Simon Pulse) Simon Pulse.

Hopkins, Cathy & Hopkins, Cathy. White Lies & Barefaced Truths. 2005. (Truth or Dare Ser.: No. 1). (ENG.). 176p. (YA). (gr. 7-12). mass mkt. 3.99 *(978-1-4169-1152-4(9)*, Simon Pulse) Simon Pulse.

Hopkins, Ellen. Tilt. (ENG., (YA). (gr. 9). 2014. Illus.). 624p. pap. 13.99 *(978-1-4169-8331-6(7))* 2012. 608p. 18.99 *(978-1-4169-8330-9(9))* McElderry, Margaret K. Bks. (McElderry, Margaret K. Bks.).

Hopkins, Ellen, ed. A New Dawn: Your Favorite Authors on Stephenie Meyer's Twilight Series: Completely Unauthorized. 2009. (Illus.). 200p. (J). (gr. 9-12). pap. 12.95 *(978-1-933771-93-9(3)*, SmartPop) BenBella Bks.

Houck, Colleen. Recreated. 2017. (Reawakened Ser.: 2). (ENG.). 416p. (YA). (gr. 9). pap. 14.99 *(978-0-385-37663-1(4)*, Ember) Random Hse. Children's Bks.

Houde, Monique. Blinded by Love. 2004. (YA). pap. 14.95 *(978-0-9748689-0-5(6))* Choices For Tomorrow.

Houran, Lori Haskins. Warts & All: A Book of Unconditional Love. Hanson, Sydney, illus. 2017. (ENG.). 32p. (J). (gr. -1-3). 15.99 *(978-0-8075-8658-7(7)*, 807586587) Whitman, Albert & Co.

House, Catherine. Little Elephant. Whelan, Olwyn, illus. 2007. 32p. pap. 11.95 *(978-1-59325-093-5(2))* Word Among Us Pr.

Houston, Meradeth. Colors Like Memories. 2013. 178p. pap. *(978-1-77127-371-8(2))* MuseItUp Publishing.

Howard, A. G. Ensnared. 2015. (Splintered Ser.). (ENG.). 384p. (YA). (gr. 9-17). pap. 8.95 *(978-1-4197-1504-4(6))* Abrams, Inc.

—Ensnared (Splintered Series #3) 2015. (ENG.). 416p. (J). (gr. 9-17). 17.95 *(978-1-4197-1229-6(2)*, 1079501, Amulet Bks.) Abrams, Inc.

—Ensnared (Splintered Series #3) Splintered Book Three. 2015. (Splintered Ser.). (ENG.). 416p. (YA). (gr. 8-17). pap. 10.99 *(978-1-4197-1675-1(1)*, 1079503, Amulet Bks.) Abrams, Inc.

Howat, Irene. Adoniram Judson: Danger on the Streets of Gold. 2007. (Trail Blazers Ser.). (ENG.). 160p. (J). mass mkt. 8.99 *(978-1-85792-660-6(9)*, 2a933e1b-d4a5-4d42-99d7-2a3a91a6ce21) Christian Focus Pubns. GBR. Dist: Baker & Taylor Publisher Services (BTPS).

Howe, James. Otter & Odder: A Love Story. Raschka, Chris, illus. 2012. (ENG.). 40p. (J). (gr. 1-4). 14.00 *(978-0-7636-4174-0(X))* Candlewick Pr.

Howells, Amanda. The Summer of Skinny Dipping. (YA). 2019. 320p. (gr. 8-12). pap. 10.99 *(978-1-4926-9671-1(4))* 2010. (ENG.). 304p. (gr. 7-12). pap. 9.99 *(978-1-4022-3862-8(2))* Sourcebooks, Inc.

Howson, Imogen. Linked. 2014. (ENG., Illus.). 384p. (YA). (gr. 7). pap. 9.99 *(978-1-4424-4660-1(9)*, Simon & Schuster Bks. For Young Readers) Simon & Schuster Bks. For Young Readers.

—Unravel. 2014. (ENG., Illus.). 480p. (YA). (gr. 7). 17.99 *(978-1-4424-4658-8(7)*, Simon & Schuster Bks. For Young Readers) Simon & Schuster Bks. For Young Readers.

Hubbard, Kirsten. Wanderlove. 2013. (ENG.). 352p. (YA). (gr. 9). pap. 9.99 *(978-0-385-73938-2(9)*, Ember) Random Hse. Children's Bks.

Hubert. Adrian & the Tree of Secrets. Caillou, Marie, illus. 2014. 128p. (gr. 6). pap. 18.95 *(978-1-55152-556-3(9))* Arsenal Pulp Pr. CAN. Dist: Consortium Bk. Sales & Distribution.

Huffman, Jared. The Lost Piece. Huffman, Jared & Rampley, Leigh, illus. 2011. 36p. pap. 24.95 *(978-1-4626-1784-5(0))* America Star Bks.

Hugger, M. A. Danny Malloy & His Mississippi River Samurai. 2008. 132p. 21.95 *(978-0-595-49382-1(3))*; pap. 11.95 *(978-0-595-48462-1(X))* iUniverse, Inc.

Hughes, Lynn Gordon. To Live a Truer Life: A Story of the Hopedale Community. Lindro, illus. 2003. 32p. (J). 10.00 *(978-0-9725017-2-9(X))* Blackstone Editions.

Hughes, Mark Peter. I Am the Wallpaper. 2007. (ENG.). 256p. (YA). (gr. 7-11). pap. 8.99 *(978-0-440-42046-0(6)*, Delacorte Bks. for Young Readers) Random Hse. Children's Bks.

Hui Lee, Kris. Out of Left Field. 2018. (ENG.). 320p. (YA). (gr. 8-12). pap. 10.99 *(978-1-4926-6385-0(9))* Sourcebooks, Inc.

Hulslander, Dyan. I Just Love You So Much. Heaton, Jr., illus. 2009. 28p. pap. 14.49 *(978-1-4490-0454-5(7))* AuthorHouse.

Humphrey, Eleanor Cairns. Building Santa's Work Shop from Tales of the Crystal Cave. 2012. 268p. pap. 27.95 *(978-1-4626-7820-4(3))* America Star Bks.

Humphrey, T. Lewis. The Price of Love. 2003. 332p. (YA). pap. 18.95 *(978-0-595-27260-0(6)*, Writers Club Pr.) iUniverse, Inc.

Hunter, C. C. Chosen at Nightfall. 2013. (Shadow Falls Novel Ser.: 5). (ENG.). 416p. (YA). (gr. 7). pap. 12.99 *(978-1-250-01289-0(9)*, 900084503, St. Martin's Griffin) St. Martin's Pr.

—Eternal. unabr. ed. 2014. (Shadow Falls: after Dark Ser.: 2). (ENG.). 400p. (YA). (gr. 7-12). 19.99 *(978-1-250-05630-6(6)*, 900138741, St. Martin's Griffin) St. Martin's Pr.

—Eternal: Shadow Falls: after Dark. 2014. (Shadow Falls: after Dark Ser.: 2). (ENG.). 400p. (YA). (gr. 7-12). pap. 12.99 *(978-1-250-04461-7(8)*, 900127030, St. Martin's Griffin) St. Martin's Pr.

—Taken at Dusk. 2012. (Shadow Falls Novel Ser.: 3). (ENG.). 400p. (YA). (gr. 7-12). pap. 14.00 *(978-0-312-62469-9(7)*, 900066454, St. Martin's Griffin) St. Martin's Pr.

Hurley Deriso, Christine. Things I'd Rather Do Than Die. 2018. (ENG.). 304p. (YA). (gr. 9-12). pap. 14.99 *(978-1-63583-022-4(2)*, 1635830222, Flux) North Star Editions.

Hurley, Jeanette Clinger. The Crystal Prince: Love Is the Only Way. 2010. (Illus.). 77p. pap. 32.95 *(978-0-578-03963-3(X))* Outskirts Pr., Inc.

Hurley, Suzanne M. To the Stars. Josephsen, Laura, ed. Judson, Gemini, illus. 2016. (ENG.). 242p. (J). pap. 16.99 *(978-1-61160-891-5(0)*, Whiskey Creek Pr.) Whiskey Creek Pr., LLC.

Husby, Greg. The Zoebirds. 2008. 40p. pap. 21.99 *(978-1-4363-4941-3(9))* Xlibris Corp.

Huskins, Suzanne Hallier, illus. No Matter What! 2004. (J). *(978-1-887905-93-0(6))* Parkway Pubs., Inc.

Hutchinson, Shaun David. Fml. 2013. (ENG.). 304p. (YA). (gr. 9). pap. 9.99 *(978-1-4424-3287-1(X))*; (Illus.). 17.99 *(978-1-4424-8318-7(0))* Simon Pulse. (Simon Pulse).

Hyde, Spencer. Waiting for Fitz. 2019. (ENG.). 256p. (YA). (gr. 9). 17.99 *(978-1-62972-527-7(7)*, 5211772, Shadow Mountain) Shadow Mountain Publishing.

Ignatow, Amy. The Popularity Papers: Book Six: Love & Other Fiascos with Lydia Goldblatt & Julie Graham-Chang, Bk. 6. 2015. (Popularity Papers). (ENG., Illus.). 206p. (J). (gr. 3-7). pap. 9.95 *(978-1-4197-1356-9(6)*, 1046703, Amulet Bks.) Abrams, Inc.

Imes, Jarod. Age Ain't Nothing but a Number. 2007. 148p. (YA). pap. 10.99 *(978-1-934195-04-8(9))* Write Sing Work, Inc.

Imes, Jarold. Never Too Much - the Remix. 2007. (YA). per. 10.99 *(978-1-934195-07-9(3))* Write Sing Work, Inc.

Imes, Jarold, adapted by. U Can't Break Me. 2007. 148p. (YA). pap. 10.99 *(978-1-934195-03-1(0))* Write Sing Work, Inc.

Inoue, Kazurou. Midori Days. Inoue, Kazurou, illus. 2006. (Midori Days Ser.). (ENG., Illus.). 208p. Vol. 6. pap. 9.99 *(978-1-4215-0495-7(2))* Vol. 7. pap. 9.99 *(978-1-4215-0496-4(0))* Viz Media.

Ius, Dawn. Anne & Henry. 2015. (ENG., Illus.). 304p. (YA). (gr. 9). 18.99 *(978-1-4814-3941-1(3)*, Simon Pulse) Simon Pulse.

Jackson, G. A. Twelve Yellow Ducks. 2011. 28p. (gr. -1 — 1). pap. 13.59 *(978-1-4567-4268-3(X))* AuthorHouse.

Jackson, Helen Hunt. Ramona. 2017. (ENG., Illus.). (J). 28.95 *(978-1-374-83920-5(5))* Capital Communications, Inc.

—Ramona. 2015. (ENG., Illus.). (J). 28.95 *(978-1-298-66942-1(1))* Creative Media Partners, LLC.

Jacobson, Jennifer Richard. Andy Shane Is Not in Love. 2009. (Andy Shane Ser.: 4). lib. bdg. 14.75 *(978-0-606-06618-1(7))* Turtleback.

James, Jenni. Pride & Popularity. 2011. (Jane Austen Diaries). (ENG.). 238p. (YA). (gr. 8-12). pap. 11.99 *(978-0-9838293-0-0(6))* Inkberry Pr.

James, Lauren. The Loneliest Girl in the Universe. (ENG.). 320p. (YA). (gr. 9). 2019. pap. 15.99 *(978-0-06-266026-8(8))* 2018. 17.99 *(978-0-06-266025-1(X))* HarperCollins Pubs. (HarperTeen).

—The Next Together. 2017. (ENG., Illus.). 368p. (J). (gr. 8-8). 17.99 *(978-1-5107-1021-4(3)*, Sky Pony Pr.) Skyhorse Publishing Co., Inc.

James, Melody. Signs of Love: Destiny Date. 2013. (ENG.). 176p. (J). pap. 7.99 *(978-0-85707-328-0(1)*, Simon & Schuster Children's) Simon & Schuster, Ltd. GBR. Dist: Simon & Schuster, Inc.

Jansson, Tove. Moomin & the Golden Tail. 2014. (Moomin Ser.). (ENG., Illus.). 56p. (J). (gr. 4-7). pap. 9.95 *(978-1-77046-133-8(7)*, 900125201) Drawn & Quarterly Pubns. CAN. Dist: Macmillan.

Jaskulka, Marie. The Lost Marble Notebook of Forgotten Girl & Random Boy. 2015. (ENG.). 272p. (J). (gr. 6-6). 16.99 *(978-1-63220-426-4(6)*, Sky Pony Pr.) Skyhorse Publishing Co., Inc.

Jay, Stacey. Juliet Immortal. 2012. (Juliet Immortal Ser.: 1). 320p. (YA). (gr. 9). pap. 9.99 *(978-0-385-74017-3(4)*, Ember) Random Hse. Children's Bks.

—Romeo Redeemed. 2013. (Juliet Immortal Ser.). 384p. (YA). (gr. 9). pap. 10.99 *(978-0-385-74019-7(0)*, Ember) Random Hse. Children's Bks.

Jaysree. Drama. 2004. 134p. (YA). pap. 11.95 *(978-0-595-29662-0(9))* iUniverse, Inc.

Jeffers, Karen. Tosh. 2013. 26p. pap. 13.95 *(978-1-4787-0255-9(9))* Outskirts Pr., Inc.

Jefferson, Patti Brassard. How Long Will You Love Me? Jefferson, Patti Brassard, illus. 2013. (Illus.). 28p. pap. 12.95 *(978-1-61244-178-8(5))* Halo Publishing International.

Jeffs, Dixie. A Baby to Love. 2012. 20p. pap. 24.95 *(978-1-4626-6780-2(5))* America Star Bks.

Jenisch, Betty. Rennie. 2007. 9.00 *(978-0-8059-8947-2(1))* Dorrance Publishing Co., Inc.

Jenkyns, Brenda. Ever After. 2012. pap. 11.95 *(978-0-7414-7620-3(7))* Infinity Publishing.

Jennings, Carol E. Marshall & Satchmo. 2008. 40p. pap. 21.32 *(978-1-4363-7117-9(1))* Xlibris Corp.

Jensen, Kathryn. Splash! 2007. 193p. pap. 24.95 *(978-1-4241-9903-7(4))* America Star Bks.

Johns, Eric. Just Let Go. 2007. (ENG.). 164p. (YA). pap. 16.95 *(978-1-84753-321-0(3))* Lulu Pr., Inc.

Johnson, Alaya Dawn. The Summer Prince, 1 vol. 2014. (ENG.). 304p. (YA). (gr. 9). pap. 12.99 *(978-0-545-41780-8(5)*, Levine, Arthur A. Bks.) Scholastic, Inc.

Johnson, Christine. The Gathering Dark. (ENG., (YA). (gr. 9). 2014. Illus.). 528p. pap. 9.99 *(978-1-4424-3904-7(1))* 2013. 512p. 16.99 *(978-1-4424-3903-0(3))* Simon Pulse. (Simon Pulse).

Johnson, Elana. Abandon: A Possession Novel. 2013. (ENG.). 464p. (YA). (gr. 9). 17.99 *(978-1-4424-8482-5(9)*, Simon Pulse) Simon Pulse.

Johnson, Gerald J. J. Bessie's Little Mouse Day Care. Miltenberger, Dave & Miltenberger, Jeri, illus. 2012. 32p. pap. 24.95 *(978-1-62709-430-6(X))* America Star Bks.

—Buffy Bunny. Miltenberger, Jeri & Miltenberger, Dave, illus. 2011. 32p. pap. 24.95 *(978-1-4512-5292-7(7))* America Star Bks.

Johnston, Tony. Spencer & Vincent, the Jellyfish Brothers. Dove, Emily, illus. 2019. (ENG.). 40p. (J). (gr. -1-3). 19.99 *(978-1-5344-1208-8(5)*, Simon & Schuster/Paula Wiseman Bks.) Simon & Schuster/Paula Wiseman Bks.

Jones, Jasmine. Head over Heels. 2004. 152p. (J). lib. bdg. 16.92 *(978-1-4242-0677-3(4))* Fitzgerald Bks.

Jones, Jasmine, adapted by. Head over Heels. 2004. (Lizzie Mcguire Ser.). (Illus.). 152p. (J). 12.65 *(978-0-7569-2723-3(4))* Perfection Learning Corp.

Jones, Patrick. Heart or Mind. 2016. (Unbarred Ser.). (ENG.). 120p. (YA). (gr. 6-12). E-Book 42.65 *(978-1-5124-0092-2(0)*, Darby Creek) Lerner Publishing Group.

Jones Yang, Dori. Daughter of Xanadu. 2012. (ENG.). 352p. (YA). (gr. 7). pap. 9.99 *(978-0-385-73924-5(9)*, Ember) Random Hse. Children's Bks.

Joosse, Barbara M. Papa, Do You Love Me? Lavallee, Barbara, illus. 2005. (Mama & Papa, Do You Love Me? Ser.: MAMA). (ENG.). 36p. (J). (gr. -1-7). 15.99 *(978-0-8118-4265-5(7))* Chronicle Bks. LLC.

Jordan, Deloris. Did I Tell You I Love You Today? Evans, Shane W., illus. 2004. (ENG.). 32p. (J). (gr. -1-3). 19.99 *(978-0-689-85271-8(1)*, Simon & Schuster/Paula Wiseman Bks.) Simon & Schuster/Paula Wiseman Bks.

Jordan, Sophie. Hidden. (Firelight Ser.: 3). (ENG.). (YA). (gr. 8). 2013. 288p. pap. 9.99 *(978-0-06-193513-8(1))* 2012. 272p. 17.99 *(978-0-06-193512-1(3))* HarperCollins Pubs. (HarperCollins).

Joseph, Lynn. Flowers in the Sky. 2013. (ENG.). 240p. (YA). (gr. 8). 17.99 *(978-0-06-029794-7(8)*, HarperTeen) HarperCollins Pubs.

Jue, Thea. Remember the Love. Lenz, Mary, illus. 2013. 36p. pap. 13.95 *(978-0-9827753-3-2(4))* Interdimensional Pr.

Kade, Stacey. For This Life Only. 2016. (ENG., Illus.). 320p. (YA). (gr. 9). 17.99 *(978-1-4814-3248-1(6)*, Simon & Schuster Bks. For Young Readers) Simon & Schuster Bks. For Young Readers.

Kadohata, Cynthia. Half a World Away. 2015. (ENG., Illus.). 256p. (J). (gr. 5-9). pap. 7.99 *(978-1-4424-1276-7(3)*, Atheneum Bks. for Young Readers) Simon & Schuster Children's Publishing.

—Half a World Away. 2014. 240p. 16.99 *(978-1-4814-1806-5(8))* Simon & Schuster, Inc.

Kagawa, Julie. The Iron King. Chan, Lidia, illus. 2017. (Iron King Ser.). (SPA.). (YA). (gr. 7-12). pap. 19.99 *(978-1-948216-67-8(1))* TidalWave Productions.

—The Iron King. 2010. (Iron Fey Ser.: 1). (J). lib. bdg. 20.85 *(978-0-606-14909-9(0))* Turtleback.

—The Iron Knight. 2011. (Iron Fey Ser.: 4). (J). lib. bdg. 20.85 *(978-0-606-23259-3(1))* Turtleback.

—The Iron Legends. 2012. (Iron Fey Ser.: 5). (J). lib. bdg. 20.85 *(978-0-606-26516-4(3))* Turtleback.

—The Iron Traitor. 2013. (Iron Fey Ser.: 6). (J). lib. bdg. 20.85 *(978-0-606-35037-2(3))* Turtleback.

Kahaney, Amelia. The Brokenhearted. 2014. (Brokenhearted Ser.: 1). (ENG.). 368p. (YA). (gr. 8). pap. 9.99 *(978-0-06-223093-5(X)*, HarperTeen) HarperCollins Pubs.

Kala & Kol. Where Your Love Is: For Peace Is in This Place. 2012. 60p. pap. 31.99 *(978-1-4691-5926-3(0))* Xlibris Corp.

Kalman, Maira. Ooh-La-La (Max in Love) 2018. (Illus.). 48p. (J). (gr. k-3). 18.95 *(978-1-68137-245-7(2)*, NYR Children's Collection) New York Review of Bks., Inc., The.

Kamio, Yoko. Boys over Flowers, Vol. 18. Kamio, Yoko, illus. 2006. (Boys over Flowers Ser.). (ENG., Illus.). 208p. pap. 9.99 *(978-1-4215-0532-9(0))* Viz Media.

Kapur, Saba. Lucky Me. 2nd ed. 2018. (Lucky Us Ser.). (ENG.). 368p. (YA). (gr. 7-12). pap. 12.99 *(978-1-948705-01-1(X))* Amberjack Publishing Co.

Karalius, Kimberly. Love Fortunes & Other Disasters. 2015. (Grimbaud Ser.: 1). (ENG.). 368p. (YA). (gr. 7). pap. 17.99 *(978-1-250-04720-5(X)*, 900132070) Feiwel & Friends.

Karst, Patrice. The Invisible Web: An Invisible String Story Celebrating Love & Universal Connection. Lew-Vriethoff, Joanne, illus. 2020. (Invisible String Ser.: 4). (ENG.). 32p. (J). (gr. -1-3). 17.99 *(978-0-316-52496-4(4))* Little, Brown Bks. for Young Readers.

Kasza, Keiko. A Mother for Choco. 2003. (ENG.). 30p. (J). (gr. -1 — 1). bds. 7.99 *(978-0-399-24191-8(4)*, G.P. Putnam's Sons Books for Young Readers) Penguin Young Readers Group.

Katcher, Brian. Deacon Locke Went to Prom. 2017. (ENG.). 400p. (YA). (gr. 8). 17.99 *(978-0-06-242252-1(9)*, Tegen, Katherine Bks) HarperCollins Pubs.

Kate, Lauren. Fallen. (Fallen Ser.: 1). (ENG.). (YA). (gr. 7). 2010. 480p. pap. 12.99 *(978-0-385-73913-9(3)*, Ember) 2009. 464p. 18.99 *(978-0-385-73893-4(5)*, Delacorte Pr.) Random Hse. Children's Bks.

—Fallen. 2010. (Fallen Ser.: 1). lib. bdg. 22.10 *(978-0-606-15168-9(0))* Turtleback.

—Fallen in Love. 2012. (Fallen Ser.). (ENG.). 224p. (YA). (gr. 7). pap. 10.99 *(978-0-385-74262-7(2)*, Ember) Random Hse. Children's Bks.

—Passion. (Fallen Ser.: 3). (ENG.). (YA). (gr. 7). 2012. 448p. pap. 13.99 *(978-0-385-73917-7(6)*, Ember) 2011. 432p. 18.99 *(978-0-385-73916-0(8)*, Delacorte Pr.) Random Hse. Children's Bks.

—Passion. 2012. (Fallen Ser.: 3). lib. bdg. 22.10 *(978-0-606-26410-5(8))* Turtleback.

—Rapture. (Fallen Ser.: 4). (ENG.). (YA). (gr. 7). 2014. 480p. pap. 10.99 *(978-0-385-73919-1(2)*, Ember) 2012. 464p. 17.99 *(978-0-385-73918-4(4)*, Delacorte Pr.) Random Hse. Children's Bks.

—Teardrop. 2013. 441p. (YA). *(978-0-385-38372-1(X))*; *(978-0-385-37491-0(7))* Random House Publishing Group. (Delacorte Pr).

—Teardrop. 2014. (Teardrop Ser.: 1). (ENG.). 480p. (YA). (gr. 7). pap. 10.99 *(978-0-385-74266-5(5)*, Ember) Random Hse. Children's Bks.

—Torment. (Fallen Ser.: 2). (ENG.). (YA). (gr. 7). 2011. 480p. pap. 10.99 *(978-0-385-73915-3(X)*, Ember) 2010. 464p. 17.99 *(978-0-385-73914-6(1)*, Delacorte Pr.) Random Hse. Children's Bks.

—Torment. 2011. (Fallen Ser.: 2). lib. bdg. 22.10 *(978-0-606-22247-1(2))* Turtleback.

—Unforgiven. 2016. (Fallen Ser.). (ENG.). 368p. (YA). (gr. 7). pap. 10.99 *(978-0-385-74264-1(9)*, Ember) Random Hse. Children's Bks.

Katrana, Carol. Charlie, the Christmas Camel: A Christmas Story to Remember. 2012. 120p. (gr. 4-6). pap. 16.95 *(978-1-4772-7710-2(2))* AuthorHouse.

Katschke, Judy. The Facts about Flirting. 2003. (Two of a Kind Ser.: Vol. 27). (Illus.). 112p. mass mkt. 4.99 *(978-0-06-009323-5(4)*, Harper Entertainment) HarperCollins Pubs.

Katz, Karen. Mommy Hugs. 2006. (ENG., Illus.). 32p. (J). (gr. -1-3). 19.99 *(978-0-689-87772-8(2)*, McElderry, Margaret K. Bks.) McElderry, Margaret K. Bks.

Kaufman, Amie & Spooner, Meagan. Their Fractured Light. 2016. (Starbound Trilogy Ser.: 3). (ENG.). 432p. (YA). (gr. 7-12). pap. 19.99 *(978-1-4847-4783-4(6))* Hyperion Pr.

Kay, L. M. Frederick's Birthday Surprise. 2009. 36p. pap. 24.95 *(978-1-60836-944-7(7))* America Star Bks.

Kaye, Marilyn. Finders Keepers, 4. 2010. (Gifted Ser.). (ENG.). 240p. (YA). (gr. 6-8). pap. 22.44 *(978-0-7534-1953-3(X)*, 9780753419533) Kingfisher Publications, plc GBR. Dist: Children's Plus, Inc.

Keating, Lucy. Literally. 2018. (ENG.). 272p. (YA). (gr. 8). pap. 9.99 *(978-0-06-238005-0(2)*, HarperTeen) HarperCollins Pubs.

Keefer, Mikal. All Day Long, God Loves Me. Perez, Nomar, illus. 2017. (Best of Li'l Buddies Ser.). (ENG.). 16p. (J). bds. 6.99 *(978-1-4707-4859-3(2))* Group Publishing, Inc.

Keil, Melissa. The Incredible Adventures of Cinnamon Girl. Lawrence, Mike, illus. 2018. (ENG.). 352p. (YA). (gr. 7-12). pap. 9.95 *(978-1-68263-041-9(2))* Peachtree Publishing Co. Inc.

Keith, Donna. I Love You All the Same, 1 vol. 2014. (ENG., Illus.). 20p. (J). bds. 9.99 *(978-0-529-10204-1(8)*, Tommy Nelson) Nelson, Thomas Inc.

Keith, Patty J. Will You Be My Friend? Even If I Am Different from You. Keith, Patty J., photos by. 2013. (Illus.). 36p. pap. 12.95 *(978-0-615-78050-4(4))* Patty's Blooming Words.

Kelly, Allison Palmer. The Power of Words. 2013. 20p. 24.95 *(978-1-4759-6745-6(4))*; pap. 14.95 *(978-1-4759-6743-2(8))* iUniverse, Inc.

Kemmerer, Brigid. Letters to the Lost. (ENG.). (YA). 2018. 416p. pap. 10.99 *(978-1-68119-591-9(7)*, 900179018) 2017. 400p. 18.99 *(978-1-68119-008-2(7)*, 900154802) Bloomsbury Publishing USA. (Bloomsbury USA Childrens).

Kenneally, Miranda. Breathe, Annie, Breathe. 2015. (Hundred Oaks Ser.: 5). 336p. (YA). (gr. 8-12). pap. 14.99 *(978-1-4926-0866-0(1)*, 9781492608660) Sourcebooks, Inc.

—Coming up for Air. 2017. (Hundred Oaks Ser.: 8). 304p. (YA). (gr. 8-12). pap. 10.99 *(978-1-4926-3011-1(X))* Sourcebooks, Inc.

—Defending Taylor. 2016. (Hundred Oaks Ser.: 7). 304p. (YA). (gr. 8-12). pap. 12.99 *(978-1-4926-3008-1(X)*, 9781492630081) Sourcebooks, Inc.

—Racing Savannah, 1 vol. unabr. ed. 2015. (Hundred Oaks Ser.: Bk. 4). (ENG.). (YA). (gr. 7-9). 14.99 *(978-1-5012-1560-5(4)*, 9781501215605, Audible Studios on Brilliance Audio) Brilliance Publishing, Inc.

—Racing Savannah. 2013. (Hundred Oaks Ser.: 4). 304p. (YA). (gr. 7-12). pap. 14.99 *(978-1-4022-8476-2(4)*, 9781402284762) Sourcebooks, Inc.

Kennedy, C. Slaying Isidore's Dragons. (ENG., Illus.). 2016. (J). 32.99 *(978-1-63533-073-1(4))* 2015. 350p. (YA). pap. 17.99 *(978-1-63476-001-0(8))* Dreamspinner Pr. (Harmony Ink Pr.).

Kennedy, Patricia Moran. The Loving Tree A Story of Love, Loss, & Transformation for All Ages. 2004. (Illus.). 64p. (YA). (gr. 5-18). per. 14.95 *(978-0-9749848-0-3(9))* Dancer's Publishing.

Kennedy, Richard. Crazy in Love. Date not set. 48p. (J). (gr. -1-3). 14.99 *(978-0-06-027213-5(9))*; lib. bdg. 15.89 *(978-0-06-027214-2(7))* HarperCollins Pubs. (Geringer, Laura Book).

Kephart, Beth. Undercover. 2009. (ENG.). 304p. (YA). (gr. 8). pap. 8.99 *(978-0-06-123895-6(3)*, HarperTeen) HarperCollins Pubs.

Khurram, Murad. The Longing Heart. 2007. (ENG., Illus.). 28p. (J). pap. 3.95 *(978-0-86037-138-0(7))* Kube Publishing Ltd. GBR. Dist: Consortium Bk. Sales & Distribution.

Kiely, Brendan. The Last True Love Story. (ENG., Illus.). 288p. (YA). (gr. 9). 2017. pap. 11.99 *(978-1-4814-2989-4(2))* 2016. 17.99 *(978-1-4814-2988-7(4))* McElderry, Margaret K. Bks. (McElderry, Margaret K. Bks.).

Kimaya. All the Flavours of Love. 2012. 40p. pap. 13.95 *(978-1-4525-0649-4(3))* Balboa Pr.

Kimmelman, Leslie. How Do I Love You? McCue, Lisa, illus. 2005. 32p. (J). lib. bdg. 16.89 *(978-0-06-001201-4(3))* HarperCollins Pubs.

King, A. S. Ask the Passengers. 2013. (ENG.). 336p. (YA). (gr. 10-17). pap. 18.99 *(978-0-316-19467-9(0))* Little, Brown Bks. for Young Readers.

King, Deja. Ride Wit' Me: A Novel. 2010. (ENG.). 151p. (YA). 29.94 *(978-0-9755811-9-3(8))* King Production, A.

Kirby, Jessi. Golden. (ENG.). 288p. (YA). (gr. 7). 2014. pap. 9.99 *(978-1-4424-5218-3(8))* 2013. 16.99 *(978-1-4424-5216-9(1))* Simon & Schuster Bks. For Young Readers. (Simon & Schuster Bks. For Young Readers).

—Things We Know by Heart. (ENG.). 304p. (YA). (gr. 9). 2016. pap. 11.99 *(978-0-06-229944-4(1))* 2015. 17.99 *(978-0-06-229943-7(3))* HarperCollins Pubs. (HarperTeen).

Kirchner, Janette. I Love You So Much. 2011. 20p. pap. 24.95 *(978-1-4137-5952-5(1))* America Star Bks.

Kirkpatrick, Teresa. Roscoe's Forest Adventures. 2008. 177p. pap. 24.95 *(978-1-60672-328-9(6))* America Star Bks.

Kirsch, Vincent. From Archie to Zack. 2020. (ENG., Illus.). 40p. (J). (gr. -1-3). 17.99 *(978-1-4197-4367-2(8)*, 1685701, Abrams Bks. for Young Readers) Abrams, Inc.

Klein, Jen. Hearts Made for Breaking. 2019. 320p. (YA). (gr. 7). pap. 9.99 *(978-1-5247-0008-9(8)*, Random Hse. Bks. for Young Readers) Random Hse. Children's Bks.

—Shuffle, Repeat. 2017. 352p. (YA). (gr. 7). pap. 9.99 *(978-0-553-50985-4(3)*, Ember) Random Hse. Children's Bks.

Klise, James. Love Drugged. 2010. (ENG.). 312p. (YA). (gr. 9-12). pap. 9.95 *(978-0-7387-2175-0(1)*, 0738721751, Flux) North Star Editions.

Kloeck-Lim, Christine. Disintegrate. 2013. 206p. pap. *(978-1-77130-367-5(0))* Evernight Publishing.

Koehn, Wendel. Love Problematic: And Other Stories. 2012. 24p. pap. 14.93 *(978-1-4669-1851-1(9))* Trafford Publishing.

Kollar, J. P. Three Tomato Brand. 2005. 127p. per. 12.95 *(978-1-59879-076-4(5))* Lifevest Publishing, Inc.

Konen, Leah. Happy Messy Scary Love. 2019. (ENG., Illus.). 336p. (YA). (gr. 8-17). 18.99 *(978-1-4197-3489-2(X)*, 1149101, Amulet Bks.) Abrams, Inc.

—The Romantics. (ENG.). 336p. (gr. 8-17). 2017. (J). pap. 9.99 *(978-1-4197-2750-4(8)*, 1149003) 2016. (YA). 18.95 *(978-1-4197-2193-9(3)*, 1149001) Abrams, Inc. (Amulet Bks.).

Konigsburg, E. L. Journey to an 800 Number. 2008. (ENG.). 160p. (J). (gr. 4-8). pap. 7.99 *(978-1-4169-5875-8(4)*, Atheneum Bks. for Young Readers) Simon & Schuster Children's Publishing.

Kouga, Yun. Crown of Love, Vol. 1. 2010. (Crown of Love Ser.: 1). (ENG., Illus.). 192p. pap. 9.99 *(978-1-4215-3[illegible]93-9(3))* Viz Media.

—Crown of Love, Vol. 2. 2010. (Crown of Love Se[illegible] 2). (ENG., Illus.). 200p. pap. 9.99 *(978-1-4215-3194-6(1)*[illegible] Media.

Krackow, Eric T. Bill the Snowman, 1 vol. 2009. [illegible] Illus.). 64p. (J). (gr. -1-3). 16.99 *(978-0-7643-3219-7(8)*, [illegible]573) Schiffer Publishing, Ltd.

Kraevskaya, Tatiyana. Wings for Little Turtle. 2012. 16p. pap. 12.68 *(978-1-4669-0733-1(9))* Trafford Publishing.

Kranz, Linda. Love You When. 2013. (Illus.). 32p. (J). (gr. -1-1). 7.95 *(978-1-58979-907-3(0))* Taylor Trade Publishing.

Krauss, Ruth. Big & Little. Szilagyi, Mary, illus. 2003. (J). pap. 12.95 *(978-0-590-40698-7(1))* Scholastic, Inc.

Krulik, Nancy. Puppy Love. 2011. (Romantic Comedies Ser.). (ENG.). 224p. (YA). (gr. 7). pap. 12.99 *(978-1-4424-3079-2(6)*, Simon Pulse) Simon Pulse.

—Ripped at the Seams. 2004. (Romantic Comedies Ser.). (ENG.). 336p. (YA). (gr. 9). mass mkt. 6.99 *(978-0-689-86771-2(9)*, Simon Pulse) Simon Pulse.

—She's Got the Beat. 2010. (Romantic Comedies Ser.). (ENG.). 320p. (YA). (gr. 9). pap. 14.99 *(978-1-4424-1419-8(7)*, Simon Pulse) Simon Pulse.

Kuper, Tonya. Anomaly. 2014. (Schrodinger's Consortium Ser.: 1). (ENG.). 400p. (YA). (gr. 7-12). pap. 9.99 *(978-1-62266-405-4(1)*, 9781622664054) Entangled Publishing, LLC.

Lacek, Carolyn. Destiny Awakened. 2009. 52p. pap. 18.25 *(978-1-60860-736-5(4)*, Eloquent Bks.) Strategic Book Publishing & Rights Agency (SBPRA).

LaFevers, Robin. Dark Triumph. 2018. (His Fair Assassin Ser.: 2). (ENG., Illus.). 416p. (YA). (gr. 9). pap. 10.99 *(978-1-328-56766-6(4)*, 1726823, Clarion Bks.) HarperCollins Pubs.

—Dark Triumph, 10 vols. 2013. (His Fair Assassin Ser.: 2). (YA). *(978-1-4640-2397-2(2))* Recorded Bks., Inc.

—Mortal Heart. 2018. (His Fair Assassin Ser.: 3). (ENG., Illus.). 496p. (YA). (gr. 9). pap. 15.99 *(978-1-328-56767-3(2)*, 1726824, Clarion Bks.) HarperCollins Pubs.

LaFleur, John & Dubin, Shawn. Dreary & Naughty: Friday the 13th of February: Friday the 13th of February, 1 vol. 2013. (ENG., Illus.). 64p. (YA). (gr. 8-12). 14.99 *(978-0-7643-4495-4(1)*, 4929) Schiffer Publishing, Ltd.

Lake, Nick. Whisper to Me. 2016. (ENG.). 544p. (YA). 17.99 *(978-1-61963-456-5(2)*, 900137473, Bloomsbury USA Childrens) Bloomsbury Publishing USA.

LaMarche, Una. Like No Other. 2015. 384p. (YA). (gr. 7). pap. 10.99 *(978-1-59514-675-5(X)*, Razorbill) Penguin Young Readers Group.

Lambert, Teres. Mommy, Do You Love Me? 2008. 20p. pap. 24.95 *(978-1-60441-911-5(3))* America Star Bks.

Lane, Amy. Triane's Son Fighting. 2nd ed. (ENG., 2016. Illus.). (J). 32.99 *(978-1-63477-982-1(7))* 2014. (Bitter Moon Saga Ser.: Bk. 3). 350p. (YA). pap. 17.99 *(978-1-62798-340-2(6))* Dreamspinner Pr. (Harmony Ink Pr.).

Lane, Dakota. Orpheus Obsession. 2005. (Illus.). 288p. (J). lib. bdg. 17.89 *(978-0-06-074174-7(0)*, HarperTeen) HarperCollins Pubs.

—The Orpheus Obsession. 2008. (ENG., Illus.). 288p. (YA). (gr. 9). pap. 8.99 *(978-0-06-074175-4(9)*, HarperTeen) HarperCollins Pubs.

Lane, Ronald. Avina's Song: A Children's Story. 2007. (ENG.). 48p. per. 16.95 *(978-1-4241-6252-9(1))* America Star Bks.

Lange, Sue. The Perpetual Motion Club. 2013. 208p. pap. 14.95 *(978-0-9887488-6-6(X))* Perpetual Motion Machine Publishing.

Lara, Mike. A Boy & a Horse. 2011. 40p. pap. 21.99 *(978-1-4628-8024-9(X))* Xlibris Corp.

Lark, Jane. I Found You. 2014. (ENG.). 392p. pap. 11.99 *(978-0-00-757776-7(1)*, One More Chapter) HarperCollins Pubs. Ltd. GBR. Dist: HarperCollins Pubs.

Larkin, Angela & Haverlock, Catina. Before. 2018. (ENG.). 256p. (YA). pap. 17.99 *(978-1-4621-2205-9(1)*, Sweetwater Bks.) Cedar Fort, Inc./CFI Distribution.

Larkin, Susan. All the Ways I Love You. East, Jacqueline, illus. 2014. (J). *(978-1-4351-5821-4(0))* Barnes & Noble, Inc.

—All the Ways I Love You. Trotter, Stuart, illus. 2012. 16p. (J). *(978-1-4351-3857-5(0))* Barnes & Noble, Inc.

Larsen, Angela Sage. Broken Record, Bk. 4. 2013. (Fifties Chix Ser.: 4). (ENG., Illus.). 200p. (YA). pap. 9.95 *(978-1-60746-446-4(2)*, Premiere) FastPrncl, Inc.

—Keeping Secrets, Bk. 2. 2012. (Fifties Chix Ser.: 2). (ENG.). 220p. (YA). pap. 9.95 *(978-1-60746-367-2(9)*, Premiere) FastPrncl, Inc.

Larson, Angela. Anthony Smoochiano: First Loves. 2012. pap. *(978-1-4507-7998-2(0))* Independent Pub.

Larson, Heidi. Love the Lord Your God! 2012. 32p. pap. 13.99 *(978-1-4624-0295-3(X)*, Inspiring Voices) Author Solutions, LLC.

Laskin, Pamela L. Ronit & Jamil. 2017. (ENG.). 192p. (YA). (gr. 8). 17.99 *(978-0-06-245854-4(X)*, Tegen, Katherine Bks) HarperCollins Pubs.

Laudati, Joe. Faela: A Fairy's Tale. 2008. 190p. pap. 14.50 *(978-0-615-20324-9(8))* Laudati, Joe.

Laura Grey Wahl. The Magic Town of Stuart Easterly. 2009. 16p. pap. 15.00 *(978-1-4389-4703-7(8))* AuthorHouse.

Laure, Estelle. But Then I Came Back. 2018. (ENG.). 320p. (YA). (gr. 9). pap. 9.99 *(978-1-328-86931-9(8)*, 1696695, Clarion Bks.) HarperCollins Pubs.

Laurens, Jennifer. Falling for Romeo. 2007. (YA). per. 12.95 *(978-1-933963-94-5(8))* Grove Creek Publishing, LLC.

—Magic Hands. 2007. (YA). per. 12.95 *(978-1-933963-97-6(2))* Grove Creek Publishing, LLC.

Laurie, Victoria. Forever, Again. (ENG.). 368p. (J). (gr. 7-12). 2017. pap. 9.99 *(978-1-4847-0151-5(8))* 2016. 17.99 *(978-1-4847-0009-9(0))* Hyperion Bks. for Children.

Lawler, Janet. If Kisses Were Colors Board Book. Jay, Alison, illus. 2010. (ENG.). 22p. (J). (gr. -1 — 1). bds. 7.99 *(978-0-8037-3530-9(8)*, Dial Bks) Penguin Young Readers Group.

Lawrence, Kelly. Unconditional. 2014. (ENG., Illus.). 162p. (J). (gr. -1-12). pap. 11.95 *(978-1-78279-394-6(1)*, Lodestone Bks.) Hunt, John Publishing Ltd. GBR. Dist: National Bk. Network.

LaZebnik, Claire. The Last Best Kiss. 2014. (ENG.). 384p. (YA). (gr. 8). pap. 9.99 *(978-0-06-225228-9(3)*, HarperTeen) HarperCollins Pubs.

—Wrong about the Guy. 2015. (ENG.). 368p. (YA). (gr. 8). pap. 9.99 *(978-0-06-225230-2(5)*, HarperTeen) HarperCollins Pubs.

Le Blanc, Lennie. The Minnesota Summer. 2011. 116p. (gr. 4-6). pap. 10.95 *(978-1-4620-3887-9(5))* iUniverse, Inc.

Leathers, Rain. Purple Mountain. 2008. 36p. pap. 20.95 *(978-1-4327-2685-0(4))* Outskirts Pr., Inc.

Leavitt, Martine. Keturah & Lord Death. 2012. (ENG.). 224p. (YA). (gr. 4-7). pap. 9.95 *(978-1-59078-949-0(0)*, Astra Young Readers) Astra Publishing Hse.

Leder, Meg. The Museum of Heartbreak. (ENG., Illus.). 288p. (YA). 2017. (gr. 7). pap. 10.99 *(978-1-4814-3211-5(7))* 2016. (gr. 9). 17.99 *(978-1-4814-3210-8(9))* Simon Pulse. (Simon Pulse).

Lee, Calee M. I Love You! Tharp, Tricia, illus. 2013. (ENG.). 32p. (J). (gr. -1-k). pap. 9.99 *(978-1-62395-471-0(1))* Xist Publishing.

Lee, Darrien. Denim Diaries 1: 16 Going On 21. 2008. (Denim Diaries: 1). (ENG., Illus.). 181p. (YA). (gr. 9). 17.00 *(978-1-933967-71-4(4)*, Urban Renaissance) Kensington Publishing Corp.

Lee, Edith. Romeo & Julie Square. 2012. 28p. pap. *(978-0-9881235-0-2(9))* Bound Publishing.

Lee, M. C. You Don't Know Jack. 2016. (ENG., Illus.). (J). 24.99 *(978-1-63477-999-9(1)*, Harmony Ink Pr.) Dreamspinner Pr.

Leech, Caroline. In Another Time. 2018. (ENG.). 384p. (YA). (gr. 8). 17.99 *(978-0-06-245991-6(0)*, HarperTeen) HarperCollins Pubs.

—Wait for Me. (ENG.). (YA). (gr. 8). 2018. 400p. pap. 9.99 *(978-0-06-245989-3(9))* 2017. 384p. 17.99 *(978-0-06-245988-6(0))* HarperCollins Pubs. (HarperTeen).

Lefall, Kathy. Stargaze. 2003. 346p. (YA). pap. 18.95 *(978-0-595-26878-8(1))* iUniverse, Inc.

Lehrman, Maggie. The Last Best Story. 2018. (ENG.). 352p. (YA). (gr. 9). 17.99 *(978-0-06-232077-3(7)*, Balzer & Bray) HarperCollins Pubs.

J
K
L

L'Engle, Madeleine. A House Like a Lotus. 2012. (Polly O'Keefe Ser.: 3). (ENG.). 336p. (YA). (gr. 7-12). pap. 13.99 *(978-0-312-54798-1(6)*, 900074325) Square Fish.

Lenzi, Christy. Stone Field: A Novel. 2016. (ENG.). 320p. (YA). 29.99 *(978-1-62672-069-5(X)*, 900134314) Roaring Brook Pr.

LeRoye, Dee. Crossfire. 2003. 137p. (YA). per. 5.99 *(978-0-9727056-0-8(0))* Dakota Rose.

Lester, Julius. Cupid: A Tale of Love & Desire. 2007. (ENG., Illus.). 208p. (YA). (gr. 7-12). 17.00 *(978-0-15-202056-9(X)*, 1191683, Clarion Bks.) HarperCollins Pubs.

Leung, Helen. Toni. 2006. 251p. pap. 27.95 *(978-1-4137-8990-4(0))* PublishAmerica, Inc.

Levenseller, Tricia. Daughter of the Pirate King. 2018. (Daughter of the Pirate King Ser.: 1). (ENG.). 336p. (YA). pap. 10.99 *(978-1-250-14422-5(1)*, 900160921) Square Fish.

Levithan, David. Another Day. 2015. (ENG.). 336p. (YA). (gr. 7-12). 18.99 *(978-0-385-75620-4(8)*, Knopf Bks. for Young Readers) Random Hse. Children's Bks.

—Every Day. 2015. (KOR.). 424p. (J). pap. *(978-89-374-3204-0(8))* Min-eumsa Publishing Co., Ltd.

—Every Day. (ENG.). (YA). (gr. 7). 2013. 400p. pap. 12.99 *(978-0-307-93189-4(7)*, Ember) 2012. 336p. 18.99 *(978-0-307-93188-7(9)*, Knopf Bks. for Young Readers) Random Hse. Children's Bks.

—Every Day. 2013. (Every Day Ser.: 1). (SWE.). lib. bdg. 20.85 *(978-0-606-32238-6(8))* Turtleback.

—Hold Me Closer: The Tiny Cooper Story. 2016. lib. bdg. 22.10 *(978-0-606-38390-5(5))* Turtleback.

—How They Met & Other Stories. 2009. (ENG.). 256p. (YA). (gr. 9). pap. 9.99 *(978-0-375-84323-5(X)*, Knopf Bks. for Young Readers) Random Hse. Children's Bks.

—Marly's Ghost. Selznick, Brian, illus. 2007. (ENG.). 208p. (YA). (gr. 7-18). 7.99 *(978-0-14-240912-1(X)*, Speak) Penguin Young Readers Group.

—Someday. 2018. 394p. (YA). *(978-0-525-70816-2(2))* Knopf, Alfred A. Inc.

—Someday. (ENG.). 400p. (YA). (gr. 7). 2019. pap. 11.99 *(978-0-399-55308-0(8)*, Ember) 2018. 18.99 *(978-0-399-55305-9(3)*, Knopf Bks. for Young Readers) Random Hse. Children's Bks.

—Two Boys Kissing. 2015. (ENG.). 224p. (YA). (gr. 9). pap. 10.99 *(978-0-307-93191-7(9)*, Ember) Random Hse. Children's Bks.

—Two Boys Kissing. 2015. lib. bdg. 20.85 *(978-0-606-37273-2(3))* Turtleback.

Lewis, Gill. I Love You More Each Day. Ho, Louise, illus. 2017. (Padded Board Books for Babies Ser.). (ENG.). 20p. (J). (gr. -1 — 1). bds. 6.99 *(978-1-68412-042-0(X)*, Silver Dolphin Bks.) Printers Row Publishing Group.

Lewis, Linda. All for the Love of That Boy. 2007. (ENG.). 224p. (YA). (gr. 7). pap. 12.95 *(978-1-4169-6142-0(9)*, Simon Pulse) Simon Pulse.

—Is There Life after Boys? 2007. (ENG.). 176p. (YA). (gr. 7). pap. 10.95 *(978-1-4169-6143-7(7)*, Simon Pulse) Simon Pulse.

—Loving Two Is Hard to Do. 2008. (ENG.). 160p. (YA). (gr. 7). pap. 8.95 *(978-1-4169-7534-2(9)*, Simon Pulse) Simon Pulse.

—My Heart Belongs to That Boy. 2008. (ENG.). 176p. (Orig.). (YA). (gr. 7). pap. 9.95 *(978-1-4169-7536-6(5)*, Simon Pulse) Simon Pulse.

—We Hate Everything but Boys. 2008. (ENG.). 160p. (YA). (gr. 7). pap. 8.95 *(978-1-4169-7537-3(3)*, Simon Pulse) Simon Pulse.

—We Love Only Older Boys. 2008. (ENG.). 160p. (Orig.). (YA). (gr. 7). pap. 8.95 *(978-1-4169-7535-9(7)*, Simon Pulse) Simon Pulse.

Lewis, Paeony. I'll Always Love You. Ives, Penny, illus. 2013. (ENG.). 32p. (J). (gr. -1-2). pap. 3.99 *(978-1-58925-441-1(4))* Tiger Tales.

Lewis, Stewart. You Have Seven Messages. 2012. (ENG.). 304p. (YA). (gr. 7). pap. 11.99 *(978-0-385-74029-6(8)*, Ember) Random Hse. Children's Bks.

Lewman, David. Lovestruck! Fruchter, Jason, illus. 2004. (Fairly Oddparents Ser.). (J). (gr. -1-3). 11.15 *(978-0-7569-1992-4(4))* Perfection Learning Corp.

Liang, Kuan & Yung, Kao. Magic Lover's Tower, Vol. 1. 2008. (ENG., Illus.). 176p. (YA). pap. 9.95 *(978-1-59796-153-0(1))* DrMaster Pubns. Inc.

Liberty, Anita. The Center of the Universe: Yep, That Would Be Me. 2008. (ENG.). 304p. (YA). (gr. 7-18). pap. 9.99 *(978-1-4169-5789-8(8)*, Simon Pulse) Simon Pulse.

Liggett, Kim. The Grace Year: A Novel. (ENG., Illus.). 416p. (YA). 2020. pap. 11.99 *(978-1-250-14545-1(7)*, 900181039) 2019. 16.99 *(978-1-250-14544-4(9)*, 900181038) St. Martin's Pr. (Wednesday Bks.).

Light, Kelly. Louise Loves Bake Sales. 2018. (I Can Read Level 1 Ser.). (ENG., Illus.). 32p. (J). (gr. -1-3). 16.99 *(978-0-06-236366-4(2)*, Balzer & Bray) HarperCollins Pubs.

—Louise Loves Bake Sales. Light, Kelly, illus. 2018. (I Can Read Level 1 Ser.). (ENG., Illus.). 32p. (J). (gr. -1-3). pap. 4.99 *(978-0-06-236365-7(4)*, Balzer & Bray) HarperCollins Pubs.

Lilly, Suzanne. Untellable. 2013. 158p. pap. 9.99 *(978-1-62237-218-8(2))* Turquoise Morning Pr.

Limke, Jeff. Tristan & Isolde: The Warrior & the Princess [a British Legend]. Randall, Ron, illus. 2009. (Graphic Myths & Legends Ser.). (ENG.). 48p. (J). (gr. 4-8). pap. 9.99 *(978-1-58013-889-5(6)*, 3b9182fb-99e4-4b65-8c7d-c5eba12bd802, Graphic Universe™) Lerner Publishing Group.

Lindner, April. Catherine. 2014. (ENG.). 336p. (YA). (gr. 10-17). pap. 10.00 *(978-0-316-19693-2(2)*, Poppy) Little, Brown Bks. for Young Readers.

—Love, Lucy. 2016. (ENG.). 304p. (YA). (gr. 10-17). pap. 9.99 *(978-0-316-40068-8(8)*, Poppy) Little, Brown Bks. for Young Readers.

Lindquist, N. J. A Friend in Need. 2016. (Circle of Friends Ser.: Vol. 3). (ENG., Illus.). (YA). pap. *(978-1-927692-06-6(7))* That's Life! Communications.

—More Than a Friend. 2016. (Circle of Friends Ser.: Vol. 4). (ENG., Illus.). (YA). pap. *(978-1-927692-07-3(5))* That's Life! Communications.

Lindsey, Julie Anne. What She Wanted. 2016. (ENG., Illus.). 220p. (J). pap. 15.00 *(978-1-60183-489-8(6))* Kensington Publishing Corp.

Linka, Catherine. A Girl Called Fearless: A Novel. 2014. (Girl Called Fearless Ser.: 1). (ENG.). 368p. (YA). (gr. 7). 34.99 *(978-1-250-03929-3(0)*, 900123214, St. Martin's Griffin) St. Martin's Pr.

Linmark, R. Zamora. The Importance of Being Wilde at Heart. 2019. 352p. (YA). (gr. 7). 17.99 *(978-1-101-93821-8(8)*, Delacorte Pr.) Random Hse. Children's Bks.

Lippincott, Rachael. Five Feet Apart. (ENG.). 304p. (YA). (gr. 7). 2022. pap. 11.99 *(978-1-6659-0496-4(8))* 2018. (Illus.). 18.99 *(978-1-5344-3733-3(9))* 2019. (Illus.). 18.99 *(978-1-5344-5156-8(0))* Simon & Schuster Bks. For Young Readers. (Simon & Schuster Bks. For Young Readers).

Lippincott, Rachael, et al. Five Feet Apart. 2019. (ENG., Illus.). 288p. (J). *(978-1-4711-8509-0(5))*; *(978-1-4711-8231-0(2))* Simon & Schuster Children's Publishing.

Little, Kimberley Griffiths. Returned. 2017. (Forbidden Ser.: 3). (ENG.). 384p. (YA). (gr. 9). 17.99 *(978-0-06-219504-3(2)*, HarperCollins) HarperCollins Pubs.

Lloyd-Caldwell, Mariana. Dancing Watermelon Babies & Mr Mouse's Good Deed. 2008. 44p. pap. 18.49 *(978-1-4343-9555-9(3))* AuthorHouse.

Lloyd-Jones, Emily. The Hearts We Sold. 2019. (ENG., Illus.). 416p. (YA). (gr. 9-17). pap. 10.99 *(978-0-316-31455-8(2))* Little, Brown Bks. for Young Readers.

Lloyd-Jones, Sally. Just Because You're Mine. Endersby, Frank, illus. 2011. (ENG.). 32p. (J). (gr. -1-2). 17.99 *(978-0-06-201476-4(5)*, HarperCollins) HarperCollins Pubs.

Lo, Malinda. Adaptation. 2013. (ENG.). 416p. (YA). (gr. 10-17). pap. 19.99 *(978-0-316-19798-4(X))* Little, Brown Bks. for Young Readers.

—Ash. 10th ed. 2019. (ENG.). 304p. (YA). (gr. 8-17). pap. 10.99 *(978-0-316-53131-3(6))* Little, Brown Bks. for Young Readers.

—Huntress. 2012. (ENG.). 416p. (YA). (gr. 9-17). pap. 11.99 *(978-0-316-03999-4(3))* Little, Brown Bks. for Young Readers.

—Inheritance. 2014. (ENG.). 480p. (YA). (gr. 10-17). pap. 21.99 *(978-0-316-19799-1(8))* Little, Brown Bks. for Young Readers.

Lobo, Julia. Will You Be My Sunshine. Cottage Door Press, ed. Slater, Nicola, illus. 2015. (ENG.). 18p. (J). (gr. -1-1). bds. 9.99 *(978-1-68052-027-9(X)*, 1000280) Cottage Door Pr.

Lockhart, E. We Were Liars. 2014. (Illus.). 227p. (YA). *(978-0-385-39009-5(2)*, Delacorte Pr) Random House Publishing Group.

—We Were Liars. (ENG.). (YA). (gr. 7). 2018. 320p. pap. 10.99 *(978-0-385-74127-9(8)*, Ember) 2014. (Illus.). 256p. 18.99 *(978-0-385-74126-2(X)*, Delacorte Pr.) Random Hse. Children's Bks.

London, Kiara. Kiss Cam. 2016. (ENG.). 272p. (YA). pap. 22.99 *(978-1-250-07096-8(1)*, 900149131) Feiwel & Friends.

Long, Ethan. Valensteins. (ENG., Illus.). (J). 2018. 30p. bds. 7.99 *(978-1-68119-894-1(0)*, 900191673, Bloomsbury Children's Bks.) 2017. 32p. 17.99 *(978-1-61963-433-6(3)*, 900135962, Bloomsbury USA Childrens) Bloomsbury Publishing USA.

Lopez, Patricia A. Carly & Boey. 2009. 56p. pap. 16.95 *(978-1-61546-836-2(6))* America Star Bks.

Lord, Emery. The Names They Gave Us. 2017. (ENG.). 400p. (YA). 17.99 *(978-1-61963-958-4(0)*, 900153588, Bloomsbury USA Childrens) Bloomsbury Publishing USA.

—Open Road Summer. 2018. (ENG.). 368p. (YA). pap. 10.99 *(978-1-68119-593-3(3)*, 900179020, Bloomsbury USA Childrens) Bloomsbury Publishing USA.

—When We Collided. 2016. (ENG.). 352p. (YA). 17.99 *(978-1-61963-845-7(2)*, 900150257, Bloomsbury USA Childrens) Bloomsbury Publishing USA.

Lore, Pittacus. I Am Number Four. (Lorien Legacies Ser.: 1). (ENG.). (YA). (gr. 9). 2011. 496p. pap. 15.99 *(978-0-06-196957-7(5))* 2010. 443p. 18.99 *(978-0-06-196955-3(9))* HarperCollins Pubs. (HarperCollins).

—I Am Number Four. 2009. (Lorien Legacies Ser.: Bk. 1). 11.04 *(978-0-7848-3715-3(5)*, Everbind) Marco Bk. Co.

—I Am Number Four. 2011. (I Am Number Four Ser.: Vol. 1). (ENG.). 440p. (gr. 9-12). 20.00 *(978-1-61383-207-3(9))* Perfection Learning Corp.

—I Am Number Four. 2011. (Lorien Legacies Ser.: 1). (YA). lib. bdg. 20.85 *(978-0-606-23545-7(0))* Turtleback.

—I Am Number Four Movie Tie-In Edition. movie tie-in ed. 2011. (Lorien Legacies Ser.: 1). (ENG.). (YA). (gr. 9). 496p. pap. 9.99 *(978-0-06-211655-0(X))*; 480p. 17.99 *(978-0-06-202624-8(0))* HarperCollins Pubs. (HarperCollins).

—I Am Number Four: the Lost Files: Rebel Allies. 2015. (Lorien Legacies: the Lost Files Ser.). (ENG.). 416p. (YA). (gr. 9). pap. 10.99 *(978-0-06-236404-3(9)*, HarperCollins) HarperCollins Pubs.

—I Am Number Four: the Lost Files: Secret Histories. 2013. (Lorien Legacies: the Lost Files Ser.). (ENG.). 416p. (YA). (gr. 9). pap. 10.99 *(978-0-06-222367-8(4)*, HarperCollins) HarperCollins Pubs.

—I Am Number Four: the Lost Files: Zero Hour. 2016. (Lorien Legacies: the Lost Files Ser.). (ENG.). 416p. (YA). (gr. 9). pap. 11.99 *(978-0-06-238771-4(5)*, HarperCollins) HarperCollins Pubs.

—Secret Histories. 2013. (Lorien Legacies: the Lost Files Ser.). (YA). lib. bdg. 20.85 *(978-0-606-31823-5(2))* Turtleback.

Lorentzen, Bent. Krona: Dragons of Nistaia. 2009. 266p. (J). pap. 18.95 *(978-1-60619-091-3(1))* Twilight Times Bks.

Loughran, Kelley. A Crab Called Mouse. 2006. (Illus.). (J). (gr. -1-3). pap. 9.50 *(978-0-9787995-2-6(6))* High-Pitched Hum Inc.

Love in Bloom. 64p. (YA). (gr. 6-12). pap. *(978-0-8224-2380-5(4))* Globe Fearon Educational Publishing.

Love, Katie. Fruit to Live By..., 1 vol. 2009. 62p. pap. 16.95 *(978-1-60836-122-9(5))* PublishAmerica, Inc.

Lu, Marie. Champion: A Legend Novel. (Legend Ser.: 3). (ENG.). (YA). (gr. 7). 2014. 416p. pap. 12.99 *(978-0-14-751228-4(X)*, Speak) 2013. (Illus.). 384p. 19.99 *(978-0-399-25677-6(6)*, G.P. Putnam's Sons Books for Young Readers) Penguin Young Readers Group.

Lubach, Vanessa, illus. Wuthering Heights, 1 vol. 2009. (Real Reads Ser.). (ENG.). 64p. (J). (gr. 5-5). 33.93 *(978-1-60754-670-2(1)*, c5655b0e-aea4-4242-aabb-4ef7549e50d5, Windmill Bks.) Rosen Publishing Group, Inc., The.

Luder, Doreen. Dax the Last Dragon. 2012. 24p. pap. 24.95 *(978-1-62709-988-2(3))* America Star Bks.

Lund, Fiauna. Indigo. 2013. 268p. pap. 13.99 *(978-1-936850-82-2(6))* Rhemalda Publishing.

Lundquist, Jenny. The Opal Crown. 2014. (ENG., Illus.). 368p. (J). (gr. 7-17). pap. 9.95 *(978-0-7624-5422-8(9)*, Running Pr. Kids) Running Pr.

Lyles, Whitney. Love Off-Limits. 2009. (Romantic Comedies Ser.). (ENG.). 304p. (YA). (gr. 7-18). mass mkt. 6.99 *(978-1-4169-7508-3(X)*, Simon Pulse) Simon Pulse.

Lynch, Janet Nichols. Addicted to Her. 2010. (ENG.). 256p. (YA). (gr. 7-18). pap. 17.95 *(978-0-8234-2186-2(4))* Holiday Hse., Inc.

Lynn, Kelly. The Princess Transformation, 1 vol. 2010. 132p. pap. 24.95 *(978-1-4512-1417-8(0))* America Star Bks.

Lynn, Tracy. Snow: A Retelling of "Snow White & the Seven Dwarfs" 2006. (Once upon a Time Ser.). (ENG.). 272p. (YA). (gr. 9-12). mass mkt. 7.99 *(978-1-4169-4015-9(4)*, Simon Pulse) Simon Pulse.

Lytton, Deborah. Silence. 2015. (ENG.). 320p. (YA). (gr. 7). 17.99 *(978-1-60907-945-1(0)*, 5125977, Shadow Mountain) Shadow Mountain Publishing.

Ma, Jyoti & Devi, Chandra. Sparkling Together: Starbright & His Earthling Friends. 2004. (ENG., Illus.). 96p. (J). pap. 19.95 *(978-0-932040-54-1(3)*, ddc1ee5d-f71a-4c3b-8b79-8b3ee127a8bb) Integral Yoga Pubns.

Maas, Sarah J. A Court of Thorns & Roses. 2020. (Court of Thorns & Roses Ser.: 1). (ENG.). 448p. pap. 19.00 *(978-1-63557-556-9(7)*, 900227029) Bloomsbury Publishing USA.

—A Court of Thorns & Roses. 2016. lib. bdg. 22.10 *(978-0-606-38548-0(7))* Turtleback.

—Crown of Midnight. 2014. (Throne of Glass Ser.: 2). (YA). lib. bdg. 22.10 *(978-0-606-36441-6(2))* Turtleback.

—Empire of Storms. 2017. (Throne of Glass Ser.: 5). (YA). lib. bdg. 22.10 *(978-0-606-40598-0(4))* Turtleback.

Maberry, Jonathan. Mars One. 2017. (ENG., Illus.). 448p. (YA). (gr. 7). 19.99 *(978-1-4814-6161-0(3)*, Simon & Schuster Bks. For Young Readers) Simon & Schuster Bks. For Young Readers.

Mabry, Samantha. All the Wind in the World. 2018. (ENG.). 272p. (gr. 9-12). pap. 13.99 *(978-1-61620-855-4(4)*, 73855) Algonquin Young Readers.

Mac, Carrie. Crush, 1 vol. 2006. (Orca Soundings Ser.). (ENG.). 136p. (YA). (gr. 8-12). per. 9.95 *(978-1-55143-526-8(8))* Orca Bk. Pubs. USA.

Macdangereuse, T. T. The Untamed Scoundrel. 2014. (Epic Tales from Adventure Time Ser.). lib. bdg. 17.20 *(978-0-606-35718-0(1))* Turtleback.

MacDonald, George. Light Princess & Other Fairy Stories. 2006. 132p. per. 10.95 *(978-1-59818-618-5(3))*; 24.95 *(978-1-59818-236-1(6))* Aegypan.

MacKenzie, Catherine. The Lonely Grey Dog at No. 6: Tammy & Jake Learn about Love & Loyalty. 2005. (Tales from Canterbury Place Ser.). (ENG., Illus.). 160p. (J). per. 6.99 *(978-1-84550-103-7(9)*, a4bd088c-1dae-4739-9ad1-c7f64ed9439d) Christian Focus Pubns. GBR. Dist: Baker & Taylor Publisher Services (BTPS).

MacKenzie, Lachlan. The Duke's Daughter. 2008. (Story Time Ser.). (ENG., Illus.). 24p. (J). (gr. -1-3). 7.99 *(978-1-84550-326-0(0)*, 55c39b86-6732-4df2-a209-0be940187130) Christian Focus Pubns. GBR. Dist: Baker & Taylor Publisher Services (BTPS).

Maetani, Valynne. Ink & Ashes, 1 vol. 2015. (ENG.). 368p. (YA). (gr. 7-12). 19.95 *(978-1-62014-211-0(2)*, leelowtu, Tu Bks.) Lee & Low Bks., Inc.

Mafi, Tahereh. Ignite Me. 2014. (Shatter Me Ser.: 3). (ENG.). 416p. (YA). (gr. 9). pap. 15.99 *(978-0-06-208558-0(1))*; 19.99 *(978-0-06-208557-3(3))* HarperCollins Pubs. (HarperCollins).

—Restore Me. 2018. 435p. (YA). *(978-0-06-284176-6(9))* Harper & Row Ltd.

—Restore Me. 2019. (Shatter Me Ser.: 4). (ENG.). 464p. (YA). (gr. 9). pap. 15.99 *(978-0-06-267637-5(7)*, HarperCollins) HarperCollins Pubs.

—Shatter Me. 2018. (Shatter Me Ser.: 1). (ENG.). (YA). (gr. 9). 448p. 21.99 *(978-0-06-274173-8(X))*; 368p. pap. 15.99 *(978-0-06-208550-4(6))* HarperCollins Pubs. (HarperCollins).

—Shatter Me. 2012. (Shatter Me Ser.: 1). (YA). lib. bdg. 20.85 *(978-0-606-26868-4(5))* Turtleback.

—Unravel Me. 2013. (Shatter Me Ser.: 2). (ENG.). (YA). (gr. 9). 496p. pap. 15.99 *(978-0-06-208554-2(9))*; 480p. 19.99 *(978-0-06-208553-5(0))* HarperCollins Pubs. (HarperCollins).

—Unravel Me. 2013. (Shatter Me Ser.: 2). (YA). lib. bdg. 20.85 *(978-0-606-35049-5(7))* Turtleback.

Magnolia, B. Beautiful Wild Rose Girl. Hugel, William K., ed. Keba, Jamila, illus. 2012. 34p. pap. 7.95 *(978-0-9854289-0-7(2))* Mystic World Pr.

Magor, Dianne M. Ed. Lauren's Wish. 2012. 32p. (-18). pap. 21.99 *(978-1-4691-3986-9(3))* Xlibris Corp.

Magsamen, Sandra. Baby Love. Magsamen, Sandra, illus. 2019. (ENG., Illus.). 10p. (J). (gr. -1 — 1). bds. 8.99 *(978-1-338-24320-8(9)*, Cartwheel Bks.) Scholastic, Inc.

—Owl Always Love You! Magsamen, Sandra, illus. 2018. (ENG.). 10p. (J). (gr. -1 — 1). bds. 7.99 *(978-0-545-92800-7(1)*, Cartwheel Bks.) Scholastic, Inc.

Maid of Deception. 2014. (Maids of Honor Ser.). (ENG., Illus.). 416p. (YA). (gr. 7). 17.99 *(978-1-4424-4141-5(0)*, Simon & Schuster Bks. For Young Readers) Simon & Schuster Bks. For Young Readers.

Maizel, Rebecca. A Season for Fireflies. 2016. (ENG.). 256p. (YA). (gr. 9). 17.99 *(978-0-06-232764-2(X)*, HarperTeen) HarperCollins Pubs.

—Stolen Nights: A Vampire Queen Novel. 2013. (Vampire Queen Ser.: 2). (ENG.). 320p. (YA). (gr. 7-12). pap. 16.99 *(978-0-312-64992-0(4)*, 900069067, St. Martin's Griffin) St. Martin's Pr.

Malcolm, Jahnna N. The Write Stuff. 2011. (Love Letters Ser.). (ENG.). 192p. (YA). (gr. 7). pap. 9.99 *(978-1-4424-3100-3(8)*, Simon Pulse) Simon Pulse.

Malkin, Nina. Swear. (ENG.). 480p. (YA). (gr. 11). 2012. pap. 9.99 *(978-1-4424-2111-0(8))* 2011. 17.99 *(978-1-4424-2110-3(X))* Simon Pulse. (Simon Pulse).

—Swoon. 2010. (ENG.). 432p. (YA). (gr. 11). pap. 9.99 *(978-1-4169-9801-3(2)*, Simon Pulse) Simon Pulse.

Mancuso, Rudy. How to Be Famous in Six Seconds. 2016. (YA). pap. *(978-1-5011-2767-0(5)*, Keywords Press) Atria Bks.

Mandelkorn, Carole. Grandma, Will You Clap! Phillips, Laverne, illus. 2013. 16p. pap. 10.95 *(978-1-61493-196-6(8))* Peppertree Pr., The.

Mannering, Rose. Feathers: The Tales Trilogy, Book 2. 2016. (Tales Trilogy Ser.). (ENG.). 288p. (J). (gr. 6-6). 17.99 *(978-1-63450-165-1(9)*, Sky Pony Pr.) Skyhorse Publishing Co., Inc.

Manners, Tyler. Continental Change of Heart. 2006. 65p. pap. 16.95 *(978-1-4137-9483-0(1))* PublishAmerica, Inc.

Manning, Sarra. Adorkable. 2013. (ENG.). 400p. (YA). (gr. 9). pap. 13.99 *(978-1-907411-00-7(3)*, Atom Books) Little, Brown Book Group Ltd. GBR. Dist: Hachette Bk. Group.

—Guitar Girl. 2003. (ENG.). 256p. (YA). pap. *(978-0-340-86071-7(5))* Hodder & Stoughton.

Manwiller, S. A. The Adventures of Jack & Max: The Truliest Meaning of Christmas. Manwiller, S. A. & Overley, Kristen V., illus. 2013. (ENG.). 38p. (J). 24.99 *(978-0-9838427-7-4(9))* Sevenhorns Publishing.

Manz Simon, Mary. With Love, from Me to You, 1 vol. Ice, Corinna, illus. 2017. (ENG.). 18p. (J). bds. 8.99 *(978-0-310-75815-0(7))* Zonderkidz.

Marineau, Michele. Lean Mean Machines, 1 vol. 2003. (ENG., Illus.). 128p. (J). (gr. 7-9). pap. 6.95 *(978-0-88995-230-0(2)*, 78bf4573-3ccf-457b-8c3e-fc1f2ee4d79f) Red Deer Pr. CAN. Dist: Firefly Bks., Ltd.

Marquardt, Marie. Dream Things True: A Novel. 2018. (ENG.). 352p. (YA). pap. 25.99 *(978-1-250-13536-0(2)*, 900160838, Wednesday Bks.) St. Martin's Pr.

—The Radius of Us: A Novel. 2017. (ENG., Illus.). 304p. (YA). 19.99 *(978-1-250-09689-0(8)*, 900160892, St. Martin's Griffin) St. Martin's Pr.

Marsoli, Lisa Ann. Puppy Love. Durk, Jim, illus. 2003. pap. *(978-0-439-61116-9(4))* Scholastic, Inc.

Martin, Emily. The Year We Fell Apart. 2016. (ENG.). 320p. (YA). (gr. 9). 17.99 *(978-1-4814-3841-4(7)*, Simon Pulse) Simon Pulse.

Martin, LaJoyce. The Silver Ghost. 2004. (Illus.). 161p. (J). pap. 9.99 *(978-1-56722-643-0(4))* Word Aflame Pr.

Martinez, Jessica. The Vow. 2014. (ENG., Illus.). 448p. (YA). (gr. 9). pap. 11.99 *(978-1-4424-5865-9(8)*, Simon Pulse) Simon Pulse.

Masciola, Carol. The Yearbook. 2015. (ENG.). 224p. (YA). 17.99 *(978-1-4405-8897-6(X)*, Simon Pulse) Simon Pulse.

Maskame, Estelle. Did I Mention I Need You? 2016. (Did I Mention I Love You (DIMILY) Ser.: 2). (ENG.). 384p. (YA). (gr. 8-12). pap. 10.99 *(978-1-4926-3218-4(X)*, 9781492632184) Sourcebooks, Inc.

Mason, Mimi Canda. Lola's Cane. 2009. 48p. pap. 19.95 *(978-1-4389-1464-0(4))* AuthorHouse.

Matson, Morgan. Second Chance Summer. 2013. (ENG.). 496p. (YA). (gr. 7). pap. 12.99 *(978-1-4169-9068-0(2)*, Simon & Schuster Bks. For Young Readers) Simon & Schuster Bks. For Young Readers.

—Second Chance Summer. 2012. (ENG.). 480p. (YA). (gr. 7). 19.99 *(978-1-4169-9067-3(4))* Simon & Schuster, Inc.

—The Unexpected Everything. 2016. (ENG.). (YA). (gr. 7). pap. 12.99 *(978-1-4814-8207-3(6))* Simon & Schuster.

—The Unexpected Everything. 2017. (ENG., Illus.). 560p. (YA). (gr. 7). pap. 9.99 *(978-1-4814-0455-6(5)*, Simon & Schuster Bks. For Young Readers) Simon & Schuster Bks. For Young Readers.

Matsumoto, Reiko Odate. The Princess with the Magic Bowl: As retold from the Japanese folk tale By. 2008. 48p. pap. 22.49 *(978-1-4389-1225-7(0))* AuthorHouse.

Matthews, Andrew. Shakespeare Stories: The Tempest. Ross, Tony, illus. 2003. (ENG.). 64p. (J). (gr. 4-6). pap. 6.99 *(978-1-84121-346-0(2)*, Orchard Bks.) Hachette Children's Group GBR. Dist: Hachette Bk. Group.

Mayer, Mercer. Little Critter: Just a Little Love. Mayer, Mercer, illus. 2013. (My First I Can Read Ser.). (ENG., Illus.). 32p. (J). (gr. -1-3). 16.99 *(978-0-06-207196-5(3))*; pap. 4.99 *(978-0-06-147815-4(6))* HarperCollins Pubs. (HarperCollins).

Mazer, Norma Fox. When We First Met. 2015. (ENG., Illus.). 208p. (YA). (gr. 7). pap. 14.99 *(978-1-4814-5103-1(0)*, Atheneum Bks. for Young Readers) Simon & Schuster Children's Publishing.

Mba, Ogochukwu. The Roaches, 1 vol. 2010. 20p. 24.95 *(978-1-4489-3951-0(8))* PublishAmerica, Inc.

McBay, Bruce & Heneghan, James. Waiting for Sarah. 2004. 170p. (gr. 7). 17.95 *(978-0-7569-4567-1(4))* Perfection Learning Corp.

McBratney, Sam. Guess How Much I Love You. Jeram, Anita, illus. 2005. 34p. (J). bds. 19.95 *(978-0-9769313-1-7(1))* BrailleInk.

—Guess How Much I Love You. Jeram, Anita, illus. (Guess How Much I Love You Ser.). (J). (gr. -1 — 1). 2014. (ENG.). 40p. 17.99 *(978-0-7636-7448-9(6))* 2006. 32p. 15.99 *(978-0-7636-3503-9(0))* Candlewick Pr.

—Guess How Much I Love You: Baby Book. Jeram, Anita, illus. 2014. (Guess How Much I Love You Ser.). (ENG.). 64p. (J). (gr. -1 — 1). 16.99 *(978-0-7636-7023-8(5))* Candlewick Pr.

—Guess How Much I Love You Padded Board Book. Jeram, Anita, illus. 2019. (Guess How Much I Love You Ser.). (ENG.). 30p. (J). (— 1). bds. 10.99 *(978-1-5362-1062-0(5))* Candlewick Pr.

—Guess How Much I Love You: Pop-Up. Jeram, Anita, illus. 2011. (Guess How Much I Love You Ser.). (ENG.). 16p. (J). (gr. -1-2). 21.99 *(978-0-7636-5378-1(0))* Candlewick Pr.

McBride, Martha J. And You Love Me. 2003. 346p. (YA). per. 5.99 *(978-1-59196-391-2(5))* Instant Pub.

McCarry, Sarah. All Our Pretty Songs: A Novel. 2013. (Metamorphoses Trilogy Ser.: 1). (ENG.). 240p. (YA). (gr. 8-12). pap. 19.99 *(978-1-250-02708-5(X)*, 900098096, St. Martin's Griffin) St. Martin's Pr.

—Dirty Wings: A Novel. 2014. (Metamorphoses Trilogy Ser.: 2). (ENG.). 288p. (YA). (gr. 8-12). 24.99 *(978-1-250-04938-4(5)*, 900098104, St. Martin's Griffin) St. Martin's Pr.

McClymer, Kelly. Getting to Third Date. 2006. (Romantic Comedies Ser.). (ENG., Illus.). 304p. (YA). (gr. 9-18). mass

mkt. 6.99 *(978-1-4169-1479-2(X)*, Simon Pulse) Simon Pulse.
McCreedy, J. L. The Orphan of Torundi. 2014. (ENG.). 300p. (YA). pap. 10.99 *(978-0-9882369-2-9(3))* Penelope Pipp Publishing.
McDaniel, Lurlene. The Girl with the Broken Heart. 2018. (ENG.). 288p. (YA). (gr. 7). 17.99 *(978-1-5247-1948-7(X)*, Delacorte Pr.) Random Hse. Children's Bks.
—True Love: Three Novels. 2009. (ENG.). 672p. (YA). (gr. 7). pap. 10.99 *(978-0-375-86148-2(3)*, Ember) Random Hse. Children's Bks.
—The Year of Chasing Dreams. 2015. (Luminous Love Ser.). (ENG.). 336p. (YA). (gr. 7). pap. 9.99 *(978-0-385-74174-3(X)*, Ember) Random Hse. Children's Bks.
McDonald, Abby. Getting over Garrett Delaney. 2012. (ENG.). 336p. (YA). (gr. 9). pap. 7.99 *(978-0-7636-6332-2(8))*; (Illus.). 16.99 *(978-0-7636-5507-5(4))* Candlewick Pr.
—Sophomore Switch. 2010. (ENG., Illus.). 304p. (YA). (gr. 9). pap. 8.99 *(978-0-7636-4774-2(8))* Candlewick Pr.
McDonald, Brenda. How Do You Love A Big Dog? 2007. 18.00 *(978-0-8059-7314-3(1))* Dorrance Publishing Co., Inc.
McGarry, Katie. Dare You To. 2014. (Pushing the Limits Ser.: 2). (ENG.). 480p. (YA). pap. 12.99 *(978-0-373-21098-5(1)*, Harlequin Teen) Harlequin Enterprises ULC CAN. Dist: HarperCollins Pubs.
—Only a Breath Apart: A Novel. 2020. (ENG.). 384p. (YA). pap. 9.99 *(978-1-250-19386-5(9))*, 900193472, Tor Teen) Doherty, Tom Assocs., LLC.
—Pushing the Limits. 2013. (Pushing the Limits Ser.: 1). (ENG.). 416p. (YA). pap. 9.99 *(978-0-373-21086-2(8)*, Harlequin Teen) Harlequin Enterprises ULC CAN. Dist: HarperCollins Pubs.
McGee, Katharine. American Royals II: Majesty. (American Royals Ser.: 2). (ENG.). (YA). (gr. 9). 2022. 400p. pap. 12.99 *(978-1-9848-3024-1(4)*, Ember) 2020. 384p. 18.99 *(978-1-9848-3021-0(X)*, Random Hse. Bks. for Young Readers) Random Hse. Children's Bks.
McGee, Krista. Revolutionary, 1 vol. 2014. (Anomaly Ser.: 3). (ENG.). 320p. (YA). pap. 14.99 *(978-1-4016-8876-9(4))* Nelson, Thomas Inc.
McGhee, Alison. All Rivers Flow to the Sea. 2005. (ENG.). 176p. (YA). (gr. 9-12). 15.99 *(978-0-7636-2591-7(4))* Candlewick Pr.
McGoran, Jon. Spiked. 2020. (Spliced Ser.: 3). 352p. (YA). (gr. 9). 18.99 *(978-0-8234-4091-7(5))* Holiday Hse., Inc.
McGovern, Cammie. Say What You Will. 2015. (ENG.). 368p. (YA). (gr. 9). pap. 9.99 *(978-0-06-227111-2(3)*, HarperTeen) HarperCollins Pubs.
McGowan, Jennifer. Maid of Secrets. (Maids of Honor Ser.). (ENG.). (YA). (gr. 7). 2014. 432p. pap. 9.99 *(978-1-4424-4139-2(9))* 2013. 416p. 17.99 *(978-1-4424-4138-5(0))* Simon & Schuster Bks. For Young Readers. (Simon & Schuster Bks. For Young Readers).
McGrellis, Barbara. Love Never Fails. 2013. 24p. pap. 10.99 *(978-1-4624-0745-3(5)*, Inspiring Voices) Author Solutions, LLC.
McKay, Emily. Weddings, Crushes & Other Dramas. 2017. (ENG., Illus.). (YA). pap. 14.99 *(978-1-68281-423-9(8))* Entangled Publishing, LLC.
McKay, Hilary. The Exiles in Love. 2007. (ENG., Illus.). 176p. (J). (gr. 3-7). pap. 9.95 *(978-1-4169-6797-2(4)*, McElderry, Margaret K. Bks.) McElderry, Margaret K. Bks.
McKellop, Holly R. To the Moon. 2012. 32p. pap. 24.95 *(978-1-4626-8034-4(8))* America Star Bks.
McKenney, M. W. Roosevelt Junior High. 2008. 73p. pap. 19.95 *(978-1-60672-157-5(7))* America Star Bks.
McLaren, Heather. Mythos. 2013. (ENG.). 260p. pap. 17.95 *(978-1-60619-093-7(8))* Twilight Times Bks.
McLaughlin, Emma & Kraus, Nicola. Over You. 2013. (ENG.). 304p. (YA). (gr. 9). pap. 9.99 *(978-0-06-172045-1(3)*, HarperTeen) HarperCollins Pubs.
McLemore, Anna-Marie. Wild Beauty: A Novel. 2018. (ENG.). 368p. (YA). pap. 15.99 *(978-1-250-18073-5(2)*, 900190253) Square Fish.
McMahon, Kara. Elmo's World: Love! (Sesame Street) Nelson, Mary Beth, illus. 2004. (Sesame Street(R) Elmos World(TM) Ser.). (ENG.). 12p. (J). (— 1). bds. 4.99 *(978-0-375-82843-0(5)*, Random Hse. Bks. for Young Readers) Random Hse. Children's Bks.
McMann, Lisa. Bang. (Visions Ser.: 2). (ENG., (YA). (gr. 9). 2014. Illus.). 272p. pap. 9.99 *(978-1-4424-6628-9(6))* 2013. 256p. 16.99 *(978-1-4424-6625-8(1))* Simon Pulse. (Simon Pulse).
—Crash. 2013. (Visions Ser.: 1). (ENG.). 256p. (YA). (gr. 9). 19.99 *(978-1-4424-0391-8(8)*, Simon Pulse) Simon Pulse.
—Gone. (Wake Ser.: Bk. 3). (ENG.). (YA). (gr. 9). 2011. 240p. pap. 11.99 *(978-1-4169-7921-0(2))* 2010. 224p. 17.99 *(978-1-4169-7918-0(2))* Simon Pulse. (Simon Pulse).
McNally, Janet. Girls in the Moon. (ENG.). (YA). (gr. 8). 2018. 368p. pap. 9.99 *(978-0-06-243625-2(2))* 2016. 352p. 17.99 *(978-0-06-243624-5(4))* HarperCollins Pubs. (HarperTeen).
McNamara, Brian. Bottled up Secret. 2014. (ENG.). 264p. (J). (gr. 7). pap. 11.95 *(978-1-62639-209-0(9))* Bold Strokes Bks.
McNaughton, Janet. To Dance at the Palais Royale. 2006. (ENG.). 252p. (J). (gr. 5-8). mass mkt. 6.99 *(978-0-00-639541-6(4)*, Harper Trophy) HarperCollins Pubs.
McNeil, Gretchen. I'm Not Your Manic Pixie Dream Girl. 2016. (ENG.). 352p. (YA). (gr. 8). 17.99 *(978-0-06-240911-9(5)*, Balzer & Bray) HarperCollins Pubs.
McQuestion, Karen. From a Distant Star, 0 vols. 2015. (ENG.). 280p. (YA). (gr. 7-12). pap. 9.99 *(978-1-4778-3016-1(2)*, 9781477830161, Skyscape) Amazon Publishing.
McStay, Moriah. Everything That Makes You. 2017. (ENG.). 352p. (YA). (gr. 8). pap. 9.99 *(978-0-06-229549-1(7)*, HarperCollins) HarperCollins Pubs.
McVoy, Terra Elan. Criminal. (ENG., (YA). (gr. 9). 2014. Illus.). 304p. pap. 9.99 *(978-1-4424-2163-9(0))* 2013. 288p. 16.99 *(978-1-4424-2162-2(2))* Simon Pulse. (Simon Pulse).
Mead, Richelle. The Emerald Sea. 2018. (Glittering Court Ser.: 3). (ENG.). 496p. (YA). (gr. 7). 19.99 *(978-1-59514-845-2(0)*, Razorbill) Penguin Young Readers Group.
—Midnight Jewel. 2017. (Glittering Court Ser.: 2). (ENG.). 416p. (YA). (gr. 7). 19.99 *(978-1-59514-843-8(4)*, Razorbill) Penguin Young Readers Group.
—Silver Shadows: A Bloodlines Novel. 2015. (Bloodlines Ser.: 5). (ENG.). 416p. (YA). (gr. 7). pap. 12.99 *(978-1-59514-632-8(6)*, Razorbill) Penguin Young Readers Group.
—Soundless. l.t. ed. 2016. (ENG.). 352p. 25.99 *(978-1-4104-8817-6(9))* Cengage Gale.
—Soundless. 2018. (SPA.). 271p. (YA). (gr. 7). pap. 17.95 *(978-987-609-642-3(7))* Editorial de Nuevo Extremo S.A. ARG. Dist: Independent Pubs. Group.
Mear, Shirley A. Feathers from Heaven. 2013. 24p. (J). pap. *(978-1-78148-567-5(4))* Grosvenor Hse. Publishing Ltd.
Mehta, Shyam. Stories for Children. 2009. 68p. pap. 8.47 *(978-1-4092-8990-6(7))* Lulu Pr., Inc.
Melean, Mary & Lascaris, Alexia. The Adventures of Don Quixote of la Mancha. 2011. 44p. pap. 18.46 *(978-1-4567-6131-8(5))* AuthorHouse.
Meléndez, Claudia. A Fighting Chance. 2015. (ENG.). 256p. (YA). (gr. 6). pap. 10.95 *(978-1-55885-818-3(0)*, Piñata Books) Arte Publico Pr.
Melmed, Laura Krauss. Before We Met. Tsong, Jing Jing, illus. 2016. (ENG.). 32p. (J). (gr. -1-3). 17.99 *(978-1-4424-4156-9(9)*, Beach Lane Bks.) Beach Lane Bks.
Mendelsohn, Jeffrey. Grumpalina. 2012. (ENG.). 30p. (J). 25.95 *(978-1-4327-7830-9(7))* Outskirts Pr., Inc.
Merrell, Billy. Vanilla. (ENG.). 320p. (YA). (gr. 9-9). 2019. pap. 12.99 *(978-1-338-10101-0(3))* 2017. 17.99 *(978-1-338-10092-1(0)*, PUSH) Scholastic, Inc.
Mesrobian, Carrie. Cut Both Ways. 2017. (ENG.). 368p. (YA). (gr. 9). pap. 9.99 *(978-0-06-234989-7(9)*, HarperCollins) HarperCollins Pubs.
Messenger, Shannon. Let the Storm Break. 2014. (Sky Fall Ser.: 2). (ENG., Illus.). 400p. (YA). (gr. 7). 17.99 *(978-1-4424-5044-8(4)*, Simon Pulse) Simon Pulse.
—Let the Wind Rise. (Sky Fall Ser.: 3). (ENG., Illus.). (YA). (gr. 7). 2017. 432p. pap. 12.99 *(978-1-4814-4655-6(X))* 2016. 416p. 19.99 *(978-1-4814-4654-9(1))* Simon Pulse. (Simon Pulse).
Metallinos, Sophia. The Heavenly Place. l.t. ed. 2016. (ENG., Illus.). (J). pap. 9.99 *(978-1-58169-640-0(X)*, Axiom Pr.) Genesis Communications, Inc.
Metcalf, Dawn. Indelible. 2013. (Twixt Ser.: 1). (ENG.). 384p. (YA). pap. 9.99 *(978-0-373-21073-2(6)*, Harlequin Teen) Harlequin Enterprises ULC CAN. Dist: HarperCollins Pubs.
—Invisible. 2014. (Twixt Ser.: 2). (ENG.). 384p. (YA). pap. 12.99 *(978-0-373-21107-4(4)*, Harlequin Teen) Harlequin Enterprises ULC CAN. Dist: HarperCollins Pubs.
Metzger, Lois. Change Places with Me. 2016. (ENG.). 224p. (YA). (gr. 9). 17.99 *(978-0-06-238553-6(4)*, Balzer & Bray) HarperCollins Pubs.
Meyer, L. A. Wild Rover No More: Being the Last Recorded Account of the Life & Times of Jacky Faber. (Bloody Jack Adventures Ser.). (ENG.). 368p. (YA). (gr. 9). 2016. pap. 9.99 *(978-0-544-66842-3(1)*, 1625456) 2014. 17.99 *(978-0-544-21777-5(2)*, 1561983) HarperCollins Pubs. (Clarion Bks.).
Meyer, Marissa. Heartless. 2016. (ENG.). 464p. (YA). 22.99 *(978-1-250-04465-5(0)*, 900128559) Feiwel & Friends.
—Heartless. 2018. (ENG.). 480p. (YA). pap. 12.99 *(978-1-250-14818-6(9)*, 900181891) Square Fish.
—Heartless. 2016. (ENG.). (YA). (gr. 8-12). pap. 12.99 *(978-1-250-11486-0(1))* St. Martin's Pr.
—Heartless. 2018. (YA). lib. bdg. 22.10 *(978-0-606-41089-2(9))* Turtleback.
—Heartless. 2017. 592p. (YA). pap. 17.99 *(978-987-747-254-7(6))* V&R Editoras.
Meyer, Stephenie. Amanecer / Breaking Dawn. 2008. (Saga Crepusculo / the Twilight Saga Ser.: 4).Tr. of Breaking Dawn. (SPA.). 832p. (YA). (gr. 9-12). pap. 23.95 *(978-607-11-0033-7(X)*, Alfaguara) Penguin Random House Grupo Editorial ESP. Dist: Penguin Random Hse. LLC.
—Eclipse. 2007. (Twilight Saga Ser.: 3). (ENG.). 640p. (YA). (gr. 7-17). 22.99 *(978-0-316-16020-9(2))* Little, Brown Bks. for Young Readers.
—Eclipse. 2008. 576p. *(978-1-904233-91-6(0)*, Atom Books) Little, Brown Book Group Ltd.
—Eclipse. 2011. (Twilight Saga: Bk. 3). 13.08 *(978-0-7848-3531-9(4)*, Everbind) Marco Bk. Co.
—Eclipse. 2010. (Twilight Saga: Bk. 3). 629p. (YA). (gr. 9-12). 22.10 *(978-1-60686-303-9(7))* Perfection Learning Corp.
—Eclipse. 2007. (Twilight Saga Spanish Ser.: 3). (SPA.). 637p. (gr. 7-12). lib. bdg. 28.15 *(978-1-4177-9862-9(9))* Turtleback.
—New Moon. 2008. (Twilight Saga: Bk. 2). 563p. (gr. 9-12). 21.00 *(978-1-60686-336-7(3))* Perfection Learning Corp.
—New Moon. 2006. (Twilight Saga Ser.: 2). (ENG.). 608p. (J). (gr. 7-17). 24.99 *(978-0-316-16019-3(9))* Little, Brown Bks. for Young Readers.
—New Moon. 2011. (Twilight Saga: Bk. 2). 11.72 *(978-0-7848-3535-7(7)*, Everbind) Marco Bk. Co.
—The Short Second Life of Bree Tanner: An Eclipse Novella. 2010. (Twilight Saga Ser.). (ENG.). 192p. (YA). (gr. 7-17). 17.99 *(978-0-316-12558-1(X))* Little, Brown Bks. for Young Readers.
—Twilight. 2008. (Twilight Saga: Bk. 1). (CHI.). 375p. (YA). pap. *(978-7-5448-0333-5(3))* Jieli Publishing Hse.
—Twilight. 2005. (Twilight Saga Ser.: 1). (ENG.). 544p. (YA). (gr. 7-17). 24.99 *(978-0-316-16017-9(2))* Little, Brown Bks. for Young Readers.
—Twilight. 2008. 480p. pap. *(978-1-905654-34-5(0)*, Atom Books) Little, Brown Book Group Ltd.
—Twilight. 2009. (Twilight Saga: Bk. 1). 11.72 *(978-0-7848-1934-0(3)*, Everbind) Marco Bk. Co.
—Twilight. (Twilight Saga: Bk. 1). 2010. 498p. (YA). (gr. 9-12). 20.10 *(978-1-60686-352-7(5))* 2006. 21.00 *(978-0-7569-6825-0(9))* Perfection Learning Corp.
—Twilight. (Twilight Ser.: 1). (YA). 2007. 1.25 *(978-1-4193-9974-6(8))* 2006. 87.75 *(978-1-4193-9975-6(6))* Recorded Bks., Inc.
—Twilight. 2006. (Twilight Saga Ser.: 1). (Illus.). 498p. (YA). (gr. 9-12). lib. bdg. 28.15 *(978-1-4177-5591-2(1))* Turtleback.
—The Twilight Saga Collection Set, 4 vols. 2008. (ENG.). 2560p. (YA). (gr. 7-17). 92.00 *(978-0-316-03184-4(4))* Little, Brown Bks. for Young Readers.
—Twilight Tenth Anniversary / Life & Death Dual Edition. 2015. (Twilight Saga Ser.). (YA). lib. bdg. 35.50 *(978-0-606-37801-7(4))* Turtleback.
Michaels, Robbie. Caught. 2016. (ENG., Illus.). (J). 24.99 *(978-1-63477-950-0(9)*, Harmony Ink Pr.) Dreamspinner Pr.
—A Star Is Born. 2016. (ENG., Illus.). (J). 24.99 *(978-1-63477-930-2(4)*, Harmony Ink Pr.) Dreamspinner Pr.
Michelle, Sara. The Beginning: Book 5, 1 vol., 5. unabr. ed. 2012. (My New Normal Ser.: 5). (ENG.). 97p. (YA). (gr. 9-12). pap. 10.75 *(978-1-61651-785-4(9))* Saddleback Educational Publishing, Inc.
Michot, Fabienne. Maki, I Love to Kiss You. braille ed. 2004. (J). (gr. 1). spiral bd., bds. *(978-0-616-07268-4(6))* Canadian National Institute for the Blind/Institut National Canadien pour les Aveugles.
Mifae. 2013. 200p. *(978-1-4602-2049-8(8))* FriesenPress.
Miller, Barnabas. The Girl with the Wrong Name. 2016. (Illus.). 272p. (YA). (gr. 9). pap. 10.99 *(978-1-61695-704-9(2)*, Soho Teen) Soho Pr., Inc.
Miller, Jonathan. Kim's Introductions. 2009. 48p. pap. 21.99 *(978-1-4389-0856-4(3))* AuthorHouse.
Miller, Leah Rae. Romancing the Nerd. 2016. (ENG.). 352p. (YA). pap. 9.99 *(978-1-63375-225-2(9)*, 9781633752252) Entangled Publishing, LLC.
Miller, Pat Zietlow. Loretta's Gift. Marley, Alea, illus. 2018. (ENG.). 40p. (J). (gr. -1-3). 17.99 *(978-1-4998-0[illegible]1-6(7))* Little Bee Books Inc.
Miller, Tiwana Mutch. Praying Time. 2008. (YA). [illegible]0.00 *(978-0-9788937-8-1(6))* Amani Publishing, LLC.
Millmann, Anita Sutherland. Zitta & Nelli. 2011. 24p. pap. 15.14 *(978-1-4634-0036-1(5))* AuthorHouse.
Mills, Wendy. All We Have Left. 2017. (ENG.). 368p. (YA). pap. 10.99 *(978-1-68119-432-5(5)*, 900172651, Bloomsbury USA Childrens) Bloomsbury Publishing USA.
Mirabelli, Eugene. The Queen of the Rain Was in Love with the Prince of the Sky. 2008. pap. 5.00 *(978-0-935891-08-9(0))* Spring Harbor Pr.
Mitchell, Melanie, illus. Who Do You Love? 2008. (ENG.). 6p. (J). bds. 5.95 *(978-1-58117-707-7(0)*, Intervisual/Piggy Toes) Bendon, Inc.
Mitchell, Saundra. The Springsweet. 2013. (ENG.). 304p. (YA). (gr. 7). pap. 16.99 *(978-0-544-00327-9(6)*, 1526369, Clarion Bks.) HarperCollins Pubs.
Mittal, Amitabh. The Heir Apparent. 2009. 32p. pap. 14.99 *(978-1-4389-7845-1(6))* AuthorHouse.
Miura, Taro. Hello, Love! (Board Books for Baby, Baby Books on Love an Friendship) 2018. (ENG., Illus.). 22p. (J). (gr. -1 — 1). bds. 6.99 *(978-1-4521-7087-9(8))* Chronicle Bks. LLC.
Moffitt, Debra. Girls in Charge. 2011. (Pink Locker Society Novels Ser.: 4). (ENG.). 208p. (J). (gr. 3-7). pap. 18.99 *(978-0-312-64506-9(6)*, 900068660, St. Martin's Griffin) St. Martin's Pr.
Molesworth. The Tapestry Room: A Child's Romance. 2017. (ENG., Illus.). (J). 23.95 *(978-1-374-82098-2(9))*; pap. 13.95 *(978-1-374-82097-5(0))* Capital Communications, Inc.
Molesworth, Mary Louisa S. The Tapestry Room. 2008. 116p. 22.95 *(978-1-60664-990-9(6))*; per. 9.95 *(978-1-60312-540-6(X))* Aegypan.
Monir, Alexandra. Timekeeper. 2014. (Timeless Ser.). (ENG.). 304p. (YA). (gr. 7). pap. 9.99 *(978-0-385-73841-5(2)*, Ember) Random Hse. Children's Bks.
Montgomery, L. M. The Blue Castle. Date not set. (J). 22.95 *(978-0-8488-2370-2(2))* Amereon Ltd.
Moore, A. C. Always Room for Dessert. 2nd ed. 2004. 304p. (YA). per. 13.95 *(978-0-9744060-0-8(7))* Moore, Ammanuel.
Moore, Katrina. One Hug. Woolf, Julia, illus. 2019. (ENG.). 32p. (J). (gr. -1 — 1). 14.99 *(978-0-06-284954-0(9)*, Tegen, Katherine Bks) HarperCollins Pubs.
Moore, Kelly, et al. Neverwas. 2014. (YA). pap. *(978-0-545-43419-5(X))* Scholastic, Inc.
Moore, Stephen. Dancing in the Arms of Orion. 2004. 366p. (YA). 30.95 *(978-0-595-66335-4(4))* iUniverse, Inc.
Moroney, Trace. When I'm Feeling Love. 2018. (Feelings Ser.). (ENG., Illus.). 24p. (J). (— 1). 10.99 *(978-1-76068-066-4(4))* Bonnier Publishing GBR. Dist: Independent Pubs. Group.
Morrill, Stephanie. Within These Lines, 1 vol. 2019. (ENG.). 352p. (YA). 17.99 *(978-0-310-76523-3(4))* Blink.
Mosher, Richard. Zazoo. 2004. (ENG.). 272p. (YA). (gr. 7-18). reprint ed. pap. 15.95 *(978-0-618-43904-1(8))* Houghton Mifflin Harcourt Publishing Co.
Moskowitz, Hannah & Helgeson, Kat. Gena/Finn. 2016. (ENG., Illus.). 292p. (YA). (gr. 7-12). 17.99 *(978-1-4521-3839-8(7))* Chronicle Bks. LLC.
Moss, Marissa. Amelia's Summer Survival Guide: Amelia's Longest, Biggest, Most-Fights-Ever Family Reunion; Amelia's Itchy-Twitchy, Lovey-Dovey Summer at Camp Mosquito. Moss, Marissa, illus. 2011. (Amelia Ser.). (ENG., Illus.). 160p. (J). (gr. 5-8). 12.99 *(978-1-4424-2331-2(5)*, Simon & Schuster/Paula Wiseman Bks.) Simon & Schuster/Paula Wiseman Bks.
Moulton, Courtney Allison. Shadows in the Silence. 2014. (Angelfire Ser.: 3). (ENG.). 480p. (YA). (gr. 9). pap. 9.99 *(978-0-06-200241-9(4)*, Tegen, Katherine Bks) HarperCollins Pubs.
Moyer, Jenny. Flashfall. 2016. (Flashfall Ser.: 1). (ENG., Illus.). 352p. (YA). 29.99 *(978-1-62779-481-7(6)*, 900152138, Holt, Henry & Co. Bks. For Young Readers) Holt, Henry & Co.
Ms. G. Mommy, Why Can't I Be Rich? Dade, Raheem, illus. 2005. 20p. (J). 7.00 *(978-0-9724621-1-2(2))* Unlimited Possibilities Publishing, LLC.
Munsch, Robert. Love You Forever. McGraw, Sheila, illus. 2018. (ENG.). 32p. (J). (gr. -1-1). bds. 8.95 *(978-0-2281-0104-8(2)*, 93279bc2-9280-4ed0-8e4f-216516529c98) Firefly Bks., Ltd.
—Love You Forever Pop-Up Edition. McGraw, Sheila, illus. 2017. (ENG.). 14p. (J). (gr. -1-1). 29.95 *(978-1-77085-965-4(9)*, a9e2dca8-f177-424e-8b80-a3c02dd73a41) Firefly Bks., Ltd.
—Siempre Te Querre. 2004. (SPA., Illus.). (J). (gr. k-3). spiral bd. *(978-0-616-14608-8(6))* Canadian National Institute for the Blind/Institut National Canadien pour les Aveugles.
Murphy, Julie. Side Effects May Vary. 2014. (ENG.). 336p. (YA). (gr. 9). 17.99 *(978-0-06-224535-9(X)*, Balzer & Bray) HarperCollins Pubs.
Murphy, Lisa. Secret Smile. 2008. 52p. pap. 11.95 *(978-1-4092-2767-0(7))* Lulu Pr., Inc.
Murphy, Mary. Utterly Lovely One. 2012. (ENG., Illus.). 32p. (J). (gr. -1-k). 16.99 *(978-0-7636-5267-8(9))* Candlewick Pr.
Myers, Jason. Dead End. 2011. (ENG.). 384p. (YA). (gr. 10-18). pap. 9.99 *(978-1-4424-1430-3(8)*, Simon Pulse) Simon Pulse.
—Exit Here. 2007. (ENG.). 464p. (YA). (gr. 10-12). pap. 13.99 *(978-1-4169-1748-9(9)*, Simon Pulse) Simon Pulse.
—Run the Game. 2012. (ENG.). 544p. (YA). (gr. 10). pap. 9.99 *(978-1-4424-1432-7(4)*, Simon Pulse) Simon Pulse.
Myers, Walter Dean. Street Love. (ENG.). 2007. 160p. (YA). (gr. 8-18). pap. 15.99 *(978-0-06-440732-8(2))* 2006. 144p. (J). (gr. 7-18). 15.99 *(978-0-06-028079-6(4))* HarperCollins Pubs. (Amistad).
—Street Love. 2007. 19.00 *(978-0-7569-8102-0(6))* Perfection Learning Corp.
—What They Found: Love on 145th Street. 2011. 10.54 *(978-0-7848-3386-5(9))*; 10.54 *(978-0-7848-3499-2(7))* Marco Bk. Co. (Everbind).
—What They Found: Love on 145th Street. (ENG.). (YA). (gr. 9). 2009. 256p. pap. 9.99 *(978-0-375-84545-1(3))* 2007. 243p. lib. bdg. 22.44 *(978-0-375-93709-5(9))* Random Hse. Children's Bks. (Lamb, Wendy Bks.).
Mystic. Talon Hawke: A Journey Through Darkness. 2007. 228p. per. 15.95 *(978-0-595-46386-2(X))* iUniverse, Inc.
Na, An. Wait for Me. 2006. (ENG.). 176p. (J). (gr. 7-18). 22.44 *(978-0-399-24275-5(9))* Penguin Young Readers Group.
Nadin, Joanna. Paradise. 2012. (ENG., Illus.). 272p. (YA). (gr. 9). 16.99 *(978-0-7636-5713-0(1))* Candlewick Pr.
Nahall Nikoo Fells. Drowning in the Mainstream: Confessions of a Sister. 2010. 284p. pap. 17.95 *(978-1-4502-0554-2(2))* iUniverse, Inc.
Nanette. Tootie the Green Kitten. 2004. (Life on Granny's Farm Ser.). (J). 12.95 *(978-0-9741269-7-5(7))* St. Bernard Publishing, LLC.
Napoli, Donna Jo. Skin, 0 vols. 2013. (ENG.). 352p. (YA). (gr. 9-12). pap. 9.99 *(978-1-4778-1690-5(9)*, 9781477816905, Skyscape) Amazon Publishing.
Narayhan, Manjula. The Green Green Pear. 2009. (Illus.). 32p. pap. 14.49 *(978-1-4389-6957-2(0))* AuthorHouse.
Nayeri, Daniel. Straw House, Wood House, Brick House, Blow: Four Novellas by Daniel Nayeri. 2011. (ENG., Illus.). 432p. (YA). (gr. 9). 19.99 *(978-0-7636-5526-6(0))* Candlewick Pr.
Nazemian, Abdi. The Authentics. 2017. (ENG.). 288p. (YA). (gr. 8). 17.99 *(978-0-06-248646-2(2)*, Balzer & Bray) HarperCollins Pubs.
Neely, Judith. And Even More. 2009. 24p. pap. 11.49 *(978-1-4389-5649-7(5))* AuthorHouse.
Neenan, Colin. Idiot! A Love Story with Drama, Betrayal & E-mail. 2004. (Illus.). 152p. (YA). (gr. 7-13). per. 8.95 *(978-0-9746481-1-8(6))* Brown Barn Bks.
Neighbour, Leona. Fairly Ballerina Princess. 2003. 26p. per. 10.95 *(978-1-932344-42-4(X))* Thornton Publishing, Inc.
Nelson, Jan. Signs of Love. Bohart, Lisa, illus. 2009. 24p. pap. 12.95 *(978-1-936051-54-0(0))* Peppertree Pr., The.
Nelson, Sarah. Just for You. 2012. 20p. (-18). pap. 10.95 *(978-1-4497-7017-4(7)*, WestBow Pr.) Author Solutions, LLC.
Nelson, Suzanne. Heart & Salsa. 2006. (S. A. S. S. Ser.). (Illus.). 224p. (YA). (gr. 7-18). 6.99 *(978-0-14-240647-2(3)*, Speak) Penguin Young Readers Group.
—You're Bacon Me Crazy: a Wish Novel. 2017. (ENG.). 256p. (J). (gr. 4-7). pap. 7.99 *(978-1-338-09919-5(1)*, Scholastic Paperbacks) Scholastic, Inc.
Neumann, A. C. The Drawer's Gift. 2010. 60p. pap. 25.95 *(978-1-935340-62-1(X))* Worthy Shorts.
Newland, Laura. Nicky Boy, I Love You. 2009. 24p. pap. 14.99 *(978-1-4389-2210-2(8))* AuthorHouse.
Nex, Anthony, photos by. Little Hands Love. 2009. (ENG., Illus.). 12p. (J). 8.95 *(978-1-58117-851-7(4)*, Intervisual/Piggy Toes) Bendon, Inc.
Nielsen, Susin. Optimists Die First. 2018. (ENG.). 256p. (YA). (gr. 7). pap. 9.99 *(978-0-553-49693-2(X)*, Ember) Random Hse. Children's Bks.
Night, P. J. Don't Drink the Punch! 2012. (You're Invited to a Creepover Ser.: 11). (ENG.). 160p. (J). (gr. 3-7). pap. 6.99 *(978-1-4424-5287-9(0)*, Simon Spotlight) Simon Spotlight.
Niven, Jennifer. Holding up the Universe. l.t. ed. 2018. (ENG.). 646p. (YA). 22.99 *(978-1-4328-5132-3(2))* Cengage Gale.
—Holding up the Universe. (ENG.). (YA). (gr. 9). 2018. 416p. pap. 10.99 *(978-0-385-75595-5(3)*, Ember) 2016. 400p. 17.99 *(978-0-385-75592-4(9)*, Knopf Bks. for Young Readers) Random Hse. Children's Bks.
Nix, Garth. Newt's Emerald. 2015. (ENG.). 304p. (YA). (gr. 8-12). 18.99 *(978-0-06-236004-5(3)*, Tegen, Katherine Bks) HarperCollins Pubs.
Noel, Alyson. Everlasting: A Novel. 2013. (Immortals Ser.: 6). (ENG.). 352p. (YA). (gr. 7-12). pap. 13.99 *(978-1-250-02517-3(6)*, 900097463, St. Martin's Griffin) St. Martin's Pr.
—Mystic. 2013. (Soul Seekers Ser.: 3). (ENG.). 320p. (YA). (gr. 7). pap. 24.00 *(978-0-312-57567-0(X)*, 900075091, St. Martin's Griffin) St. Martin's Pr.
—Unrivaled. 2017. (Beautiful Idols Ser.: 1). (ENG.). 448p. (YA). (gr. 9). pap. 9.99 *(978-0-06-232453-5(5)*, Tegen, Katherine Bks) HarperCollins Pubs.
Nolan, Allia Zobel. God's Rainbow. Chung, Chi, illus. 2007. 16p. (J). 12.99 *(978-0-8254-5537-7(5))* Kregel Pubns.
Norac, Carl. Las Palabras Dulces. 2003. (SPA., Illus.). 32p. (J). *(978-84-95150-05-9(0)*, COR1690) Corimbo, Editorial S.L. ESP. Dist: Lectorum Pubns., Inc.
North, Phoebe. Starbreak. 2014. (Starglass Sequence Ser.). (ENG., Illus.). 432p. (YA). (gr. 7). 17.99 *(978-1-4424-5956-4(5)*, Simon & Schuster Bks. For Young Readers) Simon & Schuster Bks. For Young Readers.
Novel Units. My Antonia Novel Units Student Packet. 2019. (ENG.). (YA). pap. 13.99 *(978-1-56137-759-6(7))*, Novel Units, Inc.) Classroom Library Co.
Nowlin, Laura. If He Had Been with Me. 2019. (ENG.). 400p. (YA). (gr. 8-12). pap. 10.99 *(978-1-7282-0548-9(4))* Sourcebooks, Inc.
—This Song Is (Not) for You. 2016. 240p. (YA). (gr. 8-12). pap. 12.99 *(978-1-4926-0290-3(6)*, 9781492602903) Sourcebooks, Inc.
Numeroff, Laura. Happy Valentine's Day, Mouse! Bond, Felicia, illus. 2019. (If You Give... Ser.). (ENG.). 24p. (J). (gr. -1 — 1). bds. 7.99 *(978-0-06-180432-8(0)*, HarperFestival) HarperCollins Pubs.
Nunes, Lygia Bojunga. El Sofa Estampado. (SPA.). 184p. (YA). (gr. 5-8). *(978-84-239-2748-7(2)*, EC2752) Espasa Calpe, S.A. ESP. Dist: Lectorum Pubns., Inc.
Oaklee, Mammy. Mailbox Kitten. 2012. 56p. pap. *(978-1-77097-643-6(4))* FriesenPress.
O'Brien, Lara. Chesca & the Spirit of Grace. 2013. 316p. pap. 13.99 *(978-0-9896752-0-8(3))* O'Brien, Lara Publishing.

J K L

Ockler, Sarah. The Book of Broken Hearts. (ENG., Illus.). (YA). (gr. 9). 2014. 384p. pap. 11.99 *(978-1-4424-3039-6(7))* 2013. 368p. 17.99 *(978-1-4424-3038-9(9))* Simon Pulse. (Simon Pulse).

—#scandal. 2014. (ENG., Illus.). 416p. (YA). (gr. 9). 17.99 *(978-1-4814-0124-1(6),* Simon Pulse) Simon Pulse.

O'Dare, Helen. Love. O'Byrne, Nicola, illus. 2016. (ENG.). 26p. (J). (gr. -1 — 1). bds. 6.99 *(978-1-62686-677-5(5),* Silver Dolphin Bks.) Printers Row Publishing Group.

Odom, Leslie, Jr. & Robinson, Nicolette. I Love You More Than You'll Ever Know. Ruiz, Joy Hwang, illus. 2023. (ENG.). 32p. (J). 17.99 *(978-1-250-26564-7(9),* 900222067) Feiwel & Friends.

Ohlin, Nancy. Consent. 2015. (ENG., Illus.). 288p. (YA). (gr. 9). 17.99 *(978-1-4424-6490-2(9),* Simon Pulse) Simon Pulse.

Oliver, Amanda Eaddy. Cheyenne the Cat. 2010. 28p. 13.99 *(978-1-4520-6218-1(8))* AuthorHouse.

Oliver, Lauren. Delirium, 1. 2016. (Delirium Trilogy Ser.: 1). (ENG.). 480p. (YA). (gr. 9-12). pap. 15.99 *(978-0-06-172683-5(4),* HarperCollins) HarperCollins Pubs.

—Delirium. 2016. (Delirium Ser.: 1). (YA). lib. bdg. 20.85 *(978-0-606-23575-4(2))* Turtleback.

—Delirium Stories: Hana, Annabel, Raven & Alex. (Delirium Ser.). (YA). 2016. lib. bdg. 20.85 *(978-0-606-38920-4(2))* 2013. lib. bdg. 20.85 *(978-0-606-31834-1(8))* Turtleback.

—Delirium Stories: Hana, Annabel, & Raven. 2013. (Delirium Trilogy Ser.). (ENG.). 224p. (YA). (gr. 9). pap. 9.99 *(978-0-06-226778-8(7),* HarperCollins) HarperCollins Pubs.

—Delirium Stories: Hana, Annabel, Raven, & Alex. 2016. (Delirium Story Ser.). (ENG.). 224p. (YA). (gr. 9). pap. 9.99 *(978-0-06-248432-1(X),* HarperCollins) HarperCollins Pubs.

—Delirium: the Special Edition. 2011. (Delirium Trilogy Ser.: 1). (ENG.). 480p. (YA). (gr. 9). 17.99 *(978-0-06-211243-9(0),* HarperCollins) HarperCollins Pubs.

—Pandemonium. (YA). 2016. (Delirium Trilogy Ser.: 2). (ENG.). 400p. (gr. 9). pap. 11.99 *(978-0-06-197807-4(8),* HarperCollins) 2012. (Delirium Trilogy Ser.: 2). (ENG.). 384p. (gr. 9-18). 18.99 *(978-0-06-197806-7(X),* HarperCollins) 2012. (Delirium Trilogy: Bk. 2). 375p. *(978-0-06-213008-2(0))* HarperCollins Pubs.

—Pandemonium. 2016. (Delirium Ser.: 2). (YA). lib. bdg. 20.85 *(978-0-606-27141-7(4))* Turtleback.

—Requiem. 2013. (Delirium Trilogy Ser.: 3). (ENG.). 432p. (YA). (gr. 9). 18.99 *(978-0-06-201453-5(6),* HarperCollins) HarperCollins Pubs.

Olivieri, Laura. Where Are You: A Child's Book about Loss. 2007. 28p. 13.94 *(978-1-4357-0091-8(0))* Lulu Pr., Inc.

Olsen, Kaki. Swan & Shadow: A Swan Lake Story. 2016. (ENG.). 299p. (YA). pap. 18.99 *(978-1-4621-1814-4(3),* Sweetwater Bks.) Cedar Fort, Inc./CFI Distribution.

Olsen, Mary-Kate & Olsen, Ashley. The Facts about Flirting. 2005. (ENG., Illus.). 112p. *(978-0-00-715883-6(1),* HarperCollins Children's Bks.) HarperCollins Pubs. Ltd.

—Secret Crush. 2003. (ENG., Illus.). 128p. *(978-0-00-714452-5(0),* HarperCollins Children's Bks.) HarperCollins Pubs. Ltd.

Olsen, Nora. Frenemy of the People. 2014. (ENG.). 264p. (J). (gr. 7). pap. 11.95 *(978-1-62639-063-8(0))* Bold Strokes Bks.

—Maxine Wore Black. 2014. (ENG.). 264p. (J). (gr. 7). pap. 11.95 *(978-1-62639-208-3(0))* Bold Strokes Bks.

—Swans & Klons. 2013. (ENG.). 192p. (gr. 7). pap. 11.95 *(978-1-60282-874-2(1))* Bold Strokes Bks.

Omololu, C. J. Transcendence. 2012. (ENG.). 336p. (YA). (gr. 8-12). 26.19 *(978-0-8027-2370-3(5),* 9780802723703) Walker & Co.

One, Hitoshi. Fireworks, Should We See It from the Side or the Bottom? (light Novel) 2018. (ENG., Illus.). 208p. (YA). (gr. 8-17). 20.00 *(978-1-9753-5326-1(9),* 9781975353261, Yen Pr.) Yen Pr. LLC.

Oppel, Kenneth. Every Hidden Thing. (ENG., Illus.). 368p. (YA). (gr. 9). 2017. pap. 11.99 *(978-1-4814-6417-8(5))* 2016. 17.99 *(978-1-4814-6416-1(7))* Simon & Schuster Bks. For Young Readers. (Simon & Schuster Bks. For Young Readers).

Orczy, Emmuska. The Nest of the Sparrowhawk. 2008. 236p. pap. 15.95 *(978-1-60664-232-0(4))* Rodgers, Alan Bks.

—Unto Caesar. 2008. 260p. 29.95 *(978-1-60664-863-6(2));* pap. 15.95 *(978-1-60664-110-1(7))* Aegypan.

Ormand, Kate. Dark Days. 2014. (ENG.). 256p. (J). (gr. 6-6). 16.95 *(978-1-62873-594-9(5),* Sky Pony Pr.) Skyhorse Publishing Co., Inc.

Ormsbee, Kathryn. Lucky Few. (ENG., Illus.). (YA). (gr. 9). 2017. 400p. pap. 10.99 *(978-1-4814-5529-9(X))* 2016. 384p. 17.99 *(978-1-4814-5528-2(1))* Simon & Schuster Bks. For Young Readers. (Simon & Schuster Bks. For Young Readers).

O'Rourke, Erica. Resonance. 2015. (Dissonance Ser.). (ENG., Illus.). 448p. (YA). (gr. 7). 18.99 *(978-1-4424-6027-0(X),* Simon & Schuster Bks. For Young Readers) Simon & Schuster Bks. For Young Readers.

O'Shea, M.J. Blood Moon [Library Edition]. 3rd ed. 2014. 160p. pap. 14.99 *(978-1-62798-454-6(2),* Harmony Ink Pr.) Dreamspinner Pr.

Owens, Robert. Butterfly Love. 2008. (ENG.). 34p. pap. 16.70 *(978-0-557-01168-1(X))* Lulu Pr., Inc.

Owens, Robert & Owens, Donna. The Misadventures of Our Son Henry. Bollinger, Carol, illus. 2007. 52p. per. 16.95 *(978-1-4241-8721-8(4))* America Star Bks.

Page, Nick & Claire. Snow White. 2006. (Read with Me (Make Believe Ideas) Ser.). (Illus.). 32p. (J). (gr. k-2). *(978-1-84610-163-2(8))* Make Believe Ideas.

Paige, Danielle. Stealing Snow. (Stealing Snow Ser.). (ENG.). 384p. (YA). 2018. pap. 10.99 *(978-1-68119-546-9(1),* 900177244, Bloomsbury Young Adult) 2016. (gr. 9-12). 18.99 *(978-1-68119-076-1(1),* 900158388, Bloomsbury USA Childrens) Bloomsbury Publishing USA.

—Stealing Snow (Spanish Edition) Anguio Fernández, María, tr. 2017. (SPA.). 386p. (J). (gr. 9). 18.95 *(978-84-16700-68-4(0))* Penguin Random House Grupo Editorial ESP. Dist: Penguin Random Hse. LLC.

—Yellow Brick War. 2017. (Dorothy Must Die Ser.: 3). (ENG.). 304p. (YA). (gr. 9). pap. 11.99 *(978-0-06-228074-9(0),* HarperCollins) HarperCollins Pubs.

Palmer, Larry Schwarz,Iva-Marie. Romeo, Juliet & Jim: Book 1, Bk. 1. 2017. (ENG., Illus.). 288p. (YA). 34.99 *(978-1-62779-250-9(3),* 900143896, Holt, Henry & Co. Bks. For Young Readers) Holt, Henry & Co.

Panaitescu, Simona. The Unseen Paths of the Forest: 13 Tales about Love & Friendship. Moscal, Manuela, illus. 2012. (ENG.). 263p. pap. 14.95 *(978-1-4327-7908-5(7))* Outskirts Pr., Inc.

Pandell, Karen. I Love You Sun / I Love You Moon: Te Amo Sol / Te Amo Luna. dePaola, Tomie, illus. 2003.Tr. of I Love You, Sun - I Love You, Moon. 12p. (J). (gr. -1 — 1). bds. 7.99 *(978-0-399-24165-9(5),* G.P. Putnam's Sons Books for Young Readers) Penguin Young Readers Group.

Parish, Herman. Amelia Bedelia Ties the Knot. 2016. (Amelia Bedelia Chapter Book Ser.: 10). (J). lib. bdg. 14.75 *(978-0-606-38762-0(5))* Turtleback.

Parker, Madison. Play Me, I'm Yours. (ENG., 2016. Illus.). (J). 24.99 *(978-1-63533-062-5(9))* 2013. 244p. (YA). pap. 14.99 *(978-1-62380-449-7(3))* Dreamspinner Pr. (Harmony Ink Pr.).

—Play Me, I'm Yours [Library Edition]. 2013. 244p. pap. 14.99 *(978-1-62380-919-5(3),* Harmony Ink Pr.) Dreamspinner Pr.

Parker, Marjorie Blain. I Love You near & Far. Henry, Jed, illus. 2015. 24p. (J). (gr. -1-1). 9.95 *(978-1-4549-0507-3(7))* Sterling Publishing Co., Inc.

Parker, Natalie C., et al. Three Sides of a Heart: Stories about Love Triangles. (ENG.). 448p. (YA). (gr. 9). 2018. pap. 9.99 *(978-0-06-242448-8(3))* 2017. 17.99 *(978-0-06-242447-1(5))* HarperCollins Pubs. (HarperTeen).

Parker, S. M. The Girl Who Fell. (ENG., Illus.). (YA). (gr. 11). 2017. 384p. pap. 12.99 *(978-1-4814-3724-0(0))* 2016. 368p. 17.99 *(978-1-4814-3725-7(9))* Simon Pulse. (Simon Pulse).

Parks, M. Elizabeth. The Sea Cow. 2013. (Illus.). 44p. pap. 16.95 *(978-0-9824565-2-1(2))* Sibyl Merritt.

Parr, todd. The I LOVE YOU Book. (ENG., Illus.). (J). (gr. -1 — 1). 2013. 28p. bds. 7.99 *(978-0-316-24756-6(1))* 2009. 32p. 14.99 *(978-0-316-01985-9(2))* Little, Brown Bks. for Young Readers.

—Love the World. 2019. (ENG., Illus.). 22p. (J). (gr. -1 — 1). bds. 7.99 *(978-0-316-45716-3(7))* Little, Brown Bks. for Young Readers.

—Love the World. Parr, todd, illus. 2019. (Todd Parr Picture Bks.). (ENG., Illus.). 32p. (J). (gr. -1-2). 31.36 *(978-1-5321-4376-2(1),* 31826, Picture Bk.) Spotlight.

Patricelli, Leslie. Huggy Kissy. Patricelli, Leslie, illus. 2012. (Leslie Patricelli Board Bks.). (ENG., Illus.). 26p. (J). (gr. -1 — 1). bds. 7.99 *(978-0-7636-3246-5(5))* Candlewick Pr.

—Huggy Kissy: Padded Board Book. Patricelli, Leslie, illus. 2019. (Leslie Patricelli Board Bks.). (ENG., Illus.). 26p. (J). (— 1). bds. 9.99 *(978-1-5362-1135-1(4))* Candlewick Pr.

Patterson, Horace. Ernie the Ermine. Parker, Jack, illus. 2007. 28p. per. 7.99 *(978-1-58942-374-9(7))* R.H. Boyd Publishing Corp.

Patterson, James & Dembowski, Jill. The Kiss. 2013. (Witch & Wizard Ser.: 4). (ENG.). 384p. (YA). (gr. 7-17). pap. 10.99 *(978-0-316-10176-9(1),* Jimmy Patterson) Little Brown & Co.

Patterson, James & Paetro, Maxine. Confessions: the Paris Mysteries. 2014. (Confessions Ser.: 3). (ENG.). (YA). (gr. 7-17). 320p. 33.99 *(978-0-316-37084-4(3));* 352p. 35.99 *(978-0-316-40963-6(4))* Little Brown & Co. (Jimmy Patterson).

—The Paris Mysteries. 2015. (Confessions Ser.: 3). (YA). lib. bdg. 20.85 *(978-0-606-37526-9(0))* Turtleback.

—The Private School Murders. 2014. (Confessions Ser.: 2). (YA). lib. bdg. 20.85 *(978-0-606-35945-0(1))* Turtleback.

Patterson, James & Raymond, Emily. First Love. (ENG., 2014. Illus.). 288p. 33.99 *(978-0-316-20704-1(7))* 2015. (Illus.). 336p. (gr. 10-17). pap. 9.99 *(978-0-316-20703-4(9))* 2014. 560p. pap. 16.00 *(978-1-4555-8501-4(7))* Little Brown & Co. (Jimmy Patterson).

—First Love. 2014. (YA). lib. bdg. 28.20 *(978-0-606-35894-1(3))* Turtleback.

Patterson, Shannon. The Princess & the Cheese. 2010. 43p. pap. 19.95 *(978-0-557-51615-5(3))* Lulu Pr., Inc.

Paul & Juliana: A Novel. 2003. (ENG.). 188p. (J). 19.95 *(978-1-890862-33-6(9),* 3a4b7b92-f233-4386-9bd5-6fb939e47eb8) Bancroft Pr.

Paul, Ann Whitford. If Animals Said I Love You. Walker, David, illus. 2017. (If Animals Kissed Good Night Ser.). (ENG.). 32p. (J). 16.99 *(978-0-374-30602-1(8),* 900173498, Farrar, Straus & Giroux (BYR)) Farrar, Straus & Giroux.

Paulsen, Gary. Crush: The Theory, Practice & Destructive Properties of Love. 2013. (Liar Liar Ser.). (ENG.). 144p. (J). (gr. 4-7). pap. 7.99 *(978-0-385-74231-3(2),* Yearling) Random Hse. Children's Bks.

Payne, K. E. Another 365 Days. 2013. (ENG.). 264p. (J). (gr. 7). pap. 11.95 *(978-1-60282-775-2(3))* Bold Strokes Bks.

—Before. 2016. (ENG.). 240p. (J). (gr. 7). pap. 11.95 *(978-1-62639-677-7(9))* Bold Strokes Bks.

—Me@You.com. 2012. (ENG.). 288p. (J). (gr. 7). pap. 13.95 *(978-1-60282-592-5(0))* Bold Strokes Bks.

Pearson, Mary E. The Beauty of Darkness: The Remnant Chronicles, Book Three. 2017. (Remnant Chronicles Ser.: 3). (ENG.). 688p. (YA). pap. 14.99 *(978-1-250-11531-7(0),* 900157585) Square Fish.

—The Heart of Betrayal: The Remnant Chronicles, Book Two. 2015. (Remnant Chronicles Ser.: 2). (ENG.). 480p. (YA). (gr. 9). 21.99 *(978-0-8050-9924-9(7),* 900126079, Holt, Henry & Co. Bks. For Young Readers) Holt, Henry & Co.

—The Heart of Betrayal: The Remnant Chronicles, Book Two. 2016. (Remnant Chronicles Ser.: 2). (ENG.). 496p. (YA). pap. 12.99 *(978-1-250-08002-8(9),* 900154651) Square Fish.

—The Kiss of Deception: The Remnant Chronicles, Book One. 2014. (Remnant Chronicles Ser.: 1). (ENG.). 496p. (YA). (gr. 9-12). E-Book *(978-1-62779-218-9(X),* 900141518, Holt, Henry & Co. Bks. For Young Readers) Holt, Henry & Co.

—The Kiss of Deception: The Remnant Chronicles, Book One. 2015. (Remnant Chronicles Ser.: 1). (ENG.). 512p. (YA). (gr. 9-12). pap. 12.99 *(978-1-250-06315-1(9),* 900142660) Square Fish.

Pearson, Susan. Slugs in Love, 0 vols. O'Malley, Kevin, illus. 2012. (ENG.). 34p. (J). (gr. -1-3). pap. 7.99 *(978-0-7614-6248-4(1),* 9780761462484, Two Lions) Amazon Publishing.

Pechero-Loewen, Mariella. I Want to Know How You Found Me. 2004. 39p. pap. 24.95 *(978-1-4137-2955-9(X))* PublishAmerica, Inc.

Peckham, Lori, ed. Guide's Greatest Animal Stories. 2006. 143p. (J). (gr. 5-9). per. 10.99 *(978-0-8280-1944-6(4))* Review & Herald Publishing Assn.

Pelton, Lisa. Logos & Adoption: Remi's Journey. 2012. 40p. pap. 14.95 *(978-1-4497-5378-8(7),* WestBow Pr.) Author Solutions, LLC.

Penn, Audrey. A Pocket Full of Kisses. Gibson, Barbara Leonard, illus. 2004. (New Child & Family Press Titles Ser.). 32p. (J). (gr. -1-1). 16.95 *(978-0-87868-894-4(3),* 8943, Child & Family Pr.) Child Welfare League of America, Inc.

—A Pocket Full of Kisses. Gibson, Barbara, illus. 2006. (Kissing Hand Ser.). (ENG.). 32p. (J). (gr. -1-3). 18.99 *(978-1-933718-02-6(1))* Tanglewood Pr.

Pennington, Jessica. Love Songs & Other Lies. 2019. (ENG.). 288p. (YA). pap. 9.99 *(978-0-7653-9229-9(1),* 900173333, Tor Teen) Doherty, Tom Assocs., LLC.

Pennypacker, Sara. Pax, Journey Home. Klassen, Jon, illus. 2021. 246p. (J). *(978-0-06-314400-2(X));* *(978-0-06-320674-8(9))* Addison Wesley.

—Pax, Journey Home. Klassen, Jon, illus. (Pax Ser.). (ENG.). (J). (gr. 3-7). 2023. 272p. pap. 9.99 *(978-0-06-293036-1(2))* 2021. 272p. E-Book *(978-0-06-293037-8(0),* 9780062930378) 2021. 256p. 17.99 *(978-0-06-293034-7(6))* HarperCollins Pubs. (Balzer & Bray).

Pepper, Cally. Bird Without Wings: Faebles. 2013. (ENG., Illus.). 283p. (J). (gr. -1-12). pap. 12.95 *(978-1-78099-902-9(X),* Lodestone Bks.) Hunt, John Publishing Ltd. GBR. Dist: National Bk. Network.

Perkins, Kevin John. The Circlet. 2010. 316p. pap. *(978-1-907211-33-1(0))* Grosvenor Hse. Publishing Ltd.

Perkins, Stephanie. Isla & the Happily Ever After. 2015. (ENG.). 368p. (YA). (gr. 9-12). pap. 10.99 *(978-0-14-242627-2(X),* Speak) Penguin Young Readers Group.

—Summer Days & Summer Nights: Twelve Love Stories. 2017. (ENG.). 400p. (YA). pap. 17.99 *(978-1-250-07913-8(6),* 900154306, St. Martin's Griffin) St. Martin's Pr.

Perrault, Charles. Cinderella. Innocenti, Roberto, illus. 2013. (ENG.). 32p. (J). (gr. 2-5). pap. 7.99 *(978-0-89812-828-4(5),* 22040, Creative Paperbacks) Creative Co., The.

Perry, Jolene. The Next Door Boys. 2011. 266p. (YA). *(978-1-59955-910-0(2),* Bonneville Bks.) Cedar Fort, Inc./CFI Distribution.

Perry, Laurie. Hello World, This Is Me!, 1 vol. 2009. 55p. pap. 16.95 *(978-1-4489-2013-6(2))* PublishAmerica, Inc.

Peter, Dawn. Mark the Remarkable & Can't Say Can't. 2012. 24p. pap. *(978-1-77067-033-4(5))* FriesenPress.

Peterfreund, Diana. For Darkness Shows the Stars. 2013. (Stars Ser.: 1). (ENG.). 448p. (YA). (gr. 8). pap. 10.99 *(978-0-06-200615-8(0),* Balzer & Bray) HarperCollins Pubs.

Peters, Julie Anne. Lies My Girlfriend Told Me. 2017. (ENG.). 256p. (YA). (gr. 10-17). pap. 14.99 *(978-0-316-23495-5(8))* Little, Brown Bks. for Young Readers.

Petersen, David. Snowy Valentine. Petersen, David, illus. 2011. (ENG., Illus.). 32p. (J). (gr. -1-3). 14.99 *(978-0-06-146378-5(7),* HarperCollins) HarperCollins Pubs.

Petty, Heather W. Final Fall. (Lock & Mori Ser.). (ENG.). 208p. (YA). (gr. 9). 2018. pap. 11.99 *(978-1-4814-2310-6(X))* 2017. (Illus.). 18.99 *(978-1-4814-2309-0(6))* Simon & Schuster Bks. For Young Readers. (Simon & Schuster Bks. For Young Readers).

—Lock & Mori. 2016. (Lock & Mori Ser.). (ENG.). 272p. (YA). (gr. 9). pap. 10.99 *(978-1-4814-2304-5(5))* Simon & Schuster, Inc.

—Mind Games. (Lock & Mori Ser.). (ENG.). (YA). (gr. 9). 2017. 320p. pap. 11.99 *(978-1-4814-2307-6(X))* 2016. (Illus.). 304p. 17.99 *(978-1-4814-2306-9(1))* Simon & Schuster Bks. For Young Readers. (Simon & Schuster Bks. For Young Readers).

Peyton, Kim. Far from Home. 2014. (ENG., Illus.). 183p. (J). (gr. 4-7). pap. 5.99 *(978-0-7945-3292-5(6),* Usborne) EDC Publishing.

Pham, LeUyen. All the Things I Love about You. Pham, LeUyen, illus. 2010. (ENG., Illus.). 40p. (J). (gr. -1-3). 14.99 *(978-0-06-199029-8(9),* Balzer & Bray) HarperCollins Pubs.

Philips, L. Sometime after Midnight. 2018. 400p. (YA). (gr. 9). 18.99 *(978-0-425-29163-4(4),* Viking Books for Young Readers) Penguin Young Readers Group.

Phipps, Alisha. Growing up with Allie: The Dance. 2005. 58p. pap. 16.95 *(978-1-4137-9713-8(X))* PublishAmerica, Inc.

Picoult, Jodi & van Leer, Samantha. Off the Page. Gilbert, Yvonne, illus. 2015. (YA). lib. bdg. *(978-0-553-53557-0(9),* Delacorte Pr) Random House Publishing Group.

—Off the Page. Gilbert, Yvonne, illus. 2016. (ENG.). 368p. (YA). (gr. 7). pap. 10.99 *(978-0-553-53559-4(5),* Ember) Random Hse. Children's Bks.

Pierce, Terry. Mama Loves You So. Shin, Simone, illus. 2017. (New Books for Newborns Ser.). (ENG.). 16p. (J). (gr. -1 — 1). bds. 7.99 *(978-1-4814-8159-5(2),* Little Simon) Little Simon.

Piggy Toes Press, creator. Five Little Kisses. 2007. (ENG., Illus.). 10p. (J). (gr. -1-3). 9.95 *(978-1-58117-683-4(X),* Intervisual/Piggy Toes) Bendon, Inc.

Pike, Christopher, pseud. Black Knight. 2014. (Witch World Ser.: 2). (ENG., Illus.). 464p. (YA). (gr. 9). 19.99 *(978-1-4424-6733-0(9));* pap. 11.99 *(978-1-4424-6734-7(7))* Simon Pulse. (Simon Pulse).

—Red Queen. 2014. (Witch World Ser.: 1). (ENG., Illus.). 560p. (YA). (gr. 9). pap. 11.99 *(978-1-4424-3029-7(X),* Simon Pulse) Simon Pulse.

—Strange Girl. 2015. (ENG., Illus.). 432p. (YA). (gr. 9). pap. 12.99 *(978-1-4814-5058-4(1),* Simon Pulse) Simon Pulse.

—Thirst (Boxed Set) Thirst No. 1; Thirst No. 2; Thirst No. 3, 3 vols. 2013. (Thirst Ser.). (ENG.). 1744p. (YA). (gr. 9). pap. 30.99 *(978-1-4424-8375-0(X),* Simon Pulse) Simon Pulse.

—Thirst No. 1: The Last Vampire, Black Blood, Red Dice. 2009. (Thirst Ser.: 1). (ENG., Illus.). 624p. (YA). (gr. 9). pap. 14.99 *(978-1-4169-8308-8(2),* Simon Pulse) Simon Pulse.

—Thirst No. 2 No. 2: Phantom, Evil Thirst, Creatures of Forever, Bk. 2. 2010. (Thirst Ser.: 2). (ENG.). 608p. (YA). (gr. 9). pap. 14.99 *(978-1-4169-8309-5(0),* Simon Pulse) Simon Pulse.

—Thirst No. 3: The Eternal Dawn. 2010. (Thirst Ser.: 3). (ENG.). 512p. (YA). (gr. 9-18). pap. 14.99 *(978-1-4424-1317-7(4),* Simon Pulse) Simon Pulse.

—Thirst No. 4: The Shadow of Death, 4. 2011. (Thirst Ser.: 4). (ENG., Illus.). 528p. (YA). (gr. 9). pap. 10.99 *(978-1-4424-1319-1(0),* Simon Pulse) Simon Pulse.

—Witch World. 2012. (Witch World Ser.: 1). (ENG.). 528p. (YA). (gr. 9). 17.99 *(978-1-4424-3028-0(1),* Simon Pulse) Simon Pulse.

Pinto, Dan. Hedgehug: a Sharp Lesson in Love. Pinto, Dan, illus. 2011. (ENG., Illus.). 40p. (J). (gr. -1-2). 9.99 *(978-0-06-196101-4(9),* HarperCollins) HarperCollins Pubs.

Piper, Noël & Piper, Noël. Most of All, Jesus Loves You! Anderson, Debby, illus. 2004. (ENG.). 24p. (J). 11.99 *(978-1-58134-630-5(1))* Crossway.

Pisano, Maryann. The Decision. 2003. 66p. (YA). pap. 8.95 *(978-0-595-29262-2(3))* iUniverse, Inc.

Plank, Alex & Plank, Lisa. How Bad Could It Be? 2007. (ENG.). 64p. per. 19.95 *(978-1-4241-6217-8(3))* America Star Bks.

Platt, Cynthia. Little Bit of Love. Whitty, Hannah, illus. 2011. (ENG.). 32p. (J). (gr. -1-2). pap. 7.95 *(978-1-58925-426-8(0))* Tiger Tales.

Plum, Amy. Die for Me. (Die for Me Ser.: 1). (ENG.). (YA). (gr. 9). 2012. 368p. pap. 8.99 *(978-0-06-200402-4(6))* 2011. 352p. 17.99 *(978-0-06-200401-7(8))* HarperCollins Pubs. (HarperTeen).

—Until I Die. 2013. (Die for Me Ser.: 2). (ENG.). 384p. (YA). (gr. 9). pap. 10.99 *(978-0-06-200405-5(0),* HarperTeen) HarperCollins Pubs.

—Until the Beginning. 2015. (After the End Ser.: 2). (ENG.). 336p. (YA). (gr. 8). 17.99 *(978-0-06-222563-4(4),* HarperTeen) HarperCollins Pubs.

Polisner, Gae. The Memory of Things. 2017. (YA). lib. bdg. 22.10 *(978-0-606-40599-7(2))* Turtleback.

—The Memory of Things: A Novel. 2017. (ENG.). 288p. (YA). pap. 12.99 *(978-1-250-14442-3(6),* 900180643, Wednesday Bks.) St. Martin's Pr.

Ponti, Jamie. Sea of Love. 2008. (Romantic Comedies Ser.). (ENG.). 272p. (YA). (gr. 7-18). mass mkt. 6.99 *(978-1-4169-6791-0(5),* Simon Pulse) Simon Pulse.

Poole, Susie. All These Things: Based on 1 Corinthians 13:4-7. 2012. (ENG., Illus.). 26p. bds. 7.99 *(978-1-904637-27-1(2),* 1904637272, Pupfish) Authentic Media GBR. Dist: EMI CMG Distribution.

Porras, Javier Fernando, illus. Historias de Amores y Desvarios en America. 2004. (Literatura Juvenil (Panamericana Editorial) Ser.). (SPA.). 179p. (J). (gr. -1-7). pap. *(978-958-30-0569-5(X),* PV4378) Centro de Informacion y Desarrollo de la Comunicacion y la Literatura MEX. Dist: Lectorum Pubns., Inc.

Porter, Sarah. Waking Storms. 2013. (Lost Voices Trilogy Ser.: 2). (ENG.). 416p. (YA). (gr. 7). pap. 8.99 *(978-0-547-48254-5(X),* 1439697, Clarion Bks.) HarperCollins Pubs.

Poston, Ashley. Geekerella: A Fangirl Fairy Tale. 2018. (Once upon a Con Ser.: 1). 336p. (YA). (gr. 9). pap. 10.99 *(978-1-68369-043-6(5))* 2017. 320p. *(978-1-59474-993-3(0))* Quirk Bks.

Prasadam-Halls, Smriti. I Love You Night & Day. Brown, Alison, illus. 2014. (ENG.). 32p. (J). (gr. -1-1). 16.99 *(978-1-61963-222-6(5),* 900127512, Bloomsbury USA Childrens) Bloomsbury Publishing USA.

—I'll Never Let You Go. Brown, Alison, illus. 2015. (ENG.). 32p. (J). 16.99 *(978-1-61963-922-5(X),* 900152078, Bloomsbury USA Childrens) Bloomsbury Publishing USA.

—Kiss It Better. Massini, Sarah, illus. 2017. (ENG.). 26p. (J). bds. 7.99 *(978-1-68119-164-5(4),* 900161040, Bloomsbury USA Childrens) Bloomsbury Publishing USA.

Pratchett, Terry. Dodger. (ENG.). 368p. (YA). (gr. 8). 2013. pap. 10.99 *(978-0-06-200951-7(6))* 2012. 17.99 *(978-0-06-200949-4(4))* HarperCollins Pubs. (Clarion Bks.).

Preble, Joy. It Wasn't Always Like This. 2017. 256p. (YA). (gr. 9). pap. 10.99 *(978-1-61695-777-3(8),* Soho Teen) Soho Pr., Inc.

Prendergast, G. S. Cold Falling White. (Nahx Invasions Ser.: 2). (ENG.). 576p. (YA). (gr. 9). 2020. pap. 13.99 *(978-1-4814-8188-5(6))* 2019. 19.99 *(978-1-4814-8187-8(8))* Simon & Schuster Bks. For Young Readers. (Simon & Schuster Bks. For Young Readers).

—Cold Falling White. 2019. (ENG.). 368p. (YA). *(978-1-5011-4714-2(5))* Simon & Schuster Children's Publishing.

—Zero Repeat Forever. (Nahx Invasions Ser.: 1). (ENG.). (YA). (gr. 9). 2019. 512p. pap. 13.99 *(978-1-4814-8185-4(1))* 2017. (Illus.). 496p. 17.99 *(978-1-4814-8184-7(3))* Simon & Schuster Bks. For Young Readers. (Simon & Schuster Bks. For Young Readers).

Prendergast, Gabrielle. Capricious, 1 vol. 2017. (ENG., Illus.). 352p. (YA). (gr. 8-12). pap. 14.95 *(978-1-4598-1428-8(2))* Orca Bk. Pubs. USA.

Preston, Natasha. Awake. 2015. 336p. (YA). (gr. 9-12). pap. 10.99 *(978-1-4926-1852-2(7),* 9781492618522) Sourcebooks, Inc.

Price, David. Sly the Fox & Advice from la Princessa Roja. 2008. (Illus.). 34p. (J). 14.95 *(978-0-9779701-2-4(4))* Wishingstone Publishing.

Price, Jennifer L. Half Moon: Phases of the Moon: Book 2, 1 vol. 2009. 252p. pap. 27.95 *(978-1-4489-2193-5(7))* PublishAmerica, Inc.

Price, Kevin, ed. Fields of Wheat: And other Romance Stories. 2012. 200p. pap. *(978-0-9872559-4-5(0),* Crotchet Quaver) Logorythm.

—Ice Castles: A Born Storytellers Collection of Teen Fiction & Romance. 2013. (Illus.). 226p. pap. *(978-0-9872559-8-3(3),* Crotchet Quaver) Logorythm.

Priddy, Roger. Shiny Shapes: Love You Always. 2016. (Shiny Shapes Ser.). (ENG.). 10p. (J). bds. 7.99 *(978-0-312-52053-3(0),* 900161214) St. Martin's Pr.

Purtill, C. Leigh. FaceSpace Face-Off! 2010. 240p. pap. 5.95 *(978-1-60747-781-5(5),* Pickwick Pr.) Phoenix Bks., Inc.

Pushkin, Alexksandr Sergeevich. The Daughter of the Commandant. 2017. (ENG., Illus.). (J). (gr. -1-7). 22.95 *(978-1-374-95089-4(0));* pap. 12.95 *(978-1-374-95088-7(2))* Capital Communications, Inc.

Pyros, Andrea. My Year of Epic Rock: How to Survive 7th Grade: Make Some Noise. 2014. (ENG.). 208p. (J). (gr. 4-8). pap. 10.99 *(978-1-4022-9300-9(3),* 9781402293009) Sourcebooks, Inc.

Qualey, Marsha. Come in from the Cold. 2008. (ENG.). 224p. (YA). (gr. 7). pap. 14.95 *(978-0-547-01439-5(2),* 1030986, Clarion Bks.) HarperCollins Pubs.

Quinn, Paul Michael. The Love Flute. 2013. 24p. pap. 24.95 *(978-1-63000-705-8(6))* America Star Bks.
Rae, Kristin. Wish You Were Italian: An If Only Novel. 2014. (If Only... Ser.). (ENG.). 352p. (YA). (gr. 7). pap. 9.99 *(978-1-61963-286-8(1),* 900131800, Bloomsbury USA Childrens) Bloomsbury Publishing USA.
Rajadel, Fernando López. False Love, True Love/Amor Falso, Amor Verdadero: The Alfambra Woman Buried Alive & the Lovers of Teruel. 2010.Tr. of Amor Falso, Amor Verdadero: La enterrada viva de Alfambra & Los amantes de Teruel. (SPA.). 164p. pap. 44.48 *(978-1-4251-8920-4(2))* Trafford Publishing.
Ramey, Stacie. The Secrets We Bury. 2018. (ENG.). 304p. (YA). (gr. 7-12). 12.99 *(978-1-4926-5420-9(5))* Sourcebooks, Inc.
Ramos, Maria Cristina. Del Amor Nacen Los Rios. (SPA.). pap. 9.95 *(978-950-07-1351-1(9))* Editorial Sudamericana S.A. ARG. Dist: Distribooks, Inc.
Ramos, Marielly. The Fast Getting Married Ugly Changing Bear. 2012. 24p. pap. 17.99 *(978-1-4772-8581-7(4))* AuthorHouse.
Ramsey, Jo. Ball Caps & Khakis. 2016. (ENG., Illus.). (YA). 24.99 *(978-1-63477-938-8(X),* Harmony Ink Pr.) Dreamspinner Pr.
Rautenberg, Karen Rita. Ballerina Detective & the Missing Jeweled Tiara. 2009. (ENG.). 198p. (J). (gr. 5-8). pap. *(978-1-933255-47-7(1))* DNA Pr.
Rawls, Wilson. Where the Red Fern Grows. l.t. ed. 2017. (ENG.). 378p. 22.99 *(978-1-4328-3845-4(8))* Cengage Gale.
Rayburn, Tricia. Maggie Bean in Love. 2009. (ENG.). 288p. (J). (gr. 4-8). pap. 6.99 *(978-1-4169-8700-0(2))* Simon & Schuster, Inc.
Raymond, Patrick. Daniel & Esther. 2007. (ENG.). 176p. (J). (gr. 3-7). pap. 9.95 *(978-1-4169-6798-9(2),* Simon & Schuster/Paula Wiseman Bks.) Simon & Schuster/Paula Wiseman Bks.
RealBuzz Studios Staff. Let There Be Lighten Up! 2007. (Goofyfoot Gurl Ser.: No. 1). 96p. (YA). pap. 4.97 *(978-1-59789-573-6(3),* Barbour Bks.) Barbour Publishing, Inc.
Redwine, C. J. Defiance. 2013. (Defiance Trilogy Ser.: 1). (ENG.). 432p. (YA). (gr. 8). pap. 9.99 *(978-0-06-211717-5(3),* Balzer & Bray) HarperCollins Pubs.
Reed, Amy. Invincible. 2015. (ENG.). 336p. (YA). (gr. 9). 17.99 *(978-0-06-229957-4(3),* Tegen, Katherine Bks) HarperCollins Pubs.
Reekles, Beth. The Kissing Booth. 2013. (Kissing Booth Ser.: 1). (ENG.). 448p. (YA). (gr. 9). pap. 12.99 *(978-0-385-37868-0(8),* Ember) Random Hse. Children's Bks.
Reese, Jacob. Copperweight. 2008. 231p. pap. 24.95 *(978-1-60813-240-9(4))* America Star Bks.
Reimer, Charlotte. Problems with Pies. 2008. (ENG.). 69p. (YA). pap. 13.50 *(978-1-4116-7646-6(7))* Lulu Pr., Inc.
Reisfeld, Randi. All Access. rev. ed. 2007. (ENG.). 288p. (gr. 7-12). pap. 8.99 *(978-1-4231-0503-9(6))* Hyperion Pr.
Rendina, Donna Rae. The Golden Leaf. Bronowski, Karen Kmetz, illus. 2011. 24p. 20.00 *(978-1-61170-014-5(0))* Robertson Publishing.
Rennison, Louise. Love Is a Many Trousered Thing. (Confessions of Georgia Nicolson Ser.: 8). (YA). 2008. (ENG.). 304p. (gr. 8). pap. 9.99 *(978-0-06-085389-1(1))* 2007. 256p. (gr. 7-12). 16.99 *(978-0-06-085387-7(5))* HarperCollins Pubs. (HarperTeen).
Revis, Beth. Shades of Earth. 2013. (Across the Universe Trilogy: 3). lib. bdg. 20.85 *(978-0-606-32117-4(9))* Turtleback.
Rex, Adam. Xo, Ox: A Love Story. Campbell, Scott, illus. 2017. (ENG.). 40p. (J). 17.99 *(978-1-62672-288-0(9),* 900149172) Roaring Brook Pr.
Reyl, Hilary. Kids Like Us. 2018. (ENG.). 288p. (YA). pap. 18.99 *(978-1-250-18069-8(4),* 900175055) Square Fish.
Reynolds, Alison. Why I Love My Mom. Geddes, Serena, illus. 2015. (ENG.). 22p. (J). (gr. -1-1). 9.99 *(978-1-4998-0020-3(7))* Little Bee Books Inc.
Reynolds, Justin A. Opposite of Always. (ENG.). (YA). (gr. 9). 2020. 480p. pap. 11.99 *(978-0-06-274838-6(6))* 2019. 464p. 17.99 *(978-0-06-274837-9(8))* HarperCollins Pubs. (Tegen, Katherine Bks).
Reynolds Naylor, Phyllis. Achingly Alice. 2012. (Alice Ser.: 10). (ENG., Illus.). 176p. (J). (gr. 5-9). pap. 7.99 *(978-1-4424-3494-3(5),* Atheneum Bks. for Young Readers) Simon & Schuster Children's Publishing.
—Alice in Rapture, Sort Of. 2011. (Alice Ser.: 2). (ENG.). 208p. (J). (gr. 5-9). pap. 7.99 *(978-1-4424-2362-6(5),* Atheneum Bks. for Young Readers) Simon & Schuster Children's Publishing.
Rhine, Linda H. The Ivory Buttons, 1 vol. 2010. 30p. 24.95 *(978-1-4512-1745-2(5))* PublishAmerica, Inc.
Rich, Jamie S. Love the Way You Love. Ellerby, Marc, illus. 2006. (J). *(978-1-932664-52-2(1))* Oni Pr., Inc.
Richmond, Marianne. Dear Sister: A Message of Love. 2008. (Illus.). 40p. (J). 15.95 *(978-1-934082-46-1(5),* Marianne Richmond Studios, Inc.) Sourcebooks, Inc.
Rider, Catherine. Kiss Me in Paris. 2018. (ENG.). 216p. (YA). (gr. 9-12). pap. 10.99 *(978-1-5253-0142-1(X))* Kids Can Pr., Ltd. CAN. Dist: Hachette Bk. Group.
Rigaud, Debbie. Perfect Shot. 2019. (Romantic Comedies Ser.). (ENG.). 304p. (YA). (gr. 7). pap. 14.99 *(978-1-5344-5173-5(0),* Simon Pulse) Simon Pulse.
—Truly Madly Royally. 2019. (ENG.). 304p. (YA). (gr. 7-7). pap. 9.99 *(978-1-338-33272-8(4))* Scholastic, Inc.
Rikkers, Don. Jesus Loves Me. 2009. 16p. 6.95 *(978-1-60349-025-2(6),* Marimba Bks.) Just Us Bks., Inc.
Rinaldi, Ann. Brooklyn Rose. 2006. (ENG., Illus.). 240p. (J). (gr. 5-7). reprint ed. pap. 15.95 *(978-0-15-205538-7(X),* 1196655, Clarion Bks.) HarperCollins Pubs.
Rivadeneira, Alexa. Confessions from the Heart of a Teenage Girl. 2007. 248p. per. 16.95 *(978-0-595-42432-0(5))* iUniverse, Inc.
Rivera, Jeff. Forever My Lady: Young Adult. 2005. (YA). per. 12.95 *(978-0-9762838-1-2(6))* Gumbo Multimedia Entertainment.
Rivera, Lilliam. The Education of Margot Sanchez. 2017. (ENG., Illus.). 304p. (YA). (gr. 9). 19.99 *(978-1-4814-7211-1(9),* Simon & Schuster Bks. For Young Readers) Simon & Schuster Bks. For Young Readers.
Rivers, Rae. The Keepers: Declan (the Keepers, Book 2), Book 2. 2014. (Keepers Ser.: 2). (ENG.). 336p. pap. 11.99 *(978-0-00-810443-6(3),* One More Chapter) HarperCollins Pubs. Ltd. GBR. Dist: HarperCollins Pubs.
Roberts, Dina. Thirty Cats. 2003. 162p. (YA). pap. 12.95 *(978-0-595-29775-7(7))* iUniverse, Inc.
Roberts, Lisa Brown. Resisting the Rebel. 2016. (ENG., Illus.). 270p. (YA). pap. 14.99 *(978-1-68281-254-9(5))* Entangled Publishing, LLC.
Roberts, Pauline. Oh! I Wish. Bates, Lindsey E. & Wiggan, Desmond, illus. 2012. 24p. pap. 9.95 *(978-0-9848243-3-5(2))* Beckham Pubns. Co.
Robertson, Andrea. Bloodrose: A Nightshade Novel. 2012. (Nightshade Ser.: 3). (ENG.). 432p. (YA). (gr. 9). pap. 12.99 *(978-0-14-242370-7(X),* Speak) Penguin Young Readers Group.
Rock, Brian. With All My Heart. Banta, Susan, illus. 2012. (ENG.). 24p. (J). *(978-1-58925-648-4(4))* Tiger Tales.
Röder, Marlene & Röder, Marlene. In the River Darkness, 1 vol. 2014. (Scarlet Voyage Ser.). (ENG., Illus.). 224p. (YA). (gr. 9-10). pap. 13.88 *(978-1-62324-011-0(5),* 91fd001a-28d6-42a3-b57b-2ac27625e82c) Enslow Publishing, LLC.
Rodrigues, Carmen. The Universal Laws of Marco. 2019. (ENG., Illus.). 432p. (YA). (gr. 7). 18.99 *(978-1-4424-8509-9(4),* Simon Pulse) Simon Pulse.
Rodriguez, A.J. Cycle of Life. 2009. 20p. pap. 12.49 *(978-1-4389-5528-5(6))* AuthorHouse.
Rodriguez, Bobbie. How I Love My Dad. 2013. 40p. 22.99 *(978-1-62697-112-7(9));* pap. 11.99 *(978-1-62509-995-2(9))* Salem Author Services.
Rogerson, Margaret. An Enchantment of Ravens. (ENG., Illus.). (YA). (gr. 9). 2018. 320p. pap. 12.99 *(978-1-4814-9759-6(6))* 2017. 304p. 19.99 *(978-1-4814-9758-9(8))* McElderry, Margaret K. Bks. (McElderry, Margaret K. Bks.).
Romanoff, Zan. Grace & the Fever. 2017. (ENG.). 352p. (YA). (gr. 7). 17.99 *(978-1-5247-2084-1(4),* Knopf Bks. for Young Readers) Random Hse. Children's Bks.
Ron, Berry. Daddy Do You Love Me. 2009. (ENG.). 20p. bds. 5.99 *(978-0-8249-1423-3(6),* Ideals Pubns.) Worthy Publishing.
—Mommy Do You Love Me. 2009. (ENG.). 20p. bds. 5.99 *(978-0-8249-1422-6(8),* Ideals Pubns.) Worthy Publishing.
Rosa-Mendoza, Gladys. Lola. 2007. (Englishspanish Story Book Ser.). (ENG & SPA., Illus.). 32p. (J). (gr. -1-3). 13.95 *(978-1-931398-51-0(8))* Me+Mi Publishing.
Rose, Nancy. The Secret Life of Squirrels: a Love Story. 2016. (ENG., Illus.). 32p. (J). (gr. -1-3). 16.99 *(978-0-316-27263-6(9))* Little, Brown Bks. for Young Readers.
Rose, R. M. & Leuzinger, Shannon. Guardians or Demons. 2017. (ENG.). 419p. (YA). pap. 15.95 *(978-1-78612-746-4(6),* 1250bce7-2cc5-4844-8e09-9c8a726c6786) Austin Macauley Pubs. Ltd. GBR. Dist: Baker & Taylor Publisher Services (BTPS).
Rosenthal, Amy Krouse. Plant a Kiss. Reynolds, Peter H., illus. 2011. (ENG.). 40p. (J). (gr. -1-3). 15.99 *(978-0-06-198675-8(5),* HarperCollins) HarperCollins Pubs.
—Plant a Kiss Board Book. Reynolds, Peter H., illus. 2015. (ENG.). 36p. (J). (gr. -1 — 1). bds. 7.99 *(978-0-06-241652-0(9),* HarperFestival) HarperCollins Pubs.
—Sugar Cookies. Dyer, Jane & Dyer, Brooke, illus. 2009. (ENG.). 40p. (J). (gr. k-5). 12.99 *(978-0-06-174072-5(1),* HarperCollins) HarperCollins Pubs.
—That's Me Loving You. White, Teagan, illus. 2016. 40p. (J). (gr. -1-2). 18.99 *(978-1-101-93238-4(4),* Random Hse. Bks. for Young Readers) Random Hse. Children's Bks.
—That's Me Loving You. White, Teagan, illus. 2018. 28p. (J). (— 1). bds. 8.99 *(978-1-9848-4773-7(2),* Random Hse. Bks. for Young Readers) Random Hse. Children's Bks.
Rosland, Linsey. How Much Do I Love You? 2012. 20p. pap. 14.99 *(978-1-4567-4880-7(7))* AuthorHouse.
Rosoff, Meg. There Is No Dog. l.t. ed. 2012. (ENG.). 392p. (J). (gr. 7-12). 23.99 *(978-1-4104-4707-4(3))* Thorndike Pr.
Ross, Leanna. Julie Simone. 2004. 194p. (YA). pap. 14.95 *(978-0-595-30376-2(5))* iUniverse, Inc.
Ross, Margaret Clark. Jumpy the Frog Learns the Meaning of Love, 1 vol. McNeely, William, illus. 2010. 20p. pap. 24.95 *(978-1-4489-8370-4(3))* PublishAmerica, Inc.
Ross, Marlene. The Adventures of Donny the Doorknob. Hallam, Colleen and Peggy, illus. 2009. 32p. pap. 24.95 *(978-1-61546-539-2(1))* America Star Bks.
Rossetti-Shustak, Bernadette. I Love You Through & Through. Church, Caroline Jayne, illus. 2005. (ENG.). 24p. (J). (gr. -1 — 1). bds. 8.95 *(978-0-439-67363-1(1),* Cartwheel Bks.) Scholastic, Inc.
—I Love You Through & Through / Te Quiero, Yo Te Quiero (Bilingual) (Bilingual Edition) Church, Caroline Jayne, illus. 2013. (SPA.). 24p. (J). (gr. -1 — 1). bds. 8.95 *(978-0-545-58416-6(7))* Scholastic, Inc.
Rossi, Veronica. Through the Ever Night. 2013. 341p. (YA). *(978-0-06-224710-0(7))* Harper & Row Ltd.
Roth, Susan L. Mi Amor Por Ti/My Love for You. 2003. (Illus.). 26p. (J). (gr. -1 — 1). bds. 6.99 *(978-0-8037-2944-5(8),* Dial Bks) Penguin Young Readers Group.
Rothenberg, Jess. The Kingdom. 2019. (Illus.). 340p. (YA). *(978-1-250-25935-6(5))* Holt, Henry & Co.
Roy, Oscar. I Was Captured by Pirates. 2013. 110p. pap. 11.00 *(978-1-62212-790-0(0),* Strategic Bk. Publishing) Strategic Book Publishing & Rights Agency (SBPRA).
RR. Priscilla. 2008. 32p. pap. 24.95 *(978-1-60813-213-3(7))* America Star Bks.
Rubens, Michael. The Bad Decisions Playlist. 2017. (ENG.). 304p. (YA). (gr. 9). pap. 9.99 *(978-1-328-74208-7(3),* 1677324, Clarion Bks.) HarperCollins Pubs.
Rumbaugh, Melinda. Somebunny Loves You! 2015. (ENG., Illus.). 16p. (J). bds. 13.99 *(978-0-8249-1950-4(5),* Worthy Kids/Ideals) Worthy Publishing.
Rusackas, Francesca. Daddy All Day Long. Burris, Priscilla, tr. Burris, Priscilla, illus. 2004. 32p. (J). (gr. -1-k). lib. bdg. 13.89 *(978-0-06-050285-0(1))* HarperCollins Pubs.
Rush, Jennifer. Devils & Thieves. 2017. (Devils & Thieves Ser.: 1). (ENG.). 336p. (YA). (gr. 9-17). 17.99 *(978-0-316-39089-7(5))* Little, Brown Bks. for Young Readers.
Russo, Meredith. If I Was Your Girl. 2016. (ENG.). 288p. (YA). 18.99 *(978-1-250-07840-7(7),* 900153639) Flatiron Bks.
Rutkoski, Marie. The Winner's Curse. 2015. (Winner's Trilogy Ser.: 1). (ENG.). 384p. (YA). (gr. 7). pap. 15.99 *(978-1-250-05697-9(7),* 900139106) Square Fish.
Rutland, J. I Love You No Matter What: A Prince Chirpio Story, 1 vol. 2013. (ENG., Illus.). 32p. (J). 9.99 *(978-1-4003-2195-7(6),* Tommy Nelson) Nelson, Thomas Inc.
Ryder, Chloe. Princess Ponies 12: an Enchanted Heart. 2019. (Princess Ponies Ser.). (ENG., Illus.). 128p. (J). pap. 5.99 *(978-1-5476-0190-5(6),* 900203169, Bloomsbury Children's Bks.) Bloomsbury Publishing USA.
Ryder, Joanne. Won't You Be My Hugaroo? Board Book. Sweet, Melissa, illus. 2008. (ENG.). 30p. (J). (gr. -1 — 1). bds. 6.95 *(978-0-15-206298-9(X),* 1198872, Clarion Bks.) HarperCollins Pubs.
Saijyo, Shinji. Iron Wok Jan!, Vol. 13. 2005. (Iron Wok Jan! Ser.). (ENG., Illus.). 200p. (YA). pap. 9.95 *(978-1-59796-031-1(4))* DrMaster Pubns. Inc.
Sainsbury, Adam. The Coin. 2005. 84p. (YA). pap. 9.96 *(978-1-4116-5358-0(0))* Lulu Pr., Inc.
Salerni, Dianne K. The Caged Graves. 2014. (ENG.). 336p. (YA). (gr. 7). pap. 10.99 *(978-0-544-33622-3(4),* 1584168, Clarion Bks.) HarperCollins Pubs.
Salisbury, Melinda. The Sin Eater's Daughter (Unabridged Edition), 1 vol. unabr. ed. 2015. (ENG.). 2p. (J). (gr. 9). audio compact disk 39.99 *(978-0-545-83830-6(4))* Scholastic, Inc.
Sama, Kent. Fruit of the Spirit - Love. Moody, Julie, illus. 2005. (J). bds. 9.99 *(978-1-4183-0060-9(8))* Christ Inspired, Inc.
Samples, Suzanne. Pivot. 2011. 208p. pap. 13.00 *(978-1-257-03969-2(5))* Lulu Pr., Inc.
Sanders, Russell J. Colors. 2016. (ENG., Illus.). (J). 24.99 *(978-1-63477-956-2(8),* Harmony Ink Pr.) Dreamspinner Pr.
—Special Effect. 2016. (ENG., Illus.). (J). 24.99 *(978-1-63533-074-8(2),* Harmony Ink Pr.) Dreamspinner Pr.
Sandoval, John. The Witches of Ruidoso. 2013. (ENG.). 120p. (YA). pap. 12.95 *(978-1-55885-766-7(4),* Piñata Books) Arte Publico Pr.
Sarnella, Jeanette. Santini's Magic Castle. 2010. 28p. 15.49 *(978-1-4520-4908-3(4))* AuthorHouse.
Sauceda, Vickie. Doobie Kind & Mean Gene. 2013. 22p. pap. 9.99 *(978-1-62697-509-5(4))* Salem Author Services.
Sava, Scott Christian. Gary the Pirate. 2008. (Illus.). 112p. 12.95 *(978-0-9789168-5-5(9))* Blue Dream Studios.
Scaperrotta, Kirstyn. I Lost My Cracker to the Big Cheese: A Collection of Voices. 2003. 126p. (YA). pap. 10.95 *(978-0-595-26478-0(6),* Writers Club Pr.) iUniverse, Inc.
Scelsa, Kate. Fans of the Impossible Life. 2017. (ENG.). 368p. (YA). (gr. 9). pap. 9.99 *(978-0-06-233176-2(0),* Balzer & Bray) HarperCollins Pubs.
Scheid, Petra Maria. DIARY for lovers: Tagebuch für Verliebte. 2011. (GER.). 120p. pap. 15.90 *(978-3-8423-7899-5(8))* Bks. on Demand.
Scheier, Leah. Your Voice Is All I Hear. 2015. 336p. (YA). (gr. 8-12). pap. 9.99 *(978-1-4926-1441-8(6))* Sourcebooks, Inc.
Schertle, Alice. When the Moon Is High. 2003. (Illus.). 32p. (J). 16.89 *(978-0-688-15144-7(2))* HarperCollins Pubs.
Scheuer, Benjamin. Hibernate with Me. Williams, Jemima, illus. 2019. (ENG.). 40p. (J). (gr. -1-3). 17.99 *(978-1-5344-3217-8(5),* Simon & Schuster Bks. For Young Readers) Simon & Schuster Bks. For Young Readers.
Schneider, Robyn. Extraordinary Means. 2016. (ENG.). 352p. (YA). (gr. 8). pap. 9.99 *(978-0-06-221717-2(8),* Tegen, Katherine Bks) HarperCollins Pubs.
Schombs, James. The Little Boy in a Dog Suit, 1 vol. Weidman, James, illus. 2010. 28p. pap. 24.95 *(978-1-61582-053-5(1))* PublishAmerica, Inc.
Schraff, Anne. A Matter of Trust. 2007. (Bluford High — Scholastic Ser.: 2). lib. bdg. 16.00 *(978-1-4177-7142-4(9))* Turtleback.
—Please Don't Ask Me to Love You. 2008. (Passages Contemporary Ser.). 115p. (J). lib. bdg. 13.95 *(978-0-7569-8372-7(X))* Perfection Learning Corp.
—Secrets in the Shadows. 2007. (Bluford High — Scholastic Ser.: 3). lib. bdg. 16.00 *(978-1-4177-7149-3(6))* Turtleback.
—Someone to Love Me. 2007. (Bluford High — Scholastic Ser.: 4). lib. bdg. 16.00 *(978-1-4177-7151-6(8))* Turtleback.
Schraff, Anne E. Bad Blood. 2014. (Urban Underground — Cesar Chavez High School Ser.). (YA). lib. bdg. 20.80 *(978-0-606-35591-9(X))* Turtleback.
—Misjudged. 2014. (Urban Underground — Cesar Chavez High School Ser.). (YA). lib. bdg. 20.80 *(978-0-606-35589-6(8))* Turtleback.
Schreiber, Ellen. Teenage Mermaid. 2003. 160p. (J). (gr. 4-18). lib. bdg. 16.89 *(978-0-06-008205-5(4))* HarperCollins Pubs.
—Vampire Kisses 9: Immortal Hearts, 9. 2013. (Vampire Kisses Ser.: 9). (ENG.). 272p. (YA). (gr. 8-12). pap. 10.99 *(978-0-06-207009-8(6),* Tegen, Katherine Bks) HarperCollins Pubs.
Schroeder, Lisa. I Heart You, You Haunt Me. 2008. (ENG.). 240p. (YA). (gr. 9). pap. 11.99 *(978-1-4169-5520-7(8),* Simon Pulse) Simon Pulse.
Schur, Maxine Rose. Sacred Shadows. 2005. (ENG.). 224p. pap. 14.95 *(978-0-595-36793-1(3),* Backinprint.com) iUniverse, Inc.
Schwab, V. E. This Savage Song. (Monsters of Verity Ser.: 1). (ENG.). (YA). (gr. 9). 2020. 480p. pap. 14.99 *(978-0-06-298339-8(3))* 2016. 464p. 17.99 *(978-0-06-238085-2(0))* HarperCollins Pubs. (Greenwillow Bks.).
Schwab, Victoria. This Savage Song. 2017. (Monsters of Verity Ser.: 1). (ENG.). 480p. (YA). (gr. 9). pap. 10.99 *(978-0-06-238086-9(9),* Greenwillow Bks.) HarperCollins Pubs.
—This Savage Song. 2017. (Monsters of Verity Ser.: 1). (YA). lib. bdg. 20.85 *(978-0-606-40071-8(0))* Turtleback.
Scott, B. L. The Adventures of Babadoodle Kit Kit. 2008. 52p. pap. 22.99 *(978-1-4389-1812-9(7))* AuthorHouse.
Scott, Elizabeth. Bloom. 2007. (ENG.). 240p. (YA). (gr. 7-12). pap. 8.99 *(978-1-4169-2683-2(6),* Simon Pulse) Simon Pulse.
—Perfect You. 2008. (ENG.). 304p. (YA). (gr. 9-12). pap. 9.99 *(978-1-4169-5355-5(8),* Simon Pulse) Simon Pulse.
—Something, Maybe. 2010. (ENG.). 240p. (YA). (gr. 9). pap. 9.99 *(978-1-4169-5356-2(6),* Simon Pulse) Simon Pulse.
Scott, Kieran. A Non-Blonde Cheerleader in Love. 2008. (ENG.). 272p. (YA). (gr. 7-18). 8.99 *(978-0-14-241186-5(8),* Speak) Penguin Young Readers Group.
—Only Everything. 2014. (True Love Ser.: 1). (ENG., Illus.). 352p. (YA). (gr. 7). pap. 9.99 *(978-1-4424-7716-2(4),* Simon & Schuster Bks. For Young Readers) Simon & Schuster Bks. For Young Readers.
Scott, Shirley A. The Adventures of Jack & Dobbie: The Beginning. 2009. 32p. pap. 13.95 *(978-1-4389-4840-9(9))* AuthorHouse.
Second Look. 64p. (YA). (gr. 6-12). pap. *(978-0-8224-2385-0(5))* Globe Fearon Educational Publishing.
Sedgwick, Marcus. Midwinterblood. 2014. (ENG., Illus.). 288p. (YA). (gr. 7). pap. 14.99 *(978-1-250-04007-7(6),* 900123710) Square Fish.
—Midwinterblood. 2014. (YA). lib. bdg. 20.85 *(978-0-606-35221-5(X))* Turtleback.
Seduction. 2014. (Legacy Ser.). (ENG., Illus.). 416p. (YA). (gr. 9). 17.99 *(978-1-4814-0023-7(1),* Simon & Schuster/Paula Wiseman Bks.) Simon & Schuster/Paula Wiseman Bks.
Serle, Rebecca. Famous in Love. 2014. (ENG.). 336p. (YA). (gr. 7-17). 18.00 *(978-0-316-36632-8(3),* Poppy) Little, Brown Bks. for Young Readers.
—Truly Madly Famously. 2015. (Famous in Love Ser.: 2). (ENG.). 320p. (YA). (gr. 7-17). 18.00 *(978-0-316-36640-3(4),* Poppy) Little, Brown Bks. for Young Readers.
Sesame Workshop. Love: From Sesame Street. 2018. (Sesame Street Scribbles Ser.: 0). (ENG., Illus.). 32p. (J). (gr. k-3). 12.99 *(978-1-4926-7749-9(3))* Sourcebooks, Inc.
Sevigny, Alisha. Summer Constellations. 2018. (ENG.). 264p. (J). (gr. 9-12). pap. 10.99 *(978-1-5253-0043-1(1))* Kids Can Pr., Ltd. CAN. Dist: Hachette Bk. Group.
Shakespeare, William. A Midsummer Night's Dream the Graphic Novel: Original Text. Nicholson, Kat, illus. 2012. (ENG.). 144p. (gr. 6). lib. bdg. 24.95 *(978-1-907127-44-1(5))* Classical Comics GBR. Dist: Publishers Group West (PGW).
—Romeo & Juliet, 1 vol. Cabrera, Eva, illus. 2011. (Shakespeare Graphics Ser.). (ENG.). 88p. (J). (gr. 5-9). pap. 7.15 *(978-1-4342-3448-3(7),* 116469, Stone Arch Bks.) Capstone.
—Romeo & Juliet: The Graphic Novel, 1 vol. 2011. (Classic Graphic Novel Collection). (ENG., Illus.). 168p. (gr. 7-10). lib. bdg. 41.03 *(978-1-4205-0631-0(5),* cce53f3d-222c-4b3a-aa77-2b1188cff1bc, Lucent Pr.) Greenhaven Publishing LLC.
Shakespeare, William & Gabel, Claudia. Romeo & Juliet & Vampires. 2010. (ENG.). 256p. (YA). (gr. 9-18). pap. 9.99 *(978-0-06-197624-7(5),* HarperTeen) HarperCollins Pubs.
Shalant, Phyllis. Beware of Kissing Lizard Lips. 2010. 196p. pap. 13.95 *(978-1-4401-8339-3(2))* iUniverse, Inc.
Shalhout, Ahlam. For the Love of My Dreams, 1. 2004. 95p. per. 14.95 *(978-0-9668179-2-8(3))* Expressions Woven.
Shanker, Tarun & Zekas, Kelly. These Ruthless Deeds. 2017. (These Vicious Masks Ser.: 2). (ENG.). 320p. (YA). pap. 10.99 *(978-1-250-12795-2(5),* 900175610) Feiwel & Friends.
—These Vicious Masks. 2016. (These Vicious Masks Ser.: 1). (ENG.). 320p. (YA). pap. 15.99 *(978-1-250-07389-1(8),* 900150894) Feiwel & Friends.
Shankman, Adam & Sullivan, Laura L. Girl about Town: A Lulu Kelly Mystery. 2016. (ENG., Illus.). 336p. (YA). (gr. 9). 17.99 *(978-1-4814-4787-4(4),* Atheneum Bks. for Young Readers) Simon & Schuster Children's Publishing.
Shapiro, Jane. Daddy, What Is Love? Robinson, Don, illus. 2008. (ENG.). 28p. (J). (gr. -1-3). *(978-1-59700-244-8(5))* Island Heritage Publishing.
Sharp, Laura. The Key Prince. 2012. 24p. pap. 24.95 *(978-1-4626-8959-0(0))* America Star Bks.
Sheehan, Monica. Love Is You & Me. Sheehan, Monica, illus. (ENG., Illus.). (J). (gr. -1-3). 2013. 48p. 14.99 *(978-1-4424-3607-7(7))* 2010. 38p. bds. 8.99 *(978-1-4424-0765-7(4))* Little Simon. (Little Simon).
Sheldon, Dyan. Just Friends. 2018. (ENG.). 288p. (YA). (gr. 7). 16.99 *(978-0-7636-9354-1(5))* Candlewick Pr.
—One or Two Things I Learned about Love. (ENG.). 304p. (YA). (gr. 7). 2015. pap. 8.99 *(978-0-7636-7677-3(2))* 2013. 15.99 *(978-0-7636-6665-1(3))* Candlewick Pr.
Shepard, Sara. The Amateurs. 2016. (Amateurs Ser.: 1). (ENG.). 320p. (YA). (gr. 9-17). 17.99 *(978-1-4847-4227-3(3))* Little, Brown Bks. for Young Readers.
—Pretty Little Liars. 2006. (Pretty Little Liars Ser.: No. 1). (ENG.). 304p. (YA). (gr. 9-12). 16.99 *(978-0-06-088730-8(3),* HarperTeen) HarperCollins Pubs.
Sherman, Paulette Kouffman. Shekhinah. Vine, Rachel Shana, illus. 2013. 26p. pap. 10.95 *(978-0-9852469-5-2(2))* Parachute Jump Publishing.
Shields, Gillian. Eternal. 2012. (Immortal Ser.: 3). (ENG.). 384p. (YA). (gr. 8). pap. 9.99 *(978-0-06-200040-8(3),* Tegen, Katherine Bks) HarperCollins Pubs.
—Immortal. 2010. (Immortal Ser.: 1). (ENG.). 384p. (YA). (gr. 8-12). pap. 8.99 *(978-0-06-137583-5(7),* Tegen, Katherine Bks) HarperCollins Pubs.
Shifflett, Stephen. Josie Unlimited. 2007. 136p. (YA). per. 11.95 *(978-0-595-43013-0(9))* iUniverse, Inc.
Shimalla, Jen. Heaven Cent. 2013. 24p. pap. 10.95 *(978-1-4525-8042-5(1),* Balboa Pr.) Author Solutions, LLC.
Shine, Joe. I Become Shadow. 2015. (ENG.). 336p. (YA). (gr. 9). pap. 10.99 *(978-1-61695-537-3(6),* Soho Teen) Soho Pr., Inc.
Shirvington, Jessica. Corruption. 2017. (Disruption Ser.: 02). 448p. 9.99 *(978-1-4607-5219-7(8),* HarperCollins) HarperCollins Pubs.
—Endless. 2014. (Embrace Ser.: 4). (ENG.). 480p. (YA). (gr. 7-12). pap. 15.99 *(978-1-4022-8945-3(6))* Sourcebooks, Inc.
Short, Carol. Robert & the Princess. 2008. 16p. pap. 9.94 *(978-1-4389-2203-4(5))* AuthorHouse.
Showalter, Gena. Alice in Zombieland. 2013. (White Rabbit Chronicles Ser.: 1). (ENG.). 416p. pap. 10.99 *(978-0-373-21089-3(2),* Harlequin Teen) Harlequin Enterprises ULC CAN. Dist: HarperCollins Pubs.
—Alice in Zombieland. 2013. (J). lib. bdg. 20.85 *(978-0-606-31712-2(0))* Turtleback.
—A Mad Zombie Party. 2015. (White Rabbit Chronicles Ser.: 4). (ENG.). 448p. (YA). 18.99 *(978-0-373-21182-1(1),* Harlequin Teen) Harlequin Enterprises ULC CAN. Dist: HarperCollins Pubs.

J
K
L

—The Queen of Zombie Hearts. 2014. (White Rabbit Chronicles Ser.: 3). (ENG.). 464p. (YA). 18.99 *(978-0-373-21131-9(7)*, Harlequin Teen) Harlequin Enterprises ULC CAN. Dist: HarperCollins Pubs.
—Through the Zombie Glass. 2014. (White Rabbit Chronicles Ser.: 2). (ENG.). 480p. (YA). pap. 12.99 *(978-0-373-21129-6(5)*, Harlequin Teen) Harlequin Enterprises ULC CAN. Dist: HarperCollins Pubs.
—Twisted. 2011. (Intertwined Novel Ser.: 3). (ENG.). 576p. 18.99 *(978-0-373-21038-1(8)*, Harlequin Teen) Harlequin Enterprises ULC CAN. Dist: HarperCollins Pubs.
Shrum, Brianna R. The Art of French Kissing. 2018. (ENG.). 256p. (YA). (gr. 8-12). pap. 8.99 *(978-1-5107-3205-6(5)*, Sky Pony Pr.) Skyhorse Publishing Co., Inc.
Shubuck, Sheila. I Love You All Year Round. Padron, Alicia, illus. 2008. (ENG.). 16p. (J). (gr. -1). 10.95 *(978-1-58117-786-2(0)*, Intervisual/Piggy Toes) Bendon, Inc.
Silva, Abbey. She Came to Heal. 2008. 136p. pap. 11.50 *(978-1-4389-1086-4(X))* AuthorHouse.
Silver, Ruth. Aberrant. 2013. 250p. pap. 14.99 *(978-0-9917897-8-8(4))* Patchwork Pr.
—Isaura. 2013. 242p. pap. 14.99 *(978-1-927940-02-0(8))* Patchwork Pr.
Silvera, Adam. They Both Die at the End. l.t. ed. 2022. (ENG.). 516p. lib. bdg. 24.99 Cengage Gale.
—They Both Die at the End. (YA). 2018. (ENG.). 416p. (gr. 8). pap. 12.99 *(978-0-06-245780-6(2)*, Quill Tree Bks.) 2017. (ENG.). 384p. (gr. 8). 21.99 *(978-0-06-245779-0(9)*, Quill Tree Bks.) 2017. 373p. *(978-0-06-268851-4(0)*, HarperTeen) HarperCollins Pubs.
—They Both Die at the End. 2019. (YA). lib. bdg. 22.10 *(978-0-606-41431-9(2))* Turtleback.
Silverstein, Shel. The Giving Tree. Silverstein, Shel, illus. gif. ed. 2007. (Illus.). 64p. 16.99 *(978-0-06-124001-0(X))* HarperCollins Pubs.
Sima, Jessie. Love, Z. Sima, Jessie, illus. 2018. (ENG., Illus.). 48p. (J). (gr. -1-3). 17.99 *(978-1-4814-9677-3(8)*, Simon & Schuster Bks. For Young Readers) Simon & Schuster Bks. For Young Readers.
Simendinger, Ted. 12 Miles to Paradise: A People Story about Horses & Horseracing. 2nd ed. 2004. 364p. per. 12.95 *(978-0-9702405-4-5(6))* Airplane Reader Publishing.
Simon, Mary Manz. Bunny Loves Others. Stott, Dorothy, illus. 2006. (First Virtues for Toddlers Ser.). 20p. (J). 5.99 *(978-0-7847-1409-6(6)*, 04037) Standard Publishing.
Singh, Jay. Once upon a Time in a Forest Far Away. 2009. 394p. pap. 33.12 *(978-1-4251-9122-1(3))* Trafford Publishing.
Singleton, David & Martin, Loyce. Us Mail. 2008. 132p. pap. 11.95 *(978-0-595-52437-2(0))* iUniverse, Inc.
Sise, Katie. The Academy. 2018. (ENG.). 288p. (YA). (gr. 8). 17.99 *(978-0-06-240414-5(8)*, Balzer & Bray) HarperCollins Pubs.
Skidmore, Lauren. What Is Lost. 2015. 217p. (YA). pap. 16.99 *(978-1-4621-1621-8(3))* Cedar Fort, Inc./CFI Distribution.
Skillchecks for Romance. 2005. (Double Fastback Ser.). (J). (gr. 6-12). 64p. pap. 5.95 *(978-0-13-024474-1(0))*; 32p. pap. 5.95 *(978-0-13-024457-4(0))* Globe Fearon Educational Publishing.
Sky, Rebecca. Arrowheart. 2020. (Love Curse Ser.: 1). (ENG.). 352p. (YA). (gr. 7-17). pap. 10.99 *(978-1-4449-4005-3(8))* Hachette Children's Group GBR. Dist: Hachette Bk. Group.
Slater, Teddy. Beauty & the Beast (Disney Beauty & the Beast) Gonzalez, Ric & Dias, Ron, illus. 2004. (Little Golden Book Ser.). (ENG.). 24p. (J). (gr. -1-2). 5.99 *(978-0-7364-2197-3(1)*, Golden/Disney) Random Hse. Children's Bks.
Smith Annie, Laura. Whispers in the Wind. 2006. 144p. pap. 12.95 *(978-1-59113-914-0(7))* Booklocker.com, Inc.
Smith, Heather. Baygirl. 1 vol. 2013. (ENG.). 288p. (YA). (gr. 8-12). pap. 12.95 *(978-1-4598-0274-2(8))* Orca Bk. Pubs. USA.
Smith, Jennifer E. Hello, Goodbye, & Everything in Between. 2015. (ENG.). 256p. (YA). (gr. 7-17). 18.00 *(978-0-316-33442-6(1)*, Poppy) Little, Brown Bks. for Young Readers.
—The Statistical Probability of Love at First Sight. 2013. (ENG.). 272p. (YA). (gr. 7-17). pap. 11.99 *(978-0-316-12239-9(4)*, Poppy) Little, Brown Bks. for Young Readers.
—This Is What Happy Looks Like. 2013. (ENG.). 432p. (YA). (gr. 7-17). pap. 19.99 *(978-0-316-21281-6(4)*, Poppy) Little, Brown Bks. for Young Readers.
—Windfall. (ENG.). 432p. (YA). (gr. 7). 2018. pap. 10.99 *(978-0-399-55940-2(X)*, Ember) 2017. 18.99 *(978-0-399-55937-2(X)*, Delacorte Pr.) Random Hse. Children's Bks.
Smith, L. J. Daughters of Darkness. 2016. (Night World Ser.: 2). (ENG., Illus.). 256p. (YA). (gr. 9). 13.99 *(978-1-4814-7964-6(4)*, Simon Pulse) Simon Pulse.
—The Secret Circle: The Initiation & the Captive Part I TV Tie-In Edition. movie tie-in ed. 2011. (Secret Circle Ser.). (ENG.). 416p. (YA). (gr. 8). pap. 9.99 *(978-0-06-211900-1(1)*, HarperTeen) HarperCollins Pubs.
—The Secret Circle: the Captive Part II & the Power. 2012. (Secret Circle Ser.: Vols. 1-2). (ENG.). 416p. (YA). (gr. 8). pap. 10.99 *(978-0-06-167135-7(5)*, HarperTeen) HarperCollins Pubs.
—The Secret Circle: the Divide, Vol. 4. 2013. (Secret Circle Ser.: 4). (ENG.). 320p. (YA). (gr. 8). pap. 10.99 *(978-0-06-213041-9(2)*, HarperTeen) HarperCollins Pubs.
—Spellbinder. 2016. (Night World Ser.: 3). (ENG., Illus.). 256p. (YA). (gr. 9). 13.99 *(978-1-4814-8681-1(0)*, Simon Pulse) Simon Pulse.
Smith-Ready, Jeri. Shine. 2012. (ENG.). 416p. (YA). (gr. 9). pap. 9.99 *(978-1-4424-3946-7(7)*, Simon Pulse) Simon Pulse.
Smithem, Beth. Cocoa Bean & Squirt. 2010. 68p. pap. 10.49 *(978-1-4520-1929-1(0))* AuthorHouse.
Sniegoski, Thomas E. The Fallen 4: Forsaken. 2012. (Fallen Ser.: 4). (ENG.). 416p. (YA). (gr. 9). pap. 13.99 *(978-1-4424-4699-1(4)*, Simon Pulse) Simon Pulse.
—The Fallen 5: Armageddon. 2013. (Fallen Ser.: 5). (ENG., Illus.). 592p. (YA). (gr. 9). pap. 13.99 *(978-1-4424-6005-8(9)*, Simon Pulse) Simon Pulse.
Sobat, Gail Sidonie. Chance to Dance for You. 2011. (ENG.). 176p. pap. 14.95 *(978-1-926531-11-3(6)*, Great Plains Teen Fiction) Great Plains Pubns. CAN. Dist: Publishers Group Canada.
Solomon, Rachel Lynn. Our Year of Maybe. 2019. (ENG., Illus.). 384p. (YA). (gr. 9). 18.99 *(978-1-4814-9776-3(6)*, Simon Pulse) Simon Pulse.
Sones, Sonya. What My Girlfriend Doesn't Know. 2008. (ENG.). 320p. (YA). (gr. 7-18). pap. 8.99 *(978-0-689-87603-5(3)*, Simon & Schuster Bks. For Young Readers) Simon & Schuster Bks. For Young Readers.
—What My Mother Doesn't Know. 2004. 259p. (gr. 7-12). 19.00 *(978-0-7569-4268-7(3))* Perfection Learning Corp.
—What My Mother Doesn't Know. (ENG., Illus.). (YA). 2013. 288p. (gr. 7). pap. 12.99 *(978-1-4424-9385-8(2))* 2003. 272p. pap. 8.99 *(978-0-689-85553-5(2))* Simon & Schuster Bks. For Young Readers. (Simon & Schuster Bks. For Young Readers).
Soto, Gary. Accidental Love. 2008. (ENG., Illus.). 192p. (YA). (gr. 7). pap. 9.99 *(978-0-15-206113-5(4)*, 1198363, Clarion Bks.) HarperCollins Pubs.
Sowles, Joann I. Martin. Darkness (the Brookehaven Vampires Series #2) The Brookehaven Vampires. 2011. (YA). *(978-0-9844867-3-1(9))* Brookehaven Publishing.
Sparks, Favre. Agnes, the Eggless Quail. 2009. 28p. pap. 16.50 *(978-1-60693-491-3(0)*, Strategic Bk. Publishing) Strategic Book Publishing & Rights Agency (SBPRA).
Spaziano, Layna. Shane & Molly's Magical Journey, 1 vol. 2010. 28p. pap. 24.95 *(978-1-4489-6261-7(7))* PublishAmerica, Inc.
Spinelli, Eileen. Love You Always. Flint, Gillian, illus. 2018. (ENG.). 22p. (J). (gr. -1-k). bds. 7.99 *(978-0-8249-1667-1(0))* Worthy Publishing.
Spinelli, Jerry. Love, Stargirl. 2009. (Stargirl Ser.: 2). (ENG.). 288p. (YA). (gr. 7). pap. 9.99 *(978-0-375-85644-0(7)*, Ember) Random Hse. Children's Bks.
St. Aubin, Anne. Drafus the Daring Dragon. 2008. 24p. pap. 16.49 *(978-1-4343-8875-9(1))* AuthorHouse.
Staehli, Melissa. I Love You to the Moon. 2013. 28p. 15.95 *(978-1-61244-205-1(6))* Halo Publishing International.
Stamaty, Mark Alan. Who Needs Donuts? 2003. (ENG., Illus.). 40p. (J). (gr. -1-2). 17.99 *(978-0-375-82550-7(9)*, Knopf Bks. for Young Readers) Random Hse. Children's Bks.
Stamper, Phil. The Gravity of Us. 2020. (ENG.). 320p. (YA). 17.99 *(978-1-5476-0014-4(4)*, 900195006, Bloomsbury Young Adult) Bloomsbury Publishing USA.
Stampler, Ann Redisch. How to Disappear. 2016. (ENG., Illus.). 416p. (YA). (gr. 9). 18.99 *(978-1-4814-4393-7(3)*, Simon Pulse) Simon Pulse.
Staniszewski, Anna. Finders Reapers. 2016. (Switched at First Kiss Ser.: 2). 272p. (J). (gr. 5-8). pap. 7.99 *(978-1-4926-1549-1(8))* Sourcebooks, Inc.
—I'm with Cupid. 2015. (Switched at First Kiss Ser.: 1). 240p. (J). (gr. 5-8). pap. 7.99 *(978-1-4926-1546-0(3)*, 9781492615460) Sourcebooks, Inc.
—Match Me If You Can. 2017. (Switched at First Kiss Ser.: 3). 240p. (J). (gr. 5-8). pap. 12.99 *(978-1-4926-1552-1(8)*, 9781492615521) Sourcebooks, Inc.
Stanley, Mandy. Who Do You Love? Stanley, Mandy, illus. 2007. (ENG., Illus.). 24p. (J). (gr. -1 — 1). bds. 8.99 *(978-1-4169-3929-0(6)*, Little Simon) Little Simon.
Stapleton, Rhonda. Pucker Up. 2010. (ENG.). 272p. (YA). (gr. 7-18). pap. 9.99 *(978-1-4169-7466-6(0)*, Simon Pulse) Simon Pulse.
Staub, Leslie. How Do You Say I Love You, Dewey Dew? Mack, Jeff, illus. 2017. (ENG.). 32p. (J). (gr. -1-3). 17.95 *(978-1-62979-497-6(X)*, Astra Young Readers) Astra Publishing Hse.
Steiger, A. J. When My Heart Joins the Thousand. 2018. (ENG.). 352p. (YA). (gr. 9). 17.99 *(978-0-06-265647-6(3)*, HarperTeen) HarperCollins Pubs.
Steinkellner, Teddy. Two Roads from Here. 2017. (ENG., Illus.). 448p. (YA). (gr. 9). 17.99 *(978-1-4814-3061-6(0)*, Simon & Schuster Bks. For Young Readers) Simon & Schuster Bks. For Young Readers.
Stephenson, Stone. Somewhere among the Stars & Snowflakes. 2013. 40p. pap. 20.99 *(978-1-4520-5629-6(3))* AuthorHouse.
Stepp, Shirley. Santa Lost His Cell Phone. 2012. 24p. 24.95 *(978-1-4626-5479-6(7))* America Star Bks.
Stevens, Jennifer. Love You More. 2013. 24p. pap. 24.95 *(978-1-63004-655-2(8))* America Star Bks.
Stevenson, Peggy. Meet the Spencers & the Smart Knots. 2009. 48p. pap. 16.95 *(978-1-60813-517-2(9))* America Star Bks.
Stiefvater, Maggie. Forever (Shiver, Book 3) 2014. (Shiver Ser.: 3). (ENG.). 416p. (YA). (gr. 9). pap. 10.99 *(978-0-545-68280-0(0))* Scholastic, Inc.
—Linger. 2014. (Shiver Ser.). (ENG.). (YA). (gr. 9). lib. bdg. 20.60 *(978-1-68065-091-4(2))* Perfection Learning Corp.
—Linger. l.t. ed. 2011. (Shiver Trilogy: Bk. 2). (ENG.). 488p. pap. 23.99 *(978-1-4104-3447-0(8))* Thorndike Pr.
—Linger (Shiver, Book 2). 1 vol. 2014. (Shiver Ser.: 2). (ENG.). 384p. (YA). (gr. 9). pap. 10.99 *(978-0-545-68279-4(7))* Scholastic, Inc.
—The Raven King. 2016. 439p. (J). *(978-0-605-90184-1(8)*, Scholastic Pr.) Scholastic, Inc.
—The Raven King (the Raven Cycle, Book 4) (Raven Cycle Ser.: 4). (ENG.). (YA). (gr. 9-9). 2016. 448p. 18.99 *(978-0-545-42498-1(4))*IV. 2018. 480p. pap. 12.99 *(978-0-545-42499-8(2))* Scholastic, Inc. (Scholastic Pr.).
—The Raven King (the Raven Cycle, Book 4) (Unabridged Edition), 1 vol. unabr. ed. 2016. (Raven Cycle Ser.: 4). (ENG.). 1p. (YA). (gr. 7). audio compact disk 39.99 *(978-0-545-64908-7(0))* Scholastic, Inc.
—The Scorpio Races, 1 vol. 2011. (ENG.). 416p. (YA). (gr. 8). 19.99 *(978-0-545-22490-1(X)*, Scholastic Pr.) Scholastic, Inc.
—The Scorpio Races (Unabridged Edition), 1 vol. unabr. ed. 2011. (ENG.). 5p. (J). audio compact disk 79.99 *(978-0-545-35705-0(5))* Scholastic, Inc.
Stilton, Geronimo. All Because of a Cup of Coffee (Geronimo Stilton #10), Volume 10. 2004. (Geronimo Stilton Ser.: 10). (ENG., Illus.). 128p. (J). (gr. 2-5). pap. 7.99 *(978-0-439-55972-0(3)*, Scholastic Paperbacks) Scholastic, Inc.
Stine, R. L. The New Girl. 2006. (Fear Street Ser.: Bk. 1). (ENG., Illus.). 176p. (YA). (gr. 7-12). mass mkt. 7.99 *(978-1-4169-1810-3(8)*, Simon Pulse) Simon Pulse.
Stirling, Joss. Shaken. 2017. 332p. (YA). (gr. 9-12). pap. 16.99 *(978-987-747-242-4(2))* V&R Editoras.
Stoehr, Shelley. Tomorrow Wendy: A Love Story. 2003. 176p. pap. 14.95 *(978-0-595-26954-9(0)*, Backinprint.com) iUniverse, Inc.
Stoffels, Karlijn. Heartsinger. 2009. (YA). pap. *(978-0-545-06968-7(8)*, Levine, Arthur A. Bks.) Scholastic, Inc.
Stone, Amy Wingrove. I Love You Every Minute. Lennhoff, Andrew, illus. 2006. pap. 18.00 *(978-0-8059-9119-2(0)*, RoseDog Bks.) Dorrance Publishing Co., Inc.
Stone, Danika. Internet Famous. 2017. (ENG.). 336p. (YA). pap. 17.99 *(978-1-250-11437-2(3)*, 900171419) Feiwel & Friends.
Stone, Juliana. Some Kind of Normal. 2015. (ENG.). 304p. (YA). (gr. 8-12). pap. 9.99 *(978-1-4926-1871-3(3))* Sourcebooks, Inc.
Stone, Tamara Ireland. Every Last Word. 2017. (ENG.). (YA). (gr. 7-12). lib. bdg. 20.85 *(978-0-606-39885-5(6))* Turtleback.
—Time after Time. 2014. (ENG.). 368p. (J). (gr. 7-12). pap. 18.99 *(978-1-4231-5981-0(0))* Hyperion Bks. for Children.
—Time & Time Again. 2017. (ENG.). 736p. (YA). (gr. 7-12). pap. 11.99 *(978-1-4847-8133-3(3))* Hyperion Bks. for Children.
—Time Between Us. 2013. (ENG.). 384p. (J). (gr. 7-12). pap. 19.99 *(978-1-4231-5977-3(2))* Hyperion Pr.
Storms, Patricia. Never Let You Go. 2018. (ENG., Illus.). 32p. (J). (gr. -1-1). 14.99 *(978-1-5107-3871-3(1)*, Sky Pony Pr.) Skyhorse Publishing Co., Inc.
Stott, Ann. Always. Phelan, Matt, illus. 2008. (ENG.). 32p. (J). (gr. k-k). 15.99 *(978-0-7636-3232-8(5))* Candlewick Pr.
Stout, Katie M. Hello, I Love You. 2015. (ENG.). 304p. (YA). pap. *(978-1-250-08195-7(5)*, St. Martin's Griffin) St. Martin's Pr.
Strange, Derek. Level 1: Girl Meets Boy. 2nd ed. 2008. (Pearson English Graded Readers Ser.). (ENG., Illus.). 32p. pap. 11.99 *(978-1-4058-6971-3(2)*, Pearson ELT) Pearson Education.
Strasnick, Lauren. 16 Ways to Break a Heart. 2017. (ENG.). 208p. (YA). (gr. 9). 17.99 *(978-0-06-241872-2(6)*, Tegen, Katherine Bks) HarperCollins Pubs.
Strasser, Todd. Blood on My Hands. 2011. (ENG.). 304p. (YA). (gr. 9-12). pap. 8.99 *(978-1-60684-228-7(5)*, fc739d70-6a40-42fa-b8e1-d93dc4d8aac1, Carolrhoda Lab™) Lerner Publishing Group.
—For Money & Love. 2007. (Mob Princess Ser.: 1). (ENG.). 208p. (YA). (gr. 9-18). pap. 10.99 *(978-1-4169-3533-9(9)*, Simon Pulse) Simon Pulse.
Studio Mouse Editorial. Belle: The Power of Love. 2008. (ENG., Illus.). 36p. (gr. -1-k). 7.99 *(978-1-59069-435-0(X))* Studio Mouse LLC.
StVil, Yves Lola. Girls Like Me. 2016. (ENG.). 320p. (YA). (gr. 7). 17.99 *(978-0-544-70674-3(9)*, 1628646, Clarion Bks.) HarperCollins Pubs.
Sublime. 2014. (ENG., Illus.). 336p. (YA). (gr. 9). 17.99 *(978-1-4814-1368-8(6)*, Simon & Schuster Bks. For Young Readers) Simon & Schuster Bks. For Young Readers.
Sugg, Zoe. Girl Online. 2018. (VIE.). (YA). (gr. 7). pap. *(978-604-1-11129-5(5))* Kim Dong Publishing Hse.
Sullivan, Mary Jo. The Wonder of Us, 1 vol. 2010. 16p. 24.95 *(978-1-4489-2600-8(9))* PublishAmerica, Inc.
Summers, Natalie. The Noweos: Neighbors One with Each Other. 2009. 20p. pap. 12.99 *(978-1-4490-3710-9(0))* AuthorHouse.
Sun, Amanda. Ink. 2013. (Paper Gods Ser.: 2). (ENG., Illus.). 384p. (YA). pap. 9.99 *(978-0-373-21071-8(X)*, Harlequin Teen) Harlequin Enterprises ULC CAN. Dist: HarperCollins Pubs.
—Storm. 2015. (Paper Gods Ser.: 5). (ENG.). 304p. (YA). pap. 9.99 *(978-0-373-21174-6(0)*, Harlequin Teen) Harlequin Enterprises ULC CAN. Dist: HarperCollins Pubs.
Sundberg, Ingrid. All We Left Behind. 2015. (ENG.). 432p. (YA). (gr. 9). 17.99 *(978-1-4814-3742-4(9)*, Simon Pulse) Simon Pulse.
Sunderland, Margot. The Frog Who Longed for the Moon to Smile: A Story for Children Who Yearn for Someone They Love, 2 vols. 2017. (Helping Children with Feelings Ser.). (ENG., Illus.). 28p. (C). pap. 17.95 *(978-0-86388-495-5(4)*, Y330286) Routledge.
Sunseri, Heather. Mindsiege. 2013. (ENG.). 374p. (YA). pap. 14.00 *(978-0-9887153-5-6(X))* Sunseri, Heather.
Surace, Joan. The Story of Lucia. Rockford, Nancy, illus. 2006. (YA). pap. 8.00 *(978-0-8059-7062-3(2))* Dorrance Publishing Co., Inc.
Surmelis, Angelo. The Dangerous Art of Blending In. 2019. (ENG.). 336p. (YA). (gr. 8). pap. 11.99 *(978-0-06-265901-9(4)*, Balzer & Bray) HarperCollins Pubs.
Suzuki, Mamoru. You Belong to Me. 2016. (ENG., Illus.). 32p. (J). (gr. -1-k). 12.99 *(978-1-940842-12-7(3))* Museyon.
Swain, Heather. Me, My Elf & I. 2009. (ENG.). 256p. (YA). (gr. 7-12). 22.44 *(978-0-14-241255-8(4))* Penguin Young Readers Group.
Sybesma, Lila Jeanne Elliot. Yours: The Civil War, a Love Triangle, & the Steamboat Sultana. 2019. (Illus.). xiii, 307p. (YA). pap. *(978-0-87195-431-2(1))* Indiana Historical Society.
Tahir, Sabaa. An Ember in the Ashes. l.t. ed. (Ember in the Ashes Ser.: 1). 2018. (ENG.). pap. 15.99 *(978-1-4328-5034-0(2))* 2016. 648p. 25.99 *(978-1-4104-8875-6(6))* Cengage Gale.
—An Ember in the Ashes. (Ember in the Ashes Ser.: 1). (ENG.). (YA). 2016. 480p. (gr. 7). pap. 12.99 *(978-1-59514-804-9(3))* 2015. 464p. (gr. 9). 21.95 *(978-1-59514-803-2(5))* Penguin Young Readers Group. (Razorbill).
—An Ember in the Ashes. 2016. 464p. lib. bdg. 23.30 *(978-0-606-38848-1(6))* Turtleback.
—A Reaper at the Gates. 2018. (Ember in the Ashes Ser.: 3). (ENG.). 480p. (YA). (gr. 9). 19.95 *(978-0-448-49450-0(7)*, Razorbill) Penguin Young Readers Group.
—A Torch Against the Night. l.t. ed. 2016. (Ember in the Ashes Ser.: 2). (ENG.). (YA). (gr. 9-12). 22.99 *(978-1-4104-8925-8(6))* Cengage Gale.
—A Torch Against the Night. (Ember in the Ashes Ser.: 2). (ENG.). (YA). (gr. 9). 2017. 496p. pap. 12.99 *(978-1-101-99888-5(1))* 2016. (Illus.). 464p. 19.95 *(978-1-101-99887-8(3))* Penguin Young Readers Group. (Razorbill).
—A Torch Against the Night. 2017. (Ember in the Ashes Ser.: 2). lib. bdg. 23.30 *(978-0-606-40085-5(0))* Turtleback.
Take a Hike, Romeo. (Full House Ser.). 96p. (J). (gr. 4-6). pap. 3.95 *(978-0-938753-75-9(4)*, PP4) Parachute Publishing, LLC.
Talbott, Shawn M. Springtime Robins. 2006. (J). lib. bdg. 19.95 *(978-1-933732-05-3(9))* Big Ransom Studio.
Tammi, Elizabeth. Outrun the Wind. 2018. (ENG.). 304p. (YA). (gr. 9-12). pap. 11.99 *(978-1-63583-026-2(5)*, 1635830265, Flux) North Star Editions.
Tanco, Miguel. Mom & Me, Me & Mom (Mother Daughter Gifts, Mother Daughter Books, Books for Moms, Motherhood Books) 2019. (You & Me, Me & You Ser.). (ENG., Illus.). 36p. (J). (gr. -1-k). 12.99 *(978-1-4521-7190-6(4))* Chronicle Bks. LLC.
Tash, Sarvenaz. The Geek's Guide to Unrequited Love. 2016. (ENG., Illus.). 256p. (YA). (gr. 9). 19.99 *(978-1-4814-5653-1(9)*, Simon & Schuster Bks. For Young Readers) Simon & Schuster Bks. For Young Readers.
Taub, Melinda. Still Star-Crossed. 2017. (SPA.). 376p. (YA). (gr. 9-12). pap. *(978-987-747-262-2(7))* V&R Editoras.
Taylor, Janet B. Sparks of Light. 2018. (ENG.). 448p. (YA). (gr. 9). pap. 9.99 *(978-1-328-91526-9(3)*, 1701811, Clarion Bks.) HarperCollins Pubs.
Taylor, Jessica. Wandering Wild. (ENG.). 368p. 2017. (YA). (gr. 9-9). pap. 9.99 *(978-1-5107-2657-4(8))* 2016. (J). (gr. 8-8). 17.99 *(978-1-5107-0400-8(0))* Skyhorse Publishing Co., Inc. (Sky Pony Pr.).
Taylor, Laini. Lips Touch: Three Times. Di Bartolo, Jim, illus. 2011. (ENG.). 288p. (YA). (gr. 7-7). pap. 14.99 *(978-0-545-05586-4(5)*, Levine, Arthur A. Bks.) Scholastic, Inc.
Taylor, Whitney. Definitions of Indefinable Things. (ENG.). 336p. (YA). (gr. 9). 2019. pap. 9.99 *(978-1-328-49801-4(8)*, 1717859) 2017. 17.99 *(978-0-544-80504-0(6)*, 1640946) HarperCollins Pubs. (Clarion Bks.).
Teis, Kyra. The Magic Flute, 1 vol. Teis, Kyra, illus. 2008. (ENG., Illus.). 32p. (J). (gr. k-9). 17.95 *(978-1-59572-058-0(8))* Star Bright Bks., Inc.
Telep, Trisha, ed. Kiss Me Deadly: 13 Tales of Paranormal Love. 2010. (ENG.). 432p. (YA). (gr. 9-17). pap. 19.99 *(978-0-7624-3949-2(1)*, Running Pr. Kids) Running Pr.
Tetzlaff, Wendy Jo. A Girl Named Frannie. 2008. 28p. pap. 24.95 *(978-1-60703-055-3(1))* America Star Bks.
Theobald the Iron Hearted or Love to Ene. 2004. reprint ed. pap. 15.95 *(978-1-4191-8941-8(7))* Kessinger Publishing, LLC.
Theobald the Iron Hearted or Love to Enemies. 2004. reprint ed. pap. 1.99 *(978-1-4192-8941-5(1))* Kessinger Publishing, LLC.
Thomas, Cynthia. Promise Ring: The Promise. 2013. (ENG.). 82p. (YA). pap. 12.95 *(978-1-4787-1008-0(X))* Outskirts Pr., Inc.
Thomas, Isabel & Thomas, Marilyn. Stargazing from Nowhere. 2013. 448p. pap. *(978-0-9880448-0-7(3))* Do Art Publishing.
Thomes, William Henry. The Bushrangers a Yankee's Adventures During His Second Visit to Australia by William H Thomes. 2006. 420p. per. 26.99 *(978-1-4255-4567-3(X))* Michigan Publishing.
Thompson, Karri. Ascendancy. 2015. (ENG., Illus.). 248p. (YA). (gr. 7). pap. 15.99 *(978-1-68281-024-8(0))* Entangled Publishing, LLC.
Thompson, Kelly. Lasting. 2005. 120p. pap. 19.95 *(978-1-4137-9653-7(2))* PublishAmerica, Inc.
Thomson, Celia. The Stolen. 2004. (Nine Lives of Chloe King Ser.: 2). (ENG.). 288p. (YA). (gr. 8). pap. 13.99 *(978-0-689-86659-3(3)*, Simon Pulse) Simon Pulse.
Thornburgh, Blair. Who's That Girl. 2017. (ENG.). 400p. (YA). (gr. 8). 17.99 *(978-0-06-244777-7(7)*, HarperTeen) HarperCollins Pubs.
Thorne, Bella. Autumn's Kiss. 2016. (Autumn Falls Ser.: 2). (ENG.). 256p. (YA). (gr. 7). pap. 9.99 *(978-0-385-74436-2(6)*, Ember) Random Hse. Children's Bks.
Thornhorn. The Kestrel Waters: A Tale of Love & Devil. 2014. (ENG.). 33.39 *(978-0-9916496-4-8(8))*; pap. 19.95 *(978-0-615-96746-2(9))* Rosasharn Pr.
Tiernan, Cate. Eternally Yours. 2013. (Immortal Beloved Ser.: 3). (ENG.). 464p. (YA). (gr. 7-17). pap. 21.99 *(978-0-316-03595-8(5)*, Poppy) Little, Brown Bks. for Young Readers.
Tillit, L. B. 2 Days. 2012. (Gravel Road Ser.). (YA). lib. bdg. 20.80 *(978-0-606-25252-2(5))* Turtleback.
Tillman, Nancy. The Spirit of Christmas. Tillman, Nancy, illus. 2009. (ENG., Illus.). 32p. (J). (gr. -1-3). 17.99 *(978-0-312-54965-7(2)*, 900055822) Feiwel & Friends.
—Wherever You Are: My Love Will Find You. Tillman, Nancy, illus. (ENG., Illus.). 32p. (J). (gr. -1-3). 2012. bds. 8.99 *(978-1-250-01797-0(1)*, 900087504) 2010. 18.99 *(978-0-312-54966-4(0)*, 900055823) Feiwel & Friends.
Tinetti, Elizabeth Ordaz. Love Is Patient. 2012. 32p. pap. 16.99 *(978-1-4634-3862-3(1))* AuthorHouse.
Tintera, Amy. Ruined. (Ruined Ser.: 1). (ENG.). (YA). (gr. 8). 2017. 384p. pap. 10.99 *(978-0-06-239660-0(9))* 2016. 368p. 17.99 *(978-0-06-239660-0(9))* HarperCollins Pubs. (HarperTeen).
Tolcser, Sarah. Whisper of the Tide. 2018. (ENG., Illus.). 416p. (YA). 17.99 *(978-1-68119-299-4(3)*, 900165542, Bloomsbury Young Adult) Bloomsbury Publishing USA.
Toliver, Wendy. Miss Match. 2009. (Romantic Comedies Ser.). (ENG.). 304p. (YA). (gr. 7-18). mass mkt. 6.99 *(978-1-4169-6413-1(4)*, Simon Pulse) Simon Pulse.
—The Secret Life of a Teenage Siren. 2007. (Romantic Comedies Ser.). (ENG.). 304p. (YA). (gr. 7-12). mass mkt. 6.99 *(978-1-4169-5065-3(6)*, Simon Pulse) Simon Pulse.
Tomlin, Chris. Good Good Father, 1 vol. 2016. (ENG., Illus.). 32p. (J). 17.99 *(978-0-7180-8695-4(3)*, Tommy Nelson) Nelson, Thomas Inc.
Tozer, Gabrielle. Remind Me How This Ends. 2022. 352p. 9.99 *(978-1-4607-5168-8(X)*, HarperCollins) HarperCollins Pubs.
Tracy, Roseann. Do You Love Me When I Am Upside Down? 2008. 28p. pap. 12.99 *(978-1-4389-0503-7(3))* AuthorHouse.
Tregay, Sarah. Fan Art. DeJesus, Melissa, illus. 2014. (ENG.). 368p. (YA). (gr. 8). 17.99 *(978-0-06-224315-7(2)*, Tegen, Katherine Bks) HarperCollins Pubs.
Tremblay, Carole. Romeo, le Rat Romantique. 2004. (FRE., Illus.). (J). (gr. -1-3). spiral bd. *(978-0-616-07266-0(X))*

Canadian National Institute for the Blind/Institut National Canadien pour les Aveugles.

Triana, Gaby. Summer of Yesterday. 2014. (ENG., Illus.). 272p. (YA). (gr. 9). pap. 9.99 (978-1-4814-0130-2(0), Simon Pulse) Simon Pulse.

Tsahiridis, Van. Peree' & the Magic Fish: Fairy Tale from Pontos. 2010. 64p. pap. 10.16 (978-1-4269-2335-7(X)) Trafford Publishing.

Tuorto, Diana. Janie's New Legs. 2008. (ENG.). 48p. pap. 11.99 (978-1-4196-9142-3(2)) CreateSpace Independent Publishing Platform.

Two Lies & a Spy. 2014. (ENG., Illus.). 272p. (YA). (gr. 9). pap. 12.99 (978-1-4424-8173-2(0), Simon & Schuster Bks. For Young Readers) Simon & Schuster Bks. For Young Readers.

Tyrrell, Melissa. Beauty & the Beast. McMullen, Nigel, illus. 2005. (Fairytale Friends Ser.). 12p. (J). bds. 5.95 (978-1-58117-153-2(6), Intervisual/Piggy Toes) Bendon, Inc.

Ueda, Rinko. Tail of the Moon, Vol. 4. 2007. (Tail of the Moon Ser.: 4). (ENG., Illus.). 200p. (gr. 11). pap. 8.99 (978-1-4215-0816-0(8)) Viz Media.

Umansky, Kaye. The Romantic Giant. Weir, Doffy, illus. 2006. 29p. (J). (gr. k-2). pap. 6.95 (978-1-903015-25-4(1)) Barn Owl Bks, London GBR. Dist: Independent Pubs. Group.

Upperman, Katy. Kissing Max Holden. 2018. (ENG.). 320p. (YA). pap. 17.99 (978-1-250-15896-3(6), 900185542) Square Fish.

Urbanek Reese, Dorothy. When Mice Sing — the Story of Mei & Yu. 2008. 138p. pap. 13.95 (978-1-4357-6104-9(9)) Lulu Pr., Inc.

Urda, Gary. Love You More. Bell, Jennifer A., illus. 2018. (ENG.). 40p. (J). (gr. -1-3). 17.99 (978-1-4998-0652-6(3)) Little Bee Books Inc.

Ure, Jean. Love & Kisses. 2009. (ENG.). 192p. (J). (gr. 4-7). pap. 9.99 (978-0-00-728172-5(2), HarperCollins Children's Bks.) HarperCollins Pubs. Ltd. GBR. Dist: HarperCollins Pubs.

—Strawberry Crush. 2016. (ENG.). 224p. (J). 6.99 (978-0-00-755396-9(X), HarperCollins Children's Bks.) HarperCollins Pubs. Ltd. GBR. Dist: HarperCollins Pubs.

Usera, Christian. The Ones. 2007. (ENG.). 35p. (978-0-615-14645-4(7)) Usera, Christian.

Vail, Rachel. Kiss Me Again. 2013. (If We Kiss Ser.: 2). (ENG.). 272p. (YA). (gr. 8). pap. 9.99 (978-0-06-194719-3(9), HarperTeen) HarperCollins Pubs.

Valdes, Alisa. Perdition: A Kindred Novel. 2013. (YA). pap. (978-0-06-202421-3(3), HarperTeen) HarperCollins Pubs.

Valdivia, Benjamín. The Cage of the Different People: A Story of Brotherly Love. Gabriel, Andrea K., illus. 2009. (ENG.). 46p. pap. 21.99 (978-1-4771-0343-2(0)) Xlibris Corp.

Van Buren, David. I Love You As Big As the World. Warnes, Tim, illus. 2013. (ENG.). 22p. (J). (-k). bds. 8.95 (978-1-58925-603-3(4)) Tiger Tales.

van Diepen, Allison. Raven. 2010. (ENG.). 304p. (YA). (gr. 9). pap. 12.99 (978-1-4169-7468-0(7), Simon Pulse) Simon Pulse.

Van Draanen, Wendelin. Flipped. 2003. (gr. 5-8). 20.85 (978-0-613-62948-5(5)) Turtleback.

Van Duzen, Fisher. Searching for Sand Dollars. 2013. 416p. 19.99 (978-0-9896335-0-5(0)) PoorHse. Publishing LLC.

Vars, Elle Márjá. The Most Beautiful Dawn. Janda, Laura A., tr. Guttormsen, Trygve Lund, illus. 2013. 80p. (J). pap. 17.99 (978-0-9772714-6-7(3)) Nordic Studies Pr.

Vaval, Fisepe. The Blueprint. Bubsy, Nancy, ed. 2003. 270p. (YA). pap. 15.00 (978-0-9743207-0-0(6)) Tayes Bks.

Verday, Jessica. The Haunted. (ENG.). (YA). (gr. 9). 2011. 496p. pap. 14.99 (978-1-4169-7896-1(8)) 2010. 480p. 17.99 (978-1-4169-7895-4(X)) Simon Pulse. (Simon Pulse).

Verde, Susan. I Am Love: A Book of Compassion. Reynolds, Peter H., illus. (I Am Bks.). (ENG.). (J). (gr. -1 — 1). 2021. 22p. bds., bds. 8.99 (978-1-4197-4237-8(X), 1277610, Abrams Appleseed) 2019. 32p. 14.99 (978-1-4197-3726-8(0), 1277601) Abrams, Inc.

Vernick, Shirley Reva. The Black Butterfly, 1 vol. 2014. (ENG.). 226p. (J). (gr. 8-12). 19.95 (978-1-935955-79-5(9), 23353382, Cinco Puntos Press) Lee & Low Bks., Inc.

—The Blood Lie. (ENG.). 144p. (YA). (gr. 9-12). 2015. pap. 16.95 (978-1-941026-09-0(5), 23353382) 2011. 15.95 (978-1-933693-84-2(3), 23353382) Lee & Low Bks., Inc. (Cinco Puntos Press).

Viguié, Debbie. The Summer of Cotton Candy, 1 vol. 2008. (Sweet Seasons Novel Ser.: 1). (ENG., Illus.). 224p. (YA). (gr. 8-11). pap. 9.99 (978-0-310-71558-0(X)) Zondervan.

Viguié, Debbie & Viguié, Debbie. Midnight Pearls: A Retelling of "the Little Mermaid" 2006. (Once upon a Time Ser.). (ENG., Illus.). 208p. (YA). (gr. 9-12). mass mkt. 7.99 (978-1-4169-4016-6(2), Simon Pulse) Simon Pulse.

Villani, Donna. The Capture of Art. 2008. 244p. pap. 14.95 (978-1-60693-104-2(0), Eloquent Bks.) Strategic Book Publishing & Rights Agency (SBPRA).

Vincent, Rachel. Brave New Girl. 2017. 272p. (YA). (gr. 7). 17.99 (978-0-399-55245-8(6), Delacorte Pr.) Random Hse. Children's Bks.

Vinesse, Cecilia. The Summer of Us. 2019. (ENG.). 336p. (YA). (gr. 9-17). pap. 10.99 (978-0-316-39114-6(X), Poppy) Little, Brown Bks. for Young Readers.

Viselman, Kenn. I Love You Bunches. 2004. (Illus.). 28p. 14.98 (978-0-9722361-0-2(4)) Viselman, Kenn Presents...

Vision, David & Vision, Mutiya Sahar. Daddy Loves His Baby Girl. Vision, Mutiya Sahar, illus. 2009. (Illus.). 32p. 16.00 (978-0-9659538-7-0(4)) Visor Bks.

Vivian, Siobhan. The Last Boy & Girl in the World. 2016. (ENG., Illus.). 432p. (YA). (gr. 9). 17.99 (978-1-4814-5229-8(0), Simon & Schuster Bks. For Young Readers) Simon & Schuster Bks. For Young Readers.

Voss, Dawn. Avenging Aja. 2007. (ENG.). 52p. pap. 15.00 (978-0-615-15324-7(0)) Voss, Dawn L.

Vrabel, Beth. Camp Dork. 2016. (Pack of Dorks Ser.: 2). (ENG.). 240p. (J). (gr. 2-7). 16.99 (978-1-63450-181-1(0), Sky Pony Pr.) Skyhorse Publishing Co., Inc.

Wagner, Paul. Just One Mo. 2003. 130p. (YA). pap. 10.95 (978-0-595-27223-5(1), Writers Club Pr.) iUniverse, Inc.

Wakefield, Beth. The Cleaner. 2010. 151p. pap. 14.50 (978-1-4457-6809-0(7)) Lulu Pr., Inc.

Wakefield, Nelida. Little Flathead & the Black Pearl. Smith, Nathan, illus. 2009. 36p. pap. 12.99 (978-1-59858-828-6(1)) Dog Ear Publishing, LLC.

Wakefield, Vikki. In-Between Days. 2016. (ENG., Illus.). 352p. (YA). (gr. 9). 17.99 (978-1-4424-8656-0(2), Simon & Schuster Bks. For Young Readers) Simon & Schuster Bks. For Young Readers.

Walker, Melissa. Ashes to Ashes. 2015. (ENG.). 352p. (YA). (gr. 8). pap. 9.99 (978-0-06-207735-6(X), Tegen, Katherine Bks) HarperCollins Pubs.

—Dust to Dust. 2016. (ENG.). 320p. (YA). (gr. 8). pap. 9.99 (978-0-06-207738-7(4), Tegen, Katherine Bks) HarperCollins Pubs.

Wallach, Tommy. Thanks for the Trouble. 2016. (ENG., Illus.). 288p. (YA). (gr. 9). 17.99 (978-1-4814-1880-5(7), Simon & Schuster Bks. For Young Readers) Simon & Schuster Bks. For Young Readers.

Walsh, Joanna. The Biggest Kiss. Abbot, Judi, illus. 2011. (ENG.). 32p. (J). (gr. -1-3). 14.99 (978-1-4424-2769-3(8), Simon & Schuster/Paula Wiseman Bks.) Simon & Schuster/Paula Wiseman Bks.

Walsh, Meg. Mama, Won't You Play with Me? 2009. 28p. pap. 13.99 (978-1-4490-1424-7(0)) AuthorHouse.

Walton, A. E. What Should I Do with My Love for You? 2009. 24p. pap. 11.49 (978-1-4389-8532-9(0)) AuthorHouse.

Wan, Joyce. Hug You, Kiss You, Love You. Wan, Joyce, illus. 2013. (ENG., Illus.). 14p. (J). (— 1). bds. 7.99 (978-0-545-54045-2(3), Cartwheel Bks.) Scholastic, Inc.

—My Lucky Little Dragon. Wan, Joyce, illus. 2014. (ENG., Illus.). 14p. (J). (— 1). bds. 6.99 (978-0-545-54046-9(1), Cartwheel Bks.) Scholastic, Inc.

—You Are My Cupcake. Wan, Joyce, illus. 2011. (ENG., Illus.). 14p. (J). (gr. k — 1). bds. 6.99 (978-0-545-30741-3(4), Cartwheel Bks.) Scholastic, Inc.

Wang, Dorothea DePrisco & Imperato, Teresa. All the Ways I Love You. Downing, Julie, illus. 2005. (ENG.). 10p. (J). bds. 8.95 (978-1-58117-190-7(0), Intervisual/Piggy Toes) Bendon, Inc.

Warburton, Carol. Edge of Night: A Novel. 2004. (Illus.). 278p. pap. 14.95 (978-1-59156-013-5(6)) Covenant Communications, Inc.

Ward, Heather Patricia & Ward, Heather Patricia. I Promise I'll Find You. McGraw, Sheila & McGraw, Sheila, illus. 2005. (ENG.). 32p. (J). (gr. -1-2). pap. 6.95 (978-1-55209-094-7(9), 53401c50-b9a8-447e-8d14-0c9c07c96875) Firefly Bks., Ltd.

Ward, Nick. The Ice Child. Bailey, Peter, tr. Bailey, Peter, illus. 2003. 32p. (YA). (978-1-84365-004-1(5), Pavilion Children's Books) Pavilion Bks.

Wardlaw, Lee. Coreys Fire. 2006. pap. 12.95 (978-0-595-40170-3(8), Backinprint.com) iUniverse, Inc.

Watase, Yuu. Absolute Boyfriend, Vol. 3, 6 vols. 2007. (Absolute Boyfriend Ser.: 3). (ENG., Illus.). 200p. pap. 9.99 (978-1-4215-1003-3(0)) Viz Media.

Watson, Kate. Lovestruck. 2019. (ENG.). 352p. (YA). (gr. 9-12). pap. 14.99 (978-1-63583-030-9(3), 1635830303, Flux) North Star Editions.

Watt, Fiona. I Love You, Baby. MacKinnon, Catherine-Anne, illus. 2008. (Snuggletime Touchy-Feely Ser.). 10p. (J). (gr. -1-k). bds. 8.99 (978-0-7945-2071-7(5), Usborne) EDC Publishing.

Watts, Frances. Kisses for Daddy. Legge, David, illus. 2008. (ENG.). 24p. (J). bds. (978-1-921272-56-1(2)) Little Hare Bks. AUS. Dist: HarperCollins Pubs. Australia.

Weatherly, L. A. Angel Burn. 2011. (Angel Ser.: 1). (ENG., Illus.). 464p. (YA). (gr. 9). pap. 9.99 (978-0-7636-5846-5(4)); 17.99 (978-0-7636-5652-2(6)) Candlewick Pr.

—Angel Fever. 2013. (Angel Ser.: 3). (ENG.). 496p. (YA). (gr. 9). 17.99 (978-0-7636-5680-5(1)) Candlewick Pr.

—Angel Fire. 2012. (Angel Ser.: 2). (ENG., Illus.). 656p. (YA). (gr. 9). 17.99 (978-0-7636-5679-9(8)) Candlewick Pr.

Webster, Jean. Daddy-Long-Legs. 2004. reprint ed. pap. 1.99 (978-1-4192-1490-5(X)); pap. 19.95 (978-1-4191-1490-8(5)) Kessinger Publishing, LLC.

—Jerry Junior. 2005. pap. (978-1-4065-0014-1(3)) Dodo Pr.

Weimer, Heidi. You're My Little Love Bug! 2013. (ENG., Illus.). 12p. (gr. -1). bds. 12.99 (978-1-891100-29-1(7), Smart Kids) Penton Overseas, Inc.

Weimer, Heidi R. Love from My Heart: To a Precious Sweet Little Girl. 2005. (ENG., Illus.). 14p. (J). (gr. -1-3). bds. 12.99 (978-0-8249-6655-3(4), Ideals Pubns.) Worthy Publishing.

—Love from My Heart: To a Snuggly Cuddly Little Boy. 2005. (Parent Love Letters Ser.). (ENG., Illus.). 14p. (J). (gr. -1-3). bds. 12.99 (978-0-8249-6654-6(6), Ideals Pubns.) Worthy Publishing.

Weinberg, Jennifer Liberts. Princess Hearts (Disney Princess) Legramandi, Francesco, illus. 2012. (Step into Reading Ser.). (ENG.). 32p. (J). (gr. -1-1). pap. 5.99 (978-0-7364-3013-5(X), RH/Disney) Random Hse. Children's Bks.

Weingarten, Lynn. The Book of Love. 2013. (ENG.). 272p. (YA). (gr. 8). 17.99 (978-0-06-192620-4(5), HarperTeen) HarperCollins Pubs.

—The Secret Sisterhood of Heartbreakers. 2011. (ENG.). 352p. (YA). (gr. 8). 17.99 (978-0-06-192618-1(3), HarperTeen) HarperCollins Pubs.

Weisenberg, Marit. Select Few. 2018. (Select Ser.: 2). 384p. (YA). (gr. 9). 17.99 (978-1-58089-829-4(7), Charlesbridge Teen) Charlesbridge Publishing, Inc.

Weiss, Sonya. Reckoning. 2016. (ENG., Illus.). 210p. (J). pap. 15.00 (978-1-60183-730-1(5)) Kensington Publishing Corp.

—Rising. 2017. (ENG., Illus.). (YA). pap. 15.00 (978-1-5161-0028-6(X)) Kensington Publishing Corp.

Wekelo, Kerry Alison. Audrey's Journey: Playful Namaste. 2012. 16p. pap. 15.99 (978-1-4772-7207-7(0)) AuthorHouse.

Welch, Jenna Evans. Love & Gelato. (ENG., Illus.). 400p. (YA). (gr. 7). 2017. pap. 11.99 (978-1-4814-3255-9(9)) 2016. 19.99 (978-1-4814-3254-2(0)) Simon Pulse. (Simon Pulse).

Welford, Sue. Secret Love. l.t. ed. 2006. pap. (978-1-905665-10-5(5)) Pollinger In Print.

Wells, Carolyn. Patty at Home. 2007. (ENG.). 204p. per. 12.95 (978-1-4218-3321-7(2)) 1st World Publishing, Inc.

Wells, Rosemary. Love Waves. Wells, Rosemary, illus. 2011. (ENG., Illus.). 32p. (J). (gr. -1-2). 15.99 (978-0-7636-4989-0(9)) Candlewick Pr.

—Love Waves: Midi Edition. Wells, Rosemary, illus. 2012. (ENG., Illus.). 32p. (J). (gr. k — 1). 8.99 (978-0-7636-6224-0(0)) Candlewick Pr.

West, Casey. To Nicole with Love. Miller, Fujiko, illus. 2003. (Romance Ser.). 60p. (J). pap. 4.95 (978-1-58659-188-5(6)) Artesian Pr.

West, Kasie. By Your Side. 2017. (ENG.). 352p. (YA). (gr. 8). pap. 12.99 (978-0-06-245586-4(9), HarperTeen) HarperCollins Pubs.

—Maybe This Time. 2019. (ENG., Illus.). 368p. (YA). (gr. 7-7). 17.99 (978-1-338-21008-8(4)) Scholastic, Inc.

—Pivot Point. 2013. (Pivot Point Ser.: 1). (ENG.). 384p. (YA). (gr. 8). pap. 9.99 (978-0-06-211736-6(X), HarperTeen) HarperCollins Pubs.

Westerfeld, Scott. Afterworlds. 2014. (ENG., Illus.). 608p. (YA). (gr. 9). 19.99 (978-1-4814-2234-5(0), Simon Pulse) Simon Pulse.

—Afterworlds. 2015. lib. bdg. 24.50 (978-0-606-37860-4(X)) Turtleback.

Westover, Steve. A Nothing Named Silas. 2013. 304p. (J). 17.99 (978-1-4621-1165-7(3)) Cedar Fort, Inc./CFI Distribution.

Wettersten, Laura. My Faire Lady. 2014. (ENG., Illus.). 352p. (YA). (gr. 7). 17.99 (978-1-4424-8933-2(2), Simon & Schuster Bks. For Young Readers) Simon & Schuster Bks. For Young Readers.

Weyland, Jack. Brianna, My Brother, & the Blog. 2009. (YA). (978-1-60641-140-7(3)) Deseret Bk. Co.

Weyn, Suzanne & Gonzalez, Diana. South Beach Sizzle. 2005. (Romantic Comedies Ser.). (ENG.). 272p. (YA). (gr. 9). mass mkt. 5.99 (978-1-4169-0011-5(X), Simon Pulse) Simon Pulse.

What Is Hidden. 2014. 281p. (YA). pap. 16.99 (978-1-4621-1429-0(6)) Cedar Fort, Inc./CFI Distribution.

Whitcomb, Laura. Under the Light. (ENG.). 256p. (YA). (gr. 7). 2014. pap. 8.99 (978-0-544-30294-5(X), 1578440) 2013. 17.99 (978-0-547-36754-5(6), 1422685) HarperCollins Pubs. (Clarion Bks.).

White Driscoll, Heather. He Calls Me Harp. 2013. 456p. 26.95 (978-1-4575-2229-1(2)); pap. 19.95 (978-1-4575-2086-0(9)) Dog Ear Publishing, LLC.

White, E. B. & DiCamillo, Kate. Charlotte's Web: a Harper Classic. Williams, Garth, illus. 2017. (Harper Classic Ser.). (ENG.). 208p. (J). (gr. 3-7). 16.99 (978-0-06-265875-3(1), HarperCollins) HarperCollins Pubs.

White, Sarah. Let Me List the Ways. 2018. (ENG.). 304p. (YA). (gr. 9). pap. 9.99 (978-0-06-247315-8(8), HarperCollins) HarperCollins Pubs.

Widmayer, Paul E. Bessie & Bo: The Story of a Mother's Love. 2013. 20p. pap. 12.45 (978-1-4908-0300-5(9), WestBow Pr.) Author Solutions, LLC.

Wiggin, Kate Douglas. The Old Peabody Pew. 2009. 60p. pap. 7.95 (978-1-60664-315-0(0)) Rodgers, Alan Bks.

Wilde, Jen. Queens of Geek. 2017. (ENG.). 288p. (YA). pap. 12.99 (978-1-250-11139-5(0), 900169956) Feiwel & Friends.

Wildsmith, Sarah. Princess Charming. 2013. (ENG., Illus.). 32p. (-12). pap. 14.99 (978-1-62380-970-6(3), Harmony Ink Pr.) Dreamspinner Pr.

Wilhelm, Hans. Yo Siempre te Quierre. (SPA.). 296p. (J). 13.95 (978-84-261-2404-3(6)) Juventud, Editorial ESP. Dist: AIMS International Bks., Inc.

Wilkerson, L. Kobie, 3rd, reader. Fred & Mary. 2008. (Illus.). 32p. (J). 24.95 incl. DVD, audio compact disk (978-0-9796679-0-9(9)) Love II Learn Bks.

Wilkinson, Lili. Green Valentine. 2016. (ENG.). 288p. (YA). (gr. 9-12). 12.99 (978-1-76011-027-7(2)) Allen & Unwin AUS. Dist: Independent Pubs. Group.

Wilkinson, Simon. Noah's Ark Black & White Visual Development Book for Babies. 2008. 34p. pap. 17.95 (978-1-4092-4702-9(3)) Lulu Pr., Inc.

Williams, Alison. Pink Cat Blue Cat. 2009. (Illus.). 32p. pap. 14.49 (978-1-4389-4623-8(6)) AuthorHouse.

Williams, Avery. The Alchemy of Forever. 2012. (ENG.). 368p. (YA). (gr. 7). pap. 9.99 (978-1-4424-4317-4(0), Simon & Schuster Bks. For Young Readers) Simon & Schuster Bks. For Young Readers.

Williams, C. B. Walkers. 2012. 118p. pap. 6.95 (978-0-9881814-0-3(1)) ALCHEMY RANCH STUDIOS LLC.

Williams, Erika. Through the Shattered Glass, 1 vol. 2010. 62p. pap. 19.95 (978-1-4489-5149-9(6)) America Star Bks.

Williams, Jamie L. Mommy's Little Helper, 1 vol. 2010. 26p. 24.95 (978-1-4512-9232-9(5)) PublishAmerica, Inc.

Williams, Margery. The Velveteen Rabbit. Berg, Maria, illus. 2018. (ENG.). 36p. (J). (gr. k-5). 24.95 (978-1-60025-124-5(2)) Bassett, Maurice.

—The Velveteen Rabbit. 2017. (ENG., Illus.). (J). (gr. k-2). pap. 4.95 (978-1-68422-087-8(4)) Martino Fine Bks.

—The Velveteen Rabbit. 2018. (ENG., Illus.). 24p. (J). 9.99 (978-1-5154-2926-5(1)) Wilder Pubns., Corp.

—Velveteen Rabbit. Nicholson, William, illus. ed. 2022. (ENG.). 48p. (J). (gr. -1-k). pap. 8.99 (978-1-4052-1054-6(0)) Farshore GBR. Dist: HarperCollins Pubs.

Williams, Nicole. Almost Impossible. 2018. 272p. (YA). (gr. 9). pap. 9.99 (978-0-553-49881-3(9), Crown Books For Young Readers) Random Hse. Children's Bks.

—Clash, 2. 2012. (Crash Ser.: 2). (ENG.). 288p. (YA). (gr. 11). pap. 9.99 (978-0-06-226715-3(9), HarperCollins) HarperCollins Pubs.

—Crash, 1. 2012. (Crash Ser.: 1). (ENG.). 384p. (YA). (gr. 11). pap. 9.99 (978-0-06-226714-6(0), HarperCollins) HarperCollins Pubs.

—Crush, 3. 2013. (Crash Ser.: 3). (ENG.). 400p. (YA). (gr. 11). pap. 9.99 (978-0-06-226717-7(5), HarperCollins) HarperCollins Pubs.

Willis, Jeanne. Never Too Little to Love. Fearnley, Jan, illus. 2013. (ENG.). 32p. (J). (gr. -1-2). 9.99 (978-0-7636-6656-9(4)) Candlewick Pr.

Wilson, Barbara Rogers. Deva & the Soul Snatcher an Environmental Fantasy. 2nd ed. 2013. 216p. pap. 11.95 (978-0-9834956-9-7(6), SpiritBooks) Portal Ctr. Pr.

Wilson, Budge. The Courtship, 1 vol. unabr. ed. 2003. (ENG.). 160p. (YA). (gr. 7-18). mass mkt. (978-0-7736-7456-1(X)) Fitzhenry & Whiteside, Ltd.

Wilson, Jacqueline. Kiss: A Novel. 2010. (ENG., Illus.). 256p. (YA). (gr. 7-12). 33.99 (978-1-59643-242-0(X), 900042189) Roaring Brook Pr.

Wilson, Ricky Derail. Mirror of Hope Mirror of Fame. 2007. 32p. per. 12.95 (978-1-4327-1391-1(4)) Outskirts Pr., Inc.

Wilson, W. Shane. War for Ice. 2010. 158p. pap. 13.99 (978-0-557-23572-8(3)) Lulu Pr., Inc.

Wind, Chuck T. The Test of Love. 2011. 24p. pap. 24.95 (978-1-4626-2398-3(0)) America Star Bks.

Winegardner, Suze. Anya & the Shy Guy. 2015. (ENG., Illus.). 230p. (J). pap. 15.49 (978-1-943336-62-3(8)) Entangled Publishing, LLC.

Wise, Rachel. Breaking News. 2013. (Dear Know-It-All Ser.: 10). (ENG., Illus.). 160p. (J). (gr. 3-7). 15.99 (978-1-4424-8965-3(0)); pap. 7.99 (978-1-4424-8964-6(2)) Simon Spotlight. (Simon Spotlight).

—Cast Your Ballot! 2013. (Dear Know-It-All Ser.: 9). (ENG., Illus.). 160p. (J). (gr. 3-7). 15.99 (978-1-4424-8793-2(3)); pap. 5.99 (978-1-4424-8792-5(5)) Simon Spotlight. (Simon Spotlight).

Wittlinger, Ellen. Lombardo's Law. 2003. (ENG.). 144p. (J). (gr. 5-7). pap. 10.95 (978-0-618-31108-8(4), 498750, Clarion Bks.) HarperCollins Pubs.

—Razzle. 2003. (ENG.). 256p. (YA). (gr. 7). pap. 12.99 (978-0-689-85600-6(8), Simon & Schuster Bks. For Young Readers) Simon & Schuster Bks. For Young Readers.

Wolf, Ema. 18 Cuentos de Amor.Tr. of 18 Short Love Stories. (SPA.). (J). pap. (978-950-07-1107-4(9)) Editorial Sudamericana S.A.

Wolf, Sara. Love Me Never. 2016. (Lovely Vicious Ser.: 1). (ENG.). 304p. (J). pap. 9.99 (978-1-63375-229-0(1), 900154724) Entangled Publishing, LLC.

Wood, Douglas. When a Dad Says "I Love You" Bell, Jennifer A., illus. 2013. (ENG.). 32p. (J). (gr. -1-3). 19.99 (978-0-689-87532-8(0), Simon & Schuster Bks. For Young Readers) Simon & Schuster Bks. For Young Readers.

—When a Grandpa Says "I Love You" Bell, Jennifer A., illus. 2014. (ENG.). 32p. (J). (gr. -1-3). 18.99 (978-0-689-81512-6(3), Simon & Schuster Bks. For Young Readers) Simon & Schuster Bks. For Young Readers.

Woods, Darcy. Summer of Supernovas. 2017. 352p. (YA). (gr. 9). 9.99 (978-0-553-53706-2(7), Ember) Random Hse. Children's Bks.

Woodson, Jacqueline. If You Come Softly. 2010. (ENG.). 224p. (YA). (gr. 7-18). 9.99 (978-0-14-241522-1(7), Penguin Books) Penguin Young Readers Group.

X, Sulayman & Sulayman, X. Tears of a Dragon. 2nd ed. 2016. (ENG., Illus.). (J). 29.99 (978-1-63533-079-3(3), Harmony Ink Pr.) Dreamspinner Pr.

Yasko, Carmen R. Buddy & His Buddies. 2012. 40p. pap. 22.65 (978-1-4797-4710-8(6)) Xlibris Corp.

Yolen, Jane. How Do Dinosaurs Say I Love You? Teague, Mark, illus. (J). 2020. (ENG.). 34p. (gr. -1 — 1). bds. 7.99 (978-1-338-71282-7(9), Cartwheel Bks.) 2011. pap. (978-0-545-33076-3(9)) 2009. (ENG.). 40p. (gr. -1 — 1). 17.99 (978-0-545-14314-1(4), Blue Sky Pr., The) Scholastic, Inc.

Yoon, Nicola. Everything, Everything. (ENG.). (YA). (gr. 7). 2017. 352p. pap. 13.99 (978-0-553-49667-3(0), Ember) 2015. (Illus.). 336p. 18.99 (978-0-553-49664-2(6), Delacorte Pr.) Random Hse. Children's Bks.

—Everything, Everything. 2017. lib. bdg. 22.10 (978-0-606-40341-2(8)) Turtleback.

—The Sun Is Also a Star. (ENG.). 384p. (YA). (gr. 7). 2019. pap. 12.99 (978-0-553-49671-0(9), Ember) 2016. 19.99 (978-0-553-49668-0(9), Delacorte Pr.) Random Hse. Children's Bks.

—The Sun Is Also a Star Movie Tie-In Edition. 2019. (ENG.). 384p. (YA). (gr. 7). pap. 12.99 (978-1-9848-4939-7(5), Ember) Random Hse. Children's Bks.

Yoon, Salina. Penguin in Love. (Penguin Ser.). (ENG., Illus.). (J). (gr. -1-1). 2014. 34p. bds. 7.99 (978-0-8027-3758-8(7), 900135684) 2013. 40p. 14.99 (978-0-8027-3600-0(9), 900123419) Bloomsbury Publishing USA. (Bloomsbury USA Childrens).

Young, Adrienne. Sky in the Deep. (Sky & Sea Ser.: 1). (ENG.). (YA). 2019. 368p. pap. 11.99 (978-1-250-16846-7(5), 900187700) 2018. 352p. 18.99 (978-1-250-16845-0(7), 900187699) St. Martin's Pr. (Wednesday Bks.).

—Sky in the Deep. l.t. ed. 2020. (Sky & Sea Ser.: 1). (ENG.). lib. bdg. 22.99 (978-1-4328-7818-4(2)) Thorndike Pr.

Young, Ann Eastman. Once Blue. 2011. (ENG.). 108p. pap. 15.00 (978-0-557-71193-2(2)) Lulu Pr., Inc.

Young, Leslie. Plaid: A Tale of Compassion. 2006. (Illus.). 15p. 9.00 (978-1-4120-2793-9(4)) Trafford Publishing.

Young, Suzanne. The Adjustment. 2017. (Program Ser.: 5). (ENG., Illus.). 416p. (YA). (gr. 9). 19.99 (978-1-4814-7132-9(5), Simon Pulse) Simon Pulse.

—The Adjustment. 2018. (Program Ser.: 5). (ENG., Illus.). 480p. (YA). (gr. 9). pap. 12.99 (978-1-4814-7133-6(3), Simon Pulse) Simon Pulse.

—The Complication. (Program Ser.: 6). (ENG.). (YA). (gr. 9). 2019. 496p. pap. 12.99 (978-1-4814-7136-7(8)) 2018. (Illus.). 464p. 17.99 (978-1-4814-7135-0(X)) Simon Pulse. (Simon Pulse).

—The Program. (Program Ser.: 1). (ENG., Illus.). (YA). (gr. 9). 2014. 432p. pap. 12.99 (978-1-4424-4581-9(5)) 2013. 416p. 19.99 (978-1-4424-4580-2(7)) Simon Pulse. (Simon Pulse).

—The Treatment. (Program Ser.: 2). (ENG., Illus.). (YA). (gr. 9). 2015. 368p. pap. 12.99 (978-1-4424-4584-0(X)) 2014. 352p. 19.99 (978-1-4424-4583-3(1)) Simon Pulse. (Simon Pulse).

Young, T. M. What's Love Got to Do with It. Vickie Washington and Carla Watts, ed. Cromwell, Danielle, illus. 2013. 32p. pap. 24.95 (978-1-4626-0889-8(2)) America Star Bks.

Young, Tonya. Here's to the Nights. 2011. 190p. pap. 19.99 (978-1-4628-8707-1(4)) Xlibris Corp.

Younge-Ullman, Danielle. Lola Carlyle's 12-Step Romance. 2015. (ENG.). 304p. (YA). pap. 9.99 (978-1-62266-785-7(9), 9781622667857) Entangled Publishing, LLC.

Yung, Kao & Liang, Kuan. Magic Lover's Tower, Vol. 2. 2008. (Magic Lover's Tower Ser.). (ENG., Illus.). 176p. (YA). (gr. 8). pap. 9.95 (978-1-59796-154-7(X)) DrMaster Pubns. Inc.

Yunisa. Schoolaholic Princess 2: Romansa Singapura. 2008. 232p. pap. 14.88 (978-1-4357-6044-8(1)) Lulu Pr., Inc.

Zafon, Carlos. Marina. 2011. (FRE.). (YA). (gr. 8-12). pap. (978-2-266-21302-8(4)) Le Robert.

Zafon, Carlos Ruiz. Marina. 2014. (ENG.). 336p. (YA). (gr. 7-17). 34.99 (978-0-316-04471-4(7)) Little, Brown Bks. for Young Readers.

Zink, Michelle. A Walk in the Sun. 2016. (ENG.). 336p. (YA). (gr. 8). 17.99 (978-0-06-243446-3(2), HarperTeen) HarperCollins Pubs.

Zuckerman, Linda. I Will Hold You 'Til You Sleep. Muth, Jon J., illus. 2006. (J). *(978-0-439-43421-8(1),* Levine, Arthur A. Bks.) Scholastic, Inc.

LOVE (THEOLOGY)

Boynton, Jeannette. God Loves Variety. Boynton, Jeannette & Holdeen, Bonnie, illus. 2007. (J). per. 10.99 *(978-1-59879-264-5(4))* Lifevest Publishing, Inc.

Cope, Dorothy. The Day Star: A Love Spirit, 1 vol. 2009. 30p. pap. 24.95 *(978-1-60749-729-5(8))* America Star Bks.

Murad, Khurram. Love at Home. 2007. (ENG., Illus.). 48p. pap. 3.95 *(978-0-86037-122-9(0))* Kube Publishing Ltd. GBR. Dist: Consortium Bk. Sales & Distribution.

Student Life Staff. 31 Verses - Love: Every Teenager Should Know. 2008. 76p. (YA). pap. 4.99 *(978-1-935040-11-8(1))* NavPress Publishing Group.

LOVE POETRY

Berry, George B. The Compassionate Side of a Common Man: Love Poems from the Heart, Vol. 3. unabr. ed. 2004. 120p. (YA). pap. 12.99 *(978-0-9720308-6-1(7))* Mindfull Publishing Co.

Berry, Ron. The 123s of How I Love You. Sharp, Chris, illus. 2012. 24p. (J). bds. 12.99 *(978-0-8249-1601-5(8),* Ideals Pubns.) Worthy Publishing.

Boynton, Sandra. Consider Love. Boynton, Sandra, illus. 2013. (ENG., Illus.). 32p. (J). (gr. -1-3). 14.99 *(978-1-4424-9465-7(4))* Simon & Schuster, Inc.

Nino, Jairo Anibal. La Alegría de Querer: Poemas de Amor para Ninos. Acosta, Patricia, illus. 2010. (Literatura Juvenil (Panamericana Editorial) Ser.). (SPA.). 70p. (gr. 4-6). pap. 9.99 *(978-958-30-0293-9(3),* PV30142) Panamericana Editorial COL. Dist: Lectorum Pubns., Inc.

Prelutsky, Jack. It's Valentine's Day! 2013. (I Can Read! Level 3 Ser.). (J). lib. bdg. 13.55 *(978-0-606-32174-7(8))* Turtleback.

Weeks, Sarah. Be Mine, Be Mine, Sweet Valentine. Kosaka, Fumi, illus. 2005. (ENG.). 20p. (J). (gr. -1-k). 9.99 *(978-0-694-01514-6(8),* HarperFestival) HarperCollins Pubs.

Young, Ed. Should You Be a River: A Poem about Love. 2015. (ENG.). 40p. (J). (gr. -1-3). 18.00 *(978-0-316-23089-6(8))* Little, Brown Bks. for Young Readers.

LOW, JULIETTE GORDON, 1860-1927

Aller, Susan Bivin. Juliette Low. 2007. (History Maker Biographies Ser.). (Illus.). 48p. (J). (gr. 3-7). lib. bdg. 26.60 *(978-0-8225-6580-2(3),* Lerner Pubns.) Lerner Publishing Group.

Corey, Shana. Here Come the Girl Scouts!: the Amazing All-True Story of Juliette 'Daisy' Gordon Low & Her Great Adventure. Hooper, Hadley, illus. 2012. (ENG.). 40p. (J). (gr. -1-3). 18.99 *(978-0-545-34278-0(3),* Scholastic Pr.) Scholastic, Inc.

Hally, Ashleigh. Juliette Gordon Low. 2012. (Illus.). 24p. (J). *(978-1-935884-77-4(8));* pap. *(978-1-935884-83-5(2))* State Standards Publishing, LLC.

LOW TEMPERATURES

Strazzabosco, John. Extreme Temperatures: Learning about Positive & Negative Numbers, 1 vol. (Math for the REAL World Ser.). (ENG., 32p. (gr. 4-5). 2010. illus.). pap. 10.00 *(978-0-8239-8927-0(5),* dbc52991-0b18-498d-a2c9-4c78dfd2c7cd, PowerKids Pr.) 2004. 47.50 *(978-0-8239-7649-2(1))* Rosen Publishing Group, Inc., The.

LOYALTY

Raatma, Lucia. Loyalty. 2009. (21st Century Junior Library: Character Education Ser.). (ENG., Illus.). 24p. (gr. 2-5). lib. bdg. 29.21 *(978-1-60279-326-2(3),* 200222) Cherry Lake Publishing.

LOYALTY—FICTION

Barchers, Suzanne. The Brave Servant: A Tale from China. Han, Yu-Mei, illus. 2013. (Tales of Honor Ser.). (ENG.). 32p. (J). (gr. 1-3). pap. 8.99 *(978-1-937529-57-4(6),* 5347fe48-e5c0-4a2c-8c2c-1f6f58064513); E-Book 39.99 *(978-1-936163-89-2(6))* Red Chair Pr.

Bates, Michelle. Dream Pony. 2010. (Sandy Lane Stables Ser.). 100p. (J). pap. 4.99 *(978-0-7945-2537-8(7),* Usborne) EDC Publishing.

Bowser, Ken. Hal & Al: Self-Esteem. Bowser, Ken, illus. 2016. (Funny Bone Readers (tm) — Truck Pals on the Job Ser.). (ENG., Illus.). 24p. (J). (gr. k-2). E-Book 30.65 *(978-1-63440-070-1(4))* Red Chair Pr.

Castner, K. D. Daughters of Ruin. 2017. (ENG.). 320p. (YA). (gr. 9). pap. 11.99 *(978-1-4814-3666-3(X),* McElderry, Margaret K. Bks.) McElderry, Margaret K. Bks.

Charles, Rie. No More Dragons. 2010. (ENG., Illus.). 112p. (J). (gr. 5-7). pap. 9.95 *(978-1-926607-12-2(0),* Napoleon & Co.) Dundurn Pr. CAN. Dist: Publishers Group West (PGW).

Clements, Andrew. Lost & Found. Elliott, Mark, illus. 2008. (ENG.). 176p. (J). (gr. 3-7). 18.99 *(978-1-4169-0985-9(0),* Atheneum Bks. for Young Readers) Simon & Schuster Children's Publishing.

Cleveland, Rob. The Bear, the Bat & the Dove: Three Stories from Aesop. Hoffmire, Baird, illus. 2006. (Story Cove Ser.). (ENG.). 32p. (J). (gr. -1-3). pap. 3.95 *(978-0-87483-810-7(X))* August Hse. Pubs., Inc.

Daley, Pj. Roger & the Giant People: Roger meets Giant People. 2011. 20p. pap. *(978-1-4269-6824-2(8))* Trafford Publishing (UK) Ltd.

Elliott, David. This Orq. (He Cave Boy.) Nichols, Lori, illus. 2014. (ENG.). 40p. (J). (gr. -1-2). 15.95 *(978-1-62091-521-9(9),* Astra Young Readers) Astra Publishing Hse.

Ellis, Deborah. The Breadwinner. 2015. (Breadwinner Ser.: 1). lib. bdg. 20.80 *(978-0-606-37232-9(6))* Turtleback.

Gallant, Mark D. Christmas at Wildwood Farm. 2010. 140p. 22.49 *(978-1-4520-2808-8(7));* pap. 11.99 *(978-1-4520-2807-1(9))* AuthorHouse.

Gosling, Cherie & Disney Storybook Artists Staff. Mulan Is Loyal: Merida Is Brave. 2017. (Illus.). 24p. (J). *(978-1-5379-5745-6(7))* Random Hse., Inc.

Gunderson, Jessica. Full Court Pressure, 1 vol. Ruiz, Jose, illus. 2010. (Sports Illustrated Kids Graphic Novels Ser.). (ENG.). 56p. (J). (gr. 3-8). 26.65 *(978-1-4342-1911-4(9),* 102370); pap. 7.19 *(978-1-4342-2291-6(8),* 103160) Capstone. (Stone Arch Bks.)

Gunnery, Sylvia. Out of Bounds. 2004. (Sports Stories Ser.). (ENG.). 104p. (J). (gr. 3-8). *(978-1-55028-827-8(X))* James Lorimer & Co. Ltd., Pubs. CAN. Dist: Casemate Pubs. & Bk. Distributors, LLC.

Harbo, Christopher. Batman Is Loyal. Schigiel, Gregg, illus. 2019. (DC Super Heroes Character Education Ser.). (ENG.). 24p. (J). (gr. k-2). lib. bdg. 27.32 *(978-1-5158-4019-0(0),* 139806, Stone Arch Bks.) Capstone.

Jack, Gordon. The Boomerang Effect. 2018. (ENG.). 368p. (YA). (gr. 9). pap. 11.99 *(978-0-06-239940-3(3),* HarperTeen) HarperCollins Pubs.

Jebiwool Art Museum Staff. Destination Blackbeard: Destinations in Time, Book 2, 1 vol. 2009. 101p. pap. 19.95 *(978-1-60749-626-7(7))* America Star Bks.

Keeble, Helen. Fang Girl. 2012. (ENG.). 352p. (YA). (gr. 8). pap. 9.99 *(978-0-06-208225-1(6),* HarperTeen) HarperCollins Pubs.

Kraatz, Jeramey. The Cloak Society. (Cloak Society Ser.: 1). (ENG.). (J). (gr. 3-7). 2013. 304p. pap. 7.99 *(978-0-06-209548-0(X))* 2012. 288p. 16.99 *(978-0-06-209547-3(1))* HarperCollins Pubs. (HarperCollins).

—Villains Rising. 2013. (Cloak Society Ser.: 2). (ENG.). 320p. (J). (gr. 3-7). 16.99 *(978-0-06-209550-3(1),* HarperCollins) HarperCollins Pubs.

Lackey, Mercedes & Edghill, Rosemary. Shadow Grail #3: Sacrifices. 2013. (Shadow Grail Ser.: 3). (ENG.). 304p. (YA). (gr. 8-12). pap. 17.99 *(978-0-7653-1763-6(X),* 900041776, Tor Teen) Doherty, Tom Assocs., LLC.

Lavender, William. Just Jane: A Daughter of England Caught in the Struggle of the American Revolution. 2005. (Great Episodes Ser.). (ENG.). 336p. (YA). (gr. 7-12). pap. 15.95 *(978-0-15-205472-4(3),* 1196465, Clarion Bks.) HarperCollins Pubs.

Leibenkop, T. The Sovereign of the Northern Winds. 2009. 30p. pap. 13.50 *(978-1-60693-847-8(9),* Eloquent Bks.) Strategic Book Publishing & Rights Agency (SBPRA).

MacKenzie, Catherine. The Lonely Grey Dog at No. 6: Tammy & Jake Learn about Love & Loyalty. 2005. (Tales from Canterbury Place Ser.). (ENG., Illus.). 160p. (J). per. 6.99 *(978-1-84550-103-7(9),* a4bd088c-1dae-4739-9ad1-c7f64ed9439d) Christian Focus Pubns. GBR. Dist: Baker & Taylor Publisher Services (BTPS).

Maddox, Jake. Tae Kwon Do Clash. 2016. (Jake Maddox JV Ser.). (ENG., Illus.). 96p. (J). (gr. 4-6). lib. bdg. 26.65 *(978-1-4965-3981-6(8),* 133204, Stone Arch Bks.) Capstone.

Marchetta, Melina. Quintana of Charyn: The Lumatere Chronicles. 2013. (Lumatere Chronicles Ser.: 3). (ENG.). 528p. (YA). (gr. 9). 18.99 *(978-0-7636-5835-9(9))* Candlewick Pr.

Milan, Maura. Eclipse the Skies. 2019. (Ignite the Stars Ser.: 2). (ENG.). 400p. (YA). (gr. 8-12). 17.99 *(978-0-8075-3636-4(5),* 807536385) Whitman, Albert & Co.

—Ignite the Stars. (Ignite the Stars Ser.: 1). (ENG.). 400p. (YA). (gr. 8-12). 2019. pap. 9.99 *(978-0-8075-3627-8(X),* 080753627X) 2018. 17.99 *(978-0-8075-3625-4(3),* 807536253) Whitman, Albert & Co.

Orietta, Susan. The Day Tyson Became a Hero. 2011. 24p. pap. 15.99 *(978-1-4628-6823-0(1))* Xlibris Corp.

Ott, Alexandra. The Shadow Thieves. 2018. (Rules for Thieves Ser.: 2). (ENG., Illus.). 400p. (J). (gr. 3-7). 17.99 *(978-1-4814-7277-7(1),* Aladdin) Simon & Schuster Children's Publishing.

Pantelides, Sherry. It's Blue Like You! A Story about Loyalty. Perez, Debi, illus. 2007. 32p. (J). 12.99 *(978-0-9771076-1-2(2))* Lacey Productions.

Park, Linda Sue. When My Name Was Keoko. 2004. 199p. (J). (gr. 5). 14.65 *(978-0-7569-2928-2(8))* Perfection Learning Corp.

Patterson, James & Dembowski, Jill. The Kiss. 2013. (Witch & Wizard Ser.: 4). (ENG.). 368p. (YA). (gr. 7-17). 35.99 *(978-0-316-10191-2(5),* Jimmy Patterson) Little Brown & Co.

Porter, Pamela. The Crazy Man. 2013. 164p. pap. *(978-1-4596-6446-3(9))* ReadHowYouWant.com, Ltd.

Purday, Paul. The Two Lands. 2006. 310p. (J). pap. *(978-1-905809-11-0(5))* Pneuma Springs Publishing.

Schick, Joel, illus. The Jungle Book: A Story about Loyalty. 2006. (J). 6.99 *(978-1-59939-023-9(X))* Cornerstone Pr.

Shemtov, Yael. Sadie's Funny Feeling. 2009. 24p. pap. 16.99 *(978-1-4389-6023-4(9))* AuthorHouse.

Soto, Gary. Chato Goes Cruisin' Guevara, Susan, illus. 2008. (Chato Ser.). (J). 25.95 incl. audio *(978-1-59519-906-5(3))* Live Oak Media.

—Chato Goes Cruisin' Guevara, Susan, illus. 2007. (Chato Ser.). (J). (gr. -1-3). 14.65 *(978-0-7569-8147-1(6))* Perfection Learning Corp.

Standish, Burt L. Frank Merriwell's Faith. Rudman, Jack, ed. 2003. (Frank Merriwell Ser.). 29.95 *(978-0-8373-9360-5(4));* pap. 9.95 *(978-0-8373-9060-4(5))* Merriwell, Frank Inc.

Townsend, Jessica. Wundersmith: The Calling of Morrigan Crow. (Nevermoor Ser.: 2) (ENG.). (J). (gr. 3-7). 2019. 560p. pap. 8.99 *(978-0-316-50892-6(6))* 2018. 544p. 17.99 *(978-0-316-50891-9(8))* 2018. 720p. 48.99 *(978-0-316-41990-1(7))* Little, Brown Bks. for Young Readers.

Turner, Megan Whalen. The King of Attolia. (Queen's Thief Ser.: 3). (ENG.). (YA). (gr. 8). 2017. 432p. pap. 10.99 *(978-0-06-264298-1(7))* 2007. 432p. pap. 7.99 *(978-0-06-083579-8(6))* 2006. 400p. 17.99 *(978-0-06-083577-4(X))* HarperCollins Pubs. (Greenwillow Bks.).

—The King of Attolia. 2007. (Queen's Thief Ser.: BK.3). 387p. (YA). 18.00 *(978-0-7569-8106-8(9))* Perfection Learning Corp.

—The King of Attolia. (YA). 2008. (Queen's Thief Ser.: BK.3). (ENG.). 84.49 *(978-1-4281-8027-7(3))* 2007. (Attolia Ser.: 3). 119.75 *(978-1-4281-1722-8(9))* 2007. (Queen's Thief Ser.: BK.3). (ENG.). 92.75 *(978-1-4281-1716-7(4))* 2006. (Queen's Thief Ser.: BK.3). (ENG.). 90.75 *(978-1-4281-1718-1(0))* 2006. (Queen's Thief Ser.: BK.3). (ENG.). 122.75 *(978-1-4281-1720-4(2))* 2006. (Queen's Thief Ser.: BK.3). (ENG.). 1.25 *(978-1-4281-1713-6(X))* 2006. (Queen's Thief Ser.: BK.3). 281.75 *(978-1-4281-1721-1(0))* 2006. (Queen's Thief Ser.: BK.3). (ENG.). 251.75 *(978-1-4281-1717-4(2))* Recorded Bks., Inc.

Van Gorder, Vivian Ezeife. Master Kofi & Friskey the Dog. 2012. 20p. pap. 17.99 *(978-1-4772-6817-9(0))* AuthorHouse.

Vrabel, Beth. Pack of Dorks. 2014. (Pack of Dorks Ser.: 1). (ENG.). 240p. (J). (gr. 2-7). 15.95 *(978-1-62914-623-2(4),* Sky Pony Pr.) Skyhorse Publishing Co., Inc.

Wibberley, Leonard. Peter Treegate's War. 2009. (ENG.). 134p. (J). (gr. 10-12). pap. 12.95 *(978-1-932350-21-0(7))* Ignatius Pr.

Wilson, John. Battle Scars: The American Civil War, Part Two. 2016. (Fields of Conflict Ser.). (ENG.). 192p. (YA). (gr. 8-12). pap. 12.95 *(978-1-77203-093-8(7),* Wandering Fox) Heritage Hse. CAN. Dist: Orca Bk. Pubs. USA.

Yeamans Simrell, Elizabeth. Only Mr. Bromley Will Do. 2008. 26p. 14.25 *(978-0-615-22279-0(X))* Dash & Doodles Productions.

Young, Adrienne. Sky in the Deep. (Sky & Sea Ser.: 1). (ENG.). (YA). 2019. 368p. pap. 11.99 *(978-1-250-16846-7(5),* 900187700) 2018. 352p. 18.99 *(978-1-250-16845-0(7),* 900187699) St. Martin's Pr. (Wednesday Bks.).

—Sky in the Deep. Lt. ed. 2020. (Sky & Sea Ser.: 1). (ENG.). lib. bdg. 22.99 *(978-1-4328-7818-4(2))* Thorndike Pr.

LOYOLA, IGNACIO DE, SAINT, 1491-1556

see Ignatius, of Loyola, Saint, 1491-1556

LSD (DRUG)

LeVert, Suzanne. The Facts about Facts about LSD, 1 vol. 2007. (Facts about Drugs Ser.). (ENG., Illus.). 128p. (gr. 6-6). 45.50 *(978-0-7614-1974-7(8),* 204d61f5-f9a4-40e5-827d-97284bbdcc7d) Cavendish Square Publishing LLC.

Petechuk, David. LSD. 2004. (Drug Education Library). (Illus.). 112p. (J). (gr. 7-10). 32.45 *(978-1-59018-417-2(3))* Cengage Gale.

LUDINGTON, SYBIL, 1761-1839

Marsico, Katie. Sybil Ludington's Revolutionary War Story. Girard, Thomas, illus. 2018. (Narrative Nonfiction: Kids in War Ser.). (ENG.). 32p. (J). (gr. 2-4). pap. 9.99 *(978-1-5415-1194-1(8),* cec45b0f-080d-4da3-ab6d-0c870f19cc2b); lib. bdg. 27.99 *(978-1-5124-5676-9(4),* 5eb11b74-cf07-4032-890a-7cd3011602d0, Lerner Pubns.) Lerner Publishing Group.

Schiffman, Jessica, illus. Sybil Ludington: Freedom's Brave Rider. 2005. 32p. (J). pap. *(978-0-7367-2931-4(3))* Zaner-Bloser, Inc.

LULLABIES

Aigner-Clark, Julie. Baby Einstein: Lullabies & Sweet Dreams. 2007. (Baby Einstein Ser.). (ENG.). (J). (gr. -1). *(978-0-7634-2151-9(0))* Walt Disney Records.

Balmer, Paul & Music Sales Corporation Staff. Lullaby Songbook. 2009. (ENG., Illus.). 104p. (J). 9.95 *(978-1-84772-582-0(1),* AM993861) Wise Pubns. GBR. Dist: Music Sales Corp.

Bang, Molly. Ten, Nine, Eight: A Caldecott Honor Award Winner. Bang, Molly, illus. 2003. (ENG., Illus.). 24p. (J). (gr. -1-3). reprint ed. pap. 7.99 *(978-0-688-10480-1(0));* 20th ed. 16.99 *(978-0-688-00906-9(9))* HarperCollins Pubs. (Greenwillow Bks.).

Barber, Jill. Baby's Lullaby, 1 vol. Rose, Hilda, illus. 2010. (ENG.). 16p. (J). (gr. -1 — 1). bds. 8.95 *(978-1-55109-795-4(8),* 8de545f4-8d17-4cd1-b9eb-6ee864ca5d34) Nimbus Publishing, Ltd. CAN. Dist: Baker & Taylor Publisher Services (BTPS).

Baxter, Nicola. Bedtime Lullabies: Fall Asleep to Your Free Cd. Finn, Rebecca, illus. 2014. 12p. (J). (gr. -1-12). bds. 14.99 *(978-1-86147-360-8(5),* Armadillo) Anness Publishing GBR. Dist: National Bk. Network.

Beaton, Clare. Mrs. Moon: Lullabies for Bedtime. 2003. (ENG., Illus.). 48p. (J). 19.99 *(978-1-84148-176-0(9))* Barefoot Bks., Inc.

Brown, Petra, illus. Hush, Little Baby. 2007. (Padded Hardcover Ser.). 18p. (J). 8.95 *(978-1-58925-819-8(3))* Tiger Tales.

Chatelain, Jeremy. May the Stars Drip Down. McClure, Nikki, illus. 2014. (ENG.). 40p. (J). (gr. -1-2). 17.95 *(978-1-4197-1024-7(9),* 698101, Abrams Bks. for Young Readers) Abrams, Inc.

DaySpring Greeting Card Staff & Jensen, Bonnie Rickner. Really Woolly Nighttime Lullabies, 1 vol. 2015. (Really Woolly Ser.). (ENG., Illus.). 40p. (J). bds. 9.99 *(978-0-7180-2295-2(5),* Tommy Nelson) Nelson, Thomas Inc.

Delacre, Lulu. Arrorro, Mi Nino: Latino Lullabies & Gentle Games, 1 vol. 2004. (ENG., Illus.). 32p. (J). 16.95 *(978-1-58430-159-2(7))* Lee & Low Bks., Inc.

Dorrian, James G., contrib. by. Lullabys for Starry Nights. (J). pap. 10.98 *(978-0-9647786-1-0(0),* 3001-4) Baby Music Boom, Inc.

God Is with You in Sleep. Date not set. 44p. (J). (gr. -1-5). 16.99 incl. audio compact disk *(978-0-9702219-0-2(8))* Bowden Music Co.

Heath, Beverly C. A Bedtime Lullaby. Floyd, John, Jr., illus. 2006. 9p. (J). (gr. -1). bds. 5.95 *(978-0-9752860-1-2(3))* OurRainbow Pr., LLC.

Ho, Minfong. Hush! A Thai Lullaby. 2004. (Illus.). (J). (gr. -1-1). spiral bd. *(978-0-616-08497-7(8))* Canadian National Institute for the Blind/Institut National Canadien pour les Aveugles.

Ho, Mingfong. Hush! A Thai Lullaby. Meade, Holly, illus. 2004. (J). (gr. -1-1). spiral bd. *(978-0-616-07255-4(4))* Canadian National Institute for the Blind/Institut National Canadien pour les Aveugles.

Hodges, Lynn & Buchanan, Sue. I Love You This Much, 1 vol. Bendall-Brunello, John, illus. (ENG.). (J). 2010. 36p. pap. 6.99 *(978-0-310-72265-6(9))* 2005. 16p. (gr. -1). bds. 8.99 *(978-0-310-70961-9(X))* Zonderkidz.

Hogan, Micki. A Midnight's Lullaby: Volume One. Brown, Bobby, illus. 2011. 40p. pap. 24.95 *(978-1-4560-2090-3(0))* America Star Bks.

Hughes, Langston. Lullaby (for a Black Mother) Qualls, Sean, illus. 2013. (ENG.). 32p. (J). (gr. -1-3). 17.99 *(978-0-547-36265-6(X),* 1421855, Clarion Bks.) HarperCollins Pubs.

Lacoursiere, Patrick. Dream Songs Night Songs: From Mali to Louisiana. Bourbonnière, Sylvie & Bourbonnière, Sylvie, illus. 2006. (ENG.). 36p. (J). (gr. -1-2). 16.95 *(978-2-923163-06-2(0))* La Montagne Secrete CAN. Dist: Independent Pubs. Group.

López, Oscar J., illus. Sing along with Abuelita Rosa: Hispanic Lullabies = Canciones de Cuna. 2006. (ENG & SPA.). 13p. (J). *(978-0-9788379-0-7(8))* Baby Abuelita Productions, Inc.

Myers, Stephanie L. Bedtime Lullaby for Baby. 2008. 16p. pap. 10.49 *(978-1-4389-0278-4(6))* AuthorHouse.

Nelson, Alexis Andria. Sing Mommie Sing: Lullabies from the Heart. 2010. 36p. 21.99 *(978-1-4490-9405-8(8))* AuthorHouse.

Our Time: Lullabies for those special Moments. 2010. 56p. pap. 23.99 *(978-1-4490-8172-0(X))* AuthorHouse.

Seeger, Pete. One Grain of Sand: A Lullaby. Wingerter, Linda, illus. 2005. 30p. (J). (gr. -1-4). reprint ed. 16.00 *(978-0-7567-8586-4(3))* DIANE Publishing Co.

Stohs, Anita Reith. Hush, Little One: A Lullaby for God's Children. Kanzler, John, tr. Kanzler, John, illus. 2004. 32p. (J). 12.99 *(978-0-570-07144-0(5))* Concordia Publishing Hse.

—Hush Little One: A Lullaby for God's Children. Kanzler, John, illus. 2006. 20p. (J). (gr. -1). bds. 5.49 *(978-0-7586-0861-1(6))* Concordia Publishing Hse.

Stuart, Kelly. Cancion de Cuna de la Virgen de Guadalupe. Caban, Carlos, tr. from ENG. Caban, Carlos, illus. 2003. (SPA.). 28p. (J). *(978-1-931721-18-9(1))* Night Heron Media.

Studio Mouse Staff. Mother Goose Lullabies. de La Cour, Gary et al, illus. rev. ed. 2007. (ENG.). 24p. (J). 4.99 *(978-1-59069-559-3(3))* Studio Mouse LLC.

Tucker, Jill C. Dylan Rides the Sleepy Town Express, 1 vol. 2010. 43p. pap. 24.95 *(978-1-4489-2165-2(1))* PublishAmerica, Inc.

Van Camp, Richard. Welcome Song for Baby: A Lullaby for Newborns, 1 vol. 2007. (ENG., Illus.). 24p. (J). (gr. -1 — 1). bds. 12.95 *(978-1-55143-661-6(2))* Orca Bk. Pubs. USA.

Watt, Fiona. Baby's First Christmas. 2009. (Baby Board Books with CD Ser.). 10p. (J). (gr. -1). bds. 14.99 *(978-0-7945-1902-5(4),* Usborne) EDC Publishing.

Williams, Sarajane. Dreamtime: Lullabies for Lever & Pedal Harp, 1 vol. 2004. (ENG., Illus.). 32p. pap. 14.99 *(978-0-7866-7192-2(0))* Mel Bay Pubns., Inc.

Zoboli, Giovanna. The Big Book of Slumber. Mulazzani, Simona, illus. 2014. (ENG.). 26p. (J). 16.00 *(978-0-8028-5439-1(7),* Eerdmans Bks For Young Readers) Eerdmans, William B. Publishing Co.

LUMBER AND LUMBERING

see also Forests and Forestry; Trees; Wood

Brainard, Jason. Operating Farms & Logging Companies, 1 vol. 2018. (Impacting Earth: How People Change the Land Ser.). (ENG.). 24p. (gr. 2-2). pap. 9.25 *(978-1-5383-4196-4(4),* c2c4485d-829c-4e46-8a4b-6aa585861b9f, PowerKids Pr.) Rosen Publishing Group, Inc., The.

Cowan, Mary Morton. Timberrr! A History of Logging in New England. 2003. (Women at War Ser.). (Illus.). 128p. (gr. 5-18). lib. bdg. 25.90 *(978-0-7613-1866-8(6),* Twenty-First Century Bks.) Lerner Publishing Group.

Gordon, Nick. Lumberjack. 2012. (Dangerous Jobs Ser.). (ENG., Illus.). 24p. (J). (gr. 3-7). lib. bdg. 26.95 *(978-1-60014-780-7(1),* Torque Bks.) Bellwether Media.

Hamlin, John. Tales of an Old Lumber Camp: A Story of Early Days in A Great Industry. Bernard, C. E. B., illus. 2011. 188p. 42.95 *(978-1-258-04052-9(2))* Literary Licensing, LLC.

Johnston, Marianne. Paul Bunyan. 2009. (American Legends Ser.). 24p. (gr. 3-3). 42.50 *(978-1-61511-385-9(1),* PowerKids Pr.) Rosen Publishing Group, Inc., The.

Kostecki-Shaw, Jenny Sue. Luna & Me: The True Story of a Girl Who Lived in a Tree to Save a Forest. Kostecki-Shaw, Jenny Sue, illus. 2015. (ENG., Illus.). 40p. (J). (gr. k-4). 19.99 *(978-0-8050-9976-8(X),* 900128928, Holt, Henry & Co. Bks. For Young Readers) Holt, Henry & Co.

McClure, Jason & Whelan, Piper. Forests. 2017. (Illus.). 24p. (J). *(978-1-5105-1054-8(0))* SmartBook Media, Inc.

Nagle, Jeanne. A Career in Mining & Logging, 1 vol. 2018. (Jobs for Rebuilding America Ser.). (ENG.). 80p. (gr. 6-6). 38.80 *(978-1-5081-7999-3(9),* 43187897-4a54-4c22-8525-37e4cea72418) Rosen Publishing Group, Inc., The.

Rae, Alison. Trees & Timber Products. 2010. (Development Without Damage Ser.). (YA). (gr. 5-9). 34.25 *(978-1-59920-247-1(6))* Black Rabbit Bks.

Thomas, Aaron. Logs & Lumber: From the Forest to Your Home, 1 vol. 2008. (Real Life Readers Ser.). (ENG.). 16p. (gr. 2-3). pap. 7.05 *(978-1-4358-0069-4(9),* 5250cc63-b038-47a8-86e9-4376af506465, Rosen Classroom) Rosen Publishing Group, Inc., The.

Zimm, John. John Nelligan: Wisconsin Lumberjack. 2015. (Badger Biographies Ser.). (ENG., Illus.). 80p. (J). (gr. 4-6). pap. 12.95 *(978-0-87020-698-6(2))* Wisconsin Historical Society.

LUMBER AND LUMBERING—FICTION

Briggs, Andy. Tarzan: The Greystoke Legacy. 2011. (ENG.). 304p. pap. 8.99 *(978-0-571-27238-9(X))* Faber & Faber, Ltd.

Horne, Constance. The Tenth Pupil. 2005. (ENG., Illus.). 160p. (J). (gr. 3-9). pap., tchr. ed. 8.95 *(978-0-921870-86-9(8))* Ronsdale Pr. CAN. Dist: Literary Pr. Group of Canada.

Jennings, Patrick. Wish Riders. 2008. (ENG.). 288p. pap. 6.99 *(978-1-4231-0015-7(8))* Hyperion Pr.

Johnson, Lois Walfrid. Trouble at Wild River. 2009. (J). 8.99 *(978-0-88062-279-0(2))* Mott Media.

LUMINESCENCE, ANIMAL

see Bioluminescence

LUNAR EXPEDITIONS

see Space Flight to the Moon

LUNAR EXPLORATION

see Moon—Exploration

LUNAR PROBES

see also names of space projects, e.g. Mariner Project; etc.

Morey, Allan. Lunar Probes. 2017. (Space Tech Ser.). (ENG., Illus.). 24p. (J). (gr. 3-7). lib. bdg. 26.95 *(978-1-62617-702-4(3),* Epic Bks.) Bellwether Media.

LUNCH ROOMS

see Restaurants

LUNCHEONS

Arnez, Lynda. We Make Lunch, 1 vol. 2019. (We Can Be Responsible! Ser.). (ENG.). 24p. (gr. k-k). pap. 9.15 *(978-1-5382-3915-5(9),* 9a36f03d-86ac-4c3e-b79b-e2e2f291de12) Stevens, Gareth Publishing LLLP.

Aunt Louisa is coming for Lunch: Individual Title Six-Packs. (gr. 1-2). 25.00 *(978-0-7635-9128-1(9))* Rigby Education.

Chambers, Catherine. What's for Lunch? White Band. 2017. (Cambridge Reading Adventures Ser.). (ENG., Illus.). 24p. pap. 8.60 *(978-1-108-41187-5(8))* Cambridge Univ. Pr.

Greathouse, Lisa. What's for Lunch?, 1 vol. 2nd rev. ed. 2011. (TIME for KIDS(r): Informational Text Ser.). (ENG., Illus.). 28p. (gr. 2-3). pap. 10.99 *(978-1-4333-3639-3(1))* Teacher Created Materials, Inc.

Green, Gail & Peschke, Marci. Lunch Recipe Queen. Mourning, Tuesday, illus. 2018. (Kylie Jean Recipe Queen Ser.). (ENG.). 32p. (J). (gr. 1-3). lib. bdg. 27.99 *(978-1-5158-2848-8(4),* 138397, Picture Window Bks.) Capstone.

Griffin Llanas, Sheila. Easy Lunches from Around the World, 1 vol. 2011. (Easy Cookbooks for Kids Ser.). (ENG., Illus.). 48p. (gr. 3-3). pap. 11.53 *(978-1-59845-272-3(X),* 7921eaae-6a2c-4fe8-af7f-439caf5f783a); lib. bdg. 27.93 *(978-0-7660-3708-3(8),* 8643ec25-7895-41c2-9043-0d07d5940eae) Enslow Publishing, LLC. (Enslow Elementary).

Kalman, Bobbie. Lunch Munch: Step-by-Step Recipes. 2003. (Kid Power Ser.). (ENG., Illus.). 32p. (J). (gr. 3). pap. *(978-0-7787-1273-2(7));* lib. bdg. *(978-0-7787-1251-0(6))* Crabtree Publishing Co.

Lunch Around the World: Inside the U. S. A. 2009. (Inside the USA Ser.). (Illus.). 16p. (C). pap. 14.95 *(978-0-7362-7060-1(4))* National Geographic School Publishing, Inc.

Storey, Rita. A Tasty Lunch. 2014. (Plan, Prepare, Cook Ser.). 32p. (gr. 3-6). 31.35 *(978-1-59920-954-8(3))* Black Rabbit Bks.

Thomson, Sarah L. What's for Lunch? Aye, Nila, illus. 2016. (Let's-Read-And-Find-Out Science 1 Ser.). (ENG.). 40p. (J). (gr. -1-3). pap. 6.99 *(978-0-06-233137-3(X),* HarperCollins) HarperCollins Pubs.

Vega, Ali. Tombstone Sandwiches & Other Horrifying Lunches. 2017. (Little Kitchen of Horrors Ser.). (ENG., Illus.). 32p. (J). (gr. 2-5). 26.65 *(978-1-5124-2577-2(X),* e4c1b81e-4c10-47b6-818e-1302cef9b067); E-Book 39.99 *(978-1-5124-3773-7(5),* 9781512437737); E-Book 39.99 *(978-1-5124-2807-0(8));* E-Book 26.65 *(978-1-5124-3774-4(3),* 9781512437744) Lerner Publishing Group. (Lerner Pubns.).

LUTHER, MARTIN, 1483-1546

Baden, Marian. Martin Luther: Life & Legacy - Grade 3-4 Student Book. 2017. (ENG.). (J). pap. 5.25 *(978-0-7586-5918-7(0))* Concordia Publishing Hse.

—Martin Luther: Life & Legacy - Grade 5-6 Student Book. 2017. (ENG.). (J). pap. 5.25 *(978-0-7586-5919-4(9))* Concordia Publishing Hse.

—Martin Luther: Life & Legacy - Grade 7-8 Student Book. 2017. (ENG.). (J). pap. 5.25 *(978-0-7586-5920-0(2))* Concordia Publishing Hse.

—Martin Luther: Life & Legacy - K-2 Student Book. 2017. (ENG.). (J). pap. 5.25 *(978-0-7586-5917-0(2))* Concordia Publishing Hse.

Bodden, Valerie. The Assassination of Martin Luther King Jr. 2016. (Turning Points Ser.). (ENG., Illus.). 48p. (J). (gr. 4-7). pap. 12.00 *(978-1-62832-334-6(4),* 20805, Creative Paperbacks) Creative Co., The.

Hollingsworth, Tamara. Martin Luther: A Reforming Spirit, 1 vol. rev. ed. 2012. (Social Studies: Informational Text Ser.). (ENG.). 32p. (gr. 4-8). pap. 11.99 *(978-1-4333-5010-8(6))* Teacher Created Materials, Inc.

Nohl, Frederick. Martin Luther: Hero of Faith. Hook, Richard, illus. 2003. 160p. (YA). pap. 9.99 *(978-0-7586-0592-4(7))* Concordia Publishing Hse.

Rijswijk, Cor van. Martin Shows the Way. 2004. (Illus.). 43p. (J). *(978-1-894666-80-0(1))* Inheritance Pubns.

Roth-Beck, Meike. The Life & Times of Martin Luther. Ensikat, Klaus, illus. 2017. (ENG.). 44p. (J). *(978-0-8028-5495-7(8),* Eerdmans Bks For Young Readers) Eerdmans, William B. Publishing Co.

Seymour, Michaela. Why Do We Celebrate Martin Luther King Jr. Day?, 1 vol. 2018. (Celebrating U. S. Holidays Ser.). (ENG.). 24p. (gr. 1-1). 25.27 *(978-1-5081-6655-9(2),* fc5617b7-c6c0-4ab7-82d6-af2a94468e64, PowerKids Pr.) Rosen Publishing Group, Inc., The.

LUTZ, FRANK EUGENE, 1879-1943

Pallister, John C. In the Steps of the Great American Entomologist. Elgin, Kathleen, illus. 2014. (ENG.). 128p. (J). (gr. 2-6). pap. 11.95 *(978-1-59077-364-2(0))* Evans, M. & Co., Inc.

LUXEMBOURG

Sheehan, Patricia. Luxembourg, 1 vol. 2017. (Cultures of the World (Third Edition)(r) Ser.). (ENG.). 144p. (gr. 5-5). lib. bdg. 48.79 *(978-1-5026-2743-8(4),* f879082e-a69c-4d09-8843-23c1f71f9901) Cavendish Square Publishing LLC.

Sheehan, Patricia & Dhilawala, Sakina. Luxembourg, 1 vol. 2nd rev. ed. 2008. (Cultures of the World (Second Edition)(r) Ser.). (ENG.). 144p. (gr. 5-5). lib. bdg. 49.79 *(978-0-7614-2088-0(6),* 30837f8d-b58b-47d1-8b79-ff148c49c507) Cavendish Square Publishing LLC.

Simons, Rae. Luxembourg. 2007. (European Union Ser.). (Illus.). 88p. (YA). (gr. 3-7). lib. bdg. 21.95 *(978-1-4222-0055-1(8))* Mason Crest.

Simons, Rae & Indovino, Shaina Carmel. Luxembourg. 2012. (J). *(978-1-4222-2251-5(9));* pap. *(978-1-4222-2282-9(9))* Mason Crest.

LYING

see Truthfulness and Falsehood

LYLE THE CROCODILE (FICTITIOUS CHARACTER)—FICTION

Novel Units. Lyle, Lyle, Crocodile Novel Units Teacher Guide. 2019. (Lyle the Crocodile Ser.). (ENG.). (J). (gr. -1-3). pap., tchr. ed. 12.99 *(978-1-56137-327-7(3),* Novel Units, Inc.) Classroom Library Co.

Waber, Bernard. Lyle, Lyle, Crocodile. 2022. (Lyle the Crocodile Ser.). (ENG., Illus.). 48p. (J). (gr. -1-3). pap. 7.99 *(978-0-395-13720-8(9),* 497521); tchr. ed. 19.99 *(978-0-395-16995-7(X),* 597524) HarperCollins Pubs. (Clarion Bks.).

LYME DISEASE

Donelly, Karen. Coping with Lyme Disease. 2009. (Coping Ser.). 192p. (gr. 7-12). 63.90 *(978-1-61512-002-4(5))* Rosen Publishing Group, Inc., The.

Fox, Nancy. Hide & Seek, No Ticks Please: No Ticks, Please. Seward, Daniel, illus. 2014. (ENG.). 42p. (gr. k-6). pap. 9.95 *(978-1-61448-705-0(7))* Morgan James Publishing.

Kelly, Shannon. Lyme Disease, 1 vol. 2011. (Diseases & Disorders Ser.). (ENG., Illus.). 104p. (gr. 7-7). lib. bdg. 41.53 *(978-1-4205-0635-8(8),* 540ca494-b324-4d8f-ae56-78b40bb8427a, Lucent Pr.) Greenhaven Publishing LLC.

Williams, Mary E., ed. Lyme Disease, 1 vol. 2011. (Perspectives on Diseases & Disorders Ser.). (ENG., Illus.). 152p. (gr. 10-12). 45.93 *(978-0-7377-5777-4(9),* 77dfd24b-cf01-4177-8a6d-a9097e736f8a, Greenhaven Publishing) Greenhaven Publishing LLC.

LYNX

Borgert-Spaniol, Megan. Canada Lynx. 2017. (North American Animals Ser.). (ENG., Illus.). 24p. (J). (gr. k-3). lib. bdg. 26.95 *(978-1-62617-635-5(3),* Blastoff! Readers) Bellwether Media.

Haakonsen, Jens. Lynx Chase, Hares Dash, 1 vol. 2017. (Hunter & Hunted: Animal Survival Ser.). (ENG.). 24p. (J). (gr. 3-3). 25.27 *(978-1-5081-5664-2(6),* 17f2f6ae-49fe-4b7b-9cc7-12f4efaf168c, PowerKids Pr.) Rosen Publishing Group, Inc., The.

Klukow, Mary Ellen. A Wild Cat's Shrinking Home. Pinilla, Albert, illus. 2019. (Animal Habitats at Risk Ser.). (ENG.). 24p. (J). (gr. 1-3). pap. 9.99 *(978-1-68152-488-7(0),* 11074) Amicus.

Parker, Barbara Keevil & Parker, Duane F. Lynxes. 2005. (Early Bird Nature Bks.). (ENG., Illus.). 48p. (gr. 2-5). lib. bdg. 26.60 *(978-0-8225-2871-5(1),* Lerner Pubns.) Lerner Publishing Group.

Randall, Henry. Lynxes, 1 vol. 2011. (Cats of the Wild Ser.). (ENG.). 24p. (J). (gr. 1-2). pap. 9.25 *(978-1-4488-2619-3(5),* adeca459-cd27-4d45-8de3-74eb9c2da67d); lib. bdg. 26.27 *(978-1-4488-2517-2(2),* 3064b6f0-9c5b-4ff2-b97a-b997c3dc4464) Rosen Publishing Group, Inc., The. (PowerKids Pr.).

—Lynxes: Linces, 1 vol. 2011. (Cats of the Wild / Felinos Salvajes Ser.). (SPA & ENG., Illus.). 24p. (gr. 1-2). lib. bdg. 26.27 *(978-1-4488-3129-6(6),* 4d53a55f-0df1-4f6d-89bb-42fb25580468) Rosen Publishing Group, Inc., The.

LYNX—FICTION

Fox, L. B. The Adventures of Marky, Slash & Levy. 2006. (ENG.). 184p. per. 24.95 *(978-1-4241-4992-6(4))* PublishAmerica, Inc.

LYSERGIC ACID DIETHYLAMIDE

see LSD (Drug)

M

MACARTHUR, DOUGLAS, 1880-1964

Benge, Janet & Benge, Geoff. Heroes of History - Douglas MacArthur: What Greater Honor. 2005. (ENG., Illus.). 205p. (YA). pap. 11.99 *(978-1-932096-15-6(9))* Emerald Bks.

McPherson, Stephanie Sammartino. Douglas MacArthur. 2005. (History Maker Bios Ser.). (Illus.). 48p. (J). 26.60 *(978-0-8225-2434-2(1))* Lerner Publishing Group.

MACCABEES

Balsley, Tilda. Maccabee! The Story of Hanukkah. Harrington, David, illus. 2010. (ENG.). 32p. (J). (gr. -1-2). pap. 7.95 *(978-0-7613-4508-4(6),* 95a9a473-6004-474c-b632-f61511ce963d, Kar-Ben Publishing) Lerner Publishing Group.

Raabe, Emily. A Hanukkah Holiday Cookbook. 2009. (Festive Foods for the Holidays Ser.). 24p. (gr. 3-3). 42.50 *(978-1-61512-595-1(7),* PowerKids Pr.) Rosen Publishing Group, Inc., The.

MCCAIN, JOHN, 1936-2018

Falk, Laine. Meet President John McCain. 2009. (J). *(978-0-531-23650-5(1))* Children's Pr., Ltd.

Horn, Geoffrey M. John Mccain, 1 vol. 2009. (People We Should Know (Second Series) Ser.). (ENG., Illus.). 32p. (J). (gr. 3-5). pap. 11.50 *(978-1-4339-0160-7(9),* fbdf5273-8ceb-4a6e-93dd-e54d3db41f8f); lib. bdg. 33.67 *(978-1-4339-0020-4(3),* 9a51add1-6bb7-4cac-bcd4-e17aafea87d6) Stevens, Gareth Publishing LLLP. (Gareth Stevens Learning Library).

Robinson, Tom. Barack Obama: 44th U. S. President, 1 vol. 2009. (Essential Lives Set 3 Ser.). (ENG., Illus.). 112p. (YA). (gr. 6-12). lib. bdg. 41.36 *(978-1-60453-527-3(X),* 6683, Essential Library) ABDO Publishing Co.

Schwartz, Heather E. John Mccain: The Courage of Conviction. 2018. (Gateway Biographies Ser.). (ENG., Illus.). 48p. (J). (gr. 4-8). lib. bdg. 31.99 *(978-1-5415-3839-9(0),* 1189939d-de06-4a0c-a070-19dbd43e5cbf, Lerner Pubns.) Lerner Publishing Group.

Wells, Catherine. John McCain. 2008. (Political Profiles Ser.). (Illus.). 112p. (YA). (gr. 5-9). lib. bdg. 27.95 *(978-1-59935-046-2(7))* Reynolds, Morgan Inc.

Wizner, Kira. John Mccain: Profile of a Leading Republican. 2007. 116p. (gr. 3-7). pap. 31.95 *(978-1-4358-3790-4(8))* Rosen Publishing Group, Inc., The.

MCCARTHY, JOSEPH, 1908-1957

Cunningham, Jesse G., ed. The McCarthy Hearings. 2003. (At Issue in History Ser.). (Illus.). 144p. (YA). (gr. 7-10). pap. 18.70 *(978-0-7377-1347-3(X),* Greenhaven Pr., Inc.) Cengage Gale.

Giblin, James Cross. The Rise & Fall of Senator Joe Mccarthy. 2009. (ENG., Illus.). 304p. (YA). (gr. 7-18). 22.00 *(978-0-618-61058-7(8),* 100444, Clarion Bks.) HarperCollins Pubs.

Hudak, Heather C. McCarthyism & the Red Scare. 2017. (Uncovering the Past: Analyzing Primary Sources Ser.). 48p. (J). (gr. 5-6). *(978-0-7787-3939-5(2))* Crabtree Publishing Co.

Immell, Myra, ed. The Mccarthy Era, 1 vol. 2011. (Perspectives on Modern World History Ser.). (ENG.). 184p. (gr. 10-12). lib. bdg. 49.43 *(978-0-7377-5260-1(2),* 9f2a225c-bbae-4f14-8e0c-b4f9b0d5cbd1, Greenhaven Publishing) Greenhaven Publishing LLC.

Tracy, Kathleen. The McCarthy Era. 2008. (Monumental Milestones Ser.). (Illus.). 48p. (YA). (gr. 4-7). lib. bdg. 29.95 *(978-1-58415-694-9(5))* Mitchell Lane Pubs.

Zeinert, Karen. McCarthyism & the Communist Scare in United States History, 1 vol. 2014. (In United States History Ser.). (ENG.). 96p. (gr. 5-5). 31.61 *(978-0-7660-6345-7(3),* 857a7b48-4b29-4d4e-8449-2f1fbc9ce0a8); pap. 13.88 *(978-0-7660-6346-4(1),* 4c26452c-05a6-48ab-91dc-21b46a12e8e8) Enslow Publishing, LLC.

MCCAULEY, MARY (LUDWIG) HAYS, 1754-1832

Marsh, Carole. Molly Pitcher. 2004. 12p. (gr. k-4). 2.95 *(978-0-635-02375-9(X))* Gallopade International.

MCCORMICK, CYRUS HALL, 1809-1884

Aldrich, Lisa J. Cyrus McCormick: And the Mechanical Reaper. 2004. (American Business Leaders Ser.). (Illus.). 112p. (YA). (gr. 6-12). 23.95 *(978-1-883846-91-6(9),* First Biographies) Reynolds, Morgan Inc.

Welch, Catherine A. Farmland Innovator: A Story about Cyrus Mccormick. Jones, Jan Naimo, illus. 2007. (Creative Minds Biographies Ser.). (ENG.). 64p. (gr. 4-8). lib. bdg. 22.60 *(978-0-8225-5988-7(9))* Lerner Publishing Group.

MCDUCK, SCROOGE (FICTITIOUS CHARACTER)—FICTION

Barks, Carl, et al. Uncle Scrooge #387. 2009. 64p. pap. 7.99 *(978-1-60360-087-3(6))* Gemstone Publishing, Inc.

—Uncle Scrooge #389. 2009. 64p. pap. 7.99 *(978-1-60360-089-7(2))* Gemstone Publishing, Inc.

—Walt Disney's Vacation Parade Volume 5. Clark, John, ed. 2008. (ENG., Illus.). 80p. pap. 9.95 *(978-1-60360-031-6(0),* 9781603600316) Gemstone Publishing, Inc.

Barosso, Abramo, et al. Uncle Scrooge #386. 2009. 64p. pap. 7.99 *(978-1-60360-086-6(8))* Gemstone Publishing, Inc.

Bottaro, Luciano & Chendi, Carlo. Disney Masters Vol. 2: Luciano Bottaro: Walt Disney's Donald Duck: Uncle Scrooge's Money Rocket. 2018. (Disney Masters Collection: 0). (ENG., Illus.). 192p. 29.99 *(978-1-68396-109-3(9),* 683109) Fantagraphics Bks.

McGreal, Pat & McGreal, Carol. Uncle Scrooge #385. 2008. 64p. pap. 7.99 *(978-1-60360-062-0(0))* Gemstone Publishing, Inc.

McGreal, Pat, et al. Uncle Scrooge #390. 2009. 64p. pap. 7.99 *(978-1-60360-090-3(6))* Gemstone Publishing, Inc.

Murry, Paul & Fallberg, Carl. Disney Masters Vol. 3: Paul Murry: Walt Disney's Mickey Mouse: the Case of the Vanishing Bandit. 2018. (Disney Masters Collection: 0). (ENG., Illus.). 184p. 29.99 *(978-1-68396-113-0(7),* 683113) Fantagraphics Bks.

Pujol, Miquel, et al. Uncle Scrooge #388. 2009. 64p. pap. 7.99 *(978-1-60360-088-0(4))* Gemstone Publishing, Inc.

Rosa, Don. Walt Disney Uncle Scrooge & Donald Duck: The Don Rosa Library Vol. 9: the Three Caballeros Ride Again! 2018. (Don Rosa Library: 0). (ENG., Illus.). 224p. 29.99 *(978-1-68396-102-4(1),* 683102) Fantagraphics Bks.

—Walt Disney Uncle Scrooge & Donald Duck: Treasure under Glass: The Don Rosa Library Vol. 3. 2015. (Don Rosa Library: 3). (ENG., Illus.). 192p. 29.99 *(978-1-60699-836-6(6),* 699836) Fantagraphics Bks.

MACEDONIA

Knowlton, MaryLee & Nevins, Debbie. North Macedonia, 1 vol. 3rd ed. 2020. (Cultures of the World (Third Edition)(r) Ser.). (ENG.). 144p. (J). (gr. 5-5). 48.79 *(978-1-5026-5589-9(6),* 451d5998-7f63-43b7-af20-c6918dcf18a3) Cavendish Square Publishing LLC.

MCGUIRE, LIZZIE (FICTITIOUS CHARACTER)—FICTION

Alfonsi, Alice. Lizzie for President. 2004. 149p. (J). lib. bdg. 16.92 *(978-1-4242-0681-0(2))* Fitzgerald Bks.

Alfonsi, Alice, adapted by. 'Rents: Lizzie Mcguire. 2005. 134p. (J). lib. bdg. 16.92 *(978-1-4242-0689-6(8))* Fitzgerald Bks.

Banim, Lisa. Hands off My Crush-Boy! 2004. 125p. (J). lib. bdg. 16.92 *(978-1-4242-0684-1(7))* Fitzgerald Bks.

—In the Doghouse. 2005. 124p. (J). lib. bdg. 16.92 *(978-1-4242-0685-8(5))* Fitzgerald Bks.

Banim, Lisa & Minsky, Terri. The Case of the Kate Haters. 2005. (Illus.). 124p. (J). *(978-1-4156-3927-6(2))* Disney Pr.

Jones, Jasmine, adapted by. The Importance of Being Gordo. 2005. (Illus.). 138p. (J). *(978-1-4155-7362-4(X))* Disney Pr.

—Importance of Being Gordo. 2005. 138p. (J). lib. bdg. 16.92 *(978-1-4242-0688-9(X))* Fitzgerald Bks.

—Just Like Lizzie. 2003. (Lizzie Mcguire Ser.). (Illus.). 153p. (J). 12.65 *(978-0-7569-2720-2(X))* Perfection Learning Corp.

—Oh, Brother! 2005. 146p. (J). lib. bdg. 16.92 *(978-1-4242-0682-7(0))* Fitzgerald Bks.

Jones, Jasmine & Alfonsi, Alice. My Second Way Cool, Set. 2nd gif. novel rev. ed. 2004. (ENG.). 144p. (gr. 3-7). 12.99 *(978-0-7868-4678-8(X))* Disney Pr.

Minsky, Terri. All over It! 2005. (Illus.). 138p. (J). *(978-1-4156-0271-3(9))* Disney Pr.

Minsky, Terri, creator. Lizzie McGuire Cine-Manga Vol. 2: Rumors & I've Got Rhythmic, 7 vols. 2003. (Lizzie McGuire Ser.: Vol. 2). (Illus.). 96p. (gr. 2-18). pap. 14.99 *(978-1-59182-148-9(7),* Tokyopop Kids) TOKYOPOP, Inc.

Papademetriou, Lisa. On the Job. 2005. (On the Job Ser.). (Illus.). 32p. (gr. 2-4). 138.00 *(978-0-7910-7408-4(0),* Facts On File) Infobase Holdings, Inc.

Papademetriou, Lisa & Minsky, Terri. A Very Lizzie Summer. 2005. (Lizzie Mcguire Super Special Ser.). (Illus.). 265p. (J). *(978-1-4155-9625-8(5))* Disney Pr.

MCGWIRE, MARK, 1963-

Kirkpatrick, Rob. Mark Mcgwire: Record Breaker/Rompe Records. 2009. (Power Players / Deportistas de Poder Ser.). (ENG & SPA.). 24p. (gr. 1-2). 42.50 *(978-1-60851-332-1(7),* Editorial Buenas Letras) Rosen Publishing Group, Inc., The.

—Mark Mcgwire: Rompe Récords (Record Breaker) 2009. (Deportistas de Poder (Power Players) Ser.). (SPA.). 24p. (gr. 1-1). 42.50 *(978-1-61512-159-5(5),* Editorial Buenas Letras) Rosen Publishing Group, Inc., The.

—Mark Mcgwire: The Home Run King. 2009. (Great Record Breakers in Sports Ser.). 24p. (gr. 3-3). 42.50 *(978-1-61513-188-4(4),* PowerKids Pr.) Rosen Publishing Group, Inc., The.

Rains, Rob & Smith, Ozzie. Cardinals Sports Heroes Block: City Block St. Louis: Mark Mcgwire, Ozzie Smith. 2004. (Illus.). 5.98 *(978-1-58261-858-6(5))* Sports Publishing, LLC.

Savage, Jeff. Mark McGwire: Home Run King. 2003. (Sports Achievers Biographies Ser.). (Illus.). 64p. (YA). (gr. 4-9). pap. 5.95 *(978-0-8225-9845-9(0),* Carolrhoda Bks.) Lerner Publishing Group.

MACHINERY

see also Agricultural Machinery; Engines; Inventions; Locomotives; Mechanical Drawing; Mechanics; Steam-Engines

ABDO Publishing Company Staff. Mighty Movers. 2005. (Mighty Movers Ser.). (gr. k-4). 153.90 *(978-1-59197-824-4(6),* Buddy Bks.) ABDO Publishing Co.

Abramovitz, Melissa & Alpert, Barbara. Military Machines. 2012. (Military Machines Ser.). (ENG.). 24p. (gr. k-1). pap. 250.20 *(978-1-4296-8319-7(8),* Capstone Pr.) Capstone.

Adams, Simon, et al. Discover the Savage World. 2013. (Illus.). 224p. (J). *(978-1-4351-4990-8(4))* Barnes & Noble, Inc.

Addison, D. R. Diggers at Work, 1 vol. 2009. (Big Trucks Ser.). (ENG., Illus.). 24p. (gr. 1-1). lib. bdg. 26.27 *(978-1-4358-2700-4(7),* 04601aa8-976a-4f08-a247-a1b8c607ce09) Rosen Publishing Group, Inc., The.

Adkins, Jan. Moving Heavy Things. Adkins, Jan, illus. 2004. (ENG., Illus.). 48p. (J). (gr. -1-3). pap. 13.95 *(978-0-937822-82-1(5))* WoodenBoat Pubns.

Adler, David A. Simple Machines: Wheels, Levers, & Pulleys. Raff, Anna, illus. (ENG.). 32p. (J). (gr. -1-3). 2016. 8.99 *(978-0-8234-3572-2(5))* 2015. 17.95 *(978-0-8234-3309-4(9))* Holiday Hse., Inc.

Allan, John. Let's Look at Monster Machines. 2019. (Illus.). 24p. (J). *(978-1-912108-16-9(X));* (ENG., (gr. 1-3). lib. bdg. 26.65 *(978-1-5415-5531-0(7),* e7a9cc92-4539-4b0e-a235-eb457f604693, Hungry Tomato (r)) Lerner Publishing Group.

Amazing Machines. 2004. (Sticker Timelines Ser.). (Illus.). 12p. (J). pap. *(978-1-84229-844-2(5))* Top That! Publishing PLC.

Ardagh, Philip. A Hole in the Road. (Illus.). 32p. (J). lib. bdg. 24.25 *(978-1-931983-02-0(X))* Chrysalis Education.

Arnold, Nick. Funtastic Forces & Incredible Machines. 2018. (STEM Quest Ser.). lib. bdg. 22.10 *(978-0-606-41261-2(1))* Turtleback.

Arnold, Quinn M. Backhoes. 2018. (Amazing Machines Ser.). (ENG., Illus.). 24p. (J). (gr. 1-4). *(978-1-60818-885-7(X),* 19498, Creative Education); pap. 8.99 *(978-1-62832-501-0(1),* 19496, Creative Paperbacks) Creative Co., The.

—Concrete Mixers. 2018. (Amazing Machines Ser.). (ENG., Illus.). 24p. (J). (gr. 1-3). pap. 10.99 *(978-1-62832-503-4(8),* 19523, Creative Paperbacks); *(978-1-60818-887-1(6),* 19525, Creative Education) Creative Co., The.

—Excavators. 2018. (Amazing Machines Ser.). (ENG., Illus.). 24p. (J). (gr. 1-3). pap. 10.99 *(978-1-62832-505-8(4),* 19563, Creative Paperbacks); *(978-1-60818-889-5(2),* 19562, Creative Education) Creative Co., The.

—Krupp Digging Machine. 2016. (Now That's Big! Ser.). (ENG., Illus.). 24p. (J). (gr. 1-3). *(978-1-60818-713-3(6),* 20638, Creative Education) Creative Co., The.

—Overburden Conveyor Bridge F60. 2016. (Now That's Big! Ser.). (ENG., Illus.). 24p. (J). (gr. 1-3). *(978-1-60818-716-4(0),* 20650, Creative Education) Creative Co., The.

AZ Books, creator. Construction Machines. 2012. (Lively Machines Ser.). (ENG., Illus.). 10p. (J). (gr. -1-k). bds. 10.95 *(978-1-61889-324-6(6))* AZ Bks. LLC.

—Everyday Machines. 2012. (Peep Inside Ser.). (ENG.). 10p. (J). (gr. -1-k). 12.95 *(978-1-61889-099-3(9))* AZ Bks. LLC.

—Magic Machines. 2012. (Baby Book Ser.). (ENG., Illus.). 10p. (J). (gr. -1 — 1). bds. 4.95 *(978-1-61889-286-7(X))* AZ Bks. LLC.

—Powerful Machines. 2012. (Peep Inside Ser.). (ENG., Illus.). 10p. (J). (gr. -1-k). 12.95 *(978-1-61889-102-0(2))* AZ Bks. LLC.

—Rescue Machines. 2012. (Peep Inside Ser.). (ENG., Illus.). 10p. (J). (gr. -1-k). 12.95 *(978-1-61889-100-6(6))* AZ Bks. LLC.

Bailey, Gerry. Powerful Machines, 1 vol. 2009. (Simply Science Ser.). (ENG., Illus.). 32p. (YA). (gr. 3-5). lib. bdg. 28.67 *(978-1-4339-0035-8(1),* 690398c4-ebd0-45df-971d-ecec03844ea5) Stevens, Gareth Publishing LLLP.

—Pressing Down: The Lever. Spoor, Mike, illus. 2014. (Robotx Get Help from Simple Machines Ser.). (ENG.). 32p. (J). (gr. 2-3). *(978-0-7787-0416-4(5));* pap. *(978-0-7787-0422-5(X))* Crabtree Publishing Co.

—Pulling Up: The Pulley. Spoor, Mike, illus. 2014. (Robotx Get Help from Simple Machines Ser.). (ENG.). 32p. (J). (gr. 2-3). *(978-0-7787-0417-1(3));* pap. *(978-0-7787-0423-2(8))* Crabtree Publishing Co.

—Rolling Along: Wheels & Axles. Spoor, Mike, illus. 2014. (Robotx Get Help from Simple Machines Ser.). (ENG.). 32p. (J). (gr. 2-3). *(978-0-7787-0418-8(1));* pap. *(978-0-7787-0424-9(6))* Crabtree Publishing Co.

—Splitting Apart: The Wedge. Spoor, Mike, illus. 2014. (Robotx Get Help from Simple Machines Ser.). (ENG.). 32p. (J). (gr. 2-3). *(978-0-7787-0420-1(3));* pap. *(978-0-7787-0426-3(2))* Crabtree Publishing Co.

—Winding Around: The Screw. Spoor, Mike, illus. 2014. (Robotx Get Help from Simple Machines Ser.). (ENG.). 32p. (J). (gr. 2-3). *(978-0-7787-0421-8(1));* pap. *(978-0-7787-0427-0(0))* Crabtree Publishing Co.

Bailey, Gerry & Law, Felicia. Sloping up & Down: The Ramp. Spoor, Mike, illus. 2014. (Robotx Get Help from Simple Machines Ser.). (ENG.). 32p. (J). (gr. 2-3). *(978-0-7787-0419-5(X));* pap. *(978-0-7787-0425-6(4))* Crabtree Publishing Co.

Baker, Wendy. Experimenta - Maquinas. (SPA.). 52p. (J). *(978-84-348-3997-7(0))* SM Ediciones.

M
N
O

Believe It Or Not!, Ripleys, compiled by. Ripley Twists PB: Mighty Machines. 2018. (Twist Ser.: 2). (ENG.). 48p. (J). pap. 7.99 *(978-1-60991-229-1(2))* Ripley Entertainment, Inc.

Bell, Samantha. Excavator. 2018. (21st Century Basic Skills Library: Level 1: Welcome to the Construction Site Ser.). (ENG., Illus.). 24p. (J). (gr. k-3). lib. bdg. 30.64 *(978-1-5341-2917-7(0)*, 211712) Cherry Lake Publishing.

—Road Roller. 2018. (21st Century Basic Skills Library: Level 1: Welcome to the Construction Site Ser.). (ENG., Illus.). 24p. (J). (gr. k-3). lib. bdg. 30.64 *(978-1-5341-2920-7(0)*, 211724) Cherry Lake Publishing.

Bender, Lionel. Diggers & Tractors. 2006. (J). *(978-1-59389-267-8(5))* Chrysalis Education.

Big Machines, 8 vols. 2016. (Big Machines Ser.). 32p. (ENG.). (gr. 1-2). 115.72 *(978-1-4994-8095-5(4)*, bc1a1026-5b02-4b60-b8dd-1f2de585ad31); (gr. 2-1). pap. 40.00 *(978-1-5081-9269-5(3))* Rosen Publishing Group, Inc., The. (Windmill Bks.).

Bodden, Valerie. Inclined Planes. 2011. (Simple Machine Ser.). 24p. (J). (gr. 1-3). 24.25 *(978-1-60818-008-0(5))* Creative Co., The.

—Levers. 2011. (Simple Machine Ser.). 24p. (J). (gr. 1-3). 24.25 *(978-1-60818-009-7(3))* Creative Co., The.

—Pulleys. 2011. (Simple Machine Ser.). 24p. (J). (gr. 1-3). 24.25 *(978-1-60818-010-3(7))* Creative Co., The.

—Screws. 2011. (Simple Machines Ser.). (ENG.). 24p. (J). (gr. 1-4). 24.25 *(978-1-60818-011-0(5)*, 22287) Creative Co., The.

—Wedges. 2011. (Simple Machines Ser.). (ENG.). 24p. (J). (gr. 1-4). 24.25 *(978-1-60818-012-7(3)*, 22288) Creative Co., The.

Bowman, Chris. Backhoes. 2017. (Mighty Machines in Action Ser.). (ENG., Illus.). 24p. (J). (gr. k-3). lib. bdg. 26.95 *(978-1-62617-600-3(0)*, Blastoff! Readers) Bellwether Media.

Braun, Eric. Curious Pearl Tinkers with Simple Machines: 4D an Augmented Reading Science Experience. Lewis, Anthony, illus. 2018. (Curious Pearl, Science Girl 4D Ser.). (ENG.). 24p. (J). (gr. k-2). lib. bdg. 25.99 *(978-1-5158-2973-7(1)*, 138575, Picture Window Bks.) Capstone.

Brooks, Felicity. Diggers Lift-and-Look. 2005. (Illus.). 12p. (J). (gr. -1-k). per., bds. 9.95 *(978-0-7945-1067-1(1)*, Usborne) EDC Publishing.

Brown Bear Books. Power & Energy. 2012. (Invention & Technology Ser.). (ENG.). 64p. (J). (gr. 8-11). lib. bdg. 39.95 *(978-1-936333-39-4(2)*, 16525) Brown Bear Bks.

Bruning, Matt. Mighty Machines Picture Puzzles, 1 vol. 2009. (Look, Look Again Ser.). (ENG.). 32p. (J). (gr. -1-2). lib. bdg. 27.99 *(978-1-4296-3289-8(5)*, 95698, Capstone Pr.) Capstone.

Bryant-Mole, Karen. Dot-to-Dot Machines. Tyler, Jenny, ed. Round, Graham, illus. rev. ed. 2006. (Dot to Dot Ser.). 22p. (J). (gr. -1-2). pap. 3.99 *(978-0-7945-1495-2(2)*, Usborne) EDC Publishing.

Buehr, Walter. The First Book of Machines. Buehr, Walter, illus. 2017. (ENG., Illus.). (J). (gr. 4-6). pap. 12.95 *(978-0-692-97395-0(8))* Living Library Pr.

Butterfield, Moira. Bulldozers & Other Construction Machines. Lyon, Chris & Biggin, Gary, illus. 32p. (J). mass mkt. 8.99 *(978-0-590-24556-2(2))* Scholastic, Inc.

Capici, Gaetano. What Does It Do? Cement Mixer. 2011. (Community Connections: What Does It Do? Ser.). (ENG., Illus.). 24p. (gr. 2-5). lib. bdg. 29.21 *(978-1-60279-973-8(3)*, 200972) Cherry Lake Publishing.

Carrière, Nicholle. Excavators & Diggers, 1 vol. 2016. (Mega Machines Ser.). (ENG., Illus.). 64p. (J). pap. 6.99 *(978-1-926700-65-6(1)*, 5a3ef9dc-5c6c-446f-b3dd-db1cb0843e64) Blue Bike Bks. CAN. Dist: Lone Pine Publishing USA.

Challen, Paul. Get to Know Screws. 2009. (Get to Know Simple Machines Ser.). (ENG., Illus.). 32p. (J). (gr. 2-3). pap. *(978-0-7787-4486-3(8))*; lib. bdg. *(978-0-7787-4469-6(8))* Crabtree Publishing Co.

—Get to Know Wheels & Axles. 2009. (Get to Know Simple Machines Ser.). (ENG., Illus.). 32p. (J). (gr. 2-3). pap. *(978-0-7787-4488-7(4))* Crabtree Publishing Co.

Christiansen, Jennifer. Get to Know Inclined Planes. 2009. (Get to Know Simple Machines Ser.). (ENG., Illus.). 32p. (J). (gr. 2-3). pap. *(978-0-7787-4483-2(3))* Crabtree Publishing Co.

—Get to Know Wedges. 2009. (ENG.). 32p. (J). lib. bdg. *(978-0-7787-4470-2(1))*; (Illus.). (gr. 2-3). pap. *(978-0-7787-4487-0(6))* Crabtree Publishing Co.

Clay, Kathryn. Backhoes. 2016. (Construction Vehicles at Work Ser.). (ENG., Illus.). 24p. (J). (gr. -1-2). lib. bdg. 22.65 *(978-1-5157-2527-5(8)*, 132898, Capstone Pr.) Capstone.

—Concrete Mixers. 2017. (Construction Vehicles at Work Ser.). (ENG., Illus.). 24p. (J). (gr. -1-2). pap. 6.95 *(978-1-5157-8018-2(X)*, 136057, Pebble) Capstone.

—Construction Vehicles. 2015. (Wild about Wheels Ser.). (ENG., Illus.). 24p. (J). (gr. -1-2). lib. bdg. 27.32 *(978-1-4914-2117-8(7)*, 127600, Capstone Pr.) Capstone.

—Cranes. 2016. (Construction Vehicles at Work Ser.). (ENG., Illus.). 24p. (J). (gr. -1-2). lib. bdg. 22.65 *(978-1-5157-2528-2(6)*, 132899, Pebble) Capstone.

—Excavators. 2017. (Construction Vehicles at Work Ser.). (ENG., Illus.). 24p. (J). (gr. -1-2). lib. bdg. 22.65 *(978-1-5157-8015-1(5)*, 136054, Pebble) Capstone.

Claybourne, Anna. Recreate Machine Innovations. 2018. (Recreate Scientific Discoveries Ser.). (Illus.). 32p. (J). (gr. 4-5). *(978-0-7787-5063-5(9))* Crabtree Publishing Co.

The Clean Machine: Individual Title Six-Packs. (gr. k-1). 23.00 *(978-0-7635-9077-2(0))* Rigby Education.

Close, Edward. Force & Motion, 1 vol., 1. 2014. (Discovery Education: How It Works). (ENG.). 32p. (gr. 4-5). 28.93 *(978-1-4777-6317-9(1)*, eebde530-eb2d-4ed6-9a19-ebf34d7aec72, PowerKids Pr.) Rosen Publishing Group, Inc., The.

Collander, Hope. Inclined Planes, 1 vol. 2013. (Simple Machine Science Ser.). (ENG., Illus.). 24p. (J). (gr. 1-2). pap. 9.15 *(978-1-4339-8132-6(7)*, 7c6d2ac1-fda2-4607-9701-e013b3e191b5); lib. bdg. 25.27 *(978-1-4339-8131-9(9)*, b04dfaa6-e44e-4c24-8351-d972a1025c0a) Stevens, Gareth Publishing LLLP.

Corporate Contibutor & Snedden, Robert. Mechanical Engineering & Simple Machines. 2012. (ENG.). 32p. (J). *(978-0-7787-7498-3(8))* Crabtree Publishing Co.

Crane, Cody. Simple Machines (Rookie Read-About Science: Physical Science) (Library Edition) 2019. (Rookie Read-About Science Ser.). (ENG., Illus.). 32p. (J). (gr. 1-2). lib. bdg. 25.00 *(978-0-531-13406-1(7)*, Children's Pr.) Scholastic Library Publishing.

Davis, Caroline. Diggers. Davis, Caroline, illus. 2010. (ENG., Illus.). 20p. (J). bds. *(978-1-4083-0785-4(5)*, Orchard Bks.) Hachette Children's Group GBR. Dist: Hachette Bk. Group.

Dayton, Connor. Cherry Pickers. 24p. (J). 2012. 49.50 *(978-1-4488-5071-6(1))* 2011. (ENG.). (gr. 1-1). pap. 9.25 *(978-1-4488-5070-9(3)*, 2d04d9f5-75e6-4430-bf71-00762d09f73c) 2011. (ENG.). (gr. 1-1). lib. bdg. 26.27 *(978-1-4488-4960-4(8)*, 47e4f237-3ef9-4aaa-a4f1-4802255d14fd) Rosen Publishing Group, Inc., The. (PowerKids Pr.).

—Jackhammers. (J). 2012. 49.50 *(978-1-4488-5065-5(7))* 2011. (ENG.). 24p. (gr. 1-1). pap. 9.25 *(978-1-4488-5064-8(9)*, 1935afbe-5a30-41b4-9dc0-e739cda08429) 2011. (ENG.). 24p. (gr. 1-1). lib. bdg. 26.27 *(978-1-4488-4957-4(8)*, 22598c3d-a75c-473b-bb4c-7772dcc8c616) Rosen Publishing Group, Inc., The. (PowerKids Pr.).

De Medeiros, J. Pulleys. 2009. (Science Matters Ser.). (Illus.). 24p. (J). (gr. 3-5). pap. 8.95 *(978-1-60596-042-5(X))* Weigl Pubs., Inc.

De Medeiros, James. Pulleys. (J). 2013. *(978-1-62127-426-1(8))* 2013. pap. *(978-1-62127-432-2(2))* 2009. (Illus.). 24p. (gr. 3-5). lib. bdg. 24.45 *(978-1-60596-041-8(1))* Weigl Pubs., Inc.

De Medeiros, M. Screws. 2009. (Science Matters Ser.). (Illus.). 24p. (J). (gr. 3-5). pap. 10.95 *(978-1-60596-040-1(3))* Weigl Pubs., Inc.

De Medeiros, Michael. Screws. (J). 2013. *(978-1-62127-427-8(6))* 2013. pap. *(978-1-62127-433-9(0))* 2009. (Illus.). 24p. (gr. 3-5). lib. bdg. 24.45 *(978-1-60596-039-5(X))* Weigl Pubs., Inc.

Deane-Pratt, Ade. Simple Machines, 1 vol. 2011. (How Things Work Ser.). (ENG., Illus.). 32p. (J). (gr. 4-4). lib. bdg. 30.27 *(978-1-4488-5279-6(X)*, 5c85d800-5b08-41c4-823f-9ce47c2f55de) Rosen Publishing Group, Inc., The.

Dickmann, Nancy. Levers. 2018. (Simple Machines Ser.). (ENG., Illus.). 24p. (J). (gr. 2-4). *(978-1-78121-398-8(4)*, 16686) Brown Bear Bks.

—Pulleys. 2018. (Simple Machines Ser.). (ENG., Illus.). 24p. (J). (gr. 2-4). *(978-1-78121-399-5(2)*, 23011) Brown Bear Bks.

—Screws. 2018. (Simple Machines Ser.). (ENG., Illus.). 24p. (J). (gr. 2-4). *(978-1-78121-401-5(8)*, 16689) Brown Bear Bks.

—Wedges. 2018. (Simple Machines Ser.). (ENG., Illus.). 24p. (J). (gr. 2-4). 28.50 *(978-1-78121-402-2(6)*, 16690) Brown Bear Bks.

Dittmer, Lori. Cultivators. 2018. (Seedlings Ser.). (ENG., Illus.). 24p. (J). (gr. -1-1). pap. 7.99 *(978-1-62832-524-9(0)*, 19529, Creative Paperbacks); *(978-1-60818-908-3(2)*, 19531, Creative Education) Creative Co., The.

—Harvesters. 2018. (Seedlings Ser.). (ENG., Illus.). 24p. (J). (gr. -1-1). pap. 7.99 *(978-1-62832-525-6(9)*, 19570, Creative Paperbacks); *(978-1-60818-909-0(0)*, 19572, Creative Education) Creative Co., The.

—Plows. 2018. (Seedlings Ser.). (ENG., Illus.). 24p. (J). (gr. -1-1). pap. 7.99 *(978-1-62832-526-3(7)*, 19634, Creative Paperbacks); *(978-1-60818-910-6(4)*, 19636, Creative Education) Creative Co., The.

—Seeders. 2018. (Seedlings Ser.). (ENG., Illus.). 24p. (J). (gr. -1-1). pap. 7.99 *(978-1-62832-527-0(5)*, 19648, Creative Paperbacks); *(978-1-60818-911-3(2)*, 19650, Creative Education) Creative Co., The.

DK. Diggers. 2009. (ENG.). 10p. (J). (gr. -1-k). bds. 8.99 *(978-0-7566-5229-6(4)*, DK Children) Dorling Kindersley Publishing, Inc.

Doman, Mary Kate. Earthmovers & Diggers, 1 vol. 2011. (All about Big Machines Ser.). (ENG., Illus.). 24p. (gr. -1-1). pap. 10.35 *(978-1-59845-245-7(2)*, 4906814e-819a-44d4-bd98-1df9e8705b40, Enslow Publishing) Enslow Publishing, LLC.

Dos Santos, Julie. Diggers, 1 vol. 2010. (Amazing Machines Ser.). (ENG.). 32p. (gr. 2-2). 31.21 *(978-0-7614-4402-2(5)*, f207d7e5-956d-4c25-a662-c6ed9296af48) Cavendish Square Publishing LLC.

Doudna, Kelly. The Kids' Book of Simple Machines. 2015. (ENG., Illus.). 144p. (J). (gr k-4). pap. 14.95 *(978-1-938063-59-6(7)*, Mighty Media Kids) Mighty Media Pr.

—The Kids' Book of Simple Machines: Cool Projects & Activities That Make Science Fun! 2015. (Illus.). 144p. (J). *(978-1-938063-60-2(0))* Mighty Media Pr.

Edison, Erin & Troupe, Thomas Kingsley. Crush It!, 1 vol. 2013. (Destruction Ser.). (ENG.). 24p. (J). (gr. -1-2). lib. bdg. 27.32 *(978-1-4765-2088-9(7)*, 122816, Capstone Pr.) Capstone.

Eggleton, Jill. The Amazing Machine. Kieley, Rob, illus. (Sails Literacy Ser.). 24p. (gr. 3-18). 27.00 *(978-0-7578-6979-2(3))*;Pack. 57.00 *(978-0-7578-6995-2(5))* Rigby Education.

—The Amazing Machine: 6 Small Books. Kieley, Rob, illus. (Sails Literacy Ser.). 24p. (gr. 3-18). 25.00 *(978-0-7578-6987-7(4))* Rigby Education.

Eldridge, Jim. The Digger 2 Wayfarers. Cook, Euan, illus. 2017. (Cambridge Reading Adventures Ser.). (ENG.). 32p. pap. 7.35 *(978-1-108-40093-0(0))* Cambridge Univ. Pr.

Enz, Tammy. Super Cool Mechanical Activities with Max Axiom. Baez, Marcelo, illus. 2015. (Max Axiom Science & Engineering Activities Ser.). (ENG.). 32p. (J). (gr. 3-9). lib. bdg. 31.32 *(978-1-4914-2080-5(4)*, 127558, Capstone Pr.) Capstone.

—Zoom It: Invent New Machines That Move. 2012. (Invent It Ser.). (ENG.). 32p. (gr. 3-4). pap. 47.70 *(978-1-4296-8458-3(5))*; (J). pap. 8.10 *(978-1-4296-7984-8(0)*, 118316); (J). lib. bdg. 27.99 *(978-1-4296-7634-2(5)*, 117231) Capstone. (Capstone Pr.).

Enz, Tammy Laura Lynn. Simple Machines at the Amusement Park. 2019. (Amusement Park Science Ser.). (ENG., Illus.). 32p. (J). (gr. 3-6). pap. 7.95 *(978-1-5435-7526-2(9)*, 141056) Capstone.

Extreme Machines. 2015. (Extreme Machines Ser.). (ENG.). 32p. (J). (gr. 3-4). pap., pap., pap. 360.00 *(978-1-4994-1369-4(6)*, PowerKids Pr.) Rosen Publishing Group, Inc., The.

Farndon, John. Stickmen's Guide to Gigantic Machines. Paul de Quay, John, illus. 2016. (Stickmen's Guides to How Everything Works). (ENG.). 32p. (J). (gr. 3-6). lib. bdg. 27.99 *(978-1-4677-9361-2(2)*, ef86552b-68cc-48fb-8652-4d2895fcd8e6); E-Book 42.65 *(978-1-4677-9596-8(8))* Lerner Publishing Group. (Hungry Tomato (r)).

Feldman, Roseann & Walker, Sally M. Put Inclined Planes to the Test. 2011. (Searchlight Books How Do Simple Machines Work Ser.). (ENG., Illus.). (gr. 3-5). pap. 51.01 *(978-0-7613-8397-0(2))* Lerner Publishing Group.

—Put Levers to the Test. 2011. (Searchlight Books How Do Simple Machines Work Ser.). (ENG., Illus.). (gr. 3-5). pap. 51.01 *(978-0-7613-8398-7(0))* Lerner Publishing Group.

—Put Pulleys to the Test. 2011. (Searchlight Books How Do Simple Machines Work Ser.). (ENG., Illus.). (gr. 3-5). pap. 51.01 *(978-0-7613-8399-4(9))* Lerner Publishing Group.

—Put Screws to the Test. 2011. (Searchlight Books How Do Simple Machines Work Ser.). (ENG., Illus.). (gr. 3-5). pap. 51.01 *(978-0-7613-8400-7(6))* Lerner Publishing Group.

—Put Wedges to the Test. 2011. (Searchlight Books How Do Simple Machines Work Ser.). (ENG., Illus.). (gr. 3-5). pap. 51.01 *(978-0-7613-8401-4(4))* Lerner Publishing Group.

Feldmann, Roseann & Walker, Sally M. Put Levers to the Test. 2011. (Searchlight Books (tm) — How Do Simple Machines Work? Ser.). (ENG., Illus.). 40p. (J). (gr. 3-5). pap. 9.99 *(978-0-7613-7866-2(9)*, 26f803ba-7d7f-4ee2-97f7-1005821e5a30) Lerner Publishing Group.

—Trabajo (Work) King, Andy, photos by. 2005. (Libros de Física para Madrugadores (Early Bird Physics) Ser.). (SPA., Illus.). 48p. (J). (gr. 3-6). lib. bdg. 26.65 *(978-0-8225-2984-2(X)*, 3d141b04-f130-4bc9-8f29-316c0a288cbe, Ediciones Lerner) Lerner Publishing Group.

Freed, Kira. Tools We Use. 2017. (Text Connections Guided Close Reading Ser.). (J). (gr. 2). *(978-1-4900-1831-7(X))* Benchmark Education Co.

French, Cathy. From Axes to Zippers: Simple Machines & Del hacha al Cierre: 6 English, 6 Spanish Adaptations: Las máquinas Simples. 2011. (ENG & SPA.). (J). 89.00 net. *(978-1-4108-5672-2(0))* Benchmark Education Co.

French, Kathy. From Axes to Zippers Simple Machines: Set Of 6. 2010. (Navigators Ser.). (J). pap. 44.00 net. *(978-1-4108-0413-6(5))* Benchmark Education Co.

Frisch, Aaron. Diggers. 2013. (Seedlings Ser.). (ENG.). 24p. (J). (gr. -1-k). 22.85 *(978-1-60818-340-1(8)*, 21671) Creative Co., The.

—Seedlings: Diggers. 2014. (Seedlings Ser.). (ENG.). 24p. (J). (gr. -1-k). pap. 10.99 *(978-0-89812-885-7(4)*, 21672, Creative Paperbacks) Creative Co., The.

Gardner, Charlie. Digger. 2009. (Illus.). (J). *(978-1-4654-5513-0(2))* Dorling Kindersley Publishing, Inc.

Gardner, Robert. Simple Machine Experiments Using Seesaws, Wheels, Pulleys, & More: One Hour or Less Science Experiments, 1 vol. 2012. (Last-Minute Science Projects Ser.). (ENG.). 48p. (gr. 5-6). 27.93 *(978-0-7660-3957-5(9)*, c71e592f-1768-45fd-8ff8-e7bb096193fc) Enslow Publishing, LLC.

Gilbert, Sara. Concrete Mixers. 2009. (Machines That Build Ser.). (J). (gr. 1-5). 24.25 *(978-1-58341-726-3(5)*, Creative Education) Creative Co., The.

—Diggers. 2009. (Machines That Build Ser.). (J). (gr. 1-5). 24.25 *(978-1-58341-728-7(1)*, Creative Education) Creative Co., The.

—Drilling Machines. 2009. (Machines That Build Ser.). (J). (gr. 1-5). 24.25 *(978-1-58341-729-4(X)*, Creative Education) Creative Co., The.

—Dump Trucks. 2009. (Machines That Build Ser.). (J). (gr. 1-5). 24.25 *(978-1-58341-730-0(3)*, Creative Education) Creative Co., The.

Glover, David & Barnes, Jon. Machines. (Make It Work! Ser.). (Illus.). 48p. (J). pap. 7.95 *(978-0-590-24401-5(9))* Scholastic, Inc.

Glover, David & Glover, Penny. Digging Machines in Action, 1 vol. 2007. (On the Go Ser.). (ENG., Illus.). 24p. (J). (gr. 1-2). lib. bdg. 26.27 *(978-1-4042-4307-1(0)*, f2f59bb9-c45b-4285-a0d2-76e811c33409, PowerKids Pr.) Rosen Publishing Group, Inc., The.

Good, Keith. Gear Up! Marvelous Machine Projects. 2008. (Design It! Ser.). pap. 6.95 *(978-0-8225-9925-8(2))* Lerner Publishing Group.

Gordon, Nick. Monster Diggers. 2013. (Monster Machines Ser.). (ENG., Illus.). 24p. (J). (gr. k-3). lib. bdg. 26.95 *(978-1-60014-937-5(5)*, Blastoff! Readers) Bellwether Media.

Gosman, Gillian. Inclined Planes in Action, 1 vol. 2010. (Simple Machines at Work Ser.). (ENG.). 24p. (J). (gr. 2-3). pap. 9.25 *(978-1-4488-1303-2(4)*, 46b0086f-57b7-414c-a709-d2029b3a08bd); lib. bdg. 26.27 *(978-1-4488-0685-0(2)*, 671bf95e-2e9e-48df-b47c-7494923eac98) Rosen Publishing Group, Inc., The. (PowerKids Pr.).

—Levers in Action, 1 vol. 2010. (Simple Machines at Work Ser.). (ENG.). 24p. (J). (gr. 2-3). pap. 9.25 *(978-1-4488-1297-4(6)*, 16601bbc-b7b6-4a9f-a5e0-026e151e598a); lib. bdg. 26.27 *(978-1-4488-0682-9(8)*, 0108f3a1-5fcc-4296-9e94-e4d716889f7c) Rosen Publishing Group, Inc., The. (PowerKids Pr.).

—Pulleys in Action, 1 vol. 2010. (Simple Machines at Work Ser.). (ENG.). 24p. (J). (gr. 2-3). pap. 9.25 *(978-1-4488-1294-3(1)*, 16b79d70-1ce0-46a4-9dd2-f9c68215515b); lib. bdg. 26.27 *(978-1-4488-0681-2(X)*, 85da98c9-4bdf-43f1-adff-ce2a985827ab) Rosen Publishing Group, Inc., The. (PowerKids Pr.).

—Screws in Action, 1 vol. 2010. (Simple Machines at Work Ser.). (ENG.). 24p. (J). (gr. 2-3). pap. 9.25 *(978-1-4488-1305-6(0)*, 15607edf-39d5-4cb3-8420-eaa06f05bde3); lib. bdg. 26.27 *(978-1-4488-0686-7(0)*, 31ed86f1-4082-4fa2-b661-124b7435f0a7) Rosen Publishing Group, Inc., The. (PowerKids Pr.).

—Simple Machines & Holidays. 2014. (Simple Machines Everywhere Ser.). 24p. (J). (gr. k-3). pap. 49.50 *(978-1-4777-6643-9(X)*, PowerKids Pr.) Rosen Publishing Group, Inc., The.

—Simple Machines in Sports, 1 vol. 2014. (Simple Machines Everywhere Ser.). (ENG., Illus.). 24p. (J). (gr. 2-3). 25.27 *(978-1-4777-6829-7(7)*, 34603074-eae7-45c7-b80f-b288e150f932, PowerKids Pr.) Rosen Publishing Group, Inc., The.

—Simple Machines in the Great Outdoors, 1 vol. 2014. (Simple Machines Everywhere Ser.). (ENG., Illus.). 24p. (J). (gr. 2-3). pap. 9.25 *(978-1-4777-6838-9(6)*, b6dcc283-0896-4b16-bda1-1028cc8aa009, PowerKids Pr.) Rosen Publishing Group, Inc., The.

—Simple Machines in the Military, 1 vol. 2014. (Simple Machines Everywhere Ser.). (ENG., Illus.). 24p. (J). (gr. 2-3). pap. 9.25 *(978-1-4777-6834-1(3)*, e5bdae66-ccd0-4093-8cf2-8d1058b6769f, PowerKids Pr.) Rosen Publishing Group, Inc., The.

—Simple Machines in Your Home. 2014. (Simple Machines Everywhere Ser.). 24p. (J). (gr. k-3). pap. 49.50 *(978-1-4777-6644-6(8)*, PowerKids Pr.) Rosen Publishing Group, Inc., The.

—Wedges in Action, 1 vol. 2010. (Simple Machines at Work Ser.). (ENG.). 24p. (J). (gr. 2-3). pap. 9.25 *(978-1-4488-1299-8(2)*, 7b85957a-1ad9-437e-aa9e-72a9de8f97ea); lib. bdg. 26.27 *(978-1-4488-0683-6(6)*, 84324b5d-de94-4476-8392-6f700f5fdc8a) Rosen Publishing Group, Inc., The. (PowerKids Pr.).

Graham, Ian. Emergency Vehicles. 2009. (How Machines Work Ser.). (ENG., Illus.). 32p. (J). pap. *(978-1-897563-42-7(6))* Saunders Bk. Co.

—Mighty Machines. (Ripley Twists Ser.). (Illus.). 48p. (J). (gr. 3-18). 2010. lib. bdg. 19.95 *(978-1-4222-1831-0(7)*, 1318260) 2009. pap. 8.95 *(978-1-4222-2069-6(9)*, 1318260) Mason Crest.

—On the Water. 2006. (QEB Machines at Work Ser.). (Illus.). 36p. (J). lib. bdg. 16.95 *(978-1-59566-190-6(5))* QEB Publishing Inc.

Graubart, Norman D. Cement Mixers, 1 vol. 2014. (Giants on the Road Ser.). (ENG.). 24p. (J). (gr. 1-2). lib. bdg. 25.27 *(978-1-4994-0053-3(5)*, 60e14eec-32a2-450a-83b5-b98a27152e17, PowerKids Pr.) Rosen Publishing Group, Inc., The.

Greathead, Helen. Megamachines, 1 vol. 2016. (What Would You Choose? Ser.). (ENG.). 32p. (J). (gr. 4-5). pap. 11.50 *(978-1-4824-6079-7(3)*, 68c22d6e-2c31-46d4-b9e4-06230aabe365) Stevens, Gareth Publishing LLLP.

Gregory, Helen. How Things Move, 1 vol. 2011. (Wonder Readers Early Level Ser.). (ENG.). 16p. (gr. -1-1). (J). pap. 6.25 *(978-1-4296-7814-8(3)*, 117986); pap. 35.94 *(978-1-4296-8096-7(2))* Capstone. (Capstone Pr.).

Gulkin, Sidney & Notkin, Jerome J. The How & Why Wonder Book of MacHines. Zaffo, George J., illus. 2011. 48p. pap. 35.95 *(978-1-258-10533-4(0))* Literary Licensing, LLC.

Gunn, Richard. Monster Movers, 1 vol. 2006. (Cool Wheels Ser.). (ENG., Illus.). 32p. (gr. 3-5). lib. bdg. 28.67 *(978-0-8368-6827-2(7)*, 58c25124-f996-4397-a42a-a55a89692800, Gareth Stevens Learning Library) Stevens, Gareth Publishing LLLP.

Hankin, Rosie. Cut & Paste Trucks, Trains, & Big Machines, 1 vol. 2007. (Cut, Paste, & Create Ser.). (ENG., Illus.). 32p. (gr. 1-3). lib. bdg. 28.67 *(978-0-8368-7721-2(7)*, 36f28e3c-f97d-453a-af3c-291be27279ba, Gareth Stevens Learning Library) Stevens, Gareth Publishing LLLP.

Hansen, Grace. Machines to Thrill You!, 1 vol. 2015. (Seeing Is Believing Ser.). (ENG., Illus.). 24p. (J). (gr. -1-2). lib. bdg. 32.79 *(978-1-62970-732-7(5)*, 17281, Abdo Kids) ABDO Publishing Co.

—Machines to Thrill You! 2017. (Seeing Is Believing Ser.). (ENG.). 24p. (J). (gr. -1-2). pap. 7.95 *(978-1-4966-1317-2(1)*, 135029, Capstone Classroom) Capstone.

—Maquinas Asombrosas! (Machines to Thrill You!) 2016. (Ver para Creer (Seeing Is Believing) Ser.). (SPA., Illus.). 24p. (J). (gr. -1-2). lib. bdg. 32.79 *(978-1-68080-769-1(2)*, 22700, Abdo Kids) ABDO Publishing Co.

Harris, Patricia. Understanding Coding with Lego Wedo(tm), 1 vol., 1. 2015. (Spotlight on Kids Can Code Ser.). (ENG., Illus.). 24p. (J). (gr. 4-5). pap. 12.75 *(978-1-5081-4466-3(4)*, 7c8821f2-b29f-4f57-8f95-6eb7c9b92d48, PowerKids Pr.) Rosen Publishing Group, Inc., The.

Hayes, Amy. Big Diggers, 1 vol. 2015. (Machines That Work Ser.). (ENG., Illus.). 24p. (gr. 1-1). pap. 9.23 *(978-1-5026-0391-3(8)*, ec61079a-3514-479b-a7fe-c67f8eae1ff8) Cavendish Square Publishing LLC.

—Big Loaders, 1 vol. 2015. (Machines That Work Ser.). (ENG., Illus.). 24p. (gr. 1-1). pap. 9.23 *(978-1-5026-0397-5(7)*, d063e21e-3d52-4b6b-aae9-e98f09e59613) Cavendish Square Publishing LLC.

Heitkamp, Kristina Lyn. Fab Lab Creating with Digital Sewing Machines, 1 vol. 2016. (Getting Creative with Fab Lab Ser.). (ENG., Illus.). 64p. (J). (gr. 6-6). 36.13 *(978-1-4994-6508-2(4)*, 9278c82f-b150-4f25-97bf-8320b4e68f37) Rosen Publishing Group, Inc., The.

Hennessy, B. G. Road Builders. Taback, Simms, illus. 2018. 32p. (J). (— 1). bds. 7.99 *(978-0-425-29121-4(9)*, Viking Books for Young Readers) Penguin Young Readers Group.

Hill, Lee Sullivan. Earthmovers on the Move. 2010. (Lightning Bolt Books (r) — Vroom-Vroom Ser.). (ENG., Illus.). 32p. (J). (gr. 1-3). lib. bdg. 29.32 *(978-0-7613-3918-2(3)*, c69c124d-1972-4fd0-9bf6-eb978a540d90, Lerner Pubns.) Lerner Publishing Group.

How Machines Help, 6 vols. (Sunshinetm Science Ser.). 24p. (gr. 1-2). 36.95 *(978-0-7802-0552-9(9))*; 31.50 *(978-0-7802-0301-3(1))* Wright Group/McGraw-Hill.

Howse, Jennifer. Inclined Planes. (J). 2013. *(978-1-62127-424-7(1))* 2013. pap. *(978-1-62127-430-8(6))* 2009. (Illus.). 24p. (gr. 3-5). pap. 8.95 *(978-1-60596-036-4(5))* 2009. (Illus.). 24p. (gr. 3-5). lib. bdg. 24.45 *(978-1-60596-035-7(7))* Weigl Pubs., Inc.

—Levers. (J). 2013. 27.13 (978-1-62127-425-4(X)) 2013. pap. 12.95 (978-1-62127-431-5(4)) 2009. (Illus.). 24p. (gr. 3-5). pap. 8.95 (978-1-60596-032-6(2)) 2009. (Illus.). 24p. (gr. 3-5). lib. bdg. 24.45 (978-1-60596-031-9(4)) Weigl Pubs., Inc.

—Wedges. 2009. (Science Matters Ser.). (Illus.). 24p. (J). (gr. 3-5). lib. bdg. 24.45 (978-1-60596-037-1(3)) Weigl Pubs., Inc.

Huff, Regan A. Eli Whitney: The Cotton Gin & American Manufacturing. 2009. (Library of American Lives & Times Ser.). 112p. (gr. 5-5). 69.20 (978-1-60853-478-4(2)) Rosen Publishing Group, Inc., The.

Inside Machines, 12 vols. 2017. (Inside Machines Ser.). 24p. (ENG.). (gr. 3-3). 157.62 (978-1-4994-8376-5(7), aa1049e1-8627-4d90-a691-5e97f5f37777); (gr. 8-8). pap. 49.50 (978-1-4994-8384-0(8)) Rosen Publishing Group, Inc., The. (Windmill Bks.).

Jefferis, David. Extreme Structures: Mega-Constructions of the 21st Century. 2006. (Science Frontiers Ser.). (ENG., Illus.). 32p. (J). (gr. 3-7). pap. (978-0-7787-2872-6(2)) Crabtree Publishing Co.

—Micro Machines: Ultra-Small World of Nanotechnology. 2006. (Science Frontiers Ser.). (ENG., Illus.). 32p. (J). (gr. 4-7). pap. (978-0-7787-2873-3(0)) Crabtree Publishing Co.

Kalman, Bobbie & MacAulay, Kelley. Fantásticos Vehiculos para la Construccion. 2007. (Vehículos en Acción Ser.). (SPA & ENG., Illus.). 32p. (J). lib. bdg. (978-0-7787-8304-6(9)) Crabtree Publishing Co.

Kawa, Katie. Loaders, 1 vol. 2011. (Big Machines Ser.). (ENG., Illus.). 24p. (J). (gr. k-k). pap. 9.15 (978-1-4339-5568-6(7), de5783a6-6fe5-4178-9c46-08f7ea917e06); lib. bdg. 25.27 (978-1-4339-5566-2(0), f85a0f10-1ef9-4221-b678-195c14b76f42) Stevens, Gareth Publishing LLLP.

—Loaders / Palas Cargadoras, 1 vol. 2011. (Big Machines / Grandes Máquinas Ser.). (SPA & ENG., Illus.). 24p. (J). (gr. k-k). lib. bdg. 25.27 (978-1-4339-5582-2(2), e8b637bc-4e72-453c-a83f-c4a592abfa2f) Stevens, Gareth Publishing LLLP.

Koehntopp, James. Hydraulics for Kids. 2019. (J). 27.99 (978-0-578-61820-3(6)) Koehntopp, James.

Kramer, Jon. Learning about Simple Machines with Graphic Organizers, 1 vol. 2006. (Graphic Organizers in Science Ser.). (ENG.). 24p. (J). (gr. 3-4). pap. 9.25 (978-1-4358-3277-0(9), b2ebbae2-fa31-4c62-9bae-7959806c9a39, PowerKids Pr.) Rosen Publishing Group, Inc., The.

Kravetz, Jonathan. Learning about Simple Machines with Graphic Organizers, 1 vol. 2006. (Graphic Organizers in Science Ser.: Vol. 3). (ENG., Illus.). 24p. (J). (gr. 3-4). lib. bdg. 26.27 (978-1-4042-3411-6(X), 869c6af7-ba0f-4528-925e-2c926907ca97) Rosen Publishing Group, Inc., The.

Kulling, Monica. All Aboard! Elijah Mccoy's Steam Engine. Slavin, Bill, illus. 2013. (Great Idea Ser.: 2). 32p. (J). (gr. k-3). pap. 7.95 (978-1-77049-514-2(2), Tundra Bks.) Tundra Bks. CAN. Dist: Penguin Random Hse. LLC.

Lacey, Minna. Big Book of Big Machines. 2010. (Big Book of Big Machines Ser.). 14p. (J). 13.99 (978-0-7945-2764-8(7), Usborne) EDC Publishing.

LaMachia, Dawn. Inclined Planes at Work, 1 vol. 2015. (Zoom in on Simple Machines Ser.). (ENG.). 24p. (gr. 2-2). pap. 10.95 (978-0-7660-6726-4(2), 117f7f5d-8801-4edc-b117-f06a84f5cf44); (Illus.). 25.60 (978-0-7660-6728-8(9), d9a7fa19-8adb-47ae-9b2b-c05110eb95f5) Enslow Publishing, LLC.

—Levers at Work, 1 vol. 2015. (Zoom in on Simple Machines Ser.). (ENG.). 24p. (gr. 2-2). 25.60 (978-0-7660-6732-5(7), bfd135f4-46f8-46d0-b2d5-d74c2f3390b6); pap. 10.95 (978-0-7660-6730-1(0), 3fbf740e-0664-4a4d-93ab-9582792cc407) Enslow Publishing, LLC.

—Pulleys at Work, 1 vol. 2015. (Zoom in on Simple Machines Ser.). (ENG.). 24p. (gr. 2-2). pap. 10.95 (978-0-7660-6734-9(3), 00c18f3d-9ea5-4057-b8cb-fb3c4862bc14) Enslow Publishing, LLC.

—Screws at Work, 1 vol. 2015. (Zoom in on Simple Machines Ser.). (ENG.). 24p. (gr. 2-2). 25.60 (978-0-7660-6740-0(8), 08f43d7f-5841-49a2-bfe8-51e0ae9ddb2d); pap. 10.95 (978-0-7660-6738-7(6), 340bb947-ec64-4e00-ac87-4a4a04cb41a5) Enslow Publishing, LLC.

—Wedges at Work, 1 vol. 2015. (Zoom in on Simple Machines Ser.). (ENG.). 24p. (gr. 2-2). 25.60 (978-0-7660-6744-8(0), 1ea31cee-866a-427a-8a00-be751f3f8ac8); pap. 10.95 (978-0-7660-6742-4(4), d4ca7434-2744-4439-9d8b-87eddb98b7b5) Enslow Publishing, LLC.

—Wheels & Axles at Work, 1 vol. 2015. (Zoom in on Simple Machines Ser.). (ENG.). 24p. (gr. 2-2). 25.60 (978-0-7660-6748-6(3), 078e701e-b15e-4c0f-bc7d-363a0888df7f); pap. 10.95 (978-0-7660-6746-2(7), 5cee8c48-c518-4c40-aae1-f3523b988988) Enslow Publishing, LLC.

Lancaster, Juliana. PBIS- Building Big Things. 2005. pap., stu. ed. 8.00 (978-1-58591-565-1(3)) It's About Time, Herff Jones Education Div.

Langley, Andrew. Diggers. 2010. (Machines on the Move Ser.). (ENG.). 32p. (J). (gr. 1-3). lib. bdg. 28.50 (978-1-60753-058-9(9), 17211) Amicus.

—Diggers. 2012. (ENG., Illus.). 32p. (gr. 1-3). pap. 8.95 (978-1-926722-68-9(X)) Saunders Bk. Co. CAN. Dist: RiverStream Publishing.

Latour, Pierre. Where Do Big Machines Work? 2012. (Level B Ser.). (ENG., Illus.). 16p. (J). (gr. k-2). pap. 7.95 (978-1-927136-12-6(1), 19444) RiverStream Publishing.

Law, Felicia. Simple Machines. 2015. (Stone Age Science Ser.). (ENG., Illus.). 32p. (J). (gr. 4-5). lib. bdg. (978-0-7787-1890-1(5)) Crabtree Publishing Co.

Lawrence, Debbie & Lawrence, Richard. Machines & Motion: God's Design for the Physical World. 2005. (Illus.). 160p. per. (978-0-9725365-9-2(0)) Boarding House Publishing.

Leaf, Christina. Mechanics. 2018. (Community Helpers Ser.). (ENG., Illus.). 24p. (J). (gr. k-3). lib. bdg. 26.95 (978-1-62617-900-4(X), Blastoff! Readers) Bellwether Media.

Lennie, Charles. Concrete Mixers, 1 vol. 2014. (Construction Machines Ser.). (ENG.). 24p. (J). (gr. -1-2). lib. bdg. 32.79 (978-1-62970-016-8(9), 1253, Abdo Kids) ABDO Publishing Co.

Lindeen, Mary. Graders. 2007. (Mighty Machines Ser.). (ENG., Illus.). 24p. (J). (gr. k-3). lib. bdg. 26.95 (978-1-60014-118-8(8)) Bellwether Media.

Litchfield, Jo & Brooks, Felicity. Diggers. 2004. (Chunky Board Bks.). (ENG., Illus.). 6p. (J). bds. 4.95 (978-0-7945-0350-5(0), Usborne) EDC Publishing.

Lowery, Lawrence F. Michael's Racing Machine. 2014. (I Wonder Why Ser.). (ENG., Illus.). 36p. (J). (gr. k-3). pap. 11.95 (978-1-941316-05-4(0), P241372) National Science Teachers Assn.

MacAulay, Kelley & Kalman, Bobbie. Cool Construction Vehicles. 2007. (Vehicles on the Move Ser.). (ENG., Illus.). 32p. (J). (gr. 3-7). lib. bdg. (978-0-7787-3042-2(5)); (gr. 1-5). pap. (978-0-7787-3056-9(5)) Crabtree Publishing Co.

—Fantasticos Vehiculos para la Construccion. 2007. (Vehículos en Acción Ser.). (SPA & ENG., Illus.). 32p. (J). (gr. 6-10). pap. (978-0-7787-8314-5(6)) Crabtree Publishing Co.

MacHines. (Make it Work Ser.). 42p. (J). (gr. 4-8). pap. (978-1-882210-48-0(4)) Action Publishing, Inc.

Machines: Big Book: Level E. 8p. 20.95 (978-0-322-00344-6(X)) Wright Group/McGraw-Hill.

Machines at Sea, 10 vols. 2017. (Machines at Sea Ser.). 32p. (ENG.). (gr. 4-5). 139.65 (978-1-4994-3401-9(4), b3e0d11f-fd58-410b-be7f-9a88ef6720db); (gr. 9-10). pap. 50.00 (978-1-5081-5429-7(5)) Rosen Publishing Group, Inc., The. (PowerKids Pr.).

Machines in Motion, 12 vols. 2013. (Machines in Motion Ser.). 48p. (J). (gr. 3-3). (ENG.). 207.66 (978-1-4339-9685-6(5), 9b3e3af5-cdfa-48b4-973c-a17669d5c953); pap. 505.80 (978-1-4339-9818-8(1)); pap. 84.30 (978-1-4339-9817-1(3)) Stevens, Gareth Publishing LLLP.

Machines in the Home: Individual Title Six-Packs. (gr. k-1). 23.00 (978-0-7635-9075-8(4)) Rigby Education.

Machines That Work. 2015. (Machines That Work Ser.). (ENG.). 24p. (J). (gr. 1-1). pap., pap., pap. 49.32 (978-1-5026-0693-8(3)); lib. bdg. 155.58 (978-1-5026-0350-0(0), 9b996e56-585f-43cf-ac79-858a51ecc42a) Cavendish Square Publishing LLC. (Cavendish Square).

Machut, Ronald. Working with Inclined Planes, 1 vol. 2019. (Doing Work with Simple Machines Ser.). (ENG.). 24p. (gr. 3-3). 25.27 (978-1-5383-4360-9(6), a71eebfd-1c6a-4ba3-b96e-10629b5d976a, PowerKids Pr.) Rosen Publishing Group, Inc., The.

—Working with Levers, 1 vol. 2019. (Doing Work with Simple Machines Ser.). (ENG.). 24p. (gr. 3-3). 25.27 (978-1-5383-4361-6(4), 205d5399-8465-49bf-bd34-5295c6086df6, PowerKids Pr.) Rosen Publishing Group, Inc., The.

Macken, JoAnn Early. Simple Machines. 2010. (Everyday Science Ser.). 24p. (J). (gr. k-3). 25.65 (978-1-60753-016-9(3)) Amicus Learning.

Manolis, Kay. Levers. 2009. (Simple Machines Ser.). (ENG., Illus.). 24p. (J). (gr. 2-5). lib. bdg. 26.95 (978-1-60014-325-0(3), Blastoff! Readers) Bellwether Media.

—Pulleys. 2009. (Simple Machines Ser.). (ENG., Illus.). 24p. (J). (gr. 2-5). lib. bdg. 26.95 (978-1-60014-324-3(5), Blastoff! Readers) Bellwether Media.

—Skid Steer Loaders. 2008. (Mighty Machines Ser.). (ENG., Illus.). 24p. (J). (gr. k-3). lib. bdg. 26.95 (978-1-60014-181-2(1)) Bellwether Media.

Marsico, Katie. Simple Machines. Bane, Jeff, illus. 2018. (My Early Library: My World of Science Ser.). (ENG.). 24p. (J). (gr. k-1). lib. bdg. 30.64 (978-1-5341-2892-7(1), 211612) Cherry Lake Publishing.

Martin, M. T. Earth Movers. 2006. (Mighty Machines Ser.). (ENG., Illus.). 24p. (J). (gr. k-3). lib. bdg. 26.95 (978-1-60014-047-1(5)) Bellwether Media.

Mason, Conrad. See Inside How Things Work. 2010. (See Inside Board Bks). 16p. (J). bds. 12.99 (978-0-7945-2406-7(0), Usborne) EDC Publishing.

Masters, Nancy Robinson. Heavy Equipment Operator. 2010. (21st Century Skills Library: Cool Careers Ser.). (ENG., Illus.). 32p. (gr. 4-8). lib. bdg. 32.07 (978-1-60279-941-7(5), 200627) Cherry Lake Publishing.

Mattern, Joanne. Inclined Planes. 2019. (Simple Machines Fun! Ser.). (ENG., Illus.). 24p. (J). (gr. k-3). lib. bdg. 26.95 (978-1-62617-991-2(3), Blastoff! Readers) Bellwether Media.

—Levers. 2019. (Simple Machines Fun! Ser.). (ENG., Illus.). 24p. (J). (gr. k-3). lib. bdg. 26.95 (978-1-62617-992-9(1), Blastoff! Readers) Bellwether Media.

—Pulleys. 2019. (Simple Machines Fun! Ser.). (ENG., Illus.). 24p. (J). (gr. k-3). lib. bdg. 26.95 (978-1-62617-993-6(X), Blastoff! Readers) Bellwether Media.

—Screws. 2019. (Simple Machines Fun! Ser.). (ENG., Illus.). 24p. (J). (gr. k-3). lib. bdg. 26.95 (978-1-62617-994-3(8), Blastoff! Readers) Bellwether Media.

—Wedges. 2019. (Simple Machines Fun! Ser.). (ENG., Illus.). 24p. (J). (gr. k-3). lib. bdg. 26.95 (978-1-62617-995-0(6), Blastoff! Readers) Bellwether Media.

McBride, Carol. Making Magnificent Machines: Fun with Math, Science, & Engineering. 2008. (ENG.). 128p. (gr. k-8). pap. 19.95 (978-1-59363-337-0(8)) Prufrock Pr.

McClellan, Ray. Backhoes. 2006. (Mighty Machines Ser.). (ENG., Illus.). 24p. (J). (gr. k-3). lib. bdg. 26.95 (978-1-60014-042-6(4)) Bellwether Media.

—Concrete Mixers. 2006. (Mighty Machines Ser.). (ENG., Illus.). 24p. (J). (gr. k-3). lib. bdg. 26.95 (978-1-60014-044-0(0)) Bellwether Media.

Mega Machines. 2004. (Illus.). 64p. (J). pap. (978-2-7643-0202-6(9)) Phidal Publishing, Inc./Editions Phidal, Inc.

Meister, Cari. Backhoes. 2013. (ENG., Illus.). 24p. (J). lib. bdg. 25.65 (978-1-62031-042-7(2)) Jump! Inc.

Mezzanotte, Jim. Cargadores (Giant Loaders), 1 vol. 2005. (Vehículos Gigantes (Giant Vehicles) Ser.). (SPA.). 24p. (gr. 2-4). pap. 9.15 (978-0-8368-5994-2(4), 865b2ebb-8663-4c13-95e5-b2f05ab22bea); lib. bdg. 25.67 (978-0-8368-5987-4(1), aba37f91-8add-4afe-8fbd-f5617bf7dee8) Stevens, Gareth Publishing LLLP. (Gareth Stevens Learning Library).

—Cómo Funcionan Las Rampas, Las Cuñas y Los Tornillos (How Ramps, Wedges, & Screws Work), 1 vol. 2006. (Cómo Funcionan Las Máquinas Simples (How Simple Machines Work) Ser.). (SPA., Illus.). 24p. (gr. 2-4). pap. 9.15 (978-0-8368-7450-1(1), 00d6fd03-071c-450d-89a6-c0e99e1f5909); lib. bdg. 24.67 (978-0-8368-7445-7(5), 8efc33a7-b535-4abe-8311-cb567c89b6f4) Stevens, Gareth Publishing LLLP. (Weekly Reader Leveled Readers).

—Cómo Funcionan Las Ruedas y Los Ejes (How Wheels & Axles Work), 1 vol. 2006. (Cómo Funcionan Las Máquinas Simples (How Simple Machines Work) Ser.). (SPA., Illus.). 24p. (gr. 2-4). pap. 9.15 (978-0-8368-7451-8(X), 298f3066-2824-456c-81ae-b84d8a98ce55); lib. bdg. 24.67 (978-0-8368-7446-4(3), 635d35a0-7760-4abe-8808-7eb0c7e5572f) Stevens, Gareth Publishing LLLP. (Weekly Reader Leveled Readers).

—Excavadoras (Giant Diggers), 1 vol. 2005. (Vehículos Gigantes (Giant Vehicles) Ser.). (SPA., Illus.). 24p. (gr. 2-4). lib. bdg. 25.67 (978-0-8368-5988-1(X), a5153680-ce6b-42c6-a5ce-96dd7f62acb1, Gareth Stevens Learning Library) Stevens, Gareth Publishing LLLP.

—Giant Diggers, 1 vol. 2005. (Giant Vehicles Ser.). (ENG., Illus.). 24p. (gr. 2-4). pap. 9.15 (978-0-8368-4918-9(3), 8ece21f4-855f-41cc-ae85-6f2dfa47b27c); lib. bdg. 25.67 (978-0-8368-4911-0(6), 84d4b372-306a-45dc-878d-d6b19fdba6f4) Stevens, Gareth Publishing LLLP. (Gareth Stevens Learning Library).

—Giant Loaders, 1 vol. 2005. (Giant Vehicles Ser.). (ENG., Illus.). 24p. (gr. 2-4). pap. 9.15 (978-0-8368-4920-2(5), 86628ff8-40ee-49d8-96c8-498181c9ad87); lib. bdg. 25.67 (978-0-8368-4913-4(2), 70512ffb-5116-445c-9157-fd086162b4f5) Stevens, Gareth Publishing LLLP. (Gareth Stevens Learning Library).

—Giant Scrapers, 1 vol. 2005. (Giant Vehicles Ser.). (ENG., Illus.). 24p. (gr. 2-4). pap. 9.15 (978-0-8368-4921-9(3), 81fb3163-45f5-4178-b797-1a3fd0fd53d5); lib. bdg. 25.67 (978-0-8368-4914-1(0), 5cc16064-5e8c-4f38-b3d2-579c20e31125) Stevens, Gareth Publishing LLLP. (Gareth Stevens Learning Library).

—How Levers Work, 1 vol. 2006. (How Simple Machines Work Ser.). (ENG., Illus.). 24p. (gr. 2-4). pap. 9.15 (978-0-8368-7352-8(1), 7ab0c880-2395-4618-9ee8-d223dfb30f0c); lib. bdg. 24.67 (978-0-8368-7347-4(5), 9559e5f0-4b86-4662-ad2f-f279d32a3c5f) Stevens, Gareth Publishing LLLP. (Weekly Reader Leveled Readers).

—How Pulleys Work, 1 vol. 2006. (How Simple Machines Work Ser.). (ENG., Illus.). 24p. (gr. 2-4). lib. bdg. 24.67 (978-0-8368-7348-1(3), dcaadf68-8718-4736-b817-a4348fbf6486, Weekly Reader Leveled Readers) Stevens, Gareth Publishing LLLP.

—How Ramps, Wedges, & Screws Work, 1 vol. (How Simple Machines Work Ser.). (ENG., Illus.). 24p. (gr. 2-4). 2007. lib. bdg. 24.67 (978-0-8368-7349-8(1), 20418366-bb9d-41b6-9476-d2ad6b1f5921) 2006. pap. 9.15 (978-0-8368-7354-2(8), 94a798eb-82dd-431f-9884-54940ee5f491) Stevens, Gareth Publishing LLLP. (Weekly Reader Leveled Readers).

—Raspadores (Giant Scrapers), 1 vol. 2005. (Vehículos Gigantes (Giant Vehicles) Ser.). (SPA.). 24p. (gr. 2-4). lib. bdg. 25.67 (978-0-8368-5990-4(1), ca6f6731-c0e0-4d92-b364-3551cc88ae04, Gareth Stevens Learning Library) Stevens, Gareth Publishing LLLP.

Michele, Tracey. Big Machines. 2011. (Learn-Abouts Ser.). (Illus.). 16p. (J). pap. 7.95 (978-1-59920-610-3(2)) Black Rabbit Bks.

Mighty Machines: A Lego Adventure in the Real World. 2017. (Illus.). 32p. (J). (978-1-5182-4494-0(7)) Scholastic, Inc.

Mighty Machines (6 book Set) [NASCO]. 2012. (Mighty Machines Ser.). (ENG.). 24p. pap. 41.70 (978-1-62065-473-6(3), Capstone Pr.) Capstone.

Miller, Jake. Screws, 1 vol. 2013. (Simple Machine Science Ser.). (ENG., Illus.). 24p. (J). (gr. 1-2). pap. 9.15 (978-1-4339-8147-0(5), 924face0-14a3-4b68-b583-121af7e8a6e1); lib. bdg. 25.27 (978-1-4339-8146-3(7), 87fd1fd9-73af-4b00-9476-6154b46b0485) Stevens, Gareth Publishing LLLP.

Miller, Malinda. Modern Mechanics: Maintaining Tomorrow's Green Vehicles. 2010. (New Careers for the 21st Century Ser.). (Illus.). 64p. (YA). (gr. 7-18). lib. bdg. 22.95 (978-1-4222-1818-1(X)) Mason Crest.

Miller, Marie. Pulleys, 1 vol. 2013. (Simple Machine Science Ser.). (ENG., Illus.). 24p. (gr. 1-2). 25.27 (978-1-4339-8141-8(6), 7e684a22-a8ab-421c-aeb8-cd7d22e32caf); pap. 9.15 (978-1-4339-8142-5(4), a5b70808-7497-4a94-a01a-9362b80df9b4) Stevens, Gareth Publishing LLLP.

Miller, Tim & Sjonger, Rebecca. Levers in My Makerspace, 1 vol. 2017. (Simple Machines in My Makerspace Ser.). (ENG., Illus.). 32p. (J). (gr. 3-4). pap. (978-0-7787-3377-5(7)) Crabtree Publishing Co.

Mitton, Tony. Amazing Machines Cool Cars Activity Book. Parker, Ant, illus. 2017. (Amazing Machines Ser.). (ENG.). 24p. (J). pap. 5.99 (978-0-7534-7296-5(1), 900161205, Kingfisher) Roaring Brook Pr.

Mitton, Tony & Parker, Ant. Amazing Machines Jigsaw Book. 2018. (Amazing Machines Ser.). (ENG.). 10p. (J). bds. 12.99 (978-0-7534-7391-7(7), 900183782, Kingfisher) Roaring Brook Pr.

—Tough Trucks. 2018. (Amazing Machines Ser.). (ENG.). 20p. (J). bds. 6.99 (978-0-7534-7397-9(6), 900183781, Kingfisher) Roaring Brook Pr.

Monroe, Tilda. What Do You Know about Simple Machines?, 1 vol. 2010. (20 Questions: Physical Science Ser.). (ENG.). 24p. (J). (gr. 2-3). pap. 9.25 (978-1-4488-1257-8(7), fa28147f-8367-47a2-a187-8af3709a55e0, PowerKids Pr.); lib. bdg. 26.27 (978-1-4488-0674-4(7), e2201e78-de61-4cc2-9da8-bd8d2cdd343c) Rosen Publishing Group, Inc., The.

El Mundo de las Maquinas. (Coleccion Lo Sabias?). (SPA., Illus.). 44p. (J). 12.95 (978-950-11-0939-9(9), SGM9399) Sigmar ARG. Dist: Continental Bk. Co., Inc.

Murphy, Patricia J. Simple Machines. 2006. (Rosen Real Readers Big Bookstm Ser.). (ENG.). 16p. (gr. 2-3). 37.95 (978-1-4042-6220-1(2)) Rosen Publishing Group, Inc., The.

Murray, Julie. Excavators. 2018. (Construction Machines (Dash!) Ser.). (ENG., Illus.). 24p. (J). (gr. k-4). lib. bdg. 31.36 (978-1-5321-2517-1(8), 30043, Abdo Zoom-Dash) ABDO Publishing Co.

National Geographic Learning. Language, Literacy & Vocabulary - Reading Expeditions (Physical Science): Machines: Simple & Compound. 2007. (ENG., Illus.). 36p. (J). pap. 20.95 (978-0-7922-5439-3(2)) CENGAGE Learning.

O'Brien, Cynthia. Parts Work Together. 2019. (Full STEAM Ahead! - Technology Time Ser.). (Illus.). 24p. (J). (gr. 1-1). (978-0-7787-6201-0(7)); pap. (978-0-7787-6238-6(6)) Crabtree Publishing Co.

Oliver, Simone G. Tools Make Work Easier. 2017. (Text Connections Guided Close Reading Ser.). (J). (gr. k). (978-1-4900-1768-6(2)) Benchmark Education Co.

Oxlade, Chris. Construction Machines. 2018. (ENG., Illus.). 48p. (J). (gr. 1-5). pap. 6.95 (978-0-2281-0111-6(5), 7cf8e4b1-dfd2-4ec1-b6ca-b474b215b4f4) Firefly Bks., Ltd.

—Cool Machines: Ten Fire Engines & Emergency Vehicles. 2019. (Cool Machines Ser.). (ENG., Illus.). 32p. (J). (gr. k-2). pap. 10.99 (978-1-4451-5511-1(7), Franklin Watts) Hachette Children's Group GBR. Dist: Hachette Bk. Group.

—Find Out about Machines. 2013. (Illus.). 64p. (J). (gr. 3-7). 9.99 (978-1-84322-973-5(0)) Anness Publishing GBR. Dist: National Bk. Network.

—Levers. 2009. (Simple Machines (Smart Apple Media Paperback) Ser.). (Illus.). 32p. (J). (gr. k-2). pap. 7.95 (978-1-59920-200-6(X)) Black Rabbit Bks.

—Pulleys. 2009. (Simple Machines (Smart Apple Media Paperback) Ser.). (Illus.). 32p. (J). (gr. k-2). pap. 7.95 (978-1-59920-201-3(8)) Black Rabbit Bks.

—Simple Experiments with Inclined Planes, 1 vol. 2013. (Science Experiments with Simple Machines Ser.). (ENG.). 32p. (J). (gr. 2-3). 31.17 (978-1-61533-752-1(0), 2c1b48f5-4d72-4d74-885c-1fe571cab294); pap. 12.75 (978-1-61533-821-4(7), 81808ed5-9e4b-4eac-b4d7-a06c9973b73f) Rosen Publishing Group, Inc., The. (Windmill Bks.).

—Simple Experiments with Inclined Planes. 2013. (Science Experiments with Simple Machines Ser.). 32p. (J). (gr. k-3). pap. 70.50 (978-1-61533-822-1(5)) Windmill Bks.

—This Is My Digger. Laila, Christine, photos by. 2008. (Mega Machine Drivers Ser.). (Illus.). 30p. (J). (gr. k). lib. bdg. 28.50 (978-1-59771-104-3(7)) Sea-To-Sea Pubns.

—This Is My Dump Truck. Crawford, Andy, photos by. 2008. (Mega Machine Drivers Ser.). (Illus.). 30p. (J). (gr. k). lib. bdg. 28.50 (978-1-59771-105-0(5)) Sea-To-Sea Pubns.

—Wedges & Ramps. 2009. (Simple Machines (Smart Apple Media Paperback) Ser.). (Illus.). 32p. (J). (gr. 4-7). pap. 7.95 (978-1-59920-203-7(4)) Black Rabbit Bks.

Oxlade, Chris & Peacock, Graham. Machines: Gears, Levers, Pulleys, Engines. 2016. (Illus.). 64p. (J). (gr. -1-12). 12.99 (978-1-86147-490-2(3), Armadillo) Anness Publishing GBR. Dist: National Bk. Network.

Paes, Rob, illus. Mighty Machines. 2003. 12p. (J). (gr. k-3). 20.00 (978-0-7567-6652-8(4)) DIANE Publishing Co.

Palas Mecánicas (Earthmovers) 2006. (J). pap. 6.95 (978-0-8225-6644-1(3), Ediciones Lerner) Lerner Publishing Group.

Pang, Alex, illus. Machines Close-Up, 12 vols., Set. Incl. Military Vehicles. Gilpin, Daniel. 31.21 (978-1-60870-109-4(3), 14a3a8bb-2574-46e7-aa93-863cf03f9611); Modern Military Aircraft. Gilpin, Daniel. 31.21 (978-1-60870-108-7(5), 747283ab-fe32-435c-a207-73801e7bb1ca); Modern Warships & Submarines. West, David. 31.21 (978-1-60870-110-0(7), 4bec0be5-c9bd-4986-8690-2b3f3a283437); Record Breakers. Gilpin, Daniel. 31.21 (978-1-60870-113-1(1), 4582474e-2edb-4155-a62a-6f9144194f4c); Rescue Vehicles. Gilpin, Daniel. 31.21 (978-1-60870-111-7(5), 2b5c3164-2cb9-466b-80f6-484ba3f35644); Spacecraft. Gilpin, Daniel. 31.21 (978-1-60870-112-4(3), 3d924006-0a5a-4d82-a29b-abe9a8227f78); (Illus.). 32p. (gr. 4-4). (Machines Close-Up Ser.). (ENG.). 2011. Set lib. bdg. 187.26 (978-1-60870-107-0(7), c80e0190-38d1-4e7e-8d6a-efb456074e84, Cavendish Square) Cavendish Square Publishing LLC.

Parker, Janice. Machines. 2016. (Illus.). 24p. (J). (978-1-5105-2241-1(7)) SmartBook Media, Inc.

—Machines. 2008. (Science Q & A Ser.). (Illus.). 48p. (YA). (gr. 5-8). pap. 10.95 (978-1-59036-951-7(3)); lib. bdg. 29.05 (978-1-59036-950-0(5)) Weigl Pubs., Inc.

—Machines Q & A. 2013. (J). (978-1-62127-416-2(0)); pap. (978-1-62127-422-3(5)) Weigl Pubs., Inc.

Parker, Steve. Giant Machines. 2010. (How It Works Ser.). 40p. (J). (gr. 3-18). lib. bdg. 19.95 (978-1-4222-1796-2(5)) Mason Crest.

—On the Building Site. 2010. (J). 28.50 (978-1-59920-288-4(3)) Black Rabbit Bks.

Peppas, Lynn. Road Makers & Breakers. 2012. (ENG.). 32p. (J). (978-0-7787-3020-0(4)); pap. (978-0-7787-3025-5(5)) Crabtree Publishing Co.

Perritano, John. The Revolution in Industry: How Machines Changed America. 2008. (Graphic America Ser.). (ENG., Illus.). 32p. (J). (gr. 3-6). lib. bdg. (978-0-7787-4189-3(3)) Crabtree Publishing Co.

Petruccio, Steven. At the Construction Site (en el Sitio de Construccion) Gongora, Oscar, tr. 2011. (Dover Bilingual Books for Kids Ser.). (ENG., Illus.). 32p. (J). (gr. k-6). pap. 3.99 (978-0-486-46368-1(0), 463680) Dover Pubns., Inc.

Pettiford, Rebecca. Concrete Mixers. 2017. (Mighty Machines in Action Ser.). (ENG., Illus.). 24p. (J). (gr. k-3). lib. bdg. 26.95 (978-1-62617-630-0(2), Blastoff! Readers) Bellwether Media.

—Earth Movers. 2017. (Mighty Machines in Action Ser.). (ENG., Illus.). 24p. (J). (gr. k-3). lib. bdg. 26.95 (978-1-62617-631-7(0), Blastoff! Readers) Bellwether Media.

Phillips, Jessica, illus. Zoom along at the Construction Site. 2018. (Zoom Along Ser.: 2). (ENG.). 16p. (J). (gr. -1 — 1). bds. 15.99 (978-1-77138-886-3(2)) Kids Can Pr., Ltd. CAN. Dist: Hachette Bk. Group.

Porterfield, Jason. Fab Lab Creating with Milling Machines, 1 vol. 2016. (Getting Creative with Fab Lab Ser.). (ENG., Illus.).

64p. (J). (gr. 6-6). 36.13 *(978-1-4994-6506-8(3),* f2dfca2b-df76-4290-afb7-e8b8f62e1045) Rosen Publishing Group, Inc., The.

Priddy, Roger. Big Board First 100 Trucks & Things That Go. 2006. (First 100 Ser.). (ENG., Illus.). 14p. (J). (gr. -1 — 1). bds. 10.99 *(978-0-312-49806-1(3),* 900041003) St. Martin's Pr.

Randolph, Joanne. Inclined Planes in My World. 2009. (My World of Science Ser.). 24p. (gr. 2-2). 37.50 *(978-1-61514-723-6(3),* PowerKids Pr.) Rosen Publishing Group, Inc., The.

—Inclined Planes in My World/Planos inclinados en mi Mundo. 2009. (My World of Science/la ciencia en mi mundo Ser.). 48p. (gr. 2-2). 37.50 *(978-1-61514-735-9(7),* Editorial Buenas Letras) Rosen Publishing Group, Inc., The.

—Levers in My World. (My World of Science Ser.). 24p. 2009. (gr. 2-2). 37.50 *(978-1-61514-724-3(1),* PowerKids Pr.) 2005. (ENG.). (gr. k-2). pap. 7.05 *(978-1-4042-8424-1(9),* 4464f224-230d-436e-82b1-e349398f3f20, Rosen Classroom) Rosen Publishing Group, Inc., The.

—Levers in My World/Palancas en mi Mundo. 2009. (My World of Science/la ciencia en mi mundo Ser.). 48p. (gr. 2-2). 37.50 *(978-1-61514-736-6(5),* Editorial Buenas Letras) Rosen Publishing Group, Inc., The.

—Pulleys in My World. 2009. (My World of Science Ser.). 24p. (gr. 2-2). 37.50 *(978-1-61514-727-4(6),* PowerKids Pr.) Rosen Publishing Group, Inc., The.

—Pulleys in My World/Poleas en mi Mundo. 2009. (My World of Science/la ciencia en mi mundo Ser.). (ENG & SPA.). 48p. (gr. 2-2). 37.50 *(978-1-61514-739-7(X),* Editorial Buenas Letras) Rosen Publishing Group, Inc., The.

—Wedges in My World. 2009. (My World of Science Ser.). 24p. (gr. 2-2). 37.50 *(978-1-61514-730-4(6),* PowerKids Pr.) Rosen Publishing Group, Inc., The.

—Wedges in My World/Cunas en mi Mundo. 2009. (My World of Science/la ciencia en mi mundo Ser.). (ENG & SPA.). 48p. (gr. 2-2). 37.50 *(978-1-61514-742-7(X),* Editorial Buenas Letras) Rosen Publishing Group, Inc., The.

—Wheel Loaders. 2009. (Earth Movers Ser.). 24p. (gr. k-1). 37.50 *(978-1-61512-237-0(0),* PowerKids Pr.) Rosen Publishing Group, Inc., The.

—Wheels & Axels in My World/Ejes y ruedas en mi Mundo. 2009. (My World of Science/la ciencia en mi mundo Ser.). (ENG & SPA.). 48p. (gr. 2-2). 37.50 *(978-1-61514-743-4(8),* Editorial Buenas Letras) Rosen Publishing Group, Inc., The.

—Wheels & Axles in My World. (My World of Science Ser.). 24p. 2009. (gr. 2-2). 37.50 *(978-1-61514-731-1(4),* PowerKids Pr.) 2006. (ENG.). (gr. k-2). pap. 7.05 *(978-1-4042-8427-2(3),* 27fa068d-8e9a-4d09-80a0-b6ac1c5228d2, Rosen Classroom) Rosen Publishing Group, Inc., The.

—Wheels & Axles in My World: Ejes y Ruedas en Mi Mundo, 1 vol. 2005. (My World of Science / la Ciencia en Mi Mundo Ser.). (ENG & SPA.). 24p. (J). (gr. 2-2). 22.27 *(978-1-4042-3325-6(3),* 7a96327d-1324-482a-8470-843977f3d90d) Rosen Publishing Group, Inc., The.

Rau, Dana Meachen. Simple Machines. 2011. (True Book(tm), a — Physical Science Ser.). (ENG., Illus.). 48p. (J). lib. bdg. 31.00 *(978-0-531-26324-2(X));* pap. 6.95 *(978-0-531-26586-4(2))* Scholastic Library Publishing. (Children's Pr.).

Rauf, Don. Careers in Machine Maintenance, 1 vol. 2019. (Makerspace Careers Ser.). (ENG., Illus.). 80p. (J). (gr. 7-7). pap. 16.30 *(978-1-5081-8806-3(8),* a0192b5f-34b6-4928-9d07-945b58b77d09) Rosen Publishing Group, Inc., The.

Reinke, Beth Bence. Front Loaders Scoop! 2017. (Bumba Books (r) — Construction Zone Ser.). (ENG., Illus.). 24p. (J). (gr. -1-1). 26.65 *(978-1-5124-3360-9(8),* 864c08a5-46f0-46a6-8ffe-963bf7212d4f, Lerner Pubns.) Lerner Publishing Group.

Resler, T. J. How Things Work: Then & Now. 2018. (Illus.). 208p. (J). (gr. 3-7). 19.99 *(978-1-4263-3166-4(5),* National Geographic Kids) Disney Publishing Worldwide.

Rice, Dona Herweck. Creative Machines. rev. ed. 2019. (Smithsonian: Informational Text Ser.). (ENG., Illus.). 32p. (J). (gr. 2-3). pap. 10.99 *(978-1-4938-6668-7(0))* Teacher Created Materials, Inc.

Richards, Jon. Forces & Simple Machines. (Science Factory Ser.). 32p. (gr. 4-5). 2009. 50.50 *(978-1-60853-021-2(3),* PowerKids Pr.) 2007. (ENG., Illus.). (YA). lib. bdg. 30.27 *(978-1-4042-3908-1(1),* e432f193-c484-444f-bbef-54a5d26f799d) Rosen Publishing Group, Inc., The.

Richards, Jon & Simkins, Ed. Machines & Motors, 1 vol. 2017. (Infographics: How It Works). (ENG.). 32p. (J). (gr. 4-5). pap. 11.50 *(978-1-5382-1352-0(4),* ec665422-f59b-47fb-93db-570b05c9d393); lib. bdg. 28.27 *(978-1-5382-1354-4(0),* 8f15fddf-3331-4963-8450-21fa57723952) Stevens, Gareth Publishing LLLP.

Rigby Education Staff. Machines Around Your Home. (Illus.). 8p. (J). bds. 3.95 *(978-0-7635-6491-9(5),* 764915C99) Rigby Education.

Rinkel, Ken, illus. Giant Machines. 2003. 12p. (J). (gr. k-3). 20.00 *(978-0-7567-6653-5(2))* DIANE Publishing Co.

Ripley's Believe It Or Not! Ripley Twists: Mighty Machines PORTRAIT EDN. 2014. (Twist Ser.). (ENG.). 48p. (J). 12.95 *(978-1-893951-85-3(5))* Ripley Entertainment, Inc.

Rissman, Rebecca. Simple Machines: Real Size Science, 1 vol. 2013. (Real Size Science Ser.). (ENG.). 24p. (J). (gr. -1-1). pap. 6.95 *(978-1-4329-7884-6(5),* 122824, Heinemann) Capstone.

Rooney, Anne. You Wouldn't Want to Live Without Simple Machines! (You Wouldn't Want to Live Without...) (Library Edition) Bergin, Mark, illus. 2018. (You Wouldn't Want to Live Without... Ser.). (ENG.). 32p. (J). (gr. 3). lib. bdg. 29.00 *(978-0-531-12815-2(6),* Watts, Franklin) Scholastic Library Publishing.

Roza, Greg. Wedges, 1 vol. 2013. (Simple Machine Science Ser.). (ENG., Illus.). 24p. (J). (gr. 1-2). 25.27 *(978-1-4339-8151-7(3),* be4b6f06-2369-420f-bc78-05fb85a05b2c); pap. 9.15 *(978-1-4339-8152-4(1),* 3373a7fa-f632-41a2-b01b-92a7f271e3a6) Stevens, Gareth Publishing LLLP.

Ruck, Colleen. Diggers. 2011. (My Favorite Machines Ser.). (ENG.). 24p. (J). (gr. 1-4). 28.50 *(978-1-59920-674-5(9),* 17347) Black Rabbit Bks.

Rustad, Martha E. H. Pulleys. 2018. (Simple Machines Ser.). (ENG., Illus.). 24p. (J). (gr. -1-2). lib. bdg. 22.65 *(978-1-5435-0074-5(9),* 137023, Pebble) Capstone.

Sadler, Wendy. Using Levers, 6 vols. 2005. (Raintree Perspectives Ser.). (Illus.). *(978-1-4109-1449-1(6)); (978-1-4109-1453-8(4)); (978-1-4109-1451-4(8)); (978-1-4109-1450-7(X)); (978-1-4109-1452-1(6)); (978-1-4109-1454-5(2))* Steck-Vaughn.

Samuels, Charlie. The Rise of Industry (1700 - 1800), 1 vol. 2010. (Science Highlights: a Gareth Stevens Timeline Ser.). (ENG.). 48p. (J). (gr. 6-8). pap. 15.05 *(978-1-4339-4146-7(5),* 1aef8a49-1ce9-49d1-9444-dcb41634169e); lib. bdg. 34.60 *(978-1-4339-4145-0(7),* acde0dd0-8818-4e17-a792-3e7f632f6be1) Stevens, Gareth Publishing LLLP. (Gareth Stevens Secondary Library).

Scheff, Matt. Mighty Military Machines. 2018. (Mighty Military Machines Ser.). (ENG.). 24p. (J). (gr. -1-2). 147.90 *(978-1-9771-0133-4(X),* 28311, Pebble) Capstone.

—Speed Machines, 7 vols. 2015. (Speed Machines Ser.: 8). (ENG.). 32p. (J). (gr. 3-6). lib. bdg. 229.53 *(978-1-62403-607-1(4),* 17291, SportsZone) ABDO Publishing Co.

Scholastic Clubs US Machines at Work Set #1: Machines at Work. 2006. (J). 39.80 *(978-1-59566-321-4(5))* QEB Publishing Inc.

Scholastic Clubs US Machines at Work Set #2: Machines at Work. 2006. 39.80 *(978-1-59566-322-1(3))* QEB Publishing Inc.

Schuh, Mari. Concrete Mixers. (Spot Ser.). (ENG.). 16p. (J). (gr. -1-1). 2018. pap. 7.99 *(978-1-68152-209-8(8),* 14741) 2017. 17.95 *(978-1-68151-098-9(7),* 14622) Amicus.

—Diggers. (Spot Ser.). (ENG.). 16p. (J). (gr. -1-1). 2018. pap. 7.99 *(978-1-68152-212-8(8),* 14743) 2017. 17.95 *(978-1-68151-101-6(0),* 14624) Amicus.

—Hauling a Pumpkin: Wheels & Axles vs. Lever. 2015. (First Step Nonfiction — Simple Machines to the Rescue Ser.). (ENG., Illus.). 24p. (J). (gr. k-2). pap. 6.99 *(978-1-4677-8304-0(8),* e7f4a3c6-fb07-4757-abc5-aeecbf1664db) Lerner Publishing Group.

—Holding a Door Open: Wedge vs. Wheels & Axles. 2015. (First Step Nonfiction — Simple Machines to the Rescue Ser.). (ENG., Illus.). 24p. (J). (gr. k-2). E-Book 35.99 *(978-1-4677-8303-3(X),* Lerner Pubns.) Lerner Publishing Group.

—Las Cargadoras (Loaders) 2017. (Spot Mighty Machines Ser.). (ENG & SPA., Illus.). 16p. (J). (gr. k-3). 17.95 *(978-1-68151-269-3(6),* Amicus Readers) Amicus Learning.

—Las Excavadoras (Diggers) 2017. (Spot Mighty Machines Ser.). (ENG & SPA., Illus.). 16p. (J). (gr. k-3). 17.95 *(978-1-68151-267-9(X),* Amicus Readers) Amicus Learning.

—Las Mezcladoras de Concreto. 2017. (Máquinas Poderosas Ser.). (Illus.). 16p. (J). (gr. -1-2). lib. bdg. 17.95 *(978-1-68151-265-5(3),* 14706) Amicus.

—Loaders. (Spot Ser.). (ENG., Illus.). 16p. (J). (gr. -1-1). 2018. pap. 7.99 *(978-1-68152-214-2(4),* 14745) 2017. lib. bdg. 17.95 *(978-1-68151-103-0(7),* 14626) Amicus.

—Making a Salad: Wedge vs. Inclined Plane. 2015. (First Step Nonfiction — Simple Machines to the Rescue Ser.). (ENG., Illus.). 24p. (J). (gr. k-2). E-Book 35.99 *(978-1-4677-8295-1(5),* Lerner Pubns.) Lerner Publishing Group.

—Raising a Bag of Toys: Pulley vs. Inclined Plane. 2015. (First Step Nonfiction — Simple Machines to the Rescue Ser.). (ENG., Illus.). 24p. (J). (gr. k-2). 23.99 *(978-1-4677-8024-7(3),* 23efc321-98d9-4b26-933e-55675eaeba98, Lerner Pubns.) Lerner Publishing Group.

Science Experiments with Simple Machines. 2013. (Science Experiments with Simple Machines Ser.). 32p. (J). (gr. k-3). 159.00 *(978-1-61533-871-9(3));* pap. 423.00 *(978-1-61533-879-5(9))* Windmill Bks.

Seagraves, Erin & Baker, Heather. My Neighbors & Their Simple Machines. 2016. (Illus.). 18p. (J). *(978-1-60617-727-3(3))* Teaching Strategies, LLC.

Secrets of the Fun Park, 6 Packs. (gr. k-1). 23.00 *(978-0-7635-9080-2(0))* Rigby Education.

Selwyn, Josephine. Who Uses This Machine? 2012. (Level C Ser.). (ENG., Illus.). 16p. (J). (gr. k-2). pap. 7.95 *(978-1-927136-29-4(6),* 19456) RiverStream Publishing.

Shand, Jennifer. Why Do Tractors Have Such Big Tires? 2015. (Why Do... ? Ser.). lib. bdg. 19.65 *(978-1-4867-0624-2(X))* Turtleback.

—Why Do Tractors Have Such Big Tires? Stem. Fabbri, Daniele, illus. 2014. (ENG.). 20p. (J). (gr. k-4). 8.99 *(978-1-4867-0382-1(8))* Flowerpot Children's Pr. Inc. CAN. Dist: Cardinal Pubs. Group.

Silverman, Buffy. I Use Simple Machines. 2011. (My Science Library). (ENG., Illus.). 24p. (gr. k-1). pap. 9.95 *(978-1-61741-930-0(3),* 9781617419300) Rourke Educational Media.

—Simple Machines: Forces in Action. rev. ed. 2016. (Do It Yourself Ser.). (ENG.). 48p. (J). (gr. 3-6). pap. 8.99 *(978-1-4846-3640-4(6),* 134036, Heinemann) Capstone.

Simple Machines. 2004. (Illus.). lib. bdg. 7.95 *(978-0-8225-3352-8(9))*Set. 2006. (J). (gr. 2-4). 46.95 *(978-0-8225-3353-5(7))* Lerner Publishing Group.

Simple Machines - English Take Home Book. 2007. (Journeys Ser.). (J). pap. 20.00 *(978-1-4042-9493-6(7),* Rosen Classroom) Rosen Publishing Group, Inc., The.

Simple Machines Everywhere. 2014. (Simple Machines Everywhere Ser.). 24p. (J). (gr. k-3). pap. 49.50 *(978-1-4777-7246-1(4));* (ENG.). (gr. 2-3). 151.62 *(978-1-4777-6646-0(4),* de80bc71-78a9-4372-afd4-71132eeee77b) Rosen Publishing Group, Inc., The. (PowerKids Pr.).

Slingerland, Janet. Construction Vehicles. 2018. (Vehicles on the Job Ser.). (ENG., Illus.). 24p. (J). (gr. 1-3). 25.27 *(978-1-59953-942-3(X))* Norwood Hse. Pr.

Small, Cathleen. Fab Lab Creating with Vinyl Cutters, 1 vol. 2016. (Getting Creative with Fab Lab Ser.). (ENG.). 64p. (J). (gr. 6-6). 36.13 *(978-1-5081-7350-2(8),* e849f08c-76ad-4558-a5ef-9a99fbad08d7) Rosen Publishing Group, Inc., The.

Small Machines Sets: 1 Each of 3 Big Books. (Sunshinetm Science Ser.). (gr. 1-2). 93.95 *(978-0-7802-0531-4(6))* Wright Group/McGraw-Hill.

Small Machines Sets: 1 Each of 3 Student Books. (Sunshinetm Science Ser.). (gr. 1-2). 17.95 *(978-0-7802-0272-6(4))* Wright Group/McGraw-Hill.

Sohn, Emily. Levers & Pulleys. 2019. (iScience Ser.). (ENG., Illus.). 48p. (J). (gr. 5-6). 23.94 *(978-1-68450-949-2(1));* pap. 13.26 *(978-1-68404-403-0(0))* Norwood Hse. Pr.

Speed Machines Sticker Book. Date not set. (Illus.). 12p. (J). 3.98 *(978-1-4054-0499-0(X))* Parragon, Inc.

Spilsbury, Louise. Inclined Planes, 1 vol. 2018. (Technology in Action Ser.). (ENG.). 32p. (gr. 3-3). 27.93 *(978-1-5383-3749-3(5),* b3befd4c-d216-42ec-8d36-79d156added7, PowerKids Pr.) Rosen Publishing Group, Inc., The.

—Levers, 1 vol. 2018. (Technology in Action Ser.). (ENG.). 32p. (gr. 3-3). 27.93 *(978-1-5383-3753-0(3),* 54beca23-9760-474e-b283-092101adac05, PowerKids Pr.) Rosen Publishing Group, Inc., The.

—Pulleys, 1 vol. 2018. (Technology in Action Ser.). (ENG.). 32p. (gr. 3-3). 27.93 *(978-1-5383-3757-8(6),* cf89cbe5-d114-4c2a-a994-f42e688942bb, PowerKids Pr.) Rosen Publishing Group, Inc., The.

—Wedges, 1 vol. 2018. (Technology in Action Ser.). (ENG.). 32p. (gr. 3-3). 27.93 *(978-1-5383-3765-3(7),* 30fab7be-18db-4ba1-b308-51e69a58dd1f, PowerKids Pr.) Rosen Publishing Group, Inc., The.

Stilwell, Debra. Levers, 1 vol. 2013. (Simple Machine Science Ser.). (ENG., Illus.). 24p. (gr. 1-2). 25.27 *(978-1-4339-8136-4(X),* 782d5154-8222-41a0-be1c-f3de93947c00); pap. 9.15 *(978-1-4339-8137-1(8),* fe381f25-c4ed-4134-82a8-7f5457f910cb) Stevens, Gareth Publishing LLLP.

Stone, Tanya Lee. P Is for Passover. Lucas, Margeaux, illus. 2003. 32p. (J). (gr. -1-k). mass mkt. 5.99 *(978-0-8431-0238-3(1),* Price Stern Sloan) Penguin Young Readers Group.

Sundance/Newbridge LLC Staff. Simple Machines. 2007. (Early Science Ser.). (gr. k-3). 18.95 *(978-1-4007-6612-3(5));* pap. 6.10 *(978-1-4007-6608-6(7))* Sundance/Newbridge Educational Publishing.

—Six Simple Machines. 2004. (Reading PowerWorks Ser.). (gr. 1-3). 37.50 *(978-0-7608-9735-5(2));* pap. 6.10 *(978-0-7608-9736-2(0))* Sundance/Newbridge Educational Publishing.

Ticktock Media, Ltd. Staff. Extreme Machines. 2010. (Top Tens Ser.). (ENG.). 32p. (J). (gr. 1-3). pap. 6.95 *(978-1-84898-197-3(X),* TickTock Books) Octopus Publishing Group GBR. Dist: Independent Pubs. Group.

Tieck, Sarah. Earthmovers. 2005. (Buddy Book Ser.). (Illus.). 24p. (gr. k-4). 25.65 *(978-1-59197-826-8(2),* Buddy Bks.) ABDO Publishing Co.

—Inclined Planes, 1 vol. 2006. (Simple Machines Ser.). (ENG., Illus.). 24p. (gr. -1-3). 25.65 *(978-1-59679-818-2(1),* Buddy Bks.) ABDO Publishing Co.

—Levers, 1 vol. 2006. (Simple Machines Ser.). (ENG., Illus.). 24p. (gr. -1-3). 25.65 *(978-1-59679-814-4(9),* Buddy Bks.) ABDO Publishing Co.

—Pulleys, 1 vol. 2006. (Simple Machines Ser.). (ENG., Illus.). 24p. (gr. -1-3). 25.65 *(978-1-59679-815-1(7),* Buddy Bks.) ABDO Publishing Co.

—Simple Machines, 6 vols., Set. Incl. Inclined Planes. 25.65 *(978-1-59679-818-2(1));* Levers. 25.65 *(978-1-59679-814-4(9));* Pulleys. 25.65 *(978-1-59679-815-1(7));* Screws. 25.65 *(978-1-59679-817-5(3));* Wedges. 25.65 *(978-1-59679-816-8(5));* Wheels & Axles. 25.65 *(978-1-59679-819-9(X));* (Illus.). 24p. (gr. -1-3). (Simple Machines Ser.). 2006. 153.90 *(978-1-59679-813-7(0),* Buddy Bks.) ABDO Publishing Co.

—Wedges, 1 vol. 2006. (Simple Machines Ser.). (ENG., Illus.). 24p. (gr. -1-3). 25.65 *(978-1-59679-816-8(5),* Buddy Bks.) ABDO Publishing Co.

Tiner, John Hudson. Levers. 2003. (Simple Machines Ser.). (Illus.). 24p. (J). lib. bdg. 21.35 *(978-1-58340-135-4(0))* Black Rabbit Bks.

—Pulleys. 2003. (Simple Machines Ser.). (Illus.). 23p. (J). lib. bdg. 21.35 *(978-1-58340-136-1(9))* Black Rabbit Bks.

Tomljanovic, Tatiana. Wedges. (J). 2013. *(978-1-62127-428-5(4))* 2013. pap. *(978-1-62127-434-6(9))* 2009. (Illus.). 24p. (gr. 3-5). pap. 8.59 *(978-1-60596-038-8(1))* Weigl Pubs., Inc.

TOOLS & MACHINES. 2010. (ENG., Illus.). 184p. (gr. 6-12). 35.00 *(978-1-60413-171-0(3),* P179241, Facts On File) Infobase Holdings, Inc.

Top That Publishing Staff, ed. Real Spies. 2004. (I-Quest Ser.). (Illus.). 48p. (J). per. *(978-1-84510-134-3(0))* Top That! Publishing PLC.

Troupe, Thomas Kingsley. Keep It Simple, Rapunzel! The Fairy-Tale Physics of Simple Machines. Tejido, Jomike, illus. 2018. (STEM-Twisted Fairy Tales Ser.). (ENG.). 32p. (J). (gr. k-3). pap. 7.95 *(978-1-5158-2899-0(9),* 138421); lib. bdg. 27.99 *(978-1-5158-2895-2(6),* 138417) Capstone. (Picture Window Bks.).

VanVoorst, Jenny Fretland. Bicycles. 2016. (Early Physics Fun). (Illus.). 24p. (J). (gr. 2-5). lib. bdg. *(978-1-62031-314-5(6),* Pogo) Jump! Inc.

Veitch, Catherine. Big Machines Float!, 1 vol. 2014. (Big Machines Ser.). (ENG., Illus.). 24p. (J). (gr. -1-1). 25.99 *(978-1-4846-0587-5(X),* 126689, Heinemann) Capstone.

Volpe, Karen. Get to Know Levers. 2009. (Get to Know Simple Machines Ser.). (ENG., Illus.). 32p. (J). (gr. 2-3). pap. *(978-0-7787-4484-9(1));* lib. bdg. *(978-0-7787-4467-2(1))* Crabtree Publishing Co.

—Get to Know Pulleys. 2009. (Get to Know Simple Machines Ser.). (ENG., Illus.). 32p. (J). (gr. 2-3). pap. *(978-0-7787-4485-6(X));* lib. bdg. *(978-0-7787-4468-9(X))* Crabtree Publishing Co.

Walker, Sally M. & Feldmann, Roseann. Levers. 2005. (Early Bird Physics Ser.). (Illus.). 48p. (gr. 3-6). lib. bdg. 25.26 *(978-0-8225-2218-8(7))* Lerner Publishing Group.

—Planos Inclinados. King, Andy, photos by. 2009. (Libros de Fisica para Madrugadores Ser.). (SPA., Illus.). 47p. (J). (gr. 3-7). pap. 11.95 *(978-0-8225-2971-2(8))* Lerner Publishing Group.

—Poleas. King, Andy, photos by. 2005. (Libros de Física para Madrugadores (Early Bird Physics) Ser.). (SPA & ENG., Illus.). 48p. (J). (gr. 3-6). lib. bdg. 26.60 *(978-0-8225-2980-4(7),* Ediciones Lerner) Lerner Publishing Group.

—Tornillos. King, Andy, photos by. 2009. (Libros de Fisica para Madrugadores Ser.). (SPA., Illus.). 47p. (J). (gr. 3-7). pap. 11.95 *(978-0-8225-2979-8(3))* Lerner Publishing Group.

Walker, Sally M., et al. Work. 2005. (Early Bird Physics Ser.). (Illus.). 48p. (gr. 3-6). lib. bdg. 25.26 *(978-0-8225-2217-1(9))* Lerner Publishing Group.

Ward, D. J. Simple Machines. Lowery, Mike, illus. 2015. (Let's-Read-And-Find-Out Science 2 Ser.). (ENG.). 40p. (J). (gr. -1-3). pap. 8.99 *(978-0-06-232147-3(1),* HarperCollins) HarperCollins Pubs.

Watt, Fiona & Wells, Rachel. Diggers. 2004. (Ultimate Touchy-Feely Ser.). (Illus.). 10p. (J). 15.95 *(978-0-7945-0340-6(3),* Usborne) EDC Publishing.

Weakland, Mark. Flintstones Explain Simple Machines. 2016. (Flintstones Explain Simple Machines Ser.). (ENG., Illus.). 24p. (J). (gr. k-2). 179.94 *(978-1-4914-8485-2(3),* 24127) Capstone.

—Fred Flintstone's Adventures with Inclined Planes: A Rampin' Good Time. Brown, Alan, illus. 2016. (Flintstones Explain Simple Machines Ser.). (ENG.). 24p. (J). (gr. k-2). lib. bdg. 27.99 *(978-1-4914-8476-0(4),* 130926) Capstone.

—Fred Flintstone's Adventures with Levers: Lift That Load! Cornia, Christian, illus. 2016. (Flintstones Explain Simple Machines Ser.). (ENG.). 24p. (J). (gr. k-2). lib. bdg. 27.99 *(978-1-4914-8473-9(X),* 130922) Capstone.

—Fred Flintstone's Adventures with Pulleys: Work Smarter, Not Harder. Sordo, Paco, illus. 2016. (Flintstones Explain Simple Machines Ser.). (ENG.). 24p. (J). (gr. k-2). lib. bdg. 27.99 *(978-1-4914-8475-3(6),* 130925) Capstone.

—Fred Flintstone's Adventures with Screws: Righty Tighty, Lefty Loosey. Billiau, Loic, illus. 2016. (Flintstones Explain Simple Machines Ser.). (ENG.). 24p. (J). (gr. k-2). lib. bdg. 27.99 *(978-1-4914-8478-4(0),* 130928) Capstone.

—Fred Flintstone's Adventures with Wedges: Just Split! 2016. (Flintstones Explain Simple Machines Ser.). (ENG., Illus.). 24p. (J). (gr. k-2). lib. bdg. 27.99 *(978-1-4914-8477-7(2),* 130927) Capstone.

—Fred Flintstone's Adventures with Wheels & Axles: Bedrock & Roll! Brown, Alan, illus. 2016. (Flintstones Explain Simple Machines Ser.). (ENG.). 24p. (J). (gr. k-2). lib. bdg. 27.99 *(978-1-4914-8474-6(8),* 130923) Capstone.

—Gears Go, Wheels Roll, 1 vol. 2010. (Science Starts Ser.). (ENG., Illus.). 32p. (J). (gr. -1-2). pap. 8.10 *(978-1-4296-6143-0(7),* 115294, Capstone Pr.) Capstone.

—Smash! Wile E. Coyote Experiments with Simple Machines, 1 vol. Cornia, Christian, illus. 2014. (Wile E. Coyote, Physical Science Genius Ser.). (ENG.). 32p. (J). (gr. 3-6). 31.32 *(978-1-4765-4222-5(8),* 124334, Capstone Pr.) Capstone.

What Does It Do? (Set), 10 vols., Set. Incl. What Does It Do? Ambulance. Gregory, Josh. lib. bdg. 29.21 *(978-1-60279-969-1(5),* 200970); What Does It Do? Bulldozer. Capici, Gaetano. lib. bdg. 29.21 *(978-1-60279-972-1(5),* 200966); What Does It Do? Cement Mixer. Capici, Gaetano. lib. bdg. 29.21 *(978-1-60279-973-8(3),* 200972); What Does It Do? Combine. Friedman, Mark. lib. bdg. 29.21 *(978-1-61080-117-1(2),* 201124); What Does It Do? Crane. Gregory, Josh. lib. bdg. 29.21 *(978-1-60279-967-7(9),* 200958); What Does It Do? Digger. Zeiger, Jennifer. lib. bdg. 29.21 *(978-1-60279-968-4(7),* 200968); What Does It Do? Dump Truck. Zeiger, Jennifer. lib. bdg. 29.21 *(978-1-60279-974-5(1),* 200962); What Does It Do? Fire Truck. Gregory, Josh. lib. bdg. 29.21 *(978-1-60279-971-4(7),* 200964); What Does It Do? Tractor. Gregory, Josh. lib. bdg. 29.21 *(978-1-60279-970-7(9),* 200960); What Does It Do? Windmill. Friedman, Mark. lib. bdg. 29.21 *(978-1-61080-118-8(0),* 201126); (gr. 2-5). (Community Connections: What Does It Do? Ser.). (ENG., Illus.). 24p. 2011. 292.10 *(978-1-61080-152-2(0),* 201022) Cherry Lake Publishing.

Whitehouse, Patty. Moving Machines. 2006. (Construction Forces Discovery Library). (Illus.). 24p. (J). (gr. k-2). lib. bdg. 22.79 *(978-1-60044-192-9(0))* Rourke Educational Media.

—Pushes & Pulls. 2006. (Construction Forces Discovery Library). (Illus.). 24p. (J). (gr. k-2). lib. bdg. 22.79 *(978-1-60044-193-6(9))* Rourke Educational Media.

The World's Most Powerful Machines, 10 vols. 2016. (World's Most Powerful Machines Ser.). (ENG.). 00224p. (YA). (gr. 9-9). 234.00 *(978-1-4994-6563-1(7),* 85833897-56e6-48b2-8994-dcec0e128411, Rosen Young Adult) Rosen Publishing Group, Inc., The.

Wright, Nicola. Diggers. 2006. (Illus.). 24p. (YA). (gr. 1-18). lib. bdg. 22.80 *(978-1-931983-57-0(7))* Chrysalis Education.

Yasuda, Anita. Simple Machines! With 25 Science Projects for Kids. Stone, Bryan, illus. 2019. (Explore Your World Ser.). 96p. (J). (gr. 3-4). 19.95 *(978-1-61930-814-5(2),* c033c893-858b-4507-851a-093bf1c90a91); (ENG.). pap. 14.95 *(978-1-61930-817-6(7),* f9b8bb54-9c0a-4988-a549-0c9060787e78) Nomad Pr.

Young, Caroline & Castor, Harriet. The Usborne Book of Machines That Work. Lyon, Chris, illus. 2004. (Young MacHines Ser.). 95p. (J). (gr. k). lib. bdg. 22.95 *(978-1-58086-031-4(1),* Usborne) EDC Publishing.

Zeiger, Jennifer. What Does It Do? Digger. 2011. (Community Connections: What Does It Do? Ser.). (ENG., Illus.). 24p. (gr. 2-5). lib. bdg. 29.21 *(978-1-60279-968-4(7),* 200968) Cherry Lake Publishing.

Zobel, Derek. Blastoff! Readers - Mighty Machines, 4 vols., Set. Incl. Bucket Trucks. 20.00 *(978-0-531-21707-8(8));* Diggers. 20.00 *(978-0-531-21708-5(6));* Pickup Trucks. 20.00 *(978-0-531-21709-2(4));* Wheel Loaders. 20.00 *(978-0-531-21710-8(8));* (Illus.). 24p. (J). (gr. k-3). 2009. 2009. Set lib. bdg. 80.00 *(978-0-531-26127-9(1),* Children's Pr.) Scholastic Library Publishing.

—Diggers. 2009. (Mighty Machines Ser.). (ENG., Illus.). 24p. (J). (gr. k-3). lib. bdg. 26.95 *(978-1-60014-235-2(4))* Bellwether Media.

—Diggers. 2009. (Blastoff! Readers Ser.). (ENG., Illus.). 24p. (J). (gr. k-3). 20.00 *(978-0-531-21708-5(6),* Children's Pr.) Scholastic Library Publishing.

—Scrapers. 2009. (Mighty Machines Ser.). (ENG., Illus.). 24p. (J). (gr. k-3). lib. bdg. 26.95 (978-1-60014-271-0(0)) Bellwether Media.
—Wheel Loaders. 2009. (Blastoff! Readers Ser.). (ENG., Illus.). 24p. (J). (gr. k-3). 20.00 (978-0-531-21710-8(8)), Children's Pr.) Scholastic Library Publishing.
Zoom in on Simple Machines. 2015. (Zoom in on Simple Machines Ser.). (ENG.). 24p. (J). (gr. 2-2). pap., pap., pap. 56.10 (978-0-7660-7052-3(2)); pap., pap., pap. 336.60 (978-0-7660-6675-5(4)); lib. bdg. 153.60 (978-0-7660-6674-8(6), d1c95895-40bd-4ba6-9b2a-683bac76025e) Enslow Publishing, LLC.

MACHINERY, AUTOMATIC
see Automation

MACHINERY—FICTION
Angleberger, Tom. McToad Mows Tiny Island. Hendrix, John, illus. 2015. (ENG.). 40p. (J). (gr. -1-3). 16.95 (978-1-4197-1650-8(6), 1088401, Abrams Bks. for Young Readers) Abrams, Inc.
Auerbach, Annie. Junkyard Dig! Building from a to Z. Shannon, David et al, illus. 2010. (Jon Scieszka's Trucktown Ser.). (ENG.). 26p. (J). (gr. -1-k). bds. 5.99 (978-1-4169-4187-3(8), Little Simon) Little Simon.
AZ Books Staff. Musical Machines. Tulup, Natalia, ed. 2012. (Tra-La-la Ser.). (ENG.). 14p. (J). (-k). bds. 10.95 (978-1-61889-055-9(7)) AZ Bks. LLC.
Berrios, Frank. Let's Be Firefighters! (Blaze & the Monster Machines) Foley, Niki, illus. 2016. (Little Golden Book Ser.). (ENG.). 24p. (J). (-k). 5.99 (978-0-399-55351-6(7), Golden Bks.) Random Hse. Children's Bks.
Bruss, Deborah. Good Morning, Snowplow! Johnson, Steve & Fancher, Lou, illus. 2018. (ENG.). 32p. (J). (gr. -1 — 1). 17.99 (978-1-338-08949-3(8), Levine, Arthur A. Bks.) Scholastic, Inc.
Castrataro, Kristen. Grandpa's Farm Has Lots of Saws. 2012. 32p. (-18). pap. 19.99 (978-1-4772-8636-4(5)) AuthorHouse.
Côté, Geneviève. Mr. King's Machine. Côté, Geneviève, illus. 2016. (Mr. King Ser.). (ENG., Illus.). 32p. (J). (gr. -1-2). 16.95 (978-1-77138-021-8(7)) Kids Can Pr., Ltd. CAN. Dist: Hachette Bk. Group.
Dover, Ilana. The Talking MacHine: The Story of Alexander Graham Bell. 2012. 36p. pap. 17.49 (978-1-4691-8328-2(5)) Xlibris Corp.
Foofy the Friendly Crane. 2013. 24p. pap. (978-965-550-219-0(8)) Contento De Semrik.
Goetz, Steve. Old MacDonald Had a Truck. Kaban, Eda, illus. 2019. (ENG.). 30p. (J). (gr. -1-k). bds. 8.99 (978-1-4521-8176-9(4)) Chronicle Bks. LLC.
—Old MacDonald Had a Truck: (Preschool Read Aloud Books, Books for Kids, Kids Construction Books) Kaban, Eda, illus. 2016. (ENG.). 40p. (J). (gr. -1-k). 16.99 (978-1-4521-3260-0(7)) Chronicle Bks. LLC.
Golden Books. Championship Colors! (Blaze & the Monster Machines) Golden Books, illus. 2017. (ENG., Illus.). 224p. (J). (gr. -1-2). pap. 6.99 (978-1-5247-6558-3(9), Golden Bks.) Random Hse. Children's Bks.
Grant, Gavin J. & Link, Kelly, eds. Steampunk! an Anthology of Fantastically Rich & Strange Stories. 2013. (ENG.). 432p. (YA). (gr. 9). pap. 19.99 (978-0-7636-5797-0(2)) Candlewick Pr.
Koehler, Lora. The Little Snowplow. Parker, Jake, illus. (ENG.). (J). 2022. 32p. (gr. -1-2). 7.99 (978-1-5362-2777-2(3)) 2018. 30p. (— 1). bds. 8.99 (978-1-5362-0340-0(8)) 2015. 32p. (gr. -1-2). 17.99 (978-0-7636-7074-0(X)) Candlewick Pr.
Kyung, Hyewon. Bigger Than You. 2018. (ENG., Illus.). 32p. (J). (gr. -1-3). 17.99 (978-0-06-268312-0(8), Greenwillow Bks.) HarperCollins Pubs.
Langridge, Roger. Family Reunion. Langridge, Roger & Mebberson, Amy, illus. 2010. (Muppet Show Ser.). (ENG.). 112p. (J). pap. 9.99 (978-1-60886-587-1(8)) BOOM! Studios.
McCully, Emily Arnold. Min Makes a Machine. 2018. (I Like to Read Ser.). (Illus.). 32p. (J). (gr. -1-3). 14.99 (978-0-8234-3970-6(4)) Holiday Hse., Inc.
Merry, Margaret. The Lonely Digger. 2009. 72p. pap. 21.50 (978-1-60860-144-8(7), Strategic Bk. Publishing) Strategic Book Publishing & Rights Agency (SBPRA).
Publications International Ltd. Staff. Steering Wheel Sound Thomas the Tank. 2007. 12p. (J). bds. 17.98 (978-1-4127-6811-5(X)) Phoenix International Publications, Inc.
Random House. Meet the Machines! (Blaze & the Monster Machines) 4 Board Books, 4 vols. Random House, illus. 2016. (ENG., Illus.). 48p. (J). (— 1). bds. 10.99 (978-1-101-93678-8(9), Random Hse. Bks. for Young Readers) Random Hse. Children's Bks.
Roadbloc. Vending MacHine Lunch. 2012. 172p. pap. (978-0-9570633-4-1(2)) Fragged Publishing.
Spangler, Lois. Fort on Fourth Street, the: a Story about the Six Simple Machines, 1 vol. Wald, Christina, illus. 2013. (ENG.). 32p. (J). (gr. 2-3). pap. 10.95 (978-1-60718-632-8(2), 3251b480-d1c0-4b93-9f0f-9102cce9cf79) Arbordale Publishing.
—The Fort on Fourth Street, the: a Story about the Six Simple Machines, 1 vol. Wald, Christina, illus. 2013. (ENG.). 32p. (J). (gr. 1-4). 17.95 (978-1-60718-620-5(9)) Arbordale Publishing.
Sutton, Sally. Dig, Dump, Roll. Lovelock, Brian, illus. (Construction Crew Ser.). (ENG.). (J). 2019. 28p. (-k). bds. 8.99 (978-1-5362-0902-0(3)) 2018. 32p. (gr. -1-2). 16.99 (978-1-5362-0391-2(2)) Candlewick Pr.
—Roadwork. Lovelock, Brian, illus. 2017. (Construction Crew Ser.). (ENG.). 32p. (J). (-k). 7.99 (978-0-7636-9870-6(9)) Candlewick Pr.
Swinburne, Minnie. Laz's Perfect State Machine. 2011. (Illus.). 52p. (gr. 4-6). pap. 11.76 (978-1-4567-9293-0(8)) AuthorHouse.
Taplin, Sam. Noisy Diggers. 2012. (Noisy Bks). 10p. (J). bds. 18.99 (978-0-7945-3264-2(0), Usborne) EDC Publishing.
Tillworth, Mary. Bubble Trouble! (Blaze & the Monster Machines) Kobasic, Kevin, illus. 2016. (Step into Reading Ser.). (ENG.). 24p. (J). (gr. -1-1). 4.99 (978-1-101-93680-1(0), Random Hse. Bks. for Young Readers) Random Hse. Children's Bks.
—Dino Parade! (Blaze & the Monster Machines) Martinez, Heather, illus. 2017. (Little Golden Book Ser.). (ENG.). 24p. (J). (-k). 5.99 (978-0-399-55795-8(4), Golden Bks.) Random Hse. Children's Bks.
—Zeg & the Egg (Blaze & the Monster Machines) Foley, Niki, illus. 2016. (Step into Reading Ser.). (ENG.). 24p. (J). (gr. -1-1). 4.99 (978-0-553-53935-6(3), Random Hse. Bks. for Young Readers) Random Hse. Children's Bks.
Uribe, Denise. Queen MacHine. 2012. 24p. pap. 12.56 (978-1-4669-6083-1(3)) Trafford Publishing.
Wojtowycz, David. Scoop, the Digger! 2003. (Illus.). (J). (978-0-439-74269-6(2)) Scholastic, Inc.
Zimmerman, Andrea & Clemesha, David. Dig! Rosenthal, Marc, illus. 2014. (ENG.). 30p. (J). (— 1). bds. 8.99 (978-0-544-17388-0(0), 1552172, Clarion Bks.) HarperCollins Pubs.

MACHINERY—HISTORY
The History of Machines: Individual Title Six-Packs. (gr. k-1). 23.00 (978-0-7635-9079-6(7)) Rigby Education.
Perritano, John. The Revolution in Industry: How Machines Changed America. 2008. (Graphic America Ser.). (ENG., Illus.). 32p. (J). (gr. 3-6). pap. (978-0-7787-4216-6(4)) Crabtree Publishing Co.
Resler, T. J. How Things Work: Then & Now. 2018. (ENG., Illus.). 208p. (J). (gr. 3-7). lib. bdg. 29.90 (978-1-4263-3167-1(3), National Geographic Kids) Disney Publishing Worldwide.
Woods, Michael & Woods, Mary B. Ancient Machines: From Wedges to Waterwheels. 2005. (Ancient Technology Ser.). (Illus.). 96p. (J). (gr. 6-12). 25.26 (978-0-8225-2994-1(7)) Lerner Publishing Group.

MACHINERY—MODELS
see also Airplanes—Models; Automobiles—Models; Railroads—Models
Balmer, Alden. Doc Fizzix Mousetrap Racers: The Complete Builder's Manual. 2008. (ENG., Illus.). 144p. (gr. 7-18). pap. 14.95 (978-1-56523-359-1(X), 3591D) Fox Chapel Publishing Co., Inc.

MACHINERY IN THE WORKPLACE
Addison, D. R. Cement Mixers at Work. 2009. (Big Trucks Ser.). 24p. (gr. 1-1). 42.50 (978-1-61511-576-1(5), PowerKids Pr.) Rosen Publishing Group, Inc., The.

MACHINES
see Machinery

MACKINAC ISLAND (MICH.)—FICTION
Panagopoulos, Janie Lynn. A Castle at the Straits. Evans, Laura, illus. 2003. 48p. (J). (gr. 1-6). (978-0-911872-83-5(3)) Mackinac State Historic Parks.
Whelan, Gloria, et al. Bernida: a Michigan Sailing Legend: A Michigan Sailing Legend. Miles, David, illus. 2014. (ENG.). 32p. (J). (gr. 1-4). 16.99 (978-1-58536-904-1(7), 203553) Sleeping Bear Pr.

MCKINLEY, WILLIAM, 1843-1901
Bailey, Diane & Nash, Philip. William Mckinley, the 25th President. 2016. (First Look at America's Presidents Ser.). (ENG., Illus.). 24p. (J). (gr. -1-3). 26.99 (978-1-944102-68-5(X)) Bearport Publishing Co., Inc.
Edge, Laura Bufano. William Mckinley. 2007. (Presidential Leaders Ser.). (Illus.). 112p. (J). (gr. 3-7). lib. bdg. 29.27 (978-0-8225-1508-1(3), Twenty-First Century Bks.) Lerner Publishing Group.
Gunderson, Jessica. President Mckinley's Killer & the America He Left Behind: The Assassin, the Crime, Teddy Roosevelt's Rise, & the Dawn of the American Century. 2018. (Assassins' America Ser.). (ENG., Illus.). 64p. (J). (gr. 4-9). lib. bdg. 30.65 (978-0-7565-5714-0(3), 137213, Compass Point Bks.) Capstone.
Parker, Lewis. How to Draw the Life & Times of William Mckinley. 2009. (Kid's Guide to Drawing the Presidents of the United States of America Ser.). 32p. (gr. 4-4). 50.50 (978-1-61511-167-1(0), PowerKids Pr.) Rosen Publishing Group, Inc., The.
Parker, Lewis K. How to Draw the Life & Times of William McKinley, 1 vol. 2005. (Kid's Guide to Drawing the Presidents of the United States of America Ser.). (ENG., Illus.). 32p. (YA). (gr. 4-4). 30.27 (978-1-4042-3001-9(7), 4b41591a-019f-47db-a80e-4e2ffb0aff5b) Rosen Publishing Group, Inc., The.
Venezia, Mike. William McKinley. Venezia, Mike, illus. 2006. (Getting to Know the U. S. Presidents Ser.). (ENG., Illus.). 32p. (J). (gr. 3-7). lib. bdg. 28.00 (978-0-516-22629-3(0), Children's Pr.) Scholastic Library Publishing.
Wilson, Antoine. The Assassination of William McKinley. 2009. (Library of Political Assassinations Ser.). 64p. (gr. 5-5). 58.50 (978-1-60853-830-0(3)) Rosen Publishing Group, Inc., The.

MCKINLEY, MOUNT (ALASKA)
Establishment of Mount McKinley Park. (Shorey Historical Ser.). (Illus.). 32p. (J). reprint ed. pap. 10.00 (978-0-8466-0015-2(3), S15) Shorey's Bookstore.
Gill, Shelley. Up on Denali: Alaska's Wild Mountain. Cartwright, Shannon, illus. 2006. (Paws IV Ser.). (ENG.). 32p. (J). (gr. -1-2). pap. 11.99 (978-1-57061-365-4(6), Little Bigfoot) Sasquatch Bks.

MACRAME
Boase, Petra. Friendship Bracelets & Beading Fun: 25 Knotty, Dotty, Stripey & Sparkly Designs to Make! 2014. (ENG., Illus.). 64p. (J). (gr. -1-6). 9.99 (978-1-84322-944-5(7), Armadillo) Anness Publishing GBR. Dist: National Bk. Network.
Johnson, Anne Akers. Pulseras Rusticas. 2005. (SPA., Illus.). 32p. (J). (gr. 1). 17.95 (978-968-5528-11-5(X)) Klutz Latino MEX. Dist: Independent Pubs. Group.
Rau, Dana Meachen. Making Knot Projects. Petelinsek, Kathleen, illus. 2016. (How-To Library). (ENG.). 32p. (J). (gr. 3-6). 32.07 (978-1-63471-420-4(2), 208459) Cherry Lake Publishing.
Torres, Laura. Brazaletes de la Amistad. 2005. (SPA., Illus.). 57p. (J). (gr. 3). 17.95 (978-968-5528-05-4(5)) Klutz Latino MEX. Dist: Independent Pubs. Group.

MACY, ANNE SULLIVAN, 1866-1936
see Sullivan, Annie, 1866-1936

MADAGASCAR
Aronin, Miriam. Aye-Aye: An Evil Omen. 2016. (Uncommon Animals Ser.). (ENG., Illus.). 32p. (J). (gr. 2-7). pap. 7.99 (978-1-944998-60-8(8)) Bearport Publishing Co., Inc.
Frazel, Ellen. Madagascar. 2013. (Exploring Countries Ser.). (ENG., Illus.). 32p. (J). (gr. 3-7). lib. bdg. 27.95 (978-1-60014-861-3(1), Blastoff! Readers) Bellwether Media.
Gagne, Tammy. We Visit Madagascar. 2012. (J). lib. bdg. 33.95 (978-1-61228-305-0(5)) Mitchell Lane Pubs.
Heale, Jay & Latif, Zawiah Abdul. Madagascar, 1 vol. 2nd rev. ed. 2009. (Cultures of the World (Second Edition)(r) Ser.). (ENG.). 144p. (gr. 5-5). lib. bdg. 49.79 (978-0-7614-3036-0(9), e7588014-6bfd-49ae-833c-b606567f70df) Cavendish Square Publishing LLC.
Heale, Jay, et al. Madagascar, 1 vol. 2017. (Cultures of the World (Third Edition)(r) Ser.). (ENG.). 144p. (gr. 5-5). lib. bdg. 48.79 (978-1-5026-3242-5(X), 5e1571f8-33be-43bb-a449-67cf421ff889) Cavendish Square Publishing LLC.
Kabana, Joni. Torina's World: A Child's Life in Madagascar. 2nd ed. 2007. (ENG., Illus.). 52p. (J). 14.95 (978-0-9794771-4-0(X)) ACS, LLC Amica Creative Services.
Kocienda, Genevieve. Madagascar Low Intermediate Book with Online Access, 1 vol. 2014. (ENG., Illus.). 24p. (J). pap., E-Book, E-Book 9.50 (978-1-107-62940-0(3)) Cambridge Univ. Pr.
Oluonye, Mary N. Madagascar. 2005. (Ticket to Ser.). (Illus.). 48p. (gr. 2-4). 22.60 (978-1-57505-145-1(1)) Lerner Publishing Group.

MADAGASCAR—FICTION
Cunningham, Elaine. Missing in Madagascar. 2006. 32p. 4.50 (978-0-8341-2230-7(8)) Beacon Hill Pr. of Kansas City.
Dennard, Deborah. Lemur Landing: A Story of a Madagascan Dry Tropical Forest. Kest, Kristin, illus. 2005. (Wild Habitats Ser.). (ENG.). 32p. (J). (gr. 1-4). 19.95 (978-1-56899-980-7(1)) Soundprints.
Dennard, Deborah & Kest, Kristin. Lemur Landing: A Story of a Madagascan Dry Tropical Forest. 2005. (Wild Habitats Ser.). (ENG., Illus.). 32p. (J). (gr. 1-4). pap. 6.95 (978-1-56899-979-1(8), S7019) Soundprints.
Gunby, Stephanie. The Clever Clouds. 2010. 56p. pap. 24.20 (978-1-4269-3902-0(7)) Trafford Publishing.
Lumry, Amanda & Hurwitz, Laura. Adventures of Riley: Mission to Madagascar. McIntyre, Sarah, illus. 2005. 36p. (gr. 2-3). 15.95 (978-0-9748411-2-0(9)) Eaglemont Pr.
Marcy Wirth's Second Grade Class, compiled by. A Journey to Madagascar. 2010. (Illus.). 38p. (YA). pap. 6.25 (978-0-9619407-8-2(6)) Country Messenger Pr. Publishing Group, LLC.
Meredith Books Staff, ed. Madagascar Activity Book & Floor Puzzle. 10p. (J). bds. 12.95 (978-0-696-22701-1(0)) Meredith Bks.
—Madagascar Stencil Activity Book with Stickers. 22p. (J). bds. 12.95 (978-0-696-22702-8(9)) Meredith Bks.

MADELINE (FICTITIOUS CHARACTER)—FICTION
Bemelmans, Ludwig. Madeline. l.t. ed. 2018. (ENG., Illus.). 54p. (J). (gr. k-6). pap. (978-4-87187-929-3(1)) Ishi Pr., Inc., The.
—Madeline. 2012. (Madeline Ser.). 36p. (J). (gr. -1-k). bds. 9.99 (978-0-670-01407-1(9), Viking Books for Young Readers) Penguin Young Readers Group.
—Madeline: Activity Book with Stickers. 2012. (Madeline Ser.). 32p. (J). (gr. k-3). act. bk. ed. 8.99 (978-0-448-45903-5(5), Grosset & Dunlap) Penguin Young Readers Group.
Marciano, John Bemelmans. Madeline & the Cats of Rome. 2008. (Madeline Ser.). (ENG.). 48p. (J). (gr. 1-3). 19.99 (978-0-670-06297-3(9), Viking Books for Young Readers) Penguin Young Readers Group.
—Madeline at the White House. (Madeline Ser.). (Illus.). (J). (gr. -1-2). 2020. 34p. bds. 9.99 (978-0-593-11800-9(6), Viking Books for Young Readers) 2016. 48p. pap. 9.99 (978-1-101-99780-2(X), Puffin Books) 2011. 48p. 19.99 (978-0-670-01228-2(9), Viking Books for Young Readers) Penguin Young Readers Group.
—Madeline at the White House. 2016. (Madeline Ser.). lib. bdg. 19.65 (978-0-606-38845-0(1)) Turtleback.

MADISON, DOLLEY, 1768-1849
Ashby, Ruth. James & Dolley Madison, 1 vol. 2005. (Presidents & First Ladies Ser.). (ENG., Illus.). 48p. (gr. 5-8). lib. bdg. 33.67 (978-0-8368-5757-3(7), 479a0864-fbda-4f8c-9f0a-e044e1df8fb2, Gareth Stevens Secondary Library) Stevens, Gareth Publishing LLLP.
Carosella, Melissa. Dolley Madison: First Lady of the United States. rev. ed. 2011. (Social Studies: Informational Text Ser.). (ENG.). 32p. (gr. 4-8). pap. 11.99 (978-1-4333-1504-6(1)) Teacher Created Materials, Inc.
Figley, Marty Rhodes. Washington Is Burning. Orback, Craig, illus. (On My Own History Ser.). 48p. (J). (gr. 2-4). 2007. (ENG.). per. 8.99 (978-0-8225-6050-0(X), 220511bf-9018-498f-8ff3-a73d591dfbeb, First Avenue Editions) 2006. lib. bdg. 25.26 (978-1-57505-875-7(8)) Lerner Publishing Group.
Kent, Zachary A. Dolley Madison: The Enemy Cannot Frighten a Free People, 1 vol. 2008. (Americans: the Spirit of a Nation Ser.). (ENG., Illus.). 128p. (gr. 5-6). lib. bdg. 35.93 (978-0-7660-3356-6(2), 578bdc34-0b85-4900-a190-8fc4d183b93a) Enslow Publishing, LLC.
Krull, Kathleen. Women Who Broke the Rules: Dolley Madison. Johnson, Steve & Fancher, Lou, illus. 2015. (Women Who Broke the Rules Ser.). (ENG.). 48p. (J). (gr. 1-4). 16.99 (978-0-8027-3793-9(5), 900139089, Bloomsbury USA Childrens) Bloomsbury Publishing USA.
Larkin, Tanya. What Was Cooking in Dolley Madison's White House? 2009. (Cooking Throughout American History Ser.). 24p. (gr. 3-3). 42.50 (978-1-61511-950-9(7), PowerKids Pr.) Rosen Publishing Group, Inc., The.
Loh-Hagan, Virginia. The Real Dolley Madison. 2018. (History Uncut Ser.). (ENG., Illus.). 32p. (J). (gr. 4-8). lib. bdg. 32.07 (978-1-5341-2952-8(9), 211852, 45th Parallel Press) Cherry Lake Publishing.
Shulman, Holly. Dolley Madison: Her Life, Letters, & Legacy. 2009. (Library of American Lives & Times Ser.). 112p. (gr. 5-5). 69.20 (978-1-60853-477-7(4)) Rosen Publishing Group, Inc., The.
Weatherly, Myra. Dolley Madison: America's First Lady. 2004. (Notable Americans Ser.). (Illus.). 128p. (YA). (gr. 6-12). 23.95 (978-1-883846-95-4(1), First Biographies) Reynolds, Morgan Inc.

MADISON, JAMES, 1751-1836
Ashby, Ruth. James & Dolley Madison, 1 vol. 2005. (Presidents & First Ladies Ser.). (ENG., Illus.). 48p. (gr. 5-8). lib. bdg. 33.67 (978-0-8368-5757-3(7), 479a0864-fbda-4f8c-9f0a-e044e1df8fb2, Gareth Stevens Secondary Library) Stevens, Gareth Publishing LLLP.
Britton, Arthur K. 20 Fun Facts about James Madison. 2017. (Fun Fact File: Founding Fathers Ser.). 32p. (gr. 2-3). pap. 63.00 (978-1-5382-0273-9(5)) Stevens, Gareth Publishing LLLP.
Dooling, Sandra. James Madison, 1 vol. 2012. (Jr. Graphic Founding Fathers Ser.). (ENG., Illus.). 24p. (J). (gr. 2-3). pap. 11.60 (978-1-4488-7992-2(2), f4d38373-b864-4032-9f27-d95f85561fd1); lib. bdg. 28.93 (978-1-4488-7898-7(5), b0da6c67-4e46-4e62-98f3-3e24bfa5e3b4) Rosen Publishing Group, Inc., The. (PowerKids Pr.).
Elish, Dan. James Madison, 1 vol. 2008. (Presidents & Their Times Ser.). (ENG., Illus.). 96p. (gr. 6-6). lib. bdg. 36.93 (978-0-7614-2432-1(6), fa0cbdb0-9a1c-489c-b7b7-cf602998b5fc) Cavendish Square Publishing LLC.
Gregory, Josh & Bose, Meenekshi. James Madison: The 4th President. 2015. (First Look at America's Presidents Ser.). (ENG.). 24p. (J). (gr. -1-3). lib. bdg. 26.99 (978-1-62724-559-3(6)) Bearport Publishing Co., Inc.
Gunderson, Megan M. James Madison, 1 vol. 2016. (United States Presidents *2017 Ser.). (ENG., Illus.). 40p. (J). (gr. 2-5). lib. bdg. 35.64 (978-1-68078-107-6(3), 21831, Big Buddy Bks.) ABDO Publishing Co.
Kozleski, Lisa. James Madison. 2004. (Childhoods of the Presidents Ser.). (Illus.). 48p. (J). (gr. 4-18). lib. bdg. 17.95 (978-1-59084-269-0(3)) Mason Crest.
Loh-Hagan, Virginia. The Real Dolley Madison. 2018. (History Uncut Ser.). (ENG., Illus.). 32p. (J). (gr. 4-8). lib. bdg. 32.07 (978-1-5341-2952-8(9), 211852, 45th Parallel Press) Cherry Lake Publishing.
Lusted, Marcia Amidon. Revolution & the New Nation: 1750-Early 1800s. 2007. (Presidents of the United States Ser.). (Illus.). 48p. (J). (gr. 4-7). lib. bdg. 29.05 (978-1-59036-739-1(1)); per. 10.95 (978-1-59036-740-7(5)) Weigl Pubs., Inc.
Maloof, Torrey. James Madison & the Making of the United States. rev. ed. 2017. (Social Studies: Informational Text Ser.). (ENG., Illus.). 32p. (gr. 4-8). pap. 11.99 (978-1-4938-3795-3(8)) Teacher Created Materials, Inc.
Mattern, David B. James Madison: Patriot, Politician, & President, 1 vol. 2004. (Library of American Lives & Times Ser.). (ENG., Illus.). 112p. (gr. 5-5). lib. bdg. 38.27 (978-1-4042-2648-7(6), 897734e1-fb85-40c8-bb97-6177b50e76ca) Rosen Publishing Group, Inc., The.
McDowell, Pamela. James Madison. 2015. (Padres Fundadores Ser.). (SPA.). (J). lib. bdg. 27.13 (978-1-4896-2796-4(0), AV2 by Weigl) Weigl Pubs., Inc.
Mulhall, Jill K. James Madison, 1 vol. rev. ed. 2005. (Social Studies: Informational Text Ser.). (ENG.). 24p. (gr. 4-8). pap. 10.99 (978-0-7439-8908-4(2)) Teacher Created Materials, Inc.
Naden, Corinne & Flum Galvin, Irene. Marbury V. Madison: The Court's Foundation, 1 vol. 2006. (Supreme Court Milestones Ser.). (ENG., Illus.). 128p. (YA). (gr. 8-8). 45.50 (978-0-7614-1840-5(7), 76516cd7-d560-4af1-a357-98dc26318a2e) Cavendish Square Publishing LLC.
Randolph, Ryan. Marbury V. Madison: The New Supreme Court Gets More Powers. 2009. (Life in the New American Nation Ser.). 32p. (gr. 4-4). 47.90 (978-1-61514-277-4(0)) Rosen Publishing Group, Inc., The.
Ransom, Candice. James Madison. 2018. (Founding Fathers Ser.). (ENG., Illus.). 24p. (J). (gr. 1-1). pap. 8.95 (978-1-63517-816-6(9), 1635178169) North Star Editions.
—James Madison. 2018. (Founding Fathers Ser.). (ENG., Illus.). 24p. (J). (gr. k-3). lib. bdg. 31.36 (978-1-5321-6021-9(6), 28674, Pop! Cody Koala) Pop!
Roberts, Jeremy. James Madison. 2004. (Presidential Leaders Ser.). (Illus.). 112p. (J). (gr. 6-12). lib. bdg. 29.27 (978-0-8225-0823-6(0)) Lerner Publishing Group.
Schmidt, Roderic. How to Draw the Life & Times of James Madison. (Kid's Guide to Drawing the Presidents of the United States of America Ser.). 32p. (gr. 4-4). 2009. 50.50 (978-1-61511-148-0(4), PowerKids Pr.) 2005. (ENG.). (YA). 30.27 (978-1-4042-2981-5(7), 36be9f8b-f29f-4ed2-8bcd-cc4e76561da3) Rosen Publishing Group, Inc., The.
Smith-Llera, Danielle. The Real James Madison: The Truth Behind the Legend. 2019. (Real Revolutionaries Ser.). (ENG., Illus.). 64p. (J). (gr. 5-9). lib. bdg. 34.65 (978-0-7565-6252-6(X), 141185, Compass Point Bks.) Capstone.
Somervill, Barbara A. The Life & Times of James Madison. 2008. (Profiles in American History Ser.). (Illus.). 48p. (J). (gr. 4-7). lib. bdg. 29.95 (978-1-58415-530-0(2)) Mitchell Lane Pubs.
Wittekind, Erika. James Madison's Presidency. 2016. (Presidential Powerhouses Ser.). (ENG., Illus.). 104p. (YA). (gr. 6-12). 35.99 (978-1-4677-7929-6(6), e13b2ba0-3b43-4bfa-ba26-961be1313ce5); E-Book 54.65 (978-1-4677-8599-0(7)) Lerner Publishing Group. (Lerner Pubns.).

MADONNA
see Mary, Blessed Virgin, Saint

MAFIA
Bockmann, Melanie Scherencel. In the Shadow of the Mob/Melanie Scherencel Bockmann. 2011. (J). (978-0-8280-2583-6(5)) Review & Herald Publishing Assn.
Loh-Hagan, Virginia. Yakuza vs. Mafia. 2019. (Battle Royale: Lethal Warriors Ser.). (ENG., Illus.). 32p. (J). (gr. 4-8). pap. 14.21 (978-1-5341-5055-3(2), 213527); lib. bdg. 32.07 (978-1-5341-4769-0(1), 213526) Cherry Lake Publishing. (45th Parallel Press).

MAFIA—FICTION
Blumenthal, Deborah. Mafia Girl. 2014. (ENG.). 272p. (YA). (gr. 8-12). 16.99 (978-0-8075-4911-7(8), 807549118) Whitman, Albert & Co.

Côté, Denis. La Machination du Scorpion Noir. 2004. (Mon Roman Ser.). (FRE.). 160p. (J). (gr. 2). pap. *(978-2-89021-667-9(5))* Diffusion du livre Mirabel (DLM).

Cox, M. M. Accidental Mobster. 2012. 252p. pap. *(978-1-927134-89-4(7))* Bluewood Publishing, Ltd.

Green, Tim. Football Hero. (Football Genius Ser.: 2). (ENG.). (J). (gr. 3-7). 2009. 320p. pap. 9.99 *(978-0-06-112276-7(9))* 2008. (Illus.). 304p. 16.99 *(978-0-06-112274-3(2))* HarperCollins Pubs. (HarperCollins).

—Football Hero. l.t. ed. 2008. (YA). 23.95 *(978-1-4104-1116-7(8))* Thorndike Pr.

Shakespeare, William. Manga Shakespeare: Romeo & Juliet. Leong, Sonia, illus. 2007. (ENG.). 208p. (J). (gr. 2-8). pap. 16.99 *(978-0-8109-9325-9(2)*, Abrams Bks. for Young Readers) Abrams, Inc.

Trenchard, Robert. The Famous Frog Fiasco. 2008. 265p. (J). pap. 13.99 *(978-0-615-20974-6(2))* Soxwings Publishing.

MAGALHAES, FERNAO DE, -1521

Burnett, Betty. Ferdinand Magellan: The First Voyage Around the World. 2009. (Library of Explorers & Exploration Ser.). 112p. (gr. 5-8). 66.50 *(978-1-60853-602-3(5)*, Rosen Reference) Rosen Publishing Group, Inc., The.

Fandel, Jennifer. Ferdinand Magellan. 2003. (Explorers of the Unknown Ser.). (J). *(978-1-58417-036-5(0))*; pap. *(978-1-58417-099-0(9))* Lake Street Pubs.

Gould, Jane H. Ferdinand Magellan, 1 vol. 2013. (Jr. Graphic Famous Explorers Ser.). (ENG., Illus.). 24p. (J). (gr. 2-3). pap. 11.60 *(978-1-4777-0123-2(0)*, e3cb2c07-ada3-43c9-aede-62dac39b22fe); lib. bdg. 28.93 *(978-1-4777-0069-3(2)*, 3784f612-3280-40e5-9727-85860ff7d0c1) Rosen Publishing Group, Inc., The. (PowerKids Pr.).

Hoogenboom, Lynn. Ferdinand Magellan. 2009. (Primary Source Library of Famous Explorers Ser.). 24p. (gr. 4-4). 42.50 *(978-1-60854-120-1(7)*, PowerKids Pr.) Rosen Publishing Group, Inc., The.

Koestler-Grack, Rachel A. Ferdinand Magellan. 2009. (Great Explorers Ser.). (ENG., Illus.). 112p. (gr. 6-12). 30.00 *(978-1-60413-422-3(4)*, P173421, Facts On File) Infobase Holdings, Inc.

Kramer, S. A. & Who HQ. Who Was Ferdinand Magellan? 2004. (Who Was? Ser.). (Illus.). 112p. (J). (gr. 3-7). pap. 6.99 *(978-0-448-43105-5(X)*, Penguin Workshop) Penguin Young Readers Group.

Kramer, Sydelle. Who Was Ferdinand Magellan? Wolf, Elizabeth, illus. 2004. (Who Was... ? Ser.). 105p. (J). (gr. 3-7). 12.65 *(978-0-7569-4615-9(8))* Perfection Learning Corp.

Landau, Elaine. Ferdinand Magellan. 2005. (History Maker Bios Ser.). (Illus.). 48p. (J). (gr. 3-7). lib. bdg. 26.60 *(978-0-8225-2942-2(4)*, Lerner Pubns.) Lerner Publishing Group.

Macdonald, Fiona. The Story of Magellan. Mark Bergin, illus. 2017. (Explorers Ser.). 32p. (gr. 3-6). 31.35 *(978-1-910706-90-9(6))* Book Hse. GBR. Dist: Black Rabbit Bks.

Marsh, Carole. Ferdinand Magellan, World Voyager. 2004. 12p. (gr. k-4). 2.95 *(978-0-635-02373-5(3))* Gallopade International.

Meyer, Susan. Ferdinand Magellan, 1 vol. 2016. (Spotlight on Explorers & Colonization Ser.). (ENG., Illus.). 48p. (J). (gr. 6-6). pap. 12.75 *(978-1-4777-8800-4(X)*, 6615c7db-b16f-4a3f-9c78-51e8a7c1dae2) Rosen Publishing Group, Inc., The.

Morlock, Rachael. Magellan Sails Around the World, 1 vol. 2018. (Real-Life Scientific Adventures Ser.). (ENG.). 32p. (gr. 4-5). 29.27 *(978-1-5081-6854-6(7)*, e078633b-3d16-45f3-9e72-0d445088ecc0, PowerKids Pr.) Rosen Publishing Group, Inc., The.

Powell, Marie. Explore with Ferdinand Magellan. 2014. (Travel with the Great Explorers Ser.). (ENG., Illus.). 32p. (J). (gr. 4-5). *(978-0-7787-1425-5(X))* Crabtree Publishing Co.

Strand, Jennifer. Ferdinand Magellan. 2016. (Pioneering Explorers Ser.). (ENG., Illus.). 24p. (J). (gr. -1-2). 49.94 *(978-1-68079-409-0(4)*, 23030, Abdo Zoom-Launch) ABDO Publishing Co.

Waldman, Stuart. Magellan's World. Manchess, Gregory, illus. 2007. (Great Explorers Ser.). (ENG.). 48p. (J). (gr. 4-8). 22.95 *(978-1-931414-19-7(X)*, 53d8c30d-8502-40e6-85b4-31411556e104) Mikaya Pr.

Whiting, Jim. Ferdinand Magellan. 2006. (What's So Great About... ? Ser.). (Illus.). 32p. (J). (gr. 2-4). lib. bdg. 25.70 *(978-1-58415-480-8(2))* Mitchell Lane Pubs.

MAGALHAES, FERNAO DE, -1521—FICTION

Johnson, Vargie. Ferdinand Magellan the Explorer: What Made Them Famous? 2006. 156p. (J). per. 15.00 *(978-1-931195-92-8(7))* KiwE Publishing, Ltd.

MAGAZINES

see Periodicals

MAGELLAN, FERDINAND, -1521

see Magalhaes, Fernao de, -1521

MAGIC

Here are entered works on the use of charms, spells, etc., believed to have supernatural power to produce or prevent a particular result considered unobtainable by natural means. Works on performance of sleight of hand or tricks involving various types of illusion for purposes of entertainment are entered under Magic Tricks.

see also Card Tricks; Occultism

Andrews, Ted. Faerie Charms. 2005. (Young Person's School of Magic & Mystery Ser.: Vol. 6). (Illus.). 255p. (YA). (gr. 8-12). 18.95 *(978-1-888767-42-1(1))* Dragonhawk Publishing.

Austin, John. Labcraft Wizards: Magical Projects & Experiments. 2016. (ENG., Illus.). 256p. (J) (gr. 4). pap. 16.99 *(978-1-61373-621-0(5))* Chicago Review Pr., Inc.

Barnhart, Norm. Magic Manuals. 2013. (Magic Manuals Ser.). (ENG.). 32p. (J). (gr. 3-9). 122.60 *(978-1-62065-972-4(7)*, 19551, Capstone Pr.) Capstone.

Beahm, George. The Whimsic Alley Book of Spells: Mythical Incantations for Wizards of All Ages. Goldin, Stan, ed. 2007. (ENG., Illus.). 192p. (YA). pap. 14.95 *(978-1-57174-535-4(1))* Hampton Roads Publishing Co., Inc.

Blackstone, Gay. Around the House Magic. (Illus.). (J). *(978-1-59093-000-7(2)*, Eager Minds Pr.) Warehousing & Fulfillment Specialists, LLC (WFS, LLC).

Blaine, Victor. Mi Trineo / My Sled, 1 vol. 2014. (¡Mírame, Ahí Voy! / Watch Me Go! Ser.). (ENG & SPA.). 24p. (J). (gr. 1-2). 25.27 *(978-1-4994-0284-1(8)*, 34b64cb7-5695-48fa-8c53-5f91fd6382b5, PowerKids Pr.) Rosen Publishing Group, Inc., The.

Dale, Elizabeth. Izzy! Wizzy! Forshaw, Louise, illus. 2019. (Early Bird Readers — Yellow (Early Bird Stories (tm)) Ser.). (ENG.). 32p. (J). (gr. -1-2). 30.65 *(978-1-5415-4168-9(5)*, 2354fe56-b64a-4c1d-b804-7c3af26990dc, Lerner Pubns.) Lerner Publishing Group.

Della, Jamie. The Book of Spells: The Magick of Witchcraft [a Spell Book for Witches]. rev. ed. 2019. (Illus.). 224p. (gr. 7). 15.99 *(978-1-9848-5702-6(9)*, Ten Speed Pr.) Potter/Ten Speed/Harmony/Rodale.

Denne, Ben. Magia Para Todos. 2005. (Titles in Spanish Ser.). (SPA.). 32p. (J). pap. 8.95 *(978-0-7460-6394-1(6)*, Usborne) EDC Publishing.

Dooling, Sandra. Sorcerers, Spells, & Magic!, 1 vol., 1. 2013. (Jr. Graphic Monster Stories Ser.). (ENG.). 24p. (J). (gr. 2-3). 28.93 *(978-1-4777-6211-0(6)*, 3647e898-4c6a-4fa0-952d-13c56c8fc89d, PowerKids Pr.) Rosen Publishing Group, Inc., The.

Editors of Klutz & Chorba, April. Prankster Magic: With Real Fake Gum. 2015. (ENG., Illus.). 60p. (J). (gr. 3). pap. 12.99 *(978-0-545-80545-2(7))* Klutz.

Eldin, Peter. Great Box of Magic. 2008. 48p. (gr. 2-10). pap. 34.95 *(978-1-905339-03-7(8)*, Red Kite Bks.) Haldane Mason, Ltd. GBR. Dist: Trans-Atlantic Pubns., Inc.

Hayward, Mark Brauner. I'm a Magician's Helper. 2012. 24p. pap. 17.99 *(978-1-4772-4107-3(8))* AuthorHouse.

Horsley, Kathryn. Investigating Magic, 1 vol. 2016. (Understanding the Paranormal Ser.). (ENG., Illus.). 48p. (J). (gr. 5-5). lib. bdg. 28.41 *(978-1-68048-575-2(X)*, 389ccb8e-2b9e-4314-9d6f-f655953dc91e, Britannica Educational Publishing) Rosen Publishing Group, Inc., The.

Kallmeyer-Mehlhorn, Margarete. The Wondrous Ball of Yarn: A Facsimile of the Previously Unpublished Manuscript. 2008.Tr. of Wunderknaul. (ENG & GER., Illus.). 40p. 41.00 *(978-0-9745168-2-0(1))* Cotsen Occasional Pr.

Kilby, Janice Eaton & Taylor, Terry. The Book of Wizard Magic: In Which the Apprentice Finds Marvelous Magic Tricks, Mystifying Illusions & Astonishing Tales. Burnett, Lindy, illus. 2019. (Books of Wizard Craft Ser.: 3). 144p. (J). (gr. 3-7). lthr. 19.95 *(978-1-4549-3548-3(0))* Sterling Publishing Co., Inc.

Kilby, Janice Eaton, et al. The Book of Wizard Craft: In Which the Apprentice Finds Spells, Potions, Fantastic Tales & 50 Enchanting Things to Make. Burnett, Lindy, illus. 2019. (Books of Wizard Craft Ser.: 1). 144p. (J). (gr. 3-7). lthr. 19.95 *(978-1-4549-3547-6(2))* Sterling Publishing Co., Inc.

Kiraithe, Jackie. Magic Links: Manual. Gonzales, Linda, ed. 200p. (J). 48.00 *(978-0-942787-95-5(1))* Binet International.

Kronzek, Allan Zola & Kronzek, Elizabeth. Diccionario del Mago. Paula Vicens, Ines Belasategui, tr. 2005. (Escritura desatada Ser.). (SPA.). 368p. (J). 17.95 *(978-970-710-056-5(7))* Ediciones B ESP. Dist: Independent Pubs. Group.

Marsico, Katie. Magic Monsters: From Witches to Goblins. 2017. (Monster Mania Ser.). (ENG., Illus.). 32p. (J). (gr. 2-5). 26.65 *(978-1-5124-2595-6(6)*, 6ee6e0ef-68ff-4a76-ab82-2ae5adf99180); E-Book 39.99 *(978-1-5124-3822-2(7)*, 9781512438222); E-Book 4.99 *(978-1-5124-3821-5(9)*, 9781512438215); E-Book 39.99 *(978-1-5124-2815-5(9))* Lerner Publishing Group. (Lerner Pubns.).

Maurer, Tracy Nelson. Chilling Ancient Curses. 2017. (Searchlight Books (tm) — Fear Fest Ser.). (ENG., Illus.). 32p. (J). (gr. 3-5). 30.65 *(978-1-5124-3403-3(5)*, 6a03d50a-51f0-4a35-8568-28812bfa4dce, Lerner Pubns.) Lerner Publishing Group.

Muten, Burleigh. Goddesses: A World of Myth & Magic. Guay, Rebecca, illus. 2003. (ENG.). 80p. (J). 19.99 *(978-1-84148-075-6(4))* Barefoot Bks., Inc.

Orme, Helen. Magic. 2011. (Fact to Fiction Grafx Ser.). (ENG., Illus.). 36p. (J). (gr. 4-7). lib. bdg. 17.45 *(978-1-61384-020-7(9))* Perfection Learning Corp.

Roleff, Tamara L., ed. Black Magic & Witches. 2003. (Illus.). 127p. (J). pap. 18.70 *(978-0-7377-1319-0(4)*, Greenhaven Pr., Inc.) Cengage Gale.

Ross, Brad. Hocus Pocus Al I Mi Choo. Arnold, Michael, illus. 2012. 62p. pap. 19.95 *(978-0-9834201-0-1(6))* Illusionary Magic LLC.

Savage, Candace. Wizards: An Amazing Journey Through the Last Great Age of Magic. 2003. (ENG., Illus.). 80p. (J). (gr. 4-7). 17.95 *(978-1-55054-943-0(X))* Greystone Books Ltd. CAN. Dist: Publishers Group West (PGW).

Scott, Carey. Magic & Mystery. 2010. (Unpredictable Nature Ser.). (Illus.). 48p. (J). (gr. 3-18). lib. bdg. 19.95 *(978-1-4222-2001-6(X))* Mason Crest.

Top That. Fun Kits Amazing Magic. 2008. *(978-1-84666-592-9(2))* Top That! Publishing PLC.

Walton, Rick & Walton, Ann. Magical Mischief: Jokes That Shock & Amaze. Gable, Brian, illus. 2005. (Make Me Laugh! Ser.). 32p. (J). (gr. k-3). lib. bdg. 19.93 *(978-1-57505-664-7(X))* Lerner Publishing Group.

Wood, John. Classic Magic, 1 vol. 2018. (Magic Tricks Ser.). (ENG.). 32p. (J). (gr. 3-4). lib. bdg. 28.27 *(978-1-5382-2591-2(3)*, 15886394-8e2b-4113-ad81-f90c21d68d22) Stevens, Gareth Publishing LLLP.

Ytreeide, Arnold. Ishtar's Odyssey: A Storybook for Advent, 1 vol. 2015. 176p. (J). pap. 16.99 *(978-0-8254-4393-0(8))* Kregel Pubns.

MAGIC—FICTION

Abbott, Tony. The Chariot of Queen Zara (the Secrets of Droon #27) Merrell, David, illus. 2004. (Geronimo Stilton Ser.: 27). (ENG.). 128p. (J). (gr. 2-5). E-Book 7.99 *(978-0-545-41840-9(2)*, Scholastic Paperbacks) Scholastic, Inc.

—City in the Clouds. Jessell, Tim, illus. 2004. (Secrets of Droon Ser.: No. 4). 88p. 15.00 *(978-0-7569-3930-4(5))* Perfection Learning Corp.

—Escape from Jabar-Loo (the Secrets of Droon #30) Merrell, David, illus. 2016. (Star Wars: Jedi Academy Ser.: 30). (ENG.). 128p. (J). (gr. 3-7). E-Book 12.99 *(978-0-545-41843-0(7)*, Scholastic Paperbacks) Scholastic, Inc.

—The Hawk Bandits of Tarkoom (the Secrets of Droon #11) Jessell, Tim, illus. 2018. (True Book (Relaunch) Ser.: 11). (ENG.). 128p. (J). (gr. 3-5). E-Book 31.00 *(978-0-545-41824-9(0)*, Scholastic Paperbacks) Scholastic, Inc.

—The Hidden Stairs & the Magic Carpet. Jessell, Tim, illus. 2004. (Secrets of Droon Ser.: No. 1). 80p. (gr. 2-5). 15.00 *(978-0-7569-3939-7(9))* Perfection Learning Corp.

—Knights of the Ruby Wand, 36. Fitzgerald, Royce & Jessell, Tim, illus. 2010. (Secrets of Droon Ser.: 36). (ENG.). 128p. (J). (gr. 2-4). 17.44 *(978-0-545-09886-1(6))* Scholastic, Inc.

—The Lost Empire of Koomba (the Secrets of Droon #35) 2018. (True Book (Relaunch) Ser.: 35). (ENG.). 128p. (J). (gr. 3-5). E-Book 7.95 *(978-0-545-41849-2(6)*, Scholastic Paperbacks) Scholastic, Inc.

—The Magic Escapes. Jessell, Tim, illus. 2004. (Secrets of Droon Ser.: No. 1). 161p. (gr. 2-5). 16.00 *(978-0-7569-3944-1(5))* Perfection Learning Corp.

—The Mask of Maliban (the Secrets of Droon #13) Jessell, Tim, illus. 2018. (Math Counts, New & Updated Ser.: 13). (ENG.). 128p. (J). (gr. k-3). E-Book 25.00 *(978-0-545-41826-3(7)*, Scholastic Paperbacks) Scholastic, Inc.

—The Moon Scroll. Jessell, Tim, illus. 2004. (Secrets of Droon Ser.: No. 15). 129p. (gr. 2-5). 15.00 *(978-0-7569-3946-5(1))* Perfection Learning Corp.

—The Mysterious Island (the Secrets of Droon #3) Jessell, Tim, illus. 2016. (Lector de Scholastic, Nivel 2 Ser.: 3). (ENG.). 96p. (J). (gr. k-2). E-Book 4.99 *(978-0-545-83340-0(X)*, Scholastic Paperbacks) Scholastic, Inc.

—Queen of Shadowthorn (the Secrets of Droon #31) 2018. (True Book (Relaunch) Ser.: 31). (ENG.). 128p. (J). (gr. 3-5). E-Book 31.00 *(978-0-545-41844-7(5)*, Scholastic Paperbacks) Scholastic, Inc.

—The Riddle of Zorfendorf Castle. Merrell, David, illus. 2005. (Secrets of Droon Ser.: No. 25). 124p. (J). lib. bdg. 15.38 *(978-1-4242-0310-9(4))* Fitzgerald Bks.

—The Tower of the Elf King, 9. Merrell, David & Jessell, Tim, illus. 2010. (Secrets of Droon Ser.: 9). (ENG.). 100p. (J). (gr. 2-4). 16.19 *(978-0-439-20772-0(X))* Scholastic, Inc.

—Voyagers of the Silver Sand (the Secrets of Droon: Special Edition #3) Merrell, David, illus. 2022. (Five Nights at Freddy's Ser.: 3). (ENG.). 192p. (YA). (gr. 7-5). E-Book 12.99 *(978-0-545-41860-7(7)*, Scholastic Paperbacks) Scholastic, Inc.

Abrahams, Peter. The Outlaws of Sherwood Street: Stealing from the Rich. 2013. 320p. (J). (gr. 5). 7.99 *(978-0-14-242438-4(2)*, Puffin Books) Penguin Young Readers Group.

Abrahamson, Jean. Manners Are Magic. 2005. (Illus.). 48p. 6.99 *(978-1-57860-231-5(9)*, Clerisy Pr.) AdventureKEEN.

Abrahamson, Ruth Ann. The Adventures of Magic Cookie Bean: A Precocious Calico Shares Christian-Principled Tales; Purrfect for Ages 5 & Up! 2010. 24p. pap. 10.95 *(978-1-4497-0640-1(1)*, WestBow Pr.) Author Solutions, LLC.

—Paris & the Purple Purse: Continuing Adventures of Magic Cookie Bean. 2011. 40p. (gr. 1-2). pap. 13.95 *(978-1-4497-1665-3(2)*, WestBow Pr.) Author Solutions, LLC.

Abromovitz, Jaime. Zazzy-Q Ding-A-Ling: Ding-A-Lings: the Magic Wand. 2004. (Illus.). (J). per. 9.95 *(978-0-9762587-2-8(2))* StoryGirl Productions, LLC.

Abshire, Lisa D. Sam's Magical Day. 2006. 48p. pap. 16.95 *(978-1-4241-1484-9(5))* PublishAmerica, Inc.

Adams, Alane. The Raven God: The Legends of Orkney Series. 2017. (Legends of Orkney Ser.: 3). (ENG., Illus.). 344p. (J). (gr. 4-7). pap. 16.95 *(978-1-943006-36-6(9))* SparkPr. (a Bks.parks Imprint).

—The Red Sun. 2015. (Legends of Orkney Ser.: 1). (ENG., Illus.). 346p. (J). pap. 17.00 *(978-1-940716-24-4(1))* SparkPr. (a Bks.parks Imprint).

Adams, Jackie. Without a Blink. 2008. 40p. (J). 10.99 *(978-0-9800327-0-3(9))* Speranza's Pr.

Addino, Victoria. Sadie's Wish: Three Little Elves. Garafalo, Beatrice, illus. 2012. 32p. (-18). pap. 24.95 *(978-1-4626-9907-0(3))* America Star Bks.

Adeyemi, Tomi. Children of Blood & Bone. 2019. (KOR.). (YA). (gr. 9-12). pap. *(978-89-7478-418-8(1))* Daseot Sure.

—Children of Blood & Bone. 2018. (Legacy of Orisha Ser.). (ENG.). (YA). (gr. 9-13). pap. 10.99 *(978-1-250-19412-1(1))*; (Illus.). 544p. 21.99 *(978-1-250-17097-2(4)*, 900188178, Holt, Henry & Co. Bks. For Young Readers) Holt, Henry & Co.

Adler, David A. Young Cam Jansen & the Magic Bird Mystery. Natti, Susanna, illus. 2013. (Young Cam Jansen Ser.: 18). (ENG.). 32p. (J). (gr. 1-3). pap. 4.99 *(978-0-448-46613-2(9)*, Penguin Young Readers) Penguin Young Readers Group.

Agee, Jon. Milo's Hat Trick. 2017. (Illus.). 40p. (J). (gr. k-3). 17.99 *(978-0-7352-2987-7(2)*, Dial Bks) Penguin Young Readers Group.

Agraso, Alberto & Dojeiji, Mony. Je Suis Heureuse. Agraso, Alberto, illus. 2013. (Illus.). 36p. pap. *(978-1-927803-01-1(2))* Walking for Peace Publishing.

—Soy Feliz. 2012. 36p. pap. 14.95 *(978-1-62141-690-6(9))* Booklocker.com, Inc.

Aguiar, Nadia. The Great Wave of Tamarind. 2018. (Book of Tamarind Ser.: 3). (ENG.). 384p. (J). pap. 16.99 *(978-1-250-14394-5(2)*, 900177169) Square Fish.

Ahdieh, Renée. The Rose & the Dagger. (Wrath & the Dawn Ser.: 2). (ENG., Illus.). (YA). (gr. 7). 2017. 448p. pap. 12.99 *(978-0-14-751386-1(3)*, Penguin Books) 2016. 432p. 18.99 *(978-0-399-17162-8(2)*, G.P. Putnam's Sons Books for Young Readers) Penguin Young Readers Group.

—The Rose & the Dagger. 2017. (Wrath & the Dawn Ser.: 2). lib. bdg. 22.10 *(978-0-606-40106-7(7))* Turtleback.

Ahlers, Oly. Following My Magical Dream, 1 vol. 2010. 48p. pap. 16.95 *(978-1-61582-758-9(7))* America Star Bks.

Ahour, Paravish. All Children of the World Smile in the Same Language: Iran, the Cradle of Civilization. 2006. (Illus.). 103p. (J). (gr. 4-7). per. 16.95 *(978-1-60002-015-5(1)*, 3593) Mountain Valley Publishing, LLC.

Aiken, Joan. A Necklace of Raindrops & Other Stories. Hawkes, Kevin, illus. 2003. 84p. (J). (gr. 1-5). 13.15 *(978-0-7569-5686-8(2))* Perfection Learning Corp.

—The Serial Garden. 2012. (ENG.). 320p. (J). (gr. 4). pap. 16.00 *(978-1-931520-82-9(8)*, Big Mouth Hse.) Small Beer Pr.

Albert, Melissa. The Hazel Wood. l.t. ed. 2018. (ENG.). 458p. 21.99 *(978-1-4328-4617-6(5))* Cengage Gale.

—The Hazel Wood: A Novel. (Hazel Wood Ser.: 1). (ENG., Illus.). (YA). 2019. 400p. pap. 10.99 *(978-1-250-14793-6(X)*, 900181824) 2018. 368p. 16.99 *(978-1-250-14790-5(5)*, 900181823) Flatiron Bks.

Alcántara, Ricardo. Mauro Ojos Brillantes. 9th ed. 2003. (SPA., Illus.). 48p. *(978-84-236-2865-0(5)*, ED6279) Edebé ESP. Dist: Lectorum Pubns., Inc.

Alcántara Sgarbi, Ricardo. TOMÁS Y EL LÁPIZ MÁGICO. 2007. (SPA., Illus.). 46p. per. 10.50 *(978-84-263-4829-6(7))* Vives, Luis Editorial (Edelvives) ESP. Dist: Lectorum Pubns., Inc.

Aldrick, Shirley H. F. Tobias & the Pale, Pale Leprechaun. 2009. 52p. pap. 19.50 *(978-1-60693-959-8(9)*, Strategic Bk. Publishing) Strategic Book Publishing & Rights Agency (SBPRA).

Aldridge, Ethan M. Estranged. Aldridge, Ethan M., illus. 2018. (ENG., Illus.). 224p. (J). (gr. 3-7). 21.99 *(978-0-06-265387-1(3))*; pap. 13.99 *(978-0-06-265386-4(5))* HarperCollins Pubs. (Quill Tree Bks.).

Alexander, Alma. Gift of the Unmage. 2007. (Worldweavers Ser.: Bk. 1). (ENG.). 400p. (J). (gr. 7-12). 16.99 *(978-0-06-083955-0(4))* HarperCollins Pubs.

—Spellspam. 2008. (Worldweavers Ser.: Bk. 2). (YA). (gr. 7-18). (ENG.). 448p. 17.99 *(978-0-06-083958-1(9))*; 437p. lib. bdg. 18.89 *(978-0-06-083959-8(7))* HarperCollins Pubs. (Eos).

Alexander, Annette M. Snow Magic & the Sad Little Christmas Tree. 2011. (Illus.). 32p. 14.66 *(978-1-4567-7182-9(5))* AuthorHouse.

Alexander, Lloyd. The High King. 2006. (Chronicles of Prydain: Bk. 5). (Illus.). 253p. (gr. 3-7). 17.00 *(978-0-7569-6816-8(X))* Perfection Learning Corp.

Alexander, Michael. Until Wishes Are Fulfilled II: Alec's Story. 2007. 204p. per. 15.50 *(978-1-84426-468-1(8))* Upfront Publishing Ltd. GBR. Dist: Printondemand-worldwide.com.

Alexander, R. C. Unfamiliar Magic. 2011. 368p. (J). (gr. 3-7). pap. 8.99 *(978-0-375-85855-0(5)*, Yearling) Random Hse. Children's Bks.

Alexander, Susanne L. Adventures of the Pixies of Penny Brook Village: Reeza's Revenge. 2007. 174p. (J). pap. 12.95 *(978-0-7414-4292-5(2))* Infinity Publishing.

Alexander, William. Goblin Secrets. (ENG., Illus.). (J). (gr. 3-7). 2013. 256p. pap. 7.99 *(978-1-4424-2727-3(2))* 2012. 240p. 19.99 *(978-1-4424-2726-6(4))* McElderry, Margaret K. Bks. (McElderry, Margaret K. Bks.).

Aliaga, Roberto. A Night Time Story. Brokenbrow, Jon, tr. Wimmer, Sonja, illus. 2012. 24p. (J). (gr. k-3). 14.95 *(978-84-15241-98-0(4))* Cuento de Luz SL ESP. Dist: Publishers Group West (PGW).

Allan, Delores. Magical Moments with Roy & Toni: Come on Lets Go. 2011. 24p. (gr. 1-2). pap. 12.79 *(978-1-4634-0950-0(8))* AuthorHouse.

—Magical Moments with Roy & Toni: Do You Ever Wonder. 2012. 24p. pap. 17.99 *(978-1-4772-8910-5(0))* AuthorHouse.

Allen, Elise & Stanford, Halle. Jim Henson's Enchanted Sisters: Autumn's Secret Gift. 2014. (Enchanted Sisters Ser.). (ENG., Illus.). 128p. (J). (gr. 2-4). pap. 5.99 *(978-1-61963-254-7(3)*, 900131787, Bloomsbury USA Childrens) Bloomsbury Publishing USA.

—Winter's Flurry Adventure. Pooler, Paige, illus. 2014. (Enchanted Sisters Ser.: 2). (YA). lib. bdg. 16.00 *(978-0-606-36217-7(7))* Turtleback.

Allen, F. M. Brayhard. 2009. 268p. pap. 30.95 *(978-1-4092-7639-5(2))* Lulu Pr., Inc.

Allman, Joy. Hailey's Magic Stone. 2010. (ENG., Illus.). 32p. pap. 12.99 *(978-1-4389-1264-6(1))* AuthorHouse.

Allman-Varty, Faye. The Kitten Tales of Pumpkin & Parsnip 'Fairy Fields. Knott, Stephen, illus. 2008. 20p. pap. *(978-1-905553-28-0(5))* BookPublishingWorld.

Alston, B. B. Amari & the Great Game. (Supernatural Investigations Ser.). (ENG.). 432p. 2023. (gr. 4-7). 28.69 ***(978-1-5364-8191-4(2))*** 2023. (J). (gr. 3-7). pap. 10.99 ***(978-0-06-297520-1(X))*** 2022. (Illus.). (J). (gr. 3-7). 18.99 *(978-0-06-297519-5(6))* HarperCollins Pubs. (Balzer & Bray).

—Amari & the Night Brothers. (Supernatural Investigations Ser.: 1). (ENG.). 2022. 432p. (J). (gr. 3-7). pap. 11.99 *(978-0-06-297517-1(X))* 2021. (Illus.). 416p. (J). (gr. 3-7). 17.99 *(978-0-06-297516-4(1))*1. 2022. 432p. (gr. 4-7). 29.94 *(978-1-5364-7242-4(5))* HarperCollins Pubs. (Balzer & Bray).

Alston, B. B. Amari y Los Hermanos de la Noche / Amari & the Night Brothers. 2023. (Amari Ser.). (SPA.). 448p. (J). (gr. 4-7). pap. 14.95 ***(978-1-64473-875-7(9))*** Penguin Random House Grupo Editorial ESP. Dist: Penguin Random Hse. LLC.

Alton, Steve. The Firehills. 2005. (ENG.). 192p. (YA). (gr. 5-12). 15.95 *(978-1-57505-798-9(0)*, Carolrhoda Bks.) Lerner Publishing Group.

—The Malifex. 2003. (Middle Readers Ser.). (Illus.). 182p. (J). (gr. 3-7). 14.95 *(978-0-8225-0959-2(8))* Lerner Publishing Group.

Alward, Amy. Going Viral. (Potion Diaries). (ENG., Illus.). 352p. (gr. 7). 2018. (J). pap. 11.99 *(978-1-4814-4385-2(2))* 2017. (YA). 18.99 *(978-1-4814-4384-5(4))* Simon & Schuster Bks. For Young Readers. (Simon & Schuster Bks. For Young Readers).

—Royal Tour. 2017. (Potion Diaries). (ENG., Illus.). 432p. (YA). (gr. 7). pap. 11.99 *(978-1-4814-4382-1(8)*, Simon & Schuster Bks. For Young Readers) Simon & Schuster Bks. For Young Readers.

Amara, Phil. The Treehouse Heroes: The Forgotten Beast. Chau, Alina, illus. 2012. (ENG.). 36p. (J). (gr. -1-3). 15.95 *(978-1-59702-034-3(6))* Immedium.

Amato, Mary. The Word Eater. Ryniak, Christopher, illus. 2005. (ENG.). 151p. (J). (gr. 3-7). reprint ed. pap. 7.99 *(978-0-8234-1940-1(1))* Holiday Hse., Inc.

Ambau, Getty. Desta & the Winds of Washaa Umera: The Winds of Washaa Umera, vols. 7, vol. 2. 2nd ed. 2013.

(ENG., Illus.). 454p. (YA). pap. 15.95 *(978-1-884459-03-0(X))* Falcon Pr. International.

Amestoy, Jennifer. Junkyard Junction: The Story of the Magic Microwave. 2008. 32p. pap. 14.75 *(978-1-4389-1755-9(4))* AuthorHouse.

Amundson, Sandi. Zach & Dougie Dragonfly's Adventure. 2011. 55p. pap. 23.95 *(978-1-4327-3536-4(5))* Outskirts Pr., Inc.

Ananda, Linda. Rainbow Childrenr-Magical Moving Stories: Stories with Movement, Dance, Yoga, & Song. 2012. 152p. pap. 47.95 *(978-1-4525-5475-4(7))* Balboa Pr.

and Film Studio, Shanghai Animation & Tang, Sanmu. Nezha Conquers the Dragon King. Yawtsong, Lee, tr. from CHI. 2010. (Favorite Childrens Cartoons from China Ser.). (ENG., Illus.). 32p. (gr. -1-3). pap. 5.95 *(978-1-60220-975-6(8))* Shanghai Pr.

Andersen, Alan Lance. Wizard Academies - Rumpots, Crackpots, & Pooka-Mazed Halfwits. 2007. (ENG.). 174p. pap. 19.96 *(978-0-615-18594-1(0))* Wizard Academies, LLC.

Anderson, Al. Adventures with Bingo Borden. Agora Publications Staff, tr. Kurzycka, Krystyna Emilia, illus. 2010. 77p. (J). pap. 9.50 *(978-1-887250-46-7(8))* Agora Pubns., Inc.

Anderson, AnnMarie. Attack of the Plants. 2019. (Branches Early Ch Bks). (ENG., Illus.). 96p. (J). (gr. 2-4). 15.96 *(978-1-64310-823-0(9))* Penworthy Co., LLC, The.

—The Attack of the Plants (the Magic School Bus Rides Again #5) 2018. (Magic School Bus Rides Again Ser.: 5). (ENG., Illus.). 96p. (J). (gr. 1-3). pap. 5.99 *(978-1-338-29079-0(7))* Scholastic, Inc.

Anderson, Cassie. Extraordinary: a Story of an Ordinary Princess. 2019. (ENG., Illus.). 200p. (J). (gr. 3-7). pap. 12.99 *(978-1-5067-1027-3(1)*, Dark Horse Books) Dark Horse Comics.

Anderson, Hans Christian. The Snow Queen: A Story in Seven Parts. Holmes, Sally, illus. 2019. 64p. (J). (gr. -1-12). 13.00 *(978-1-86147-856-6(9)*, Armadillo) Anness Publishing GBR. Dist: National Bk. Network.

Anderson, Hans Christian & Fowler, Gloria. The Red Shoes. Yung Yoo, Sun, illus. 2008. (ENG.). 32p. (J). (gr. -1-3). 16.95 *(978-1-934429-06-8(6))* AMMO Bks., LLC.

Anderson, Jodi Lynn. Tiger Lily. (ENG.). 304p. (YA). (gr. 8). 2013. pap. 9.99 *(978-0-06-200326-3(7))* 2012. 17.99 *(978-0-06-200325-6(9))* HarperCollins Pubs. (HarperCollins).

Anderson, Matt & Lambert, Chad. Kung Fu Panda Vol. 2: It's Elemental & Other Stories. 2012. (ENG., Illus.). 24p. pap., pap. 6.95 *(978-1-936340-56-9(9)*, 9781936340569) Ape Entertainment.

Anderson, R. J. A Little Taste of Poison. 2016. (ENG., Illus.). 368p. (J). (gr. 4-7). 18.99 *(978-1-4814-3774-5(7)*, Atheneum Bks. for Young Readers) Simon & Schuster Children's Publishing.

—A Pocket Full of Murder. 2015. (ENG., Illus.). 352p. (J). (gr. 4-7). 18.99 *(978-1-4814-3771-4(2))* Simon & Schuster Children's Publishing.

—Spell Hunter. 2009. (Faery Rebels Ser.). (ENG.). 336p. (J). (gr. 8-18). 16.99 *(978-0-06-155474-2(X))* HarperCollins Pubs.

—Wayfarer. 2010. (ENG.). 304p. (J). (gr. 8-18). 16.99 *(978-0-06-155477-3(4)*, HarperTeen) HarperCollins Pubs.

Andrew-Kollmann, Marcia. Blinky the Magical Elf. Dittus, Jade Moon, illus. 2012. 28p. pap. 24.95 *(978-1-4626-5345-4(6))* America Star Bks.

Andrews, Randall. The Last Guardian of Magic. 2008. 448p. (YA). per. 23.95 *(978-0-595-47345-8(8))* iUniverse, Inc.

Anna, Holly. Pop Goes the Bubble Trouble. Santos, Genevieve, illus. 2018. (Daisy Dreamer Ser.: 8). (ENG.). 128p. (J). (gr. k-4). 17.99 *(978-1-5344-2653-5(1))*; pap. 6.99 *(978-1-5344-2652-8(3))* Little Simon. (Little Simon).

—Posey, the Class Pest. Santos, Genevieve, illus. 2018. (Daisy Dreamer Ser.: 7). (ENG.). 128p. (J). (gr. k-4). 16.99 *(978-1-5344-1269-9(7))*; pap. 6.99 *(978-1-5344-1268-2(9))* Little Simon. (Little Simon).

Arbuthnott, Gill. The Chaos Clock, 40 vols. 2003. (Kelpies Ser.). (ENG.). 160p. 10.00 *(978-0-86315-422-5(0))* Floris Bks. GBR. Dist: SteinerBooks, Inc.

Archer, Chris. Aftershock. 2010. (Mindwarp Ser.: 6). (ENG.). 144p. (YA). (gr. 11). pap. 8.99 *(978-1-4424-1415-0(4)*, Simon Pulse) Simon Pulse.

Arden, Alys. The Romeo Catchers. 2017. (Casquette Girls Ser.: 2). (ENG., Illus.). 604p. (YA). (gr. 7-12). pap. 12.95 *(978-1-5039-4000-0(4)*, 9781503940000, Skyscape) Amazon Publishing.

Arevalo, Luis Paquime. Juan & the Magic Shoes. 2005. (J). per. 3.99 *(978-0-9748598-1-1(8))* L. A. Eng Bks.

Arevamirp, Esile & Primavera, Elise. Fred & Anthony Meet the Demented Super-Degerm-O Zombie. Primavera, Elise, illus. 2007. (ENG., Illus.). 128p. (J). (gr. 2-6). pap. 4.99 *(978-0-7868-3680-2(6))* Hyperion Pr.

Arias, Carlos Ballesteros. The Magic Forest. 2006. (J). pap. 8.00 *(978-0-8059-7022-7(3))* Dorrance Publishing Co., Inc.

Arkin, Alan. Cosmo: A Cautionary Tale. Richards, Jon, illus. 2005. 40p. (J). 19.95 *(978-1-929115-12-9(1))* Azro Pr., Inc.

Armenteros, Sarah. Emma & the Mashed Potato Monster. 2009. (ENG., Illus.). 44p. (J). 18.99 *(978-1-59092-384-9(7))* Blue Forge Pr.

Armentrout, Jennifer L. Every Last Breath. 2019. (Dark Elements Ser.: 3). (ENG.). 384p. (YA). pap. 10.99 *(978-1-335-00921-0(3))* Harlequin Enterprises ULC CAN. Dist: HarperCollins Pubs.

Armstrong, Kelley. The Awakening. (Darkest Powers Ser.: 2). (ENG.). (YA). (gr. 8-18). 2009. 368p. 17.99 *(978-0-06-166276-8(3))*2. 2010. 384p. pap. 11.99 *(978-0-06-145055-6(3))* HarperCollins Pubs. (HarperCollins).

—The Awakening, 7 vols. 2009. (Darkest Powers Ser.: 2). (YA). 133.75 *(978-1-4407-3103-7(9))*; 103.75 *(978-1-4407-3099-3(7))* Recorded Bks., Inc.

—The Reckoning. 2011. (Darkest Powers Ser.: 3). (ENG.). 416p. (YA). (gr. 8). pap. 10.99 *(978-0-06-145056-3(1)*, HarperCollins) HarperCollins Pubs.

Arnauld, D. S. Zertelo & the Road of Fire: Book Two. Scott, Sara, ed. 2007. 210p. (J). per. 9.95 *(978-0-9801408-1-1(1))* Heroes & Leaders.

Arnett, Mindee. The Nightmare Dilemma. 2015. (Arkwell Academy Ser.: 2). (ENG.). 400p. (YA). (gr. 8-12). pap. 10.99 *(978-0-7653-3337-7(6)*, 900084950, Tor Teen) Doherty, Tom Assocs., LLC.

—Onyx & Ivory. (ENG.). (YA). (gr. 9). 2019. 528p. pap. 12.99 *(978-0-06-265267-6(2))* 2018. (Illus.). 512p. 17.99 *(978-0-06-265266-9(4))* HarperCollins Pubs. (Balzer & Bray).

—Shadow & Flame. (ENG.). 496p. (YA). (gr. 9). 2020. pap. 12.99 *(978-0-06-265271-3(0))* 2019. (Illus.). 17.99 *(978-0-06-265269-0(9))* HarperCollins Pubs. (Balzer & Bray).

Arnold, Elizabeth. The Parsley Parcel. 2006. 212p. per. *(978-1-904529-22-4(4)*, Back to Front) Solidus.

Aronson, Sarah. Halfway to Happily Ever after (the Wish List #3) 2018. (Wish List Ser.: 3). (ENG., Illus.). 192p. (J). (gr. 3-7). 14.99 *(978-0-545-94162-4(8)*, Scholastic Pr.) Scholastic, Inc.

—The Worst Fairy Godmother Ever! (the Wish List #1) (Wish List Ser.: 1). (ENG.). 176p. (J). (gr. 3-7). 2018. pap. 5.99 *(978-1-338-14148-1(1))* 2017. 14.99 *(978-0-545-94151-8(2)*, Scholastic Pr.) Scholastic, Inc.

Aros, Angela. Aunt Emma's Secret Recipe, 1 vol. 2009. 15p. pap. 19.95 *(978-1-60813-862-3(3))* PublishAmerica, Inc.

Arrathroon, Leigh A. Magical Adventures in Michigan. 2003. (Illus.). viii, 349p. *(978-1-893047-10-5(5))* Archus Pr., LLC.

Artz, D. M. Maggie & the Magic Sparkle Seed. 2007. 30p. 16.95 *(978-1-4357-0152-6(6))* Lulu Pr., Inc.

Asbroek, Karen. The Adventures of Princess Jordan 1: Forest Magic — Believe! Paradero, Shannen Marie, illus. 2017. (ENG.). 24p. (J). pap. 20.69 *(978-1-5434-0578-1(9))*; 34.49 *(978-1-5434-0579-8(7))* Xlibris Corp.

—The Adventures of Princess Jordan 2: Green Grass Romp. Paradero, Shannen Marie, illus. 2017. (ENG.). 24p. pap. 20.69 *(978-1-5434-0581-1(9))* Xlibris Corp.

—The Adventures of Princess Jordan 3: Cloud Hopping. Paradero, Shannen Marie, illus. 2017. (ENG.). 24p. pap. 20.69 *(978-1-5434-0583-5(5))* Xlibris Corp.

Asphyxia. The Grimstones Collection. Asphyxia, illus. 2015. (Grimstones Ser.). (ENG., Illus.). 488p. (J). (gr. 3-7). pap. 17.99 *(978-1-76011-391-9(3))* Allen & Unwin AUS. Dist: Independent Pubs. Group.

Atamer, Billie. The Magic Sleigh. 2013. 28p. pap. 13.95 *(978-1-61244-213-6(7))* Halo Publishing International.

Atwater-Rhodes, Amelia. Wolfcry. 2008. (Kiesha'ra Ser.: Bk. 4). (ENG.). 208p. (YA). (gr. 9-12). pap. 7.99 *(978-0-440-23886-7(2)*, Delacorte Pr.) Random Hse. Children's Bks.

Atwell, A. Erika Laura. 2008. 157p. pap. 24.95 *(978-1-60703-006-5(3))* PublishAmerica, Inc.

Atwood, Megan. Molly Discovers Magic (Then Wants to un-Discover It) Fleming, Lucy, illus. 2016. (Dear Molly, Dear Olive Ser.). (ENG.). 96p. (J). (gr. 1-3). lib. bdg. 21.99 *(978-1-4795-8694-3(3)*, 130930, Picture Window Bks.) Capstone.

—Molly Discovers Magic (Then Wants to Un-Discover It) Fleming, Lucy, illus. 2017. (Dear Molly, Dear Olive Ser.). (ENG.). 96p. (J). (gr. 1-3). pap. 5.95 *(978-1-62370-616-6(5)*, 130934, Capstone Young Readers) Capstone.

Augenstein, Marianne R. The Quest for Kair, 1 vol. 2009. 152p. pap. 24.95 *(978-1-60813-899-9(2))* America Star Bks.

August, John. Arlo Finch in the Valley of Fire. 2019. (Arlo Finch Ser.: 1). (ENG.). 352p. (J). pap. 8.99 *(978-1-250-29425-8(8)*, 900174830) Square Fish.

Aumuller, Kimberly. Dragon's Hope: Tale of the Guardians. 2009. 224p. 25.95 *(978-0-595-50945-4(2))*; pap. 15.95 *(978-0-595-52209-5(2))* iUniverse, Inc.

Auxier, Jonathan. Peter Nimble & His Fantastic Eyes. 2012. (ENG.). 400p. (YA). (gr. 5-17). pap. 9.95 *(978-1-4197-0421-5(4)*, 693403, Amulet Bks.) Abrams, Inc.

—Sophie Quire & the Last Storyguard: A Peter Nimble Adventure. (ENG.). 464p. (gr. 3-7). 2017. (J). pap. 10.99 *(978-1-4197-2202-8(6)*, 1114103) 2016. (YA). 18.95 *(978-1-4197-1747-5(2)*, 1114101, Amulet Bks.) Abrams, Inc.

AZ Books Staff. Cinderella. Zyl, Olga, ed. 2012. (Classic Fairy Tales Ser.). (ENG.). 10p. (J). (gr. -1-k). bds. 9.95 *(978-1-61889-007-8(7))* AZ Bks. LLC.

—Horse's Farm. Potapenko, Olga, ed. 2012. (Talking Plush Animals Ser.). (ENG.). 10p. (J). (gr. -1-k). bds. 10.95 *(978-1-61889-112-9(X))* AZ Bks. LLC.

—Little Thumb. Zyl, Olga, ed. 2012. (Classic Fairy Tales Ser.). (ENG.). 10p. (J). (gr. -1-k). bds. 9.95 *(978-1-61889-008-5(5))* AZ Bks. LLC.

Azad, Nafiza. The Candle & the Flame. 2019. (ENG.). 416p. (YA). (gr. 7-7). 18.99 *(978-1-338-30604-0(9)*, Scholastic Pr.) Scholastic, Inc.

Babbitt, Natalie. Elsie Times Eight. Babbitt, Natalie, illus. 2005. (Illus.). 26p. (J). (gr. k-4). reprint ed. 16.00 *(978-0-7567-9640-2(7))* DIANE Publishing Co.

Baccalario, P. D. Suitcase of Stars, 1 vol. Pernigotti, Chiara, tr. Bruno, Iacopo, illus. 2014. (Enchanted Emporium Ser.). (ENG.). 240p. (J). (gr. 4-8). 26.65 *(978-1-4342-6516-6(1)*, 124272, Stone Arch Bks.) Capstone.

Baccalario, Pierdomenico. Compass of Dreams, 1 vol. Pernigotti, Chiara, tr. Bruno, Iacopo, illus. 2014. (Enchanted Emporium Ser.). (ENG.). 240p. (J). (gr. 4-8). 26.65 *(978-1-4342-6517-3(X)*, 124273, Stone Arch Bks.) Capstone.

—Map of the Passages. McGuinness, Nanette, tr. Bruno, Iacopo, illus. 2015. (Enchanted Emporium Ser.). (ENG.). 240p. (J). (gr. 4-8). 12.95 *(978-1-62370-204-5(6)*, 127181, Capstone Young Readers) Capstone.

Bach, Richard & Gardner, Sally. La Niña Más Pequeña del Mundo. Tapia, Sonia, tr. 2005. (Niños Mágicos Ser.).Tr. of One. (SPA & ENG., Illus.). 128p. (J). (gr. 2-4). pap. 7.95 *(978-84-666-1339-2(0))* Ediciones B ESP. Dist: Independent Pubs. Group.

Bach, Shelby. Of Enemies & Endings. 2015. (Ever Afters Ser.: 4). (ENG., Illus.). 400p. (J). (gr. 3-7). 16.99 *(978-1-4424-9787-0(4)*, Simon & Schuster Bks. For Young Readers) Simon & Schuster Bks. For Young Readers.

—Of Giants & Ice. 2013. (Ever Afters Ser.: 1). (ENG., Illus.). 368p. (J). (gr. 3-7). pap. 7.99 *(978-1-4424-3147-8(4)*, Simon & Schuster Bks. For Young Readers) Simon & Schuster Bks. For Young Readers.

—Of Sorcery & Snow. 2015. (Ever Afters Ser.: 3). (ENG., Illus.). 352p. (J). (gr. 3-7). pap. 8.99 *(978-1-4424-9785-6(8)*, Simon & Schuster Bks. For Young Readers) Simon & Schuster Bks. For Young Readers.

—Of Witches & Wind. (Ever Afters Ser.: 2). (ENG., Illus.). (J). (gr. 3-7). 2014. 416p. pap. 8.99 *(978-1-4424-3150-8(4))* 2013. 400p. 15.99 *(978-1-4424-3149-2(0))* Simon & Schuster Bks. For Young Readers. (Simon & Schuster Bks. For Young Readers).

Bachmann, Stefan. The Peculiar. (Peculiar Ser.: 1). (ENG.). (J). (gr. 4). 2013. 400p. pap. 8.99 *(978-0-06-219519-7(0))* 2012. 384p. 16.99 *(978-0-06-219518-0(2))* HarperCollins Pubs. (Greenwillow Bks.).

—The Whatnot. 2013. 421p. (J). *(978-0-06-228630-7(7)*, Harper Design) HarperCollins Pubs.

Backus, Leatha F. Annie & Timmy's Magic Pebbles. 2008. 32p. per. 24.95 *(978-1-4241-9513-8(6))* America Star Bks.

Badger, Meredith. Fairy School Dropout Undercover. 2011. (Fairy School Ser.: 2). (ENG., Illus.). 160p. (J). (gr. 2-4). pap. 15.99 *(978-0-312-61951-0(0)*, 900065967) Square Fish.

Baggott, Julianna. The Ever Breath. 2011. (ENG.). 240p. (J). (gr. 4-6). lib. bdg. 21.19 *(978-0-385-90676-0(5)*, Delacorte Pr.) Random Hse. Children's Bks.

Bagley, Conor. Ziggy McFinster's Nantucket Adventure. Bernard Westcott, Nadine, illus. 2008. (ENG.). 40p. (J). (gr. -1-3). 16.95 *(978-1-56625-315-4(2))* Bonus Bks., Inc.

Bailey, Kristin. Into the Nightfell Wood. 2018. (ENG.). 368p. (J). (gr. 3-7). 16.99 *(978-0-06-239860-4(1)*, Tegen, Katherine Bks) HarperCollins Pubs.

Baker, E. D. Dragon's Breath: Read-Along/Homework Pack. 6 vols. unabr. ed. 2005. (Frog Princess Ser.: 2). (SPA.). (J). (gr. 5-8). 78.75 *(978-1-4193-3563-1(4)*, 42041) Recorded Bks., Inc.

—Magic Animal Rescue 1: Maggie & the Flying Horse. Manuzak, Lisa, illus. 2017. (ENG.). 128p. (J). pap. 5.99 *(978-1-68119-141-6(5)*, 900159887, Bloomsbury USA Childrens) Bloomsbury Publishing USA.

—Magic Animal Rescue 4: Maggie & the Flying Pigs. 2017. (ENG., Illus.). 128p. (J). 16.99 *(978-1-68119-489-9(9)*, 900175461); pap. 5.99 *(978-1-68119-485-1(6)*, 900175433) Bloomsbury Publishing USA. (Bloomsbury USA Childrens).

—More Than a Princess. (More Than a Princess Ser.). (ENG.). (J). 2019. 304p. pap. 8.99 *(978-1-5476-0211-7(2)*, 900203281) 2018. 288p. 16.99 *(978-1-68119-768-5(5)*, 900185875) Bloomsbury Publishing USA. (Bloomsbury Children's Bks.).

—Power of a Princess. 2019. (More Than a Princess Ser.). (ENG.). 304p. (J). 16.99 *(978-1-68119-769-2(3)*, 900185870, Bloomsbury Children's Bks.) Bloomsbury Publishing USA.

—Princess in Disguise: A Tale of the Wide-Awake Princess. (Wide-Awake Princess Ser.: 4). (ENG.). 240p. (J). pap. 8.99 *(978-1-61963-934-8(3)*, 900152548) 2015. 224p. (YA). (gr. 3-6). 16.99 *(978-1-61963-573-9(9)*, 900140973) Bloomsbury Publishing USA. (Bloomsbury USA Childrens).

—Unlocking the Spell: A Tale of the Wide-Awake Princess. 2014. (Wide-Awake Princess Ser.: 2). (ENG.). 288p. (YA). (gr. 5-6). pap. 9.99 *(978-1-61963-194-6(6)*, 900125844, Bloomsbury USA Childrens) Bloomsbury Publishing USA.

—The Wide-Awake Princess. 2012. (Wide-Awake Princess Ser.: 1). (ENG.). 288p. (J). (gr. 5-14). pap. 8.99 *(978-1-59990-658-4(9)*, 900074739, Bloomsbury USA Childrens) Bloomsbury Publishing USA.

Baker, Keith. Cookies: A Mr. & Mrs. Green Adventure. 2012. (ENG., Illus.). 24p. (J). (gr. -1-3). pap. 4.99 *(978-0-547-74561-9(3)*, 1486285, Clarion Bks.) HarperCollins Pubs.

Baldacci, David. The Keeper. 2015. 428p. (YA). *(978-0-545-88230-9(3)*, Scholastic Pr.) Scholastic, Inc.

—The Keeper. 2016. (Vega Jane Ser.: 2). (ENG.). 428p. (J). (gr. 5-9). 20.85 *(978-0-606-39127-6(4))* Turtleback.

—The Keeper (Vega Jane, Book 2) 2016. (Vega Jane Ser.: 2). (ENG.). 448p. (J). (gr. 5-9). pap. 10.99 *(978-0-545-83195-6(4)*, Scholastic Pr.) Scholastic, Inc.

—The Keeper (Vega Jane, Book 2) (Unabridged Edition), 1 vol. unabr. ed. 2015. (Vega Jane Ser.: 2). (ENG.). 2p. (J). (gr. 5-9). audio compact disk 44.99 *(978-0-545-88154-8(4))* Scholastic, Inc.

—The Width of the World. 2018. (Vega Jane Ser.: 3). lib. bdg. 20.85 *(978-0-606-41137-0(2))* Turtleback.

—The Width of the World (Vega Jane, Book 3) 2018. (Vega Jane Ser.: 3). (ENG.). 448p. (J). (gr. 4-7). pap. 7.99 *(978-1-338-23559-3(1))*; (gr. 5-9). 9.99 *(978-0-545-83197-0(0))* Scholastic, Inc.

Baldwin, J. R. The Magic Jammies, 1 vol. 2010. 24p. 24.95 *(978-1-4512-9442-2(5))* PublishAmerica, Inc.

Balfour, Melissa, et al. Yr Olion Traed Hud. 2005. (WEL., Illus.). 48p. pap. *(978-1-85596-677-2(8))* Dref Wen.

Balian, Lorna. Sweet Touch, 1 vol. Balian, Lecia, illus. 2005. (ENG.). 32p. (J). (gr. -1-3). 16.95 *(978-1-59572-017-7(0))* Star Bright Bks., Inc.

Ball, Georgia & Disney Editors. Disney Frozen Comics Collection. 2016. (ENG.). 96p. (J). (gr. 4-7). 20.85 *(978-0-606-39075-0(8))* Turtleback.

Ballerina Magic Shoes. (Ballerina Charm Book Ser.). (Illus.). 32p. (J). *(978-1-4054-1144-8(9))* Parragon, Inc.

Banda, Rey A. The Magical City of Northopolis; a Christmas Story. Patlan, Alyssa A., illus. 2012. 50p. (-18). pap. 16.95 *(978-0-615-69125-1(0))* Northopolis.

Banks, Angelica. Finding Serendipity. Lewis, Stevie, illus. 2016. (Tuesday Mcgillycuddy Adventures Ser.). (ENG.). 304p. (J). pap. 10.99 *(978-1-250-07337-2(5)*, 900150766) Square Fish.

Banks, Lynne Reid. The Indian in the Cupboard. 2011. 9.14 *(978-0-7848-3449-7(0)*, Everbind) Marco Bk. Co.

—The Indian in the Cupboard. 2010. (Indian in the Cupboard Ser.). (ENG.). 240p. (J). (gr. 3-7). 8.99 *(978-0-375-84753-0(7)*, Yearling) Random Hse. Children's Bks.

—The Key to the Indian. 2004. (Indian in the Cupboard Ser.: 5). (J). (gr. 3-6). lib. bdg. 17.20 *(978-0-613-23006-3(X))* Turtleback.

—The Mystery of the Cupboard. Newsom, Tom, illus. 2004. (ENG.). 256p. (J). (gr. 4-18). pap. 7.99 *(978-0-380-72013-2(2)*, HarperCollins) HarperCollins Pubs.

—The Return of the Indian. 2010. (Indian in the Cupboard Ser.). (ENG.). 208p. (J). (gr. 3-7). 7.99 *(978-0-375-85523-8(8)*, Yearling) Random Hse. Children's Bks.

—The Secret of the Indian. 2010. (Indian in the Cupboard Ser.). (ENG.). 192p. (J). (gr. 3-7). 7.99 *(978-0-375-85524-5(6)*, Yearling) Random Hse. Children's Bks.

—Secret of the Indian. 2003. (ENG., Illus.). 160p. pap. *(978-0-00-714900-1(X)*, Collins) HarperCollins Pubs. Ltd.

Banks, Lynne Reid & Banks, L. The Return of the Indian. 2010. (Indian in the Cupboard Ser.: 2). (gr. 3-6). lib. bdg. 17.20 *(978-0-8335-0902-4(0))* Turtleback.

Banks, Rosie. Enchanted Palace. 2014. (Secret Kingdom Ser.: 1). lib. bdg. 14.75 *(978-0-606-35390-8(9))* Turtleback.

—Glitter Beach. 2015. (Secret Kingdom Ser.: 6). lib. bdg. 14.75 *(978-0-606-36349-5(1))* Turtleback.

—Magic Mountain. 2014. (Secret Kingdom Ser.: 5). lib. bdg. 14.75 *(978-0-606-36062-3(X))* Turtleback.

—Mermaid Reef. 2014. (Secret Kingdom Ser.: 4). lib. bdg. 14.75 *(978-0-606-35842-2(0))* Turtleback.

—Secret Kingdom: Starlight Adventure. 2017. (Secret Kingdom Ser.). (ENG., Illus.). 208p. (J). (gr. k-2). pap. 5.99 *(978-1-4083-2918-4(2)*, Orchard Bks.) Hachette Children's Group GBR. Dist: Hachette Bk. Group.

Banks, Tyra. Modelland. 2011. 569p. (YA). (gr. 7). 17.99 *(978-0-375-97259-1(5)*, Delacorte Pr) Random House Publishing Group.

Baptiste, Tracey. The Jumbies. 2015. (Jumbies Ser.). (ENG.). 240p. (J). (gr. 4-7). 16.95 *(978-1-61620-414-3(1)*, 73414) Algonquin Young Readers.

Baratz-Logsted, Lauren. Durinda's Dangers. 2. Weber, Lisa K., illus. 2008. (Sisters 8 Ser.: 2). (ENG.). 128p. (J). (gr. 2-4). 18.69 *(978-0-547-13347-8(2))* Houghton Mifflin Harcourt Publishing Co.

—The Final Battle... for Now Bk. 9. 2012. (Sisters Eight Ser.: 9). (ENG., Illus.). 160p. (J). (gr. 1-4). pap. 6.99 *(978-0-547-55441-9(9)*, 1452177, Clarion Bks.) HarperCollins Pubs.

Bardugo, Leigh. King of Scars. 2019. (Illus.). 528p. (J). *(978-1-5101-0445-7(3))* ETT Imprint.

—King of Scars. 2019. (ENG., Illus.). 514p. (J). (gr. 9-13). pap. 11.99 *(978-1-250-23107-9(8))* ImPrint.

—King of Scars. 2019. (King of Scars Duology Ser.: 1). (ENG., Illus.). 528p. (YA). 19.99 *(978-1-250-14228-3(8)*, 900180180) Imprint IND. Dist: Macmillan.

—King of Scars. 2020. (King of Scars Duology Ser.: 1). (ENG., Illus.). 528p. (YA). pap. 12.99 *(978-1-250-61897-9(5)*, 900180181) Square Fish.

—The Language of Thorns: Midnight Tales & Dangerous Magic. 2017. (ENG.). (YA). (gr. 8-12). pap. 11.99 *(978-1-250-17392-8(2))* ImPrint.

—The Language of Thorns: Midnight Tales & Dangerous Magic. Kipin, Sara, illus. 2017. (ENG.). 288p. (YA). 24.99 *(978-1-250-12252-0(X)*, 900173718) Imprint IND. Dist: Macmillan.

—Ruin & Rising. 2014. (Shadow & Bone Trilogy Ser.: 3). (ENG., Illus.). 432p. (YA). (gr. 7-12). 19.99 *(978-0-8050-9461-9(X)*, 900078589, Holt, Henry & Co. Bks. For Young Readers) Holt, Henry & Co.

—Ruin & Rising. 2015. (Grisha Trilogy Ser.: 3). (YA). lib. bdg. 22.10 *(978-0-606-37283-1(0))* Turtleback.

—Shadow & Bone. 2012. (Shadow & Bone Trilogy Ser.: 1). (ENG.). 368p. (YA). (gr. 7-12). 19.99 *(978-0-8050-9459-6(8)*, 900078585, Holt, Henry & Co. Bks. For Young Readers) Holt, Henry & Co.

—Shadow & Bone. 2013. (Shadow & Bone Trilogy Ser.: 1). (ENG.). 416p. (YA). (gr. 7-12). pap. 10.99 *(978-1-250-02743-6(8)*, 900098315) Square Fish.

—Shadow & Bone. 2013. (Grisha Trilogy Ser.: 1). (YA). lib. bdg. 22.10 *(978-0-606-31903-4(4))* Turtleback.

—Siege & Storm. 2013. (Shadow & Bone Trilogy Ser.: 2). (ENG., Illus.). 448p. (YA). (gr. 7). 19.99 *(978-0-8050-9460-2(1)*, 900078587, Holt, Henry & Co. Bks. For Young Readers) Holt, Henry & Co.

—Siege & Storm. 2014. (Shadow & Bone Trilogy Ser.: 2). (ENG.). 496p. (YA). (gr. 7). pap. 10.99 *(978-1-250-04443-3(X)*, 900128342) Square Fish.

Barker, Cicely Mary. Flower Fairies Magical Doors. 2009. (Flower Fairies Ser.). (ENG.). 16p. (J). (gr. k-4). 29.99 *(978-0-7232-6351-7(5)*, Warne) Penguin Young Readers Group.

—Magical Secret Garden. 2010. (Flower Fairies Ser.). (ENG.). 24p. (J). (gr. k-3). 19.99 *(978-0-7232-6440-8(6)*, Warne) Penguin Young Readers Group.

Barnard, Sarah. The Map & the Stone. 2nd ed. 2010. (Illus.). 142p. pap. 16.95 *(978-0-9556887-2-0(8))* Ethics Trading GBR. Dist: Lulu Pr., Inc.

Barnett, Brandi. Glamour. 2008. 231p. 19.95 *(978-1-930709-68-3(4))* HAWK Publishing Group.

Barnett, Mac. The Magic Word. Parsley, Elise, illus. 2016. (ENG.). 40p. (J). (gr. -1-3). 17.99 *(978-0-06-235484-6(1)*, Balzer & Bray) HarperCollins Pubs.

Barnhill, Kelly. The Girl Who Drank the Moon (Winner of the 2017 Newbery Medal) (ENG.). 400p. (J). (gr. 5-9). 2019. pap. 9.95 *(978-1-61620-746-5(9)*, 73746) 2016. 18.99 *(978-1-61620-567-6(9)*, 73567) Algonquin Young Readers.

—The Girl Who Drank the Moon (Winner of the 2017 Newbery Medal) - Gift Edition. 2019. (ENG., Illus.). 416p. (gr. 5-9). 19.95 *(978-1-61620-997-1(6)*, 73997) Algonquin Young Readers.

—The Mostly True Story of Jack. 2012. (ENG.). 352p. (J). (gr. 3-7). pap. 18.99 *(978-0-316-05672-4(3))* Little, Brown Bks. for Young Readers.

—La Niña Que Bebió la Luna. Onoda, Yuta, illus. 2018.Tr. of Girl Who Drank the Moon. (SPA.). 424p. pap. 17.95 *(978-1-64101-210-2(2)*, Loqueleo) Santillana USA Publishing Co., Inc.

—The Witch's Boy. 2014. (ENG.). 400p. (J). (gr. 4-7). 37.99 *(978-1-61620-351-1(X)*, 73351) Algonquin Young Readers.

Barnholdt, Lauren. Hailey Twitch & the Campground Itch. Beaky, Suzanne, illus. 2011. (Hailey Twitch Ser.: 3). 144p. (J). (gr. 2-4). pap. 8.99 *(978-1-4022-2446-1(X)*, Sourcebooks Jabberwocky) Sourcebooks, Inc.

Barnholdt, Lauren & Beaky, Suzanne. Hailey Twitch & the Wedding Glitch. 2011. (Hailey Twitch Ser.: 4). (Illus.). 144p. (J). (gr. 2-4). pap. 10.99 *(978-1-4022-2447-8(8)*, Sourcebooks Jabberwocky) Sourcebooks, Inc.

Barr, Mary. The Trouble with Filly Tucker. 2010. 112p. (gr. 4-6). 20.95 *(978-1-4502-3517-4(4))*; pap. 10.95 *(978-1-4502-3515-0(8))* iUniverse, Inc.

Barron, T. A. Doomraga's Revenge: Book 7, 7 vols., Bk. 7. 2011. (Merlin Saga Ser.: 7). (ENG.). 272p. (J). (gr. 5-18). 8.99 *(978-0-14-241925-0(7)*, Puffin Books) Penguin Young Readers Group.

M N O

—The Eternal Flame: Book 11, 11 vols. 2011. (Merlin Saga Ser.: 11). (ENG.). 416p. (J). (gr. 5-18). 9.99 (978-0-14-241929-8(X), Puffin Books) Penguin Young Readers Group.

—The Great Tree of Avalon: Book 9, 9 vols. 2011. (Merlin Saga Ser.: 9). (ENG.). 464p. (J). (gr. 5-18). 8.99 (978-0-14-241927-4(3), Puffin Books) Penguin Young Readers Group.

—The Mirror of Fate: Book 4, Bk. 4. 2011. (Merlin Saga Ser.: 4). (ENG.). 272p. (J). (gr. 5-18). 8.99 (978-0-14-241922-9(2), Puffin Books) Penguin Young Readers Group.

—Ultimate Magic: Book 8, 8 vols., Bk. 8. 2011. (Merlin Saga Ser.: 8). (ENG.). 256p. (J). (gr. 5-18). 8.99 (978-0-14-241926-7(5), Puffin Books) Penguin Young Readers Group.

Barrowman, John & Barrowman, Carole. Conjuror. 2016. (Orion Chronicles Ser.). (ENG.). 320p. (YA). (gr. 7). 16.99 (978-1-78185-637-6(0)) Head of Zeus GBR. Dist: Independent Pubs. Group.

Barrowman, John & Barrowman, Carole E. Bone Quill. 2014. (Hollow Earth Ser.). (ENG., Illus.). 304p. (J). (gr. 3-7). pap. 8.99 (978-1-4424-8929-5(4), Aladdin) Simon & Schuster Children's Publishing.

—Hollow Earth. 2013. (Hollow Earth Ser.). (ENG., Illus.). 416p. (J). (gr. 3-7). pap. 8.99 (978-1-4424-5853-6(4), Aladdin) Simon & Schuster Children's Publishing.

Barrows, Annie. Magic in the Mix. 2015. (ENG.). 288p. (YA). (gr. 3-6). pap. 8.99 (978-1-61963-798-6(7), 900148899, Bloomsbury USA Childrens) Bloomsbury Publishing USA.

Barry, Dave. Peter & the Sword of Mercy. 4. 2011. (Peter & the Starcatchers Ser.: Bk. 4). (ENG., Illus.). 528p. (J). (gr. 5-9). pap. 9.99 (978-1-4231-3070-3(7), Disney-Hyperion) Disney Publishing Worldwide.

Barton, Bree. Heart of Thorns. 2019. (Heart of Thorns Ser.: 1). (ENG.). 480p. (YA). (gr. 8). pap. 11.99 (978-0-06-244769-2(6)) 2018. (Heart of Thorns Ser.: 1). (ENG., Illus.). 464p. (YA). (gr. 8). 17.99 (978-0-06-244768-5(8)) 2018. (Illus.). 464p. (J). (978-0-06-288917-1(6)) HarperCollins Pubs. (Tegen, Katherine Bks).

Baruch, M. P. Spend the Day with Me. Arscott, Dean, illus. 2009. 20p. pap. 10.95 (978-1-936051-27-4(3)) Peppertree Pr., The.

Barulich-Liederbach, Terri & Liederbach, Tom. The Memory Chair. 2010. 48p. pap. 19.49 (978-1-4520-5672-2(2)) AuthorHouse.

Bass, Patrik Henry. The Zero Degree Zombie Zone. Craft, Jerry, illus. 2014. (ENG.). 144p. (J). (gr. 3-7). 16.99 (978-0-545-13210-7(X), Scholastic Pr.) Scholastic, Inc.

Bassett, Alisa Cuthbertson. Threads of Time. 2013. 24p. pap. 24.95 (978-1-63000-063-9(9)) America Star Bks.

Batham, Matthew. Lightsleep. 2006. 167p. pap. (978-1-904623-39-7(5)) WritersPrintShop.

Baucom, Ian. Through the Skylight. Gerard, Justin, illus. (ENG.). 400p. (J). (gr. 4-8). 2014. pap. 6.99 (978-1-4424-8167-1(6)) 2013. 17.99 (978-1-4169-1777-9(2)) Simon & Schuster Children's Publishing. (Atheneum Bks. for Young Readers).

Bauer, Deidre. Silver Mountain. 2008. 38p. pap. 8.00 (978-0-8059-7672-4(8)) Dorrance Publishing Co., Inc.

Baum, L. Frank. Adventures in Oz: Dorothy & the Wizard in Oz, the Road to Oz, the Emerald City of Oz. 2007. 296p. 24.95 (978-1-60459-017-3(3)); per. 12.95 (978-1-60459-016-6(5)) Wilder Pubns., Corp.

—Adventures in Oz: The Tin Woodman of Oz, the Magic of Oz, Glinda of Oz. 2007. 284p. 24.95 (978-1-60459-023-4(8)) Wilder Pubns., Corp.

—The Magic of Oz. 2007. 108p. (gr. 4-7). per. 9.95 (978-1-60312-334-1(2)); 22.95 (978-1-60312-671-7(6)) Aegypan.

—The Marvelous Land of Oz. 2007. 120p. per. 10.95 (978-1-60312-149-1(8)) Aegypan.

—Sky Island. 2007. 144p. (gr. 4-7). per. 11.95 (978-1-60312-253-5(2)) Aegypan.

—Sky Island. 2004. (Twelve-Point Ser.). lib. bdg. 24.00 (978-1-58287-280-3(5)); lib. bdg. 25.00 (978-1-58287-792-1(0)) North Bks.

Baum, L. Frank & Thompson, Ruth Plumly. The Royal Book of Oz. 2009. 112p. pap. 8.99 (978-1-60459-763-9(1)) Wilder Pubns., Corp.

Baum, L. Frank, et al. A Children's Treasury. 2007. 792p. per. 24.95 (978-1-60459-011-1(4)) Wilder Pubns., Corp.

Baxter, Nicola. Dreamland Fairies: Magical Bedtime Stories from Fairyland. Manson, Beverlie, illus. 2012. 80p. (J). (gr. k-4). pap. 9.99 (978-1-84322-806-6(8)) Anness Publishing GBR. Dist: National Bk. Network.

—My Treasury of Fairies & Elves: A Collection of 20 Magical Stories. Manson, Beverlie, illus. 2012. 240p. (J). (gr. k-4). 18.99 (978-1-84322-835-6(1)) Anness Publishing GBR. Dist: National Bk. Network.

—Witches, Wizards & Magicians. Morton, Ken, illus. 2012. 80p. (J). (gr. k-4). pap. 9.99 (978-1-84322-807-3(6)) Anness Publishing GBR. Dist: National Bk. Network.

Beamish, Diane. Grandma's Magic Button Necklace. 2006. 25p. 12.16 (978-1-4116-5487-7(0)) Lulu Pr., Inc.

Bear, F. T. Connor Finn: The Secret of Snow. 2013. 258p. pap. (978-0-646-91485-5(5)) F. T. Bear.

Beardslee, Nellie L. The Glenn's of Newberry Hills. 2008. 164p. pap. 24.95 (978-1-60703-471-1(9)) America Star Bks.

Beasley, Cassie. Circus Mirandus. 2016. (SPA.). 25.99 (978-84-246-5686-7(5)) La Galera, S.A. Editorial ESP. Dist: Lectorum Pubns., Inc.

—Circus Mirandus. 2016. (ENG., Illus.). 320p. (J). (gr. 4-7). pap. 8.99 (978-0-14-751554-4(8), Puffin Books) Penguin Young Readers Group.

—Circus Mirandus. Lt. ed. 2020. (ENG.). lib. bdg. 22.99 (978-1-4328-7834-4(4)) Thorndike Pr.

—Circus Mirandus. 2016. (ENG.). 304p. (J). (gr. 3-7). 19.65 (978-0-606-39311-9(0)) Turtleback.

Beatty, Robert. Willa of Dark Hollow. (Willa of the Wood Ser.). (ENG.). (J). (gr. 3-7). 2022. 384p. pap. 7.99 (978-1-368-00948-5(4)) 2021. (Illus.). 368p. 17.99 (978-1-368-00760-3(0)) Disney Publishing Worldwide. (Disney-Hyperion).

Becker, Aaron. Return. Becker, Aaron, illus. 2016. (ENG., Illus.). 40p. (J). (gr. -1-3). 17.99 (978-0-7636-7730-5(2)) Candlewick Pr.

Becker, Bonny. The Magical Ms. Plum. Portnoy, Amy, illus. 2011. (ENG.). 112p. (J). (gr. 1-4). 7.99 (978-0-375-84760-8(X), Yearling) Random Hse. Children's Bks.

Becker, Jaqueline H. Listen, There Are More Than Seven Dwarfs. 2012. pap. 11.95 (978-0-7414-7037-9(3)) Infinity Publishing.

Begler, Pete. The Fearless Travelers' Guide to Wicked Places. 2017. (ENG., Illus.). 384p. (J) (gr. 4-8). 14.95 (978-1-62370-799-6(4), 133339, Capstone Young Readers) Capstone.

Belanger, Kathleen. Cooldog's Holiday Adventures. Baker, David, illus. 2012. 48p. 24.95 (978-1-4626-3045-5(6)) America Star Bks.

Bell, Anita & Bell, Belinda. 'Twas Ever. 2011. 210p. pap. 11.99 (978-1-257-00131-6(0)) 2010. (ENG.). 207p. 28.99 (978-0-557-41894-7(1)) Lulu Pr., Inc.

Bell, Braden. The Kindling. 2012. (YA). (978-1-4621-1027-8(4)) Cedar Fort, Inc./CFI Distribution.

—Luminescence. 2014. pap. 14.99 (978-1-4621-1405-4(9), Horizon Pubs.) Cedar Fort, Inc./CFI Distribution.

—Penumbras. 2013. (Middle School Magic Ser.). (ENG.). 305p. (J). (gr. 3-7). 14.99 (978-1-4621-1220-3(X), Sweetwater Bks.) Cedar Fort, Inc./CFI Distribution.

Bell, Frank. Ma Jong & the Magic Carpet. Seaman, Paul, illus. 2004. 24p. pap. 7.00 (978-1-84161-070-2(4)) Ravette Publishing, Ltd. GBR. Dist: Parkwest Pubns., Inc.

Bell, Hilari. Fall of a Kingdom. 2005. (Farsala Trilogy Ser.: 1). (ENG.). 448p. (YA). (gr. 7). pap. 6.99 (978-0-689-85414-9(5), Simon Pulse) Simon Pulse.

—The Goblin Gate. (ENG.). (YA). (gr. 8). 2011. 400p. pap. 8.99 (978-0-06-165104-5(4)) 2010. 384p. 16.99 (978-0-06-165102-1(8)) HarperCollins Pubs. (HarperTeen).

—The Goblin War. 2011. (ENG.). 304p. (J). (gr. 8). 17.99 (978-0-06-165105-2(2), HarperTeen) HarperCollins Pubs.

—The Goblin Wood. 2004. (Illus.). 371p. (J). (gr. 5-9). 14.65 (978-0-7569-3253-4(X)) Perfection Learning Corp.

—The Prophecy. 2006. (ENG., Illus.). 208p. (J). (gr. 5-9). 15.99 (978-0-06-059943-0(X)) HarperCollins Pubs.

—Trickster's Girl: The Raven Duet Book #1. 2011. (Raven Duet Ser.). (ENG.). 288p. (YA). (gr. 7). pap. 15.99 (978-0-547-57724-1(9), 1458522, Clarion Bks.) HarperCollins Pubs.

Bell, Jennifer. The Uncommoners #1: the Crooked Sixpence. (Uncommoners Ser.: 1). (ENG., Illus.). (J). (gr. 3-7). 2018. 336p. 7.99 (978-0-553-49846-2(0), Yearling) 2017. 320p. 16.99 (978-0-553-49843-1(6), Crown Books For Young Readers) Random Hse. Children's Bks.

Bell, P. G. The Train to Impossible Places: a Cursed Delivery. 2019. (Train to Impossible Places Ser.: 1). (ENG.). 400p. (J). pap. 7.99 (978-1-250-21142-2(5), 900192256) Square Fish.

Bell, Parker. Tale of the Hundred. 2012. (ENG.). pap. (978-1-4675-2062-1(4)) Independent Pub.

Bellairs, John. The Chessmen of Doom (A Johnny Dixon Mystery: Book Seven) 2011. 114p. pap. 14.95 (978-1-61756-348-5(X)) Open Road Integrated Media, Inc.

—The House with a Clock in Its Walls. Gorey, Edward, illus. 2004. (Lewis Barnavelt Ser.: Bk. 1). (ENG.). 192p. (J). (gr. 3-7). pap. 7.99 (978-0-14-240257-3(5), Puffin Books) Penguin Young Readers Group.

—The House with a Clock in Its Walls. Gorey, Edward, illus. 2004. (John Bellairs Mysteries Ser.). 179p. (J). (gr. 3-7). 13.65 (978-0-7569-5257-0(3)) Perfection Learning Corp.

—The House with a Clock in Its Walls. (Lewis Barnavelt Ser.: Bk. 1). 179p. (J). (gr. 4-6). pap. 4.50 (978-0-8072-1423-7(X), Listening Library) Random Hse. Audio Publishing Group.

—The House with a Clock in Its Walls. 2004. 17.20 (978-1-4176-3513-9(4)) Turtleback.

—The Spell of the Sorcerer's Skull. Gorey, Edward, illus. 2004. 170p. (J). (gr. 4-7). 13.65 (978-0-7569-4965-5(3)) Perfection Learning Corp.

Benko, Kamilla. Fire in the Star. 2020. (Unicorn Quest Ser.). (ENG., Illus.). 384p. (J). 16.99 (978-1-68119-249-9(7), 900164375, Bloomsbury Children's Bks.) Bloomsbury Publishing USA.

—Secret in the Stone. (Unicorn Quest Ser.). (ENG.). (J). 2020. 352p. pap. 8.99 (978-1-5476-0310-7(0), 900211266) 2019. (Illus.). 336p. 16.99 (978-1-68119-247-5(0), 900164378) Bloomsbury Publishing USA. (Bloomsbury Children's Bks.).

—The Unicorn Quest. (Unicorn Quest Ser.). (ENG.). 336p. (J). 2019. pap. 8.99 (978-1-68119-983-2(1), 900194729, Bloomsbury Children's Bks.) 2018. 16.99 (978-1-68119-245-1(4), 900164376, Bloomsbury USA Childrens) Bloomsbury Publishing USA.

Bennett, Jeffrey. El Mago Que Salvó el Mundo. Collier-Morales, Roberta, illus. 2011. (SPA.). 32p. (J). (gr. 2-4). 15.00 (978-0-9721819-5-2(4)) Big Kid Science.

—The Wizard Who Saved the World. Collier-Morales, Roberta, illus. 2011. (ENG.). 32p. (J). (gr. 2-4). 15.00 (978-0-9721819-4-5(6)) Big Kid Science.

Bennett, Jenn. The Lady Rogue. 2019. (ENG., Illus.). 384p. (YA). (gr. 9). 18.99 (978-1-5344-3199-7(3), Simon Pulse) Simon Pulse.

Benoff-Nadel, Phyllis. The Magical Garden. 2013. 32p. pap. 16.99 (978-1-4525-7445-5(6), Balboa Pr.) Author Solutions, LLC.

Bentley, Nancy Kaye. Mema's back Yard. 2010. 39p. pap. 17.95 (978-0-557-68242-3(8)) Lulu Pr., Inc.

Bentley, Sue. Chocolate Wishes #1. Swan, Angela, illus. 2013. (Magic Bunny Ser.: 1). (ENG.). 128p. (J). (gr. 1-3). pap. 6.99 (978-0-448-46727-6(5), Grosset & Dunlap) Penguin Young Readers Group.

—A Christmas Surprise. Swan, Angela, illus. 2008. (Magic Kitten Ser.). (ENG.). 128p. (J). (gr. 1-3). pap. 5.99 (978-0-448-45001-8(1), Grosset & Dunlap) Penguin Young Readers Group.

—Circus Surprise #7. Swan, Angela, illus. 2014. (Magic Ponies Ser.: 7). (ENG.). 128p. (J). (gr. 1-3). 6.99 (978-0-448-46734-4(8), Grosset & Dunlap) Penguin Young Readers Group.

—A Circus Wish. 2009. (Magic Kitten Ser.: 6). lib. bdg. 14.75 (978-0-606-06970-0(4)) Turtleback.

—A Circus Wish #6, 6 vols. Swan, Angela, illus. 2009. (Magic Kitten Ser.: 6). (ENG.). 128p. (J). (gr. 1-3). pap. 6.99 (978-0-448-45062-9(3), Grosset & Dunlap) Penguin Young Readers Group.

—Classroom Capers. 2014. (Magic Bunny Ser.: 4). lib. bdg. 14.75 (978-0-606-34134-9(X)) Turtleback.

—Classroom Capers #4. Swan, Angela, illus. 2014. (Magic Bunny Ser.: 4). (ENG.). 128p. (J). (gr. 1-3). 6.99 (978-0-448-46792-4(5), Grosset & Dunlap) Penguin Young Readers Group.

—Classroom Chaos #2, 2 vols. Swan, Angela, illus. 2008. (Magic Kitten Ser.: 2). (ENG.). 128p. (J). (gr. 1-3). pap. 6.99 (978-0-448-44999-9(4), Grosset & Dunlap) Penguin Young Readers Group.

—Classroom Princess. 2013. (Magic Puppy Ser.: 9). lib. bdg. 16.00 (978-0-606-32122-8(5)) Turtleback.

—Classroom Princess #9. Swan, Angela, illus. 2013. (Magic Puppy Ser.: 9). (ENG.). 128p. (J). (gr. 1-3). 6.99 (978-0-448-46732-0(1), Grosset & Dunlap) Penguin Young Readers Group.

—Cloud Capers. 2009. (Magic Puppy Ser.: 3). lib. bdg. 14.75 (978-0-606-06977-9(1)) Turtleback.

—Cloud Capers #3, 3 vols., 3. Swan, Angela, illus. 2009. (Magic Puppy Ser.: 3). (ENG.). 128p. (J). (gr. 1-3). 6.99 (978-0-448-45046-9(1), Grosset & Dunlap) Penguin Young Readers Group.

—Dancing Days. 2014. (Magic Bunny Ser.: 5). lib. bdg. 14.75 (978-0-606-34135-6(8)) Turtleback.

—Dancing Days #5. Swan, Angela, illus. 2014. (Magic Bunny Ser.: 5). (ENG.). 128p. (J). (gr. 1-3). 5.99 (978-0-448-46793-1(3), Grosset & Dunlap) Penguin Young Readers Group.

—Double Trouble. 2009. (Magic Kitten Ser.: 4). lib. bdg. 16.00 (978-0-606-06004-2(9)) Turtleback.

—Double Trouble #4, 4 vols. Swan, Angela, illus. 2009. (Magic Kitten Ser.: 4). (ENG.). 128p. (J). (gr. 1-3). pap. 6.99 (978-0-448-45060-5(7), Grosset & Dunlap) Penguin Young Readers Group.

—Firelight Friends. 2014. (Magic Kitten Ser.: 10). lib. bdg. 14.75 (978-0-606-34136-3(6)) Turtleback.

—Firelight Friends #10. Swan, Angela, illus. 2014. (Magic Kitten Ser.: 10). (ENG.). 128p. (J). (gr. 1-3). 6.99 (978-0-448-46788-7(7), Grosset & Dunlap) Penguin Young Readers Group.

—Friendship Forever. 2013. (Magic Puppy Ser.: 10). lib. bdg. 14.75 (978-0-606-32123-5(3)) Turtleback.

—Friendship Forever #10. Swan, Angela, illus. 2013. (Magic Puppy Ser.: 10). (ENG.). 128p. (J). (gr. 1-3). 6.99 (978-0-448-46733-7(X), Grosset & Dunlap) Penguin Young Readers Group.

—A Glittering Gallop. 2013. (Magic Kitten Ser.: 8). lib. bdg. 16.00 (978-0-606-32120-4(9)) Turtleback.

—A Glittering Gallop #8, No. 8. Swan, Angela, illus. 2013. (Magic Kitten Ser.: 8). (ENG.). 128p. (J). (gr. 1-3). 6.99 (978-0-448-46730-6(5), Grosset & Dunlap) Penguin Young Readers Group.

—Magic Puppy - A New Beginning. 2009. (Magic Puppy Ser.: 1). lib. bdg. 16.00 (978-0-606-06017-2(0)) Turtleback.

—Magic Puppy #5 Party Dreams. 5th ed. 2008. (Illus.). 128p. (J). pap. (978-0-14-132379-4(5), Puffin) Penguin Bks., Ltd.

—Magic Puppy #6 a Forest Charm. 2008. (Illus.). 128p. (J). pap. (978-0-14-132380-0(9), Puffin) Penguin Bks., Ltd.

—Magic Puppy: Books 1-3. Swan, Angela, illus. 2014. (Magic Puppy Ser.). (ENG.). 368p. (J). (gr. 1-3). 11.99 (978-0-448-48460-0(9), Grosset & Dunlap) Penguin Young Readers Group.

—Muddy Paws. 2009. (Magic Puppy Ser.: 2). lib. bdg. 14.75 (978-0-606-06021-9(9)) Turtleback.

—Muddy Paws #2, No. 2. Swan, Angela, illus. 2009. (Magic Puppy Ser.: 2). (ENG.). 128p. (J). (gr. 1-3). pap. 6.99 (978-0-448-45045-2(3), Grosset & Dunlap) Penguin Young Readers Group.

—A New Beginning #1, No. 1. Swan, Angela, illus. 2009. (Magic Puppy Ser.: 1). (ENG.). 128p. (J). (gr. 1-3). pap. 6.99 (978-0-448-45044-5(5), Grosset & Dunlap) Penguin Young Readers Group.

—A New Friend. 2013. (Magic Ponies Ser.: 1). lib. bdg. 16.00 (978-0-606-29584-0(4)) Turtleback.

—A New Friend #1. 1. Swan, Angela, illus. 2013. (Magic Ponies Ser.: 1). (ENG.). 128p. (J). (gr. 1-3). 6.99 (978-0-448-46205-9(2), Grosset & Dunlap) Penguin Young Readers Group.

—Party Dreams #5, 5 vols., 5. Swan, Angela, illus. 2010. (Magic Puppy Ser.: 5). (ENG.). 128p. (J). (gr. 1-3). 5.99 (978-0-448-45064-3(X), Grosset & Dunlap) Penguin Young Readers Group.

—The Perfect Secret. 2014. (Magic Puppy Ser.: 14). lib. bdg. 14.75 (978-0-606-35686-2(X)) Turtleback.

—The Perfect Secret #14. Swan, Angela, illus. 2014. (Magic Puppy Ser.: 14). (ENG.). 128p. (J). (gr. 1-3). 6.99 (978-0-448-46799-3(2), Grosset & Dunlap) Penguin Young Readers Group.

—Picture Perfect #13. Swan, Angela, illus. 2014. (Magic Kitten Ser.: 13). (ENG.). 128p. (J). (gr. 1-3). 5.99 (978-0-448-46796-2(8), Grosset & Dunlap) Penguin Young Readers Group.

—Pony Camp. 2014. (Magic Ponies Ser.: 8). lib. bdg. 16.00 (978-0-606-34139-4(0)) Turtleback.

—Pony Camp #8. Swan, Angela, illus. 2014. (Magic Ponies Ser.: 8). (ENG.). 128p. (J). (gr. 1-3). 6.99 (978-0-448-46787-0(9), Grosset & Dunlap) Penguin Young Readers Group.

—A Puzzle of Paws. 2014. (Magic Kitten Ser.: 12). lib. bdg. 14.75 (978-0-606-35682-4(7)) Turtleback.

—A Puzzle of Paws #12. Swan, Angela, illus. 2014. (Magic Kitten Ser.: 12). (ENG.). 128p. (J). (gr. 1-3). 5.99 (978-0-448-46795-5(X), Grosset & Dunlap) Penguin Young Readers Group.

—Riding Rescue #6. Swan, Angela, illus. 2013. (Magic Ponies Ser.: 6). (ENG.). 128p. (J). (gr. 1-3). 6.99 (978-0-448-46735-1(6), Grosset & Dunlap) Penguin Young Readers Group.

—School of Mischief #8, 8 vols., 8. Swan, Angela, illus. 2010. (Magic Puppy Ser.: 8). (ENG.). 128p. (J). (gr. 1-3). 5.99 (978-0-448-45067-4(4), Grosset & Dunlap) Penguin Young Readers Group.

—Seaside Mystery. 2013. (Magic Kitten Ser.: 9). lib. bdg. 16.00 (978-0-606-32121-1(7)) Turtleback.

—Seaside Mystery #9. Swan, Angela, illus. 2013. (Magic Kitten Ser.: 9). (ENG.). 128p. (J). (gr. 1-3). 5.99 (978-0-448-46731-3(3), Grosset & Dunlap) Penguin Young Readers Group.

—A Shimmering Splash. 2014. (Magic Kitten Ser.: 11). lib. bdg. 14.75 (978-0-606-34137-0(4)) Turtleback.

—A Shimmering Splash #11. Swan, Angela, illus. 2014. (Magic Kitten Ser.: 11). (ENG.). 128p. (J). (gr. 1-3). 6.99 (978-0-448-46789-4(5), Grosset & Dunlap) Penguin Young Readers Group.

—Show-Jumping Dreams. 2013. (Magic Ponies Ser.: 4). lib. bdg. 14.75 (978-0-606-31679-8(5)) Turtleback.

—Show-Jumping Dreams #4. Swan, Angela, illus. 2013. (Magic Ponies Ser.: 4). (ENG.). 128p. (J). (gr. 1-3). pap. 5.99 (978-0-448-46208-0(7), Grosset & Dunlap) Penguin Young Readers Group.

—Snowy Wishes. Swan, Angela, illus. 2013. (Magic Puppy Ser.). (ENG.). 128p. (J). (gr. 1-3). 6.99 (978-0-448-46737-5(2), Grosset & Dunlap) Penguin Young Readers Group.

—Snowy Wishes. 2013. (Magic Puppy Ser.). lib. bdg. 16.00 (978-0-606-32124-2(1)) Turtleback.

—Sparkling Skates. 2014. (Magic Puppy Ser.: 13). lib. bdg. 14.75 (978-0-606-35685-5(1)) Turtleback.

—Sparkling Skates #13. Swan, Angela, illus. 2014. (Magic Puppy Ser.: 13). (ENG.). 128p. (J). (gr. 1-3). 5.99 (978-0-448-46798-6(4), Grosset & Dunlap) Penguin Young Readers Group.

—Sparkling Steps. 7th ed. 2007. (ENG., Illus.). 128p. (J). pap. (978-0-14-132155-4(5), Puffin) Penguin Publishing Group.

—Sparkling Steps #7, 7 vols., 7. Swan, Angela, illus. 2009. (Magic Kitten Ser.: 7). (ENG.). 128p. (J). (gr. 1-3). 5.99 (978-0-448-45063-6(1), Grosset & Dunlap) Penguin Young Readers Group.

—A Special Wish. 2013. (Magic Ponies Ser.: 2). lib. bdg. 14.75 (978-0-606-29758-5(8)) Turtleback.

—A Special Wish #2, No. 2. Swan, Angela, illus. 2013. (Magic Ponies Ser.: 2). (ENG.). 128p. (J). (gr. 1-3). pap. 6.99 (978-0-448-46206-6(0), Grosset & Dunlap) Penguin Young Readers Group.

—Spellbound at School. 2014. (Magic Puppy Ser.: 11). lib. bdg. 16.00 (978-0-606-34140-0(4)) Turtleback.

—Spellbound at School #11. Swan, Angela, illus. 2014. (Magic Puppy Ser.: 11). (ENG.). 128p. (J). (gr. 1-3). 5.99 (978-0-448-46790-0(9), Grosset & Dunlap) Penguin Young Readers Group.

—A Splash of Forever. 2014. (Magic Kitten Ser.: 14). lib. bdg. 16.00 (978-0-606-35684-8(3)) Turtleback.

—A Splash of Forever #14. Swan, Angela, illus. 2014. (Magic Kitten Ser.: 14). (ENG.). 128p. (J). (gr. 1-3). 6.99 (978-0-448-46797-9(6), Grosset & Dunlap) Penguin Young Readers Group.

—A Splash of Magic. 2013. (Magic Bunny Ser.: 3). lib. bdg. 14.75 (978-0-606-31677-4(9)) Turtleback.

—A Splash of Magic #3. Swan, Angela, illus. 2013. (Magic Bunny Ser.: 3). (ENG.). 128p. (J). (gr. 1-3). pap. 6.99 (978-0-448-46729-0(1), Grosset & Dunlap) Penguin Young Readers Group.

—Star Dreams #3, 3 vols. Swan, Angela, illus. 2008. (Magic Kitten Ser.: 3). (ENG.). 128p. (J). (gr. 1-3). pap. 6.99 (978-0-448-45000-1(3), Grosset & Dunlap) Penguin Young Readers Group.

—Star of the Show. 2009. (Magic Puppy Ser.: 4). lib. bdg. 16.00 (978-0-606-06978-6(X)) Turtleback.

—Star of the Show #4, 4 vols. Swan, Angela, illus. 2009. (Magic Puppy Ser.: 4). (ENG.). 128p. (J). (gr. 1-3). pap. 6.99 (978-0-448-45047-6(X), Grosset & Dunlap) Penguin Young Readers Group.

—A Summer Spell #1. Swan, Angela, illus. 2008. (Magic Kitten Ser.: 1). (ENG.). 128p. (J). (gr. 1-3). pap. 6.99 (978-0-448-44998-2(6), Grosset & Dunlap) Penguin Young Readers Group.

—Sunshine Shimmers. 2014. (Magic Puppy Ser.: 12). lib. bdg. 14.75 (978-0-606-34141-7(2)) Turtleback.

—A Twinkle of Hooves. 2013. (Magic Ponies Ser.: 3). lib. bdg. 14.75 (978-0-606-31678-1(7)) Turtleback.

—A Twinkle of Hooves #3. Swan, Angela, illus. 2013. (Magic Ponies Ser.: 3). (ENG.). 128p. (J). (gr. 1-3). pap. 5.99 (978-0-448-46207-3(9), Grosset & Dunlap) Penguin Young Readers Group.

—Twirling Tails #7, 7 vols. Swan, Angela, illus. 2010. (Magic Puppy Ser.: 7). (ENG.). 128p. (J). (gr. 1-3). pap. 5.99 (978-0-448-45066-7(6), Grosset & Dunlap) Penguin Young Readers Group.

—Vacation Dreams. 2013. (Magic Bunny Ser.: 2). lib. bdg. 16.00 (978-0-606-31676-7(0)) Turtleback.

—Vacation Dreams #2. Swan, Angela, illus. 2013. (Magic Bunny Ser.: 2). (ENG.). 128p. (J). (gr. 1-3). pap. 6.99 (978-0-448-46728-3(3), Grosset & Dunlap) Penguin Young Readers Group.

—Winter Wonderland. 2013. (Magic Ponies Ser.: 5). lib. bdg. 16.00 (978-0-606-32118-1(7)) Turtleback.

—Winter Wonderland #5. Swan, Angela, illus. 2013. (Magic Ponies Ser.: 5). (ENG.). 128p. (J). (gr. 1-3). 6.99 (978-0-448-46786-3(0), Grosset & Dunlap) Penguin Young Readers Group.

Benz, Derek & Lewis, J. S. Grey Griffins: the Brimstone Key. 2011. (Grey Griffins: the Clockwork Chronicles Ser.: 1). (ENG.). 400p. (J). (gr. 3-7). pap. 19.99 (978-0-316-04521-6(7)) Little, Brown Bks. for Young Readers.

—Grey Griffins: the Relic Hunters. 2012. (Grey Griffins: the Clockwork Chronicles Ser.: 2). (ENG.). 384p. (J). (gr. 3-7). pap. 19.99 (978-0-316-04520-9(9)) Little, Brown Bks. for Young Readers.

Beobi & the Magic Coloring Book ABC First Words. 2005. (J). cd-rom 15.99 (978-0-9743847-8-8(X)) Cohn, Tricia.

Beobi & the Magic Coloring Book at the Horse Stables. 2006. (J). 3.99 (978-0-9743847-5-7(5)) Cohn, Tricia.

Beobi & the Magic Coloring Book Funland. 2006. (Illus.). 24p. (J). 3.99 (978-0-9743847-7-1(1)) Cohn, Tricia.

Beobi & the Magic Coloring Book in the Universe. 2006. (J). 3.99 (978-0-9743847-4-0(7)) Cohn, Tricia.

BEOBI & the Magic Coloring Book Our First Adventure. 2005. (J). cd-rom 15.99 (978-0-9743847-9-5(8)) Cohn, Tricia.

Beobi & the Magic Coloring Book Our First Adventure. 2005. (J). 3.99 (978-0-9743847-2-6(0)) Cohn, Tricia.

Bergsma, Jody. Wizard. 2nd ed. 2008. (Illus.). 32p. (J). 15.95 (978-0-9740190-9-3(7)) Illumination Arts Publishing Co., Inc.

Bergstrom, Sarah. Desert Dwellers Born by Fire: The First Book in the Paintbrush Saga. 2015. (ENG., Illus.). 312p. (J). (gr. -1-12). pap. 12.95 (978-1-78279-587-2(1), Lodestone Bks.) Hunt, John Publishing Ltd. GBR. Dist: National Bk. Network.

Bergstrom, William. The Magic Telescope. 2006. 9.95 (978-0-9787648-0-7(3)) Bergstrom Bks.

Berman, Ali. Misdirected: A Novel. 2014. (Illus.). 288p. (YA). (gr. 7). 18.95 (978-1-60980-573-9(9), Triangle Square) Seven Stories Pr.

Bernatene, Poly, illus. The Sorcerer's Apprentice. 2007. (Usborne Young Reading: Series One Ser.). 47p. (J). (gr. -1-3). 8.99 (978-0-7945-1589-8(4), Usborne) EDC Publishing.

Bernstein, Danielle V. The Magic in a Mermaid's Tear. 2013. 28p. pap. 24.95 (978-1-62709-604-1(3)) America Star Bks.

Bernstein, David D. The Enchanted Rope. 2010. 25p. (J). pap. 13.95 (978-1-4327-5175-3(1)) Outskirts Pr., Inc.

Bernstein, Nina. Magic by the Book, 4 vols. unabr. ed. 2005. (J). 65.75 (978-1-4193-3607-2(X), 42048) Recorded Bks., Inc.

Berquist, Emma. Missing, Presumed Dead. 2019. (ENG.). 384p. (YA). (gr. 9). 17.99 (978-0-06-264281-3(2), Greenwillow Bks.) HarperCollins Pubs.

Berry, Julie. The Emperor's Ostrich. 2018. (J). lib. bdg. 18.40 (978-0-606-41103-5(8)) Turtleback.

Berry, Kit. Moondance at Stonewylde. 2011. (ENG.). 304p. (gr. 13-17). 13.99 (978-0-575-09885-5(6), Gollancz) Orion Publishing Group, Ltd. GBR. Dist: Hachette Bk. Group.

—Shadows at Stonewylde. 2013. (ENG.). 432p. 13.99 (978-0-575-09891-6(0), Gollancz) Orion Publishing Group, Ltd. GBR. Dist: Hachette Bk. Group.

Berry, Nessa. Protectors of Little Africa. 2005. 108p. per. 9.99 (978-1-58832-132-9(0)) Unlimited Publishing LLC.

Bessen, Luc. Arthur & the Minimoys. Sowchek, Ellen, tr. from FRE. 2005. (ENG.). 240p. (J). 15.99 (978-0-06-059623-1(6)) HarperCollins Pubs.

Besson, Luc. Arthur & the Forbidden City. Sowchek, Ellen, tr. 2006. (ENG., Illus.). 192p. (J). (gr. 3-7). pap., pap. 5.99 (978-0-06-059628-6(7), Harper Trophy) HarperCollins Pubs.

—Arthur & the Forbidden City. 2005. (ENG., Illus.). 192p. (J). 15.99 (978-0-06-059626-2(0)) HarperCollins Pubs.

—Arthur & the Minimoys. 2005. (Illus.). 240p. (J). lib. bdg. 16.89 (978-0-06-059624-8(4)) HarperCollins Pubs.

Binding, Tim. Sylvie & the Songman. 2011. (ENG.). 352p. (J). (gr. 4-6). lib. bdg. 22.44 (978-0-385-75159-9(1), Yearling) Random Hse. Children's Bks.

Bingham, Laura. Ălvor. 2009. 277p. (J). pap. 17.99 (978-1-59955-272-9(8)) Cedar Fort, Inc./CFI Distribution.

—Wings of Light. 2011. 240p. (J). pap. 15.99 (978-1-59955-492-1(5), Sweetwater Bks.) Cedar Fort, Inc./CFI Distribution.

Bird, Benjamin. Magic Monsters! Levins, Tim, illus. 2015. (Amazing Adventures of Superman! Ser.). (ENG.). 32p. (J). (gr. k-2). pap. 3.95 (978-1-4795-6525-2(3), 128514, Stone Arch Bks.) Capstone.

Bishop, Helena Edwards. Lucille Tinderbox. 2012. (ENG., Illus.). 38p. 18.95 (978-1-4710-6053-3(5)) Lulu Pr., Inc.

Black, Holly. The Darkest Part of the Forest. 2019. (ENG.). 368p. (YA). (gr. 9-17). pap. 12.99 (978-0-316-53621-9(0)) Little, Brown Bks. for Young Readers.

—The Darkest Part of the Forest. 2016. (YA). lib. bdg. 22.10 (978-0-606-37533-7(3)) Turtleback.

—The Iron Trial. 2014. (Magisterium Ser.: Bk. 1). pap. (978-0-545-84067-5(8), Scholastic Pr.) Scholastic, Inc.

—Ironside: A Modern Faerie Tale. 2020. (Modern Faerie Tales Ser.). (ENG.). 288p. (YA). (gr. 9). 19.99 (978-1-5344-8455-9(8)); pap. 11.99 (978-1-5344-8454-2(X)) McElderry, Margaret K. Bks. (McElderry, Margaret K. Bks.).

—Red Glove. 2012. (Curse Workers Ser.: 2). (ENG.). 352p. (YA). (gr. 9). pap. 12.99 (978-1-4424-0340-6(3), McElderry, Margaret K. Bks.) McElderry, Margaret K. Bks.

—Red Glove, 2. 2011. (Curse Workers Ser.: 2). (ENG.). 336p. (YA). (gr. 9-12). 19.99 (978-1-4424-0339-0(X)) Simon & Schuster, Inc.

—Tithe: A Modern Faerie Tale. 2020. (Modern Faerie Tales Ser.). (ENG.). 272p. (YA). (gr. 9). 19.99 (978-1-5344-8450-4(7)); pap. 11.99 (978-1-5344-8451-1(5)) McElderry, Margaret K. Bks. (McElderry, Margaret K. Bks.).

—Valiant: A Modern Faerie Tale. 2020. (Modern Faerie Tales Ser.). (ENG.). 256p. (YA). (gr. 9). 19.99 (978-1-5344-8453-5(1)); pap. 11.99 (978-1-5344-8452-8(3)) McElderry, Margaret K. Bks. (McElderry, Margaret K. Bks.).

—White Cat. (Curse Workers Ser.: 1). (ENG.). (YA). (gr. 9). 2011. 336p. pap. 11.99 (978-1-4169-6397-4(9)) 2010. 320p. 17.99 (978-1-4169-6396-7(0)) McElderry, Margaret K. Bks. (McElderry, Margaret K. Bks.).

Black, Holly & Clare, Cassandra. The Bronze Key (Magisterium #3), 1 vol. 2017. (Magisterium Ser.: 3). (ENG., Illus.). 256p. (J). (gr. 3-7). pap. 8.99 (978-0-545-52232-8(3), Scholastic Pr.) Scholastic, Inc.

—The Copper Gauntlet. 2016. (Magisterium Ser.). (ENG.). (J). (gr. 4-7). lib. bdg. 18.40 (978-0-606-38811-5(7)) Turtleback.

—The Copper Gauntlet (Magisterium #2), 1 vol. (Magisterium Ser.: 2). (ENG.). 272p. (J). (gr. 3-7). 2016. pap. 8.99 (978-0-545-52229-8(3)) 2015. 17.99 (978-0-545-52228-1(5), Scholastic Pr.) Scholastic, Inc.

—The Golden Tower (Magisterium #5) 2018. (Magisterium Ser.: 5). (ENG., Illus.). 256p. (J). (gr. 3-7). 17.99 (978-0-545-52240-3(4), Scholastic Pr.) Scholastic, Inc.

—The Iron Trial. 2014. (ENG., Illus.). 320p. (J). (978-0-85753-250-3(2), Scholastic Pr.) Scholastic, Inc.

—The Iron Trial. 2015. (Magisterium Ser.: 1). lib. bdg. 18.40 (978-0-606-37028-8(5)) Turtleback.

—The Iron Trial (Magisterium #1), 1 vol. 2015. (Magisterium Ser.: 1). (ENG.). 304p. (J). (gr. 3-7). pap. 8.99 (978-0-545-52226-7(9), Scholastic Pr.) Scholastic, Inc.

—The Silver Mask (Magisterium #4) (Magisterium Ser.: 4). (ENG.). 240p. (J). (gr. 3-7). 2018. pap. 8.99 (978-0-545-52238-0(2)) 2017. (Illus.). 17.99 (978-0-545-52236-6(6)) Scholastic, Inc. (Scholastic Pr.).

Black, Holly & DiTerlizzi, Tony. Care & Feeding of Sprites. DiTerlizzi, Tony, illus. 2006. (Spiderwick Chronicles Ser.). (ENG., Illus.). 48p. (J). (gr. 2-7). 19.99 (978-1-4169-2757-0(3), Simon & Schuster Bks. For Young Readers) Simon & Schuster Bks. For Young Readers.

—The Wrath of Mulgarath. l.t. ed. 2006. (Spiderwick Chronicles: Bk. 5). (Illus.). 183p. (J). (gr. 3-7). 23.95 (978-0-7862-8579-2(6)) Thorndike Pr.

Blackburn, Sheila M. Stewie Scraps & the Super Sleigh. 2008. 72p. pap. (978-1-903853-89-4(3)) Brilliant Pubns.

Blacker, Terence & Ross, Tony. Estrella de la Tele. 2003. (Serafina the Little Witch Ser.). (SPA.). 80p. (J). 7.95 (978-84-8453-066-4(3)) Ediciones del Bronce ESP. Dist: Planeta Publishing Corp.

—Fuera de Control. 2003. (Serafina the Little Witch Ser.). (SPA., Illus.). 72p. (J). 7.95 (978-84-8453-049-7(3)) Ediciones del Bronce ESP. Dist: Planeta Publishing Corp.

—Una Intrusa en el Hospital. 2003. (Serafina the Little Witch Ser.). (SPA., Illus.). 72p. (J). 7.95 (978-84-8453-010-7(8)) Ediciones del Bronce ESP. Dist: Planeta Publishing Corp.

—Un Mundo de Problemas. 2003. (Serafina the Little Witch Ser.). (SPA.). 80p. (J). 7.95 (978-84-8453-009-1(4)) Ediciones del Bronce ESP. Dist: Planeta Publishing Corp.

Blackford, Ami. Quest for the Dragon Stone: A Duncan Family Adventure. Blackford, Ami, illus. 2006. (Illus.). 48p. (J). (gr. 3-7). 16.95 (978-1-60108-008-0(5), 1265253) Red Cygnet Pr.

—Quest for the Elfin Elixir: A Duncan Family Adventure Book 2. Blackford, Ami, illus. 2007. (Illus.). 79p. (J). (gr. 3-7). 16.95 (978-1-60108-021-9(2)) Red Cygnet Pr.

Blackwood, Gary L. Second Sight. 2007. (Illus.). 279p. (J). (gr. 5-9). 14.65 (978-0-7569-8132-7(8)) Perfection Learning Corp.

Blackwood, Sage. Jinx. 2013. (Jinx Ser.: 1). (ENG.). 368p. (J). (gr. 3-7). 16.99 (978-0-06-212990-1(2), HarperCollins) HarperCollins Pubs.

—Jinx's Fire. (Jinx Ser.: 3). (ENG.). 400p. (J). (gr. 3-7). 2016. pap. 9.99 (978-0-06-212997-0(X)) 2015. 16.99 (978-0-06-212996-3(1)) HarperCollins Pubs. (Tegen, Katherine Bks).

—Jinx's Magic. 2014. (Jinx Ser.: 2). (ENG.). 400p. (J). (gr. 3-7). 16.99 (978-0-06-212993-2(7), Tegen, Katherine Bks) HarperCollins Pubs.

Blaha-Black, Caroline. Anika & the Magic Top. 2008. 60p. pap. 11.95 (978-1-4357-1194-5(7)) Lulu Pr., Inc.

Blair, Eric. Rumpelstiltskin: Versión Del Cuento de Los Hermanos Grimm. Abello, Patricia, tr. Shaw, David, illus. 2006. (Read-It! Readers en Español: Cuentos de Hadas Ser.). (SPA.). 32p. (J). (gr. k-3). 22.65 (978-1-4048-1637-4(2), 91749, Picture Window Bks.) Capstone.

Blair, Katharyn. The Beckoning Shadow. 2019. (ENG.). 480p. (YA). (gr. 9). 17.99 (978-0-06-265761-9(5), Tegen, Katherine Bks) HarperCollins Pubs.

Blair, Marion E. Just Beyond a Finger's Reach. 2013. (ENG.). 54p. (YA). pap. 21.95 (978-1-4787-1396-8(8)) Outskirts Pr., Inc.

Blake, Drew. Engineer's Spell. 2007. 380p. per. 21.95 (978-0-595-45249-1(3)) iUniverse, Inc.

Blake, Elly. Frostblood. 2017. (Frostblood Saga Ser.: 1). (ENG.). 400p. (YA). (gr. 7-17). pap. 11.99 (978-0-316-27318-3(X)) Little, Brown Bks. for Young Readers.

—Nightblood. 2019. (Frostblood Saga Ser.: 3). (ENG.). 448p. (YA). (gr. 7-17). pap. 11.99 (978-0-316-27336-7(8)) Little, Brown Bks. for Young Readers.

Blake, Kendare. One Dark Throne. (YA). 2019. (Three Dark Crowns Ser.: 2). (ENG.). 480p. (gr. 9). pap. 12.99 (978-0-06-238547-5(X), Quill Tree Bks.) 2017. (Three Dark Crowns Ser.: 2). (ENG., Illus.). 464p. (gr. 9). 18.99 (978-0-06-238546-8(1), Quill Tree Bks.) 2017. (Illus.). 448p. (978-0-06-269045-6(0), HarperTeen) 2017. (Illus.). 448p. (978-0-06-269935-0(0), HarperTeen) 2017. (Illus.). 448p. (978-0-06-279729-2(8), HarperTeen) 2017. (Illus.). 448p. (978-0-06-274764-8(9), HarperTeen) 2017. (Illus.). 448p. (978-0-06-269730-1(7), HarperTeen) HarperCollins Pubs.

—Three Dark Crowns. (Three Dark Crowns Ser.: 1). (ENG.). (YA). (gr. 9). 2018. 432p. pap. 15.99 (978-0-06-238544-4(5)) 2016. (Illus.). 416p. 17.99 (978-0-06-238543-7(7)) HarperCollins Pubs. (Quill Tree Bks.).

—Three Dark Crowns. 2018. (YA). lib. bdg. 22.10 (978-0-606-40404-4(X)) Turtleback.

—Two Dark Reigns. 2018. (Three Dark Crowns Ser.: 3). (ENG., Illus.). 464p. (YA). (gr. 9). 18.99 (978-0-06-268614-5(3), Quill Tree Bks.) HarperCollins Pubs.

—Two Dark Reigns: Three Dark Crowns Book 3. 2018. (ENG., Illus.). 432p. (J). (978-1-5098-7649-5(9), HarperTeen) HarperCollins Pubs.

Blatchford, David. The Story of Mr Tomkins. 2012. (Illus.). 50p. pap. (978-1-908773-29-6(4)) Iponymous Publishing, Ltd.

Bliss, Bob, illus. The Hardest Lessons: The Lost Babies Series #3. 2007. 118p. (J). per. 5.99 (978-0-9792499-2-1(9)) Eagle Tree Pr.

—The Ruby Hind: The Lost Babies Series #1. 2007. 116p. (J). per. 5.99 (978-0-9792499-0-7(2)) Eagle Tree Pr.

—Too Many Parents: The Lost Babies Series #2. 2007. 109p. (J). per. 5.99 (978-0-9792499-1-4(0)) Eagle Tree Pr.

Bliss, Emily. Unicorn Princesses 2: Flash's Dash. Hanson, Sydney, illus. 2017. (Unicorn Princesses Ser.: 2). (ENG.). 128p. (J). 15.99 (978-1-68119-329-8(9), 900170030, Bloomsbury USA Childrens) Bloomsbury Publishing USA.

—Unicorn Princesses 3: Bloom's Ball. Hanson, Sydney, illus. 2017. (Unicorn Princesses Ser.: 3). (ENG.). 128p. (J). pap. 5.99 (978-1-68119-334-2(5), 900170042, Bloomsbury USA Childrens) Bloomsbury Publishing USA.

—Unicorn Princesses 4: Prism's Paint. Hanson, Sydney, illus. 2017. (Unicorn Princesses Ser.: 4). (ENG.). 128p. (J). pap. 5.99 (978-1-68119-338-0(8), 900170045, Bloomsbury USA Childrens) Bloomsbury Publishing USA.

—Unicorn Princesses 5: Breeze's Blast. Hanson, Sydney, illus. 2018. (Unicorn Princesses Ser.: 5). (ENG.). 128p. (J). 16.99 (978-1-68119-650-3(6), 900179833); pap. 5.99 (978-1-68119-649-7(2), 900179849) Bloomsbury Publishing USA. (Bloomsbury USA Childrens).

—Unicorn Princesses 6: Moon's Dance. Hanson, Sydney, illus. 2018. (Unicorn Princesses Ser.: 6). (ENG.). 128p. (J). pap. 6.99 (978-1-68119-652-7(2), 900179844, Bloomsbury USA Childrens) Bloomsbury Publishing USA.

—Unicorn Princesses 7: Firefly's Glow. Hanson, Sydney, illus. 2018. (Unicorn Princesses Ser.: 7). (ENG.). 128p. (J). 16.99 (978-1-68119-927-6(0), 900192376); pap. 5.99 (978-1-68119-926-9(2), 900192401) Bloomsbury Publishing USA. (Bloomsbury Children's Bks.).

—Unicorn Princesses 8: Feather's Flight. Hanson, Sydney, illus. 2018. (Unicorn Princesses Ser.: 8). (ENG.). 128p. (J). 16.99 (978-1-68119-930-6(0), 900192387); pap. 5.99 (978-1-68119-929-0(7), 900192375) Bloomsbury Publishing USA. (Bloomsbury Children's Bks.).

Block, Betty Mitchell. The Magic Pork Chop Bone. 2013. (ENG.). 76p. (YA). pap. 8.95 (978-1-4787-1482-8(4)) Outskirts Pr., Inc.

Bloomberg, Sandi. Ava & the Magic Tutu. 2008. 40p. per. 13.95 (978-1-59800-248-5(1)) Outskirts Pr., Inc.

—Veronica & the Magic Fountain. 2010. (Illus.). 32p. (J). pap. 13.95 (978-1-935268-66-6(X)) Halo Publishing International.

Bloomfield, Glynis. Jake's Secret. 2011. 194p. pap. 13.95 (978-1-60976-615-3(6), Strategic Bk. Publishing) Strategic Book Publishing & Rights Agency (SBPRA).

Blubaugh, Penny. Serendipity Market. 2011. (ENG.). 304p. (YA). (gr. 8). pap. 8.99 (978-0-06-146877-3(0), HarperTeen) HarperCollins Pubs.

Blueraven, Solaris. Mr. Sun & the Halloween Ball. 2010. (ENG.). 24p. pap. 13.99 (978-1-4520-0431-0(5)) AuthorHouse.

Blumer, J. Michael. The Book of Second Chances, Bk. 1. 2006. (Secret Books of Gabendoor Ser.). 284p. per. 14.99 (978-1-59092-317-7(0)) Blue Forge Pr.

Blunden, Alan. Tommy & the Garden Shed. 2008. 104p. pap. (978-1-84923-111-4(7)) YouWriteOn.

Blyton, Enid. The Goblin Aeroplane. (Illus.). 144p. (J). (gr. k-6). pap. 5.95 (978-0-09-973590-8(3)) Penguin Random Hse. GBR. Dist: Trafalgar Square Publishing.

Bobulski, Chelsea. The Wood. 2017. (ENG.). 320p. (YA). 27.99 (978-1-250-09426-1(7), 900160379) Feiwel & Friends.

Bode, N. E. The Anybodies. 2005. (ENG., Illus.). 288p. (J). (gr. 5-8). reprint ed. pap. 7.99 (978-0-06-055737-9(0), HarperCollins) HarperCollins Pubs.

Boehnert, Ernest. The Magic Christmas Train. 2010. (ENG.). 24p. pap. 14.93 (978-1-4269-4447-5(0)) Trafford Publishing.

Boen, Sherry. The Fish Who Made a Magical Wish, 1 vol. 2009. 21p. pap. 24.95 (978-1-61582-726-8(9)) America Star Bks.

Bolander, Sharon Miller. At the Stroke of Midnight. 2012. 40p. pap. 24.95 (978-1-4626-8905-7(1)) America Star Bks.

Bond, Gwenda. Girl in the Shadows, 0 vols. 2016. (Cirque American Ser.: 2). (ENG.). 380p. (YA). (gr. 9-13). pap. 9.99 (978-1-5039-5393-2(9), 9781503953932, Skyscape) Amazon Publishing.

Bond, Michael. Paddington & the Magic Trick. Alley, R. W., illus. 2016. (I Can Read Level 1 Ser.). (ENG.). 32p. (J). (gr. -1-3). pap. 4.99 (978-0-06-243067-0(X), HarperCollins) HarperCollins Pubs.

Bongiovanni, Debbie. It's All about Magic or Is It?, 1 vol. 2009. 55p. pap. 16.95 (978-1-61546-875-1(7)) America Star Bks.

Booraem, Ellen. Small Persons with Wings. 2012. (ENG.). 304p. (J). (gr. 6-8). 21.19 (978-0-8037-3471-5(9)) Penguin Young Readers Group.

Booth, Anne. The Christmas Fairy. Beardshaw, Rosalind, illus. 2017. (ENG.). 32p. (J). (gr. -1-2). 15.99 (978-0-7636-9629-0(3)) Candlewick Pr.

Borchini, Ernest. Three Stories about Jonathan, the Computer, & Little Kitty: Three Short Stories about a Boy & His Magic Cat. 2013. 36p. (gr. -1). pap. 15.49 (978-1-4669-6636-9(X)) Trafford Publishing.

Bosch, Pseudonymous. Bad Luck. 2017. (Bad Bks.: 2). (ENG., Illus.). 304p. (J). (gr. 3-7). pap. 8.99 (978-0-316-32044-3(7)) Little, Brown Bks. for Young Readers.

—Bad Luck. 2017. (Bad Bks.: 2). (J). lib. bdg. 18.40 (978-0-606-39475-8(3)) Turtleback.

—Bad Magic. 2014. (Bad Bks.: 1). (ENG.). 400p. (J). (gr. 3-7). 17.00 (978-0-316-32038-2(2)) Little, Brown Bks. for Young Readers.

—Bad Magic. 2015. (Bad Bks.: 1). (J). lib. bdg. 18.45 (978-0-606-37522-1(8)) Turtleback.

—Bad Magic 9c Solid Floor Display. 2014. (ENG.). 384p. (J). (gr. 3-7). 153.00 (978-0-316-37696-9(5)) Little, Brown Bks. for Young Readers.

—If You're Reading This, It's Too Late. 2009. (Secret Ser.: 2). (ENG.). 400p. (J). (gr. 3-7). pap. 9.99 (978-0-316-11368-7(9)) Little, Brown Bks. for Young Readers.

—This Isn't What It Looks Like. 2011. (Secret Ser.: 4). (ENG.). 448p. (J). (gr. 3-7). pap. 9.99 (978-0-316-07624-1(4)) Little, Brown Bks. for Young Readers.

—You Have to Stop This. (Secret Ser.: 5). (ENG.). (J). (gr. 3-7). 2012. 368p. pap. 9.99 (978-0-316-07627-2(9)) 2011. 352p. 17.99 (978-0-316-07626-5(0)) Little, Brown Bks. for Young Readers.

—You Have to Stop This. 2012. (Secret Ser.: 5). (J). lib. bdg. 18.45 (978-0-606-26695-6(X)) Turtleback.

Boston, L. M. The Stones of Green Knowe. Boston, Peter, illus. 2006. (Green Knowe Ser.: 6). (ENG.). 144p. (J). (gr. 3-7). 17.00 (978-0-15-205560-8(6), 1196721); pap. 10.95 (978-0-15-205566-0(5), 1196740) HarperCollins Pubs. (Clarion Bks.).

Botha, Si. Goosala Goop. 2009. 48p. pap. 16.50 (978-1-60860-124-0(2), Strategic Bk. Publishing) Strategic Book Publishing & Rights Agency (SBPRA).

Bottner, Barbara & Kruglik, Gerald. Pish & Posh. Bottner, Barbara, illus. 2004. (I Can Read Bks.). (Illus.). 48p. (J). (gr. k-3). pap. 15.99 (978-0-06-051416-7(7)) HarperCollins Pubs.

—Pish & Posh Wish for Fairy Wings. Bottner, Barbara, illus. (I Can Read Level 2 Ser.). (Illus.). 48p. (J). 2007. (ENG.). (gr. k-3). pap. 4.99 (978-0-06-051421-1(3), Tegen, Katherine Bks) 2006. (gr. -1-3). lib. bdg. 16.89 (978-0-06-051420-4(5)) HarperCollins Pubs.

Boukov, Lubima. The Magic Swing, 1 vol. 2009. 15p. pap. 24.95 (978-1-60749-612-0(7)) America Star Bks.

Bover, Annie. Mooncorn. 2013. (Illus.). 20p. pap. (978-1-909465-18-3(6)) Cloister Hse. Pr., The.

Bowers, Chuck. Leprechaun Legacy. 2009. 156p. pap. 12.95 (978-1-4401-2248-4(2)) iUniverse, Inc.

Bowles, David. Rise of the Halfling King, 1 vol. Bowles, Charlene, illus. 2020. (Tales of the Feathered Serpent Ser.: 1). (ENG.). 64p. (J). (gr. 4-8). pap. 14.95 (978-1-947627-37-6(6), 23353382, Cinco Puntos Press) Lee & Low Bks., Inc.

Bowles, David & Bowles, Charlene, illus. The Rise of the Halfling King. 2021. 63p. (J). (978-1-947627-36-9(8), Cinco Puntos Press) Lee & Low Bks., Inc.

Bowman, Mare. The Magic Shell. 2011. 108p. (gr. -1). 21.49 (978-1-4520-5738-5(9)); pap. 10.99 (978-1-4520-5113-0(5)) AuthorHouse.

Bowser, D. M. The Enchanting Tales of Lilith. 2011. 54p. pap. 16.95 (978-1-4560-9570-3(6)) America Star Bks.

Bowyer, Clifford B. The Darkness Within: The Imperium Saga: the Adventures of Kyria, 12 vols., Vol. 9. Brigman, June, illus. 2009. (Imperium Saga: 9). (ENG.). (J). 5.99 (978-0-9787782-4-8(3)) Silver Leaf Bks., LLC.

The Boy Who Went to the North Wind: Individual Title Six-Packs. (Literatura 2000 Ser.). (gr. 2-3). 33.00 (978-0-7635-0217-1(0)) Rigby Education.

Boyce, Frank Cottrell. Chitty Chitty Bang Bang & the Race Against Time. Berger, Joe, illus. (Chitty Chitty Bang Bang Ser.: 3). (ENG.). 240p. (J). (gr. 4-7). 2014. pap. 6.99 (978-0-7636-6931-7(8)) 2013. 15.99 (978-0-7636-5982-0(7)) Candlewick Pr.

—Chitty Chitty Bang Bang Flies Again. Berger, Joe, illus. 2013. (Chitty Chitty Bang Bang Ser.: 2). (ENG.). 224p. (J). (gr. 4-7). pap. 6.99 (978-0-7636-6353-7(0)) Candlewick Pr.

—Desirable. 2012. (Stoke Books Titles Ser.). 64p. (J). (gr. 5-8). pap. 45.32 (978-0-7613-9216-3(5)) Stoke Bks.

Boyd, Cathy. The Little Snowman's New Hat. 2011. 28p. pap. 24.95 (978-1-4560-2751-3(4)) PublishAmerica, Inc.

Boyd, G. A. Alchemy Jones & the Source of Magic. 2011. 324p. (gr. -1). 29.95 (978-1-4620-2234-2(0)); pap. 19.95 (978-1-4620-2232-8(4)) iUniverse, Inc.

Bozarth, Jan. Zally's Book, 3. Burden, Andrea, illus. 2010. (Fairy Godmother Academy Ser.: No. 3). (ENG.). 208p. (J). (gr. 4-6). lib. bdg. 22.44 (978-0-375-95185-5(7)) Random House Publishing Group.

Bracken, Beth & Fraser, Kay. Believe, 1 vol. Sawyer, Odessa, illus. 2014. (Faerieground Ser.). (ENG.). 288p. (J). (gr. 4-8). 12.95 (978-1-62370-113-0(9), 125670, Capstone Young Readers) Capstone.

Bracken, Beth, et al. The Fate of the Willow Queen. Sawyer, Odessa, illus. 2013. (Faerieground Ser.). (ENG.). 96p. (J). (gr. 5-9). 23.99 (978-1-4342-4492-5(X), 120491, Stone Arch Bks.) Capstone.

—The Two Mothers. Sawyer, Odessa, illus. 2013. (Faerieground Ser.). (ENG.). 96p. (J). (gr. 5-9). 23.99 (978-1-4342-4490-1(3), 120489, Stone Arch Bks.) Capstone.

Bradfield, Jolly Roger. Benjamin Dilley's Thirsty Camel. Bradfield, Jolly Roger, illus. 2012. (ENG., Illus.). 64p. (J). (gr. 4-7). 18.95 (978-1-930900-60-8(0)) Purple Hse. Pr.

Bradman, Tony. Flora the Fairy's Magic Spells: Green Banana (Reading Ladder Level 1) Carlow, Emma, illus. 2nd ed. 2016. (Reading Ladder Level 1 Ser.). (ENG.). 48p. (gr. k-2). 4.99 (978-1-4052-8227-7(4), Reading Ladder) Farshore GBR. Dist: HarperCollins Pubs.

—Snow White & the Magic Mirror (after Happily Ever After) Warburton, Sarah, illus. 2014. (After Happily Ever After Ser.). (ENG.). 56p. (J). (gr. 3-6). pap. 4.95 (978-1-4342-7956-9(1), 124704); lib. bdg. 25.99 (978-1-4342-7950-7(2), 124698) Capstone. (Stone Arch Bks.).

Braithwaite, Lisa. Lucy Goes into the Wild. 2012. 28p. pap. 15.99 (978-1-4771-4341-4(6)) Xlibris Corp.

Bramlett, Timothy A. Thomas in the Land of the Blips. 2012. 26p. pap. 19.99 (978-1-4772-9576-2(3)) AuthorHouse.

Braswell, Liz. As Old As Time: A Twisted Tale. (Twisted Tale Ser.). (ENG.). (YA). (gr. 7-12). 2018. 512p. pap. 10.99 (978-1-4847-0731-9(1)) 2016. 496p. 17.99 (978-1-4847-0728-9(1)) Disney Publishing Worldwide. (Disney-Hyperion).

—As Old As Time: A Twisted Tale. 2018. (YA). lib. bdg. 20.85 (978-0-606-39964-7(X)) Turtleback.

—A Whole New World: A Twisted Tale. 2016. (Twisted Tale Ser.). (YA). lib. bdg. 20.85 (978-0-606-38511-4(8)) Turtleback.

—A Whole New World-A Twisted Tale. 2016. (Twisted Tale Ser.). (ENG.). 400p. (YA). (gr. 7-12). pap. 9.99 (978-1-4847-0732-6(X), Disney-Hyperion) Disney Publishing Worldwide.

Braun, Eric. Rumpelstiltskin: An Interactive Fairy Tale Adventure. Brown, Alan, illus. 2017. (You Choose: Fractured Fairy Tales Ser.). (ENG.). 112p. (J). (gr. 3-7). pap. 6.95 (978-1-5157-8777-8(X), 136328); lib. bdg. 32.65 (978-1-5157-8775-4(3), 136326) Capstone. (Capstone Pr.).

Bray, Libba. A Great & Terrible Beauty. 2005. (Gemma Doyle Trilogy Ser.: 1). (ENG.). 432p. (YA). (gr. 7). reprint ed. pap. 10.99 (978-0-385-73231-4(7), Ember) Random Hse. Children's Bks.

—Rebel Angels. 2006. (Gemma Doyle Trilogy Ser.: 2). (ENG.). 576p. (YA). (gr. 7-12). pap. 16.99 (978-0-385-73341-0(0), Ember) Random Hse. Children's Bks.

—The Sweet Far Thing. 2009. (Gemma Doyle Trilogy Ser.: 3). (ENG.). 848p. (YA). (gr. 7). pap. 14.99 (978-0-440-23777-8(7), Ember) Random Hse. Children's Bks.

Breece, Beverly. The Curwood Acorns. DeWeese, Susan, illus. 2012. 40p. pap. 24.95 (978-1-4626-8202-7(2)) America Star Bks.

Brennan, Sarah Rees. Tell the Wind & Fire. 2017. (ENG.). 368p. (YA). (gr. 7). pap. 9.99 (978-0-544-93887-8(9), 1658467, Clarion Bks.) HarperCollins Pubs.

Brent, Isabelle. The Christmas Horse & the Three Wise Men. 2016. (Illus.). 28p. (J). (gr. k-3). 17.95 (978-1-937786-61-8(7), Wisdom Tales) World Wisdom, Inc.

Breslin, Jayne. The Princess Jelly Tutu Adventures. 2011. (Illus.). 28p. (gr. -1). pap. 14.09 (978-1-4567-7611-4(8)) AuthorHouse.

Brett, James. Infaeter. Englund, Jonathon, illus. 2nd ed. 2013. 238p. pap. (978-1-908462-03-9(5)) New Dawn Pubs.

Brett, Jan. Jan Brett's the Nutcracker. Brett, Jan, illus. 2021. (Illus.). 32p. (J). (gr. -1-3). 18.99 (978-0-593-10982-3(1), G.P. Putnam's Sons Books for Young Readers) Penguin Young Readers Group.

Brewin, Barbara. Sidney Snail's Wonderful World of Adventure. 2009. (Illus.). 32p. pap. 14.49 (978-1-4389-4100-4(5)) AuthorHouse.

Bridge, George. Jack & the Beanstalk. Flowerpot Press, ed. 2012. (Illus.). 20p. (J). (978-1-77093-127-5(9)) Flowerpot Children's Pr. Inc.

Bridgman, Rae. Kingdom of Trolls: A Middlegate Book. 2010. (Illus.). 287p. (J). pap. 15.00 (978-0-9864974-1-4(X)) Sybertooth, Inc. CAN. Dist: Ingram Content Group.

Brignole, Giancarla, tr. El Pulpo Campanero. Meconni, Beppe, illus. (Fabulas De Familia Ser.). (SPA.). 32p. (978-970-20-0262-8(1)) Castillo, Ediciones, S. A. de C. V.

Brignull, Irena. The Hawkweed Prophecy. 2017. (Hawkweed Ser.: 1). (ENG.). 384p. (YA). (gr. 7-17). pap. 10.99 (978-1-60286-313-2(X)) Hachette Bk. Group.

Brittain, Bill. The Wish Giver: A Newbery Honor Award Winner. Glass, Andrew, illus. 2019. (ENG.). 192p. (J). (gr. 3-7). pap. 6.99 (978-0-06-440168-5(5), HarperCollins) HarperCollins Pubs.

Brodhead, Kimberly. Gaden's Tower: Book One. 2007. 164p. per. 24.95 (978-1-60441-038-9(8)) America Star Bks.

Brodien-Jones, Christine. The Owl Keeper. Kneen, Maggie, illus. 2011. (ENG.). 320p. (J). (gr. 3-7). 8.99 (978-0-385-73815-6(3), Yearling) Random Hse. Children's Bks.

Brody, Jessica. Addie Bell's Shortcut to Growing Up. 2018. 368p. (J). (gr. 5). 7.99 (978-0-399-55513-8(7), Yearling) Random Hse. Children's Bks.

Brondos, Pam. The Last Remnant, 0 vols. 2016. (Fourline Trilogy Ser.: 3). (ENG.). 320p. (YA). (gr. 8-12). pap. 9.99 (978-1-61218-470-8(7), 9781612184708, Skyscape) Amazon Publishing.

—On the Meldon Plain, 0 vols. 2016. (Fourline Trilogy Ser.: 2). (ENG.). 364p. (YA). (gr. 9-13). pap. 9.99 (978-1-5039-5320-8(3), 9781503953208, Skyscape) Amazon Publishing.

Brooke, Jasmine. Jack & the Beanstalk: Chart Your Magic Bean's Life Cycle! 2017. (Fairy Tale Fixers: Fixing Fairy Tale Problems with STEM Ser.). 32p. (gr. 3-4). pap. 63.00 (978-1-5382-0666-9(8)) Stevens, Gareth Publishing LLLP.

Brooks, Charlie. Greystone Valley. Grundy, Jessica, illus. 2013. 166p. 17.99 (978-1-938821-33-2(5)); 198p. pap. 9.99 (978-1-938821-41-7(6)) Grey Gecko Pr.

Brooks, Donna. The Golden Spindle. 2010. 112p. pap. 30.00 (978-1-60860-852-2(2), Eloquent Bks.) Strategic Book Publishing & Rights Agency (SBPRA).

Brothers, Marilee. Moonstone. 2008. 236p. (YA). pap. 14.95 (978-0-9802453-4-9(6), Bell Bridge Bks.) BelleBks., Inc.

Brown, Alan James. Michael & the Monkey King. 2008. (ENG.). 177p. pap. 16.95 (978-1-4092-0241-7(0)) Lulu Pr., Inc.

Brown, E.A. Gossamer. 2012. 24p. pap. 24.95 (978-1-4626-5043-9(0)) America Star Bks.

Brown, Jason Robert. Tickety Tock. GrandPré, Mary, illus. 2008. 32p. (J). (gr. -1-3). lib. bdg. 18.89 (978-0-06-078753-0(8), Geringer, Laura Book) HarperCollins Pubs.

Brown, Jeff. Stanley & the Magic Lamp. Pamintuan, Macky, illus. 2009. (Flat Stanley Ser.). (ENG.). 128p. (J). (gr. 2-5). pap. 4.99 (978-0-06-009793-6(0), HarperCollins) HarperCollins Pubs.

—Stanley & the Magic Lamp. 2009. (Flat Stanley Ser.). (J). (gr. k-3). lib. bdg. 14.75 (978-0-613-68465-1(6)) Turtleback.

Brown, Marc. D. W. the Big Boss. 2005. (ENG., Illus.). 24p. (J). (gr. -1-1). per. 3.99 (978-0-316-73395-3(4)) Little, Brown Bks. for Young Readers.

Brownlow, Brooke. The Magic of Old Oak Hill. 2005. 48p. pap. 16.95 (978-1-4241-0223-5(5)) PublishAmerica, Inc.

Bruckner, Tai. Lemon Path Encounter, 1 vol. Bruckner, Wes, illus. 2009. 15p. pap. 24.95 (978-1-60836-407-7(0)) America Star Bks.

Bruno, Cristina. The Mother Store. 2009. 52p. pap. 30.00 (978-1-4389-2875-3(0)) AuthorHouse.

Bryant, Anne. The Fantasy Soccer Wall. 2015. (Race Further with Reading Ser.). (ENG., Illus.). 48p. (J). (gr. 3-3). (978-0-7787-2061-4(6)) Crabtree Publishing Co.

Buchanan, Johnny & Conway, Beth. Rachel & the Magic Beads. Bosak, Virginia, illus. 2007. 16p. (YA). pap. 7.99 (978-0-9768772-9-5(5)) Wise Guides, LLC.

Buck, Alicia. Out of the Ashes. 2015. 281p. (YA). pap. 17.99 (978-1-4621-1727-7(9)) Cedar Fort, Inc./CFI Distribution.

Buckley, Michael. The Council of Mirrors. (Sisters Grimm Ser.: 9). 2018. lib. bdg. 19.65 (978-0-606-41062-5(7)) 2013. (J). lib. bdg. 18.40 (978-0-606-31650-7(7)) Turtleback.

—The Council of Mirrors (the Sisters Grimm #9) 10th Anniversary Edition. 10th ed. 2018. (Sisters Grimm Ser.). (ENG., Illus.). 304p. (J). (gr. 3-7). pap. 9.99 (978-1-4197-2009-3(0), 696406, Amulet Bks.) Abrams, Inc.

—The Everafter War. 2018. (Sisters Grimm Ser.: 7). (J). lib. bdg. 19.65 (978-0-606-41064-9(3)) Turtleback.

—The Everafter War (the Sisters Grimm #7) 10th Anniversary Edition. 10th ed. 2018. (Sisters Grimm Ser.). (ENG., Illus.). 272p. (J). (gr. 3-7). pap. 8.99 (978-1-4197-2011-6(2), 660206, Amulet Bks.) Abrams, Inc.

—The Inside Story, 6 vols. 2010. (Sisters Grimm Ser.: 8). (J). 89.75 (978-1-4498-1969-9(9)); 72.75 (978-1-4498-1967-5(2)); 87.75 (978-1-4498-1971-2(0)); 1.25 (978-1-4498-1973-6(7)); 219.75 (978-1-4498-1966-8(4)) Recorded Bks., Inc.

—The Inside Story (the Sisters Grimm #8) 10th Anniversary Edition. 10th ed. 2018. (Sisters Grimm Ser.). (ENG., Illus.). 240p. (J). (gr. 3-7). pap. 9.99 (978-1-4197-2006-2(6), 660306, Amulet Bks.) Abrams, Inc.

—Magic & Other Misdemeanors (the Sisters Grimm #5) 10th Anniversary Edition. Ferguson, Peter, illus. 10th ed. 2017. (Sisters Grimm Ser.). (ENG.). 280p. (J). (gr. 3-7). pap. 9.99 (978-1-4197-2010-9(4), 608806, Amulet Bks.) Abrams, Inc.

—Once upon a Crime (the Sisters Grimm #4) 10th Anniversary Edition. Ferguson, Peter, illus. 10th anniv. ed. 2017. (Sisters Grimm Ser.). (ENG.). 272p. (J). (gr. 3-7). pap. 9.99 (978-1-4197-2007-9(4), 608706, Amulet Bks.) Abrams, Inc.

—The Problem Child: The Sisters Grimm. 2007. (Sisters Grimm Ser.: 3). (YA). lib. bdg. 18.40 (978-1-4178-0733-8(4)) Turtleback.

—Tales from the Hood (the Sisters Grimm #6) 10th Anniversary Edition. 10th ed. 2017. (Sisters Grimm Ser.). (ENG., Illus.). 256p. (J). (gr. 3-7). pap. 8.99 (978-1-4197-2012-3(0), 608906, Amulet Bks.) Abrams, Inc.

—A Very Grimm Guide. Ferguson, Peter, illus. 2012. (Sisters Grimm Ser.). (ENG.). 128p. (J). (gr. 3-7). 17.99 (978-1-4197-0201-3(7), 1019601, Amulet Bks.) Abrams, Inc.

Buckmaster, Heath L. Box of Hair: A Fairy Tale, 3 bks., Bk. 1. (Illus.). (YA). 2007. 102p. pap. 12.99 (978-0-9771802-5-7(5)) 2008. 108p. lib. bdg. 25.00 (978-0-9771802-4-0(7)) Transaltar Publishing.

—Box of Hair: A Fairy Tale. 2008. 104p. pap. 12.50 (978-1-4357-2690-1(1)) Lulu Pr., Inc.

—The Venus Diary. 2008. 136p. pap. 13.50 (978-0-615-20678-3(6)) Transaltar Publishing.

Budreau, Craig. Trail Map: Barton Creek Greenbelt — Loop 360 to Zilker Park. 2006. (J). per. 5.00 (978-1-932196-26-9(9)) WordWright.biz, Inc.

Bugg, Ann T. Into the Forest & down the Tower. Kramin, Valerie, illus. 2012. 136p. pap. (978-1-927044-24-7(3)) Writers AMuse Me.

Bunce, Elizabeth C. Liar's Moon. 2011. (YA). pap. (978-0-545-13607-5(5), Levine, Arthur A. Bks.) Scholastic, Inc.

—StarCrossed. 2011. (ENG.). 368p. (YA). pap. 9.99 (978-0-545-13606-8(7), Levine, Arthur A. Bks.) Scholastic, Inc.

Burden, Meg. The King Commands. 2010. (Tales of the Borderlands Ser.: Bk. 2). 312p. (YA). (gr. 7-18). pap. 8.95 (978-0-9798824-1-8(9)) Brown Barn Bks.

Burgis, Stephanie. Kat, Incorrigible. 2012. (Kat, Incorrigible Ser.: 1). (ENG., Illus.). 320p. (J). (gr. 5-9). pap. 8.99 (978-1-4169-9448-0(3), Atheneum Bks. for Young Readers) Simon & Schuster Children's Publishing.

—Kat, Incorrigible, 1. 2011. (Kat, Incorrigible Ser.: 1). (ENG., Illus.). 304p. (J). (gr. 5-9). 16.99 (978-1-4169-9447-3(5)) Simon & Schuster, Inc.

—The Princess Who Flew with Dragons. 2019. (Dragon Heart Ser.: 3). (ENG.). 224p. (J). 16.99 (978-1-5476-0207-0(4), 900203278, Bloomsbury Children's Bks.) Bloomsbury Publishing USA.

—Renegade Magic, 2. 2012. (Kat, Incorrigible Ser.: 2). (ENG., Illus.). 336p. (J). (gr. 5-9). 16.99 (978-1-4169-9449-7(1), Atheneum Bks. for Young Readers) Simon & Schuster Children's Publishing.

—Stolen Magic. (Kat, Incorrigible Ser.: 3). (ENG., Illus.). 400p. (J). (gr. 5-8). 2014. pap. 7.99 (978-1-4169-9452-7(1)) 2013. 17.99 (978-1-4169-9451-0(3), Atheneum Bks. for Young Readers) Simon & Schuster Children's Publishing.

Burke, Ellinor Rozecki. Susana Worrywart & the Magical Teddy Bear Balloon. Perciopelo, illus. 2003. 32p. (J). 17.99 (978-0-9741586-3-1(1)) Comfort Tales, LLC.

—Susana Worrywart & the Magical Teddy Bear Balloon: With CD for Relaxation. Perciopelo, illus. 2003. 32p. (J). 27.00 incl. audio compact disk (978-0-9741586-0-0(7)) Comfort Tales, LLC.

Burkhart, Jessica. Unicorn Magic 3-Books-In-1! Bella's Birthday Unicorn; Where's Glimmer?; Green with Envy, 3 Bks. in 1. Ying, Victoria, illus. 2018. (Unicorn Magic Ser.). (ENG.). 384p. (J). (gr. 1-4). pap. 8.99 (978-1-5344-0998-9(X), Aladdin) Simon & Schuster Children's Publishing.

Burnell, Cerrie. Harper & the Scarlet Umbrella. Anderson, Laura Ellen, illus. 2017. (ENG.). 128p. (J). (gr. 1-4). 14.99 (978-1-5107-1566-0(5), Sky Pony Pr.) Skyhorse Publishing Co., Inc.

Burns, Laura J. Bewitched in Oz, 1 vol. 2014. (Bewitched in Oz Ser.). (ENG., Illus.). 256p. (J). (gr. 4-8). 12.95 (978-1-62370-129-1(5), 125714, Capstone Young Readers); lib. bdg. 30.65 (978-1-4342-9207-0(X), 125712, Stone Arch Bks.) Capstone.

—Magic Below. 2016. (Bewitched in Oz Ser.). (ENG.). 240p. (J). (gr. 4-8). lib. bdg. 30.65 (978-1-4965-2603-8(1), 130909, Stone Arch Bks.) Capstone.

Burns, Mary Gore. The Magic Room: Mandy & the Lily Pond. 2011. 48p. pap. 17.30 (978-1-4634-2642-2(9)) AuthorHouse.

Burton, Elizabeth K. The Everdark Gate: The Everdark Wars Book 3. 2008. (ENG.). 280p. pap. 15.50 (978-1-934135-79-2(8), Zumaya Otherworlds) Zumaya Pubns. LLC.

Busse, R. R., adapted by. Meet Kubo. 2016. (Illus.). 32p. (J). (978-1-5182-3471-2(2)) Little Brown & Co.

Bussell, Darcey. Christmas in Enchantia (Magic Ballerina) 2010. (Magic Ballerina Ser.). (ENG., Illus.). 144p. (J). (gr. k-2). pap. 9.99 (978-0-00-734800-8(2), HarperCollins Children's Bks.) HarperCollins Pubs. Ltd. GBR. Dist: HarperCollins Pubs.

—Delphie & the Glass Slippers (Magic Ballerina, Book 4), Book 4. 2008. (Magic Ballerina Ser.: 4). (ENG., Illus.). 96p. (J). (gr. k-2). pap. 6.99 (978-0-00-728617-1(1), HarperCollins Children's Bks.) HarperCollins Pubs. Ltd. GBR. Dist: HarperCollins Pubs.

—Delphie & the Masked Ball (Magic Ballerina, Book 3), Book 3. 2008. (Magic Ballerina Ser.: 3). (ENG., Illus.). 96p. (J). (gr. k-2). pap. 6.99 (978-0-00-728610-2(4), HarperCollins Children's Bks.) HarperCollins Pubs. Ltd. GBR. Dist: HarperCollins Pubs.

—Summer in Enchantia (Magic Ballerina) 2009. (Magic Ballerina Ser.). (ENG., Illus.). 144p. (J). (gr. k-2). pap. 9.99 (978-0-00-731721-9(2)) HarperCollins Pubs. Ltd. GBR. Dist: Independent Pubs. Group.

Butler, Kynora. Knowing Is Believing in Reading: Facing Your Fears. 2007. 48p. per. 16.95 (978-1-4241-7559-8(3)) America Star Bks.

Byrne, Jean Livingstone. Legends of Newgrange. 2014. 54p. pap. 12.99 (978-1-84386-818-7(0)) Vanguard Pr.

Cabell, Robert W. The Mermaid Adventures of Princess Miranda: Volume One. Cabell, Robert W., illus. 2013. (Illus.). 128p. pap. 7.95 (978-0-9890974-3-7(9), Oceanus Bks.) Warrington Pubns.

Cabrini, Joe. Chicco's Nicedream Van - Daniel's Winning Goal. Cabrini, Joe, illus. 2007. (Illus.). 32p. per. (978-0-7552-0300-0(3)) Authors OnLine, Ltd.

—Chicco's Nicedream Van - Jessica the Superstar. Cabrini, Joe, illus. 2007. (Illus.). 32p. per. (978-0-7552-0301-7(1)) Authors OnLine, Ltd.

Caine, Rachel, pseud & Vincent, Rachel. Immortal: Love Stories with Bite. Cast, P.c., ed. 2009. (Illus.). 280p. (J). (gr. 9-12). pap. 8.95 (978-1-933771-92-2(5)) BenBella Bks.

Cajoleas, Jimmy. Goldeline. (ENG.). (J). (gr. 5). 2019. 272p. pap. 6.99 (978-0-06-249876-2(2)) 2017. 256p. 16.99 (978-0-06-249875-5(4)) HarperCollins Pubs. (HarperCollins).

—The Rambling. 2019. (ENG.). 304p. (J). (gr. 3-7). 16.99 (978-0-06-249878-6(9), HarperCollins) HarperCollins Pubs.

Calhoun, Dia. Avielle of Rhia, 1 vol. 2006. (ENG.). 400p. (J). (gr. 6). 16.99 (978-0-7614-5320-8(2)) Marshall Cavendish Corp.

Calhoun, Megan. Oscar the Pig: Mommy Goes to Work. 2008. 32p. 18.50 (978-0-615-25193-6(5)) Silly String Media.

Callaghan, Cindy. Just Add Magic. 2010. (Just Add Magic Ser.: 1). (ENG., Illus.). 240p. (J). (gr. 4-8). pap. 8.99 (978-1-4424-0268-3(7)) Simon & Schuster, Inc.

—Potion Problems. 2018. (Just Add Magic Ser.: 2). (ENG., Illus.). 224p. (J). (gr. 4-8). pap. 8.99 (978-1-5344-1741-0(9), Aladdin) Simon & Schuster Children's Publishing.

Calmenson, Stephanie. The Frog Principal. Brunkus, Denise, illus. 2006. (ENG.). 32p. (J). pap. 5.99 (978-0-439-81217-7(8), Scholastic Paperbacks) Scholastic, Inc.

—Our Principal Is a Frog! A QUIX Book. Blecha, Aaron, illus. 2018. (Our Principal Ser.). (ENG.). 64p. (J). (gr. k-3). 17.99 (978-1-4814-6667-7(4)); pap. 5.99 (978-1-4814-6665-3(8)) Simon & Schuster Children's Publishing. (Aladdin).

Calvert, Pam. The Multiplying Menace Divides. Geehan, Wayne, illus. 2011. (Charlesbridge Math Adventures Ser.). (ENG.). 32p. (J). (gr. 2-5). pap. 7.99 (978-1-57091-782-0(5)) Charlesbridge Publishing, Inc.

Cameron, Anne. The Lightning Catcher. Jamieson, Victoria, illus. 2013. (Lightning Catcher Ser.: 1). (ENG.). 432p. (J). (gr. 3-7). 16.99 (978-0-06-211276-7(7), Greenwillow Bks.) HarperCollins Pubs.

Cammuso, Frank. Cookie Catastrophe. 2014. (Misadventures of Salem Hyde Ser.: 3). (J). lib. bdg. 17.15 (978-0-606-36149-1(9)) Turtleback.

—The Misadventures of Salem Hyde: Book Two: Big Birthday Bash. 2014. (Misadventures of Salem Hyde Ser.). (ENG., Illus.). 96p. (J). (gr. 1-4). 14.95 (978-1-4197-1025-4(7), 1044801, Amulet Bks.) Abrams, Inc.

—The Misadventures of Salem Hyde: Spelling Trouble. 2013. (Misadventures of Salem Hyde Ser.: 1). (J). lib. bdg. 17.15 (978-0-606-33440-2(8)) Turtleback.

Camp, Bryan. The City of Lost Fortunes. 2018. (Crescent City Novel Ser.). (ENG., Illus.). 384p. 24.00 (978-1-328-81079-3(8), 1687328, Harper Voyager) HarperCollins Pubs.

Campbell, Chelsea M. Dragonbound. 2016. (ENG.). 288p. (YA). (gr. 7-11). pap. 9.99 (978-1-5039-3609-6(0), 9781503936096, Skyscape) Amazon Publishing.

Campbell, Isaiah. AbrakaPOW. Perillo, Dave, illus. 2016. (ENG.). 400p. (J). (gr. 3-7). 16.99 (978-1-4814-2634-3(6), Simon & Schuster Bks. For Young Readers) Simon & Schuster Bks. For Young Readers.

Campbell, R. W. Merrick Tumbledorf: The Last Talcomite Dragon. 2013. (ENG.). 250p. (YA). pap. 15.95 (978-1-4787-1312-8(7)) Outskirts Pr., Inc.

Cannistra, Meg. The Trouble with Shooting Stars. 2019. (ENG., Illus.). 336p. (J). (gr. 3-7). 17.99 (978-1-5344-2896-6(8), Simon & Schuster Bks. For Young Readers) Simon & Schuster Bks. For Young Readers.

Caple, Kathy. Frog & Ball. 2021. (I Like to Read Comics Ser.). (Illus.). 40p. (J). (gr. -1-3). 14.99 (978-0-8234-4341-3(8)) Holiday Hse., Inc.

Caprara, Rebecca. The Magic of Melwick Orchard. 2018. (ENG.). 376p. (J). (gr. 4-8). 17.99 (978-1-5124-6687-4(5), cbdf4843-d3d6-457a-9fa0-9e41212c3008, Carolrhoda Bks.) Lerner Publishing Group.

Caprin, K. F. The Adventures of the Little Savages. 2009. (ENG.). 167p. pap. 16.95 (978-1-4092-3379-4(0)) Lulu Pr., Inc.

Carbone, Courtney. Dragon Pox! (Shimmer & Shine) Cartobaleno, illus. 2018. (Little Golden Book Ser.). (ENG.). 24p. (J). (-k). 4.99 (978-1-5247-6798-3(0), Golden Bks.) Random Hse. Children's Bks.

—Snow Day! 2014. (Step into Reading Level 2 Ser.). lib. bdg. 13.55 (978-0-606-36009-8(3)) Turtleback.

Card, Orson Scott. Stonefather. Kidd, Tom, illus. 2008. 112p. 35.00 (978-1-59606-194-1(4)) Subterranean Pr.

Cardwell, Helen. Amber Janusson: Protector of the Magic Lands. 2003. 136p. pap. 11.95 (978-0-595-29436-7(7)) iUniverse, Inc.

Carlson, Caroline. The Buccaneers' Code. (Very Nearly Honorable League of Pirates Ser.: 3). (ENG.). 320p. (J). (gr. 3-7). 2016. pap. 7.99 (978-0-06-219440-4(2)) 2015. 16.99 (978-0-06-219439-8(9)) HarperCollins Pubs. (HarperCollins).

—The Door at the End of the World. 2019. (ENG.). 304p. (J). (gr. 3-7). 16.99 (978-0-06-236830-0(3), HarperCollins) HarperCollins Pubs.

—Magic Marks the Spot. Phillips, Dave, illus. 2014. (Very Nearly Honorable League of Pirates Ser.: 1). (ENG.). 384p. (J). (gr. 3-7). pap. 9.99 (978-0-06-219435-0(6), HarperCollins) HarperCollins Pubs.

—The Terror of the Southlands. Phillips, Dave, illus. 2014. (ENG.). 336p. (J). pap. (978-0-06-236178-3(3)) Harper & Row Ltd.

—The Terror of the Southlands. Phillips, Dave, illus. 2015. (Very Nearly Honorable League of Pirates Ser.: 2). (ENG.). 352p. (J). (gr. 3-7). pap. 8.99 (978-0-06-219437-4(2), HarperCollins) HarperCollins Pubs.

Carman, Patrick. Into the Mist, 5. 2011. (Land of Elyon Ser.: Bk. 4). 304p. (J). (gr. 4-6). 18.69 (978-0-439-89998-7(2)) Scholastic, Inc.

—Mr. Gedrick & Me. 2017. (ENG.). 224p. (J). (gr. 3-7). 16.99 (978-0-06-242160-9(3), Tegen, Katherine Bks) HarperCollins Pubs.

Carr, Lawrence. Under the Peach Tree. 2006. pap. 8.00 (978-0-8059-7019-7(3)) Dorrance Publishing Co., Inc.

Carris, Joan. Magic at the Bed & Biscuit. Jones, Noah Z., illus. (ENG.). (J). (gr. 1-4). 2012. 112p. pap. 5.99 (978-0-7636-5849-6(9)) 2011. 128p. 15.99 (978-0-7636-4306-5(8)) Candlewick Pr.

Carroll, D. L. Sir Licksalot & the Island Fools. 2012. 120p. pap. 19.95 (978-1-4626-8092-4(5)) America Star Bks.

Carroll, Emma. In Darkling Wood. 2018. (ENG.). 256p. (J). (gr. 5). 6.99 (978-0-399-55604-3(4), Yearling) Random Hse. Children's Bks.

Carryl, Charles E. The Admiral's Caravan: A Tale Inspired by Lewis Carroll's Wonderland. 2011. 110p. pap. (978-1-904808-66-4(2)) Evertype.

Carson, Rae. The Crown of Embers. (Girl of Fire & Thorns Ser.: 2). (ENG.). (YA). (gr. 8). 2019. 432p. pap. 10.99 (978-0-06-202653-8(4)) 2012. 416p. 17.99 (978-0-06-202651-4(8)) HarperCollins Pubs. (Greenwillow Bks.).

—The Girl of Fire & Thorns. (Girl of Fire & Thorns Ser.: 1). (ENG.). (YA). (gr. 8). 2019. 448p. pap. 11.99 (978-0-06-202650-7(X)) 2011. 432p. 17.99 (978-0-06-202648-4(8)) HarperCollins Pubs. (Greenwillow Bks.).

—Like a River Glorious. Hendrix, John, illus. (Gold Seer Trilogy Ser.: 2). (ENG.). (YA). (gr. 8). 2017. 432p. pap. 10.99 (978-0-06-224295-2(4)) 2016. 416p. 17.99 (978-0-06-224294-5(6)) HarperCollins Pubs. (Greenwillow Bks.).

—Walk on Earth a Stranger. (Gold Seer Trilogy Ser.: 1). (ENG.). (YA). (gr. 8). 2016. 464p. pap. 10.99 (978-0-06-224292-1(X)) 2015. 448p. 17.99 (978-0-06-224291-4(1)) HarperCollins Pubs. (Greenwillow Bks.).

Carter, David. The Nutters of Pendle Forest - Part 1 the Enchanted Valley. 2012. (Illus.). 222p. pap. (978-1-908098-54-2(6)) 2QT, Ltd. (Publishing).

carter, robert bob. The Magic Eye. 2009. 106p. pap. 12.95 (978-0-557-05597-5(0)) Lulu Pr., Inc.

Carter, Scott William. Wooden Bones. (ENG., Illus.). 160p. (J). (gr. 3-7). 2013. pap. 6.99 (978-1-4424-2752-5(3)) 2012. 15.99 (978-1-4424-2751-8(5)) Simon & Schuster Bks. For Young Readers. (Simon & Schuster Bks. For Young Readers).

Cartmell, C. J. The Magic Mailbox. 2011. 28p. pap. 15.99 (978-1-4568-4525-4(X)) Xlibris Corp.

Cash, M. A. Edward of Canterbury & the King of Red. Adams, Craig, illus. 2003. (J). (978-0-9772711-0-8(2)) Jama Kids.

Cashore, Kristin. Fire. 2011. (Graceling Realm Ser.). (ENG.). (YA). 512p. (gr. 7-18). pap. 13.99 (978-0-14-241591-7(X), Penguin Books);2. 480p. (gr. 9-12). 28.69 (978-0-8037-3461-6(1)) Penguin Young Readers Group.

—Fire. 2011. (Graceling Realm Ser.: 2). lib. bdg. 22.10 (978-0-606-23085-8(8)) Turtleback.

Caspian. The Magician in the Attic. 2014. (ENG., Illus.). 352p. (YA). pap. (978-1-908168-42-9(0), Elsewhen Pr.) Alnpete Ltd.

Cassidy, Sara. The Great Googlini, 1 vol. Chua, Charlene, illus. 2018. (Orca Echoes Ser.). (ENG.). 112p. (J). (gr. 1-3). pap. 7.95 (978-1-4598-1703-6(6)) Orca Bk. Pubs. USA.

Cast, P. C. Moon Chosen. l.t. ed. 2017. (Tales of a New World Ser.). (ENG.). 896p. lib. bdg. 22.99 (978-1-4328-4325-0(7)) Cengage Gale.

—Moon Chosen: Tales of a New World. 2017. (Tales of a New World Ser.: 1). (ENG.). 624p. (YA). pap. 15.00 (978-1-250-10073-3(9), 900162486, Wednesday Bks.) St. Martin's Pr.

—Sun Warrior: Tales of a New World. 2018. (Tales of a New World Ser.: 2). (ENG., Illus.). 576p. (YA). pap. 11.99 (978-1-250-10076-4(3), 900162489, Wednesday Bks.) St. Martin's Pr.

Cast, P. C. & Cast, Kristin. Lost. unabr. ed. (House of Night Other World Ser.: 2). (ENG.). 2019. 416p. pap. 14.99 (978-1-9825-4647-2(6), PBahrs) 2018. 408p. (YA). 18.99 (978-1-5384-4074-2(1), HCahrs) Blackstone Audio, Inc.

—Redeemed: A House of Night Novel. 2014. (YA). 310p. (978-1-250-05952-9(6)); (House of Night Novels Ser.: 12). (ENG.). 320p. (gr. 7-12). 21.99 (978-0-312-59444-2(5), 900062751, St. Martin's Griffin) St. Martin's Pr.

Castle, Amber. Spell Sisters: Olivia the Otter Sister. Hall, Mary, illus. 2013. (ENG.). 160p. (J). (gr. 2-4). pap. 7.99 (978-0-85707-253-5(6), Simon & Schuster Children's) Simon & Schuster, Ltd. GBR. Dist: Simon & Schuster, Inc.

Castle, Jennifer. Butterfly Wishes 1: the Wishing Wings. 2017. (Butterfly Wishes Ser.). (ENG., Illus.). 128p. (J). 15.99 (978-1-68119-491-2(0), 9781681194912, Bloomsbury USA Childrens) Bloomsbury Publishing USA.

—Butterfly Wishes 2: Tiger Streak's Tale. 2017. (Butterfly Wishes Ser.). (ENG.). 128p. (J). pap. 5.99 (978-1-68119-373-1(6), 900171778, Bloomsbury USA Childrens) Bloomsbury Publishing USA.

—Butterfly Wishes 3: Blue Rain's Adventure. 2018. (Butterfly Wishes Ser.). (ENG., Illus.). 128p. (J). 16.99 (978-1-68119-691-6(3), 900182258); pap. 5.99 (978-1-68119-375-5(2), 900171781) Bloomsbury Publishing USA. (Bloomsbury USA Childrens).

Castle, M. E. Fakespeare: Something Stinks in Hamlet. Jennewein, Daniel, illus. 2017. 261p. (J). pap. (978-1-250-10157-0(3)) St. Martin's Pr.

—Fakespeare: Starcrossed in Romeo & Juliet. Jennewein, Daniel, illus. 2017. 295p. (J). pap. (978-1-250-10160-0(3)) St. Martin's Pr.

Catanese, P. W. Happenstance Found, 1. 2009. (Books of Umber Ser.: 1). (ENG.). 352p. (J). (gr. 3-7). 16.99 (978-1-4169-7519-9(5), Aladdin) Simon & Schuster Children's Publishing.

—The Mirror's Tale. 2017. (ENG., Illus.). 304p. (J). (gr. 4-8). 17.99 (978-1-4814-7636-2(X)); pap. 8.99 (978-1-4814-7635-5(1)) Simon & Schuster/Paula Wiseman Bks. (Simon & Schuster/Paula Wiseman Bks.).

Catasús Jennings, Terry. Magnetic Magic, 1 vol. Gabriel, Andrea, illus. 2016. (ENG.). 32p. (J). (gr. k-3). 17.95 (978-1-62855-861-6(X)) Arbordale Publishing.

Cate, Annette LeBlanc. The Magic Rabbit. Cate, Annette LeBlanc, illus. 2013. (ENG., Illus.). 32p. (J). (gr. -1-3). 7.99 (978-0-7636-6685-9(8)) Candlewick Pr.

Caterer, Claire M. The Key & the Flame. (ENG.). (J). (gr. 3-7). 2015. 496p. pap. 7.99 (978-1-4424-5742-3(2)) 2013. 480p. 17.99 (978-1-4424-5741-6(4)) McElderry, Margaret K. Bks. (McElderry, Margaret K. Bks.).

Catipon, Atreyu. The Wizard's Magic Hat. 2012. 26p. 16.00 (978-1-61863-390-3(2)) Bookstand Publishing.

Caveney, Philip. Spy Another Day. 2013. (ENG.). 240p. (J). (gr. 4-6). pap. 10.99 (978-1-84939-417-8(2)) Andersen Pr. GBR. Dist: Independent Pubs. Group.

Cestari, Crystal. The Fairest Kind of Love. 2019. (Windy City Magic Ser.: 3). (ENG.). 320p. (YA). (gr. 7-17). 17.99 (978-1-368-03884-3(0)) Hyperion Bks. for Children.

—The Sweetest Kind of Fate. 2018. (Windy City Magic Ser.: 2). (ENG.). 320p. (YA). (gr. 7-12). pap. 9.99 (978-1-4847-7569-1(4)) Hyperion Bks. for Children.

Chabon, Michael. Summerland. l.t. ed. 2003. 615p. (J). 25.95 (978-0-7862-5143-8(3)) Thorndike Pr.

Chadwick, J. R. Thomas & the Dragon's Pearl. 2008. (Illus.). v, 181p. pap. *(978-0-7552-0430-4(1))* Authors OnLine, Ltd.
Chadwick, Jennie. The Peach Tree Kids: Circus Fleas. 2012. 96p. pap. 9.99 *(978-1-61897-455-6(6)*, Strategic Bk. Publishing) Strategic Book Publishing & Rights Agency (SBPRA).
Chainani, Soman. A Crystal of Time. Bruno, Iacopo, illus. 2019. 624p. (J). *(978-0-06-289559-2(1)); (978-0-06-290764-6(6)); (978-0-06-290697-7(6)); (978-0-06-288641-5(X))* Harper & Row Ltd.
—A Crystal of Time. 2019. (School for Good & Evil Ser.: 5). (ENG., Illus.). 640p. (J). (gr. 3-7). pap. 10.50 *(978-0-06-288575-3(8)*, HarperCollins) HarperCollins Pubs. Ltd. GBR. Dist: HarperCollins Pubs.
Chaisson, Kristen. Dreamland. 2013. 28p. pap. 24.95 *(978-1-63000-664-8(5))* America Star Bks.
Chamberlain, Nick. The Adventures of Papillon. 2008. 176p. pap. 15.95 *(978-1-60290-092-9(2))* Nassau-Street.com.
Chance, Kim. Keeper. 2018. (Keeper Duology Ser.). (ENG.). 408p. (YA). (gr. 9-12). pap. 14.99 *(978-1-63583-012-5(5)*, 1635830125, Flux) North Star Editions.
—Keeper. 2018. lib. bdg. 26.95 *(978-0-606-41244-5(1))* Turtleback.
Chang, Mi-Kyoung. Mina's White Canvas. Yi, Hyon-Ju, illus. 2015. (ENG.). 38p. (J). 17.99 *(978-1-4413-1826-8(7)*, 0c6f777b-887d-44cf-babd-93b24358c92e) Peter Pauper Pr. Inc.
Chapman, Lara. Accidentally Evil. 2015. (Mix Ser.). (ENG., Illus.). 240p. (J). (gr. 4-8). pap. 7.99 *(978-1-4814-0110-4(6)*, Aladdin) Simon & Schuster Children's Publishing.
—The XYZs of Being Wicked. 2014. (Mix Ser.). (ENG., Illus.). 272p. (J). (gr. 4-8). pap. 6.99 *(978-1-4814-0107-4(6)*, Aladdin) Simon & Schuster Children's Publishing.
—The XYZs of Being Wicked. 2014. (Mix Ser.). (ENG., Illus.). 272p. (J). (gr. 4-8). 17.99 *(978-1-4814-0108-1(4)*, Simon & Schuster/Paula Wiseman Bks.) Simon & Schuster/Paula Wiseman Bks.
Charman, Katrina. The Crystal Caverns: a Branches Book (the Last Firehawk #2) (Library Edition) Norton, Jeremy, illus. 2017. (Last Firehawk Ser.: 2). (ENG.). 96p. (J). (gr. 1-3). 15.99 *(978-1-338-12252-7(5))* Scholastic, Inc.
—The Ember Stone: a Branches Book (the Last Firehawk #1) Norton, Jeremy, illus. 2017. (Last Firehawk Ser.: 1). (ENG.). 96p. (J). (gr. 1-3). pap. 5.99 *(978-1-338-12213-8(4))* Scholastic, Inc.
—Lullaby Lake: a Branches Book (the Last Firehawk #4) Norton, Jeremy, illus. 2018. (Last Firehawk Ser.: 4). (ENG.). 96p. (J). (gr. 1-3). pap. 5.99 *(978-1-338-12267-1(3))* Scholastic, Inc.
—Lullaby Lake: a Branches Book (the Last Firehawk #4) (Library Edition), Vol. 4. Norton, Jeremy, illus. 2018. (Last Firehawk Ser.: 4). (ENG.). 96p. (J). (gr. 1-3). lib. bdg. 24.99 *(978-1-338-12271-8(1))* Scholastic, Inc.
—The Whispering Oak: a Branches Book (the Last Firehawk #3), 1 vol., Vol. 3. Norton, Jeremy, illus. 2018. (Last Firehawk Ser.: 3). (ENG.). 96p. (J). (gr. 1-3). pap. 5.99 *(978-1-338-12255-8(X))* Scholastic, Inc.
Chartrand, Lili. Taming Horrible Harry. Ouriou, Susan, tr. from FRE. Roge, illus. 2006. (ENG.). 32p. (J). (gr. -1-3). 16.95 *(978-0-88776-772-2(9)*, Tundra Bks.) Tundra Bks. CAN. Dist: Penguin Random Hse. LLC.
Chen, Eva. Juno Valentine & the Magical Shoes. Desierto, Derek, illus. 2018. (Juno Valentine Ser.). (ENG.). 32p. (J). 18.99 *(978-1-250-29726-6(5)*, 900195905) Feiwel & Friends.
Chen, Wei Dong. Monkey King: The Sacred Tree. Peng, Chao, illus. 2012. (Monkey King Ser.: 6). (ENG.). 176p. (gr. 5-8). lib. bdg. 29.27 *(978-89-94208-74-9(7))* JR Comics KOR. Dist: Lerner Publishing Group.
Chesterfield, Sadie. Mysticons: Prophecy of Evil. 2018. (Mysticons Ser.). (ENG., Illus.). 128p. (J). pap. 6.99 *(978-1-250-16512-1(1)*, 900186941) Imprint IND. Dist: Macmillan.
—Prophecy of Evil. 2018. (Illus.). 118p. (J). *(978-1-5490-7800-2(3))* Follett School Solutions.
Cheverton, Mark. Herobrine's War: The Birth of Herobrine Book Three: a Gameknight999 Adventure: an Unofficial Minecrafter's Adventure. 2017. (Gameknight999 Ser.). 272p. (J). (gr. 3-3). pap. 9.99 *(978-1-5107-0996-6(7)*, Sky Pony Pr.) Skyhorse Publishing Co., Inc.
Chew, Ruth. A Matter-Of-Fact Magic Book: Witch's Broom. 2015. (Matter-Of-Fact Magic Book Ser.). (Illus.). 144p. (J). (gr. 2-5). pap. 5.99 *(978-0-449-81578-6(1)*, Random Hse. Bks. for Young Readers) Random Hse. Children's Bks.
Chewins, Hayley. The Turnaway Girls. 2018. (ENG.). 272p. (J). (gr. 5-9). 16.99 *(978-0-7636-9792-1(3))* Candlewick Pr.
Chick, Bryan. Riddles & Danger. 2011. (Secret Zoo Ser.: 3). (ENG.). 288p. (J). (gr. 3-7). 16.99 *(978-0-06-198927-8(4)*, Greenwillow Bks.) HarperCollins Pubs.
Child, Lydia Maria. The Magician's Show Box & Other Stories. 2007. (ENG.). 124p. per. *(978-1-4065-1354-7(7))* Dodo Pr.
—The Magician's Show Box, & Other Stories by the Author of Rainbows for Children. 2006. 312p. per. 23.99 *(978-1-4255-2973-4(9))* Michigan Publishing.
Chima, Cinda Williams. Deathcaster. 656p. (YA). 2020. (Shattered Realms Ser.: 4). (ENG.). (gr. 8). pap. 11.99 *(978-0-06-238104-0(0))* 2019. (Illus.). *(978-0-06-290591-8(0))* 2019. (Shattered Realms Ser.: 4). (ENG., Illus.). (gr. 8). 18.99 *(978-0-06-238103-3(2))* HarperCollins Pubs. (HarperTeen).
—The Dragon Heir. 2009. (Heir Chronicles Ser.: 3). (ENG., Illus.). 528p. (YA). (gr. 7-17). pap. 11.99 *(978-1-4231-1071-2(4))* Little, Brown Bks. for Young Readers.
—The Enchanter Heir. 2013. (Heir Chronicles Ser.: 4). (ENG.). 464p. (YA). (gr. 7-12). E-Book 45.00 *(978-1-4231-8789-9(X))* Little, Brown Bks. for Young Readers.
—Flamecaster. (Shattered Realms Ser.: 1). (gr. 8). 2017. (ENG.). 560p. (YA). pap. 10.99 *(978-0-06-238095-1(8))* 2016. 544p. (J). pap. 12.00 *(978-0-06-245490-4(0))* 2016. (ENG.). 544p. (YA). 18.99 *(978-0-06-238094-4(X))* HarperCollins Pubs. (HarperTeen).
—The Sorcerer Heir. 2016. (Heir Chronicles Ser.: 5). (ENG.). 560p. (YA). (gr. 7-12). pap. 11.99 *(978-1-4231-9475-0(6))* Little, Brown Bks. for Young Readers.
—Stormcaster. (Shattered Realms Ser.: 3). (ENG.). (YA). (gr. 8). 2019. 560p. pap. 10.99 *(978-0-06-238101-9(6))* 2018. 544p. 18.99 *(978-0-06-238100-2(8))* HarperCollins Pubs. (HarperTeen).
—The Warrior Heir. 2007. (Heir Chronicles Ser.: 1). (ENG.). 448p. (YA). (gr. 7-17). pap. 11.99 *(978-0-7868-3917-9(1))* Little, Brown Bks. for Young Readers.
—The Warrior Heir. 2006. (Heir Chronicles: No. 1). 1.00 *(978-1-4294-0323-8(3))* Recorded Bks., Inc.
—The Wizard Heir. 2008. (Heir Chronicles Ser.: 2). (ENG.). 480p. (YA). (gr. 7-17). pap. 12.99 *(978-1-4231-0488-9(9))* Little, Brown Bks. for Young Readers.
Chime, P. K. Moonrise. 2013. 452p. pap. *(978-1-78299-644-6(3))* FeedARead.com.
Chipman, Laura. Dragonspeaker. 2005. 76p. pap. 19.95 *(978-1-4241-0136-8(0))* America Star Bks.
Chizuru, Mio. The Pirate & the Princess Volume 1: the Timelight Stone: The Timelight Stone. 2017. 110p. (J). pap. 5.99 *(978-1-933164-43-4(3))* Seven Seas Entertainment, LLC.
The Chocolate Moose. 2007. (Illus.). 48p. (J). per. 13.00 *(978-0-9767189-5-6(2))* Better Day Publishing.
Chokshi, Roshani. The Gilded Wolves: A Novel. (Gilded Wolves Ser.: 1). (ENG., Illus.). (YA). 2020. 416p. pap. 11.99 *(978-1-250-14455-3(8)*, 900180661) 2019. 400p. 19.99 *(978-1-250-14454-6(X)*, 900180660) St. Martin's Pr. (Wednesday Bks.).
—The Star-Touched Queen. 2017. (Star-Touched Ser.: 1). (ENG.). 368p. (YA). pap. 11.99 *(978-1-250-10020-7(8)*, 900162432, St. Martin's Griffin) St. Martin's Pr.
Christen, Dennis H. Lundon's Bridge & the Three Keys. 2008. 221p. (J). pap. 12.95 *(978-0-9718151-5-5(1))* C-It Entertainment Group, LLC.
Chubbs-Rogers, Shannon. Listen... Can You Hear It? 2013. 40p. pap. *(978-1-4602-1980-5(5))* FriesenPress.
Chupeco, Rin. The Heart Forger: Bone Witch #2. (Bone Witch Ser.: 2). (YA). (gr. 8-12). 2019. 544p. pap. 10.99 *(978-1-4926-6808-4(7))* 2018. (ENG., Illus.). 528p. 17.99 *(978-1-4926-3585-7(5))* Sourcebooks, Inc.
—The Shadowglass: Bone Witch #3. (Bone Witch Ser.: 3). 480p. (YA). (gr. 8-12). 2020. pap. 12.99 *(978-1-4926-9332-1(4))* 2019. (ENG., Illus.). 17.99 *(978-1-4926-6060-6(4))* Sourcebooks, Inc.
Ciccone, Tiziana. Tooth Fairy Trouble. 2013. 36p. pap. 13.95 *(978-1-62857-176-9(4)*, Strategic Bk. Publishing) Strategic Book Publishing & Rights Agency (SBPRA).
Ciccone, Tiziana & Linardi, Franca. Lucinda, Queen of Everything. Cannavicci, Luigi A., illus. 2012. 36p. pap. 13.95 *(978-1-61897-719-9(9)*, Strategic Bk. Publishing) Strategic Book Publishing & Rights Agency (SBPRA).
Ciddor, Anna. Wolfspell: Viking Magic Book 2. 2007. (Viking Magic Ser.). (ENG., Illus.). 192p. (J). (gr. 4-7). pap. 12.99 *(978-1-74114-013-2(7))* Allen & Unwin AUS. Dist: Independent Pubs. Group.
Ciencin, Scott & Burge, Constance M. Luck Be a Lady. 2004. (Charmed Ser.). (ENG., Illus.). 224p. (YA). pap. 16.95 *(978-0-689-85793-5(4)*, Gallery Bks.) Gallery Bks.
Cirrone, Dorian. The First Last Day. (ENG., Illus.). 240p. (J). (gr. 3-7). 2017. pap. 8.99 *(978-1-4814-5814-6(0))* 2016. 17.99 *(978-1-4814-5813-9(2))* Simon & Schuster Children's Publishing. (Aladdin).
C.J. Elgert. The Elder Brothers & the Padstow Crystals. 2009. 284p. 27.95 *(978-1-4401-7678-4(7))*; pap. 17.95 *(978-1-4401-7676-0(0))* iUniverse, Inc.
Clare, Cassandra. City of Ashes. 2008. (Mortal Instruments Ser.: Bk. 2). (YA). (gr. 9). 64.99 *(978-1-60640-964-0(6))* Findaway World, LLC.
—City of Ashes. 2008. (YA). (Mortal Instruments Ser.: 2). (ENG.). 464p. (gr. 9-12). 24.99 *(978-1-4169-1429-7(3))*; 416p. pap. *(978-1-4063-1849-4(3))* McElderry, Margaret K. Bks. (McElderry, Margaret K. Bks.).
—City of Fallen Angels. 2011. (Mortal Instruments Ser.: 4). (ENG.). 432p. (YA). (gr. 9-18). 24.99 *(978-1-4424-0354-3(3)*, McElderry, Margaret K. Bks.) McElderry, Margaret K. Bks.
—City of Fallen Angels, 11 vols. (Mortal Instruments Ser.: 4). (YA). 2012. 133.75 *(978-1-4618-0638-7(0))* 2011. 135.75 *(978-1-4618-0637-0(2))* 2011. 1.25 *(978-1-4640-2483-2(9))* 2011. 317.75 *(978-1-4618-0642-4(9))* 2011. 133.75 *(978-1-4618-0641-7(0))* Recorded Bks., Inc.
—City of Glass. (Mortal Instruments Ser.: 3). (ENG., (YA). (gr. 9). 2015. Illus.). 592p. pap. 14.99 *(978-1-4814-5598-5(2))* 2009. 560p. 24.99 *(978-1-4169-1430-3(7))* McElderry, Margaret K. Bks. (McElderry, Margaret K. Bks.).
—City of Glass. 2010. 23.00 *(978-1-60686-827-0(6))* Perfection Learning Corp.
—City of Glass. 2009. pap. *(978-1-4424-9308-7(9))* Simon & Schuster.
—City of Glass. 2015. (Mortal Instruments Ser.: Bk. 3). (Illus.). 592p. (J). lib. bdg. 25.75 *(978-0-606-37733-1(6))* Turtleback.
—City of Heavenly Fire. 2014. (Mortal Instruments Ser.: 6). (ENG., Illus.). 752p. (YA). (gr. 9). 24.99 *(978-1-4424-1689-5(0)*, McElderry, Margaret K. Bks.) McElderry, Margaret K. Bks.
—City of Lost Souls. (Mortal Instruments Ser.: 5). (ENG., (YA). (gr. 9). 2015. Illus.). 592p. pap. 14.99 *(978-1-4814-5600-5(8))* 2012. 544p. 24.99 *(978-1-4424-1686-4(6))* McElderry, Margaret K. Bks. (McElderry, Margaret K. Bks.).
—City of Lost Souls, 16 vols. 2012. (Mortal Instruments Ser.: Bk. 5). (YA). 135.75 *(978-1-4640-3948-5(8))*; 133.75 *(978-1-4640-3952-2(6))*; 317.75 *(978-1-4640-3949-2(6))*; 133.75 *(978-1-4640-3951-5(8))* Recorded Bks., Inc.
—City of Lost Souls. 2015. (Mortal Instruments Ser.: Bk. 5). 592p. (YA). lib. bdg. 25.75 *(978-0-606-37736-2(0))* Turtleback.
—City of Lost Souls. 2012. 512p. pap. *(978-1-4063-3760-0(9))* Walker Bks., Ltd.
—The Dark Artifices, the Complete Collection: Lady Midnight; Lord of Shadows; Queen of Air & Darkness. 2019. (Dark Artifices Ser.). (ENG., Illus.). 2288p. (YA). (gr. 9). 74.99 *(978-1-5344-4954-1(X)*, McElderry, Margaret K. Bks.) McElderry, Margaret K. Bks.
—Lady Midnight. 2016. (Dark Artifices Ser.: 1). (ENG., Illus.). 688p. (YA). (gr. 9-12). 24.99 *(978-1-4424-6835-1(1)*, McElderry, Margaret K. Bks.) McElderry, Margaret K. Bks.
—Lady Midnight. 2017. lib. bdg. 26.95 *(978-0-606-40535-5(6))* Turtleback.
—Lord of Shadows. (YA). 2018. (Dark Artifices Ser.: 2). (ENG., Illus.). 752p. (gr. 9). pap. 14.99 *(978-1-4424-6841-2(6))* 2017. (Dark Artifices Ser.: 2). (ENG., Illus.). 720p. (gr. 9). 24.99 *(978-1-4424-6840-5(8))* 2017. 699p. *(978-1-5344-0617-9(4))* McElderry, Margaret K. Bks. (McElderry, Margaret K. Bks.).
—Queen of Air & Darkness. 2018. (Dark Artifices Ser.: 3). (ENG., Illus.). 912p. (YA). (gr. 9). 24.99 *(978-1-4424-6843-6(2))*; E-Book *(978-1-4424-6845-0(9))* McElderry, Margaret K. Bks. (McElderry, Margaret K. Bks.).
Clare, Cassandra & Chu, Wesley. The Red Scrolls of Magic. 2020. (Eldest Curses Ser.: 1). (ENG.). 384p. (YA). (gr. 9). pap. 14.99 *(978-1-4814-9509-7(7)*, McElderry, Margaret K. Bks.) McElderry, Margaret K. Bks.
—The Red Scrolls of Magic. 2019. (Eldest Curses Ser.: 1). (ENG., Illus.). 368p. (YA). (gr. 9). 24.99 *(978-1-4814-9508-0(9)*, SAGA Press) Simon & Schuster Bks. For Young Readers.
Clare, Cassandra & Lewis, Joshua. The Shadowhunter's Codex. 2013. (Mortal Instruments Ser.). (ENG., Illus.). 288p. (YA). (gr. 9). 24.99 *(978-1-4424-1692-5(0))*; 49.99 *(978-1-4424-9682-8(7))* McElderry, Margaret K. Bks. (McElderry, Margaret K. Bks.).
Clare, Cassandra, et al. The Bane Chronicles. Clare, Cassandra, ed. 2014. (Bane Chronicles Ser.). (ENG., Illus.). 528p. (YA). (gr. 9). 24.99 *(978-1-4424-9599-9(5)*, McElderry, Margaret K. Bks.) McElderry, Margaret K. Bks.
—Tales from the Shadowhunter Academy. (Tales from the Shadowhunter Academy Ser.). (ENG.). (YA). (gr. 9). 2017. 704p. pap. 14.99 *(978-1-4814-4326-5(7))* 2016. (Illus.). 672p. 24.99 *(978-1-4814-4325-8(9))* McElderry, Margaret K. Bks. (McElderry, Margaret K. Bks.).
Clarion Books, Clarion. Girl Power 5-Minute Stories. 2015. (5-Minute Stories Ser.). (ENG., Illus.). 224p. (J). (gr. -1-3). 12.99 *(978-0-544-33925-5(8)*, 1584496, Clarion Bks.) HarperCollins Pubs.
Clarizio, Laura. If I Had a Magic Carpet. 2005. 48p. pap. 16.95 *(978-1-4137-8557-9(3))* America Star Bks.
—If I Had a Magic Carpet II: Key to Kindness. 2006. (ENG.). 48p. per. 16.95 *(978-1-4241-3985-9(6))* America Star Bks.
—If I Had a Magic Carpet III: Haunted Holidays. 2008. 73p. pap. 19.95 *(978-1-60563-240-7(6))* America Star Bks.
—Traveling Through Time: If I Had a Magic Carpet IV. 2012. 100p. 21.95 *(978-1-4489-3229-0(7))* 2010. 98p. pap. 16.95 *(978-1-4489-5428-5(2))* America Star Bks.
Clark, Chris Elliott. Hazel's Secret. 2008. 64p. pap. 19.95 *(978-1-60474-500-9(2))* America Star Bks.
Clark, Hannah L. Uncovering Cobbogoth. 2014. pap. 17.99 *(978-1-4621-1426-9(1))* Cedar Fort, Inc./CFI Distribution.
Clark, Isabelle. The Enchanted Forest of Hope. 2009. 44p. pap. 18.50 *(978-1-4389-7781-2(6))* AuthorHouse.
Clark, Jr. Metrognomes. 2007. 292p. per. 17.95 *(978-0-595-42973-8(4))* iUniverse, Inc.
Clark, Kristina. The Great Adventures of Ella: The Magic Desk. 2010. 28p. 12.95 *(978-1-4520-2412-7(X))* AuthorHouse.
Clark, Platte F. Bad Unicorn. (Bad Unicorn Trilogy Ser.: 1). (ENG., Illus.). (J). (gr. 3-7). 2014. 448p. pap. 7.99 *(978-1-4424-5013-4(4))* 2013. 432p. 18.99 *(978-1-4424-5012-7(6))* Simon & Schuster Children's Publishing. (Aladdin).
Clark, William. Magic Raindrops. 2013. 24p. pap. 14.93 *(978-1-4669-7414-2(1))* Trafford Publishing.
Clarke, Christie. Star Spirit. 2013. 118p. pap. *(978-0-9917348-2-5(3))* RedemptionHse. Publishing.
Clarke, Lizzy. The Spirit of the Jaguar. 2013. 92p. pap. 11.38 *(978-1-4907-0600-9(3))*; (gr. -1). 21.38 *(978-1-4907-0602-3(X))* Trafford Publishing.
Clarkson, Kelly. River Rose & the Magical Christmas. Fleming, Lucy, illus. 2017. (J). *(978-0-06-274098-4(9))* Harper & Row Ltd.
—River Rose & the Magical Lullaby. Hughes, Laura, illus. 2016. (ENG.). 32p. (J). (gr. -1-3). 18.99 *(978-0-06-242756-4(3)*, HarperCollins) HarperCollins Pubs.
Clement-Davies, David. The Telling Pool. 2007. (ENG., Illus.). 382p. (YA). (gr. 7-17). per. 8.95 *(978-0-8109-9257-3(4))* Abrams, Inc.
—The Telling Pool. 2006. 1.00 *(978-1-4237-6417-5(X))* Recorded Bks., Inc.
Clickard, Carrie. Magic for Sale. Shelley, John, illus. 2017. (ENG.). 32p. (J). (gr. -1-3). 16.95 *(978-0-8234-3559-3(8))* Holiday Hse., Inc.
Clifford, Leah. A Touch Morbid. 2012. (Touch Mortal Trilogy Ser.: 2). (ENG.). 304p. (YA). (gr. 9). 16.99 *(978-0-06-200502-1(2)*, Greenwillow Bks.) HarperCollins Pubs.
Cluess, Jessica. A Poison Dark & Drowning (Kingdom on Fire, Book Two) (Kingdom on Fire Ser.: 2). (ENG.). (YA). (gr. 7). 2018. 448p. pap. 10.99 *(978-0-553-53597-6(8)*, Ember) 2017. 432p. 17.99 *(978-0-553-53594-5(3)*, Random Hse. Bks. for Young Readers) Random Hse. Children's Bks.
—A Shadow Bright & Burning (Kingdom on Fire, Book One) 2017. (Kingdom on Fire Ser.: 1). (ENG.). 432p. (YA). (gr. 7). pap. 9.99 *(978-0-553-53593-8(5)*, Ember) Random Hse. Children's Bks.
—A Sorrow Fierce & Falling (Kingdom on Fire, Book Three) 2018. (Kingdom on Fire Ser.: 3). (ENG.). 416p. (YA). (gr. 7). 17.99 *(978-0-553-53598-3(6)*, Random Hse. Bks. for Young Readers) Random Hse. Children's Bks.
Chockaert, Cindy. The Magical Stones. 2011. 36p. pap. 16.86 *(978-1-4389-8929-7(6))* AuthorHouse.
Coakley, Lena. Wicked Nix. Zollars, Jaime, illus. (ENG.). (J). (gr. 3-7). 2019. 176p. pap. 8.99 *(978-1-4197-3703-9(1)*, 1197603) 2018. 160p. 16.99 *(978-1-4197-2869-3(5)*, 1197601) Abrams, Inc. (Amulet Bks.).
Coats, J. Anderson. The Green Children of Woolpit. 2020. (ENG.). 272p. (J). (gr. 5). pap. 7.99 *(978-1-5344-2791-4(0))* Simon & Schuster Children's Publishing.
Cody, Matthew. The Secrets of the Pied Piper 3: the Piper's Apprentice. 2017. (Secrets of the Pied Piper Ser.: 3). (ENG., Illus.). 288p. (J). (gr. 3-7). 16.99 *(978-0-385-75530-6(9)*, Knopf Bks. for Young Readers) Random Hse. Children's Bks.
Coe, Catherine. A Magical Beginning. 2016. (Illus.). 83p. (J). *(978-0-545-92890-8(7))* Scholastic, Inc.
Coe, Mary. The Prince of Betherland. 2007. 100p. pap. 9.95 *(978-1-4303-2521-5(6))* Lulu Pr., Inc.
Cofer, Amadeus. Aloha Adventure: The Magic of Imagination on a Rainy Day. l.t. ed. 2004. (Illus.). 36p. (J). 14.00 *(978-1-932957-01-3(4))* Legacy Pubs.
Coggan, Helena. The Reaction: The Wars of Angels Book Two. 2017. (War of Angels Ser.). (ENG.). 464p. (YA). (gr. 9). 18.99 *(978-0-7636-8973-5(4))* Candlewick Pr.
Cohen, Lawrence J. The Dragon's Familiar. 2008. 236p. (YA). pap. 15.95 *(978-0-595-51413-7(8))* iUniverse, Inc.
Cohen, Leah. The Magic Pond: How a Small Flock of Birds Brought Life & Cheer to a Lonely Pond. 2010. 36p. 15.49 *(978-1-4520-1082-3(X))* AuthorHouse.
Cohen, Lee. Find the Magic: A Rip Squeak Book. 2008. (Illus.). 32p. (J). 16.95 *(978-0-9747825-2-2(1)*, Rip Squeak Pr.) Rip Squeak, Inc.
Cole, Frank L. Potion Masters: The Eternity Elixir. 2018. (Potion Masters Ser.: 1). (ENG., Illus.). 304p. (J). (gr. 5). 16.99 *(978-1-62972-358-7(4)*, 5182305, Shadow Mountain) Shadow Mountain Publishing.
—The Transparency Tonic. 2019. (Potion Masters Ser.: 2). (ENG., Illus.). 384p. (J). (gr. 5). 16.99 *(978-1-62972-488-1(2)*, 5206082, Shadow Mountain) Shadow Mountain Publishing.
Cole, Myke. The Wildsidhe Chronicles Bk. 6: Car Trouble. 2003. (J). pap. 7.99 *(978-1-890096-18-2(0))* Padwolf Publishing Inc.
Cole, Penelope Ann. Magical Matthew. Collier, Kevin Scott, illus. 2012. 24p. pap. 10.95 *(978-1-61633-326-3(X))* Guardian Angel Publishing, Inc.
Cole, Penelope Anne. Magical Matthew. Collier, Kevin Scott, illus. 2012. 24p. 19.95 *(978-1-61633-325-6(1))* Guardian Angel Publishing, Inc.
—Magical Mea. Collier, Kevin, illus. 2013. 24p. 19.95 *(978-1-61633-394-2(4))*; pap. 10.95 *(978-1-61633-395-9(2))* Guardian Angel Publishing, Inc.
Colebourn, Craig. The Knights of Videnland: Passing the Torch. 2007. 428p. per. 23.95 *(978-0-595-46989-5(2))* iUniverse, Inc.
Colfer, Chris. Adventures from the Land of Stories Boxed Set: The Mother Goose Diaries & Queen Red Riding Hood's Guide to Royalty. 2015. (Land of Stories Ser.). (ENG.). 256p. (J). (gr. 3-7). 22.00 *(978-0-316-26151-7(3))* Little, Brown Bks. for Young Readers.
—An Author's Odyssey. 2016. (Land of Stories Ser.: 5). (ENG.). 496p. (J). (gr. 3-7). pap. 11.99 *(978-0-316-27214-8(0))* Little, Brown Bks. for Young Readers.
—The Curvy Tree: A Tale from the Land of Stories. Dorman, Brandon, illus. 2015. (Land of Stories Ser.). (ENG.). 32p. (J). (gr. -1-3). 18.99 *(978-0-316-40685-7(6))* Little, Brown Bks. for Young Readers.
—The Enchantress Returns. 2014. (Land of Stories Ser.: 2). (J). lib. bdg. 20.85 *(978-0-606-37229-9(6))* Turtleback.
—A Grimm Warning. 2015. (Land of Stories Ser.: 3). (J). lib. bdg. 20.85 *(978-0-606-37230-5(X))* Turtleback.
—The Land of Stories: a Grimm Warning. (Land of Stories Ser.: 3). (ENG.). (J). (gr. 3-7). 2015. 496p. pap. 9.99 *(978-0-316-40682-6(1))* 2014. 480p. 19.99 *(978-0-316-40681-9(3))* 2014. 768p. 50.99 *(978-0-316-40964-3(2))* Little, Brown Bks. for Young Readers.
—The Land of Stories: an Author's Odyssey. (Land of Stories Ser.: 5). (ENG., Illus.). 464p. (J). (gr. 3-7). 2017. pap. 9.99 *(978-0-316-38321-9(X))* 2016. 19.99 *(978-0-316-38329-5(5))* Little, Brown Bks. for Young Readers.
—The Land of Stories: Beyond the Kingdoms. 2015. (Land of Stories Ser.: 4). (ENG., Illus.). (J). (gr. 3-7). 432p. 19.99 *(978-0-316-40689-5(9))*; 624p. 45.99 *(978-0-316-33938-4(5))* Little, Brown Bks. for Young Readers.
—The Land of Stories: the Enchantress Returns. (Land of Stories Ser.: 2). (ENG.). (J). (gr. 3-7). 2014. 544p. pap. 9.99 *(978-0-316-20155-1(3))* 2013. (Illus.). 528p. 19.99 *(978-0-316-20154-4(5))* 2013. 832p. 52.99 *(978-0-316-24235-6(7))* Little, Brown Bks. for Young Readers.
—The Land of Stories: the Wishing Spell. (Land of Stories Ser.: 1). (ENG., Illus.). (J). (gr. 3-7). 2013. 464p. pap. 9.99 *(978-0-316-20156-8(1))* 2012. 448p. 19.99 *(978-0-316-20157-5(X))* 2013. 672p. pap. 28.99 *(978-0-316-24236-3(5))* Little, Brown Bks. for Young Readers.
—The Land of Stories: Worlds Collide. 2018. (Land of Stories Ser.: 6). (ENG.). 464p. (J). (gr. 3-7). pap. 9.99 *(978-0-316-35588-9(7))* Little, Brown Bks. for Young Readers.
—The Mother Goose Diaries. Dorman, Brandon et al, illus. 2015. 121p. (J). *(978-0-316-38332-5(5))* Little Brown & Co.
—Queen Red Riding Hood's Guide to Royalty. Dorman, Brandon, illus. 2015. 118p. (J). *(978-0-316-38339-4(2))* Little Brown & Co.
—A Tale of Magic... (Tale of Magic... Ser.: 1). (ENG.). (J). (gr. 3-7). 2020. 512p. pap. 9.99 *(978-0-316-52351-6(8))* 2019. (Illus.). 496p. 18.99 *(978-0-316-52347-9(X))* 2019. 720p. pap. 30.99 *(978-0-316-42633-6(4))* Little, Brown Bks. for Young Readers.
—A Tale of Sorcery... 2021. (ENG., (J). (gr. 3-7). (Tale of Magic... Ser.: 3). Illus.). 496p. 18.99 *(978-0-316-05599-4(9))*; 576p. 20.99 *(978-0-316-30096-4(9))* Little, Brown Bks. for Young Readers.
—A Tale of Witchcraft... Dorman, Brandon, illus. 2020. 432p. (J). *(978-0-316-59120-1(3))* Little Brown & Co.
—A Tale of Witchcraft... (Tale of Magic... Ser.: 2). (ENG.). (J). (gr. 3-7). 2021. 464p. pap. 9.99 *(978-0-316-52354-7(2))* 2020. (Illus.). 448p. 18.99 *(978-0-316-52356-1(9))* 2020. 528p. pap. 26.99 *(978-0-316-54175-6(3))* Little, Brown Bks. for Young Readers.
—The Wishing Spell. Dorman, Brandon, illus. 2012. 438p. (J). pap. *(978-0-316-45393-6(5))* Little Brown & Co.
—The Wishing Spell. 2013. (Land of Stories Ser.: 1). (J). lib. bdg. 20.85 *(978-0-606-31746-7(5))* Turtleback.
—Worlds Collide. Dorman, Brandon, illus. 2017. 434p. (J). *(978-0-316-43920-6(7))* Little Brown & Co.
Colfer, Chris & Dorman, Brandon. The Land of Stories the Wishing Spell. 2013. pap. *(978-0-545-64793-9(2))* Scholastic, Inc.
Colfer, Eoin. Artemis Fowl, 3 vols., Set. 2010. (Artemis Fowl Ser.). (ENG.). 944p. (J). (gr. 5-17). pap. 19.99 *(978-1-4231-3681-1(0))* Disney Pr.
—Artemis Fowl. (Artemis Fowl Ser.: Bk. 1). (FRE.). pap. 34.95 *(978-2-07-054681-7(0))* Gallimard, Editions FRA. Dist: Distribooks, Inc.

MNO

—Artemis Fowl. (Artemis Fowl Ser.: Bk. 1). pap. 34.95 *(978-88-04-49788-2(2))* Mondadori ITA. Dist: Distribooks, Inc.

—Artemis Fowl. (Artemis Fowl Ser.: 1). (YA). 2007. 1.25 *(978-1-4193-6020-6(5))* 2006. 52.75 *(978-1-4193-6023-7(X))* 2006. 54.75 *(978-1-4193-6021-3(3))* 2006. 54.75 *(978-1-4193-6026-8(4))* 2006. 132.75 *(978-1-4193-6022-0(1))* 2005. 56.75 *(978-1-4193-6024-4(8))* Recorded Bks., Inc.

—Artemis Fowl. 2009. (Artemis Fowl Ser.: 1). (J). (gr. 5-8). lib. bdg. 19.65 *(978-0-613-60637-0(X))* Turtleback.

—The Atlantis Complex. 2012. (Artemis Fowl Ser.: 7). (J). lib. bdg. 19.65 *(978-0-606-23614-0(7))* Turtleback.

—Eoin Colfer: Artemis Fowl: the Graphic Novel. 2019. (Artemis Fowl Ser.). (ENG., Illus.). 128p. (J). (gr. 3-7). 21.99 *(978-1-368-04314-4(3)*, Disney-Hyperion) Disney Publishing Worldwide.

—Fowl Twins, the-A Fowl Twins Novel, Book 1. 2019. (Artemis Fowl Ser.). (ENG.). 368p. (J). (gr. 5-9). 18.99 *(978-1-368-04375-5(5)*, Disney-Hyperion) Disney Publishing Worldwide.

—The Last Guardian. 2014. (Artemis Fowl Ser.: 8). (J). lib. bdg. 19.65 *(978-0-606-32288-1(4))* Turtleback.

—EL MUNDO SUBTERRÁNEO (ARTEMIS FOWL 1) (Artemis Fowl Ser.: Bk. 1). (SPA.). 288p. pap. *(978-84-8441-115-4(X)*, MO31567) Grijalbo Mondadori, S.A.-Montena.

—The Opal Deception. 2006. (Artemis Fowl Ser.: Bk. 4). 17.10 *(978-0-7569-6828-1(3))* Disney Pr.

—The Opal Deception. (Artemis Fowl Ser.: 4). (J). 2007. 1.25 *(978-1-4193-6041-1(8))* 2006. 69.75 *(978-1-4193-6047-3(7))* 2006. 72.75 *(978-1-4193-6045-9(0))* Recorded Bks., Inc.

—The Time Paradox. 2009. (Artemis Fowl Ser.: 6). (J). lib. bdg. 19.65 *(978-0-606-10579-8(4))* Turtleback.

Compestine, Ying Chang. The Runaway Wok: A Chinese New Year Tale. Serra, Sebastia, illus. 2011. 32p. (J). (gr. 1-3). 17.99 *(978-0-525-42068-2(1)*, Dutton Books for Young Readers) Penguin Young Readers Group.

Condenzio, John. Cocoa the Witch Cat. 2013. 20p. pap. 24.95 *(978-1-62709-264-7(1))* America Star Bks.

Conlon, Mara. Nutcracker Ballet: A Book, Theater, & Paper Doll Foldout Play Set. Gershman, Jo, illus. 2007. (Foldout Playset Ser.). 30p. (J). 17.99 *(978-1-59359-885-3(8))* Peter Pauper Pr. Inc.

Connolly, MarcyKate. Comet Rising. 2019. (Shadow Weaver Ser.: 2). (ENG.). (J). (gr. 3-9). 320p. pap. 12.99 *(978-1-4926-9152-5(6))*; 304p. 16.99 *(978-1-4926-4998-4(8))* Sourcebooks, Inc.

—Monstrous. 2016. (J). lib. bdg. 18.40 *(978-0-606-38136-9(8))* Turtleback.

—Shadow Weaver. 2018. (Shadow Weaver Ser.: 1). (ENG.). 336p. (J). (gr. 3-9). pap. 7.99 *(978-1-4926-6798-8(6))* Sourcebooks, Inc.

Connolly, Tina. Seriously Wicked. 2016. (YA). lib. bdg. 20.85 *(978-0-606-38783-5(8))* Turtleback.

Cook, Eileen. Gnome Invasion, 3. 2011. (Fourth Grade Fairy Ser.: 3). (ENG.). 160p. (J). (gr. 3-7). pap. 6.99 *(978-1-4169-9813-6(6))* Simon & Schuster, Inc.

Cook, Jeremy. Illusion Meets Reality. 2008. 116p. pap. 19.95 *(978-1-60813-059-7(2))* America Star Bks.

—The Illusion Stick. 2008. 115p. pap. 19.95 *(978-1-60474-705-8(6))* America Star Bks.

Cook, Maureen McNamee. Is There Magic in the Mountains, Mamma? Connell, Jacqueline, illus. 2008. 23p. pap. 24.95 *(978-1-60672-673-0(0))* America Star Bks.

Coomber, Suzanne. The Magic Sandcastle. 2011. 16p. 8.32 *(978-1-4520-9612-4(0))* AuthorHouse.

Coombs, Kate. The Runaway Princess. l.t. ed. 2007. (Literacy Bridge Middle Reader Ser.). 325p. (J). (gr. 3-7). 22.95 *(978-0-7862-9633-0(X))* Thorndike Pr.

Cooper, Abby. Friend or Fiction. 2019. (ENG.). 272p. (J). (gr. 5). 16.99 *(978-1-62354-108-8(5))* Charlesbridge Publishing, Inc.

Cooper, Brigitte Henry. Creepy Customers. Napoli, Elena, illus. 2018. (Odd Jobs Ser.). (ENG.). 48p. (J). (gr. 3-7). lib. bdg. 34.21 *(978-1-5321-3188-2(7)*, 28481, Spellbound) Magic Wagon.

—Peculiar Packages. Napoli, Elena, illus. 2018. (Odd Jobs Ser.). (ENG.). 48p. (J). (gr. 3-7). lib. bdg. 34.21 *(978-1-5321-3189-9(5)*, 28483, Spellbound) Magic Wagon.

Cooper, Catherine. The Golden Acorn. 2nd rev. ed. 2010. (Adventures of Jack Brenin Ser.). (ENG., Illus.). 376p. (J). pap. *(978-1-906821-65-4(8))* Infinite Ideas.

—The Lost Treasure of Annwn. 2012. (ENG., Illus.). 320p. (J). pap. *(978-1-908984-04-3(X))* Infinite Ideas.

Cooper, Susan. The Boggart. 2018. (Boggart Ser.). (ENG.). 240p. (J). (gr. 3-7). pap. 7.99 *(978-1-5344-2011-3(8)*, McElderry, Margaret K. Bks.) McElderry, Margaret K. Bks.

—The Boggart. 2004. 196p. (gr. 3-7). 17.00 *(978-0-7569-3932-8(1))* Perfection Learning Corp.

—The Boggart Fights Back. 2018. (Boggart Ser.). (ENG., Illus.). 224p. (J). (gr. 3-7). 16.99 *(978-1-5344-0629-2(8)*, McElderry, Margaret K. Bks.) McElderry, Margaret K. Bks.

—The Dark Is Rising. 2009. 7.64 *(978-0-7348-2212-8(3)*, Everbind) Marco Bk. Co.

—The Dark Is Rising. 15.85 *(978-0-7569-8464-9(5))* Perfection Learning Corp.

—The Dark Is Rising. (Dark Is Rising Sequence Ser.). 244p. (YA). (gr. 5-18). pap. 4.99 *(978-0-8072-1533-3(3)*, Listening Library) Random Hse. Audio Publishing Group.

—Over Sea, under Stone. 2013. (Dark Is Rising Sequence Ser.: 1). (ENG., Illus.). 288p. (J). (gr. 3-7). 19.99 *(978-1-4424-9592-0(8)*, McElderry, Margaret K. Bks.) McElderry, Margaret K. Bks.

Coppock, Phil & Bower's 2008-2009 4th Grade Class. Rubber Tuesday. 2010. 70p. pap. 12.95 *(978-1-4327-5751-9(2))* Outskirts Pr., Inc.

Corbett, Sue. 12 Again. 2007. 240p. (J). (gr. 5-18). 6.99 *(978-0-14-240729-5(1)*, Puffin Books) Penguin Young Readers Group.

Córdova, Zoraida. Bruja Born. 2019. (Brooklyn Brujas Ser.: 2). (ENG.). 352p. (YA). (gr. 8-12). pap. 10.99 *(978-1-7282-0986-9(2))* Sourcebooks, Inc.

—Labyrinth Lost. 2017. (Brooklyn Brujas Ser.: 1). (ENG.). 352p. (YA). (gr. 8-12). pap. 10.99 *(978-1-4926-2316-8(4))* Sourcebooks, Inc.

Corlett, William. The Door in the Tree. 2010. (Magician's House Quartet Ser.: 2). (ENG.). 304p. (YA). (gr. 5-8). pap. 13.99 *(978-1-4424-1414-3(6)*, Simon Pulse) Simon Pulse.

—The Steps up the Chimney. 2011. (Magician's House Quartet Ser.: 1). (ENG.). 288p. (YA). (gr. 7). pap. 13.99 *(978-1-4424-2935-2(6)*, Simon Pulse) Simon Pulse.

Cornelia, Funke. Igraine the Brave. Bell, Anthea, tr. Cornelia, Funke, illus. l.t. ed. 2008. (Thorndike Literacy Bridge Middle Reader Ser.). (Illus.). 259p. (J). (gr. 4-7). 23.95 *(978-1-4104-0341-4(6))* Thorndike Pr.

—Inkheart Trilogy Boxed Set: Inkheart, Inkspell, Inkdeath. 2003. (Inkheart Trilogy: Bks. 1-3). 544p. (J). 60.00 *(978-0-439-61671-3(9)*, Chicken Hse., The) Scholastic, Inc.

—Inkspell. Bell, Anthea, tr. from GER. 2007. (Illus.). 653p. (gr. 3-7). 21.00 *(978-0-7569-7917-1(X))* Perfection Learning Corp.

—Inkspell. 2007. (Inkheart Trilogy Ser.: 2). lib. bdg. 22.10 *(978-1-4177-7471-5(1))* Turtleback.

Cornwell, Betsy. Mechanica. 2016. (ENG.). 320p. (YA). (gr. 7). pap. 8.99 *(978-0-544-66868-3(5)*, 1625494, Clarion Bks.) HarperCollins Pubs.

—Mechanica. 2016. lib. bdg. 19.65 *(978-0-606-37999-1(1))* Turtleback.

—Venturess. 2018. (ENG.). 336p. (YA). (gr. 7). pap. 9.99 *(978-1-328-94164-0(7)*, 1705019, Clarion Bks.) HarperCollins Pubs.

—Venturess. 2018. lib. bdg. 20.85 *(978-0-606-40995-7(5))* Turtleback.

Cossanteli, Veronica. The Extincts. Muradov, Roman, illus. 2016. (ENG.). 240p. (J). 27.99 *(978-1-62779-403-9(4)*, 900149181, Holt, Henry & Co. Bks. For Young Readers) Holt, Henry & Co.

Coughlin, Jennie Rose. The Purple Scarf. Howes, Bryan Arthur, illus. 2008. 20p. per. 24.95 *(978-1-60441-733-3(1))* America Star Bks.

Coutinho, Lucy M. The Rangers of Andor: The Beginning. 2011. 278p. pap. 27.95 *(978-1-4626-1014-3(5))* America Star Bks.

Coven, Wanda. Heidi Heckelbeck 3 Books In 1! Heidi Heckelbeck Has a Secret; Heidi Heckelbeck Casts a Spell; Heidi Heckelbeck & the Cookie Contest. Burris, Priscilla, illus. 2014. (Heidi Heckelbeck Ser.). (ENG.). 384p. (J). (gr. k-4). pap. 8.99 *(978-1-4814-2771-5(7)*, Little Simon) Little Simon.

—Heidi Heckelbeck & the Big Mix-Up. Burris, Priscilla, illus. 2016. (Heidi Heckelbeck Ser.: 18). (ENG.). 128p. (J). (gr. k-4). pap. 5.99 *(978-1-4814-7169-5(4)*, Little Simon) Little Simon.

—Heidi Heckelbeck & the Christmas Surprise. Burris, Priscilla, illus. 2013. (Heidi Heckelbeck Ser.: 9). (ENG.). 128p. (J). (gr. k-2). 17.99 *(978-1-4424-8125-1(0))*; pap. 6.99 *(978-1-4424-8124-4(2))* Little Simon. (Little Simon).

—Heidi Heckelbeck & the Christmas Surprise. 2013. (Heidi Heckelbeck Ser.: 9). lib. bdg. 14.75 *(978-0-606-32325-3(2))* Turtleback.

—Heidi Heckelbeck & the Cookie Contest. Burris, Priscilla, illus. 2012. (Heidi Heckelbeck Ser.: 3). (ENG.). 128p. (J). (gr. k-4). 17.99 *(978-1-4424-4166-8(6))*; pap. 6.99 *(978-1-4424-4165-1(8))* Little Simon. (Little Simon).

—Heidi Heckelbeck & the Cookie Contest. 2012. (Heidi Heckelbeck Ser.: 3). lib. bdg. 16.00 *(978-0-606-26328-3(4))* Turtleback.

—Heidi Heckelbeck & the Magic Puppy. Burris, Priscilla, illus. 2017. (Heidi Heckelbeck Ser.: 20). (ENG.). 128p. (J). (gr. k-4). pap. 5.99 *(978-1-4814-9521-9(6)*, Little Simon) Little Simon.

—Heidi Heckelbeck & the Never-Ending Day. Burris, Priscilla, illus. 2017. (Heidi Heckelbeck Ser.: 21). (ENG.). 128p. (J). (gr. k-4). 17.99 *(978-1-4814-9525-7(9))*; pap. 6.99 *(978-1-4814-9524-0(0))* Little Simon. (Little Simon).

—Heidi Heckelbeck & the Tie-Dyed Bunny. 2014. (Heidi Heckelbeck Ser.: 10). lib. bdg. 16.00 *(978-0-606-35429-5(8))* Turtleback.

—Heidi Heckelbeck Goes to Camp! Burris, Priscilla, illus. 2013. (Heidi Heckelbeck Ser.: 8). (ENG.). 128p. (J). (gr. k-4). 17.99 *(978-1-4424-6481-0(X))*; pap. 6.99 *(978-1-4424-6480-3(1))* Little Simon. (Little Simon).

—Heidi Heckelbeck Goes to Camp! 2013. (Heidi Heckelbeck Ser.: 8). lib. bdg. 16.00 *(978-0-606-32031-3(8))* Turtleback.

—Heidi Heckelbeck Has a New Best Friend. Burris, Priscilla, illus. 2018. (Heidi Heckelbeck Ser.: 22). (ENG.). 128p. (J). (gr. k-4). 17.99 *(978-1-5344-1108-1(9))*; pap. 6.99 *(978-1-5344-1107-4(0))* Little Simon. (Little Simon).

—Heidi Heckelbeck in Disguise. Burris, Priscilla, illus. 2012. (Heidi Heckelbeck Ser.: 4). (ENG.). 128p. (J). (gr. k-2). 17.99 *(978-1-4424-4169-9(0))*; pap. 6.99 *(978-1-4424-4168-2(2))* Little Simon. (Little Simon).

—Heidi Heckelbeck in Disguise. 2012. (Heidi Heckelbeck Ser.: 4). lib. bdg. 16.00 *(978-0-606-26329-0(2))* Turtleback.

—Heidi Heckelbeck Is Not a Thief! Burris, Priscilla, illus. 2015. (Heidi Heckelbeck Ser.: 13). (ENG.). 128p. (J). (gr. k-4). pap. 5.99 *(978-1-4814-2324-3(X)*, Little Simon) Little Simon.

—Heidi Heckelbeck Is So Totally Grounded! Burris, Priscilla, illus. 2018. (Heidi Heckelbeck Ser.: 24). (ENG.). 128p. (J). (gr. k-4). 16.99 *(978-1-5344-2645-0(0))*; pap. 5.99 *(978-1-5344-2644-3(2))* Little Simon. (Little Simon).

—Heidi Heckelbeck Is the Bestest Babysitter! Burris, Priscilla, illus. 2015. (Heidi Heckelbeck Ser.: 16). (ENG.). 128p. (J). (gr. k-4). pap. 6.99 *(978-1-4814-4630-3(4)*, Little Simon) Little Simon.

—Heidi Heckelbeck Makes a Wish. 2016. (Heidi Heckelbeck Ser.: 17). lib. bdg. 16.00 *(978-0-606-38962-4(8))* Turtleback.

—Heidi Heckelbeck Makes a Wish: Super Special! Burris, Priscilla, illus. 2016. (Hedi Heckelbeck Ser.: 17). (ENG.). 160p. (J). (gr. k-4). pap. 6.99 *(978-1-4814-6613-4(5)*, Little Simon) Little Simon.

—Heidi Heckelbeck Says "Cheese!" Burris, Priscilla, illus. 2015. (Heidi Heckelbeck Ser.: 14). (ENG.). 128p. (J). (gr. k-4). pap. 6.99 *(978-1-4814-2327-4(4)*, Little Simon) Little Simon.

—Heidi Heckelbeck Tries Out for the Team. Burris, Priscilla, illus. 2017. (Heidi Heckelbeck Ser.: 19). (ENG.). 128p. (J). (gr. k-4). pap. 6.99 *(978-1-4814-7172-5(4)*, Little Simon) Little Simon.

Coville, Bruce. Cursed. 2016. (Enchanted Files Ser.: 1). lib. bdg. 17.20 *(978-0-606-38460-5(X))* Turtleback.

—Goblins in the Castle. Coville, Katherine, illus. 2015. (ENG.). 208p. (J). (gr. 3-7). 17.99 *(978-1-4814-3900-8(6)*, Aladdin) Simon & Schuster Children's Publishing.

—Goblins on the Prowl. 2015. (ENG., Illus.). 272p. (J). (gr. 3-7). 17.99 *(978-1-4169-1440-2(4)*, Aladdin) Simon & Schuster Children's Publishing.

—Jennifer Murdley's Toad: A Magic Shop Book. Lippincott, Gary A., illus. 2007. (Magic Shop Book Ser.: 3). (ENG.). 176p. (J). (gr. 5-7). pap. 9.99 *(978-0-15-206246-0(7)*, 1198731, Clarion Bks.) HarperCollins Pubs.

—The Monster's Ring: A Magic Shop Book. Coville, Katherine, illus. 2008. (Magic Shop Book Ser.: 1). (ENG.). 128p. (J). (gr. 5-7). pap. 7.99 *(978-0-15-206442-6(7)*, 1199254, Clarion Bks.) HarperCollins Pubs.

—The Skull of Truth. (Magic Shop Bks.). 208p. (J). (gr. 5-7). pap. 3.99 *(978-0-8072-1538-8(4)*, Listening Library) Random Hse. Audio Publishing Group.

Cowey, James. William Snottengrout - Gangor's Reign. 2006. 104p. per. *(978-1-84667-006-0(3))* Derwent Pr., The.

—William Snottengrout - Quapta's Revenge. 2006. 104p. per. *(978-1-84667-023-7(3))* Derwent Pr., The.

Cowsar, Susan. The Magic Flower. 2013. 58p. pap. 10.99 *(978-1-62697-943-7(X))* Salem Author Services.

COX, Margaret. The Emerald-fire. 2010. 166p. pap. 11.50 *(978-1-4461-3379-8(6))* Lulu Pr., Inc.

—The Soul-pearl. 2010. (ENG.). 169p. pap. 11.50 *(978-1-4457-5679-0(X))* Lulu Pr., Inc.

Cox, R. The Lonely Wizard Named Wizzy: The Apprentice. 2009. 16p. pap. 8.49 *(978-1-4490-2236-5(7))* AuthorHouse.

Crabtree, Julie. Discovering Pig Magic. 2008. (ENG.). 144p. (J). (gr. 2-8). 16.95 *(978-1-57131-683-7(3))*; pap. 6.95 *(978-1-57131-684-4(1))* Milkweed Editions.

Craig, Barbara J. Santa's Magical Key. 2010. 20p. 10.49 *(978-1-4520-4399-9(X))* AuthorHouse.

Crawford, Hannah. The Fight for Light by Hannah Crawford. 2012. (ENG., Illus.). 86p. pap. 8.50 *(978-1-78035-335-7(9)*, Fastprint Publishing) Upfront Publishing Ltd. GBR. Dist: Printondemand-worldwide.com.

—The Fight with Darkness. 2013. (ENG., Illus.). 79p. pap. 8.49 *(978-1-78035-586-3(6)*, Fastprint Publishing) Upfront Publishing Ltd. GBR. Dist: Printondemand-worldwide.com.

Creamer, Joan Klatil. The Magic Sceptre - the Legend of Blue Santa Claus. Creamer, Joan Klatil, illus. 2006. (Illus.). 32p. (J). 16.95 *(978-0-9778476-3-1(2))* Silver Snowflake Publishing.

—The Magic Sceptre & Reginald the Rabbit. 2007. (Illus.). 32p. (J). 16.95 *(978-0-9778476-5-5(9))* Silver Snowflake Publishing.

Croggon, Alison. The Bone Queen: Pellinor: Cadvan's Story. 2018. (Pellinor Ser.). (ENG.). 416p. (J). (gr. 7). pap. 12.99 *(978-1-5362-0370-7(X))* Candlewick Pr.

—The Riddle: Book Two of Pellinor. 2017. (Pellinor Ser.). (ENG.). 512p. (J). (gr. 7). pap. 9.99 *(978-0-7636-9444-9(4))* Candlewick Pr.

—The Singing: Book Four of Pellinor. 2017. (Pellinor Ser.). (ENG.). 496p. (J). (gr. 7). pap. 9.99 *(978-0-7636-9446-3(0))* Candlewick Pr.

Crommett, Lora. The Blue Witch Who Dared to Be Different. 2013. 64p. 14.99 *(978-1-62951-025-5(4))* Mockingbird Lane Pr.

Cronin, Doreen. Bloom. Small, David, illus. 2016. (ENG.). 40p. (J). (gr. -1-3). 17.99 *(978-1-4424-0620-9(8))* Simon & Schuster Children's Publishing.

Crossley-Holland, Kevin. At the Crossing-Places. 2004. (Arthur Trilogy). (Illus.). 394p. (YA). (gr. 7-12). 15.65 *(978-0-7569-3182-7(7))* Perfection Learning Corp.

Crowder, Melanie. A Nearer Moon. 2019. (Penworthy Picks Middle School Ser.). (ENG.). 160p. (J). (gr. 4-5). 18.96 *(978-1-64310-941-1(3))* Penworthy Co., LLC, The.

—A Nearer Moon. (ENG., Illus.). (J). (gr. 3-7). 2016. 176p. pap. 7.99 *(978-1-4814-4149-0(3)*, Atheneum Bks. for Young Readers) 2015. 160p. 16.99 *(978-1-4814-4148-3(5))* Simon & Schuster Children's Publishing.

—A Nearer Moon. 2016. (ENG.). 176p. (J). (gr. 3-7). 18.40 *(978-0-606-39238-9(6))* Turtleback.

—A Way Between Worlds. 2020. (Lighthouse Keepers Ser.). (ENG.). 224p. (J). (gr. 3-7). pap. 7.99 *(978-1-5344-0519-6(4))* Simon & Schuster Children's Publishing.

Cruz, Wilfredo. Charlie's Box: A Story about a Boy & His Magical Box. 2013. 24p. pap. 24.95 *(978-1-63000-514-6(2))* America Star Bks.

Culpepper, R. B. W. Ellena & the Magic Lamp. 2011. 182p. pap. 24.95 *(978-1-4626-2830-8(3))* America Star Bks.

Cumyn, Alan. After Sylvia. 2nd ed. 2008. (ENG.). 200p. (J). (gr. 3-6). pap. 8.95 *(978-0-88899-868-2(6))* Groundwood Bks. CAN. Dist: Publishers Group West (PGW).

Cunningham, Mary. Cynthias Attic Magicians Castle. 2009. 158p. pap. 10.99 *(978-1-59080-656-2(5))* Echelon Press Publishing.

Curnin, V. J. Millie's Magic Wellies. 2009. (Illus.). 20p. pap. 10.49 *(978-1-4389-8258-8(5))* AuthorHouse.

Curry, Kenneth. The Legend of the Dancing Trees: An African American Folk Tale. 2007. 111p. (J). per. 14.95 *(978-0-9798364-0-4(9))* Curry Brothers Publishing Group.

Curry, Kenneth, et al. The Legend of the Dancing Tees Teachers Resource: The Legend of the Dancing Trees. 2007.Tr. of Teachers Resource. per. 19.95 *(978-0-9798364-1-1(7))* Curry Brothers Publishing Group.

Curtis, Jillian M. The Little Prince & His Magic Wand. 2005. (Illus.). 28p. (J). 24.95 *(978-1-59858-015-0(9))*; pap. 16.95 *(978-1-59858-010-5(8))* Dog Ear Publishing, LLC.

Cushman, Karen. Grayling's Song. 2020. (ENG.). 240p. (J). (gr. 3-7). pap. 7.99 *(978-0-358-09748-8(7)*, 1747604, Clarion Bks.) HarperCollins Pubs.

Cussler, Clive. The Adventures of Hotsy Totsy. 2011. (ENG., Illus.). 166p. (J). (gr. 3-7). 7.99 *(978-0-14-241873-4(0)*, Puffin Books) Penguin Young Readers Group.

Cyber. The Transdimensional War Series. 2006. 67p. pap. 16.95 *(978-1-4241-2778-8(5))* PublishAmerica, Inc.

Cypess, Leah. Death Sworn. 2015. (ENG.). 368p. (YA). (gr. 8). pap. 9.99 *(978-0-06-222122-3(1)*, Greenwillow Bks.) HarperCollins Pubs.

Cyprus, Naomi. Sisters of Glass. (Sisters of Glass Ser.: 1). (ENG.). (J). (gr. 3-7). 2018. 400p. pap. 9.99 *(978-0-06-245849-0(3))* 2017. 384p. 16.99 *(978-0-06-245847-6(7))* HarperCollins Pubs. (HarperCollins).

Cyrus, Kurt. Be a Good Dragon. Cyrus, Kurt, illus. 2018. (ENG., Illus.). 32p. (J). (gr. k-3). 16.99 *(978-1-58536-383-4(9)*, 204395) Sleeping Bear Pr.

Daffern, Brian. Prince Albert Bk. 2: The Beast School. 2005. 160p. (YA). per. 10.95 *(978-0-9709104-6-2(0))* Hickory Tales Publishing.

Dahl, Michael. The Assistant Vanishes!, 1 vol. Weber, Lisa K., illus. 2013. (Hocus Pocus Hotel Ser.). (ENG.). 112p. (J). (gr. 3-6). lib. bdg. 25.32 *(978-1-4342-4101-6(7)*, 119822, Stone Arch Bks.) Capstone.

—Shadow Shoes: And Other Scary Tales. Bonet, Xavier, illus. 2017. (Michael Dahl's Really Scary Stories Ser.). (ENG.). 72p. (J). (gr. 1-3). lib. bdg. 25.32 *(978-1-4965-4900-6(7)*, 135652, Stone Arch Bks.) Capstone.

Dahl, Roald. El Dedo Magico. Marriot, Pat, illus.Tr. of Magic Finger. (SPA.). 74p. (J). (gr. 3-5). 9.95 *(978-968-19-0621-4(7))* Aguilar Editorial MEX. Dist: Santillana USA Publishing Co., Inc.

—George's Marvelous Medicine. Blake, Quentin, illus. 2007. (ENG.). 112p. (J). (gr. 3-7). 7.99 *(978-0-14-241035-6(7)*, Puffin Books) Penguin Young Readers Group.

—George's Marvelous Medicine. Blake, Quentin, illus. 2008. 88p. (gr. 4-7). 18.00 *(978-0-7569-8777-0(6))* Perfection Learning Corp.

—George's Marvelous Medicine. 2007. lib. bdg. 18.40 *(978-1-4177-8619-0(1))* Turtleback.

—James et la Grosse Peche.Tr. of James & the Giant Peach. (FRE.). (J). pap. 17.95 *(978-2-07-051374-1(2))* Gallimard, Editions FRA. Dist: Distribooks, Inc.

—The Magic Finger. Blake, Quentin, illus. 2009. (ENG.). 96p. (J). (gr. 3-7). 7.99 *(978-0-14-241385-2(2)*, Puffin Books) Penguin Young Readers Group.

—The Magic Finger. Blake, Quentin, illus. 2003. (CHI.). 133p. (J). pap. 11.70 *(978-957-574-476-2(4))* Youth Cultural Publishing Co. CHN. Dist: Chinasprout, Inc.

Daily, Lorrie Ann. The Castlewood Twins, the Magic Begins. 2008. 196p. pap. 12.95 *(978-0-9820479-8-9(3))* Peppertree Pr., The.

Daines, Julie. Unraveled: A Tale of True Love. 2014. 192p. (J). pap. 14.99 *(978-1-62108-627-7(5))* Covenant Communications, Inc.

Dalon, Phillip A. Clanwickie: Life High in the Kabalas. 2011. 232p. pap. 24.95 *(978-1-4626-4033-1(8))* America Star Bks.

Dalton, Kippy. Nanna's Magic Globe. 2016. (Spring Forward Ser.). (J). (gr. k). *(978-1-4900-2253-6(8))* Benchmark Education Co.

Dalton, Susan. The Magic Glasses. 2012. 36p. pap. 19.95 *(978-1-4685-2586-1(7))* AuthorHouse.

Daly, Stuart. The Final Battle. 2016. (Brotherhood of Thieves Ser.: 3). 288p. (J). (gr. 4-7). pap. 9.99 *(978-0-85798-538-5(8))* Random Hse. Australia AUS. Dist: Independent Pubs. Group.

Damitz, Charlie. Diving for el Corazon. Diefendorf, Cathy, illus. 2007. (ENG.). 101p. (J). pap. 10.95 *(978-0-9744446-3-5(4))* All About Kids Publishing.

D'Angelo, Elaina R. The Magic Book of E, 1 vol. 2010. 48p. pap. 16.95 *(978-1-4489-3949-7(6))* America Star Bks.

Daniels, Linda. The Magic Gazebo. 2012. 36p. pap. 18.41 *(978-1-4669-6165-4(1))* Trafford Publishing.

Danielski, A. The Nick & Austin Chronicles: The Pirate Ship's Magic & a New Home. 2013. 28p. pap. 24.95 *(978-1-4626-7709-2(6))* America Star Bks.

Dao, Julie C. Kingdom of the Blazing Phoenix. 2019. (Rise of the Empress Ser.: 2). 384p. (YA). (gr. 9). pap. 10.99 *(978-1-5247-3834-1(4)*, Penguin Books) Penguin Young Readers Group.

Darcy, Kate. Winnie Windmill: The Village Fete. 2012. (Illus.). 52p. pap. 24.40 *(978-1-4678-8382-5(4))* AuthorHouse.

Dark, Gregory. Susie & the Snow-it-alls. 2011. (ENG., Illus.). 286p. (J). (gr. -1-12). pap. 24.95 *(978-1-84694-881-7(9))* Hunt, John Publishing Ltd. GBR. Dist: National Bk. Network.

Darlison, Aleesah. Ellabeth's Light. Brailsford, Jill, illus. 2017. (Unicorn Riders Ser.). (ENG.). 112p. (J). (gr. 3-5). pap. 5.95 *(978-1-4795-6559-7(8)*, 128549, Picture Window Bks.) Capstone.

—Ellabeth's Test. Brailsford, Jill, illus. 2017. (Unicorn Riders Ser.). (ENG.). 112p. (J). (gr. 3-5). pap. 5.95 *(978-1-4795-6555-9(5)*, 128545, Picture Window Bks.) Capstone.

—Krystal's Charge. Brailsford, Jill, illus. 2017. (Unicorn Riders Ser.). (ENG.). 112p. (J). (gr. 3-5). pap. 5.95 *(978-1-4795-6558-0(X)*, 128548, Picture Window Bks.) Capstone.

—Krystal's Choice. Brailsford, Jill, illus. 2017. (Unicorn Riders Ser.). (ENG.). 112p. (J). (gr. 3-5). pap. 5.95 *(978-1-4795-6554-2(7)*, 128544, Picture Window Bks.) Capstone.

—Quinn's Riddles. Brailsford, Jill, illus. 2017. (Unicorn Riders Ser.). (ENG.). 112p. (J). (gr. 3-5). pap. 5.95 *(978-1-4795-6552-8(0)*, 128542, Picture Window Bks.) Capstone.

—Quinn's Truth. Brailsford, Jill, illus. 2017. (Unicorn Riders Ser.). (ENG.). 112p. (J). (gr. 3-5). pap. 5.95 *(978-1-4795-6556-6(3)*, 128546, Picture Window Bks.) Capstone.

—Willow's Challenge. Brailsford, Jill, illus. 2017. (Unicorn Riders Ser.). (ENG.). 112p. (J). (gr. 3-5). pap. 5.95 *(978-1-4795-6553-5(9)*, 128543, Picture Window Bks.) Capstone.

—Willow's Victory. Brailsford, Jill, illus. 2017. (Unicorn Riders Ser.). (ENG.). 112p. (J). (gr. 3-5). pap. 5.95 *(978-1-4795-6557-3(1)*, 128547, Picture Window Bks.) Capstone.

DasGupta, Sayantani. Game of Stars (Kiranmala & the Kingdom Beyond #2) (Kiranmala & the Kingdom Beyond Ser.: 2). (ENG.). 384p. (J). (gr. 3-7). 2020. pap. 8.99 *(978-1-338-18574-4(8))* 2019. (Illus.). 17.99 *(978-1-338-18573-7(X))* Scholastic, Inc. (Scholastic Pr.).

—The Serpent's Secret (Kiranmala & the Kingdom Beyond #1) (Kiranmala & the Kingdom Beyond Ser.: 1). (ENG.). 368p. (J). (gr. 3-7). 2019. pap. 8.99 *(978-1-338-18571-3(3))* 2018. 18.99 *(978-1-338-18570-6(5))* Scholastic, Inc. (Scholastic Pr.).

Dashney, John. The Adventures of Walter the Weremouse; the Adventures of Mishka the Mousewere. Somerville, Sheila, illus. 2005. 202p. (J). pap. *(978-0-9633236-7-5(9))* Storm Peak Pr.

Davenport, Kelly. Do Hotdogs Grow on Trees? 2010. 32p. pap. 17.99 *(978-1-4520-6636-3(1))* AuthorHouse.

Davidson, Susanna. Stories of Dolls. Wanert, Amandine, illus. 2006. 48p. (J). (gr. 2-5). 8.99 *(978-0-7945-1327-6(1),* Usborne) EDC Publishing.

—Stories of Magic Ponies. Costa, Jana, illus. 2007. (Young Reading Series 1 Gift Bks). 48p. (J). 8.99 *(978-0-7945-1790-8(0),* Usborne) EDC Publishing.

Davies, Jacqueline. The Magic Trap. 2014. (Lemonade War Ser.: 5). (ENG., Illus.). 272p. (J). (gr. 3-7). 18.99 *(978-0-544-05289-5(7),* 1533150, Clarion Bks.) HarperCollins Pubs.

Davies, Peter. Molly's Magic Pencil: The Blue Genie. 2011. 28p. (gr. 1-2). 14.99 *(978-1-4567-3018-5(5))* AuthorHouse.

—Molly's Magic Pencil: The Flying Carpet. 2010. 32p. 14.99 *(978-1-4520-4830-7(4))* AuthorHouse.

Davis, Graeme. Re-Read Harry Potter & the Chamber of Secrets Today! an Unauthorized Guide. 2008. 112p. pap. 15.49 *(978-1-934840-72-6(5))* Nimble Bks. LLC.

Davis, Kent. A Riddle in Ruby #2: the Changer's Key. 2016. (Riddle in Ruby Ser.: 2). (ENG.). 448p. (J). (gr. 3-7). 17.99 *(978-0-06-236837-9(0),* Greenwillow Bks.) HarperCollins Pubs.

Davis, Marshall L. Og the Magical Green Frog. 2012. (ENG.). (J). pap. *(978-1-4675-4055-1(2))* Independent Pub.

Davis, Martine. There's a Red Hippo at My Door. 2012. 24p. pap. 13.99 *(978-1-4772-8070-6(7))* AuthorHouse.

Dawley, Linda. The Tooth Fairy's Mistake. 2nd ed. 2014. (ENG.). 114p. (J). pap. *(978-0-9941011-6-7(3),* The Little Red Hen Community Pr.) CCB Publishing.

Day, K. The Silver Bullet: Tour of the Universe. 2010. 120p. pap. 12.49 *(978-1-4490-6534-8(1))* AuthorHouse.

de Becerra, Katya. What the Woods Keep. 2018. (ENG.). 384p. (J). pap. *(978-1-76063-730-9(0))* ETT Imprint.

—What the Woods Keep. 2019. (ENG.). 400p. (YA). pap. 10.99 *(978-1-250-21167-5(0),* 900174375) Square Fish.

De Campi, Alex, et al. My Little Pony: Friends Forever Omnibus, Vol. 1, Vol. 1. 2016. (MLP FF Omnibus Ser.: 1). (Illus.). 292p. (J). (gr. 4-7). pap. 24.99 *(978-1-63140-771-0(6),* 9781631407710) Idea & Design Works, LLC.

De Jesus, Opal. The Magical Purple-Blue Frog, 1 vol. Pagona, Aurora, illus. 2010. 16p. pap. 24.95 *(978-1-4489-5925-9(X))* PublishAmerica, Inc.

De la Cruz, Melissa. The Isle of the Lost. 2017. (Descendants Ser.: 1). (J). lib. bdg. 20.85 *(978-0-606-41118-9(6))* Turtleback.

de la Cruz, Melissa. Isle of the Lost, the-A Descendants Novel, Book 1: A Descendants Novel. 2017. (Descendants Ser.: 1). (ENG.). 336p. (J). (gr. 3-7). pap. 9.99 *(978-1-4847-2544-3(1),* Disney-Hyperion) Disney Publishing Worldwide.

—Isle of the Lost, the-A Descendants Novel, Vol. 1: A Descendants Novel. 2015. (Descendants Ser.: 1). (ENG.). 316p. (J). (gr. 3-7). 17.99 *(978-1-4847-2097-4(0),* Disney-Hyperion) Disney Publishing Worldwide.

De la Cruz, Melissa. Return to the Isle of the Lost. 2018. (Descendants Ser.: 2). (J). lib. bdg. 20.85 *(978-0-606-41123-3(2))* Turtleback.

—Return to the Isle of the Lost: A Descendants Novel. 2016. (Descendants Ser.). (ENG.). 320p. (J). (gr. 4-7). 17.99 *(978-1-4847-8520-1(7));* 17.99 *(978-1-4847-8521-8(5));* 17.99 *(978-1-4847-8522-5(3))* Hyperion Bks. for Children.

de la Cruz, Melissa. Return to the Isle of the Lost-A Descendants Novel, Book 2: A Descendants Novel. (Descendants Ser.: 2). (ENG.). (J). (gr. 5-9). 2018. 336p. pap. 9.99 *(978-1-368-02136-4(0))* 2016. (Illus.). 320p. 17.99 *(978-1-4847-5071-1(3))* Disney Publishing Worldwide. (Disney-Hyperion).

—The Ring & the Crown (Extended Edition): the Ring & the Crown, Book 1. 2017. (ENG.). 480p. (J). (gr. 9-12). pap. 10.99 *(978-1-4847-9925-3(9),* Disney-Hyperion) Disney Publishing Worldwide.

—Rise of the Isle of the Lost-A Descendants Novel: A Descendants Novel. 2017. (Descendants Ser.: 3). (ENG.). 304p. (J). (gr. 3-7). 17.99 *(978-1-4847-8128-9(7),* Disney-Hyperion) Disney Publishing Worldwide.

—Rise of the Isle of the Lost-A Descendants Novel, Book 3: A Descendants Novel. 2018. (Descendants Ser.: 3). (ENG.). 304p. (J). (gr. 3-7). pap. 9.99 *(978-1-368-02831-8(4),* Disney-Hyperion) Disney Publishing Worldwide.

De Lint, Charles. The Cats of Tanglewood Forest. 2014. (J). lib. bdg. 22.10 *(978-0-606-36532-1(X))* Turtleback.

De Matos, Isabel Freire. El Pececito Magico. Torres, Walter, illus. 2004. (SPA.). 22p. (J). pap. 6.95 *(978-1-57581-578-7(8))* Santillana USA Publishing Co., Inc.

De Valera, Sinead. The Magic Gifts: Classic Irish Fairytales. (Illus.). 224p. 16.95 *(978-0-86327-822-8(1))* Wolfhound Pr. IRL. Dist: Irish Bks. & Media, Inc.

De Witt, Peter. Toaster Pond. 2006. (ENG.). 248p. (YA). (gr. 7-12). per. *(978-1-933255-21-7(8))* DNA Pr.

Dean, James & Dean, Kimberly. Pete the Cat & His Magic Sunglasses. Dean, James, illus. 2013. (Pete the Cat Ser.). (ENG., Illus.). 40p. (J). (gr. -1-3). lib. bdg. 18.89 *(978-0-06-227557-8(7),* HarperCollins) HarperCollins Pubs.

Debono, Angelo. The Magic in You. 2011. 36p. pap. 13.95 *(978-1-61204-783-6(1),* Strategic Bk. Publishing) Strategic Book Publishing & Rights Agency (SBPRA).

Deep Trouble (Book 5) 2017. (Secret Mermaid Ser.). (ENG.). (J). pap. 4.99 *(978-0-7945-3685-5(9),* Usborne) EDC Publishing.

Defabio, Richard Bryan. The Magic Spoon. 2011. 42p. pap. 21.99 *(978-1-4568-1773-2(6))* Xlibris Corp.

Defreitas, Henrietta. Henratty Mortimer: The Meerville Myth. (Illus.). 2012. 84p. pap. 32.03 *(978-1-4772-3867-7(0))* 2011. 88p. pap. 28.14 *(978-1-4520-8237-0(5))* AuthorHouse.

deGroat, Diane. Trick or Treat, Smell My Feet. deGroat, Diane, illus. 2008. (Illus.). (J). (gr. -1-7). pap. 16.95 incl. audio *(978-1-4301-0425-4(2))* Live Oak Media.

DeKeyser, Stacy. The Brixen Witch. Nickle, John, illus. (ENG.). 208p. (J). (gr. 3-7). 2013. pap. 6.99 *(978-1-4424-3329-8(9))* 2012. 15.99 *(978-1-4424-3328-1(0))* McElderry, Margaret K. Bks. (McElderry, Margaret K. Bks.).

del Rio, Tania. Sabrina the Teenage Witch: the Magic Within 4. 2014. (Sabrina Manga Ser.: 4). (Illus.). 272p. (J). (gr. 4-7). pap. 10.99 *(978-1-936975-76-1(9))* Archie Comic Pubns., Inc.

Delacre, Lulu. Rafi & Rosi. 2004. (Illus.). 64p. (J). lib. bdg. 13.85 *(978-1-4242-0596-7(4))* Fitzgerald Bks.

DeLaney, Edgar Azell. The Magical Hammock. DeLaney, Edgar Azell, illus. 2004. (ENG., Illus.). 83p. (J). 19.95 *(978-0-9759013-0-4(3))* Special Edition Studios, Inc.

Delaney, Joseph. The Last Apprentice: Slither (Book 11), Bk. 11. 2014. (Last Apprentice Ser.: 11). (ENG.). 432p. (YA). (gr. 8). pap. 11.99 *(978-0-06-219235-6(3),* Greenwillow Bks.) HarperCollins Pubs.

Delporte, Yvan & Peyo. The Smurfs #2: The Smurfs & the Magic Flute. 2010. (Smurfs Graphic Novels Ser.: 2). (ENG., Illus.). 64p. (J). (gr. 2-5). pap. 5.99 *(978-1-59707-208-3(7),* 900070210, Papercutz) Mad Cave Studios.

Delrusso, Diana. Pages, the Book-Maker Elf. Schwab, Jordan, illus. 2008. 68p. pap. 23.49 *(978-1-4343-9844-4(7))* AuthorHouse.

Deluca, Alison. Christmas O'Clock: A Collection. Daly, Lisa, illus. 2013. 198p. pap. 9.99 *(978-1-939296-98-6(6))* Myrddin Publishing Group.

Dematteis, J. M. The Puppet, the Professor, & the Prophet. Ploog, Mike, illus. 3rd rev. ed. 2007. 144p. (J). (gr. 4-7). 9.99 *(978-1-4231-0063-8(8))* Hyperion Pr.

—Stardust Kid. Ploog, Mike, illus. 2008. (ENG.). 128p. pap. 14.99 *(978-1-934506-04-2(4))* BOOM! Studios.

Demetrios, Heather. Blood Passage. 2016. (Dark Caravan Cycle Ser.: 2). (ENG.). 512p. (YA). (gr. 8). 17.99 *(978-0-06-231859-6(4),* Balzer & Bray) HarperCollins Pubs.

Demi. The Magic Pillow. Demi, illus. 2008. (ENG., Illus.). 40p. (J). (gr. 2-5). 24.99 *(978-1-4169-2470-8(1),* McElderry, Margaret K. Bks.) McElderry, Margaret K. Bks.

Demolin, G. The Blaue Hexe. 2010. (Illus.). 44p. pap. 21.22 *(978-1-4520-5516-9(5))* AuthorHouse.

DeMonte, Joe. Lucy & the Magic Factory. 2008. 79p. pap. 19.95 *(978-1-60813-119-8(X))* America Star Bks.

Denman, K. L. Perfect Revenge, 1 vol. 2009. (Orca Currents Ser.). (ENG.). 128p. (J). (gr. 4-7). pap. 9.95 *(978-1-55469-102-9(8))* Orca Bk. Pubs. USA.

—La Revanche Parfaite, 1 vol. 2011. (Orca Currents en Français Ser.). (FRE.). 144p. (J). (gr. 4-7). pap. 9.95 *(978-1-55469-853-0(7))* Orca Bk. Pubs. USA.

Dennard, Susan. Truthwitch. 2016. (Witchlands Ser.: Vol. 1). (ENG.). (gr. 8-12). pap. 12.99 *(978-0-7653-9022-6(1),* Tor Teen) Doherty, Tom Assocs., LLC.

—Truthwitch. 2017. (Witchlands Ser.: 1). (YA). lib. bdg. 20.85 *(978-0-606-39586-1(5))* Turtleback.

—Truthwitch: The Witchlands. 2017. (Witchlands Ser.: 1). (ENG.). 432p. (YA). pap. 10.99 *(978-0-7653-7929-0(5),* 900141949, Tor Teen) Doherty, Tom Assocs., LLC.

—Windwitch. 2017. (Witchlands Ser.). (ENG., Illus.). 380p. (gr. 8-12). pap. 12.99 *(978-0-7653-9579-5(7),* Tor Teen) Doherty, Tom Assocs., LLC.

—Windwitch: The Witchlands. (Witchlands Ser.: 2). (ENG.). (YA). 2018. 400p. pap. 10.99 *(978-0-7653-7931-3(7),* 900141951) 2017. (Illus.). 384p. 18.99 *(978-0-7653-7930-6(9),* 900141950) Doherty, Tom Assocs., LLC. (Tor Teen).

dePaola, Tomie. Strega Nona's Gift. dePaola, Tomie, illus. 2011. (Illus.). 32p. (J). (gr. -1-3). 17.99 *(978-0-399-25649-3(0),* Nancy Paulsen Books) Penguin Young Readers Group.

—Strega Nona's Harvest. dePaola, Tomie, illus. (Illus.). 32p. (J). (gr. -1-3). 2012. (ENG.). mass mkt. 8.99 *(978-0-14-242338-7(6),* Puffin Books) 2009. 17.99 *(978-0-399-25291-4(6),* G.P. Putnam's Sons Books for Young Readers) Penguin Young Readers Group.

—Strega Nona's Magic Lessons. dePaola, Tomie, illus. 2017. (Strega Nona Book Ser.). (ENG., Illus.). 32p. (J). (gr. -1-3). 17.99 *(978-1-4814-7759-8(5),* Simon & Schuster Bks. For Young Readers) Simon & Schuster Bks. For Young Readers.

—Strega Nona's Magic Ring. dePaola, Tomie, illus. (Strega Nona Book Ser.). (ENG., Illus.). 32p. (J). (gr. -1-3). 2019. 7.99 *(978-1-5344-3017-4(2))* 2018. 17.99 *(978-1-4814-7761-1(7))* Simon & Schuster Bks. For Young Readers. (Simon & Schuster Bks. For Young Readers).

dePaola, Tomie, illus. Strega Nona & the Twins. 2017. (J). *(978-1-5379-5057-0(6),* Simon Spotlight) Simon Spotlight.

Depken, Kristen L. Fairytale Magic. 2014. (Dora the Explorer Step into Reading Ser.). lib. bdg. 13.55 *(978-0-606-36011-1(5))* Turtleback.

DeStefano, Lauren. The Glass Spare. (Glass Spare Ser.: 1). (ENG.). (YA). (gr. 8). 2018. 432p. pap. 9.99 *(978-0-06-249129-9(6))* 2017. 416p. 17.99 *(978-0-06-249128-2(8))* HarperCollins Pubs. (Balzer & Bray).

Deutsch, Stacia. Quest for the Keys. 2015. (LEGO Elves Chapter Book Ser.: 1). lib. bdg. 16.00 *(978-0-606-37769-0(7))* Turtleback.

Dey, Frederic Van Re. The Magic Story. 2004. reprint ed. pap. 15.95 *(978-0-7661-8653-8(9))* Kessinger Publishing, LLC.

D.G., Gigi. Cucumber Quest: the Doughnut Kingdom. 2017. (Cucumber Quest Ser.: 1). (ENG., Illus.). 192p. (J). pap. 14.99 *(978-1-62672-832-5(1),* 900175241, First Second Bks.) Roaring Brook Pr.

Dharma Publishing Staff. The King Who Understood Animals: A Story about Using Knowledge Wisely. 2nd ed. 2013. (Jataka Tales Ser.). (Illus.). 36p. (gr. -1-7). pap. 8.95 *(978-0-89800-520-2(5))* Dharma Publishing.

Diamond, Kathryn. Rachel's Magic Swing. 2009. 80p. pap. 11.00 *(978-0-557-06497-7(X))* Lulu Pr., Inc.

Dickens, Rosie. Illustrated Stories of Horses & Ponies. 2018. (Illustrated Stories Ser.). (ENG.). 280p. 19.99 *(978-0-7945-4026-5(0),* Usborne) EDC Publishing.

Dickinson, Peter. The Ropemaker. Andrew, Ian, illus. 2004. 375p. (gr. 7). 17.95 *(978-0-7569-1935-1(5))* Perfection Learning Corp.

Dickson, Diane. 3 Things That Might Have Happened. 2010. 100p. pap. 15.50 *(978-1-4452-3414-4(9))* Lulu Pr., Inc.

DiGerolamo, Tony. The Wildsidhe Chronicles Bk. 5: The Undercover Dragon. 2003. (J). pap. 7.99 *(978-1-890096-17-5(2))* Padwolf Publishing Inc.

DiMarco, Carol. The Magical Child. 3rd rev. ed. 2009. (ENG., Illus.). 44p. (J). 10.99 *(978-1-59092-273-6(5))* Blue Forge Pr.

DiMartino, Michael Dante. Rebel Geniuses. (Rebel Geniuses Ser.: 1). (ENG., Illus.). 400p. (J). pap. 8.99 *(978-1-250-12974-1(5),* 900176115) Square Fish.

Disbro, Laura M. Adventures with Miss Lol: The Magic Paper Ride. 2011. 28p. pap. 15.99 *(978-1-4628-9072-9(5))* Xlibris Corp.

Disney. Frozen Cinestory, Volume 1. 2014. lib. bdg. 26.95 *(978-0-606-36645-8(8))* Turtleback.

Disney Books. Fairest of All-Villains, Book 1. 2009. (Villains Ser.: 1). (ENG., Illus.). 256p. (YA). (gr. 7-12). 17.99 *(978-1-4231-0629-6(6),* Disney Press Books) Disney Publishing Worldwide.

—Frozen ReadAlong Storybook & CD. 2013. (Read-Along Storybook & CD Ser.). (ENG., Illus.). 32p. (J). (gr. -1-k). pap. 6.99 *(978-1-4231-7064-8(4),* Disney Press Books) Disney Publishing Worldwide.

Disney Editors. Beauty & the Beast Novelization. 2017. 275p. (J). lib. bdg. 19.65 *(978-0-606-40201-9(2))* Turtleback.

—Disney Descendants Wicked World Cinestory Comic, Volume 3, 3. 2017. (J). lib. bdg. 20.85 *(978-0-606-39833-6(3))* Turtleback.

—Disney Tangled Movie Comic. 2017. (ENG.). 64p. (J). (gr. 4-7). 18.40 *(978-0-606-39085-9(5))* Turtleback.

—Frozen. 2013. lib. bdg. 14.75 *(978-0-606-32207-2(8))* Turtleback.

—Frozen - Anna's Icy Adventure. 2013. lib. bdg. 14.75 *(978-0-606-32206-5(X))* Turtleback.

Disney Press Editors. Riches to Rags. 2015. (Sofia the First World of Reading Ser.). (J). lib. bdg. 13.55 *(978-0-606-36901-5(5))* Turtleback.

Distler, Christine A. Pegasus: The Introduction. 2005. 84p. pap. 11.95 *(978-1-59113-763-4(2))* Booklocker.com, Inc.

Divakaruni, Chitra Banerjee. The Mirror of Fire & Dreaming. 2007. (ENG.). 336p. (J). (gr. 3-7). pap. 14.99 *(978-1-4169-1768-7(3),* Aladdin) Simon & Schuster Children's Publishing.

Dixon, Andy. Sword Quest. Brooks, Felicity, ed. Boni, Simone, illus. rev. ed. 2005. (Usborne Fantasy Puzzle Bks.). 31p. (J). (gr. 3-7). pap., pap. 7.95 *(978-0-7945-1096-1(5),* Usborne) EDC Publishing.

Dixon, Danielle. Project: Purest. 2012. 370p. pap. 19.99 *(978-1-4691-8247-6(5))* Xlibris Corp.

Dixon, Heather. Entwined. 2012. (ENG.). 480p. (YA). (gr. 8). pap. 10.99 *(978-0-06-200104-7(3),* Greenwillow Bks.) HarperCollins Pubs.

d'Lacey, Chris. Dark Wyng (the Erth Dragons #2) 2018. (Erth Dragons Ser.: 2). (ENG.). 352p. (J). (gr. 3-7). pap. 7.99 *(978-0-545-90058-4(1));* 16.99 *(978-0-545-90057-7(3),* Scholastic Pr.) Scholastic, Inc.

—The New Age (the Erth Dragons #3) 2019. (Erth Dragons Ser.: 3). (ENG.). 368p. (J). (gr. 3-7). 16.99 *(978-1-338-29192-6(0),* Scholastic Pr.) Scholastic, Inc.

D'lacey, Chris. The Wearle. 2018. (Erth Dragons Ser.: 1). lib. bdg. 18.40 *(978-0-606-41129-5(1))* Turtleback.

Dodd, Emma. Foxy. Dodd, Emma, illus. 2012. (ENG., Illus.). 40p. (J). (gr. -1-2). 14.99 *(978-0-06-201419-1(6),* HarperCollins) HarperCollins Pubs.

—Foxy in Love. Dodd, Emma, illus. 2013. (ENG., Illus.). 40p. (J). (gr. -1-3). 17.99 *(978-0-06-201422-1(6),* HarperCollins) HarperCollins Pubs.

—Foxy in Love. 2013. (Illus.). (J). lib. bdg. *(978-0-06-201423-8(4))* HarperCollins Pubs.

Dodd, Susan. Dreaming the Dreams That Only Cats Can Dream. 2013. 150p. pap. *(978-1-78148-654-2(9))* Grosvenor Hse. Publishing Ltd.

Doerrfeld, Cori. Créele a Tus Ojos (Believe Your Eyes) Libro 1 (Book 1) Doerrfeld, Cori & Page, Tyler, illus. 2020. (Cici: un Cuento de Hada (Cici: a Fairy's Tale) Ser.). (SPA.). 48p. (J). (gr. 2-5). 26.65 *(978-1-5415-7935-4(6),* d7aa239d-55fd-4e3a-b777-c15f12a8bd8d, Graphic Universe™) Lerner Publishing Group.

—A Perfect View: Book 3. Doerrfeld, Cori & Page, Tyler, illus. 2017. (Cici: a Fairy's Tale Ser.: 3). (ENG.). 48p. (J). (gr. 2-5). E-Book 39.99 *(978-1-5124-2700-4(4),* 9781512427004);No. 3. pap. 7.99 *(978-1-5124-3068-4(4),* 61c1d407-bd3b-4707-b0cd-60fa50eb1528) Lerner Publishing Group. (Graphic Universe™).

—Truth in Sight: Book 2, No. 2. Doerrfeld, Cori & Page, Tyler, illus. 2016. (Cici: a Fairy's Tale Ser.: 2). (ENG.). 48p. (J). (gr. 2-5). lib. bdg. 26.65 *(978-1-4677-6153-6(2),* e6bba0b4-2fa7-4a1e-9099-fe73b146e422, Graphic Universe™) Lerner Publishing Group.

Doherty, Glen. The Magic Sucker or How Love Really Works. 2012. 24p. pap. 12.99 *(978-1-4797-0978-6(6))* Xlibris Corp.

Dokey, Cameron. Golden: A Retelling Of "Rapunzel" 2007. (Once upon a Time Ser.). (ENG.). 192p. (YA). (gr. 7-9). mass mkt. 8.99 *(978-1-4169-3926-9(1),* Simon Pulse) Simon Pulse.

Dolamore, Jaclyn. Glittering Shadows. 2016. (Dark Metropolis Ser.). (ENG., Illus.). 448p. (J). (gr. 7-12). pap. 9.99 *(978-1-4231-6477-7(6))* Hyperion Bks. for Children.

Dolbeck, Andrew. Fever Jenny, Bk. 1. 2006. 120p. pap. 10.99 *(978-1-59092-324-5(3))* Blue Forge Pr.

Donaldson, Babette. Emma Lea's Magic Teapot. Van Dijk, Jerianne, illus. 2007. 32p. (J). lib. bdg. 16.95 *(978-0-9792612-1-3(X))* Blue Gate Bks.

Donfrancesco, Anna. Keepers of the Dream. 2007. (Illus.). 92p. per. *(978-1-84549-238-0(2))* arima publishing.

Donnelly, Jennifer. Waterfire Saga, Book Four: Sea Spell. 2017. (Waterfire Saga Ser.). (ENG.). 368p. (J). (gr. 7-12). pap. 9.99 *(978-1-4847-1303-7(6),* Disney-Hyperion) Disney Publishing Worldwide.

Dora's Magical Adventures, Set. 2008. (Dora the Explorer Ser.). (ENG.). 144p. (J). pap. 10.99 *(978-1-4169-7583-0(7),* Simon Spotlight/Nickelodeon) Simon Spotlight/Nickelodeon.

Dorison, Xavier & Nury, Fabian. Century Club. Ross, C., illus. 2012. (Spooks Ser.: 2). (ENG.). 56p. (J). (gr. 10-12). pap. 13.95 *(978-1-84918-129-7(2))* CineBook GBR. Dist: National Bk. Network.

Dorothy, Grandma. Magic, Mystery, Adventure: Wild Animals Talk to Us. 2009. 196p. 24.99 *(978-1-4490-3578-5(7));* pap. 14.99 *(978-1-4490-3579-2(5))* AuthorHouse.

Doucette, Christina. Gordon's Treasure! A Sparkle Cove Adventure. 2011. 44p. (gr. 1-2). pap. 19.99 *(978-1-4634-0487-1(5))* AuthorHouse.

Dougherty, John. Stinkbomb & Ketchup-Face & the Quest for the Magic Porcupine. Ricks, Sam, illus. 2019. (Stinkbomb & Ketchup-Face Ser.: 2). (ENG.). 176p. (J). (gr. 3-7). 7.99 *(978-1-101-99666-9(8),* Puffin Books) Penguin Young Readers Group.

Downer, Ann. The Dragon of Never-Was. Rayyan, Omar, illus. 2008. (ENG.). 320p. (J). (gr. 3-6). pap. 14.99 *(978-1-4169-5453-8(8),* Atheneum Bks. for Young Readers) Simon & Schuster Children's Publishing.

—Hatching Magic. Rayyan, Omar, illus. 2004. 242p. 16.00 *(978-0-7569-3481-1(8))* Perfection Learning Corp.

—Hatching Magic. 2004. (ENG.). 256p. (J). (gr. 3-7). reprint ed. pap. 15.99 *(978-0-689-87057-6(4),* Atheneum Bks. for Young Readers) Simon & Schuster Children's Publishing.

Downes, Alice. Lucy & the Magic Loom: A Rainbow Loomer's Adventure Story. 2015. (ENG.). 112p. (J). (gr. k-5). pap. 7.99 *(978-1-63450-137-8(3),* Sky Pony Pr.) Skyhorse Publishing Co., Inc.

Downes, Kit. Zal & Zara & the Great Race of Azamed. 2009. 1.00 *(978-1-4074-4352-2(6))* Recorded Bks., Inc.

Downest, Madeline. Lucy & the Magic Loom: the Daring Rescue: A Rainbow Loomer's Adventure Story. 2016. (ENG.). 112p. (J). (gr. k-5). pap. 7.99 *(978-1-63450-215-3(9),* Sky Pony Pr.) Skyhorse Publishing Co., Inc.

Doyle, Bill. Attack of the Shark-Headed Zombie. Altman, Scott, illus. 2011. (Stepping Stone Book(TM) Ser.). (ENG.). 112p. (J). (gr. 1-4). 5.99 *(978-0-375-86675-3(2),* Random Hse. Bks. for Young Readers) Random Hse. Children's Bks.

Doyle, Catherine. The Lost Tide Warriors. 2020. (Storm Keeper's Island Ser.: 2). (ENG.). 320p. (J). 16.99 *(978-1-5476-0272-8(4),* 900209549, Bloomsbury Children's Bks.) Bloomsbury Publishing USA.

Doyle, Marissa. Betraying Season. 2010. (ENG.). 336p. (YA). (gr. 9-13). pap. 19.99 *(978-0-312-62916-8(8),* 900066880) Square Fish.

—Bewitching Season. 2009. (ENG.). 368p. (YA). (gr. 9-12). 24.94 *(978-0-312-59695-8(2),* 9780312596958) Square Fish.

—Courtship & Curses. 2013. (ENG.). 368p. (YA). (gr. 9-13). pap. 19.99 *(978-1-250-02744-3(6),* 900098317) Square Fish.

Drischel, Candy L. Restless with the Dark Moon Rising. 2008. 105p. pap. 19.95 *(978-1-60610-421-7(7))* America Star Bks.

Driscoll, Roger K. Echo Mccool, Outlaw Through Time. 2011. 190p. pap. *(978-1-908105-26-4(7))* Grosvenor Hse. Publishing Ltd.

The Drums of Legenderry. 2006. (J). per. *(978-0-9776967-0-3(7))* Legenderry.com.

Duane, Diane. Games Wizards Play. 2017. (Young Wizards Ser.: 10). (ENG.). 640p. (YA). (gr. 7). pap. 8.99 *(978-0-544-81323-6(5),* 1641929, Clarion Bks.) HarperCollins Pubs.

Duce, Gillian. Magic & Mayhem. 2006. (ENG.). 212p. per. *(978-1-894936-64-4(7))* Saga Bks.

Due, Kirsten L. Bearen Bear & the Bunbury Tales. Berends, Jenny, illus. 2013. 194p. pap. *(978-0-9884916-3-2(X))* Roxby Media Ltd.

Duerr, Doug. The Adventures of Jazz & Elliott: Danielle goes to the Magical Land of Roop-E-Doo. 2010. 29p. (J). pap. 17.95 *(978-1-4327-5405-1(X))* Outskirts Pr., Inc.

Duey, Kathleen. Following Magic. Tang, Sandara, illus. 2010. (Faeries' Promise Ser.: 2). (ENG.). 128p. (J). (gr. 2-5). pap. 6.99 *(978-1-4169-8459-7(3),* Aladdin) Simon & Schuster Children's Publishing.

—Following Magic. Tang, Sandara, illus. 2010. (Faeries' Promise Ser.: 2). (ENG.). 128p. (J). (gr. 2-5). 15.99 *(978-1-4169-8458-0(5),* Simon & Schuster/Paula Wiseman Bks.) Simon & Schuster/Paula Wiseman Bks.

—The Full Moon. Tang, Sandara, illus. 2011. (Faeries' Promise Ser.: 4). (ENG.). 128p. (J). (gr. 2-5). pap. 5.99 *(978-1-4169-8463-4(1));4.* lib. bdg. 15.99 *(978-1-4169-8462-7(3))* Simon & Schuster Children's Publishing. (Aladdin).

—Sacred Scars, No. 2. Rayyan, Sheila, illus. 2009. (Resurrection of Magic Ser.: 2). (ENG.). 560p. (YA). (gr. 7-18). 18.99 *(978-0-689-84095-1(0),* Atheneum Bks. for Young Readers) Simon & Schuster Children's Publishing.

—Silence & Stone. Tang, Sandara, illus. 2010. (Faeries' Promise Ser.: 1). (ENG.). 128p. (J). (gr. 2-5). pap. 6.99 *(978-1-4169-8457-3(7),* Aladdin) Simon & Schuster Children's Publishing.

—Silence & Stone. Tang, Sandara, illus. 2010. (Faeries' Promise Ser.: 1). (ENG.). 128p. (J). (gr. 2-5). 15.99 *(978-1-4169-8456-6(9),* Simon & Schuster/Paula Wiseman Bks.) Simon & Schuster/Paula Wiseman Bks.

—Skin Hunger. 2008. (Resurrection of Magic Ser.: 1). (ENG.). 368p. (YA). (gr. 7-7). pap. 12.99 *(978-0-689-84094-4(2),* Atheneum Bks. for Young Readers) Simon & Schuster Children's Publishing.

—Skin Hunger, 1. Rayyan, Sheila, illus. 2007. (Resurrection of Magic Ser.: Bk. 1). (ENG.). 357p. (YA). (gr. 7-12). 24.94 *(978-0-689-84093-7(4))* Simon & Schuster, Inc.

—Wishes & Wings. Tang, Sandara, illus. 2011. (Faeries' Promise Ser.: 3). (ENG.). 128p. (J). (gr. 2-5). pap. 4.99 *(978-1-4169-8461-0(5),* Aladdin) Simon & Schuster Children's Publishing.

—Wishes & Wings. Tang, Sandara, illus. 2011. (Faeries' Promise Ser.: 3). (ENG.). 128p. (J). (gr. 2-5). 15.99 *(978-1-4169-8460-3(7),* Simon & Schuster/Paula Wiseman Bks.) Simon & Schuster/Paula Wiseman Bks.

Duncan, Emily A. Ruthless Gods: A Novel. 2020. (Something Dark & Holy Ser.: 2). (ENG., Illus.). 544p. (YA). 18.99 *(978-1-250-19569-2(1),* 900193806, Wednesday Bks.) St. Martin's Pr.

Duncan, Jasmin. The Unicorn Legacy. 2013. 100p. pap. *(978-1-909402-12-6(5));* pap. *(978-1-909402-11-9(7))* Vamptasy Publishing.

Dunkle, Clare B. Close Kin: Book II — the Hollow Kingdom Trilogy. 2nd rev. ed. 2006. (Hollow Kingdom Trilogy Ser.: 2). (ENG.). 224p. (J). (gr. 6-9). pap. 12.99 *(978-0-8050-8109-1(7),* 900039577, Holt, Henry & Co. Bks. For Young Readers) Holt, Henry & Co.

—The Hollow Kingdom: Book I — the Hollow Kingdom Trilogy. 2006. (Hollow Kingdom Trilogy Ser.: 1). (ENG.). 240p. (J). (gr. 6-9). reprint ed. pap. 16.99 *(978-0-8050-8108-4(9),* 900039576, Holt, Henry & Co. Bks. For Young Readers) Holt, Henry & Co.

—In the Coils of the Snake: Book III — the Hollow Kingdom Trilogy. 3rd rev. ed. 2006. (Hollow Kingdom Trilogy Ser.: 3). (ENG.). 240p. (J). (gr. 6-9). 15.99 *(978-0-8050-8110-7(0),* 900039578, Holt, Henry & Co. Bks. For Young Readers) Holt, Henry & Co.

Dunseith, Peter. Bird of Heaven: The Story of a Swazi Sangoma. 2010. (Illus.). 257p. pap. *(978-0-624-04557-1(9))* NB Pubs. Ltd.

Dunston, Marc. The Magic of Giving, 1 vol. Cantrell, Katie, illus. 2010. (ENG.). 32p. (J). (gr. k-3). 16.99 *(978-1-58980-805-8(3)*, Pelican Publishing) Arcadia Publishing.

Durst, Sarah Beth. Enchanted Ivy. (ENG.). (YA). (gr. 7). 2011. 336p. pap. 9.99 *(978-1-4169-8646-1(4))* 2010. 320p. 16.99 *(978-1-4169-8645-4(6))* McElderry, Margaret K. Bks. (McElderry, Margaret K. Bks.).

Dye, Troy & Kelesides, Tom. Goblin Chronicles 01A. 2008. (YA). 3.50 *(978-0-9801314-0-6(5))* Ape Entertainment.

—Goblin Chronicles #1B. 2008. (YA). 3.50 *(978-0-9801314-1-3(3))* Ape Entertainment.

—Goblin Chronicles #2A. 2008. (Illus.). 32p. (J). 3.50 *(978-0-9801314-2-0(1))* Ape Entertainment.

—Goblin Chronicles #2B. 2008. (Illus.). 32p. (J). 3.50 *(978-0-9801314-3-7(X))* Ape Entertainment.

Eager, Edward. Half Magic. l.t. ed. 2005. (ENG., Illus.). 216p. (J). (gr. 4-7). pap. 15.99 *(978-0-7862-7952-4(4))* Cengage Gale.

—Half Magic. 192p. (J). (gr. 2-4). pap. 6.00 *(978-0-8072-1534-0(1)*, Listening Library) Random Hse. Audio Publishing Group.

—Magic by the Lake. Bodecker, N. M., illus. 2016. (Tales of Magic Ser.: 2). (ENG.). 224p. (J). (gr. 3-7). pap. 7.99 *(978-0-544-67170-6(8)*, 1625816, Clarion Bks.) HarperCollins Pubs.

—The Well-Wishers. Bodecker, N. M., illus. 2016. (Tales of Magic Ser.: 6). (ENG.). 240p. (J). (gr. 3-7). pap. 7.99 *(978-0-544-67167-6(8)*, 1625810, Clarion Bks.) HarperCollins Pubs.

Easley, Sean. The Hotel Between. 2018. (ENG., Illus.). 352p. (J). (gr. 4-7). 19.99 *(978-1-5344-1697-0(8)*, Simon & Schuster Bks. For Young Readers) Simon & Schuster Bks. For Young Readers.

—The Key of Lost Things. 2020. (ENG.). 400p. (J). (gr. 4-7). pap. 8.99 *(978-1-5344-3788-3(6)*, Simon & Schuster Bks. For Young Readers) Simon & Schuster Bks. For Young Readers.

Ebel, Sherry. Cassie's Magic Doors. 2008. 28p. pap. 15.99 *(978-1-4363-2970-5(1))* Xlibris Corp.

—Cassie's Magic Doors the Butterfly Garden. 2012. 36p. pap. 21.99 *(978-1-4797-0108-7(4))* Xlibris Corp.

Eberly, Chelsea. Magic Friends. 2014. (Barbie Step into Reading Level 2 Ser.). lib. bdg. 13.55 *(978-0-606-35991-7(5))* Turtleback.

—Magic Friends (Barbie & the Secret Door) 2014. (Step into Reading Ser.). (ENG., Illus.). 32p. (J). (gr. -1-1). 5.99 *(978-0-385-38296-0(0)*, Random Hse. Bks. for Young Readers) Random Hse. Children's Bks.

Ecton, Emily. Night of the Living Lawn Ornaments. 2009. (ENG.). 240p. (J). (gr. 3-7). pap. 5.99 *(978-1-4169-6451-3(7)*, Aladdin) Simon & Schuster Children's Publishing.

EDCON Publishing Group Staff. Jack & the Beanstalk - The Stubborn Witch - Rapunzel - Betsy - The Magic Bus. l.t. ed. 2008. (Classic Children's Tales Ser.). 32p. (gr. k-4). pap. 8.95 *(978-1-55576-551-4(3))* EDCON Publishing Group.

—Little Toot - The Story of White Satin - Five Peas in a Pod - Rumpelstiltskin - The Little Magic Pot. l.t. ed. 2008. (Classic Children's Tales Ser.). 32p. (gr. k-4). pap. 8.95 *(978-1-55576-552-1(1))* EDCON Publishing Group.

Edgar, Amy. Pet Charms #3: Here, Kitty, Kitty (Scholastic Reader, Level 2) Tejido, Jomike, illus. 2017. (Scholastic Reader, Level 2 Ser.). (ENG.). 32p. (J). (gr. k-2). pap. 5.99 *(978-1-338-04591-8(1))* Scholastic, Inc.

Ediciones B (Firm) Staff & Outhwaite, Ida Rentoul. La Magia de las Hadas. 2005. (SPA & ENG., Illus.). 64p. (J). (gr. 2-4). 12.95 *(978-84-666-1610-2(1))* Ediciones B ESP. Dist: Independent Pubs. Group.

Edmondson, Frank. Mr. Frank's Magic School Bus: Rainbow's End Adventure. Edmondson, Brad, illus. 2007. 20p. per. 24.95 *(978-1-4241-8617-4(X))* America Star Bks.

—Mr. Frank's Magic School Bus: Rainbow's End Adventure, 1 vol. Edmondson, Brad, illus. 2010. 20p. 24.95 *(978-1-4512-1042-2(6))* PublishAmerica, Inc.

Edmondson, Matt. The Greatest Magician in the World. 2018. (ENG., Illus.). 40p. (J). (gr. 1-5). 21.99 *(978-1-5098-0618-8(0))* Pan Macmillan GBR. Dist: Independent Pubs. Group.

Edwards, Christine. The Charmed Enchanted Book. 2010. 24p. pap. 16.49 *(978-1-4490-7091-5(4))* AuthorHouse.

Edwards, Garth. The Magic Boots. Stasyuk, Max, illus. 2011. (Adventures of Titch & Mitch Ser.). (J). pap. *(978-0-9567449-8-2(2))* Inside Pocket Publishing, Ltd.

—The #04 Magic Boots. Stasyuk, Max, illus. 2011. (Adventures of Titch & Mitch, the Ser.). (J). pap. *(978-0-7613-8424-3(3))* Inside Pocket Publishing, Ltd.

Edwards, R. G. Eafin Lokdore & the Altar of the Sun Book II. 2007. (ENG.). 264p. pap. 19.96 *(978-0-615-17785-4(9))* Edwards, R. G. Publishing.

—Eafin Lokdore & the Magician's Lost Medallion: Book I of the Eafin Lokdore Trilogy. 2007. (Illus.). 268p. pap. 19.95 *(978-0-615-16739-8(X))*; (J). 35.95 *(978-0-615-13336-2(3))* Edwards, R. G. Publishing.

Edwards, Wayne. Ali & the Magic Ball. Golden, Rayna, illus. 2009. 24p. pap. 12.50 *(978-1-60860-367-1(9)*, Eloquent Bks.) Strategic Book Publishing & Rights Agency (SBPRA).

Egan, Kate, adapted by. World's Apart. 2005. (W. I. T. C. H. Ser.: Bk. 14). 134p. (J). lib. bdg. 16.92 *(978-1-4242-0788-6(6))* Fitzgerald Bks.

Eldredge, Jan. Evangeline of the Bayou. Kuefler, Joseph, illus. 2018. (ENG.). 320p. (J). (gr. 3-7). 16.99 *(978-0-06-268034-1(X)*, Balzer & Bray) HarperCollins Pubs.

Eldridge, Jim. The Final Showdown: Match Six. Bielecki, Jan, illus. 2016. (Wrestling Trolls Ser.: 6). (ENG.). 176p. (J). (gr. k-3). pap. 9.99 *(978-1-4714-0269-2(X))* Bonnier Publishing GBR. Dist: Independent Pubs. Group.

Elgert, C. J. The Elder Brothers & the Padstow Crystals. 2013. 208p. *(978-1-4602-1788-7(8))*; pap. *(978-1-4602-1789-4(6))* FriesenPress.

Eliot, Ethel. The Little House in the Fairy Wood. 2006. 108p. per. 9.95 *(978-1-59818-097-8(5))*; 22.95 *(978-1-59818-343-6(5))* Aegypan.

Eliot, Ethel Cook. The Little House in the Fairy Wood. 2017. (ENG., Illus.). (J). 22.95 *(978-1-374-81790-6(2))* Capital Communications, Inc.

—The Little House in the Fairy Wood. 2015. (ENG., Illus.). (J). 22.95 *(978-1-297-76874-3(4))* Creative Media Partners, LLC.

Elliott, Linda. When Little Pinkie Gets Her Wings. Switzer, Bobbi, illus. 2007. 28p. per. 11.95 *(978-1-59800-871-5(4))* Outskirts Pr., Inc.

Elliott, M. G. The Magic Wheel: And the Adventures of Ding-How, Ah-So, & Mi-Tu. 2011. 220p. (gr. 4-6). 33.95 *(978-1-4497-3050-5(7))*; pap. 17.95 *(978-1-4497-3049-9(3))* Author Solutions, LLC. (WestBow Pr.).

Elliott, Zetta. The Dragon Thief. Geneva B, Geneva, illus. 2019. (Dragons in a Bag Ser.: 2). 176p. (J). (gr. 3-7). 16.99 *(978-1-5247-7049-5(3)*, Random Hse. Bks. for Young Readers) Random Hse. Children's Bks.

—Dragons in a Bag. Geneva B. Geneva, illus. 2018. (Dragons in a Bag Ser.: 1). 160p. (J). (gr. 3-7). 16.99 *(978-1-5247-7045-7(0)*, Random Hse. Bks. for Young Readers) Random Hse. Children's Bks.

Ellsworth, Theo. Eyes of War. 2006. 385p. (YA). pap. 14.99 *(978-0-9776114-0-9(X))* Hidden Talent Pr.

Emmett, Jonathan. The Conjuror's Cookbook Vol. I: Goblin Stew. (Illus.). 64p. (J). pap. 7.99 *(978-0-7475-4403-6(4))* Bloomsbury Publishing Plc GBR. Dist: Trafalgar Square Publishing.

—The Conjuror's Cookbook Vol. II: Serpent Soup. (Illus.). 64p. (J). pap. 7.99 *(978-0-7475-4408-1(5))* Bloomsbury Publishing Plc GBR. Dist: Trafalgar Square Publishing.

—The Conjuror's Cookbook Vol. III: Ghostly Goulash. (Illus.). 64p. (J). pap. 7.99 *(978-0-7475-4413-5(1))* Bloomsbury Publishing Plc GBR. Dist: Trafalgar Square Publishing.

Endacott, C. R. Afflatus. 2006. 232p. pap. 15.95 *(978-0-595-52418-1(4))* iUniverse, Inc.

Ende, Michael. The Night of Wishes: Or the Satanarchaeolidealcohellish Notion Potion. Schwarzbauer, Heike & Takvorian, Rick, trs. Kehn, Regina, illus. 2017. 216p. (J). (gr. 3-7). 16.95 *(978-1-58137-188-7(X)*, NYR Children's Collection) New York Review of Bks., Inc., The.

Endicott, Megan. In the Hall of the Mountain King. 2013. 48p. pap. 20.95 *(978-1-4582-0789-0(7)*, Abbott Pr.) Author Solutions, LLC.

Endou, Asari. Magical Girl Raising Project, Vol. 2 (light Novel) Restart I. 2017. (Magical Girl Raising Project (light Novel) Ser.: 2). (ENG., Illus.). 208p. (gr. 11-17). pap. 14.00 *(978-0-316-55991-1(1)*, Yen Pr.) Yen Pr. LLC.

—Magical Girl Raising Project, Vol. 3 (light Novel) Restart II. 2018. (Magical Girl Raising Project (light Novel) Ser.: 3). (ENG., Illus.). 212p. (gr. 11-17). pap. 14.00 *(978-0-316-55996-6(2)*, Yen Pr.) Yen Pr. LLC.

Ennis-Hill, Jessica. The Clocktower Charm, Bk. 5. Caldecott, Elen, illus. 2022. (Evie's Magic Bracelet Ser.). (ENG.). 144p. (J). (gr. 2-4). pap. 9.99 *(978-1-4449-3443-4(0))* Hachette Children's Group GBR. Dist: Hachette Bk. Group.

—The Sprites' Den, Bk. 3. Caldecott, Elen, illus. 2022. (Evie's Magic Bracelet Ser.). (ENG.). 144p. (J). (gr. 2-4). pap. 9.99 *(978-1-4449-3441-0(4))* Hachette Children's Group GBR. Dist: Hachette Bk. Group.

Enyi, Patricia Nmukoso. Marcus the Magician: At the Beach. 2010. 38p. pap. 15.50 *(978-1-60911-447-3(7)*, Eloquent Bks.) Strategic Book Publishing & Rights Agency (SBPRA).

Ephron, Amy. Carnival Magic. 2019. (Other Side Ser.). (Illus.). 288p. (J). (gr. 3-7). 8.99 *(978-1-5247-4023-8(3)*, Puffin Books) Penguin Young Readers Group.

—The Castle in the Mist. 2018. (Other Side Ser.). 208p. (J). (gr. 3-7). 8.99 *(978-0-399-54700-3(2)*, Puffin Books) Penguin Young Readers Group.

—The Castle in the Mist. 2018. lib. bdg. 19.65 *(978-0-606-40670-7(3))* Turtleback.

Epner, Paul. Herbert Hilligan & His Magical Lunchbox. Kuon, Vuthy & Nguyen, Duke, illus. rev. ed. (Herbert Hilligan Ser.). 15.95 *(978-1-57168-549-0(9))* Eakin Pr.

—Herbert Hilligan's Lone Star Adventure. Kuon, Vuthy & Nguyen, Duke, illus. 2003. 32p. (J). 15.95 *(978-0-9743335-3-3(0))* Imaginative Publishing, Ltd.

—Herbert Hilligan's Tropical Adventure. Kuon, Vuthy & Nguyen, Duke, illus. 2003. 32p. (J). 15.95 *(978-0-9743335-2-6(2))* Imaginative Publishing, Ltd.

Epstein, Adam Jay & Jacobson, Andrew. Circle of Heroes. (Familiars Ser.: 3). (ENG.). 336p. (J). (gr. 3-7). 2013. pap. 7.99 *(978-0-06-196116-8(7))* 2012. (Illus.). 16.99 *(978-0-06-196114-4(0))* HarperCollins Pubs. (HarperCollins).

—The Familiars. (Familiars Ser.: 1). (ENG.). (J). (gr. 3-7). 2011. 384p. pap. 9.99 *(978-0-06-196110-6(8))* 2010. (Illus.). 368p. 17.99 *(978-0-06-196108-3(6))* HarperCollins Pubs. (HarperCollins).

—Palace of Dreams. Phillips, Dave, illus. (Familiars Ser.: 4). (ENG.). 336p. (J). (gr. 3-7). 2015. pap. 9.99 *(978-0-06-212031-1(X))*No. 4. 2013. 16.99 *(978-0-06-212029-8(8))* HarperCollins Pubs. (HarperCollins).

—Secrets of the Crown. (Familiars Ser.: 2). (ENG.). (J). (gr. 3-7). 2012. 400p. pap. 7.99 *(978-0-06-196113-7(2))* 2011. 384p. 16.99 *(978-0-06-196111-3(6))* HarperCollins Pubs. (HarperCollins).

Epstein, Alex. The Circle Cast: The Lost Years of Morgan le Fey, 1 vol. 2011. (ENG., Illus.). 240p. (YA). (gr. 8-12). pap. 12.95 *(978-1-896580-63-0(7))* Tradewind Bks. CAN. Dist: Orca Bk. Pubs. USA.

Erich, James. Dreams of Fire & Gods: Dreams. 2016. (ENG., Illus.). (J). 27.99 *(978-1-63533-005-2(X)*, Harmony Ink Pr.) Dreamspinner Pr.

—Dreams of Fire & Gods: Fire. 2016. (ENG., Illus.). (J). 24.99 *(978-1-63533-006-9(8)*, Harmony Ink Pr.) Dreamspinner Pr.

—Dreams of Fire & Gods: Gods. 2016. (ENG., Illus.). (J). 24.99 *(978-1-63533-007-6(6)*, Harmony Ink Pr.) Dreamspinner Pr.

Erickson, Melissa. When the Tooth Fairy Comes... Erickson, Melissa, illus. 2007. (Illus.). 15p. (J). (gr. -1-3). 10.99 *(978-1-59879-369-7(1))* Lifevest Publishing, Inc.

Errico, Jessica / C. Grandpa's Magical Accordion. Star, Brenda, illus. 2007. 28p. (J). pap. 17.95 incl. cd-rom *(978-0-9800577-0-6(1))* Three Part Harmony LLC.

Eschler, Linda. The Strawberry Fairies & the Secret of Mystery Island. 2008. 57p. pap. 16.95 *(978-1-60610-960-1(X))* America Star Bks.

Escondete y Grita, Vol. II. (Fantasmas de Fear Street Coleccion: No. 1). (SPA.). (J). (gr. 4-7). pap. 7.95 *(978-950-04-1999-4(8)*, EM4474) Emecé Editores S.A. ARG. Dist: Lectorum Pubns., Inc., Planeta Publishing Corp.

Eshed, Tina. The Adventures of Bunzy: The Beginning. 2009. 60p. pap. 24.49 *(978-1-4389-2673-5(1))* AuthorHouse.

Estep, Jennifer. Bright Blaze of Magic. 2016. (Black Blade Ser.: 3). (ENG.). 320p. (YA). (gr. 9). pap. 18.00 *(978-1-61773-828-9(X))* Kensington Publishing Corp.

Eubank, Patricia Reeder. The Princess & the Snails. Eubank, Patricia Reeder, illus. 2006. (ENG., Illus.). 32p. (J). (gr. k-3). 16.95 *(978-0-8249-5536-6(6)*, Ideals Pubns.) Worthy Publishing.

Evans, Florence Adèle. Alice's Adventures in Pictureland: A Tale Inspired by Lewis Carroll's Wonderland. 2011. (Illus.). 152p. pap. *(978-1-904808-63-3(8))* Evertype.

Evans, Pamela. Tina Queen of the Dragons. 2006. 101p. pap. 16.95 *(978-1-4241-3356-7(4))* PublishAmerica, Inc.

Evans, Richard Paul. The Christmas Candle. Collins, Jacob, illus. (ENG.). 32p. (J). (gr. -1-3). 2007. 14.99 *(978-1-4169-5047-9(8))* 2006. 9.99 *(978-1-4169-2682-5(8))* Simon & Schuster Bks. For Young Readers. (Simon & Schuster Bks. For Young Readers).

Evans, Robert J. The Magic Sneakers. 2007. (ENG.). 88p. (J). pap. 11.95 *(978-0-615-14106-0(4))* R. C. Bk. Publishing.

Evans, Rosemary R. The Little Princesses Magial Party. Taylor, Erin, illus. 2012. 40p. (J). 16.95 *(978-1-60743-759-8(7))* Wink Publishing.

Eve, Laure. Graces. 2016. (Graces Novel Ser.). (ENG.). 352p. (YA). (gr. 8-17). 18.95 *(978-1-4197-2123-6(2)*, 1138101, Amulet Bks.) Abrams, Inc.

Everburg, R. S. Audrika's Magic. 2011. 264p. 29.99 *(978-1-4628-5596-4(2))*; pap. 19.99 *(978-1-4628-5595-7(4))* Xlibris Corp.

Everest, D. D. Archie Greene & the Magician's Secret. 2016. (Archie Greene Ser.: 1). (ENG.). 336p. (J). (gr. 3-7). pap. 6.99 *(978-0-06-231212-9(X)*, HarperCollins) HarperCollins Pubs.

Eves, Rosalyn. Blood Rose Rebellion. (Blood Rose Rebellion Ser.: 1). (ENG.). (YA). (gr. 7). 2018. 432p. pap. 11.99 *(978-1-101-93602-3(9)*, Ember) 2017. 416p. 17.99 *(978-1-101-93599-6(5)*, Knopf Bks. for Young Readers) Random Hse. Children's Bks.

—Lost Crow Conspiracy (Blood Rose Rebellion, Book 2) (Blood Rose Rebellion Ser.). (ENG.). 464p. (YA). (gr. 7). 2019. pap. 10.99 *(978-1-101-93610-8(X)*, Ember) 2018. 18.99 *(978-1-101-93607-8(X)*, Knopf Bks. for Young Readers) Random Hse. Children's Bks.

Ewert, Marcus. Mr. Pack Rat Really Wants That. Stark, Kayla, illus. 2018. 40p. (J). (gr. -1-3). 14.95 *(978-1-946764-25-6(6)*, Plum Blossom Bks.) Parallax Pr.

Ewing, Amy. The Cerulean. (ENG.). (YA). (gr. 9). 2020. 512p. pap. 11.99 *(978-0-06-249000-1(1))* 2019. 496p. 17.99 *(978-0-06-248998-2(4))* HarperCollins Pubs. (HarperTeen).

—The Jewel. (Lone City Trilogy Ser.: 1). (ENG.). (YA). (gr. 9). 2015. 400p. pap. 10.99 *(978-0-06-223578-7(8))* 2014. 368p. 17.99 *(978-0-06-223579-4(6))* HarperCollins Pubs. (HarperTeen).

Faircloth, Sean. The Enchanted Globe. 2016. (ENG., Illus.). 224p. (J). (gr. 4-7). pap. 12.95 *(978-1-63431-101-4(9))* Pitchstone LLC.

Fairy Gardens Magic Painting Book. 2017. (Magic Painting Bks.). (ENG.). (J). pap. 9.99 *(978-0-7945-3798-2(7)*, Usborne) EDC Publishing.

Fairy Palaces Magic Painting Book. 2017. (Magic Painting Bks.). (ENG.). (J). pap. 9.99 *(978-0-7945-3876-7(2)*, Usborne) EDC Publishing.

Fairy Tale Fixers: Fixing Fairy Tale Problems with STEM. 2017. (Fairy Tale Fixers: Fixing Fairy Tale Problems with STEM Ser.). 32p. (gr. 3-4). pap. 42.00 *(978-1-5382-0614-0(5))*; (ENG.). lib. bdg. 113.08 *(978-1-5382-0616-4(1)*, bb98f596-7294-46d1-83f9-61dead4b335e) Stevens, Gareth Publishing LLLP.

Faizal, Hafsah. We Hunt the Flame. 2019. (Sands of Arawiya Ser.: 1). (ENG., Illus.). 480p. (YA). 18.99 *(978-0-374-31154-4(4)*, 900195159, Farrar, Straus & Giroux (BYR)) Farrar, Straus & Giroux.

—We Hunt the Flame. 2020. (Sands of Arawiya Ser.: 1). (ENG., Illus.). 480p. (YA). pap. 12.99 *(978-1-250-25079-7(X)*, 900195160) Square Fish.

Fajardo, Alexis E. Kid Beowulf: The Song of Roland. 2017. lib. bdg. 24.50 *(978-0-606-40301-6(9))* Turtleback.

Falcon Press International. Desta & King Solomon's Coin of Magic & Fortune: And king solomon's coinof of magic & Fortune, nos. 7, no. 2. 2nd ed. 2010. (ENG., Illus.). 430p. (YA). pap. 15.95 *(978-1-884459-01-6(3))* Falcon Pr. International.

Falter, Laury. Residue. 2013. (Residue Ser.: bk.1). 306p. pap. 12.99 *(978-0-9855110-0-5(1))* William & William Publishing.

Farley, Christina. The Princess & the Page. 2017. (J). (ENG.). 240p. (gr. 3-7). 17.99 *(978-0-545-92409-2(X))*; 228p. *(978-1-338-18120-3(3))* Scholastic, Inc. (Scholastic Pr.).

Farooqi, Imran A. The Spell of the Witch-Queen. 2006. (Illus.). 60p. pap. *(978-1-84401-816-1(4))* Athena Pr.

Farr, Dan. Mr. Finnegan's Giving Chest. 2005. (Illus.). 32p. (J). (gr. -1-3). 19.95 incl. audio compact disk *(978-1-59038-555-5(1)*, Shadow Mountain) Shadow Mountain Publishing.

Farrey, Brian. The Vengekeep Prophecies. Helquist, Brett, illus. 2013. (Vengekeep Prophecies Ser.: 1). (ENG.). 416p. (J). (gr. 3-7). pap. 7.99 *(978-0-06-204929-2(1)*, HarperCollins) HarperCollins Pubs.

Farrow, G. & Farrow, George. The Mysterious Shin Shira. 2007. 116p. per. 10.95 *(978-1-60312-225-2(7))* Aegypan.

Farrow, George Edward. The Mysterious Shin Shira. 2017. (ENG., Illus.). (J). 22.95 *(978-1-374-87008-6(0))*; pap. 12.95 *(978-1-374-87007-9(2))* Capital Communications, Inc.

Faust, Lauren. My Little Pony: the Magic Begins, Vol. 1. 2013. (MLP Episode Adaptations Ser.). (Illus.). 112p. (J). (gr. 1-3). pap. 7.99 *(978-1-61377-754-1(X)*, 9781613777541) Idea & Design Works, LLC.

Fayers, Claire. The Book of Unwyse Magic. 2019. (ENG.). 320p. (J). 16.99 *(978-1-62779-422-0(0)*, 900150100, Holt, Henry & Co. Bks. For Young Readers) Holt, Henry & Co.

—The Voyage to Magical North. 2016. (Accidental Pirates Ser.: 1). (ENG.). 320p. (J). 27.99 *(978-1-62779-420-6(4)*, 900150098, Holt, Henry & Co. Bks. For Young Readers) Holt, Henry & Co.

Feldman, Lowell S. Little Falabella the Magical Horse. 2006. 92p. (gr. 1-1). pap. 31.99 *(978-1-4257-1869-5(8))* Xlibris Corp.

Feldmann, Claudia, tr. ARTEMIS FOWL. (Artemis Fowl Ser.: Bk. 1). (GER.). pap. 24.95 *(978-3-548-60320-9(3))* Ullstein-Taschenbuch-Verlag DEU. Dist: Distribooks, Inc.

Fénelon, Marie Jirlande. The Two Best Friends & the Old Lady. 2004. (Illus.). 28p. (J). bds. 19.00 *(978-1-58432-128-6(8))* Educa Vision Inc.

Ferguson, Sarah. Little Red's Autumn Adventure. Williams, Sam, illus. 2009. (ENG.). 40p. (J). (gr. -1-1). 19.99 *(978-0-689-84341-9(0)*, Simon & Schuster/Paula Wiseman Bks.) Simon & Schuster/Paula Wiseman Bks.

Fernandez, David R. Lady Godiva & the Legend of the Black Rose. 2008. (Illus.). 32p. (J). pap. 8.99 *(978-0-9817521-4-3(4))* Mirror Publishing.

Fernandez, Eugenia. Astria & the Missing Prince. 2009. (Illus.). 39p. (J). 31.99 *(978-1-4363-7543-6(6))* Xlibris Corp.

Fernandez, Giselle. Gigi & the Birthday Ring. Petersen, Sheli, illus. 2005. (J). *(978-1-56492-358-5(4))* Laredo Publishing Co., Inc.

Fforde, Jasper. The Last Dragonslayer. 2011. (ENG.). 352p. pap. *(978-1-4447-0720-5(5)*, Hodder Faith) Hodder & Stoughton.

—The Last Dragonslayer: The Chronicles of Kazam, Book 1. 2013. (Chronicles of Kazam Ser.). (ENG.). 304p. (J). (gr. 5-7). pap. 7.99 *(978-0-544-10471-6(4)*, 1540786, Clarion Bks.) HarperCollins Pubs.

—The Song of the Quarkbeast: The Chronicles of Kazam, Book 2. 2014. (Chronicles of Kazam Ser.). (ENG.). 304p. (J). (gr. 5-7). pap. 7.99 *(978-0-544-33662-9(3)*, 1584184, Clarion Bks.) HarperCollins Pubs.

Field, Brett. Screno Magic Medieval Collision. 2007. 52p. per. 10.00 *(978-1-4257-4700-8(0))* Xlibris Corp.

Fienberg, Anna, et al. Tashi & the Dancing Shoes. 8th ed. 2007. (Tashi Ser.). (ENG., Illus.). 64p. (Orig.). (J). (gr. k-2). pap. 8.99 *(978-1-74114-972-2(X))* Allen & Unwin AUS. Dist: Independent Pubs. Group.

—Tashi & the Royal Tomb. 10th ed. 2007. (Tashi Ser.: 10). (ENG., Illus.). 64p. (Orig.). (J). (gr. k-2). pap. 8.99 *(978-1-74114-973-9(8))* Allen & Unwin AUS. Dist: Independent Pubs. Group.

Fiford, Tanya. Robin & the Pocket Dragon. 2009. (Illus.). 24p. pap. 11.49 *(978-1-4389-9610-3(1))* AuthorHouse.

Figueroa, M. A. & Figueroa, P. A. Melissa & the Magic Pen. Barnoski, Karel, illus. 2004. 36p. pap. 24.95 *(978-1-4137-3441-6(3))* PublishAmerica, Inc.

Filaretos, William. The Potion of Time: A Story of Demetrios. 2006. per. 12.95 *(978-0-9724520-0-7(1))* Filaretos, William.

Findlay, Andrew. Roddy & the Magic Mattress. 2005. 54p. pap. 5.61 *(978-1-4116-3612-5(0))* Lulu Pr., Inc.

Fine, Sarah. The Cursed Queen. 2017. (Impostor Queen Ser.: 2). (ENG., Illus.). 432p. (YA). (gr. 7). 19.99 *(978-1-4814-4193-3(0)*, McElderry, Margaret K. Bks.) McElderry, Margaret K. Bks.

—The Impostor Queen. (Impostor Queen Ser.: 1). (ENG., Illus.). (YA). (gr. 7). 2017. 448p. pap. 13.99 *(978-1-4814-4191-9(4))* 2016. 432p. 18.99 *(978-1-4814-4190-2(6))* McElderry, Margaret K. Bks. (McElderry, Margaret K. Bks.).

—The True Queen. 2018. (Impostor Queen Ser.: 3). (ENG., Illus.). 384p. (YA). (gr. 7). 19.99 *(978-1-4814-9060-3(5)*, McElderry, Margaret K. Bks.) McElderry, Margaret K. Bks.

Finke, Margot. Ruthie & the Hippo's Fat Behind. Snider, K. C., illus. 2010. 16p. pap. 10.95 *(978-1-61633-059-0(7))* Guardian Angel Publishing, Inc.

Finley, Leah. The One & Only Mr C. 2009. 82p. pap. 8.95 *(978-1-935118-75-6(7))* Bellissima Publishing, LLC.

Finn McCool The Magic Leprechaun Cat. Irish Holiday Fairy Tales: Volume 1. 2012. 44p. pap. 19.95 *(978-1-4772-1331-5(7))* AuthorHouse.

Firtha, Gizella. Spookybrooke. 2011. 58p. pap. 16.95 *(978-1-4512-5822-6(4))* America Star Bks.

Fischel, Ana. The Twelve Quests - Book 2, a Dragon's Tooth. 2009. 158p. pap. *(978-1-84923-874-8(X))* YouWriteOn.

—The Twelve Quests - Book 3, the Pied Piper's Flute. 2009. 158p. pap. *(978-1-84923-875-5(8))* YouWriteOn.

—The Twelve Quests - Book 5, a Firebird's Feather. 2009. 158p. pap. *(978-1-84923-877-9(4))* YouWriteOn.

—The Twelve Quests - Book 6, the Enchanted Harp. 2009. 158p. pap. *(978-1-84923-878-6(2))* YouWriteOn.

Fischer, David. Heir to Oswyn. 2011. 66p. pap. 19.95 *(978-1-4626-2581-9(9))* America Star Bks.

Fisher, Catherine. Corbenic. 2006. 281p. (YA). (gr. 7). lib. bdg. 17.89 *(978-0-06-072471-9(4))* HarperCollins Pubs.

—Darkhenge. 2006. 340p. (YA). (gr. 7-12). 15.99 *(978-0-06-078582-6(9))* HarperCollins Pubs.

Fisher, Edward J. The Little Girl with the Magic Shoes: And Other Delights. 2008. 40p. 31.99 *(978-1-4363-4210-0(4))* Xlibris Corp.

Fisher, Justin. The Gold Thief (Ned's Circus of Marvels, Book 2) 2018. (Ned's Circus of Marvels Ser.: 2). (ENG.). 432p. (J). 6.99 *(978-0-00-826221-1(7)*, HarperCollins Children's Bks.) HarperCollins Pubs. Ltd. GBR. Dist: HarperCollins Pubs.

Fisher, Maire & Beautement, Tiah, eds. Follow the Road. 2015. (ENG., Illus.). 154p. (J). pap. *(978-1-920590-98-7(6))* Modjaji Bks.

Fisscher, Tiny. RUBY & MAGIC TWIG. 2008. (ENG.). 48p. (J). (gr. 1-7). 11.95 *(978-1-60136-013-7(4))* Audio Holdings, LLC.

Fitzgerald, D. M. The True Story of the Big Red Onion. Cudd, Savannah, illus. 2013. 36p. 18.99 *(978-0-9890288-7-5(9))*; pap. 10.99 *(978-0-9890288-5-1(2))* Mindstir Media.

Flaker, Tracey. Around the Corner: Gwenever's Quest. 2006. 55p. pap. 16.95 *(978-1-4241-1886-1(7))* PublishAmerica, Inc.

Flanagan, John. The Outcasts. 2011. (Brotherband Chronicles: Bk. 1). (ENG.). (J). (gr. 3-7). 54.99 *(978-1-61657-043-9(1))* Findaway World, LLC.

—The Outcasts. 2012. (Brotherband Chronicles Ser.: 1). lib. bdg. 19.65 *(978-0-606-26636-9(4))* Turtleback.

—The Outcasts: Brotherband Chronicles, Book 1. (Brotherband Chronicles Ser.: 1). (ENG., Illus.). (J). (gr. 5). 2012. 464p. pap. 9.99 *(978-0-14-242194-9(4)*, Puffin Books) 2011. 448p. 18.99 *(978-0-399-25619-6(9)*, Philomel Bks.) Penguin Young Readers Group.

—The Royal Ranger: a New Beginning. 2014. (Ranger's Apprentice: the Royal Ranger Ser.: 1). (ENG.). 480p. (J). (gr. 5). pap. 9.99 (978-0-14-242731-6(4), Viking Books for Young Readers) Penguin Young Readers Group.

—The Sorcerer of the North. 2009. (Ranger's Apprentice Ser.: 5). lib. bdg. 19.65 (978-0-606-02237-8(6)) Turtleback.

Flanagan, John A. The Tournament at Gorlan. 2016. (Ranger's Apprentice the Early Years Ser.: 1). lib. bdg. 19.65 (978-0-606-39332-4(3)) Turtleback.

Flavin, Teresa. The Crimson Shard. (ENG.). (J). (gr. 4-7). 2015. 288p. pap. 6.99 (978-0-7636-7172-3(X)) 2012. (Illus.). 256p. 15.99 (978-0-7636-6093-2(0)) Candlewick Pr. (Templar).

Fleming, Ian. Chitty Chitty Bang Bang: the Magical Car. Berger, Joe, illus. 2013. (Chitty Chitty Bang Bang Ser.: 1). (ENG.). 160p. (J). (gr. 4-7). pap. 8.99 (978-0-7636-6666-8(1)) Candlewick Pr.

Flinn, Alex. Beheld. 2018. (ENG.). 368p. (YA). (gr. 8). pap. 9.99 (978-0-06-213456-1(6), HarperTeen) HarperCollins Pubs.

—Cloaked. (YA). 2012. (ENG.). 368p. (gr. 8). pap. 9.99 (978-0-06-087424-7(4)) 2011. 341p. lib. bdg. 17.89 (978-0-06-087423-0(6)) HarperCollins Pubs. (HarperTeen).

—Towering. 2013. 296p. (YA). (978-0-06-227632-2(8)) HarperCollins Pubs.

Flitcroft, Jean. The Loch Ness Monster. 2010. (Cryptid Files Ser.: No. 1). xii, 176p. (J). pap. (978-1-84840-940-8(0)) Little Island.

Flounders, Anne; DuFalla, ed. Sumac & the Magic Lake. DuFalla, Anita, illus. 2004. (Reader's Theater Content-Area Concepts Ser.). (ENG.). (J). (gr. 1-2). 5.00 net. (978-1-4108-2291-8(5), A22915) Benchmark Education Co.

Födi, Lee Edward. Kendra Kandlestar & the Crack in Kazah. 2011. (ENG., Illus.). 294p. (J). pap. 8.95 (978-1-61254-019-1(8)) Brown Books Publishing Group.

—Kendra Kandlestar & the Crack in Kazah. Födi, Lee Edward, illus. 2011. (ENG., Illus.). 282p. (J). (gr. 4-7). 16.95 (978-1-61254-018-4(X)) Brown Books Publishing Group.

Foley, Greg. Willoughby & the Lion. 2009. (ENG., Illus.). 40p. (J). (gr. -1-2). 17.99 (978-0-06-154750-8(6)) HarperCollins Pubs.

Folz, Alexandra. Indigo's Bracelet. 2010. 84p. pap. 9.95 (978-1-4525-0058-4(4)) Get Published.

Food Fight Frenzy. 2008. (ENG., Illus.). 32p. pap. 15.95 (978-1-933300-65-8(5)) Wandering Sage Pubns., LLC.

Forbes, Anne. The Underground City, 32 vols. 2008. (Contemporary Kelpies Ser.). (ENG.). 272p. (J). pap. (978-0-86315-637-3(1)) Floris Bks.

Ford, Adam B. The Six Sisters & Their Flying Carpets. 2017. (ENG., Illus.). (J). (gr. k-2). pap. 10.95 (978-0-9794104-7-5(9)) H Bar Pr.

—The Six Sisters & Their Flying Carpets. Abbott, Kristin, illus. 2012. 34p. (-18). 20.95 (978-0-9794104-6-8(0)) H Bar Pr.

Ford, Laura. Buster Brown & Tige in Misfit Heroes. 2004. (Illus.). 320p. (J). 19.95 (978-1-881554-28-8(7)) Skyward Publishing Co.

Ford, RoShawn T. Marty & the Magical Christmas Tree. 2012. 24p. pap. 17.99 (978-1-4772-3719-9(4)) AuthorHouse.

Fordham, Walter. Ilian. Krizmanic, Tatjana, illus. 2012. 42p. pap. (978-0-9813889-5-3(7)) Publish Yourself.

Forman, M. L. Adventurers Wanted, Book 1: Slathbog's Gold. 2011. (Adventurers Wanted Ser.: 1). (ENG.). 416p. (J). (gr. 5). mass mkt. 9.99 (978-1-60641-681-5(2), 5053131, Shadow Mountain) Shadow Mountain Publishing.

—Adventurers Wanted, Book 2: The Horn of Moran. 2011. 400p. 39.99 (978-1-60641-255-8(8)) Deseret Bk. Co.

—Adventurers Wanted, Book 2: The Horn of Moran. 2012. (Adventurers Wanted Ser.: 2). (ENG.). 384p. (J). (gr. 5). pap. 9.99 (978-1-60908-911-5(1), 5069125, Shadow Mountain) Shadow Mountain Publishing.

—Adventurers Wanted, Book 3: Albrek's Tomb. 2013. (Adventurers Wanted Ser.: 3). (ENG.). 504p. (J). (gr. 5). pap. 9.99 (978-1-60907-339-8(8), 5097801, Shadow Mountain) Shadow Mountain Publishing.

—Adventurers Wanted, Book 4: Sands of Nezza. 2013. (Adventurers Wanted Ser.: 4). (ENG.). 400p. (J). (gr. 5). 19.99 (978-1-60907-329-9(0), 5097486, Shadow Mountain) Shadow Mountain Publishing.

—Adventures Wanted, Book 3: Albrek's Tomb. 2012. x, 494p. (YA). 19.99 (978-1-60908-892-7(1)) Deseret Bk. Co.

Forman, Mark. The Horn of Moran. 2011. 400p. (YA). (gr. 3-18). 18.99 (978-1-60641-226-8(4), Shadow Mountain) Shadow Mountain Publishing.

Forsyth, Kate. Battle of the Heroes. 2016. (Illus.). 188p. (J). pap. 5.99 (978-1-61067-418-8(9)) Kane Miller.

—The Beast of Blackmoor Bog. 2016. (Illus.). 183p. (J). pap. 5.99 (978-1-61067-416-4(2)) Kane Miller.

—The Drowned Kingdom. 2016. (Illus.). 185p. (J). pap. 5.99 (978-1-61067-417-1(0)) Kane Miller.

—Escape from Wolfhaven Castle. 2016. (Illus.). 185p. (J). pap. 5.99 (978-1-61067-414-0(6)) Kane Miller.

—Wolves of the Witchwood. 2016. (Illus.). 188p. (J). pap. 5.99 (978-1-61067-415-7(4)) Kane Miller.

Foster, D. S. The Stone Heart. Lewis, Jesse, illus. 2012. (J). pap. 12.99 (978-1-937331-14-6(8)) ShadeTree Publishing, LLC.

Foster, Emily. The Drowning Eyes. 2016. (ENG.). 144p. pap. 13.99 (978-0-7653-8768-4(9), 900161511, Tor.com) Doherty, Tom Assocs., LLC.

Fouch, Robert L. Christmas Carol & the Defenders of Claus. 2017. (Christmas Carol Adventure Ser.: 1). (ENG.). 256p. (J). 15.99 (978-1-5107-2452-5(4), Sky Pony Pr.) Skyhorse Publishing Co., Inc.

Fox, Alex. Windsock Wesley & His Wild & Wonderful Weather MacHine, Living in Cloud. Bazzoni, Lainie M. A., illus. 2010. 48p. pap. 16.50 (978-1-60911-873-0(1), Eloquent Bks.) Strategic Book Publishing & Rights Agency (SBPRA).

Fox, Janet. The Charmed Children of Rookskill Castle. 2017. lib. bdg. 19.65 (978-0-606-39785-8(X)) Turtleback.

Fox, Lucy. Keeper of the Enchanted Pool. 2009. 184p. pap. (978-1-84923-437-5(X)) YouWriteOn.

Fox, R. J. Stuart & His Incredibly Obnoxious Magical Book: Soccer, 1 vol. 2009. 86p. pap. 19.95 (978-1-4489-9833-3(6)) America Star Bks.

Foxlee, Karen. A Most Magical Girl. 2017. (ENG.). 304p. (J). (gr. 3-7). 8.99 (978-0-553-51288-5(9), Yearling) Random Hse. Children's Bks.

Frabetti, Carlo. La Magia Mas Poderosa. 11th ed. 2003. (SPA., Illus.). 120p. (J). 15.95 (978-84-204-4844-2(3)) Ediciones Alfaguara ESP. Dist: Santillana USA Publishing Co., Inc.

Francesca, Sieglinde De. A Donsy of Gnomes. 2009. pap. (978-1-61623-243-6(9)) Independent Pub.

Francis-Harris, Annabel. The Other Side of the Forest. 2006. pap. 19.95 (978-1-59526-458-9(2)) Aeon Publishing Inc.

Frank, Hannah. If I Had Three Wishes. 2008. 56p. pap. 23.99 (978-1-4343-7529-2(3)) AuthorHouse.

Franklin, Cathy. Pinta & Polly Go to the Moon, 1 vol. Poole, Tracy, illus. 2009. 27p. pap. 24.95 (978-1-60813-861-6(5)) America Star Bks.

Freeman, Faith L. Beyond the Magic Waterfall. 2006. 79p. pap. 26.38 (978-1-4116-8202-3(5)) Lulu Pr., Inc.

Freeman, Richard. The Legend of Booga Bearia. 2004. 117p. pap. 19.95 (978-1-4137-2016-7(1)) America Star Bks.

French, Vivian. The Bag of Bones: The Second Tale from the Five Kingdoms. Collins, Ross, illus. 2009. (Tales from the Five Kingdoms Ser.: 2). (ENG.). 256p. (J). (gr. 3-7). 14.99 (978-0-7636-4255-6(X)) Candlewick Pr.

—Princess Charlotte & the Enchanted Rose. Gibb, Sarah, illus. 2007. (Tiara Club Ser.: No. 7). 80p. (J). (gr. 1-4). pap. 3.99 (978-0-06-112441-9(9), Tegen, Katherine Bks) HarperCollins Pubs.

—Princess Katie & the Silver Pony. Gibb, Sarah, illus. 2007. (Tiara Club Ser.: No.2). 80p. (J). (gr. 1-4). 15.99 (978-0-06-112432-7(X), Tegen, Katherine Bks) HarperCollins Pubs.

—The Robe of Skulls: The First Tale from the Five Kingdoms. Collins, Ross, illus. 2009. (Tales from the Five Kingdoms Ser.: 1). (ENG.). 208p. (J). (gr. 3-7). pap. 8.99 (978-0-7636-4364-5(5)) Candlewick Pr.

Fridolfs, Derek. Darkseid & the Fires of Apokolips. Levins, Tim, illus. 2017. (Justice League Ser.). (ENG.). 88p. (J). (gr. 2-6). lib. bdg. 26.65 (978-1-4965-5157-3(5), 136170, Stone Arch Bks.) Capstone.

Friesner, Esther. Spirit's Chosen. 2014. (Princesses of Myth Ser.). (ENG., Illus.). 512p. (YA). (gr. 7). pap. 10.99 (978-0-375-87316-4(3), Ember) Random Hse. Children's Bks.

Friesner, Esther M. Spirit's Princess. 2012. 449p. (YA). (978-0-375-87315-7(5)) Random Hse., Inc.

Frost, C. Amethyst. Mourning under the Bridge. 2012. 280p. pap. 9.99 (978-0-9847236-2-1(5)) Frost, C. A.

Frost, Libby. Princess Snowbelle & the Snow Games. 2018. (ENG., Illus.). 32p. (J). 16.99 (978-1-5476-0025-0(X), 900195204, Bloomsbury Children's Bks.) Bloomsbury Publishing USA.

Funaro, Gregory. Alistair Grim's Odd Aquaticum. 2016. (Alistair Grim Ser.: 2). (ENG.). 448p. (J). (gr. 3-7). pap. 7.99 (978-1-4847-0900-9(4)) Hyperion Bks. for Children.

—Alistair Grim's Odditorium. 2015. (J). lib. bdg. 18.40 (978-0-606-37399-9(3)) Turtleback.

—Watch Hollow. Griffin, Matthew, illus. (Watch Hollow Ser.: 1). (ENG.). (J). (gr. 3-7). 2020. 272p. pap. 7.99 (978-0-06-264346-9(0)) 2019. 256p. 16.99 (978-0-06-264345-2(2)) HarperCollins Pubs. (HarperCollins).

Funke, Cornelia. Inkdeath (Inkheart Trilogy, Book 3) 2010. (Inkheart Ser.: 3).Tr. of Tintentod. (ENG.). 704p. (J). (gr. 3-8). 12.99 (978-0-439-86629-3(4), Scholastic Paperbacks) Scholastic, Inc.

—Inkheart (Inkheart Trilogy, Book 1) Bell, Anthea, tr. 2005. (Inkheart Ser.: 1).Tr. of Tintenherz. (ENG., Illus.). 576p. (J). (gr. 4-7). pap. 10.99 (978-0-439-70910-1(5)) Scholastic, Inc.

—Inkspell (Inkheart Trilogy, Book 2) 2007. (Inkheart Ser.: 2). (ENG., Illus.). 672p. (J). (gr. 4-7). pap. 10.99 (978-0-439-55401-5(2), Chicken Hse., The) Scholastic, Inc.

Funny, Ania. The Power of Ania to Change the World of Bullying. 2012. 28p. pap. 15.99 (978-1-4797-4599-9(5)) Xlibris Corp.

Furman, Ben. Sam's Quest. 2008. 240p. pap. 8.95 (978-0-9778731-4-2(5)) Black Hawk Pr., Inc., The.

Furuya, Michael, illus. Keoni's Special Gift. 2009. (J). (978-1-56647-915-8(0)) Mutual Publishing LLC.

Gabriel, Thora. Chessie Bligh & the Scroll of Andelthor. 2006. 284p. (J). 27.95 (978-0-595-83579-9(1)) iUniverse, Inc.

Gailey, Sarah. When We Were Magic. 2020. (ENG.). 352p. (YA). (gr. 9). 18.99 (978-1-5344-3287-1(6), Simon Pulse) Simon Pulse.

Gaiman, Neil, et al. Eternity's Wheel. (InterWorld Trilogy Ser.: 3). (ENG.). 288p. (YA). (gr. 8). 2016. pap. 9.99 (978-0-06-206800-2(8)) 2015. 17.99 (978-0-06-206799-9(0)) HarperCollins Pubs. (HarperTeen).

Gale, Audra. The Adventures of Buddy & Me. 2007. 32p. (YA). pap. 8.00 (978-0-8059-7277-1(3)) Dorrance Publishing Co., Inc.

Gale, Eric Kahn. The Wizard's Dog Fetches the Grail. 2018. (ENG., Illus.). 288p. (J). (gr. 3-7). 16.99 (978-0-553-53740-6(7), Crown Books For Young Readers) Random Hse. Children's Bks.

Gallego García, Laura & Peden, Margaret Sayers. The Valley of the Wolves. 2006. 247p. (J). pap. (978-0-439-58554-5(6), Levine, Arthur A. Bks.) Scholastic, Inc.

Galliez, Roxane Marie. Give Me Moon. Delanssay, Cathy, illus. 2009. 44p. (J). (gr. -1-3). 14.99 (978-0-8416-7138-6(9)) Hammond World Atlas Corp.

Garber, Stephanie. Legendary. 2018. (CHI.). (YA). (gr. 8-12). pap. (978-986-235-684-5(7)) Faces Pubns.

—Legendary. 2018. (Caraval Ser.). (ENG., Illus.). 495p. (YA). (gr. 8-13). pap. 11.99 (978-1-250-19222-6(6)) Flatiron Bks.

—Legendary. 2018. (Illus.). 451p. (YA). (978-1-250-30129-1(7)); (978-1-250-30127-7(0)) St. Martin's Pr.

—Legendary: A Caraval Novel. (Caraval Ser.: 2). (ENG., Illus.). (YA). 2019. 512p. pap. 11.99 (978-1-250-09532-9(8), 900160660) 2018. 464p. 19.99 (978-1-250-09531-2(X), 900160659) Flatiron Bks.

Garcia, Gloria. Magia. (SPA.). 8p. 9.95 (978-84-272-7275-0(8)) Molino, Editorial ESP. Dist: Distribooks, Inc.

Gardner, Lyn. Out of the Woods. 2011. (Eden Sisters Ser.). (ENG., Illus.). 368p. (J). (gr. 3-7). 8.99 (978-0-385-75226-8(1), Yearling) Random Hse. Children's Bks.

Gardner, Sally. I, Coriander. 2007. (ENG., Illus.). 288p. (J). (gr. 5-18). 7.99 (978-0-14-240763-9(1), Puffin Books) Penguin Young Readers Group.

—Operation Bunny: Book One. Roberts, David, illus. 2014. (Wings & Co Ser.: 1). (ENG.). 208p. (J). (gr. 2-5). pap. 8.99 (978-1-250-05053-3(7), 900134108) Square Fish.

—The Red Necklace. 2009. (ENG.). 400p. (YA). (gr. 7-18). 8.99 (978-0-14-241488-0(3), Speak) Penguin Young Readers Group.

—The Red Necklace: A Story of the French Revolution. 2009. (ENG.). 378p. (YA). (gr. 7). lib. bdg. 19.80 (978-1-5311-8287-8(9)) Perfection Learning Corp.

—The Red Necklace: A Story of the French Revolution. l.t. ed. 2008. 583p. 23.95 (978-1-4104-1016-0(1)) Thorndike Pr.

—The Silver Blade. 2010. (ENG.). 384p. (YA). (gr. 7-18). 8.99 (978-0-14-241731-7(9), Speak) Penguin Young Readers Group.

Garis, Howard R. Umboo, the Elephant. 2008. 108p. pap. 9.95 (978-1-60664-156-9(5)) Aegypan.

Garland, Michael. Miss Smith & the Haunted Library. 2012. 32p. (J). (gr. -1-2). 7.99 (978-0-14-242122-2(7), Puffin Books) Penguin Young Readers Group.

—Miss Smith Reads Again! 2006. (Illus.). (J). (978-1-4156-8098-8(1), Dutton Juvenile) Penguin Publishing Group.

—Miss Smith's Incredible Storybook. Garland, Michael, illus. 2005. (Illus.). 32p. (J). (gr. -1-2). pap. 8.99 (978-0-14-240282-5(6), Puffin Books) Penguin Young Readers Group.

—Miss Smith's Incredible Storybook. 2007. 29.95 incl. audio compact disk (978-0-8045-4159-6(0)); 27.95 incl. audio (978-0-8045-6945-3(2)) Spoken Arts, Inc.

Garner, Alan. The Weirdstone of Brisingamen: A Tale of Alderley. 2006. (ENG., Illus.). 288p. (J). (gr. 4-8). pap. 16.95 (978-0-15-205636-0(X)) Houghton Mifflin Harcourt Publishing Co.

Garrido, Pedro Gelabert. El Libro del Abuelo: Un Mundo de Aventuras Entre la Realidad y la Fantasma. Velert, Miriam, illus. 2003. (Ficcion Interactiva Ser.). (SPA.). 160p. pap. 14.95 (978-84-89984-11-0(5)) Recursos, Ediciones ESP. Dist: Independent Pubs. Group.

Gary R Kirby. Stories of Sunshine & Funtime of Wonder & Thunder of Mystery & Magic for the Young to Grow On. 2009. 404p. pap. 22.95 (978-1-4401-8640-0(5)) iUniverse, Inc.

Garza, Carmen Lomas. Magic Windows: Ventanas Magicas, 1 vol. Garza, Carmen Lomas, illus. 2013. (Magic Windows Ser.). (ENG., Illus.). 32p. (J). (gr. 2-5). pap. 10.95 (978-0-89239-183-7(9), leelowcbp, Children's Book Press) Lee & Low Bks., Inc.

Gates, J. Gabriel & Keel, Charlene. Ghost Crown. 2012. (Tracks Ser.). (ENG.). 456p. (YA). (gr. 6-12). pap. 9.95 (978-0-7573-1594-7(1), HCI Teens) Health Communications, Inc.

Geiger, Kay. Treasure. 2010. 36p. pap. 19.95 (978-1-4457-6383-5(4)) Lulu Pr., Inc.

Gentry, Brad. The Hollywood Princess. 2009. 40p. pap. 20.99 (978-1-4490-3545-7(0)) AuthorHouse.

George, Jessica Day. Princess of Glass. 2011. (Twelve Dancing Princesses Ser.). (ENG.). 272p. (YA). (gr. 7). pap. 10.99 (978-1-59990-659-1(7), 900074740, Bloomsbury USA Childrens) Bloomsbury Publishing USA.

—Princess of the Midnight Ball. 2010. (Twelve Dancing Princesses Ser.). (ENG.). 304p. (YA). (gr. 7-9). pap. 10.99 (978-1-59990-455-9(1), 900064161, Bloomsbury USA Childrens) Bloomsbury Publishing USA.

—Saturdays at Sea. 2018. (Tuesdays at the Castle Ser.). (ENG.). 288p. (J). pap. 8.99 (978-1-68119-606-0(9), 900179030, Bloomsbury USA Childrens) Bloomsbury Publishing USA.

George, Kallie. Clover's Luck. 2015. (Magical Animal Adoption Agency Ser.: 1). (J). lib. bdg. 16.00 (978-0-606-37504-7(X)) Turtleback.

—The Enchanted Egg. 2015. (Magical Animal Adoption Agency Ser.: 2). (J). lib. bdg. 26.95 (978-0-606-38337-0(9)) Turtleback.

—The Missing Magic. 2017. (Magical Animal Adoption Agency Ser.: 3). (J). lib. bdg. 16.00 (978-0-606-39973-9(9)) Turtleback.

Geragotelis, Brittany. Life's a Witch. 2013. (Life's a Witch Ser.). (ENG., Illus.). 320p. (YA). (gr. 9). 16.99 (978-1-4424-6655-5(3), Simon & Schuster Bks. For Young Readers) Simon & Schuster Bks. For Young Readers.

—What the Spell. (Life's a Witch Ser.). (ENG., Illus.). (YA). (gr. 9). 2014. 352p. pap. 9.99 (978-1-4424-6707-1(X)) 2013. 336p. 16.99 (978-1-4424-6815-3(7)) Simon & Schuster Bks. For Young Readers. (Simon & Schuster Bks. For Young Readers).

—The Witch Is Back. 2014. (Life's a Witch Ser.). (ENG., Illus.). 352p. (YA). (gr. 9). 17.99 (978-1-4424-6688-3(X), Simon & Schuster Bks. For Young Readers) Simon & Schuster Bks. For Young Readers.

—The Witch Is Back. 2015. (Life's a Witch Ser.). (ENG., Illus.). 352p. (YA). (gr. 9). pap. 11.99 (978-1-4424-6691-3(X)) Simon & Schuster Children's Publishing.

Geron, Eric. The Hocus Pocus Spell Book. 2022. (ENG.). 240p. (J). (gr. 3-7). 14.99 (978-1-368-07669-2(6), Disney Press Books) Disney Publishing Worldwide.

Gewirtz, Allen. The Magic Turtle. 2008. (ENG.). 42p. per. 16.99 (978-1-4257-9134-6(4)) Xlibris Corp.

Ghazwah, Sura, illus. Aladdin & His Magic Lamp: One Thousand & One Nights. 2016. (ENG.). 64p. pap. 7.95 (978-1-911091-00-4(X)) Real Reads Ltd. GBR. Dist: Casemate Pubs. & Bk. Distributors, LLC.

—Ali Baba & the Forty Thieves: One Thousand & One Nights. 2016. (ENG.). 64p. pap. 7.95 (978-1-911091-01-1(8)) Real Reads Ltd. GBR. Dist: Casemate Pubs. & Bk. Distributors, LLC.

Gibbins, Desiree. The Book Keeper's Oracle. 2008. 212p. pap. 14.49 (978-1-4389-0791-8(5)) AuthorHouse.

Gidwitz, Adam. The Inquisitor's Tale: Or, the Three Magical Children & Their Holy Dog. Aly, Hatem, illus. (ENG.). (J). (gr. 5). 2018. 400p. 9.99 (978-0-14-242737-8(3), Puffin Books) 2016. 384p. 18.99 (978-0-525-42616-5(7), Dutton Books for Young Readers) Penguin Young Readers Group.

—The Inquisitor's Tale: Or, the Three Magical Children & Their Holy Dog. 2018. lib. bdg. 20.85 (978-0-606-40873-8(8)) Turtleback.

Giles, Chauncey. The Magic Spectacles: A Fairy Story. 2004. reprint ed. pap. 22.95 (978-0-7661-8731-3(4)) Kessinger Publishing, LLC.

Gillrie Fraser, Marg. The Dolphin Way. 2011. 156p. (gr. -1 — 1). 22.95 (978-1-4502-8225-3(3)); pap. 12.95 (978-1-4502-8224-6(5)) iUniverse, Inc.

Gilman, Laura Anne. The Camelot Spell. 2006. (Grail Quest Ser.: No. 1). 291p. (J). (gr. 5-9). 10.99 (978-0-06-077279-6(4)) HarperCollins Pubs.

Gilman, Phoebe. The Balloon Tree. 2011. (ENG., Illus.). 32p. (J). (gr. -1-k). 16.95 (978-1-61608-454-7(5), 608454, Sky Pony Pr.) Skyhorse Publishing Co., Inc.

Gilson. Melusine - Hocus Pocus. Clarke & Clarke, illus. 2007. (Melusine Ser.: 1). 48p. (J). (gr. -1-12). per. 9.99 (978-1-905460-20-5(1)) CineBook GBR. Dist: National Bk. Network.

Ginoschio De Osceola, Ibrahim. Enter the Corn Bunny, Vol. 1. 2007. 56p. per. 8.95 (978-0-595-45273-6(6)) iUniverse, Inc.

Giordano, Anne. Spencer, the Magic Rabbit. 2009. 40p. pap. 16.99 (978-1-4490-3296-8(6)) AuthorHouse.

Giorgio, Marg. Maxi's Magical Dream. 2011. 24p. pap. 12.79 (978-1-4634-4491-4(5)) AuthorHouse.

Glass, Calliope. Tiana: The Stolen Jewel. 2013. (Disney Princess Early Chapter Bks.). (J). lib. bdg. 14.75 (978-0-606-32291-1(4)) Turtleback.

Glencoe Staff. Magic Times. (J). (gr. 2). wbk. ed. (978-0-02-132490-3(5)) Macmillan Publishing Co., Inc.

Glenn Marsh, Sarah. Reign of the Fallen. 2019. (Reign of the Fallen Ser.: 1). 400p. (YA). (gr. 7). pap. 10.99 (978-0-448-49440-1(X), Razorbill) Penguin Young Readers Group.

Glennon, Michelle. My Big Green Teacher: Don't Rock the Boat: Saving Our Oceans. Glennon, Michelle, illus. 2008. (Illus.). 32p. (J). 19.95 (978-0-9796625-2-2(4)) GDG Publishing.

—My Big Green Teacher: Seven Generations from Now. Glennon, Michelle, illus. 2008. (Illus.). (J). 19.95 (978-0-9797952-1-3(4)) GDG Publishing.

—My Big Green Teacher: Take a Deep Breath: Saving Our Rainforests. Glennon, Michelle, illus. 2008. (ENG., Illus.). 32p. (J). 19.95 (978-0-9797952-0-6(6)) GDG Publishing.

Glessner, Gordon. Water Wars, Secrets Revealed. 2012. 24p. 12.00 (978-0-9859603-0-8(2)) Laughing Rhino Bks.

Glewwe, Eleanor. Sparkers. 2014. 336p. (J). (gr. 5-8). 16.99 (978-0-451-46876-5(7), Viking Books for Young Readers) Penguin Young Readers Group.

Gliori, Debi. Witch Baby & Me. 2010. (Illus.). 256p. (J). (gr. 2-4). pap. 12.99 (978-0-552-55676-7(9)) Transworld Publishers Ltd. GBR. Dist: Independent Pubs. Group.

Glover, Ruth E. The Lost Labyrinth. 2008. 239p. pap. 15.95 (978-1-4092-1076-4(6)) Lulu Pr., Inc.

Goelman, Ari. The Path of Names. 2013. (Illus.). 339p. (J). pap. (978-0-545-47431-3(0), Levine, Arthur A. Bks.) Scholastic, Inc.

Gogolewski, Kathe, illus. Tato. 2008. (J). (978-0-9800064-2-1(2)) Red Engine Pr.

Going, K. L. The Garden of Eve. 2009. (ENG., Illus.). 240p. (J). (gr. 3-7). pap. 14.95 (978-0-15-206614-7(4), 1099005, Clarion Bks.) HarperCollins Pubs.

Gold, Gina. Minnie: Hocus Bow-Cus! 2014. (Mickey & Friends World of Reading Ser.). (J). lib. bdg. 13.55 (978-0-606-35270-3(8)) Turtleback.

Golden Books. Christmas Magic! (Frosty the Snowman) Golden Books, illus. 2016. (ENG., Illus.). 128p. (J). (gr. -1-2). pap. 9.99 (978-0-399-55224-3(3), Golden Bks.) Random Hse. Children's Bks.

—Genie Magic! (Shimmer & Shine) Golden Books, illus. 2016. (ENG., Illus.). 48p. (J). (gr. -1-2). pap. 5.99 (978-0-553-52205-1(1), Golden Bks.) Random Hse. Children's Bks.

Gollahon, Carleen Anderson. Sophie & the Mysterious Ring. 2012. 62p. (gr. 4-18). pap. 8.99 (978-1-4624-0379-0(4), Inspiring Voices) Author Solutions, LLC.

Gollub, Matthew. The Twenty-Five Mixtec Cats. Martinez, Leovigildo, illus. 2004. (J). (978-1-889910-30-7(9)) Tortuga Pr.

Goode, Suzi. The Lost Wizard Series Bk 1. 2007. pap. 11.95 (978-1-59374-817-3(5)) Whiskey Creek Pr., LLC.

Gooderham, Chris. Even More Wicked Rhymes. 2008. 68p. pap. 13.95 (978-1-4092-1753-4(1)) Lulu Pr., Inc.

Goodman, Alison. Eon. 2010. Orig. Title: The Two Pearls of Wisdom. (ENG.). 576p. (YA). (gr. 7-18). 13.99 (978-0-14-241711-9(4), Firebird) Penguin Young Readers Group.

—Eon: Dragoneye Reborn. 2010. (Eon Ser.: 1). lib. bdg. 22.10 (978-0-606-23647-8(3)) Turtleback.

—The Last Dragoneye. 2012. (Eon Ser.: 2). lib. bdg. 23.30 (978-0-606-23648-5(1)) Turtleback.

Goodman, John. Percy's Magical Adventures. 2005. (Illus.). 170p. pap. (978-1-84401-556-6(4)) Athena Pr.

Goodnight, Lora. Ivy Tales: The First Irish Fairy. Goins, Heather Lea, illus. 2012. 28p. pap. 24.95 (978-1-4626-9484-6(5)) America Star Bks.

Goodyear-Brown, Paris. Gabby the Gecko. 2003. per. (978-1-932203-54-7(0)) Sundog, Ltd.

Gordon, Judy Ann. Grammie's Magical Garden: Beyond the Gate. 2012. 68p. pap. 28.99 (978-1-4772-7973-1(3)) AuthorHouse.

Gordon, Mike & Gordon, Carl, illus. The Magic Porridge Pot. 2008. (Usborne First Reading: Level 3 Ser.). 48p. (J). (gr. -1-3). 8.99 (978-0-7945-1883-7(4), Usborne) EDC Publishing.

Gordon, Sylvia. Further Adventures of the Potty Wizard & His Cat, Muddles. 2009. (Illus.). 60p. pap. 10.49 (978-1-4389-6819-3(1)) AuthorHouse.

Gorman, Zac. Thisby Thestoop & the Wretched Scrattle. Bosma, Sam, illus. 2019. (ENG.). 384p. (J). (gr. 3-7). 16.99 (978-0-06-249574-7(7), HarperCollins) HarperCollins Pubs.

Gormley, Greg. Grandad's Busy Day. 2007. (Fantastic Phones Ser.). (Illus.). 12p. (J). (gr. k-k). bds. 9.99 (978-0-7475-8377-6(3)) Bloomsbury Publishing Plc GBR. Dist: Independent Pubs. Group.

Gormon: The Sentinel Awakes. 2004. per. 2.75 (978-0-9762294-0-7(4)) Corbett Features.

Gos. The Smurfs #7: The Astrosmurf. 2011. (Smurfs Graphic Novels Ser.: 7). (ENG., Illus.). 56p. (J). (gr. 2-5). pap. 5.99

(978-1-59707-250-2(8), 900075394, Papercutz) Mad Cave Studios.

Gos & Delporte, Yvan. The Smurfs #6: Smurfs & the Howlibird: The Smurfs & the Howlibird, Vol. 6. 2011. (Smurfs Graphic Novels Ser.: 6). (ENG., Illus.). 56p. (J). (gr. 2-5). pap. 5.99 *(978-1-59707-260-1(5)*, 900075410, Papercutz) Mad Cave Studios.

—The Smurfs #6: Smurfs & the Howlibird: The Smurfs & the Howlibird, Vol. 6. 2011. (Smurfs Graphic Novels Ser.: 6). (ENG., Illus.). 56p. (J). (gr. 2-5). 10.99 *(978-1-59707-261-8(3)*, 900075411, Papercutz) Mad Cave Studios.

Gosine, Aarti. The Magic Cave: A Cascade Children's Book. 2011. (Illus.). 100p. pap. 12.52 *(978-1-4567-7050-1(0))* AuthorHouse.

Goudge, Elizabeth. The Little White Horse. movie tie-in ed. 2008. (ENG., Illus.). 224p. (J). (gr. 4-7). pap. *(978-0-7459-6118-7(5))* Lion Hudson PLC GBR. Dist: Independent Pubs. Group.

Graegin, Stephanie. Little Fox in the Forest. Graegin, Stephanie, illus. 2017. (Illus.). 40p. (J). (gr. -1-3). 17.99 *(978-0-553-53789-5(X)*, Schwartz & Wade Bks.) Random Hse. Children's Bks.

Graham, Deborah. The Magic Comes Back: A Max & Sam Adventure. 2012. 66p. (gr. 2-4). pap. 8.95 *(978-1-4759-4758-8(5))* iUniverse, Inc.

Graham-Larkin, Debbie. Magic in the Air. 2005. (Graham Cracker Kids Adventure Ser.). (Illus.). (J). pap. 12.95 *(978-0-9716475-1-0(8))* Graham Cracker Kids.

Grahame, Howard. The Wishing Book 2 - Return to Mars. 2009. 102p. (J). pap. *(978-1-905809-80-6(6))* Pneuma Springs Publishing.

Gramp's Magic Gift. 2011. 98p. 24.99 *(978-1-4628-2980-4(5))*; pap. 15.99 *(978-1-4628-2979-8(1))* Xlibris Corp.

Grandma's Magical Storybook. 2003. (Illus.). 256p. (J). 12.98 *(978-1-4054-0968-1(1))* Parragon, Inc.

Grant, John. Littlenose the Magician. Collins, Ross, illus. 2009. (ENG.). 112p. (J). (gr. k-12). pap. 5.99 *(978-1-84738-201-6(0)*, Simon & Schuster Children's) Simon & Schuster, Ltd. GBR. Dist: Simon & Schuster, Inc.

Grant, Joyce. Gabby Drama Queen, 1 vol. Dolby, Jan, illus. 2013. (ENG.). 32p. (J). (gr. -1-1). 18.95 *(978-1-55455-310-5(5)*, 554faacb-7160-42da-a385-593b934b19c6) Trifolium Bks., Inc. CAN. Dist: Firefly Bks., Ltd.

Gratton, Tessa. Blood Magic. 2012. (Blood Journals). (ENG.). 416p. (YA). (gr. 8-12). lib. bdg. 26.19 *(978-0-375-96733-7(8))* Random House Publishing Group.

—Blood Magic. 2011. 408p. (YA). pap. *(978-0-375-86486-5(5))* Random Hse. Children's Bks.

Graves, Jonathan. Isabella Propeller & the Magic Beanie. Haley, Gail E., illus. 2011. (J). 15.95 *(978-1-933251-74-5(3))* Parkway Pubs., Inc.

Graves, Peter, tr. from SWE. Nils Holgersson's Wonderful Journey Through Sweden, 2 vols. 2013. (ENG., Illus.). 382p. pap. 32.00 *(978-1-870041-97-3(6))*; 360p. pap. 32.00 *(978-1-870041-96-6(8))* Norvik Pr. GBR. Dist: Dufour Editions, Inc.

Graves, Robert. The Big Green Book. Sendak, Maurice, illus. 2018. (ENG.). 64p. (J). (gr. -1-3). 18.95 *(978-0-06-264483-1(1)*, HarperCollins) HarperCollins Pubs.

Graves, Sue. Harry & the Horse. 2011. (Tadpoles Ser.). (ENG., Illus.). 24p. (J). (gr. k-2). *(978-0-7787-0579-6(X))*; pap. *(978-0-7787-0590-1(0))* Crabtree Publishing Co.

Gravett, Emily. Spells. Gravett, Emily, illus. 2009. (ENG., Illus.). 32p. (J). (gr. -1-3). 16.99 *(978-1-4169-8270-8(1)*, Simon & Schuster Bks. For Young Readers) Simon & Schuster Bks. For Young Readers.

Gray, Betty. The Legend of CaseyRock. 2007. (Illus.). 40p. (J). per. 12.00 *(978-0-9779601-2-5(9))* Neighborhood Pubs.

Gray, Christopher. There Be Goblins in the Wood! 2012. 112p. (gr. 2-4). 23.99 *(978-1-4772-6994-7(0))*; pap. 14.95 *(978-1-4772-6995-4(9))* AuthorHouse.

Gray, Claudia. Steadfast. 2015. (Spellcaster Ser.: 2). (ENG.). 368p. (YA). (gr. 8). pap. 9.99 *(978-0-06-196123-6(X)*, HarperTeen) HarperCollins Pubs.

Graziani, Maria. A Black Cat on Halloween: Un Gato Negro en Dia de Brujas. Elejalde, Eliana, illus. l.t. ed. 2004. (SPA.). 23p. (J). 7.00 *(978-0-9762361-1-5(7))* Ed. Acespanish S.A.C.- Lima, Peru.

Greban, Tanguy. Sarah So Small. Greban, Quentin, illus. 2004. (ENG.). 32p. (J). (gr. 4-7). 16.95 *(978-1-59687-179-3(2))* IBks., Inc.

Green, Katie May. Seen & Not Heard. Green, Katie May, illus. 2015. (ENG., Illus.). 32p. (J). (gr. k-3). 15.99 *(978-0-7636-7612-4(8))* Candlewick Pr.

Green with Envy. 2014. (Unicorn Magic Ser.: 3). (ENG., Illus.). 144p. (J). (gr. 1-4). pap. 6.99 *(978-1-4424-9826-6(9)*, Aladdin) Simon & Schuster Children's Publishing.

Greenawalt, Kelly. Princess Truly in My Magical, Sparkling Curls. Rauscher, Amariah, illus. 2018. (Princess Truly Ser.). (ENG.). 40p. (J). (gr. -1-k). 18.99 *(978-1-338-16719-1(7)*, Orchard Bks.) Scholastic, Inc.

Greenberg, Nicki. Zelda Stitch Term Two: Too Much Witch. 2019. (ENG.). 288p. (J). (gr. 2-6). pap. 12.99 *(978-1-76052-367-1(4)*, A&U Children's) Allen & Unwin AUS. Dist: Independent Pubs. Group.

Greene, Montrell. The Magic in Me Series #1: Magical Me. 2011. 16p. (gr. -1). pap. 12.95 *(978-1-4567-5785-4(7))* AuthorHouse.

Greene, Montrell & Greene, Robie. The Magic in Me Series #2: Imagine Me. 2011. 16p. (gr. -1). pap. 12.95 *(978-1-4567-5783-0(0))* AuthorHouse.

Greene, Stephanie. Princess Posey & the Christmas Magic. 2013. (Princess Posey, First Grader Ser.: 7). 96p. (J). (gr. k-3). pap. 5.99 *(978-0-14-242734-7(9)*, Puffin Books) Penguin Young Readers Group.

Greenfield, Amy Butler. Chantress Alchemy. 2015. (Chantress Ser.). (ENG., Illus.). 368p. (YA). (gr. 7). pap. 10.99 *(978-1-4424-5708-9(2)*, McElderry, Margaret K. Bks.) McElderry, Margaret K. Bks.

Greenspan, Deborah. Kids' Day. 2004. (J). pap. 10.95 *(978-1-59526-197-7(4))* Aeon Publishing Inc.

Greer, Hannah. The Castle Ivengless: The Velvet Bag Memoirs, Bk. 3. 2009. 145p. pap. 24.95 *(978-1-60749-105-7(2))* America Star Bks.

—The Velvet Bag Memoirs, Bk. 1. 2008. 132p. pap. 24.95 *(978-1-60672-190-2(9))* America Star Bks.

Gregorich, Barbara. It's Magic, Level 3. Hoffman, Joan, ed. Pape, Richard, illus. 3rd ed. 2011. (ENG.). 16p. (J). (gr. -1-2). pap. 3.49 *(978-0-88743-029-9(5)*, 72588415-8d9c-494d-907c-097ed9e20a52) School Zone Publishing Co.

Grey, Melissa. The Savage Dawn. 2017. (Girl at Midnight Ser.: 3). (ENG.). 496p. (YA). (gr. 9). 17.99 *(978-0-385-74469-0(2))*; lib. bdg. 20.99 *(978-0-375-99181-3(6))* Random Hse. Children's Bks. (Delacorte Pr.)

Griffin, Lydia. BeBa & the Curious Creature Catchers. Lostimolo, Stephanie, illus. l.t. ed. 2006. 32p. (J). 16.95 *(978-0-9770516-0-1(9))* Laffin Minor Pr.

Griffin, Sammy. Mighty Meg 1: Mighty Meg & the Magical Ring. Player, Micah, illus. 2019. (Mighty Meg Ser.: 1). (ENG.). 112p. (J). (gr. k-3). 17.99 *(978-1-4998-0832-2(1))*; pap. 6.99 *(978-1-4998-0831-5(3))* Little Bee Books Inc.

Griffin, Sarah Maria. Other Words for Smoke. 2019. (ENG.). 352p. (YA). (gr. 9). 17.99 *(978-0-06-240891-4(7)*, Greenwillow Bks.) HarperCollins Pubs.

Griffith, Diane. Granny's Magic Garden. 2010. 66p. pap. 19.95 *(978-1-60693-925-3(4)*, Eloquent Bks.) Strategic Book Publishing & Rights Agency (SBPRA).

Griggs, Terry. Nieve. Griggs-Burr, Alexander, illus. 2010. 264p. (J). (gr. 4-10). pap. 14.95 *(978-1-897231-87-6(3))* Biblioasis CAN. Dist: Consortium Bk. Sales & Distribution.

Grime, L. L. Do You Love Me? 2006. (ENG.). 48p. pap. 22.95 *(978-1-4357-1364-2(8))* Lulu Pr., Inc.

Grimm, Brothers. Sleeping Beauty. Dusíková, Maja, illus. 2012. (ENG.). 32p. (J). (gr. -1-3). 17.95 *(978-0-7358-4087-4(3))* North-South Bks., Inc.

Grinti, Mike & Grinti, Rachel. Claws. 2012. (J). *(978-0-545-43314-3(2)*, Chicken Hse., The) Scholastic, Inc.

Gripari, Pierre. Le Gentil Petit Diable: Et Autres Contes de la Rue Broca. Rosado, Puig, illus. 2007. (Folio Junior Ser.). 142p. (J). per. *(978-2-07-061255-0(4))* National Round Table on the Environment & the Economy (NRTEE)/Table ronde nationale sur l'environnement et l'economie (TRNEE).

Grossman, Lev. The Silver Arrow. (ENG.). (J). (gr. 3-7). 2021. 272p. pap. 8.99 *(978-0-316-53954-8(6))* 2020. (Illus.). 272p. 16.99 *(978-0-316-53953-1(8))* 2020. (Illus.). 288p. 32.99 *(978-0-316-54170-1(2))* Little, Brown Bks. for Young Readers.

—The Silver Arrow. 2022. (Penworthy Picks YA Fiction Ser.). (ENG., Illus.). 259p. (J). (gr. 4-5). 19.46 *(978-1-68505-117-4(0))* Penworthy Co., LLC, The.

Gruber, Daveda. Castle of Ice. 2008. 51p. pap. 10.94 *(978-1-4357-3251-3(0))* Lulu Pr., Inc.

Gudsnuk, Kristen. Making Friends: a Graphic Novel (Making Friends #1) Gudsnuk, Kristen, illus. 2018. (Making Friends Ser.: 1). (ENG., Illus.). 272p. (J). (gr. 3-7). pap. 12.99 *(978-1-338-13921-1(5))*; Vol. 1. 24.99 *(978-1-338-13922-8(3))* Scholastic, Inc. (Graphix).

Guess, Catherine Ritch. Rudy & the Magic Sleigh. 2006. (Rudy the Red Pig Ser.). (ENG., Illus.). 32p. 14.95 *(978-1-933341-18-7(1))* CRM.

Guillain, Adam. Bella Balistica & the Temple of Tikal, 1 vol. 2004. (Bella Balistica Ser.). (ENG., Illus.). 288p. (J). (gr. 4-7). pap. 9.95 *(978-1-84059-394-5(6))* Milet Publishing.

Gummelt, Donna & Melchiorre, Dondino. Michelina the Magical Musical Good Witch of the Forest. Wall, Randy Hugh, ed. Varela, Juan D., tr. Varela, Juan D., illus. 2006. (SPA.). 34p. (J). 14.95 *(978-0-9764798-6-4(9))* Story Store Collection Publishing.

Gunderson, Jessica. Truthfully, Something Smelled Fishy! The Story of the Fisherman & His Wife As Told by the Wife. Guerlais, Gérald, illus. 2018. (Other Side of the Story Ser.). (ENG.). 24p. (J). (gr. -1-3). lib. bdg. 27.99 *(978-1-5158-2298-1(2)*, 137007, Picture Window Bks.) Capstone.

Guru Animation Studio Ltd., illus. True & the Rainbow Kingdom: the Magical Flower. 2019. 24p. (J). (gr. -1-1). 3.99 *(978-2-89802-034-6(6)*, CrackBoom! Bks.) Chouette Publishing CAN. Dist: Publishers Group West (PGW).

Guterson, Ben. The Secrets of Winterhouse. Bristol, Chloe, illus. 2019. (Winterhouse Ser.: 2). (ENG.). 400p. (J). pap. 9.99 *(978-1-250-23352-3(6)*, 900174324) Square Fish.

—Winterhouse. Bristol, Chloe, illus. 2018. (Winterhouse Ser.: 1). (ENG.). 400p. (J). pap. 8.99 *(978-1-250-29419-7(3)*, 900174321) Square Fish.

Gwyer, Gillian K. Podnockery Forest - Owl & the Trickster. 2013. 40p. *(978-1-4602-3974-2(1))* FriesenPress.

Haesche, Richard Paul, Sr. The Magic of the Leprechaun. 2007. (ENG.). 182p. (YA). *(978-0-9798536-3-0(X))* Kreative X-Pressions Pubns.

Hagen, George. Gabriel Finley & the Lord of Air & Darkness. 2017. 288p. (J). (gr. 4-7). 16.99 *(978-0-399-55347-9(9)*, Schwartz & Wade Bks.) Random Hse. Children's Bks.

Hahner, Aaron. The Magic of Midnight. 2004. per. 8.95 *(978-1-932560-58-9(0))* Aeon Publishing Inc.

Hahnke. Through the Eyes of a Raptor. 2007. 424p. per. 19.95 *(978-0-595-42609-6(3))* iUniverse, Inc.

Haig, Matt. To Be a Cat. Curtis, Stacy, illus. (ENG.). 304p. (J). (gr. 3-7). 2014. pap. 3.99 *(978-1-4424-5406-4(7))* 2013. 16.99 *(978-1-4424-5405-7(9))* Simon & Schuster Children's Publishing.

Haile, Carol J. The Princess Tree: A Tale of Fairies, Elves & Magic. l.t. ed. 2005. (ESK., Illus.). 32p. (J). 19.95 *(978-0-9711236-1-8(6))* Firenze Pr.

Haining, Peter. Magicians' Circle. 2012. 348p. (-18). pap. *(978-1-4596-4365-9(8))* ReadHowYouWant.com, Ltd.

Halbrook, K. D. Smoke & Mirrors. 2018. (ENG., Illus.). 240p. (J). (gr. 3-7). 16.99 *(978-1-5344-0504-2(6)*, Simon & Schuster/Paula Wiseman Bks.) Simon & Schuster/Paula Wiseman Bks.

Haldane, Rachael. Nymphas' World. 2009. 392p. pap. 13.99 *(978-1-61667-003-0(7))* Raider Publishing International.

Hale, Bruce. Fat Cat of Underwhere. Hillman, Shane, illus. 2009. (Underwhere Ser.). 176p. (J). pap. 5.99 *(978-0-06-085135-4(X))* HarperCollins Pubs.

—Pirates of Underwhere. Hillman, Shane, illus. 2008. (Underwhere Ser.). 164p. (J). (gr. 3-7). lib. bdg. 16.89 *(978-0-06-085128-6(7))* HarperCollins Pubs.

—Prince of Underwhere. Hillman, Shane, illus. 2009. (Underwhere Ser.: 1). (ENG.). 176p. (J). (gr. 3-7). pap. 5.99 *(978-0-06-085126-2(0)*, HarperCollins) HarperCollins Pubs.

Hale, Susan Elizabeth. Emma Oliver & the Song of Creation. 2016. (ENG., Illus.). 178p. (J). (gr. -1-12). pap. 11.95 *(978-1-78535-386-4(1)*, Our Street Bks.) Hunt, John Publishing Ltd. GBR. Dist: National Bk. Network.

Hall, Kirsten. Revamp Your Room. 2005. (Illus.). 48p. pap. *(978-0-439-80296-3(2))* Scholastic, Inc.

Hall, Traci. Wiccan Cool. 2010. (Rhiannon Godfrey Ser.). (ENG.). 264p. pap. 15.00 *(978-1-60504-611-2(6))* Samhain Publishing, LTD.

Hamilton, C. After Ever Happily. 2006. 80p. pap. 16.95 *(978-1-4241-3190-7(1))* PublishAmerica, Inc.

Hamilton, John. Dog Friday. 2010. (Illus.). 60p. pap. 21.99 *(978-1-4490-9468-3(6))* AuthorHouse.

Hamilton, Kersten. In the Forests of the Night. 2. 2013. (Goblin Wars Ser.). (ENG.). 288p. (YA). (gr. 7-12). 24.94 *(978-0-547-43560-2(6)*, Clarion Bks.) HarperCollins Pubs.

Hampton, Patrick. Down by the Mulberry Tree, 1 vol. 2009. 15p. pap. 24.95 *(978-1-60703-672-2(X))* America Star Bks.

Han, Jia. My Name Is Zedonk. 2017. (Illus.). 40p. (J). (gr. -1-2). 16.95 *(978-1-941529-53-9(4)*, Plum Blossom Bks.) Parallax Pr.

Hanley, Victoria. Violet Wings. 2009. (ENG.). 368p. (J). (gr. 6-8). lib. bdg. 21.19 *(978-1-60684-039-9(8))* Farshore GBR. Dist: Children's Plus, Inc.

Hanna, Kevin & Fagan, Dave. Creature Academy GN. 2011. (Illus.). 80p. (YA). pap. 14.95 *(978-1-897548-53-0(2))* Arcana Studio, Inc.

Hao, K. T. The Magic Book. Ferri, Giuliano, illus. 2008. (ENG.). 32p. (J). (gr. -1). 16.50 *(978-1-933327-44-0(8))*; 15.95 *(978-1-933327-43-3(X))* Purple Bear Bks., Inc.

Hapka, Catherine, pseud. Dolphin School: Echo's New Pet. 2017. (ENG., Illus.). 107p. (J). pap. 4.99 *(978-1-338-05374-6(4))* Scholastic, Inc.

—Don't Meddle with Miss Nettle. 2014. (Sofia the First Ser.). (J). lib. bdg. 24.50 *(978-0-606-34101-1(3))* Turtleback.

Hardinge, Frances. Verdigris Deep. 2018. (ENG.). 304p. (gr. 8-17). pap. 10.99 *(978-1-4197-2878-5(4)*, 1172203, Amulet Bks.) Abrams, Inc.

Hardwell, Gary D. A Boo Bears' Story: Stormy Night. 2007. (Illus.). 36p. per. 10.00 *(978-0-9792016-9-1(1))* Professional Publishing Hse. LLC.

Hargreaves, Roger. Mr. Stingy. 2011. (Mr. Men & Little Miss Ser.). (ENG.). 32p. (J). (gr. -1-2). mass mkt. 4.99 *(978-0-8431-9959-8(8)*, Price Stern Sloan) Penguin Young Readers Group.

Harkey, Faith. Genuine Sweet. 2016. (ENG.). 288p. (J). (gr. 5-7). pap. 6.99 *(978-0-544-66853-9(7)*, 1625478, Clarion Bks.) HarperCollins Pubs.

Harper, Benjamin. Bird Boy: A Grimm & Gross Retelling. Banks, Timothy, illus. 2018. (Michael Dahl Presents: Grimm & Gross Ser.). (ENG.). 64p. (J). (gr. 3-5). lib. bdg. 21.99 *(978-1-4965-7317-9(X)*, 138921, Stone Arch Bks.) Capstone.

Harrington, Claudia. Book 3: Yum-Yum the Very Spoiled Fish. Syed, Anoosha, illus. 2016. (Hank the Pet Sitter Ser.). (ENG.). 32p. (J). (gr. -1-3). lib. bdg. 32.79 *(978-1-62402-189-3(1)*, 24557, Calico Chapter Bks) Magic Wagon.

Harris, Neil Patrick. The Magic Misfits. Martin, Lissy & Hilton, Kyle, illus. (Magic Misfits Ser.: 1). (ENG.). (J). (gr. 3-7). 2018. 288p. pap. 8.99 *(978-0-316-35557-5(7))* 2017. 272p. 16.99 *(978-0-316-39182-5(4))* 2017. 336p. 34.99 *(978-0-316-43984-8(3))* Little, Brown Bks. for Young Readers.

—The Magic Misfits: the Minor Third. 2019. (Magic Misfits Ser.: 3). (ENG., (J). (gr. 3-7). Illus.). 336p. 16.99 *(978-0-316-39187-0(5))*; 400p. 36.99 *(978-0-316-42589-6(3))* Little, Brown Bks. for Young Readers.

—The Magic Misfits: the Second Story. Martin, Lissy & Hilton, Kyle, illus. (Magic Misfits Ser.: 2). (ENG.). (J). (gr. 3-7). 2019. 352p. pap. 8.99 *(978-0-316-39184-9(0))* 2018. 336p. 16.99 *(978-0-316-39185-6(9))* 2018. 400p. 37.99 *(978-0-316-41986-4(9))* Little, Brown Bks. for Young Readers.

Harris, Neil Patrick & Azam, Alec. The Magic Misfits: The Second Story. Martin, Lissy, illus. 2018. xii, 312p. (J). *(978-0-316-52639-5(8))*; *(978-0-316-48724-5(4))* Little Brown & Co.

Harris, Patricia. Rosalina Becomes a Flower Fairy, 1 vol. 2017. (Rosalina's Flower Garden Ser.). (ENG.). 24p. (gr. 1-1). pap. 9.25 *(978-1-5383-2109-6(2)*, 95c68d68-32c5-4094-b5a9-c3882c0ac697, PowerKids Pr.) Rosen Publishing Group, Inc., The.

—Rosalina Learns Magic Games, 1 vol. 2017. (Rosalina's Flower Garden Ser.). (ENG.). 24p. (gr. 1-1). pap. 9.25 *(978-1-5383-2113-3(0)*, 136d091a-bca0-4bc0-996e-832ef36c113b, PowerKids Pr.) Rosen Publishing Group, Inc., The.

Harrison, Mette Ivie. The Princess & the Hound. (YA). 2008. (ENG.). 432p. (gr. 8). pap. 8.99 *(978-0-06-113189-9(X)*, HarperTeen) 2007. 410p. (gr. 7-18). lib. bdg. 18.89 *(978-0-06-113188-2(1)*, Eos) HarperCollins Pubs.

Harrison, Michelle. One Wish. 2016. (13 Treasures Trilogy Ser.: Prequel). (ENG.). 384p. (J). (gr. 3-7). 17.00 *(978-0-316-33529-4(0))* Little, Brown Bks. for Young Readers.

—13 Curses. 2012. (13 Treasures Trilogy Ser.: 2). (ENG.). 512p. (J). (gr. 5-9). pap. 23.99 *(978-0-316-04149-2(1))* Little, Brown Bks. for Young Readers.

—13 Curses. 2012. (13 Treasures Ser.: 2). (J). lib. bdg. 19.65 *(978-0-606-26160-9(5))* Turtleback.

Harrison, Paula. The Magic Fox. Williams, Sophy, illus. 2017. (Secret Rescuers Ser.: 4). (ENG.). 112p. (J). (gr. 2-5). 16.99 *(978-1-4814-7620-1(3))*; pap. 6.99 *(978-1-4814-7619-5(X))* Simon & Schuster Children's Publishing. (Aladdin).

—The Star Wolf. Williams, Sophy, illus. 2018. (Secret Rescuers Ser.: 5). (ENG.). 112p. (J). (gr. 2-5). 16.99 *(978-1-4814-7617-1(3))*; pap. 5.99 *(978-1-4814-7616-4(5))* Simon & Schuster Children's Publishing. (Aladdin).

Harrold, A. F. The Song from Somewhere Else. Pinfold, Levi, illus. 2017. (ENG.). 240p. (J). 16.99 *(978-1-68119-401-1(5)*, 900172517, Bloomsbury USA Childrens) Bloomsbury Publishing USA.

—The Song from Somewhere Else. 2018. (J). lib. bdg. 19.65 *(978-0-606-41074-8(0))* Turtleback.

Hartwell, David G., ed. Christmas Magic: Short Stories from Award-Winning Fantasy Writers. 2016. (ENG.). 496p. (Orig.). pap. 22.99 *(978-0-7653-1580-9(7)*, 900038089, Tor Bks.) Doherty, Tom Assocs., LLC.

Hartwright, Gianna. The Befana Drama. 2013. 352p. pap. *(978-0-9575697-6-8(9))* Gianna Della Luna Publishing.

Harvey, Keith. Oscar & the Magic Table: A Story about a Little Boy Who For got His Table Manners. 2015. (ENG., Illus.). 24p. pap. 8.99 *(978-1-84135-922-9(X))* Award Pubns. Ltd. GBR. Dist: Parkwest Pubns., Inc.

Harwell, Andrew. The Spider Ring. 2015. (ENG.). 224p. (J). (gr. 3-7). 16.99 *(978-0-545-68290-9(8)*, Scholastic Pr.) Scholastic, Inc.

Hasbro. Gift of Maud Pie. 2016. (Passport to Reading Level 2 Ser.). (J). lib. bdg. 13.55 *(978-0-606-39194-8(0))* Turtleback.

Haselhuhn, Hugo & Cowdell, Luke. Lucas Lightfoot & the Fire Crystal. 2016. (ENG., Illus.). 180p. (J). pap. 12.95 *(978-1-63047-783-7(4))* Morgan James Publishing.

Hashimoto, Meika. The Magic Cake Shop. Masse, Josée, illus. 2012. (ENG.). 176p. (J). (gr. 4-6). lib. bdg. 21.19 *(978-0-375-96822-8(9))* Random House Publishing Group.

Haskell, Merrie. The Princess Curse. 2013. (ENG.). 352p. (J). (gr. 3-7). pap. 7.99 *(978-0-06-200815-2(3)*, HarperCollins) HarperCollins Pubs.

Hauman, Carrie. Zoe the Magic Love Dog. 2003. (Illus.). 32p. (J). 16.00 *(978-0-9746333-8-1(0))* Alma Pr.

Hawkins, Delta Michelle. Cassandra's Journey. 2012. 28p. pap. 24.95 *(978-1-4626-9566-9(3))* America Star Bks.

Hawkins, Rachel. Demonglass, 2. 2012. (Hex Hall Novel Ser.: 2). (ENG.). 384p. (J). (gr. 5-9). pap. 8.99 *(978-1-4231-2844-1(3))* Hyperion Bks. for Children.

—Spell Bound, 3. 2013. (Hex Hall Novel Ser.: 3). (ENG.). 352p. (J). (gr. 7-17). pap. 10.99 *(978-1-4231-2140-4(6))* Hyperion Bks. for Children.

Hawley, Bobby. Matt & the Wonder of Wishes, 1 vol. 2009. 165p. pap. 24.95 *(978-1-60836-743-6(6))* America Star Bks.

Hay, Sam. Knit-Knotters. Tran, Turine, illus. 2016. (Stella & the Night Sprites Ser.: 1). (ENG.). 96p. (J). (gr. 1-3). pap. 4.99 *(978-0-545-81998-5(9))* Scholastic, Inc.

—Stella & the Night Sprites: Tooth Bandits, Vol. 2. Manuzak, Lisa, illus. 2016. (Stella & the Night Sprites Ser.: 2). (ENG.). 96p. (J). (gr. 1-3). 15.99 *(978-0-545-82001-1(4))* Scholastic, Inc.

Hayden, Jeanne. Last Minute Wilma & Her Toad Soup. 2009. 24p. pap. 14.95 *(978-1-4327-3857-0(7))* Outskirts Pr., Inc.

Haydu, Corey Ann. The Someday Suitcase. (ENG.). (J). (gr. 3-7). 2019. 320p. pap. 9.99 *(978-0-06-235276-7(8))* 2017. 304p. 16.99 *(978-0-06-235275-0(X))* HarperCollins Pubs. (Tegen, Katherine Bks).

Hayes, John C. Splurge & the Theatre of Magic. 2008. 348p. pap. 22.00 *(978-1-84426-500-8(5))* Upfront Publishing Ltd. GBR. Dist: Printondemand-worldwide.com.

Hayes, Kathryn. The Balloon Fairy. 2009. 30p. pap. 13.99 *(978-1-4389-6857-5(4))* AuthorHouse.

Hayes, Sean & Icenogle, Scott. Plum. Thompson, Robin, illus. 2018. (ENG.). 48p. (J). (gr. -1-3). 17.99 *(978-1-5344-0404-5(X)*, Simon & Schuster Bks. For Young Readers) Simon & Schuster Bks. For Young Readers.

Hayter, Rhonda. The Witchy Worries of Abbie Adams. 2011. (ENG.). 224p. (gr. 4-6). 21.19 *(978-0-8037-3468-5(9))* Penguin Young Readers Group.

Heacock, David & Giles, Inga. Child of Oz. 2010. (J). pap. *(978-0-88092-479-5(9))* Royal Fireworks Publishing Co.

Hearne, Betsy. Wishes, Kisses, & Pigs. 2003. (ENG.). 144p. (J). (gr. 3-7). pap. 6.99 *(978-0-689-86347-9(0)*, Simon & Schuster/Paula Wiseman Bks.) Simon & Schuster/Paula Wiseman Bks.

Heible, Beverly. A Christmas Party on River Row. 2012. 98p. 22.95 *(978-1-62709-018-6(5))*; pap. 17.95 *(978-1-4626-9575-1(2))* America Star Bks.

Heidi Heckelbeck Gets the Sniffles. 2014. (Heidi Heckelbeck Ser.: 12). (ENG., Illus.). 128p. (J). (gr. k-4). pap. 6.99 *(978-1-4814-1362-6(7)*, Little Simon) Little Simon.

Heilig, Heidi. For a Muse of Fire. (ENG.). (YA). (gr. 8). 2019. 528p. pap. 10.99 *(978-0-06-238082-1(6))* 2018. (Illus.). 512p. 17.99 *(978-0-06-238081-4(8))* HarperCollins Pubs. (Greenwillow Bks.).

Helgerson, Joseph. Horns & Wrinkles. Ceccoli, Nicoletta, illus. 2008. (ENG.). 240p. (J). (gr. 5-7). pap. 7.99 *(978-0-618-98178-6(0)*, 1025446, Clarion Bks.) HarperCollins Pubs.

Heller, Donna & Payne, James. The Enchanted Tree. Zamboni, David, illus. 2007. 44p. per. 14.95 *(978-1-934246-72-6(7))* Peppertree Pr., The.

Helliwell, Sheila. Gammy. Hawthorn, Paul & Hopkins, Simon, illus. 2nd ed. 2013. 70p. pap. *(978-0-9560331-4-7(8))* Children' Story Pubs.

—Hoonraki Moon: The Murphy Stories. 2006. (J). pap. 9.00 *(978-0-8059-7027-2(4))* Dorrance Publishing Co., Inc.

Hemmings, Lisa & O'Keefe, Allan. Imagine Me with the Three Owls: Feeling Great. 2012. 32p. pap. 13.95 *(978-1-4525-0551-0(9))* Balboa Pr.

Hemmingway, Tracy Hayden. The Magic Flower. George, Alex, illus. 2003. (ENG.). 24p. pap. 9.00 *(978-1-4120-0984-3(7))* Trafford Publishing.

Hendesi, Roya. The Ancient Queendom. 2011. 52p. pap. 29.05 *(978-1-4568-2783-0(9))* Xlibris Corp.

Henighan, Tom. Mercury Man. 2004. (ENG.). 200p. (YA). (gr. 6). pap. 9.99 *(978-1-55002-508-8(2))* Dundurn Pr. CAN. Dist: Publishers Group West (PGW).

Henning, Sarah. Sea Witch. (ENG.). 2019. 384p. (YA). (gr. 8). pap. 10.99 *(978-0-06-243880-5(8))* 2018. 368p. (YA). (gr. 8). 17.99 *(978-0-06-243877-5(8))* 2018. 368p. (J). *(978-0-00-830084-5(4))* HarperCollins Pubs. (Tegen, Katherine Bks).

—Sea Witch Rising. 2019. (ENG.). 416p. (YA). (gr. 8). 17.99 *(978-0-06-293147-4(4)*, Tegen, Katherine Bks) HarperCollins Pubs.

Henry, Emily. A Million Junes. 2018. 400p. (YA). (gr. 7). pap. 12.99 *(978-0-448-49397-8(7)*, Razorbill) Penguin Young Readers Group.

Henry, Heather French. Claire's Magic Sades. Henry, Heather French, illus. 2004. (Claire's Everyday Adventures Ser.). (Illus.). 32p. (J). (gr. k-4). pap. 8.95 *(978-0-9706341-7-7(X)*, 1231609) Cubbie Blue Publishing.

Henry, James. The Cabinet of Curiosities. 2010. 240p. pap. 21.50 *(978-0-9559851-0-2(2))* Blue Cat GBR. Dist: Lulu Pr., Inc.

Henry, William. Tir Na Nog: A New Adventure. Arnault, Delphine, illus. 2009. (ENG.). 128p. (J). pap. 25.95 *(978-1-85635-597-1(7))* Mercier Pr., Ltd., The IRL. Dist: Dufour Editions, Inc.

Heppermann, Christine & Koertge, Ron. Sadie's Story. Marcero, Deborah, illus. 2016. (Backyard Witch Ser.: 1). (ENG.). 176p. (J). (gr. 3-7). pap. 5.99 *(978-0-06-233839-6(0)*, Greenwillow Bks.) HarperCollins Pubs.

Herbert, Frances. Fran's Van & the Magic Box. Herbert, Frances, illus. 2013. (Illus.). 24p. pap. *(978-1-78222-085-5(2))* Paragon Publishing, Rothersthorpe.

Herbert Hilligan & His Magical Adventure Curriculum Guide. 2004. ring bd. 24.95 *(978-0-9743335-4-0(9))* Imaginative Publishing, Ltd.

Herbert Hilligan's Lone Star Adventure Curriculum Guide. 2004. ring bd. 24.95 *(978-0-9743335-7-1(3))* Imaginative Publishing, Ltd.

Herbert Hilligan's Tropical Adventure Curriculum Guide. 2004. ring bd. 24.95 *(978-0-9743335-6-4(5))* Imaginative Publishing, Ltd.

Herda, Frank A. The Cup of Death: Cronicles of the Dragons of the Magi. 2007. 180p. 16.95 *(978-1-4327-0922-8(4))*; 212p. per. 9.95 *(978-1-4327-1412-3(0))* Outskirts Pr., Inc.

Hernandez, Janice. Lisa & the Light Dancer. 2009. 48p. pap. 9.95 *(978-1-60860-243-8(5)*, Eloquent Bks.) Strategic Book Publishing & Rights Agency (SBPRA).

Hernandez, Vince. Soulfire - Shadow Magic, Vol. 1. 2018. (ENG., Illus.). 152p. (YA). pap. 14.99 *(978-0-9823628-7-7(0)*, 964981b5-5390-431c-bc1f-edbc91ceed0f) Aspen MLT, Inc.

Herrera, Joaquin. Horris, Little Eli & the Lens of Truth. 2007. (DreamFever Chronicles Ser.: Bk. 1). 208p. *(978-1-59258-245-7(1))* Hylas Publishing.

Hess, Brian F. Lynquest & the Search for Greatness. 2006. (ENG.). 116p. per. 19.95 *(978-1-4241-4503-4(1))* PublishAmerica, Inc.

Hewett, Katherine. Magic Bubble Bath. 2012. 40p. pap. 25.10 *(978-0-578-09202-7(6))* Hewett, Katherine J.E.

Higgins, Jim. The Enchanted Nursery: Heather & Hamish, Fun in Florida, Reggie Rabbit at the Seaside, Percy Penguin's Friends. 2009. (Illus.). 36p. pap. 15.49 *(978-1-4389-9904-3(6))* AuthorHouse.

Highway, Tomson. Caribou Song, 1 vol. Rombough, John, illus. 2016. (Songs of the North Wind Ser.). (ENG.). 32p. (J). (gr. 1-4). 14.95 *(978-1-927083-49-9(4)*, 9d41b559-5302-4793-8992-0810706e2291) Fifth Hse. Pubs. CAN. Dist: Firefly Bks., Ltd.

Hildahl, Violetta R. Peacock of Taj Mahal. 2011. 28p. (gr. -1). pap. 13.59 *(978-1-4520-0259-0(2))* AuthorHouse.

Hill, Amanda Rawson. The Three Rules of Everyday Magic. 2018. (ENG.). 192p. (J). (gr. 3-7). 17.95 *(978-1-62979-940-7(8)*, Astra Young Readers) Astra Publishing Hse.

Hill, Sarah. Posie Pixie & the Lost Matchbox. O'Gorman, Sarah, ed. Mauchline, Sarah, illus. 2013. 60p. pap. *(978-1-909302-31-0(7))* Abela Publishing.

Hill, Tony. The Curse of the Crooked Spire & Other Fairy Tales. 2013. (Illus.). 230p. pap. *(978-0-9568409-3-6(0))* Northern Lights Lit.

Hillyer, Rhonda. Butterfly Magic. Wood, Steve, illus. 2013. 84p. pap. 12.00 *(978-1-62212-306-3(9)*, Strategic Bk. Publishing) Strategic Book Publishing & Rights Agency (SBPRA).

Hilton, Marcel. The Magical Web. 2007. 38p. 19.50 *(978-1-4303-2678-6(6))* Lulu Pr., Inc.

Hilton, N. E. The Spell. 2010. (Illus.). 216p. pap. 15.95 *(978-1-4452-7791-2(3))* Lulu Pr., Inc.

hines, j. Finding Raven. 2007. 101p. pap. 8.95 *(978-0-615-17723-6(9))* Hines, Jerry.

Hinkler Books, ed. Ghostly Glow in the Haunted House. 2012. (Glow & Learn Ser.). (Illus.). 16p. (J). bds. 12.99 *(978-1-74308-808-1(6))* Hinkler Bks. Pty, Ltd. AUS. Dist: Ideals Pubns.

Hliva, Diana. My Pet Lunecat. 2010. 36p. pap. 18.41 *(978-1-4269-3208-3(1))* Trafford Publishing.

Hobbs, Will. Kokopelli's Flute. 2005. 148p. (gr. 5-9). 17.00 *(978-0-7569-5503-8(3))* Perfection Learning Corp.

—Kokopelli's Flute. 2005. (ENG.). 160p. (J). (gr. 5-9). pap. 7.99 *(978-1-4169-0250-8(3)*, Simon & Schuster/Paula Wiseman Bks.) Simon & Schuster/Paula Wiseman Bks.

Hodge, Rosamund. Endless Water, Starless Sky. 2019. (Bright Smoke, Cold Fire Ser.: 2). (ENG.). 448p. (YA). (gr. 8). pap. 10.99 *(978-0-06-236945-1(8)*, Balzer & Bray) HarperCollins Pubs.

Hodgson, Julie. Earth Child. 2008. 81p. pap. 6.95 *(978-1-4092-2764-9(2))* Lulu Pr., Inc.

Hodgson, Sandra. The Toof Fairies. 2011. (Illus.). 44p. (gr. -1). pap. 16.76 *(978-1-4567-7978-8(8))* AuthorHouse.

Hoena, Blake. The Horrible Hex. Bardin, Dave, illus. 2018. (Monster Heroes Ser.). (ENG.). 32p. (J). (gr. k-2). lib. bdg. 21.32 *(978-1-4965-6413-9(8)*, 138260, Stone Arch Bks.) Capstone.

—Witch's Brew. Bardin, Dave, illus. 2016. (Monster Heroes Ser.). (ENG.). 32p. (J). (gr. k-2). lib. bdg. 21.32 *(978-1-4965-3756-0(4)*, 133082, Stone Arch Bks.) Capstone.

Holbrook, John Robert. Gingerbread Jimmi: Magical Storybook. Scott, Catherine, ed. Stensaas, Martin & Strasburg, Sunny, illus. 2004. (J). 19.95 *(978-0-9762440-0-4(4))* Holbrook Studios.

Holbrook, L. E. Victoria & the Door to Travarnis. 2007. 108p. per. 19.95 *(978-1-4241-6934-4(8))* America Star Bks.

Holder, Nancy. Spirited. 2004. (Once upon a Time Ser.). (ENG.). 272p. (YA). (gr. 9). pap. 13.95 *(978-0-689-87063-7(9)*, Simon Pulse) Simon Pulse.

Holder, Nancy, et al. Resurrection. 2009. (Wicked Ser.). (ENG.). 416p. (YA). (gr. 9-18). pap. 9.99 *(978-1-4169-7227-3(7)*, Simon Pulse) Simon Pulse.

—Wicked 2: Legacy & Spellbound. 2008. (Wicked Ser.). (ENG.). 672p. (YA). (gr. 9). pap. 13.99 *(978-1-4169-7117-7(3)*, Simon Pulse) Simon Pulse.

Holland, Dwayne K. Princess Laura & the Magic Waterfall. 2010. 42p. pap. 15.50 *(978-1-60860-744-0(5)*, Strategic Bk. Publishing) Strategic Book Publishing & Rights Agency (SBPRA).

Holland, Sara. Havenfall. 2020. (Havenfall Ser.: 1). (ENG.). 320p. (YA). 18.99 *(978-1-5476-0379-4(8)*, 900215313, Bloomsbury Young Adult) Bloomsbury Publishing USA.

Holmes, Anna. Emmet's Awesome Day. Scholastic, Inc. Staff, illus. 2014. (LEGO: the LEGO Movie Ser.). (ENG.). 32p. (J). (gr. 1-3). pap. 3.99 *(978-0-545-79539-5(7))* Scholastic, Inc.

Holmes-Merritt, Angela. LINK Fairflies & Fairies. 2008. 36p. 17.50 *(978-0-615-17415-0(9))* AngiesInk.

Holmes, Sara. The Wolf Hour. 2017. 310p. (J). pap. *(978-0-545-10798-3(9)*, Levine, Arthur A. Bks.) Scholastic, Inc.

Holmes, Sara Lewis. The Wolf Hour. 2017. (ENG.). 320p. (J). (gr. 3-7). 16.99 *(978-0-545-10797-6(0)*, Levine, Arthur A. Bks.) Scholastic, Inc.

Holthaus, Abbey. The Treasures of Christmas. Downs, Braden, illus. 2008. 126p. pap. 19.95 *(978-1-60672-152-0(6))* America Star Bks.

Holub, Joan & Williams, Suzanne. Freya & the Magic Jewel. 2018. (Thunder Girls Ser.: 1). (ENG., Illus.). 272p. (J). (gr. 3-7). 16.99 *(978-1-4814-9640-7(9)*, Aladdin) Simon & Schuster Children's Publishing.

—Freya & the Magic Jewel. 2019. (Thunder Girls Ser.: 1). (ENG.). 288p. (J). (gr. 3-7). pap. 7.99 *(978-1-4814-9639-1(5)*, Simon & Schuster/Paula Wiseman Bks.) Simon & Schuster/Paula Wiseman Bks.

—Medea the Enchantress. 2017. (Goddess Girls Ser.: 23). (ENG.). 272p. (J). (gr. 3-7). 17.99 *(978-1-4814-7018-6(3))*; (Illus.). pap. 8.99 *(978-1-4814-7017-9(5))* Simon & Schuster Children's Publishing. (Aladdin).

—Snow White Lucks Out. 2014. (Grimmtastic Girls Ser.: 3). lib. bdg. 16.00 *(978-0-606-35852-1(8))* Turtleback.

Holyoak, Kathleen & Summers, Sherry. Flowers in Heaven. 2009. 32p. pap. 14.49 *(978-1-4389-4607-8(4))* AuthorHouse.

Homeyer, Henry. Wobar & the Quest for the Magic Calumet. Yunger, Joshua, illus. 2012. (ENG.). 144p. (YA). (gr. 3-9). 19.95 *(978-1-59373-108-3(6))* Bunker Hill Publishing, Inc.

Hong, Lily Toy, illus. & retold by. Two of Everything. Hong, Lily Toy, retold by. 2012. (J). *(978-1-61913-138-5(2))* Weigl Pubs., Inc.

Honigsberg, Peter Jan. Pillow of Dreams. Morse, Tony, illus. 2004. 32p. (gr. k-4). 17.95 *(978-1-57143-076-2(8))* RDR Bks.

Hook, Derek. He Walked & He Walked & He Walked. 2012. 110p. 23.95 *(978-1-937902-08-7(0))* Karina Library Pr.

Hoover, Leighnne W. Festus & his Fest Favorites. 2010. pap. 11.99 *(978-0-578-05051-5(X))* Word of Mouth Pr.

Hope, Harry S. The Elements of Lore - Volume 1 of the Books of Lore. 2008. 272p. pap. *(978-1-906210-83-0(7))* Grosvenor Hse. Publishing Ltd.

Hopkins, Jeanette. The Juggler. 2011. (Illus.). 32p. (J). 16.95 *(978-1-888160-58-1(6))* Ice Cube Pr., LLC.

Hoppe, Bethany A. Molly B. Golly's Wonderful Dancing Debut. Ayotte, Andie C., illus. 2013. 32p. 28.00 *(978-1-937763-85-5(4))* Published by Westview, Inc.

Horn, Sandra. Silkie. (ENG., Illus.). 89p. pap. 7.95 *(978-0-340-67265-5(X))* Hodder & Stoughton GBR. Dist: Trafalgar Square Publishing.

—The Silkie. Perks, Anne-Marie, illus. 2017. (ENG.). 46p. (J). pap. *(978-1-909568-11-2(2))* Clucket Pr., The.

Horowitz, Alena Netia. The Tlytiettlym Tree. Horowitz, Alena Netia & De La Fuente, Mary, illus. l.t. ed. 2003. 64p. (J). per. 12.95 *(978-0-923550-42-4(9))* Tetrahedron Publishing LLC.

Horwitz, Sarah Jean. The Dark Lord Clementine. 2019. (ENG.). 336p. (J). (gr. 4-8). 17.95 *(978-1-61620-894-3(5)*, 73894) Algonquin Young Readers.

Houle, Kelly. Gracie's Gallery: A Magic Mirror Book. 2008. (ENG., Illus.). 28p. (J). (gr. -1). 14.95 *(978-1-58117-784-8(4)*, Intervisual/Piggy Toes) Bendon, Inc.

Hounam, Donald. A Dangerous Magic. 2017. (ENG., Illus.). 352p. (YA). (gr. 5-12). 17.99 *(978-1-5124-3232-9(6)*, ce27e1d0-1960-495f-a52b-2d7bd78c0eca, Carolrhoda Lab™) Lerner Publishing Group.

Howard, A. G. Untamed: a Splintered Companion. 2015. (Splintered Ser.). (ENG.). 288p. (YA). (gr. 9-17). pap. 7.95 *(978-1-4197-1926-4(2))* Abrams, Inc.

Howard, Cheryl L. Mikhael the Mighty: Be True to Who You Are & You Can Never Go Wrong. 2009. 52p. pap. 18.50 *(978-1-60860-760-0(7)*, Strategic Bk. Publishing) Strategic Book Publishing & Rights Agency (SBPRA).

Howard, Grahame. The Wishing Book 3 - Extermination. 2010. 170p. (J). pap. *(978-1-905809-90-5(5))* Pneuma Springs Publishing.

Howard, Peggy Ann. Zorees: Land of Dreams. 2007. (YA). per. 16.95 *(978-0-9795519-0-1(0))* Dream Scape Publishing, LLC.

Howell, Heather. Emily's Ballet Recital. 2010. 32p. pap. 12.99 *(978-1-4490-8457-8(5))* AuthorHouse.

Howells, Andrea. Finding Peace & the True Soul. 2006. 60p. (J). per. *(978-0-9765072-4-6(2))* Tribute Bks.

Howland, Naomi. Latkes, Latkes, Good to Eat: A Hanukkah Holiday Book for Kids. 2004. (ENG., Illus.). 32p. (J). (gr. -1-3). pap. 7.99 *(978-0-618-49295-4(X)*, 100396, Clarion Bks.) HarperCollins Pubs.

Hoyle, K. B. The Enchanted. 2016. (ENG., Illus.). (J). 29.99 *(978-1-61213-399-7(1))* Writer's Coffee Shop, The.

Hoylie, Gerry. Byron Unleashed. 2005. 60p. pap. 14.95 *(978-1-59113-670-5(9))* Booklocker.com, Inc.

Hru, Dakari. Joshua's Masai Mask, 1 vol. Rich, Anna, illus. 2013. (ENG.). 32p. (J). (gr. 1-4). pap. 11.95 *(978-1-880000-32-8(6)*, leelowbooks) Lee & Low Bks., Inc.

Hubbard, L. Ron, contrib. by. If I Were You: Literature Guide for Teachers & Librarians, Based on Common Core ELA Standards for Classrooms 6-9. 2013. (Stories from the Golden Age Ser.). (ENG.). 35p. (gr. 6-9). pap., tchr. ed. 14.95 *(978-1-61986-201-2(8))* Galaxy Pr., LLC.

Hubbell, Mary A. The Miracle of Annie's Ring. 2010. 138p. pap. 11.50 *(978-1-60911-530-2(9)*, Eloquent Bks.) Strategic Book Publishing & Rights Agency (SBPRA).

Hudson, Margaret Parker. The Blue Umbrella. 2005. (Illus.). (J). 15.95 *(978-0-9771301-0-8(X))* FayRe Pr.

Hudson, Wade. Places I Love to Go. 2008. (Illus.). 24p. (J). (gr. -1-3). 3.99 *(978-1-60349-008-5(6)*, Marimba Bks.) Just Us Bks., Inc.

Huggett, Christopher. The Magic Man. 2011. 216p. pap. 24.95 *(978-1-4560-6701-4(X))* America Star Bks.

Hughes, Hollie. The Girl & the Dinosaur. Massini, Sarah, illus. 2020. (ENG.). 32p. (J). 17.99 *(978-1-5476-0322-0(4)*, 900211339, Bloomsbury Children's Bks.) Bloomsbury Publishing USA.

Hughley-Edwards, Phyllis. Nana's Magical Closet: First Edition. 2012. 24p. pap. 15.99 *(978-1-4797-3573-0(6))* Xlibris Corp.

Hult, Robert William. Time Dancer. 2004. (Illus.). (YA). pap. 14.00 *(978-0-9754114-0-7(3))* Hegemony Pr.

Humphreys, Neil. Picking up a Penguin's Egg Really Got Me into Trouble. Cheng, Puay Koon, illus. 2014. (Abbie Rose & the Magic Suitcase Ser.). (ENG.). 24p. (J). (gr. -1 — 1). pap. 13.99 *(978-981-4484-18-3(0))* Marshall Cavendish International (Asia) Private Ltd. SGP. Dist: Independent Pubs. Group.

Hunt, Julie. Shine Mountain. 2019. (ENG.). 288p. (J). (gr. 4-7). pap. 14.99 *(978-1-76029-150-1(1))* Allen & Unwin AUS. Dist: Independent Pubs. Group.

Hunt, Leo. Eight Rivers of Shadow. (ENG.). 368p. (YA). (gr. 9). 2017. pap. 9.99 *(978-0-7636-9457-9(6))* 2016. 17.99 *(978-0-7636-8994-0(7))* Candlewick Pr.

Hunt, Zoe Paton. Azrael's Magical Moment. 2008. 24p. pap. 18.95 *(978-1-60693-070-0(2)*, Strategic Bk. Publishing) Strategic Book Publishing & Rights Agency (SBPRA).

Hunter, Erin. The Burning Horizon. 2016. (Seekers: Return to the Wild Ser.: 5). (J). lib. bdg. 18.40 *(978-0-606-38147-5(3))* Turtleback.

—Shadows of the Clans. 2016. (Warriors Ser.). (J). lib. bdg. 18.40 *(978-0-606-38146-8(5))* Turtleback.

—Thunder Rising. McLoughlin, Wayne & Douglas, Allen, illus. 2014. (Warriors: Dawn of the Clans Ser.: 2). 368p. (J). (gr. 3-7). pap. 7.99 *(978-0-06-206352-6(9))* HarperCollins Pubs.

—Warriors: The New Prophecy #2: Moonrise. 2015. (Warriors: the New Prophecy Ser.: 2). (ENG., Illus.). 336p. (J). (gr. 3-7). pap. 9.99 *(978-0-06-236703-7(X)*, HarperCollins) HarperCollins Pubs.

Hunter, Erin & Jolley, Dan. Bramblestar's Storm. 2016. (Warriors Super Edition Ser.). (J). lib. bdg. 18.40 *(978-0-606-38180-2(5))* Turtleback.

Hunter, Mollie. A Stranger Came Ashore, 30 vols. 2012. (Classic Kelpies Ser.). 192p. (J). 9.95 *(978-0-86315-883-4(8)*, Kelpies) Floris Bks. GBR. Dist: Consortium Bk. Sales & Distribution.

Huntley, Tex. Catch a Wishing Star (Shimmer & Shine) Cartobaleno, illus. 2017. (Little Golden Book Ser.). (ENG.). 24p. (J). (-k). 4.99 *(978-1-5247-1667-7(7)*, Golden Bks.) Random Hse. Children's Bks.

Hurwitz, Johanna. Magical Monty. McGrory, Anik, illus. 2013. (Monty Ser.: 4). (ENG.). 112p. (J). (gr. k-4). pap. 5.99 *(978-0-7636-6457-2(X))* Candlewick Pr.

Hyperion Staff. Walt Disney World: Where Magic Lives 2006. 2006. (ENG.). 96p. (gr. -1-17). pap. 9.95 *(978-1-4231-0257-1(6)*, Disney Editions) Disney Pr.

I Am a Wish. 2013. 36p. pap. 16.99 *(978-1-4808-0094-6(5))* Archway Publishing.

Ifueko, Jordan. Raybearer. (Raybearer Ser.). (ENG., Illus.). (YA). (gr. 7-17). 2021. 400p. pap. 10.99 *(978-1-4197-3983-5(2)*, 1297003) 2020. 368p. 18.99 *(978-1-4197-3982-8(4)*, 1297001) Abrams, Inc.

Ikegami, Aiko. Seed Man. Ikegami, Aiko, illus. 2018. (ENG., Illus.). 32p. (J). (gr. k-3). 17.99 *(978-1-58536-379-7(0)*, 204403) Sleeping Bear Pr.

The Indian in the Cupboard. 2004. (J). *(978-1-59564-280-6(3))* Steps To Literacy, LLC.

Insight Editions. Harry Potter: Magical Film Projections: Quidditch. 2017. (Harry Potter Ser.). (ENG.). 16p. (J). (gr. 2-5). 16.99 *(978-0-7636-9587-3(4))* Candlewick Pr.

Insight Editions, compiled by. J. K. Rowling's Wizarding World: Magical Film Projections: Creatures. 2017. (J. K. Rowling's Wizarding World Ser.). (ENG.). 16p. (J). (gr. 2-5). 16.99 *(978-0-7636-9585-9(8))* Candlewick Pr.

Irvine, Kitty & MacPherson-Irvine, Julie. Mysterious Moorings with Mouse. 2017. (ENG.). 96p. (J). pap. 11.95 *(978-1-78693-220-4(2)*, b4497a1c-0581-417e-a47b-bb389a574432) Austin Macauley Pubs. Ltd. GBR. Dist: Baker & Taylor Publisher Services (BTPS).

Iserles, Inbali. The Elders. 2016. (Illus.). 281p. (J). *(978-1-338-13298-4(9)*, Scholastic Pr.) Scholastic, Inc.

Isern, Susanna. The Magic Ball of Wool. Brokenbrow, Jon, tr. Hilb, Nora, illus. (ENG.). 32p. (J). 2019. (gr. -1-k). 11.95 *(978-84-16733-66-8(X))* 2013. (gr. k-3). 16.95 *(978-84-15619-89-5(8))* Cuento de Luz SL ESP. Dist: Publishers Group West (PGW).

Island, Fiona. Wishbone's Magic Garden. 2006. (Illus.). 120p. pap. *(978-1-84401-733-1(8))* Athena Pr.

Island of Legends. 2014. (Unwanteds Ser.: 4). (ENG., Illus.). 496p. (J). (gr. 3-7). 19.99 *(978-1-4424-9328-5(3)*, Aladdin) Simon & Schuster Children's Publishing.

Ivanoff, George. Gamers' Quest. 2009. (Gamers Ser.: Bk. 1). (ENG.). 172p. (YA). pap. *(978-1-876462-86-4(8))* Ford Street Publishing Pty, Limited.

Jackson, Amy. Cassandra & the Night Sky. 2018. (ENG., Illus.). 32p. (J). pap. 10.95 *(978-1-942945-74-1(4)*, 050c55fd-3ef5-48dd-9731-52687da7d266) Night Heron Media.

—Cassandra & the Night Sky. Paredes, Donna, illus. 2017. (ENG.). 32p. (J). 18.95 *(978-1-942945-40-6(X)*, cfabfbd7-de57-4a43-a5b5-40be4e93f2f3) Night Heron Media.

Jackson, Kristen. Tales of Taneslan the Greatest Secret. 2006. (ENG.). 235p. pap. 19.90 *(978-0-615-13580-9(3))* Jackson, Kristen M.

Jackson, Ruth Montgomery. A Bit of Magic with Wee Willie & Double Trouble. 2011. 76p. pap. 27.50 *(978-1-4567-0050-8(2))* AuthorHouse.

Jackson, Shirley. Nine Magic Wishes. 2015. (ENG., Illus.). 48p. pap. 9.99 *(978-0-486-79808-0(9)*, 798089) Dover Pubns., Inc.

Jackson, Stephen. Mundoespejo. 2005. (SPA., Illus.). 28p. (J). (gr. 2-4). 15.95 *(978-84-666-1495-5(8))* Ediciones B ESP. Dist: Independent Pubs. Group.

James, Bethany & Shady, Leigh. Matilda Turnip's Endless Belly Button. 2010. (Illus.). 32p. (J). 12.99 *(978-1-60706-187-8(2))* Image Comics.

James, Greg & Smith, Chris. Kid Normal. Salcedo, Erica, illus. (Kid Normal Ser.). (ENG.). 400p. (J). 2019. pap. 7.99 *(978-1-5476-0267-4(8)*, 900209369) 2018. 13.99 *(978-1-68119-709-8(X)*, 900182253) Bloomsbury Publishing USA. (Bloomsbury Children's Bks.).

James, Montague Rhodes. The Five Jars. 2008. 96p. pap. *(978-1-84830-112-2(X)*, Wildhern Pr.) Echo Library.

Janesh, Ron. Ariela Aparecida E O Vale Da Neblina Da Cachoeir. Gonçalves da Silva, Fabio, illus. 2012. 56p. pap. 20.50 *(978-1-60976-925-3(2)*, Strategic Bk. Publishing) Strategic Book Publishing & Rights Agency (SBPRA).

Jardine, Kathy & Jardine, Ashley. The Durples: Go to School. 2010. 28p. pap. 17.99 *(978-1-4490-3405-4(5))* AuthorHouse.

Jarman, Julia. The Magic Backpack. Gon, Adriano, illus. 2003. (Flying Foxes Ser.). (ENG.). 48p. (J). lib. bdg. *(978-0-7787-1487-3(X))* Crabtree Publishing Co.

Jaycox, Jaclyn. Witch's Stew. Gatti, Giada, illus. 2019. (Boo Bks.). (ENG.). 32p. (J). (gr. k-2). lib. bdg. 21.32 *(978-1-5158-4482-2(X)*, 140578, Picture Window Bks.) Capstone.

Jeffers, Susan. The Nutcracker. Jeffers, Susan, illus. 2007. (Illus.). 40p. (J). (gr. -1-3). 17.89 *(978-0-06-074387-1(5))* HarperCollins Pubs.

—The Nutcracker. 2007. (ENG., Illus.). 40p. (J). (gr. -1-3). 18.99 *(978-0-06-074386-4(7)*, HarperCollins) HarperCollins Pubs.

—The Twelve Days of Christmas: A Christmas Holiday Book for Kids. Jeffers, Susan, illus. 2013. (ENG., Illus.). 40p. (J). (gr. -1-3). 17.99 *(978-0-06-206615-2(3)*, HarperCollins) HarperCollins Pubs.

Jeffers, Susan, illus. The Twelve Days of Christmas. 2013. (J). *(978-0-06-206616-9(1))* Harper & Row Ltd.

Jefferson, Barbara. The Luck of the Dragonfly. Jefferson, Daniel E., illus. 2008. 31p. pap. 24.95 *(978-1-60672-283-1(2))* America Star Bks.

Jenkins, Gloria. Storm: The Peace Maker. 2006. (J). pap. 8.00 *(978-0-8059-7116-3(5))* Dorrance Publishing Co., Inc.

Jennings, Rashad. Arcade & the Golden Travel Guide, 1 vol. 2019. (Coin Slot Chronicles Ser.: 2). (ENG., Illus.). 240p. (J). 16.99 *(978-0-310-76743-5(1))* Zonderkidz.

—Arcade & the Triple T Token, 1 vol. 2019. (Coin Slot Chronicles Ser.). (ENG., Illus.). 256p. (J). 16.99 *(978-0-310-76741-1(5))* Zonderkidz.

Jensen, Michael R. & King, David Powers. Woven. 2015. (Illus.). 344p. (J). *(978-0-545-83117-8(2)*, Scholastic Pr.) Scholastic, Inc.

Jerome, Louie. Peter & the Black Dog. 2009. 120p. 22.50 *(978-1-60693-737-2(5)*, Strategic Bk. Publishing) Strategic Book Publishing & Rights Agency (SBPRA).

Jesperson, Per. Wonder & Magic: The David Tales. 2003. 50p. pap. *(978-1-84401-017-2(1))* Athena Pr.

Jian, Li. The Little Monkey King's Journey: Retold in English & Chinese (Stories of the Chinese Zodiac) Wert, Yijin, tr. Li, Jian, illus. 2012. (Stories of the Chinese Zodiac Ser.). 48p. (gr. -1-3). 16.95 *(978-1-60220-981-7(2))* Shanghai Pr.

Joe Thomson-Swift. The Magic Stone. 2011. 92p. pap. *(978-1-908105-83-7(6))* Grosvenor Hse. Publishing Ltd.

Johnson, D. B. Magritte's Marvelous Hat. Johnson, D. B., illus. 2012. (ENG., Illus.). 32p. (J). (gr. -1-3). 17.99 *(978-0-547-55864-6(3)*, 1453619, Clarion Bks.) HarperCollins Pubs.

Johnson, Gerald J. J. A Boy Called Tiny Tim. 2013. 20p. pap. 24.95 *(978-1-62709-865-6(8))* America Star Bks.

Johnson, Gillian. Thora. Johnson, Gillian, illus. 2003. (Illus.). 128p. *(978-0-207-19815-1(2))* HarperCollins Pubs. Australia.

Johnson, Jane. Legends of the Shadow World: The Secret Country; the Shadow World; Dragon's Fire. Stower, Adam, illus. 2010. (ENG.). 1120p. (J). (gr. 3-7). pap. 14.99 *(978-1-4169-9082-6(8)*, Simon & Schuster Bks. For Young Readers) Simon & Schuster Bks. For Young Readers.

—The Secret Country. Stower, Adam, illus. 2007. (Eidolon Chronicles Ser.: 1). (ENG.). 336p. (J). (gr. 3-7). per. 15.99 *(978-1-4169-3815-6(X)*, Simon & Schuster Bks. For Young Readers) Simon & Schuster Bks. For Young Readers.

Johnson, Pete. Bug Brother. Gordon, Mike, illus. 2019. 107p. (J). pap. 4.99 *(978-1-61067-742-4(0))* Kane Miller.

—Detective Brother. Philips, Mike, illus. 2019. 106p. (J). pap. 4.99 *(978-1-61067-744-8(7))* Kane Miller.

—Pirate Brother. Gordon, Mike, illus. 2019. 111p. (J). pap. 4.99 *(978-1-61067-745-5(5))* Kane Miller.

Johnson, Sandi. Dittle's Christmas Wish. Durant, Sybrina, ed. Sturgen, Bobbi, illus. 2014. 40p. (J). (gr. k-5). pap. 12.99 *(978-1-929063-65-9(2)*, 164) Moons & Stars Publishing For Children.

Johnson, Sarah Blake. Crossings. 2017. 309p. (YA). pap. 17.99 *(978-1-4621-1957-8(3))* Cedar Fort, Inc./CFI Distribution.

Johnston, E. K. Spindle. 2017. (ENG.). 384p. (YA). (gr. 9-17). pap. 9.99 *(978-1-4847-7618-6(6))* Hyperion Bks. for Children.

—A Thousand Nights. 2015. (ENG.). 336p. (J). (gr. 9-17). 18.99 *(978-1-4847-2227-5(2))* Hyperion Bks. for Children.

Johnston, Tony. The Spoon in the Bathroom Wall. 2006. (ENG., Illus.). 144p. (J). (gr. 3-7). pap. 10.95 *(978-0-15-205625-4(4)*, 1196920, Clarion Bks.) HarperCollins Pubs.

Johnstone, G. L. Sleep Tight Nancy... 2012. (Illus.). 12p. pap. 18.30 *(978-1-4772-1517-3(4))* AuthorHouse.

Jolley, Dan. The Shadow City. 2018. (Five Elements Ser.: 2). (J). lib. bdg. 17.20 *(978-0-606-41026-7(0))* Turtleback.

Jonell, Lynne. Grasshopper Magic. Dorman, Brandon, illus. 2014. (Magical Mix-Ups Ser.: 3). (ENG.). 112p. (J). (gr. 1-4). pap. 4.99 *(978-0-307-93123-8(4)*, Random Hse. Bks. for Young Readers) Random Hse. Children's Bks.

—Hamster Magic. Dorman, Brandon, illus. 2012. (Magical Mix-Ups Ser.: 1). (ENG.). 112p. (J). (gr. 1-4). pap. 6.99 *(978-0-375-86616-6(7)*, Random Hse. Bks. for Young Readers) Random Hse. Children's Bks.

Jones, Alexandra. Moon Magic. 2012. 28p. pap. 21.99 *(978-1-4771-3995-0(8))* Xlibris Corp.

Jones, Carrie. Quest for the Golden Arrow. 2017. (Time Stoppers Ser.). (ENG.). 464p. (J). 16.99 *(978-1-61963-863-1(0)*, 900150699, Bloomsbury USA Childrens) Bloomsbury Publishing USA.

—Time Stoppers. 2016. (Time Stoppers Ser.). (ENG.). 384p. (J). 16.99 *(978-1-61963-861-7(4)*, 900150704, Bloomsbury USA Childrens) Bloomsbury Publishing USA.

Jones, Christianne C. How the Camel Got Its Hump, 1 vol. Rooney, Veronica, illus. 2011. (My First Classic Story Ser.). (ENG.). 32p. (J). (gr. k-3). pap. 7.10 *(978-1-4048-7358-2(9)*, 118574, Picture Window Bks.) Capstone.

Jones, Diana Wynne. Castle in the Air. 2008. (World of Howl Ser.: 2). (ENG.). 400p. (J). (gr. 3-7). pap. 9.99 *(978-0-06-147877-2(6)*, Greenwillow Bks.) HarperCollins Pubs.

—Castle in the Air, 7 vols. 2009. (J). 91.75 *(978-1-4361-6121-3(5))*; 94.75 *(978-1-4361-6119-0(3))*; 156.75 *(978-1-4361-6116-9(9))*; 73.75 *(978-1-4361-6115-2(0))*; 1.25 *(978-1-4361-6112-1(6))*; 70.75 *(978-1-4361-6117-6(7))* Recorded Bks., Inc.

—The Chronicles of Chrestomanci Vol. 1: Charmed Life; The Lives of Christopher Chant, Vol. 1. 2007. (Chrestomanci Ser.). (YA). (gr. 5-8). lib. bdg. 19.65 *(978-0-613-31070-3(5))* Turtleback.

—The Chronicles of Chrestomanci, Volume I, Vol. 1. 2007. (Chronicles of Chrestomanci Ser.: Nos. 1-2). (ENG.). 608p. (YA). (gr. 8-12). pap. 10.99 *(978-0-06-447268-5(X)*, Greenwillow Bks.) HarperCollins Pubs.

—The Chronicles of Chrestomanci, Volume II, Vol. 2. 2007. (Chronicles of Chrestomanci Ser.: Nos. 3-4). (ENG.). 560p. (YA). (gr. 8-12). pap. 8.99 *(978-0-06-447269-2(8)*, Greenwillow Bks.) HarperCollins Pubs.

—The Chronicles of Chrestomanci, Volume III, Vol. 3. 2008. (Chronicles of Chrestomanci Ser.: 3). (ENG.). 688p. (YA). (gr. 8-18). pap. 8.99 *(978-0-06-114832-3(6)*, Greenwillow Bks.) HarperCollins Pubs.

—Conrad's Fate. 2006. (ENG., Illus.). 352p. *(978-0-00-719087-4(5))* HarperCollins Children's Bks.

—Conrad's Fate. (J). 2006. (Chronicles of Chrestomanci Ser.: 3). (ENG.). 400p. (gr. 3-7). per. 6.99 *(978-0-06-074745-9(5)*, Greenwillow Bks.) 2005. (Chrestomanci Ser.: No. 5). 384p. (gr. k-17). lib. bdg. 17.89 *(978-0-06-074744-2(7))* 2005. (Chrestomanci Ser.: No. 5). 384p. (gr. 5-18). 16.99 *(978-0-06-074743-5(9))* HarperCollins Pubs.

—Conrad's Fate: Read-Along/Homework Pack, 6 vols. 2005. (Chrestomanci Ser.: No. 5). (J). (gr. 5-8). 86.75 *(978-1-4193-3551-8(0)*, 42039) Recorded Bks., Inc.

—Earwig & the Witch. Zelinsky, Paul O., illus. 2012. (ENG.). 128p. (J). (gr. 3-7). 15.99 *(978-0-06-207511-6(X)*, Greenwillow Bks.) HarperCollins Pubs.

—Enchanted Glass. 2011. (ENG.). 304p. (J). (gr. 3-7). pap. 7.99 *(978-0-06-186685-2(7)*, Greenwillow Bks.) HarperCollins Pubs.

—House of Many Ways. 2008. 404p. (J). 9.99 *(978-0-06-147798-0(2)*, Greenwillow Bks.) HarperCollins Pubs.

—House of Many Ways, 7 vols. 2009. (J). 79.75 *(978-1-4361-6128-2(2))*; 100.75 *(978-1-4361-6132-9(0))*; 245.75 *(978-1-4361-6127-5(4))*; 102.75 *(978-1-4361-6130-5(4))*; 1.25 *(978-1-4361-6123-7(1))* Recorded Bks., Inc.

—The Merlin Conspiracy. 480p. (J). 2004. (Magids Ser.: 2). (ENG.). (gr. 3-7). pap. 9.99 *(978-0-06-052320-6(4)*, Greenwillow Bks.) 2003. (gr. 5-18). 17.89 *(978-0-06-052319-0(0))* HarperCollins Pubs.

—The Pinhoe Egg. (J). 2007. (Chronicles of Chrestomanci Ser.: 6). (ENG.). 480p. (gr. 3-7). per. 7.99 *(978-0-06-113126-4(1)*, Greenwillow Bks.) 2006. (Chrestomanci Ser.: No. 6). 528p. lib. bdg. 18.89 *(978-0-06-113125-7(3))* HarperCollins Pubs.

Jones, Diana Wynne & Jones, Ursula. The Islands of Chaldea. 2015. (ENG.). 368p. (J). (gr. 3-7). pap. 10.99 *(978-0-06-229508-8(X)*, Greenwillow Bks.) HarperCollins Pubs.

Jones, Elwynn. Frank's Frantic Friday. 2010. 40p. pap. 16.95 *(978-1-60911-750-4(6)*, Eloquent Bks.) Strategic Book Publishing & Rights Agency (SBPRA).

Jones, Frewin. The Faerie Path #3: the Seventh Daughter. 2009. (Faerie Path Ser.: 3). (ENG.). 352p. (YA). (gr. 8). pap. 9.99 *(978-0-06-087110-9(5)*, HarperTeen) HarperCollins Pubs.

—Warrior Princess. 2009. (YA). 346p. lib. bdg. 17.89 *(978-0-06-087144-4(X))*; (ENG.). 352p. (gr. 7-18). 16.99 *(978-0-06-087143-7(1))* HarperCollins Pubs. (Eos).

—Warrior Princess #2: Destiny's Path. 2010. (Warrior Princess Ser.: 2). (ENG.). 352p. (YA). (gr. 8). pap. 8.99 *(978-0-06-087148-2(2)*, HarperTeen) HarperCollins Pubs.

—Warrior Princess #3: the Emerald Flame. 2010. (Warrior Princess Ser.: 3). (ENG.). 352p. (YA). (gr. 8-18). 16.99 *(978-0-06-087149-9(0)*, HarperTeen) HarperCollins Pubs.

Jones, Guy. The Ice Garden. 2019. (ENG.). 272p. (J). (gr. 3-7). 17.99 *(978-1-338-28533-8(5)*, Chicken Hse., The) Scholastic, Inc.

Jones, Kelly. The Adventure Tree - Branch II "the Royal Magic Show" McDowell, Tina, illus. 2005. (ENG.). 34p. pap. 15.99 *(978-1-4134-7448-0(9))* Xlibris Corp.

Jones, Marcia & Dadey, Debbie. The Other Side of Magic, 2. 2009. (Keyholders Ser.: 2). (ENG.). 144p. (J). (gr. 4-7). 17.44 *(978-0-7653-5983-4(9)*, 9780765359834) Doherty, Tom Assocs., LLC.

—This Side of Magic, 1. Stower, Adam, illus. 2009. (Keyholders Ser.: 1). (ENG.). 144p. (J). (gr. 4-7). 17.44 *(978-0-7653-5982-7(0)*, 900050018) Doherty, Tom Assocs., LLC.

—Wizards Do Roast Turkeys. Dreidemy, Joëlle, illus. 2007. 64p. (J). pap. *(978-0-545-00235-6(4))* Scholastic, Inc.

Jordan, Claire. Fanakapan & the Fairies - a Children's Fairy Story. Skou, Nick, illus. 2013. 52p. pap. *(978-1-78148-648-1(4))* Grosvenor Hse. Publishing Ltd.

Joyce, Jan. The Wizard Visits Magic School. 2018. (ENG., Illus.). 50p. (J). *(978-1-5289-2388-0(X))*; pap. *(978-1-5289-2389-7(8))* Austin Macauley Pubs. Ltd.

Joyce, Marie. Thunder Rules! 2005. (ENG.). 183p. (J). pap. 12.95 *(978-1-4116-2178-7(6))* Lulu Pr., Inc.

Juster, Norton. Casello Magico. pap. 19.95 *(978-88-452-3854-3(7))* Fabbri Editori - RCS Libri ITA. Dist: Distribooks, Inc.

Kaaberbøl, Lene. Heartbreak Island. 2005. (W. I. T. C. H. Adventures Ser.: Bk. 3). (Illus.). 105p. (J). lib. bdg. 11.00 *(978-1-4242-0786-2(X))* Fitzgerald Bks.

Kaaberbøl, Lene. Wildwitch 4 - Bloodling. 2017. (Wildwitch Ser.: 4). (ENG., Illus.). 200p. (J). (gr. 3-7). pap. 9.99 *(978-1-78269-086-3(7)*, Pushkin Children's Bks.) Steerforth Pr.

Kaczka, Fallon. What about Oysters. 2010. 24p. 13.00 *(978-1-4520-2066-2(3))* AuthorHouse.

Kadono, Eiko. Kiki's Delivery Service: The Classic That Inspired the Beloved Animated Film. Balistrieri, Emily, tr. from JPN. Onoda, Yuta, illus. 2020. (ENG.). 208p. (J). (gr. 5). 16.99 *(978-1-9848-9666-7(0))*; lib. bdg. 19.99 *(978-1-9848-9668-1(7))* Random Hse. Children's Bks. (Delacorte Bks. for Young Readers).

Kagawa, Julie. The Iron Legends. 2012. (Iron Fey Ser.: 5). (J). lib. bdg. 20.85 *(978-0-606-26516-4(3))* Turtleback.

Kagna, Barbara. Magic of Masara. Gonzalez, Ashley, illus. 2010. 24p. pap. 12.50 *(978-1-4490-5651-3(2))* AuthorHouse.

Kamachi, Kazuma. A Certain Magical Index, Vol. 1 (light Novel), Vol. 1. Haimura, Kiyotaka, illus. 2014. (Certain Magical Index Ser.: 1). (ENG.). 224p. (gr. 8-17). 14.00 *(978-0-316-33912-4(1)*, Yen Pr.) Yen Pr. LLC.

—A Certain Magical Index, Vol. 14 (light Novel) Haimura, Kiyotaka, illus. 2018. (Certain Magical Index Ser.: 14). (ENG.). 192p. (gr. 8-17). pap. 14.00 *(978-0-316-44270-1(4)*, Yen Pr.) Yen Pr. LLC.

Kamon. Hooty & the Magic Power. Krit, Joey, illus. 2011. 36p. pap. 14.39 *(978-1-4634-1042-1(5))* AuthorHouse.

Kann, Victoria. Emeraldalicious. A Springtime Book for Kids. Kann, Victoria, illus. 2013. (Pinkalicious Ser.). (ENG., Illus.). 40p. (J). (gr. -1-3). 19.99 *(978-0-06-178126-1(6))*; lib. bdg. 18.89 *(978-0-06-178127-8(4))* HarperCollins Pubs. (HarperCollins).

Kaplan, Arie. Doctor Strange Little Golden Book (Marvel: Doctor Strange) Atiyeh, Michael & Borkowski, Michael, illus. 2017. (Little Golden Book Ser.). (ENG.). 24p. (J). (-k). 4.99 *(978-1-101-93865-2(X)*, Golden Bks.) Random Hse. Children's Bks.

Karalius, Kimberly. Love Fortunes & Other Disasters. 2015. (Grimbaud Ser.: 1). (ENG.). 368p. (YA). (gr. 7). pap. 17.99 *(978-1-250-04720-5(X)*, 900132070) Feiwel & Friends.

Karcz, Lauren. The Gallery of Unfinished Girls. 2017. (ENG.). 352p. (YA). (gr. 8). 17.99 *(978-0-06-246777-5(8)*, HarperTeen) HarperCollins Pubs.

Karre, Elizabeth. All You Are. 2014. (Gift Ser.). (ENG.). 120p. (YA). (gr. 6-12). pap. 7.95 *(978-1-4677-4477-5(8)*, eb718cc1-6713-4a48-b567-548e6a7ebfcf, Darby Creek) Lerner Publishing Group.

—Certain Signals. 2014. (Gift Ser.). (ENG.). 112p. (YA). (gr. 6-12). pap. 7.95 *(978-1-4677-4479-9(4)*, c7e0be5a-2e55-4339-9db4-7405e8913c8c); lib. bdg. 27.99 *(978-1-4677-3511-7(6)*, eb702a74-7dbd-4cb2-9b02-79165c604231) Lerner Publishing Group. (Darby Creek).

Kassem, Amirah. The Magical Land of Birthdays. 2019. (Magical Land of Birthdays Ser.). (ENG., Illus.). 192p. (J). (gr. 2-6). 14.99 *(978-1-4197-3743-5(0)*, 1280101, Amulet Bks.) Abrams, Inc.

Kassner, Heather. The Bone Garden. Saunders, Matt, illus. 2020. (ENG.). 288p. (J). pap. 7.99 *(978-1-250-25053-7(6)*, 900195831) Square Fish.

Kate, Lauren. Teardrop. 2013. 441p. (YA). *(978-0-385-37491-0(7))*; *(978-0-385-38372-1(X))* Random House Publishing Group. (Delacorte Pr).

—Teardrop. 2014. (Teardrop Ser.: 1). (ENG.). 480p. (YA). (gr. 7). pap. 10.99 *(978-0-385-74266-5(5)*, Ember) Random Hse. Children's Bks.

Kats, Jewel. Cinderella's Magical Wheelchair: An Empowering Fairy Tale. Kinra, Richa, illus. 2012. (J). 24p. 29.95 *(978-1-61599-113-6(1))*; 20p. pap. 16.95 *(978-1-61599-112-9(3))* Loving Healing Pr., Inc.

Katz, Bebe Weinberg. Princess Claudia & the Freckles. 2007. 48p. per. 16.95 *(978-1-4241-6446-2(X))* America Star Bks.

Kauffman, Tracy. Gwendolyn's Wish. 2012. 24p. (-18). 24.95 *(978-1-62709-555-6(1))* America Star Bks.

Kaylor, J. Garcia. Animal Magic Coloring Pages. 2012. (ENG.). pap. 11.99 *(978-1-4675-2458-2(1))* Independent Pub.

Kelley, Marty. Magic Molly. 2018. (Molly Mac Ser.). (ENG., Illus.). 56p. (J). (gr. k-2). lib. bdg. 22.65 *(978-1-5158-2384-1(9)*, 137198, Picture Window Bks.) Capstone.

Kelly, Diana. Tamla Bear & the Magic Goblin. Walker, Jack, illus. 2013. 30p. pap. *(978-1-78148-182-0(2))* Grosvenor Hse. Publishing Ltd.

Kelly, Kevin Vincent. Hattie Mcdimple Makes a Wish. 2012. 20p. pap. 24.95 *(978-1-4626-8310-9(X))* America Star Bks.

Kelly, Tess. Buko's Journey. 2004. 262p. (YA). 26.95 *(978-0-595-66864-9(X))* iUniverse, Inc.

Kemler, Nancy. Dragon Box: The Key to Magic. 2005. 108p. pap. 19.95 *(978-1-4137-8445-9(3))* America Star Bks.

Kendall, Jack. The Magic Apple Tree. Bostrom, Sally, illus. l.t. ed. 2006. (ENG.). 48p. (J). per. 9.95 *(978-0-9787740-4-2(3))* Peppertree Pr., The.

Kennedy, Kim & Kennedy, Doug. Hee-Haw-Dini & the Great Zambini. 2009. (ENG., Illus.). 32p. (J). (gr. k-2). 15.95 *(978-0-8109-7025-0(2)*, 586001, Abrams Bks. for Young Readers) Abrams, Inc.

Kent, Jaden. Ella & Owen 1: the Cave of Aaaaah! Doom! Bodnaruk, Iryna, illus. 2017. (Ella & Owen Ser.: 1). (ENG.). 112p. (J). (gr. k-3). pap. 5.99 *(978-1-4998-0368-6(0))* Little Bee Books Inc.

—Ella & Owen 10: the Dragon Games! Bodnaruk, Iryna, illus. 2018. (Ella & Owen Ser.: 10). (ENG.). 112p. (J). (gr. k-3). 16.99 *(978-1-4998-0617-5(5))*; pap. 5.99 *(978-1-4998-0616-8(7))* Little Bee Books Inc.

—Ella & Owen 2: Attack of the Stinky Fish Monster! Bodnaruk, Iryna, illus. 2017. (Ella & Owen Ser.: 2). (ENG.). 112p. (J). (gr. k-3). pap. 5.99 *(978-1-4998-0369-3(9))* Little Bee Books Inc.

—Ella & Owen 5: the Great Troll Quest. Bodnaruk, Iryna, illus. 2017. (Ella & Owen Ser.: 5). (ENG.). 112p. (J). (gr. k-3). 16.99 *(978-1-4998-0474-4(1))*; pap. 5.99 *(978-1-4998-0473-7(3))* Little Bee Books Inc.

—Ella & Owen 8: the Worst Pet. Bodnaruk, Iryna, illus. 2018. (Ella & Owen Ser.: 8). (ENG.). 112p. (J). (gr. k-3). 16.99 *(978-1-4998-0613-7(2))*; pap. 5.99 *(978-1-4998-0612-0(4))* Little Bee Books Inc.

Kessler, Liz. Emily Windsnap: Six Swishy Tails of Land & Sea: Books 1-6, 6 vols. 2016. (Emily Windsnap Ser.). (ENG.). 1552p. (J). (gr. 3-7). pap. 41.00 *(978-0-7636-9223-0(9))* Candlewick Pr.

—Philippa Fisher & the Dream-Maker's Daughter. 2015. (Philippa Fisher Ser.: 2). (ENG.). 288p. (J). (gr. 3-7). pap. 7.99 *(978-0-7636-7460-1(5))* Candlewick Pr.

—Philippa Fisher & the Fairy Godsister. 2015. (Philippa Fisher Ser.: 1). (ENG.). 288p. (J). (gr. 3-7). pap. 8.99 *(978-0-7636-7462-5(1))* Candlewick Pr.

—Philippa Fisher & the Fairy's Promise. (Philippa Fisher Ser.: 3). (ENG.). 288p. (J). (gr. 3-7). 2015. pap. 7.99 *(978-0-7636-7461-8(3))* 2010. (Illus.). 15.99 *(978-0-7636-5031-5(5))* Candlewick Pr.

Khan, Joshua. Dream Magic. 2018. (Shadow Magic Novel Ser.). (ENG.). 352p. (J). (gr. 3-7). pap. 6.99 *(978-1-4847-3798-9(9))* Hyperion Bks. for Children.

—Shadow Magic. Hibon, Ben, illus. 2017. (Shadow Magic Novel Ser.: 1). (ENG.). 352p. (J). (gr. 3-7). pap. 6.99 *(978-1-4847-3788-0(1))* Little, Brown Bks. for Young Readers.

Kharbanda, Priya. Flumpa & Bosly Learn the Magic Three Rs: Reduce, Reuse & Recycle. 2010. 32p. pap. 23.50 *(978-1-4461-3602-7(7))* Lulu Pr., Inc.

Khoury, Jessica. The Forbidden Wish. 352p. (YA). (gr. 7). 2017. pap. 10.99 *(978-1-59514-768-4(3))* 2016. 17.99 *(978-1-59514-767-7(5))* Penguin Young Readers Group. (Razorbill).

—The Mystwick School of Musicraft. 2020. (ENG., Illus.). 368p. (J). (gr. 5-7). 16.99 *(978-1-328-62563-2(X)*, 1734231, Clarion Bks.) HarperCollins Pubs.

Kibuishi, Kazu. Escape from Lucien, 6. 2018. (Amulet Ser.). (ENG.). 213p. (J). (gr. 4-5). 23.96 *(978-1-64310-260-3(5))* Penworthy Co., LLC, The.

—Escape from Lucien. 2014. (Amulet Ser.: 6). lib. bdg. 24.50 *(978-0-606-36039-5(5))* Turtleback.

—Escape from Lucien: a Graphic Novel (Amulet #6) Kibuishi, Kazu, illus. (Amulet Ser.: 6). (ENG., Illus.). 224p. (J). (gr. 3-7). 2015. 24.99 *(978-0-545-84899-2(7))* 6. 2014. pap. 12.99 *(978-0-545-43315-0(0))* Scholastic, Inc. (Graphix).

—Firelight, 7. 2018. (Amulet Ser.). (ENG.). 197p. (J). (gr. 4-5). 23.96 *(978-1-64310-261-0(3))* Penworthy Co., LLC, The.

—Firelight. 2016. (Amulet Ser.: 7). (ENG., Illus.). 224p. (J). (gr. 3-7). lib. bdg. 24.50 *(978-0-606-38070-6(1))* Turtleback.

—Firelight: a Graphic Novel (Amulet #7) Kibuishi, Kazu, illus. 2016. (Amulet Ser.: 7). (ENG., Illus.). 208p. (J). (gr. 3-7). 24.99 *(978-0-545-83966-2(1))*; pap. 12.99 *(978-0-545-43316-7(9))* Scholastic, Inc. (Graphix).

—The Last Council, 4. 2018. (Amulet Ser.). (ENG.). 207p. (J). (gr. 4-5). 23.96 *(978-1-64310-258-0(3))* Penworthy Co., LLC, The.

—The Last Council. 2011. (Amulet Ser.: 4). lib. bdg. 24.50 *(978-0-606-23209-8(5))* Turtleback.

—The Last Council: a Graphic Novel (Amulet #4) 2015. (Amulet Ser.: 4). (ENG.). 224p. (J). (gr. 3-7). 24.99 *(978-0-545-20686-4(6)*, Graphix) Scholastic, Inc.

—The Last Council: a Graphic Novel (Amulet #4) Kibuishi, Kazu, illus. 2011. (Amulet Ser.: 4). (ENG., Illus.). 224p. (J). (gr. 4-7). pap. 12.99 *(978-0-545-20887-1(4)*, Graphix) Scholastic, Inc.

—Prince of the Elves, 5. 2018. (Amulet Ser.). (ENG.). 187p. (J). (gr. 4-5). 23.96 *(978-1-64310-259-7(1))* Penworthy Co., LLC, The.

—Prince of the Elves. 2012. (Amulet Ser.: 5). lib. bdg. 24.50 *(978-0-606-26499-0(X))* Turtleback.

—Prince of the Elves: a Graphic Novel (Amulet #5) Kibuishi, Kazu, illus. (Amulet Ser.: 5). (ENG.). 208p. (J). (gr. 3-7). 2015. 24.99 *(978-0-545-20888-8(2))* 2012. (Illus.). pap. 12.99 *(978-0-545-20889-5(0))* Scholastic, Inc. (Graphix).

—The Stonekeeper's Curse. 2009. (Amulet Ser.: 2). lib. bdg. 24.50 *(978-0-606-10671-9(5))* Turtleback.

—The Stonekeeper's Curse: a Graphic Novel (Amulet #2) Kibuishi, Kazu, illus. (Amulet Ser.: 2). (ENG., Illus.). 224p. (J). 2015. (gr. 3-7). 24.99 *(978-0-439-84682-0(X))* 2009. (gr. 4-7). pap. 12.99 *(978-0-439-84683-7(8))* Scholastic, Inc. (Graphix).

Kibuishi, Kazu, illus. Firelight. 2016. 197p. (J). *(978-1-4806-9909-0(8))* Baker & Taylor, CATS.

Killen, Nicola. The Little Rabbit. Killen, Nicola, illus. 2019. (My Little Animal Friend Ser.). (ENG., Illus.). 32p. (J). (gr. -1-3). 17.99 *(978-1-5344-3828-6(9)*, Simon & Schuster/Paula Wiseman Bks.) Simon & Schuster/Paula Wiseman Bks.

Kimmel, Eric A. Anansi & the Magic Stick. Stevens, Janet, illus. 2003. (J). 25.95 incl. audio *(978-1-59112-482-5(4))*; pap. 37.95 incl. audio *(978-1-59112-483-2(2))*; pap. 39.95 incl. audio compact disk *(978-1-59112-519-8(7))* Live Oak Media.

Kimmons, Janet M. The Jewel in the Attic & the Adventures of Tiger. Farmer, Zoe, illus. 2007. 108p. (J). (gr. 1-3). pap. *(978-1-58690-028-1(5))* Mould, Paul Publishing.

King, J. R. Arianna Kelt & the Renegades of Time: Signature Edition, Wizards of Skyhall Book 2. 2008. (ENG.). 256p. (J). 18.95 *(978-1-57545-165-7(4)*, Reagent Pr. Echo) RP Media.

—Arianna Kelt & the Wizards of Skyhall: Deluxe Edition, Wizards of Skyhall Book 1. 2008. (ENG.). 200p. (YA). per. 14.95 *(978-1-57545-170-1(0))* RP Media.

KING, R. O. N. S. The emerald Fire. 2010. 166p. pap. 11.50 *(978-1-4461-3748-2(1))* Lulu Pr., Inc.

—The Soul-pearl. 2010. 169p. pap. 11.50 *(978-1-4457-5542-7(4))* Lulu Pr., Inc.

King, Zach. Zach King: The Magical Mix-Up. Arce, Beverly, illus. 2018. 192p. (J). *(978-0-241-32188-1(3))* Harper & Row Ltd.

—Zach King: My Magical Life. (ENG.). 208p. (J). (gr. 3-7). 2018. pap. 9.99 *(978-0-06-267719-8(5))* 2017. (Illus.). 18.99 *(978-0-06-267718-1(7))* HarperCollins Pubs. (HarperCollins).

—Zach King: the Magical Mix-Up. 2018. (ENG., Illus.). 192p. (J). (gr. 3-7). 18.99 *(978-0-06-267721-1(7)*, HarperCollins) HarperCollins Pubs.

Kingsley, Kaza. The Dragon's Eye. 2007. (Erec Rex Ser.). (Illus.). 384p. (J). (gr. 3-7). per. 9.99 *(978-0-9786555-3-2(2))* Firelight Press, Inc.

—The Dragon's Eye. Grant, Melvyn, illus. 2009. (Erec Rex Ser.: 1). (ENG.). 368p. (J). (gr. 5-9). pap. 12.99 *(978-1-4169-7933-3(6)*, Simon & Schuster Bks. For Young Readers) Simon & Schuster Bks. For Young Readers.

—Erec Rex: The Dragon's Eye. Payne, John, ed. Grant, Melvyn, illus. 2006. 360p. (J). 17.99 *(978-0-9786555-6-3(7))* Firelight Press, Inc.

Kingsley Troupe, Thomas. Swamp of Lost Souls. Ivy, Maggie, illus. 2019. (Haunted States of America Set 2 Ser.). (ENG.). 136p. (J). (gr. 3-4). pap. 7.99 *(978-1-63163-356-0(2)*, 1631633562); lib. bdg. 27.13 *(978-1-63163-355-3(4)*, 1631633554) North Star Editions. (Jolly Fish Pr.).

Kinra, Richa, illus. The Princess Panda Tea Party: A Cerebral Palsy Fairy Tale. 2014. 45p. (J). pap. 14.95 *(978-1-61599-219-5(7))* Loving Healing Pr., Inc.

Kinsella, Sophie, pseud. Fairy Mom & Me #1. Kissi, Marta, illus. 2019. (Fairy Mom & Me Ser.: 1). (ENG.). 160p. (J). (gr. 2-5). pap. 5.99 *(978-1-5247-6993-2(2)*, Yearling) Random Hse. Children's Bks.

Kintz, Elizabeth. The Magic Hose. 2012. 30p. 16.95 *(978-1-4575-1087-8(1))*; pap. 14.00 *(978-1-4575-0948-3(2))* Dog Ear Publishing, LLC.

Kirk, Daniel. Elf Realm: The High Road. 2010. (ENG., Illus.). 576p. (YA). (gr. 7-17). pap. 8.95 *(978-0-8109-8979-5(4)*, 647503, Amulet Bks.) Abrams, Inc.

—Elf Realm: The Road's End. 2011. (ENG., Illus.). 496p. (YA). (gr. 7-17). 18.95 *(978-0-8109-8978-8(6)*, 647601, Amulet Bks.) Abrams, Inc.

Kirov, Erica. Magickeepers: The Eternal Hourglass. Fortune, Eric, illus. 2010. 256p. (J). (gr. 4-7). pap. 10.99 *(978-1-4022-3855-0(X))* Sourcebooks, Inc.

Kisinger, E. Jean. Firebug & the Mind Spark. Marta, Diana M., illus. 2012. 42p. pap. 12.50 *(978-0-615-58954-1(5))* Firebug Fairy Tales.

Kitamura, Satoshi. Me & My Cat? Kitamura, Satoshi, illus. 2009. (ENG., Illus.). 32p. (J). (gr. k-k). pap. 12.95 *(978-1-84270-775-3(2))* Andersen Pr. GBR. Dist: Independent Pubs. Group.

Klein, Abby. Ready, Freddy! #5: Talent Show Scardey-Pants: Talent Show Scardey-Pants. McKinley, John, illus. 5th ed. 2005. (Ready, Freddy! Ser.: 5). (ENG.). 96p. (J). (gr. -1-3). 5.99 *(978-0-439-55604-0(X))* Scholastic, Inc.

Klein Bernstein, Sandy. The Door in the Sky. 2012. 268p. pap. 12.95 *(978-1-4575-1111-0(8))* Dog Ear Publishing, LLC.

Klimo, Kate. The Dragon in the Driveway, 2. Shroades, John, illus. 2009. (Dragon Keepers Ser.). (ENG.). 176p. (J). (gr. 4-6). lib. bdg. 21.19 *(978-0-375-95589-1(5))* Random House Publishing Group.

—The Dragon in the Library, 3. Shroades, John, illus. 2011. (Dragon Keepers Ser.: No. 3). (ENG.). 224p. (J). (gr. 4-6). lib. bdg. 21.19 *(978-0-375-95591-4(7)*, Yearling) Random Hse. Children's Bks.

—The Dragon in the Sea, 5. Shroades, John, illus. 2012. (Dragon Keepers Ser.). (ENG.). 224p. (J). (gr. 4-6). lib. bdg. 22.44 *(978-0-375-97065-8(7))* Random Hse. Bks. for Young Readers.

—Dragon Keepers #2: the Dragon in the Driveway. Shroades, John, illus. 2010. (Dragon Keepers Ser.: 2). 176p. (J). (gr. 3-7). pap. 7.99 *(978-0-375-85590-0(4)*, Yearling) Random Hse. Children's Bks.

—Dragon Keepers #3: the Dragon in the Library. Shroades, John, illus. 2011. (Dragon Keepers Ser.: 3). 240p. (J). (gr. 3-7). 7.99 *(978-0-375-85592-4(0)*, Yearling) Random Hse. Children's Bks.

—Dragon Keepers #4: the Dragon in the Volcano. Shroades, John, illus. 2012. (Dragon Keepers Ser.: 4). (ENG.). 256p. (J). (gr. 3-7). 7.99 *(978-0-375-86688-3(4)*, Yearling) Random Hse. Children's Bks.

—Dragon Keepers #5: the Dragon in the Sea. Shroades, John, illus. 2013. (Dragon Keepers Ser.: 5). 224p. (J). (gr. 3-7). 7.99 *(978-0-375-87116-0(0)*, Yearling) Random Hse. Children's Bks.

—Dragon Keepers #6: the Dragon at the North Pole. Shroades, John, illus. 2014. (Dragon Keepers Ser.: 6). 176p. (J). (gr. 3-7). 6.99 *(978-0-375-87117-7(9)*, Yearling) Random Hse. Children's Bks.

Kline, Lisa Williams. Write Before Your Eyes. 2010. (ENG.). 192p. (J). (gr. 3-7). 6.99 *(978-0-440-42251-8(5)*, Yearling) Random Hse. Children's Bks.

Klingele, Lindsey. The Broken World. (ENG.). (YA). (gr. 8). 2018. 448p. pap. 9.99 *(978-0-06-238037-1(0))* 2017. 432p. 17.99 *(978-0-06-238036-4(2))* HarperCollins Pubs. (HarperTeen).

K.M. Mohr, John Kelley and. Waking Dalifi. 2005. 72p. pap. 9.95 *(978-1-4116-6364-0(0))* Lulu Pr., Inc.

Knickerbocker, S. J. King of the Ball. 2008. 24p. pap. 13.50 *(978-1-60693-215-5(2)*, Eloquent Bks.) Strategic Book Publishing & Rights Agency (SBPRA).

Knight, Aya. The Chronicles of Kale: Dawn of Retribution. 2012. 456p. 28.95 *(978-1-938083-13-6(X))*; pap. 15.95 *(978-1-938083-12-9(1))* Black Forge.

Knox nee Ramsamugh, Lorna. Fire the Wolf & His Magical Kingdom, 1 vol. 2010. 24p. pap. 24.95 *(978-1-4489-6677-6(9))* PublishAmerica, Inc.

Knudsen, Michelle. The Dragon of Trelian. (Trelian Ser.: 1). (ENG.). 416p. (J). (gr. 5). 2017. pap. 9.99 *(978-0-7636-9454-8(1))* 2009. (Illus.). 16.99 *(978-0-7636-3455-1(7))* Candlewick Pr.

—The Mage of Trelian. 2016. (Trelian Ser.: 3). (ENG.). 432p. (J). (gr. 5). 17.99 *(978-0-7636-7436-6(2))* Candlewick Pr.

—The Princess of Trelian. (Trelian Ser.: 2). (ENG.). 448p. (J). (gr. 5). 2017. pap. 9.99 *(978-0-7636-9455-5(X))* 2012. (Illus.). 16.99 *(978-0-7636-5062-9(5))* Candlewick Pr.

Koch, Claus. The Three Little Wolves & the Big Bad Boar. 2011. 68p. pap. 9.99 *(978-1-4520-5321-9(9))* AuthorHouse.

Kodaka, Nao, illus. Disney Manga: the Princess & the Frog. 2018. (Disney Manga: the Princess & the Frog Ser.). 144p. (J). (gr. 1-1). pap. 10.99 *(978-1-4278-5805-4(5)*, d01665f8-0bde-448c-873c-a2c43af43635, TOKYOPOP Manga) TOKYOPOP, Inc.

Koehler, Hanne Lore & Laraya-Coutts, Corie. A Tale of a Malipayon Warrior. 2010. 128p. 21.95 *(978-1-4502-1344-8(8))*; pap. 11.95 *(978-1-4502-1346-2(4))* iUniverse, Inc.

Kohl, T. Michelle. The Magical Adventures of Bailey Boo the Cockatoo: When the Family's Away, the Parrots Will Play! 2012. 24p. pap. 24.95 *(978-1-4626-6215-9(3))* America Star Bks.

Kok, Gemma. Explore. 2008. 44p. pap. 18.50 *(978-1-4092-2058-9(3))* Lulu Pr., Inc.

—Explore (Printed in black & White) 2008. 44p. pap. 8.00 *(978-1-4092-2530-0(5))* Lulu Pr., Inc.

Koller, Jackie French. The Wizard's Scepter. 2012. (ENG., Illus.). 176p. (J). (gr. 3-7). pap. 9.99 *(978-0-689-85593-1(1)*, Aladdin) Simon & Schuster Children's Publishing.

Komorn, Julie, adapted by. Out of the Dark. 2004. (W. I. T. C. H. Ser.: Bk. 8). (Illus.). 128p. (J). lib. bdg. 16.92 *(978-1-4242-0789-3(4))* Fitzgerald Bks.

Komorn, Julie & Lenhard, Elizabeth, adapted by. The Light of Meridian. 2004. (W. I. T. C. H. Ser.: Bk. 7). (Illus.). 144p. (J). lib. bdg. 16.92 *(978-1-4242-0794-7(0))* Fitzgerald Bks.

Kongyin. Gooby & the Dreamwalker. 2011. 296p. pap. *(978-0-9869858-4-3(8))* Kima Global Pubs.

Korczak, Janusz. Kaytek the Wizard. Lloyd-Jones, Antonia, tr. 2012. (ENG.). 272p. (J). (gr. 4-7). 17.95 *(978-0-9838685-0-7(6))* Flashlight Pr.

Korelitz, Jean Hanff. Interference Powder, 0 vols. 2006. (ENG.). 146p. (J). (gr. 4-6). pap. 7.99 *(978-0-7614-5275-1(3)*, 9780761452751, Two Lions) Amazon Publishing.

—Interference Powder, 1 vol. 2003. (ENG.). 300p. (J). 15.95 *(978-0-7614-5139-6(0))* Marshall Cavendish Corp.

Korté, Steve. The Man of Steel: Superman vs. Mr. Mxyzptlk. Levins, Tim, illus. 2013. (Man of Steel Ser.). (ENG.). 88p. (J). (gr. 3-7). pap. 5.95 *(978-1-4342-4826-8(7)*, 121742, Stone Arch Bks.) Capstone.

Kova, Elise. Water's Wrath (Air Awakens Series Book 4) 2016. (ENG., Illus.). 378p. pap. 14.99 *(978-1-61984-425-4(7))* Gatekeeper Pr.

Kovalkova-McKenna, Svetlana & McKenna, Konstantin. Oberon. 2009. 44p. pap. 7.26 *(978-0-557-06114-3(8))* Lulu Pr., Inc.

Kozlowsky, M. P. The Dyerville Tales. Thompson, Brian, illus. 2014. (ENG.). 336p. (J). (gr. 3-7). 16.99 *(978-0-06-199871-3(0)*, Waldon Pond Pr.) HarperCollins Pubs.

Krakower, Harold. Sugarland: Josh & his magic Bed. 2011. 24p. (gr. -1). pap. 11.32 *(978-1-4567-2957-8(8))* AuthorHouse.

—Sugarland: Princess Sarafina. 2011. 32p. (gr. 1-2). pap. 12.77 *(978-1-4634-0123-8(X))* AuthorHouse.

Kramer, Stacy & Thomas, Valerie. Karma Bites. 2010. (ENG.). 348p. (J). (gr. 5-7). pap. 18.99 *(978-0-547-36301-1(X)*, 1422027, Clarion Bks.) HarperCollins Pubs.

Kravitz, Cathy. The Art Box. 2012. 30p. pap. 11.95 *(978-1-4575-1262-9(9))* Dog Ear Publishing, LLC.

Krensky, Stephen. The Magic Pomegranate: A Jewish Folktale. 2009. pap. 40.95 *(978-0-7613-4818-4(2))* Lerner Publishing Group.

—Too Many Leprechauns: Or How That Pot o' Gold Got to the End of the Rainbow. Andreasen, Dan, illus. 2007. (ENG.). 32p. (J). (gr. -1-1). 12.99 *(978-0-689-85112-4(X)*, Simon & Schuster Bks. For Young Readers) Simon & Schuster Bks. For Young Readers.

Kretzer, Kimberly. The Mystic Valley Adventures of Kody & Kory: The Journey Begins. 2008. 25p. pap. 24.95 *(978-1-60610-692-1(9))* America Star Bks.

Krouskop, Adrienne. The Bakers Moon. 2013. 24p. pap. 10.50 *(978-1-938743-92-4(X))* Reimann Bks.

Krulik, Nancy. Any Way You Slice It #9. John and Wendy, illus. 9th ed. 2003. (Katie Kazoo, Switcheroo Ser.: 9). 80p. (J). (gr. 2-4). pap. 6.99 *(978-0-448-43204-5(8)*, Grosset & Dunlap) Penguin Young Readers Group.

—Attack of the Tighty Whities! 2012. (George Brown, Class Clown Ser.: 7). lib. bdg. 14.75 *(978-0-606-23651-5(1))* Turtleback.

—Attack of the Tighty Whities! #7. Blecha, Aaron, illus. 2012. (George Brown, Class Clown Ser.: 7). 128p. (J). (gr. 2-4). pap. 6.99 *(978-0-448-45575-4(7)*, Grosset & Dunlap) Penguin Young Readers Group.

—Be Careful What You Sniff For. 2013. (Magic Bone Ser.: 1). lib. bdg. 16.00 *(978-0-606-31680-4(9))* Turtleback.

—Be Careful What You Sniff For #1, No. 1. Braun, Sebastien, illus. 2013. (Magic Bone Ser.: 1). 128p. (J). (gr. 1-3). pap. 6.99 *(978-0-448-46399-5(7)*, Grosset & Dunlap) Penguin Young Readers Group.

—Broadway Doggie. 2016. (Magic Bone Ser.: 10). lib. bdg. 14.75 *(978-0-606-38416-2(2))* Turtleback.

—Camp Rules! Super Special. John and Wendy, illus. 2007. (Katie Kazoo, Switcheroo Ser.: No. 5). 160p. (J). (gr. 2-4). pap. 7.99 *(978-0-448-44542-7(5)*, Grosset & Dunlap) Penguin Young Readers Group.

—Catch That Wave. 2013. (Magic Bone Ser.: 2). lib. bdg. 14.75 *(978-0-606-31681-1(7))* Turtleback.

—Catch That Wave #2. Braun, Sebastien, illus. 2013. (Magic Bone Ser.: 2). 128p. (J). (gr. 1-3). pap. 6.99 *(978-0-448-46444-2(6)*, Grosset & Dunlap) Penguin Young Readers Group.

—Dance Your Pants Off! 2013. (George Brown, Class Clown Ser.: 9). lib. bdg. 14.75 *(978-0-606-29802-5(9))* Turtleback.

—Dance Your Pants Off! #9, No. 9. Blecha, Aaron, illus. 2013. (George Brown, Class Clown Ser.: 9). 128p. (J). (gr. 2-4). pap. 6.99 *(978-0-448-45679-9(6)*, Grosset & Dunlap) Penguin Young Readers Group.

—Doggone It! #8. John and Wendy, illus. 8th ed. 2006. (Katie Kazoo, Switcheroo Ser.: 8). (ENG.). 80p. (J). (gr. 2-4). 6.99 *(978-0-448-43172-7(6)*, Grosset & Dunlap) Penguin Young Readers Group.

—Dogs Don't Have Webbed Feet #7. Braun, Sebastien, illus. 2015. (Magic Bone Ser.: 7). 128p. (J). (gr. 1-3). bds. 6.99 *(978-0-448-48096-1(4)*, Grosset & Dunlap) Penguin Young Readers Group.

—Don't Be Such a Turkey! John and Wendy, illus. 2010. (Katie Kazoo, Switcheroo Ser.). 160p. (J). (gr. 2-4). pap. 6.99 *(978-0-448-45448-1(3)*, Grosset & Dunlap) Penguin Young Readers Group.

—Don't Mess with the Ninja Puppy! 2014. (Magic Bone Ser.: 6). lib. bdg. 14.75 *(978-0-606-36162-0(6))* Turtleback.

—Don't Mess with the Ninja Puppy! #6, No. 6. Braun, Sebastien, illus. 2014. (Magic Bone Ser.: 6). 128p. (J). (gr. 1-3). 6.99 *(978-0-448-48095-4(6)*, Grosset & Dunlap) Penguin Young Readers Group.

—Eww! What's on My Shoe? 2013. (George Brown, Class Clown Ser.: 11). lib. bdg. 14.75 *(978-0-606-32126-6(8))* Turtleback.

—Flower Power. John and Wendy Staff, illus. 2008. (Katie Kazoo, Switcheroo Ser.). 78p. (gr. 2-5). 14.00 *(978-0-7569-8806-7(3))* Perfection Learning Corp.

—Follow That Furball. 2013. (Magic Bone Ser.: 3). lib. bdg. 16.00 *(978-0-606-32127-3(6))* Turtleback.

—Free the Worms! John & Wendy, illus. 2008. (Katie Kazoo, Switcheroo Ser.). 78p. (J). 11.65 *(978-0-7569-8807-4(1))* Perfection Learning Corp.

—Friends for Never #14, 14 vols., 14. John and Wendy, illus. 2004. (Katie Kazoo, Switcheroo Ser.: 14). 80p. (J). (gr. 2-4). 6.99 *(978-0-448-43606-7(X)*, Grosset & Dunlap) Penguin Young Readers Group.

—Get Lost! #6, 6 vols. John and Wendy, illus. 6th ed. 2006. (Katie Kazoo, Switcheroo Ser.: 6). 80p. (J). (gr. 2-4). 6.99 *(978-0-448-43101-7(7)*, Grosset & Dunlap) Penguin Young Readers Group.

—Go Fetch! 2014. (Magic Bone Ser.: 5). (Illus.). 111p. (J). lib. bdg. 14.75 *(978-0-606-35701-2(7))* Turtleback.

—Go Fetch! #5. Braun, Sebastien, illus. 2014. (Magic Bone Ser.: 5). 128p. (J). (gr. 1-3). 6.99 *(978-0-448-48094-7(8)*, Grosset & Dunlap) Penguin Young Readers Group.

—Hey! Who Stole the Toilet? 2012. (George Brown, Class Clown Ser.: 8). lib. bdg. 14.75 *(978-0-606-26075-6(7))* Turtleback.

—Hey! Who Stole the Toilet? #8, 8 vols. Blecha, Aaron, illus. 2012. (George Brown, Class Clown Ser.: 8). 128p. (J). (gr. 2-4). pap. 6.99 *(978-0-448-45576-1(5)*, Grosset & Dunlap) Penguin Young Readers Group.

—I Hate Rules! #5. John and Wendy, illus. 5th ed. 2006. (Katie Kazoo, Switcheroo Ser.: 5). 80p. (J). (gr. 2-4). pap. 6.99 *(978-0-448-43100-0(9)*, Grosset & Dunlap) Penguin Young Readers Group.

—Never Box with a Kangaroo #11. Braun, Sebastien, illus. 2016. (Magic Bone Ser.: 11). 128p. (J). (gr. 1-3). 5.99 *(978-0-448-48876-9(0)*, Grosset & Dunlap) Penguin Young Readers Group.

—Nice Snowing You! 2014. (Magic Bone Ser.: 4). lib. bdg. 14.75 *(978-0-606-34145-5(5))* Turtleback.

—Nice Snowing You! #4. Braun, Sebastien, illus. 2014. (Magic Bone Ser.: 4). 128p. (J). (gr. 1-3). 6.99 *(978-0-448-46446-6(2)*, Grosset & Dunlap) Penguin Young Readers Group.

—Quiet on the Set! #10. John and Wendy, illus. 10th ed. 2003. (Katie Kazoo, Switcheroo Ser.: 10). 80p. (J). (gr. 2-4). pap. 6.99 *(978-0-448-43214-4(5)*, Grosset & Dunlap) Penguin Young Readers Group.

—Return to the Scene of the Burp #19. Blecha, Aaron, illus. 2017. (George Brown, Class Clown Ser.: 19). 128p. (J). (gr. 1-3). 5.99 *(978-0-448-48287-3(8)*, Grosset & Dunlap) Penguin Young Readers Group.

—Rootin' Tootin' Cow Dog #8. Braun, Sebastien, illus. 2015. (Magic Bone Ser.: 8). 128p. (J). (gr. 1-3). bds. 5.99 *(978-0-448-48097-8(2)*, Grosset & Dunlap) Penguin Young Readers Group.

—Something's Fishy. John & Wendy, illus. 2008. (Katie Kazoo, Switcheroo Ser.). 76p. 14.00 *(978-0-7569-8348-2(7))* Perfection Learning Corp.

—Super Burp! #1, No. 1. Blecha, Aaron, illus. 2010. (George Brown, Class Clown Ser.: 1). 128p. (J). (gr. 2-4). pap. 6.99 *(978-0-448-45367-5(3)*, Grosset & Dunlap) Penguin Young Readers Group.

—Super Special: Going Overboard! John and Wendy, illus. 2012. (Katie Kazoo, Switcheroo Ser.: No. 9). 144p. (J). (gr. 2-4). pap. 6.99 *(978-0-448-45681-2(8)*, Grosset & Dunlap) Penguin Young Readers Group.

—Super Special: Two Tales. One Dog. Braun, Sebastien, illus. 2016. (Magic Bone Ser.: 12). 192p. (J). (gr. 1-3). 6.99 *(978-0-448-48877-6(9)*, Grosset & Dunlap) Penguin Young Readers Group.

—Three Cheers For... Who? #35. John and Wendy, illus. 2011. (Katie Kazoo, Switcheroo Ser.: 35). (ENG.). 80p. (J). (gr. 2-4). pap. 5.99 *(978-0-448-45449-8(1)*, Grosset & Dunlap) Penguin Young Readers Group.

—Trouble Magnet #2. Blecha, Aaron, illus. 2010. (George Brown, Class Clown Ser.: 2). 128p. (J). (gr. 2-4). pap. 6.99 *(978-0-448-45368-2(1)*, Grosset & Dunlap) Penguin Young Readers Group.

—The Twelve Burps of Christmas. 2012. (George Brown, Class Clown Ser.: No. 1). lib. bdg. 16.00 *(978-0-606-26652-9(6))* Turtleback.

—Wet & Wild! #5, 5 vols. Blecha, Aaron, illus. 2011. (George Brown, Class Clown Ser.: 5). 128p. (J). (gr. 2-4). pap. 6.99 *(978-0-448-45570-9(6)*, Grosset & Dunlap) Penguin Young Readers Group.

—What's Black & White & Stinks All Over? #4. Blecha, Aaron, illus. 2011. (George Brown, Class Clown Ser.: 4). (ENG.). 128p. (J). (gr. 2-4). pap. 6.99 *(978-0-448-45370-5(3)*, Grosset & Dunlap) Penguin Young Readers Group.

—Witch Switch: Super Special. John and Wendy, illus. 2006. (Katie Kazoo, Switcheroo Ser.: No. 4). (ENG.). 160p. (J). (gr. 2-4). pap. 4.99 *(978-0-448-44330-0(9)*, Grosset & Dunlap) Penguin Young Readers Group.

—World's Worst Wedgie #3, 3. Blecha, Aaron, illus. 2010. (George Brown, Class Clown Ser.: 3). 128p. (J). (gr. 2-4). 6.99 *(978-0-448-45369-9(X)*, Grosset & Dunlap) Penguin Young Readers Group.

Krulik, Nancy E. Nice Snowing You! Braun, Sébastien, illus. 2014. 108p. (J). *(978-1-62565-236-2(4)*, Grosset & Dunlap) Penguin Publishing Group.

Kuenzler, Lou. Bella Broomstick #1: Magic Mistakes. 2018. (Bella Broomstick Ser.: 1). (ENG., Illus.). 208p. (J). (gr. 3-7). 7.99 *(978-1-5247-6780-8(8)*, Random Hse. Bks. for Young Readers) Random Hse. Children's Bks.

—Bella Broomstick #2: School Spells. 2019. (Bella Broomstick Ser.: 2). (ENG., Illus.). 224p. (J). (gr. 3-7). pap. 7.99 *(978-1-5247-6783-9(2)*, Random Hse. Bks. for Young Readers) Random Hse. Children's Bks.

Kuipers, Alice. Polly Diamond & the Magic Book: Book 1. Toledano, Diana, illus. 2018. (Polly Diamond Ser.). (ENG.). 160p. (J). (gr. 1-4). 14.99 *(978-1-4521-5232-5(2))* Chronicle Bks. LLC.

—Polly Diamond & the Magic Book: Book 1 (Book Series for Elementary School Kids, Children's Chapter Book for Bookworms) Toledano, Diana, illus. 2019. (Polly Diamond Ser.). (ENG.). 112p. (J). (gr. 1-4). pap. 6.99 *(978-1-4521-8221-6(3))* Chronicle Bks. LLC.

—Polly Diamond & the Super Stunning Spectacular School Fair: Book 2 (Book Series for Kids, Polly Diamond Book Series, Books for Elementary School Kids) Book 2, Bk. 2. Toledano, Diana, illus. 2019. (Polly Diamond Ser.). (ENG.). 112p. (J). (gr. 2-5). 14.99 *(978-1-4521-5233-2(0))* Chronicle Bks. LLC.

Kuipers, Jennifer L. Lynn's Magic Trunk: An Adventure in King Arthur's Court. 2007. 76p. per. 19.95 *(978-1-4241-9860-3(7))* America Star Bks.

Kulick Triscila, Verne. Joel & the Magic Toy Tree. 2005. 36p. (J). 11.99 *(978-1-4116-6985-7(1))* Lulu Pr., Inc.

Kulper, Kendall. Drift & Dagger. 2015. (ENG.). 368p. (YA). (gr. 7-17). 18.00 *(978-0-316-40453-2(5))* Little, Brown Bks. for Young Readers.

—Salt & Storm. 2014. (ENG.). 416p. (YA). E-Book *(978-0-316-40456-3(X))* Little Brown & Co.

Kumin, Maxine & Sexton, Anne. The Wizard's Tears. Katz, Keren, illus. 2019. 48p. (J). (gr. k-4). 18.95 *(978-1-60980-875-4(4)*, Triangle Square) Seven Stories Pr.

Kunkel, Mike. Billy Batson & the Magic of Shazam! 2015. (Billy Batson & the Magic of Shazam! Ser.). (ENG., Illus.). 32p. (J). (gr. 3-6). 95.96 *(978-1-4965-0290-2(6)*, 22750, Stone Arch Bks.) Capstone.

—Brother vs. Brother!, 1 vol. 2014. (Billy Batson & the Magic of Shazam! Ser.). (ENG., Illus.). 32p. (J). (gr. 3-6). 22.60 *(978-1-4342-9228-5(2)*, 125735, Stone Arch Bks.) Capstone.

—Magic Words!, 1 vol. 2014. (Billy Batson & the Magic of Shazam! Ser.). (ENG., Illus.). 32p. (J). (gr. 3-6). 22.60 *(978-1-4342-9209-4(6)*, 125716, Stone Arch Bks.) Capstone.

—The World's Mightiest Mortal!, 1 vol. 2014. (Billy Batson & the Magic of Shazam! Ser.). (ENG., Illus.). 32p. (J). (gr. 3-6). 22.60 *(978-1-4342-9226-1(6)*, 125733, Stone Arch Bks.) Capstone.

Kurtagich, Dawn. Teeth in the Mist. 2019. (ENG., Illus.). 464p. (J). (gr. 9-17). 18.99 *(978-0-316-47847-2(4))* Little, Brown Bks. for Young Readers.

Kurzweil, Allen. Leon & the Champion Chip. Bertholf, Bret, illus. 2005. 352p. (J). lib. bdg. 16.89 *(978-0-06-053934-4(8))* HarperCollins Pubs.

—Leon & the Spitting Image. Bertholf, Bret, illus. (ENG.). 320p. (J). (gr. 3-18). 2005. pap. 7.99 *(978-0-06-053932-0(1)*, Greenwillow Bks.) 2003. 16.99 *(978-0-06-053930-6(5))* HarperCollins Pubs.

Lacamara, Laura. Dalia's Wondrous Hair / el Maravilloso Cabello de Dalia. Baeza Ventura, Gabriela, tr. from SPA. Lacamara, Laura, illus. 2014. (ENG & SPA., Illus.). (J). 17.95 *(978-1-55885-789-6(3)*, Piñata Books) Arte Publico Pr.

Lachmann, Carola. Gayo, a young pirate on a treasure Hunt. 2007. (ENG.). 68p. pap. 41.95 *(978-1-84753-250-3(0))* Lulu Pr., Inc.

Lackey, Mercedes & Edghill, Rosemary. Shadow Grail #2: Conspiracies: Conspiracies. 2011. (Shadow Grail Ser.: 2). (ENG.). 352p. (YA). (gr. 8-12). pap. 18.99 *(978-0-7653-1762-9(1)*, 900041774, Tor Teen) Doherty, Tom Assocs., LLC.

—Shadow Grail #3: Sacrifices. 2013. (Shadow Grail Ser.: 3). (ENG.). 304p. (YA). (gr. 8-12). pap. 17.99 *(978-0-7653-1763-6(X)*, 900041776, Tor Teen) Doherty, Tom Assocs., LLC.

Ladybird. The Magic Paintbrush Activity Book - Ladybird Readers Level 2. 2019. (Ladybird Readers Ser.). (ENG., Illus.). 16p. (J). (gr. k-2). pap. 5.99 *(978-0-241-35823-8(X))* Penguin Random Hse. AUS. Dist: Independent Pubs. Group.

—The Magic Porridge Pot: Ladybird Readers Level 1. 2016. (Ladybird Readers Ser.). (Illus.). 48p. (J). pap. 9.99 *(978-0-241-25406-6(X))* Penguin Bks., Ltd. GBR. Dist: Independent Pubs. Group.

LaFevers, R. L. Theodosia & the Eyes of Horus. Tanaka, Yoko, illus. 2011. (Theodosia Ser.: 3). (ENG.). 384p. (J). (gr. 3-7). pap. 7.99 *(978-0-547-55011-4(1)*, 1450219, Clarion Bks.) HarperCollins Pubs.

—Theodosia & the Last Pharaoh, 4. Tanaka, Yoko, illus. 2012. (Theodosia Ser.: 4). (ENG.). 400p. (J). (gr. 4-6). 21.19 *(978-0-547-39018-5(1))* Houghton Mifflin Harcourt Publishing Co.

—Theodosia & the Serpents of Chaos. Tanaka, Yoko, illus. 2008. (Theodosia Ser.: 1). (ENG.). 352p. (J). (gr. 3-7). pap. 8.99 *(978-0-618-99976-7(0)*, 1027887, Clarion Bks.) HarperCollins Pubs.

—Theodosia & the Serpents of Chaos, 1. Tanaka, Yoko, illus. 2007. (Theodosia Ser.). (ENG.). 352p. (J). (gr. 4-6). 22.44 *(978-0-618-75638-4(8))* Houghton Mifflin Harcourt Publishing Co.

Lagonegro, Melissa. Outside My Window (Disney Tangled) Orpinas, Jean-Paul et al, illus. 2010. (Step into Reading Ser.). (ENG.). 32p. (J). (gr. k-3). pap. 5.99 *(978-0-7364-2688-6(4)*, RH/Disney) Random Hse. Children's Bks.

Lagrow, Victoria. The Adventures of the Magical Hubcap Kid. 2005. pap. 33.49 *(978-1-4208-7981-0(2))* AuthorHouse.

Laird, Donivee M. Ula Li'i & the Magic Shark. Jossem, Carol, illus. 2003. 49p. (J). (gr. k-3). 9.95 *(978-0-940350-23-6(8))* Barnaby Bks., Inc.

Lalicki, Tom. Danger in the Dark: A Houdini & Nate Mystery, 1. 2010. (Houdini & Nate Mysteries Ser.: 1). (ENG.). 208p. (J). (gr. 6-8). pap. 15.99 *(978-0-312-60214-7(6)*, 900064229) Square Fish.

Lallemand, Orianne & Strickland, Tessa. The Blue Bird's Palace. Hénaff, Carole, illus. 2016. (J). *(978-1-78285-308-4(1))* Barefoot Bks., Inc.

Lamb, Charles & Lamb, Mary. Tales from Shakespeare: "A Midsummer Night's Dream" Strang, Kay, ed. Andrews, Gary, illus. rev. ed. 2005. 39p. pap. 4.95 *(978-0-9542905-3-5(4))* Capercaillie Bks., Ltd GBR. Dist: Gatewood Pr.

Lambert, Shirley. Tales of Beaver Hollow: The Magic Flute, 1 vol. 2009. 31p. pap. 24.95 *(978-1-60836-705-4(3))* America Star Bks.

Lamere, Jill. The King's Crown. 2007. (Illus.). 5p. (J). (gr. -1). vinyl bd. 14.95 *(978-0-9772320-2-4(6))* Minikin Pr.

Lanagan, Margo. The Brides of Rollrock Island. 2013. (ENG.). 320p. (YA). (gr. 9). pap. 9.99 *(978-0-375-87336-2(8)*, Ember) Random Hse. Children's Bks.

Lancett, Peter. Dark Words. 2007. (Dark Man Ser.). (ENG.). 36p. pap. *(978-1-84167-602-9(0))* Ransom Publishing Ltd.

Landy, Derek. And He's the Good Guy. Percival, Tom, illus. 2007. (Skulduggery Pleasant Ser.: 1). (ENG.). 400p. (J). (gr. 5-7). 17.99 *(978-0-06-123115-5(0))* HarperCollins Pubs.

—Dark Days (Skulduggery Pleasant, Book 4) 2018. (Skulduggery Pleasant Ser.: 4). (ENG.). 416p. (J). 7.99 *(978-0-00-826634-9(4)*, HarperCollins Children's Bks.) HarperCollins Pubs. Ltd. GBR. Dist: HarperCollins Pubs.

—The Faceless Ones. (Skulduggery Pleasant Ser.: 3). (ENG.). 432p. (J). (gr. 5). 2010. pap. 7.99 *(978-0-06-124093-5(1))* 2009. 16.99 *(978-0-06-124091-1(5))* HarperCollins Pubs.

—Mortal Coil (Skulduggery Pleasant, Book 5) 2018. (Skulduggery Pleasant Ser.: 5). (ENG.). 576p. (J). 7.99 *(978-0-00-826636-3(0)*, HarperCollins Children's Bks.) HarperCollins Pubs. Ltd. GBR. Dist: HarperCollins Pubs.

—Playing with Fire. 2008. (Skulduggery Pleasant Ser.: 2). (ENG.). 400p. (J). (gr. 5-9). 16.99 *(978-0-06-124088-1(5))* HarperCollins Pubs.

—Scepter of the Ancients. Percival, Tom, illus. 2008. (Skulduggery Pleasant Ser.: 1). (ENG.). 416p. (J). (gr. 5). pap. 7.99 *(978-0-06-123117-9(7))* HarperCollins Pubs.

Lane, Jessica E. The Secret of the Swans. 2009. 52p. pap. 31.99 *(978-1-4415-5517-5(X))* Xlibris Corp.

Lane, Leonie. The Retford Witch Catchers. 2005. 144p. per. *(978-1-84667-002-2(0))* Derwent Pr., The.

Lane, Nickel. The Ferret Crusaders: Quest of the Wish A Pod. 2nd ed. 2004. 73p. (J). per. 8.49 *(978-1-4116-0459-9(8))* Lulu Pr., Inc.

Lang, Andrew. The Violet Fairy Book. 2005. 404p. pap. 16.95 *(978-1-4218-0107-0(8)*, 1st World Library - Literary Society) 1st World Publishing, Inc.

Langton, Jane. The Dragon Tree. 2008. (Hall Family Chronicles). 176p. (J). (gr. 3-7). lib. bdg. 16.89 *(978-0-06-082342-9(9))* HarperCollins Pubs.

Larbalestier, Justine. Magic's Child. 2007. (Magic or Madness Trilogy). 291p. (YA). *(978-1-4287-3603-0(4)*, Razorbill) Penguin Publishing Group.

LaRocca, Rajani. Midsummer's Mayhem. 2019. (ENG., Illus.). 352p. (J). (gr. 3-7). 17.99 *(978-1-4998-0888-9(7)*, Yellow Jacket) Bonnier Publishing USA.

Larsen, C. S. The Chronicles of Marvin Archibald Trekker: Boy Magician Book 1 - Penguins of Choice. Lt. ed. 2006. (Illus.). 163p. (YA). per. 5.99 *(978-0-9779844-1-1(9))* KnowledgeGain.

Larson, Sara B. Bright Burns the Night. 2018. (ENG., Illus.). 320p. (YA). (gr. 7-7). 17.99 *(978-1-338-06878-8(4)*, Scholastic Pr.) Scholastic, Inc.

—Dark Breaks the Dawn. (ENG.). 320p. (YA). (gr. 7-7). 2018. pap. 9.99 *(978-1-338-06870-2(9))* 2017. 17.99 *(978-1-338-06869-6(5)*, Scholastic Pr.) Scholastic, Inc.

Lasaracina, Barbara. Mermaid Tears: A Magical Sea Tale. Peer, Nancy, illus. 2010. 28p. pap. 11.99 *(978-1-60844-451-9(1))* Dog Ear Publishing, LLC.

Laura Beth. Two Girls 2 Cats: A Magical Mystery, 1 vol. 2010. 130p. pap. 24.95 *(978-1-4489-4235-0(7))* PublishAmerica, Inc.

Laura Grey Wahl. The Magic Town of Stuart Easterly. 2009. 16p. pap. 15.00 *(978-1-4389-4703-7(8))* AuthorHouse.

Law, Ingrid. Savvy. 2011. 9.68 *(978-0-7848-3575-3(6)*, Everbind) Marco Bk. Co.

—Savvy. 2010. (Illus.). 368p. (J). (gr. 4-7). 9.99 *(978-0-14-241433-0(6)*, Puffin Books) Penguin Young Readers Group.

—Savvy. l.t. ed. 2011. (ENG.). 500p. 23.99 *(978-1-4104-3530-9(X))* Thorndike Pr.

—Savvy. 2010. lib. bdg. 18.40 *(978-0-606-14394-3(7))* Turtleback.

—Scumble. 2011. 432p. (J). (gr. 3-7). 9.99 *(978-0-14-241962-5(1)*, Puffin Books) Penguin Young Readers Group.

—Scumble. l.t. ed. 2011. (Companion to the Newberry Honor Winner Savvy Ser.). (ENG.). 575p. 23.99 *(978-1-4104-3531-6(8))* Thorndike Pr.

—Switch. 2015. (ENG.). 368p. (J). (gr. 3-7). 16.99 *(978-0-8037-3862-1(5)*, Dial Bks) Penguin Young Readers Group.

Lawhorn, Mary Joyce. When Annie Dreams. 2012. 74p. pap. 8.95 *(978-1-4697-8819-7(5))* iUniverse, Inc.

Lawlor, Ashley. Ashley & the First Day of School. 2012. 24p. pap. 24.95 *(978-1-4626-6518-1(7))* America Star Bks.

Lawson, Barbara. Huff the Magicless Dragon, 1 vol. Swope, Brenda, illus. 2009. 35p. pap. 24.95 *(978-1-61546-419-7(0))* PublishAmerica, Inc.

Lay, Kathryn. Time & Space. Bardin, Dave, illus. 2016. (Time Twisters Ser.). (ENG.). 112p. (J). (gr. 2-5). lib. bdg. 38.50 *(978-1-62402-177-0(8)*, 24533, Calico Chapter Bks.) ABDO Publishing Co.

Layton, Roxanne A. Henry & His Amazing MacHine. 2012. 32p. pap. 24.95 *(978-1-4626-6550-1(0))* America Star Bks.

Le Gallienne, Richard. The Book Bills of Narcissus. 2004. reprint ed. pap. 1.99 *(978-1-4192-5479-6(0))*; pap. 15.95 *(978-1-4191-5479-9(6))* Kessinger Publishing, LLC.

Le Guin, Ursula K. Tehanu. 2012. (Earthsea Cycle Ser.: 4). (ENG., Illus.). 288p. (gr. k-k). 18.99 *(978-1-4424-5995-3(6)*, SAGA Press) Simon & Schuster Bks. For Young Readers.

Le Guin, Úrsula K. A Wizard of Earthsea. 2012. (Earthsea Cycle Ser.: Vol. 1). (ENG.). (YA). (gr. 7). lib. bdg. 19.60 *(978-1-68065-210-9(9))* Perfection Learning Corp.

Le Guin, Ursula. K. A Wizard of Earthsea. 2012. (Earthsea Cycle Ser.: 1). (ENG., Illus.). (YA). (gr. 7). 240p. 19.99 *(978-0-547-85139-6(1)*, 1501135); 320p. mass mkt. 10.99 *(978-0-547-77374-2(9)*, 1490754) HarperCollins Pubs. (Clarion Bks.).

Le Guin, Ursula K. A Wizard of Earthsea. 2012. (Earthsea Cycle Ser.: 1). (ENG., Illus.). 264p. (YA). (gr. 7). pap. 15.99 *(978-0-547-72202-3(8)*, 1482458, Clarion Bks.) HarperCollins Pubs.

Le Guin, Úrsula K. A Wizard of Earthsea. 2012. (Earthsea Ser.: 1). lib. bdg. 19.65 *(978-0-606-26624-6(0))* Turtleback.

Ledford, Mary"Aunt Sissy"Ledlowtranette. Cowboy Will & the Magic Rope. 2012. 32p. pap. 19.99 *(978-1-4772-5167-6(7))* AuthorHouse.

Ledger, Kate. Twin Magic: School Bully, Beware! 2013. (Scholastic Reader Level 2 Ser.: 1). (Illus.). 32p. (J). lib. bdg. 13.55 *(978-0-606-31972-0(7))* Turtleback.

Lee, Brian. Bouncey the Elf & Friends - Bedtime St. 2005. (ENG., Illus.). 53p. pap. *(978-0-7552-1023-7(9))* Authors OnLine, Ltd.

Lee, Honest & Gilbert, Matthew J. The Happy & Heinous Halloween of Classroom 13. Dreidemy, Joëlle, illus. 2018. (Classroom 13 Ser.: 5). (ENG.). 128p. (J). (gr. 1-5). pap. 9.99 *(978-0-316-50115-6(8))* Little, Brown Bks. for Young Readers.

Lee, Howard. Jamshid & the Lost Mountain of Light. 2008. (ENG.). 248p. pap. 14.99 *(978-1-4196-8958-1(4))* CreateSpace Independent Publishing Platform.

M N O

Lee, Karin. Zangadoo Kangaroo & the Mysterious Boomerang. Porterfield, Scott, illus. 2012. 94p. pap. 6.99 *(978-0-9847428-2-0(4))* Zangadoo Entertainment.

Lee, Shell. Teenie's Treehouse Adventures: The Magic Begins. 2004. 37p. pap. 24.95 *(978-1-4137-2879-8(0))* PublishAmerica, Inc.

Lee, Stacey. The Secret of a Heart Note. 2016. (ENG.). 384p. (YA). (gr. 8). 17.99 *(978-0-06-242832-5(2)*, Tegen, Katherine Bks) HarperCollins Pubs.

Lee, Stan. The Dragon's Return. 2017. (Zodiac Legacy Ser.: 2). (J). lib. bdg. 20.85 *(978-0-606-39500-7(8))* Turtleback.

—The Zodiac Legacy: the Dragon's Return. 2017. (Zodiac Ser.). (ENG., Illus.). 448p. (J). (gr. 3-7). pap. 9.99 *(978-1-4847-5255-5(4)*, Disney Press Books) Disney Publishing Worldwide.

Lee, Yoon. Dragon Pearl. 2019. (ENG.). 320p. lib. bdg. 18.80 *(978-1-6636-2730-8(4))* Perfection Learning Corp.

—Rick Riordan Presents Dragon Pearl (a Thousand Worlds Novel, Book 1) 2019. (ENG., Illus.). 320p. (J). (gr. 3-7). 16.99 *(978-1-368-01335-2(X)*, Riordan, Rick) Disney Publishing Worldwide.

—Rick Riordan Presents Dragon Pearl (a Thousand Worlds Novel Book 1) 2020. 320p. (J). (gr. 3-7). pap. 8.99 *(978-1-368-01474-8(7)*, Riordan, Rick) Disney Publishing Worldwide.

Lee, Yoon Ha. Dragon Pearl. 2020. (Thousand Worlds (Trade) Ser.). (ENG.). 320p. (gr. 4-7). 24.94 *(978-1-5364-6113-8(X)*, Riordan, Rick) Disney Pr.

—Dragon Pearl. 2019. 320p. 16.99 *(978-1-368-01519-6(0))* Disney Publishing Worldwide.

LeGette, M. L. The Unicorn Girl. 2008. (ENG.). 416p. pap. 10.00 *(978-1-4196-8696-2(8))* CreateSpace Independent Publishing Platform.

Legrand, Claire. Foxheart. Zollars, Jaime, illus. 2016. (ENG.). 480p. (J). (gr. 3-7). 16.99 *(978-0-06-242773-1(3)*, Greenwillow Bks.) HarperCollins Pubs.

—Furyborn. 2018. (Empirium Trilogy Ser.: 1). (ENG.). 512p. (YA). (gr. 8-12). 18.99 *(978-1-4926-5662-3(3))* Sourcebooks, Inc.

—Furyborn: The Empirium Trilogy Book 1. 2019. (Empirium Trilogy Ser.: 1). 496p. (YA). (gr. 8-12). pap. 12.99 *(978-1-4926-7877-9(5))* Sourcebooks, Inc.

Lehane, Pearse. The Train That Never Came. 2008. 328p. pap. *(978-1-84923-249-4(0))* YouWriteOn.

Lehman, Seth. The Color Pets. 2006. (Illus.). 52p. (J). 7.00 net. *(978-0-9787986-0-4(0))* 4All Ages LLC.

Lehrman, Maggie. The Cost of All Things. 2015. (ENG.). 416p. (YA). (gr. 9). 17.99 *(978-0-06-232074-2(2)*, Balzer & Bray) HarperCollins Pubs.

Lemire, Lillie. A Young Witch's Magical Adventure. 2006. (ENG.). 48p. per. 16.95 *(978-1-4241-5413-5(8))* America Star Bks.

Lemke, Donald. The Mightiest Magic. 2015. (Justice League Classic 8X8 Ser.). (J). lib. bdg. 13.55 *(978-0-606-37619-8(4))* Turtleback.

Lenhard, Elizabeth. A Bridge Between Worlds. 2004. (W. I. T. C. H. Ser.: Bk. 10). 158p. (J). lib. bdg. 16.92 *(978-1-4242-0796-1(7))* Fitzgerald Bks.

—Different Path. 2004. (W. I. T. C. H. Ser.: Bk. 13). 158p. (J). lib. bdg. 16.92 *(978-1-4242-0791-6(6))* Fitzgerald Bks.

—The Disappearance. 2004. (W. I. T. C. H. Ser.: Bk. 2). 158p. (J). lib. bdg. 16.92 *(978-1-4242-0799-2(1))* Fitzgerald Bks.

—Finding Meridian. 2004. (W. I. T. C. H. Ser.: Bk. 3). 158p. (J). lib. bdg. 16.92 *(978-1-4242-0801-2(7))* Fitzgerald Bks.

—Power of Five. 2004. 158p. (J). lib. bdg. 16.92 *(978-1-4242-0795-4(9))* Fitzgerald Bks.

Lenhard, Elizabeth, adapted by. The Disappearance. 2004. (W. I. T. C. H. Ser.). (Illus.). 144p. (J). 12.65 *(978-0-7569-4620-3(4))* Perfection Learning Corp.

—The Return of a Queen. 2004. (W. I. T. C. H. Ser.: Bk. 12). 152p. (J). lib. bdg. 16.92 *(978-1-4242-0797-8(5))* Fitzgerald Bks.

Lennon, Thomas. Ronan Boyle & the Bridge of Riddles (Ronan Boyle #1) Hendrix, John, illus. (Ronan Boyle Ser.). (ENG.). (J). (gr. 5-9). 2020. 336p. pap. 8.99 *(978-1-4197-4093-0(8)*, 1266903) 2019. 304p. 17.99 *(978-1-4197-3491-5(1)*, 1266901) Abrams, Inc. (Amulet Bks.).

—Ronan Boyle & the Bridge of Riddles (Ronan Boyle #1) 2019. (ENG., Illus.). 304p. (J). pap. *(978-1-4197-3905-7(0)*, Amulet Bks.) Abrams, Inc.

Lerangis, Peter. Whoa! Amusement Park Gone Wild! Talbot, Jim, illus. 2003. (Abracadabra Ser.: No. 7). (ENG.). 112p. (J). pap. 3.99 *(978-0-439-38938-9(0)*, Scholastic Paperbacks) Scholastic, Inc.

—Wow! Blast from the Past! Talbot, Jim, illus. 2003. (Abracadabra Ser.: No. 8). (ENG.). 112p. (J). pap. 3.99 *(978-0-439-38939-6(9)*, Scholastic Paperbacks) Scholastic, Inc.

Lesler, Rebecca. The Magic Stone: Return of Two Kings. 2008. 73p. pap. 19.95 *(978-1-60610-101-8(3))* America Star Bks.

—The Truth of the Magic Stone, 1 vol. 2009. 107p. pap. 19.95 *(978-1-60836-422-0(4))* America Star Bks.

Lessing, Edeltraut B. Amber & Flax. 2009. *(978-1-61623-777-6(5))* Independent Pub.

Lester, Helen. The Wizard, the Fairy, & the Magic Chicken. Munsinger, Lynn, illus. 2014. (Laugh-Along Lessons Ser.). (ENG.). 32p. (J). (gr. -1-3). 8.99 *(978-0-544-22064-5(1)*, 1562393, Clarion Bks.) HarperCollins Pubs.

Lethcoe, Jason. Der Geheimnisvolle Mr. Spines - Wings, 1. Altmann, Scott, illus. 2010. (Mysterious Mr. Spines Ser.: 1). 256p. (J). (gr. 6-8). 21.19 *(978-0-448-44653-0(7))* Penguin Young Readers Group.

Lethcoe, Jason, illus. You Wish. 2007. 215p. (J). *(978-1-4287-1806-7(0)*, Grosset & Dunlap) Penguin Publishing Group.

Levine, Gail Carson. The Two Princesses of Bamarre. (J). 2012. (ENG.). 272p. (gr. 3-7). pap. 9.99 *(978-0-06-440966-7(X)*, HarperCollins) 2004. (Illus.). 304p. (gr. 7-18). reprint ed. pap. 6.99 *(978-0-06-057580-9(8))* HarperCollins Pubs.

Levinson, Marilyn. Rufus & Magic Run Amok, 1 vol. 2005. (ENG.). 32p. (YA). pap. 5.95 *(978-0-7614-5176-1(5))* Marshall Cavendish Corp.

Levy, Carol L. Elphy Grey. 2012. 24p. pap. 17.99 *(978-1-4772-6687-8(9))* AuthorHouse.

Lewis, C. S. Las Cronicas de Narnia: The Chronicles of Narnia (Spanish Edition), 1 vol. 2006. (Las Cronicas de Narnia Ser.). (SPA., Illus.). 816p. (J). (gr. 3-7). pap. 21.99 *(978-0-06-119900-4(1))* HarperCollins Español.

Lewis, Regina N. The Smallest Schoolhouse. Moore, P. M., illus. 2007. 56p. (J). pap. 12.95 *(978-0-9776958-3-6(2))* CyPress Pubns.

—The Smallest Toy Store, A Christmas Story. Moore, Phyllis M., illus. 2004. 44p. (J). per. 12.95 *(978-0-9672585-8-4(8))* CyPress Pubns.

Leyva, Barbara. Henry & the Magic Window. Leyva, Barbara, illus. l.t. ed. 2003. (Illus.). 50p. (J). 3.50 *(978-0-9729056-0-2(X)*, 0, Balticbard Publishing) Leyva, Barbara.

Liberto, Lorenzo. Matt the Rat & His Sister Maggie (Raton Mateo y Su Hermana Maggie) When I Grow Up (Cuando Yo Crezca) Gomez, Rocio, ed. Torres, Irving, illus. 2003. (Matt the Rat Ser. / La Serie de Ratón Mateo). (SPA & ENG.). 40p. (J). lib. bdg. 20.00 *(978-0-9743668-1-4(1))* Harvest Sun Pr., LLC.

Liess, Claudia Schmidt. Henry the Magical, Mythical Dragon. 2008. 74p. pap. 19.95 *(978-1-60672-956-4(X))* America Star Bks.

Lim, Tiffany. The Scavenger's Scheme: The April Fool's Apprentice. 2019. (ENG.). 112p. (J). pap. 12.95 *(978-981-4794-91-6(0))* Marshall Cavendish International (Asia) Private Ltd. SGP. Dist: Independent Pubs. Group.

Limb, Lisa. The Wishing Wheelchair. 2009. 40p. pap. 16.99 *(978-1-4389-4205-6(2))* AuthorHouse.

Lindsay, Elizabeth. Annie Saves the Day. Eastwood, John, illus. 2003. 92p. (J). *(978-0-439-44651-8(1))* Scholastic, Inc.

—Unicorn Dreams (Book 1) 2011. (Silverlake Fairy School Ser.). 96p. (J). pap. 4.99 *(978-0-7945-3062-4(1)*, Usborne) EDC Publishing.

Lindsey, Norman. The Magic Pudding. 2011. 126p. *(978-1-84902-497-6(9))* Benediction Classics.

Link, Kelly. Pretty Monsters. 2010. (ENG., Illus.). 416p. (YA). (gr. 7-12). pap. 11.99 *(978-0-14-241672-3(X)*, Speak) Penguin Young Readers Group.

Lipka, Francine. Balloon Babies Inside Our Rainbows. 2009. 32p. (gr. -1). pap. 14.49 *(978-1-4490-3118-3(8))* AuthorHouse.

Litke, Erin. Crystal Shards. 2007. 528p. per. 16.95 *(978-1-4327-1548-9(8))* Outskirts Pr., Inc.

Little, Judy. Yody & Bippy the Boo: Friends for Life. 2010. 28p. pap. 12.49 *(978-1-4389-7145-2(1))* AuthorHouse.

Littlewood, Kathryn. Bite-Sized Magic. McGuire, Erin, illus. 2015. (Bliss Bakery Trilogy Ser.: 3). (ENG.). 432p. (J). (gr. 3-7). pap. 7.99 *(978-0-06-208427-9(5)*, Tegen, Katherine Bks) HarperCollins Pubs.

—Bliss. (Bliss Bakery Trilogy Ser.: 1). (ENG.). (J). (gr. 3-7). 2013. 400p. pap. 8.99 *(978-0-06-208424-8(0))* 2012. (Illus.). 384p. 16.99 *(978-0-06-208423-1(2))* HarperCollins Pubs. (Tegen, Katherine Bks).

Littman, Sarah Darer. Charmed, I'm Sure. 2016. (ENG., Illus.). 208p. (J). (gr. 3-7). 17.99 *(978-1-4814-5127-7(8)*, Aladdin) Simon & Schuster Children's Publishing.

—Charmed, I'm Sure. 2017. (ENG., Illus.). 224p. (J). (gr. 3-7). pap. 8.99 *(978-1-4814-5126-0(X)*, Simon & Schuster/Paula Wiseman Bks.) Simon & Schuster/Paula Wiseman Bks.

Lloyd, Natalie. A Snicker of Magic. 2015. lib. bdg. 17.20 *(978-0-606-37089-9(7))* Turtleback.

—A Snicker of Magic (Scholastic Gold) 2015. (ENG.). 336p. (J). (gr. 3-7). pap. 7.99 *(978-0-545-55273-8(7)*, Scholastic Pr.) Scholastic, Inc.

—A Snicker of Magic (Scholastic Gold) (Unabridged Edition), 2 vols. unabr. ed. 2014. (ENG.). 2p. (J). (gr. 3-7). audio compact disk 34.99 *(978-0-545-70679-7(3))* Scholastic, Inc.

Lloyd, Natalie, et al. A Snicker of Magic. 2014. (ENG.). mass mkt. *(978-0-545-68447-7(1))* Scholastic, Inc.

Locke, Katherine. The Girl with the Red Balloon. 2017. (Balloonmakers Ser.: 1). (ENG.). 288p. (YA). (gr. 8-12). pap. 9.99 *(978-0-8075-2937-9(0)*, 807529370) Whitman, Albert & Co.

—The Spy with the Red Balloon. 2019. (Balloonmakers Ser.: 2). (ENG.). 368p. (YA). (gr. 8-12). pap. 9.99 *(978-0-8075-2938-6(9)*, 807529389) Whitman, Albert & Co.

Locurto, Ian N. The Christmas Penny. 2010. 20p. 11.99 *(978-1-4490-7100-4(7))* AuthorHouse.

Loehr, Mallory. Unicorn Wings. Silin-Palmer, Pamela, illus. 2006. (Step into Reading Ser.: Vol. 1). 32p. (J). (gr. -1-1). per. 4.99 *(978-0-375-83117-1(7)*, Random Hse. Bks. for Young Readers) Random Hse. Children's Bks.

Loftin, Nikki. Nightingale's Nest. 2015. 272p. (J). (gr. 3-7). pap. 8.99 *(978-1-59514-623-6(7)*, Razorbill) Penguin Young Readers Group.

Logan, Christopher. Daphne. 2008. 145p. pap. 18.95 *(978-1-4357-5038-8(1))* Lulu Pr., Inc.

Loiske, Jennifer. Black Diamond. 2013. (ENG.). 246p. (J). pap. *(978-1-291-30145-8(3))* Lulu Pr., Inc.

Loiske, Jennifer, et al. Tales of an Old Wizard. 2013. (ENG.). 116p. pap. 10.58 *(978-1-291-30601-9(3))* Lulu Pr., Inc.

Loman, Sam. The Magical Unicorn Activity Book. Loman, Sam, illus. 2019. (ENG., Illus.). 176p. (J). pap. 16.99 *(978-1-78950-829-1(0)*, d39a6a67-509e-4b02-804f-ad3b61056380) Arcturus Publishing GBR. Dist: Baker & Taylor Publisher Services (BTPS).

—The Magical Unicorn Activity Book. 2018. (ENG.). 96p. (J). pap. 9.99 *(978-1-78828-715-9(0)*, acfc23f5-38d6-4207-8211-870d8e1a26cb) Arcturus Publishing GBR. Dist: Baker & Taylor Publisher Services (BTPS).

Long, Loren & Bildner, Phil. Game 3. Long, Loren, illus. 2008. (ENG., Illus.). 208p. (J). (gr. 2-5). 10.99 *(978-1-4169-1865-3(5)*, Simon & Schuster Bks. For Young Readers) Simon & Schuster Bks. For Young Readers.

—Great Balls of Fire. Long, Loren, illus. 2009. (Sluggers Ser.: 3). (ENG., Illus.). 224p. (J). (gr. 3-7). pap. 7.99 *(978-1-4169-1889-9(2)*, Simon & Schuster Bks. For Young Readers) Simon & Schuster Bks. For Young Readers.

Long, Susan Hill. The Magic Mirror: Concerning a Lonely Princess, a Foundling Girl, a Scheming King & a Pickpocket Squirrel. 2016. (ENG., Illus.). 320p. (J). (gr. 3-7). 16.99 *(978-0-553-51134-5(3)*, Knopf Bks. for Young Readers) Random Hse. Children's Bks.

Longus. The ADVENTURES of SILVANA & the MAGIC UNICORN. 2008. 48p. 18.95 *(978-1-4357-1877-7(1))* Lulu Pr., Inc.

Look, Lenore. Ruby Lu, Brave & True. Wilsdorf, Anne, illus. 2006. (Ruby Lu Ser.). 105p. (J). (gr. 1-5). 11.65 *(978-0-7569-6553-2(5))* Perfection Learning Corp.

Lopez, David Mark. Run Like a Fugitive. 2006. (J). (gr. 4-8). *(978-0-9744097-2-6(3))* Lopez, David.

—Walk Like an Egyptian. 2006. (J). (gr. 3-7). *(978-0-9744097-0-2(7))* Lopez, David.

Love, D. Anne. The Secret Prince. 2012. (ENG.). 240p. (J). (gr. 3-7). pap. 11.99 *(978-1-4424-5931-1(X)*, McElderry, Margaret K. Bks.) McElderry, Margaret K. Bks.

Love, Emily. The Beginning of Freedom. 2010. (ENG.). 81p. pap. 9.00 *(978-0-557-56598-6(7))* Lulu Pr., Inc.

Loveridge, Pamela. The Knife of Blood. 2012. 28p. pap. 32.70 *(978-1-4797-4804-4(8))* Xlibris Corp.

Lovhaug, Lewis J. Angel Armor: The Cassandra Conflict. 2004. 188p. (YA). pap. 13.95 *(978-0-595-30869-9(4))* iUniverse, Inc.

Lowe, Natasha. The Courage of Cat Campbell. 2015. (Poppy Pendle Ser.). (ENG., Illus.). 288p. (J). (gr. 3-7). 16.99 *(978-1-4814-1870-6(X)*, Simon & Schuster/Paula Wiseman Bks.) Simon & Schuster/Paula Wiseman Bks.

—The Marvelous Magic of Miss Mabel. (Poppy Pendle Ser.). (ENG.). (J). (gr. 3-7). 2017. 304p. pap. 8.99 *(978-1-4814-6534-2(1))* 2016. (Illus.). 288p. 16.99 *(978-1-4814-6533-5(3))* Simon & Schuster/Paula Wiseman Bks. (Simon & Schuster/Paula Wiseman Bks.).

—The Power of Poppy Pendle. (Poppy Pendle Ser.). (ENG., 272p. (J). (gr. 3-7). 2013. Illus.). pap. 8.99 *(978-1-4424-4926-8(8))* 2012. 16.99 *(978-1-4424-4679-3(X))* Simon & Schuster/Paula Wiseman Bks. (Simon & Schuster/Paula Wiseman Bks.).

Lowe, Wesley. The Griffin's Gauntlet. 2003. (Illus.). (YA). per. 14.95 *(978-0-9723011-2-1(7))* Helm Publishing.

Lowes, Sarah. The Snow Queen. Clara, Miss, illus. 2013. 64p. (J). 17.99 *(978-1-84686-964-8(1))* Barefoot Bks., Inc.

Lubar, David. Meltdown Madness: a Branches Book (Looniverse #2) Loveridge, Matt, illus. 2013. (Looniverse Ser.: 2). (ENG.). 96p. (J). (gr. 1-3). pap. 4.99 *(978-0-545-49604-9(7))* Scholastic, Inc.

—Stranger Things. Loveridge, Matt, illus. 2013. (Looniverse Ser.: 1). (ENG.). 96p. (J). (gr. 1-3). pap. 4.99 *(978-0-545-49602-5(0))* Scholastic, Inc.

—Stranger Things. 2013. (Looniverse Ser.: 1). lib. bdg. 14.75 *(978-0-606-31982-9(4))* Turtleback.

Lucas, David. The Lying Carpet. Lucas, David, illus. 2013. (ENG., Illus.). 80p. (J). (gr. 4-7). pap. 10.99 *(978-1-84939-017-0(7))* Andersen Pr. GBR. Dist: Independent Pubs. Group.

Luciano, Sonia. Mr. I Forgot. 2009. 48p. pap. 16.95 *(978-1-61582-765-7(X))* America Star Bks.

Lück, Stefanie. Carla's Worlds. 2010. 222p. pap. 20.90 *(978-3-8391-4857-0(X))* Bks. on Demand.

Luiken, Nicole. In Truth & Ashes. 2016. (ENG., Illus.). (YA). pap. 19.99 *(978-1-68281-388-1(6))* Entangled Publishing, LLC.

Lundquist, Jenny. Seeing Cinderella. 2012. (Mix Ser.). (ENG.). 240p. (J). (gr. 4-8). pap. 6.99 *(978-1-4424-2926-0(7)*, Aladdin) Simon & Schuster Children's Publishing.

—Seeing Cinderella. 2012. (Mix Ser.). (ENG.). 240p. (J). (gr. 4-8). 16.99 *(978-1-4424-4550-5(5))* Simon & Schuster, Inc.

Lunetta, Demitria. Bad Blood. 2017. 272p. (YA). (gr. 7). 17.99 *(978-1-101-93805-8(6)*, Delacorte Pr.) Random Hse. Children's Bks.

Luper, Eric. Battle of the Bots. 2018. (Key Hunters Ser.: 7). (ENG., Illus.). 128p. (J). (gr. 2-5). pap. 4.99 *(978-1-338-21233-4(8)*, Scholastic Paperbacks) Scholastic, Inc.

—The Haunted Howl. Weber, Lisa K., illus. 2016. (Key Hunters Ser.: 3). (ENG.). 128p. (J). (gr. 2-5). pap. 4.99 *(978-0-545-82211-4(4)*, Scholastic Paperbacks) Scholastic, Inc.

—The Mysterious Moonstone (Key Hunters #1) 2016. (Key Hunters Ser.: 1). (ENG., Illus.). 128p. (J). (gr. 2-5). pap. 5.99 *(978-0-545-82204-6(1))* Scholastic, Inc.

—The Risky Rescue (Key Hunters #6) 2017. (Key Hunters Ser.: 6). (ENG., Illus.). 128p. (J). (gr. 2-5). pap. 5.99 *(978-1-338-21229-7(X)*, Scholastic Paperbacks) Scholastic, Inc.

—The Spy's Secret (Key Hunters #2) 2016. (Key Hunters Ser.: 2). (ENG.). 128p. (J). (gr. 2-5). pap. 5.99 *(978-0-545-82206-0(8))* Scholastic, Inc.

—The Wizard's War (Key Hunters #4) 2017. (Key Hunters Ser.: 4). (ENG., Illus.). 128p. (J). (gr. 2-5). pap. 5.99 *(978-0-545-82213-8(0)*, Scholastic Paperbacks) Scholastic, Inc.

Lupton, Hugh. Tales of Mystery & Magic. Baruzzi, Agnese, illus. 2019. (ENG.). 64p. (J). (gr. k-3). pap. 16.99 ***(978-1-78285-860-7(1))*** Barefoot Bks., Inc.

Lupton, Hugh & Barefoot Books. Tales of Mystery & Magic. Baruzzi, Agnese, illus. 2015. 64p. (J). (gr. -1-2). 16.99 *(978-1-78285-254-4(9))* Barefoot Bks., Inc.

Lurie, Craig. Butterflies, Ladybugs, & Bumble Bees & the wonderful world this could Be ... . 2011. 36p. (gr. -1). pap. 14.95 *(978-1-4567-6300-8(8))* AuthorHouse.

Lynn, Deidre. Treasure Delight: A Sweet Story about the Joy in Sharing. Morris, Jessica, illus. 2013. 36p. pap. 12.95 *(978-0-9893181-0-5(9))* LoveLight Media.

Lyons Stroud, Patricia. The Seven Keys to Adventure. 2007. 148p. 23.00 *(978-1-59048-252-0(2))* Long Riders' Guild Pr., The.

Maberry, Jonathan. The Orphan Army. 2015. (Nightsiders Ser.: 1). (ENG., Illus.). 400p. (J). (gr. 3-7). 16.99 *(978-1-4814-1575-0(1)*, Simon & Schuster Bks. For Young Readers) Simon & Schuster Bks. For Young Readers.

—The Orphan Army. 2016. (Nightsiders Ser.: 1). lib. bdg. 18.40 *(978-0-606-38959-4(8))* Turtleback.

—Vault of Shadows. (Nightsiders Ser.: 2). (ENG.). 464p. (J). (gr. 3-7). 2017. pap. 8.99 *(978-1-4814-1579-8(4))* 2016. (Illus.). 16.99 *(978-1-4814-1578-1(6))* Simon & Schuster Bks. For Young Readers. (Simon & Schuster Bks. For Young Readers).

MacDonald, Betty. Hello, Mrs. Piggle-Wiggle. Boiger, Alexandra, illus. 2007. (ENG.). 176p. (J). (gr. 3-7). pap. 7.99 *(978-0-06-440149-4(9)*, HarperCollins) HarperCollins Pubs.

—Hello, Mrs. Piggle Wiggle. Boiger, Alexandra, illus. 2007. (ENG.). 176p. (J). (gr. 3-7). 16.99 *(978-0-397-31715-8(8)*, HarperCollins) HarperCollins Pubs.

—Mrs. Piggle-Wiggle's Magic. Boiger, Alexandra, illus. 2007. (ENG.). 192p. (J). (gr. 3-7). pap. 6.99 *(978-0-06-440151-7(0)*, HarperCollins) HarperCollins Pubs.

MacDonald, George. The Light Princess. 110p. (J). (gr. 4-5). pap. 5.95 *(978-0-8072-1396-4(9)*, Listening Library) Random Hse. Audio Publishing Group.

—Light Princess. l.t. ed. 2006. pap. *(978-1-84702-350-6(9))* Echo Library.

Macinnis, Katherine. Kelsar. 2006. pap. 12.95 *(978-1-58939-876-4(9))* Virtualbookworm.com Publishing, Inc.

Mack, Karen. The Magical Adventures of Sun Beams. 2009. 42p. 31.99 *(978-1-4415-3636-5(1))* Xlibris Corp.

Mack, Michele. Henry Fickle & the Secret Laboratory. 2005. (Illus.). 112p. (J). 18.00 *(978-0-9667747-1-9(X)*, 1239658) Skylar Doreal.

MacKenzie, Ross. Zac & the Dream Stealers. 2013. 297p. (J). *(978-0-545-40107-4(0)*, Chicken Hse., The) Scholastic, Inc.

Madden, Michelle. The Butterfly Garden. 2008. 24p. pap. 24.95 *(978-1-60813-375-8(3))* America Star Bks.

Madrid, Bo. The Lunar Express. 2010. (Illus.). 32p. 12.99 *(978-1-4490-6949-0(5))* AuthorHouse.

Madsen, W. J. Arkeepers: Episode One. 2012. 142p. pap. 7.95 *(978-0-9830487-0-1(3))* little m Bks.

—Arkeepers: Episode Two. 2012. 206p. pap. 9.30 *(978-0-9830487-1-8(1))* little m Bks.

Mafi, Tahereh. Furthermore. 2017. (ENG.). 432p. (J). (gr. 4-7). 9.99 *(978-1-101-99477-1(0)*, Puffin Books) Penguin Young Readers Group.

—Furthermore. 2017. (Furthermore Ser.: 1). lib. bdg. 19.65 *(978-0-606-40493-8(7))* Turtleback.

—Whichwood. (YA). 2018. 384p. (gr. 7). pap. 11.99 *(978-1-101-99480-1(0)*, Speak) 2017. 368p. (gr. 5). 17.99 *(978-1-101-99479-5(7)*, Dutton Books for Young Readers) Penguin Young Readers Group.

Magic Box. (ARA., Illus.). 100p. (YA). pap. 5.95 *(978-0-86685-743-7(5)*, LDL946) Librairie du Liban Pubns. FRA. Dist: International Bk. Ctr., Inc.

The Magic King. 2003. (J). *(978-1-4120-3345-9(4))* Black Dot Pubns.

The Magic of Tobias Twissle. 2003. (J). lib. bdg. *(978-0-9744923-0-8(2))* Purple Plume Pr.

Magic Painting Jungle. 2017. (Magic Painting Bks.). (ENG.). (J). pap. 9.99 *(978-0-7945-3982-5(3)*, Usborne) EDC Publishing.

Magic Wand Disney Princess. 2005. (Illus.). 10p. (J). bds. 16.98 *(978-1-4127-3537-7(8)*, 7263500) Publications International, Ltd.

The Magical Horses Vol. 2000: A Fairy Tale for the Young & the Young at Heart. l.t. ed. 2005. (Illus.). 127p. (J). per. *(978-0-9738625-0-8(5))* Blue Cat Publishing.

Magical Max Makes Friends. 2005. (Adventures of Magical Max, Scarlet Feather & Little Lilly Woo-Woo Ser.). (Illus.). 16p. (J). (gr. k-4). 14.95 *(978-0-9762408-0-8(7))* Lead Life Pr., LLC.

The Magical Singing Wood. 2017. (ENG., Illus.). 176p. (J). 9.00 *(978-1-78270-141-5(9))* Award Pubns. Ltd. GBR. Dist: Parkwest Pubns., Inc.

Magness, Lee. Silver Dasher. 2003. 164p. pap. 12.95 *(978-0-595-29043-7(4))* iUniverse, Inc.

Mahabeer, Rishen. Anna & Timothy. 2012. 20p. pap. 13.77 *(978-1-4669-5509-7(0))* Trafford Publishing.

Mahon, Matthew. The Defenders of All Thats Fall. 2008. 56p. pap. 24.95 *(978-1-4327-3169-4(6))* Outskirts Pr., Inc.

Mahoney, Jerry. My Rotten Stepbrother Ruined Cinderella. Bitskoff, Aleksei, illus. 2017. (My Rotten Stepbrother Ruined Fairy Tales Ser.). (ENG.). 160p. (J). (gr. 3-6). lib. bdg. 26.65 *(978-1-4965-4466-7(8)*, 134771, Stone Arch Bks.) Capstone.

—My Rotten Stepbrother Ruined Snow White. Bitskoff, Aleksei, illus. 2017. (My Rotten Stepbrother Ruined Fairy Tales Ser.). (ENG.). 160p. (J). (gr. 3-6). pap. 8.95 *(978-1-4965-4467-4(6)*, 134772); lib. bdg. 26.65 *(978-1-4965-4463-6(3)*, 134768) Capstone. (Stone Arch Bks.).

—My Stupid Stepbrother Ruined Aladdin. Bitskoff, Aleksei, illus. 2017. (My Rotten Stepbrother Ruined Fairy Tales Ser.). (ENG.). 160p. (J). (gr. 3-6). lib. bdg. 26.65 *(978-1-4965-4464-3(1)*, 134769, Stone Arch Bks.) Capstone.

—My Stupid Stepbrother Ruined Beauty & the Beast. Bitskoff, Aleksei, illus. 2017. (My Rotten Stepbrother Ruined Fairy Tales Ser.). (ENG.). 160p. (J). (gr. 3-6). lib. bdg. 26.65 *(978-1-4965-4465-0(X)*, 134770, Stone Arch Bks.) Capstone.

Mahy, Margaret. Maddigan's Fantasia. 2012. (ENG.). 512p. (J). (gr. 5-9). pap. 22.99 *(978-1-4424-6053-9(9)*, McElderry, Margaret K. Bks.) McElderry, Margaret K. Bks.

Maisel, Eric & Maisel, Natalya. The Magic of Sleep Thinking: How to Solve Problems, Reduce Stress, & Increase Creativity While You Sleep. 2018. (ENG.). 240p. pap. 14.95 *(978-0-486-82428-4(4)*, 824284, Ixia Pr.) Dover Pubns., Inc.

Makinen, Kirsti, ed. The Kalevala: Tales of Magic & Adventure. Brooks, Kaarina, tr. Surojegin, Pirkko-Liisa, illus. 2009. (ENG.). 214p. (YA). (gr. 4-18). 24.95 *(978-1-897476-00-0(0))* Simply Read Bks. CAN. Dist: Ingram Publisher Services.

Malbrough, Mike. Marigold Finds the Magic Words. Malbrough, Mike, illus. 2019. (Illus.). 40p. (J). (gr. -1-2). 17.99 *(978-1-5247-3743-6(7))* Flamingo Bks.

Malchow, Hal & Malchow, Alex. The Sword of Darrow. 2011. 372p. (J). (gr. 3-7). pap. 12.99 *(978-1-935618-47-8(4))* BenBella Bks.

Malloy, Chris. Wizard Academies - A Special Kind of Talent. 2007. (ENG.). 142p. pap. 19.95 *(978-0-615-18505-7(3))* Wizard Academies, LLC.

Malone, Marianne. The Pirate's Coin: a Sixty-Eight Rooms Adventure. Call, Greg, illus. 2014. (Sixty-Eight Rooms Adventures Ser.: 3). (ENG.). 240p. (J). (gr. 3-7). 7.99 *(978-0-307-97720-5(X)*, Yearling) Random Hse. Children's Bks.

—The Secret of the Key: a Sixty-Eight Rooms Adventure. 2015. (Sixty-Eight Rooms Adventures Ser.: 4). (ENG., Illus.). 256p. (J). (gr. 3-7). 8.99 *(978-0-307-97724-3(2)*, Yearling) Random Hse. Children's Bks.

—The Sixty-Eight Rooms, 1. Triplett, Gina & Call, Greg, illus. 2011. (Sixty-Eight Rooms Adventures Ser.). (ENG.). 288p. (J). (gr. 4-6). lib. bdg. 22.44 *(978-0-375-95710-9(3))* Random House Publishing Group.
—The Sixty-Eight Rooms. Call, Greg, illus. 2011. (Sixty-Eight Rooms Adventures Ser.: 1). (ENG.). 288p. (J). (gr. 3-7). pap. 9.99 *(978-0-375-85711-9(7),* Yearling) Random Hse. Children's Bks.
—Stealing Magic, 2. Call, Greg, illus. 2013. (Sixty-Eight Rooms Adventures Ser.). (ENG.). 272p. (J). (gr. 4-6). lib. bdg. 21.19 *(978-0-375-96819-8(9),* Yearling) Random Hse. Children's Bks.
—Stealing Magic: a Sixty-Eight Rooms Adventure. Call, Greg, illus. 2013. (Sixty-Eight Rooms Adventures Ser.: 2). (ENG.). 272p. (J). (gr. 3-7). pap. 9.99 *(978-0-375-86790-3(2),* Yearling) Random Hse. Children's Bks.
Mama Doo. Zachary & the Magic Pumpkin Seeds, 1 vol. 2007. (ENG.). 35p. 24.95 *(978-1-4241-8579-5(3))* America Star Bks.
Mancil, Arlene. The Garden Fairy. 2008. 32p. pap. 24.95 *(978-1-60441-735-7(8))* PublishAmerica, Inc.
Maniscalco, Kerri. Escaping from Houdini. (Stalking Jack the Ripper Ser.: 3). (ENG., Illus.). (YA). (gr. 10-17). 2019. 480p. pap. 12.99 *(978-0-316-55172-4(4))* 2018. 448p. 19.99 *(978-0-316-55170-0(8))* Little Brown & Co. (Jimmy Patterson).
Manning, Matthew K. Magic Smells Awful. Ellis, Joey, illus. 2018. (Xander & the Rainbow-Barfing Unicorns Ser.). (ENG.). 128p. (J). (gr. 3-5). pap. 7.95 *(978-1-4965-5719-3(0),* 136708); lib. bdg. 22.65 *(978-1-4965-5715-5(8),* 136704) Capstone. (Stone Arch Bks.).
—Return to Pegasia. Ellis, Joey, illus. 2018. (Xander & the Rainbow-Barfing Unicorns Ser.). (ENG.). 128p. (J). (gr. 3-5). pap. 7.95 *(978-1-4965-5718-6(2),* 136707, Stone Arch Bks.) Capstone.
—Revenge of the One-Trick Pony. Ellis, Joey, illus. 2018. (Xander & the Rainbow-Barfing Unicorns Ser.). (ENG.). 128p. (J). (gr. 3-5). pap. 7.95 *(978-1-4965-5716-2(6),* 136705, Stone Arch Bks.) Capstone.
—The Search for Stalor. Ellis, Joey, illus. 2018. (Xander & the Rainbow-Barfing Unicorns Ser.). (ENG.). 128p. (J). (gr. 3-5). pap. 7.95 *(978-1-4965-5717-9(4),* 136706); lib. bdg. 22.65 *(978-1-4965-5713-1(1),* 136702) Capstone. (Stone Arch Bks.).
Mantchev, Lisa. Eyes Like Stars: Theatre Illuminata, Act I. 2010. (Theatre Illuminata Ser.: 1). (ENG.). 384p. (YA). (gr. 7-12). pap. 17.99 *(978-0-312-60866-8(7),* 900065167) Square Fish.
—Perchance to Dream: Theatre Illuminata #2, 2. 2011. (Theatre Illuminata Ser.: 2). (ENG.). 368p. (YA). (gr. 7-12). pap. 17.99 *(978-0-312-67510-3(0),* 900072953) Square Fish.
Marciano, John Bemelmans. The Secret Janara. Blackall, Sophie, illus. 2019. (Witches of Benevento Ser.: 6). 144p. (J). (gr. 3-7). 13.99 *(978-0-425-29154-2(5),* Viking Books for Young Readers) Penguin Young Readers Group.
Margo's Magic Trunk. 2006. (Illus.). 32p. (J). pap. 6.95 *(978-0-9789016-0-8(6))* Jodaviste Publishing.
Mariconda, Barbara. The Voyage of Lucy P. Simmons. 2012. (Voyage of Lucy P. Simmons Ser.: 1). (ENG.). 256p. (J). (gr. 3-7). 16.99 *(978-0-06-211979-7(6),* Tegen, Katherine Bks) HarperCollins Pubs.
Marie, Jill Jana. Anna Lee Enis Bee. 2010. 24p. pap. 11.00 *(978-1-60860-907-9(3),* Eloquent Bks.) Strategic Book Publishing & Rights Agency (SBPRA).
Marillier, Juliet. Cybele's Secret. 2011. (Wildwood Dancing Ser.: 2). (ENG.). 448p. (YA). (gr. 7). pap. 9.99 *(978-0-553-49486-0(4),* Knopf Bks. for Young Readers) Random Hse. Children's Bks.
—Raven Flight: A Shadowfell Novel. 2014. (Shadowfell Ser.). (ENG.). 416p. (YA). (gr. 7). pap. 9.99 *(978-0-375-87197-9(7),* Ember) Random Hse. Children's Bks.
—Shadowfell. 2013. (Shadowfell Ser.). (ENG., Illus.). 416p. (YA). (gr. 7). pap. 14.99 *(978-0-375-87196-2(9),* Ember) Random Hse. Children's Bks.
—Wildwood Dancing. 2008. (Wildwood Dancing Ser.: 1). (ENG.). 432p. (YA). (gr. 7). pap. 16.99 *(978-0-375-84474-4(0),* Knopf Bks. for Young Readers) Random Hse. Children's Bks.
Marinsky, Jane, illus. The Goat-Faced Girl: A Classic Italian Folktale. 2009. (ENG.). 32p. (J). (gr. 1-4). 16.95 *(978-1-56792-393-3(3))* Godine, David R. Pub.
Mariotte, Jeff. Dark Vengeance Vol. 1: Summer, Fall. 2011. (ENG.). 512p. (YA). (gr. 9). pap. 9.99 *(978-1-4424-2975-8(5),* Simon Pulse) Simon Pulse.
Marr, Melissa. Untamed City: Carnival of Secrets Signed 8c Carton. 2012. (ENG.). 320p. (J). pap. 143.92 *(978-0-06-221668-7(6),* Harper) HarperCollins Pubs.
Marrone, Amanda. Master of Mirrors. 2011. (Magic Repair Shop Ser.: 3). (ENG.). 192p. (J). (gr. 3-7). pap. 5.99 *(978-1-4169-9035-2(6),* Aladdin) Simon & Schuster Children's Publishing.
—Only the Stars Know Her Name: Salem's Lost Story of Tituba's Daughter. 2019. (ENG.). 304p. (J). (gr. 4-9). 16.99 *(978-1-4998-0890-2(9),* Yellow Jacket) Bonnier Publishing USA.
—Revealers. 2008. (ENG.). 288p. (YA). (gr. 9-18). pap. 8.99 *(978-1-4169-5874-1(6),* Simon Pulse) Simon Pulse.
Marsh, Richard Phillip. Mattress People Go to Bear Park. 2009. 44p. pap. 10.95 *(978-1-935125-39-6(7))* Robertson Publishing.
Marsh, Sarah Glenn. Fear the Drowning Deep. (ENG.). 312p. (gr. 6-12). 2018. (YA). pap. 8.99 *(978-1-5107-2658-1(6))* 2016. (J). 16.99 *(978-1-5107-0348-3(9))* Skyhorse Publishing Co., Inc. (Sky Pony Pr.).
Marshall, Heidi Amenda. Petra's Adventure in Nievenheim. Marshall, Heidi Amenda, illus. l.t. ed. 2003. (Illus.). 57p. (J). per. 7.99 *(978-0-9747445-0-6(6))* Landfall Co., The.
Marshall, Linda Elovitz. The Mitzvah Magician. Engel, Christiane, illus. 2012. (ENG.). 24p. (J). (gr. -1-2). lib. bdg. 7.95 *(978-0-7613-5655-4(X),* 7ba9f681-643a-4044-bd26-5b8cae01eeae, Kar-Ben Publishing) Lerner Publishing Group.
Marsham, Liz. Wonder Woman: Maze of Magic. 2017. (I Can Read! Level 2 Ser.). (Illus.). 32p. (J). lib. bdg. 13.55 *(978-0-606-40057-2(5))* Turtleback.
—Wonder Woman Classic: Maze of Magic. Ferguson, Lee, illus. 2017. (I Can Read Level 2 Ser.). 32p. (J). (gr. -1-3). pap. 3.99 *(978-0-06-236093-9(0))* HarperCollins Pubs.
Martin, Alison. Princess of Tabaria. 2004. (Illus.). 104p. pap. *(978-1-84401-151-3(8))* Athena Pr.
Martin, Ann M. & Parnell, Annie. Missy Piggle-Wiggle & the Sticky-Fingers Cure. Hatke, Ben, illus. 2019. (Missy Piggle-Wiggle Ser.: 3). (ENG.). 240p. (J). pap. 11.99 *(978-1-250-21139-2(5),* 900176808) Square Fish.
—Missy Piggle-Wiggle & the Won't-Walk-The-Dog Cure. Hatke, Ben, illus. 2018. (Missy Piggle-Wiggle Ser.: 2). (ENG.). 256p. (J). pap. 11.99 *(978-1-250-17903-6(3),* 900189918) Square Fish.
Martin, Emily Winfield. Snow & Rose. (Illus.). 224p. (J). (gr. 3-7). 2019. pap. 9.99 *(978-0-553-53821-2(7),* Yearling) 2017. 17.99 *(978-0-553-53818-2(7),* Random Hse. Bks. for Young Readers) Random Hse. Children's Bks.
Martin, Gary. The Witch of Endor, 1 vol. Cariello, Sergio, illus. 2008. (Z Graphic Novels / Son of Samson Ser.). (ENG.). 160p. (J). pap. 6.99 *(978-0-310-71283-1(1))* Zonderkidz.
Martineck, Michael J. The Wrong Channel. 2005. 160p. (J). (gr. 4-8). 8.00 *(978-0-9720978-1-9(3))* Our Little Secret Pr.
Masessa, Ed. Wandmaker. 2016. (ENG.). 336p. (J). (gr. 3-7). 12.99 *(978-0-545-86174-8(8),* Scholastic Pr.) Scholastic, Inc.
Masi, Sue. A Journey Through Fantasy Forest. 2012. 44p. pap. 21.99 *(978-1-4691-4837-3(4))* Xlibris Corp.
Mason, Aaron & Warr, Doug. Baffelgagging Blundernagging Brothers in the Curse of the Bog Frog. Walton, Jason, illus. 2008. (ENG.). 192p. (YA). 29.95 *(978-0-9800274-0-2(3))* Whirlwhim.
Mason, Alexis. Just an Ordinary Little Dog: Barnaby's Story. Bunch, Paul, illus. 2010. (J). *(978-0-9755280-4-4(1))* Insight Technical Education.
Mason-Black, Jennifer. Devil & the Bluebird. 2016. (ENG.). 336p. (J). (gr. 8-17). 17.95 *(978-1-4197-2000-0(7),* 1135901, Amulet Bks.) Abrams, Inc.
Mason, Conrad. The Watchmen of Port Fayt. 2015. (ENG.). 400p. (J). (gr. 3-7). 17.99 *(978-0-545-83308-0(6))* Scholastic, Inc.
Mass, Wendy. Escape from Egypt: a Branches Book (Time Jumpers #2) Vidal, Oriol, illus. 2018. (Time Jumpers Ser.: 2). (ENG.). 96p. (J). (gr. 1-3). pap. 5.99 *(978-1-338-21739-1(9))* Scholastic, Inc.
—Fast-Forward to the Future!: a Branches Book (Time Jumpers #3), Vol. 3. Vidal, Oriol, illus. 2019. (Time Jumpers Ser.: 3). (ENG.). 96p. (J). (gr. 1-3). pap. 5.99 *(978-1-338-21742-1(9))* Scholastic, Inc.
—Graceful. 2015. (ENG.). 256p. (J). (gr. 3-7). 16.99 *(978-0-545-77313-3(X),* Scholastic Pr.) Scholastic, Inc.
—The Last Present. 2015. (Willow Falls Ser.: 4). lib. bdg. 17.20 *(978-0-606-37015-8(3))* Turtleback.
—Stealing the Sword: a Branches Book (Time Jumpers #1) Vidal, Oriol, illus. 2018. (Time Jumpers Ser.: 1). (ENG.). 96p. (J). (gr. 1-3). pap. 5.99 *(978-1-338-21736-0(4))* Scholastic, Inc.
Master Merlin. Wizardology: The Book of the Secrets of Merlin. Steer, Dugald A., ed. gif. ed. 2005. (Ologies Ser.). (ENG., Illus.). 32p. (J). (gr. 3-7). 29.99 *(978-0-7636-2895-6(6))* Candlewick Pr.
Mastro, M. L. Return to Baladah. 2011. 88p. (gr. 10-12). pap. 9.99 *(978-1-4520-7377-4(5))* AuthorHouse.
Matharu, Taran. The Battlemage. 2017. 390p. (YA). *(978-1-250-15426-2(X))* Feiwel & Friends.
—The Battlemage. 2018. (Summoner Ser.: 3). (YA). lib. bdg. 22.10 *(978-0-606-41115-8(1))* Turtleback.
—The Battlemage: Summoner, Book Three. 2018. (Summoner Trilogy Ser.: 3). (ENG.). 384p. (YA). pap. 11.99 *(978-1-250-15863-5(X),* 900185524) Square Fish.
—The Inquisition. 2017. (Summoner Ser.: 2). (YA). lib. bdg. 22.10 *(978-0-606-39945-6(3))* Turtleback.
—The Inquisition: Summoner: Book Two. 2017. (Summoner Trilogy Ser.: 2). (ENG.). 384p. (YA). pap. 10.99 *(978-1-250-11521-8(3),* 900171654) Square Fish.
Matheos, George P. Pure Magic. 2011. 156p. (gr. 2-4). 22.95 *(978-1-4620-1619-8(7))*; pap. 12.95 *(978-1-4620-1617-4(0))* iUniverse, Inc.
Mather, Adriana. Haunting the Deep. (ENG.). (YA). (gr. 7). 2018. 368p. pap. 9.99 *(978-0-553-53954-7(X),* Ember) 2017. 352p. lib. bdg. 20.99 *(978-0-553-53952-3(3),* Knopf Bks. for Young Readers) Random Hse. Children's Bks.
Matheson, Christie. Tap the Magic Tree Board Book. Matheson, Christie, illus. 2016. (ENG., Illus.). 42p. (J). (gr. -1-3). bds. 7.99 *(978-0-06-227446-5(5),* Greenwillow Bks.) HarperCollins Pubs.
Matthews, Caitlín, et al. Tales from Celtic Lands. Whelan, Olwyn, illus. 2008. 80p. (J). (gr. -1-3). 21.99 *(978-1-84686-213-7(2))* Barefoot Bks., Inc.
Matthews, John. The Barefoot Book of Giants, Ghosts, & Goblins. Manna, Giovanni, illus. 2008. 80p. (J). 21.99 *(978-1-84686-235-9(3))* Barefoot Bks., Inc.
Maxwell, Lisa. The Devil's Thief. 2018. (Last Magician Ser.: 2). (ENG., Illus.). 704p. (YA). (gr. 9). 18.99 *(978-1-4814-9445-8(7),* Simon Pulse) Simon Pulse.
—The Last Magician. (Last Magician Ser.: 1). (ENG., Illus.). (YA). (gr. 9). 2018. 528p. pap. 13.99 *(978-1-4814-3208-5(7))* 2017. 512p. 21.99 *(978-1-4814-3207-8(9))* Simon Pulse. (Simon Pulse).
May, Tallulah, adapted by. Crystal Heart Kisses. 2016. (Illus.). (J). *(978-1-5182-3830-7(0))* Little, Brown Bks. for Young Readers.
Mayer, Shannon & Breene, K. F. Shadowspell Academy: the Culling Trials. 2019. 576p. (YA). (gr. 9-12). 16.99 *(978-1-5107-5510-9(1),* Sky Pony Pr.) Skyhorse Publishing Co., Inc.
Mazer, Anne. Mabel on the Move, 6. Brown, Bill, illus. 2009. (Sister Magic Ser.: 6). (ENG.). 128p. (J). (gr. 3-6). pap. 16.19 *(978-0-439-87251-5(0))* Scholastic, Inc.
Mbalia, Kwame. Rick Riordan Presents Tristan Strong Destroys the World (a Tristan Strong Novel, Book 2) (Tristan Strong Ser.: 2). (J). (gr. 3-7). 2021. 48p. pap. 8.99 *(978-1-368-04240-6(6))* 2020. (Illus.). 12p. 17.99 *(978-1-368-04238-3(4))* Disney Publishing Worldwide. (Riordan, Rick).
Mcallister, Bruce. The Village Sang to the Sea. 2013. 172p. pap. *(978-0-9534784-9-1(1))* Aeon Pr.
McBrier, Page. Abracadabra Tut. 2014. (ENG.). (J). pap. 9.99 *(978-0-9960794-0-2(8))* Palm Canyon Pr.
McBroom, Danielle Loiselle. A Painted Dream. 2008. 20p. pap. 24.95 *(978-1-60441-694-7(7))* America Star Bks.
McCarthy, Jenna & Evans, Carolyn. Maggie Malone Makes a Splash. 2015. (Maggie Malone Ser.: 3). (ENG.). 192p. (J). (gr. 4-7). pap. 8.99 *(978-1-4022-9312-2(7))* Sourcebooks, Inc.
McCartney, Paul. Hey Grandude! Durst, Kathryn, illus. 2019. (ENG.). 32p. (J). (gr. -1-1). 17.99 *(978-0-525-64867-3(4),* Random Hse. Bks. for Young Readers) Random Hse. Children's Bks.
McCaughrean, Geraldine. Peter Pan de Rojo Escarlata. Gonzalez-Gallarza, Isabel, tr. Wyatt, David, illus. 2006. 296p. (J). (gr. 5-8). 17.95 *(978-958-704-467-6(3))* Ediciones Alfaguara ESP. Dist: Santillana USA Publishing Co., Inc.
—Peter Pan in Scarlet. Fischer, Scott M., illus. 2008. (ENG.). 320p. (J). (gr. 4-9). pap. 8.99 *(978-1-4169-1809-7(4),* McElderry, Margaret K. Bks.) McElderry, Margaret K. Bks.
McCorvie, D. Lawrence. Timothy Hunt: The Great Candy Caper. 2007. 232p. 30.00 *(978-1-4251-3618-5(4))* Trafford Publishing.
McDonagh, Christelle, et al. Mission Magic Bubble. 2009. (Illus.). 56p. pap. 23.99 *(978-1-4389-0640-9(4))* AuthorHouse.
McDonald, Ann-Eve. The Tale of the Black Square. 2004. (J). *(978-0-9770158-2-5(3))* BeachWalk Bks. Inc.
McDonald, Fiona. Ghost Doll & Jasper. 2012. (ENG., Illus.). 112p. (J). (gr. 2-7). 12.95 *(978-1-62087-174-4(2),* 620174, Sky Pony Pr.) Skyhorse Publishing Co., Inc.
Mcdonald, Megan. Judy Moody, Mood Martian. 2015. (Judy Moody Ser.: 12). lib. bdg. 16.00 *(978-0-606-36876-6(0))* Turtleback.
McDonald, Megan. Judy Moody, Mood Martian. Reynolds, Peter H., illus. 2018. (Judy Moody Ser.: 12). (ENG.). 208p. (J). (gr. 1-4). pap. 5.99 *(978-1-5362-0081-2(6))* Candlewick Pr.
McFarland, Kim. A Refugee in Oz. 2010. 164p. pap. 11.95 *(978-0-557-48706-6(4))* Lulu Pr., Inc.
Mcfaul, Jason & Macdonald, Eric. What A Trip. 2007. pap. 77.53 *(978-0-7575-4014-1(7))* Kendall Hunt Publishing Co.
McGalliard, Julie. Waking up Naked in Strange Places. 2015. (YA). 24.99 *(978-1-941662-09-0(9))* Jakal LLC.
—Waking Up Naked in Strange Places. 2015. (YA). pap. 14.99 *(978-1-941662-10-6(2))* Jakal LLC.
McGann, Erika. The Midnight Carnival: Step Right up, Don't Be Shy. 2015. (ENG.). 320p. (J). 12.99 *(978-1-84717-740-7(9))* O'Brien Pr., Ltd., The. IRL. Dist: Casemate Pubs. & Bk. Distributors, LLC.
McGaw, Wayne T. T-Boy of the Bayou. Crespo, George, illus. 2003. 32p. (J). (gr. -1-3). 15.95 *(978-0-87614-648-4(5),* Carolrhoda Bks.) Lerner Publishing Group.
McGee, Helen. Ikky Dikky Dak: Magical Adventures with Googler! Book Two. Kaltenborn, Karl, illus. 2011. pap. 21.95 *(978-1-60494-573-7(7))* Wheatmark, Inc.
McGowan, Maureen. Cinderella: Ninja Warrior. 2010. 320p. pap. 8.95 *(978-1-60747-778-5(5),* Pickwick Pr.) Phoenix Bks., Inc.
McGregor, Suzy. Moon Leopard. 2013. 40p. pap. 11.95 *(978-0-9824926-5-9(0))* Lollipop Media Productions, LP.
McGriff, Shawna A. Princess Pink: Princess Pink Saves the Girls of Lahappyville. 2010. 44p. pap. 18.49 *(978-1-4520-3936-7(4))* AuthorHouse.
McGuire, Jeremy. O'shaughnessey: Boy & His Leprechaun. 2007. 140p. per. 14.95 *(978-1-4327-0892-4(9))* Outskirts Pr., Inc.
Mcintyre, Mel. Flutter Bunnies. Grady, Kit, illus. 2008. 24p. pap. 10.95 *(978-1-933090-68-9(5))* Guardian Angel Publishing, Inc.
McKay, Hilary. The Time of Green Magic. (ENG., Illus.). (J). (gr. 3-7). 2021. 272p. pap. 7.99 *(978-1-5344-6277-9(5))* 2020. 240p. 17.99 *(978-1-5344-6276-2(7))* McElderry, Margaret K. Bks. (McElderry, Margaret K. Bks.).
McKellar, Danica. Ten Magic Butterflies. Bricking, Jen, illus. (McKellar Math Ser.). (J). 2019. 38p. (— 1). bds. 8.99 *(978-1-101-93385-5(2))* 2018. (ENG.). 40p. (gr. -1-1). 17.99 *(978-1-101-93382-4(8))* Random Hse. Children's Bks. (Crown Books For Young Readers).
Mckenzie, Riford. The Witches of Dredmoore Hollow, 0 vols. unabr. ed. 2013. (ENG.). 274p. (J). (gr. 5-7). pap. 9.99 *(978-1-4778-1702-5(6),* 9781477817025, Two Lions) Amazon Publishing.
McKinley, Robin. Shadows. 2013. 356p. (YA). *(978-0-399-25625-7(3))* Penguin Publishing Group.
McLaren, Clemence. Aphrodite's Blessing. 2008. (ENG.). 208p. (YA). (gr. 7). pap. 10.99 *(978-1-4169-7860-2(7),* Simon Pulse) Simon Pulse.
McLelland, Brad & Sylvester, Louis. The Fang of Bonfire Crossing: Legends of the Lost Causes. 2020. (Legends of the Lost Causes Ser.: 2). (ENG.). 400p. (J). pap. 20.99 *(978-1-250-23360-8(7),* 900174394) Square Fish.
McLemore, Anna-Marie. The Weight of Feathers. 2017. (ENG.). 320p. (YA). pap. 13.99 *(978-1-250-11599-7(X),* 900171736, Wednesday Bks.) St. Martin's Pr.
—When the Moon Was Ours: A Novel. 2018. (ENG.). 288p. (YA). pap. 10.99 *(978-1-250-16010-2(3),* 900185827, Wednesday Bks.) St. Martin's Pr.
—Wild Beauty: A Novel. 2018. (ENG.). 368p. (YA). pap. 15.99 *(978-1-250-18073-5(2),* 900190253) Square Fish.
McMann, Lisa. Dragon Bones. (Unwanteds Quests Ser.: 2). (ENG., Illus.). (J). (gr. 3-7). 2019. 432p. pap. 9.99 *(978-1-4814-5685-2(7))* 2018. 416p. 19.99 *(978-1-4814-5684-5(9))* Simon & Schuster Children's Publishing. (Aladdin).
—Dragon Captives. 2017. (Unwanteds Quests Ser.: 1). (ENG., Illus.). 432p. (J). (gr. 3-7). 19.99 *(978-1-4814-5681-4(4),* Simon & Schuster/Paula Wiseman Bks.) Simon & Schuster/Paula Wiseman Bks.
—Dragon Captives. 2018. (Unwanteds Quests Ser.: 1). lib. bdg. 18.40 *(978-0-606-40846-2(0))* Turtleback.
—Dragon Curse. 2019. (Unwanteds Quests Ser.: 4). (ENG., Illus.). 432p. (J). (gr. 3-7). 18.99 *(978-1-5344-1601-7(3),* Simon & Schuster/Paula Wiseman Bks.) Simon & Schuster/Paula Wiseman Bks.
—Dragon Ghosts. 2019. (Unwanteds Quests Ser.: 3). (ENG., Illus.). 528p. (J). (gr. 3-7). 19.99 *(978-1-5344-1598-0(X),* Aladdin) Simon & Schuster Children's Publishing.
—Island of Dragons. (Unwanteds Ser.: 7). (ENG., Illus.). 544p. (J). (gr. 3-7). 2017. pap. 9.99 *(978-1-4424-9338-4(0))* 2016. 19.99 *(978-1-4424-9337-7(2))* Simon & Schuster Children's Publishing. (Aladdin).
—Island of Graves. (Unwanteds Ser.: 6). (ENG., Illus.). (J). (gr. 3-7). 2016. 560p. pap. 9.99 *(978-1-4424-9335-3(6))* 2015. 528p. 21.99 *(978-1-4424-9334-6(8))* Simon & Schuster Children's Publishing. (Aladdin).
—Island of Graves. 2016. (Unwanteds Ser.: 6). lib. bdg. 19.65 *(978-0-606-38497-1(9))* Turtleback.
—Island of Silence. (Unwanteds Ser.: 2). (ENG., (J). (gr. 3-7). 2013. Illus.). 432p. pap. 8.99 *(978-1-4424-0772-5(7))* 2012. 416p. 19.99 *(978-1-4424-0771-8(9))* Simon & Schuster Children's Publishing. (Aladdin).
—Island of Silence. 2013. (Unwanteds Ser.: 2). lib. bdg. 18.40 *(978-0-606-32044-3(X))* Turtleback.
—The Unwanteds. 2011. (Unwanteds Ser.: Bk. 1). (J). 1.25 *(978-1-4640-2489-4(8))* Recorded Bks., Inc.
—The Unwanteds. (Unwanteds Ser.: 1). (ENG., Illus.). (J). (gr. 3-7). 2012. 416p. pap. 8.99 *(978-1-4424-0769-5(7))* 2011. 400p. 19.99 *(978-1-4424-0768-8(9))* Simon & Schuster Children's Publishing. (Aladdin).
—The Unwanteds. 2012. (Unwanteds Ser.: 1). lib. bdg. 18.40 *(978-0-606-26953-7(3))* Turtleback.
McMullan, Kate. The New Kid at School #1. Basso, Bill, illus. 2003. (Dragon Slayers' Academy Ser.: 1). (ENG.). 112p. (J). (gr. 2-5). mass mkt. 6.99 *(978-0-448-43108-6(4),* Grosset & Dunlap) Penguin Young Readers Group.
McNabb, Linda. Dragons' Bane. 2008. 208p. *(978-1-86950-655-1(3))* HarperCollins Pubs. Australia.
McNamara, Margaret. The Fairy Bell Sisters #4: Clara & the Magical Charms. Denos, Julia, illus. 2013. (Fairy Bell Sisters Ser.: 4). (ENG.). 128p. (J). (gr. 1-5). pap. 4.99 *(978-0-06-222810-9(2),* Balzer & Bray) HarperCollins Pubs.
—The Fairy Bell Sisters #5: Sylva & the Lost Treasure. Collingridge, Catharine, illus. 2014. (Fairy Bell Sisters Ser.: 5). (ENG.). 144p. (J). (gr. 1-5). pap. 4.99 *(978-0-06-226720-7(5),* Balzer & Bray) HarperCollins Pubs.
—The Fairy Bell Sisters #6: Christmas Fairy Magic. Collingridge, Catharine, illus. 2014. (Fairy Bell Sisters Ser.: 6). (ENG.). 144p. (J). (gr. 1-5). pap. 4.99 *(978-0-06-226723-8(X),* Balzer & Bray) HarperCollins Pubs.
McNiff, Dawn. Worry Magic. 2016. (ENG.). 256p. (J). (gr. 4-7). pap. 9.99 *(978-1-4714-0371-2(8))* Bonnier Publishing GBR. Dist: Independent Pubs. Group.
McOmber, Rachel B., ed. McOmber Phonics Storybooks: The Magic "E" rev. ed. (Illus.). (J). *(978-0-944991-37-4(8))* Swift Learning Resources.
—McOmber Phonics Storybooks: The Neat Trick. rev. ed. (Illus.). (J). *(978-0-944991-55-8(6))* Swift Learning Resources.
—McOmber Phonics Storybooks: The Prime Time Trick. rev. ed. (Illus.). (J). *(978-0-944991-56-5(4))* Swift Learning Resources.
McPhate, Paul J. The Puggle King. 2008. 52p. pap. 16.95 *(978-1-60703-709-5(2))* America Star Bks.
McQuerry, Maureen Doyle. Time Out of Time: Book One: Beyond the Door. 2014. (Time Out of Time Ser.). (ENG., Illus.). 384p. (J). (gr. 3-7). 16.95 *(978-1-4197-1016-2(8),* 683301, Amulet Bks.) Abrams, Inc.
Mcshane, Pol. The Magic Elevator: The Adventures of Johnny & Joey. 2005. 129p. pap. 19.95 *(978-1-4241-0014-9(3))* PublishAmerica, Inc.
Mead, Richelle. Frostbite: A Vampire Academy Novel. 2008. (Vampire Academy Ser.: 2). 336p. (YA). (gr. 7-18). pap. 12.99 *(978-1-59514-175-0(8),* Razorbill) Penguin Young Readers Group.
—Shadow Kiss. 2013. (Vampire Academy (Graphic Novels) Ser.: 3). lib. bdg. 24.50 *(978-0-606-34129-5(3))* Turtleback.
—Vampire Academy. 2007. (Vampire Academy Ser.: 1). 336p. (YA). (gr. 7-18). 11.99 *(978-1-59514-174-3(X),* Razorbill) Penguin Young Readers Group.
—Vampire Academy: A Graphic Novel. Vieceli, Emma, illus. 2011. (Vampire Academy Ser.: 1). 144p. (YA). (gr. 7-18). pap. 12.99 *(978-1-59514-429-4(3),* Razorbill) Penguin Young Readers Group.
—Vampire Academy 10th Anniversary Edition. 10th ed. 2016. (Vampire Academy Ser.). 512p. (YA). (gr. 7). pap. 11.99 *(978-0-448-49429-6(9),* Razorbill) Penguin Young Readers Group.
—Vampire Academy Box Set 1-6, 6 vols. 2013. (Vampire Academy Ser.). (ENG.). 2784p. (YA). (gr. 7). pap., pap., pap. 77.94 *(978-1-59514-758-5(6),* Razorbill) Penguin Young Readers Group.
Meadows, Daisy. Addison the April Fool's Day Fairy. 2014. (Rainbow Magic — Special Edition Ser.). lib. bdg. 17.20 *(978-0-606-35378-6(X))* Turtleback.
—Aisha the Princess & the Pea Fairy. 2016. (Illus.). 62p. (J). *(978-0-545-88741-0(0))* Scholastic, Inc.
—Alicia the Snow Queen Fairy. 2017. (Illus.). 159p. (J). *(978-1-5182-2779-0(1))* Scholastic, Inc.
—Alicia the Snow Queen Fairy. 2016. (Rainbow Magic — Special Edition Ser.). (Illus.). 159p. (J). lib. bdg. 17.20 *(978-0-606-39728-5(0))* Turtleback.
—Alison the Art Fairy. 2018. 65p. (J). (gr. 1-4). 15.36 *(978-1-64310-182-8(X))* Penworthy Co., LLC, The.
—Alison the Art Fairy. 2016. (Illus.). 65p. (J). *(978-0-545-95523-2(8))* Scholastic, Inc.
—Ally the Dolphin Fairy. 2011. (Illus.). 63p. (J). *(978-0-545-28871-2(1))* Scholastic, Inc.
—Alyssa the Star-Spotter Fairy. 2013. (Rainbow Magic — the Superstar Fairies Ser.: 6). lib. bdg. 14.75 *(978-0-606-31518-0(7))* Turtleback.
—Amelie the Seal Fairy. 2011. (Illus.). 65p. (J). *(978-0-545-28872-9(X))* Scholastic, Inc.
—Ashley the Dragon Fairy. 2012. (Illus.). 65p. (J). *(978-0-545-42595-7(6))* Scholastic, Inc.
—Autumn the Falling Leaves Fairy. 2013. (Rainbow Magic — Special Edition Ser.). lib. bdg. 17.20 *(978-0-606-32370-3(8))* Turtleback.
—Ava the Sunset Fairy. 2011. (Illus.). 63p. (J). *(978-0-545-38040-9(5))* Scholastic, Inc.
—Belle the Birthday Fairy. 2012. (Rainbow Magic — Special Edition Ser.). lib. bdg. 17.20 *(978-0-606-23726-0(7))* Turtleback.
—Brianna the Tooth Fairy. 2013. (Rainbow Magic — Special Edition Ser.). lib. bdg. 17.20 *(978-0-606-31990-4(5))* Turtleback.

M
N
O

—Caitlin the Ice Bear Fairy. 2012. (Illus.). 65p. (J). *(978-0-545-42602-2(2))* Scholastic, Inc.

—Cara the Camp Fairy. 2011. (Illus.). 165p. (J). *(978-0-545-31656-9(1))* Scholastic, Inc.

—Carmen the Cheerleading Fairy. 2017. (Illus.). 145p. (J). *(978-1-5182-3956-4(0))* Scholastic, Inc.

—Cassidy the Costume Fairy. 2012. (Rainbow Magic — the Princess Fairies Ser.: 2). lib. bdg. 14.75 *(978-0-606-26170-8(2))* Turtleback.

—Clare the Caring Fairy. 2017. (Illus.). 65p. (J). *(978-1-5379-1839-6(7))* Scholastic, Inc.

—Coral the Reef Fairy. 2014. (Rainbow Magic — the Earth Fairies Ser.). lib. bdg. 14.75 *(978-0-606-35833-0(1))* Turtleback.

—Courtney the Clownfish Fairy. 2011. (Illus.). 62p. (J). *(978-0-545-28877-4(0))* Scholastic, Inc.

—Debbie the Duckling Fairy. 2018. (Illus.). 65p. (J). *(978-1-5490-0260-1(0))* Scholastic, Inc.

—Edie the Garden Fairy. 2014. (Rainbow Magic — the Earth Fairies Ser.). lib. bdg. 14.75 *(978-0-606-35832-3(3))* Turtleback.

—Eleanor the Snow White Fairy. 2016. (Illus.). 65p. (J). *(978-0-545-88738-0(0))* Scholastic, Inc.

—Elisa the Royal Adventure Fairy. 2012. (Rainbow Magic — the Princess Fairies Ser.: 4). lib. bdg. 14.75 *(978-0-606-26172-2(9))* Turtleback.

—Elle the Thumbelina Fairy. 2017. (Illus.). 63p. (J). *(978-1-5182-3952-6(8))* Scholastic, Inc.

—Ellie Featherbill All Alone. 2015. (Magic Animal Friends Ser.: 3). lib. bdg. 14.75 *(978-0-606-37047-9(1))* Turtleback.

—Emily, the Emerald Fairy. Ripper, Georgie, illus. 2005. 65p. (J). pap. *(978-0-545-01190-7(6))* Scholastic, Inc.

—Erin the Phoenix Fairy. 2012. (Illus.). 64p. (J). *(978-0-545-42597-1(2))* Scholastic, Inc.

—Esther the Kindness Fairy. 2017. (Illus.). 65p. (J). *(978-1-5379-1854-9(0))* Scholastic, Inc.

—Eva the Enchanted Ball Fairy. 2012. (Rainbow Magic — the Princess Fairies Ser.: 7). lib. bdg. 14.75 *(978-0-606-26175-3(3))* Turtleback.

—Evie Scruffypup's Big Surprise (Magic Animal Friends #10), 1 vol. 2016. (Magic Animal Friends Ser.: 1). (ENG., Illus.). 112p. (J). (gr. 2-5). pap. 4.99 *(978-0-545-94077-1(X),* Scholastic Paperbacks) Scholastic, Inc.

—Evie Scruffypup's Surprise. 2016. (Magic Animal Friends Ser.: 10). lib. bdg. 14.75 *(978-0-606-38800-9(1))* Turtleback.

—The Fairy Treasure Hunt. 2012. (Rainbow Magic — Scholastic Reader Ser.). lib. bdg. 13.55 *(978-0-606-23912-7(X))* Turtleback.

—A Fairyland Costume Ball. 2012. (Rainbow Magic — Scholastic Reader Ser.). lib. bdg. 13.55 *(978-0-606-26235-4(0))* Turtleback.

—Frankie the Makeup Fairy. 2013. (Rainbow Magic — the Superstar Fairies Ser.: 5). lib. bdg. 14.75 *(978-0-606-31517-3(9))* Turtleback.

—Georgia the Guinea Pig Fairy. Ripper, Georgie, illus. 2008. (Rainbow Magic — the Pet Fairies Ser.). 65p. (gr. 3). lib. bdg. 14.75 *(978-1-4178-2997-2(4))* Turtleback.

—Grace Woollyhop's Musical Mystery. 2016. (Magic Animal Friends Ser.: 12). lib. bdg. 14.75 *(978-0-606-38802-3(8))* Turtleback.

—Gwen the Beauty & the Beast Fairy. 2016. (Illus.). 67p. (J). *(978-1-5182-1018-1(X))* Scholastic, Inc.

—Isabella the Air Fairy: Rainbow Magic. 2014. (Rainbow Magic — the Earth Fairies Ser.). lib. bdg. 14.75 *(978-0-606-35831-6(5))* Turtleback.

—Julia the Sleeping Beauty Fairy. 2016. (Illus.). 65p. (J). *(978-0-545-88737-3(2))* Scholastic, Inc.

—Kathryn the Gym Fairy. 2018. 65p. (J). (gr. 1-4). 15.36 *(978-1-64310-186-6(2))* Penworthy Co., LLC, The.

—Kathryn the Gym Fairy. 2016. (Rainbow Magic — the School Day Fairies Ser.: 4). lib. bdg. 14.75 *(978-0-606-38792-7(7))* Turtleback.

—Katie the Kitten Fairy. Ripper, Georgie, illus. 2008. 65p. (J). pap. *(978-0-545-13320-3(3))* Scholastic, Inc.

—Katie the Kitten Fairy. Ripper, Georgie. illus. 2008. (Rainbow Magic — the Pet Fairies Ser.). 65p. (gr. 1-4). lib. bdg. 14.75 *(978-1-4178-2999-6(0))* Turtleback.

—Lara the Black Cat Fairy. 2012. (Illus.). 65p. (J). *(978-0-545-42596-4(4))* Scholastic, Inc.

—Leona the Unicorn Fairy. 2012. (Illus.). 65p. (J). *(978-0-545-42601-5(4))* Scholastic, Inc.

—Libby the Writing Fairy. 2014. (Illus.). 65p. (J). *(978-0-545-72414-2(7))* Scholastic, Inc.

—Lily the Rain Forest Fairy. 2014. (Rainbow Magic — the Earth Fairies Ser.). lib. bdg. 14.75 *(978-0-606-35834-7(X))* Turtleback.

—Lizzie the Sweet Treats Fairy. 2012. (Rainbow Magic — the Princess Fairies Ser.: 5). lib. bdg. 14.75 *(978-0-606-26173-9(7))* Turtleback.

—Lucy Longwhiskers Gets Lost. 2015. (Magic Animal Friends Ser.: 1). lib. bdg. 14.75 *(978-0-606-37045-5(5))* Turtleback.

—Mariana the Goldilocks Fairy. 2017. (Illus.). 65p. (J). *(978-1-5182-3953-3(6))* Scholastic, Inc.

—Mary the Sharing Fairy. 2017. (Illus.). 65p. (J). *(978-1-5379-1875-4(3))* Scholastic, Inc.

—Michelle the Winter Wonderland Fairy. 2017. (Illus.). 150p. (J). *(978-1-5379-5586-5(1))* Scholastic, Inc.

—Miley the Stylist Fairy. 2013. (Rainbow Magic — the Superstar Fairies Ser.: 4). lib. bdg. 14.75 *(978-0-606-31516-6(0))* Turtleback.

—Milly the River Fairy. 2014. (Rainbow Magic — the Earth Fairies Ser.). lib. bdg. 14.75 *(978-0-606-35835-4(8))* Turtleback.

—Molly Twinkletail Runs Away. 2015. (Magic Animal Friends Ser.: 2). lib. bdg. 14.75 *(978-0-606-37046-2(3))* Turtleback.

—Nicole the Beach Fairy. 2014. (Rainbow Magic — the Earth Fairies Ser.). lib. bdg. 14.75 *(978-0-606-35830-9(7))* Turtleback.

—Olympia: The Games Fairy. 2012. (Rainbow Magic — Special Edition Ser.). lib. bdg. 17.20 *(978-0-606-26541-6(4))* Turtleback.

—Penelope the Foal Fairy. 2018. (Illus.). 65p. (J). *(978-1-5490-0262-5(7))* Scholastic, Inc.

—Pia the Penguin Fairy. 2011. (J). (Rainbow Magic: Ocean Fairies Ser.: 3). (ENG.). 80p. (gr. 1-4). 17.44 *(978-0-545-27038-0(3));* (Illus.). 63p. *(978-0-545-28873-6(8))* Scholastic, Inc.

—Rihanna the Seahorse Fairy. 2012. (Illus.). 65p. (J). *(978-0-545-42599-5(9))* Scholastic, Inc.

—Ruth the Red Riding Hood Fairy. 2017. (Illus.). 65p. (J). *(978-1-5182-3955-7(2))* Scholastic, Inc.

—Skyler the Fireworks Fairy. 2016. (Illus.). 182p. (J). *(978-1-5182-1487-5(8))* Scholastic, Inc.

—Sophia the Snow Swan Fairy. 2012. (Illus.). 65p. (J). *(978-0-545-42600-8(6))* Scholastic, Inc.

—Stephanie the Starfish Fairy. 2011. (Illus.). 65p. (J). *(978-0-545-28875-0(4))* Scholastic, Inc.

—Tess the Sea Turtle Fairy. 2011. (Illus.). 65p. (J). *(978-0-545-28874-3(6))* Scholastic, Inc.

—Vanessa the Choreography Fairy. 2013. (Rainbow Magic — the Superstar Fairies Ser.: 3). lib. bdg. 14.75 *(978-0-606-31515-9(2))* Turtleback.

—Violet the Painting Fairy. 2015. (Illus.). 65p. (J). *(978-0-545-72413-5(9))* Scholastic, Inc.

—Whitney the Whale Fairy. 2011. (Illus.). 64p. (J). *(978-0-545-28876-7(2))* Scholastic, Inc.

—Zadie the Sewing Fairy. 2015. (Illus.). 65p. (J). *(978-0-545-72411-1(2))* Scholastic, Inc.

Meadows, Jodi. Before She Ignites. (Fallen Isles Ser.: 1). (ENG.). 496p. (YA). (gr. 8). 2018. 10.99 *(978-0-06-246941-0(X))* 2017. 17.99 *(978-0-06-246940-3(1))* HarperCollins Pubs. (Tegen, Katherine Bks).

Meadows, Melissa. What's the Word, Thunderbird? 2008. (ENG., Illus.). 80p. (J). *(978-1-934517-01-7(1))* Firelight Press, Inc.

—What's the Word, Thunderbird? Book A: the Alamo. 2007. (Wishing Well Ser.). (Illus.). 81p. (J). (gr. k-3). per. 4.99 *(978-1-934517-00-0(3))* Firelight Press, Inc.

Meeks, John R. Dugan's Magical Island. 2011. (ENG.). 26p. pap. 12.40 *(978-1-4567-3947-8(6))* AuthorHouse.

Meer, Pippa Lee. Matilda's Marvellous Monday. 2008. 32p. pap. 14.49 *(978-1-4389-0421-4(5))* AuthorHouse.

Megerdichian, Janet. Pine Needle Pedro. Adams, Allysa, illus. 2010. 36p. pap. 16.99 *(978-1-4520-4422-4(8))* AuthorHouse.

Melki-Wegner, Skye. The Hush. 2017. (ENG.). 386p. (J). (gr. 6-6). 16.99 *(978-1-5107-1248-5(8),* Sky Pony Pr.) Skyhorse Publishing Co., Inc.

Mello, Alondra. Alanora's Magic Tree: Alanora's Spirit Journey. 2007. 48p. per. 12.97 *(978-1-932344-77-6(2))* Thornton Publishing, Inc.

Meredith, Susan Markowitz. The Magical Simon & Roxie. 2016. (Spring Forward Ser.). (J). (gr. 2). *(978-1-4900-9469-4(5))* Benchmark Education Co.

Meriano, Anna. Love Sugar Magic: a Dash of Trouble. Ortega, Mirelle, illus. (Love Sugar Magic Ser.: 1). (ENG.). (J). (gr. 3-7). 2019. 336p. pap. 7.99 *(978-0-06-249847-2(9))* 2018. 320p. 16.99 *(978-0-06-249846-5(0))* HarperCollins Pubs. (Waldon Pond Pr.).

—Love Sugar Magic: a Sprinkle of Spirits. Ortega, Mirelle, illus. (Love Sugar Magic Ser.: 2). (ENG.). (J). (gr. 3-7). 2020. 336p. pap. 9.99 *(978-0-06-249852-6(5))* 2019. 320p. 16.99 *(978-0-06-249849-6(5))* HarperCollins Pubs. (Waldon Pond Pr.).

Merrick, M.R. Endure. 2013. 382p. pap. *(978-0-9917862-4-4(6))* Merrick, M.R.

Meshach, Joanna. The Land of the Magical Mirrors. 2012. 32p. pap. 32.70 *(978-1-4771-2595-3(7))* Xlibris Corp.

Mesibere, Ellen. The Magic Log. Naime, Sophie, ed. Joseph, Albert, illus. 2012. 24p. pap. *(978-9980-945-68-6(0))* Univ. of Papua New Guinea Pr.

Messenger, Lois. Fairy Magic & the Healing Rainbow Colours. 2013. 36p. pap. 15.95 *(978-1-4525-7663-3(7),* Balboa Pr.) Author Solutions, LLC.

Messner, Kate. The Seventh Wish. 2017. (ENG.). 256p. (J). pap. 8.99 *(978-1-68119-431-8(7),* 900172647, Bloomsbury USA Childrens) Bloomsbury Publishing USA.

Metcalf, Dan. The Egyptian Enchantment: A Lottie Lipton Adventure. Panagarry, Rachelle, illus. 2017. (Adventures of Lottie Lipton Ser.). (ENG.). 96p. (J). (gr. 2-5). pap. 6.99 *(978-1-5124-8188-4(2),* 4fed1583-9683-4856-8a90-024c82752f05); lib. bdg. 25.32 *(978-1-5124-8182-2(3),* b8fef38d-820d-4af0-a6d3-a069159248c1) Lerner Publishing Group. (Darby Creek).

Metz, Diana. Brinn & the Dragons of Pallan Cliffs. 2003. 352p. (J). pap. *(978-0-9718431-2-7(0))* M.O.T.H.E.R. Publishing Co., Inc., The.

Meyer, Kai. Dark Reflections: The Water Mirror; the Stone Light; the Glass Word. Crawford, Elizabeth D., tr. 2010. (Dark Reflections Trilogy Ser.). (ENG.). 896p. (YA). (gr. 7). pap. 9.99 *(978-1-4424-0938-5(X),* McElderry, Margaret K. Bks.) McElderry, Margaret K. Bks.

—The Glass Word. Crawford, Elizabeth D., tr. 2008. (ENG.). 288p. (YA). (gr. 7). (Dark Reflections Trilogy Ser.: 3). pap. 9.99 *(978-0-689-87792-6(7));* (Dark Reflections Trilogy: Bk. 3). 16.99 *(978-0-689-87791-9(9))* McElderry, Margaret K. Bks. (McElderry, Margaret K. Bks.).

—Pirate Wars. Crawford, Elizabeth D., tr. 2008. (Wave Walkers Ser.: 3). (ENG.). 384p. (J). (gr. 5-9). pap. 8.99 *(978-1-4169-2477-7(9),* McElderry, Margaret K. Bks.) McElderry, Margaret K. Bks.

—The Stone Light. Crawford, Elizabeth D., tr. 2007. (Dark Reflections Trilogy Ser.: 2). (ENG.). 384p. (YA). (gr. 7-12). pap. 8.99 *(978-0-689-87790-2(0),* McElderry, Margaret K. Bks.) McElderry, Margaret K. Bks.

Meyer, Linda Ross. The Recipe Box. 2010. 73p. pap. 7.99 *(978-0-557-54210-9(3))* Lulu Pr., Inc.

Michael, Alexander. Until Wishes Are Fulfilled. 2007. (ENG.). 154p. per. 13.50 *(978-1-84426-408-7(4))* Upfront Publishing Ltd. GBR. Dist: Printondemand-worldwide.com.

Mientus, Andy. The Backstagers & the Ghost Light (Backstagers #1) Sygh, Rian, illus. 2018. (Backstagers Ser.). (ENG.). 208p. (J). (gr. 5-9). 14.99 *(978-1-4197-3120-4(3),* 1220801, Amulet Bks.) Abrams, Inc.

—The Backstagers & the Theater of the Ancients (Backstagers #2) Sygh, Rian & BOOM! Studios, illus. 2019. (Backstagers Ser.). (ENG.). 192p. (YA). (gr. 5-9). 14.99 *(978-1-4197-3365-9(6),* 1262501, Amulet Bks.) Abrams, Inc.

Mikalatos, Matt. The Crescent Stone. 2018. (Sunlit Lands Ser.: 1). (ENG., Illus.). 448p. (YA). 24.99 *(978-1-4964-3170-7(7),* 20_31146, Wander) Tyndale Hse. Pubs.

—The Heartwood Crown. 2019. (Sunlit Lands Ser.: 2). (ENG., Illus.). 416p. (YA). pap. 15.99 *(978-1-4964-3176-9(6),* 20_31152, Wander) Tyndale Hse. Pubs.

Miles, Cindy. Forevermore. 2013. (ENG.). 288p. (YA). (gr. 7). pap. 9.99 *(978-0-545-42622-0(7))* Scholastic, Inc.

Milford, Kate. Greenglass House. 2015. (CHI.). 352p. (J). (gr. 5-7). pap. *(978-986-320-886-0(8))* Commonwealth Publishing Co., Ltd.

—Greenglass House. 2016. (Greenglass House Ser.: 1). lib. bdg. 18.40 *(978-0-606-38908-2(3))* Turtleback.

—Greenglass House: A National Book Award Nominee. Zollars, Jaime, illus. (Greenglass House Ser.). (ENG.). (J). (gr. 5-7). 2016. 400p. pap. 8.99 *(978-0-544-54028-6(X),* 1608839) 2014. 384p. 18.99 *(978-0-544-05270-3(6),* 1533148) HarperCollins Pubs. (Clarion Bks.).

—The Left-Handed Fate. Wheeler, Eliza, illus. 2017. (ENG.). 384p. (J). pap. 13.99 *(978-1-250-12183-7(3),* 900157594) Square Fish.

Miller, Amanda. The Library's Secret: A Hidden Adventure. 2010. 88p. pap. 10.49 *(978-1-4520-7012-4(1))* AuthorHouse.

Miller, Chris & Miller, Allan. Hunter Brown & the Consuming Fire, 3 bks., Bk.2. 2009. (ENG., Illus.). 352p. (J). pap. 13.99 *(978-1-59317-357-9(1))* Warner Pr., Inc.

Miller, Christopher & Miller, Allan. Hunter Brown & the Eye of Ends, 3 bks., Bk.3. 2011. (J). pap. 13.99 *(978-1-59317-400-2(4))* Warner Pr., Inc.

—Hunter Brown & the Secret of the Shadow, 3 bks., Bk.1. 2008. (ENG., Illus.). 384p. (J). (gr. 9-18). pap. 13.99 *(978-1-59317-328-9(8))* Warner Pr., Inc.

Miller, Jennifer. Best Friends for Life. Choi Sung Hwan, Aragon Noel, illus. 2006. (Trollz Ser.). (ENG.). 120p. (J). pap. 4.99 *(978-0-439-80311-3(X))* Scholastic, Inc.

Miller, Olive Beaupr. The Magic Garden of My Book House. 2005. reprint ed. pap. 24.95 *(978-1-4191-4169-0(4))* Kessinger Publishing, LLC.

Miller, Sibley. The Horse Must Go On: A Sumatra Story. Chang, Tara Larsen & Gershman, Jo, illus. 2008. (Wind Dancers Ser.: 3). (ENG.). 80p. (J). (gr. 1-4). pap. 12.99 *(978-0-312-38282-7(0),* 900051214) Feiwel & Friends.

—A Horse, of Course! A Sumatra Story. 2009. (Wind Dancers Ser.: 7). (ENG., Illus.). 80p. (J). (gr. 1-4). pap. 16.99 *(978-0-312-56402-5(3),* 900059061) Feiwel & Friends.

—Horses' Night Out: A Sirocco Story. Chang, Tara Larsen & Gershman, Jo, illus. 2008. (Wind Dancers Ser.: 4). (ENG.). 80p. (J). (gr. 1-4). pap. 16.99 *(978-0-312-38283-4(9),* 900051215) Feiwel & Friends.

—Horsey Trails: A Sumatra Story. Chang, Tara Larsen & Gershman, Jo, illus. 2011. (Wind Dancers Ser.: 11). (ENG.). 80p. (J). (gr. 1-4). pap. 16.99 *(978-0-312-60544-5(7),* 900064395) Feiwel & Friends.

—Magic Horses - or Not? A Sirocco Story. Chang, Tara Larsen & Gershman, Jo, illus. 2011. (Wind Dancers Ser.: 12). (ENG.). 80p. (J). (gr. 1-4). pap. 16.99 *(978-0-312-60545-2(5),* 900064396) Feiwel & Friends.

Miller, Toby. The Magic Word. 2011. (Illus.). 24p. pap. 14.09 *(978-1-4567-7793-7(9))* AuthorHouse.

Milligan, Domino. The Sandman. Spiller, Michael, illus. 2008. 16p. pap. 24.95 *(978-1-60703-728-6(9))* America Star Bks.

Milliner, Naomi. Super Jake & the King of Chaos. 2019. (ENG.). 288p. (J). (gr. 3-7). 16.99 *(978-0-7624-6615-3(4),* Running Pr. Kids) Running Pr.

Minami, Natsuki, illus. Disney Manga: Descendants - Rotten to the Core, Book 2: The Rotten to the Core Trilogy, Bk. 2. 2017. (Disney Manga: Descendants - the Rotten to the Core Trilogy Ser.: 2). (ENG.). 80p. (J). (gr. 3-1). pap. 10.99 *(978-1-4278-5689-0(3),* 793adea8-abae-4a59-91c8-7d530cde05b3, TOKYOPOP Manga) TOKYOPOP, Inc.

Mincks, Margaret. President of Poplar Lane. 2019. 288p. (J). (gr. 3-7). 16.99 *(978-0-425-29093-4(X),* Viking Books for Young Readers) Penguin Young Readers Group.

Misra, Michelle. Birthday Surprise. Chaffey, Samantha, illus. 2016. (Angel Wings Ser.: 2). (ENG.). 128p. (J). (gr. 1-4). pap. 5.99 *(978-1-4814-5800-9(0),* Aladdin) Simon & Schuster Children's Publishing.

—Rainbows & Halos. Chaffey, Samantha, illus. 2017. (Angel Wings Ser.: 4). (ENG.). 112p. (J). (gr. 1-4). pap. 5.99 *(978-1-4814-5806-1(X),* Simon & Schuster/Paula Wiseman Bks.) Simon & Schuster/Paula Wiseman Bks.

Miyazaki, Hayao. Ponyo Film Comic, Vol. 1. movie tie-in ed. 2009. (Ponyo Film Comics Ser.: 1). (ENG., Illus.). 172p. (J). pap. 9.99 *(978-1-4215-3077-2(5))* Viz Media.

—Ponyo Film Comic, Vol. 2. movie tie-in ed. 2009. (Ponyo Film Comics Ser.: 2). (ENG., Illus.). 152p. (J). pap. 9.99 *(978-1-4215-3078-9(3))* Viz Media.

—Ponyo Film Comic, Vol. 3. movie tie-in ed. 2009. (Ponyo Film Comics Ser.: 3). (ENG., Illus.). 152p. (J). pap. 9.99 *(978-1-4215-3079-6(1))* Viz Media.

—Ponyo Film Comic, Vol. 4. movie tie-in ed. 2009. (Ponyo Film Comics Ser.: 4). (ENG., Illus.). 168p. (J). pap. 9.99 *(978-1-4215-3080-2(5))* Viz Media.

—Ponyo Picture Book. 2009. (Ponyo Picture Book Ser.). (ENG., Illus.). 152p. (J). (gr. 2-7). 19.99 *(978-1-4215-3065-9(1))* Viz Media.

Mlynowski, Sarah. Abby in Wonderland (Whatever after Special Edition), 1 vol., Vol. 1. 2018. (Whatever After Ser.: 1). (ENG.). 256p. (J). (gr. 3-7). pap. 7.99 *(978-0-545-74667-0(1))* Scholastic, Inc.

—Cold As Ice (Whatever After #6) 2015. (Whatever After Ser.: 6). (ENG.). 176p. (J). (gr. 3-7). pap. 5.99 *(978-0-545-62736-8(2),* Scholastic Pr.) Scholastic, Inc.

—Dream on (Whatever After #4) 2014. (Whatever After Ser.: 4). (ENG.). 176p. (J). (gr. 3-7). pap. 5.99 *(978-0-545-41572-9(1),* Scholastic Paperbacks) Scholastic, Inc.

—Fairest of All (Whatever After #1) 2013. (Whatever After Ser.: 1). (ENG.). 176p. (J). (gr. 3-7). pap. 6.99 *(978-0-545-48571-5(1),* Scholastic Pr.) Scholastic, Inc.

—Frogs & French Kisses. 2007. (Magic in Manhattan Ser.: 2). (ENG.). 304p. (YA). (gr. 7). pap. 8.99 *(978-0-385-73185-0(X),* Delacorte Pr.) Random Hse. Children's Bks.

—If the Shoe Fits. 2013. 176p. 14.99 *(978-0-545-50465-2(1))* Scholastic, Inc.

—If the Shoe Fits (Whatever After #2) 2013. (Whatever After Ser.: 2). (ENG.). 176p. (J). (gr. 3-7). pap. 6.99 *(978-0-545-41568-2(3),* Scholastic Pr.) Scholastic, Inc.

—Magic in Manhattan: Bras & Broomsticks & Frogs & French Kisses. 2012. (Magic in Manhattan Ser.). (ENG.). 608p. (YA). (gr. 7). pap. 11.99 *(978-0-385-74232-0(0),* Ember) Random Hse. Children's Bks.

—Sink or Swim. 2013. (Whatever After Ser.: No. 3). 165p. (J). *(978-0-545-53316-4(3),* Scholastic Pr.) Scholastic, Inc.

—Sink or Swim (Whatever After #3) 2014. (Whatever After Ser.: 3). (ENG.). 176p. (J). (gr. 3-7). pap. 6.99 *(978-0-545-41570-5(5),* Scholastic Pr.) Scholastic, Inc.

—Spill the Beans (Whatever After #13) 2019. (Whatever After Ser.: 13). (ENG.). 176p. (J). (gr. 3-7). 14.99 *(978-1-338-16297-4(7),* Scholastic Pr.) Scholastic, Inc.

—Sugar & Spice (Whatever After #10) 2018. (Whatever After Ser.: 10). (ENG.). 176p. (J). (gr. 3-7). pap. 6.99 *(978-0-545-85107-7(6))* Scholastic, Inc.

—Two Peas in a Pod (Whatever After #11) (Whatever After Ser.: 11). (ENG.). 176p. (J). (gr. 3-7). 2019. pap. 6.99 *(978-1-338-16291-2(8))* 2018. 14.99 *(978-1-338-16289-9(6),* Scholastic Pr.) Scholastic, Inc.

—Whatever after Books 1-3, Bks. 1-3. 2016. (Whatever After Ser.). (ENG.). 528p. (J). (gr. 3-7). pap. 9.99 *(978-1-338-10175-1(7))* Scholastic, Inc.

Mlynowski, Sarah & Rigaud, Debbie. The Sister Switch (Best Wishes #2) Vee, Maxine, illus. 2023. (Best Wishes Ser.). (ENG.). 192p. (J). (gr. 3-7). 15.99 *(978-1-338-62828-9(3),* Scholastic Pr.) Scholastic, Inc.

Mlynowski, Sarah, et al. Dragon Overnight (Upside-Down Magic #4), 1 vol. (Upside-Down Magic Ser.: 4). (ENG.). 192p. (J). (gr. 3-7). 2019. pap. 5.99 *(978-1-338-11116-3(7))* 2018. 14.99 *(978-1-338-11115-6(9),* Scholastic Pr.) Scholastic, Inc.

—Dragon Overnight (Upside-Down Magic #4) (Unabridged Edition), 1 vol. unabr. ed. 2018. (Upside-Down Magic Ser.: 4). (ENG.). 1p. (J). (gr. 3-7). audio compact disk 24.99 *(978-1-338-22741-3(6))* Scholastic, Inc.

—Showing off (Upside-Down Magic #3), 1 vol. (Upside-Down Magic Ser.: 3). (ENG.). 208p. (J). (gr. 3-7). 2018. pap. 5.99 *(978-0-545-80054-9(4))* 2016. 14.99 *(978-0-545-80053-2(6),* Scholastic Pr.) Scholastic, Inc.

—Sticks & Stones (Upside-Down Magic #2), 1 vol. (Upside-Down Magic Ser.: 2). (ENG.). 208p. (J). (gr. 3-7). 2017. pap. 5.99 *(978-0-545-80050-1(1))* 2016. 14.99 *(978-0-545-80049-5(8),* Scholastic Pr.) Scholastic, Inc.

—Upside-Down Magic. 2015. 196p. (J). pap. *(978-0-545-90822-1(1),* Scholastic Pr.) Scholastic, Inc.

—Upside-Down Magic (Upside-down Magic #1), 1 vol. 2016. (Upside-Down Magic Ser.: 1). (ENG.). 208p. (J). (gr. 3-7). pap. 5.99 *(978-0-545-80046-4(3))* Scholastic, Inc.

—Weather or Not (Upside-Down Magic #5), 1 vol. (Upside-Down Magic Ser.: 5). (ENG.). 192p. (J). (gr. 3-7). 2019. pap. 5.99 *(978-1-338-22148-0(5))* 2018. 14.99 *(978-1-338-22147-3(7),* Scholastic Pr.) Scholastic, Inc.

Modesto, Michelle. Revenge & the Wild. 2016. (ENG.). 384p. (YA). (gr. 9). 17.99 *(978-0-06-236615-3(7),* Balzer & Bray) HarperCollins Pubs.

Moffit, Linda L. The Magic Mirror. 2003. (Illus.). 80p. (Orig.). (gr. k-7). 10.95 *(978-0-87516-615-5(6),* Devorss Pubns.) DeVorss & Co.

Molesworth. Cuckoo Clock. 2006. 216p. per. *(978-1-4067-1668-9(5),* Hesperides Pr.) Read Bks.

Molesworth, Mary Louisa. The Cuckoo Clock. 2004. reprint ed. pap. 1.99 *(978-1-4192-5839-8(7));* pap. 19.95 *(978-1-4191-5839-1(2))* Kessinger Publishing, LLC.

Molesworth, Mary Louisa S. The Palace in the Garden. 2011. 148p. 25.95 *(978-1-4638-9525-9(9))* Rodgers, Alan Bks.

Monaghan, Joseph. The Boy Who Loved Trees. 2013. (Illus.). 24p. pap. 19.82 *(978-1-4817-8225-8(8))* AuthorHouse.

Monahan, Hillary. The Hollow Girl. 2017. ix, 261p. (YA). *(978-1-5247-0188-8(2),* Delacorte Pr.) Random Hse. Children's Bks.

Mongredien, Sue. Oliver Moon & the Dragon Disaster. 2011. (Oliver Moon Ser.). 94p. (J). pap. 4.99 *(978-0-7945-3036-5(2),* Usborne) EDC Publishing.

—Oliver Moon & the Monster Mystery. 2011. (Oliver Moon, Junior Wizard Ser.). (ENG.). 89p. (J). (gr. 2-5). 17.44 *(978-0-7945-3095-2(8))* EDC Publishing.

—Oliver Moon & the Nipperbat Nightmare. 2011. (Oliver Moon, Junior Wizard Ser.). (ENG.). 94p. (J). (gr. 2-5). 17.44 *(978-0-7945-3037-2(0))* EDC Publishing.

—Oliver Moon & the Spell Off. 2011. (Oliver Moon, Junior Wizard Ser.). (ENG.). 93p. (J). (gr. 2-5). 17.44 *(978-0-7945-3093-8(1))* EDC Publishing.

Monsef, Kiyash. Once There Was. 2023. (Once There Was Ser.). (ENG., Illus.). 416p. (J). (gr. 5). 18.99 *(978-1-6659-2850-2(6),* Simon & Schuster Bks. For Young Readers) Simon & Schuster Bks. For Young Readers.

Moone, Colin. Wonderful Adventures of the Magicans: The One Bad Apple. 2003. 164p. pap. *(978-1-84426-189-5(1))* Upfront Publishing Ltd.

Moonheart, Ella. Kitty's Magic 1: Misty the Scared Kitten. 2018. (Kitty's Magic Ser.). (ENG., Illus.). 128p. (J). pap. 6.99 *(978-1-68119-385-4(X),* 900172065, Bloomsbury USA Childrens) Bloomsbury Publishing USA.

—Kitty's Magic 3: Ruby the Runaway Kitten. 2018. (Kitty's Magic Ser.). (ENG., Illus.). 128p. (J). pap. 5.99 *(978-1-68119-389-2(2),* 900172064, Bloomsbury Children's Bks.) Bloomsbury Publishing USA.

—Kitty's Magic 4: Star the Little Farm Cat. 2018. (Kitty's Magic Ser.). (ENG., Illus.). 128p. (J). 15.99 *(978-1-68119-703-6(0),* 900182274); pap. 5.99 *(978-1-68119-391-5(4),* 900172066) Bloomsbury Publishing USA. (Bloomsbury Children's Bks.).

—Kitty's Magic 5: Frost & Snowdrop the Stray Kittens. 2018. (Kitty's Magic Ser.). (ENG., Illus.). 128p. (J). 15.99 *(978-1-68119-908-5(4),* 900191749); pap. 5.99 *(978-1-68119-907-8(6),* 900191744) Bloomsbury Publishing USA. (Bloomsbury Children's Bks.).

—Kitty's Magic 6: Sooty the Birthday Cat. 2018. (Kitty's Magic Ser.). (ENG., Illus.). 128p. (J). 15.99 *(978-1-68119-911-5(4),* 900191748, Bloomsbury Children's Bks.) Bloomsbury Publishing USA.

Moore, Clement C. Magie de Noel. pap. 16.95 *(978-2-07-054886-6(4))* Gallimard, Editions FRA. Dist: Distribooks, Inc.

Moore, Rosey. Dreams. 2010. 228p. pap. 14.49 (978-1-4520-7485-6(2)) AuthorHouse.

Moore, Stuart, et al. The Dragon's Return. 2016. (978-1-4847-7415-1(9)) Disney Publishing Worldwide.

Moore, Victor L. The Pentacle of Northumbria. 2013. 432p. pap. (978-1-78222-073-2(9)) Paragon Publishing, Rothersthorpe.

Morales, Rebecca Lynn. Walter Plume & the Dehydrated Imagination. 2016. (ENG.). viii, 150p. (J). pap. 11.99 (978-1-4621-1780-2(5), Sweetwater Bks.) Cedar Fort, Inc./CFI Distribution.

Morgan, C. M. Silver Doorway #6: The Alchemist's Girl. 2008. 108p. pap. 6.99 (978-0-9771005-2-1(9)) Sabledrake Enterprises.

Morgan, Marlee. Soujon's Journey. 2010. 380p. (J). pap. 10.00 (978-0-9789247-6-8(2), INDI Best) INDI, LLC.

Morgan, Melissa J. Charmed Forces #19: Super Special. 2008. (Camp Confidential Ser.: 19). 256p. (J). (gr. 3-7). pap. 5.99 (978-0-448-44722-3(3), Grosset & Dunlap) Penguin Young Readers Group.

Morgan, Nikki. Mithendrove: Escaping Callendae. 2003. 110p. (YA). pap. 9.95 (978-0-595-27138-2(3), Writer's Showcase Pr.) iUniverse, Inc.

Moriarty, Chris. The Inquisitor's Apprentice. Geyer, Mark Edward, illus. 2013. (ENG.). 352p. (J). (gr. 5-7). pap. 7.99 (978-0-547-85084-9(0), 1501042, Clarion Bks.) HarperCollins Pubs.

—The Watcher in the Shadows. Geyer, Mark Edward, illus. 2014. (ENG.). 336p. (J). (gr. 5-7). pap. 18.99 (978-0-544-22776-7(X), 1563388, Clarion Bks.) HarperCollins Pubs.

Moriarty, Jaclyn. A Corner of White (the Colors of Madeleine, Book 1) 2013. (Colors of Madeleine Ser.: 1). (ENG.). 384p. (YA). (gr. 7-7). 18.99 (978-0-545-39736-0(7), Levine, Arthur A. Bks.) Scholastic, Inc.

—The Extremely Inconvenient Adventures of Bronte Mettlestone. 2018. (ENG., Illus.). 384p. (J). (gr. 3-7). 17.99 (978-1-338-25584-3(3), Levine, Arthur A. Bks.) Scholastic, Inc.

—The Spell Book of Listen Taylor. 2007. (YA). (978-0-439-84679-0(X), Levine, Arthur A. Bks.) Scholastic, Inc.

—A Tangle of Gold (the Colors of Madeleine, Book 3) 2016. (Colors of Madeleine Ser.: 3). (ENG.). 480p. (YA). (gr. 7-7). 18.99 (978-0-545-39740-7(5), Levine, Arthur A. Bks.) Scholastic, Inc.

Morlock, Theresa. Fairy & Leprechaun Legends, 1 vol. 2017. (Famous Legends Ser.). (ENG.). 32p. (J). (gr. 2-3). pap. 11.50 (978-1-5382-0353-8(7), 17dd33ff-d363-4e5b-8d53-92440a397f14) Stevens, Gareth Publishing LLLP.

Morpurgo, Michael. Toto: the Dog-Gone Amazing Story of the Wizard of Oz. Chichester Clark, Emma, illus. 2017. (ENG.). 284p. (J). 17.99 (978-0-00-825256-4(4), HarperCollins Children's Bks.) HarperCollins Pubs. Ltd. GBR. Dist: HarperCollins Pubs.

Morris, Gerald. The Squire's Tale. 2008. (Squire's Tales Ser.: 1). (ENG.). 224p. (J). (gr. 5-7). pap. 7.99 (978-0-618-73743-7(X), 410325, Clarion Bks.) HarperCollins Pubs.

Morris, J. S. The Jewel. 2007. (ENG.). 204p. pap. 22.95 (978-1-4357-0140-3(2)) Lulu Pr., Inc.

Morrisette, Sharon. Toads & Tessellations. O'Neill, Philomena, illus. 2012. (Charlesbridge Math Adventures Ser.). 32p. (J). (gr. 2-5). 16.95 (978-1-58089-354-1(6)) Charlesbridge Publishing, Inc.

Morrison, Megan. Disenchanted: the Trials of Cinderella (Tyme #2) 2019. (Tyme Ser.: 2). (ENG.). 432p. (J). (gr. 3-7). pap. 8.99 (978-0-545-64272-9(8), Levine, Arthur A. Bks.) Scholastic, Inc.

—Grounded: The Tale of Rapunzel. 2015. (Illus.). 374p. (J). (978-0-545-75468-2(2)) Scholastic, Inc.

—Transformed: the Perils of the Frog Prince (Tyme #3) 2019. (Tyme Ser.: 3). (ENG.). 368p. (J). (gr. 3-7). 17.99 (978-1-338-11392-1(5), Levine, Arthur A. Bks.) Scholastic, Inc.

Morrissey, Dean & Krensky, Stephen. The Wizard Mouse. Morrissey, Dean, illus. 2011. (ENG., Illus.). 32p. (J). (gr. k-4). 16.99 (978-0-06-008066-2(3)) HarperCollins Pubs.

Moser, Fiadhnait. The Serendipity of Flightless Things. 2019. (ENG.). 320p. (J). (gr. 4-9). 16.99 (978-1-4998-0843-8(7), Yellow Jacket) Bonnier Publishing USA.

Mosley, Walter. 47. 2006. (ENG., Illus.). 272p. (J). (gr. 7-17). reprint ed. per. 11.99 (978-0-316-01635-3(7)) Little, Brown Bks. for Young Readers.

Moss, J. P. The Kind Fairy Adventures: 3 Loving Fairy Tales from the Land of the Faye. 2010. (Illus.). 52p. pap. 22.99 (978-1-4520-3868-1(6)) AuthorHouse.

Moss, Ronald. The Wizard Next Door. 2009. 198p. pap. 14.95 (978-1-60911-077-2(3), Eloquent Bks.) Strategic Book Publishing & Rights Agency (SBPRA).

Motayne, Maya. Nocturna. (Nocturna Ser.: 1). (ENG.). (YA). (gr. 8). 2020. 496p. pap. 11.99 (978-0-06-284274-9(9)) 2019. (Illus.). 480p. 18.99 (978-0-06-284273-2(0)) HarperCollins Pubs. (Balzer & Bray).

Motley, T., illus. The Golden Ass: Of Lucius Apuleius. 2011. (ENG.). 85p. (J). 17.95 (978-1-56792-418-3(2)) Godine, David R. Pub.

Mudenda, Duly & Nagunga, Kansi. Syankombo. 2004. (Illus.). 20p. 16.95 (978-1-77936-005-2(3)) Africa Community Publishing & Development Trust ZWE. Dist: Michigan State Univ. Pr.

Muir, Suzanne. The Magic Tile. 2007. (Illus.). 48p. (J). lib. bdg. 15.00 (978-1-4242-1619-2(2)) Dingles & Co.

Mulholland, Marie. A Study Guide for the Necklace of Terrersylvanous. 2007. 38p. (J). ring bd. 11.95 (978-0-9797715-0-7(1)) Sonic Sword Productions.

mulholland, robin. Bolivia & the sunshine King. 2008. (ENG.). 147p. pap. 14.98 (978-0-557-01401-9(8)) Lulu Pr., Inc.

Mull, Brandon. Arcade Catastrophe. 2014. (Candy Shop War Ser.: 2). lib. bdg. 18.40 (978-0-606-35795-1(5)) Turtleback.

—Beyonders the Complete Set (Boxed Set) A World Without Heroes; Seeds of Rebellion; Chasing the Prophecy, Set. 2013. (Beyonders Ser.). (ENG., Illus.). 1456p. (J). (gr. 3-7). 59.99 (978-1-4424-8593-8(0), Aladdin) Simon & Schuster Children's Publishing.

—The Candy Shop War. 2007. (Candy Shop War Ser.: 1). (ENG.). 400p. (gr. 3-8). E-Book 18.95 (978-1-60641-649-5(9)) Deseret Bk. Co.

—The Candy Shop War. (Candy Shop War Ser.: Bk. 1). 2008. 368p. pap. 6.99 (978-1-59038-970-6(0)) 2007. (ENG., Illus.). 416p. (J). (gr. 3-8). 19.99 (978-1-59038-783-2(X), 4988540) Shadow Mountain Publishing. (Shadow Mountain).

—The Candy Shop War. 2014. (Candy Shop War Ser.: 1). lib. bdg. 18.40 (978-0-606-35794-4(7)) Turtleback.

—Chasing the Prophecy. (Beyonders Ser.: 3). (ENG.). (J). (gr. 3-7). 2014. 528p. pap. 9.99 (978-1-4169-9797-9(0)) 2013. 512p. 21.99 (978-1-4169-9796-2(2)) Simon & Schuster Children's Publishing. (Aladdin).

—Crystal Keepers. (Five Kingdoms Ser.: 3). (ENG., Illus.). (J). (gr. 3-7). 2016. 512p. pap. 9.99 (978-1-4424-9707-8(6), Aladdin) 2015. 496p. 19.99 (978-1-4424-9706-1(8), Aladdin Library) Simon & Schuster Children's Publishing.

—Crystal Keepers. 2016. (Five Kingdoms Ser.: 3). lib. bdg. 18.40 (978-0-606-38253-3(4)) Turtleback.

—Dragonwatch. 2017. (Dragonwatch Ser.: 1). (ENG., Illus.). 384p. (J). (gr. 3). 18.99 (978-1-62972-256-6(1), 5158440, Shadow Mountain) Shadow Mountain Publishing.

—Dragonwatch. 2018. (Dragonwatch Ser.: 1). lib. bdg. 19.65 (978-0-606-40838-7(X)) Turtleback.

—Dragonwatch: A Fablehaven Adventure. Dorman, Brandon, illus. 2018. (Dragonwatch Ser.: 1). (ENG.). 384p. (J). (gr. 3-8). pap. 9.99 (978-1-4814-8502-9(4), Aladdin) Simon & Schuster Children's Publishing.

—Dragonwatch Complete Boxed Set: Dragonwatch; Wrath of the Dragon King; Master of the Phantom Isle; Champions of the Titan Games; Return of the Dragon Slayers. 2021. (Dragonwatch Ser.). (ENG.). 2448p. (J). (gr. 3-6). 99.99 (978-1-62972-936-7(1), 5252623, Shadow Mountain) Deseret Bk. Co.

—Fablehaven. 2006. (ENG., Illus.). 351p. (J). lib. bdg. 20.00 (978-1-4242-4831-5(0)) Fitzgerald Bks.

—Fablehaven. 2009. (SPA.). 306p. (YA). (gr. 5-8). 24.95 (978-84-9918-033-5(7)) Roca Editorial ESP. Dist: Spanish Pubs., LLC.

—Fablehaven. 2006. (Fablehaven Ser.: 1). (ENG., Illus.). 368p. (J). (gr. 3-7). 19.99 (978-1-59038-581-4(0), 4961111, Shadow Mountain) Shadow Mountain Publishing.

—Fablehaven. Dorman, Brandon, illus. 2007. (Fablehaven Ser.: 1). (ENG.). 384p. (J). (gr. 3-8). pap. 9.99 (978-1-4169-4720-2(5), Aladdin) Simon & Schuster Children's Publishing.

—Fablehaven. 2007. (Fablehaven Ser.: 01). lib. bdg. 18.40 (978-1-4177-9328-0(7)) Turtleback.

—Fablehaven: Las Llaves de la Prision de los Demonios. 2012. (SPA.). 466p. (YA). 24.95 (978-84-9918-438-8(3)) Roca Editorial ESP. Dist: Spanish Pubs., LLC.

—Fablehaven Complete Boxed Set: Rise of the Evening Star; Grip of the Shadow Plague; Secrets of the Dragon Sanctuary; Keys to the Demon Prison. 2010. (Fablehaven Ser.: Bks. 1-3). (ENG.). 2512p. (gr. 3-6). 99.99 (978-1-60641-832-1(7), 5046909, Shadow Mountain) Shadow Mountain Publishing.

—Fablehaven Complete Set (Boxed Set) Set: Fablehaven; Rise of the Evening Star; Grip of the Shadow Plague; Secrets of the Dragon Sanctuary; Keys to the Demon Prison. Dorman, Brandon, illus. 2011. (Fablehaven Ser.). (ENG.). 2512p. (J). (gr. 3-8). pap. 49.99 (978-1-4424-2977-2(1), Aladdin) Simon & Schuster Children's Publishing.

—Grip of the Shadow Plague. Dorman, Brandon, illus. 2008. (Fablehaven Ser.: 3). (ENG.). 480p. (J). (gr. 3-7). 19.99 (978-1-59038-898-3(4), 5004776, Shadow Mountain) Shadow Mountain Publishing.

—Keys to the Demon Prison. Dorman, Brandon, illus. 2011. (Fablehaven Ser.: 5). (ENG.). 640p. (J). (gr. 3-8). pap. 9.99 (978-1-4169-9029-1(1), Aladdin) Simon & Schuster Children's Publishing.

—Master of the Phantom Isle. 2019. (Dragonwatch Ser.: 3). (ENG., Illus.). 496p. (J). (gr. 5). 18.99 (978-1-62972-604-5(4), 5222032, Shadow Mountain) Deseret Bk. Co.

—Master of the Phantom Isle: A Fablehaven Adventure. 2020. (Dragonwatch Ser.: 3). (ENG., Illus.). 496p. (J). (gr. 3-8). pap. 9.99 (978-1-4814-8506-7(7), Aladdin) Simon & Schuster Children's Publishing.

—Return of the Dragon Slayers. 2021. (Dragonwatch Ser.: 5). (ENG., Illus.). 624p. (J). (gr. 3-6). 21.99 (978-1-62972-930-5(2), 5252621, Shadow Mountain) Deseret Bk. Co.

—Rise of the Evening Star. Dorman, Brandon, illus. 2007. (Fablehaven Ser.: 2). (ENG.). 456p. (J). (gr. 3-7). 19.99 (978-1-59038-742-9(2), 4981432, Shadow Mountain) Shadow Mountain Publishing.

—Rise of the Evening Star. Dorman, Brandon, illus. 2008. (Fablehaven Ser.: 2). (ENG.). 480p. (J). (gr. 3-8). pap. 8.99 (978-1-4169-5770-6(7), Aladdin) Simon & Schuster Children's Publishing.

—Rogue Knight. (Five Kingdoms Ser.: 2). (ENG., Illus.). (J). (gr. 3-7). 2015. 496p. pap. 9.99 (978-1-4424-9704-7(1)) 2014. 480p. 19.99 (978-1-4424-9703-0(3)) Simon & Schuster Children's Publishing. (Aladdin).

—Rogue Knight. 2015. (Five Kingdoms Ser.: 2). lib. bdg. 19.65 (978-0-606-38254-0(2)) Turtleback.

—Secrets of the Dragon Sanctuary. Dorman, Brandon, illus. 2010. (Fablehaven Ser.: 4). (ENG.). 560p. (J). (gr. 3-8). pap. 9.99 (978-1-4169-9028-4(3), Aladdin) Simon & Schuster Children's Publishing.

—Secrets of the Dragon Sanctuary. 2010. (Fablehaven Ser.: 4). lib. bdg. 19.65 (978-0-606-10685-6(5)) Turtleback.

—Seeds of Rebellion. (Beyonders Ser.: 2). (ENG., Illus.). 512p. (J). (gr. 3-7). 2013. pap. 9.99 (978-1-4169-9795-5(4)) 2012. 21.99 (978-1-4169-9794-8(6)) Simon & Schuster Children's Publishing. (Aladdin).

—Seeds of Rebellion. 2012. (Beyonders Ser.: Bk. 2). (ENG., Illus.). 512p. (J). pap. 10.99 (978-1-4424-4965-7(9), Simon & Schuster/Paula Wiseman Bks.) Simon & Schuster/Paula Wiseman Bks.

—Seeds of Rebellion. 2013. (Beyonders Ser.: 2). lib. bdg. 19.65 (978-0-606-27030-4(2)) Turtleback.

—Time Jumpers. (Five Kingdoms Ser.: 5). (ENG.). (J). (gr. 3-7). 2019. 464p. pap. 9.99 (978-1-4424-9713-9(0)) 2018. (Illus.). 448p. 18.99 (978-1-4424-9712-2(2)) Simon & Schuster Children's Publishing. (Aladdin).

—A World Without Heroes. (J). 2011. (Beyonders Ser.: 1). 1.25 (978-1-4640-0920-4(1)) (Beyonders Ser.: 1). 92.75 (978-1-4618-0338-6(1)) 2011. (Beyonders Ser.: 1). 124.75 (978-1-4618-0353-9(5)) 2011. 122.75 (978-1-4618-0363-8(2)) Recorded Bks., Inc.

—A World Without Heroes. (Beyonders Ser.: 1). (ENG.). (J). (gr. 3-7). 2012. 512p. pap. 9.99 (978-1-4169-9793-1(8)) 2011. 464p. 21.99 (978-1-4169-9792-4(X)) Simon & Schuster Children's Publishing. (Aladdin).

—A World Without Heroes. 2011. (Beyonders Ser.: Bk. 1). (ENG.). 464p. (J). pap. 10.99 (978-1-4424-3530-8(5), Simon & Schuster/Paula Wiseman Bks.) Simon & Schuster/Paula Wiseman Bks.

—A World Without Heroes. 2012. (Beyonders Ser.: 1). lib. bdg. 19.65 (978-0-606-23675-1(9)) Turtleback.

—Wrath of the Dragon King. 2018. (Dragonwatch Ser.: 2). (ENG., Illus.). 416p. (J). (gr. 5). 18.99 (978-1-62972-486-7(6), 5206080) Deseret Bk. Co.

—Wrath of the Dragon King: A Fablehaven Adventure. 2019. (Dragonwatch Ser.: 2). (ENG., Illus.). 432p. (J). (gr. 3-8). pap. 9.99 (978-1-4814-8505-0(9), Aladdin) Simon & Schuster Children's Publishing.

Muncaster, Harriet. Isadora Moon Has a Birthday. 2018. (Isadora Moon Ser.: 4). (ENG., Illus.). 128p. (J). (gr. 1-4). 6.99 (978-0-399-55835-1(7)); 14.99 (978-0-399-55833-7(0)) Random Hse. Children's Bks. (Random Hse. Bks. for Young Readers).

Muneefa. My Tales for Children. 2006. 90p. (J). pap. 13.95 (978-1-58909-339-3(9)) Bookstand Publishing.

Munsch, Robert. MMM, Cookies. 2007. (J). 12.65 (978-0-7569-7657-6(X)) Perfection Learning Corp.

Murdock, Catherine Gilbert. Princess Ben. 2009. (ENG.). 352p. (YA). (gr. 7). pap. 9.99 (978-0-547-22325-4(0), 1061789, Clarion Bks.) HarperCollins Pubs.

Murtagh, Ciaran. Megastar: the Fincredible Diary of Fin Spencer. Wesson, Tim, illus. 2016. (Fincredible Diary of Fin Spencer Ser.: 2). (ENG.). 224p. (J). (gr. 4-7). pap. 7.99 (978-1-84812-447-9(3)) Bonnier Publishing GBR. Dist: Independent Pubs. Group.

Murty, Sudha. Bird with Golden Wings. 2016. (ENG., Illus.). 136p. (J). pap. 8.99 (978-0-14-333425-5(5), Puffin) Penguin Bks. India PVT, Ltd IND. Dist: Independent Pubs. Group.

Muscia, Marilena Carrubba. Misses Cowy to the Rescue. 2011. 24p. (gr. -1). 12.99 (978-1-4567-3582-1(9)) AuthorHouse.

Musgrove, Marianne. Forget-me-not Fairies Story Collection. MacCarthy, Patricia, illus. 2013. (ENG.). 192p. (J). (gr. -1-3). (978-1-74308-536-3(2)) Hinkler Bks. Pty, Ltd.

My Amazing Pet Snail. 2013. (Illus.). (J). (978-1-4351-4755-3(3)) Barnes & Noble, Inc.

Myers, Tim. Basho & the River Stones, 0 vols. Han, Oki S., illus. 2013. (ENG.). 34p. (J). (gr. 1-3). pap. 9.99 (978-1-4778-1682-0(8), 9781477816820, Two Lions) Amazon Publishing.

Myklusch, Matt. Order of the Majestic. 2019. (Order of the Majestic Ser.: 1). (ENG., Illus.). 432p. (J). (gr. 3-7). 18.99 (978-1-5344-2487-6(3), Aladdin) Simon & Schuster Children's Publishing.

Myracle, Lauren. The Backward Season. (Wishing Day Ser.: 3). (ENG.). 304p. (J). (gr. 3-7). 2019. pap. 6.99 (978-0-06-234213-3(4)) 2018. 16.99 (978-0-06-234212-6(6)) HarperCollins Pubs. (Tegen, Katherine Bks).

!Myster?Ous M! & Courageous $Oul. The Lonely Flower. Courageous $oul, illus. 2011. 20p. pap. 24.95 (978-1-4560-6950-6(0)) America Star Bks.

Na'Shae. The Magic Chronicles: Ice. 2008. 80p. pap. 9.99 (978-0-9814650-6-7(4)) G Publishing LLC.

Nathan, Sarah. Sofia's Magic Lesson. 2014. (Sofia the First Ser.). (J). lib. bdg. 13.55 (978-0-606-35258-1(9)) Turtleback.

Nation, Kaleb. Bran Hambric: The Farfield Curse. 2010. (ENG.). 464p. (J). (gr. 4-6). 24.94 (978-1-4022-4397-4(9)) Sourcebooks, Inc.

—Bran Hambric: The Specter Key. 2010. 352p. (J). (gr. 4-7). pap. 11.99 (978-1-4022-4059-1(7)) Sourcebooks, Inc.

Nayeri, Daniel. Sasha & Puck & the Brew for Brainwash. Lourenço, Estrela, illus. 2020. (Elixir Fixers Ser.: 4). (ENG.). 128p. (J). (gr. 1-5). 14.99 (978-0-8075-7246-7(2), 807572462) Whitman, Albert & Co.

Nazemi, Mary. Kaveh, Jolly & the Super Giant. 2006. (J). pap. 15.00 (978-0-8059-7001-2(0)) Dorrance Publishing Co., Inc.

Nefcy, Daron. Star vs. the Forces of Evil: the Magic Book of Spells. 2018. (ENG., Illus.). 256p. (J). (gr. 3-7). 19.99 (978-1-368-02050-3(X), Disney Press Books) Disney Publishing Worldwide.

Neff, Henry H. The Fiend & the Forge: Book Three of the Tapestry. 2011. (Tapestry Ser.: 3). (ENG., Illus.). 560p. (J). (gr. 3-7). 9.99 (978-0-375-83899-6(6), Yearling) Random Hse. Children's Bks.

—The Hound of Rowan, 1. Neff, Henry H., illus. 2007. (Tapestry Ser.: Bk. 1). (ENG., Illus.). 432p. (J). (gr. 4-6). lib. bdg. 24.94 (978-0-375-93894-8(X)) Random House Publishing Group.

—The Hound of Rowan: Book One of the Tapestry. 2008. (Tapestry Ser.: 1). (ENG., Illus.). 448p. (J). (gr. 3-7). 9.99 (978-0-375-83895-8(3), Yearling) Random Hse. Children's Bks.

—The Maelstrom: Book Four of the Tapestry, Bk. 4. Neff, Henry H., illus. 2013. (Tapestry Ser.: 4). (Illus.). 480p. (J). (gr. 3-7). 8.99 (978-0-375-87148-1(9), Yearling) Random Hse. Children's Bks.

—The Second Siege: Book Two of the Tapestry. 2010. (Tapestry Ser.: 2). (ENG., Illus.). 512p. (J). (gr. 3-7). 9.99 (978-0-375-83897-2(X), Yearling) Random Hse. Children's Bks.

Negrin, Fabian, illus. Wizard Tales. 2003. 96p. 19.95 (978-1-55285-558-4(9)) Whitecap Bks., Ltd. CAN. Dist: Graphic Arts Ctr. Publishing Co.

Neill, Chloe. Charmfall: A Novel of the Dark Elite. 2012. (Dark Elite Ser.: 3). (ENG.). 288p. (YA). (gr. 9). 9.99 (978-0-451-23080-5(9), Berkley) Penguin Publishing Group.

Neilson, G. E. F. Cosmic Aviators - Nathaniel's 1st Adventure. 2013. 332p. pap. (978-0-9576132-0-1(2)) Buzzword Pr.

Nelson, Brett Alan. The Magical Forest. Ueda, Kumiko, illus. 2020. (ENG.). 42p. (J). (gr. k-4). 19.95 (978-0-9655078-7-5(4)) Windsong Publishing Co.

Nelson, S. D. Coyote Christmas: A Lakota Story. 2007. (ENG., Illus.). 40p. (J). (gr. 1-4). 18.95 (978-0-8109-9367-9(8), Abrams Bks. for Young Readers) Abrams, Inc.

Neno, Michael. The Children's Magical Adventure: 1 the Rescue. 2011. (Illus.). 48p. (gr. -1). pap. 19.59 (978-1-4567-7887-3(0)) AuthorHouse.

Nesbet, Anne. The Cabinet of Earths, 1. 2013. (ENG.). 288p. (J). (gr. 3-7). pap. 6.99 (978-0-06-196319-3(4), HarperCollins) HarperCollins Pubs.

—The Wrinkled Crown. 2015. (ENG.). 400p. (J). (gr. 3-7). 17.99 (978-0-06-210429-8(2), HarperCollins) HarperCollins Pubs.

Nesbit, E. The Enchanted Castle. l.t. ed. 2005. 388p. pap. (978-1-84637-202-5(X)) Echo Library.

—Harding's Luck. 2006. 164p. (gr. 4-7). 25.95 (978-1-59818-170-8(X)) Aegypan.

—The House of Arden. 2006. 184p. (gr. 3-7). per. 14.95 (978-1-59818-967-4(0)); 26.95 (978-1-59818-181-4(5)) Aegypan.

—The Magic City. 2008. 144p. (gr. 4-7). 24.95 (978-1-60664-925-1(6)); pap. 11.95 (978-1-60664-045-6(3)) Aegypan.

—The Magic City. 2018. (ENG., Illus.). 204p. (YA). (gr. 7-12). pap. (978-93-5329-314-7(6)) Alpha Editions.

—The Magic City. 2017. (ENG., Illus.). (J). 24.95 (978-1-374-92012-5(6)); pap. 14.95 (978-1-374-92011-8(8)) Capital Communications, Inc.

—The Magic City. (ENG., 2019. Illus.). 414p. (YA). (gr. 7-12). pap. 26.99 (978-1-6942-5021-6(0)) 2019. 646p. (YA). (gr. 7-12). pap. 42.99 (978-1-0895-7478-1(9)) 2019. 426p. (YA). (gr. 7-12). pap. 25.99 (978-1-0870-1955-0(9)) 2019. 270p. (YA). (gr. 7-12). pap. 16.99 (978-1-0859-6244-5(X)) 2019. 272p. (YA). (gr. 7-12). pap. 16.99 (978-1-0709-4705-1(9)) 2019. 646p. (YA). (gr. 7-12). pap. 36.99 (978-1-0997-8430-9(1)) 2019. 422p. (YA). (gr. 7-12). pap. 24.99 (978-1-0989-2791-2(5)) 2019. 426p. (YA). (gr. 7-12). pap. 24.99 (978-1-0918-5303-4(7)) 2018. (Illus.). 194p. (J). pap. 14.99 (978-1-7919-6765-9(5)) Independently Published.

—The Magic City. 2018. (ENG.). 194p. (J). (978-3-7340-4691-9(2)); pap. (978-3-7340-4690-2(4)) Outlook Verlagsgesellschaft mbH.

—The Magic World. 2006. 156p. (gr. -1-7). 24.95 (978-1-59818-176-0(9)) Aegypan.

—The Magic World. 2019. (ENG.). (J). 138p. pap. 6.99 (978-1-6532-4009-8(1)); (Illus.). 326p. pap. 21.99 (978-1-6942-5023-0(7)) Independently Published.

—Magic World. 2006. 156p. (gr. -1-7). per. 12.95 (978-1-59818-966-7(2)) Aegypan.

—The Phoenix & the Carpet. 2009. 156p. pap. 4.95 (978-1-60459-693-9(7)) Wilder Pubns., Corp.

—The Red House. 2006. 140p. per. 11.95 (978-1-59818-965-0(4)) Aegypan.

—The Seven Dragons & Other Stories. 2006. 140p. 24.95 (978-1-59818-171-5(8)) Aegypan.

—The Story of the Amulet. 2009. 176p. (gr. -1-7). pap. 4.95 (978-1-60459-694-6(5)) Wilder Pubns., Corp.

—The Story of the Treasure Seekers. 2009. 128p. (gr. 4-7). pap. 5.50 (978-1-60459-695-3(3)) Wilder Pubns., Corp.

—Wet Magic. 2006. 200p. (gr. -1-7). per. (978-1-84350-095-7(7)) Soft Editions Ltd.

—7 Books in 1 - "The Railway Children", "Five Children & It", "The Phoenix & the Carpet", "The Story of the Amulet", "The Story of the Treasure-Seekers", "The Would-Be-Goods" & "The Enchanted Castle" 2004. 472p. pap. (978-0-9548401-0-5(0)) Shoes & Ships & Sealing Wax Ltd.

Nesbit, Edith. The Magic City. 2018. (ENG., Illus.). (J). 782p. pap. 49.99 (978-1-7917-1791-9(8)); 356p. pap. 24.99 (978-1-7918-0087-1(4)) Independently Published.

—The Magic City. 2018. (ENG., Illus.). 160p. (J). 14.99 (978-1-5154-3189-3(4)) Wilder Pubns., Corp.

—The Magic World. 2018. (ENG., Illus.). 156p. (J). 19.99 (978-1-5154-3188-6(6)) Wilder Pubns., Corp.

Nestell, Mark. Gordon & the Magic Fishbowl, 1 vol. Daley-Prado, M. J., illus. 2010. 26p. pap. 24.95 (978-1-4489-8495-4(5)) America Star Bks.

Neumeier, Rachel. The Floating Islands. 2012. (ENG.). 400p. (YA). (gr. 7). pap. 9.99 (978-0-440-24060-0(3)) Random Hse. Children's Bks.

Newcomb, Victoria. Gathering Grace. 2008. 250p. (YA). pap. 15.95 (978-1-59275-009-2(5)) Hanford Mead Pubs., Inc.

Newman, Samantha. Sammy Skizzors & the Rainbow Knight. 2010. 32p. 14.99 (978-1-4520-9976-7(6)) AuthorHouse.

Nicoll, Maxwell & Smith, Matthew. Slamdown Town. 2020. (ENG., Illus.). 320p. (YA). (gr. 3-7). 14.99 (978-1-4197-3885-2(2), 1291701, Amulet Bks.) Abrams, Inc.

Nielsen, Jennifer A. Mark of the Thief (Mark of the Thief, Book 1) 2015. (Mark of the Thief Ser.: 1). (ENG.). 352p. (J). (gr. 4-7). pap. 8.99 (978-0-545-56155-6(8), Scholastic Paperbacks) Scholastic, Inc.

—Rise of the Wolf. 2016. (Mark of the Thief Ser.: 2). lib. bdg. 18.40 (978-0-606-39707-0(8)) Turtleback.

—Rise of the Wolf (Mark of the Thief, Book 2) 2016. (Mark of the Thief Ser.: 2). (ENG.). 352p. (J). (gr. 4-7). pap. 8.99 (978-0-545-56205-8(8), Scholastic Pr.) Scholastic, Inc.

—Wrath of the Storm (Mark of the Thief, Book 3) (Mark of the Thief Ser.: 3). (ENG.). 352p. (J). (gr. 4-7). 2018. pap. 8.99 (978-0-545-56208-9(2)) 2017. 16.99 (978-0-545-56207-2(4), Scholastic Pr.) Scholastic, Inc.

Nielson, Kelli S. Stone Mage Wars, Book 1: Journey to the Fringe. 2011. (YA). 17.99 (978-1-60908-833-0(6)) Deseret Bk. Co.

Niemi, Renee. Because Gage Believed. 2013. 20p. pap. 24.95 (978-1-62709-730-7(9)) America Star Bks.

Night, P. J. No Trick-Or-Treating! 2012. (Creepover Ser.: 9). lib. bdg. 17.20 (978-0-606-26337-5(3)) Turtleback.

—Read It & Weep! 2013. (You're Invited to a Creepover Ser.: 13). (ENG., Illus.). 160p. (J). (gr. 3-7). pap. 6.99 (978-1-4424-5987-8(5), Simon Spotlight) Simon Spotlight.

—Read It & Weep! 2013. (Creepover Ser.: 13). lib. bdg. 16.00 (978-0-606-27039-7(6)) Turtleback.

Nimmo, Jenny. Charlie Bone & the Red Knight (Children of the Red King #8) (Unabridged Edition), 1 vol. unabr. ed. 2010. (Children of the Red King Ser.: 8). Tr. of #8. (ENG.). 1p. (J). (gr. 4-7). audio compact disk 34.99 (978-0-545-07856-6(3)) Scholastic, Inc.

—Midnight for Charlie Bone. 2003. (Children of the Red King Ser.: Bk. 1). (J). (gr. 2-6). per. 4.99 *(978-0-439-48839-6(7))* Scholastic, Inc.
Nishi, Yoshiyuki. Muhyo & Roji's Bureau of Supernatural Investigation, Vol. 18. 2010. (Muhyo & Roji's Bureau of Supernatural Investigation Ser.: 18). (ENG., Illus.). 192p. pap. 9.99 *(978-1-4215-2840-3(1))* Viz Media.
Nix, Garth. Across the Wall: A Tale of the Abhorsen & Other Stories. 2006. (ENG.). 432p. (YA). (gr. 8-12). pap. 10.99 *(978-0-06-074715-2(3),* HarperTeen) HarperCollins Pubs.
—Clariel: The Lost Abhorsen. 2014. (Old Kingdom Ser.: 4). (ENG., Illus.). 400p. (YA). (gr. 8). 18.99 *(978-0-06-156155-9(X),* HarperCollins) HarperCollins Pubs.
—Frogkisser! 2019. (ENG.). 384p. (YA). (gr. 7-7). pap. 12.99 *(978-1-338-05209-1(8))* Scholastic, Inc.
—Goldenhand. (Old Kingdom Ser.: 5). (ENG.). (YA). (gr. 8). 2019. 384p. pap. 10.99 *(978-0-06-156160-3(6))* 2016. (Illus.). 368p. 19.99 *(978-0-06-156158-0(4))* HarperCollins Pubs. (HarperCollins).
—Lirael. 2014. (Old Kingdom Ser.: 2). (ENG.). 512p. (YA). (gr. 8). pap. 12.99 *(978-0-06-231556-4(0),* HarperCollins) HarperCollins Pubs.
—Lirael, Daughter of the Clayr. 2009. 9.68 *(978-0-7848-2612-6(9),* Everbind) Marco Bk. Co.
—Mister Monday (the Keys to the Kingdom #1) 2018. (Keys to the Kingdom Ser.: 1). (ENG.). 368p. (J). (gr. 2-5). pap. 8.99 *(978-1-338-21613-4(9))* Scholastic, Inc.
—Newt's Emerald. 2015. (ENG.). 304p. (YA). (gr. 8-12). 18.99 *(978-0-06-236004-5(3),* Tegen, Katherine Bks) HarperCollins Pubs.
—Sir Thursday. 2007. (Keys to the Kingdom Ser.: No. 4). 344p. (gr. 4-7). 18.00 *(978-0-7569-8121-1(2))* Perfection Learning Corp.
—The Violet Keystone. 2004. (Seventh Tower Ser.: Bk. 6). 233p. (gr. 4-7). 17.00 *(978-0-7569-3506-1(7))* Perfection Learning Corp.
Nixon, Joan Lowery. A Deadly Game of Magic. 2004. (ENG.). 240p. (YA). (gr. 7-12). pap. 7.99 *(978-0-15-205030-6(2),* 1195191, Clarion Bks.) HarperCollins Pubs.
—A Deadly Game of Magic. 2004. 228p. (YA). (gr. 7). 13.60 *(978-0-7569-7230-1(2))* Perfection Learning Corp.
Noel, Alyson. Dark Flame: A Novel. 2012. (Immortals Ser.: 4). (ENG.). 336p. (YA). (gr. 7-12). pap. 15.00 *(978-0-312-58375-0(3),* 900075111, St. Martin's Griffin) St. Martin's Pr.
Nojima, Kazushige. Final Fantasy VII: on the Way to a Smile. 2018. (ENG., Illus.). 204p. (YA). (gr. 8-17). pap. 14.00 *(978-1-9753-8235-3(8),* 9781975382353, Yen Pr.) Yen Pr. LLC.
Nolan, Lucy A. A Fairy in a Dairy. 0 vols. Bryant, Laura J., illus. 2013. (ENG.). 33p. (J). (gr. -1-2). pap. 9.99 *(978-1-4778-1678-3(X),* 9781477816783, Two Lions) Amazon Publishing.
Noland, Charles. The Adventures of Drew & Ellie: The Daring Rescue. Moyer, Tom, illus. 2nd ed. 2006. 92p. (J). per. 7.95 *(978-0-9789297-2-5(1))* TMD Enterprises.
Norris, Christine. The Ankh of Isis. 2017. (Library of Athena Ser.: bk.2). (J). pap. *(978-1-61271-332-8(7))* Zumaya Pubns. LLC.
—The Crown of Zeus. 2017. (Library of Athena Ser.: bk.1). 241p. (J). pap. *(978-1-61271-335-9(1))* Zumaya Pubns. LLC.
—The Sword of Danu. 2012. (Library of Athena Ser.: bk.4). (J). 268p. (gr. 3-7). pap. 14.99 *(978-1-61271-095-2(6)); (978-1-61271-097-6(2)); (978-1-61271-096-9(4))* Zumaya Pubns. LLC.
—Talisman of Zandria, 1. Nagy, Robert, illus. 2005. 187p. (YA). pap. 14.95 *(978-1-885093-44-8(6),* LBF/Hadrosaur) Hadrosaur Pr.
—The Talisman of Zandria. 2013. 240p. pap. 14.99 *(978-1-61271-220-8(7))* Zumaya Pubns. LLC.
North, Laura. The Boy with the Pudding Touch. Chapman, Neil, illus. 2014. (Race Ahead with Reading Ser.). (ENG.). 32p. (J). pap. *(978-0-7787-1364-7(4))* Crabtree Publishing Co.
Northrop, Michael. Amulet Keepers (TombQuest, Book 2) 2015. (TombQuest Ser.: 2). (ENG., Illus.). 192p. (J). (gr. 3-7). 12.99 *(978-0-545-72339-8(6),* Scholastic Pr.) Scholastic, Inc.
—Book of the Dead. 2015. (TombQuest Ser.: Bk. 1). (J). 197p. *(978-1-76015-315-1(X));* 208p. pap. *(978-1-74362-924-6(9))* Scholastic, Inc.
—Book of the Dead (TombQuest, Book 1) 2015. (TombQuest Ser.: 1). (ENG.). 208p. (J). (gr. 3-7). 12.99 *(978-0-545-72338-1(8),* Scholastic Pr.) Scholastic, Inc.
—The Final Kingdom (TombQuest, Book 5) 2016. (TombQuest Ser.: 5). (ENG.). 192p. (J). (gr. 3-7). 16.99 *(978-0-545-87111-2(5),* Scholastic Pr.) Scholastic, Inc.
—The Stone Warriors (TombQuest, Book 4) 2015. (TombQuest Ser.: 4). (ENG.). 192p. (J). (gr. 3-7). 12.99 *(978-0-545-72341-1(8),* Scholastic Pr.) Scholastic, Inc.
—Valley of Kings (TombQuest, Book 3) 2015. (TombQuest Ser.: 3). (ENG.). 192p. (J). (gr. 3-7). 12.99 *(978-0-545-72340-4(X),* Scholastic Pr.) Scholastic, Inc.
Norton, Tamra. Shayla Witherwood: A Half-Faerie Tale. 2012. pap. 16.99 *(978-1-59955-963-6(3))* Cedar Fort, Inc./CFI Distribution.
Novel Units. Harry Potter & the Prisoner of Azkaban Novel Units Student Packet. 2019. (Harry Potter Ser.: Year 3). (ENG.). (J). pap., stu. ed. 13.99 *(978-1-58130-657-6(1),* Novel Units, Inc.) Classroom Library Co.
—Harry Potter & the Prisoner of Azkaban Novel Units Teacher Guide. 2019. (Harry Potter Ser.: Year 3). (ENG.). (J). pap., tchr. ed. 12.99 *(978-1-58130-656-9(3),* Novel Units, Inc.) Classroom Library Co.
—The Indian in the Cupboard Novel Units Student Packet. 2019. (Indian in the Cupboard Ser.: No. 1). (ENG.). (J). (gr. 4-7). pap. 13.99 *(978-1-56137-693-3(0),* NU6930SP, Novel Units, Inc.) Classroom Library Co.
—The Indian in the Cupboard Novel Units Teacher Guide. 2019. (Indian in the Cupboard Ser.: No. 1). (ENG.). (J). (gr. 4-7). pap. 12.99 *(978-1-56137-225-6(0),* Novel Units, Inc.) Classroom Library Co.
Nowicki, Colin J. Lamia High: Moon of Destiny, 1 vol. 2010. 186p. pap. 24.95 *(978-1-4512-8561-1(2))* America Star Bks.
Noyes, Deborah, ed. Sideshow: Ten Original Tales of Freaks, Illusionists & Other Matters Odd & Magical. 2009. (ENG., Illus.). 240p. (YA). (gr. 9-18). 16.99 *(978-0-7636-3752-1(1))* Candlewick Pr.
Nugent, Cynthia. Francesca & the Magic Bike. 2005. 4p. (J). pap., tchr. ed. *(978-1-55192-825-8(6))* Raincoast Bk. Distribution CAN. Dist: Publishers Group West (PGW).
Nuno, Fran. The Great Magician of the World. Brokenbrow, Jon, tr. Quevedo, Enrique, illus. 2012. (ENG.). 24p. (J). (gr. k-3). 14.95 *(978-84-15241-11-9(9))* Cuento de Luz SL ESP. Dist: Publishers Group West (PGW).
Nye, Barry. Hannah & the Magic Blanket - Land of the Dinosaurs. 2008. (ENG.). 40p. pap. 18.50 *(978-0-557-03682-0(8))* Lulu Pr., Inc.
Oakes, Colleen. Queen of Hearts. 2016. (Queen of Hearts Ser.: 1). (ENG.). 320p. (YA). (gr. 8). 17.99 *(978-0-06-240972-0(7),* HarperTeen) HarperCollins Pubs.
Oakes, Cory Putman. Witchtown. 2017. (ENG.). 320p. (YA). (gr. 7). 17.99 *(978-0-544-76557-3(5),* 1635515, Clarion Bks.) HarperCollins Pubs.
O'Brien, Joe. Alfie Green & the Bee-Bottle Gang. Texier, Jean, illus. 2nd rev. ed. 2007. (Alfie Green Ser.). (ENG.). 80p. (J). pap. 13.00 *(978-1-84717-054-5(4))* O'Brien Pr., Ltd., The IRL. Dist: Dufour Editions, Inc.
—Alfie Green & the Conker King. Texier, Jean, illus. 2012. (Alfie Green Ser.). (ENG.). 80p. (J). pap. 13.00 *(978-1-84717-283-9(0))* O'Brien Pr., Ltd., The IRL. Dist: Dufour Editions, Inc.
O'Callaghan, G. Sorcerers Apprentice. 2007. 244p. per. *(978-1-84693-024-9(3))* Best Global Publishing Ltd.
—Tektite. 2007. 144p. per. *(978-1-84693-025-6(1))* Best Global Publishing Ltd.
Ocasio, David. The Magical Reindeer. Carmi, Giora, illus. 2004. (ENG.). 32p. per. 14.99 *(978-1-4134-2896-4(7))* Xlibris Corp.
Ochse, Bobbie Colliton. Nana's Magic Closet. 2010. 40p. pap. 16.99 *(978-1-4520-7663-8(4))* AuthorHouse.
O'Connor, Jane. Fancy Nancy: Jojo & the Magic Trick. Glasser, Robin Preiss, illus. 2017. (My First I Can Read Ser.). (ENG.). 32p. (J). (gr. -1-3). pap. 5.99 *(978-0-06-237795-1(7),* HarperCollins) HarperCollins Pubs.
—JoJo & the Magic Trick. 2017. (Fancy Nancy - I Can Read! Ser.). (J). lib. bdg. 13.55 *(978-0-606-39638-7(1))* Turtleback.
O'Dell, Kathleen. The Aviary. 2012. (ENG.). 352p. (J). (gr. 3-7). 7.99 *(978-0-375-85226-8(3)* Yearling) Random Hse. Children's Bks.
Ogilvy, Ian. Measle & the Dragodon. 2006. 344p. (J). (gr. 3-8). per. 6.99 *(978-0-06-058690-4(7),* Harper Trophy) HarperCollins Pubs.
Oginga, Effua. Morgan Erika Pearl. 2012. 20p. pap. 16.20 *(978-1-4670-4194-2(7))* AuthorHouse.
Okorafor, Nnedi. Akata Warrior. 2018. (Nsibidi Scripts Ser.: 2). (ENG.). 512p. (YA). (gr. 7). pap. 12.99 *(978-0-14-242585-5(0),* Speak) Penguin Young Readers Group.
—Akata Witch. (Nsibidi Scripts Ser.: 1). (ENG.). (YA). (gr. 7). 2017. 384p. pap. 11.99 *(978-0-14-242091-1(3),* Speak) 2011. 368p. 18.99 *(978-0-670-01196-4(7),* Viking Books for Young Readers) Penguin Young Readers Group.
—Akata Witch. 2017. (Akata Witch Ser.: 1). lib. bdg. 22.10 *(978-0-606-40101-2(6))* Turtleback.
—Akata Woman. 2022. (Nsibidi Scripts Ser.: 3). (Illus.). 416p. (J). (gr. 7). 18.99 *(978-0-451-48058-3(9),* Viking Books for Young Readers) Penguin Young Readers Group.
—Ikenga. 2020. 240p. (J). (gr. 5). 16.99 *(978-0-593-11352-3(7),* Viking Books for Young Readers) Penguin Young Readers Group.
Oladokun, Alexander. Acrux Manor: The Prodigal's Curse (Hardcover) 2013. (ENG.). 204p. 28.50 *(978-1-300-68651-4(0))* Lulu Pr., Inc.
Older, Daniel José. Shadowhouse Fall (the Shadowshaper Cypher, Book 2) 2017. (Shadowshaper Cypher Ser.: 2). (ENG., Illus.). 368p. (YA). (gr. 9-9). 18.99 *(978-0-545-95282-8(4),* Levine, Arthur A. Bks.) Scholastic, Inc.
—Shadowshaper (the Shadowshaper Cypher, Book 1) 2016. (Shadowshaper Cypher Ser.: 1). (ENG.). 320p. (YA). (gr. 9-9). pap. 12.99 *(978-1-338-03247-5(X))* Scholastic, Inc.
Olding, Lori. The Origami Nun. 2012. 80p. pap. *(978-1-908505-74-3(5))* Vamptasy Publishing.
Oliver, Lauren. Liesl & Po. Acedera, Kei, illus. 2012. (ENG.). 336p. (J). (gr. 3-7). pap. 7.99 *(978-0-06-201452-8(8),* HarperCollins) HarperCollins Pubs.
—Liesl & Po. 2012. (J). lib. bdg. 17.20 *(978-0-606-26853-0(7))* Turtleback.
Ollweiler, Angela Messina. The Strange Wish. Ollweiler, D. R., illus. 2010. 112p. pap. 10.95 *(978-1-60844-274-4(8))* Dog Ear Publishing, LLC.
Olmstead, Kathleen. The Sorcerer's Apprentice. Olafsdottir, Linda, illus. 2015. (J). *(978-1-4027-8350-0(7))* Sterling Publishing Co., Inc.
Olsen, Erik. Garden of the Lost Souls. 2012. (J). *(978-1-4621-1010-0(X))* Cedar Fort, Inc./CFI Distribution.
Olsen, J. J. The Mystic Kingdom: A Jenny Dewberry Series. 2008. 400p. pap. 17.99 *(978-1-4389-2598-1(0))* AuthorHouse.
O'Neill, Richard & Quarmby, Katharine. Yokki & the Parno Gry. Nelissen, Marieke, illus. 2017. (Travellers Tales Ser.). (ENG.). 32p. (J). *(978-1-84643-927-8(2))* Child's Play International Ltd.
Onyebuchi, Tochi. Crown of Thunder. 320p. 2019. (ENG.). (YA). (gr. 7). pap. 9.99 *(978-0-448-49394-7(2))* 2018. (J). *(978-0-451-48131-3(3))* 2018. (YA). (gr. 7). 17.99 *(978-0-448-49393-0(4),* Penguin Young Readers Group. (Razorbill).
Oracle of the Horses. 2005. (YA). per. *(978-0-615-12836-8(X))* Miller, Don G.
O'Reilly, Avril. A Fairy in the Family. 2009. 32p. pap. 22.50 *(978-1-4092-8061-3(6))* Lulu Pr., Inc.
Ormondroyd, Edward. Time at the Top & All in Good Time: Two Novels. Ericksen, Barb et al, illus. 2011. (ENG.). 379p. (J). (gr. 4-7). pap. 12.95 *(978-1-930900-55-4(4))* Purple Hse. Pr.
Ormsbee, K. E. The Doorway & the Deep. 2016. (Water & the Wild Ser.: 2). (ENG., Illus.). 480p. (J). (gr. 3-7). 16.99 *(978-1-4521-3636-3(X))* Chronicle Bks. LLC.
—The Water & the Wild. Mora, Elsa, illus. 2015. (Water & the Wild Ser.). (ENG.). 448p. (J). (gr. 3-7). 16.99 *(978-1-4521-1386-9(6))* Chronicle Bks. LLC.
Orsi, Tea. Tinker Bell & the Legend of the NeverBeast. 2015. (Disney Fairies Graphic Novels Ser.: 17). (J). lib. bdg. 18.40 *(978-0-606-37295-4(4))* Turtleback.
Ortega, Claribel A. The Golden Frog Games (Witchlings 2) 2023. (Witchlings Ser.). (ENG.). 384p. (J). (gr. 3-7). 17.99 *(978-1-338-74579-5(4),* Scholastic Pr.) Scholastic, Inc.
Ortiz, Andrea. Snowflakes in June. Ortega, James, illus. 2013. 36p. 14.00 *(978-0-9884237-9-4(0))* CLF Publishing.
Osborne, Mary A. Nonna's Book of Mysteries. 2010. (ENG., Illus.). 352p. (gr. 8-17). pap. 16.95 *(978-1-936181-16-2(9))* Lake Street Pr.
Osborne, Mary Pope. Abe Lincoln at Last! Murdocca, Sal, illus. 2013. (Magic Tree House (R) Merlin Mission Ser.: 19). 144p. (J). (gr. 2-5). 6.99 *(978-0-375-86797-2(X),* Random Hse. Bks. for Young Readers) Random Hse. Children's Bks.
—Abe Lincoln at Last! 2013. (Magic Tree House Merlin Missions Ser.: 19). lib. bdg. 16.00 *(978-0-606-35563-6(4))* Turtleback.
—Barcos Vikingos Al Amanecer. Brovelli, Marcela, tr. from ENG. Murdocca, Sal, illus. 2007. (Casa del Arbol Ser.: 15). (SPA.). 73p. (J). per. 6.99 *(978-1-933032-21-4(9))* Lectorum Pubns., Inc.
—A Big Day for Baseball. Ford, A. G., illus. 2017. (Magic Tree House (R) Ser.: 29). (J). (gr. 1-4). 80p. 13.99 *(978-1-5247-1308-9(2));* (ENG.). 96p. lib. bdg. 16.99 *(978-1-5247-1309-6(0))* Random Hse. Children's Bks. (Random Hse. Bks. for Young Readers).
—Blizzard of the Blue Moon. Murdocca, Sal, illus. 2007. (Magic Tree House (R) Merlin Mission Ser.: 8). 144p. (J). (gr. 2-5). 5.99 *(978-0-375-83038-9(3),* Random Hse. Bks. for Young Readers) Random Hse. Children's Bks.
—Buffalo Before Breakfast. 2004. (Magic Tree House Ser.: No. 18). 72p. (J). (gr. k-3). pap. 17.00 incl. audio *(978-0-8072-0927-1(9),* Listening Library) Random Hse. Audio Publishing Group.
—Carnival at Candlelight, Vol. 5. Murdocca, Sal, illus. 2006. (Magic Tree House (R) Merlin Mission Ser.: 5). 144p. (J). (gr. 2-5). 6.99 *(978-0-375-83034-1(0),* Random Hse. Bks. for Young Readers) Random Hse. Children's Bks.
—Christmas in Camelot. Murdocca, Sal, illus. 2009. (Magic Tree House (R) Merlin Mission Ser.: 1). 144p. (J). (gr. 2-5). 6.99 *(978-0-375-85812-3(1),* Random Hse. Bks. for Young Readers) Random Hse. Children's Bks.
—Christmas in Camelot. 2009. (Magic Tree House Merlin Missions Ser.: 1). lib. bdg. 16.00 *(978-0-606-06386-9(2))* Turtleback.
—Civil War on Sunday. unabr. ed. 2004. (Magic Tree House Ser.: No. 21). 76p. (J). (gr. k-3). pap. 17.00 incl. audio *(978-0-8072-0930-1(9),* S FTR 253 SP, Listening Library) Random Hse. Audio Publishing Group.
—A Crazy Day with Cobras. Murdocca, Sal, illus. 2012. (Magic Tree House (R) Merlin Mission Ser.: 17). 144p. (J). (gr. 2-5). 5.99 *(978-0-375-86795-8(3),* Random Hse. Bks. for Young Readers) Random Hse. Children's Bks.
—A Crazy Day with Cobras. 2012. (Magic Tree House Merlin Missions Ser.: 17). lib. bdg. 16.00 *(978-0-606-26997-1(5))* Turtleback.
—Dark Day in the Deep Sea. Murdocca, Sal, illus. 2009. (Magic Tree House (R) Merlin Mission Ser.: 11). 144p. (J). (gr. 2-5). 6.99 *(978-0-375-83732-6(9),* Random Hse. Bks. for Young Readers) Random Hse. Children's Bks.
—Dark Day in the Deep Sea. 2009. (Magic Tree House Merlin Missions Ser.: 11). lib. bdg. 16.00 *(978-0-606-01778-7(X))* Turtleback.
—Das magische Baumhaus 09. Der Ruf der Delfine. 18.95 *(978-3-7855-4185-2(6))* Loewe Verlag GmbH DEU. Dist: Distribooks, Inc.
—Day of the Dragon King. unabr. ed. 2004. (Magic Tree House Ser.: No. 14). 68p. (J). (gr. k-3). pap. 17.00 incl. audio *(978-0-8072-0783-3(7),* S FTR 242 SP, Listening Library) Random Hse. Audio Publishing Group.
—Dinosaurs Before Dark. unabr. ed. 2004. (Magic Tree House Ser.: No. 1). 68p. (J). (gr. k-5). pap. 17.00 incl. audio *(978-0-8072-0330-9(0),* FTR208SP, Listening Library) Random Hse. Audio Publishing Group.
—Dogs in the Dead of Night, Bk. 18. Murdocca, Sal, illus. 2013. (Magic Tree House (R) Merlin Mission Ser.: 18). 144p. (J). (gr. 2-5). 6.99 *(978-0-375-86796-5(1),* Random Hse. Bks. for Young Readers) Random Hse. Children's Bks.
—Dogs in the Dead of Night. 2013. (Magic Tree House Merlin Missions Ser.: 18). lib. bdg. 16.00 *(978-0-606-31939-3(5))* Turtleback.
—Dragon of the Red Dawn. Murdocca, Sal, illus. 2008. (Magic Tree House (R) Merlin Mission Ser.: 9). 144p. (J). (gr. 2-5). 6.99 *(978-0-375-83728-9(0),* Random Hse. Bks. for Young Readers) Random Hse. Children's Bks.
—Earthquake in the Early Morning. unabr. ed. 2004. (Magic Tree House Ser.: No. 24). 71p. (J). (gr. k-3). pap. 17.00 incl. audio *(978-0-8072-0933-2(3),* S FTR 256 SP, Listening Library) Random Hse. Audio Publishing Group.
—Eve of the Emperor Penguin. Murdocca, Sal, illus. 2009. (Magic Tree House (R) Merlin Mission Ser.: 12). (ENG.). 144p. (J). (gr. 2-5). 6.99 *(978-0-375-83734-0(5),* Random Hse. Bks. for Young Readers) Random Hse. Children's Bks.
—A Ghost Tale for Christmas Time. Murdocca, Sal, illus. 2012. (Magic Tree House (R) Merlin Mission Ser.: 16). 144p. (J). (gr. 2-5). pap. 6.99 *(978-0-375-85653-2(6),* Random Hse. Bks. for Young Readers) Random Hse. Children's Bks.
—A Ghost Tale for Christmas Time. 2012. (Magic Tree House Merlin Missions Ser.: 16). lib. bdg. 16.00 *(978-0-606-26808-0(1))* Turtleback.
—Ghost Town at Sundown. unabr. ed. 2004. (Magic Tree House Ser.: No. 10). 73p. (J). (gr. k-3). pap. 17.00 incl. audio *(978-0-8072-0535-8(4),* Listening Library) Random Hse. Audio Publishing Group.
—A Good Night for Ghosts. 2010. (Magic Tree House Merlin Missions Ser.: No. 14). (Illus.). 157p. (J). pap. *(978-4-8401-3411-8(1))* Fukuinkan Shoten.
—A Good Night for Ghosts. Murdocca, Sal, illus. 2011. (Magic Tree House (R) Merlin Mission Ser.: 14). 144p. (J). (gr. 2-5). 5.99 *(978-0-375-85649-5(8),* Random Hse. Bks. for Young Readers) Random Hse. Children's Bks.
—Haunted Castle on Hallows Eve. Murdocca, Sal, illus. 2010. (Magic Tree House (R) Merlin Mission Ser.: 2). 144p. (J). (gr. 2-5). pap. 5.99 *(978-0-375-86090-4(8),* Random Hse. Bks. for Young Readers) Random Hse. Children's Bks.
—Haunted Castle on Hallows Eve. 2010. (Magic Tree House Merlin Missions Ser.: 2). lib. bdg. 16.00 *(978-0-606-13992-2(3))* Turtleback.
—High Tide in Hawaii. Murdocca, Sal, illus. 2003. (Magic Tree House (R) Ser.: 28). 96p. (J). (gr. 1-4). pap. 6.99 *(978-0-375-80616-2(4),* Random Hse. Bks. for Young Readers) Random Hse. Children's Bks.
—High Tide in Hawaii. 2003. (Magic Tree House Ser.: 28). (gr. k-3). lib. bdg. 16.00 *(978-0-613-62386-5(X))* Turtleback.
—La Hora de Los Juegos Olimpicos. Brovelli, Marcela, tr. Murdocca, Sal, illus. 2007. (Casa del Arbol Ser.: 16).Tr. of Hour of the Olympics Games. (ENG & SPA.). 68p. (J). per. 6.99 *(978-1-933032-22-1(7))* Lectorum Pubns., Inc.
—Hour of the Olympics. unabr. ed. 2004. (Magic Tree House Ser.: No. 16). 70p. (J). (gr. k-3). pap. 17.00 incl. audio *(978-0-8072-0785-7(3),* LFTR 244 SP, Listening Library) Random Hse. Audio Publishing Group.
—Hurricane Heroes in Texas. Ford, A. G., illus. 2018. (Magic Tree House (R) Ser.: 30). 112p. (J). (gr. 1-4). 13.99 *(978-1-5247-1312-6(0),* Random Hse. Bks. for Young Readers) Random Hse. Children's Bks.
—El Invierno Del Hechicero Del Hielo. 2015. (Casa De árbol Ser.: 32). (SPA., Illus.). 144p. (J). (gr. 2-4). pap. 6.99 *(978-1-63245-535-2(8))* Lectorum Pubns., Inc.
—The Knight at Dawn. unabr. ed. 2004. (Magic Tree House Ser.: No. 2). 66p. (J). (gr. k-3). pap. 17.00 incl. audio *(978-0-8072-0331-6(9),* Listening Library) Random Hse. Audio Publishing Group.
—Leprechaun in Late Winter. Murdocca, Sal, illus. 2012. (Magic Tree House (R) Merlin Mission Ser.: 15). 144p. (J). (gr. 2-5). 6.99 *(978-0-375-85651-8(X),* Random Hse. Bks. for Young Readers) Random Hse. Children's Bks.
—Leprechaun in Late Winter. 2012. (Magic Tree House Merlin Missions Ser.: 15). lib. bdg. 16.00 *(978-0-606-23860-1(3))* Turtleback.
—Magic Tree House Books 17-20 Boxed Set: The Mystery of the Enchanted Dog, 4 vols., Bks. 17-20. Murdocca, Sal, illus. 2009. (Magic Tree House (R) Ser.). 96p. (J). (gr. 1-4). 27.96 *(978-0-375-85811-6(3),* Random Hse. Bks. for Young Readers) Random Hse. Children's Bks.
—Midnight on the Moon. unabr. ed. 2004. (Magic Tree House Ser.: No. 8). 70p. (J). (gr. k-3). pap. 17.00 incl. audio *(978-0-8072-0341-5(6),* Listening Library) Random Hse. Audio Publishing Group.
—Una Momia Al Amanecer. 2004. (Casa del Arbol Ser.: 3). (SPA.). (J). pap. 6.99 *(978-1-930332-51-5(3))* Lectorum Pubns., Inc.
—Una Momia en la Manana. 2003. (Magic Tree House Ser.: 3). (SPA.). (gr. 3-6). lib. bdg. 16.00 *(978-0-613-64609-3(6))* Turtleback.
—Monday with a Mad Genius. Murdocca, Sal, illus. 2009. (Magic Tree House (R) Merlin Mission Ser.: 10). 144p. (J). (gr. 2-5). 5.99 *(978-0-375-83730-2(2),* Random Hse. Bks. for Young Readers) Random Hse. Children's Bks.
—Monday with a Mad Genius. 2009. (Magic Tree House Merlin Missions Ser.: 10). lib. bdg. 16.00 *(978-0-606-01777-0(1))* Turtleback.
—Moonlight on the Magic Flute, Bk. 13. Murdocca, Sal, illus. 2010. (Magic Tree House (R) Merlin Mission Ser.: 13). 144p. (J). (gr. 2-5). pap. 5.99 *(978-0-375-85647-1(1),* Random Hse. Bks. for Young Readers) Random Hse. Children's Bks.
—Navidad en Camelot. 2015. (Casa De árbol Ser.: 29). (SPA., Illus.). 144p. (J). (gr. 2-4). pap. 6.99 *(978-1-63245-532-1(3))* Lectorum Pubns., Inc.
—Night of the New Magicians. 2007. (Magic Tree House Merlin Missions Ser.: 7). lib. bdg. 16.00 *(978-1-4177-9108-8(X))* Turtleback.
—Night of the Ninth Dragon. Murdocca, Sal, illus. (Magic Tree House (R) Merlin Mission Ser.: 27). 144p. (J). (gr. 2-5). 2018. 6.99 *(978-0-553-51092-8(4))* 2016. 13.99 *(978-0-553-51089-8(4))* Random Hse. Children's Bks. (Random Hse. Bks. for Young Readers).
—La Noche de Los Ninjas. 2004. (Casa del Arbol Ser.: 5).Tr. of Night of the Ninjas. (SPA., Illus.). (J). pap. 6.99 *(978-1-930332-66-9(1))* Lectorum Pubns., Inc.
—Osos Polares Despues de la Medianoche. 2005. (Casa del Arbol Ser.: 12).Tr. of Polar Bears Past Bedtime. (SPA., Illus.). 71p. (J). pap. 6.99 *(978-1-930332-99-7(8))* Lectorum Pubns., Inc.
—A Perfect Time for Pandas, Bk. 20. Murdocca, Sal, illus. 2014. (Magic Tree House (R) Merlin Mission Ser.: 20). (ENG.). 144p. (J). (gr. 2-5). pap. 6.99 *(978-0-375-86798-9(8),* Random Hse. Bks. for Young Readers) Random Hse. Children's Bks.
—A Perfect Time for Pandas. 2014. (Magic Tree House Merlin Missions Ser.: 20). lib. bdg. 16.00 *(978-0-606-35564-3(2))* Turtleback.
—Revolutionary War on Wednesday. unabr. ed. 2004. (Magic Tree House Ser.: No. 22). 69p. (J). (gr. k-3). pap. 17.00 incl. audio *(978-0-8072-0931-8(7),* S FTR 254 SP, Listening Library) Random Hse. Audio Publishing Group.
—Season of the Sandstorms. 2014. (Magic Tree House Merlin Missions Ser.: No. 6). 15.00 *(978-1-63419-681-9(3))* Perfection Learning Corp.
—Season of the Sandstorms, Bk. 6. Murdocca, Sal, illus. 2006. (Magic Tree House (R) Merlin Mission Ser.: 6). 144p. (J). (gr. 2-5). 6.99 *(978-0-375-83032-7(4),* Random Hse. Bks. for Young Readers) Random Hse. Children's Bks.
—Shadow of the Shark. Murdocca, Sal, illus. 2017. (Magic Tree House (R) Merlin Mission Ser.: 25). 144p. (J). (gr. 2-5). 5.99 *(978-0-553-51084-3(3),* Random Hse. Bks. for Young Readers) Random Hse. Children's Bks.
—Soccer on Sunday. Murdocca, Sal, illus. 2016. (Magic Tree House (R) Merlin Mission Ser.: 24). 144p. (J). (gr. 2-5). 6.99 *(978-0-307-98056-4(1),* Random Hse. Bks. for Young Readers) Random Hse. Children's Bks.
—Stallion by Starlight. Murdocca, Sal, illus. 2014. (Magic Tree House (R) Merlin Mission Ser.: 21). 144p. (J). (gr. 2-5). pap. 5.99 *(978-0-307-98044-1(8),* Random Hse. Bks. for Young Readers) Random Hse. Children's Bks.
—Stallion by Starlight. 2014. (Magic Tree House Merlin Missions Ser.: 21). lib. bdg. 16.00 *(978-0-606-36411-9(0))* Turtleback.
—Summer of the Sea Serpent, Bk. 3. Murdocca, Sal, illus. 2011. (Magic Tree House (R) Merlin Mission Ser.: 3). 144p. (J). (gr. 2-5). 6.99 *(978-0-375-86491-9(1),* Random Hse. Bks. for Young Readers) Random Hse. Children's Bks.

—Una Tarde en el Amazonas. 2004. (Casa del Arbol Ser.: 6).Tr. of Afternoon on the Amazon. (SPA., Illus.). 66p. (J). pap. 6.99 *(978-1-930332-67-6(X))* Lectorum Pubns., Inc.
—Tigers at Twilight. unabr. ed. 2004. (Magic Tree House Ser.: No. 19). 72p. (J). (gr. k-3). pap. 17.00 incl. audio *(978-0-8072-0928-8(7),* S FTR 251 SP, Listening Library) Random Hse. Audio Publishing Group.
—Un Tigre Dientes de Sable en el Ocaso. 2004. (Casa del Arbol Ser.: 7).Tr. of Sunset of the Sabretooth. (SPA., Illus.). (J). pap. 6.99 *(978-1-930332-68-3(8))* Lectorum Pubns., Inc.
—To the Future, Ben Franklin! Ford, A. G., illus. 2019. (Magic Tree House (R) Ser.: 32). (J). (gr. 1-4). 96p. 13.99 *(978-0-525-64832-1(1));* (ENG.). 112p. lib. bdg. 16.99 *(978-0-525-64833-8(X))* Random Hse. Children's Bks. (Random Hse. Bks. for Young Readers).
—Tonight on the Titanic. unabr. ed. 2004. (Magic Tree House Ser.: No. 17). 71p. (J). (gr. k-3). pap. 17.00 incl. audio *(978-0-8072-0926-4(0),* S FTR 249 SP, Listening Library) Random Hse. Audio Publishing Group.
—Twister on Tuesday. 2004. (Magic Tree House Ser.: No. 23). 70p. (J). (gr. k-3). pap. 17.00 incl. audio *(978-0-8072-9932-6(4),* Listening Library) Random Hse. Audio Publishing Group.
—El Verano de la Serpiente Marina. 2015. (Casa De árbol Ser.: 31). (SPA., Illus.). 144p. (J). (gr. 2-4). pap. 6.99 *(978-1-63245-534-5(X))* Lectorum Pubns., Inc.
—Viking Ships at Sunrise. unabr. ed. 2004. (Magic Tree House Ser.: No. 15). 71p. (J). (gr. k-3). pap. 17.00 incl. audio *(978-0-8072-0784-0(5),* LFTR 243 SP, Listening Library) Random Hse. Audio Publishing Group.
—Winter of the Ice Wizard. Murdocca, Sal, illus. 2011. (Magic Tree House (R) Merlin Mission Ser.: 4). 144p. (J). (gr. 2-5). 6.99 *(978-0-375-87395-9(3),* Random Hse. Bks. for Young Readers) Random Hse. Children's Bks.
Osborne, Mary Pope & Murdocca, Sal. Esta Noche en el Titanic. Murdocca, Sal, illus. 2008. (Casa del Arbol Ser.: 17).Tr. of Tonight on the Titanic. (SPA., Illus.). (J). (gr. 2-4). pap. 6.99 *(978-1-933032-47-4(2))* Lectorum Pubns., Inc.
Osborne, Mary Pope & PLC Editors Staff. Carnival at Candlelight. Murdocca, Sal, illus. 2006. (Magic Tree House Merlin Missions Ser.: No. 5). 105p. (gr. 2-6). 15.00 *(978-0-7569-6690-4(6))* Perfection Learning Corp.
Osborne, Mary Pope, et al. Buenos Días, Gorilas. Murdocca, Sal, illus. 2014. (SPA.). 88p. (J). (gr. 2-4). pap. 6.99 *(978-1-933032-93-1(6))* Lectorum Pubns., Inc.
—Búfalos Antes Del Desayuno. Murdocca, Sal, illus. 2008. (Casa del Arbol Ser.: 18).Tr. of Buffalo Before Breakfast. (SPA.). (J). (gr. 2-4). pap. 6.99 *(978-1-933032-48-1(0))* Lectorum Pubns., Inc.
—Carnaval a Media Luz. Murdocca, Sal, illus. 2016. (SPA.). 113p. (J). (gr. 2-4). pap. 6.99 *(978-1-63245-643-4(5))* Lectorum Pubns., Inc.
—Día Negro en el Fondo Del Mar. Murdocca, Sal, illus. 2018. (SPA.). 118p. (J). (gr. 2-4). pap. 6.99 *(978-1-63245-682-3(6))* Lectorum Pubns., Inc.
—La Estación de Las Tormentas de Arena. Murdocca, Sal, illus. 2016. (SPA.). 107p. (J). (gr. 2-4). pap. 5.99 *(978-1-63245-644-1(3))* Lectorum Pubns., Inc.
—The Fun Starts Here! Four Favorite Chapter Books in One: Junie B. Jones, Magic Tree House, Purrmaids, & a to Z Mysteries. Murdocca, Sal, illus. 2018. (ENG.). 336p. (J). (gr. 1-4). 9.99 *(978-1-9848-3059-3(7),* Random Hse. Bks. for Young Readers) Random Hse. Children's Bks.
—Maremoto en Hawái. Murdocca, Sal, illus. 2014. (SPA.). 88p. (J). (gr. 2-4). pap. 6.99 *(978-1-933032-95-5(2))* Lectorum Pubns., Inc.
—Miedo Escénico en una Noche de Verano. Murdocca, Sal, illus. 2014. (SPA.). 86p. (J). (gr. 2-4). pap. 6.99 *(978-1-933032-92-4(8))* Lectorum Pubns., Inc.
—La Noche de Los Nuevos Magos. Murdocca, Sal, illus. 2016. (SPA.). 111p. (J). (gr. 2-4). pap. 6.99 *(978-1-63245-645-8(1))* Lectorum Pubns., Inc.
—Perros Salvajes a la Hora de la Cena. Murdocca, Sal, illus. 2008. (Casa del Arbol Ser.: 20).Tr. of Dingoes at Dinnertime. (SPA.). (J). (gr. 2-4). pap. 6.99 *(978-1-933032-50-4(2))* Lectorum Pubns., Inc.
—El Regalo Del Pingüino Emperador. Murdocca, Sal, illus. 2018. (SPA.). 118p. (J). (gr. 2-4). pap. 6.99 *(978-1-63245-683-0(4))* Lectorum Pubns., Inc.
—Tigres Al Anochecer. Murdocca, Sal, illus. 2008. (Casa del Arbol Ser.: 19).Tr. of Tigers at Twilight. (SPA.). (J). (gr. 2-4). pap. 8.99 *(978-1-933032-49-8(9))* Lectorum Pubns., Inc.
—Tormenta de Nieve en Luna Azul. Murdocca, Sal, illus. 2016. (SPA.). (J). (gr. 2-4). pap. 6.99 *(978-1-63245-646-5(X))* Lectorum Pubns., Inc.
O'Sullivan, Helen. The Magic Piano. Busuttil, Conor, illus. 2013. 34p. pap. *(978-1-908773-36-4(7))* Iponymous Publishing, Ltd.
Ott, Alexandra. Rules for Thieves. 2017. (Rules for Thieves Ser.: 1). (ENG., Illus.). 320p. (J). (gr. 3-7). 17.99 *(978-1-4814-7274-6(7),* Aladdin) Simon & Schuster Children's Publishing.
—Rules for Thieves. 2018. (Rules for Thieves Ser.: 1). (ENG.). 336p. (J). (gr. 3-7). pap. 8.99 *(978-1-4814-7275-3(5),* Simon & Schuster/Paula Wiseman Bks.) Simon & Schuster/Paula Wiseman Bks.
—The Shadow Thieves. 2018. (Rules for Thieves Ser.: 2). (ENG., Illus.). 400p. (J). (gr. 3-7). 17.99 *(978-1-4814-7277-7(1),* Aladdin) Simon & Schuster Children's Publishing.
Outram, Evelyn. Sav & Josh O Lucky's Christmas Adventure & Magic Street. 2010. 56p. pap. 17.95 *(978-1-60911-876-1(6),* Eloquent Bks.) Strategic Book Publishing & Rights Agency (SBPRA).
Ovani, Germano, illus. The Monkey King. 2007. (Young Reading Series 1 Gift Bks). 47p. (J). (gr. -1-3). 8.99 *(978-0-7945-1593-5(2),* Usborne) EDC Publishing.
Pabbaraju, S. Adventures of Andreux: Book One - Aranya. 2008. 176p. 23.95 *(978-1-4401-0075-8(6));* pap. 13.95 *(978-0-595-40964-8(4))* iUniverse, Inc.
Page, Lynda. Caley's Secret Garden. 2012. 28p. pap. 32.70 *(978-1-4771-0605-1(7))* Xlibris Corp.
Page, Nathan. The Montague Twins: the Witch's Hand: (a Graphic Novel) Shannon, Drew, illus. 2020. (Montague Twins Ser.: 1). 352p. (YA). (gr. 7). pap. 17.99 *(978-0-525-64677-8(9),* Knopf Bks. for Young Readers) Random Hse. Children's Bks.
Page, P. K. The Old Woman & the Hen. 2008. (ENG., Illus.). 32p. (J). pap. 10.95 *(978-0-88984-309-7(0))* Porcupine's Quill, Inc. CAN. Dist: Univ. of Toronto Pr.
Paige, Danielle. Stealing Snow. (Stealing Snow Ser.). (ENG.). 384p. (YA). 2018. pap. 10.99 *(978-1-68119-546-9(1),* 900177244, Bloomsbury Young Adult) 2016. (gr. 9-12). 18.99 *(978-1-68119-076-1(1),* 900158388, Bloomsbury USA Childrens) Bloomsbury Publishing USA.
—Stealing Snow (Spanish Edition) Angulo Fernández, María, tr. 2017. (SPA.). 386p. (J). (gr. 9). 18.95 *(978-84-16700-68-4(0))* Penguin Random House Grupo Editorial ESP. Dist: Penguin Random House, LLC.
—Yellow Brick War. 2016. *(978-0-06-245860-5(4));* (Dorothy Must Die Ser.: 3). (ENG.). 288p. (YA). (gr. 9-12). 18.99 *(978-0-06-228073-2(2),* HarperCollins) HarperCollins Pubs.
Panamkat, Matthew. Karan Quma & the Meluha Tree. 2007. 348p. per. 19.95 *(978-0-595-41816-9(3))* iUniverse, Inc.
Pandora. Ankh: Conquering the Seven Deadly Sins. 2013. 100p. pap. 10.95 *(978-1-62212-908-9(3),* Strategic Bk. Publishing) Strategic Book Publishing & Rights Agency (SBPRA).
Pangalos, Carol B. Gabriella & the Magic Stars. 2011. 36p. (gr. -1). pap. 15.14 *(978-1-4634-1108-4(1))* AuthorHouse.
Papademetriou, Lisa. A Tale of Highly Unusual Magic. (ENG.). (J). (gr. 3-7). 2017. 336p. pap. 6.99 *(978-0-06-237106-5(1))* 2015. 320p. 16.99 *(978-0-06-237121-8(5))* HarperCollins Pubs. (HarperCollins).
Paradise, Elizabeth. The Lost Dreamer. 2013. 192p. pap. 9.99 *(978-0-615-77563-0(2))* EJMP.
Parcus, Stephanie, illus. Jupiter Storm. gif. ltd. ed. 2017. 256p. (J). (gr. 3-6). pap. 14.99 *(978-1-943169-31-3(4))* Plum Street Press.
Park, Linda Sue. Archer's Quest. 2018. (ENG., Illus.). 176p. (J). (gr. 5-7). pap. 7.99 *(978-1-328-89575-2(0),* 1699653, Clarion Bks.) HarperCollins Pubs.
—Wing & Claw #1: Forest of Wonders. Madsen, Jim, illus. 2017. (Wing & Claw Ser.: 1). (ENG.). 352p. (J). (gr. 3-7). pap. 7.99 *(978-0-06-232739-0(9),* HarperCollins) HarperCollins Pubs.
—Wing & Claw #2: Cavern of Secrets. Madsen, Jim, illus. 2017. (Wing & Claw Ser.: 2). (ENG.). 320p. (J). (gr. 3-7). 16.99 *(978-0-06-232741-3(0),* HarperCollins) HarperCollins Pubs.
Parker, Emma. The Magic Show. 2010. (Illus.). pap. *(978-1-877561-23-8(1))* First Edition Ltd.
—The Magic Snow Globe. 2010. (Illus.). pap. *(978-1-877561-30-6(4))* First Edition Ltd.
Parker, Patti. Book of Ominook: The Journey Begins. 2012. 28p. pap. 9.95 *(978-1-936587-98-8(X))* Brighton Publishing LLC.
Parkhouse, David. Lucy's Spoons. 2004. 52p. pap. *(978-1-84401-276-3(X))* Athena Pr.
Parsons, Julie. Julianne & the Jinn, the Evil Genie. 2008. 56p. pap. 16.95 *(978-1-60703-984-6(2))* America Star Bks.
Pascoe, Sara. Being a Witch, & Other Things I Didn't Ask For. Lindsey, Alexander, ed. 2nd ed. 2017. (Historicalnovelsociety. Org/Reviews/Ratchet-The-Rel Ser.). (ENG., Illus.). 369p. (YA). (gr. 7-12). pap. *(978-0-9935747-3-4(3))* Trindles & Green, Ltd.
Pasillo, Susan. The Perfect Pumpkin. 2006. (J). lib. bdg. 20.95 *(978-1-933732-14-5(8))* Big Ransom Studio.
Paterson, Katherine & Paterson, John. The Flint Heart. Rocco, John, illus. 2018. (ENG.). 288p. (J). (gr. 2-5). pap. 7.99 *(978-1-5362-0371-4(8))* Candlewick Pr.
Patrick, Ruthven. Prisoners under Glass. 2005. (YA). per. *(978-0-9735422-2-6(5))* Scroll Pr.
Patterson, Eric. Nature Boy. Wright, Christopher, illus. 2007. 112p. (J). pap. 6.95 *(978-0-9797106-0-5(X))* Avid Readers Publishing Group.
Patterson, James. The Gift. 2010. (Witch & Wizard Ser.: No. 2). (J). 59.99 *(978-1-60941-012-4(2))* Findaway World, LLC.
—The Gift. 2014. lthr. 79.00 *(978-1-62715-523-6(6))* Leatherbound Bestsellers.
—Nevermore: The Final Maximum Ride Adventure. 2012. (Maximum Ride Ser.: 8). (ENG.). (YA). (gr. 5-17). 384p. 36.99 *(978-0-316-10184-4(2));* 448p. 30.99 *(978-0-316-20811-6(6))* Little Brown & Co. (Jimmy Patterson).
—Witch & Wizard. 2010. (Witch & Wizard Ser.: 1). (YA). lib. bdg. 20.85 *(978-0-606-15119-1(2))* Turtleback.
Patterson, James & Dembowski, Jill. The Fire. 2013. (Witch & Wizard Ser.: 3). (ENG.). 352p. (YA). (gr. 5-17). mass mkt. 8.00 *(978-1-4555-2152-4(3),* Jimmy Patterson) Little Brown & Co.
—The Fire. 2012. (Witch & Wizard Ser.: 3). (YA). lib. bdg. 20.85 *(978-0-606-26698-7(4))* Turtleback.
—The Kiss. 2013. (YA). (Witch & Wizard Ser.: 4). (ENG.). 368p. (gr. 7-17). 35.99 *(978-0-316-10191-2(5),* Jimmy Patterson); 357p. *(978-0-316-22640-0(8))* Little Brown & Co.
Patterson, James & Raymond, Emily. The Lost. (YA). 2015. (Witch & Wizard Ser.: 5). (ENG.). 384p. (gr. 7-17). pap. 10.99 *(978-0-316-20774-4(8),* Jimmy Patterson) 2014. (Witch & Wizard Ser.: 5). (ENG.). 384p. (gr. 7-17). 36.99 *(978-0-316-20770-6(5),* Jimmy Patterson) 2014. 355p. *(978-0-316-24266-0(7))* 2014. (Witch & Wizard Ser.: 5). (ENG.). 480p. (gr. 7-17). 39.99 *(978-0-316-24002-4(8),* Jimmy Patterson) Little Brown & Co.
—The Lost. 2015. (Witch & Wizard Ser.: 5). (YA). lib. bdg. 20.85 *(978-0-606-37528-3(7))* Turtleback.
Patterson, James & Rust, Ned. The Gift. (Witch & Wizard Ser.: 2). (ENG.). (gr. 5-17). 2012. 352p. mass mkt. 7.99 *(978-0-446-56245-4(9))* 2011. 400p. pap. 10.99 *(978-0-316-03835-5(0))* 2010. 352p. 17.99 *(978-0-316-03625-2(0))* Little Brown & Co. (Jimmy Patterson).
—The Gift. 2012. (Witch & Wizard Ser.: 2). lib. bdg. 18.40 *(978-0-606-26451-8(5))* Turtleback.
Patton, Chris. A Totally True Princess Story. Wellman, Mike, ed. St. Aubin, Claude, illus. 2009. 72p. 12.99 *(978-0-615-27602-1(4))* Atomic Basement.
Pau Preto, Nicki. Crown of Feathers. 2019. (Crown of Feathers Ser.). (ENG., Illus.). 496p. (YA). (gr. 7). 21.99 *(978-1-5344-2462-3(8),* Simon Pulse) Simon Pulse.
Paulk, William. The Creatures of Vision City: Pokie's Party, Book One. 2009. 48p. pap. 10.99 *(978-1-4389-5659-6(2))* AuthorHouse.
Payton, Nicole. Dragon Savior. 2007. 212p. per. 24.95 *(978-1-4241-5498-2(7))* America Star Bks.
Peachey, Ted. The Adventures of Ryan & His Magic Carrot. 2010. 90p. pap. 9.99 *(978-1-60911-222-6(9),* Eloquent Bks.) Strategic Book Publishing & Rights Agency (SBPRA).
Pearce, Jackson & Stiefvater, Maggie. Pip Bartlett's Guide to Magical Creatures (Pip Bartlett #1) Stiefvater, Maggie, illus. 2016. (Pip Bartlett Ser.: 1). (ENG.). 192p. (J). (gr. 3-7). 9.99 *(978-1-338-08815-1(7),* Scholastic Pr.) Scholastic, Inc.
Pearce, Philippa. A Finder's Magic. Craig, Helen, illus. 2009. (ENG.). 128p. (J). (gr. 2-4). 15.99 *(978-0-7636-4072-9(7))* Candlewick Pr.
—The Little Gentleman. Pohrt, Tom, illus. 2004. 208p. (J). (gr. 3-18). lib. bdg. 16.89 *(978-0-06-073161-8(3))* HarperCollins Pubs.
Pearl, Alexa. Tales of Sasha 2: Journey Beyond the Trees. Sordo, Paco, illus. 2017. (Tales of Sasha Ser.: 2). (ENG.). 112p. (J). (gr. k-3). pap. 5.99 *(978-1-4998-0391-4(5))* Little Bee Books Inc.
Pearson, Kimberly Ann. Mystling Glen Book I: The Tale of A Prince. 2009. 207p. pap. 14.95 *(978-1-4327-4169-3(1))* Outskirts Pr., Inc.
Pearson, Maggie. Rumpelstiltskin Returns. Stone, Steve, illus. 2014. (Race Ahead with Reading Ser.). (ENG.). 32p. (J). (gr. 2-2). *(978-0-7787-1332-6(6))* Crabtree Publishing Co.
Pearson, Ridley. Legacy of Secrets. 2017. (Kingdom Keepers - the Return Ser.: 2). (J). lib. bdg. 19.65 *(978-0-606-39497-0(4))* Turtleback.
—Peter & the Starcatchers-Peter & the Starcatchers, Book One. rev. ed. 2006. (Peter & the Starcatchers Ser.: 1). (ENG., Illus.). 480p. (J). (gr. 5-9). reprint ed. pap. 9.99 *(978-0-7868-4907-9(X),* Disney-Hyperion) Disney Publishing Worldwide.
Pedersen, Peggy A. Jasmine & the Magic Squirrel. 2008. 12p. pap. 24.95 *(978-1-60474-052-3(3))* America Star Bks.
Peeler, Gail. Jackson's Magic Wishing Well. 2008. 25p. 35.50 *(978-1-4357-2950-6(1))* Lulu Pr., Inc.
Peirce, Lincoln. Max & the Midknights: Battle of the Bodkins. 2020. (Max & the Midknights Ser.: 2). (ENG., Illus.). 272p. (J). (gr. 3-7). 13.99 *(978-0-593-12590-8(8));* E-Book *(978-0-593-12592-2(4))* Random Hse. Children's Bks. (Crown Books For Young Readers).
—Max & the Midknights: the Tower of Time. 2022. (Illus.). 262p. (J). *(978-0-593-37792-5(3))* Bantam Doubleday Dell Large Print Group, Inc.
—Max & the Midknights: the Tower of Time. 2022. (Max & the Midknights Ser.: 3). (Illus.). 272p. (J). (gr. 3-7). 13.99 *(978-0-593-37789-5(3),* Crown Books For Young Readers) Random Hse. Children's Bks.
Pendergrass, D. Louis. a Blue Dragon. 2009. 32p. pap. 15.00 *(978-1-4389-9036-1(7))* AuthorHouse.
Penick Phillips-Cermak, Mosetta. The Wishing Flower. 2007. 24p. 16.50 *(978-0-615-15573-9(1))* PM Moon Pub., LLC.
Pennypacker, Sara. Stuart Goes to School. Matje, Martin, illus. 2005. (ENG.). 64p. (gr. -1-3). reprint ed. pap. 5.99 *(978-0-439-30183-1(1))* Scholastic, Inc.
Pentz, Jane A. Horatio's Magical Journeys - the Secret. 2007. 108p. pap. 10.00 *(978-1-892426-11-6(0))* LMA Publishing.
Percival, Tom. The Genie's Curse. 2017. (Little Legends Ser.: 3). (ENG., Illus.). 208p. (J). (gr. 2-5). pap. 8.99 *(978-1-4926-4256-5(8),* 9781492642565, Sourcebooks Jabberwocky) Sourcebooks, Inc.
—The Magic Looking Glass. 2017. (Little Legends Ser.: 4). (ENG.). 192p. (J). (gr. 2-5). pap. 8.99 *(978-1-4926-4259-6(2),* Sourcebooks Jabberwocky) Sourcebooks, Inc.
—The Secret Mountain. 2018. (Little Legends Ser.: 5). (ENG., Illus.). 192p. (J). (gr. 2-5). pap. 8.99 *(978-1-4926-6570-0(3),* Sourcebooks Jabberwocky) Sourcebooks, Inc.
—The Story Tree. 2018. (Little Legends Ser.: 6). (ENG., Illus.). 192p. (J). (gr. 2-5). pap. 8.99 *(978-1-4926-6573-1(8),* Sourcebooks Jabberwocky) Sourcebooks, Inc.
Pereira, Chritine M. Madilynn Rose Rhyming Fairy: Volume 1, 1 vol. 2010. 44p. pap. 24.95 *(978-1-61546-591-0(X))* PublishAmerica, Inc.
Perelman, Helen. Gooey Goblins: Halloween Special. Waters, Erica-Jane, illus. 2011. (Candy Fairies Ser.). (ENG.). 176p. (J). (gr. 2-5). pap. 6.99 *(978-1-4424-2213-1(0),* Aladdin) Simon & Schuster Children's Publishing.
—Gooey Goblins: Halloween Special. Waters, Erica-Jane, illus. 2013. (Candy Fairies Ser.). (ENG.). 176p. (J). (gr. 2-5). 15.99 *(978-1-4424-6495-7(X),* Simon & Schuster/Paula Wiseman Bks.) Simon & Schuster/Paula Wiseman Bks.
—The Sugar Ball. Waters, Erica-Jane, illus. 2013. (Candy Fairies Ser.: 6). (ENG.). 128p. (J). (gr. 2-5). 15.99 *(978-1-4424-6498-8(4),* Simon & Schuster/Paula Wiseman Bks.) Simon & Schuster/Paula Wiseman Bks.
Perkins, Kevin John. The Circlet. 2010. 316p. pap. *(978-1-907211-33-1(0))* Grosvenor Hse. Publishing Ltd.
Perone, S. P. Star of the Future. 2010. 176p. 23.95 *(978-1-4502-6861-5(7));* pap. 13.95 *(978-1-4502-6859-2(5))* iUniverse, Inc.
Perrault, Charles. Cinderella. Innocenti, Roberto, illus. 2013. (ENG.). 32p. (J). (gr. 2-5). pap. 7.99 *(978-0-89812-828-4(5),* 22040, Creative Paperbacks) Creative Co., The.
Perry, Adam. The Magicians of Elephant County. Perry, Adam, illus. 2018. (ENG., Illus.). 384p. (J). (gr. 3-7). 16.99 *(978-0-06-279535-9(X),* HarperCollins) HarperCollins Pubs.
Perry, Fred. Gold Digger Platinum, Vol. 4. 2012. (ENG., Illus.). 132p. (YA). pap. 14.95 *(978-0-9850925-0-4(5),* 6eb5c744-1c7a-4d40-beaf-42788e2bbd6c) Antarctic Pr., Inc.
Perry, Valerie J. Trilby Learns a Lesson. 2011. 26p. pap. 14.00 *(978-1-60976-659-7(8),* Eloquent Bks.) Strategic Book Publishing & Rights Agency (SBPRA).
Peters, Jackie. Mary Maybelieve. 2011. (Illus.). 92p. pap. 30.63 *(978-1-4567-7283-3(X))* AuthorHouse.
Peters, Karen Lynn. If I Only Had a Horse. 2013. 36p. 16.99 *(978-0-9894748-4-9(4))* Mindstir Media.
Peters, Stephanie True. Sleeping Beauty, Magic Master: A Graphic Novel. López, Álex, illus. 2016. (Far Out Fairy Tales Ser.). (ENG.). 40p. (J). (gr. 3-6). lib. bdg. 26.65 *(978-1-4965-3784-3(X),* 133107, Stone Arch Bks.) Capstone.
Peterson, Alyson. The Cursed Dagger. 2016. 308p. (YA). pap. *(978-1-4621-1865-6(8))* Cedar Fort, Inc./CFI Distribution.
—The Exiled Prince. 2017. (ENG.). (YA). (gr. 8-12). pap. 17.99 *(978-1-4621-2035-2(0),* Sweetwater Bks.) Cedar Fort, Inc./CFI Distribution.
—Ian Quicksilver: The Warrior's Return. 2015. viii, 309p. (YA). pap. 17.99 *(978-1-4621-1629-4(9))* Cedar Fort, Inc./CFI Distribution.
Peyo & Delporte, Yvan. The Smurfs Graphic Novels Boxed Set: Vol. #1 - 3, 3 Vols., Vol. 1. 2011. (Smurfs Graphic Novels Ser.). (ENG., Illus.). 184p. (J). (gr. 2-5). pap. 17.99 *(978-1-59707-273-1(7),* 900078889, Papercutz) Mad Cave Studios.
Pfeiffer, Kathleen. Spartacus Sprout, Please Watch Out! 2011. (ENG.). 31p. 15.99 *(978-1-257-50163-2(1))* Lulu Pr., Inc.
Phillips, Liam & Plumm, Gabi. Mumble & Jumble & the Great Corpsicle Conundrum. 2009. 278p. pap. 24.50 *(978-1-4092-5577-2(8))* Lulu Pr., Inc.
Phoenix International Staff, illus. Princess Sofia. 2013. (Play-A-Sound Ser.). (ENG.). 14p. (J). bds., bds. *(978-1-4508-6822-8(3),* 8877f18f-6f50-4b01-bcb0-36932429420b) Phoenix International Publications, Inc.
Phoenix, Three. Daughter of the Sun. 2012. 36p. pap. 11.99 *(978-0-9830686-3-1(1))* Capital Apple Pr.
Picado, Gail. Magical Bandages. 2008. 32p. per. 24.95 *(978-1-4241-8851-2(2))* America Star Bks.
Pierce, Angelica. Wizard in Blue Jeans. 2006. (ENG.). 184p. pap. 10.95 *(978-1-4303-0647-4(5))* Lulu Pr., Inc.
Pierce, Tamora. The Immortals Quartet (Boxed Set) Wild Magic; Wolf-Speaker; Emperor Mage; the Realms of the Gods. 2015. (Immortals Ser.). (ENG., Illus.). 1440p. (YA). (gr. 7). pap. 51.99 *(978-1-4814-4030-1(6),* Atheneum Bks. for Young Readers) Simon & Schuster Children's Publishing.
—Magic Steps. 2006. (Circle Opens Ser.: No. 1). 264p. 18.00 *(978-0-7569-6588-4(8))* Perfection Learning Corp.
—Mastiff, 3. 2012. (Beka Cooper Ser.: Bk. 3). (ENG.). 608p. (J). (gr. 7-12). lib. bdg. 26.19 *(978-0-375-91470-6(6))* Random Hse. Bks. for Young Readers.
—Melting Stones. 2010. (Circle Reforged Ser.: Bk. 2). (ENG.). 320p. (J). (gr. 9-12). 24.94 *(978-0-545-05265-8(3))* Scholastic, Inc.
—Tempests & Slaughter (the Numair Chronicles, Book One) (Numair Chronicles Ser.: 1). (ENG.). (YA). (gr. 7). 2019. 496p. pap. 11.99 *(978-0-375-84712-7(X),* Ember) 2018. 480p. 18.99 *(978-0-375-84711-0(1),* Random Hse. Bks. for Young Readers) 2018. 480p. lib. bdg. 21.99 *(978-0-375-94711-7(6),* Random Hse. Bks. for Young Readers) Random Hse. Children's Bks.
—Terrier: The Legend of Beka Cooper #1. 2007. (Beka Cooper Ser.: 1). (ENG., Illus.). 608p. (YA). (gr. 7-11). pap. 11.99 *(978-0-375-83816-3(3),* Ember) Random Hse. Children's Bks.
—Tortall & Other Lands: a Collection of Tales. 2012. (ENG.). 400p. (YA). (gr. 7). pap. 10.99 *(978-0-375-86633-3(7),* Ember) Random Hse. Children's Bks.
Pierce, Walter. Dreams Unseen: The Dragon of Mists. 2007. 260p. (YA). per. 16.95 *(978-0-595-45171-5(3))* iUniverse, Inc.
Pike, Christopher, pseud. Pan's Realm. 2015. (Spooksville Ser.: 8). (ENG., Illus.). 128p. (J). (gr. 3-7). pap. 6.99 *(978-1-4814-1079-3(2),* Aladdin) Simon & Schuster Children's Publishing.
—Thirst (Boxed Set) Thirst No. 1; Thirst No. 2; Thirst No. 3, 3 vols. 2013. (Thirst Ser.). (ENG.). 1744p. (YA). (gr. 9). pap. 30.99 *(978-1-4424-8375-0(X),* Simon Pulse) Simon Pulse.
—Thirst No. 1: The Last Vampire, Black Blood, Red Dice. 2009. (Thirst Ser.: 1). (ENG., Illus.). 624p. (YA). (gr. 9). pap. 14.99 *(978-1-4169-8308-8(2),* Simon Pulse) Simon Pulse.
—Thirst No. 2 No. 2: Phantom, Evil Thirst, Creatures of Forever, Bk. 2. 2010. (Thirst Ser.: 2). (ENG.). 608p. (YA). (gr. 9). pap. 14.99 *(978-1-4169-8309-5(0),* Simon Pulse) Simon Pulse.
—Thirst No. 3: The Eternal Dawn. 2010. (Thirst Ser.: 3). (ENG.). 512p. (YA). (gr. 9-18). pap. 14.99 *(978-1-4424-1317-7(4),* Simon Pulse) Simon Pulse.
—Thirst No. 4: The Shadow of Death, 4. 2011. (Thirst Ser.: 4). (ENG., Illus.). 528p. (YA). (gr. 9). pap. 10.99 *(978-1-4424-1319-1(0),* Simon Pulse) Simon Pulse.
Pilumeli, Tanya. The Dragonfly Keeper. 2008. 264p. (J). per. 12.95 *(978-0-9801396-0-0(0))* FAVA Pr.
Plant, Marilyn. Trinka's Magic Bracelet. 2012. 40p. pap. *(978-1-77067-956-6(1))* FriesenPress.
Plotz, John. Time & the Tapestry. Saroff, Phyllis, illus. 2014. (ENG.). 192p. (YA). (gr. 4-11). 18.50 *(978-1-59373-145-8(0))* Bunker Hill Publishing, Inc.
Plourde, Lynn. The Blizzard Wizard. Aardema, John, illus. 2010. (ENG.). 32p. (J). (gr. -1-3). 16.95 *(978-0-89272-789-6(6))* Down East Bks.
Plourde, Paulette. My Magic Pillow. 2005. (Illus.). 40p. (J). per. 8.99 *(978-1-932338-76-8(4))* Lifevest Publishing, Inc.
Polanco, Amparo. The Magical Forest. 2016. (ENG., Illus.). (J). 16.95 *(978-1-5069-0268-5(5));* pap. 12.95 *(978-1-5069-0269-2(3))* First Edition Design Publishing.
Poltera, Anne. Castle Magic & the Sinister Encroaching Fir Wood. 2012. (Illus.). 256p. (-18). pap. 19.76 *(978-1-4772-3943-8(X))* AuthorHouse.
Pontacoloni, Edward. The Adventures of Firstyr the Younger Knight Errata of Cort: Bed Time Stories for First Year Lawyers. 2008. (ENG.). 36p. per. 15.99 *(978-1-4257-6527-9(0))* Xlibris Corp.
Pool, Catherine. Catrina's Journey to Her Musical Friends, 1 vol. 2010. 18p. pap. 24.95 *(978-1-4489-7237-1(X))* PublishAmerica, Inc.
Poole, Philip. The Trouble with Time. 2012. (Illus.). 24p. pap. 19.82 *(978-1-4772-3459-4(4))* AuthorHouse.
Pope, Paul. Battling Boy. Pope, Paul, illus. 2013. (Battling Boy Ser.: 1). (ENG., Illus.). 208p. (J). (gr. 5-12). pap. 25.99 *(978-1-59643-145-4(8),* 900034672, First Second Bks.) Roaring Brook Pr.
Popovic, Lana. Wicked Like a Wildfire. (ENG.). (YA). (gr. 9). 2018. 432p. 10.99 *(978-0-06-243684-9(8))* 2017. 416p. 17.99 *(978-0-06-243683-2(X))* HarperCollins Pubs. (Tegen, Katherine Bks).
Posner-Sanchez, Andrea. I Am Belle (Disney Beauty & the Beast) Batson, Alan, illus. 2017. (Little Golden Book Ser.). (ENG.). 24p. (J). (-k). 5.99 *(978-0-7364-3905-3(6),* Golden/Disney) Random Hse. Children's Bks.

M N O

—I Am the Beast (Disney Beauty & the Beast) Batson, Alan, illus. 2017. (Little Golden Book Ser.). (ENG.). 24p. (J). (-k). 4.99 *(978-0-7364-3907-7(2)*, Golden/Disney) Random Hse. Children's Bks.

Potter, Kay. I Hate Fairies! the Adventures of Katie James. 2013. 140p. pap. 13.97 *(978-1-62212-127-4(9)*, Strategic Bk. Publishing) Strategic Book Publishing & Rights Agency (SBPRA).

Potter, Tony, des. Finn & the Magic Harp. 2004. (ENG., Illus.). 12p. (J). 10.95 *(978-0-7171-3767-1(8))* M.H. Gill & Co. U. C. IRL. Dist: Dufour Editions, Inc.

Pounder, Sibéal & Pounder, Sibéal. Witch Wars. Anderson, Laura Ellen, illus. 2016. (Witch Wars Ser.). (ENG.). 272p. (J). 16.99 *(978-1-61963-925-6(4)*, 900152463, Bloomsbury USA Childrens) Bloomsbury Publishing USA.

Powell-Tuck, Maudie. Last Stop on the Reindeer Express. Mountford, Karl James, illus. 2018. (ENG.). 32p. (J). (gr. -1-2). 18.99 *(978-1-5247-7166-9(X)*, Doubleday Bks. for Young Readers) Random Hse. Children's Bks.

Power, Nicholas D. Paudie's Magical Adventures. 2009. 236p. 24.75 *(978-1-60693-534-7(8)*, Strategic Bk. Publishing) Strategic Book Publishing & Rights Agency (SBPRA).

Prasad, Sunayna. Alyssa Mccarthy's Magical Missions: Book 1. 2013. 216p. pap. *(978-1-4602-0701-7(7))* FriesenPress.

Preble, Joy. Dreaming Anastasia. 2009. (Dreaming Anastasia Ser.: 1). 320p. (YA). (gr. 7-12). pap. 13.99 *(978-1-4022-1817-0(6))* Sourcebooks, Inc.

—Haunted, 2. 2011. (Dreaming Anastasia Ser.: 2). 304p. (YA). (gr. 7-12). pap. 9.99 *(978-1-4022-4468-1(1))* Sourcebooks, Inc.

Preble, Laura. Lica's Angel. 2003. 142p. (YA). 21.95 *(978-0-595-74914-0(3))*; pap. 11.95 *(978-0-595-28253-1(9))* iUniverse, Inc.

Preussler, Otfried. The Little Witch. Bell, Anthea, tr. Gebhardt-Gayler, Winnie, illus. 2015. (ENG.). 144p. (J). (gr. k-4). 16.95 *(978-1-59017-934-5(X)*, NYR Children's Collection) New York Review of Bks., Inc., The.

Price, Ellen Ann. Gladly's Magic. 2011. 160p. 27.50 *(978-0-557-71561-9(X))*; (ENG.). pap. 18.00 *(978-1-257-10561-8(2))*; pap. 55.00 *(978-1-4583-6372-5(4))* Lulu Pr., Inc.

The Princess & the Magic Locket. (My Tooth Is Loose!). (Illus.). 32p. (J). *(978-1-4054-1022-9(1))* Parragon, Inc.

Prineas, Sarah. Lost. 2009. (Magic Thief Ser.: 2). (J). 88.75 *(978-1-4407-3133-4(0))*; 130.75 *(978-1-4407-3129-7(2))*; 110.75 *(978-1-4407-3125-9(X))*; 112.75 *(978-1-4407-3123-5(3))*; (SPA.). 265.75 *(978-1-4407-3124-2(1))*; 132.75 *(978-1-4407-3127-3(6))*; 1.25 *(978-1-4407-3131-0(4))* Recorded Bks., Inc.

—The Magic Thief. Caparo, Antonio Javier, illus. (Magic Thief Ser.: 1). (ENG.). (J). (gr. 5-9). 2008. 432p. 16.99 *(978-0-06-137587-3(X))*1. 2009. 448p. pap. 7.99 *(978-0-06-137590-3(X))* HarperCollins Pubs. (HarperCollins).

—The Magic Thief: Found. Caparo, Antonio Javier, illus. 2011. (Magic Thief Ser.: 3). (ENG.). 384p. (J). (gr. 5). pap. 7.99 *(978-0-06-137595-8(0)*, HarperCollins) HarperCollins Pubs.

—The Magic Thief: Home. Caparo, Antonio Javier, illus. 2015. (Magic Thief Ser.: 4). (ENG.). 416p. (J). (gr. 3-7). pap. 8.99 *(978-0-06-220956-6(6)*, HarperCollins) HarperCollins Pubs.

—The Magic Thief: Lost. Caparo, Antonio Javier, illus. (Magic Thief Ser.: 2). (ENG.). (J). (gr. 5-18). 2009. 400p. 17.99 *(978-0-06-137589-7(6))*2. 2010. 416p. pap. 8.99 *(978-0-06-137592-7(6))* HarperCollins Pubs. (HarperCollins).

—Moonkind. 2014. (Summerlands Ser.: 3). (ENG.). 272p. (J). (gr. 3-7). pap. 6.99 *(978-0-06-192111-7(4)*, HarperCollins) HarperCollins Pubs.

—Summerkin. 2013. (Summerlands Ser.: 2). (ENG.). 288p. (J). (gr. 3-7). pap. 7.99 *(978-0-06-192108-7(4)*, HarperCollins) HarperCollins Pubs.

—Winterling. 2013. (Summerlands Ser.: 1). (ENG.). 272p. (J). (gr. 5-7). pap. 6.99 *(978-0-06-192105-6(X)*, HarperCollins) HarperCollins Pubs.

—Winterling, 5 vols. 2012. (Winterling Ser.: 1). (J). 75.75 *(978-1-4640-1032-3(3))*; 230.75 *(978-1-4640-1034-7(X))*; 73.75 *(978-1-4640-1037-8(4))*; 73.75 *(978-1-4640-1036-1(6))* Recorded Bks., Inc.

Pritchard, David. Ghost of Spring. 2010. 228p. pap. *(978-1-907652-11-0(6))* Grosvenor Hse. Publishing Ltd.

Provencher, Olga J. Joey & Mup. 2005. 134p. per. 9.95 *(978-1-59824-048-1(X))* E-BookTime LLC.

Pruitt, Lisa A. Savanna & the Magic Boots. 2011. 24p. (gr. 1-2). pap. 11.32 *(978-1-4634-0090-3(X))* AuthorHouse.

Pryce, Trevor. Amphibians' End (a Kulipari Novel #3) Greene, Sanford, illus. 2016. (Kulipari Ser.). (ENG.). 304p. (J). (gr. 3-7). pap. 8.95 *(978-1-4197-2194-6(1)*, 1088803) Abrams, Inc.

Pryce, Trevor & Naftali, Joel. The Rainbow Serpent: A Kulipari Novel. Greene, Sanford, illus. 2014. (ENG.). 301p. (J). (gr. 3-7). 15.95 *(978-1-4197-1309-5(4)*, 1088701, Amulet Bks.) Abrams, Inc.

Psilopoulou, Koralia. The Magic Amulets. 2012. 24p. pap. 17.99 *(978-1-4389-6654-0(7))* AuthorHouse.

Publications International Ltd. Staff, creator. Fairy Tales: Keepsake Collection. 2007. (Illus.). 96p. 12.98 *(978-1-4127-7453-6(5))* Publications International, Ltd.

Publications International Ltd. Staff, ed. Disney Princess Storybook & Magic Bracelet. 2010. 12p. (J). bds. 12.98 *(978-1-4127-9912-6(0))* Phoenix International Publications, Inc.

—Princess Magic. 2010. (My First Look & Find Ser.). (Illus.). 12p. (gr. -1). bds. 7.98 *(978-1-4127-3074-7(0)*, 7227000) Phoenix International Publications, Inc.

Pullman, Philip. Das Magische Messer. (GER.). pap. 22.95 *(978-3-453-15227-4(1))* Verlag Wilhelm Heyne DEU. Dist: Distribooks, Inc.

Purday, Paul. The Two Lands. 2006. 310p. (J). pap. *(978-1-905809-11-0(5))* Pneuma Springs Publishing.

Purdie, Kathryn. Burning Glass. (Burning Glass Ser.: 1). (ENG.). (YA). (gr. 9). 2017. 528p. pap. 9.99 *(978-0-06-241237-9(X))* 2016. (Illus.). 512p. 17.99 *(978-0-06-241236-2(1))* HarperCollins Pubs. (Tegen, Katherine Bks).

—Crystal Blade. (Burning Glass Ser.: 2). (ENG.). (YA). (gr. 9). 2018. 384p. pap. 9.99 *(978-0-06-241240-9(X))* 2017. (Illus.). 368p. 17.99 *(978-0-06-241239-3(6))* HarperCollins Pubs. (Tegen, Katherine Bks).

Quest, Stacy. Sad Sam & the Magic Cookies. Wertheimer, Beverly & Ronsley, Jill, eds. Morris, Michael, illus. 2006. (ENG.). (J). 16.95 *(978-1-932367-01-0(2))* BookBound Publishing.

Quinn, Jordan. The False Fairy. McPhillips, Robert, illus. 2016. (Kingdom of Wrenly Ser.: 11). (ENG.). 128p. (J). (gr. k-4). pap. 6.99 *(978-1-4814-8586-9(5)*, Little Simon) Little Simon.

—The Sorcerer's Shadow. McPhillips, Robert, illus. 2017. (Kingdom of Wrenly Ser.: 12). (ENG.). 128p. (J). (gr. k-4). 17.99 *(978-1-5344-0000-9(1))*; pap. 6.99 *(978-1-4814-9999-6(8))* Little Simon. (Little Simon).

—The Witch's Curse. McPhillips, Robert, illus. 2014. (Kingdom of Wrenly Ser.: 4). (ENG.). 128p. (J). (gr. k-4). pap. 6.99 *(978-1-4814-0075-6(4)*, Little Simon) Little Simon.

Raasch, Sara. Frost Like Night. (Snow Like Ashes Ser.: 3). (ENG.). (YA). (gr. 9). 2017. 512p. pap. 10.99 *(978-0-06-228699-4(4))* 2016. (Illus.). 496p. 17.99 *(978-0-06-228698-7(6))* HarperCollins Pubs. (Balzer & Bray).

—Ice Like Fire. (Illus.). (YA). 2016. (Snow Like Ashes Ser.: 2). (ENG.). 512p. (gr. 9). pap. 9.99 *(978-0-06-228696-3(X)*, Balzer & Bray) 2015. (Snow Like Ashes Ser.: 2). (ENG., 496p. (gr. 9-12). 17.99 *(978-0-06-228695-6(1)*, Balzer & Bray) 2015. 496p. pap. *(978-0-06-242793-9(8))* HarperCollins Pubs.

—These Rebel Waves. 2018. (Illus.). 480p. (YA). *(978-0-06-284272-5(2))* Addison Wesley.

—These Rebel Waves. (These Rebel Waves Ser.: 1). (ENG.). (YA). (gr. 8). 2019. 496p. pap. 11.99 *(978-0-06-247151-2(1))* 2018. (Illus.). 480p. 17.99 *(978-0-06-247150-5(3))* HarperCollins Pubs. (Balzer & Bray).

Rabe, Tish. Frozen. 2013. (Disney Princess Step into Reading Ser.). lib. bdg. 13.55 *(978-0-606-32203-4(5))* Turtleback.

Racaniello, P. Marcella & the Magic Hat. 2012. 20p. pap. 9.99 *(978-1-105-02672-0(8))* Lulu Pr., Inc.

A Ragged Magic. 2014. (ENG.). (YA). 24.95 *(978-1-941662-03-8(X))* Jakal LLC.

Rallison, Janette. My Fair Godmother. 2009. (ENG.). 384p. (J). (gr. 6-8). 21.19 *(978-0-8027-9780-3(6)*, 900051897) Walker & Co.

—My Unfair Godmother. 2012. (ENG.). 352p. (YA). (gr. 7-12). 26.19 *(978-0-8027-2236-2(9)*, 9780802722362) Bloomsbury Publishing USA.

Rand, Johnathan. Freddie Fernortner #8: Chippers Crazy Carnival. 2008. 96p. (J). pap. 4.99 *(978-1-893699-77-9(3))* AudioCraft Publishing, Inc.

Rand, Jonathan. Freddie Fernortner #7 Bk 7: Fearless First Grader: the Magical Wading Pool. 2007. pap. 4.99 *(978-1-893699-91-5(9))* AudioCraft Publishing, Inc.

Random House. Magical Mermaids! (Shimmer & Shine) Aikins, Dave, illus. 2017. (Step into Reading Ser.). (ENG.). 24p. (J). (gr. -1-1). pap. 4.99 *(978-0-399-55886-3(1)*, Random Hse. Bks. for Young Readers) Random Hse. Children's Bks.

—Meet Shimmer & Shine! (Shimmer & Shine) Cardona, Jose Maria, illus. 2016. (Step into Reading Ser.). (ENG.). 24p. (J). (gr. -1-1). 4.99 *(978-0-553-52203-7(5)*, Random Hse. Bks. for Young Readers) Random Hse. Children's Bks.

—Six Magical Tales! (Shimmer & Shine) Random House, illus. 2018. (Step into Reading Ser.). (ENG., Illus.). 144p. (J). (gr. -1-1). pap. 8.99 *(978-1-5247-7278-9(X)*, Random Hse. Bks. for Young Readers) Random Hse. Children's Bks.

Ranjalkar, Shreyans. My Sunny British Days - Stories for Children by a Child. 2013. (Illus.). 70p. pap. *(978-1-78148-596-5(8))* Grosvenor Hse. Publishing Ltd.

Ranson, Erin. Woodland Fairies. Top That Publishing Staff, ed. Richards, Kirsten, illus. 2008. (Magnetic Story & Play Scene Ser.). 9p. (J). (gr. -1). bds *(978-1-84666-440-3(3)*, Tide Mill Pr.) Top That! Publishing PLC.

Rao, Chatura. Amie & the Chawl of Colour. Pathak, Ashutosh, illus. 2004. 100p. pap. *(978-0-14-333592-4(8)*, Puffin) Penguin Publishing Group.

Rao, Lisa. Dora's Magic Watering Can. Miller, Victoria, illus. 2008. (Dora the Explorer Ser.). (ENG.). 16p. (J). (gr. -1-1). pap. 4.99 *(978-1-4169-4772-1(8)*, Simon Spotlight/Nickelodeon) Simon Spotlight/Nickelodeon.

Raynor, Michelle. A Magical World. 2011. 20p. pap. 11.99 *(978-1-257-65025-5(4))* Lulu Pr., Inc.

Reader, Gwendolin. The Life Cycle of A Snowman. 2010. 24p. pap. 12.50 *(978-1-4520-7686-7(3))* AuthorHouse.

Reardon, A. C. Galish: The adventure of Isabelle & Eva. 2011. 168p. pap. 14.69 *(978-1-4567-7818-7(8))* AuthorHouse.

Reaves, Esther R. Gammy's Snow Queen. 2011. 24p. pap. 12.79 *(978-1-4520-7153-9(6))* AuthorHouse.

The Rebel Princess. 2014. pap. 12.99 *(978-1-4621-1430-6(X))* Cedar Fort, Inc./CFI Distribution.

Redwine, C. J. The Blood Spell. (Ravenspire Ser.: 4). (ENG.). 448p. (YA). (gr. 8). 2020. pap. 10.99 *(978-0-06-265302-4(4))* 2019. 17.99 *(978-0-06-265301-7(6))* HarperCollins Pubs. (Balzer & Bray).

—The Shadow Queen. 2016. (Ravenspire Ser.: 1). (ENG.). (YA). (gr. 8). 416p. pap. 10.99 *(978-0-06-236025-0(6))*; (Illus.). 400p. 17.99 *(978-0-06-236024-3(8))* HarperCollins Pubs. (Balzer & Bray).

—The Shadow Queen. 2016. (Ravenspire Ser.: 1). (YA). lib. bdg. 20.85 *(978-0-606-39615-8(2))* Turtleback.

Reef Rescue (Book 4) 2017. (Secret Mermaid Ser.). (ENG.). (J). pap. 4.99 *(978-0-7945-3686-2(7)*, Usborne) EDC Publishing.

Rees Brennan, Sarah. The Demon's Covenant. (Demon's Lexicon Trilogy Ser.: 2). (ENG., Illus.). (YA). (gr. 9). 2011. 464p. pap. 12.99 *(978-1-4169-6382-0(0))* 2010. 448p. 17.99 *(978-1-4169-6381-3(2))* McElderry, Margaret K. Bks. (McElderry, Margaret K. Bks.).

—The Demon's Lexicon. (Demon's Lexicon Trilogy Ser.: 1). (ENG., Illus.). (YA). (gr. 9). 2010. 352p. pap. 12.99 *(978-1-4169-6380-6(4))* 2009. 336p. 18.99 *(978-1-4169-6379-0(0))* McElderry, Margaret K. Bks. (McElderry, Margaret K. Bks.).

—The Demon's Surrender. 2012. (Demon's Lexicon Trilogy Ser.: 3). (ENG., Illus.). 400p. (YA). (gr. 9). pap. 9.99 *(978-1-4169-6384-4(7)*, McElderry, Margaret K. Bks.) McElderry, Margaret K. Bks.

—Unspoken (the Lynburn Legacy Book 1). Bk. 1. 2013. (Lynburn Legacy Ser.: 1). (ENG.). 400p. (YA). (gr. 7). pap. 13.99 *(978-0-375-87103-0(9)*, Ember) Random Hse. Children's Bks.

—Untold (the Lynburn Legacy Book 2) 2014. (Lynburn Legacy Ser.: 2). (ENG., Illus.). 400p. (YA). (gr. 7). pap. 10.99 *(978-0-375-87104-7(7)*, Ember) Random Hse. Children's Bks.

Reeve, Philip. Here Lies Arthur. 2010. lib. bdg. 19.65 *(978-0-606-10557-6(3))* Turtleback.

Reh, Rusalka. Pizzicato: The Abduction of the Magic Violin, 0 vols. Wilson, David Henry, tr. 2011. (ENG.). 132p. (J). (gr. 4-6). pap. 9.95 *(978-1-61109-004-8(0)*, 9781611090048, Two Lions) Amazon Publishing.

—The Secret of the Water Knight, 0 vols. Derbyshire, Katy, tr. unabr. ed. 2011. (ENG.). 100p. (J). (gr. 4-7). pap. 9.95 *(978-1-61109-006-2(7)*, 9781611090062, Two Lions) Amazon Publishing.

Reihs, Linda. The Adventures of Maddy Morphis. 2012. 34p. pap. 9.99 *(978-0-9819648-1-2(8))* Mindstir Media.

Reilly, Carmel & Hopkinson, Courtney. Magic Tricks. 2008. (Rigby Focus Forward: Level F Ser.). (Illus.). 24p. (J). (gr. 4-7). pap. *(978-1-4190-3697-2(1)*, Rigby) Pearson Education Australia.

—New Tricks. 2008. (Rigby Focus Forward: Level J Ser.). (Illus.). 24p. (J). (gr. 4-7). pap. *(978-1-4190-3766-5(8)*, Rigby) Pearson Education Australia.

Reisfeld, Randi. Trouble with Trix (Winx Club), 2. Golden Books, illus. 2012. (Winx Club: Chapter Bks.). (ENG.). 128p. (J). (gr. 2-5). 17.44 *(978-0-307-97995-7(4))* Random House Publishing Group.

—Welcome to Alfea, 1. Golden Books, illus. 2012. (Winx Club: Chapter Bks.). (ENG.). 128p. (J). (gr. 2-5). 17.44 *(978-0-307-97994-0(6))* Random House Publishing Group.

Reiss, Kathryn. Paint by Magic. 2003. (ENG.). 288p. (J). (gr. 5-7). pap. 17.95 *(978-0-15-204925-6(8)*, 1194872, Clarion Bks.) HarperCollins Pubs.

Return of the Dark Queen (Book 6) 2017. (Secret Mermaid Ser.). (ENG.). (J). pap. 4.99 *(978-0-7945-3684-8(0)*, Usborne) EDC Publishing.

Reviejo, Carlos & Reviejo, Carlos. Dejame Que te Cuente: Cincuenta Cuentos de Animales para Ninos. 2003. (SPA., Illus.). 212p. *(978-84-348-7166-3(1)*, SM31147) SM Ediciones ESP. Dist: Lectorum Pubns., Inc.

Revis, Beth. Give the Dark My Love. 2019. (ENG.). 384p. (YA). (gr. 7). pap. 10.99 *(978-1-59514-718-9(7)*, Razorbill) Penguin Young Readers Group.

Rex, Adam. Cold Cereal, 1. 2013. (Cold Cereal Saga Ser.: 1). (ENG.). 448p. (J). (gr. 3-7). pap. 7.99 *(978-0-06-206003-7(1)*, Balzer & Bray) HarperCollins Pubs.

Reynolds, Caroline. Bead Street-the Fable of Red Clover. 2009. 116p. 22.50 *(978-1-60693-579-8(8)*, Eloquent Bks.) Strategic Book Publishing & Rights Agency (SBPRA).

Reynolds, Mariem. The World in Between. 2008. 87p. pap. 16.95 *(978-1-60672-144-5(5))* PublishAmerica, Inc.

Rhodes, Jewell Parker. Bayou Magic. 2016. (ENG.). 272p. (J). (gr. 3-7). pap. 7.99 *(978-0-316-22485-7(5))* Little, Brown Bks. for Young Readers.

Rhodes, Morgan. Crystal Storm: A Falling Kingdoms Novel. (Falling Kingdoms Ser.: 5). (Illus.). (YA). (gr. 7). 2017. 416p. pap. 11.99 *(978-1-59514-823-0(X))* 2016. 368p. 18.99 *(978-1-59514-822-3(1))* Penguin Young Readers Group. (Razorbill).

—Gathering Darkness: A Falling Kingdoms Novel. 2015. (Falling Kingdoms Ser.: 3). 448p. (YA). (gr. 7). 11.99 *(978-1-59514-706-6(3)*, Razorbill) Penguin Young Readers Group.

—Immortal Reign: A Falling Kingdoms Novel. 2018. (Falling Kingdoms Ser.: 6). (YA). (gr. 7). 416p. pap. 11.99 *(978-1-59514-825-4(6))*; 400p. 18.99 *(978-1-59514-824-7(8))* Penguin Young Readers Group. (Razorbill).

Riazi, Karuna. The Battle. 2019. (ENG., Illus.). 304p. (J). (gr. 3-7). 17.99 *(978-1-5344-2872-0(0)*, Salaam Reads) Simon & Schuster Bks. For Young Readers.

—The Gauntlet. 2018. (ENG., Illus.). 304p. (J). (gr. 3-7). pap. 8.99 *(978-1-4814-8697-2(7)*, Salaam Reads) Simon & Schuster Bks. For Young Readers.

Rice, Morgan. A Reign of Steel (Book #11 in the Sorcerer's Ring) 2014. 216p. (YA). pap. 15.99 *(978-1-939416-76-6(0)*, Morgan Rice) Morgan Rice Bks.

Richard Richtmyer. A Bit of Magic: A Novel. 2009. 116p. pap. 10.95 *(978-1-4401-5565-9(8))* iUniverse, Inc.

Richards, Chip & De Alessi, O. B. Flutes in the Garden. 2015. (ENG.). 68p. pap. 13.95 *(978-0-7387-4658-6(4))* Llewellyn Pubns.

Richemont, Enid. The Big Purple Wonderbook, 1 vol. Waldek, Kelly, illus. 2009. (Go! Readers Ser.). (ENG.). 48p. (J). (gr. 1-2). pap. 13.85 *(978-1-60754-279-7(X)*, 14e93d66-490a-43a0-9f0b-266e1423a85a); lib. bdg. 33.93 *(978-1-60754-278-0(1)*, faf51c0d-aad4-4512-bfad-000e351971ed) Rosen Publishing Group, Inc., The. (Windmill Bks.).

Rickis, Andrew. The Magic Oak: (A Baseball Story) A Novel for Young Adults. 2003. 114p. pap. 19.95 *(978-1-4137-0665-9(7))* America Star Bks.

Riggs, Mary L. Dragon Forge the Ballad of Beighn. 2009. 110p. pap. 9.95 *(978-1-60860-499-9(3)*, Strategic Bk. Publishing) Strategic Book Publishing & Rights Agency (SBPRA).

Riley, James. The Last Dragon. 2020. (Revenge of Magic Ser.: 2). (ENG.). 400p. (J). (gr. 3-7). pap. 8.99 *(978-1-5344-2573-6(X)*, Aladdin) Simon & Schuster Children's Publishing.

—The Last Dragon. 2019. (Revenge of Magic Ser.: 2). (ENG., Illus.). 384p. (J). (gr. 3-7). 18.99 *(978-1-5344-2572-9(1)*, Simon & Schuster/Paula Wiseman Bks.) Simon & Schuster/Paula Wiseman Bks.

—Pick the Plot. (Story Thieves Ser.: 4). (ENG.). (J). (gr. 3-7). 2018. 400p. pap. 9.99 *(978-1-4814-6129-0(X))* 2017. (Illus.). 384p. 17.99 *(978-1-4814-6128-3(1))* Simon & Schuster Children's Publishing. (Aladdin).

—The Revenge of Magic. 2019. (Revenge of Magic Ser.: 1). (ENG., Illus.). 416p. (J). (gr. 3-7). 18.99 *(978-1-4814-8577-7(6)*, Simon & Schuster/Paula Wiseman Bks.) Simon & Schuster/Paula Wiseman Bks.

—Secret Origins. 2017. (Story Thieves Ser.: 3). (ENG., Illus.). 400p. (J). (gr. 3-7). pap. 9.99 *(978-1-4814-6126-9(5)*, Aladdin) Simon & Schuster Children's Publishing.

—Secret Origins. 2017. (Story Thieves Ser.: 3). (ENG., Illus.). 384p. (J). (gr. 3-7). 18.99 *(978-1-4814-6125-2(7)*, Simon & Schuster/Paula Wiseman Bks.) Simon & Schuster/Paula Wiseman Bks.

—The Stolen Chapters. Eliopoulos, Chris, illus. 2016. (Story Thieves Ser.: 2). (ENG.). 368p. (J). (gr. 3-7). 19.99 *(978-1-4814-0922-3(0)*, Aladdin) Simon & Schuster Children's Publishing.

—Story Thieves. 2015. (Story Thieves Ser.: 1). (ENG., Illus.). (J). (gr. 3-7). 416p. pap. 8.99 *(978-1-4814-0920-9(4))*; 400p. 19.99 *(978-1-4814-0919-3(0))* Simon & Schuster Children's Publishing. (Aladdin).

—Story Thieves. 2015. (Story Thieves Ser.: Vol. 1). (ENG.). (J). (gr. 3-7). lib. bdg. 18.40 *(978-0-606-39444-4(3))* Turtleback.

—Worlds Apart. (Story Thieves Ser.: 5). (ENG.). (J). (gr. 3-7). 2019. 512p. pap. 9.99 *(978-1-4814-8575-3(X))* 2018. (Illus.). 496p. 17.99 *(978-1-4814-8574-6(1))* Simon & Schuster Children's Publishing. (Aladdin).

Ringwald, Whitaker. Secret Box (2) The Secret Cipher. 2016. (Secret Box Ser.: 2). (ENG.). 272p. (J). (gr. 3-7). pap. 6.99 *(978-0-06-221618-2(X)*, Tegen, Katherine Bks) HarperCollins Pubs.

Riordan, Rick. Demigods & Magicians: Percy & Annabeth Meet the Kanes. 2016. (ENG.). 224p. (J). (gr. 3-7). 14.99 *(978-1-4847-3278-6(2)*, Disney-Hyperion) Disney Publishing Worldwide.

—From the Kane Chronicles: Brooklyn House Magician's Manual-An Official Rick Riordan Companion Book: Your Guide to Egyptian Gods & Creatures, Glyphs & Spells, & More. 2018. (Kane Chronicles Ser.). (ENG., Illus.). 192p. (J). (gr. 3-7). 9.99 *(978-1-4847-8553-9(3)*, Disney-Hyperion) Disney Publishing Worldwide.

—Kane Chronicles, the, Book One: Red Pyramid: the Graphic Novel, the-Kane Chronicles, the, Book One, Bk. 1. 2012. (Kane Chronicles Ser.: 1). (ENG., Illus.). 192p. (J). (gr. 5-9). pap. 12.99 *(978-1-4231-5069-5(4)*, Disney-Hyperion) Disney Publishing Worldwide.

—Kane Chronicles, the, Book One: Red Pyramid, the-Kane Chronicles, the, Book One. 2010. (Kane Chronicles Ser.: 1). (ENG., Illus.). 528p. (J). (gr. 5-9). 19.99 *(978-1-4231-1338-6(1)*, Disney-Hyperion) Disney Publishing Worldwide.

—Kane Chronicles, the, Book Three: Serpent's Shadow: the Graphic Novel, the-Kane Chronicles, the, Book Three. 2017. (Kane Chronicles Ser.). (ENG., Illus.). 160p. (J). (gr. 5-9). 21.99 *(978-1-4847-8132-6(5))*; pap. 14.99 *(978-1-4847-8234-7(8))* Disney Publishing Worldwide. (Disney-Hyperion).

—Kane Chronicles, the Book Three: Serpent's Shadow, the-Kane Chronicles, the Book Three. 2018. (Kane Chronicles Ser.: 3). (ENG., Illus.). 496p. (J). (gr. 5-9). pap. 9.99 *(978-1-368-01357-4(0)*, Disney-Hyperion) Disney Publishing Worldwide.

—Kane Chronicles, the, Book Three: Serpent's Shadow, the-Kane Chronicles, the, Book Three, Bk. 3. 2012. (Kane Chronicles Ser.: 3). (ENG.). 416p. (J). (gr. 5-9). 19.99 *(978-1-4231-4057-3(5)*, Disney-Hyperion) Disney Publishing Worldwide.

—Kane Chronicles, the, Book Two: Throne of Fire, the-Kane Chronicles, the, Book Two. (Kane Chronicles Ser.: 2). (ENG., (J). (gr. 5-9). 2018. Illus.). 528p. pap. 9.99 *(978-1-368-01359-8(7))*Bk. 2. 2011. 464p. 18.99 *(978-1-4231-4056-6(7))* Disney Publishing Worldwide. (Disney-Hyperion).

—The Red Pyramid. l.t. ed. 2018. (Kane Chronicles Ser.: 1). (ENG.). (J). pap. 15.99 *(978-1-4328-5029-6(6))* Cengage Gale.

—The Red Pyramid. 2009. (Kane Chronicles: Bk. 1). 11.04 *(978-0-7848-3733-7(3)*, Everbind) Marco Bk. Co.

—The Red Pyramid. 2012. 20.00 *(978-1-61383-660-6(0))* Perfection Learning Corp.

—The Red Pyramid. 2010. pap. *(978-0-545-40016-9(3))* Scholastic, Inc.

—The Red Pyramid. l.t. ed. 2010. (Kane Chronicles: Bk. 1). (ENG.). 671p. 23.95 *(978-1-4104-2536-2(3))* Thorndike Pr.

—The Red Pyramid. (Kane Chronicles Ser.: 1). (J). 2018. lib. bdg. 20.85 *(978-0-606-41205-6(0))* 2012. lib. bdg. 24.50 *(978-0-606-37510-8(4))* 2011. lib. bdg. 20.85 *(978-0-606-39216-7(5))* Turtleback.

—The Serpent's Shadow. 2012. 416p. *(978-0-14-133568-1(8)*, Puffin) Penguin Bks., Ltd.

—The Serpent's Shadow. l.t. ed. 2012. (Kane Chronicles: Bk. 3). (ENG.). 521p. (gr. 5-12). 23.99 *(978-1-4104-4789-0(8))* Thorndike Pr.

—The Serpent's Shadow. 2018. (Kane Chronicles Ser.: 3). (J). lib. bdg. 20.85 *(978-0-606-41206-3(9))* Turtleback.

—The Throne of Fire. l.t. ed. 2011. (Kane Chronicles Ser.: 2). (ENG.). 591p. lib. bdg. 23.99 *(978-1-4328-4405-9(9))* Cengage Gale.

—The Throne of Fire. 2011. (Kane Chronicles: Bk. 2). 452p. (J). pap. *(978-1-4231-5059-6(7))* Disney Pr.

—The Throne of Fire. 2nd ed. 2012. (ENG.). 464p. (YA). (gr. 5-9). pap. 9.99 *(978-1-4231-6703-7(1))* Hyperion Bks. for Children.

—The Throne of Fire. 2011. (Kane Chronicles: Bk. 2). (ENG., Illus.). 451p. 28.25 *(978-0-85757-231-8(8))*; 2nd ed. 554p. pap. *(978-0-14-133566-7(1))* Penguin Publishing Group. (Puffin).

—The Throne of Fire. l.t. ed. 2011. (Kane Chronicles: Bk. 2). (ENG.). 589p. 23.99 *(978-1-4104-3607-8(1))* Thorndike Pr.

—The Throne of Fire. (Kane Chronicles Graphic Novels Ser.: 2). 2015. lib. bdg. 24.50 *(978-0-606-37509-2(0))* 2018. (J). lib. bdg. 20.85 *(978-0-606-41204-9(2))* 2012. (J). lib. bdg. 20.85 *(978-0-606-39217-4(3))* Turtleback.

Riordan, Rick & Collar, Orpheus. Serpent's Shadow. 2017. (Kane Chronicles Graphic Novels Ser.: 3). (J). lib. bdg. 24.50 *(978-0-606-40604-8(2))* Turtleback.

Rissi, Anica Mrose. Anna, Banana, & the Magic Show Mix-Up. Kuo, Cassey, illus. 2019. (Anna, Banana Ser.: 8). (ENG.). 160p. (J). (gr. 1-5). 17.99 *(978-1-5344-1722-9(2))*; pap. 5.99 *(978-1-5344-1721-2(4))* Simon & Schuster Bks. For Young Readers. (Simon & Schuster Bks. For Young Readers).

Riva, Jim. Marvin Mallard & the Magic Medallion. Steinmark, Sharyl, illus. 2004. 64p. (YA). pap. 14.95 *(978-1-891262-03-6(3))* Soaring Sparrow Pr.

Rivers, Phoebe. Yesterday & Today. 2013. (Saranormal Ser.: 11). (ENG., Illus.). 160p. (J). (gr. 3-7). 15.99 *(978-1-4424-8962-2(6))*; pap. 5.99 *(978-1-4424-8961-5(8))* Simon Spotlight. (Simon Spotlight).

Robbins, Karen. Care for Our World Play Set. 2012. (ENG.). (J). 34.95 *(978-1-935414-63-6(1))* Casemate Pubs. & Bk. Distributors, LLC.

Roberts, Rachel. All That Glitters. 2007. (Avalon Ser.: Bk. 2). 175p. (J). (gr. 3-7). 9.99 *(978-1-933164-65-6(4))* Seven Seas Entertainment, LLC.

Roberts, Roxanne. Angel Wings, Faery Dust & Other Magical Things: A Story about Witches, Warlocks & Such. 2011. 24p. pap. 11.50 *(978-1-61204-072-1(1)*, Eloquent Bks.) Strategic Book Publishing & Rights Agency (SBPRA).

Roberts, Stacey. Reggie He Came from Zarzieville. 2006. (ENG.). 74p. pap. 25.99 *(978-1-4257-1120-7(0))* Xlibris Corp.

Robichaud, Yves. Tomes of Tan: Kaylen's Rising. 2013. 240p. *(978-1-4602-0526-6(X))*; pap. *(978-1-4602-0524-2(3))* FriesenPress.

Robinson, Hilary. Cinderella & the Beanstalk. Sanfilippo, Simona, illus. 2013. (ENG.). 32p. (J). *(978-0-7787-1156-8(0))* Crabtree Publishing Co.

Robinson, Hilary & Catling, Andy. Aladdin & the Lamp. 2009. (Hopscotch Adventures Ser.). (Illus.). 31p. (J). (gr. 1). lib. bdg. 25.65 *(978-1-59771-181-4(0))* Sea-To-Sea Pubns.

Robinson, Kathleen Marie. The Magic Doorknob. 1 vol. 2009. 56p. pap. 16.95 *(978-1-60813-362-8(1))* America Star Bks.

Robinson, Steve. Tool Town. 2010. 85p. pap. 17.95 *(978-1-4452-4457-0(8))* Lulu Pr., Inc.

Rockwood, Roy. The Wizard of the Se. 2008. 124p. 23.95 *(978-1-60664-931-2(0))*; pap. 10.95 *(978-1-60664-051-7(8))* Aegypan.

Rodda, Emily. The Charm Bracelet. Vitale, Raoul, illus. 2003. (Fairy Realm Ser.). 128p. (J). (gr. 2-5). 8.99 *(978-0-06-009583-3(0))* HarperCollins Pubs.

—Deltora Quest 1. Niwano, Makoto, illus. 2011. (Deltora Quest Ser.: 1). 208p. (gr. 8-12). pap. 10.99 *(978-1-935429-28-9(0))* Kodansha America, Inc.

—Deltora Quest 2. Niwano, Makoto, illus. 2011. (Deltora Quest Ser.: 2). 208p. (gr. 8-12). pap. 10.99 *(978-1-935429-29-6(9))* Kodansha America, Inc.

—Deltora Quest 3. Niwano, Makoto, illus. 2011. (Deltora Quest Ser.: 3). 208p. (gr. 8-12). pap. 10.99 *(978-1-935429-30-2(2))* Kodansha America, Inc.

—Fairy Realm #1: the Charm Bracelet Bk. 1. Vitale, Raoul, illus. 2009. (ENG.). 128p. (J). (gr. 2-5). pap. 4.99 *(978-0-06-009585-7(7)*, HarperCollins) HarperCollins Pubs.

—Fairy Realm #2: the Flower Fairies. Vitale, Raoul, illus. 2009. (ENG.). 128p. (J). (gr. 2-5). pap. 4.99 *(978-0-06-009588-8(1)*, HarperCollins) HarperCollins Pubs.

—The Flower Fairies. Vitale, Raoul, illus. 2003. (Fairy Realm Ser.). 128p. (J). 8.99 *(978-0-06-009586-4(5))* HarperCollins Pubs.

—Isle of the Dead. 2004. (Dragons of Deltora Ser.: No. 3). 195p. (J). lib. bdg. 16.92 *(978-1-4242-0273-7(6))* Fitzgerald Bks.

—Pigs Might Fly. 2019. (Illus.). 128p. 7.99 *(978-1-4607-5374-3(7)*, HarperCollins) HarperCollins Pubs.

—Shadowgate. 2004. (Dragons of Deltora Ser.: No. 2). 195p. (J). lib. bdg. 16.92 *(978-1-4242-0274-4(4))* Fitzgerald Bks.

—The Silver Door. 2013. (Illus.). 278p. (J). pap. *(978-0-545-42993-1(5)*, Scholastic Pr.) Scholastic, Inc.

—The Third Door. 2013. (J). pap. *(978-0-545-42995-5(1)*, Scholastic Pr.) Scholastic, Inc.

Roderman, Anna Marie. Two Tales of Courage. 2004. 116p. (YA). pap. 7.95 *(978-0-87714-318-5(8))* i-5 Publishing LLC.

Rodriguez, AJ. A Cajun Crawfish Tale. 2009. 20p. pap. 12.49 *(978-1-4389-5529-2(4))* AuthorHouse.

Rodriguez, Sergio R. Little Santa & Snowboy: The Childhood Adventures of Santa Claus. 2007. (Illus.). 32p. (J). pap. 8.95 *(978-0-615-17411-2(6))* Little Santa Bks., Inc.

Rogers, Anne. The magic rainbow large Print. 2008. 332p. pap. 30.95 *(978-1-4092-3059-5(7))* Lulu Pr., Inc.

—The magic rainbow very large Print. 2008. 502p. pap. 39.50 *(978-1-4092-3065-6(1))* Lulu Pr., Inc.

Rogers, Derek G. Monstrous Myths & Fabulous Fables. 2012. 184p. pap. *(978-1-78176-741-2(6))* FeedARead.com.

Rogers, Suzanne J. Cody Meets A Butterfly. 2008. 72p. pap. 19.95 *(978-1-4327-2069-8(4))* Outskirts Pr., Inc.

Rogers, Tom, adapted by. The Secret Spell Book. 2017. (Illus.). 31p. (J). *(978-1-5182-3831-4(9))* Disney Publishing Worldwide.

Rogerson, Margaret. Sorcery of Thorns. 2019. (ENG., Illus.). 464p. (YA). (gr. 9). 19.99 *(978-1-4814-9761-9(8)*, McElderry, Margaret K. Bks.) McElderry, Margaret K. Bks.

Rohan, Julia K. Weaverworld: Grimsnipe's Revenge. 2012. 382p. 31.95 *(978-1-4697-0031-1(X))*; pap. 21.95 *(978-1-4697-0032-8(8))* iUniverse, Inc.

Rolly's Magic Pencil. 2005. (J). per. 6.99 *(978-0-9769985-0-1(5)*, 1-206-818-9769) Grace Publishing.

Roman, Javier. Adventures of Tinturu & Kumachan the M. 2007. (Illus.). 48p. pap. 16.95 *(978-1-4241-1626-3(0))* PublishAmerica, Inc.

Romero, R. M. The Dollmaker of Krakow. 2017. (ENG.). 336p. (J). (gr. 3-7). lib. bdg. 19.99 *(978-1-5247-1540-3(9)*, Delacorte Bks. for Young Readers) Random Hse. Children's Bks.

Ronne, Susan. Webster the Spelling Dog. 2012. (ENG.). (J). pap. *(978-1-4675-1184-1(6))* Independent Pub.

Rooney-Freedman, Isabelle. Angus MacDream & the Roktopus Rogue. 2011. 206p. pap. 11.95 *(978-0-9843064-3-5(9))* Word with You Pr., A.

Roop, Peter. Houdini: Prince of Air. 2003. (ENG., Illus.). (J). spiral bd. 14.95 *(978-1-59319-023-1(9)*, LeapFrog Schl. Hse.) LeapFrog Enterprises, Inc.

Rosario, Joann. The Trick That Turned into Poop! Rosario, Joann, illus. 2004. (Illus.). 20p. (J). (gr. -1-13). pap. 10.00 *(978-0-9758746-5-3(9)*, 1246169) J.G.R. Enterprises.

Rosasco, Jose Luis. La Mariposa Negra y Otros Cuentos. 2003. (SPA.). pap. *(978-956-13-1661-4(7)*, AB12831) Bello, Andres CHL. Dist: Lectorum Pubns., Inc.

Rose, Simon. The Alchemist's Portrait. 1 vol. 2003. (ENG., Illus.). 120p. (J). (gr. 4-7). per. 6.95 *(978-1-896580-29-6(7))* Tradewind Bks. CAN. Dist: Orca Bk. Pubs. USA.

Ross, Joel. Beast & Crown. 2017. (ENG.). 384p. (J). (gr. 3-7). 16.99 *(978-0-06-248459-8(1)*, HarperCollins) HarperCollins Pubs.

Ross, K. N. Daughters of the Lost World. 2012. 132p. 29.99 *(978-1-4653-8397-6(2))*; pap. 19.99 *(978-1-4653-8396-9(4))* Xlibris Corp.

Ross, Marlene. The Adventures of Donny the Doorknob. Hallam, Colleen and Peggy, illus. 2009. 32p. pap. 24.95 *(978-1-61546-539-2(1))* America Star Bks.

Rossell, Judith. Withering-By-Sea. Rossell, Judith, illus. 2017. (ENG., Illus.). 288p. (J). (gr. 3-7). pap. 8.99 *(978-1-4814-4368-5(2))* Simon & Schuster Children's Publishing.

Rossitto, Tamara. Alura. 2007. 127p. pap. 10.95 *(978-1-4357-0421-3(5))* Lulu Pr., Inc.

Rothenberger, Charlene. Kara's Kapers with Katy Pillar. Rothenberger, Boyd & Bays, Gail, illus. 2006. 64p. per. 9.99 *(978-0-9776260-6-9(7))* Bearhead Publishing, LLC.

Rouncville, Bibi. Bog Nymphs & Tiger Stones. 2008. 52p. pap. 15.50 *(978-1-4357-3966-6(3))* Lulu Pr., Inc.

—Trouble at Binka Bridge. 2009. (ENG.). 52p. pap. 9.50 *(978-0-557-16051-8(0))* Lulu Pr., Inc.

Round, Suzanne. The Dragonfire Crystal. 2011. 154p. pap. *(978-0-7552-1359-7(9))* Authors OnLine, Ltd.

Rounds, Harriet. The Magic Stairway. 1 vol. 2009. 48p. pap. 16.95 *(978-1-60749-707-3(7))* America Star Bks.

Rowe, W. W. The Wand Goes Wild. 2011. 120p. (gr. 3-7). pap. 12.95 *(978-0-9843754-4-8(9))* Sanctuary Publishing, Inc.

Rowling, J. K. Harrius Potter et Philosophi Lapis: (Harry Potter & the Philosopher's Stone) 2003. (Harry Potter Ser.).Tr. of Harry Potter & the Philosopher's Stone. (LAT., Illus.). 256p. (YA). (gr. 7). 29.99 *(978-1-58234-825-4(1)*, 900020066, Bloomsbury USA Childrens) Bloomsbury Publishing USA.

—Harry Potter & the Chamber of Secrets. 2009. 9.64 *(978-0-7848-1444-4(9)*, Everbind) Marco Bk. Co.

—Harry Potter & the Chamber of Secrets. unabr. ed. 2004. (Harry Potter Ser.: Year 2). 352p. (J). (gr. 3-18). pap. 46.00 incl. audio *(978-0-8072-8207-6(3)*, S YA 137 SP, Listening Library) Random Hse. Audio Publishing Group.

—Harry Potter & the Chamber of Secrets. (Harry Potter Ser.: 2). (J). 2006. 1.25 *(978-1-4193-8079-2(6))* 2003. 78.75 *(978-1-4025-6698-1(0))* Recorded Bks., Inc.

—Harry Potter & the Chamber of Secrets. (Harry Potter Ser.: Year 2). (RUS., Illus.). 28.95 *(978-5-8451-0947-7(7))* Rosmen-Izdat RUS. Dist: Distribooks, Inc.

—Harry Potter & the Chamber of Secrets, Bk. 2. Selznick, Brian & GrandPré, Mary, illus. 2018. (Harry Potter Ser.: 2). (ENG.). 368p. (J). (gr. 3). pap. 12.99 *(978-1-338-29915-1(8)*, Levine, Arthur A. Bks.) Scholastic, Inc.

—Harry Potter & the Chamber of Secrets, Bk. 2. Kay, Jim, illus. 2016. (Harry Potter Ser.: 2). (ENG.). 272p. (J). (gr. 3). 39.99 *(978-0-545-79132-8(4)*, Levine, Arthur A. Bks.) Scholastic, Inc.

—Harry Potter & the Chamber of Secrets. l.t. ed. 2003. (Harry Potter Ser.: Year 2). (ENG.). 466p. pap. 13.95 *(978-1-59413-001-4(9))* Thorndike Pr.

—Harry Potter & the Deathly Hallows. (Illus.). 2008. 832p. pap. *(978-0-7475-9586-1(0))* 2007. (ENG., 608p. *(978-0-7475-9106-1(7))* Bloomsbury Publishing Plc.

—Harry Potter & the Deathly Hallows. Ménard, Jean-François, tr. 2017. (FRE.). 896p. (J). (gr. 4-10). pap. *(978-2-07-058523-6(9))* Gallimard, Editions.

—Harry Potter & the Deathly Hallows. braille ed. 2007. (Harry Potter Ser.: Year 7). (J). (gr. 4-7). 34.99 *(978-0-939173-57-0(3))* National Braille Pr.

—Harry Potter & the Deathly Hallows. 2010. 25.00 *(978-1-60686-882-9(9))* Perfection Learning Corp.

—Harry Potter & the Deathly Hallows. 17 vols. 2007. (Harry Potter Ser.: 7). (YA). 131.75 *(978-1-4281-6652-3(1))*; 129.79 *(978-1-4281-6654-7(8))* Recorded Bks., Inc.

—Harry Potter & the Deathly Hallows, Bk. 7. Selznick, Brian & GrandPré, Mary, illus. 2018. (Harry Potter Ser.: 7). (ENG.). 784p. (J). (gr. 3). pap. 16.99 *(978-1-338-29920-5(4)*, Levine, Arthur A. Bks.) Scholastic, Inc.

—Harry Potter & the Deathly Hallows, 7 vols., Bk. 7. GrandPré, Mary, illus. 2007. (Harry Potter Ser.: 7). (ENG.). 784p. (J). (gr. 3-9). 37.99 *(978-0-545-01022-1(5)*, Levine, Arthur A. Bks.) Scholastic, Inc.

—Harry Potter & the Deathly Hallows. l.t. ed. 2009. (ENG.). 970p. pap. 14.95 *(978-1-59413-355-8(7)*, Large Print Pr.) 2007. (Harry Potter Ser.: Year 7). (Illus.). 969p. (J). (gr. 4-7). 34.95 *(978-0-7862-9665-1(8))* Thorndike Pr.

—Harry Potter & the Deathly Hallows. (Harry Potter (Kazu Kibuishi Illustrations) Ser.: 7). 2013. lib. bdg. 29.40 *(978-0-606-32351-2(1))* 2009. lib. bdg. 26.95 *(978-0-606-00420-6(3))* Turtleback.

—Harry Potter & the Deathly Hallows. Bar-hillel, Gili, tr. from ENG. 2007. (Harry Potter Ser.: Year 7). (HEB., Illus.). 568p. (J). (gr. 4-7). pap. *(978-965-482-635-8(6))* Yediot Aharonot Bks., Miscal.

—Harry Potter & the Goblet of Fire. 2009. 10.24 *(978-0-7848-1587-8(9)*, Everbind) Marco Bk. Co.

—Harry Potter & the Goblet of Fire. (Harry Potter Ser.: 4). (J). 2006. 1.25 *(978-1-4193-8531-5(3))* 2003. 101.75 *(978-1-4025-6702-5(2))* Recorded Bks., Inc.

—Harry Potter & the Goblet of Fire. Kay, Jim, illus. 2019. (Harry Potter Ser.: 4). (ENG.). 464p. (J). (gr. 3). 47.99 *(978-0-545-79142-7(1)*, Levine, Arthur A. Bks.) Scholastic, Inc.

—Harry Potter & the Goblet of Fire, Bk. 4. Selznick, Brian & GrandPré, Mary, illus. 2018. (Harry Potter Ser.: 4). (ENG.). 768p. (J). (gr. 3). pap. 14.99 *(978-1-338-29917-5(4)*, Levine, Arthur A. Bks.) Scholastic, Inc.

—Harry Potter & the Goblet of Fire. GrandPré, Mary, illus. l.t. ed. 2003. (Harry Potter Ser.: Vol. 4). (ENG.). 936p. pap. 11.66 *(978-1-59413-003-8(5))* Thorndike Pr.

—Harry Potter & the Half-Blood Prince. 2005. audio compact disk *(978-0-7475-8258-8(0))* Bloomsbury Publishing Plc.

—Harry Potter & the Half-Blood Prince, 9 vols. braille ed. 2005. (Harry Potter Ser.: Year 6). (J). (gr. 4-8). 29.99 *(978-0-939173-39-6(5)*, HALF) National Braille Pr.

—Harry Potter & the Half-Blood Prince. GrandPré, Mary, illus. 2006. (Harry Potter Ser.: Year 6). 652p. (gr. 4-8). 23.00 *(978-0-7569-6765-9(1))* Perfection Learning Corp.

—Harry Potter & the Half-Blood Prince. (Harry Potter Ser.: 6). (J). 2007. 1.25 *(978-1-4193-5430-4(2))* 2006. 110.75 *(978-1-4193-5436-6(1))* 2006. 193.75 *(978-1-4193-5432-8(9))* 2005. 113.75 *(978-1-4193-5434-2(5))* Recorded Bks., Inc.

—Harry Potter & the Half-Blood Prince, Bk. 6. Selznick, Brian & GrandPré, Mary, illus. 2018. (Harry Potter Ser.: 6). (ENG.). 688p. (J). (gr. 3). pap. 14.99 *(978-1-338-29919-9(0)*, Levine, Arthur A. Bks.) Scholastic, Inc.

—Harry Potter & the Half-Blood Prince, Bk. 6. GrandPré, Mary, illus. 2005. (Harry Potter Ser.: 6). (ENG.). 672p. (J). (gr. 3-8). 32.99 *(978-0-439-78454-2(9)*, Levine, Arthur A. Bks.) Scholastic, Inc.

—Harry Potter & the Half-Blood Prince. l.t. ed. (Illus.). (J). (gr. 4-7). 2007. (ENG.). 832p. per. 14.95 *(978-1-59413-221-6(6))* 2005. (Harry Potter Ser.: Year 6). 831p. 29.95 *(978-0-7862-7745-2(9))* Thorndike Pr. (Large Print Pr.).

—Harry Potter & the Half-Blood Prince. 2013. (Harry Potter (Kazu Kibuishi Illustrations) Ser.: 6). lib. bdg. 26.95 *(978-0-606-32350-5(3))* Turtleback.

—Harry Potter & the Half Blood Prince - Chinese Language. 2005. (Harry Potter Ser.: Year 6). (CHI.). 496p. (YA). (gr. 4-8). pap. 28.95 *(978-7-02-005323-0(8)*, HAP06) People's Literature Publishing Hse. CHN. Dist: Chinasprout, Inc.

—Harry Potter & the Order of the Phoenix. 768p. (J). (gr. 6-10). pap. *(978-0-7475-6107-1(9))* Bloomsbury Publishing Plc.

—Harry Potter & the Order of the Phoenix, 13 vols. braille ed. 2003. (Harry Potter Ser.: Year 5). (YA). 29.99 *(978-0-939173-38-9(7))* National Braille Pr.

—Harry Potter & the Order of the Phoenix. 2003. (Harry Potter Ser.: Year 5). (CHI.). 575p. (YA). pap. 26.95 *(978-7-02-004327-9(5)*, HAP05) People's Literature Publishing Hse. CHN. Dist: Chinasprout, Inc.

—Harry Potter & the Order of the Phoenix. 2004. (Harry Potter Ser.). 870p. (gr. 4-6). 16.49 *(978-0-7569-4163-5(6))* Perfection Learning Corp.

—Harry Potter & the Order of the Phoenix. 2003. (ENG.). 768p. *(978-1-55192-570-7(2))* Raincoast Bk. Distribution.

—Harry Potter & the Order of the Phoenix. 2004. (JPN.). (J). (gr. 6-10). *(978-4-915512-51-3(7))* Sayzansha.

—Harry Potter & the Order of the Phoenix, Bk. 5. Selznick, Brian & GrandPré, Mary, illus. 2018. (Harry Potter Ser.: 5). (ENG.). 912p. (J). (gr. 3). pap. 14.99 *(978-1-338-29918-2(2)*, Levine, Arthur A. Bks.) Scholastic, Inc.

—Harry Potter & the Order of the Phoenix, Bk. 5. GrandPré, Mary, illus. 2003. (Harry Potter Ser.: 5). (ENG.). 896p. (gr. 3-7). 32.99 *(978-0-439-35806-4(X)*, Levine, Arthur A. Bks.) Scholastic, Inc.

—Harry Potter & the Order of the Phoenix. l.t. ed. 2003. (Harry Potter Ser.: Year 5). 1093p. 29.95 *(978-0-7862-5778-2(4)*, Large Print Pr.) Thorndike Pr.

—Harry Potter & the Order of the Phoenix. GrandPré, Mary, illus. l.t. ed. 2003. (Thorndike Young Adult Ser.). (ENG.). 1232p. (J). (gr. 4-7). per. 14.95 *(978-1-59413-112-7(0)*, Large Print Pr.) Thorndike Pr.

—Harry Potter & the Order of the Phoenix. 2004. (Harry Potter Ser.: 5). lib. bdg. 24.50 *(978-0-613-99916-8(9))* Turtleback.

—Harry Potter & the Philosopher's Stone. 2014. (ENG., Illus.). 352p. *(978-1-4088-5589-8(5))* Bloomsbury Publishing Plc.

—Harry Potter & the Philosopher's Stone (Irish) 2015. (ENG.). 272p. (J). *(978-1-4088-6619-1(6)*, 283017, Bloomsbury Children's Bks.) Bloomsbury Publishing Plc.

—Harry Potter & the Philosopher's Stone (Latin) Harrius Potter et Philosophi Lapis (Latin) Needham, Peter, tr. 2015. (LAT.). 256p. (J). *(978-1-4088-6618-4(8)*, 283019, Bloomsbury Children's Bks.) Bloomsbury Publishing Plc.

—Harry Potter & the Prisoner of Azkaban. 2009. 9.64 *(978-0-7848-1542-7(9)*, Everbind) Marco Bk. Co.

—Harry Potter & the Prisoner of Azkaban. 2005. (Harry Potter Ser.: Year 3). (CHI.). 260p. (YA). pap. 16.95 *(978-7-02-003345-4(8)*, HAP03) People's Literature Publishing Hse. CHN. Dist: Chinasprout, Inc.

—Harry Potter & the Prisoner of Azkaban, 10 vols. 2003. (Harry Potter Ser.: 3). (J). 84.75 *(978-1-4025-6700-1(6))* Recorded Bks., Inc.

—Harry Potter & the Prisoner of Azkaban, Bk. 3. Selznick, Brian & GrandPré, Mary, illus. 2018. (Harry Potter Ser.: 3). (ENG.). 464p. (J). (gr. 3). pap. 12.99 *(978-1-338-29916-8(6)*, Levine, Arthur A. Bks.) Scholastic, Inc.

—Harry Potter & the Prisoner of Azkaban. l.t. ed. 2003. (Harry Potter Ser.: Year 3). (ENG.). 592p. pap. 13.95 *(978-1-59413-002-1(7)*, Large Print Pr.) Thorndike Pr.

—Harry Potter & the Prisoner of Azkaban. 2013. (Harry Potter (Kazu Kibuishi Illustrations) Ser.: 3). lib. bdg. 24.50 *(978-0-606-32347-5(3))* Turtleback.

—Harry Potter & the Sorcerer's Stone. 2014. (ENG.). lthr. 79.00 *(978-1-62715-772-8(7))* Leatherbound Bestsellers.

—Harry Potter & the Sorcerer's Stone. 2009. 8.44 *(978-0-7848-2438-2(X))*; 10.84 *(978-0-7848-1357-7(4))* Marco Bk. Co. (Everbind).

—Harry Potter & the Sorcerer's Stone. 2003. (Harry Potter Ser.: Year 1). (CHI.). 191p. (YA). pap. 14.95 *(978-7-02-003343-0(1)*, HAP01) People's Literature Publishing Hse. CHN. Dist: Chinasprout, Inc.

—Harry Potter & the Sorcerer's Stone. (Harry Potter Ser.: 1). (J). 2004. 1.25 *(978-1-4025-6757-5(X))* 2003. 80.75 *(978-1-4025-6696-7(4))* Recorded Bks., Inc.

—Harry Potter & the Sorcerer's Stone, Bk. 1. Selznick, Brian & GrandPré, Mary, illus. 2018. (Harry Potter Ser.: 1). (ENG.). 336p. (J). (gr. 3). pap. 12.99 *(978-1-338-29914-4(X)*, Levine, Arthur A. Bks.) Scholastic, Inc.

—Harry Potter & the Sorcerer's Stone, Bk. 1. Kay, Jim, illus. 2015. (Harry Potter Ser.: 1). (ENG.). 256p. (J). (gr. 3). 39.99 *(978-0-545-79035-2(2)*, Levine, Arthur A. Bks.) Scholastic, Inc.

—Harry Potter & the Sorcerer's Stone. 2013. (Harry Potter (Kazu Kibuishi Illustrations) Ser.: 1). lib. bdg. 24.50 *(978-0-606-32345-1(7))* Turtleback.

—Harry Potter e a Camara Secreta. (Harry Potter Ser.: Year 2).Tr. of Harry Potter & the Chamber of Secrets. (POR.). pap. 28.95 *(978-85-325-1166-9(X))* Rocco, Editora, Ltda BRA. Dist: Distribooks, Inc.

—Harry Potter Signature Hardback Boxed Set X 7, 7 vols., Set. 2011. (ENG.). 7p. *(978-1-4088-2594-5(5))* Bloomsbury Publishing Plc.

—Harry Potter y el Prisionero de Azkaban. 2015. (Harry Potter Spanish Ser.: 3).Tr. of Harry Potter & the Prisoner of Azkaban. (SPA.). (gr. 3-6). lib. bdg. 28.10 *(978-0-613-35958-0(5))* Turtleback.

—Harry Potter Y la Orden del Fenix. 2004. (Harry Potter Ser.: Year 5).Tr. of Harry Potter & the Order of the Phoenix. (SPA.). 893p. (YA). 23.99 *(978-84-7888-901-3(9))* Emece Editores ESP. Dist: Lectorum Pubns., Inc.

—Harry Potter Y la Orden del Fenix. Ortega, Gemma Rovira, tr. from ENG. 2004. (Harry Potter Ser.: Year 5).Tr. of Harry Potter & the Order of the Phoenix. (SPA.). 893p. (YA). pap. 17.99 *(978-84-7888-884-9(5))* Emece Editores ESP. Dist: Lectorum Pubns., Inc.

—The Tales of Beedle the Bard. Rowling, J. K., illus. 2008. (ENG., Illus.). 128p. *(978-0-7475-9987-6(4))* Bloomsbury Publishing Plc.

—The Tales of Beedle the Bard. GrandPré, Mary, illus. collector's ed. 2008. 184p. *(978-0-9560109-0-2(3))* Children's High Level Group.

—The Tales of Beedle the Bard. 2017. (ENG.). 128p. (J). (gr. 3-3). 12.99 *(978-1-338-12568-9(0)*, Levine, Arthur A. Bks.) Scholastic, Inc.

—The Tales of Beedle the Bard. 2017. (ENG.). (J). (gr. 3). lib. bdg. 24.50 *(978-0-606-39695-0(0))* Turtleback.

Rowling, J. K. & Xocuasvili, Cico. Hari Poteri Da Sikvdilis Sacukrebi. 2008. (GEO.). 636p. (J). *(978-9941-403-14-9(7))* Georgian Biographic Ctr., Ltd.

Rowling, J.k. Harry Potter y el cáliz de fuego (Harry Potter 4) 2004. (Harry Potter Ser.: Year 4). (SPA., Illus.). 240p. (YA). 19.95 *(978-84-7888-645-6(1)*, SAL30169) Emece Editores ESP. Dist: Lectorum Pubns., Inc.

—Harry Potter y el prisionero de Azkaban (Harry Potter 3) 2004. (Harry Potter Ser.: Year 3). (SPA., Illus.). 360p. (gr. 3-18). 17.95 *(978-84-7888-519-0(6)*, SAL1889) Emece Editores ESP. Dist: Lectorum Pubns., Inc.

—Harry Potter y la cámara secreta (Harry Potter 2) 2004. (Harry Potter Ser.: Year 2). (SPA., Illus.). 288p. (YA). (gr. 3-18). 15.95 *(978-84-7888-495-7(5)*, SAL4595) Emece Editores ESP. Dist: Lectorum Pubns., Inc.

—Harry Potter y la piedra filosofal (Harry Potter 1) 2004. (Harry Potter Ser.: Year 1). (SPA., Illus.). 256p. (YA). (gr. 7-18). 15.95 *(978-84-7888-445-2(9)*, SAL2819) Emece Editores ESP. Dist: Lectorum Pubns., Inc.

Rowntree, G. M. Wizards Spell Magic in the Legends of Mere Leander. 2010. 291p. pap. 32.50 *(978-1-4452-6812-5(4))* Lulu Pr., Inc.

—Wizards Spell Magic in the Legends of Mere Leander - US Trade Size. 2010. (ENG.). 291p. pap. 24.95 *(978-1-4452-9266-3(1))* Lulu Pr., Inc.

Rubens, Michael. Emily & the Spellstone. 2017. (ENG.). 288p. (J). (gr. 5-7). 16.99 *(978-0-544-79086-5(3)*, 1639147, Clarion Bks.) HarperCollins Pubs.

Rudden, Dave. The Forever Court (Knights of the Borrowed Dark, Book 2) 2017. (Knights of the Borrowed Dark Ser.: 2). (ENG.). 432p. (J). (gr. 5). 16.99 *(978-0-553-52301-0(5)*, Random Hse. Bks. for Young Readers) Random Hse. Children's Bks.

Rue, Ginger. Aleca Zamm Fools Them All. 2018. (Aleca Zamm Ser.: 3). (ENG.). 160p. (J). (gr. 2-5). 16.99 *(978-1-4814-7067-4(1))*; (Illus.). pap. 6.99 *(978-1-4814-7066-7(3))* Simon & Schuster Children's Publishing. (Aladdin).

—Aleca Zamm Is a Wonder. 2017. (Aleca Zamm Ser.: 1). (ENG., Illus.). 160p. (J). (gr. 2-5). 16.99 *(978-1-4814-7061-2(2)*, Aladdin) Simon & Schuster Children's Publishing.

—Aleca Zamm Is Ahead of Her Time. 2017. (Aleca Zamm Ser.: 2). (ENG., Illus.). 128p. (J). (gr. 2-5). pap. 6.99 *(978-1-4814-7063-6(9)*, Aladdin) Simon & Schuster Children's Publishing.

—Aleca Zamm Travels Through Time. 2018. (Aleca Zamm Ser.: 4). (ENG.). 112p. (J). (gr. 2-5). 17.99 *(978-1-4814-7070-4(1))*; (Illus.). pap. 6.99 *(978-1-4814-7069-8(8))* Simon & Schuster Children's Publishing. (Aladdin).

Rundell, Katherine. One Christmas Wish. Sutton, Emily, illus. 2018. (ENG.). 64p. (J). (gr. k-4). 18.99 *(978-1-4814-9161-7(X)*, Simon & Schuster Bks. For Young Readers) Simon & Schuster Bks. For Young Readers.

Rupp, Rebecca. The Dragon of Lonely Island. 2006. (Dragon of Lonely Island Ser.: 1). (ENG.). 192p. (J). (gr. 4-7). 8.99 *(978-0-7636-2805-5(0))* Candlewick Pr.

Rush, Jennifer. Devils & Thieves. 2017. (Devils & Thieves Ser.: 1). (ENG.). 336p. (YA). (gr. 9-17). 17.99 *(978-0-316-39089-7(5))* Little, Brown Bks. for Young Readers.

Russell, Sharman Apt. Teresa of the New World. 2015. (ENG.). 192p. (gr. 6-6). 14.99 *(978-1-63158-042-0(6)*, Yucca Publishing) Skyhorse Publishing Co., Inc.

Russo, Bud. The Magic Picture. 2007. (ENG.). 156p. pap. 10.95 *(978-1-4357-0110-6(0))* Lulu Pr., Inc.

Russon, Penni. Breathe. 2007. (ENG., Illus.). 368p. (YA). (gr. 9-18). 16.99 *(978-0-06-079393-7(7))* HarperCollins Pubs.

Rusu, Meredith. Charmer Girls Rock! 2016. (Scholastic Reader, Level 1 Ser.). (ENG.). 32p. (J). (gr. -1-1). pap. 5.99 *(978-1-338-03730-2(7))* Scholastic, Inc.

Ruth, Nick. The Breezes of Inspire. Concannon, Sue, illus. 2005. (Remin Chronicles: 2). (ENG.). 264p. (J). (gr. 3-7). 16.95 *(978-0-9745603-3-5(2))* Imaginator Pr.

Rutkoski, Marie. The Cabinet of Wonders: The Kronos Chronicles: Book I. 2013. (Kronos Chronicles Ser.: 1). (ENG.). 288p. (J). (gr. 5-9). pap. 21.99 *(978-1-250-01804-5(8)*, 900087537) Square Fish.

—The Celestial Globe: The Kronos Chronicles: Book II. 2013. (Kronos Chronicles Ser.: 2). (ENG.). 320p. (J). (gr. 5-9). pap. 23.99 *(978-1-250-02732-0(2)*, 900098304) Square Fish.

—The Jewel of the Kalderash: The Kronos Chronicles: Book III. 2013. (Kronos Chronicles Ser.: 3). (ENG.). 336p. (J). (gr. 5-9). pap. 18.99 *(978-1-250-01025-4(X)*, 900084763) Square Fish.

Ryan, Brittney. The Legend of Holly Claus. Long, Laurel, illus. 2004. (Julie Andrews Collection). 544p. (J). (gr. 4-18). 16.99 *(978-0-06-058511-2(0))*; lib. bdg. 17.89 *(978-0-06-058514-3(5))* HarperCollins Pubs. (Julie Andrews Collection).

Ryan, Carrie & Davis, John Parke. City of Thirst. (Map to Everywhere Ser.: 2). (ENG., Illus.). (J). (gr. 3-7). 2016. 416p. pap. 19.99 *(978-0-316-24082-6(6))* 2015. 400p. 17.00 *(978-0-316-24084-0(2))* Little, Brown Bks. for Young Readers.

Ryan, Pam Muñoz. Mañanaland. 2020. (ENG., Illus.). 256p. (J). (gr. 3-7). 18.99 *(978-1-338-15786-4(8)*, Scholastic Pr.) Scholastic, Inc.

—Mañanaland (Spanish Edition) 2020. (SPA.). 288p. (J). (gr. 3-7). pap. 8.99 *(978-1-338-67009-7(3)*, Scholastic en Espanol) Scholastic, Inc.

Ryder, Chloe. Princess Ponies 1: a Magical Friend. 2014. (Princess Ponies Ser.). (ENG., Illus.). 128p. (J). (gr. 1-3).

M
N
O

pap. 5.99 (978-1-61963-165-6(2), 900123295, Bloomsbury USA Childrens) Bloomsbury Publishing USA.

—Princess Ponies 10: the Pumpkin Ghost. 2019. (Princess Ponies Ser.). (ENG., Illus.). 128p. (J). pap. 5.99 (978-1-5476-0166-0(3), 900201119, Bloomsbury Children's Bks.) Bloomsbury Publishing USA.

—Princess Ponies 12: an Enchanted Heart. 2019. (Princess Ponies Ser.). (ENG., Illus.). 128p. (J). pap. 5.99 (978-1-5476-0190-5(6), 900203169, Bloomsbury Children's Bks.) Bloomsbury Publishing USA.

—Princess Ponies 2: a Dream Come True. 2014. (Princess Ponies Ser.). (ENG., Illus.). 128p. (J). (gr. 1-3). pap. 6.99 (978-1-61963-167-0(9), 900123305, Bloomsbury USA Childrens) Bloomsbury Publishing USA.

—Princess Ponies 3: the Special Secret. 2014. (Princess Ponies Ser.). (ENG., Illus.). 128p. (J). (gr. 2-4). pap. 6.99 (978-1-61963-237-0(3), 900128207, Bloomsbury USA Childrens) Bloomsbury Publishing USA.

—Princess Ponies 4: a Unicorn Adventure! 2014. (Princess Ponies Ser.). (ENG., Illus.). 128p. (J). (gr. 2-4). pap. 6.99 (978-1-61963-294-3(2), 900132055, Bloomsbury USA Childrens) Bloomsbury Publishing USA.

—Princess Ponies 5: an Amazing Rescue. 2015. (Princess Ponies Ser.). (ENG., Illus.). 128p. (J). (gr. 2-4). pap. 6.99 (978-1-61963-403-9(1), 900135708, Bloomsbury USA Childrens) Bloomsbury Publishing USA.

—Princess Ponies 6: Best Friends Forever! 2015. (Princess Ponies Ser.). (ENG., Illus.). 128p. (J). (gr. 2-4). pap. 5.99 (978-1-61963-405-3(8), 900135710, Bloomsbury USA Childrens) Bloomsbury Publishing USA.

—Princess Ponies 7: a Special Surprise. 2015. (Princess Ponies Ser.). (ENG., Illus.). 128p. (J). (gr. 2-4). pap. 5.99 (978-1-61963-565-4(8), 900140702, Bloomsbury USA Childrens) Bloomsbury Publishing USA.

—Princess Ponies 8: a Singing Star. 2015. (Princess Ponies Ser.). (ENG., Illus.). 128p. (J). (gr. 2-4). pap. 5.99 (978-1-61963-567-8(4), 900140704, Bloomsbury USA Childrens) Bloomsbury Publishing USA.

—Princess Ponies 9: the Lucky Horseshoe. 2019. (Princess Ponies Ser.). (ENG., Illus.). 128p. (J). pap. 5.99 (978-1-5476-0164-6(7), 900201120, Bloomsbury Children's Bks.) Bloomsbury Publishing USA.

Rylander, Chris. The Legend of Greg. 2018. (Epic Series of Failures Ser.: 1). (ENG.). 352p. (J). (gr. 3-7). 16.99 (978-1-5247-3972-0(3), G.P. Putnam's Sons Books for Young Readers) Penguin Young Readers Group.

Rylant, Cynthia. The Van Gogh Cafe. 2006. (ENG., Illus.). 64p. (J). (gr. 3-7). pap. 8.99 (978-0-15-205750-3(1), 1197281, Clarion Bks.) HarperCollins Pubs.

—The Van Gogh Café. 2015. 64p. pap. 7.00 (978-1-61003-500-2(3)) Center for the Collaborative Classroom.

Sabo-Western, Deborah. Peter Penny: Discovers the Gift. 2007. (ENG.). 46p. pap. 15.99 (978-1-4196-8115-8(X)) CreateSpace Independent Publishing Platform.

Saccheri, Josephine. Magic on the Wall, 1 vol. Carrescia, Reid, illus. 2009. 11p. pap. 24.95 (978-1-61546-374-9(7)) America Star Bks.

—The Secret to Easter Eggs. Saccheri, Briana, illus. 2008. 28p. pap. 24.95 (978-1-60474-210-7(0)) America Star Bks.

Sackier, Shelley. The Antidote. 2019. (ENG.). 368p. (YA). (gr. 8). 17.99 (978-0-06-245347-1(5), HarperTeen) HarperCollins Pubs.

Sadler, Marilyn. P. J. Funnybunny's Bag of Tricks. Bollen, Roger, illus. 2005. (Step into Reading Ser.). 32p. 14.00 (978-0-7569-5405-5(3)) Perfection Learning Corp.

—P. J. Funnybunny's Bag of Tricks. Bollen, Roger, illus. 2004. (Step into Reading Ser.). 32p. (J). (gr. -1-1). pap. 4.99 (978-0-375-82444-9(8), Random Hse. Bks. for Young Readers) Random Hse. Children's Bks.

—P. J. Funnybunny's Bag of Tricks. 2004. (Step into Reading Level 2 Ser.). (gr. -1-2). lib. bdg. 13.55 (978-0-613-83535-0(2)) Turtleback.

Sage, Angie. Darke, 12 vols. (Septimus Heap Ser.: 6). (J). 297.75 (978-1-4498-6217-6(9)); 1.25 (978-1-4498-6226-8(8)); 131.75 (978-1-4498-6218-3(7)); 2013. 92.75 (978-1-4498-6225-1(X)); 2011. 133.75 (978-1-4498-6220-6(9)); 2011. 131.75 (978-1-4498-6222-0(5)) Recorded Bks., Inc.

—Darke. Zug, Mark, illus. 2012. (Septimus Heap Ser.: 6). (J). lib. bdg. 18.40 (978-0-606-26264-4(4)) Turtleback.

—Flyte. (Septimus Heap Ser.: 2). (J). 2009. 84.49 (978-1-4361-5831-2(1)) 2008. 1.25 (978-1-4193-9383-9(9)) 2006. 114.75 (978-1-4193-9386-0(3)) 2006. 133.75 (978-1-4193-9390-7(1)) 2006. 282.75 (978-1-4193-9387-7(1)) 2006. 111.75 (978-1-4193-9388-4(X)) 2006. 131.75 (978-1-4193-9392-1(8)) Recorded Bks., Inc.

—Fyre. Zug, Mark, illus. 2013. 702p. (J). (978-0-06-224697-4(6)) HarperCollins Pubs.

—Fyre. 2014. (Septimus Heap Ser.: 7). (J). lib. bdg. 18.40 (978-0-606-35067-9(5)) Turtleback.

—Magyk. Zug, Mark, illus. 2007. (Septimus Heap Ser.: Bk. 1). 564p. (gr. 4-7). 18.00 (978-0-7569-7760-3(6)) Perfection Learning Corp.

—Magyk. (Septimus Heap Ser.: 1). (J). 2008. 79.75 (978-1-4361-0584-2(6)) 2007. 1.25 (978-1-4193-2619-6(8)) 2006. 123.75 (978-1-4193-3807-6(2)) 2005. 106.75 (978-1-4193-2622-6(8)) 2005. 126.75 (978-1-4193-3805-2(6)) 2005. 103.75 (978-1-4193-2624-0(4)) Recorded Bks., Inc.

—Magyk. 2006. (Septimus Heap Ser.: 1). (J). lib. bdg. 18.40 (978-1-4177-3321-7(7)) Turtleback.

—Pathfinder. 2015. (Septimus Heap: TodHunter Moon Ser.: 1). (J). lib. bdg. 18.40 (978-0-606-37612-9(7)) Turtleback.

—Physik, 11 vols. 2007. (Septimus Heap Ser.: 3). (J). 113.75 (978-1-4281-4576-4(1)); 133.75 (978-1-4281-4580-1(X)); (SPA.). 131.75 (978-1-4281-4582-5(6)); 1.25 (978-1-4281-4573-3(7)); 277.75 (978-1-4281-4577-1(X)); 111.75 (978-1-4281-4578-8(8)) Recorded Bks., Inc.

—Physik. 2008. (Septimus Heap Ser.: 3). (J). lib. bdg. 18.40 (978-1-4178-1565-4(5)) Turtleback.

—Queste. Zug, Mark, illus. 2009. (Septimus Heap Ser.: 4). 596p. (J). lib. bdg. 18.40 (978-0-606-02607-9(X)) Turtleback.

—Septimus Heap, Set. Zug, Mark, illus. 2007. (Septimus Heap Ser.: Bks. 1-2). (J). (gr. 4). pap. 15.99 (978-0-06-136195-1(X), Tegen, Katherine Bks) HarperCollins Pubs.

—Septimus Heap, Book Five: Syren. Zug, Mark, illus. (Septimus Heap Ser.: 5). (ENG.). (J). (gr. 4). 2011. 656p. pap. 8.99 (978-0-06-088212-9(3)) 2009. 640p. lib. bdg. 18.89 (978-0-06-088211-2(5)) 2009. 640p. 17.99 (978-0-06-088210-5(7)) HarperCollins Pubs. (Tegen, Katherine Bks).

—Septimus Heap, Book Four: Queste. Zug, Mark, illus. (Septimus Heap Ser.: 4). (ENG.). (J). (gr. 4). 2009. 624p. pap. 10.99 (978-0-06-088209-9(3)) 2008. 608p. 18.99 (978-0-06-088207-5(7)) HarperCollins Pubs. (Tegen, Katherine Bks).

—Septimus Heap, Book One: Magyk. Zug, Mark, illus. (Septimus Heap Ser.: 1). (ENG.). (J). (gr. 4-18). 2005. 576p. 18.99 (978-0-06-057731-5(2)) 2005. 576p. lib. bdg. 18.89 (978-0-06-057732-2(0)) 2006. 608p. reprint ed. pap. 7.99 (978-0-06-057733-9(9)) HarperCollins Pubs. (Tegen, Katherine Bks).

—Septimus Heap, Book Seven: Fyre. Zug, Mark, illus. 2013. (Septimus Heap Ser.: 7). (ENG.). 720p. (J). (gr. 3-7). 18.99 (978-0-06-124245-8(4), Tegen, Katherine Bks) HarperCollins Pubs.

—Septimus Heap, Book Six: Darke. Zug, Mark, illus. 2012. (Septimus Heap Ser.: 6). (ENG.). 656p. (J). (gr. 4). pap. 7.99 (978-0-06-124244-1(6), Tegen, Katherine Bks) HarperCollins Pubs.

—Septimus Heap, Book Three: Physik. Zug, Mark, illus. (Septimus Heap Ser.: 3). (ENG.). (J). (gr. 4-7). 2007. 560p. 18.99 (978-0-06-057737-7(1))Bk. 3. 2008. 576p. pap. 9.99 (978-0-06-057739-1(8)) HarperCollins Pubs. (Tegen, Katherine Bks).

—Septimus Heap, Book Two: Flyte. Zug, Mark, illus. (Septimus Heap Ser.: 2). (ENG.). 544p. (J). (gr. 4-7). 2007. pap. 8.99 (978-0-06-057736-0(3)) 2006. 17.99 (978-0-06-057734-6(7)) HarperCollins Pubs. (Tegen, Katherine Bks).

—Todhunter Moon: Sandrider. Zug, Mark, illus. 2016. (Septimus Heap: TodHunter Moon Ser.: 2). (ENG.). 496p. (J). (gr. 3-7). 18.40 (978-0-606-39255-6(6)) Turtleback.

—TodHunter Moon, Book One: PathFinder. Zug, Mark, illus. 2014. (World of Septimus Heap Ser.: 1). (ENG.). 480p. (J). (gr. 3-7). 17.99 (978-0-06-227245-4(4), Tegen, Katherine Bks) HarperCollins Pubs.

—TodHunter Moon, Book Three: StarChaser. Zug, Mark, illus. 2017. (World of Septimus Heap Ser.: 3). (ENG.). 496p. (J). (gr. 3-7). pap. 7.99 (978-0-06-227252-2(7), Tegen, Katherine Bks) HarperCollins Pubs.

—TodHunter Moon, Book Two: SandRider. Zug, Mark, illus. 2015. (World of Septimus Heap Ser.: 2). (ENG.). 480p. (J). (gr. 3-7). 17.99 (978-0-06-227248-5(9), Tegen, Katherine Bks) HarperCollins Pubs.

Sager Weinstein, Jacob & Sager Weinstein, Jacob. Hyacinth & the Stone Thief. 2018. (Hyacinth Ser.: 2). (ENG.). 320p. (J). (gr. 3-7). 16.99 (978-0-399-55321-9(5), Random Hse. Bks. for Young Readers) Random Hse. Children's Bks.

Saito, Taeko. Kiss the Frog. 2010. (Princess & the Frog Ser.). (JPN., Illus.). (J). bds. (978-4-06-262548-7(2)) Kodansha America, Inc.

Salazar, L. J. Chin & the Magic Stones: Book One - Becoming Guardians. 2009. 108p. 20.95 (978-0-595-63627-3(6)); pap. 10.95 (978-0-595-53157-8(1)) iUniverse, Inc.

Salerni, Dianne K. The Eighth Day. McClellan, David, illus. 2015. (Eighth Day Ser.: 1). (ENG.). 336p. (J). (gr. 3-7). pap. 6.99 (978-0-06-227216-4(0), HarperCollins) HarperCollins Pubs.

—The Eighth Day. 2014. (Eighth Day Ser.: 1). (ENG., Illus.). 320p. (J). (gr. 3-7). 16.99 (978-0-06-227215-7(2), HarperCollins) HarperCollins Pubs.

—The Inquisitor's Mark. 2015. (Eighth Day Ser.: 2). (ENG.). 368p. (J). (gr. 3-7). pap. 6.99 (978-0-06-227219-5(5), HarperCollins) HarperCollins Pubs.

—The Morrigan's Curse. 2016. (Eighth Day Ser.: 3). (ENG.). 400p. (J). (gr. 3-7). 16.99 (978-0-06-227221-8(7), HarperCollins) HarperCollins Pubs.

Salsi, Lynn. Jack & the Giants. Young, James, illus. 2012. (ENG.). 32p. (J). 16.95 (978-0-938467-52-6(2)) Headline Bks., Inc.

Sampson, Fay. The Sorcerer's Daughter. 2007. (ENG.). 224p. (J). (gr. 4-7). per. 7.99 (978-0-7459-6072-2(3), d4495d7a-5217-4312-b7a4-6d79658080ae, Lion Children's) Lion Hudson PLC GBR. Dist: Baker & Taylor Publisher Services (BTPS).

San Souci, Robert D. Cinderella Skeleton. Catrow, David, illus. 2004. (ENG.). 32p. (J). (gr. -1-3). reprint ed. pap. 7.99 (978-0-15-205069-6(8), 1195310, Clarion Bks.) HarperCollins Pubs.

Sanders, Ted. The Box & the Dragonfly. Bruno, Iacopo, illus. 2015. (Keepers Ser.: No. 1). 534p. (J). (978-0-06-239019-6(8), Harper & Row Ltd.

—The Keepers #3: the Portal & the Veil. Bruno, Iacopo, illus. 2017. (Keepers Ser.: 3). (ENG.). 592p. (J). (gr. 3-7). 16.99 (978-0-06-227588-2(7), HarperCollins) HarperCollins Pubs.

—The Keepers: the Box & the Dragonfly. Bruno, Iacopo, illus. 2015. (Keepers Ser.: 1). (ENG.). 544p. (J). (gr. 3-7). 16.99 (978-0-06-227582-0(8), HarperCollins) HarperCollins Pubs.

Sanderson, Brandon. The Rithmatist. McSweeney, Ben, illus. (ENG.). (YA). 2019. 443p. 14.99 (978-1-250-24271-6(1), 900211978) 2014. 384p. (gr. 7). pap. 11.99 (978-0-7653-3844-0(0), 900126287) Doherty, Tom Assocs., LLC. (Tor Teen).

—The Rithmatist. McSweeney, Ben & McSweeney, Ben, illus. 2013. (ENG.). 384p. (YA). (gr. 7). 19.99 (978-0-7653-2032-2(0), 900050488, Tor Teen) Doherty, Tom Assocs., LLC.

—The Rithmatist. 2014. (YA). lib. bdg. 22.10 (978-0-606-38512-1(6)) Turtleback.

Santa the Chimney Sweep/the Candy Cane That Found a Home: Wee Voices Collection. 2005. (Illus.). 37p. per. 6.95 (978-0-9764444-9-7(6)) E. J. Publishing.

Santiago, Shelly. The Fairies of Tythian. 2010. 40p. pap. 14.95 (978-1-60976-143-1(X), Eloquent Bks.) Strategic Book Publishing & Rights Agency (SBPRA).

Santillo, LuAnn. Look at Me. Santillo, LuAnn, ed. 2003. (Half-Pint Kids Readers Ser.). (Illus.). 7p. (J). (gr. -1-1). pap. 1.00 (978-1-59256-052-3(0)) Half-Pint Kids, Inc.

Sarrasin, Alex. The Guardians of Neoegypti: Book One. 2007. 300p. per. 18.95 (978-0-595-45710-6(X)) iUniverse, Inc.

Sataram, Nikita. Zatheria: The Hidden Realm. 2013. 194p. (gr. -1). 24.77 (978-1-4907-0938-3(X)); pap. 14.77 (978-1-4907-0936-9(3)) Trafford Publishing.

Saunders, George P. The Last Elf. 2007. 180p. per. 13.95 (978-0-595-40843-6(5)) iUniverse, Inc.

Saunders, Kate. Beswitched. 2012. (ENG.). 272p. (J). (gr. 4-7). 7.99 (978-0-375-87329-4(5), Yearling) Random Hse. Children's Bks.

—The Curse of the Chocolate Phoenix. 2016. (ENG.). 272p. (J). (gr. 5). 7.99 (978-0-385-39105-4(6), Yearling) Random Hse. Children's Bks.

—Magicalamity. 2013. (ENG.). 320p. (J). (gr. 4-7). 9.99 (978-0-385-74078-4(6), Yearling) Random Hse. Children's Bks.

—The Whizz Pop Chocolate Shop. 2014. (ENG.). 304p. (J). (gr. 5). 7.99 (978-0-385-74302-0(5), Yearling) Random Hse. Children's Bks.

Sava, Scott Christian. Animal Crackers. 2011. (Illus.). 152p. pap. 11.99 (978-1-60010-619-4(6)) Idea & Design Works, LLC.

—Magic Carpet. 2010. (Illus.). 110p. (J). pap. 11.99 (978-1-60010-563-0(7)) Idea & Design Works, LLC.

Savage, J. Scott. Land Keep. 2009. (Farworld Ser.: Bk. 2). 432p. (YA). (gr. 5-18). 18.95 (978-1-60641-164-3(0), Shadow Mountain) Shadow Mountain Publishing.

Saveley, Barb. Dusky: The Lost Unicorn. 2008. 24p. pap. 24.95 (978-1-60441-909-2(1)) America Star Bks.

Sawler, Kimberly. Rocket & the Magical Cosmic Candies. Walls, Ty, illus. 2006. 32p. (J). (gr. 4-7). 18.95 (978-1-933285-51-1(6)) Brown Books Publishing Group.

Saxon, Victoria. Frozen (Disney Frozen) Lee, Grace & Cagol, Andrea, illus. 2015. (Little Golden Book Ser.). (ENG.). 24p. (J). (-k). 5.99 (978-0-7364-3471-3(2), Golden/Disney) Random Hse. Children's Bks.

Sayre, Jill K. The Fairies of Turtle Creek. 2013. 322p. 22.17 (978-0-9885066-4-0(5)); pap. 15.70 (978-0-9885066-6-4(1)) Infinity Oak Bks.

Scaletta, Kurtis. Mudville. 2010. 272p. (J). (gr. 3-7). 8.99 (978-0-375-84472-0(4), Yearling) Random Hse. Children's Bks.

Schaefer, Lola. Easter Surprises. McCue, Lisa, illus. 2009. (ENG.). 18p. (J). (gr. -1-1). 7.99 (978-1-4169-6476-6(2), Little Simon) Little Simon.

Scheidt, Dave. Wrapped up Vol. 2. McMahon, Scoot, illus. 2018. (ENG.). 144p. (J). pap. 12.99 (978-1-941302-70-5(X), 41dfa637-7f8b-4c36-9590-b8766c99c3ec, Lion Forge) Oni Pr., Inc.

Schlesinger, Gretchen. Send Me the Soap #1: The Emerald Isle Adventure. Pietila, David, illus. 2006. (J). 11.95 (978-0-9778536-0-1(8)) Eco-thumb Publishing Co.

—Send Me the Soap #1: The Emerald Isle Adventure (lib. Bdg.) Pietila, David, illus. 2006. (J). lib. bdg. (978-0-9778536-1-8(6)) Eco-thumb Publishing Co.

Schlitz, Laura Amy. The Night Fairy. Barrett, Angela, illus. 2011. (ENG.). 128p. (J). (gr. 2-5). pap. 7.99 (978-0-7636-5295-1(4)) Candlewick Pr.

—The Night Fairy, 2 vols. unabr. ed. 2010. (J). (gr. 1-4). 54.75 (978-1-4407-6983-2(4)) Recorded Bks., Inc.

Schmatz, Pat. The Key to Every Thing. 2018. (ENG.). 208p. (J). (gr. 3-7). 16.99 (978-0-7636-9566-8(1)) Candlewick Pr.

Schmid, Susan Maupin. Ghost of a Chance. Marlin, Lissy, illus. 2017. (100 Dresses Ser.: 2). 320p. (J). (gr. 3-7). 16.99 (978-0-553-53373-6(8), Random Hse. Bks. for Young Readers) Random Hse. Children's Bks.

—If the Magic Fits. 2017. (100 Dresses Ser.: 1). 320p. (J). (gr. 3-7). 7.99 (978-0-553-53369-9(X), Yearling) Random Hse. Children's Bks.

—The Starlight Slippers. 2018. (100 Dresses Ser.: 3). (Illus.). 336p. (J). (gr. 3-7). 16.99 (978-0-553-53377-4(0), Random Hse. Bks. for Young Readers) Random Hse. Children's Bks.

Schneller, Candace. Jayden's Magic Door. Margolis, Al, illus. 2010. (ENG.). 60p. pap. 22.00 (978-1-4269-4228-0(1)) Trafford Publishing.

Schoffstall, John. Half-Witch: A Novel. 2019. (ENG.). 336p. (YA). pap. 14.95 (978-1-61873-167-8(X), Big Mouth Hse.) Small Beer Pr.

Schow, Betsy. Banished. 2018. (Storymakers Ser.: 3). (ENG.). 336p. (YA). (gr. 6-12). pap. 10.99 (978-1-4926-3602-1(9)) Sourcebooks, Inc.

—Spelled. 2015. (Storymakers Ser.: 0). (ENG.). 352p. (YA). (gr. 6-12). pap. 10.99 (978-1-4926-0871-4(8), 9781492608714) Sourcebooks, Inc.

Schrader, Racheal. Doodlebugs: Trouble On Moss Farm. Schrader, Racheal, illus. 2008. (Illus.). 156p. (YA). per. 7.99 (978-0-9815274-0-6(X)) Schrader, Racheal.

Schraff, Anne. The Magic Stone. 2015. (Red Rhino Ser.). (J). lib. bdg. 18.40 (978-0-606-37207-7(5)) Turtleback.

Schram, Kristina. The Chronicles of Anaedor. 2010. 416p. pap. 9.95 (978-1-935142-10-2(0)) Variance Author Services.

Schram, Peninnah. The Magic Pomegranate. Hall, Melanie, illus. 2007. (On My Own Folklore Ser.). 48p. (J). lib. bdg. 17.95 (978-0-8225-8856-6(0), Kar-Ben Publishing) Lerner Publishing Group.

Schrefer, Eliot. The Lost Rainforest: Mez's Magic. 2018. (Illus.). 368p. (J). (978-0-06-283959-6(4), Tegen, Katherine Bks) HarperCollins Pubs.

—The Lost Rainforest #1: Mez's Magic. Dziubak, Emilia, illus. 2018. (ENG.). (J). (gr. 3-7). 384p. pap. 6.99 (978-0-06-249113-8(X)); 368p. 16.99 (978-0-06-249107-7(5)) HarperCollins Pubs. (Tegen, Katherine Bks).

—The Lost Rainforest #2: Gogi's Gambit. Dziubak, Emilia, illus. 2019. (ENG.). (J). (gr. 3-7). 368p. pap. 6.99 (978-0-06-249115-2(6)); 352p. 16.99 (978-0-06-249111-4(3)) HarperCollins Pubs. (Tegen, Katherine Bks).

Schroeder, Lisa. Sealed with a Secret. 2016. (ENG.). 224p. (J). (gr. 3-7). 16.99 (978-0-545-90734-7(9), Scholastic Pr.) Scholastic, Inc.

Schuff, Nicolás & Fraticelli, Damin. Ana y la Maldicion de Las Pecas, Vol. 1. Mey, illus. 2013. (Coleccion Heroinas Ser.).Tr. of Ana & the Cursed Freckles. (SPA.). 96p. (J). (gr. 4-7). pap. 10.95 (978-987-1710-84-3(4)) Ediciones Urano S. A. ESP. Dist: Spanish Pubs., LLC.

Scieszka, Jon. Hey Kid, Want to Buy a Bridge? McCauley, Adam, illus. 2005. (Time Warp Trio Ser.: No. 11). 74p. (gr. 4-7). 15.00 (978-0-7569-5988-3(8)) Perfection Learning Corp.

—Marco? Polo! McCauley, Adam, illus. 2008. (Time Warp Trio Ser.: No. 16). 90p. (J). (gr. 4-6). 12.65 (978-0-7569-8923-1(X)) Perfection Learning Corp.

—Marco? Polo! #16, No. 16. McCauley, Adam, illus. 2008. (Time Warp Trio Ser.: 16). 96p. (J). (gr. 2-4). 5.99 (978-0-14-241177-3(9), Puffin Books) Penguin Young Readers Group.

—Me Oh Maya. McCauley, Adam, illus. 2005. (Time Warp Trio Ser.: No. 13). 69p. (gr. 2-6). 15.00 (978-0-7569-5060-6(0)) Perfection Learning Corp.

—Me Oh Maya #13. McCauley, Adam, illus. 2005. (Time Warp Trio Ser.: 13). 96p. (J). (gr. 2-4). 5.99 (978-0-14-240300-6(8), Puffin Books) Penguin Young Readers Group.

—Summer Reading Is Killing Me! Smith, Lane, illus. 2004. (Time Warp Trio Ser.: No. 7). 73p. (J). (gr. 4-7). 12.65 (978-0-7569-6781-9(3)) Perfection Learning Corp.

—Summer Reading Is Killing Me! #7. Smith, Lane, illus. 2004. (Time Warp Trio Ser.: 7). 80p. (J). (gr. 2-4). pap. 5.99 (978-0-14-240115-6(3), Puffin Books) Penguin Young Readers Group.

—Viking It & Liking It. McCauley, Adam, illus. 2004. (Time Warp Trio Ser.: No. 12). 73p. (gr. 2-6). 15.00 (978-0-7569-2589-5(4)) Perfection Learning Corp.

—Viking It & Liking It. 2004. (Time Warp Trio Ser.: 12). 16.00 (978-1-4176-3613-6(0)) Turtleback.

Scott, Lisa Ann. All That Glitters. Burns, Heather, illus. 2017. 117p. (J). pap. (978-1-338-13559-6(7)) Scholastic, Inc.

—Dreams That Sparkle, 4. Burns, Heather, illus. 2017. (Enchanted Pony Academy Ser.). (ENG.). 128p. (J). (gr. 1-4). 17.44 (978-1-5364-0219-3(2)) Scholastic, Inc.

—Let It Glow, 3. Burns, Heather, illus. 2017. (Enchanted Pony Academy Ser.). (ENG.). 128p. (J). (gr. 1-4). 17.44 (978-1-5364-0218-6(4)) Scholastic, Inc.

Scott, Mairghread. The City on the Other Side. 2018. (ENG., Illus.). 224p. (J). pap. 18.99 (978-1-62672-457-0(1), 900158088, First Second Bks.) Roaring Brook Pr.

Scott, Michael. The Alchemyst. 2009. (ENG., Illus.). 375p. (gr. 6-10). 19.00 (978-1-60686-514-9(5)) Perfection Learning Corp.

—The Alchemyst. (Secrets of the Immortal Nicholas Flamel Ser.: 1). (ENG.). 400p. (YA). (gr. 7). 2008. pap. 11.99 (978-0-385-73600-8(2), Ember) 2007. (Illus.). 18.99 (978-0-385-73357-1(7), Delacorte Bks. for Young Readers) Random Hse. Children's Bks.

—The Enchantress. 2013. (Secrets of the Immortal Nicholas Flamel Ser.: 6). (ENG.). 528p. (YA). (gr. 7). pap. 10.99 (978-0-385-73536-0(7), Ember) Random Hse. Children's Bks.

—The Enchantress. 2013. (Secrets of the Immortal Nicholas Flamel Ser.: 6). lib. bdg. 22.10 (978-0-606-31947-8(6)) Turtleback.

—The Magician. 2009. (Secrets of the Immortal Nicholas Flamel Ser.: 2). (ENG.). 496p. (YA). (gr. 7). pap. 11.99 (978-0-385-73728-9(9), Ember) Random Hse. Children's Bks.

—The Necromancer. 2011. (Secrets of the Immortal Nicholas Flamel Ser.: 4). (ENG.). 416p. (YA). (gr. 7). pap. 11.99 (978-0-385-73532-2(4), Ember) Random Hse. Children's Bks.

—The Necromancer. l.t. ed. 2010. (Secrets of the Immortal Nicholas Flamel Ser.). (ENG.). 690p. pap. 23.99 (978-1-4104-2851-6(6)) Thorndike Pr.

—The Sorceress. 2010. (Secrets of the Immortal Nicholas Flamel Ser.: 3). (ENG.). 512p. (YA). (gr. 7-18). pap. 11.99 (978-0-385-73530-8(8), Ember) Random Hse. Children's Bks.

—The Sorceress. 2010. (Secrets of the Immortal Nicholas Flamel Ser.: 3). lib. bdg. 22.10 (978-0-606-14133-8(2)) Turtleback.

—The Sorceress the Secrets of the Immortal Nicholas Flamel. l.t. ed. 2009. (Secrets of the Immortal Nicholas Flamel Ser.). (ENG.). 614p. (YA). 23.95 (978-1-4104-2092-3(2)) Thorndike Pr.

Scott, Molly. Broken Bones Are No Fun, but Broken Bones Won't Stop My Play! Baker, David, illus. 2012. 32p. pap. 24.95 (978-1-4626-7424-4(0)) America Star Bks.

Scotton, Rob. Russell's Christmas Magic. Scotton, Rob, illus. 2007. (Illus.). 32p. (J). (gr. -1-2). lib. bdg. 17.89 (978-0-06-059855-6(7)) HarperCollins Pubs.

Seal, Caitlin. Trinity of Bones. 2019. (Illus.). 336p. (YA). (gr. 7). lib. bdg. 17.99 (978-1-58089-808-9(4), Charlesbridge Teen) Charlesbridge Publishing, Inc.

—Twice Dead. 2019. 336p. (YA). (gr. 7). pap. 12.99 (978-1-62354-105-7(0), Charlesbridge Teen) Charlesbridge Publishing, Inc.

—Twice Dead: The Necromancer's Song. 2018. (Necromancer's Song Ser.: 1). (Illus.). 336p. (YA). (gr. 7). 17.99 (978-1-58089-807-2(6), Charlesbridge Teen) Charlesbridge Publishing, Inc.

Sealey, Philip. The Sorcerer's Tome. 2013. 254p. pap. (978-1-78407-199-8(4)) FeedARead.com.

Sedacca, Luisa M. Gigi's Magic Carpet Ride: Travels with Gigi. 2009. (ENG.). 24p. pap. 15.99 (978-1-4500-0547-0(0)) Xlibris Corp.

Sedgwick, Julian. The Black Dragon. Moffett, Patricia, illus. 2018. (Mysterium Ser.). (ENG.). 352p. (J). (gr. 4-8). pap. 9.99 (978-1-5415-1489-8(0), 6c0683dc-fa47-4097-b4fd-1f7a2d9c8e98, Carolrhoda Bks.) Lerner Publishing Group.

—The Palace of Memory, No. 2. Moffett, Patricia, illus. 2017. (Mysterium Ser.: 2). (ENG.). 352p. (J). (gr. 4-8). 18.99 (978-1-4677-7568-7(1), a33df367-d91f-4e23-aeec-f2976f2a8368, Carolrhoda Bks.) Lerner Publishing Group.

—The Wheel of Life & Death, No. 3. Moffett, Patricia, illus. 2018. (Mysterium Ser.). (ENG.). 344p. (J). (gr. 4-8). 18.99 (978-1-4677-7569-4(X), e1dc9978-31c7-4613-afa7-14b9bae2030a, Carolrhoda Bks.) Lerner Publishing Group.

Sedgwick, Marcus. The Book of Dead Days. 2006. (Book of Dead Days Ser.: 1). (ENG.). 288p. (YA). (gr. 5-12). reprint ed. per. 7.99 (978-0-385-74704-2(7), Lamb, Wendy Bks.) Random Hse. Children's Bks.

Sedoti, Chelsea. As You Wish. 2018. 432p. (YA). (gr. 7-12). 17.99 (978-1-4926-4231-2(2)) Sourcebooks, Inc.

Sellers, Kathy Lacey. Willie Chaff. 2010. pap. 10.95 (978-0-7414-6080-6(7)) Infinity Publishing.

Sexton, Shirley. Fairy with an Attitude. 2009. 142p. 22.50 (978-1-60860-616-0(3), Strategic Bk. Publishing) Strategic Book Publishing & Rights Agency (SBPRA).

Shah, Yasmin. Abby & the Feather Quest. 2010. (Illus.). 48p. pap. 10.49 (978-1-4343-9839-0(0)) AuthorHouse.

Shalant, Phyllis. When Pirates Came to Brooklyn. 2010. 224p. pap. 14.95 (978-1-4401-8338-6(4)) iUniverse, Inc.

Shan, Darren, pseud. Dark Calling. 2010. (Demonata Ser.: 9). (ENG.). 224p. (J). (gr. 10-17). pap. 13.99 (978-0-316-04872-9(0)) Little, Brown Bks. for Young Readers.

—Death's Shadow. 2009. (Demonata Ser.: 7). (ENG.). 240p. (J). (gr. 10-17). pap. 14.99 (978-0-316-00382-7(4)) Little, Brown Bks. for Young Readers.

—Slawter. 2007. (Demonata Ser.: 3). (ENG.). 240p. (J). (gr. 10-17). pap. 13.99 (978-0-316-01388-8(9)) Little, Brown Bks. for Young Readers.

Shannon, David. Alice the Fairy, 1 vol. Shannon, David, illus. 2009. (ENG., Illus.). (J). (gr. -1-k). pap. 10.99 incl. audio compact disk (978-0-545-11758-6(5)) Scholastic, Inc.

Sharkey, Niamh & Walker, Richard. Jack & the Beanstalk. Sharkey, Niamh, illus. 2006. (ENG., Illus.). 40p. (J). (gr. -1-2). pap. 10.99 (978-1-905236-69-5(7)) Barefoot Bks., Inc.

Sharp, D. L. M. A Pocket of Magic on Beechwood Street. 2004. (J). pap. (978-0-9762626-0-2(6)) Sharp, Diana Consulting.

Sharp, Margery. The Rescuers. Williams, Garth, illus. 2016. (ENG.). 160p. (J). (gr. 4-7). pap. 11.99 (978-1-68137-007-1(7), NYRB Kids) New York Review of Bks., Inc., The.

Sharpe, Gerald. Parade of Lights. Moya, Patricia, illus. 2007. (What Lies Beneath the Bed Ser.). 487p. (J). per. 11.00 (978-1-933894-01-0(6)) IJN Publishing, Inc.

Sharplin, Emory. Scrap. 2013. 352p. (J). pap. 14.95 (978-1-938416-35-4(X)) River Grove Bks.

Sheinmel, Courtney & Turetsky, Bianca. Magic on the Map #1: Let's Mooove! Lewis, Stevie, illus. 2019. (Magic on the Map Ser.: 1). 128p. (J). (gr. 2-5). 6.99 (978-1-63565-166-9(2), Random Hse. Bks. for Young Readers) Random Hse. Children's Bks.

—Magic on the Map #2: the Show Must Go On. Lewis, Stevie, illus. 2019. (Magic on the Map Ser.: 2). 128p. (J). (gr. 2-5). 5.99 (978-1-63565-169-0(7), Random Hse. Bks. for Young Readers) Random Hse. Children's Bks.

—Magic on the Map #3: Texas Treasure, 3. Lewis, Stevie, illus. 2020. (Magic on the Map Ser.: 3). 128p. (J). (gr. 2-5). 5.99 (978-1-9848-9569-1(9), Random Hse. Bks. for Young Readers) Random Hse. Children's Bks.

Shepard, Aaron. The Mountain of Marvels: A Celtic Tale of Magic, Retold from the Mabinogion. (Ancient Fantasy Ser.: Vol. 1). (J). 2017. (ENG., Illus.). (gr. 4-6). pap. 6.00 (978-1-62035-541-1(8)) 2007. 46p. pap. 6.00 (978-0-938497-36-3(7)) 2007. 46p. lib. bdg. 15.00 (978-0-938497-34-9(0)) Shepard Pubns. (Skyhook Pr.).

—The Songs of Power: A Finnish Tale of Magic, Retold from the Kalevala. 2007. (Ancient Fantasy Ser.: 2). 54p. (J). lib. bdg. 15.00 (978-0-938497-35-6(9)); lib. bdg. 6.00 (978-0-938497-37-0(5)) Shepard Pubns. (Skyhook Pr.).

Shepherd, Anita. Easter Rabbit's Magic. 2013. 48p. pap. 7.95 (978-0-9882368-2-0(6)) New Eden Publishing.

Shepherd, Megan. Grim Lovelies. (Grim Lovelies Ser.). (ENG.). (YA). (gr. 9). 2019. 448p. pap. 9.99 (978-0-358-10823-8(3), 1748887) 2018. 384p. 17.99 (978-1-328-80918-6(8), 1688543) HarperCollins Pubs. (Clarion Bks.).

—Midnight Beauties. 2019. (Grim Lovelies Ser.). (ENG.). 448p. (YA). (gr. 9). 17.99 (978-1-328-81190-5(5), 1688554, Clarion Bks.) HarperCollins Pubs.

Shin, Yujin, illus. My Magical Mermaid. 2019. (My Magical Friends Ser.). (ENG.). 8p. (J). (gr. -1 — 1). bds. 8.99 (978-1-4197-3730-5(9), 1278010, Abrams Appleseed) Abrams, Inc.

Shire, Poppy. Magic Pony Carousel #1: Sparkle the Circus Pony. Berg, Ron, illus. 2007. (Magic Pony Carousel Ser.: 1). (ENG.). 96p. (J). (gr. 2-5). pap. 3.99 (978-0-06-083779-2(9), HarperCollins) HarperCollins Pubs.

—Magic Pony Carousel #3: Star the Western Pony. Berg, Ron, illus. 2007. (Magic Pony Carousel Ser.: 3). (ENG.). 96p. (J). (gr. 2-5). pap. 3.99 (978-0-06-083785-3(3), HarperCollins) HarperCollins Pubs.

—Magic Pony Carousel #4: Jewel the Midnight Pony. Berg, Ron, illus. 2008. (Magic Pony Carousel Ser.: 4). (ENG.). 96p. (J). (gr. 2-5). pap. 4.99 (978-0-06-083788-4(8), HarperCollins) HarperCollins Pubs.

Shoesmith-Bateman, Amanda. The Magic Tree House, 1 vol. Beitz-Grant, Heather, illus. 2010. 22p. 24.95 (978-1-4489-3866-7(X)) PublishAmerica, Inc.

Shooter, Sam. The Goat in the Coat. 2012. 24p. pap. 15.99 (978-1-4691-8749-5(3)) Xlibris Corp.

Shorrock, Anne. The Secret Adventures of Amelia & Rainbow. 2008. 36p. pap. 15.95 (978-1-60693-011-3(7), Eloquent Bks.) Strategic Book Publishing & Rights Agency (SBPRA).

Shughart-Knecht, Kimberly. Princess Kiali & the Purple Box. 2010. 32p. pap. 12.99 (978-1-4490-0913-7(1)) AuthorHouse.

Shulda, Daron M. Dragon Boots. 2009. 40p. pap. 18.49 (978-1-4389-7022-6(6)) AuthorHouse.

Shulman, Polly. The Grimm Legacy. 2011. (ENG.). (J). 352p. (gr. 5-18). 8.99 (978-0-14-241904-5(4), Puffin Books);1. (Illus.). 336p. (gr. 6-8). 24.94 (978-0-399-25096-5(4)) Penguin Young Readers Group.

Shultz, D. B. The World Adventures of Sahara the Mummy: The Magical Exploration of Ancient Egypt. 2012. 28p. pap. 17.99 (978-1-4772-3310-8(5)) AuthorHouse.

Shurtliff, Liesl. Rump: the (Fairly) True Tale of Rumpelstiltskin. 2014. (ENG.). 288p. (J). (gr. 3-7). pap. 8.99 (978-0-307-97796-0(X), Yearling) Random Hse. Children's Bks.

Shusterman, Neal. The Dark Side of Nowhere. unabr. ed. 2004. 192p. (J). (gr. 4-7). pap. 36.00 incl. audio (978-0-8072-8757-6(1), YA258SP, Listening Library) Random Hse. Audio Publishing Group.

—The Eyes of Kid Midas. 2009. (ENG.). 176p. (YA). (gr. 7-8). pap. 10.99 (978-1-4169-9750-4(4)) Simon & Schuster, Inc.

Siegrist, Vicky. Our Magical House. 2008. 31p. 15.50 (978-0-615-21676-8(5)) Siegrist, Vicky.

Sierra, JulieAnn. Legacy & the Dark Prince, 1 vol. 2009. 209p. pap. 24.95 (978-1-61582-693-3(9)) America Star Bks.

Silberberg, Alan. The Awesome, Almost 100% True Adventures of Matt & Craz. Silberberg, Alan, illus. 2014. (ENG., Illus.). 336p. (J). (gr. 4-8). pap. 8.99 (978-1-4169-9433-6(5), Aladdin) Simon & Schuster Children's Publishing.

Simard, Remy. La Bottine Magique de Pipo. 2004. (FRE., Illus.). (J). (gr. k-2). spiral bd. (978-0-616-01841-5(X)) Canadian National Institute for the Blind/Institut National Canadien pour les Aveugles.

Simko, Joe. The Sweet Rot, Book 3 Book 3: The Purple Meltdown, 1 vol. 2012. (ENG., Illus.). 32p. (YA). (gr. 8-12). 19.99 (978-0-7643-3977-6(X), 4447) Schiffer Publishing, Ltd.

Simner, Janni Lee. Bones of Faerie. 2009. 247p. (YA). (978-0-375-84564-2(X)) Random Hse. Children's Bks.

—Faerie After. 2013. 264p. (YA). pap. (978-0-375-87118-4(7)) Random Hse., Inc.

—Faerie Winter, 2. 2012. (Bones of Faerie Trilogy Ser.). (ENG.). 288p. (J). (gr. 8-12). 24.94 (978-0-375-96671-2(4)) Random House Publishing Group.

Simon, Jenne. A Day at Charm School. 2016. (ENG.). 32p. (J). (gr. -1-k). pap. 3.99 (978-0-545-93224-0(6)) Scholastic, Inc.

—The Magic Charm Chase. 2016. (ENG., Illus.). 24p. (J). (gr. -1-k). 3.99 (978-0-545-94302-4(7)) Scholastic, Inc.

—Meet the Little Charmers (Little Charmers) 2015. (ENG.). 24p. (J). (gr. -1-k). 3.99 (978-0-545-85021-6(5)) Scholastic, Inc.

—Sparkle Bunny Day! (Little Charmers: 8x8) 2017. (Little Charmers Ser.: 5). (ENG.). 24p. (J). (gr. -1-k). pap. 3.99 (978-1-338-11279-5(1)) Scholastic, Inc.

Simon, Jenne, adapted by. The Magic Charm Chase. 2016. (Little Charmers Ser.). (ENG., Illus.). 24p. (J). (gr. -1-1). 16.19 (978-1-4844-8691-7(9)) Scholastic, Inc.

Simon, Raphael. The Anti-Book. 2021. (Illus.). 320p. (J). (gr. 3-7). 17.99 (978-0-525-55241-3(3), Dial Bks) Penguin Young Readers Group.

Simonet, Evan, illus. Jake & the Sailing Tree. 2009. (J). (978-1-60108-019-6(0)) Red Cygnet Pr.

Simonson, Louise. Beauty & the Dreaded Sea Beast: A Graphic Novel. Frampton, Otis, illus. 2019. (Far Out Fairy Tales Ser.). (ENG.). 40p. (J). (gr. 3-6). pap. 5.95 (978-1-4965-8442-7(2), 140967); lib. bdg. 25.32 (978-1-4965-8393-2(0), 140684) Capstone. (Stone Arch Bks.).

—Giganta's Colossal Double-Cross. Vecchio, Luciano, illus. 2018. (Wonder Woman the Amazing Amazon Ser.). (ENG.). 88p. (J). (gr. 2-7). lib. bdg. 24.65 (978-1-4965-6532-7(0), 138546, Stone Arch Bks.) Capstone.

Simpson, Dana. The Big Sparkly Box of Unicorn Magic: Phoebe & Her Unicorn Box Set Volume 1-4, 4 vols., Box set. 2017. (Phoebe & Her Unicorn Ser.). (ENG.). (J). pap. 45.00 (978-1-4494-9324-0(6)) Andrews McMeel Publishing.

—Phoebe & Her Unicorn in the Magic Storm. 2017. (Phoebe & Her Unicorn Ser.: 6). (ENG., Illus.). (J). 176p. pap. 9.99 (978-1-4494-8359-3(3)); 157p. (gr. 3-6). 33.99 (978-1-4494-9450-6(1)) Andrews McMeel Publishing.

—Phoebe & Her Unicorn in the Magic Storm. 2017. (Phoebe & Her Unicorn Ser.: 6). lib. bdg. 20.85 (978-0-606-40512-6(7)) Turtleback.

—Unicorn Bowling: Another Phoebe & Her Unicorn Adventure. 2019. (Phoebe & Her Unicorn Ser.: Vol. 9). (ENG., Illus.). (J). 178p. (gr. 3-6). 45.99 (978-1-5248-5132-3(9));Volume 9. 176p. pap. 9.99 (978-1-4494-9938-9(4)) Andrews McMeel Publishing.

Simpson, Dana, illus. Phoebe & Her Unicorn in the Magic Storm. 2017. 157p. (J). (978-1-5182-5085-9(8)) Andrews McMeel Publishing.

Sims, Lesley. The Enchanted Castle. Marks, Alan, illus. 2007. (Young Reading Series 2 Gift Bks). 62p. (J). (gr. 4-7). 8.99 (978-0-7945-1347-4(6), Usborne) EDC Publishing.

—The Magical Book. Tavares, Victor, illus. 2007. (Young Reading Series 2 Gift Bks). 64p. (J). (gr. 4-7). 8.99 (978-0-7945-1703-8(X), Usborne) EDC Publishing.

—Magical Stories for Little Children. 2012. (Picture Bks). 128p. (J). ring bd. 18.99 (978-0-7945-2919-2(4), Usborne) EDC Publishing.

Sinclair, Alison. Lightborn. 2011. (Darkborn Trilogy Ser.: 2). (Illus.). 320p. (gr. 12). 7.99 (978-0-451-46358-6(7), Ace) Penguin Publishing Group.

Singh, Rina. The Magic Braid. Zaman, Farida, illus. Date not set. 134p. (J). pap. (978-0-920813-25-6(9)) Sister Vision Pr.

Singleton, Linda Joy. Magician's Muse. 2010. (Seer Ser.: 6). (ENG.). 312p. (YA). (gr. 6-18). pap. 9.95 (978-0-7387-1957-3(9), Flux) Llewellyn Pubns.

Sire, Storma. Lessons in Magic. 2005. pap. (978-1-897242-11-7(5)) Aydy Pr.

Sister Flowers. When Boo Boo Wakes Up!, 1 vol. Smith, Brenda, illus. 2009. 36p. pap. 24.95 (978-1-61546-250-6(3)) America Star Bks.

Skelton, K. Magic from the Wishing Well. 2009. 28p. pap. 12.49 (978-1-4389-8747-7(1)) AuthorHouse.

Skelton, Matthew. Endymion Spring. 2008. (ENG.). 416p. (YA). (gr. 7). pap. 9.99 (978-0-385-73456-1(5), Delacorte Bks. for Young Readers) Random Hse. Children's Bks.

Skye, Evelyn. Circle of Shadows. 2019. (YA). (Circle of Shadows Ser.: 1). (ENG.). 480p. (gr. 8). pap. 10.99 (978-0-06-264373-5(8)); (Illus.). 464p. (978-0-06-291540-5(1)); (Circle of Shadows Ser.: 1). (ENG., Illus.). 464p. (gr. 8). 17.99 (978-0-06-264372-8(X)) HarperCollins Pubs. (Balzer & Bray).

—The Crown's Fate. (Crown's Game Ser.: 2). (ENG.). 432p. (YA). (gr. 8). 2018. pap. 10.99 (978-0-06-242262-0(6)) 2017. 17.99 (978-0-06-242261-3(8)) HarperCollins Pubs. (Balzer & Bray).

Skye, Obert. Apprentice Needed. 2019. (Wizard for Hire Ser.: 2). (ENG., Illus.). 416p. (J). (gr. 5-9). 17.99 (978-1-62972-529-1(3), 5211782, Shadow Mountain) Shadow Mountain Publishing.

—Choke. 2010. (Pillage Ser.: 2). (ENG., Illus.). 336p. (YA). (gr. 7). 17.99 (978-1-60641-653-2(7), 5040458, Shadow Mountain) Shadow Mountain Publishing.

—The Eyes of the Want. Sowards, Ben, illus. 2008. (Leven Thumps Ser.: 3). (ENG.). 464p. (J). (gr. 3-7). pap. 10.99 (978-1-4169-4719-6(1), Aladdin) Simon & Schuster Children's Publishing.

—The Gateway. 2006. (Leven Thumps Ser.: 1). (ENG., Illus.). 400p. (J). (gr. 3-7). pap. 10.99 (978-1-4169-2806-5(5), Aladdin) Simon & Schuster Children's Publishing.

—Leven Thumps 5 Volume Set. 2009. (ENG.). (J). (978-1-60641-220-6(5), Shadow Mountain) Shadow Mountain Publishing.

—Leven Thumps & the Gateway to Foo. (Leven Thumps Ser.: 1). (J). 2008. 74.75 (978-1-4361-1570-4(1)) 2007. 85.75 (978-1-4281-4616-7(4)) 2007. 112.75 (978-1-4281-4622-8(9)) 2007. 115.75 (978-1-4281-4620-4(2)) 2007. 1.25 (978-1-4281-4613-6(X)) 2007. 82.75 (978-1-4281-4618-1(0)) 2007. 178.75 (978-1-4281-4617-4(2)) Recorded Bks., Inc.

—Leven Thumps & the Gateway to Foo. 2005. (Leven Thumps Ser.: Bk. 1). (Illus.). 384p. (J). 17.95 (978-1-59038-369-8(9), Shadow Mountain) Shadow Mountain Publishing.

—Leven Thumps & the Wrath of Ezra. 2008. (Leven Thumps Ser.: Bk. 4). (Illus.). 388p. (J). 19.95 (978-1-59038-963-8(8), Shadow Mountain) Shadow Mountain Publishing.

—Pillage. 2008. (Illus.). 352p. (YA). 17.95 (978-1-59038-922-5(0), Shadow Mountain) Shadow Mountain Publishing.

—Pillagy: The Complete Trilogy. 2013. (ENG., Illus.). 712p. (YA). (gr. 6). pap. 17.99 (978-1-60907-706-8(7), 5108646, Shadow Mountain) Shadow Mountain Publishing.

—The Ruins of Alder. Sowards, Ben, illus. 2010. (Leven Thumps Ser.: 5). (ENG.). 416p. (J). (gr. 4-9). pap. 10.99 (978-1-4169-9093-2(3), Aladdin) Simon & Schuster Children's Publishing.

—The Wrath of Ezra. Sowards, Ben, illus. 2009. (Leven Thumps Ser.: 4). (ENG.). 464p. (J). (gr. 4-9). pap. 10.99 (978-1-4169-9092-5(5), Aladdin) Simon & Schuster Children's Publishing.

Slade, Arthur. Crimson. 2018. (ENG.). 288p. (J). (gr. 5-9). 16.93 (978-1-4434-1668-9(1)) HarperCollins Pubs.

Sleigh, Barbara. Carbonel: The King of the Cats. Drummond, V. H., illus. 2018. (ENG.). 192p. (J). (gr. 4-7). pap. 9.99 (978-1-68137-305-8(X), NYRB Kids) New York Review of Bks., Inc., The.

Sloat, Teri & Huffmon, Betty. Berry Magic. 2015. (ENG., Illus.). 34p. (J). 21.99 (978-1-943328-12-3(9), Alaska Northwest Bks.) West Margin Pr.

*Small World Creations. Glub, Glub! Magic Pictures Change Color in Water! Robjohns, Laura-Anne, illus. 2018. (ENG.). 8p. (J). (gr. -1-k). 5.99 (978-1-4380-7908-0(7)) Sourcebooks, Inc.

Smejkal, Kim. Ink in the Blood. 2020. (Ink in the Blood Duology Ser.). (ENG., Illus.). 448p. (YA). (gr. 9). 17.99 (978-1-328-55705-6(7), 1725524, Clarion Bks.) HarperCollins Pubs.

Smiletown's Upside Down. 2007. (J). per. 14.95 (978-0-9785132-3-8(1)) Smile-a-Lot, LLP.

Smith, Brian. The Intrepid EscapeGoat: Curse of the Buddha's Tooth. Conkling, Jon & DeVito, Michael A., eds. 2012. (ENG., Illus.). 96p. pap. 12.95 (978-0-9832161-3-1(4), ea5958fb-69f1-4383-9f0f-55bf2628a5fb) Th3rd World Studios.

Smith, Cliff. New Magical Holiday Stories. 2005. (ENG.). 70p. pap. 23.99 (978-1-4134-7971-3(5)) Xlibris Corp.

Smith, Debora Ann Baker. The Magnificent Fairy Party. 2010. (Illus.). 30p. pap. 13.00 (978-1-60911-404-6(3), Eloquent Bks.) Strategic Book Publishing & Rights Agency (SBPRA).

Smith, Eric. The Girl & the Grove. 2018. (ENG.). 368p. (YA). (gr. 9-12). pap. 11.99 (978-1-63583-018-7(4), 1635830184, Flux) North Star Editions.

—The Girl & the Grove. 2018. lib. bdg. 23.30 (978-0-606-41247-6(6)) Turtleback.

Smith, Jennifer E. The Storm Makers. Helquist, Brett, illus. 2013. (ENG.). 384p. (J). (gr. 3-7). pap. 19.99 (978-0-316-17959-1(0)) Little, Brown Bks. for Young Readers.

Smith, John C. Popee the Purple Pig-a-Saurus. 2010. 40p. pap. 16.99 (978-1-4490-9285-6(3)) AuthorHouse.

Smith, L. J. & Smith, Tom. The Night of the Solstice. 2008. (ENG.). 244p. (YA). pap. 11.99 (978-1-4169-8965-3(X), Simon & Schuster Bks. For Young Readers) Simon & Schuster Bks. For Young Readers.

Smith, Miss Diane Pearl. Princess S Magickal Christmas. 2012. 28p. pap. (978-0-9878503-0-0(X)) Rainbowchild.

Smith, Ronald L. Hoodoo. 2017. (ENG.). 224p. (J). (gr. 5-7). pap. 7.99 (978-0-544-93561-7(6), 1658342, Clarion Bks.) HarperCollins Pubs.

—Hoodoo. 2017. (ENG.). (J). (gr. 5-7). lib. bdg. 18.40 (978-0-606-39820-6(1)) Turtleback.

Smyth, Jimmy. The Magic Garden. 2013. 36p. pap. (978-0-9569314-7-4(2)) Smith, Jimmy.

Snaith, Simone. Between the Water & the Woods. Kipin, Sara, illus. 2019. 320p. (YA). (gr. 7). 18.99 (978-0-8234-4020-7(6)) Holiday Hse., Inc.

Snider, Brandon T. Cheetah Unleashed. Vecchio, Luciano, illus. 2018. (Wonder Woman the Amazing Amazon Ser.). (ENG.). 88p. (J). (gr. 2-7). lib. bdg. 24.65 (978-1-4965-6529-7(0), 138543, Stone Arch Bks.) Capstone.

—Circe's Dark Reign. Vecchio, Luciano, illus. 2018. (Wonder Woman the Amazing Amazon Ser.). (ENG.). 88p. (J). (gr. 2-7). lib. bdg. 24.65 (978-1-4965-6530-3(4), 138544, Stone Arch Bks.) Capstone.

—Doctor Strange: Mystery of the Dark Magic. 2016. (Mighty Marvel Chapter Bks.). (J). lib. bdg. 16.00 (978-0-606-39173-3(8)) Turtleback.

—Doctor Strange: Mystery of the Dark Magic. Pham, Khoi et al, illus. 2018. (Mighty Marvel Chapter Bks.). (ENG.). 128p. (J). (gr. 2-7). lib. bdg. 31.36 (978-1-5321-4215-4(3), 28552, Chapter Bks.) Spotlight.

Sniegoski, Thomas E. The Brimstone Network. 2008. (Brimstone Network Ser.: 1). (ENG.). 304p. (J). (gr. 4-8). pap. 14.99 (978-1-4169-5104-9(0), Simon & Schuster/Paula Wiseman Bks.) Simon & Schuster/Paula Wiseman Bks.

Sniegoski, Thomas E. & Golden, Christopher. Battle for Arcanum. 2013. (Magic Zero Ser.: 4). (ENG., Illus.). 240p. (J). (gr. 3-7). pap. 6.99 (978-1-4424-7315-7(0), Aladdin) Simon & Schuster Children's Publishing.

—Battle for Arcanum. 2013. (Magic Zero Ser.: 4). (ENG., Illus.). 240p. (J). (gr. 3-7). 17.99 (978-1-4424-7316-4(9), Simon & Schuster/Paula Wiseman Bks.) Simon & Schuster/Paula Wiseman Bks.

Sniegoski, Tom. Quest for the Spark. (Bone: Quest for the Spark Ser.: 3). 2013. lib. bdg. 22.10 (978-0-606-31497-8(0)) 2012. lib. bdg. 22.10 (978-0-606-23947-9(2)) Turtleback.

—Quest for the Spark: Book One: a BONE Companion, Bk. 1. Smith, Jeff, illus. 2011. (BONE: Quest for the Spark Ser.: 1).Tr. of a Bone Companion. (ENG.). 224p. (J). (gr. 4-7). 26.99 (978-0-545-14101-7(X), Graphix) Scholastic, Inc.

—Quest for the Spark: Book Three: a BONE Companion, Bk. 3. Smith, Jeff, illus. 2013. (BONE: Quest for the Spark Ser.). (ENG.). 288p. (J). (gr. 3-7). 26.99 (978-0-545-14105-5(2), Graphix) Scholastic, Inc.

—Quest for the Spark: Book Two: a BONE Companion, Bk. 2. Smith, Jeff, illus. 2012. (BONE: Quest for the Spark Ser.). (ENG.). 240p. (J). (gr. 4-7). 26.99 (978-0-545-14103-1(6), Graphix) Scholastic, Inc.

Snowe, Olivia. Dandelion & the Witch, 1 vol. Lamoreaux, Michelle, illus. 2014. (Twicetold Tales Ser.). (ENG.). 128p. (J). (gr. 3-6). 25.32 (978-1-4342-9147-9(2), 125595, Stone Arch Bks.) Capstone.

—The Sealed-Up House, 1 vol. Lamoreaux, Michelle, illus. (Twicetold Tales Ser.). (ENG.). 128p. (J). (gr. 3-6). 2014. pap. 5.95 (978-1-4342-9556-9(7), 126740) 2013. lib. bdg. 25.32 (978-1-4342-6019-2(4), 123160) Capstone. (Stone Arch Bks.).

Snyder, Laurel. Any Which Wall. Pham, LeUyen, illus. 256p. (J). 2010. (gr. 3-7). pap. 7.99 (978-0-375-85561-0(0)) 2009. (ENG.). (gr. 6-8). lib. bdg. 21.19 (978-0-375-95560-0(7)) Random Hse. Children's Bks. (Yearling).

Snyder, Maria V. Dawn Study. 2017. (Chronicles of Ixia Ser.: 9). (ENG.). 480p. pap. 19.99 (978-0-7783-1985-6(7), Mira Bks.) Harlequin Enterprises ULC CAN. Dist: HarperCollins Pubs.

Snyder, Zilpha Keatley. The Bronze Pen. 2009. (ENG.). 208p. (J). (gr. 3-7). pap. 5.99 (978-1-4169-4208-5(4), Atheneum Bks. for Young Readers) Simon & Schuster Children's Publishing.

—The Headless Cupid. Raible, Alton, illus. 2009. (Stanley Family Ser.). (ENG.). 224p. (J). (gr. 3-7). 16.99 (978-1-4169-9532-6(3), Atheneum Bks. for Young Readers) Simon & Schuster Children's Publishing.

—The Witches of Worm. 2009. 9.00 (978-0-7848-3612-5(4), Everbind) Marco Bk. Co.

—The Witches of Worm. Raible, Alton, illus. 2009. (ENG.). (J). (gr. 3-7). 192p. 19.99 (978-1-4169-9531-9(5)); 208p. pap. 8.99 (978-1-4169-9053-6(4)) Simon & Schuster Children's Publishing. (Atheneum Bks. for Young Readers).

—The Witches of Worm. 2006. 22.75 (978-0-8446-7290-8(4)) Smith, Peter Pub., Inc.

Sobat, Gail Sidonie. A Glass Darkly. 2006. (Ingamald Ser.: 3). (ENG., Illus.). 192p. (YA). (gr. 8-12). per. 14.95 (978-1-894283-69-4(4)) Great Plains Pubns. CAN. Dist: Publishers Group Canada.

—A Winter's Tale. 2004. (Ingamald Ser.: 2). (ENG.). 176p. pap. 16.95 (978-1-894283-45-8(7)) Great Plains Pubns. CAN. Dist: Publishers Group Canada.

Soderberg, Erin. The Quirks & the Quirkalicious Birthday. 2015. (Quirks Ser.). (ENG., Illus.). 208p. (J). (gr. 3-6). 13.99 (978-1-61963-370-4(1), 9781619633704, Bloomsbury USA Childrens) Bloomsbury Publishing USA.

—The Quirks in Circus Quirkus. 2014. (Quirks Ser.). (ENG., Illus.). 240p. (YA). (gr. 3-6). 13.99 (978-1-59990-790-1(9), 900080308, Bloomsbury USA Childrens) Bloomsbury Publishing USA.

Somtow, S. P. The Wizard's Apprentice. 2018. (ENG., Illus.). 144p. (YA). (gr. 7). pap. 13.00 (978-1-940999-27-2(8)); pap. 13.00 (978-1-940999-28-9(6)) Diplodocus Pr.

Soontornvat, Christina. The Changelings. 2017. (Changelings Ser.: 1). (ENG.). 304p. (J). (gr. 5-8). pap. 8.99 (978-1-4926-4795-9(0)) Sourcebooks, Inc.

Spann, Bill. The Agents of Little Woods. 2005. 116p. pap. 19.95 (978-1-4137-6574-8(2)) America Star Bks.

Spanton, Elizabeth & Bright, Laren. Golden Voyages. 2013. 84p. pap. 27.99 (978-1-4525-7213-0(5), Balboa Pr.) Author Solutions, LLC.

Spaziano, Layna. Shane & Molly's Magical Journey, 1 vol. 2010. 28p. pap. 24.95 (978-1-4489-6261-7(7)) PublishAmerica, Inc.

Specter, Baron. Hobgoblins Just Wanna Have Fun: Book 8. Boyden, Robin, illus. 2018. (Graveyard Diaries). (ENG.). 112p. (J). (gr. 2-5). lib. bdg. 38.50 (978-1-5321-3179-0(8), 28453, Calico Chapter Bks.) ABDO Publishing Co.

Speer, Cindy Lynn. Unbalanced. 2010. 241p. pap. (978-1-934841-90-7(0)) Zumaya Pubns. LLC.

Spicer, Lin. Faerie Baby. 2006. 148p. pap. 13.50 (978-1-84426-384-4(3)) Upfront Publishing Ltd. GBR. Dist: Printondemand-worldwide.com.

Spinale, Wendy. Umberland (the Everland Trilogy, Book 2) 2018. (Everland Ser.: 2). (ENG.). 304p. (YA). (gr. 7). pap. 9.99 (978-0-545-95319-1(7), Scholastic Paperbacks) Scholastic, Inc.

Spinner, Stephanie. Damosel: In Which the Lady of the Lake Renders a Frank & Often Startling Account of Her Wondrous Life & Times. 2010. (ENG.). 208p. (YA). (gr. 7-12). lib. bdg. 24.94 (978-0-375-93634-0(3)) Random House Publishing Group.

—The Magic of Merlin. Sokolova, Valerie, illus. 2004. (Stepping Stones: A Chapter Book: Fantasy Ser.). 42p. (J). 11.65 (978-0-7569-0905-5(8)) Perfection Learning Corp.

Spooner, Meagan. Lark Ascending. 2014. (Skylark Trilogy Ser.). (ENG.). 328p. (YA). (gr. 7-12). 17.95 (978-0-7613-8867-8(2), 9c8b3bbe-4f94-42e2-a78b-3a8870d6a56c, Carolrhoda Lab™) Lerner Publishing Group.

—Shadowlark. 2013. (Skylark Trilogy Ser.). (ENG.). 336p. (YA). (gr. 7-12). E-Book 27.99 (978-1-4677-1664-2(2), Carolrhoda Lab™) Lerner Publishing Group.

—Skylark. 2012. (Skylark Trilogy Ser.). (ENG.). 344p. (YA). (gr. 7-12). 17.95 (978-0-7613-8865-4(6), e83334e5-216e-4448-b5ff-af0d5f446791, Carolrhoda Lab™) Lerner Publishing Group.

Spring, Manda. Emerald & the Magic of Raynon. 2004. 118p. pap. 19.95 (978-1-4137-3708-0(0)) America Star Bks.

Stadelmann, Amy Marie. Olive & Beatrix: The Super-Smelly Moldy Blob, Vol. 2. Stadelmann, Amy Marie, illus. 2016. (Olive & Beatrix Ser.: 2). (ENG., Illus.). 80p. (J). (gr. k-2). 15.99 *(978-0-545-81485-0(5))* Scholastic, Inc.

Stainton, Sue. Christmas Magic. Melhuish, Eva, illus. 2007. 32p. (J). (gr. -1-1). lib. bdg. 16.89 *(978-0-06-078572-7(1)*, Tegen, Katherine Bks) HarperCollins Pubs.

Stan, Adrianna. The Letters. 2012. 24p. pap. *(978-1-4602-0045-2(4))* FriesenPress.

Stanek, Robert, pseud. In the Service of Dragons III: Keeper Martin's Tales, Book 7. 2005. (Keeper Martin's Tales Ser.). (Illus.). 240p. (J). (gr. 4-7). per. 14.00 *(978-1-57545-093-3(3))* RP Media.

—In the Service of Dragons IV: Keeper Martin's Tales, Book 8. 2005. (Keeper Martin's Tales Ser.). (ENG., Illus.). 240p. (YA). (gr. 8-12). per. 14.00 *(978-1-57545-094-0(1))* RP Media.

—Journey Beyond the Beyond. 2007. (ENG.). 156p. (J). per. 14.00 *(978-1-57545-132-9(8))* RP Media.

—The Kingdoms & the Elves of the Reaches. Stanek, Robert, illus. alt. gif. ed. 2004. (Illus.). 176p. (YA). pap. 10.99 *(978-1-57545-501-3(3)*, Reagent Pr. Echo) RP Media.

—The Kingdoms & the Elves of the Reaches: Keeper Martin's Tales, Book 1. deluxe ed. 2005. (Keeper Martin's Tales Ser.: Bk. 1). (Illus.). 240p. (J). pap. 14.00 *(978-1-57545-059-9(3))* RP Media.

—The Kingdoms & the Elves of the Reaches: Signature, Keeper Martin's Tales, Bk. 1. 2007. (Illus.). 240p. (YA). 35.00 *(978-1-57545-128-2(X))* RP Media.

—The Kingdoms & the Elves of the Reaches II. Stanek, Robert, illus. alt. gif. ed. 2004. (ENG., Illus.). 180p. (YA). pap. 10.99 *(978-1-57545-502-0(1)*, Reagent Pr. Echo) RP Media.

—The Kingdoms & the Elves of the Reaches II: Keeper Martin's Tales, Book 2. deluxe ed. 2005. (Keeper Martin's Tales Ser.: Bk. 2). (Illus.). 240p. (J). pap. 14.00 *(978-1-57545-060-5(7))* RP Media.

—The Kingdoms & the Elves of the Reaches Ii (Reader's Choice Edition, Keeper Martin's Tales Book 2) 2008. (Illus.). 244p. pap. 15.95 *(978-1-57545-197-8(2))* RP Media.

—The Kingdoms & the Elves of the Reaches III. Stanek, Robert, illus. alt. gif. ed. 2004. (ENG., Illus.). 172p. (YA). pap. 10.99 *(978-1-57545-503-7(X)*, Reagent Pr. Echo) RP Media.

—The Kingdoms & the Elves of the Reaches III: Keeper Martin's Tales, Book 3. deluxe ed. 2005. (Keeper Martin's Tales Ser.: Vol. 3). (Illus.). 240p. (J). pap. 14.00 *(978-1-57545-063-6(1))* RP Media.

—The Kingdoms & the Elves of the Reaches Iii (Reader's Choice Edition, Keeper Martin's Tales Book 3) 2008. (Illus.). 244p. pap. 15.95 *(978-1-57545-198-5(0))* RP Media.

—The Kingdoms & the Elves of the Reaches Iv. 2008. (Illus.). 244p. 35.00 *(978-1-57545-131-2(X))* RP Media.

—The Kingdoms & the Elves of the Reaches IV. Stanek, Robert, illus. alt. gif. ed. 2005. (Illus.). 172p. (YA). pap. 10.99 *(978-1-57545-504-4(8)*, Reagent Pr. Echo) RP Media.

—The Kingdoms & the Elves of the Reaches IV: Keeper Martin's Tales, Book 4. deluxe ed. 2005. (Keeper Martin's Tales Ser.: Vol. 4). (Illus.). 240p. (YA). pap. 14.00 *(978-1-57545-065-0(8))* RP Media.

—The Kingdoms & the Elves of the Reaches Iv (Reader's Choice Edition, Keeper Martin's Tales Book 4) 2008. (Illus.). 244p. pap. 15.95 *(978-1-57545-199-2(9))* RP Media.

—The Kingdoms & the Elves of the Reaches (Reader's Choice Edition, Keeper Martin's Tales Book 1) 2008. (Illus.). 240p. pap. 15.95 *(978-1-57545-196-1(4))* RP Media.

Stanfield, Michael. Bucky & Becky - the Magic of Wigglepoo Mountain. 2009. 144p. pap. 14.96 *(978-0-557-02614-2(8))* Lulu Pr., Inc.

Staniszewski, Anna. The Magic Mirror: a Branches Book (Once upon a Fairy Tale #1) Pamintuan, Macky, illus. 2019. (Once upon a Fairy Tale Ser.: 1). (ENG.). 96p. (J). (gr. 1-3). pap. 4.99 *(978-1-338-34971-9(6))* Scholastic, Inc.

—My Epic Fairy Tale Fail. 2013. (My Very Unfairy Tale Life Ser.: 2). (ENG.). 224p. (J). (gr. 4-7). pap. 6.99 *(978-1-4022-7930-0(2)*, 9781402279300) Sourcebooks, Inc.

—My Sort of Fairy Tale Ending. 2013. (My Very Unfairy Tale Life Ser.: 3). (ENG.). 224p. (J). (gr. 4-7). pap. 6.99 *(978-1-4022-7933-1(7))* Sourcebooks, Inc.

—The Wonder of Wildflowers. 2020. (ENG.). 192p. (J). (gr. 3-7). 17.99 *(978-1-5344-4278-8(2)*, Simon & Schuster Bks. For Young Readers) Simon & Schuster Bks. For Young Readers.

Stanley, Diane. The Cup & the Crown. 2013. (Silver Bowl Ser.: 2). (ENG.). 368p. (J). (gr. 3-7). pap. 6.99 *(978-0-06-196323-0(2)*, HarperCollins) HarperCollins Pubs.

—The Princess of Cortova. 2013. 311p. (J). lib. bdg. *(978-0-06-204731-1(0))* HarperCollins Pubs.

—The Silver Bowl. (Silver Bowl Ser.: 1). (ENG.). (J). (gr. 5). 2012. 336p. pap. 6.99 *(978-0-06-157546-4(1))* 2011. 320p. 16.99 *(978-0-06-157543-3(7))* HarperCollins Pubs. (HarperCollins).

Stanley, Pauline. The Children & the Witches Magic. 2010. (Illus.). 48p. pap. 10.49 *(978-1-4490-9544-4(5))* AuthorHouse.

Stapleton, Rhonda. Stupid Cupid. 2009. (ENG.). 272p. (YA). (gr. 7-18). pap. 9.99 *(978-1-4169-7464-2(4)*, Simon Pulse) Simon Pulse.

Starkey, R. Hawk. Mysterious Magical Circus Family Kids: The Chocolate Cake Turkey Lip Crumb Trail Mystery Adventure. 2008. 192p. pap. 13.95 *(978-1-4327-3096-3(7))* Outskirts Pr., Inc.

Steadman, A. F. Skandar & the Phantom Rider. 2023. (Illus.). (J). x, 484p. ***(978-1-6659-1277-8(4))***; (Skandar Ser.: 2). (ENG., 496p. (gr. 3-7). 18.99 *(978-1-6659-1276-1(6))* Simon & Schuster Bks. For Young Readers. (Simon & Schuster Bks. For Young Readers).

Steadman, A. F. Skandar & the Unicorn Thief. 2022. (Skandar Ser.: 1). (ENG., Illus.). 448p. (J). (gr. 3-7). 18.99 *(978-1-6659-1273-0(1)*, Simon & Schuster Bks. For Young Readers) Simon & Schuster Bks. For Young Readers.

Steig, William. Sylvester & the Magic Pebble. Steig, William, illus. 2005. (ENG., Illus.). 42p. (J). (gr. -1-3). 19.99 *(978-1-4169-0206-5(6)*, Simon & Schuster Bks. For Young Readers) Simon & Schuster Bks. For Young Readers.

—Sylvester & the Magic Pebble. Steig, William, illus. 2006. (Stories to Go! Ser.). (Illus.). 32p. (J). (gr. -1-3). 4.99 *(978-1-4169-1857-8(4)*, Simon & Schuster/Paula Wiseman Bks.) Simon & Schuster/Paula Wiseman Bks.

—Sylvester & the Magic Pebble: Book & CD. Steig, William, illus. 2012. (ENG., Illus.). 32p. (J). (gr. -1-2). pap. 10.99 *(978-1-4424-3560-5(7)*, Little Simon) Little Simon.

Stein, A. K. EZEKIEL MAYHILL & the Crystal of God. 2007. 196p. pap. 16.96 *(978-1-4303-2540-6(2))* Lulu Pr., Inc.

Stein, Uriel Von. Gretta's & Graci's Bright, Bright, Moonlit Night. 2011. 24p. pap. 12.79 *(978-1-4634-0225-9(2))* AuthorHouse.

Stephane, Nelly. Roland. Francois, Andre, illus. 2016. (ENG.). 36p. (J). (gr. -1-3). 17.95 *(978-1-59270-204-6(X))* Enchanted Lion Bks., LLC.

Stephens, Helen. Witchety Sticks & the Magic Buttons. Stephens, Helen, illus. 2010. (ENG., Illus.). 32p. (J). (gr. -1-k). pap. 8.99 *(978-1-4169-1107-4(3)*, Simon & Schuster Children's) Simon & Schuster, Ltd. GBR. Dist: Simon & Schuster, Inc.

Stephens, John. The Emerald Atlas. 2012. (Books of Beginning Ser.: 1). (ENG.). 464p. (J). (gr. 3-7). 10.99 *(978-0-375-87271-6(X)*, Yearling) Random Hse. Children's Bks.

—The Emerald Atlas. Lt. ed. 2012. (Books of Beginning Ser.). (ENG.). 547p. (J). (gr. 4-7). 23.99 *(978-1-4104-4234-5(9))* Thorndike Pr.

—The Fire Chronicle. 2012. (Illus.). 437p. (J). *(978-0-449-81015-6(1))* Knopf, Alfred A. Inc.

—The Fire Chronicle. 2013. (Books of Beginning Ser.: 2). (ENG., Illus.). 464p. (J). (gr. 3-7). 9.99 *(978-0-375-87272-3(8)*, Yearling) Random Hse. Children's Bks.

Steps To Literacy Staff, compiled by. Eragon/Eldest Box Set: Variety Pack (2 Titles, 1 Each) 2010. (ENG.). (J). pap. 23.85 *(978-1-61267-194-9(2))* Steps To Literacy, LLC.

Sterrett, Virginia. Old French Fairy Tales. 2010. (Applewood Bks.). (ENG., Illus.). 296p. (gr. -1-3). pap. 19.95 *(978-1-4290-1186-0(6))* Appewood Bks.

Stewart, Martin. Riverkeep. 2017. lib. bdg. 22.10 *(978-0-606-40100-5(8))* Turtleback.

Stewart, Shawna. Amazing Tails of Zomber Doodles & Buttons, 1 vol. 2010. 30p. pap. 24.95 *(978-1-4489-7913-4(7))* PublishAmerica, Inc.

Stewart, Trenton Lee. The Secret Keepers. Sudyka, Diana, illus. 2017. (ENG.). 512p. (J). (gr. 3-7). pap. 9.99 *(978-0-316-38954-9(4))* Little, Brown Bks. for Young Readers.

—The Secret Keepers. 2017. (J). lib. bdg. 19.65 *(978-0-606-40551-5(8))* Turtleback.

Stiefvater, Maggie. Blue Lily, Lily Blue. 2015. (Raven Cycle Ser.: 3). lib. bdg. 20.85 *(978-0-606-38004-1(3))* Turtleback.

—Blue Lily, Lily Blue (the Raven Cycle, Book 3) (Raven Cycle Ser.: 3). (ENG.). 400p. (YA). (gr. 9-9). 2015. pap. 12.99 *(978-0-545-42497-4(6))* 2014. 21.99 *(978-0-545-42496-7(8))* Scholastic, Inc. (Scholastic Pr.).

—Blue Lily, Lily Blue (the Raven Cycle, Book 3) (Unabridged Edition), 1 vol. unabr. ed. 2014. (Raven Cycle Ser.: 3). (ENG.). 2p. (YA). (gr. 7). audio compact disk 39.99 *(978-0-545-64907-0(2))* Scholastic, Inc.

—The Dream Thieves. 2014. (Raven Cycle Ser.: 2). lib. bdg. 20.85 *(978-0-606-36029-6(8))* Turtleback.

—The Dream Thieves (the Raven Cycle, Book 2) (Raven Cycle Ser.: 2). (ENG.). 448p. (YA). (gr. 9). 2014. pap. 12.99 *(978-0-545-42495-0(X)*, Scholastic Paperbacks) 2013. 19.99 *(978-0-545-42494-3(1)*, Scholastic Pr.) Scholastic, Inc.

—The Dream Thieves (the Raven Cycle, Book 2) (Unabridged Edition), 1 vol. unabr. ed. 2013. (Raven Cycle Ser.: 2). (ENG.). 2p. (YA). (gr. 9). audio compact disk 39.99 *(978-0-545-60039-2(1))* Scholastic, Inc.

—Lament: The Faerie Queen's Deception. 2008. (Lament Novel Ser.: 1). (ENG., Illus.). 336p. (YA). (gr. 9-12). pap. 9.95 *(978-0-7387-1370-0(8)*, C738713708, Flux) North Star Editions.

—The Raven Boys. 2015. 50.87 *(978-1-320-56337-6(6))* Blurb, Inc.

—The Raven Boys. 2013. (Raven Cycle Ser.: 1). 20.00 *(978-1-62765-119-6(5))* Perfection Learning Corp.

—The Raven Boys. 2016. (CHI.). 448p. (YA). (gr. 7). pap. *(978-986-361-180-6(8))* Sitak Group Holding, Ltd.

—The Raven Boys. 2013. (Raven Cycle Ser.: 1). lib. bdg. 20.85 *(978-0-606-32026-3(8))* Turtleback.

—The Raven Boys (the Raven Cycle, Book 1), 1 vol. (Raven Cycle Ser.: 1). (ENG.). 416p. (gr. 9-9). 2013. (YA). pap. 12.99 *(978-0-545-42493-6(3)*, Scholastic Paperbacks) 2012. (J). E-Book *(978-0-545-46979-1(1))* 2012. (J). 21.99 *(978-0-545-42492-9(5)*, Scholastic Pr.) Scholastic, Inc.

—The Raven Boys (the Raven Cycle, Book 1) (Unabridged Edition), 1 vol. unabr. ed. 2012. (Raven Cycle Ser.: 1). (ENG.). (J). (gr. 8). 5p. audio compact disk 79.99 *(978-0-545-46594-6(X)*; 2p. audio compact disk 39.99 *(978-0-545-46593-9(1))* Scholastic, Inc.

—The Raven King. 2016. 439p. (J). *(978-0-605-90184-1(8)*, Scholastic Pr.) Scholastic, Inc.

—The Raven King (the Raven Cycle, Book 4) (Raven Cycle Ser.: 4). (ENG.). (YA). (gr. 9-9). 2016. 448p. 18.99 *(978-0-545-42498-1(4))*IV. 2018. 480p. pap. 12.99 *(978-0-545-42499-8(2))* Scholastic, Inc. (Scholastic Pr.).

Stilton, Geronimo. The Phoenix of Destiny (Geronimo Stilton & the Kingdom of Fantasy: Special Edition) An Epic Kingdom of Fantasy Adventure. 2015. (Geronimo Stilton & the Kingdom of Fantasy Ser.). (ENG., Illus.). 592p. (J). (gr. 2-5). 19.99 *(978-0-545-82907-6(0)*, Scholastic Paperbacks) Scholastic, Inc.

—The Wizard's Wand (Geronimo Stilton & the Kingdom of Fantasy #9) 2016. (Geronimo Stilton & the Kingdom of Fantasy Ser.: 9). (ENG., Illus.). 320p. (J). (gr. 2-5). 16.99 *(978-1-338-03291-8(7)*, Scholastic Paperbacks) Scholastic, Inc.

Stilton, Thea. The Secret of the Fairies (Thea Stilton: Special Edition #2) A Geronimo Stilton Adventure. 2018. (True Book (Relaunch) Ser.). (ENG.). 320p. (J). (gr. 3-5). E-Book 7.95 *(978-0-545-55688-0(0)*, Scholastic Paperbacks) Scholastic, Inc.

Stine, Faye. The Magic Forest: The Magic of Childhood. 2009. 117p. (J). pap. 10.95 *(978-1-4327-3617-0(5))* Outskirts Pr., Inc.

Stine, Megan, et al. Now You See Him, Now You Don't. 2004. (ENG., Illus.). 112p. *(978-0-00-714446-4(6)*, HarperCollins Children's Bks.) HarperCollins Pubs. Ltd.

Stine, R. L. Betrayal: The Betrayal; the Secret; the Burning. 2015. (Fear Street Saga Ser.). (ENG., Illus.). 544p. (YA). (gr. 7). pap. 14.99 *(978-1-4814-5041-6(7)*, Simon Pulse) Simon Pulse.

—A Midsummer Night's Scream. 2014. (ENG.). 256p. (YA). (gr. 7-12). pap. 17.99 *(978-1-250-04434-1(0)*, 900128329) Square Fish.

Stockham, Jess, illus. The Frog Prince. 2007. (Flip-Up Fairy Tales Ser.). 24p. (J). *(978-1-84643-143-2(3))*; (gr. 2-2). pap. *(978-1-84643-077-0(1))* Child's Play International Ltd.

Stockton, Frank Richard. The Bee-Man of Orn & Other Fanciful Tales. 2007. (ENG.). 140p. pap. 18.99 *(978-1-4264-5788-3(X))* Creative Media Partners, LLC.

—Ting-a-Ling Tales. 2008. 88p. pap. 8.95 *(978-1-60664-056-2(9))* Aegypan.

Stolarz, Laurie Faria. Silver Is for Secrets. 2005. (Stolarz Ser.: 3). (ENG.). 288p. (YA). (gr. 9-12). pap. 11.99 *(978-0-7387-0631-3(0)*, 0738706310, Flux) North Star Editions.

—White Is for Magic. 2004. (Stolarz Ser.: 2). (ENG.). 312p. (YA). (gr. 9-12). pap. 11.99 *(978-0-7387-0443-2(1)*, 0738704431, Flux) North Star Editions.

Stone, Forrest. Loki & the Magic Hammer: A Norse Myth. 2006. (J). pap. *(978-1-4108-6178-8(3))* Benchmark Education Co.

Stone, Kelsey. The Predahil Chronicles. 2005. (YA). per. 6.49 *(978-1-59196-995-2(6))* Instant Pub.

Stones, Yvonne. Olivia's Magical Moment. 2010. 36p. pap. 16.99 *(978-1-4490-8045-7(6))* AuthorHouse.

Storer, June. Kip, Brenda & Emong's Adventure. 2013. 164p. pap. *(978-0-9923603-1-3(5))* BWM Bks.

Storm, Jeff. Petrified World, Determine Your Destiny No. 1: You Are the Hero of This Book! Chan, Harvey, illus. 2nd ed. 2014. 160p. pap. *(978-1-77143-159-0(8)*, CCB Publishing) CCB Publishing.

Storr, Catherine. Marianne Dreams. 2014. (ENG., Illus.). 224p. pap. 9.95 *(978-0-571-31327-3(2))* Faber & Faber, Inc.

Strand, Kai. The Wishing Well. 2012. 104p. 19.95 *(978-1-61633-301-0(4))*; pap. 9.95 *(978-1-61633-302-7(2))* Guardian Angel Publishing, Inc.

Strange, Jason. Faceless Friend, 1 vol. Parks, Phil, illus. 2011. (Jason Strange Ser.). (ENG.). 72p. (J). (gr. 3-6). pap. 6.25 *(978-1-4342-3431-5(2)*, 116452); lib. bdg. 25.32 *(978-1-4342-3232-8(8)*, 116204) Capstone. (Stone Arch Bks.).

—Strays, 1 vol. Kendall, Bradford & Evergreen, Nelson, illus. 2012. (Jason Strange Ser.). (ENG.). 72p. (J). (gr. 3-6). pap. 6.25 *(978-1-4342-3883-2(0)*, 118064, Stone Arch Bks.) Capstone.

—Strays, 1 vol. Evergreen, Nelson & Kendall, Bradford, illus. 2012. (Jason Strange Ser.). (ENG.). 72p. (J). (gr. 3-6). lib. bdg. 25.32 *(978-1-4342-3295-3(6)*, 116260, Stone Arch Bks.) Capstone.

Strega Nona. 2005. (J). *(978-1-59564-834-1(8))* Steps To Literacy, LLC.

Stroud, Jonathan. The Golem's Eye, Bk. 2. 2nd rev. ed. 2006. (Bartimaeus Novel Ser.: 2). (ENG.). 592p. (J). (gr. 5-9). reprint ed. per. 8.99 *(978-0-7868-3654-3(7))* Little, Brown Bks. for Young Readers.

Studio Mouse Staff. Kindness Counts. rev. ed. 2004. (Kindness Counts Ser.). (ENG., Illus.). 36p. (J). (gr. -1-3). 12.99 *(978-1-59069-364-3(7)*, 1A500) Studio Mouse LLC.

Stumpe, Jennifer. Aunt Jo Jo's Magical Gifts: Amazing Underwater Adventure. 2011. 32p. (gr. 1-2). pap. 14.95 *(978-1-4567-3160-1(2))* AuthorHouse.

—Aunt Jo Jo's Magical Gifts: Ethan's Great African Journey. 2012. 32p. pap. 17.95 *(978-1-4772-9097-2(4))* AuthorHouse.

Sturm, Ilana. The 13th Moon. 2013. 92p. pap. *(978-1-936922-61-1(4))* Roxby Media Ltd.

Stutzman, D. J. The Promise Ring. 2007. (J). pap. 9.00 *(978-0-8059-7365-5(6))* Dorrance Publishing Co., Inc.

Suarez, Sergio Lopez. Huakala! a los Miedos. Suarez, Sergio Lopez, illus. 2003. (SPA., Illus.). 32p. (J). (gr. k-3). 9.95 *(978-968-19-0556-9(3))* Aguilar, Altea, Taurus, Alfaguara, S.A. de C.V MEX. Dist: Santillana USA Publishing Co., Inc.

Suhay, Lisa. Our Fantasy Island: An Interactive Book. Hundley, Sam, illus. 2006. 30p. (J). pap. 8.00 *(978-0-9766628-0-8(9))* Fantasy Island Pr.

Suits, Barbara Bradford. The Hidden Treasure. 2013. 48p. pap. 7.95 *(978-1-61286-199-9(7))* Avid Readers Publishing Group.

Sullivan, Laura L. Delusion. 2014. (ENG.). 352p. (YA). (gr. 7). pap. 18.99 *(978-0-544-10478-5(1)*, 1540787, Clarion Bks.) HarperCollins Pubs.

Summerill, Erin. Ever the Brave. (Clash of Kingdoms Novel Ser.: bk.2). (ENG., Illus.). (YA). (gr. 7). 2018. 480p. pap. 9.99 *(978-1-328-49795-6(X)*, 1717847) 2017. 464p. 17.99 *(978-0-544-66446-3(9)*, 1625025) HarperCollins Pubs. (Clarion Bks.).

—Once a King. 2018. (Clash of Kingdoms Novel Ser.). (ENG., Illus.). 464p. (YA). (gr. 7). 17.99 *(978-1-328-94997-4(4)*, 1705582, Clarion Bks.) HarperCollins Pubs.

Sussman, Elissa. Stray. 2014. (Stray Ser.: 1). (ENG., Illus.). 384p. (YA). (gr. 8). 17.99 *(978-0-06-227455-7(4)*, Greenwillow Bks.) HarperCollins Pubs.

Sutcliffe, Charlie. Zubert. 2014. (ENG., Illus.). 32p. (J). (gr. -1-3). 18.95 *(978-1-84976-121-5(3))* Tate Publishing, Ltd. GBR. Dist: Abrams, Inc.

Sutherland, David, et al. Siriol Llywelyn A'r Salwch Chwyrlio Erchyll. Roberts, David, illus. 2005. (WEL.). 48p. pap. *(978-1-85596-679-6(4))* Dref Wen.

Sutherland, Tui T. The Hive Queen (Wings of Fire #12), 1 vol., Bk. 12. 2018. (Wings of Fire Ser.: 12). (ENG., Illus.). 320p. (J). (gr. 3-7). 16.99 *(978-1-338-21448-2(9)*, Scholastic Pr.) Scholastic, Inc.

—The Lost Continent (Wings of Fire #11) (Wings of Fire Ser.: 11). (ENG.). 336p. (J). (gr. 3-7). 2019. pap. 8.99 *(978-1-338-21444-4(6))*Bk. 11. 2018. (Illus.). 16.99 *(978-1-338-21443-7(8))* Scholastic, Inc. (Scholastic Pr.).

—The Menagerie: Krakens & Lies. 2016. (Menagerie Ser.: 3). (ENG.). 368p. (J). (gr. 3-7). pap. 9.99 *(978-0-06-078069-2(X)*, HarperCollins) HarperCollins Pubs.

—So This Is How It Ends. 2006. (Avatars Ser.: Bk. 1). 353p. (YA). (gr. 7-12). 16.99 *(978-0-06-075024-4(3)*, Eos); lib. bdg. 17.89 *(978-0-06-075028-2(6))* HarperCollins Pubs.

—Talons of Power (Wings of Fire #9) (Wings of Fire Ser.: 9). (ENG.). 336p. (J). (gr. 3-7). 2018. pap. 8.99 *(978-0-545-68543-6(5))* 2016. (Illus.). 16.99 *(978-0-545-68540-5(0)*, Scholastic Pr.) Scholastic, Inc.

Sutherland, Tui T. & Sutherland, Kari H. The Menagerie. 2013. (Menagerie Ser.: 1). (ENG., Illus.). 288p. (J). (gr. 3-7). 16.99 *(978-0-06-078064-7(9)*, HarperCollins) HarperCollins Pubs.

—The Menagerie #3: Krakens & Lies. 2015. (Menagerie Ser.: 3). (ENG., Illus.). 368p. (J). (gr. 3-7). 16.99 *(978-0-06-078067-8(3)*, HarperCollins) HarperCollins Pubs.

Sutiff, Jamie. The Elves of Owl's Head Mountain. Blumberg, Christine A., ed. Evens, Kevin C., illus. 2007. 276p. pap. 10.95 *(978-0-9712867-8-8(7))* Cold River Pubns.

—The Elves of Owl's Head Mountain. Blumberg, Christine A., ed. Evans, Kevin, illus. 2007. 280p. (gr. 8-12). 26.95 *(978-0-9712867-7-1(9))* Cold River Pubns.

—The Land of Nen-Us-Yok. Blumberg, Christine A., ed. Evans, Kevin C., illus. 2007. 256p. pap. 10.95 *(978-0-9712867-4-0(4))*; 26.95 *(978-0-9712867-6-4(0))* Cold River Pubns.

Sutton, Laurie S. Cosmic Conquest. Doescher, Erik, illus. 2018. (You Choose Stories: Justice League Ser.). (ENG.). 112p. (J). (gr. 2-6). pap. 6.95 *(978-1-4965-6559-4(2)*, 138572); lib. bdg. 32.65 *(978-1-4965-6555-6(X)*, 138568) Capstone. (Stone Arch Bks.).

—The Crystal Quest. Lozano, Omar, illus. 2019. (You Choose Stories: Wonder Woman Ser.). (ENG.). 112p. (J). (gr. 2-6). pap. 6.95 *(978-1-4965-8441-0(4)*, 140966); lib. bdg. 32.65 *(978-1-4965-8351-2(5)*, 140645) Capstone. (Stone Arch Bks.).

—Wonder Woman vs. Circe, 1 vol. Vecchio, Luciano, illus. 2013. (DC Super Heroes Ser.). (ENG.). 56p. (J). (gr. 3-6). lib. bdg. 26.65 *(978-1-4342-6014-7(3)*, 123074, Stone Arch Bks.) Capstone.

Sutton, Pamelina Jean'e. Bill Bill the Burger Boy. 2012. 24p. pap. 12.00 *(978-1-61286-108-1(3))* Avid Readers Publishing Group.

Swanson, Stan. The Misadventures of Hobart Hucklebuck. 2007. (J). 16.95 *(978-0-9787925-3-4(X))*; per. 9.95 *(978-0-9787925-2-7(1))* Stony Meadow Publishing.

Swinney, Kay. Marty Moose & the Mystical Reunion, 1 vol. 2009. 73p. pap. 19.95 *(978-1-61546-867-6(6))* America Star Bks.

Sykes, Julie. Unicorn Academy #1: Sophia & Rainbow. Truman, Lucy, illus. 2019. (Unicorn Academy Ser.: 1). (ENG.). 128p. (J). (gr. 1-4). 5.99 *(978-1-9848-5082-9(2)*, Random Hse. Bks. for Young Readers) Random Hse. Children's Bks.

—Unicorn Academy #2: Scarlett & Blaze. Truman, Lucy, illus. 2019. (Unicorn Academy Ser.: 2). (ENG.). 128p. (J). (gr. 1-4). 5.99 *(978-1-9848-5085-0(7)*, Random Hse. Bks. for Young Readers) Random Hse. Children's Bks.

—Unicorn Academy #3: Ava & Star. Truman, Lucy, illus. 2019. (Unicorn Academy Ser.: 3). (ENG.). 128p. (J). (gr. 1-4). pap. 5.99 *(978-1-9848-5088-1(1)*, Random Hse. Bks. for Young Readers) Random Hse. Children's Bks.

—Unicorn Academy #4: Isabel & Cloud. Truman, Lucy, illus. 2019. (Unicorn Academy Ser.: 4). (ENG.). 128p. (J). (gr. 1-4). pap. 5.99 *(978-1-9848-5091-1(1)*, Random Hse. Bks. for Young Readers) Random Hse. Children's Bks.

—Unicorn Academy #5: Layla & Dancer. Truman, Lucy, illus. 2019. (Unicorn Academy Ser.: 5). (ENG.). 128p. (J). (gr. 1-4). 12.99 *(978-1-9848-5168-0(3)*, Random Hse. Bks. for Young Readers) Random Hse. Children's Bks.

—Unicorn Academy #6: Olivia & Snowflake. Truman, Lucy, illus. 2019. (Unicorn Academy Ser.: 6). (ENG.). 128p. (J). (gr. 1-4). 12.99 *(978-1-9848-5171-0(3)*, Random Hse. Bks. for Young Readers) Random Hse. Children's Bks.

Sykes, Tina. Elliot Makes a Friend. 2012. 26p. 24.95 *(978-1-4626-5980-7(2))* America Star Bks.

Symes, Ruth. Bella Donna: Too Many Spells. Lindsay, Marion, illus. 2016. (ENG.). 192p. (J). (gr. 1-5). pap. 7.99 *(978-1-63450-155-2(1)*, Sky Pony Pr.) Skyhorse Publishing Co., Inc.

Szpirglas, Jeff & Saint-Onge, Danielle. Messy Miranda, 1 vol. Whamond, Dave, illus. 2013. (Orca Echoes Ser.). (ENG.). 64p. (J). (gr. 1-3). pap. 6.95 *(978-1-4598-0117-2(2))* Orca Bk. Pubs. USA.

Taddonio, Lea. The Curse of Deadwood Hill: Book 2. Trunfio, Alessia, illus. 2017. (Lucky 8 Ser.). (ENG.). 48p. (J). (gr. 3-7). lib. bdg. 34.21 *(978-1-5321-3054-0(6)*, 27061, Spellbound) Magic Wagon.

—Deadwood Hill Strikes Back: Book 3. Trunfio, Alessia, illus. 2017. (Lucky 8 Ser.). (ENG.). 48p. (J). (gr. 3-7). lib. bdg. 34.21 *(978-1-5321-3055-7(4)*, 27062, Spellbound) Magic Wagon.

Takahashi, Rumiko. Inuyasha, Vol. 44, Set. Takahashi, Rumiko, illus. 2003. (Inuyasha Ser.). (ENG., Illus.). 200p. (YA). pap. 39.98 *(978-1-59116-235-3(1)*, Viz Comics) Viz Media.

The Tale of Jackie Berry. 2005. (J). per. 12.95 *(978-0-9677047-5-3(8))* Marble Hse. Editions.

Tamura, Mitsuhisa. BakéGyamon, Vol. 1. 2009. (Bakégyamon Ser.: 1). (ENG., Illus.). 200p. (J). pap. 7.99 *(978-1-4215-1793-3(0))* Viz Media.

—BakéGyamon, Vol. 2. 2009. (Bakégyamon Ser.: 2). (ENG., Illus.). 200p. (J). pap. 7.99 *(978-1-4215-1794-0(9))* Viz Media.

Tandi's World. 2006. (J). *(978-0-9772634-0-0(1))* Hall, Monique P. Productions.

Tanguay, Dave. The Legacy of Mr. Banjo! Vaughns, Byron, illus. 2015. (Billy Batson & the Magic of Shazam! Ser.). (ENG.). 32p. (J). (gr. 3-6). lib. bdg. 22.60 *(978-1-4342-9746-4(2)*, 127078, Stone Arch Bks.) Capstone.

Tanigawa, Nagaru. The Indignation of Haruhi Suzumiya (light Novel), Volume 8. 2012. (Haruhi Suzumiya Ser.: 8). (ENG., Illus.). 232p. (YA). (gr. 10-17). pap. 18.00 *(978-0-316-03899-7(7)*, Yen Pr.) Yen Pr. LLC.

Tanner, Matthew J. The Winds of Aragon. 2013. 40p. pap. 14.95 *(978-0-9885253-0-6(5))* Tanner, Matt J.

Tapia, Rayner. The Adventures of Tom Mcguire: Morkann's Revenge. 2010. (Illus.). 156p. pap. 11.99 *(978-1-4490-8183-6(5))* AuthorHouse.

Taranta, Mary. Shimmer & Burn. 2018. (ENG.). 352p. (YA). (gr. 9). pap. 11.99 *(978-1-4814-7200-5(3)*, McElderry, Margaret K. Bks.) McElderry, Margaret K. Bks.

Tarnowska, Wafa'. The Seven Wise Princesses: A Medieval Persian Epic. Nilesh, Misty, illus. 2008. (ENG.). 96p. (J). (gr. 5-9). 19.99 *(978-1-84686-250-2(7))* Barefoot Bks., Inc.
Tarver, Monroe S. Tales from the Mapmaker: Imagia & the Magic Pearls. 2009. (ENG.). 99p. (J). (gr. 2-4). 21.19 *(978-0-9723936-5-2(X))* Wizarding World Pr.
Tarver, S., 1st. Imaga & the Magic Pearls 2nd l.t. ed. 2003. (Illus.). 20p. (J). 6.99 *(978-0-9743568-0-8(8))* Tarver, Monroe.
Tashlikowich, Natasha. The Secret of the Seven Stones. 2009. 117p. pap. 18.97 *(978-0-557-03747-6(6))* Lulu Pr., Inc.
Tate, Bernice & Andy. Funspell. 2009. 20p. pap. 14.95 *(978-1-4343-7103-4(4))* AuthorHouse.
Tate, Meredith. The Red Labyrinth. 2019. (ENG., Illus.). 352p. (YA). (gr. 9-12). pap. 14.99 *(978-1-63583-034-7(6)*, 1635830346, Flux) North Star Editions.
Tatulli, Mark. Desmond Pucket Makes Monster Magic. (ENG.). 240p. (J). 2015. pap. 9.99 *(978-1-4494-7139-2(0))* 2013. (Desmond Pucket Ser.: 1). 13.99 *(978-1-4494-3548-6(3))* Andrews McMeel Publishing.
Tawa, Renee. Tink's Magical Day. 2011. (Illus.). (J). *(978-1-4508-1707-3(6))* Publications International, Ltd.
Taylor, Dereen. The Dragon's Magic Wish. Hutchinson, Tim, illus. 2012. 12p. (J). (gr. 1-6). 16.99 *(978-1-84322-856-1(4))* Anness Publishing GBR. Dist: National Bk. Network.
Taylor, G. P. Shadowmancer: What Can Stand Against an Ancient Evil... 2004. (ENG., Illus.). 275p. 16.99 *(978-1-59185-613-9(2)*, 6132, Charisma Hse.) Charisma Media.
—The Shadowmancer Returns: The Curse of Salamander Street. 2008. (ENG.). 256p. (gr. 7-12). pap. 17.99 *(978-1-59979-084-8(X)*, 084X, Realms) Charisma Media.
—The Shadowmancer Returns: The Curse of Salamander Street. 2007. (Shadowmancer; 04 Ser.). 240p. (J). *(978-1-4287-4670-1(6)*, Putnam Juvenile) Penguin Publishing Group.
Taylor, Laini. Night of Cake & Puppets. Di Bartolo, Jim, illus. 2017. (Daughter of Smoke & Bone Ser.). (ENG.). 256p. (YA). (gr. 10-17). 16.99 *(978-0-316-43919-0(3))* Little, Brown Bks. for Young Readers.
Taylor, Phillip J. Brian, His Granddad & the Cup of Ages. 2012. 310p. pap. *(978-1-78003-422-5(9))* Pen Pr. Pubs., Ltd.
Taylor, Roy. Matilda's Magic Wand: Dreamland Adventure. 2008. 36p. (J). pap. 9.00 *(978-0-8059-7716-5(3))* Dorrance Publishing Co., Inc.
Taylor, Terry. Tim the Young Magician: Tim Discovers Magic. 2005. 48p. pap. 16.95 *(978-1-4137-6023-1(6))* America Star Bks.
Tea, Michelle. Mermaid in Chelsea Creek. Polan, Jason, illus. 2013. 240p. (J). (gr. 5-11). 19.95 *(978-1-938073-36-6(3)*, ea44eacc-0b51-4a46-b778-cae153d08009) McSweeney's Publishing.
Teague, Mark. Jack & the Beanstalk & the French Fries. Teague, Mark, illus. 2017. (ENG., Illus.). 40p. (J). (gr. -1-k). 18.99 *(978-0-545-91431-4(0)*, Orchard Bks.) Scholastic, Inc.
Teitelbaum, Michael. Tale of Zuko. Spaziante, Patrick, illus. 2008. (Avatar Ser.). (ENG.). 96p. (J). (gr. 2-6). pap. 5.99 *(978-1-4169-4984-8(4)*, Simon Spotlight/Nickelodeon) Simon Spotlight/Nickelodeon.
Tennapel, Doug. Cardboard. 2012. lib. bdg. 24.50 *(978-0-606-26212-5(1))* Turtleback.
Tercio, Ricardo, illus. Jack y Los Frijoles Magicos: La Novela Grafica. 2010. (Graphic Spin en Español Ser.). (SPA.). 40p. (J). (gr. 3-6). pap. 5.95 *(978-1-4342-2272-5(1)*, 103135); lib. bdg. 25.99 *(978-1-4342-1902-2(X)*, 102361) Capstone. (Stone Arch Bks.).
Terrell, Brandon. No Escape: A Tale of Terror. Epelbaum, Mariano, illus. 2019. (Michael Dahl Presents: Phobia Ser.). (ENG.). 72p. (J). (gr. 4-6). lib. bdg. 25.32 *(978-1-4965-7911-9(9)*, 139616, Stone Arch Bks.) Capstone.
Tewee, Laqaixit. Winterbloom & the Magical Swan: Book 1 Discovery of the Moon Treasure. 2012. 68p. pap. 31.99 *(978-1-4653-9933-5(X))* Xlibris Corp.
Tey, Rachel. Tea in Pajamas. 2019. 170p. (J). (gr. 2-4). pap. 16.95 *(978-981-4828-85-7(8))* Marshall Cavendish International (Asia) Private Ltd. SGP. Dist: Independent Pubs. Group.
Thame, Val. Witches in Deed. l.t. ed. 2007. 100p. per. *(978-1-905665-25-9(3))* Pollinger In Print.
Thomas, Beth. Jack & the Richmond Bubble. 2012. pap. 11.95 *(978-0-7414-7495-7(6))* Infinity Publishing.
Thomas, Gerry. The Umbrella Race. 2010. 25p. (J). pap. 25.95 *(978-1-4327-6006-9(8))* Outskirts Pr., Inc.
Thomas, Joyce Carol. Christmas & the Magic Pie Pan. Date not set. 32p. (J). lib. bdg. 15.89 *(978-0-06-025386-8(X)*, Cotler, Joanna Books) HarperCollins Pubs.
Thomas, Rhiannon. A Wicked Thing. (ENG.). (YA). (gr. 9). 2016. 368p. pap. 9.99 *(978-0-06-230354-7(6))* 2015. 352p. 17.99 *(978-0-06-230353-0(8))* HarperCollins Pubs. (HarperTeen).
Thomas, Scarlett. The Chosen Ones. 2018. (Worldquake Ser.: 2). (ENG., Illus.). 384p. (J). (gr. 4-7). 17.99 *(978-1-4814-9787-9(1)*, Simon & Schuster Bks. For Young Readers) Simon & Schuster Bks. For Young Readers.
—Dragon's Green. (Worldquake Ser.: 1). (ENG.). (J). (gr. 4-7). 2018. 400p. pap. 8.99 *(978-1-4814-9785-5(5))* 2017. (Illus.). 384p. 18.99 *(978-1-4814-9784-8(7))* Simon & Schuster Bks. For Young Readers. (Simon & Schuster Bks. For Young Readers).
—Galloglass. 2019. (Worldquake Ser.: 3). (ENG., Illus.). 432p. (J). (gr. 4-7). 17.99 *(978-1-4814-9790-9(1)*, Simon & Schuster Bks. For Young Readers) Simon & Schuster Bks. For Young Readers.
Thomas, Sherry. The Burning Sky. 2013. (Elemental Trilogy Ser.: 1). (ENG.). 480p. (YA). (gr. 9). 17.99 *(978-0-06-220729-6(6)*, Balzer & Bray) HarperCollins Pubs.
Thomasian, Sara. Charlie's Magical Night. Harrington, David, illus. 2007. (J). per. 11.99 *(978-1-59879-381-9(0))* Lifevest Publishing, Inc.
Thompson, Colin. The Floods #2: School Plot. Scrambly, Crab, illus. 2008. (Floods Ser.). (J). (ENG.). 224p. 15.99 *(978-0-06-113861-4(4))*; 256p. lib. bdg. 16.89 *(978-0-06-113855-3(X))* HarperCollins Pubs.
—Good Neighbors. Scrambly, Crab, illus. 2008. (Floods Ser.: No. 1). 214p. (J). (gr. 3-7). 15.99 *(978-0-06-113196-7(2))* HarperCollins Pubs.
Thompson, Jan & Sharpe, Jaime. Amara's Magical Playhouse: The Adventure Begins. 2010. 108p. pap. 37.99 *(978-1-4520-8284-4(7))* AuthorHouse.
Thompson, Jill. Magic Trixie & the Dragon. 2009. (ENG., Illus.). 96p. (J). (gr. 3-7). pap. 7.99 *(978-0-06-117050-8(X))* HarperCollins Pubs.
Thompson, John M. & Schultz, George M. Just Imagine. Wodin, illus. 2006. 32p. (J). (gr. -1-3). 16.95 *(978-0-9740190-6-2(2))* Illumination Arts Publishing Co., Inc.
Thompson, Lauren. The Christmas Magic. Muth, Jon J., illus. 2009. (ENG.). 40p. (J). (gr. -1-2). 17.99 *(978-0-439-77497-0(7)*, Scholastic Pr.) Scholastic, Inc.
Thompson, Paul B. The Battle for the Brightstone: Book III of the Brightstone Saga, 1 vol. 2014. (Brightstone Saga Ser.). (ENG.). 176p. (J). (gr. 5-6). 39.93 *(978-0-7660-3984-1(6)*, e9149e38-6bf6-4e58-a2bb-da562639cd41) Enslow Publishing, LLC.
—The Brightworking: Book I of the Brightstone Saga, 1 vol. 2013. (Brightstone Saga Ser.). (ENG.). 160p. (J). (gr. 5-6). pap. 13.88 *(978-1-4644-0169-5(1)*, db84a9c8-04aa-4944-8d71-cebeceb16135);Bk. 1. (Illus.). 39.93 *(978-0-7660-3950-6(1)*, 11174435-cc08-4bf2-900d-17644dd892b7) Enslow Publishing, LLC.
—The Fortune-Teller: Book II of the Brightstone Saga, 1 vol. 2013. (Brightstone Saga Ser.). (ENG.). 160p. (J). (gr. 5-6). 39.93 *(978-0-7660-3983-4(8)*, 33708694-74f5-4c14-b5c4-80a8adbdb9e3); pap. 13.88 *(978-1-4644-0265-4(5)*, 495c2983-5c39-40c9-9230-c735fb19d132) Enslow Publishing, LLC.
Thompson-Swift, Joseph. The Adventures of Primrose Perfect. 2011. 248p. pap. *(978-1-907652-88-2(4))* Grosvenor Hse. Publishing Ltd.
Thomson-Swift, Joe. The Monkeyboy & the Gruffits. 2011. (Illus.). 44p. pap. *(978-1-908105-63-9(1))* Grosvenor Hse. Publishing Ltd.
—The Twig People of Mossdown Woods. 2011. (Illus.). 36p. pap. *(978-1-908105-35-6(6))* Grosvenor Hse. Publishing Ltd.
Thorne, Bella. Autumn's Wish. 2017. (Autumn Falls Ser.: 3). (ENG.). 320p. (YA). (gr. 7). pap. 10.99 *(978-0-385-74438-6(2)*, Ember) Random Hse. Children's Bks.
Thorpe, Kiki. A Dandelion Wish. Christy, Jana, illus. 2013. (Never Girls Ser.: 3). lib. bdg. 16.00 *(978-0-606-32199-0(3))* Turtleback.
—The Dark Forest. 2018. (Finding Tinker Bell Ser.: 2). lib. bdg. 17.20 *(978-0-606-40952-0(1))* Turtleback.
—A Fairy's Gift (Disney: the Never Girls) Christy, Jana, illus. 2017. (Never Girls Ser.). (ENG.). 224p. (J). (gr. 1-4). 7.99 *(978-0-7364-3773-8(8)*, RH/Disney) Random Hse. Children's Bks.
—Finding Tinker Bell #2: Through the Dark Forest (Disney: the Never Girls) Christy, Jana, illus. 2018. (Never Girls Ser.: 2). (ENG.). 128p. (J). (gr. 1-4). 6.99 *(978-0-7364-3651-9(0))*; lib. bdg. 12.99 *(978-0-7364-8183-0(4))* Random Hse. Children's Bks. (RH/Disney).
—In a Blink. Christy, Jana, illus. 2013. (Never Girls Ser.: 1). lib. bdg. 16.00 *(978-0-606-26977-3(0))* Turtleback.
—Into the Waves. 2016. (Never Girls Ser.: 11). lib. bdg. 16.00 *(978-0-606-38467-4(7))* Turtleback.
—Never Girls #1: in a Blink (Disney: the Never Girls), 1 vol. Christy, Jana, illus. 2013. (Never Girls Ser.: 1). (ENG.). 128p. (J). (gr. 1-4). 6.99 *(978-0-7364-2794-4(5)*, c2a6ecc2-a3fd-4e6e-8d54-c897a10e30d1, Rosen Classroom) Random Hse. Children's Bks.
—Never Girls #10: on the Trail (Disney: the Never Girls) Christy, Jana, illus. 2015. (Never Girls Ser.: 10). (ENG.). 128p. (J). (gr. 1-4). 6.99 *(978-0-7364-3306-8(6)*, RH/Disney) Random Hse. Children's Bks.
—Never Girls #11: into the Waves (Disney: the Never Girls) Christy, Jana, illus. 2016. (Never Girls Ser.: 11). (ENG.). 128p. (J). (gr. 1-4). 6.99 *(978-0-7364-3525-3(5)*, RH/Disney) Random Hse. Children's Bks.
—Never Girls #12: in the Game (Disney: the Never Girls) Christy, Jana, illus. 2016. (Never Girls Ser.: 12). (ENG.). 128p. (J). (gr. 1-4). 6.99 *(978-0-7364-3527-7(1)*, RH/Disney) Random Hse. Children's Bks.
—Never Girls #2: the Space Between (Disney: the Never Girls) Christy, Jana, illus. 2013. (Never Girls Ser.: 2). (ENG.). 128p. (J). (gr. 1-4). 6.99 *(978-0-7364-2795-1(3)*, RH/Disney) Random Hse. Children's Bks.
—Never Girls #3: a Dandelion Wish (Disney: the Never Girls) Christy, Jana, illus. 2013. (Never Girls Ser.: 3). (ENG.). 128p. (J). (gr. 1-4). 6.99 *(978-0-7364-2796-8(1)*, RH/Disney) Random Hse. Children's Bks.
—Never Girls #4: from the Mist (Disney: the Never Girls) Christy, Jana, illus. 2013. (Never Girls Ser.: 4). (ENG.). 128p. (J). (gr. 1-4). 5.99 *(978-0-7364-2797-5(X)*, RH/Disney) Random Hse. Children's Bks.
—Never Girls #5: Wedding Wings (Disney: the Never Girls) Christy, Jana, illus. 2014. (Never Girls Ser.: 5). (ENG.). 128p. (J). (gr. 1-4). 6.99 *(978-0-7364-3077-7(6)*, RH/Disney) Random Hse. Children's Bks.
—Never Girls #6: the Woods Beyond (Disney: the Never Girls) Christy, Jana, illus. 2014. (Never Girls Ser.: 6). (ENG.). 128p. (J). (gr. 1-4). 6.99 *(978-0-7364-3096-8(2)*, RH/Disney) Random Hse. Children's Bks.
—Never Girls #7: a Pinch of Magic (Disney: the Never Girls) Christy, Jana, illus. 2014. (Never Girls Ser.: 7). (ENG.). 128p. (J). (gr. 1-4). 6.99 *(978-0-7364-3097-5(0)*, RH/Disney) Random Hse. Children's Bks.
—Never Girls #9: Before the Bell (Disney: the Never Girls) Christy, Jana, illus. 2015. (Never Girls Ser.: 9). (ENG.). 128p. (J). (gr. 1-4). 6.99 *(978-0-7364-3304-4(X))*; lib. bdg. 12.99 *(978-0-7364-8167-0(2))* Random Hse. Children's Bks. (RH/Disney).
—A Pinch of Magic. 2014. (Never Girls Ser.: 7). lib. bdg. 16.00 *(978-0-606-36008-1(5))* Turtleback.
—The Space Between. Christy, Jana, illus. 2013. (Never Girls Ser.: 2). lib. bdg. 16.00 *(978-0-606-26974-2(6))* Turtleback.
—Wedding Wings. 2014. (Never Girls Ser.: 5). lib. bdg. 16.00 *(978-0-606-35544-5(8))* Turtleback.
—The Woods Beyond. Christy, Jana, illus. 2014. (Never Girls Ser.: 6). lib. bdg. 16.00 *(978-0-606-35545-2(6))* Turtleback.
Thrasher, Amanda M. Mischief in the Mushroom Patch. 2010. 174p. pap. 10.50 *(978-1-60911-165-6(6)*, Strategic Bk. Publishing) Strategic Book Publishing & Rights Agency (SBPRA).
Tiernan, Cate. Eternally Yours. 2013. (Immortal Beloved Ser.: 3). (ENG.). 464p. (YA). (gr. 7-17). pap. 21.99 *(978-0-316-03595-8(5)*, Poppy) Little, Brown Bks. for Young Readers.
—Immortal Beloved. 2012. (Immortal Beloved Ser.: 1). (ENG.). 432p. (YA). (gr. 7-17). pap. 9.99 *(978-0-316-03591-0(2)*, Poppy) Little, Brown Bks. for Young Readers.
—Sweep: Book of Shadows, the Coven, & Blood Witch: Volume 1. 2010. (Sweep Ser.: 1). (ENG.). 592p. (YA). (gr. 7-18). 12.99 *(978-0-14-241717-1(3)*, Speak) Penguin Young Readers Group.
Tiki Machine, LLC Staff, creator. Deus Libris: An Illustrated Collection. 2011. (Illus.). 58p. 19.99 *(978-0-615-49510-1(9))* Tiki Machine, LLC.
Tilley, Laura. The Magic of the Morning. 2011. 36p. pap. 17.49 *(978-1-4568-6451-4(3))* Xlibris Corp.
Tillis, Dionne. Willameana Whitney White & the Magical Butterfly. 2012. 24p. pap. 17.99 *(978-1-4685-7286-5(5))* AuthorHouse.
Tillworth, Mary. Leah's Dream Dollhouse (Shimmer & Shine) Yum, Heekyoung & Aikins, Dave, illus. 2016. (Pictureback(R) Ser.). (ENG.). 16p. (J). (gr. -1-2). 4.99 *(978-1-101-93249-0(X)*, Random Hse. Bks. for Young Readers) Random Hse. Children's Bks.
Timroth, Stephen. Dreamhawk. 2009. 24p. pap. 12.00 *(978-1-60860-501-9(9)*, Strategic Bk. Publishing) Strategic Book Publishing & Rights Agency (SBPRA).
Toalson, R. L. The Woods. 2019. (ENG.). 480p. (J). (gr. 6). 17.99 *(978-1-4998-0957-2(3)*, Yellow Jacket) Bonnier Publishing USA.
Tobin, Irene. The Tidy Bunch. 2010. (Illus.). 58p. pap. *(978-1-84748-666-0(5))* Athena Pr.
Tomlinson, Heather. The Swan Maiden. 2008. (ENG.). 320p. (YA). (gr. 7-12). pap. 22.99 *(978-0-312-38447-0(5)*, 900053433) Square Fish.
Tooth, Lucy. Star the Tooth Fairy from Treasure Cloud Shares Secrets with You! 2010. (ENG.). 36p. 16.95 *(978-0-557-37985-9(7))* Lulu Pr., Inc.
—Star the Tooth Fairy Is Checking on You! 2010. (ENG.). 36p. 16.95 *(978-0-557-49450-7(8))* Lulu Pr., Inc.
—Star the Tooth Fairy Takes A Holiday to Visit Santa at the North Pole! 2010. (ENG.). 40p. 17.95 *(978-0-557-41623-3(X))* Lulu Pr., Inc.
—Star the Tooth Fairy Wants to Know If You Need Braces? 2010. (ENG.). 36p. 16.95 *(978-0-557-49455-2(9))* Lulu Pr., Inc.
Top That. Press Out & Play Magic Castle. 2008. *(978-1-84666-600-1(7))* Top That! Publishing PLC.
Torribio, Penelope. The Magic in You: From vacant lot to community Garden. 2011. 40p. pap. 16.46 *(978-1-4269-5723-9(8))* Trafford Publishing.
Touring Europe on a Magic Carpet. 2004. (J). ring bd. 4.50 *(978-0-9762740-9-4(4))* Smart Smiles Co., The.
Town, Nathan. Ned Stapleton & the Wrath of the Death Gods. 2006. 174p. (YA). *(978-0-9781040-0-9(5))* Emerald City Storytellers.
Townsan, Judy. The Wishing Flower, 1 vol. Rosado, Michael, illus. 2009. 13p. pap. 24.95 *(978-1-61546-179-0(5))* America Star Bks.
Townsend, Jessica. Hollowpox: the Hunt for Morrigan Crow. 2020. (Nevermoor Ser.: 3). (ENG., Illus.). 560p. (J). (gr. 3-7). 17.99 *(978-0-316-50895-7(0))* Little, Brown Bks. for Young Readers.
—Nevermoor: the Trials of Morrigan Crow. (Nevermoor Ser.: 1). (ENG.). (J). (gr. 3-7). 2018. 512p. pap. 8.99 *(978-0-316-50889-6(6))* 2017. 480p. 17.99 *(978-0-316-50888-9(8))* 2017. 640p. 45.99 *(978-0-316-43995-4(9))* Little, Brown Bks. for Young Readers.
—Wundersmith: The Calling of Morrigan Crow. (Nevermoor Ser.: 2). (ENG.). (J). (gr. 3-7). 2019. 560p. pap. 8.99 *(978-0-316-50892-6(6))* 2018. 544p. 17.99 *(978-0-316-50891-9(8))* 2018. 720p. 48.99 *(978-0-316-41990-1(7))* Little, Brown Bks. for Young Readers.
Townsend, Tamela Ann. Finding Pumpkin, 1 vol. 2010. 48p. pap. 16.95 *(978-1-4489-5983-9(7))* America Star Bks.
Tozier, Christopher. Olivia Brophie & the Pearl of Tagelus. 2013. (ENG.). 208p. (J). (gr. -1-12). pap. 12.95 *(978-1-56164-519-0(2))* Pineapple Pr., Inc.
—Olivia Brophie & the Sky Island. 2014. (ENG.). 304p. (J). (gr. -1-12). pap. 12.95 *(978-1-56164-680-7(6))* Pineapple Pr., Inc.
Tracey, Andrée. Storyland: Poppy & Her Magic Hat: A Story Coloring Book. 2015. (Dover Coloring Bks.). (ENG., Illus.). 32p. (J). (gr. k-5). pap. 3.99 *(978-0-486-79403-7(2)*, 794032) Dover Pubns., Inc.
Tracy, Judith. The Wildsidhe Chronicles Bk. 3: Dark Proposal. 2003. (J). pap. 7.99 *(978-1-890096-15-1(6))* Padwolf Publishing Inc.
Travers, P. L. Mary Poppins. Shepard, Mary, illus. 2006. (Mary Poppins Ser.: No. 1). (ENG.). 224p. (J). (gr. 5-7). 16.99 *(978-0-15-205810-4(9)*, 1197456, Clarion Bks.) HarperCollins Pubs.
—Mary Poppins in the Park. Shepard, Mary, illus. 2015. (Mary Poppins Ser.). (ENG.). 272p. (J). (gr. 5-7). pap. 7.99 *(978-0-544-51384-6(3)*, 1605889, Clarion Bks.) HarperCollins Pubs.
—Mary Poppins Opens the Door. Shepard, Mary, illus. 2015. (Mary Poppins Ser.). (ENG.). 256p. (J). (gr. 5-7). pap. 7.99 *(978-0-544-43958-0(9)*, 1596852, Clarion Bks.) HarperCollins Pubs.
—Mary Poppins: the Illustrated Gift Edition. Sardà, Júlia, illus. 2018. (Mary Poppins Ser.). (ENG.). 248p. (J). (gr. 5-7). 24.99 *(978-1-328-49884-7(0)*, 1717674, Clarion Bks.) HarperCollins Pubs.
—Mary Poppins Vintage Boxed Set: Three Enchanting Classics: Mary Poppins, Mary Poppins Comes Back, & Mary Poppins Opens the Door. 2007. (Illus.). (J). 38.85 *(978-0-15-205858-6(3))* Harcourt Children's Bks.
Trevayne, Emma. The Accidental Afterlife of Thomas Marsden. 2016. (ENG.). 272p. (J). (gr. 3-7). pap. 8.99 *(978-1-4424-9884-6(6)*, Simon & Schuster Bks. For Young Readers) Simon & Schuster Bks. For Young Readers.
—Spindrift & the Orchid. (ENG.). 256p. (J). (gr. 3-7). 2019. pap. 8.99 *(978-1-4814-6260-0(1))* 2018. (Illus.). 17.99 *(978-1-4814-6259-4(8))* Simon & Schuster Bks. For Young Readers. (Simon & Schuster Bks. For Young Readers).
Trigg, Michael J. Greanwold & the Mystery Cave: Greanwold & the Minosaurs Story Books. 2013. 148p. pap. 12.97 *(978-1-61897-466-2(1)*, Strategic Bk. Publishing) Strategic Book Publishing & Rights Agency (SBPRA).
Trini Torres Carrion. The Magic of a Strawberry Lollipop. 2009. 16p. pap. 8.49 *(978-1-4389-7900-7(2))* AuthorHouse.
Trivas, Tracy. The Wish Stealers. 2010. (ENG.). 288p. (J). (gr. 3-7). 17.99 *(978-1-4169-8725-3(8)*, Aladdin) Simon & Schuster Children's Publishing.
Trotter, Bob. The Curious Tale of Marmalade Tuttle. 2008. 116p. pap. 12.95 *(978-1-60693-014-4(1)*, Eloquent Bks.) Strategic Book Publishing & Rights Agency (SBPRA).
Troulis, Jennifer. Penelope & Priscilla: And the Enchanted House of Whispers. 2nd ed. 2004. (Illus.). 229p. per. 13.95 *(978-0-9768602-0-4(1))* Twin Monkeys Pr.
—Penelope & Priscilla & the City of the Banished. 2007. (J). per. 14.95 *(978-0-9768602-1-1(X))* Twin Monkeys Pr.
Trowell, Michelle. Magical Mermaids. Top That Publishing Staff, ed. Richards, Kirsten, illus. 2008. (Magnetic Story & Play Scene Ser.). 9p. (J). (gr. -1). *(978-1-84666-442-7(X)*, Tide Mill Pr.) Top That! Publishing PLC.
Truax, Lois. Grandmothers Are Magic. 2010. 28p. pap. 5.95 *(978-1-935355-01-4(5))* New Shelves Bks.
Trudeau, Scott & Holzbauer, David. A Treasure to Share: Adventures in Social Skills. Trudeau, Scott, illus. 2003. (Illus.). 68p. (J). *(978-0-9743805-0-6(4))* Intellipop, LLC.
Tulien, Sean. The Not-So-Evil Wizard. Cunyat, Pol, illus. 2016. (Thud & Blunder Ser.). (ENG.). 56p. (J). (gr. 1-3). lib. bdg. 23.99 *(978-1-4965-3221-3(X)*, 132416, Stone Arch Bks.) Capstone.
Turetsky, Bianca. The Time-Traveling Fashionista at the Palace of Marie Antoinette. 2013. (Time-Traveling Fashionista Ser.: 2). (ENG., Illus.). 272p. (J). (gr. 3-7). pap. 9.00 *(978-0-316-10535-4(X)*, Poppy) Little, Brown Bks. for Young Readers.
Turner, Megan Whalen. Instead of Three Wishes: Magical Short Stories. 2006. (ENG.). 160p. (J). (gr. 5-9). per. 6.99 *(978-0-06-084231-4(8)*, Greenwillow Bks.) HarperCollins Pubs.
Tyrrell, Melissa. The Gingerbread Man. McMullen, Nigel, illus. 2005. (Fairytale Friends Ser.: Vol. 8). 12p. (J). (gr. -1-k). bds. 5.95 *(978-1-58117-154-9(4)*, Intervisual/Piggy Toes) Bendon, Inc.
Tzingoker, Lilach. Sonny's Adventure in Mystery Park. 2010. 44p. pap. 19.95 *(978-1-60911-927-0(4)*, Eloquent Bks.) Strategic Book Publishing & Rights Agency (SBPRA).
Uehashi, Nahoko. The Beast Player. Hirano, Cathy, tr. 2019. (ENG., Illus.). 352p. (YA). 19.99 *(978-1-250-30746-0(5)*, 900198010, Holt, Henry & Co. Bks. For Young Readers) Holt, Henry & Co.
Ullman, Barb Bentler. Whistle Bright Magic: A Nutfolk Tale. 2010. 224p. (J). (gr. 3-7). 16.99 *(978-0-06-188286-9(0))* HarperCollins Pubs.
Umansky, Kaye. Clover Twig & the Perilous Path. Wright, Johanna, illus. 2013. (ENG.). 272p. (J). (gr. 3-7). pap. 15.99 *(978-1-250-02727-6(6)*, 900098299) Square Fish.
Uncle Bernie. Michaels Adventures in the Land of Nod Book: Michaels Trip to Orange County. 2008. 32p. pap. 12.99 *(978-1-4389-1097-0(5))* AuthorHouse.
Underwood, Kim. The Wonderful World of Sparkle Girl & Doobins. Goldman, Garnet, illus. 2009. 48p. (J). pap. 16.95 *(978-0-89587-373-6(7)*, Blair) Carolina Wren Pr.
Upton, Robert Jesten. Milo & the Dragon Cross: A Novel. 2017. (Illus.). 283p. (YA). pap. *(978-1-63293-177-1(X))* Sunstone Pr.
Urban, Linda. Milo Speck, Accidental Agent. 2017. (ENG., Illus.). 272p. (J). (gr. 3-7). pap. 7.99 *(978-0-544-93523-5(3)*, 1658130, Clarion Bks.) HarperCollins Pubs.
Ursu, Anne. Breadcrumbs. McGuire, Erin, illus. 2013. (ENG.). 336p. (J). (gr. 3-7). pap. 7.99 *(978-0-06-201506-8(0)*, Waldon Pond Pr.) HarperCollins Pubs.
—Breadcrumbs. McGuire, Erin, illus. 2012. 320p. 55.00 *(978-0-449-01400-4(2))* Random Hse., Inc.
—Breadcrumbs. 2013. (J). lib. bdg. 17.20 *(978-0-606-27130-1(9))* Turtleback.
—The Real Boy. McGuire, Erin, illus. 2015. (ENG.). 352p. (J). (gr. 3-7). pap. 7.99 *(978-0-06-201508-2(7)*, Waldon Pond Pr.) HarperCollins Pubs.
Uwuigiaren, Omoruyi. The Adventures of Nihu. Ayalomeh, Shedrach, illus. 2007. 158p. (J). (gr. 2-8). 16.95 *(978-1-934138-15-1(0))* Bouncing Ball Bks., Inc.
Valente, Catherynne M. The Girl Who Fell Beneath Fairyland & Led the Revels There. Juan, Ana, illus. 2013. (Fairyland Ser.: 2). (ENG.). 304p. (YA). (gr. 5-9). pap. 9.99 *(978-1-250-03412-0(4)*, 900120582) Square Fish.
Valentino, Serena. Mistress of All Evil-Villains, Book 4. 2017. (Villains Ser.: 4). (ENG.). 320p. (YA). (gr. 7-12). 17.99 *(978-1-368-00901-0(8)*, Disney Press Books) Disney Publishing Worldwide.
—Poor Unfortunate Soul-Villains, Book 3. 2016. (Villains Ser.: 3). (ENG., Illus.). 224p. (YA). (gr. 7-12). 17.99 *(978-1-4847-2405-7(4)*, Disney Press Books) Disney Publishing Worldwide.
Van Allsburg, Chris. Probuditi! 2009. 30p. (J). 19.00 *(978-1-4379-6940-5(2))* DIANE Publishing Co.
—Probuditi! Van Allsburg, Chris, illus. 2006. (ENG., Illus.). 32p. (J). (gr. 1-4). 18.95 *(978-0-618-75502-8(0)*, 579489, Clarion Bks.) HarperCollins Pubs.
—The Sweetest Fig. 2014. 32p. pap. 9.00 *(978-1-61003-223-0(3))* Center for the Collaborative Classroom.
Van Cleve, Kathleen. Drizzle. 2011. (ENG.). 368p. (J). (gr. 3-7). 9.99 *(978-0-14-241113-1(2)*, Puffin Books) Penguin Young Readers Group.
Van Der Watt, Tony. Balthazar, the Wolf Who Reformed. 2010. 48p. pap. 12.50 *(978-1-60911-125-0(7)*, Eloquent Bks.) Strategic Book Publishing & Rights Agency (SBPRA).
van Diepen, Allison. Raven. 2010. (ENG.). 304p. (YA). (gr. 9). pap. 12.99 *(978-1-4169-7468-0(7)*, Simon Pulse) Simon Pulse.
Van Draanen, Wendelin. The Gecko & Sticky: Sinister Substitute. Gilpin, Stephen, illus. 2011. (Gecko & Sticky Ser.:

3). (ENG.). 224p. (J). (gr. 3-7). 7.99 *(978-0-440-42244-0(2)*, Yearling) Random Hse. Children's Bks.

—The Gecko & Sticky: the Greatest Power. Gilpin, Stephen, illus. 2011. (Gecko & Sticky Ser.: 2). (ENG.). 208p. (J). (gr. 3-7). 7.99 *(978-0-440-42243-3(4)*, Yearling) Random Hse. Children's Bks.

—The Gecko & Sticky: the Power Potion. Gilpin, Stephen, illus. 2011. (Gecko & Sticky Ser.: 4). (ENG.). 240p. (J). (gr. 3-7). 7.99 *(978-0-440-42245-7(0)*, Yearling) Random Hse. Children's Bks.

Vande Velde, Vivian. Curses, Inc. & Other Stories. 2007. (ENG., Illus.). 240p. (YA). (gr. 7-12). pap. 12.95 *(978-0-15-206107-4(X)*, 1198344, Clarion Bks.) HarperCollins Pubs.

—A Hidden Magic. 176p. (J). pap. 5.00 *(978-0-8072-1519-7(8)*, Listening Library) Random Hse. Audio Publishing Group.

—Wizard at Work. 2004. (ENG., Illus.). 144p. (J). (gr. 5-7). pap. 10.95 *(978-0-15-205309-3(3)*, 1195997, Clarion Bks.) HarperCollins Pubs.

Varian, H. K. The Changer War. 2017. (Hidden World of Changers Ser.: 8). (ENG.). 176p. (J). (gr. 3-7). 17.99 *(978-1-5344-0146-4(6))*; (Illus.). pap. 6.99 *(978-1-5344-0145-7(8))* Simon Spotlight. (Simon Spotlight).

—The Emerald Mask. 2016. (Hidden World of Changers Ser.: 2). (ENG., Illus.). 176p. (J). (gr. 3-7). pap. 6.99 *(978-1-4814-6619-6(4)*, Simon Spotlight) Simon Spotlight.

—The Gathering Storm. 2016. (Hidden World of Changers Ser.: 1). (ENG., Illus.). 176p. (J). (gr. 3-7). pap. 6.99 *(978-1-4814-6616-5(X)*, Simon Spotlight) Simon Spotlight.

—The Power Within. 2016. (Hidden World of Changers Ser.: 3). (ENG., Illus.). 176p. (J). (gr. 3-7). pap. 6.99 *(978-1-4814-6963-0(0)*, Simon Spotlight) Simon Spotlight.

—The Selkie Song. 2016. (Hidden World of Changers Ser.: 4). (ENG., Illus.). 176p. (J). (gr. 3-7). pap. 6.99 *(978-1-4814-6966-1(5)*, Simon Spotlight) Simon Spotlight.

—The Spider's Curse. 2017. (Hidden World of Changers Ser.: 7). (ENG., Illus.). 176p. (J). (gr. 3-7). pap. 6.99 *(978-1-4814-9826-5(6)*, Simon Spotlight) Simon Spotlight.

—The Spirit Warrior. 2017. (Hidden World of Changers Ser.: 6). (ENG., Illus.). 176p. (J). (gr. 3-7). pap. 6.99 *(978-1-4814-8084-0(7)*, Simon Spotlight) Simon Spotlight.

Varveris, Ariana Eleni. The Adventures of Magic Island: Book I-Welcome to Magic Island. 2012. 122p. (gr. 2-2). pap. 9.95 *(978-1-4620-5751-1(9))* iUniverse, Inc.

Vaughan, Grace. Annie & the Magic Book. 2012. 30p. pap. 19.99 *(978-1-4772-5498-1(6))* AuthorHouse.

Venable, Alan. Take Me with You When You Go. Marshall, Laurie, illus. 2008. 112p. (J). 12.95 *(978-0-9777082-7-7(6))* One Monkey Bks.

Vercz, Carol A. The Magic of Hildie. (J). 6.95 *(978-0-910119-44-3(9))* S.O.C.O. Pubns.

Verhoosky, Michele. Molly Marie & the Amazing Jimmy. Verhoosky, Michele, illus. 2012. (Illus.). 34p. pap. 10.95 *(978-1-937260-22-4(4))* Sleepytown Pr.

Vickers, Tamara. Mr. Green & the Animal Kingdom: (Imagine That!) You Draw the Picture! 2007. 228p. per. 24.95 *(978-1-4241-8256-5(5))* America Star Bks.

Vinci, Leonardo Da. Leonardo's Fables & Jests. 2003. 48p. per. 14.95 *(978-0-9719898-9-4(3))* E & E Publishing.

Vitale, Brooke & Disney Storybook Artists Staff, adapted by. Disney Classics. 2017. (Illus.). (J). *(978-1-368-00668-2(X))* Disney Publishing Worldwide.

Viz Media. Fairy Dreams. 2013. (Winx Club Ser.: 5). lib. bdg. 17.20 *(978-0-606-26987-2(8))* Turtleback.

—Time for Magic. 2013. (Winx Club Ser.: 6). lib. bdg. 17.20 *(978-0-606-27022-9(1))* Turtleback.

VIZ Media Staff. WINX Club, Vol. 3, 3. 2012. (Winx Club: Graphic Novel Ser.). (ENG.). 96p. (J). (gr. 3-6). 21.19 *(978-1-4215-4161-7(0))* Viz Media.

VIZ Media Staff & Straffi, Iginio. WINX Club, Vol. 2, 2. 2012. (Winx Club: Graphic Novel Ser.). (ENG.). 96p. (J). (gr. 3-6). 18.69 *(978-1-4215-4160-0(2))* Viz Media.

Volkov, Alexander. Tales of Magic Land 1. 2010. 360p. pap. 22.95 *(978-0-557-44825-8(5))* Lulu Pr., Inc.

Vornholt, John. The Troll Treasure. 2003. (Troll King Trilogy). 185p. (J). (gr. 5-9). 12.65 *(978-0-7569-3954-0(2))* Perfection Learning Corp.

Wagman, Diana. Extraordinary October. 2016. (ENG.). 264p. (J). (gr. 6). 18.95 *(978-1-63246-036-3(X))* Ig Publishing, Inc.

Wagner, Mckenzie. The Amulet Chase. 2017. (ENG., Illus.). 215p. (J). pap. 10.99 *(978-1-4621-1983-7(2)*, Sweetwater Bks.) Cedar Fort, Inc./CFI Distribution.

—Casters of Doovik. 2015. 298p. (YA). pap. 17.99 *(978-1-4621-1757-4(0))* Cedar Fort, Inc./CFI Distribution.

—Keys to the Dream World. 2014. pap. 8.99 *(978-1-4621-1435-1(0))* Cedar Fort, Inc./CFI Distribution.

Wakem, Samantha. Milly's Magic Play House: The Hospital, 1 vol. Herridge, Debbie, illus. 2010. 20p. 24.95 *(978-1-4489-5114-7(3))* PublishAmerica, Inc.

Waldman, Thomas. 1 ! 2 ! 3 ! 4 ! Saisons. 2005. 10p. 8.53 *(978-1-4116-3332-2(6))* Lulu Pr., Inc.

Walker, Crystal. Maceys Magic Tree. 2009. 28p. pap. 12.49 *(978-1-4490-4916-4(8))* AuthorHouse.

Walker-Renner, Christa. Santa's Magic. 2009. 20p. pap. 11.00 *(978-1-4389-8206-9(2))* AuthorHouse.

Walker, Russell D. Michelle & the Magic Timepiece. 2006. 108p. pap. 19.95 *(978-1-4241-3143-3(X))* PublishAmerica, Inc.

Walker, Victoria. The Winter of Enchantment. 2007. (Illus.). 152p. (YA). (gr. 8-12). 18.95 *(978-1-930900-33-2(3))* Purple Hse. Pr.

Wallace, Becky. The Skylighter. 2017. (Keepers' Chronicles Ser.). (ENG.). 432p. (YA). (gr. 9). pap. 11.99 *(978-1-4814-0569-0(1)*, McElderry, Margaret K. Bks.) McElderry, Margaret K. Bks.

—The Storyspinner. 2015. (Keepers' Chronicles Ser.). (ENG., Illus.). 432p. (YA). (gr. 9). 17.99 *(978-1-4814-0565-2(9)*, McElderry, Margaret K. Bks.) McElderry, Margaret K. Bks.

Wallace, Kali. City of Islands. 2018. (ENG., Illus.). 336p. (J). (gr. 3-7). 16.99 *(978-0-06-249981-3(5)*, Tegen, Katherine Bks) HarperCollins Pubs.

—The Memory Trees. 2017. (ENG.). 432p. (YA). (gr. 9). 17.99 *(978-0-06-236623-8(8)*, Tegen, Katherine Bks) HarperCollins Pubs.

Wallace, Karen. Where Are My Shoes? Allwright, Deborah, illus. 2005. (Reading Corner Ser.). 24p. (J). (gr. k-3). lib. bdg. 22.80 *(978-1-59771-002-2(4))* Sea-To-Sea Pubns.

Wallace, William H. Santa's Magic Key. 2010. 20p. (J). 10.49 *(978-1-4490-8924-5(0))* AuthorHouse.

Walsh, Pat. The Crowfield Demon. 2013. 360p. (J). *(978-0-545-37350-0(6))* Scholastic, Inc.

Walsh, Sara. The Dark Light. 2013. (ENG., Illus.). 512p. (YA). (gr. 9). pap. 9.99 *(978-1-4424-3458-5(9)*, Simon Pulse) Simon Pulse.

Walter, Wendy D. & Walter, Wendy D. Return of the Dullaith: Ambril's Tale. 2012. (Illus.). 318p. (J). pap. 15.99 *(978-0-9857147-1-0(9)*, Angry Bicycle) Walter, Wendy D.

Wampol, Pam & Woodard, Heather. Oscar's Dreamzz: The Story of Santa's First Elf. 2013. 40p. pap. *(978-1-4602-0414-6(X))* FriesenPress.

Wandless, David. Natural Magic. 2010. 344p. pap. 27.50 *(978-1-4461-4163-2(2))* Lulu Pr., Inc.

—Natural Magic Book 3 - the Milk Stone & the Tauren. 2010. 134p. pap. 20.95 *(978-1-4461-5162-4(X))* Lulu Pr., Inc.

Wang, An. Anywhere but Here. 2006. 107p. (J). (gr. 6-8). per. 9.95 *(978-0-88100-140-2(6))* National Writers Pr., The.

Ward, John. The Stone of Sorrow: The Revealer of Wonders. 2004. (Fate of the Stone Ser.: Pt. 2). 256p. (YA). pap. *(978-1-55207-080-2(8))* Studio 9 Bks. and Music.

Warner, Michael N. The Titanic Game. Ordaz, Frank, illus. 2018. (ENG.). 208p. (J). pap. 11.95 *(978-0-9744446-2-8(6))* All About Kids Publishing.

Warner, Sally. Ellray Jakes Is Magic. 2014. (EllRay Jakes Ser.: 6). lib. bdg. 16.00 *(978-0-606-34215-5(X))* Turtleback.

Warren, Cindy. The Unicorn's Horn. 2011. 98p. pap. 19.95 *(978-1-4560-6987-2(X))* America Star Bks.

Watase, Yuu. Alice 19th, Vol. 1, 7 vols. 2003. (Alice 19th Ser.: 1). (ENG., Illus.). 192p. pap. 9.95 *(978-1-59116-215-5(7))* Viz Media.

—Alice 19th, Vol. 2, 7 vols. 2003. (Alice 19th Ser.: 2). (ENG., Illus.). 200p. pap. 9.95 *(978-1-59116-229-2(7))* Viz Media.

Waterfield, Susan. Spunkie's Magical Garden. 2012. 32p. pap. 14.95 *(978-1-257-77576-7(6))* Lulu Pr., Inc.

Watson, Heather M. J. L. Thistle Lodge: The Legendary Sidhe Saga. 2012. (ENG.). 224p. pap. *(978-1-78088-181-2(9))* Troubador Publishing Ltd.

Watson, M. Desmond & the Challenge on Mudwig Mountain. 2005. 109p. pap. *(978-1-84401-010-3(4))* Athena Pr.

Watson, Mary. The Wickerlight. 2019. (ENG.). 416p. (YA). 17.99 *(978-1-5476-0194-3(9)*, 900203172, Bloomsbury Young Adult) Bloomsbury Publishing USA.

—The Wren Hunt. 2018. (ENG.). 416p. (YA). 17.99 *(978-1-68119-859-0(2)*, 900189933, Bloomsbury Young Adult) Bloomsbury Publishing USA.

Weatherill, Cat. Wild Magic. 2008. (ENG., Illus.). 288p. (YA). (gr. 4-6). 21.19 *(978-0-8027-9799-5(7)*, 9780802797995) Walker & Co.

Webb, Holly. Dog Magic. 2009. (Animal Magic Ser.). (ENG.). 144p. (J). (gr. 2-4). 18.69 *(978-0-545-12415-7(8))* Scholastic, Inc.

—Rose. 2013. (Rose Ser.: 1). (ENG.). 240p. (J). (gr. 3-6). pap. 12.99 *(978-1-4022-8581-3(7)*, 9781402285813) Sourcebooks, Inc.

—Rose & the Lost Princess. 2014. (Rose Ser.: 2). (ENG.). 256p. (J). (gr. 3-6). pap. 10.99 *(978-1-4022-8584-4(1))* Sourcebooks, Inc.

—Rose & the Magician's Mask. 2014. (Rose Ser.: 3). (ENG.). 224p. (J). (gr. 3-6). pap. 10.99 *(978-1-4926-0430-3(5)*, 9781492604303) Sourcebooks, Inc.

—Rose & the Silver Ghost. 2015. (Rose Ser.: 4). (ENG.). 224p. (J). (gr. 3-6). pap. 10.99 *(978-1-4926-0433-4(X))* Sourcebooks, Inc.

Webster, Wendy. Magicus Perfecticum. 2009. (Illus.). 60p. pap. 11.49 *(978-1-4490-0765-2(1))* AuthorHouse.

Wees, Alyssa. The Waking Forest. 2019. 304p. (YA). (gr. 7). 17.99 *(978-0-525-58116-1(2)*, Delacorte Pr.) Random Hse. Children's Bks.

Weinberg, Jennifer. Surprise for a Princess. 2003. (Disney Princess Step into Reading Ser.). (gr. -1-2). 13.55 *(978-0-613-73686-2(9))* Turtleback.

Weingarten, Lynn. The Book of Love. 2013. (ENG.). 272p. (YA). (gr. 8). 17.99 *(978-0-06-192620-4(5)*, HarperTeen) HarperCollins Pubs.

—The Secret Sisterhood of Heartbreakers. 2011. (ENG.). 352p. (YA). (gr. 8). 17.99 *(978-0-06-192618-1(3)*, HarperTeen) HarperCollins Pubs.

Weinshall Liberman, Judith. The Little Fairy. 2013. 32p. 21.99 *(978-1-4575-2351-9(5))* Dog Ear Publishing, LLC.

Weinstein, Jacob Sager. Hyacinth & the Destiny Stones. 2018. 316p. (J). pap. *(978-0-399-55322-6(3))* Random Hse., Inc.

—Hyacinth & the Secrets Beneath. 2018. (Hyacinth Ser.: 1). lib. bdg. 18.40 *(978-0-606-40938-4(6))* Turtleback.

Welborn, Kathleen. The Cacklebeans, 1 vol. 2009. 33p. pap. 24.95 *(978-1-4489-1933-8(9))* America Star Bks.

Welch-Biggs, Susan. Your Magical Party. 2008. (ENG.). 36p. per. 21.99 *(978-1-4257-9181-0(6))* Xlibris Corp.

Welles, Lee. Enter the Earth. Hameister, Ann, illus. 2006. (Gaia Girls Ser.: 1). (ENG.). 336p. (YA). (gr. 4-7). 18.95 *(978-1-933609-00-3(1))* Chelsea Green Publishing.

Welling, Martin. Guardian of the Stones: Nat & Mateo Discover the Two Forces of Magic Stones. 2012. (ENG.). 40p. (J). 29.95 *(978-1-4327-7692-3(4))* Outskirts Pr., Inc.

Wells, Carolyn. Patty Fairfield. 2004. reprint ed. pap. 1.99 *(978-1-4192-4033-1(1))*; pap. 20.95 *(978-1-4191-4033-4(7))* Kessinger Publishing, LLC.

Wells, J. & L. Antares & the Zodiac. 2012. (ENG.). 256p. pap. *(978-1-78088-294-9(7))* Troubador Publishing Ltd.

Welsh, Kenneth Wilbur. Magic Chalk. 2011. 16p. pap. 12.00 *(978-1-4520-6078-1(9))* AuthorHouse.

Wendling, Peter. The Magic of the Dark Ravine. Durie, Sally, illus. 2011. 36p. pap. 13.95 *(978-1-60976-933-8(3)*, Eloquent Bks.) Strategic Book Publishing & Rights Agency (SBPRA).

Werlin, Nancy. Impossible. 2011. 11.04 *(978-0-7848-3488-6(1)*, Everbind) Marco Bk. Co.

Werner, Teresa O. A Quilt of Wishes. Tremlin, Nathan, illus. l.t. ed. 2005. 21p. (J). per. 9.99 *(978-1-59879-037-5(4))* Lifevest Publishing, Inc.

West, Hannah. Palace of Silver: A Nissera Novel. 2020. (Nissera Chronicles Ser.: 3). (Illus.). 464p. (YA). (gr. 7). 18.99 *(978-0-8234-4443-4(0))* Holiday Hse., Inc.

—Realm of Ruins: A Nissera Novel. 2018. (Nissera Chronicles Ser.: 2). (Illus.). 464p. (YA). (gr. 7). 18.99 *(978-0-8234-3986-7(0))* Holiday Hse., Inc.

West, Hilary. The Secret Kingdom. 2013. 76p. pap. 17.95 *(978-1-62709-626-3(4))* America Star Bks.

West, Jacqueline. The Collectors. 2018. (ENG.). 384p. (J). (gr. 3-7). 16.99 *(978-0-06-269169-9(4)*, Greenwillow Bks.) HarperCollins Pubs.

—The Collectors. 2019. (ENG.). 400p. (J). (gr. 3-7). pap. 7.99 *(978-0-06-269170-5(8)*, Greenwillow Bks.) HarperCollins Pubs.

—The Second Spy. 2013. (Books of Elsewhere Ser.: 3). lib. bdg. 18.40 *(978-0-606-31698-9(1))* Turtleback.

—The Second Spy: The Books of Elsewhere: Volume 3. 2013. (Books of Elsewhere Ser.: 3). (ENG., Illus.). 320p. (J). (gr. 5). pap. 9.99 *(978-0-14-242608-1(3)*, Puffin Books) Penguin Young Readers Group.

—The Shadows. l.t. ed. 2010. (Books of Elsewhere Ser.: Vol. 1). (ENG.). 268p. 23.99 *(978-1-4104-3139-4(8))* Thorndike Pr.

—The Shadows. 2011. (Books of Elsewhere Ser.: 1). lib. bdg. 17.20 *(978-0-606-23070-4(X))* Turtleback.

—The Shadows: The Books of Elsewhere: Volume 1. 2011. (Books of Elsewhere Ser.: 1). (ENG.). 272p. (J). (gr. 5-7). 8.99 *(978-0-14-241872-7(2)*, Puffin Books) Penguin Young Readers Group.

—Spellbound, 2. 2012. (Books of Elsewhere Ser.: 2). (ENG., Illus.). 304p. (J). (gr. 6-8). 21.19 *(978-0-8037-3441-8(7))* Penguin Young Readers Group.

—Spellbound. 2012. (Books of Elsewhere Ser.: 2). lib. bdg. 18.40 *(978-0-606-26082-4(X))* Turtleback.

—Spellbound: The Books of Elsewhere: Volume 2, 2 vols. 2012. (Books of Elsewhere Ser.: 2). (ENG.). 320p. (J). (gr. 5-18). pap. 8.99 *(978-0-14-242102-4(2)*, Puffin Books) Penguin Young Readers Group.

—Still Life. 2015. (Books of Elsewhere Ser.: 5). lib. bdg. 18.40 *(978-0-606-36786-8(1))* Turtleback.

—Still Life: The Books of Elsewhere: Volume 5. Bernatene, Poly, illus. 2015. (Books of Elsewhere Ser.: 5). (ENG.). 352p. (J). (gr. 5). 8.99 *(978-0-14-242297-7(5)*, Puffin Books) Penguin Young Readers Group.

—The Strangers. 2014. (Books of Elsewhere Ser.: 4). lib. bdg. 18.40 *(978-0-606-35680-0(0))* Turtleback.

—The Strangers: The Books of Elsewhere: Volume 4. Bernatene, Poly, illus. 2014. (Books of Elsewhere Ser.: 4). (ENG.). 336p. (J). (gr. 5). pap. 8.99 *(978-0-14-242575-6(3)*, Puffin Books) Penguin Young Readers Group.

West, Tracey. Call of the Sound Dragon: a Branches Book (Dragon Masters #16) Loveridge, Matt, illus. 2020. (Dragon Masters Ser.: 16). (ENG.). 96p. (J). (gr. 1-3). pap. 5.99 *(978-1-338-54028-4(9))* Scholastic, Inc.

—Call of the Sound Dragon: a Branches Book (Dragon Masters #16) (Library Edition) Loveridge, Matt, illus. 2020. (Dragon Masters Ser.: 16). (ENG.). 96p. (J). (gr. 1-3). lib. bdg. 24.99 *(978-1-338-54029-1(7))* Scholastic, Inc.

—Chill of the Ice Dragon, 9. 2019. (Branches Early Ch Bks). (ENG.). 89p. (J). (gr. 2-3). 15.36 *(978-0-87617-974-1(X))* Penworthy Co., LLC, The.

—Chill of the Ice Dragon, 9. 2018. (Branches: Dragon Masters Ser.). (ENG.). 96p. (gr. 1-4). 18.69 *(978-1-5364-3194-0(X))* Scholastic, Inc.

—Chill of the Ice Dragon: a Branches Book (Dragon Masters #9), 1 vol. de Polonia, Nina, illus. 2018. (Dragon Masters Ser.: 9). (ENG.). 96p. (J). (gr. 1-3). pap. 5.99 *(978-1-338-16986-7(6))* Scholastic, Inc.

—Dionysus & the Land of Beasts. Phillips, Craig, illus. 2017. (Heroes in Training Ser.: 14). (ENG.). 112p. (J). (gr. 1-4). 17.99 *(978-1-4814-8835-8(X))*; pap. 5.99 *(978-1-4814-8834-1(1))* Simon & Schuster Children's Publishing. (Aladdin).

—Eye of the Earthquake Dragon, 13. 2019. (Branches Early Ch Bks). (ENG.). 90p. (J). (gr. 2-3). 15.36 *(978-1-64697-098-8(5))* Penworthy Co., LLC, The.

—Eye of the Earthquake Dragon, 13. 2019. (Branches: Dragon Masters Ser.). (ENG.). 96p. (gr. 1-4). 18.69 *(978-1-5364-5484-0(2))* Scholastic, Inc.

—Eye of the Earthquake Dragon: a Branches Book (Dragon Masters #13) Griffo, Daniel, illus. 2019. (Dragon Masters Ser.: 13). (ENG.). 96p. (J). (gr. 1-3). pap. 5.99 *(978-1-338-26371-8(4))* Scholastic, Inc.

—Flight of the Moon Dragon, 6. 2016. (Branches: Dragon Masters Ser.). (ENG.). 96p. (gr. 1-4). 17.44 *(978-1-4844-9296-3(X))* Scholastic, Inc.

—Flight of the Moon Dragon. Jones, Damien, illus. 2016. (Dragon Masters Ser.: bk.6). (ENG.). 96p. (J). (gr. 1-3). 14.75 *(978-0-606-39155-9(X))* Turtleback.

—Flight of the Moon Dragon: a Branches Book (Dragon Masters #6) Jones, Damien, illus. 2016. (Dragon Masters Ser.: 6). (ENG.). 96p. (J). (gr. 1-3). pap. 4.99 *(978-0-545-91392-8(6))* Scholastic, Inc.

—Fortress of the Stone Dragon: a Branches Book (Dragon Masters #17) Loveridge, Matt, illus. 2020. (Dragon Masters Ser.). (ENG.). 96p. (J). (gr. 1-3). pap. 5.99 *(978-1-338-54031-4(9))* Scholastic, Inc.

—Fortress of the Stone Dragon: a Branches Book (Dragon Masters #17) (Library Edition) Loveridge, Matt, illus. 2020. (Dragon Masters Ser.). (ENG.). 96p. (J). (gr. 1-3). 24.99 *(978-1-338-54032-1(7))* Scholastic, Inc.

—Future of the Time Dragon, 15. 2020. (Branches: Dragon Masters Ser.). (ENG.). 96p. (gr. 1-4). 18.69 *(978-1-5364-6188-6(1))* Scholastic, Inc.

—Future of the Time Dragon: a Branches Book (Dragon Masters #15) Griffo, Daniel, illus. 2020. (Dragon Masters Ser.: 15). (ENG.). 96p. (J). (gr. 1-3). pap. 5.99 *(978-1-338-54025-3(4))* Scholastic, Inc.

—Future of the Time Dragon: a Branches Book (Dragon Masters #15) (Library Edition) Griffo, Daniel, illus. 2020. (Dragon Masters Ser.: 15). (ENG.). 96p. (J). (gr. 1-3). 24.99 *(978-1-338-54026-0(2))* Scholastic, Inc.

—Land of the Spring Dragon: a Branches Book (Dragon Masters #14) Loveridge, Matt, illus. 2019. (Dragon Masters Ser.: 14). (ENG.). 96p. (J). (gr. 1-3). pap. 4.99 *(978-1-338-26374-9(9))* Scholastic, Inc.

—Land of the Spring Dragon: a Branches Book (Dragon Masters #14) (Library Edition) Loveridge, Matt, illus. 2019. (Dragon Masters Ser.: 14). (ENG.). 96p. (J). (gr. 1-3). 24.99 *(978-1-338-26375-6(7))* Scholastic, Inc.

—Power of the Fire Dragon: a Branches Book (Dragon Masters #4) Howells, Graham, illus. 2015. (Dragon Masters Ser.: 4). (ENG.). 96p. (J). (gr. 1-3). pap. 5.99 *(978-0-545-64631-4(6))* Scholastic, Inc.

—Rise of the Earth Dragon. 2014. (Dragon Masters Ser.: 1). lib. bdg. 14.75 *(978-0-606-36050-0(6))* Turtleback.

—Rise of the Earth Dragon: a Branches Book (Dragon Masters #1) Howells, Graham, illus. 2014. (Dragon Masters Ser.: 1). (ENG.). 96p. (J). (gr. 1-3). pap. 5.99 *(978-0-545-64623-9(5))* Scholastic, Inc.

—Rise of the Earth Dragon: a Branches Book (Dragon Masters #1) (Library Edition), Vol. 1. Howells, Graham, illus. 2014. (Dragon Masters Ser.: 1). (ENG.). 96p. (J). (gr. 1-3). 24.99 *(978-0-545-64624-6(3))* Scholastic, Inc.

—Roar of the Thunder Dragon, 8. 2019. (Branches Early Ch Bks). (ENG.). 88p. (J). (gr. 2-3). 15.36 *(978-0-87617-975-8(8))* Penworthy Co., LLC, The.

—Roar of the Thunder Dragon. 2017. (Dragon Masters — Branches Ser.: 8). lib. bdg. 14.75 *(978-0-606-40668-0(9))* Turtleback.

—Roar of the Thunder Dragon: a Branches Book (Dragon Masters #8) Jones, Damien, illus. 2017. (Dragon Masters Ser.: 8). (ENG.). 96p. (J). (gr. 1-3). pap. 5.99 *(978-1-338-04292-4(0))* Scholastic, Inc.

—Roar of the Thunder Dragon: a Branches Book (Dragon Masters #8) (Library Edition) Jones, Damien, illus. 2017. (Dragon Masters Ser.: 8). (ENG.). 96p. (J). (gr. 1-3). lib. bdg. 15.99 *(978-1-338-04293-1(9))* Scholastic, Inc.

—Saving the Sun Dragon. 2014. (Dragon Masters Ser.: 2). lib. bdg. 14.75 *(978-0-606-36051-7(4))* Turtleback.

—Saving the Sun Dragon: a Branches Book (Dragon Masters #2) Jones, Damien, illus. 2014. (Dragon Masters Ser.: 2). (ENG.). 96p. (J). (gr. 1-3). pap. 5.99 *(978-0-545-64625-3(1))* Scholastic, Inc.

—Saving the Sun Dragon: a Branches Book (Dragon Masters #2) (Library Edition) Jones, Damien, illus. 2014. (Dragon Masters Ser.: 2). (ENG.). 96p. (J). (gr. 1-3). 15.99 *(978-0-545-64626-0(X))* Scholastic, Inc.

—Search for the Lightning Dragon. 2017. (Dragon Masters Ser.: 7). lib. bdg. 14.75 *(978-0-606-39713-1(2))* Turtleback.

—Search for the Lightning Dragon: a Branches Book (Dragon Masters #7) Jones, Damien, illus. 2017. (Dragon Masters Ser.: 7). (ENG.). 96p. (J). (gr. 1-3). pap. 4.99 *(978-1-338-04288-7(2))* Scholastic, Inc.

—Search for the Lightning Dragon: a Branches Book (Dragon Masters #7) (Library Edition) Jones, Damien, illus. 2017. (Dragon Masters Ser.: 7). (ENG.). 96p. (J). (gr. 1-3). lib. bdg. 24.99 *(978-1-338-04289-4(0))* Scholastic, Inc.

—Secret of the Water Dragon. 2015. (Dragon Masters Ser.: 3). lib. bdg. 14.75 *(978-0-606-39886-2(4))* Turtleback.

—Secret of the Water Dragon: a Branches Book (Dragon Masters #3) Jones, Damien, illus. 2015. (Dragon Masters Ser.: 3). (ENG.). 96p. (J). (gr. 1-3). pap. 5.99 *(978-0-545-64628-4(6))* Scholastic, Inc.

—Shine of the Silver Dragon, 11. 2019. (Branches Early Ch Bks). (ENG.). 90p. (J). (gr. 2-3). 15.36 *(978-0-87617-976-5(6))* Penworthy Co., LLC, The.

—Shine of the Silver Dragon. Polonia, Nina de, illus. 2018. (Dragon Masters Ser.: 11). (ENG.). 96p. (J). (gr. 1-3). 15.99 *(978-1-338-26366-4(8))* Scholastic, Inc.

—Shine of the Silver Dragon: a Branches Book (Dragon Masters #11) de Polonia, Nina, illus. 2018. (Dragon Masters Ser.: 11). (ENG.). 96p. (J). (gr. 1-3). pap. 4.99 *(978-1-338-26365-7(X))* Scholastic, Inc.

—Song of the Poison Dragon. 2016. (Dragon Masters Ser.: 5). lib. bdg. 14.75 *(978-0-606-38808-5(7))* Turtleback.

—Song of the Poison Dragon: a Branches Book (Dragon Masters #5) Jones, Damien, illus. 2016. (Dragon Masters Ser.: 5). (ENG.). 96p. (J). (gr. 1-3). pap. 4.99 *(978-0-545-91387-4(X))* Scholastic, Inc.

—Song of the Poison Dragon: a Branches Book (Dragon Masters #5) (Library Edition) Jones, Damien, illus. 2016. (Dragon Masters Ser.: 5). (ENG.). 96p. (J). (gr. 1-3). 15.99 *(978-0-545-91388-1(8))* Scholastic, Inc.

—Treasure of the Gold Dragon, 12. 2019. (Branches Early Ch Bks). (ENG.). 90p. (J). (gr. 2-3). 15.36 *(978-0-87617-977-2(4))* Penworthy Co., LLC, The.

—Treasure of the Gold Dragon: a Branches Book (Dragon Masters #12) Foresti, Sara, illus. 2018. (Dragon Masters Ser.: 12). (ENG.). 96p. (J). (gr. 1-3). pap. 4.99 *(978-1-338-26368-8(4))* Scholastic, Inc.

—Treasure of the Gold Dragon: a Branches Book (Dragon Masters #12) (Library Edition) Foresti, Sara, illus. 2018. (Dragon Masters Ser.: 12). (ENG.). 96p. (J). (gr. 1-3). lib. bdg. 15.99 *(978-1-338-26369-5(2))* Scholastic, Inc.

—Waking the Rainbow Dragon, 10. 2019. (Branches Early Ch Bks). (ENG.). 89p. (J). (gr. 2-3). 15.36 *(978-0-87617-978-9(2))* Penworthy Co., LLC, The.

—Waking the Rainbow Dragon: a Branches Book (Dragon Masters #10), 1 vol. Jones, Damien, illus. 2018. (Dragon Masters Ser.: 10). (ENG.). 96p. (J). (gr. 1-3). pap. 5.99 *(978-1-338-16989-8(0))* Scholastic, Inc.

—Waking the Rainbow Dragon: a Branches Book (Dragon Masters #10) (Library Edition) Jones, Damien, illus. 2018. (Dragon Masters Ser.: 10). (ENG.). 96p. (J). (gr. 1-3). lib. bdg. 24.99 *(978-1-338-16990-4(4))* Scholastic, Inc.

West, Tracey, adapted by. Phantom Unmasked. 2006. (Illus.). 62p. (J). pap. *(978-0-439-80000-6(5))* Scholastic, Inc.

West, Tracey, et al. Hermes & the Horse with Wings. 2017. (Heroes in Training Ser.: 13). lib. bdg. 16.00 *(978-0-606-39738-4(8))* Turtleback.

Weston Woods Staff, creator. Harold & the Purple Crayon. 2011. 18.95 *(978-0-439-72691-7(3))*; 38.75 *(978-0-439-72693-1(X))*; 29.95 *(978-0-439-73474-5(6))* Weston Woods Studios, Inc.

—James Marshall's Cinderella. 2011. 38.75 *(978-0-439-84886-2(5))* Weston Woods Studios, Inc.

—Possum Magic. 2011. 38.75 *(978-0-545-14784-2(0))*; 18.95 *(978-0-545-08634-9(5))* Weston Woods Studios, Inc.

—Sylvester & the Magic Pebble. 2011. 38.75 *(978-0-439-72898-0(3))*; 29.95 *(978-0-439-73522-3(X))* Weston Woods Studios, Inc.

Wexler, Django. The Fall of the Readers: The Forbidden Library: Volume 4. 2017. (Forbidden Library: 4). 368p. (J). (gr. 5). 17.99 *(978-0-399-53920-6(4)*, Kathy Dawson Books) Penguin Young Readers Group.

—The Forbidden Library. 2015. (Forbidden Library: 1). (ENG., Illus.). 400p. (J). (gr. 5). 8.99 *(978-0-14-242681-4(4),* Puffin Books) Penguin Young Readers Group.
—The Palace of Glass: The Forbidden Library: Volume 3. 2016. (Forbidden Library: 3). (ENG., Illus.). 368p. (J). (gr. 5). 16.99 *(978-0-8037-3978-9(8),* Kathy Dawson Books) Penguin Young Readers Group.
—Ship of Smoke & Steel. 2020. (Wells of Sorcery Trilogy Ser.: 1). (ENG., Illus.). 368p. (YA). pap. 18.99 *(978-0-7653-9725-6(0),* 900181138, Tor Teen) Doherty, Tom Assocs., LLC.
Weyn, Suzanne. Water Song: A Retelling of "the Frog Prince" 2012. (Once upon a Time Ser.). (ENG.). 208p. (YA). (gr. 9). pap. 10.99 *(978-1-4424-6052-2(0),* Simon Pulse) Simon Pulse.
Weyr, Garret. The Language of Spells: (Fantasy Middle Grade Novel, Magic & Wizard Book for Middle School Kids) Harnett, Katie, illus. 2018. (ENG.). 256p. (J). (gr. 5-9). 16.99 *(978-1-4521-5958-4(0))* Chronicle Bks. LLC.
Wheeler, E. B. The Haunting of Springett Hall. 2015. (ENG.). 256p. (YA). (gr. 7-13). pap. 16.99 *(978-1-4621-1672-0(8),* Sweetwater Bks.) Cedar Fort, Inc./CFI Distribution.
Wheeler, Jeff. The Hollow Crown. 2017. (Kingfountain Ser.: 4). (ENG., Illus.). 302p. pap. 14.95 *(978-1-5039-4396-4(8),* 9781503943964, 47North) Amazon Publishing.
Wheeler, Lisa. The Christmas Boot. Pinkney, Jerry, illus. 2016. 32p. (J). (gr. -1-3). 18.99 *(978-0-8037-4134-8(0),* Dial Bks) Penguin Young Readers Group.
Whelan, Olwyn. The Star Child. Maidment, Stella, illus. 2004. 40p. (J). 14.95 *(978-1-84458-039-2(3))* Avalon Publishing.
White, Amanda. Sand Sister. Morales, Yuyi, illus. 2004. (ENG.). 32p. (J). 16.99 *(978-1-84148-617-8(5))* Barefoot Bks., Inc.
White, Dorine. The Emerald Ring (Cleopatra's Legacy) 2013. 183p. (YA). pap. 13.99 *(978-1-4621-1133-6(5),* Horizon Pubs.) Cedar Fort, Inc./CFI Distribution.
White, J. A. The Thickety: Well of Witches. 2016. (Thickety Ser.: 3). (ENG., Illus.). 512p. (J). (gr. 5). 16.99 *(978-0-06-225732-1(3),* Tegen, Katherine Bks) HarperCollins Pubs.
—The Thickety #4: The Last Spell. Offermann, Andrea, illus. 2017. (Thickety Ser.: 4). (ENG.). 512p. (J). (gr. 5). 16.99 *(978-0-06-238139-2(3),* Tegen, Katherine Bks) HarperCollins Pubs.
—The Whispering Trees. Offermann, Andrea, illus. 2015. (Thickety Ser.: 2). (ENG.). 528p. (J). (gr. 5). 16.99 *(978-0-06-225729-1(3),* Tegen, Katherine Bks) HarperCollins Pubs.
White, Paul. Jungle Doctor on the Hop. 2015. (Flamingo Fiction 9-13s Ser.). (ENG., Illus.). 160p. (J). (gr. 4-7). per. 8.99 *(978-1-84550-297-3(3),* d66d650a-5d06-4ed6-9f8e-bb803656ca4a) Christian Focus Pubns. GBR. Dist: Baker & Taylor Publisher Services (BTPS).
White, Wade Albert. The Adventurer's Guide to Dragons (and Why They Keep Biting Me) (Adventurer's Guide Ser.: 2). (ENG.). (J). (gr. 3-7). 2018. 400p. pap. 8.99 *(978-0-316-30532-7(4))* 2017. 384p. 16.99 *(978-0-316-30531-0(6))* Little, Brown Bks. for Young Readers.
—The Adventurer's Guide to Treasure (and How to Steal It) 2019. (Adventurer's Guide Ser.: 3). (ENG., Illus.). 448p. (J). (gr. 3-7). 17.99 *(978-0-316-51844-4(1))* Little, Brown Bks. for Young Readers.
Whitesides, Tyler. Heroes of the Dustbin. 2015. (Janitors Ser.: 5). (ENG., Illus.). 416p. (J). (gr. 5). 18.99 *(978-1-62972-065-4(8),* 5136476, Shadow Mountain) Shadow Mountain Publishing.
—Strike of the Sweepers. 2014. (Janitors Ser.: 4). (ENG., Illus.). 400p. (J). (gr. 5). 18.99 *(978-1-60907-907-9(8),* 5121465, Shadow Mountain) Shadow Mountain Publishing.
—The Wishmakers. Warrick, Jessica, illus. 2018. (Wishmakers Ser.: 1). (ENG.). 352p. (J). (gr. 3-7). pap. 9.99 *(978-0-06-256832-8(9),* HarperCollins) HarperCollins Pubs.
—The Wishmakers. 2018. (Wishmakers Ser.: 1). (ENG., Illus.). 336p. (J). (gr. 3-7). 16.99 *(978-0-06-256831-1(0),* HarperCollins) HarperCollins Pubs.
Whitley, Jeremy. My Little Pony: Legends of Magic, Vol. 2. Fleecs, Tony, illus. 2018. (MLP Legends of Magic Ser.: 2). 144p. (J). (gr. 4-7). pap. 19.99 *(978-1-68405-158-8(4))* Idea & Design Works, LLC.
Whitley, Jeremy & Rice, Christina. My Little Pony: Friends Forever Omnibus, Vol. 2, Vol. 2. Garbowska, Agnes et al, illus. 2017. (MLP FF Omnibus Ser.: 2). 296p. (J). (gr. 4-7). pap. 24.99 *(978-1-63140-882-3(8),* 9781631408823) Idea & Design Works, LLC.
—My Little Pony: Friends Forever Omnibus, Vol. 3, Vol. 3. Fleecs, Tony et al, illus. 2018. (MLP FF Omnibus Ser.: 3). 320p. (J). (gr. 4-7). pap. 24.99 *(978-1-68405-050-5(2))* Idea & Design Works, LLC.
Whittle, J. Robert & Sandilands, Joyce. Leprechaun Magic. Galego, Ane M., illus. 2004. 64p. (J). *(978-0-9685061-2-7(7))* Whitlands Publishing, Ltd.
Whybrow, Ian. The Flying Diggers. Melling, David, illus. 2009. (J). *(978-1-4351-6500-7(4))* Barnes & Noble, Inc.
Whyman, Matt. Street Runners. 2008. (ENG.). 272p. (J). (gr. 4-7). pap. 11.95 *(978-1-84738-282-5(7))* Simon & Schuster, Ltd. GBR. Dist: Simon & Schuster, Inc.
Wicke, Ed. Akayzia Adams & the Masterdragon's Secret. 2003. 280p. (J). per. 9.99 *(978-0-9677652-3-5(4),* BlacknBlue Pr. UK) Blacknblue Pr.
Widow's Broom (25th Anniversary Edition) 25th ed. 2018. (ENG., Illus.). 32p. (J). (gr. -1-3). 18.99 *(978-1-328-47019-5(9),* 1714512, Clarion Bks.) HarperCollins Pubs.
Wiggins, Bethany. The Dragon's Curse (a Transference Novel) 2018. (Transference Trilogy Ser.: 2). 336p. (YA). (gr. 7). 17.99 *(978-0-399-55101-7(8),* Crown Books For Young Readers) Random Hse. Children's Bks.
Wilde, Fran. Riverland. 2019. (ENG., Illus.). 352p. (YA). (gr. 5-9). 17.99 *(978-1-4197-3372-7(9),* 1256101, Amulet Bks.) Abrams, Inc.
Wiley, Melissa. The Prairie Thief. Madrid, Erwin, illus. 2013. (ENG.). 224p. (J). (gr. 3-7). pap. 7.99 *(978-1-4424-4057-9(0),* McElderry, Margaret K. Bks.) McElderry, Margaret K. Bks.
Williams, Alison. Pink Cat Blue Cat. 2009. (Illus.). 32p. pap. 14.49 *(978-1-4389-4623-8(6))* AuthorHouse.
Williams, Mandi Tillotson. The Many Adventures of Mortimer Crump: Mortimer's Sweet Retreat. 2011. 28p. pap. 13.83 *(978-1-4634-2637-8(2))* AuthorHouse.
Williams, Marie Sheppard. The Magic Stories. 2012. pap. 12.95 *(978-0-7414-7280-9(5))* Infinity Publishing.
Williams, T. D. Happy Village. 2010. 24p. 13.99 *(978-1-4269-3492-6(0))* Trafford Publishing.
Williamson, B. A. The Marvelous Adventures of Gwendolyn Gray. 2018. (Chronicles of Gwendolyn Gray Ser.). (ENG., Illus.). 336p. (J). (gr. 3-7). pap. 11.99 *(978-1-63163-172-6(1),* 1631631721, Jolly Fish Pr.) North Star Editions.
—The Marvelous Adventures of Gwendolyn Gray. 2018. lib. bdg. 23.30 *(978-0-606-41248-3(4))* Turtleback.
Williamson, Hilary & Adams, Lynne. The Magic Pumpkin. 2007. (ENG.). 16p. 9.99 *(978-1-4357-0321-6(9))* Lulu Pr., Inc.
Williamson, Liza. Emily to the Rescue. Keddy, Brian, illus. 2011. 28p. pap. 24.95 *(978-1-4626-3342-5(0))* America Star Bks.
Willis, Jeanne. Shamanka. 2009. (J). pap. *(978-0-7636-3767-5(X))* Candlewick Pr.
Wilson, Amy. The Lost Frost Girl. 2017. (ENG.). 320p. (J). (gr. 3-7). 16.99 *(978-0-06-267148-6(0),* Tegen, Katherine Bks) HarperCollins Pubs.
Wilson, David Cramb. The Day that the Fairies stole Badger! 2008. (ENG.). 40p. pap. 9.95 *(978-0-557-00247-4(8))* Lulu Pr., Inc.
Wilson, Karma. Baby Cakes. Williams, Sam, illus. 2006. (ENG.). 32p. (J). (gr. -1 — 1). bds. 8.99 *(978-1-4169-0289-6(9),* Little Simon) Little Simon.
Wilson, Mary & Berrios, Frank. Disney Tales of Magic, 4 vols. 2004. (Illus.). (J). *(978-0-7364-2251-2(X)); (978-0-7364-2252-9(8)); (978-0-7364-2250-5(1)); (978-0-7364-2253-6(6))* Random Hse., Inc.
Wilson, N. D. The Chestnut King (100 Cupboards Book 3) 2011. (100 Cupboards Ser.: 3). (ENG., Illus.). 512p. (J). (gr. 3-7). 9.99 *(978-0-375-83886-6(4),* Yearling) Random Hse. Children's Bks.
—Dandelion Fire (100 Cupboards Book 2) 2009. (100 Cupboards Ser.: 2). (ENG., Illus.). 480p. (J). (gr. 3-7). 9.99 *(978-0-375-83884-2(8),* Yearling) Random Hse. Children's Bks.
—The Dragon's Tooth (Ashtown Burials #1) 2012. (Ashtown Burials Ser.: 1). (ENG.). 496p. (J). (gr. 3-7). 8.99 *(978-0-375-86396-7(6),* Yearling) Random Hse. Children's Bks.
—Outlaws of Time #3: the Last of the Lost Boys. 2018. (Outlaws of Time Ser.: 3). (ENG., Illus.). 256p. (J). (gr. 3-7). 16.99 *(978-0-06-232732-1(1),* Tegen, Katherine Bks) HarperCollins Pubs.
—Outlaws of Time: the Legend of Sam Miracle. 2017. (Outlaws of Time Ser.: 1). (ENG.). 352p. (J). (gr. 3-7). pap. 6.99 *(978-0-06-232727-7(5),* Tegen, Katherine Bks) HarperCollins Pubs.
—100 Cupboards, 1. 2007. (100 Cupboards Ser.: Bk. 1). (ENG., Illus.). 289p. (J). (gr. 4-6). lib. bdg. 22.44 *(978-0-375-93881-8(8))* Random House Publishing Group.
—100 Cupboards (100 Cupboards Book 1) 2008. (100 Cupboards Ser.: 1). (ENG.). 320p. (J). (gr. 3-7). 8.99 *(978-0-375-83882-8(1),* Yearling) Random Hse. Children's Bks.
Windsor, Justine. Goodly & Grave in a Case of Bad Magic (Goodly & Grave, Book 3) 2019. (Goodly & Grave Ser.: 3). (ENG.). 288p. (J). 6.99 *(978-0-00-829427-4(5),* HarperCollins Children's Bks.) HarperCollins Pubs. Ltd. GBR. Dist: HarperCollins Pubs.
Windsor, M. L. Jack Death. 2016. (ENG., Illus.). 163p. (J). (gr. 4-6). 12.99 *(978-1-939547-28-6(8),* 21f8be44-e783-4b5f-86f7-2ee741f8fb21) Creston Bks.
Winkler, Ashley & Winkler, Michael. One Good Quest Deserves Another: A Crown of Amaranth Story. 2009. 292p. 28.95 *(978-0-595-71039-3(5));* pap. 18.95 *(978-0-595-47365-6(2))* iUniverse, Inc.
Winkler, Henry & Oliver, Lin. Fake Snakes & Weird Wizards #4. Garrett, Scott, illus. 2015. (Here's Hank Ser.: 4). (ENG.). 128p. (J). (gr. 1-3). 6.99 *(978-0-448-48252-1(5),* Penguin Workshop) Penguin Young Readers Group.
—Niagara Falls, or Does It? 2004. (Hank Zipzer Ser.: No. 1). 128p. (J). (gr. 2-6). pap. 29.00 incl. audio *(978-1-4000-9006-8(7),* Listening Library) Random Hse. Audio Publishing Group.
Winn, Sheridan. The Sprite Sisters: Magic at Drysdale's School (Vol 7) Winn, Christopher, illus. 2013. 256p. pap. *(978-0-9574231-2-1(8))* Winn, Sheridan.
Winslade, Jayn E. Emily & Jen Dance for Deeron. 2010. 352p. pap. *(978-1-907211-48-5(9))* Grosvenor Hse. Publishing Ltd.
Winstanley, Liz. The Adventures of Abra & His Magic Carpet. 2012. 32p. pap. 14.97 *(978-1-62212-406-0(5),* Strategic Bk. Publishing) Strategic Book Publishing & Rights Agency (SBPRA).
Winterspell. 2014. (ENG., Illus.). 464p. (YA). (gr. 9). 17.99 *(978-1-4424-6598-5(0),* Simon & Schuster Bks. For Young Readers) Simon & Schuster Bks. For Young Readers.
Wittner, Shirley. Kemira & the Ancient Book of Spells. 2006. 51p. pap. 16.95 *(978-1-4241-4840-0(5))* PublishAmerica, Inc.
Wizards of Waverly Place Insider's Guide. 2009. 128p. pap. 8.99 *(978-1-4231-2473-3(1))* Disney Pr.
Wolverton, Barry. The Vanishing Island. Stevenson, Dave, illus. (Chronicles of the Black Tulip Ser.: 1). (ENG.). (J). (gr. 3-7). 2016. 368p. pap. 6.99 *(978-0-06-222191-9(4))* 2015. 352p. 16.99 *(978-0-06-222190-2(6))* HarperCollins Pubs. (Waldon Pond Pr.).
—The Vanishing Island. Stevenson, Dave, illus. 2016. (Chronicles of the Black Tulip Ser.: Vol. 1). (ENG.). 368p. (J). (gr. 3-7). 17.20 *(978-0-606-39260-0(2))* Turtleback.
Wong, Carmen L. F. Written By... 2013. 252p. (gr. 4-6). 33.25 *(978-1-4669-3179-4(5));* pap. 18.85 *(978-1-4669-3178-7(7))* Trafford Publishing.
Wood, Audrey. Magic Shoelaces. 2005. (Child's Play Library). (Illus.). 32p. (J). (gr. 1-2). pap. *(978-1-904550-51-8(7))* Child's Play International Ltd.
—Presto Change-O. 2005. (Child's Play Library). (Illus.). 32p. (J). pap. *(978-1-904550-52-5(5))* Child's Play International Ltd.
Worthington, Jennifer & Shoals, Melinda, illus. The Gift That Saved Christmas. 2008. 40p. (J). 17.00 *(978-0-9773460-1-(3))* Spritelee Enterprises.
Worthington, Lisa & Moon, Susan. My Magic Bike. Harston, Jerry, illus. 2006. (ENG.). 16p. (gr. k-2). pap. 7.95 *(978-1-57874-039-0(8),* Kaeden Bks.) Kaeden Corp.
Worthington, Michelle. Noah Chases the Wind. Cowman, Joseph, illus. 2015. (ENG.). 32p. (J). (gr. -1-3). 19.95 *(978-1-60554-356-7(X))* Redleaf Pr.
Wrede, Patricia C. Book of Enchantments. 2005. (ENG., Illus.). 256p. (J). (gr. 5-7). pap. 14.95 *(978-0-15-205508-0(8),* 1196568, Clarion Bks.) HarperCollins Pubs.
—Calling on Dragons. unabr. ed. 2004. (Enchanted Forest Chronicles: Bk. 3). 244p. (J). (gr. 6-18). pap. 38.00 incl. audio *(978-0-8072-0792-5(6),* LYA 347 SP, Listening Library) Random Hse. Audio Publishing Group.
—Talking to Dragons. unabr. ed. 2004. (Enchanted Forest Chronicles: Bk. 4). 255p. (J). (gr. 6-18). pap. 38.00 incl. audio *(978-0-8072-0983-7(X),* S YA 385 SP, Listening Library) Random Hse. Audio Publishing Group.
Wrede, Patricia C. & Stevermer, Caroline. Sorcery & Cecelia or the Enchanted Chocolate Pot: Being the Correspondence of Two Young Ladies of Quality Regarding Various Magical Scandals in London & the Country. 2004. (ENG., Illus.). 336p. (YA). (gr. 7-12). pap. 7.99 *(978-0-15-205300-0(X),* 1195969, Clarion Bks.) HarperCollins Pubs.
Wurge, B. B. Squiggle. 2009. (LeapKids Ser.). (ENG., Illus.). 152p. (J). (gr. 2-7). pap. 9.95 *(978-0-9815148-9-5(8))* Leapfrog Pr.
Wyatt, Trina. Magical Mrs Mable Comes to Green Hills. 2008. 28p. pap. 12.50 *(978-1-4389-1015-4(0))* AuthorHouse.
Wyche, Wofford, Jane. Adventures at Hi-Lonesome Ranch: The Magic Cabin, Book Two. 2014. 194p. pap. 17.95 *(978-1-4908-1824-5(3),* WestBow Pr.) Author Solutions, LLC.
Wynne, Rhys. The Magic Pencil, 1 vol. 2009. 13p. pap. 24.95 *(978-1-60749-089-0(7))* America Star Bks.
Xavier V, Sajjad. Baboonia. 2010. 191p. pap. 14.99 *(978-0-557-04174-9(0))* Lulu Pr., Inc.
Yager, Karen & Williams, Kiersten. Krickle Forest Adventures, Wizbet's Notebook. Walsh, Jennifer, illus. 2012. 60p. pap. 7.95 *(978-0-9855997-0-6(7))* Krickle Forest Adventures.
Yannuzzi, Frank M. The Magic Lacrosse Stick. 2011. 44p. pap. 21.99 *(978-1-4653-3930-0(2))* Xlibris Corp.
Yee, Wong Herbert. Abracadabra! Magic with Mouse & Mole (Reader) 2010. (Mouse & Mole Story Ser.). (ENG., Illus.). 48p. (J). (gr. -1-3). pap. 4.99 *(978-0-547-40621-3(5),* 1428499, Clarion Bks.) HarperCollins Pubs.
Yep, Laurence. The Magic Paintbrush. Wang, Suling, illus. 2003. (ENG.). 96p. (J). (gr. 3-7). pap. 6.99 *(978-0-06-440852-3(3),* HarperCollins) HarperCollins Pubs.
—The Magic Paintbrush. Wang, Suling, illus. 2003. 89p. (J). (gr. 3-7). 12.65 *(978-0-7569-1444-8(2))* Perfection Learning Corp.
—The Tiger's Apprentice. 2005. (Tiger's Apprentice Ser.: Bk. 1). 184p. (J). lib. bdg. 24.62 *(978-1-4242-0449-6(6))* Fitzgerald Bks.
—The Tiger's Apprentice. 2005. (Tiger's Apprentice (Tandem Library) Ser.). 184p. (gr. 5-9). 17.00 *(978-0-7569-5074-3(0))* Perfection Learning Corp.
—Tiger's Blood. 2005. (Tiger's Apprentice Ser.: Bk. 2). (ENG.). 240p. (J). (gr. 5-18). 15.99 *(978-0-06-001016-4(9))* HarperCollins Pubs.
Yin, Aidi. Emily & Her Dolls. 2011. 28p. pap. 15.99 *(978-1-4628-5254-3(8))* Xlibris Corp.
Yolen, Jane. Snow in Summer. 2013. (ENG.). 272p. (J). (gr. 5). pap. 7.99 *(978-0-14-242197-0(9),* Puffin Books) Penguin Young Readers Group.
—Wizard's Hall. 144p. (J). (gr. 3-5). pap. 6.00 *(978-0-8072-1544-9(9),* Listening Library) Random Hse. Audio Publishing Group.
Yoo, Tae-Eun. The Little Red Fish. 2007. (Illus.). (J). *(978-1-4287-3601-6(8),* Dial) Penguin Publishing Group.
Young, Cleous. The Magical Rug. 2004. 25p. pap. 24.95 *(978-1-4137-3555-0(X))* PublishAmerica, Inc.
Young, Helen Ann. Hellie & the Sensational Magic Carpet. Young, Tim, illus. 2013. 106p. pap. *(978-1-908353-02-3(3))* Young Editions.
Young, Julie. Dragon Stone: Dragon Cliff Trilogy Book Two. 2011. 160p. (gr. 4-6). pap. 12.95 *(978-1-4620-0682-3(5))* iUniverse, Inc.
Yourish, Meryl. Darkness Rising: Book One of the Catmage Chronicles. 2012. (ENG.). 258p. (J). pap. 13.99 *(978-0-9881804-0-6(5))* MAY Publishing.
Yü, Li, et al. The Holy Spark: Rogel & the Goddess of Liberty. 2006. (Illus.). 259p. (J). *(978-1-931907-42-2(0))* Homa & Sekey Bks.
Yu, Mimi. The Girl King. (Girl King Ser.). (ENG.). 496p. (YA). 2020. pap. 10.99 *(978-1-5476-0308-4(9),* 900211273) 2019. 17.99 *(978-1-68119-889-7(4),* 900191621) Bloomsbury Publishing USA. (Bloomsbury Young Adult).
Yun, Monokuro. The Sign: A Novel. 2019. 188p. (gr. 7-12). pap. 14.95 *(978-1-64279-116-7(4))* Morgan James Publishing.
Yurksaitis, Anne. The Ingle Bingle. Yurksaitis, Stephanie, illus. 2012. 16p. pap. 24.95 *(978-1-4626-7687-3(1))* America Star Bks.
Zafon, Carlos Ruiz. The Prince of Mist. 2011. (ENG.). 256p. (YA). (gr. 7-17). pap., pap. 14.99 *(978-0-316-04480-6(6))* Little, Brown Bks. for Young Readers.
Zagarenski, Pamela. The Whisper. 2015. (ENG., Illus.). 40p. (J). (gr. -1-3). 17.99 *(978-0-544-41686-4(4),* 1594761, Clarion Bks.) HarperCollins Pubs.
Zahler, Diane. The Marvelwood Magicians. 2017. (ENG.). 192p. (J). (gr. 3-7). 16.95 *(978-1-62979-724-3(3),* Astra Young Readers) Astra Publishing Hse.
—Sleeping Beauty's Daughters. 2013. 216p. (J). lib. bdg. *(978-0-06-200497-0(2))* Harper & Row Ltd.
—The Thirteenth Princess. 2011. (ENG.). 272p. (J). (gr. 3-7). pap. 6.99 *(978-0-06-182500-2(X),* HarperCollins) HarperCollins Pubs.
Zales, S. R. Jenny & the Hummingbird Faeries. 2012. 152p. pap. 14.95 *(978-1-4575-1330-5(7))* Dog Ear Publishing, LLC.
Zellers, Michelle. Maya's Magic Carpet. 2006. (J). per. 11.95 *(978-1-889743-48-6(8))* Robbie Dean Pr.
Zhao, Xiran Jay. Zachary Ying & the Dragon Emperor. 2022. (Zachary Ying Ser.). (ENG., Illus.). 352p. (J). (gr. 3-7). 17.99 *(978-1-6659-0070-6(9));* E-Book *(978-1-6659-0072-0(5))* McElderry, Margaret K. Bks. (McElderry, Margaret K. Bks.).
Zink, Michelle. Circle of Fire. 2012. (Prophecy of the Sisters Ser.: 3). (ENG.). 368p. (YA). (gr. 7-17). pap. 19.99 *(978-0-316-03446-3(0))* Little, Brown Bks. for Young Readers.
—Guardian of the Gate. 2011. (Prophecy of the Sisters Ser.: 2). (ENG.). 368p. (YA). (gr. 7-17). pap. 18.99 *(978-0-316-02740-3(5))* Little, Brown Bks. for Young Readers.
123 Sesame Street, ed. Abby in Wonderland. 2009. (ENG.). 20p. 16.99 *(978-1-59069-834-1(7))* Studio Mouse LLC.

MAGIC—HISTORY

Bentley, Sue. Sunshine Shimmers #12. Swan, Angela, illus. 2014. (Magic Puppy Ser.: 12). (ENG.). 128p. (J). (gr. 1-3). 5.99 *(978-0-448-46791-7(7),* Grosset & Dunlap) Penguin Young Readers Group.
Bosch, Pseudonymous. This Book Is Not Good for You. 2010. (Secret Ser.: 3). (ENG.). 416p. (J). (gr. 3-7). pap. 8.99 *(978-0-316-04085-3(1))* Little, Brown Bks. for Young Readers.
Dowswell, Paul. The Amazing History of Wizards & Witches: Discover a World of Magic & Mystery, with over 340 Exciting Pictures. 2016. (Illus.). 64p. (J). (gr. -1-12). 12.99 *(978-1-86147-731-6(7))* Anness Publishing, Inc.

MAGIC TRICKS

Here are entered works on performance of sleight of hand or tricks involving various types of illusion for purposes of entertainment. Works on the use of charms, spells, etc., believed to have supernatural power to produce or prevent a result considered unobtainable by natural means are entered under Magic.

Amazing Magic. 2004. (Fun Kits Ser.). (Illus.). 48p. (J). *(978-1-84229-859-6(3))* Top That! Publishing PLC.
Amazing Magic Tricks [Dollar General]: Apprentice Level. 2010. (Magic Tricks Ser.). 56p. pap. 0.75 *(978-1-4296-4633-8(0),* Capstone Pr.) Capstone.
Amery, Heather, et al. The Usborne Book of KnowHow. King, Colin, illus. 2008. (Usborne Book Of... Ser.). 127p. (J). (gr. 4-7). 19.99 *(978-0-7945-2040-3(5),* Usborne) EDC Publishing.
Anderson, James. The Science of Magic (Grade 6) 2nd rev. ed. 2016. (TIME(r): Informational Text Ser.). (ENG., Illus.). 64p. (gr. 5-8). pap. 13.99 *(978-1-4938-3606-2(4))* Teacher Created Materials, Inc.
Andrews, Ted. Faerie Charms. 2005. (Young Person's School of Magic & Mystery Ser.: Vol. 6). (Illus.). 255p. (YA). (gr. 8-12). 18.95 *(978-1-888767-42-1(1))* Dragonhawk Publishing.
Balloon Oriented Magic. 2004. (Illus.). 139p. (YA). spiral bd. 16.95 *(978-1-931084-01-7(7))* Balloon Magic.
Barnhart, Norm. Abracadabra! Tricks for Rookie Magicians: 4D a Magical Augmented Reading Experience. 2018. (Amazing Magic Tricks 4D! Ser.). (ENG., Illus.). 32p. (J). (gr. 2-6). lib. bdg. 33.99 *(978-1-5435-0568-9(6),* 137372, Capstone Classroom) Capstone.
—Alakazam! Tricks for Veteran Magicians: 4D a Magical Augmented Reading Experience. 2018. (Amazing Magic Tricks 4D! Ser.). (ENG., Illus.). 32p. (J). (gr. 2-6). lib. bdg. 33.99 *(978-1-5435-0571-9(6),* 137375, Capstone Classroom) Capstone.
—Amazing Magic Tricks! 2019. (ENG., Illus.). 112p. (J). (gr. 2-6). pap., pap., pap. 12.95 *(978-1-5435-0604-4(6),* 137389, Capstone Classroom) Capstone.
—Amazing Magic Tricks 4D!, 4 vols. 2018. (Amazing Magic Tricks 4D! Ser.). (ENG.). 32p. (J). (gr. 2-6). 135.96 *(978-1-5435-0572-6(4),* 27681, Capstone Classroom) Capstone.
—Amazing Magic Tricks [Home Design Alternatives]: Beginner Level. 2009. (Magic Tricks Ser.). 32p. (gr. 3-4). pap. 3.00 *(978-1-4296-3731-2(5),* Capstone Pr.) Capstone.
—Hocus Pocus! Tricks for Amateur Magicians: 4D a Magical Augmented Reading Experience. 2018. (Amazing Magic Tricks 4D! Ser.). (ENG., Illus.). 32p. (J). (gr. 2-6). lib. bdg. 33.99 *(978-1-5435-0569-6(4),* 137373, Capstone Classroom) Capstone.
—Presto Chango! Tricks for Skilled Magicians: 4D a Magical Augmented Reading Experience. 2018. (Amazing Magic Tricks 4D! Ser.). (ENG., Illus.). 32p. (J). (gr. 2-6). lib. bdg. 33.99 *(978-1-5435-0570-2(8),* 137374, Capstone Classroom) Capstone.
Barnhart, Norm & Charney, Steve. My First Guide to Magic Tricks. 2015. (My First Guides). (ENG., Illus.). 24p. (J). (gr. 1-3). lib. bdg. 27.99 *(978-1-4914-2048-5(0),* 127525, Capstone Pr.) Capstone.
Blackstone, Bellamie. Everyday Magic. *(978-1-59093-002-1(9),* Eager Minds Pr.) Warehousing & Fulfillment Specialists, LLC (WFS, LLC).
Book of Magic Tricks Kid Kit. 2004. 64p. (J). 15.99 *(978-1-58086-454-1(6))* EDC Publishing.
Bree, Loris. Kids' Magic Secrets: Simple Magic Tricks & Why They Work. Bree, Marlin, illus. 2003. (ENG.). 112p. (J). (gr. 2-6). pap. 10.99 *(978-1-892147-08-0(4))* Marlor Pr., Inc.
Capstone Press. Easy Magic Tricks, 1 vol. 2010. (Easy Magic Tricks Ser.). (ENG.). 32p. lib. bdg. 95.96 *(978-1-4296-5933-8(5),* Capstone Pr.) Capstone.
Carlson, Laurie. Harry Houdini for Kids: His Life & Adventures with 21 Magic Tricks & Illusions. 2009. (For Kids Ser.: 29). (ENG., Illus.). 144p. (J). (gr. 4-7). pap. 18.95 *(978-1-55652-782-1(9))* Chicago Review Pr., Inc.
Charney, Steve. Hocus-Jokus: 50 Funny Magic Tricks Complete with Jokes. 2003. (Illus.). ix, 132p. (J). *(978-0-88166-376-1(X))* Meadowbrook Pr.
Denne, B. Amazing Magic Tricks. 2004. (Illus.). 32p. (J). pap., act. bk. ed. 6.95 *(978-0-7945-0601-8(1))* EDC Publishing.
Denne, Ben. Amazing Magic Tricks Kid Kit. 2004. (Kid Kits Ser.). 32p. (J). 12.99 *(978-1-58086-729-0(4));* 12.99 *(978-1-58086-736-8(7))* EDC Publishing. (Usborne).
—Magic Tricks to Make & Do. 2009. (Activity Bks). 32p. (J). pap. 6.99 *(978-0-7945-2164-6(9),* Usborne) EDC Publishing.
Dunn, Anthony, illus. Completely Magi-CaLL: The TRUE Secrets of Magic: A Study of the Magician's Art. Gunther, Chat, photos by. 2009. 346p. (YA). pap. 29.95 *(978-0-9729546-8-6(6))* SMC Pubns., LLC.

M
N
O

Einhorn, Nicholas. Abracadabra! Cool Magic Tricks with Cards, 1 vol. 2012. (Inside Magic Ser.). (ENG., Illus.). 64p. (YA). (gr. 6-6). lib. bdg. 37.13 (978-1-4488-9219-8(8), 6c6b45ee-a038-438a-96f7-6b128c7cda22, Rosen Reference) Rosen Publishing Group, Inc., The.

—Alakazam! Sensational Magic Tricks with Silk, Thimbles, Paper, & Money, 1 vol. 2012. (Inside Magic Ser.). (ENG., Illus.). 64p. (YA). (gr. 6-6). 37.13 (978-1-4488-9221-1(X), ac1d220a-e785-416e-a5b9-bade43429c25, Rosen Reference) Rosen Publishing Group, Inc., The.

—Close-Up Magic, 1 vol. 2010. (Inside Magic Ser.). (ENG.). 64p. (YA). (gr. 6-6). lib. bdg. 37.13 (978-1-4358-9453-2(7), 089938a5-ef49-46d8-9bdd-d9243517f806, Rosen Reference) Rosen Publishing Group, Inc., The.

—Presto Change-O! Jaw-Dropping Magic with Dinner Table Objects, 1 vol. 2012. (Inside Magic Ser.). (ENG., Illus.). 64p. (J). (gr. 6-6). 37.13 (978-1-4488-9220-4(1), 7fda300d-804a-4b5b-8801-72423fb1a948, Rosen Reference) Rosen Publishing Group, Inc., The.

—Stand-up Magic & Optical Illusions, 1 vol. 2010. (Inside Magic Ser.). (ENG., Illus.). 64p. (YA). (gr. 6-6). 37.13 (978-1-4358-9452-5(9), 72d76f25-304f-4c37-822f-6795a1e7e82c, Rosen Reference) Rosen Publishing Group, Inc., The.

—Stunts, Puzzles, & Stage Illusions, 1 vol. 2010. (Inside Magic Ser.). (ENG.). 64p. (YA). (gr. 6-6). lib. bdg. 37.13 (978-1-4358-9454-9(5), 9354db2d-b255-405a-a857-cbce294d1983, Rosen Reference) Rosen Publishing Group, Inc., The.

Flom, Justin. Everyday Magic for Kids: 30 Amazing Magic Tricks That You Can Do Anywhere. 2018. (ENG., Illus.). 128p. (J). (gr. 3-7). pap. 12.99 (978-0-7624-9260-2(0), Running Pr. Kids) Running Pr.

Frederick, Guy. 101 Best Magic Tricks. Anderson, Doug, illus. 2012. 130p. 40.95 (978-1-258-23095-1(X)); pap. 25.95 (978-1-258-23889-6(6)) Literary Licensing, LLC.

Fullman, Joe. Mind Tricks. 2009. (Magic Handbook Ser.). (ENG., Illus.). 32p. (J). (gr. 3-12). pap. 6.95 (978-1-55407-571-3(8), 36b851b7-4af2-4efe-8370-a31d1caa813e) Firefly Bks., Ltd.

—Sleight of Hand. 2009. (Magic Handbook Ser.). (ENG., Illus.). 32p. (J). (gr. 3-12). pap. 6.95 (978-1-55407-572-0(6), 2b94c145-f23c-4162-9c30-a81990212f5e) Firefly Bks., Ltd.

Gardner, Robert. The Science Behind Magic Science Projects, 1 vol. 2013. (Exploring Hands-On Science Projects Ser.). (ENG.). 128p. (gr. 5-6). 30.60 (978-0-7660-4147-9(6), 61d4e8fc-867f-4e58-8fba-ee01fad5a7f2); pap. 13.88 (978-1-4644-0223-4(X), d309281d-6071-4681-ad53-44a2b82d6486) Enslow Publishing, LLC.

Harbo, Christopher L. Easy Magician Origami, 1 vol. 2011. (Easy Origami Ser.). (ENG.). 24p. (J). (gr. 1-3). lib. bdg. 25.99 (978-1-4296-6000-6(7), 114937, Capstone Pr.) Capstone.

Heos, Bridget. Do You Really Want to Visit Neptune? Fabbri, Daniele, illus. 2013. (Do You Really Want to Visit the Solar System? Ser.). (ENG.). 24p. (J). (gr. 1-4). 27.10 (978-1-60753-201-9(8), 16269) Amicus.

—Do You Really Want to Visit Uranus? Fabbri, Daniele, illus. 2013. (Do You Really Want to Visit the Solar System? Ser.). (ENG.). 24p. (J). (gr. 1-4). 27.10 (978-1-60753-202-6(6), 16270) Amicus.

Higginson, Sheila Sweeny. Pulling Back the Curtain on Magic! Ready-To-Read Level 3. McClurkan, Rob, illus. 2015. (Science of Fun Stuff Ser.). (ENG.). 48p. (J). (gr. 1-3). 16.99 (978-1-4814-3702-8(X), Simon Spotlight) Simon Spotlight.

Insight Editions. Harry Potter: Magical Film Projections: Patronus Charm. 2017. (Harry Potter Ser.). (ENG., Illus.). 16p. (J). (gr. 2-5). 16.99 (978-0-7636-9586-6(6)) Candlewick Pr.

Jacklin, Karl. It's Magic. (Illus.). (J). (gr. 3-6). pap. (978-1-876367-03-9(2)) Wizard Bks.

Jay, Joshua. Big Magic for Little Hands: 25 Astounding Illusions for Young Magicians. 2014. (ENG., Illus.). 112p. (J). (gr. 2-6). 21.95 (978-0-7611-8009-8(5), 18009) Workman Publishing Co., Inc.

Kelly, Kristen & Kelly, Ken. Abracadabra! Fun Magic Tricks for Kids - 30 Tricks to Make & Perform (includes Video Links) 2016. (Illus.). 96p. (J). (gr. 1-1). 14.99 (978-1-5107-0296-7(2), Sky Pony Pr.) Skyhorse Publishing Co., Inc.

Khee, Seah Wee, et al. Chemagic. 2008. (ENG.). 148p. pap. (978-981-283-707-3(8)) World Scientific Publishing Co. Pte Ltd.

Kilby, Janice Eaton & Taylor, Terry. The Book of Wizard Magic: In Which the Apprentice Finds Marvelous Magic Tricks, Mystifying Illusions & Astonishing Tales. Burnett, Lindy, illus. 2019. (Books of Wizard Craft Ser.: 3). 144p. (J). (gr. 3-7). lthr. 19.95 (978-1-4549-3548-3(0)) Sterling Publishing Co., Inc.

King, Mac. Mac King's Campfire Magic: 50 Amazing, Easy-To-Learn Tricks & Mind-Blowing Stunts Using Cards, String, Pencils, & Other Stuff from Your Knapsack. King, Bill, illus. 2010. (ENG.). 176p. (J). (gr. -1-17). pap. 13.99 (978-1-57912-829-6(7), 81829, Black Dog & Leventhal Pubs. Inc.) Hachette Bks.

Kole, Andre. Tricks & Twists. 2004. 168p. pap. (978-0-9727279-7-6(3)) Pine Hill Graphics.

Kovacs, Vic. Get into Magic. 2017. (Get-Into-It Guides). (ENG., Illus.). 32p. (J). (gr. 3-4). (978-0-7787-3401-7(3)); pap. (978-0-7787-3405-5(6)) Crabtree Publishing Co.

Lane, Mike. Close-Up Magic, 1 vol. Mostyn, David, illus. 2012. (Miraculous Magic Tricks Ser.). (ENG.). 32p. (J). (gr. 3-3). pap. 12.75 (978-1-4488-6737-0(1), 2af1466a-b822-4871-825e-79f87966e883); lib. bdg. 31.27 (978-1-61533-515-2(3), 7d353c6d-e7f3-4ec3-baaa-3f1a0436bc21) Rosen Publishing Group, Inc., The. (Windmill Bks.).

—Mind Magic, 1 vol. Mostyn, David, illus. 2012. (Miraculous Magic Tricks Ser.). (ENG.). 32p. (J). (gr. 3-3). pap. 12.75 (978-1-4488-6735-6(5), 51fc2dda-48d5-4ad0-9a6a-540289d07415); lib. bdg. 31.27 (978-1-61533-514-5(5), 1fb99e60-c039-4e8b-b558-f3207f9d9f83) Rosen Publishing Group, Inc., The. (Windmill Bks.).

Loh-Hagan, Virginia. Magic Show. 2016. (D. I. Y. Make It Happen Ser.). (ENG., Illus.). 32p. (J). (gr. 4-8). 32.07 (978-1-63470-493-9(2), 207703) Cherry Lake Publishing.

Magic Card Tricks. 2004. (Whizz Kits Ser.). (Illus.). 48p. (J). (978-1-84229-943-2(3)) Top That! Publishing PLC.

Martineau, Susan. Marvelous Magic, 1 vol. Ursell, Martin, illus. 2011. (Awesome Activities Ser.). (ENG.). 24p. (J). (gr. 4-4). lib. bdg. 29.93 (978-1-61533-368-4(1), e4b5523d-3a19-4422-973e-5a0712815d24, Windmill Bks.) Rosen Publishing Group, Inc., The.

Mason, Tom. Magic of the Masters: Learn Tricks by David Copperfield, Harry Houdini & More! 2007. (Illus.). 48p. (J). (978-0-439-90716-3(0)) Scholastic, Inc.

Mason, Tom & Danko, Dan. Food Magic: How to Do Amazing Tricks with Ordinary Food! 2007. (Illus.). 48p. (J). (978-0-439-90715-6(2)) Scholastic, Inc.

—Where Did It Go? Magic: How to Make Things Change Places! 2007. (Illus.). 48p. (J). (978-0-439-90713-2(6)) Scholastic, Inc.

Mason, Tom, et al. Disappearing Magic: How to Make Things Vanish into Thin Air! 2007. (Illus.). 48p. (J). pap. (978-0-439-90711-8(X)) Scholastic, Inc.

—Shape-Shifting Magic: How to Turn One Thing into Another. 2006. (Illus.). 48p. (J). (978-0-439-90708-8(X)) Scholastic, Inc.

Mayne, Andrew. Handbook of Super Powers: Magic Tricks that Make It Look Like You Possess Super-human Abilities. 2004. (Illus.). 96p. (YA). per. 11.95 (978-0-9715183-6-0(X)) Maynestream Pr.

Mostyn, David, illus. Amazing Magic Tricks. 2014. (ENG.). 128p. (J). (gr. 2). 9.99 (978-0-486-78034-4(1), 780341) Dover Pubns., Inc.

Nightingale, Hugh. Show Me How: I Can Make Magic: Easy Conjuring Tricks for Kids, Shown Step by Step. 2016. (Illus.). 48p. (J). (gr. -1-12). 7.99 (978-1-86147-482-7(2), Armadillo) Anness Publishing GBR. Dist: National Bk. Network.

Olson, Elsie. Magic Disappearing Acts. 2019. (Lightning Bolt Books (r) — Magic Tricks Ser.). (ENG., Illus.). 24p. (J). (gr. 1-3). pap. 9.99 (978-1-5415-4579-3(6), 0d04c662-2df5-42f7-a418-572ff891bdf3); lib. bdg. 29.32 (978-1-5415-3897-9(8), a9d6e800-dec2-4068-a8cb-ea765945e3f3, Lerner Pubns.) Lerner Publishing Group.

—Magic Tricks with Cards. 2019. (Lightning Bolt Books (r) — Magic Tricks Ser.). (ENG., Illus.). 24p. (J). (gr. 1-3). pap. 9.99 (978-1-5415-4580-9(X), 3119964f-30cb-4441-8f01-8279ebba40cd); lib. bdg. 29.32 (978-1-5415-3894-8(3), b626b322-2744-4b3a-aad1-dda995e3f93d, Lerner Pubns.) Lerner Publishing Group.

—Magic Tricks with Optical Illusions. 2019. (Lightning Bolt Books (r) — Magic Tricks Ser.). (ENG., Illus.). 24p. (J). (gr. 1-3). 29.32 (978-1-5415-3896-2(X), 86686e6c-6ceb-4c9d-8cca-e332a715d694, Lerner Pubns.); pap. 9.99 (978-1-5415-4581-6(8), 381d3a1b-ef93-40f0-8c72-6bf3e71a45ed) Lerner Publishing Group.

—Magic Tricks with Props. 2019. (Lightning Bolt Books (r) — Magic Tricks Ser.). (ENG., Illus.). 24p. (J). (gr. 1-3). 29.32 (978-1-5415-3895-5(1), 14893d78-e6f2-46e6-89ca-dd0eb8ffe9a3, Lerner Pubns.); pap. 9.99 (978-1-5415-4582-3(6), c21f82c2-8c6f-44fc-b2c0-ec5b3013d3f9) Lerner Publishing Group.

Osborne, Mary Pope & Boyce, Natalie Pope. Magic Tricks from the Tree House: A Fun Companion to Magic Tree House 50: Hurry up, Houdini! 2013. (Magic Tree House Fact Tracker Ser.: 50). lib. bdg. 14.75 (978-0-606-32476-2(3)) Turtleback.

—Magic Tricks from the Tree House: A Fun Companion to Magic Tree House Merlin Mission #22: Hurry up, Houdini! Murdocca, Sal & Vilela, Luiz, illus. 2013. (Magic Tree House (R) Ser.). 128p. (J). (gr. 2-5). 5.99 (978-0-449-81790-2(3), Random Hse. Bks. for Young Readers) Random Hse. Children's Bks.

Owen, Ruth. Kids Do Magic!, 1 vol. 2016. (Creative Kids Ser.). (ENG.). 32p. (gr. 3-3). pap. 12.75 (978-1-4994-8113-6(6), f8398427-48c2-471d-a3f2-2f513c0a7341, Windmill Bks.) Rosen Publishing Group, Inc., The.

Regan, Lisa. Magician, 1 vol. 2012. (Stage School Ser.). (ENG., Illus.). 32p. (J). (gr. 2-3). pap. 11.00 (978-1-4488-8153-6(6), 7b1932cb-6195-46df-b70f-99ef2d4637d7); lib. bdg. 29.93 (978-1-4488-8094-2(7), 51811e2d-196a-401f-9215-f599768d03f0) Rosen Publishing Group, Inc., The. (Windmill Bks.).

Stadler, Charlotte. Coin Magic. 2011. (Early Connections Ser.). (J). (978-1-61672-611-9(3)) Benchmark Education Co.

Tilden, Thomasine E. Lewis. Mind Games! Can a Psychic Tell What You're Thinking? 2011. (J). pap. (978-0-545-32943-9(4)) Scholastic, Inc.

Top That Publishing Editors, ed. Magical Mischief. Dahl, Roald, illus. 2005. 24p. (J). pap. (978-1-905359-51-6(9)) Top That! Publishing PLC.

Tremaine, Jon. Magic with Numbers. 2012. (ENG., Illus.). 32p. (gr. 3-5). pap. 8.95 (978-1-926853-82-6(2)) Saunders Bk. Co. CAN. Dist: RiverStream Publishing.

—Magical Illusions. 2012. (ENG., Illus.). 32p. (gr. 3-5). pap. 8.95 (978-1-926853-83-3(0)) Saunders Bk. Co. CAN. Dist: RiverStream Publishing.

—Paper Tricks. 2012. (ENG., Illus.). 32p. (gr. 3-5). pap. 8.95 (978-1-926853-84-0(9)) Saunders Bk. Co. CAN. Dist: RiverStream Publishing.

—Pocket Tricks. 2012. (ENG., Illus.). 32p. (gr. 3-5). pap. 8.95 (978-1-926853-85-7(7)) Saunders Bk. Co. CAN. Dist: RiverStream Publishing.

Turnbull, Stephanie. Close-Up Tricks. 2011. (ENG., Illus.). 32p. (J). pap. 10.95 (978-1-77092-042-2(0)) Saunders Bk. Co. CAN. Dist: RiverStream Publishing.

—Do You Really Want to Visit Neptune? 2011. (Secrets of Magic Ser.). 32p. (gr. 4-7). lib. bdg. 31.35 (978-1-59920-499-4(1)) Black Rabbit Bks.

—Do You Really Want to Visit Uranus? 2011. (Secrets of Magic Ser.). 32p. (gr. 4-7). lib. bdg. 31.35 (978-1-59920-498-7(3)) Black Rabbit Bks.

—Easy Dinner Table Tricks. 2014. (Beginner Magic Ser.). (ENG., Illus.). 24p. (J). (gr. 2-5). pap. 8.95 (978-1-77092-156-6(7)) Saunders Bk. Co. CAN. Dist: RiverStream Publishing.

—Easy Mind & Body Tricks. 2014. (Beginner Magic Ser.). (ENG., Illus.). 24p. (J). (gr. 2-5). pap. 8.95 (978-1-77092-157-3(5)) Saunders Bk. Co. CAN. Dist: RiverStream Publishing.

—Easy Pen & Paper Tricks. 2014. (Beginner Magic Ser.). (ENG., Illus.). 24p. (J). (gr. 2-5). pap. 8.95 (978-1-77092-158-0(3)) Saunders Bk. Co. CAN. Dist: RiverStream Publishing.

—Incredible Illusions. 2011. (ENG., Illus.). 32p. (J). pap. 10.95 (978-1-77092-043-9(9)) Saunders Bk. Co. CAN. Dist: RiverStream Publishing.

—Magic Skills. 2012. (Super Skills Ser.). (ENG., Illus.). 32p. (J). (gr. 2-5). lib. bdg. 31.35 (978-1-59920-801-5(6), 17415, Smart Apple Media) Black Rabbit Bks.

—A Magician. 2016. (How to Be ... Ser.). (ENG.). 24p. (J). (gr. 2-5). 28.50 (978-1-62588-369-8(2), 17300) Black Rabbit Bks.

—Mind-Reading Tricks. 2011. (ENG., Illus.). 32p. (J). pap. 10.95 (978-1-77092-044-6(7)) Saunders Bk. Co. CAN. Dist: RiverStream Publishing.

—Prop Tricks. 2011. (ENG., Illus.). 32p. (J). pap. 10.95 (978-1-77092-045-3(5)) Saunders Bk. Co. CAN. Dist: RiverStream Publishing.

—Transformation & Vanishing Tricks. 2011. (Secrets of Magic Ser.). 32p. (gr. 4-7). lib. bdg. 31.35 (978-1-59920-500-7(9)) Black Rabbit Bks.

—Vanishing Tricks. 2011. (ENG., Illus.). 32p. (J). pap. 10.95 (978-1-77092-046-0(3)) Saunders Bk. Co. CAN. Dist: RiverStream Publishing.

Wood, John. Card Magic, 1 vol. 2018. (Magic Tricks Ser.). (ENG.). 32p. (J). (gr. 3-4). lib. bdg. 28.27 (978-1-5382-2595-0(6), 41e64d6c-194d-4809-9355-779bfc9a2168) Stevens, Gareth Publishing LLLP.

—Coin Magic, 1 vol. 2018. (Magic Tricks Ser.). (ENG.). 32p. (J). (gr. 3-4). lib. bdg. 28.27 (978-1-5382-2602-5(2), 8b983047-7bf9-4922-91a5-90ddbd500ff2) Stevens, Gareth Publishing LLLP.

—Illusions, 1 vol. 2018. (Magic Tricks Ser.). (ENG.). 32p. (J). (gr. 3-4). lib. bdg. 28.27 (978-1-5382-2606-3(5), 6daf9cdf-1525-4786-85e2-7d24fcf5d60c) Stevens, Gareth Publishing LLLP.

—Magic Stunts, 1 vol. 2018. (Magic Tricks Ser.). (ENG.). 32p. (J). (gr. 3-4). lib. bdg. 28.27 (978-1-5382-2587-5(5), e0855f31-f7ab-4ff0-9649-99a926d8a8c2) Stevens, Gareth Publishing LLLP.

—Mind Magic, 1 vol. 2018. (Magic Tricks Ser.). (ENG.). 32p. (J). (gr. 3-4). lib. bdg. 28.27 (978-1-5382-2599-8(9), 93e2ce24-5da2-4abb-8628-51cbc1f85cdb) Stevens, Gareth Publishing LLLP.

Zenon, Paul. Magic of the Mind: Tricks for the Master Magician, 1 vol. 2007. (Amazing Magic Ser.). (ENG., Illus.). 64p. (gr. 6-6). pap. 15.05 (978-1-4042-1759-1(2), be3e352b-90f3-434e-af97-465992360432, Rosen Reference); (YA). lib. bdg. 37.13 (978-1-4042-1072-1(5), c53f3089-5588-41c4-8dad-f479a37cc51e) Rosen Publishing Group, Inc., The.

—Simple Sleight-of-Hand: Card & Coin Tricks for the Beginning Magician, 1 vol. 2007. (Amazing Magic Ser.). (ENG., Illus.). 64p. (gr. 6-6). per. 15.05 (978-1-4042-1757-7(6), 6bac0f9d-f6d2-4c43-9c67-1a16fe51f99c, Rosen Reference); (YA). lib. bdg. 37.13 (978-1-4042-1070-7(9), 889e5cb3-f6f3-4e7a-9df4-57354cac176b) Rosen Publishing Group, Inc., The.

MAGICIANS

see also Wizards

Adler, David A. & Adler, Michael S. A Picture Book of Harry Houdini. Collins, Matt, illus. 2010. (Picture Book Biography Ser.). (ENG.). 32p. (J). (gr. k-3). pap. 7.99 (978-0-8234-2302-6(6)) Holiday Hse., Inc.

Allen, John. Great Magicians & Illusionists. 2016. (ENG.). 80p. (J). (gr. 5-12). lib. bdg. (978-1-60152-998-5(8)) ReferencePoint Pr., Inc.

Bednar, Chuck. David Blaine: Illusionist & Endurance Artist. (Transcending Race in America: Biographies of Biracial Achievers Ser.). (Illus.). 64p. (YA). (gr. 5-18). 2010. lib. bdg. 22.95 (978-1-4222-1609-5(8)) 2009. pap. 9.95 (978-1-4222-1623-1(3)) Mason Crest.

Carlson, Laurie. Harry Houdini for Kids: His Life & Adventures with 21 Magic Tricks & Illusions. 2009. (For Kids Ser.: 29). (ENG., Illus.). 144p. (J). (gr. 4-7). pap. 18.95 (978-1-55652-782-1(9)) Chicago Review Pr., Inc.

Dillies, Lyn. Your Vote Is Magic! 2012. 184p. pap. 14.95 (978-0-615-66530-6(6)) Dillies, Lyn.

Dooling, Sandra. Sorcerers, Spells, & Magic!, 1 vol., 1. 2013. (Jr. Graphic Monster Stories Ser.). (ENG.). 24p. (J). (gr. 2-3). 28.93 (978-1-4777-6211-0(6), 3647e898-4c6a-4fa0-952d-13c56c8fc89d, PowerKids Pr.) Rosen Publishing Group, Inc., The.

Fleischman, Sid. Escape! The Story of the Great Houdini. (Illus.). (J). 2008. (ENG.). 240p. (gr. 3-7). pap. 8.99 (978-0-06-085096-8(5), Greenwillow Bks.) 2006. (ENG., 224p. (gr. 3-7). 19.99 (978-0-06-085094-4(9), Greenwillow Bks.) 2006. 210p. (gr. 4-8). lib. bdg. 19.89 (978-0-06-085095-1(7)) HarperCollins Pubs.

Higginson, Sheila Sweeny. Pulling Back the Curtain on Magic! Ready-To-Read Level 3. McClurkan, Rob, illus. 2015. (Science of Fun Stuff Ser.). (ENG.). 48p. (J). (gr. 1-3). 16.99 (978-1-4814-3702-8(X), Simon Spotlight) Simon Spotlight.

Hill, Douglas. Brujas y Magos. Wilson, Alex, illus. 2003. (SPA.). 64p. (J). 14.95 (978-84-372-2321-6(0)) Altea, Ediciones, S.A. - Grupo Santillana ESP. Dist: Santillana USA Publishing Co., Inc.

Jarrow, Gail. The Amazing Harry Kellar: Great American Magician. 2012. (ENG., Illus.). 96p. (J). (gr. 3-7). 17.95 (978-1-59078-865-3(6), Calkins Creek) Highlights Pr., c/o Highlights for Children, Inc.

Kacer, Kathy. The Magician of Auschwitz, 1 vol. Newland, Gillian, illus. 2014. (ENG.). 32p. (J). (gr. 3-6). 18.95 (978-1-927583-46-3(2)) Second Story Pr. CAN. Dist: Orca Bk. Pubs. USA.

Kraske, Robert. Harry Houdini. 2015. 72p. pap. 7.00 (978-1-61003-493-7(7)) Center for the Collaborative Classroom.

MacLeod, Elizabeth. Harry Houdini. Mantha, John, illus. 2009. (Kids Can Read Ser.). 32p. (J). (gr. 1-3). 14.95 (978-1-55453-298-8(1)) Kids Can Pr., Ltd. CAN. Dist: Hachette Bk. Group.

Noyes, Deborah. The Magician & the Spirits. 2017. (Illus.). 160p. (J). (gr. 5). 18.99 (978-0-8037-4018-1(2), Viking Books for Young Readers) Penguin Young Readers Group.

Piehl, Janet. Harry Houdini. 2009. (History Maker Biographies Ser.). (gr. 3-6). 26.60 (978-1-58013-705-8(9), Lerner Pubns.) Lerner Publishing Group.

Poskitt, Kjartan. Harry Houdini (the First Names Series) Ford, Geraint, illus. 2019. (First Names Ser.). (ENG.). 160p. (J). (gr. 3-7). 9.99 (978-1-4197-3862-3(3), 1279201, Abrams Bks. for Young Readers) Abrams, Inc.

Regan, Lisa. Magician, 1 vol. 2012. (Stage School Ser.). (ENG., Illus.). 32p. (J). (gr. 2-3). pap. 11.00 (978-1-4488-8153-6(6), 7b1932cb-6195-46df-b70f-99ef2d4637d7); lib. bdg. 29.93 (978-1-4488-8094-2(7), 51811e2d-196a-401f-9215-f599768d03f0) Rosen Publishing Group, Inc., The. (Windmill Bks.).

Rockliff, Mara. Anything but Ordinary Addie: The True Story of Adelaide Herrmann, Queen of Magic. Bruno, Iacopo, illus. 2016. 48p. (J). (gr. 1-4). 17.99 (978-0-7636-6841-9(9)) Candlewick Pr.

Saddleback Educational Publishing Staff, ed. Houdini, 1 vol. unabr. ed. 2007. (Graphic Biographies Ser.). (ENG., Illus.). 25p. (YA). (gr. 4-12). pap. 9.75 (978-1-59905-224-3(5)) Saddleback Educational Publishing, Inc.

Turnbull, Stephanie. A Magician. 2016. (How to Be ... Ser.). (ENG.). 24p. (J). (gr. 2-5). 28.50 (978-1-62588-369-8(2), 17300) Black Rabbit Bks.

MAGICIANS—FICTION

Afterglow. 2014. (ENG., Illus.). 336p. (YA). (gr. 9). pap. 11.99 (978-1-4424-5038-7(X), Simon & Schuster Bks. For Young Readers) Simon & Schuster Bks. For Young Readers.

Agee, Jon. Milo's Hat Trick. 2017. (Illus.). 40p. (J). (gr. k-3). 17.99 (978-0-7352-2987-7(2), Dial Bks) Penguin Young Readers Group.

Akita, Yoshinobu. Orphen, Vol. 4. 2006. (Orphen Ser.). (Illus.). 168p. (YA). pap. 9.99 (978-1-4139-0269-3(3)) ADV Manga.

Avi. Magia de Medianoche. 2004. (SPA.). 194p. (YA). 10.99 (978-84-348-9112-8(3)) SM Ediciones ESP. Dist: Lectorum Pubns., Inc.

—Murder at Midnight. 2011. (ENG.). 256p. (J). (gr. 3-7). pap. 7.99 (978-0-545-08091-0(6), Scholastic Paperbacks) Scholastic, Inc.

AZ Books, creator. Little Magician. 2012. (Millions of Inventions Ser.). (ENG., Illus.). 16p. (J). (gr. 1-3). pap. 5.95 (978-1-61889-302-4(5)) AZ Bks. LLC.

Barron, T. A. Doomraga's Revenge: Book 7, 7 vols., Bk. 7. 2011. (Merlin Saga Ser.: 7). (ENG.). 272p. (J). (gr. 5-18). 8.99 (978-0-14-241925-0(7), Puffin Books) Penguin Young Readers Group.

Beaty, Andrea. Dorko the Magnificent. 2014. (ENG.). 240p. (J). (gr. 3-7). pap. 8.99 (978-1-4197-1019-3(2), 1051003, Amulet Bks.) Abrams, Inc.

Benjamin, Sigalit. Garland of Stars. 2009. 26p. pap. 14.50 (978-1-60860-345-9(8), Eloquent Bks.) Strategic Book Publishing & Rights Agency (SBPRA).

Bernatene, Poly, illus. The Sorcerer's Apprentice. 2007. (Usborne Young Reading: Series One Ser.). 47p. (J). (gr. -1-3). 8.99 (978-0-7945-1589-8(4), Usborne) EDC Publishing.

Birney, Betty G. Humphrey's Mixed-Up Magic Trick. Burris, Priscilla, illus. 2016. (Humphrey's Tiny Tales Ser.: 5). (ENG.). 96p. (J). (gr. k-3). 6.99 (978-0-14-751461-5(4), Puffin Books) Penguin Young Readers Group.

Bond, Gwenda. Girl in the Shadows, 0 vols. 2016. (Cirque American Ser.: 2). (ENG.). 380p. (YA). (gr. 9-13). pap. 9.99 (978-1-5039-5393-2(9), 9781503953932, Skyscape) Amazon Publishing.

Brown, Teri. Born of Deception. 2014. (Born of Illusion Ser.: 2). (ENG.). 336p. (YA). (gr. 8). 17.99 (978-0-06-218757-4(0), Balzer & Bray) HarperCollins Pubs.

—Born of Illusion. 2013. (ENG.). 384p. (YA). pap. 9.99 (978-0-06-227720-6(0)) HarperCollins Pubs.

Cate, Annette LeBlanc. The Magic Rabbit. Cate, Annette LeBlanc, illus. 2013. (ENG., Illus.). 32p. (J). (gr. -1-1). 21.19 (978-0-7636-2672-3(4)) Candlewick Pr.

—The Magic Rabbit. 2013. lib. bdg. 17.20 (978-0-606-31601-9(9)) Turtleback.

Cerda, Alfredo Gomez. Manolo Multon y el Mago Guason. Antonio & Covi, illus. 2004.Tr. of Manolo Citation & Boring the Magician. (SPA.). (J). pap. 7.99 (978-84-236-6322-4(1)) Edebé ESP. Dist: Lectorum Pubns., Inc.

Child, Lydia Maria. The Magician's Show Box & Other Stories. 2007. (ENG.). 124p. per. (978-1-4065-1354-7(7)) Dodo Pr.

—The Magician's Show Box & Other Stories. 2004. reprint ed. pap. 1.99 (978-1-4192-7122-9(9)); pap. 19.95 (978-1-4191-7122-2(4)) Kessinger Publishing, LLC.

Clarke, Jane. G. E. M. Parsons, Garry, illus. 2008. (ENG.). 32p. (J). (gr. -1-k). pap. 9.95 (978-0-09-948012-9(3), Red Fox) Random House Children's Books GBR. Dist: Independent Pubs. Group.

Cole, Frank L. Potion Masters: The Eternity Elixir. 2018. (Potion Masters Ser.: 1). (ENG., Illus.). 304p. (J). (gr. 5). 16.99 (978-1-62972-358-7(4), 5182305, Shadow Mountain) Shadow Mountain Publishing.

—The Transparency Tonic. 2019. (Potion Masters Ser.: 2). (ENG., Illus.). 384p. (J). (gr. 5). 16.99 (978-1-62972-488-1(2), 5206082, Shadow Mountain) Shadow Mountain Publishing.

Cooper, Susan. The Magician's Boy. Riglietti, Serena, illus. 2006. (ENG.). 112p. (J). (gr. 3-7). pap. 9.99 (978-1-4169-1555-3(9), McElderry, Margaret K. Bks.) McElderry, Margaret K. Bks.

Corlett, William. The Bridge in the Clouds. 2010. (Magician's House Quartet Ser.: 4). (ENG.). 352p. (YA). (gr. 5-8). pap. 15.99 (978-1-4424-1412-9(X), Simon Pulse) Simon Pulse.

—The Door in the Tree. 2010. (Magician's House Quartet Ser.: 2). (ENG.). 304p. (YA). (gr. 5-8). pap. 13.99 (978-1-4424-1414-3(6), Simon Pulse) Simon Pulse.

—The Steps up the Chimney. 2011. (Magician's House Quartet Ser.: 1). (ENG.). 288p. (YA). (gr. 7). pap. 13.99 (978-1-4424-2935-2(6), Simon Pulse) Simon Pulse.

—The Tunnel Behind the Waterfall. 2010. (Magician's House Quartet Ser.: 3). (ENG.). 320p. (YA). (gr. 5-8). pap. 14.99 (978-1-4424-1413-6(8), Simon Pulse) Simon Pulse.

Coville, Bruce. The Dragon of Doom. Coville, Katherine, illus. 2005. (Moongobble & Me Ser.: Bk. 1). (ENG.). 80p. (J). (gr. 1-5). pap. 6.99 *(978-0-689-85757-7(8)*, Aladdin) Simon & Schuster Children's Publishing.

—The Evil Elves. Coville, Katherine, illus. 2006. (Moongobble & Me Ser.: Bk. 3). (ENG.). 80p. (J). (gr. 1-5). pap. 6.99 *(978-0-689-85759-1(4)*, Simon & Schuster/Paula Wiseman Bks.) Simon & Schuster/Paula Wiseman Bks.

—The Mischief Monster. Coville, Katherine, illus. 2008. (Moongobble & Me Ser.: Bk. 4). (ENG.). 80p. (J). (gr. 1-5). pap. 6.99 *(978-1-4169-0808-1(0)*, Aladdin) Simon & Schuster Children's Publishing.

—The Mischief Monster. Coville, Katherine, illus. 2007. (Moongobble & Me Ser.: Bk. 4). (ENG.). 80p. (J). (gr. 3-6). 16.19 *(978-1-4169-0807-4(2))* Simon & Schuster, Inc.

—The Naughty Nork. Coville, Katherine, illus. 2009. (Moongobble & Me Ser.). (ENG.). 128p. (J). (gr. 1-5). pap. 6.99 *(978-1-4169-0810-4(2)*, Aladdin) Simon & Schuster Children's Publishing.

—The Weeping Werewolf. Coville, Katherine, illus. 2006. (Moongobble & Me Ser.). 68p. (gr. 1-5). 16.00 *(978-0-7569-6582-2(9))* Perfection Learning Corp.

—The Weeping Werewolf. Coville, Katherine, illus. 2005. (Moongobble & Me Ser.: Bk. 2). (ENG.). 80p. (J). (gr. 1-5). pap. 6.99 *(978-0-689-85758-4(6)*, Aladdin) Simon & Schuster Children's Publishing.

Cross, Frances. Butternut Blobber & the Blue Jade. 2007. (Blobber Ser.). (ENG.). 84p. pap. *(978-1-84167-561-9(X))* Ransom Publishing Ltd.

Cunningham, Mary. Cynthias Attic Magicians Castle. 2009. 158p. pap. 10.99 *(978-1-59080-656-2(5))* Echelon Press Publishing.

Dahl, Michael. The Assistant Vanishes!, 1 vol. Weber, Lisa K., illus. 2013. (Hocus Pocus Hotel Ser.). (ENG.). 112p. (J). (gr. 3-6). lib. bdg. 25.32 *(978-1-4342-4101-6(7)*, 119822, Stone Arch Bks.) Capstone.

—Out the Rear Window, 1 vol. Weber, Lisa K., illus. 2012. (Hocus Pocus Hotel Ser.). (ENG.). 112p. (J). (gr. 3-6). lib. bdg. 25.32 *(978-1-4342-4038-5(X)*, 118479, Stone Arch Bks.) Capstone.

—The Thirteenth Mystery. Weber, Lisa K., illus. 2016. (Hocus Pocus Hotel Ser.). (ENG.). 224p. (J). (gr. 3-6). pap., pap. 7.95 *(978-1-4965-0755-6(X)*, 128800, Stone Arch Bks.) Capstone.

Davies, Margaret, et al. Y Dewin Diog. 2005. (WEL., Illus.). 32p. pap. *(978-1-85596-219-4(5))* Dref Wen.

Delgado, Luis Cabrera. Catalina la Maga. (Torre de Papel Ser.). (J). (gr. 2). 7.95 *(978-958-04-4220-2(7))* Norma S.A. COL. Dist: Distribuidora Norma, Inc.

Dickson, Louise. The Disappearing Magician. Cupples, Pat, illus. 2007. (Kids Can Read Ser.). 32p. (J). (gr. 1-2). 3.95 *(978-1-55453-034-2(2))* Kids Can Pr., Ltd. CAN. Dist: Hachette Bk. Group.

Dragt, Tonke. The Song of Seven. 2018. (ENG., Illus.). 352p. (J). (gr. 3-7). pap. 15.95 *(978-1-78269-142-6(1)*, Pushkin Children's Bks.) Steerforth Pr.

Durrant, Geraldine. Twinbane: an Appalling True History. 2010. 142p. pap. 16.95 *(978-1-4457-7998-0(6))* Lulu Pr., Inc.

Duvall, Deborah L. Rabbit & the Fingerbone Necklace. Jacob, Murv, illus. 2009. (ENG.). 32p. (J). (gr. 1). 19.95 *(978-0-8263-4723-7(1)*, P167927) Univ. of New Mexico Pr.

Edgson, Alison, illus. The Magician's Apprentice. 2011. (Flip-Up Fairy Tales Ser.). 24p. (J). (gr. 2-2). *(978-1-84643-370-2(3))* Child's Play International Ltd.

Edmondson, Matt. The Greatest Magician in the World. 2018. (ENG., Illus.). 40p. (J). (gr. 1-5). 21.99 *(978-1-5098-0618-8(0))* Pan Macmillan GBR. Dist: Independent Pubs. Group.

Edwards, R. G. Eafin Lokdore & the Altar of the Sun Book II. 2007. (ENG.). 264p. pap. 19.96 *(978-0-615-17785-4(9))* Edwards, R. G. Publishing.

Elmer, Robert. Trion Rising, 1 vol. 2008. (Shadowside Trilogy Ser.). (ENG.). 352p. (YA). (gr. 8-11). pap. 9.99 *(978-0-310-71421-7(4))* Zondervan.

Enderle, Dotti. Book 16: Abracadabra!, 1 vol. 2014. (Ghost Detectors Ser.). (ENG., Illus.). 80p. (J). (gr. 2-5). lib. bdg. 35.64 *(978-1-62402-004-9(6)*, 8834, Calico Chapter Bks.) ABDO Publishing Co.

Enyi, Patricia Nmukoso. Marcus the Magician: At the Beach. 2010. 38p. pap. 15.50 *(978-1-60911-447-3(7)*, Eloquent Bks.) Strategic Book Publishing & Rights Agency (SBPRA).

Everson, Chance. Verlin's Magical Blunder: Tales of the Mandrasaurs, Volume the Seventh. Geary, Steve, illus. 2004. cd-rom 9.95 *(978-0-9760303-6-2(5))* R.A.R.E. TALES.

Fienberg, Anna & Fienberg, Barbara. Tashi & the Wicked Magician: And Other Stories. Kelly, Geoff & Gamble, Kim, illus. 2017. (Tashi Ser.). (ENG.). 96p. (J). (gr. k-3). pap. 10.99 *(978-1-76029-050-4(5))* Allen & Unwin AUS. Dist: Independent Pubs. Group.

Frost, Andrew David. The Magician & the Priestess. 2010. 416p. pap. 17.99 *(978-1-4490-7830-0(3))* AuthorHouse.

Gauthier, Bertrand. Zunik dans le Grand Magicien. 2004. (FRE., Illus.). (J). (gr. -1-2). spiral bd. *(978-0-616-01831-6(2))* Canadian National Institute for the Blind/Institut National Canadien pour les Aveugles.

Giordano, Anne. Spencer, the Magic Rabbit. 2009. 40p. pap. 16.99 *(978-1-4490-3296-8(6))* AuthorHouse.

Gosling, Sharon. The Ruby Airship. 2015. (Diamond Thief Ser.). (ENG.). 496p. (YA). (gr. 9-12). 16.95 *(978-1-63079-004-2(4)*, 126924, Switch Pr.) Capstone.

Gutman, Dan. Houdini & Me. 2021. (ENG., Illus.). 224p. (J). (gr. 3-7). 16.99 *(978-0-8234-4515-8(1))* Holiday Hse., Inc.

Hardinge, Frances. Cuckoo Song. 2016. (ENG.). 432p. (YA). (gr. 8-17). pap. 12.99 *(978-1-4197-1939-4(4)*, 1096603, Amulet Bks.) Abrams, Inc.

Heneghan, Judith. The Magician's Apprentice. 2008. (Illus.). 168p. (J). (gr. 3-7). 16.95 *(978-0-8234-2150-3(3))* Holiday Hse., Inc.

Higgins, F. E. The Bone Magician, 2. 2011. (ENG.). 304p. (J). (gr. 6-8). pap. 18.99 *(978-0-312-65944-8(X)*, 900070542) Square Fish.

Higgins, Lawrence. Demons & Dragons: Time, Space & Magic. 2010. (ENG., Illus.). 93p. pap. 20.99 *(978-1-906791-68-1(6))* Arena Bks. GBR. Dist: Lightning Source UK, Ltd.

Hood, Ann. Prince of Air, 4. Altmann, Scott & Zilber, Denis, illus. 2012. (Treasure Chest: the Time-Traveling Adventures of the Robbins Twins Ser.: 4). 208p. (J). (gr. 4-6). 21.19 *(978-0-448-45474-0(2))* Penguin Young Readers Group.

Horwitz, Sarah Jean. Carmer & Grit, Book One: the Wingsnatchers, Volume 1. 2018. (Carmer & Grit Ser.). (ENG.). 368p. (gr. 5-9). pap. 8.99 *(978-1-61620-802-8(3)*, 73802) Algonquin Young Readers.

—Carmer & Grit, Book Two: the Crooked Castle. 2019. (Carmer & Grit Ser.). (ENG.). 368p. (gr. 4-9). pap. 8.95 *(978-1-61620-925-4(9)*, 73925) Algonquin Young Readers.

Howe, James. Rabbit-Cadabra! Ready-To-Read Level 3. Mack, Jeff, illus. (Bunnicula & Friends Ser.: 4). (ENG.). 48p. (J). (gr. 1-3). 2007. pap. 4.99 *(978-0-689-85752-2(7))* 2006. 17.99 *(978-0-689-85727-0(6))* Simon Spotlight. (Simon Spotlight).

Keene, Carolyn. The Magician's Secret. 2015. (Nancy Drew Diaries: 8). (ENG., Illus.). 176p. (J). (gr. 3-7). pap. 7.99 *(978-1-4814-1700-6(2)*, Aladdin) Simon & Schuster Children's Publishing.

Kennedy, Kim & Kennedy, Doug. Hee-Haw-Dini & the Great Zambini. 2009. (ENG., Illus.). 32p. (J). (gr. k-2). 15.95 *(978-0-8109-7025-0(2)*, 586001, Abrams Bks. for Young Readers) Abrams, Inc.

Kirov, Erica. Magickeepers: The Eternal Hourglass. Fortune, Eric, illus. 2010. 256p. (J). (gr. 4-7). pap. 10.99 *(978-1-4022-3855-0(X))* Sourcebooks, Inc.

Kova, Elise. Water's Wrath (Air Awakens Series Book 4) 2016. (ENG., Illus.). 378p. pap. 14.99 *(978-1-61984-425-4(7))* Gatekeeper Pr.

Lalicki, Tom. Danger in the Dark: A Houdini & Nate Mystery, 1. 2010. (Houdini & Nate Mysteries Ser.: 1). (ENG.). 208p. (J). (gr. 6-8). pap. 15.99 *(978-0-312-60214-7(6)*, 900064229) Square Fish.

—Shots at Sea: A Houdini & Nate Mystery. 2011. (Houdini & Nate Mysteries Ser.). 224p. (J). pap. 6.99 *(978-0-312-65920-2(2))* Square Fish.

Larson, Kirby. Audacity Jones Steals the Show (Audacity Jones #2) 2018. lib. bdg. 17.20 *(978-0-606-41131-8(3))* Turtleback.

Lawhorn, Mary Joyce. When Annie Dreams. 2012. 74p. pap. 8.95 *(978-1-4697-8819-7(5))* iUniverse, Inc.

Lee, Shell. Teenie's Treehouse Adventures: The Magic Begins. 2004. 37p. pap. 24.95 *(978-1-4137-2879-8(0))* PublishAmerica, Inc.

Lopez, Diana. Nothing up My Sleeve. 2016. (ENG.). 400p. (J). (gr. 3-7). 17.99 *(978-0-316-34087-8(1))* Little, Brown Bks. for Young Readers.

Luciano, Sonia. Mr. I Forgot. 2009. 48p. pap. 16.95 *(978-1-61582-765-7(X))* America Star Bks.

Mahy, Margaret. The Magician of Hoad. (ENG.). 432p. (YA). (gr. 9). 2010. pap. 9.99 *(978-1-4169-7808-4(9))* 2009. 18.99 *(978-1-4169-7807-7(0))* McElderry, Margaret K. Bks. (McElderry, Margaret K. Bks.).

Mason, Adrienne. The Drop of Doom. Cupples, Pat, illus. 2007. (Kids Can Read Ser.). 32p. (J). (gr. 1-2). 3.95 *(978-1-55453-036-6(9))*; 14.95 *(978-1-55453-035-9(0))* Kids Can Pr., Ltd. CAN. Dist: Hachette Bk. Group.

Matthews, Andrew. Shakespeare Stories: The Tempest. Ross, Tony, illus. 2003. (ENG.). 64p. (J). (gr. 4-6). pap. 6.99 *(978-1-84121-346-0(2)*, Orchard Bks.) Hachette Children's Group GBR. Dist: Hachette Bk. Group.

Mcdonald, Megan. Rocky Zang in the Amazing Mr. Magic. 2014. (Judy Moody & Friends Ser.: 2). lib. bdg. 14.75 *(978-0-606-35163-8(9))* Turtleback.

McLaren, Meg. Rabbit Magic. McLaren, Meg, illus. 2017. (ENG., Illus.). 40p. (J). (gr. -1-3). 16.99 *(978-0-544-78469-7(3)*, 1638303, Clarion Bks.) HarperCollins Pubs.

McSkimming, Geoffrey. Phyllis Wong & the Waking of the Wizard. 2016. (Phyllis Wong Ser.). (ENG.). 400p. (J). (gr. 3-7). pap. 12.99 *(978-1-76011-338-4(7))* Allen & Unwin AUS. Dist: Independent Pubs. Group.

Meadows, Daisy. Penelope the Foal Fairy. 2018. (Rainbow Magic — Farm Aminal Fairies Ser.). lib. bdg. 14.75 *(978-0-606-41158-5(5))* Turtleback.

Merola, Caroline. Toni Biscotti's Magic Trick. Cummins, Sarah, tr. 2006. (Formac First Novels Ser.: 60). (ENG., Illus.). 64p. (J). (gr. 2-5). 14.95 *(978-0-88780-719-0(4)*, 719) Formac Publishing Co., Ltd. CAN. Dist: Formac Lorimer Bks. Ltd.

—Toni Biscotti's Magic Trick, 1 vol. Cummins, Sarah, tr. Merola, Caroline, illus. 2006. (Formac First Novels Ser.: 60). (ENG., Illus.). 64p. (J). (gr. 2-5). 4.95 *(978-0-88780-715-2(1)*, 715) Formac Publishing Co., Ltd. CAN. Dist: Formac Lorimer Bks. Ltd.

Milgrim, David. See Zip Zap. 2019. (Ready-To-Read Ser.). (ENG.). 32p. (J). (gr. k-1). 13.89 *(978-1-64310-886-5(7))* Penworthy Co., LLC, The.

—See Zip Zap: Ready-To-Read Ready-to-Go! Milgrim, David, illus. 2018. (Adventures of Zip Ser.). (ENG., Illus.). 32p. (J). (gr. -1-k). 17.99 *(978-1-5344-1100-5(3))*; pap. 4.99 *(978-1-5344-1099-2(6))* Simon Spotlight. (Simon Spotlight).

Milliner, Naomi. Super Jake & the King of Chaos. 2019. (ENG.). 288p. (J). (gr. 3-7). 16.99 *(978-0-7624-6615-3(4)*, Running Pr. Kids) Running Pr.

Morrisette, Sharon. Toads & Tessellations. O'Neill, Philomena, illus. 2012. (Charlesbridge Math Adventures Ser.). 32p. (J). (gr. 2-5). 16.95 *(978-1-58089-354-1(6))* Charlesbridge Publishing, Inc.

Nicholson, Simon. The Magician's Fire. 2015. (Young Houdini Ser.: 1). (ENG.). 272p. (J). (gr. 4-7). pap. 7.99 *(978-1-4926-0949-0(8))* Sourcebooks, Inc.

Nuno, Fran. The Great Magician of the World. Brokenbrow, Jon, tr. Quevedo, Enrique, illus. 2012. (ENG.). 24p. (J). (gr. k-3). 14.95 *(978-84-15241-11-9(9))* Cuento de Luz SL ESP. Dist: Publishers Group West (PGW).

Osborne, Mary Pope. High Time for Heroes. Murdocca, Sal, illus. 2016. (Magic Tree House (R) Merlin Mission Ser.: 23). 144p. (J). (gr. 2-5). 6.99 *(978-0-307-98052-6(9)*, Random Hse. Bks. for Young Readers) Random Hse. Children's Bks.

—Hurry up, Houdini! 2015. (Magic Tree House Merlin Missions Ser.: 22). lib. bdg. 16.00 *(978-0-606-37718-8(2))* Turtleback.

Parker, Emma. The Magic Show. 2010. (Illus.). pap. *(978-1-877561-23-8(1))* First Edition Ltd.

Paschkis, Julie. Magic Spell. Paschkis, Julie, illus. 2017. (ENG., Illus.). 32p. (J). (gr. -1-3). 17.99 *(978-1-4814-2210-9(3)*, Simon & Schuster Bks. For Young Readers) Simon & Schuster Bks. For Young Readers.

Paul, Ruth. Hedgehog's Magic Tricks. Paul, Ruth, illus. 2013. (ENG., Illus.). 32p. (J). (gr. -1-2). 12.99 *(978-0-7636-6385-8(9))* Candlewick Pr.

Peterson, Alyson. The Cursed Dagger. 2016. 308p. (YA). pap. *(978-1-4621-1865-6(8))* Cedar Fort, Inc./CFI Distribution.

—Ian Quicksilver: The Warrior's Return. 2015. vii, 309p. (YA). pap. 17.99 *(978-1-4621-1629-4(9))* Cedar Fort, Inc./CFI Distribution.

Prineas, Sarah. The Magic Thief: Found. Caparo, Antonio Javier, illus. 2011. (Magic Thief Ser.: 3). (ENG.). 384p. (J). (gr. 5). pap. 7.99 *(978-0-06-137595-8(0)*, HarperCollins) HarperCollins Pubs.

Rees Brennan, Sarah. Unspoken (the Lynburn Legacy Book 1), Bk. 1. 2013. (Lynburn Legacy Ser.: 1). (ENG.). 400p. (YA). (gr. 7). pap. 13.99 *(978-0-375-87103-0(9)*, Ember) Random Hse. Children's Bks.

Risso, Eduardo. Mysteries of the Red Moon, Vol. 3. 2006. (SPA.). 48p. pap. 16.95 *(978-1-59497-163-1(3))* Public Square Bks.

Risso, Eduardo & Trillo, Carlos. Los Misterios de la Luna Roja Vol. 2: El Ataque del Circo. 2006. (SPA., Illus.). 72p. (J). (gr. 1). per. 16.95 *(978-1-59497-162-4(5))* Public Square Bks.

Scheid, Petra Maria. Fairy Tales, Elves & Magicans. 2009. 82p. pap. *(978-3-8391-1065-2(3))* Books on Demand GmbH.

Sedgwick, Marcus. The Book of Dead Days. 2006. (Book of Dead Days Ser.: 1). (ENG.). 288p. (YA). (gr. 5-12). reprint ed. per. 7.99 *(978-0-385-74704-2(7)*, Lamb, Wendy Bks.) Random Hse. Children's Bks.

Sheard, Jean. A Chinese Fantasy - Cave in a Casket. (ENG.). 128p. 2007. 34.95 *(978-1-84753-349-4(3))* 2006. (Illus.). pap. *(978-1-84753-249-7(7))* Lulu Pr., Inc.

Shehadeh, Y. I. The Legendary Heroes: The Beginning. 2011. 80p. pap. 13.00 *(978-1-4575-0372-6(7))* Dog Ear Publishing, LLC.

Singleton, Linda Joy. Magician's Muse. 2010. (Seer Ser.: 6). (ENG.). 312p. (YA). (gr. 6-18). pap. 9.95 *(978-0-7387-1957-3(9)*, Flux) Llewellyn Pubns.

Skye, Evelyn. The Crown's Game. 2017. (Crown's Game Ser.: 1). (ENG.). 432p. (YA). (gr. 8). pap. 9.99 *(978-0-06-242259-0(6)*, Balzer & Bray) HarperCollins Pubs.

—The Crown's Game. 2017. (Crown's Game Ser.: bk.1). (ENG.). (YA). lib. bdg. 20.85 *(978-0-606-39645-5(4))* Turtleback.

Smith, Roy. Louphole Forest Tells Its Tale of Enchantment. Magpie, ed. Burnell Walsh, Avenda, illus. 2012. 38p. *(978-1-908000-18-7(X))* Pyjama Pr.

Stephens, Juanita. Martha the Multiplying Magician. 2011. 48p. pap. 18.99 *(978-1-4634-2725-2(5))* AuthorHouse.

Stockton, Frank Richard. The Bee-Man of Orn & Other Fanciful Tales. 2004. reprint ed. pap. 20.95 *(978-1-4191-5383-9(8))*; pap. 1.99 *(978-1-4192-5383-6(2))* Kessinger Publishing, LLC.

Styles, Walker. Labra-Cadabra-dor's Revenge. Whitehouse, Ben, illus. 2017. (Rider Woofson Ser.: 7). (ENG.). 128p. (J). (gr. k-4). 16.99 *(978-1-4814-8593-7(8))*; pap. 5.99 *(978-1-4814-8592-0(X))* Little Simon. (Little Simon).

Sullivan, Laura L. Delusion. 2014. (ENG.). 352p. (YA). (gr. 7). pap. 18.99 *(978-0-544-10478-5(1)*, 1540787, Clarion Bks.) HarperCollins Pubs.

Tait, Barbara. Timothy Toot... . Finds A Hat. Margolis, Al, illus. 2011. 32p. (J). 24.95 *(978-1-58909-917-3(6))* Bookstand Publishing.

Taylor, Theodore. The Boy Who Could Fly Without a Motor. 2004. (ENG., Illus.). 168p. (J). (gr. 3-7). pap. 11.95 *(978-0-15-204767-2(0)*, 1194383, Clarion Bks.) HarperCollins Pubs.

Thompson, Colin. The Great Montefiasco. Redlich, Ben, illus. 2004. 40p. (J). (gr. -1 — 1). 16.95 *(978-1-59572-008-5(1))* Star Bright Bks., Inc.

Thomson-Swift, Joseph & Thomson-Swift, Joe. The Giant, the Antman & the Mermaid. 2011. (Illus.). 30p. pap. *(978-1-908105-50-9(X))* Grosvenor Hse. Publishing Ltd.

The Three Magicians, 6 Packs. (Literatura 2000 Ser.). (gr. 2-3). 33.00 *(978-0-7635-0241-6(3))* Rigby Education.

Tiffany, Grace. Ariel. 2005. 240p. (J). 16.99 *(978-0-06-075327-6(7))* HarperCollins Pubs.

Los tres Magos: Individual Title, 6 Packs. (Literatura 2000 Ser.). (SPA.). (gr. 2-3). 33.00 *(978-0-7635-1275-0(3))* Rigby Education.

Warren, Cindy. The Unicorn's Horn. 2011. 98p. pap. 19.95 *(978-1-4560-6987-2(X))* America Star Bks.

Watson-Dubisch, Carolyn. Andy! & the Magician's Horn, 1. l.t. ed. 2006. (Illus.). 32p. (J). per. 9.95 *(978-0-9779295-0-4(7))* Medusa Road Pr.

Whited, Wayne & Burns, Robert David. The Adventures of Orie Alexander - the Story Thief (Paperback Edition) 2010. (ENG.). 70p. pap. 7.95 *(978-0-557-63433-0(4))* Lulu Pr., Inc.

Wilson, Wendy. The First Book of Red. 2005. 99p. pap. 19.95 *(978-1-4137-5570-1(4))* America Star Bks.

Windsor, Justine. Goodly & Grave in a Case of Bad Magic (Goodly & Grave, Book 3) 2019. (Goodly & Grave Ser.: 3). (ENG.). 288p. (J). 6.99 *(978-0-00-829427-4(5)*, HarperCollins Children's Bks.) HarperCollins Pubs. Ltd. GBR. Dist: HarperCollins Pubs.

Woodbridge, Nancy Garfield. A Bouquet of Fairy Tales. 2012. 108p. 24.99 *(978-1-4771-4493-0(5))*; pap. 15.99 *(978-1-4771-4492-3(7))* Xlibris Corp.

Yoyo Books Staff. Princess Charlotte Becomes a Magician. 2005. 32p. *(978-90-5843-459-3(1))* YoYo Bks.

Zucker, Jonny. Mission 6: Short Circuit. Woodman, Ned, illus. 2013. (Max Flash Ser.: 6). (ENG.). 144p. (J). (gr. 2-5). pap. 7.95 *(978-1-4677-1480-8(1)*, c61e92f5-c442-45a0-a1a5-43191834b8d6, Darby Creek) Lerner Publishing Group.

MAGNA CARTA

Barrington, Richard. The Magna Carta. 2016. (J). lib. bdg. *(978-1-68048-549-3(0))* Windmill Bks.

Levy, Janey. The Magna Carta, 1 vol. 2013. (Documents That Shaped America Ser.). (ENG.). 32p. (J). (gr. 4-5). 29.27 *(978-1-4339-9001-4(6)*, 9d9c2f46-4760-4cdb-9249-48c4cc9a508a); pap. 11.50 *(978-1-4339-9002-1(4)*, f0a0e46d-2435-43ae-9966-dbf2e01b2079) Stevens, Gareth Publishing LLLP.

Lusted, Marcia Amidon. The Magna Carta. 2019. (Shaping the United States of America Ser.). (ENG., Illus.). 24p. (J). (gr. 1-3). pap. 7.95 *(978-1-9771-1014-5(2)*, 140957); lib. bdg. 25.99 *(978-1-9771-0915-6(2)*, 140516) Capstone. (Pebble).

The Magna Carta. 2013. (Documents That Shaped America Ser.). 32p. (J). (gr. 4-6). pap. 63.00 *(978-1-4339-9003-8(2))* Stevens, Gareth Publishing LLLP.

MAGNET WINDING

see Electromagnets

MAGNETIC RECORDERS AND RECORDING

Kenney, Karen Latchana. Make & Upload Your Own Videos. 2018. (Digital Makers (Alternator Books (r)) Ser.). (ENG., Illus.). 32p. (J). (gr. 3-6). 29.32 *(978-1-5124-8340-6(0)*, effd9500-c87a-4a19-a305-1ef5a3394743, Lerner Pubns.) Lerner Publishing Group.

MAGNETISM

see also Electricity; Electromagnetism; Electromagnets; Magnets

Adler, David A. Magnets Push, Magnets Pull. Raff, Anna, illus. 2018. 32p. (J). (gr. k-3). pap. 8.99 *(978-0-8234-4018-4(4))* Holiday Hse., Inc.

Alpert, Barbara. A Look at Magnets, 1 vol. 2011. (Science Builders Ser.). (ENG.). 24p. (J). (gr. -1-2). pap. 7.29 *(978-1-4296-7109-5(2)*, 116769, Capstone Pr.) Capstone.

Arbuthnott, Gill. Your Guide to Electricity & Magnetism. 2017. (Drawn to Science: Illustrated Guides to Key Science Concepts Ser.). (Illus.). 64p. (J). (gr. 5-5). *(978-0-7787-3398-0(X))* Crabtree Publishing Co.

Beasley, Ava. My Magnet: Fixing a Problem, 1 vol. 2017. (Computer Science for the Real World Ser.). (ENG.). 12p. (gr. 1-2). pap. *(978-1-5383-5146-8(3)*, e400cd07-a2ae-4ca5-b265-7047bd2c1830, Rosen Classroom) Rosen Publishing Group, Inc., The.

Benchmark Education Company, LLC Staff, compiled by. Electricity & Magnetism. 2006. (J). 91.00 *(978-1-4108-7035-3(9))* Benchmark Education Co.

—Electricity & Magnetism: Theme Set. 2006. (J). 131.00 *(978-1-4108-7136-7(3))* Benchmark Education Co.

Bernhardt, Carolyn. Magnetism. 2018. (Science Starters Ser.). (ENG., Illus.). 24p. (J). (gr. k-3). pap. 7.99 *(978-1-61891-465-1(0)*, 12118); lib. bdg. 26.95 *(978-1-62617-809-0(7))* Bellwether Media. (Blastoff! Readers).

Boothroyd, Jennifer. Attract & Repel. 2010. pap. 45.32 *(978-0-7613-6930-1(9))* Lerner Publishing Group.

—Attract & Repel: A Look at Magnets. 2010. (Lightning Bolt Books (r) — Exploring Physical Science Ser.). (ENG., Illus.). 32p. (J). (gr. 1-3). pap. 9.99 *(978-0-7613-6059-9(X)*, c01efc7e-c62d-4767-b524-2674bf3a3e3f) Lerner Publishing Group.

Bryan, Dale-Marie. Experiments with Magnets. 2011. (True Bk Ser.). (Illus.). 48p. (J). (ENG.). pap. 6.95 *(978-0-531-26645-8(1))*; lib. bdg. 29.00 *(978-0-531-26345-7(2))* Scholastic Library Publishing. (Children's Pr.).

Canavan, Thomas. Excellent Experiments with Electricity & Magnetism. 2017. (Mind-Blowing Science Experiments Ser.). 32p. (gr. 4-5). pap. 63.00 *(978-1-5382-0730-7(3))* Stevens, Gareth Publishing LLLP.

Cavell-Clarke, Steffi. Magnets. (First Science Ser.). (J). (gr. 1-1). 2017. pap. 49.50 *(978-1-5345-2077-6(5))* 2016. (ENG.). 24p. pap. 9.25 *(978-1-5345-2076-9(7)*, 04012681-7775-4f1d-bba3-bf56465f7aed) 2016. (ENG.). 24p. lib. bdg. 26.23 *(978-1-5345-2078-3(3)*, fb778daf-450c-4b25-ada6-e9447276a718) Greenhaven Publishing LLC. (KidHaven Publishing).

Cheshire, Gerard. Electricity & Magnetism. 2006. (Fundamental Physics Ser.). (Illus.). 48p. (YA). (gr. 5-9). lib. bdg. 34.25 *(978-1-58340-994-7(7)*, 1262672) Black Rabbit Bks.

Cobb, Vicki. Sources of Forces: Science Fun with Force Fields. Haefele, Steve, illus. 2007. (Science Fun with Vicki Cobb Ser.). 48p. (J). (gr. 4-7). per. 7.95 *(978-0-8225-7023-3(8)*, First Avenue Editions) Lerner Publishing Group.

Connors, Kathleen. Magnetism, 1 vol. 2018. (Look at Physical Science Ser.). (ENG.). 32p. (gr. 2-2). 28.27 *(978-1-5382-2155-6(1)*, 3d4265c9-bc9f-485e-bfc5-4092d76555be) Stevens, Gareth Publishing LLLP.

Cook, Trevor M. Experiments with Electricity & Magnetism, 1 vol. 2009. (Science Lab Ser.). (ENG.). 32p. (J). (gr. 4-4). lib. bdg. 30.27 *(978-1-4358-2807-0(0)*, 69da57a4-388c-42c4-a596-34b9685f2163); (Illus.). pap. 11.00 *(978-1-4358-3220-6(5)*, 0609d081-8746-4b10-b455-925f8dd81759) Rosen Publishing Group, Inc., The. (PowerKids Pr.).

Cooper, Christopher. The Basics of Magnetism, 1 vol. 2014. (Core Concepts Ser.). (ENG., Illus.). 96p. (YA). (gr. 7-7). 39.77 *(978-1-4777-7760-2(1)*, 8563f571-0c14-4ec5-8a49-c0a4de047bca) Rosen Publishing Group, Inc., The.

—Magnetism: From Pole to Pole. 2003. (Science Answers Ser.). (ENG., Illus.). 32p. pap. 7.99 *(978-1-4034-3551-4(0)*, Heinemann) Capstone.

Crane, Cody. Electricity & Magnetism (a True Book: Physical Science) (Library Edition) 2019. (True Book (Relaunch) Ser.). (ENG., Illus.). 48p. (J). (gr. 3-5). lib. bdg. 31.00 *(978-0-531-13137-4(8)*, Children's Pr.) Scholastic Library Publishing.

Dunne, Abbie. Magnetism. 2016. (Physical Science Ser.). (ENG., Illus.). 24p. (J). (gr. -1-2). lib. bdg. 27.32 *(978-1-5157-0938-1(8)*, 132237, Capstone Pr.) Capstone.

Eboch, Chris. Magnets in the Real World. 2013. (Science in the Real World Ser.). (ENG.). 48p. (J). (gr. 4-8). pap. 18.50 *(978-1-61783-792-0(X)*, 14616) ABDO Publishing Co.

Fairley, Peter. Electricity & Magnetism. 2007. (Great Ideas of Science Ser.). (Illus.). 80p. (YA). (gr. 9-12). lib. bdg. 27.93 *(978-0-8225-6605-2(2))* Twenty First Century Bks.

Felix, Rebecca. Magnetism at Work. 2016. (Science at Work Ser.). (ENG.). 24p. (J). (gr. -1-3). 48.50 *(978-1-68077-585-3(5)*, 22477, SandCastle) ABDO Publishing Co.

Forest, Christopher. Focus on Magnetism. 2017. (Hands-On STEM Ser.). (ENG., Illus.). 32p. (J). (gr. 2-3). pap. 9.95 *(978-1-63517-350-5(7)*, 1635173507); lib. bdg. 31.35 *(978-1-63517-285-0(3)*, 1635172853) North Star Editions. (Focus Readers).

Frisch-Schmoll, Joy. Magnetism. 2008. (Simple Science Ser.). (ENG., Illus.). 24p. (J). (gr. 1-4). lib. bdg. 24.25 *(978-1-58341-577-1(7),* 22290, Creative Education) Creative Co., The.

Furgang, Kathy. Working with Electricity & Magnetism & Trabajar con la electricidad y el Magnetismo: 6 English, 6 Spanish Adaptations. 2011. (ENG & SPA.). (J). 97.00 net. *(978-1-4108-5719-4(0))* Benchmark Education Co.

Galiano, Dean. Electric & Magnetic Phenomena. 1 vol. 2011. (Science Made Simple Ser.). (ENG.). 64p. (YA). (gr. 7-7). pap. 13.95 *(978-1-4488-2239-3(4),* 506aca3a-8c13-4d94-8ef5-23d1ea6b000e); (Illus.). lib. bdg. 37.13 *(978-1-4488-1231-8(3),* 14ef026a-ff3a-4419-bbf8-2246e2a92de5) Rosen Publishing Group, Inc., The. (Rosen Reference).

Gardner, Robert. Easy Genius Science Projects with Electricity & Magnetism: Great Experiments & Ideas, 1 vol. 2008. (Easy Genius Science Projects Ser.). (ENG., Illus.). 128p. (gr. 5-6). lib. bdg. 35.93 *(978-0-7660-2923-1(9),* 9961177c-44c3-4566-93d4-de7b73146222) Enslow Publishing, LLC.

—Electricity & Magnetism Science Fair Projects, Using the Scientific Method, 1 vol. 2010. (Physics Science Projects Using the Scientific Method Ser.). (ENG., Illus.). 160p. (gr. 5-6). 38.60 *(978-0-7660-3418-1(6),* b57da7f6-a4df-44a7-9e44-7597feee5c2c) Enslow Publishing, LLC.

—Experiments with Electricity & Magnetism, 1 vol. 2017. (Science Whiz Experiments Ser.). (ENG.). 128p. (gr. 5-5). 38.93 *(978-0-7660-8678-4(X),* 8673fc7d-bb50-4e2b-a503-cdf5a8fcbe1a) Enslow Publishing, LLC.

Gianopoulos, Andrea. The Attractive Story of Magnetism with Max Axiom, Super Scientist. Martin, Cynthia, illus. 2008. (Graphic Science Ser.). (ENG.). 32p. (J). (gr. 3-9). pap. 8.10 *(978-1-4296-1769-7(1),* 94816) Capstone.

—The Attractive Story of Magnetism with Max Axiom Super Scientist: 4D an Augmented Reading Science Experience. Martin, Cynthia, illus. 2018. (Graphic Science 4D Ser.). (ENG.). 32p. (J). (gr. 3-9). pap. 7.95 *(978-1-5435-2961-6(5),* 138561); lib. bdg. 36.65 *(978-1-5435-2950-0(X),* 138539) Capstone. (Capstone Pr.).

Goldsworthy, Kaite. Magnetism. 2011. (J). (gr. 4-6). pap. 12.95 *(978-1-61690-732-7(0),* AV2 by Weigl); (Illus.). 24p. (YA). (gr. 3-6). 27.13 *(978-1-61690-728-0(2))* Weigl Pubs., Inc.

—Studying Magnetism. 2016. (Illus.). 24p. (J). *(978-1-5105-1126-2(1))* SmartBook Media, Inc.

Gray, Leon. Magnetism, 1 vol. 2013. (Physical Science Ser.). 48p. (J). (gr. 4-5). (ENG.). 34.61 *(978-1-4339-9516-3(6),* 30f0e607-e6bc-4316-a51c-07ec053e55bc); (ENG.). pap. 15.05 *(978-1-4339-9517-0(4),* ca3669a2-8db9-4652-b809-53a4c58d180a); pap. 84.30 *(978-1-4339-9518-7(2))* Stevens, Gareth Publishing LLLP.

Hagler, Gina. Magnets. 2016. (J). *(978-1-4896-5286-7(8))* Weigl Pubs., Inc.

Hansen, Grace. Magnetism. 2018. (Beginning Science Ser.). (ENG., Illus.). 24p. (J). (gr. -1-2). lib. bdg. 32.79 *(978-1-5321-0810-5(9),* 28181, Abdo Kids) ABDO Publishing Co.

Holt, Rinehart and Winston Staff. Holt Science & Technology Pt. N: Electricity & Magnetism. 3rd ed. 2003. (Holt Science & Technology Ser.). (SPA.). 18.60 *(978-0-03-069329-8(2))* Holt McDougal.

Jennings, Terry. Electricidad y Magnetismo (Electricity & Magnetism) (SPA.). 32p. (J). 6.95 *(978-84-348-1741-8(1))* SM Ediciones ESP. Dist: AIMS International Bks., Inc.

—Magnets. 2009. (Science Alive Ser.). (ENG., Illus.). 32p. (J). pap. *(978-1-897563-57-1(4))* Saunders Bk. Co.

Kenney, Karen Latchana. Magnetism Investigations. 2017. (Key Questions in Physical Science (Alternator Books (r)) Ser.). (ENG., Illus.). 32p. (J). (gr. 3-6). 29.32 *(978-1-5124-4005-8(1),* 6e61acbe-b52b-447b-a5ff-8e12ccab5247, Lerner Pubns.) Lerner Publishing Group.

Kessler, Colleen. A Project Guide to Electricity & Magnetism. 2011. (Physical Science Projects for Kids Ser.). (Illus.). 48p. (J). (gr. 3-6). lib. bdg. 29.95 *(978-1-58415-966-7(9),* 1327821) Mitchell Lane Pubs.

Lachner, Elizabeth. Magnetic Forces. (Science Kaleidoscope Ser.). 32p. (gr. 4-4). 2009. 47.90 *(978-1-60853-037-3(X),* PowerKids Pr.) 2008. (ENG.). pap. 10.00 *(978-1-4358-0155-4(5),* 96da62ce-67b1-4f76-b46a-a4ce66b0565f, Rosen Classroom) Rosen Publishing Group, Inc., The.

Lawrence, Ellen. Magnets. 2014. (Science Slam: FUN-Damentals Ser.). (ENG., Illus.). 24p. (J). (gr. -1-3). lib. bdg. 26.99 *(978-1-62724-312-4(7))* Bearport Publishing Co., Inc.

Loria, Laura. What is Magnetism?, 1 vol. 2014. (Let's Find Out! Physical Science Ser.). (ENG.). 32p. (J). (gr. 2-3). 26.06 *(978-1-62275-497-7(2),* 177d4c73-45e2-4860-a148-59342e4fd141) Rosen Publishing Group, Inc., The.

Madgwick, Wendy. Magnets & Sparks: 16 Easy-to-Follow Experiments for Learning Fun - Find Out How Electricity & Magnetism Works! 2014. (Illus.). 270p. (J). (gr. -1-12). 8.99 *(978-1-86147-352-3(4),* Armadillo) Anness Publishing GBR. Dist: National Bk. Network.

Magnetic Magic. 2007. (J). pap. *(978-1-59174-381-1(8))* Klutz.

Magnetism & Electricity. (Jump Ser.). (Illus.). 32p. (J). (gr. 2-7). pap. *(978-1-882210-27-5(1))* Action Publishing, Inc.

McGregor, Harriet. Magnets & Springs, 1 vol. 2010. (Sherlock Bones Looks at Physical Science Ser.). (ENG.). 32p. (YA). (gr. 5-5). lib. bdg. 29.93 *(978-1-61533-213-7(8),* eecdc225-5aae-4c01-aa31-190466a637b6, Windmill Bks.) Rosen Publishing Group, Inc., The.

McKinnon, Elaine. Magnets Are Fun!, 1 vol. 2013. (Rosen Readers Ser.). (ENG.). 24p. (J). (gr. 2-2). pap. 8.25 *(978-1-4777-2240-4(8),* 9882fa67-a371-4081-90cf-d19d58970cb7); pap. 49.50 *(978-1-4777-2241-1(6))* Rosen Publishing Group, Inc., The. (Rosen Classroom).

McMahon, Michael. Why Do Magnets Attract? Level 4 Factbook. 2010. (Cambridge Young Readers Ser.). (ENG., Illus.). 16p. pap. 6.00 *(978-0-521-13721-8(7))* Cambridge Univ. Pr.

Meiani, Antonella. Magnetism. 2003. (Experimenting with Science Ser.). (Illus.). 40p. (J). (gr. 4-8). lib. bdg. 23.93 *(978-0-8225-0085-8(X))* Lerner Publishing Group.

Merrill, Amy French. Everyday Physical Science Experiments with Magnetism, 1 vol. 2004. (Science Surprises Ser.). (ENG., Illus.). 24p. (J). (gr. 3-4). lib. bdg. 26.27 *(978-0-8239-5800-9(0),* 339eadb1-8d5c-434c-994b-a6282c2c3e95, PowerKids Pr.) Rosen Publishing Group, Inc., The.

National Geographic Learning. World Windows 3 (Science): Magnets: Content Literacy, Nonfiction Reading, Language & Literacy. 2011. (World Windows Ser.). (ENG., Illus.). 16p. (J). stu. ed. 10.95 *(978-1-133-49266-5(5))* Cengage Heinle.

Nelson, Robin. Los Imanes; Magnets. 2008. pap. 34.95 *(978-0-8225-9898-5(1))* Lerner Publishing Group.

—Magnets. 2005. (First Step Nonfiction Ser.). (Illus.). 24p. (J). (gr. k-2). lib. bdg. 18.60 *(978-0-8225-5132-4(2))* Lerner Publishing Group.

Newson, Lesley & Wadsworth, Pamela. Trydan a Magnetedd. 2005. (WEL., Illus.). 24p. pap *(978-1-85596-225-5(X))* Dref Wen.

Oxlade, Chris. Experiments with Electricity & Magnets, 1 vol. 2014. (Excellent Science Experiments Ser.). (ENG., Illus.). 32p. (J). (gr. 4-5). pap. 12.75 *(978-1-4777-5962-2(X),* 62787578-06c9-47df-97ef-aa4f4d0cd21d, PowerKids Pr.) Rosen Publishing Group, Inc., The.

Parker, Steve. Find Out about Magnets. 2013. (Illus.). 60p. (J). (gr. 2-7). mic. form 9.99 *(978-1-84322-895-0(5))* Anness Publishing GBR. Dist: National Bk. Network.

Petersen, Kristen. Understanding Forces of Nature: Gravity, Electricity, & Magnetism. 2015. (J). lib. bdg. *(978-1-62713-437-8(9))* Cavendish Square Publishing LLC.

Project Kit for Kids: Magnetism. 2004. (Illus.). 28p. pap. 19.99 *(978-0-9724983-1-9(1))* Jazwares Distribution, Inc.

Randolph, Ryan P. Robotics, 1 vol. 2009. (Science Kaleidoscope Ser.). (ENG.). 32p. (J). (gr. 4-4). lib. bdg. 28.93 *(978-1-4358-2986-2(7),* 6fd2cfd1-20b3-46f1-bc27-ba20063162f8, PowerKids Pr.) Rosen Publishing Group, Inc., The.

Rau, Dana Meachen. Electricity & Magnetism. 2009. (21st Century Skills Library: Real World Science Ser.). (ENG., Illus.). 32p. (gr. 4-8). lib. bdg. 32.07 *(978-1-60279-459-7(6),* 200236) Cherry Lake Publishing.

Riley, Peter. Forces & Magnets, 1 vol. 2016. (Moving up with Science Ser.). (ENG., Illus.). 32p. (J). (gr. 3-4). pap. 11.00 *(978-1-4994-3141-4(4),* ef92d4cc-1c8e-4d6a-a536-32c8a8d4c6c8, PowerKids Pr.) Rosen Publishing Group, Inc., The.

Rising, Trudy L. Is It Magnetic or Nonmagnetic? 2012. (ENG., Illus.). 24p. (J). *(978-0-7787-2050-8(0));* pap. *(978-0-7787-2057-7(8))* Crabtree Publishing Co.

Schuh, Mari. Magnetism. 2007. (First Science Ser.). (ENG., Illus.). 24p. (J). (gr. 2-5). lib. bdg. 26.95 *(978-1-60014-098-3(X))* Bellwether Media.

Schuh, Mari C. Blastoff Reader: Mafnetism. 2011. (Blastoff! Readers Ser.). (ENG.). 24p. (J). pap. 5.95 *(978-0-531-28456-8(5),* Children's Pr.) Scholastic Library Publishing.

Solway, Andrew. Exploring Electricity & Magnetism, 1 vol. 2007. (Exploring Physical Science Ser.). (ENG., Illus.). 48p. (YA). (gr. 6-6). lib. bdg. 34.47 *(978-1-4042-3749-0(6),* 8b47ad5e-9f11-4db6-a031-834cd44b54f5) Rosen Publishing Group, Inc., The.

Spilsbury, Louise. The Science of Magnetism, 1 vol. 2015. (Flowchart Smart Ser.). (ENG.). 48p. (J). (gr. 4-5). pap. 15.05 *(978-1-4824-4147-5(0),* 4978b44d-8361-4c93-ae4a-62e4a2e9c956) Stevens, Gareth Publishing LLLP.

Spilsbury, Louise & Spilsbury, Richard. Magnetism, 1 vol. 2013. (Essential Physical Science Ser.). (ENG.). 48p. (J). (gr. 4-6). pap. 9.95 *(978-1-4329-8157-0(9),* 123397, Heinemann) Capstone.

Spilsbury, Richard. Investigating Magnetism. 2018. (Investigating Science Challenges Ser.). (ENG., Illus.). 32p. (J). (gr. 4-4). *(978-0-7787-4208-1(3));* pap. *(978-0-7787-4312-5(8))* Crabtree Publishing Co.

Stanley, Joseph. Magnet Magic!, 1 vol. 2013. (InfoMax Readers Ser.). (ENG.). 24p. (J). (gr. 2-2). pap. 8.25 *(978-1-4777-2341-8(2),* 7d6f1af9-7184-4e13-9658-f9b367206bb9); pap. 49.50 *(978-1-4777-2343-2(9))* Rosen Publishing Group, Inc., The. (Rosen Classroom).

Stringer, John. Magnetism: An Investigation, 1 vol. 2007. (Science Investigations Ser.). (ENG., Illus.). 32p. (YA). (gr. 4-5). lib. bdg. 30.27 *(978-1-4042-4288-3(0),* 0c207025-02ec-4590-8de7-fa857c8961dd) Rosen Publishing Group, Inc., The.

Sundance/Newbridge LLC Staff. The Mystery of Magnets. 2007. (Early Science Ser.). (gr. k-3). 18.95 *(978-1-4007-6323-8(1));* pap. 6.10 *(978-1-4007-6319-1(3))* Sundance/Newbridge Educational Publishing.

Taylor-Butler, Christine. Experiments with Magnets & Metals, 1 vol. 2011. (My Science Investigations Ser.). (ENG.). 32p. (J). (gr. 1-3). pap. 8.29 *(978-1-4329-5365-2(6),* 116078, Heinemann) Capstone.

—Junior Scientists: Experiment with Magnets. 2010. (Explorer Junior Library: Science Explorer Junior Ser.). (ENG., Illus.). 32p. (gr. 3-6). lib. bdg. 32.07 *(978-1-60279-844-1(3),* 200554) Cherry Lake Publishing.

Top That Publishing Staff, ed. Magnet Science. 2004. (Top That! Labs Ser.). (Illus.). 24p. (J). *(978-1-84510-154-1(5))* Top That! Publishing PLC.

Wadsworth, Pamela. Golwg Gyntaf Ar Drydan a Magnetau. 2005. (WEL., Illus.). 24p. pap *(978-1-85596-255-2(1))* Dref Wen.

Walker, Sally M. Investigating Magnetism. 2011. (Searchlight Books (tm) — How Does Energy Work? Ser.). (ENG., Illus.). (gr. 3-5). 40p. (J). pap. 9.99 *(978-0-7613-7874-7(X),* 3f1e9b9a-d135-40ec-b1e5-51850cf608e6); 40p. (J). lib. bdg. 30.65 *(978-0-7613-5775-9(0),* 8fcb867f-1eff-4d61-9e2b-e34a66416cc9, Lerner Pubns.); pap. 51.01 *(978-0-7613-8408-3(1))* Lerner Publishing Group.

—Magnetism. 2006. (Illus.). 48p. (J). pap. 8.95 *(978-0-8225-2843-2(6))* Lerner Publishing Group.

—Magnetism. King, Andy, photos by. 2005. (Early Bird Energy Ser.). (ENG., Illus.). 48p. (gr. 2-5). lib. bdg. 26.60 *(978-0-8225-2932-3(7),* Lerner Pubns.) Lerner Publishing Group.

—El Magnetismo. Translations.com Staff, tr. from ENG. King, Andy, photos by. 2007. (Libros de Energía para madrugadores (Early Bird Energy) Ser.). (SPA., Illus.). 48p. (J). (gr. 2-5). lib. bdg. 26.60 *(978-0-8225-7720-1(8))* Lerner Publishing Group.

—El Magnetismo; Magnetism. 2008. pap. 52.95 *(978-0-8225-9778-0(0))* Lerner Publishing Group.

Weakland, Mark. Magnets Push, Magnets Pull. 2010. (Science Starts Ser.). (ENG.). 32p. (J). (gr. 1-2). pap. 48.60 *(978-1-4296-6148-5(8),* 16037, Capstone Pr.); (Illus.). (gr. -1-2). pap. 8.10 *(978-1-4296-6147-8(X),* 115297) Capstone.

—What Is Magnetism? 2019. (Science Basics Ser.). (ENG., Illus.). 24p. (J). (gr. 1-3). pap. 7.95 *(978-1-9771-0510-3(6),* 139899, Capstone Pr.) Capstone.

Weakland, Mark & Bros., Warner. Clang! Wile E. Coyote Experiments with Magnetism. Billiau, Loic & Sordo, Paco, illus. 2017. (Wile E. Coyote, Physical Science Genius Ser.). (ENG.). 32p. (J). (gr. 3-5). lib. bdg. 31.32 *(978-1-5157-3731-5(4),* 133675, Capstone Pr.) Capstone.

Woodford, Chris. Experiments with Electricity & Magnetism, 1 vol. 2010. (Cool Science Ser.). (ENG., Illus.). 32p. (J). (gr. 4-5). pap. 11.50 *(978-1-4339-3445-2(0),* e24803d7-ad45-4777-b1b6-40c01e2267b2); lib. bdg. 30.67 *(978-1-4339-3444-5(2),* 1c799b41-836f-410d-bb27-b92337ce061d) Stevens, Gareth Publishing LLLP. (Gareth Stevens Learning Library).

World Book, Inc. Staff, contrib. by. Magnetism. 2011. (Illus.). 32p. (J). *(978-0-7166-1427-2(8))* World Bk., Inc.

MAGNETS

see also Electromagnets

Adler, David A. Magnets Push, Magnets Pull. Raff, Anna, illus. 2018. 32p. (J). (gr. k-3). pap. 8.99 *(978-0-8234-4018-4(4))* Holiday Hse., Inc.

Alpert, Barbara. A Look at Magnets. 2011. (Science Builders Ser.). (ENG.). 24p. (J). (gr. k-1). pap. 43.74 *(978-1-4296-7115-6(7),* 16696, Capstone Pr.) Capstone.

Anderson, Lynne. Fun with Magnets. 2011. (Early Connections Ser.). (J). *(978-1-61672-622-5(9))* Benchmark Education Co.

Ballard, Carol. Exploring Magnets & Springs, 1 vol. 2007. (How Does Science Work? Ser.). (ENG., Illus.). 32p. (J). (gr. 2-3). lib. bdg. 30.27 *(978-1-4042-4282-1(1),* 650b4e1d-f8e7-4dce-a98d-f0b3bfd782c0) Rosen Publishing Group, Inc., The.

Bernhardt, Carolyn. Magnetism. 2018. (Science Starters Ser.). (ENG., Illus.). 24p. (J). (gr. k-3). lib. bdg. 26.95 *(978-1-62617-809-0(7),* Blastoff! Readers) Bellwether Media.

Bodach, Vijaya Khisty. Magnets. 2008. (Discovering & Exploring Science Ser.). (Illus.). 16p. (J). (gr. -1-3). lib. bdg. 12.95 *(978-0-7569-8429-8(7))* Perfection Learning Corp.

Bradley, Doug. Magnets in My World, 1 vol. 2008. (Real Life Readers Ser.). (ENG.). 16p. (gr. 2-3). pap. 7.05 *(978-1-4358-0063-2(X),* b97d98af-6a0e-4398-8eff-fecd617fbb6a, Rosen Classroom) Rosen Publishing Group, Inc., The.

Branley, Franklyn M. What Makes a Magnet? Kelley, True, illus. rev. ed. 2016. (Let's-Read-And-Find-Out Science 2 Ser.). (ENG.). 32p. (J). (gr. -1-3). pap. 6.99 *(978-0-06-233801-3(3),* HarperCollins) HarperCollins Pubs.

—What Makes a Magnet? 2016. (Let's-Read-And-Find-Out Science: Stage 2 Ser.). (J). lib. bdg. 17.20 *(978-0-606-38144-4(9))* Turtleback.

Bryan, Dale-Marie. Experiments with Magnets. 2011. (True Bk Ser.). (Illus.). 48p. (J). (ENG.). pap. 6.95 *(978-0-531-26645-8(1));* lib. bdg. 29.00 *(978-0-531-26345-7(2))* Scholastic Library Publishing. (Children's Pr.).

Burton, Margie, et al. Using Magnets. 2011. (Early Connections Ser.). (J). *(978-1-61672-311-8(4))* Benchmark Education Co.

Cavell-Clarke, Steffi. Magnets. (First Science Ser.). (J). (gr. 1-1). 2017. pap. 49.50 *(978-1-5345-2077-6(5))* 2016. (ENG.). 24p. pap. 9.25 *(978-1-5345-2076-9(7),* 04012681-7775-4f1d-bba3-bf56465f7aed) 2016. (ENG.). 24p. lib. bdg. 26.23 *(978-1-5345-2078-3(3),* fb778daf-450c-4b25-ada6-e9447276a718) Greenhaven Publishing LLC. (KidHaven Publishing).

Dinmont, Kerry. Maria's Magic Magnet: A Book about Magnets. 2017. (My Day Readers Ser.). (ENG.). 24p. (J). (gr. -1-2). lib. bdg. 32.79 *(978-1-5038-2033-3(5),* 211866) Child's World, Inc, The.

Doherty, Paul & Cassidy, John. Magia Magnetica. 2005. (SPA., Illus.). 68p. (J). spiral bd. 15.95 *(978-987-1078-40-0(4))* Klutz Latino MEX. Dist: Independent Pubs. Group.

Dunne, Abbie. Magnetism. 2016. (Physical Science Ser.). (ENG., Illus.). 24p. (J). (gr. -1-2). lib. bdg. 27.32 *(978-1-5157-0938-1(8),* 132237, Capstone Pr.) Capstone.

Edom, H. Science Activities, Vol. 1. 2010. (Science Activities Ser.). 72p. (J). 13.99 *(978-0-7945-2752-5(3),* Usborne) EDC Publishing.

Electricidad e Imanes. (Coleccion Jugando Con la Ciencia). (SPA., Illus.). 39p. (J). pap. 9.95 *(978-950-11-0828-6(7),* SGM309) Sigmar ARG. Dist: Continental Bk. Co., Inc.

Endres, Hollie J. The Letter Tt Set: Magnets, 6 vols. 2004. (Letter Bks.). (ENG.). 8p. (gr. k-1). pap. 29.70 *(978-0-7368-4119-1(9))* Capstone.

Forest, Christopher. Focus on Magnetism. 2017. (Hands-On STEM Ser.). (ENG., Illus.). 32p. (J). (gr. 2-3). pap. 9.95 *(978-1-63517-350-5(7),* 1635173507); lib. bdg. 31.35 *(978-1-63517-285-0(3),* 1635172853) North Star Editions. (Focus Readers).

French, Cathy. People Who Use Magnets at Work. 2011. (Early Connections Ser.). (J). *(978-1-61672-241-8(X))* Benchmark Education Co.

Gianopoulos, Andrea. The Attractive Story of Magnetism with Max Axiom Super Scientist: 4D an Augmented Reading Science Experience. Martin, Cynthia, illus. 2018. (Graphic Science 4D Ser.). (ENG.). 32p. (J). (gr. 3-9). pap. 7.95 *(978-1-5435-2961-6(5),* 138561); lib. bdg. 36.65 *(978-1-5435-2950-0(X),* 138539) Capstone. (Capstone Pr.).

Hagler, Gina. Magnets. 2016. (J). *(978-1-4896-5286-7(8))* Weigl Pubs., Inc.

Hedde, Rebecca. Science with Magnets. rev. ed. 2008. (Science Activities Ser.). 24p. (J). pap. 5.99 *(978-0-7945-1406-8(5),* Usborne) EDC Publishing.

Higgins, Nadia. Mighty Magnet Site CD+Book. Martinez Ricci, Andres, illus. 2010. (Science Rocks! Set 2 Site CD+Book Ser.). 32p. lib. bdg. 84.14 incl. cd-rom *(978-1-61641-011-7(6))* ABDO Publishing Co.

Jennings, Terry. Magnets. 2009. (Science Alive Ser.). (ENG., Illus.). 32p. (J). pap. *(978-1-897563-57-1(4))* Saunders Bk. Co.

Kenney, Karen Latchana. Magnets. 2010. (Everyday Science Ser.). (ENG.). 24p. (J). (gr. k-2). lib. bdg. 25.65 *(978-1-60753-019-0(8),* 17135) Amicus.

—Super Simple Magnets: Fun & Easy-to-Make Crafts for Kids, 1 vol. 2009. (Super Simple Crafts Ser.). (ENG., Illus.). 32p. (J). (gr. -1-4). 34.21 *(978-1-60453-626-3(8),* 13934, Super SandCastle) ABDO Publishing Co.

Lawrence, Ellen. Magnets. 2014. (Science Slam: FUN-Damentals Ser.). (ENG., Illus.). 24p. (J). (gr. -1-3). lib. bdg. 26.99 *(978-1-62724-312-4(7))* Bearport Publishing Co., Inc.

McGregor, Harriet. Magnets & Springs, 1 vol. 2010. (Sherlock Bones Looks at Physical Science Ser.). (ENG.). 32p. (YA). (gr. 5-5). lib. bdg. 29.93 *(978-1-61533-213-7(8),* eecdc225-5aae-4c01-aa31-190466a637b6, Windmill Bks.) Rosen Publishing Group, Inc., The.

McKinnon, Elaine. Magnets Are Fun!, 1 vol. 2013. (Rosen Readers Ser.). (ENG.). 24p. (J). (gr. 2-2). pap. 8.25 *(978-1-4777-2240-4(8),* 9882fa67-a371-4081-90cf-d19d58970cb7); pap. 49.50 *(978-1-4777-2241-1(6))* Rosen Publishing Group, Inc., The. (Rosen Classroom).

National Geographic Learning. Reading Expeditions (Science: Physical Science): the Mystery of Magnets. 2007. (Nonfiction Reading & Writing Workshops Ser.). (ENG., Illus.). 32p. (J). pap. 18.95 *(978-0-7922-4581-0(4))* CENGAGE Learning.

—World Windows 3 (Science): Magnets: Content Literacy, Nonfiction Reading, Language & Literacy. 2011. (World Windows Ser.). (ENG., Illus.). 16p. (J). stu. ed. 10.95 *(978-1-133-49266-5(5))* Cengage Heinle.

Nelson, Robin. Los Imanes. Translations.com Staff, tr. from ENG. 2007. (Mi Primer Paso Al Mundo Real - Fuerzas y Movimiento (First Step Nonfiction - Forces & Motion) Ser.).Tr. of Magnets. (SPA., Illus.). 24p. (gr. k-2). lib. bdg. 23.93 *(978-0-8225-7809-3(3),* Ediciones Lerner) Lerner Publishing Group.

—Los Imanes; Magnets. 2008. pap. 34.95 *(978-0-8225-9898-5(1))* Lerner Publishing Group.

—Magnets. 2005. (First Step Nonfiction Ser.). (Illus.). 24p. (J). (gr. k-2). lib. bdg. 18.60 *(978-0-8225-5132-4(2))* Lerner Publishing Group.

Publications International Ltd. Staff, ed. Baby Faces. 2011. 10p. (J). bds. 12.98 *(978-1-4508-1404-1(2))* Phoenix International Publications, Inc.

Roman, Nora. Using Magnets, 1 vol. 2017. (Super Science Tools Ser.). (ENG.). 24p. (J). (gr. 1-2). pap. 9.15 *(978-1-4824-6393-4(8),* 69700df2-d95c-412d-a78d-9f7a81cfdf2d) Stevens, Gareth Publishing LLLP.

Schuh, Mari C. Blastoff Reader: Mafnetism. 2011. (Blastoff! Readers Ser.). (ENG.). 24p. (J). pap. 5.95 *(978-0-531-28456-8(5),* Children's Pr.) Scholastic Library Publishing.

Science with Magnets Kid Kit. 2004. (Kid Kits Ser.). (Illus.). 24p. (J). 14.95 *(978-1-58086-420-6(1))* EDC Publishing.

Sian Revision Magnet Magic. 2004. (Science in A Nutshell Ser.). (J). *(978-1-59242-043-8(5))* Delta Education, LLC.

Stanley, Joseph. Magnet Magic!, 1 vol. 2013. (InfoMax Readers Ser.). (ENG.). 24p. (J). (gr. 2-2). pap. 8.25 *(978-1-4777-2341-8(2),* 7d6f1af9-7184-4e13-9658-f9b367206bb9); pap. 49.50 *(978-1-4777-2343-2(9))* Rosen Publishing Group, Inc., The. (Rosen Classroom).

Stringer, John. Magnetism: An Investigation, 1 vol. 2007. (Science Investigations Ser.). (ENG., Illus.). 32p. (YA). (gr. 4-5). lib. bdg. 30.27 *(978-1-4042-4288-3(0),* 0c207025-02ec-4590-8de7-fa857c8961dd) Rosen Publishing Group, Inc., The.

Sundance/Newbridge LLC Staff. The Mystery of Magnets. 2007. (Early Science Ser.). (gr. k-3). 18.95 *(978-1-4007-6323-8(1));* pap. 6.10 *(978-1-4007-6319-1(3))* Sundance/Newbridge Educational Publishing.

Taylor-Butler, Christine. Magnets. 2009. (Explorer Library: Science Explorer Ser.). (ENG., Illus.). 32p. (gr. 4-8). lib. bdg. 32.07 *(978-1-60279-530-3(4),* 200296) Cherry Lake Publishing.

—Super Cool Science Experiments: Magnets. 2009. (Explorer Library: Science Explorer Ser.). (ENG., Illus.). 32p. (gr. 4-8). pap. 14.21 *(978-1-60279-609-6(2),* 200895) Cherry Lake Publishing.

Troupe, Thomas Kingsley. Magnet Power! Science Adventures with MAG-3000 the Origami Robot, 1 vol. Christoph, Jamey, illus. 2013. (Origami Science Adventures Ser.). (ENG.). 24p. (J). (gr. -1-3). pap. 6.95 *(978-1-4048-8070-2(4),* 121841, Picture Window Bks.) Capstone.

Walker, Sally M. Investigating Magnetism. 2011. (Searchlight Books (tm) — How Does Energy Work? Ser.). (ENG., Illus.). (gr. 3-5). 40p. (J). pap. 9.99 *(978-0-7613-7874-7(X),* 3f1e9b9a-d135-40ec-b1e5-51850cf608e6); 40p. (J). lib. bdg. 30.65 *(978-0-7613-5775-9(0),* 8fcb867f-1eff-4d61-9e2b-e34a66416cc9, Lerner Pubns.); pap. 51.01 *(978-0-7613-8408-3(1))* Lerner Publishing Group.

—Magnetism. King, Andy, photos by. 2005. (Early Bird Energy Ser.). (ENG., Illus.). 48p. (gr. 2-5). lib. bdg. 26.60 *(978-0-8225-2932-3(7),* Lerner Pubns.) Lerner Publishing Group.

—El Magnetismo. Translations.com Staff, tr. from ENG. King, Andy, photos by. 2007. (Libros de Energía para madrugadores (Early Bird Energy) Ser.). (SPA., Illus.). 48p. (J). (gr. 2-5). lib. bdg. 26.60 *(978-0-8225-7720-1(8))* Lerner Publishing Group.

—El Magnetismo; Magnetism. 2008. pap. 52.95 *(978-0-8225-9778-0(0))* Lerner Publishing Group.

Weakland, Mark. Magnets Push, Magnets Pull. 2010. (Science Starts Ser.). (ENG.). 32p. (J). (gr. 1-2). pap. 48.60 *(978-1-4296-6148-5(8),* 16037, Capstone Pr.); (Illus.). (gr. -1-2). pap. 8.10 *(978-1-4296-6147-8(X),* 115297) Capstone.

MAGPIES—FICTION

Anholt, Laurence & Coplestone, Jim. Seven for a Secret. 2006. (ENG., Illus.). 32p. (J). pap. *(978-1-84507-590-3(0),* White Lion Publishing) Quarto Publishing Group UK.

Long, Jan. Azule & the White Hummingbird: The Birth of the White Hummingbird. 2014. (Illus.). 84p. (J). pap. 9.95 *(978-1-63047-171-2(2))* Morgan James Publishing.

Restrepo, Bettina. Moose & Magpie, 1 vol. Rogers, Sherry, illus. 2009. (ENG.). 32p. (J). (gr. -1-3). 16.95 *(978-1-934359-97-6(1));* pap. 9.95 *(978-1-60718-042-5(1))* Arbordale Publishing.

Slater, Kate. Magpie's Treasure. Slater, Kate, illus. 2012. (ENG., Illus.). 32p. (J). (gr. -1 — 1). pap. 10.99 *(978-1-84939-075-0(4))* Andersen Pr. GBR. Dist: Independent Pubs. Group.

Springman, I. C. More. Lies, Brian, illus. 2019. (ENG.). 40p. (J). (gr. -1-3). pap. 7.99 *(978-0-358-11790-2(9),* 1750732, Clarion Bks.) HarperCollins Pubs.

Von Michaelis, Carol. Magpie Grows Up. 2012. 16p. pap. 15.99 *(978-1-4772-6115-6(X))* AuthorHouse.

MAINE

Brown, Jonatha A. Maine, 1 vol. 2006. (Portraits of the States Ser.). (ENG.). 32p. (gr. 3-5). pap. 11.50 *(978-0-8368-4718-5(0),* 743dbaba-c467-484c-80ec-9a145d10b543); (Illus.). lib. bdg. 28.67 *(978-0-8368-4701-7(6),* d5bbad0a-8caa-4061-89a2-195cc7e1070d) Stevens, Gareth Publishing LLLP. (Gareth Stevens Learning Library).

Cossette, Julie, illus. Maine Monsters: A Search & Find Book. 2018. (ENG.). 22p. (J). (gr. -1). bds. 9.99 *(978-2-924734-14-8(2))* City Monsters Bks. CAN. Dist: Publishers Group West (PGW).

Craig, Janet. Maine, 1 vol. 2003. (World Almanac(r) Library of the States Ser.). (ENG., Illus.). 48p. (gr. 4-6). pap. 15.05 *(978-0-8368-5322-3(9),* c81b495d-c911-47f5-a040-c6ffc376a5b9); lib. bdg. 33.67 *(978-0-8368-5151-9(X),* db11ef54-c923-4cf8-9ae9-4a1c095d8f15) Stevens, Gareth Publishing LLLP. (Gareth Stevens Learning Library).

Dean, Carol. The Hen House: A True Story of Growing up on a Maine Farm. Dunn, Sandy, illus. 2003. (ENG.). 32p. (J). (gr. -1-k). 15.95 *(978-0-89272-609-7(1))* Down East Bks.

Deinard, Jenny. How to Draw Maine's Sights & Symbols. 2009. (Kid's Guide to Drawing America Ser.). 32p. (gr. k-k). 50.50 *(978-1-61511-068-1(2),* PowerKids Pr.) Rosen Publishing Group, Inc., The.

Dornfeld, Margaret & Hart, Joyce. Maine, 1 vol. 2nd rev. ed. 2010. (Celebrate the States (Second Edition) Ser.). (ENG.). 144p. (gr. 6-6). 39.79 *(978-0-7614-4726-9(1),* bff7ec88-34a3-4ec6-82f2-2f393182440f) Cavendish Square Publishing LLC.

Engfer, LeeAnne. Maine. 2nd exp. rev. ed. 2003. (Hello U. S. A. Ser.). (Illus.). 84p. (J). (gr. 3-6). pap. 6.95 *(978-0-8225-4138-7(6))* Lerner Publishing Group.

Exploring Acadia National Park: Solve Problems Involving the Four Operations, 1 vol. 2014. (Rosen Math Readers Ser.). (ENG., Illus.). 24p. (J). (gr. 3-3). pap. 8.25 *(978-1-4777-4944-9(6),* 1703e656-a406-480c-96b7-6d85916d16ec, PowerKids Pr.) Rosen Publishing Group, Inc., The.

Fendler, Donn & Egan, Joseph. Lost on a Mountain in Maine. 2013. (ENG., Illus.). 112p. (J). (gr. 3-7). pap. 9.99 *(978-0-688-11573-9(X),* HarperCollins) HarperCollins Pubs.

Foran, Jill. Maine. 2011. (Guide to American States Ser.). (Illus.). 48p. (YA). (gr. 3-6). 29.99 *(978-1-61690-791-4(6));* (J). 29.99 *(978-1-61690-467-8(4))* Weigl Pubs., Inc.

Garry, J. W. Storm's Maine Vacation. 2011. 48p. pap. 17.50 *(978-1-4567-2874-8(1))* AuthorHouse.

Hansen, Grace. Acadia National Park. 2018. (National Parks (Abdo Kids Jumbo) Ser.). (ENG., Illus.). 24p. (J). (gr. -1-2). lib. bdg. 32.79 *(978-1-5321-8205-1(8),* 29869, Abdo Kids) ABDO Publishing Co.

Heinrichs, Ann. America the Beautiful, Third Series: Maine (Revised Edition) 2014. (America the Beautiful Ser.: 3). (ENG.). 144p. (J). lib. bdg. 40.00 *(978-0-531-24887-4(9))* Scholastic Library Publishing.

—Maine. Kania, Matt, illus. 2017. (U. S. A. Travel Guides). (ENG.). 40p. (J). (gr. 2-5). lib. bdg. 38.50 *(978-1-5038-1959-7(0),* 211596) Child's World, Inc, The.

Hicks, Terry Allan. Maine, 1 vol. Santoro, Christopher, illus. 2006. (It's My State! (First Edition)(r) Ser.). (ENG.). 80p. (gr. 4-4). lib. bdg. 34.07 *(978-0-7614-1910-5(1),* dc3ebf47-20ed-42a8-864f-2ee6fd9c4dfd) Cavendish Square Publishing LLC.

—Maine, 1 vol. 2nd rev. ed. 2013. (It's My State! (Second Edition)(r) Ser.). (ENG.). 80p. (gr. 4-4). pap. 18.64 *(978-1-62712-094-4(7),* b5190359-621a-4918-88be-616588d3cb02) Cavendish Square Publishing LLC.

Marsh, Carole. Maine Current Events Projects: 30 Cool, Activities, Crafts, Experiments & More for Kids to Do to Learn about Your State! 2003. (Maine Experience Ser.). 32p. (gr. k-8). pap. 5.95 *(978-0-635-02038-3(6),* Marsh, Carole Bks.) Gallopade International.

—Maine Geography Projects: 30 Cool, Activities, Crafts, Experiments & More for Kids to Do to Learn about Your State! 2003. (Maine Experience Ser.). 32p. (gr. k-5). pap. 5.95 *(978-0-635-01838-0(1),* Marsh, Carole Bks.) Gallopade International.

—Maine Government Projects: 30 Cool, Activities, Crafts, Experiments & More for Kids to Do to Learn about Your State! 2003. (Maine Experience Ser.). 32p. (gr. k-5). pap. 5.95 *(978-0-635-01938-7(8),* Marsh, Carole Bks.) Gallopade International.

—Maine People Projects: 30 Cool, Activities, Crafts, Experiments & More for Kids to Do to Learn about Your State! 2003. (Maine Experience Ser.). 32p. (gr. k-5). pap. 5.95 *(978-0-635-01988-2(4),* Marsh, Carole Bks.) Gallopade International.

—Maine Symbols & Facts Projects: 30 Cool, Activities, Crafts, Experiments & More for Kids to Do to Learn about Your State! 2003. (Maine Experience Ser.). 32p. (gr. k-5). pap. 5.95 *(978-0-635-01888-5(8),* Marsh, Carole Bks.) Gallopade International.

Murray, Julie. Maine, 1 vol. 2006. (United States Ser.). (ENG., Illus.). 32p. (gr. 2-4). 27.07 *(978-1-59197-678-3(2),* Buddy Bks.) ABDO Publishing Co.

Obregon, Jose Maria. Maine, 1 vol. Brusca, Maria Cristina, tr. 2005. (Bilingual Library of the United States of America Ser.: Set 1). (ENG & SPA., Illus.). 32p. (J). (gr. 2-2). lib. bdg. 28.93 *(978-1-4042-3084-2(X),* 7e9c3c16-1eec-4e5b-b35b-ce2bd2473734) Rosen Publishing Group, Inc., The.

Obregón, José María. Maine. 2009. (Bilingual Library of the United States of America Ser.). (ENG & SPA.). 32p. (gr. 2-2). 47.90 *(978-1-60853-364-0(6),* Editorial Buenas Letras) Rosen Publishing Group, Inc., The.

OGINTZ, Eileen. Kids Guide to Maine. 2018. (Illus.). 144p. (J). (gr. k-5). pap. 14.95 *(978-1-60893-982-4(0))* Down East Bks.

Peterson, Sheryl. Maine. 2008. (This Land Called America Ser.). 32p. (YA). (gr. 3-6). 22.95 *(978-1-58341-644-0(7))* Creative Co., The.

Reynolds, Cynthia Furlong. Fishing for Numbers: A Maine Number Book. Brett, Jeannie, illus. 2005. (America by the Numbers Ser.). (ENG.). 40p. (J). (gr. 1-3). 19.99 *(978-1-58536-035-2(X),* 201953) Sleeping Bear Pr.

Roop, Peter & Roop, Connie. Down East in the Ocean: A Maine Counting Book. 2011. (ENG., Illus.). 32p. (J). (gr. -1-12). 16.95 *(978-0-89272-709-4(8))* Down East Bks.

—The Stormy Adventure of Abbie Burgess, Lighthouse Keeper. 2010. pap. 51.02 *(978-0-7613-6922-6(8))* Lerner Publishing Group.

Rowan, Hope. Ten Days in the North Woods: A Kids' Hiking Guide to the Katahdin Region. Fitch, Jada, illus. 2019. (ENG.). 104p. (J). pap. 12.95 *(978-1-944762-64-3(7),* be9835ea-43a4-48ef-aa16-0a0e586681e4) Islandport Pr., Inc.

Walker, Cynthia. Maine. 2005. (Rookie Read-About Geography Ser.). (ENG., Illus.). 32p. (J). (gr. 1-2). lib. bdg. 20.50 *(978-0-516-25255-1(0),* Children's Pr.) Scholastic Library Publishing.

MAINE—FICTION

Aldridge, Janet. The Meadow-Brook Girls in the Hills: Or the Missing Pilot of the White Mountains. 2006. pap. *(978-1-4065-0694-5(X))* Dodo Pr.

Arenstam, Peter. Nicholas, a Maine Tale. Holman, Karen Busch, illus. 2015. (Nicholas Northeastern Ser.: 2). 166p. (J). (gr. k-7). pap. 8.95 *(978-1-938170-67-6(9),* Mitten Pr.) Ann Arbor Editions LLC.

Austin, Heather. Boatyard Ducklings. Austin, Heather, illus. 2008. (ENG., Illus.). 32p. (J). (gr. -1-3). 15.95 *(978-0-89272-663-9(6))* Down East Bks.

Banghart, Tracy E. What the Sea Wants. Blum, Julia C., illus. 2006. 64p. (YA). kivar 16.00 *(978-0-9779753-0-3(4))* LizStar Bks.

Beston, Henry. Chimney Farm Bedtime Stories. 2006. (Illus.). 80p. (J). pap. 13.95 *(978-0-942396-93-5(6))* Blackberry Maine.

Birdsall, Jeanne. The Penderwicks at Point Mouette. 2011. (Playaway Children Ser.). (J). (gr. k). 44.99 *(978-1-61707-434-9(9))* Findaway World, LLC.

—The Penderwicks at Point Mouette. (Penderwicks Ser.: 3). (ENG.). (J). (gr. 3-7). 2012. 320p. 8.99 *(978-0-375-85135-3(6),* Yearling) 2011. 304p. 16.99 *(978-0-375-85851-2(2),* Knopf Bks. for Young Readers) Random Hse. Children's Bks.

Blakemore, Megan Frazer. The Water Castle. 2014. (ENG.). 368p. (YA). (gr. 3-8). pap. 9.99 *(978-0-8027-3593-5(2),* 900123283, Bloomsbury USA Childrens) Bloomsbury Publishing USA.

Blume, Judy. Fudge-A-Mania. 2007. (ENG.). 176p. (J). (gr. 3-7). 8.99 *(978-0-14-240877-3(8),* Puffin Books) Penguin Young Readers Group.

Blumstein, Amy Beth. Jamie & Tallulah. 2009. 16p. pap. 12.00 *(978-1-4389-3997-1(3))* AuthorHouse.

Boat, Patty. A Disappointing Homecoming: (A Soldier's Story), 1 vol. 2009. 158p. pap. 24.95 *(978-1-61546-997-0(4))* PublishAmerica, Inc.

Brewer, Sarah. Our New Garden. Brewer, Sarah & Brewer, Dean, illus. 2013. 20p. pap. 24.95 *(978-1-63004-768-9(6))* America Star Bks.

Brown, Margaret Wise. The Little Island: (Caldecott Medal Winner) Weisgard, Leonard, illus. 2003. (ENG.). 48p. (J). (gr. -1-2). 18.99 *(978-0-385-74640-3(7),* Doubleday Bks. for Young Readers) Random Hse. Children's Bks.

Carter, Herbert. The Boy Scouts on the Trail or Scouting. 2005. pap. 27.95 *(978-1-885529-56-5(2))* Stevens Publishing.

Castonguay, Leo. Piper Peter. 2012. 44p. 24.95 *(978-1-4626-8604-9(4));* pap. 24.95 *(978-1-4626-8078-8(X))* America Star Bks.

Chenette, Roseanne V. Shellaby Willowbee. 2008. 13p. pap. 24.95 *(978-1-60672-137-7(2))* America Star Bks.

Clough, Lisa. Country Girl, City Girl. 2009. (ENG.). 192p. (YA). (gr. 7). pap. 12.95 *(978-0-547-22322-3(6),* 1061786, Clarion Bks.) HarperCollins Pubs.

Copeland, Cynthia L. Elin's Island. 2003. (Single Titles Ser.: up). (ENG.). 144p. (YA). (gr. 6-12). lib. bdg. 22.60 *(978-0-7613-2522-2(0),* Millbrook Pr.) Lerner Publishing Group.

Cornwell, Betsy. Tides. 2014. (ENG.). 304p. (YA). (gr. 7). pap. 8.99 *(978-0-544-30296-9(6),* 1578441, Clarion Bks.) HarperCollins Pubs.

Cotler, Steve. Cheesie Mack Is Cool in a Duel. McCauley, Adam, illus. 2013. (Cheesie Mack Ser.: 2). 240p. (J). (gr. 3-7). 7.99 *(978-0-375-86395-0(8),* Yearling) Random Hse. Children's Bks.

Cowan, Charlotte. Moose with Loose Poops. Neal, Penelope, illus. 2008. (Dr. Hippo Ser.). (ENG.). 32p. (J). (gr. -1-2). 17.95 *(978-0-9753516-5-9(6))* Hippocratic Pr., The.

Creech, Sharon. Moo. 2018. (Penworthy Picks Middle School Ser.). (ENG.). 278p. (J). (gr. 5-7). 17.96 *(978-1-64310-363-1(6))* Penworthy Co., LLC, The.

—Moo. 2017. (J). lib. bdg. 17.20 *(978-0-606-40402-0(3))* Turtleback.

—Moo: A Novel. (ENG.). 288p. (J). (gr. 3-7). 2017. pap. 9.99 *(978-0-06-241526-4(3))* 2016. 16.99 *(978-0-06-241524-0(7))* 2016. lib. bdg. 17.89 *(978-0-06-241525-7(5))* HarperCollins Pubs. (HarperCollins).

Cross, Mimi. Shining Sea, 0 vols. 2016. (ENG.). 432p. (YA). (gr. 9-12). pap. 9.99 *(978-1-5039-3553-2(1),* 9781503935532, Skyscape) Amazon Publishing.

Crossman, D. A. The Legend of Burial Island: A Bean & Ab Mystery. 2009. (J). pap. *(978-0-89272-812-1(4))* Down East Bks.

Crossman, David. The Legend of Burial Island: A Bean & Ab Mystery. 2009. 201p. (J). (gr. 3-7). pap. 11.95 *(978-0-89272-797-1(7))* Down East Bks.

Crowley, Peter. J T Seavey. 2012. (ENG.). 35p. (J). pap. 18.95 *(978-1-4327-8712-7(8))* Outskirts Pr., Inc.

Curtis, Alice Turner. A Little Maid of Old Maine. 2018. (ENG., Illus.). 124p. (YA). (gr. 7-12). pap. *(978-93-5297-436-8(0))* Alpha Editions.

Day, Karen. A Million Miles from Boston. 2012. (ENG.). 224p. (J). (gr. 4-6). lib. bdg. 21.19 *(978-0-385-90763-7(X),* Lamb, Wendy Bks.) Random Hse. Children's Bks.

Draper, Rochelle. The Stone Wall Dragon. Draper, Rochelle, illus. 2007. (ENG., Illus.). 32p. (J). (gr. 1-17). 15.95 *(978-0-89272-690-5(3))* Down East Bks.

Eaton, Walter Prichard. Boy Scouts in the White Mountains: the Story of a Long Hike. Merrill, Frank T., illus. 2006. (ENG.). 316p. per. 30.95 *(978-1-4286-4117-4(3))* Kessinger Publishing, LLC.

Edwards, Nicholas. Dog Whisperer: the Rescue: The Rescue. 2009. (Dog Whisperer Ser.: 1). (ENG.). 224p. (J). (gr. 3-7). pap. 10.99 *(978-0-312-36768-8(6),* 900042450) Square Fish.

Emerson, Alice B. Ruth Fielding on Cliff Island: Or, the Old Hunter's Treasure Box. 2017. (ENG., Illus.). (J). 22.95 *(978-1-374-83808-6(X))* Capital Communications, Inc.

Farish, Terry. The Good Braider, 0 vols. 2013. (ENG.). 224p. (YA). (gr. 7-12). pap. 9.99 *(978-1-4778-1628-8(3),* 9781477816288, Skyscape) Amazon Publishing.

—The Good Braider. 2014. (ENG.). 221p. (YA). (gr. 9-12). lib. bdg. 21.80 *(978-1-5311-8306-6(9))* Perfection Learning Corp.

Fendler, Donn & Plourde, Lynn. Lost Trail: Nine Days Alone in the Wilderness, 1 vol. Bishop, Ben, illus. 2011. (ENG.). 72p. (J). (gr. 4-7). pap. 14.95 *(978-0-89272-945-6(7))* Down East Bks.

Fields, Cassidy. Disaster Lake. 2011. 28p. pap. 16.09 *(978-1-4269-6053-6(0))* Trafford Publishing.

Flint, Garrison. The Butler Did It! A Raymond Masrters Mystery. 2003. (Raymond Masters Mystery: 10). 206p. per. 13.99 *(978-1-885631-72-5(3))* Hutchison, G.F. Pr.

Francis, Lee DeCora. Kunu's Basket: A Story of Indian Island, 1 vol. Drucker, Susan, illus. 2012. (ENG.). 32p. (J). 16.95 *(978-0-88448-330-4(4))* Tilbury Hse. Pubs.

French, Gillian. The Door to January, 1 vol. 2nd ed. 2019. (ENG.). 212p. (YA). pap. 14.95 *(978-1-944762-61-2(2),* bfd61ab4-190b-41be-a973-f62e0568c1f7) Islandport Pr., Inc.

Frey, Hildegard G. The Camp Fire Girls in the Maine Woods: Or the Winnebagos Go Camping. 2007. (ENG.). 152p. pap. 19.99 *(978-1-4264-9375-1(4))* Creative Media Partners, LLC.

Frey, Hildegard Gertrude. The Camp Fire Girls in the Maine Woods: Or, the Winnebagos Go Camping. 2017. (ENG., Illus.). (J). 23.95 *(978-1-374-97005-2(0));* pap. 13.95 *(978-1-374-97004-5(2))* Capital Communications, Inc.

Frey, Hildegarde Gertrude. The Camp Fire Girls in the Maine Woods; or, the Winnebagos Go Camping. 2016. (ENG., Illus.). (J). 25.95 *(978-1-359-70357-6(8))* Creative Media Partners, LLC.

Friedland, Joyce, ed. Lizzie Bright & the Buckminster Boy: Novel-Ties Study Guide. 2007. 36p. pap. 16.95 *(978-0-7675-3558-8(8))* Learning Links Inc.

Fuller, Sandy Fergus. Moon Loon. 2010. (Illus.). 32p. (J). (gr. k-17). 15.95 *(978-1-58979-453-5(2))* Taylor Trade Publishing.

Fuller, Sandy Ferguson. Moon Loon. 2010. (J). 7.95 *(978-1-58979-454-2(0));* (Illus.). 32p. pap. 7.95 *(978-1-58979-455-9(9))* Taylor Trade Publishing.

Gamble, Adam. Good Night Maine. Chan, Suwin, illus. 2007. (Good Night Our World Ser.). (ENG.). 18p. (J). (gr. k — 1). bds. 9.95 *(978-1-60219-010-8(0))* Good Night Bks.

Garfield, Henry. Tartabull's Throw. 2015. (ENG., Illus.). 272p. (YA). (gr. 7). pap. 12.99 *(978-1-4814-7510-5(X),* Atheneum Bks. for Young Readers) Simon & Schuster Children's Publishing.

Goldsberry, Booty. Scaredy-Cat, I'm Not. 2007. (ENG., Illus.). 40p. (gr. 4-7). pap. 9.95 *(978-0-9792875-0-3(2))* Goldsberry, Booty.

Griffin, N. The Whole Stupid Way We Are. (ENG., Illus.). 368p. (YA). (gr. 9). 2014. pap. 9.99 *(978-1-4424-3156-0(3))* 2013. 16.99 *(978-1-4424-3155-3(5))* Simon & Schuster Children's Publishing. (Atheneum Bks. for Young Readers).

Gutman, Dan. The Get Rich Quick Club. (ENG.). 128p. (J). 2008. (gr. 3-7). pap. 6.99 *(978-0-06-053442-4(7),* HarperCollins) 2004. 15.99 *(978-0-06-053440-0(0))* HarperCollins Pubs.

Haesche, Richard Paul, Sr. The Treasure of Pirates Cave. 2007. (ENG.). 378p. (YA). 11.99 *(978-0-9798536-7-8(2))* Kreative X-Pressions Pubns.

Hahn, Mary Downing. Look for Me by Moonlight. 2008. (ENG.). 208p. (YA). (gr. 7). pap. 7.99 *(978-0-547-07616-4(9),* 1042006, Clarion Bks.) HarperCollins Pubs.

Harlow, Joan Hiatt. Shadows on the Sea. (ENG., Illus.). (J). (gr. 3-7). 2005. 272p. pap. 7.99 *(978-0-689-84927-5(3))* 2003. 256p. 17.99 *(978-0-689-84926-8(5))* McElderry, Margaret K. Bks. (McElderry, Margaret K. Bks.).

Harpan, Gaile. The Ballad of Omar the Cat. Reddy, Sneha, illus. 2008. 28p. pap. 12.95 *(978-0-9820479-1-0(6))* Peppertree Pr., The.

Hawkes, Kevin. The Wicked Big Toddlah. 2010. 40p. (J). (gr. -1-2). pap. 7.99 *(978-0-440-41788-0(0),* Dragonfly Bks.) Random Hse. Children's Bks.

Hopkins, Howard. The Nightmare Club #2: the Deadly Dragon. 2008. (ENG.). 104p. pap. 9.98 *(978-0-578-00320-7(1))* Golden Perils Pr.

—The Nightmare Club #3: the Willow Witch. 2008. (ENG.). 104p. pap. 9.98 *(978-0-578-00361-0(9))* Golden Perils Pr.

Horvath, Polly. The Canning Season. 2012. (ENG., Illus.). 224p. (YA). (gr. 7-12). pap. 11.99 *(978-0-312-53564-3(3),* 900054742) Square Fish.

Jackson, Penny. Pepere's Little Girl. Jackson, Helston & Anderson, Betheny, illus. 2008. 27p. pap. 24.95 *(978-1-60441-881-1(8))* America Star Bks.

Jacobs, Lily. The Littlest Bunny in Maine: An Easter Adventure. Dunn, Robert, illus. 2015. (Littlest Bunny Ser.). (ENG.). 32p. (J). (gr. -1-3). 9.99 *(978-1-4926-1108-0(5),* Hometown World) Sourcebooks, Inc.

—The Littlest Bunny in Portland: An Easter Adventure. Dunn, Robert, illus. 2015. (Littlest Bunny Ser.). (ENG.). 32p. (J). (gr. -1-3). 9.99 *(978-1-4926-1186-8(7),* Hometown World) Sourcebooks, Inc.

James, Eric. Santa's Sleigh is on Its Way to Maine: A Christmas Adventure. Dunn, Robert, illus. 2016. (Santa's Sleigh is on Its Way Ser.). (ENG.). 32p. (J). (gr. k-2). 12.99 *(978-1-4926-4334-0(3),* 9781492643340, Hometown World) Sourcebooks, Inc.

—The Spooky Express Maine. Piwowarski, Marcin, illus. 2017. (Spooky Express Ser.). (ENG.). 32p. (J). (gr. k-6). 9.99 *(978-1-4926-5367-7(5),* Hometown World) Sourcebooks, Inc.

—Tiny the Maine Easter Bunny. 2018. (Tiny the Easter Bunny Ser.). (ENG.). 40p. (J). (gr. k-3). 9.99 *(978-1-4926-5934-1(7),* Hometown World) Sourcebooks, Inc.

Jones, Kimberly K. Sand Dollar Summer. 2008. (ENG., Illus.). 224p. (J). (gr. 4-8). pap. 7.99 *(978-1-4169-5834-5(7),* McElderry, Margaret K. Bks.) McElderry, Margaret K. Bks.

Jones, Molly. The Choosing Tree. 2006. 126p. pap. 19.95 *(978-1-4241-5076-2(0))* PublishAmerica, Inc.

Jordan, Evora. Annie Love: A Hannah Gray Dog Story. 2003. (Hannah Gray Mysteries). (J). per. *(978-0-9725071-2-7(4))* EvoraBooks, LLC.

Keil, James. Tiger & the Poachers. 2010. 54p. pap. 15.52 *(978-0-557-34105-4(1))* Lulu Pr., Inc.

Kinsella, Warren. Recipe for Hate: The X Gang. 2017. (X Gang Ser.: 1). (ENG.). 304p. (YA). pap. 14.99 *(978-1-4597-3906-2(X))* Dundurn Pr. CAN. Dist: Publishers Group West (PGW).

LaFaye, A. The Keening. 2010. (ENG.). 224p. (J). (gr. 2-8). 17.00 *(978-1-57131-692-9(2));* pap. 8.00 *(978-1-57131-694-3(9))* Milkweed Editions.

LaFleur, Suzanne. Listening for Lucca. 2015. (ENG.). 240p. (J). (gr. 4-7). pap. 8.99 *(978-0-307-98030-4(8),* Yearling) Random Hse. Children's Bks.

Langer, Dana. Siren Sisters. 2017. (ENG., Illus.). 256p. (J). (gr. 4-8). 17.99 *(978-1-4814-6686-8(0),* Simon & Schuster/Paula Wiseman Bks.) Simon & Schuster/Paula Wiseman Bks.

Larbalestier, Justine & Brennan, Sarah Rees. Team Human. 2012. (ENG.). 352p. (YA). (gr. 8). 17.99 *(978-0-06-208964-9(1),* HarperTeen) HarperCollins Pubs.

Lasky, Kathryn. Lucy (Daughters of the Sea #3) 2012. (Daughters of the Sea Ser.: 3). (ENG.). 320p. (J). (gr. 7). 17.99 *(978-0-439-78312-5(7),* Scholastic Pr.) Scholastic, Inc.

Leach, Cheryl. Sally to the Rescue. 2012. 36p. pap. 20.99 *(978-1-4772-9974-6(2))* AuthorHouse.

Lewis, Carolyn & DeVince, James. Hairy Beary Book Three: The Blue Ribbon Hero, 3 bks., Vol. 3. DeVince, James, ed. Porcheron, Tammy, illus. 2003. (Hairy Beary Ser.: 3). 46p. (J). pap. 9.95 *(978-0-9712641-2-0(0))* J M D's Business Services.

Libhart, Virginia B. Carrie's Dream. 2005. *(978-0-9652963-7-3(7))* Harborseal Publishing Co.

Long, Susan Hill. Josie Bloom & the Emergency of Life. 2020. (ENG., Illus.). 288p. (J). (gr. 3-7). 17.99 *(978-1-5344-4427-0(0))* Simon & Schuster.

Lord, Cynthia. Because of the Rabbit (Scholastic Gold) 2019. (ENG.). 192p. (J). (gr. 3-7). 17.99 *(978-0-545-91424-6(8),* Scholastic Pr.) Scholastic, Inc.

—Touch Blue. 2012. (ENG.). 192p. (J). (gr. 4-7). pap. 8.99 *(978-0-545-03532-3(5),* Scholastic Pr.) Scholastic, Inc.

Lubner, Susan. Lizzy & the Good Luck Girl. 2018. (ENG.). 224p. (J). (gr. 3-7). 16.99 *(978-0-7624-6502-6(6),* Running Pr. Kids) Running Pr.

Mackinnon, Bernard. The Boy Who Turned Green. 2005. 119p. pap. 19.95 *(978-1-4137-7262-3(5))* America Star Bks.

Marrone, Amanda. Slayed. 2010. (ENG., Illus.). 272p. (YA). (gr. 9-18). pap. 9.99 *(978-1-4169-9487-9(4),* Simon Pulse) Simon Pulse.

Martin, Ann M. Family Tree Book One: Better to Wish. 2014. (Family Tree Ser.: 1). (ENG.). 240p. (J). (gr. 3-7). pap. 6.99 *(978-0-545-67518-5(9))* Scholastic, Inc.

Martin-Fluet, Marie T. The Fairies' Century Celebration. 2011. 40p. pap. 18.62 *(978-1-4567-2477-1(0))* AuthorHouse.

Martin, Jacqueline Briggs. The Finest Horse in Town. Gaber, Susan, illus. 2016. (ENG.). (J). pap. 8.99 *(978-1-930900-82-0(1))* Purple Hse. Pr.

Martinez, David & Benchmark Education Co., LLC. My Whale of a Tale. 2014. (Text Connections Ser.). (J). (gr. 3). *(978-1-4509-9651-8(5))* Benchmark Education Co.

McCloskey, Robert. Blueberries for Sal. (J). (gr. -1-k). pap. 12.95 incl. audio. 2004. 29.95 *(978-1-55592-841-4(2));* 2004. (J). 38.75 *(978-1-55592-816-2(1));* 2004. (J). 18.95 *(978-1-55592-799-8(8))* Weston Woods Studios, Inc.

McCreight, Kimberly. The Outliers. (Outliers Ser.: 1). (ENG.). (YA). (gr. 9). 2017. 368p. pap. 10.99 *(978-0-06-235910-0(X))* 2016. 352p. 18.99 *(978-0-06-235909-4(6))* HarperCollins Pubs. (HarperCollins).

McKenzie, Lyn. Betsy, Girl Scout of Woodward Center 1935. 2007. 244p. (YA). pap. 17.95 net. *(978-0-9722839-0-8(0))* Just Write Bks.

McTiernan, Deborah. Lilly Noble & Actual Magic. 2013. (ENG.). 318p. (YA). pap. 14.99 *(978-0-9891807-0-2(0))* Actual Magic Enterprises, LLC.

Merrill, Karen Grill. Oh, What a State I'm In: The USA in Rhyme & Riddle, 1 vol. Grill, Gerald, illus. 2010. 48p. pap. 24.95 *(978-1-4489-7979-0(X))* PublishAmerica, Inc.

Metzger, Steve. The Turkey Train. Paillot, Jim, illus. 2013. (ENG.). 32p. (J). (gr. -1-k). 6.99 *(978-0-545-49229-4(7),* Cartwheel Bks.) Scholastic, Inc.

Morgan, G. A. Chantarelle, 1 vol. 2015. (Five Stones Trilogy Ser.: 2). (ENG.). 300p. (J). 18.95 *(978-1-939017-63-5(7),* d13ddfd9-69e5-436d-8734-e893acab42f3) Islandport Pr., Inc.

—The Fog of Forgetting, 1 vol. 2017. (Five Stones Trilogy Ser.: 1). (ENG.). 304p. (J). pap. 14.95 *(978-1-939017-87-1(4),* 41192ffb-9750-42d9-a4b2-6b01dbc01a50) Islandport Pr., Inc.

Nana B. & Brittany. Forest Friends of Maine: The Chipmunks Have an Argument. 2010. 16p. pap. 8.49 *(978-1-4490-0647-1(7))* AuthorHouse.

Nolan, Han. Pregnant Pause. 2012. (ENG.). 352p. (YA). (gr. 9). pap. 8.99 *(978-0-547-85414-4(5),* 1501157, Clarion Bks.) HarperCollins Pubs.

M N O

Northrop, Michael. On Thin Ice. 2019. (ENG.). 240p. (YA). (gr. 4-7). 17.99 (978-0-545-49590-5(3), Scholastic Pr.) Scholastic, Inc.
Nugent, Matthew. Nightmares on Goose Rocks Beach in Kennebunkport, Maine: Book 4 of the Goose Rocks Tales. 2003. (Illus.). 204p. (J). per. 14.95 (978-0-9705812-3-5(8)) CBI Pr.
O'Brien, Anne Sibley. A Path of Stars. O'Brien, Anne Sibley, illus. 2012. (Illus.). 40p. (J). (gr. k-3). 17.99 (978-1-57091-735-6(3)) Charlesbridge Publishing, Inc.
O'Brien, Thomas E. The Magic of Finbar. 2011. 68p. pap. 19.95 (978-1-4560-4235-6(1)) America Star Bks.
Ogilvie, Elizabeth. The Pigeon Pair. (J). reprint ed. lib. bdg. 19.95 (978-0-88411-336-2(1)) Amereon Ltd.
Oliver, Lauren. Delirium. 1. 2016. (Delirium Trilogy Ser.: 1). (ENG.). 480p. (YA). (gr. 9-12). pap. 15.99 (978-0-06-172683-5(4), HarperCollins) HarperCollins Pubs.
—Delirium. 2016. (Delirium Ser.: 1). (YA). lib. bdg. 20.85 (978-0-606-23575-4(2)) Turtleback.
—Delirium Stories: Hana, Annabel, Raven & Alex. (Delirium Ser.). (YA). 2016. lib. bdg. 20.85 (978-0-606-38920-4(2)) 2013. lib. bdg. 20.85 (978-0-606-31834-1(8)) Turtleback.
—Delirium Stories: Hana, Annabel, & Raven. 2013. (Delirium Trilogy Ser.). (ENG.). 224p. (YA). (gr. 9). pap. 9.99 (978-0-06-226778-8(7), HarperCollins) HarperCollins Pubs.
—Delirium Stories: Hana, Annabel, Raven, & Alex. 2016. (Delirium Story Ser.). (ENG.). 224p. (YA). (gr. 9). pap. 9.99 (978-0-06-248432-1(X), HarperCollins) HarperCollins Pubs.
—Delirium: the Special Edition. 2011. (Delirium Trilogy Ser.: 1). (ENG.). 480p. (YA). (gr. 9). 17.99 (978-0-06-211243-9(0), HarperCollins) HarperCollins Pubs.
—Requiem. 2013. (Delirium Trilogy Ser.: 3). (ENG.). 432p. (YA). (gr. 9). 18.99 (978-0-06-201453-5(6), HarperCollins) HarperCollins Pubs.
O'Neill, Elizabeth. Alfred Visits Maine. 2008. (Illus.). 24p. (J). pap. 12.00 (978-0-9799121-3-9(X)) Funny Bone Bks.
Padian, Maria. Brett McCarthy: Work in Progress. 2008. (ENG.). 288p. (J). (gr. 7-12). lib. bdg. 24.94 (978-0-375-94675-2(6), Knopf Bks. for Young Readers) Random Hse. Children's Bks.
—Brett McCarthy: Work in Progress. 2009. (ENG.). 288p. (YA). (gr. 7). pap. 8.99 (978-0-440-24055-6(7), Knopf Bks. for Young Readers) Random Hse. Children's Bks.
Perkins, T. J. Wound Too Tight. 2006. (Illus.). 141p. (YA). 10.99 (978-0-9777538-5-7(9)) GumShoe Press.
Philbrick, Rodman. Wildfire (the Wild Series) A Novel. 2019. (ENG.). 208p. (J). (gr. 3-7). 17.99 (978-1-338-26690-0(X), Blue Sky Pr., The) Scholastic, Inc.
Pochocki, Ethel. A Penny for a Hundred. Owens, Mary Beth, illus. 2005. 31p. (J). (gr. 2-5). pap. 9.95 (978-1-883937-52-2(3)) Bethlehem Bks.
—A Penny for a Hundred. 2014. (Illus.). 32p. (J). (gr. -1-3). 15.95 (978-1-60893-311-2(3)) Down East Bks.
Pohl, William L. The Amazing Flight of Daisy: A Runaway Kite Circles the World on the Back of the Wind. 2006. 72p. 20.00 (978-1-4257-0666-1(5)) Xlibris Corp.
Potter, Ellen. Piper Green & the Fairy Tree: Pie Girl. Leng, Qin, illus. 2017. (Piper Green & the Fairy Tree Ser.: 5). 144p. (J). (gr. 2-4). pap. 5.99 (978-1-101-93968-0(0), Yearling) Random Hse. Children's Bks.
Reynolds, Cynthia Furlong. Across the Reach. 2007. 269p. (J). (gr. 3-7). 16.95 (978-1-58726-518-1(4), Mitten Pr.) Ann Arbor Editions LLC.
Ross, Susan. Kiki & Jacques: A Refugee Story. 2019. (ENG.). 144p. (J). (gr. 3-7). pap. 7.99 (978-0-8234-4180-8(6)) Holiday Hse., Inc.
Roy, Ron. A to Z Mysteries: the White Wolf. Gurney, John Steven, illus. 2004. (to Z Mysteries Ser.: 23). 96p. (J). (gr. 1-4). pap. 6.99 (978-0-375-82480-7(4), Random Hse. Bks. for Young Readers) Random Hse. Children's Bks.
Scaletta, Kurtis. The Tanglewood Terror. 2012. (ENG.). 272p. (J). (gr. 4-6). lib. bdg. 18.69 (978-0-375-96758-0(3), Knopf Bks. for Young Readers) Random Hse. Children's Bks.
Schmidt, Mollie. It Happened in Maine. Wood, Madeline, illus. 2013. (ENG.). 56p. (J). pap. 10.95 (978-1-59713-137-7(7)) Goose River Pr.
Sedita, Francesco. Miss Popularity Goes Camping. 2009. (ENG.). 142p. (J). lib. bdg. 15.38 (978-1-4242-4383-9(1)) Fitzgerald Bks.
Shankman, Ed. I Met a Moose in Maine One Day. O'Neill, Dave, illus. 2008. (Shankman & O'Neill Ser.). (ENG.). 32p. (J). (gr. -1-3). 17.99 (978-1-933212-77-7(2), Commonwealth Editions) Applewood Bks.
Shue, Jenna. Animal Island. Herzog, Inge, illus. 2005. 27p. (J). (gr. -1-3). per. 14.95 (978-1-4259-0039-7(9)) AuthorHouse.
Simmons, Derek. Flash of Life. 2006. 85p. pap. 16.95 (978-1-4241-3890-6(6)) PublishAmerica, Inc.
Skurzynski, Gloria. Mysteries in Our National Parks: Out of the Deep: A Mystery in Acadia National Park. 2008. (Mysteries in Our National Park Ser.). (Illus.). 160p. (J). (gr. 3-7). pap. 4.99 (978-1-4263-0251-0(7), National Geographic Kids) Disney Publishing Worldwide.
Smith, Constance. Pea Soup Fog. Cart, Jen, illus. 2004. (ENG.). 32p. (J). (gr. -1-17). 15.95 (978-0-89272-643-1(1)) Down East Bks.
Smith, George. The Journey of the Little Red Boat: A Story from the Coast of Maine. 2nd ed. 2004. (Illus.). 50p. (J). per. 7.99 (978-0-9740434-1-8(9), 255-3716) Smith, George Publishing.
Smith, Lauren. Ashley Enright & the Mystery at Miller's Pond. 2006. (ENG.). 60p. per. 16.95 (978-1-4241-5268-1(2)) America Star Bks.
Smith, Lauren E. Ashley Enright & the Darnell Diamonds. 1 vol. 2009. 90p. pap. 19.95 (978-1-60836-332-2(5)) America Star Bks.
—Ashley Enright Investigations. 2006. 48p. pap. 16.95 (978-1-4241-2963-8(X)) America Star Bks.
Smith, Maggie. Counting Our Way to Maine. 2008. (ENG., Illus.). 32p. (J). (gr. -1-3). 15.95 (978-0-89272-775-9(6)) Down East Bks.
Sockabasin, Allen. Thanks to the Animals: 10th Anniversary Edition. 1 vol. Raye, Rebekah, illus. 2nd ed. 2014. (ENG.). 64p. (J). (gr. 1-6). 17.95 (978-0-88448-414-1(9), 884414) Tilbury Hse. Pubs.
Speare, Elizabeth George. The Sign of the Beaver. 135p. (J). (gr. 4-6). pap. 4.99 (978-0-8072-1517-3(1), Listening Library) Random Hse. Audio Publishing Group.
—The Sign of the Beaver: A Newbery Honor Award Winner. 2011. (ENG.). 144p. (J). (gr. 5-7). pap. 9.99 (978-0-547-57711-1(7), 1458459, Clarion Bks.) HarperCollins Pubs.
Spencer, Jamie. The Train to Maine. Reed, Rebecca, illus. 2008. (ENG.). 32p. (J). (gr. -1-3). 15.95 (978-0-89272-767-4(5)) Down East Bks.
Standish, Burt L. Frank Merriwell in Maine. Rudman, Jack, ed. 2003. (Frank Merriwell Ser.). (YA). (gr. 9-18). 29.95 (978-0-8373-9328-5(0)); pap. 9.95 (978-0-8373-9028-4(1), FM-028) Merriwell, Frank Inc.
Sticks Stones & Stumped. 2006. (Illus.). 26p. (J). 19.95 (978-0-9773738-0-2(0)) Bryson Taylor Publishing.
Stockwell, Jeff. Fandango: The Key to the Wind. Stockwell, Pel, illus. 2007. 58p. (YA). per. 22.50 (978-0-9785594-0-3(1)) Stockwell Publishing.
Stone, Phoebe. Romeo Blue. 2013. (ENG.). 352p. (J). (gr. 3-7). 16.99 (978-0-545-44360-9(1), Levine, Arthur A. Bks.) Scholastic, Inc.
Strohm, Stephanie Kate. Pilgrims Don't Wear Pink. 2012. (ENG.). 208p. (YA). (gr. 7-12). pap. 12.99 (978-0-547-56459-3(7), 1454809, Clarion Bks.) HarperCollins Pubs.
Strykowski, Marcia. Call Me Amy. 2013. (ENG.). 176p. (J). (gr. 3-10). 24.95 (978-1-935462-76-7(8)); pap. 14.95 (978-1-935462-75-0(X)) Luminis Bks., Inc.
Surrisi, C. M. The Maypop Kidnapping: A Quinnie Boyd Mystery. (Quinnie Boyd Mysteries Ser.). (ENG.). 304p. (J). (gr. 4-8). 2018. pap. 9.99 (978-1-5415-1490-4(4), c6bfb82b-5feb-4601-a681-edbe24d09c92) 2016. E-Book 26.65 (978-1-4677-9560-9(7)) Lerner Publishing Group. (Carolrhoda Bks.).
—A Side of Sabotage: A Quinnie Boyd Mystery. (Quinnie Boyd Mysteries Ser.). (ENG.). 280p. (J). (gr. 4-8). 2019. pap. 9.99 (978-1-5415-7758-9(2), df48a301-f493-4867-acd0-7099f5d7865c) 2018. 16.99 (978-1-5124-4836-8(2), 2f2233a9-53da-4efc-ba4d-e5c7d38d2937) Lerner Publishing Group. (Carolrhoda Bks.).
—Vampires on the Run: A Quinnie Boyd Mystery. 2017. (Quinnie Boyd Mysteries Ser.: 2). (ENG.). 296p. (J). (gr. 4-8). 16.99 (978-1-5124-1150-8(7), 7aed6910-020c-4ae6-a0b2-d7143911d482, Carolrhoda Bks.) Lerner Publishing Group.
Tata, Cb. Ernie the Eagle Goes to Maine. Hanley, Zachary, illus. 2012. 42p. 24.95 (978-1-4626-4545-9(3)) America Star Bks.
Terrell, Brandon. Don't Look Down: A Tale of Terror. Epelbaum, Mariano, illus. 2019. (Michael Dahl Presents: Phobia Ser.). (ENG.). 72p. (J). (gr. 4-6). lib. bdg. 25.32 (978-1-4965-7912-6(7), 139617, Stone Arch Bks.) Capstone.
Van Dusen, Chris. The Circus Ship. Van Dusen, Chris, illus. 2015. (ENG., Illus.). 40p. (J). (gr. -1-3). 8.99 (978-0-7636-5592-1(9)) Candlewick Pr.
Vanderpool, Clare. Navigating Early. 2014. 336p. (J). (gr. 5). pap. 8.99 (978-0-307-93065-1(3), Yearling) Random Hse. Children's Bks.
—Navigating Early. 2014. lib. bdg. 18.40 (978-0-606-36420-1(X)) Turtleback.
Vernick, Shirley Reva. The Black Butterfly. 1 vol. 2014. (ENG.). 226p. (J). (gr. 8-12). 19.95 (978-1-935955-79-5(9), 23353382, Cinco Puntos Press) Lee & Low Bks., Inc.
Voigt, Cynthia. Angus & Sadie. Leigh, Tom, illus. 2008. (ENG.). 208p. (J). (gr. 3-7). pap. 9.99 (978-0-06-074584-4(3), Greenwillow Bks.) HarperCollins Pubs.
Wait, Lea. Stopping to Home. 2003. (ENG.). 160p. (J). (gr. 3-7). pap. 8.99 (978-0-689-83849-1(2), Simon & Schuster/Paula Wiseman Bks.) Simon & Schuster/Paula Wiseman Bks.
—Wintering Well. 2006. (ENG., Illus.). 192p. (J). (gr. 3-7). pap. 8.99 (978-0-689-85647-1(4), McElderry, Margaret K. Bks.) McElderry, Margaret K. Bks.
Walker, Brian F. Black Boy White School. 2012. (ENG.). 256p. (YA). (gr. 9). 17.99 (978-0-06-191483-6(5), HarperTeen) HarperCollins Pubs.
Warne, Jude. The Big Reveal. 2017. (Crushing Ser.). (ENG.). 192p. (YA). (gr. 5-12). lib. bdg. 31.42 (978-1-68076-717-9(8), 25382, Epic Escape) EPIC Pr.
Weston Woods Staff, creator. Time of Wonder. 2011. 29.95 (978-0-439-73525-4(4)); 18.95 (978-0-439-72905-5(X)); 38.75 (978-0-439-72906-2(8)) Weston Woods Studios, Inc.
White-Adams, Beverly. The Adventures of Rusty: Rusty Goes to Maine Vol. 3. 2012. 40p. pap. 19.57 (978-1-4669-5442-7(6)) Trafford Publishing.
Whitten, A. J. The Well. 2009. (ENG., Illus.). 336p. (YA). (gr. 7-18). pap. 18.95 (978-0-547-23229-4(2), 1082742, Clarion Bks.) HarperCollins Pubs.
Wiggin, Kate Douglas. Homespun Tales. 2007. 240p. 26.95 (978-1-60312-668-7(6)); per. 14.95 (978-1-60312-410-2(1)) Aegypan.
—Rose o' the River. 2004. reprint ed. pap. 15.95 (978-1-4179-9998-9(5)); pap. 1.99 (978-1-4179-9948-4(9)) Kessinger Publishing, LLC.
Wigington, Patti. Summer's Ashes. 2007. (ENG.). 208p. (gr. 8-12). per. 15.00 (978-0-9766805-9-8(9)) Keene Publishing.
Wolf, Elaine. Camp. 2012. (ENG.). 256p. (YA). (gr. 6-6). 16.95 (978-1-61608-657-2(2), 608657, Sky Pony Pr.) Skyhorse Publishing Co., Inc.
Wolk, Lauren. Echo Mountain. 2020. (ENG.). 368p. (J). (gr. 5). 17.99 (978-0-525-55556-8(0), Dutton Books for Young Readers) Penguin Young Readers Group.

MAINE—HISTORY

Believe It Or Not!, Ripleys, compiled by. Ripley's Fun Facts & Silly Stories: the MANE EVENT. 2017. (Fun Facts Ser.: 4). (ENG., Illus.). 144p. (J). 18.95 (978-1-60991-184-3(9)) Ripley Entertainment, Inc.
Brett, Jeannie. Little Maine. Brett, Jeannie, illus. 2010. (Little State Ser.). (ENG., Illus.). 20p. (J). (gr. -1-1). bds. 9.95 (978-1-58536-497-8(5), 202242) Sleeping Bear Pr.
Doak, Robin S. Maine (a True Book: My United States) (Library Edition) 2018. (True Book (Relaunch) Ser.). (ENG., Illus.). 48p. (J). (gr. 3-5). 31.00 (978-0-531-23166-1(6), Children's Pr.) Scholastic Library Publishing.
Ehman, Ashley M., et al. Maine: The Pine Tree State, 1 vol. 2019. (It's My State! (Fourth Edition)(r) Ser.). (ENG.). 80p. (gr. 4-4). 35.93 (978-1-5026-4222-6(0), 533c59e1-906d-446f-8d54-ebeefa7affd9) Cavendish Square Publishing LLC.
Foran, Jill. Maine: The Pine Tree State. 2016. (J). (978-1-4896-4872-3(0)) Weigl Pubs., Inc.
Hamilton, John. Maine. 1 vol. 2016. (United States of America Ser.). (ENG., Illus.). 48p. (J). (gr. 5-9). 34.21 (978-1-68078-321-6(1), 21627, Abdo & Daughters) ABDO Publishing Co.
Hicks, Terry Allan. Maine. 1 vol. 2nd rev. ed. 2013. (It's My State! (Second Edition)(r) Ser.). (ENG.). 80p. (gr. 4-4). 35.93 (978-1-60870-881-9(0), 94fdbe90-8e90-4ada-9c8b-c08f90983295) Cavendish Square Publishing LLC.
Hicks, Terry Allan, et al. Maine. 2015. (J). lib. bdg. (978-1-62713-201-5(5)) Cavendish Square Publishing LLC.
Koontz, Robin Michal. Maine: The Pine Tree State, 1 vol. 2010. (Our Amazing States Ser.). (ENG., Illus.). 24p. (J). (gr. 3-3). pap. 9.25 (978-1-4488-0734-5(4), 892fa687-f829-41c3-ad57-af0750c5ae7b); lib. bdg. 26.27 (978-1-4488-0651-5(8), ad575f69-e71e-4775-b71a-42a3dd0f96d8) Rosen Publishing Group, Inc., The. (PowerKids Pr.).
Marsh, Carole. Exploring Maine Through Project-Based Learning. 2016. (Maine Experience Ser.). (ENG.). (J). pap. 9.99 (978-0-635-12343-5(6)) Gallopade International.
—I'm Reading about Maine. 2014. (Maine Experience Ser.). (ENG., Illus.). (J). pap., pap. 8.99 (978-0-635-11294-1(9)) Gallopade International.
—Maine History Projects: 30 Cool, Activities, Crafts, Experiments & More for Kids to Do to Learn about Your State! 2003. (Maine Experience Ser.). 32p. (gr. k-5). pap. 5.95 (978-0-635-01788-8(1), Marsh, Carole Bks.) Gallopade International.
Perish, Patrick. Maine. 2013. (Exploring the States Ser.). (ENG., Illus.). 32p. (J). (gr. 3-7). lib. bdg. 27.95 (978-1-62617-018-6(5), Blastoff! Readers) Bellwether Media.
Peterson, Judy Monroe. Maine: Past & Present. 1 vol. 2010. (United States: Past & Present Ser.). (ENG.). 48p. (YA). (gr. 5-5). pap. 12.75 (978-1-4358-9511-9(8), f95d04d6-302c-418e-9321-a783f32e2afc); lib. bdg. 34.47 (978-1-4358-9484-6(7), c1bca77e-0890-4bcc-beb2-09b5f6367086) Rosen Publishing Group, Inc., The. (Rosen Reference).
Schneider, Jack. Allagash River Towboat: A Maine Logging Adventure. 2003. (ENG., Illus.). 120p. (J). (gr. 4-12). pap. 10.95 (978-0-89272-601-1(6)) Down East Bks.
Smolik, Jane Petrlik. The Great State of Maine Activity Book: Over 75 Puzzles about Life in Maine. rev. ed. 2006. (Illus.). 96p. (J). (gr. 2-7). per. 11.95 (978-0-9664095-6-7(6)) MidRun Pr.
Swanson, Angie & Parker, Bridget. Maine. 2016. (States Ser.). (ENG., Illus.). 32p. (J). (gr. 3-6). lib. bdg. 27.99 (978-1-5157-0406-5(8), 132017, Capstone Pr.) Capstone.
Turner, Myra Faye. Events That Changed the Course of History: The Story of Maine Becoming a State 200 Years Later. 2019. (ENG.). 198p. (YA). pap. 19.95 (978-1-62023-542-3(0)) Atlantic Publishing Group, Inc.
Webster, Christine. From Sea to Shining Sea: Maine. 2008. (ENG.). 80p. (J). pap. 7.95 (978-0-531-20806-9(0), Children's Pr.) Scholastic Library Publishing.
—Maine. 2009. (Illus.). 80p. (J). pap. (978-0-8312-0806-6(6)) Children's Pr., Ltd.
Yasuda, Anita. Maine: The Pine Tree State. 2012. (J). (978-1-61913-357-0(1)); pap. (978-1-61913-358-7(X)) Weigl Pubs., Inc.
Ziff, John. Northern New England: Maine, New Hampshire, Vermont, Vol. 19. 2015. (Let's Explore the States Ser.). (Illus.). 64p. (J). (gr. 5). 23.95 (978-1-4222-3330-6(8)) Mason Crest.

MAINE (BATTLESHIP)

Crompton, Samuel Willard. The Sinking of the USS Maine: Declaring War Against Spain. 2009. (ENG., Illus.). 112p. (gr. 7-12). 35.00 (978-1-60413-049-2(0), P159424, Facts On File) Infobase Holdings, Inc.
McNeese, Tim. Remember the Maine! The Spanish-American War Begins. 2004. (First Battles Ser.). (Illus.). 112p. (YA). (gr. 6-12). 23.95 (978-1-883846-79-4(X), First Biographies) Reynolds, Morgan Inc.

MAISY (FICTITIOUS CHARACTER: COUSINS)—FICTION

Cousins, Lucy. Maisy Goes Camping. 2009. (Maisy First Experiences Ser.). lib. bdg. 17.20 (978-0-606-06667-9(5)) Turtleback.
—Maisy Goes on a Plane: A Maisy First Experiences Book. Cousins, Lucy, illus. 2017. (Maisy Ser.). (ENG., Illus.). 32p. (J). (-k). 7.99 (978-0-7636-9791-4(5)) Candlewick Pr.
—Maisy Goes to a Wedding. Cousins, Lucy, illus. 2019. (Maisy Ser.). (ENG., Illus.). 32p. (J). (-k). 6.99 (978-1-5362-0614-2(8)) Candlewick Pr.
—Maisy Goes to a Wedding. 2018. (Illus.). 32p. (J). (978-1-4063-7851-1(8)) Candlewick Pr.
—Maisy Goes to a Wedding. 2019. (Maisy First Experiences Pic Bks). (ENG.). 26p. (J). (gr. k-1). 17.36 (978-0-87617-298-8(2)) Penworthy Co., LLC, The.
—Maisy Goes to the Hospital. 2009. (Maisy First Experiences Ser.). lib. bdg. 17.20 (978-0-606-06686-0(1)) Turtleback.
—Maisy Goes to the Library. 2009. (Maisy First Experiences Ser.). lib. bdg. 17.20 (978-0-606-06687-7(X)) Turtleback.
—Maisy Goes to the Local Bookstore. 2018. (Maisy First Experiences Pic Bks). (ENG.). 26p. (J). (gr. -1-k). 17.36 (978-1-64310-238-2(9)) Penworthy Co., LLC, The.
—Maisy Goes to the Local Bookstore. 2018. (Maisy First Experiences Ser.). lib. bdg. 17.20 (978-0-606-40914-8(9)) Turtleback.
—Maisy Goes to the Local Bookstore: A Maisy First Experiences Book. Cousins, Lucy, illus. 2018. (Maisy Ser.). (ENG., Illus.). 32p. (J). (-k). 6.99 (978-1-5362-0085-0(9)) Candlewick Pr.
—Maisy Goes to the Movies. 2014. (Maisy First Experiences Ser.). lib. bdg. 17.20 (978-0-606-35156-0(6)) Turtleback.
—Maisy Goes to the Museum: A Maisy First Experience Book. Cousins, Lucy, illus. 2009. (Maisy Ser.). (ENG., Illus.). 32p. (J). (gr. k-k). pap. 6.99 (978-0-7636-4370-6(X)) Candlewick Pr.
—Maisy Learns to Swim: A Maisy First Experience Book. Cousins, Lucy, illus. 2015. (Maisy Ser.). (ENG., Illus.). 32p. (J). (-k). 7.99 (978-0-7636-7749-7(3)) Candlewick Pr.
—Maisy Plays Soccer. 2014. (Maisy First Experiences Ser.). lib. bdg. 17.20 (978-0-606-35155-3(8)) Turtleback.
—Maisy's Digger: A Go with Maisy Board Book. Cousins, Lucy, illus. 2015. (Maisy Ser.). (ENG., Illus.). 18p. (J). (— 1). bds. 7.99 (978-0-7636-8010-7(9)) Candlewick Pr.
—Maisy's Field Day. 2019. (Maisy First Experiences Pic Bks). (ENG.). 26p. (J). (gr. k-1). 17.36 (978-0-87617-299-5(0)) Penworthy Co., LLC, The.
—Maisy's House: Complete with Durable Play Scene: A Fold-Out & Play Book. Cousins, Lucy, illus. 2018. (Maisy Ser.). (ENG., Illus.). 16p. (J). (-k). bds. 9.99 (978-1-5362-0378-3(5)) Candlewick Pr.
—Maisy's Plane. Cousins, Lucy, illus. 2015. (Maisy Ser.). (ENG., Illus.). 18p. (J). (— 1). bds. 6.99 (978-0-7636-7304-8(8)) Candlewick Pr.
—Maisy's Tractor. Cousins, Lucy, illus. 2015. (Maisy Ser.). (ENG., Illus.). 18p. (J). (— 1). bds. 7.99 (978-0-7636-7305-5(6)) Candlewick Pr.
—Maisy's Wonderful Weather Book. Cousins, Lucy, illus. 2006. (Maisy Ser.). (ENG., Illus.). 14p. (J). (gr. -1). 11.99 (978-0-7636-2987-8(1)) Candlewick Pr.
—Where Are Maisy's Friends? A Maisy Lift-The-Flap Book. Cousins, Lucy, illus. 2010. (Maisy Ser.). (ENG., Illus.). 12p. (J). (-k). bds. 6.99 (978-0-7636-4669-1(5)) Candlewick Pr.
—Where Does Maisy Live? 2010. 12p. bds. 4.99 (978-976-3-64668-7(5)) Candlewick Pr.
—Where Does Maisy Live? A Maisy Lift-The-Flap Book. Cousins, Lucy, illus. 2010. (Maisy Ser.). (ENG., Illus.). 12p. (J). (-k). bds. 6.99 (978-0-7636-4668-4(7)) Candlewick Pr.

MAIZE

see Corn

MAKE-UP (COSMETICS)

see Cosmetics

MAKE-UP, THEATRICAL

see Theatrical Makeup

MALADJUSTED CHILDREN

see Problem Children

MALAGASY REPUBLIC

see Madagascar

MALARIA

Ciletti, Barbara. Malaria Parasites. 2016. (Awful, Disgusting Parasites Ser.). (ENG.). 32p. (J). (gr. 4-6). 31.35 (978-1-68072-008-2(2), 10253); pap. 9.99 (978-1-64466-138-3(1), 10254) Black Rabbit Bks. (Bolt).
Donaldson, Olivia. Malaria, 1 vol. 2014. (Deadliest Diseases of All Time Ser.). (ENG.). 64p. (YA). (gr. 8-8). 35.93 (978-1-5026-0095-0(1), 3eebe989-4093-471a-9291-8533eae794fa) Cavendish Square Publishing LLC.
Dziedzic, Nancy, ed. Malaria. 1 vol. 2009. (Perspectives on Diseases & Disorders Ser.). (ENG., Illus.). 152p. (gr. 10-12). 45.93 (978-0-7377-4379-1(4), 918c118d-024b-4610-9ae4-0be1d9acdb63, Greenhaven Publishing) Greenhaven Publishing LLC.
Ford, Jeanne Marie. Malaria: How a Parasite Changed History. 2019. (Infected! Ser.). (ENG., Illus.). 32p. (J). (gr. 3-9). lib. bdg. 28.65 (978-1-5435-5505-9(5), 139377, Capstone Pr.) Capstone.
Hamen, Susan E. The 12 Worst Health Disasters of All Time. 2019. (All-Time Worst Disasters Ser.). (ENG., Illus.). 32p. (J). (gr. 3-6). 14.25 (978-1-63235-602-4(3), 13919, 12-Story Library) Bookstaves, LLC.
Hardyman, Robyn. Fighting Malaria. 2014. (Tiny Battlefields Ser.). 48p. (YA). (gr. 6-8). pap. 84.30 (978-1-4824-1310-6(8)) Stevens, Gareth Publishing LLLP.
Isle, Mick. Malaria. 2009. (Epidemics Ser.). 64p. (gr. 5-5). 58.50 (978-1-61512-293-6(1)) Rosen Publishing Group, Inc., The.
Marcus, Bernard. Malaria, Second Edition. 2nd rev. ed. 2009. (Deadly Diseases & Epidemics Ser.). 128p. (C). (gr. 9-18). 34.95 (978-1-60413-281-6(7), Facts On File) Infobase Holdings, Inc.
Mitchell, Kirstin. Madame Anopheles. 2008.Tr. of Señora Anopheles. (Illus.). 26p. (J). pap. 20.00 (978-0-9816301-0-6(3)) Alexander, Raine.
Person, Stephen. Malaria: Super Killer! 2010. (Nightmare Plagues Ser.). 32p. (YA). (gr. 4-9). lib. bdg. 28.50 (978-1-936088-07-2(X)) Bearport Publishing Co., Inc.

MALAWI

DeCapua, Sarah. Malawi in Pictures. 2009. (Visual Geography Series, Second Ser.). (ENG.). 80p. (gr. 5-12). 31.93 (978-0-8225-8575-6(8)) Lerner Publishing Group.
Kamkwamba, William. The Boy Who Harnessed the Wind: Creating Currents of Electricity & Hope. 2009. 14.44 (978-0-7848-3872-3(0), Everbind) Marco Bk. Co.
Kamkwamba, William & Mealer, Bryan. The Boy Who Harnessed the Wind: Picture Book Edition. Zunon, Elizabeth, illus. 2012. 32p. (J). (gr. 1-3). 18.99 (978-0-8037-3511-8(1), Dial Bks) Penguin Young Readers Group.
—The Boy Who Harnessed the Wind: Young Readers Edition. Hymas, Anna, illus. 304p. (J). (gr. 5). 2016. (ENG.). 9.99 (978-0-14-751042-6(2), Puffin Books) 2015. 18.99 (978-0-8037-4080-8(8), Dial Bks) Penguin Young Readers Group.
Levete, Sarah. A Tale of One Well in Malawi. 2010. (Big Picture: Climate Ser.). (ENG.). 24p. (gr. 1-2). pap. 41.70 (978-1-4296-5973-4(4), Capstone Pr.) Capstone.

MALAYSIA

Broadhead, Arp Raph. Mudley Explores Kuala Lumpur: An Amazing Adventure into Mudtown. 2017. (ENG., Illus.). 64p. (J). pap. 19.95 (978-981-4721-94-3(8)) Marshall Cavendish International (Asia) Private Ltd. SGP. Dist: Independent Pubs. Group.
Currie, Stephen. The Tallest Building. 2003. (Extreme Places Ser.). (ENG., Illus.). 48p. (J). (gr. 3-5). 27.50 (978-0-7377-1374-9(7), Kidhaven) Cengage Gale.
Di Piazza, Francesca. Malaysia in Pictures. 2006. (Visual Geography Series, Second Ser.). (ENG., Illus.). 80p. (J). (gr. 5-12). 31.93 (978-0-8225-2674-2(3)) Lerner Publishing Group.
Poisson, Barbara Aoki. Malaysia. 2010. (Major Muslim Nations Ser.). 128p. (YA). (gr. 5-18). lib. bdg. 25.95 (978-1-4222-1409-1(5)) Mason Crest.
Pundyk, Grace. Welcome to Malaysia. 1 vol. 2004. (Welcome to My Country Ser.). (ENG., Illus.). 48p. (gr. 2-4). lib. bdg.

29.67 *(978-0-8368-2560-2(8),* c7c96bb5-c527-47d4-9902-602c310e8b04) Stevens, Gareth Publishing LLLP.

Sullivan, Laura L. Malaysia, 1 vol. 2018. (Exploring World Cultures (First Edition) Ser.). (ENG.). 32p. (gr. 3-3). pap. 12.16 *(978-1-5026-4342-1(1),* 79172a82-094a-449b-a1a7-bf7f04b8d679) Cavendish Square Publishing LLC.

Thomas, Mark. Las Torres Gemelas Petronas, 1 vol. 2003. (Estructuras Extraordinarias (Record-Breaking Structures) Ser.). (SPA.). 24p. (J). (gr. 2-2). lib. bdg. 26.27 *(978-0-8239-6862-6(6),* f4b302f0-c52f-4471-955c-458adbe5d854, Editorial Buenas Letras) Rosen Publishing Group, Inc., The.

—The Petronas Twin Towers: World's Tallest Buildings. 2009. (Record-Breaking Structures Ser.). 24p. (gr. 1-2). 42.50 *(978-1-60852-457-0(4),* PowerKids Pr.) Rosen Publishing Group, Inc., The.

Weil, Ann. Meet Our New Student from Malaysia. 2008. (Meet Our New Student Ser.). (Illus.). 48p. (J). (gr. 1-5). lib. bdg. 29.95 *(978-1-58415-654-3(6))* Mitchell Lane Pubs.

MALAYSIA—FICTION

Alkaf, Hanna. The Weight of Our Sky. 2019. (ENG., Illus.). 288p. (YA). (gr. 7). 19.99 *(978-1-5344-2608-5(6),* Salaam Reads) Simon & Schuster Bks. For Young Readers.

Buchmann, Stephen & Cohn, Diana. The Bee Tree, 1 vol. Mirocha, Paul, illus. 2012. (ENG.). 40p. (J). (gr. 1-6). pap. 12.95 *(978-1-935955-14-6(4),* 23353382, Cinco Puntos Press) Lee & Low Bks., Inc.

Lat. Kampung Boy. Lat, illus. rev. ed. 2006. Orig. Title: The Kampung Boy. (ENG., Illus.). 144p. (YA). (gr. 7-8). pap. 21.99 *(978-1-59643-121-8(0),* 900031942, First Second Bks.) Roaring Brook Pr.

Lowe, Dave. The Incredible Dadventure 3: the Spectacular Holly-Day. Hammond, The Boy Fitz, illus. 2018. (Incredible Dadventure Ser.: 3). (ENG.). 192p. (J). (gr. 2-4). pap. 8.99 *(978-1-84812-611-4(5))* Bonnier Publishing GBR. Dist: Independent Pubs. Group.

Zeiss, Joyce Burns. Out of the Dragon's Mouth. 2015. (ENG., Illus.). 240p. (YA). (gr. 9-12). pap. 11.99 *(978-0-7387-4196-3(5),* 0738741965, Flux) North Star Editions.

MALAYSIA—HISTORY

Choi, Eun-Mi. Where Are You, Sun Bear? Malaysia. Cowley, Joy, ed. Noh, Seong-bin, illus. 2015. (Global Kids Storybooks Ser.). (ENG.). 32p. (gr. 1-4). 7.99 *(978-1-925246-54-4(X));* 26.65 *(978-1-925246-02-5(7));* 26.65 *(978-1-925246-28-5(0))* ChoiceMaker Pty. Ltd., The AUS. (Big and SMALL). Dist: Lerner Publishing Group.

Daniels-Cowart, Catrina. Malaysia. 2019. (Asian Countries Today Ser.). (Illus.). 96p. (J). (gr. 12). lib. bdg. 34.60 *(978-1-4222-4268-1(4))* Mason Crest.

Munan, Heidi, et al. Malaysia, 1 vol. 3rd rev. ed. 2012. (Cultures of the World (Third Edition)(r) Ser.). (ENG., Illus.). 144p. (gr. 5-5). 48.79 *(978-1-60870-785-0(7),* baaf5de3-e056-4864-99c5-f3d81b97c176) Cavendish Square Publishing LLC.

Owings, Lisa. Malaysia. 2014. (Exploring Countries Ser.). (ENG., Illus.). 32p. (J). (gr. 3-7). lib. bdg. 27.95 *(978-1-62617-068-1(1),* Blastoff! Readers) Bellwether Media.

Thomas, Mark. Las Torres Gemelas Petronas: Los Edificios Más Altos del Mundo (The Petronas Twin Towers: World'S Tallest Building) 2009. (Estructuras extraordinarias (Record-Breaking Structures) Ser.). (SPA.). 24p. (gr. 1-2). 42.50 *(978-1-61512-314-8(8),* Editorial Buenas Letras) Rosen Publishing Group, Inc., The.

MALCOLM X, 1925-1965

see X, Malcolm, 1925-1965

MALE GROOMING

see Grooming for Men

MALI

Blauer, Ettagale & LeVert, Suzanne. Mali, 1 vol. 2008. (Cultures of the World (First Edition)(r) Ser.). (ENG.). 144p. (gr. 5-5). lib. bdg. 49.79 *(978-0-7614-2568-7(3),* ad7229d6-88b6-4960-aa12-3a58d395c4d6) Cavendish Square Publishing LLC.

Diakité, Baba Wagué. A Gift from Childhood, 1 vol. 2013. (ENG., Illus.). 136p. (J). (gr. 4-5). pap. 12.95 *(978-1-55498-421-3(1))* Groundwood Bks. CAN. Dist: Publishers Group West (PGW).

DiPiazza, Francesca Davis. Mali in Pictures. 2007. (Visual Geography Series, Second Ser.). (ENG., Illus.). 80p. (gr. 5-12). lib. bdg. 31.93 *(978-0-8225-6591-8(9))* Lerner Publishing Group.

Harper, Kathryn. Timbuktu 2 Wayfarers. Peinador, Angeles, illus. 2017. (Cambridge Reading Adventures Ser.). (ENG.). 24p. (J). pap. 7.35 *(978-1-108-41085-4(5))* Cambridge Univ. Pr.

Klobuchar, Lisa. Africans of the Ghana, Mali, & Songhai Empires. 2009. (J). *(978-0-7166-2134-8(7))* World Bk., Inc.

Krasner, Barbara. Mansa Musa, 1 vol. 2016. (Silk Road's Greatest Travelers Ser.). (ENG.). 112p. (J). (gr. 6-6). 38.80 *(978-1-5081-7151-5(3),* b17cbd0a-277d-43eb-90c0-166677ab31c7) Rosen Publishing Group, Inc., The.

National Geographic Learning. Reading Expeditions (Social Studies: Civilizations Past to Present): Mali. 2007. (ENG., Illus.). 24p. (J). pap. 15.95 *(978-0-7922-4539-1(3))* CENGAGE Learning.

Ogunnaike, Oludamini. Meet Our New Student from Mali. 2009. (Meet Our New Student Ser.). (Illus.). 48p. (J). (gr. 2-5). lib. bdg. 25.70 *(978-1-58415-734-2(8))* Mitchell Lane Pubs.

Wolny, Philip. Discovering the Empire of Mali, 1 vol. 2013. (Exploring African Civilizations Ser.). (ENG.). 64p. (J). (gr. 6-6). 37.12 *(978-1-4777-1883-4(4),* 64432b1a-d2cb-4192-a304-7cc1687f0963, Rosen Reference) Rosen Publishing Group, Inc., The.

Zamosky, Lisa. Mansa Musa: Leader of Mali, 1 vol. rev. ed. 2007. (Social Studies: Informational Text Ser.). (ENG.). 32p. (gr. 4-8). pap. 11.99 *(978-0-7439-0439-1(7))* Teacher Created Materials, Inc.

MALI—FICTION

Fontes, Justine & Fontes, Ron. Sunjata: Warrior King of Mali [a West African Legend]. Carruthers, Sandy, illus. 2009. (Graphic Myths & Legends Ser.). (ENG.). 48p. (J). (gr. 4-8). pap. 9.99 *(978-1-58013-891-8(8),* 3168f99e-e3e7-4b82-b6a2-3688f6c11a45, Graphic Universe™) Lerner Publishing Group.

McDowell, JOsh & Hostetler, Bob. The Truth Twisters. 2006. (Illus.). 167p. (YA). (gr. 8-12). per. 11.99 *(978-1-932587-84-5(5))* Practical Christianity Foundation.

Wingard, Lucinda. The Turn-Around Bird. 2012. 296p. pap. 16.00 *(978-0-9848400-1-4(X))* Plicata Pr. LLC.

MALLORY, GEORGE, 1886-1924

Herman, Gail & Amatrula, Michele. Climbing Everest (Totally True Adventures) How Two Friends Reached Earth's Highest Peak. 2015. (Totally True Adventures Ser.). (Illus.). 112p. (J). (gr. 2-5). 5.99 *(978-0-553-50986-1(1),* Random Hse. Bks. for Young Readers) Random Hse. Children's Bks.

MALTA

Nevins, Debbie, et al. Malta, 1 vol. 2019. (Cultures of the World (Third Edition)(r) Ser.). (ENG.). 144p. (gr. 5-5). lib. bdg. 48.79 *(978-1-5026-4748-1(6),* 1a45bacf-a54d-4aa8-9fd4-94b28576d8d9) Cavendish Square Publishing LLC.

Sheehan, Sean & Lin, Yong Jui. Malta, 1 vol. 2nd rev. ed. 2011. (Cultures of the World (Second Edition)(r) Ser.). (ENG.). 144p. (gr. 5-5). 49.79 *(978-1-60870-024-0(0),* 867483a0-5f80-4b84-9eb9-3cedf9bfe9b0) Cavendish Square Publishing LLC.

Stafford, James. Malta. 2007. (European Union Ser.). (Illus.). 88p. (YA). (gr. 3-7). lib. bdg. 21.95 *(978-1-4222-0056-8(6))* Mason Crest.

Stafford, James & Indovino, Shaina Carmel. Malta. 2012. (J). *(978-1-4222-2252-2(7));* pap. *(978-1-4222-2283-6(7))* Mason Crest.

MALTA—FICTION

Brunson, Emma. Survivor Spirit Book: Megan's Ark. 2010. 204p. pap. 13.50 *(978-1-60911-834-1(0),* Eloquent Bks.) Strategic Book Publishing & Rights Agency (SBPRA).

Evans, Margaret & Galea, Angele. Marco the Malta Bus. 2018. (ENG., Illus.). 116p. (J). (gr. 1-5). pap. *(978-1-5289-2437-5(1))* Austin Macauley Pubs. Ltd.

MAMMALS

see also Primates

also names of mammals, e.g. Bats

About Mammals / Sobre Los Mamíferos: A Guide for Children / una Guía para Niños, 1 vol. 2014. (About... Ser.: 15). (Illus.). 48p. (J). (gr. -1-2). 8.99 *(978-1-56145-800-4(7))* Peachtree Publishing Co. Inc.

Alden, Peter. Peterson Field Guide Coloring Books: Mammals. 2nd ed. 2013. (Peterson Field Guide Color-In Bks.). (ENG., Illus.). 64p. 10.99 *(978-0-544-03254-5(3),* 1530244, Mariner Bks.) HarperCollins Pubs.

Alderton, David. Mammals Around the World. 2014. (Animals Around the World Ser.). (ENG., Illus.). 32p. (J). (gr. 2-5). 31.35 *(978-1-62588-195-3(9),* 19260, Smart Apple Media) Black Rabbit Bks.

Allan, John. Mammals. 2019. (Amazing Life Cycles Ser.). (ENG., Illus.). 32p. (J). (gr. 1-3). lib. bdg. 29.32 *(978-1-912108-11-4(9),* c6e95e53-37dc-4c51-9670-33b7ca08480d, Hungry Tomato (r)) Lerner Publishing Group.

Allman, Toney. Deadliest Mammals. 2016. (ENG.). 80p. (J). (gr. 5-12). lib. bdg. *(978-1-68282-050-6(5))* ReferencePoint Pr., Inc.

Anne McBride. Ferrets, Vol. 12. 2016. (Understanding & Caring for Your Pet Ser.: Vol. 12). (ENG., Illus.). 128p. (J). (gr. 5-8). 25.95 *(978-1-4222-3695-6(1))* Mason Crest.

Anteaters. 2014. (ENG.). 48p. (J). lib. bdg. 28.00 *(978-0-531-20667-6(X))* Scholastic Library Publishing.

Antill, Sara. Giant Anteater, 1 vol. 2010. (Unusual Animals Ser.). (ENG., Illus.). 24p. (J). (gr. 2-3). pap. 9.15 *(978-1-61533-001-0(1),* 987f6cc5-5045-4965-ab72-28935411e412); lib. bdg. 27.27 *(978-1-60754-993-2(X),* 6a00972a-b924-40c4-a0a9-eabbb554de87) Rosen Publishing Group, Inc., The. (Windmill Bks.).

—Okapi, 1 vol. 2010. (Unusual Animals Ser.). (ENG., Illus.). 24p. (J). (gr. 2-3). pap. 9.15 *(978-1-61533-007-2(0),* 50ef7529-434e-48de-a1d2-a8122ca2d742); lib. bdg. 27.27 *(978-1-60754-996-3(4),* 328c26f7-ab04-4c3c-8447-dc8a771ceb3f) Rosen Publishing Group, Inc., The. (Windmill Bks.).

Bailey, Diane. Saving Marine Mammals: Whales, Dolphins, Seals, & More. 2017. (Illus.). 64p. (J). *(978-1-4222-3878-3(4))* Mason Crest.

Beaumont, Holly. Why Do Monkeys & Other Mammals Have Fur? 2015. (Animal Body Coverings Ser.). (ENG., Illus.). 24p. (J). (gr. 1-3). pap. 6.99 *(978-1-4846-2539-2(0),* 130024, Heinemann) Capstone.

Bennett, Mia. Ferrets, 1 vol. 2017. (Our Weird Pets Ser.). (ENG.). 24p. (J). (gr. 3-3). 25.27 *(978-1-5081-5416-7(3),* 6b346bcd-5358-4d2e-89a7-da0d5ac4686e, PowerKids Pr.) Rosen Publishing Group, Inc., The.

Bloom & Ronzani, Maggie. Mammals: Grades 2 Through 4. (Illus.). (J). pap., wbk. ed. 4.99 *(978-0-88743-963-6(2))* School Zone Publishing Co.

Bodden, Valerie. Le Léopard des Neiges. 2018. (Planète Animaux Ser.). (FRE., Illus.). 24p. (J). *(978-1-77092-398-0(5),* 19687) Creative Co., The.

—Le Paresseux. 2018. (Planète Animaux Ser.). (FRE., Illus.). 24p. (J). *(978-1-77092-397-3(7),* 19686) Creative Co., The.

Bowman, Chris. Pronghorn. 2015. (North American Animals Ser.). (ENG., Illus.). 24p. (J). (gr. k-3). lib. bdg. 26.95 *(978-1-62617-192-3(0),* Blastoff! Readers) Bellwether Media.

Bredeson, Carmen. Fainting Goats & Other Weird Mammals, 1 vol. 2009. (I Like Weird Animals! Ser.). (ENG., Illus.). 24p. (gr. k-2). lib. bdg. 25.27 *(978-0-7660-3122-7(5),* c4ad87a9-847c-4a8a-94fb-c3ee80574a76, Enslow Elementary) Enslow Publishing, LLC.

Brewer, Duncan. 1000 Things You Should Know about Mammals. 2004. (1000 Things You Should Know about Ser.). (Illus.). 64p. (YA). (gr. 5-18). 19.95 *(978-1-59084-467-0(X))* Mason Crest.

Brown Bear Books. Mammals of the Northern Hemisphere. 2011. (Endangered Animals Ser.). (ENG., Illus.). 64p. (J). (gr. 8-11). lib. bdg. 39.95 *(978-1-936333-34-9(1),* 16484) Brown Bear Bks.

Brown, Kathryn Keil. The Alpaca-Bet! Abc's of Alpacas. 2012. 48p. pap. 21.88 *(978-1-4669-7108-0(8))* Trafford Publishing.

Brown, Martin. Lesser Spotted Animals. 2017. (Illus.). 53p. (J). *(978-1-338-17148-8(9))* Scholastic, Inc.

Buckingham, Suzanne. Meet the Ring-Tailed Lemur, 1 vol. 2008. (Scales & Tails Ser.). (ENG., Illus.). 24p. (J). (gr. 2-3). lib. bdg. 26.27 *(978-1-4042-4501-3(4),* d913d97d-07fc-481c-a35d-92f30ad86a2d, PowerKids Pr.) Rosen Publishing Group, Inc., The.

Bulletpoints Mammals. 2005. (Illus.). (J). per. 4.99 *(978-1-933581-04-0(2))* Byeway Bks.

Burroughs, John. Squirrels & Other Fur-Bearers (Yesterday's Classics) 2006. (Illus.). 144p. (J). pap. 8.95 *(978-1-59915-070-3(0))* Yesterday's Classics.

Caputo, Christine A. Mammals. 2012. (Illus.). 32p. (J). *(978-0-545-46699-8(7))* Scholastic, Inc.

Carper, Virginia. Animal Teachings: Mammals. 2005. ring bd., wbk. ed. 20.00 *(978-0-9788858-0-9(5))* Animal Teachers Enterprises.

Carr, Aaron. Ferret. 2014. (Illus.). 24p. (J). *(978-1-62127-292-2(3))* Weigl Pubs., Inc.

Ciovacco, Justine. Meerkats, 1 vol. 2008. (Amazing Animals Ser.). (ENG.). 48p. (YA). (gr. 3-5). lib. bdg. 30.67 *(978-0-8368-9098-3(1),* 343c72cb-3801-41cb-8f15-af63d4cdb9dd) Stevens, Gareth Publishing LLLP.

Clark, Willow. Flying Lemurs, 1 vol. 2012. (Up a Tree Ser.). (ENG., Illus.). 24p. (J). (gr. 2-3). pap. 9.25 *(978-1-4488-6327-3(9),* 80c93e28-d67a-46e2-93df-3000ec48eada, PowerKids Pr.); lib. bdg. 26.27 *(978-1-4488-6184-2(5),* b6f428e0-bba3-49c5-b226-089f378d35ed) Rosen Publishing Group, Inc., The.

—Meerkats: Life in the Mob, 1 vol. 2011. (Animal Families Ser.). (ENG.). 24p. (J). (gr. 1-1). pap. 9.25 *(978-1-4488-2608-7(X),* 99d0e55e-9bd0-4362-a894-1fdc1e12229b); (Illus.). lib. bdg. 26.27 *(978-1-4488-2511-0(3),* 3ab6db97-51ab-4113-a978-4c2ec87d2b2f) Rosen Publishing Group, Inc., The. (PowerKids Pr.).

—Meerkats: Suricatas: Life in the Mob: Vida en la Colonia, 1 vol. 2011. (Animal Families / Familias de Animales Ser.). (SPA & ENG., Illus.). 24p. (gr. 1-1). lib. bdg. 26.27 *(978-1-4488-3125-8(3),* 7f634dfc-510b-491d-9b8f-01f52772c2c9, PowerKids Pr.) Rosen Publishing Group, Inc., The.

Clarke, Ginjer L. Baby Otter. Cuddy, Robin, illus. 2009. (Penguin Young Readers, Level 3 Ser.). 48p. (J). (gr. 1-3). mass mkt. 4.99 *(978-0-448-45105-3(0),* Penguin Young Readers) Penguin Young Readers Group.

Clay, Kathryn. Mammals in the Wild. 2018. (Mammals in the Wild Ser.). (ENG.). 24p. (J). (gr. -1-2). 147.90 *(978-1-9771-0100-6(3),* 28296, Pebble) Capstone.

Claybourne, Anna. A Pack of Wolves: And Other Canine Groups, 1 vol. 2012. (Animals in Groups Ser.). (ENG.). 48p. (J). (gr. 4-6). pap. 9.95 *(978-1-4329-6489-4(5),* 119076, Heinemann) Capstone.

Collinson, Clare. Nature in Your Neighbourhood: British Mammals. 2018. (Nature in Your Neighbourhood Ser.). (ENG., Illus.). 32p. (J). (gr. 2-4). pap. 9.99 *(978-1-4451-3639-4(2),* Franklin Watts) Hachette Children's Group GBR. Dist: Hachette Bk. Group.

Conklin, Wendy. Life Cycles, 1 vol. 2015. (Science: Informational Text Ser.). (ENG., Illus.). 32p. (gr. 3-4). pap. 11.99 *(978-1-4807-4637-4(1))* Teacher Created Materials, Inc.

Costain, Meredith. Mammals Great & Small, 1 vol. 2014. (Discovery Education: Animals Ser.). (ENG.). 32p. (J). (gr. 4-5). 27.93 *(978-1-4777-6940-9(4),* 038ee61f-de83-498a-8651-497d26c2181e); pap. 11.00 *(978-1-4777-6941-6(2),* 8db76486-b347-4ef0-8c83-d003087f73c1) Rosen Publishing Group, Inc., The. (PowerKids Pr.).

Dawson, Emily C. How Animals Find Water. 2010. (Amicus Readers. Our Animal World (Level 1) Ser.). (ENG.). 24p. (J). (gr. k-2). lib. bdg. 25.65 *(978-1-60753-011-4(2),* 17166) Amicus.

De la Bédoyère, Camilla. My Little Book of Baby Animals. 2016. (Illus.). 64p. (J). *(978-1-4351-6347-8(8))* Barnes & Noble, Inc.

—Why Why Why Are Orang-Utans So Hairy? 2008. (Why Why Why Ser.). (Illus.). 32p. (J). (gr. 4-7). pap. *(978-1-84810-003-9(5))* Miles Kelly Publishing, Ltd.

—Why Why Why... Are Orangutans So Hairy? 2010. (Why Why Why Ser.). (Illus.). 32p. (J). (gr. 1-3). lib. bdg. 18.95 *(978-1-4222-1570-8(9))* Mason Crest.

DK. Pocket Genius: Mammals: Facts at Your Fingertips. 2016. (Pocket Genius Ser.: 12). (ENG., Illus.). 160p. (J). (gr. 3-7). pap. 6.99 *(978-1-4654-4589-6(7),* DK Children) Dorling Kindersley Publishing, Inc.

Drumlin, Sam. Manatees, 1 vol. 2013. (PowerKids Readers: Sea Friends Ser.). (ENG., Illus.). 24p. (J). (gr. k-k). pap. 9.25 *(978-1-4488-9746-9(7),* 4cba2d30-085f-470e-9410-e3c8b5b69792); lib. bdg. 26.27 *(978-1-4488-9644-8(4),* e0e6cfa0-1fd6-4013-b524-e385d6f80e16) Rosen Publishing Group, Inc., The. (PowerKids Pr.).

—Manatees: Los Manatíes, 1 vol. Alamán, Eduardo, tr. 2013. (PowerKids Readers: Los Amigos Del Mar / Sea Friends Ser.). (SPA & ENG., Illus.). 24p. (J). (gr. k-k). lib. bdg. 26.27 *(978-1-4488-9974-6(5),* 4721f5db-b0b1-47a4-b912-f1a666e8a005, PowerKids Pr.) Rosen Publishing Group, Inc., The.

Early Macken, JoAnn. Mountain Goats / Cabra Montés, 1 vol. 2005. (Animals That Live in the Mountains / Animales de Las Montañas (First Edition) Ser.). (ENG & SPA., Illus.). 24p. (gr. 1-1). lib. bdg. 24.27 *(978-0-8368-6451-9(4),* 468e789c-de87-4eac-8fc4-621c0196165b, Weekly Reader Leveled Readers) Stevens, Gareth Publishing LLLP.

Edwards, Sue Bradford. The Evolution of Mammals. 2018. (Animal Evolution Ser.). (ENG., Illus.). 112p. (J). (gr. 6-12). lib. bdg. 41.36 *(978-1-5321-1666-7(7),* 30584, Essential Library) ABDO Publishing Co.

Einhorn, Kama. Anteater Adventure. 2019. (True Tales of Rescue Ser.). (ENG., Illus.). 144p. (J). (gr. 3-7). 14.99 *(978-1-328-76704-2(3),* 1680374, Clarion Bks.) HarperCollins Pubs.

Einstein, Tamara. Mammals of Canada, 1 vol. 2016. (KidsWorld Ser.). (ENG., Illus.). 64p. (J). pap. 6.99 *(978-0-9940069-3-6(4),* c5d02ba5-61cc-4af0-abf2-3ad9311b9119) KidsWorld Bks. CAN. Dist: Lone Pine Publishing USA.

Encyclopaedia Britannica, Inc. Staff, compiled by. Britannica Illustrated Science Library: Mammals, 16 vols. 2008. (Illus.). (J). 29.95 *(978-1-59339-393-9(8))* Encyclopaedia Britannica, Inc.

—My First Britannica: Mammals. 2008. (gr. 7-12). *(978-1-59339-412-7(8))* Encyclopaedia Britannica, Inc.

Encyclopedia Britannica Staff, creator. Mammals. 2011. (Britannica Illustrated Science Library Ser.). 104p. (J). 37.44 *(978-1-61535-466-5(2))* Encyclopaedia Britannica, Inc.

Endangered Mammals - Africa: An Educational Coloring Book. (J). (gr. 3-18). pap. 1.99 *(978-0-86545-213-8(X))* Spizzirri Pr., Inc.

Endangered Mammals - Asia & China: An Educational Coloring Book. (J). (gr. 3-18). pap. 1.99 *(978-0-86545-214-5(8))* Spizzirri Pr., Inc.

Endangered Mammals - South America: An Educational Coloring Book. (J). pap. 1.99 *(978-0-86545-215-2(6))* Spizzirri Pr., Inc.

Falchetta, Drew. Mammals Love Their Babies. 2015. (1-3Y Animals Ser.). (ENG., Illus.). 20p. (J). pap. 8.00 *(978-1-63437-623-5(4))* American Reading Co.

Feldman, Thea. Animales Migratorios: Por Tierra (Migrating Animals of the Land), 1 vol. 2007. (En Marcha: Migraciones Animales (on the Move: Animal Migration) Ser.). (SPA.). 24p. (gr. 2-4). pap. 9.15 *(978-0-8368-8433-3(7),* 4ff86505-62a7-4a2b-817e-46e5b9c1692a); (Illus.). lib. bdg. 24.67 *(978-0-8368-8428-9(0),* 942535c5-1053-4b9f-9e50-88b1309f52a2) Stevens, Gareth Publishing LLLP. (Weekly Reader Leveled Readers).

—Migrating Animals of the Land, 1 vol. 2007. (On the Move: Animal Migration Ser.). (ENG.). 24p. (gr. 2-4). pap. 9.15 *(978-0-8368-8423-4(X),* a2e26e30-2d12-4a7e-8ea7-77f43f2fcd58); (Illus.). lib. bdg. 24.67 *(978-0-8368-8418-0(3),* a00a8909-329f-4cbf-8c60-7609868f6f83) Stevens, Gareth Publishing LLLP. (Weekly Reader Leveled Readers).

Fox, Phoebe. Babies Nurse: Así Se Alimentan los Bebés. Geating, Karen Rivera, tr. Fox, Jim, illus. 2018. (ENG.). 32p. (J). (gr. -1-2). 14.95 *(978-1-930775-73-2(3))* Platypus Media, L.L.C.

—Babies Nurse / Así Se Alimentan Los Bebés. Geating, Karen Rivera, tr. Fox, Jim, illus. 2018. (ENG.). 32p. (J). (gr. -1-2). pap. 9.95 *(978-1-930775-72-5(5))* Platypus Media, L.L.C.

Furstinger, Nancy. Warthogs. 2017. (Animals of Africa Ser.). (ENG., Illus.). 32p. (J). (gr. 2-3). pap. 9.95 *(978-1-63517-333-8(7),* 1635173337); lib. bdg. 31.35 *(978-1-63517-268-3(3),* 1635172683) North Star Editions. (Focus Readers).

—12 Mammals Back from the Brink. 2015. (Back from the Brink Ser.). (ENG., Illus.). 32p. (J). (gr. 3-6). 32.80 *(978-1-63235-003-9(3),* 11530, 12-Story Library) Bookstaves, LLC.

Gagne, Tammy. Meerkats. 2017. (Animals of Africa Ser.). (ENG., Illus.). 32p. (J). (gr. 2-3). lib. bdg. 31.35 *(978-1-63517-267-6(5),* 1635172675, Focus Readers) North Star Editions.

—The Most Adorable Animals in the World. 2015. (All about Animals Ser.). (ENG., Illus.). 24p. (J). (gr. 1-3). pap. 6.95 *(978-1-4914-2239-7(4),* 127735) Capstone.

Gibbs, Maddie. Jackals, 1 vol. 2011. (Safari Animals Ser.). (ENG.). 24p. (J). (gr. 1-1). pap. 9.25 *(978-1-4488-2596-7(2),* 763ee5db-4761-4e34-9780-ae7a16a693ea); lib. bdg. 26.27 *(978-1-4488-2505-9(9),* 1aa3e14d-62fc-49cd-a803-d69480b7a768) Rosen Publishing Group, Inc., The. (PowerKids Pr.).

—Jackals: Chacales, 1 vol. 2011. (Safari Animals / Animales de Safari Ser.). (ENG & SPA.). 24p. (J). (gr. 1-1). lib. bdg. 26.27 *(978-1-4488-3119-7(9),* dc860035-599f-4b2f-9b4f-ab2058d47fc9) Rosen Publishing Group, Inc., The.

Gilbert, Sara. Giant Short-Faced Bears. 2017. (Ice Age Mega Beasts Ser.). (ENG., Illus.). 24p. (J). (gr. 1-4). pap. 8.99 *(978-1-62832-374-0(4),* 20072, Creative Paperbacks) Creative Co., The.

—Stag-Moose. 2017. (Ice Age Mega Beasts Ser.). (ENG., Illus.). 24p. (J). (gr. 1-4). pap. 8.99 *(978-1-62832-378-8(7),* 20084, Creative Paperbacks) Creative Co., The.

Gish, Melissa. Bighorn Sheep. (Living Wild Ser.). (ENG.). 48p. (J). 2016. (gr. 5-9). pap. 12.00 *(978-1-62832-165-4(2),* 20878, Creative Paperbacks) 2015. (Illus.). (gr. 4-7). *(978-1-60818-564-1(8),* 20877, Creative Education) Creative Co., The.

—Manatees. 2017. (Living Wild Ser.). (ENG., Illus.). 48p. (J). (gr. 4-7). pap. 12.00 *(978-1-62832-301-6(9),* 20611, Creative Paperbacks) Creative Co., The.

—Meerkats. 2015. (Living Wild Ser.). (ENG., Illus.). 48p. (J). (gr. 4-7). *(978-1-60818-569-6(9),* 20893, Creative Education) Creative Co., The.

Goldish, Meish. Fossa: A Fearsome Predator. 2008. (Uncommon Animals Ser.). (Illus.). 32p. (J). (gr. 2-5). lib. bdg. 28.50 *(978-1-59716-732-1(0))* Bearport Publishing Co., Inc.

—Mammal Menu. 2009. (Extreme Cuisine Ser.). (Illus.). 24p. (J). (gr. 1-4). lib. bdg. 26.99 *(978-1-59716-760-4(6))* Bearport Publishing Co., Inc.

Graham Gaines, Ann. Kids Top 10 Small Mammal Pets, 1 vol. 2014. (American Humane Association Top 10 Pets for Kids Ser.). (ENG.). 48p. (gr. 3-4). 26.93 *(978-0-7660-6650-2(9),* f9e54a01-448b-4020-a7eb-89e4fc22f5ff); pap. 11.53 *(978-0-7660-6651-9(7),* 91b75ee7-ee96-485b-a367-c17108750adc, Enslow Elementary) Enslow Publishing, LLC.

Greenwood, Mark. The Last Tiger. 2018. (History Mysteries Ser.). (Illus.). 96p. (J). (gr. 3-7). 8.99 *(978-0-14-330925-3(0))* Random Hse. Australia AUS. Dist: Independent Pubs. Group.

Gregory, Helen. All about Mammals, 1 vol. 2011. (Wonder Readers Early Level Ser.). (ENG.). 16p. (gr. -1-1). (J). pap. 6.25 *(978-1-4296-7795-0(3),* 117967); pap. 35.94 *(978-1-4296-8067-7(9))* Capstone. (Capstone Pr.).

Grucella, A. J. Bobcats, 1 vol. 2012. (Killer Cats Ser.). (ENG., Illus.). 24p. (J). (gr. 2-3). pap. 9.15 *(978-1-4339-6996-6(3),* 34e0f7a5-dab0-45b4-9979-2b2a6abea046); lib. bdg. 25.27 *(978-1-4339-6995-9(5),*

MNO

911a2413-7ec5-4538-8cda-f65d01b322e5) Stevens, Gareth Publishing LLLP.

Grzimek, Bernhard & McDade, Melissa C. Grzimek's Student Animal Life Resource. 2004. (J). (978-0-7876-9234-6(4)); (978-0-7876-9188-2(7)); (978-0-7876-9187-5(9)); (978-0-7876-9184-4(4)); (Illus.). (978-0-7876-9185-1(2)) Cengage Gale. (UXL).

—Mammals, 5 vols., Vol. 20. 2004. (Grzimek's Student Animal Life Resource Ser.). (ENG., Illus.). 1000p. (J). 557.00 (978-0-7876-9183-7(6), UXL) Cengage Gale.

Gustafson, Sarah. Whales, Dolphins, & More Marine Mammals. 2005. (Illus.). 48p. (J). pap. (978-0-439-71189-0(4)) Scholastic, Inc.

Hairy Little Critters: Individual Title Six-Packs. (Action Packs Ser.). 104p. (gr. 3-5). 44.00 (978-0-7635-8404-7(5)) Rigby Education.

Hall, Katharine. Mammals: a Compare & Contrast Book, 1 vol. 2016. (Compare & Contrast Ser.). (ENG., Illus.). 39p. (J). (gr. k-3). 17.95 (978-1-62855-729-9(X)) Arbordale Publishing.

—Mammals: a Compare & Contrast Book: Spanish, 1 vol. 2016. (SPA.). 39p. (J). (gr. k-3). pap. 11.95 (978-1-62855-743-5(5)) Arbordale Publishing.

Halls, Kelly Milner. Wild Horses: Galloping Through Time. Hallett, Mark, illus. 2008. (Darby Creek Exceptional Titles Ser.). 72p. (J). (gr. 1-7). 18.95 (978-1-58196-065-5(4), Darby Creek) Lerner Publishing Group.

Hamilton, Lynn & Gillespie, Katie. Ferret. 2015. (J). (978-1-4896-2954-8(8)) Weigl Pubs., Inc.

Hansen, Grace. Bonobos, 1 vol. 2015. (Animal Friends Ser.). (ENG., Illus.). 24p. (J). (gr. -1-2). 32.79 (978-1-62970-895-9(X), 18226, Abdo Kids) ABDO Publishing Co.

—Suricata (Meerkat) 2018. (Animales Africanos (African Animals) Ser.). (SPA., Illus.). 24p. (J). (gr. -1-2). lib. bdg. 32.79 (978-1-5321-8031-6(4), 28277, Abdo Kids) ABDO Publishing Co.

Hare, Tony. Animal Fact File: Head-To-Tail Profiles of More Than 90 Mammals. 2018. (ENG.). 192p. (J). pap. 26.95 (978-981-4779-76-0(8)) Marshall Cavendish International (Asia) Private Ltd. SGP. Dist: Independent Pubs. Group.

Harvey, Jeanne Walker. Honey Girl: the Hawaiian Monk Seal. Bersani, Shennen, illus. 2017. (ENG.). 32p. (J). (gr. k-3). pap. 9.95 (978-1-62855-922-4(5)) Arbordale Publishing.

Hay DeSimone, Corkey. Mammal Animal Board Book 2nd Edition. Hay DeSimone, Corkey, illus. 2007. (Illus.). 24p. (J). 7.95 (978-0-9777394-2-4(2)) Gentle Giraffe Pr.

—Mammal Animal Coloring & Activity Book: What Is a mammal? You are a mammal Too! 2005. (illus.). (J). pap. 4.95 (978-0-9747921-2-5(8)) Gentle Giraffe Pr.

Haynes, Danielle. Mammal Fossils, 1 vol. 2016. (Fossil Files Ser.). (ENG.). 32p. (J). (gr. 5-5). 27.93 (978-1-4994-2859-9(6), ad056739-de75-4fbc-bd76-d1cefb1310f7, PowerKids Pr.) Rosen Publishing Group, Inc., The.

Head, Honor. Amazing Mammals, 1 vol. 2008. (Amazing Life Cycles Ser.). (ENG., Illus.). 32p. (gr. 3-5). lib. bdg. 28.67 (978-0-8368-8896-6(0), af13f778-17e8-466b-9c16-e62453b60da8, Gareth Stevens Learning Library) Stevens, Gareth Publishing LLLP.

Heos, Bridget. Just Like Us! Cats. Clark, David, illus. 2019. (Just Like Us! Ser.). (ENG.). 32p. (J). (gr. -1-3). pap. 7.99 (978-0-358-00389-2(X), 1736322); 14.99 (978-1-328-79184-9(X), 1685035) HarperCollins Pubs. (Clarion Bks.).

Herriges, Ann. Manatees. 2006. (Oceans Alive Ser.). (ENG., Illus.). 24p. (J). (gr. k-3). lib. bdg. 26.95 (978-1-60014-048-8(3)) Bellwether Media.

Higgins, Melissa. Woolly Mammoths. 2015. (Ice Age Animals Ser.). (ENG., Illus.). 24p. (J). (gr. -1-2). pap. 6.95 (978-1-4914-2320-2(X), 127778, Capstone Pr.) Capstone.

Holt, Rinehart and Winston Staff. Holt Science & Technology Chapter 17: Life Science: Birds & Mammals. 5th ed. 2004. (Illus.). pap. 12.86 (978-0-03-030226-8(9)) Holt McDougal.

Housel, Debra J. Mammal Mania, 1 vol. 2nd rev. ed. 2011. (TIME for KIDS(r): Informational Text Ser.). (ENG.). 28p. (gr. 3-4). pap. 11.99 (978-1-4333-3658-4(8)) Teacher Created Materials, Inc.

Hudak, Heather C. Carnivores. 2011. (J). (gr. 4-6). pap. 12.95 (978-1-61690-713-6(4), AV2 by Weigl); (Illus.). 24p. (gr. 2-5). 27.13 (978-1-61690-707-5(X)) Weigl Pubs., Inc.

—Land Mammals. 2005. (Animal Facts Ser.). (Illus.). 24p. (J). (gr. 2-3). per. 8.95 (978-1-59036-245-7(4)); (gr. 4-7). lib. bdg. 24.45 (978-1-59036-200-6(4)) Weigl Pubs., Inc.

Hunt, Santana. Name That Mammal!, 1 vol. 2016. (Guess That Animal! Ser.). (ENG.). 24p. (J). (gr 1-2). lib. bdg. 24.27 (978-1-4824-4746-0(0), 7a75dcb3-a611-44eb-ac91-7f2d4aad4b2b) Stevens, Gareth Publishing LLLP.

Inserra, Rose. Mammals, 1 vol. 2010. (Weird, Wild, & Wonderful Ser.). (ENG., Illus.). 24p. (J). (gr. 2-3). lib. bdg. 24.67 (978-1-4339-3573-2(2), ab2011b9-0826-4fbb-8e57-6dbb59df1cf2, Gareth Stevens Learning Library) Stevens, Gareth Publishing LLLP.

Jacobs, Daniel. Big Babies. 2005. (Yellow Umbrella Fluent Level Ser.). (ENG., Illus.). 16p. (gr. k-1). pap. 35.70 (978-0-7368-5293-7(X), Capstone Pr.) Capstone.

Jacobs, Pat. Why Do Mammals Have Fur? And Other Questions about Evolution & Classification, 1 vol. 2016. (Wildlife Wonders Ser.). (ENG.). 32p. (J). (gr. 3-3). pap. 11.00 (978-1-4994-3208-4(9), f71e1fb8-144e-4520-bbe7-2c0d86111be8, PowerKids Pr.) Rosen Publishing Group, Inc., The.

Jacobson, Bray. Mammal Life Cycles, 1 vol. 2017. (Look at Life Cycles Ser.). (ENG.). 32p. (J). (gr. 2-2). pap. 11.50 (978-1-5382-1048-2(7), 69f7c8a2-c7ea-4ea7-8ed4-ccdf0817bdcb) Stevens, Gareth Publishing LLLP.

Jaycox, Jaclyn. Mammals: A 4D Book. 2018. (Little Zoologist Ser.). (ENG., Illus.). 32p. (J). (gr. -1-2). lib. bdg. 30.65 (978-1-5435-2646-2(2), 138106, Pebble) Capstone.

Jeffrey, Laura S. Choosing a Hamster, Gerbil, Guinea Pig, Rabbit, Ferret, Mouse, or Rat: How to Choose & Care for a Small Mammal, 1 vol. 2013. (American Humane Association Pet Care Ser.). (ENG.). 48p. (gr. 3-3). pap. 11.53 (978-1-4644-0217-3(5), 09cd07e0-95e5-4041-ad02-62463cf3eb9c, Enslow Elementary); lib. bdg. 27.93 (978-0-7660-4082-3(8), d3d8843b-30fd-47f5-897a-ead7dd0b568e) Enslow Publishing, LLC.

Jennings, Dorothy. Otters Smash, Crabs Pinch, 1 vol. 2017. (Hunter & Hunted: Animal Survival Ser.). (ENG.). 24p. (J). (gr. 3-3). 25.27 (978-1-5081-5662-8(X), 3981d87f-307e-4b6d-98de-eff2c9b49f78, PowerKids Pr.) Rosen Publishing Group, Inc., The.

Johnston, Coleen. Unusual Mammals from A to Z. 2008. (ENG.). 34p. pap. 19.95 (978-1-4357-5566-6(9)) Lulu Pr., Inc.

Kalman, Bobbie. Baby Carnivores. 2013. (ENG., Illus.). 24p. (J). (978-0-7787-1010-3(6)); pap. (978-0-7787-1015-8(7)) Crabtree Publishing Co.

—Baby Mammals. 2013. (ENG., Illus.). 24p. (J). (978-0-7787-1008-0(4)); pap. (978-0-7787-1013-4(0)) Crabtree Publishing Co.

—Insect Eaters, 1 vol. 2008. (Big Science Ideas Ser.). (ENG., Illus.). 32p. (J). (gr. 1-4). pap. (978-0-7787-3298-3(3), 1286308); lib. bdg. (978-0-7787-3278-5(9), 1286308) Crabtree Publishing Co.

—What Is a Carnivore? 2008. (ENG., Illus.). 32p. (J). (978-0-7787-7664-2(6)) Crabtree Publishing Co.

Kalman, Bobbie & Dyer, Hadley. Endangered Manatees. 2006. (Earth's Endangered Animals Ser.). (ENG., Illus.). 32p. (J). (gr. 3-7). lib. bdg. (978-0-7787-1868-0(9)) Crabtree Publishing Co.

Kalman, Bobbie & Johnson, Robin. Koalas & Other Marsupials. 2005. (What Kind of Animal Is It? Ser.). (ENG., Illus.). 32p. (J). (gr. 1-2). lib. bdg. (978-0-7787-2162-8(0)) Crabtree Publishing Co.

Kalman, Bobbie & Lundblad, Kristina. Animales Llamados Mamiferos. 2007. (Que Tipo de Animal Es? Ser.). (SPA., Illus.). 32p. (J). (gr. 1-2). lib. bdg. (978-0-7787-8836-2(9)); (gr. k-4). pap. (978-0-7787-8872-0(5)) Crabtree Publishing Co.

—Animals Called Mammals. 2005. (What Kind of Animal Is It? Ser.). (ENG., Illus.). 32p. (J). (gr. k-4). pap. (978-0-7787-2215-1(5)) Crabtree Publishing Co.

Kaspar, Anna. What's a Mammal?, 1 vol. 2012. (All about Animals Ser.). (ENG., Illus.). 24p. (J). (gr. 1-1). pap. 9.25 (978-1-4488-6232-0(9), 4e75e1a9-2df5-4aa2-bb77-eadaf3b3d650); lib. bdg. 26.27 (978-1-4488-6137-8(3), 01c06f25-fd36-4f93-b60d-dcccfb155117) Rosen Publishing Group, Inc., The. (PowerKids Pr.).

—What's a Mammal? Qué Es un Mamifero?, 1 vol. 2012. (All about Animals / Todo Sobre Los Animales Ser.). (SPA & ENG., Illus.). 24p. (J). (gr. 1-1). lib. bdg. 26.27 (978-1-4488-6703-5(7), 71ac5438-7816-4435-9eff-5ae9ad398d97, PowerKids Pr.) Rosen Publishing Group, Inc., The.

Kids, National Geographic. Ultimate Explorer Field Guide: Mammals. 2019. (Illus.). 160p. (J). (gr. 3-7). pap. 12.99 (978-1-4263-3369-9(2)); (ENG., lib. bdg. 22.90 (978-1-4263-3370-5(6)) Disney Publishing Worldwide. (National Geographic Kids).

King, Zelda. Manatees. (Illus.). 24p. (J). 2012. 49.50 (978-1-4488-5136-2(X), PowerKids Pr.) 2011. (ENG., (gr. 2-3). pap. 9.25 (978-1-4488-5135-5(1), 8e1630f0-c339-4d91-b923-2b41ff770cbc, PowerKids Pr.) 2011. (ENG., (gr. 2-3). lib. bdg. 26.27 (978-1-4488-5002-0(9), 4b10e016-9be0-4dd7-913e-a99e84b68d9b) Rosen Publishing Group, Inc., The.

Kobasa, Paul A. Furry Animals. 2018. (J). (978-0-7166-3573-4(9)) World Bk., Inc.

Kopp, Megan. Mammals. 2016. (Illus.). 32p. (J). (978-1-5105-1116-3(4)) SmartBook Media, Inc.

LaPlante, Walter. Manatees, 1 vol. 2019. (Ocean Animals Ser.). (ENG.). 24p. (gr. k-k). pap. 9.15 (978-1-5382-4457-9(8), 6bed7f4a-d354-43ea-afd5-69e3051be4b5) Stevens, Gareth Publishing LLLP.

Lee, David. Jackals, 1 vol. 2016. (Wild Canines Ser.). (ENG., Illus.). 24p. (J). (gr. 3-3). pap. 9.25 (978-1-4994-2027-2(7), f91ee940-a43d-4966-bb3c-3b40d28a789f, PowerKids Pr.) Rosen Publishing Group, Inc., The.

Levine, Michelle. Mammals. 2014. (Animal Kingdom Ser.). (ENG., Illus.). 32p. (J). (gr. 2-5). lib. bdg. 28.50 (978-1-60753-475-4(4), 15944) Amicus.

Levine, Sara. Tooth by Tooth: Comparing Fangs, Tusks, & Chompers. Spookytooth, T. S., illus. 2016. (Animal by Animal Ser.). (ENG.). 32p. (J). (gr. k-4). 26.65 (978-1-4677-5215-2(0), 7acaba15-e659-40a5-8cd9-127da28c5c4a); E-Book 39.99 (978-1-4677-9727-6(8)); E-Book 39.99 (978-1-5124-0732-7(1), 9781512407327) Lerner Publishing Group. (Millbrook Pr.).

Levy, Janey. Really Strange Mammals, 1 vol. 2016. (Really Strange Adaptations Ser.). (ENG.). 32p. (J). (gr. 5-5). pap. 11.00 (978-1-4994-2789-9(1), f98d6d27-7213-4445-9d90-c145074522f7, PowerKids Pr.) Rosen Publishing Group, Inc., The.

Long, Olivia. Why Don't Cats Lay Eggs? Long, Olivia, illus. Date not set. (Our Precious Planet Ser.). (Illus.). 32p. (J). (gr. -1-4). (978-1-880042-12-0(6)) Shelf-Life Bks.

Lundblad, Kristina. Les Mammifères. 2011. (FRE., Illus.). 32p. (J). pap. 9.95 (978-2-89579-393-9(X)) Bayard Canada CAN. Dist: Crabtree Publishing Co.

Lunde, Darrin. Meet the Meerkat. Wynne, Patricia J., illus. 2007. (gr. -1-1). 17.95 (978-0-7569-8047-4(X)) Perfection Learning Corp.

Lunis, Natalie. Capybara. 2018. (More SuperSized! Ser.). (ENG.). 24p. (J). (gr. k-3). 7.99 (978-1-64280-078-4(3)) Bearport Publishing Co., Inc.

Lynette, Rachel. South American Tapirs. 2013. (Jungle Babies of the Amazon Rain Forest Ser.). (Illus.). 24p. (J). (gr. -1-3). lib. bdg. 25.65 (978-1-61772-759-7(8)) Bearport Publishing Co., Inc.

MacAulay, Kelley & Kalman, Bobbie. Dolphins & Other Marine Mammals, 1 vol. 2005. (What Kind of Animal Is It? Ser.). (ENG., Illus.). 32p. (J). (gr. 1-2). pap. (978-0-7787-2222-9(8)); lib. bdg. (978-0-7787-2164-2(7)) Crabtree Publishing Co.

Machajewski, Sarah. Life of a Honey Badger, 1 vol. 2013. (InfoMax Readers Ser.). (ENG.). 24p. (J). (gr. 3-3). pap. 8.25 (978-1-4777-2515-3(6), d7692829-9be0-4d04-b94a-20117e3987b3); pap. 49.50 (978-1-4777-2516-0(4)) Rosen Publishing Group, Inc., The. (Rosen Classroom).

—The Return of the Mountain Gorilla. 2017. (Bouncing Back from Extinction Ser.). 32p. (J). (gr. 9-10). 60.00 (978-1-5081-5603-1(4), PowerKids Pr.) Rosen Publishing Group, Inc., The.

Malam, John. Pinnipeds. 2009. (Scary Creatures Ser.). (ENG., Illus.). 32p. (J). (gr. 3-5). 27.00 (978-0-531-21672-9(1), Children's Pr.) Scholastic Library Publishing.

Mamiferos Pequenos, 6 vols., Vol. 3. (Explorers. Exploradores Nonfiction Sets Ser.). (SPA.). (gr. 3-6). (978-0-7699-0651-5(6)) Shortland Pubns. (U. S. A.) Inc.

Mamiferos de Gran TamanO, 6 vols., Vol. 2. (Explorers. Exploradores Nonfiction Sets Ser.). (SPA.). 32p. (gr. 3-6). 44.95 (978-0-7699-0638-6(9)) Shortland Pubns. (U. S. A.) Inc.

Los Mamiferos Del Mar, 6 vols. (Explorers. Exploradores Nonfiction Sets Ser.). (SPA.). 32p. (gr. 3-6). 44.95 (978-0-7699-0629-4(X)) Shortland Pubns. (U. S. A.) Inc.

Mammals. 2019. (Illus.). 96p. (J). (978-0-7166-3730-1(8)) World Bk., Inc.

Mammals Set 1: Mammals of North America. 2005. (J). spiral bd. 23.40 (978-0-9770248-9-6(X)) Sidedoor Publishing LLC.

Markle, Sandra. Finding Home. Marks, Alan, illus. 2010. 32p. (J). (gr. -1-3). pap. 7.95 (978-1-58089-123-3(3)) Charlesbridge Publishing, Inc.

—Jackals. 2005. (Animal Scavengers Ser.). (ENG., Illus.). 40p. (gr. 3-6). lib. bdg. 25.26 (978-0-8225-3197-5(6), Lerner Pubns.) Lerner Publishing Group.

—Los Demonios de Tasmania; Tasmanian Devils. 2008. pap. 46.95 (978-0-8225-9452-9(8)) Lerner Publishing Group.

—The Search for Olinguito: Discovering a New Species. 2017. (Sandra Markle's Science Discoveries Ser.). (ENG., Illus.). 40p. (J). (gr. 4-6). 33.32 (978-1-5124-1015-0(2), 71251d39-42e4-4019-a21c-26f1db481b43); E-Book 47.99 (978-1-5124-3876-5(6), 9781512438765); E-Book 47.99 (978-1-5124-2842-1(6)); E-Book 9.99 (978-1-5124-3875-8(8), 9781512438758) Lerner Publishing Group. (Millbrook Pr.).

Markovics, Joyce. Mi Lengua Es Larga y Curva (Okapi) 2016. (Pistas de Animales 2/Zoo Clues 2 Ser.). (SPA.). 24p. (J). (gr. -1-3). 26.99 (978-1-944102-77-7(9)) Bearport Publishing Co., Inc.

—My Nose Is Long & Fuzzy (Anteater) 2014. (Zoo Clues Ser.). 24p. (J). (gr. -1-3). lib. bdg. 26.99 (978-1-62724-111-3(6)) Bearport Publishing Co., Inc.

Markovics, Joyce L. Deadly Venomous Mammals! 2018. (Envenomators Ser.). (ENG., Illus.). 24p. (J). (gr. 2-7). 19.45 (978-1-68402-660-9(1)) Bearport Publishing Co., Inc.

—Ringtail: Miner's Cat. 2012. (America's Hidden Animal Treasures Ser.). 32p. (J). (gr. 2-7). lib. bdg. 28.50 (978-1-61772-580-7(3)) Bearport Publishing Co., Inc.

—Warthog. 2016. (J). lib. bdg. (978-1-62724-821-1(8)) Bearport Publishing Co., Inc.

Marsh, Laura. National Geographic Readers: Meerkats. 2013. (Readers Ser.). (Illus.). 32p. (J). (gr. -1-k). pap. 5.99 (978-1-4263-1342-4(X)); (ENG., lib. bdg. 14.90 (978-1-4263-1343-1(8)) Disney Publishing Worldwide. (National Geographic Kids).

Marsico, Katie. A Manatee Calf Grows Up. 2007. (Scholastic News Nonfiction Readers Ser.). (ENG., Illus.). 24p. (J). (gr. 1-2). 22.00 (978-0-531-17479-1(4)) Scholastic Library Publishing.

Martin, Chia. Nos Gusta Amamantar / We Like to Nurse. Mithuna, Shukyu Linn, illus. 2nd alt. ed. 2016. (Family & World Health Ser.). (ENG.). 28p. (J). pap. 12.95 (978-1-942493-12-9(6)) Hohm Pr.

Martin, Isabel. Mammals: A Question & Answer Book, 1 vol. 2014. (Animal Kingdom Questions & Answers Ser.). (ENG., Illus.). 24p. (J). (gr. -1-2). pap. 6.95 (978-1-4914-0634-2(8), 125938, Capstone Pr.) Capstone.

Martin-James, Kathleen. Gentle Manatees. 2005. (Pull Ahead Bks.). (J). 22.60 (978-0-8225-2422-9(8), Lerner Pubns.); (ENG., Illus.). 32p. pap. 7.99 (978-0-8225-2441-0(4), 1de86507-c217-4ac0-bb4e-0ea2dc353b14, First Avenue Editions) Lerner Publishing Group.

Matthews, Rupert. The Illustrated Encyclopedia of Mammals. 2008. (ENG., Illus.). 80p. (J). (gr. 3-18). 19.95 (978-88-88166-59-9(9)) McRae Bks. Srl ITA. Dist: Independent Pubs. Group.

McGill, Jordan. Zarigüeyas. 2012. (SPA.). (J). (978-1-61913-194-1(3)) Weigl Pubs., Inc.

McRae, Anne & Agosta, Loredana. Mammals. Dogi, Flammetta, illus. 2007. (Back to Basics Ser.). 32p. (J). lib. bdg. (978-88-6098-047-2(X)) McRae Bks. Srl.

Meister, Cari. Do You Really Want to Meet an Anteater? Fabbri, Daniele, illus. 2018. (Do You Really Want to Meet ... ? Ser.). (ENG.). 24p. (J). (gr. 1-4). lib. bdg. (978-1-68151-394-2(3), 15035) Amicus.

Michele, Tracey. What Is a Mammal? 2011. (Learn-Abouts Ser.). (Illus.). 16p. (J). pap. 7.95 (978-1-59920-643-1(9)) Black Rabbit Bks.

Michels, Dia L. If My Mom Were a Platypus: Mammal Babies & Their Mothers. 2006. (ENG., Illus.). 64p. (J). (gr. -1-12). 16.95 (978-965-90219-6-3(8)) Platypus Media, L.L.C.

—If My Mom Were a Platypus: Mammal Babies & Their Mothers. Barthelmes, Andrew, illus. 4th ed. 2014. 64p. (J). (gr. -1-12). pap. 12.95 (978-1-938492-11-2(0)) Science, Naturally!

—If My Mom Were A Platypus- Hebrew Language Edition. Barthelmes, Andrew, illus. 2006. Orig. Title: #1488;#1501; #1488;#1502;#1497; #1492;#1497;#1514;#1492; #1508;#1500;#1496;#1497;#1508;#1493;#1505;. 64p. (J). 29.95 (978-0-9678020-9-1(1)) Science, Naturally!

—If My Mom Were a Platypus- Hebrew Language Edition. Barthelmes, Andrew, illus. 2006. Orig. Title: #1488;#1501; #1488;#1502;#1497; #1492;#1497;#1514;#1492; #1508;#1500;#1496;#1497;#1508;#1493;#1505;. (HEB.). 64p. (J). 19.95 (978-0-9678020-8-4(3)) Science, Naturally!

Mighty Mammals: Level O, 6 vols., Vol. 2. (Explorers Ser.). 32p. (gr. 3-6). 44.95 (978-0-7699-0602-7(8)) Shortland Pubns. (U. S. A.) Inc.

Miller, Sara Swan. Walruses of the Arctic, 1 vol. 2009. (Brrr! Polar Animals Ser.). (ENG., Illus.). 24p. (J). (gr. 2-3). pap. 9.25 (978-1-4358-3150-6(0), d84bb6f3-12ee-4069-9790-5f42c4cd936b, PowerKids Pr.); lib. bdg. 26.27 (978-1-4358-2746-2(5), a6a6078a-a765-41cb-94fa-ea743c2d5506) Rosen Publishing Group, Inc., The.

Mini Mammals: Level P, 6 vols., Vol. 3. (Explorers Ser.). 32p. (gr. 3-6). 44.95 (978-0-7699-0615-7(X)) Shortland Pubns. (U. S. A.) Inc.

Mitchell, Susan K. Biggest vs. Smallest Amazing Mammals, 1 vol. 2010. (Biggest vs. Smallest Animals Ser.). (ENG., Illus.). 24p. (gr. k-2). 25.27 (978-0-7660-3582-9(4), e3c16631-3421-42a2-b5d5-c2b032ef6570, Enslow Elementary) Enslow Publishing, LLC.

Munson, Victoria. Mammals, 1 vol. 2018. (My First Book of Nature Ser.). (ENG.). 24p. (gr. 2-2). 26.27 (978-1-5081-9615-0(X), 702d4457-e668-400e-a432-5e97041b562c, Windmill Bks.) Rosen Publishing Group, Inc., The.

Murray, Julie. Mammals. 2018. (Animal Classes Ser.). (ENG., Illus.). 24p. (J). (gr. k-4). lib. bdg. 31.36 (978-1-5321-2299-6(3), 28365, Abdo Zoom-Dash) ABDO Publishing Co.

Mystifying Mammals. 2016. (Illus.). 32p. (J). (978-1-4222-3523-2(8)) Mason Crest.

Niver, Heather Moore. We Need Bats, 1 vol. 2015. (Creatures We Can't Live Without Ser.). (ENG., Illus.). 24p. (J). (gr. 3-4). pap. 9.25 (978-1-4994-0979-6(6), 5fa9a3b7-f887-4055-96ba-1966d30750cf, PowerKids Pr.) Rosen Publishing Group, Inc., The.

O'Hare, Ted. Mammals. 2005. (What Is an Animal? Ser.). (Illus.). 24p. (J). (gr. 1-4). per. 5.45 (978-1-59515-734-8(4)); lib. bdg. 14.95 (978-1-59515-420-0(5)) Rourke Educational Media.

O'Reilly, Wenda. Go fish wildlife Mammals. 2007. n/ap. pap. 119.40 (978-1-59960-016-1(1)) Birdcage Pr.

—Wild Cards. 2007. n/ap. pap. 119.40 (978-1-59960-012-3(9)) Birdcage Pr.

Orr, Tamra. Care for a Pet Ferret. 2008. (How to Convince Your Parents You Can ... Ser.). (Illus.). 32p. (YA). (gr. 1-4). lib. bdg. 25.70 (978-1-58415-660-4(0)) Mitchell Lane Pubs.

Owen, Ruth. Manatee Calves. 2012. (Water Babies Ser.). 24p. (J). (gr. -1-3). lib. bdg. 25.65 (978-1-61772-599-9(4)) Bearport Publishing Co., Inc.

Pallotta, Jerry. The Sea Mammal Alphabet Book. Leonard, Tom, illus. 2019. 32p. (J). (gr. -1-2). lib. bdg. 17.99 (978-1-57091-146-0(0)) Charlesbridge Publishing, Inc.

Parker, Steve. Mamiferos. 2nd ed. Date not set. (SPA., Illus.). 64p. 14.95 (978-84-372-3714-5(9)) Santillana USA Publishing Co., Inc.

—Mammal: Eyewitness Books. Burton, Jane & King, Dave, photos by. 2004. (Illus.). 63p. (gr. 4-8). reprint ed. 16.00 (978-0-7567-7286-4(9)) DIANE Publishing Co.

—Whales & Dolphins, 1 vol. 2010. (I Love Animals Ser.). (ENG., Illus.). 24p. (J). (gr. 2-2). pap. 9.15 (978-1-61533-236-6(7), 6de635dc-a510-4470-ae2f-3f9730d68ac8); lib. bdg. 27.27 (978-1-61533-230-4(8), 040be7a7-9e9c-4f99-a74a-32c8d7a1c1e4) Rosen Publishing Group, Inc., The. (Windmill Bks.).

Pesta, K. My Ferret Dexter. 2008. 20p. per. 24.95 (978-1-4241-9137-6(8)) America Star Bks.

Petersen, Christine. A Project Guide to Mammals. 2010. (Life Science Projects for Kids Ser.). (Illus.). 48p. (J). (gr. 4-8). lib. bdg. 29.95 (978-1-58415-875-2(1)) Mitchell Lane Pubs.

Pettiford, Rebecca. Manatees. 2017. (Ocean Life up Close Ser.). (ENG., Illus.). 24p. (J). (gr. k-3). lib. bdg. 26.95 (978-1-62617-570-9(5), Blastoff! Readers) Bellwether Media.

Phillips, Dee. Mammals. 2006. (Blue Zoo Guides). (ENG., Illus.). 96p. (J). (gr. -1-2). 18.95 (978-1-58728-519-6(3)) Cooper Square Publishing Llc.

—Meerkat's Burrow. 2014. (Science Slam: the Hole Truth Ser.). 24p. (J). (gr. -1-3). lib. bdg. 26.99 (978-1-62724-092-5(6)) Bearport Publishing Co., Inc.

Platypus, Editors at. Carried & Cuddled: Consentido y Cargado. Speiser, Mike, illus. 2018. (ENG.). 32p. (J). (gr. -1-k). 14.95 (978-1-930775-96-1(2)) Platypus Media, L.L.C.

Rajczak Nelson, Kristen. Mammals, 1 vol. 2018. (Investigate Biodiversity Ser.). (ENG.). 24p. (gr. 2-2). 25.60 (978-1-9785-0195-9(1), b96517c2-77ac-4e9a-b0ef-4b3d50f91eaf) Enslow Publishing, LLC.

Rake, Jody Sullivan. Meerkats. 2010. (African Animals Ser.). (ENG.). 24p. (gr. k-1). pap. 41.70 (978-1-4296-5083-0(4), Capstone Pr.) Capstone.

—Star-Nosed Moles & Other Extreme Mammal Adaptations, 1 vol. 2014. (Extreme Adaptations Ser.). (ENG.). 32p. (J). (gr. 3-6). lib. bdg. 27.99 (978-1-4914-0167-5(2), 125772, Capstone Pr.) Capstone.

Rake, Matthew. The Rise of Mammals. Minister, Peter, illus. 2015. (Prehistoric Field Guides). (ENG.). 32p. (J). (gr. 3-6). lib. bdg. 27.99 (978-1-4677-6351-6(9), 0442d702-5646-4765-bfa8-021057759449, Hungry Tomato (r)) Lerner Publishing Group.

Randall, Henry. Wildcats: Gatos Monteses, 1 vol. 2011. (Cats of the Wild / Felinos Salvajes Ser.). (SPA & ENG., Illus.). 24p. (gr. 1-2). lib. bdg. 26.27 (978-1-4488-3133-3(4), 8dc1e891-cbbf-42a1-b120-ba5fc101a9d8) Rosen Publishing Group, Inc., The.

Randolph, Joanne. My Friend the Ferret, 1 vol. 2010. (Curious Pet Pals Ser.). (ENG., Illus.). 24p. (J). (gr. 2-3). pap. 9.15 (978-1-60754-980-2(8), 527212db-a99a-4a1f-9396-ea5c25e2a2f0); lib. bdg. 27.27 (978-1-60754-974-1(3), 4836f44d-bd50-4b59-aec4-6aafec05834b) Rosen Publishing Group, Inc., The. (Windmill Bks.).

Read, Nicholas. The Seal Garden, 1 vol. McAllister, Ian, photos by. 2018. (My Great Bear Rainforest Ser.: 3). (ENG., Illus.). 32p. (J). (gr. 1-3). 19.95 (978-1-4598-1267-3(0)) Orca Bk. Pubs. USA.

Reade, Clara. Warthogs, 1 vol. 2012. (PowerKids Readers: Safari Animals Ser.). (ENG., Illus.). 24p. (J). (gr. k-k). pap. 9.25 (978-1-4488-7473-6(4), 87b86244-7255-42eb-b5c9-6d74840fb50e); lib. bdg. 26.27 (978-1-4488-7393-7(2), 1f1cbbe4-3649-4847-aa25-52304f545208) Rosen Publishing Group, Inc., The. (PowerKids Pr.).

Reference, Marshall Cavendish Reference Staff, ed. Mammal Anatomy: an Illustrated Guide, 1 vol. 2010. (Mammal Anatomy: an Illustrated Guide Ser.). (ENG., Illus.). 288p. (YA). (gr. 7-7). 102.64 (978-0-7614-7882-9(5),

2e879e0c-b373-49b2-8f90-3f8bf80d0207) Cavendish Square Publishing LLC.

—Mammals of the Northern Hemisphere, 1 vol. 2011. (Mammals of the Northern Hemisphere Ser.). (ENG.). 208p. (YA). (gr. 7-7). lib. bdg. 88.36 *(978-0-7614-7936-9(8),* f25a5bc7-e1fe-4f90-a104-b8ba2b88520d) Cavendish Square Publishing LLC.

—Mammals of the Southern Hemisphere, 1 vol. 2011. (Mammals of the Southern Hemisphere Ser.). (ENG.). 208p. (YA). (gr. 7-7). lib. bdg. 88.36 *(978-0-7614-7937-6(6),* e7dff8eb-d0dc-469e-95f7-15b4717b4beb) Cavendish Square Publishing LLC.

Reiter, Chris & Katirgis, Jane. Endangered Blue Whales, 1 vol. 2015. (Wildlife at Risk Ser.). (ENG., Illus.). 48p. (gr. 6-6). 29.60 *(978-0-7660-6890-2(0),* 00e9f3f6-f985-47b8-a750-d0238fe2fd40) Enslow Publishing, LLC.

Richardson, Joy. Mammals, 1 vol. 2004. (Variety of Life Ser.). (ENG., Illus.). 32p. (gr. 2-4). lib. bdg. 28.67 *(978-0-8368-4506-8(4),* b2cbc719-4d2b-4beb-ae58-4c296262f40b, Gareth Stevens Learning Library) Stevens, Gareth Publishing LLLP.

Rieger, Linda. How Are We Alike? Bianchi, John, illus. 2006. 20p. (J). *(978-0-9779427-0-1(8))* Pathways into Science.

Riggs, Kate. Le Lamantin. 2018. (Planète Animaux Ser.). (FRE., Illus.). 24p. (J). *(978-1-77092-393-5(4),* 19682) Creative Co., The.

—Manatees. 2018. (Amazing Animals Ser.). (ENG., Illus.). 24p. (J). (gr. 1-4). *(978-1-60818-879-6(5),* 19606, Creative Education) Creative Co., The.

Rockwell, Lizzy. A Mammal Is an Animal. 2018. *(978-0-8234-4070-2(2));* (ENG., Illus.). 40p. (J). (gr. -1-3). 17.95 *(978-0-8234-3670-5(5))* Holiday Hse., Inc.

Rodríguez, Ana María. The Secret of the Bird's Smart Brain... & More!, 1 vol. 2017. (Animal Secrets Revealed! Ser.). (ENG.). 48p. (gr. 4-4). pap. 12.70 *(978-0-7660-8852-8(9),* c1da708f-e755-46c8-9917-9f0144554bf3); lib. bdg. 29.60 *(978-0-7660-8623-4(2),* 365f89b6-891c-41bb-a347-203b57d6459b) Enslow Publishing, LLC.

—The Secret of the Scorpion-Eating Meerkats... & More!, 1 vol. 2017. (Animal Secrets Revealed! Ser.). (ENG.). 48p. (gr. 4-4). pap. 12.70 *(978-0-7660-8848-1(0),* 1cd642e9-0cdf-409f-ab24-5bec55dd69d3); lib. bdg. 29.60 *(978-0-7660-8627-2(5),* 8f1ff151-2918-4854-a0dc-83c66a893aef) Enslow Publishing, LLC.

Royston, Angela. Mammals. (Illus.). 32p. (YA). (gr. 2-18). lib. bdg. 27.10 *(978-1-932333-37-4(1))* Chrysalis Education.

Rupp, Kristina. See the Mammals. 2010. (1-3Y Animals Ser.). (ENG., Illus.). 20p. (J). pap. 9.60 *(978-1-63437-152-0(6))* American Reading Co.

Rustad, Martha E. H. A Mob of Meerkats. 2019. (Animal Groups Ser.). (ENG., Illus.). 24p. (J). (gr. -1-2). pap. 6.95 *(978-1-9771-1044-2(4),* 141120); lib. bdg. 27.32 *(978-1-9771-0948-4(9),* 140547) Capstone. (Pebble).

Sabelko, Rebecca. Long-Tailed Weasels. 2018. (North American Animals Ser.). (ENG., Illus.). 24p. (J). (gr. k-3). lib. bdg. 26.95 *(978-1-62617-798-7(8),* Blastoff! Readers) Bellwether Media.

Sackett-Smith, Lucy. Hippos: Huge & Hungry, 1 vol. 2009. (Mighty Mammals Ser.). (ENG., Illus.). 24p. (J). (gr. 2-3). 26.27 *(978-1-4042-8105-9(3),* 30542151-3cb9-43ae-885b-ba95a097a3c5) Rosen Publishing Group, Inc., The.

Savage, Stephen. Focus on Mammals, 1 vol. 2011. (Animal Watch Ser.). (ENG.). 32p. (YA). (gr. 3-4). lib. bdg. 29.27 *(978-1-4339-5990-5(9),* ab7510d8-8e1f-44ca-8886-c2b608163b1b) Stevens, Gareth Publishing LLLP.

School Zone Publishing Company Staff. Mammals. (Illus.). (J). 19.99 incl. audio compact disk *(978-0-88743-972-8(1))* School Zone Publishing Co.

Schuetz, Kari. Mammals. 2012. (Animal Classes Ser.). (ENG., Illus.). 24p. (J). (gr. k-3). lib. bdg. 26.95 *(978-1-60014-775-3(5),* Blastoff! Readers) Bellwether Media.

—Meerkats. 2012. (Animal Safari Ser.). (ENG., Illus.). 24p. (J). (gr. k-3). lib. bdg. 26.95 *(978-1-60014-718-0(6),* Blastoff! Readers) Bellwether Media.

Schuh, Mari. The World's Biggest Mammals. 2015. (Illus.). 24p. (J). lib. bdg. *(978-1-62031-204-9(2))* Jump! Inc.

Sebastian, Emily. Moles. (Illus.). 24p. (J). 2012. 49.50 *(978-1-4488-5055-6(X),* PowerKids Pr.) 2011. (ENG., (gr. 1-1). pap. 9.25 *(978-1-4488-5054-9(1),* 4f687d14-633c-43a3-b7cf-0eb17b80dbf4, PowerKids Pr.) 2011. (ENG., (gr. 1-1). lib. bdg. 26.27 *(978-1-4488-4952-9(7),* 615c555c-925d-4f15-9cd9-c1f569fbdf86) Rosen Publishing Group, Inc., The.

—Mongooses. (Illus.). 24p. (J). 2012. 49.50 *(978-1-4488-5063-1(0),* PowerKids Pr.) 2011. (ENG., (gr. 1-1). pap. 9.25 *(978-1-4488-5062-4(2),* 53f71474-0883-4113-96f6-5e9267846364, PowerKids Pr.) 2011. (ENG., (gr. 1-1). lib. bdg. 26.27 *(978-1-4488-4956-7(X),* 2f9170e8-1416-4ae5-a998-36015d1426ba) Rosen Publishing Group, Inc., The.

Shea, Mary Molly. Being a Manatee, 1 vol. 2013. (Can You Imagine? Ser.). (ENG.). 32p. (gr. 2-3). E-Book 27.25 *(978-1-4824-6504-4(3),* 554123cd-5ece-4061-94b7-1a84af083aef) Rosen Publishing Group, Inc., The.

Shea, Nicole. Creepy Mammals, 1 vol. 2012. (Nature's Creepiest Creatures Ser.). (ENG.). 24p. (J). (gr. 2-3). pap. 9.15 *(978-1-4339-6495-4(3),* 135d86a7-3a09-4af4-86c2-00c23dab9e85); lib. bdg. 25.27 *(978-1-4339-6493-0(7),* ed077c0b-90e2-4d3b-a399-b294401196a0) Stevens, Gareth Publishing LLLP. (Gareth Stevens Learning Library).

Siemens, Jared. Ferret. 2017. (Illus.). 24p. (J). *(978-1-5105-0560-5(1))* SmartBook Media, Inc.

Sill, Cathryn. About Mammals: A Guide for Children, 1 vol. Sill, John, illus. rev. ed. 2014. (About... Ser.: 2). 48p. (J). (gr. -1-2). 16.95 *(978-1-56145-757-1(4))* Peachtree Publishing Co. Inc.

—Sobre Los Mamíferos: Una Guía para Niños. Sill, John, illus. 2019. (About... Ser.). 48p. (J). (gr. -1-2). pap. 8.95 *(978-1-68263-072-3(2))* Peachtree Publishing Co. Inc.

Silverman, Buffy. Do You Know about Mammals? 2009. (Lightning Bolt Books (r) — Meet the Animal Groups Ser.). (ENG., Illus.). 32p. (J). (gr. 1-3). pap. 9.99 *(978-1-58013-860-4(8),* f033de56-7355-44bc-9be7-0a815cde4a75); (gr. k-2). 26.60 *(978-0-8225-7539-9(6),* Lerner Pubns.) Lerner Publishing Group.

—¿Sabes Algo Sobre Mamíferos? (Do You Know about Mammals?) 2012. (Libros Rayo — Conoce Los Grupos de Animales (Lightning Bolt Books (r) — Meet the Animal Groups) Ser.). (SPA., Illus.). 32p. (J). (gr. 1-3). pap. 9.99 *(978-0-7613-9375-7(7),* 04bf035f-5d21-4aee-9ce8-7e4b5b10f5b5, Ediciones Lerner) Lerner Publishing Group.

Simmons, Nancy B., ed. Exploring the World of Mammals, 6 vols. 2008. (ENG., Illus.). 480p. (gr. 5-8). 210.00 *(978-0-7910-9651-2(3),* P144629, Facts On File) Infobase Holdings, Inc.

Smith, Lucy Sackett. Mighty Mammals, 12 vols., Set. Incl. Elephants: From Trunk to Tail. lib. bdg. 26.27 *(978-1-4042-8102-8(9),* 63822c9b-57b5-4124-af64-9537ff1133e6); Tigers: Prowling Predators. lib. bdg. 26.27 *(978-1-4042-8107-3(X),* fd8d64b8-98cd-42ce-a405-266baaf584ec); (Illus.). 24p. (J). (gr. 2-3). 2009. (Mighty Mammals Ser.). (ENG.). 2009. Set lib. bdg. 157.62 *(978-1-4358-3294-7(9),* a457b55a-c101-4256-a4b3-f3e9e274111f, PowerKids Pr.) Rosen Publishing Group, Inc., The.

Snedden, Robert. Mammals. (Living Things Ser.). (Illus.). 32p. 2009. (J). (gr. -1-3). pap. 7.95 *(978-1-59920-198-6(4))* 2007. (YA). (gr. 3-6). lib. bdg. 28.50 *(978-1-59920-081-1(3))* Black Rabbit Bks.

Somervill, Barbara A. Small Indian Mongoose. 2010. (21st Century Skills Library: Animal Invaders Ser.). (ENG., Illus.). 32p. (gr. 4-8). lib. bdg. 32.07 *(978-1-60279-630-0(0),* 200336) Cherry Lake Publishing.

Spilsbury, Louise. Superstar Mammals, 1 vol. 2014. (Nature's Got Talent Ser.). (ENG., Illus.). 32p. (J). (gr. 3-3). 27.93 *(978-1-4777-7052-8(6),* ff7b50df-1004-4283-880e-9b0381e8fa69, PowerKids Pr.) Rosen Publishing Group, Inc., The.

Squire, Ann O. Mammals. 2013. (ENG.). 48p. (J). 29.00 *(978-0-531-21754-2(X));* pap. 6.95 *(978-0-531-22339-0(6))* Scholastic Library Publishing.

Sterling Publishing Company Staff & Ward, Adam, contrib. by. Pocket Factfiles: Mammals. 2004. (Illus.). 256p. (J). 4.98 *(978-1-4027-1851-9(9))* Sterling Publishing Co., Inc.

Storad, Conrad J. Meerkats. 2007. (Early Bird Nature Books Ser.). (Illus.). 48p. (J). (gr. -1-3). lib. bdg. 25.26 *(978-0-8225-6466-9(1),* Lerner Pubns.) Lerner Publishing Group.

Sullivant, Holly. Ferrets. 2009. (Illus.). 112p. (J). 14.95 *(978-1-932904-35-2(2))* Eldorado Ink.

Sullivant, Holly J. Ferrets. 2008. (J). *(978-1-932904-27-7(1))* Eldorado Ink.

Thornhill, Jan. I Am Josephine: (and I Am a Living Thing) Lee, Jacqui, illus. 2019. (ENG.). 32p. (J). (gr. k-2). pap. 9.95 *(978-1-77147-353-8(3))* Owlkids Bks. Inc. CAN. Dist: Publishers Group West (PGW).

Torre, Cristina de la. About Mammals: A Guide for Children = Sobre Los Mamíferos: Una Guía para Niños. Sill, Cathryn P. & Sill, John, illus. 2014. (SPA & ENG.). (J). *(978-1-56145-815-8(5),* Peachtree Junior) Peachtree Publishing Co. Inc.

Vastola, P. Huge Animals: Learning the Long U Sound. 2009. (PowerPhonics Ser.). 24p. (gr. 1-1). 39.90 *(978-1-60851-445-8(5),* PowerKids Pr.) Rosen Publishing Group, Inc., The.

Walden, Katherine. Meerkats. 2009. (Safari Animals Ser.). 24p. (gr. 1-1). 42.50 *(978-1-60852-957-5(6));* (ENG.). (J). lib. bdg. 26.27 *(978-1-4358-2691-5(4),* 027331e6-b51c-40c2-b481-6e05ae048ad4); (ENG., Illus.). (J). pap. 9.25 *(978-1-4358-3065-3(2),* 65d6648c-6af3-4c95-ad34-8f9084a8c11b) Rosen Publishing Group, Inc., The. (PowerKids Pr.).

—Warthogs, 1 vol. 2009. (Safari Animals Ser.). (ENG., Illus.). 24p. (J). (gr. 1-1). pap. 9.25 *(978-1-4358-3062-2(8),* b2aa31c9-30fd-41d4-a875-cfafb9ec175f, PowerKids Pr.) Rosen Publishing Group, Inc., The.

Weber, Valerie J. Manatees, 1 vol. 2008. (Animals That Live in the Ocean Ser.). (ENG., Illus.). 24p. (J). (gr. 1-1). lib. bdg. 25.27 *(978-0-8368-9241-3(0),* b71f1422-a2e8-495b-a3be-421fdcd13fd4, Weekly Reader Leveled Readers) Stevens, Gareth Publishing LLLP.

—Manatees / Manatíes, 1 vol. 2008. (Animals That Live in the Ocean / Animales Que Viven en el Océano Ser.). (SPA & ENG.). 24p. (gr. 1-1). pap. 9.15 *(978-0-8368-9346-5(8),* 94a54f72-1e18-4b12-96b1-b4c560428fda, Weekly Reader Leveled Readers) Stevens, Gareth Publishing LLLP.

—Manatees / Manatíes, 1 vol. 2008. (Animals That Live in the Ocean / Animales Que Viven en el Océano Ser.). (SPA & ENG.). 24p. (J). (gr. 1-1). lib. bdg. 25.27 *(978-0-8368-9247-5(X),* f6ade463-b519-4816-9d1d-7d92b4e8b3a4, Weekly Reader Leveled Readers) Stevens, Gareth Publishing LLLP.

West, David. Whales & Other Mammals, 1 vol. 2017. (Inside Animals Ser.). (ENG.). 24p. (J). (gr. 3-3). 26.27 *(978-1-5081-9392-0(4),* cf834669-04b1-4c76-b99c-16c8f1fb8301, Windmill Bks.) Rosen Publishing Group, Inc., The.

West, David, contrib. by. Whales & Other Mammals, 1 vol. 2017. (Inside Animals Ser.). (ENG.). 24p. (J). (gr. 3-3). pap. 9.25 *(978-1-5081-9431-6(9),* 3a530a54-c08e-42dc-9967-b8e8d8aa04bf, Windmill Bks.) Rosen Publishing Group, Inc., The.

World Book, Inc. Staff, contrib. by. Mammals. 2009. (J). *(978-0-7166-0406-8(X))* World Bk., Inc.

—Mammals of the United States & Canada. 2004. (World Book's Science & Nature Guides Ser.). (Illus.). 80p. (J). *(978-0-7166-4215-2(8))* World Bk., Inc.

Wynne, Patricia J. Extreme Mammals. 2009. (Dover Nature Coloring Book Ser.). (ENG., Illus.). 32p. (J). (gr. 2-5). pap. 3.99 *(978-0-486-47286-7(8),* 472868) Dover Pubns., Inc.

Zabludoff, Marc. Basilosaurus, 1 vol. Bollinger, Peter, illus. 2010. (Prehistoric Beasts Ser.). (ENG.). 32p. (gr. 2-2). 32.64 *(978-0-7614-3999-8(4),* 8781e761-3a65-4818-b23e-9e7836f55c96) Cavendish Square Publishing LLC.

Zappa, Marcia. Elephant Shrews, 1 vol. 2015. (World's Weirdest Animals Ser.). (ENG., Illus.). 32p. (J). (gr. 2-5). 34.21 *(978-1-62403-774-0(7),* 17850, Big Buddy Bks.) ABDO Publishing Co.

Zoehfeld, Kathleen. National Geographic Readers: Prehistoric Mammals. 2015. (Readers Ser.). (Illus.). 32p. (J). (gr. 1-3). pap. 4.99 *(978-1-4263-1951-8(7),* National Geographic Kids) Disney Publishing Worldwide.

MAMMALS—FICTION

Anderson, Laurie Halse. Manatee Blues, No. 4. 2008. (Vet Volunteers Ser.: 4). (ENG.). 144p. (J). (gr. 3-7). 7.99 *(978-0-14-241084-4(5),* Puffin Books) Penguin Young Readers Group.

Asheida. Peach & Pun: The New Family Ferret. 2012. 28p. pap. 17.99 *(978-1-4685-8481-3(2))* AuthorHouse.

Bernay, Emma & Berne, Emma Carlson. Orca in Open Water. Madrid, Erwin, illus. 2019. (Seaside Sanctuary Ser.). (ENG.). 112p. (J). (gr. 3-7). lib. bdg. 25.99 *(978-1-4965-7862-4(7),* 139401, Stone Arch Bks.) Capstone.

Bone, Thomas H. & LeTourneau, Anthony Alex, illus. Mama, Can Armadillos Swim? 2004. (J). 17.00 *(978-0-9674602-6-0(3))* Blue Marlin Pubns.

Brett, Jan. The 3 Little Dassies. Brett, Jan, illus. 2010. (Illus.). 32p. (J). (gr. -1-k). 18.99 *(978-0-399-25499-4(4),* G.P. Putnam's Sons Books for Young Readers) Penguin Young Readers Group.

Clarke, Jane. Plodney Creeper, Supersloth. 2006. (Blue Bananas Ser.). (ENG., Illus.). 48p. (J). (gr. -1-3). *(978-0-7787-0896-4(9))* Crabtree Publishing Co.

Cosgrove, Matt. Macca the Alpaca. Cosgrove, Matt, illus. 2020. (ENG., Illus.). 24p. (J). (gr. -1-k). 14.99 *(978-1-338-60282-1(9),* Scholastic Pr.) Scholastic, Inc.

—A Stack of Alpacas. Cosgrove, Matt, illus. 2020.Tr. of Stack of Alpacas. (ENG., Illus.). 24p. (J). (gr. -1-k). 14.99 *(978-1-338-71622-1(0),* Scholastic Pr.) Scholastic, Inc.

Deal-Trainor, Carol. Marilee: A Manatee's First Journey to the Springs. 2008. 48p. pap. 16.95 *(978-1-60563-660-3(6))* America Star Bks.

Dewdney, Anna. Nelly Gnu & Daddy Too. (Illus.). (J). 2017. 36p. (-k). bds. 9.99 *(978-0-425-28977-8(X))* 2014. 32p. (gr. -1-k). 17.99 *(978-0-670-01227-5(0))* Penguin Young Readers Group. (Viking Books for Young Readers).

Dharma Publishing Staff. Golden Foot: A Story about Unselfish Love. 3rd ed. 2013. (Jataka Tales Ser.). (Illus.). 36p. (gr. -1-7). pap. 8.95 *(978-0-89800-517-2(5))* Dharma Publishing.

Elsohn Ross, Michael. Mama's Milk. Wolff, Ashley, illus. 2007. 32p. (J). (gr. -1-2). 12.95 *(978-1-58246-181-6(3),* Tricycle Pr.) Random Hse. Children's Bks.

—Mama's Milk / Mamá Me Alimenta. Wolff, Ashley, illus. (J). 2016. 24p. (-k). bds. 7.99 *(978-0-553-53874-8(8))* 2008. 32p. (gr. -1-2). pap. 6.99 *(978-1-58246-245-5(3))* Random Hse. Children's Bks. (Tricycle Pr.).

Galvin, Laura Gates & Smithsonian Institution Staff. Armadillo at Riverside Road (Armadillo en la calle Riverside) 2008. (MUL.). 16p. 14.95 *(978-1-59249-842-0(6))* Soundprints.

The Girl Who Loved Meerkats. 2005. (J). *(978-1-933248-04-2(1))* World Quest Learning.

Hawkins, Karel. Iggy Wallaby's Walkabout. 2019. (ENG.). 26p. 37.94 *(978-1-7960-0338-3(7));* (Illus.). pap. 24.14 *(978-1-7960-0337-6(9))* Xlibris Corp.

Hawkins, Wendy. Binky Goes to School. 2009. 20p. pap. 13.99 *(978-1-4389-6990-9(2))* AuthorHouse.

Hoffman, Peter. A ferret in a Garret. Olson, Cindy, illus. 2008. 36p. (J). 24.99 *(978-0-9790247-6-4(5))* Artpacks.

Howard, Abby. Mammal Takeover! (Earth Before Us #3) Journey Through the Cenozoic Era. 2019. (Earth Before Us Ser.). (ENG., Illus.). 128p. (J). (gr. 3-7). 15.99 *(978-1-4197-3624-7(8),* 1145101, Amulet Bks.) Abrams, Inc.

Hughes, Vicki Million. Growing up with Buck, 1 vol. 2009. 141p. pap. 24.95 *(978-1-61546-620-7(7))* America Star Bks.

Jones, Gareth P. Ninja Meerkats (#4): Hollywood Showdown, 4. Finlayson, Luke, illus. 2013. (Ninja Meerkats Ser.: 4). (ENG.). 128p. (J). (gr. 2-4). pap. 9.99 *(978-1-250-02932-4(5),* 900118544) Square Fish.

—Ninja Meerkats (#5): the Tomb of Doom. Finlayson, Luke, illus. 2013. (Ninja Meerkats Ser.: 5). (ENG.). 128p. (J). (gr. 2-4). pap. 16.99 *(978-1-250-03402-1(7),* 900120572) Square Fish.

—Ninja Meerkats (#6): Big City Bust-Up. Finlayson, Luke, illus. 2013. (Ninja Meerkats Ser.: 6). (ENG.). 128p. (J). (gr. 2-4). pap. 14.99 *(978-1-250-03403-8(5),* 900120573) Square Fish.

Julie, Aunt. State Symbols of Texas - Paddleduck #8. 2012. (ENG.). 50p. pap. 5.95 *(978-1-105-91163-7(2))* Lulu Pr., Inc.

Knesek, Marian. Zane & the Armadillo. Leipsic, Regina, illus. 2012. 26p. 24.95 *(978-1-4626-6685-0(X))* America Star Bks.

Law, Felicia. Alice the Armadillo: A Tale of Self Discovery, 1 vol. Messina, Lilli, illus. 2009. (Animal Fair Values Ser.). (ENG.). 32p. (J). (gr. 2-2). pap. 11.55 *(978-1-60754-809-6(7),* 8a68dd81-a5ab-4cf1-ba70-8da519c28b56); lib. bdg. 27.27 *(978-1-60754-805-8(4),* be84d1fe-62bf-4c6f-adfd-871f539a98bd) Rosen Publishing Group, Inc., The. (Windmill Bks.).

Lee, Shari. Mandie's & Mindie's Adventure under the Sea, 1 vol. 2009. 63p. pap. 19.95 *(978-1-4489-9977-4(4))* America Star Bks.

Louie, Mary. Amazing Amand. 2009. 16p. pap. 13.49 *(978-1-4389-7903-8(7))* AuthorHouse.

McClure, Beverly Stowe. Frankie's Perfect Home. Morris, Alexander, illus. 2011. 16p. pap. 9.95 *(978-1-61633-162-7(3))* Guardian Angel Publishing, Inc.

Meadows, Daisy. Mara the Meerkat Fairy. 2015. (Rainbow Magic — Baby Animal Rescue Fairies Ser.: 3). lib. bdg. 14.75 *(978-0-606-37051-6(X))* Turtleback.

Michaels, Andie. ACHOO! ACHOO! I've Got the Flu. (ENG.). (J). 2021. pap. 14.95 *(978-1-7330663-2-7(2))* 2019. 32p. 19.95 *(978-1-7330663-0-3(6))* Mulberry Street Publishing.

Miller, Pat. Substitute Groundhog, 1 vol. Ember, Kathi, illus. 2010. (ENG.). 32p. (J). (gr. -1-3). pap. 7.99 *(978-0-8075-7644-1(1),* 807576441) Whitman, Albert & Co.

Ouchley, Amy Griffin. Swamper: Letters from a Louisiana Swamp Rabbit. 2013. (ENG., Illus.). 72p. (gr. 4-7). 22.50 *(978-0-8071-5074-0(6),* 1763) Louisiana State Univ. Pr.

Rostoker-Gruber, Karen. Ferret Fun, 0 vols. de Tagyos, Paul Rátz, illus. 2012. (ENG.). 32p. (J). (gr. k-3). 17.99 *(978-0-7614-5817-3(4),* 9780761458173, Two Lions) Amazon Publishing.

Saxon, Victoria. Big Trouble in Little Rodentia. 2016. (Illus.). (J). *(978-1-5182-0883-6(5))* Random House Children's Books.

Thayer, Robert Scott. Kobee Manatee: Heading Home to Florida. Korman, Susan, ed. Gallegos, Lauren, illus. 2013. (Kobee Manatee Ser.). (ENG.). 32p. (J). (gr. k-3). 16.99 *(978-0-9883269-2-7(2))* Thompson Mill Pr.

Velástegui, Cecilia. Olinguito Speaks Up. 2013. (ENG., Illus.). 36p. (J). 19.99 *(978-0-9851769-7-6(0),* 37126aa1-04ad-4887-b51f-727981be0880) Libros Publishing.

Wallace, Nancy Elizabeth. Water! Water! Water!, 0 vols. 2014. (ENG.). 40p. (J). (gr. -1-k). 17.99 *(978-1-4778-4730-5(8),* 9781477847305, Two Lions) Amazon Publishing.

Weaver, Jo. Little Whale, 1 vol. 2018. (ENG., Illus.). 32p. (J). (gr. -1-2). 17.95 *(978-1-68263-049-5(8))* Peachtree Publishing Co. Inc.

Young, Elizabeth. The ed up Platypus. Seabrooks, Lydia, illus. 2011. 20p. pap. 24.95 *(978-1-4560-7028-1(2))* America Star Bks.

Zamenhof, Robert. The Adventures of Armadillo Baby & Annabelli. Baker, Sara, illus. 2013. 56p. pap. 9.29 *(978-0-615-80196-4(X))* RGZ Consulting.

Zoehfeld, Kathleen Weidner. Manatee Winter. Petruccio, Steven James, illus. 2005. (ENG.). 32p. (J). (gr. -1-2). 8.95 *(978-1-59249-072-1(7),* SC4003) Soundprints.

MAMMALS, FOSSIL

see also names of extinct animals, e.g. Mastodon; etc.

Brown, Charlotte Lewis. After the Dinosaurs: Mammoths & Fossil Mammals. Wilson, Phil, illus. (I Can Read Level 2 Ser.). 32p. (J). (gr. -1-3). 2007. (ENG.). pap. 4.99 *(978-0-06-053055-6(3),* HarperCollins) 2006. lib. bdg. 17.89 *(978-0-06-053054-9(5))* HarperCollins Pubs.

Clay, Kathryn. American Mastodon. 2018. (Little Paleontologist Ser.). (ENG., Illus.). 32p. (J). (gr. k-3). pap. 6.95 *(978-1-5435-0547-4(3),* 137362); lib. bdg. 28.65 *(978-1-5435-0543-6(0),* 137358) Capstone. (Capstone Pr.).

Clickard, Carrie. Thomas Jefferson & the Mammoth Hunt: The True Story of the Quest for America's Biggest Bones. Carpenter, Nancy, illus. 2019. (ENG.). 40p. (J). (gr. -1-3). 17.99 *(978-1-4814-4268-8(6),* Beach Lane Bks.) Beach Lane Bks.

de la Bédoyère, Camilla. Bone Collection: Skulls. Doyle, Sandra, illus. 2014. (ENG.). 96p. (J). (gr. 3-7). pap. 14.99 *(978-0-545-72457-9(0),* Scholastic Paperbacks) Scholastic, Inc.

Gilbert, Sara. Giant Short-Faced Bears. 2017. (Ice Age Mega Beasts Ser.). (ENG., Illus.). 24p. (J). (gr. 1-4). *(978-1-60818-766-9(7),* 20074, Creative Education) Creative Co., The.

—Stag-Moose. 2017. (Ice Age Mega Beasts Ser.). (ENG., Illus.). 24p. (J). (gr. 1-4). *(978-1-60818-770-6(5),* 20086, Creative Education) Creative Co., The.

Jeffrey, Gary. Giant Hunter. 2017. (Graphic Prehistoric Animals Ser.). (ENG., Illus.). 32p. (J). (gr. 5-8). 31.35 *(978-1-62588-408-4(7),* 19277, Smart Apple Media) Black Rabbit Bks.

—Sabertooth Tiger. 2017. (Graphic Prehistoric Animals Ser.). (ENG., Illus.). 32p. (J). (gr. 5-8). lib. bdg. 31.35 *(978-1-62588-411-4(7),* 19280, Smart Apple Media) Black Rabbit Bks.

—Woolly Mammoth. 2017. (Graphic Prehistoric Animals Ser.). (ENG., Illus.). 32p. (J). (gr. 5-8). lib. bdg. 31.35 *(978-1-62588-414-5(1),* 19283, Smart Apple Media) Black Rabbit Bks.

Mehling, Carl. Prehistoric Mammals, 1 vol. 2009. (Discovering Dinosaurs Ser.). (ENG., Illus.). 48p. (YA). (gr. 4-4). 33.93 *(978-1-60754-779-2(1),* 61682f24-64dc-45bd-8ebb-7974c16b42f5); pap. 13.85 *(978-1-60754-787-7(2),* da4e6bf7-be54-4fef-b45d-b33b3ac30e06) Rosen Publishing Group, Inc., The. (Windmill Bks.).

Oard, Beverly & Oard, Michael. What Ever Happened to the Wooly Mammoth: Life at the End of the Great Ice Age. Looney, Bill, illus. 2007. 72p. (J). 15.99 *(978-0-89051-508-2(5),* Master Books) New Leaf Publishing Group.

Parker, Steve. Ice Age Giants. 2011. (ENG., Illus.). 32p. (J). pap. 10.95 *(978-1-77092-012-5(9))* Saunders Bk. Co. CAN. Dist: RiverStream Publishing.

Rake, Matthew. The Rise of Mammals. Minister, Peter, illus. 2015. (Prehistoric Field Guides). (ENG.). 32p. (J). (gr. 3-6). lib. bdg. 27.99 *(978-1-4677-6351-6(9),* 0442d702-5646-4765-bfa8-021057759449, Hungry Tomato (r)) Lerner Publishing Group.

Staunton, Joseph & Flinthart, Dirk. Meat Eating Dinosaurs. Rey, Luis, illus. 2011. (Inside Crime Ser.). 48p. (YA). (gr. 5-9). 34.25 *(978-1-59920-395-9(2))* Black Rabbit Bks.

Thomson, Sarah L. Saber-Toothed Cat. Plant, Andrew, illus. 2014. (Ancient Animals Ser.). 32p. (J). (gr. 1-4). pap. 5.95 *(978-1-58089-407-4(0));* lib. bdg. 12.95 *(978-1-58089-400-5(3))* Charlesbridge Publishing, Inc.

West, David. Prehistoric Mammals, 1 vol., 1. 2015. (Prehistoric Animals Ser.). (ENG., Illus.). 24p. (J). (gr. 2-3). pap. 9.25 *(978-1-5081-9041-7(0),* fed2f40a-ad11-4f08-9781-f68287ed0005, Windmill Bks.) Rosen Publishing Group, Inc., The.

Worth, Bonnie. Once upon a Mastodon: All about Prehistoric Mammals. 2014. (Cat in the Hat's Learning Library). (Illus.). 48p. (J). (gr. k-3). 9.99 *(978-0-375-87075-0(X),* Random Hse. Bks. for Young Readers) Random Hse. Children's Bks.

MAMMOTHS

Agenbroad, Larry D. & Nelson, Lisa W. Mammoths: Ice-Age Giants. 2003. (Illus.). 120p. (J). (gr. 7-12). pap. 7.95 *(978-0-8225-0470-2(7))* Lerner Publishing Group.

Bailey, Gerry. Woolly Mammoth. Carr, Karen, illus. 2011. (Smithsonian Prehistoric Zone Ser.). (ENG.). 32p. (J). (gr. k-3). *(978-0-7787-1808-6(5),* 1325454); pap. *(978-0-7787-1821-5(2),* 1325454) Crabtree Publishing Co.

Clay, Kathryn. Woolly Mammoth. 2018. (Little Paleontologist Ser.). (ENG., Illus.). 32p. (J). (gr. k-3). lib. bdg. 28.65 *(978-1-5435-0541-2(4),* 137356, Capstone Pr.) Capstone.

Clickard, Carrie. Thomas Jefferson & the Mammoth Hunt: The True Story of the Quest for America's Biggest Bones. Carpenter, Nancy, illus. 2019. (ENG.). 40p. (J). (gr. -1-3).

17.99 (978-1-4814-4268-8(6), Beach Lane Bks.) Beach Lane Bks.

Frost, Helen. Woolly Mammoth [Scholastic]. Hughes, Jon, illus. 2009. (Dinosaurs & Prehistoric Animals Ser.). 24p. (gr. k-1). pap. 1.00 (978-1-4296-4250-7(5), Capstone Pr.) Capstone.

Gilbert, Sara. Mammoths. 2017. (Ice Age Mega Beasts Ser.). (ENG., Illus.). 24p. (J). (gr. 1-4). pap. 8.99 (978-1-62832-375-7(2), 20075, Creative Paperbacks); (978-1-60818-767-6(5), 20077, Creative Education) Creative Co., The.

Goecke, Michael P. Woolly Mammoth, 1 vol. 2003. (Prehistoric Animals Ser.). (ENG.). 24p. (gr. k-4). 25.65 (978-1-57765-971-6(6), Buddy Bks.) ABDO Publishing Co.

Gutman, Dan. My Weird School Fast Facts: Dinosaurs, Dodos, & Woolly Mammoths. Paillot, Jim, illus. 2018. (My Weird School Fast Facts Ser.: 6). (ENG.). 208p. (J). (gr. 1-5). pap. 5.99 (978-0-06-267309-1(2)); lib. bdg. 16.89 (978-0-06-267310-7(6)) HarperCollins Pubs. (HarperCollins).

Higgins, Melissa. Woolly Mammoths. 2015. (Ice Age Animals Ser.). (ENG., Illus.). 24p. (J). (gr. -1-2). pap. 6.95 (978-1-4914-2320-2(X), 127778, Capstone Pr.) Capstone.

Miller, Debbie S. A Woolly Mammoth Journey. 2010. (ENG., Illus.). 32p. (J). pap. 15.95 (978-1-60223-098-9(6)) Univ. of Alaska Pr.

Nelson, Lisa W. & Agenbroad, Larry D. Mammoths: Ice-Age Giants. Jansen, Paula, illus. Jansen, Paula, photos by. 2005. (Discovery! Ser.). 120p. (gr. 5-12). lib. bdg. 27.93 (978-0-8225-2862-3(2)) Lerner Publishing Group.

Orr, Tamra. Unearthing Fossils. 2018. (J). (978-1-5105-3718-7(X)) SmartBook Media, Inc.

Orr, Tamra B. Unearthing Fossils. 2014. (Explorer Library: Science Explorer Ser.). (ENG., Illus.). 32p. (J). (gr. 4-8). 32.07 (978-1-62431-781-1(2), 203320) Cherry Lake Publishing.

Philippo, Sophie. Meet the Woolly Mammoth. Dutertre, Charles, illus. 2005. (ENG.). 45p. (J). (gr. 4-7). 15.95 (978-1-58728-521-9(5)) Cooper Square Publishing Llc.

Rober, Harold. Woolly Mammoth. 2017. (Bumba Books (r) — Dinosaurs & Prehistoric Beasts Ser.). (ENG., Illus.). 24p. (J). (gr. -1-1). 26.65 (978-1-5124-2644-1(X), 8a4e432b-8a7d-456f-b476-1995865be03f); E-Book 39.99 (978-1-5124-3725-6(5), 9781512437256); E-Book 39.99 (978-1-5124-2738-7(1)); E-Book 4.99 (978-1-5124-3726-3(3), 9781512437263) Lerner Publishing Group. (Lerner Pubns.).

Sloan, Christopher. Baby Mammoth Mummy: Frozen in Time (Special Sales Edition) A Prehistoric Animal's Journey into the 21st Century. 2011. (ENG., Illus.). 48p. (J). (gr. 3-7). 17.95 (978-1-4263-0865-9(5)) National Geographic Society.

Wadsworth, Ginger. Woolly Mammoths. Zalewski, Todd, illus. 2006. (On My Own Science Ser.). (ENG.). 48p. (gr. 2-4). lib. bdg. 25.26 (978-1-57505-879-5(0), Millbrook Pr.) Lerner Publishing Group.

Zabludoff, Marc. Woolly Mammoth, 1 vol. Bollinger, Peter, illus. 2010. (Prehistoric Beasts Ser.). (ENG.). 32p. (gr. 2-2). 32.64 (978-0-7614-3996-7(X), 13700f0e-86c1-4d32-8bd1-f52db2496652) Cavendish Square Publishing LLC.

Zeiger, Jennifer. Mammoth & Mastodon. 2015. (21st Century Junior Library: Dinosaurs & Prehistoric Creatures Ser.). (ENG., Illus.). 24p. (J). (gr. 2-5). lib. bdg. 29.21 (978-1-63362-383-5(1), 206952) Cherry Lake Publishing.

MAMMOTHS—FICTION

Artful Doodlers Ltd Staff, contrib. by. Adventures of Ice Age. 2013. (Illus.). 128p. (J). (978-1-4351-5060-7(0)) Barnes & Noble, Inc.

Bentley, Dawn. Woolly Mammoth in Trouble. 2010. (Smithsonian's Prehistoric Pals Ser.). (Illus.). (J). 21.95 (978-1-59249-547-4(8)) Soundprints.

—Woolly Mammoth in Trouble. Carr, Karen, illus. (Smithsonian's Prehistoric Pals Ser.). (ENG.). 36p. (J). (gr. -1-2). 2005. 14.95 (978-1-59249-364-7(5), H2404) 2005. 2.95 (978-1-59249-367-8(X), S2454) 2005. pap. 6.95 (978-1-59249-365-4(3), S2404) 2004. 9.95 (978-1-59249-368-5(8), PS2454) 2004. 8.95 (978-1-59249-366-1(1), SD2404) Soundprints.

Clark, Patricia Nikolina. In the Shadow of the Mammoth. LeTourneau, Anthony Alex, illus. (J). 2005. 14.99 (978-0-9674602-8-4(X)) 2003. 190p. pap. 6.99 (978-0-9674602-4-6(7)) Blue Marlin Pubns.

Elliott, David. This Orq. (He Say UGH!) Nichols, Lori, illus. 2015. (ENG.). 40p. (J). (gr. -1-2). 16.95 (978-1-62091-789-3(0), Astra Young Readers) Astra Publishing Hse.

Fraser, Ian. Life with Mammoth, 0 vols. Fraser, Mary Ann, illus. (Ogg & Bob Ser.: 2). (ENG.). 64p. (J). 2013. (gr. k-3). pap. 9.99 (978-1-4778-1615-8(1), 9781477816158) 2012. (gr. 1-3). 14.99 (978-0-7614-5722-0(4), 9780761457220) Amazon Publishing. (Two Lions).

—Meet Mammoth, 0 vols. Fraser, Mary Ann, illus. 2013. (Ogg & Bob Ser.: 1). (ENG.). 64p. (J). (gr. 1-3). pap. 9.99 (978-1-4778-1617-2(8), 9781477816172, Two Lions) Amazon Publishing.

Gabriel, Andrea. Wandering Woolly, 1 vol. 2015. (ENG., Illus.). 32p. (J). (gr. 1-4). 17.95 (978-1-62855-558-5(0)) Arbordale Publishing.

Gréban, Quentin. Woolly & Me, 1 vol. 2018. (ENG., Illus.). 32p. (J). (gr. -1-2). 16.95 (978-0-88448-636-7(2), 884636) Tilbury Hse. Pubs.

Layton, Neal. The Mammoth Academy. Layton, Neal, illus. 2010. (ENG., Illus.). 176p. (J). (gr. 4-6). 21.19 (978-0-312-60882-8(9)) Square Fish.

Mezrich, Ben & Mezrich, Tonya. Charlie Numbers & the Woolly Mammoth. 2020. (Charlie Numbers Adventures Ser.). (ENG.). 192p. (J). (gr. 3-7). pap. 8.99 (978-1-5344-4101-9(8), Simon & Schuster Bks. For Young Readers) Simon & Schuster Bks. For Young Readers.

PaleoJoe & Caszatt-Allen, Wendy. Mysterious Mammoths. 2008. (PaleoJoe's Dinosaur Detective Club Ser.). (Illus.). 200p. (J). (gr. 2-5). pap. 8.95 (978-1-934133-43-9(4), Mackinac Island Press, Inc.) Charlesbridge Publishing, Inc.

Robinson, Michelle. How to Wash a Woolly Mammoth: A Picture Book. Hindley, Kate, illus. 2014. (ENG.). 32p. (J). (gr. -1-3). 21.99 (978-0-8050-9966-9(2), 900128169, Holt, Henry & Co. Bks. For Young Readers) Holt, Henry & Co.

Russell, Jesse & Cohn, Ronald, eds. Ice Age: Continental Drift. 2012. 158p. pap. (978-5-512-74544-1(1)) Books on Demand.

Smith, Suzanne & Taylor, Lindsay. The Magical Ice Palace: A Doodle Girl Adventure. Maurri, Mamie, illus. 2018. (ENG.). 32p. (J). 9.99 (978-1-4711-2319-1(7), Simon & Schuster Children's) Simon & Schuster, Ltd. GBR. Dist: Simon & Schuster, Inc.

Stead, Philip C. Samson in the Snow. 2016. (ENG., Illus.). 40p. (J). 17.99 (978-1-62672-182-1(3), 900143664) Roaring Brook Pr.

Walters, Eric. Elephant Secret. 2018. (ENG.). 352p. (J). (gr. 5-7). 16.99 (978-1-328-79617-2(5), 1685560, Clarion Bks.) HarperCollins Pubs.

MAN

see Human Beings

MAN—COLOR

see Human Skin Color

MAN, PREHISTORIC

see Prehistoric Peoples

MAN IN SPACE

see Manned Space Flight

MANAGEMENT

see also Farm Management; Industrial Management

Aikins, Anne Marie. Authority: Deal with It Before It Deals with You, 1 vol. Murray, Steven, illus. 2005. (Lorimer Deal with It Ser.). (ENG.). 32p. (J). (gr. 4-9). 12.95 (978-1-55028-869-8(5), 183476f6-554f-4567-b7a5-42a153e10bc9) James Lorimer & Co. Ltd., Pubs. CAN. Dist: Lerner Publishing Group.

Bailey, Rachel. Superstorm Sandy, 1 vol. 2013. (History's Greatest Disasters Ser.). (ENG., Illus.). 48p. (J). (gr. 4-8). lib. bdg. 34.22 (978-1-61783-961-0(2), 9493) ABDO Publishing Co.

Beasley, Ava. We Plant Vegetables: Working As a Team, 1 vol. 2017. (Computer Science for the Real World Ser.). (ENG.). 8p. (gr. k-1). pap. (978-1-5383-5063-8(7), 0ad7863c-c239-4a04-8135-e8a174486f52, Rosen Classroom) Rosen Publishing Group, Inc., The.

Bernstein, Daryl. Better Than a Lemonade Stand! Small Business Ideas for Kids. Husberg, Rob, illus. 2012. (ENG.). 224p. (J). (gr. 4-9). pap. 14.99 (978-1-58270-330-5(2)) Aladdin/Beyond Words.

Broyles, Janell. Chemical Biological Incident Response Force. 2009. (Inside Special Operations Ser.). 64p. (gr. 6-6). 58.50 (978-1-61513-551-6(0), Rosen Reference) Rosen Publishing Group, Inc., The.

Byers, Ann. Blackouts: A Practical Survival Guide. 2009. (Library of Emergency Preparedness Ser.). 64p. (gr. 6-6). 58.50 (978-1-60853-591-0(6), Rosen Reference) Rosen Publishing Group, Inc., The.

Cunningham, Kevin. Surviving Tsunamis, 1 vol. 2011. (Children's True Stories: Natural Disasters Ser.). (ENG.). 32p. (J). (gr. 3-5). 31.32 (978-1-4109-4095-7(0), 114630); pap. 8.29 (978-1-4109-4102-2(7), 114636) Capstone. (Raintree).

Donovan, Sandra. Teen Wise Guide to Time Management. 2012. (USA TODAY Teen Wise Guides: Time, Money, & Relationships Ser.). (ENG.). 64p. (gr. 8-12). lib. bdg. 31.93 (978-0-7613-7019-2(6)) Lerner Publishing Group.

Ferguson, creator. Business Managers. 2nd rev. ed. 2009. (Ferguson's Careers in Focus Ser.). (ENG.). 204p. (gr. 6-12). 32.95 (978-0-8160-7296-5(5), P179098, Ferguson Publishing Company) Infobase Holdings, Inc.

Hibbert, Clare. My Busy Day. Raga, Sylvia, illus. 2011. (Busy Times Ser.). (ENG.). 24p. (J). 19.99 (978-0-237-54263-4(3)) Evans Brothers, Ltd. GBR. Dist: Independent Pubs. Group.

Higgins, Nadia. Sequences: Order Matters! Sanchez, Sr., illus. 2018. (Code It! Ser.). (ENG.). 24p. (J). (gr. 1-3). 33.99 (978-1-68410-310-2(X), 140702) Cantata Learning.

Jeffries, Corina. We Work Together for Equality! Working As a Team, 1 vol. 2017. (Computer Science for the Real World Ser.). (ENG.). 16p. (gr. 2-3). pap. (978-1-5383-5212-0(5), 72465734-7b17-47ea-81e6-999afb1991ef, Rosen Classroom) Rosen Publishing Group, Inc., The.

La Bella, Laura. Careers in Crisis Management & Hostage Negotiation, 1 vol. 2013. (Extreme Law Enforcement Ser.). (ENG., Illus.). 112p. (YA). (gr. 7-7). 39.77 (978-1-4777-1709-7(9), dfc3d4f7-156e-4c43-b279-850e0bf6b40e) Rosen Publishing Group, Inc., The.

McCabe, Matthew. 12 Business Leaders Who Changed the World. 2016. (Change Makers Ser.). (ENG., Illus.). 32p. (J). (gr. 3-6). 32.80 (978-1-63235-145-6(5), 11935, 12-Story Library) Bookstaves, LLC.

Mitchell Haugen, Hayley & Elkins, Bruce, eds. Disaster Relief, 1 vol. 2009. (Issues That Concern You Ser.). (ENG., Illus.). 104p. (gr. 7-10). 43.63 (978-0-7377-4494-1(4), f7339766-25df-48be-8d3b-f38aa5829882, Greenhaven Publishing) Greenhaven Publishing LLC.

Murdico, Suzanne. Earthquakes: A Practical Survival Guide. 2009. (Library of Emergency Preparedness Ser.). 64p. (gr. 6-6). 58.50 (978-1-60853-593-4(2), Rosen Reference) Rosen Publishing Group, Inc., The.

Pelos, Rebecca & Greenberger, Robert. Cool Careers Without College for People Who Love Planning & Organizing, 1 vol. 2017. (Cool Careers Without College Ser.). (ENG., Illus.). 112p. (J). (gr. 7-7). 41.12 (978-1-5081-7540-7(3), 72ed9db2-9f2f-4731-aea6-ec0e04b8b59c, Rosen Young Adult) Rosen Publishing Group, Inc., The.

Raum, Elizabeth. Surviving Hurricanes, 1 vol. 2011. (Children's True Stories: Natural Disasters Ser.). (ENG.). 32p. (J). (gr. 3-5). pap. 8.29 (978-1-4109-4100-8(0), 114634, Raintree) Capstone.

—Surviving Tornadoes, 1 vol. 2011. (Children's True Stories: Natural Disasters Ser.). (ENG.). 32p. (J). (gr. 3-5). pap. 8.29 (978-1-4109-4099-5(3), 114633, Raintree) Capstone.

MANAGEMENT—EMPLOYEE PARTICIPATION

Connolly, Sean. Rights at Work. 2005. (Campaigns for Change Ser.). (Illus.). 48p. (J). (gr. 6-9). lib. bdg. 29.95 (978-1-58340-518-5(6), 1247340) Black Rabbit Bks.

MANAGEMENT, INDUSTRIAL

see Industrial Management

MANAGEMENT, SCIENTIFIC

see Management

MANAGEMENT OF CHILDREN

see Child Rearing

MANDELA, NELSON, 1918-2013

Baptiste, Tracey. Nelson Mandela: Nobel Peace Prize-Winning Champion for Hope & Harmony, 4 vols. 2015. (Britannica Beginner Bios Ser.). (ENG.). 32p. (J). (gr. 2-3). 52.12 (978-1-62275-943-9(5), a2f77d99-a713-4e04-9c46-41666fe29d1e, Britannica Educational Publishing) Rosen Publishing Group, Inc., The.

—Nelson Mandela: Nobel Peace Prize-Winning Warrior for Hope & Harmony, 1 vol. 2015. (Britannica Beginner Bios Ser.). (ENG., Illus.). 32p. (J). (gr. 2-3). 26.06 (978-1-62275-941-5(9), 9c880c74-7f67-442d-b141-497ece6499c4, Britannica Educational Publishing) Rosen Publishing Group, Inc., The.

Belviso, Meg & Pollack, Pam. Who Is Nelson Mandela? 2014. (Who Was... ? Ser.). lib. bdg. 16.00 (978-0-606-34158-5(7)) Turtleback.

Boothroyd, Jennifer. Nelson Mandela: A Life of Persistence. (Pull Ahead Books — Biographies Ser.). (ENG., Illus.). 32p. (gr. k-3). 2007. (J). pap. 7.99 (978-0-8225-6434-8(3), 4ba9e03a-1644-4461-a60e-7c4961301a45) 2006. lib. bdg. 22.60 (978-0-8225-6385-3(1), Lerner Pubns.) Lerner Publishing Group.

Crompton, Samuel Willard. Nelson Mandela. 2006. (ENG., Illus.). 112p. (gr. 9-12). 30.00 (978-0-7910-8997-2(5), P114504, Facts On File) Infobase Holdings, Inc.

Dakers, Diane. Nelson Mandela: South Africa's Anti-Apartheid Revolutionary. 2014. (Crabtree Groundbreaker Biographies Ser.). (ENG., Illus.). 112p. (J). (gr. 6-6). (978-0-7787-1241-1(9)) Crabtree Publishing Co.

Denenberg, Barry. Nelson Mandela: No Easy Walk to Freedom. 2014. (ENG.). 240p. (J). (gr. 4-7). pap. 7.99 (978-0-545-66911-5(1)) Scholastic, Inc.

Doeden, Matt. Nelson Mandela: World Leader for Human Rights. 2014. (Gateway Biographies Ser.). (ENG., Illus.). 48p. (J). (gr. 4-8). lib. bdg. 31.99 (978-1-4677-5197-1(9), d0f1c40a-f447-4632-a27b-fd7328cbc513, Lerner Pubns.) Lerner Publishing Group.

Finlayson, Reggie. Nelson Mandela. pap. 9.95 (978-0-8225-5743-2(6)); 2005. (ENG., Illus.). 112p. (gr. 5-12). lib. bdg. 27.93 (978-0-8225-2644-5(1), Lerner Pubns.) Lerner Publishing Group.

Gormley, Beatrice. Nelson Mandela: South African Revolutionary. 2015. (Real-Life Story Ser.). (ENG., Illus.). 256p. (J). (gr. 3-7). 17.99 (978-1-4814-2059-4(3), Aladdin) Simon & Schuster Children's Publishing.

Graham Gaines Rodriguez, Ann. Nelson Mandela & the End of Apartheid, 1 vol. 2015. (People & Events That Changed the World Ser.). (ENG., Illus.). 128p. (J). (gr. 7-8). 38.93 (978-0-7660-7300-5(9), a27ea591-870c-45ea-8587-10e2d5002b79) Enslow Publishing, LLC.

Grant, Karima. Nelson Mandela. 2006. (Rookie Biographies Ser.). (ENG., Illus.). 32p. (J). (gr. 1-2). per. 4.95 (978-0-516-25537-8(1), Children's Pr.) Scholastic Library Publishing.

Holland, Gini & O'Hern, Kerri. Nelson Mandela, 1 vol. (Biografías Gráficas (Graphic Biographies) Ser.). (Illus.). 32p. (gr. 3-3). 2007. (SPA.). pap. 11.50 (978-0-8368-7888-2(4), c0856dc9-2ca1-4644-99c6-dd783962ddac) 2007. (SPA., lib. bdg. 29.67 (978-0-8368-7881-3(7), b3c04f14-f5db-498a-8d90-9e9bb7ba5e50) 2005. (ENG., pap. 11.50 (978-0-8368-6249-2(X), 187ebf93-9b41-4f9e-8153-9c4bdab7a428) Stevens, Gareth Publishing LLLP.

Hollingsworth, Tamara. Nelson Mandela: Leading the Way, 1 vol. 2nd rev. ed. (TIME for KIDS(r): Informational Text Ser.). (ENG., Illus.). 48p. (gr. 4-5). 2013. (J). lib. bdg. 29.96 (978-1-4807-1116-7(0)) 2012. pap. 11.99 (978-1-4333-4864-8(0)) Teacher Created Materials, Inc.

Josephson, Judith P. Nelson Mandela. 2009. (History Maker Biographies Ser.). (ENG.). 48p. (gr. 3-6). 27.93 (978-1-58013-703-4(2), Lerner Pubns.) Lerner Publishing Group.

Keller, Bill. Tree Shaker: The Life of Nelson Mandela. 2013. (New York Times Ser.). (ENG., Illus.). 128p. (J). (gr. 5-9). pap. 14.99 (978-1-59643-533-9(X), 900061088) Square Fish.

Kramer, Ann. World History Biographies: Mandela: The Hero Who Led His Nation to Freedom. 2008. (National Geographic World History Biographies Ser.). (Illus.). 64p. (J). (gr. 3-7). pap. 7.99 (978-1-4263-0173-5(1), National Geographic Kids) Disney Publishing Worldwide.

Kramer, Barbara. National Geographic Readers: Nelson Mandela. 2014. (Readers Bios Ser.). (Illus.). 48p. (J). (gr. 1-3). pap. 4.99 (978-1-4263-1763-7(8), National Geographic Kids) Disney Publishing Worldwide.

Magoon, Kekla. Nelson Mandela: A Leader for Freedom, 1 vol. 2008. (Essential Lives Set 2 Ser.). (ENG., Illus.). 112p. (YA). (gr. 6-12). lib. bdg. 41.36 (978-1-60453-038-4(3), 6657, Essential Library) ABDO Publishing Co.

Malaspina, Ann. Nelson Mandela: Fighting to Dismantle Apartheid, 1 vol. 2017. (Rebels with a Cause Ser.). (ENG.). 128p. (YA). (gr. 8-8). lib. bdg. 38.93 (978-0-7660-8517-6(1), 0b4489f0-6cb5-4f8d-9265-b48760337c0e) Enslow Publishing, LLC.

Meyer, Susan. Nelson Mandela: South African President & Anti-Apartheid Activist. 2017. (Spotlight on Civic Courage: Heroes of Conscience Ser.). 48p. (J). (gr. 10-15). 70.50 (978-1-5383-8089-5(7)); (ENG.). (gr. 6-6). pap. 12.75 (978-1-5383-8088-8(9), d7b4d779-7010-4b28-9fdf-11e0b9b95b88) Rosen Publishing Group, Inc., The. (Rosen Young Adult).

Morini, Manuel & Segesso, Ignacio. Nelson Mandela. 2017. (Graphic Lives Ser.). (ENG., Illus.). 80p. (J). (gr. 3-9). lib. bdg. 32.65 (978-1-5157-9164-5(5), 136606, Capstone Pr.) Capstone.

Nelson, Kadir. Nelson Mandela. Nelson, Kadir, illus. (ENG., Illus.). 40p. (J). (gr. -1-3). 2019. pap. 9.99 (978-0-06-178377-7(3)) 2013. 17.99 (978-0-06-178374-6(9)) 2013. lib. bdg. 18.89 (978-0-06-178376-0(5)) HarperCollins Pubs. (Tegen, Katherine Bks).

—Nelson Mandela. 2014. (SPA.). (J). (gr. 2-4). 21.99 (978-84-261-4069-2(6)) Juventud, Editorial ESP. Dist: Lectorum Pubns., Inc.

O'Neill, John R. Mahatma Gandhi, Nelson Mandela. 2011. (Readers' & Writers' Genre Workshop Ser.). (YA). pap. (978-1-4509-3024-6(7)) Benchmark Education Co.

Pollack, Pam & Who HQ. Who Was Nelson Mandela? Marchesi, Stephen, illus. 2014. (Who Was? Ser.). 112p. (J). (gr. 3-7). 5.99 (978-0-448-47933-0(8), Penguin Workshop) Penguin Young Readers Group.

Rajczak Nelson, Kristen. Nelson Mandela, 1 vol. 2015. (Heroes of Black History Ser.). (ENG., Illus.). 32p. (J). (gr. 3-4). pap. 11.50 (978-1-4824-2908-4(X), b39b2d5c-3cb7-42ed-81f5-4043e85c1433) Stevens, Gareth Publishing LLLP.

Riggs, Kate. The Release of Nelson Mandela. 2009. (Days of Change Ser.). (ENG., Illus.). 48p. (J). (gr. 5-8). 22.95 (978-1-58341-736-2(2), 22145) Creative Co., The.

Rose, Simon. Nelson Mandela. 2010. (Remarkable People Ser.). (Illus.). 24p. (J). (gr. 3-5). lib. bdg. 25.70 (978-1-61690-172-1(1)); (gr. 4-6). pap. 11.95 (978-1-61690-173-8(X)) Weigl Pubs., Inc.

Schuldt, Lori Meek. Martin Luther King, Jr: With Profiles of Mohandas K. Gandhi & Nelson Mandela. 2006. (Biographical Connections Ser.). (Illus.). 112p. (J). (978-0-7166-1822-5(2)) World Bk., Inc.

Senker, Cath. Nelson Mandela. 2015. (Against the Odds Biographies Ser.). (ENG., Illus.). 48p. (J). (gr. 3-6). 35.99 (978-1-4846-2465-4(3), 129623, Heinemann) Capstone.

Shone, Rob. Nelson Mandela: The Life of an African Statesman. 2009. (Graphic Nonfiction Biographies Ser.). (ENG.). 48p. (YA). (gr. 4-5). 58.50 (978-1-61513-023-8(3), Rosen Reference) Rosen Publishing Group, Inc., The.

—Nelson Mandela: The Life of an African Statesman, 1 vol. Reed, Neil, illus. 2006. (Graphic Nonfiction Biographies Ser.). (ENG.). 48p. (gr. 4-5). (J). lib. bdg. 37.13 (978-1-4042-0860-5(7), 7a196e9f-b30e-495d-9ddc-967f20e6af60); pap. 14.05 (978-1-4042-0923-7(9), 6dc1dd53-2e23-47a5-933c-762eb0508d10) Rosen Publishing Group, Inc., The.

Stamper, G. C. Nelson Mandela. 2005. (Illus.). 32p. (J). pap. (978-0-7367-2922-2(4)) Zaner-Bloser, Inc.

Strand, Jennifer. Nelson Mandela. 2016. (Legendary Leaders Ser.). (ENG.). 24p. (J). (gr. -1-2). 49.94 (978-1-68079-407-6(8), 23028, Abdo Zoom-Launch) ABDO Publishing Co.

Toufexis, George. Nelson Mandela Coloring Book. 2014. (Dover Black History Coloring Bks.). (ENG.). 32p. (J). (gr. 3-8). pap. 3.99 (978-0-486-78813-5(X), 78813X) Dover Pubns., Inc.

Trussell-Cullen, Alan. Nelson Mandela. 2009. pap. 13.25 (978-1-60559-067-7(3)) Hameray Publishing Group, Inc.

Turner, Myra Faye. People That Changed the Course of History: The Story of Nelson Mandela 100 Years after His Birth. 2017. (J). (978-1-62023-450-1(5)) Atlantic Publishing Group, Inc.

—People Who Changed the Course of History: The Story of Nelson Mandela 100 Years after His Birth. 2018. (ENG.). 238p. (YA). pap. 19.95 (978-1-62023-446-4(7), 0df6c692-20ee-481c-b071-04ecc3e6f8e5) Atlantic Publishing Group, Inc.

Woll, Kris. Nelson Mandela: South African President & Civil Rights Activist, 1 vol. 2015. (Newsmakers Ser.). (ENG., Illus.). 48p. (J). (gr. 4-8). lib. bdg. 35.64 (978-1-62403-643-9(0), 17185) ABDO Publishing Co.

MANET, EDOUARD, 1832-1883

Mis, Melody S. Edouard Manet. (Meet the Artist Ser.). 24p. (gr. 2-3). 2009. 42.50 (978-1-61514-629-1(6), PowerKids Pr.) 2007. (ENG., Illus.). (J). lib. bdg. 26.27 (978-1-4042-3841-1(7), 41a9fc1c-05de-4cd4-bd9a-614ed331338d) Rosen Publishing Group, Inc., The.

Tracy, Kathleen. Edouard Manet. 2009. (Art Profiles for Kids Ser.). (Illus.). 48p. (YA). (gr. 4-7). lib. bdg. 29.95 (978-1-58415-746-5(1)) Mitchell Lane Pubs.

Zaczek, Iain. Édouard Manet, 1 vol. 2014. (Great Artists Ser.). (ENG., Illus.). 32p. (J). (gr. 4-4). pap. 11.50 (978-1-4824-1217-8(9), 6dcfd654-b353-41b8-adeb-81dfa8799daa) Stevens, Gareth Publishing LLLP.

MANGROVE

Levy, Janey. Mangroves Grow in Salt Water!, 1 vol. 2019. (World's Weirdest Plants Ser.). (ENG.). 24p. (gr. 2-3). pap. 9.15 (978-1-5382-4646-7(5), 20d5018f-9360-4ab3-b2f3-b3e677b18e08) Stevens, Gareth Publishing LLLP.

Roth, Susan L. & Trumbore, Cindy. The Mangrove Tree: Planting Trees to Feed Families. Roth, Susan L., illus. 2011. (ENG., Illus.). 40p. (J). (gr. 1-6). 19.95 (978-1-60060-459-1(5)) Lee & Low Bks., Inc.

MANNED SPACE FLIGHT

see also Astronauts; Outer Space—Exploration; Space Medicine

also names of projects, e.g. Gemini Project; etc.

Amstutz, Lisa J. NASA & the Astronauts. 2018. (Destination Space Ser.). (ENG., Illus.). 48p. (J). (gr. 5-6). pap. 11.95 (978-1-63517-569-1(0), 1635175690); lib. bdg. 34.21 (978-1-63517-497-7(X), 163517497X) North Star Editions. (Focus Readers).

Anderson, Rane. Stem: Mission to Mars: Problem Solving (Grade 3) 2017. (Mathematics in the Real World Ser.). (ENG., Illus.). 32p. (J). (gr. 3-4). pap. 11.99 (978-1-4807-5801-8(9)) Teacher Created Materials, Inc.

Barghoorn, Linda. Mae Jemison: Trailblazing Astronaut, Doctor, & Teacher. 2016. (Remarkable Lives Revealed Ser.). (ENG., Illus.). 32p. (J). (gr. 2-5). (978-0-7787-2693-7(2)) Crabtree Publishing Co.

Brake, Mark. Lonely Planet Kids How to Be a Space Explorer 1: Your Out-Of-this-World Adventure. 2014. (Lonely Planet Kids Ser.). (ENG., Illus.). 160p. (J). (gr. 4-7). 17.99 (978-1-74360-434-2(3), 4798) Lonely Planet Global Ltd. IRL. Dist: Hachette Bk. Group.

Bredeson, Carmen. Living on a Space Shuttle. 2003. (Rookie Read-About Science: Space Science Ser.). (ENG., Illus.). 32p. (J). (gr. 1-2). 17.44 (978-0-516-22528-9(6), Children's Pr.) Scholastic Library Publishing.

Bredeson, Carmen & Dyson, Marianne. Astronauts Explore the Galaxy, 1 vol. 2015. (Launch into Space! Ser.). (ENG.).

32p. (gr. 3-4). pap. 11.52 *(978-0-7660-6813-1(7),* 00d8f81b-f083-40b8-973d-f9b231a12e9f); (Illus.). 26.93 *(978-0-7660-6815-5(3),* f403da6b-59be-4669-b4df-051d43179460) Enslow Publishing, LLC.

Clay, Kathryn. Space Flights. 2017. (Little Astronauts Ser.). (ENG., Illus.). 32p. (J). (gr. -1-2). lib. bdg. 28.65 *(978-1-5157-3659-2(8),* 133644, Capstone Pr.) Capstone.

—Spacewalks. 2017. (Little Astronauts Ser.). (ENG., Illus.). 32p. (J). (gr. -1-2). lib. bdg. 28.65 *(978-1-5157-3658-5(X),* 133643, Capstone Pr.) Capstone.

Dickmann, Nancy. Exploring the Inner Planets, 1 vol. 2015. (Spectacular Space Science Ser.). (ENG., Illus.). 48p. (J). (gr. 5-6). 33.47 *(978-1-4994-3629-7(7),* ab513eb5-c984-4eb0-b82d-98012308a5f4, Rosen Central) Rosen Publishing Group, Inc., The.

Dugan, Christine. Living in Space, 1 vol. 2nd rev. ed. 2012. (TIME for KIDS(r): Informational Text Ser.). (ENG.). 32p. (gr. 3-5). pap. 12.99 *(978-1-4333-3675-1(8))* Teacher Created Materials, Inc.

—Space Exploration, 1 vol. 2nd rev. ed. 2014. (TIME for KIDS(r): Informational Text Ser.). (ENG., Illus.). 32p. (J). (gr. 3-5). lib. bdg. 25.96 *(978-1-4807-1083-2(0))* Teacher Created Materials, Inc.

Ertle-Rickard, Stephen & Rickard, Steve. Astronaut. 2008. (321 Go! Ser.). (ENG., Illus.). 36p. pap. *(978-1-84167-781-1(7))* Ransom Publishing Ltd.

Freedman, Jeri. Interstellar Manned Space Travel, 1 vol. 2018. (Sci-Fi or STEM? Ser.). (ENG., Illus.). 64p. (gr. 7-7). 36.13 *(978-1-5081-8037-1(7),* cffae283-98a5-4c46-859b-ed0bc8410878) Rosen Publishing Group, Inc., The.

Furgang, Adam. Human Spaceflight, 1 vol. 2017. (From Earth to the Stars Ser.). (ENG.). 48p. (gr. 6-7). pap. 15.05 *(978-1-68048-669-8(1),* 0dee7fa1-36a8-4491-ace1-54cb3d373420, Britannica Educational Publishing) Rosen Publishing Group, Inc., The.

Goldstein, Margaret J. Astronauts: A Space Discovery Guide. 2017. (Space Discovery Guides). (ENG., Illus.). 48p. (J). (gr. 4-6). 31.99 *(978-1-5124-2588-8(5),* f66640b4-d476-4f07-bf0d-2992b97f5148); E-Book 4.99 *(978-1-5124-3800-0(6),* 9781512438000); E-Book 47.99 *(978-1-5124-3801-7(4),* 9781512438017) Lerner Publishing Group. (Lerner Pubns.).

—Private Space Travel: A Space Discovery Guide. 2017. (Space Discovery Guides). (ENG., Illus.). 48p. (J). (gr. 4-6). 31.99 *(978-1-5124-2589-5(3),* 2d08579d-21f9-4260-89cd-5ffef4d2d88d); E-Book 4.99 *(978-1-5124-3816-1(2),* 9781512438161); E-Book 47.99 *(978-1-5124-2797-4(7));* E-Book 47.99 *(978-1-5124-3815-4(4),* 9781512438154) Lerner Publishing Group. (Lerner Pubns.).

Goodman, Susan E. How Do You Burp in Space? And Other Tips Every Space Tourist Needs to Know. Slack, Michael, illus. 2013. (ENG.). 80p. (J). (gr. 3-6). 17.99 *(978-1-59990-068-1(8),* 900042509, Bloomsbury USA Childrens) Bloomsbury Publishing USA.

Grack, Rachel. Space Travel from Then to Now. 2019. (Sequence Developments in Technology Ser.). (ENG.). 32p. (J). (gr. 2-5). pap. 9.99 *(978-1-68152-473-3(2),* 11057); lib. bdg. *(978-1-68151-687-5(X),* 10817) Amicus.

Hirsch, Rebecca E. Space Gear in Action (an Augmented Reality Experience) 2020. (Space in Action: Augmented Reality (Alternator Books (r)) Ser.). (ENG., Illus.). 32p. (J). (gr. 3-6). 31.99 *(978-1-5415-7884-5(8),* 105df6d6-45f6-4a72-b667-271012aaa93f, Lerner Pubns.) Lerner Publishing Group.

Holden, Henry M. The Coolest Job in the Universe: Working Aboard the International Space Station, 1 vol. 2012. (American Space Missions: Astronauts, Exploration, & Discovery Ser.). (ENG., Illus.). 48p. (gr. 5-7). lib. bdg. 27.93 *(978-0-7660-4074-8(7),* 2a655c2e-ef54-4c2c-9324-2b92f1c91bec) Enslow Publishing, LLC.

Hubbard, Ben. Yuri Gagarin & the Race to Space. 2015. (Adventures in Space Ser.). (ENG., Illus.). 48p. (J). (gr. 4-6). 35.99 *(978-1-4846-2514-9(5),* 130011, Heinemann) Capstone.

Ingebretsen, Karen, et al. Human Space Exploration. 2006. (World Book's Solar System & Space Exploration Library). (Illus.). 63p. (J). *(978-0-7166-9509-7(X))* World Bk., Inc.

Jefferis, David. Dreams of Space: Before Apollo. 2019. (Moon Flight Atlas Ser.). (Illus.). 32p. (J). (gr. 5-5). *(978-0-7787-5408-4(1));* pap. *(978-0-7787-5417-6(0))* Crabtree Publishing Co.

Jefferis, David & Irvine, Mat. Flight into Orbit. 2007. (Humans in Space Ser.). (ENG., Illus.). 32p. (J). (gr. 3-7). lib. bdg. *(978-0-7787-3101-6(4));* pap. *(978-0-7787-3115-3(4))* Crabtree Publishing Co.

Jemison, Mae & Rau, Dana Meachen. The 100 Year Starship. 2013. (True Book™—Dr. Mae Jemison & 100 Year Starship™ Ser.). (ENG.). 48p. (J). 29.00 *(978-0-531-25500-1(X),* Children's Pr.) Scholastic Library Publishing.

Kerrod, Robin. Space Pioneers, 1 vol. 2004. (History of Space Exploration Ser.). (ENG., Illus.). 48p. (gr. 5-8). lib. bdg. 33.67 *(978-0-8368-5707-8(0),* 9cecd3d7-b1b4-4fa1-8e4f-6c5a7f4d01fc) Stevens, Gareth Publishing LLLP.

Kluger, Jeffrey. Disaster Strikes! The Most Dangerous Space Missions of All Time. 2019. (ENG., Illus.). 224p. (J). (gr. 3-7). 18.99 *(978-1-9848-1275-9(0),* Philomel Bks.) Penguin Young Readers Group.

Kopp, Megan. Journeys to Outer Space. 2019. (Mission: Space Science Ser.). (Illus.). 48p. (J). (gr. 5-5). *(978-0-7787-5393-3(X));* pap. *(978-0-7787-5404-6(9))* Crabtree Publishing Co.

Kruesi, Liz. Discover Space Exploration. 2016. (Searchlight Books (tm) — What's Cool about Science? Ser.). (ENG., Illus.). 40p. (J). (gr. 3-5). 30.65 *(978-1-5124-0811-9(5),* 1fb5a99a-38ad-49de-bf70-ed8d315026f8, Lerner Pubns.) Lerner Publishing Group.

Kurtz, Kevin. Cutting-Edge Space Tourism. 2019. (Searchlight Books (tm) — New Frontiers of Space Ser.). (ENG., Illus.). 32p. (J). (gr. 3-5). pap. 9.99 *(978-1-5415-7486-1(9),* c0323055-a890-4581-8d18-e493505a8663); lib. bdg. 30.65 *(978-1-5415-5744-4(1),* 41826025-3a04-4f45-ac6e-e861b4f83121) Lerner Publishing Group. (Lerner Pubns.).

Littlejohn, Randy. Life in Outer Space, 1 vol. 2003. (Life in Extreme Environments Ser.). (ENG., Illus.). 64p. (gr. 5-8). lib. bdg. 37.13 *(978-0-8239-3989-3(8),* e1a48f16-b307-4fad-a22f-dde0324840fa, Rosen Reference) Rosen Publishing Group, Inc., The.

Mahoney, Emily. How Will People Travel to Mars?, 1 vol. 2018. (Space Mysteries Ser.). (ENG.). 32p. (gr. 2-3). 29.27 *(978-1-5382-1951-5(4),* ed057ffc-398c-4986-abc7-31accd2388bf) Stevens, Gareth Publishing LLLP.

Mallick, Nita. Space Exploration, 1 vol. 2016. (Study of Science Ser.). (ENG., Illus.). 124p. (J). (gr. 8-8). lib. bdg. 37.82 *(978-1-5081-0427-8(1),* c0f0da99-b423-4e52-b0f5-89e423be5633) Rosen Publishing Group, Inc., The.

Nelson, Maria. Life on the International Space Station, 1 vol. 2013. (Extreme Jobs in Extreme Places Ser.). (ENG., Illus.). 32p. (gr. 3-4). 29.27 *(978-1-4339-8507-2(1),* d1ef007e-e8eb-4c99-99cf-a50558078d80); pap. 11.50 *(978-1-4339-8508-9(X),* 3eb56929-5cdf-4d0e-afc2-7ab7615d1778) Stevens, Gareth Publishing LLLP. (Gareth Stevens Learning Library).

Newland, Sonya. Space Exploration: Triumphs & Tragedies, 1 vol. 2016. (Crabtree Chrome Ser.). (ENG., Illus.). 48p. (J). (gr. 6-9). pap. *(978-0-7787-2231-1(7))* Crabtree Publishing Co.

Parker, Steve. Space Pioneers. West, David, illus. 2015. (Story of Space Ser.). (ENG.). 32p. (J). (gr. 3-6). 31.35 *(978-1-62588-080-2(4),* 1389452) Black Rabbit Bks.

Parker, Steve & Snedding, Robert. A Brief Illustrated History of Space Exploration. 2017. (Brief Illustrated History Ser.). (ENG., Illus.). 32p. (J). (gr. 3-6). lib. bdg. 27.99 *(978-1-5157-2519-0(7),* Capstone Pr.) Capstone.

Peterson, Megan Cooley & Rustad, Martha E. H. The First Space Missions, 1 vol. 2014. (Famous Firsts Ser.). (ENG., Illus.). 24p. (J). (gr. -1-2). 27.32 *(978-1-4914-0576-5(7),* 125914, Capstone Pr.) Capstone.

Raketen und Raumfahrt. (GER.). 40p. *(978-3-411-08191-2(0))* Bibliographisches Institut & F. A. Brockhaus AG DEU. Dist: I. b. d., Ltd.

Rice, Dona Herweck. ¡Locos por insectos y Arañas! 2nd rev. ed. 2012. (TIME for KIDS(r): Informational Text Ser.).Tr. of Going Buggy. (SPA.). 20p. (gr. 1-2). 8.99 *(978-1-4333-4424-4(6))* Teacher Created Materials, Inc.

Rice Jr., Earle. The Orion Spacecraft. 2018. lib. bdg. 29.95 *(978-1-68020-168-0(9))* Mitchell Lane Pubs.

Royston, Angela. Space Blog. 2010. (ENG., Illus.). 32p. (J). *(978-0-7787-9910-8(7));* pap. *(978-0-7787-9931-3(X))* Crabtree Publishing Co.

Rustad, Martha E. H. Life in Space. 2018. (Astronaut's Life Ser.). (ENG., Illus.). 24p. (J). (gr. -1-2). lib. bdg. 27.32 *(978-1-5157-9817-0(8),* 136883, Capstone Pr.) Capstone.

—Working in Space. 2018. (Astronaut's Life Ser.). (ENG., Illus.). 24p. (J). (gr. -1-2). lib. bdg. 27.32 *(978-1-5157-9820-0(8),* 136888, Capstone Pr.) Capstone.

Sipe, Nicole. Living & Working in Space. rev. ed. 2018. (Smithsonian: Informational Text Ser.). (ENG., Illus.). 32p. (J). (gr. 4-8). pap. 11.99 *(978-1-4938-6712-7(1))* Teacher Created Materials, Inc.

Space Explorers, 12 vols. 2017. (Space Explorers Ser.). (ENG.). (J). (gr. 2-2). lib. bdg. 161.58 *(978-0-7660-9269-3(0),* f55d26b1-1ce0-4562-8ac8-4bbf3d89d258) Enslow Publishing, LLC.

Sparrow, Giles, et al. Shuttles & Space Missions, 1 vol. 2015. (Discoveries in Space Science Ser.). (ENG., Illus.). 80p. (YA). (gr. 9-9). lib. bdg. 37.36 *(978-1-5026-1016-4(7),* 69c4d247-85f3-419b-99f3-58f67e00afea) Cavendish Square Publishing LLC.

Waxman, Laura Hamilton. Exploring Space Travel. 2011. (Searchlight Books (tm) — What's Amazing about Space? Ser.). (ENG., Illus.). (gr. 3-5). 40p. (J). pap. 9.99 *(978-0-7613-7881-5(2),* f2bffb52-23b6-48b4-ba5c-fae20415e1ce); pap. 51.01 *(978-0-7613-8418-2(9))* Lerner Publishing Group.

West, David. Lots of Things You Want to Know about Astronauts. 2015. (Lots of Things You Want to Know About Ser.). (ENG., Illus.). 24p. (J). 28.50 *(978-1-62588-088-8(X),* 19299, Smart Apple Media) Black Rabbit Bks.

World Book, Inc. Staff, contrib. by. Human Space Exploration. 2nd ed. 2006. (World Book's Solar System & Space Exploration Library). (Illus.). 64p. (J). *(978-0-7166-9514-1(6))* World Bk., Inc.

—Space Exploration. 2011. (J). *(978-0-7166-1792-1(7))* World Bk., Inc.

Zelon, Helen. The Endeavor Mission STS-61: Fixing the Hubble Space Telescope. 2009. (Space Missions Ser.). 24p. (gr. 3-4). 42.50 *(978-1-60853-117-2(1),* PowerKids Pr.) Rosen Publishing Group, Inc., The.

—The Gemini IV Mission: The First American Space Walk. 2009. (Space Missions Ser.). 24p. (gr. 3-4). 42.50 *(978-1-60853-119-6(8),* PowerKids Pr.) Rosen Publishing Group, Inc., The.

MANNED SPACE FLIGHT—FICTION

Hunt, Elizabeth Singer. Secret Agent Jack Stalwart: Book 9: the Deadly Race to Space: Russia. 2009. (Secret Agent Jack Stalwart Ser.: 9). (ENG.). 144p. (J). (gr. 1-4). pap. 5.99 *(978-1-60286-078-0(5))* Hachette Bk. Group.

Krasner, Nick. My Bed Is a Spaceship: The Globbus. White, Charlotte, illus. 2013. 122p. pap. *(978-1-909593-34-3(6))* Legend Pr.

Olivas, John D. Endeavour's Long Journey. Roski, Gayle Garner, illus. 2013. (J). *(978-0-9856237-2-2(1))* East West Discovery Pr.

—Endeavour's Long Journey: Celebrating 19 Years of Space Exploration. Roski, Gayle Garner, illus. 2013. (J). pap. *(978-0-9856237-3-9(X))* East West Discovery Pr.

Slivensky, Katie. The Countdown Conspiracy. (ENG.). (J). (gr. 3-7). 2018. 352p. pap. 7.99 *(978-0-06-246260-2(1))* 2017. 336p. 16.99 *(978-0-06-246255-8(5))* HarperCollins Pubs. (HarperCollins).

MANNERS

see Courtesy; Etiquette

MANNERS AND CUSTOMS

see also Chivalry; Clothing and Dress; Costume; Etiquette; Food Habits; Funeral Rites and Ceremonies; Holidays; Marriage Customs and Rites; Social Classes; Travel

Ajmera, Maya & Ivanko, John D. To Be a Kid. 2004. (Global Fund for Children Bks.). (ENG., Illus.). 26p. (J). (-k). bds. 7.95 *(978-1-57091-371-6(4))* Charlesbridge Publishing, Inc.

Alexander, Florence & Alexander, Stanley. Come with Me & See... Children of the World. I.t. ed. 2003. (ENG & SPA., Illus.). 32p. (J). 9.99 *(978-0-9648313-9-1(2))* Ebon Research Systems Publishing, LLC.

Aloian, Molly. What Does It Mean to Go Green? 2013. (ENG., Illus.). 24p. (J). *(978-0-7787-0275-7(8));* pap. *(978-0-7787-0286-3(3))* Crabtree Publishing Co.

Amery, Heather. Then & Now. Firmin, Peter, illus. 2008. (Then & Now Ser.). 24p. (J). (gr. -1-3). pap. 4.99 *(978-0-7945-2211-7(4),* Usborne) EDC Publishing.

Before You Say Yes to a Guest. 2003. (YA). *(978-0-9729586-0-8(6))* Imani-MCHS.

Berry, Joy. Bad Habits. 3rd ed. 2005. (Winning skills series, get over It! Ser.). (ENG., Illus.). 48p. (J). pap. 3.95 *(978-1-57687-280-2(7),* PowerHouse Kids) powerHse. Bks.

Bradford, Wade. Around the World in a Bathtub: Bathing All over the Globe. Archer, Micha, illus. 2017. 32p. (J). (gr. -1-2). lib. bdg. 16.99 *(978-1-58089-544-6(1))* Charlesbridge Publishing, Inc.

Butterfield, Moira. Schools Around the World, 1 vol. 2015. (Children Like Us Ser.). (ENG., Illus.). 32p. (gr. 3-3). pap. 11.58 *(978-1-5026-0846-8(4),* 0ae31151-9fe8-45f3-b1f4-5dcae825631a) Cavendish Square Publishing LLC.

Cain, Marie Mowery. Celebrate Cinco de Mayo. 2013. (Big Books, Red Ser.). (ENG & SPA., Illus.). 16p. pap. 33.00 *(978-1-59246-222-3(7))* Big Books, by George!

Chancellor, Deborah. Good Manners. 2009. (Now We Know About... Ser.). (ENG., Illus.). 24p. (J). (gr. k-3). pap. *(978-0-7787-4736-9(0));* lib. bdg. *(978-0-7787-4719-2(0))* Crabtree Publishing Co.

Cohen, Robert Z. Body Piercing & Tattooing: Making Smart Choices, 1 vol. 2013. (Helpline: Teen Issues & Answers Ser.). (ENG.). 80p. (YA). (gr. 5-6). 38.41 *(978-1-4488-9451-2(4),* ea323f8d-e81f-408d-a0ed-774d51994caf) Rosen Publishing Group, Inc., The.

Collins, Savina. Who Makes Rules? 2018. (My World Ser.). (ENG., Illus.). 16p. (gr. -1-2). lib. bdg. 28.50 *(978-1-64156-174-7(2),* 9781641561747) Rourke Educational Media.

Coppendale, Jean. Life & Death. 2006. (Illus.). 32p. (YA). (gr. 1-18). lib. bdg. 27.10 *(978-1-931983-99-0(2))* Chrysalis Education.

Cultures of the World, 12 vols. 2nd ed. 2005. (Cultures of the World (Second Edition)(r) Ser.). (ENG., Illus.). 144p. (gr. 5-5). lib. bdg. 298.74 *(978-0-7614-1664-7(1),* 369efdb6-86ac-4724-b108-8d5271702780, Cavendish Square) Cavendish Square Publishing LLC.

Cultures of the World - Group 14. 2nd rev. ed. Incl. Algeria. Kagda, Falaq & Latif, Zawiah Abdul. lib. bdg. 49.79 *(978-0-7614-2085-9(1),* fbb05ac8-8b54-4072-84bb-9a4758a4f80c); Armenia. Dhilawala, Sakina. (Illus.). lib. bdg. 49.79 *(978-0-7614-2029-3(0),* cd0eb998-f5ae-4695-95c2-2e470291129b); Lithuania. Kagda, Sakina & Latif, Zawiah Abdul. lib. bdg. 49.79 *(978-0-7614-2087-3(8),* ec57c5ad-1d37-488f-bd72-5635fecc4be3); Luxembourg. Sheehan, Patricia & Dhilawala, Sakina. lib. bdg. 49.79 *(978-0-7614-2088-0(6),* 30837f8d-b58b-47d1-8b79-ff148c49c507); Tahiti. NgCheong-Lum, Roseline. lib. bdg. 49.79 *(978-0-7614-2089-7(4),* 478ad83a-72bc-49c5-9ad3-e38d186950e8); Ukraine. Bassis, Volodymyr & Dhilawala, Sakina. lib. bdg. 49.79 *(978-0-7614-2090-3(8),* 9ecdef87-d7cd-41eb-89de-9a9a91e9b69a); 144p. (gr. 5-5). 2008. (Cultures of the World 14 Ser.). 2007. lib. bdg. *(978-0-7614-2084-2(3),* Cavendish Square) Cavendish Square Publishing LLC.

Cultures of the World - Group 6, 12 vols. 2nd ed. 2004. (Cultures of the World (Second Edition)(r) Ser.). (ENG., Illus.). 144p. (gr. 5-5). lib. bdg. 298.74 *(978-0-7614-1700-2(1),* 1012ec4b-5b6c-4d09-9d00-0d8753cd7208, Cavendish Square) Cavendish Square Publishing LLC.

Delea, Pattie. Wisdom for Young Hearts Volume 1 Wisdom's Foundation. DeLea, Ray and Daniella, ed. Herman, Scott, illus. 2011. 114p. pap. 20.00 *(978-1-61286-030-5(3))* Avid Readers Publishing Group.

—Wisdom for Young Hearts Volume 2 - Applications of Wisdom. Gammage, Dana, illus. 2011. 126p. pap. 20.00 *(978-1-61286-058-9(3))* Avid Readers Publishing Group.

Do, Elisa Shipon-Blum. Understanding Katie: A Day in the Life Of. Salus, Diane, illus. 2003. 28p. (J). (gr. -1-18). pap. *(978-0-9714800-3-2(6))* Selective Mutism Anxiety Research & Treatment Ctr.

Doherty, Gillian & Claybourne, Anna. Peoples of the World. rev. ed. 2012. (World Cultures Ser.). 96p. (J). pap. 14.99 *(978-0-7945-3280-2(2),* Usborne) EDC Publishing.

Dover & Tattoos. Moustache Tattoos: For Your Face or Finger! 2013. (Dover Tattoos Ser.). (ENG., Illus.). 2p. (J). (gr. 3-4). pap. 3.50 *(978-0-486-49329-9(6),* 493296) Dover Pubns., Inc.

Dragon School. 2015. (Dragon School Ser.). (ENG.). 32p. (J). (gr. 1-2). pap., pap., pap. 240.00 *(978-1-4777-5689-8(2),* Windmill Bks.) Rosen Publishing Group, Inc., The.

Dyan, Penelope. Ladies First, Please! a Kid's Most Important & Fun Guide to Good Manners. Dyan, Penelope, illus. 2009. (Illus.). 106p. pap. 8.95 *(978-1-935118-67-1(6))* Bellissima Publishing, LLC.

East, Jacqueline, illus. Learn Good Habits with Jessica: Above All, Don't Behave Like Zoe!, 1 vol. 2008. (ENG.). 28p. (J). (gr. -1-3). 6.95 *(978-1-59496-163-2(8))* Teora USA LLC.

—Learn Good Manners with Charles: Above All, Don't Behave Like Trevor!, 1 vol. 2008. (ENG.). 28p. (J). (gr. -1-3). 6.95 *(978-1-59496-162-5(X))* Teora USA LLC.

Ever Wonder What to Do Manners. 2004. pap. 1.50 *(978-0-87162-918-0(6))* Warner Pr., Inc.

Faulkner, Nicholas & Nagle, Jeanne. Express Yourself: Why People Get Body Art, 1 vol. 2018. (Body Arts: the History of Tattooing & Body Modification Ser.). (ENG.). 64p. (gr. 7-7). 36.13 *(978-1-5081-8073-9(3),* 8f39fc93-fcd5-4d60-b28a-6e7fdd3ad503) Rosen Publishing Group, Inc., The.

Flynn, Claire E. Running with the Bulls, 1 vol. 2013. (Thrill Seekers Ser.). (ENG., Illus.). 32p. (J). (gr. 3-4). pap. 11.50 *(978-1-4824-3294-7(3),* 11be7de3-8e16-4ae6-8805-62e5d3a09286) Rosen Publishing Group, Inc., The.

Fulcher, Roz. Mind Your Manners! 2013. (Dover Kids Coloring Bks.). (ENG.). 48p. (J). (gr. 1-5). pap. 4.99 *(978-0-486-49883-6(2),* 498832) Dover Pubns., Inc.

Gale Cengage Learning Staff, ed. Worldmark Encyclopedia of Cultures & Daily Life: 5 Volume Set, 5 vols. 3rd ed. 2016. (Worldmark Encyclopedia of Cultures & Daily Life Ser.). (ENG., Illus.). 2800p. (J). 845.00 *(978-1-4103-3896-9(7))* Cengage Gale.

—Worldmark Encyclopedia of Cultures & Daily Life: Africa. 3rd ed. 2016. (Worldmark Encyclopedia of Cultures & Daily Life Ser.: 1). (ENG., Illus.). 768p. (J). 234.00 *(978-1-4103-5525-6(X))* Cengage Gale.

—Worldmark Encyclopedia of Cultures & Daily Life: America. 3rd ed. 2016. (Worldmark Encyclopedia of Cultures & Daily Life Ser.: 2). (ENG., Illus.). 704p. (J). 234.00 *(978-1-4103-5539-3(X))* Cengage Gale.

—Worldmark Encyclopedia of Cultures & Daily Life: Asia, Part 1. 3rd ed. 2016. (Worldmark Encyclopedia of Cultures & Daily Life Ser.: 3). (ENG., Illus.). 736p. (J). 234.00 *(978-1-4103-5542-3(X))* Cengage Gale.

—Worldmark Encyclopedia of Cultures & Daily Life: Asia, Part 2. 3rd ed. 2016. (Worldmark Encyclopedia of Cultures & Daily Life Ser.: 4). (ENG., Illus.). 720p. (J). 234.00 *(978-1-4103-5556-0(X))* Cengage Gale.

—Worldmark Encyclopedia of Cultures & Daily Life: Europe. 3rd ed. 2016. (Worldmark Encyclopedia of Cultures & Daily Life Ser.: 5). (ENG., Illus.). 608p. (J). 234.00 *(978-1-4103-5573-7(X))* Cengage Gale.

Ganeri, Anita. Remembering the Dead Around the World. 2015. (Cultures & Customs Ser.). (ENG., Illus.). 32p. (J). (gr. 2-5). 33.32 *(978-1-4109-8018-2(9),* 130050, Raintree) Capstone.

Giles, Sophie, et al. The Children's Book of Manners. East, Jacqueline, illus. 2014. (ENG.). 32p. (J). pap. 10.00 *(978-1-84135-971-7(8))* Award Pubns. Ltd. GBR. Dist: Parkwest Pubns., Inc.

Gilmour, Barbara, et al. Cool Kind Kid Camp Kit 4-6: Social Skills Shaping Futures. 2007. (J). spiral bd. *(978-0-9743499-7-8(6))* CKK Educational, LLC.

Gray, Carolyn. All about M. E. Manners & Etiquette for TWEENS & TEENS. 2007. 28p. (J). pap. 12.95 *(978-1-60131-010-1(2))* Big Tent Bks.

Gregson, Agatha. Traditions, 1 vol. 2019. (Cultures Connect Us! Ser.). (ENG.). 24p. (J). (gr. 1-2). pap. 9.15 *(978-1-5382-3854-7(3),* 1c5f43c4-95ae-4f0a-a457-fd9dfeef7268) Stevens, Gareth Publishing LLLP.

Groves, Marsha. Manners & Customs in the Middle Ages, 1 vol. 2005. (Medieval World Ser.). (ENG., Illus.). 32p. (J). (gr. 5-9). pap. *(978-0-7787-1389-0(X))* Crabtree Publishing Co.

Gurkow, Malkie. Building a Better Me: Student's Workbook. 2005. 29p. pap., wbk. ed. 7.50 *(978-1-878895-44-8(3))* Torah Umesorah Pubns.

Gustafson, Angela. Imagine a House: A Journey to Fascinating Houses Around the World. 2003. (What a World We Live in Ser.). (Illus.). 32p. (J). (gr. k-6). lib. bdg. 16.95 *(978-0-9726849-0-3(5))* Out of the Box.

Guy, John. Victorian Life. 2004. (Illus.). 32p. (J). (gr. 4-7). pap. 5.95 *(978-1-86007-005-1(1),* TickTock Books) Octopus Publishing Group GBR. Dist: Independent Pubs. Group.

Harris, Lisa Delmedico. The Official Princess Handbook: A Little Girl's Guide to Beauty, Poise, & Righteousness. 2010. (ENG.). 96p. (J). pap. 9.99 *(978-1-60683-025-3(2))* Harrison House Pubs.

Harrison, Paul. Ancient Roman Clothes, 1 vol. 2010. (Ancient Communities: Roman Life Ser.). (ENG., Illus.). 32p. (J). (gr. 4-4). lib. bdg. 30.27 *(978-1-61532-304-3(X),* 1e01ca0a-378c-4439-aaff-e822399c2242, PowerKids Pr.) Rosen Publishing Group, Inc., The.

Haywood, John. Home, Family & Everyday Life Through the Ages: Compare the Food, Homes & Daily Lives of Ancient People from All the Major Civilizations. 2008. (Illus.). 64p. (J). (gr. 4-7). pap. 12.99 *(978-1-84476-602-4(0))* Anness Publishing GBR. Dist: National Bk. Network.

Hibbert, Clare. Our Busy Lives. Raga, Sylvia, illus. 2011. (Busy Times Ser.). (ENG.). 24p. (J). 19.99 *(978-0-237-54266-5(8))* Evans Brothers, Ltd. GBR. Dist: Independent Pubs. Group.

Hillstead, McKensy & Gonzales, Brittany. One Day. 2012. 28p. pap. 16.09 *(978-1-4669-5171-6(0))* Trafford Publishing.

Hogan, Wes. Balloons. Hogan, Wes & Hogan, Tom, illus. 2008. 24p. pap. 13.99 *(978-1-4389-0206-7(9))* AuthorHouse.

Howell, Des. The Abcs of Good Manners. 2009. 20p. pap. 13.00 *(978-1-4389-1837-2(2))* AuthorHouse.

Jackson, Abby. Fancy Feet. 2005. (Yellow Umbrella Fluent Level Ser.). (ENG.). 16p. (gr. k-1). pap. 35.70 *(978-0-7368-5313-2(8),* Capstone Pr.) Capstone.

Jno-Lewis, Jason. The Thank You Book: A Thank-You Goes a Long Way. 2012. 28p. pap. 13.95 *(978-1-4582-0345-8(X),* Abbott Pr.) Author Solutions, LLC.

Jones, M. b. & Jones, M. B. Manners Are Free. 2011. 24p. pap. 11.95 *(978-1-4634-1307-1(6))* AuthorHouse.

King, Elizabeth. Quinceanera: Celebrating Fifteen. King, Elizabeth, photos by. 2006. (Illus.). 40p. (YA). (gr. 8-11). reprint ed. 17.00 *(978-1-4223-5728-6(7))* DIANE Publishing Co.

Krasner, Barbara. A Career As an Event Coordinator, 1 vol. 2014. (Essential Careers Ser.). (ENG., Illus.). 80p. (J). (gr. 6-6). 37.47 *(978-1-4777-7878-4(0),* d594664b-2574-47ef-8986-92106bb1e72f, Rosen Young Adult) Rosen Publishing Group, Inc., The.

Leaf, Munro. How to Speak Politely & Why. 2005. (ENG., Illus.). 56p. (J). (gr. k-4). 14.95 *(978-0-7893-1352-2(9))* Universe Publishing.

MNO

Lindeen, Mary. Where People Live, 1 vol. 2011. (Wonder Readers Fluent Level Ser.). (ENG.). 16p. (gr. -1-2). (J). pap. 6.25 (978-1-4296-7975-6(1), 118307); pap. 35.94 (978-1-4296-8207-7(8)) Capstone. (Capstone Pr.).

Loewen, Nancy. Kids Talk, 12 vols. Wesley, Omarr, illus. Incl. We Live Here Too! Kids Talk about Good Citizenship. (ENG., Illus.). 32p. (J). (gr. 2-5). 2002. lib. bdg. 28.65 (978-1-4048-0035-9(2), 90388, Picture Window Bks.); (Kids Talk Ser.). (ENG.). Illus.). 32p. 2004. 85.95 o.p. (978-1-4048-0635-1(0), 164893, Picture Window Bks.) Capstone.

Love, Mary A. Learning Through Symbolism & Celebrations. Flournoy, L. Diana, illus. 2nd rev. ed. 2011. (ENG.). 168p. pap. 24.00 (978-1-929548-00-2(1)) Love's Creative Resources.

Lowenstein Niven, Felicia. Fabulous Fashions of The 1920s, 1 vol. 2011. (Fabulous Fashions of the Decades Ser.). (ENG., Illus.). 48p. (gr. 5-6). lib. bdg. 27.93 (978-0-7660-3551-5(4), 35e5c0c0-8742-46e0-926c-0c8465c4441c) Enslow Publishing, LLC.

—Fabulous Fashions of The 1930s, 1 vol. 2011. (Fabulous Fashions of the Decades Ser.). (ENG., Illus.). 48p. (J). (gr. 5-6). lib. bdg. 27.93 (978-0-7660-3824-0(6), 9c359f21-d7ca-4610-9aee-16645d9228fe) Enslow Publishing, LLC.

—Fabulous Fashions of The 1940s, 1 vol. 2011. (Fabulous Fashions of the Decades Ser.). (ENG., Illus.). 48p. (J). (gr. 5-6). lib. bdg. 27.93 (978-0-7660-3552-2(2), a6a210a7-3adb-4ad2-b385-9817a13d9fd8) Enslow Publishing, LLC.

—Fabulous Fashions of The 1950s, 1 vol. 2011. (Fabulous Fashions of the Decades Ser.). (ENG., Illus.). 48p. (J). (gr. 5-6). lib. bdg. 27.93 (978-0-7660-3825-7(4), 4e300690-1dae-4785-a490-3a2b752692f2) Enslow Publishing, LLC.

—Fabulous Fashions of The 1960s, 1 vol. 2011. (Fabulous Fashions of the Decades Ser.). (ENG., Illus.). 48p. (J). (gr. 5-6). lib. bdg. 27.93 (978-0-7660-3553-9(0), 25156601-c1df-49ec-b998-bbf6117ddd34) Enslow Publishing, LLC.

—Fabulous Fashions of The 1970s, 1 vol. 2011. (Fabulous Fashions of the Decades Ser.). (ENG., Illus.). 48p. (J). (gr. 5-6). lib. bdg. 27.93 (978-0-7660-3826-4(2), d952d1a4-d768-45af-aa44-6f21b42fb7fb) Enslow Publishing, LLC.

—Fabulous Fashions of The 1980s, 1 vol. 2011. (Fabulous Fashions of the Decades Ser.). (ENG., Illus.). 48p. (J). (gr. 5-6). lib. bdg. 27.93 (978-0-7660-3554-6(9), 7fdaab64-2a28-4853-8a7b-09ec11f1f6b8) Enslow Publishing, LLC.

—Fabulous Fashions of The 1990s, 1 vol. 2011. (Fabulous Fashions of the Decades Ser.). (ENG., Illus.). 48p. (J). (gr. 5-6). lib. bdg. 27.93 (978-0-7660-3827-1(0), 72f93e87-814e-41bc-9109-efeaebcdf638) Enslow Publishing, LLC.

MacDonald, Fiona. History of Culture. 2004. (Culture Encyclopedia Ser.). (Illus.). 40p. (YA). (gr. 5-18). lib. bdg. 19.95 (978-1-59084-477-9(7)) Mason Crest.

Mair, J. Samia. Zak & His Little Lies. Burgess, Omar, illus. 2018. (ENG.). 32p. (J). (gr. -1-2). 12.95 (978-0-86037-627-9(3)) Kube Publishing Ltd. GBR. Dist: Consortium Bk. Sales & Distribution.

Manners Matter, 8 vols. 2017. (Manners Matter Ser.). 24p. (ENG.). (gr. 1-1). 101.08 (978-1-5081-5788-5(X), 00372387-8992-4a5f-83cd-a6c0389e49e5); (gr. 4-6). pap. 33.00 (978-1-5081-5799-1(5)) Rosen Publishing Group, Inc., The. (PowerKids Pr.).

Marsh, Carole. Christmas Traditions Around the World. 2003. 12p. (J). (gr. k-4). pap. 2.95 (978-0-635-02154-0(4)) Gallopade International.

—Why Do We Hang Christmas Stockings. 2003. 12p. (J). (gr. k-4). pap. 2.95 (978-0-635-02152-6(8)) Gallopade International.

Marshall, Shelley. Molly the Great Misses the Bus: A Book about Being on Time, 1 vol. 2010. (Character Education with Super Ben & Molly the Great Ser.). (ENG., Illus.). 24p. (J). (gr. k-2). pap. 10.35 (978-0-7660-3743-4(6), a2f520a3-9dba-4b32-a3fd-8f7816991257, Enslow Elementary) Enslow Publishing, LLC.

Mattern, Joanne. Getting Ready for School / Me Preparo para Ir a la Escuela, 1 vol. 2006. (My Day at School / Mi día en la Escuela Ser.). (ENG & SPA., Illus.). 24p. (gr. k-2). pap. 9.15 (978-0-8368-7366-5(1), bea46c8e-c078-4d95-b924-c8115c263d9a); lib. bdg. 24.67 (978-0-8368-7359-7(9), 0e4754d6-2f8d-45c3-9830-336a29708d3c) Stevens, Gareth Publishing LLLP. (Weekly Reader Leveled Readers).

Mauzy, Barbara E. Don't Be a Schwoe: Manners, 1 vol. 2010. (ENG., Illus.). 64p. (J). (gr. -1-3). 14.99 (978-0-7643-3428-3(X), 3784) Schiffer Publishing, Ltd.

Meiners, Cheri J. Respect & Take Care of Things / Respetar y Cuidar Las Cosas. Johnson, Meredith, illus. 2015. (Learning to Get Along(r) Ser.). (ENG.). 48p. (J). (gr. -1-3). pap. 12.99 (978-1-63198-036-7(X)) Free Spirit Publishing Inc.

Menges, Jeff A. Tall Ships Tattoos. 2018. (Dover Tattoos Ser.). (ENG., Illus.). 2p. pap. 1.99 (978-0-486-81983-9(3), 819833) Dover Pubns., Inc.

Minding Our Manners, 12 vols. 2014. (Minding Our Manners Ser.). (ENG.). 24p. (J). (gr. -1-k). lib. bdg. 145.62 (978-1-4824-1628-2(X), d28ec00c-2308-4678-bbec-643de7463fa7) Stevens, Gareth Publishing LLLP.

Montanari, Donata, illus. Children Around the World. 2004. (Around the World Ser.). (ENG.). 32p. (J). (gr. -1-2). pap. 8.99 (978-1-55337-684-2(6)) Kids Can Pr., Ltd. CAN. Dist: Hachette Bk. Group.

—Children Around the World. 2004. (Around the World Ser.). (ENG.). 32p. (J). (gr. -1-2). 19.80 (978-1-5311-7658-7(5)) Perfection Learning Corp.

Morris, Taylor. Surviving a First Date, 1 vol. 2017. (Teen Survival Guide Ser.). (ENG.). 48p. (gr. 6-6). 29.60 (978-0-7660-9191-7(0), 7c8b76a1-118e-4e6f-a6dc-54228493b173) Enslow Publishing, LLC.

Mulcahy, William. Zach Makes Mistakes. McKee, Darren, illus. 2016. (Zach Rules Ser.). (ENG.). 32p. (J). (gr. -1-3). 15.99 (978-1-63198-110-4(2)) Free Spirit Publishing Inc.

Mundy, Michaelene. Saying Good-Bye, Saying Hello... When Your Family Is Moving. Alley, R. W., illus. 2005. (Elf-Help Books for Kids). 32p. (J). (gr. -1-3). per. 7.95 (978-0-87029-393-1(1)) Abbey Pr.

Neely, Judith. Never Too Big for Monkey Hugs. Joslin, Irene, illus. 2009. 16p. pap. 8.49 (978-1-4389-7289-3(X)) AuthorHouse.

Newcomer, Ruth. Silly Songs for Little People. 2004. (Illus.). 42p. (J). spiral bd. 18.00 (978-1-883911-63-8(X)) Brandylane Pubs., Inc.

One City, One School, Many Foods: Six-Pack. (Greetings Ser.: Vol. 1). (gr. 3-5). 31.00 (978-0-7635-1797-7(6)) Rigby Education.

Ornstein, Esther. Middos Man Book & CD. Judowitz, Yoel, illus. 2013. 33p. 19.95 (978-1-60091-257-3(5)) Israel Bookshop Pubns.

Pacileo, Cindy, creator. The Virtues Activity & Coloring Book, Ages 5-7. 2005. (J). 4.50 (978-0-9741930-0-7(3)) Changing-Times.net.

—The Virtues Activity & Coloring Book, Ages 8-10. 2005. (J). 4.50 (978-0-9741930-1-4(1)) Changing-Times.net.

Parish, Scott. Tiger at the Table. 2005. 14p. (J). 10.00 (978-1-4116-4704-6(1)) Lulu Pr., Inc.

Phelan, Thomas. 1-2-3 Magia para Niños: Ayudando a Sus Hijos a Entender las Nuevas Reglas. 2010. 112p. (J). (gr. -1). pap. 9.95 (978-1-889140-42-1(2)) Sourcebooks, Inc.

PoliteKids 101. . . Social Skills Your Child Needs for Success in Life! 2004. (J). (978-0-9729706-7-9(3)); wbk. ed. (978-0-9729706-8-6(1)) Production 101, Inc.

Ricciuti, Edward R. We Are Kind, 1 vol. 2007. (Ready for School Ser.). (ENG., Illus.). 24p. (gr. k-1). lib. bdg. 25.50 (978-0-7614-1992-1(6), 2af08c6d-8c94-46b4-9f91-f2fd93c16f15, Cavendish Square) Cavendish Square Publishing LLC.

Riggs, Kate. Le Tatou. 2018. (Planète Animaux Ser.). (FRE., Illus.). 24p. (J). (978-1-77092-391-1(8), 19680) Creative Co., The.

Ring, Susan. Places We Live. 2005. (Yellow Umbrella Fluent Level Ser.). (ENG.). 16p. (gr. k-1). pap. 35.70 (978-0-7368-5316-3(2), Capstone Pr.) Capstone.

Rosson, Denise & Tumblacer, Margaret. Tadpole Dreams Etiquette & Good Manners Program Handbook. 2005. 25p. (J). 12.95 (978-0-9769320-1-7(6), ss0002) Smith, S. Pubns.

Rotner, Shelley. Different Kinds of Good-Byes. 2013. (Shelley Rotner's World Ser.). (ENG.). 32p. (gr. 1-2). pap. 47.70 (978-1-62065-751-5(1), Capstone Pr.) Capstone.

School Students, Tuttle Elementary. Respect, a Global Vision by the Students of Tuttle Elementary School. 2010. 32p. pap. 12.95 (978-1-936051-85-4(0)) Peppertree Pr., The.

Schwartz, Sara Leah. Let's Use Them Right: Social Skills for My Hands, Feet, & Mouth. David, Racheli, illus. 2013. 39p. 16.95 (978-1-60091-276-4(1)) Israel Bookshop Pubns.

Sesame Street Staff, creator. Sesame Street: My First Manners Boxed Set. 2011. 72p. (J). bds. 12.99 (978-1-60745-238-6(3)) Flying Frog Pubs.

Sonnier, Suzanne. Shinto, Spirits, & Shrines: Religion in Japan, 1 vol. 2007. (Lucent Library of Historical Eras Ser.). (ENG., Illus.). 96p. (gr. 7-10). lib. bdg. 41.03 (978-1-4205-0029-5(5), 2ab6c961-ed73-4308-b303-170e93f8da89, Lucent Pr.) Greenhaven Publishing LLC.

Steele, Philip. I Wonder Why Countries Fly Flags. 2012. (I Wonder Why Ser.). (ENG., Illus.). 32p. (J). (gr. k-3). 6.99 (978-0-7534-6793-0(3), 900085101, Kingfisher) Roaring Brook Pr.

Stefoff, Rebecca. The Medieval World, 1 vol. 2006. (World Historical Atlases Ser.). (ENG., Illus.). 48p. (gr. 5-5). 34.07 (978-0-7614-1642-5(0), c305c035-8e42-4726-9717-97f3d919f6b8) Cavendish Square Publishing LLC

Stephens, Chris S. A Christmas Box. 2003. (ENG.). 48p. pap. 20.95 (978-1-84323-306-0(1)) Beekman Bks., Inc.

Summers, Jean. The Kids' Guide to Writing Great Thank-You Notes. 2010. (Illus.). 48p. (J). 9.95 (978-1-59411-125-9(1)) Writers' Collective, The

Swain, Gwenyth. Bedtime! 2011. (Small World Ser.). (Illus.). 24p. bds. (978-1-84089-673-2(6)) Zero to Ten, Ltd.

—Celebrating. 2011. (Small World Ser.). (Illus.). 24p. bds. (978-1-84089-674-9(4)) Zero to Ten, Ltd.

Tadpole Dreams Etiquette & Good Manners Curriculum. 2005. (YA). ring bd. 249.95 (978-0-9769320-0-0(8), ss0001) Smith, S. Pubns.

Tourville, Amanda Doering. Manners at a Friend's House, 1 vol. Lensch, Chris, illus. 2009. (Way to Be!: Manners Ser.). (ENG.). 24p. (J). (gr. -1-2). pap. 7.95 (978-1-4048-5306-5(5), 95539); lib. bdg. 27.32 (978-1-4048-5305-8(7), 95537) Capstone. (Picture Window Bks.).

Washington, L. Manners First - G I F T S. 2007. 88p. pap. 14.99 (978-0-88144-273-1(9)) Yorkshire Publishing Group.

What Really Matters. 2007. (J). per. 10.00 (978-1-930052-35-2(9)) Cherokee Bks.

Whiteside, Doug. Thank You... No, Thank You! 2009. 80p. pap. 10.49 (978-1-4389-8173-4(2)) AuthorHouse.

Whyte, Daniel, III. Money under the Car Seat: And Other Things to Thank God For. 2008. (ENG., Illus.). 251p. per. 13.99 (978-0-9763487-0-2(5)) Torch Legacy Pubns.

World Book, Inc. Staff, contrib. by. Cumulative Glossary & Index. 46p. (J). 2009. (978-0-7166-5051-5(7)) 2003. (978-0-7166-5017-1(7)) World Bk., Inc.

—Everyday Celebrations & Rituals. (Illus.). 46p. (J). 2009. (978-0-7166-5050-8(9)) 2003. (978-0-7166-5016-4(9)) World Bk., Inc.

—Marriage Celebrations. 2009. (Illus.). 46p. (J). (978-0-7166-5046-1(0)) World Bk., Inc.

Worthy of Honor. 2003. (Humble Heart Ser.). (J). spiral bd., wbk. ed. (978-0-9746148-2-3(3)) Common Courtesy.

MANNERS AND CUSTOMS—FICTION

Abraham, Holly. Good Manners at a Friend's House, 1 vol. 2017. (Manners Matter Ser.). (ENG.). 24p. (gr. 1-1). 25.27 (978-1-5081-5731-1(6), da0118ff-e614-432e-a442-68df58e9a47b, PowerKids Pr.) Rosen Publishing Group, Inc., The.

Adler, David A. Cam Jansen & the Graduation Day Mystery. 2012. (Cam Jansen Ser.: 31). lib. bdg. 14.75 (978-0-606-26663-5(1)) Turtleback.

Alegria, Malin. Estrella's Quinceañera. 2006. (ENG., Illus.). 272p. (J). (gr. 7). 15.99 (978-0-689-87809-1(5), Simon & Schuster Bks. For Young Readers) Simon & Schuster Bks. For Young Readers.

Alexander, Mary Helen. Please & Thank You. 2005. 23p. pap. 24.95 (978-1-4137-6240-2(9)) PublishAmerica, Inc.

Ana, Reverend & Binkow, Howard. Howard B. Wigglebottom Learns to Listen. Cornelison, Susan F., illus. 2008. (Howard B. Wigglebottom Ser.). (ENG.). 32p. (J). (gr. -1-3). 15.00 (978-0-9715390-1-3(4), df6c8ae2-f1da-4aaa-a6cb-27d0ee9d8149, We Do Listen) We Do Listen Foundation.

Aunt Judy. Chickens on the Go! Chickens from different locations around the World. Aunt Judy, illus. 2nd ed. 2006. (Illus.). 40p. (J). pap. 7.00 (978-0-9780693-0-8(7)) McEwen, Judith A.

Bauer, Joan. Best Foot Forward. 2006. 183p. (gr. 7-12). 18.00 (978-0-7569-6767-3(8)) Perfection Learning Corp.

Beek, Rosheena. Mommy Says! Maye, Warren L., illus. 2nd ed. 2013. (ENG.). 24p. pap. (978-1-927750-20-9(2)) Bermuda National Trust.

Beers, Gary. Pumpkinroo. 2013. 32p. pap. 24.95 (978-1-63004-258-5(7)) America Star Bks.

Birt, Pat. Ian Wakes Up. 2009. 28p. pap. 12.49 (978-1-4490-1213-7(2)) AuthorHouse.

Björkman, Steve. Dinosaurs Don't, Dinosaurs Do. 2012. (I Like to Read Ser.). (ENG., Illus.). 24p. (J). (gr. -1-3). pap. 7.99 (978-0-8234-2640-9(8)) Holiday Hse., Inc.

Blessing, Victor. Santa Claus Got Sick Because. 2009. 24p. pap. 12.99 (978-1-4490-1126-0(8)) AuthorHouse.

Bloom, Becky. Leo & Lester. Biet, Pascal, illus. 2003. (J). 32p. 15.95 (978-1-59034-582-5(7)); 33p. pap. (978-1-59034-583-2(5)) Mondo Publishing.

Brown, Linnet. Keep Your Eyes on the Goal. 2013. 48p. pap. (978-1-4602-1828-0(0)) FriesenPress.

Bruce, David. Manners I. Care. Delehanty, Joan M., illus. 2006. 32p. (J). 16.95 (978-0-9771143-2-0(5)) Child Life Bks., LLC.

Buckley, Charlie. How to Wash Your Hands. 2007. (Show Jo Language Development Ser.). (Illus.). 16p. (J). (gr. -1-1). per., bds. 14.95 (978-1-933669-09-0(8)) Literary Architects, LLC.

Bunny, Hull. The Hidden Treasure. Fleming, Kye, illus. 2007. (Young Masters Ser.). (J). (gr. -1). 13.95 incl. audio compact disk (978-0-9721478-8-0(8)) BrassHeart Music.

Byrum, Isabel C. How John Became a Man Life Story of a Motherless Boy. 2005. reprint ed. pap. 15.95 (978-1-4179-0742-7(8)) Kessinger Publishing, LLC.

Catanzarite, Lisa. What the World Is Like to Bea Moore: The Treasure. Miller, Heidi, illus. 2009. 56p. pap. 17.26 (978-1-4251-6321-1(1)) Trafford Publishing.

Chambers, Robert W. The Purple Emperor. 2004. reprint ed. pap. 1.99 (978-1-4192-7947-8(5)); pap. 15.95 (978-1-4191-7947-1(0)) Kessinger Publishing, LLC.

Champier, Jacqueline. The Little Piggy Goes South. 2012. 28p. pap. 19.99 (978-1-4772-8976-1(3)) AuthorHouse.

Chi Omega - My First Board Book. 2006. (J). bds. 10.95 (978-0-9776627-1-5(3)) Captus, LLC.

Chou, Joey, illus. Olaf's Frozen Adventure. 2017. (J). (978-1-5379-5893-4(3), Golden Bks.) Random Hse. Children's Bks.

Clark, Jeanne B. The Second Encounter: With the Snake Named Bully. 2012. 40p. pap. 24.99 (978-1-4772-1568-5(9)) AuthorHouse.

Coach B. Kingdom College. 2009. 48p. pap. 19.49 (978-1-4389-5181-2(7)) AuthorHouse.

Coates-Smith, Renee. Bobby's Secret Is Out. 2007. (Illus.). 43p. (J). 12.95 (978-0-615-14325-5(3)) Imani Productions.

Cochran, Jean M. Your Tummy's Talking! Gullens, Lee M., illus. 2008. (ENG.). 32p. (J). (gr. -1-k). 16.95 (978-0-9792035-3-4(8)) Pleasant St. Pr.

Consugar, Beth. Swanee Day. Rottinger, Amy, illus. 2013. 24p. pap. 12.95 (978-1-61244-176-4(9)) Halo Publishing International.

Crow, Marilee. A Pocketful of Manners. Snider, K. C., illus. 2011. 16p. pap. 9.95 (978-1-61633-176-4(3)) Guardian Angel Publishing, Inc.

Davis, G. M. You Can Change Almost Anything! Go Challenge the Old Status Quo. 2013. 20p. pap. 12.45 (978-1-4908-0028-8(X), WestBow Pr.) Author Solutions, LLC.

Dean Van Scoyoc, Andrea. Graveyard katie & her Pals. 2008. 52p. pap. 20.00 (978-0-557-01337-1(2)) Lulu Pr., Inc.

Delta Delta Delta - My First Board Book. 2006. (J). bds. 10.95 (978-0-9776627-3-9(X)) Captus, LLC.

DiCicco, Sue. Manners. DiCicco, Sue, illus. 2010. (Illus.). 10p. 9.95 (978-1-60747-749-5(1), Pickwick Pr.) Phoenix Bks., Inc.

Dickens, Charles. Great Expectations. 2019. (ENG.). 470p. (YA). (gr. 7). pap. 19.89 (978-1-7274-9559-1(4)) CreateSpace Independent Publishing Platform.

—Great Expectations. 2020. (ENG.). 416p. (J). (gr. 3-7). pap. (978-1-77426-072-2(7)) East India Publishing Co.

—Great Expectations. 2019. (ENG.). 552p. (J). (gr. 3-7). pap. 21.99 (978-1-7036-4774-7(2)); 498p. (YA). (gr. 7). pap. 32.99 (978-1-0890-6847-1(6)); 552p. (YA). (gr. 7). pap. 30.99 (978-1-6867-1072-8(0)); 552p. (YA). (gr. 7). pap. 34.99 (978-1-0810-7252-0(0)); 552p. (YA). (gr. 7). pap. 30.99 (978-1-0713-5331-8(4)); 668p. (YA). (gr. 7). pap. 24.95 (978-1-0703-4968-8(2)) Independently Published.

—Great Expectations. 2013. (Differentiated Timeless Classics Ser.). (ENG.). 80p. (YA). (gr. 4-12). 14.95 (978-1-62250-718-4(5)) Saddleback Educational Publishing, Inc.

—Great Expectations. 2018. (ENG., Illus.). 466p. (J). (gr. 4-6). 24.99 (978-1-5154-2681-3(5)) Wilder Pubns., Corp.

Disney Books. Olaf's Frozen Adventure Read-Along Storybook & CD. Disney Storybook Art Team, Disney Storybook, illus. 2017. (Read-Along Storybook & CD Ser.). (ENG.). 32p. (J). (gr. 1-3). pap. 6.99 (978-1-4847-8491-4(X), Disney Press Books) Disney Publishing Worldwide.

English, Karen. Nadia's Hands. Weiner, Jonathan, illus. 2009. (ENG.). 32p. (J). (gr. k-2). pap. 9.99 (978-1-59078-784-7(6), Astra Young Readers) Astra Publishing Hse.

Feder, Joel A. Kokomo Superhero. 2011. 32p. pap. 14.99 (978-1-4634-4748-9(5)) AuthorHouse.

Ferguson, Scott. The Itty Bitty It. Rudd, Benton, illus. 2012. 26p. pap. 9.99 (978-0-9858398-1-9(3)) Mindstir Media.

Fett, Ruth E. Goldilocks & the Three Bears: Baxter Bee Teaches about Respect. 2011. 24p. (gr. 1-2). 13.99 (978-1-4567-6192-9(7)) AuthorHouse.

Freeman, Emily. God Bless Your Way: A Christmas Journey. Burr, Dan, illus. 2007. 32p. (J). (gr. -1-3). 19.95 incl. audio compact disk (978-1-59038-806-8(2)) Deseret Bk. Co.

Galán, Ana. Qué Cosas Dice Mi Abuela (the Things My Grandmother Says) Pino, Pablo, illus. 2013. (SPA.). 32p. (J). (gr. -1-3). 4.99 (978-0-545-32863-0(2), Scholastic en Espanol) Scholastic, Inc.

Gales, Rick. Granny Puckerlips: Keepin' It Real with Kindness & Respect. 2013. 108p. (gr. 9-12). 28.95 (978-1-4908-0438-5(2)); pap. 11.95 (978-1-4908-0437-8(4)) Author Solutions, LLC. (WestBow Pr.).

Gallegos, Eligio Stephen. Nothing Is Nothing. 2013. 144p. pap. 6.99 (978-0-944164-24-2(2)) Moon Bear Pr.

Gallo, Tina. Master of Manners. 2016. (Kung Fu Panda 8x8 Ser.). lib. bdg. 13.55 (978-0-606-38996-9(2)) Turtleback.

Gilmore, Rachna. When-I-Was-A-Little-Girl, 1 vol. Benoit, Renné, illus. 2006. (ENG.). 24p. (J). (gr. -1-2). 14.95 (978-1-897187-12-8(2)) Second Story Pr. CAN. Dist: Orca Bk. Pubs. USA.

Goldberg, Barbara. Mindy's Passover Parsley. 2008. 24p. per. 24.95 (978-1-4241-9779-8(1)) America Star Bks.

Graham, Mary. Good Manners at the Table, 1 vol. 2017. (Manners Matter Ser.). (ENG.). 24p. (gr. 1-1). 25.27 (978-1-5081-5730-4(8), 933aa713-ce27-43ba-8eb3-d2e7c25f27b0, PowerKids Pr.) Rosen Publishing Group, Inc., The.

Graham, Tamara. Little Miss Litterbug. 2008. 24p. pap. 12.99 (978-1-4389-2519-6(0)) AuthorHouse.

Greig, Elna. Bye-Bye! 2005. (Illus.). 16p. pap. 7.95 (978-1-932915-13-6(3)) Sandvik Publishing.

—Hello! 2005. (Illus.). 16p. pap. 7.95 (978-1-932915-12-9(5)) Sandvik Publishing.

Hargreaves, Roger. Little Miss Quick. 2009. (Mr. Men & Little Miss Ser.). (ENG.). 32p. (J). (gr. -1-2). mass mkt. 4.99 (978-0-8431-8956-8(8), Price Stern Sloan) Penguin Young Readers Group.

—Mr. Nervous. 2009. (Mr. Men & Little Miss Ser.). (ENG., Illus.). 32p. (J). (gr. -1-2). mass mkt. 4.99 (978-0-8431-8957-5(6), Price Stern Sloan) Penguin Young Readers Group.

Harland, Richard. Worldshaker. 2010. (ENG.). 400p. (YA). (gr. 7-18). 16.99 (978-1-4169-9552-4(8), Simon & Schuster Bks. For Young Readers) Simon & Schuster Bks. For Young Readers.

Harris, Patrice. Grandma Asks: Were You Good at School Today? Harrison, Nicholas, illus. 2013. 26p. pap. 10.00 (978-0-9892358-5-3(8)) CLF Publishing.

Harvey, Keith. Oscar & the Magic Table: A Story about a Little Boy Who For got His Table Manners. 2015. (ENG., Illus.). 24p. pap. 8.99 (978-1-84135-922-9(X)) Award Pubns. Ltd. GBR. Dist: Parkwest Pubns., Inc.

Hawley, Richard And Elizabeth. There's a Monster in My Nose. Hawley, R. Spencer, illus. 2009. 36p. pap. 24.95 (978-1-61546-177-6(9)) America Star Bks.

Hickey, Barbara. Ms Sincerely Kind Goes Out & About: (Where Good Manners Matter) 2008. 76p. pap. 24.99 (978-1-4389-0851-9(2)) AuthorHouse.

Holliday, Anne. No More Puppet Shows. 2011. 20p. pap. 12.99 (978-1-4634-2354-4(3)) AuthorHouse.

Holm, Jennifer L. Wilderness Days. unabr. ed. 2004. (Boston Jane Ser.: No. 2). 288p. (J). (gr. 5-9). pap. 38.00 incl. audio (978-0-8072-0787-1(X), S YA 307 SP, Listening Library) Random Hse. Audio Publishing Group.

Jacober, Virginia. Trail Followers in India. 2013. pap. 12.95 (978-0-7414-8181-8(2)) Infinity Publishing.

Johnston, Annie Fellows. Mary Ware the Little Colonel's Chum. Barry, Etheldred B., illus. 2004. reprint ed. pap. 30.95 (978-1-4179-1704-4(0)) Kessinger Publishing, LLC.

Kappa Alpha Theta - My First Board Book. 2006. (J). bds. 10.95 (978-0-9776627-4-6(8)) Captus, LLC.

Kappa Delta - My First Board Book. 2006. (J). bds. 10.95 (978-0-9776627-5-3(6)) Captus, LLC.

Katinszky, Harold. Billy Learns Manners. 2008. (ENG.). 40p. pap. 16.99 (978-1-4134-9670-3(9)) Xlibris Corp.

Katz, Karin Jill. There's a Fly in My Soup. 2012. 16p. pap. 15.99 (978-1-4772-6331-0(4)) AuthorHouse.

Krueger, T. W. Donkeys Are Special & So Are You! Bohart, Lisa, illus. 2013. (ENG.). 46p. (J). 12.99 (978-0-9887454-0-7(2)) Donkey Publishing.

Lorraine, Loria. Wild about Manners. Bonnie, Spino, illus. 2013. 36p. 17.99 (978-0-9881889-1-4(0)) Piccolo Tales.

MacKey, Cindy. The Girl Who Blamed the World. Chiang, Shirley, illus. 2013. 50p. pap. 16.50 (978-0-9892699-0-2(6)) Cyrano Bks.

Mackey, Cindy. The Girl Who Blamed the World. 2017. (ROA., Illus.). (J). (gr. k-4). pap. 10.99 (978-0-9990993-3-9(7)) Cyrano Bks.

Madore, Michele. Rudee Goes Bananas for Manners. Gravitt, Bill, illus. 2006. (ENG.). 38p. (J). pap. 6.95 (978-0-615-17967-4(3)) Manners Toy Co., LLC.

Magi, Aria. The Lulilites: And the Star of Seven Rays. l.t. ed. 2005. (Illus.). 34p. (J). (gr. -1-3). 19.95 (978-0-9759631-0-4(4)) Lulilite Productions.

Manners I. Care. 2005. (J). pap. 5.99 (978-0-9771143-4-4(1)) Child Life Bks., LLC.

Marie, Tina. Isabella Learns Her Manners. 2011. 24p. 12.95 (978-1-4567-2000-1(7)) AuthorHouse.

Matchett, Gillian. The Adventures of Weston Super Cat with Activities. 2009. (Illus.). 92p. pap. 30.49 (978-1-4389-2241-6(8)) AuthorHouse.

Mcdoogle, Farrah. Thank You Day. 2014. (Daniel Tiger's Neighborhood Ready-To-Read Ser.). lib. bdg. 13.55 (978-0-606-35449-3(2)) Turtleback.

McGuirk, Leslie & Von Bidder, Alex. Wiggens Learns His Manners at the Four Seasons Restaurant. McGuirk, Leslie, illus. 2009. (ENG., Illus.). 32p. (J). (gr. -1-2). 16.99 (978-0-7636-4014-9(X)) Candlewick Pr.

McLellan, Sean. The Red Booted Chicken. 2009. 48p. (J). pap. 17.49 (978-1-4389-5610-7(X)) AuthorHouse.

Morel, John Henry. Is It True. 2009. 144p. 24.99 (978-1-935436-40-9(6)) Rodaian Pr.

Morrissey, Donna. What Beautiful Mistake Did You Make Today? 2012. 24p. pap. 13.95 (978-1-4772-5669-5(5)) AuthorHouse.

Munson, Kyle Lloyd. The King They Call Dumm. 2008. 32p. per. 24.95 (978-1-60441-215-4(1)) America Star Bks.

Nicholson, Wanda. Mr Henry's Grass. Webb, Shamore, illus. 2008. 76p. pap. 20.95 *(978-1-59800-665-0(7))* Outskirts Pr., Inc.
O'Connor, Jane. Apples Galore! 2013. (Fancy Nancy - I Can Read! Ser.). (J). lib. bdg. 13.55 *(978-0-606-32150-1(0))* Turtleback.
—Fancy Nancy. Glasser, Robin Preiss, illus. 2005. (Fancy Nancy Ser.). (ENG.). 32p. (J). (gr. -1-3). 17.89 *(978-0-06-054210-8(1))*; 17.99 *(978-0-06-054209-2(8))* HarperCollins Pubs. (HarperCollins).
—Fancy Nancy: Too Many Tutus. 2012. (I Can Read Level 1 Ser.). (ENG., Illus.). 32p. (J). (gr. -1-3). pap. 4.99 *(978-0-06-208307-4(4))*, HarperCollins) HarperCollins Pubs.
—Fancy Nancy & the Posh Puppy. Glasser, Robin Preiss, illus. 2007. (Fancy Nancy Ser.). (ENG.). 32p. (J). (gr. -1-2). 17.99 *(978-0-06-054213-9(6))*, HarperCollins) HarperCollins Pubs.
—Fancy Nancy: Too Many Tutus. Glasser, Robin Preiss, illus. 2012. (I Can Read Level 1 Ser.). (ENG.). 32p. (J). (gr. -1-3). 16.99 *(978-0-06-208308-1(2))*, HarperCollins) HarperCollins Pubs.
—Nancy la Elegante: Fancy Nancy (Spanish Edition). 1 vol. Glasser, Robin Preiss, illus. 2008. (Fancy Nancy Ser.). (SPA.). 32p. (J). (gr. -1-3). 17.99 *(978-0-06-143528-7(7))* HarperCollins Español.
Olsen, Leigh & S. I. International. What Do You Say? A Book about Manners. 2009. (Playskool Ser.). (ENG.). 16p. (J). (gr. -1). pap. 6.99 *(978-1-4169-8518-1(2))*, Simon Spotlight) Simon Spotlight.
Orozco, Maria. Lizards on 41st Street. 2011. 28p. pap. 13.59 *(978-1-4567-2412-2(6))* AuthorHouse.
Parish, Scott. Tigre a la Mesa. 2005. 14p. (J). 10.00 *(978-1-4116-6003-8(X))* Lulu Pr., Inc.
Pashilk, Meri. Pearl the Turtle. 2013. 32p. pap. 13.99 *(978-1-4525-6658-0(5))* Balboa Pr.
Patterson, James. Give Thank You a Try. 2017. (Give Please a Chance Ser.: 2). (ENG., Illus.). 56p. (J). (gr. -1-1). 17.99 *(978-0-316-44042-4(6))*, Jimmy Patterson) Little Brown & Co.
The Pledge of Allegiance. 2006. (J). bds. 7.95 *(978-0-9776627-2-2(1))* Captus, LLC.
Posner-Sanchez, Andrea. Olaf's Frozen Adventure Little Golden Book (Disney Frozen) Chou, Joey, illus. 2017. (Little Golden Book Ser.). (ENG.). 24p. (J). (-k). 4.99 *(978-0-7364-3835-3(1))*, Golden/Disney) Random Hse. Children's Bks.
Prignano, Barbara. The Tiny Tomato & His Terrific Manners. Kalpart, illus. 2013. 32p. pap. 12.95 *(978-1-62857-080-9(6))*, Strategic Bk. Publishing) Strategic Book Publishing & Rights Agency (SBPRA).
Racaniello, P. Emilia & Emma Say Please. 2011. 20p. pap. 9.99 *(978-1-257-65455-0(1))* Lulu Pr., Inc.
—Emilia & Emma Say Sorry. 2012. 20p. pap. 9.99 *(978-1-257-63118-6(7))* Lulu Pr., Inc.
—Emilia & Emma Say Thank You. 2012. 20p. pap. 9.99 *(978-1-257-63119-3(5))* Lulu Pr., Inc.
Ricci, Christine. Dora's Book of Manners. Hall, Susan, illus. 2005. (Dora the Explorer Ser.: No. 7). 22p. (J). lib. bdg. 15.00 *(978-1-59054-793-9(4))* Fitzgerald Bks.
Riddle, Sharon Kay & Sanders, Nancylda. The King's Silverware. Lowe, Frank Allen, illus. 2007. 32p. (J). pap. 15.00 *(978-0-9761583-5-6(3))* Olive Leaf Pubns.
Rodriguez, Emma Vera & Scogin, Connie. Blanca Rosa's Quinceaner. 2011. 34p. pap. 13.50 *(978-1-60911-444-2(2))*, Eloquent Bks.) Strategic Book Publishing & Rights Agency (SBPRA).
Rose, Hayley. The Do's & Don'ts. 2013. 38p. 16.50 *(978-1-939625-38-0(6))* Inkwell Books LLC.
Santos, Gloria. Good Manners at the Library. 1 vol. 2017. (Manners Matter Ser.). (ENG.). 24p. (gr. 1-1). 25.27 *(978-1-5081-5728-1(6))*, de535bed-0895-4d4d-819d-7227ca94ceb1, PowerKids Pr.) Rosen Publishing Group, Inc., The.
Scandora, Julie. Rules Are Rules. 2008. (ENG., Illus.). 32p. (gr. -1). 17.95 *(978-1-887542-64-7(7))* Scandora.
Schaefer, Lola. Please Pass the Manners! Mealtime Tips for Everyone. Lewis, Kellie, illus. 2009. (ENG.). 12p. (J). (gr. -1-1). 7.99 *(978-1-4169-4826-1(0))*, Little Simon) Little Simon.
Shofner, Melissa Raé. Good Manners at the Playground. 1 vol. 2017. (Manners Matter Ser.). (ENG.). 24p. (gr. 1-1). 25.27 *(978-1-5081-5729-8(4))*, 38ee01ac-b6f5-4c76-9b5f-c136d5205eae, PowerKids Pr.) Rosen Publishing Group, Inc., The.
Sigma Kappa - My First Board Book. 2006. (J). bds. 10.95 *(978-0-9776627-6-0(4))* Captus, LLC.
Smith, C. Michelle. Skeeter Uses Manners. Foreman, A., illus. 2010. 28p. pap. 17.36 *(978-1-60888-017-1(6))* Nimble Bks. LLC.
Sposito, Pipi, illus. Charles Dickens: Great Expectations. 2021. (Sweet Cherry Easy Classics Ser.: 2). (ENG.). 96p. (J). 6.95 *(978-1-78226-744-7(1))*, aae9966f-3007-42ff-b8c1-f8dedf20addc) Sweet Cherry Publishing GBR. Dist: Baker & Taylor Publisher Services (BTPS).
Stanek, Robert, pseud. Bugville Critters Remember Their Manners. 2011. (Illus.). 46p. pap. 6.99 *(978-1-57545-260-9(X))*, Reagent Pr. Bks. for Young Readers) RP Media.
—Remember Their Manners. 2010. 46p. pap. 11.99 *(978-1-57545-177-0(8))*, Reagent Pr. Bks. for Young Readers) RP Media.
Swafford, Trona Muse. The Country Bunnies & Friends. 2008. (ENG.). 32p. per. 21.99 *(978-1-4363-0016-2(9))* Xlibris Corp.
Swanson Sateren, Shelley. Max & Zoe at the Library. 1 vol. Sullivan, Mary, illus. 2013. (Max & Zoe Ser.). (ENG.). 32p. (J). (gr. k-2). pap. 5.19 *(978-1-4048-8058-0(5))*, 121734, Picture Window Bks.) Capstone.
Taylor, Kyle. Friends That Care Always Share. 2012. 24p. pap. 14.93 *(978-1-4669-4183-0(9))* Trafford Publishing.
Terrell, Andrea M. The Adventures of Sammy the Squirrel: Buying Shoes. Mitchell, Anthony W., illus. 2008. (ENG.). 28p. pap. 13.99 *(978-1-4343-5608-6(6))* AuthorHouse.
Thaler, Mike. Earth Day from the Black Lagoon. Lee, Jared D., illus. 2013. 64p. (J). *(978-0-545-47669-0(0))* Scholastic, Inc.
Tissot Lcsw, Jennifer. Grateful Gracie: A Story about Gratitude. Washburn, Cecilia, illus. 2013. 34p. pap. 14.95 *(978-0-9882804-1-0(8))* Grateful Day Pr.
Toombs, Robert. Dottie the Bus Driver in Bicycle Safety. Barnett, Linda, illus. 2013. 24p. pap. 9.99 *(978-0-9885180-6-3(6))* Mindstir Media.
Tracy, Roseann. Do You Love Me When I Am Upside Down? 2008. 28p. pap. 12.99 *(978-1-4389-0503-7(3))* AuthorHouse.
Tym, Kate. Say Please. 2008. (Manners Ser.). (Illus.). 24p. (J). (gr. -1-1). lib. bdg. 16.95 *(978-1-59566-589-8(7))* QEB Publishing Inc.
VanDenhoven, Godelieve. Louis in Kindergarten. 2009. 40p. pap. 14.50 *(978-1-60693-752-5(9))*, Eloquent Bks.) Strategic Book Publishing & Rights Agency (SBPRA).
Walton, Evangeline. The Misadventures of Rufus & Misha: Two Dogs Who Are Smart Enough to Go to School. 2013. 24p. pap. 14.93 *(978-1-4669-9970-1(5))* Trafford Publishing.
Weimer, Heidi R. How Do I Kiss You? Sharp, Chris, illus. 2008. (ENG.). 18p. (J). (gr. -1-k). bds. 12.99 *(978-0-8249-1814-9(2))*, Ideals Pubns.) Worthy Publishing.
Williams, Felisha. I'm No Bully, Am I? 2012. 24p. (-18). pap. 15.99 *(978-1-4797-0973-1(5))* Xlibris Corp.
Wong-Avery, Sally. Chinese Manners. 2007. (Illus.). (J). pap. *(978-0-9798874-0-6(2))* Tsui Wong-Avery, Sally.
Zima, Gordon. Sunbirds & Evergreens. 2006. (J). 16.00 *(978-0-9742894-5-8(0))* Hutton Electronic Publishing.
Zima, Gordon & Zima, Paula, illus. Sun Birds & Evergreens: The Nuk-Chuk Stories. 2005. (J). *(978-0-9742894-3-4(4))* Hutton Electronic Publishing.

MANPOWER POLICY

Canetti, Yanitzia. When Times Are Tough. Keating, Alison, tr. Willy, Romont, illus. 2009. 32p. (J). (gr. k-2). 8.99 *(978-1-59835-103-3(6))* Cambridge BrickHouse, Inc.
Haugen, David M. & Musser, Susan, eds. Unemployment. 1 vol. 2011. (Opposing Viewpoints Ser.). (ENG.). 208p. (gr. 10-12). pap. 34.80 *(978-0-7377-5248-9(3))*, bf7f1c30-bbea-4b9c-9f95-d49557f9cc78); lib. bdg. 50.43 *(978-0-7377-5247-2(5))*, 8bb3fda4-ddff-4ec1-9f34-aa13c2fc09f1) Greenhaven Publishing LLC. (Greenhaven Publishing).
Merino, Noel, ed. Unemployment. 1 vol. 2014. (Global Viewpoints Ser.). (ENG., Illus.). 216p. (gr. 10-12). pap. 32.70 *(978-0-7377-6917-3(3))*, ee2ab1c9-9b0d-4f55-94d2-21b48d44202d, Greenhaven Publishing) Greenhaven Publishing LLC.
—Unemployment. 1 vol. 2014. (Global Viewpoints Ser.). (ENG., Illus.). 216p. (gr. 10-12). lib. bdg. 47.83 *(978-0-7377-6916-6(5))*, 8d5998d1-8dc7-42c3-8286-afcdfc3fac4b, Greenhaven Publishing) Greenhaven Publishing LLC.
Stewart, Sheila. When My Dad Lost His Job. (Kids Have Troubles Too Ser.). (Illus.). 48p. (YA). (gr. 5-18). 2010. lib. bdg. 19.95 *(978-1-4222-1703-0(5))* 2009. pap. 7.95 *(978-1-4222-1916-4(X))* Mason Crest.

MANTLE, MICKEY, 1931-1995

Glueckstein, Fred. Mickey Mantle: Rookie in Pinstripes. 2008. (ENG.). 170p. 25.95 *(978-0-595-70936-6(2))*; pap. 15.95 *(978-0-595-46921-5(3))* iUniverse, Inc.
Marlin, John. Mickey Mantle. 2004. (Sports Heroes & Legends Ser.). (ENG., Illus.). 112p. (gr. 5-12). lib. bdg. 30.60 *(978-0-8225-1796-2(5))* Lerner Publishing Group.
Reis, Ronald A. Mickey Mantle. 2009. (Baseball Superstars Ser.). (ENG.). 136p. (gr. 6-12). pap. 11.95 *(978-0-7910-9900-1(6))*, P160503, Checkmark Bks.) Infobase Holdings, Inc.
Weinstein, Howard. Mickey Mantle. 2009. (Baseball Hall of Famers Ser.). 112p. (gr. 5-8). 63.90 *(978-1-61511-513-6(7))*, Rosen Reference) Rosen Publishing Group, Inc., The.
Winter, Jonah. Mickey Mantle: the Commerce Comet. Payne, C. F., illus. 2017. 40p. (J). (gr. -1-3). 17.99 *(978-1-101-93352-7(6))*, Schwartz & Wade Bks.) Random Hse. Children's Bks.

MANUFACTURES

see also Machinery; Waste Products

Abrams, Dennis. Invention of the Moving Assembly Line. 2011. (ENG., Illus.). 120p. (gr. 6-12). 35.00 *(978-1-60413-772-9(X))*, P189894, Facts On File) Infobase Holdings, Inc.
Andrews, Carolyn. What Are Goods & Services?. 1 vol. 2008. (Economics in Action Ser.). (ENG., Illus.). 32p. (J). (gr. 3-7). pap. *(978-0-7787-4260-9(1))* Crabtree Publishing Co.
Bethea, Nikole Brooks. The Invention of the Assembly Line. 2017. (Engineering That Made America Ser.). (ENG.). 32p. (J). (gr. 3-6). lib. bdg. 35.64 *(978-1-5038-1636-7(2))*, 211156) Child's World, Inc, The.
Cardenas, Ernesto A. Wholes & Parts. 2009. pap. 4.95 *(978-1-60698-078-1(5))* Milo Educational Bks. & Resources.
Carr, Aaron. Natural o Hecho Por el Hombre. 2013. (SPA., Illus.). 24p. (J). *(978-1-62127-607-4(4))* Weigl Pubs., Inc.
—Natural or Man-Made, with Code. 2012. (Science Kids Ser.). (ENG., Illus.). 24p. (J). (gr. -1-1). pap. 12.95 *(978-1-61913-757-8(7))*; lib. bdg. 27.13 *(978-1-61913-067-6(4))* Weigl Pubs., Inc. (AV2 by Weigl).
CDs Super Glue & Salsa. 6 vols. 2004. (ENG.). 522.00 *(978-1-4144-0521-6(9))*, UXL) Cengage Gale.
Duling, Kaitlyn. Coding Careers in Manufacturing. 1 vol. 2019. (Coding Careers for Tomorrow Ser.). (ENG.). 80p. (gr. 8-8). lib. bdg. 37.36 *(978-1-5026-4585-2(6))*, db120459-70e2-450c-a695-1a11a5c95aff) Cavendish Square Publishing LLC.
Eagen, Rachel. Meeting Needs in Our Community. 2018. (Money Sense: an Introduction to Financial Literacy Ser.). 24p. (J). (gr. 2-2). *(978-0-7787-5185-4(6))* Crabtree Publishing Co.
Gagne, Tammy. Teen Guide to Buying Goods & Services. 2014. (Illus.). 48p. (gr. 4-8). lib. bdg. 29.95 *(978-1-61228-472-9(8))* Mitchell Lane Pubs.
Greek, Joe. Incredible Projects Using 3D Printing. 1 vol. 2014. (Digital & Information Literacy Ser.). (ENG.). 48p. (YA). (gr. 5-5). 33.47 *(978-1-4777-7946-0(9))*, 2103b671-a65e-4dde-8236-18c725cc2e78); pap. 12.75 *(978-1-4777-7947-7(7))*, 3388c8a4-44d6-4861-97f0-bc1b27dc4f49) Rosen Publishing Group, Inc., The. (Rosen Reference).
Houghton, Gillian. Goods & Services. 2009. (Invest Kids Ser.). 24p. (gr. 2-3). 42.50 *(978-1-61513-617-9(7))*; (ENG., Illus.). (J). pap. 9.25 *(978-1-4358-3210-7(8))*, f8895fab-da59-4a48-8d13-f1613b5804f7); (ENG., Illus.). (J). lib. bdg. 26.27 *(978-1-4358-2775-2(9))*, b7b07655-5df7-4a23-afdf-0d3cadb35cf5) Rosen Publishing Group, Inc., The. (PowerKids Pr.).
Hustad, Douglas. How Can We Reduce Manufacturing Pollution? 2016. (Searchlight Books (tm) — What Can We Do about Pollution? Ser.). (ENG., Illus.). 40p. (J). (gr. 3-5). 30.65 *(978-1-4677-9518-0(6))*, adce80d6-7d6f-4168-8fa2-f709ff6fc26b, Lerner Pubns.) Lerner Publishing Group.
Jd, Duchess Harris & Cornell, Kari A. The Future of Work in America. 2018. (Class in America Ser.). (ENG., Illus.). 112p. (J). (gr. 6-12). lib. bdg. 41.36 *(978-1-5321-1408-3(7))*, 28798, Essential Library) ABDO Publishing Co.
Johnson, Martin. Critical World Issues: Consumerism, Vol. 16. 2016. (Critical World Issues Ser.: Vol. 16). (ENG., Illus.). 112p. (J). (gr. 7-12). 25.95 *(978-1-4222-3650-5(1))* Mason Crest.
Kamberg, Mary-Lane. Working with Tech in Manufacturing. 1 vol. 2020. (Technology in the Workplace Ser.). (ENG.). 80p. (gr. 7-7). pap. 16.30 *(978-1-7253-4164-7(6))*, 1cc98266-9c71-40cb-ad2b-78ec780950f1) Rosen Publishing Group, Inc., The.
La Bella, Laura. What Are Goods & Services? 2016. (Let's Find Out! Ser.). (ENG.). 32p. (J). (gr. 3-7). 23.70 *(978-1-5311-8661-6(0))* Perfection Learning Corp.
—What Are Goods & Services?. 1 vol. 2016. (Let's Find Out! Community Economics Ser.). (ENG.). 32p. (J). (gr. 2-3). lib. bdg. 26.06 *(978-1-68048-400-7(1))*, 083af074-6bef-4b63-b275-cf2619bf5d08) Rosen Publishing Group, Inc., The.
Lafferty, Peter. How Things Are Made. 2004. (Knowledge Masters Plus Ser.). (Illus.). 32p. (YA). pap. incl. cd-rom *(978-1-903954-42-3(8))*, Pavilion Children's Books) Pavilion Bks.
Lewis, Daniel. Transportation & Manufacturing, Vol. 10. 2018. (Careers in Demand for High School Graduates Ser.). 112p. (J). (gr. 7). 34.60 *(978-1-4222-4139-4(4))* Mason Crest.
Manufacturing TCG. 3rd rev. ed. 2004. 48p. pap. *(978-0-86657-513-3(8))* Lab-Volt Systems, Inc.
Marsico, Katie. Working at a Factory. 2008. (21st Century Junior Library: Careers Ser.). (ENG., Illus.). 24p. (gr. 2-5). lib. bdg. 29.21 *(978-1-60279-268-5(2))*, 200173) Cherry Lake Publishing.
McCarthy, Cecilia Pinto. How 3D Printing Will Impact Society. 2018. (Technology's Impact Ser.). (ENG.). 80p. (YA). (gr. 6-12). 39.93 *(978-1-68282-499-3(3))* ReferencePoint Pr., Inc.
Meister, Cari. From Wax to Crayons. Pinilla, Albert, illus. 2019. (Who Made My Stuff? Ser.). (ENG.). 24p. (J). (gr. 1-4). lib. bdg. *(978-1-68151-698-1(5))*, 10850) Amicus.
Miller, Raymond H. Milton Bradley. 2004. (Inventors & Creators Ser.). (ENG., Illus.). 48p. (J). (gr. 4-7). lib. bdg. 27.50 *(978-0-7377-2613-8(X))*, Greenhaven Pr., Inc.) Cengage Gale.
Morganelli, Adrianna. Dream Jobs in Manufacturing. 2018. (ENG.). (J). (gr. 3-7). *(978-1-4271-2030-4(7))*; (Illus.). 32p. (gr. 5-5). *(978-0-7787-4439-9(6))*; (Illus.). 32p. (gr. 5-5). pap. *(978-0-7787-4450-4(7))* Crabtree Publishing Co.
Morlock, Theresa. The Amazing Assembly Line: Working at the Same Time. 1 vol. 2017. (Computer Kids: Powered by Computational Thinking Ser.). (ENG.). 24p. (J). (gr. 4-5). 25.27 *(978-1-5383-2431-8(8))*, e6984085-0204-4d6d-bd51-204852cebe98, PowerKids Pr.); pap. *(978-1-5081-3752-8(8))*, 096f4718-22ac-4967-b5db-73173a5e8ca1, Rosen Classroom) Rosen Publishing Group, Inc., The.
Mortensen, Lori. Peek Inside a Pencil. 2018. (Let's Learn Ser.). (ENG., Illus.). 16p. (gr. -1-2). lib. bdg. 28.50 *(978-1-64156-164-8(5))*, 9781641561648) Rourke Educational Media.
Nelson, Robin. What Do We Buy? A Look at Goods & Services. 2010. (Lightning Bolt Books (r) — Exploring Economics Ser.). (ENG., Illus.). 32p. (J). (gr. 1-3). pap. 9.99 *(978-0-7613-5667-7(3))*, e3526cd3-d305-4aa0-a9fc-d041aeb7400d) Lerner Publishing Group.
Prentzas, G. S. Gps. 2009. (21st Century Skills Library: Global Products Ser.). (ENG., Illus.). 32p. (gr. 4-8). lib. bdg. 32.07 *(978-1-60279-506-8(1))*, 200321) Cherry Lake Publishing.
Production of Goods & Services. 16 vols. 2011. (Dollars & Sense: a Guide to Financial Literacy Ser.). (ENG.). (J). (gr. 5-5). 297.04 *(978-1-4488-4860-7(1))*, c3b077bc-4cba-4770-8e0b-89175e49b06c) Rosen Publishing Group, Inc., The.
Reeves, Diane Lindsey. Career Ideas for Teens in Manufacturing. 2005. (Career Ideas for Teens Ser.). (Illus.). 192p. (gr. 6-12). 40.00 *(978-0-8160-5294-3(8))*, Ferguson Publishing Company) Infobase Holdings, Inc.
—Manufacturing. 2017. (Bright Futures Press: World of Work Ser.). (ENG., Illus.). 32p. (J). (gr. 4-7). lib. bdg. 32.07 *(978-1-63472-627-6(8))*, 209542) Cherry Lake Publishing.
Rice, Dona Herweck. Making Crayons. rev. ed. 2019. (Smithsonian: Informational Text Ser.). (ENG., Illus.). 20p. (J). (gr. k-1). 7.99 *(978-1-4938-6637-3(0))* Teacher Created Materials, Inc.
Royston, Angela. Pencil. 2005. (How Are Things Made? Ser.). (ENG., Illus.). 32p. (J). tchr. ed. *(978-0-431-05045-4(7))*; pap. *(978-0-431-05052-2(X))* Steck-Vaughn.
Shaw, Jessica. Careers in Manufacturing. 1 vol. 2019. (Makerspace Careers Ser.). (ENG., Illus.). 80p. (J). (gr. 7-7). 37.47 *(978-1-5081-8810-0(6))*, 45533b31-b26d-46c9-8a78-73dbb10bef96) Rosen Publishing Group, Inc., The.
Slavin, Bill. Transformed: How Everyday Things Are Made. Slavin, Bill, illus. 2007. (ENG., Illus.). 160p. (J). (gr. 3-7). pap. 18.99 *(978-1-55453-244-5(2))* Kids Can Pr., Ltd. CAN. Dist: Hachette Bk. Group.
Sylvester, Kevin & Hlinka, Michael. Follow Your Stuff: Who Makes It, Where Does It Come from, How Does It Get to You? 2019. (Illus.). 100p. (J). (gr. 6). pap. 12.95 *(978-1-77321-253-1(2))* Annick Pr., Ltd. CAN. Dist: Publishers Group West (PGW).
Turner, Donald R. & Tillema, Juliana O. Production of Goods & Services. 1 vol. 2011. (Dollars & Sense: a Guide to Financial Literacy Ser.). (ENG.). 64p. (gr. 5-5). (J). pap. 13.95 *(978-1-4488-4721-1(4))*, 44756545-d62e-4a06-a4a5-cb998bc1b443); (YA). lib. bdg. 37.13 *(978-1-4488-4711-2(7))*, 95cba78f-7a41-4dc8-a186-ccaa8075bd8e) Rosen Publishing Group, Inc., The.
World Book, Inc. Staff, contrib. by. Consumable Goods. 2008. (J). *(978-0-7166-1407-4(3))* World Bk., Inc.

MAO, TSE-TUNG, 1893-1976

see Mao, Zedong, 1893-1976

MAO, ZEDONG, 1893-1976

Gardner, April B. Mao: Boy of Stone. 2012. 24p. 24.95 *(978-1-4626-9867-7(0))*; pap. 24.95 *(978-1-4626-8244-7(8))* America Star Bks.
Heuston, Kimberley. Mao Zedong. 2010. (Wicked History Ser.). (ENG.). 128p. (J). (gr. 6-12). pap. 5.95 *(978-0-531-22356-7(6))*, Watts, Franklin) Scholastic Library Publishing.
Heuston, Kimberley Burton. Mao Zedong. 2010. (Wicked History Ser.). (ENG., Illus.). 128p. (J). (gr. 5-8). 31.00 *(978-0-531-20756-7(0))* Scholastic Library Publishing.
Malaspina, Ann. Mao Zedong & the Chinese Revolution. 1 vol. 2015. (People & Events That Changed the World Ser.). (ENG., Illus.). 128p. (gr. 7-8). lib. bdg. 38.93 *(978-0-7660-7292-3(4))*, a6376b76-b4a7-4ec2-b29b-6db67609e41e) Enslow Publishing, LLC.

MAORI (NEW ZEALAND PEOPLE)

Amery, Heather, et al. First Hundred Words in Maori. 2008. (MAO., Illus.). 40p. pap. 14.00 *(978-1-86969-304-6(3))* Huia Pubs. NZL. Dist: Univ. of Hawaii Pr.
Bekkering, Annalise. Great Lakes. 2012. (J). *(978-1-61913-526-0(4))*; (Illus.). 32p. pap. *(978-1-61913-440-9(3))* Weigl Pubs., Inc.
McClellan, Ray. Maori Warriors. 2012. (History's Greatest Warriors Ser.). (ENG., Illus.). 24p. (J). (gr. 3-7). lib. bdg. 26.95 *(978-1-60014-745-6(3))*, Torque Bks.) Bellwether Media.
Meredith, Courtney Sina. The Adventures of Tupaia. Tait, Mat, illus. 2019. (ENG.). 64p. (J). (gr. 3-7). 22.99 *(978-1-988547-14-5(8))* Allen & Unwin AUS. Dist: Independent Pubs. Group.
Strudwick, Leslie. Maori. 32p. 2012. (Illus.). (J). *(978-1-61913-095-1(5))* 2005. pap. 9.95 *(978-1-59036-256-3(X))* 2004. (Illus.). (J). lib. bdg. 24.45 *(978-1-59036-221-1(7))* Weigl Pubs., Inc.
—Maori with Code. 2012. (World Cultures Ser.). (ENG., Illus.). 32p. (J). (gr. 3-7). pap. 13.95 *(978-1-61913-532-1(9))*, AV2 by Weigl) Weigl Pubs., Inc.
Theunissen, Steve. The Maori of New Zealand. 2005. (First Peoples Ser.). (Illus.). 48p. (J). (gr. 4-8). lib. bdg. 23.95 *(978-0-8225-0665-2(3))* Lerner Publishing Group.
World Book, Inc. Staff, contrib. by. The Maori. 2009. (Illus.). 63p. (J). *(978-0-7166-2143-0(6))* World Bk., Inc.

MAORI (NEW ZEALAND PEOPLE)—FICTION

Alden, Raymond MacDonald. Once There Was a King: A Tournament of Stories. Copelman, Evelyn, illus. 2011. 194p. 42.95 *(978-1-258-08031-0(1))* Literary Licensing, LLC.
Barker, Stephen Elliot. The Secret of Spirits Bay. 2008. (Illus.). 224p. *(978-1-86950-725-1(8))* HarperCollins Pubs. Australia.
Bixley, Donovan. How Maui Fished Up the North Island. 2018. (Illus.). 24p. (J). (gr. k-2). pap. 15.99 *(978-1-988516-18-9(8))* Upstart Pr. NZL. Dist: Independent Pubs. Group.
Dauphin, Vaya. The Greenstone Garden: The Elementals of Aotearoa, Vol. 2. 2013. viii, 297p. pap. *(978-1-74284-346-9(8))* ReadOnTime.
Dawe, Ted. Into the River. 2016. (ENG.). 304p. (J). (gr. 7). 17.99 *(978-1-943818-19-8(3))* Polis Bks.
Kapai, Tommy. Cuzzies Find the Rainbow's End. Henry, Mike, illus. 2006. (ENG.). 32p. (gr. -1-3). pap. 9.00 *(978-0-9582517-0-9(3))*, 2990) Huia Pubs. NZL. Dist: Univ. of Hawaii Pr.
—Cuzzies Meet the Motuhoa Shark. Henry, Mike, illus. 2006. (Cuzzies Adventures Ser.). (MAO & ENG.). 32p. (J). (gr. -1-3). pap. 9.00 *(978-1-86969-100-4(8))* Huia Pubs. NZL. Dist: Univ. of Hawaii Pr.
McConchie, Lyn. Winter of Waiting. 2015. (YA). (gr. 5-18). pap. 15.00 *(978-1-936021-55-0(2))*, Banana Oil Bks.) Cyberwizard Productions.
Rolleston-Cummins, Toni. The Seven Stars of Matariki. Slade-Robinson, Nikki, illus. 2009. (ENG.). 28p. pap. 12.00 *(978-1-86969-327-5(2))*, 4346) Huia Pubs. NZL. Dist: Univ. of Hawaii Pr.
Summer of Dreaming. 2010. (Illus.). 157p. (YA). pap. *(978-1-936021-22-2(6))*, Banana Oil Bks.) Cyberwizard Productions.
Waerea, James. Pukunui. FireHydrant Creative Studios, ed. Waerea, James & Waerea, Mitch, illus. 2010. (ENG & MAO.). 26p. (J). pap. 14.95 *(978-0-9826066-0-5(5))* FireHydrant Creative Studios, Inc.

MAORI (NEW ZEALAND PEOPLE)—FOLKLORE

Croy, Anita. Myths & Legends of Australia, New Zealand, & Pacific Islands. 2015. (Illus.). 64p. (J). *(978-0-7166-2629-9(2))* World Bk., Inc.
Kahukiwa, Robyn. Ngā Atua: Māori Gods. Hammond, Kiwa, tr. Kahukiwa, Robyn, illus. 2017. (Illus.). 32p. (J). 19.00 *(978-0-947506-26-1(8))*, 13416, Oratia Bks.) Oratia Media NZL. Dist: Univ. of Hawaii Pr.
Tipene, Tim. Māui: Sun Catcher. Ruha, Rob, tr. Waipara, Zak, illus. 2016. 32p. (J). 19.00 *(978-0-947506-14-8(4))*, 13417, Oratia Bks.) Oratia Media NZL. Dist: Univ. of Hawaii Pr.

MAP DRAWING

see also Atlases

Bandrova, Temenoujka, et al. Children Map the World Vol. 2: Selections from the Barbara Petchenik Children's World Map Competition. 2009. (ENG., Illus.). 136p. (J). pap. 29.95 *(978-1-58948-246-3(8))*, ESRI Pr.) ESRI, Inc.
Quinlan, Julia J. How to Draw a Map. 2012. (How to Use Maps Ser.). (ENG.). 24p. (J). (gr. 3-5). 19.05 *(978-1-5311-8664-7(5))* Perfection Learning Corp.
—How to Draw a Map. 1 vol. 2012. (How to Use Maps Ser.). (ENG.). 24p. (J). (gr. 2-3). pap. 9.25 *(978-1-4488-6274-0(4))*, 3fc599a4-bbdd-4e72-af18-2e662588f9f1, PowerKids Pr.); lib. bdg. 26.27 *(978-1-4488-6158-3(6))*, 61745ae5-6e9e-40d6-83e9-200b5a168536) Rosen Publishing Group, Inc., The.
Torpie, Kate. Drawing Maps. 1 vol. 2008. (ENG., Illus.). 32p. (J). (gr. 1-4). pap. *(978-0-7787-4272-2(5))* Crabtree Publishing Co.

MNO

—Drawing Maps. 2008. (All over the Map Ser.). (ENG.). 32p. (J). (gr. 3-6). 19.75 *(978-1-5311-7651-8(8))* Perfection Learning Corp.

MAP-MAKING

see Cartography

MAPLE

George, Gale. The Life Cycle of a Maple Tree, 1 vol. 2015. (Watch Them Grow! Ser.). (ENG.). 24p. (J). (gr. 1-1). pap. 9.25 *(978-1-4994-0677-1(0),* 40a9dbeb-ea08-4333-bcb6-b18ec627c8f2, PowerKids Pr.) Rosen Publishing Group, Inc., The.

Glaser, Rebecca. Maple Tree. 2012. (ENG., Illus.). 24p. (J). lib. bdg. 25.65 *(978-1-62031-026-7(0))* Jump! Inc.

Hansen, Grace. How Is Maple Syrup Made? 2018. (How Is It Made? Ser.). (ENG., Illus.). 24p. (J). (gr. -1-2). lib. bdg. 32.79 *(978-1-5321-8195-5(7),* 29905, Abdo Kids) ABDO Publishing Co.

Mitchell, Melanie. From Maple Tree to Syrup. (gr. k-3). 2012. (Start to Finish, Second Ser.: No. 2). (ENG., Illus.). 24p. (J). pap. 7.99 *(978-1-58013-967-0(1),* ff3d08e3-3917-4df9-b0cf-16deb40d184a) 2004. pap. 5.95 *(978-0-8225-2144-0(X))* Lerner Publishing Group.

Moore, Elizabeth. Making Maple Syrup, 1 vol. 2011. (Wonder Readers Early Level Ser.). (ENG.). 16p. (gr. -1-1). (J). pap. 6.25 *(978-1-4296-7866-7(6),* 118195); pap. 35.94 *(978-1-4296-8124-7(1),* Capstone Pr.) Capstone.

Morgan, Emily. Next Time You See a Maple Seed. 2014. (Next Time You See Ser.). (ENG.). 32p. (J). (gr. -1-k). 13.99 *(978-1-938946-35-6(9))* National Science Teachers Assn.

Stockland, Patricia M. Look at a Maple Tree. 2012. (First Step Nonfiction — Look at Trees Ser.). (ENG., Illus.). 8p. (J). (gr. k-2). pap. 5.99 *(978-1-4677-0522-6(5),* d4f4dcb4-70d0-48ec-97e4-be0a17f891f6) Lerner Publishing Group.

MAPS

Here are entered works about maps. Works on the mapping of small areas and the drawing of maps in elementary schools are entered under Map Drawing. Works on the general science of map-making, including map projection and the mapping of large areas are entered under Cartography.

Aberg, Rebecca. Claves de Mapas. 2005. (Rookie Espaanol Geografia Ser.). (SPA., Illus.). 32p. (J). (gr. k-2). lib. bdg. 19.50 *(978-0-516-25242-1(9),* Children's Pr.) Scholastic Library Publishing.

Ashcroft, Minnie. Marvelous Map Activities for Young Learners. 2003. (ENG.). 64p. pap. 11.95 *(978-0-439-17887-7(8))* Scholastic, Inc.

Autumn Publishing Staff, illus. World Map. 2004. (Wall Charts Ser.). (J). pap. 4.99 *(978-1-85997-235-9(7))* Byeway Bks.

Ball, Jacqueline A. & Ball, Jacqueline A. Mapping Earth, 1 vol. 2004. (Discovery Channel School Science: Our Planet Earth Ser.). (ENG., Illus.). 32p. (gr. 5-7). lib. bdg. 28.67 *(978-0-8368-3382-9(1),* 98a338d2-49cf-4812-8ef6-fdef5bbcd57c, Gareth Stevens Learning Library) Stevens, Gareth Publishing LLLP.

Besel, Jennifer M. Compass Roses & Directions, 1 vol. 2013. (Maps Ser.). (ENG.). 24p. (J). (gr. -1-2). pap. 6.95 *(978-1-4765-3524-1(8),* 123574) Capstone.

—Maps. 2013. (Maps Ser.). (ENG.). 24p. (J). (gr. -1-2). pap., pap., pap. 34.75 *(978-1-4765-3711-5(9),* 20207, Pebble) Capstone.

—Symbols & Keys, 1 vol. 2013. (Maps Ser.). (ENG.). 24p. (J). (gr. -1-2). 27.32 *(978-1-4765-3082-6(3),* 123056, Capstone Pr.); pap. 6.95 *(978-1-4765-3522-7(1),* 123572, Pebble) Capstone.

—Types of Maps, 1 vol. 2013. (Maps Ser.). (ENG.). 24p. (J). (gr. -1-2). 27.32 *(978-1-4765-3124-3(2),* 123108, Capstone Pr.); pap. 6.95 *(978-1-4765-3525-8(6),* 123575, Pebble) Capstone.

—What Is a Map?, 1 vol. 2013. (Maps Ser.). (ENG.). 24p. (J). (gr. -1-2). 27.32 *(978-1-4765-3081-9(5),* 123054); pap. 6.95 *(978-1-4765-3521-0(3),* 123571) Capstone.

Bluthenthal, Todd. The Equator, 1 vol. 2017. (Where on Earth? Mapping Parts of the World Ser.). (ENG.). 24p. (gr. 1-2). pap. 9.15 *(978-1-4824-6421-4(7),* d702983b-fc2c-4ed5-b2d0-39258a1918fc) Stevens, Gareth Publishing LLLP.

—Making Maps, 1 vol. 2017. (Where on Earth? Mapping Parts of the World Ser.). (ENG.). 24p. (gr. 1-2). pap. 9.15 *(978-1-4824-6425-2(X),* 65f4beff-36d1-44d4-be23-cd34866a6db3) Stevens, Gareth Publishing LLLP.

Boothroyd, Jennifer. Map My Continent. 2013. (First Step Nonfiction — Map It Out Ser.). (ENG., Illus.). 24p. (J). (gr. k-2). pap. 6.99 *(978-1-4677-1529-4(8),* 3805183a-355b-47c7-88c9-e6c7a84c6fd4); lib. bdg. 23.99 *(978-1-4677-1114-2(4),* be0fe6df-4877-4299-a3c3-e11ea1481c08, Lerner Pubns.) Lerner Publishing Group.

—Map My Country. 2013. (First Step Nonfiction — Map It Out Ser.). (ENG., Illus.). 24p. (J). (gr. k-2). lib. bdg. 23.99 *(978-1-4677-1113-5(6),* 058d8d9b-a60a-47e0-bf6d-a59e6620f655, Lerner Pubns.) Lerner Publishing Group.

—Map My Home. 2013. (First Step Nonfiction — Map It Out Ser.). (ENG., Illus.). 24p. (J). (gr. k-2). pap. 6.99 *(978-1-4677-1530-0(1),* c1e58b75-3aa4-43ae-9cc9-b43ce28ba0d2) Lerner Publishing Group.

—Map My Neighborhood. 2013. (First Step Nonfiction — Map It Out Ser.). (ENG., Illus.). 24p. (J). (gr. k-2). pap. 6.99 *(978-1-4677-1531-7(X),* 75c8b4a9-1061-4ce4-98d3-8afcc981c7af) Lerner Publishing Group.

—Map My Room. 2013. (First Step Nonfiction — Map It Out Ser.). (ENG., Illus.). 24p. (J). (gr. k-2). pap. 6.99 *(978-1-4677-1532-4(8),* 067461ce-06d1-4d29-9670-c27cafd77435) Lerner Publishing Group.

—Map My State. 2013. (First Step Nonfiction — Map It Out Ser.). (ENG., Illus.). 24p. (J). (gr. k-2). lib. bdg. 23.99 *(978-1-4677-1112-8(8),* 27358fd2-1a5e-4504-ad37-e0d709f0ccc9, Lerner Pubns.) Lerner Publishing Group.

Boswell, Kelly. Maps, Maps, Maps!, 1 vol. 2013. (Displaying Information Ser.). (ENG.). 32p. (J). (gr. -1-2). pap. 8.95 *(978-1-4765-3339-1(3),* 123456, Capstone Pr.) Capstone.

Bredeson, Carmen. Mapas y Globos Terraqueos. 2005. (Rookie Espaanol Geografia Ser.). (SPA., Illus.). 32p. (J). (gr. k-2). lib. bdg. 19.50 *(978-0-516-25241-4(0),* Children's Pr.) Scholastic Library Publishing.

Brennan, Linda Crotta. Maps: What You Need to Know. 2017. (Fact Files Ser.). (ENG., Illus.). 24p. (J). (gr. 1-3). lib. bdg. 27.99 *(978-1-5157-8109-7(7),* 136116, Capstone Pr.) Capstone.

Brundle, Harriet. Map My Community. 2018. (Mapping My World Ser.). (Illus.). 24p. (J). (gr. 2-2). *(978-0-7787-5001-7(9))* Crabtree Publishing Co.

—Map My Country. 2018. (Mapping My World Ser.). (Illus.). 24p. (J). (gr. 2-2). *(978-0-7787-5002-4(7))* Crabtree Publishing Co.

—Map My Planet. 2018. (Mapping My World Ser.). (Illus.). 24p. (J). (gr. 2-2). *(978-0-7787-5003-1(5))* Crabtree Publishing Co.

—Map My School. 2018. (Mapping My World Ser.). (Illus.). 24p. (J). (gr. 2-2). *(978-0-7787-5000-0(0))* Crabtree Publishing Co.

Cator, David. Map Symbols, 1 vol. 2008. (Real Life Readers Ser.). (ENG.). 16p. (gr. 2-3). pap. 7.05 *(978-1-4358-0075-5(3),* 2ba52477-9677-4afd-81dd-c53100155165, Rosen Classroom) Rosen Publishing Group, Inc., The.

Chapman, Joan. Maps, Maps, Maps. 2006. (Rosen Real Readers Big Bookstm Ser.). (ENG.). 8p. (gr. k-1). 29.95 *(978-1-4042-6211-9(3))* Rosen Publishing Group, Inc., The.

Cicciarelli, Joellyn T. Maps. 2017. (Learn-To-Read Ser.). (ENG., Illus.). (J). pap. 3.49 *(978-1-68310-251-9(7))* Pacific Learning, Inc.

Collins Maps & Scoffham, Stephen. UK in Maps Activities - CANCELLED. 2nd rev. ed. 2018. (Collins Primary Atlases Ser.). (ENG.). 80p. (J). (gr. 3-6). pap. 58.95 *(978-0-00-827174-9(7))* HarperCollins Pubs. Ltd. GBR. Dist: Independent Pubs. Group.

—World in Maps Activities - CANCELLED. 2nd rev. ed. 2018. (Collins Primary Atlases Ser.). (ENG.). 80p. (J). (gr. 3-6). pap. 59.95 *(978-0-00-827176-3(3))* HarperCollins Pubs. Ltd. GBR. Dist: Independent Pubs. Group.

Comire, S. Joshua & Porter, Malcolm. Atlas of Australia & the Pacific, 1 vol. 2010. (Atlases of the World Ser.). (ENG., Illus.). 48p. (YA). (gr. 5-5). 34.47 *(978-1-4358-8456-4(6),* 1671208c-0c67-4fc3-99fb-590f6130c402, Rosen Reference) Rosen Publishing Group, Inc., The.

Como Ser un Experto en Mapas. (Coleccion Ciencia y Proyectos). (SPA., Illus.). (YA). (gr. 5-8). pap. *(978-950-724-562-6(6),* LMA8239) Lumen ARG. Dist: Lectorum Pubns., Inc.

Cooke, Tim. The Changing Face of Maps. 2017. (Mapping in the Modern World Ser.). (Illus.). 32p. (J). (gr. 5-5). *(978-0-7787-3221-1(5))* Crabtree Publishing Co.

—Maps & Mapping the World, 1 vol. 2010. (Understanding Maps of Our World Ser.). (ENG.). 48p. (gr. 6-8). (YA). lib. bdg. 33.67 *(978-1-4339-3498-8(1),* 741ebbc0-6cec-4310-bb66-210c170a61d2); (Illus.). pap. 15.05 *(978-1-4339-3501-5(5),* 9e6fdc51-60a4-4679-9c6b-dcc702033ad7, Gareth Stevens Secondary Library) Stevens, Gareth Publishing LLLP.

—Maps Today, 1 vol. 2010. (Understanding Maps of Our World Ser.). (ENG., Illus.). 48p. (J). (gr. 6-8). pap. 15.05 *(978-1-4339-3522-0(8),* 42fea597-b3b5-48d1-bc15-7b563299fd91, Gareth Stevens Secondary Library); lib. bdg. 33.67 *(978-1-4339-3521-3(X),* fb945606-1673-4a47-9ee5-a3b839224381) Stevens, Gareth Publishing LLLP.

—Travel Maps, 1 vol. 2010. (Understanding Maps of Our World Ser.). (ENG., Illus.). 48p. (gr. 6-8). (J). pap. 15.05 *(978-1-4339-3507-7(4),* 20ec9ae5-551d-4ae2-acaa-b7d013a642e6, Gareth Stevens Secondary Library); (YA). lib. bdg. 33.67 *(978-1-4339-3506-0(6),* 6b06a8ed-c7f1-4182-b4ea-f75a1f43f975) Stevens, Gareth Publishing LLLP.

—Understanding Maps of Our World, 16 vols., Set. Incl. Government Maps. (YA). lib. bdg. 33.67 *(978-1-4339-3515-2(5),* d45875e3-62b7-439f-88a5-f806b9870baa); Maps & Cities. (YA). lib. bdg. 33.67 *(978-1-4339-3518-3(X),* 40a978d2-70ba-4235-924c-63e27ab0c59c); Maps & Exploration. (YA). lib. bdg. 33.67 *(978-1-4339-3512-1(0),* 9538bc5b-4a7e-4b35-9a78-c98d259ffa7); Maps & Mapping the World. (YA). lib. bdg. 33.67 *(978-1-4339-3498-8(1),* 741ebbc0-6cec-4310-bb66-210c170a61d2); Maps & Measurement. (Illus.). (YA). lib. bdg. 33.67 *(978-1-4339-3503-9(1),* 17e4fd02-53df-4af4-9130-b4fc3f650368); Maps & Navigation. (YA). lib. bdg. 33.67 *(978-1-4339-3509-1(0),* c0086775-66f2-4347-965e-dd2c09e205f5); Maps Today. (Illus.). (J). lib. bdg. 33.67 *(978-1-4339-3521-3(X),* fb945606-1673-4a47-9ee5-a3b839224381); Travel Maps. (Illus.). (YA). lib. bdg. 33.67 *(978-1-4339-3506-0(6),* 6b06a8ed-c7f1-4182-b4ea-f75a1f43f975); (gr. 6-8). (Understanding Maps of Our World Ser.). (ENG.). 48p. 2010. Set lib. bdg. 269.36 *(978-1-4339-3589-3(9),* 805c0f69-e7cd-4840-a459-b9d9bf4cd7b0, Gareth Stevens Secondary Library) Stevens, Gareth Publishing LLLP.

Cooper, Alison & McRae, Anne. The Children's Pictorial Atlas of the World. De Luca, Daniela, illus. 2008. (ENG.). 45p. (J). (gr. -1-3). 17.95 *(978-88-88166-05-6(X))* McRae Bks. Srl ITA. Dist: Independent Pubs. Group.

Corporate Contributor Staff & O'Brien, Cynthia. Climate Maps. 2012. (ENG.). 32p. (J). pap. *(978-0-7787-4496-2(5))*; lib. bdg. *(978-0-7787-4491-7(4))* Crabtree Publishing Co.

Corporate Contributor Staff & Pegis, Jessica. Political Maps. 2012. (ENG.). 32p. (J). pap. *(978-0-7787-4498-6(1))*; lib. bdg. *(978-0-7787-4493-1(0))* Crabtree Publishing Co.

Corporate Contributor Staff & Rodger, Ellen. Physical Maps. 2012. (ENG.). 32p. (J). pap. *(978-0-7787-4497-9(3))*; lib. bdg. *(978-0-7787-4492-4(2))* Crabtree Publishing Co.

Dispenzio, Michael A. Map Mania: Discovering Where You Are & Getting to Where You Aren't. Garbot, Dave, illus. 2006. 80p. (J). (gr. 4-8). reprint ed. 20.00 *(978-0-7567-9893-2(0))* DIANE Publishing Co.

Edson, Ann & Insel, Eunice. Reading Maps, Globes, Charts, Graphs. (J). (gr. 4-6). stu. ed., instr.'s gde. ed. 39.00 incl. audio *(978-0-89525-175-6(2),* AKC 356) Educational Activities, Inc.

Endres, Hollie J. The Letter Rr Set, 6 vols. Maps. 2004. (Letter Bks.). (ENG.). 8p. (gr. k-1). pap. 29.70 *(978-0-7368-4117-7(2))* Capstone.

Fun with Map Skills, 12 vols. 2014. (Fun with Map Skills Ser.). (ENG.). 32p. (J). (gr. 4-4). 167.58 *(978-1-4777-6985-0(4),* 41bfa25d-d989-4709-88df-0eb62ea60db1, PowerKids Pr.) Rosen Publishing Group, Inc., The.

Furgang, Kathy. Zoom in on Satellite & Street Maps, 1 vol. 2017. (Zoom in on Maps Ser.). (ENG.). 24p. (gr. 2-2). 25.60 *(978-0-7660-9225-9(9),* 6ff3469e-a0cc-4c24-b5db-da4bfba08ea5) Enslow Publishing, LLC.

Furgang, Kathy, rev. Zoom in on Climate Maps, 1 vol. 2017. (Zoom in on Maps Ser.). (ENG.). 24p. (gr. 2-2). 25.60 *(978-0-7660-9222-8(4),* c9b90c87-430d-47b8-a5ec-5e376fbd3bf9) Enslow Publishing, LLC.

—Zoom in on Physical Maps, 1 vol. 2017. (Zoom in on Maps Ser.). (ENG.). 24p. (gr. 2-2). 25.60 *(978-0-7660-9219-8(4),* da4f66b4-1033-41ca-8e71-293f074f1c2f) Enslow Publishing, LLC.

—Zoom in on Political Maps, 1 vol. 2017. (Zoom in on Maps Ser.). (ENG.). 24p. (gr. 2-2). 25.60 *(978-0-7660-9220-4(8),* 3e9bf756-0cbc-4519-9883-56ecd76a57e1) Enslow Publishing, LLC.

—Zoom in on Road Maps, 1 vol. 2017. (Zoom in on Maps Ser.). (ENG.). 24p. (gr. 2-2). 25.60 *(978-0-7660-9223-5(2),* d24d408f-bb4b-4203-b69c-8ba01660e034) Enslow Publishing, LLC.

—Zoom in on Topographic Maps, 1 vol. 2017. (Zoom in on Maps Ser.). (ENG.). 24p. (gr. 2-2). 25.60 *(978-0-7660-9221-1(6),* ca361d20-086e-4334-8b68-1f6dd1dd947b) Enslow Publishing, LLC.

—Zoom in on Weather Maps, 1 vol. 2017. (Zoom in on Maps Ser.). (ENG.). 24p. (gr. 2-2). 25.60 *(978-0-7660-9224-2(0),* 85b035de-646e-47b5-9229-581a69128d55) Enslow Publishing, LLC.

Gillis, Jennifer B. You Are Here. 2006. (My Neighborhood Ser.). (Illus.). 24p. (gr. k-2). 18.00 *(978-0-7569-6931-8(X))* Perfection Learning Corp.

Gillis, Jennifer Blizin. Estas Aqui/You Are Here. Duque, Olga, tr. 2006. (My Neighborhood Discovery Library). (SPA & ENG., Illus.). 24p. (J). (gr. 3-7). lib. bdg. 22.79 *(978-1-60044-294-0(3))* Rourke Educational Media.

Gonzales, Doreen. Up North & down South: Using Map Directions. rev. ed. 2016. (Map Mania Ser.). (ENG.). 24p. (J). (gr. 1-3). pap. 7.29 *(978-1-5157-4219-7(9),* 133982) Capstone.

Greve, Meg. Maps Are Flat, Globes Are Round. 2009. (Little World Geography Ser.). (ENG.). 24p. (J). (gr. k-2). 19.75 *(978-1-5311-7666-2(6))* Perfection Learning Corp.

Hammond World Atlas Corporation Staff, ed. Globes in a Box. 2008. (Hammond Ser.). 64p. (J). (gr. 5-18). 19.95 *(978-0-8437-1825-6(0))* Hammond World Atlas Corp.

—Planet Earth: Our Planet as You've Never Seen It Before. 2008. 168p. (J). (gr. 3-7). 19.99 *(978-0-8437-1834-8(X))* Hammond World Atlas Corp.

Hewitt, Sally. Maps. 2010. (Starting Geography Ser.). 32p. (J). (gr. 2-5). 28.50 *(978-1-60753-126-5(7))* Amicus Learning.

—Maps. 2012. (Deadly & Incredible Animals Ser.). 32p. (gr. 2-6). 27.10 *(978-1-59920-412-3(6))* Black Rabbit Bks.

Hibbert, Clare. Around the World in 80 Maps. 2017. (ENG., Illus.). 96p. (J). (gr. 3-7). 19.95 *(978-0-2281-0010-2(0),* c549c60a-0fa0-4376-ab54-404881f6a49c) Firefly Bks., Ltd.

Hicer, Nancy. Maps & New York City, 1 vol. 2011. (My Community Ser.). (ENG.). 12p. (gr. 2-2). pap. 6.95 *(978-1-4488-5732-6(5),* 9a11f075-0ce3-4587-9ceb-882143a5d414) Rosen Publishing Group, Inc., The.

Hirsch, Rebecca E. Using Climate Maps. 2016. (Searchlight Books (tm) — What Do You Know about Maps? Ser.). (ENG., Illus.). 40p. (J). (gr. 3-5). 30.65 *(978-1-5124-0950-5(2),* 3911df2a-67ab-44f8-bb0d-ae78ee67b509, Lerner Pubns.) Lerner Publishing Group.

—Using Physical Maps. 2016. (Searchlight Books (tm) — What Do You Know about Maps? Ser.). (ENG., Illus.). 40p. (J). (gr. 3-5). 30.65 *(978-1-5124-0949-9(9),* b4136701-0ce6-4667-b5ee-d7b2ba8392ad, Lerner Pubns.) Lerner Publishing Group.

—Using Political Maps. 2016. (Searchlight Books (tm) — What Do You Know about Maps? Ser.). (ENG., Illus.). 40p. (J). (gr. 3-5). 30.65 *(978-1-5124-0947-5(2),* d581336c-a189-49ce-933c-5a6be13d7534, Lerner Pubns.) Lerner Publishing Group.

Home & School. (J). (gr. k-1). *(978-84-342-2416-2(X),* PR30570) Parramon Ediciones S.A. ESP. Dist: Lectorum Pubns., Inc.

Home & School. (J). (gr. 1). 3.80 *(978-0-8374-1450-8(4),* 401) Weekly Reader Corp.

Hudak, Heather C. Mapping. 2007. (Social Studies Essential Skills Ser.). (Illus.). 24p. (J). (gr. 4-7). lib. bdg. 24.45 *(978-1-59036-761-2(8))*; per. 8.95 *(978-1-59036-762-9(6))* Weigl Pubs., Inc.

In the World. (J). (gr. 6). 3.80 *(978-0-8374-1455-3(5),* 406) Weekly Reader Corp.

Jennings, Ken. Maps & Geography. Lowery, Mike, illus. 2014. (Ken Jennings' Junior Genius Guides). (ENG.). 160p. (J). (gr. 3-5). pap. 9.99 *(978-1-4424-7328-7(2),* Little Simon) Little Simon.

Kachur, Matthew. Making Maps: Set Of 6. 2011. (Navigators Ser.). (J). pap. 48.00 net. *(978-1-4108-0416-7(X))* Benchmark Education Co.

Kalman, Bobbie. Rapping about Directions on Earth. 2012. (ENG.). 24p. (J). *(978-0-7787-2796-5(3))*; pap. *(978-0-7787-2803-0(X))* Crabtree Publishing Co.

Kalz, Jill. Farm Adventure. Cerato, Mattia, illus. 2010. (A-MAZE-Ing Adventures Ser.). (ENG.). 32p. (J). (gr. -1-2). lib. bdg. 27.32 *(978-1-4048-6038-4(X),* 102997, Picture Window Bks.) Capstone.

Klimchuk, Karen. Manuel Makes a Map!, 1 vol. 2013. (Rosen Readers Ser.). (ENG.). 24p. (J). (gr. 2-2). pap. 8.25 *(978-1-4777-2319-7(6),* b901b21a-deab-4d1a-924b-0e9329470db0); pap. 49.50 *(978-1-4777-2320-3(X))* Rosen Publishing Group, Inc., The. (Rosen Classroom).

Lavagno, Enrico. Maps of the World: An Illustrated Children's Atlas of Adventure, Culture, & Discovery. Vallarino, Sacco, illus. 2018. (ENG.). 136p. (J). (gr. 1-5). 24.99 *(978-0-316-41770-9(X),* Black Dog & Leventhal Pubs. Inc.) Running Pr.

Lawson, Barbara Spilman. Maps Show Where to Go. 2016. (Spring Forward Ser.). (J). (gr. 2). *(978-1-4900-2245-1(7))* Benchmark Education Co.

Leithauser, Jessica. Maps Show Us the Way. 2006. (Rosen Real Readers Big Bookstm Ser.). (ENG., Illus.). 12p. (gr. 1-2). 33.50 *(978-1-4042-6218-8(0))* Rosen Publishing Group, Inc., The.

Levy, Janey. Mapping Australia, 1 vol. 2013. (Mapping the World Ser.). (ENG.). 24p. (J). (gr. 2-3). 25.27 *(978-1-4339-9104-2(7),* d0c35460-9e35-4d32-984c-c7e9bc6ff0e5) Stevens, Gareth Publishing LLLP.

—The Silk Road: Using a Map Scale to Measure Distances, 1 vol. 2010. (Math for the REAL World Ser.). (ENG., Illus.). 32p. (gr. 5-6). pap. 10.00 *(978-1-4042-5140-3(5),* 799bfe4c-ef04-44b8-9d05-f9cd0955f09d) Rosen Publishing Group, Inc., The.

—The Silk Road: Using A Map Scale to Measure Distances, 1 vol. 2004. (PowerMath: Proficiency Plus Ser.). (ENG., Illus.). 32p. (J). (gr. 5-6). lib. bdg. 28.93 *(978-1-4042-2938-9(8),* ba7efad1-2e8e-4dc2-ae37-00966f217408, PowerKids Pr.) Rosen Publishing Group, Inc., The.

Linde, Barbara. Mapping Europe. 2013. (Mapping the World Ser.). 24p. (J). (gr. 2-5). pap. 48.90 *(978-1-4339-9111-0(X))* Stevens, Gareth Publishing LLLP.

Linde, Barbara M. All about Climate Maps, 1 vol. 2018. (Map Basics Ser.). (ENG.). 24p. (gr. 2-3). lib. bdg. 24.27 *(978-1-5382-2915-6(3),* 5e44992b-f78b-4fa4-afd4-c6ea54152156) Stevens, Gareth Publishing LLLP.

—All about Physical Maps, 1 vol. 2018. (Map Basics Ser.). (ENG.). 24p. (gr. 2-3). lib. bdg. 24.27 *(978-1-5382-2916-3(1),* 7db9cc59-3dfc-46f1-8787-5ff135a268bc) Stevens, Gareth Publishing LLLP.

—All about Political Maps, 1 vol. 2018. (Map Basics Ser.). (ENG.). 24p. (gr. 2-3). lib. bdg. 24.27 *(978-1-5382-2917-0(X),* 273c0401-c4cd-4be6-9c03-e6c19984430b) Stevens, Gareth Publishing LLLP.

—All about Resource Maps, 1 vol. 2018. (Map Basics Ser.). (ENG.). 24p. (gr. 2-3). lib. bdg. 24.27 *(978-1-5382-2918-7(8),* 5002bfa9-e33f-44bb-8978-edd1de8072f0) Stevens, Gareth Publishing LLLP.

—All about Topographic Maps, 1 vol. 2018. (Map Basics Ser.). (ENG.). 24p. (gr. 2-3). lib. bdg. 24.27 *(978-1-5382-2920-0(X),* 2ff296d8-cd2e-47d7-a10a-9dab13927a8f) Stevens, Gareth Publishing LLLP.

—Mapping Africa. 2013. (Mapping the World Ser.). 24p. (J). (gr. 2-5). pap. 48.90 *(978-1-4339-9091-5(1))*; (ENG., Illus.). 25.27 *(978-1-4339-9089-2(X),* 4362a3e5-70af-4c34-aa2b-57f69628d211); (ENG., Illus.). pap. 9.15 *(978-1-4339-9090-8(3),* 2722cc9a-48b1-49aa-a234-08bb83d6fc42) Stevens, Gareth Publishing LLLP.

—Mapping Asia, 1 vol. 2013. (Mapping the World Ser.). 24p. (J). (gr. 2-3). (ENG.). 25.27 *(978-1-4339-9099-1(7),* 52a5e1c7-f58d-4e07-8a82-82a40b4a90f3); (ENG.). pap. 9.15 *(978-1-4339-9100-4(4),* c3bcd377-10be-45f2-bff5-c08183045020); pap. 48.90 *(978-1-4339-9101-1(2))* Stevens, Gareth Publishing LLLP.

—Mapping Europe, 1 vol. 2013. (Mapping the World Ser.). (ENG., Illus.). 24p. (J). (gr. 2-3). 25.27 *(978-1-4339-9109-7(8),* 12c47551-5b6a-46a5-8f23-68d3515ce64f); pap. 9.15 *(978-1-4339-9110-3(1),* d34cb65e-bace-4e20-b706-399d354c058b) Stevens, Gareth Publishing LLLP.

Lucas, Bruce. North America on the Map. 2013. (InfoMax Readers Ser.). (ENG.). 24p. (J). (gr. 2-3). pap. 49.50 *(978-1-4777-2432-3(X))*; (Illus.). pap. 8.25 *(978-1-4777-2431-6(1),* d802f550-008c-47c9-b3d8-c309294f6d41) Rosen Publishing Group, Inc., The. (Rosen Classroom).

MacReady, R. J. We Can Use a Map, 1 vol. 2012. (InfoMax Readers Ser.). (ENG., Illus.). 16p. (J). (gr. k-k). pap. 7.00 *(978-1-4488-8935-8(9),* 8d6a079e-01e1-42ac-8e40-e2b4a87d33be, Rosen Classroom) Rosen Publishing Group, Inc., The.

Mahaney, Ian F. Climate Maps. 2009. (Map It! Ser.). 24p. (gr. 3-4). 42.50 *(978-1-61514-354-2(8),* PowerKids Pr.) Rosen Publishing Group, Inc., The.

—Physical Maps. (Map It! Ser.). 24p. (gr. 3-4). 2009. 42.50 *(978-1-61514-355-9(6),* PowerKids Pr.) 2006. (ENG., Illus.). (YA). lib. bdg. 26.27 *(978-1-4042-3054-5(8),* 41849798-859d-4271-b8ee-9b6f469f2661) Rosen Publishing Group, Inc., The.

—Political Maps. (Map It! Ser.). 24p. (gr. 3-4). 2009. 42.50 *(978-1-61514-356-6(4),* PowerKids Pr.) 2006. (ENG., Illus.). (YA). lib. bdg. 26.27 *(978-1-4042-3055-2(6),* e19a72c5-1a68-43e6-a44c-4a2e671f4db4) Rosen Publishing Group, Inc., The.

—Road Maps. 2009. (Map It! Ser.). 24p. (gr. 3-4). 42.50 *(978-1-61514-357-3(2),* PowerKids Pr.) Rosen Publishing Group, Inc., The.

—Topographic Maps. (Map It! Ser.). 24p. (gr. 3-4). 2009. 42.50 *(978-1-61514-358-0(0),* PowerKids Pr.) 2006. (ENG., Illus.). (YA). lib. bdg. 26.27 *(978-1-4042-3053-8(X),* 5978b795-85c3-4042-a78b-344be404a65e) Rosen Publishing Group, Inc., The.

—Weather Maps. 2009. (Map It! Ser.). 24p. (gr. 3-4). 42.50 *(978-1-61514-359-7(9),* PowerKids Pr.) Rosen Publishing Group, Inc., The.

Make It Work Geography, 4 vol. set. 2003. (gr. 4-8). 59.00 *(978-0-7166-5124-6(6))* World Bk., Inc.

Map Basics, 12 vols. 2014. (Map Basics Ser.). 24p. (J). (gr. 2-3). (ENG.). 145.62 *(978-1-4824-1062-4(1),*

805ae259-1a4e-42bc-99bf-a1332e34e670); pap. 48.90 *(978-1-4824-1573-5(9))* Stevens, Gareth Publishing LLLP.
Map Mysteries, 6 vols., Pack. (gr. k-1). 23.00 *(978-0-7635-9071-0(1))* Rigby Education.
Map Skills for Today Gr. 1 -revised 2003- rev. ed. 2003. (YA). *(978-0-8374-0000-6(7))* Weekly Reader Corp.
Mapping Antarctica. 2013. (Mapping the World Ser.). 24p. (J). (gr. 2-5). pap. 48.90 *(978-1-4339-9096-0(2))* Stevens, Gareth Publishing LLLP.
Mapping Australia. 2013. (Mapping the World Ser.). 24p. (J). (gr. 2-5). pap. 48.90 *(978-1-4339-9106-6(3))* Stevens, Gareth Publishing LLLP.
Mapping Specialists. US & World Map Outlines, Vol. 8305. 2004. (Power Practice Ser.). (Illus.). 128p. (J). pap. 12.99 *(978-1-59198-075-9(5)*, 8305) Creative Teaching Pr., Inc.
Mapping The World, 14 vols. 2013. (Mapping the World Ser.). 24p. (J). (gr. 2-3). (ENG.). 176.89 *(978-1-4339-9674-0(X)*, d7085ee4-20f3-497f-9915-58980e1a523c); pap. 57.05 *(978-1-4339-9759-4(2))*; pap. 342.30 *(978-1-4339-9760-0(6))* Stevens, Gareth Publishing LLLP.
Matteson, Adrienne. Using Digital Maps. Petelinsek, Kathleen, illus. 2013. (Explorer Library: Information Explorer Ser.). (ENG.). 32p. (J). (gr. 4-8). 32.07 *(978-1-62431-129-1(6)*, 202836); pap. 14.21 *(978-1-62431-261-8(6)*, 202838) Cherry Lake Publishing.
Maurer, Tracy Nelson. Using Economic & Resource Maps. 2016. (Searchlight Books (tm) — What Do You Know about Maps? Ser.). (ENG., Illus.). 40p. (J). (gr. 3-5). 30.65 *(978-1-5124-0951-2(0)*, 13bcb8a7-1238-4e73-bbee-ce32e6ebde1a, Lerner Pubns.) Lerner Publishing Group.
—Using Road Maps & GPS. 2016. (Searchlight Books (tm) — What Do You Know about Maps? Ser.). (ENG., Illus.). 40p. (J). (gr. 3-5). 30.65 *(978-1-5124-0952-9(9)*, 446c684c-5165-4c8f-a3ca-bca4f3c9073b, Lerner Pubns.) Lerner Publishing Group.
—Using Topographic Maps. 2016. (Searchlight Books (tm) — What Do You Know about Maps? Ser.). (ENG., Illus.). 40p. (J). (gr. 3-5). 30.65 *(978-1-5124-0948-2(0)*, 3922ad54-c647-4ca6-8db0-052267630b9c, Lerner Pubns.) Lerner Publishing Group.
McAneney, Caitie. The Compass Rose & Cardinal Directions, 1 vol. 2014. (Map Basics Ser.). (ENG.). 24p. (J). (gr. 2-3). 24.27 *(978-1-4824-1083-9(4)*, cc159901-e5cc-42be-bbb2-807ec3b9b6b7) Stevens, Gareth Publishing LLLP.
McKay, Sindy. We Both Read-My Town. Johnson, Meredith, illus. 2007. (We Both Read Ser.). 44p. (J). (gr. -1-2). 9.95 *(978-1-60115-001-1(6))*; pap. 5.99 *(978-1-60115-002-8(4))* Treasure Bay, Inc.
McRae, Anne. The Animal Atlas. De Luca, Daniela, illus. 2008. (ENG.). 29p. (J). (gr. -1-3). 16.95 *(978-88-88166-38-4(6))* McRae Bks. Srl ITA. Dist: Independent Pubs. Group.
Meachen Rau, Dana. Los Mapas / Maps, 1 vol. 2010. (Nuestro Planeta Es Importante / Earth Matters Ser.). (ENG & SPA.). 32p. (gr. 1-2). lib. bdg. 25.50 *(978-0-7614-3493-1(3)*, 8a57ae17-e33f-413e-978d-8517be711a70) Cavendish Square Publishing LLC.
—Los Mapas (Maps), 1 vol. 2010. (Nuestro Planeta Es Importante (Earth Matters) Ser.). (SPA.). 32p. (gr. 1-2). lib. bdg. 25.50 *(978-0-7614-3468-9(2)*, d150f204-d06a-47de-b638-de54d0a98829) Cavendish Square Publishing LLC.
—Maps, 1 vol. 2009. (Earth Matters Ser.). (ENG.). 32p. (gr. 1-2). pap. 9.23 *(978-0-7614-3571-6(9)*, 64f03cee-94b6-4ad7-8918-ce757713ed9a); lib. bdg. 25.50 *(978-0-7614-3046-9(6)*, 5c028b62-2e3a-424b-a75b-6611a6b9bbe2) Cavendish Square Publishing LLC.
Meredith, Susan Markowitz. Maps Are Useful. 2016. (Spring Forward Ser.). (J). (gr. 2). *(978-1-4900-9431-1(8))* Benchmark Education Co.
Michele, Tracey. Follow the Road Map. 2011. (Learn-Abouts Ser.). (Illus.). 16p. (J). pap. 7.95 *(978-1-59920-638-7(2))* Black Rabbit Bks.
Miles, Justin. Ultimate Mapping Guide for Kids. 2016. (ENG., Illus.). 96p. (J). (gr. 5-8). pap. 9.95 *(978-1-77085-741-4(9)*, 2bfe77db-577a-42b9-8824-14a7c0ac5b22) Firefly Bks., Ltd.
Mizielinska, Aleksandra & Mizielinski, Daniel. Maps. 2013. (ENG.). 112p. (J). (gr. 5-12). 37.99 *(978-0-7636-6896-9(6)*, Big Picture Press) Candlewick Pr.
—Maps Activity Book. 2015. (ENG., Illus.). 72p. (J). (gr. 2-5). 19.99 *(978-0-7636-7771-8(X)*, Big Picture Press) Candlewick Pr.
—Maps Poster Book. 2016. (ENG.). 56p. (J). (gr. 2-4). 22.00 *(978-0-7636-8835-6(5)*, Big Picture Press) Candlewick Pr.
Morris, Neil. The Atlas of Ancient Civilizations. De Luca, Daniela, illus. 2008. (ENG.). 28p. (J). (gr. -1-3). 17.95 *(978-88-900466-0-5(0))* McRae Bks. Srl ITA. Dist: Independent Pubs. Group.
Neighborhood. (J). (gr. 2). 3.80 *(978-0-8374-1451-5(2)*, 402) Weekly Reader Corp.
Nelson, Robin. Maps. 2005. (First Step Nonfiction — Geography Ser.). (ENG., Illus.). 8p. (J). (gr. k-2). pap. 5.99 *(978-0-8225-5393-9(7)*, 3a4c72ba-f27e-44dc-920a-5146f251b696) Lerner Publishing Group.
Oleksy, Walter. Maps in History. 2003. (Watts Library). (ENG., Illus.). 64p. (J). (gr. 5-7). pap. 8.95 *(978-0-531-16633-8(3)*, Watts, Franklin) Scholastic Library Publishing.
Olien, Rebecca. Looking at Maps & Globes (Rookie Read-About Geography: Map Skills) 2012. (Rookie Read-About Geography Ser.). (ENG., Illus.). 32p. (J). (gr. 1-2). pap. 5.95 *(978-0-531-29288-4(6)*, Children's Pr.) Scholastic Library Publishing.
—Map Keys (Rookie Read-About Geography: Map Skills) 2012. (Rookie Read-About Geography Ser.). (ENG.). 32p. (J). (gr. 1-2). pap. 5.95 *(978-0-531-29289-1(4)*, Children's Pr.) Scholastic Library Publishing.
—Map Keys (Rookie Read-About Geography: Map Skills) (Library Edition) 2012. (Rookie Read-About Geography Ser.). (ENG.). 32p. (J). (gr. 1-2). lib. bdg. 25.00 *(978-0-531-28965-5(6)*, Children's Pr.) Scholastic Library Publishing.
On the Right Track, 6, Pack. (gr. k-1). 23.00 *(978-0-7635-9070-3(3))* Rigby Education.
Our Book of Maps: Individual Title Six-Packs. (Discovery World Ser.). 24p. (gr. 1-2). 33.00 *(978-0-7635-8470-2(3))* Rigby Education.
Panchyk, Richard. Charting the World: Geography & Maps from Cave Paintings to GPS with 21 Activities. 2011. (For Kids Ser.: 36). (ENG.). 144p. (J). (gr. 4). pap. 19.99 *(978-1-56976-344-5(5))* Chicago Review Pr., Inc.
Pearson, Claudia. This Way, Watson! A Map & Directions Primer, 1 vol. 2017. (ENG.). 32p. (J). 12.99 *(978-1-4236-4765-2(3))* Gibbs Smith, Publisher.
Petersen, David & Petersen, Christine A. Maps & Globes. 2004. (True Bks.). (Illus.). (J). lib. bdg. 24.00 *(978-0-516-22044-4(6)*, Children's Pr.) Scholastic Library Publishing.
Phoenix Learning Resources Staff, ed. Exploring Maps Volume 1. 2009. (ENG.). pap., stu. ed. 11.95 *(978-0-7915-1539-6(7))* Phoenix Learning Resources, LLC.
Prior, Jennifer Overend. Map Skills, Grade 4. 2003. (Practice Makes Perfect Ser.). (ENG., Illus.). 48p. (gr. 4). pap. 5.99 *(978-0-7439-3729-0(5))* Teacher Created Resources, Inc.
Quinlan, Julia. Different Kinds of Maps. 2012. (How to Use Maps (Powerkids) Ser.). (ENG.). 24p. (J). (gr. 3-5). 19.05 *(978-1-5311-8666-1(1))* Perfection Learning Corp.
Quinlan, Julia J. Different Kinds of Maps, 1 vol. 2012. (How to Use Maps Ser.). (ENG.). 24p. (J). (gr. 2-3). pap. 9.25 *(978-1-4488-6268-9(X)*, 47cd5baf-f854-4e6f-9614-482fa728f126, PowerKids Pr.); lib. bdg. 26.27 *(978-1-4488-6155-2(1)*, 7eeb0131-8607-4145-889b-2cbc3036da94) Rosen Publishing Group, Inc., The.
—Keys, Legends, & Symbols in Maps. 2012. (How to Use Maps (Powerkids) Ser.). (ENG.). 24p. (J). (gr. 3-5). 19.05 *(978-1-5311-8665-4(3))* Perfection Learning Corp.
—Keys, Legends, & Symbols in Maps, 1 vol. 2012. (How to Use Maps Ser.). (ENG.). 24p. (J). (gr. 2-3). pap. 9.25 *(978-1-4488-6266-5(3)*, 5e6e0459-1e3e-468e-aa6c-c35d17e04ecc, PowerKids Pr.); lib. bdg. 26.27 *(978-1-4488-6154-5(3)*, e6095254-b505-4c99-9c8e-c32a705fc3fc) Rosen Publishing Group, Inc., The.
—Scale & Distance in Maps, 1 vol. 2012. (How to Use Maps Ser.). (ENG.). 24p. (J). (gr. 2-3). pap. 9.25 *(978-1-4488-6270-2(1)*, 79dc7d6c-0c82-4280-9fd8-474e4f3a3ac6, PowerKids Pr.); lib. bdg. 26.27 *(978-1-4488-6156-9(X)*, e5cc1a0c-e33b-4647-9a17-91a0d153ae0a) Rosen Publishing Group, Inc., The.
Rajczak, Kristen. Climate Zones. 2014. (Map Basics Ser.). (ENG.). 24p. (J). (gr. 2-5). 18.95 *(978-1-5311-8604-3(1))* Perfection Learning Corp.
—Types of Maps. 2014. (Map Basics Ser.). (ENG.). 24p. (J). (gr. 2-5). 18.95 *(978-1-5311-8603-6(3))* Perfection Learning Corp.
Rajczak Nelson, Kristen. The Climate Zones, 1 vol. 2014. (Map Basics Ser.). (ENG., Illus.). 24p. (J). (gr. 2-3). 24.27 *(978-1-4824-0800-3(7)*, d948cec8-f849-4113-bbdb-19a4cd9bddf6) Stevens, Gareth Publishing LLLP.
—Latitude & Longitude, 1 vol. 2014. (Map Basics Ser.). (ENG., Illus.). 24p. (J). (gr. 2-3). 24.27 *(978-1-4824-1078-5(8)*, 1695ff72-beb5-4be2-ab8f-fa657978a59b) Stevens, Gareth Publishing LLLP.
—Types of Maps, 1 vol. 2014. (Map Basics Ser.). (ENG., Illus.). 24p. (J). (gr. 2-3). 24.27 *(978-1-4824-1063-1(X)*, 6f5c7520-6be2-4483-af26-eec526c42699) Stevens, Gareth Publishing LLLP.
Rand McNally. Map It! Jr Landforms Boardbook. 2018. (ENG., Illus.). (J). bds. *(978-0-528-02089-6(7))* Rand McNally Canada.
—Map It! Jr Waterways Boardbook. 2018. (Map It! Jr Ser.). (ENG., Illus.). 20p. (J). bds. *(978-0-528-02034-6(X))* Rand McNally Canada.
Rand McNally Staff. Atlas Schoolhouse Beginner's Workbook. 2005. 128p. (J). pap. 7.95 *(978-0-528-93469-8(4))* Rand McNally.
—Atlas Schoolhouse Illustrated World Atlas. 2005. 112p. (J). 9.95 *(978-0-528-93458-2(9))* Rand McNally.
—Atlas Schoolhouse Intermediate World Atlas. 2005. 128p. (J). pap. 6.95 *(978-0-528-93460-5(0))* Rand McNally.
—Atlas Scoolhouse Beginner's World Atlas. 2005. 48p. (J). pap. 5.95 *(978-0-528-93463-6(5))* Rand McNally.
Rand McNally Staff, creator. Intermediate Geography & Map Activities. 2005. (Rand Mcnally Schoolhouse Ser.). (Illus.). 128p. per. 7.95 *(978-0-528-93470-4(8))* Rand McNally.
Ray, Kurt. A Historical Atlas of Kuwait, 1 vol. 2003. (Historical Atlases of South Asia, Central Asia, & the Middle East Ser.). (ENG., Illus.). 64p. (gr. 6-6). lib. bdg. 37.13 *(978-0-8239-3981-7(2)*, 843b5c28-1c1d-44ca-93ff-576bf656c840) Rosen Publishing Group, Inc., The.
Rice, Dona Herweck. Maps & Globes. rev. ed. 2018. (Social Studies: Informational Text Ser.). (ENG., Illus.). 24p. (J). (gr. 1-3). pap. 10.99 *(978-1-4258-2515-7(X))* Teacher Created Materials, Inc.
Ritchie, Scot. Follow That Map! A First Book of Mapping Skills. Ritchie, Scot, illus. 2009. (ENG., Illus.). 32p. (J). (gr. -1-2). 19.99 *(978-1-55453-274-2(4))* Kids Can Pr., Ltd. CAN. Dist: Hachette Bk. Group.
Roza, Greg. Mapping Antarctica, 1 vol. 2013. (Mapping the World Ser.). (ENG.). 24p. (J). (gr. 2-3). 25.27 *(978-1-4339-9094-6(6)*, dbc37a3b-8b48-4fc6-b81e-568110263a86); pap. 9.15 *(978-1-4339-9095-3(4)*, e4a3116d-4edd-4f00-8c0d-b6345cfdf14f) Stevens, Gareth Publishing LLLP.
—Tony Stewart, 1 vol. 2006. (NASCAR Champions Ser.). (ENG., Illus.). 24p. (J). (gr. 1-2). lib. bdg. 26.27 *(978-1-4042-3456-7(X)*, 66f5e9ac-162a-4988-837b-dea3f72d8da2) Rosen Publishing Group, Inc., The.
Rudgers, Stephanie. How We Use Maps, 1 vol. 2008. (Real Life Readers Ser.). (ENG.). 12p. (gr. 1-2). pap. 5.90 *(978-1-4042-7907-0(5)*, 84068124-6c73-4db2-b032-80b21d470e50, Rosen Classroom) Rosen Publishing Group, Inc., The.
Rusinek, Catherine. So Many Maps! Reading Different Kinds of Maps, 1 vol. 2008. (Real Life Readers Ser.). (ENG.). 24p. (gr. 3-4). pap. 8.25 *(978-1-4358-0133-2(4)*, d005468e-e785-4f7a-9c3e-eddf0edb3575, Rosen Classroom) Rosen Publishing Group, Inc., The.
Shannon, Terry Miller. The Key to City Maps. 2016. (Spring Forward Ser.). (J). (gr. 2). *(978-1-4900-9450-2(4))* Benchmark Education Co.
—Maps & More Maps. 2016. (Spring Forward Ser.). (J). (gr. 1). *(978-1-4900-9381-9(8))* Benchmark Education Co.
Shea, Therese M. Reading Map Keys, 1 vol. 2014. (Map Basics Ser.). (ENG.). 24p. (J). (gr. 2-3). 24.27 *(978-1-4824-1073-0(7)*, d513cf23-6d13-4f06-bbf5-561528a931e5) Stevens, Gareth Publishing LLLP.
Simons, Lisa M. Bolt. How to Read a Map. 2018. (Understanding the Basics Ser.). (ENG.). 24p. (J). (gr. 1-4). lib. bdg. 32.79 *(978-1-5038-2328-0(8)*, 212203) Child's World, Inc, The.
Sundance/Newbridge LLC Staff. Maps & Globes. 2004. (Reading PowerWorks Ser.). (gr. 1-3). 37.50 *(978-0-7608-9747-8(6))*; pap. 6.10 *(978-0-7608-9748-5(4))* Sundance/Newbridge Educational Publishing.
Sweeney, Joan. Me on the Map. 2019. (Me... Books! Ser.). (ENG.). 32p. (J). (gr. k-2). 18.96 *(978-1-64310-820-9(4))* Penworthy Co., LLC, The.
—Me on the Map. Leng, Qin, illus. 2018. 32p. (J). (gr. -1-2). 14.99 *(978-1-5247-7200-0(3)*, Knopf Bks. for Young Readers); pap. 8.99 *(978-1-5247-7201-7(1)*, Dragonfly Bks.) Random Hse. Children's Bks.
Taylor, Barbara. Looking at Maps. 2007. (Geography Skills/Watts Ser.). (Illus.). 46p. (J). (gr. 4-7). lib. bdg. 32.80 *(978-1-59920-050-7(3))* Black Rabbit Bks.
The Atlas of the Seven Continents, 10 vols. 2003. (Atlas of the Seven Continents Ser.). (ENG., Illus.). (J). (gr. 3-3). 131.35 *(978-0-8239-6996-8(7)*, 70e3b7cf-2a7a-4f09-aa39-2d8d3f437b72) Rosen Publishing Group, Inc., The.
Thomas, Isabel. You Are Here; Maps & Why We Use Them: Band 12/Copper. 2017. (Collins Big Cat Ser.). (ENG., Illus.). 32p. (J). pap. 9.99 *(978-0-00-820874-5(3))* HarperCollins Pubs. Ltd. GBR. Dist: Independent Pubs. Group.
Thompson, Sharon. Map Skills: Grade 1. Poitras, Tara & Brooks, Whitney, eds. 2003. (Basic Skills & Beyond Ser.). 48p. (gr. 1-1). pap. 7.99 *(978-0-88724-959-4(0)*, CD-4700) Carson-Dellosa Publishing, LLC.
—Map Skills: Grade 3. Poitras, Tara & Brooks, Whitney, eds. 2003. (Basic Skills & Beyond Ser.). 48p. (gr. 3-3). pap. 7.99 *(978-0-88724-961-7(2)*, CD-4702) Carson-Dellosa Publishing, LLC.
—Map Skills: Grade 5. Poitras, Tara & Brooks, Whitney, eds. 2003. (Basic Skills & Beyond Ser.). 48p. (gr. 5-5). pap. 7.99 *(978-0-88724-963-1(9)*, CD-4704) Carson-Dellosa Publishing, LLC.
Torpie, Kate. Map Parts, 1 vol. 2008. (ENG., Illus.). 32p. (J). (gr. 1-4). pap. *(978-0-7787-4273-9(3))* Crabtree Publishing Co.
Torpie, Kate & Becker, Ann. Map Types, 1 vol. 2008. (ENG., Illus.). 32p. (J). (gr. 1-4). pap. *(978-0-7787-4274-6(1))* Crabtree Publishing Co.
Torpie, Kate & Sandvold, Rolf. Reading Maps, 1 vol. 2008. (All over the Map Ser.). (ENG., Illus.). 32p. (J). (gr. 1-4). pap. *(978-0-7787-4275-3(X))* Crabtree Publishing Co.
Vierow, Wendy. Africa, 1 vol. 2003. (Atlas of the Seven Continents Ser.). (ENG., Illus.). 24p. (YA). (gr. 3-3). lib. bdg. 26.27 *(978-0-8239-6687-5(9)*, 0ee1b8d3-3926-4bda-ad03-230ef0931a1d) Rosen Publishing Group, Inc., The.
—Asia, 1 vol. 2003. (Atlas of the Seven Continents Ser.). (ENG., Illus.). 24p. (YA). (gr. 3-3). lib. bdg. 26.27 *(978-0-8239-6689-9(5)*, e7190bc9-26c7-4a95-8753-6ea5ab6529f8) Rosen Publishing Group, Inc., The.
—North America. 2009. (Atlas of the Seven Continents Ser.). 24p. (gr. 3-3). 42.50 *(978-1-61511-481-8(5)*, PowerKids Pr.) Rosen Publishing Group, Inc., The.
Wade, Mary Dodson. Map Scales. 2012. (Rookie Read-About Geography Ser.). (ENG., Illus.). 32p. (J). pap. 5.95 *(978-0-531-29290-7(8))* Scholastic Library Publishing.
—Tipos de Mapas. 2005. (Rookie Espanol Geografia Ser.). (SPA., Illus.). 32p. (J). (gr. k-2). lib. bdg. 19.50 *(978-0-516-25243-8(7)*, Children's Pr.) Scholastic Library Publishing.
Waldron, Melanie. Mapping the World, 1 vol. 2013. (Let's Get Mapping! Ser.). (ENG., Illus.). 32p. (J). (gr. 2-4). pap. 8.29 *(978-1-4109-4910-3(9)*, 120892, Raintree) Capstone.
—Types of Maps, 1 vol. 2013. (Let's Get Mapping! Ser.). (ENG., Illus.). 32p. (J). (gr. 2-4). pap. 8.29 *(978-1-4109-4911-0(7)*, 120893, Raintree) Capstone.
Walker, Rob. Mapping Towns & Cities, 1 vol. 2011. (Mapping Our World Ser.). (ENG.). 32p. (gr. 4-4). 31.21 *(978-1-60870-120-9(4)*, e4bbbf46-62d4-4609-8b0a-8784a2f876ee) Cavendish Square Publishing LLC.
Wallace, Karen. Collins Big Cat Phonics for Letters & Sounds - Maps: Band 04/Blue, Bd. 4. Bacchin, Giorgio, illus. 2018. (Collins Big Cat Phonics Ser.). (ENG.). 16p. (J). (gr. k-1). pap. 6.99 *(978-0-00-825165-9(7))* HarperCollins Pubs. Ltd. GBR. Dist: Independent Pubs. Group.
Waxman, Malcolm & Porter, Malcolm. Atlas of South America & Antarctica, 1 vol. 2010. (Atlases of the World Ser.). (ENG., Illus.). 48p. (YA). (gr. 5-5). 34.47 *(978-1-4358-8459-5(0)*, 507e3b28-3aa1-479a-b0ab-d765ce01bedb, Rosen Reference) Rosen Publishing Group, Inc., The.
The Western Hemisphere Through the Five Themes of Geography Map Activities Book plus 5 Transparencies. 2005. (Western Hemisphere Through the Five Themes of Geography Ser.). 16p. 55.95 *(978-1-4042-5159-5(6)*, Rosen Classroom) Rosen Publishing Group, Inc., The.
Where on Earth? Mapping Parts of the World. 2017. (Where on Earth? Mapping Parts of the World Ser.). 24p. (gr. 1-2). pap. 48.90 *(978-1-5382-0239-5(5))*; (ENG.). lib. bdg. 145.62 *(978-1-5382-0238-8(7)*, 51fc173e-fe3e-44f7-bb4f-069adbb25f60) Stevens, Gareth Publishing LLLP.
The Whole World in Your Hands. (Discovery Readers Ser.). 48p. (J). pap. 3.95 *(978-0-8249-5315-7(0)*, Ideals Pubns.) Worthy Publishing.
Williams, Rozanne. Can You Read a Map? 2017. (Learn-To-Read Ser.). (ENG., Illus.). (J). pap. 3.49 *(978-1-68310-239-7(8))* Pacific Learning, Inc.
Wolny, Philip. How Do You Read Maps?, 1 vol. 2018. (Let's Find Out! Social Studies Skills Ser.). (ENG.). 32p. (gr. 2-3). lib. bdg. 26.06 *(978-1-5081-0701-9(7)*, 8a0f10c4-9d85-4f86-98dd-028d7a17c207, Britannica Educational Publishing) Rosen Publishing Group, Inc., The.
Wood, Alix. Dinosaurs on the Map, 1 vol. 2014. (Fun with Map Skills Ser.). (ENG., Illus.). 32p. (J). (gr. 4-4). lib. bdg. 27.93 *(978-1-4777-6960-7(9)*, fbd7958b-2f4e-4621-91ed-cd3e6126ba14, PowerKids Pr.) Rosen Publishing Group, Inc., The.
—Disasters on the Map, 1 vol. 2014. (Fun with Map Skills Ser.). (ENG., Illus.). 32p. (J). (gr. 4-4). lib. bdg. 27.93 *(978-1-4777-6976-8(5)*, 83fbca92-d2f6-48fe-b323-ba803fef9377, PowerKids Pr.) Rosen Publishing Group, Inc., The.
—Hunting on the Map, 1 vol. 2014. (Fun with Map Skills Ser.). (ENG., Illus.). 32p. (J). (gr. 4-4). lib. bdg. 27.93 *(978-1-4777-6980-5(3)*, 4e639af8-69d8-445c-a9d8-68e05650343a, PowerKids Pr.) Rosen Publishing Group, Inc., The.
—The Military on the Map, 1 vol. 2014. (Fun with Map Skills Ser.). (ENG., Illus.). 32p. (J). (gr. 4-4). lib. bdg. 27.93 *(978-1-4777-6968-3(4)*, 9bc2927d-4876-4d11-8bcf-ea6cb7f98eb9, PowerKids Pr.) Rosen Publishing Group, Inc., The.
—Pirates on the Map, 1 vol. 2014. (Fun with Map Skills Ser.). (ENG.). 32p. (J). (gr. 4-4). lib. bdg. 27.93 *(978-1-4777-6964-5(1)*, fec8c55f-d565-4b07-9de6-666ba09f7e0d, PowerKids Pr.) Rosen Publishing Group, Inc., The.
—Sports on the Map, 1 vol. 2014. (Fun with Map Skills Ser.). (ENG., Illus.). 32p. (J). (gr. 4-4). lib. bdg. 27.93 *(978-1-4777-6972-0(2)*, 00276323-63ed-4b71-9d5d-285a2dddebc8, PowerKids Pr.) Rosen Publishing Group, Inc., The.
X Marks the Spot, 6 Packs. (gr. k-1). 23.00 *(978-0-7635-9064-2(9))* Rigby Education.
Your Community. (J). (gr. 3). 3.80 *(978-0-8374-1452-2(0)*, 403) Weekly Reader Corp.
Zelon, Helen. The Endeavor SRTM: Mapping the Earth. 2009. (Space Missions Ser.). 24p. (gr. 3-4). 42.50 *(978-1-60853-118-9(X)*, PowerKids Pr.) Rosen Publishing Group, Inc., The.
Zoom in on Maps, 14 vols. 2017. (Zoom in on Maps Ser.). (ENG.). (J). (gr. 2-2). lib. bdg. 179.20 *(978-0-7660-9239-6(9)*, 4674625c-0ba1-44a3-97c7-eb805b47668b) Enslow Publishing, LLC.
Zuravicky, Orli. Map Math: Learning about Latitude & Longitude Using Coordinate Systems, 1 vol. 2010. (Math for the REAL World Ser.). (ENG.). 32p. (gr. 5-6). pap. 10.00 *(978-1-4042-5133-5(2)*, 6fe8d50d-49cd-4352-a9d0-83948f8ab6a8, PowerKids Pr.) Rosen Publishing Group, Inc., The.

MAPS, HISTORICAL

see Historical Geography—Maps

MARATHON, BATTLE OF, GREECE, 490 B.C.

Rice, Earle, Jr. Battle of Marathon. 2011. (Technologies & Strategies in Battle Ser.). (Illus.). 48p. (J). (gr. 4-7). lib. bdg. 29.95 *(978-1-61228-077-6(3))* Mitchell Lane Pubs.

MARCH FAMILY (FICTITIOUS CHARACTERS)

Novel Units. Little Women Novel Units Student Packet. 2019. (ENG.). (YA). pap. 13.99 *(978-1-58130-631-6(8)*, Novel Units, Inc.) Classroom Library Co.
—Little Women Novel Units Teacher Guide. 2019. (ENG.). (YA). pap. 12.99 *(978-1-58130-630-9(X)*, Novel Units, Inc.) Classroom Library Co.

MARCH FAMILY (FICTITIOUS CHARACTERS)—FICTION

Alcott, Louisa. Jo's Boys. 2013. (Works of Louisa May Alcott). 366p. reprint ed. lthr. 79.00 *(978-0-7812-1642-5(7))* Reprint Services Corp.
—Little Women. 2007. 264p. (YA). 11.95 *(978-1-933486-01-7(5))* Core Knowledge Foundation.
—Little Women. unabr. ed. 2004. (Chrysalis Childrens Classics Ser.). (Illus.). 190p. (YA). pap. *(978-1-84365-049-2(5)*, Pavilion Children's Books) Pavilion Bks.
—Little Women. 2013. (Works of Louisa May Alcott). 451p. reprint ed. lthr. 79.00 *(978-0-7812-1627-2(3))* Reprint Services Corp.
—Little Women. 2008. (Puffin Classics Ser.). (gr. k-3). lib. bdg. 19.65 *(978-0-613-86261-5(9))* Turtleback.
—Little Women: Bring the Classics to Life. 2008. (Bring the Classics to Life Ser.). (Illus.). 72p. (gr. 1-12). pap., act. bk. ed. 10.95 *(978-1-55576-047-2(3)*, EDCTR-103B) EDCON Publishing Group.
—Mujercitas.Tr. of Little Women. (SPA., Illus.). 192p. (YA). 11.95 *(978-84-7281-101-0(8)*, AF1101) Auriga, Ediciones S.A. ESP. Dist: Continental Bk. Co., Inc.
—Mujercitas. 2004.Tr. of Little Women. (SPA.). lib. bdg. *(978-1-4135-2067-5(7))* El Cid Editor Incorporated.
—Mujercitas. (Coleccion Estrella).Tr. of Little Women. (SPA., Illus.). 64p. (J). 14.95 *(978-950-11-0010-5(3)*, SGM010) Sigmar ARG. Dist: Continental Bk. Co., Inc.
Alcott, Louisa May. The Annotated Little Women. 2015. (Annotated Bks.: 0). (ENG., Illus.). 744p. (gr. 11-17). 39.95 *(978-0-393-07219-8(3)*, 7219) Norton, W. W. & Co., Inc.
—Good Wives. 2013. (Vintage Children's Classics Ser.). 464p. (J). (gr. 4-7). pap. 11.99 *(978-0-09-957369-2(5))* Penguin Random Hse. GBR. Dist: Independent Pubs. Group.
—Little Women. 2013. (Vintage Children's Classics Ser.). (Illus.). 432p. (J). (gr. 4-7). pap. 10.99 *(978-0-09-957296-1(6))* Penguin Random Hse. GBR. Dist: Independent Pubs. Group.
Dale, Katie. Little Women: Band 18/Pearl (Collins Big Cat) Selivanova, Elena, illus. 2016. (Collins Big Cat Ser.). (ENG.). 80p. (J). pap. 11.99 *(978-0-00-814737-2(X))* HarperCollins Pubs. Ltd. GBR. Dist: Independent Pubs. Group.
Eiselein, Gregory, et al. Little Women. 2003. (Norton Critical Editions Ser.: 0). (ENG., Illus.). 688p. (C). pap. 13.00 *(978-0-393-97614-4(9)*, 97614) Norton, W. W. & Co., Inc.
Francis, Pauline & Alcott, Louisa. Little Women. 2003. (Fast Track Classics Ser.). (Illus.). 48p. (YA). pap. *(978-0-237-52533-0(X))* Evans Brothers, Ltd.

MNO

Lauter, Richard, illus. Little Women. (Young Collector's Illustrated Classics Ser.). 192p. (J). 9.95 *(978-1-56156-371-5(4))* Kidsbooks, LLC.
Lindskoog, Kathryn, ed. Little Women. Chitouras, Barbara, illus. 2003. (Classics for Young Readers Ser.). 432p. (J). per. 12.99 *(978-0-87552-734-5(5))* P & R Publishing.

MARCONI, GUGLIELMO, 1874-1937

Auch, Allison. Electrifying Personalities & Personalidades Electrizantes: 6 English, 6 Spanish Adaptations. 2011. (ENG & SPA.). (J). 97.00 net. *(978-1-4108-5713-2(1))* Benchmark Education Co.
Kulling, Monica. Making Contact! Marconi Goes Wireless. Rudnicki, Richard, illus. (Great Idea Ser.: 5). 32p. (J). (gr. k-3). 2016. pap. 6.99 *(978-1-101-91842-5(X))* 2013. 17.95 *(978-1-77049-378-0(6))* Tundra Bks. CAN. (Tundra Bks.). Dist: Penguin Random Hse. LLC.
Zannos, Susan. Guglielmo Marconi & Radio Waves. 2004. (Uncharted, Unexplored, & Unexplained Ser.). (Illus.). 48p. (J). (gr. 4-8). lib. bdg. 29.95 *(978-1-58415-265-1(6))* Mitchell Lane Pubs.

MARFAN SYNDROME

Mitchell, Lori, illus. & compiled by. Marfan Syndrome A-Z. Mitchell, Lori, compiled by. 2007. 36p. (J). pap. *(978-0-918335-14-2(0))* National Marfan Foundation, The.

MARIE ANTOINETTE, QUEEN, CONSORT OF LOUIS XVI, KING OF FRANCE, 1755-1793

Daynes, Katie. Marie Antoinette. Mistry, Nilesh, illus. 2005. 64p. (J). 8.95 *(978-0-7945-1049-7(3)*, Usborne) EDC Publishing.
Hockinson, Liz. Marie Antoinette "Madame Deficit" Malone, Peter, illus. 2011. (Thinking Girl's Treasury of Dastardly Dames Ser.). (ENG.). 32p. (J). (gr. 3-8). 18.95 *(978-0-9834256-4-9(7))* Goosebottom Bks. LLC.
Lotz, Nancy & Phillips, Carlene. Marie Antoinette & the Decline of French Monarchy. 2004. (World Leaders Ser.). (Illus.). 160p. (YA). (gr. 6-12). lib. bdg. 26.95 *(978-1-931798-28-0(1))* Reynolds, Morgan Inc.
Rau, Dana Meachen. Who Was Marie Antoinette? 2015. (Who Was... ? Ser.). lib. bdg. 16.00 *(978-0-606-37554-2(6))* Turtleback.
Rau, Dana Meachen & Who HQ. Who Was Marie Antoinette? O'Brien, John, illus. 2015. (Who Was? Ser.). 112p. (J). (gr. 3-7). 6.99 *(978-0-448-48310-8(6)*, Penguin Workshop) Penguin Young Readers Group.
Schwartz, Heather. Marie Antoinette: The Controversial Queen of France, 1 vol. rev. ed. 2012. (Social Studies: Informational Text Ser.). (ENG.). 32p. (J). (gr. 4-8). pap. 11.99 *(978-1-4333-5012-2(2))* Teacher Created Materials, Inc.
Webb, Sarah Powers. Marie Antoinette: Fashionable Queen or Greedy Royal? 2015. (Perspectives on History Ser.). (ENG., Illus.). 32p. (J). (gr. 3-6). pap. 7.95 *(978-1-4914-2216-8(5)*, 127727) Capstone.

MARIE ANTOINETTE, QUEEN, CONSORT OF LOUIS XVI, KING OF FRANCE, 1755-1793—FICTION

Turetsky, Bianca. The Time-Traveling Fashionista at the Palace of Marie Antoinette. 2013. (Time-Traveling Fashionista Ser.: 2). (ENG., Illus.). 272p. (J). (gr. 3-7). pap. 9.00 *(978-0-316-10535-4(X)*, Poppy) Little, Brown Bks. for Young Readers.

MARIJUANA

Allen, John. Thinking Critically: Legalizing Marijuana. 2015. (ENG., Illus.). 80p. (J). lib. bdg. *(978-1-60152-782-0(9))* ReferencePoint Pr., Inc.
Barbour, Scott. Should Marijuana Be Legalized? 2010. (In Controversy Ser.). 96p. (YA). (gr. 7-12). 41.27 *(978-1-60152-106-4(5))* ReferencePoint Pr., Inc.
Benjamin, Daniel. Marijuana, 1 vol. 2013. (Dangerous Drugs Ser.). (ENG.). 64p. (gr. 6-6). 36.93 *(978-1-60870-825-3(X)*, b73a9391-ef6f-4495-a3c9-9b6c896e7f64); pap. 16.28 *(978-1-62712-061-6(0)*, b33d2273-f84a-4a86-94e3-5f04948ab872) Cavendish Square Publishing LLC.
bjornlund, lydia. Marijuana. 2011. (Compact Research Ser.). 96p. (YA). (gr. 7-12). lib. bdg. 43.93 *(978-1-60152-160-6(X))* ReferencePoint Pr., Inc.
Claybome, Leigh. The Benefits of Medical Marijuana: From Cancer to PTSD, Vol. 5. 2018. (Marijuana Today Ser.). 80p. (J). (gr. 7). lib. bdg. 33.27 *(978-1-4222-4108-0(4))* Mason Crest.
—Marijuana: Facts, Figures, & Opinions, Vol. 5. 2018. (Marijuana Today Ser.). 80p. (J). (gr. 7). lib. bdg. 33.27 *(978-1-4222-4106-6(8))* Mason Crest.
Collins, Anna & Marcovitz, Hal. Marijuana: Abuse & Legalization, 1 vol. 2016. (Drug Education Library). (ENG.). 104p. (YA). (gr. 7-7). lib. bdg. 39.08 *(978-1-5345-6001-7(7)*, b9302d17-39b4-4329-b8cf-c6807c0aba7d, Lucent Pr.) Greenhaven Publishing LLC.
Connolly, Sean. Marijuana. 2009. (Straight Talking Ser.). (ENG., Illus.). 48p. (YA). (gr. 8-12). pap. *(978-1-895058-54-3(6))* Saunders Bk. Co.
Cornell, Kari A. Marijuana & Its Dangers. 2019. (Drugs & Their Dangers Ser.). (ENG.). 80p. (YA). (gr. 6-12). 41.27 *(978-1-68282-709-3(7)*, BrightPoint Pr.) ReferencePoint Pr., Inc.
Cunningham, Anne C. Critical Perspectives on Legalizing Marijuana, 1 vol. 2016. (Analyzing the Issues Ser.). (ENG.). 208p. (gr. 8-8). 50.93 *(978-0-7660-7669-3(5)*, 3d0fb791-907a-4c69-a4bf-f22a82eac5e7) Enslow Publishing, LLC.
Eboch, M. M., ed. Legalization of Marijuana, 1 vol. 2019. (Introducing Issues with Opposing Viewpoints Ser.). (ENG.). 120p. (gr. 7-10). pap. 29.30 *(978-1-5345-0668-8(3)*, 1cb02d88-1607-4e5e-b438-b8ee0b11d190) Greenhaven Publishing LLC.
Giddens, Sandra. Everything You Need to Know about the Risks of Marijuana, 1 vol. 2019. (Need to Know Library). (ENG., Illus.). 64p. (J). (gr. 6-6). pap. 13.95 *(978-1-5081-8767-7(3)*, 58077fea-8d57-4bcc-b461-0f401d92ba6b) Rosen Publishing Group, Inc., The.
Gillard, Arthur, ed. Marijuana, 1 vol. 2009 (At Issue Ser.). (ENG., Illus.). 128p. (J). (gr. 10-12). 41.03 *(978-0-7377-4432-3(4)*, 5e9477aa-9baa-468a-a093-9490f683f26a);No. 9. pap. 28.80 *(978-0-7377-4433-0(2)*, e746fa93-6d65-47fc-9a0a-8dd5ae578977) Greenhaven Publishing LLC. (Greenhaven Publishing).
—Medical Marijuana, 1 vol. 2013. (Issues That Concern You Ser.). (ENG., Illus.). 104p. (gr. 7-10). lib. bdg. 43.63 *(978-0-7377-6297-6(7)*, b5d67577-ac6c-45f2-aeed-31cfdcad1f5b, Greenhaven Publishing) Greenhaven Publishing LLC.
Goldstein, Margaret J. Legalizing Marijuana: Promises & Pitfalls. 2016. (ENG., Illus.). 104p. (YA). (gr. 7-12). 35.99 *(978-1-4677-9243-1(8)*, 669a1146-d4dc-454d-a890-47244eaba116); E-Book 54.65 *(978-1-5124-1144-7(2))* Lerner Publishing Group. (Twenty-First Century Bks.).
Gottfried, Ted & Harkrader, Lisa. Marijuana, 1 vol. 2010. (Drug Facts Ser.). (ENG.). 32p. (gr. 5-5). 31.21 *(978-0-7614-4351-3(7)*, 502d8204-c470-4086-8a97-f92c43d1c1aa) Cavendish Square Publishing LLC.
Gross, Frederick C. & Chace, Reeve. The Truth about Marijuana, 1 vol. 2011. (Drugs & Consequences Ser.). (ENG.). 64p. (YA). (gr. 5-5). lib. bdg. 37.13 *(978-1-4488-4639-9(0)*, 13d9efb5-ca58-4208-8002-0fcfe78632bc) Rosen Publishing Group, Inc., The.
Hand, Carol. Marijuana. 2018. (Drugs in Real Life Ser.). (ENG., Illus.). 112p. (J). (gr. 6-12). lib. bdg. 41.36 *(978-1-5321-1417-5(6)*, 28816, Essential Library) ABDO Publishing Co.
Harrison Adams, Troon & Harrison, Troon. Marijuana. 2011. (ENG.). 48p. (J). pap. *(978-0-7787-5516-6(9))*; (gr. 4-7). lib. bdg. *(978-0-7787-5509-8(6))* Crabtree Publishing Co.
Heing, Bridey. Marijuana Abuse, 1 vol. 2018. (Overcoming Addiction Ser.). (ENG.). 64p. (gr. 7-7). 36.13 *(978-1-5081-7944-3(1)*, 96097747-d6d9-4c10-b093-c510e0ce03fe) Rosen Publishing Group, Inc., The.
Hillstrom, Kevin. Medical Marijuana, 1 vol. 2014. (Hot Topics Ser.). (ENG., Illus.). 104p. (gr. 7-7). lib. bdg. 41.03 *(978-1-4205-0871-0(7)*, a05bb82e-a259-485a-9327-814116a4eb69, Lucent Pr.) Greenhaven Publishing LLC.
Ingram, Scott. Marijuana. 2008. (Junior Drug Awareness Ser.). (ENG., Illus.). 110p. (gr. 5-8). lib. bdg. 30.00 *(978-0-7910-9695-6(5)*, P145754, Facts On File) Infobase Holdings, Inc.
Morkes, Andrew. Growing Career Opportunities in the Marijuana Industry, Vol. 5. 2018. (Marijuana Today Ser.). 80p. (J). (gr. 7). lib. bdg. 33.27 *(978-1-4222-4104-2(1))* Mason Crest.
Nelson, Julie. Marijuana in Society, Vol. 5. 2018. (Marijuana Today Ser.). 80p. (J). (gr. 7). lib. bdg. 33.27 *(978-1-4222-4105-9(X))* Mason Crest.
—Marijuana's Harmful Effects on Youth, Vol. 5. 2018. (Marijuana Today Ser.). 80p. (J). (gr. 7). lib. bdg. 33.27 *(978-1-4222-4107-3(6))* Mason Crest.
Netzley, Patricia D. Is Legalized Marijuana Good for Society? 2015. (ENG., Illus.). 96p. (J). lib. bdg. *(978-1-60152-774-5(8))* ReferencePoint Pr., Inc.
Perritano, John. Marijuana & Synthetics, Vol. 13. Becker, Sara, ed. 2016. (Drug Addiction & Recovery Ser.). (Illus.). 64p. (J). (gr. 7). 23.95 *(978-1-4222-3606-2(4))* Mason Crest.
Sanna, E. J. Marijuana: Mind-Altering Weed. Henningfield, Jack E., ed. 2012. (Illicit & Misused Drugs Ser.). 128p. (J). (gr. 7). 24.95 *(978-1-4222-2435-9(X))*; pap. 14.95 *(978-1-4222-2454-0(6))* Mason Crest.
—Marijuana: Mind-Altering Weed. 2009. (Illicit & Misused Drugs Ser.). (Illus.). 128p. (J). (gr. 7-18). lib. bdg. 24.95 *(978-1-4222-0158-9(9))* Mason Crest.
Steffens, Bradley. Is Marijuana Harmful? 2016. (ENG.). 80p. (J). (gr. 5-12). lib. bdg. *(978-1-68282-097-1(1))* ReferencePoint Pr., Inc.
Tardiff, Joseph, ed. Marijuana, 1 vol. 2007. (Contemporary Issues Companion Ser.). (ENG., Illus.). 216p. (gr. 10-12). lib. bdg. 42.53 *(978-0-7377-2775-3(6)*, 0c55b51f-eeed-4934-8dbe-4623ee74a9eb, Greenhaven Publishing) Greenhaven Publishing LLC.
Ventura, Marne. The Debate about Legalizing Marijuana. 2018. (Pros & Cons Ser.). (ENG., Illus.). 48p. (J). (gr. 5-6). pap. 11.95 *(978-1-63517-594-3(1)*, 1635175941); lib. bdg. 34.21 *(978-1-63517-522-6(4)*, 1635175224) North Star Editions. (Focus Readers).
—Legalizing Marijuana. 2018. (Illus.). 48p. (J). *(978-1-4896-9599-4(0)*, AV2 by Weigl) Weigl Pubs., Inc.
Waters, Rosa. Legal & Developmental Consequences. Borus, Joshua, ed. 2014. (Downside of Drugs Ser.). 48p. (J). (gr. 5-18). pap. 10.95 *(978-1-4222-3192-0(5))* Mason Crest.
—Marijuana: Legal & Developmental Consequences. Borus, Joshua, ed. 2014. (Downside of Drugs Ser.). (ENG., Illus.). 48p. (J). (gr. 5-18). lib. bdg. 20.95 *(978-1-4222-3022-0(8))* Mason Crest.

MARIJUANA—FICTION

Bussereth, Bianca. Sky Rod. 2010. 80p. pap. 6.95 *(978-1-60594-391-6(6)*, Llumina Pr.) Aeon Publishing Inc.
Dirkes, Craig. Sucktown, Alaska. 2017. (ENG.). 352p. (YA). (gr. 9-12). 17.95 *(978-1-63079-055-4(9)*, 132182, Switch Pr.) Capstone.
France, Emily. Zen & Gone. 2019. (ENG.). 1p. (YA). (gr. 9). pap. 10.99 *(978-1-64129-031-9(5)*, Soho Teen) Soho Pr., Inc.
It's Just a Plant: A Children's Story about Marijuana. 2nd rev. ed. 2006.Tr. of Www. justaplant. com. (J). per. 20.00 *(978-0-9760117-2-9(7))* Magic Propaganda Mill.
Stone, Heather Duffy. Over the Tracks. 2015. (Suspended Ser.). (ENG.). 96p. (YA). (gr. 6-12). 27.99 *(978-1-4677-5711-9(X)*, a27c9ee2-e68b-48fe-b301-4ac7ea30dcaa, Darby Creek) Lerner Publishing Group.

MARINE ANIMALS

see also Corals; Fishes; Freshwater Animals

Alderton, David. Ocean Animals Around the World. 2014. (Animals Around the World Ser.). (ENG., Illus.). 32p. (J). (gr. 2-5). 31.35 *(978-1-62588-199-1(1)*, 19261, Smart Apple Media) Black Rabbit Bks.
—Sharks & Sea Creatures Around the World. 2014. (Animals Around the World Ser.). (ENG., Illus.). 32p. (J). (gr. 2-5). 31.35 *(978-1-62588-196-0(7)*, 19262, Smart Apple Media) Black Rabbit Bks.
Alkire, Jessie. Harp Seals. 2018. (Arctic Animals at Risk Ser.). (ENG., Illus.). 32p. (J). (gr. 3-6). lib. bdg. 32.79 *(978-1-5321-1696-4(9)*, 30680, Checkerboard Library) ABDO Publishing Co.
—Narwhals. 2018. (Arctic Animals at Risk Ser.). (ENG., Illus.). 32p. (J). (gr. 3-6). lib. bdg. 32.79 *(978-1-5321-1698-8(5)*, 30684, Checkerboard Library) ABDO Publishing Co.
Allen, Francesca, illus. Under the Sea. 2005. 10p. (J). 4.99 *(978-0-7945-0857-9(X)*, Usborne) EDC Publishing.
Allen, Nancy Kelly. What Sea Creature Is This? Brown, Gloria, illus. 2012. (J). *(978-1-933176-41-3(5))* Red Rock Pr., Inc.
Allgor, Marie. Endangered Ocean Animals, 1 vol. 2012. (Save Earth's Animals! Ser.). (ENG., Illus.). 24p. (J). (gr. 2-3). pap. 9.25 *(978-1-4488-7493-4(9)*, 5ec8bb72-e43f-43da-8122-870a8f7e979a, PowerKids Pr.) Rosen Publishing Group, Inc., The.
American Museum of Natural History, American Museum. ABC Oceans. 2014. (AMNH ABC Board Bks.). (Illus.). 18p. (J). (gr. -1-k). bds. 9.95 *(978-1-4549-1195-1(6))* Sterling Publishing Co., Inc.
Anastasio, Dina. Hiding in the Sea & Escondidos en el Mar: 6 English, 6 Spanish Adaptations. 2011. (ENG & SPA.). (J). 75.00 net. *(978-1-4108-5643-2(7))* Benchmark Education Co.
Anderson, Sheila. What Can Live in the Ocean? 2010. (First Step Nonfiction — Animal Adaptations Ser.). (gr. k-2). (ENG., Illus.). 24p. (J). pap. 6.99 *(978-0-7613-5673-8(8)*, 22ecf9d3-99ce-4c4c-a759-2b8891204f4d); pap. 33.92 *(978-0-7613-6906-6(6))* Lerner Publishing Group.
Animales Marinos, 6 vols. (Explorers. Exploradores Nonfiction Sets Ser.).Tr. of Marine Animals. (SPA.). 32p. (gr. 3-6). 44.95 *(978-0-7699-0627-0(3))* Shortland Pubns. (U. S. A.) Inc.
Animales Marinos. 2005. (Collection Abre Tus Ojos, Collection Eye Openers Ser.).Tr. of Marine Animals. (SPA.). (J). (gr. k-2). 6.95 *(978-950-11-0966-5(6))* Sigmar ARG. Dist: Iaconi, Mariuccia Bk. Imports.
Animals of the Ocean Series (Illus.). (J). (gr. 2-6). lib. bdg. 44.85 *(978-1-56674-947-3(6))* Forest Hse. Publishing Co., Inc.
Arnold, Quinn M. Seedlings: Stingrays. 2017. (Seedlings Ser.). (ENG., Illus.). 24p. (J). (gr. -1-1). pap. 10.99 *(978-1-62832-402-0(3)*, 20156, Creative Paperbacks) Creative Co., The.
Arnosky, Jim. All about Manatees. Arnosky, Jim, illus. 2008. (ENG., Illus.). 32p. (J). (gr. -1-3). pap. 6.99 *(978-0-439-90361-5(0)*, Scholastic Nonfiction) Scholastic, Inc.
AZ Books, creator. Lake Animals Moving & Talking. 2012. (Funny Trails Ser.). (ENG., Illus.). 10p. (J). (gr. -1-k). bds. 9.95 *(978-1-61889-216-4(9))* AZ Bks. LLC.
—Water Animals. 2013. (Sounds Around Us Ser.). (ENG., Illus.). 16p. (J). (gr. 1-3). bds. 17.95 *(978-1-61889-283-6(5))* AZ Bks. LLC.
—Who Lives in the Ocean? 2012. (Funny Animals Ser.). (ENG., Illus.). 10p. (J). (gr. -1-k). bds. 8.95 *(978-1-61889-210-2(X))* AZ Bks. LLC.
AZ Books Staff. Exploring the Ocean. Vasilkova, Elena, ed. 2012. (Wild Theater Ser.). (ENG.). 8p. (J). (gr. -1-3). bds. 17.95 *(978-1-61889-020-7(4))* AZ Bks. LLC.
—In the Sea & Ocean. Efimova, Tatiana, ed. 2012. (Animal Sounds Ser.). (ENG.). 14p. (J). (-k). bds. 7.95 *(978-1-61889-127-3(8))* AZ Bks. LLC.
—Living Book of the Ocean. Aksinovich, Natalia, ed. 2012. (Our Amazing World Ser.). (ENG.). 12p. (J). (gr. 1-3). bds. 19.95 *(978-1-61889-021-4(2))* AZ Bks. LLC.
—Ocean Animals. Gorojan, Elena, ed. 2012. (My First Library). (ENG.). 12p. (J). (gr. -1-k). bds. 8.95 *(978-1-61889-119-8(7))* AZ Bks. LLC.
—Visiting the Ocean. Lukjanenko, Anna, ed. 2012. (Lively Pictures Ser.). (ENG.). 10p. (J). (gr. -1-1). bds. 9.95 *(978-1-61889-180-8(4))* AZ Bks. LLC.
Baggott, Stella. Glug, Glug, Glug. Cartwright, Mary, illus. 2007. (Bath Bks.). 5p. (J). (gr. -1-k). 14.99 *(978-0-7945-1784-7(6)*, Usborne) EDC Publishing.
Barraclough, Susan. Sharks & Other Creatures of the Deep. 2007. (Illus.). 192p. (J). *(978-0-7607-9143-1(0))* Barnes & Noble, Inc.
Beaton, Kathryn. Discover Moray Eels. 2015. (21st Century Basic Skills Library: Splash! Ser.). (ENG., Illus.). 24p. (J). (gr. 2-4). 26.35 *(978-1-63362-601-0(6)*, 206588) Cherry Lake Publishing.
Beck, W. H. Glow: Animals with Their Own Night-Lights. 2015. (ENG., Illus.). 32p. (J). (gr. -1-3). 18.99 *(978-0-544-41666-6(X)*, 1594755, Clarion Bks.) HarperCollins Pubs.
Bedoyere, Camilla. Monsters of the Deep. 2014. (ENG., Illus.). 80p. (J). (gr. 3-6). pap. 9.95 *(978-1-77085-465-9(7)*, 713b1e19-b5f2-4993-99c3-f3d98834b481) Firefly Bks., Ltd.
Believe It Or Not!, Ripleys, compiled by. Ripley Twists PB: Sharks & Other Scary Sea Creatures. 2018. (Twist Ser.: 9). (ENG.). 48p. (J). pap. 7.99 *(978-1-60991-231-4(4))* Ripley Entertainment, Inc.
Benchmark Education Company, LLC Staff, compiled by. Watery World & Animal Adaptations. 2005. spiral bd. 225.00 *(978-1-4108-5814-6(6))* Benchmark Education Co.
Bennett, Doraine. Atlantic Ocean. 2009. (J). *(978-1-935077-34-3(1))*; pap. *(978-1-935077-39-8(2))* State Standards Publishing, LLC.
Bennett, Elizabeth. Counting in the Ocean. 2014. (Illus.). (J). pap. *(978-0-545-61302-6(7))* Scholastic, Inc.
Berger, Melvin & Berger, Gilda. Manta Rays. 2003. (Illus.). (J). pap. *(978-0-439-47393-4(4))* Scholastic, Inc.
Beringer Mckissack, Lisa. Counting in the Oceans, 1 vol. 2009. (Counting in the Biomes Ser.). (ENG., Illus.). 32p. (gr. k-2). lib. bdg. 26.60 *(978-0-7660-2994-1(8)*, b0e6b41e-3eaf-4b3a-9a39-27bd997cf58a, Enslow Elementary) Enslow Publishing, LLC.
Bessesen, Brooke. Look Who Lives in the Ocean: Splashing & Dashing, Nibbling & Quibbling, Blending & Fending. 2009. (Illus.). 48p. (J). (gr. k-4). 19.95 *(978-1-932082-82-1(4))* Arizona Highways.
Bishop, Celeste. Wandering Woodlice, 1 vol. 2015. (Icky Animals! Small & Gross Ser.). (ENG.). 24p. (J). (gr. 1-1). pap. 9.25 *(978-1-4994-0724-2(6)*, 258fc45c-a54f-4592-b5a9-cfbd8a02f7ac, PowerKids Pr.) Rosen Publishing Group, Inc., The.
Blocksma, Mary. What's on the Beach? A Great Lakes Treasure Hunt. Blocksma, Mary, illus. 2003. (Great Lakes Treasure Hunts Ser.: No. 1). (Illus.). 48p. (J). pap. 9.95 *(978-0-9708575-1-4(9))* Beaver Island Arts.
Blyton, Enid, et al. Under the Sea. 2013. 10p. (J). bds. 9.95 *(978-1-84135-723-2(5))* Parkwest Pubns., Inc.
Boelts, Maribeth. Amazing Ocean Animals. 2016. (Spring Forward Ser.). (J). (gr. 1). *(978-1-4900-2244-4(9))* Benchmark Education Co.
Bradley, Timothy J. Demons of the Deep, 1 vol. 2nd rev. ed. 2013. (TIME for KIDS(r): Informational Text Ser.). (ENG., Illus.). 64p. (J). (gr. 4-8). pap. 14.99 *(978-1-4333-4896-9(9))* Teacher Created Materials, Inc.
Brecke, Nicole & Stockland, Patricia M. Sea Creatures You Can Draw. Brecke, Nicole, illus. 2010. (Ready, Set, Draw! Ser.). (ENG., Illus.). 32p. (gr. 2-4). lib. bdg. 25.26 *(978-0-7613-4168-0(4)*, Millbrook Pr.) Lerner Publishing Group.
Bredeson, Carmen. Baby Animals of the Ocean, 1 vol. 2009. (Nature's Baby Animals Ser.). (ENG., Illus.). 24p. (gr. k-2). pap. 10.35 *(978-1-59845-407-9(2)*, a290c4e9-33df-4459-87f1-525fc70591b7, Enslow Elementary); lib. bdg. 25.27 *(978-0-7660-3003-9(2)*, 00e5aebe-eb27-419e-9adc-9278cf46b579) Enslow Publishing, LLC.
—Leafy Sea Dragons & Other Weird Sea Creatures, 1 vol. 2009. (I Like Weird Animals! Ser.). (ENG., Illus.). 24p. (gr. k-2). lib. bdg. 25.27 *(978-0-7660-3125-8(X)*, 6b7d6579-5320-47db-b1d4-ac5323e5ee40, Enslow Elementary) Enslow Publishing, LLC.
Brewster, Joy. Animals of the Sea & Animales del Mar: 6 English, 6 Spanish Adaptations, 122 vols., Vol. 2. 2011. (SPA.). (J). instr.'s gde. ed. 97.00 net. *(978-1-4108-2397-7(0)*, 23970) Benchmark Education Co.
Brookes, Olivia. A Shark & Other Sea Creatures, 1 vol. 2008. (Ask Ser.). (ENG., Illus.). 32p. (J). (gr. 3-3). lib. bdg. 30.27 *(978-1-4358-2515-4(2)*, 78174a4b-3420-4988-b9b0-0d48e9ff4b5e, PowerKids Pr.) Rosen Publishing Group, Inc., The.
Brooks, Susie. Ocean Emporium: A Compilation of Creatures. COOPER, Dawn, illus. 2019. (ENG.). 64p. (J). (gr. k-4). lib. bdg. 18.99 *(978-1-58089-828-7(9))* Charlesbridge Publishing, Inc.
Brown Bear Books (Firm) Staff, contrib. by. Ocean Life. 2007. (J). *(978-1-933834-16-0(1))* Brown Bear Books.
Brown, Laaren. Icky Sticky Readers: Splendid Sea Creatures (Scholastic Reader, Level 2) 2017. (Scholastic Reader, Level 2 Ser.). (ENG.). 32p. (J). (gr. 1-3). pap. 4.99 *(978-1-338-14416-1(2))* Scholastic, Inc.
Buchanan, Shelly. The Powerful Ocean. 2015. (Science: Informational Text Ser.). (ENG., Illus.). 32p. (gr. 4-8). pap. 11.99 *(978-1-4807-4726-5(2))* Teacher Created Materials, Inc.
Bull, Peter. Under the Sea. 2008. (Quick Draw Ser.). (ENG., Illus.). 32p. (J). (gr. -1-3). 18.69 *(978-0-7534-6199-0(4)*, 9780753461990) Kingfisher Publications, plc GBR. Dist: Children's Plus, Inc.
Bull, Peter, illus. Under the Sea. 2004. (Out & about Ser.). 12p. (J). bds. 4.99 *(978-1-85997-806-1(1))* Byeway Bks.
—Under the Sea. (Magnets on the Move Ser.). (J). 8p. bds. *(978-2-7643-0146-3(4))*; 10p. bds. *(978-2-89393-938-4(4))* Phidal Publishing, Inc./Editions Phidal, Inc.
Butler, John Marius, et al, illus. The Awesome Book of Monsters of the Deep: Awesome. 2013. (World of Wonder: the Awesome Book Of Ser.). (ENG.). 32p. (J). (gr. 3-7). 7.99 *(978-1-77093-777-2(3))* Flowerpot Pr.
Calver, Paul & Reynolds, Toby. First Sticker Art: in the Ocean: Use Stickers to Create 20 Cute Ocean Animals. Savva, Ksenya, illus. 2019. (First Sticker Art Ser.). (ENG.). 64p. (J). (gr. -1-2). pap. 9.99 *(978-1-4380-1247-6(0))* Sourcebooks, Inc.
—How to Draw Incredible Sharks & Other Ocean Giants: Packed with over 80 Creatures of the Sea. Gowen, Fiona, illus. 2016. (How to Draw Ser.). (ENG.). 32p. (J). (gr. 2-6). pap. 6.99 *(978-1-4380-0853-0(8))* Sourcebooks, Inc.
Cando, Kinder. Creatures under the Sea Take Home. (J). 7.95 *(978-0-8136-0667-5(5))* Modern Curriculum Pr.
Castellano, Peter. Sea Creatures, 1 vol. 2015. (Monsters! Ser.). (ENG., Illus.). 32p. (J). (gr. 1-2). pap. 11.50 *(978-1-4824-4091-1(1)*, cce35b69-a069-43f9-8035-f80766ebbbd8) Stevens, Gareth Publishing LLLP.
Cecchini, Marie E. Under the Sea: A Cross-Curricular Unit for Grades 1-3. Mitchell, Judy & Lindeen, Mary, eds. Armbrust, Janet & Skiles, Janet, illus. 2007. 32p. (J). pap. 6.95 *(978-1-57310-529-3(5))* Teaching & Learning Co.
Centore, Michael. Saving Ocean Animals: Sharks, Turtles, Coral, & Fish. 2017. (Illus.). 64p. (J). *(978-1-4222-3879-0(2))* Mason Crest.
Cerullo, Mary M. & Simmons, Beth E. Sea Secrets: Tiny Clues to a Big Mystery. Carlson, Kirsten., illus. 2015. (Long Term Ecological Research Ser.). 32p. (J). (gr. 1-5). pap. 9.95 *(978-1-63076-075-5(7))* Taylor Trade Publishing.
Chagollan, Samantha. Ocean Friends: A Step-By-step Drawing & Story Book. Ho, Jannie, illus. 2019. (Watch Me Read & Draw Ser.). (ENG.). 32p. (J). (gr. -1-2). lib. bdg. 26.65 *(978-1-60058-799-3(2)*, 170b111b-c345-4066-a803-a512a65a453e, Walter Foster Jr) Quarto Publishing Group USA.
Christiansen, Per. Terrifying & Ugly Sea Creatures, 1 vol. 2008. (Nature's Monsters: Water Creatures Ser.). (ENG., Illus.). 32p. (YA). (gr. 3-5). lib. bdg. 28.67 *(978-0-8368-9221-5(6)*, d52eb100-06c5-44c3-96c5-84f53da49680) Stevens, Gareth Publishing LLLP.
Clark, Willow. Asian Dolphins & Other Marine Mammals, 1 vol. 2012. (Animals of Asia Ser.). (ENG., Illus.). 24p. (J). (gr. 2-3). 26.27 *(978-1-4488-7419-4(X)*, 8a443a83-846e-4a30-94c6-552cabc99d17); pap. 9.25 *(978-1-4488-7492-7(0)*, b6437700-9ec8-47e1-a20a-8355814cf12b) Rosen Publishing Group, Inc., The. (PowerKids Pr.).
Clarke, Phillip. Seas & Oceans Sticker Atlas. Le Rolland, Leonard, illus. 2006. 24p. (J). pap. 8.95 *(978-0-7945-1218-7(6)*, Usborne) EDC Publishing.
Cleave, Andrew. Giants of the Sea. 2019. (Creatures of the Ocean Ser.). (Illus.). 80p. (J). (gr. 12). lib. bdg. 34.60 *(978-1-4222-4306-0(0))* Mason Crest.

Cocoretto, illus. Peekaboo! in the Ocean! 2016. (Peekaboo! Ser.: 4). 12p. (J). spiral bd. *(978-1-84643-867-7(5))* Child's Play International Ltd.

Cole, Joanna. The Magic School Bus on the Ocean Floor, 1 vol. Degen, Bruce, illus. 2010. (Magic School Bus Ser.). (ENG.). (J). (gr. 2-5). pap. 10.99 *(978-0-545-22751-3(8))* Scholastic, Inc.

—Sea Creatures. 2014. (Magic School Bus Presents Ser.). lib. bdg. 17.20 *(978-0-606-35814-9(5))* Turtleback.

Coleman, Miriam. Swimming with Manatees, 1 vol. 2009. (Flippers & Fins Ser.). (ENG., Illus.). 24p. (J). (gr. 2-3). pap. 9.25 *(978-1-4358-3241-1(8),* 73a583db-e236-4132-9302-86cb72b670ea, PowerKids Pr.); lib. bdg. 26.27 *(978-1-4042-8092-2(8),* 9eb83b6b-b6b4-455b-8e20-6e2b6ef15e9e) Rosen Publishing Group, Inc., The.

Collard, Sneed B., III. The Deep-Sea Floor. Wenzel, Gregory, illus. 2003. 32p. (J). (gr. 1-4). pap. 7.95 *(978-1-57091-403-4(6))* Charlesbridge Publishing, Inc.

—One Night in the Coral Sea. Brickman, Robin, illus. 2006. 32p. (J). (gr. 1-4). pap. 7.95 *(978-1-57091-390-7(0))* Charlesbridge Publishing, Inc.

—One Night in the Coral Sea. Brickman, Robin, illus. 2006. 32p. (gr. 3-7). 17.95 *(978-0-7569-6969-1(7))* Perfection Learning Corp.

Collins Kids. Oceans (Collins Fascinating Facts) 2016. (Collins Fascinating Facts Ser.). (ENG.). 72p. (J). (gr. 1-3). pap. 10.99 *(978-0-00-816924-4(1))* HarperCollins Pubs. Ltd. GBR. Dist: Independent Pubs. Group.

Collins, Sarah Jean. God Made the Ocean. Collins, Sarah Jean, illus. 2019. (God Made Ser.). (ENG., Illus.). 22p. (J). bds. 7.99 *(978-1-4964-3633-7(4),* 20_32104, Tyndale Kids) Tyndale Hse. Pubs.

Colosi, Rosie. National Geographic Readers: Alien Ocean Animals (L3) 2020. (Readers Ser.). (Illus.). 48p. (J). (gr. 3-7). (ENG.). 14.90 *(978-1-4263-3706-2(X))*; pap. 4.99 *(978-1-4263-3705-5(1))* Disney Publishing Worldwide. (National Geographic Kids).

Confalone, Nick & Confalone, Chelsea. Ocean Monsters. 2013. (Penguin Young Readers, Level 4 Ser.). 48p. (J). (gr. 3-4). pap. 4.99 *(978-0-448-46723-8(2),* Penguin Young Readers) Penguin Young Readers Group.

Crenson, Victoria. Horseshoe Crabs & Shorebirds: The Story of a Food Web, 0 vols. Cannon, Annie, illus. unabr. ed. 2009. (ENG.). 42p. (J). (gr. 3-5). pap. 9.99 *(978-0-7614-5552-3(3),* 9780761455523, Two Lions) Amazon Publishing.

Crow, Marilee. Down by the Shore. Roberts, Mary Sue, photos by. 2011. (Illus.). 30p. 19.95 *(978-1-61633-087-3(2))* Guardian Angel Publishing, Inc.

Daubney, Kate. Sea Creatures, 1 vol. 2018. (Fantastic Fingerprint Art Ser.). (ENG.). 32p. (J). (gr. k-k). 30.27 *(978-1-5081-9530-6(7),* e57ff42a-b268-4a41-8591-c074a8dbeef8, Windmill Bks.) Rosen Publishing Group, Inc., The.

Davies, Monika. How Deep in the Ocean? Ocean Animal Habitats. Marti, Romina, illus. 2018. (Animals Measure Up Ser.). (ENG.). 24p. (J). (gr. 1-4). pap. 9.99 *(978-1-68152-304-0(3),* 15018); lib. bdg. *(978-1-68151-384-3(6),* 15012) Amicus.

Dawson, Emily C. Ocean Animals. 2010. (Our Animal World Ser.). 24p. (J). 25.65 *(978-1-60753-013-8(9))* Amicus Learning.

Daynes, Katie. 1001 Things to Spot in the Sea. Gower, Teri, illus. 2009. (1001 Things to Spot Ser.). 32p. (J). (gr. 1). 9.99 *(978-0-7945-2615-3(2),* Usborne) EDC Publishing.

—1001 Things to Spot in the Sea. 2004. (1001 Things to Spot Ser.). 32p. (J). pap. 6.95 *(978-0-7945-0229-4(6))* EDC Publishing.

De la Bédoyère, Camilla. Deep Ocean. 2010. (Unpredictable Nature Ser.). (Illus.). 48p. (J). (gr. 3-18). lib. bdg. 19.95 *(978-1-4222-1997-3(6))* Mason Crest.

—On the Trail of the Whale. Kelly, Richard, ed. Watson, Richard, illus. 2017. (ENG.). 24p. (J). pap. 9.95 *(978-1-78209-983-3(2))* Miles Kelly Publishing, Ltd. GBR. Dist: Parkwest Pubns., Inc.

De la Bédoyère, Camilla & Kelly, Miles. Spot 50 Seashore. Kelly, Richard, ed. 2013. (Illus.). 560p. (J). pap. 9.95 *(978-1-84810-906-3(7))* Miles Kelly Publishing, Ltd. GBR. Dist: Parkwest Pubns., Inc.

De la Bédoyère, Camilla & Philip, Claire. Seashore. Kelly, Richard, ed. 2017. (ENG., Illus.). 96p. (J). pap. 9.95 *(978-1-78209-168-4(8))* Miles Kelly Publishing, Ltd. GBR. Dist: Parkwest Pubns., Inc.

Delano, Marfe Ferguson. Sea Monsters: A Prehistoric Adventure. 2007. (Illus.). 32p. (J). (gr. 3-7). pap. 6.95 *(978-1-4263-0162-9(6),* National Geographic Kids) Disney Publishing Worldwide.

Dembicki, Matt, ed. Wild Ocean: Sharks, Whales, Rays, & Other Endangered Sea Creatures. 2014. (ENG., Illus.). 156p. (YA). (gr. 7). pap. 19.95 *(978-1-938486-38-8(2))* Fulcrum Publishing.

Denne, B. First Encyclopedia of Seas & Oceans II. rev. ed. 2011. (First Encyclopedias Ser.). 64p. (J). pap. 9.99 *(978-0-7945-3048-8(6),* Usborne) EDC Publishing.

Devera, Czeena. Animals of the Beach. 2019. (Wild Things Ser.). (ENG.). 16p. (J). (gr. -1-2). pap. 11.36 *(978-1-5341-4982-3(1),* 213235, Cherry Blossom Press) Cherry Lake Publishing.

—Animals of the Ocean. 2019. (Wild Things Ser.). (ENG.). 16p. (J). (gr. -1-2). pap. 11.36 *(978-1-5341-4980-9(5),* 213229, Cherry Blossom Press) Cherry Lake Publishing.

Diamond, Claudia. What's under the Sea? 2009. (Reading Room Collection 2 Ser.). 24p. (gr. 3-4). 42.50 *(978-1-60852-002-2(1),* PowerKids Pr.) Rosen Publishing Group, Inc., The.

Dickmann, Nancy. Sea Otters. 2019. (Animals in Danger Ser.). (ENG.). 24p. (J). (gr. 2-4). lib. bdg. *(978-1-78121-445-9(X),* 16563) Brown Bear Bks.

Dickmann, Nancy, text. A Curious Collection of Ocean Life & Other Watery Wonders. 2016. (Illus.). 64p. (J). *(978-1-4351-6572-4(1))* Barnes & Noble, Inc.

Dils, Tracey E. Under the Sea 1, 2, 3: An Ocean Counting Book. 2015. (1, 2, 3 Count with Me Ser.). (ENG., Illus.). 24p. (J). (gr. k-2). lib. bdg. 19.95 *(978-1-60753-717-5(6),* 15249) Amicus.

DK. Sharks & Other Deadly Ocean Creatures Visual Encyclopedia. 2016. (DK Children's Visual Encyclopedias Ser.). (ENG., Illus.). 208p. (J). (gr. 4-7). 17.99 *(978-1-4654-5084-5(X),* DK Children) Dorling Kindersley Publishing, Inc.

—Super Tiburones (Super Shark Encyclopedia) Y Otras Criaturas de Las Profundidades. 2018. (DK Super Nature Encyclopedias Ser.). Orig. Title: Super Shark Encyclopedia. (SPA., Illus.). 208p. (J). (gr. 3-7). 24.99 *(978-1-4654-7924-2(4),* DK Children) Dorling Kindersley Publishing, Inc.

—Ultimate Sticker Book: Glow in the Dark: Ocean Creatures: Create Your Own Picture Book. 2003. (Ultimate Sticker Book Ser.). (ENG., Illus.). 16p. (J). (gr. k-3). pap. 6.99 *(978-0-7894-9277-7(6),* DK Children) Dorling Kindersley Publishing, Inc.

Donaldson, Chelsea. Great White Shark: An Up-Close Look at Senses. 2014. (Illus.). 16p. (J). pap. *(978-0-545-75172-8(1))* Scholastic, Inc.

Dunn, Joeming & Denham, Brian. Shamu: The 1st Killer Whale in Captivity, 1 vol. 2011. (Famous Firsts: Animals Making History Ser.). (ENG., Illus.). 32p. (J). (gr. 3-8). 32.79 *(978-1-61641-642-3(4),* 1332269, Graphic Planet - Fiction) Magic Wagon.

duopress labs, concept. Hello, Ocean Friends. 2015. (High-Contrast Bks.). (Illus.). 20p. (J). (-k). bds. 7.99 *(978-1-938093-41-8(0),* 809341) Duo Pr. LLC.

Early Macken, JoAnn. Rivers / Ríos, 1 vol. 2005. (Water Habitats / Hábitats Acuáticos Ser.). (SPA & ENG.). 24p. (gr. k-2). pap. 9.15 *(978-0-8368-6038-2(1),* e1f114b5-579a-44ca-8032-72b7bf52fd1e, Weekly Reader Leveled Readers) Stevens, Gareth Publishing LLLP.

—Sea Lions / Los Leones Marinos, 1 vol. 2004. (Animals I See at the Zoo / Animales Que Veo en el Zoológico Ser.). (ENG & SPA., Illus.). 24p. (gr. k-2). lib. bdg. 24.67 *(978-0-8368-4384-2(3),* 72c2cb3b-fe15-4dbc-8be3-0ddddc27741f) Stevens, Gareth Publishing LLLP.

Eggleton, Jill. The Deep Ocean. 2007. (Connectors Ser.). (gr. 2-5). pap. *(978-1-877453-02-1(1))* Global Education Systems Ltd.

Encyclopaedia Britannica Publishers, Inc. Staff. Creatures of the Waters. 2003. (Illus.). 64p. 14.95 *(978-1-59339-014-3(9))* Encyclopaedia Britannica, Inc.

Evans, Topper. 200-Year-Old Red Sea Urchins!, 1 vol. 2016. (World's Longest-Living Animals Ser.). (ENG., Illus.). 24p. (J). (gr. 1-2). lib. bdg. 24.27 *(978-1-4824-5597-7(8),* 4c7226f0-114a-49d7-849d-0c9aec5f19ef) Stevens, Gareth Publishing LLLP.

Farrell, Russell & Fisher, Diana, illus. All about Drawing Sea Creatures & Animals. 2010. (All about Drawing Ser.). 80p. (J). 34.25 *(978-1-936309-08-5(4))* Quarto Publishing Group USA.

Faundez, Anne. Sea Creatures. 2004. (QEB Start Reading Ser.). (Illus.). 24p. (J). lib. bdg. 15.95 *(978-1-59566-008-4(9))* QEB Publishing Inc.

Fiedler, Heidi. Sea Swimmers: A Close-Up Photographic Look Inside Your World. 2017. (Up Close Ser.). (ENG., Illus.). 32p. (J). (gr. k-6). lib. bdg. 27.99 *(978-1-942875-34-5(7),* dd816102-a195-4d1f-a62d-15f916573bab, Walter Foster Jr) Quarto Publishing Group USA.

Firth, Alex & Lacey, Minna. Big Book of Big Sea Creatures. 2012. (Big Bks). 16p. (J). ring bd. 14.99 *(978-0-7945-3244-4(6),* Usborne) EDC Publishing.

Fish, Lori Flying. One Shining Starfish. Fish, Lori Flying, illus. 2010. (Illus.). 16p. pap. 9.95 *(978-1-936343-12-6(6))* Peppertree Pr., The.

Fleisher, Paul. Ocean Food Webs in Action. 2013. (Searchlight Books (tm) — What Is a Food Web? Ser.). (ENG., Illus.). 40p. (J). (gr. 3-5). pap. 9.99 *(978-1-4677-1556-0(5),* fe99e355-c570-430b-9c79-44e051e6ea8f) Lerner Publishing Group.

Fokina, N. N., et al. Lipidnyi Sostav Midii Mytilus Edulis L. Belogo Moria: Vliianie Nekotorykh Faktorov Sredy Obitaniia. 2010. (RUS., Illus.). 241p. pap. *(978-5-9274-0405-6(7))* Karel'skij nauchnyj centr Rossijskoj akademii nauk.

Franklin, Carolyn. Ocean Life. Franklin, Carolyn, illus. 2013. (World of Wonder Ser.). (Illus.). 32p. (gr. 1-3). 31.35 *(978-1-904642-63-3(2))* Book Hse. GBR. Dist: Black Rabbit Bks.

Franklin, Carolyn & Stewart, David. Ocean Life. Franklin, Carolyn, illus. 2008. (World of Wonder Ser.). (ENG., Illus.). 32p. (J). (gr. 1-4). 29.00 *(978-0-531-20451-1(0),* Children's Pr.) Scholastic Library Publishing.

Furstinger, Nancy. 12 Marine Animals Back from the Brink. 2015. (Back from the Brink Ser.). (ENG., Illus.). 32p. (J). (gr. 3-6). 32.80 *(978-1-63235-004-6(1),* 11531, 12-Story Library) Bookstaves, LLC.

Galvin, Laura Gates. Alphabet of Ocean Animals. Petruccio, Steven James et al, illus. 2009. (ENG.). 40p. 9.95 *(978-1-60727-024-9(2))* Soundprints.

—Alphabet of Ocean Animals. Petruccio, Steven James et al, illus. 2007. (ENG.). 40p. (J). (gr. k-2). 15.95 *(978-1-59249-690-7(3))* Soundprints.

Ganeri, Anita. I Wonder Why the Sea Is Salty. 2014. 32p. pap. 7.00 *(978-1-61003-352-7(3))* Center for the Collaborative Classroom.

—I Wonder Why the Sea Is Salty: And Other Questions about the Oceans. 2011. (I Wonder Why Ser.). (ENG., Illus.). 32p. (J). (gr. k-3). pap. 6.99 *(978-0-7534-6521-9(3),* 900070301, Kingfisher) Roaring Brook Pr.

Gardeski, Christina Mia. All about Oceans. 2017. (Habitats Ser.). (ENG., Illus.). 24p. (J). (gr. -1-2). lib. bdg. 22.65 *(978-1-5157-7644-4(1),* 135929, Pebble) Capstone.

Garrett, Ann & Higney, Gene-Michael. Fins & Flippers, Scales & Nippers. 2003. (Illus.). 32p. (J). pap. *(978-1-59034-871-0(0))*; 15.95 *(978-1-59034-869-7(9))* Mondo Publishing.

Gigantes marinos de la época de los dinosaurios (Sea Giants of Dinosaur Time) 2006. (J). pap. 6.95 *(978-0-8225-6638-0(9),* Ediciones Lerner) Lerner Publishing Group.

Gish, Ashley. Walruses. 2019. (X-Books: Marine Mammals Ser.). (ENG.). 32p. (J). (gr. 3-5). pap. 9.99 *(978-1-62832-756-4(1),* 19225, Creative Paperbacks) Creative Co., The.

Gish, Melissa. Coral Reef Communities. 2018. (Down in the Ocean Ser.). (ENG.). 48p. (J). (gr. 4-7). pap. 12.00 *(978-1-62832-550-8(X),* 19737, Creative Paperbacks) Creative Co., The.

—Deep-Sea Mysteries. 2018. (Down in the Ocean Ser.). (ENG.). 48p. (J). (gr. 4-7). pap. 12.00 *(978-1-62832-551-5(8),* 19738, Creative Paperbacks) Creative Co., The.

—Manatees. 2016. (Living Wild Ser.). (ENG., Illus.). 48p. (J). (gr. 4-7). *(978-1-60818-705-8(5),* 20613, Creative Education) Creative Co., The.

—Seafloor Scavengers. 2018. (Down in the Ocean Ser.). (ENG.). 48p. (J). (gr. 4-7). *(978-1-60818-998-4(8),* 19734, Creative Education) Creative Co., The.

—Spineless Sea Creatures. 2018. (Down in the Ocean Ser.). (ENG.). 48p. (J). (gr. 4-7). *(978-1-60818-999-1(6),* 19735, Creative Education) Creative Co., The.

Golding, Elizabeth. Moonlight Ocean. Lodge, Ali, illus. 2012. (ENG.). 12p. (J). (gr. -1-3). 14.99 *(978-0-7624-4486-1(X),* Running Pr. Kids) Running Pr.

Goldish, Meish. Florida Manatees: Warm Water Miracles. 2007. (America's Animal Comebacks Ser.). (Illus.). 32p. (YA). (gr. 2-5). lib. bdg. 28.50 *(978-1-59716-507-5(7))* Bearport Publishing Co., Inc.

Goldsack, Gaby. Ocean Animals. Bampton, Bob, illus. (J). *(978-1-57755-508-7(2))* Flying Frog Publishing, Inc.

Gordon, Sharon. Animales Del Mar (Ocean Animals), 1 vol. 2010. (Animales Salvajes (Wild Animals) Ser.). (SPA.). 24p. (gr. k-1). lib. bdg. 25.50 *(978-0-7614-3431-3(3),* 5b6b0964-cedf-4666-a82a-c524a54ae7ac) Cavendish Square Publishing LLC.

—Ocean Animals, 1 vol. 2009. (Wild Animals Ser.). (ENG.). 24p. (gr. k-1). pap. 9.23 *(978-0-7614-3509-9(3),* 26ffdedc-dd0c-4b4b-8cf6-8d5fc5c36497); lib. bdg. 25.50 *(978-0-7614-2903-6(4),* b5f2e3a5-60e8-46f2-9d59-a3ce5407205a) Cavendish Square Publishing LLC.

Grady, Colin. The Ocean Biome, 1 vol. 2016. (Zoom in on Biomes Ser.). (ENG.). 24p. (gr. 2-2). pap. 10.95 *(978-0-7660-7785-0(3),* df432bb7-472b-42b5-b97a-6f824d6f0f37) Enslow Publishing, LLC.

Greenaway, Theresa, ed. Ocean: A Foldout Book & Wall Chart. 2005. (Illus.). 12p. (J). (gr. k-4). reprint ed. 10.00 *(978-0-7567-8533-8(2))* DIANE Publishing Co.

Gresham, Jennifer. Sea Creatures. 2013. (Illus.). (J). *(978-1-58865-831-9(7))* Kidsbooks, LLC.

Grodzicki, Jenna. I See Sea Food: Sea Creatures That Look Like Food. 2019. (ENG., Illus.). 32p. (J). (gr. -1-3). lib. bdg. 27.99 *(978-1-5415-5463-4(9),* dfac9b81-511d-4dea-8cec-cdf7924ddb04, Millbrook Pr.) Lerner Publishing Group.

Gross, Miriam J. The Moray Eel, 1 vol. 2005. (Weird Sea Creatures Ser.). (ENG., Illus.). 24p. (J). (gr. 3-3). lib. bdg. 26.27 *(978-1-4042-3189-4(7),* 639b1890-d68c-4422-8dc2-0615fe463513) Rosen Publishing Group, Inc., The.

—The Octopus, 1 vol. 2005. (Weird Sea Creatures Ser.). (ENG., Illus.). 24p. (J). (gr. 3-3). lib. bdg. 26.27 *(978-1-4042-3188-7(9),* 930cefed-0443-46bb-a119-22d927628be2, PowerKids Pr.) Rosen Publishing Group, Inc., The.

—The Sea Slug: Nudibranchs, 1 vol. 2005. (Weird Sea Creatures Ser.). (ENG., Illus.). 24p. (J). (gr. 3-3). lib. bdg. 26.27 *(978-1-4042-3191-7(9),* beb319db-2950-444d-a7a5-763551b3e282, PowerKids Pr.) Rosen Publishing Group, Inc., The.

—The Stingray, 1 vol. 2005. (Weird Sea Creatures Ser.). (ENG., Illus.). 24p. (J). (gr. 3-3). lib. bdg. 26.27 *(978-1-4042-3190-0(0),* 11b1f3c0-bc13-473a-8c35-7c6d37a93c85, PowerKids Pr.) Rosen Publishing Group, Inc., The.

Group/McGraw-Hill, Wright. Under the Sea, 6 vols. (Wildcats Ser.). 32p. (gr. 2-8). *(978-0-322-05862-0(7))* Wright Group/McGraw-Hill.

Gulberson, Brenda Z. The Most Amazing Creature in the Sea. Spirin, Gennady, illus. 2015. (ENG.). 32p. (J). (gr. -1-3). 18.99 *(978-0-8050-9961-4(1),* 900127879, Holt, Henry & Co. Bks. For Young Readers) Holt, Henry & Co.

Hale, Wendy A. & Lantz, Peggy. The Oceans of Florida. 2014. (Florida Water Story Ser.). (Illus.). 36p. (J). (gr. -1-12). pap. 6.95 *(978-1-56164-704-0(7))* Pineapple Pr., Inc.

Hall, Howard. The Secrets of Kelp Forests: Life's Ebb & Flow in the Sea's Richest Habitat. Leon, Vicki, ed. 2nd ed. 2007. (Jean-Michel Cousteau Presents Ser.). (ENG., Illus.). 48p. (J). (gr. 3-9). pap. 9.95 *(978-0-9766134-9-7(2))* London Town Pr.

Hall, Stephen. Exploring the Oceans. 2012. (ENG., Illus.). 48p. (J). 15.00 *(978-1-899762-79-8(5))* Award Pubns. Ltd. GBR. Dist: Parkwest Pubns., Inc.

Hansen, Judith. Seashells in My Pocket: AMC's Family Guide to Exploring the Coast from Maine to Florida. Sabaka, Donna, illus. 3rd ed. 2008. (ENG.). 160p. (gr. 3-7). per. 14.95 *(978-1-929173-61-7(X))* Appalachian Mountain Club Bks.

Hardy, A. S. Sea Stories for Wonder Eyes. 2005. reprint ed. pap. 21.95 *(978-1-4191-0670-5(8))* Kessinger Publishing, LLC.

Harris, Nicholas, text. Panoramas: Ocean Life. 2006. (Illus.). 23p. (J). *(978-0-7607-8156-2(7))* backpackbook.

Harrison, Paul. Sea Monsters. (Up Close Ser.). 24p. (gr. 3-3). 2009. 47.90 *(978-1-60854-701-2(9))* 2007. (ENG., Illus.). (J). lib. bdg. 28.93 *(978-1-4042-4224-1(4),* 2812d95a-b355-4ba1-857f-1cfa3f97309e) Rosen Publishing Group, Inc., The. (PowerKids Pr.).

Heos, Bridget. Do You Really Want a Hamster? Longhi, Katya, illus. 2013. (Do You Really Want a Pet? Ser.). (ENG.). 24p. (J). (gr. 1-4). 27.10 *(978-1-60753-206-4(9),* 16248) Amicus.

Herndon, Ryan, compiled by. 3-D Deep-Sea Creatures! 2007. (Illus.). 31p. (J). *(978-0-439-02696-3(2))* Scholastic, Inc.

Hirschi, Ron. Winter Is for Whales: A Book of Hawaiian Seasons. Green, Yuko, illus. 2007. (ENG.). 36p. (J). (gr. -1-3). 16.95 *(978-1-59700-504-3(5))* Island Heritage Publishing.

Hodgkins, Fran. Do Seals Ever... ? Leggitt, Marjorie, illus. 2017. 32p. (J). (gr. -1-3). 16.95 *(978-1-60893-467-6(5))* Down East Bks.

Holden, Pam. Watch Me Swim, 1 vol. Hansen, Christine, illus. 2009. (Red Rocket Readers Ser.). (ENG.). 16p. (gr. -1-1). pap. *(978-1-877363-31-3(6),* Red Rocket Readers) Flying Start Bks.

Hopgood, Sally & Hinton, Stephanie. Under the Waves: A Pull-The-Tab Book. 2014. (Illus.). (J). *(978-1-4351-5691-3(9))* Barnes & Noble, Inc.

Hopkins, Therese. Underwater Homes, 1 vol. 2009. (Home Sweet Home Ser.). (ENG.). 24p. (J). (gr. 1-1). lib. bdg. 26.27 *(978-1-4358-2694-6(9),* 4b5eeabc-0fd7-4e61-9ad9-f97c44157024); (Illus.). pap. 9.25 *(978-1-4358-3068-4(7),* 7000e282-bb96-4ab1-b81c-dcd7cd43d384, PowerKids Pr.) Rosen Publishing Group, Inc., The.

Horning, Nicole. Let's Explore the Ocean!, 1 vol. 2020. (Earth Science Explorers Ser.). (ENG.). 24p. (gr. 1-2). pap. 9.22 *(978-1-5026-5625-4(6),* cebf5f4c-07a8-43af-8bad-d5d3033d73a3) Cavendish Square Publishing LLC.

Horsman, Paul. Out of the Blue: A Journey Through the World's Oceans. Seapics.com Staff, photos by. 2005. (ENG., Illus.). 160p. (gr. 17). 32.95 *(978-0-262-08341-6(8),* 0262083418) MIT Pr.

Hoyt, Erich. Weird Sea Creatures. 2013. (ENG., Illus.). 64p. (J). (gr. 5-12). 19.95 *(978-1-77085-197-9(6),* 446946d0-ad7f-4705-9e78-68b02c8f46fa); pap. 9.95 *(978-1-77085-191-7(7),* 41d932ab-f9fb-46a5-af77-85944a0e831b) Firefly Bks., Ltd.

Hubbell, Patricia. Papa Fish's Lullaby. Eaddy, Susan, illus. 2007. (ENG.). 32p. (J). (gr. -1-1). 16.95 *(978-1-55971-965-0(6))* Cooper Square Publishing Llc.

Hudak, Heather C. Epic Migrations by Water. 2019. (Epic Animal Journeys Ser.). (ENG.). 32p. (J). (gr. 4-5). pap. *(978-0-7787-6373-4(0),* 71748963-42f0-4217-aa0a-907b66cf4aa6); lib. bdg. *(978-0-7787-6369-7(2),* 9d38b793-1833-456d-8ed9-78c6048dbd54) Crabtree Publishing Co.

—Marine Mammals. (Animal Facts Ser.). (Illus.). 24p. (J). 2005. (gr. 2-3). per. 8.95 *(978-1-59036-247-1(0))* 2004. lib. bdg. 24.45 *(978-1-59036-201-3(2))* Weigl Pubs., Inc.

Hughes, Mónica. Swimming Giants. 2007. (I Love Reading Ser.). (Illus.). 24p. (J). (gr. -1-2). lib. bdg. 25.65 *(978-1-59716-542-6(5))* Bearport Publishing Co., Inc.

Hyde, Natalie. Deep Sea Extremes. 2008. (Extreme Nature Ser.). (ENG., Illus.). 32p. (J). (gr. 2-3). pap. *(978-0-7787-4518-1(X))*; lib. bdg. *(978-0-7787-4501-3(5))* Crabtree Publishing Co.

Ipcar, Dahlov. Deep Sea Farm. 2014. (Illus.). 40p. (J). (gr. -1-3). 17.95 *(978-1-60893-317-4(2))* Down East Bks.

Ishak, Lauren. Map & Track Oceans. 2019. (Map & Track Biomes & Animals Ser.). (ENG.). 32p. (J). (gr. 4-5). *(978-0-7787-5369-8(7))*; pap. *(978-0-7787-5381-0(6))* Crabtree Publishing Co.

Jackson, Tom. Scary Sea Monsters, 1 vol. 2010. (Dangerous Animals Ser.). (ENG.). 32p. (gr. 2-4). (J). pap. 11.50 *(978-1-4339-4047-7(7),* e49c0dd1-c61b-4aaf-9d9d-c055e53675f4, Gareth Stevens Learning Library); (YA). lib. bdg. 29.27 *(978-1-4339-4046-0(9),* 1b7f7af5-b46c-42dd-80f7-5e06edfb9b17) Stevens, Gareth Publishing LLLP.

—Sea Creatures. Bracken, Carolyn, illus. 2014. (Magic School Bus Presents Ser.). (ENG.). 32p. (J). (gr. -1-3). pap. 6.99 *(978-0-545-68366-1(1),* Scholastic Paperbacks) Scholastic, Inc.

Jango-Cohen, Judith. Real-Life Sea Monsters. 2009. pap. 40.95 *(978-0-7613-4820-7(4))* Lerner Publishing Group.

—Real-Life Sea Monsters. Burney, Ryan, illus. 2007. (On My Own Science Ser.). 48p. (J). (gr. 3-7). lib. bdg. 25.26 *(978-0-8225-6747-9(4),* Millbrook Pr.) Lerner Publishing Group.

—Real-life Sea Monsters. 2008. 48p. (J). pap. 6.95 *(978-0-8225-6750-9(4),* First Avenue Editions) Lerner Publishing Group.

Jeffrey, Gary. Mega Shark. 2017. (Graphic Prehistoric Animals Ser.). (ENG., Illus.). 32p. (J). (gr. 5-8). lib. bdg. 31.35 *(978-1-62588-410-7(9),* 19279, Smart Apple Media) Black Rabbit Bks.

Jenkins, Steve & Page, Robin. Flying Frogs & Walking Fish: Leaping Lemurs, Tumbling Toads, Jet-Propelled Jellyfish, & More Surprising Ways That Animals Move. Jenkins, Steve, illus. 2016. (ENG., Illus.). 40p. (J). (gr. -1-3). 17.99 *(978-0-544-63090-1(4),* 1619566, Clarion Bks.) HarperCollins Pubs.

Jennings, Dorothy. Otters Smash, Crabs Pinch, 1 vol. 2017. (Hunter & Hunted: Animal Survival Ser.). (ENG.). 24p. (J). (gr. 3-3). 25.27 *(978-1-5081-5662-8(X),* 3981d87f-307e-4b6d-98de-eff2c9b49f78, PowerKids Pr.) Rosen Publishing Group, Inc., The.

Johnson, Gee. Orcas. 2011. (Power 100 - Marine Life Ser.). 24p. (J). (gr. k-2). pap. 6.95 *(978-1-61541-403-1(7))* American Reading Co.

Johnson, Jinny. Coral Reef Life. 2011. (Watery Worlds Ser.). 32p. (gr. 3-6). 31.35 *(978-1-59920-502-1(5))* Black Rabbit Bks.

—Deep Sea Life. 2011. (Watery Worlds Ser.). 32p. (gr. 3-6). 31.35 *(978-1-59920-503-8(3))* Black Rabbit Bks.

—Ocean Life. 2011. (Watery Worlds Ser.). 32p. (gr. 3-6). 31.35 *(978-1-59920-504-5(1))* Black Rabbit Bks.

—Seashore Life. 2011. (Watery Worlds Ser.). 32p. (gr. 3-6). lib. bdg. 31.35 *(978-1-59920-501-4(7))* Black Rabbit Bks.

Johnson, Rebecca L. Journey into the Deep: Discovering New Ocean Creatures. 2010. (ENG., Illus.). 64p. (J). (gr. 4-8). lib. bdg. 31.99 *(978-0-7613-4148-2(X),* f2f61c84-d06a-4e20-80f6-33973b2f5e36, Millbrook Pr.) Lerner Publishing Group.

Kainen, Dan & Kaufmann, Carol. Ocean: A Photicular Book. 2014. (Photicular Ser.). (ENG., Illus.). 28p. 26.99 *(978-0-7611-8051-7(6),* 18051) Workman Publishing Co., Inc.

Kalman, Bobbie. Baby Animals in Ocean Habitats. 2011. (Habitats of Baby Animals Ser.). (ENG.). 24p. (J). (gr. k-3). *(978-0-7787-7729-8(4))*; pap. *(978-0-7787-7742-7(1))* Crabtree Publishing Co.

Kalman, Bobbie & Dyer, Hadley. Endangered Manatees. 2006. (Earth's Endangered Animals Ser.). (ENG., Illus.). 32p. (J). (gr. 3-7). pap. *(978-0-7787-1914-4(6))* Crabtree Publishing Co.

Kalman, Bobbie & Langille, Jacqueline. Les Mammifères Marins. 2003. (Petit Monde Vivant Ser.). (FRE., Illus.). 32p.

M
N
O

(J). pap. 9.95 *(978-2-920660-97-7(7))* Bayard Canada Livres CAN. Dist: Crabtree Publishing Co.
Karst, Ken. Sea Monsters. 2018. (Enduring Mysteries Ser.). (ENG.). 48p. (J). (gr. 4-7). pap. 12.00 *(978-1-62832-559-1(3),* 19756, Creative Paperbacks) Creative Co., The.
Kavanagh, James & Waterford Press Staff. My First Seashores: Nature Activity Book. Leung, Raymond, illus. 2013. (Nature Activity Book Ser.). (ENG.). 32p. (J). (gr. -1-12). pap., act. bk. ed. 6.95 *(978-1-58355-590-3(0))* Waterford Pr., Inc.
—Seashore Wildlife: Nature Activity Book. Leung, Raymond, illus. 2nd ed. 2013. (Nature Activity Book Ser.). (ENG.). 32p. (J). (gr. -1-8). pap., act. bk. ed. 6.95 *(978-1-58355-584-2(6))* Waterford Pr., Inc.
Kavanaugh, Missy & Gurman, Sarah, texts. Sea Creatures. 2009. (Illus.). (J). *(978-1-4351-1785-3(9))* Barnes & Noble, Inc.
Kelley, K. C. Snorkel Coral Reefs. 2018. (Amazing Adventures Ser.). (ENG.). 16p. (J). (gr. k-2). pap. 7.99 *(978-1-68152-266-1(7),* 14891) Amicus.
Kelly, Richard. Ultimate Guide - Ocean: Contains 5 See-Through Feature Pages. 2017. 69p. (J). 24.95 *(978-1-78209-991-8(3))* Miles Kelly Publishing, Ltd. GBR. Dist: Parkwest Pubns., Inc.
Kenan, Tessa. ¡Mira, una Raya! (Look, a Ray!) 2017. (Bumba Books (r) en Español — Veo Animales Marinos (I See Ocean Animals) Ser.). (SPA., Illus.). 24p. (J). (gr. -1-1). 26.65 *(978-1-5124-2867-4(1),* fe75fbf1-fa17-489a-bf4e-daeab3569c45, Ediciones Lerner) Lerner Publishing Group.
Kidpressions! Sea Creature Creations: A Hand Print Discovery Book. Uting, Justin, illus. 2008. 32p. pap. 24.95 *(978-1-60610-853-6(0))* America Star Bks.
Kids, National Geographic. National Geographic Kids Little Kids First Board Book: Ocean. 2019. (First Board Bks.). (Illus.). 26p. (J). (gr. -1 — 1). bds. 7.99 *(978-1-4263-3468-9(0),* National Geographic Kids) Disney Publishing Worldwide.
King, Trey. Training Academy: Sharks & Other Sea Life! (Illus.). 32p. (J). *(978-1-5182-4448-3(3),* Reagan Arthur Bks.) Little Brown & Co.
Kingsley, Charles. Glaucus: The Wonders of the Shore. 2006. (ENG.). 122p. pap. 18.99 *(978-1-4264-0318-7(6));* 116p. pap. 19.99 *(978-1-4264-0369-9(0))* Creative Media Partners, LLC.
Kranking, Kathy & Carrano, Matthew T. Swimming with Saurs. 2006. 32p. (J). *(978-0-439-83875-7(4))* Scholastic, Inc.
Kravetz, Jonathan. Ticks, 1 vol. 2005. (Gross Bugs Ser.). (ENG., Illus.). 24p. (J). (gr. 3-4). lib. bdg. 26.27 *(978-1-4042-3046-0(7),* 6b08c82f-b37d-4142-9e89-92400e7d5c72, PowerKids Pr.) Rosen Publishing Group, Inc., The.
Kroll, Jennifer. Mighty Micros: Little Things Big Results, 1 vol. 2nd rev. ed. 2013. (TIME for KIDS(r): Informational Text Ser.). (ENG., Illus.). 64p. (J). (gr. 4-8). lib. bdg. 31.96 *(978-1-4333-7447-0(1))* Teacher Created Materials, Inc.
Kronstadt, Jonathan. Ocean Extremes: Life in the Darkest Depths & under the Ice. 2005. (Illus.). 48p. (J). *(978-0-439-71190-6(8))* Scholastic, Inc.
KUBU. Ocean Friends: A Journey Beneath the Sea. 2016. (Kubu Ser.: 1). (Illus.). 32p. (J). (gr. -1-2). pap. 5.99 *(978-1-57826-468-1(5),* Hatherleigh Pr.) Hatherleigh Co., Ltd., The.
Kulavis, Allyson. Sea-Sational. 2013. (Science with Stuff Ser.: 5). (ENG.). 48p. (J). (gr. 1). 11.99 *(978-1-935703-55-6(2))* Downtown Bookworks.
Kurtz, Kevin. A Day in the Deep, 1 vol. Hunter, Erin E., illus. 2013. (Day in the Habitat Ser.). (ENG.). 32p. (J). (gr. 1-4). 17.95 *(978-1-60718-617-5(9));* (gr. 2-3). pap. 10.95 *(978-1-60718-629-8(2),* fe76080c-89f1-4b76-bbe7-68dc7e024e0f) Arbordale Publishing.
—Un Día en la Profundidad, 1 vol. Hunter, Erin E., illus. 2013. (SPA.). 32p. (J). (gr. 1-4). 17.95 *(978-1-60718-715-8(9))* Arbordale Publishing.
—Sharks & Dolphins: a Compare & Contrast Book, 1 vol. 2016. (Compare & Contrast Ser.). (ENG., Illus.). 39p. (J). (gr. k-3). 17.95 *(978-1-62855-732-9(X))* Arbordale Publishing.
—Sharks & Dolphins: a Compare & Contrast Book: Spanish, 1 vol. 2016. (SPA., Illus.). 39p. (J). (gr. k-1). pap. 11.95 *(978-1-62855-746-6(X),* 676a6ffd-b416-4bb7-862f-9797937f72e6) Arbordale Publishing.
Labella, Susan. Animales Migratorios: en el Agua (Migrating Animals of the Water), 1 vol. 2007. (En Marcha: Migraciones Animales (on the Move: Animal Migration) Ser.). (SPA., Illus.). 24p. (gr. 2-4). pap. 9.15 *(978-0-8368-8431-9(0),* 875cb8d8-77ab-4639-ba08-dbec0434737b); lib. bdg. 24.67 *(978-0-8368-8426-5(4),* d9a2a914-b2e6-47ac-93de-7411a0c77c06) Stevens, Gareth Publishing LLLP. (Weekly Reader Leveled Readers).
—Migrating Animals of the Water, 1 vol. 2007. (On the Move: Animal Migration Ser.). (ENG.). 24p. (gr. 2-4). pap. 9.15 *(978-0-8368-8424-1(8),* 903c3030-d01c-4eb8-95b9-039f31b6408a); (Illus.). lib. bdg. 24.67 *(978-0-8368-8419-7(1),* 057bfc81-588d-43e5-9b9a-2460e4b351d4) Stevens, Gareth Publishing LLLP. (Weekly Reader Leveled Readers).
Lambert, Nat. Sharks & Other Predators. Top That Publishing Staff, ed. 2004. (ENG., Illus.). 1p. (J). (gr. 2-4). pap. 5.99 *(978-1-84510-117-6(0))* Top That! Publishing PLC GBR. Dist: Independent Pubs. Group.
Langer Karwoski, Gail. Water Beds: Sleeping in the Ocean, 1 vol. McLennan, Connie, illus. 2005. (ENG.). 32p. (J). (gr. -1-3). 15.95 *(978-0-9764943-1-7(0));* pap. 9.95 *(978-1-934359-01-3(7),* 9781934359013) Arbordale Publishing.
LaPlante, Walter. Sea Anemones, 1 vol. 2015. (Things That Sting Ser.). (ENG., Illus.). 24p. (J). (gr. 2-3). lib. bdg. 24.27 *(978-1-4824-1710-4(3),* c491c1e8-86b9-4858-8298-2e0c2ceb64e3) Stevens, Gareth Publishing LLLP.
Lassen, Christian Riese, illus. Moon Dance. 2005. 16p. (J). (gr. -1-3). bds. 8.95 *(978-1-74047-591-4(7),* Penton Kids) Penton Overseas, Inc.
Lawler, Janet. Ocean Counting. Skerry, Brian, photos by. 2013. (ENG., Illus.). 32p. (J). (gr. -1-k). lib. bdg. 25.90 *(978-1-4263-1117-8(6),* National Geographic Children's Bks.) National Geographic Society.
Lawrence, Ellen. Beach Fleas & Other Tiny Sand Animals. 2018. (Day at the Beach: Animal Life on the Shore Ser.). (ENG.). 24p. (J). (gr. -1-3). 17.95 *(978-1-68402-449-0(8))* Bearport Publishing Co., Inc.
—Bloodworms & Other Wriggly Beach Dwellers. 2018. (Day at the Beach: Animal Life on the Shore Ser.). (ENG.). 24p. (J). (gr. -1-3). lib. bdg. 26.99 *(978-1-68402-444-5(7))* Bearport Publishing Co., Inc.
Leardi, Jeanette. Southern Sea Otters: Fur-Tastrophe Avoided. 2007. (America's Animal Comebacks Ser.). (Illus.). 32p. (YA). (gr. 2-5). lib. bdg. 28.50 *(978-1-59716-534-1(4))* Bearport Publishing Co., Inc.
Lensch, Chris, illus. Coral Reef: Hide & Seek. 2005. (ENG.). 10p. (J). bds. 7.95 *(978-1-58117-362-8(8),* Intervisual/Piggy Toes) Bendon, Inc.
Leon, Vicki. A Raft of Sea Otters: The Playful Life of a Furry Survivor. 2nd ed. 2005. (Jean-Michel Cousteau Presents Ser.). (ENG., Illus.). 48p. (J). pap. 9.95 *(978-0-9666490-4-8(4))* London Town Pr.
—The Secrets of Tidepools: The Bright World of the Rocky Shoreline. 2nd ed. 2006. (Jean-Michel Cousteau Presents Ser.). (ENG., Illus.). 48p. (J). (gr. 4). pap. 9.95 *(978-0-9766134-6-6(8))* London Town Pr.
Lessem, Don. Sea Giants of Dinosaur Time. Bindon, John, illus. 2005. 32p. (J). (gr. 2-5). pap. 6.95 *(978-0-8225-2623-0(9));* (gr. 3-7). lib. bdg. 23.93 *(978-0-8225-1425-1(7))* Lerner Publishing Group.
Let's Find Out! Marine Life, 12 vols. 2016. (Let's Find Out! Marine Life Ser.). (ENG.). 00032p. (J). (gr. 2-3). 156.36 *(978-1-5081-0284-7(8),* 2bf6c9dc-a02f-4775-a247-415d84b81181, Britannica Educational Publishing) Rosen Publishing Group, Inc., The.
Lindeen, Carol K. & Sullivan, Jody. Under the Sea (8 book Set) [NASCO]. 2012. (Under the Sea Ser.). (ENG.). 24p. (gr. k-1). pap. 55.60 *(978-1-62065-475-0(X),* Capstone Pr.) Capstone.
Lindeen, Mary. Crayola (r) Ocean Colors. 2020. (Crayola (r) Colorful Biomes Ser.). (ENG., Illus.). 32p. (J). (gr. k-3). 29.32 *(978-1-5415-7754-1(X),* f088d48b-7ab5-4854-826b-91151e2194eb, Lerner Pubns.) Lerner Publishing Group.
Lithgow, John & Blackaby, Susan. Sea Cows Don't Moo! Level 3. 2007. (Palooza Readers Level 3: Confident Reader Ser.). (ENG., Illus.). 32p. (J). (gr. 1-2). 16.19 *(978-0-7696-4243-7(8))* School Specialty, Incorporated.
Llewellyn, Claire. In the Sea Red Band. Belcher, Andy, photos by. 2016. (Cambridge Reading Adventures Ser.). (ENG., Illus.). 16p. pap. 7.95 *(978-1-107-57578-3(8))* Cambridge Univ. Pr.
—Sea Animals. 2005. (I Know That! Ser.). (Illus.). 24p. (J). (gr. 1-3). lib. bdg. 22.80 *(978-1-932889-32-1(9))* Sea-To-Sea Pubns.
Lourie, Peter. The Manatee Scientists: Saving Vulnerable Species. 2016. (Scientists in the Field Ser.). (ENG., Illus.). 80p. (J). (gr. 5-7). pap. 10.99 *(978-0-544-22529-9(5),* 1563372, Clarion Bks.) HarperCollins Pubs.
Lunis, Natalie. Slimy Sea Slugs. 2007. (No Backbone! Ser.). (Illus.). 24p. (J). (gr. k-3). lib. bdg. 26.99 *(978-1-59716-511-2(5))* Bearport Publishing Co., Inc.
Magby, Meryl. Sea Urchins, 1 vol. 2012. (Under the Sea Ser.). (ENG., Illus.). 24p. (J). (gr. 2-3). pap. 9.25 *(978-1-4488-7479-8(3),* 856dd58f-d197-4bc5-a2bf-bfdec8998459); lib. bdg. 26.27 *(978-1-4488-7400-2(9),* 2e19ecb2-39d8-4889-bfc6-d9ea5afb58c1) Rosen Publishing Group, Inc., The. (PowerKids Pr.).
Makowski, Robin Lee, illus. Sea Creatures. 2004. (J). *(978-1-59203-090-3(4))* Learning Challenge, Inc.
Mammals of the Sea: Level N, 6 vols. (Explorers Ser.). 32p. (gr. 3-6). 44.95 *(978-0-7699-0593-8(5))* Shortland Pubns. (U. S. A.) Inc.
Marine Debris Program (U.S.), Office of Response and Restoration, ed. Understanding Marine Debris: Games & Activities for Kids of All Ages: Marine Debris 101: Games & Activities for Kids of All Ages: Marine Debris 101. 2012. (ENG.). 23p. 7.00 *(978-0-16-091362-4(4),* National Marine Fisheries Service) United States Government Printing Office.
Marsh, Laura. National Geographic Readers: Manatees. 2014. (Readers Ser.). (Illus.). 32p. (J). (gr. 1-3). pap. 4.99 *(978-1-4263-1472-8(8),* National Geographic Kids) Disney Publishing Worldwide.
—National Geographic Readers: Weird Sea Creatures. 2012. (Readers Ser.). (Illus.). 32p. (J). (gr. 1-3). pap. 4.99 *(978-1-4263-1047-8(1));* (ENG., lib. bdg. 14.90 *(978-1-4263-1048-5(X))* Disney Publishing Worldwide. (National Geographic Kids).
Marsico, Katie. A Baby Lobster Grows Up. Marsico, Katie, illus. 2007. (Scholastic News Nonfiction Readers Ser.). (ENG., Illus.). 24p. (J). (gr. 1-2). 22.00 *(978-0-531-17475-3(1))* Scholastic Library Publishing.
—Manatees. 2012. (Nature's Children Ser.). (ENG., Illus.). 48p. (J). pap. 6.95 *(978-0-531-25480-6(1));* lib. bdg. 28.00 *(978-0-531-26835-3(7))* Scholastic Library Publishing.
Martin, Claudia. The Complete Guide to Ocean Life. 2016. (Illus.). 144p. (J). *(978-1-4351-6357-7(5))* Barnes & Noble, Inc.
—Complete Guides Ocean Life. 2012. (ENG.). 144p. (J). *(978-1-4351-4408-8(2))* Barnes & Noble, Inc.
Martin, Justin McCory. Deep-Sea Creatures. 2011. (Illus.). 16p. (J). *(978-0-545-24789-4(6))* Scholastic, Inc.
Marx, Christy. Life in the Ocean Depths. (Life in Extreme Environments Ser.). 64p. (gr. 5-8). 2009. 53.00 *(978-1-61514-272-9(X))* 2003. (ENG.). (YA). pap. 13.95 *(978-1-4358-3265-7(5),* cf7d2f7a-5334-4406-9410-309b306f5853) Rosen Publishing Group, Inc., The. (Rosen Reference).
Mason, Janeen. Ocean Commotion: Life on the Reef, 1 vol. Mason, Janeen, illus. 2010. (ENG., Illus.). 32p. (J). (gr. k-3). 16.99 *(978-1-58980-783-9(9),* Pelican Publishing) Arcadia Publishing.
Massey, Kay. What Do You See in the Sea? Canals, Sonia & O'Toole, Jeanette, illus. 2009. (Little Green Footprints Ser.). 12p. (J). (gr. -1-k). bds. 11.40 *(978-1-60754-698-6(1))* Windmill Bks.
Mattern, Joanne. What River Animals Eat / ¿Qué Comen Los Animales de Los Ríos?, 1 vol. 2006. (Nature's Food Chains / Las Cadenas Alimentarias en la Naturaleza Ser.). (Illus.). 24p. (gr. 1-3). (ENG & SPA.). pap. 9.15 *(978-0-8368-7382-5(3),* 24157320-235d-4262-9cd2-5c3e286badb0); (SPA & ENG., lib. bdg. 24.67 *(978-0-8368-7375-7(0),* e010ad87-6cce-4837-b862-542888c54c0b) Stevens, Gareth Publishing LLLP. (Weekly Reader Leveled Readers).
—What Sea Animals Eat, 1 vol. 2006. (Nature's Food Chains Ser.). (ENG., Illus.). 24p. (gr. 1-3). lib. bdg. 24.67 *(978-0-8368-6875-3(7),* 7c90712e-3adf-496e-bc8a-f5ff936a22e0, Weekly Reader Leveled Readers) Stevens, Gareth Publishing LLLP.
—What Sea Animals Eat / ¿Qué Comen Los Animales Del Mar?, 1 vol. 2006. (Nature's Food Chains / Las Cadenas Alimentarias en la Naturaleza Ser.). (ENG & SPA., Illus.). 24p. (gr. 1-3). pap. 9.15 *(978-0-8368-7383-2(1),* 029ffafd-2831-4a99-bfd1-e75bcf5cd466, Weekly Reader Leveled Readers) Stevens, Gareth Publishing LLLP.
McAneney, Caitie. Freaky Stories from Beneath the Sea, 1 vol. 2015. (Freaky True Science Ser.). (ENG.). 32p. (J). (gr. 4-5). pap. 11.50 *(978-1-4824-2964-0(0),* f93ef275-ee93-4a0d-948f-7987ea744a4e); lib. bdg. 28.27 *(978-1-4824-2966-4(7),* 1be3a7af-3193-476a-adb1-8aea41b3e5ab) Stevens, Gareth Publishing LLLP.
—Really Strange Marine Animals, 1 vol. 2016. (Really Strange Adaptations Ser.). (ENG.). 32p. (J). (gr. 5-5). 27.93 *(978-1-4994-2853-7(7),* c543515b-b436-4752-8f71-518738ea50ce); pap. 11.00 *(978-1-4994-2738-7(7),* bf15534f-2112-41eb-b8c1-64d4ec3ff1c9) Rosen Publishing Group, Inc., The. (PowerKids Pr.).
McCall, Gerrie. Fierce Water Creatures, 1 vol. 2005. (Nature's Monsters: Water Creatures Ser.). (ENG., Illus.). 32p. (gr. 3-5). lib. bdg. 28.67 *(978-0-8368-6177-8(9),* 145b2311-2333-4ac3-a74d-8ae137375423, Gareth Stevens Learning Library) Stevens, Gareth Publishing LLLP.
McCune, Jamie. First Look at Ocean Animals. 2010. (First Look At Ser.). (ENG.). 16p. (J). (gr. -1). 6.95 *(978-1-60727-138-3(9))* Soundprints.
McCurry, Kristen & Jackson, Aimee. Ocean Babies. NorthWord Books for Young Readers Staff, ed. 2004. (Animal Babies Ser.). (ENG., Illus.). 22p. (J). (gr. -1 — 1). bds. 9.95 *(978-1-55971-898-1(6))* Cooper Square Publishing Llc.
McElligott, Matthew. Mad Scientist Academy: the Ocean Disaster. 2019. (Mad Scientist Academy Ser.). (ENG., Illus.). 40p. (J). (gr. k-3). lib. bdg. 20.99 *(978-1-5247-6720-4(4),* Crown Books For Young Readers) Random Hse. Children's Bks.
McGinlay, Richard. My First Encyclopedia of Fish: A Great Big Book of Amazing Aquatic Creatures to Discover. 2017. (Illus.). 24p. (J). (gr. -1-12). pap. 7.99 *(978-1-86147-824-5(0),* Armadillo) Anness Publishing GBR. Dist: National Bk. Network.
Mcginty, Alice B. Ocean Animals. 2015. (Illus.). 16p. (J). pap. *(978-0-545-85887-8(9))* Scholastic, Inc.
McKnight, Diane. The Lost Seal. Emerling, Dorothy, illus. 2006. (Long Term Ecological Research Ser.). (ENG.). 40p. (J). (gr. 4-7). 19.95 *(978-0-9723422-7-8(3))* Taylor Trade Publishing.
McNeil, Niki, et al. HOCPP 1077 Predators of the Deep. 2006. spiral bd. 16.50 *(978-1-60308-077-4(5))* In the Hands of a Child.
Mead, Brian. Creatures of the Deep Coloring Book. 2003. 32p. (J). (gr. -1-3). pap. 3.99 *(978-0-9717509-3-7(9))* Mead, Brian Publishing.
Mehling, Carl. Prehistoric Creatures of the Sea & Skies, 1 vol. 2009. (Discovering Dinosaurs Ser.). (ENG., Illus.). 48p. (YA). (gr. 4-4). 33.93 *(978-1-60754-773-0(2),* 8b15e4e7-ad82-497a-81a6-a15219d7b366); pap. 13.85 *(978-1-60754-781-5(3),* 55fc2f9a-4afd-4478-bca0-a8ddc26b8ebf) Rosen Publishing Group, Inc., The. (Windmill Bks.).
Meister, Cari. Do You Really Want to Meet an Octopus? Fabbri, Daniele, illus. 2018. (Do You Really Want to Meet ... ? Ser.). (ENG.). 24p. (J). (gr. 1-4). pap. 9.99 *(978-1-68152-315-6(9),* 15042); lib. bdg. *(978-1-68151-395-9(1),* 15036) Amicus.
—Sea Dragons. 2014. (Illus.). 24p. (J). lib. bdg. 25.65 *(978-1-62031-101-1(1),* Bullfrog Bks.) Jump! Inc.
—Totally Wacky Facts about Sea Animals. 2015. (Mind Benders Ser.). (ENG., Illus.). 112p. (J). (gr. 3-6). lib. bdg. 23.99 *(978-1-4914-6521-9(2),* 129020, Capstone Pr.) Capstone.
Merlino, Kim. Ocean Life: Grades 2 Through 4. (Illus.). (J). pap., wbk. ed. 4.99 *(978-0-88743-966-7(7))* School Zone Publishing Co.
Mihaltchev, Atanas. Kid-Agami — Sea Life: Kiragami for Kids: Easy-To-Make Paper Toys. 2013. (Dover Kids Activity Bks.). (ENG.). 24p. (J). (gr. 1-5). pap. 9.99 *(978-0-486-49744-0(5),* 497445) Dover Pubns., Inc.
Milbourne, Anna. Under the Sea. Shimmen, Cathy, illus. 2007. (Picture Bks). 32p. (J). 9.99 *(978-0-7945-1801-1(X),* Usborne) EDC Publishing.
Miles, Lisa. Origami Sea Creatures, 1 vol. 2013. (Amazing Origami Ser.). 32p. (J). (gr. 2-3). (ENG.). pap. 11.50 *(978-1-4339-9661-0(8),* 90f44aac-29ae-44b4-93bd-e966b71226e8); pap. 63.00 *(978-1-4339-9662-7(6));* (ENG., Illus.). lib. bdg. 29.27 *(978-1-4339-9660-3(X),* a11891c0-4854-4ac1-bac3-b849f7c98e9f) Stevens, Gareth Publishing LLLP.
Miller, Tessa. Inventions Inspired by Oceanic Animals. 2019. (J). *(978-1-7911-1820-4(8),* AV2 by Weigl) Weigl Pubs., Inc.
Miller, Tori. Eels, 1 vol. 2009. (Freaky Fish Ser.). (ENG.). 24p. (J). (gr. 2-3). lib. bdg. 26.27 *(978-1-4358-2754-7(6),* cc7560b7-42eb-452f-9567-1216b340e28f) Rosen Publishing Group, Inc., The.
Milner, Charlotte. The Sea Book. Milner, Charlotte, illus. 2019. (Conservation for Kids Ser.). (ENG., Illus.). 48p. (J). (gr. k-3). 15.99 *(978-1-4654-7882-5(5),* DK Children) Dorling Kindersley Publishing, Inc.
Mineo, Ella. Sea Otters in Danger, 1 vol. 2013. (Animals at Risk Ser.). 24p. (J). (gr. 2-3). (ENG.). pap. 9.15 *(978-1-4339-9170-7(5),* a80b7a85-4dfb-42a0-b3f8-c8e6f582f971); pap. 48.90 *(978-1-4339-9171-4(3));* (ENG., Illus.). lib. bdg. 25.27 *(978-1-4339-9169-1(1),* 9163a4d9-9435-4656-8baf-0428ffdbe032) Stevens, Gareth Publishing LLLP.
Montgomery, Heather L. Little Monsters of the Ocean: Metamorphosis under the Waves. 2019. (ENG., Illus.). 56p. (J). (gr. 4-8). 33.32 *(978-1-5415-2898-7(0),* 082f2d0f-0aad-4900-b551-bdf5d8606244, Millbrook Pr.) Lerner Publishing Group.
Moore, David. National Geographic Science 1-2 (Life Science: Habitats): Explore on Your Own: Watch Out! 2007. 16p. (C). pap. 8.95 *(978-0-7362-5372-7(6))* National Geographic School Publishing, Inc.
Moore Niver, Heather. 20 Fun Facts about Moray Eels, 1 vol. 2012. (Fun Fact File: Fierce Fish! Ser.). (ENG., Illus.). 32p. (J). (gr. 2-3). pap. 11.50 *(978-1-4339-6984-3(X),* eb4bfbf7-13f2-41d8-9727-a1434782a20f); lib. bdg. 27.93 *(978-1-4339-6983-6(1),* 9e391783-f476-449a-af1e-a00cf610e257) Stevens, Gareth Publishing LLLP.
Morgan, Sally & De la Bédoyère, Camilla. Under the Sea. 2014. (Illus.). 120p. (J). *(978-1-4351-5536-7(X))* Barnes & Noble, Inc.
Murphy, Julie. Ocean Animal Adaptations, 1 vol. 2011. (Amazing Animal Adaptations Ser.). (ENG.). 32p. (J). (gr. -1-2). pap. 8.10 *(978-1-4296-7029-6(0),* 116741); (gr. -1-2). lib. bdg. 27.99 *(978-1-4296-6029-7(5),* 114972); (gr. 1-2). pap. 49.60 *(978-1-4296-7036-4(3),* 16660) Capstone. (Capstone Pr.).
Murray, Aaron R. Counting in the Oceans 1-2-3, 1 vol. 2012. (All about Counting in the Biomes Ser.). (ENG., Illus.). 24p. (gr. -1-1). 25.27 *(978-0-7660-4052-6(6),* 24d648a6-f224-4734-b329-775b917c402e, Enslow Publishing) Enslow Publishing, LLC.
Nagle, Kerry. Marine Creatures, 1 vol. 2010. (Weird, Wild, & Wonderful Ser.). (ENG., Illus.). 24p. (J). (gr. 2-3). lib. bdg. 24.67 *(978-1-4339-3581-7(3),* 8cf0dd06-639b-43d3-82c9-d94911f630f7, Gareth Stevens Learning Library) Stevens, Gareth Publishing LLLP.
—Marine Minibeasts, 1 vol. 2010. (Weird, Wild, & Wonderful Ser.). (ENG.). 24p. (J). (gr. 2-3). lib. bdg. 24.67 *(978-1-4339-3571-8(6),* f8ba0dfd-3745-478a-8184-2c4dac0b2772, Gareth Stevens Learning Library) Stevens, Gareth Publishing LLLP.
Nakamura, May. If You Love Dolphins, You Could Be... Ready-To-Read Level 2. Kwee, Natalie, illus. 2019. (If You Love Ser.). (ENG.). 32p. (J). (gr. k-2). 17.99 *(978-1-5344-4469-0(6));* pap. 4.99 *(978-1-5344-4468-3(8))* Simon Spotlight. (Simon Spotlight).
National Geographic Kids. National Geographic Kids Beach Day: Sticker Activity Book. 2017. (NG Sticker Activity Bks.). 56p. (J). (gr. -1-k). pap. 6.99 *(978-1-4263-2776-6(5),* National Geographic Kids) Disney Publishing Worldwide.
—National Geographic Kids Look & Learn: Ocean Creatures. 2015. (Look & Learn Ser.). (Illus.). 24p. (J). (gr. -1-k). bds. 6.99 *(978-1-4263-2063-7(9),* National Geographic Kids) Disney Publishing Worldwide.
—National Geographic Kids Ocean Animals Sticker Activity Book: Over 1,000 Stickers! 2016. (NG Sticker Activity Bks.). 56p. (J). (gr. -1-k). pap., act. bk. ed. 6.99 *(978-1-4263-2424-6(3),* National Geographic Kids) Disney Publishing Worldwide.
—National Geographic Readers - Ocean Animals Collection. 2015. (Readers Ser.). (Illus.). 128p. (J). (gr. -1-k). pap. 8.99 *(978-1-4263-2273-0(9),* National Geographic Kids) Disney Publishing Worldwide.
National Geographic Learning. Reading Expeditions (Science: Everyday Science): Science at the Sandy Shore. 2006. (ENG., Illus.). 24p. (J). pap. 15.95 *(978-0-7922-8625-7(1))* CENGAGE Learning.
Nature Series Books 25 & 26: Activities. 2004. (J). pap., instr.'s gde. ed. 2.95 *(978-1-878405-48-7(9))* Nags Head Art, Inc.
Needham, Kate. Usborne the Great Undersea Search. Brooks, Felicity, ed. Jackson, Ian, illus. rev. ed. 2006. (Great Searches Ser.). 32p. (J). (gr. -1-3). per. 7.99 *(978-0-7945-1228-6(3),* Usborne) EDC Publishing.
Nelson, Robert Lyn. Ocean Friends. 2003. (ENG., Illus.). 32p. (J). (gr. -1-3). 15.95 *(978-1-55971-840-0(4))* Cooper Square Publishing Llc.
Newland, Sonya. Ocean Animals. 2011. (Saving Wildlife Ser.). 32p. (YA). (gr. 3-6). lib. bdg. 28.50 *(978-1-59920-658-5(7))* Black Rabbit Bks.
Nichols, Catherine. One Big Ocean, 1 vol. 2003. (We Can Read about Nature! Ser.). (ENG., Illus.). 32p. (gr. 1-2). 25.50 *(978-0-7614-1433-9(9),* debc88b0-db8c-4d89-9916-8b72a7b9ebee) Cavendish Square Publishing LLC.
NorthWord Books for Young Readers Editors. Ocean Babies. 2005. (SPA.). (J). bds. 5.95 *(978-1-55971-908-7(7),* NorthWord Bks. for Young Readers) T&N Children's Publishing.
Ocean Animals. 2004. (Illus.). lib. bdg. 7.95 *(978-0-8225-4511-8(X))* Lerner Publishing Group.
Ocean Animals. Date not set. (Illus.). 16p. (J). 5.98 *(978-0-7525-7698-5(4));* 2.98 *(978-0-7525-9762-1(0))* Parragon, Inc.
Octopuses & Squids: Level N, 6 vols. (Wonder Worldtm Ser.). 48p. 34.95 *(978-0-7802-2902-0(9))* Wright Group/McGraw-Hill.
O'Donnell, Kerri. Ugly Sea Creatures. (Ugly Animals Ser.). 24p. (gr. 2-3). 2009. 42.50 *(978-1-60854-604-6(7),* PowerKids Pr.) 2006. (ENG., Illus.). (J). lib. bdg. 26.27 *(978-1-4042-3528-1(0),* d9db517f-1c2b-49c4-95f5-ff6406539690) Rosen Publishing Group, Inc., The.
O'Reilly, Wenda. Go fish wildlife sea Creatures. 2007. n/ap. pap. 119.40 *(978-1-59960-020-8(X))* Birdcage Pr.
Osborne, Mary Pope & Boyce, Natalie Pope. Sea Monsters: A Nonfiction Companion to Dark Day in the Deep Sea. Murdocca, Sal, illus. 2008. (Magic Tree House Research Guides: No. 17). 121p. (J). (gr. 1-5). 12.65 *(978-0-7569-8809-8(8))* Perfection Learning Corp.
—Sea Monsters: A Nonfiction Companion to Magic Tree House Merlin Mission #11: Dark Day in the Deep Sea. Murdocca, Sal, illus. 2008. (Magic Tree House (R) Fact Tracker Ser.: 17). 128p. (J). (gr. 2-5). 6.99

(978-0-375-84663-2(8), Random Hse. Bks. for Young Readers) Random Hse. Children's Bks.

Otfinoski, Steven. Manatees, 1 vol. 2011. (Animals, Animals Ser.). (ENG.). 48p. (gr. 5-5). 32.64 *(978-0-7614-4842-6(X)*, 9d954d06-cc5a-47f5-b801-3a21bc02f658) Cavendish Square Publishing LLC.

Ottina, Laura. In the Sea, 1 vol. 2009. (Learn with Animals Ser.). (ENG., Illus.). 24p. (J). (gr. k-1). pap. 9.15 *(978-1-4339-2091-2(3)*, d97bd269-052a-4dfc-81f8-991e30f0a68d); lib. bdg. 24.67 *(978-1-4339-1914-5(1)*, 551b0f35-5531-4a55-b7bf-0a90f9758d09) Stevens, Gareth Publishing LLLP. (Weekly Reader Leveled Readers).

Owen, Ruth. Marvelous Marine Mammals, 1 vol. 2012. (Eye to Eye with Animals Ser.). (ENG., Illus.). 32p. (J). (gr. 2-2). 29.93 *(978-1-4488-8070-6(X)*, 18ba854a-0ec5-475b-97e3-98891d524100); pap. 11.00 *(978-1-4488-8106-2(4)*, e7b9795c-8edd-4e88-b9ff-874367abbf13) Rosen Publishing Group, Inc., The. (Windmill Bks.).

—Sea Otter Pups. 2012. (Water Babies Ser.). 24p. (J). (gr. -1-3). lib. bdg. 25.65 *(978-1-61772-601-9(X))* Bearport Publishing Co., Inc.

Pallotta, Jerry. The Ocean Alphabet Board Book. Mazzola, Frank, Jr., illus. 2003. 28p. (J). (-k). bds. 7.95 *(978-1-57091-524-6(5))* Charlesbridge Publishing, Inc.

—Sea Mammal Alphabet Book. 2012. (ENG.). (J). 16.95 *(978-0-9852032-5-2(0))* Who Would Win?

—The Sea Mammal Alphabet Book. Leonard, Tom, illus. 2019. 32p. (J). (gr. -1-2). pap. 7.99 *(978-1-57091-149-1(5))* Charlesbridge Publishing, Inc.

—Ultimate Ocean Rumble (Who Would Win?) Bolster, Rob, illus. 2020. (Who Would Win? Ser.: 14). (ENG.). 32p. (J). (gr. 1-4). pap. 4.99 *(978-0-545-68118-6(9))* Scholastic, Inc.

Parker, Steve. Sea Monsters. 2011. (ENG., Illus.). 32p. (J). pap. 10.95 *(978-1-77092-014-9(5))* Saunders Bk. Co. CAN. Dist: RiverStream Publishing.

Patterson, Caroline. Fish Do WHAT in the Water? The Secret Lives of Marine Animals. Rath, Robert, illus. 2012. 48p. (J). 14.95 *(978-1-56037-519-7(1))* Farcountry Pr.

Peacock, L. A. The Truth (and Myths) about Sea Monsters. Wigsby, Nick, illus. 2015. 93p. (J). pap. *(978-0-545-70566-0(5))* Scholastic, Inc.

Perkins, Wendy. Sea Cucumbers. (Weird & Unusual Animals Ser.). (ENG., Illus.). 24p. (J). (gr. 1-4). 2018. pap. 8.99 *(978-1-68152-191-6(1)*, 16102) 2017. 20.95 *(978-1-68151-160-3(6)*, 14702) Amicus.

—Sea Dragons. 2018. (Weird & Unusual Animals Ser.). (ENG., Illus.). 24p. (J). (gr. 1-4). pap. 8.99 *(978-1-68152-190-9(3)*, 16103) Amicus.

Person, Stephen. The Coral Reef: A Giant City under the Sea. 2009. (Spectacular Animal Towns Ser.). (Illus.). 32p. (J). (gr. 2-7). lib. bdg. 28.50 *(978-1-59716-869-4(6))* Bearport Publishing Co., Inc.

Peters, Katie. I See the Ocean. 2019. (Let's Look at Animal Habitats (Pull Ahead Readers — Nonfiction) Ser.). (ENG., Illus.). 16p. (J). (gr. -1-1). pap. 8.99 *(978-1-5415-7312-3(9)*, 0296c2d8-acc5-4b58-b4bc-a3f6813dcce6, Lerner Pubns.) Lerner Publishing Group.

Pettiford, Rebecca. Ocean Food Chains. 2016. (Who Eats What?). (Illus.). 24p. (J). (gr. 2-5). lib. bdg. 25.65 *(978-1-62031-302-2(2)*, Pogo) Jump! Inc.

Phillips, Dee. Find It at the Beach, 1 vol. 2005. (Can You Find It? Ser.). (ENG., Illus.). 24p. (gr. 1-3). lib. bdg. 25.67 *(978-0-8368-6298-0(8)*, 216f63c2-856b-469d-a25f-537172c27f1a, Gareth Stevens Learning Library) Stevens, Gareth Publishing LLLP.

Piddock, Charles. Creeps of the Deep: Explore the Ocean's Strangest Creatures. 2009. (Current Science Ser.). (ENG.). 48p. (J). (gr. 4-6). pap. 8.95 *(978-1-4339-2130-8(8)*, Gareth Stevens Learning Library) Stevens, Gareth Publishing LLLP.

—Creeps of the Deep: Explore the Ocean's Strangest Creatures, 1 vol. 2009. (Current Science Ser.). (ENG.). 48p. (YA). (gr. 4-6). lib. bdg. 33.67 *(978-1-4339-2059-2(X)*, 7609817c-486b-49d7-b927-cfedea0622d4) Stevens, Gareth Publishing LLLP.

Pierce, Terry & Kofsky, Kristen. Dangerous Sea Creatures A to Z Coloring Book. 2004. (Illus.). 24p. pap. 4.95 *(978-1-57306-177-3(8))* Bess Pr., Inc.

Pipe, Jim. Scary Creatures of the Deep. Bergin, Mark et al, illus. 2009. (Scary Creatures Ser.). (ENG.). 32p. (J). (gr. k-3). 24.94 *(978-0-531-21822-8(8))* Scholastic Library Publishing.

Pirotta. Baby's First Sea Creatures. 2017. (Illus.). (J). bds. 7.98 *(978-1-946000-07-1(8))* Starry Forest Bks., Inc.

Potter, William. Under the Sea, 1 vol. Scott, Matthew, illus. 2017. (Spot & Discover Ser.). (ENG.). 24p. (J). (gr. 1-2). 26.27 *(978-1-5081-9341-8(X)*, 243fdf16-e31e-4083-b686-c262aacaf876); pap. 9.25 *(978-1-5081-9345-6(2)*, 4ddd6319-3968-400e-abe8-d114a965e2f0) Rosen Publishing Group, Inc., The. (Windmill Bks.).

Prager, Ellen. Sea Slime: It's Eeuwy, Gooey & under the Sea, 1 vol. Bersani, Shennen, illus. 2014. 32p. (J). (ENG.). (gr. 1-4). 17.95 *(978-1-62855-210-2(7))*; (SPA.). (gr. 2-3). pap. 11.95 *(978-1-62855-228-7(X)*, df16d99e-3bc6-4651-8e30-f0140234780f) Arbordale Publishing.

Pratt-Serafini, Kristin Joy. A Swim Through the Sea: Board Book, 1 vol. Pratt-Serafini, Kristin Joy, illus. 2006. (Illus.). 26p. (J). (gr. k-6). bds. 7.99 *(978-1-58469-080-1(1)*, Dawn Pubns.) Sourcebooks, Inc.

Press, Judy. Little Hands Sea Life Art & Activities: Creative Learning Experiences for 3-7-Year Olds. 2004. (Williamson's Little Hands Book Ser.). (Illus.). 128p. (J). pap. 12.95 *(978-1-885593-94-8(5)*, Ideals Pubns.) Worthy Publishing.

Prince, Savannah. Manny the Mol. 2012. 40p. pap. 19.57 *(978-1-4669-2968-5(5))* Trafford Publishing.

QEB Start Reading Together National Book Stores Edition: Sea Creatures. 2006. (J). per. *(978-1-59566-258-3(8))* QEB Publishing Inc.

Quinlan, Julia J. What Are Sea Invertebrates?, 4 vols. 2016. (Let's Find Out! Marine Life Ser.). (ENG.). 32p. (J). (gr. 2-3). 52.12 *(978-1-5081-0460-5(3)*, 697f7aaf-81a2-46ef-91e2-41a1f0fe501d); (Illus.). 26.06 *(978-1-5081-0389-9(5)*, 535fed49-aeb8-4926-86d2-710b48e33cfc, Britannica Educational Publishing) Rosen Publishing Group, Inc., The.

Rajczak, Michael. Sea Urchins, 1 vol. 2015. (Things That Sting Ser.). (ENG., Illus.). 24p. (J). (gr. 2-3). pap. 9.15 *(978-1-4824-1719-7(7)*, c5ef9bfd-dd98-4d19-8f08-feeacb9c0d29) Stevens, Gareth Publishing LLLP.

Rake, Jody S. Faceless, Spineless, & Brainless Ocean Animals. 2016. (Faceless, Spineless, & Brainless Ocean Animals Ser.). (ENG.). 24p. (J). (gr. 1-3). 111.96 *(978-1-5157-2164-2(7)*, 25073, Capstone Pr.) Capstone.

—Kings of the Oceans. 2017. (Animal Rulers Ser.). (ENG.). 24p. (J). (gr. 1-3). lib. bdg. 27.99 *(978-1-5157-8066-3(X)*, 136071, Capstone Pr.) Capstone.

—Sea Anemones. 2016. (Faceless, Spineless, & Brainless Ocean Animals Ser.). (ENG., Illus.). 24p. (J). (gr. 1-3). 27.99 *(978-1-5157-2139-0(6)*, 132713, Capstone Pr.) Capstone.

—Sea Cucumbers. 2016. (Faceless, Spineless, & Brainless Ocean Animals Ser.). (ENG., Illus.). 24p. (J). (gr. 1-3). 27.99 *(978-1-5157-2140-6(X)*, 132714, Capstone Pr.) Capstone.

—Sea Urchins. 2016. (Faceless, Spineless, & Brainless Ocean Animals Ser.). (ENG., Illus.). 24p. (J). (gr. 1-3). lib. bdg. 27.99 *(978-1-5157-2142-0(6)*, 132716, Capstone Pr.) Capstone.

Rake, Matthew. Prehistoric Sea Beasts. Mendez, Simon, illus. 2017. (If Extinct Beasts Came to Life Ser.). (ENG.). 32p. (J). (gr. 3-6). 7.99 *(978-1-5124-1158-4(2)*, cc477503-e896-49c1-a50c-de9b770a000b); E-Book 42.65 *(978-1-5124-3617-4(8)*, 9781512436174); E-Book 42.65 *(978-1-5124-0909-3(X))*; E-Book 4.99 *(978-1-5124-3618-1(6)*, 9781512436181) Lerner Publishing Group. (Hungry Tomato (r)).

Ranson, Erin & Imagine That. Ocean Animals. Green, Barry, illus. 2017. (Soft Felt Play Bks.). (ENG.). 10p. (J). (gr. -1-k). 12.99 *(978-1-78700-084-1(2))* Top That! Publishing PLC GBR. Dist: Independent Pubs. Group.

Read, Nicholas. The Seal Garden. McAllister, Ian, photos by. 2018. (My Great Bear Rainforest Ser.: 3). (ENG., Illus.). 32p. (J). (gr. 1-3). E-Book *(978-1-4598-1269-7(7))* Orca Bk. Pubs.

Redmond, Shirley Raye. Tentacles! Tales of the Giant Squid. Barnard, Bryn, illus. 2003. (Step into Reading Ser.). 48p. (J). (gr. k-3). pap. 5.99 *(978-0-375-81307-8(1)*, Random Hse. Bks. for Young Readers) Random Hse. Children's Bks.

Rennocks, Sam. Under the Sea ABC. 2018. (Padded Board Bks.). (ENG., Illus.). 28p. (J). (gr. -1-k). bds. 9.99 *(978-1-78700-452-8(X))* Top That! Publishing PLC GBR. Dist: Independent Pubs. Group.

Reyes, Blanca Matilde. Sea Animals. 2006. (Illus.). 16p. (J). 0.75 *(978-1-933984-03-2(1))* Two Lands.

Rhodes, Mary Jo & Hall, David. Dolphins, Seals, & Other Sea Mammals. 2006. (Undersea Encounters Ser.). (ENG., Illus.). 48p. (J). (gr. 3-7). 27.00 *(978-0-516-24392-4(6)*, Children's Pr.) Scholastic Library Publishing.

—Partners in the Sea. Hall, David, photos by. 2006. (Undersea Encounters Ser.). (ENG., Illus.). 48p. (J). (gr. 3-7). per. 6.95 *(978-0-516-25492-0(8)*, Children's Pr.) Scholastic Library Publishing.

—Predators of the Sea. 2006. (Undersea Encounters Ser.). (ENG., Illus.). 48p. (J). (gr. 3-7). lib. bdg. 27.00 *(978-0-516-24399-3(3)*, Children's Pr.) Scholastic Library Publishing.

—Undersea Encounters: Predators of the Sea. 2007. (Undersea Encounters Ser.). (ENG., Illus.). 48p. (J). (gr. 3-7). pap. 6.95 *(978-0-516-25465-4(0)*, Children's Pr.) Scholastic Library Publishing.

Ricciuti, Edward R. Adivina Quién Atrapa (Guess Who Grabs), 1 vol. 2008. (Adivina Quién (Guess Who?) Ser.). (SPA., Illus.). 32p. (gr. k-2). lib. bdg. 25.50 *(978-0-7614-2383-6(4)*, 2432c2fa-766a-48e6-9509-f541a0032e4e) Cavendish Square Publishing LLC.

Rice, Dona. Crazy Creatures: Deep Ocean. 2020. (J). pap. *(978-1-64290-723-0(5))* Teacher Created Materials, Inc.

Rice, William B. Endangered Animals of the Sea, 1 vol. 2nd rev. ed. 2013. (TIME for KIDS(r): Informational Text Ser.). (ENG., Illus.). 64p. (J). (gr. 4-8). pap. 14.99 *(978-1-4333-4935-5(3))*; lib. bdg. 31.96 *(978-1-4333-7434-0(X))* Teacher Created Materials, Inc.

Richmond, Ben. Why Is the Sea Salty? And Other Questions about Oceans. Azhderian, Cecelia, illus. 2014. (Good Question! Ser.). 32p. (J). (gr. 1). pap. 5.95 *(978-1-4549-0677-3(4))* Sterling Publishing Co., Inc.

Riggs, Kate. Manatees. 2018. (Amazing Animals Ser.). (ENG., Illus.). 24p. (J). (gr. 1-4). *(978-1-60818-879-6(5)*, 19606, Creative Education) Creative Co., The.

Rin, Bo. What Lives in the Sea? Marine Life. Park, Yeong Jin, illus. 2015. (Science Storybooks Ser.). (ENG.). 32p. (J). (gr. k-4). 27.99 *(978-1-925233-63-6(4)*, 8d12a99c-8c53-4923-a6de-ce72f6254068, Big and SMALL) ChoiceMaker Pty. Ltd., The AUS. Dist: Lerner Publishing Group.

Ripley's Believe It Or Not, Ripley's Believe. Ripley Twists: Sharks: And Other Scary Sea Creatures. 2013. (Twist Ser.: 9). (ENG.). 48p. (J). (gr. 1-4). 12.95 *(978-1-60991-083-9(4))* Ripley Entertainment, Inc.

Rissman, Rebecca. Counting in the Ocean, 1 vol. 2012. (I Can Count! Ser.). (ENG.). 24p. (gr. -1-k). pap. 9.95 *(978-1-4329-6701-7(0)*, Heinemann) Capstone.

—Living & Nonliving in the Ocean, 1 vol. 2013. (Is It Living or Nonliving? Ser.). (ENG., Illus.). 24p. (J). (gr. k-2). 25.99 *(978-1-4109-5381-0(5)*, 123310); pap. 6.95 *(978-1-4109-5388-9(2)*, 123328) Capstone. (Raintree).

Rivera, Sheila. Ocean. 2005. (Illus.). 24p. (J). pap. 5.95 *(978-0-8225-5372-4(4))* Lerner Publishing Group.

Rizzo, Johnna. Ocean Animals: Who's Who in the Deep Blue. 2016. (Illus.). 112p. (J). (gr. 3-7). pap. 12.99 *(978-1-4263-2506-9(1)*, National Geographic Kids) Disney Publishing Worldwide.

Roderick, Stacey. Ocean Animals from Head to Tail. Moriya, Kwanchai, illus. 2016. (Head to Tail Ser.). (ENG.). 36p. (J). (gr. -1-2). 16.95 *(978-1-77138-345-5(3))* Kids Can Pr., Ltd. CAN. Dist: Hachette Bk. Group.

Rodríguez, Ana María. Leatherback Turtles, Giant Squids, & Other Mysterious Animals of the Deepest Seas, 1 vol. 2012. (Extreme Animals in Extreme Environments Ser.). (ENG., Illus.). 48p. (gr. 5-7). pap. 11.53 *(978-1-4644-0019-3(9)*, 32a9cba7-04ad-4d2f-b562-47e58e0090de) Enslow Publishing, LLC.

—The Secret of the Squiggly Green Bombers... & More!, 1 vol. 2017. (Animal Secrets Revealed! Ser.). (ENG.). 48p. (gr. 4-4). lib. bdg. 29.60 *(978-0-7660-8631-9(3)*, 4585a1ef-1be2-4811-bfe7-1a0a22ae7be4) Enslow Publishing, LLC.

Rodríguez, Ana María & Rodríguez, Ana María. Leatherback Turtles, Giant Squids, & Other Mysterious Animals of the Deepest Seas, 1 vol. 2012. (Extreme Animals in Extreme Environments Ser.). (ENG., Illus.). 48p. (gr. 5-7). 27.93 *(978-0-7660-3696-3(0)*, 7e31be71-5b07-42a4-b871-9470224cb3d3) Enslow Publishing, LLC.

—Secret of the Sleepless Whales... & More!, 1 vol. 2008. (Animal Secrets Revealed! Ser.). (ENG., Illus.). 48p. (gr. 5-7). lib. bdg. 27.93 *(978-0-7660-2957-6(3)*, 5c784a96-e8f1-4b02-9ff2-68dd3fe147e2) Enslow Publishing, LLC.

Rogan, Bernie. Creatures of the Sea: Can You Guess Me. 2012. 52p. pap. 10.99 *(978-1-61904-758-7(6))* Salem Author Services.

Rogers, Kirsteen. Under the Sea Jigsaw Book. Scott, Peter, illus. 2007. (Luxury Jigsaw Bks.). 14p. (J). bds. 14.99 *(978-0-7945-1330-6(1)*, Usborne) EDC Publishing.

Rudolph, Jessica. Mi Cuerpo Es Rayado y Parece Lleno de Hojas. 2015. (Pistas de Animales Ser.). (SPA.). 24p. (J). (gr. -1-3). lib. bdg. 26.99 *(978-1-62724-577-7(4))* Bearport Publishing Co., Inc.

Rustad, Martha E. H. Sea Anemones. 2007. (Oceans Alive Ser.). (ENG., Illus.). 24p. (J). (gr. k-3). lib. bdg. 26.95 *(978-1-60014-081-5(5))* Bellwether Media.

—Sea Urchins. 2007. (Oceans Alive Ser.). (ENG., Illus.). 24p. (J). (gr. k-3). lib. bdg. 26.95 *(978-1-60014-109-6(9))* Bellwether Media.

—Stingrays. 2007. (Oceans Alive Ser.). (ENG., Illus.). 24p. (J). (gr. k-3). lib. bdg. 26.95 *(978-1-60014-080-8(7))* Bellwether Media.

Sabuda, Robert & Reinhart, Matthew. Encyclopedia Prehistorica Sharks & Other Sea Monsters Pop-Up. Sabuda, Robert & Reinhart, Matthew, illus. 2006. (Encyclopedia Prehistorica Ser.: 2). (ENG., Illus.). 12p. (J). (gr. k-4). 49.99 *(978-0-7636-2229-9(X))* Candlewick Pr.

Sakanakun. Gensundai Suizokukan. Matsuzawa, Yoji, photos by. 2010. (JPN., Illus.). 48p. (J). *(978-4-09-217253-1(2))* Shogakukan.

Samuel, Nigel. Creatures of the Deep. 2007. (Steck-Vaughn BOLDPRINT Anthologies Ser.). (ENG., Illus.). 48p. (gr. 4-7). pap. 16.90 *(978-1-4190-4021-4(9))* Houghton Mifflin Harcourt Publishing Co.

Sandy Creek (Firm) Staff, contrib. by. My First Book of Ocean Creatures: Learn about Jellyfish, Sharks, Deep Sea Creatures, & More with Fun Facts! 2016. (Illus.). 51p. (J). *(978-1-4351-6406-2(7))* Barnes & Noble, Inc.

Santillo, LuAnn. Under the Sea, 6 vols. Santillo, LuAnn, ed. 2003. (Half-Pint Kids Readers Ser.). (Illus.). 42p. (J). (gr. -1-1). pap. 6.95 *(978-1-59256-091-2(1))* Half-Pint Kids, Inc.

Sayre, April Pulley & Sayre, Jeff. One Is a Snail, Ten Is a Crab Big Book: A Counting by Feet Book. Cecil, Randy, illus. 2010. (ENG.). 40p. (J). (gr. k-3). pap. 24.99 *(978-0-7636-4790-2(X))* Candlewick Pr.

Schach, David. Sea Dragons. 2007. (Oceans Alive Ser.). (ENG., Illus.). 24p. (J). (gr. k-3). lib. bdg. 26.95 *(978-1-60014-055-6(6))* Bellwether Media.

Schoeller, Jen. Biggest, Baddest Book of Sea Creatures, 1 vol. 2015. (Biggest, Baddest Bks.). (ENG.). 24p. (J). (gr. k-4). 32.79 *(978-1-62403-517-3(5)*, 16685, Super SandCastle) ABDO Publishing Co.

Schomp, Virginia. Kronosaurus & Other Sea Creatures, 1 vol. 2005. (Prehistoric World Ser.). (ENG., Illus.). 32p. (gr. 3-3). lib. bdg. 32.64 *(978-0-7614-1543-5(2)*, ad13eb8b-e93d-4dcf-9530-c364374cc0d9) Cavendish Square Publishing LLC.

Schuh, Mari. Manatees. 2015. (Illus.). 24p. (J). lib. bdg. *(978-1-62031-189-9(5)*, Bullfrog Bks.) Jump! Inc.

—Sea Anemones. 2017. (Ocean Life up Close Ser.). (ENG., Illus.). 24p. (J). (gr. k-3). lib. bdg. 26.95 *(978-1-62617-573-0(X)*, Blastoff! Readers) Bellwether Media.

—Sea Slugs. 2015. (Illus.). 24p. (J). lib. bdg. *(978-1-62031-192-9(5)*, Bullfrog Bks.) Jump! Inc.

—Sea Turtles. 2018. (Spot Ocean Animals Ser.). (ENG.). 16p. (J). (gr. -1-2). pap. 7.99 *(978-1-68152-302-6(7)*, 15004); lib. bdg. *(978-1-68151-382-9(X)*, 14998) Amicus.

Scott, Janine. An Ocean of Animals. 2011. (Habitats Around the World Ser.). (ENG.). 24p. (J). (gr. k-1). pap. 44.74 *(978-1-4296-7155-2(6)*, 16719); (Illus.). (gr. -1-2). pap. 7.29 *(978-1-4296-7151-4(3)*, 116785) Capstone. (Capstone Pr.).

Sea Creatures Pack [Scholastic]. 2011. (Under the Sea Ser.). pap. 3.00 *(978-1-4296-6304-5(9)*, Capstone Pr.) Capstone.

Sea Mammals. (Illus.). (J). (gr. -1-6). pap., act. bk. ed. 2.95 *(978-0-565-00974-8(5))* Natural History Museum Pubns. GBR. Dist: Parkwest Pubns., Inc.

Sea Shapes. (Illus.). 12p. (J). *(978-2-7643-0150-0(2))* Phidal Publishing, Inc./Editions Phidal, Inc.

Sea Splash. (My Animal Library). (Illus.). 10p. (J). *(978-2-7643-0103-6(0))* Phidal Publishing, Inc./Editions Phidal, Inc.

Sexton, Colleen. Blastoff! Readers - Oceans Alive, 6 vols., Set. Incl. Angelfish. 20.00 *(978-0-531-21711-5(6))*; Frogfish. 20.00 *(978-0-531-21712-2(4))*; Lionfish. 20.00 *(978-0-531-21713-9(2))*; Puffins. 20.00 *(978-0-531-21714-6(0))*; Shrimp. 20.00 *(978-0-531-21716-0(7))*; Swordfish. 20.00 *(978-0-531-21715-3(9))*; (Illus.). 24p. (J). (gr. k-3). 2009. 2009. Set lib. bdg. 120.00 *(978-0-531-26128-6(X)*, Children's Pr.) Scholastic Library Publishing.

—Coral Reefs. 2011. (Blastoff! Readers Ser.). 24p. (J). pap. 5.95 *(978-0-531-26026-5(7)*, Children's Pr.) Scholastic Library Publishing.

—Cuttlefish. 2009. (Oceans Alive Ser.). (ENG., Illus.). 24p. (J). (gr. k-3). lib. bdg. 26.95 *(978-1-60014-273-4(7))* Bellwether Media.

—Sponges. 2009. (Oceans Alive Ser.). (ENG., Illus.). 24p. (J). (gr. k-3). lib. bdg. 26.95 *(978-1-60014-268-0(0))* Bellwether Media.

Shea, Mary Molly. Being a Manatee, 1 vol., Vol. 1. 2013. (Can You Imagine? Ser.). (ENG., Illus.). 32p. (J). (gr. 2-3). 27.92 *(978-1-4824-0127-1(4)*, eceac665-0e5e-4c48-9148-a63c96c2f757) Stevens, Gareth Publishing LLLP.

Shea, Nicole. Creepy Sea Creatures, 1 vol. 2012. (Nature's Creepiest Creatures Ser.). (ENG., Illus.). 24p. (J). (gr. 2-3). pap. 9.15 *(978-1-4339-6503-6(8)*, 86764d8c-9937-46d7-abf3-875c8b5c9a1b); lib. bdg. 25.27 *(978-1-4339-6501-2(1)*, 584f53d7-2fa8-4712-9fd9-fcea8d81025b) Stevens, Gareth Publishing LLLP. (Gareth Stevens Learning Library).

Shea, Therese. What Are Crustaceans?, 1 vol. 2016. (Let's Find Out! Marine Life Ser.). (ENG.). 32p. (J). (gr. 2-3). pap. 13.90 *(978-1-5081-0386-8(0)*, 3185449f-bff6-46e2-9541-6cd833718440, Britannica Educational Publishing) Rosen Publishing Group, Inc., The.

Shocking Sea Creatures. 2016. (Illus.). 32p. (J). *(978-1-4222-3528-7(9))* Mason Crest.

Shore, Diane Z. & Calvert, Deanna. Riddle Diddle Ocean. Bauer, Stephanie, illus. 2019. (Riddle Diddle Dumplings Ser.). (ENG.). 10p. (J). (gr. -1-1). bds. 9.99 *(978-1-68152-499-3(6)*, 10867) Amicus.

Sill, Cathryn. About Crustaceans: A Guide for Children, 1 vol. Sill, John, illus. (About... Ser.: 8). 40p. (J). (gr. -1-2). 2007. pap. 8.99 *(978-1-56145-405-1(2))* 2004. 16.95 *(978-1-56145-301-6(3))* Peachtree Publishing Co. Inc.

—About Marine Mammals: A Guide for Children, 1 vol. Sill, John, illus. 2016. (About... Ser.: 19). 48p. (J). (gr. -1-2). 16.95 *(978-1-56145-906-3(2))* Peachtree Publishing Co. Inc.

Silver Dolphin en Español Editors. El Mundo a Mi Alrededor: El Oceano. Zaidi, Nadeem, illus. 2007. (Baby Einstein Ser.). (SPA.). 12p. (J). (gr. -1). bds. *(978-970-718-457-2(4)*, Silver Dolphin en Español) Advanced Marketing, S. de R. L. de C. V.

Simon, Seymour. Sea Creatures. 2018. (ENG., Illus.). 40p. (J). (gr. 1-5). 17.99 *(978-0-06-228921-6(7))*; pap. 6.99 *(978-0-06-228920-9(9))* HarperCollins Pubs. (HarperCollins).

—Under the Sea. 2008. (Illus.). 24p. (J). *(978-0-439-86656-9(1))* Scholastic, Inc.

Skerry, Brian & Zoehfeld, Kathleen Weidner. National Geographic Kids Chapters: the Whale Who Won Hearts: And More True Stories of Amazing Animal Adventures. 2014. (NGK Chapters Ser.). (Illus.). 112p. (J). (gr. 3-7). pap. 5.99 *(978-1-4263-1520-6(1)*, National Geographic Kids) Disney Publishing Worldwide.

Slade, Suzanne. What Eats What in an Ocean Food Chain, 1 vol. McLaughlin, Zack, illus. 2012. (Food Chains Ser.). (ENG.). 24p. (J). (gr. 2-4). pap. 8.95 *(978-1-4048-7696-5(0)*, 120443, Picture Window Bks.) Capstone.

Smith, Alastair & Howell, Laura. On the Beach. 2004. (Lift-the-Flap Learners Ser.). (Illus.). 16p. (J). (gr. 1-18). pap. 8.95 *(978-0-7945-0213-3(X)*, Usborne) EDC Publishing.

Smith, Alastair & Tachell, Judy. Under the Sea. Scott, Peter David, illus. 2007. (J). *(978-0-545-03305-3(5))* Scholastic, Inc.

Smith, Carrie & Swain, Cameron. Life at the Beach. 2006. (Early Explorers Ser.). (J). pap. *(978-1-4108-6020-0(5))* Benchmark Education Co.

Sovak, Jan. Let's Explore! Sea Animals. 2011. (Dover Sea Life Coloring Bks.). (ENG.). 32p. (J). (gr. 1-5). pap. 7.99 *(978-0-486-47895-1(5)*, 478955) Dover Pubns., Inc.

—Manatees Coloring Book. 2010. (Dover Sea Life Coloring Bks.). (ENG., Illus.). 32p. (J). (gr. 2-5). pap. 3.99 *(978-0-486-47390-1(2)*, 473902) Dover Pubns., Inc.

Spilsbury, Louise. A Day in the Life: Sea Animals Set. Incl. Jellyfish. (ENG.). 24p. (J). (gr. k-2). 2010. pap. 6.79 *(978-1-4329-4007-2(4)*, 113127, Heinemann); (Day in the Life: Sea Animals Ser.). (ENG.). 24p. 2010. pap., pap., pap. 27.16 o.p. *(978-1-4329-4012-6(0)*, 15032, Heinemann) Capstone.

Spilsbury, Richard & Spilsbury, Louise. At Home in the Ocean, 1 vol., 1. 2015. (Home in the Biome Ser.). (ENG.). 32p. (J). (gr. 3-4). 27.93 *(978-1-5081-4567-7(9)*, 3dfd6065-6470-412d-864f-6295e8b27447, PowerKids Pr.) Rosen Publishing Group, Inc., The.

Spizzirri, Linda, ed. Prehistoric Sea Life. Kohn, Arnie, illus. 32p. (J). (gr. 1-8). pap. 4.98 incl. audio *(978-0-86545-020-2(X))* Spizzirri Pr., Inc.

Staunton, Joseph. Dinosaurs in the Sea. 2010. (Discover the Dinosaurs Ser.). 32p. (J). (gr. 2-5). 28.50 *(978-1-60753-107-4(0))* Amicus Learning.

Staunton, Joseph & Flinthart, Dirk. Dinosaurs in the Sea. Rey, Luis, illus. 2011. (Inside Crime Ser.). 48p. (YA). (gr. 5-9). 34.25 *(978-1-59920-393-5(6))* Black Rabbit Bks.

Stefoff, Rebecca. Sea Mammals, 1 vol. 2009. (Family Trees Ser.). (ENG.). 96p. (gr. 6-6). lib. bdg. 36.93 *(978-0-7614-3072-8(5)*, 64b026e3-2f6b-4d1c-a0fd-54277b534bc7) Cavendish Square Publishing LLC.

Stewart, Melissa. Extreme Coral Reef! 2008. (Smithsonian Q & A Ser.). (Illus.). 48p. (J). (gr. k-4). 16.99 *(978-0-06-111577-6(0))* Smithsonian Bks.

Stone, Lynn. How Do Animals Use Their Flippers? 2007. (How Do Animals Use (Discovery Library) Ser.). (Illus.). 24p. (J). (gr. -1-3). lib. bdg. 22.79 *(978-1-60044-505-7(5))* Rourke Educational Media.

Sullivan, Laura. Saltwater & Freshwater Creatures Explained, 1 vol. 2016. (Distinctions in Nature Ser.). (ENG.). 32p. (gr. 3-3). pap. 11.58 *(978-1-5026-2185-6(1)*, b8b35d52-36e0-40c7-b4a8-20c333541ddf) Cavendish Square Publishing LLC.

Swan Miller, Sara. Secret Lives of Deep-Sea Creatures, 1 vol. 2011. (Secret Lives Ser.). (ENG.). 48p. (gr. 4-4). 32.64 *(978-0-7614-4226-4(X)*, 2a382f2e-3fe6-4107-bc3c-827213ed694f) Cavendish Square Publishing LLC.

Swanson, Diane. Safari Beneath the Sea: The Wonder World of the North Pacific Coast, 1 vol. Royal British Columbia Museum Staff, photos by. (ENG., Illus.). 64p. (J). pap. 12.95 *(978-1-55110-441-6(5))* Whitecap Bks., Ltd. CAN. Dist: Graphic Arts Ctr. Publishing Co.

Swanson, Maggie. SPARK Sea Life Designs Coloring Book. 2016. (Dover Sea Life Coloring Bks.). (ENG.). 64p. (J). (gr. 1-4). pap. 5.99 *(978-0-486-81025-6(9)*, 810259) Dover Pubns., Inc.

Swinburne, Stephen R. Ocean Soup: Tide-Pool Poems. Peterson, Mary, illus. 2009. (ENG.). 32p. (J). (gr. k-3). 22.44 *(978-1-58089-200-1(0))* Charlesbridge Publishing, Inc.

Szymanski, Jennifer. National Geographic Readers: in the Ocean (L1/Coreader) 2018. (Readers Ser.). (Illus.). 48p. (J).

(gr. -1-k). pap. 4.99 *(978-1-4263-3235-7(1)*, National Geographic Kids) Disney Publishing Worldwide.

Taylor, Trace, et al. In the Ocean. Reese, Jonathan, illus. 2012. (1-3Y Ecosystems Ser.). (ENG.). 16p. (J). (gr. k-1). pap. 8.00 *(978-1-59301-438-4(4))* American Reading Co.

Teora, creator. Sea Animals, 1 vol. 2007. (My First Sticker Encyclopedia Ser.). (ENG., Illus.). 16p. (J). (gr. -1-3). pap. 5.95 *(978-1-59496-148-9(4))* Teora USA LLC.

Toufexis, George. River Monsters of the World. 2014. (Dover Sea Life Coloring Bks.). (ENG., Illus.). 32p. (J). (gr. 3-8). pap. 3.99 *(978-0-486-49627-6(9)*, 496279) Dover Pubns., Inc.

Troup, Roxanne. Deep-Sea Creatures, 1 vol. 2019. (Creepy, Kooky Science Ser.). (ENG.). 48p. (gr. 5-5). pap. 12.70 *(978-1-9785-1371-6(2)*, c5dd90f0-910b-420f-b308-4ac755a1336b) Enslow Publishing, LLC.

Twist, Clint. 1000 Things You Should Know about Oceans. 2008. (1000 Things You Should Know about (Miles Kelley) Ser.). (Illus.). 61p. (J). pap. *(978-1-84236-852-7(4))* Miles Kelly Publishing, Ltd.

Under the Sea [Scholastic]. 2010. (Under the Sea Ser.). pap. 3.12 *(978-1-4296-5068-7(0)*, Capstone Pr.) Capstone.

Underwater Animals: Level O, 6 vols. (Explorers Ser.). 32p. (gr. 3-6). 44.95 *(978-0-7699-0591-4(9))* Shortland Pubns. (U. S. A.) Inc.

Underwood, Deborah. Hiding in Oceans, 1 vol. 2010. (Creature Camouflage Ser.). (ENG., Illus.). 32p. (J). (gr. 1-3). pap. 8.29 *(978-1-4329-4029-4(5)*, 113174, Heinemann) Capstone.

Van Zandt, Steve & Zecca, Katherine. River Song: With the Banana Slug String Band. 2007. (Illus.). 32p. (J). (gr. k-4). 9.99 *(978-1-58469-094-8(1)*, 1268621, Dawn Pubns.) Sourcebooks, Inc.

—River Song: With the Banana Slug String Band (Includes Music CD) 2007. (Illus.). 32p. (J). (gr. k-4). 17.99 *(978-1-58469-093-1(3)*, 1268621, Dawn Pubns.) Sourcebooks, Inc.

Vink, Amanda. Sea Urchins Are Brainless!, 1 vol. 2019. (Animals Without Brains! Ser.). (ENG.). 24p. (J). (gr. 1-2). pap. 9.15 *(978-1-5382-4598-9(1)*, 72fed99f-2d5c-4395-8e2a-7126a91277b5) Stevens, Gareth Publishing LLLP.

Wade, Laura. Sea & Sealife. 2003. (Knowledge Masters Ser.). (Illus.). 32p. (YA). pap. incl. cd-rom *(978-1-903954-10-2(X)*, Pavilion Children's Books) Pavilion Bks.

Wagner, Karen. Mosasaurus: Mighty Ruler of the Sea. 2008. (ENG., Illus.). 36p. (J). (gr. k-2). pap. 6.95 *(978-1-59249-781-2(0))* Soundprints.

—Mosasaurus: Mighty Ruler of the Sea. Carr, Karen, illus. 2008. (ENG.). 36p. (J). (gr. k-2). 8.95 *(978-1-59249-782-9(9))*; 2.95 *(978-1-59249-783-6(7))*; 9.95 *(978-1-59249-784-3(5))*; 14.95 *(978-1-59249-780-5(2))* Soundprints.

Walden, Libby. Hidden World: Ocean. Coleman, Stephanie Fizer, illus. 2018. (ENG.). 18p. (J). (gr. -1-2). 14.99 *(978-1-944530-15-0(0)*, 360 Degrees) Tiger Tales.

Walker Harvey, Jeanne. Astro: the Steller Sea Lion, 1 vol. Bersani, Shennen, illus. 2010. (ENG.). 32p. (J). (gr. 2-3). pap. 10.95 *(978-1-60718-874-2(0)*, bfba7161-c404-4b8d-bbeb-72553eefc543) Arbordale Publishing.

Walter Foster Creative Team. Sea Creatures: Step-by-Step Insructions for 25 Ocean Animals. Farrell, Russell, illus. 2011. (Learn to Draw Ser.). 32p. (J). (gr. 1-4). 28.50 *(978-1-936309-19-1(X))* Quarto Publishing Group USA.

Walters, Peter. The Hungriest Mouth in the Sea, 1 vol. 2015. (ENG., Illus.). 32p. (J). (gr. k-3). pap. 9.95 *(978-1-62855-636-0(6))* Arbordale Publishing.

Waters, Kate. Ocean Giants. 2009. (Illus.). 32p. (J). pap. *(978-0-545-07233-5(6))* Scholastic, Inc.

Watt, Fiona. Under the Sea Baby Jigsaw Book. 2010. (Baby Jigsaw Bks.). (Illus.). 10p. (J). bds. 9.99 *(978-0-7945-1314-6(X)*, Usborne) EDC Publishing.

Waxman, Laura Hamilton. Let's Look at Sea Otters. 2010. (Lightning Bolt Books (r) — Animal Close-Ups Ser.). (ENG., Illus.). 32p. (J). (gr. 1-3). pap. 9.99 *(978-1-58013-864-2(0)*, bee80c25-f04e-4388-94c2-54ed96fccde5) Lerner Publishing Group.

Wearing, Judy. World of Wonder: Underwater Life, 4 vols., Set. Incl. Jellyfish. (gr. k-3). lib. bdg. 24.45 *(978-1-60596-100-2(0))*; Manta Rays. (gr. 2-4). lib. bdg. 24.45 *(978-1-60596-104-0(3)*, 1305023); Sea Turtles. (gr. 2-4). lib. bdg. 24.45 *(978-1-60596-106-4(X))*; Seahorses. (gr. 2-4). lib. bdg. 24.45 *(978-1-60596-102-6(7))*; (Illus.). 24p. (J). 2009. 2010. Set lib. bdg. 97.80 *(978-1-60596-669-4(X))* Weigl Pubs., Inc.

Webb, Sophie. Far from Shore: Chronicles of an Open Ocean Voyage. 2011. (ENG., Illus.). 80p. (J). (gr. 5-7). 18.99 *(978-0-618-59729-1(8)*, 567897, Clarion Bks.) HarperCollins Pubs.

Weber, Valerie J. Animals That Live in the Ocean, 14 vols., Set. Incl. Dolphins. lib. bdg. 25.27 *(978-0-8368-9240-6(2)*, 8daefe29-3ff1-45cc-b6e7-f47d327db16e); Manatees. lib. bdg. 25.27 *(978-0-8368-9241-3(0)*, b71f1422-a2e8-495b-a3be-421fdcd13fd4); Octopuses & Squids. lib. bdg. 25.27 *(978-0-8368-9242-0(9)*, 4b2b859f-1912-446c-a41a-50ed9e5ab7f3); Sea Horses. lib. bdg. 25.27 *(978-0-8368-9243-7(7)*, 2508d9e5-03c2-4b25-ae74-62b349e87293); Sea Turtles. lib. bdg. 25.27 *(978-0-8368-9244-4(5)*, ae2dd165-8622-4bff-8450-bb29abd5b218); Sharks. lib. bdg. 25.27 *(978-0-8368-9245-1(3)*, 0fcac860-e40d-4c1d-b378-ac7b6807ab64); Walruses. lib. bdg. 25.27 *(978-0-8368-9566-7(5)*, 9116a86c-886d-4dc7-9fd9-ecfd261739f9); Whales. lib. bdg. 25.27 *(978-0-8368-9567-4(3)*, 62d23f93-cad3-44d7-a5ce-e810e6a55ff7); (Illus.). (J). (gr. 1-1). (Animals That Live in the Ocean Ser.). (ENG.). 24p. 2008. Set lib. bdg. 176.89 *(978-0-8368-9314-4(X)*, 963b77ac-8ee7-4743-9339-fe316149dd6d, Weekly Reader Leveled Readers) Stevens, Gareth Publishing LLLP.

—Animals That Live in the Ocean/Animales Que Viven en el Océano, 12 vols., Set. Incl. Dolphins / Delfines. lib. bdg. 25.27 *(978-0-8368-9246-8(1)*, 7576a41b-fbaf-4e5f-9d63-ee4a468f58a4); Manatees / Manatíes. lib. bdg. 25.27 *(978-0-8368-9247-5(X)*, f6ade463-b519-4816-9d1d-7d92b4e8b3a4); Octopuses & Squids / Pulpos y Calamares. lib. bdg. 25.27 *(978-0-8368-9248-2(8)*, f7699b10-e49f-41af-b08b-444ac4153781); Sea Horses / Caballitos de Mar. lib. bdg. 25.27 *(978-0-8368-9249-9(6)*, 559f6309-9aa6-4121-950f-9d7d1e9b3015); Sea Turtles / Tortugas Marinas. lib. bdg. 25.27 *(978-0-8368-9250-5(X)*, d833269d-dc68-452e-b9eb-7011da8449ec); Sharks / Tiburones. lib. bdg. 25.27 *(978-0-8368-9251-2(8)*, dca0805d-5f9e-4b75-8034-4b6c5df4a5ef); Walruses / Morsas. lib. bdg. 25.27 *(978-0-8368-9568-1(1)*, 1de07039-9504-4536-8a12-576eab82686f); Whales / Ballenas. lib. bdg. 25.27 *(978-0-8368-9569-8(X)*, abd00aaa-37d5-4f85-a775-f8a7ad79666f); (J). (gr. 1-1). (Animals That Live in the Ocean / Animales Que Viven en el Océano Ser.). (SPA & ENG.). 24p. 2008. Set lib. bdg. 151.62 *(978-0-8368-9315-1(8)*, 2a6eb847-96cb-49e5-863f-e4f61e7442f6, Weekly Reader Leveled Readers) Stevens, Gareth Publishing LLLP.

—Manatees / Manatíes, 1 vol. 2008. (Animals That Live in the Ocean / Animales Que Viven en el Océano Ser.). (SPA & ENG.). 24p. (J). (gr. 1-1). lib. bdg. 25.27 *(978-0-8368-9247-5(X)*, f6ade463-b519-4816-9d1d-7d92b4e8b3a4, Weekly Reader Leveled Readers) Stevens, Gareth Publishing LLLP.

—Sea Slugs, 1 vol. 2004. (Weird Wonders of the Deep Ser.). (ENG., Illus.). 24p. (gr. 2-4). lib. bdg. 25.67 *(978-0-8368-4563-1(3)*, bbd0626f-c3b9-48f4-a92d-88271c8b5ca4, Gareth Stevens Learning Library) Stevens, Gareth Publishing LLLP.

—Squids, 1 vol. 2004. (Weird Wonders of the Deep Ser.). (ENG., Illus.). 24p. (gr. 2-4). lib. bdg. 25.67 *(978-0-8368-4564-8(1)*, 8042743c-1b81-495d-a18f-ba1102c97149, Gareth Stevens Learning Library) Stevens, Gareth Publishing LLLP.

Weird Sea Creatures, 12 vols. 2005. (Weird Sea Creatures Ser.). (ENG., Illus.). (J). (gr. 3-3). 157.62 *(978-1-4042-3298-3(2)*, a479a7a8-4128-4cf9-8584-c82a4a3ef28b) Rosen Publishing Group, Inc., The.

Weiss, Sabrina. Ocean: Secrets of the Deep. De Amicis, Giulia, illus. 2019. (ENG.). 72p. (J). (gr. 2-6). 19.99 *(978-1-9999680-7-6(7))* What on Earth Bks GBR. Dist: Ingram Publisher Services.

West, David. Ocean Animals. 2015. (Safari Sam's Wild Animals Ser.). (ENG.). 24p. (J). (gr. k-3). 28.50 *(978-1-62588-075-8(8)*, 19365, Smart Apple Media) Black Rabbit Bks.

—Tide Pool Animals. 2014. (Nora the Naturalist's Animals Ser.). 24p. (gr. k-3). pap. 8.95 *(978-1-62588-054-3(5))* Black Rabbit Bks.

Westerskov, Kim, photos by. Friends in the Sea. 2004. (Illus.). 32p. (J). *(978-0-7685-2112-2(2))* Dominie Pr., Inc.

—Ocean Travelers. 2004. (ENG., Illus.). 32p. (J). (gr. 5-5). pap. 7.47 net. *(978-0-7685-2118-4(1)*, Dominie Elementary) Savvas Learning Co.

Who Lives in the Coral Reef. 2004. (J). 6.95 *(978-0-931548-12-3(8))* Island Heritage Publishing.

Wicker, Jan L. Those Magical Manatees. Weaver, Steve, illus. 2008. (Those Amazing Animals Ser.). (ENG.). 56p. (J). (gr. -1-12). pap. 16.95 *(978-1-56164-383-7(1))* Pineapple Pr., Inc.

Wicker, Jan Lee. Those Magical Manatees. Weaver, Steve, illus. 2008. (Those Amazing Animals Ser.). (ENG.). 55p. (J). (gr. -1-12). lib. bdg. 14.95 *(978-1-56164-382-0(3))* Pineapple Pr., Inc.

Wieland, Carl. Dragons of the Deep: Ocean Monsters Past & Present. Wiskur, Darrell, illus. 2005. 78p. (J). 16.99 *(978-0-89051-424-5(0)*, Master Books) New Leaf Publishing Group.

Wilkins, Mary-Jane. Deep Sea. 2017. (Who Lives Here? Ser.). (ENG., Illus.). 24p. (J). (gr. 2-4). 28.50 *(978-1-78121-345-2(3)*, 16710) Brown Bear Bks.

Williams, Brenda. Home for a Penguin, Home for a Whale. Beghelli, Annalisa, illus. 2019. (ENG.). 32p. (J). (gr. -1-3). 16.99 *(978-1-78285-743-3(5))* Barefoot Bks., Inc.

Williams, Lily. If Sharks Disappeared. Williams, Lily, illus. 2017. (If Animals Disappeared Ser.). (ENG., Illus.). 40p. (J). 18.99 *(978-1-62672-413-6(X)*, 900156281) Roaring Brook Pr.

Winkelman, Barbara Gaines. Puffer's Surprise. Petruccio, Steven James, illus. 2003. (Smithsonian Oceanic Collection). (ENG.). 32p. (J). (gr. -1-3). 8.95 *(978-1-59249-062-2(X)*, SC4024) Soundprints.

World Book, Inc. Staff, contrib. by. Endangered Animals of the Oceans. 2014. (J). *(978-0-7166-5627-2(2))* World Bk., Inc.

—Mollusks & Similar Sea Creatures. 2009. (J). *(978-0-7166-0407-5(8))* World Bk., Inc.

—Oceans. 2012. (J). *(978-0-7166-0447-1(7))* World Bk., Inc.

—The Sea & Its Marvels. 2011. (Illus.). 64p. (J). *(978-0-7166-1791-4(9))* World Bk., Inc.

—Under the Sea. 2007. (J). *(978-0-7166-7731-4(8))* World Bk., Inc.

Wright, Craig, ed. Dolphin Readers: Level 4: 625-Word Vocabulary in the Ocean Activity Book. 2010. (ENG., Illus.). 16p. act. bk. ed. 5.00 *(978-0-19-440174-6(X))* Oxford Univ. Pr., Inc.

Wrird Wonders of the Deep, 8 vols., Set. 2004. (Weird Wonders of the Deep Ser.). (ENG.). 24p. (gr. 2-4). lib. bdg. 102.68 *(978-0-8368-4559-4(5)*, cc241f24-44e8-4bbd-9c6b-91e26810aa44, Gareth Stevens Learning Library) Stevens, Gareth Publishing LLLP.

Wunderlich, Rick. Math on the Job: Caring for Marine Animals. 2016. (ENG., Illus.). 32p. (J). *(978-0-7787-2358-5(5))* Crabtree Publishing Co.

Wyland: Ocean Life. 2010. (Illus.). 24p. (J). pap. 6.95 *(978-1-884840-91-3(4))* Wyland Worldwide, LLC.

Yasuda, Anita. Oceans & Seas! With 25 Science Projects for Kids. Casteel, Tom, illus. 2018. (Explore Your World Ser.). (ENG.). 96p. (J). (gr. 3-4). 19.95 *(978-1-61930-696-7(4)*, b4b88235-a5a5-43cc-bff0-576376e10876) Nomad Pr.

Yelagalawadi, Jyoti. Deep Sea Creatures. Nagaraju, Harsha, illus. 2004. 32p. (J). 14.99 *(978-0-9725901-2-9(9))* Lekha Pubs., LLC.

Yoon, Salina. Deep Sea Dive. 2012. (Lift-The-Flap Adventures Ser.). (Illus.). 12p. (J). (gr. -1-2). bds. 9.99 *(978-1-4027-8525-2(9))* Sterling Publishing Co., Inc.

Yoon, Salina, creator. Sea Creatures: A Sparkling Little Colors Book, 4 vols. 2005. (ENG., Illus.). 12p. (J). bds. 5.95 *(978-1-58117-169-3(2)*, Intervisual/Piggy Toes) Bendon, Inc.

Young, Mary. We Like to Nurse Too. Parker, Zac, illus. 2009. (ENG.). 32p. (J). (gr. -1). pap. 9.95 *(978-1-890772-98-7(4))* Hohm Pr.

Young, Mary & Parker, Zac. También a Nosotros Nos Gusta Amamantar We Like to Nurse Too. 2009. (SPA.). 32p. pap. 10.95 *(978-1-890772-99-4(2))* Hohm Pr.

Zeiger, Jennifer. Nature's Children: Stingrays. 2012. (Nature's Children Ser.). (ENG., Illus.). 48p. (J). pap. 6.95 *(978-0-531-25483-7(6))* Scholastic Library Publishing.

—Stingrays. 2012. (Nature's Children Ser.). (ENG., Illus.). 48p. (J). lib. bdg. 28.00 *(978-0-531-26838-4(1))* Scholastic Library Publishing.

Zommer, Yuval. The Big Book of the Blue. 2018. (Big Book Ser.: 0). (ENG., Illus.). 64p. (J). (gr. -1-3). 19.95 *(978-0-500-65119-3(1)*, 565119) Thames & Hudson.

Zondervan Staff. Sea Creatures, 1 vol. 2011. (I Can Read! / Made by God Ser.). (ENG., Illus.). 32p. (J). (gr. -1-2). pap. 4.99 *(978-0-310-72183-3(0))* Zonderkidz.

199 Things under the Sea. 2017. (199 Things to Spot Ser.). (ENG.). (J). bds. 8.99 *(978-0-7945-3998-6(X)*, Usborne) EDC Publishing.

MARINE ANIMALS—FICTION

Aldrich, Sandra D. Danny Dolphin. 2012. 30p. 19.95 *(978-1-4626-6594-5(2))* America Star Bks.

Allen, Elaine Ann. Olly's Treasure, 1 vol. 2011. (ENG., Illus.). 40p. (J). (gr. -1-3). 16.99 *(978-0-7643-3772-7(6)*, 4107, Schiffer Publishing Ltd) Schiffer Publishing, Ltd.

Allen-Fletcher, Carly. Goodnight, Seahorse. 2018. (Illus.). 22p. (J). (gr. -1-1). bds. 11.95 *(978-1-63076-333-6(0))* Muddy Boots Pr.

Ann Scott, Lisa. Goodnight Lagoon. Sordo, Paco, illus. 2019. (ENG.). 40p. (J). (gr. -1-3). 17.99 *(978-1-4998-0845-2(3))* Little Bee Books Inc.

Ann, Shilo. Silly the Selfish Shellfish & Clara the Clumsy Clam. Whittier, Donna, illus. 2006. (ENG.). 56p. pap. 26.49 *(978-1-4208-4654-6(X))* AuthorHouse.

Anthony, Roger. Rindin the Puffer. 2007. (Crocponds Ser.). (Illus.). 32p. (J). (gr. -1-3). 19.95 *(978-0-9798297-0-3(4))* Crocodiles Not Waterlilies Entertainment.

Applegate, Katherine. Odder. 2023. (SPA.). 296p. (J). (gr. 4-7). pap. 15.95 ***(978-607-557-713-5(0))*** Editorial Oceano de Mexico MEX. Dist: Independent Pubs. Group.

—Odder. Santoso, Charles, illus. 2022. (ENG.). 288p. (J). 16.99 *(978-1-250-14742-4(5)*, 900181554) Feiwel & Friends.

Arone, Cathleen. Seababies Come Ashore. Date not set. (J). (gr. -1-3). 15.95 *(978-0-915009-60-2(9))* World Leisure Marketing Ltd GBR. Dist: Midpoint Trade Bks., Inc.

Artifact Group Staff & Artifact Group, The. Atlantis SquarePantis. 2007. (SpongeBob SquarePants Ser.). (ENG., Illus.). 24p. (J). (gr. k-3). pap. 3.99 *(978-1-4169-3799-9(4)*, Simon Spotlight/Nickelodeon) Simon Spotlight/Nickelodeon.

Auerbach, Annie. Spongebob Superstar, Vol. 5. 2004. 64p. (J). (gr. 2-5). pap. 17.00 incl. audio *(978-1-4000-8628-3(0)*, Listening Library) Random Hse. Audio Publishing Group.

Babypants, Caspar. Ocean Motions. Endle, Kate, illus. 2018. 20p. (J). (— 1). bds. 10.99 *(978-1-63217-131-3(7)*, Little Bigfoot) Sasquatch Bks.

Baker, Deirdre. Becca at Sea, 1 vol. 2018. (ENG.). 168p. (J). (gr. 4-7). pap. 8.95 *(978-0-88899-738-8(8))* Groundwood Bks. CAN. Dist: Publishers Group West (PGW).

Baltazar, Art. Starro & the Space Dolphins, 1 vol. Baltazar, Art, illus. 2012. (DC Super-Pets Ser.). (ENG., Illus.). 56p. (J). (gr. 1-3). pap. 4.95 *(978-1-4048-7217-2(5)*, 118035, Stone Arch Bks.) Capstone.

Banks, Steven. The Big Halloween Scare. Martinez, Heather, illus. 2003. (SpongeBob SquarePants Ser.: Vol. 1). (ENG.). 32p. (J). (gr. k-2). pap. 3.99 *(978-0-689-84196-5(5)*, Simon Spotlight/Nickelodeon) Simon Spotlight/Nickelodeon.

—Lost in Time. The Artifact Group, illus. 2006. 22p. (J). lib. bdg. 15.00 *(978-1-4242-0977-4(3))* Fitzgerald Bks.

—Show Me the Bunny! Greenblatt, C. H. & Reiss, William, illus. 2004. (Spongebob Squarepants Ser.). 32p. (J). 11.65 *(978-0-7569-5643-1(9))* Perfection Learning Corp.

—Special Delivery! DePorter, Vince, illus. 2003. (SpongeBob SquarePants Ser.: Vol. 2). (ENG.). 32p. (J). pap. 3.99 *(978-0-689-85887-1(6)*, Simon Spotlight/Nickelodeon) Simon Spotlight/Nickelodeon.

—Spongebob Goes to the Doctor. Saunders, Zina, illus. 2005. 22p. (J). lib. bdg. 15.00 *(978-1-4242-0976-7(5))* Fitzgerald Bks.

—Stop the Presses! DePorter, Vince, illus. 2005. 22p. (J). lib. bdg. 15.00 *(978-1-4242-0973-6(0))* Fitzgerald Bks.

Banks, Steven & Hillenburg, Stephen. Show Me the Bunny! Greenblatt, C. H. & Reiss, William, illus. 2004. (SpongeBob SquarePants Ser.: 3). (ENG.). 32p. (J). pap. 3.99 *(978-0-689-86485-8(X)*, Simon Spotlight/Nickelodeon) Simon Spotlight/Nickelodeon.

Banks, Steven, et al. For the Love of Bubbles. Osterhold, Jared, illus. 2006. (SpongeBob SquarePants Ser.: 12). (ENG.). 64p. (J). pap. 4.99 *(978-1-4169-1633-8(4)*, Simon Spotlight/Nickelodeon) Simon Spotlight/Nickelodeon.

Barefoot Books. Out of the Blue. Jay, Alison, illus. 2014. (ENG.). 32p. (J). (gr. -1-k). 16.99 *(978-1-78285-042-7(2))* Barefoot Bks., Inc.

Barland, Dj. The Little Ray's Big Rescue. 2013. 40p. pap. 15.99 *(978-1-4808-0284-1(0))* Archway Publishing.

Baum, L. Frank. The Sea Fairies. I.t. ed. 2004. (Large Print Ser.). lib. bdg. 25.00 *(978-1-58287-793-8(9))* North Bks.

Berenstain, Mike. The Berenstain Bears under the Sea. 2016. (Illus.). (J). *(978-1-5182-2637-3(X))* Baker & Taylor, CATS.

Berk, Ari. The Secret History of Mermaids & Creatures of the Deep. 2009. (ENG., Illus.). 48p. (J). (gr. 3-7). 22.99 *(978-0-7636-4515-1(X))* Candlewick Pr.

Blackstone, Stella. Secret Seahorse. Beaton, Clare, illus. 2005. (ENG.). (J). (gr. -1-2). 24p. bds. 8.99 *(978-1-905236-15-2(8))*; 24p. 15.99 *(978-1-84148-704-5(X))*; 32p. pap. 9.99 *(978-1-84148-937-7(9))* Barefoot Bks., Inc.

Boehler, Ren'Ae L. The Unicorn Fish Are Having a Party. 2008. (ENG.). 26p. per. 15.99 *(978-1-4257-9945-8(0))* Xlibris Corp.

Bonnell, Kris. Down in the Sea. 2006. (J). pap. 5.95 *(978-1-933727-38-7(1))* Reading Reading Bks., LLC.

—Mudskipper & the Water. 2006. (J). pap. 3.95 *(978-1-933727-21-9(7))* Reading Reading Bks., LLC.

Book Company Staff. Ocean Friends. Lassen, Christian R., illus. 2003. (Puzzles Ser.). (J). bds. 14.95 *(978-1-74047-381-1(7))* Book Co. Publishing Pty, Ltd., The AUS. Dist: Penton Overseas, Inc.

—Treasures of the Sea: Birthday & Address Book. Lassen, Christian R., illus. 2003. (Stationery Ser.). (J). 14.95 *(978-1-86309-793-2(7))* Book Co. Publishing Pty, Ltd., The AUS. Dist: Penton Overseas, Inc.

Botterill, Ron E. Big, Green & Mean, Ogie, the Misunderstood Monster. 2009. 28p. pap. 13.00 *(978-1-60860-712-9(7)*, Eloquent Bks.) Strategic Book Publishing & Rights Agency (SBPRA).

Bringsvaerd, Tor Age. Ruffen: The Sea Serpent Who Couldn't Swim. Hansen, Thore, illus. 2008. (Ruffen Ser.). 64p. (J). (gr. -1-3). 16.95 *(978-0-9790347-9-4(5))* Mackenzie Smiles, LLC.

Brooks, David. You Can Count at the Ocean. 2005. (You Can Count Ser.). (ENG., Illus.). 24p. (J). (gr. -1 — 1). bds. 7.95 *(978-1-55971-930-8(3))* Cooper Square Publishing Llc.

Brooks, Felicity. Under the Sea Lift & Look. 2010. (Lift & Look Board Bks). 12p. (J). bds. 9.99 *(978-0-7945-2576-7(8)*, Usborne) EDC Publishing.

Brooks, John. Balloons, Sea Creatures, & Me. 2006. 34p. (J). 14.58 *(978-0-9661789-3-7(9))* Lulu Pr., Inc.

Brunellière, Lucie. Deep in the Ocean. 2019. (ENG., Illus.). 14p. (J). (gr. -1-k). bds. 15.99 *(978-1-4197-3356-7(7)*, 1254910, Abrams Appleseed) Abrams, Inc.

Burns, Joanne. Ollie Oyster's Ouch. 2005. 21p. 8.99 *(978-1-4116-5337-5(8))* Lulu Pr., Inc.

Cafaro, Phyllis. The Legend of Captain McFinn & Friends. 2012. (ENG.). 24p. (J). 17.99 *(978-0-9799283-3-8(8)*, 9780979928338) Captain McFinn and Friends LLC, McFinn Pr.

Carle, Eric. A House for Hermit Crab: Book & CD. Carle, Eric, illus. 2013. (World of Eric Carle Ser.). (ENG., Illus.). 32p. (J). (gr. -1-2). pap. 10.99 *(978-1-4424-7224-2(3)*, Little Simon) Little Simon.

—A House for Hermit Crab/Ready-To-Read Level 2. Carle, Eric, illus. 2014. (World of Eric Carle Ser.). (ENG., Illus.). 32p. (J). (gr. k-2). pap. 4.99 *(978-1-4814-0915-5(8)*, Simon Spotlight) Simon Spotlight.

Carpenter, L. J. Out of the Tank. 2012. 24p. pap. 15.99 *(978-1-4685-9633-5(0))* AuthorHouse.

Chaisson, Samuel Jam. Larry & Joe's Detective Agency. 2005. pap. 26.50 *(978-1-4184-6878-1(9))* AuthorHouse.

Chanda, J-P. Happy Birthday, SpongeBob! Martinez, Heather, illus. 2005. (SpongeBob SquarePants Ser.). (ENG.). 24p. (J). pap. 3.99 *(978-0-689-87674-5(2)*, Simon Spotlight/Nickelodeon) Simon Spotlight/Nickelodeon.

Chipponeri, Kelli. SpongeBob Rocks! Martinez, Heather, illus. 2006. (SpongeBob SquarePants Ser.: 9). (ENG.). 32p. (J). (gr. -1-3). pap. 3.99 *(978-1-4169-1314-6(9)*, Simon Spotlight/Nickelodeon) Simon Spotlight/Nickelodeon.

Clanton, Ben. Narwhal: Unicorn of the Sea, 1. 2018. (ENG.). 64p. (J). (gr. -1-1). 17.96 *(978-1-64310-522-2(1))* Penworthy Co., LLC, The.

—Narwhal: Unicorn of the Sea (a Narwhal & Jelly Book #1) 2016. (Narwhal & Jelly Book Ser.: 1). (ENG., Illus.). 64p. (J). (gr. 1-4). pap. 7.99 *(978-1-101-91871-5(3)*, Tundra Bks.) Tundra Bks. CAN. Dist: Penguin Random Hse. LLC.

Collins, Terry. Tea at the Treedome. 2004. 64p. (J). (gr. 2-5). pap. 17.00 incl. audio *(978-0-8072-1986-7(X)*, Listening Library) Random Hse. Audio Publishing Group.

Conrique, Samantha. The Pod-Poppers. 2007. (J). pap. 8.00 *(978-0-8059-7200-9(5))* Dorrance Publishing Co., Inc.

CortAs, Ricardo. Sea Creatures from the Sky. 2018. (ENG., Illus.). 48p. (J). 16.95 *(978-1-61775-616-0(4)*, Black Sheep) Akashic Bks.

Cousteau, Fabien & Fraioli, James O. Great White Shark Adventure. St.Pierre, Joe, illus. 2019. (Fabien Cousteau Expeditions Ser.). (ENG.). 112p. (J). (gr. 3-7). 12.99 *(978-1-5344-2087-8(8)*, McElderry, Margaret K. Bks.) McElderry, Margaret K. Bks.

Craipeau, Jean-Lou & Dutrieux, Brigitte. Half & Half-Giants of the Ocean: Great Story & Cool Facts. Hyman, Miles & Alibert, Eric, illus. 2009. 56p. (J). pap. 4.99 *(978-1-60115-212-1(4))* Treasure Bay, Inc.

Craipeau, Jean-Lou & Dutrieux, Julien. Half & Half-Giants of the Ocean: Great Story & Cool Facts. Hyman, Miles & Alibert, Eric, illus. 2009. 56p. (J). 9.95 *(978-1-60115-211-4(6))* Treasure Bay, Inc.

Crow, Marilee. Down by the Shore. Roberts, MarySue, photos by. 2008. (Illus.). 28p. pap. 10.95 *(978-1-933090-39-9(1))* Guardian Angel Publishing, Inc.

Cuasay, Alison Taimanglo. Tasi & Matina: The Story of the First Clown Fish. 2010. 28p. pap. 12.99 *(978-1-4520-6672-1(8))* AuthorHouse.

Cummings, Priscilla. Meet Chadwick & His Chesapeake Bay Friends, 1 vol. 2019. (ENG., Illus.). 32p. (J). pap. 9.99 *(978-0-7643-5700-8(X)*, 16396) Schiffer Publishing, Ltd.

Curious George Discovers the Ocean. 2015. (Curious George Ser.). (ENG., Illus.). 32p. (J). (gr. -1-3). 6.99 *(978-0-544-43065-5(4)*, 1595740, Clarion Bks.) HarperCollins Pubs.

Davies, Nicola. Manatee Rescue. Wright, Annabel, illus. 2016. (Heroes of the Wild Ser.). (ENG.). 112p. (J). (gr. 2-5). 16.99 *(978-0-7636-7830-2(9))* Candlewick Pr.

Davis, Caroline. Animals in the Water. 2009. (My First Noisy Bath Bks.). (ENG.). 8p. (J). (gr. -1-k). 6.99 *(978-0-7641-9591-4(3))* Sourcebooks, Inc.

Dean, James, illus. Pete the Cat: Scuba-Cat. 2016. (I Can Read Book: My First Ser.). (ENG.). 32p. (J). (gr. -1-1). 17.44 *(978-1-4844-7052-7(4))* HarperCollins Pubs.

Dean, James & Dean, Kimberly. Pete the Cat: Scuba-Cat. Dean, James, illus. 2016. (My First I Can Read Ser.). (ENG., Illus.). 32p. (J). (gr. -1-3). pap. 4.99 *(978-0-06-230388-2(0)*, HarperCollins) HarperCollins Pubs.

DePrisco, Dorothea. Who's in the Ocean? Gilvan-Cartwright, Chris, illus. 2006. (ENG.). 10p. (gr. -1-k). bds. 4.95 *(978-1-58117-509-7(4)*, Intervisual/Piggy Toes) Bendon, Inc.

Derrick, David G., Jr. Sid the Squid: And the Search for the Perfect Job. 2010. (ENG., Illus.). 36p. (J). (gr. -1-3). 15.95 *(978-1-59702-021-3(4))* Immedium.

Diesen, Deborah. The Not Very Merry Pout-Pout Fish. Hanna, Dan, illus. (Pout-Pout Fish Adventure Ser.). (ENG.). (J). 2017. 34p. bds. 8.99 *(978-0-374-30459-1(9)*, 900159459)

2015. 32p. (gr. -1-1). 17.99 (978-0-374-35549-4(5), 900122565) Farrar, Straus & Giroux. (Farrar, Straus & Giroux (BYR)).

—The Pout-Pout Fish. Hanna, Dan, illus. 2018. (Pout-Pout Fish Adventure Ser.: 1). (ENG.). 32p. (J). bds. 12.99 (978-0-374-31219-0(2), 900199885, Farrar, Straus & Giroux (BYR)) Farrar, Straus & Giroux.

—The Pout-Pout Fish. Hanna, Dan & Hanna, Dan, illus. 2013. (Pout-Pout Fish Adventure Ser.: 1). (ENG.). 32p. (J). (gr. -1 — 1). bds. 7.99 (978-0-374-36097-9(9), 900075215, Farrar, Straus & Giroux (BYR)) Farrar, Straus & Giroux.

—The Pout-Pout Fish. Hanna, Dan, illus. 2008. (Pout-Pout Fish Adventure Ser.: 1). (ENG.). 32p. (J). (gr. -1-1). 18.99 (978-0-374-36096-2(0), 900031428, Farrar, Straus & Giroux (BYR)) Farrar, Straus & Giroux.

—The Pout-Pout Fish & the Can't-Sleep Blues. Hanna, Dan, illus. 2018. (Pout-Pout Fish Adventure Ser.). (ENG.). 32p. (J). 18.99 (978-0-374-30403-4(3), 900158633, Farrar, Straus & Giroux (BYR)) Farrar, Straus & Giroux.

—The Pout-Pout Fish Cleans up the Ocean. Hanna, Dan, illus. 2019. (Pout-Pout Fish Adventure Ser.: 4). (ENG.). 32p. (J). 18.99 (978-0-374-30934-3(5), 900189997, Farrar, Straus & Giroux (BYR)) Farrar, Straus & Giroux.

—Pout-Pout Fish: Easter Surprise. Hanna, Dan, illus. 2018. (Pout-Pout Fish Paperback Adventure Ser.). (ENG.). 24p. (J). 5.99 (978-0-374-31051-6(3), 900193163, Farrar, Straus & Giroux (BYR)) Farrar, Straus & Giroux.

—The Pout-Pout Fish in the Big-Big Dark. Hanna, Dan, illus. (Pout-Pout Fish Adventure Ser.: 2). (ENG.). 32p. (J). (gr. -1-1). 2015. bds. 8.99 (978-0-374-30189-7(1), 900141680) 2010. 18.99 (978-0-374-30798-1(9), 900064075) Farrar, Straus & Giroux. (Farrar, Straus & Giroux (BYR)).

—Pout-Pout Fish: Lucky Leprechaun. Hanna, Dan, illus. 2019. (Pout-Pout Fish Paperback Adventure Ser.). (ENG.). 24p. (J). 6.99 (978-0-374-31054-7(8), 900193165, Farrar, Straus & Giroux (BYR)) Farrar, Straus & Giroux.

—Smile, Pout-Pout Fish. Hanna, Dan, illus. 2014. (Pout-Pout Fish Mini Adventure Ser.: 1). (ENG.). 12p. (J). (gr. -1 — 1). bds. 5.99 (978-0-374-37084-8(2), 900122559, Farrar, Straus & Giroux (BYR)) Farrar, Straus & Giroux.

—You Can Do It, Pout-Pout Fish! 2019. (Pout-Pout Fish Readers Ser.). (ENG.). 24p. (J). (gr. k-1). 14.49 (978-0-87617-547-7(7)) Penworthy Co., LLC, The.

—You Can Make a Friend, Pout-Pout Fish! 2019. (Pout-Pout Fish Readers Ser.). (ENG.). 24p. (J). (gr. k-1). 14.49 (978-0-87617-548-4(5)) Penworthy Co., LLC, The.

Diesen, Deborah & Hanna, Dan. You Can Do It, Pout-Pout Fish! 2019. (Pout-Pout Fish Reader Ser.: 1). (ENG., Illus.). 24p. (J). pap. 5.99 (978-1-250-06427-1(9), 900143686, Farrar, Straus & Giroux (BYR)) Farrar, Straus & Giroux.

—You Can Make a Friend, Pout-Pout Fish! 2019. (Pout-Pout Fish Reader Ser.: 2). (ENG., Illus.). 24p. (J). pap. 5.99 (978-1-250-06428-8(7), 900143688, Farrar, Straus & Giroux (BYR)) Farrar, Straus & Giroux.

DK. Pop-Up Peekaboo: under the Sea. 2018. (Pop-Up Peekaboo! Ser.). (ENG.). 12p. (J). (— 1). bds. 12.99 (978-1-4654-7316-5(5), DK Children) Dorling Kindersley Publishing, Inc.

Dobell, Darcy. The Oyster Who Looked at the Sky. 2008. (ENG., Illus.). 32p. 16.95 (978-0-88982-250-4(6)) Oolichan Bks. CAN. Dist: Univ. of Toronto Pr.

Dombek, Jeff. How the Oysters Saved the Bay, 1 vol. 2013. (ENG., Illus.). 32p. (J). (gr. -1-3). 16.99 (978-0-7643-4283-7(5), 4791) Schiffer Publishing, Ltd.

Donovan, Gail. !Listos... Ya! Clar, David Austin, illus. 2003. (Rainbow Fish & Friends Ser.). 24p. (J). mass mkt. 3.99 (978-1-59014-123-6(7)) Night Sky Bks.

Downer, Ann. Shark Baby, 1 vol. Bersani, Shennen, illus. 2013. 32p. (J). (ENG.). (gr. -1-3). 17.95 (978-1-60718-622-9(5)); (ENG.). (gr. -1-3). pap. 9.95 (978-1-60718-634-2(9)); (SPA.). (gr. 2-3). pap. 11.95 (978-1-62855-351-2(0), 30d907ee-6c53-4f54-ab9f-06d37fefc8ad) Arbordale Publishing.

Downing, Johnette. Why the Oyster Has the Pearl, 1 vol. Hill, Bethanne, illus. 2011. (ENG.). 32p. (J). (gr. k-3). 16.99 (978-1-4556-1460-8(2), Pelican Publishing) Arcadia Publishing.

Dunn, Catherine. Oscar & Solomon. 2008. 40p. pap. 21.99 (978-1-4363-6977-0(0)) Xlibris Corp.

Dyckman, Ame. Misunderstood Shark. Magoon, Scott, illus. 2018. (ENG.). 48p. (J). (gr. -1-k). 18.99 (978-1-338-11247-4(3), Orchard Bks.) Scholastic, Inc.

—Misunderstood Shark: Friends Don't Eat Friends. Magoon, Scott, illus. 2019. (ENG.). 48p. (J). (gr. -1-k). 17.99 (978-1-338-11388-4(7), Orchard Bks.) Scholastic, Inc.

Edgemon, Darcie. Seamore, the Very Forgetful Porpoise. Seibold, J. Otto, illus. 2008. (J). 48p. (gr. -1-3). lib. bdg. 17.89 (978-0-06-085076-0(0)); (978-0-06-085075-3(2)) HarperCollins Pubs.

Ferris, Aimee. Girl Overboard. 2007. (S. A. S. S. Ser.). (Illus.). 224p. (YA). (gr. 7-18). 7.99 (978-0-14-240799-8(2), Speak) Penguin Young Readers Group.

Fletcher, Corina. Playbook Pirates. Teckentrup, Britta, illus. 2013. (ENG.). 12p. (J). (gr. -1-2). 24.00 (978-0-7636-6606-4(8)) Candlewick Pr.

Fogle, Llynda, et al. A Pond Full of Feelings. Bicking, Judy, illus. 2005. (SPA.). (J). (978-0-9760282-9-1(8)) RAPC - Sparkle & Shine Project.

Foreman, Grindley -. La playa de Pedro. 2003. (SPA., Illus.). 32p. (J). (gr. 1-3). 19.99 (978-84-261-3314-4(2)) Juventud, Editorial ESP. Dist: Lectorum Pubns., Inc.

Fry, Sonali. Under the Sea. Blanco, Migy, illus. 2014. (Dream Doodle Draw! Ser.). (ENG.). 96p. (J). (gr. -1-2). pap. 7.99 (978-1-4814-0453-2(9), Little Simon) Little Simon.

Galloway, Ruth. Smiley Shark. Galloway, Ruth, illus. (Illus.). 32p. (J). 2005. 6.95 (978-1-58925-391-9(4)) 2003. tchr. ed. 15.95 (978-1-58925-028-4(1)) Tiger Tales.

Gamble, Adam & Jasper, Mark. Good Night Whales. Stevenson, Harvey, illus. 2016. (Good Night Our World Ser.). (ENG.). 20p. (J). (— 1). bds. 9.95 (978-1-60219-507-3(2)) Good Night Bks.

Gantry, Chris. The Underwater Orchestra. Burns, Theresa, illus. 2013. 38p. (J). 16.98 (978-1-940224-19-0(5)) Taylor and Seale Publishing.

Garton, Sam. Otter: Hello, Sea Friends! 2016. (My First I Can Read Ser.). (ENG., Illus.). 32p. (J). (gr. -1-3). pap. 4.99 (978-0-06-236660-3(2), Balzer & Bray) HarperCollins Pubs.

Garton, Sam, illus. Otter: Hello, Sea Friends! 2016. 32p. (J). (978-1-5182-2257-3(9), Balzer & Bray) HarperCollins Pubs.

Gelin, Antoinette. Captain Underfish: Superhero for the Underworld. 2011. 40p. pap. 25.95 (978-1-4634-2662-0(3)) AuthorHouse.

Gladwell, Michael. Slappers Maui Vacation. 2008. 32p. pap. 6.95 (978-0-615-21549-5(1)) Hawaii Fine Art Studio.

Goodrich, Carter. The Hermit Crab. Goodrich, Carter, illus. 2009. (ENG., Illus.). 40p. (J). (gr. 1-5). 16.99 (978-1-4169-3892-7(3), Simon & Schuster Bks. For Young Readers) Simon & Schuster Bks. For Young Readers.

Gould, Robert. Sea Creatures. 2005. (Big Stuff Ser.: 8). (ENG., Illus.). 16p. (J). bds. 7.95 (978-1-929945-59-7(0)) Big Guy Bks., Inc.

Greenburg, J. C. Andrew Lost #5: under Water. Reed, Mike, illus. 2003. (Andrew Lost Ser.: 5). (ENG.). 96p. (J). (gr. 1-4). mass mkt. 4.99 (978-0-375-82523-1(1), Random Hse. Bks. for Young Readers) Random Hse. Children's Bks.

—Andrew Lost #7: on the Reef. Gerardi, Jan, illus. 2004. (Andrew Lost Ser.: 7). 96p. (J). (gr. 1-4). 6.99 (978-0-375-82525-5(8), Random Hse. Bks. for Young Readers) Random Hse. Children's Bks.

—Andrew Lost #8: in the Deep. Gerardi, Jan, illus. 2004. (Andrew Lost Ser.: 8). (ENG.). 96p. (J). (gr. 1-4). 6.99 (978-0-375-82526-2(6), Random Hse. Bks. for Young Readers) Random Hse. Children's Bks.

Hale, Bruce. Clark the Shark. Francis, Guy, illus. 2013. (Clark the Shark Ser.). (ENG.). 32p. (J). (gr. -1-3). 18.99 (978-0-06-219226-4(4), HarperCollins) HarperCollins Pubs.

—Clark the Shark: Tooth Trouble. Francis, Guy, illus. 2014. (I Can Read Level 1 Ser.). (ENG.). 32p. (J). (gr. -1-3). 16.99 (978-0-06-227908-8(4), HarperCollins) HarperCollins Pubs.

—Clark the Shark: Afraid of the Dark. Francis, Guy, illus. 2015. (Clark the Shark Ser.). (ENG.). 32p. (J). (gr. -1-3). 18.99 (978-0-06-237450-9(8), HarperCollins) HarperCollins Pubs.

—Clark the Shark Dares to Share. Francis, Guy, illus. 2013. (Clark the Shark Ser.). (ENG.). 32p. (J). (gr. -1-3). 17.99 (978-0-06-227905-7(X), HarperCollins) HarperCollins Pubs.

—Clark the Shark Takes Heart. Francis, Guy, illus. 2014. (Clark the Shark Ser.). (ENG.). 32p. (J). (gr. -1-3). 17.99 (978-0-06-219227-1(2), HarperCollins) HarperCollins Pubs.

—Clark the Shark: Tooth Trouble. Francis, Guy, illus. 2014. (I Can Read Level 1 Ser.). (ENG.). 32p. (J). (gr. -1-3). pap. 4.99 (978-0-06-227906-4(8), HarperCollins) HarperCollins Pubs.

Halter, Loretta. Lacy's Journey: The Life of a Decorator Crab. 2010. (ENG., Illus.). 64p. (J). 19.95 (978-0-9822942-1-5(2)) Nature's Hopes & Heroes.

Hawk, J. L. If I Were a Creature under the Seaà. 2008. 12p. pap. 24.95 (978-1-60703-378-3(X)) America Star Bks.

Herz, Henry. How the Squid Got Two Long Arms, 1 vol. Graber, Luke, illus. 2018. (ENG.). 32p. (J). (gr. -1-3). 16.99 (978-1-4556-2388-4(1), Pelican Publishing) Arcadia Publishing.

Higginson, Sheila Sweeny. Diego rescata al bebé manatí (Diego's Manatee Rescue) McGee, Warner, illus. 2009. (Go, Diego, Go! Ser.). (SPA.). 24p. (J). pap. 3.99 (978-1-4169-7983-8(2), Libros Para Ninos) Libros Para Ninos.

Hogan, Barbora. How Ryan & Aiden Saved the Ocean. 2013. 36p. pap. 16.99 (978-1-4525-7776-0(5), Balboa Pr.) Author Solutions, LLC.

Holden, Pam, et al. Míra Como Nado, 1 vol. Hansen, Christine, illus. 2012.Tr. of Watch Me Swim. (ENG.). 16p. (gr. -1-1). pap. (978-1-877506-90-1(7), Red Rocket Readers) Flying Start Bks.

Holmes, Steve, illus. Animales Marinos: Mezcla y Diviertete. 2005. (Mezcla y Diviertete Ser.). (SPA.). 5p. (J). (gr. -1-7). (978-970-718-291-2(1), Silver Dolphin en Español) Advanced Marketing, S. de R. L. de C. V.

Holtfreter, Nastja. Colorful World: Sea. Holtfreter, Nastja, illus. 2017. (ENG., Illus.). 14p. (J). bds. 5.99 (978-1-61067-576-5(2)) Kane Miller.

Howard, Abby. Ocean Renegades! (Earth Before Us #2) Journey Through the Paleozoic Era. 2018. (Earth Before Us Ser.). (ENG., Illus.). 128p. (J). (gr. 3-7). 15.99 (978-1-4197-3136-5(X), 1145001, Amulet Bks.) Abrams, Inc.

Howard, Ruth I. Crabby Crab. Hunter, Helen D., illus. 2004. (ENG.). 24p. (YA). pap. 9.00 (978-1-4120-1432-8(8)) Trafford Publishing.

Humann, Amanda. Deep Water Hotel. 2016. (Tartan House Ser.). (ENG.). 96p. (J). (gr. 3-6). (978-1-63235-160-9(9), 11891, 12-Story Library) Bookstaves, LLC.

Jarkins, Sheila. The Adventures of Marco Flamingo in the Jungle. Jarkins, Sheila, illus. 2012. (Illus.). 32p. (J). 1.99 (978-1-936299-31-7(3), Raven Tree Pr.) Delta Systems Company, Inc.

Jarman, Julia. Class Three at Sea. Chapman, Lynne, illus. 2008. (ENG.). 32p. (J). (gr. k-3). 16.95 (978-0-8225-7617-4(1), Carolrhoda Bks.) Lerner Publishing Group.

Jefferson, E. Louis. Terry-The Little Tadpole-Making New Friends. 2013. (ENG.). 89p. pap. 35.00 (978-1-300-61843-0(4)) Lulu Pr., Inc.

Johnston, Tony. Spencer & Vincent, the Jellyfish Brothers. Dove, Emily, illus. 2019. (ENG.). 40p. (J). (gr. -1-3). 19.99 (978-1-5344-1208-8(5), Simon & Schuster/Paula Wiseman Bks.) Simon & Schuster/Paula Wiseman Bks.

Kaplan, Osman. Animal Wonders of the Water. Kalender, Oznur, illus. 2009. (Amazing Animals Ser.). (ENG.). 56p. (J). (gr. 2-4). 9.95 (978-1-59784-200-6(1), Tughra Bks.) Blue Dome, Inc.

King, Kerrigan. At the Aquarium, 1 vol. 2006. (Neighborhood Readers Ser.). (ENG., Illus.). 12p. (gr. k-1). pap. 5.90 (978-1-4042-6726-8(3), d928f38a-259f-4b3e-baa5-57ca4431f765, Rosen Classroom) Rosen Publishing Group, Inc., The.

Knife & Packer, creator. Deep-Sea Dash. 2016. (Illus.). 93p. (J). pap. 6.99 (978-1-61067-398-3(0)) Kane Miller.

Korman, Susan. Swordfish Returns. Stegos, Daniel J., illus. 2011. (Smithsonian Oceanic Collection Ser.). (ENG.). 32p. (J). (gr. -1-3). 8.95 (978-1-60727-666-1(6)); 19.95 (978-1-60727-665-4(8)) Soundprints.

—Swordfish Returns. Stegos, Daniel, illus. (ENG.). 32p. (J). 2005. (gr. -1-2). 9.95 (978-1-59249-132-2(4), PB4075) 2005. (gr. -1-2). 4.95 (978-1-59249-126-1(X), B4075) 2004. (gr. 2-2). pap. 6.95 (978-1-59249-127-8(8), S4025) 2003. (gr. -1-2). 8.95 (978-1-59249-129-2(4), SC4025) 2003. (gr. -1-2). 19.95 (978-1-59249-128-5(6), BC4025) Soundprints.

—Swordfish Returns. Stegos, Daniel J., illus. 2003. (Smithsonian Oceanic Collection). (ENG.). 32p. (J). (gr. 2-2). 15.95 (978-1-59249-125-4(1), B4025) Soundprints.

Kuperman, Marina. Turtle Feet, Surfer's Beat. 2007. 164p. (J). pap. 9.99 (978-0-9801109-0-6(4)) Kuperman, Marina.

Kyung, Hyewon. Save Your Friends! Kyung, Hyewon, illus. 2019. (ENG., Illus.). 32p. (J). (gr. -1-3). 16.99 (978-0-06-268315-1(2), Greenwillow Bks.) HarperCollins Pubs.

Landrón, Rafael & Landrón, José Rafael. Beba y la Isla Nena: Beba & the Little Island. Ordóñez, María Antonia, illus. 2010. (SPA & ENG.). 32p. (J). (978-1-934370-05-6(3), Campanita Bks.) Editorial Campana.

Larsen, Kirsten. Dora & the Baby Crab. Roper, Robert, illus. 2008. (Dora the Explorer Ser.: 17). (ENG.). 24p. (J). (gr. -1-1). pap. 3.99 (978-1-4169-5451-4(1), Simon Spotlight/Nickelodeon) Simon Spotlight/Nickelodeon.

Lavin, Christine & Franco-Feeney, Betsy. Hole in the Bottom of the Sea. McHugh, Patricia & Feeney, Kathryn, eds. Franco-Feeney, Betsy, illus. 2012. (ENG., Illus.). 32p. (J). 18.95 incl. audio compact disk (978-0-9726487-8-3(X)) Puddle Jump Pr., Ltd.

Leaf, Autumn. Coto, Child of the Ocean. 2008. 122p. pap. 19.95 (978-1-60703-843-6(9)) America Star Bks.

Leopold, Nikia Speliakos Clark. Adam's Crayons. Nemett, Barry & Nemett, Laini, illus. 2011. (J). (978-0-9817519-1-7(1)) Galileo Pr.

Litton, Jonathan. Planet Pop-Up: Shark Makes a Splash! Anderson, Nicola, illus. 2015. (Planet Pop-Up Ser.). (ENG.). 12p. (J). (gr. -1). 12.95 (978-1-62686-353-8(9), Silver Dolphin Bks.) Readerlink Distribution Services, LLC.

Long, Ethan. Clara & Clem under the Sea. Long, Ethan, illus. 2014. (Penguin Young Readers, Level 1 Ser.). (Illus.). 32p. (J). (gr. k-1). pap. 5.99 (978-0-448-47812-8(9), Penguin Young Readers) Penguin Young Readers Group.

Lucas, Nancy T. Peppy's Coral Kingdom. 2008. (ENG.). 24p. pap. 12.99 (978-1-4196-9046-4(9)) CreateSpace Independent Publishing Platform.

Lumry, Amanda & Hurwitz, Laura. Adventures of Riley: Dolphins in Danger. McIntyre, Sarah, illus. 2005. 36p. (J). 15.95 (978-0-9748411-1-3(0)) Eaglemont Pr.

MacGregor, Doug, creator. Ochre the Smoker: A fantastic Fable. 2007. (Illus.). 48p. (J). per. 14.95 (978-0-9654843-2-9(7)) MacGregor, Doug.

MacVeety, Sue Maney. Singing Sea/el Mar Que Canta. Zantay, Valerie, tr. 2005. (ENG., Illus.). 36p. per. 15.99 (978-1-4134-7275-2(3)) Xlibris Corp.

Mae, Darcie. Sammy & Robert Discover the Ocean, 1 vol. 2009. 39p. pap. 24.95 (978-1-61546-827-0(7)) America Star Bks.

A Manatee Christmas. 2007. (Illus.). 32p. (J). lib. bdg. 15.99 (978-0-9771059-7-7(0)) Thomas Expressions, LLC.

Marston, Hope Irvin. My Little Book of Manatees. Mirocha, Stephanie, illus. 2007. (ENG.). 32p. (J). (gr. k-5). pap. 7.95 (978-0-89317-065-3(8), Windward Publishing) Finney Co., Inc.

Mayer, Mercer. Going to the Sea Park. 2009. (Little Critter: I Can Read! Ser.). (J). lib. bdg. 13.55 (978-0-606-06964-9(X)) Turtleback.

—Little Critter: Just Critters Who Care. Mayer, Mercer, illus. 2010. (My First I Can Read Ser.). (ENG., Illus.). 32p. (J). (gr. -1-3). 16.99 (978-0-06-083560-6(5)); pap. 4.99 (978-0-06-083559-0(1)) HarperCollins Pubs. (HarperCollins).

Mayfield, Sue. Under the Sea (Reading Ladder Level 1) Hendra, Sue, illus. 2nd ed. 2016. (Reading Ladder Level 1 Ser.). (ENG.). 48p. (gr. k-2). 7.99 (978-1-4052-8230-7(4), Reading Ladder) Farshore GBR. Dist: Independent Pubs. Group, HarperCollins Pubs.

McClure, Nikki. Waiting for High Tide. 2016. (ENG., Illus.). 48p. (J). (gr. k-2). 19.95 (978-1-4197-1656-0(5), 1090101, Abrams Bks. for Young Readers) Abrams, Inc.

McDonnell, Patrick. Shine! 2017. (ENG., Illus.). 40p. (J). (gr. -1-3). 16.99 (978-0-316-26278-1(1)) Little, Brown Bks. for Young Readers.

McDuffie, Linda. The Underwater Adventures of Little Ki. 2008. (ENG.). 28p. per. 21.99 (978-1-4257-8392-1(9)) Xlibris Corp.

McGee, Warner, illus. Ariel's Song. 2007. (Play a Tune Tale Ser.). 16p. (gr. -1-k). 12.98 (978-1-4127-8829-8(3)) Publications International, Ltd.

Meadows, Daisy. Ally the Dolphin Fairy. 2011. (Illus.). 63p. (J). (978-0-545-28871-2(1)) Scholastic, Inc.

—Courtney the Clownfish Fairy. 2011. (Illus.). 62p. (J). (978-0-545-28877-4(0)) Scholastic, Inc.

—Tess the Sea Turtle Fairy. 2011. (Illus.). 65p. (J). (978-0-545-28874-3(6)) Scholastic, Inc.

—Whitney the Whale Fairy. 2011. (Illus.). 64p. (J). (978-0-545-28876-7(2)) Scholastic, Inc.

Meister, Cari. Shark in the Library!, 1 vol. Simard, Rémy, illus. (My First Graphic Novel Ser.). (ENG.). 32p. (J). (gr. k-2). 2011. pap. 6.25 (978-1-4342-3104-8(6), 114744) 2010. 24.65 (978-1-4342-2058-5(3), 102802) Capstone. (Stone Arch Bks.).

Meng, Cece. Always Remember. Jago, illus. 2016. 32p. (J). (gr. -1-2). 17.99 (978-0-399-16809-3(5), Philomel Bks.) Penguin Young Readers Group.

Meyer, Bryce L. Dolphin & Manatee Friends End to End: Formerly Grant's Book of Manatees & Dolphins. 2009. 32p. pap. 16.99 (978-1-4269-1678-6(7)) Trafford Publishing.

Milbourne, Anna. How Deep Is the Sea? Riglietti, Serena, illus. 2010. (Picture Bks). 24p. (J). 10.99 (978-0-7945-2311-4(0)) EDC Publishing.

Moore, Angel. Squinky the Squid, 1 vol. 2010. 26p. pap. 24.95 (978-1-4489-8111-3(5)) PublishAmerica, Inc.

Moore, Carol Hair. Busy Bumble Bee Rides the Waves. Harrell, Michael, illus. 2009. (I Wish You Ice Cream & Cake Ser.: 2). (ENG.). 32p. (J). lib. bdg. 15.95 (978-1-935083-06-1(6)) CyPress Pubns.

Mora, Ebie. Kai: The Honu Didn't Know He Was Brave. Tackett, Mike, illus. 2005. 24p. (J). 12.95 (978-1-56647-755-0(7)) Mutual Publishing LLC.

Moriarty, Ros. Who Saw Turtle? 2019. (ENG., Illus.). 24p. (J). (gr. -1-k). pap. 9.99 (978-1-76029-780-0(1)) Allen & Unwin AUS. Dist: Independent Pubs. Group.

Napoli, Donna Jo. Fish Girl. 2017. (ENG.). (J). (gr. 5-7). lib. bdg. 30.60 (978-0-606-39824-4(4)) Turtleback.

Napoli, Donna Jo & Wiesner, David. Fish Girl. Wiesner, David, illus. 2017. (ENG., Illus.). 192p. (J). (gr. 5-7). pap. 17.99 (978-0-547-48393-1(7), 1439924, Clarion Bks.) HarperCollins Pubs.

Narvick, the Whark (or a Shwale) 2003. (J). 8.95 (978-0-9729703-1-0(2)) Kidderature Publishing.

Nerlove, Miriam, illus. Dot, Stripe, Squiggle. 2018. (ENG.). 28p. (J). (gr. -1-1). bds. 9.99 (978-1-56846-325-4(1), 19710, Creative Editions) Creative Co., The.

Nickelodeon Staff. Party Time! 2013. (Spongebob Squarepants Step into Reading Ser.). lib. bdg. 13.55 (978-0-606-32221-8(3)) Turtleback.

Nickelodeon Staff & Nickelodeon / LeapFrog. Go Diego Go! Underwater Mystery. 2008. (J). 13.99 (978-1-59319-925-8(2)) LeapFrog Enterprises, Inc.

Nosy Crow. Flip Flap Ocean. Scheffler, Axel, illus. 2018. (Flip Flap Bks.). (ENG.). 28p. (J). (gr. -1-2). 11.99 (978-0-7636-9942-0(X), Nosy Crow) Candlewick Pr.

Ocean, Davy. Long Fin Silver. Blecha, Aaron, illus. 2018. (Shark School Ser.: 9). (ENG.). 144p. (J). (gr. 1-4). 16.99 (978-1-4814-6553-3(8)); pap. 6.99 (978-1-4814-6552-6(X)) Simon & Schuster Children's Publishing. (Aladdin).

October the Octopus: A Huggable Concept Book about the Months of the Year. 2014. (ENG., Illus.). 28p. (J). (gr. -1-k). 24.99 (978-1-4814-2047-1(X), Simon & Schuster/Paula Wiseman Bks.) Simon & Schuster/Paula Wiseman Bks.

O'Neill, Michael Patrick. Fishy Friends: A Journey Through the Coral Kingdom. O'Neill, Michael Patrick, photos by. 2003. (Illus.). 64p. (J). 19.95 (978-0-9728653-0-2(6)) Batfish Bks.

Orodan, Mike. Peek-A-Baby: Ocean: Peekaboo Flaps Inside! 2019. (Peek-A-Baby Ser.). (ENG., Illus.). 14p. (J). (gr. -1 — 1). bds. 9.99 (978-1-4521-6646-9(3)) Chronicle Bks. LLC.

Osborne, Mary Pope. Das magische Baumhaus 09. Der Ruf der Delfine. 18.95 (978-3-7855-4185-2(6)) Loewe Verlag GmbH DEU. Dist: Distribooks, Inc.

Packer. Deep-Sea Dash. Knife, illus. 2016. 93p. (J). (978-1-61067-478-2(2)) Kane Miller.

Pallotta, Jerry. Dory Story. Biedrzycki, David, illus. 2006. 32p. (J). (gr. -1-3). pap. 7.95 (978-0-88106-076-8(3)) Charlesbridge Publishing, Inc.

Paquette, Ammi-Joan. The Tiptoe Guide to Tracking Mermaids. LeTourneau, Marie, illus. 2012. (ENG.). 32p. (J). (gr. k-5). 16.95 (978-1-933718-59-0(5)) Tanglewood Pr.

Pass, Erica. Hooray for Dads! 2014. (SpongeBob Squarepants 8X8 Ser.). lib. bdg. 14.75 (978-0-606-35560-5(X)) Turtleback.

Pass, Erica & Artifact Group Staff. Hooray for Dads! 2007. (SpongeBob SquarePants Ser.: 14). (ENG., Illus.). 24p. (J). (gr. k-2). pap. 3.99 (978-1-4169-2782-2(4), Simon Spotlight/Nickelodeon) Simon Spotlight/Nickelodeon.

Patterson, James. Max: A Maximum Ride Novel. 2009. (Maximum Ride Ser.: 5). (ENG.). (YA). (gr. 5-17). 352p. pap. 11.99 (978-0-316-00290-5(9)); 416p. 38.99 (978-0-316-03759-4(1)) Little Brown & Co. (Jimmy Patterson).

—Saving the World & Other Extreme Sports. l.t. ed. 2007. (Maximum Ride Ser.: No. 3). 489p. (J). (gr. 3-7). 23.95 (978-0-7862-9887-7(1)) Thorndike Pr.

—Saving the World & Other Extreme Sports: A Maximum Ride Novel. 3rd ed. (Maximum Ride Ser.: 3). (ENG.). (J). (gr. 5-17). 2007. 416p. 37.99 (978-0-316-15560-1(8)) 2008. 432p. pap. 10.99 (978-0-316-15427-7(X)) Little Brown & Co. (Jimmy Patterson).

Peck, Jan. Way down Deep in the Deep Blue Sea. 2004. (ENG., Illus.). 32p. (J). (gr. -1-3). 18.99 (978-0-689-85110-0(3), Simon & Schuster Bks. For Young Readers) Simon & Schuster Bks. For Young Readers.

Pfister, Marcus. Rainbow Fish & the Big Blue Whale. 2012. (Rainbow Fish Ser.). Orig. Title: Regenbogenfisch und Grosser Blauer Wal. (ENG., Illus.). 32p. (J). (gr. -1-2). pap. 10.95 (978-3-314-01669-1(7)) North-South Bks., Inc.

Piggy Toes Press, creator. Crayola Sea Life: Counting Sea Life. 2011. (Crayola (Piggy Toes Press) Ser.). (ENG., Illus.). 6p. (gr. -1). bds. 5.95 (978-1-61524-289-4(9), Intervisual/Piggy Toes) Bendon, Inc.

Pledger, Maurice, illus. Noisy Nature: in the Ocean. 2015. (Noisy Nature Ser.). (ENG.). 12p. (J). (gr. -1). 16.95 (978-1-62686-105-3(6), Silver Dolphin Bks.) Readerlink Distribution Services, LLC.

Poitier, Anton. Flippy Floppy Ocean Animals. Touliatou, Sophia, illus. 2015. 10p. (J). 12.99 (978-1-61067-346-4(8)) Kane Miller.

Prager, Ellen. The Shark Whisperer. Caparo, Antonio Javier, illus. 2014. (Tristan Hunt & the Sea Guardians Ser.). (ENG.). 288p. (J). (gr. 3-7). pap. 9.95 (978-1-938063-44-2(9), Mighty Media Junior Readers) Mighty Media Pr.

—Stingray City. Caparo, Antonio Javier, illus. 2016. (Tristan Hunt & the Sea Guardians Ser.: 3). (ENG.). 292p. (J). (gr. 2-7). pap. 9.95 (978-1-938063-70-1(8), Mighty Media Junior Readers) Mighty Media Pr.

R, J. Ff: The Weedy Sea Dragon Coloring Book (Standard Version) 2013. 38p. (J). pap. 9.95 (978-1-935734-53-6(9)) Kitanie Bks.

Random House. Five Undersea Stories (SpongeBob SquarePants) Random House, illus. 2015. (Step into Reading Ser.). (ENG., Illus.). 160p. (J). (gr. -1-1). 8.99 (978-0-553-50860-4(1), Random Hse. Bks. for Young Readers) Random Hse. Children's Bks.

Random House Staff. You're Fired! 2014. (SpongeBob Squarepants 8X8 Ser.). lib. bdg. 13.55 (978-0-606-35204-8(X)) Turtleback.

Ranson, Erin. Ocean Wonders. Wood, Hannah, illus. 2007. (Sparkling Slide Nature Bks.). (ENG.). 12p. (J). (gr. -1). 9.99 (978-1-84666-167-9(6)) Top That! Publishing PLC GBR. Dist: Independent Pubs. Group.

Raschka, Chris, illus. Clammy Clam. 2014. (Thingy Things Ser.). (ENG.). 24p. (J). (gr. -1-k). 6.95 (978-1-4197-1201-2(2), 1072601, Abrams Appleseed) Abrams, Inc.

Rathmell, Donna & Rathmell, Doreen. Octavia & Her Purple Ink Cloud, 1 vol. McLennan, Connie, illus. 2006. (ENG.). 32p. (J). (gr. -1-2). 15.95 (978-0-9764943-5-5(3)) Arbordale Publishing.

Reasoner, Charles. Ocean Tails. Nelson, Judy, illus. 2011. (Tail Spin Bks.). (ENG.). 14p. (J). (gr. -1-3). bds. 9.99 (978-1-934650-92-9(7)) Just For Kids Pr., LLC.

Reed, Lynn Rowe. Benny Shark Goes to Friend School. Montijo, Rhode, illus. 2017. (ENG.). 32p. (J). (gr. -1-2). 17.99 *(978-1-4778-2803-8(6)*, 9781477828038, Two Lions) Amazon Publishing.

Reeve, Philip. Oliver & the Sea Monkeys. McIntyre, Sarah, illus. 2016. (Not-So-Impossible Tale Ser.). (ENG.). 224p. (J). (gr. 2-5). pap. 7.99 *(978-0-385-38789-7(X)*, Yearling) Random Hse. Children's Bks.

Reid, James. Ready, Set, Go!, 1 vol. rev. ed. 2013. (Literary Text Ser.). (ENG., Illus.). 20p. (gr. 1-2). (J). lib. bdg. 15.96 *(978-1-4807-1144-0(6))*; 7.99 *(978-1-4333-5438-5(8))* Teacher Created Materials, Inc.

Rey, H. A. Curious George at the Aquarium/Jorge el Curioso Visita el Acuario: Bilingual English-Spanish. 2010. (Curious George Ser.).Tr. of Curious George at the Aquarium. (ENG., Illus.). 24p. (J). (gr. -1-3). pap. 6.99 *(978-0-547-29963-1(X)*, 1413256, Clarion Bks.) HarperCollins Pubs.

Rey, H. A. & Rey, Margret. Curious George at the Aquarium. 2014. (Curious George Ser.). (ENG., Illus.). 24p. (J). (gr. -1-3). pap. 4.99 *(978-0-544-17674-4(X)*, 1556495, Clarion Bks.) HarperCollins Pubs.

RH Disney. Finding Dory Little Golden Book (Disney/Pixar Finding Dory) RH Disney, illus. 2016. (Little Golden Book Ser.). (ENG., Illus.). 24p. (J). (-k). 5.99 *(978-0-7364-3511-6(5)*, Golden/Disney) Random Hse. Children's Bks.

Riddle, Jamie. Beach Bum Babies & Sand Sisters Stormy. 2006. 48p. pap. 16.95 *(978-1-4241-3600-1(3))* PublishAmerica, Inc.

Romeu, Emma. My Manatee Friend. Vigil, Luis Gerardo Sanchez & Broeck, Fabricio Vanden, illus. 2004. (Colección Animales de América / Animals of the Americas Ser.). (SPA.). 24p. (gr. 3-5). pap. 11.95 *(978-1-59437-845-4(2))* Santillana USA Publishing Co., Inc.

Rovetch, L. Bob. 1,2,3 Octopus & Me. Gévry, Claudine, illus. 2006. (J). *(978-1-58987-011-6(5))* Kindermusik International.

Salton, Liz. Eelfish, a Rock & Roll King. Hathaway, Karen, illus. 2004. 38p. pap. 24.95 *(978-1-4137-1847-8(7))* PublishAmerica, Inc.

Saunders, Zina, illus. Trouble at the Krusty Krab! 2004. (SpongeBob SquarePants Ser.). (ENG.). 32p. (J). pap. 3.99 *(978-0-689-86838-2(3)*, Simon Spotlight/Nickelodeon) Simon Spotlight/Nickelodeon.

Schlegl, Stacey Lynn & Schlegl, Abigail. MerMountain. 2012. 84p. (J). pap. 11.95 *(978-0-9850272-2-3(3))* Jan-Carol Publishing, INC.

Schwarz, Viviane. Shark & Lobster's Amazing Undersea Adventure. Stewart, Joel, illus. 2006. 34p. (J). *(978-1-4156-8140-4(6))* Candlewick Pr.

Scollon, Bill. Ocean of Color (Disney/Pixar Finding Dory) The Disney Storybook Art Team, illus. 2016. (Step into Reading Ser.). (ENG.). 24p. (J). (gr. -1-1). 4.99 *(978-0-7364-3519-2(0)*, RH/Disney) Random Hse. Children's Bks.

Shepherd, Jodie. Guess Who Ocean Friends. Ovresat, Laura, illus. 2007. (Guess Who Ser.). (ENG.). 12p. (J). (gr. -1-k). bds. 8.99 *(978-0-7944-1122-0(3)*, Studio Fun International) Printers Row Publishing Group.

Sherry, Kevin. I'm the Best Artist in the Ocean! 2008. (ENG.). 24p. (J). (gr. -1-3). 16.99 *(978-0-8037-3255-1(4)*, Dial Bks) Penguin Young Readers Group.

—I'm the Biggest Thing in the Ocean! (J). (gr. -1 — 1). 2010. 28p. bds. 8.99 *(978-0-8037-3529-3(4))* 2007. (ENG., Illus.). 32p. 18.99 *(978-0-8037-3192-9(2))* Penguin Young Readers Group. (Dial Bks).

Sierra, Judy. Ballyhoo Bay. Anderson, Derek, illus. 2009. (ENG.). 40p. (J). (gr. -1-3). 19.99 *(978-1-4169-5888-8(6)*, Simon & Schuster/Paula Wiseman Bks.) Simon & Schuster/Paula Wiseman Bks.

Silver Dolphin en Español Editors. Amigos del Mar. 2006. (Magnets on the Move Ser.). (Illus.). 8p. (J). (gr. -1). bds. *(978-970-718-368-1(3)*, Silver Dolphin en Español) Advanced Marketing, S. de R. L. de C. V.

Siminovich, Lorena, illus. You Are My Baby: Ocean. 2014. (You Are My Baby Ser.). (ENG.). 10p. (J). (gr. -1 — 1). bds. 8.99 *(978-1-4521-2650-0(X))* Chronicle Bks. LLC.

Slate, Jenny & Fleischer-Camp, Dean. Marcel the Shell with Shoes On: Things about Me, 1 vol. 2011. (Marcel the Shell Ser.: 1). 48p. (J). (gr. k-3). 19.99 *(978-1-59514-455-3(2)*, Razorbill) Penguin Young Readers Group.

Slezak, Roy E. Marsha the Manatee. 2012. 32p. (-18). pap. 24.95 *(978-1-4626-9465-5(9))* America Star Bks.

Smith, Danna. Swallow the Leader. Sherry, Kevin, illus. 2016. (ENG.). 32p. (J). (gr. -1-3). 16.99 *(978-0-544-10518-8(4)*, 1540594, Clarion Bks.) HarperCollins Pubs.

Sohn, Emily. Astro the Alien Visits Ocean Animals. 2018. (BeginningtoRead Ser.). (ENG., Illus.). 32p. (J). (gr. 1-2). 22.60 *(978-1-59953-916-4(0))* Norwood Hse. Pr.

Soileau, Hodges, illus. The Great Shark Mystery. 2003. (Boxcar Children Special Ser.). 130p. (gr. 4-7). 15.50 *(978-0-7569-1616-9(X))* Perfection Learning Corp.

Sollinger, Emily. Diego's Ocean Adventure: A Book of Facts about Ocean Animals. Mawhinney, Art, illus. 2008. (Go, Diego, Go! Ser.). (ENG.). 16p. (J). (gr. -1-2). pap. 6.99 *(978-1-4169-4781-3(7)*, Simon Spotlight/Nickelodeon) Simon Spotlight/Nickelodeon.

Soundprints Staff. Ocean Adventures: Story-Time Treasury. 2005. (Smithsonian Institution Story-Time Treasures Ser.). (Illus.). 256p. (J). (gr. -1-2). 14.95 *(978-1-59069-226-4(8)*, HT1001) Studio Mouse LLC.

Srinivasan, Divya. Octopus Alone. 2013. (Illus.). 40p. (J). (gr. -1-k). 18.99 *(978-0-670-78515-5(6)*, Viking Books for Young Readers) Penguin Young Readers Group.

Steele, Kathleen Marie. The Legend of the Angel Wing Shell. Chylak, Jolie Catherine, illus. 2009. 20p. pap. 24.95 *(978-1-60749-134-7(6))* America Star Bks.

Stine, R. L. Rotten School #3: the Good, the Bad & the Very Slimy. Park, Trip, illus. 2008. (Rotten School Ser.: 3). (ENG.). 128p. (J). (gr. 3-7). pap. 5.99 *(978-0-06-078594-9(2)*, HarperCollins) HarperCollins Pubs.

Swift, Ginger. Little Blue Boat. Cottage Door Press, ed. Persico, Zoe, illus. 2016. (ENG.). 12p. (J). (gr. -1 — 1). bds. 7.99 *(978-1-68052-077-4(6)*, 1000300) Cottage Door Pr.

Sycamore, Beth. Who Needs a Hug? A Finding Dory Story. Disney Storybook Artists, illus. 2018. (Disney Learning Everyday Stories Ser.). (ENG.). 32p. (J). (gr. k-3). pap. 8.99 *(978-1-5415-3296-0(1)*, Lerner Pubns.) Lerner Publishing Group.

—Who Needs a Hug? A Finding Dory Story. Disney Storybook Artists, Disney Storybook, illus. 2018. (Disney Learning Everyday Stories Ser.). (ENG.). 32p. (J). (gr. k-3). lib. bdg. 31.99 *(978-1-5415-3254-0(6)*, Lerner Pubns.) Lerner Publishing Group.

Tate, Suzanne. Sandy Seal: A Tale of Sea Dogs. Melvin, James, illus. l.t. ed. 2004. (Suzanne Tate's Nature Ser.: No. 27). 28p. (J). pap. 4.95 *(978-1-878405-49-4(7))* Nags Head Art, Inc.

Teevee, Ningeokuluk. Alego, 1 vol. 2009. (ENG., Illus.). 24p. (J). (gr. -1-2). 17.99 *(978-0-88899-943-6(7))* Groundwood Bks. CAN. Dist: Publishers Group West (PGW).

Theule, Larissa. How Do You Do? Marino, Gianna, illus. 2019. (ENG.). 40p. (J). 17.99 *(978-1-61963-807-5(X)*, 900149147, Bloomsbury Children's Bks.) Bloomsbury Publishing USA.

Ticktock Media, Ltd. Staff. Ocean. 2009. (Animal Fun Touch & Feel Ser.). (ENG.). 10p. (J). (gr. -1-k). bds. 4.95 *(978-1-84696-830-3(5)*, TickTock Books) Octopus Publishing Group GBR. Dist: Independent Pubs. Group.

Todd-Stanton, Joe. The Secret of Black Rock. 2017. (ENG., Illus.). 40p. (J). (gr. -1-2). 16.95 *(978-1-911171-25-6(9))* Flying Eye Bks. GBR. Dist: Penguin Random Hse. LLC.

Tsurumi, Andrea. Crab Cake: Turning the Tide Together. 2019. (ENG., Illus.). 48p. (J). (gr. -1-3). 18.99 *(978-0-544-95900-2(0)*, 1661279, Clarion Bks.) HarperCollins Pubs.

Tunks, Karyn. Jubilee!, 1 vol. Buckner, Julie, illus. 2012. (ENG.). 32p. (J). (gr. k-3). 16.99 *(978-1-58980-880-5(0)*, Pelican Publishing) Arcadia Publishing.

Van Tassel, Mary A. Beach Ball's Discovery. 2013. 24p. pap. 24.95 *(978-1-4626-9698-7(8))* America Star Bks.

Vanier, Jolie. Puwaii Adventures with Joliea & Friends. 2006. 16.95 *(978-0-9787949-1-0(5))* Puwaii International, LLC.

Vernon, Ursula. Dragonbreath. 2009. (Dragonbreath Ser.: 1). (Illus.). 160p. (J). (gr. 3-7). 14.99 *(978-0-8037-3363-3(1)*, Dial Bks) Penguin Young Readers Group.

—Dragonbreath. 2012. (Dragonbreath Ser.: 1). lib. bdg. 17.20 *(978-0-606-26665-9(8))* Turtleback.

—Dragonbreath #1. 2012. (Dragonbreath Ser.: 1). (Illus.). 160p. (J). (gr. 3-7). pap. 8.99 *(978-0-14-242095-9(6)*, Puffin Books) Penguin Young Readers Group.

The Water Park, 6 Pack. (Sails Literacy Ser.). 16p. (gr. k-18). 27.00 *(978-0-7635-4415-7(9))* Rigby Education.

Watt, Fiona. Baby's Very First Slide & See under the Sea. 2015. (Baby's Very First Slide & See Board Bks.). (ENG.). 10p. (J). 14.99 *(978-0-7945-3482-0(1)*, Usborne) EDC Publishing.

Webster, Christy. Big Fish, Little Fish (Disney/Pixar Finding Dory) The Disney Storybook Art Team, illus. 2016. (Step into Reading Ser.). (ENG.). 24p. (J). (gr. -1-1). E-Book *(978-0-7364-3705-9(3)*, RH/Disney) Random Hse. Children's Bks.

Whiteley, Jason. Tales from the Tacklebox: Escape from the Crooked Tree. 2012. 48p. 23.99 *(978-1-4575-1152-3(5))*; pap. 14.99 *(978-1-4575-1150-9(9))* Dog Ear Publishing, LLC.

Wilson, Sarah. Moms Are the Best! 2014. (Spongebob Squarepants Step into Reading Ser.). lib. bdg. 13.55 *(978-0-606-35203-1(1))* Turtleback.

MARINE ARCHITECTURE

see Shipbuilding

MARINE BIOLOGY

see also Freshwater Biology; Marine Animals; Marine Ecology; Marine Plants; Marine Resources

Baker, Beth. Sylvia Earle. 2006. (Just the Facts Biographies Ser.). (ENG., Illus.). 112p. (gr. 5-12). 27.93 *(978-0-8225-3422-8(3)*, Lerner Pubns.) Lerner Publishing Group.

Bensinger, Lou. Tiny Invaders in the Water, 1 vol. 2010. (Tiny Invaders Ser.). (ENG., Illus.). 24p. (J). (gr. 2-3). pap. 9.25 *(978-1-4358-9852-3(4)*, df5d6ac4-090d-486a-8982-cc3dd4e96a95); lib. bdg. 26.27 *(978-1-4358-9380-1(8)*, f9aaad7d-fc44-4524-9e43-263843909207) Rosen Publishing Group, Inc., The. (PowerKids Pr.).

Bush Gibson, Karen. Marine Biology: Cool Women Who Dive. Chandhok, Lena, illus. 2016. (Girls in Science Ser.). (ENG.). 112p. (J). (gr. 3-7). 19.95 *(978-1-61930-431-4(7)*, 5e4bf935-9b66-4bec-bee7-4693c99466ed) Nomad Pr.

Crowson, Andrew. Flip Flap Ocean. 2003. (Illus.). 12p. bds. *(978-1-85602-431-0(8)*, Pavilion Children's Books) Pavilion Bks.

Cummings, Priscillia. The Chadwick Coloring Book, 1 vol. 2009. (ENG., Illus.). 32p. (J). (gr. -1-3). pap. 3.95 *(978-0-87033-389-7(5)*, 3617, Cornell Maritime Pr./Tidewater Pubs.) Schiffer Publishing, Ltd.

Davies, Kate. See under the Sea. 2008. (See Inside Board Bks). 16p. (J). (gr. 2). bds. 12.99 *(978-0-7945-2238-4(6)*, Usborne) EDC Publishing.

DK. Super Tiburones (Super Shark Encyclopedia) Y Otras Criaturas de Las Profundidades. 2018. (DK Super Nature Encyclopedias Ser.). Orig. Title: Super Shark Encyclopedia. (SPA., Illus.). 208p. (J). (gr. 3-7). 24.99 *(978-1-4654-7924-2(4)*, DK Children) Dorling Kindersley Publishing, Inc.

Evans, Topper. 100-Year-Old Tuataras!, 1 vol. 2016. (World's Longest-Living Animals Ser.). (ENG., Illus.). 24p. (J). (gr. 1-2). pap. 9.15 *(978-1-4824-5624-0(9)*, dbf01c56-30dc-4901-a7c7-cf6eec31027e) Stevens, Gareth Publishing LLLP.

Exploring Creation Marine Biology. 2006. cd-rom 58.50 *(978-1-932012-66-8(4))* Apologia Educational Ministries, Inc.

Exploring Creation Marine Biology Companion CD-ROM. 2006. cd-rom 13.50 *(978-1-932012-67-5(2))* Apologia Educational Ministries, Inc.

Field, Conrad. Alaska Ocean ABCs. Field, Conrad, illus. 2008. (Illus.). 32p. (J). pap. 9.95 *(978-0-9797442-2-8(9))* Alaska Independent Pubs.

Field, Nancy H. Discovering Sharks & Rays. Maydak, Michael S., illus. 2003. (Discovering Nature Library). 40p. (J). (gr. 2-6). pap. 7.95 *(978-0-941042-33-8(2))* Dog-Eared Pubns.

Frantz, Jennifer & Price, Roger. Under the Sea Mad Libs Junior: World's Greatest Word Game. 2005. (Mad Libs Junior Ser.). 48p. (J). (gr. k-3). mass mkt. 6.99 *(978-0-8431-1350-1(2)*, Mad Libs) Penguin Young Readers Group.

Ganeri, Anita. Protecting Ocean Habitats, 1 vol. 2005. (Protecting Habitats Ser.). (ENG., Illus.). 32p. (gr. 4-6). lib. bdg. 28.67 *(978-0-8368-4992-9(2)*, 82d0090f-bada-4da2-846f-0b7f0cceefa6, Gareth Stevens Learning Library) Stevens, Gareth Publishing LLLP.

Gilvan-Cartwright, Chris, illus. Who's in the Ocean? 2005. (Lift-The-Flap 'n' Learn Ser.). 10p. (J). 9.95 *(978-1-58117-213-3(3)*, Intervisual/Piggy Toes) Bendon, Inc.

Hale, Wendy A. & Lantz, Peggy. The Coral Reefs of Florida. 2014. (Florida Water Story Ser.). (Illus.). 36p. (J). (gr. -1-12). pap. 6.95 *(978-1-56164-703-3(9)*, 9781561647033) Pineapple Pr., Inc.

Hand, Carol. Marine Science in the Real World. 2016. (STEM in the Real World Set 2 Ser.). (ENG., Illus.). 48p. (J). (gr. 4-8). lib. bdg. 35.64 *(978-1-68078-480-0(3)*, 23897) ABDO Publishing Co.

Hemmel, David Lee & Knutson, Janette C. Alexis' Island: Growing up in the Tropical Paradise of Key West. 2006. (J). per. 14.95 *(978-0-9745637-2-5(2))* Duval Publishing.

Hopkins, Therese. Underwater Homes. 2009. (Home Sweet Home Ser.). 24p. (gr. 1-1). 42.50 *(978-1-61513-408-3(5)*, PowerKids Pr.) Rosen Publishing Group, Inc., The.

Kalman, Bobbie. Le Biome Marin. 2012. (FRE.). 32p. (J). pap. 10.95 *(978-2-89579-478-3(2))* Bayard Canada CAN. Dist: Crabtree Publishing Co.

—Los Océanos de la Tierra. 2009. (SPA.). 32p. (J). *(978-0-7787-8243-8(3))*; pap. *(978-0-7787-8260-5(3))* Crabtree Publishing Co.

Kalman, Bobbie & Aloian, Molly. Les Océans Polaires. 2009. (FRE., Illus.). 32p. (J). pap. 9.95 *(978-2-89579-248-2(8))* Bayard Canada Livres CAN. Dist: Crabtree Publishing Co.

Kalman, Bobbie & Macaulay, Kelly. Les Mers Tropicales. Briere, Marie-Josee, tr. from ENG. 2008. (Petit Monde Vivant Ser.). (FRE., Illus.). 32p. (J). (gr. 3-7). pap. 9.95 *(978-2-89579-182-9(1))* Bayard Canada Livres CAN. Dist: Crabtree Publishing Co.

Kelley, K. C. Marine Biologists!, Vol. 10. 2015. (Scientists in Action Ser.). (Illus.). 48p. (J). (gr. 5). 20.95 *(978-1-4222-3425-9(8))* Mason Crest.

Kelly, Richard. Ultimate Guide - Ocean: Contains 5 See-Through Feature Pages. 2017. 69p. (J). 24.95 *(978-1-78209-991-8(3))* Miles Kelly Publishing, Ltd. GBR. Dist: Parkwest Pubns., Inc.

Leardi, Jeanette. Protecting Our Oceans: Text Pairs. 2008. (Bridges/Navigators Ser.). (J). (gr. 6). 89.00 *(978-1-4108-8447-3(3))* Benchmark Education Co.

Look Who's Popping Up: Under the Sea. 2003. (J). (gr. -1-k). 4.98 *(978-0-7525-8904-6(0))* Parragon, Inc.

MacAulay, Kelley & Kalman, Bobbie. Tropical Oceans. 2005. (Living Ocean Ser.). (ENG., Illus.). 32p. (J). (gr. 3-4). lib. bdg. *(978-0-7787-1300-5(8))* Crabtree Publishing Co.

Malnig, Anita. Tide Pools: Life at the Edge of the Sea. rev. ed. 2009. (Nature Watch Ser.). (YA). (gr. 3-6). 27.93 *(978-1-58013-945-8(0))* Lerner Publishing Group.

Martin, Claudia. The Complete Guide to Ocean Life. 2016. (Illus.). 144p. (J). *(978-1-4351-6357-7(5))* Barnes & Noble, Inc.

—Complete Guides Ocean Life. 2012. (ENG.). 144p. (J). *(978-1-4351-4408-8(2))* Barnes & Noble, Inc.

Marx, Christy. Life in the Ocean Depths, 1 vol. 2003. (Life in Extreme Environments Ser.). (ENG.). 64p. (YA). (gr. 5-8). pap. 13.95 *(978-1-4358-3265-7(5)*, cf7d2f7a-5334-4406-9410-309b306f5853, Rosen Reference) Rosen Publishing Group, Inc., The.

McElligott, Matthew. Mad Scientist Academy: the Ocean Disaster. 2019. (Mad Scientist Academy Ser.). (ENG., Illus.). 40p. (J). (gr. k-3). lib. bdg. 20.99 *(978-1-5247-6720-4(4)*, Crown Books For Young Readers) Random Hse. Children's Bks.

National Geographic Learning. Language, Literacy & Vocabulary - Reading Expeditions (Earth Science): Ocean Exploration. 2007. (Avenues Ser.). (ENG., Illus.). 36p. (J). pap. 20.95 *(978-0-7922-5430-0(9))* CENGAGE Learning.

—Reading Expeditions (Science: Scientists in the Field): Sylvia Earle: Protecting the Seas. 2007. (Nonfiction Reading & Writing Workshops Ser.). (ENG., Illus.). 32p. (J). pap. 18.95 *(978-0-7922-8879-4(3))* CENGAGE Learning.

Ocean Life: Level Q, 6 vols., Vol. 2. (Explorers Ser.). 32p. (gr. 3-6). 44.95 *(978-0-7699-0604-1(4))* Shortland Pubns. (U. S. A.) Inc.

A Ocean Life, Set. 2005. (Ocean Life Ser.). (YA). (gr. k-3). 267.30 *(978-0-7368-4214-3(4)*, Pebble) Capstone.

Ocean Life, Set B. 2005. (Ocean Life Ser.). (YA). (gr. k-3). 267.30 *(978-0-7368-4215-0(2)*, Pebble) Capstone.

Owen, Ruth. Marine Biologists. 2013. (Out of the Lab: Extreme Jobs in Science Ser.). 32p. (J). (gr. 3-6). pap. 60.00 *(978-1-4777-1386-0(7))*; (ENG.). (gr. 4-5). pap. 11.00 *(978-1-4777-1381-5(6)*, 5a9acbb8-9c54-4208-8a68-65ab5d187441); (ENG.). (gr. 4-5). pap. 11.00 *(978-1-4777-1381-5(6)*, 5a9acbb8-9c54-4208-8a68-65ab5d187441); (ENG.). (gr. 4-5). lib. bdg. 28.93 *(978-1-4777-1291-7(7)*, 99da8f07-6bd6-4951-b3c1-1ad4c78d0211) Rosen Publishing Group, Inc., The. (PowerKids Pr.).

Patchett, Fiona. Under the Sea. Kushii, Tetsuo & Wray, Zoe, illus. 2006. (Beginners Nature: Level 1 Ser.). 32p. (J). (gr. k-2). 4.99 *(978-0-7945-1336-8(0)*, Usborne) EDC Publishing.

—Under the Sea. Kushii, Tetsuo, illus. 2006. (Usborne Beginners Ser.). 32p. (J). (gr. 1). lib. bdg. 12.99 *(978-1-58086-931-7(9)*, Usborne) EDC Publishing.

Pebble Books: Ocean Life. 2005. (YA). (gr. k-3). 534.60 *(978-0-7368-4223-5(3)*, Pebble) Capstone.

Perdew, Laura. The Great Pacific Garbage Patch. 2017. (Ecological Disasters Ser.). (ENG.). 112p. (J). (gr. 6-12). lib. bdg. 41.36 *(978-1-5321-1023-8(5)*, 25622, Essential Library) ABDO Publishing Co.

Peterson, Christy. Into the Deep: Science, Technology, & the Quest to Protect the Ocean. 2020. (ENG., Illus.). 152p. (YA). (gr. 6-12). lib. bdg. 39.99 *(978-1-5415-5555-6(4)*, 146760ff-0ad5-44c7-8434-6d8a84d3d8ab, Twenty-First Century Bks.) Lerner Publishing Group.

Peterson, Judy Monroe. Underwater Explorers: Marine Biologists. (Extreme Scientists Ser.). 24p. (gr. 2-3). 2009. 42.50 *(978-1-61512-453-4(5)*, PowerKids Pr.) 2008. (ENG., Illus.). (YA). lib. bdg. 26.27 *(978-1-4042-4526-6(X)*, e5708052-f6ba-4088-a012-c2f3a5d06e0d) Rosen Publishing Group, Inc., The.

Piano, Maureen. My Adventure with Tidepools. 2009. (ENG.). 44p. (J). 8.99 *(978-1-59092-473-0(8))* Blue Forge Pr.

Read, Nicholas. The Great Bear Sea: Exploring the Marine Life of a Pacific Paradise, 1 vol. McAllister, Ian, photos by. 2013. (ENG., Illus.). 128p. (J). (gr. 4-7). pap. 19.95 *(978-1-4598-0019-9(2))* Orca Bk. Pubs. USA.

Reid, Emily. Underwater Claymation, 1 vol. 2016. (Claymation Sensation Ser.). (ENG.). 32p. (gr. 3-3). pap. 12.75 *(978-1-4994-8108-2(X)*, b759d63d-1754-4945-80f4-3f1bf763355e, Windmill Bks.) Rosen Publishing Group, Inc., The.

Rizzo, Johnna. Oceans: Dolphins, Sharks, Penguins, & More! 2010. (Illus.). 64p. (J). (gr. 3-7). 14.95 *(978-1-4263-0686-0(5)*, National Geographic Kids) Disney Publishing Worldwide.

Roumanis, Alexis. Oceans. 2014. (Illus.). 24p. (J). *(978-1-4896-3014-8(7))* Weigl Pubs., Inc.

Salt, Zelda. Be a Marine Biologist, 1 vol. 2018. (Be a Scientist! Ser.). (ENG.). 32p. (gr. 3-4). 28.27 *(978-1-5382-2997-2(8)*, 5454289c-cc80-402e-a458-7b0b33492e7d) Stevens, Gareth Publishing LLLP.

Schuh, Mari. Sea Life. 2015. (Sea Life Ser.). (ENG.). 24p. (gr. k-1). 109.28 *(978-1-4914-6937-8(4)*, Capstone Pr.) Capstone.

Seligson, Sherri. Exploring Creation with Marine Biology. Wile, Jay L., ed. 2005. stu. ed., per. 20.00 *(978-1-932012-59-0(1))*;Set. 85.00 *(978-1-932012-60-6(5))* Apologia Educational Ministries, Inc.

—Exploring Creation with Marine Biology: Student Text. Wile, Jay L., ed. 2005. 65.00 *(978-1-932012-58-3(3))* Apologia Educational Ministries, Inc.

Sexton, Colleen. Blastoff! Readers - Oceans Alive, 6 vols., Set. Incl. Angelfish. 20.00 *(978-0-531-21711-5(6))*; Frogfish. 20.00 *(978-0-531-21712-2(4))*; Lionfish. 20.00 *(978-0-531-21713-9(2))*; Puffins. 20.00 *(978-0-531-21714-6(0))*; Shrimp. 20.00 *(978-0-531-21716-0(7))*; Swordfish. 20.00 *(978-0-531-21715-3(9))*; (Illus.). 24p. (J). (gr. k-3). 2009. 2009. Set lib. bdg. 120.00 *(978-0-531-26128-6(X)*, Children's Pr.) Scholastic Library Publishing.

Smith, Roland & Smith, Marie. W Is for Waves: An Ocean Alphabet. Megahan, John, illus. 2008. (Science Alphabet Ser.). (ENG.). 40p. (J). (gr. 1-4). 17.95 *(978-1-58536-254-7(9)*, 202070) Sleeping Bear Pr.

Smithyman, Kathryn & Kalman, Bobbie. El Bioma Marino. 2006. (Libro de Bobbie Kalman Ser.). (SPA., Illus.). 32p. (J). (gr. 3-7). pap. *(978-0-7787-8414-2(2))*; lib. bdg. *(978-0-7787-8400-5(2))* Crabtree Publishing Co.

Somervill, Barbara A. Marine Biologist. 2009. (21st Century Skills Library: Cool Science Careers Ser.). (ENG., Illus.). 32p. (gr. 4-8). lib. bdg. 32.07 *(978-1-60279-504-4(5)*, 200306) Cherry Lake Publishing.

Spilsbury, Richard & Spilsbury, Louise. At Home in the Ocean, 1 vol., 1. 2015. (Home in the Biome Ser.). (ENG.). 32p. (J). (gr. 3-4). 27.93 *(978-1-5081-4567-7(9)*, 3dfd6065-6470-412d-864f-6295e8b27447, PowerKids Pr.) Rosen Publishing Group, Inc., The.

Swanson, Diane. Safari Beneath the Sea: The Wonder World of the North Pacific Coast, 1 vol. Royal British Columbia Museum Staff, photos by. (ENG., Illus.). 64p. (J). pap. 12.95 *(978-1-55110-441-6(5))* Whitecap Bks., Ltd. CAN. Dist: Graphic Arts Ctr. Publishing Co.

Tahta, Sophie. What's under the Sea? Trotter, Stuart, illus. rev. ed. 2006. (Starting Point Science Ser.). 24p. (J). (gr. 4-7). pap. 4.99 *(978-0-7945-1409-9(X)*, Usborne) EDC Publishing.

Tejido, Jomike, illus. Jumbo Stickers for Little Hands: under the Sea: Includes 75 Stickers. 2017. (Jumbo Stickers for Little Hands Ser.). (ENG.). 24p. (J). (gr. -1-k). pap. 7.95 *(978-1-63322-156-7(3)*, 224360, Moondance) Quarto Publishing Group USA.

Thomas, William David. Marine Biologist, 1 vol. 2009. (Cool Careers: Cutting Edge Ser.). (ENG., Illus.). 32p. (J). (gr. 3-3). pap. 11.50 *(978-1-4339-2156-8(1)*, 80994c2a-1031-49c8-936a-3bfbe27203b8); lib. bdg. 28.67 *(978-1-4339-1957-2(5)*, 1655f66a-f139-4886-a668-8148d44cef98) Stevens, Gareth Publishing LLLP.

Ventura, Marne. Marine Biologist. 2019. (Jobs with Animals Ser.). (ENG., Illus.). 32p. (J). (gr. 4-6). pap. 7.95 *(978-1-5435-6046-6(6)*, 140091); lib. bdg. 28.65 *(978-1-5435-5784-8(8)*, 139740) Capstone.

Vogel, Carole Garbuny. Savage Waters. 2003. (Restless Sea Ser.). (ENG., Illus.). 80p. (gr. 5-8). pap. 12.95 *(978-0-531-16682-6(1)*, Watts, Franklin) Scholastic Library Publishing.

Westerskov, Kim, photos by. Life in a Frozen Sea. 2004. (Illus.). 32p. (J). pap. *(978-0-7685-2114-6(9))* Dominie Pr., Inc.

Woodward, John. Under the Waves. 2010. (Oceans Alive! Ser.). (ENG.). 32p. (J). (gr. 4-7). lib. bdg. 28.50 *(978-1-933834-62-7(5)*, 16774) Brown Bear Bks.

MARINE BIOLOGY—FICTION

Baldwin, Robert F. The Fish House Door. Sheckels, Astrid, illus. 2010. (ENG.). 36p. (J). 16.95 *(978-1-934031-30-8(5)*, 4e2fdddb-0133-414a-8d2f-864fa8aeaa26) Islandport Pr., Inc.

Crowley, Peter. J T Seavey. 2012. (ENG.). 35p. (J). pap. 18.95 *(978-1-4327-8712-7(8))* Outskirts Pr., Inc.

Mihalek, Alex, et al. The Adventures of Captain Fishhook Waterflea: the Invasion of Lake Champlain. 2009. (ENG.). 34p. pap. 13.98 *(978-0-557-12868-6(4))* Lulu Pr., Inc.

Riordan, Rick. Daughter of the Deep. Naidu, Lavanya, illus. 2021. xii, 336p. (J). ***(978-1-368-08084-2(7))*** Disney Pr.

—Daughter of the Deep. (ENG.). 2023. 368p. (J). (gr. 5-9). pap. 9.99 *(978-1-368-07793-4(5)*, Disney-Hyperion) 2023. 368p. (gr. 6-8). 26.19 ***(978-1-5364-7874-7(1))*** 2021. (Illus.). 352p. (J). (gr. 5-9). 19.99 *(978-1-368-07792-7(7)*, Disney-Hyperion) Disney Publishing Worldwide.

Snively, Gloria. Explore the Rocky Shore with Sam & Crystal, 1 vol. Gillmore, Karen, illus. 2018. (Explore with Sam & Crystal Ser.: 2). (ENG.). 64p. (J). (gr. 4-7). 18.95 *(978-1-77203-236-9(0))* Heritage Hse. CAN. Dist: Orca Bk. Pubs. USA.

—Explore the Wild Coast with Sam & Crystal, 1 vol. Gillmore, Karen, illus. 2018. (Explore with Sam & Crystal Ser.: 1).

(ENG.). 64p. (J). (gr. 4-7). 18.95 (978-1-77203-167-6(4)) Heritage Hse. CAN. Dist: Orca Bk. Pubs. USA.

Stilton, Thea. Thea Stilton & the Ghost of the Shipwreck (Thea Stilton #3) A Geronimo Stilton Adventure. 2010. (Thea Stilton Ser.: 3). Orig. Title: Il Vascello Fantasma. (ENG., Illus.). 176p. (J). (gr. 2-5). pap. 8.99 (978-0-545-15059-0(0), Scholastic Paperbacks) Scholastic, Inc.

Treasures of the Barrier Reef. 2005. (J). audio, cd-rom 24.95 (978-0-9771381-7-3(8)) Williams, Geoffrey T.

Wild, Ailsa, et al. Zobi & the Zoox: A Story of Coral Bleaching. 2018. (Stories of Partnership & Cooperation in Nature Ser.: 1). (Illus.). 44p. (J). (gr. 3-7). 19.95 (978-1-4863-0960-3(7)) CSIRO Publishing AUS. Dist: Stylus Publishing, LLC.

MARINE ECOLOGY

Aitken, Stephen. Ocean Life, 1 vol. 2013. (Climate Crisis Ser.). (ENG., Illus.). 64p. (gr. 5-5). 34.07 (978-1-60870-460-6(2), 02bc06a1-ccb0-42ae-bde1-78be054a8e51); pap. 16.28 (978-1-62712-040-1(8), d6a34bb5-7ab0-4582-9527-17f543de7cb1) Cavendish Square Publishing LLC.

Aloian, Molly & Kalman, Bobbie. Habitats Acuaticos. 2007. (Introduction a Los Habitats Ser.). (SPA., Illus.). 32p. (J). (gr. 3-7). lib. bdg. (978-0-7787-8325-1(1)); (gr. k-3). pap. (978-0-7787-8349-7(9)) Crabtree Publishing Co.

—Water Habitats, 1 vol. 2006. (Introducing Habitats Ser.). (ENG., Illus.). 32p. (J). (gr. 3-7). pap. (978-0-7787-2977-8(X)) Crabtree Publishing Co.

Anderson, Sheila. Coasts. 2015. (First Step Nonfiction — Landforms Ser.). (ENG., Illus.). 24p. (J). (gr. k-2). E-Book 35.99 (978-1-5124-1041-9(1), Lerner Pubns.) Lerner Publishing Group.

Animals of the Ocean Series (Illus.). (J). (gr. 2-6). lib. bdg. 44.85 (978-1-56674-947-3(6)) Forest Hse. Publishing Co., Inc.

Basher, Simon & Green, Dan. Oceans: Making Waves! Basher, Simon, illus. 2012. (Basher Science Ser.). (ENG., Illus.). 128p. (J). (gr. 5-9). pap. 9.99 (978-0-7534-6822-7(0), 900081821, Kingfisher) Roaring Brook Pr.

Bayrock, Fiona. The Ocean Explorer's Handbook. 2005. (Undersea University Ser.). (Illus.). 48p. (J). pap. (978-0-439-71184-5(3)) Scholastic, Inc.

Beaton, Clare & Haig, Rudi. Read, Learn & Create — The Ocean Craft Book. Beaton, Clare, illus. 2019. (ENG., Illus.). 32p. (J). (gr. 1-4). 17.99 (978-1-58089-941-3(2)) Charlesbridge Publishing, Inc.

Bennett, Doraine. Atlantic Ocean. 2009. (J). (978-1-935077-34-3(1)) State Standards Publishing, LLC.

—Coast. 2009. (J). (978-1-935077-35-0(X)); pap. (978-1-935077-40-4(6)) State Standards Publishing, LLC.

—Coastal Plain. 2009. (J). (978-1-935077-51-0(1)); pap. (978-1-935077-52-7(X)) State Standards Publishing, LLC.

Beringer Mckissack, Lisa. Counting in the Oceans, 1 vol. 2009. (Counting in the Biomes Ser.). (ENG., Illus.). 32p. (gr. k-2). lib. bdg. 26.60 (978-0-7660-2994-1(8), b0e6b41e-3eaf-4b3a-9a39-27bd997cf58a, Enslow Elementary) Enslow Publishing, LLC.

Blocksma, Mary. What's on the Beach? A Great Lakes Treasure Hunt. Blocksma, Mary, illus. 2003. (Great Lakes Treasure Hunts Ser.: No. 1). (Illus.). 48p. (J). pap. 9.95 (978-0-9708575-1-4(9)) Beaver Island Arts.

Bodden, Valerie. Great Barrier Reef. 2010. (Big Outdoors Ser.). 24p. (J). (gr. k-3). 16.95 (978-1-58341-816-1(4)) Creative Co., The.

Boothroyd, Jennifer. Let's Visit the Ocean. 2016. (Lightning Bolt Books (r) — Biome Explorers Ser.). (ENG., Illus.). 32p. (J). (gr. 1-3). 29.32 (978-1-5124-1194-2(9), cdf4ca2e-6b12-4d4d-bfb5-04b8aebf1395, Lerner Pubns.) Lerner Publishing Group.

Brooks, Susie. Ocean Emporium: A Compilation of Creatures. COOPER, Dawn, illus. 2019. (ENG.). 64p. (J). (gr. k-4). lib. bdg. 18.99 (978-1-58089-828-7(9)) Charlesbridge Publishing, Inc.

Brown, Carron. Secrets of the Seashore. 2014. (ENG., Illus.). 36p. (J). 12.99 (978-1-61067-309-9(3)) Kane Miller.

Butterfield, Moira. Who Eats Who at the Seashore? 2006. (Food Chains in Action Ser.). (Illus.). 32p. (YA). (gr. 4-7). lib. bdg. 28.50 (978-1-58340-963-3(7), 1262631) Black Rabbit Bks.

Cain, Marie Mowery. Under the Waves. 2013. (Big Books, Blue Ser.). (ENG & SPA., Illus.). 16p. pap. 33.00 (978-1-59246-005-2(4)) Big Books, by George!

Cefrey, Holly. Oceans. 2009. (Biomes Ser.). 24p. (gr. 2-3). 42.50 (978-1-61511-592-1(7), PowerKids Pr.) Rosen Publishing Group, Inc., The.

Centore, Michael. Saving Ocean Animals: Sharks, Turtles, Coral, & Fish. 2017. (Illus.). 64p. (J). (978-1-4222-3879-0(2)) Mason Crest.

Cerullo, Mary M. & Simmons, Beth E. Sea Secrets: Tiny Clues to a Big Mystery. Carlson, Kirsten., illus. 2015. (Long Term Ecological Research Ser.). 32p. (J). (gr. 1-5). pap. 9.95 (978-1-63076-075-5(7)) Taylor Trade Publishing.

Channing, Margot. Seas & Oceans. 2014. (Closer Look At... Ser.). (Illus.). 32p. (gr. 3-6). 31.35 (978-1-905087-07-5(1)) Book Hse. GBR. Dist: Black Rabbit Bks.

Charles, Patrick. Ocean Food Chains, 1 vol. 2008. (Real Life Readers Ser.). (ENG.). 16p. (gr. 2-3). pap. 7.05 (978-1-4358-0065-6(6), c16f7949-ee15-48d3-896e-d9ca9f18dfcf, Rosen Classroom) Rosen Publishing Group, Inc., The.

Crenson, Victoria. Horseshoe Crabs & Shorebirds: The Story of a Food Web, 0 vols. Cannon, Annie, illus. unabr. ed. 2009. (ENG.). 42p. (J). (gr. 3-5). pap. 9.99 (978-0-7614-5552-3(3), 9780761455523, Two Lions) Amazon Publishing.

Crossingham, John & Kalman, Bobbie. Cadenas Alimentarias de la Costa Marina. 2006. (Cadenas Alimentarias Ser.). (SPA., Illus.). 32p. (J). (gr. 3-7). lib. bdg. (978-0-7787-8531-6(9)) Crabtree Publishing Co.

Davies, Nicola. Oceans & Seas. 2014. 48p. pap. 7.00 (978-1-61003-360-2(4)) Center for the Collaborative Classroom.

Dichter, Paul. The Ocean World: A Finding Dory Discovery Book. Disney Storybook Artists, illus. 2018. (Disney Learning Discovery Bks.). (ENG.). 48p. (J). (gr. 2-5). pap. 8.99 (978-1-5415-3272-4(4), Lerner Pubns.) Lerner Publishing Group.

—The Ocean World: A Finding Dory Discovery Book. Disney Storybook Artists, Disney Storybook, illus. 2018. (Disney Learning Discovery Bks.). (ENG.). 48p. (J). (gr. 2-5). lib. bdg. 31.99 (978-1-5415-3259-5(7), Lerner Pubns.) Lerner Publishing Group.

Dichter, Paul & Heiman, Larry. The Magic of Our World: From the Night Sky to the Pacific Islands with Favorite Disney Characters. 2018. (ENG., Illus.). 176p. (J). (gr. 2-5). pap. 14.99 (978-1-5415-4250-1(9), Lerner Pubns.) Lerner Publishing Group.

Editors of Storey Publishing. Under the Sea Poster Book. 2005. (ENG., Illus.). 64p. (J). (gr. 2-7). pap. 9.95 (978-1-58017-623-1(2), 67623) Storey Publishing, LLC.

Encyclopaedia Britannica, Inc. Staff, compiled by. Beginning of the Food Chain. 2008. 49.95 (978-1-59339-555-1(8)) Encyclopaedia Britannica, Inc.

Fleisher, Paul. Lake & Pond Food Webs. 2008. pap. 52.95 (978-0-8225-9352-2(1)) Lerner Publishing Group.

—Ocean Food Webs. 2008. pap. 52.95 (978-0-8225-9353-9(X)) Lerner Publishing Group.

—Ocean Food Webs in Action. 2013. (Searchlight Books (tm) — What Is a Food Web? Ser.). (ENG., Illus.). 40p. (J). (gr. 3-5). pap. 9.99 (978-1-4677-1556-0(5), fe99e355-c570-430b-9c79-44e051e6ea8f) Lerner Publishing Group.

Franklin, Carolyn. Ocean Life. Franklin, Carolyn, illus. 2013. (World of Wonder Ser.). (Illus.). 32p. (gr. 1-3). 31.35 (978-1-904642-63-3(2)) Book Hse. GBR. Dist: Black Rabbit Bks.

Gagne, Tammy. Marine Ecosystems. 2018. (Earth's Ecosystems Ser.). (ENG., Illus.). 32p. (J). (gr. 3-6). 32.80 (978-1-63235-458-7(6), 13870, 12-Story Library) Bookstaves, LLC.

Gamble, Adam & Jasper, Mark. Good Night Seashore. Kelly, Cooper, illus. 2019. (Good Night Our World Ser.). 26p. (J). (— 1). bds. 9.95 (978-1-60219-665-0(6)) Good Night Bks.

Ganeri, Anita. I Wonder Why the Sea Is Salty. 2014. 32p. pap. 7.00 (978-1-61003-352-7(3)) Center for the Collaborative Classroom.

—I Wonder Why the Sea Is Salty: And Other Questions about the Oceans. 2011. (I Wonder Why Ser.). (ENG., Illus.). 32p. (J). (gr. k-3). pap. 6.99 (978-0-7534-6521-9(3), 900070301, Kingfisher) Roaring Brook Pr.

Gardeski, Christina Mia. All about Oceans. 2017. (Habitats Ser.). (ENG., Illus.). 24p. (J). (gr. -1-2). lib. bdg. 22.65 (978-1-5157-7644-4(1), 135929, Pebble) Capstone.

Gaydos, Joseph K. & DeLella Benedict, Audrey. Explore the Salish Sea: A Nature Guide for Kids. 2018. (Illus.). 64p. (J). (gr. 2-5). 19.99 (978-1-63217-095-8(7), Little Bigfoot) Sasquatch Bks.

George, Lynn. Coral: Reef Builders, 1 vol. 2010. (Animal Architects Ser.). (ENG.). 24p. (J). (gr. 2-3). pap. 9.25 (978-1-4488-1349-0(2), c9d77d9c-ef4d-4212-8207-8ab975a3a438); lib. bdg. 26.27 (978-1-4488-0694-2(1), 6d041307-dcc2-4fd3-aee4-f65c97412761) Rosen Publishing Group, Inc., The. (PowerKids Pr.).

Gish, Melissa. Coral Reef Communities. 2018. (Down in the Ocean Ser.). (ENG.). 48p. (J). (gr. 4-7). pap. 12.00 (978-1-62832-550-8(X), 19737, Creative Paperbacks) Creative Co., The.

—Deep-Sea Mysteries. 2018. (Down in the Ocean Ser.). (ENG.). 48p. (J). (gr. 4-7). pap. 12.00 (978-1-62832-551-5(8), 19738, Creative Paperbacks) Creative Co., The.

—Seafloor Scavengers. 2018. (Down in the Ocean Ser.). (ENG.). 48p. (J). (gr. 4-7). (978-1-60818-998-4(8), 19734, Creative Education) Creative Co., The.

Gottlieb. Water Life. 2004. (Wonders of Science Ser.). (ENG., Illus.). 144p. (gr. 7-12). pap. 24.55 (978-0-7398-9178-0(2)) Houghton Mifflin Harcourt Publishing Co.

Grady, Colin. The Ocean Biome, 1 vol. 2016. (Zoom in on Biomes Ser.). (ENG.). 24p. (gr. 2-2). pap. 10.95 (978-0-7660-7785-0(3), df432bb7-472b-42b5-b97a-6f824d6f0f37) Enslow Publishing, LLC.

Gray, Leon. Oceans. 2015. (Amazing Biomes Ser.). (ENG., Illus.). 32p. (J). (gr. 3-6). 31.35 (978-1-78121-243-1(0), 16390) Brown Bear Bks.

Green, Jen. Life in a Coral Reef, 1 vol. 2010. (Nature in Focus Ser.). (ENG., Illus.). 32p. (gr. 3-4). (J). pap. 11.50 (978-1-4339-3424-7(8), 5f5a4679-bd59-4e83-af37-dffe7c860b72, Gareth Stevens Learning Library); (YA). lib. bdg. 28.67 (978-1-4339-3423-0(X), 780d3128-bd53-47bc-8e3e-c0cbf7135050) Stevens, Gareth Publishing LLLP.

Group/McGraw-Hill, Wright. La Vida en el Oceano, 6 vols., Vol. 2. (Explorers. Exploradores Nonfiction Sets Ser.). (SPA.). 32p. (gr. 3-6). 44.95 (978-0-7699-0740-6(7)) Shortland Pubns. (U. S. A.) Inc.

Hale, Wendy A. & Lantz, Peggy. The Coral Reefs of Florida. 2014. (Florida Water Story Ser.). (Illus.). 36p. (J). (gr. -1-12). pap. 6.95 (978-1-56164-703-3(9), 9781561647033) Pineapple Pr., Inc.

—The Oceans of Florida. 2014. (Florida Water Story Ser.). (Illus.). 36p. (J). (gr. -1-12). pap. 6.95 (978-1-56164-704-0(7)) Pineapple Pr., Inc.

Haugen, Hayley Mitchell. Life in a Coral Reef. 2003. (Ecosystems Library). (Illus.). 48p. (J). 23.70 (978-0-7377-1370-1(4), Greenhaven Pr., Inc.) Cengage Gale.

Head, Honor. Poisoned Oceans, 1 vol. 2018. (Totally Toxic Ser.). (ENG.). 48p. (gr. 4-5). pap. 15.05 (978-1-5382-3494-5(7), b5c78486-9c4b-4b67-8c9b-c5cfa11ff3f5) Stevens, Gareth Publishing LLLP.

Hidden World: Level P, 6 vols., Vol. 3. (Explorers Ser.). 32p. (gr. 3-6). 44.95 (978-0-7699-0616-4(8)) Shortland Pubns. (U. S. A.) Inc.

Higgins, Melissa. Ocean Ecosystems, 1 vol. 2015. (Ecosystems of the World Ser.). (ENG., Illus.). 48p. (J). (gr. 4-8). 35.64 (978-1-62403-855-6(7), 18080) ABDO Publishing Co.

Hirschi, Ron. Ocean Seasons, 1 vol. Carlson, Kirsten., illus. 2007. (ENG.). 32p. (J). (gr. k-4). 15.95 (978-0-9777423-2-5(6)); pap. 10.95 (978-1-60718-863-6(5)) Arbordale Publishing.

Holewa, Lisa. Using Marine Microbes. rev. ed. 2018. (Smithsonian: Informational Text Ser.). (ENG., Illus.). 32p. (J). (gr. 4-8). pap. 11.99 (978-1-4938-6720-2(2)) Teacher Created Materials, Inc.

Hudak, Heather C. Oceans. (Illus.). 32p. (J). 2017. (978-1-5105-0878-1(3)) 2016. (978-1-5105-0876-7(7)) SmartBook Media, Inc.

—Oceans. 2005. (Biomes Ser.). (Illus.). 32p. (J). (gr. 4-6). lib. bdg. 24.45 (978-1-59036-348-5(5)) Weigl Pubs., Inc.

Hulick, Kathryn. Coral Reefs. 2018. (Animal Engineers Ser.). (ENG., Illus.). 32p. (J). (gr. 2-3). pap. 9.95 (978-1-63517-962-0(9), 1635179629); lib. bdg. 31.35 (978-1-63517-861-6(4), 1635178614) North Star Editions. (Focus Readers).

—Coral Reefs. 2018. (Illus.). 32p. (J). pap. (978-1-4896-9750-9(0), AV2 by Weigl) Weigl Pubs., Inc.

Hyde, Natalie. Deep Sea Extremes. 2008. (Extreme Nature Ser.). (ENG., Illus.). 32p. (J). (gr. 2-3). pap. (978-0-7787-4518-1(X)); lib. bdg. (978-0-7787-4501-3(5)) Crabtree Publishing Co.

—Great Barrier Reef Research Journal. 2017. (Ecosystems Research Journal Ser.). (Illus.). 32p. (J). (gr. 4-5). (978-0-7787-3470-3(6)); (ENG., pap. (978-0-7787-3495-6(1)) Crabtree Publishing Co.

Inskipp, Carol. Healthy Seas. 2006. (Sustainable Futures Ser.). (Illus.). 48p. (YA). (gr. 5-9). lib. bdg. 31.35 (978-1-58340-980-0(7), 1262623) Black Rabbit Bks.

Ishak, Lauren. Map & Track Oceans. 2019. (Map & Track Biomes & Animals Ser.). (Illus.). 32p. (J). (gr. 4-5). (978-0-7787-5369-8(7)); pap. (978-0-7787-5381-0(6)) Crabtree Publishing Co.

Johnson, Jinny. Deep Sea Life. 2011. (Watery Worlds Ser.). 32p. (gr. 3-6). 31.35 (978-1-59920-503-8(3)) Black Rabbit Bks.

Johnson, Rebecca L. Journey into the Deep: Discovering New Ocean Creatures. 2010. (ENG., Illus.). 64p. (J). (gr. 4-8). lib. bdg. 31.99 (978-0-7613-4148-2(X), f2f61c84-d06a-4e20-80f6-33973b2f5e36, Millbrook Pr.) Lerner Publishing Group.

—A Journey into the Ocean. Saroff, Phyllis V., illus. 2004. (Biomes of North America Ser.). (ENG.). 48p. (gr. 3-6). lib. bdg. 23.93 (978-1-57505-591-6(0)) Lerner Publishing Group.

Johnson, Robin. Oceans Inside Out. 2014. (Ecosystems Inside Out Ser.). (ENG., Illus.). 32p. (J). (gr. 4-5). (978-0-7787-0635-9(4)) Crabtree Publishing Co.

Joyce, John. Black John the Bogus Pirate - Cartoon Workbook of Marine Beasts. Joyce, John, illus. 2012. (ENG., Illus.). 20p. (J). (978-0-9557637-8-6(9)) Sprindrift Pr.

Kalman, Bobbie. Le Biome Marin. 2012. (FRE.). 32p. (J). pap. 10.95 (978-2-89579-478-3(2)) Bayard Canada CAN. Dist: Crabtree Publishing Co.

Kalman, Bobbie & Aloian, Molly. Les Océans Polaires. 2009. (FRE., Illus.). 32p. (J). pap. 9.95 (978-2-89579-248-2(8)) Bayard Canada Livres CAN. Dist: Crabtree Publishing Co.

King, Zelda. Examining Tide Pool Habitats. 2009. (Graphic Organizers: Habitats Ser.). 24p. (gr. 2-3). 42.50 (978-1-61513-103-7(5), PowerKids Pr.) Rosen Publishing Group, Inc., The.

Kortemeier, Todd. Exploring the Depths of the Ocean. 2017. (Science Frontiers Ser.). (ENG., Illus.). 32p. (J). (gr. 3-6). 32.80 (978-1-63235-377-1(6), 11871); pap. 9.95 (978-1-63235-394-8(6), 11879) Bookstaves, LLC. (12-Story Library).

Kurtz, Kevin. A Day in the Salt Marsh, 1 vol. Powell, Consie, illus. 2007. (ENG.). 32p. (J). (gr. 2-3). pap. 10.95 (978-1-934359-19-8(X), e88c19aa-d7c4-4170-a5dc-46f581ff8a89) Arbordale Publishing.

Lawrence, Ellen. Polluted Oceans. 2014. (Science Slam: Green World, Clean World Ser.). 24p. (J). (gr. -1-3). lib. bdg. 26.99 (978-1-62724-236-3(8)) Bearport Publishing Co., Inc.

Levy, Janey. Discovering Coral Reefs. 2009. (World Habitats Ser.). 32p. (gr. 4-5). 47.90 (978-1-60854-834-7(1), PowerKids Pr.) Rosen Publishing Group, Inc., The.

Lindop, Laurie. Venturing the Deep Sea. 2005. (Science on the Edge Ser.). (ENG., Illus.). 80p. (gr. 5-12). 27.93 (978-0-7613-2701-1(0)) Lerner Publishing Group.

Llewellyn, Claire. In the Sea Red Band. Belcher, Andy, photos by. 2016. (Cambridge Reading Adventures Ser.). (ENG., Illus.). 16p. pap. 7.95 (978-1-107-57578-3(8)) Cambridge Univ. Pr.

Lynch, Seth. There's an Ocean in My Backyard!, 1 vol. 2016. (Backyard Biomes Ser.). (ENG., Illus.). 24p. (J). (gr. 1-2). pap. 9.15 (978-1-4824-5567-0(6), d5ba91f5-a394-4037-8095-1e9ef18bce59) Stevens, Gareth Publishing LLLP.

Martin, Claudia. The Complete Guide to Ocean Life. 2016. (Illus.). 144p. (J). (978-1-4351-6357-7(5)) Barnes & Noble, Inc.

Mason, Janeen. Ocean Commotion: Life on the Reef, 1 vol. Mason, Janeen, illus. 2010. (ENG., Illus.). 32p. (J). (gr. k-3). 16.99 (978-1-58980-783-9(9), Pelican Publishing) Arcadia Publishing.

McFadzean, Lesley. Ocean Habitats. 2013. (Discovery Education: Habitats Ser.). 32p. (J). (gr. 3-6). pap. 60.00 (978-1-4777-1480-5(4)); (ENG.). (gr. 4-5). 28.93 (978-1-4777-1322-8(0), 96a1a577-3ee1-4511-b2c7-a29335e5ae0c); (ENG.). (gr. 4-5). pap. 11.00 (978-1-4777-1479-9(0), 11a44e58-1dd0-4334-8886-5422085dc012) Rosen Publishing Group, Inc., The. (PowerKids Pr.).

Meachen Rau, Dana. Coral Reefs, 1 vol. 2008. (Wonders of Nature Ser.). (ENG.). 32p. (gr. 1-2). pap. 9.23 (978-0-7614-3326-2(0), 058caa36-2647-4923-96ab-e5a2179c3939) Cavendish Square Publishing LLC.

Meltzer Kleinhenz, Sydnie. Coral Reefs. 2004. (ENG., Illus.). 32p. (J). (gr. 4-4). pap. 12.29 (978-0-7652-5223-4(6), Celebration Pr.) Savvas Learning Co.

Milbourne, Anna. Peek Inside the Sea. 2018. (Peek Inside Board Bks.). (ENG.). 14p. (J). 11.99 (978-0-7945-4038-8(4), Usborne) EDC Publishing.

—Under the Sea. Shimmen, Cathy, illus. 2007. (Picture Bks). 32p. (J). 9.99 (978-0-7945-1801-1(X), Usborne) EDC Publishing.

Miller-Schroeder, Patricia. Underwater Life. 2007. (Life Science (Weigl Hardcover) Ser.). (Illus.). 32p. (J). (gr. 4-7). lib. bdg. 26.00 (978-1-59036-713-1(8)); per. 9.95 (978-1-59036-714-8(6)) Weigl Pubs., Inc.

Milner, Charlotte. The Sea Book. Milner, Charlotte, illus. 2019. (Conservation for Kids Ser.). (ENG., Illus.). 48p. (J). (gr. k-3). 15.99 (978-1-4654-7882-5(5), DK Children) Dorling Kindersley Publishing, Inc.

Morey, Allan. Ocean Food Chains. 2003. (What Eats What? Ser.). (J). pap. (978-1-58417-219-2(3)); lib. bdg. (978-1-58417-218-5(5)) Lake Street Pubs.

Murray, Aaron R. Counting in the Oceans 1-2-3, 1 vol. 2012. (All about Counting in the Biomes Ser.). (ENG., Illus.). 24p. (gr. -1-1). 25.27 (978-0-7660-4052-6(6), 24d648a6-f224-4734-b329-775b917c402e, Enslow Publishing) Enslow Publishing, LLC.

Newman, Patricia. Sea Otter Heroes: The Predators That Saved an Ecosystem. 2017. (ENG., Illus.). 56p. (J). (gr. 4-8). 33.32 (978-1-5124-2631-1(8), bdb5dec7-eab1-434b-9e98-f6d597589e5d); E-Book 47.99 (978-1-5124-3885-7(5), 9781512438857); E-Book 47.99 (978-1-5124-2844-5(2)); E-Book 9.99 (978-1-5124-3884-0(7), 9781512438840) Lerner Publishing Group. (Millbrook Pr.).

O'Neill, Michael Patrick, photos by. Ocean Magic. O'Neill, Michael Patrick, . 2008. (Illus.). 48p. (J). (gr. 1-4). 19.95 (978-0-9728653-5-7(7)) Batfish Bks.

Orr, Tamra B. Ocean Discoveries. 2018. (Marvelous Discoveries Ser.). (ENG., Illus.). 32p. (J). (gr. 2-5). lib. bdg. 28.65 (978-1-5435-2617-2(9), 138088, Capstone Pr.) Capstone.

Pettiford, Rebecca. Ocean Food Chains. 2016. (Who Eats What?). (Illus.). 24p. (J). (gr. 2-5). lib. bdg. 25.65 (978-1-62031-302-2(2), Pogo) Jump! Inc.

Pratt-Serafini, Kristin Joy. A Swim Through the Sea: Board Book, 1 vol. Pratt-Serafini, Kristin Joy, illus. 2006. (Illus.). 26p. (J). (gr. k-6). bds. 7.99 (978-1-58469-080-1(1), Dawn Pubns.) Sourcebooks, Inc.

Pyers, Greg. Biodiversity of Oceans & Seas, 1 vol. 2012. (Biodiversity Ser.). (ENG.). 32p. (gr. 4-4). 31.21 (978-1-60870-530-6(7), 511857e6-9c7c-4e82-8c21-9adbfadbf6f1) Cavendish Square Publishing LLC.

—Biodiversity of Rivers, 1 vol. 2012. (Biodiversity Ser.). (ENG.). 32p. (gr. 4-4). 31.21 (978-1-60870-531-3(5), d20c2886-2e1f-4892-87ff-72189c16a0be) Cavendish Square Publishing LLC.

Rice, Dona. Crazy Creatures: Deep Ocean. 2020. (J). pap. (978-1-64290-723-0(5)) Teacher Created Materials, Inc.

Rigby Education Staff. Gardens of the Sea. (Sails Literacy Ser.). (Illus.). 16p. (gr. 1-2). 27.00 (978-0-7635-9923-2(9), 699239C99) Rigby Education.

Riggs, Kate. Le Lamantin. 2018. (Planète Animaux Ser.). (FRE., Illus.). 24p. (J). (978-1-77092-393-5(4), 19682) Creative Co., The.

—Oceans. (Seedlings Ser.). 24p. (J). 2016. (ENG., Illus.). (gr. -1-k). (978-1-60818-743-0(8), 20739) 2010. (gr. 1-4). 16.95 (978-1-58341-828-4(8)) Creative Co., The. (Creative Education).

Rissman, Rebecca. Living & Nonliving in the Ocean, 1 vol. 2013. (Is It Living or Nonliving? Ser.). (ENG., Illus.). 24p. (J). (gr. k-2). 25.99 (978-1-4109-5381-0(5), 123310); pap. 6.95 (978-1-4109-5388-9(2), 123328) Capstone. (Raintree).

Rivera, Sheila. Ocean. 2005. (Illus.). 24p. (J). pap. 5.95 (978-0-8225-5372-4(4)) Lerner Publishing Group.

Royston, Angela. Ocean - It's My Home! 2011. (ENG., Illus.). 24p. (J). pap. (978-0-7787-7873-8(8)) Crabtree Publishing Co.

—Ocean It's My Home! 2011. (Crabtree Connections Ser.). (ENG., Illus.). 24p. (J). (gr. 3-6). (978-0-7787-7851-6(7)) Crabtree Publishing Co.

Shocking Sea Creatures. 2016. (Illus.). 32p. (J). (978-1-4222-3528-7(9)) Mason Crest.

Sidabras, Kimberly. Oceans, Vol. 5. 2018. (World's Biomes Ser.). (Illus.). 80p. (J). (gr. 7). 33.27 (978-1-4222-4038-0(X)) Mason Crest.

Siddell, Robert. Sea Life 3D. 2013. (Illus.). 27p. 19.99 (978-0-9830127-4-0(1)) Digital Tech Frontier, LLC.

Sill, Cathryn. About Habitats: Oceans, 1 vol. Sill, John, illus. 2012. (About Habitats Ser.: 5). 48p. (J). (gr. -1-2). 16.95 (978-1-56145-618-5(7)) Peachtree Publishing Co. Inc.

Simon, Seymour. Coral Reefs. 2013. (ENG.). 32p. (J). (gr. 1-5). pap. 7.99 (978-0-06-191496-6(7), HarperCollins) HarperCollins Pubs.

Simpson, Phillip. Marine Biomes Around the World. 2019. (Exploring Earth's Biomes Ser.). (ENG., Illus.). 32p. (J). (gr. 3-6). pap. 7.95 (978-1-5435-7535-4(8), 141066); lib. bdg. 29.99 (978-1-5435-7234-6(0), 140518) Capstone.

Slade, Suzanne. What Eats What in an Ocean Food Chain, 1 vol. McLaughlin, Zack, illus. 2012. (Food Chains Ser.). (ENG.). 24p. (J). (gr. 2-4). pap. 8.95 (978-1-4048-7696-5(0), 120443, Picture Window Bks.) Capstone.

—What If There Were No Sea Otters? A Book about the Ocean Ecosystem, 1 vol. Schwartz, Carol, illus. 2010. (Food Chain Reactions Ser.). (ENG.). 24p. (J). (gr. 2-4). pap. 9.95 (978-1-4048-6397-2(4), 114148, Picture Window Bks.) Capstone.

Smith, Alastair & Tachell, Judy. Under the Sea. Scott, Peter David, illus. 2007. (J). (978-0-545-03305-3(5)) Scholastic, Inc.

Smithyman, Kathryn & Kalman, Bobbie. El Bioma Marino. 2006. (Libro de Bobbie Kalman Ser.). (SPA., Illus.). 32p. (J). (gr. 3-7). pap. (978-0-7787-8414-2(2)); lib. bdg. (978-0-7787-8400-5(2)) Crabtree Publishing Co.

Spilsbury, Louise & Spilsbury, Richard. Marine Biomes. 2018. (Earth's Natural Biomes Ser.). (Illus.). 32p. (J). (gr. 4-4). (978-0-7787-3996-8(1)) Crabtree Publishing Co.

Spilsbury, Louise & Spilsbury, Richard, contrib. by. MARINE BIOMES. 2018. (Earth's Natural Biomes Ser.). (Illus.). 32p. (J). (gr. 4-4). pap. (978-0-7787-4181-7(8)) Crabtree Publishing Co.

Spilsbury, Richard & Spilsbury, Louise. At Home in the Ocean, 1 vol., 1. 2015. (Home in the Biome Ser.). (ENG.). 32p. (J). (gr. 3-4). 27.93 (978-1-5081-4567-7(9), 3dfd6065-6470-412d-864f-6295e8b27447, PowerKids Pr.) Rosen Publishing Group, Inc., The.

Stewart, Melissa. Extreme Coral Reef! 2008. (Smithsonian Q & A Ser.). (Illus.). 48p. (J). (gr. k-4). 16.99 (978-0-06-111577-6(0)) Smithsonian Bks.

—A Place for Fish, 1 vol. Bond, Higgins, illus. 32p. (J). 2011. (ENG.). (gr. 1-5). 16.95 (978-1-56145-562-1(8)) 2018. (Place For... Ser.: 4). (gr. 2-6). pap. 7.95 (978-1-68263-012-9(9)) Peachtree Publishing Co. Inc.

Stone, Lynn M. Oceans. 2003. (Illus.). 24p. (J). 20.64 (978-1-58952-686-0(4)) Rourke Educational Media.

Sullivan, Laura. 24 Hours in the Ocean, 1 vol. 2017. (Day in an Ecosystem Ser.). (ENG., Illus.). 48p. (J). (gr. 4-4). 33.07 (978-1-5026-2478-9(8), 37e3cff0-09b5-49ba-9b0b-260fde1298f2) Cavendish Square Publishing LLC.

Sundance/Newbridge LLC Staff. Life in the Sea. 2007. (Early Science Ser.). (gr. k-3). 18.95 (978-1-4007-6386-3(X)); pap. 6.10 (978-1-4007-6382-5(7)) Sundance/Newbridge Educational Publishing.

Tarbox, A. D. An Ocean Food Chain. 2009. (Nature's Bounty Ser.). (ENG.). 48p. (J). (gr. 5-8). pap. 12.00 (978-0-89812-740-9(8), 22693, Creative Paperbacks) Creative Co., The.

—An Ocean Food Chain: Nature's Bounty. 2015. (Odysseys in Nature Ser.). (ENG., Illus.). 80p. (J). (gr. 7-10). (978-1-60818-541-2(9), 20971, Creative Education) Creative Co., The.

Tocci, Salvatore. Marine Habitats: Life in Saltwater. 2004. (Watts Library). (ENG.). (J). 25.50 (978-0-531-12306-5(5), Watts, Franklin) Scholastic Library Publishing.

Wade, Laura. Sea & Sealife. 2003. (Knowledge Masters Ser.). (Illus.). 32p. (YA). pap. incl. cd-rom (978-1-903954-10-2(X), Pavilion Children's Books) Pavilion Bks.

Walker, Rachel. Help Our Oceans, 1 vol. 2015. (ENG., Illus.). 16p. (-2). pap. (978-1-77654-138-6(3), Red Rocket Readers) Flying Start Bks.

Water Habitats, 8 vols. 2005. (Water Habitats Ser.). (ENG.). 24p. (gr. k-2). lib. bdg. 98.68 (978-0-8368-4881-6(0), d5073f74-f9cd-4944-aafc-3dc637db2586, Weekly Reader Leveled Readers) Stevens, Gareth Publishing LLLP.

Water Habitats/Hábitats Acuáticos: Set of 6, 8 vols. 2005. (Water Habitats / Hábitats Acuáticos Ser.). (SPA & ENG.). 24p. (gr. k-2). lib. bdg. 98.68 (978-0-8368-6026-9(8), 5793011e-6315-4fb5-bd40-5900c6333cbb, Weekly Reader Leveled Readers) Stevens, Gareth Publishing LLLP.

Weiss, Sabrina. Ocean: Secrets of the Deep. De Amicis, Giulia, illus. 2019. (ENG.). 72p. (J). (gr. 2-6). 19.99 (978-1-9999680-7-6(7)) What on Earth Bks GBR. Dist: Ingram Publisher Services.

West, David. Tide Pool Animals. 2014. (Nora the Naturalist's Animals Ser.). 24p. (gr. k-3). pap. 8.95 (978-1-62588-054-3(5)) Black Rabbit Bks.

West, Krista, ed. Critical Perspectives on the Oceans. (Scientific American Critical Anthologies on Environment & Climate Ser.). 208p. (gr. 9-9). 2009. 63.90 (978-1-60853-070-0(1)) 2006. (ENG., Illus.). (J). 42.47 (978-1-4042-0692-2(2), a8a33de8-d2a0-460c-bd0e-765d504b6865) Rosen Publishing Group, Inc., The.

Westerskov, Kim, photos by. Forests in the Sea. 2004. (Illus.). 32p. (J). (978-0-7685-2387-4(7)); pap. (978-0-7685-2116-0(5)) Dominie Pr., Inc.

Woolf, Alex. Sailing the Great Barrier Reef. 2014. (Traveling Wild Ser.). 32p. (J). (gr. 3-6). pap. 63.00 (978-1-4824-1252-9(7)) Stevens, Gareth Publishing LLLP.

Working on Water: Individual Title Six-Packs. (gr. k-1). 23.00 (978-0-7635-8853-3(9)) Rigby Education.

World Book, Inc. Staff, contrib. by. Oceans. 2012. (J). (978-0-7166-0447-1(7)) World Bk., Inc.

—Oceans, Islands, & Polar Regions. 2008. (J). (978-0-7166-1402-9(2)) World Bk., Inc.

Yasuda, Anita. Oceans & Seas! With 25 Science Projects for Kids. Casteel, Tom, illus. 2018. (Explore Your World Ser.). (ENG.). 96p. (J). (gr. 3-4). 19.95 (978-1-61930-696-7(4), b4b88235-a5a5-43cc-bff0-576376e10876) Nomad Pr.

MARINE FAUNA

see Marine Animals

MARINE FLORA

see Marine Plants

MARINE GEOLOGY

see Submarine Geology

MARINE PAINTING

Baumbusch, Brigitte. Oceans in Art, 1 vol. 2004. (What Makes a Masterpiece? Ser.). (ENG., Illus.). 32p. (gr. 2-4). lib. bdg. 25.67 (978-0-8368-4782-6(2), 7e409b0d-36a5-4401-b1c8-26db556befa0, Gareth Stevens Learning Library) Stevens, Gareth Publishing LLLP.

MARINE PLANTS

see also Algae; Freshwater Plants

De la Bédoyère, Camilla & Kelly, Miles. Spot 50 Seashore. Kelly, Richard, ed. 2013. (Illus.). 560p. (J). pap. 9.95 (978-1-84810-906-3(7)) Miles Kelly Publishing, Ltd. GBR. Dist: Parkwest Pubns., Inc.

De la Bédoyère, Camilla & Philip, Claire. Seashore. Kelly, Richard, ed. 2017. (ENG., Illus.). 96p. (J). pap. 9.95 (978-1-78209-168-4(8)) Miles Kelly Publishing, Ltd. GBR. Dist: Parkwest Pubns., Inc.

Diamond, Claudia. What's under the Sea? 2009. (Reading Room Collection 2 Ser.). 24p. (gr. 3-4). 42.50 (978-1-60852-002-2(1), PowerKids Pr.) Rosen Publishing Group, Inc., The.

Fleisher, Paul. Ocean Food Webs in Action. 2013. (Searchlight Books (tm) — What Is a Food Web? Ser.). (ENG., Illus.). 40p. (J). (gr. 3-5). pap. 9.99 (978-1-4677-1556-0(5), fe99e355-c570-430b-9c79-44e051e6ea8f) Lerner Publishing Group.

Hardy, A. S. Sea Stories for Wonder Eyes. 2005. reprint ed. pap. 21.95 (978-1-4191-0670-5(8)) Kessinger Publishing, LLC.

Horsman, Paul. Out of the Blue: A Journey Through the World's Oceans. Seapics.com Staff, photos by. 2005. (ENG., Illus.). 160p. (gr. 17). 32.95 (978-0-262-08341-6(8), 0262083418) MIT Pr.

Kavanagh, James & Waterford Press Staff. My First Seashores: Nature Activity Book. Leung, Raymond, illus. 2013. (Nature Activity Book Ser.). (ENG.). 32p. (J). (gr. -1-12). pap., act. bk. ed. 6.95 (978-1-58355-590-3(0)) Waterford Pr., Inc.

Llewellyn, Claire. In the Sea Red Band. Belcher, Andy, photos by. 2016. (Cambridge Reading Adventures Ser.). (ENG., Illus.). 16p. pap. 7.95 (978-1-107-57578-3(8)) Cambridge Univ. Pr.

Merlino, Kim. Ocean Life: Grades 2 Through 4. (Illus.). (J). pap., wbk. ed. 4.99 (978-0-88743-966-7(7)) School Zone Publishing Co.

Richmond, Ben. Why Is the Sea Salty? And Other Questions about Oceans. Azhderian, Cecelia, illus. 2014. (Good Question! Ser.). 32p. (J). (gr. 1). pap. 5.95 (978-1-4549-0677-3(4)) Sterling Publishing Co., Inc.

Rissman, Rebecca. Living & Nonliving in the Ocean, 1 vol. 2013. (Is It Living or Nonliving? Ser.). (ENG., Illus.). 24p. (J). (gr. k-2). 25.99 (978-1-4109-5381-0(5), 123310); pap. 6.95 (978-1-4109-5388-9(2), 123328) Capstone. (Raintree).

Rivera, Sheila. Ocean. 2005. (Illus.). 24p. (J). pap. 5.95 (978-0-8225-5372-4(4)) Lerner Publishing Group.

Rushworth, Gary. The Life Cycle of Water Plants: Text Pairs. 2008. (Bridges/Navigators Ser.). (J). (gr. 3). 89.00 (978-1-4108-8365-0(5)) Benchmark Education Co.

Swanson, Diane. Safari Beneath the Sea: The Wonder World of the North Pacific Coast, 1 vol. Royal British Columbia Museum Staff, photos by. (ENG., Illus.). 64p. (J). pap. 12.95 (978-1-55110-441-6(5)) Whitecap Bks., Ltd. CAN. Dist: Graphic Arts Ctr. Publishing Co.

Twist, Clint. 1000 Things You Should Know about Oceans. 2008. (1000 Things You Should Know about (Miles Kelley) Ser.). (Illus.). 61p. (J). pap. (978-1-84236-852-7(4)) Miles Kelly Publishing, Ltd.

Walden, Libby. Hidden World: Ocean. Coleman, Stephanie Fizer, illus. 2018. (ENG.). 18p. (J). (gr. -1-2). 14.99 (978-1-944530-15-0(0), 360 Degrees) Tiger Tales.

World Book, Inc. Staff, contrib. by. The Sea & Its Marvels. 2011. (Illus.). 64p. (J). (978-0-7166-1791-4(9)) World Bk., Inc.

MARINE RESOURCES

see also Fisheries

Hand, Carol. Bringing Back Our Oceans. 2017. (Conservation Success Stories Ser.). (ENG., Illus.). 112p. (J). (gr. 6-12). lib. bdg. 41.36 (978-1-5321-1315-4(3), 27523, Essential Library) ABDO Publishing Co.

Harper, Joel. All the Way to the Ocean. Spusta, Marq, illus. 2006. (J). 14.95 (978-0-9714254-1-5(8)) Freedom Three Publishing.

Mallory, Kenneth. A Home by the Sea: Protecting Coastal Wildlife. 2003. (Illus.). 64p. (YA). (gr. 4-8). reprint ed. 20.00 (978-0-7567-6562-0(5)) DIANE Publishing Co.

Marine Debris Program (U.S.), Office of Response and Restoration, ed. Understanding Marine Debris: Games & Activities for Kids of All Ages: Marine Debris 101: Games & Activities for Kids of All Ages: Marine Debris 101. 2012. (ENG.). 23p. 7.00 (978-0-16-091362-4(4), National Marine Fisheries Service) United States Government Printing Office.

Milner, Charlotte. The Sea Book. Milner, Charlotte, illus. 2019. (Conservation for Kids Ser.). (ENG., Illus.). 48p. (J). (gr. k-3). 15.99 (978-1-4654-7882-5(5), DK Children) Dorling Kindersley Publishing, Inc.

Perritano, John. Marine Resources, Vol. 12. 2015. (North American Natural Resources Ser.). (Illus.). 64p. (J). (gr. 7). lib. bdg. 23.95 (978-1-4222-3384-9(7)) Mason Crest.

Peterson, Christy. Into the Deep: Science, Technology, & the Quest to Protect the Ocean. 2020. (ENG., Illus.). 152p. (YA). (gr. 6-12). lib. bdg. 39.99 (978-1-5415-5555-6(4), 146760ff-0ad5-44c7-8434-6d8a84d3d8ab, Twenty-First Century Bks.) Lerner Publishing Group.

Spilsbury, Louise & Spilsbury, Richard. Marine Biomes. 2018. (Earth's Natural Biomes Ser.). (Illus.). 32p. (J). (gr. 4-4). (978-0-7787-3996-8(1)) Crabtree Publishing Co.

Spilsbury, Louise & Spilsbury, Richard, contrib. by. MARINE BIOMES. 2018. (Earth's Natural Biomes Ser.). (Illus.). 32p. (J). (gr. 4-4). pap. (978-0-7787-4181-7(8)) Crabtree Publishing Co.

MARINE ZOOLOGY

see Marine Animals

MARINERS

see Sailors

MARION, FRANCIS, 1732-1795

Kauffman, Scott. Francis Marion: Swamp Fox of South Carolina. 2006. (Forgotten Heroes of the American Revolution Ser.). (Illus.). 88p. (YA). (gr. 5-11). lib. bdg. 23.95 (978-1-59556-014-8(9)) OTTN Publishing.

MARION, FRANCIS, 1732-1795—FICTION

Gunderson, Jessica. A Rebel among Redcoats: A Revolutionary War Novel. 2015. (Revolutionary War Ser.). (ENG., Illus.). 96p. (J). (gr. 3-5). lib. bdg. 26.65 (978-1-4342-9701-3(2), 127020, Stone Arch Bks.) Capstone.

MARIONETTES

Anderson, Lynne. Make a Marionette. 2011. (Early Connections Ser.). (J). (978-1-61672-556-3(7)) Benchmark Education Co.

MARITIME DISCOVERIES

see Discoveries in Geography

MARK, SAINT

Woodman, Ros. Bible Detectives Mark. 2005. (Activity Ser.). (ENG.). 58p. (J). pap., act. bk. ed. 7.99 (978-1-85792-674-3(9), 2bdbde8b-e366-4790-8638-4af88b76af2f) Christian Focus Pubns. GBR. Dist: Baker & Taylor Publisher Services (BTPS).

MARKET GARDENING

see Vegetable Gardening

MARKETING

Capaccio, George. Advertising & Marketing in Theater, 1 vol. 2017. (Exploring Theater Ser.). (ENG.). 96p. (YA). (gr. 7-7). pap. 20.99 (978-1-5026-3430-6(9), ac3bb200-766c-43cb-bb86-efa25b4f99f6); lib. bdg. 44.50 (978-1-5026-2999-9(2), e0024756-f406-4e49-93e5-d9e59cc2c8c4) Cavendish Square Publishing LLC.

Caraccilo, Dominic. E-Tailing: Careers Selling over the Web. 2009. (Library of E-Commerce & Internet Careers Ser.). 64p. (gr. 5-5). 58.50 (978-1-60853-587-3(8)) Rosen Publishing Group, Inc., The.

Cohn, Jessica. Fashion Buyer, 1 vol. 2009. (Cool Careers: on the Go Ser.). (ENG.). 32p. (gr. 3-3). pap. 11.50 (978-1-4339-0166-9(8), be55eaaf-6b85-4abb-a579-cd4816c59684); (YA). lib. bdg. 28.67 (978-1-4339-0002-0(5), 46fd3cff-e78c-41c4-9057-cd4a91aa9dec) Stevens, Gareth Publishing LLLP.

Earl, C. F. Marketing Your Business. Madrian, Brigitte, ed. 2013. (Young Adult Library of Small Business & Finance Ser.: 10). 64p. (J). (gr. 7-18). 22.95 (978-1-4222-2919-4(X)) Mason Crest.

Etzel. Marketing: Student Study Guide. 13th rev. ed. 2004. 368p. (gr. 6-12). pap. (978-0-07-283785-8(3)) Glencoe/McGraw-Hill.

Harris, Duchess & Edwards, Sue Bradford. Advertising Overload. 2017. (News Literacy Ser.). (ENG., Illus.). 48p. (J). (gr. 4-8). lib. bdg. 35.64 (978-1-5321-1387-1(0), 27685) ABDO Publishing Co.

Jovin, Michelle. Your World: Shopping Secrets: Multiplication (Grade 3) 2017. (Mathematics in the Real World Ser.). (ENG., Illus.). 32p. (J). (gr. 3-4). pap. 11.99 (978-1-4807-5796-7(9)) Teacher Created Materials, Inc.

Lewis, Daniel. Sales, Marketing & Finance, Vol. 10. 2018. (Careers in Demand for High School Graduates Ser.). 112p. (J). (gr. 7). 34.60 (978-1-4222-4142-4(4)) Mason Crest.

Loftus, Jennifer. Buying & Selling at the Yard Sale, 1 vol. 2008. (Real Life Readers Ser.). (ENG.). 12p. (gr. 1-2). pap. 5.90 (978-1-4042-7913-1(X), fc59b9f4-d85d-4c2a-9087-3af7ba76dac0, Rosen Classroom) Rosen Publishing Group, Inc., The.

MacDonald, Margaret. Bargaining at the Market. 2011. (Learn-Abouts Ser.). (Illus.). 16p. (J). pap. 7.95 (978-1-59920-647-9(1)) Black Rabbit Bks.

Malaspina, Ann. False Images, Deadly Promises: Smoking & the Media. 2007. (Tobacco: the Deadly Drug Ser.). (Illus.). 112p. (YA). pap. 12.95 (978-1-4222-0812-0(5)) Mason Crest.

Meyer, Susan. Branding: Creating an Identity on the Web. 2014. (Digital & Information Literacy Ser.). (Illus.). 48p. (J). (gr. 5-8). pap. 70.50 (978-1-4777-7650-6(8)); (ENG., (gr. 6-6). 33.47 (978-1-4777-7647-6(8), 1b5d73a4-bdd4-4564-8234-0ed3007c06d0); (ENG., (gr. 6-6). pap. 12.75 (978-1-4777-7649-0(4), efbd977e-d62e-4f83-a1ca-b87e67b9141d) Rosen Publishing Group, Inc., The.

Mortensen, Lori. Buyers & Sellers. 2016. (Spring Forward Ser.). (J). (gr. 1). (978-1-4900-9376-5(1)) Benchmark Education Co.

Murley, Leon & Wilson, Antoine. The Distribution of Goods & Services. 2011. 77.70 (978-1-4488-4750-1(8), Rosen Reference); (ENG.). 64p. (YA). (gr. 5-5). pap. 13.95 (978-1-4488-4718-1(4), 487c8387-924b-4f01-b82b-d2be73e678cf, Rosen Reference); (ENG.). 64p. (YA). (gr. 5-5). lib. bdg. 37.13 (978-1-4488-4710-5(9), a24898d1-9ff3-47ba-8f02-cc7f364f5f1b) Rosen Publishing Group, Inc., The.

Nieuwland, Jackson. Careers for Tech Girls in E-Commerce, 1 vol. 2018. (Tech Girls Ser.). (ENG.). 80p. (J). (gr. 7-7). 37.47 (978-1-5081-8017-3(2), fad7bb4b-91dc-45e2-a432-ddd5aab7686e) Rosen Publishing Group, Inc., The.

Orr, Tamra. Blogging. 2019. (21st Century Skills Library: Global Citizens: Social Media Ser.). (ENG., Illus.). 32p. (J). (gr. 4-7). pap. 14.21 (978-1-5341-3962-6(1), 212677); lib. bdg. 32.07 (978-1-5341-4306-7(8), 212676) Cherry Lake Publishing.

Reeves, Diane Lindsey. Marketing, Sales & Service. 2017. (Bright Futures Press: World of Work Ser.). (ENG., Illus.). 32p. (J). (gr. 4-7). lib. bdg. 32.07 (978-1-5341-0177-7(2), 210178) Cherry Lake Publishing.

Rice, Dona Herweck. Legacy: The Names Behind the Brands. 2018. (TIME(r): Informational Text Ser.). (ENG., Illus.). 48p. (J). (gr. 5-8). pap. 13.99 (978-1-4258-4995-5(4)) Teacher Created Materials, Inc.

Sheen, Barbara. Careers in Sales & Marketing. 2015. (ENG., Illus.). 80p. (YA). lib. bdg. (978-1-60152-812-4(4)) ReferencePoint Pr., Inc.

Sichol, Lowey Bundy. From an Idea to Disney: How Imagination Built a World of Magic. Jennings, C. S., illus. 2019. (From an Idea To Ser.). (ENG.). 112p. (J). (gr. 1-5). 16.99 (978-1-328-45360-0(X), 1711801); pap. 6.99 (978-1-328-45361-7(8), 1711803) HarperCollins Pubs. (Clarion Bks.).

Wittekind, Erika. The Big Push: How Popular Culture Is Always Selling, 1 vol. 2012. (Exploring Media Literacy Ser.). (ENG.). 80p. (J). (gr. 5-8). pap. 9.10 (978-0-7565-4535-2(8), 118367); lib. bdg. 35.32 (978-0-7565-4518-5(8), 117099) Capstone. (Compass Point Bks.).

MARKETING—VOCATIONAL GUIDANCE

Ferguson, creator. Advertising & Marketing. 2nd rev. ed. 2009. (Ferguson's Careers in Focus Ser.). (ENG.). 202p. (gr. 6-12). 32.95 (978-0-8160-7295-8(7), P179097, Ferguson Publishing Company) Infobase Holdings, Inc.

Haegele, Katie. E-Advertising & E-Marketing Online Opportunities. 2009. (Library of E-Commerce & Internet Careers Ser.). 64p. (gr. 5-5). 58.50 (978-1-60853-585-9(1)) Rosen Publishing Group, Inc., The.

Harmon, Daniel E. Careers As a Marketing & Public Relations Specialist, 1 vol. 2013. (Essential Careers Ser.). (ENG.). 80p. (YA). (gr. 6-6). 37.47 (978-1-4777-1793-6(5), 272a2c97-ae58-47e9-8018-f86ab7fd8afe) Rosen Publishing Group, Inc., The.

Nagle, Jeanne. Careers in Internet Advertising & Marketing, 1 vol. 2013. (Careers in Computer Technology Ser.). (ENG.). 80p. (YA). (gr. 8-8). 38.47 (978-1-4488-9596-0(0), 4de9a860-bf1f-42c9-82f8-4695ec80b2d3) Rosen Publishing Group, Inc., The.

MARKETING (HOME ECONOMICS)

see Shopping

MARKETING OF FARM PRODUCE

see Farm Produce—Marketing

MARKETS

see also Fairs

Bailey, Diane. How Markets Work, 1 vol. 2011. (Real World Economics Ser.). (ENG.). 80p. (YA). (gr. 7-7). lib. bdg. 38.47 (978-1-4488-5564-3(0), 7cdb1923-d814-4d73-834c-87c41d9ff9ad) Rosen Publishing Group, Inc., The.

Brinker, Spencer. At the Market. 2019. (I Spy Ser.). (ENG., Illus.). 16p. (J). (gr. -1-1). 6.99 (978-1-64280-398-3(7)) Bearport Publishing Co., Inc.

Chambers, Catherine. A Day at an Indian Market. 2011. (Big Picture: Food Ser.). (ENG.). 24p. (gr. 1-2). pap. 41.70 (978-1-4296-6725-8(7), Capstone Pr.) Capstone.

Francis, Amy, ed. The Local Food Movement, 1 vol. 2010. (At Issue Ser.). (ENG.). 160p. (gr. 10-12). 41.03 (978-0-7377-4888-8(5), 6fe1c1fe-be46-4f19-86e6-8d736c660a46); pap. 28.80 (978-0-7377-4889-5(3), 1e81c7be-6b76-4797-9831-b4453f810fa5) Greenhaven Publishing LLC. (Greenhaven Publishing).

Hawes, Alison. At the Market. Cambridge Reading Adventures. Pink B Band. Robert, LeyHonor, illus. 2016. (Cambridge Reading Adventures Ser.). (ENG.). 16p. pap. 7.95 (978-1-107-54993-7(0)) Cambridge Univ. Pr.

Laks Gorman, Jacqueline. The Shopping Mall / el Centro Comercial, 1 vol. 2004. (I Like to Visit / Me Gusta Visitar Ser.). (ENG & SPA., Illus.). 24p. (gr. k-2). pap. 9.15 (978-0-8368-4606-5(0), ec033e9a-a6c6-452f-9d23-363c0915c3d4); lib. bdg. 24.67 (978-0-8368-4599-0(4), ba7ad4e3-e187-46fd-a4bf-bb537b371fdd) Stevens, Gareth Publishing LLLP. (Weekly Reader Leveled Readers).

Munro, Roxie. Market Maze. 2015. (978-0-8234-3358-2(7)) Holiday Hse., Inc.

Petersen, Null Casey. Markets Around the World, 1 vol. 2nd rev. ed. (TIME for KIDS(r): Informational Text Ser.). (ENG., 28p. (gr. 3-4). 2014. Illus.). (J). lib. bdg. 25.96 (978-1-4807-1067-2(9)) 2011. pap. 11.99 (978-1-4333-3652-2(9)) Teacher Created Materials, Inc.

Rauen, Amy. Counting at the Market, 1 vol. 2008. (Getting Started with Math Ser.). (ENG., Illus.). 16p. (gr. k-1). lib. bdg. 21.67 (978-0-8368-8981-9(9), ac3553e2-1c64-4aad-800d-8e2e3acd6dc8, Weekly Reader Leveled Readers) Stevens, Gareth Publishing LLLP.

—Vamos a Contar en el Mercado (Counting at the Market), 1 vol. 2008. (Matemáticas para Empezar (Getting Started with Math) Ser.).Tr. of Counting at the Market. (SPA., Illus.). 16p. (gr. k-1). pap. 6.30 (978-0-8368-8996-3(7), 849c410a-2e01-4b57-8a24-dde919fdfded); lib. bdg. 21.67 (978-0-8368-8991-8(6), 3ccaec65-3d92-4258-b9cf-ec28b619d2ad) Stevens, Gareth Publishing LLLP. (Weekly Reader Leveled Readers).

Wolfe, Mike & Sprengelmeyer, Lily. Kid Pickers: How to Turn Junk into Treasure. Right, Mike, illus. 2013. (ENG.). 128p. (J). (gr. 2-7). 19.99 (978-1-250-00848-0(4), 900083576); pap. 16.99 (978-1-250-01930-1(3), 900087856) Feiwel & Friends.

MARKETS—FICTION

Alakija, Polly. Catch That Goat! Alakija, Polly, illus. 2007. (ENG., Illus.). 40p. (J). (gr. -1-3). pap. 9.99 (978-1-84686-057-7(1)) Barefoot Bks., Inc.

Alfaro, Manuel. Griego el Magnifico y la Gotita Verde Golosa Pegajos. Harrington, David, illus. 2007. (SPA.). 36p. per. 15.50 (978-1-59858-337-3(9)) Dog Ear Publishing, LLC.

Amollo, Regina. When Mother Leaves Home. 2004. (Illus.). 35p. pap. (978-9970-02-435-3(3)) Fountain Pubs. Ltd. UGA. Dist: Michigan State Univ. Pr.

Averbeck, Jim. The Market Bowl. Averbeck, Jim, illus. 2013. (Illus.). 32p. (J). (gr. -1-3). lib. bdg. 16.95 (978-1-58089-368-8(6)) Charlesbridge Publishing, Inc.

Baker, Jeannie. Mirror. Baker, Jeannie, illus. 2010. (ENG., Illus.). 48p. (J). (gr. k-4). 21.99 (978-0-7636-4848-0(5)) Candlewick Pr.

Capucilli, Alyssa Satin. Monkey Play. 2012. (Step into Reading Ser.). (Illus.). 32p. (J). (gr. -1-1). pap. 5.99 (978-0-375-86993-8(X), Random Hse. Bks. for Young Readers) Random Hse. Children's Bks.

Charles, Bob. A Trip to the Market: Set Of 6. 2010. (Early Connections Ser.). (J). 37.00 net. (978-1-4108-1359-6(2)) Benchmark Education Co.

—A Trip to the Market & una visita al Mercado: 6 English, 6 Spanish Adaptations. 2011. (ENG & SPA.). (J). 75.00 net. (978-1-4108-5642-5(9)) Benchmark Education Co.

Clarke, Lorin. Our Last Trip to the Market. Vane, Mitch, illus. 2017. (ENG.). 32p. (J). (-k). 18.99 (978-1-925266-96-2(6)) Allen & Unwin AUS. Dist: Independent Pubs. Group.

Conn, Marla. At the Market with Dear Dragon, 10 vols. David Schimmell, illus. 2019. (Dear Dragon Developing Readers Ser.). (ENG.). 24p. (J). (gr. k-k). pap. 11.94 (978-1-68404-316-3(6)) Norwood Hse. Pr.

Davies, Lewis. Tai, Troll & the Black & White Cow. 2009. (ENG., Illus.). 30p. (J). pap. 7.95 (978-1-905762-64-4(X)) Parthian Bks. GBR. Dist: Independent Pubs. Group.

Get Together Girls - Going to the Mall. 2005. (J). bds. (978-1-4194-0087-2(8)) Paradise Pr., Inc.

Janice Turner & Colleen Connelly. Colleen Goes to the Farmer's Market. Ron Frazier, photos by. 2009. (Illus.). 20p. pap. 12.49 (978-1-4389-6085-2(9)) AuthorHouse.

Leto, Frank & Scelsa, Greg. Let's Go to the Market. Faulkner, Stacey, ed. 2006. (J). pap. 2.99 (978-1-59198-317-0(7)) Creative Teaching Pr., Inc.

Lindman. Flicka, Ricka, Dicka Go to Market. Lindman, illus. 2012. (Flicka, Ricka, Dicka Ser.). (ENG., Illus.). 32p. (J). (gr. -1-3). 9.99 (978-0-8075-2478-7(6), 807524786) Whitman, Albert & Co.

Randolph, Robert. Ben Goes to the Farmer's Market, 1 vol. 2009. 37p. pap. 24.95 (978-1-4489-1934-5(7)) PublishAmerica, Inc.

Raúl the Third, Raúl the, III. ¡Vamos! Let's Go to the Market. Raúl the Third, Raúl the, III, illus. 2019. (World Of ¡Vamos! Ser.). (ENG., Illus.). 48p. (J). (gr. k-3). 14.99 (978-1-328-55726-1(X), 1725405, Versify) HarperCollins Pubs.

Rocky Porch Moore. It's Farm Market Day! 2009. 24p. pap. 12.99 (978-1-4490-2854-1(3)) AuthorHouse.

Taylor, Chloë. Sewing in Circles. Zhang, Nancy, illus. 2015. (Sew Zoey Ser.: 13). (ENG.). 176p. (J). (gr. 3-7). pap. 6.99 (978-1-4814-4032-5(2), Simon Spotlight) Simon Spotlight.

Taylor, W. Y. Baby Goes to Market. 2009. (ENG.). 12p. bds. 3.95 (978-1-58117-897-5(2), Intervisual/Piggy Toes) Bendon, Inc.

Turnbull, Elizabeth. Janjak & Freda Go to the Iron Market. Turnbull, Wally, tr. Jones, Mark, illus. 2013. 36p. 18.95 (978-1-61153-072-8(5)) Light Messages Publishing.

Turnbull, Elizabeth J. Janjak & Freda Go to the Iron Market. Turnbull, Wally R., tr. Jones, Mark, illus. 2013. 36p. pap. 12.95 *(978-1-61153-062-9(8))* Light Messages Publishing.
Vonthron, Satanta C. Caillou Visits the Farmer's Market. Meier, Kerry L., illus. l.t. ed. 2005. (HRL Board Book Ser.). (J). (gr. -1-k). pap. 10.95 *(978-1-57332-310-9(1),* HighReach Learning, Incorporated) Carson-Dellosa Publishing, LLC.
Wellington, Monica. Ana Cultiva Manzanas / Apple Farmer Annie. del Risco, Eida, tr. 2004. (Illus.). 32p. (J). (gr. -1-2). 16.99 *(978-0-525-47252-0(5),* Dutton Books for Young Readers) Penguin Young Readers Group.
—Apple Farmer Annie Board Book. 2012. (Illus.). 26p. (J). (gr. -1 — 1). bds. 7.99 *(978-0-8037-3888-1(9),* Dial Bks) Penguin Young Readers Group.

MARKSMANSHIP
see Shooting

MARLEY, BOB, 1945-1981
Ellison, Katie. Who Was Bob Marley? 2017. (Who Was... ? Ser.). lib. bdg. 16.00 *(978-0-606-40115-9(6))* Turtleback.
Ellison, Katie & Who HQ. Who Was Bob Marley? Copeland, Gregory, illus. 2017. (Who Was? Ser.). 112p. (J). (gr. 3-7). 6.99 *(978-0-448-48919-3(8),* Penguin Workshop) Penguin Young Readers Group.
Jeffrey, Gary. Bob Marley: The Life of a Musical Legend, 1 vol. Riley, Terry, illus. 2006. (Graphic Nonfiction Biographies Ser.). (ENG.). 48p. (YA). (gr. 4-5). lib. bdg. 37.13 *(978-1-4042-0854-4(2),* 5d207acf-32f4-451c-baac-fa0ec9578448) Rosen Publishing Group, Inc., The.
Medina, Tony. I & I: Bob Marley. Watson, Jesse Joshua, illus. 2009. (ENG.). 48p. (J). (gr. 3-6). 19.95 *(978-1-60060-257-3(6))* Lee & Low Bks., Inc.
—I & I Bob Marley, 1 vol. Watson, Jesse Joshua, illus. 2009. (ENG.). 48p. (J). (gr. 3-8). pap. 12.95 *(978-1-62014-030-7(6),* leelowbooks) Lee & Low Bks., Inc.
Miller, Calvin Craig. Reggae Poet: The Story of Bob Marley. 2007. (Modern Music Masters Ser.). (Illus.). 128p. (YA). (gr. 9-18). lib. bdg. 27.95 *(978-1-59935-071-4(8))* Reynolds, Morgan Inc.
Waters, Rosa. Bob Marley & the Wailers. (Pop Rock Ser.). (Illus.). 64p. (YA). 2008. (gr. 7-18). lib. bdg. 22.95 *(978-1-4222-0192-3(9))* 2007. pap. 7.95 *(978-1-4222-0317-0(4))* Mason Crest.

MARMOTS
see also Woodchuck
Beer, Amy-Jane. Woodchucks. 2008. (Nature's Children Ser.). (Illus.). 52p. (J). *(978-0-7172-6267-0(7))* Grolier, Ltd.

MARMOTS—FICTION
Burchfield, Cindy. Gimme, Gimme Moocher Marmots. Burchfield, Cindy, illus. 2007. (Illus.). 48p. per. 18.95 *(978-1-59858-457-8(X))* Dog Ear Publishing, LLC.
Mitchell, George. The Marmots of Lenk & the Long Sleep. 2011. (ENG.). 108p. 25.50 *(978-1-105-61600-6(2));* 66p. pap. 20.95 *(978-1-4476-2895-8(0))* Lulu Pr., Inc.

MARQUETTE, JACQUES, 1637-1675
Donaldson-Forbes, Jeff. Jacques Marquette & Louis Jolliet. 2009. (Primary Source Library of Famous Explorers Ser.). 24p. (gr. 4-4). 42.50 *(978-1-60854-127-0(4),* PowerKids Pr.) Rosen Publishing Group, Inc., The.
Harkins, Susan Sales & Harkins, William H. The Life & Times of Father Jacques Marquette. 2008. (Profiles in American History Ser.). (Illus.). 48p. (J). (gr. 4-8). lib. bdg. 29.95 *(978-1-58415-528-7(0))* Mitchell Lane Pubs.
Larkin, Tanya. Jacques Marquette & Louis Jolliet: Explorers of the Mississippi. 2009. (Library of Explorers & Exploration Ser.). 112p. (gr. 5-8). 66.50 *(978-1-60853-608-5(4),* Rosen Reference) Rosen Publishing Group, Inc., The.
O'Brien, Cynthia. Explore with Marquette & Jolliet. 2016. (Travel with the Great Explorers Ser.). (ENG., Illus.). 32p. (J). (gr. 3-6). *(978-0-7787-2850-4(1))* Crabtree Publishing Co.
Zelenyi, Alexander & Zelenyj, Alexander. Marquette & Jolliet: Quest for the Mississippi. 2006. (In the Footsteps of Explorers Ser.). (ENG., Illus.). 32p. (J). (gr. 4-7). pap. *(978-0-7787-2467-4(0));* lib. bdg. *(978-0-7787-2431-5(X))* Crabtree Publishing Co.

MARRIAGE
see also Dating (Social Customs); Domestic Relations; Family; Family Life; Family Life Education; Intermarriage; Sex; Sexual Ethics
Ascension Press, creator. Theology of the Body for Teens Student Workbook: Discovering God's Plan for Love & Life. 2006. (Illus.). 210p. per. 14.95 *(978-1-932927-86-3(7))* Ascension Pr.
Ayer, Eleanor H. Todo lo que necesitas saber sobre el matrimonio adolescente (Everything You Need to Know about Teen Marriage) 2009. (Todo lo que necesitas (the Need to Know Library) Ser.). (SPA.). 64p. (gr. 6-6). 58.50 *(978-1-60854-408-0(7),* Editorial Buenas Letras) Rosen Publishing Group, Inc., The.
Boehme, Gerry. Same-Sex Marriage: Obergefell V. Hodges, 1 vol. 2018. (Courting History Ser.). (ENG.). 64p. (gr. 6-6). lib. bdg. 37.36 *(978-1-5026-3592-1(5),* dc1b96e3-98de-4bda-884e-3d10404269bd) Cavendish Square Publishing LLC.
Brown, Kyle. My Wedding Activity Book. 2009. (ENG.). 48p. pap. 9.95 *(978-0-557-06217-1(9))* Lulu Pr., Inc.
Brown, Tracy. Frequently Asked Questions about Same-Sex Marriage & When a Parent Is Gay, 1 vol. 2012. (FAQ: Teen Life Ser.). (ENG., Illus.). 64p. (J). (gr. 5-6). lib. bdg. 37.13 *(978-1-4488-8330-1(X),* 7736c889-cf0c-4b68-b022-ac7bf27b69be) Rosen Publishing Group, Inc., The.
Center for Learning Network Staff. Charming Billy/at Weddings & Wakes: Curriculum Unit. 2005. (Novel Ser.). 64p. (YA). tchr. ed., spiral bd. 19.95 *(978-1-56077-788-5(5))* Center for Learning, The.
Chastain, Zachary. From the Parlor to the Altar: Romance & Marriage in The 1800s. 2009. (Daily Life in America in the 1800s Ser.). 64p. (YA). (gr. 7-18). pap. 9.95 *(978-1-4222-1852-5(X));* lib. bdg. 22.95 *(978-1-4222-1779-5(5))* Mason Crest.
Don, Katherine. Nujood Ali & the Fight Against Child Marriage. 2014. (J). *(978-1-59935-466-8(7))* Reynolds, Morgan Inc.
Hillstrom, Kevin. Gay Marriage, 1 vol. 2014. (Hot Topics Ser.). (ENG., Illus.). 104p. (gr. 7-7). lib. bdg. 41.03 *(978-1-4205-0870-3(9),* 87d55f9c-e12b-43f8-8a2e-86bb9fdd00e8, Lucent Pr.) Greenhaven Publishing LLC.
Hollander, Barbara Gottfried. Marriage Rights & Gay Rights: Interpreting the Constitution, 1 vol. 2014. (Understanding the United States Constitution Ser.). (ENG., Illus.). 112p. (J). (gr. 7-7). 38.80 *(978-1-4777-7514-1(5),* 5e882933-2bd2-415a-a480-3d5a39cd6d4f) Rosen Publishing Group, Inc., The.
Hossier, Margaret. Spenser Rose Is Born. 2003. 32p. 12.99 *(978-0-9650491-4-6(0))* Send The Light Distribution LLC.
Hunnicutt, M. E. The Wedding Wonderful. 2013. 24p. pap. 24.95 *(978-1-62709-035-3(5))* America Star Bks.
Kiesbye, Stefan, ed. Polygamy, 1 vol. 2012. (At Issue Ser.). (ENG.). 96p. (gr. 10-12). pap. 28.80 *(978-0-7377-6194-8(6),* 120c350d-4231-4299-9d5f-4960f918648c); lib. bdg. 41.03 *(978-0-7377-6193-1(8),* d6d05f9f-b00c-4cb4-93b1-7ad437ce700e) Greenhaven Publishing LLC. (Greenhaven Publishing).
McCoy, Erin L. & Stemgass, Jon. Same-Sex Marriage: Cause for Concern or Celebration?, 1 vol. 2019. (Today's Debates Ser.). (ENG.). 144p. (gr. 7-7). pap. 22.16 *(978-1-5026-4486-2(X),* 44a6e6e3-a9bf-4b7e-92a2-0bafac315607); lib. bdg. 47.36 *(978-1-5026-4487-9(8),* 0db9d9da-7b0d-4efc-850f-87dfe88d87de) Cavendish Square Publishing LLC.
Meredith, Samantha & Wyk, Hanri van, illus. Weddings Sticker Color Book. 2011. (First Sticker Coloring Bks). 20p. (J). pap. 5.99 *(978-0-7945-3108-9(3),* Usborne) EDC Publishing.
Open for Debate - Group 5, 8 vols., Set. Incl. National Health Care. Kowalski, Kathiann M. lib. bdg. 45.50 *(978-0-7614-2943-2(3),* edaa0977-a53f-47fe-aa23-2e0389c5e727); Political Campaigns. Naden, Corinne. lib. bdg. 45.50 *(978-0-7614-2944-9(1),* 9d2e64a5-2c0c-4a63-9836-204d64ed8840); Religious Fundamentalism. Fridell, Ron. lib. bdg. 45.50 *(978-0-7614-2945-6(X),* d9d1f5c0-2b35-4938-9b69-3cde347cd370); Right to Die. Stefoff, Rebecca. lib. bdg. 45.50 *(978-0-7614-2948-7(4),* bcbd0407-c7ba-4a50-9da6-fe926a35d042); 144p. (YA). (gr. 8-8). (Open for Debate Ser.). (ENG.). 2009. Set lib. bdg. 182.00 *(978-0-7614-2940-1(9),* dee07674-67e9-492f-9ba3-039659ed2638, Cavendish Square) Cavendish Square Publishing LLC.
Parys, Sabrina. The Road to Marriage Equality, 1 vol. 2018. (History of the LGBTQ+ Rights Movement Ser.). (ENG., Illus.). 112p. (J). (gr. 7-7). 38.80 *(978-1-5383-8132-8(X),* 0468df57-0537-4965-ac4f-2970e42600da) Rosen Publishing Group, Inc., The.
Scherer, Lauri S., ed. Gay Marriage, 1 vol. 2014. (Introducing Issues with Opposing Viewpoints Ser.). (ENG., Illus.). 128p. (gr. 7-10). lib. bdg. 43.63 *(978-0-7377-6923-4(8),* 65c532bd-ae39-454a-b1dc-483907501d70, Greenhaven Publishing) Greenhaven Publishing LLC.
Snyder, Gail. Marriage & Family Issues. 2008. (Gallup Major Trends & Events Ser.). (Illus.). 118p. (YA). (gr. 7-18). lib. bdg. 22.95 *(978-1-59084-966-8(3),* 1260831) Mason Crest.
Spilsbury, Louise. Same-Sex Marriage, 1 vol. 2011. (Ethical Debates Ser.). (ENG., Illus.). 48p. (YA). (gr. 5-5). pap. 12.75 *(978-1-4488-7013-4(5),* 1760b080-3845-4b7c-b45d-5b9b5bdc94cc); lib. bdg. 34.47 *(978-1-4488-6020-3(2),* 106876c1-c3d4-426e-9417-c7f647b891e0) Rosen Publishing Group, Inc., The. (Rosen Reference).
Stern, Zoe & Stern, Evan. Divorce Is Not the End of the World: Zoe's & Evan's Coping Guide for Kids. 2nd rev. ed. 2008. (Illus.). 112p. (J). (gr. 3-7). pap. 9.99 *(978-1-58246-241-7(0),* Tricycle Pr.) Random Hse. Children's Bks.
Sterngass, Jon. Same-Sex Marriage, 1 vol. 2012. (Controversy! Ser.). (ENG.). 112p. (YA). (gr. 8-8). 39.79 *(978-1-60870-490-3(4),* e6911bc9-12d4-4b1d-ad20-64cbe273650d) Cavendish Square Publishing LLC.
Stewart, Sheila & Simons, Rae. I Live in Two Homes: Adjusting to Divorce & Remarriage. 2010. (Kids Have Troubles Too Ser.). 48p. (YA). (gr. 5-18). lib. bdg. 19.95 *(978-1-4222-1694-1(2))* Mason Crest.

MARRIAGE—FICTION
Ahdieh, Renée. Smoke in the Sun. 2018. (Flame in the Mist Ser.: 2). (ENG.). 432p. (YA). (gr. 7). 18.99 *(978-1-5247-3814-3(X),* G.P. Putnam's Sons Books for Young Readers) Penguin Young Readers Group.
Alcott, Louisa. Kitty's Class Day, & Other Stories. 2013. 178p. (J). pap. 8.75 *(978-1-61720-920-8(1))* Wilder Pubns., Corp.
Anderson, Hans Christian. The Little Mermaid Retold. Charlotte, J. M., illus. 2013. 48p. 18.00 *(978-0-9895422-0-3(9))* MHC Ministries.
Andrews, V. C. Garden of Shadows. 2010. (Dollanganger Ser.). (ENG.). 368p. (YA). (gr. 9). pap. 12.99 *(978-1-4424-0643-8(7),* Simon Pulse) Simon Pulse.
App, Linda Hoogeveen. Emma Pearl, Flower Girl. 2012. 34p. pap. 16.95 *(978-1-4497-6619-1(6),* WestBow Pr.) Author Solutions, LLC.
Ariel Make Believe Bride. 2008. (Disney 8*8 Ser.). 24p. pap. *(978-1-4075-1620-2(5))* Parragon, Inc.
Armstrong, Rachel. Fair Folk in Knob's End. 2013. 274p. pap. 14.99 *(978-1-60820-851-7(6))* MLR Pr., LLC.
Artigas de Sierra, Ione M. Las Bodas del Gallo Perico. (Superbks./Superlibros). (SPA.). (J). (gr. k-1). 21.95 *(978-0-88272-488-1(6));* pap. 6.95 *(978-0-88272-489-8(4))* Santillana USA Publishing Co., Inc.
—On the Way to the Wedding. (Superbks./Superlibros). (Illus.). 16p. (J). (gr. k-3). pap. 6.95 *(978-0-88272-491-1(6))* Santillana USA Publishing Co., Inc.
Austrian, J. J. Worm Loves Worm. Curato, Mike, illus. 2016. (ENG.). 32p. (J). (gr. -1-3). 17.99 *(978-0-06-238633-5(6),* Balzer & Bray) HarperCollins Pubs.
Baker, E. D. Princess in Disguise: A Tale of the Wide-Awake Princess. 2015. (Wide-Awake Princess Ser.: 4). (ENG.). 224p. (YA). (gr. 3-6). 16.99 *(978-1-61963-573-9(9),* 900140973, Bloomsbury USA Childrens) Bloomsbury Publishing USA.
Barkley, Callie. Amy Meets Her Stepsister. Riti, Marsha, illus. 2013. (Critter Club Ser.: 5). (ENG.). 128p. (J). (gr. k-2). 17.99 *(978-1-4424-8216-6(8));* pap. 6.99 *(978-1-4424-8215-9(X))* Little Simon. (Little Simon).
—Ellie the Flower Girl. Bishop, Tracy, illus. 2016. (Critter Club Ser.: 14). (ENG.). 128p. (J). (gr. k-4). pap. 6.99 *(978-1-4814-6718-6(2),* Little Simon) Little Simon.
Barnholdt, Lauren. Fake Me a Match. 2012. (Mix Ser.). (ENG.). 304p. (J). (gr. 4-8). pap. 6.99 *(978-1-4424-2259-9(9),* Aladdin) Simon & Schuster Children's Publishing.
Beach, Kathleen H. & Weeber, Stephanie B. Madison's Mixed-up Flower Girl Magic & Aiden's Amazing Ring Bearer Act Aiden's Amazing Ring Bearer Act. Baisley, Maryann Leake, illus. 2009. 32p. pap. 19.95 *(978-1-4251-7059-2(5))* Trafford Publishing.
Beaty, Erin. The Traitor's Kiss. 2018. (Traitor's Trilogy Ser.: 1). (ENG.). 368p. (YA). pap. 12.99 *(978-1-250-15884-0(2),* 900172348) Square Fish.
Beauvais, Clémentine & Beauvais, Clémentine. The Royal Wedding Crashers. Moor, Becka, illus. 2015. (Holy Moly Holiday Ser.). (ENG.). 240p. (J). (gr. 1-3). pap. *(978-1-4088-5544-7(5),* 256248, Bloomsbury Children's Bks.) Bloomsbury Publishing Plc.
Berk, Sheryl & Berk, Carrie. The Cupcake Club: Icing on the Cake. 2013. (Cupcake Club Ser.: 4). 160p. (J). (gr. 3-7). pap. 9.99 *(978-1-4022-8327-7(X))* Sourcebooks, Inc.
Birchall, Katy. The It Girl. 2016. (It Girl Ser.: 1). (ENG., Illus.). 352p. (J). (gr. 4-8). 16.99 *(978-1-4814-6362-1(4),* Aladdin) Simon & Schuster Children's Publishing.
Boat, Patty. A Disappointing Homecoming: (A Soldier's Story), 1 vol. 2009. 158p. pap. 24.95 *(978-1-61546-997-0(4))* PublishAmerica, Inc.
Bottner, Barbara. Flower Girl, 0 vols. Grier, Laura, photos by. 2012. (ENG., Illus.). 32p. (J). (gr. -1-2). 16.99 *(978-0-7614-6119-7(1),* 9780761461197, Two Lions) Amazon Publishing.
Bower, Gary. The Person I Marry. Bower, Jan, illus. 2008. 32p. (J). pap. 11.99 *(978-0-9704621-7-6(4))* Storybook Meadow Publishing.
Bradbury, Bianca. Flight into Spring. 2005. (ENG.). 190p. (gr. 7). per. 11.95 *(978-1-932350-01-2(2))* Ignatius Pr.
Bradley, Debby. Sophie Wonders about Marriage. Guzman, Lula, illus. 2013. (Sophie Wonders about the Sacraments Ser.). (ENG.). 31p. (J). pap. 4.99 *(978-0-7648-2351-0(5))* Liguori Pubns.
Brandon, Demi. Princess Shakina's Locks. 2007. 48p. per. 16.95 *(978-1-4241-7195-8(4))* America Star Bks.
Brennan-Nelson, Denise. Willow & the Wedding. Moore, Cyd, illus. 2017. (ENG.). 32p. (J). (gr. k-3). 16.99 *(978-1-58536-966-9(7),* 204236) Sleeping Bear Pr.
Bronte, Jules. The Royal Wedding Adventure. 2012. (Illus.). 188p. pap. *(978-1-908804-01-3(7))* Bingham Mayne & Smith, Ltd.
Buehner, Caralyn & Buehner, Mark. Fanny's Dream. Buehner, Caralyn & Buehner, Mark, illus. 2003. (Illus.). 32p. (J). (gr. k-3). 8.99 *(978-0-14-250060-6(7),* Puffin Books) Penguin Young Readers Group.
Bunting, Eve. My Mom's Wedding. Papp, Lisa, illus. 2006. (ENG.). 32p. (J). (gr. 1-4). 16.95 *(978-1-58536-288-2(3),* 202099) Sleeping Bear Pr.
Burgis, Stephanie. Renegade Magic, 2. 2012. (Kat, Incorrigible Ser.: 2). (ENG., Illus.). 336p. (J). (gr. 5-9). 16.99 *(978-1-4169-9449-7(1),* Atheneum Bks. for Young Readers) Simon & Schuster Children's Publishing.
—Stolen Magic. (Kat, Incorrigible Ser.: 3). (ENG., Illus.). 400p. (J). (gr. 5-8). 2014. pap. 7.99 *(978-1-4169-9452-7(1))* 2013. 17.99 *(978-1-4169-9451-0(3),* Atheneum Bks. for Young Readers) Simon & Schuster Children's Publishing.
Caletti, Deb. The Story of Us. (ENG.). 400p. (YA). (gr. 7). 2013. pap. 13.99 *(978-1-4424-2347-3(1))* 2012. 16.99 *(978-1-4424-2346-6(3))* Simon Pulse. (Simon Pulse).
Campbell, Chelsea M. Dragonbound. 2016. (ENG.). 288p. (YA). (gr. 7-11). pap. 9.99 *(978-1-5039-3609-6(0),* 9781503936096, Skyscape) Amazon Publishing.
Capucilli, Alyssa Satin. Katy Duck, Flower Girl: Ready-To-Read Level 1. Cole, Henry, illus. 2013. (Katy Duck Ser.). (ENG.). 24p. (J). (gr. -1-1). 16.99 *(978-1-4424-7279-2(0));* pap. 3.99 *(978-1-4424-7278-5(2))* Simon Spotlight. (Simon Spotlight).
Carter, Caela. My Best Friend, Maybe. 2014. (ENG.). 352p. (YA). (gr. 9). 17.99 *(978-1-59990-970-7(7),* 900095590, Bloomsbury USA Childrens) Bloomsbury Publishing USA.
Cass, Kiera. The Elite. (Selection Ser.: 2). (ENG.). (YA). (gr. 8). 2014. 352p. pap. 12.99 *(978-0-06-205997-0(1))* 2013. 336p. 19.99 *(978-0-06-205996-3(3))* HarperCollins Pubs. (HarperTeen).
—The Elite. 2014. (Selection Ser.: 2). (YA). lib. bdg. 20.85 *(978-0-606-35489-1(7))* Turtleback.
—La Elite / the Elite, Vol. 1. 2013. (SelecciÓn / the Selection Ser.: 2). (SPA.). 224p. (YA). (gr. 8-12). pap. 20.95 *(978-84-9918-613-9(0))* Penguin Random House Grupo Editorial ESP. Dist: Penguin Random Hse. LLC.
—La Elite/ the Elite, Vol. 2. 2017. (SelecciÓn / the Selection Ser.: 2). (SPA.). 224p. (J). (gr. 8-12). pap. 12.95 *(978-84-16240-61-6(2))* Penguin Random House Grupo Editorial ESP. Dist: Penguin Random Hse. LLC.
—Happily Ever After. 2015. (ENG., Illus.). 416p. (YA). *(978-0-00-814366-4(8))* HarperCollins Pubs.
—Happily Ever After: Companion to the Selection Series. 2016. (Selection Ser.). (YA). lib. bdg. 20.85 *(978-0-606-38919-8(9))* Turtleback.
—Happily Ever after: Companion to the Selection Series. 2015. (Selection Novella Ser.). (ENG., Illus.). 416p. (YA). (gr. 8). 18.99 *(978-0-06-241408-3(9),* HarperTeen) HarperCollins Pubs.
—The Heir. 2015. (ENG.). 368p. (YA). (Selection Ser.: 4). (gr. 8). 19.99 *(978-0-06-234985-9(6),* HarperTeen); pap. *(978-0-06-239130-8(5))* HarperCollins Pubs.
—The One. (Selection Ser.: 3). (ENG.). (YA). (gr. 8). 2015. 368p. pap. 12.99 *(978-0-06-206000-6(7))* 2014. 336p. 19.99 *(978-0-06-205999-4(8))* HarperCollins Pubs. (HarperTeen).
—The Selection. (Selection Ser.: 1). (ENG.). (YA). (gr. 8). 2013. 352p. pap. 12.99 *(978-0-06-205994-9(7))* 2012. 336p. 19.99 *(978-0-06-205993-2(9))* HarperCollins Pubs. (HarperTeen).
—The Selection, Book 1. (ENG.). 336p. pap. *(978-0-00-746669-6(2),* HarperCollins Children's Bks.) HarperCollins Pubs. Ltd.
—The Selection. 2013. (Selection Ser.: 1). (YA). lib. bdg. 20.85 *(978-0-606-35488-2(3))* Turtleback.
—The Selection. 2013. (Selection Ser.: Vol. 1). (CHI & ENG.). 288p. (YA). (gr. 8). pap. *(978-986-133-471-4(8))* Yuan Shen Pr. Co., Ltd.
—The Selection Stories: the Prince & the Guard. 2014. (Selection Novella Ser.). (ENG.). 240p. (YA). (gr. 8). pap. 15.99 *(978-0-06-231832-9(2),* HarperTeen) HarperCollins Pubs.
Chambers, Pamela G. My Mommy's Getting Married. Stewart, Muriel, illus. 2009. 32p. (gr. -1-3). 17.95 *(978-0-9799487-0-1(3))* Infinity Publishing Co.
Childs, Karin Alfelt. The Balm of Gilead. 2007. 356p. (YA). 15.95 *(978-0-9748423-7-0(0))* Fountain Publishing.
Chokshi, Roshani. The Star-Touched Queen. 2017. (Star-Touched Ser.: 1). (ENG.). 368p. (YA). pap. 11.99 *(978-1-250-10020-7(8),* 900162432, St. Martin's Griffin) St. Martin's Pr.
Chopin, Kate. The Awakening. 2014. (American Classics Ser.). (ENG., Illus.). 64p. pap. 7.95 *(978-1-906230-78-4(1))* Real Reads Ltd. GBR. Dist: Casemate Pubs. & Bk. Distributors, LLC.
Ciddor, Anna. The Family with Two Front Doors. 2018. (ENG., Illus.). 208p. (J). (gr. 3-6). 12.99 *(978-1-5415-0011-2(3),* cde459b6-6cee-4eae-8964-4b6e58cdfefc); pap. 6.99 *(978-1-5415-0012-9(1),* 7bf0f625-be94-4f2c-aa3e-8be52aaf66e4) Lerner Publishing Group. (Kar-Ben Publishing).
Cleary, Beverly. Sister of the Bride. 2007. (ENG., Illus.). 272p. (J). (gr. 5-18). pap. 9.99 *(978-0-380-72807-7(9),* HarperCollins) HarperCollins Pubs.
Coe, Mary E. The Prince of Betherland. 2008. 117p. 24.95 *(978-0-557-03112-2(5))* Lulu Pr., Inc.
—The Prince of Betherland A Wonderful World of Fantasy. 2009. 66p. pap. 9.95 *(978-0-557-08499-9(7))* Lulu Pr., Inc.
—The Prince of Betherland A Wonderful World of Fantasy. 2009. 112p. pap. 9.95 *(978-0-557-09297-0(3))* Lulu Pr., Inc.
Cohn, Rachel. Two Steps Forward. 2013. (ENG., Illus.). 240p. (YA). (gr. 7). pap. 11.99 *(978-1-4424-9615-6(0),* Simon & Schuster Bks. For Young Readers) Simon & Schuster Bks. For Young Readers.
Condie, Ally. Crossed. (Matched Ser.: 2). (ENG.). (YA). (gr. 7). 2013. 416p. pap. 12.99 *(978-0-14-242171-0(5),* Penguin Books) 2011. 384p. 19.99 *(978-0-525-42365-2(6),* Dutton Books for Young Readers) Penguin Young Readers Group.
—Crossed. l.t. ed. 2011. (Matched Trilogy: Bk. 2). (ENG.). 448p. (J). 23.99 *(978-1-4104-4325-0(6))* Thorndike Pr.
—Crossed. 2013. (Matched Trilogy Ser.: 2). lib. bdg. 20.85 *(978-0-606-26634-5(8))* Turtleback.
—Juntos. 2011.Tr. of Matched. (SPA.). lib. bdg. 22.05 *(978-0-606-26417-4(5))* Turtleback.
—Matched. 2009. (Matched Trilogy: Bk. 1). 11.04 *(978-0-7848-3716-0(3),* Everbind) Marco Bk. Co.
—Matched. (Matched Ser.: 1). (ENG.). (YA). (gr. 7-18). 2011. 416p. 12.99 *(978-0-14-241977-9(X),* Penguin Books) 2010. 384p. 19.99 *(978-0-525-42364-5(8),* Dutton Books for Young Readers) Penguin Young Readers Group.
—Matched. 2011. pap. *(978-0-545-39990-6(4))* Scholastic, Inc.
—Matched. l.t. ed. 2011. (Matched Trilogy: Bk. 1). (ENG.). 449p. 23.99 *(978-1-4104-3954-3(2))* Thorndike Pr.
—Matched. 2011. (Matched Trilogy Ser.: 1). lib. bdg. 20.85 *(978-0-606-23140-4(4))* Turtleback.
—Reached. 2012. (Matched Ser.: 3). (ENG.). 528p. (YA). (gr. 7-18). 19.99 *(978-0-525-42366-9(4),* Dutton Books for Young Readers) Penguin Young Readers Group.
—Reached. l.t. ed. 2012. (Matched Trilogy: Bk. 3). (ENG.). 614p. 23.99 *(978-1-4104-5366-2(9))* Thorndike Pr.
Cook, Eileen. Unraveling Isobel. 2012. (ENG.). 320p. (YA). (gr. 9). pap. 9.99 *(978-1-4424-1328-3(X),* Simon Pulse) Simon Pulse.
—Wishes for Beginners. 2011. (Fourth Grade Fairy Ser.: 2). (ENG.). 160p. (J). (gr. 3-7). pap. 6.99 *(978-1-4169-9812-9(8),* Aladdin) Simon & Schuster Children's Publishing.
Coolidge, Susan. Clover. 2017. (ENG., Illus.). (J). 23.95 *(978-1-374-96593-5(6))* Capital Communications, Inc.
—Clover. 2016. (ENG., Illus.). (J). 26.95 *(978-1-359-71234-9(8))* Creative Media Partners, LLC.
Cooper, Floyd. The Ring Bearer. Cooper, Floyd, illus. 2017. (Illus.). 32p. (J). (gr. -1-2). 17.99 *(978-0-399-16740-9(4),* Philomel Bks.) Penguin Young Readers Group.
Couloumbis, Audrey. Lexie. Denos, Julia, illus. 2012. (ENG.). 208p. (J). (gr. 3-7). pap. 6.99 *(978-0-375-85633-4(1),* Yearling) Random Hse. Children's Bks.
Cousins, Lucy. Maisy Goes to a Wedding: A Maisy First Experiences Book. Cousins, Lucy, illus. 2018. (Maisy Ser.). (ENG., Illus.). 32p. (J). (-k). 12.99 *(978-1-5362-0011-9(5))* Candlewick Pr.
Coven, Wanda. Heidi Heckelbeck Is a Flower Girl. Burris, Priscilla, illus. 2014. (Heidi Heckelbeck Ser.: 11). (ENG.). 128p. (J). (gr. k-4). pap. 6.99 *(978-1-4814-0498-3(9),* Little Simon) Little Simon.
Cushman, Karen. El Libro de Catherine. 2003.Tr. of Catherine, Called Birdy. (SPA.). 237p. *(978-84-236-4600-5(9),* ED8017) Edebé ESP. Dist: Lectorum Pubns., Inc.
Dadey, Debbie. Flower Girl Dreams. Avakyan, Tatevik, illus. 2017. (Mermaid Tales Ser.: 16). (ENG.). 128p. (J). (gr. 1-4). pap. 5.99 *(978-1-4814-4084-4(5),* Simon & Schuster/Paula Wiseman Bks.) Simon & Schuster/Paula Wiseman Bks.
Danziger, Paula. Forever Amber Brown. 2008. (Amber Brown Ser.: 5). (ENG.). 128p. (J). (gr. 2-5). 6.99 *(978-0-14-241201-5(5),* Puffin Books) Penguin Young Readers Group.
Danziger, Paula, et al. Amber Brown Is Tickled Pink. Ross, Tony, illus. 2013. (Amber Brown Ser.: 10). (ENG.). 176p. (J). (gr. 2-5). pap. 7.99 *(978-0-14-242757-6(8),* Puffin Books) Penguin Young Readers Group.
Daswani, Kavita. Lovetorn. 2012. (ENG.). 256p. (YA). (gr. 8). 17.99 *(978-0-06-167311-5(0),* HarperTeen) HarperCollins Pubs.
de la Cruz, Melissa. All for One. 2019. (Alex & Eliza Trilogy Ser.: 3). 400p. (YA). (gr. 7). 17.99 *(978-0-525-51588-3(7),* G.P. Putnam's Sons Books for Young Readers) Penguin Young Readers Group.
—Love & War. 2018. (Alex & Eliza Trilogy Ser.: 2). 384p. (YA). (gr. 7). 18.99 *(978-1-5247-3965-2(0),* G.P. Putnam's Sons Books for Young Readers) Penguin Young Readers Group.
Demas, Corinne. Returning to Shore. 2014. (ENG.). 208p. (YA). (gr. 6-12). 17.95 *(978-1-4677-1328-3(7),* f1305577-556b-4ab1-bbd3-6087cb98b8e1, Carolrhoda Lab™) Lerner Publishing Group.

MNO

DeStefano, Lauren. Wither, 9 vols. (Chemical Garden Ser.: 1). (YA). 256.75 *(978-1-4561-2059-7(X))*; 90.75 *(978-1-4561-2060-3(3))*; 1.25 *(978-1-4561-2064-1(6))*; 2011. 122.75 *(978-1-4561-2061-0(1))*; 2011. 120.75 *(978-1-4561-2063-4(8))* Recorded Bks., Inc.

—Wither. 2011. (Chemical Garden Trilogy Ser.: 1). (ENG.). 384p. (YA). (gr. 9). pap. 13.99 *(978-1-4424-0906-4(1)*, Simon & Schuster Bks. For Young Readers) Simon & Schuster Bks. For Young Readers.

Dhami, Narinder & Dhami, Narinder. Bhangra Babes. 2006. (Bindi Babes Ser.). (ENG.). 185p. (J). (gr. 4-6). 18.69 *(978-0-440-42106-1(3))* Random House Publishing Group.

Dillon-Hreha, Denise & Mathews, Sheri. The Wedding of Q & U. 2007. (ENG., Illus.). 48p. per. 16.99 *(978-1-4259-8040-5(6))* AuthorHouse.

Donaldson, Julia. The Scarecrows' Wedding. Scheffler, Axel, illus. 2014. (ENG.). 32p. (J). (gr. -1-3). 18.99 *(978-0-545-72606-1(9)*, Levine, Arthur A. Bks.) Scholastic, Inc.

Doty, Linda. Hydrangea Hill: A New Home for Amy Manchester. 2008. 182p. pap. 24.95 *(978-1-60610-840-6(9))* America Star Bks.

DuJardin, Rosamond. Wedding in the Family. 2003. (YA). pap. 12.95 *(978-1-930009-72-1(0)*, 800-691-7779) Image Cascade Publishing.

Dunkle, Clare B. Close Kin: Book II — the Hollow Kingdom Trilogy. 2nd rev. ed. 2006. (Hollow Kingdom Trilogy Ser.: 2). (ENG.). 224p. (J). (gr. 6-9). pap. 12.99 *(978-0-8050-8109-1(7)*, 900039577, Holt, Henry & Co. Bks. For Young Readers) Holt, Henry & Co.

—In the Coils of the Snake: Book III — the Hollow Kingdom Trilogy. 3rd rev. ed. 2006. (Hollow Kingdom Trilogy Ser.: 3). (ENG.). 240p. (J). (gr. 6-9). pap. 15.99 *(978-0-8050-8110-7(0)*, 900039578, Holt, Henry & Co. Bks. For Young Readers) Holt, Henry & Co.

Dyan, Penelope. Someone's Getting Married! 2011. 34p. pap. 11.95 *(978-1-935630-64-7(4))* Bellissima Publishing, LLC.

Elias, Megan J. Stir It Up: Home Economics in American Culture. 2010. (ENG., Illus.). 240p. (C). pap. 29.95 *(978-0-8122-2121-3(4)*, 6611) Univ. of Pennsylvania Pr.

Elliott, Rebecca. A Woodland Wedding. 2016. (Owl Diaries: 3). (ENG.). 80p. (J). (gr. k-2). lib. bdg. 14.75 *(978-0-606-38068-3(X))* Turtleback.

—A Woodland Wedding: a Branches Book (Owl Diaries #3) (Library Edition), Vol. 3. Elliott, Rebecca, illus. 2016. (Owl Diaries: 3). (ENG., Illus.). 80p. (J). (gr. k-2). 24.99 *(978-0-545-82558-0(X))* Scholastic, Inc.

English, Karen. Nadia's Hands. Weiner, Jonathan, illus. 2009. (ENG.). 32p. (J). (gr. k-2). pap. 9.99 *(978-1-59078-784-7(6)*, Astra Young Readers) Astra Publishing Hse.

—Nikki & Deja: Wedding Drama. Freeman, Laura, illus. 2013. (Nikki & Deja Ser.). (ENG.). 112p. (J). (gr. 1-4). pap. 6.99 *(978-0-544-00324-8(1)*, 1526366, Clarion Bks.) HarperCollins Pubs.

Essama, Molly Jane. The Prince & the Three Ugly Hags. 2010. 28p. pap. 16.95 *(978-1-4490-5587-5(7))* AuthorHouse.

Finchler, Judy & O'Malley, Kevin. Congratulations, Miss Malarkey! O'Malley, Kevin, illus. 2011. (Miss Malarkey Ser.). (ENG., Illus.). 32p. (J). (gr. k-2). 21.19 *(978-0-8027-9836-7(5)*, 9780802798367) Walker & Co.

Finley, Martha. Elsie at Home. 2006. 27.95 *(978-1-4218-2989-0(4))*; pap. 12.95 *(978-1-4218-3089-6(2))* 1st World Publishing, Inc.

—Elsie at Home. 2018. (ENG., Illus.). 162p. (YA). (gr. 7-12). pap. *(978-93-5297-351-4(8))* Alpha Editions.

—Elsie at Home. (ENG., Illus.). (J). 2018. 304p. pap. 16.95 *(978-1-376-41190-4(3))* 2015. 26.95 *(978-1-297-88807-6(3))* Creative Media Partners, LLC.

—Elsie's Young Folks. 2008. 296p. 34.99 *(978-1-58960-287-8(0))* Sovereign Grace Pubs., Inc.

Fisch, Sholly & Kane, Bob. The Bride & the Bold. 2015. (All-New Batman: the Brave & the Bold Ser.). (ENG., Illus.). 32p. (J). (gr. 2-5). lib. bdg. 22.60 *(978-1-4342-9661-0(X)*, 126962, Stone Arch Bks.) Capstone.

Francoise. Fanchette & Jeannot: A Little Story with Pictures. 2011. 26p. 35.95 *(978-1-258-07322-0(6))* Literary Licensing, LLC.

Frederick, Heather Vogel. Wish You Were Eyre. 2013. (Mother-Daughter Book Club Ser.). (ENG.). 480p. (J). (gr. 4-9). pap. 8.99 *(978-1-4424-3065-5(6)*, Simon & Schuster Bks. For Young Readers) Simon & Schuster Bks. For Young Readers.

Friedman, Laurie. Heart to Heart with Mallory. Pollak, Barbara, illus. (Mallory Ser.: 6). (ENG.). 160p. (J). (gr. 2-5). 2007. per. 7.99 *(978-0-8225-7133-9(1)*, b2c6ea4e-9452-4902-bcd8-b84c16b1ce2f, Darby Creek) 2006. lib. bdg. 15.95 *(978-1-57505-932-7(0)*, Twenty-First Century Bks.) Lerner Publishing Group.

—Mallory on Board. 2008. pap. 34.95 *(978-0-8225-9440-6(4))* Lerner Publishing Group.

—Mallory on Board. Pollak, Barbara, illus. 2007. (Mallory Ser.: 7). (ENG.). 176p. (J). (gr. 2-5). 15.95 *(978-0-8225-6194-1(8)*, Carolrhoda Bks.) Lerner Publishing Group.

—A Style All Her Own. Watts, Sharon, illus. 2005. 32p. (J). (gr. -1-3). lib. bdg. 15.95 *(978-1-57505-599-2(6))* Lerner Publishing Group.

Friesen, Gayle. For Now. 2007. 248p. (J). (gr. 5-9). 7.95 *(978-1-55453-133-2(0))* Kids Can Pr., Ltd. CAN. Dist: Hachette Bk. Group.

Gail, Becky. How the Little White Monkey Became a Woman. 2008. 19p. pap. 24.95 *(978-1-60563-471-5(9))* America Star Bks.

Garber, Stephanie. Caraval. l.t. ed. 2017. (Caraval Ser.). (ENG.). 510p. 24.95 *(978-1-4328-4221-5(8))* Cengage Gale.

—Caraval. (ENG.). (YA). 2018. (Caraval Ser.: 1). 448p. pap. 11.99 *(978-1-250-09526-8(3)*, 900160654) 2017. (gr. 8-12). pap. 11.99 *(978-1-250-14149-1(4))* 2017. (Caraval Ser.: 1). 416p. 18.99 *(978-1-250-09525-1(5)*, 900160653) Flatiron Bks.

—Caraval. 2018. (YA). lib. bdg. 22.10 *(978-0-606-41093-9(7))* Turtleback.

—Legendary. 2018. (CHI.). (YA). (gr. 8-12). pap. *(978-986-235-684-5(7))* Faces Pubns.

—Legendary. 2018. (Caraval Ser.). (ENG., Illus.). 495p. (YA). (gr. 8-13). pap. 11.99 *(978-1-250-19222-6(6))* Flatiron Bks.

—Legendary. 2018. (Illus.). 451p. (YA). *(978-1-250-30129-1(7))*; *(978-1-250-30127-7(0))* St. Martin's Pr.

—Legendary: A Caraval Novel. (Caraval Ser.: 2). (ENG., Illus.). (YA). 2019. 512p. pap. 11.99 *(978-1-250-09532-9(8)*, 900160660) 2018. 464p. 19.99 *(978-1-250-09531-2(X)*, 900160659) Flatiron Bks.

Graff, Lisa. Lost in the Sun. 2016. lib. bdg. 19.65 *(978-0-606-38835-1(4))* Turtleback.

Griffith, Linda, illus. The Best Ever Ring Bearer: All the Best Things about Being in a Wedding. 2010. (ENG.). 24p. 10.99 *(978-1-4022-3818-5(5))* Sourcebooks, Inc.

—The Most Special Flower Girl: All the Best Things about Being in a Wedding. 2010. (ENG.). 24p. 10.99 *(978-1-4022-3817-8(7))* Sourcebooks, Inc.

Grogan, John. Marley: Thanks, Mom & Dad! Cowdrey, Richard, illus. 2011. (Marley Ser.). (ENG.). 24p. (J). (gr. -1-2). 3.99 *(978-0-06-185381-4(X)*, HarperFestival) HarperCollins Pubs.

Hamilton, Elizabeth L. Date with Responsibility. 2004. (Character-in-Action Ser.: No. 2). (Illus.). 384p. (YA). per. 19.95 *(978-0-9713749-0-4(2)*, Character-in-Action) Quiet Impact, Inc.

Han, Jenny. Always & Forever, Lara Jean. 2018. (To All the Boys I've Loved Before Ser.: 3). (ENG., Illus.). 336p. (YA). (gr. 7). pap. 10.99 *(978-1-4814-3049-4(1)*, Simon & Schuster Bks. For Young Readers) Simon & Schuster Bks. For Young Readers.

Hand, Cynthia, et al. My Plain Jane. (Lady Janies Ser.). (ENG.). (YA). (gr. 8). 2019. 480p. pap. 10.99 *(978-0-06-265278-2(8))* 2018. 464p. 17.99 *(978-0-06-265277-5(X))* HarperCollins Pubs. (HarperTeen).

Hargreaves, Roger. Little Miss Princess & the Very Special Wedding. 2011. (Mr. Men & Little Miss Ser.). (ENG., Illus.). 24p. (J). (gr. -1-3). *(978-1-4052-5996-5(5))* Farshore.

Harper, Charise Mericle & Malk, Steven. Just Grace & the Flower Girl Power. Harper, Charise Mericle, illus. 2013. (Just Grace Ser.). (ENG., Illus.). 208p. (J). (gr. 1-4). pap. 7.99 *(978-0-544-02283-6(1)*, 1528504, Clarion Bks.) HarperCollins Pubs.

Hartt-Sussman, Heather. Nana's Getting Married. Graham, Georgia, illus. 2010. 32p. (J). (gr. -1-1). 17.95 *(978-0-88776-911-5(X)*, Tundra Bks.) Tundra Bks. CAN. Dist: Penguin Random Hse. LLC.

Harvey, Jacqueline. Clementine Rose & the Wedding Wobbles. 2017. (Clementine Rose Ser.: 13). (ENG.). 160p. (J). (gr. 2-4). 8.99 *(978-0-85798-790-7(9))* Random Hse. Australia AUS. Dist: Independent Pubs. Group.

Henkes, Kevin. El Gran día de Lily: Lily's Big Day (Spanish Edition), 1 vol. Henkes, Kevin, illus. 2008. (SPA., Illus.). 40p. (J). (gr. -1-3). 17.99 *(978-0-06-136316-0(2))* HarperCollins Español.

—Lilly's Big Day. Henkes, Kevin, illus. (ENG., Illus.). 40p. (J). (gr. -1-3). 2014. pap. 8.99 *(978-0-06-231358-4(4))* 2006. 18.99 *(978-0-06-074236-2(4))* 2006. lib. bdg. 18.89 *(978-0-06-074237-9(2))* HarperCollins Pubs. (Greenwillow Bks.).

—Lilly's Big Day. 2014. (J). lib. bdg. 17.20 *(978-0-606-35472-1(7))* Turtleback.

Hermes, Patricia. Emma Dilemma, the Nanny, & the Wedding, 0 vols. Carter, Abby, illus. 2012. (Emma Dilemma Ser.: 7). (ENG.). 144p. (J). (gr. 3-6). 16.99 *(978-0-7614-6210-1(4)*, 9780761462101, Two Lions) Amazon Publishing.

Hicks, Betty. Out of Order. 2007. (ENG.). 176p. (J). (gr. 3-7). pap. 15.99 *(978-0-312-37355-9(4)*, 900045404) Square Fish.

Hidaka, Banri. V. B. Rose Volume 10. 2010. (Illus.). 208p. pap. 10.99 *(978-1-4278-1160-8(1))* TOKYOPOP, Inc.

—V. B. Rose Volume 9. 2010. (Illus.). 192p. pap. 10.99 *(978-1-4278-0927-8(5))* TOKYOPOP, Inc.

Hingoro, Samira, creator. A Marriage Proposal. 2003. (YA). per. 12.95 *(978-0-9743167-0-3(9))* Faith Pubns.

Hirahara, Naomi. 1001 Cranes. 2009. (ENG.). 240p. (J). (gr. 3-7). 7.99 *(978-0-440-42234-1(5)*, Yearling) Random Hse. Children's Bks.

Hodge, Rosamund. Cruel Beauty. (ENG.). (YA). (gr. 8). 2015. 368p. pap. 10.99 *(978-0-06-222474-3(3))* 2014. 352p. 17.99 *(978-0-06-222473-6(5))* HarperCollins Pubs. (Balzer & Bray).

Hoffman, Amalia. Klezmer Bunch. 2009. (ENG.). 36p. 15.95 *(978-965-229-447-0(0))* Gefen Publishing Hse., Ltd ISR. Dist: Strauss Consultants.

Hoffman, Mary. Bravo, Grace! 2011. (ENG.). 112p. (J). (gr. 3-7). 5.99 *(978-0-14-241850-5(1)*, Puffin Books) Penguin Young Readers Group.

Holland, Sara. Everless. 2018. (ENG.). 368p. (YA). (gr. 8). 17.99 *(978-0-06-265365-9(2)*, HarperTeen) HarperCollins Pubs.

Holm, Jennifer L. Middle School Is Worse Than Meatloaf: A Year Told Through Stuff. Castaldi, Elicia, illus. 2011. (ENG.). 128p. (J). (gr. 3-7). pap. 9.99 *(978-1-4424-3663-3(8)*, Atheneum Bks. for Young Readers) Simon & Schuster Children's Publishing.

Holt, Catherine. Midnight Reynolds & the Agency of Spectral Protection. 2018. (Midnight Reynolds Ser.: 2). (ENG.). 264p. (J). (gr. 3-7). 14.99 *(978-0-8075-5128-8(7)*, 807551287) Whitman, Albert & Co.

Hook, Jacqueline A. You're Going to Be a Flower Girl. 2005. (J). per. *(978-0-9664783-3-4(9))* Jacqueline Beverly Hills.

Hooper, Mary. Katie: The Revolting Bridesmaid. Vayssiere, Frederique, illus. 2007. (Katie Ser.). 80p. (J). (gr. 2-4). per. 8.95 *(978-0-7475-8611-1(X))* Bloomsbury Publishing Plc GBR. Dist: Independent Pubs. Group.

—The Revolting Wedding. Vayssiere, Frederique, illus. 2007. (Katie Ser.). 96p. (J). (gr. 2-4). per. 8.95 *(978-0-7475-8612-8(8))* Bloomsbury Publishing Plc GBR. Dist: Independent Pubs. Group.

Howard, Annabelle. As the Mayan Calendars Turn. 2005. (J). pap. *(978-1-4108-4223-7(1))* Benchmark Education Co.

Howard, Elizabeth Fitzgerald. Flower Girl Butterflies. Kromer, Christiane, illus. 2004. 32p. (J). 16.89 *(978-0-688-17810-9(3))* HarperCollins Pubs.

Howitt, Mary Botham. Strive & Thrive a Tale by Mary Howitt. 2006. 180p. per. 18.99 *(978-1-4255-1426-6(X))* Michigan Publishing.

Ingalls, Laura. Los Cuatro Primeros Años. 2006. (Little House Bks.). (SPA., Illus.). 126p. (gr. 5-8). pap. 12.99 *(978-84-279-3259-3(6))* Lectorum Pubns., Inc.

Johnson, Annabel & Johnson, Edgar. Wilderness Bride. 2003. 232p. (J). 12.95 *(978-0-9714612-7-7(9))* Green Mansion Pr. LLC.

Jones, Faith. Sprouting Wings, 1 vol. 2010. 96p. pap. 16.95 *(978-1-4489-6366-9(4))* PublishAmerica, Inc.

Jones, Jen. Maren's New Family. Franco, Paula, illus. 2015. (Sleepover Girls Ser.). (ENG.). 128p. (J). (gr. 3-5). lib. bdg. 22.65 *(978-1-4965-0540-8(9)*, 128612, Stone Arch Bks.) Capstone.

Joyce, Melaine. Cinderella. 2009. (Fairydust Fairytales Ser.). (ENG.). 5p. (J). (gr. -1-k). bds. 6.95 *(978-1-84696-964-5(6)*, TickTock Books) Octopus Publishing Group GBR. Dist: Independent Pubs. Group.

Katherine's Story 1848. 2014. (Secrets of the Manor Ser.: 4). (ENG., Illus.). 160p. (J). (gr. 3-7). pap. 6.99 *(978-1-4814-1843-0(2)*, Simon Spotlight) Simon Spotlight.

Katies Choice. 2005. (YA). per. *(978-1-59872-217-8(4))* Instant Pub.

Kaupp, Rosemarie. The Amberella Tales: Amberella & Double Double Trouble. 2013. 144p. (gr. 2-4). 20.77 *(978-1-4669-9233-7(6))*; pap. 10.77 *(978-1-4669-9234-4(4))* Trafford Publishing.

Keene, Carolyn. Puppy Love Prank. Francis, Peter, illus. 2020. (Nancy Drew Clue Book Ser.: 13). (ENG.). 112p. (J). (gr. 1-4). 16.99 *(978-1-5344-3134-8(9)*, Simon & Schuster/Paula Wiseman Bks.) Simon & Schuster/Paula Wiseman Bks.

—Wedding Day Disaster. Pamintuan, Macky, illus. 2008. (Nancy Drew & the Clue Crew Ser.: 17). (ENG.). 96p. (J). (gr. 1-4). pap. 5.99 *(978-1-4169-6778-1(8)*, Aladdin) Simon & Schuster Children's Publishing.

Kelly, Jamie & Benton, Jim. Never Underestimate Your Dumbness. 2008. (Dear Dumb Diary Ser.). (Illus.). 150p. (gr. 4-7). 16.00 *(978-0-7569-8814-2(4))* Perfection Learning Corp.

Kiser, Dolores White. The Marriage of White Rabbit. 2005. (J). 10.00 net. *(978-0-9766648-3-3(6))* White Kiser, Dolores.

Kline, Suzy. Horrible Harry & the Wedding Spies. 2016. (Horrible Harry Ser.: 32). lib. bdg. 14.75 *(978-0-606-38389-9(1))* Turtleback.

Konigsburg, E. L. Journey to an 800 Number. 2008. (ENG.). 160p. (J). (gr. 4-8). pap. 7.99 *(978-1-4169-5875-8(4)*, Atheneum Bks. for Young Readers) Simon & Schuster Children's Publishing.

Korba, Joanna. Rough-Face Girl: A Native American Cinderella Tale. 2006. (J). pap. *(978-1-4108-6163-4(5))* Benchmark Education Co.

Kraus, Joanna H. A Night of Tamales & Roses. Caravela, Elena, illus. 2007. (ENG.). 32p. (J). (gr. -1-3). 15.95 *(978-0-9726614-4-7(1))* Shenanigan Bks.

Krider, Dave. Do Animals Go to Heaven?, 1 vol. 2009. 49p. pap. 16.95 *(978-1-61546-049-6(7))* America Star Bks.

Leavitt, Lindsey. The Chapel Wars. 2014. (ENG.). 304p. (YA). (gr. 7). 17.99 *(978-1-59990-788-8(7)*, 9781599907888, Bloomsbury USA Childrens) Bloomsbury Publishing USA.

Lee, Kyanna Shanae. Stepdad? No Thanks...! 2008. 60p. pap. 19.95 *(978-1-60563-422-7(0))* America Star Bks.

Levins, Sandra. Do You Sing Twinkle? A Story about Remarriage & New Family. Langdo, Bryan, illus. 2009. 32p. (J). (gr. -1-3). (ENG.). 14.95 *(978-1-4338-0539-4(1))*; pap. 9.95 *(978-1-4338-0551-6(0))* American Psychological Assn. (Magination Pr.).

Lollino, Jessica. Lily & the Big Italian Wedding. Lollino, Jessica, ed. 2008. (Little Lily Mays Ser.: vol. 2). (ENG., Illus.). 32p. (J). pap. 12.95 *(978-0-9712383-2-9(4))* Culturatti Ink.

Looper, Grace W. Great-Grandpa's Hidden Treasure. 2006. (YA). pap. *(978-1-933523-18-7(2))* Bella Rosa Bks.

Lynne, Kimberlee, illus. The Frog & the Mouse. 2011. (First Steps in Music Ser.). (ENG.). 32p. (J). (gr. k-2). 17.95 *(978-1-57999-802-8(X))* G I A Pubns., Inc.

Lyons, Kelly Starling. Ellen's Broom. Minter, Daniel, illus. 2012. (ENG.). 32p. (J). (gr. k-3). 17.99 *(978-0-399-25003-3(4)*, G.P. Putnam's Sons Books for Young Readers) Penguin Young Readers Group.

MacKenzie, Lachlan. The Duke's Daughter. 2008. (Story Time Ser.). (ENG., Illus.). 24p. (J). (gr. -1-3). 7.99 *(978-1-84550-326-0(0)*, 55c39b86-6732-4df2-a209-0be940187130) Christian Focus Pubns. GBR. Dist: Baker & Taylor Publisher Services (BTPS).

Malone, Jen & Nall, Gail. You're Invited Too. 2016. (Mix Ser.). (ENG., Illus.). 304p. (J). (gr. 4-8). pap. 7.99 *(978-1-4814-3199-6(4)*, Aladdin) Simon & Schuster Children's Publishing.

Martin, C. K. Kelly. The Lighter Side of Life & Death. 2010. (YA). pap. *(978-0-375-84590-1(9))* Random Hse. Children's Bks.

Matson, Morgan. Save the Date. 2018. (ENG., Illus.). 432p. (YA). (gr. 7). 17.99 *(978-1-4814-0457-0(1)*, Simon & Schuster Bks. For Young Readers) Simon & Schuster Bks. For Young Readers.

Mayer, Pamela. Don't Sneeze at the Wedding. Avilés, Martha Graciela, illus. 2013. (ENG.). 32p. (J). (gr. k-3). E-Book 23.99 *(978-1-4677-1641-3(3)*, Kar-Ben Publishing) Lerner Publishing Group.

McDougal-Littell Publishing Staff, creator. Picture Bride & Related Readings. 2006. (Literature Connections Ser.). 314p. (gr. 6-12). *(978-0-395-77540-0(X)*, 2-80109) Holt McDougal.

McKay, Hilary. Caddy Ever After. 2007. (ENG.). 240p. (J). (gr. 4-8). per. 7.99 *(978-1-4169-0931-6(1)*, McElderry, Margaret K. Bks.) McElderry, Margaret K. Bks.

Mead, Richelle. The Emerald Sea. 2018. (Glittering Court Ser.: 3). (ENG.). 496p. (YA). (gr. 7). 19.99 *(978-1-59514-845-2(0)*, Razorbill) Penguin Young Readers Group.

—The Glittering Court. 2016. 416p. (YA). pap. *(978-0-448-49385-5(3)*, Razorbill) Penguin Publishing Group.

—The Glittering Court. (Glittering Court Ser.: 1). (ENG.). (YA). (gr. 7). 2017. 432p. pap. 11.99 *(978-1-59514-842-1(6))* 2016. 416p. 19.99 *(978-1-59514-841-4(8))* Penguin Young Readers Group. (Razorbill).

Mejia, Tehlor Kay. We Set the Dark on Fire. (ENG.). (YA). (gr. 9). 2020. 400p. pap. 11.99 *(978-0-06-269132-3(5))* 2019. 384p. 17.99 *(978-0-06-269131-6(7))* HarperCollins Pubs. (Tegen, Katherine Bks).

Mejuto Rial, Eva. RUN PUMPKIN, RUN. 2007. (ENG., Illus.). 36p. (J). 17.95 *(978-84-96788-88-6(1))* OQO, Editora ESP. Dist: Baker & Taylor Bks.

Menon, Sandhya. When Dimple Met Rishi. 2021. (ENG.). 432p. (YA). (gr. 7). pap. 12.99 *(978-1-5344-9479-4(0)*, Simon & Schuster Bks. For Young Readers) Simon & Schuster Bks. For Young Readers.

—When Dimple Met Rishi. (ENG.). (YA). (gr. 7). 2018. 400p. pap. 12.99 *(978-1-4814-7869-4(9))* 2017. (Illus.). 384p. 19.99 *(978-1-4814-7868-7(0))* Simon Pulse. (Simon Pulse).

—When Dimple Met Rishi. 2018. lib. bdg. 23.30 *(978-0-606-41411-1(8))* Turtleback.

Meyer, Stephenie. Breaking Dawn. 2008. (Twilight Saga Ser.: 4). (ENG.). 768p. (YA). (gr. 7-17). 24.99 *(978-0-316-06792-8(X))* Little, Brown Bks. for Young Readers.

—Breaking Dawn. 2010. (Twilight Saga Ser.: 4). (YA). lib. bdg. 29.40 *(978-0-606-23108-4(0))* Turtleback.

Milan, D. S. A Year of Starless Nights. 2013. 154p. pap. 14.95 *(978-1-62432-012-5(0))* Loose Leaves Publishing.

Milde, Jeanette. Once upon a Wedding. Sandin, Joan, tr. from SWE. 2004. (Illus.). 32p. (J). 15.00 *(978-91-29-66048-7(3))* R & S Bks. SWE. Dist: Macmillan.

Minke, Shari. The Airplane Story: A Blended Family's Journey. 2010. pap. 12.99 *(978-1-61579-944-2(3))* Salem Author Services.

Monnar, Ana. Heart of Stone. Michaud, Nancy, illus. 2007. 24p. (J). per. 11.99 *(978-0-9768035-5-3(0))* Readers Are Leaders U.S.A.

Mun-Ensor, Michelle. The Ten Bridesmaids. 2011. 28p. pap. 24.95 *(978-1-4560-9003-6(8))* America Star Bks.

Munsch, Robert. Ribbon Rescue. 2004. (Illus.). (J). (gr. k-3). spiral bd. *(978-0-616-01742-5(1))*; spiral bd. *(978-0-616-01743-2(X))* Canadian National Institute for the Blind/Institut National Canadien pour les Aveugles.

—Ribbon Rescue. 2007. (J). 12.65 *(978-0-7569-7466-4(6))* Perfection Learning Corp.

Newhall, Mary & Campbell, Joanna. Bridal Dreams. 2005. (Thoroughbred Ser.). (Illus.). 163p. (gr. 3-7). 15.00 *(978-0-7569-5359-1(6))* Perfection Learning Corp.

Newman, Leslea. Donovan's Big Day. Dutton, Mike, illus. 2011. (ENG.). 32p. (J). (gr. -1-2). 17.99 *(978-1-58246-332-2(8)*, Tricycle Pr.) Random Hse. Children's Bks.

Nolan, Han. Pregnant Pause. 2012. (ENG.). 352p. (YA). (gr. 9). pap. 8.99 *(978-0-547-85414-4(5)*, 1501157, Clarion Bks.) HarperCollins Pubs.

North, Laura. The Princess & the Frozen Peas. Dreidemy, Joelle, illus. 2014. (Tadpoles: Fairytale Twists Ser.). (ENG.). 32p. (J). (gr. 1-2). *(978-0-7787-0446-1(7))*; pap. *(978-0-7787-0481-2(5))* Crabtree Publishing Co.

Ohtaka, Shinobu, creator. Sumomomo, Momomo, Vol. 12: The Strongest Bride on Earth, 12 vols. 2012. (Sumomomo, Momomo Ser.: 12). (ENG., Illus.). 240p. (gr. 11-17). pap. 13.00 *(978-0-316-20470-5(6))* Yen Pr. LLC.

Oliver, Lauren. Requiem. 2013. (Delirium Trilogy Ser.: 3). (ENG.). 432p. (YA). (gr. 9). 18.99 *(978-0-06-201453-5(6)*, HarperCollins) HarperCollins Pubs.

Palmer, Robin. Love You Like a Sister. 2017. (Mix Ser.). (ENG., Illus.). 256p. (J). (gr. 4-8). pap. 7.99 *(978-1-4814-6642-4(9)*, Aladdin) Simon & Schuster Children's Publishing.

Paratore, Coleen Murtagh. Willa by Heart. 2008. (Wedding Planner's Daughter Ser.). (ENG.). 240p. (J). (gr. 3-7). 15.99 *(978-1-4169-4076-0(6)*, Simon & Schuster Bks. For Young Readers) Simon & Schuster Bks. For Young Readers.

—Willa by Heart. 2009. (Wedding Planner's Daughter Ser.). (ENG.). 240p. (J). (gr. 4-8). pap. 6.99 *(978-1-4169-7470-3(9)*, Aladdin) Simon & Schuster Children's Publishing.

Parish, Herman. Amelia Bedelia Chapter Book #10: Amelia Bedelia Ties the Knot. Avril, Lynne, illus. 2016. (Amelia Bedelia Ser.). (ENG.). 160p. (J). (gr. 1-5). pap. 6.99 *(978-0-06-233416-9(6)*, Greenwillow Bks.) HarperCollins Pubs.

—Amelia Bedelia Ties the Knot. 2016. (Amelia Bedelia Chapter Book Ser.: 10). (J). lib. bdg. 14.75 *(978-0-606-38762-0(5))* Turtleback.

Parker, Emma. The Wedding Day. 2010. (Illus.). 16p. pap. *(978-1-877561-51-1(7))* First Edition Ltd.

Pate, Ginger. Would You Invite a Skunk to Your Wedding? Blanski, Maribeth, illus. 2009. 32p. (J). 16.95 *(978-1-880851-73-9(3))* Greene Bark Pr., Inc.

Peck, Richard. The Best Man. 2017. (ENG.). 256p. (J). (gr. 4-7). 8.99 *(978-0-14-751579-7(3)*, Puffin Books) Penguin Young Readers Group.

Peterson, John & Slater, Teddy. The Littles Have a Happy Valentine's Day. Rogers, Jacqueline, illus. 2003. (Littles First Readers Ser.: No. 11). (ENG.). 32p. (J). (gr. k-2). pap. 3.99 *(978-0-439-42499-8(2)*, Scholastic Paperbacks) Scholastic, Inc.

Pike, Olly. The Prince & the Frog: A Story to Help Children Learn about Same-Sex Relationships. 2018. (Illus.). 48p. (J). 18.95 *(978-1-78592-382-1(X)*, 696646) Kingsley, Jessica Pubs. GBR. Dist: Hachette UK Distribution.

Porter, Eleanor H. Miss Billy - Married. 2006. pap. *(978-1-4068-3238-9(3))* Echo Library.

—Miss Billy's Decision. 2006. pap. *(978-1-4068-3240-2(5))* Echo Library.

Powell, Joyce. The Greatest Marriage Ever. Schacher, Tracey, illus. 2011. 26p. pap. 11.95 *(978-1-4575-0215-6(1))* Dog Ear Publishing, LLC.

Prosek, James. The Day My Mother Left. Prosek, James, illus. 2009. (ENG., Illus.). 304p. (J). (gr. 4-7). pap. 7.99 *(978-1-4169-0771-8(8)*, Simon & Schuster Bks. For Young Readers) Simon & Schuster Bks. For Young Readers.

Rajadel, Fernando López. False Love, True Love/Amor Falso, Amor Verdadero: The Alfambra Woman Buried Alive & the Lovers of Teruel. 2010.Tr. of Amor Falso, Amor Verdadero: La enterrada viva de Alfambra & Los amantes de Teruel. (SPA.). 164p. pap. 44.48 *(978-1-4251-8920-4(2))* Trafford Publishing.

Ray, Christie Jones & Ray, Christie Jones. Eliza Celebrates a Royal Wedding. 2012. (Illus.). 48p. pap. 15.00 *(978-0-9853223-6-6(5))* Rose Water Cottage Pr.

Reiter, David P. Bringing down the Wall. Babajanyan, Sona, illus. 2012. (ENG.). 38p. (J). pap. 18.00 *(978-1-922120-19-9(7)*, IP Kidz) Interactive Pubns. Pty. Ltd. AUS. Dist: Ingram Content Group.

Remington, Laurel. Cake & Confessions. 2019. (Secret Recipe Book Ser.: 2). (ENG.). 304p. (J). (gr. 3-7). pap. 7.99 *(978-1-4926-6967-8(9))* Sourcebooks, Inc.

Reynolds Naylor, Phyllis. I Like Him, He Likes Her: Alice Alone; Simply Alice; Patiently Alice. 2010. (Alice Ser.). (ENG.). 640p. (J). (gr. 7). pap. 12.99 *(978-1-4424-0978-1(9),* Atheneum Bks. for Young Readers) Simon & Schuster Children's Publishing.

—Including Alice. 2005. (Alice McKinley Ser.: No. 16). 277p. (J). (gr. 4-7). 13.65 *(978-0-7569-5460-4(6))* Perfection Learning Corp.

Rinaldi, Ann. Brooklyn Rose. 2006. (ENG., Illus.). 240p. (J). (gr. 5-7). reprint ed. pap. 15.95 *(978-0-15-205538-7(X),* 1196655, Clarion Bks.) HarperCollins Pubs.

Rouss, Sylvia A. Sammy Spider's First Wedding. Kahn, Katherine Janus, illus. 2019. (ENG.). 32p. (J). (gr. -1-3). 12.99 *(978-1-5124-8366-6(4),* a2b8388f-a654-45a7-b287-15c8d6352996, Kar-Ben Publishing) Lerner Publishing Group.

Rowley, Deborah Pace. My Wedding Day. Harmon, Glenn, illus. 2007. 24p. (J). (gr. -1-3). 15.99 *(978-1-59955-016-9(4))* Cedar Fort, Inc./CFI Distribution.

Roy, Jennifer. Cordially Uninvited. 2012. (ENG., Illus.). 256p. (J). (gr. 3-7). 15.99 *(978-1-4424-3920-7(3))* Simon & Schuster, Inc.

Roy, Ron. Capital Mysteries #4: a Spy in the White House. Bush, Timothy, illus. 2004. (Capital Mysteries Ser.: 4). 96p. (J). (gr. 1-4). 6.99 *(978-0-375-82557-6(6),* Random Hse. Bks. for Young Readers) Random Hse. Children's Bks.

—A Spy in the White House, 4. Bush, Timothy, tr. Bush, Timothy, illus. 2004. (Capital Mysteries Ser.: No. 4). (ENG.). 86p. (J). (gr. 2-4). lib. bdg. 17.44 *(978-0-375-92557-3(0))* Random House Publishing Group.

Rylant, Cynthia. Wedding Flowers. Halperin, Wendy Anderson, illus. 2003. (Cobble Street Cousins Ser.). 72p. (gr. 2-5). 15.00 *(978-0-7569-1476-9(0))* Perfection Learning Corp.

—Wedding Flowers. Halperin, Wendy Anderson, illus. 2003. (Cobble Street Cousins Ser.: 6). (ENG.). 80p. (J). (gr. 2-5). pap. 5.99 *(978-0-689-83418-9(7),* Aladdin) Simon & Schuster Children's Publishing.

Saint, Mimi. The Bride's Price. Wendt, Yohanna, illus. 2013. 16p. pap. 24.95 *(978-1-4241-4249-1(0))* America Star Bks.

Salerni, Dianne K. The Caged Graves. 2014. (ENG.). 336p. (YA). (gr. 7). pap. 10.99 *(978-0-544-33622-3(4),* 1584168, Clarion Bks.) HarperCollins Pubs.

Saseen, Sharon, illus. Patience & the Flower Girl. 2004. *(978-0-9748425-0-9(8))* Saseen, Sharon.

Sateren, Shelley Swanson. Mudball Molly. Melmon, Deborah, illus. 2015. (Adventures at Hound Hotel Ser.). (ENG.). 72p. (J). (gr. 1-3). lib. bdg. 25.32 *(978-1-4795-5900-8(8),* 127046, Picture Window Bks.) Capstone.

Scott, Elizabeth. Perfect You. 2008. (ENG.). 304p. (YA). (gr. 9-12). pap. 9.99 *(978-1-4169-5355-5(8),* Simon Pulse) Simon Pulse.

Shacter, Sara F. Heading to the Wedding: You're Invited to Join Patrick & Evie on the Great Adventure of Becoming (Almost) Perfect Guests. Thornton, Christine, illus. 2006. (ENG.). 32p. (J). (gr. -1-3). 18.95 *(978-1-933176-05-5(9))* Red Rock Pr., Inc.

Sheth, Kashmira. Keeping Corner. 2009. (ENG.). 304p. (J). (gr. 5-9). pap. 16.99 *(978-0-7868-3860-8(4))* Hyperion Pr.

Simmonds, Posy. Lulu & the Chocolate Wedding. 2016. (ENG., Illus.). 32p. (J). (-k). pap. 12.99 *(978-1-78344-407-6(X))* Andersen Pr. GBR. Dist: Independent Pubs. Group.

Simon, Coco. Emma: Lights! Camera! Cupcakes! 2014. (Cupcake Diaries: 19). lib. bdg. 17.20 *(978-0-606-35437-0(9))* Turtleback.

—Emma: Lights! Camera! Cupcakes! 2014. (Cupcake Diaries: 19). (ENG., Illus.). 160p. (J). (gr. 3-7). pap. 6.99 *(978-1-4424-9930-0(3),* Simon Spotlight) Simon Spotlight.

—Emma on Thin Icing. 2013. (Cupcake Diaries: 3). (ENG., Illus.). 160p. (J). (gr. 3-7). 17.99 *(978-1-4424-7492-5(0),* Simon Spotlight) Simon Spotlight.

—Emma on Thin Icing. 2011. (Cupcake Diaries: 3). lib. bdg. 17.20 *(978-0-606-23734-5(8))* Turtleback.

Slater, David Michael. Westley the Wicked & the Rascally Ring Bear. Brooks, S. G., illus. 2012. 36p. pap. 10.95 *(978-1-61413-028-4(0))* Puddletown Publishing Group, Inc.

Smith, Jennifer E. The Statistical Probability of Love at First Sight. 2013. (ENG.). 272p. (YA). (gr. 7-17). pap. 11.99 *(978-0-316-12239-9(4),* Poppy) Little, Brown Bks. for Young Readers.

Smith, Roland. Independence Hall. 2009. (I, Q Ser.: Bk. 1). (ENG., Illus.). 312p. (YA). (gr. 6-8). 15.95 *(978-1-58536-468-8(1),* 202188) Sleeping Bear Pr.

Soentpiet, Chris K. & McGill, Alice. Molly Bannaky. 2009. (ENG., Illus.). 32p. (J). (gr. -1-3). pap. 9.99 *(978-0-547-07676-8(2),* 1042032, Clarion Bks.) HarperCollins Pubs.

Springer, Nancy. Enola Holmes: the Case of the Peculiar Pink Fan. 2010. (Enola Holmes Mystery Ser.: 4). (ENG.). 192p. (J). (gr. 3-7). 7.99 *(978-0-14-241517-7(0),* Puffin Books) Penguin Young Readers Group.

Standish, Burt L. Frank Merriwell's Marriage. Rudman, Jack, ed. 2003. (Frank Merriwell Ser.). pap. 9.95 *(978-0-8373-9125-0(3))* Merriwell, Frank Inc.

Stapleton, Rhonda. Stupid Cupid. 2009. (ENG.). 272p. (YA). (gr. 7-18). pap. 9.99 *(978-1-4169-7464-2(4),* Simon Pulse) Simon Pulse.

Stead, Rebecca. The List of Things That Will Not Change. (ENG.). (J). (gr. 3-7). 2022. 240p. pap. 8.99 *(978-1-101-93812-6(9),* Yearling) 2020. 224p. 16.99 *(978-1-101-93809-6(9),* Lamb, Wendy Bks.) Random Hse. Children's Bks.

Stern, A. J. Here Comes The... Trouble! Marts, Doreen Mulryan, illus. 2012. (Frankly, Frannie Ser.: 9). 128p. (J). (gr. 1-3). pap. 6.99 *(978-0-448-45752-9(0),* Grosset & Dunlap) Penguin Young Readers Group.

—Here Comes the... Trouble!, 9. Marts, Doreen Mulryan, illus. 2012. (Frankly, Frannie Ser.: 9). (ENG.). 128p. (J). (gr. 2-5). 18.69 *(978-0-448-45753-6(9))* Penguin Young Readers Group.

Sticker Dolly Dressing Weddings (Revised) 2017. (Sticker Dolly Dressing Ser.). (ENG.). (J). pap. 9.99 *(978-0-7945-3785-2(5),* Usborne) EDC Publishing.

Stier, Catherine. Welcome to America, Champ. Ettlinger, Doris, illus. 2013. (Tales of the World Ser.). (ENG.). 32p. (J). (gr. 1-4). 17.95 *(978-1-58536-606-4(4),* 202360) Sleeping Bear Pr.

Strom, Yale. The Wedding That Saved a Town. Prosmitsky, Jenya, illus. 2008. (J). (gr. -1). 17.95 *(978-0-8225-7376-0(8),* Kar-Ben Publishing) Lerner Publishing Group.

Studio Mouse Staff. Wedding Countdown. 2008. (ENG.). 36p. (J). (gr. -1). 12.99 *(978-1-59069-740-5(5))* Studio Mouse LLC.

Suma, Nova Ren. Fade Out. 2012. (ENG.). 288p. (YA). (gr. 7). pap. 9.99 *(978-1-4169-7565-6(9),* Simon Pulse) Simon Pulse.

Surace, Joan. The Story of Lucia. Rockford, Nancy, illus. 2006. (YA). pap. 8.00 *(978-0-8059-7062-3(2))* Dorrance Publishing Co., Inc.

Sutton, Margaret. Discovery at Dragon's Mouth #31, No. 31. 2008. (Judy Bolton Ser.). (ENG., Illus.). 196p. (gr. 4-7). pap. 14.95 *(978-1-4290-9051-3(0))* Applewood Bks.

Sypolt, Carl W. Adventures of David the Honeybee. 2003. 51p. pap. 9.95 *(978-0-7414-1526-4(7))* Infinity Publishing.

Tammi, Elizabeth. Outrun the Wind. 2018. (ENG.). 304p. (YA). (gr. 9-12). pap. 11.99 *(978-1-63583-026-2(5),* 1635830265, Flux) North Star Editions.

Taylor, Chloë. Bursting at the Seams. Zhang, Nancy, illus. 2014. (Sew Zoey Ser.: 10). (ENG.). 176p. (J). (gr. 3-7). pap. 6.99 *(978-1-4814-1964-2(1),* Simon Spotlight) Simon Spotlight.

Thiel, Annie. Cosmos' Blended Family. Edwards, William M., illus. 2007. (Playdate Kids: Let's Be Friends! Ser.). 27p. (J). (gr. -1-3). per. 6.95 *(978-1-933721-23-1(5))* Playdate Kids Publishing.

Thiel Annie. Playdate Kids Cosmos' Blended Family. 2007. 32p. 12.95 *(978-1-933721-10-1(3))* Playdate Kids Publishing.

Thompson, Kay & Knight, Hilary. Eloise Ready-To-Read Value Pack: Eloise's Summer Vacation; Eloise at the Wedding; Eloise & the Very Secret Room; Eloise Visits the Zoo; Eloise Throws a Party!; Eloise's Pirate Adventure, Pack. 2012. (Eloise Ser.). (ENG.). 192p. (J). (gr. -1-1). pap. 17.96 *(978-1-4424-4949-7(7),* Simon Spotlight) Simon Spotlight.

The Three Sillies, 6, Pack. (Literatura 2000 Ser.). (gr. 2-3). 33.00 *(978-0-7635-0242-3(1))* Rigby Education.

Tolcser, Sarah. Whisper of the Tide. 2018. (ENG., Illus.). 416p. (YA). 17.99 *(978-1-68119-299-4(3),* 900165542, Bloomsbury Young Adult) Bloomsbury Publishing USA.

Tucker, Patricia Wright. The Princess Who Couldn't Laugh. 2012. 24p. pap. 24.95 *(978-1-4626-8133-4(6))* America Star Bks.

Upham, Linda. Divided Loyalties. Littlejohn, Anna, illus. 2007. 188p. per. *(978-0-7552-0302-4(X))* Authors OnLine, Ltd.

Van Draanen, Wendelin. Sammy Keyes & the Wedding Crasher. 2011. (Sammy Keyes Ser.: 13). (ENG.). 320p. (J). (gr. 5). 8.99 *(978-0-375-85456-9(8),* Yearling) Random Hse. Children's Bks.

Venkatraman, Padma. Climbing the Stairs. 2010. (ENG., Illus.). 254p. (YA). (gr. 7-18). 10.99 *(978-0-14-241490-3(5),* Speak) Penguin Young Readers Group.

Vorster, Nicola. A Monkeys' Wedding. 2012. (Illus.). 24p. pap. 21.35 *(978-1-4772-3126-5(9))* AuthorHouse.

Wakeman, Lars. Prince Harry the Hairy Prince: A hairy fairy Tale. 2011. 24p. (gr. -1). pap. 12.56 *(978-1-4269-6304-9(1))* Trafford Publishing.

The Wedding of the Mouse: An Asian Folktale. 2006. (J). 17.95 *(978-0-9790033-0-1(X))* Playground Pr.

West, Kathryn E. Garden of Roses. 2007. 328p. per. 19.95 *(978-0-595-45295-8(7))* iUniverse, Inc.

Westaway, Kylie. Why Can't I Be a Dinosaur? Jellett, Tom, illus. 2017. (ENG.). 32p. (J). (gr. -1-k). 19.99 *(978-1-76029-472-4(1),* A&U Children's) Allen & Unwin AUS. Dist: Independent Pubs. Group.

Wojciechowski, Susan. Beany & the Dreaded Wedding. Natti, Susanna, illus. 2005. (Beany Adventures Ser.). 121p. (J). 13.65 *(978-0-7569-6498-6(9))* Perfection Learning Corp.

Zalben, Jane Breskin. Brenda Berman, Wedding Expert. Chess, Victoria, illus. 2009. (ENG.). 48p. (J). (gr. 1-4). 16.00 *(978-0-618-31321-1(4),* 111298, Clarion Bks.) HarperCollins Pubs.

Zepeda, Gwendolyn. Maya & Annie on Saturdays & Sundays: Los Sábados y Domingos de Maya y Annie. 2018. (ENG & SPA., Illus.). 32p. (J). (gr. 1-4). 17.95 *(978-1-55885-859-6(8))* Arte Publico Pr.

MARRIAGE, INTERRACIAL

see Interracial Marriage

MARRIAGE, MIXED

see Intermarriage

MARRIAGE CUSTOMS AND RITES

Dawson, Emily C. Weddings Around the World. 2010. (Special Days Ser.). (ENG.). 24p. (J). (gr. k-2). lib. bdg. 25.65 *(978-1-60753-031-2(7),* 17191) Amicus.

Hook, Jacqueline A. You're Going to Be a Ring Bearer. 2005. (J). per. *(978-0-9664783-4-1(7))* Jacqueline Beverly Hills.

Keyser, Amber J. Tying the Knot: A World History of Marriage. 2018. (ENG., Illus.). 104p. (YA). (gr. 6-12). 35.99 *(978-1-4677-9242-4(X),* d59dcc18-2fb0-4049-97c3-d510f78b4e36, Twenty-First Century Bks.) Lerner Publishing Group.

Mattox, Brenda Sneathen. Wedding Traditions from Around the World Coloring Book. 2007. (Dover Fashion Coloring Book Ser.). (ENG., Illus.). 32p. (J). (gr. 3-5). 3.99 *(978-0-486-46232-5(3),* 462323) Dover Pubns., Inc.

World Book, Inc. Staff, contrib. by. Marriage Celebrations. 2003. (World Book's Celebrations & Rituals Around the World Ser.). (Illus.). 46p. (J). *(978-0-7166-5012-6(6))* World Bk., Inc.

MARRIAGE CUSTOMS AND RITES—FICTION

Herman, Gail. Flower Girl. Billin-Frye, Paige, illus. 2012. (Penguin Young Readers: Level 3 Ser.: Level 2). (ENG.). 48p. (J). (gr. 1-3). 16.19 *(978-0-448-41108-8(3))* Penguin Young Readers Group.

O'Connor, Jane. Fancy Nancy & the Wedding of the Century. Glasser, Robin Preiss, illus. 2014. (Fancy Nancy Ser.). (ENG.). 32p. (J). (gr. -1-3). 19.99 *(978-0-06-208319-7(8));* lib. bdg. 18.89 *(978-0-06-208320-3(1))* HarperCollins Pubs. (HarperCollins).

Staples, Suzanne Fisher. Shabanu: Daughter of the Wind. 3rd ed. (J). pap. 3.99 *(978-0-13-800053-0(0))* Prentice Hall (Schl. Div.).

Thorpe, Kiki. Never Girls #5: Wedding Wings (Disney: the Never Girls) Christy, Jana, illus. 2014. (Never Girls Ser.: 5). (ENG.). 128p. (J). (gr. 1-4). 6.99 *(978-0-7364-3077-7(6),* RH/Disney) Random Hse. Children's Bks.

—Wedding Wings. 2014. (Never Girls Ser.: 5). lib. bdg. 16.00 *(978-0-606-35544-5(8))* Turtleback.

MARS (PLANET)

Adamson, Thomas K. Do You Really Want to Visit Mars? Fabbri, Daniele, illus. 2013. (Do You Really Want to Visit the Solar System? Ser.). (ENG.). 24p. (J). (gr. 1-4). 27.10 *(978-1-60753-198-2(4),* 16265) Amicus.

—Mars [Scholastic]: Revised Edition. 2010. (Exploring the Galaxy Ser.). (ENG.). 24p. pap. 0.49 *(978-1-4296-5811-9(8),* Capstone Pr.) Capstone.

Allan, John. Journey to Mars. 2019. (Math Adventures (Step 1) Ser.). (ENG., Illus.). 32p. (J). (gr. 1-3). lib. bdg. 29.32 *(978-1-912108-23-7(2),* ff5cfee6-9b6a-4353-b54c-fa4a04ca2719, Hungry Tomato (r)) Lerner Publishing Group.

Allien Cave Explorers: Meet NASA Inventor William "Red" Whittaker & His Team's. 2017. (J). *(978-0-7166-6163-4(2))* World Bk., Inc.

Anderson, Rane. Stem: Mission to Mars: Problem Solving (Grade 3) 2017. (Mathematics in the Real World Ser.). (ENG., Illus.). 32p. (J). (gr. 3-4). pap. 11.99 *(978-1-4807-5801-8(9))* Teacher Created Materials, Inc.

Arnold, Quinn M. Mars. 2018. (Graines de Savoir Ser.). (Illus.). 24p. (J). (FRE.). *(978-1-77092-407-9(8),* 19696); (ENG., (gr. -1-k). *(978-1-60818-915-1(5),* 19609, Creative Education); (ENG., (gr. -1-k). pap. 8.99 *(978-1-62832-531-7(3),* 19607, Creative Paperbacks) Creative Co., The.

Baker, David. Inside the Mars Rover, 1 vol. 2017. (Geek's Guide to Space Ser.). (ENG., Illus.). 192p. (J). (gr. 9-9). 46.27 *(978-1-4994-6700-0(1),* d3176c4b-251c-4d08-86a6-0b764dfce75d, Rosen Young Adult) Rosen Publishing Group, Inc., The.

Baker, David & Kissock, Heather. Journey to Mars. (Illus.). 32p. (J). 2016. *(978-1-4896-5827-2(0),* AV2 by Weigl) 2009. (gr. 2-4). pap. 9.95 *(978-1-60596-030-2(6))* 2009. (gr. 2-4). lib. bdg. 26.00 *(978-1-60596-029-6(2))* Weigl Pubs., Inc.

Bellisario, Gina. To Mars! Moran, Mike, illus. 2017. (Cloverleaf Books (tm) — Space Adventures Ser.). (ENG.). 24p. (J). (gr. k-2). 25.32 *(978-1-5124-2539-0(7),* df57e8ce-22db-41b2-9a4c-913f1808335c); E-Book 38.65 *(978-1-5124-2832-2(9));* E-Book 4.99 *(978-1-5124-3888-8(X),* 9781512438888); E-Book 38.65 *(978-1-5124-3887-1(1),* 9781512438871) Lerner Publishing Group. (Millbrook Pr.).

Berger, Melvin & Carson, Mary Kay. Discovering Mars: The Amazing Story of the Red Planet. 2015. lib. bdg. 16.00 *(978-0-606-37755-3(7))* Turtleback.

—Discovering Mars: the Amazing Story of the Red Planet. Holub, Joan, illus. 2015. (ENG.). 64p. (J). (gr. 2-5). pap. 5.99 *(978-0-545-83960-0(2),* Scholastic Nonfiction) Scholastic, Inc.

Beth, Georgia. Discover Mars. 2018. (Searchlight Books (tm) — Discover Planets Ser.). (ENG., Illus.). 32p. (J). (gr. 3-5). 30.65 *(978-1-5415-2338-8(5),* a8fb55ab-660d-4ca4-929b-52a7a41ef766, Lerner Pubns.) Lerner Publishing Group.

Bloom, J. P. Mars, 1 vol. 2015. (Planets Ser.). (ENG., Illus.). 24p. (J). (gr. -1-2). lib. bdg. 32.79 *(978-1-62970-717-4(1),* 17233, Abdo Kids) ABDO Publishing Co.

—Mars. 2017. (Planets Ser.). (ENG.). 24p. (J). (gr. -1-2). pap. 7.95 *(978-1-4966-1282-3(5),* 135014, Capstone Classroom) Capstone.

—Marte (Mars), 1 vol. 2016. (Planetas (Planets) Ser.). (SPA., Illus.). 24p. (J). (gr. -1-2). lib. bdg. 32.79 *(978-1-68080-754-7(4),* 22670, Abdo Kids) ABDO Publishing Co.

Bridges, Andrew. The Inside Story of Mars. 2006. (J). 7.80 *(978-0-9753920-8-9(5))* Sally Ride Science.

Capaccio, George. Mars, 1 vol. 2010. (Space! Ser.). (ENG.). 64p. (gr. 5-5). lib. bdg. 35.50 *(978-0-7614-4247-9(2),* 67891272-d4ac-40cc-af7f-6b78d9b98751) Cavendish Square Publishing LLC.

Capstone Classroom & Stead, Tony. I'm Moving to Mars! 2017. (What's the Point? Reading & Writing Expository Text Ser.). (ENG., Illus.). 32p. (J). (gr. 5-5). pap. 7.95 *(978-1-4966-0734-8(1),* 132369, Capstone Classroom) Capstone.

Carney, Elizabeth. National Geographic Kids: Mars: The Red Planet. 2016. (Illus.). 32p. (J). (gr. 1-3). pap. 7.99 *(978-1-4263-2754-4(4),* National Geographic Kids) Disney Publishing Worldwide.

—National Geographic Readers: Mars. 2014. (Readers Ser.). (Illus.). 48p. (J). (gr. 1-3). pap. 4.99 *(978-1-4263-1747-7(6),* National Geographic Kids) Disney Publishing Worldwide.

Carson, Mary Kay. Far-Out Guide to Mars, 1 vol. 2010. (Far-Out Guide to the Solar System Ser.). (ENG.). 48p. (gr. 4-6). 27.93 *(978-0-7660-3183-8(7),* 7d349ac4-2183-49c2-8f16-66babd497cf1); (Illus.). pap. 11.53 *(978-1-59845-185-6(5),* 66d79d97-21a4-4979-a50c-96e67ab5898c, Enslow Elementary) Enslow Publishing, LLC.

—Mission to Mars. 2018. (Beyond Planet Earth Ser.). (Illus.). 32p. (J). (gr. 1). 16.95 *(978-1-4549-2351-0(2))* Sterling Publishing Co., Inc.

Chrismer, Melanie. Mars. 2007. (Scholastic News Nonfiction Readers Ser.). (ENG., Illus.). 24p. (J). (gr. 1-2). 22.00 *(978-0-531-14697-2(9))* Scholastic Library Publishing.

Christopher, Nick. Exploring Mars. 2017. (Journey Through Our Solar System Ser.). 24p. (gr. 1-2). 49.50 *(978-1-5345-2255-8(7),* KidHaven Publishing); (ENG.). pap. 9.25 *(978-1-5345-2286-2(7),* ff4635fd-000c-4409-9360-1bb29d65bc51); (ENG.). lib. bdg. 26.23 *(978-1-5345-2270-1(0),* cc35390c-fdfe-4489-9c72-8ae0e53d241c) Greenhaven Publishing LLC.

Cobb, Allan B. Mars. (Library of Planets Ser.). 48p. (gr. 5-8). 2009. 55.90 *(978-1-60853-817-1(6),* Rosen Reference) 2004. (ENG., Illus.). (J). lib. bdg. 34.47 *(978-1-4042-0169-9(6),* 4b97d94a-2700-4e2a-8e5a-3d600cd3c291) Rosen Publishing Group, Inc., The.

Collins, Ailynn. Mars or Bust! Orion & the Mission to Deep Space. 2019. (Future Space Ser.). (ENG., Illus.). 32p. (J). (gr. 3-9). pap. 7.95 *(978-1-5435-7514-9(5),* 141045); lib. bdg. 28.65 *(978-1-5435-7268-1(5),* 140599) Capstone.

Coming Soon. Mars. 2018. (Eyediscover Ser.). (ENG., Illus.). 24p. (J). (gr. k-2). 28.55 *(978-1-4896-8009-9(8),* AV2 by Weigl) Weigl Pubs., Inc.

Cornell, Karl. Mars Science Lab Engineer Diana Trujillo. 2016. (STEM Trailblazer Bios Ser.). (ENG., Illus.). 32p. (J). (gr. 2-5). pap. 8.99 *(978-1-4677-9721-4(9),* a151d2de-059c-425b-9844-3dfc69db621c) Lerner Publishing Group.

Cutting, Robert. Mars Colony. Jeevan, Dhamindra, illus. 2007. 48p. (J). lib. bdg. 23.08 *(978-1-4242-1630-7(3))* Fitzgerald Bks.

Dickmann, Nancy. Exploring the Inner Planets, 1 vol. 2015. (Spectacular Space Science Ser.). (ENG., Illus.). 48p. (J). (gr. 5-6). 33.47 *(978-1-4994-3629-7(7),* ab513eb5-c984-4eb0-b82d-98012308a5f4, Rosen Central) Rosen Publishing Group, Inc., The.

Doyle, Bill. The Space Explorer's Guide to Mars — in 3-D! 2004. (Space University Ser.). (Illus.). 47p. (J). *(978-0-439-55748-1(8))* Scholastic, Inc.

Dunn, Mary R. A Look at Mars. 2009. (Astronomy Now! Ser.). 24p. (gr. 2-3). 42.50 *(978-1-61511-469-6(6),* PowerKids Pr.) Rosen Publishing Group, Inc., The.

Goldstein, Margaret J. Mars. 2005. (Pull Ahead Bks.). (Illus.). 32p. (gr. 2-4). lib. bdg. 22.60 *(978-0-8225-4651-1(5))* Lerner Publishing Group.

Gruber, Lorin. Journey to Mars. 32p. (J). 2015. (Illus.). *(978-1-4898-5169-7(0))* 2014. (ENG.). (gr. 5-5). pap. 12.75 *(978-1-4994-0371-8(2),* 011b8071-024b-42a0-8dbb-4347e318378d, PowerKids Pr.) Rosen Publishing Group, Inc., The.

Hamilton, John. Curiosity Rover: Searching for Life on Mars. 2017. (Xtreme Spacecraft Ser.). (ENG., Illus.). 32p. (J). (gr. 3-9). lib. bdg. 32.79 *(978-1-5321-1009-2(X),* 25594, Abdo & Daughters) ABDO Publishing Co.

—Humans to Mars. 2018. (Mission to Mars Ser.). (ENG., Illus.). 48p. (J). (gr. 5-9). lib. bdg. 34.21 *(978-1-5321-1592-9(X),* 28760, Abdo & Daughters) ABDO Publishing Co.

—Mars: The Red Planet. 2018. (Mission to Mars Ser.). (ENG., Illus.). 48p. (J). (gr. 5-9). lib. bdg. 34.21 *(978-1-5321-1597-4(0),* 28770, Abdo & Daughters) ABDO Publishing Co.

—Mars Landers. 2018. (Mission to Mars Ser.). (ENG.). 48p. (J). (gr. 5-9). lib. bdg. 34.21 *(978-1-5321-1593-6(8),* 28762, Abdo & Daughters) ABDO Publishing Co.

—Mars Myths & Legends. 2018. (Mission to Mars Ser.). (ENG., Illus.). 48p. (J). (gr. 5-9). lib. bdg. 34.21 *(978-1-5321-1594-3(6),* 28764, Abdo & Daughters) ABDO Publishing Co.

Hawksett, David. Living on Mars: Can You Colonize a Planet?, 1 vol. 2017. (Be a Space Scientist! Ser.). (ENG.). 48p. (J). (gr. 5-6). 31.93 *(978-1-5383-2205-5(6),* 364ab89d-04a4-4a62-92d7-407629468fc4); pap. 12.75 *(978-1-5383-2298-7(6),* cba58767-1d72-4f5d-9fe0-28747d343e18) Rosen Publishing Group, Inc., The. (PowerKids Pr.).

Hirsch, Rebecca E. Mysteries of Mars. 2020. (Searchlight Books (tm) — Space Mysteries Ser.). (ENG., Illus.). 32p. (J). (gr. 3-5). 30.65 *(978-1-5415-9736-5(2),* d9ca6a02-f520-4fec-a7f0-ff404c5e922b, Lerner Pubns.) Lerner Publishing Group.

Hollar, Sherman. The Inner Planets: Mercury, Venus, & Mars, 1 vol. 2011. (Solar System Ser.). (ENG., Illus.). 96p. (J). (gr. 8-8). 35.29 *(978-1-61530-512-4(2),* d524e35f-a616-40a6-a97b-953a5b929220) Rosen Publishing Group, Inc., The.

James, Lincoln. Mars, 1 vol. 2010. (Our Solar System Ser.). (ENG.). 24p. (J). (gr. k-2). pap. 9.15 *(978-1-4339-3825-2(1),* 95a5137e-648d-4cfa-9968-42709ad05eab); (Illus.). lib. bdg. 25.27 *(978-1-4339-3824-5(3),* 916a509c-d805-4302-bf5f-91e3b88fe74b) Stevens, Gareth Publishing LLLP.

Jefferis, David. Mars: Distant Red Planet. 2008. (Exploring Our Solar System Ser.). (ENG., Illus.). 32p. (J). (gr. 3-7). pap. *(978-0-7787-3748-3(9))* Crabtree Publishing Co.

Jefferis, David & Irvine, Mat. Exploring Planet Mars. 2007. (Humans in Space Ser.). (ENG., Illus.). 32p. (J). (gr. 4-7). lib. bdg. *(978-0-7787-3100-9(6));* pap. *(978-0-7787-3114-6(6))* Crabtree Publishing Co.

Kenney, Karen Latchana. Cutting-Edge Journey to Mars. 2019. (Searchlight Books (tm) — New Frontiers of Space Ser.). (ENG., Illus.). 32p. (J). (gr. 3-5). pap. 9.99 *(978-1-5415-7485-4(0),* b8ec822a-c817-4ca7-91e2-00d114dfacf1); lib. bdg. 30.65 *(978-1-5415-5745-1(X),* 307656cb-9ae5-40cd-b8fa-e8d4b19b269e) Lerner Publishing Group. (Lerner Pubns.).

Khan, Hena & Borgenicht, David. Mars: You Decide How to Survive! 2015. (Worst-Case Scenario Ultimate Adventure Ser.). (ENG., Illus.). 204p. (J). (gr. 3-8). 47.10 *(978-1-59920-979-1(9),* 19402, Smart Apple Media) Black Rabbit Bks.

Kortenkamp, Steve. Mars Exploration Rovers: An Interactive Space Exploration Adventure. 2016. (You Choose: Space Ser.). (ENG., Illus.). 112p. (J). (gr. 3-7). lib. bdg. 32.65 *(978-1-4914-8106-6(4),* 130589, Capstone Pr.) Capstone.

Lendroth, Susan. Hey-Ho, to Mars We'll Go! A Space-Age Version of the Farmer in the Dell. Kolar, Bob, illus. 40p. (J). (gr. -1-3). 2019. pap. 8.99 *(978-1-62354-100-2(X))* 2018. 16.99 *(978-1-58089-744-0(4))* Charlesbridge Publishing, Inc.

Lomberg, Michelle. Mars. (J). 2013. 27.13 *(978-1-62127-265-6(6))* 2013. pap. 12.95 *(978-1-62127-274-8(5))* 2004. (Illus.). pap. 8.95 *(978-1-59036-226-6(8))* 2004. (Illus.). 24p. (gr. 4-7). lib. bdg. 24.45 *(978-1-59036-099-6(0))* Weigl Pubs., Inc.

Lomberg, Michelle & Willis, John. Mars. 2016. (Illus.). 24p. (J). *(978-1-5105-0977-1(1))* SmartBook Media, Inc.

MacCarald, Clara. Colonizing Mars. 2019. (Science for the Future Ser.). (ENG., Illus.). 48p. (J). (gr. 5-6). pap. 11.95 *(978-1-64185-847-2(8),* 1641858478); lib. bdg. 34.21 *(978-1-64185-778-9(1),* 1641857781) North Star Editions. (Focus Readers).

MNO

—How Did Robots Land on Mars? 2018. (How'd They Do That? Ser.). (ENG., Illus.). 32p. (J). (gr. 4-6). lib. bdg. 28.65 *(978-1-5435-4136-6(4)*, 139090, Capstone Pr.) Capstone.
Mahoney, Emily. How Will People Travel to Mars?, 1 vol. 2018. (Space Mysteries Ser.). (ENG.). 32p. (gr. 2-3). 29.27 *(978-1-5382-1951-5(4)*, ed057ffc-398c-4986-abc7-31accd2388bf) Stevens, Gareth Publishing LLLP.
Markovics, Joyce. Marte: Rocas y Polvo Rojos. 2015. (Fuera de Este Mundo Ser.). (SPA., Illus.). 24p. (J). (gr. -1-3). lib. bdg. 26.99 *(978-1-62724-591-3(X))* Bearport Publishing Co., Inc.
Markovics, Joyce L. Mars: Red Rocks & Dust. 2015. (Out of This World Ser.). (ENG.). 24p. (J). (gr. -1-3). lib. bdg. 23.93 *(978-1-62724-564-7(2))* Bearport Publishing Co., Inc.
Miller, Ron. Curiosity's Mission on Mars: Exploring the Red Planet. 2014. (ENG., Illus.). 64p. (YA). (gr. 6-12). lib. bdg. 33.32 *(978-1-4677-1087-9(3)*, 8419b4eb-818c-4707-bc6e-2594a790ff60, Twenty-First Century Bks.) Lerner Publishing Group.
—Mars. 2006. (Worlds Beyond Ser.). (Illus.). 96p. (YA). (gr. 5-9). 27.93 *(978-0-7613-2362-4(7))* Lerner Publishing Group.
Morey, Allan. Mars Rovers. 2017. (Space Tech Ser.). (ENG., Illus.). 24p. (J). (gr. 3-7). lib. bdg. 26.95 *(978-1-62617-703-1(1)*, Epic Bks.) Bellwether Media.
Motum, Markus. Curiosity: the Story of a Mars Rover. Motum, Markus, illus. 2018. (ENG., Illus.). 56p. (J). (gr. 3-7). 22.99 *(978-0-7636-9504-0(1))* Candlewick Pr.
O'Brien, Patrick. You Are the First Kid on Mars. O'Brien, Patrick, illus. 2009. (Illus.). 32p. (J). (gr. k-3). 17.99 *(978-0-399-24634-0(7)*, G.P. Putnam's Sons Books for Young Readers) Penguin Young Readers Group.
Orme, Helen & Orme, David. Let's Explore Mars, 1 vol. 2007. (Space Launch! Ser.). (ENG., Illus.). 24p. (gr. 2-4). lib. bdg. 25.67 *(978-0-8368-7941-4(4)*, 78382eb2-0ac4-4b98-b24d-08a15981dc25, Gareth Stevens Learning Library) Stevens, Gareth Publishing LLLP.
Owen, Ruth. Mars, 1 vol. 2013. (Explore Outer Space Ser.). (ENG.). 32p. (J). (gr. 2-3). pap. 11.00 *(978-1-61533-767-5(9)*, 848e0ecd-0269-45c3-a97b-61d922cea715); lib. bdg. 29.93 *(978-1-61533-725-5(3)*, 427e476e-5d18-4262-b9ff-3ca1333b5f79) Rosen Publishing Group, Inc., The. (Windmill Bks.).
—Mars. 2013. (Explore Outer Space Ser.). 32p. (J). (gr. 3-6). pap. 60.00 *(978-1-61533-768-2(7))* Windmill Bks.
Oxlade, Chris. Mercury, Mars, & Other Inner Planets, 1 vol. 2007. (Earth & Space Ser.). (ENG., Illus.). 48p. (YA). (gr. 6-6). lib. bdg. 34.47 *(978-1-4042-3735-3(6)*, 69b00a7b-f6f7-4e68-a243-b4d1bb8e955a) Rosen Publishing Group, Inc., The.
Portman, Michael. Is There Life on Mars?, 1 vol. 2013. (Space Mysteries Ser.). (ENG., Illus.). 32p. (J). (gr. 2-3). 29.27 *(978-1-4339-8272-9(2)*, e5c1ea31-d67a-4dd0-a633-ad634732257e); pap. 11.50 *(978-1-4339-8273-6(0)*, a4e69fe5-ed91-4867-84dc-426bca60476b) Stevens, Gareth Publishing LLLP. (Gareth Stevens Learning Library).
Radomski, Kassandra. The Secrets of Mars. 2015. (Planets Ser.). (ENG., Illus.). 32p. (J). (gr. 2-4). lib. bdg. 32.65 *(978-1-4914-5865-5(8)*, 128828) Capstone.
Romero, Libby. Discover Mars & Venus. 2006. (J). pap. *(978-1-4108-6507-6(X))* Benchmark Education Co.
—Mars & Venus. 2006. (J). pap. *(978-1-4108-6504-5(5))* Benchmark Education Co.
Roumanis, Alexis. Mars. 2016. (J). *(978-1-5105-2049-3(X))* SmartBook Media, Inc.
—Mars. 2015. (J). *(978-1-4896-3288-3(3))* Weigl Pubs., Inc.
Rusch, Elizabeth. The Mighty Mars Rovers: The Incredible Adventures of Spirit & Opportunity. (Scientists in the Field Ser.). (ENG., Illus.). 80p. (J). (gr. 5-7). 2017. pap. 11.99 *(978-0-544-93246-3(3)*, 1657955) 2012. 18.99 *(978-0-547-47881-4(X)*, 1439105) HarperCollins Pubs. (Clarion Bks.).
—The Mighty Mars Rovers: The Incredible Adventures of Spirit & Opportunity. 2017. (Scientists in the Field Ser.). (ENG.). (J). (gr. 5-7). lib. bdg. 20.85 *(978-0-606-39812-1(0))* Turtleback.
Scott, Elaine. Mars & the Search for Life. 2008. (ENG., Illus.). 64p. (J). (gr. 5-7). 17.00 *(978-0-618-76695-6(2)*, 100538, Clarion Bks.) HarperCollins Pubs.
Silverman, Buffy. Mars Missions: A Space Discovery Guide. 2017. (Space Discovery Guides). (ENG., Illus.). 48p. (J). (gr. 4-6). 31.99 *(978-1-5124-2585-7(0)*, 72b2d712-8724-4432-84d7-5be2d3aacef4); E-Book 47.99 *(978-1-5124-2795-0(0))*; E-Book 47.99 *(978-1-5124-3810-9(3)*, 9781512438109); E-Book 4.99 *(978-1-5124-3809-3(X)*, 9781512438093) Lerner Publishing Group. (Lerner Pubns.).
Simon, Charnan. Mars. 2011. (21st Century Junior Library: Solar System Ser.). (ENG., Illus.). 24p. (J). (gr. 2-5). lib. bdg. 29.21 *(978-1-61080-082-2(6)*, 201074) Cherry Lake Publishing.
Simon, Seymour. Destination: Mars. 2016. (ENG.). 32p. (J). (gr. 1-5). 17.20 *(978-0-606-39251-8(3))* Turtleback.
Siy, Alexandra. Cars on Mars: Roving the Red Planet. 2011. (Illus.). 64p. (J). (gr. 3-7). pap. 9.95 *(978-1-57091-463-8(X))* Charlesbridge Publishing, Inc.
Smith-Llera, Danielle. Mars Rover: How a Self-Portrait Captured the Power of Curiosity. 2017. (Captured Science History Ser.). (ENG., Illus.). 64p. (J). (gr. 5-9). lib. bdg. 35.32 *(978-0-7565-5641-9(4)*, 136081, Compass Point Bks.) Capstone.
Sommer, Nathan. Mars. 2019. (Space Science Ser.). (ENG., Illus.). 24p. (J). (gr. 3-7). lib. bdg. 26.95 *(978-1-62617-973-8(5)*, Torque Bks.) Bellwether Media.
Sparrow, Giles. Destination Mars, 1 vol. 2009. (Destination Solar System Ser.). (ENG., Illus.). 32p. (J). (gr. 3-4). pap. 11.00 *(978-1-4358-3459-0(3)*, fbad798e-9438-4b98-8603-3bfdce8eb4c9); lib. bdg. 28.93 *(978-1-4358-3443-9(7)*, d68da343-bd95-4d14-b8cb-7ebaddfd7ed1) Rosen Publishing Group, Inc., The. (PowerKids Pr.).
Squire, Ann O. Planet Mars. 2014. (True Book — Space (Revised Edition) Ser.). (ENG.). 48p. (J). lib. bdg. 29.00 *(978-0-531-21152-6(5))* Scholastic Library Publishing.
Steinkraus, Kyla. Planetas Rocosos - Mercurio, Venus, la Tierra y Marte. 2017. (Inside Outer Space Ser.). Tr. of Rocky Planets - Mercury, Venus, Earth, & Mars. (SPA.). 24p. (gr. k-3). pap. 9.95 *(978-1-68342-262-4(7)*, 9781683422624) Rourke Educational Media.
Storad, Conrad J. Mars. 2009. (Early Bird Astronomy Ser.). (ENG.). 48p. (gr. 2-5). lib. bdg. 26.60 *(978-0-7613-4152-9(8))*; (Illus.). pap. 8.95 *(978-0-7613-4980-8(4)*, Lerner Pubns.) Lerner Publishing Group.
Sumners, Carolyn T. & Handron, Kerry. An Earthling's Guide to Mars: Travel to Mars with Pathfinder. 2003. (Illus.). 138p. (YA). (gr. 4-7). pap. 12.95 *(978-0-07-069635-8(7))* McGraw-Hill Trade.
Teitelbaum, Michael. Mars & Venus Space Exploration: Set Of 6. 2011. (Navigators Ser.). (J). pap. 50.00 net. *(978-1-4108-6243-3(7))* Benchmark Education Co.
Vogt, Gregory. Missions to Mars. 2018. (Illus.). 48p. (J). pap. *(978-1-4896-9818-6(3)*, AV2 by Weigl) Weigl Pubs., Inc.
Vogt, Gregory L. Missions to Mars. 2018. (Destination Space Ser.). (ENG., Illus.). 48p. (J). (gr. 5-6). pap. 11.95 *(978-1-63517-568-4(2)*, 1635175682); lib. bdg. 34.21 *(978-1-63517-496-0(1)*, 1635174961) North Star Editions. (Focus Readers).
Wimmer, Teresa. Mars. 2007. (My First Look at: Planets Ser.). (Illus.). 24p. (J). (gr. -1-3). lib. bdg. 24.25 *(978-1-58341-518-4(1)*, Creative Education) Creative Co., The.
Wittenberg, John C. The Amazing Adventures of Spirit & Opportunity. 2004. (Illus.). 20p. *(978-0-9705150-1-8(4))* Aerospace 1 Pubns.
World Book, Inc. Staff, contrib. by. Mars. (J). 2010. *(978-0-7166-9536-3(7))* 2nd ed. 2006. (Illus.). 64p. *(978-0-7166-9516-5(2))* World Bk., Inc.
Zobel, Derek. Mars. 2010. (Exploring Space Ser.). (ENG., Illus.). 24p. (J). (gr. k-3). lib. bdg. 26.95 *(978-1-60014-405-9(5)*, Blastoff! Readers) Bellwether Media.

MARS (PLANET)—FICTION

Adams, John Joseph, ed. Under the Moons of Mars: New Adventures on Barsoom. (ENG., Illus.). 368p. (YA). (gr. 7). 2013. pap. 9.99 *(978-1-4424-2030-4(8))* 2012. 16.99 *(978-1-4424-2029-8(4))* Simon & Schuster Bks. For Young Readers. (Simon & Schuster Bks. For Young Readers).
Agee, Jon. Life on Mars. 2017. (ENG., Illus.). 32p. (J). (gr. -1-3). 18.99 *(978-0-399-53852-0(6)*, Dial Bks) Penguin Young Readers Group.
Barrett, Judith. Cloudy with a Chance of Meatballs 3: Planet of the Pies. Mones, Isidre, illus. 2013. (ENG.). 32p. (J). (gr. -1-3). 18.99 *(978-1-4424-9027-7(6)*, Atheneum Bks. for Young Readers) Simon & Schuster Children's Publishing.
Bean, Raymond. The Curse of Mars. Vimislik, Matthew, illus. 2016. (Out of This World Ser.). (ENG.). 112p. (J). (gr. 2-5). lib. bdg. 32.65 *(978-1-4965-3615-0(0)*, 132831, Stone Arch Bks.) Capstone.
Bennett, Jeffrey. Max Goes to Mars: A Science Adventure with Max the Dog. Okamoto, Alan, illus. 2015. (Science Adventures with Max the Dog Ser.). (ENG.). 32p. (J). (gr. 2-4). 15.00 *(978-1-937548-44-5(9))* Big Kid Science.
Bily, Ro. My Red Island in the Sky. 2012. 530p. 34.95 *(978-1-4626-6645-4(0))*; pap. 34.95 *(978-1-4626-6971-4(9))* America Star Bks.
Brockington, Drew. CatStronauts: Race to Mars. 2017. (CatStronauts Ser.: 2). (J). lib. bdg. 18.40 *(978-0-606-39901-2(1))* Turtleback.
Brouwer, Sigmund. Death Trap. 2009. (Robot Wars Ser.: 1). (ENG.). 288p. (J). pap. 7.99 *(978-1-4143-2309-1(3)*, 4601299, Tyndale Kids) Tyndale Hse. Pubs.
Burroughs, Edgar Rice. Mars Trilogy: A Princess of Mars; the Gods of Mars; the Warlord of Mars. Fischer, Scott M. et al, illus. 2012. (ENG.). 704p. (gr. 7). pap. 18.99 *(978-1-4424-2387-9(0)*, Simon & Schuster Bks. For Young Readers) Simon & Schuster Bks. For Young Readers.
Cahill, Byron. Space Pox. 2005. (J). pap. *(978-1-4108-4220-6(7))* Benchmark Education Co.
Catlow, Nikalas & Wesson, Tim. Mega Mash-Up: Romans vs. Dinosaurs on Mars. Catlow, Nikalas & Wesson, Tim, illus. 2011. (Mega Mash-Up Ser.: 3). (ENG., Illus.). 96p. (J). (gr. 2-5). pap. 6.99 *(978-0-7636-5872-4(3))* Candlewick Pr.
Collins, A. L. Asylum: Refugees of Mars. Tikulin, Tomislav, illus. 2018. (Redworld Ser.). (ENG.). 128p. (J). (gr. 3-8). lib. bdg. 25.99 *(978-1-4965-5886-2(3)*, 137024, Stone Arch Bks.) Capstone.
—Homestead: A New Life on Mars. Tikulin, Tomislav, illus. 2017. (Redworld Ser.). (ENG.). 128p. (J). (gr. 3-8). lib. bdg. 25.99 *(978-1-4965-4819-1(1)*, 135341, Stone Arch Bks.) Capstone.
—Legacy: Relics of Mars. Tikulin, Tomislav, illus. 2017. (Redworld Ser.). (ENG.). 128p. (J). (gr. 3-8). lib. bdg. 25.99 *(978-1-4965-4822-1(1)*, 135344, Stone Arch Bks.) Capstone.
—Outcry: Defenders of Mars. Tikulin, Tomislav, illus. 2018. (Redworld Ser.). (ENG.). 128p. (J). (gr. 3-8). lib. bdg. 25.99 *(978-1-4965-5887-9(1)*, 137025, Stone Arch Bks.) Capstone.
—Raiders: Water Thieves of Mars. Tikulin, Tomislav, illus. 2017. (Redworld Ser.). (ENG.). 128p. (J). (gr. 3-8). lib. bdg. 25.99 *(978-1-4965-4820-7(5)*, 135342, Stone Arch Bks.) Capstone.
—Redworld: Year One. Tikulin, Tomislav, illus. 2018. (Redworld Ser.). (ENG.). 320p. (J). (gr. 3-8). pap., pap., pap. 8.95 *(978-1-62370-986-0(5)*, 137317, Capstone Young Readers) Capstone.
—Tharsis City: The Wonder of Mars. Tikulin, Tomislav, illus. 2017. (Redworld Ser.). (ENG.). 128p. (J). (gr. 3-8). lib. bdg. 25.99 *(978-1-4965-4821-4(3)*, 135343, Stone Arch Bks.) Capstone.
Collins, Tim. The Long-Lost Secret Diary of the World's Worst Astronaut. 2018. (Long-Lost Secret Diary Ser.). (ENG., Illus.). 216p. (J). (gr. 4-5). pap. 9.99 *(978-1-63163-192-4(6)*, 1631631926); lib. bdg. 28.50 *(978-1-63163-191-7(8)*, 1631631918) North Star Editions. (Jolly Fish Pr.).
Davis, Pat. Estelle & the Escape from Mars: A Children's Novel By. 2009. 136p. pap. 10.99 *(978-1-4389-5432-5(8))* AuthorHouse.
Dinardo, Jeff. Field Trip to Mars (Book 1) Clegg, Dave, illus. 2018. (Funny Bone Books (tm) First Chapters — the Jupiter Twins Ser.). (ENG.). 32p. (J). (gr. k-2). pap. 4.99 *(978-1-63440-253-8(7)*, a36c3066-7240-49c6-8199-6603c4e655a8); lib. bdg. 19.99 *(978-1-63440-249-1(9)*, 6e39dd05-728c-4f2b-a77c-a147a05d70b4) Red Chair Pr.
Dingman, Matthew. The Very Different Animal from Mars. 2013. 24p. pap. 24.95 *(978-1-63000-730-0(7))* America Star Bks.
Duffett-Smith, James. A Curious Robot on Mars! Straker, Bethany, illus. 2013. (ENG.). 32p. (J). (gr. -1-k). 14.95 *(978-1-62087-994-8(8)*, 620994, Sky Pony Pr.) Skyhorse Publishing Co., Inc.
Elam Jr., Richard M. Young Visitor to Mars. Geer, Charles, illus. 2011. 256p. 47.95 *(978-1-258-09909-1(8))* Literary Licensing, LLC.
Gill, David Macinnis. Black Hole Sun. 2012. (Black Hole Sun Ser.: 1). (ENG.). 368p. (YA). (gr. 9). pap. 8.99 *(978-0-06-167306-1(4)*, Greenwillow Bks.) HarperCollins Pubs.
—Invisible Sun. 2013. (Black Hole Sun Ser.: 2). (ENG.). 400p. (YA). (gr. 9). pap. 9.99 *(978-0-06-207333-4(8)*, Greenwillow Bks.) HarperCollins Pubs.
—Shadow on the Sun. 2013. (Black Hole Sun Ser.: 3). (ENG.). 432p. (YA). (gr. 9). 17.99 *(978-0-06-207335-8(4)*, Greenwillow Bks.) HarperCollins Pubs.
Grahame, Howard. The Wishing Book. 2009. 110p. (J). pap. *(978-1-905809-64-6(6))* Pneuma Springs Publishing.
—The Wishing Book 2 - Return to Mars. 2009. 102p. (J). pap. *(978-1-905809-80-6(8))* Pneuma Springs Publishing.
Guettier, Nancy. Mermaids on Mars. 2013. (ENG.). 36p. (-3). pap. 9.95 *(978-1-61448-670-1(0))*; (Illus.). (gr. 1-3). 19.95 *(978-1-61448-640-4(9))* Morgan James Publishing.
Gutman, Dan. Rappy Goes to Mars. Bowers, Tim, illus. 2017. (I Can Read Level 2 Ser.). (ENG.). 32p. (J). (gr. -1-3). 16.99 *(978-0-06-225269-2(0))*; pap. 4.99 *(978-0-06-225268-5(2))* HarperCollins Pubs. (HarperCollins).
Hays, Barrett K. Mars, Jimmy & Me. 2011. 24p. (J). (gr. 4-6). pap. 11.32 *(978-1-4567-4164-8(0))* AuthorHouse.
Hirschfeld, Robert. Martians Are People, Too. 2011. (Navigators Ser.). (J). pap. *(978-1-61672-969-1(4))* Benchmark Education Co.
Howard, Grahame. The Wishing Book 3 - Extermination. 2010. 170p. (J). pap. *(978-1-905809-90-5(5))* Pneuma Springs Publishing.
Hunt, Elizabeth Singer. Secret Agent Jack Stalwart: Book 9: the Deadly Race to Space: Russia. 2009. (Secret Agent Jack Stalwart Ser.: 9). (ENG.). 144p. (J). (gr. 1-4). pap. 5.99 *(978-1-60286-078-0(5))* Hachette Bk. Group.
The Imaginer: Individual Title Six-Packs. (Bookweb Ser.). 32p. (gr. 6-18). 34.00 *(978-0-7578-0900-2(6))* Rigby Education.
Kelly, Mark. Mousetronaut Goes to Mars. Payne, C. F., illus. 2013. (Mousetronaut Ser.). (ENG.). 40p. (J). (gr. -1-3). 19.99 *(978-1-4424-8426-9(8)*, Simon & Schuster/Paula Wiseman Bks.) Simon & Schuster/Paula Wiseman Bks.
Lathrop, Brandy. Jalen Goes to Mars. 2008. 22p. pap. 24.95 *(978-1-4241-9010-2(X))* America Star Bks.
Marsh, Carole. Adventure to the Planet Mars! 2007. (Field Trips (Gallopade International) Ser.). (Illus.). 114p. (J). (gr. 2-9). 14.95 *(978-0-635-06392-2(1))* Gallopade International.
McDougall, Sophia. Mars Evacuees. (ENG.). (J). (gr. 3-7). 2016. 432p. pap. 7.99 *(978-0-06-229400-5(8))* 2015. 416p. 16.99 *(978-0-06-229399-2(0))* HarperCollins Pubs. (HarperCollins).
McGee, Warner, illus. Mission to Mars. 2006. (Backyardigans Ser.: 4). (ENG.). 24p. (J). (gr. -1-2). pap. 3.99 *(978-1-4169-1486-0(2)*, Simon Spotlight/Nickelodeon) Simon Spotlight/Nickelodeon.
Metz, Melinda. S. M. A. R. T. S. & the Mars Mission Mayhem. McKenzie, Heath, illus. 2016. (S. M. A. R. T. S. Ser.). (ENG.). 128p. (J). (gr. 3-6). lib. bdg. 22.65 *(978-1-4965-3016-5(0)*, 131903, Stone Arch Bks.) Capstone.
Oakes, Cory Putman. Dinosaur Boy Saves Mars. 2016. (Dinosaur Boy Ser.: 2). (ENG.). 224p. (J). (gr. 3-7). 18.40 *(978-0-606-39306-5(4))* Turtleback.
Pilkey, Dav. Ricky Ricotta's Mighty Robot vs. the Mecha-Monkeys from Mars (Ricky Ricotta's Mighty Robot #4) Santat, Dan, illus. 2014. (Ricky Ricotta's Mighty Robot Ser.: 4). (ENG.). 144p. (J). (gr. -1-3). pap. 5.99 *(978-0-545-63012-2(6))* Scholastic, Inc.
Preston, L. M. The Pack. 2010. (ENG.). 316p. (J). pap. 14.99 *(978-0-9841989-7-9(0))* Phenomenal One Pr.
—The Pack - Retribution: Retribution. 2012. (ENG.). 250p. (YA). (gr. 8-12). pap. 11.99 *(978-0-9850251-0-6(7))* Phenomenal One Pr.
Rockwood, Roy. Lost on the Moon. 2008. 132p. pap. 10.95 *(978-1-60664-236-8(7))* Rodgers, Alan Bks.
Sayres, Brianna Caplan. Night Night, Curiosity. O'Rourke, Ryan, illus. 2020. 32p. (J). (gr. -1-2). lib. bdg. 16.99 *(978-1-58089-893-5(9))* Charlesbridge Publishing, Inc.
Schachner, Judy. Skippyjon Jones, Lost in Spice. Schachner, Judy, illus. 2009. (Skippyjon Jones Ser.). (Illus.). 32p. (J). (gr. -1-k). 17.99 *(978-0-525-47965-9(1)*, Dutton Books for Young Readers) Penguin Young Readers Group.
—Skippyjon Jones, Lost in Spice. 2009. (Skippyjon Jones Ser.). (J). 1.25 *(978-1-4407-6563-6(4))*; 37.75 *(978-1-4407-6558-2(8))*; 192.75 *(978-1-4407-6557-5(X))* Recorded Bks., Inc.
Slivensky, Katie. The Countdown Conspiracy. (ENG.). (J). (gr. 3-7). 2018. 352p. pap. 7.99 *(978-0-06-246260-2(1))* 2017. 336p. 16.99 *(978-0-06-246255-8(5))* HarperCollins Pubs. (HarperCollins).
Summers, Kim. Senor Mundo & Me: A Happy Birthday Story. Mariscal, Javier, illus. 2004. 31p. (J). (gr. k-4). 20.00 *(978-0-7567-7759-3(3))* DIANE Publishing Co.
Todd, Ruthven. Space Cat Meets Mars. Galdone, Paul, illus. 2018. (ENG.). 80p. (gr. 1-5). 16.95 *(978-0-486-82274-7(5)*, 822745) Dover Pubns., Inc.
Trimble, Marcia J. Marsby & the Martian Detectives. Hayden, Jennifer H., illus. 2004. 56p. (J). per. 9.95 *(978-1-891577-52-9(2)*, SAN299-4844) Images Pr.
Warga, Jasmine. A Rover's Story. 2022. (ENG., Illus.). 320p. (J). (gr. 3-7). 19.99 *(978-0-06-311392-3(9)*, Balzer & Bray) HarperCollins Pubs.
Wolff, Tracy. Book 4: Arrival. Kinsella, Pat, illus. 2016. (Mars Bound Ser.). (ENG.). 48p. (J). (gr. 3-8). lib. bdg. 34.21 *(978-1-62402-200-5(6)*, 24579, Spellbound) Magic Wagon.

MARSH, OTHNIEL CHARLES, 1831-1899

Enik, Ted. Sticks 'n' Stones 'n' Dinosaur Bones: Being a Whimsical Take on a (pre)Historical Event, 1 vol. Newland, G. F., illus. 2017. (Unhinged History Ser.: 1). (ENG.). 48p. (J). (gr. -1-3). 16.99 *(978-0-7643-5394-9(2)*, 7730) Schiffer Publishing, Ltd.
Goldish, Meish. The Fossil Feud: Marsh & Cope's Bone Wars. 2006. (Fossil Hunters Ser.). (Illus.). 32p. (YA). (gr. 2-5). lib. bdg. 28.50 *(978-1-59716-256-2(6))* Bearport Publishing Co., Inc.

MARSHALL, GEORGE C. (GEORGE CATLETT), 1880-1959

Gimpel, Lee. Fighting Wars, Planning for Peace: The Story of George C. Marshall. 2005. (World Leaders Ser.). (Illus.). 176p. (J). (gr. 6-12). lib. bdg. 26.95 *(978-1-931798-66-2(4))* Reynolds, Morgan Inc.
Welch, Catherine A. George C. Marshall. (History Maker Bios Ser.). 48p. (J). 2006. (Illus.). (gr. 3-7). lib. bdg. 26.60 *(978-0-8225-2435-9(X)*, Lerner Pubns.) 2005. pap. 8.95 *(978-0-8225-5460-8(7))* Lerner Publishing Group.

MARSHALL, JOHN, 1755-1835

Corrigan, Jim. John Marshall: The Story of John Marshall. 2011. (Supreme Court Justices Ser.). (Illus.). 112p. (J). 28.95 *(978-1-59935-159-9(5))* Reynolds, Morgan Inc.
Wetterer, Charles M. & Wetterer, Margaret K. Chief Justice. Walters, Kurt K. C., illus. 2005. 32p. (J). *(978-1-59336-306-2(0))*; pap. *(978-1-59336-307-9(9))* Mondo Publishing.

MARSHALL, THURGOOD, 1908-1993

Aaron, Lance. Thurgood Marshall, Vol. 9. 2018. (Civil Rights Leaders Ser.). 144p. (J). (gr. 7). lib. bdg. 35.93 *(978-1-4222-4013-7(4))* Mason Crest.
Aldred, Lisa. Thurgood Marshall. 2004. (Black Americans of Achievement Legacy Edition Ser.). (ENG., Illus.). 112p. (gr. 6-12). 35.00 *(978-0-7910-8163-1(X)*, P114167, Facts On File) Infobase Holdings, Inc.
Boerst, William J. Galileo Galilei & the Science of Motion. 2004. (Profiles in Science Ser.). (Illus.). 144p. (YA). (gr. 6-12). lib. bdg. 26.95 *(978-1-931798-00-6(1))* Reynolds, Morgan Inc.
Carey Rohan, Rebecca. Thurgood Marshall: The First African-American Supreme Court Justice, 1 vol. 2016. (Great American Thinkers Ser.). (ENG.). 128p. (J). (gr. 9-9). 47.36 *(978-1-5026-1932-7(6)*, 756c9265-9225-4c4f-8b5b-6445c19afc2c) Cavendish Square Publishing LLC.
Chavez, Emilio. Thurgood Marshall: Supreme Court Justice, 1 vol. 2013. (InfoMax Readers Ser.). (ENG.). 24p. (J). (gr. 3-3). pap. 8.25 *(978-1-4777-2599-3(7)*, 11ef806a-272f-4544-86d4-42b9491905cd); pap. 49.50 *(978-1-4777-2600-6(4))* Rosen Publishing Group, Inc., The. (Rosen Classroom).
Collins, Luke. Thurgood Marshall, 1 vol. 2014. (Great African-Americans Ser.). (ENG., Illus.). 24p. (J). (gr. -1-2). lib. bdg. 24.65 *(978-1-4765-3956-0(1)*, 123955, Capstone Pr.) Capstone.
Horn, Geoffrey M. Thurgood Marshall, 1 vol. 2004. (Trailblazers of the Modern World Ser.). (ENG., Illus.). 48p. (gr. 5-8). pap. 15.05 *(978-0-8368-5258-5(3)*, 0eaf0b52-0726-4be3-b1fa-870937b22719); lib. bdg. 33.67 *(978-0-8368-5098-7(X)*, 243d2da1-a59e-4bd5-a401-db59905c50c5) Stevens, Gareth Publishing LLLP. (Gareth Stevens Secondary Library).
Kanefield, Teri. Thurgood Marshall: The Making of America #6. 2020. (Making of America Ser.). (ENG., Illus.). 256p. (J). (gr. 5-9). 16.99 *(978-1-4197-4104-3(7)*, 1264101, Abrams Bks. for Young Readers) Abrams, Inc.
Keiser, Cody. Thurgood Marshall: Civil Rights Leader, 1 vol. 2013. (Rosen Readers Ser.). (ENG.). 24p. (J). (gr. 3-3). pap. 8.25 *(978-1-4777-2545-0(8)*, 6b5ba441-2af5-458d-9bea-ace2e6770bd7); pap. 49.50 *(978-1-4777-2546-7(6))* Rosen Publishing Group, Inc., The. (Rosen Classroom).
Kemp, Kristin. Amazing Americans: Thurgood Marshall, 1 vol. rev. ed. 2014. (Social Studies: Informational Text Ser.). (ENG., Illus.). 32p. (gr. 3-4). pap. 11.99 *(978-1-4333-7374-9(2))* Teacher Created Materials, Inc.
Mara, Wil. Thurgood Marshall: Champion for Civil Rights. 2004. (Great Life Stories Ser.). (ENG., Illus.). 128p. (J). 30.50 *(978-0-531-12058-3(9)*, Watts, Franklin) Scholastic Library Publishing.
Stoltman, Joan. Thurgood Marshall, 1 vol. 2018. (Heroes of Black History Ser.). (ENG.). 32p. (gr. 3-4). 28.27 *(978-1-5382-3021-3(6)*, 9e41f34f-bc53-4ad9-9b23-60da96338bda) Stevens, Gareth Publishing LLLP.
Wheeler, Jill C. Thurgood Marshall. 2003. (Breaking Barriers Ser.). 64p. (gr. 3-8). lib. bdg. 27.07 *(978-1-57765-907-5(4)*, Abdo & Daughters) ABDO Publishing Co.
Whitelaw, Nancy. Mr. Civil Rights: The Story of Thurgood Marshall. 2nd rev. exp. ed. 2004. (Notable Americans Ser.). (Illus.). 144p. (YA). (gr. 6-12). 23.95 *(978-1-931798-02-0(8))* Reynolds, Morgan Inc.
—Thurgood Marshall. 2011. (Supreme Court Justices Ser.). (Illus.). 128p. 28.95 *(978-1-59935-157-5(9))* Reynolds, Morgan Inc.
Winter, Jonah. Thurgood. Collier, Bryan, illus. 2019. 40p. (J). (gr. k-4). 17.99 *(978-1-5247-6533-0(3)*, Schwartz & Wade Bks.) Random Hse. Children's Bks.

MARSHES

Bennett, Doraine. Marsh & Swamp. 2009. (J). *(978-1-935077-36-7(8))*; pap. *(978-1-935077-41-1(4))* State Standards Publishing, LLC.
Carlone, Sydney. Life in a Marsh, 1 vol. 2013. (Rosen Readers Ser.). (ENG.). 24p. (J). (gr. 3-3). pap. 8.25 *(978-1-4777-2533-7(4)*, 03151638-ed8b-4135-a5cc-e5cb177cd775); pap. 49.50 *(978-1-4777-2534-4(2))* Rosen Publishing Group, Inc., The. (Rosen Classroom).
Cheshire, Gerard. Day & Night in Swamp. Camm, Martin, illus. 2009. 38p. (J). (gr. 2-5). 14.99 *(978-0-8437-0974-2(X))* Hammond World Atlas Corp.
Declus, Jennifer. What Might I Find in a Swamp. Kalasea, illus. 2004. (J). *(978-0-9743690-3-7(9))* Britt Allcroft Productions.

Lion, David C. A Home in the Swamp. 2006. (Scholastic News Nonfiction Readers Ser.). (ENG., Illus.). 24p. (J). (gr. 1-2). lib. bdg. 22.00 *(978-0-516-25349-7(2))* Scholastic Library Publishing.

—La Vida en el Pantano. 2008. (Scholastic News Nonfiction Readers en Espanol Ser.). 24p. (J). pap. 6.95 *(978-0-531-20648-5(3))*; (SPA., Illus.). 22.00 *(978-0-531-20714-7(5))* Scholastic Library Publishing. (Children's Pr.).

Marais, Vivian. Life in a Swamp: A Wetlands Habitat. (Look at Life Science Ser.). 24p. (gr. 3-3). 2009. 42.50 *(978-1-61511-215-9(4)*, PowerKids Pr.) 2008. (ENG.). pap. 8.25 *(978-1-4358-0141-7(5)*, bf64001c-344b-4fcc-8dc3-f99daa53a6a7, Rosen Classroom) Rosen Publishing Group, Inc., The.

Marais, Vivien. Life in a Swamp: A Wetlands Habitat, 1 vol. 2009. (Look at Life Science Ser.). (ENG.). 24p. (J). (gr. 3-3). lib. bdg. 26.27 *(978-1-4358-2972-5(7)*, 3bfd7ab3-d338-4e21-b741-5600be8d78be, PowerKids Pr.) Rosen Publishing Group, Inc., The.

Meister, Cari. Do You Really Want to Meet a Swan? Fabbri, Daniele, illus. 2014. (Do You Really Want to Meet ... ? Ser.). (ENG.). 24p. (J). (gr. 1-4). lib. bdg. 27.10 *(978-1-60753-458-7(4)*, 15900) Amicus.

Peterson, Christy. 24 Hours in a Salt Marsh, 1 vol. 2017. (Day in an Ecosystem Ser.). (ENG.). 48p. (gr. 4-4). 33.07 *(978-1-5026-2479-6(6)*, 0cb47c3a-8e1d-4ca1-988a-a72a04c3f07a) Cavendish Square Publishing LLC.

MARSHES—FICTION

Appelt, Kathi. The True Blue Scouts of Sugar Man Swamp. (ENG., Illus.). (J). (gr. 3-7). 2014. 352p. pap. 8.99 *(978-1-4424-2108-0(8)*, Atheneum Bks. for Young Readers) 2013. 336p. 19.99 *(978-1-4424-2105-9(3))* Simon & Schuster Children's Publishing.

—The True Blue Scouts of Sugar Man Swamp. 2014. lib. bdg. 19.65 *(978-0-606-35793-7(9))* Turtleback.

Bracegirdle, P. J. Fiendish Deeds. 2009. (Joy of Spooking Ser.: 1). (ENG.). 224p. (J). (gr. 3-7). pap. 5.99 *(978-1-4169-3417-2(0)*, McElderry, Margaret K. Bks.) McElderry, Margaret K. Bks.

Cali, Davide. The Call of the Swamp. Somà, Marco, illus. 2017. (ENG.). 32p. (J). 16.00 *(978-0-8028-5486-5(9)*, Eerdmans Bks For Young Readers) Eerdmans, William B. Publishing Co.

Crochet, Pat. Randolph Saves Christmas, 1 vol. Gramelspacher, Sarah, illus. 2018. (ENG.). 32p. (J). (gr. -1-3). 16.99 *(978-1-4556-2269-6(9)*, Pelican Publishing) Arcadia Publishing.

Hurd, Thacher. Mama Don't Allow 25th Anniversary Edition. Hurd, Thacher, illus. 25th anniv. ed. 2008. (ENG., Illus.). 40p. (J). (gr. -1-3). pap. 8.99 *(978-0-06-443078-4(2)*, HarperCollins) HarperCollins Pubs.

Hurd, Thacher & Hurd, T. Mama Don't Allow. 2008. (Illus.). (J). (gr. -1-2). 17.20 *(978-0-8085-3698-7(2))* Turtleback.

Jaz. Lost Lake: An Adventure for Kids of All Ages. 2008. 172p. pap. 24.95 *(978-1-60703-398-1(4))* America Star Bks.

Jones, C. B. The Cats' Meow. Green, Chris, illus. 2017. (Bog Hollow Boys Ser.). (ENG.). 72p. (J). (gr. 4-8). lib. bdg. 25.32 *(978-1-4965-4057-7(3)*, 133365, Stone Arch Bks.) Capstone.

—Gone to the Buzzards. Green, Chris, illus. 2017. (Bog Hollow Boys Ser.). (ENG.). 72p. (J). (gr. 4-8). lib. bdg. 25.32 *(978-1-4965-4058-4(1)*, 133366, Stone Arch Bks.) Capstone.

King, Trey & Kiernan, Kenny. Cops, Crocs, & Crooks! 2015. (LEGO City Ser.). (ENG., Illus.). 24p. (J). (gr. -1-3). pap. 3.99 *(978-0-545-78525-9(1))* Scholastic, Inc.

Kurtz, Kevin. A Day in the Salt Marsh, 1 vol. Powell, Consie, illus. 2007. (Day in the Habitat Ser.). (ENG.). 32p. (J). (gr. -1-3). 15.95 *(978-0-9768823-5-0(3))* Arbordale Publishing.

London, Lewis. Wesley Owl. 2010. (Illus.). 36p. (J). pap. 16.99 *(978-1-4490-6122-7(2))* AuthorHouse.

Ouchley, Amy Griffin. Swamper: Letters from a Louisiana Swamp Rabbit. 2013. (ENG., Illus.). 72p. (gr. 4-7). 22.50 *(978-0-8071-5074-0(6)*, 1763) Louisiana State Univ. Pr.

Prins, Piet. The Flying Phantom. 2006. (Illus.). 142p. (J). pap. *(978-1-894666-45-9(3))* Inheritance Pubns.

Roberts, Daniel. The Ghost of Froggy's Swamp. 2012. 36p. pap. 18.99 *(978-1-4772-0316-3(8))* AuthorHouse.

Sazaklis, John. Swamp Thing vs the Zombie Pets, 1 vol. Baltazar, Art, illus. 2012. (DC Super-Pets Ser.). (ENG.). 56p. (J). (gr. 1-3). pap. 4.95 *(978-1-4048-7667-5(7)*, 120254, Stone Arch Bks.) Capstone.

Stine, R. L. Here Comes the Shaggedy. 2016. (Goosebumps Most Wanted Ser.: 9). (Illus.). 140p. (J). lib. bdg. 17.20 *(978-0-606-38587-9(8))* Turtleback.

Stratton-Porter, Gene. Freckles. l.t. ed. 2007. (ENG.). 248p. pap. 22.99 *(978-1-4264-5654-1(9))* Creative Media Partners, LLC.

—Freckles. 2006. 236p. (YA). 19.95 *(978-1-934169-32-2(3))*; pap. 8.95 *(978-1-934169-33-9(1))* Norilana Bks.

—A Girl of the Limberlost. 2006. 336p. (YA). 21.95 *(978-1-934169-30-8(7))*; pap. 10.95 *(978-1-934169-31-5(5))* Norilana Bks.

Turley/Alber. And the Tide Comes In. 2012. (Long Term Ecological Research Ser.). (ENG., Illus.). 32p. (J). (gr. 3-7). 15.95 *(978-0-9817700-5-5(3))* Taylor Trade Publishing.

Vanholme, Virginie. The Vampire from the Marshes. Mauricet, illus. 2008. (Scared to Death Ser.: 1). 46p. pap. 11.95 *(978-1-905460-47-2(3))* CineBook GBR. Dist: National Bk. Network.

Weeks, Sarah. Catfish Kate & the Sweet Swamp Band. Smith, Elwood H., illus. 2009. (ENG.). 32p. (J). (gr. -1-3). 19.99 *(978-1-4169-4026-5(X)*, Atheneum Bks. for Young Readers) Simon & Schuster Children's Publishing.

MARSUPIALS

Bishop, Nic. Nic Bishop: Marsupials. Bishop, Nic, photos by. 2009. (ENG., Illus.). 48p. (J). (gr. -1-3). 17.99 *(978-0-439-87758-9(X)*, Scholastic Nonfiction) Scholastic, Inc.

Bjorklund, Ruth. Tasmanian Devils. 2013. (Nature's Children Ser.). (ENG.). 48p. (J). pap. 6.95 *(978-0-531-24308-4(7)*, Children's Pr.) Scholastic Library Publishing.

Cleave, Rohan & Tulloch, Coral. Bouncing Back: An Eastern Barred Bandicoot Story. 2018. (Illus.). 32p. (J). (gr. 1-4). 18.95 *(978-1-4863-0827-9(9))* CSIRO Publishing AUS. Dist: Stylus Publishing, LLC.

Esbaum, Jill. Explore My World: Kangaroos. 2018. (Explore My World Ser.). (Illus.). 32p. (J). (gr. -1-k). pap. 4.99 *(978-1-4263-3157-2(6)*, National Geographic Kids) Disney Publishing Worldwide.

Fishman, Jon M. Meet a Baby Tasmanian Devil. 2017. (Lightning Bolt Books (r) — Baby Australian Animals Ser.). (ENG., Illus.). 24p. (J). (gr. 1-3). 29.32 *(978-1-5124-3385-2(3)*, cfab2a3a-fc42-4698-9e11-fe01a0743a54, Lerner Pubns.) Lerner Publishing Group.

Kalman, Bobbie. Baby Marsupials. 2012. (ENG., Illus.). 24p. (J). *(978-0-7787-4074-2(9))*; pap. *(978-0-7787-4079-7(X))* Crabtree Publishing Co.

Kenah, Katharine. Super Marsupials: Kangaroos, Koalas, Wombats, & More. Coleman, Stephanie Fizer, illus. 2019. (Let's-Read-And-Find-Out Science 1 Ser.). (ENG.). 40p. (J). (gr. -1-3). pap. 6.99 *(978-0-06-249529-7(1)*, HarperCollins) HarperCollins Pubs.

Lusted, Marcia Amidon. Tasmanian Devil: Savage Island Scavenger. 2017. (Real Monsters Ser.). (ENG., Illus.). 32p. (J). (gr. 3-6). 51.35 *(978-1-68079-776-3(X)*, 24008, Checkerboard Library) ABDO Publishing Co.

Markovics, Joyce L. Tasmanian Devil: Nighttime Scavenger. 2008. (Uncommon Animals Ser.). (Illus.). 32p. (YA). (gr. 2-5). lib. bdg. 25.27 *(978-1-59716-733-8(9)*, 1284366) Bearport Publishing Co., Inc.

Morgan, Sally. Marsupials. 2004. (J). lib. bdg. 27.10 *(978-1-59389-175-6(X))* Chrysalis Education.

Murray, Julie. Sugar Gliders. 2017. (Nocturnal Animals (Abdo Kids Junior) Ser.). (ENG.). 24p. (J). (gr. -1-2). lib. bdg. 31.36 *(978-1-5321-0407-7(3)*, 26533, Abdo Kids) ABDO Publishing Co.

Racanelli, Marie. Animals with Pockets. 2010. (Crazy Nature Ser.). 24p. (J). (gr. 1-5). lib. bdg., E-Book 42.50 *(978-1-4488-0155-8(9))*; (ENG., Illus.). (gr. 2-3). pap. 9.25 *(978-1-4358-9862-2(1)*, 1b4dbad7-db1b-49d8-8799-474867669915, PowerKids Pr.); (ENG., Illus.). (gr. 2-3). lib. bdg. 26.27 *(978-1-4358-9385-6(9)*, 304fc356-b80f-4327-8599-d03e8a3c40e5) Rosen Publishing Group, Inc., The.

Roza, Greg. Tasmanian Devil vs. Hyena, 1 vol. 2015. (Bizarre Beast Battles Ser.). (ENG.). 24p. (J). (gr. 2-3). 24.27 *(978-1-4824-2798-1(2)*, f0306ddf-9759-4b98-8bc0-0278d0f6aa62) Stevens, Gareth Publishing LLLP.

Rustad, Martha E. H. Baby Animals in Pouches. 2017. (Baby Animals & Their Homes Ser.). (ENG., Illus.). 24p. (J). (gr. -1-2). lib. bdg. 22.65 *(978-1-5157-3829-9(9)*, 133722, Pebble) Capstone.

Saxby, Claire. Koala. Vivas, Julie, illus. 2019. (Read & Wonder Ser.). (ENG.). 32p. (J). (gr. -1-3). 7.99 *(978-1-5362-0896-2(5))* Candlewick Pr.

Sill, Cathryn. About Marsupials: A Guide for Children, 1 vol. Sill, John, illus. (About... Ser.: 10). 48p. (J). (gr. -1-2). 2009. pap. 7.95 *(978-1-56145-407-5(9))* 2006. 15.95 *(978-1-56145-358-0(7))* Peachtree Publishing Co. Inc.

Stefoff, Rebecca. The Marsupial Order, 1 vol. 2008. (Family Trees Ser.). (ENG., Illus.). 96p. (gr. 6-6). lib. bdg. 36.93 *(978-0-7614-2697-4(3)*, e3b63167-eed1-4b87-b8f1-48c96435170e) Cavendish Square Publishing LLC.

Tatlock, Ann. Backyard Jungle Safari Opossums: Opossums. 2015. (ENG., Illus.). 32p. (J). 26.50 *(978-1-62469-100-3(5))* Purple Toad Publishing, Inc.

Wilson, Paula M. Sugar Gliders. 2018. (Cute & Unusual Pets Ser.). (ENG., Illus.). 32p. (J). (gr. 3-9). lib. bdg. 28.65 *(978-1-5435-3057-5(5)*, 138631, Capstone Pr.) Capstone.

Zondervan Staff. Curious Creatures down Under, 1 vol. 2011. (I Can Read! / Made by God Ser.). (ENG., Illus.). 32p. (J). pap. 4.99 *(978-0-310-72187-1(3))* Zonderkidz.

MARTHA'S VINEYARD (MASS.)

The Greatest Place on Earth: A Children's Story, A History Lesson, A Scrapbook, A Lifetime Keepsake. 2006. (J). 18.95 *(978-0-9777882-0-0(2)*, Light Works Publishing) I.M. Enterprises.

MARTHA'S VINEYARD (MASS.)—FICTION

Leahy, Sandy & Tarentino, Kathy. The Hibernating House. 2013. 26p. 19.95 *(978-1-4575-1753-2(1))*; pap. 12.95 *(978-1-4575-1670-2(5))* Dog Ear Publishing, LLC.

Schaal, Patty. Nighttide on a Vineyard Farm. Datz, Margot, illus. 2010. (J). *(978-0-9827146-1-4(0))* Vineyard Stories.

Stewart, Jane. The Island Escapade. 2003. 102p. (YA). pap. 9.95 *(978-0-595-27734-6(9))* iUniverse, Inc.

MARTIAL ARTS

see also Archery; Self-Defense

The ABCs of Tae Kwon Do. 2004. (J). 5.95 *(978-0-9754345-0-5(0))* Cannady, John.

Abdo, Kenny. Conor Mcgregor. 2018. (Sports Biographies Ser.). (ENG., Illus.). 24p. (J). (gr. 2-8). lib. bdg. 31.36 *(978-1-5321-2477-8(5)*, 28427, Abdo Zoom-Fly) ABDO Publishing Co.

Adams, Colleen. Kelly Clarkson, 1 vol. 2006. (Stars in the Spotlight Ser.: Vol. 3). (ENG., Illus.). 32p. (YA). (gr. 4-4). lib. bdg. 28.93 *(978-1-4042-3515-1(9)*, 1a05ba88-1b4e-4350-8b37-79433156d265) Rosen Publishing Group, Inc., The.

Amerland, David. Tae Kwon Do, 1 vol. 2004. (Martial Arts Ser.). (ENG.). 32p. (gr. 3-5). lib. bdg. 28.67 *(978-0-8368-4195-4(6)*, a9c45a99-1668-44f2-956b-ad4fe85fd891, Gareth Stevens Learning Library) Stevens, Gareth Publishing LLLP.

Bagnulo, Giancarlo. A Complete Guide to Ju Jitsu, 1 vol. 2017. (Mastering Martial Arts Ser.). (ENG.). 128p. (gr. 6-6). lib. bdg. 38.93 *(978-0-7660-8545-9(7)*, 67a230bd-370e-40e3-9cf8-87af4a47f9ad) Enslow Publishing, LLC.

Binder, C. F. Black Belt Attitude. 2003. (Illus.). 16p. (J). 7.70 *(978-1-4120-0351-3(2))* Trafford Publishing.

Bjorklund, Ruth. Aikido, 1 vol. 2012. (Martial Arts in Action Ser.). (ENG., Illus.). 48p. (gr. 5-5). lib. bdg. 32.64 *(978-0-7614-4931-7(0)*, 2442f5ae-22a8-4c91-b250-1716c271b5a9) Cavendish Square Publishing LLC.

Castellano, Peter. Mma, 1 vol. 2015. (Daredevil Sports Ser.). (ENG., Illus.). 32p. (J). (gr. 1-1). pap. 11.50 *(978-1-4824-2981-7(0)*, 2db908f6-a619-4261-a7b5-c447e2ee8016); lib. bdg. 28.27 *(978-1-4824-2982-4(9)*, 00edb684-1ba5-410f-810d-256a8d1cd22c) Stevens, Gareth Publishing LLLP.

Chaline, Eric. Martial Arts for Athletic Conditioning. 2003. (Martial & Fighting Arts Ser.). (Illus.). 96p. (J). (gr. 7-18). lib. bdg. *(978-1-59084-397-0(5))* Mason Crest.

—Martial Arts for Athletic Conditioning: Winning Ways. James, Adam, ed. 2015. (Mastering Martial Arts Ser.). (Illus.). 96p. (J). (gr. 5). lib. bdg. 24.95 *(978-1-4222-3241-5(7))* Mason Crest.

—Martial Arts for Women: Winning Ways. James, Adam, ed. 2015. (Mastering Martial Arts Ser.). (Illus.). 96p. (J). (gr. 5). lib. bdg. 24.95 *(978-1-4222-3243-9(3))* Mason Crest.

—Ninjutsu. 2004. (Martial & Fighting Arts Ser.). (Illus.). 96p. (YA). (gr. 7-18). lib. bdg. 22.95 *(978-1-59084-398-7(3))* Mason Crest.

—Ninjutsu: Winning Ways. James, Adam, ed. 2015. (Mastering Martial Arts Ser.). 96p. (J). (gr. 5). lib. bdg. 24.95 *(978-1-4222-3244-6(1))* Mason Crest.

Corporate Contributor. Taylor Lautner. 2012. (ENG.). 32p. (J). *(978-0-7787-7619-2(0))*; pap. *(978-0-7787-7632-1(8))* Crabtree Publishing Co.

Crabtree, Marc. Meet My Neighbor, the Taekwondo Master. 2009. (Meet my Neighbor Ser.). (ENG., Illus.). 24p. (J). (gr. k-2). pap. *(978-0-7787-4582-2(1))* Crabtree Publishing Co.

Crossingham, John & Kalman, Bobbie. High Flying Martial Arts. 2008. (Sports Starters Ser.). (ENG., Illus.). 32p. (J). (gr. 3-7). pap. *(978-0-7787-3172-6(3))*; lib. bdg. *(978-0-7787-3140-5(5))* Crabtree Publishing Co.

Dancer, Audrey & Falk, Laine. Let's Talk Tae Kwon Do. 2009. (Scholastic News Nonfiction Readers: Sports Talk Ser.). (ENG., Illus.). 24p. (J). (gr. k-3). 21.19 *(978-0-531-13828-1(3))* Scholastic Library Publishing.

Dawson, Patricia. Ninjas: Masters of Stealth & Secrecy. 2015. (J). lib. bdg. *(978-1-62713-413-2(1))* Cavendish Square Publishing LLC.

Dawson, Patricia A. Ninjas: Masters of Stealth & Secrecy, 1 vol. 2014. (History's Greatest Warriors Ser.). (ENG., Illus.). 48p. (gr. 4-4). 33.07 *(978-1-5026-0122-3(2)*, 674e71ec-964a-4a87-9ab4-c559c302a5e2) Cavendish Square Publishing LLC.

Doeden, Matt. Combat Sports. 2015. (Summer Olympic Sports Ser.). (ENG., Illus.). 32p. (J). (gr. 2-4). 19.95 *(978-1-60753-807-3(5))* Amicus Learning.

—Life as a Ninja: An Interactive History Adventure. 2010. (You Choose: Warriors Ser.). (ENG.). 112p. (gr. 3-4). pap. 41.70 *(978-1-4296-5099-1(0)*, Capstone Pr.) Capstone.

Dougherty, Martin. Secrets of Martial Arts Masters. 2010. (Extreme! Ser.). (ENG.). 32p. (gr. 3-4). pap. 47.70 *(978-1-4296-5116-5(4)*, Capstone Pr.) Capstone.

Durrie, Karen. Artes Marciales. 2012. (J). 27.13 *(978-1-61913-202-3(8))* Weigl Pubs., Inc.

—Martial Arts. 2011. (J). 27.13 *(978-1-61690-941-3(2))* Weigl Pubs., Inc.

Ellis, Carol & Bredeson, Carmen. Kendo, 1 vol. 2011. (Martial Arts in Action Ser.). (ENG.). 48p. (gr. 5-5). lib. bdg. 32.64 *(978-0-7614-4935-5(3)*, 9242bcb6-b4f3-4d21-965c-3c60c69ec505) Cavendish Square Publishing LLC.

Etingoff, Kim. All Around Good Habits. 2013. (Junior Martial Arts Ser.: 9). 32p. (J). (gr. 4-18). 19.95 *(978-1-4222-2732-9(4))* Mason Crest.

—Concentration. 2013. (Junior Martial Arts Ser.: 9). 32p. (J). (gr. 4-18). 19.95 *(978-1-4222-2733-6(2))* Mason Crest.

—Confidence. 2013. (Junior Martial Arts Ser.: 9). 32p. (J). (gr. 4-18). 19.95 *(978-1-4222-2734-3(0))* Mason Crest.

—Hand-Eye Coordination. 2013. (Junior Martial Arts Ser.: 9). 32p. (J). (gr. 4-18). 19.95 *(978-1-4222-2735-0(9))* Mason Crest.

—Handling Peer Pressure. 2013. (Junior Martial Arts Ser.: 9). 32p. (J). (gr. 4-18). 19.95 *(978-1-4222-2736-7(7))* Mason Crest.

—Junior Martial Arts, 9 vols. 2014. (Illus.). 9p. (J). *(978-1-4222-2731-2(6))* Mason Crest.

Fishman, Jon M. Ninja Weapons. 2020. (Lightning Bolt Books (r) — Ninja Mania Ser.). (ENG., Illus.). 24p. (J). (gr. 1-3). pap. 9.99 *(978-1-5415-8917-9(3)*, 899f3989-2a75-4596-a16d-e9da79f73a36); lib. bdg. 29.32 *(978-1-5415-7708-4(6)*, 7fe4e6e9-d672-47e5-802a-7d1ca9cbdbac) Lerner Publishing Group. (Lerner Pubns.).

—Real-Life Ninja. 2020. (Lightning Bolt Books (r) — Ninja Mania Ser.). (ENG., Illus.). 24p. (J). (gr. 1-3). pap. 9.99 *(978-1-5415-8918-6(1)*, 41eb8370-8018-4d11-86a3-52cdfdd4a47b); lib. bdg. 29.32 *(978-1-5415-7706-0(X)*, acd1fef7-a396-47e3-86cc-eec57033aba1) Lerner Publishing Group. (Lerner Pubns.).

—Ronda Rousey. 2016. (Amazing Athletes Ser.). (ENG., Illus.). 32p. (J). (gr. 2-5). 26.65 *(978-1-5124-1333-5(X)*, c558c02e-c55c-4334-afb5-be33a0b09be8, Lerner Pubns.) Lerner Publishing Group.

FitzPatrick, Bill. The Shaolin Action Principles. 2004. Orig. Title: 100 Action Principles of the Shaolin. 128p. pap. 20.00 *(978-1-884864-22-3(8))* American Success Institute, Inc.

Gagne, Tammy. Trends in Martial Arts. 2014. 48p. (gr. 4-8). 29.95 *(978-1-61228-553-5(8))* Mitchell Lane Pubs.

Gifford, Clive. Combat Sports. 2011. (Olympic Sports Ser.). (ENG.). 32p. (J). (gr. 4-8). lib. bdg. 28.50 *(978-1-60753-189-0(5)*, 17104) Amicus.

—Combat Sports. 2011. (ENG., Illus.). 32p. (J). pap. 10.95 *(978-1-77092-036-1(6))* Saunders Bk. Co. CAN. Dist: RiverStream Publishing.

—Martial Arts, 1 vol. 2010. (Tell Me about Sports Ser.). (ENG.). 32p. (gr. 4-4). 31.21 *(978-0-7614-4457-2(2)*, 860d3c39-ca9a-4240-b9c7-f0b79739ab29) Cavendish Square Publishing LLC.

—Martial Arts Legends. 2009. (ENG., Illus.). 32p. (J). (gr. 4-7). lib. bdg. *(978-0-7787-3776-6(4))* Crabtree Publishing Co.

Gitlin, Martin. Martial Arts & Its Greatest Fighters, 1 vol. 2014. (Inside Sports Ser.). (ENG.). 80p. (J). (gr. 6-6). 35.29 *(978-1-62275-588-2(X)*, ddfad8c1-8fc7-439a-99aa-2d027ab4986d, Britannica Educational Publishing) Rosen Publishing Group, Inc., The.

Group/McGraw-Hill, Wright. Formas de Moverse, 6 vols. (First Explorers. Primeros Exploradores Nonfiction Sets Ser.). (SPA.). (gr. 1-2). 29.95 *(978-0-7699-1473-2(X))* Shortland Pubns. (U. S. A.) Inc.

Haney-Withrow, Anna. Tae Kwon Do, 1 vol. 2012. (Martial Arts in Action Ser.). (ENG.). 48p. (gr. 5-5). lib. bdg. 32.64 *(978-0-7614-4940-9(X)*, 05e6f628-76da-40a3-96fc-fbbc0944c22e) Cavendish Square Publishing LLC.

Harbo, Christopher L. The Secrets of Martial Arts: An Isabel Soto History Adventure. 2010. (Graphic Expeditions Ser.). (ENG., Illus.). 32p. (J). (gr. 3-9). lib. bdg. 31.32 *(978-1-4296-3973-6(3)*, 102583, Capstone Pr.) Capstone.

Hillson, Ted. Tae Kwon Do Classic Forms: 21 Hyung — Novice White Belt Through Advanced Black Belt. Kligge, Elizabeth, illus. 2003. 232p. (YA). spiral bd. 22.50 *(978-0-9729293-0-1(4))* Double Dagger Pr.

Hyde, Natalie. Ninjas. 2014. (Crabtree Chrome Ser.). (ENG., Illus.). 48p. (J). (gr. 2-2). *(978-0-7787-1365-4(2))* Crabtree Publishing Co.

Inside Martial Arts, 6 vols. 2015. (Inside Martial Arts Ser.: 6). (ENG.). 48p. (J). (gr. 3-6). lib. bdg. 205.32 *(978-1-62403-600-2(7)*, 17067, SportsZone) ABDO Publishing Co.

James, Sara. Safety. 2013. (Junior Martial Arts Ser.: 9). 32p. (J). (gr. 4-18). 19.95 *(978-1-4222-2737-4(5))* Mason Crest.

—Self-Defense. 2013. (Junior Martial Arts Ser.: 9). 32p. (J). (gr. 4-18). 19.95 *(978-1-4222-2738-1(3))* Mason Crest.

—Self-Discipline. 2013. (Junior Martial Arts Ser.: 9). 32p. (J). (gr. 4-18). 19.95 *(978-1-4222-2739-8(1))* Mason Crest.

—Self-Esteem. 2013. (Junior Martial Arts Ser.: 9). 32p. (J). (gr. 4-18). 19.95 *(978-1-4222-2740-4(5))* Mason Crest.

Johnson, Nathan. Jujutsu: Winning Ways. James, Adam, ed. 2015. (Mastering Martial Arts Ser.). (Illus.). 96p. (J). (gr. 5). lib. bdg. 24.95 *(978-1-4222-3237-8(9))* Mason Crest.

—Kickboxing & MMA: Winning Ways. James, Adam, ed. 2015. (Mastering Martial Arts Ser.). 96p. (J). (gr. 5). lib. bdg. 24.95 *(978-1-4222-3239-2(5))* Mason Crest.

—Martial Arts for Children: Winning Ways. James, Adam, ed. 2015. (Mastering Martial Arts Ser.). (Illus.). 96p. (J). (gr. 5). lib. bdg. 24.95 *(978-1-4222-3242-2(5))* Mason Crest.

Jones, Patrick. Ultimate Fighting: The Brains & Brawn of Mixed Martial Arts. 2013. (Spectacular Sports Ser.). (ENG., Illus.). 64p. (J). (gr. 5-8). lib. bdg. 34.65 *(978-1-4677-0934-7(4)*, ed778620-7039-409d-a72e-ba8eb7329db4, Millbrook Pr.) Lerner Publishing Group.

Jones, Richard & Santillan, Jorge. Manga Martial Arts Figures, 1 vol. 2012. (Learn to Draw Manga Ser.). (ENG., Illus.). 32p. (J). (gr. 4-5). pap. 12.75 *(978-1-4488-7946-5(9)*, 5aeedcb5-393e-47d3-a1f7-55539121b638); lib. bdg. 30.27 *(978-1-4488-7875-8(6)*, 9ba79e5c-5e1a-4957-9767-eefa83373931) Rosen Publishing Group, Inc., The. (PowerKids Pr.).

Kennedy, Robert. Would You Dare Be an MMA Fighter?, 1 vol. 2016. (Would You Dare? Ser.). (ENG., Illus.). 32p. (J). (gr. 1-2). pap. 11.50 *(978-1-4824-5814-5(4)*, f9065e93-21be-4e17-b392-7a4afad83be0) Stevens, Gareth Publishing LLLP.

Klimchuk, David. Aikido, 1 vol. 2019. (Enter the Dojo! Martial Arts for Kids Ser.). (ENG.). 24p. (gr. 3-4). pap. 9.25 *(978-1-7253-0998-2(X)*, 51d28fd8-889a-4016-a7e8-ffa95ea2aabb, PowerKids Pr.) Rosen Publishing Group, Inc., The.

Kortemeier, Todd. Superstars of the UFC. 2016. (Pro Sports Superstars Ser.). (ENG.). 24p. (J). (gr. 1-4). lib. bdg. 20.95 *(978-1-60753-939-1(X)*, 15669) Amicus.

Lacey, Saskia. Deportes Espectaculares: Comparacion de Números. rev. ed. 2018. (Mathematics in the Real World Ser.). (SPA., Illus.). 32p. (J). (gr. 2-3). pap. 10.99 *(978-1-4258-2862-2(0))* Teacher Created Materials, Inc.

—Spectacular Sports: Martial Arts: Comparing Numbers (Grade 2) 2018. (Mathematics in the Real World Ser.). (ENG., Illus.). 32p. (J). (gr. 2-3). pap. 10.99 *(978-1-4258-5745-5(0))* Teacher Created Materials, Inc.

Levigne, Heather. Les Arts Martiaux. Briere, Marie-Josee, tr. from ENG. Rouse, Bonna, illus. 2007. (Sans Limites Ser.). (FRE.). 32p. (J). pap. 9.95 *(978-2-89579-168-3(6))* Bayard Canada Livres CAN. Dist: Crabtree Publishing Co.

Litmanovich, Ellina. Ronda Rousey: Champion Mixed Martial Arts Star, 1 vol. 2017. (Sports Star Champions Ser.). (ENG.). 48p. (gr. 5-6). lib. bdg. 29.60 *(978-0-7660-8696-8(8)*, a7ddf10b-19f6-4e1c-863d-8ffc98f92aa1) Enslow Publishing, LLC.

Lorini, Walter. A Complete Guide to Tai Chi, 1 vol. 2017. (Mastering Martial Arts Ser.). (ENG.). 128p. (gr. 6-6). lib. bdg. 38.93 *(978-0-7660-8537-4(6)*, 3c861bfd-5c91-404a-9bea-9c21a7596112) Enslow Publishing, LLC.

MacAulay, Kelley & Kalman, Bobbie. Taekwondo in Action. Crabtree, Marc, photos by. 2004. (Sports in Action Ser.). (ENG., Illus.). 32p. (J). pap. *(978-0-7787-0358-7(4))* Crabtree Publishing Co.

Mapua, Jeff. Martial Arts for Fun & Fitness, 1 vol. 2019. (Sports for Fun & Fitness Ser.). (ENG.). 32p. (gr. 3-3). pap. 11.53 *(978-1-9785-1341-9(0)*, 6cb453a7-887b-4976-a482-58981ba76c5a) Enslow Publishing, LLC.

Martial Arts Sports Zone: Spring 2012 New Releases. 2012. (Martial Arts Sports Zone Ser.). 32p. (gr. 4-8). lib. bdg. 159.60 *(978-0-7613-8901-9(6)*, Lerner Pubns.) Lerner Publishing Group.

Mason, Paul. Tae Kwon Do. 2010. (Combat Sports Ser.). 32p. (J). (gr. 2-5). lib. bdg. 28.50 *(978-1-59771-277-4(9))* Sea-To-Sea Pubns.

Mastering Martial Arts, 12 vols. 2017. (Mastering Martial Arts Ser.). (ENG.). 128p. (gr. 6-6). lib. bdg. 233.58 *(978-0-7660-8595-4(3)*, 1496b4bb-688f-4758-adca-4cb3e6d5c800) Enslow Publishing, LLC.

Mattern, Joanne. Kickboxing. 2008. (Illus.). 24p. (J). lib. bdg. *(978-1-60472-395-3(5))* Rourke Educational Media.

Matthews, Rupert. Ninjas, 1 vol. 2015. (History's Fearless Fighters Ser.). (ENG., Illus.). 48p. (J). (gr. 5-6). pap. 15.05 *(978-1-4824-3173-5(4)*,

56235f88-f04b-43cd-8a48-1dd575b9022a) Stevens, Gareth Publishing LLLP.

McFee, Shane. Let's Learn Martial Arts. (Let's Get Active Ser.). 24p. (gr. 2-3). 2009. 42.50 *(978-1-61514-250-7(9))* 2008. (ENG., Illus.). (J). lib. bdg. 26.27 *(978-1-4042-4196-1(5),* 6eac7299-e520-4f20-a8ab-2d83d540379c) Rosen Publishing Group, Inc., The. (PowerKids Pr.).

McIntosh, J. S. Martial Arts. 2010. (Getting the Edge Ser.). 96p. (YA). lib. bdg. 24.95 *(978-1-4222-1738-2(8))* Mason Crest.

McNab, Chris. Martial Arts for People with Disabilities. 2004. (Martial & Fighting Arts Ser.). (Illus.). 96p. (YA). (gr. 7). lib. bdg. 22.95 *(978-1-59084-399-4(1))* Mason Crest.

Mochizuki, Ken. Be Water, My Friend, 1 vol. Lee, Dom, illus. 2006. (ENG.). 32p. (J). 16.95 *(978-1-58430-265-0(8))* Lee & Low Bks., Inc.

Monnig, Alex. Aikido, 1 vol. 2015. (Inside Martial Arts Ser.). (ENG., Illus.). 48p. (J). (gr. 3-6). lib. bdg. 34.21 *(978-1-62403-601-9(5),* 17069, SportsZone) ABDO Publishing Co.

Montanha. The Brazilian Jiu-Jitsu Mind Set: To Submit Your Opponent from Any Position ! 2004. (Illus.). 108p. per. 12.95 *(978-0-9743380-0-2(1))* Montanha Pr.

Mooney, Carla. Ninjas. 2013. (Great Warriors Ser.). (ENG., Illus.). 48p. (J). (gr. 4-8). pap. 18.50 *(978-1-61783-776-0(8),* 10808) ABDO Publishing Co.

Mostofizadeh, Hoomaz. MMA Coloring Book: Mixed Martial Arts Coloring Book. 2012. (ENG.). 52p. pap. 5.99 *(978-1-937981-60-0(6))* Mikazuki Publishing Hse.

Nishida, Masaki. Drawing Manga Martial Arts Figures. (How to Draw Manga Ser.). 24p. (gr. 3-3). 2009. 47.90 *(978-1-61513-440-3(9),* PowerKids Pr.) 2007. (ENG., Illus.). (J). lib. bdg. 28.93 *(978-1-4042-3850-3(6),* 899dc180-5f59-4a11-8ecb-4cdab25e6a29) Rosen Publishing Group, Inc., The.

Noll, Elizabeth. Mixed Martial Artists. 2016. (Rank It! Ser.). (ENG.). 32p. (J). (gr. 4-6). 31.35 *(978-1-68072-061-7(9),* 10235); pap. 9.99 *(978-1-64466-133-8(0),* 10236) Black Rabbit Bks. (Bolt).

Osborne, M. K. Combat Sports. 2020. (Summer Olympic Sports Ser.). (ENG.). 32p. (J). (gr. 2-5). lib. bdg. *(978-1-68151-822-0(8),* 10696) Amicus.

—Los Deportes de Combate. 2020. (Deportes Olímpicos de Verano Ser.). (SPA.). 32p. (J). (gr. 2-5). lib. bdg. *(978-1-68151-896-1(1),* 10706) Amicus.

O'Shei, Tim. Kendo [Scholastic]. 2011. (Martial Arts Ser.). 32p. pap. 1.00 *(978-1-4296-6484-4(3),* Capstone Pr.) Capstone.

Page, Jason. Martial Arts, Boxing, & Other Combat Sports: Fencing, Judo, Wrestling, Taekwondo, & a Whole Lot More, 1 vol. 2008. (Olympic Sports Ser.). (ENG., Illus.). 32p. (J). (gr. 3-7). pap. *(978-0-7787-4033-9(1));* lib. bdg. *(978-0-7787-4016-2(1))* Crabtree Publishing Co.

Park, Y. H. Taekwondo for Kids. Tok, Stephanie, illus. 2005. (Martial Arts for Kids Ser.). 48p. (J). (gr. k-3). 13.95 *(978-0-8048-3631-9(0))* Tuttle Publishing.

Pawlett, Mark & Pawlett, Ray. The Tae Kwon Do Handbook, 1 vol. 2008. (Martial Arts Ser.). (ENG., Illus.). 256p. (YA). (gr. 8-8). lib. bdg. 47.80 *(978-1-4042-1396-8(1),* 36e33bec-9e98-417a-9d1d-1090fa1418d3) Rosen Publishing Group, Inc., The.

Rielly, Robin L. Karate for Kids. Tok, Stephanie & Tok, Stephanie, illus. 2004. (Martial Arts for Kids Ser.). 48p. (J). (gr. k-3). 13.95 *(978-0-8048-3534-3(9))* Tuttle Publishing.

Roytman, Arkady. Martial Arts Coloring Book. 2013. (Dover Sports Coloring Bks.). (ENG., Illus.). 32p. (J). (gr. 3-5). pap. 3.99 *(978-0-486-49023-6(8),* 490238) Dover Pubns., Inc.

Roza, Greg. Judo, 1 vol. 2019. (Enter the Dojo! Martial Arts for Kids Ser.). (ENG.). 24p. (gr. 3-4). pap. 9.25 *(978-1-7253-1010-0(4),* 670a95f6-7a72-453f-b110-64f3c8372875, PowerKids Pr.) Rosen Publishing Group, Inc., The.

Rumpf, Wolfgang. Taekwondo Kids: From White Belt to Yellow/Green Belt. Dornemann, Volker, illus. 2007. 136p. (J). pap. 14.95 *(978-1-84126-214-7(5))* Meyer & Meyer Sport, Ltd. GBR. Dist: Cardinal Pubs. Group.

Rumpf, Wolfgang & Dornemann, Volker. Taekwondo Kids Volume 2: From Green Belt to Blue Belt. 2008. (Illus.). 144p. (J). (gr. 4-7). pap. 14.95 *(978-1-84126-240-6(4))* Meyer & Meyer Sport, Ltd. GBR. Dist: Cardinal Pubs. Group.

Safe Kids USA Staff. Self-Defense for Kids: Learn Practical & Effective Techniques to Help You Defend Yourself. 2004. (Illus.). 48p. (J). (gr. -1-12). pap. 6.95 *(978-0-9718609-5-7(5))* Escher, Ursula.

Sherman, Jill. Ronda Rousey. 2019. (Pro Sports Biographies Ser.). (ENG.). 24p. (J). (gr. 1-3). pap. 8.99 *(978-1-68152-451-1(1),* 11037) Amicus.

Snow, Kevin. Ronda Rousey: Conquering New Ground, 1 vol. 2017. (At the Top of Their Game Ser.). (ENG., Illus.). 112p. (YA). (gr. 9-9). 44.50 *(978-1-5026-2832-9(5),* 200ad270-ab9f-4a63-89a5-a1de9d8892d8) Cavendish Square Publishing LLC.

Streissguth, Thomas. Kickboxing. 2008. (Action Sports Ser.). (ENG., Illus.). 24p. (J). (gr. 3-7). lib. bdg. 26.95 *(978-1-60014-140-9(4))* Bellwether Media.

Tometich, Annabelle. Mixed Martial Arts, 1 vol. 2015. (Inside Martial Arts Ser.). (ENG., Illus.). 48p. (J). (gr. 3-6). lib. bdg. 34.21 *(978-1-62403-605-7(8),* 17077, SportsZone) ABDO Publishing Co.

Trimble, Aidan, contrib. by. Martial & Fighting Arts, 13 vols., Set. (Illus.). 96p. (YA). (gr. 7-18). lib. bdg. *(978-1-59084-387-1(8))* Mason Crest.

Turnbull, Stephen. Real Ninja: Over 20 True Stories of Japan's Secret Assassins, 1 vol. Field, James, illus. 2009. (Real Adventurers Ser.). (ENG.). 48p. (J). (gr. 3-3). 25.50 *(978-1-59270-081-3(0),* d8656722-10af-4444-86bb-a28667bdb08d, Cavendish Square) Cavendish Square Publishing LLC.

Uschan, Michael V. Jet Li, 1 vol. 2011. (People in the News Ser.). (ENG., Illus.). 96p. (gr. 7-7). lib. bdg. 41.03 *(978-1-4205-0731-7(1),* c9bfb396-2c14-4c5d-9866-277ca19f5b07, Lucent Pr.) Greenhaven Publishing LLC.

Warr, Peter. The Kung Fu Handbook. 2009. (Martial Arts Ser.). 256p. (gr. 8-8). 79.90 *(978-1-61514-369-6(6))* Rosen Publishing Group, Inc., The.

Waxman, Laura Hamilton. Ninja Competitions. 2020. (Lightning Bolt Books (r) — Ninja Mania Ser.). (ENG., Illus.). 24p. (J). (gr. 1-3). pap. 9.99 *(978-1-5415-8916-2(5),* 0ad7bc1d-8113-4512-ba60-ff93601bb746); lib. bdg. 29.32 *(978-1-5415-7705-3(1),* 599eb8cc-4258-4a9b-8059-f648655ed580) Lerner Publishing Group. (Lerner Pubns.).

Weiss, Bobbi J. G. & Weiss, David Cody. Phonic Comics - Hiro Dragon Warrior: Fight or Flight Level 2, Issue 3. 2011. (ENG., Illus.). 24p. (J). (gr. 1-17). pap. 3.99 *(978-1-60169-111-8(4))* Innovative Kids.

Whiting, Jim. Mixed Martial Arts. 2018. (Odysseys in Extreme Sports Ser.). (ENG.). 80p. (J). (gr. 7-10). *(978-1-60818-692-1(X),* 19876, Creative Education) Creative Co., The.

Wiseman, Blaine. UFC Championship. 2010. (Sporting Championships Ser.). 32p. (J). (gr. 4-6). lib. bdg. 27.13 *(978-1-61690-130-1(6))* Weigl Pubs., Inc.

—UFC Championship: Sporting Championships. 2010. (J). pap. 10.95 *(978-1-61690-131-8(4))* Weigl Pubs., Inc.

Wood, Alix. Dueling, 1 vol. Wood, Alix, illus. 2013. (Why'd They Do That? Strange Customs of the Past Ser.). (Illus.). 32p. (J). (gr. 4-5). (ENG.). pap. 11.50 *(978-1-4339-9577-4(8),* 86a97d52-f938-4ab3-a7fd-7cfa004afbb2); (ENG., lib. bdg. 29.27 *(978-1-4339-9576-7(X),* a0d3f328-0009-416f-8cb5-29a959de8e73); pap. 63.00 *(978-1-4339-9578-1(6))* Stevens, Gareth Publishing LLLP.

—You Can Be a Martial Artist, 1 vol., Vol. 1. 2013. (Let's Get Moving! Ser.). (ENG.). 32p. (J). (gr. 3-4). 29.27 *(978-1-4824-0279-7(3),* 176efd3d-83a6-4730-9a28-e86bfb70eab2) Stevens, Gareth Publishing LLLP.

MARTIAL ARTS—FICTION

Adam D. Levine. Knights: Reign of Hellfire. 2010. (ENG.). 184p. 23.95 *(978-1-4401-7614-2(0));* pap. 13.95 *(978-1-4401-7618-0(3))* iUniverse, Inc.

Asai, Carrie. The Book of the Pearl. Alarcão, Renato, illus. 2003. (Samurai Girl Ser.: 3). (ENG.). 240p. (YA). (gr. 11). pap. 6.99 *(978-0-689-86432-2(9),* Simon Pulse) Simon Pulse.

—The Book of the Wind. Alarcão, Renato & Alarcão, Renato, illus. 2003. (Samurai Girl Ser.: 4). (ENG.). 224p. (YA). (gr. 11). pap. 6.99 *(978-0-689-86433-9(7),* Simon Pulse) Simon Pulse.

Barnes, Dawn. Seven Wheels of Power. Chang, Bernard, illus. 2005. (Black Belt Club Ser.: No. 1). (ENG.). 173p. (J). (gr. 3-6). 17.44 *(978-0-439-63936-1(0))* Scholastic, Inc.

Binfet, Eric. The Ninja with Bunny Rabbit Slippers. 2012. 34p. pap. 19.99 *(978-1-105-44896-6(7))* Lulu.com GBR. Dist: Lulu Pr., Inc.

Boltonwood-Castle, Tony. Ben,Jay & Ricardo Karate Adventure: The Night the Thieves Came Calling. 2010. 80p. pap. 10.49 *(978-1-4520-8114-4(X))* AuthorHouse.

Bradford, Chris. Bodyguard: Hostage (Book 2), Bk. 2. 2017. (Bodyguard Ser.: 2). (ENG.). 224p. (J). (gr. 5). pap. 8.99 *(978-1-5247-3699-6(6),* Philomel Bks.) Penguin Young Readers Group.

—Bodyguard: Ransom (Book 4), Bk. 4. 2017. (Bodyguard Ser.: 4). (ENG.). 224p. (J). (gr. 5). pap. 9.99 *(978-1-5247-3703-0(8),* Philomel Bks.) Penguin Young Readers Group.

—Bodyguard: Recruit (Book 1), Bk. 1. 2017. (Bodyguard Ser.: 1). (ENG.). 272p. (J). (gr. 5). pap. 8.99 *(978-1-5247-3697-2(X),* Philomel Bks.) Penguin Young Readers Group.

—Bodyguard: Target (Book 7) 2018. (Bodyguard Ser.: 7). (ENG.). 288p. (J). (gr. 5). pap. 8.99 *(978-1-5247-3935-5(9),* Philomel Bks.) Penguin Young Readers Group.

—Bodyguard: Traitor (Book 8) 2018. (Bodyguard Ser.: 8). (ENG., Illus.). 224p. (J). (gr. 5). pap. 8.99 *(978-1-5247-3937-9(5),* Philomel Bks.) Penguin Young Readers Group.

—Ninja: First Mission. 2012. (Stoke Books Titles Ser.). 64p. (J). (gr. 5-8). pap. 7.95 *(978-1-78112-022-4(6));* pap. 45.32 *(978-0-7613-9221-7(1));* lib. bdg. 22.60 *(978-1-78112-021-7(8))* Stoke Bks.

—The Way of the Dragon, 3. 2012. (Young Samurai Ser.). (ENG.). 512p. (J). (gr. 6-8). 22.44 *(978-1-4231-3779-5(5))* Hyperion Bks. for Children.

—The Way of the Dragon. Lt. ed. 2012. (Young Samurai Ser.). (ENG.). 448p. (J). (gr. 9-12). 23.99 *(978-1-4104-4466-0(X))* Thorndike Pr.

—The Way of the Sword. Lt. ed. 2012. (Young Samurai Ser.). (ENG.). 547p. (J). (gr. 6-9). 23.99 *(978-1-4104-4404-2(X))* Thorndike Pr.

—The Way of the Warrior, 1. 2008. (Young Samurai Ser.). (ENG.). 384p. (J). (gr. 6-8). 22.44 *(978-1-4231-1986-9(X))* Hyperion Bks. for Children.

—The Way of the Warrior. Lt. ed. 2011. (Young Samurai Ser.). (ENG.). 328p. (J). 23.99 *(978-1-4104-4329-8(9))* Thorndike Pr.

—Young Samurai: the Way of the Sword, 2. 2011. (Young Samurai Ser.). (ENG.). 448p. (gr. 6-8). 22.44 *(978-1-4231-2937-0(7))* Hyperion Bks. for Children.

—Young Samurai the Way of the Warrior: The Way of the Warrior, Bk. 1. 2008. (Young Samurai Ser.: 1). (Illus.). 352p. (J). (gr. 6-10). pap. 12.99 *(978-0-14-132430-2(9))* Penguin Bks., Ltd. GBR. Dist: Independent Pubs. Group.

Brown, K. T. The Adventures of Peter Tucker: Introduction of the Tiger. 2011. 82p. pap. 15.99 *(978-1-4628-7856-7(3))* Xlibris Corp.

Bruchac, Joseph. The Way. 2013. (ENG.). 160p. (YA). (gr. 6-12). pap. 9.95 *(978-1-4677-0862-3(3),* dd3043d8-11f7-4c45-a484-7bef255f2f84) 2007. 156p. (J). (gr. 4-7). 16.95 *(978-1-58196-062-4(X))* Lerner Publishing Group. (Darby Creek).

Caputo, Kenneth. The Adventures of Jay & Tay: Our First Karate Class. 2011. 32p. pap. 14.99 *(978-1-4567-1999-9(8))* AuthorHouse.

Cha, Louis. The Legendary Couple, Vol. 4. Wong, Tony, illus. 2003. 120p. (YA). (gr. 8-18). pap. 13.95 *(978-1-58899-233-8(0))* ComicsOne Corp./Dr. Masters.

Chanda, J-P. Turtle Rescue! Redondo, Jesus, illus. 2004. (Teenage Mutant Ninja Turtles Ser.). 32p. (J). (gr. 4-7). 11.65 *(978-0-7569-5371-3(5))* Perfection Learning Corp.

Chin, Oliver. Julie Black Belt: the Belt of Fire. Chua, Charlene, illus. 2013. (Julie Black Belt Ser.). (ENG.). 40p. (J). (gr. -1-3). 15.95 *(978-1-59702-079-4(6))* Immedium.

Colossal, Eric. Feasts of Fury. 2016. (Rutabaga the Adventure Chef Ser.: 2). (Illus.). 124p. (J). lib. bdg. 20.80 *(978-0-606-38205-2(4))* Turtleback.

DaCosta, Barbara. Nighttime Ninja. 2012. (ENG., Illus.). 32p. (J). (gr. -1-3). 18.99 *(978-0-316-20384-5(X))* Little, Brown Bks. for Young Readers.

Davis, Jacky. Black Belt Bunny. Fleck, Jay, illus. 2017. 40p. (J). (-k). 16.99 *(978-0-525-42902-9(6),* Dial Bks) Penguin Young Readers Group.

Devine, Eric. Tap Out. 2012. (ENG.). 320p. (YA). (gr. 8-17). pap. 17.99 *(978-0-7624-4569-1(6),* Running Pr. Kids) Running Pr.

DreamWorks. Kung Fu Panda: Po's Tasty Training. 2008. (J). 13.99 *(978-1-59319-981-4(3))* LeapFrog Enterprises, Inc.

DreamWorks & DreamWorks / LeapFrog. Kung Fu Panda: L'Entrainement Gourmand. 2008. (J). 20.79 *(978-1-59319-946-3(5))* LeapFrog Enterprises, Inc.

Gallo, Tina. Like Father, Like Po. 2015. (Kung Fu Panda 8x8 Ser.). lib. bdg. 13.55 *(978-0-606-38257-1(7))* Turtleback.

Gerver, Jane E. The Santa Snatcher. Spaziante, Patrick, illus. 2004. 32p. (J). lib. bdg. 15.00 *(978-1-4242-0959-0(5))* Fitzgerald Bks.

Goh, Colin & Woo, Yen Yen. Enter the Dumpling, Vol. 1. Lee, Soo, illus. 2013. (ENG.). 144p. (J). pap. 12.99 *(978-0-9881899-0-4(9),* e7f45ba0-9304-4f0a-8a11-6f00e368a06a) Yumcha Studios LLC.

Higgins, Simon. Moonshadow: Rise of the Ninja. 2011. (Moonshadow Ser.: 1). (ENG.). 352p. (J). (gr. 3-7). pap. 18.99 *(978-0-316-05532-1(8))* Little, Brown Bks. for Young Readers.

—Moonshadow: the Nightmare Ninja. 2012. (Moonshadow Ser.: 2). (ENG.). 384p. (J). (gr. 3-7). pap. 19.99 *(978-0-316-05534-5(4))* Little, Brown Bks. for Young Readers.

Himmelman, John. Bunjitsu Bunny Jumps to the Moon. Himmelman, John, illus. 2017. (Bunjitsu Bunny Ser.: 3). (ENG., Illus.). 144p. (J). pap. 6.99 *(978-1-250-12940-6(0),* 900158780) Square Fish.

—Bunjitsu Bunny vs. Bunjitsu Bunny. Himmelman, John, illus. 2018. (Bunjitsu Bunny Ser.: 4). (ENG., Illus.). 128p. (J). pap. 8.99 *(978-1-250-17720-9(0),* 900158783) Square Fish.

Holt, Alex. Kung-Fu Frogs: From the Planet Intellectica. 2012. 40p. pap. 19.57 *(978-1-4669-1973-0(6))* Trafford Publishing.

Ishida, Sanae. Chibi Samurai Wants a Pet: An Adventure with Little Kunoichi the Ninja Girl. 2017. (Little Kunoichi the Ninja Girl Ser.). (Illus.). 32p. (J). (gr. -1-2). 16.99 *(978-1-63217-117-7(1),* Little Bigfoot) Sasquatch Bks.

—Little Kunoichi the Ninja Girl. 2015. (Little Kunoichi the Ninja Girl Ser.). (ENG., Illus.). 32p. (J). (gr. -1-2). 16.99 *(978-1-57061-954-0(9),* Little Bigfoot) Sasquatch Bks.

James, Hollis. Mikey's Monster (Teenage Mutant Ninja Turtles) Spaziante, Patrick, illus. 2013. (Step into Reading Ser.). (ENG.). 48p. (J). (gr. k-3). 5.99 *(978-0-449-81826-8(8),* Random Hse. Bks. for Young Readers) Random Hse. Children's Bks.

Jiang Hong, Chen. Little Eagle. 2007. (ENG., Illus.). 32p. (J). (gr. -1-3). 16.95 *(978-1-59270-071-4(3))* Enchanted Lion Bks., LLC.

Johnson, Lauren. Beastly Basketball, 1 vol. Garcia, Eduardo, illus. 2014. (Sports Illustrated Kids Graphic Novels Ser.). (ENG.). 72p. (J). (gr. 3-8). lib. bdg. 26.65 *(978-1-4342-6490-9(4),* 124178, Stone Arch Bks.) Capstone.

Jones, Patrick. Body Shot. 2013. (Dojo Ser.). (ENG.). 112p. (YA). (gr. 6-12). pap. 7.95 *(978-1-4677-1490-7(9),* 609b64c8-d5a6-4a67-8b8d-c25607ed4236, Darby Creek) Lerner Publishing Group.

—Triangle Choke. 2013. (Dojo Ser.). (ENG.). 136p. (YA). (gr. 6-12). pap. 7.95 *(978-1-4677-1487-7(9),* 4d46aae7-575c-4173-bdff-a916d8555b03, Darby Creek) Lerner Publishing Group.

Kakakios, Melissa. I Love Taekwondo: My First Taekwondo Books. 2013. 28p. pap. 16.95 *(978-1-4525-7668-8(8),* Balboa Pr.) Author Solutions, LLC.

—The Spirit of Courage: My First Tae Kwon Do Books. 2013. 28p. pap. 16.95 *(978-1-4525-8284-9(X),* Balboa Pr.) Author Solutions, LLC.

Katzenberger, Lisa. A Triceratops Would NOT Make a Good Ninja. Calvert, Steph, illus. 2018. (Dinosaur Daydreams Ser.). (ENG.). 24p. (J). (gr. -1-2). pap. 7.95 *(978-1-5158-2131-1(5),* 136735, Picture Window Bks.) Capstone.

Kishimoto, Masashi. Naruto: Chapter Book, Vol. 11: The Tenth Question. 2010. (Naruto: Chapter Bks.: 11). (ENG., Illus.). 80p. (J). pap. 4.99 *(978-1-4215-3041-3(4))* Viz Media.

—Naruto: Chapter Book, Vol. 12: Coward. 2010. (Naruto: Chapter Bks.: 12). (ENG., Illus.). 80p. (J). pap. 4.99 *(978-1-4215-3042-0(2))* Viz Media.

—Naruto: Chapter Book, Vol. 13: Beauty Is the Beast. 2010. (Naruto: Chapter Bks.: 13). (ENG., Illus.). 80p. (J). pap. 4.99 *(978-1-4215-3043-7(0))* Viz Media.

—Naruto: Chapter Book, Vol. 15: The Last Chance. 2010. (Naruto: Chapter Bks.: 15). (ENG., Illus.). 80p. (J). (gr. 1-4). pap. 4.99 *(978-1-4215-3045-1(7))* Viz Media.

Laflamme, Mark. Guys Named Jack. 2013. 308p. pap. 17.95 *(978-1-62646-391-2(3))* Booklocker.com, Inc.

Leibold, Jay. Secret of the Ninja. Nugent, Suzanne, illus. 2006. (ENG.). 144p. (J). (gr. 4-8). per. 7.99 *(978-1-933390-16-1(6))* Chooseco LLC.

Leigh, C. J. The Ninjabread Man. Gall, Chris, illus. 2016. (ENG.). 40p. (J). (gr. -1-k). 18.99 *(978-0-545-81430-0(8))* Scholastic, Inc.

Lien, Henry. Peasprout Chen, Future Legend of Skate & Sword. 2019. (Peasprout Chen Ser.: 1). (ENG., Illus.). 352p. (J). pap. 12.99 *(978-1-250-29436-4(3),* 900187110) Square Fish.

Ling, L. M. ZOEY LEE Schoolyard Scuffle. 2011. (ENG., illus.). 160p. pap. 9.99 *(978-1-937861-00-1(7))* Fear2love Pr.

Ma, Wing Shing. Storm Riders Vol. 1: Invading Sun. 2003. (ENG., Illus.). 128p. pap. 9.95 *(978-1-58899-359-5(0))* ComicsOne Corp./Dr. Masters.

Ma, Wing Shing & Lau, Ding Kin. Chinese Hero Vol. 3: Tales of the Blood Sword. Yang, Sue & Stone, Benjamin, eds. Zhao, Yun, tr. from CHI. 2007. (ENG., Illus.). 280p. (YA). pap. 19.95 *(978-1-59796-117-2(5))* DrMaster Pubns. Inc.

Mah, Adeline Yen. Chinese Cinderella & the Secret Dragon Society. 2006. (ENG., Illus.). 256p. (J). (gr. 5-9). pap. 7.99 *(978-0-06-056736-1(8),* HarperCollins) HarperCollins Pubs.

Mauser McCord, Pat. A Bundle of Sticks. 2nd ed. 2004. (ENG., Illus.). 170p. (J). pap. 6.99 *(978-1-880336-86-1(3),* BOS) Turtle Pr.

McCann, James. Flying Feet, 1 vol. 2010. (Orca Sports Ser.). (ENG., Illus.). 152p. (J). (gr. 4-7). pap. 9.95 *(978-1-55469-290-3(3))* Orca Bk. Pubs. USA.

Montgomery, R. A. Tattoo of Death. Cannella, Marco, illus. 2007. (ENG.). 144p. (J). (gr. 4-8). pap. 7.99 *(978-1-933390-22-2(0))* Chooseco LLC.

Ohtaka, Shinobu, creator. Sumomomo, Momomo, Vol. 12: The Strongest Bride on Earth, 12 vols. 2012. (Sumomomo, Momomo Ser.: 12). (ENG., Illus.). 240p. (gr. 11-17). pap. 13.00 *(978-0-316-20470-5(6))* Yen Pr. LLC.

Pierce, Terry. Tae Kwon Do! Bonita, Todd, illus. 2006. (Step into Reading: Step 1 Ser.). (ENG.). 32p. (J). (gr. -1-1). lib. bdg. 16.19 *(978-0-375-93448-3(0))* Random House Publishing Group.

—Tae Kwon Do! Bonita, Todd, illus. 2006. (Step into Reading Ser.). 32p. (J). (gr. -1-1). per. 5.99 *(978-0-375-83448-6(6),* Random Hse. Bks. for Young Readers) Random Hse. Children's Bks.

Ray, Joanna Z. 'elaran! Isithan!' 2008. (ENG.). 91p. (YA). per. *(978-1-4116-9393-7(0))* Lulu Pr., Inc.

Richard, Laurent. Ninjas & Knock Outs! Book 2, No. 2. Ryser, Nicolas, illus. 2014. (Tao, the Little Samurai Ser.: 2). (ENG.). 64p. (J). (gr. 2-5). lib. bdg. 29.32 *(978-1-4677-3272-7(9),* e5d02ec4-9e15-490c-a5e7-a8fd6247b4c7, Graphic Universe™) Lerner Publishing Group.

Roman, Annette. Passage 2: HIV/AIDS — First Love. Ng, Leandro, illus. 2005. (1 World Manga Ser.: Vol. 2). (ENG.). 40p. (J). pap. 3.99 *(978-0-8213-6406-2(5))* World Bank Pubns.

Schwartz, Corey Rosen. Ninja Red Riding Hood. Santat, Dan, illus. 2014. 40p. (J). (gr. k-3). 18.99 *(978-0-399-16354-8(9),* G.P. Putnam's Sons Books for Young Readers) Penguin Young Readers Group.

—The Three Ninja Pigs. Santat, Dan, illus. 2012. 40p. (J). (gr. k-3). 18.99 *(978-0-399-25514-4(1),* G.P. Putnam's Sons Books for Young Readers) Penguin Young Readers Group.

Schwartz, Corey Rosen & Gomez, Rebecca J. Hensel & Gretel: Ninja Chicks. Santat, Dan, illus. 2016. 40p. (J). (gr. k-3). 18.99 *(978-0-399-17626-5(8),* G.P. Putnam's Sons Books for Young Readers) Penguin Young Readers Group.

Sensei Teaches Focus. 2004. (J). 10.00 *(978-0-9767483-0-4(4))* Wright's Way Inc.

Siu-Chong, Ken. Street Fighter Legends Volume 1: Sakura: Sakura. 2007. (ENG., Illus.). 128p. pap. 11.95 *(978-0-9781386-4-6(3),* 4616f794-70aa-47c9-bc3d-789015ec918f) URON Entertainment Corp. CAN. Dist: Diamond Comic Distributors, Inc.

Stevens, B. K. Fighting Chance. 2015. (ENG.). 336p. (YA). pap. 18.99 *(978-1-929345-14-4(3),* Poisoned Pen Press) Sourcebooks, Inc.

Styles, Walker. Ghosts & Goblins & Ninja, Oh My! Whitehouse, Ben, illus. 2016. (Rider Woofson Ser.: 4). (ENG.). 128p. (J). (gr. k-4). pap. 5.99 *(978-1-4814-6306-5(3),* Little Simon) Little Simon.

Teitelbaum, Michael. Trial by Fire. 2010. (Avatar: the Last Airbender Ser.). (ENG.). 64p. (J). (gr. 3-6). 18.69 *(978-1-4424-0290-4(3),* Simon Spotlight) Simon & Schuster Children's Publishing.

Thielbar, Melinda. The Ancient Formula: A Mystery with Fractions. Pantoja, Maria Kristina Sb., illus. 2011. (Manga Math Mysteries Ser.: 5). (ENG.). 48p. (J). (gr. 3-5). pap. 6.95 *(978-0-7613-8134-1(1),* 1c74d365-5757-4fe3-8be4-721e1b06585d, Graphic Universe™) Lerner Publishing Group.

—#5 the Ancient Formula: A Mystery with Fractions. Pantoja, Tintin, illus. 2011. (Manga Math Mysteries Set II Ser.). pap. 39.62 *(978-0-7613-8362-8(X),* Graphic Universe™) Lerner Publishing Group.

Thomas, Jim. Super Slam Turtles! Spaziante, Patrick, illus. 2005. 22p. (J). lib. bdg. 15.00 *(978-1-4242-0971-2(4))* Fitzgerald Bks.

Toriyama, Akira. Dragon Ball Full Color Freeza Arc, Volume 1. 2016. (Dragon Ball Freeza Ser.: 1). lib. bdg. 33.05 *(978-0-606-38706-4(4))* Turtleback.

—Dragon Ball Full Color Freeza Arc, Volume 2. 2016. (Dragon Ball Freeza Ser.: 2). lib. bdg. 33.05 *(978-0-606-38934-1(2))* Turtleback.

—Dragon Ball Z (VIZBIG Edition), Vol. 8. 2010. (Dragon Ball Z VIZBIG Edition Ser.: 8). (ENG., Illus.). 560p. pap. 19.99 *(978-1-4215-2071-1(0))* Viz Media.

Toriyama, Akira, creator. Dragon Ball: Chapter Book, Vol. 7: Let the Tournament Begin! 2010. (Dragon Ball: Chapter Bks.: 7). (ENG., Illus.). 80p. (J). pap. 4.99 *(978-1-4215-3123-6(2))* Viz Media.

—Dragon Ball: Chapter Book, Vol. 8: Fight to the Finish! 2010. (Dragon Ball: Chapter Bks.: 8). (ENG., Illus.). 80p. (J). pap. 4.99 *(978-1-4215-3124-3(0))* Viz Media.

Van Vleet, Carmella. Eliza Bing Is (Not) a Big, Fat Quitter. 2017. (Eliza Bing Ser.). (ENG.). 176p. (J). (gr. 2-5). pap. 7.99 *(978-0-8234-3878-5(3))* Holiday Hse., Inc.

Vernon, Ursula. Attack of the Ninja Frogs. 2012. (Dragonbreath Ser.: 2). lib. bdg. 17.20 *(978-0-606-26666-6(5))* Turtleback.

—Dragonbreath #2: Attack of the Ninja Frogs. 2nd ed. 2010. (Dragonbreath Ser.: 2). 208p. (J). (gr. 3-7). 14.99 *(978-0-8037-3365-7(8),* Dial Bks) Penguin Young Readers Group.

Wax, Wendy. Meet Leatherhead. Spaziante, Patrick, illus. 2005. 22p. (J). lib. bdg. 15.00 *(978-1-4242-0972-9(2))* Fitzgerald Bks.

Webster, Christy. Green Team! (Teenage Mutant Ninja Turtles) Spaziante, Patrick, illus. 2012. (Step into Reading Ser.). (ENG.). 48p. (J). (gr. k-3). pap. 5.99 *(978-0-307-98070-0(7),* Random Hse. Bks. for Young Readers) Random Hse. Children's Bks.

West, Tracey. Kung Fu Panda 3 Movie Novelization. 2015. lib. bdg. 17.20 *(978-0-606-38260-1(7))* Turtleback.

—A Ninja's Path. 2012. (Ninjago Readers Ser.: 5). lib. bdg. 13.55 *(978-0-606-26771-7(9))* Turtleback.

MARTIN DE PORRES, SAINT, 1579-1639

Schmidt, Gary D. Martin de Porres: The Rose in the Desert. Diaz, David, illus. 2012. (ENG.). 32p. (J). (gr. 1-4). lib. bdg. 19.99 (978-0-547-61218-8(4), 1464622, Clarion Bks.) HarperCollins Pubs.

MARTINIQUE—FICTION

Cendrillon.Tr. of Cinderella. (FRE.). 48p. pap. 12.95 incl. audio compact disk (978-2-89558-065-2(0)) Coffragants CAN. Dist: Penton Overseas, Inc.

MARX, KARL, 1818-1883

Cates, David. Karl Marx: Philosopher & Revolutionary, 1 vol. 2011. (Essential Lives Set 7 Ser.). (ENG., Illus.). 112p. (YA). (gr. 6-12). lib. bdg. 41.36 (978-1-61783-005-1(4), 6749, Essential Library) ABDO Publishing Co.

Rössig, Wolfgang. Karl Marx. 2009. (Profiles in Economics Ser.). 112p. (YA). lib. bdg. 28.95 (978-1-59935-132-2(3)) Reynolds, Morgan Inc.

MARXISM

see Communism; Socialism

MARY, BLESSED VIRGIN, SAINT

Aston, Al. A Message for Mary. Hutchinson, Joy, illus. 2005. 16p. 2.00 (978-1-84427-176-4(5)) Scripture Union GBR. Dist: Send The Light Distribution LLC.

La Casa de Maria.Tr. of Mary's House. (SPA.). (J). (978-0-7899-0875-9(1), 496234) Editorial Unilit.

Ficocelli, Elizabeth. Child's Guide to the Rosary. Blake, Anne Catharine, illus. 2009. (ENG.). 32p. (J). 10.95 (978-0-8091-6736-4(0)) Paulist Pr.

Gormally, Elenor. The Three Visitors: The Story of Knock. Croatto, Barbara, illus. 2014. (ENG.). 32p. (J). pap. 11.00 (978-1-84730-554-1(7)) Veritas Pubns. IRL. Dist: Casemate Pubs. & Bk. Distributors, LLC.

Grandgirard, Mélanie. Mary's Story. 2017. (ENG., Illus.). 20p. (J). (gr. -1 — 1). bds. 14.99 (978-1-61261-916-3(9)) Paraclete Pr., Inc.

Lumsden, Colin, illus. Story of Mary. 2003. (Bible Colour & Learn Ser.). 32p. pap. 2.50 (978-1-903087-43-5(0)) DayOne Pubns. GBR. Dist: Send The Light Distribution LLC.

MacKenzie, Carine. Martha & Mary: Friends of Jesus. rev. ed. 2014. (Bible Time Ser.). (ENG., Illus.). 32p. (J). (gr. -1-2). pap. 4.50 (978-1-84550-167-9(5), f22c98ee-85f0-4e6f-a18a-e80bf784357e) Christian Focus Pubns. GBR. Dist: Baker & Taylor Publisher Services (BTPS).

—Mary: Mother of Jesus. rev. ed. 2012. (Bible Time Ser.). (ENG., Illus.). 32p. (J). (gr. -1-2). pap. 4.50 (978-1-84550-168-6(3), 15cf069f-45a6-4494-888a-1ee06f166a54) Christian Focus Pubns. GBR. Dist: Baker & Taylor Publisher Services (BTPS).

Moore, Alan & Tavner, Gill. Mary of Galilee. Donnelly, Karen, illus. 2014. (New Testament Ser.). (ENG.). 64p. pap. 7.95 (978-1-906230-25-8(0)) Real Reads Ltd. GBR. Dist: Casemate Pubs. & Bk. Distributors, LLC.

Orfeo, Christine Virginia. My First Book about Mary. Darrenkamp, Julia Mary, illus. 2007. 63p. (Orig.). (J). (gr. 3-7). per. 7.95 (978-0-8198-4861-1(1)) Pauline Bks. & Media.

Pingry, Patricia A. The Story of Mary. Venturi-Pickett, Stacy, illus. 2006. (ENG.). 32p. (J). (gr. -1-3). pap. 3.95 (978-0-8249-5546-5(3), Ideals Pubns.) Worthy Publishing.

Ronchi, Ermes. Hail Mary. 2013. (ENG., Illus.). 40p. (J). 12.95 (978-0-8091-6768-5(9)) Paulist Pr.

Serrano, Francisco. La Virgen de Guadalupe. Dávalos, Felipe, illus.Tr. of Virgin of Guadalupe. (SPA.). (J). (gr. 2-4). 18.00 (978-968-494-070-3(X)) Centro de Informacion y Desarrollo de la Comunicacion y la Literatura MEX. Dist: Lectorum Pubns., Inc.

MARY, QUEEN OF SCOTS, 1542-1587

Burnett, Alan & Burnett, Allan. Mary Queen of Scots & All That. Anderson, Scoular, illus. 2016. (and All That Ser.). 112p. (gr. 4-8). pap. 7.95 (978-1-78027-388-4(6)) Birlinn, Ltd. GBR. Dist: Casemate Pubs. & Bk. Distributors, LLC.

Carruth, J. A., text. Mary Queen of Scots. (Scotland in Words & Pictures Ser.). (Illus.). 32p. pap. 3.95 (978-0-7117-0147-2(4)) Jarrold Publishing GBR. Dist: 7 Hills Bk. Distributors.

MacDonald, Fiona. You Wouldn't Want to Be Mary Queen of Scots. Antram, David, illus. 2008. (You Wouldn't Want to...: History of the World Ser.). (ENG.). 32p. (J). (gr. 2-5). pap. 9.95 (978-0-531-14853-2(X), Watts, Franklin) Scholastic Library Publishing.

—You Wouldn't Want to Be Mary Queen of Scots: A Ruler Who Really Lost Her Head. Antram, David, illus. 2008. (You Wouldn't Want to Ser.). (ENG.). 32p. (J). (gr. 4-7). 29.00 (978-0-531-13912-7(3)) Scholastic Library Publishing.

Roxburgh, Ellis. Elizabeth I of England vs. Mary, Queen of Scots: Battle for the Throne, 1 vol. 2015. (History's Greatest Rivals Ser.). (ENG., Illus.). 48p. (J). (gr. 6-8). pap. 15.05 (978-1-4824-4227-4(2), e752310b-61d4-4f48-873e-92177ec42d69) Stevens, Gareth Publishing LLLP.

MARY, QUEEN OF SCOTS, 1542-1587—FICTION

Bowling, Nicholas. Witch Born. 2018. (ENG., Illus.). 320p. (YA). (gr. 7-7). 18.99 (978-1-338-27753-1(7), Chicken Hse., The) Scholastic, Inc.

Breslin, Theresa. Mary, Queen of Scots: Escape from Lochleven Castle, 48 vols. Martinez, Teresa, illus. 2018. (Traditional Scottish Tales Ser.). 32p. (J). 14.95 (978-1-78250-512-9(1), Kelpies) Floris Bks. GBR. Dist: Consortium Bk. Sales & Distribution.

Hendry, Frances. Quest for a Queen: The Falcon. 2006. pap. (978-1-905665-06-8(7)) Pollinger In Print.

—Quest for a Queen: The Jackdaw. 2006. pap. (978-1-905665-05-1(9)) Pollinger In Print.

—Quest for a Queen: The Lark. 2006. (Illus.). 251p. pap. (978-1-905665-04-4(0)) Pollinger In Print.

Meyer, Carolyn. The Wild Queen: The Days & Nights of Mary, Queen of Scots. 2013. (Young Royals Ser.). (ENG.). 432p. (YA). (gr. 7). pap. 8.99 (978-0-544-02219-5(X), 1528477, Clarion Bks.) HarperCollins Pubs.

MARYLAND

Blashfield, Jean F. America the Beautiful, Third Series: Maryland (Revised Edition) 2014. (America the Beautiful Ser.: 3). (ENG., Illus.). 144p. (J). lib. bdg. 40.00 (978-0-531-24888-1(7)) Scholastic Library Publishing.

Brown, Jonatha A. Maryland, 1 vol. 2005. (Portraits of the States Ser.). (ENG., Illus.). 32p. (gr. 3-5). pap. 11.50 (978-0-8368-4687-4(7), 3e7cc4de-cf47-42fa-9bc4-7271abd443db); lib. bdg. 28.67 (978-0-8368-4668-3(0), da5aee3e-5cf8-48ff-95fb-12ee05380472) Stevens, Gareth Publishing LLLP. (Gareth Stevens Learning Library).

Brown, Vanessa. Maryland, 1 vol. 2005. (Bilingual Library of the United States of America Ser.: Set 1). (ENG & SPA., Illus.). 32p. (J). (gr. 2-2). lib. bdg. 28.93 (978-1-4042-3085-9(8), 19454942-553e-4774-b66c-ca35f77464b7) Rosen Publishing Group, Inc., The.

Bunting, Elaine. Counties of Central Maryland, 1 vol. 2009. (ENG., Illus.). 160p. (gr. 3-6). 19.95 (978-0-87033-503-7(0), 3611, Cornell Maritime Pr./Tidewater Pubs.) Schiffer Publishing, Ltd.

—Counties of Maryland's Lower Eastern Shore, 1 vol. 2009. (ENG., Illus.). 168p. (gr. 3-6). 19.95 (978-0-87033-555-6(3), 3668, Cornell Maritime Pr./Tidewater Pubs.) Schiffer Publishing, Ltd.

—Counties of Southern Maryland, 1 vol. 2009. (ENG., Illus.). 144p. (gr. 3-6). 19.95 (978-0-87033-535-8(9), 3730, Cornell Maritime Pr./Tidewater Pubs.) Schiffer Publishing, Ltd.

Connors, Kathleen. People of the Chesapeake Bay, 1 vol. 2013. (Exploring the Chesapeake Bay Ser.). 32p. (J). (gr. 3-4). (ENG.). 29.27 (978-1-4339-9776-1(2), b014a0dd-f22c-4e40-b5e8-e0ba0fb7d94d); (ENG.). pap. 11.50 (978-1-4339-9777-8(0), ec648a77-65b4-4a69-a88d-725db1b04be8); pap. 63.00 (978-1-4339-9778-5(9)) Stevens, Gareth Publishing LLLP.

—Plants & Animals of the Chesapeake Bay, 1 vol. 2013. (Exploring the Chesapeake Bay Ser.). 32p. (J). (gr. 3-4). (ENG.). 29.27 (978-1-4339-9780-8(0), c90dd9f0-6246-4367-9b8c-3b8ff12f1933); (ENG.). pap. 11.50 (978-1-4339-9781-5(9), e24a2ae6-ddf3-4b6f-a605-7ccff7ce0b53); pap. 63.00 (978-1-4339-9782-2(7)) Stevens, Gareth Publishing LLLP.

Craats, Rennay. Maryland. 2011. (Guide to American States Ser.). (J). (Illus.). 48p. (gr. 3-6). 29.99 (978-1-61690-792-1(4)); (978-1-61690-468-5(2)) Weigl Pubs., Inc.

Deinard, Jenny. How to Draw Maryland's Sights & Symbols. 2009. (Kid's Guide to Drawing America Ser.). 32p. (gr. k-k). 50.50 (978-1-61511-069-8(0), PowerKids Pr.) Rosen Publishing Group, Inc., The.

Franchino, Vicky. Maryland (a True Book: My United States) 2017. (True Book (Relaunch) Ser.). (ENG., Illus.). 48p. (J). (gr. 3-5). pap. 7.95 (978-0-531-23288-0(3), Children's Pr.) Scholastic Library Publishing.

Gelletly, LeeAnne. The Mid-Atlantic States: Delaware, Maryland, & Washington, D. C. 2015. (Let's Explore the States Ser.). (Illus.). 64p. (J). (gr. 5). 23.95 (978-1-4222-3327-6(8)) Mason Crest.

Johnston, Joyce. Maryland. 2012. (J). lib. bdg. 25.26 (978-0-7613-4537-4(X), Lerner Pubns.) Lerner Publishing Group.

Labella, Susan. Maryland. 2005. (Rookie Read-About Geography Ser.). (ENG., Illus.). 32p. (J). (gr. 1-2). lib. bdg. 20.50 (978-0-516-25256-8(9), Children's Pr.) Scholastic Library Publishing.

Latta, Sara L. Who Fixed Babies' Hearts? Vivien Thomas, 1 vol. 2012. (I Like Inventors! Ser.). (ENG., Illus.). 24p. (gr. k-2). lib. bdg. 25.27 (978-0-7660-3963-6(3), fd287b4f-ca26-449a-b765-71d34ec150fe, Enslow Elementary) Enslow Publishing, LLC.

Levy, Debbie & Panza, Rosana. Dozer's Run: A True Story of a Dog & His Race. Opie, David, illus. 2014. (ENG.). 32p. (J). (gr. 1-4). 16.99 (978-1-58536-896-9(2), 203665) Sleeping Bear Pr.

Marsh, Carole. The Marvelous Maryland Coloring Book! 2004. (Maryland Experience! Ser.). (Illus.). 32p. (J). (gr. k-2). pap. 3.95 (978-0-7933-9615-3(8)) Gallopade International.

—Maryland Current Events Projects: 30 Cool, Activities, Crafts, Experiments & More for Kids to Do to Learn about Your State! 2003. (Maryland Experience Ser.). 32p. (gr. k-8). pap. 5.95 (978-0-635-02039-0(4), Marsh, Carole Bks.) Gallopade International.

—Maryland Geography Projects: 30 Cool, Activities, Crafts, Experiments & More for Kids to Do to Learn about Your State! 2003. (Maryland Experience Ser.). 32p. (gr. k-5). pap. 5.95 (978-0-635-01839-7(X), Marsh, Carole Bks.) Gallopade International.

—Maryland Government Projects: 30 Cool, Activities, Crafts, Experiments & More for Kids to Do to Learn about Your State! 2003. (Maryland Experience Ser.). 32p. (gr. k-5). pap. 5.95 (978-0-635-01939-4(6), Marsh, Carole Bks.) Gallopade International.

—Maryland Jeopardy! Answers & Questions about Our State! 2004. (Maryland Experience! Ser.). (Illus.). 32p. (J). (gr. 3-8). pap. 7.95 (978-0-7933-9612-2(3)) Gallopade International.

—Maryland "Jography" A Fun Run Thru Our State! 2004. (Maryland Experience! Ser.). (Illus.). 32p. (J). (gr. 3-8). pap. 7.95 (978-0-7933-9613-9(1)) Gallopade International.

—Maryland People Projects: 30 Cool, Activities, Crafts, Experiments & More for Kids to Do to Learn about Your State! 2003. (Maryland Experience Ser.). 32p. (gr. k-5). pap. 5.95 (978-0-635-01989-9(2), Marsh, Carole Bks.) Gallopade International.

—Maryland Symbols & Facts Projects: 30 Cool, Activities, Crafts, Experiments & More for Kids to Do to Learn about Your State! 2003. (Maryland Experience Ser.). 32p. (gr. k-5). pap. 5.95 (978-0-635-01889-2(6), Marsh, Carole Bks.) Gallopade International.

—My First Book about Maryland. 2004. (Maryland Experience! Ser.). (Illus.). 32p. (J). (gr. k-4). pap. 7.95 (978-0-7933-9611-5(5)) Gallopade International.

—My First Pocket Guide: Maryland. 2004. (Maryland Experience! Ser.). (Illus.). 96p. (J). (gr. 3-8). per. 6.95 (978-0-7933-9610-8(7)) Gallopade International.

Menendez, Shirley C. B Is for Blue Crab: A Maryland Alphabet. Stutzman, Laura, illus. 2004. (Discover America State by State Ser.). (ENG.). 40p. (J). (gr. 1-3). 18.99 (978-1-58536-160-1(7), 202020) Sleeping Bear Pr.

Miller, Derek, et al. Maryland: The Old Line State, 1 vol. 3rd ed. 2018. (It's My State! (Fourth Edition)(r) Ser.). (ENG.). 80p. (gr. 4-4). pap. 18.64 (978-1-5026-4442-8(8), 7a81bf66-2600-406c-ad26-25945253e076) Cavendish Square Publishing LLC.

Murray, Julie. Maryland, 1 vol. 2006. (Buddy Book Ser.). (ENG., Illus.). 32p. (gr. 2-4). 27.07 (978-1-59197-679-0(0), Buddy Bks.) ABDO Publishing Co.

Otfinoski, Steven. Maryland, 1 vol. Santoro, Christopher, illus. 2003. (It's My State! (First Edition)(r) Ser.). (ENG.). 80p. (gr. 4-4). 34.07 (978-0-7614-1421-6(5), e44a4836-9ef1-44bb-ad0c-b62b81602623) Cavendish Square Publishing LLC.

Saving the Chesapeake Bay. 2013. (Exploring the Chesapeake Bay Ser.). 32p. (J). (gr. 3-6). pap. 63.00 (978-1-4339-9786-0(X)) Stevens, Gareth Publishing LLLP.

Somervill, Barbara A. Maryland. 2003. (From Sea to Shining Sea Ser.: 2). (ENG., Illus.). 80p. (J). 30.50 (978-0-516-22384-1(4), Children's Pr.) Scholastic Library Publishing.

Swanson, Angie & Parker, Bridget. Maryland. 2016. (States Ser.). (ENG., Illus.). 32p. (J). (gr. 3-6). lib. bdg. 27.99 (978-1-5157-0407-2(6), 132018, Capstone Pr.) Capstone.

Wimmer, Teresa. Maryland. 2008. (This Land Called America Ser.). 32p. (YA). (gr. 3-6). 22.95 (978-1-58341-645-7(5)) Creative Co., The.

MARYLAND—FICTION

Allbritton, Stacy Demoran. The Diary of Marie Landry, Acadian Exile, 1 vol. Haynes, Joyce, illus. 2012. (ENG.). 160p. (J). (gr. 3-7). pap. 14.95 (978-1-58980-865-2(7), Pelican Publishing) Arcadia Publishing.

Allen, Elaine Ann. Olly's Treasure, 1 vol. 2011. (ENG., Illus.). 40p. (J). (gr. -1-3). 16.99 (978-0-7643-3772-7(6), 4107, Schiffer Publishing Ltd) Schiffer Publishing, Ltd.

Altsheler, Joseph A. The Sword of Antietam: A Story of the Nation's Crisis. 2006. (Civil War Ser.: Vol. 4). 296p. (J). reprint ed. 28.95 (978-1-4218-1776-7(4)); pap. 13.95 (978-1-4218-1876-4(0)) 1st World Publishing, Inc. (1st World Library - Literary Society).

—The Sword of Antietam: A Story of the Nation's Crisis. l.t. ed. (Civil War Ser.: Vol. 4). (J). reprint ed. 2006. 262p. pap. 23.99 (978-1-4264-2714-5(X)) 2011. 358p. (gr. 4-7). pap. 32.75 (978-1-245-13385-2(3)) 2008. 264p. 28.99 (978-0-554-22582-1(4)) 2008. 264p. 25.99 (978-0-554-31885-1(7)) 2007. (ENG.). 242p. pap. 20.99 (978-1-4264-2657-5(7)) Creative Media Partners, LLC.

—The Sword of Antietam: A Story of the Nation's Crisis. 2006. (Civil War Ser.: Vol. 4). (J). reprint ed. pap. (978-1-4065-0825-3(X)) Dodo Pr.

—The Sword of Antietam: A Story of the Nation's Crisis. 2007. (Civil War Ser.: Vol. 4). 176p. (J). reprint ed. per. (978-1-4068-1690-7(6)) Echo Library.

—The Sword of Antietam: A Story of the Nation's Crisis. 2010. (Civil War Ser.: Vol. 4). (Illus.). 160p. (J). (gr. 4-7). reprint ed. pap. 19.99 (978-1-153-72276-6(3)) General Bks. LLC.

—The Sword of Antietam: A Story of the Nation's Crisis. 2010. (Civil War Ser.: Vol. 4). 224p. (J). reprint ed. pap. (978-1-4076-4642-8(7)) HardPr.

—The Sword of Antietam: A Story of the Nation's Crisis. (Civil War Ser.: Vol. 4). (J). reprint ed. 2011. 352p. (gr. 4-7). 46.95 (978-1-169-87969-0(1)) 2010. 352p. (gr. 4-7). 37.56 (978-1-163-20537-2(0)) 2010. 352p. (gr. 4-7). pap. 25.56 (978-1-162-77564-7(5)) 2005. 352p. 46.95 (978-1-4326-1485-0(1)) 2005. pap. 31.95 (978-0-7661-9405-2(1)) 2004. pap. 1.99 (978-1-4192-8469-4(X)) Kessinger Publishing, LLC.

—The Sword of Antietam: A Story of the Nation's Crisis. 2009. (Civil War Ser.: Vol. 4). (J). reprint ed. pap. 16.95 (978-1-933573-85-4(6)) Zeezok Publishing, LLC.

—The Sword of Antietam: A Story of the Nation's Crisis. 2011. (Civil War Ser.: Vol. 4). 264p. (J). (gr. 4-7). reprint ed. pap. (978-3-8424-3211-6(9)) tredition Verlag.

Baker, Monica S. Freestyle, 1 vol. 2010. (ENG., Illus.). 160p. (gr. 3-6). 14.99 (978-0-7643-3538-9(3), 3791) Schiffer Publishing, Ltd.

Basham, Tom. Sailing Home. Calvert, Lissa, illus. 2012. 168p. (978-1-77097-370-1(2)) FriesenPress.

Basham, Tom & Calvert, Lissa. Sailing Home. 2012. 168p. pap. (978-1-77097-371-8(0)) FriesenPress.

Brashares, Ann. 3 Willows: The Sisterhood Grows. 2009. (JPN.). 339p. (YA). (gr. 7). pap. (978-4-652-07950-8(8)) Riron-Sha.

Broach, Elise. Shakespeare's Secret. 2007. (Illus.). 258p. (gr. 4-9). 17.00 (978-0-7569-8204-1(9)) Perfection Learning Corp.

—Shakespeare's Secret. l.t. ed. 2006. (Thorndike Literacy Bridge Ser.). (Illus.). 263p. (J). (gr. 5-10). 22.95 (978-0-7862-8735-2(7)) Thorndike Pr.

Buffington, Cecil. High School Super-Star: The Junior Year. 2008. 244p. pap. 16.95 (978-0-595-51914-9(8)) iUniverse, Inc.

Cummings, Priscilla. A Face First. 2003. 208p. (J). (gr. 4-7). 6.99 (978-0-14-230247-7(3), Puffin Books) Penguin Young Readers Group.

—A Face First. 2003. 197p. (gr. 7-12). 17.00 (978-0-7569-1547-6(3)) Perfection Learning Corp.

—The Journey Back. 2013. 272p. (J). (gr. 5). pap. 8.99 (978-0-14-242290-8(8), Puffin Books) Penguin Young Readers Group.

Delacre, Lulu. Alicia Afterimage, 1 vol. (ENG.). 144p. (YA). (gr. 7-12). 2017. pap. 18.95 (978-1-62014-578-4(2), leelowbooks) 2008. 19.95 (978-1-60060-242-9(8)) Lee & Low Bks., Inc.

Eisner, Fern. Saba's Room. 2009. 28p. pap. 15.99 (978-1-4415-1843-9(6)) Xlibris Corp.

Furtney, Charles S. Tryconnel: An Antebellum Adventure along the C & O Canal. 2004. (Illus.). iii, 156p. (J). pap. (978-0-9711835-3-7(8)) Local History Co., The.

Gamble, Adam & Jasper, Mark. Good Night Maryland. Rosen, Anne, illus. 2011. (Good Night Our World Ser.). (ENG.). 20p. (J). (gr. k — 1). bds. 9.95 (978-1-60219-046-7(1)) Good Night Bks.

Hahn, Mary Downing. Promises to the Dead. 2009. (ENG.). 208p. (J). (gr. 5-7). pap. 7.99 (978-0-547-25838-6(0), 1402071, Clarion Bks.) HarperCollins Pubs.

Hancock, H. Irving. Dave Darrin's First Year at Annapolis. 2018. (ENG., Illus.). 168p. (YA). (gr. 7-12). pap. (978-93-5297-335-4(6)) Alpha Editions.

—Dave Darrin's First Year at Annapolis. 2017. (ENG., Illus.). (J). 23.95 (978-1-374-94527-2(7)) Capital Communications, Inc.

—Dave Darrin's First Year at Annapolis. 2007. 180p. per. (978-1-4065-1974-7(X)) Dodo Pr.

—Dave Darrin's Fourth Year at Annapolis. 2018. (ENG., Illus.). 174p. (YA). (gr. 7-12). pap. (978-93-5297-338-5(0)) Alpha Editions.

—Dave Darrin's Second Year at Annapolis. 2018. (ENG., Illus.). 144p. (YA). (gr. 7-12). pap. (978-93-5297-336-1(4)) Alpha Editions.

—Dave Darrin's Second Year at Annapolis. 2007. 152p. per. (978-1-4065-1976-1(6)) Dodo Pr.

Hollenbeck, Kathleen M. Dancing on the Sand: A Story of an Atlantic Blue Crab. 2005. (ENG., Illus.). 32p. (J). (gr. -1-2). 8.95 (978-1-59249-234-3(7), SC4017) Soundprints.

Jackson, Gabrielle E. Peggy Stewart. 2007. 176p. per. (978-1-4065-1803-0(4)) Dodo Pr.

Jacobs, Lily. The Littlest Bunny in Maryland: An Easter Adventure. Dunn, Robert, illus. 2015. (Littlest Bunny Ser.). (ENG.). 32p. (J). (gr. -1-3). 9.99 (978-1-4926-1111-0(5), Hometown World) Sourcebooks, Inc.

James, Eric. Santa's Sleigh Is on Its Way to Maryland: A Christmas Adventure. Dunn, Robert, illus. 2016. (Santa's Sleigh Is on Its Way Ser.). (ENG.). 32p. (J). (gr. k-2). 12.99 (978-1-4926-4335-7(1), 9781492643357, Hometown World) Sourcebooks, Inc.

—The Spooky Express Maryland. Piwowarski, Marcin, illus. 2017. (Spooky Express Ser.). (ENG.). 32p. (J). (gr. k-6). 9.99 (978-1-4926-5368-4(3), Hometown World) Sourcebooks, Inc.

—Tiny the Maryland Easter Bunny. 2018. (Tiny the Easter Bunny Ser.). (ENG.). 40p. (J). (gr. k-3). 9.99 (978-1-4926-5935-8(5), Hometown World) Sourcebooks, Inc.

Johnson-Simon. Anaya Visits the James E Lewis Museum of Art at Morgan State University. 2009. 40p. pap. 16.99 (978-1-4490-1884-9(X)) AuthorHouse.

Kehne, Carroll Harrison, Jr. & Kehne, Carroll Harrison. Buried Treasure, a Pirate's Tale, 1 vol. 2009. (ENG., Illus.). 34p. (J). (gr. 3-7). 12.95 (978-0-87033-601-0(0), 3602, Cornell Maritime Pr./Tidewater Pubs.) Schiffer Publishing, Ltd.

LeFlore, Lyah B. The World Is Mine. Warfield, D. L., illus. 2009. (Come Up Ser.). (ENG.). 304p. (YA). (gr. 9-18). pap. 8.99 (978-1-4169-7963-0(8), Simon Pulse) Simon Pulse.

Litzenberg, Corinne M. The Sand Lady: An Ocean City, Maryland, Tale, 1 vol. 2007. (ENG., Illus.). 32p. (gr. 3-6). 14.95 (978-0-7643-2684-4(8), 2975) Schiffer Publishing, Ltd.

Lockhart, Barbara & Lynne. Rambling Raft, 1 vol. 2009. (ENG., Illus.). 30p. (J). (gr. -1-3). 7.95 (978-0-87033-392-7(5), 3706, Cornell Maritime Pr./Tidewater Pubs.) Schiffer Publishing, Ltd.

Lorton, Barbara. Sidney Seagull Marks Lighthouses & Buoys of the Chesapeake. 2013. (Illus.). 28p. pap. 16.99 (978-1-4582-1055-5(3), Abbott Pr.) Author Solutions, LLC.

Lyga, Barry. Hero-Type. 2009. (ENG.). 312p. (YA). (gr. 7). pap. 17.99 (978-0-547-24877-6(6), 1100781, Clarion Bks.) HarperCollins Pubs.

Mair, J. Samia. The Great Race to Sycamore Street. 2013. (ENG., Illus.). 196p. (J). (gr. 3-6). pap. 12.99 (978-1-84774-057-1(X)) Kube Publishing Ltd. GBR. Dist: Consortium Bk. Sales & Distribution.

Maxson, H. A. & Young, Claudia H. Tea Party at Chestertown. Kosits, Andrew, illus. 2003. (Magical History Tours Ser.). 55p. (J). per. 8.95 (978-0-9741713-0-2(1)) Bay Oak Pubs., Ltd.

Messner, Kate. Long Road to Freedom (Ranger in Time #3) McMorris, Kelley, illus. 2015. (Ranger in Time Ser.: 3). (ENG.). 160p. (J). (gr. 2-5). pap. 5.99 (978-0-545-63920-0(4), Scholastic Pr.) Scholastic, Inc.

Mills, Charles. Storm on Shadow Mountain. 2003. 127p. (J). 7.99 (978-0-8163-1993-0(6)) Pacific Pr. Publishing Assn.

Molinari, Laurice Elehwany. The Ether: Vero Rising, 1 vol. 2014. (Ether Novel Ser.: 1). (ENG.). 368p. (J). pap. 8.99 (978-0-310-73561-8(0)) Zonderkidz.

—Pillars of Fire, 1 vol. 2016. (Ether Novel Ser.: 2). (ENG.). 368p. (J). pap. 8.99 (978-0-310-73562-5(9)) Zonderkidz.

Moore, Kelly, et al. Neverwas. 2014. (YA). pap. (978-0-545-43419-5(X)) Scholastic, Inc.

Now I'll Tell You Everything. 2014. (Alice Ser.: 25). (ENG., Illus.). 544p. (YA). (gr. 9). pap. 12.99 (978-1-4424-4591-8(2), Atheneum Bks. for Young Readers) Simon & Schuster Children's Publishing.

Oneill, Elizabeth. Alfred Visits Maryland. 2008. 24p. (J). pap. 12.00 (978-0-9799121-7-7(2)) Funny Bone Bks.

Otis, James. Calvert of Maryland A Story of Lord Baltimore's Colony. 2005. reprint ed. pap. 21.95 (978-1-4179-3369-3(0)) Kessinger Publishing, LLC.

Papp, Lisa. The Town That Fooled the British: A War of 1812 Story. Papp, Lisa, illus. 2011. (Tales of Young Americans Ser.). (ENG., Illus.). 32p. (J). (gr. 1-4). 18.99 (978-1-58536-484-8(3), 202192) Sleeping Bear Pr.

Reynolds Naylor, Phyllis. Alice in Charge. (Alice Ser.: 22). (ENG., (YA). (gr. 9). 2011. Illus.). 304p. pap. 8.99 (978-1-4169-7555-7(1)) 2010. 336p. 16.99 (978-1-4169-7552-6(7)) Simon & Schuster Children's Publishing. (Atheneum Bks. for Young Readers).

—Alice on Board. 2012. (Alice Ser.: 24). (ENG., Illus.). 288p. (YA). (gr. 9). 17.99 (978-1-4424-4588-8(2), Atheneum Bks. for Young Readers) Simon & Schuster Children's Publishing.

—Dangerously Alice. 2007. (Alice Ser.: 19). (ENG.). 304p. (YA). (gr. 9-12). 15.99 (978-0-689-87094-1(9), Atheneum Bks. for Young Readers) Simon & Schuster Children's Publishing.

—Dangerously Alice. 2008. (Alice Ser.: No. 19). (ENG.). 320p. (YA). mass mkt. 6.99 (978-0-689-87095-8(7), Simon Pulse) Simon Pulse.

—Incredibly Alice. (Alice Ser.: 23). (ENG., (YA). (gr. 9). 2012. Illus.). 304p. pap. 8.99 (978-1-4169-7556-4(X)) 2011. 288p. 16.99 (978-1-4169-7553-3(5)) Simon & Schuster Children's Publishing. (Atheneum Bks. for Young Readers).

—Intensely Alice. 2009. (Alice Ser.: 21). (ENG.). 288p. (YA). (gr. 9-18). 16.99 (978-1-4169-7551-9(9), Atheneum Bks. for Young Readers) Simon & Schuster Children's Publishing.

—Lovingly Alice. 2004. (Alice Bks.). 166p. (J). (gr. 4-6). 13.65 (978-0-7569-6604-1(3)) Perfection Learning Corp.

—Lovingly Alice. 2006. (Alice Ser.). (ENG., Illus.). 176p. (J). (gr. 4-7). pap. 5.99 *(978-0-689-84400-3(X),* Atheneum Bks. for Young Readers) Simon & Schuster Children's Publishing.
—Now I'll Tell You Everything. 2013. (Alice Ser.: 25). (ENG., Illus.). 528p. (YA). (gr. 9). 17.99 *(978-1-4424-4590-1(4))* Simon & Schuster Children's Publishing.
—Please Don't Be True: Dangerously Alice; Almost Alice; Intensely Alice. 2011. (Alice Ser.). (ENG., Illus.). 768p. (YA). (gr. 9). pap. 12.99 *(978-1-4424-1721-2(8),* Atheneum Bks. for Young Readers) Simon & Schuster Children's Publishing.
—You & Me & the Space in Between: Alice in Charge; Incredibly Alice; Alice on Board. 2013. (Alice Ser.). (ENG., Illus.). 880p. (YA). (gr. 9). pap. 10.99 *(978-1-4424-8664-5(3),* Atheneum Bks. for Young Readers) Simon & Schuster Children's Publishing.
Rosenthal, Betsy R. Looking for Me: ... in This Great Big Family. 2013. (ENG., Illus.). 176p. (J). (gr. 5-7). pap. 7.99 *(978-0-544-02271-3(8),* 1528493, Clarion Bks.) HarperCollins Pubs.
Roy, Ron. Capital Mysteries #12: the Ghost at Camp David. Bush, Timothy, illus. 2010. (Capital Mysteries Ser.: 12). 96p. (J). (gr. 1-4). pap. 5.99 *(978-0-375-85925-0(X),* Random Hse. Bks. for Young Readers) Random Hse. Children's Bks.
—The Ghost at Camp David. 2010. (Capital Mysteries Ser.: 12). lib. bdg. 14.75 *(978-0-606-14010-2(7))* Turtleback.
Sharpe, Susan. Waterman's Boy. 2007. (ENG.). 176p. (J). (gr. 3-7). pap. 11.95 *(978-1-4169-6453-7(3),* Simon & Schuster/Paula Wiseman Bks.) Simon & Schuster/Paula Wiseman Bks.
Siwak, Brenda S. Counting on the Bay. Dodge, Barbara A., illus. 2006. (J). per. 14.95 *(978-0-9790906-0-8(1))* Pleasant Plains Pr.
Smith, Nikki Shannon. Ann Fights for Freedom: An Underground Railroad Survival Story. Trunfio, Alessia, illus. 2019. (Girls Survive Ser.). (ENG.). 112p. (J). (gr. 3-7). lib. bdg. 25.99 *(978-1-4965-7853-2(8),* 139371, Stone Arch Bks.) Capstone.
Soentpiet, Chris K. & McGill, Alice. Molly Bannaky. 2009. (ENG., Illus.). 32p. (J). (gr. -1-3). pap. 9.99 *(978-0-547-07676-8(2),* 1042032, Clarion Bks.) HarperCollins Pubs.
Spotswood, Jessica. The Last Summer of the Garrett Girls. 2018. 368p. (YA). (gr. 8-12). pap. 10.99 *(978-1-4926-2219-2(2))* Sourcebooks, Inc.
Standiford, Natalie. The Secret Tree. 2012. 245p. (J). pap. *(978-0-545-48976-8(8),* Scholastic Pr.) Scholastic, Inc.
Step Up 2 - The Streets. 2008. 160p. pap. 4.99 *(978-1-4231-1319-5(5))* Disney Pr.
Stout, Shawn K. Ballerina Weather Girl. Martini, Angela, illus. 2013. (Not-So-Ordinary Girl Ser.: 1). (ENG.). 192p. (J). (gr. 1-5). pap. 6.99 *(978-1-4424-7401-7(7),* Aladdin) Simon & Schuster Children's Publishing.
—Ballerina Weather Girl. Martini, Angela, illus. 2013. (Not-So-Ordinary Girl Ser.: 1). (ENG.). 192p. (J). (gr. 1-5). 15.99 *(978-1-4424-7402-4(5),* Simon & Schuster/Paula Wiseman Bks.) Simon & Schuster/Paula Wiseman Bks.
—Don't Chicken Out. Ying, Victoria, illus. 2013. (Not-So-Ordinary Girl Ser.: 3). (ENG.). 176p. (J). (gr. 1-5). pap. 5.99 *(978-1-4169-7111-5(4),* Aladdin) Simon & Schuster Children's Publishing.
—Don't Chicken Out. Ying, Victoria, illus. 2013. (Not-So-Ordinary Girl Ser.: 3). (ENG.). 176p. (J). (gr. 1-5). 15.99 *(978-1-4169-7929-6(8),* Simon & Schuster/Paula Wiseman Bks.) Simon & Schuster/Paula Wiseman Bks.
—Fiona Finkelstein, Big-Time Ballerina!! Martini, Angela, illus. 2010. (ENG.). 192p. (J). pap. 4.99 *(978-1-4169-7109-2(2),* Simon & Schuster/Paula Wiseman Bks.) Simon & Schuster/Paula Wiseman Bks.
—Miss Matched. Martini, Angela, illus. 2013. (Not-So-Ordinary Girl Ser.: 2). (ENG.). 176p. (J). (gr. 1-5). pap. 5.99 *(978-1-4424-7404-8(1),* Aladdin) Simon & Schuster Children's Publishing.
—Miss Matched. Martini, Angela, illus. 2013. (Not-So-Ordinary Girl Ser.: 2). (ENG.). 160p. (J). (gr. 1-5). 15.99 *(978-1-4424-7405-5(X),* Simon & Schuster/Paula Wiseman Bks.) Simon & Schuster/Paula Wiseman Bks.
Sully, Katherine. Night-Night Maryland. Poole, Helen, illus. 2017. (Night-Night Ser.). (ENG.). 20p. (J). (gr. -1-1). bds. 9.99 *(978-1-4926-4768-3(3),* 9781492647683, Hometown World) Sourcebooks, Inc.
Szymanski, Lois. Grandfather's Secret, 1 vol. 2010. (ENG., Illus.). 64p. (gr. 3-6). pap. 12.99 *(978-0-7643-3535-8(9),* 3790) Schiffer Publishing, Ltd.
Thompson, Kimberly. Toulouse Tangled up in Lights. Easey, Chris, illus. 2011. 64p. (J). 19.95 *(978-0-9818976-1-5(4))* Little Pigeon Bks.
Trimper, Marty. Hermione: Shipwrecked! in Ocean City, Maryland. Amy, Holloway, illus. 2004. (J). *(978-1-886068-28-5(3))* Fruitbearer Publishing, LLC.
Troeger, Virginia B. Secret along the St. Mary's. Swisher, Michael-Che, tr. Swisher, Michael-Che, illus. 2003. (Mysteries in Time Ser.). 92p. (gr. 4). 14.95 *(978-1-893110-35-9(4))* Silver Moon Pr.
Winstead, Amy. The Star-Spangled Banner. Dacey, Bob & Bandelin, Debra, illus. 2003. (ENG.). 32p. (J). 18.65 *(978-0-8249-5462-8(9),* Ideals Pubns.) Worthy Publishing.

MARYLAND—HISTORY

Bachmann, Elaine Rice. While a Tree Grew, the Story of Maryland's Wye Oak, 1 vol. 2009. (ENG., Illus.). 30p. (gr. -1-3). 10.00 *(978-0-87033-577-8(4),* 7335, Cornell Maritime Pr./Tidewater Pubs.) Schiffer Publishing, Ltd.
Brown, Vanessa. Maryland. 2009. (Bilingual Library of the United States of America Ser.). (ENG & SPA.). 32p. (gr. 2-2). 47.90 *(978-1-60853-365-7(4),* Editorial Buenas Letras) Rosen Publishing Group, Inc., The.
Bunting, Elaine. Counties of Northern Maryland, 1 vol. 2010. (ENG., Illus.). 176p. (gr. 3-6). 19.95 *(978-0-87033-520-4(0),* 3691, Cornell Maritime Pr./Tidewater Pubs.) Schiffer Publishing, Ltd.
Connors, Kathleen. Visiting the Chesapeake Bay, 1 vol. 2013. (Exploring the Chesapeake Bay Ser.). (ENG.). 32p. (J). (gr. 3-4). 29.27 *(978-1-4339-9788-4(6),* 4aa416ed-5360-4c89-8a93-881be3375abc); pap. 11.50 *(978-1-4339-9789-1(4),* 51081937-2d4f-45c8-b32e-8aed4adb132c) Stevens, Gareth Publishing LLLP.
Craats, Rennay. Maryland: The Old Line State. 2016. (J). *(978-1-4896-4875-4(5))* Weigl Pubs., Inc.
Cunningham, Kevin. The Maryland Colony. 2011. (True Bk Ser.). (ENG., Illus.). 48p. (J). pap. 6.95 *(978-0-531-26603-8(6));* lib. bdg. 29.00 *(978-0-531-25390-8(2))* Scholastic Library Publishing. (Children's Pr.).
Damanda, Lori. The Story of the "Star-Spangled Banner", 1 vol. (American History Milestones Ser.). (ENG.). 32p. (J). (gr. 5-5). 2009. lib. bdg. 28.93 *(978-1-4358-3015-8(6),* f2e5f903-40c2-4903-afa4-1d952dbeb193) 2008. (Illus.). pap. 10.00 *(978-1-4358-0205-6(5),* 4f301343-44f2-47a1-9f74-353cdd17b026) Rosen Publishing Group, Inc., The. (PowerKids Pr.).
Dans, Peter E. Sergeant Bill & His Horse Bob. Corpus, Mary-Grace, illus. 2015.Tr. of 28. (ENG.). (J). 17.95 *(978-1-933822-97-6(X))* Camino Bks., Inc.
Doak, Robin S. Exploring the Maryland Colony. 2016. (Exploring the 13 Colonies Ser.). (ENG., Illus.). 48p. (J). (gr. 3-6). lib. bdg. 34.65 *(978-1-5157-2238-0(4),* 132762) Capstone.
Exploring the Chesapeake Bay, 12 vols. 2013. (Exploring the Chesapeake Bay Ser.). 32p. (J). (gr. 3-4). (ENG.). 175.62 *(978-1-4339-9843-0(2),* 3dbf9bdb-3190-4d9b-96e4-ce1612f28569); pap. 378.00 *(978-1-4339-9845-4(9));* pap. 63.00 *(978-1-4339-9844-7(0))* Stevens, Gareth Publishing LLLP.
Friddell, Claudia. Goliath: Hero of the Great Baltimore Fire. Howell, Troy, illus. 2010. (True Stories Ser.). (ENG.). 32p. (J). (gr. 1-4). 17.95 *(978-1-58536-455-8(X),* 202179) Sleeping Bear Pr.
Grau, Maritta, ed. The ABCs of Frederick Maryland: A Historic Coloring Book. Grau, Ryon, illus. 2007. 32p. 8.95 *(978-0-9772559-0-0(5))* Grau, Ryon.
Hama, Larry. The Battle of Antietam: The Bloodiest Day of Battle. 2009. (Graphic Civil War Battles Ser.). (ENG.). 48p. (YA). (gr. 4-5). 58.50 *(978-1-61512-897-6(2),* Rosen Reference) Rosen Publishing Group, Inc., The.
—The Battle of Antietam: The Bloodiest Day of Battle, 1 vol. Moore, Scott, illus. 2006. (Graphic Battles of the Civil War Ser.). (ENG.). 48p. (YA). (gr. 5-6). lib. bdg. 37.13 *(978-1-4042-0775-2(9),* 9d711419-32c5-49c3-9dc1-bc0c5704efe0) Rosen Publishing Group, Inc., The.
—The Battle of Antietam: The Bloodiest Day of Battle, 1 vol. 2006. (Graphic Battles of the Civil War Ser.). (ENG., Illus.). 48p. (gr. 5-6). pap. 14.05 *(978-1-4042-6475-5(2),* 0e51d26f-d2cf-4848-a286-5ee9ad9f3afa, Rosen Classroom) Rosen Publishing Group, Inc., The.
Hamilton, John. Maryland, 1 vol. 2016. (United States of America Ser.). (ENG., Illus.). 48p. (J). (gr. 5-9). 34.21 *(978-1-68078-322-3(X),* 21629, Abdo & Daughters) ABDO Publishing Co.
Heinrichs, Ann. Maryland. Kania, Matt, illus. 2017. (U. S. A. Travel Guides). (ENG.). 40p. (J). (gr. 2-5). lib. bdg. 38.50 *(978-1-5038-1960-3(4),* 211597) Child's World, Inc, The.
History of the Chesapeake Bay. 2013. (Exploring the Chesapeake Bay Ser.). 32p. (J). (gr. 3-6). pap. 63.00 *(978-1-4339-9774-7(6))* Stevens, Gareth Publishing LLLP.
Jensen, Ann. The World Turned Upside Down: Children Of 1776, 1 vol. 2009. (ENG., Illus.). 80p. (gr. 3-6). pap. 9.95 *(978-0-87033-534-1(0),* 3745, Cornell Maritime Pr./Tidewater Pubs.) Schiffer Publishing, Ltd.
Jerome, Kate B. Lucky to Live in Maryland. 2017. (Arcadia Kids Ser.). (ENG., Illus.). 32p. (J). 16.99 *(978-0-7385-2785-7(8))* Arcadia Publishing.
—The Wise Animal Handbook Maryland. 2017. (Arcadia Kids Ser.). (ENG., Illus.). 32p. (J). 16.99 *(978-0-7385-2824-3(2))* Arcadia Publishing.
Loker, Aleck. The Murder of Joseph Henry Ching: A Legend Examined. 2003. (Illus.). 28p. 6.00 *(978-1-928874-04-1(5))* Solitude Pr.
Lusted, Marcia Amidon. Maryland: The Old Line State, 1 vol. 2010. (Our Amazing States Ser.). (ENG., Illus.). 24p. (J). (gr. 3-3). pap. 9.25 *(978-1-4358-9794-6(3),* 1307045); lib. bdg. 26.27 *(978-1-4358-9350-4(6),* 1307045) Rosen Publishing Group, Inc., The. (PowerKids Pr.).
Marsh, Carole. Exploring Maryland Through Project-Based Learning. 2016. (Maryland Experience Ser.). (ENG.). (J). pap. 9.99 *(978-0-635-12344-2(4))* Gallopade International.
—I'm Reading about Maryland. 2014. (Maryland Experience Ser.). (ENG., Illus.). (J). pap., pap. 8.99 *(978-0-635-11295-8(7))* Gallopade International.
—Let's Discover Maryland! 2004. (J). (gr. 2-8). cd-rom 14.95 *(978-0-7933-9617-4(7))* Gallopade International.
—Lords of Baltimore, Founders of Maryland. 2004. 12p. (gr. k-4). 2.95 *(978-0-635-02368-1(7))* Gallopade International.
—Maryland History Projects: 30 Cool, Activities, Crafts, Experiments & More for Kids to Do to Learn about Your State! 2003. (Maryland Experience Ser.). 32p. (gr. k-5). pap. 5.95 *(978-0-635-01789-5(X),* Marsh, Carole Bks.) Gallopade International.
Marsico, Katie. The Chesapeake Bay. 2013. (Explorer Library: Social Studies Explorer Ser.). (ENG.). 32p. (gr. 4-8). pap. 14.21 *(978-1-62431-037-9(0),* 202505); (Illus.). lib. bdg. 32.07 *(978-1-62431-013-3(3),* 202503) Cherry Lake Publishing.
The Maryland Adventure: New Maryland 4th Grade, 1 vol. l.t. ed. 2009. 360p. (gr. 4-4). 47.95 *(978-1-4236-0583-6(7))* Gibbs Smith, Publisher.
The Maryland Adventure Program Kit: All program components for the Maryland Adventure, 1 vol. 2009. pap. 169.95 *(978-1-4236-0719-9(8))* Gibbs Smith, Publisher.
Mattern, Joanne. Maryland: Past & Present, 1 vol. 2010. (United States: Past & Present Ser.). (ENG., Illus.). 48p. (J). (gr. 5-5). pap. 12.75 *(978-1-4358-8488-5(4),* 826212b4-a8cd-4d2d-994b-1c0deaf26bab); lib. bdg. 34.47 *(978-1-4358-3519-1(0),* 714bbe8f-12d1-4ac8-81b0-0ab66eda2008) Rosen Publishing Group, Inc., The. (Rosen Reference).
McDowell, Pamela. Maryland: The Old Line State. 2012. (J). *(978-1-61913-359-4(8));* pap. *(978-1-61913-360-0(1))* Weigl Pubs., Inc.
Miller, Derek, et al. Maryland: The Old Line State, 1 vol. 3rd ed. 2018. (It's My State! (Fourth Edition)(r) Ser.). (ENG.). 80p. (gr. 4-4). 35.93 *(978-1-5026-2631-8(4),* df623c09-8413-400f-839e-156bdc6b08a6) Cavendish Square Publishing LLC.
Mis, Melody S. The Colony of Maryland: A Primary Source History. (Primary Source Library of the Thirteen Colonies & the Lost Colony Ser.). 24p. (gr. 3-4). 2009. 42.50 *(978-1-60854-139-3(8))* 2006. (ENG., Illus.). (J). lib. bdg. 26.27 *(978-1-4042-3434-5(9),* 92983857-5adb-4e9d-bfc4-191cba771595) Rosen Publishing Group, Inc., The. (PowerKids Pr.).
Moore Niver, Heather. Tributaries of the Chesapeake Bay, 1 vol. 2013. (Exploring the Chesapeake Bay Ser.). (ENG., Illus.). 32p. (J). (gr. 3-4). pap. 11.50 *(978-1-4339-9793-8(2),* 8f35a463-4c01-4bd1-be38-71cdffd395a9); lib. bdg. 29.27 *(978-1-4339-9792-1(4),* b6919ea1-67a9-4fe2-84e6-b1114a0590bf) Stevens, Gareth Publishing LLLP.
Murphy, Jim. A Savage Thunder: Antietam & the Bloody Road to Freedom. 2009. (ENG.). 112p. (J). (gr. 3-7). 19.99 *(978-0-689-87633-2(5),* McElderry, Margaret K. Bks.) McElderry, Margaret K. Bks.
Nagelhout, Ryan. Saving the Chesapeake Bay, 1 vol. 2013. (Exploring the Chesapeake Bay Ser.). (ENG., Illus.). 32p. (J). (gr. 3-4). pap. 11.50 *(978-1-4339-9785-3(1),* 8d856c30-b5c6-4731-a3b6-785bfd7a2aea); lib. bdg. 29.27 *(978-1-4339-9784-6(3),* 49d2e09a-fd80-4a58-8dd1-de1f29a70604) Stevens, Gareth Publishing LLLP.
Otfinoski, Steven & Steinitz, Andy. Maryland, 1 vol. (It's My State! (Second Edition)(r) Ser.). (ENG.). 80p. (gr. 4-4). 2nd rev. ed. 2011. lib. bdg. 34.07 *(978-1-60870-052-3(6),* 973de8b9-fdb9-46d2-a87d-64f6b7f4beae) 3rd rev. ed. 2014. (Illus.). lib. bdg. 35.93 *(978-1-62712-743-1(7),* ed270434-c28f-4ae7-abd0-89de9349d884) Cavendish Square Publishing LLC.
Pietrzyk, Leslie & Kneib, Martha. Maryland, 1 vol. 2nd rev. ed. 2009. (Celebrate the States (Second Edition) Ser.). (ENG.). 144p. (gr. 6-6). lib. bdg. 39.79 *(978-0-7614-3004-9(0),* 14d2469d-638c-46e1-97f4-9b6577a17792) Cavendish Square Publishing LLC.
Shea, Therese M. History of the Chesapeake Bay, 1 vol. 2013. (Exploring the Chesapeake Bay Ser.). (ENG.). 32p. (J). (gr. 3-4). 29.27 *(978-1-4339-9772-3(X),* 4b26b1f6-9d40-49cd-9a6c-95298f24e328); pap. 11.50 *(978-1-4339-9773-0(8),* 4f0c2f97-5c60-466c-a859-ad37cf84580e) Stevens, Gareth Publishing LLLP.
Somervill, Barbara A. From Sea to Shining Sea: Maryland. 2008. (ENG.). 80p. (J). pap. 7.95 *(978-0-531-20807-6(9),* Children's Pr.) Scholastic Library Publishing.
Sonneborn, Liz. The Colony of Maryland, 1 vol. 2005. (Primary Sources of the Thirteen Colonies & the Lost Colony Ser.). (ENG., Illus.). 64p. (gr. 4-6). per. 12.95 *(978-1-4042-0672-4(8),* d6e3a297-a25e-4040-9ddd-6eba4b1913d3) Rosen Publishing Group, Inc., The.
—A Primary Source History of the Colony of Maryland. (Primary Sources of the Thirteen Colonies & the Lost Colony Ser.). 64p. 2009. (gr. 5-8). 58.50 *(978-1-60851-879-1(5))* 2005. (ENG., Illus.). (YA). (gr. 4-6). lib. bdg. 37.13 *(978-1-4042-0427-0(X),* a2084cfc-8741-463f-9d1e-ae2c3e66f660) Rosen Publishing Group, Inc., The.
Tributaries of the Chesapeake Bay. 2013. (Exploring the Chesapeake Bay Ser.). 32p. (J). (gr. 3-6). pap. 63.00 *(978-1-4339-9794-5(0))* Stevens, Gareth Publishing LLLP.
Visiting the Chesapeake Bay. 2013. (Exploring the Chesapeake Bay Ser.). 32p. (J). (gr. 3-6). pap. 63.00 *(978-1-4339-9790-7(8))* Stevens, Gareth Publishing LLLP.
Walker, Sally M. Ghost Walls: The Story of a 17th-Century Colonial Homestead. 2014. (ENG., Illus.). 136p. (J). (gr. 5-8). lib. bdg. 20.95 *(978-0-7613-5408-6(5),* 6238a30f-4da2-4abe-8468-663f92628278, Carolrhoda Bks.) Lerner Publishing Group.
Whiting, Jim. The Maryland Colony: Lord Baltimore. 2007. (Building America Ser.). (Illus.). 48p. (J). (gr. 4-8). lib. bdg. 29.95 *(978-1-58415-547-8(7))* Mitchell Lane Pubs.
Wyckoff, Edwin Brit. The African-American Heart Surgery Pioneer: The Genius of Vivien Thomas, 1 vol. 2013. (Genius Inventors & Their Great Ideas Ser.). (ENG.). 48p. (gr. 3-3). pap. 11.53 *(978-1-4644-0210-4(8),* 2b8ef94c-a9ea-46db-8f27-258b06589a23, Enslow Elementary) Enslow Publishing, LLC.
Yasuda, Anita. What's Great about Maryland? 2015. (Our Great States Ser.). (ENG., Illus.). 32p. (J). (gr. 2-5). 26.65 *(978-1-4677-3875-0(1),* 603b3212-3388-413b-baec-5dfe5087f2fc, Lerner Pubns.) Lerner Publishing Group.

MASAI (AFRICAN PEOPLE)

Alexander, Florence & Alexander, Stanley. Come with Me & See— African People: Venga Conmigo y Vea— la Gente de Africa. 2003. (SPA & ENG., Illus.). 34p. (J). *(978-964-8313-41-3(5))* Ebon Research Systems Publishing, LLC.
—Come with Me & See... African People. l.t. ed. 2003. (ENG & SPA., Illus.). 13p. (J). 3.99 *(978-0-9648313-8-4(4))* Ebon Research Systems Publishing, LLC.
Craats, Rennay. Maasai. (Indigenous Peoples Ser.). 32p. 2005. pap. 9.95 *(978-1-59036-255-6(1))* 2004. (Illus.). (J). lib. bdg. 26.00 *(978-1-59036-219-8(5))* Weigl Pubs., Inc.
Deedy, Carmen Agra. 14 Cows for America, 1 vol. Gonzalez, Thomas, illus. 36p. (J). (gr. 2-5). 2016. pap. 8.99 *(978-1-56145-961-2(5))* 2009. 17.99 *(978-1-56145-490-7(7))* Peachtree Publishing Co. Inc.
—14 Cows for America. Gonzalez, Thomas, illus. 2016. (ENG.). 36p. (J). (gr. -1-3). lib. bdg. 19.60 *(978-0-606-39065-1(0))* Turtleback.
Scott, Jonathan & Scott, Angela. The Maasai: Tribe of Warriors: Band 15/Emerald (Collins Big Cat) Scott, Jonathan & Scott, Angela, illus. 2007. (Collins Big Cat Ser.). (ENG., Illus.). 48p. (J). (gr. 3-4). pap. 11.99 *(978-0-00-723097-6(4))* HarperCollins Pubs. Ltd. GBR. Dist: Independent Pubs. Group.

MASAI (AFRICAN PEOPLE)—FICTION

Barasch, Lynne. First Come the Zebra. Barasch, Lynne, illus. 2009. (ENG., Illus.). 40p. (J). (gr. 1-6). 18.95 *(978-1-60060-365-5(3))* Lee & Low Bks., Inc.
—First Come the Zebra, 1 vol. 2005. (ENG., Illus.). 40p. (J). (gr. 1-4). pap. 12.95 *(978-1-62014-029-1(2),* leelowbooks) Lee & Low Bks., Inc.
Joosse, Barbara M. Papa, Do You Love Me? Lavallee, Barbara, illus. 2005. (Mama & Papa, Do You Love Me? Ser.: MAMA). (ENG.). 36p. (J). (gr. -1-7). 15.99 *(978-0-8118-4265-5(7))* Chronicle Bks. LLC.

MASERS, OPTICAL

see Lasers

MASKS

Anastasio, Dina. Mask Making Around the World. 2011. (Early Connections Ser.). (J). *(978-1-61672-588-4(5))* Benchmark Education Co.
—Mask Making Around the World: Set Of 6. 2011. (Early Connections Ser.). (J). pap. 37.00 net. *(978-1-4108-1069-4(0))* Benchmark Education Co.
Cryan, Mary Beth. Make Your Own Masks: Tear Them, Share Them, Color & Wear Them! 2015. (Dover Kids Activity Bks.). (ENG.). 64p. (J). (gr. 1-4). pap. 7.99 *(978-0-486-79406-8(7),* 794067) Dover Pubns., Inc.
D'Cruz, Anna-Marie. Make Your Own Masks, 1 vol. (Do It Yourself Projects! Ser.). (ENG.). 24p. (J). (gr. 4-4). 2009. pap. 10.40 *(978-1-4358-2923-7(9),* 4cea656d-709e-4634-a2f1-8719a50128e6) 2008. lib. bdg. 28.93 *(978-1-4358-2853-7(4),* 76b8b4e5-d971-4384-ab94-a474720fca70) Rosen Publishing Group, Inc., The. (PowerKids Pr.).
Doney, Meryl. Masks, 1 vol. 2004. (Crafts from Many Cultures Ser.). (ENG., Illus.). 32p. (gr. 3-5). lib. bdg. 28.67 *(978-0-8368-4044-5(5),* 779e87c2-f40a-4618-9f69-aacfd0437fa9, Gareth Stevens Learning Library) Stevens, Gareth Publishing LLLP.
Hodge, Susie. Masks. 2006. (Design & Make Ser.). (Illus.). 32p. (J). (gr. 4-7). lib. bdg. 28.50 *(978-1-58340-952-7(1))* Black Rabbit Bks.
Holden, Pam. Masks, 1 vol. 2009. (Red Rocket Readers Ser.). (ENG., Illus.). 16p. (gr. 1-1). pap. *(978-1-877490-19-4(9))* Flying Start Bks.
Humphrey, Paul. How to Make a Mask. Fairclough, Chris, photos by. 2007. (Crafty Kids Ser.). (Illus.). 24p. (J). (gr. -1-3). lib. bdg. 24.25 *(978-1-59771-101-2(2))* Sea-To-Sea Pubns.
Kenney, Karen Latchana. Super Simple Masks: Fun & Easy-to-Make Crafts for Kids, 1 vol. Craig, Diane, ed. 2009. (Super Simple Crafts Ser.). (ENG., Illus.). 32p. (J). (gr. -1-4). 34.21 *(978-1-60453-627-0(6),* 13936, Super SandCastle) ABDO Publishing Co.
LaFosse, Michael G. Making Origami Masks Step by Step. 2009. (Kid's Guide to Origami Ser.). 24p. (gr. 3-4). 47.90 *(978-1-61511-188-6(3),* PowerKids Pr.) Rosen Publishing Group, Inc., The.
Morris, Ting & Morris, Neil. Masks. 2006. (Sticky Fingers Ser.). (Illus.). 32p. (J). lib. bdg. 28.50 *(978-1-59771-030-5(X),* 1268892) Sea-To-Sea Pubns.
Rudolph, Nancy Lyn. Paper Animal Masks from Northwest Tribal Tales. 2004. (Illus.). 80p. (J). (gr. 4-8). reprint ed. 20.00 *(978-0-7567-7073-0(4))* DIANE Publishing Co.
Smith, A. G. Masks of the World Coloring Book. 2003. (Dover Design Coloring Bks.). (ENG., Illus.). 32p. (J). (gr. 3-8). pap. 3.99 *(978-0-486-43039-3(1),* 430391) Dover Pubns., Inc.
Smith, Thomasina. Amazing Masks to Make Yourself: 25 Projects for Funny & Frightening Faces to Wear! 2014. (ENG., Illus.). 64p. (J). (gr. 3-8). 9.99 *(978-1-84322-913-1(7),* Armadillo) Anness Publishing GBR. Dist: National Bk. Network.
Storey, Rita. Masks. Rhodes, Harry, illus. Rhodes, Harry, photos by. 2014. (J). lib. bdg. 26.60 *(978-1-4677-4195-8(7),* Lerner Pubns.) Lerner Publishing Group.
Yates, Jane. Paper-Mache Masks, 1 vol. 2016. (Cool Crafts for Kids Ser.). (ENG.). 32p. (J). (gr. 3-3). pap. 12.75 *(978-1-4994-8234-8(5),* 2eee5d46-4a78-4831-ace0-530457fc0557, Windmill Bks.) Rosen Publishing Group, Inc., The.

MASONRY

Mara, Wil. Be a Mason. 2019. (21st Century Skills Library: Guide to the Trades Ser.). (ENG., Illus.). 32p. (J). (gr. 4-7). pap. 14.21 *(978-1-5341-5109-3(5),* 213743); lib. bdg. 32.07 *(978-1-5341-4823-9(X),* 213742) Cherry Lake Publishing.
Morkes, Andrew. Masonry Worker, Vol. 10. 2018. (Careers in the Building Trades: a Growing Demand Ser.). 80p. (J). (gr. 7). lib. bdg. 33.27 *(978-1-4222-4117-2(3))* Mason Crest.
Willett, Edward. A Career As a Mason, 1 vol., 1. 2015. (Essential Careers Ser.). (ENG.). 80p. (J). (gr. 6-6). 37.47 *(978-1-4994-6217-3(4),* 6982f387-98b7-484b-9350-c54dcd1ee915, Rosen Young Adult) Rosen Publishing Group, Inc., The.

MASS COMMUNICATION

see Communication

MASS MEDIA

Abdo, Kenny. Jason Voorhees. 2019. (Hollywood Monsters Ser.). (ENG., Illus.). 24p. (J). (gr. 2-8). lib. bdg. 31.36 *(978-1-5321-2746-5(4),* 31699, Abdo Zoom-Fly) ABDO Publishing Co.
—Leatherface. 2019. (Hollywood Monsters Ser.). (ENG., Illus.). 24p. (J). (gr. 2-8). lib. bdg. 31.36 *(978-1-5321-2747-2(2),* 31701, Abdo Zoom-Fly) ABDO Publishing Co.
Adams, Simon. Politics. 2010. (Media Power Ser.). 48p. (YA). (gr. 5-9). 35.65 *(978-1-60753-114-2(3))* Amicus Learning.
Ali, Dominic. Media Madness: An Insider's Guide to Media. Cho, Michael, illus. 2005. 64p. (J). (gr. 5-9). 9.95 *(978-1-55337-175-5(5))* Kids Can Pr., Ltd. CAN. Dist: Hachette Bk. Group.
Anderson, Jennifer Joline. Exploring Media & Government. 2019. (Searchlight Books (tm) — Getting into Government Ser.). (ENG., Illus.). 32p. (J). (gr. 3-5). 30.65 *(978-1-5415-5586-0(4),* 1ccc0c28-82c5-47a0-ae1d-0b21811eac43, Lerner Pubns.) Lerner Publishing Group.
Anderson, Judith. Celebrity & Fame. 2010. (Media Power Ser.). 48p. (YA). (gr. 5-9). 35.65 *(978-1-60753-112-8(7))* Amicus Learning.
—Celebrity & Fame. 2011. (Inside Crime Ser.). 48p. (YA). (gr. 5-9). lib. bdg. 34.25 *(978-1-59920-398-0(7))* Black Rabbit Bks.
—Crime. 2010. (Media Power Ser.). 48p. (YA). (gr. 5-9). 35.65 *(978-1-60753-113-5(5))* Amicus Learning.

—War & Conflict. 2010. (Media Power Ser.). 48p. (J). 35.65 (978-1-60753-116-6(X)) Amicus Learning.

Anderson, Judith & Flinthart, Dirk. War & Conflict. 2011. (Inside Crime Ser.). 48p. (YA). (gr. 5-9). lib. bdg. 34.25 (978-1-59920-399-7(5)) Black Rabbit Bks.

Anderson, Judith & Vaughan, Jenny. Crime. 2011. (Inside Crime Ser.). 48p. (YA). (gr. 5-9). lib. bdg. 34.25 (978-1-59920-400-0(2)) Black Rabbit Bks.

Ball, Jacqueline A., et al. Communication Inventions: From Hieroglyphics to DVDs. 2006. (Which Came First? Ser.). (Illus.). 32p. (YA). (gr. 3-6). lib. bdg. 28.50 (978-1-59716-129-9(2)) Bearport Publishing Co., Inc.

Barber, Phil. Football & Player Safety. 2017. (Illus.). 64p. (J). (978-1-4222-3576-8(9)) Mason Crest.

Berlatsky, Noah, ed. Media Violence, 1 vol. 2012. (Opposing Viewpoints Ser.). (ENG., Illus.). 208p. (gr. 10-12). 50.43 (978-0-7377-6328-7(0), 6e957719-1c2c-4c21-bc38-1a84fe3f9b41); pap. 34.80 (978-0-7377-6329-4(9), 4ad3e688-4335-4b3a-b1ac-5984519d23ce) Greenhaven Publishing LLC. (Greenhaven Publishing).

Bernay, Emma, et al. Cracking the Media Literacy Code. 2018. (Cracking the Media Literacy Code Ser.). (ENG.). 32p. (J). (gr. 3-6). 119.96 (978-1-5435-2724-7(8), 28205, Capstone Pr.) Capstone.

Botzakis, Stergios. Mastering Media, 1 vol., Set. Incl. Entertainment & Gaming. (ENG., Illus.). 56p. (J). (gr. 6-10). 2010. 37.32 (978-1-4109-3844-2(1), 112982, Raintree); (Mastering Media Ser.). (ENG.). 56p. 2010. 70.64 o.p. (978-1-4109-3846-6(8), 14977, Raintree) Capstone.

Bozzo, Linda. Staying in Touch in the Past, Present, & Future, 1 vol. 2010. (Imagining the Future Ser.). (ENG., Illus.). 24p. (gr. k-2). lib. bdg. 25.27 (978-0-7660-3438-9(0), e955973c-d2ad-4139-a7b3-ce0d3774d7a5, Enslow Elementary) Enslow Publishing, LLC.

Brezina, Corona. Careers in Digital Media, 1 vol. 2017. (Essential Careers Ser.). (ENG., Illus.). 80p. (J). (gr. 6-6). pap. 16.30 (978-1-5081-7874-3(7), 06f73835-6ebf-4c63-9c29-0e457e142955) Rosen Publishing Group, Inc., The.

Brophy Down, Susan. Free Press & Censorship. 2018. (Why Does Media Literacy Matter? Ser.). (ENG., Illus.). 48p. (J). (gr. 6-6). (978-0-7787-4543-3(0)); pap. (978-0-7787-4547-1(3)) Crabtree Publishing Co.

—Power & Persuasion in Media & Advertising. 2018. (Why Does Media Literacy Matter? Ser.). (ENG., Illus.). 48p. (J). (gr. 6-6). (978-0-7787-4544-0(9)); pap. (978-0-7787-4548-8(1)) Crabtree Publishing Co.

Cooper, Alison. Media Power? 2005. (Viewpoints (Sea to Sea) Ser.). (Illus.). 32p. (J). (gr. 5-9). lib. bdg. 27.10 (978-1-932889-61-1(2)) Sea-To-Sea Pubns.

Cornell, Kari A. Fake News. 2019. (In Focus Ser.). (ENG.). 80p. (YA). (gr. 6-12). 41.27 (978-1-68282-715-4(1), BrightPoint Pr.) ReferencePoint Pr., Inc.

Currie, Stephen. Sharing Posts: The Spread of Fake News. 2017. (ENG.). 80p. (YA). (gr. 5-12). (978-1-68282-297-5(4)) ReferencePoint Pr., Inc.

Dakers, Diane. Representation in Media. 2018. (Why Does Media Literacy Matter? Ser.). (ENG., Illus.). 48p. (J). (gr. 6-6). (978-0-7787-4545-7(7)); pap. (978-0-7787-4549-5(X)) Crabtree Publishing Co.

Dell, Pamela. Understanding Social Media. 2018. (Cracking the Media Literacy Code Ser.). (ENG., Illus.). 32p. (J). (gr. 3-6). lib. bdg. 27.99 (978-1-5435-2706-3(X), 138142, Capstone Pr.) Capstone.

—Understanding the News. 2018. (Cracking the Media Literacy Code Ser.). (ENG., Illus.). 32p. (J). (gr. 3-6). lib. bdg. 27.99 (978-1-5435-2704-9(3), 138140, Capstone Pr.) Capstone.

Donovan, Sandy. Media: From News Coverage to Political Advertising. 2015. (Inside Elections Ser.). (ENG., Illus.). 64p. (J). (gr. 6-8). 26.65 (978-1-4677-7909-8(1), 8d62d2f6-7515-4cea-b10d-aedb95571a8d, Lerner Pubns.) Lerner Publishing Group.

Dugan, Christine. Tech World: The Language of Social Media (Level 5) 2017. (TIME for KIDS(r): Informational Text Ser.). (ENG., Illus.). 48p. (J). (gr. 4-8). pap. 13.99 (978-1-4258-4989-4(X)) Teacher Created Materials, Inc.

Duhig, Holly. Media & the News. 2018. (Our Values - Level 3 Ser.). (Illus.). 32p. (J). (gr. 5-6). (978-0-7787-5434-3(0)) Crabtree Publishing Co.

Edwards, Claire. Social Media & Mental Health: Handbook for Teens. 2018. (Pulling the Trigger Ser.). (ENG., Illus.). 80p. (J). (gr. 3-7). pap. 9.95 (978-1-911246-37-4(2)) Welbeck Publishing Group Ltd. GBR. Dist: Two Rivers Distribution.

Endich, Roberta. Media Literacy: Activities for Understanding the Scripted World, 1 vol. 2003. (ENG., Illus.). 150p. pap. 34.95 (978-1-58683-094-6(5), 900303814, Linworth Publishing, Inc.) ABC-CLIO, LLC.

Evans, Christine. Objectification of Women in the Media. 2019. (Women & Society Ser.). (ENG.). 80p. (J). (gr. 6-12). (978-1-68282-543-3(4)) ReferencePoint Pr., Inc.

Garner, Gerald W. News Media Relations for Law Enforcement Leaders. 2nd ed. 2018. 230p. pap. 34.95 (978-0-398-09243-6(5)) Thomas, Charles C. Pub., Ltd.

Gifford, Clive. Violence on the Screen. 2010. (Voices Ser.). (Illus.). 48p. pap. (978-0-237-54218-4(8)) Evans Brothers, Ltd.

Gitlin, Martin. Online News. 2019. (21st Century Skills Innovation Library: Disruptors in Tech Ser.). (ENG.). 32p. (J). (gr. 4-8). pap. 14.21 (978-1-5341-5043-0(9), 213479); (Illus.). lib. bdg. 32.07 (978-1-5341-4757-7(8), 213478) Cherry Lake Publishing.

Gregory, Josh. Posting on Social Media (a True Book: Get Ready to Code) (Library Edition) 2019. (True Book (Relaunch) Ser.). (ENG., Illus.). 48p. (J). (gr. 3-5). lib. bdg. 31.00 (978-0-531-12734-6(6), Children's Pr.) Scholastic Library Publishing.

Haerens, Margaret & Zott, Lynn M., eds. Mass Media, 1 vol. 2014. (Opposing Viewpoints Ser.). (ENG.). 208p. (gr. 10-12). lib. bdg. 50.43 (978-0-7377-6660-8(3), e76e0d68-27f1-458c-a815-79144b35ba27); (Illus.). pap. 34.80 (978-0-7377-6661-5(1), 92110fc1-ce49-46b8-a061-0d10de9364cc) Greenhaven Publishing LLC. (Greenhaven Publishing).

Hand, Carol. Everything You Need to Know about Fake News & Propaganda, 1 vol. 2017. (Need to Know Library). (ENG., Illus.). 64p. (J). (gr. 6-6). 36.13 (978-1-5081-7664-0(7), 799fea4f-744d-45f4-8793-c5079a391511); pap. 13.95 (978-1-5081-7663-3(9), 01943e45-b23c-4e46-89dc-3af4c5477b00) Rosen Publishing Group, Inc., The. (Rosen Young Adult).

—Getting Paid to Produce Videos, 1 vol. 2016. (Turning Your Tech Hobbies into a Career Ser.). (ENG., Illus.). 80p. (J). (gr. 7-7). 37.47 (978-1-5081-7292-5(7), b40702c0-9655-4b46-b648-65d67ecf36a2) Rosen Publishing Group, Inc., The.

Harmon, Daniel E. Dream Jobs in Sports Media, 1 vol. 2014. (Great Careers in the Sports Industry Ser.). (ENG., Illus.). 160p. (YA). (gr. 7-7). 44.13 (978-1-4777-7523-3(4), 6de7c3ad-b871-4de4-8d68-e8012cb3b257) Rosen Publishing Group, Inc., The.

Harper, Leslie. Cómo Mantenerse Informado. 2014. (Sé un líder de la Comunidad (Be a Community Leader) Ser.). (SPA.). 32p. (J). (gr. 4-6). pap. 60.00 (978-1-4777-6923-2(4), PowerKids Pr.) Rosen Publishing Group, Inc., The.

—Cómo Mantenerse Informados, 1 vol. 2014. (Sé un líder de la Comunidad (Be a Community Leader) Ser.). (SPA.). 32p. (J). (gr. 5-5). lib. bdg. 27.93 (978-1-4777-6921-8(8), 829dbc4b-55b0-4ea3-a1f3-e1095203f601, PowerKids Pr.) Rosen Publishing Group, Inc., The.

—How to Stay Informed, 1 vol. 2014. (Be a Community Leader Ser.). (ENG.). 32p. (J). (gr. 5-5). lib. bdg. 27.93 (978-1-4777-6701-6(0), 4a2c32a5-e6f5-4ed4-b05f-5f02918f88db, PowerKids Pr.) Rosen Publishing Group, Inc., The.

Harris, Duchess. The Fake News Phenomenon. 2017. (News Literacy Ser.). (ENG., Illus.). 48p. (J). (gr. 4-8). lib. bdg. 35.64 (978-1-5321-1388-8(9), 27686) ABDO Publishing Co.

Harris, Duchess & Morris, Rebecca. The Silence Breakers & the #MeToo Movement. 2018. (Special Reports). (ENG., Illus.). 112p. (J). (gr. 6-12). lib. bdg. 41.36 (978-1-5321-1683-4(7), 30618, Essential Library) ABDO Publishing Co.

Hermansson, Casie. Parental Guidance Ratings. 2013. (Hot Topics in Media Ser.). (ENG.). 48p. (J). (gr. 4-8). pap. 18.50 (978-1-61783-784-5(9), 10758) ABDO Publishing Co.

Hernández, Roger E. Teens & the Media. 2008. (Gallup Youth Survey, Major Issues & Trends Ser.). (Illus.). 112,128p. (YA). lib. bdg. 22.95 (978-1-59084-874-6(8)) Mason Crest.

Hernandez, Roger E. Teens & the Media. Developed in Association with the Gallup Organization Staff, ed. 2013. (Gallup Youth Survey: Major Issues & Trends Ser.: 14). 112p. (J). (gr. 7-18). 24.95 (978-1-4222-2954-5(8)) Mason Crest.

Horn, Geoffrey M. Political Parties, Interest Groups, & the Media, 1 vol. 2003. (World Almanac(r) Library of American Government Ser.). (ENG., Illus.). 48p. (gr. 5-8). pap. 15.05 (978-0-8368-5483-1(7), 97efc7c4-510b-4e32-8f0f-c646243b1f7f, Gareth Stevens Secondary Library) Stevens, Gareth Publishing LLLP.

Idzikowski, Lisa, ed. Celebrities in Politics, 1 vol. 2019. (At Issue Ser.). (ENG.). 128p. (gr. 10-12). pap. 28.80 (978-1-5345-0519-3(9), 903513f2-5e4f-43ab-b93d-c1c1f7df18b0) Greenhaven Publishing LLC.

Jennings, Brien J. Fact, Fiction, & Opinions: The Differences Between Ads, Blogs, News Reports, & Other Media. 2018. (All about Media Ser.). (ENG., Illus.). 24p. (J). (gr. 1-3). lib. bdg. 27.99 (978-1-5435-0222-0(9), 137140, Capstone Pr.) Capstone.

Jones, Grace. Body Image & the Media. 2018. (Our Values - Level 3 Ser.). (Illus.). 32p. (J). (gr. 5-6). (978-0-7787-5189-2(9)) Crabtree Publishing Co.

Kawa, Katie. Should We Trust the News?, 1 vol. 2019. (Points of View Ser.). (ENG.). 24p. (gr. 3-3). 26.23 (978-1-5345-6723-8(2), 1068dce2-d56e-4fd8-b902-5edc655cce39, KidHaven Publishing) Greenhaven Publishing LLC.

Keppeler, Jill. The Media's Role in Democracy, 1 vol. 2018. (Young Citizen's Guide to News Literacy Ser.). (ENG.). 32p. (gr. 4-5). 27.93 (978-1-5383-4502-3(1), 791e4e9d-c1c5-457e-aa26-574ed8593f8a, PowerKids Pr.) Rosen Publishing Group, Inc., The.

Kerr, Jim. Sports. 2010. (Media Power Ser.). 48p. (YA). (gr. 5-9). 35.65 (978-1-60753-115-9(1)) Amicus Learning.

Krajna, Cheryl. Blurred Lines: News or Advertisements?, 1 vol. 2018. (Young Citizen's Guide to News Literacy Ser.). (ENG.). 32p. (gr. 4-5). 27.93 (978-1-5383-4497-2(1), 8a994da0-7f70-4eb3-956c-4802d399ab51, PowerKids Pr.) Rosen Publishing Group, Inc., The.

Ledbetter, Ebonie, ed. Media Bias, 1 vol. 2015. (Introducing Issues with Opposing Viewpoints Ser.). (ENG., Illus.). 160p. (gr. 7-10). 43.63 (978-0-7377-7236-4(0), 8f7337b6-eee7-4ea1-815e-ea338dbbd430, Greenhaven Publishing) Greenhaven Publishing LLC.

Lewis, Clare. Entertainment Through the Years: How Having Fun Has Changed in Living Memory. 2015. (History in Living Memory Ser.). (ENG., Illus.). 24p. (J). (gr. k-2). 25.99 (978-1-4846-0923-1(9), 128022, Heinemann) Capstone.

Malaspina, Ann. False Images, Deadly Promises: Smoking & the Media. 2007. (Tobacco: the Deadly Drug Ser.). (Illus.). 112p. (YA). pap. 12.95 (978-1-4222-0812-0(5)) Mason Crest.

Mara, Wil. Body Image in the Media. 2018. (21st Century Skills Library: Global Citizens: Modern Media Ser.). (ENG., Illus.). 32p. (J). (gr. 4-7). lib. bdg. 32.07 (978-1-5341-2925-2(1), 211744) Cherry Lake Publishing.

—Mainstream News. 2018. (21st Century Skills Library: Global Citizens: Modern Media Ser.). (ENG.). 32p. (J). (gr. 4-7). pap. 14.21 (978-1-5341-3251-1(1), 211769); (Illus.). lib. bdg. 32.07 (978-1-5341-2931-3(6), 211768) Cherry Lake Publishing.

—Politics & the Media. 2018. (21st Century Skills Library: Global Citizens: Modern Media Ser.). (ENG., Illus.). 32p. (J). (gr. 4-7). lib. bdg. 32.07 (978-1-5341-2929-0(4), 211760) Cherry Lake Publishing.

Merino, Noël, ed. Media Violence, 1 vol. 2010. (Introducing Issues with Opposing Viewpoints Ser.). (ENG., Illus.). 128p. (gr. 7-10). 43.63 (978-0-7377-4480-4(4), 5446fb51-4774-43e9-9848-a64bfb9d1478, Greenhaven Publishing) Greenhaven Publishing LLC.

Murray, Laura K. & Harris, Duchess. Uncovering Bias in the News. 2017. (News Literacy Ser.). (ENG., Illus.). 48p. (J). (gr. 4-8). lib. bdg. 35.64 (978-1-5321-1390-1(0), 27688) ABDO Publishing Co.

Ogden, Charlie. Censorship & Privacy. 2018. (Our Values - Level 3 Ser.). 32p. (J). (gr. 5-6). (978-0-7787-4731-4(X)) Crabtree Publishing Co.

Open for Debate - Group 5, 8 vols., Set. Incl. National Health Care. Kowalski, Kathiann M. lib. bdg. 45.50 (978-0-7614-2943-2(3), edaa0977-a53f-47fe-aa23-2e0389c5e727); Political Campaigns. Naden, Corinne. lib. bdg. 45.50 (978-0-7614-2944-9(1), 9d2e64a5-2c0c-4a63-9836-204d64ed8840); Religious Fundamentalism. Fridell, Ron. lib. bdg. 45.50 (978-0-7614-2945-6(X), d9d1f5c0-2b35-4938-9b69-3cde347cd370); Right to Die. Stefoff, Rebecca. lib. bdg. 45.50 (978-0-7614-2948-7(4), bcbd0407-c7ba-4a50-9da6-fe926a35d042); 144p. (YA). (gr. 8-8). (Open for Debate Ser.). (ENG.). 2009. Set lib. bdg. 182.00 (978-0-7614-2940-1(9), dee07674-67e9-492f-9ba3-039659ed2638, Cavendish Square) Cavendish Square Publishing LLC.

Orr, Tamra. Image Sharing. 2019. (21st Century Skills Library: Global Citizens: Social Media Ser.). (ENG., Illus.). 32p. (J). (gr. 4-7). pap. 14.21 (978-1-5341-3964-0(8), 212685); lib. bdg. 32.07 (978-1-5341-4308-1(4), 212684) Cherry Lake Publishing.

—Video Sharing. 2019. (21st Century Skills Library: Global Citizens: Social Media Ser.). (ENG.). 32p. (J). (gr. 4-7). pap. 14.21 (978-1-5341-3965-7(6), 212689); (Illus.). lib. bdg. 32.07 (978-1-5341-4309-8(2), 212688) Cherry Lake Publishing.

Pelusey, Michael & Pelusey, Jane. The Media. 2005. (ENG., Illus.). 32p. (gr. 5-8). 131.70 (978-0-7910-9093-0(0), P196816, Facts On File) Infobase Holdings, Inc.

Peters, Jennifer, ed. Critical Perspectives on Media Bias, 1 vol. 2017. (Analyzing the Issues Ser.). (ENG.). 224p. (gr. 8-8). 50.93 (978-0-7660-9169-6(4), 19cef3b9-e6f0-486f-bd11-64599a70ac1a); pap. 26.23 (978-0-7660-9560-1(6), 5f9be1e4-32ff-46a0-8fbd-420dd9986633) Enslow Publishing, LLC.

Radley, Gail. Facebook. 2018. (Tech Titans Ser.). (ENG., Illus.). 112p. (J). (gr. 6-12). lib. bdg. 41.36 (978-1-5321-1687-2(X), 30626, Essential Library) ABDO Publishing Co.

Reeves, Diane Lindsey. Arts & Communication. 2017. (Bright Futures Press: World of Work Ser.). (ENG., Illus.). 32p. (J). (gr. 4-7). lib. bdg. 32.07 (978-1-5341-0170-8(5), 210150) Cherry Lake Publishing.

Regulating Violence in Entertainment. 2010. (ENG., Illus.). 152p. (gr. 9-18). 35.00 (978-1-60413-510-7(7), P178899, Facts On File) Infobase Holdings, Inc.

Rooney, Anne. Creative & Media Careers. 2010. (In the Workplace Ser.). 48p. (J). lib. bdg. 34.25 (978-1-60753-090-9(2)) Amicus Learning.

Rooney, Anne & Savery, Annabel. Creative & Media Careers. 2011. (Been There! Ser.). 32p. (J). (gr. 3-6). lib. bdg. 28.50 (978-1-59920-470-3(3)) Black Rabbit Bks.

Rustad, Martha E. H. Learning about Fact & Opinion. 2015. (Media Literacy for Kids Ser.). (ENG., Illus.). 24p. (J). (gr. -1-2). lib. bdg. 27.32 (978-1-4914-1831-4(1), 127273, Capstone Pr.) Capstone.

Ryan, Aidan M. Recognizing Bias, 1 vol. 2018. (News Literacy Ser.). (ENG.). 64p. (gr. 5-5). pap. 16.28 (978-1-5026-4143-4(7), cbbff8b7-4b82-48ee-86f5-95ce9d136d30) Cavendish Square Publishing LLC.

Saedi Bocci, Goali. The Social Media Workbook for Teens: Skills to Help You Balance Screen Time, Manage Stress, & Take Charge of Your Life. 2019. (ENG.). 152p. (YA). (gr. 5-12). pap. 21.95 (978-1-68403-190-0(7), 41900, Instant Help Books) New Harbinger Pubns.

Smith, Devlin. Coping with Fake News & Disinformation, 1 vol. 2019. (Coping Ser.). (ENG.). 112p. (gr. 7-7). pap. 19.24 (978-1-7253-4119-7(0), f3f2708b-6c1a-412b-bd62-c972c70b43f5) Rosen Publishing Group, Inc., The.

Summers, Sue L. Media Alert! 200 Activities to Create Media-Savvy Kids. (J). pap. 15.00 (978-0-9676616-0-5(9)) Media Alert!

Vander Hook, Sue. Rupert Murdoch: News Corporation Magnate, 1 vol. 2011. (Essential Lives Set 6 Ser.). (ENG., Illus.). 112p. (J). (gr. 6-12). lib. bdg. 41.36 (978-1-61714-782-1(6), 6729, Essential Library) ABDO Publishing Co.

Vaughan, Jenny. Causes & Campaigns. 2010. (Media Power Ser.). 48p. (YA). (gr. 5-9). 35.65 (978-1-60753-111-1(9)) Amicus Learning.

Way, Steve & Bailey, Gerry. Communication, 1 vol. 2008. (Simply Science Ser.). (ENG., Illus.). 32p. (YA). (gr. 3-5). lib. bdg. 28.67 (978-0-8368-9226-0(7), 3fefc888-023f-4f35-af08-4fba711bb4aa) Stevens, Gareth Publishing LLLP.

Wilson, Rosie. Media & Communications Industry, 1 vol. 2010. (Closer Look: Global Industries Ser.). (ENG.). 48p. (YA). (gr. 7-7). lib. bdg. 34.47 (978-1-4358-9632-1(7), 90241992-e4fa-4cd7-9037-48009a16c551, Rosen Reference) Rosen Publishing Group, Inc., The.

Wittekind, Erika. Violence as Entertainment: Why Aggression Sells. 2012. (Exploring Media Literacy Ser.). (ENG.). 80p. (J). (gr. 5-8). pap. 9.10 (978-0-7565-4536-9(6), 118368); lib. bdg. 35.32 (978-0-7565-4520-8(X), 117101) Capstone. (Compass Point Bks.).

MASSACHUSETTS

Baker, Helen. Shopping the Cape, 1 book. 2003. 160p. per. 12.95 (978-0-9743511-0-0(5)) Baker, Helen Interiors, Inc.

Bjorklund, Ruth. Massachusetts, 1 vol. Santoro, Christopher, illus. 2003. (It's My State! (First Edition)(r) Ser.). (ENG.). 80p. (gr. 4-4). 34.07 (978-0-7614-1418-6(5), 7d725e7a-cf42-4453-b870-b824b1d231ab) Cavendish Square Publishing LLC.

Brown, Jonatha A. & Fairley, Melissa. Massachusetts, 1 vol. 2005. (Portraits of the States Ser.). (ENG., Illus.). 32p. (gr. 3-5). pap. 11.50 (978-0-8368-4645-4(1), 232f7eba-2aff-45d9-9148-60032344dbb8); lib. bdg. 28.67 (978-0-8368-4626-3(5), 56e2c48f-65c0-451e-a397-e8d241788d60) Stevens, Gareth Publishing LLLP. (Gareth Stevens Learning Library).

Bruun, Erik. State Shapes: Massachusetts. 2006. (ENG., Illus.). 48p. (J). (gr. -1-17). 9.95 (978-1-57912-230-0(2), 81230, Black Dog & Leventhal Pubs. Inc.) Hachette Bks.

Cusolito, Michelle. Flying Deep: Climb Inside Deep-Sea Submersible Alvin. Wong, Nicole, illus. 2018. 32p. (J). (gr. k-4). pap. 7.99 (978-1-58089-841-6(6)) Charlesbridge Publishing, Inc.

Deinard, Jenny. How to Draw Massachusetts's Sights & Symbols. 2009. (Kid's Guide to Drawing America Ser.). 32p. (gr. k-k). 50.50 (978-1-61511-070-4(4), PowerKids Pr.) Rosen Publishing Group, Inc., The.

Ewing, Juliana Horatia. Story of A Short Life. 2006. pap. 24.95 (978-1-4286-3593-7(9)) Kessinger Publishing, LLC.

Freedman, Jeri. Massachusetts: Past & Present. 2009. (J). 70.50 (978-1-4358-5587-8(6)); (ENG.). 48p. (J). (gr. 5-5). pap. 12.75 (978-1-4358-5586-1(8), 4e4f2c3a-5f71-402f-9393-d060f40fb859); (ENG., Illus.). 48p. (YA). (gr. 5-5). lib. bdg. 34.47 (978-1-4358-5294-5(X), 2e78acf6-8060-4fd5-a705-f15e7c3316c7) Rosen Publishing Group, Inc., The. (Rosen Reference).

Hale, Kate. Little Massachusetts. Brett, Jeannie, illus. 2016. (Little State Ser.). (ENG.). 20p. (J). (gr. -1-k). bds. 9.95 (978-1-58536-949-2(7), 204035) Sleeping Bear Pr.

Heinrichs, Ann. Massachusetts. Kania, Matt, illus. 2017. (U. S. A. Travel Guides). (ENG.). 40p. (J). (gr. 2-5). lib. bdg. 38.50 (978-1-5038-1961-0(2), 211598) Child's World, Inc, The.

Jerome, Kate Boehm. Massachusetts: What's So Great about This State? 2011. (Arcadia Kids Ser.). (ENG., Illus.). 32p. (J). pap. 9.99 (978-1-58973-019-9(4)) Arcadia Publishing.

Knudsen, Shannon. Alice Ray & the Salem Witch Trials. Palmer, Ruth, illus. 2011. (History Speaks: Picture Books Plus Reader's Theater Ser.). 48p. pap. 56.72 (978-0-7613-7629-3(1)); (ENG.). (gr. 2-4). pap. 9.95 (978-0-7613-7114-4(1)) Lerner Publishing Group.

Marsh, Carole. Massachusetts Current Events Projects: 30 Cool, Activities, Crafts, Experiments & More for Kids to Do to Learn about Your State! 2003. (Massachusetts Experience Ser.). 32p. (gr. k-8). pap. 5.95 (978-0-635-02040-6(8), Marsh, Carole Bks.) Gallopade International.

—Massachusetts Geography Projects: 30 Cool, Activities, Crafts, Experiments & More for Kids to Do to Learn about Your State! 2003. (Massachusetts Experience Ser.). 32p. (gr. k-5). pap. 5.95 (978-0-635-01840-3(3), Marsh, Carole Bks.) Gallopade International.

—Massachusetts Government Projects: 30 Cool, Activities, Crafts, Experiments & More for Kids to Do to Learn about Your State! 2003. (Massachusetts Experience Ser.). 32p. (gr. k-5). pap. 5.95 (978-0-635-01940-0(X), Marsh, Carole Bks.) Gallopade International.

—Massachusetts People Projects: 30 Cool, Activities, Crafts, Experiments & More for Kids to Do to Learn about Your State! 2003. (Massachusetts Experience Ser.). 32p. (gr. k-5). pap. 5.95 (978-0-635-01990-5(6), Marsh, Carole Bks.) Gallopade International.

—Massachusetts Symbols & Facts Projects: 30 Cool, Activities, Crafts, Experiments & More for Kids to Do to Learn about Your State! 2003. (Massachusetts Experience Ser.). 32p. (gr. k-5). pap. 5.95 (978-0-635-01890-8(X), Marsh, Carole Bks.) Gallopade International.

Massachusetts. 2003. (Switched on Schoolhouse Ser.). cd-rom 24.95 (978-0-7403-0645-7(6)) Alpha Omega Pubns., Inc.

McDowell, Pamela. Massachusetts: The Bay Btate. 2012. (J). (978-1-61913-361-7(X)); pap. (978-1-61913-362-4(8)) Weigl Pubs., Inc.

Murray, Julie. Massachusetts, 1 vol. 2006. (Buddy Book Ser.). (ENG., Illus.). 32p. (gr. 2-4). 27.07 (978-1-59197-680-6(4), Buddy Bks.) ABDO Publishing Co.

Obregon, Jose Maria. Massachusetts, 1 vol. Brusca, Maria Cristina, tr. 2005. (Bilingual Library of the United States of America Ser.: Set 1). (ENG & SPA., Illus.). 32p. (J). (gr. 2-2). lib. bdg. 28.93 (978-1-4042-3086-6(6), 395e73de-93de-4414-a9c1-b965a85843f3) Rosen Publishing Group, Inc., The.

Pezzi, Bryan. Massachusetts. 2011. (Guide to American States Ser.). (Illus.). 48p. (YA). (gr. 3-6). 29.99 (978-1-61690-793-8(2)); (J). (978-1-61690-469-2(0)) Weigl Pubs., Inc.

Schmermund, Elizabeth, et al. Massachusetts: The Bay State, 1 vol. 2018. (It's My State! (Fourth Edition)(r) Ser.). (ENG.). 80p. (gr. 4-4). 35.93 (978-1-5026-2630-1(6), e22730a5-d636-44c4-9a6c-0a3302ac6e51) Cavendish Square Publishing LLC.

Stemple, Heidi E. Y. One If by Land: A Massachusetts Number Book. Brett, Jeannie, illus. 2006. (America by the Numbers Ser.). (ENG.). 40p. (J). (gr. 1-3). 17.95 (978-1-58536-186-1(0), 202032) Sleeping Bear Pr.

Troupe, Thomas Kingsley. Paul Revere's Ride: a Fly on the Wall History. Tejido, Jomike, illus. 2017. (Fly on the Wall History Ser.). (ENG.). 32p. (J). (gr. 1-3). lib. bdg. 27.99 (978-1-4795-9785-7(6), 133407, Picture Window Bks.) Capstone.

Trueit, Trudi Strain. America the Beautiful, Third Series: Massachusetts (Revised Edition) 2014. (America the Beautiful Ser.: 3). (ENG.). 144p. (J). lib. bdg. 40.00 (978-0-531-24889-8(5)) Scholastic Library Publishing.

—Massachusetts. 2011. (America the Beautiful, Third Ser.). (Illus.). 144p. (J). pap. 12.95 (978-0-531-22920-0(3), Children's Pr.) Scholastic Library Publishing.

Warner, J. F. Massachusetts. 2012. (J). lib. bdg. 25.26 (978-0-7613-4538-1(8), Lerner Pubns.) Lerner Publishing Group.

Wimmer, Teresa. Massachusetts. 2008. (This Land Called America Ser.). 32p. (YA). (gr. 3-6). 22.95 (978-1-58341-646-4(3)) Creative Co., The.

Winter, Jonah. Paul Revere & the Bell Ringers: Ready-To-Read Level 2. Dodson, Bert, illus. 2003. (Ready-To-Read Childhood of Famous Americans Ser.). (ENG.). 32p. (J). (gr. k-2). pap. 4.99 (978-0-689-85635-8(0), Simon Spotlight) Simon Spotlight.

MASSACHUSETTS—FICTION

Alderson, Sarah. The Sound. 2014. (ENG., Illus.). 320p. (YA). (gr. 9). 17.99 (978-1-4424-9933-1(8), Simon Pulse) Simon Pulse.

Allen, Kate. The Line Tender. 2019. (Illus.). 384p. (J). (gr. 5). 17.99 (978-0-7352-3160-3(5), Dutton Books for Young Readers) Penguin Young Readers Group.

Armistead, Cal. Being Henry David. (ENG.). 312p. (YA). (gr. 8-12). 2014. pap. 9.99 *(978-0-8075-0616-5(8)*, 807506168) 2013. 16.99 *(978-0-8075-0615-8(X)*, 080750615X) Whitman, Albert & Co.
Atkinson, Elizabeth. From Alice to Zen & Everyone in Between. 2008. (Exceptional Reading & Language Arts Titles for Intermediate Grades Ser.). 247p. (YA). (gr. 4-7). 16.95 *(978-0-8225-7271-8(0))* Lerner Publishing Group.
—I, Emma Freke. 2012. (ENG.). 240p. (J). (gr. 4-7). 10.99 *(978-0-7613-8500-4(2)*, 4c09ccbf-9456-48aa-8415-47bb3cfd891b, Carolrhoda Bks.) Lerner Publishing Group.
Barnhart, Judy. Sand Angels in the Snow. 2007. 68p. per. 8.95 *(978-0-595-45154-8(3))* iUniverse, Inc.
Barnholdt, Lauren & Beaky, Suzanne. Hailey Twitch & the Great Teacher Switch. 2010. (Hailey Twitch Ser.: 2). (Illus.). 176p. (J). (gr. 2-4). pap. 10.99 *(978-1-4022-2445-4(1)*, Sourcebooks Jabberwocky) Sourcebooks, Inc.
—Hailey Twitch Is Not a Snitch. 2010. (Hailey Twitch Ser.: 1). (Illus.). 160p. (J). (gr. 2-4). pap. 6.99 *(978-1-4022-2444-7(3)*, Sourcebooks Jabberwocky) Sourcebooks, Inc.
Bestul, Nancy M. The Final Clue: An Historical Novel. 2014. (Illus.). 150p. (J). pap. *(978-1-4951-1481-6(3))* Independent Pub.
Birdsall, Jeanne. The Penderwicks: A Summer Tale of Four Sisters, Two Rabbits, & a Very Interesting Boy. (Penderwicks Ser.: 1). (ENG.). (J). (gr. 3-7). 2007. 288p. 8.99 *(978-0-440-42047-7(4)*, Yearling) 2005. 272p. 17.99 *(978-0-375-83143-0(6)*, Knopf Bks. for Young Readers) Random Hse. Children's Bks.
—The Penderwicks: A Summer Tale of Four Sisters, Two Rabbits & a Very Interesting Boy. 2007. (Penderwicks (Hardback) Ser.). 262p. (gr. 3-7). 18.00 *(978-0-7569-7798-6(3))* Perfection Learning Corp.
—The Penderwicks: A Summer Tale of Four Sisters, Two Rabbits, & a Very Interesting Boy. 2007. (Penderwicks Ser.: 1). (Illus.). 262p. (gr. 4-7). lib. bdg. 18.40 *(978-1-4177-7275-9(1))* Turtleback.
—The Penderwicks: A Summer Tale of Four Sisters, Two Rabbits & a Very Interesting Boy. 2009. 8.80 *(978-0-7848-2826-7(1)*, Everbind) Marco Bk. Co.
—The Penderwicks: A Summer Tale of Four Sisters, Two Rabbits & a Very Interesting Boy. l.t. ed. 2006. (Penderwick Ser.). 304p. (J). (gr. 3-7). 23.95 *(978-0-7862-8897-7(3))* Thorndike Pr.
—The Penderwicks in Spring. 2015. (Penderwicks Ser.: 4). (ENG.). 352p. (J). (gr. 3-7). 16.99 *(978-0-375-87077-4(6)*, Knopf Bks. for Young Readers) Random Hse. Children's Bks.
—The Penderwicks on Gardam Street. 2011. (Playaway Children Ser.). (J). (gr. 3-6). 44.99 *(978-1-61707-435-6(7))* Findaway World, LLC.
—The Penderwicks on Gardam Street. 2010. (Penderwicks Ser.: 2). (ENG.). 336p. (J). (gr. 3-7). 8.99 *(978-0-440-42203-7(5)*, Yearling) Random Hse. Children's Bks.
—The Penderwicks on Gardam Street. 2010. (Penderwicks Ser.: 2). lib. bdg. 18.40 *(978-0-606-14418-6(8))* Turtleback.
Bruchac, Joseph. Squanto's Journey: The Story of the First Thanksgiving. Shed, Greg, illus. 2007. (ENG.). 32p. (J). (gr. -1-3). pap. 7.99 *(978-0-15-206044-2(8)*, 1198153, Clarion Bks.) HarperCollins Pubs.
Bryant, Annie. Ghost Town. 2007. (Beacon Street Girls Ser.: No. 11). (Illus.). 217p. (J). (gr. 4-7). per. 7.10 *(978-1-933566-09-2(4))* B*tween Productions, Inc.
—Just Kidding. 2007. (Beacon Street Girls Ser.: No. 10). (Illus.). 247p. (J). (gr. 3-8). per. 7.99 *(978-1-933566-07-8(8))* B*tween Productions, Inc.
Burnham, Niki. Sticky Fingers. 2005. (ENG.). 288p. (YA). (gr. 9-18). pap. 7.99 *(978-0-689-87649-3(1)*, Simon Pulse) Simon Pulse.
Chetkowski, Emily. Amasa Walker's Splendid Garment. Peterson, Dawn, illus. 2003. (ENG.). 48p. (gr. 5-8). reprint ed. pap. 9.95 *(978-0-911469-21-9(4))* Hood, Alan C. & Co., Inc.
Clark, Eleanor Linton, et al. Dodo's Dream Boat or the Voyage of the Seven Seas. 2008. (Illus.). 45p. (J). *(978-0-9816873-2-2(6))* West Barnstable Pr.
Clements, Andrew. In Harm's Way. Stower, Adam, illus. (Benjamin Pratt & the Keepers of the School Ser.: 4). (ENG.). (J). (gr. 2-5). 2014. 240p. pap. 8.99 *(978-1-4169-3910-8(5))* 2013. 224p. 14.99 *(978-1-4169-3889-7(3))* Simon & Schuster Children's Publishing. (Atheneum Bks. for Young Readers).
Cochran, Molly. Legacy, 1. 2011. (Legacy Ser.). (ENG.). 432p. (YA). (gr. 9-12). 17.99 *(978-1-4424-1739-7(0))* Simon & Schuster, Inc.
—Poison. 2012. (Legacy Ser.). (ENG.). 368p. (YA). (gr. 9). 17.99 *(978-1-4424-5050-9(9)*, Simon & Schuster/Paula Wiseman Bks.) Simon & Schuster/Paula Wiseman Bks.
Cooper, Susan. Ghost Hawk. 2014. (ENG., Illus.). 352p. (J). (gr. 5-9). pap. 8.99 *(978-1-4424-8142-8(0)*, McElderry, Margaret K. Bks.) McElderry, Margaret K. Bks.
Cotler, Steve. Cheesie Mack Is Not a Genius or Anything, 1. McCauley, Adam, illus. 2012. (Cheesie Mack Ser.). (ENG.). 240p. (J). (gr. 4-6). lib. bdg. 21.19 *(978-0-375-96437-4(1))* Random House Publishing Group.
—Cheesie Mack Is Not a Genius or Anything. McCauley, Adam, illus. 2012. (Cheesie Mack Ser.: 1). 240p. (J). (gr. 3-7). 6.99 *(978-0-375-86394-3(X)*, Yearling) Random Hse. Children's Bks.
Cusick, John M. Girl Parts. 2010. (ENG., Illus.). 240p. (YA). (gr. 9-18). 16.99 *(978-0-7636-4930-2(9))* Candlewick Pr.
Daneshvari, Gitty. School of Fear: Class Is Not Dismissed! 2011. (School of Fear Ser.: 2). (ENG.). 336p. (J). (gr. 3-7). pap. 17.99 *(978-0-316-03329-9(4))* Little, Brown Bks. for Young Readers.
—The School of Fear: the Final Exam. (School of Fear Ser.: 3). (ENG.). (J). (gr. 3-7). 2012. 352p. pap. 18.99 *(978-0-316-18285-0(0))* 2011. (Illus.). 336p. 16.99 *(978-0-316-18287-4(7))* Little, Brown Bks. for Young Readers.
Davis, Rachel. My Life at Mapleleaf Cabin. 2nd ed. 2004. (YA). per. 10.00 *(978-0-9741176-8-3(4))* Wu Li Turtle Corp.
Diver, Lucienne. Fangtabulous. 2017. (Vamped Ser.: Vol. 4). (ENG., Illus.). (YA). pap. 14.95 *(978-1-62268-121-1(5))* Bella Rosa Bks.
Dixon, Franklin. Thrill Ride. 2005. 154p. (J). lib. bdg. 16.92 *(978-1-4242-0386-4(4))* Fitzgerald Bks.
Dorato, A. P. Arthur, Donna, & the Magic Crown of Tiabora. 2006. pap. 24.95 *(978-1-4137-8898-3(X))* PublishAmerica, Inc.
Douglas, Amanda Minnie. A Little Girl in Old Salem. 2018. (ENG., Illus.). 216p. (YA). (gr. 7-12). pap. *(978-93-5297-434-4(4))* Alpha Editions.
Durst, Sarah Beth. Into the Wild. 2007. (ENG.). 278p. (J). (gr. 6-8). 22.44 *(978-1-59514-156-9(1)*, Razorbill) Penguin Young Readers Group.
Easer, Katherine. Vicious Little Darlings. 2012. (ENG.). 320p. (YA). (gr. 9-12). pap. 9.99 *(978-1-59990-854-0(9)*, 900081571, Bloomsbury USA Childrens) Bloomsbury Publishing USA.
Ehrlich, Esther. Nest. 2016. (ENG.). 336p. (J). (gr. 5). pap. 9.99 *(978-0-385-38610-4(9)*, Yearling) Random Hse. Children's Bks.
Firkins, Jacqueline. Hearts, Strings, & Other Breakable Things. 2019. (ENG.). 384p. (YA). (gr. 9). 17.99 *(978-1-328-63519-8(8)*, 1735318, Clarion Bks.) HarperCollins Pubs.
Foard, Judith P. Senior Year. 2013. 416p. pap. 16.95 *(978-1-4759-6552-0(4))*; (gr. 10-12). 26.95 *(978-1-4759-6554-4(0))* iUniverse, Inc.
Frederick, Heather Vogel. The Mother-Daughter Book Club. (Mother-Daughter Book Club Ser.). (ENG.). (J). 2008. 288p. (gr. 4-7). pap. 8.99 *(978-1-4169-7079-8(7))* 2007. (Illus.). 256p. (gr. 5-7). 19.99 *(978-0-689-86412-4(4))* Simon & Schuster Bks. For Young Readers. (Simon & Schuster Bks. For Young Readers).
—Pies & Prejudice. 2010. (Mother-Daughter Book Club Ser.). (ENG.). 384p. (J). (gr. 4-7). 15.99 *(978-1-4169-7431-4(8)*, Simon & Schuster Bks. For Young Readers) Simon & Schuster Bks. For Young Readers.
Friend, Natasha. For Keeps. 2011. (YA). (ENG.). 256p. (gr. 8-12). 22.44 *(978-0-670-01190-2(8))*; 272p. (gr. 7-18). 7.99 *(978-0-14-241846-8(3)*, Speak) Penguin Young Readers Group.
—How We Roll. 2019. (ENG.). 272p. (YA). pap. 10.99 *(978-1-250-30881-8(X)*, 900164411) Square Fish.
Gagnon, Mary. Are Those Your Shoes? 2008. 120p. pap. 11.95 *(978-1-4357-2942-1(0))* Lulu Pr., Inc.
Gaylord, Glance. Culm Rock, the Story of a Year: What it Brought & What it Taught. 2007. (Illus.). 188p. per. *(978-1-4065-2819-0(6))* Dodo Pr.
Gleason, Barbara. My Hometown: Barnstable. 2010. 28p. pap. 15.99 *(978-1-4490-6928-5(2))* AuthorHouse.
Goldstein, Meredith. Chemistry Lessons. 2018. (ENG.). 256p. (YA). (gr. 7). 17.99 *(978-1-328-76464-5(8)*, 1681106, Clarion Bks.) HarperCollins Pubs.
Grab, Daphne. Halftime. 2010. (J). *(978-0-385-90693-7(5))*; *(978-0-385-73783-8(1))* Random House Publishing Group. (Delacorte Pr).
Green, Jacqueline. Kiss & Tell. 2015. (Truth or Dare Ser.: 3). (ENG.). 288p. (YA). (gr. 10-17). 18.00 *(978-0-316-22033-0(7)*, Poppy) Little, Brown Bks. for Young Readers.
—Secrets & Lies. 2014. (Truth or Dare Ser.: 2). (ENG.). 336p. (YA). (gr. 10-17). pap. 17.99 *(978-0-316-22030-9(2)*, Poppy) Little, Brown Bks. for Young Readers.
—Truth or Dare. (Truth or Dare Ser.: 1). (ENG.). (YA). (gr. 10-17). 2014. 416p. pap. 19.99 *(978-0-316-22035-4(3))* 2013. 400p. 18.00 *(978-0-316-22036-1(1))* Little, Brown Bks. for Young Readers. (Poppy).
Greenburg, Dan. It's Itchcraft! Davis, Jack E., illus. 2004. (Zack Files Ser.). 118p. lib. bdg. 15.00 *(978-0-7569-2238-2(0))* Perfection Learning Corp.
Greenspan, Paul. Crystal of Dreams. 2006. (ENG.). 192p. pap. 12.96 *(978-0-615-13477-2(7))* Flying Cloud Bks.
Griffin, Adele. Amandine. 2003. (ENG.). 208p. (gr. 5-9). pap. 6.99 *(978-0-7868-1441-1(1))* Disney Pr.
Harrington, Kim. Revenge of the Red Club. 2020. (ENG., Illus.). 256p. (J). (gr. 4-8). pap. 8.99 *(978-1-5344-3573-5(5)*, Simon & Schuster/Paula Wiseman Bks.) Simon & Schuster/Paula Wiseman Bks.
Hoffmann, Alice. Nightbird. 2016. (ENG., Illus.). 208p. (J). (gr. 5). pap. 7.99 *(978-0-385-38961-7(2)*, Yearling) Random Hse. Children's Bks.
—Nightbird. 2016. lib. bdg. 18.40 *(978-0-606-38451-3(0))* Turtleback.
Horvath, Polly. Northward to the Moon. 2012. (My One Hundred Adventures Ser.). (ENG.). 256p. (J). (gr. 6-8). lib. bdg. 22.44 *(978-0-375-96110-6(0))* Random House Publishing Group.
—Northward to the Moon. 2012. (My One Hundred Adventures Ser.: 2). 256p. (J). (gr. 5-8). 7.99 *(978-0-307-92980-8(9)*, Yearling) Random Hse. Children's Bks.
Howe, Katherine. Conversion. 2015. (ENG.). 432p. (YA). (gr. 7). pap. 11.99 *(978-0-14-751155-3(0)*, Speak) Penguin Young Readers Group.
Hughes, Lynn Gordon. To Live a Truer Life: A Story of the Hopedale Community. Lindro, illus. 2003. 32p. (J). 10.00 *(978-0-9725017-2-9(X))* Blackstone Editions.
Ius, Dawn. Lizzie. 2018. (ENG., Illus.). 336p. (YA). (gr. 7). 18.99 *(978-1-4814-9076-4(1)*, Simon Pulse) Simon Pulse.
Jacobs, Lily. The Littlest Bunny in Massachusetts: An Easter Adventure. Dunn, Robert, illus. 2015. (Littlest Bunny Ser.). (ENG.). 32p. (J). (gr. -1-3). 9.99 *(978-1-4926-1114-1(X)*, Hometown World) Sourcebooks, Inc.
James, Eric. Santa's Sleigh Is on Its Way to Massachusetts: A Christmas Adventure. Dunn, Robert, illus. 2016. (Santa's Sleigh Is on Its Way Ser.). (ENG.). 32p. (J). (gr. k-2). 12.99 *(978-1-4926-4336-4(X)*, 9781492643364, Hometown World) Sourcebooks, Inc.
—The Spooky Express Massachusetts. Piwowarski, Marcin, illus. 2017. (Spooky Express Ser.). (ENG.). 32p. (J). (gr. k-6). 9.99 *(978-1-4926-5369-1(1)*, Hometown World) Sourcebooks, Inc.
—Tiny the Massachusetts Easter Bunny. 2018. (Tiny the Easter Bunny Ser.). (ENG.). 40p. (J). (gr. k-3). 9.99 *(978-1-4926-5936-5(3)*, Hometown World) Sourcebooks, Inc.
Jantha, A. W. Hocus Pocus & the AllNew Sequel. 2018. (ENG., Illus.). 528p. (YA). (gr. 9-12). 12.99 *(978-1-368-02003-9(8)*, Disney-Hyperion) Disney Publishing Worldwide.
Katherine, Paterson. Lyddie. 2014. (Puffin Modern Classics Ser.). (ENG.). 192p. (J). (gr. 1-4). 11.24 *(978-1-63245-222-1(7))* Lectorum Pubns., Inc.
Klausner, Julie. Art Girls Are Easy. 2013. (ENG.). 240p. (YA). (gr. 10-17). pap. 13.99 *(978-0-316-24362-9(0)*, Poppy) Little, Brown Bks. for Young Readers.
Koller, Jackie French. Someday. 2010. 228p. pap. 14.95 *(978-1-4401-8675-2(8))* iUniverse, Inc.
Konigsberg, Bill. Openly Straight. 2013. (ENG.). 336p. (YA). (gr. 9). 17.99 *(978-0-545-50989-3(0)*, Levine, Arthur A. Bks.) Scholastic, Inc.
Kurtz, Jane. Lanie, Bk. 1. Hirsch, Jennifer, ed. Papp, Robert, illus. 2010. (American Girl: Lanie Ser.). (ENG.). 112p. (J). (gr. 2-4). pap. 21.19 *(978-1-59369-682-5(5))* American Girl Publishing, Inc.
—Lanie's Real Adventures. Papp, Robert, illus. 2010. (American Girl Today Ser.). (ENG.). 112p. (YA). (gr. 3-18). 12.95 *(978-1-59369-685-6(X))* American Girl Publishing, Inc.
Lehr, Dick. Trell. 2017. (ENG.). 320p. (YA). (gr. 7). 17.99 *(978-0-7636-9275-9(1))* Candlewick Pr.
—Trell: Nothing but the Truth. 2019. (ENG.). 320p. (J). (gr. 7). pap. 8.99 *(978-1-5362-0490-2(0))* Candlewick Pr.
Lenzi, Danielle E. My Search for Prince Charming's Normal Brother. 2011. 136p. pap. 25.70 *(978-1-4634-0446-8(8))*; (gr. 10-12). 33.70 *(978-1-4634-0445-1(X))* AuthorHouse.
Lewis, Maggie. Morgy Coast to Coast. Chesworth, Michael, illus. (ENG.). 144p. (J). 2008. (gr. 1-4). pap. 4.95 *(978-0-618-96641-7(2)*, 1023073) 2005. (gr. 3-7). 15.00 *(978-0-618-44896-8(9)*, 589876) HarperCollins Pubs. (Clarion Bks.).
Lewis, Michael. The Great Thanksgiving Food Fight, 1 vol. Jaskiel, Stan, illus. 2017. (ENG.). 32p. (J). (gr. -1-3). 16.99 *(978-1-4556-2285-6(0)*, Pelican Publishing) Arcadia Publishing.
Lo, Malinda. A Line in the Dark. 2017. 288p. (YA). (gr. 9). 17.99 *(978-0-7352-2742-2(X)*, Dutton Books for Young Readers) Penguin Young Readers Group.
Lockhart, E. We Were Liars. 2014. (Illus.). 227p. (YA). *(978-0-385-39009-5(2)*, Delacorte Pr) Random House Publishing Group.
—We Were Liars. (ENG.). (YA). (gr. 7). 2018. 320p. pap. 10.99 *(978-0-385-74127-9(8)*, Ember) 2014. (Illus.). 256p. 18.99 *(978-0-385-74126-2(X)*, Delacorte Pr.) Random Hse. Children's Bks.
Look, Lenore. Alvin Ho: Allergic to Babies, Burglars, & Other Bumps in the Night. Pham, LeUyen, illus. 2014. (Alvin Ho Ser.: 5). 192p. (J). (gr. 1-4). 7.99 *(978-0-385-38600-5(1)*, Yearling) Random Hse. Children's Bks.
—Alvin Ho: Allergic to Birthday Parties, Science Projects, & Other Man-Made Catastrophes. Pham, LeUyen, illus. 2011. (Alvin Ho Ser.: 3). 192p. (J). (gr. 1-4). 7.99 *(978-0-375-87369-0(4)*, Yearling) Random Hse. Children's Bks.
—Alvin Ho: Allergic to Camping, Hiking, & Other Natural Disasters. Pham, LeUyen, illus. 2010. (Alvin Ho Ser.: 2). 192p. (J). (gr. 1-4). 7.99 *(978-0-375-85750-8(8)*, Yearling) Random Hse. Children's Bks.
—Alvin Ho: Allergic to Dead Bodies, Funerals, & Other Fatal Circumstances. Pham, LeUyen, illus. 2012. (Alvin Ho Ser.: 4). 208p. (J). (gr. 1-4). 6.99 *(978-0-307-97695-6(5)*, Yearling) Random Hse. Children's Bks.
Lowe, Natasha. Lucy Castor Finds Her Sparkle. 2018. (ENG., Illus.). 240p. (J). (gr. 3-7). 16.99 *(978-1-5344-0196-9(2)*, Simon & Schuster/Paula Wiseman Bks.) Simon & Schuster/Paula Wiseman Bks.
Lupica, Mike. Million-Dollar Throw. 2010. (ENG.). 272p. (J). (gr. 5-18). 8.99 *(978-0-14-241558-0(8)*, Puffin Books) Penguin Young Readers Group.
—Million-Dollar Throw. 2010. (Million Dollar Sports Ser.). lib. bdg. 18.40 *(978-0-606-25316-1(5))* Turtleback.
MacColl, Michaela. Nobody's Secret. 2014. (ENG.). 256p. (YA). (gr. 7-17). pap. 9.99 *(978-1-4521-2854-2(5))* Chronicle Bks. LLC.
—The Revelation of Louisa May: A Novel of Intrigue & Romance. 2015. (ENG.). 272p. (J). (gr. 7-12). 16.99 *(978-1-4521-3357-7(3))* Chronicle Bks. LLC.
Malone, Lee Gjertsen. The Last Boy at St. Edith's. 2017. lib. bdg. 18.40 *(978-0-606-40157-9(1))* Turtleback.
Mancusi, Mari. Gamer Girl. 2010. 256p. (YA). (gr. 7-18). 7.99 *(978-0-14-241509-2(X)*, Speak) Penguin Young Readers Group.
Manning, Matthew K. The Salem Witch Showdown. Neely, Scott, illus. 2017. (You Choose Stories: Scooby-Doo Ser.). (ENG.). 112p. (J). (gr. 2-6). lib. bdg. 32.65 *(978-1-4965-4334-9(3)*, 134223, Stone Arch Bks.) Capstone.
Marshall, Peter, et al. Mercy Clifton: Pilgrim Girl. 2007. 208p. (J). pap. 9.99 *(978-0-8054-4395-0(9)*, B&H Bks.) B&H Publishing Group.
Martin, Ann M. Needle & Thread. Andreasen, Dan, illus. 2007. 205p. (J). pap. *(978-0-545-03660-3(7))* Scholastic, Inc.
—Tis the Season. 2007. (Main Street Ser.). (Illus.). 195p. (J). (gr. 4-7). 14.65 *(978-0-7569-8327-7(4))* Perfection Learning Corp.
Mather, Adriana. Haunting the Deep. (ENG.). (YA). (gr. 7). 2018. 368p. pap. 9.99 *(978-0-553-53954-7(X)*, Ember) 2017. 352p. lib. bdg. 20.99 *(978-0-553-53952-3(3)*, Knopf Bks. for Young Readers) Random Hse. Children's Bks.
McCoy, Chris. Scurvy Goonda. 2011. (ENG.). 336p. (J). (gr. 6-8). lib. bdg. 22.44 *(978-0-375-95598-3(4)*, Knopf Bks. for Young Readers) Random Hse. Children's Bks.
McGuire, Roberta Libby. The Adventures of the Cape Cod Bear. 2012. 24p. pap. 15.99 *(978-1-4771-5266-9(0))* Xlibris Corp.
Miceli, Mary Anne. Boston North Shore's ... Salem's Golden Broomstick. 2013. 44p. pap. 20.00 *(978-0-9888654-0-2(8))* Miceli, Mary Anne.
Montague, Gay & Wise, Erin. Peace Is a Bright Delight. 2008. 28p. pap. 13.99 *(978-1-4389-2153-2(5))* AuthorHouse.
Nardone, Frank. Something's Brewing in Salem. 2013. 164p. pap. 9.99 *(978-0-9884024-1-6(6))* Dragon Tree Bks.
Novel Units. The Scarlet Letter Novel Units Student Packet. 2019. (ENG.). (YA). pap. 13.99 *(978-1-56137-339-0(7)*, NU3397SP, Novel Units, Inc.) Classroom Library Co.
—The Scarlet Letter Novel Units Teacher Guide. 2019. (ENG.). (YA). pap. 12.99 *(978-1-56137-338-3(9)*, NU3389, Novel Units, Inc.) Classroom Library Co.
O'Neill, Elizabeth. Alfred Visits Massachusetts. 2006. (Illus.). 24p. (J). (gr. -1-3). pap. 12.00 *(978-0-9771836-7-8(X))* Funny Bone Bks.
Osborne, Mary Pope, et al. Jueves de Acción de Gracias. Murdocca, Sal, illus. 2014. (SPA.). 88p. (J). (gr. 2-4). pap. 6.99 *(978-1-933032-94-8(4))* Lectorum Pubns., Inc.
Otis, James. Ruth of Boston: A story of the Massachusetts Bay Colony. 2007. 140p. per. 9.95 *(978-0-9790876-3-9(5))* Living Bks. Pr.
Paratore, Coleen Murtagh. The Funeral Director's Son. 2008. (Funeral Director's Son Ser.). (ENG.). 144p. (J). (gr. 3-7). 15.99 *(978-1-4169-3594-0(0)*, Simon & Schuster Bks. For Young Readers) Simon & Schuster Bks. For Young Readers.
—Kip Campbell's Gift. 2009. (ENG.). 160p. (J). (gr. 3-7). 15.99 *(978-1-4169-3596-4(7)*, Simon & Schuster Bks. For Young Readers) Simon & Schuster Bks. For Young Readers.
—The Wedding Planner's Daughter. McGregor, Barbara, illus. 2006. (Wedding Planner's Daughter Ser.). (ENG.). 208p. (J). (gr. 3-8). reprint ed. pap. 7.99 *(978-1-4169-1854-7(X)*, Simon & Schuster Bks. For Young Readers) Simon & Schuster Bks. For Young Readers.
Parra, B. A. Tyler Trio Adventure Salem Witch Hunt. 2007. (ENG.). 124p. pap. *(978-0-615-14720-8(8))* Parra, Beverly.
Phillips, Merrill. Tell Me Again Grampa. 2013. 172p. pap. 13.96 *(978-1-4669-9676-2(5))* Trafford Publishing.
Ramsey, Jo. Shoulder Pads & Flannel. 2016. (ENG., Illus.). (J). 24.99 *(978-1-63533-072-4(6)*, Harmony Ink Pr.) Dreamspinner Pr.
Rees, Douglas. Vampire High. 2010. (ENG.). 240p. (YA). (gr. 6-8). lib. bdg. 24.94 *(978-0-385-90143-7(7))* Random House Publishing Group.
—Vampire High. 2010. (Vampire High Ser.). 240p. (YA). (gr. 7-18). pap. 9.99 *(978-0-385-73920-7(6)*, Delacorte Bks. for Young Readers) Random Hse. Children's Bks.
Reinhardt, Dana. A Brief Chapter in My Impossible Life. 2007. (ENG.). 256p. (YA). (gr. 9-12). pap. 8.99 *(978-0-375-84691-5(3)*, Ember) Random Hse. Children's Bks.
Rohr, Rebecca. Flocks: A Buster Bird Adventure. 2011. pap. 8.95 *(978-0-7414-6735-5(6))* Infinity Publishing.
Sales, Leila. Mostly Good Girls. (ENG.). 368p. (YA). (gr. 9). 2011. pap. 9.99 *(978-1-4424-0680-3(1))* 2010. 17.99 *(978-1-4424-0679-7(8))* Simon Pulse. (Simon Pulse).
Schmidt, Gary D. What Came from the Stars. 2014. (ENG.). 304p. (J). (gr. 5-7). pap. 7.99 *(978-0-544-33636-0(4)*, 1584182, Clarion Bks.) HarperCollins Pubs.
Schorr, Melissa. Identity Crisis. 2017. (ENG.). 240p. (YA). (gr. 8-12). pap. 11.99 *(978-1-5344-1874-5(1)*, Simon Pulse) Simon Pulse.
Shults, Sylvia. Double Double Love & Trouble. 2013. 150p. pap. 12.99 *(978-0-9848931-3-3(X))* Dark Continents Publishing.
Sinel, Natasha. Soulstruck. 2018. (ENG.). 304p. (YA). 16.99 *(978-1-5107-3118-9(0)*, Sky Pony Pr.) Skyhorse Publishing Co., Inc.
Speare, Elizabeth George. The Witch of Blackbird Pond. 2004. 223p. (J). (gr. 4-7). pap., tchr.'s planning gde. ed. 38.00 incl. audio *(978-0-8072-0862-5(0)*, Listening Library) Random Hse. Audio Publishing Group.
Stanley, Diane. Thanksgiving on Plymouth Plantation. Berry, Holly, illus. 2004. (ENG.). 48p. (J). (gr. k-5). 17.99 *(978-0-06-027069-8(1)*, HarperCollins) HarperCollins Pubs.
Stewart, Whitney. Marshall, the Sea Dog. 2010. (ENG.). 56p. (J). (gr. 4-7). 17.95 *(978-1-60727-183-3(4))* Soundprints.
Stone, Phoebe. The Boy on Cinnamon Street. 2012. 234p. (J). *(978-0-545-43368-6(1)*, Levine, Arthur A. Bks.) Scholastic, Inc.
Sully, Katherine. Night-Night Massachusetts. Poole, Helen, illus. 2017. (Night-Night Ser.). (ENG.). 20p. (J). (gr. -1-1). bds. 9.99 *(978-1-4926-5485-8(X)*, Hometown World) Sourcebooks, Inc.
Tashjian, Janet. Larry & the Meaning of Life. 2014. (Larry Ser.: 3). (ENG., Illus.). 240p. (YA). (gr. 7-12). pap. 15.99 *(978-1-250-05035-9(9)*, 900133985) Square Fish.
Tea, Michelle. Girl at the Bottom of the Sea. Verwey, Amanda, illus. 2015. 240p. (J). (gr. 6). 19.95 *(978-1-940450-00-1(4)*, 3f4b9717-9960-4c67-8ef0-24515f98345f) McSweeney's Publishing.
—Mermaid in Chelsea Creek. Polan, Jason, illus. 2013. 240p. (J). (gr. 5-11). 19.95 *(978-1-938073-36-6(3)*, ea44eacc-0b51-4a46-b778-cae153d08009) McSweeney's Publishing.
Tiernan, Cate. Immortal Beloved. 2012. (Immortal Beloved Ser.: 1). (ENG.). 432p. (YA). (gr. 7-17). pap. 9.99 *(978-0-316-03591-0(2)*, Poppy) Little, Brown Bks. for Young Readers.
Vrettos, Adrienne Maria. Best Friends for Never. 2016. (ENG.). 240p. (J). (gr. 3-7). 16.99 *(978-0-545-56149-5(3)*, Scholastic Pr.) Scholastic, Inc.
Whitney, A. D. T. A Summer in Leslie Goldthwaite's Life. 2017. (ENG., Illus.). (J). 23.95 *(978-1-374-97625-2(3))*; pap. 13.95 *(978-1-374-97624-5(5))* Capital Communications, Inc.
—A Summer in Leslie Goldthwaite's Life. 2017. (ENG., Illus.). (J). pap. *(978-0-649-27040-8(1))* Trieste Publishing Pty Ltd.
Wittlinger, Ellen. Blind Faith. 2007. (ENG.). 304p. (YA). (gr. 7-12). pap. 9.99 *(978-1-4169-4906-0(2)*, Simon & Schuster Bks. For Young Readers) Simon & Schuster Bks. For Young Readers.
—Love & Lies: Marisol's Story. (ENG.). (YA). 2009. 272p. (gr. 7). pap. 8.99 *(978-1-4169-7914-2(X))* 2008. 256p. (gr. 9-18). 16.99 *(978-1-4169-1623-9(7))* Simon & Schuster Bks. For Young Readers. (Simon & Schuster Bks. For Young Readers).
Young, Janet Ruth. The Babysitter Murders. 2011. (ENG., Illus.). 336p. (YA). (gr. 9-18). 16.99 *(978-1-4169-5944-1(0)*, Atheneum Bks. for Young Readers) Simon & Schuster Children's Publishing.
—My Beautiful Failure. (ENG., Illus.). 320p. (YA). (gr. 7). 2013. pap. 9.99 *(978-1-4424-8269-2(9))* 2012. 16.99 *(978-1-4169-5489-7(9))* Simon & Schuster Children's Publishing. (Atheneum Bks. for Young Readers).

MASSACHUSETTS—HISTORY

Allen, David. Early Maps of Greenfield, Massachusetts, 1717-1918. 2003. (Illus.). 64p. cd-rom 27.95 *(978-0-911653-10-6(4))* Old Maps.

Arenstam, Peter. The Mighty Mastiff of the Mayflower. Holman, Karen Busch, illus. 2012. Orig. Title: The Mighty Mastiff of the Mayflower. (ENG.). 112p. 16.99 *(978-1-60949-609-8(4),* History Pr., The) Arcadia Publishing.

Aretha, David. Mitt Romney. 2012. (Illus.). 112p. (J). *(978-1-59935-344-9(X))* Reynolds, Morgan Inc.

Bailey, Budd. Plymouth & the Settlement of New England, 1 vol. 2017. (Primary Sources of Colonial America Ser.). (ENG.). 64p. (gr. 6-6). 35.93 *(978-1-5026-3140-4(7),* ee943d94-d3c5-41c3-a484-dfbd813384cd); pap. 16.28 *(978-1-5026-3457-3(0),* 01ec0b91-6764-4305-ab12-d8280bde9a1b) Cavendish Square Publishing LLC.

Baxter, Roberta. The Battle of Gettysburg: A History Perspectives Book. 2013. (Perspectives Library). (ENG., Illus.). 32p. (J). (gr. 4-8). 32.07 *(978-1-62431-415-5(5),* 202780); pap. 14.21 *(978-1-62431-491-9(0),* 202782) Cherry Lake Publishing.

Benge, Janet & Benge, Geoff. Heroes of History - William Bradford: Plymouth's Rock. 2016. (ENG., Illus.). 200p. (YA). pap. 11.99 *(978-1-62486-092-8(3))* Emerald Bks.

Bjorklund, Ruth & Fitzgerald, Stephanie. Massachusetts, 1 vol. (It's My State! (Second Edition)(r) Ser.). (ENG.). 80p. (gr. 4-4). 2nd rev. ed. 2011. lib. bdg. 34.07 *(978-1-60870-053-0(4),* 237a2166-2825-40ef-b466-a8155ccf2bab) 3rd rev. ed. 2014. lib. bdg. 35.93 *(978-1-62712-500-0(0),* 21f7b903-2a58-4c64-8549-5deecc1df3bd) Cavendish Square Publishing LLC.

Brandt, Keith & Macken, JoAnn Early. Paul Revere, Son of Liberty. Livingston, Francis, illus. 2007. 50p. (J). *(978-0-439-02017-6(4))* Scholastic, Inc.

Brindell Fradin, Dennis. The Mayflower Compact, 1 vol. 2007. (Turning Points in U. S. History Ser.). (ENG., Illus.). 48p. (gr. 4-4). lib. bdg. 34.07 *(978-0-7614-2125-2(4),* 047805e0-f50c-4cca-90d8-3562f332da95) Cavendish Square Publishing LLC.

Caswell, Max. My Life in the Plymouth Colony. 2017. (My Place in History Ser.). 24p. (J). (gr. 2-3). pap. 48.90 *(978-1-5382-0306-4(5));* (ENG.). pap. 9.15 *(978-1-5382-0305-7(7),* df02096f-11bd-46ba-b238-e6a666baecc2) Stevens, Gareth Publishing LLLP.

Cherry, Lynne. A River Ran Wild. 2005. 17.00 *(978-0-7569-5231-0(X))* Perfection Learning Corp.

Clark, Mary. Biographical Sketches of the Fathers of New England. 2003. 180p. 89.00 *(978-0-7950-4738-1(X))* New Library Press LLC.

Colonel Edward Howland Robinson Green & the World He Created at Round Hill. 2003. 39.95 *(978-0-9743731-0-2(9),* 2500) Bedell, Barbara F.

Connors, Kathleen. The First Thanksgiving, 1 vol., Vol. 1. 2013. (What You Didn't Know about History Ser.). (ENG., Illus.). 24p. (J). (gr. 2-3). 25.27 *(978-1-4824-0581-1(4),* a32acce5-2977-40eb-a4fe-4662b029fe08); pap. 9.15 *(978-1-4824-0582-8(2),* 2da75e09-1664-42bc-8b67-0924117edce0) Stevens, Gareth Publishing LLLP.

Cook, Peter & Whelan, Kevin. You Wouldn't Want to Sail on the Mayflower! A Trip That Took Entirely Too Long. rev. ed. 2013. (ENG.). 32p. (J). 29.00 *(978-0-531-27107-0(2),* Watts, Franklin) Scholastic Library Publishing.

Cox, Clinton. Undying Glory: The Story of the Massachusetts 54th Regiment. 2007. 196p. (YA). (gr. 4-7). per. 15.95 *(978-0-595-45116-6(0),* Backinprint.com) iUniverse, Inc.

Cusolito, Michelle. Flying Deep: Climb Inside Deep-Sea Submersible Alvin. Wong, Nicole, illus. 2018. 32p. (J). (gr. k-4). 17.99 *(978-1-58089-811-9(4))* Charlesbridge Publishing, Inc.

Davidson, Tish. Southern New England: Connecticut, Massachusetts, Rhode Island, Vol. 19. 2015. (Let's Explore the States Ser.). (Illus.). 64p. (J). (gr. 5). 23.95 *(978-1-4222-3333-7(2))* Mason Crest.

Downey, Tika. Massachusetts: The Bay State, 1 vol. 2009. (Our Amazing States Ser.). (ENG., Illus.). 24p. (J). (gr. 3-3). pap. 9.25 *(978-1-4358-3342-5(2),* 93b17a5f-ad12-4af9-869f-862541cdbf0e); lib. bdg. 26.27 *(978-1-4042-8111-0(8),* e59364a9-926f-4192-aae0-5a55a526376c) Rosen Publishing Group, Inc., The. (PowerKids Pr.).

Dreyer, Ellen. A Band of Brave Men: The Story of the 54th Massachusetts Regiment. 2004. (ENG., Illus.). 31p. (J). (gr. 5-5). pap. 12.00 net. *(978-0-7652-5247-0(3))* Celebration Pr.

Duris, Joan & Jones, Gillian. B Is for Berkshires. 2015. (ENG., Illus.). 32p. (J). 17.95 *(978-1-939017-51-2(3),* 055ef89e-3af9-42d0-b6cd-a0d85dfd87f5) Islandport Pr., Inc.

Edwards, Roberta & Who HQ. Who Was Paul Revere? O'Brien, John, illus. 2011. (Who Was? Ser.). 112p. (J). (gr. 3-7). pap. 6.99 *(978-0-448-45715-4(6),* Penguin Workshop) Penguin Young Readers Group.

Englar, Mary. The Pilgrims & the First Thanksgiving, 1 vol. McDonnell, Peter, illus. 2006. (Graphic History Ser.). (ENG.). 32p. (J). (gr. 3-9). 8.10 *(978-0-7368-9656-6(2),* 93441, Capstone Pr.) Capstone.

Ford, Barbara. Paul Revere: American Patriot, 1 vol. 2014. (Legendary American Biographies Ser.). (ENG.). 96p. (gr. 6-6). pap. 13.88 *(978-0-7660-6486-7(7),* 16fec7fd-cdf8-4057-83a8-a000c6afe506) Enslow Publishing, LLC.

Gamble, Adam & Jasper, Mark. Good Night Massachusetts. 2013. (Good Night Our World Ser.). (ENG., Illus.). 20p. (J). (— 1). bds. 9.95 *(978-1-60219-084-9(4))* Good Night Bks.

Gleason, Barbara. My Hometown: Mashpee. 2009. 28p. pap. 14.99 *(978-1-4389-9984-5(4))* AuthorHouse.

Golden, Nancy. The British Are Coming! The Midnight Ride of Paul Revere. 2009. (Great Moments in American History Ser.). 32p. (gr. 3-3). 47.90 *(978-1-61513-136-5(1))* Rosen Publishing Group, Inc., The.

The Greatest Place on Earth: A Children's Story, A History Lesson, A Scrapbook, A Lifetime Keepsake. 2006. (J). 18.95 *(978-0-9777882-0-0(2),* Light Works Publishing) I.M. Enterprises.

Griffis, William Elliot. Young People's History of the Pilgrims. 353p. reprint ed. 98.00 *(978-0-7222-6679-3(0))* Library Reprints, Inc.

Gunderson, Jessica. Life on the Mayflower, 1 vol. Dumm, Brian Caleb, illus. 2010. (Thanksgiving Ser.). (ENG.). 24p. (J). (gr. k-3). pap. 7.95 *(978-1-4048-6719-2(8),* 115518, Picture Window Bks.) Capstone.

—The Pilgrims' First Thanksgiving, 1 vol. Lucke, Deb, illus. 2010. (Thanksgiving Ser.). (ENG.). 24p. (J). (gr. k-3). pap. 8.95 *(978-1-4048-6720-8(1),* 115519, Picture Window Bks.) Capstone.

Hamilton, John. Massachusetts, 1 vol. 2016. (United States of America Ser.). (ENG., Illus.). 48p. (J). (gr. 5-9). 34.21 *(978-1-68078-323-0(8),* 21631, Abdo & Daughters) ABDO Publishing Co.

Harness, Cheryl. The Adventurous Life of Myles Standish: And the Amazing-but-True Survival Story of Plymouth Colony. 2006. (Cheryl Harness Histories Ser.). (Illus.). 144p. (J). (gr. 5-9). 16.95 *(978-0-7922-5918-3(1),* National Geographic Kids) Disney Publishing Worldwide.

Hicks, Dwayne. Paul Revere: American Patriot, 1 vol. 2012. (Beginning Biographies Ser.). (ENG., Illus.). 24p. (J). (gr. 1-2). 26.27 *(978-1-4488-8599-2(X),* 2aa1337b-5524-4b90-af85-b8dbee02d41d, PowerKids Pr.) Rosen Publishing Group, Inc., The.

Hinman, Bonnie. The Massachusetts Bay Colony: The Puritans Arrive from England. 2006. (Building America Ser.). (Illus.). 48p. (J). (gr. 3-7). lib. bdg. 29.95 *(978-1-58415-460-0(8))* Mitchell Lane Pubs.

Holub, Joan. What Was the First Thanksgiving? 2013. (What Was... Ser.). lib. bdg. 16.00 *(978-0-606-31687-3(6))* Turtleback.

Honders, Christine. Mayflower Compact, 1 vol. 2016. (Documents of American Democracy Ser.). (ENG., Illus.). 32p. (J). (gr. 5-5). pap. 11.00 *(978-1-4994-2085-2(4),* 4d5a8336-b006-4995-923b-a2b9c7947e57, PowerKids Pr.) Rosen Publishing Group, Inc., The.

Jeffrey, Gary. Paul Revere & His Midnight Ride, 1 vol. 2011. (Graphic Heroes of the American Revolution Ser.). (ENG.). 24p. (J). (gr. 3-3). pap. 9.15 *(978-1-4339-6020-8(6),* 0981fe11-ad56-49bb-ba3e-6601372ad8b3, Gareth Stevens Learning Library); lib. bdg. 26.60 *(978-1-4339-6019-2(2),* c3cd73f3-b213-499a-b80e-d68ebc2109bb) Stevens, Gareth Publishing LLLP.

Jerome, Kate B. Lucky to Live in Massachusetts. 2017. (Arcadia Kids Ser.). (ENG., Illus.). 32p. (J). 16.99 *(978-0-7385-2795-6(5))* Arcadia Publishing.

—The Wise Animal Handbook Massachusetts. 2017. (Arcadia Kids Ser.). (ENG., Illus.). 32p. (J). 16.99 *(978-0-7385-2825-0(0))* Arcadia Publishing.

Kallio, Jamie. Mayflower Compact, 1 vol. 2013. (Foundations of Our Nation Ser.). (ENG.). 48p. (J). (gr. 4-8). lib. bdg. 35.64 *(978-1-61783-711-1(3),* 7820) ABDO Publishing Co.

Kamma, Anne. If You Lived at the Time of Squanto. Johnson, Pamela Ford, illus. 2006. 63p. (J). pap. *(978-0-439-87628-5(1))* Scholastic, Inc.

Katirgis, Jane & McCarthy, Rose. Meet Paul Revere: Revolutionary Hero, 1 vol. 2019. (Introducing Famous Americans Ser.). (ENG.). 32p. (gr. 3-4). pap. 11.53 *(978-1-9785-1130-9(2),* aabbf4d0-c3b3-4ca2-86a7-db6ef8ac5f6d) Enslow Publishing, LLC.

Keller, Susanna. The True Story of Paul Revere's Ride, 1 vol. 2013. (What Really Happened? Ser.). (ENG., Illus.). 24p. (J). (gr. 2-3). pap. 9.25 *(978-1-4488-9838-1(2),* efd634f7-c46f-44be-a810-8952a3a1d7af); lib. bdg. 26.27 *(978-1-4488-9690-5(8),* b9df1cc6-fbb3-44a4-8594-63505b0e3628) Rosen Publishing Group, Inc., The. (PowerKids Pr.).

Landau, Elaine. Sacco & Vanzetti. 2004. (Cornerstones of Freedom Ser.). (ENG., Illus.). 48p. (YA). (gr. 4-7). 26.00 *(978-0-516-24237-8(7))* Scholastic Library Publishing.

Lanser, Amanda. What's Great about Massachusetts? 2014. (Our Great States Ser.). (ENG., Illus.). 32p. (J). (gr. 2-5). pap. 7.95 *(978-1-4677-4525-3(1),* 7e08a34b-b9ff-4dd3-afbc-99df9b83ed4d) Lerner Publishing Group.

LeVert, Suzanne & Orr, Tamra B. Massachusetts, 1 vol. 2nd rev. ed. 2009. (Celebrate the States (Second Edition) Ser.). (ENG.). 144p. (gr. 6-6). lib. bdg. 39.79 *(978-0-7614-3005-6(9),* 35891fa0-4a8f-492e-be4a-874fd890fc94) Cavendish Square Publishing LLC.

Lusted, Marcia Amidon. The Battle of Bunker Hill: A History Perspectives Book. 2013. (Perspectives Library). (ENG., Illus.). 32p. (J). (gr. 4-8). 32.07 *(978-1-62431-414-8(7),* 202776); pap. 14.21 *(978-1-62431-490-2(2),* 202778) Cherry Lake Publishing.

—The Mayflower Compact. 2019. (Shaping the United States of America Ser.). (ENG., Illus.). 24p. (J). (gr. 1-3). pap. 7.95 *(978-1-9771-1015-2(0),* 140958); lib. bdg. 25.99 *(978-1-9771-0916-3(0),* 140517) Capstone. (Pebble).

Mara, Wil. Rookie Biographies: Paul Revere. 2005. (Rookie Biographies Ser.). (ENG., Illus.). 32p. (J). (gr. 1-2). pap. 4.95 *(978-0-516-25820-1(6),* Children's Pr.) Scholastic Library Publishing.

Marie, June. Harry the Plum Island Fisherman. 2012. 24p. pap. 15.99 *(978-1-4797-0009-7(6))* Xlibris Corp.

Marsh, Carole. Exploring Massachusetts Through Project-Based Learning: Geography, History, Government, Economics & More. 2016. (Massachusetts Experience Ser.). (ENG.). (J). pap. 9.99 *(978-0-635-12345-9(2))* Gallopade International.

—I'm Reading about Massachusetts. 2014. (Massachusetts Experience Ser.). (ENG., Illus.). (J). pap., pap. 8.99 *(978-0-635-11296-5(5))* Gallopade International.

—Massachusetts History Projects: 30 Cool, Activities, Crafts, Experiments & More for Kids to Do to Learn about Your State! 2003. (Massachusetts Experience Ser.). 32p. (gr. k-5). pap. 5.95 *(978-0-635-01790-1(3),* Marsh, Carole Bks.) Gallopade International.

Maseres, Francis. Spencer: a Sense of Heritage. 2009. (Applewood Bks.). (ENG.). 108p. pap. 19.95 *(978-1-4290-9110-7(X))* Applewood Bks.

McCarthy, Rose. Paul Revere: Freedom Rider. 2009. (Primary Sources of Famous People in American History Ser.). 32p. (gr. 2-3). 47.90 *(978-1-60851-714-5(4))* Rosen Publishing Group, Inc., The.

—Paul Revere: Freedom Rider / Jinete de la causa Revolucionaria. 2009. (Famous People in American History/Grandes personajes en la historia de los Estados Unidos Ser.). (ENG & SPA.). 32p. (gr. 2-3). 47.90 *(978-1-61512-553-1(1),* Editorial Buenas Letras) Rosen Publishing Group, Inc., The.

—Paul Revere: Jinete de la causa revolucionaria (Paul Revere: Freedom Rider) 2009. (Grandes personajes en la historia de los Estados Unidos (Famous People in American History) Ser.). (SPA.). 32p. (gr. 2-3). 47.90 *(978-1-61512-806-8(9),* Editorial Buenas Letras) Rosen Publishing Group, Inc., The.

McNeil, Tom & Benchmark Education Co. Staff. Take-Off: A Pilot's Memoir. 2014. (Text Connections Ser.). (J). (gr. 6). *(978-1-4900-1536-1(1))* Benchmark Education Co.

Mills, Jordan & Parker, Bridget. Massachusetts. 2016. (States Ser.). (ENG., Illus.). 32p. (J). (gr. 3-6). lib. bdg. 27.99 *(978-1-5157-0408-9(4),* 132019, Capstone Pr.) Capstone.

Mills, Nathan & Hicks, Dwayne. Paul Revere: American Patriot, 1 vol. 2012. (Rosen Readers Ser.). (ENG., Illus.). 24p. (J). (gr. 1-2). pap. 8.25 *(978-1-4488-8836-8(0),* 134af41f-53e0-4456-a0f8-6e74a2a5ae8e, Rosen Classroom) Rosen Publishing Group, Inc., The.

Min, Ellen. The Midnight Ride of Paul Revere: One If by Land, Two If by Sea, 1 vol. 2015. (Spotlight on American History Ser.). (ENG., Illus.). 24p. (J). (gr. 4-6). pap. 11.00 *(978-1-4994-1734-0(9),* 6ebe0528-c359-4a33-b22f-cde39d20f9ee, PowerKids Pr.) Rosen Publishing Group, Inc., The.

Moussavi, Sam. It's Great to Be a Fan in Massachusetts. 2018. (Sports Nation Ser.). (ENG., Illus.). 48p. (J). (gr. 5-6). pap. 11.95 *(978-1-64185-032-2(9),* 1641850329); lib. bdg. 34.21 *(978-1-63517-930-9(0),* 1635179300) North Star Editions. (Focus Readers).

National Geographic Learning. Reading Expeditions (Social Studies: Documents of Freedom): the Mayflower Compact. 2007. (ENG., Illus.). 32p. (J). pap. 18.95 *(978-0-7922-4553-7(9))* CENGAGE Learning.

Nelson, Maria. The Life of Paul Revere, 1 vol. 2012. (Famous Lives Ser.). (ENG.). 24p. (J). (gr. 1-2). pap. 9.15 *(978-1-4339-6355-1(8),* 28f1d255-6234-4269-a325-eee483bc787f); lib. bdg. 25.27 *(978-1-4339-6353-7(1),* 94adfa60-b92a-4642-bf87-ccb0fbd3bbd7) Stevens, Gareth Publishing LLLP.

—The Life of Paul Revere / la Vida de Paul Revere, 1 vol. 2012. (Famous Lives / Vidas Extraordinarias Ser.). (ENG & SPA., Illus.). 24p. (J). (gr. 1-2). 25.27 *(978-1-4339-6657-6(3),* aa338b1b-e2d8-4616-9737-e97b8dd61403) Stevens, Gareth Publishing LLLP.

Obregón, José María. Massachusetts. 2009. (Bilingual Library of the United States of America Ser.). (ENG & SPA.). 32p. (gr. 2-2). 47.90 *(978-1-60853-366-4(2),* Editorial Buenas Letras) Rosen Publishing Group, Inc., The.

Oney, Yannick. First American Colonies. 2004. (World Discovery History Readers Ser.). (Illus.). 32p. (J). pap. *(978-0-439-66555-1(8))* Scholastic, Inc.

Osborne, Mary Pope & Boyce, Natalie Pope. Pilgrims: A Nonfiction Companion to Magic Tree House #27: Thanksgiving on Thursday. Murdocca, Sal, illus. 2005. (Magic Tree House (R) Fact Tracker Ser.: 13). 128p. (J). (gr. 2-5). 6.99 *(978-0-375-83219-2(X),* Random Hse. Bks. for Young Readers) Random Hse. Children's Bks.

Owens, L. L. Pilgrims in America. 2006. (Events in American History Ser.). (Illus.). 48p. (J). (gr. -1-1). lib. bdg. 31.36 *(978-1-60044-122-6(X))* Rourke Educational Media.

Pezzi, Bryan. Massachusetts: The Bay State. 2016. (J). *(978-1-4896-4878-5(X))* Weigl Pubs., Inc.

Philbrick, Nathaniel. In the Heart of the Sea (Young Readers Edition) The True Story of the Whaleship Essex. 2015. (Illus.). 208p. (J). (gr. 3-7). 8.99 *(978-1-101-99776-5(1),* Puffin Books) Penguin Young Readers Group.

—The Mayflower & the Pilgrims' New World. 2009. (ENG.). 368p. (J). (gr. 5-18). 9.99 *(978-0-14-241458-3(1),* Puffin Books) Penguin Young Readers Group.

Plimoth Plantation, et al. Mayflower 1620: A New Look at a Pilgrim Voyage. 2007. (Illus.). 48p. (J). (gr. 3-7). per. 6.95 *(978-0-7922-6276-3(X),* National Geographic Kids) Disney Publishing Worldwide.

Poolos, J. The Mayflower: A Primary Source History of the Pilgrims' Journey to the New World. 2009. (Primary Sources in American History Ser.). 64p. (gr. 5-8). 58.50 *(978-1-60851-499-1(4))* Rosen Publishing Group, Inc., The.

Rajczak, Michael. Life on the Mayflower, 1 vol., Vol. 1. 2013. (What You Didn't Know about History Ser.). (ENG.). 24p. (J). (gr. 2-3). 25.27 *(978-1-4824-0591-0(1),* 2e562962-9b3b-4209-98f1-f0e1f723e9f5) Stevens, Gareth Publishing LLLP.

Raum, Elizabeth. The Mayflower Compact, 1 vol. 2012. (Documenting U. S. History Ser.). (ENG.). 48p. (J). (gr. 3-6). lib. bdg. 33.32 *(978-1-4329-6750-5(9),* 119381, Heinemann) Capstone.

Rechner, Amy. Massachusetts. 2013. (Exploring the States Ser.). (ENG., Illus.). 32p. (J). (gr. 3-7). lib. bdg. 27.95 *(978-1-62617-020-9(7),* Blastoff! Readers) Bellwether Media.

Riehecky, Janet & Williams, Gianna. La Colonia de Plymouth (the Settling of Plymouth), 1 vol. 2006. (Hitos de la Historia de Estados Unidos (Landmark Events in American History) Ser.). (SPA.). 48p. (gr. 5-8). pap. 12.70 *(978-0-8368-7471-6(4),* c4b0334d-2730-428d-b1e9-b4c540c786ce, Gareth Stevens Learning Library); (Illus.). lib. bdg. 29.67 *(978-0-8368-7464-8(1),* 08ac8c60-625b-40a5-bde2-463bc20e4058, Gareth Stevens Secondary Library) Stevens, Gareth Publishing LLLP.

Rooney, Thomas L. Tobey Boland & the Blackstone Canal. Donovan, Patte, illus. 2005. 30p. (J). *(978-1-929039-30-2(1))* Ambassador Bks., Inc.

Russo, Kristin J. Viewpoints on the Battle of Bunker Hill. 2018. (Perspectives Library: Viewpoints & Perspectives Ser.). (ENG., Illus.). 48p. (J). (gr. 5-8). lib. bdg. 39.21 *(978-1-5341-2965-8(0),* 211904) Cherry Lake Publishing.

Santella, Andrew. Cornerstones of Freedom: the First Thanksgiving. 2003. (Cornerstones of Freedom Ser.). (ENG., Illus.). 48p. (YA). (gr. 4-7). 26.00 *(978-0-516-24204-0(0))* Scholastic Library Publishing.

Schmermund, Elizabeth, et al. Massachusetts: The Bay State, 1 vol. 2018. (It's My State! (Fourth Edition)(r) Ser.). (ENG.). 80p. (gr. 4-4). pap. 18.64 *(978-1-5026-4443-5(6),* 5c4ac018-d0d2-4c3d-a3de-6f9720739971) Cavendish Square Publishing LLC.

Schulte, Mary. The Dover Demon, 1 vol. 2009. (Mysterious Encounters Ser.). (ENG., Illus.). 48p. (gr. 4-8). 35.23 *(978-0-7377-4570-2(3),* 662c62b6-291d-489d-861b-7a8c091f651f, KidHaven Publishing) Greenhaven Publishing LLC.

Shardlow, Alice L. Crossing Completed: How the People of Eastham Saved Nauset Light. Sabin, Shirley C., photos by. 2006. (ENG.). 38p. pap. 15.99 *(978-1-4257-1638-7(5))* Xlibris Corp.

Shea, Therese M. The Boston Massacre, 1 vol., Vol. 1. 2014. (What You Didn't Know about History Ser.). (ENG.). 24p. (J). (gr. 2-3). 25.27 *(978-1-4824-0580-4(6),* 401d50b2-d2ce-442f-960f-82efce892bef) Stevens, Gareth Publishing LLLP.

Shepard, Ray Anthony. Now or Never! Fifty-Fourth Massachusetts Infantry's War to End Slavery. 2017. (ENG., Illus.). 144p. (J). (gr. 5-12). 17.95 *(978-1-62979-340-5(X),* Calkins Creek) Highlights Pr., c/o Highlights for Children, Inc.

Smith, Andrea P. A Day in the Life of Colonial Silversmith Paul Revere. (Illus.). 24p. (J). 2012. 63.60 *(978-1-4488-5217-8(X))* 2011. (ENG., (gr. 2-3). pap. 11.60 *(978-1-4488-5216-1(1),* 222487a5-1e5c-4e48-abee-09b3e5f95238) 2011. (ENG., (gr. 2-3). lib. bdg. 28.93 *(978-1-4488-5189-8(0),* 2bb3a4f9-0113-4e50-be2f-9f17eb9f5dd4) Rosen Publishing Group, Inc., The. (PowerKids Pr.).

—The First Thanksgiving. (Illus.). 24p. (J). 2012. 63.60 *(978-1-4488-5213-0(7))* 2011. (ENG., (gr. 2-3). pap. 11.60 *(978-1-4488-5212-3(9),* 29193eb1-58fc-449e-8ffd-c34f8ba58a56) 2011. (ENG., (gr. 2-3). lib. bdg. 28.93 *(978-1-4488-5187-4(4),* 558ed541-f06a-434a-870b-4905820ff6a9) Rosen Publishing Group, Inc., The. (PowerKids Pr.).

—The Journey of the Mayflower. (Illus.). 24p. (J). 2012. 63.60 *(978-1-4488-5211-6(0))* 2011. (ENG., (gr. 2-3). pap. 11.60 *(978-1-4488-5210-9(2),* ffb71748-c78c-4612-9f75-48faa5dd7d69) 2011. (ENG., (gr. 2-3). lib. bdg. 28.93 *(978-1-4488-5186-7(6),* aa04b287-2d9d-4f9d-b874-70411c20e5e6) Rosen Publishing Group, Inc., The. (PowerKids Pr.).

—The Salem Witch Trials. (Illus.). 24p. 2012. 63.60 *(978-1-4488-5215-4(3))* 2011. (ENG., (gr. 2-3). pap. 11.60 *(978-1-4488-5214-7(5),* 361277c1-75d9-4d13-aef9-4cbffbd3e9c5) 2011. (ENG., (gr. 2-3). lib. bdg. 28.93 *(978-1-4488-5188-1(2),* f2f49013-fd8c-4d4a-b602-c5f1b365aff3) Rosen Publishing Group, Inc., The. (PowerKids Pr.).

Smolik, Jane Petrlik. The Great Massachusetts Puzzle Book: Over 75 Puzzles about Life in the Bay State. rev. ed. 2005. (Illus.). 96p. (J). (gr. 2-7). per. 11.95 *(978-0-9664095-5-0(8))* MidRun Pr.

Son, John. If You Were a Kid on the Mayflower (If You Were a Kid) (Library Edition) Zanni, Roger, illus. 2018. (If You Were a Kid Ser.). (ENG.). 32p. (J). (gr. 2-4). lib. bdg. 26.00 *(978-0-531-23216-3(6),* Children's Pr.) Scholastic Library Publishing.

Spooner, J. B. The Little Black Dog Has Puppies. Seeley, Terre Lamb, illus. 2011. (Little Black Dog Ser.). (ENG.). 32p. (J). (gr. -1-k). 16.95 *(978-1-61145-006-4(3),* 611006, Arcade Publishing) Skyhorse Publishing Co., Inc.

Streissguth, Tom. The Mayflower Story. 2017. (Famous Ships Ser.). (ENG., Illus.). 112p. (J). (gr. 6-12). lib. bdg. 41.36 *(978-1-5321-1320-8(X),* 27528, Essential Library) ABDO Publishing Co.

Sullivan, Laura. The Colonial Minuteman, 1 vol. 2015. (Colonial People Ser.). (ENG., Illus.). 48p. (gr. 4-4). lib. bdg. 34.07 *(978-1-5026-0478-1(7),* fc45001f-bcae-4b28-ad4c-3e4e49cdfb65) Cavendish Square Publishing LLC.

—Life As a Passenger on the Mayflower, 1 vol. 2016. (Life As... Ser.). (ENG., Illus.). 32p. (gr. 3-3). 30.21 *(978-1-5026-1789-7(7),* a10a046e-70bc-4514-9d97-a1c7631ba2da) Cavendish Square Publishing LLC.

Tougias, Michael J. & Sherman, Casey. The Finest Hours. 2015. (True Rescue Ser.). (ENG., Illus.). 208p. (J). (gr. 4-8). pap. 7.99 *(978-1-250-04423-5(5),* 900128311) Square Fish.

—The Finest Hours (Young Readers Edition) The True Story of a Heroic Sea Rescue. 2014. (True Rescue Ser.). (ENG., Illus.). 176p. (J). (gr. 4-8). 19.99 *(978-0-8050-9764-1(3),* 900118783, Holt, Henry & Co. Bks. For Young Readers) Holt, Henry & Co.

Tracy, Kathleen. The Plymouth Colony: The Pilgrims Settle in New England. 2006. (Building America Ser.). (Illus.). 48p. (J). (gr. 3-7). lib. bdg. 29.95 *(978-1-58415-459-4(4))* Mitchell Lane Pubs.

Uhl, Xina M. & Poolos, Jamie. A Primary Source Investigation of the Mayflower, 1 vol. 2018. (Uncovering American History Ser.). (ENG.). 64p. (gr. 6-6). pap. 13.95 *(978-1-5081-8420-1(8),* 6638331e-e847-4929-9ddb-0edf86412945, Rosen Reference) Rosen Publishing Group, Inc., The.

Vierow, Wendy. The Assault on Fort Wagner: Black Union Soldiers Make a Stand in South Carolina Battle, 1 vol. 2004. (Headlines from History Ser.). (ENG., Illus.). 24p. (YA). (gr. 3-3). lib. bdg. 26.27 *(978-0-8239-6223-5(7),* ed030bee-610d-49db-bef8-b95145c9aa14) Rosen Publishing Group, Inc., The.

Wagner. William Bradford (Leaders of the Colonial Era) 2010. (ENG.). 120p. (gr. 5-8). 35.00 *(978-1-60413-743-9(6),* P200195, Facts On File) Infobase Holdings, Inc.

Waters, Kate. Sarah Morton's Day: a Day in the Life of a Pilgrim Girl. Kendall, Russ, illus. 2008. (Scholastic Bookshelf Ser.). (ENG.). 32p. (J). (gr. -1-3). pap. 7.99 *(978-0-439-81220-7(8),* Scholastic Paperbacks) Scholastic, Inc.

Waxman, Laura Hamilton. Why Did the Pilgrims Come to the New World? & Other Questions about the Plymouth Colony. 2010. pap. 56.72 *(978-0-7613-6951-6(1))* Lerner Publishing Group.

MNO

Weintraub, Aileen. Boston Light: The First Lighthouse in North America. 2009. (Great Lighthouses of North America Ser.). 24p. (gr. 3-3). 42.50 *(978-1-61513-128-0(0)*, PowerKids Pr.) Rosen Publishing Group, Inc., The.

Whitcraft, Melissa. The Mayflower Compact. 2008. (Cornerstones of Freedom Ser.). (ENG., Illus.). 48p. (YA). (gr. 3-6). 18.69 *(978-0-516-24203-3(2))* Scholastic Library Publishing.

Whitehurst, Susan. The Mayflower. 2009. (Library of the Pilgrims Ser.). 24p. (gr. 3-4). 42.50 *(978-1-60853-914-7(8)*, PowerKids Pr.) Rosen Publishing Group, Inc., The.

—The Pilgrims Before the Mayflower. 2009. (Library of the Pilgrims Ser.). 24p. (gr. 3-4). 42.50 *(978-1-60853-915-4(6)*, PowerKids Pr.) Rosen Publishing Group, Inc., The.

—Plymouth Partnership: Pilgrims & Native Americans. 2009. (Library of the Pilgrims Ser.). 24p. (gr. 3-4). 42.50 *(978-1-60853-912-3(1)*, PowerKids Pr.) Rosen Publishing Group, Inc., The.

—William Bradford & Plymouth: A Colony Grows. 2009. (Library of the Pilgrims Ser.). 24p. (gr. 3-4). 42.50 *(978-1-60853-916-1(4)*, PowerKids Pr.) Rosen Publishing Group, Inc., The.

Williams, Heather. 2013 Boston Marathon. 2018. (21st Century Skills Library: Sports Unite Us Ser.). (ENG., Illus.). 32p. (J). (gr. 3-6). lib. bdg. 32.07 *(978-1-5341-2961-0(8)*, 211888) Cherry Lake Publishing.

Woelfle, Gretchen. Mumbet's Declaration of Independence. Delinois, Alix, illus. 2014. (ENG.). 32p. (J). (gr. 1-4). 19.99 *(978-0-7613-6589-1(3)*, 67deb318-9dc6-42ef-9909-b3bfab8d493f, Carolrhoda Bks.) Lerner Publishing Group.

MASSACHUSETTS—HISTORY—COLONIAL PERIOD, CA. 1600-1775

Aller, Susan Bivin. Anne Hutchinson. 2010. (History Maker Biographies Ser.). (ENG.). 48p. (gr. 3-6). lib. bdg. 27.93 *(978-0-7613-5208-2(2)*, Lerner Pubns.) Lerner Publishing Group.

Avett, Harper. The Colony of Massachusetts, 1 vol. 2015. (Spotlight on the 13 Colonies: Birth of a Nation Ser.). (ENG., Illus.). 24p. (J). (gr. 4-6). pap. 11.00 *(978-1-4994-0511-8(1)*, f539ff16-996e-4933-bfe9-d57f6e683033, PowerKids Pr.) Rosen Publishing Group, Inc., The.

Byers, Ann. Massachusetts Body of Liberties, 1 vol. 2018. (America's Most Important Documents: Inquiry into Historical Sources Ser.). (ENG.). 64p. (gr. 6-6). lib. bdg. 37.36 *(978-1-5026-3613-3(1)*, ff55a05c-256f-492b-a265-0c54b6489c05) Cavendish Square Publishing LLC.

Cunningham, Kevin. The Massachusetts Colony. 2011. (True Book-the Thirteen Colonies Ser.). (ENG., Illus.). 48p. (J). lib. bdg. 29.00 *(978-0-531-25391-5(0)*, Children's Pr.) Scholastic Library Publishing.

Englar, Mary. The Pilgrims & the First Thanksgiving, 1 vol. McDonnell, Peter, illus. 2006. (Graphic History Ser.). (ENG.). 32p. (J). (gr. 3-9). 31.32 *(978-0-7368-5492-4(4)*, 90729, Capstone Pr.) Capstone.

Freedman, Jeri. A Primary Source History of the Colony of Massachusetts. (Primary Sources of the Thirteen Colonies & the Lost Colony Ser.). 64p. 2009. (gr. 5-8). 58.50 *(978-1-60851-880-7(9))* 2005. (ENG., Illus.). (gr. 4-6). per. 12.95 *(978-1-4042-0671-7(X)*, f60d6f65-a7ef-4c57-8684-9ab6112e6e9d) 2005. (ENG., Illus.). (YA). (gr. 4-6). lib. bdg. 37.13 *(978-1-4042-0428-7(8)*, 98284cbc-871e-4f69-8d0d-ba291fb0be3c) Rosen Publishing Group, Inc., The.

Harness, Cheryl. The Adventurous Life of Myles Standish: And the Amazing-but-True Survival Story of Plymouth Colony. 2008. (Cheryl Harness Histories Ser.). (Illus.). 144p. (J). (gr. 5-9). 9.95 *(978-1-4263-0284-8(3)*, National Geographic Kids) Disney Publishing Worldwide.

Hawthorne, Nathaniel. Grandfather's Chair: A History for Youth. 2010. (Applewood Bks.). (ENG.). 292p. pap. 17.95 *(978-1-4290-4522-3(1))* Applewood Bks.

Kiely Miller, Barbara. Anne Hutchinson, 1 vol. 2007. (Great Americans Ser.). 24p. (gr. 2-4). (ENG.). pap. 9.15 *(978-0-8368-8324-4(1)*, a8df2685-f3b6-403c-834f-c5e9c37c8aad); (SPA.). pap. 9.15 *(978-0-8368-8337-4(3)*, af384a82-389a-4771-b553-52471853289d); (SPA., Illus.). lib. bdg. 24.67 *(978-0-8368-8330-5(6)*, 14749122-7836-4305-8205-4305cf766f9f); (ENG., Illus.). lib. bdg. 24.67 *(978-0-8368-8317-6(9)*, 349e5929-1415-4b48-9fa4-586b925a16be) Stevens, Gareth Publishing LLLP. (Weekly Reader Leveled Readers).

Lynch, P. J. The Boy Who Fell off the Mayflower, or John Howland's Good Fortune. Lynch, P. J., illus. (ENG., Illus.). 64p. (J). (gr. 2-5). 2018. 9.99 *(978-1-5362-0296-0(7))* 2015. 18.99 *(978-0-7636-6584-5(3))* Candlewick Pr.

Marsh, Carole. Anne Hutchinson. 2004. 12p. (gr. k-4). 2.95 *(978-0-635-02370-4(9))* Gallopade International.

Miller, Jake. The Colony of Massachusetts: A Primary Source History. 2009. (Primary Source Library of the Thirteen Colonies & the Lost Colony Ser.). 24p. (gr. 3-4). 42.50 *(978-1-60854-142-3(8)*, PowerKids Pr.) Rosen Publishing Group, Inc., The.

Shea, Therese M. The Boston Massacre, 1 vol., Vol. 1. 2014. (What You Didn't Know about History Ser.). (ENG.). 24p. (J). (gr. 2-3). pap. 9.15 *(978-1-4824-3328-9(1)*, c2537e01-8573-4e86-848f-0585e13b1797) Stevens, Gareth Publishing LLLP.

Wolfe, James & Moe, Barbara. Understanding the Charter of the Massachusetts Bay Colony, 1 vol. 2015. (Primary Sources of American Political Documents Ser.). (ENG., Illus.). 112p. (gr. 7-7). 38.93 *(978-0-7660-6870-4(6)*, cf8f12b6-5051-4cd0-bd46-d235ab795a09) Enslow Publishing, LLC.

MASSACHUSETTS—HISTORY—FICTION

Alger, Horatio. Do & Dare: Or, A Brave Boy's Fight for Fortune. 2006. 182p. pap. 19.99 *(978-1-4264-0880-9(3))*; 170p. pap. 21.99 *(978-1-4264-0861-8(7))* Creative Media Partners, LLC.

—Do & Dare: Or, A Brave Boy's Fight for Fortune. 2006. pap. *(978-1-4065-0701-0(6))* Dodo Pr.

Anderson, M. T. The Astonishing Life of Octavian Nothing, Traitor to the Nation, Volume I: The Pox Party, Vol. 1. 2008. (ENG., Illus.). 384p. (YA). (gr. 9-12). pap. 13.99 *(978-0-7636-3679-1(7))* Candlewick Pr.

—The Serpent Came to Gloucester. Ibatoulline, Bagram, illus. 2005. (ENG.). 40p. (J). (gr. 1-4). 19.99 *(978-0-7636-2038-7(6))* Candlewick Pr.

Anderson, Matthew. The Astonishing Life of Octavian Nothing, Traitor to the Nation, Volume I: The Pox Party. 2009. (Astonishing Life of Octavian Nothing, Traitor to the Nation Ser.: Vol. 1). 11.94 *(978-0-7848-1900-5(9)*, Everbind) Marco Bk. Co.

—The Astonishing Life of Octavian Nothing, Traitor to the Nation, Volume I: The Pox Party. 2011. 22.00 *(978-1-60686-925-3(6))* Perfection Learning Corp.

—The Astonishing Life of Octavian Nothing, Traitor to the Nation, Volume I: The Pox Party. l.t. ed. 2020. (ENG.). pap. 15.99 *(978-1-4328-7401-8(2))* Thorndike Pr.

—The Astonishing Life of Octavian Nothing, Traitor to the Nation, Volume II: The Kingdom on the Waves. 2009. (ENG., Illus.). 592p. (YA). (gr. 9). pap. 12.99 *(978-0-7636-4626-4(1))* Candlewick Pr.

—The Astonishing Life of Octavian Nothing, Traitor to the Nation, Volume II: The Kingdom on the Waves. 2011. 24.00 *(978-1-60686-926-0(4))* Perfection Learning Corp.

Brodeur, Tom. Regina Silsby's Phantom Militia. 2005. (Illus.). 267p. (J). (gr. 3-7). 7.49 *(978-1-59166-385-0(7))* BJU Pr.

Cooney, Caroline B. The Ransom of Mercy Carter. 2011. (ENG.). 256p. (YA). (gr. 7-7). 8.99 *(978-0-385-74046-3(8)*, Ember) Random Hse. Children's Bks.

Cooper, Susan. Ghost Hawk. 2013. (ENG.). 336p. (J). (gr. 5-9). 16.99 *(978-1-4424-8141-1(2)*, McElderry, Margaret K. Bks.) McElderry, Margaret K. Bks.

Fama, Elizabeth. Monstrous Beauty. 2013. (ENG.). 352p. (YA). (gr. 7-12). pap. 17.99 *(978-1-250-03425-0(6)*, 900120598) Square Fish.

Figley, Marty Rhodes. Emily & Carlo. Stock, Catherine, illus. 2012. 32p. (J). (gr. k-3). 15.95 *(978-1-58089-274-2(4))* Charlesbridge Publishing, Inc.

Gibbs, Gretchen. The Book of Maggie Bradstreet. 2012. (Bradstreet Chronicles). (ENG.). 183p. (YA). pap. 9.99 *(978-0-9852948-0-9(9))* Glenmere Pr.

Gomes, Linda Nunes. Special Words: A Story about Multicultural Families & Their Pets. Levine, Lenora D., illus. 2007. (YA). per. 12.99 *(978-1-934400-02-9(5))* Rock Village Publishing.

Harlow, Joan Hiatt. Midnight Rider. 2006. (ENG.). 384p. (J). (gr. 4-9). pap. 8.99 *(978-0-689-87010-1(8)*, McElderry, Margaret K. Bks.) McElderry, Margaret K. Bks.

Hearn, Julie. The Minister's Daughter. 2006. (ENG.). 272p. (YA). (gr. 7-12). pap. 7.99 *(978-0-689-87691-2(2)*, Atheneum Bks. for Young Readers) Simon & Schuster Children's Publishing.

Hurst, Carol Otis. Terrible Storm. 2007. (Illus.). 32p. (J). (gr. k-3). lib. bdg. 17.89 *(978-0-06-009002-9(2))* HarperCollins Pubs.

Klimo, Kate. Dog Diaries #5: Dash. Bk. 5. Jessell, Tim, illus. 2014. (Dog Diaries: 5). 160p. (J). (gr. 2-5). pap. 7.99 *(978-0-385-37338-8(4)*, Random Hse. Bks. for Young Readers) Random Hse. Children's Bks.

Latham, Jean Lee & Walsh, Mary R. Carry on, Mr. Bowditch: A Newbery Award Winner. 2003. (ENG., Illus.). 256p. (YA). (gr. 7). pap. 9.99 *(978-0-618-25074-5(3)*, 489709, Clarion Bks.) HarperCollins Pubs.

LeZotte, Ann Clare. Show Me a Sign (Show Me a Sign, Book 1), 1 vol., Vol. 1. (Show Me a Sign Ser.). (ENG.). (J). (gr. 3-7). 2021. 304p. pap. 8.99 *(978-1-338-25582-9(7))* 2020. 288p. 18.99 *(978-1-338-25581-2(9)*, Scholastic Pr.) Scholastic, Inc.

Limbaugh, Rush. Rush Revere & the Brave Pilgrims: Time-Travel Adventures with Exceptional Americans. 2013. (Rush Revere Ser.: 1). (ENG., Illus.). 224p. 21.00 *(978-1-4767-5586-1(8)*, Threshold Editions) Threshold Editions.

Moody Publishing Staff & Lawton, Wendy G. Freedom's Pen: A Story Based on the Life of Freed Slave & Author Phillis Wheatley 2009. (Daughters of the Faith Ser.). (ENG.). 144p. (J). (gr. 3-3). pap. 8.99 *(978-0-8024-7639-5(2))* Moody Pubs.

Parker, Robert. Edenville Owls. 2008. 194p. (gr. 4-6). 18.00 *(978-0-7569-8920-0(5))* Perfection Learning Corp.

Paterson, Katherine. Bread & Roses, Too. (ENG.). 288p. (J). 2008. (gr. 5-7). pap. 7.99 *(978-0-547-07651-5(7)*, 1042025) 2006. (gr. 4-6). 22.44 *(978-0-618-65479-6(8))* HarperCollins Pubs. (Clarion Bks.).

Rees, Celia. Witch Child. unabr. ed. 2004. (Young Adult Cassette Librariestm Ser.). 304p. (J). (gr. 5-9). pap. 40.00 incl. audio *(978-0-8072-1198-4(2)*, S YA 343 SP, Listening Library) Random Hse. Audio Publishing Group.

Rinaldi, Ann. Hang a Thousand Trees with Ribbons: The Story of Phillis Wheatley. 2005. (Great Episodes Ser.). (ENG.). 352p. (YA). (gr. 7-8). pap. 10.99 *(978-0-15-205393-2(X)*, 1196235, Clarion Bks.) HarperCollins Pubs.

—Hang a Thousand Trees with Ribbons: The Story of Phillis Wheatley. 2005. (Great Episodes Ser.). 336p. (gr. 5-9). 18.00 *(978-0-7569-5018-7(X))* Perfection Learning Corp.

Roy, Ron. Mayflower Treasure Hunt. Gurney, John, illus. 2007. (to Z Mysteries Ser.: 28). 114p. (gr. 4-7). lib. bdg. 16.00 *(978-1-4177-9141-5(1))* Turtleback.

—A to Z Mysteries Super Edition 2: Mayflower Treasure Hunt. Gurney, John Steven, illus. 2nd ed. 2007. (to Z Mysteries Ser.: 2). 128p. (J). (gr. 1-4). per. 6.99 *(978-0-375-83937-5(2)*, Random Hse. Bks. for Young Readers) Random Hse. Children's Bks.

Sheely, Robert. In the Hands of the Enemy. Killcoyne, Hope L., ed. Martin, John F., illus. 2003. (Adventures in America Ser.: Vol. 8). 75p. (gr. 4). 14.95 *(978-1-893110-31-1(1))* Silver Moon Pr.

Smith, Mary P. Boy Captive of Old Deerfield. (Illus.). (J). (gr. 5-6). reprint ed. lib. bdg. 22.95 *(978-0-89190-961-3(3)*, Rivercity Pr.) Amereon Ltd.

Strohmeier, Lenice. Mingo, 1 vol. Farnsworth, Bill, illus. 2003. (ENG.). 32p. (J). 16.95 *(978-0-7614-5111-2(0))* Marshall Cavendish Corp.

Thomas, Carroll, creator. Under the Open Sky: A Matty Trescott Novel. 2005. (Illus.). 184p. (J). per. 12.95 *(978-0-9762091-2-6(5))* Antrim Hse.

Thompson, Paul B. The Devil's Door: A Salem Witchcraft Story, 1 vol. 2011. (Historical Fiction Adventures Ser.). (ENG., Illus.). 160p. (J). (gr. 3-5). 31.93 *(978-0-7660-3387-0(2)*, b032300a-5660-4f10-8e33-a57d5745824e); pap. 13.88 *(978-1-59845-214-3(2)*, b6288c2c-d77e-4e8d-8d6c-4dae679dbf24) Enslow Publishing, LLC.

—Liberty's Son: A Spy Story of the American Revolution, 1 vol. 2010. (Historical Fiction Adventures Ser.). (ENG., Illus.). 160p. (J). (gr. 3-5). lib. bdg. 31.93 *(978-0-7660-3309-2(0)*, d55f9c9c-b247-45b8-ab6e-3092d697d744) Enslow Publishing, LLC.

Warburton, Carol. Edge of Night: A Novel. 2004. (Illus.). 278p. pap. 14.95 *(978-1-59156-013-5(6))* Covenant Communications, Inc.

Wiley, Melissa. Little House by Boston Bay. 2007. (Little House Prequel Ser.). (ENG.). 160p. (J). (gr. 3-7). pap. 7.99 *(978-0-06-114828-6(8)*, HarperCollins) HarperCollins Pubs.

Wolk, Lauren. Beyond the Bright Sea. 2017. (ENG.). 304p. (J). (gr. 5). 18.99 *(978-1-101-99485-6(1)*, Dutton Books for Young Readers) Penguin Young Readers Group.

MASSACHUSETTS—POLITICS AND GOVERNMENT

Marsh, Carole. Exploring Massachusetts Through Project-Based Learning: Geography, History, Government, Economics & More. 2016. (Massachusetts Experience Ser.). (ENG.). (J). pap. 9.99 *(978-0-635-12345-9(2))* Gallopade International.

MASTODON

Clay, Kathryn. American Mastodon. 2018. (Little Paleontologist Ser.). (ENG., Illus.). 32p. (J). (gr. k-3). pap. 6.95 *(978-1-5435-0547-4(3)*, 137362); lib. bdg. 28.65 *(978-1-5435-0543-6(0)*, 137358) Capstone. (Capstone Pr.).

Goecke, Michael P. American Mastodon, 1 vol. 2003. (Prehistoric Animals Set II Ser.). (ENG., Illus.). 24p. (gr. k-4). 25.65 *(978-1-57765-973-0(2)*, Buddy Bks.) ABDO Publishing Co.

Ransom, Candice. Bones in the White House: Thomas Jefferson's Mammoth. Christoph, Jamey, illus. 2020. 40p. (J). (gr. -1-2). 17.99 *(978-0-525-64607-5(8)*, Doubleday Bks. for Young Readers) Random Hse. Children's Bks.

MATERIA MEDICA

see also Poisons

Claybourne, Anna. Sick at Sea? Cure It or Cut It Off! 2010. (ENG.). 32p. (J). *(978-0-7787-9901-6(8))* Crabtree Publishing Co.

Lawrence, Ellen. Healing Plants. 2015. (Plant-Ology Ser.). (ENG., Illus.). 24p. (J). (gr. -1-3). lib. bdg. 26.99 *(978-1-62724-866-2(8))* Bearport Publishing Co., Inc.

Woods, Michael & Woods, Mary B. Ancient Medical Technology: From Herbs to Scalpels. 2011. (Technology in Ancient Cultures Ser.). (ENG.). 96p. (gr. 6-12). lib. bdg. 31.93 *(978-0-7613-6522-8(2))* Lerner Publishing Group.

MATERIALS

Addison, D. R. Cement Mixers at Work, 1 vol. 2009. (Big Trucks Ser.). (ENG., Illus.). 24p. (J). (gr. 1-1). pap. 9.25 *(978-1-4358-3087-5(3)*, 4cd9040a-e2fd-4fc8-b079-a4bca56254aa, PowerKids Pr.) Rosen Publishing Group, Inc., The.

Ballard, Carol. Exploring Natural & Man-Made Materials, 1 vol. 2007. (How Does Science Work? Ser.). (ENG., Illus.). 32p. (J). (gr. 2-3). lib. bdg. 30.27 *(978-1-4042-4278-4(3)*, f6a1c680-c25a-4476-8143-6473932afea7, PowerKids Pr.) Rosen Publishing Group, Inc., The.

Barton, Chris. The Day-Glo Brothers: The True Story of Bob & Joe Switzer's Bright Ideas & Brand-New Colors. Persiani, Tony, illus. 2009. (ENG.). 44p. (J). (gr. 2-5). 21.99 *(978-1-57091-673-1(X))* Charlesbridge Publishing, Inc.

Bell, Samantha. Concrete Mixer. 2018. (21st Century Basic Skills Library: Level 1: Welcome to the Construction Site Ser.). (ENG., Illus.). 24p. (J). (gr. k-3). lib. bdg. 30.64 *(978-1-5341-2921-4(9)*, 211728) Cherry Lake Publishing.

Bentley, Joyce. Rough. 2006. (Things Around Us Ser.). (J). *(978-1-59389-276-0(4))* Chrysalis Education.

—Smooth. 2006. (Things Around Us Ser.). (J). *(978-1-59389-277-7(2))* Chrysalis Education.

Best, Arthur. Texture, 1 vol. 2018. (Properties of Matter Ser.). (ENG.). 24p. (J). (gr. 1-1). 25.93 *(978-1-5026-4275-2(1)*, 619644d5-28ea-4c88-8fed-6a40cddeea5b) Cavendish Square Publishing LLC.

Brill, Marlene Targ. Concrete Mixers. 2006. (Pull Ahead Books-Mighty Movers Ser.). (ENG., Illus.). 32p. (gr. k-3). lib. bdg. 22.60 *(978-0-8225-6011-1(9)*, Lerner Pubns.) Lerner Publishing Group.

Canavan, Thomas. Magnificent Experiments with Materials. Linley, Adam, illus. 2017. (Mind-Blowing Science Experiments Ser.). 32p. (gr. 4-5). pap. 63.00 *(978-1-5382-0732-1(X))* Stevens, Gareth Publishing LLLP.

Carr, Aaron. Natural o Hecho Por el Hombre. 2013. (SPA., Illus.). 24p. (J). *(978-1-62127-607-4(4))* Weigl Pubs., Inc.

Claybourne, Anna. Materials: Makes Science Make Sense. 2012. (ENG., Illus.). 24p. (gr. k-4). pap. 7.95 *(978-1-926853-58-1(X))* Saunders Bk. Co. CAN. Dist: RiverStream Publishing.

Dawson, Emily C. Rough & Smooth. 2011. (Amicus Readers. Let's Compare (Level A) Ser.). (ENG.). 24p. (J). (gr. -1-2). lib. bdg. 25.65 *(978-1-60753-002-2(3)*, 17023) Amicus.

Enz, Tammy. Bend It! 2017. (Shaping Materials Ser.). (ENG., Illus.). 24p. (J). (gr. k-2). pap. 6.95 *(978-1-4846-4101-9(9)*, 135862); lib. bdg. 25.99 *(978-1-4846-4097-5(7)*, 135857) Capstone. (Heinemann).

—Stretch It! 2017. (Shaping Materials Ser.). (ENG., Illus.). 24p. (J). (gr. k-2). lib. bdg. 25.99 *(978-1-4846-4094-4(2)*, 135850, Heinemann) Capstone.

—Twist It! 2017. (Shaping Materials Ser.). (ENG., Illus.). 24p. (J). (gr. k-2). lib. bdg. 25.99 *(978-1-4846-4096-8(9)*, 135856, Heinemann) Capstone.

Faulkner, Nicholas & Johanson, Paula. Nonrenewable Resources & You, 1 vol. 2018. (How Our Choices Impact Earth Ser.). (ENG.). 64p. (gr. 6-6). 36.13 *(978-1-5081-8150-7(0)*, f428a863-b2c1-4734-b905-b4459b1453a2, Rosen Reference) Rosen Publishing Group, Inc., The.

Hawkins, Jay. Material World: The Science of Matter, 1 vol. 2013. (Big Bang Science Experiments Ser.). (ENG., Illus.). 32p. (gr. 4-5). pap. 12.75 *(978-1-4777-0367-0(5)*, 545b97cc-cc04-4059-a600-fc75349632d7, Windmill Bks.) Rosen Publishing Group, Inc., The.

Hibbert, Clare. Matter & Materials, 1 vol. 2018. (Science Explorers Ser.). (ENG.). 32p. (gr. 3-3). lib. bdg. 26.93 *(978-1-9785-0645-9(7)*, 51126745-b992-4093-830d-45a0a0dffb7f) Enslow Publishing, LLC.

Hughes, Susan. Is It Transparent or Opaque? 2012. (ENG., Illus.). 24p. (J). *(978-0-7787-2052-2(7))*; pap. *(978-0-7787-2059-1(4))* Crabtree Publishing Co.

Is It Natural or Human-Made? 2014. (What's the Matter? Ser.). (ENG., Illus.). 24p. (J). (gr. 1-2). *(978-0-7787-0535-2(8))* Crabtree Publishing Co.

Issues, Evidence & You - Water Mega Module Complete Materials Package. 2003. (Illus.). tchr. ed., ring bd. *(978-1-887725-42-2(3))*; (YA). tchr. ed., stu. ed., per. *(978-1-887725-60-6(1))* Lab-Aids, Inc.

Issues, Evidence & You Complete Materials Package. 2003. (Illus.). (YA). tchr. ed., ring bd. *(978-1-887725-71-2(7))* Lab-Aids, Inc.

Issues, Evidence & You Complete Materials Package: Includes Teacher's Guide & Student Books. 2003. (Illus.). (YA). *(978-1-887725-72-9(5))* Lab-Aids, Inc.

Jennings, Terry. Materials. 2009. (Science Alive Ser.). (ENG., Illus.). 32p. (J). (gr. 4-7). pap. *(978-1-897563-58-8(2))* Saunders Bk. Co.

Kalman, Bobbie. What Is It Made From? 2011. (ENG.). 16p. (J). lib. bdg. *(978-0-7787-9562-9(4))*; (My World Ser.: No. 60). pap. *(978-0-7787-9587-2(X))* Crabtree Publishing Co.

Kerrod, Robin. New Materials. 2003. (21st Century Science Ser.). 48p. (J). lib. bdg. 27.10 *(978-1-58340-353-2(1))* Black Rabbit Bks.

Langley, Andrew. Everyday Materials. 2008. (ENG., Illus.). 24p. (J). (gr. 4-7). *(978-0-7787-4125-1(7))* Crabtree Publishing Co.

Law, Felicia. Materials. 2015. (Stone Age Science Ser.). (ENG., Illus.). 32p. (J). (gr. 4). *(978-0-7787-1889-5(1))* Crabtree Publishing Co.

Lindeen, Mary. Texture. 2018. (Beginning-To-Read Ser.). (ENG.). 32p. (J). (gr. k-2). pap. 13.26 *(978-1-68404-151-0(1))*; (Illus.). (gr. -1-2). lib. bdg. 22.60 *(978-1-59953-904-1(7))* Norwood Hse. Pr.

Lunis, Natalie. Squishy Sponges. 2007. (No Backbone! Ser.). (Illus.). 24p. (J). (gr. k-3). lib. bdg. 26.99 *(978-1-59716-512-9(3))* Bearport Publishing Co., Inc.

Lüsted, Marcia Amidon. Bit Rot: Preserving the Documents Most Important to You, 1 vol. 2016. (Digital & Information Literacy Ser.). (ENG., Illus.). 48p. (J). (gr. 6-6). pap. 12.75 *(978-1-4994-6515-0(7)*, 79c26bb4-e820-49f4-a027-e8d0c5b26fb6) Rosen Publishing Group, Inc., The.

Martin, Claudia. Materials. 2018. (Adventures in STEAM Ser.). (ENG., Illus.). 48p. (J). (gr. 3-6). lib. bdg. 27.99 *(978-1-5435-3230-2(6)*, 138828, Capstone Pr.) Capstone.

Martin, Emmett. What Is Bumpy?, 1 vol. 2019. (Let's Learn Textures! Ser.). (ENG.). 24p. (gr. k-k). pap. 9.15 *(978-1-5382-4429-6(2)*, 7bfe9387-d511-4a1c-b596-1a1e9d2ceed3) Stevens, Gareth Publishing LLLP.

—What Is Dry?, 1 vol. 2019. (Let's Learn Textures! Ser.). (ENG.). 24p. (gr. k-k). pap. 9.15 *(978-1-5382-4433-3(0)*, 55251ddf-43b9-478f-af69-3fc0f662c89d) Stevens, Gareth Publishing LLLP.

—What Is Hard?, 1 vol. 2019. (Let's Learn Textures! Ser.). (ENG.). 24p. (gr. k-k). pap. 9.15 *(978-1-5382-4437-1(3)*, 911d9051-2268-4529-ae5e-2c9b1c9dab93) Stevens, Gareth Publishing LLLP.

—What Is Smooth?, 1 vol. 2019. (Let's Learn Textures! Ser.). (ENG.). 24p. (gr. k-k). pap. 9.15 *(978-1-5382-4441-8(1)*, fe49cbf7-5b44-4db5-aa60-f7653e3cdaf0) Stevens, Gareth Publishing LLLP.

—What Is Soft?, 1 vol. 2019. (Let's Learn Textures! Ser.). (ENG.). 24p. (gr. k-k). pap. 9.15 *(978-1-5382-4445-6(4)*, 26b88374-d01c-4977-b64b-83e64604873a) Stevens, Gareth Publishing LLLP.

—What Is Wet?, 1 vol. 2019. (Let's Learn Textures! Ser.). (ENG.). 24p. (gr. k-k). pap. 9.15 *(978-1-5382-4449-4(7)*, 3a394020-31ee-4211-b648-265a2e4bffa0) Stevens, Gareth Publishing LLLP.

Mason, Adrienne. Touch It! Materials, Matter & You. Dávila, Claudia, illus. 2005. (Primary Physical Science Ser.). (ENG.). 32p. (J). (gr. -1-2). 8.99 *(978-1-55337-761-0(3))* Kids Can Pr., Ltd. CAN. Dist: Hachette Bk. Group.

Materials. 2004. (Illus.). lib. bdg. 7.95 *(978-0-8225-4789-1(9))* Lerner Publishing Group.

Materials & Their Uses, 6 vols., Pack. (Discovery World Ser.). 24p. (gr. 1-2). 33.00 *(978-0-7635-8479-5(7))* Rigby Education.

Meachen Rau, Dana. Builders, 1 vol. 2008. (Tools We Use Ser.). (ENG.). 32p. (gr. k-1). pap. 9.23 *(978-0-7614-3289-0(2)*, 9a74bc42-2a53-4d58-8347-97b1343fd1dc) Cavendish Square Publishing LLC.

Miller, Shannon & Hoena, B. A. A Low-Tech Mission. 2018. (J). *(978-1-68410-227-3(8))* Cantata Learning.

Mooney, Carla. Becoming Invisible: From Camouflage to Cloaks. 2010. (Great Idea Ser.). 48p. (J). (gr. 4-6). lib. bdg. 26.60 *(978-1-59953-378-0(2))* Norwood Hse. Pr.

Newson, Lesley & Wadsworth, Pamela. Defnyddiau. 2005. (WEL., Illus.). 24p. pap. *(978-1-85596-235-4(7))* Dref Wen.

—Rhagor Am Ddefnyddiau. 2005. (WEL., Illus.). 24p. pap. *(978-1-85596-236-1(5))* Dref Wen.

O'Hara, Nicholas. Sort It by Texture, 1 vol. 2015. (Sort It Out! Ser.). (ENG.). 24p. (J). (gr. k-1). pap. 9.15 *(978-1-4824-2581-9(5)*, 609b0199-75e0-4b34-bb73-1b52876c896e) Stevens, Gareth Publishing LLLP.

Orme, Helen. What Things Are Made Of. 2010. (Science Everywhere! Ser.). 24p. 24.25 *(978-1-84898-298-7(4))* Black Rabbit Bks.

Owen, Ruth. Let's Investigate Everyday Materials. 2017. (Get Started with STEM Ser.). (ENG., Illus.). 32p. (J). (gr. k-3). 9.99 *(978-1-78856-117-4(1)*, 09e921ef-1aa6-4b6b-8040-2f41477cea24) Ruby Tuesday Books Limited GBR. Dist: Lerner Publishing Group.

Oxlade, Chris. Changing Materials. 2007. (Working with Materials Ser.). (ENG., Illus.). 32p. (J). (gr. -1-3). pap. *(978-0-7787-3648-6(2))* Crabtree Publishing Co.

—Experiments with Matter & Materials, 1 vol. 2014. (Excellent Science Experiments Ser.). (ENG.). 32p. (J). (gr. 4-5). lib. bdg. 29.27 *(978-1-4777-5969-1(7)*,

4f23ee91-dd3d-42e7-843a-f7f824ef9bc8, PowerKids Pr.) Rosen Publishing Group, Inc., The.

—Joining Materials. 2007. (Working with Materials Ser.). (ENG.). 32p. (J). pap. *(978-0-7787-3649-3(0))*; (Illus.). (gr. -1-3). lib. bdg. *(978-0-7787-3639-4(3))* Crabtree Publishing Co.

—Shaping Materials. 2007. (Working with Materials Ser.). (ENG., Illus.). 32p. (J). (gr. -1-3). pap. *(978-0-7787-3651-6(2))* Crabtree Publishing Co.

Rector, Rebecca Kraft. Texture, 1 vol. 2019. (Let's Learn about Matter Ser.). (ENG.). 24p. (gr. 1-2). 24.27 *(978-1-9785-0755-5(0)*, c809329e-e139-4114-9784-60b47756f5b2) Enslow Publishing, LLC.

Rigby Education Staff. Discovery World Red Materials. (Discovery World Ser.). 12p. (gr. 1-2). 31.00 *(978-0-7635-2706-8(8))* Rigby Education.

Riley, Peter D. Materials. 2011. (Real Scientist Investigates Ser.). (Illus.). 32p. (J). (gr. 3-5). lib. bdg. 28.50 *(978-1-59771-282-8(5))* Sea-To-Sea Pubns.

Rising, Heather. Is It Smooth or Rough? 2012. (ENG., Illus.). 24p. (J). *(978-0-7787-2051-5(9))*; pap. *(978-0-7787-2058-4(6))* Crabtree Publishing Co.

Rissman, Rebecca. Materials: Real Size Science, 1 vol. 2013. (Real Size Science Ser.). (ENG.). 24p. (J). (gr. -1-1). pap. 6.95 *(978-1-4329-7885-3(3)*, 122825, Heinemann) Capstone.

Rivera, Andrea. Cloth. 2017. (Materials Ser.). (ENG., Illus.). 24p. (J). (gr. -1-2). lib. bdg. 31.36 *(978-1-5321-2029-9(X)*, 25294, Abdo Zoom-Launch) ABDO Publishing Co.

—Paper. 2017. (Materials Ser.). (ENG., Illus.). 24p. (J). (gr. -1-2). lib. bdg. 31.36 *(978-1-5321-2032-9(X)*, 25300, Abdo Zoom-Launch) ABDO Publishing Co.

Rivera, Sheila. How Does It Feel? (First Step Nonfiction — Properties of Matter Ser.). (J). (gr. k-2). 2005. (ENG., Illus.). 8p. pap. 5.99 *(978-0-8225-5405-9(4)*, a79cc4f6-a319-4fc8-bd7c-ab320b171dbb) 2004. lib. bdg. 23.99 *(978-0-8225-2863-0(0)*, Lerner Pubns.) Lerner Publishing Group.

Rustad, Martha E. H. What Is It Made Of? Noticing Types of Materials. Schneider, Christine M., illus. 2015. (Cloverleaf Books (tm) — Nature's Patterns Ser.). (ENG.). 24p. (J). (gr. k-2). 25.32 *(978-1-4677-8561-7(X)*, ebb0e7d3-e4dc-4a76-9355-d7c5c5020e6b, Millbrook Pr.) Lerner Publishing Group.

Sjonger, Rebecca. Exploring Materials in My Makerspace. 2018. (Matter & Materials in My Makerspace Ser.). 32p. (J). (gr. 2-3). *(978-0-7787-4607-2(0))* Crabtree Publishing Co.

—Joining Materials in My Makerspace. 2018. (Matter & Materials in My Makerspace Ser.). 32p. (J). (gr. 2-3). *(978-0-7787-4620-1(8))* Crabtree Publishing Co.

—Mixing & Separating Materials in My Makerspace. 2018. (Matter & Materials in My Makerspace Ser.). 32p. (J). (gr. 2-3). *(978-0-7787-4619-5(4))* Crabtree Publishing Co.

—Shaping Materials in My Makerspace. 2018. (Matter & Materials in My Makerspace Ser.). 32p. (J). (gr. 2-3). *(978-0-7787-4621-8(6))* Crabtree Publishing Co.

—Testing Materials in My Makerspace. 2018. (Matter & Materials in My Makerspace Ser.). 32p. (J). (gr. 2-3). *(978-0-7787-4608-9(9))* Crabtree Publishing Co.

Smith, A. Materials. 2004. (Internet-Linked Library of Science). 64p. (J). pap. 9.95 *(978-0-7945-0085-6(4)*, Usborne) EDC Publishing.

Snedden, Robert. Materials Engineering & Exploring Properties. 2015. (Engineering in Action Ser.). (ENG., Illus.). 32p. (J). (gr. 5-5). *(978-0-7787-7514-0(3))* Crabtree Publishing Co.

Sundance/Newbridge LLC Staff. Properties of Materials. 2007. (Early Science Ser.). (gr. k-3). 18.95 *(978-1-4007-6576-8(5))*; pap. 6.10 *(978-1-4007-6572-0(2))* Sundance/Newbridge Educational Publishing.

Wadsworth, Pamela. Golwg Gyntaf Ar Ddefnyddiau. 2005. (WEL., Illus.). 24p. pap. *(978-1-85596-251-4(9))* Dref Wen.

Waldman, Loretta. 3D Materials & Construction Possibilities, 1 vol. 2017. (Project Learning with 3D Printing Ser.). (ENG.). 128p. (YA). (gr. 9-9). pap. 22.16 *(978-1-5026-3423-8(6)*, dec26203-fbff-4e74-a1f7-88e2282bf18f); lib. bdg. 47.36 *(978-1-5026-3146-6(6)*, 878ab302-2001-4c74-add2-ba28e422968c) Cavendish Square Publishing LLC.

Ward, D. J. Materials Science. 2009. pap. 52.95 *(978-0-7613-4784-2(4))* 2008. (ENG.). 48p. (gr. 4-8). 27.93 *(978-0-8225-7588-7(4))* Lerner Publishing Group.

Way, Steve. Materials, 1 vol. 2009. (Simply Science Ser.). (ENG., Illus.). 32p. (YA). (gr. 3-5). lib. bdg. 28.67 *(978-1-4339-0033-4(5)*, a8705e69-5c1b-4ae8-80eb-7c27fc292ae4) Stevens, Gareth Publishing LLLP.

Wood & Other Materials: Individual Title Six-Packs. (Discovery World Ser.). 16p. (gr. 1-2). 28.00 *(978-0-7635-8460-3(6))* Rigby Education.

York, M. J. Henry Ford: Manufacturing Mogul, 1 vol. 2010. (Essential Lives Set 5 Ser.). (ENG.). 112p. (YA). (gr. 6-12). lib. bdg. 41.36 *(978-1-61613-514-0(X)*, 6711, Essential Library) ABDO Publishing Co.

MATERNITY

see Mothers

MATHEMATICAL DRAWING

see Geometrical Drawing; Mechanical Drawing

MATHEMATICAL RECREATIONS

Activity Guide Feast of Fracts. 2004. 40p. (J). *(978-1-59242-147-3(4))* Delta Education, LLC.

Activity Guide Fraction Burger. 2004. 92p. (J). *(978-1-59242-146-6(6))* Delta Education, LLC.

Big Book of English & Math. 2003. (Bumper Gold Stars Ser.). (Illus.). 240p. (J). 9.98 *(978-1-4054-1720-4(X))*; 9.98 *(978-1-4054-1719-8(6))* Parragon, Inc.

Blakely, April. Math Brainteasers. 2nd ed. 2005. (Illus.). 90p. (YA). (gr. 8-12). per. 12.95 *(978-1-59647-036-1(4))* Good Year Bks.

Blum, Raymond. Mathamusements. Date not set. (J). 5.95 *(978-0-8069-3190-6(6))* Sterling Publishing Co., Inc.

Blum, Raymond, et al. Giant Book of Science Fun/Giant Book of Math Fun: Flip Book. Sterling Publishing Company Staff, ed. (Illus.). 512p. pap. 9.98 *(978-1-4027-0469-7(0))* Sterling Publishing Co., Inc.

Burstein, John. Math Monsters(tm), 6 vols. Incl. Making Tens: Groups of Gollywomples. lib. bdg. 23.67 *(978-0-8368-3812-1(2)*, e90bf9ab-0acd-4329-9fae-a29bd57c7b6a); Measuring: the Perfect Playhouse. lib. bdg. 23.67 *(978-0-8368-3813-8(0)*, 6c1a556e-e974-443a-9179-5431e8939af3); Patterns: What's on the Wall? lib. bdg. 23.67 *(978-0-8368-3816-9(5)*, 0733a693-f036-41b1-b427-79065a52fe8b); Using Computers: Machine with a Mouse. lib. bdg. 23.67 *(978-0-8368-3817-6(3)*, 0413d44c-96bc-47dd-bcdf-f9a77de90bb4); (J). (gr. k-3). (Math Monsters(tm) Ser.). (ENG., Illus.). 24p. 2003. Set lib. bdg. 71.01 *(978-0-8368-3803-9(3)*, a1d67c9d-a8ed-436c-982e-fa6207c51948, Weekly Reader Leveled Readers) Stevens, Gareth Publishing LLLP.

Cameron, Antonia & Fosnot, Catherine Twomey. Games for Early Number Sense: A Yearlong Resource. 2008. (ENG.). 96p. (gr. k-1). pap. 31.25 *(978-0-325-01009-0(9)*, E01009, Firsthand) Heinemann.

Canavan, Thomas. Computation Skills: 50 Math Super Puzzles, 1 vol. 2011. (Math Standards Workout Ser.). (ENG., Illus.). 48p. (YA). (gr. 5-5). pap. 12.75 *(978-1-4488-6680-9(4)*, aeb86af7-cbfa-4ddf-ba50-5f218b75d327, Rosen Reference) Rosen Publishing Group, Inc., The.

—Making Connections: 50 Math Super Puzzles, 1 vol. 2011. (Math Standards Workout Ser.). (ENG., Illus.). 48p. (YA). (gr. 5-5). pap. 12.75 *(978-1-4488-6681-6(2)*, a0b24b7f-b078-43d7-9f7f-4f6a6ae9dbd9, Rosen Reference); lib. bdg. 34.47 *(978-1-4488-6674-8(X)*, 04fcdfce-74f5-40e8-a862-3e893fc30c4b) Rosen Publishing Group, Inc., The.

—Mental Math: 50 Math Super Puzzles, 1 vol. 2011. (Math Standards Workout Ser.). (ENG., Illus.). 48p. (YA). (gr. 5-5). pap. 12.75 *(978-1-4488-6684-7(7)*, 46b41be4-11cc-4ed7-b788-1e54fd6e3e41, Rosen Reference) Rosen Publishing Group, Inc., The.

—Problem Solving: 50 Math Super Puzzles, 1 vol. 2011. (Math Standards Workout Ser.). (ENG., Illus.). 48p. (YA). (gr. 5-5). pap. 12.75 *(978-1-4488-6682-3(0)*, 10f83779-c434-4db6-9a4c-98eb802ce2fc, Rosen Reference) Rosen Publishing Group, Inc., The.

—Shapes & Symmetry: 50 Math Super Puzzles, 1 vol. 2011. (Math Standards Workout Ser.). (ENG., Illus.). 48p. (YA). (gr. 5-5). pap. 12.75 *(978-1-4488-6683-0(9)*, 2b0eec55-5545-4658-a254-4a03e92130c9, Rosen Reference) Rosen Publishing Group, Inc., The.

—Symbols & Algebra: 50 Math Super Puzzles, 1 vol. 2011. (Math Standards Workout Ser.). (ENG., Illus.). 48p. (YA). (gr. 5-5). pap. 12.75 *(978-1-4488-6685-4(5)*, 0429ede5-5938-48fa-9d3e-3a1e55b694aa, Rosen Reference) Rosen Publishing Group, Inc., The.

Clemens, Meg, et al. The Everything Kids' Math Puzzles Book: Brain Teasers, Games, & Activities for Hours of Fun. 2003. (Everything(r) Kids Ser.). (ENG., Illus.). 144p. pap. 9.99 *(978-1-58062-773-3(0)*, Everything) Adams Media Corp.

Dot-to-Dot 1-100+ Spanish Version. 2007. (J). per. *(978-1-58232-163-9(9))* ECS Learning Systems, Inc.

Eastaway, Rob & Wyndham. Why Do Buses Come in Threes? 2004. (Illus.). 156p. pap. *(978-1-86105-247-6(2)*, Robson Bks. Ltd.) Pavilion Bks.

English/Math 3-4. 2003. (Illus.). 48p. (J). wbk. ed. 7.98 *(978-1-4054-1264-3(X))* Parragon, Inc.

English/Math 4-5. 2003. (Illus.). 48p. (J). wbk. ed. 7.98 *(978-1-4054-1265-0(8))* Parragon, Inc.

English/Math 5-6. 2003. (Illus.). 48p. (J). wbk. ed. 7.98 *(978-1-4054-1266-7(6))* Parragon, Inc.

English/Math 6-7. 2003. (Illus.). 48p. (YA). wbk. ed. 7.98 *(978-1-4054-1267-4(4))* Parragon, Inc.

Faulkner, Keith & Holmes, Stephen. Animal ? Math. Faulkner, Keith & Holmes, Stephen, illus. 2003. (Illus.). (J). *(978-0-439-62755-9(9))* Scholastic, Inc.

Ferrell, Karen, et al. Estimating & Measuring. 2008. (Adventures in Mathopolis Ser.). (ENG., Illus.). 172p. (J). (gr. 4-7). 21.19 *(978-0-7641-3867-6(7)*, B.E.S. Publishing) Peterson's.

Freudenthal. Reflections on Numbers. 3rd ed. 2003. (Math in Context Ser.). (Illus.). 7.86 *(978-0-03-071704-8(3))* Holt McDougal.

Ganesan, C. T. Fun with Maths. 2005. (Illus.). 188p. (gr. 4-7). per. *(978-1-84549-027-0(4))* arima publishing.

Gardner, Martin. Mental Magic: Surefire Tricks to Amaze Your Friends. Sinclair, Jeff, illus. 2010. (Dover Kids Activity Bks.). (ENG.). 96p. (J). (gr. 3-5). pap. 4.99 *(978-0-486-47495-3(X)*, 47495X) Dover Pubns., Inc.

Gave, Marc. Number Games Around the World & Juegos de números alrededor del Mundo: 6 English, 6 Spanish Adaptations 2011. (Navigators Ser.). (ENG & SPA.). (J). instr.'s gde. ed. 97.00 net. *(978-1-4108-1765-5(2))* Benchmark Education Co.

George, Rebecca. Super Smart Math: 180 Warm-Ups & Challenging Activities. 2006. (ENG., Illus.). 220p. per. 19.95 *(978-1-59363-200-7(2))* Prufrock Pr.

Hanson, Anders & Mann, Elissa. Cool Flexagon Art: Creative Activities That Make Math & Science Fun for Kids! 2013. (Cool Art with Math & Science Ser.). (ENG.). 32p. (J). (gr. 3-6). lib. bdg. 34.21 *(978-1-61783-821-7(7)*, 4588, Checkerboard Library) ABDO Publishing Co.

Hanson, Anders Mann & Mann, Elissa. Cool String Art: Creative Activities That Make Math & Science Fun for Kids! 2013. (Cool Art with Math & Science Ser.). (ENG.). 32p. (J). (gr. 3-6). lib. bdg. 34.21 *(978-1-61783-824-8(1)*, 4594, Checkerboard Library) ABDO Publishing Co.

—Cool Structures: Creative Activities That Make Math & Science Fun for Kids! 2013. (Cool Art with Math & Science Ser.). (ENG.). 32p. (J). (gr. 3-6). lib. bdg. 34.21 *(978-1-61783-825-5(X)*, 4596, Checkerboard Library) ABDO Publishing Co.

—Cool Tessellations: Creative Activities That Make Math & Science Fun for Kids! 2013. (Cool Art with Math & Science Ser.). (ENG.). 32p. (J). (gr. 3-6). lib. bdg. 34.21 *(978-1-61783-826-2(8)*, 4598, Checkerboard Library) ABDO Publishing Co.

Highling, Erin. Take Me Out to the Math Game: Home Run Activities, Big League Word Problems & Hard Ball Quizzes — A Fun Workbook for 4-6th Graders. 2018. (Books for Teachers Ser.). (ENG., Illus.). 128p. (J). (gr. 4-6). pap. 11.95 *(978-1-61243-787-3(7))* Ulysses Pr.

Leech, Bonnie Coulter. Mesopotamia: Creating & Solving Word Puzzles. 2006. (Math Big Bookstm Ser.). (ENG.). 32p. (gr. 6-7). 47.50 *(978-1-4042-6364-2(0))* Rosen Publishing Group, Inc., The.

Levy, Janey. At Sea on a Viking Ship: Solving Problems of Length & Weight Using the Four Math Operations, 1 vol. 2010. (Math for the REAL World Ser.). (ENG., Illus.). 24p. (gr. 3-4). pap. 8.25 *(978-0-8239-8922-5(4)*, eea2e498-a9d8-46c5-badc-b0088a52f6bd, PowerKids Pr.) Rosen Publishing Group, Inc., The.

Lewis, J. Patrick. Arithme-Tickle: An Even Number of Odd Riddle-Rhymes. Remkiewicz, Frank, illus. 2007. (ENG.). 32p. (J). (gr. k-3). 18.69 *(978-0-15-216418-8(9))* Harcourt Children's Bks.

—Arithme-Tickle: An Even Number of Odd Riddle-Rhymes. Remkiewicz, Frank, illus. 2007. (ENG.). 32p. (J). (gr. 1-4). pap. 7.99 *(978-0-15-205848-7(6)*, 1197563, Clarion Bks.) HarperCollins Pubs.

Linde, Barbara M. & Lechner, Judith. Working at the Farmer's Market: Solving Money Problems Involving the Four Math Operations, 1 vol. 2010. (Math for the REAL World Ser.). (ENG., Illus.). 24p. (gr. 3-4). pap. 8.25 *(978-0-8239-8920-1(8)*, dd240558-7fe6-4148-9371-71170d3f27b6, PowerKids Pr.) Rosen Publishing Group, Inc., The.

Lund, Charles. Math Games & Activies with Cards. 2008. (ENG.). 64p. tchr. ed. 14.95 *(978-1-934218-01-3(4)*, EM 500) IPMG Publishing.

—Math games & activities with Dice. 2008. (ENG.). 84p. pap. 14.95 *(978-1-934218-03-7(0)*, EM 590) IPMG Publishing.

—Place Mat Math, 1. 2009. (ENG.). 14.95 *(978-1-934218-04-4(9)*, EM 595) IPMG Publishing.

Mental Math. 2004. (Help with Homework Ser.). 32p. (J). (gr. 1-4). wbk. ed. 3.99 *(978-1-904586-26-5(0))* Byeway Bks.

Morgan, Rowland. Brain Bafflers. 2003. (Illus.). 96p. (J). pap. 3.99 *(978-0-330-36783-7(8)*, Macmillan Children's Bks.) Pan Macmillan GBR. Dist: Trafalgar Square Publishing.

National Geographic Kids. By the Numbers 3. 14: 110. 01 Cool Infographics Packed with Stats & Figures. 2017. (Illus.). 256p. (J). (gr. 3-7). (ENG.). 19.90 *(978-1-4263-2866-4(4))*; pap. 9.99 *(978-1-4263-2865-7(6))* Disney Publishing Worldwide. (National Geographic Kids).

Neuschwander, Cindy. Sir Cumference & the Sword in the Cone. Geehan, Wayne, illus. 2003. (Sir Cumference Ser.). (ENG.). 32p. (J). (gr. 3-7). pap. 7.99 *(978-1-57091-601-4(2))* Charlesbridge Publishing, Inc.

Newman-D'Amico, Fran. My First Book of Number Fun. 2006. (Dover Kids Activity Bks.). (ENG., Illus.). 64p. (J). (gr. -1-2). per. 4.95 *(978-0-486-45226-5(3)*, 452263) Dover Pubns., Inc.

Niederman, Derrick. Mind-Stretching Math Puzzles. 2005. (Illus.). 112p. (J). *(978-1-4156-0492-2(4))* Sterling Publishing Co., Inc.

Nobleman, Marc Tyler. Math Puzzles: Grades 3 & 4. (Illus.). (J). pap., wbk. ed. 4.99 *(978-0-88743-846-2(6))* School Zone Publishing Co.

Overdeck, Laura. Bedtime Math: a Fun Excuse to Stay up Late. Paillot, Jim, illus. 2013. (Bedtime Math Ser.). (ENG.). 96p. (J). (gr. -1-2). 17.99 *(978-1-250-03585-1(6)*, 900121845) Feiwel & Friends.

—Bedtime Math: This Time It's Personal: This Time It's Personal. Paillot, Jim, illus. 2014. (Bedtime Math Ser.). (ENG.). 96p. (J). (gr. -1-2). 17.99 *(978-1-250-04096-1(5)*, 900125483) Feiwel & Friends.

Paré, Roger. Les Chiffres. 2004. (Livres-jeux Ser.). (FRE.). 12p. (J). (gr. -1). pap. *(978-2-89021-654-9(3))* Diffusion du livre Mirabel (DLM).

Rooney, Anne. 50 Amazing Things Kids Need to Know about Math. 2012. (ENG., Illus.). 192p. (J). (gr. 2-7). pap. 12.95 *(978-1-61608-507-0(X)*, 608507, Sky Pony Pr.) Skyhorse Publishing Co., Inc.

Ruffin, Frances E. Creating a City Park: Dividing Three-Digit Numbers by One-Digit Numbers Without Remainders, 1 vol. (Math for the REAL World Ser.). (ENG., Illus.). 24p. (gr. 3-4). 2010. pap. 8.25 *(978-0-8239-8926-3(7)*, f61a8142-e5e0-4c07-8230-f8afd68bf7c1, PowerKids Pr.) 2003. (J). lib. bdg. 26.27 *(978-0-8239-8978-2(X)*, 5324d1f2-d5b9-4ced-84ec-eb50ec765e3a) Rosen Publishing Group, Inc., The.

—Creating a City Park: Dividing Three-digit Numbers by One-digit Numbers Without Remainders. 2009. (PowerMath: Intermediate Ser.). 24p. (gr. 3-4). 45.00 *(978-1-60851-380-2(7)*, PowerKids Pr.) Rosen Publishing Group, Inc., The.

Sargent, Brian. Grandfather's Shape Story. 2006. (Rookie Read-About Math Ser.). (ENG., Illus.). 32p. (J). (gr. -1-3). 20.50 *(978-0-516-29919-8(0)*, Children's Pr.) Scholastic Library Publishing.

School Zone Publishing Company Staff. Math War Multiplication: Multiplication, 56 vols. rev. ed. 2019. (ENG.). 56p. (J). (gr. 3-5). 3.49 *(978-0-88743-287-3(5)*, 0e0251ab-1fc5-48a9-a6a8-aa02b7648602) School Zone Publishing Co.

Schwartz, Linda. Math Critical Thinking, Grades 2-4: Creative Puzzles to Challenge the Brain. VanBlaricum, Pam, ed. Armstrong, Bev & Grayson, Rick, illus. 2005. 64p. (J). pap. 11.99 *(978-0-88160-383-5(X)*, LW-422) Creative Teaching Pr., Inc.

Steck-Vaughn Staff. Math Level H-J: How Big Is a Cat? 2003. (Illus.). pap. *(978-0-7398-7657-2(0))* Steck-Vaughn.

Super Sticker Math. Date not set. 64p. (J). 3.98 *(978-0-7525-9774-4(4))* Parragon, Inc.

Tang, Greg. The Grapes of Math. Briggs, Harry, illus. 2004. (Scholastic Bookshelf Ser.). (ENG.). 40p. (J). (gr. 2-5). pap. 7.99 *(978-0-439-59840-8(0)*, Scholastic Paperbacks) Scholastic, Inc.

—The Grapes of Math: Mind-Stretching Math Riddles. Briggs, Harry, illus. 2004. (Scholastic Bookshelf Ser.). (gr. 2-5). 17.00 *(978-0-7569-3195-7(9))* Perfection Learning Corp.

Thompson, Helen. Travel Math. 2013. (Math 24/7 Ser.: 10). 48p. (J). (gr. 5-18). 19.95 *(978-1-4222-2911-8(4))* Mason Crest.

Tremaine, Jon. Magic with Numbers. 2012. (ENG., Illus.). 32p. (gr. 3-5). pap. 8.95 *(978-1-926853-82-6(2))* Saunders Bk. Co. CAN. Dist: RiverStream Publishing.

Weiss, Ellen. Scholastic News Nonfiction Readers: Math on the Playground. 2007. (Scholastic News Nonfiction Readers Ser.). (ENG., Illus.). 24p. (J). (gr. 1-2). 22.00 *(978-0-531-18533-9(8))* Scholastic Library Publishing.

Yoder, Eric & Yoder, Natalie. One Minute Mysteries: 65 Short Mysteries You Solve with Math! 2010. (One Minute Mysteries Ser.). (ENG., Illus.). 192p. (J). (gr. 5-9). pap. 12.95 *(978-0-9678020-0-8(8))* Platypus Media, L.L.C.

Zaslavsky, Claudia. More Math Games & Activities from Around the World: From Around the World. 2003. (ENG.). 176p. (J). (gr. 4). pap. 16.95 *(978-1-55652-501-8(X))* Chicago Review Pr., Inc.

MATHEMATICAL SETS

see Set Theory

MATHEMATICIANS

Bailey, Gerry & Foster, Karen. Galileo's Telescope. Noyes, Leighton & Radford, Karen, illus. 2008. (Stories of Great People Ser.). (ENG.). 40p. (J). (gr. 3-6). lib. bdg. *(978-0-7787-3694-3(6))*; pap. *(978-0-7787-3716-2(0))* Crabtree Publishing Co.

Bardoe, Cheryl. Nothing Stopped Sophie: The Story of Unshakable Mathematician Sophie Germain. McClintock, Barbara, illus. 2018. (ENG.). 40p. (J). (gr. -1-3). 18.99 *(978-0-316-27820-1(3))* Little, Brown Bks. for Young Readers.

Becker, Helaine. Counting on Katherine: How Katherine Johnson Saved Apollo 13. Phumiruk, Dow, illus. 2018. (ENG.). 40p. (J). 18.99 *(978-1-250-13752-4(7)*, 900178843, Holt, Henry & Co. Bks. For Young Readers) Holt, Henry & Co.

Boone, Mary. Ada Lovelace: A 4D Book. 2018. (STEM Scientists & Inventors Ser.). (ENG., Illus.). 24p. (J). (gr. 1-3). lib. bdg. 27.99 *(978-1-5435-2772-8(8)*, 138222, Capstone Pr.) Capstone.

Borgert-Spaniol, Megan. Math You Can Munch. 2018. (Super Simple Science You Can Snack On Ser.). (ENG., Illus.). 32p. (J). (gr. k-4). lib. bdg. 34.21 *(978-1-5321-1726-8(4)*, 30740, Super SandCastle) ABDO Publishing Co.

Campbell, Josette & Hayhurst, Chris. Euclid: The Father of Geometry, 1 vol. 2015. (Greatest Greek Philosophers Ser.). (ENG., Illus.). 112p. (J). (gr. 7-8). 38.80 *(978-1-4994-6128-2(3)*, 9c535a26-e466-40fe-acb6-9f2504fca345, Rosen Young Adult) Rosen Publishing Group, Inc., The.

Cline-Ransome, Lesa. Counting the Stars: The Story of Katherine Johnson, NASA Mathematician. ón, Raúl, illus. 2019. (ENG.). 32p. (J). (gr. -1-3). 17.99 *(978-1-5344-0475-5(9)*, Simon & Schuster Bks. For Young Readers) Simon & Schuster Bks. For Young Readers.

Coakley, Louis C., ed. Top 101 Mathematicians, 1 vol. 2016. (People You Should Know Ser.). (ENG.). 184p. (J). (gr. 8-8). lib. bdg. 38.84 *(978-1-68048-508-0(3)*, ca783ffd-050d-43fe-8912-1d2454234f83) Rosen Publishing Group, Inc., The.

Coakley, Louis C. & Karamanides, Dimitra. Pythagoras: Mathematician & Mystic, 1 vol. 2015. (Greatest Greek Philosophers Ser.). (ENG., Illus.). 112p. (J). (gr. 7-8). 38.80 *(978-1-4994-6132-9(1)*, ecf0f4c9-b0e9-4345-a709-89fab1ccae09, Rosen Young Adult) Rosen Publishing Group, Inc., The.

Collier, Bruce & Maclachlan, James. Charles Babbage & the Engines of Perfection. 2006. (Illus.). 123p. reprint ed. pap. 12.00 *(978-1-4223-5040-9(1))* DIANE Publishing Co.

Corrigan, Jim. Alan Turing. 2007. (Profiles in Mathematics Ser.). (Illus.). 112p. (J). (gr. 4-7). lib. bdg. 28.95 *(978-1-59935-064-6(5))* Reynolds, Morgan Inc.

Doudna, Kelly. Ada Lovelace: Pioneering Computer Programming. 2017. (STEM Superstar Women Ser.). (ENG., Illus.). 32p. (J). (gr. 3-6). lib. bdg. 32.79 *(978-1-5321-1283-6(1)*, 27607, Checkerboard Library) ABDO Publishing Co.

Faulkner, Nicholas & Hosch, William L., eds. Algebra & Trigonometry, 1 vol. 2017. (Foundations of Math Ser.). (ENG., Illus.). 312p. (J). (gr. 10-10). lib. bdg. 55.59 *(978-1-68048-774-9(4)*, 2cdca200-24cf-448b-8a3d-0b0ffe8f85a3) Rosen Publishing Group, Inc., The.

Feldman, Thea. Katherine Johnson. 2019. (Ready-To-Read Ser.). (ENG.). 47p. (J). (gr. 2-3). 13.89 *(978-1-64310-883-4(2))* Penworthy Co., LLC, The.

—Katherine Johnson. Petersen, Alyssa, illus. 2017. 47p. (J). *(978-1-5182-5284-6(2)*, Simon Spotlight) Simon Spotlight.

—Katherine Johnson: Ready-To-Read Level 3. Petersen, Alyssa, illus. 2017. (You Should Meet Ser.). (ENG.). 48p. (J). (gr. 1-3). 17.99 *(978-1-5344-0341-3(8))*; pap. 4.99 *(978-1-5344-0340-6(X))* Simon Spotlight. (Simon Spotlight).

Gitlin, Marty. A Dream Job As a Sports Statistician, 1 vol. 2017. (Great Careers in the Sports Industry Ser.). (ENG., Illus.). 128p. (J). (gr. 7-7). pap. 21.00 *(978-1-5081-7861-3(5)*, 636db28e-6189-4bec-98f3-c9c860619426) Rosen Publishing Group, Inc., The.

Gow, Mary. Archimedes: Genius Mathematician, 1 vol. 2014. (Genius Scientists & Their Genius Ideas Ser.). (ENG.). 96p. (gr. 5-5). 29.60 *(978-0-7660-6530-7(8)*, 66d31456-42ef-4583-86d3-30cc12bf5526); pap. 13.88 *(978-0-7660-6531-4(6)*, 17475f79-43f4-431a-b7f5-05d0d570eacd) Enslow Publishing, LLC.

—Measuring the Earth: Eratosthenes & His Celestial Geometry, 1 vol. 2009. (Great Minds of Ancient Science & Math Ser.). (ENG., Illus.). 128p. (gr. 4-6). lib. bdg. 35.93 *(978-0-7660-3120-3(9)*, 2a395b0d-971b-4783-8120-df6fdeafd56e) Enslow Publishing, LLC.

Graham, Amy. Astonishing Ancient World Scientists: Eight Great Brains, 1 vol. 2009. (Great Scientists & Famous Inventors Ser.). (ENG., Illus.). 128p. (gr. 6-7). lib. bdg. 37.27 *(978-1-59845-079-8(4)*, 4e5b556f-9694-404a-a25e-3fa0eafcb78a) Enslow Publishing, LLC.

Gunzehauser, Kelly. Find Your Future in Mathematics. 2016. (Bright Futures Press: Find Your Future in STEAM Ser.). (ENG., Illus.). 32p. (J). (gr. 4-6). 32.07 *(978-1-63471-902-5(6)*, 208929) Cherry Lake Publishing.

Hagler, Gina. ADA Lovelace, 1 vol., 1. 2015. (Tech Pioneers Ser.). (ENG.). 112p. (J). (gr. 7-7). 38.80 *(978-1-4994-6282-1(4)*, 8a1c46ec-e990-431e-bbf1-ba5447a98b42, Rosen Young Adult) Rosen Publishing Group, Inc., The.

—Careers for Tech Girls in Math, 1 vol. 2015. (Tech Girls Ser.). (ENG., Illus.). 80p. (J). (gr. 7-8). 37.47 *(978-1-4994-6101-5(1),* bf5e6087-d18f-4787-9e77-9f9903e93af2, Rosen Young Adult) Rosen Publishing Group, Inc., The.

Harris, Duchess & Rowell, Rebecca. Hidden Heroes: The Human Computers of NASA. 2018. (Freedom's Promise Ser.). (ENG.). 48p. (J). (gr. 4-8). lib. bdg. 35.64 *(978-1-5321-1770-1(1),* 30828) ABDO Publishing Co.

Hasan, Heather. Archimedes: The Father of Mathematics. (Library of Greek Philosophers Ser.). 112p. (gr. 6-6). 2009. 66.50 *(978-1-60853-657-3(2),* Rosen Reference) 2005. (ENG., Illus.). (YA). lib. bdg. 39.80 *(978-1-4042-0774-5(0),* 2675632a-6223-4967-9510-cafeed061c03) Rosen Publishing Group, Inc., The.

Heiligman, Deborah. The Boy Who Loved Math: The Improbable Life of Paul Erdos. Pham, LeUyen, illus. 2013. (ENG.). 48p. (J). (gr. -1-2). 19.99 *(978-1-59643-307-6(8),* 900045300) Roaring Brook Pr.

Hightower, Paul W. The Father of Geometry: Euclid & His 3-D World, 1 vol. 2010. (Great Minds of Ancient Science & Math Ser.). (ENG.). 112p. (gr. 4-6). 35.93 *(978-0-7660-3409-9(7),* ec20092a-3330-4214-ba7f-9a705aa08b15) Enslow Publishing, LLC.

—The Greatest Mathematician: Archimedes & His Eureka! Moment, 1 vol. 2009. (Great Minds of Ancient Science & Math Ser.). (ENG., Illus.). 128p. (gr. 4-6). lib. bdg. 35.93 *(978-0-7660-3408-2(9),* 774a4915-ec1a-4510-bf7f-aa0624df4715) Enslow Publishing, LLC.

Hurt, Avery Elizabeth. Ada Lovelace: Computer Programmer & Mathematician, 1 vol. 2017. (History Makers Ser.). (ENG.). 144p. (YA). (gr. 9-9). 47.36 *(978-1-5026-3295-1(0),* 147e5b8d-a96e-41a0-a052-0fc3ae0b6591) Cavendish Square Publishing LLC.

Johnson, Katherine. Reaching for the Moon: The Autobiography of NASA Mathematician Katherine Johnson. 2020. (ENG., Illus.). 272p. (J). (gr. 5). pap. 8.99 *(978-1-5344-4084-5(4),* Atheneum Bks. for Young Readers) Simon & Schuster Children's Publishing.

Jones, Viola & Hasan, Heather. Archimedes: Innovative Mathematician, Engineer, & Inventor, 1 vol. 2015. (Greatest Greek Philosophers Ser.). (ENG., Illus.). 112p. (J). (gr. 7-8). 38.80 *(978-1-4994-6124-4(0),* d67ff58c-961f-4a84-8672-79fea36ce271, Rosen Young Adult) Rosen Publishing Group, Inc., The.

Keating, Susan. Archimedes: Ancient Greek Mathematician. 2013. (People of Importance Ser.: 21). (Illus.). 32p. (J). (gr. 4-18). 19.95 *(978-1-4222-2841-8(X))* Mason Crest.

Kraft Rector, Rebecca. Alan Turing, 1 vol., 1. 2015. (Tech Pioneers Ser.). (ENG.). 112p. (J). (gr. 7-7). 38.80 *(978-1-4994-6280-7(8),* 3eec5ae5-0253-486e-bf62-5554f45c9c4c, Rosen Young Adult) Rosen Publishing Group, Inc., The.

Labrecque, Ellen. Ada Lovelace & Computer Algorithms. 2017. (21st Century Junior Library: Women Innovators Ser.). (ENG., Illus.). 24p. (J). (gr. 2-5). lib. bdg. 29.21 *(978-1-63472-177-6(2),* 209280) Cherry Lake Publishing.

Leech, Bonnie. Geometry's Great Thinkers: The History of Geometry. 2009. (PowerMath: Advanced Proficiency Plus Ser.). 32p. (gr. 5-5). 47.90 *(978-1-60851-355-0(6),* PowerKids Pr.) Rosen Publishing Group, Inc., The.

Leech, Bonnie Coulter. Geometry's Great Thinkers: The History of Geometry, 1 vol. (Math for the REAL World Ser.). (ENG., Illus.). 32p. (gr. 5-5). 2009. pap. 10.00 *(978-1-4042-6073-3(0),* b01ef50a-8904-4c1a-bc1b-a439350b5192) 2006. (YA). lib. bdg. 28.93 *(978-1-4042-3360-7(1),* c7c132fb-5c1a-40da-b703-4428463d1692) Rosen Publishing Group, Inc., The.

Lew, Kristi. ADA Lovelace: Mathematician & First Programmer. 2017. (Britannica Beginner Bios Ser.). (Illus.). 32p. (J). (gr. 6-10). 77.40 *(978-1-5383-0022-0(2))* Rosen Publishing Group, Inc., The.

Lim, Bridget & Brezina, Corona. Al-Khwarizmi, 1 vol. 2016. (Physicians, Scientists, & Mathematicians of the Islamic World Ser.). (ENG., Illus.). 112p. (J). (gr. 6-6). 38.80 *(978-1-5081-7144-7(0),* 56e58821-10bc-41db-9b97-a6b30d1c4887) Rosen Publishing Group, Inc., The.

Loh-Hagan, Virginia. Ada Lovelace. Bane, Jeff, illus. 2018. (Mi Mini Biografía (My Itty-Bitty Bio): My Early Library). (ENG.). 24p. (J). (gr. k-1). pap. 12.79 *(978-1-5341-0815-8(7),* 210624); lib. bdg. 30.64 *(978-1-5341-0716-8(9),* 210623) Cherry Lake Publishing.

—Dorothy Vaughan. Bane, Jeff, illus. 2018. (Mi Mini Biografía (My Itty-Bitty Bio): My Early Library). (ENG.). 24p. (J). (gr. k-1). pap. 12.79 *(978-1-5341-0810-3(6),* 210604); lib. bdg. 30.64 *(978-1-5341-0711-3(8),* 210603) Cherry Lake Publishing.

—Katherine Johnson. Bane, Jeff, illus. 2018. (Mi Mini Biografía (My Itty-Bitty Bio): My Early Library). (ENG.). 24p. (J). (gr. k-1). pap. 12.79 *(978-1-5341-0809-7(2),* 210600); lib. bdg. 30.64 *(978-1-5341-0710-6(X),* 210599) Cherry Lake Publishing.

—Mary Jackson. Bane, Jeff, illus. 2018. (Mi Mini Biografía (My Itty-Bitty Bio): My Early Library). (ENG.). 24p. (J). (gr. k-1). pap. 12.79 *(978-1-5341-0811-0(4),* 210608); lib. bdg. 30.64 *(978-1-5341-0712-0(6),* 210607) Cherry Lake Publishing.

Lucas, Eileen. Charles Babbage & ADA Lovelace: The Pen Pals Who Imagined the First Computer. 2020. (J). pap. *(978-1-9785-1449-2(2))* Enslow Publishing, LLC.

Nichols, Susan. Al-Karaji: Tenth Century Mathematician & Engineer, 1 vol. 2016. (Physicians, Scientists, & Mathematicians of the Islamic World Ser.). (ENG.). 112p. (J). (gr. 6-6). lib. bdg. 38.80 *(978-1-5081-7143-0(2),* feec6450-8f3f-4ba8-81fe-9722e950492a) Rosen Publishing Group, Inc., The.

Pierce, Nick. Ada Lovelace (Women in Science) (Library Edition) Lundie, Isobel, illus. 2019. (Women in Science Ser.). (ENG.). 32p. (J). (gr. 2-3). lib. bdg. 29.00 *(978-0-531-23534-8(3),* Watts, Franklin) Scholastic Library Publishing.

Profiles in Mathematics, vols. 7, vol. 7. Incl. Alan Turing. Corrigan, Jim. 112p. 2007. lib. bdg. 28.95 *(978-1-59935-064-6(5))*; Carl Friedrich Gauss. West, Krista. 112p. 2008. lib. bdg. 28.95 *(978-1-59935-063-9(7))*; René Descartes. Gimbel, Steven. 128p. 2008. lib. bdg. 28.95 *(978-1-59935-060-8(2))*; Sophie Germain. Ornes, Stephen. 112p. 2008. lib. bdg. 28.95 *(978-1-59935-062-2(9))*; Women Mathematicians. Venkatraman, Padma. 160p. 2008. lib. bdg. 28.95 *(978-1-59935-091-2(2))*; (Illus.). (J). (gr. 4-7). 2008. Set lib. bdg. 202.65 *(978-1-59935-093-6(9))* Reynolds, Morgan Inc.

Reed, Jennifer. Computer Scientist Jean Bartik. 2016. (STEM Trailblazer Bios Ser.). (ENG., Illus.). 32p. (J). (gr. 2-5). 26.65 *(978-1-5124-0789-1(5),* 88b6a19d-1254-48db-ba2f-68fcdb02dcb3, Lerner Pubns.) Lerner Publishing Group.

Rissman, Rebecca. Hidden Women: The African-American Mathematicians of NASA Who Helped America Win the Space Race. 2018. (Encounter: Narrative Nonfiction Stories Ser.). (ENG., Illus.). 112p. (J). (gr. 3-7). pap. 9.95 *(978-1-5157-9963-4(8),* 136958, Capstone Pr.) Capstone.

Robinson, Fiona. Ada's Ideas: The Story of Ada Lovelace, the World's First Computer Programmer. 2016. (ENG., Illus.). 40p. (J). (gr. 1-4). 17.95 *(978-1-4197-1872-4(X),* 1103001, Abrams Bks. for Young Readers) Abrams, Inc.

Rooney, Anne. Alan Turing & His Binary Computer Code. 2012. (Miracle Makers Ser.). (ENG., Illus.). 48p. (YA). (gr. 5-8). 27.95 *(978-1-4488-6037-1(7),* Rosen Reference) Rosen Publishing Group, Inc., The.

Schwartz, Heather E. NASA Mathematician Katherine Johnson. 2017. (STEM Trailblazer Bios Ser.). (ENG., Illus.). 32p. (J). (gr. 2-5). 26.65 *(978-1-5124-5703-2(5),* 4b873c43-8f8b-4233-b212-0f0ee2d34fe9, Lerner Pubns.) Lerner Publishing Group.

Shaffer, Jody Jensen. Benjamin Banneker: Self-Made Man. rev. ed. 2016. (Social Studies: Informational Text Ser.). (ENG., Illus.). 32p. (gr. 4-8). pap. 11.99 *(978-1-4938-3082-4(1))* Teacher Created Materials, Inc.

Sheen, Barbara. Careers If You Like Math. 2016. (ENG., Illus.). 80p. (J). (gr. 5-12). *(978-1-68282-004-9(1))* ReferencePoint Pr., Inc.

Sherman, Josepha. Charles Babbage & the Story of the First Computer. 2005. (Uncharted, Unexplored, & Unexplained Ser.). (Illus.). 48p. (J). (gr. 4-8). lib. bdg. 29.95 *(978-1-58415-372-6(5))* Mitchell Lane Pubs.

Shetterly, Margot Lee. Hidden Figures. 2016. (Illus.). 231p. (J). lib. bdg. 18.40 *(978-0-606-39623-3(3))* Turtleback.

—Hidden Figures: The True Story of Four Black Women & the Space Race. Freeman, Laura, illus. 2018. (ENG.). 40p. (J). (gr. -1-3). 18.99 *(978-0-06-274246-9(9),* HarperCollins) HarperCollins Pubs.

—Hidden Figures Young Readers' Edition. 2016. (ENG., Illus.). 240p. (J). (gr. 3-7). 16.99 *(978-0-06-266238-5(4))*; pap. 9.99 *(978-0-06-266237-8(6))* HarperCollins Pubs. (HarperCollins).

Slade, Suzanne. A Computer Called Katherine: How Katherine Johnson Helped Put America on the Moon. Miller Jamison, Veronica, illus. 2019. (ENG.). 40p. (J). (gr. -1-3). 18.99 *(978-0-316-43517-8(1))* Little, Brown Bks. for Young Readers.

Stanley, Diane. Ada Lovelace, Poet of Science: The First Computer Programmer. Hartland, Jessie, illus. 2016. (ENG.). 40p. (J). (gr. -1-3). 18.99 *(978-1-4814-5249-6(5),* Simon & Schuster Bks. For Young Readers) Simon & Schuster Bks. For Young Readers.

Steffens, Bradley. Big Data Analyst. 2017. (ENG.). 64p. (YA). (gr. 5-12). *(978-1-68282-176-3(5))* ReferencePoint Pr., Inc.

Sullivan, Anne Marie. Sir Isaac Newton: Famous English Scientist. 2013. (People of Importance Ser.: 21). (Illus.). 32p. (J). (gr. 4-18). 19.95 *(978-1-4222-2856-2(8))* Mason Crest.

Sullivan, Erin. Mathematical Thinkers & Los Matemáticos: 6 English, 6 Spanish Adaptations, 122 vols., Vol. 2. 2011. (Navigators Ser.). (ENG & SPA.). (J). instr.'s gde. ed. 97.00 net. *(978-1-4108-1773-0(3),* 17733) Benchmark Education Co.

Tent, M. B. W. Emmy Noether: The Mother of Modern Algebra. 2008. (ENG., Illus.). 184p. (C). 40.95 *(978-1-56881-430-8(5),* K00391) AK Peters, Ltd.

Wallmark, Laurie. Ada Byron Lovelace & the Thinking Machine. Chu, April, illus. 2015. (ENG.). 36p. (J). (gr. -1-6). 17.99 *(978-1-939547-20-0(2),* b54fe7fb-0836-4718-bae8-0320acba85be) Creston Bks.

Zannos, Susan. The Life & Times of Archimedes. 2004. (Biography from Ancient Civilizations Ser.). (Illus.). 48p. (J). (gr. 4-8). lib. bdg. 29.95 *(978-1-58415-242-2(7))* Mitchell Lane Pubs.

MATHEMATICS

see also Algebra; Arithmetic; Binary System (Mathematics); Calculus; Geometry; Measurement; Mechanics; Number Theory; Set Theory; Trigonometry

ABDO Publishing Company Staff & Kompelien, Tracy. Math Made Fun. 2007. (Math Made Fun Ser.: 24). 24p. (J). (gr. k-3). 581.04 *(978-1-59928-503-0(7),* SandCastle) ABDO Publishing Co.

Aboff, Marcie. If You Were a Set [LTD Commodities]. Dillard, Sarah, illus. 2010. (Math Fun Ser.). 24p. pap. 3.50 *(978-1-4048-6258-6(7),* Picture Window Bks.) Capstone.

—Math Fun, 6 vols., Set. Dillard, Sarah, illus. Incl. If You Were an Even Number. (ENG., Illus.). 24p. (J). (gr. 2-4). 2008. 28.65 *(978-1-4048-4796-5(0),* 95275, Picture Window Bks.); (Math Fun Ser.). (ENG.). 24p. 2008. 85.95 o.p. *(978-1-4048-4803-0(7),* 151452, Picture Window Bks.) Capstone.

Abramson, Marcie. Painless Math Word Problems. 2nd rev. ed. 2010. (Barron's Painless Ser.). (ENG.). 288p. (YA). (gr. 6-9). pap. 11.99 *(978-0-7641-4335-9(2),* Barron's Educational Series, Inc.) Kaplan Publishing.

Accelerated Curriculum for Mathematics Grade 11 Exit TAKS Teacher Edition. 2005. (Region IV ESC Resources for Mathematics Ser.). spiral bd. *(978-1-932797-25-1(4))* Region 4 Education Service Ctr.

Accelerated Curriculum for Mathematics Grade 5 Student Edition Spanish. 2005. (Region IV ESC Resources for Mathematics Ser.). (SPA.). (J). (gr. 5). stu. ed., spiral bd. *(978-1-932797-83-1(1))* Region 4 Education Service Ctr.

Accelerated Math Learning Cards - Basic Math. 2004. 199.00 *(978-1-59455-122-2(7))* Renaissance Learning, Inc.

Accelerated Math West Virginia State Tagged Grade 3 Library. 2004. cd-rom 1199.00 *(978-1-59455-107-9(3))* Renaissance Learning, Inc.

Accelerated Math West Virginia State Tagged Grade 5 Library. 2004. cd-rom 1199.00 *(978-1-59455-109-3(X))* Renaissance Learning, Inc.

Accelerated Math West Virginia State Tagged Grade 6 Library. 2004. cd-rom 1199.00 *(978-1-59455-110-9(3))* Renaissance Learning, Inc.

Accelerated Math West Virginia State Tagged Grade 7 Library. 2004. cd-rom 1199.00 *(978-1-59455-111-6(1))* Renaissance Learning, Inc.

Accelerated Math West Virginia State Tagged Pre-Algebra Library. 2004. cd-rom 1199.00 *(978-1-59455-112-3(X))* Renaissance Learning, Inc.

ACT Mathematics Victory Student Textbook. 2nd ed. 2005. per. *(978-1-58894-031-5(4))* Cambridge Educational Services, Inc.

Activities for Base Ten Blocks. rev. ed. 2004. (J). per. 9.95 *(978-1-56911-547-3(8))* Learning Resources, Inc.

Activity Cards for Equivalency Cubes. 2004. (J). 12.95 *(978-1-56911-925-9(2))* Learning Resources, Inc.

Adams, Jim, Sr., creator. Math Made Easy As 1+2+3= 2003. (Illus.). 24p. spiral bd. 16.99 *(978-0-9729189-4-7(9))* Adams Publishing.

Adams, Presley. Let's Go to Acadia National Park: Solve Problems Involving the Four Operations, 1 vol. 2014. (InfoMax Math Readers Ser.). (ENG.). 24p. (J). (gr. 3-3). pap. 8.25 *(978-1-4777-4687-5(0),* 8d710430-dae1-4bfa-bb99-3e94c3e59eb3, Rosen Classroom) Rosen Publishing Group, Inc., The.

Adams, Scott. Ben's Bug Collection: Understanding Addition. 2013. (Rosen Math Readers Ser.). (ENG.). 16p. (J). (gr. k-1). pap. 42.00 *(978-1-4777-1621-2(1))*; (Illus.). pap. 7.00 *(978-1-4777-1620-5(3),* 1a95f066-0d4c-4cc1-89e6-e0f0ae8e816d) Rosen Publishing Group, Inc., The. (Rosen Classroom).

AdB?ge, Emma. Outdoor Math: Fun Activities for Every Season. AdB?ge, Emma, illus. 2016. (ENG., Illus.). 26p. (J). (gr. k-3). 15.95 *(978-1-77138-612-8(6))* Kids Can Pr., Ltd. CAN. Dist: Hachette Bk. Group.

Add-On Package. 2003. 129.95 *(978-0-673-76011-1(1))*; 187.95 *(978-0-673-76007-4(3))*; 187.95 *(978-0-673-76009-8(X))* Celebration Pr.

Adding. 2003. (Gold Star Workbooks Ser.). (Illus.). 32p. (J). 2.98 *(978-1-4054-1190-5(2))*; 2.98 *(978-1-4054-1191-2(0))* Parragon, Inc.

Adler, David A. Fun with Roman Numerals. 2009. (ENG., Illus.). 32p. (J). (gr. 1-4). pap. 7.99 *(978-0-8234-2255-5(0))* Holiday Hse., Inc.

—Let's Estimate: A Book about Estimating & Rounding Numbers. Miller, Edward, illus. 32p. (J). (gr. 1-4). 2018. pap. 8.99 *(978-0-8234-4017-7(6))* 2017. (ENG.). 17.95 *(978-0-8234-3668-2(3))* Holiday Hse., Inc.

Advanced Mathematics: Precalculus with Discrete Mathematics & Data Analysis. 2003. (gr. 11-12). tchr. ed. *(978-0-618-25039-4(5),* 2-06020) Holt McDougal.

Alaina, Maria. Adding Animals, 1 vol. 2013. (Wonder Readers Next Steps: Math Ser.). (ENG.). 20p. (J). (gr. -1-1). lib. bdg. 25.32 *(978-1-4765-0032-4(0),* 121950, Capstone Pr.) Capstone.

—Both Sides Are the Same, 1 vol. 2011. (Wonder Readers Early Level Ser.). (ENG.). 16p. (J). (gr. -1-1). pap. 6.25 *(978-1-4296-7797-4(X),* 117969) Capstone.

—Estimating, 1 vol. 2011. (Wonder Readers Early Level Ser.). (ENG.). 16p. (J). (gr. -1-1). pap. 6.25 *(978-1-4296-7802-5(X),* 117974, Capstone Pr.) Capstone.

—Patterns in Nature, 1 vol. 2011. (Wonder Readers Early Level Ser.). (ENG.). 16p. (gr. -1-1). (J). pap. 6.25 *(978-1-4296-7815-5(1),* 117987); pap. 35.94 *(978-1-4296-8138-4(1),* Capstone Pr.) Capstone.

Alexander, Emmett. Tamaños / Sort It by Size, 1 vol. de la Vega, Eida, tr. 2015. (Vamos a Agrupar Por... / Sort It Out! Ser.). (ENG & SPA., Illus.). 24p. (J). (gr. k-1). lib. bdg. 24.27 *(978-1-4824-3219-0(6),* ba554819-0105-4b24-8f22-acbe2285b754) Stevens, Gareth Publishing LLLP.

Alpha Omega Publishing Staff. Mathematics, 2 bks., Set. 2004. (Illus.). pap. 59.95 *(978-0-7403-0313-5(9),* JKC120, Horizons) Alpha Omega Pubns., Inc.

Amazing World of Science & Math. 2016. (Amazing World of Science & Math Ser.). 48p. (gr. 5-5). pap. 56.20 *(978-1-4824-5335-5(5))*; (ENG.). lib. bdg. 134.40 *(978-1-4824-4970-9(6),* 9d4e086f-e589-40ba-ae53-e2fd73bdddf3) Stevens, Gareth Publishing LLLP.

America's Math Teacher. Mastering Essential Math Skills Book Two: Middle Grades/High School: 20 Minutes a Day to Success. 2007. (Mastering Essential Math Skills Ser.). (Illus.). 127p. (J). (gr. 6-13). pap. 39.95 *(978-0-9821901-1-1(5))* Math Essentials.

An, Vickie. First Responders: Expressions, Equations, & Inequalities. 2019. (Mathematics in the Real World Ser.). (ENG., Illus.). 32p. (gr. 5-8). pap. 11.99 *(978-1-4258-5886-5(4))* Teacher Created Materials, Inc.

Analysis II: Differenzierbarkeit von Funktionen und Kurvendiskussion. (Duden Abiturhilfen Ser.). (GER.). 112p. (YA). (gr. 11-12). *(978-3-411-70172-8(2))* Bibliographisches Institut & F. A. Brockhaus AG DEU. Dist: International Bk. Import Service, Inc.

Anderson, Lynne. The Aquarium Adds Up: Set Of 6. 2011. (Early Connections Ser.). (J). pap. 37.00 net. *(978-1-4108-1070-0(4))* Benchmark Education Co.

Andreescu, Titu & Kisacanin, Branislav. Math Leads for Mathletes, Book 2. 2018. (ENG., Illus.). 230p. 49.95 *(978-0-9968745-5-7(0),* P583111) XYZ Pr.

Andres, Ken & Johnson, Diane. Math Go Figure Student Book. 2004. 160p. per. *(978-1-59318-179-6(5))* Cambium Education, Inc.

Andrews, Ken & Johnson, Diane. You Can Be Algebra Ready. 2003. Pt. 1. 244p. spiral bd. *(978-1-57035-848-7(6),* 185STU1)Pt. 2. 256p. spiral bd. *(978-1-57035-849-4(4),* 185STU2) Cambium Education, Inc.

Andriani, Renee. Mall Mania. 2006. (MathStart 2 Ser.). (ENG., Illus.). 40p. (J). (gr. 1-4). pap. 6.99 *(978-0-06-055777-5(X),* HarperCollins) HarperCollins Pubs.

Anghileri, Julia. Children's Mathematical Thinking in Primary Years. 2005. (ENG., Illus.). 192p. 39.95 *(978-0-8264-7911-2(1),* 900099431, Continuum) Bloomsbury Academic & Professional.

Apple, Michael W. Rosie the Counting Rabbit. (J). (gr. k-2). 75.00 *(978-0-669-13447-6(3))* Houghton Mifflin Harcourt School Pubs.

Applied Mathematics, 12 vols. 2016. (Applied Mathematics Ser.). (ENG.). 128p. (gr. 9-9). lib. bdg. 284.16 *(978-1-5026-2003-3(0),* 6e8f867e-e3c5-4104-b299-8a73d04295aa, Cavendish Square) Cavendish Square Publishing LLC.

Arroyo, Sheri L. & Stewart, Rhea A. How Crime Fighters Use Math. 2009. (Math in the Real World Ser.). (ENG.). 32p. (gr. 4-6). 28.00 *(978-1-60413-602-9(2),* P466912, Chelsea Clubhse.) Infobase Holdings, Inc.

—How Race Car Drivers Use Math. 2009. (Math in the Real World Ser.). (ENG.). 32p. (gr. 4-6). 28.00 *(978-1-60413-609-8(X),* P466917, Chelsea Clubhse.) Infobase Holdings, Inc.

Arthur's Christmas Cookies. 2003. 22.95 *(978-0-673-75906-1(7))* Celebration Pr.

Aseervatham, Aloysius & Aseervatham, Leslie. Graduated Numerical Skills: For the Young Scholar. 2011. (Illus.). 268p. pap. 74.94 *(978-1-4567-7355-7(0))* AuthorHouse.

Asker, Nick & Morrison, Karen. GCSE Mathematics for OCR Foundation Homework Book. 2015. (GCSE Mathematics OCR Ser.). (ENG., Illus.). 118p. pap. 12.65 *(978-1-107-49700-9(0))* Cambridge Univ. Pr.

Atkinson, Sue. New Cambridge Mathematics. 2005. (WEL., Illus.). 32p. pap. *(978-1-86085-267-1(X))* ICA Video.

Austin, Judi. Making My Breakfast: Learning the Sequential Steps of a Process, 1 vol. 2010. (Math for the REAL World Ser.). (ENG.). 12p. (gr. 1-2). pap. 5.90 *(978-0-8239-8889-1(9),* b7f9c684-22c8-47c3-9aeb-4f436191fd13, Rosen Classroom) Rosen Publishing Group, Inc., The.

Avenues PreK Level: Plastic Magnetic Numbers. (gr. -1-12). 11.04 *(978-0-7362-2467-3(X))* CENGAGE Learning.

Awal, Pia. Travel Math, 1 vol. 2009. (Math Alive! Ser.). (ENG., Illus.). 32p. (J). (gr. 4-4). lib. bdg. 31.21 *(978-0-7614-3217-3(5),* d4112795-25d1-4f4b-819b-d56afdd269e8) Cavendish Square Publishing LLC.

Baker, David & Kervegant, Ffion. Allwedd Mathemateg 71. 2005. (WEL., Illus.). 416p. pap. *(978-1-85644-427-9(9))* CAA.

—Allwedd Mathemateg 83. 2005. (WEL., Illus.). 382p. pap. *(978-1-85644-576-4(3))* CAA.

—Allwedd Mathemateg TGAU. 2005. (WEL., Illus.). 508p. pap. *(978-1-85644-862-8(2))* CAA.

Baker, David, et al. Allwedd Mathemateg TGAU. Jones, Eirian, ed. Kervegant, Ffion, tr. 2005. (WEL., Illus.). 468p. pap. *(978-1-85644-863-5(0))* CAA.

Baker, Linda R. Learning Division with Puppies & Kittens, 1 vol. 2017. (Math Fun with Puppies & Kittens Ser.). (ENG.). 32p. (gr. 1-2). pap. 11.52 *(978-0-7660-9073-6(6),* d9007288-0d3a-42fc-b035-337beb19ccbc) Enslow Publishing, LLC.

—Learning Multiplication with Puppies & Kittens, 1 vol. 2017. (Math Fun with Puppies & Kittens Ser.). (ENG.). 32p. (gr. 1-2). pap. 11.52 *(978-0-7660-9072-9(8),* 019ce23a-19a4-45c0-8d15-7bdec445e714) Enslow Publishing, LLC.

Baker, Linda R., contrib. by. Using Math in Cooking, 1 vol. 2017. (Math You Will Actually Use Ser.). (ENG.). 48p. (J). (gr. 5-5). pap. 12.75 *(978-1-4994-3856-7(7),* 208c3c56-303c-4442-a1a8-99381c822832, Rosen Central) Rosen Publishing Group, Inc., The.

Ball, Barbara & Ball, Derek. Task Maths Interactive 1: Sequence Machines. 2005. (ENG.). cd-rom 190.00 *(978-1-84565-124-4(3))* Cambridge Univ. Pr.

—Task Maths Interactive 3: Is it Possible? 2006. (ENG.). cd-rom 190.00 *(978-1-84565-946-2(5))* Cambridge Univ. Pr.

—Task Maths Interactive 4: Number Pyramids. 2006. (ENG.). cd-rom 177.00 *(978-1-84565-947-9(3))* Cambridge Univ. Pr.

Ball, Susan, et al. Formula One Mathematics Gold. 2003. (ENG., Illus.). 216p. pap., pupil's gde. ed. 39.50 *(978-0-340-86932-1(1),* Hodder Education) Hodder Education Group GBR. Dist: Trans-Atlantic Pubns., Inc.

—Formula One Maths Gold B. 2004. (ENG., Illus.). 240p. pap., pupil's gde. ed. 39.50 *(978-0-340-86933-8(X),* Hodder Education) Hodder Education Group GBR. Dist: Trans-Atlantic Pubns., Inc.

Bando Irvin, Barbara. Math Readiness K-1. deluxe ed. 2019. (ENG.). 64p. (J). (gr. k-1). pap. 4.49 *(978-1-58947-322-5(1),* a06aa833-1210-4cc2-aa8a-a13436ffd617) School Zone Publishing Co.

Bardos, Lazlo C. Amazing Math Projects. Carbaugh, Samuel, illus. 2010. (Build It Yourself Ser.). (ENG.). 128p. (J). (gr. 3-7). pap. 15.95 *(978-1-934670-57-6(X),* aeb8a97c-7d69-4cd6-8e36-5baae1e1c550) Nomad Pr.

—Amazing Math Projects: Projects You Can Build Yourself. Carbaugh, Samuel, illus. 2010. (Build It Yourself Ser.). (ENG.). 128p. (J). (gr. 3-7). 21.95 *(978-1-934670-58-3(8),* 9a5e5e78-ab61-443d-919d-dac567c0ae62) Nomad Pr.

Barker, Lori & Quinlan, Nola. On the Road: Ratios & Proportions. rev. ed. 2012. (Mathematics in the Real World Ser.). (ENG.). 32p. (gr. 5-8). pap. 11.99 *(978-1-4333-3450-4(X))* Teacher Created Materials, Inc.

—Our New Car. rev. ed. 2012. (Mathematics in the Real World Ser.). (ENG.). 32p. (gr. 5-8). pap. 11.99 *(978-1-4333-3451-1(8))* Teacher Created Materials, Inc.

Barnes, John, et al. Science, Maths & Technology. 2003. (ENG., Illus.). 184p. pap. *(978-0-7487-7121-9(2))* Nelson Thornes Ltd.

Barnett, Carne S., et al. General Math. 128p. (YA). (gr. 7-12). pap. 33.95 *(978-0-201-25188-3(4))* Globe Fearon Educational Publishing.

—Pre-Algebra. 152p. (YA). (gr. 7-12). pap. 33.95 *(978-0-201-25976-6(1))* Globe Fearon Educational Publishing.

Baron, Jessica. What's in the Garden? Learning to Compare Two Sets of Objects, 1 vol. 2010. (Math for the REAL World Ser.). (ENG., Illus.). 8p. (gr. k-1). pap. 5.15 *(978-0-8239-8860-0(0),* b191e9d6-405e-412d-b552-eee25bfe1bde) Rosen Publishing Group, Inc., The.

Barron's Educational Series, Barron's Educational. Common Core Success Grade 1 Math: Preparing Students for a Brilliant Future. 2015. (Barron's Common Core Success

Ser.). (ENG., Illus.). 144p. (gr. 1-1). pap. 12.99 *(978-1-4380-0670-3(5)*, Barron's Educational Series, Inc.) Kaplan Publishing.

—Common Core Success Grade 2 Math: Preparing Students for a Brilliant Future. 2015. (Barron's Common Core Success Ser.). (ENG., Illus.). 144p. (gr. 2-2). pap. 12.99 *(978-1-4380-0672-7(1)*, Barron's Educational Series, Inc.) Kaplan Publishing.

—Common Core Success Grade 6 Math: Preparing Students for a Brilliant Future. 2015. (Barron's Common Core Success Ser.). (ENG., Illus.). 208p. (gr. 6-6). pap. 12.99 *(978-1-4380-0680-2(2)*, Barron's Educational Series, Inc.) Kaplan Publishing.

Barth, April. Mira nuestros Patrones. 2010. (Rising Readers Ser.). (SPA.). (J). 3.49 *(978-1-60719-661-7(1))* Newmark Learning LLC.

Baseball Math Kindergarten Workbook. 2006. (J). *(978-0-9787458-0-6(9))* Sport Workbooks.

Basher, Simon & Green, Dan. Basher Basics: Math: A Book You Can Count On. Basher, Simon, illus. 2010. (Basher Basics Ser.). (ENG., Illus.). 64p. (J). (gr. 3-7). pap. 8.99 *(978-0-7534-6419-9(5)*, 900066948, Kingfisher) Roaring Brook Pr.

Basic Facts To 18 (Gr. 2-3) 2003. (J). *(978-1-58232-084-7(5))* ECS Learning Systems, Inc.

Basic Facts to 18 Spanish Version. 2007. (J). per. *(978-1-58232-153-0(1))* ECS Learning Systems, Inc.

Basic Math Skills, Chapter 2, Activities. 2005. (Illus.). 52p. (YA). pap. 5.00 *(978-1-59476-036-5(5))* Paradigm Accelerated Curriculum.

Basic Math Skills, Chapter 2, Text. 2005. (Illus.). 72p. (YA). pap. 7.00 *(978-1-59476-024-2(1))* Paradigm Accelerated Curriculum.

Basic Math Skills, Chapter 3, Activities. 2005. (Illus.). 42p. (YA). pap. 5.00 *(978-1-59476-037-2(3))* Paradigm Accelerated Curriculum.

Basic Math Skills, Chapter 3, Text. 2005. (Illus.). 68p. (YA). pap. 7.00 *(978-1-59476-025-9(X))* Paradigm Accelerated Curriculum.

Basic Math Skills, Chapter 4, Activities. 2005. (Illus.). 48p. (YA). pap. 5.00 *(978-1-59476-038-9(1))* Paradigm Accelerated Curriculum.

Basic Math Skills, Chapter 4, Text. 2005. (Illus.). 70p. (YA). pap. 7.00 *(978-1-59476-026-6(8))* Paradigm Accelerated Curriculum.

Basic Math Skills, Chapter 5, Activities. 2005. (Illus.). 40p. (YA). pap. 5.00 *(978-1-59476-039-6(X))* Paradigm Accelerated Curriculum.

Basic Math Skills, Chapter 5, Text. 2005. (Illus.). 62p. (YA). pap. 7.00 *(978-1-59476-027-3(6))* Paradigm Accelerated Curriculum.

Basic Math Skills, Chapter 6, Activities. 2005. (Illus.). 52p. (YA). pap. 5.00 *(978-1-59476-040-2(3))* Paradigm Accelerated Curriculum.

Basic Math Skills, Chapter 6, Text. 2005. (Illus.). 70p. (YA). pap. 7.00 *(978-1-59476-028-0(4))* Paradigm Accelerated Curriculum.

Basiswissen Mathematik zur Physik. (Duden Abiturhilfen Ser.). (GER.). 96p. (YA). (gr. 11-13). *(978-3-411-04841-0(7))* Bibliographisches Institut & F. A. Brockhaus AG DEU. Dist: International Bk. Import Service, Inc.

Bear's Book of Numbers. 2004. 12p. (J). bds. 2.99 *(978-1-85997-429-2(5))* Byeway Bks.

Beck, Esther & Doudna, Kelly. Please Don't Laugh, I Can Use a Graph! 2007. (Science Made Simple Ser.). (Illus.). 24p. (J). (gr. k-3). lib. bdg. 24.21 *(978-1-59928-614-3(9)*, SandCastle) ABDO Publishing Co.

Beck, Ray, et al. Practicing Basic Skills in Math: Grades 2-3. 2004. (One-Minute Fluency Builders Ser.). 560p. (gr. 2-3). per. 62.95 *(978-1-59318-001-0(2)*, 237MATH2-3) Cambium Education, Inc.

—Practicing Basic Skills in Math: Grades 4-5. 2004. (One-Minute Fluency Builders Ser.). 592p. (gr. 4-5). per. 62.95 *(978-1-59318-002-7(0)*, 237MATH4-5) Cambium Education, Inc.

—Practicing Basic Skills in Math: Grades 6-8. 2004. (One-Minute Fluency Builders Ser.). 558p. (gr. 6-8). per. 62.95 *(978-1-59318-003-4(9)*, 237MATH6-8) Cambium Education, Inc.

—Practicing Basic Skills in Math: Grades K-1. 2004. (One-Minute Fluency Builders Ser.). 352p. (gr. k-1). per. 49.95 *(978-1-59318-000-3(4)*, 237MATHK-1) Cambium Education, Inc.

—Practicing Basic Skills in Math: Secondary Remedial. 2004. (One-Minute Fluency Builders Ser.). 766p. per. 69.49 *(978-1-59318-004-1(7)*, 237MATHREM) Cambium Education, Inc.

Becker, Helaine. Lines, Bars & Circles: How William Playfair Invented Graphs. Tremblay, Marie-Eve & Tremblay, Marie-Ève, illus. 2017. (ENG.). 36p. (J). (gr. 1-4). 17.95 *(978-1-77138-570-1(7))* Kids Can Pr., Ltd. CAN. Dist: Hachette Bk. Group.

Beers, Jack. Anchors Grade 1. 2003. (Voyages Ser.). (J). (gr. 1). stu. ed., per. 11.95 *(978-1-58830-345-5(4))* Metropolitan Teaching & Learning Co.

—Anchors Grade 1 SP. 2004. (Voyages Ser.). (J). (gr. 1). stu. ed., per. 16.53 *(978-1-58830-990-7(8))* Metropolitan Teaching & Learning Co.

—Anchors Grade 2. 2003. (Voyages Ser.). (J). (gr. 2). stu. ed., per. 13.95 *(978-1-58830-346-2(2))* Metropolitan Teaching & Learning Co.

—Anchors Grade 2 SP. 2004. (Voyages Ser.). (J). (gr. 2). stu. ed., per. 16.53 *(978-1-58830-991-4(6))* Metropolitan Teaching & Learning Co.

—Anchors Grade 3. 2003. (Voyages Ser.). (J). (gr. 3). stu. ed., per. 13.95 *(978-1-58830-347-9(0))* Metropolitan Teaching & Learning Co.

—Anchors Grade 3 SP. 2004. (Voyages Ser.). (J). (gr. 3). stu. ed., per. 16.53 *(978-1-58830-992-1(4))* Metropolitan Teaching & Learning Co.

—Anchors Grade 4. 2003. (Voyages Ser.). (J). (gr. 4). stu. ed., per. 13.95 *(978-1-58830-348-6(9))* Metropolitan Teaching & Learning Co.

—Anchors Grade 5 Student Edition. 2003. (Voyages Ser.). (J). (gr. 5). per. 13.95 *(978-1-58830-470-4(1))* Metropolitan Teaching & Learning Co.

—Bridges-Blue. 2003. (Metro Math Bridges Ser.). (J). (gr. 8). stu. ed., per. 13.95 *(978-1-58830-191-8(5))* Metropolitan Teaching & Learning Co.

—Bridges-Gold. 2003. (Metro Math Bridges Ser.). (gr. 7). tchr. ed., per. 19.95 *(978-1-58830-613-5(5))* Metropolitan Teaching & Learning Co.

—Bridges-Red. 2003. (Metro Math Bridges Ser.). (J). (gr. 6). stu. ed., per. 13.95 *(978-1-58830-190-1(7))* Metropolitan Teaching & Learning Co.

Beissinger, Janet. The Cryptoclub Workbook: Using Mathematics to Make & Break Secret Codes. 2018. (ENG.). 144p. (C). 215.00 *(978-1-138-41314-6(3)*, K36351) AK Peters, Ltd.

Beissinger, Janet & Pless, Vera. The Cryptoclub: Using Mathematics to Make & Break Secret Codes. 2006. (ENG., Illus.). 200p. (C). pap. 66.00 *(978-1-56881-223-6(X)*, K00700, A K Peters/CRC Pr.) CRC Pr. LLC.

Bellos, Alex & Harriss, Edmund. Visions of the Universe: A Coloring Journey Through Math's Great Mysteries. 2016. (ENG., Illus.). 144p. pap. 14.95 *(978-1-61519-367-7(7)*, 779367) Experiment LLC, The.

Benchmark Education Company, LLC Staff, compiled by. Math Standards Set. 2005. spiral bd. 3950.00 *(978-1-4108-5456-8(6))* Benchmark Education Co.

—Math Strands Set. 2005. spiral bd. 695.00 *(978-1-4108-5561-9(9))*; spiral bd. 2580.00 *(978-1-4108-5458-2(2))* Benchmark Education Co.

—Math Texts Set. 2005. spiral bd. 750.00 *(978-1-4108-3827-8(7))*; spiral bd. 95.00 *(978-1-4108-3837-7(4))*; spiral bd. 100.00 *(978-1-4108-3836-0(6))*; spiral bd. 335.00 *(978-1-4108-3834-6(X))*; spiral bd. 835.00 *(978-1-4108-3832-2(3))*; spiral bd. 3685.00 *(978-1-4108-3821-6(8))*; (J). spiral bd. 575.00 *(978-1-4108-5332-5(2))* Benchmark Education Co.

—My First Reader's Theater Lap Books. 2009. (My First Reader's Theater Ser.). (J). (gr. k-1). 575.00 *(978-1-4108-8455-8(4))* Benchmark Education Co.

—Numbers & Operations. 2005. spiral bd. 615.00 *(978-1-4108-3881-0(1))*; spiral bd. 120.00 *(978-1-4108-5448-3(5))*; spiral bd. 120.00 *(978-1-4108-5859-7(6))*; spiral bd. 905.00 *(978-1-4108-5858-0(8))*; spiral bd. 95.00 *(978-1-4108-3911-4(7))*; spiral bd. 75.00 *(978-1-4108-3912-1(5))*; spiral bd. 50.00 *(978-1-4108-3907-7(9))*; spiral bd. 75.00 *(978-1-4108-3906-0(0))*; spiral bd. 75.00 *(978-1-4108-3905-3(2))*; spiral bd. 75.00 *(978-1-4108-3904-6(4))*; spiral bd. 370.00 *(978-1-4108-3890-2(0))*; spiral bd. 695.00 *(978-1-4108-3889-6(7))*; spiral bd. 420.00 *(978-1-4108-3882-7(X))*; spiral bd. 1020.00 *(978-1-4108-4509-2(5))*; spiral bd. 1095.00 *(978-1-4108-5447-6(7))* Benchmark Education Co.

—Numbers & Operations: Theme Set. 2006. (J). spiral bd. 258.00 *(978-1-4108-7094-0(4))* Benchmark Education Co.

—Spanish Math Standard Sets. 2005. spiral bd. 2775.00 *(978-1-4108-5867-2(7))* Benchmark Education Co.

—Using Maps, Graphs & Charts: Theme Set. 2006. (J). 109.00 *(978-1-4108-7091-9(X))* Benchmark Education Co.

Bennett, Clinton. Math: Chapter Resource: Indiana Middle School Edition. 4th ed. 2004. (J). 60.40 *(978-0-03-070979-1(2))* Harcourt Schl. Pubs.

—Math: Chapter Resources: Illinois Middle School Edition. 4th ed. 2004. (J). 58.60 *(978-0-03-070978-4(4))* Harcourt Schl. Pubs.

—Math: Chapter Resources: New York Middle School Edition. 4th ed. 2004. (J). 58.60 *(978-0-03-070981-4(4))* Harcourt Schl. Pubs.

—Math: Chapter Resourses: Florida Middle School Edition. 4th ed. 2004. (J). 60.40 *(978-0-03-070977-7(6))* Harcourt Schl. Pubs.

Bernardo, Kat. Stem: The Science of Travel: Multiplication (Grade 3) 2017. (Mathematics in the Real World Ser.). (ENG., Illus.). 32p. (J). (gr. 3-4). pap. 11.99 *(978-1-4807-5797-4(7))* Teacher Created Materials, Inc.

Berry, Minta. Building Sets of Ten. Crabtree Publishing Staff, ed. 2011. (My Path to Math Ser.: No. 36). (ENG.). 24p. (J). pap. *(978-0-7787-5266-0(6))* Crabtree Publishing Co.

Bertola, Linda, ed. Mad for Math, Grade 5. Baruzzi, Agnese, illus. 2018. (Math Adventures Ser.). (ENG.). 72p. (J). (gr. 5). pap. 9.95 *(978-1-4114-7909-8(2)*, Spark Publishing Group) Sterling Publishing Co., Inc.

Bertoletti, John C. & Stewart, Rhea A. How Baseball Managers Use Math. 2009. (Math in the Real World Ser.). (ENG.). 32p. (gr. 4-6). 28.00 *(978-1-60413-604-3(9)*, P466910, Chelsea Clubhse.) Infobase Holdings, Inc.

—How Fashion Designers Use Math. 2009. (Math in the Real World Ser.). (ENG.). 32p. (gr. 4-6). 28.00 *(978-1-60413-606-7(5)*, P466914, Chelsea Clubhse.) Infobase Holdings, Inc.

Besel, Jennifer M. Lions & Tigers & Graphs! Oh My! 2011. (Data Mania Ser.). (ENG.). 24p. (gr. 1-2). pap. 41.70 *(978-1-4296-6466-0(5)*, Capstone Pr.) Capstone.

Beth, Georgia & Marzocchi, Alison. Money Matters: School Fundraisers: Problem Solving with Ratios. 2019. (Mathematics in the Real World Ser.). (ENG., Illus.). 32p. (gr. 5-8). pap. 11.99 *(978-1-4258-5880-3(5))* Teacher Created Materials, Inc.

Big Book Tote Bag, 2, Pack. 2003. (Metro Reading Ser.). (J). (gr. 12). 26.45 *(978-1-58120-613-5(5))* Metropolitan Teaching & Learning Co.

Blanchard, Emma. Seeds I See: Work with 11-19 to Gain Foundations for Place Value. 2013. (Rosen Math Readers Ser.). (ENG.). 16p. (J). (gr. k-1). pap. 42.00 *(978-1-4777-1606-9(8))*; (Illus.). pap. 7.00 *(978-1-4777-1605-2(X)*, 1d65d968-7ed5-4152-aedc-77b62fd3c96e) Rosen Publishing Group, Inc., The. (Rosen Classroom).

Blane, Francisco. Stripes at the Beach: Lap Book. 2009. (My First Reader's Theater Set B Ser.). (J). 28.00 *(978-1-60634-988-5(0))* Benchmark Education Co.

Blask, Tina. I Can Help My Teacher: Use Place Value & Properties of Operation to Add, 1 vol. 2013. (InfoMax Math Readers Ser.). (ENG.). 24p. (J). (gr. 1-1). pap. 8.25 *(978-1-4777-2198-8(3)*, 07054a84-9bbc-4105-ad48-eccefc64263a, Rosen Classroom) Rosen Publishing Group, Inc., The.

—I Can Help My Teacher: Use Place Value & Properties of Operations to Add. 2013. (InfoMax Math Readers Ser.). (ENG.). 24p. (J). (gr. 1-2). pap. 49.50 *(978-1-4777-2199-5(1)*, Rosen Classroom) Rosen Publishing Group, Inc., The.

Block, Cathy Collins & Mangieri, John N. Scholastic Success with Reading & Math Jumbo Workbook, 1 vol. 2005. (ENG.). 320p. (gr. 3-3). pap., wbk. ed. 14.99 *(978-0-439-78602-7(9))*; (Illus.). (gr. 2-2). pap., wbk. ed. 14.99 *(978-0-439-78601-0(0))* Scholastic, Inc. (Teaching Resources).

Blundell, Gillian & Graham, Noel. Problem Solving Activities with Mottik. (Illus.). 64p. (J). (gr. k-4). pap. 12.50 *(978-1-871098-21-1(1))* Claire Pubns. GBR. Dist: Parkwest Pubns., Inc.

Bodach, Vijaya Khisty. Gráficas Circulares. 2012. (Hacer Gráficas/Making Graphs Ser.).Tr. of Pie Graphs. (MUL.). 32p. (gr. 1-2). pap. 47.70 *(978-1-4296-8540-5(9)*, Capstone Pr.) Capstone.

—Gráficas Circulares/Pie Graphs. 2012. (Hacer Gráficas/Making Graphs Ser.).Tr. of Pie Graphs. (MUL.). 32p. (J). (gr. -1-2). pap. 8.10 *(978-1-4296-8539-9(5)*, 118520, Capstone Pr.) Capstone.

—Gráficas de Barras. 2012. (Hacer Gráficas/Making Graphs Ser.).Tr. of Bar Graphs. (MUL.). 32p. (gr. 1-2). pap. 47.70 *(978-1-4296-8543-6(3)*, Capstone Pr.) Capstone.

—Gráficas de Barras/Bar Graphs. (Hacer Gráficas/Making Graphs Ser.). (MUL.). 32p. (J). (gr. -1-2). 2012. pap. 8.10 *(978-1-4296-8542-9(5)*, 118521) 2010. lib. bdg. 27.99 *(978-1-4296-6100-3(3)*, 115124) Capstone. (Capstone Pr.).

—Hacer Gráficas. 2012. (Hacer Gráficas/Making Graphs Ser.).Tr. of Making Graphs. (MUL.). 32p. (gr. 1-2). pap. 190.80 *(978-1-4296-8549-8(2)*, Capstone Pr.) Capstone.

—Pictografías/Pictographs. 2012. (Hacer Gráficas/Making Graphs Ser.). (MUL.). 32p. (gr. 1-2). pap. 47.70 *(978-1-4296-8545-0(X)*, Capstone Pr.) Capstone.

—Tableros de Conteo. 2012. (Hacer Gráficas/Making Graphs Ser.).Tr. of Tally Charts. (MUL.). 32p. (gr. 1-2). pap. 47.70 *(978-1-4296-8547-4(6)*, Capstone Pr.) Capstone.

—Tableros de Conteo/Tally Charts. 2012. (Hacer Gráficas/Making Graphs Ser.). (MUL.). 32p. (J). (gr. -1-2). pap. 8.10 *(978-1-4296-8546-7(8)*, 118523, Capstone Pr.) Capstone.

Bolster. Mathematics Grade 3. (Illus.). (J). pap., stu. ed. 6.59 *(978-0-673-11812-7(6))* Addison-Wesley Educational Pubs., Inc.

Book Company, Popular. Complete Math Workout, Volume 7. 2008. 271p. (J). pap. *(978-1-897164-49-5(1))* Popular Bk. Co. (Canada) Ltd.

—Complete Math Workout, Volume 8. 2008. 271p. (J). pap. *(978-1-897164-50-1(5))* Popular Bk. Co. (Canada) Ltd.

Books are Fun Exclusive Start Math, 4, Bk. 2, Set. 2005. (J). lib. bdg. *(978-1-59566-163-0(8))* QEB Publishing Inc.

Boothroyd, Jennifer. Grouping. 2007. (First Step Nonfiction — Early Math Ser.). (ENG., Illus.). 8p. (J). (gr. k-2). pap. 5.99 *(978-0-8225-6826-1(8)*, 3591667f-1fbe-461c-9c2c-a508440b5178) Lerner Publishing Group.

Borgert-Spaniol, Megan. Math You Can Munch. 2018. (Super Simple Science You Can Snack On Ser.). (ENG., Illus.). 32p. (J). (gr. k-4). lib. bdg. 34.21 *(978-1-5321-1726-8(4)*, 30740, Super SandCastle) ABDO Publishing Co.

Borovsky, Ivan. Our Trip to the Ocean: Understand Place Value. 2013. (InfoMax Math Readers Ser.). (ENG.). 24p. (J). (gr. 1-2). pap. 49.50 *(978-1-4777-2131-5(2))*; (Illus.). pap. 8.25 *(978-1-4777-2130-8(4)*, 8ebd59e0-ca22-419f-b98f-f915545febad) Rosen Publishing Group, Inc., The. (Rosen Classroom).

Boswell, Shannon. Savannah's Snorkeling Adventure! Use Place Value Understanding, 1 vol. 2014. (InfoMax Math Readers Ser.). (ENG.). 24p. (J). (gr. 3-3). pap. 8.25 *(978-1-4777-4681-3(1)*, dbb55518-21d0-450d-9f67-702c8a91979a, Rosen Classroom) Rosen Publishing Group, Inc., The.

Boyd, Amanda. Near & Far at the Beach: Learning Spatial Awareness Concepts, 1 vol. 2010. (Math for the REAL World Ser.). (ENG., Illus.). 8p. (gr. k-1). pap. 5.15 *(978-0-8239-8911-9(9)*, a6f410b7-01b3-49fc-b9b2-4d47cda0fa4e) Rosen Publishing Group, Inc., The.

—A Trip Around Town: Learning to Add 3 One-Digit Numbers, 1 vol. 2010. (Math for the REAL World Ser.). (ENG.). 12p. (gr. 1-2). pap. 5.90 *(978-0-8239-8915-7(1)*, 019ed2b9-f7a9-44ab-93d6-9f285dc36ec3, Rosen Classroom) Rosen Publishing Group, Inc., The.

Braidich, Victoria. Shapes at Home: Learning to Recognize Basic Geometric Shapes, 1 vol. 2010. (Math for the REAL World Ser.). (ENG.). 12p. (gr. 1-2). pap. 5.90 *(978-0-8239-8863-1(5)*, 708eec44-6c1c-4d02-ac1c-55dc27784d2f, Rosen Classroom) Rosen Publishing Group, Inc., The.

Brennan, Linda Crotta. Understanding Taxes. 2015. (21st Century Skills Library: Real World Math Ser.). (ENG., Illus.). 32p. (J). (gr. 4-7). 32.07 *(978-1-63362-577-8(X)*, 206492) Cherry Lake Publishing.

Brezina, Corona. Top STEM Careers in Math. 2014. (Cutting-Edge STEM Careers Ser.). (Illus.). 128p. (J). (gr. 9-12). pap. 113.10 *(978-1-4777-7679-7(6))* Rosen Publishing Group, Inc., The.

Bridger, Maggie. What Time Is It? A Content Area Reader-math. 2005. (Emergent/Early (Prek-2) Math Package Ser.). 16p. (gr. k-2). 25.20 *(978-0-8215-7824-7(3))* Sadlier, William H. Inc.

Briggs, D. Sharon. Mysteries in Knowledge Challenge Your Children: Complete Multiplication Tables. 2006. (J). per. 75.00 *(978-0-615-13051-4(8))* Briggs, Sharon.

Bright & Beyond - Math. 2004. (J). *(978-0-9763648-0-1(8))* Pal Toys, LLC.

Broadbent, Paul. Being A Cartoonist. 2007. (Trackers-Math Ser.). (gr. 2-5). pap. 5.00 *(978-1-59055-937-6(1))* Pacific Learning, Inc.

—Beneath Our Feet. 2007. (Trackers-Math Ser.). (gr. 2-5). pap. 5.00 *(978-1-59055-929-1(0))* Pacific Learning, Inc.

—Dance Fever. 2007. (Trackers-Math Ser.). (gr. 2-5). pap. 5.00 *(978-1-59055-930-7(4))* Pacific Learning, Inc.

—Detective Work. 2007. (Trackers-Math Ser.). (gr. 2-5). pap. 5.00 *(978-1-59055-931-4(2))* Pacific Learning, Inc.

—Down under Vacation. 2007. (Trackers-Math Ser.). (gr. 2-5). pap. 5.00 *(978-1-59055-940-6(1))* Pacific Learning, Inc.

—Rock Stars. 2007. (Trackers-Math Ser.). (gr. 2-5). pap. 5.00 *(978-1-59055-939-0(8))* Pacific Learning, Inc.

—Scuba Diving. 2007. (Trackers-Math Ser.). (gr. 2-5). pap. 5.00 *(978-1-59055-938-3(X))* Pacific Learning, Inc.

—What Are You Scared Of? 2007. (Trackers-Math Ser.). (gr. 2-5). pap. 5.00 *(978-1-59055-928-4(2))* Pacific Learning, Inc.

Brookie, Anna, et al. Mathematics & Statistics for the New Zealand Curriculum Year 9. 2nd ed. 2013. (Cambridge Mathematics & Statistics for the New Zealand Curriculum Ser.). (ENG.). pap., stu. ed. *(978-1-107-62840-3(7))* Cambridge Univ. Pr.

Brooks, Felicity. Lift-The-Flap First Math. 2017. (Lift-The-Flap Board Bks.). (ENG.). 16p. (J). 13.99 *(978-0-7945-3926-9(2)*, Usborne) EDC Publishing.

Brown, Melony A. Solving Word Problems for Life, Grades 6-8, 1 vol. 2009. (ENG., Illus.). 160p. pap. 32.00 *(978-1-59158-947-1(9)*, 900312469, Libraries Unlimited) ABC-CLIO, LLC.

Brown, Robin. Practice Papers: Advanced Maths. 2nd ed. (ENG., Illus.). 32p. (YA). pap. *(978-0-340-72690-7(3))* Hodder & Stoughton.

—Practice Papers: Maths. 2nd ed. (ENG., Illus.). 32p. (YA). pap. *(978-0-340-72689-1(X))* Hodder & Stoughton.

Brownlee, Joan, et al. Geofinity. 2003. (J). spiral bd. 15.95 *(978-1-931334-26-6(9))* Pieces of Learning.

Bruchgleichungen und Bruchungleichungen. (Duden-Schuelerhilfen Ser.). (GER.). 96p. (YA). (gr. 8). *(978-3-411-02614-2(6))* Bibliographisches Institut & F. A. Brockhaus AG DEU. Dist: International Bk. Import Service, Inc.

Brueche. (Duden-Schuelerhilfen Ser.). (GER.). 112gerp. (YA). (gr. 6-7). *(978-3-411-70692-1(9))* Bibliographisches Institut & F. A. Brockhaus AG DEU. Dist: International Bk. Import Service, Inc.

Brunner- Jass, Renata. Finding the Treasure: Coordinate Grids. 2013. (IMath Ser.). (ENG., Illus.). 48p. (J). (gr. 5-6). pap. 13.26 *(978-1-60357-512-6(X))* Norwood Hse. Pr.

—Winning the Game: Putting Miles in Their Place. 2013. (IMath Ser.). (ENG., Illus.). 48p. (J). (gr. 5-6). pap. 13.26 *(978-1-60357-506-5(5))* Norwood Hse. Pr.

Buckley, Jr., James. It's a Numbers Game! Soccer: The Math Behind the Perfect Goal, the Game-Winning Save, & So Much More! 2020. (It's a Numbers Game! Ser.). (ENG., Illus.). 128p. (J). (gr. 3-7). 14.99 *(978-1-4263-3923-3(2)*, National Geographic Kids) Disney Publishing Worldwide.

Buckley, Jr, James. It's a Numbers Game! Soccer: The Math Behind the Perfect Goal, the Game-Winning Save, & So Much More! 2020. (It's a Numbers Game! Ser.). (ENG.). 128p. (J). (gr. 3-7). 24.90 *(978-1-4263-3924-0(0)*, National Geographic Kids) Disney Publishing Worldwide.

Burncrot, Curt & Burncrot, Jenny. Achieving Peak Performance New Edition. Krischke, Nikki, ed. 2nd rev. ed. 2003. 19p. (gr. 2-18). pap. 5.00 *(978-1-888786-39-2(6))* Basic Skills Assessment & Educational Services.

Burganti, Darien. Fun at the Dojo: Use Place Value Understanding & Properties of Operations to Add, 1 vol. 2014. (Math Masters: Number & Operations in Base Ten Ser.). (ENG.). 24p. (J). (gr. 2-2). 25.27 *(978-1-4777-6433-6(X)*, 64973b18-6e5a-4674-adf3-d864a8bd9d58); pap. 8.25 *(978-1-4777-4717-9(6)*, 6b389a19-76ab-4c6a-978b-b3d23f0ed2ba) Rosen Publishing Group, Inc., The. (Rosen Classroom).

Burgess, Lynne. Shapes: Individual Title Six-Packs. (Discovery World Ser.). 12p. (gr. k-1). 28.00 *(978-0-7635-8446-7(0))* Rigby Education.

Burnett, Betty. Cool Careers Without College for Math & Science Wizards. 2009. (Cool Careers Without College Ser.). 144p. (gr. 6-6). 66.50 *(978-1-61511-959-2(0))* Rosen Publishing Group, Inc., The.

Burnett, James & Irons, Calvin. A Dozen Dizzy Dinosaurs: A Book about Division (Equal Groups) 2012. (J). *(978-1-921959-30-1(4))* Origo Education.

—How Many Legs? A Book about Number Combinations. 2012. (J). *(978-1-921358-97-5(1))* Origo Education.

Burns, Kylie. Roman Numerals & Ordinals. 2010. (ENG., Illus.). 24p. (J). *(978-0-7787-5250-9(X))*; pap. *(978-0-7787-5297-4(6))* Crabtree Publishing Co.

Burrill, Gail F., et al. Advanced Modeling & Matrices. (Data-Driven Mathematics Ser.). 136p. (YA). (gr. 7-12). pap., stu. ed. 18.95 *(978-1-57232-255-4(1))* Seymour, Dale Pubns.

—Exploring Symbols. (Data-Driven Mathematics Ser.). 120p. (YA). (gr. 7-12). pap., stu. ed. 18.95 *(978-1-57232-230-1(6))* Seymour, Dale Pubns.

Burstein, John. Doubling: Circus Stars, 1 vol. 2003. (Math Monsters(tm) Ser.). (ENG., Illus.). 24p. (J). (gr. k-3). pap. 9.15 *(978-0-8368-3822-0(X)*, 640ed958-093e-47a1-bb6e-709580aa7204, Weekly Reader Leveled Readers) Stevens, Gareth Publishing LLLP.

Burton, Margie, et al. Looking for Numbers. 2011. (Early Connections Ser.). (J). *(978-1-61672-300-2(9))* Benchmark Education Co.

—What Comes in Twos? 2011. (Early Connections Ser.). (J). *(978-1-61672-276-0(2))* Benchmark Education Co.

Bussell, Linda. Las Matemáticas en Nuestro Mundo - Nivel 3 (Math in Our World - Level 3), 14 vols., Set. Incl. MULTIPLICAR para Planear una Fiesta (MULTIPLY to Make Party Plans) lib. bdg. 24.67 *(978-0-8368-9293-2(3)*, ee2326c6-6d40-4040-a4b9-9febc851c8ef); Pizza Por Partes: ¡FRACCIONES! (Pizza Parts: FRACTIONS!) lib. bdg. 24.67 *(978-0-8368-9297-0(6)*, 02e03679-cad5-4ef2-886b-a644c46040b8); PROBABILIDAD con Juegos y Diversión (PROBABILITY with Fun & Games) lib. bdg. 24.67 *(978-0-8368-9298-7(4)*, ae050957-934b-4452-bbe6-53608ca225f8); Trabajemos con NÚMEROS en Las Noticias (Working with NUMBERS in the News) lib. bdg. 24.67 *(978-0-8368-9292-5(5)*, 9e717c71-dbc5-4ad3-993c-9ce031fb3c33); Vamos a Explorar CUERPOS SÓLIDOS en la Red (Exploring SOLID FIGURES on the Web) lib. bdg. 24.67 *(978-0-8368-9295-6(X)*, 7d31651f-3db0-42cd-94ad-72e07887e5d6); Vamos a

MEDIR en el Estanque (MEASURING at the Pond) lib. bdg. 24.67 *(978-0-8368-9299-4(2),* 22257668-c140-48b0-a6a5-00d45e66050e); Vamos a Usar DATOS de DIVISIÓN en el Jardín (Using DIVISION FACTS in the Garden) lib. bdg. 24.67 *(978-0-8368-9294-9(1),* 40172f98-2255-4fbc-8117-67769e80bf93); Vamos a Usar la DIVISIÓN en el Campamento de Deportes (Using DIVISION at Sports Camp) lib. bdg. 24.67 *(978-0-8368-9296-3(8),* ea493467-e6c7-445d-aa7f-4c08e14e11a4); (J). (gr. 3-3). (Las Matemáticas en Nuestro Mundo - Nivel 3 (Math in Our World - Level 3) Ser.). (SPA.). 24p. 2008. Set lib. bdg. 172.02 *(978-0-8368-9323-6(9),* aa77ef0c-7ac4-4fe4-8ed0-034a2628b48f, Weekly Reader Leveled Readers) Stevens, Gareth Publishing LLLP.

—Math in Our World: Level 3, 16 vols., Set. Incl. Exploring SOLID FIGURES on the Web. lib. bdg. 24.67 *(978-0-8368-9287-1(9),* 5a49f005-e334-4429-ba7a-24e6b2e17a0d); MEASURING at the Pond. lib. bdg. 24.67 *(978-0-8368-9291-8(7),* bb1ceb8d-2254-4043-9dd0-9f35cea088e1); MULTIPLY to Make Party Plans. lib. bdg. 24.67 *(978-0-8368-9285-7(2),* ed01e3d7-7007-40ae-a1e3-c412a8d959a6); Pizza Parts: FRACTIONS! lib. bdg. 24.67 *(978-0-8368-9289-5(5),* 44c6755f-0a03-48a2-985d-0f4bd705a851); PROBABILITY with Fun & Games. lib. bdg. 24.67 *(978-0-8368-9290-1(9),* 53568c5b-9ae3-4143-9389-fc460707475e); Using DIVISION at Sports Camp. (Illus.). lib. bdg. 24.67 *(978-0-8368-9288-8(7),* f3e8c88d-8a1c-46b7-a88c-c6e7c26b2f7e); Using DIVISION FACTS in the Garden. (Illus.). lib. bdg. 24.67 *(978-0-8368-9286-4(0),* 91462ee1-73e8-4f34-92b6-a9b7b5662b10); Working with Numbers in the News. (Illus.). lib. bdg. 24.67 *(978-0-8368-9284-0(4),* e3359afe-c0e8-42cb-89b9-6fc62638b3c5); (J). (gr. 3-3). (Math in Our World - Level 3 Ser.). (ENG.). 24p. 2008. Set lib. bdg. 197.36 *(978-0-8368-9322-9(0),* 5dc772ed-4a75-4cb9-be2d-93340d631e0b, Weekly Reader Leveled Readers) Stevens, Gareth Publishing LLLP.

—Vamos a Usar DATOS de DIVISIÓN en el Jardín (Using DIVISION FACTS in the Garden), 1 vol. 2008. (Las Matemáticas en Nuestro Mundo - Nivel 3 (Math in Our World - Level 3) Ser.). (SPA.). 24p. (gr. 3-3). pap. 9.15 *(978-0-8368-9393-9(X),* bb98f7f2-7fe7-4ee3-a337-db1459c025eb, Weekly Reader Leveled Readers) Stevens, Gareth Publishing LLLP.

—Vamos a Usar la DIVISIÓN en el Campamento de Deportes (Using DIVISION at Sports Camp), 1 vol. 2008. (Las Matemáticas en Nuestro Mundo - Nivel 3 (Math in Our World - Level 3) Ser.). (SPA.). 24p. (gr. 3-3). (J). lib. bdg. 24.67 *(978-0-8368-9296-3(8),* ea493467-e6c7-445d-aa7f-4c08e14e11a4); pap. 9.15 *(978-0-8368-9395-3(6),* c6a01d97-4738-49ff-8be0-f9038f414673) Stevens, Gareth Publishing LLLP. (Weekly Reader Leveled Readers).

Bussiere, Desireé. Bowling by the Numbers, 1 vol. 2013. (Sports by the Numbers Ser.). (ENG.). 24p. (J). (gr. k-3). lib. bdg. 29.93 *(978-1-61783-842-2(X),* 13698, SandCastle) ABDO Publishing Co.

—Gymnastics by the Numbers, 1 vol. 2013. (Sports by the Numbers Ser.). (ENG.). 24p. (J). (gr. k-3). lib. bdg. 29.93 *(978-1-61783-844-6(6),* 13702, SandCastle) ABDO Publishing Co.

Callella, Trisha. I Have, Who Has? Math, Grades 3-4: 38 Interactive Card Games. Hamaguchi, Carla, ed. Hillam, Corbin, illus. 2006. (I Have, Who Has? Ser.). 204p. (J). (gr. 3-4). per. 19.99 *(978-1-59198-230-2(8),* 2208) Creative Teaching Pr., Inc.

Campbell, Sarah C. Mysterious Patterns: Finding Fractals in Nature. Campbell, Richard P., photos by. 2014. (ENG., Illus.). 32p. (J). (gr. 2-5). 17.99 *(978-1-62091-627-8(4),* Astra Young Readers) Astra Publishing Hse.

Canavan, Thomas. Making Connections: 50 Math Super Puzzles, 1 vol. 2011. (Math Standards Workout Ser.). (ENG., Illus.). 48p. (YA). (gr. 5-5). lib. bdg. 34.47 *(978-1-4488-6674-8(X),* 04fcdfce-74f5-40e8-a862-3e893fc30c4b) Rosen Publishing Group, Inc., The.

—Math Adds Up, 1 vol. 2016. (Amazing World of Science & Math Ser.). (ENG.). 48p. (gr. 5-5). pap. 15.05 *(978-1-4824-4986-0(2),* f32c7a7b-30cf-42f1-baf1-947aa32763d5) Stevens, Gareth Publishing LLLP.

—Mental Math: 50 Math Super Puzzles, 1 vol. 2011. (Math Standards Workout Ser.). (ENG., Illus.). 48p. (YA). (gr. 5-5). pap. 12.75 *(978-1-4488-6684-7(7),* 46b41be4-11cc-4ed7-b788-1e54fd6e3e41, Rosen Reference) Rosen Publishing Group, Inc., The.

Canetti, Yanitzia. Rhyming Tongue-Twisters Math. 2010. 32p. (J). pap. 6.99 *(978-1-59835-263-4(6),* BrickHouse Education) Cambridge BrickHouse, Inc.

Capstone Press. Data Mania. 2010. (Data Mania Ser.). (ENG.). 32p. lib. bdg. 95.96 *(978-1-4296-5929-1(7),* Capstone Pr.) Capstone.

—Real World Math, 1 vol. 2010. (Real World Math - Level 4 Ser.). (ENG.). 32p. lib. bdg. 405.12 *(978-1-4296-5915-4(7))* Capstone.

Captain B's Boat, 6 vols. (Sunshinetm Ser.). 16p. (gr. k-18). 29.50 *(978-0-7802-5441-1(4))* Wright Group/McGraw-Hill.

Caron, Lucille. Addition & Subtraction Smarts!, 1 vol. 2011. (Math Smarts! Ser.). (ENG., Illus.). 64p. (gr. 5-6). pap. 11.53 *(978-1-59845-318-8(1),* 7a9c5b74-d7aa-4777-ac07-e0578279cd28); lib. bdg. 31.93 *(978-0-7660-3939-1(0),* afcb8019-ddc6-468a-ba6c-487943bf5777) Enslow Publishing, LLC.

—Pre-Algebra & Algebra Smarts!, 1 vol. 2011. (Math Smarts! Ser.). (ENG., Illus.). 64p. (gr. 5-6). pap. 11.53 *(978-1-59845-319-5(X),* 2260c136-960e-4e29-99be-56888a124e66); lib. bdg. 31.93 *(978-0-7660-3938-4(2),* f6faff8a-c451-472a-b786-86d28746183a) Enslow Publishing, LLC.

Carroll, Danielle. Tiling with Shapes. 2005. (Yellow Umbrella Fluent Level Ser.). (ENG., Illus.). 16p. (gr. k-1). pap. 35.70 *(978-0-7368-5323-1(5),* Capstone Pr.) Capstone.

Carson-Dellosa Publishing Staff. Beginning Math, Grade 1. 2010. (Home Workbooks Ser.: 2). (ENG.). 64p. (gr. 1-1). pap. 4.49 *(978-1-60418-790-8(5),* 104359) Carson-Dellosa Publishing, LLC.

Carson, Janet. In the Forest: Learning Directional Concepts, 1 vol. (Math for the REAL World Ser.). (ENG.). 12p. (gr. 1-2). 2010. pap. 5.90 *(978-0-8239-8916-4(X),* 0383b22b-3eed-4983-8e78-c40859900db4, Rosen Classroom) 2004. 33.50 *(978-0-8239-7634-8(3))* Rosen Publishing Group, Inc., The.

Carter, Denine, ed. Gotta Have Graphs. 2003. 144p. (gr. 1-6). 16.95 *(978-1-56234-573-0(7),* Mailbox Bks., The) Education Ctr., Inc.

Cartogna, Eileen. Jobs Around Town: Learning to Sort & Classify, 1 vol. (Math for the REAL World Ser.). (ENG., Illus.). 8p. (gr. k-1). 2009. pap. 5.15 *(978-0-8239-8910-2(0),* 46186454-1f29-4ea0-a646-f19141e6c3cc) 2004. 29.95 *(978-0-8239-7629-4(7))* Rosen Publishing Group, Inc., The.

Cernak, Kim & Williams, Rozanne Lanczak. Build-a-Skill Instant Books Math Facts To 20. Faulkner, Stacey, ed. Campbell, Jenny, illus. 2007. (J). 4.99 *(978-1-59198-418-4(1))* Creative Teaching Pr., Inc.

Challen, Paul & Peppas, Lynn. Math Words & Symbols. 2009. (ENG.). 24p. (J). lib. bdg. *(978-0-7787-4347-7(0));* pap. *(978-0-7787-4365-1(9))* Crabtree Publishing Co.

Chambers, Jo. All about Cars. 2007. (Trackers-Math Ser.). (gr. 2-5). pap. 5.00 *(978-1-59055-923-9(1))* Pacific Learning, Inc.

—Art Gallery. 2007. (Trackers-Math Ser.). (gr. 2-5). pap. 5.00 *(978-1-59055-927-7(4))* Pacific Learning, Inc.

—Caring for Wild Animals. 2007. (Trackers-Math Ser.). (gr. 2-5). pap. 5.00 *(978-1-59055-933-8(9))* Pacific Learning, Inc.

—Discovering India. 2007. (Trackers-Math Ser.). (gr. 2-5). pap. 5.00 *(978-1-59055-926-0(6))* Pacific Learning, Inc.

—Extreme Earth. 2007. (Trackers-Math Ser.). (gr. 2-5). pap. 5.00 *(978-1-59055-913-0(4))* Pacific Learning, Inc.

—High Tech. 2007. (Trackers-Math Ser.). (gr. 2-5). pap. 5.00 *(978-1-59055-934-5(7))* Pacific Learning, Inc.

—Making Movies. 2007. (Trackers-Math Ser.). (gr. 2-5). pap. 5.00 *(978-1-59055-932-1(0))* Pacific Learning, Inc.

—That's Extreme. 2007. (Trackers-Math Ser.). (gr. 2-5). pap. 5.00 *(978-1-59055-936-9(3))* Pacific Learning, Inc.

—Tropical Rainforest. 2007. (Trackers-Math Ser.). (gr. 2-5). pap. 5.00 *(978-1-59055-924-6(X))* Pacific Learning, Inc.

Chapman, Joan. Heavy & Light: Learning to Compare Weights of Objects, 1 vol. 2010. (Math for the REAL World Ser.). (ENG., Illus.). 8p. (gr. k-1). pap. 5.15 *(978-0-8239-8844-0(9),* d813d4e2-b543-4c4e-97a3-f529b5258d53) Rosen Publishing Group, Inc., The.

Charles, et al. Problem-Solving Experiences in Mathematics. 2003. (gr. 7-8). suppl. ed. 30.95 *(978-0-201-20688-3(9))* Seymour, Dale Pubns.

Charles, R., et al. Problem-Solving Experience in Mathematics. 2003. 30.95 *(978-0-201-20689-0(7));* (gr. 3). 30.95 *(978-0-201-20684-5(6));* (gr. 4). 30.95 *(978-0-201-20685-2(4));* (gr. 5). 30.95 *(978-0-201-20686-9(2));* (gr. 6). 30.95 *(978-0-201-20687-6(0))* Seymour, Dale Pubns.

—Problem-Solving Experiences in Mathematics. 2nd ed. 2003. 16.50 *(978-0-201-49361-0(6))* Seymour, Dale Pubns.

—Problem-Solving Experiences in Mathematics, Grade 2, BLM. Anderson, Cathy & Apple, Mali, eds. 2nd ed. 2003. (Illus.). 17.50 *(978-0-201-49363-4(2))* Seymour, Dale Pubns.

Charles, Randall I. & Prentice Hall Directories Staff. Pre-Algebra, 3 vols. 5th ed. 2003. (ENG.). 954p. (YA). (gr. 7-9). 477.00 *(978-0-13-068608-4(5),* Prentice Hall) Savvas Learning Co.

Charles, Randall I. & Prentice-Hall Staff. Prentice Hall Mathematics, 3 vols. 2003. (ENG.). 828p. (YA). (gr. 6-8). 414.00 *(978-0-13-063136-7(1),* Prentice Hall) Savvas Learning Co.

Charles, Randall I., et al. Problem-Solving Experiences in Mathematics: Prob Solv Exper. 2005. (Problem Solving Experiences Ser.). (J). (gr. k-8). stu. ed. 56.95 *(978-0-7690-3250-4(8));* (gr. 4-18). stu. ed. 56.95 *(978-0-7690-3251-1(6))* Seymour, Dale Pubns.

Chen, John. Helping at the Book Sale: Represent & Solve Subtraction Problems, 1 vol. 2013. (Rosen Math Readers Ser.). (ENG.). 24p. (J). (gr. 1-1). pap. 8.25 *(978-1-4777-2052-3(9),* 229f418a-975e-4dab-a66d-ab3f2af20682, Rosen Classroom); lib. bdg. 26.27 *(978-1-4777-2208-4(4),* ab1586a8-0da5-4c88-ab84-2dff69b3885d8, PowerKids Pr.); pap. 49.50 *(978-1-4777-2053-0(7),* Rosen Classroom) Rosen Publishing Group, Inc., The.

Chilson, Martin. Carmen Cooks Healthy! Represent & Solve Problems Involving Division, 1 vol. 2014. (Math Masters: Operations & Algebraic Thinking Ser.). (ENG.). 24p. (J). (gr. 3-3). 25.27 *(978-1-4777-6410-7(0),* 30978d13-6971-4be8-938d-fdfceab3c4c3); pap. 8.25 *(978-1-4777-4965-4(9),* e8da09b2-f71e-4394-956e-d555e06ccd20) Rosen Publishing Group, Inc., The. (Rosen Classroom).

Chrismer, Melanie. Odd & Even Socks. 2005. (Rookie Read-About Math Ser.). (ENG., Illus.). 32p. (J). (gr. 1-2). lib. bdg. 20.50 *(978-0-516-25265-0(8),* Children's Pr.) Scholastic Library Publishing.

Cipriano, Jeri S. It's Time!, 6 vols., Set. 2003. (Yellow Umbrella Early Level Ser.). (ENG.). 16p. (gr. k-1). pap. 35.70 *(978-0-7368-2993-9(8),* Capstone Pr.) Capstone.

—Making a Difference. 2003. (Shutterbug Books: Social Studies). (Illus.). 16p. (J). (gr. -1-3). pap. 4.10 *(978-0-7398-7647-3(3))* Steck-Vaughn.

Claire, Linda. Arte y Cultura: Comparación de Grupos. rev. ed. 2019. (Mathematics in the Real World Ser.). (SPA., Illus.). 20p. (J). (gr. k-1). 8.99 *(978-1-4258-2821-9(3))* Teacher Created Materials, Inc.

—Cuestion de Dinero: Conocimientos Financieros. rev. ed. 2019. (Mathematics in the Real World Ser.). (SPA.). 20p. (J). (gr. k-1). 8.99 *(978-1-4258-2825-7(6))* Teacher Created Materials, Inc.

—Las Sillas Musicales. rev. ed. 2019. (Mathematics in the Real World Ser.). (SPA.). 20p. (J). (gr. k-1). 8.99 *(978-1-4258-2828-8(0))* Teacher Created Materials, Inc.

Cleary, Brian P. A-B-A-B-A: A Book of Pattern Play. Gable, Brian, illus. 2010. (Math Is CATegorical (r) Ser.). (ENG.). 32p. (J). (gr. k-3). lib. bdg. 16.95 *(978-0-8225-7880-2(8))* Lerner Publishing Group.

—A-B-A-B-a — a Book of Pattern Play. Gable, Brian, illus. 2012. (Math Is CATegorical (r) Ser.). (ENG.). 32p. (J). (gr. k-3). pap. 7.99 *(978-0-7613-8502-8(9),* 79264e81-c9a9-414b-8889-184d34a4cd5c, Millbrook Pr.) Lerner Publishing Group.

—The Action of Subtraction. Gable, Brian, illus. 2008. (Math Is CATegorical (r) Ser.). (ENG.). 32p. (J). (gr. k-3). pap. 8.99 *(978-1-58013-843-7(8),* 27584f6c-a1d8-4a8e-8ddc-72a4608599e5, Millbrook Pr.) Lerner Publishing Group.

Clement, Rod. Counting on Frank, 1 vol. 2019. (Counting on Frank Ser.). (ENG.). 32p. (J). (gr. 1-3). pap. 10.50 *(978-1-5382-4973-4(1))* Stevens, Gareth Publishing LLLP.

Clements, Andrew. A Million Dots. Reed, Mike, illus. 2006. (ENG.). 48p. (J). (gr. -1-3). 19.99 *(978-0-689-85824-6(8),* Atheneum Bks. for Young Readers) Simon & Schuster Children's Publishing.

Clemson, David & Clemson, Wendy. Digging for Dinosaurs, 1 vol. 2007. (Math Adventures Ser.). (ENG., Illus.). 32p. (gr. 2-4). pap. 11.50 *(978-0-8368-8137-0(0),* 97475f30-9658-4c4d-8d8d-4235a2613b28, Gareth Stevens Learning Library) Stevens, Gareth Publishing LLLP.

—Rocket to the Moon, 1 vol. 2007. (Math Adventures Ser.). (ENG., Illus.). 32p. (gr. 2-4). pap. 11.50 *(978-0-8368-8140-0(0),* 37d1f896-b8a2-4d35-9744-0e62b9b8e6d7, Gareth Stevens Learning Library) Stevens, Gareth Publishing LLLP.

—Treasure Hunt in the Jungle, 1 vol. 2007. (Math Adventures Ser.). (ENG., Illus.). 32p. (gr. 2-4). pap. 11.50 *(978-0-8368-8141-7(9),* 0a614af1-042a-424d-8c51-9a25b494b76c, Gareth Stevens Learning Library) Stevens, Gareth Publishing LLLP.

Clemson, Wendy & Clemson, David. Times Tables! (Illus.). 32p. (J). pap. 11.99 *(978-0-590-24755-9(7))* Scholastic, Inc.

Clissold, Caroline. All about Pirates. 2007. (Trackers-Math Ser.). (gr. 2-5). pap. 5.00 *(978-1-59055-918-5(5))* Pacific Learning, Inc.

—Dinosaur. 2007. (Trackers-Math Ser.). (gr. 2-5). pap. 5.00 *(978-1-59055-914-7(2))* Pacific Learning, Inc.

—Extreme Earth. 2007. (Trackers-Math Ser.). (gr. 2-5). pap. 5.00 *(978-1-59055-912-3(6))* Pacific Learning, Inc.

—Food Around the World. 2007. (Trackers-Math Ser.). (gr. 2-5). pap. 5.00 *(978-1-59055-910-9(X))* Pacific Learning, Inc.

—Out of This World. 2007. (Trackers-Math Ser.). (gr. 2-5). pap. 5.00 *(978-1-59055-917-8(7))* Pacific Learning, Inc.

CMSP Projects Staff. Applied Math Concepts: Lines & Perimeters Area & Volume. rev. ed. (Illus.). 91p. (YA). reprint ed. pap. *(978-0-942851-01-4(3))* CMSP Projects.

Cocca, Lisa Colozza. Bar Graphs. 2013. (Explorer Junior Library: Math Explorer Junior Ser.). (ENG.). 24p. (gr. 1-4). pap. 12.79 *(978-1-61080-936-8(X),* 202625); (Illus.). 32.07 *(978-1-61080-911-5(4),* 202623) Cherry Lake Publishing.

—Graphing Story Problems. 2013. (Explorer Junior Library: Math Explorer Junior Ser.). (ENG.). 24p. (gr. 1-4). (J). pap. 12.79 *(978-1-61080-939-9(4),* 202637); (Illus.). 32.07 *(978-1-61080-914-6(9),* 202635); (Illus.). E-Book 49.21 *(978-1-61080-989-4(0),* 202638) Cherry Lake Publishing.

—Line Graphs. 2013. (Explorer Junior Library: Math Explorer Junior Ser.). (ENG.). 24p. (gr. 1-4). (J). pap. 12.79 *(978-1-61080-937-5(8),* 202629); (Illus.). 32.07 *(978-1-61080-912-2(2),* 202627); (Illus.). E-Book 49.21 *(978-1-61080-987-0(4),* 202630) Cherry Lake Publishing.

—Pie Graphs. 2013. (Explorer Junior Library: Math Explorer Junior Ser.). (ENG.). 24p. (gr. 1-4). (J). pap. 12.79 *(978-1-61080-940-5(8),* 202641); (Illus.). 32.07 *(978-1-61080-915-3(7),* 202639); (Illus.). E-Book 49.21 *(978-1-61080-990-0(4),* 202642) Cherry Lake Publishing.

Cognitive Tutor (R) Integrated Math II Software Manual. 2003. spiral bd. *(978-1-930804-43-2(1))* Carnegie Learning Inc.

Cognitive Tutor (R) Integrated Math II Student. 2003. per. *(978-1-930804-54-8(7))* Carnegie Learning Inc.

Cohen, Marina. Money Problems. 2010. (ENG.). 24p. (J). *(978-0-7787-6782-4(5));* pap. *(978-0-7787-6791-6(4))* Crabtree Publishing Co.

Collins. Year 3. 2019. (ENG., Illus.). 96p. (J). (gr. k-3). pap. 115.00 *(978-0-00-831116-2(1))* HarperCollins Pubs. Ltd. GBR. Dist: Independent Pubs. Group.

—Year 5. 2019. (ENG., Illus.). 96p. (J). (gr. k-3). pap. 115.00 *(978-0-00-831118-6(8))* HarperCollins Pubs. Ltd. GBR. Dist: Independent Pubs. Group.

—5 Minute Maths Mastery Book 6. 2019. (ENG., Illus.). 96p. (J). (gr. k-3). pap. 115.00 *(978-0-00-831119-3(6))* HarperCollins Pubs. Ltd. GBR. Dist: Independent Pubs. Group.

Collins Easy Learning. Maths Ages 8-10: Ideal for Home Learning. 2014. (Collins Easy Learning Ser.). (ENG.). 48p. (J). (gr. 3-5). pap. 7.99 *(978-0-00-755982-4(8))* HarperCollins Pubs. Ltd. GBR. Dist: Independent Pubs. Group.

—Maths Ages 9-11: Ideal for Home Learning. 2014. (Collins Easy Learning Ser.). (ENG.). 48p. (J). (gr. 4-6). pap. 7.99 *(978-0-00-755983-1(6))* HarperCollins Pubs. Ltd. GBR. Dist: Independent Pubs. Group.

Collins, Kathleen. On the Trail with Lewis & Clark: Learning to Use Line Graphs. 2004. (Math Big Bookstm Ser.). (ENG.). 16p. (gr. 2-3). 37.95 *(978-0-8239-7639-3(4))* Rosen Publishing Group, Inc., The.

Collins KS2. Year 6 Maths KS2 SATs Targeted Practice Workbook: For the 2024 Tests. 2016. (Collins KS2 SATs Revision & Practice Ser.). (ENG.). 128p. (J). (gr. 5-6). pap. 9.95 *(978-0-00-817549-8(7))* HarperCollins Pubs. Ltd. GBR. Dist: Independent Pubs. Group.

—Year 6 Maths Reasoning - Algebra for Papers 2 & 3: for the 2020 Tests (Collins KS2 SATs Smashers) 2017. (Collins KS2 SATs Smashers Ser.). (ENG., Illus.). 32p. (J). (gr. 5-6). pap. 3.95 *(978-0-00-825953-2(4))* HarperCollins Pubs. Ltd. GBR. Dist: Independent Pubs. Group.

Collins KS2, Collins. Year 6 Maths Reasoning - Fractions, Decimals & Percentages for Papers 2 & 3: for the 2020 Tests (Collins KS2 SATs Smashers) 2017. (Collins KS2 SATs Smashers Ser.). (ENG., Illus.). 32p. (J). (gr. 5-6). pap. 3.95 *(978-0-00-825952-5(6))* HarperCollins Pubs. Ltd. GBR. Dist: Independent Pubs. Group.

Collins KS3. KS3 Maths Higher Level Revision Guide: Ideal for Years 7, 8 And 9. 2014. (ENG., Illus.). 144p. (YA). (gr. 6-9). pap. 12.95 *(978-0-00-756278-7(0))* HarperCollins Pubs. Ltd. GBR. Dist: Independent Pubs. Group.

—KS3 Maths Year 7 Workbook: Ideal for Year 7. 2014. (ENG., Illus.). 80p. (J). (gr. 6-7). pap., wbk. ed. 8.95 *(978-0-00-756266-4(7))* HarperCollins Pubs. Ltd. GBR. Dist: Independent Pubs. Group.

—KS3 Maths Year 9 Workbook: Ideal for Year 9. 2014. (ENG., Illus.). 80p. (YA). (gr. 8-9). pap., wbk. ed. 8.95 *(978-0-00-756268-8(3))* HarperCollins Pubs. Ltd. GBR. Dist: Independent Pubs. Group.

Collins KS3, Collins. KS3 Maths Higher Level All-In-One Complete Revision & Practice: Ideal for Years 7, 8 And 9. 2014. (ENG., Illus.). 216p. (YA). (gr. 6-9). pap. 16.95 *(978-0-00-756279-4(9))* HarperCollins Pubs. Ltd. GBR. Dist: Independent Pubs. Group.

Collins UK. Student Book - CfE Advanced Higher Maths Student Book. 2017. (ENG., Illus.). 392p. (YA). (gr. 8). pap. 45.00 *(978-0-00-820903-2(0))* HarperCollins Pubs. Ltd. GBR. Dist: Independent Pubs. Group.

Collins 11+. Collins 11+ Practice - 11+ Maths Quick Practice Tests Age 9-10 (Year 5): for the 2023 CEM Tests. 2016. (Letts 11+ Success Ser.). (ENG.). 80p. (J). (gr. 4-5). pap. 9.95 *(978-1-84419-890-0(1))* HarperCollins Pubs. Ltd. GBR. Dist: Independent Pubs. Group.

Colson, Rob. Super Sums: Addition, Subtraction, Multiplication, & Division (Math Everywhere) (Library Edition) 2017. (Math Everywhere Ser.). (ENG., Illus.). 32p. (J). (gr. 5-8). lib. bdg. 27.00 *(978-0-531-22884-5(3),* Children's Pr.) Scholastic Library Publishing.

Cominskey, Michael J. The Number System & Common & Decimal Fractions, 1 vol. 2014. (Story of Math Ser.). (ENG.). 64p. (J). (gr. 8-8). 34.29 *(978-1-62275-524-0(3),* cb22ff5c-73a7-4357-a797-85d9211b4544, Britannica Educational Publishing) Rosen Publishing Group, Inc., The.

Concentrate on! — Grades 7, 8. 2003. (J). spiral bd. 15.95 *(978-1-58123-333-9(7))* Larson Learning, Inc.

Concentrate on! Grades 6/7. 2003. (J). spiral bd. 15.95 *(978-1-58123-335-3(3))* Larson Learning, Inc.

Concentrate on! Prealgebra. 2003. spiral bd. 15.95 *(978-1-58123-334-6(5))* Larson Learning, Inc.

Connecting People Pattern Cards. 2003. (J). 7.95 *(978-1-56911-144-4(8))* Learning Resources, Inc.

Connolly, Techla & Meyers, Carrie. Core Focus Grade 7: Test Practice for Common Core. 2015. (ENG., Illus.). 216p. pap. 14.99 *(978-1-4380-0706-9(X),* Barron's Educational Series, Inc.) Kaplan Publishing.

Cooper, Bob. Little Leonardo's Fascinating World of Math, 1 vol. Paprocki, Greg, illus. 2018. (ENG.). 24p. (J). (gr. -1-3). 12.99 *(978-1-4236-4936-6(2))* Gibbs Smith, Publisher.

Core Math Skills: Numbers & Operations in Base 10, 12 vols. 2013. (Core Math Skills: Numbers & Operations in Base 10 Ser.). (ENG.). 24p. (J). (gr. 1-1). 157.62 *(978-1-4777-2235-0(1),* 50d2dea1-6950-4e43-9ae4-17dd7049f4c8, Rosen Classroom) Rosen Publishing Group, Inc., The.

Core Math Skills (Grades 1 - 2), 36 vols. 2013. (Core Math Skills Ser.). (ENG.). 24p. (J). (gr. 1-1). 472.86 *(978-1-4777-2374-6(9),* 53238004-3a4f-4ef4-b9d1-de625785ea0f, Rosen Classroom) Rosen Publishing Group, Inc., The.

Cortina, Janice. The Lonely Sixteenth. 2010. (Illus.). 40p. 16.99 *(978-1-4520-2406-6(5))* AuthorHouse.

Costa, David. What's the Difference? Frink, Phil, photos by. 2004. (Illus.). 24p. (J). per. 26.99 *(978-1-4134-4855-9(0))* Xlibris Corp.

The Cotton Tale. abr. ed. 2004. (Thrilling Tales in Time Ser.: Vol. 41). (J). 19.95 *(978-1-58123-372-8(8))* Larson Learning, Inc.

Count down to Math Grade 5. 2005. (ENG.). *(978-0-9766802-9-1(7))* Educational Tools, Inc.

Counting Cards Staff. LP-Counting: Level 1 Math. 2004. (ENG.). (J). 9.99 *(978-1-59204-013-1(6))* Learning Wrap-Ups, Inc.

Cozens, Gaynor & Thomas, Cheryl Ann. Numeracy Matters, Grade 3. 2003. (AFR.). 48p. pap., wbk. ed. 2.05 *(978-0-521-53879-4(3))* Cambridge Univ. Pr.

Crabtree Publishing, creator. My Path to Math: Math Concepts Made Simple. 2008. (J). pap. *(978-0-7787-4354-5(3))* Crabtree Publishing Co.

Critical Thinking Publishing Staff & Husted, Terri. Math Detective A1: Higher-Order Thinking Reading Writing in Mathematics. 2010. (Math Detective Ser.). 128p. (gr. 5-6). pap. 19.99 *(978-0-89455-803-0(X))* Critical Thinking Co., The.

—Math Detective Beginning: Higher-Order Thinking Reading Writing in Mathematics. 2013. (Math Detective Ser.). 112p. (gr. 3-4). pap. 19.99 *(978-0-89455-802-3(1))* Critical Thinking Co., The.

Crum, Anna-Maria. Math to Build On: Set Of 6. 2011. (Navigators Ser.). (J). pap. 48.00 net. *(978-1-4108-0421-1(6))* Benchmark Education Co.

—Math to Build on & Matemáticas para Construir: 6 English, 6 Spanish Adaptations. 2011. (ENG & SPA.). (J). 97.00 net. *(978-1-4108-5696-8(8))* Benchmark Education Co.

Cuenta Conmigo. (Mathematics Ser.). (SPA.). (J). *(978-958-04-7725-9(6)); (978-958-04-7727-3(2)); (978-958-04-7726-6(4))* Norma S.A. COL. Dist: Distribuidora Norma, Inc.

Cuisenaire Rods Addition & Subtraction Activity Cards. 2003. (J). 19.95 *(978-1-56911-140-6(5))* Learning Resources, Inc.

Cuisenaire Rods Fractions & Decimals Activity Cards. 2003. (J). 19.95 *(978-1-56911-142-0(1))* Learning Resources, Inc.

Cuisenaire Rods Multiplication & Division Activity Cards. 2003. (J). 19.95 *(978-1-56911-141-3(3))* Learning Resources, Inc.

Curriculum Associates Staff. Ready New York CCLS Common Core Math Instruction 2014: Grade 4. 2014. pap. *(978-0-7609-8433-8(6))* Curriculum Assocs., LLC.

Dacey, Linda. Strategies to Integrate the Arts in Mathematics, 1 vol. rev. ed. 2013. (Strategies to Integrate the Arts Ser.). (ENG.). 280p. (gr. k-12). pap. 45.99 *(978-1-4258-1088-7(8))* Shell Educational Publishing.

Dale Seymour Staff. Mathematics: Problem Solving Activities. (J). 69p. 12.95 net. *(978-0-86651-256-5(X),* DSO1529); 77p. (gr. 3). 12.95 net. *(978-0-86651-254-1(3),* DSO1527); 71p. (gr. 6). 13.95 net. *(978-0-86651-257-2(8),* DSO1530) Seymour, Dale Pubns.

Dalton, Julie. Patterns Everywhere. 2006. (Rookie Read-About Math Ser.). (ENG., Illus.). 32p. (J). (gr. 1-2). per. 5.95

(978-0-516-25367-1(0), Children's Pr.) Scholastic Library Publishing.

Danellis, Charles W., ed. Group Theory: Classes, Representation & Connections, & Applications. 2010. (Mathematics Research Developments Ser.). (ENG., Illus.). 331p. (J). 145.00 *(978-1-60876-175-3(4))* Nova Science Pubs., Inc.

Danielson, Christopher. How Many? a Counting Book. 2018. (ENG., Illus.). 36p. (gr. -1-5). 20.00 *(978-1-62531-182-5(6))* Stenhouse Pubs.

Daronco, Mickey. Circus in the City: Set Of 6. 2011. (BuildUp Ser.). (J). pap. 27.00 net. *(978-1-4108-0774-8(6))* Benchmark Education Co.

Daronco, Mickey & Ohanesian, Diane. The Big Clock: Set Of 6. 2nd rev. ed. 2004. (BuildUp Ser.). (J). pap. 27.00 net. *(978-1-4108-1526-2(9))* Benchmark Education Co.

—Can We Pick It? Set Of 6. 2nd rev. ed. 2004. (BuildUp Ser.). (J). pap. 27.00 net. *(978-1-4108-1534-7(X))* Benchmark Education Co.

—Is It Big? Set Of 6. 2nd rev. ed. 2004. (BuildUp Ser.). (J). pap. 27.00 net. *(978-1-4108-1530-9(7))* Benchmark Education Co.

—More Corn: Set of 6. 2nd rev. ed. 2003. (BuildUp Ser.). (J). pap. 22.00 *(978-1-4108-0766-3(5))* Benchmark Education Co.

—My Turn to Fit: Set Of 6. 2nd rev. ed. 2011. (BuildUp Ser.). Orig. Title: Will It or Will It Not? (J). pap. 27.00 net. *(978-1-4108-0765-6(7))* Benchmark Education Co.

—One to Ten: Set Of 6. 2nd rev. ed. 2004. (BuildUp Ser.). (J). pap. 27.00 net. *(978-1-4108-1527-9(7))* Benchmark Education Co.

—Two by Two: Set Of 6. 2nd rev. ed. 2004. (BuildUp Ser.). (J). pap. 27.00 net. *(978-1-4108-1535-4(8))* Benchmark Education Co.

Daronco, Mickey & Presti, Lori. Instrumentos para Medir: Set Of 6. 2011. (Primeras Conexiones Ser.).Tr. of Measuring Tools. (SPA.). (J). 40.00 net. *(978-1-4108-0330-6(9))* Benchmark Education Co.

Davies, Ann & Ne, Harriet. Sum Fun. (Illus.). 40p. (J). 19.95 *(978-1-85479-226-6(1))* O'Mara, Michael Bks., Ltd. GBR. Dist: Trans-Atlantic Pubns., Inc.

Davis, Graeme. Earthquakes. 2012. (21st Century Skills Library: Real World Math Ser.). (ENG., Illus.). 32p. (gr. 4-8). (J). pap. 14.21 *(978-1-61080-411-0(2)*, 201343); lib. bdg. 32.07 *(978-1-61080-323-6(X)*, 201308) Cherry Lake Publishing.

—Floods. 2012. (21st Century Skills Library: Real World Math Ser.). (ENG., Illus.). 32p. (gr. 4-8). (J). pap. 14.21 *(978-1-61080-409-7(0)*, 201341); lib. bdg. 32.07 *(978-1-61080-324-3(8)*, 201304) Cherry Lake Publishing.

Day Two PSAE Student Textbook. 3rd ed. 2005. per. *(978-1-58894-035-3(7))* Cambridge Educational Services, Inc.

De Long, Ron, et al. Dream-Makers Mathematics: Art & Mathematics. De Long, Ron et al, eds. 2007. (Illus.). 104p. spiral bd. 9.99 *(978-0-86696-327-5(8))* Binney & Smith, Inc.

Dean, Arlan. Mathematical Thinking Ideas Procedures, 1 vol. 2003. (BrainBuilders Ser.). (ENG.). 48p. (gr. k-4). pap. 5.25 *(978-1-4042-8528-6(8)*, 8ed9ae97-9150-4949-a81f-dd5c7ed31598) Rosen Publishing Group, Inc., The.

Decoding Math Word Problems - Grade 3. 2004. (J). pap. 14.95 *(978-1-56911-156-7(1))* Learning Resources, Inc.

Decoding Math Word Problems - Grade 4. 2004. (J). pap. 14.95 *(978-1-56911-157-4(X))* Learning Resources, Inc.

Decoding Math Word Problems - Grade 5. 2004. (J). pap. 14.95 *(978-1-56911-158-1(8))* Learning Resources, Inc.

Dee, Nora. Making Circle Graphs, 1 vol. 2014. (Graph It! Ser.). (ENG.). 24p. (J). (gr. 1-2). 24.27 *(978-1-4824-0829-4(5)*, b44d4cf3-4b6a-4e92-b9c3-0e5315eb109b) Stevens, Gareth Publishing LLLP.

Deen, Marilyn. Tiling Shapes. 2011. (Wonder Readers Fluent Level Ser.). (ENG.). 16p. (gr. -1-2). pap. 35.94 *(978-1-4296-8188-9(8)*, Capstone Pr.) Capstone.

Delrose, Julian. Feeding Time at the Farm, 1 vol. 2013. (Core Math Skills: Numbers & Operations in Base 10 Ser.). (ENG.). 24p. (J). (gr. 1-1). 26.27 *(978-1-4777-2226-8(2)*, 9fc16a67-90f7-46a8-bc39-5ca68f7eb451, Rosen Classroom) Rosen Publishing Group, Inc., The.

—Feeding Time at the Farm: Use Place Value & Properties of Operation to Subtract, 1 vol. 2013. (Rosen Math Readers Ser.). (ENG.). 24p. (J). (gr. 1-1). pap. 8.25 *(978-1-4777-2043-1(X)*, 334df257-738a-4ebf-b411-21b5c3f7d0c6, Rosen Classroom) Rosen Publishing Group, Inc., The.

—Feeding Time at the Farm: Use Place Value & Properties of Operations to Subtract. 2013. (Rosen Math Readers Ser.). (ENG.). 24p. (J). (gr. 1-2). pap. 49.50 *(978-1-4777-2044-8(8)*, Rosen Classroom) Rosen Publishing Group, Inc., The.

Denman, Gregory. Mathematics: Strategies for Explaining Thinking. rev. ed. 2013. (Think It Show It Ser.). (ENG.). 192p. (gr. 3-8). pap. 45.99 *(978-1-4258-1051-1(9))* Shell Educational Publishing.

Dessen, Maci. Let's Go Snorkeling! Use Place Value Understanding, 1 vol. 2014. (Rosen Math Readers Ser.). (ENG.). 24p. (J). (gr. 3-3). pap. 8.25 *(978-1-4777-4938-8(1)*, 26966a10-3115-47d8-8850-09ce66334c7c, Rosen Classroom) Rosen Publishing Group, Inc., The.

Developmental Studies Center Staff. AfterSchool KidzMath 3-6 Games. ldr.'s ed. 2005. spiral bd. 70.00 *(978-1-57621-452-7(4))* Center for the Collaborative Classroom.

Dezimalbrueche. (Duden-Schuelerhilfen Ser.). (GER.). 112p. (J). (gr. 6). *(978-3-411-70112-4(9))* Bibliographisches Institut & F. A. Brockhaus AG DEU. Dist: International Bk. Import Service, Inc.

Dickmann, Nancy. Math in Nature. 2018. (Amazing World of Math Ser.). (ENG., Illus.). 32p. (J). (gr. 3-6). 27.99 *(978-1-5415-0099-0(7)*, 057e2314-88ef-4141-98d0-68eb52e22443, Hungry Tomato (r)) Lerner Publishing Group.

—Math in Science. 2018. (Amazing World of Math Ser.). (ENG., Illus.). 32p. (J). (gr. 3-6). 27.99 *(978-1-5415-0098-3(9)*, 107634eb-aaa6-4d65-9088-50fdb7b09ca8, Hungry Tomato (r)) Lerner Publishing Group.

—Math in Space. 2018. (Amazing World of Math Ser.). (ENG., Illus.). 32p. (J). (gr. 3-6). 27.99 *(978-1-5415-0100-3(4)*, 5717b2a1-3b14-4d24-ae55-e5a375d9cf44, Hungry Tomato (r)) Lerner Publishing Group.

Disbrow, Sheri. Math Warm-Ups: Developing Fluency in Math. 2005. (Math Warm-Ups Ser.). (ENG.). 82p. (gr. 2-2). pap. 14.95 *(978-1-59363-103-1(0))*; 82p. (gr. 3-3). pap. 14.95 *(978-1-59363-104-8(9))*; 80p. (gr. 4-4). pap. 14.95 *(978-1-59363-105-5(7))* Prufrock Pr.

—Math Warm-Ups, Grade 2. 2004. per. 12.95 *(978-1-883055-64-6(4))* Dandy Lion Pubns.

—Math Warm-Ups, Grade 3. 2004. per. 12.95 *(978-1-883055-65-3(2))* Dandy Lion Pubns.

—Math Warm-Ups, Grade 4. 2004. per. 12.95 *(978-1-883055-66-0(0))* Dandy Lion Pubns.

Dise, Molly. A Math Hike. 2011. (Wonder Readers Ser.). (ENG.). 16p. (J). (gr. -1-1). 25.95 *(978-1-4296-8541-2(7)*, 195207) Capstone.

Dix, Colton. The Popcorn Sale: Understand Place Value. 2013. (Rosen Math Readers Ser.). (ENG.). 24p. (J). (gr. 1-2). pap. 49.50 *(978-1-4777-2095-0(2))*; (Illus.). pap. 8.25 *(978-1-4777-2094-3(4)*, 9afcec61-6a47-43cb-b4be-959c3c791ebf) Rosen Publishing Group, Inc., The. (Rosen Classroom).

DK. Amazing Visual Math. 2014. (ENG.). 18p. (J). (gr. 3-7). 16.99 *(978-1-4654-2017-6(7)*, DK Children) Dorling Kindersley Publishing, Inc.

—How to Be Good at Math: Your Brilliant Brain & How to Train It. 2016. (DK How to Be Good At Ser.). (ENG., Illus.). 320p. (J). (gr. 2-5). pap. 19.99 *(978-1-4654-3575-0(1)*, DK Children) Dorling Kindersley Publishing, Inc.

—The Incredible Math Games Book. 2015. (ENG.). 16p. (J). (gr. 1-4). 16.99 *(978-1-4654-3628-3(6)*, DK Children) Dorling Kindersley Publishing, Inc.

Dockery, L. D. The Multiplication Song Book. 2012. 24p. pap. 17.99 *(978-1-4772-6900-8(2))* AuthorHouse.

Donovan, Barbara. Numbers Everywhere: A Content Area Reader-math. 2005. (Sadlier Phonics Reading Program). 12p. (gr. k-2). 25.20 *(978-0-8215-7823-0(5))* Sadlier, William H. Inc.

Dooley, Virginia. Reading & Math Jumbo Workbook: Grade PreK, 1 vol. 2005. (ENG.). 320p. (gr. -1 — 1). pap., wbk. ed. 14.99 *(978-0-439-78598-3(7)*, Teaching Resources) Scholastic, Inc.

—Scholastic Success with Reading & Math Jumbo Workbook. 2005. (ENG.). 320p. (gr. 1-1). pap., wbk. ed. 14.99 *(978-0-439-78600-3(2)*, Teaching Resources) Scholastic, Inc.

Dot-to-Dot 1-100+ (Gr. 2-4) 2003. (J). *(978-1-58232-104-2(3))* ECS Learning Systems, Inc.

Dowdy, Penny. Body Math, 1 vol. 2009. (Math Alive! Ser.). (ENG.). 32p. (gr. 4-4). lib. bdg. 31.21 *(978-0-7614-3215-9(9)*, 4d2d3d89-5c88-4f87-a837-035d2c8f7ca7) Cavendish Square Publishing LLC.

—Estimation. 2008. (My Path to Math Ser.). (ENG., Illus.). 24p. (J). (gr. k-3). pap. *(978-0-7787-4355-2(1))* Crabtree Publishing Co.

—Nature Math, 1 vol. 2009. (Math Alive! Ser.). (ENG.). 32p. (gr. 4-4). lib. bdg. 31.21 *(978-0-7614-3214-2(0)*, d8d75ca1-dbbf-4d9c-aae0-7f17b28f7fa0) Cavendish Square Publishing LLC.

Dowdy, Penny & Becker, Ann. Subtraction. 2009. (My Path to Math Ser.). (ENG.). 24p. (J). (gr. k-1). pap. *(978-0-7787-4368-2(3))* Crabtree Publishing Co.

Draze, Dianne. The Loose Caboose & Other Math Mysteries. 2005. 64p. 11.95 *(978-1-59363-136-9(7))* Prufrock Pr.

—Math-a-Logic. 2005. (ENG.). 81p. (gr. 5-8). pap. 14.95 *(978-1-59363-107-9(3))* Prufrock Pr.

Dreieckskonstruktionen. (Duden-Schuelerhilfen Ser.). (GER.). 112p. (YA). (gr. 7-8). *(978-3-411-05671-2(1))* Bibliographisches Institut & F. A. Brockhaus AG DEU. Dist: International Bk. Import Service, Inc.

Dreisatz, Prozente, Zinsen. (Duden-Schuelerhilfen Ser.). (GER.). 112p. (YA). (gr. 6-8). *(978-3-411-70762-1(3))* Bibliographisches Institut & F. A. Brockhaus AG DEU. Dist: International Bk. Import Service, Inc.

Drill, Practice, & Apply (Gr. 1-2) 2003. (J). *(978-1-58232-100-4(0))* ECS Learning Systems, Inc.

Drill, Practice, & Apply Gr. 1-2 Spanish Version. 2007. (J). per. *(978-1-58232-159-2(0))* ECS Learning Systems, Inc.

Drill, Practice, & Apply (Gr. 2-3) 2003. (J). *(978-1-58232-101-1(9))* ECS Learning Systems, Inc.

Drill, Practice, & Apply Gr. 2-3 Spanish Version. 2007. (J). per. *(978-1-58232-160-8(4))* ECS Learning Systems, Inc.

Drill, Practice, & Apply (Gr. 3-4) 2003. (J). *(978-1-58232-102-8(7))* ECS Learning Systems, Inc.

Drill, Practice, & Apply Gr. 3-4 Spanish Version. 2007. (J). per. *(978-1-58232-161-5(2))* ECS Learning Systems, Inc.

Drill, Practice, & Apply (Gr. 4-5) 2003. (J). *(978-1-58232-103-5(5))* ECS Learning Systems, Inc.

Drill, Practice, & Apply Gr. 4-5 Spanish Version. 2007. (J). per. *(978-1-58232-162-2(0))* ECS Learning Systems, Inc.

Dugan, Christine & Lane, Chloe. Pack It Up: Surface Area & Volume. rev. ed. 2012. (Mathematics in the Real World Ser.). (ENG.). 32p. (gr. 5-8). pap. 11.99 *(978-1-4333-3461-0(5))* Teacher Created Materials, Inc.

Duncan, Neil, et al. Cambridge Checkpoints HSC General Mathematics 2014. 2013. (Cambridge Checkpoints Ser.). (ENG.). pap. *(978-1-107-64370-3(8))* Cambridge Univ. Pr.

—Cambridge Checkpoints HSC Mathematics Extension 1 2014. 2013. (Cambridge Checkpoints Ser.). (ENG.). pap. *(978-1-107-64350-5(3))* Cambridge Univ. Pr.

—HSC Mathematics 2014. 2013. (Cambridge Checkpoints Ser.). (ENG.). pap. *(978-1-107-69277-0(6))* Cambridge Univ. Pr.

DynaNotes Grade 9 Math Review Guide Transparency Set. 2006. (YA). trans. *(978-1-933854-34-2(0))* DynaStudy, Inc.

DynaNotes Grade 9 Math TAKS Review Guide. 2006. (YA). pap. *(978-1-933854-30-4(8))* DynaStudy, Inc.

Eastaway, Rob & Askew, Mike. Maths on the Go: 101 Fun Ways to Play with Maths. 2016. (ENG., Illus.). 208p. 21.95 *(978-0-224-10162-2(5))* Penguin Random Hse. GBR. Dist: Independent Pubs. Group.

Edson, Ann & Schwartz, Allan A. Read & Solve Math Problems, Vol. 2. (J). (gr. 4-6). pap., act. bk. ed., pupil's gde. ed. 79.00 incl. audio *(978-0-89525-196-1(5)*, AKC 319) Educational Activities, Inc.

Educational Development Center, Inc. Staff, et al, contrib. by. Working with Data: Facilitator's Package. 2003. (Developing Mathematical Ideas Ser.). (ENG.). 81.50 *(978-0-7690-2905-4(1))* Seymour, Dale Pubns.

Education.com. All That Math: A Workbook of Basic Operations & Small Numbers. 2015. (ENG.). 128p. (J). (gr. 3-3). pap. 7.99 *(978-0-486-80268-8(X))* Dover Pubns., Inc.

—Count It: A Workbook of Patterning, Counting, & Addition. 2015. (ENG.). 128p. (J). (gr. 1-1). pap. 7.99 *(978-0-486-80260-2(4))* Dover Pubns., Inc.

—Creatures & Counting: A Workbook of Counting, Sorting, & Discovery. 2015. (ENG.). 128p. (J). (gr. -1-k). pap. 7.99 *(978-0-486-80274-9(4))* Dover Pubns., Inc.

—Earth & Sky: A Workbook of Science Facts & Math Practice. 2015. (Dover Science for Kids Ser.). (ENG.). 112p. (J). (gr. 3-3). pap. 7.99 *(978-0-486-80269-5(8)*, 802698) Dover Pubns., Inc.

Edwards, Roy. School Mathematics Project 11-16, Llyfr 1. 2005. (WEL., Illus.). 64p. *(978-1-86085-065-3(0))* ICA Video.

Edwards, Roy, et al. Mathemateg Cynradd Caergrawnt. 2005. (WEL., Illus.). 128p. pap. *(978-1-86085-070-7(7))* ICA Video.

Egan, Jill & Stewart, Rhea A. How Video Game Designers Use Math. 2009. (Math in the Real World Ser.). 32p. (gr. 4-6). 28.00 *(978-1-60413-603-6(0)*, Chelsea Clubhse.) Infobase Holdings, Inc.

Eikum, John. The 4th Dimension & Beyond: Imagining Worlds with 0, 1, 2, 3, 4 Dimensions & More. 2007. 120p. (J). per. 16.95 *(978-1-59298-172-4(0))* Beaver's Pond Pr., Inc.

Elementary Mathematics for Diverse Learners - Training Kit. 2004. (Region IV ESC Resources for Special Education Ser.). cd-rom *(978-1-932797-04-6(1))* Region 4 Education Service Ctr.

Encyclopaedia Britannica, Inc. Staff, compiled by. Britannica Math in Context Test & Practice Generator with Examview Assessment Suite. 2010. cd-rom 175.00 *(978-1-61535-441-2(7))* Encyclopaedia Britannica, Inc.

Encyclopaedia Britannica Publishers, Inc. Staff. Math in Context. 6th ed. 2005. (Math in Context Ser.). Level 1. 79.73 *(978-0-03-040374-3(X))*Level 2. 79.73 *(978-0-03-040377-4(4))*Level 3. 79.73 *(978-0-03-040378-1(2))* Harcourt Schl. Pubs.

—Math in Context: Building Formulas. 6th ed. 2005. (Math in Context Ser.). pap. 10.60 *(978-0-03-038559-9(8))* Harcourt Schl. Pubs.

—Math in Context: Dealing with Data. 6th ed. 2005. (Math in Context Ser.). pap. 10.60 *(978-0-03-038566-7(0))* Harcourt Schl. Pubs.

—Math in Context: Facts & Factors. 6th ed. 2005. (Math in Context Ser.). pap. 10.60 *(978-0-03-038564-3(4))* Harcourt Schl. Pubs.

—Math in Context: Great Predictions. 6th ed. 2005. (Math in Context Ser.). pap. 10.60 *(978-0-03-038572-8(5))* Harcourt Schl. Pubs.

—Math in Context: It's All the Same. 6th ed. 2005. (Math in Context Ser.). (gr. 8). pap. 10.60 *(978-0-03-038567-4(9))* Harcourt Schl. Pubs.

—Math in Context: Made to Measure. 6th ed. 2005. (Math in Context Ser.). (gr. 7). pap. 10.60 *(978-0-03-042404-5(6))* Harcourt Schl. Pubs.

—Math in Context: More or Less. 6th ed. 2006. (Math in Context Ser.). pap. 10.60 *(978-0-03-039618-2(2))* Harcourt Schl. Pubs.

—Math in Context: Number Tools. 6th ed. 2006. (Math in Context Ser.). pap., wbk. ed. 12.70 *(978-0-03-040384-2(7))* Harcourt Schl. Pubs.

—Math in Context: Operations. 6th ed. 2005. (Math in Context Ser.). pap. 10.60 *(978-0-03-038561-2(X))* Harcourt Schl. Pubs.

—Math in Context: Ratios & Rates. 6th ed. 2005. (Math in Context Ser.). (gr. 7). pap. 10.60 *(978-0-03-039629-8(8))* Harcourt Schl. Pubs.

—Math in Context: Reallotment. 6th ed. 2005. (Math in Context Ser.). pap. 10.60 *(978-0-03-039614-4(X))* Harcourt Schl. Pubs.

—Math in Context: Second Chance. 6th ed. 2005. (Math in Context Ser.). (gr. 7). pap. 10.60 *(978-0-03-038558-2(X))* Harcourt Schl. Pubs.

—Math in Context: Take a Chance. 6th ed. 2006. (Math in Context Ser.). (gr. 6). pap. 10.60 *(978-0-03-039613-7(1))* Harcourt Schl. Pubs.

—Math in Context: Ups & Downs. 6th ed. 2005. (Math in Context Ser.). pap. 10.60 *(978-0-03-038576-6(8))* Harcourt Schl. Pubs.

Enderle, Dotti. Storytime Discoveries: Math. Ginger Illustrations Staff, illus. 2004. 64p. (J). pap. 9.95 *(978-1-57310-440-1(X))* Teaching & Learning Co.

Essential Words Math Activity Book (Elementary) Elementary. 2006. (J). 8.95 *(978-1-933655-04-8(6))* New Leaf Educ., Inc.

Essential Words Math Activity Book (Intermediate) Intermediate/Middle School. 2005. (Illus.). 42p. (J). 8.95 *(978-0-9722452-9-6(4))* New Leaf Educ., Inc.

Evan-Moor. Math Centers, Grades 2-3. 2004. (ENG., Illus.). 192p. (J). (gr. 2-3). pap. 21.99 *(978-1-55799-978-8(3)*, EMC 3021) Evan-Moor Educational Pubs.

—Math Centers, Grades 3-4. 2004. (ENG., Illus.). 192p. (J). (gr. 3-4). pap. 21.99 *(978-1-55799-979-5(1)*, EMC 3022) Evan-Moor Educational Pubs.

Evan-Moor Educational Publishers. Basic Math Skills Grade 1. 2003. (Basic Math Skills Ser.). (ENG., Illus.). 304p. (J). (gr. 1-1). pap., tchr. ed. 29.99 *(978-1-55799-896-5(5)*, EMC 3014) Evan-Moor Educational Pubs.

—Basic Math Skills Grade 2. 2003. (Basic Math Skills Ser.). (ENG., Illus.). 304p. (J). (gr. 2-2). pap., tchr. ed. 29.99 *(978-1-55799-897-2(3)*, EMC 3015) Evan-Moor Educational Pubs.

—Basic Math Skills Grade 3. 2003. (Basic Math Skills Ser.). (ENG., Illus.). 304p. (J). (gr. 3-3). pap., tchr. ed. 29.99 *(978-1-55799-898-9(1)*, EMC 3016) Evan-Moor Educational Pubs.

—Basic Math Skills Grade 4. 2003. (Basic Math Skills Ser.). (ENG., Illus.). 304p. (J). (gr. 4-4). pap., tchr. ed. 29.99 *(978-1-55799-937-5(6)*, EMC 3017) Evan-Moor Educational Pubs.

Evans, Karen. Math Basics 6: Grade 6. deluxe ed. 2017. (ENG., Illus.). 64p. (J). (gr. 6-6). mass mkt., wbk. ed. 4.49 *(978-0-88743-142-5(9)*, 9e7cba0c-3833-4aa8-9b8b-1194b3149e65) School Zone Publishing Co.

Evans, Kevin, et al. GCSE Maths Edexcel Foundation Student Book. 4th rev. ed. 2015. (Collins GCSE Maths Ser.). (ENG.). 700p. (YA). (gr. 9-11). pap., stu. ed. 31.95 *(978-0-00-811382-7(3))* HarperCollins Pubs. Ltd. GBR. Dist: Independent Pubs. Group.

—KS3 Maths Pupil Book 3. 3. 3rd ed. 2014. (Maths Frameworking Ser.). (ENG., Illus.). 360p. (YA). (gr. 9-9). pap. 28.95 *(978-0-00-753779-2(4))* HarperCollins Pubs. Ltd. GBR. Dist: Independent Pubs. Group.

Evans, Lesli. Transport Math, 1 vol. 2009. (Math Alive! Ser.). (ENG.). 32p. (gr. 4-4). lib. bdg. 31.21 *(978-0-7614-3211-1(6)*, f815c05c-ff16-4bb7-8c4a-9970b7b8027a) Cavendish Square Publishing LLC.

Exploring Acadia National Park: Solve Problems Involving the Four Operations, 1 vol. 2014. (Rosen Math Readers Ser.). (ENG., Illus.). 24p. (J). (gr. 3-3). pap. 8.25 *(978-1-4777-4944-9(6)*, 1703e656-a406-480c-96b7-6d85916d16ec, PowerKids Pr.) Rosen Publishing Group, Inc., The.

Exploring Geometric Solids. 2004. (J). per. 4.95 *(978-1-56911-538-1(9))* Learning Resources, Inc.

Extend the Day! a Guide to Using Larson's Intermediate Math in Before-School & after-School Programs. 2003. spiral bd. 0.00 *(978-1-58123-339-1(6))* Larson Learning, Inc.

Extend the Day! a Guide to Using Larson's Prealgebra & Larson's Algebra 1 in Before-School & after-School Programs. 2003. spiral bd. 0.00 *(978-1-58123-340-7(X))* Larson Learning, Inc.

Fact Families Staff. LP-Fact Families: Level 1 Math. 2004. (ENG.) (J). 9.99 *(978-1-59204-016-2(0))* Learning Wrap-Ups, Inc.

Falvo, David C. Passport to Mathematics Practice Workbook: Book 1. 2006. (Illus.). 87p. (gr. 6-12). stu. ed., per., wbk. ed. *(978-0-395-89626-6(6)*, 2-77680) Holt McDougal.

Fan, Professor Lianghuo. Practice Book Year 8: for the English National Curriculum (the Shanghai Maths Project), Bk. 8. 2018. (Shanghai Maths Ser.). (ENG., Illus.). 288p. (J). pap., wbk. ed. 13.95 *(978-0-00-814469-2(9))* HarperCollins Pubs. Ltd. GBR. Dist: Independent Pubs. Group.

Fannon, Paul, et al. Mathematics Higher Level - Discrete Mathematics for the IB Diploma. 2013. (IB Diploma Ser.). (ENG., Illus.). 187p. pap. 23.20 *(978-1-107-66694-8(5))* Cambridge Univ. Pr.

—Mathematics Higher Level for the IB Diploma Option Topic 8 Sets, Relations & Groups. 2013. (IB Diploma Ser.). (ENG., Illus.). 148p. pap. 23.20 *(978-1-107-64628-5(6))* Cambridge Univ. Pr.

—Mathematics Higher Level Statistics & Probability for the IB Diploma. 2013. (IB Diploma Ser.). (ENG., Illus.). 172p. pap. 23.20 *(978-1-107-68226-9(6))* Cambridge Univ. Pr.

Farrell, Peter. Math Adventures with Python: An Illustrated Guide to Exploring Math with Code. 2019. (Illus.). 304p. (gr. 5). pap. 29.99 *(978-1-59327-867-0(5))* No Starch Pr., Inc.

Faulkner, Nicholas & Gregersen, Erik, eds. Analysis & Calculus, 1 vol. 2017. (Foundations of Math Ser.). (ENG., Illus.). 352p. (J). (gr. 10-10). 55.59 *(978-1-68048-775-6(2)*, 75bd0dd4-6c82-4edc-b82d-deb12c694857) Rosen Publishing Group, Inc., The.

Feldman, Jean & Karapetkova, Holly. Math Songs. unabr. ed. 2010. (ENG.). 16p. (gr. -1-k). 12.99 *(978-1-61741-588-3(X))* Rourke Educational Media.

Feldman, Sarah. Symmetry in Our World: Set Of 6. 2011. (Early Connections Ser.). (J). pap. 39.00 net. *(978-1-4108-1545-3(5))* Benchmark Education Co.

Ferniano, Robert. Dr. Funster's Quick Thinks Math C1: Fun Math Brain Teasers. 2003. (Dr. Funster's Ser.). 44p. (gr. 8-10). pap. 3.99 *(978-0-89455-831-3(5))* Critical Thinking Co., The.

Ferguson, creator. Math. 2nd rev. ed. 2008. (Discovering Careers for Your Future Ser.). (ENG.). 91p. (gr. 4-9). 21.95 *(978-0-8160-7278-1(7)*, P179083, Ferguson Publishing Company) Infobase Holdings, Inc.

—Mathematics & Physics. 2nd rev. ed. 2008. (Ferguson's Careers in Focus Ser.). (ENG.). 202p. (gr. 6-12). 32.95 *(978-0-8160-7274-3(4)*, P179081, Ferguson Publishing Company) Infobase Holdings, Inc.

Ferrie, Chris. ABCs of Mathematics. 2017. (Baby University Ser.: 0). (Illus.). 26p. (J). (gr. -1-k). bds. 9.99 *(978-1-4926-5628-9(3))* Sourcebooks, Inc.

First-Glance Finance, 12 vols. 2014. (First-Glance Finance Ser.). (ENG.). 48p. (J). (gr. 4-4). lib. bdg. 198.42 *(978-1-5026-0292-3(X)*, 2acad7d6-e5e4-4ae1-b41e-ff11a3c8b4b4, Cavendish Square) Cavendish Square Publishing LLC.

First Number Skills Spanish Version. 2007. (J). per. *(978-1-58232-150-9(7))* ECS Learning Systems, Inc.

First Picture Math. 2007. (First Picture Board Bks). (Illus.). 16p. (J). (gr. -1-k). bds. 11.99 *(978-0-7945-1642-0(4)*, Usborne) EDC Publishing.

First, Rachel. Weigh It! Fun with Weight, 1 vol. 2015. (Math Beginnings Ser.). (ENG., Illus.). 24p. (J). (gr. -1-3). 29.93 *(978-1-62403-936-2(7)*, 19299, SandCastle) ABDO Publishing Co.

Fisher, Richard W. Mastering Essential Math Skills, Book One: Grades 4 And 5: 20 Minutes a Day to Success. 2007. (Mastering Essential Math Skills Ser.). (Illus.). 142p. (J). (gr. 6-13). pap. 19.95 *(978-0-9821901-0-4(7))* Math Essentials.

Fishman, Seth. A Hundred Billion Trillion Stars. Greenberg, Isabel, illus. 2017. (ENG.). 40p. (J). (gr. -1-3). 17.99 *(978-0-06-245578-9(8)*, Greenwillow Bks.) HarperCollins Pubs.

Fitzsimmons, Jim & Whiteford, Rhona. Maths Tests. (ENG., Illus.). 32p. (J). pap. 6.99 *(978-0-340-68070-4(9))* Hodder & Stoughton GBR. Dist: Trafalgar Square Publishing.

Fix, Natalie. Graphing Death Valley: Represent & Interpret Data, 1 vol. 2014. (InfoMax Math Readers Ser.). (ENG.). 24p. (J). (gr. 3-3). pap. 8.25 *(978-1-4777-4600-4(5)*, dacda751-ee58-4a49-9458-52e7cde5b717, Rosen Classroom) Rosen Publishing Group, Inc., The.

Flash Kids Editors, ed. Math Drills: Grade 1 (Flash Skills) 2010. (Flash Skills Ser.). (ENG.). 64p. (J). pap. 3.95 *(978-1-4114-3460-8(9)*, Spark Publishing Group) Sterling Publishing Co., Inc.

—Multiplication Activities: Grade 3 (Flash Skills) 2010. (Flash Skills Ser.). (ENG.). 64p. (J). pap. 3.95

MNO

(978-1-4114-3452-3(8), Spark Publishing Group) Sterling Publishing Co., Inc.

—Number Puzzles & Games: Grade Pre-K-K (Flash Skills) 2010. (Flash Skills Ser.). (ENG.). 64p. (J). pap. 3.95 *(978-1-4114-3464-6(1)*, Spark Publishing Group) Sterling Publishing Co., Inc.

—Place Value: Grade 1 (Flash Skills) 2010. (Flash Skills Ser.). (ENG.). 64p. (J). pap. 3.95 *(978-1-4114-3455-4(2)*, Spark Publishing Group) Sterling Publishing Co., Inc.

Flash Kids Editors, Flash Kids, ed. Summer Study, Grade 3. 2016. (Summer Study Ser.). (ENG., Illus.). 160p. (J). (gr. 3-3). pap. 9.95 *(978-1-4114-7859-6(2)*, Spark Publishing Group) Sterling Publishing Co., Inc.

—Summer Study, Grade 4. 2016. (Summer Study Ser.). (ENG., Illus.). 160p. (J). (gr. 4-4). pap. 9.95 *(978-1-4114-7860-2(6)*, Spark Publishing Group) Sterling Publishing Co., Inc.

—Summer Study, Grade 5. 2016. (Summer Study Ser.). (ENG., Illus.). 160p. (J). (gr. 5-5). pap. 9.95 *(978-1-4114-7861-9(4)*, Spark Publishing Group) Sterling Publishing Co., Inc.

Flatt, Lizann. Line Graphs. 2016. (Get Graphing! Building Data Literacy Skills Ser.). (ENG., Illus.). 24p. (J). (gr. 1-3). *(978-0-7787-2625-8(8))* Crabtree Publishing Co.

Flip over Math: Addition & Subtraction. 2004. (J). spiral bd. 14.95 *(978-1-56911-540-4(0))* Learning Resources, Inc.

Flip over Math: Multiplication & Division. 2004. (J). spiral bd. 14.95 *(978-1-56911-541-1(9))* Learning Resources, Inc.

Flip over Math: Story Problems. 2004. (J). spiral bd. 14.95 *(978-1-56911-542-8(7))* Learning Resources, Inc.

Foresman, Scott. Scott Foresman - Addison Wesley Mathematics: Additional Resources. 2003. (ENG.). (gr. k-2). 46.97 net. *(978-0-328-08111-0(6))*; (gr. 5-6). 45.47 net. *(978-0-328-08113-4(2))* Savvas Learning Co. (Scott Foresman).

—Scott Foresman-Addison Wesley Mathematics. 2003. (ENG.). (gr. k-k). pap., stu. ed. 28.47 net. *(978-0-328-07586-7(8))*; (gr. k-k). pap., wbk. ed. 10.47 net. *(978-0-328-04931-8(X))*; (gr. k-k). pap., wbk. ed. 6.97 net. *(978-0-328-04952-3(2))*; (gr. 1-1). pap., stu. ed. 57.00 net. *(978-0-328-03016-3(3))* Savvas Learning Co. (Scott Foresman).

—Scott Foresman-Addison Wesley Mathematics: Pre-K Mathematics. 2003. (ENG.). (gr. -1 — 1). 62.47 net. *(978-0-328-09168-3(5))*; (gr. 1-1). 24.97 net. *(978-0-328-09365-6(3))*; (gr. 1-1). 26.97 net. *(978-0-328-09227-7(4))*; (gr. k-6). cd-rom 50.97 net. *(978-0-328-08590-3(1))*; (gr. 1-1). 26.97 net. *(978-0-328-08088-5(8))* Savvas Learning Co. (Scott Foresman).

—Scott Foresman-Addison Wesley Mathematics: Pupil Edition. 2003. (ENG.). (gr. 2-2). pap. 57.00 net. *(978-0-328-03017-0(1)*, Scott Foresman) Savvas Learning Co.

—Scott Foresman-Addison Wesley Mathematics: Workbooks. 2003. (ENG.). (gr. 1-1). pap., wbk. ed. 15.00 net. *(978-0-328-07556-0(6))*; (gr. 2-2). pap., wbk. ed. 15.00 net. *(978-0-328-07557-7(4))*; (gr. 3-3). pap., wbk. ed. 10.97 net. *(978-0-328-07558-4(2))*; (gr. 4-4). pap., wbk. ed. 10.97 net. *(978-0-328-07559-1(0))*; (gr. 5-5). pap., wbk. ed. 10.97 net. *(978-0-328-07560-7(4))*; (gr. 6-6). pap., wbk. ed. 15.00 net. *(978-0-328-07561-4(2))*; (gr. 1-1). pap., wbk. ed. 10.97 net. *(978-0-328-04932-5(8))*; (gr. 1-1). pap., wbk. ed. 10.00 net. *(978-0-328-04953-0(0))*; (gr. 1-1). pap., wbk. ed. 7.47 net. *(978-0-328-04959-2(X))*; (gr. 2-2). pap., wbk. ed. 15.00 net. *(978-0-328-04933-2(6))*; (gr. 2-2). pap., wbk. ed. 11.50 net. *(978-0-328-04966-0(2))*; (gr. 2-2). pap., wbk. ed. 7.47 net. *(978-0-328-04960-8(3))*; (gr. 2-2). pap., wbk. ed. 10.00 net. *(978-0-328-04954-7(9))*; (gr. 3-3). pap., wbk. ed. 10.97 net. *(978-0-328-04934-9(4))*; (gr. 3-3). pap., wbk. ed. 7.47 net. *(978-0-328-04961-5(1))*; (gr. 3-3). pap., wbk. ed. 10.00 net. *(978-0-328-04955-4(7))*; (gr. 3-3). pap., wbk. ed. 10.97 net. *(978-0-328-04967-7(0))*; (gr. 4-4). pap., wbk. ed. 10.00 net. *(978-0-328-04956-1(5))*; (gr. 4-4). pap., wbk. ed. 10.00 net. *(978-0-328-04962-2(X))*; (gr. 4-4). pap., wbk. ed. 10.97 net. *(978-0-328-04935-6(2))*; (gr. 4-4). pap., wbk. ed. 9.47 net. *(978-0-328-04968-4(9))*; (gr. 5-5). pap., wbk. ed. 10.00 net. *(978-0-328-04963-9(8))*; (gr. 5-5). pap., wbk. ed. 10.47 net. *(978-0-328-04936-3(0))*; (gr. 5-5). pap., wbk. ed. 10.97 net. *(978-0-328-04969-1(7))*; (gr. 5-5). pap., wbk. ed. 10.00 net. *(978-0-328-04957-8(3))*; (gr. 6-6). pap., wbk. ed. 7.47 net. *(978-0-328-04964-6(6))*; (gr. 6-6). pap., wbk. ed. 9.97 net. *(978-0-328-04937-0(9))*; (gr. 6-6). pap., wbk. ed. 10.00 net. *(978-0-328-04958-5(1))*; (gr. 6-6). pap., wbk. ed. 9.47 net. *(978-0-328-04970-7(0))* Savvas Learning Co. (Scott Foresman).

—Scott Foresman-Addison Wesley Mathematics 2. 2003. (ENG.). (gr. k-k). stu. ed. 175.97 net. *(978-0-328-06321-5(5)*, Scott Foresman) Savvas Learning Co.

—Scott Foresman-Addison Wesley Mathematics 3. 2003. (ENG.). (gr. k-k). stu. ed. 175.97 net. *(978-0-328-06322-2(3)*, Scott Foresman) Savvas Learning Co.

—Scott Foresman-Addison Wesley Mathematics 4. 2003. (ENG.). (gr. k-k). stu. ed. 175.97 net. *(978-0-328-06323-9(1)*, Scott Foresman) Savvas Learning Co.

—Scott Foresman-Addison Wesley Mathematics 1. 2003. (ENG.). (gr. k-k). stu. ed. 175.97 net. *(978-0-328-06320-8(7)*, Scott Foresman) Savvas Learning Co.

—Scott Foresman Math Around the Clock. 2003. (ENG.). (gr. 1-1). pap., wbk. ed. 46.47 net. *(978-0-328-06427-4(0))*; (gr. 1-1). pap., wbk. ed. 46.47 net. *(978-0-328-06428-1(9))*; (gr. 1-1). pap., wbk. ed. 46.47 net. *(978-0-328-06429-8(7))*; (gr. 1-1). pap., wbk. ed. 46.47 net. *(978-0-328-06430-4(0))*; (gr. 1-1). pap., wbk. ed. 46.47 net. *(978-0-328-06431-1(9))*; (gr. 1-1). pap., wbk. ed. 46.47 net. *(978-0-328-06432-8(7))*; (gr. 1-1). pap., wbk. ed. 46.47 net. *(978-0-328-06433-5(5))*; (gr. 1-1). pap., wbk. ed. 46.47 net. *(978-0-328-06426-7(2))*; (gr. 2-2). pap., wbk. ed. 46.47 net. *(978-0-328-06434-2(3))*; (gr. 2-2). pap., wbk. ed. 46.47 net. *(978-0-328-06435-9(1))*; (gr. 2-2). pap., wbk. ed. 46.47 net. *(978-0-328-06436-6(X))*; (gr. 2-2). pap., wbk. ed. 46.47 net. *(978-0-328-06437-3(8))*; (gr. 2-2). pap., wbk. ed. 46.47 net. *(978-0-328-06438-0(6))*; (gr. 2-2). pap., wbk. ed. 46.47 net. *(978-0-328-06439-7(4))*; (gr. 2-2). pap., wbk. ed. 46.47 net. *(978-0-328-06440-3(8))*; (gr. 3-3). pap., wbk. ed. 46.47 net. *(978-0-328-06448-9(3))*; (gr. 3-3). pap., wbk. ed. 46.47 net. *(978-0-328-06447-2(5))*; (gr. 3-3). pap., wbk. ed. 46.47 net. *(978-0-328-06446-5(7))*; (gr. 3-3). pap., wbk. ed. 46.47 net. *(978-0-328-06445-8(9))*; (gr. 3-3). pap., wbk. ed. 46.47 net. *(978-0-328-06444-1(0))*; (gr. 3-3). pap., wbk. ed. 46.47 net. *(978-0-328-06443-4(2))*; (gr. 3-3). pap., wbk. ed. 46.47 net. *(978-0-328-06442-7(4))*; (gr. 3-3). pap., wbk. ed. 46.47 net. *(978-0-328-06441-0(6))*; (gr. 4-4). pap., wbk. ed. 46.47 net. *(978-0-328-06455-7(6))*; (gr. 4-4). pap., wbk. ed. 46.47 net. *(978-0-328-06454-0(8))*; (gr. 4-4). pap., wbk. ed. 46.47 net. *(978-0-328-06453-3(X))*; (gr. 4-4). pap., wbk. ed. 46.47 net. *(978-0-328-06451-9(3))*; (gr. 4-4). pap., wbk. ed. 46.47 net. *(978-0-328-06450-2(5))*; (gr. 4-4). pap., wbk. ed. 46.47 net. *(978-0-328-06449-6(1))*; (gr. 5-5). pap., wbk. ed. 46.47 net. *(978-0-328-06456-4(4))*; (gr. 5-5). pap., wbk. ed. 46.47 net. *(978-0-328-06463-2(7))*; (gr. 5-5). pap., wbk. ed. 46.47 net. *(978-0-328-06462-5(9))*; (gr. 5-5). pap., wbk. ed. 46.47 net. *(978-0-328-06461-8(0))*; (gr. 5-5). pap., wbk. ed. 46.47 net. *(978-0-328-06460-1(2))*; (gr. 5-5). pap., wbk. ed. 46.47 net. *(978-0-328-06459-5(9))*; (gr. 5-5). pap., wbk. ed. 46.47 net. *(978-0-328-06458-8(0))*; (gr. 5-5). pap., wbk. ed. 46.47 net. *(978-0-328-06457-1(2))*; (gr. 6-6). pap., wbk. ed. 46.47 net. *(978-0-328-06464-9(5))*; (gr. 6-6). pap., wbk. ed. 46.47 net. *(978-0-328-06465-6(3))*; (gr. 6-6). pap., wbk. ed. 46.47 net. *(978-0-328-06466-3(1))*; (gr. 6-6). pap., wbk. ed. 46.47 net. *(978-0-328-06467-0(X))*; (gr. 6-6). pap., wbk. ed. 46.47 net. *(978-0-328-06468-7(8))*; (gr. 6-6). pap., wbk. ed. 46.47 net. *(978-0-328-06469-4(6))*; (gr. 6-6). pap., wbk. ed. 46.47 net. *(978-0-328-06470-0(X))* Savvas Learning Co. (Scott Foresman).

Forest, Anne. My Lemonade Stand: Represent & Interpret Data. 2013. (InfoMax Math Readers Ser.). (ENG.). 24p. (J). (gr. 1-2). pap. 49.50 *(978-1-4777-2173-5(8))*; (Illus.). pap. 8.25 *(978-1-4777-2172-8(X)*, 22bcdc55-f882-4e53-8b50-0adfbb59109e) Rosen Publishing Group, Inc., The. (Rosen Classroom).

Forte, Imogene. Ready to Learn Beginning Math. 2003. (Illus.). 64p. per. 7.95 *(978-0-86530-594-6(3))* Incentive Pubns., Inc.

Fortunado, Hector. Jose's Hardware Store: Understand Place Value, 1 vol. 2013. (InfoMax Math Readers Ser.). (ENG., Illus.). 24p. (J). (gr. 1-1). pap. 8.25 *(978-1-4777-2192-6(4)*, 0d0909b4-ab5c-4e43-9938-8592d17405bc, Rosen Classroom) Rosen Publishing Group, Inc., The.

—Jos's Hardware Store: Understand Place Value. 2013. (InfoMax Math Readers Ser.). (ENG.). 24p. (J). (gr. 1-2). pap. 49.50 *(978-1-4777-2193-3(2)*, Rosen Classroom) Rosen Publishing Group, Inc., The.

Fosnot, Catherine Twomey & Lent, Patricia. Trades, Jumps, & Stops: Early Algebra. 2008. (ENG.). 96p. (gr. 1-2). pap. 31.25 *(978-0-325-01015-1(3)*, E01015, Firsthand) Heinemann.

Franchino, Vicky. Droughts. 2012. (21st Century Skills Library: Real World Math Ser.). (ENG., Illus.). 32p. (gr. 4-8). (J). pap. 14.21 *(978-1-61080-407-3(4)*, 201339); lib. bdg. 32.07 *(978-1-61080-322-9(1)*, 201300) Cherry Lake Publishing.

Frary, Mark. Mathematics Explained, 1 vol., 1. 2013. (Guide for Curious Minds Ser.). (ENG.). 133p. (YA). (gr. 8-8). 42.41 *(978-1-4777-2971-7(2)*, d97ade58-f7a8-445e-945d-13eecd4b7c88) Rosen Publishing Group, Inc., The.

Freese, Joan. TABLAS y GRÁFICAS de Cosas Saludables (TABLES & GRAPHS of Healthy Things), 1 vol. 2007. (Las Matemáticas en Nuestro Mundo - Nivel 1 (Math in Our World - Level 1) Ser.). (SPA.). 24p. (gr. 1-1). pap. 9.15 *(978-0-8368-8498-2(1)*, 3c47c38c-642a-44c5-ba11-2337bc8649a2); (Illus.). lib. bdg. 24.67 *(978-0-8368-8489-0(2)*, 96ed401d-b09a-4a3d-aff0-bcf2ddb231fa) Stevens, Gareth Publishing LLLP. (Weekly Reader Leveled Readers).

—TABLES & GRAPHS of Healthy Things, 1 vol. 2007. (Math in Our World - Level 1 Ser.). (ENG.). 24p. (gr. 1-1). pap. 9.15 *(978-0-8368-8480-7(9)*, 9e43a208-12e1-458d-908f-c34490f4ae54); (Illus.). lib. bdg. 24.67 *(978-0-8368-8471-5(X)*, 66e458b0-93b3-4dc1-bd13-1ade8e9e05f7) Stevens, Gareth Publishing LLLP. (Weekly Reader Leveled Readers).

French. Consumer Mathematics. (J). (gr. 7-12). 32.97 *(978-0-13-166729-7(7))* Prentice Hall (Schl. Div.).

Freudentha, H. Powers of Ten: Math Context. 3rd ed. 2003. (Math in Context Ser.). 8.33 *(978-0-03-071529-7(6))* Holt McDougal.

—Re-Allotment Math/Context. 3rd ed. 2003. (Math in Context Ser.). 8.33 *(978-0-03-071511-2(3))* Holt McDougal.

Freudenthal. Expressions & Formulas. 3rd ed. 2003. (Math in Context Ser.). (Illus.). 8.33 *(978-0-03-071444-3(3))* Holt McDougal.

—Growth. 3rd ed. 2003. (Math in Context Ser.). (Illus.). 8.33 *(978-0-03-071667-6(5))* Holt McDougal.

—Patterns & Symbols. 3rd ed. 2003. (Math in Context Ser.). (Illus.). 8.33 *(978-0-03-071283-8(1))* Holt McDougal.

—Percentage Sense. 3rd ed. 2003. (Math in Context Ser.). (Illus.). 8.33 *(978-0-03-071286-9(6))* Holt McDougal.

Frith, Alex. What's Math All About? 2012. (What's Math All about? Ser.). 96p. (J). pap. 10.99 *(978-0-7945-3126-3(1)*, Usborne) EDC Publishing.

Frith, Alex & Lacey, Minna. See Inside Math - Internet Referenced. 2008. (See Inside Board Bks). 16p. (J). bds. 12.99 *(978-0-7945-2093-9(6)*, Usborne) EDC Publishing.

Fronczak, Blaine. Haley Helps at School, 1 vol. 2013. (Core Math Skills: Numbers & Operations in Base 10 Ser.). (ENG.). 24p. (J). (gr. 1-1). 26.27 *(978-1-4777-2225-1(4)*, fe2374ab-7523-47c6-bbb2-7940c865478a); pap. 8.25 *(978-1-4777-2097-4(9)*, 4a879267-fd94-431b-85ea-d6ecdafc7033) Rosen Publishing Group, Inc., The. (Rosen Classroom).

—Haley Helps at School: Use Place Value & Properties of Operations to Add. 2013. (Rosen Math Readers Ser.). (ENG.). 24p. (J). (gr. 1-2). pap. 49.50 *(978-1-4777-2098-1(7)*, Rosen Classroom) Rosen Publishing Group, Inc., The.

Fuerst, Jeffrey B. Sorting at My Desk: Lap Book. 2009. (My First Reader's Theater Set B Ser.). (J). 28.00 *(978-1-60634-987-8(2))* Benchmark Education Co.

Fuller, Jill. Rookie Read-About Math: Springtime Addition. 2005. (Rookie Read-About Math Ser.). (ENG., Illus.). 32p. (J). (gr. 1-2). pap. 5.95 *(978-0-516-24668-0(2)*, Children's Pr.) Scholastic Library Publishing.

—Toy Box Subtraction. 2004. (Rookie Read-About Math Ser.). (J). 20.50 *(978-0-516-24423-5(X)*, Children's Pr.) Scholastic Library Publishing.

Furgang, Kathy. Math Fun at the Fair. 2011. (Early Connections Ser.). (J). *(978-1-61672-589-1(3))* Benchmark Education Co.

—Math Fun at the Fair: Set Of 6. 2011. (Early Connections Ser.). (J). pap. 37.00 net. *(978-1-4108-1076-2(3))* Benchmark Education Co.

—Pizza Parts: Set Of 6. 2011. (Early Connections Ser.). (J). pap. 39.00 net. *(978-1-4108-1548-4(X))* Benchmark Education Co.

Furstinger, Nancy. Discovering Cylinders. 2016. (J). *(978-1-4896-4980-5(8))* Weigl Pubs., Inc.

Ganesan, C. T. Fun with Maths. 2005. (Illus.). 188p. (gr. 4-7). per. *(978-1-84549-027-0(4))* arima publishing.

Gannett, Barbara. Count Your Money: A Content Area Reader-math. 2005. (Emergent/Early (Prek-2) Math Package Ser.). 20p. (gr. k-2). 25.20 *(978-0-8215-7821-6(9))* Sadlier, William H. Inc.

Gardner, Colin. Pythagorean Triangle Properties & Attributes Samples (Enlarged), As Independently Discovered by Colin Gardner, Physicist: Pythagorean triples are everwhere, & have an application in nearly every math lesson(6th grade thru College. 2nd ed. 2004. Orig. Title: Pythagorean Triangle Properties & Attributes Samples. (Illus.). 6p. (YA). (gr. 6-18). 7.95 *(978-0-9720348-5-2(4))* Gardner, Colin.

Gardner, Harvey. Fun in Fall: Work with Addition & Subtraction Equations. 2013. (Rosen Math Readers Ser.). (ENG.). 24p. (J). (gr. 1-2). pap. 49.50 *(978-1-4777-2035-6(9))*; (Illus.). pap. 8.25 *(978-1-4777-2034-9(0)*, f4433b32-6e79-46df-9bea-a168c0b7f496) Rosen Publishing Group, Inc., The. (Rosen Classroom).

Gave, Marc. Number Games Around the World & Juegos de números alrededor del Mundo: 6 English, 6 Spanish Adaptations 2011. (Navigators Ser.). (ENG & SPA.). (J). instr.'s gde. ed. 97.00 net. *(978-1-4108-1765-5(2))* Benchmark Education Co.

Gaydos, Nora. Math Madness. Independent. 2003. (Now I'm Reading!). (Illus.). 128p. (J). 14.99 *(978-1-58476-248-5(9))* Innovative Kids.

Gensmer, Laura. Score One for Math! 2011. (Wonder Readers Ser.). (ENG.). 16p. (J). (gr. -1-1). 25.95 *(978-1-4296-8671-6(5)*, 195212, Capstone Pr.) Capstone.

GER Math Tool Kit A. 2006. (J). 19.95 *(978-1-934046-10-4(8))* Global Education Resources, LLC.

Ghim, John Y. Ghim's Critical Exercises of High School Math. 2004. (Illus.). 340p. (YA). (gr. 9-12). pap. 35.99 *(978-0-9656864-1-9(8))* Ghim, John Yun.

—Ghim's Critical Exercises of High School Math Answers & Explanations. 2004. (YA). per. 12.95 *(978-0-9656864-2-6(6))* Ghim, John Yun.

Giganti, Paul. Numeros Importantes. Grbich, Aaron, illus. (SPA.). (J). (gr. 1-3). pap. 3.16 net. *(978-0-590-48700-9(0)*, Scholastic Pr.) Scholastic, Inc.

Ginsburg, Herbert P., et al. Acorn Hunt. 2003. (Illus.). 9.95 *(978-0-7690-3046-3(7))* Seymour, Dale Pubns.

—Big Math for Little Kids: Classroom Manipulative Kit. 2003. (Illus.). 251.50 *(978-0-7690-3064-7(5))* Seymour, Dale Pubns.

—Dobee Doubler. 2003. (Illus.). 9.95 *(978-0-7690-3042-5(4))* Seymour, Dale Pubns.

—Jenny Saves the Day. 2003. (Illus.). 9.95 *(978-0-7690-3047-0(5))* Seymour, Dale Pubns.

—Leftover Muffins. 2003. (Illus.). 9.95 *(978-0-7690-3040-1(8))* Seymour, Dale Pubns.

—Rafael's Messy Room. 2003. (Illus.). 9.95 *(978-0-7690-3045-6(9))* Seymour, Dale Pubns.

—So Many Fives! 2003. (Illus.). 9.95 *(978-0-7690-3044-9(0))* Seymour, Dale Pubns.

—The Table of Phinneas Fable. 2003. (Illus.). 9.95 *(978-0-7690-3048-7(3))* Seymour, Dale Pubns.

—Tick-Tock! 2003. (Illus.). 9.95 *(978-0-7690-3041-8(6))* Seymour, Dale Pubns.

—The Trees of Mrs. Mcgee. 2003. (Illus.). 9.95 *(978-0-7690-3049-4(1))* Seymour, Dale Pubns.

Girard, Robert. The American Flag: Learning to Identify Two-Digit Numbers up To 50. 2004. (Math Big Bookstm Ser.). (ENG.). 12p. (gr. 1-2). 33.50 *(978-0-8239-7632-4(7))* Rosen Publishing Group, Inc., The.

Glasscock, Sarah & Stewart, Rhea A. How Nurses Use Math. 2009. (Math in the Real World Ser.). (ENG.). 32p. (gr. 4-6). 28.00 *(978-1-60413-607-4(3)*, P466916, Chelsea Clubhse.) Infobase Holdings, Inc.

Gleichungen mit zwei Unbekannten. (Duden-Schuelerhilfen Ser.). (GER.). 96p. (YA). (gr. 8-9). *(978-3-411-02622-7(7))* Bibliographisches Institut & F. A. Brockhaus AG DEU. Dist: International Bk. Import Service, Inc.

Gleichungen und Ungleichungen 1. 2nd ed. (Duden-Schuelerhilfen Ser.). (GER.). 112p. (J). (gr. 5-6). *(978-3-411-70872-7(7))* Bibliographisches Institut & F. A. Brockhaus AG DEU. Dist: International Bk. Import Service, Inc.

Gleichungen und Ungleichungen 2. (Duden-Schuelerhilfen Ser.). (GER.). 112p. (YA). (gr. 7-8). *(978-3-411-70682-2(1))* Bibliographisches Institut & F. A. Brockhaus AG DEU. Dist: International Bk. Import Service, Inc.

Goba, Busisiwe, et al. Mathematics for Zambia Basic Education Grade 7 Pupil's Book. 2007. (ENG., Illus.). 184p. pap., stu. ed. *(978-0-521-70345-1(X))* Cambridge Univ. Pr.

Goldie, Sophie, et al. Formula One Maths Gold. 2004. (ENG., Illus.). 228p. pap., pupil's gde. ed. 39.50 *(978-0-340-86934-5(8)*, Hodder Education) Hodder Education Group GBR. Dist: Trans-Atlantic Pubns., Inc.

Goldsmith, Mike. I Wish I Knew That. 2012. (J). *(978-1-60652-474-9(7))* Reader's Digest Assn., Inc., The.

—This Book Thinks You're a Maths Genius: Imagine · Experiment · Create. 2017. (ENG., Illus.). 96p. (J). (gr. 2-8). pap. 14.95 *(978-0-500-65117-9(5)*, 565117) Thames & Hudson.

Goldstone, Bruce. Great Estimations. Goldstone, Bruce, illus. 2010. (ENG., Illus.). 32p. (J). (gr. 2-5). pap. 8.99 *(978-0-312-60887-3(X)*, 900065182) Square Fish.

Gottwald, Siegfried, et al. Meyers Kleine Enzyklopädie Mathematik. 14th ed. (GER., Illus.). 810p. *(978-3-411-07771-7(9))* Bibliographisches Institut & F. A. Brockhaus AG DEU. Dist: i. b. d., Ltd.

Graham, Amy. Astonishing Ancient World Scientists: Eight Great Brains, 1 vol. 2009. (Great Scientists & Famous Inventors Ser.). (ENG., Illus.). 128p. (gr. 6-7). lib. bdg. 37.27 *(978-1-59845-079-8(4)*, 4e5b556f-9694-404a-a25e-3fa0eafcb78a) Enslow Publishing, LLC.

Graham, Noel & Blundell, Graham. Graph Pack. (Illus.). 22p. (J). (gr. k-3). 10.00 *(978-1-871098-29-7(7))* Claire Pubns. GBR. Dist: Parkwest Pubns., Inc.

Graham, Roland. Let's Vote! Learning to Use Simple Bar Graphs, 1 vol. (Math for the REAL World Ser.). (ENG.). 12p. (gr. 1-2). 2010. (C). pap. *(978-0-8239-8864-8(3)*, af1b82c3-93f9-4ffe-a2ec-32cbcac5a85b, Rosen Classroom) 2004. 33.50 *(978-0-8239-7635-5(1))* Rosen Publishing Group, Inc., The.

Grant, Mackensey. Roman's Road Trip: Understand Place Value, 1 vol. 2014. (Rosen Math Readers Ser.). (ENG., 24p. (J). (gr. 2-2). Illus.). pap. 8.25 *(978-1-4777-4657-8(9)*, 9ea1f4c2-2371-433d-836b-90ee19b073b9); 25.27 *(978-1-4777-6429-9(1)*, c5953bfa-fd16-43b2-a631-78f5cc2fe184) Rosen Publishing Group, Inc., The. (Rosen Classroom).

The Great Big Book of Math Kindergarten Costco Edition. 2008. (J). pap. *(978-1-59566-624-6(9))* QEB Publishing Inc.

The Great Big Book of Math Preschool Costco Edition. 2008. (J). pap. *(978-1-59566-625-3(7))* QEB Publishing Inc.

Great Source Education Group Staff. Math on Call. 2nd ed. 2003. (Math on Call Ser.). (ENG.). 480p. (gr. 6-8). 30.45 *(978-0-669-50818-5(7))* Great Source Education Group, Inc.

—Math on Call: A Mathematics Handbook. 2003. (gr. 5-8). lib. bdg. 41.10 *(978-0-613-73010-5(0))* Turtleback.

Great Source Education Group Staff, creator. Math to Know Book A: Problem Solving. 2007. (Illus.). 123p. per. 22.50 *(978-0-669-50047-9(X))* Great Source Education Group, Inc.

Greene, Lila. Henry Ford's Fantastic Factory: Identify & Explain Patterns in Arithmetic, 1 vol. 2014. (Rosen Math Readers Ser.). (ENG., Illus.). 24p. (J). (gr. 3-3). pap. 8.25 *(978-1-4777-4941-8(1)*, 0d6a7f22-4723-42d1-acf1-862d97e36d77, Rosen Classroom) Rosen Publishing Group, Inc., The.

Greenway, Karen. English for Mathematics: Book A, Bk. A. 2016. (ENG., Illus.). 80p. (J). pap. 9.95 *(978-0-00-813570-6(3))* HarperCollins Pubs. Ltd. GBR. Dist: Independent Pubs. Group.

Greg, Byrd. Cambridge Checkpoint Mathematics. Coursebook. Stage 7. Per le Scuole Superiori. Con Espansione Online, 1 vol. 2018. (ENG., Illus.). 200p. pap., E-Book 40.55 *(978-1-108-61589-1(9))* Cambridge Univ. Pr.

Greg, Tang. Un, DOS, tres, el año se fue. Acertijos matemáticos para despertar la mente. 2003. (SPA., Illus.). 40p. (J). (gr. 2-3). 14.99 *(978-84-241-8074-4(7))* Everest Editora ESP. Dist: Lectorum Pubns., Inc.

Gregorich, Barbara & DeYoung, Lorie. Math Basics 2. Koontz, Robin Michal, illus. deluxe ed. 2019. (ENG.). 64p. (J). (gr. 2-2). pap., wbk. ed. 4.49 *(978-0-88743-138-8(0)*, 5355bf1c-7ede-4815-9766-a653b3b12d5d) School Zone Publishing Co.

Gregorich, Barbara & Jennison, Christopher. Racing Math: Cherckered Flag Activities & Projects for Grades 4-8. 2nd ed. 2005. (Good Year Bks.). (Illus.). 160p. (YA). (gr. 9-14). per. 12.95 *(978-1-59647-060-6(7))* Good Year Bks.

Group/McGraw-Hill, Wright. Wonder World Complete Sets: Math Set - 1 Each of 30 Titles. (Wonder Worldtm Ser.). (gr. k-6). 153.95 *(978-0-322-06715-8(4))* Wright Group/McGraw-Hill.

—Wonder World Early & Upper Emergent Sets: Math Set - 1 Each of 20 Titles. (Wonder Worldtm Ser.). (gr. k-6). 92.50 *(978-0-322-06722-6(7))* Wright Group/McGraw-Hill.

—Wonder World Early Fluency & Fluency: Math Set - 1 Each of 10 Titles. (Wonder Worldtm Ser.). (gr. k-6). 61.95 *(978-0-322-06718-9(9))* Wright Group/McGraw-Hill.

Gunzehauser, Kelly. Find Your Future in Mathematics. 2016. (Bright Futures Press: Find Your Future in STEAM Ser.). (ENG., Illus.). 32p. (J). (gr. 4-6). 32.07 *(978-1-63471-902-5(6)*, 208929) Cherry Lake Publishing.

Gunzi, Christiane, contrib. by. Los Colores. 2004. (My Very First Look At Ser.).Tr. of Colors. (SPA., Illus.). 24p. (J). (gr. -1-k). 9.95 *(978-1-58728-270-6(4))* Cooper Square Publishing Llc.

Guzman, Sienna. Visiting Death Valley: Represent & Interpret Data, 1 vol. 2014. (Rosen Math Readers Ser.). (ENG.). 24p. (J). (gr. 3-3). pap. 8.25 *(978-1-4777-4909-8(8)*, d0cc44a4-b303-4206-9fb7-c70a9d65cda9, Rosen Classroom) Rosen Publishing Group, Inc., The.

Hagler, Gina. Careers for Tech Girls in Math, 1 vol. 2015. (Tech Girls Ser.). (ENG., Illus.). 80p. (J). (gr. 7-8). 37.47 *(978-1-4994-6101-5(1)*, bf5e6087-d18f-4787-9e77-9f9903e93af2, Rosen Young Adult) Rosen Publishing Group, Inc., The.

Hake, Stephen & Saxon, John. Saxon Math 5/4: An Incremental Development. 3rd ed. 2003. (Saxon Math 5/4 Ser.). (ENG., Illus.). 640p. (gr. 4-4). stu. ed. 75.40 *(978-1-56577-503-9(1)*, 503) Houghton Mifflin Harcourt Publishing Co.

—Saxon Math 7/6. 4th ed. 2003. (Saxon Math 7/6 Ser.). (ENG., Illus.). 756p. (gr. 6-6). stu. ed. 78.35 *(978-1-56577-507-7(4)*, 5074) Houghton Mifflin Harcourt Publishing Co.

—Saxon Math 8/7. 3rd ed. 2003. (Saxon Math 8/7 Ser.). (ENG., Illus.). 944p. (gr. 7-7). stu. ed. 81.40 *(978-1-56577-509-1(0)*, 509-0) Houghton Mifflin Harcourt Publishing Co.

Hakizimana, Laurence. Quadrature: Pi, at Last, a Rational Number Equal to 3.125. 2004. 63p. pap. 19.95 *(978-1-4137-4558-0(X))* America Star Bks.

Hammelef, Danielle S. Fun with Fives. 2006. (Early Explorers Ser.). (J). pap. *(978-1-4108-6116-0(3))* Benchmark Education Co.

Hands: Level B, 6 vols. 8p. 24.95 *(978-0-7802-8915-4(3))* Wright Group/McGraw-Hill.

Hankes, Judith E. & Fast, Gerald R. Lost & Found & Found Again: A Math Adventure. 2005. (Illus.). 167p. per. 15.00 *(978-0-9758592-1-6(8))* Mindsong Math.

Hanson, Anders Mann & Mann, Elissa. Cool Tessellations: Creative Activities That Make Math & Science Fun for Kids! 2013. (Cool Art with Math & Science Ser.). (ENG.). 32p. (J). (gr. 3-6). lib. bdg. 34.21 *(978-1-61783-826-2(8)*, 4598, Checkerboard Library) ABDO Publishing Co.

Harasymiw, R. P. Problem Solving with Pigs, 1 vol. 2013. (Animal Math Ser.). (ENG.). 24p. (J). (gr. 1-2). pap. 9.15

(978-1-4339-9324-4(4), 5d0db16d-001a-4fe5-a268-8051cf8d7637); (Illus.). lib. bdg. 25.27 (978-1-4339-9323-7(6), c3c3704c-7c10-4e54-99b1-070f7fc39daf) Stevens, Gareth Publishing LLLP.

Harasymiw, Raymond. Problem Solving with Pigs. 2013. (Animal Math Ser.). 24p. (J). (gr. 1-3). pap. 48.90 (978-1-4339-9325-1(2)) Stevens, Gareth Publishing LLLP.

Harasymiw, Therese. Making Venn Diagrams, 1 vol. 2014. (Graph It! Ser.). (ENG.). 24p. (J). (gr. 1-2). 24.27 (978-1-4824-0934-5(8), cb0b8868-f432-41e0-ab8a-fd384c3e20d0) Stevens, Gareth Publishing LLLP.

Harcourt, creator. Achieve Arizona Mathematics 5. 2007. (Illus.). 61p. (J). (gr. 4-7). per. (978-1-4190-0486-5(7)) Harcourt.

—I Know Big & Small: Math Concept Reader. 2007. (Illus.). (J). pap. 31.53 (978-0-15-379897-9(1)) Houghton Mifflin Harcourt School Pubs.

—Summertime Math: Math Concept Reader. 2007. (Illus.). (J). pap. 31.53 (978-0-15-379898-6(X)) Houghton Mifflin Harcourt School Pubs.

Harcourt Achieve, creator. Top Line Math: Data, Tables & Graphs. 2005. (Top Line Math Ser.). (Illus.). 53p. pap. 5.49 (978-1-4190-0371-4(2)) Steck-Vaughn.

Harcourt School Publishers, creator. Professional Development for Math: Fraction Operations, Grades 3-6. 2004. (ENG.). 219.27 (978-0-15-341946-1(6)) Harcourt Schl. Pubs.

Harcourt School Publishers Staff. Harcourt Matematicas: CA & National Family Involvement Activities. 2nd ed. 2003. (Harcourt Matematicas Ser.). (SPA., Illus.). (gr. k-6). 25.30 (978-0-15-321566-7(6)); (gr. 1-18). 31.10 (978-0-15-321567-4(4)); (gr. 2-18). 31.10 (978-0-15-321568-1(2)); (gr. 3-18). 35.80 (978-0-15-321569-8(0)); (gr. 4-18). 35.80 (978-0-15-321570-4(4)); (gr. 5-18). 35.80 (978-0-15-321571-1(2)); (gr. 6-18). 36.20 (978-0-15-321572-8(0)) Harcourt Schl. Pubs.

—Harcourt Matematicas: Challenge Workbook. 2nd ed. 2003. (Harcourt Matematicas Ser.). (SPA., Illus.). (gr. k-6). wbk. ed., pupil's gde. ed. 11.80 (978-0-15-321642-8(5)); (gr. 1-18). wbk. ed. 12.50 (978-0-15-321643-5(3)); (gr. 2-18). wbk. ed. 12.50 (978-0-15-321644-2(1)); (gr. 3-18). wbk. ed. 13.50 (978-0-15-321645-9(X)); (gr. 4-18). wbk. ed. 13.50 (978-0-15-321646-6(8)); (gr. 5-18). wbk. ed. 13.50 (978-0-15-321647-3(6)); (gr. 6-18). wbk. ed. 14.50 (978-0-15-321648-0(4)) Harcourt Schl. Pubs.

—Harcourt Matematicas: Checklilst for Knowledge Enrichment. 2nd ed. 2003. (Harcourt Matematicas Ser.). (SPA., Illus.). (gr. 5-18). 13.10 (978-0-15-326116-9(1)) Harcourt Schl. Pubs.

—Harcourt Matematicas: Practice Workbook. 2nd ed. 2003. (Harcourt Matematicas Ser.). (SPA., Illus.). (gr. 3-18). wbk. ed. 11.60 (978-0-15-321631-2(X)); (gr. 4-18). wbk. ed. 11.60 (978-0-15-321632-9(8)); (gr. 5-18). wbk. ed. 11.60 (978-0-15-321633-6(6)); (gr. 6-18). wbk. ed. 12.00 (978-0-15-321634-3(4)) Harcourt Schl. Pubs.

—Harcourt Matematicas: Problem Solving & Reading Strategies Workbook. 2nd ed. 2003. (Harcourt Matematicas Ser.). (SPA., Illus.). (gr. 1-18). wbk. ed. 11.00 (978-0-15-321668-8(9)); (gr. 2-18). wbk. ed. 11.00 (978-0-15-321669-5(7)); (gr. 3-18). wbk. ed. 12.00 (978-0-15-321670-1(0)); (gr. 4-18). wbk. ed. 12.00 (978-0-15-321671-8(9)); (gr. 5-18). wbk. ed. 12.00 (978-0-15-321672-5(7)); (gr. 6-18). wbk. ed. 12.50 (978-0-15-321673-2(5)) Harcourt Schl. Pubs.

—Harcourt Matematicas: Resource Package. 2nd ed. 2003. (Harcourt Matematicas Ser.). (SPA., Illus.). (gr. k-6). 992.20 (978-0-15-321844-6(4)) Harcourt Schl. Pubs.

—Harcourt Matemáticas Práctica. 4th ed. 2004. (Harcourt Matematicas Ser.). (SPA.). 168p. (gr. 3-3). pap., wbk. ed. 14.10 (978-0-15-341132-8(5)) Harcourt Schl. Pubs.

—Harcourt Math. 4th ed. 2004. (Harcourt Matematicas Ser.). (SPA.). Vol. 1. 544p. (gr. k-k). tchr. ed., spiral bd. 197.25 (978-0-15-341109-0(0)) Vol. 1. 588p. (gr. 5-5). tchr. ed., spiral bd. 131.55 (978-0-15-341123-6(6)) Vol. 2. 400p. (gr. k-k). tchr. ed., spiral bd. 197.25 (978-0-15-341110-6(4)) Vol. 2. 540p. (gr. 5-5). tchr. ed., spiral bd. 131.55 (978-0-15-341124-3(4)) Vol. 3. 432p. (gr. 2-2). tchr. ed. 121.55 (978-0-15-341116-8(3)) Vol. 3. 564p. (gr. 5-5). tchr. ed., spiral bd. 131.55 (978-0-15-341125-0(2)) Harcourt Schl. Pubs.

—Harcourt Math: MEAP Resource Book. 3rd ed. 2003. (gr. 1). pap. 7.50 (978-0-15-340989-9(4)); (gr. 2). pap. 7.50 (978-0-15-340990-5(8)); (gr. 3). pap. 9.60 (978-0-15-340991-2(6)); (gr. 4). pap. 9.60 (978-0-15-340992-9(4)); (gr. 5). pap. 9.60 (978-0-15-340993-6(2)); (gr. 6). pap. 9.60 (978-0-15-340994-3(0)) Harcourt Schl. Pubs.

—Harcourt Math Collection, Grade 1, Vols. 1-3. 3rd ed. 2003. tchr. ed. 276.00 (978-0-15-338863-7(3)) Harcourt Schl. Pubs.

—Harcourt Math Collection, Grade 2, Vols. 1-3. 3rd ed. 2003. tchr. ed. 276.00 (978-0-15-338864-4(1)) Harcourt Schl. Pubs.

—Harcourt Math Collection, Grade 3, Vols. 1-3. 3rd ed. 2003. tchr. ed. 276.00 (978-0-15-338865-1(X)) Harcourt Schl. Pubs.

—Harcourt Math Collection, Grade 4, Vols. 1-3. 3rd ed. 2003. tchr. ed. 276.00 (978-0-15-338866-8(8)) Harcourt Schl. Pubs.

—Harcourt Math Collection, Grade 5, Vols. 1-3. 3rd ed. 2003. tchr. ed. 276.00 (978-0-15-338867-5(6)) Harcourt Schl. Pubs.

—Harcourt Math Collection, Grade 6, Vols. 1-3. 3rd ed. 2003. tchr. ed. 276.00 (978-0-15-338868-2(4)) Harcourt Schl. Pubs.

—Harcourt Math, Grade 1. 4th ed. 2004. (Harcourt Matematicas Ser.). (SPA.). (gr. 1-1). Vol. 1. 504p. tchr. ed., spiral bd. 131.55 (978-0-15-341111-3(2)) Vol. 2. 528p. tchr. ed., spiral bd. 131.55 (978-0-15-341112-0(0)) Vol. 3. 456p. tchr. ed., spiral bd. 131.55 (978-0-15-341113-7(9)) Harcourt Schl. Pubs.

—Harcourt Math, Grade 3. 4th ed. 2004. (Harcourt Matematicas Ser.). (SPA.). (gr. 3-3). Vol. 1. 672p. tchr. ed., spiral bd. 131.55 (978-0-15-341117-5(1)) Vol. 2. 528p. tchr. ed., spiral bd. 131.55 (978-0-15-341118-2(X)) Vol. 3. 420p. tchr. ed., spiral bd. 131.55 (978-0-15-341119-9(8)) Harcourt Schl. Pubs.

—Harcourt Math, Grade 6. 4th ed. 2004. (Harcourt Matematicas Ser.). (SPA.). (gr. 6-6). Vol. 1. 688p. tchr. ed., spiral bd. 131.55 (978-0-15-341126-7(0)) Vol. 2. 504p. tchr. ed., spiral bd. 131.55 (978-0-15-341127-4(9)) Vol. 3. 480p. tchr. ed., spiral bd. 131.55 (978-0-15-341128-1(7)) Harcourt Schl. Pubs.

—Harcourt Math, Grade K Vol. 2. 3rd ed. 2003. tchr. ed. 138.00 (978-0-15-338908-5(7)) Harcourt Schl. Pubs.

—Harcourt School Publishers Matematicas. 4th ed. 2004. (Harcourt Matematicas Ser.). (SPA.). 396p. (gr. k-k). pap., stu. ed. 39.45 (978-0-15-341102-1(3)); 600p. (gr. 1-1). pap., stu. ed. 53.95 (978-0-15-341103-8(1)); 160p. (gr. 1-1). pap., wbk. ed. 14.10 (978-0-15-341130-4(9)); 624p. (gr. 2-2). pap., stu. ed. 53.95 (978-0-15-341104-5(X)); 176p. (gr. 2-2). pap., wbk. ed. 14.10 (978-0-15-341131-1(7)); 736p. (gr. 3-3). stu. ed. 98.65 (978-0-15-341105-2(8)); 168p. (gr. 4-4). pap., wbk. ed. 14.10 (978-0-15-341133-5(3)); 176p. (gr. 5-5). pap., wbk. ed. 14.10 (978-0-15-341134-2(1)); 144p. (gr. 6-6). pap., wbk. ed. 14.10 (978-0-15-341135-9(X)) Harcourt Schl. Pubs.

—Matemáticas. 4th ed. 2004. (Harcourt Matematicas Ser.). (SPA.). 104p. (gr. k-k). pap., stu. ed., wbk. ed. 13.90 (978-0-15-341129-8(5)) Harcourt Schl. Pubs.

—Matematicas 2005, Vol. 2. 4th ed. 2004. (Harcourt School Publishers Matematicas Ser.). (SPA.). 444p. (gr. 2-2). tchr. ed. 121.55 (978-0-15-341115-1(5)) Harcourt Schl. Pubs.

—Mathemáticas. 4th ed. 2004. (Harcourt School Publishers Matematicas Ser.). (SPA.). 768p. (gr. 4-4). stu. ed. 98.65 (978-0-15-341106-9(6)) Harcourt Schl. Pubs.

—Problem Solving. 4th ed. 2004. pap., tchr.'s training gde. ed. 54.90 (978-0-15-341942-3(3)); (ENG.). 120p. (gr. 6-6). pap., pupil's gde. ed. 15.45 (978-0-15-341943-0(1)) Harcourt Schl. Pubs.

Hardyman, Robyn. Exploring Amazing Adaptations with Math, 1 vol. 2016. (Math Attack: Exploring Life Science with Math Ser.). (ENG.). 32p. (J). (gr. 3-4). pap. 11.00 (978-1-4994-3113-1(9), d51eebfe-865a-41f5-b6cd-d2900b3832ee, PowerKids Pr.) Rosen Publishing Group, Inc., The.

—Exploring Awesome Animal Bodies with Math, 1 vol. 2016. (Math Attack: Exploring Life Science with Math Ser.). (ENG.). 32p. (J). (gr. 3-4). pap. 11.00 (978-1-4994-3117-9(1), d99ee94b-5c6c-4687-a54f-236b0a58e8b7, PowerKids Pr.) Rosen Publishing Group, Inc., The.

—Exploring Deadly Habitats with Math, 1 vol. 2016. (Math Attack: Exploring Life Science with Math Ser.). (ENG.). 32p. (J). (gr. 3-4). pap. 11.00 (978-1-4994-3121-6(X), e518c45e-4ea2-47de-b1fa-69e20658ec48, PowerKids Pr.) Rosen Publishing Group, Inc., The.

—Exploring Food Chains with Math, 1 vol. 2016. (Math Attack: Exploring Life Science with Math Ser.). (ENG.). 32p. (J). (gr. 3-4). pap. 11.00 (978-1-4994-3125-4(2), 280e1ce6-efa1-425e-8ccd-95cfd3cd86d6, PowerKids Pr.) Rosen Publishing Group, Inc., The.

—Exploring Killer Plants with Math, 1 vol. 2016. (Math Attack: Exploring Life Science with Math Ser.). (ENG.). 32p. (J). (gr. 3-4). pap. 11.00 (978-1-4994-3129-2(5), 4d6aa75f-3293-4e21-b97b-0fcbfd237bf6, PowerKids Pr.) Rosen Publishing Group, Inc., The.

—Exploring Lethal Life Cycles with Math, 1 vol. 2016. (Math Attack: Exploring Life Science with Math Ser.). (ENG.). 32p. (J). (gr. 3-4). pap. 11.00 (978-1-4994-3133-9(3), 3934772d-62c5-431a-a805-ebb34d1a6a66, PowerKids Pr.) Rosen Publishing Group, Inc., The.

Harnadek, Anita. Math Word Problems Level C: Mixed Concepts: Whole Numbers to Percents. 2006. (Math Word Problems Ser.). 96p. (gr. 5-10). pap. 14.99 (978-0-89455-822-1(6)) Critical Thinking Co., The.

Harris, Beatrice. We Love Cylinders!, 1 vol. 2018. (Our Favorite Shapes Ser.). (ENG.). 24p. (gr. k-k). 24.27 (978-1-5382-2869-2(6), c5cd5be3-19a9-48ce-bc92-c38bb525ac5d) Stevens, Gareth Publishing LLLP.

—We Love Rectangles!, 1 vol. 2017. (Our Favorite Shapes Ser.). (ENG.). 24p. (J). (gr. k-k). pap. 9.15 (978-1-5382-0997-4(7), b93dd855-5d18-41a6-891e-08b73d26a61f) Stevens, Gareth Publishing LLLP.

—We Love Squares!, 1 vol. 2017. (Our Favorite Shapes Ser.). (ENG.). 24p. (J). (gr. k-k). pap. 9.15 (978-1-5382-1001-7(0), b162d0de-f0b3-401c-b66e-4de9db94bc45) Stevens, Gareth Publishing LLLP.

—We Love Triangles!, 1 vol. 2017. (Our Favorite Shapes Ser.). (ENG.). 24p. (J). (gr. k-k). pap. 9.15 (978-1-5382-1005-5(3), 00491618-6a76-479e-b2ca-0d4dc91d55a2) Stevens, Gareth Publishing LLLP.

Harris, Brooke. Playing at My House: Lap Book. 2009. (My First Reader's Theater Set B Ser.). (J). 28.00 (978-1-60634-986-1(4)) Benchmark Education Co.

Harris, Janelle. Bree's Building Blocks: Work with 11-19 to Gain Foundations for Place Value. 2013. (Rosen Math Readers Ser.). (ENG.). 16p. (J). (gr. k-1). pap. 42.00 (978-1-4777-1672-4(6)); (Illus.). pap. 7.00 (978-1-4777-1671-7(8), 5f7f61d5-5ff8-4d6f-aeac-ee3a6fcd0c6d) Rosen Publishing Group, Inc., The. (Rosen Classroom).

Harrison, Paul & Mumford, Jeannette. Math Extension Activities for Year 6. 2004. (6 Plus Ser.). (ENG., Illus.). 144p. pap., stu. ed. 22.80 (978-0-521-54290-6(1)) Cambridge Univ. Pr.

Harrison, Sharon, et al. Mathemateg Newydd Caergrawnt. 2005. (WEL., Illus.). 32p. pap. (978-1-86085-272-5(6)) ICA Video.

Hausmann, Gisela. Hands on Mathemagical Dice. 2005. (Illus.). 30p. (J). cd-rom 13.00 (978-0-9664217-4-3(4)) Educ-Easy Bks.

Havelka, Jacqueline. STEM in Basketball. 2019. (Connecting STEM & Sports Ser.). (Illus.). 80p. (J). (gr. 12). lib. bdg. 34.60 (978-1-4222-4332-9(X)) Mason Crest.

—STEM in Football. 2019. (Connecting STEM & Sports Ser.). (Illus.). 80p. (J). (gr. 12). lib. bdg. 34.60 (978-1-4222-4334-3(6)) Mason Crest.

—STEM in Gymnastics. 2019. (Connecting STEM & Sports Ser.). (Illus.). 80p. (J). (gr. 12). lib. bdg. 34.60 (978-1-4222-4335-0(4)) Mason Crest.

—STEM in Soccer. 2019. (Connecting STEM & Sports Ser.). (Illus.). 80p. (J). (gr. 12). lib. bdg. 34.60 (978-1-4222-4337-4(0)) Mason Crest.

—STEM in Track & Field. 2019. (Connecting STEM & Sports Ser.). (Illus.). 80p. (J). (gr. 12). lib. bdg. 34.60 (978-1-4222-4338-1(9)) Mason Crest.

Hayhurst, Chris. Euclid: The Great Geometer. 2009. (Library of Greek Philosophers Ser.). 112p. (gr. 6-6). 66.50 (978-1-60853-659-7(9), Rosen Reference) Rosen Publishing Group, Inc., The.

Head, Debby & Pollett, Libby. Bby Practice Pages: 04-Addition Facts 0-10. 2004. (ENG., Illus.). 93p. spiral bd. 37.00 (978-1-885775-20-7(2)) bby Publications at The University of West Alabama.

—Bby Practice Pages: 05-Subtraction Facts 0-10. 2004. (ENG., Illus.). spiral bd. 37.00 (978-1-885775-21-4(0)) bby Publications at The University of West Alabama.

—Bby Practice Pages: 08-Beginning Addition 0-10. 2004. (ENG.). spiral bd. 37.00 (978-1-885775-24-5(5)) bby Publications at The University of West Alabama.

—Bby Practice Pages: 10-Addition Facts 11-20. 2004. (ENG., Illus.). spiral bd. 37.00 (978-1-885775-26-9(1)) bby Publications at The University of West Alabama.

—Bby Practice Pages: 11-Subtraction Facts 11-20. 2004. (ENG., Illus.). spiral bd. 37.00 (978-1-885775-27-6(X)) bby Publications at The University of West Alabama.

—Bby Practice Pages: 12-Making Change Through $1. 00. 2004. (ENG., Illus.). spiral bd. 37.00 (978-1-885775-28-3(8)) bby Publications at The University of West Alabama.

Heaney, Shane. Food from Around the World: Represent & Solve Problems Involving Division. 2014. (Rosen Math Readers Ser.). (ENG.). 24p. (J). (gr. 3-4). pap. 49.50 (978-1-4777-4978-4(0), Rosen Classroom); (Illus.). pap. 8.25 (978-1-4777-4977-7(2), 44a64148-37d0-40b5-9d16-140ba30b652e, PowerKids Pr.); (Illus.). lib. bdg. 25.27 (978-1-4777-6446-6(1), df2177f8-af05-4b75-9b19-0e7c1024d021, PowerKids Pr.) Rosen Publishing Group, Inc., The.

Heath Mathematics. (J). (gr. 1). wbk. ed. 10.44 (978-0-669-10473-8(6)); wbk. ed. (978-0-669-10502-5(3)) Houghton Mifflin Harcourt School Pubs.

Hein, Marilyn B. Math Phonics Pre-Algebra. Wheeler, Ron, illus. 2004. 96p. (J). pap. 10.65 (978-1-57310-438-8(8)) Teaching & Learning Co.

Hellebuyck, Adam & Medvinsky, Mike. Patterns & Numbers in Minecraft. 2019. (21st Century Skills Innovation Library: Minecraft & STEAM Ser.). (ENG., Illus.). 32p. (J). (gr. 4-8). pap. 14.21 (978-1-5341-3972-5(9), 212717) Cherry Lake Publishing.

—Patterns & Numbers in Minecraft: Math. 2019. (21st Century Skills Innovation Library: Minecraft & STEAM Ser.). (ENG., Illus.). 32p. (J). (gr. 4-8). lib. bdg. 32.07 (978-1-5341-4316-6(5), 212716) Cherry Lake Publishing.

Hennings, Mark. Cambridge Pre-U Mathematics Coursebook. 2017. (Pre-U Ser.). (ENG., Illus.). 788p. pap. 79.75 (978-1-316-63575-9(9)) Cambridge Univ. Pr.

Hense, Mary & Stewart, Rhea A. How Astronauts Use Math. 2009. (Math in the Real World Ser.). (ENG.). 32p. (gr. 4-6). 28.00 (978-1-60413-610-4(3), P466909, Chelsea Clubhse.) Infobase Holdings, Inc.

—How Fighter Pilots Use Math. 2009. (Math in the Real World Ser.). (ENG.). 32p. (gr. 4-6). 28.00 (978-1-60413-605-0(7), P466915, Chelsea Clubhse.) Infobase Holdings, Inc.

Heos, Bridget. Making Graphs. Longhi, Katya, illus. 2014. (Math World Ser.). (ENG.). 24p. (J). (gr. 1-4). lib. bdg. 27.10 (978-1-60753-463-1(0), 15914) Amicus.

Herbst, Kailee. Lots of Clocks: Learning about Tools That Measure Time, 1 vol. 2010. (Math for the REAL World Ser.). (ENG., Illus.). 8p. (gr. k-1). pap. 5.15 (978-0-8239-8858-7(9), b4b1b111-535f-4784-95ea-0d39415d298b) Rosen Publishing Group, Inc., The.

Hessel-Mial, Michael. How STEM Built the Chinese Dynasties, 1 vol. 2019. (How STEM Built Empires Ser.). (ENG.). 80p. (gr. 7-7). pap. 16.30 (978-1-7253-4137-1(9), 52c40482-3afd-4b12-b46b-eb95bffaa821) Rosen Publishing Group, Inc., The.

—How STEM Built the Incan Empire, 1 vol. 2019. (How STEM Built Empires Ser.). (ENG.). 80p. (gr. 7-7). pap. 16.30 (978-1-7253-4146-3(8), 8e00ab78-4c0f-4950-9a94-e3ae4af76b2e) Rosen Publishing Group, Inc., The.

Hicer, Nancy. Pennies, Nickles, & Dimes, 1 vol. 2015. (Rosen REAL Readers: STEM & STEAM Collection). (ENG.). 8p. (gr. k-1). pap. 5.46 (978-1-4994-9723-6(7), effd0bd7-a443-41e7-8177-2e477331c1b7, Rosen Classroom) Rosen Publishing Group, Inc., The.

Highling, Erin. Take Me Out to the Math Game: Home Run Activities, Big League Word Problems & Hard Ball Quizzes — A Fun Workbook for 4-6th Graders. 2018. (Books for Teachers Ser.). (ENG., Illus.). 128p. (J). (gr. 4-6). pap. 11.95 (978-1-61243-787-3(7)) Ulysses Pr.

Hinkler Books Staff, ed. Early Math. 2009. (ENG.). 24p. (J). 9.99 (978-0-8249-1401-1(5), Ideals Pubns.) Worthy Publishing.

Hinkler Studios Staff., ed. Cars: Numbers & Early Math. 2011. 12p. 9.99 (978-1-74183-870-1(3)) Hinkler Bks. Pty, Ltd. AUS. Dist: Ideals Pubns.

Hinton, John. Hot or Cold? Describe & Compare Measurable Attributes. 2013. (Rosen Math Readers Ser.). (ENG.). 16p. (J). (gr. k-1). pap. 42.00 (978-1-4777-1627-4(0)); (Illus.). pap. 7.00 (978-1-4777-1626-7(2), c6de2be7-9017-4b59-97c6-7e012ef85fea) Rosen Publishing Group, Inc., The. (Rosen Classroom).

Hironaka, Heisuke & Sugiyama, Yoshishige, eds. Tokyo Shoseki's Mathematics 4 for Elementary School (Grade 4A & 4B, 2 vol. Set) 2006. Orig. Title: Atarashii Sansuu 4 (Jo/Ge). pap. 24.99 (978-1-934046-04-3(3)) Global Education Resources, LLC.

—Tokyo Shoseki's Mathematics 5 for Elementary School (Grades 5A & 5B, 2 vol. Set) 2006. Orig. Title: Atarashii Sansuu 5 (Jo/Ge). pap. 24.99 (978-1-934046-05-0(1)) Global Education Resources, LLC.

—Tokyo Shoseki's Mathematics 6 for Elementary School (Grade 6A & 6B, 2 vol. Set) 2006. Orig. Title: Atarashii Sansuu 6 (Jo/Ge). pap. 24.99 (978-1-934046-06-7(X)) Global Education Resources, LLC.

Hobbs, Chris & Perryman, Richard. The Largest Number Smaller Than Five. 2007. (ENG.). 128p. per. 19.99 (978-1-4303-0630-6(0)) Lulu Pr., Inc.

Hoena, Blake. Algorithms: Solve a Problem! Sanchez, Sr., illus. 2018. (Code It! Ser.). (ENG.). 24p. (C). (gr. 1-3). lib. bdg. 33.99 (978-1-68410-383-6(5), 140357) Cantata Learning.

Hollenbeck, Kathleen M. Scholastic Success with Reading & Math Jumbo Workbook, 1 vol. 2005. (ENG.). 320p. (gr. k-k). pap., wbk. ed. 14.99 (978-0-439-78599-0(5), Teaching Resources) Scholastic, Inc.

Hollis, Matthew. Jada Makes Jewelry: Use Place Value Understanding & Properties of Operations to Add & Subtract, 1 vol. 2014. (Math Masters: Number & Operations in Base Ten Ser.). (ENG.). 24p. (J). (gr. 2-2). 25.27 (978-1-4777-6402-2(X), cf151c5c-c94c-4be3-a733-616ea8a4f546); pap. 8.25 (978-1-4777-4742-1(7), e0c5e66a-a3c4-4044-8ab9-97eb6be982c0) Rosen Publishing Group, Inc., The. (Rosen Classroom).

Holmes, Rebecca. Allie's Art Class: Analyze, Compare, Create, & Compose Shapes. 2013. (Rosen Math Readers Ser.). (ENG.). 16p. (J). (gr. k-1). pap. 42.00 (978-1-4777-1645-8(9)); (Illus.). pap. 7.00 (978-1-4777-1644-1(0), 58236cf3-bb36-4098-baea-0296a63a8521) Rosen Publishing Group, Inc., The. (Rosen Classroom).

HOLT MCDOUGAL. Go Math! Student Interactive Worktext Accelerated 7 2014. 2013. (Go Math! Ser.). (ENG.). 840p. (gr. 7-7). pap. 34.10 (978-0-544-14716-4(2)) Big Ideas Learning, LLC.

Holt, Rinehart and Winston Staff. Decision Making: Math Context. 3rd ed. 2003. tchr. ed. 33.53 (978-0-03-071523-5(7)) Holt McDougal.

—Math: CIM Test Preparation Book: Oregon High School Edition: 3rd ed. 2003. (YA). pap. 12.16 (978-0-03-070452-9(9)) Holt, Rinehart & Winston of Canada, Ltd. CAN. Dist: Harcourt Canada, Ltd.

—Math: Middle School: Interactive Posters & Worksheets. 4th ed. 2004. (Illus.). pap. 55.66 (978-0-03-068634-4(2)) Holt McDougal.

—Math Course 1: Middle School: Chapter Resources. 4th ed. Date not set. pap. 367.00 (978-0-03-070832-9(X)) Holt McDougal.

—Math Course 1: Middle School: Interactive Posters & Worksheets. 4th ed. 2004. (Illus.). pap. 55.66 (978-0-03-068623-8(7)) Holt McDougal.

—Math Course 2: Middle School: Chapter Resources. 4th ed. Date not set. pap. 367.00 (978-0-03-070833-6(8)) Holt McDougal.

—Math Course 2: Middle School: Standard Test Practice. 4th ed. Date not set. (YA). pap., wbk. ed. 8.40 (978-0-03-070821-3(4)) Holt McDougal.

—Math Course 2: Middle School: Standard Test Practice with Answer Key. 4th ed. Date not set. pap., wbk. ed. 12.60 (978-0-03-070822-0(2)) Holt McDougal.

—Math Course 3: Middle School: Chapter Resources. 4th ed. Date not set. pap. 367.00 (978-0-03-070834-3(6)) Holt McDougal.

—Math Course 3: Middle School: Interactive Posters & Worksheets. 4th ed. 2004. (Illus.). pap. 55.66 (978-0-03-068646-7(6)) Holt McDougal.

—Math Course 3: Middle School: Standard Test Practice. 4th ed. Date not set. pap., wbk. ed. 8.40 (978-0-03-070823-7(0)) Holt McDougal.

—Math Chapter Resources: Arizona Edition. 4th ed. 2004. (YA). tchr. ed. 110.60 (978-0-03-073509-7(2)) Holt McDougal.

—Math Chapter Resources: Maine Edition. 4th ed. 2004. (YA). tchr. ed. 110.60 (978-0-03-073292-8(1)); tchr. ed. 110.60 (978-0-03-073291-1(3)) Holt McDougal.

—Math Chapter Resources: New Jersey Edition. 4th ed. 2004. (YA). 110.60 (978-0-03-073289-8(1)); tchr. ed. 110.60 (978-0-03-073288-1(3)) Holt McDougal.

—Math Chapter Resources: Pennsylvania Edition. 4th ed. 2004. (YA). tchr. ed. 110.60 (978-0-03-073492-2(4)); tchr. ed. 110.60 (978-0-03-073493-9(2)); tchr. ed. 110.60 (978-0-03-073491-5(6)) Holt McDougal.

—Math Know-It Notebook: Middle School. 4th ed. 2004. (Holt Mathematics Ser.). (ENG., Illus.). 272p. (gr. 6-6). pap. 15.50 (978-0-03-038016-7(2)); 272p. (gr. 7-7). pap. 15.50 (978-0-03-038017-4(0)); 256p. (gr. 8-8). pap. 15.50 (978-0-03-038018-1(9)) Houghton Mifflin Harcourt Publishing Co.

—Middle School Math: New York Review & Test Preparation Workbook. 4th ed. (Holt Middle School Math Ser.). 2004. pap. 8.40 (978-0-03-070812-1(5)) 2003. pap. 8.40 (978-0-03-070811-4(7)) 2003. pap. 8.40 (978-0-03-070809-1(5)) Holt McDougal.

—Middle School Math Chapter 4: Resource Book. 4th ed. 2004. pap. 38.33 (978-0-03-067962-9(1)) Holt McDougal.

—Middle School Math Chapter 5: Resource Book. 4th ed. 2004. pap. 38.33 (978-0-03-067963-6(X)) Holt McDougal.

—Middle School Math Chapter 6: Resource Book. 4th ed. 2004. pap. 38.33 (978-0-03-067964-3(8)) Holt McDougal.

—Middle School Math Chapter 7: Resource Book. 4th ed. 2004. pap. 38.33 (978-0-03-067966-7(4)) Holt McDougal.

—Middle School Math Chapter 8: Resource Book. 4th ed. 2004. pap. 38.33 (978-0-03-067967-4(2)) Holt McDougal.

—Middle School Math Chapter 9: Resource Book. 4th ed. 2004. pap. 38.33 (978-0-03-067968-1(0)) Holt McDougal.

—Middle School Math Chapter 10: Resource Book. 4th ed. 2004. pap. 38.33 (978-0-03-067969-8(9)) Holt McDougal.

—Middle School Math Chapter 11: Resource Book. 4th ed. 2004. pap. 38.33 (978-0-03-067971-1(0)) Holt McDougal.

—Middle School Math Chapter 12: Resource Book. 4th ed. 2004. pap. 38.33 (978-0-03-067972-8(9)) Holt McDougal.

—Middle School Math Course 1: Chapter Resources: Oregon Edition. 4th ed. 2004. (YA). tchr. ed. 110.60 (978-0-03-073513-4(0)) Holt McDougal.

—Middle School Math Course 2: Chapter Resources: Oregon Edition. 4th ed. 2004. (YA). tchr. ed. 110.60 (978-0-03-073514-1(9)) Holt McDougal.

—Middle School Math Course 2: Maryland Edition. 4th ed. 2004. (J). tchr. ed. 110.60 (978-0-03-072832-7(0)) Holt McDougal.

—Middle School Math Course 3: Chapter Resources: Oregon Edition. 4th ed. 2004. (YA). tchr. ed. 110.60 (978-0-03-073516-5(5)) Holt McDougal.

—Middle School Math Course 3: Consumer/Career Mathematics. 4th ed. 2004. (Illus.). pap. 22.26 (978-0-03-066231-7(1)) Holt McDougal.

—Middle School Math Course 3: Homework/Practice Workbook with Answer Key - Spanish Edition. 4th ed. Date not set. pap. 11.00 (978-0-03-068296-4(7)) Holt McDougal.

—Middle School Math Course 3: Maryland Edition. 4th annot. ed. 2004. (J). tchr. ed. 110.60 (978-0-03-072833-4(9)) Holt McDougal.

—Middle School Math Course 3: Success for English Language Students. 4th ed. Date not set. pap. 79.53 (978-0-03-066257-7(5)) Holt McDougal.

—Middle School Math 2: Spanish Homework & Practice Workbook. 4th ed. Date not set. (Holt Mathematics Ser.). pap. 8.40 (978-0-03-067973-5(7)) Holt McDougal.

—New in Numbers. 3rd ed. 2003. (Math in Context Ser.). (Illus.). pap. 15.05 (978-0-03-072432-9(5)) Holt McDougal.

—Pre-Algebra: Hands-on Lab Activities with Answer Key. 4th ed. 2004. pap. 21.53 (978-0-03-069698-5(4)) Holt McDougal.

—Pre-Algebra: Tech Lab Activities with Answer Key. 4th ed. 2003. pap. 21.53 (978-0-03-069861-3(8)) Holt McDougal.

—Pre-Algebra: Test Preparation Tool Kit. 4th ed. 2004. pap. 264.66 (978-0-03-069616-9(X)) Holt McDougal.

—Pre-Algebra Chptr. 4: Resource Book with Answer Key. 4th ed. 2004. pap. 38.86 (978-0-03-069683-1(6)) Holt McDougal.

—Pre-Algebra Chptr. 5: Resource Book with Answer Key. 4th ed. 2004. pap. 38.86 (978-0-03-069684-8(4)) Holt McDougal.

—Science Spectrum: Physics Math Skills. 4th ed. 2004. pap., wbk. ed. 11.13 (978-0-03-067084-8(5)) Holt McDougal.

HOP LLC Staff. Hooked on Math - Addition & Subtraction. 2005. (J). (gr. 6-7). 64.99 (978-1-931020-50-3(7)) HOP, LLC.

Hore, Rosie. Lift-The-Flap Adding & Subtracting. 2018. (Advanced Lift-The-Flap Board Bks.). (ENG.). 16p. 14.99 (978-0-7945-4233-7(6), Usborne) EDC Publishing.

Houghton Mifflin Company Staff, creator. Math Practice Workbook, Grade 3. 2003. (Houghton Mifflin Math Ser.). (ENG., Illus.). 160p. (gr. 3-3). pap. 12.30 (978-0-618-38959-9(8)) Houghton Mifflin Harcourt Publishing Co.

—Math-Trips, Grades 4-6. 2011. (Steck-Vaughn School Supply Ser.). (ENG., Illus.). 79p. (J). pap. 14.99 (978-0-547-62559-1(6)) Houghton Mifflin Harcourt Trade & Reference Pubs.

Hughes, Haley. What's near & Far? Describe & Compare Measurable Attributes, 1 vol. 2013. (InfoMax Math Readers Ser.). (ENG.). 16p. (J). (gr. k-k). pap. 7.00 (978-1-4777-1925-1(3), c0b8aa77-a53d-4937-aae9-9e881af391c5, Rosen Classroom) Rosen Publishing Group, Inc., The.

Hughes, Holly. What's near & Far? Describe & Compare Measurable Attributes. 2013. (InfoMax Math Readers Ser.). (ENG.). 16p. (J). (gr. k-1). pap. 42.00 (978-1-4777-1926-8(1), Rosen Classroom) Rosen Publishing Group, Inc., The.

Hulme, Joy N. Wild Fibonacci: Nature's Secret Code Revealed. Schwartz, Carol, illus. 2010. (ENG.). 32p. (J). (gr. -1-2). pap. 8.99 (978-1-58246-324-7(7), Tricycle Pr.) Random Hse. Children's Bks.

Hunt, Darleen L. Dad's Pancakes: Number Reduction. Komarck, Michael, illus. 2003. (Sherman's Math Corner Ser.). (J). (gr. -1-3). (978-1-929591-04-6(7)) Reading Rock, Inc.

—Dog & Cat Compare: Comparing Amounts. Komarck, Michael, illus. 2003. (Sherman's Math Corner Ser.). (J). (gr. -1-3). (978-1-929591-09-1(8)) Reading Rock, Inc.

—Dog's Dollars: Patterns. Komarck, Michael, illus. 2003. (Sherman's Math Corner Ser.). (J). (gr. -1-3). (978-1-929591-08-4(X)) Reading Rock, Inc.

—Harvey T. Crow Puts It All Together: Addition. Komarck, Michael, illus. 2003. (Sherman's Math Corner Ser.). (J). (gr. -1-3). (978-1-929591-02-2(0)) Reading Rock, Inc.

—Samanta Uses Patterns: Patterns. Komarck, Michael, illus. 2003. (Sherman's Math Corner Ser.). (J). (gr. -1-3). (978-1-929591-10-7(1)) Reading Rock, Inc.

—Spider Inventories: Count & Record. Komarck, Michael, illus. 2003. (Sherman's Math Corner Ser.). (J). (gr. -1-3). (978-1-929591-05-3(5)) Reading Rock, Inc.

Hunt, Santana. Making Desserts with Math!, 1 vol. 2019. (Cooking with Math! Ser.). (ENG.). 24p. (gr. 1-2). pap. 9.15 (978-1-5382-4553-8(1), e1d53aeb-b4ea-4c5b-a4f7-416ede5e3532) Stevens, Gareth Publishing LLLP.

—Making Pasta with Math!, 1 vol. 2019. (Cooking with Math! Ser.). (ENG.). 24p. (gr. 1-2). pap. 9.15 (978-1-5382-4557-6(4), 0075e2c6-bf0c-4f8c-abc9-9e9bdfc87ee4) Stevens, Gareth Publishing LLLP.

—Making Pizza with Math!, 1 vol. 2019. (Cooking with Math! Ser.). (ENG.). 24p. (gr. 1-2). pap. 9.15 (978-1-5382-4562-0(0), 613786fe-fef2-442d-acd2-a769a8a51327) Stevens, Gareth Publishing LLLP.

—Making Snacks with Math!, 1 vol. 2019. (Cooking with Math! Ser.). (ENG.). 24p. (gr. 1-2). pap. 9.15 (978-1-5382-4574-3(4), b5200501-7554-41d2-bcc8-fcafc5f54237) Stevens, Gareth Publishing LLLP.

—Making Soups with Math!, 1 vol. 2019. (Cooking with Math! Ser.). (ENG.). 24p. (gr. 1-2). pap. 9.15 (978-1-5382-4566-8(3), a6c99a70-f44c-498b-8e82-8234daf701be) Stevens, Gareth Publishing LLLP.

Husted, Terri. Math Detective B1: Higher-Order Thinking Reading Writing in Mathematics. 2013. (Math Detective Ser.). 136p. (gr. 7-8). pap. 19.99 (978-0-89455-864-1(1)) Critical Thinking Co., The.

Hutton, Kallie, et al. Mathematics for Zambia Basic Education Grade 5 Pupil's Book. 2008. (ENG., Illus.). 128p. pap. 3.99 (978-0-521-69868-9(5)) Cambridge Univ. Pr.

Hynson, Colin. Dream Jobs in Math. 2017. (Cutting-Edge Careers in STEM Ser.). (Illus.). 32p. (J). (978-0-7787-2963-1(X)) Crabtree Publishing Co.

I Love Math Series, 12 bks. Incl. Alice in Numberland: Fantasy Math. Time-Life Books Editors. Mark, Sara et al, eds. 1993. 16.95 (978-0-8094-9978-6(9)); Case of the Missing Zebra Stripes: Zoo Math. Time-Life Books Editors. Daniels, Patricia et al, eds. 1992. 16.95 (978-0-8094-9954-0(1)); From Head to Toe: Body Math. Time-Life Books Editors. Daniels, Patricia & Crawford, Jean B., eds. 1992. 16.95 (978-0-8094-9966-3(5)); How Do Octopi Eat Pizza Pie? Pizza Math. Time-Life Books Editors. Daniels, Patricia et al, eds. 1992. 16.95 (978-0-8094-9950-2(9)); Mystery Mansion: House Math. Mark, Sara, ed. 1993. 16.95 (978-0-8094-9986-1(X)); Pterodactyl Tunnel: Amusement Park Math. Crawford, Jean B., ed. 1993. 16.95 (978-0-8094-9990-8(8)); Search for the Mystery Planet: Space Math. Time-Life Books Editors. Crawford, Jean B., ed. 1993. 16.95 (978-0-8094-9982-3(7)); (Illus.). 64p. (J). (gr. 1-4). 172.89 (978-0-8094-9991-5(6)) Time-Life, Inc.

I Use Math, 8 vols. 2005. (I Use Math Ser.). (ENG.). 24p. (gr. k-2). lib. bdg. 98.68 (978-0-8368-4853-3(5), 85f57b42-c905-4d5b-a372-ac0ef5c998c7, Weekly Reader Leveled Readers) Stevens, Gareth Publishing LLLP.

Ikids Staff. Fast Facts - Division. 2005. (ENG.). 14p. (J). (gr. 2-17). 7.99 (978-1-58476-315-4(9)) Innovative Kids.

—Fast Facts - Multiplication. 2005. (ENG.). 14p. (J). (gr. 2-17). 7.99 (978-1-58476-314-7(0)) Innovative Kids.

—Math Gear: Fast Facts - Addition. 2005. (ENG.). 14p. (J). (gr. 2-17). 9.99 (978-1-58476-326-0(4)) Innovative Kids.

—Math Gear: Fast Facts - Subtraction. 2005. (ENG.). 14p. (J). (gr. 2-17). 9.99 (978-1-58476-327-7(2)) Innovative Kids.

In Step with the Standards - Computation & Estimation. 2005. (J). spiral bd. 15.95 (978-1-58123-376-6(0)) Larson Learning, Inc.

In Step with the Standards - Data, Statistics, & Probability. 2005. (J). spiral bd. 15.95 (978-1-58123-378-0(7)) Larson Learning, Inc.

Inchworms Activity Cards. 2003. (J). 17.95 (978-1-56911-143-7(X)) Learning Resources, Inc.

Infomax Common Core Math Readers: Levels a - D. 2013. (InfoMax Math Readers Ser.). 16p. (J). (gr. k-1). pap. 1683.00 (978-1-4777-2215-2(7)); pap. 280.50 (978-1-4777-2216-9(5)) Rosen Publishing Group, Inc., The. (Rosen Classroom).

Infomax Common Core Math Readers: Levels d - I. 2013. (InfoMax Math Readers Ser.). 24p. (J). (gr. 1-2). pap. 255.75 (978-1-4777-2217-6(3)); pap. 1534.50 (978-1-4777-2218-3(1)) Rosen Publishing Group, Inc., The. (Rosen Classroom).

Integrating Grade 11 TAKS Geometry into Algebra II Student Edition. 2004. (Region IV ESC Resources for Mathematics Ser.). pap. (978-1-932797-71-8(8)) Region 4 Education Service Ctr.

Intermediate Math Skills, Chapter 1, Activities. 2005. (Illus.). 50p. (YA). per. 7.00 (978-1-59476-041-9(1)) Paradigm Accelerated Curriculum.

Intermediate Math Skills, Chapter 1, Text. 2005. (Illus.). 50p. (YA). pap. 7.00 (978-1-59476-029-7(2)) Paradigm Accelerated Curriculum.

Intermediate Math Skills, Chapter 2, Activities. 2005. (Illus.). 58p. (YA). pap. 5.00 (978-1-59476-042-6(X)) Paradigm Accelerated Curriculum.

Intermediate Math Skills, Chapter 2, Text. 2005. (Illus.). 64p. (YA). pap. 7.00 (978-1-59476-030-3(6)) Paradigm Accelerated Curriculum.

Intermediate Math Skills, Chapter 3, Activities. 2005. (Illus.). 52p. (YA). pap. 5.00 (978-1-59476-043-3(8)) Paradigm Accelerated Curriculum.

Intermediate Math Skills, Chapter 3, Text. 2005. (Illus.). 62p. (YA). pap. 7.00 (978-1-59476-031-0(4)) Paradigm Accelerated Curriculum.

Intermediate Math Skills, Chapter 4, Activities. 2005. (Illus.). 60p. (YA). pap. 5.00 (978-1-59476-044-0(6)) Paradigm Accelerated Curriculum.

Intermediate Math Skills, Chapter 4, Text. 2005. (Illus.). 70p. (YA). pap. 7.00 (978-1-59476-032-7(2)) Paradigm Accelerated Curriculum.

Intermediate Math Skills, Chapter 5, Activities. 2005. (Illus.). 68p. (YA). pap. 5.00 (978-1-59476-045-7(4)) Paradigm Accelerated Curriculum.

Intermediate Math Skills, Chapter 5, Text. 2005. (Illus.). 56p. (YA). pap. 7.00 (978-1-59476-033-4(0)) Paradigm Accelerated Curriculum.

Intermediate Math Skills, Chapter 6, Activities. 2005. 68p. (YA). pap. 5.00 (978-1-59476-046-4(2)) Paradigm Accelerated Curriculum.

Intermediate Math Skills, Chapter 6, Text. 2005. (Illus.). 68p. (YA). pap. 7.00 (978-1-59476-034-1(9)) Paradigm Accelerated Curriculum.

Intermediate Math Skills Full Course Kit with TRK & CD-ROM. 2005. (Illus.). 1042p. (YA). 87.00 (978-1-59476-203-1(1)) Paradigm Accelerated Curriculum.

Investigations in Number, Data, & Space. 2004. (gr. k-5). (978-0-328-01881-9(3), Scott Foresman) Addison-Wesley Educational Pubs., Inc.

Investigations in Number, Data, & Space: Complete Program. 2004. (gr. k-18). (978-0-201-37792-7(6)); (gr. 1-18). (978-0-201-37793-4(4)); (gr. 2-18). (978-0-201-37794-1(2)); (gr. 3-18). (978-0-201-37795-8(0)); (gr. 4-18). (978-0-201-37796-5(9)); (gr. 5-18). (978-0-201-37797-2(7)) Addison-Wesley Educational Pubs., Inc. (Scott Foresman).

Investigations in Number, Data, & Space: Individual Components (Additional Resources) 2004. (gr. k-18). (978-0-328-01882-6(1)); (gr. k-18). (978-0-328-01883-3(X)); (gr. k-2). (978-0-201-43436-1(9)); (gr. 2-18). (978-0-201-37586-2(9)); (gr. 3-5). (978-0-201-43438-5(5)) Addison-Wesley Educational Pubs., Inc. (Scott Foresman).

Irvin, Barbara Bando. Multiplication Facts Made Easy 3-4. Boyer, Robin, illus. 2018. (ENG.). 64p. (J). (gr. 3-4). pap. 4.49 (978-1-58947-328-7(0), a79231ee-2ffb-4ca0-b788-fea1079eca4e) School Zone Publishing Co.

Irvin, Barbara Bando, et al. Math Basics 3: Grade 3. Reinke, David et al, illus. deluxe ed. 2019. (ENG.). 64p. (J). (gr. 3-3). pap., wbk. ed. 4.49 (978-0-88743-139-5(9), 6d21ac7e-be5f-4f11-a3b6-b561d2ac98cd) School Zone Publishing Co.

Jackson, Dona. Let's Get Moving! Tell & Write Time. 2013. (InfoMax Math Readers Ser.). (ENG.). 24p. (J). (gr. 1-2). pap. 49.50 (978-1-4777-2176-6(2)); (Illus.). pap. 8.25 (978-1-4777-2175-9(4), ab890231-5cda-40e4-8274-c2c4dc7a97c5) Rosen Publishing Group, Inc., The. (Rosen Classroom).

Jackson, Richelle. Running for Class President: Represent & Solve Problems Involving Division. 2014. (Rosen Math Readers Ser.). (ENG.). 24p. (J). (gr. 3-4). pap. 49.50 (978-1-4777-4960-9(8), Rosen Classroom); (Illus.). pap. 8.25 (978-1-4777-4959-3(4), 6641ec75-943e-4c1e-b21f-0ed1defbe40b, PowerKids Pr.); (Illus.). lib. bdg. 25.27 (978-1-4777-6448-0(8), 0724bd52-c31a-4490-9329-d3e5fd61c642, PowerKids Pr.) Rosen Publishing Group, Inc., The.

Jacobs, Daniel. City Shapes, 6 vols., Set. 2003. (Yellow Umbrella Early Level Ser.). (ENG.). 16p. (gr. k-1). pap. 35.70 (978-0-7368-2992-2(X), Capstone Pr.) Capstone.

—Count Your Chickens, 6 vols., Set. 2003. (Yellow Umbrella Early Level Ser.). (ENG.). 16p. (gr. k-1). pap. 35.70 (978-0-7368-2995-3(4), Capstone Pr.) Capstone.

Jacobs, Russell F. Math by Design, Year 1-2, Grade 2. Naughton, Abbey L. & Bobbett, Victor M., eds. 2017. (ENG., Illus.). 48p. (J). (gr. 2-3). pap., wbk. ed. 19.95 (978-0-918272-30-0(0), 169) Tessellations.

—Math by Design, Year 2-3, Grade 3. 2017. (ENG.). 48p. (J). (gr. 3-4). pap., wbk. ed. 19.95 (978-0-918272-31-7(9), 1691) Tessellations.

—Pre-Algebra - by Design. 2017. (ENG.). 24p. (J). pap. 23.50 (978-0-918272-41-6(6)) Tessellations.

Jacobson, Jennifer. Scholastic Success with Reading & Math Jumbo Workbook, 1 vol. 2005. (ENG.). 320p. (gr. 4-4). pap., wbk. ed. 14.99 (978-0-439-78603-4(7), Teaching Resources) Scholastic, Inc.

Jason Math Adventure: Proportional Reasoning & the Disappearing Wetlands. 2004. (J). (978-0-9763809-3-1(5)) JASON Project, The.

Jennison, Christopher. Baseball Math: Grandslam Activities & Projects. 3rd ed. 2005. (Illus.). 104p. (J). (gr. 4-8). per. 12.95 (978-1-59647-007-1(0)) Good Year Bks.

Jeopardy Math Grade 3. 2006. (J). 28.00 (978-1-933178-56-1(6)) Pflaum Publishing Group.

Jeopardy Math Grade 4. 2006. (J). 28.00 (978-1-933178-57-8(4)) Pflaum Publishing Group.

Jeopardy Math Grade 5. 2006. (J). 28.00 (978-1-933178-58-5(2)) Pflaum Publishing Group.

Johns, Bobbie. Secure Year 6 Maths Pupil Resource Pack: A Primary Maths Intervention Programme, 1 vol. 2017. (ENG.). 144p. (J). pap. 89.99 incl. cd-rom (978-0-00-822152-2(9)) HarperCollins Pubs. Ltd. GBR. Dist: Independent Pubs. Group.

Johnson, Virginia. Hands-on Math, Grades K-1: Manipulative Activities for the Classroom. Hamaguchi, Carla, ed. Weller, Linda, illus. 2nd ed. 2006. 144p. (J). (gr. k-1). per. 19.99 (978-1-59198-232-6(4), 2568) Creative Teaching Pr., Inc.

Johnstone, Drummond & Wakefield, Chris. Numbers Game, Theparent Booklet: It's a Real Cure for Maths Fright. 2013. (ENG.). 26p. pap. 3.25 (978-1-85741-181-2(1)) Southgate Pubs. GBR. Dist: Parkwest Pubns., Inc.

Jones, Dee. Winston Wonders about Capacity: A mathematical Story. Klaus, Machelle, illus. 2010. 36p. pap. 14.95 (978-1-60844-181-5(4)) Dog Ear Publishing, LLC.

Jones, Otis. Geonopolis, the Shapely City of Geometry. 2003. (ENG., Illus.). 21p. (J). (978-0-9744123-0-6(9)) Jeb Cool Kids Entertainment, Inc.

Jones, Rob Lee. Mathematics 1 for Young Catholics. 2013. pap. 15.00 (978-1-60704-113-9(8)) Seton Pr.

Jovin, Michelle. Your World: Shopping Secrets: Multiplication (Grade 3) 2017. (Mathematics in the Real World Ser.). (ENG., Illus.). 32p. (J). (gr. 3-4). pap. 11.99 (978-1-4807-5796-7(9)) Teacher Created Materials, Inc.

Kaplan, Andrew & DeBold, Carol. Math on Call: A Mathematics Handbook. 2nd ed. 2003. (Math on Call Ser.). (ENG., Illus.). 480p. (gr. 6-8). pap. 31.60 (978-0-669-50819-2(5)) Great Source Education Group, Inc.

Karapetian, Marjam. Bilingual Content Dictionary/Basic Math Including Algebra & Geometry: English to Spanish. 2004. (SPA & ENG., Illus.). 4.95 (978-0-9764829-0-1(8)) WizdomInc.

Karapetkova, Holly & Robertson, J. Jean. ?un Cuadrado? ! un Rectangulo! A Square? a Rectangle! 2008. (ENG & SPA., Illus.). 24p. (J). 19.44 (978-1-60472-506-3(0)) Rourke Educational Media.

Kay, Stephanie. Let's Go to the Parade! Understand Place Value. 2013. (InfoMax Math Readers Ser.). (ENG.). 24p. (J). (gr. 1-2). pap. 49.50 (978-1-4777-2164-3(9)); (Illus.). pap. 8.25 (978-1-4777-2163-6(0), 18ef636e-5d82-4cfd-907a-00b23ba49566) Rosen Publishing Group, Inc., The. (Rosen Classroom).

Keeler, Renee. Our Pumpkin. 2017. (Learn-To-Read Ser.). (ENG., Illus.). (J). (gr. k-2). pap. 3.49 (978-1-68310-223-6(1)) Pacific Learning, Inc.

Keen Kite Books, Keen Kite. KS2 Maths SATs Practice Test Papers: Maths KS2. 2017. (ENG.). 128p. (J). (gr. 5-6). pap. 113.99 (978-0-00-824195-7(3)) HarperCollins Pubs. Ltd. GBR. Dist: Independent Pubs. Group.

Kelly, Lynne. Maths Wizard. (Illus.). (J). (gr. 2-6). pap. (978-1-876367-35-0(0)) Wizard Bks.

Kennedy Shea, Bobby. Patterns with Pandas, 1 vol. 2013. (Animal Math Ser.). (ENG.). 24p. (J). (gr. 1-2). pap. 9.15 (978-1-4339-9319-0(8), c05f70c0-c50a-4c4f-bcb1-6a5ab18aee27); (Illus.). lib. bdg. 25.27 (978-1-4339-9318-3(X), ff6b0c97-0f78-40e9-a979-00b688142e6e) Stevens, Gareth Publishing LLLP.

Kernan, Elizabeth. How Long Is It? Learning to Measure with Nonstandard Units, 1 vol. 2010. (Math for the REAL World Ser.). (ENG., Illus.). 8p. (gr. k-1). pap. 5.15 (978-0-8239-8843-3(0), 1dbf9ccf-271c-45ec-bd57-21c05ac62a0d) Rosen Publishing Group, Inc., The.

Kessler, Colleen. Math Problem Solvers: Using Word Problems to Enhance Mathematical Problem Solving. 2005. (ENG.). 44p. 14.95 (978-1-59363-026-3(3)) Prufrock Pr.

Kids Can Press Staff. Math Stories: Subtraction. 2003. (Kids Can Learn with Franklin Ser.). (Illus.). 32p. (J). (gr. 1-3). 3.95 (978-1-55337-597-5(1)) Kids Can Pr., Ltd. CAN. Dist: Hachette Bk. Group.

Kidzup Productions Staff. Addition & Subtraction. 2003. (Interactive Learning Kits Ser.). (Illus.). 24p. (J). (gr. k-2). audio, audio compact disk 13.99 (978-1-894281-01-0(2)) Kidzup Productions.

Kim, Hy. The Complete Book of Multiplication & Division: Basic Facts & Advanced Number Theories. Applebaum, Teri L. & Rous, Sheri, eds. 2004. (Illus.). 144p. (J). pap. 16.99 (978-1-59198-035-3(6), CTP 2572) Creative Teaching Pr., Inc.

—The Complete Book of Multiplication & Division: Grades 2-3. Applebaum, Teri L. & Rous, Sheri, eds. Hillam, Corbin, illus. 2004. 144p. per. 16.99 (978-1-59198-034-6(8), CTP 2571) Creative Teaching Pr., Inc.

—Math Cycles: Problems & Quizzes that Strengthen Math Skills. 2008. pap. 24.95 (978-1-59647-141-2(7)) Good Year Bks.

Kirk, Karly. All My Cousins: Understand & Apply Properties of Operations. 2013. (InfoMax Math Readers Ser.). (ENG.). 24p. (J). (gr. 1-2). pap. 49.50 (978-1-4777-2184-1(3)); (Illus.). pap. 8.25 (978-1-4777-2183-4(5), d9f08f09-4b8c-4eee-b831-446cf04b33d2) Rosen Publishing Group, Inc., The. (Rosen Classroom).

Kirkman, Steve & McAlister, Kerrie. Maths in Practice. 2013. (ENG.). pap., stu. ed. (978-1-107-63382-7(6)) Cambridge Univ. Pr.

—Maths in Practice Workbook 2. 2013. (ENG.). pap., stu. ed. (978-1-107-62846-5(6)) Cambridge Univ. Pr.

Kleist, Nick. Super Sports Numbers: Understand Place Value, 1 vol. 2014. (Math Masters: Number & Operations in Base Ten Ser.). (ENG.). 24p. (J). (gr. 2-2). 25.27 (978-1-4777-6401-5(1), 2ccfad17-15d1-436e-814a-4d96a3abb0fd); pap. 8.25 (978-1-4777-4666-0(8), 87bbad0d-8297-443f-9552-a8111c462add) Rosen Publishing Group, Inc., The. (Rosen Classroom).

Koenig, Jenaya. Jumping Animals! Relate Addition & Subtraction to Length, 1 vol. 2014. (Math Masters: Measurement & Data Ser.). (ENG., 24p. (J). (gr. 2-2). Illus.). 25.27 (978-1-4777-6439-8(9), 8a4ef7b3-6e7f-427d-822b-1a870b7e6943); pap. 8.25 (978-1-4777-4816-9(4), 8c407a36-8ae5-4b2d-9c24-d6bc6d1dd9ac) Rosen Publishing Group, Inc., The. (Rosen Classroom).

Kofman, Victoria. Guni-Pi Academy, Math & Logic: Hands-On Textbook for 4 - 7 Year Olds. 2006. spiral bd. (978-0-9777171-0-1(0)) VK Publishing, Inc.

—Guni-Pi Academy, Math & Logic: Hands-on Textbook for 4 - 7 Year Olds - Non-Laminated. 2006. spiral bd. (978-0-9777171-2-5(7)) VK Publishing, Inc.

Koizim, Jessica. Mathematical Thinking Expressing Ideas Strategies, 1 vol. 2003. (BrainBuilders Ser.). (ENG.). 48p. (gr. k-4). pap. 5.25 (978-1-4042-8523-1(7), 0a104b8e-165c-43d4-94ea-501af82fb106) Rosen Publishing Group, Inc., The.

—Mathematical Thinking Linking Math to Everyday Life, 1 vol. 2003. (BrainBuilders Ser.). (ENG.). 48p. (gr. k-4). pap. 5.25 (978-1-4042-8524-8(5), 922d69c1-8d85-4dde-b24b-9a5bb49901f5) Rosen Publishing Group, Inc., The.

Koll, Hilary & Mills, Steve. A Math Journey Around the Wonders of the World. 2016. (ENG., Illus.). 32p. (J). (978-0-7787-2321-9(6)) Crabtree Publishing Co.

—A Math Journey Through Computer Games. 2016. (ENG.). 32p. (J). (978-0-7787-2311-0(9)) Crabtree Publishing Co.

—A Math Journey Through Extreme Sports. 2016. (ENG., Illus.). 32p. (J). (978-0-7787-2313-4(5)) Crabtree Publishing Co.

—A Math Journey under the Ocean. 2016. (ENG., Illus.). 32p. (J). (978-0-7787-2315-8(1)) Crabtree Publishing Co.

—Using Math in the ER, 1 vol. 2006. (Mathworks! Ser.). (ENG., Illus.). 32p. (gr. 3-5). lib. bdg. 28.67 (978-0-8368-6762-6(9), 0adc0164-9476-4f78-8bea-981fbfd9fecb, Gareth Stevens Learning Library) Stevens, Gareth Publishing LLLP.

—Using Math to Build a Skyscraper, 1 vol. 2006. (Mathworks! Ser.). (ENG., Illus.). 32p. (gr. 3-5). lib. bdg. 28.67 (978-0-8368-6764-0(5), e094c3b7-2641-4555-973a-9726d3ab9994, Gareth Stevens Learning Library) Stevens, Gareth Publishing LLLP.

—Using Math to Design a Roller Coaster, 1 vol. 2006. (Mathworks! Ser.). (ENG., Illus.). 32p. (gr. 3-5). lib. bdg. 28.67 (978-0-8368-6766-4(1), 43c248d6-0621-4f4a-893c-0380c75648e1, Gareth Stevens Learning Library) Stevens, Gareth Publishing LLLP.

Kompelien, Tracy. Lets Sort, Its a Real Sport!, 1 vol. 2007. (Math Made Fun Ser.). (Illus.). 24p. (J). (gr. k-3). lib. bdg. 24.21 (978-1-59928-539-9(8), SandCastle) ABDO Publishing Co.

Kramer, Alan; Hirschfeld. In Search of Numbers - You're Right There! Hirschfeld, Pam, ed. 2004. (Reader's Theater Content-Area Concepts Ser.). (ENG.). (J). (gr. 3). 5.00 net. (978-1-4108-1137-0(9)) Benchmark Education Co.

—No Math Day at School. Hirschfeld, Pam, ed. 2004. (Reader's Theater Content-Area Concepts Ser.). (ENG.). (J). (gr. 1). 5.00 net. (978-1-4108-0792-2(4)) Benchmark Education Co.

Kreloff, Elliot, illus. Matching Puzzle Cards - Numbers. 2012. (ENG.). 36p. (J). (gr. k-12). 9.99 (978-1-60905-221-8(8)) Blue Apple Bks.

Krolikowski, Steven A. SBAC Grade 6 Math: Smarter Balanced. 2017. (Barron's Test Prep Ser.). (ENG.). 304p. (gr. 6-6). pap. 14.99 (978-1-4380-1029-8(X), Barron's Educational Series, Inc.) Kaplan Publishing.

Kumon. Focus on Multiplication & Division with Decimals. 2012. (ENG., Illus.). 64p. (J). pap. 5.95 (978-1-935800-42-2(6)) Kumon Publishing North America, Inc.

—Grade 3 Multiplication. 2008. (ENG.). 80p. (J). per. 7.95 (978-1-933241-54-8(3)) Kumon Publishing North America, Inc.

—My Book of Number Games: 1-70. 2004. (ENG., Illus.). 80p. (J). per. 7.95 (978-4-7743-0759-6(9)) Kumon Publishing North America, Inc.

—My Book of Simple Multiplication. 2007. (Kumon Workbooks Ser.). (ENG., Illus.). 80p. (J). (gr. 1-3). per. 7.95 (978-1-933241-41-8(1)) Kumon Publishing North America, Inc.

Kumon Publishing, ed. Focus on Multiplication & Division with Decimals. 2012. (ENG., Illus.). 64p. (J). pap. 5.95 *(978-4-7743-0025-2(X))* Kumon Publishing North America, Inc.

—Focus on Multiplication Numbers 1-10. 2012. (ENG., Illus.). 64p. (J). pap. 5.95 *(978-4-7743-0023-8(3))* Kumon Publishing North America, Inc.

—Velocity, Proportion & Ratio. 2012. (ENG., Illus.). 64p. (J). pap. 5.95 *(978-4-7743-0024-5(1))* Kumon Publishing North America, Inc.

Kumon Publishing North America. Grade 1 Addition: Kumon Math Workbooks. 2008. (ENG.). 96p. (J). per. 7.95 *(978-1-933241-49-4(7))* Kumon Publishing North America, Inc.

—Grade 1 Subtraction: Kumon Math Workbooks. 2008. (ENG.). 96p. (J). per. 7.95 *(978-1-933241-50-0(0))* Kumon Publishing North America, Inc.

—Grade 3 Addition & Subtraction: Kumon Math Workbooks. 2008. (ENG.). 96p. (J). per. 7.95 *(978-1-933241-53-1(5))* Kumon Publishing North America, Inc.

—Grade 4 Division: Kumon Math Workbooks. 2008. (ENG.). 96p. (J). per. 7.95 *(978-1-933241-57-9(8))* Kumon Publishing North America, Inc.

—Grade 4 Multiplication: Kumon Math Workbooks. 2008. (ENG.). 96p. (J). per. 7.95 *(978-1-933241-56-2(X))* Kumon Publishing North America, Inc.

Kumon Publishing North America, creator. Addition Grade 2: Kumon Math Workbooks. Kumon Publishing North America, . 2008. (Kumon Workbooks Ser.). (ENG.). 96p. (J). (gr. -1-3). pap. 7.95 *(978-1-933241-51-7(9))* Kumon Publishing North America, Inc.

Kumon Publishing North America, ed. Grade 2 Subtraction: Kumon Math Workbooks. Kumon Publishing North America, . 2008. (ENG., Illus.). 96p. (J). (gr. 2). pap. 7.95 *(978-1-933241-52-4(7))* Kumon Publishing North America, Inc.

Kumon Publishing North America. Grade 3 Division: Kumon Math Workbooks. 2008. (ENG.). 96p. (J). per. 7.95 *(978-1-933241-55-5(1))* Kumon Publishing North America, Inc.

LaCompte, Angie. Math for Fun. 2011. (Wonder Readers Ser.). (ENG.). 16p. (J). (gr. -1-1). 25.95 *(978-1-4296-8669-3(3)*, 195210, Capstone Pr.) Capstone.

Lalley, Kristine. How Many Legs? Learning to Multiply Using Repeated Addition. 2009. (PowerMath: Beginning Ser.). 16p. (gr. 2-2). 37.50 *(978-1-60851-373-4(4)*, PowerKids Pr.) Rosen Publishing Group, Inc., The.

Lanczak Williams, Rozanne. Adding, 1 vol. 2004. (I Can Do Math Ser.). (ENG., Illus.). 24p. (gr. k-2). lib. bdg. 24.67 *(978-0-8368-4108-4(5)*, 6eba23fa-e38a-4fb2-8804-18798a265270, Gareth Stevens Learning Library) Stevens, Gareth Publishing LLLP.

—I Can Do Math, 6 vols. Incl. Adding. lib. bdg. 24.67 *(978-0-8368-4108-4(5)*, 6eba23fa-e38a-4fb2-8804-18798a265270); Crayola Counting. lib. bdg. 24.67 *(978-0-8368-4109-1(3)*, 0974a32c-a255-4f82-8f85-8ce30a10b2a4); Subtracting. lib. bdg. 24.67 *(978-0-8368-4113-8(1)*, 0d3c0599-51f6-4e00-b571-95ea4466ae4f); (gr. k-2). (I Can Do Math Ser.). (ENG., Illus.). 24p. 2004. Set lib. bdg. 74.01 *(978-0-8368-4107-7(7)*, 8515ccc1-73ec-4392-9805-9c53e97d90e6, Gareth Stevens Learning Library) Stevens, Gareth Publishing LLLP.

—Subtracting, 1 vol. 2004. (I Can Do Math Ser.). (ENG., Illus.). 24p. (gr. k-2). lib. bdg. 24.67 *(978-0-8368-4113-8(1)*, 0d3c0599-51f6-4e00-b571-95ea4466ae4f, Gareth Stevens Learning Library) Stevens, Gareth Publishing LLLP.

Lane, Chloe. Package Design. rev. ed. 2012. (Mathematics in the Real World Ser.). (ENG.). 32p. (gr. 5-8). pap. 11.99 *(978-1-4333-3460-3(7))* Teacher Created Materials, Inc.

Lane County Mathematics Project Staff. Problem Solving in Mathematics. 432p. (J). (gr. 4). pap. 27.95 *(978-0-86651-181-0(4)*, DSO1407); (YA). (gr. 8). pap. 27.95 *(978-0-86651-185-8(7)*, DSO1411) Globe Fearon Educational Publishing.

Lappan, Glenda. Connected Mathematics, 3 vols. 2004. 760p. (YA). (gr. 6-18). 380.00 *(978-0-13-180833-1(8))* Prentice Hall Pr.

Lappan, Glenda & Prentice-Hall Staff. Connected Mathematics, 2 vols. 2003. (ENG.). 676p. (YA). (gr. 8-8). 338.00 *(978-0-13-180835-5(4)*, Prentice Hall) Savvas Learning Co.

Large, Tori. Illustrated Dictionary of Math: Internet-Linked. 2004. (Illustrated Dictionaries Ser.). 128p. (J). lib. bdg. 20.99 *(978-1-58086-645-3(X)*, Usborne) EDC Publishing.

—The Usborne Illustrated Dictionary of Math. 2004. (Illustrated Dictionaries Ser.). (ENG., Illus.). 128p. (J). pap. 12.99 *(978-0-7945-0662-9(3)*, Usborne) EDC Publishing.

Larson, Nancy. Lesson Planner Instruction. Saxon Publishers Staff, tr. 2nd rev. ed. 2003. (gr. k-4). incl. cd-rom *(978-1-59141-299-1(4)*, 2994) Saxon Pubs., Inc.

—Teacher Resource Instruction. Saxon Publishers Staff, tr. 2nd rev. ed. 2003. (gr. k-4). tchr. ed. incl. audio compact disk *(978-1-59141-298-4(6)*, 2986) Saxon Pubs., Inc.

Larson, Ron. Middle School Math, Course 2. l.t. ed. 2004. (McDougal Littell Math Ser.). (YA). (gr. 6-9). stu. ed. 63.96 *(978-0-618-24974-9(5)*, 2-06002) Holt McDougal.

—Precalculus Advanced Placement. 6th ed. 2003. (YA). (gr. 11-12). 161.56 *(978-0-618-31435-5(0)*, 332741) CENGAGE Learning.

Larson, Ron, et al. McDougal Littell Middle School Math Course 3. l.t. ed. 2006. (Illus.). 797p. (gr. 6-9). lib. bdg., stu. ed. 66.12 *(978-0-618-25000-4(X)*, 2-06003) Holt McDougal.

—Passport to Mathematics, Vol. 2. 2006. (Illus.). 706p. (gr. 6-12). lib. bdg., stu. ed. *(978-0-618-18599-3(2)*, 2-05511) Holt McDougal.

Lawrence, Paul. Communicator Mathematics#8482; Content Series — Fraction Addition & Subtraction Teacher Guide: W/DVD Book G. 2005. 368p. spiral bd. 45.95 *(978-1-59699-177-4(1))* Lawrence Educational Services, Inc.

—Communicator Mathematics#8482; Content Series - Concepts of Fractions & Decimals Teacher Guide: W/DVD Book F. 2005. 268p. spiral bd. 45.95 *(978-1-59699-170-5(4))* Lawrence Educational Services, Inc.

—Communicator Mathematics#8482; Content Series - Whole Number Addition & Subtraction Teacher Guide: W/DVD Book C. 2005. 436p. spiral bd. 51.95 *(978-1-59699-167-5(4))* Lawrence Educational Services, Inc.

—Communicator Mathematics#8482; Content Series - Whole Numbers: Multiplication & Division Beyond Facts Teacher Guide: W/DVD Book E. 2005. 408p. spiral bd. 51.95 *(978-1-59699-169-9(0))* Lawrence Educational Services, Inc.

—Communicator Mathematics#8482; Content Series - Whole Numbers: Understanding & Mastering Multiplication & Division Facts Teacher Guide: W/DVD Book D. 2005. 464p. spiral bd. 49.95 *(978-1-59699-168-2(2))* Lawrence Educational Services, Inc.

—Communicator Mathematics#8482; Content Series- Decimal Addition & Subtraction Teacher Guide I: W/DVD Book I. 2005. 210p. spiral bd. 42.95 *(978-1-59699-171-2(2))* Lawrence Educational Services, Inc.

—Communicator Mathematics#8482; Content Series Fractions & Decimals - Decimals Multiplication & Division Teacher Guide: W/DVD Book J. 2005. 148p. spiral bd. 40.95 *(978-1-59699-176-7(3))* Lawrence Educational Services, Inc.

—Communicator Mathematics#8482; Fractions Multiplacation & Division Teacher Guide: W/DVD Book H. 2005. 262p. spiral bd. 45.95 *(978-1-59699-178-1(X))* Lawrence Educational Services, Inc.

—Communicator#8482; Mathematics Content Series— Decimal Multiplication & Division: Book J Student Pak. 2005. 88p. ring bd. 3.95 *(978-1-59699-352-5(9))* Lawrence Educational Services, Inc.

—Communicator#8482; Mathematics Content Series- Concepts of Fractions & Decimals: Book F Student Pak. 2005. 144p. spiral bd. 4.95 *(978-1-59699-353-2(7))* Lawrence Educational Services, Inc.

—Communicator#8482; Mathematics Content Series- Fraction Multiplication & Division: Book H Student Pak. 2005. 120p. spiral bd. 3.95 *(978-1-59699-355-6(3))* Lawrence Educational Services, Inc.

—Communicator#8482; Mathematics Content Series- Perspective on Numbers Assessment: Book B Student Pak. 2005. 232p. spiral bd. 6.95 *(978-1-59699-347-1(2))* Lawrence Educational Services, Inc.

—Communicator#8482; Mathematics Content Series- Whole Number Addition & Subtraction: Book C Student Pak. 2005. 208p. spiral bd. 7.95 *(978-1-59699-348-8(0))* Lawrence Educational Services, Inc.

—Communicator#8482; Mathematics Content Series- Whole Numbers: Multiplication & Division Beyond Facts: Book E Student Pak. 2005. 232p. spiral bd. 7.95 *(978-1-59699-350-1(2))* Lawrence Educational Services, Inc.

—Communicator#8482; Mathematics Content Series- Whole Numbers: Understanding & Mastering Multiplication & Division Facts: Book D Student Pak. 2005. 312p. spiral bd. 7.95 *(978-1-59699-349-5(9))* Lawrence Educational Services, Inc.

—Communicator#8482; Mathematics Content Series-Decimal Addition & Subtraction: Book I Student Pak. 2005. 152p. spiral bd. 4.95 *(978-1-59699-351-8(0))* Lawrence Educational Services, Inc.

Lawrence, Paul R. Question Quest HSPA Math - Level A, 1 volume. 2003. (Illus.). (YA). pap. 10.95 *(978-1-931104-20-3(4))* L L Teach.

—Question Quest HSPA Math - Level B, 1 volume. 2003. (Illus.). (YA). pap. 10.95 *(978-1-931104-22-7(0))* L L Teach.

—Question Quest HSPA Math Algebra Companion, 1 volume. 2003. (Illus.). (YA). pap. 8.95 *(978-1-931104-18-0(2))* L L Teach.

—Question Quest HSPA Math Geometry Companion. 2003. (Illus.). (YA). pap. 8.95 *(978-1-931104-16-6(6))* L L Teach.

Learning Company Books Staff, ed. Mighty Math: Money & Decimals. 2003. (Illus.). (J). 32p. pap., wbk. ed. *(978-0-7630-7631-3(7))*; 32p. pap., wbk. ed. *(978-0-7630-7632-0(5))*; 320p. (gr. 2-3). pap., wbk. ed. *(978-0-7630-7636-8(8))* Magma.

—Reader Rabbit Math: Addition & Subtraction. 2003. (Illus.). (J). 32p. pap., wbk. ed. *(978-0-7630-7639-9(2))*; 32p. pap., wbk. ed. *(978-0-7630-7638-2(4))*; 320p. pap., wbk. ed. *(978-0-7630-7637-5(6))* Magma.

Learning Wrap Ups Palette Base. 2004. (ENG.). (J). 14.99 *(978-1-59204-000-1(4))* Learning Wrap-Ups, Inc.

Leavitt, Amie Jane. How STEM Built the Aztec Empire, 1 vol. 2019. (How STEM Built Empires Ser.). (ENG.). 80p. (gr. 7-7). pap. 16.30 *(978-1-7253-4134-0(4)*, 4018fd21-706c-4ecc-975f-0a94efc7e4c3) Rosen Publishing Group, Inc., The.

—How STEM Built the Mayan Empire, 1 vol. 2019. (How STEM Built Empires Ser.). (ENG.). 80p. (gr. 7-7). pap. 16.30 *(978-1-7253-4149-4(2)*, ccee7b83-7ab1-4a52-8605-764ba3b58500) Rosen Publishing Group, Inc., The.

Lechner, Judith. Our New Fish Tank: Learning to Estimate & Round Numbers to the Nearest Ones, Tens, & Hundreds Places. 2004. (Math Big Bookstm Ser.). (ENG.). 16p. (gr. 2-3). 37.95 *(978-0-8239-7640-9(8))* Rosen Publishing Group, Inc., The.

Lechner, Judith & Collins, Kathleen. Our New Fish Tank: Learning to Estimate & Round Numbers to the Nearest Ones, Tens, & Hundreds Places, 1 vol. 2010. (Math for the REAL World Ser.). (ENG.). 16p. (gr. 2-3). pap. 7.05 *(978-0-8239-8881-5(3)*, 46087ae1-2f23-4ba2-8d3f-78adc6058b53, Rosen Classroom) Rosen Publishing Group, Inc., The.

Lee, Cora & O'Reilly, Gillian. The Great Number Rumble: A Story of Math in Surprising Places. Crump, Lil, illus. 2nd ed. 2016. (ENG.). 104p. (J). (gr. 3-7). pap. 12.95 *(978-1-55451-849-4(0))* Annick Pr., Ltd. CAN. Dist: Publishers Group West (PGW).

Lee Stone, Tanya. Who Says Women Can't Be Computer Programmers? The Story of Ada Lovelace. Priceman, Marjorie, illus. 2018. (ENG.). 40p. (J). 18.99 *(978-1-62779-299-8(6)*, 900145930, Holt, Henry & Co. Bks. For Young Readers) Holt, Henry & Co.

Leech, Bonnie. Mesopotamia: Creating & Solving World Problems. 2009. (PowerMath: Advanced Proficiency Plus Ser.). 32p. (gr. 5-5). 47.90 *(978-1-60851-362-8(9)*, PowerKids Pr.) Rosen Publishing Group, Inc., The.

Leech, Bonnie Coulter. Mesopotamia: Creating & Solving Word Problems, 1 vol. (Math for the REAL World Ser.). (ENG., Illus.). 32p. (gr. 5-5). 2009. pap. 10.00 *(978-1-4042-6067-2(6)*, 31bfbb46-3e70-4b1c-89a8-c4e945953187) 2006. (YA). lib. bdg. 28.93 *(978-1-4042-3357-7(1)*, b9714b7e-d02f-478a-8828-a71b29e811f7) Rosen Publishing Group, Inc., The.

Lehoczky, Sandor & Rusczyk, Richard. The Art of Problem Solving Vol. 1: The Basics. Date not set. 361p. (YA). (gr. 7-12). pap. 29.00 *(978-1-885875-01-3(0))* Mu Alpha Theta, National High Schl. Mathematics Club.

Leigh, Autumn. On the Ball: Learning to Identify the Place Values of Ones & Tens, 1 vol. 2010. (Math for the REAL World Ser.). (ENG., Illus.). 8p. (gr. k-1). pap. 5.15 *(978-0-8239-8859-4(7)*, d4c98b27-ecd2-456f-88a7-69c0af5ffbe5) Rosen Publishing Group, Inc., The.

—Signs on the Road: Learning to Identify the Four Basic Geometric Shapes, 1 vol. 2010. (Math for the REAL World Ser.). (ENG., Illus.). 8p. (gr. k-1). pap. 5.15 *(978-0-8239-8857-0(0)*, f5253939-6466-46b7-a4e0-107d37c64b88) Rosen Publishing Group, Inc., The.

LernerClassroom Editors. First Step Nonfiction-Early Math Teaching Guide. 2009. pap. 7.95 *(978-0-8225-6881-0(0))* Lerner Publishing Group.

Letts Cambridge IGCSE. Cambridge IGCSE(tm) Maths Revision Guide (Letts Cambridge IGCSE(tm) Revision) rev. ed. 2017. (ENG.). 168p. (YA). (gr. 9-11). pap. 18.99 *(978-0-00-821034-2(9))* HarperCollins Pubs. Ltd. GBR. Dist: Independent Pubs. Group.

Letts KS2, Letts. KS2 Maths SATs Revision Guide: for the 2021 Tests (Letts KS2 SATs Success) 2017. (Letts KS3 Revision Success Ser.). (ENG.). 96p. (J). (gr. 2-6). pap. 9.99 *(978-1-84419-924-2(X))* HarperCollins Pubs. Ltd. GBR. Dist: Independent Pubs. Group.

Levit, Joe. Let's Explore Math. 2018. (Bumba Books (r) — a First Look at STEM Ser.). (ENG., Illus.). 24p. (J). (gr. -1-1). pap. 8.99 *(978-1-5415-2700-3(3)*, dc501376-92cf-4c8f-a57b-8823ffdb78e1) Lerner Publishing Group.

Levy, Janey. A Journey along the Erie Canal: Dividing Multidigit Numbers by a One-Digit Number Without Remainders, 1 vol. (Math for the REAL World Ser.). (ENG., Illus.). 32p. (gr. 4-5). 2010. pap. 10.00 *(978-0-8239-8904-1(6)*, e2319c42-24f2-41f0-9a61-e02d57fe6df9) 2003. (J). lib. bdg. 28.93 *(978-0-8239-8991-1(7)*, 6a88d465-da70-46ce-b9be-d67b57870a2a) Rosen Publishing Group, Inc., The.

Lift-The-Flap Fractions & Decimals IR. 2017. (Advanced Lift-The-Flap BDs* Ser.). (ENG.). (J). bds. 14.99 *(978-0-7945-3727-2(8)*, Usborne) EDC Publishing.

Linde, Barbara. Math in Our Solar System: Applying Problem-Solving Strategies. 2009. (PowerMath: Proficiency Plus Ser.). 32p. (gr. 4-5). 47.90 *(978-1-60851-413-7(7)*, PowerKids Pr.) Rosen Publishing Group, Inc., The.

Linde, Barbara M. Math in Our Solar System: Applying Problem-Solving Strategies, 1 vol. (Math for the REAL World Ser.). (ENG.). 32p. (gr. 5-6). 2009. pap. 10.00 *(978-1-4042-5135-9(9)*, 47c1cfe1-7782-47b5-8a24-378e22c6764a) 2004. (Illus.). (J). lib. bdg. 28.93 *(978-1-4042-2936-5(1)*, 381f9a73-425d-4ac2-aeb8-53eda63581f4, PowerKids Pr.) Rosen Publishing Group, Inc., The.

—A Shopping Trip: Learning to Add Dollars & Cents up to $10.00 Without Regrouping, 1 vol. 2010. (Math for the REAL World Ser.). (ENG.). 16p. (gr. 2-3). pap. 7.05 *(978-0-8239-8900-3(3)*, bd150635-7edf-4382-b9b6-c435b7e17e9e, Rosen Classroom) Rosen Publishing Group, Inc., The.

—Working at the Post Office: Learning to Subtract 2 Three-Digit Numbers Without Renaming, 1 vol. 2010. (Math for the REAL World Ser.). (ENG.). 16p. (gr. 2-3). pap. 7.05 *(978-0-8239-8855-6(4)*, 8f15937e-ed02-4e87-821d-42417fa601dd, Rosen Classroom) Rosen Publishing Group, Inc., The.

Lindsay, Kristine. Basic Math Practice 5 - Rounding, Reasonableness & Estimating. 2005. (YA). ring bd. 49.95 *(978-1-58804-405-1(X))* P C I Education.

—Coupon Math. 2004. (YA). ring bd. 59.95 *(978-1-58804-355-9(X))* P C I Education.

Literacy & Math Centers. 2005. (J). pap. *(978-1-60015-019-7(5))* Steps To Literacy, LLC.

Litton, Jonathan. Mesmerizing Math. Flintham, Thomas, illus. 2013. (ENG.). 16p. (J). (gr. 2-5). 18.99 *(978-0-7636-6881-5(8)*, Templar) Candlewick Pr.

Llewellyn, Claire & Holden, Arianne. It's Great to Play & Fun to Learn: A Stimulating Play-And-Learn Book with over 130 Amazing Facts, Exercises & Projects, & More Than 5000 Bright Action-Packed Photographs. 2014. (ENG., Illus.). 256p. (J). (gr. k-4). 16.99 *(978-1-84322-981-0(1)*, Armadillo) Anness Publishing GBR. Dist: National Bk. Network.

Lockerd, Jodi. Nocturnal Animals: Represent & Solve Problems Involving Multiplication, 1 vol. 2014. (Rosen Math Readers Ser.). (ENG., Illus.). 24p. (J). (gr. 3-3). pap. 8.25 *(978-1-4777-4968-5(3)*, ab2c62c8-5022-4622-bef0-875403ae5ee2); lib. bdg. 25.27 *(978-1-4777-6447-3(X)*, aae32665-9dc9-43d1-a470-3c22e71b5ec0) Rosen Publishing Group, Inc., The. (PowerKids Pr.).

Loesen von Sachaufgaben. (Duden-Schuelerhilfen Ser.). (GER.). 112p. (J). (gr. 5-6). *(978-3-411-04872-4(7))* Bibliographisches Institut & F. A. Brockhaus AG DEU. Dist: International Bk. Import Service, Inc.

Logarithmen und Exponentialgleichungen. (Duden-Schuelerhilfen Ser.). (GER.). 112p. (YA). (gr. 10). *(978-3-411-05661-3(4))* Bibliographisches Institut & F. A. Brockhaus AG DEU. Dist: International Bk. Import Service, Inc.

Logue, Damien. Favorite Foods: Classify & Count Objects in Each Category. 2013. (Rosen Math Readers Ser.). (ENG.). 16p. (J). (gr. k-1). pap. 42.00 *(978-1-4777-1654-0(8))*; (Illus.). pap. 7.00 *(978-1-4777-1653-3(X)*, 04c13285-84b8-4bc9-b0ce-29654c9e2751) Rosen Publishing Group, Inc., The. (Rosen Classroom).

Long, Lynette. Math Smarts: Tips, Tricks, & Secrets for Making Math More Fun! McGuinness, Tracy, illus. 2004. (AmericanGirl Library). (ENG.). 64p. (J). pap. 8.95 *(978-1-58485-875-1(3))* American Girl Publishing, Inc.

Loop, Katherine. Principles of Mathematics Book 1 Set. 2016. (ENG.). (J). pap. 79.98 *(978-0-89051-914-1(5)*, Master Books) New Leaf Publishing Group.

Loughran, Donna. Herding a Hundred: Counting the Sheep. 2013. (IMath Ser.). (Illus.). 24p. (J). (gr. k-2). lib. bdg. 21.27 *(978-1-59953-547-0(5))* Norwood Hse. Pr.

—On the Playground: How Do You Build Place Value? 2013. (IMath Ser.). (ENG., Illus.). 24p. (J). (gr. k-2). pap. 13.26 *(978-1-60357-488-4(3))* Norwood Hse. Pr.

—Toy Tally: How Many Toys Are There? 2013. (IMath Ser.). (Illus.). 24p. (J). (gr. k-2). (ENG.). pap. 13.26 *(978-1-60357-492-1(1))*; lib. bdg. 21.27 *(978-1-59953-553-1(X))* Norwood Hse. Pr.

Loughran, Donna & Brunner-Jass, Renata. Finding the Treasure: Coordinate Grids. 2013. (IMath Ser.). (Illus.). 48p. (J). (gr. 5-6). lib. bdg. 23.94 *(978-1-59953-573-9(4))* Norwood Hse. Pr.

—Winning the Game: Putting Miles in Their Place. 2013. (IMath Ser.). (Illus.). 48p. (J). (gr. 5-6). lib. bdg. 23.94 *(978-1-59953-567-8(X))* Norwood Hse. Pr.

Low, Emma. Cambridge Primary Mathematics: Learner's Book Stage 5. 2014. (Cambridge Primary Maths Ser.). (ENG., Illus.). 129p. pap. 24.50 *(978-1-107-63822-8(4))* Cambridge Univ. Pr.

—Cambridge Primary Mathematics. Learner's Book Stage 6. 2014. (Cambridge Primary Maths Ser.). (ENG., Illus.). 131p. pap. 24.50 *(978-1-107-61859-6(2))* Cambridge Univ. Pr.

LP-Addition: Level 2 Math. 2004. (ENG.). (J). 9.99 *(978-1-59204-018-6(7))* Learning Wrap-Ups, Inc.

LP-Blends & Digraphs: Level 1 Reading. 2004. (ENG.). (J). 9.99 *(978-1-59204-005-6(5))* Learning Wrap-Ups, Inc.

LP-Capitalization & Punctuation: Level 2 Reading. 2004. (ENG.). (J). 9.99 *(978-1-59204-009-4(8))* Learning Wrap-Ups, Inc.

LP-Place Value: Level 2 Math. 2004. (ENG.). (J). 9.99 *(978-1-59204-017-9(9))* Learning Wrap-Ups, Inc.

LP-Reading Comprehension: Level 2 Reading. 2004. (ENG.). (J). 9.99 *(978-1-59204-011-7(X))* Learning Wrap-Ups, Inc.

LP-Subtraction: Level 2 Math. 2004. (ENG.). (J). 9.99 *(978-1-59204-019-3(5))* Learning Wrap-Ups, Inc.

Luke, Andrew. STEM in Ice Hockey. 2019. (Connecting STEM & Sports Ser.). (Illus.). 80p. (J). (gr. 12). lib. bdg. 34.60 *(978-1-4222-4336-7(2))* Mason Crest.

MacFarlane, Katherine. The Father of the Atom: Democritus & the Nature of Matter, 1 vol. 2009. (Great Minds of Ancient Science & Math Ser.). (ENG., Illus.). 112p. (gr. 4-6). lib. bdg. 35.93 *(978-0-7660-3410-5(0)*, 7b71ef35-cafc-4b9f-9833-a968fd6b3d9b) Enslow Publishing, LLC.

MacGillivray, Helen & Petocz, Peter. Statistics & Probability in the Australian Curriculum Years 7 And 8. 2013. (ENG.). pap. 18.00 *(978-1-107-61421-5(X))* Cambridge Univ. Pr.

MacGregor, Helen. Songbooks - Tom Thumb's Musical Maths: Developing Maths Skills with Simple Songs. Sanderson, Ana, ed. Evans, Michael, illus. 2005. (Songbooks Ser.). (ENG.). 64p. (J). pap. 22.95 *(978-0-7136-7295-4(1))* HarperCollins Pubs. Ltd. GBR. Dist: Independent Pubs. Group.

MacPhee, K. M. Maths & English: Basics Manual for Young People. 2010. 254p. pap. *(978-0-7552-0482-3(4))* Authors OnLine, Ltd.

Mahaney, Ian F. The Math of Basketball, 1 vol. 2011. (Sports Math Ser.). (ENG.). 24p. (J). (gr. 2-3). pap. 9.25 *(978-1-4488-2694-0(2)*, 37b81a89-8586-4e30-9d59-73b84178ffb2, PowerKids Pr.); (ENG.). 24p. (J). (gr. 2-3). lib. bdg. 26.27 *(978-1-4488-2593-6(8)*, 1438cb7a-de60-4337-9cd6-592a6992a977); (J). 49.50 *(978-1-4488-2695-7(0)*, PowerKids Pr.) Rosen Publishing Group, Inc., The.

Making Connection with Measurement, Grade 11 TAKS - Student. 2004. (Region IV ESC Resources for Mathematics Ser.). pap., wbk. ed. *(978-1-932797-53-4(X))* Region 4 Education Service Ctr.

Making Connections with Measurement, Grade 1 - Student Workbook - Spanish. 2004. (Region IV ESC Resources for Mathematics Ser.). pap. *(978-1-932797-62-6(9))* Region 4 Education Service Ctr.

Making Connections with Measurement, Grade 1 TEKS - Student Workbook. 2004. (Region IV ESC Resources for Mathematics Ser.). pap. *(978-1-932797-43-5(2))* Region 4 Education Service Ctr.

Making Connections with Measurement, Grade 10 TAKS - Student Workbook. 2004. (Region IV ESC Resources for Mathematics Ser.). pap. *(978-1-932797-52-7(1))* Region 4 Education Service Ctr.

Making Connections with Measurement, Grade 2 TEKS - Student Workbook. 2004. (Region IV ESC Resources for Mathematics Ser.). pap. *(978-1-932797-44-2(0))* Region 4 Education Service Ctr.

Making Connections with Measurement, Grade 3 TAKS - Student Workbook. 2004. (Region IV ESC Resources for Mathematics Ser.). pap. *(978-1-932797-45-9(9))* Region 4 Education Service Ctr.

Making Connections with Measurement, Grade 4 TEKS - Student Workbook. 2004. (Region IV ESC Resources for Mathematics Ser.). pap. *(978-1-932797-46-6(7))* Region 4 Education Service Ctr.

Making Connections with Measurement, Grade 5 TAKS - Student Workbook. 2004. (Region IV ESC Resources for Mathematics Ser.). pap. *(978-1-932797-47-3(5))* Region 4 Education Service Ctr.

Making Connections with Measurement, Grade 5 TAKS - Teacher Edition. 2004. (Region IV ESC Resources for Mathematics Ser.). spiral bd. *(978-1-932797-35-0(1))* Region 4 Education Service Ctr.

Making Connections with Measurement, Grade 6 TAKS - Student Workbook. 2004. (Region IV ESC Resources for Mathematics Ser.). pap. *(978-1-932797-48-0(3))* Region 4 Education Service Ctr.

Making Connections with Measurement, Grade 7 TAKS - Student Workbook. 2004. (Region IV ESC Resources for Mathematics Ser.). pap. *(978-1-932797-49-7(1))* Region 4 Education Service Ctr.

Making Connections with Measurement, Grade 8 TAKS - Student Workbook. 2004. (Region IV ESC Resources for

Mathematics Ser.). pap. (978-1-932797-50-3(5)) Region 4 Education Service Ctr.

Making Connections with Measurement, Grade 9 TAKS - Student Workbook. 2004. (Region IV ESC Resources for Mathematics Ser.). pap. (978-1-932797-51-0(3)) Region 4 Education Service Ctr.

Making Connections with Measurement, Grade K TEKS - Student Workbook. 2004. (Region IV ESC Resources for Mathematics Ser.). pap. (978-1-932797-42-8(4)) Region 4 Education Service Ctr.

Making Connections with Measurement, Grade K TEKS - Student Workbook Spanish. 2004. (Region IV ESC Resources for Mathematics Ser.). pap. (978-1-932797-61-9(0)) Region 4 Education Service Ctr.

Making Connections with Measurement, TAKS Preparation Grade 2 - Student Workbook. 2004. (Region IV ESC Resources for Mathematics Ser.). pap. (978-1-932797-63-3(7)) Region 4 Education Service Ctr.

Malchik, E. The Great Depression by the Numbers & Los números de la Gran Depresión: 6 English, 6 Spanish Adaptations. 2011. (ENG & SPA.). (J). 101.00 net. (978-1-4108-5730-9(1)) Benchmark Education Co.

Malue, Jenna. Recycling Plastic: Understand Place Value, 1 vol. 2014. (Math Masters: Number & Operations in Base Ten Ser.). (ENG., Illus.). 24p. (J). (gr. 2-2). 25.27 (978-1-4777-6427-5(5), 6cacfd0c-4026-462f-acd8-f3d5ad0a19dc); pap. 8.25 (978-1-4777-4651-6(X), c66434b2-cbd6-4407-aef6-31e2ef3b6079) Rosen Publishing Group, Inc., The. (Rosen Classroom).

Mansk, Anne. You Can Measure: A Content Area Reader-math. 2005. (Emergent/Early (Prek-2) Math Package Ser.). 16p. (YA). (gr. -1-2). 25.20 (978-0-8215-7825-4(1)) Sadlier, William H. Inc.

Mapua, Jeff. Using Math in Science, 1 vol. 2017. (Math You Will Actually Use Ser.). (ENG.). 48p. (J). (gr. 5-5). pap. 12.75 (978-1-4994-3868-0(0), ced7c2a7-f849-4a61-81e9-e7da43dcf020, Rosen Central) Rosen Publishing Group, Inc., The.

Marrewa, Jennifer. Graphing Favorite Things, 1 vol. 2008. (Math in Our World - Level 2 Ser.). (ENG.). 24p. (gr. 2-2). pap. 9.15 (978-0-8368-9017-4(5), 2896bd54-7a49-4934-a805-2fea812e8f23); (Illus.). lib. bdg. 24.67 (978-0-8368-9008-2(6), 725540d5-431d-43a3-8df6-c60249c82483) Stevens, Gareth Publishing LLLP. (Weekly Reader Leveled Readers).

—Vamos a HACER GRÁFICAS de Nuestras Cosas Favoritas (GRAPHING Favorite Things), 1 vol. 2008. (Las Matemáticas en Nuestro Mundo - Nivel 2 (Math in Our World - Level 2) Ser.). (SPA.). 24p. (gr. 2-2). pap. 9.15 (978-0-8368-9035-8(3), b7f698c1-e5b8-4ff0-acc0-eaa68cf60920); (Illus.). lib. bdg. 24.67 (978-0-8368-9026-6(4), 745298ce-7e7a-471b-b42b-9a12f6c7c8a6); (Illus.). lib. bdg. 24.67 (978-0-8368-9026-6(4), 745298ce-7e7a-471b-b42b-9a12f6c7c8a6) Stevens, Gareth Publishing LLLP. (Weekly Reader Leveled Readers).

Marsh, Carole. Math for Girls Grades 3-6: The Book with the Number to Help Girls Love & Excel in Math! Beard, Chad, ed. 2004. (Math Ser.). (Illus.). 32p. (J). (gr. 2-6). pap. 7.95 (978-0-635-02445-9(4)) Gallopade International.

Marsico, Katie. Investing: Making Your Money Work for You. 2015. (21st Century Skills Library: Real World Math Ser.). (ENG., Illus.). 32p. (J). (gr. 4-7). 32.07 (978-1-63362-571-6(0), 206468) Cherry Lake Publishing.

—Using Credit Wisely. 2015. (21st Century Skills Library: Real World Math Ser.). (ENG., Illus.). 32p. (J). (gr. 4-7). 32.07 (978-1-63362-578-5(8), 206496) Cherry Lake Publishing.

Martin, Elena. Look at Both Sides, 6 vols., Set. 2003. (Yellow Umbrella Early Level Ser.). (ENG.). 16p. (gr. k-1). pap. 35.70 (978-0-7368-3013-3(8), Capstone Pr.) Capstone.

Martin, Hope. Career Math. 2007. 100p. per. 9.95 (978-1-59647-253-2(7)) Good Year Bks.

Martin, Sandra. Mathopedia Level 1. 2003. (Illus.). 118p. spiral bd. 49.99 (978-0-9718488-1-8(5)) Specialty Educational Pubs.

Mastering Math Word Problems. 2016. (Mastering Math Word Problems Ser.). 48p. (J). pap. 70.20 (978-0-7660-8401-8(9)) Enslow Publishing, LLC.

Masters, Nancy Robinson. Volcanic Eruptions. 2012. (21st Century Skills Library: Real World Math Ser.). (ENG., Illus.). 32p. (gr. 4-8). (J). pap. 14.21 (978-1-61080-414-1(7), 201346); lib. bdg. 32.07 (978-1-61080-328-1(0), 201314) Cherry Lake Publishing.

Matematicas 2000. (SPA.). (YA). (gr. 10). pap. 19.95 (978-958-02-0533-3(7), 0333); (SPA.). (YA). (gr. 11). pap. 19.95 (978-958-02-0534-0(5), 0334); (J). (gr. 6). pap. 19.95 (978-958-02-0529-6(9), 0329); (SPA.). (J). (gr. 7). pap. 19.95 (978-958-02-0530-2(2), 0330); (SPA.). (YA). (gr. 8). pap. 19.95 (978-958-02-0531-9(0), 0331); (SPA.). (YA). (gr. 9). pap. 19.95 (978-958-02-0532-6(9), 0332) Norma S.A. COL. Dist: Continental Bk. Co., Inc.

Las Matemáticas en Nuestro Mundo - Nivel 2, 14 vols., Set. Incl. ¿a Qué Distancia? Vamos a COMPARAR Viajes (How Far Away? COMPARING Trips) Marrewa, Jennifer & Marrewa, Jennifer. lib. bdg. 24.67 (978-0-8368-9024-2(8), 15a63c75-d8e2-4cec-867e-684446a1fc71); Diversión con DOBLES en la Granja (DOUBLES Fun on the Farm) Freese, Joan. lib. bdg. 24.67 (978-0-8368-9020-4(5), 7c44bc1d-99fd-4070-977b-05265b79cf6c); MIDIENDO para una Búsqueda Del Tesoro (MEASURING on a Treasure Hunt) Marrewa, Jennifer & Marrewa, Jennifer. lib. bdg. 24.67 (978-0-8368-9025-9(6), 9eb6e282-9c60-4a30-9325-82dc3267bbdc); Vamos a DECIR la HORA Todo el Tiempo (TELLING TIME All the Time) Sharp, Jean & Sharp, Jean. lib. bdg. 24.67 (978-0-8368-9019-8(1), 9f3e2b85-8de9-4b5d-9c03-6f88d72e5880); Vamos a HACER GRÁFICAS de Nuestras Cosas Favoritas (GRAPHING Favorite Things) Marrewa, Jennifer & Marrewa, Jennifer. lib. bdg. 24.67 (978-0-8368-9026-6(4), 745298ce-7e7a-471b-b42b-9a12f6c7c8a6); Vamos a Hacer una Maqueta con FIGURAS SÓLIDAS (Making a Model with SOLID FIGURES) Marrewa, Jennifer. lib. bdg. 24.67 (978-0-8368-9023-5(X), 32b42e0e-d27d-436f-982b-25ce673ad623); Vamos a Planear una Fiesta con MATEMÁTICAS (USING MATH to Make Party Plans) Freese, Joan & Freese, Joan. lib. bdg. 24.67 (978-0-8368-9021-1(3), 1fef69da-0867-404f-bca6-a21aa76a8d20); Vamos a USAR DINERO en un Viaje de Compras (USING MONEY on a Shopping Trip) Marrewa, Jennifer & Marrewa, Jennifer. lib. bdg. 24.67 (978-0-8368-9022-8(1), 469afe3a-36ad-4e49-895f-3c97fe96c86a); (Illus.). (gr. 2-2). (Las Matemáticas en Nuestro Mundo - Nivel 2 (Math in Our World - Level 2) Ser.). (SPA.). 24p. 2008. Set lib. bdg. 172.02 (978-0-8368-9018-1(3), 26f9994f-4430-4c43-840b-83bc5d93270d, Weekly Reader Leveled Readers) Stevens, Gareth Publishing LLLP.

El Matematico de Primaria 1. (Matematicos Ser.). (SPA.). (J). 15.50 (978-968-416-840-4(3), 5101) Fernandez USA Publishing.

El Matematico de Primaria 2. (Matematicos Ser.). (SPA.). (J). 15.50 (978-968-416-841-1(1), FN8411) Fernandez USA Publishing.

El Matematico de Primaria 3. (Matematicos Ser.). (SPA.). (J). 15.50 (978-968-416-842-8(X), 5103) Fernandez USA Publishing.

El Matematico de Primaria 4, Level 4. (Matematicos Ser.). (SPA.). (J). 15.50 (978-968-416-843-5(8), 5104) Fernandez USA Publishing.

El Matematico de Primaria 5, Level 5. (SPA.). (J). 15.50 (978-968-416-844-2(6), 5105) Fernandez USA Publishing.

El Matematico Preescolar Avanzado. (Matematicos Ser.). (SPA.). (J). 11.95 (978-970-03-1141-8(4), FN4736) Fernandez USA Publishing.

El Matematico Preescolar Basic. (Matematicos Ser.). (SPA.). (J). 11.95 (978-970-03-1140-1(6), FN4728) Fernandez USA Publishing.

El Matematico Preescolar Inicial. (Matematicos Ser.). (SPA.). (J). 11.95 (978-970-03-1139-5(2), FN471X) Fernandez USA Publishing.

Math. 2011. (ENG., Illus.). 128p. (gr. 4-9). 24.95 (978-0-8160-8052-6(6), P189798, Ferguson Publishing Company) Infobase Holdings, Inc.

Math: Grades 5 & 6. (Illus.). (J). pap., wbk. ed. 4.99 (978-0-88743-847-9(4)) School Zone Publishing Co.

Math: Student Testing Kit. 2004. (gr. 1-8). pap., stu. ed. 5.00 (978-1-58095-815-8(X), MD001); (gr. 7-12). pap., stu. ed. 5.00 (978-1-58095-817-2(6), MD002) Alpha Omega Pubns., Inc. (Lifepac).

Math 1 Reviews. 3rd ed. 2006. pap., act. bk. ed. 14.00 (978-1-59166-322-5(9)) BJU Pr.

Math 1 Student Manipulatives. 3rd ed. 2006. (J). 12.00 (978-1-59166-325-6(3)) BJU Pr.

Math 1 Testpack. 3rd ed. 2006. 10.00 (978-1-59166-326-3(1)) BJU Pr.

Math 4: Version 3. 1, 2 vols. 2003. (gr. 6-12). stu. ed. 40.00 (978-1-885145-48-2(9), M4-489) CPM Educational Program.

Math 5: Version 3. 0, 2 vols. 2003. (gr. 6-12). stu. ed. 50.00 (978-1-931287-28-9(7), M5-287) CPM Educational Program.

Math Activities (Gr. 1) 2003. (J). (978-1-58232-046-5(2)) ECS Learning Systems, Inc.

Math Activities (K) 2003. (J). (978-1-58232-044-1(6)) ECS Learning Systems, Inc.

Math Ad Libs: Addition & Subtraction. 2004. (J). per. 9.95 (978-1-56911-543-5(5)) Learning Resources, Inc.

Math Ad Libs: Fractions & Decimals. 2004. (J). per. 9.95 (978-1-56911-545-9(1)) Learning Resources, Inc.

Math Ad Libs: Multiplication & Division. 2004. (J). per. 9.95 (978-1-56911-544-2(3)) Learning Resources, Inc.

Math Alive!, 12 vols., Set. Incl. Body Math. Dowdy, Penny. lib. bdg. 31.21 (978-0-7614-3215-9(9), 4d2d3d89-5c88-4f87-a837-035d2c8f7ca7); Building Math. Perritano, John. lib. bdg. 31.21 (978-0-7614-3210-4(8), dc6f6038-5386-4a52-b44c-d6c2100cde10); Nature Math. Dowdy, Penny. lib. bdg. 31.21 (978-0-7614-3214-2(0), d8d75ca1-dbbf-4d9c-aae0-7f17b28f7fa0); Science Math. Stosch, Dawn. lib. bdg. 31.21 (978-0-7614-3213-5(2), 1bc024e4-895e-47f2-b8a6-27b25f284992); Transport Math. Evans, Lesli. lib. bdg. 31.21 (978-0-7614-3211-1(6), f815c05c-ff16-4bb7-8c4a-9970b7b8027a); Travel Math. Awal, Pia. (Illus.). (J). lib. bdg. 31.21 (978-0-7614-3217-3(5), d4112795-25d1-4f4b-819b-d56afdd269e8); 32p. (gr. 4-4). (Math Alive! Ser.). (ENG.). 2009. Set lib. bdg. 187.26 (978-0-7614-3208-1(6), 334bf0ce-0c6f-48f0-8e0f-c0f6f32f67ce, Cavendish Square) Cavendish Square Publishing LLC.

Math Around Us. (Math Around Us Ser.). (ENG.). 24p. (J). (gr. 1-1). 2015. 49.32 (978-1-5026-0329-6(2)) 2014. lib. bdg. 155.58 (978-1-5026-0301-2(2), ba4376d3-2ce4-4ddb-b8c7-87ec80d39e05) Cavendish Square Publishing LLC. (Cavendish Square).

Math Art (Gr. 1-2) 2003. (J). (978-1-58232-105-9(1)) ECS Learning Systems, Inc.

Math Art (Gr. 2-3) 2003. (J). (978-1-58232-106-6(X)) ECS Learning Systems, Inc.

Math Beginnings, 6 vols. 2015. (Math Beginnings Ser.: 6). (ENG.). 24p. (J). (gr. -1-3). lib. bdg. 179.58 (978-1-62403-931-7(6), 19289, SandCastle) ABDO Publishing Co.

Math Exploration: Using Math to Learn about the Continents. 2015. (Math Exploration: Using Math to Learn about the Continents Ser.). (ENG.). 32p. (J). (gr. 3-4). pap., pap., pap. 360.00 (978-1-4994-1304-5(1), PowerKids Pr.) Rosen Publishing Group, Inc., The.

Math Exploration: Using Math to Learn about the Continents Set, 12 vols. 2015. (Math Exploration: Using Math to Learn about the Continents Ser.). (ENG.). 32p. (J). (gr. 3-4). lib. bdg. 167.58 (978-1-4994-0706-8(8), 1665faee-44a6-4af5-b3c6-818d9d371b79, PowerKids Pr.) Rosen Publishing Group, Inc., The.

Math Fun with Puppies & Kittens, 12 vols. 2017. (Math Fun with Puppies & Kittens Ser.). (ENG.). (J). (gr. 1-2). lib. bdg. 161.58 (978-0-7660-9156-6(2), 95402269-81eb-42b8-b309-cec1a4d5459a) Enslow Publishing, LLC.

Math Grade Eight. 2004. (ACSI Elementary Mathmatics). tchr. ed., ring bd. (978-1-58331-198-1(X), 7225) Assn. of Christian Schls. International.

Math in Our World, 14 vols., Set. Incl. ADDING & SUBTRACTING in Math Club. Ayers, Amy. lib. bdg. 24.67 (978-0-8368-8470-8(1), 11260360-a12f-47fb-8913-cd7f1aae9bd2); Counting at the Zoo. Ayers, Amy. lib. bdg. 24.67 (978-0-8368-8469-2(8), 36c9139b-11a9-47fe-9b3a-5067032a5db5); Counting in the City. Sharp, Jean. lib. bdg. 24.67 (978-0-8368-8468-5(X), 04ef9b3b-3822-4f74-928b-07f9f555e442); MEASURING at the Dog Show. Ayers, Amy. lib. bdg. 24.67 (978-0-8368-8474-6(4), f6793012-2417-4a3c-8679-212167eb30c4); PATTERNS on Parade. Freese, Joan. lib. bdg. 24.67 (978-0-8368-8473-9(6), 6f51b3eb-24ff-430e-b55f-43ec61f82411); TABLES & GRAPHS of Healthy Things. Freese, Joan. lib. bdg. 24.67 (978-0-8368-8471-5(X), 66e458b0-93b3-4dc1-bd13-1ade8e9e05f7); USING MATH at the Class Party. Ayers, Amy. lib. bdg. 24.67 (978-0-8368-8475-3(2), f8399466-c15f-4e2c-8bee-0b56ae9caf31); USING MONEY at the Lemonade Stand. Ayers, Amy. lib. bdg. 24.67 (978-0-8368-8472-2(8), 6f742241-06fa-4018-8f8b-da23ce255790); (Illus.). (gr. 1-1). (Math in Our World - Level 1 Ser.). (ENG.). 24p. 2007. Set lib. bdg. 172.02 (978-0-8368-8467-8(1), 60cccaba-9a1b-4a6f-ab78-d1106aca9829, Weekly Reader Leveled Readers) Stevens, Gareth Publishing LLLP.

Math in Our World - Level 2, 16 vols., Set. Incl. DOUBLES Fun on the Farm. Freese, Joan. lib. bdg. 24.67 (978-0-8368-9002-0(7), 1c747ad7-1a43-4b94-89a4-fb74e95585da); Graphing Favorite Things. Marrewa, Jennifer. lib. bdg. 24.67 (978-0-8368-9008-2(6), 725540d5-431d-43a3-8df6-c60249c82483); How Far Away? COMPARING Trips. Marrewa, Jennifer. lib. bdg. 24.67 (978-0-8368-9006-8(X), 91a57017-be36-4084-98fb-e55c4a8059ee); Making a Model with SOLID FIGURES. Marrewa, Jennifer. lib. bdg. 24.67 (978-0-8368-9005-1(1), b8144a98-4e78-4067-a199-4a6b88b3c855); MEASURING on a Treasure Hunt. Marrewa, Jennifer. lib. bdg. 24.67 (978-0-8368-9007-5(8), 7b6ad788-1c44-4279-b1dc-90121ac40165); TELLING TIME All the Time. Sharp, Jean & Sharp, Jean. lib. bdg. 24.67 (978-0-8368-9001-3(9), c9609b20-6b2a-4e85-8d9e-f6d30554debc); Using Math to Make Party Plans. Freese, Joan & Freese, Joan. lib. bdg. 24.67 (978-0-8368-9003-7(5), 9f1dcf54-e8c7-49b0-890f-201f48c7a1f5); USING MONEY on a Shopping Trip. Marrewa, Jennifer. lib. bdg. 24.67 (978-0-8368-9004-4(3), d98ca260-9cc2-457e-a0fc-87cf69862017); (Illus.). (gr. 2-2). (Math in Our World - Level 2 Ser.). (ENG.). 24p. 2008. Set lib. bdg. 197.36 (978-0-8368-9000-6(0), 90b5f96e-752c-4e20-ac16-8c3930fcfc07, Weekly Reader Leveled Readers) Stevens, Gareth Publishing LLLP.

Math Is Everywhere, 6 vols. (Sunshinetm Ser.). 16p. (gr. k-18). 29.50 (978-0-7802-5442-8(2)) Wright Group/McGraw-Hill.

Math Is Everywhere! Set 1. 2016. (Math Is Everywhere! Ser.). 24p. (gr. k-k). pap. 48.90 (978-1-4824-5290-7(1)); (ENG.). lib. bdg. 145.62 (978-1-4824-4520-6(4), 74567234-58c0-48b1-b19a-3e876ab3aa6c) Stevens, Gareth Publishing LLLP.

Math Is Everywhere! Set 2, 12 vols. 2016. (Math Is Everywhere! Ser.). (ENG.). 00024p. (J). (gr. k-k). lib. bdg. 145.62 (978-1-4824-5543-4(9), 8eddbc42-6687-4bff-b242-17bfacd561ad) Stevens, Gareth Publishing LLLP.

Math Is Fun. 2004. (Play & Learn Pads Ser.). 48p. (J). 3.99 (978-1-85997-720-0(0)) Byeway Bks.

Math Journal. 2004. (J). pap. 19.95 (978-1-56911-182-6(0)) Learning Resources, Inc.

Math on Target for Grade 3. 2005. (J). stu. ed., per. 10.95 (978-1-59230-064-8(2)) Englefield & Assocs., Inc.

Math on Target for Grade 4: Student Workbook. 2006. (J). per. 10.95 (978-1-59230-161-4(4)) Englefield & Assocs., Inc.

Math on Target for Grade 5: Student Workbook. 2005. (J). stu. ed., per. 10.95 (978-1-59230-111-9(8)) Englefield & Assocs., Inc.

Math Plus Literature, Set. (J). (gr. 2). pap. (978-0-8136-8824-4(8)) Modern Curriculum Pr.

Math Program, Early Level. 2003. (Yellow Umbrella Early Level Ser.). (ENG.). 16p. (gr. k-1). pap. 453.35 (978-0-7368-3064-5(2), Capstone Pr.) Capstone.

Math Puzzle Pad (was Math Games Pad) 2017. (Tear-Off Pads Ser.). (ENG.). (J). pap. 5.99 (978-0-7945-3805-7(3), Usborne) EDC Publishing.

Math Rod Activity Cards - Addition & Subtraction. 2004. (J). 9.95 (978-1-56911-164-2(2)) Learning Resources, Inc.

Math Rod Activity Cards - Kindergarten. 2004. (J). 9.95 (978-1-56911-163-5(4)) Learning Resources, Inc.

Math Rod Activity Cards - Multiplication & Division. 2004. (J). 9.95 (978-1-56911-165-9(0)) Learning Resources, Inc.

Math Shark. 2005. (J). (978-1-60015-034-0(9)) Steps To Literacy, LLC.

Math Spanish Content Area Standard Set. 2005. spiral bd. 2095.00 (978-1-4108-4532-0(X)) Benchmark Education Co.

Math Student Text: Grade 7. 2004. 32.00 (978-0-89084-842-5(4)) BJU Pr.

Math You Will Actually Use. 2017. (Math You Will Actually Use Ser.). 48p. (gr. 10-10). pap. 70.50 (978-1-4777-8989-6(8)); (ENG.). (gr. 5-5). 200.82 (978-1-4777-8987-2(1), 29a09305-d22b-459a-8b8c-ce64a0401d37) Rosen Publishing Group, Inc., The. (Rosen Central).

Mathematics. 2004. (Illus.). (gr. 5). tchr. ed., stu. ed. 47.95 (978-1-58095-725-0(0), MAT0515);Set. (gr. 2). tchr. ed., stu. ed. 47.95 (978-1-58095-716-8(1), MAT0215) Alpha Omega Pubns., Inc. (Lifepac).

Mathematics: Algebra II, 11 vols., Set. 2004. (Illus.). (gr. 11-12). tchr. ed., stu. ed. 52.95 (978-1-58095-743-4(9), MAT1115, Lifepac) Alpha Omega Pubns., Inc.

Mathematics: Trigonometry, 11 vols., Set. 2004. (Illus.). (gr. 12). tchr. ed., stu. ed. 52.95 (978-1-58095-746-5(3), MAT1215, Lifepac) Alpha Omega Pubns., Inc.

Mathematik I. (Duden-Schuelerduden Ser.). (GER., Illus.). 544p. (YA). (978-3-411-04206-7(0)) Bibliographisches Institut & F. A. Brockhaus AG DEU. Dist: International Bk. Import Service, Inc.

Mathematik II. 4th ed. (Duden-Schuelerduden Ser.). (GER.). 480p. (YA). (978-3-411-04274-6(5)) Bibliographisches Institut & F. A. Brockhaus AG DEU. Dist: International Bk. Import Service, Inc.

Maths 3-4. Date not set. (Illus.). 32p. (J). 2.98 (978-0-7525-9560-3(1)) Parragon, Inc.

Maths 4-5. Date not set. (Gold Stars Workbook Ser.). (Illus.). 32p. (J). 2.98 (978-0-7525-9561-0(X)) Parragon, Inc.

Maths 5-6. Date not set. (Gold Stars Workbook Ser.). (Illus.). 32p. (J). 2.98 (978-0-7525-9562-7(8)) Parragon, Inc.

Maths 6-7. Date not set. (Gold Stars Workbook Ser.). (Illus.). 32p. (J). 2.98 (978-0-7525-9563-4(6)) Parragon, Inc.

Matrix Math: Innovative Educational Software for Grades 1 Thru 8+ 2004. (J). cd-rom (978-0-9763833-0-7(6)) Stellar Learning.

Mattern, Joanne. At the Football Game: Learning the Symbols , And =, 1 vol. 2010. (Math for the REAL World Ser.). (ENG.). 16p. (gr. 2-3). pap. 7.05 (978-0-8239-8875-4(9), 75a3d101-e531-4df0-bad7-8190e0af2c8f, Rosen Classroom) Rosen Publishing Group, Inc., The.

Matthews, Jean, et al. Formula One Maths. 2003. (ENG., Illus.). Vol. 1. 96p. pap. 18.50 (978-0-340-85928-5(8)) Vol. 1. 96p. pap. 18.50 (978-0-340-85926-1(1)) Vol. 2. 96p. (J). pap. 18.50 (978-0-340-85929-2(6)) Vol. 2. 88p. pap. 18.50 (978-0-340-85927-8(X)) Vol. 2. 96p. pap. 18.50 (978-0-340-85925-4(3)) Vol. 3. 96p. pap. 18.50 (978-0-340-85930-8(X)) Hodder Education Group GBR. (Hodder Education). Dist: Trans-Atlantic Pubns., Inc.

Mayfield-Ingram, Karen. The Journey Through Middle School Math. Humphrey Williams, Ann, illus. Crews, Elizabeth, photos by. 2005. (Equals Ser.). 140p. pap. 18.95 (978-0-912511-31-3(1), EQUALS) Univ. of California, Berkeley, Lawrence Hall of Science.

McAneney, Caitlin. North American Birds: Represent & Solve Problems Involving Multiplication, 1 vol. 2014. (Rosen Math Readers Ser.). (ENG., Illus.). 24p. (J). (gr. 3-3). pap. 8.25 (978-1-4777-4971-5(3), 20d66ff6-9866-48af-be2e-8884ab8c615a); lib. bdg. 25.27 (978-1-4777-6445-9(3), 6e82c6fd-ade5-4fe9-b5a6-7d09069015ad) Rosen Publishing Group, Inc., The. (PowerKids Pr.).

McDonnell, Rory. Matemáticas con el Tiempo / Math with Weather, 1 vol. de la Vega, Eida, tr. 2016. (¡Matemáticas en Todas Partes! / Math Is Everywhere! Ser.). (ENG & SPA.). 24p. (gr. k-k). lib. bdg. 24.27 (978-1-4824-5212-9(X), 8f9cd20b-92eb-4f25-937d-14a8e1f8e051) Stevens, Gareth Publishing LLLP.

—Matemáticas con Juguetes / Math with Toys, 1 vol. de la Vega, Eida, tr. 2016. (¡Matemáticas en Todas Partes! / Math Is Everywhere! Ser.). (ENG & SPA.). 24p. (gr. k-k). lib. bdg. 24.27 (978-1-4824-5214-3(6), 1109dbd5-1304-4cf2-b0e2-5317273a8a78) Stevens, Gareth Publishing LLLP.

—Matemáticas con Ruedas / Math with Wheels, 1 vol. de la Vega, Eida, tr. 2016. (¡Matemáticas en Todas Partes! / Math Is Everywhere! Ser.). (ENG & SPA.). 24p. (gr. k-k). lib. bdg. 24.27 (978-1-4824-5218-1(9), 7ca60409-5b23-4987-9b1c-f3729bb494cf) Stevens, Gareth Publishing LLLP.

—Word Problems with Wolves, 1 vol. 2017. (Animal Math Ser.). (ENG.). 24p. (J). (gr. 1-2). pap. 9.15 (978-1-5382-0868-7(7), 528811d4-0b4b-40f3-9742-31d35fc5b8ab) Stevens, Gareth Publishing LLLP.

McDougal-Littell Publishing Staff. McDougal Littell Middle School Math: Notetaking Guide. 2003. (McDougal Littell Middle School Math Ser.). (ENG.). 304p. (gr. 7-7). pap. 12.20 (978-0-618-25618-1(0), 2-06021) Great Source Education Group, Inc.

—Middle School Math. 2003. (McDougal Littell Middle School Math Ser.). (ENG.). 304p. (gr. 8-8). pap. 12.20 (978-0-618-25656-3(3), 2-06022) Great Source Education Group, Inc.

—Middle School Math: Practice Workbook. 2003. (McDougal Littell Middle School Math Ser.). (ENG.). 192p. (gr. 8-8). pap. 4.90 (978-0-618-25757-7(8), 2-06027); (gr. 7-7). pap. 4.90 (978-0-618-25755-3(1), 2-06026) Great Source Education Group, Inc.

—Middle School Math, Course 1: Notetaking Guide. 2003. (McDougal Littell Middle School Math Ser.). (ENG.). 320p. (gr. 6-6). pap. 12.20 (978-0-618-25035-6(2), 2-06018) Great Source Education Group, Inc.

—Middle School Math, Course 1: Practice Workbook, PE. 2003. (McDougal Littell Middle School Math, Course 1 Ser.). (ENG.). 192p. (gr. 6-6). pap. 4.90 (978-0-618-25754-6(3), 2-06025) Great Source Education Group, Inc.

—Notetaking Guide: Pre-Algebra. 2004. (McDougal Littell Middle School Math Ser.). (ENG.). 312p. (gr. 7-8). per. 12.20 (978-0-618-25657-0(1), 2-06023) Great Source Education Group, Inc.

—Pre-Algebra. 2004. (McDougal Littell Middle School Math Ser.). (ENG.). 208p. (gr. 7-8). pap., wbk. ed. 4.90 (978-0-618-25752-2(7), 2-06024) Great Source Education Group, Inc.

—Pre-Algebra: Exercises in Spanish. 2004. (McDougal Littell Middle School Math Ser.). (SPA.). 304p. (gr. 7-8). pap. 25.70 (978-0-618-43362-9(7), 2-05834) Great Source Education Group, Inc.

McFadden, Jesse. Franklin's Farm Stand: Understand Place Value, 1 vol. 2014. (Math Masters: Number & Operations in Base Ten Ser.). (ENG., Illus.). 24p. (J). (gr. 2-2). 25.27 (978-1-4777-6428-2(3), 9fd35e8b-3a0e-45a3-8113-9663a7223e9c); pap. 8.25 (978-1-4777-4654-7(4), eff5ea19-9741-440b-ad4d-946e9f9f49b4) Rosen Publishing Group, Inc., The. (Rosen Classroom).

McGrath, Barbara Barbieri. Teddy Bear Math. Nihoff, Tim, illus. 2011. (McGrath Math Ser.: 2). 32p. (J). (gr. k-3). 16.95 (978-1-58089-283-4(3)); pap. 7.95 (978-1-58089-284-1(1)) Charlesbridge Publishing, Inc.

McGraw Hill. Contemporary Mathematics in Context: a Unified Approach, Course 4, Part a, Student Edition Pt. A. 2nd ed. 2003. (Elc: Core Plus Ser.). (ENG., Illus.). 392p. (gr. 11-12). 57.16 (978-0-07-827549-4(0), 0078275490) McGraw-Hill Education.

—Key to Algebra, Book 7: Adding & Subtracting Rational Expressions, Bk. 7. 2012. (Key To... workbooks Ser.: Bk. 7). (ENG., Illus.). 48p. (gr. 6-8). spiral bd. 6.32

(978-1-55953-007-1(3), 1559530073) McGraw-Hill Education.

—Key to Fractions, Book 3: Adding & Subtracting, BK. 3. 2012. (Key To... workbooks Ser.: Bk. 3). (ENG.). 48p. (gr. 6-8). spiral bd., wbk. ed. 6.32 *(978-0-913684-93-1(7)*, 0913684937) McGraw-Hill Education.

—Key to Percents, Book 1: Percent Concepts, Bk. 1. 2012. (Key To... workbooks Ser.: Bk. 1). (ENG.). 48p. (gr. 6-8). spiral bd. 6.32 *(978-0-913684-57-3(0)*, 0913684570) McGraw-Hill Education.

—Key to Percents, Book 2: Percents & Fractions, Bk. 2. 2012. (Key To... workbooks Ser.: Bk. 2). (ENG.). 48p. (gr. 6-8). spiral bd., wbk. ed. 6.32 *(978-0-913684-58-0(9)*, 0913684589) McGraw-Hill Education.

—Key to Percents, Book 3: Percents & Decimals, Bk. 3. 2012. (Key To... workbooks Ser.: Bk. 3). (ENG.). 48p. (gr. 6-8). spiral bd. 6.32 *(978-0-913684-59-7(7)*, 0913684597) McGraw-Hill Education.

—Macmillan/McGraw-Hill Math, Grade 1, Pupil Edition (2 Volume Consumable Set) 2004. (Mmgh Mathematics Ser.). (ENG.). (gr. 1-1). pap., stu. ed. 67.56 *(978-0-02-105012-3(0)*, 0021050120) McGraw-Hill Education.

—Macmillan/McGraw-Hill Math, Grade 2, Pupil Edition (2 Volume Consumable Set) 2004. (Mmgh Mathematics Ser.). (ENG.). (gr. 2-2). pap. 67.56 *(978-0-02-105015-4(5)*, 0021050155) McGraw-Hill Education.

—Macmillan/McGraw-Hill Math, Grades 4-6, Overhead Manipulative Kit. 2003. (Mmgh Mathematics Ser.). (ENG.). (gr. 4-4). 233.40 *(978-0-02-104468-9(6)*, 0021044686) McGraw-Hill Education.

—Math Skills Maintenance Workbook, Course 1. 2003. (Elc: Impact Math Ser.). (ENG.). 104p. (gr. 6-8). spiral bd., wbk. ed. 8.60 *(978-0-07-860721-9(3)*, 0078607213) McGraw-Hill Education.

—Math Skills Maintenance Workbook, Course 2. 2003. (Elc: Impact Math Ser.). (ENG.). 88p. (gr. 6-8). spiral bd., wbk. ed. 8.44 *(978-0-07-860727-1(2)*, 0078607272) McGraw-Hill Education.

—Math Skills Maintenance Workbook, Course 3. 2005. (Elc: Impact Math Ser.). (ENG., Illus.). 88p. (gr. 6-8). spiral bd., wbk. ed. 8.44 *(978-0-07-860733-2(7)*, 0078607337) McGraw-Hill Education.

—Mathematics: Applications & Concepts, Course 1, Practice Skills Workbook. 2003. (MATH APPLIC & CONN CRSE Ser.). (ENG., Illus.). 96p. (gr. 6-8). spiral bd., wbk. ed. 8.60 *(978-0-07-860086-9(3)*, 0078600863) McGraw-Hill Education.

—Mathematics: Applications & Concepts, Course 1, Practice: Word Problems Workbook. 2003. (MATH APPLIC & CONN CRSE Ser.). (ENG., Illus.). 96p. (gr. 6-8). spiral bd. 8.16 *(978-0-07-860087-6(1)*, 0078600871) McGraw-Hill Education.

—Mathematics: Applications & Concepts, Course 1, Spanish Practice Skills Workbook. 2003. (MATH APPLIC & CONN CRSE Ser.). (SPA., Illus.). 96p. (gr. 5-6). spiral bd., wbk. ed. 7.92 *(978-0-07-860092-0(8)*, 0078600928) McGraw-Hill Education.

—Mathematics: Applications & Concepts, Course 1, Student Edition. (MATH APPLIC & CONN CRSE Ser.). (ENG., Illus.). 2004. 736p. (gr. 5-6). stu. ed. 114.44 *(978-0-07-865253-0(7)*, 0078652537) 2003. 720p. (gr. 6-8). lib. bdg., stu. ed. 114.44 *(978-0-07-829631-4(5)*, 0078296315) McGraw-Hill Education.

—Mathematics: Applications & Concepts, Course 1, Study Guide & Intervention Workbook. 2003. (MATH APPLIC & CONN CRSE Ser.). (ENG., Illus.). 96p. (gr. 6-8). spiral bd., wbk. ed. 8.60 *(978-0-07-860085-2(5)*, 0078600855) McGraw-Hill Education.

—Mathematics: Applications & Concepts, Course 2, Noteables: Interactive Study Notebook with Foldables. 2004. (MATH APPLIC & CONN CRSE Ser.). (ENG., Illus.). 304p. (gr. 6-7). per. 37.56 *(978-0-07-868215-5(0)*, 0078682150) McGraw-Hill Education.

—Mathematics: Applications & Concepts, Course 2, Practice Skills Workbook. 2nd ed. 2003. (MATH APPLIC & CONN CRSE Ser.). (ENG., Illus.). 104p. (gr. 6-8). spiral bd., wbk. ed. 8.60 *(978-0-07-860129-3(0)*, 0078601290) McGraw-Hill Education.

—Mathematics: Applications & Concepts, Course 2, Practice: Word Problems Workbook. 2003. (MATH APPLIC & CONN CRSE Ser.). (ENG., Illus.). 104p. (gr. 6-8). spiral bd. 8.16 *(978-0-07-860130-9(4)*, 0078601304) McGraw-Hill Education.

—Mathematics: Applications & Concepts, Course 2, Student Edition. 2006. (MATH APPLIC & CONN CRSE Ser.). (ENG., Illus.). 704p. (gr. 6-8). lib. bdg., stu. ed. 116.32 *(978-0-07-865263-9(4)*, 0078652634) McGraw-Hill Education.

—Mathematics: Applications & Concepts, Course 2, StudentWorks CD-ROM. 2003. (MATH APPLIC & CONN CRSE Ser.). (ENG.). (gr. 6-7). 130.24 *(978-0-07-860279-5(3)*, 0078602793) McGraw-Hill Education.

—Mathematics: Applications & Concepts, Course 3, Practice Skills Workbook. 2003. (MATH APPLIC & CONN CRSE Ser.). (ENG., Illus.). 104p. (gr. 6-8). spiral bd. 8.16 *(978-0-07-860163-7(0)*, 0078601630) McGraw-Hill Education.

—Mathematics: Applications & Concepts, Course 3, Practice: Word Problems Workbook. 2003. (MATH APPLIC & CONN CRSE Ser.). (ENG., Illus.). 104p. (gr. 7-8). spiral bd. 7.92 *(978-0-07-860164-4(9)*, 0078601649) McGraw-Hill Education.

—Mathematics: Applications & Concepts, Course 3, Student Edition. 2004. (MATH APPLIC & CONN CRSE Ser.). (ENG., Illus.). 784p. (gr. 6-8). lib. bdg., stu. ed. 116.32 *(978-0-07-865265-3(0)*, 0078652650) McGraw-Hill Education.

—MathScape: Seeing & Thinking Mathematically, Course 1, Beside the Point, Student Guide. 2004. (Creative Pub: Mathscape Ser.). (ENG., Illus.). 66p. (gr. 6-6). stu. ed., per. 17.40 *(978-0-07-866800-5(X)*, 007866800X) McGraw-Hill Education.

—MathScape: Seeing & Thinking Mathematically, Course 1, Designing Spaces, Student Guide. 2004. (Creative Pub: Mathscape Ser.). (ENG., Illus.). 40p. (gr. 6-6). stu. ed., per. 17.40 *(978-0-07-866798-5(4)*, 0078667984) McGraw-Hill Education.

—MathScape: Seeing & Thinking Mathematically, Course 1, from Whole to Parts, Student Guide. 2004. (Creative Pub: Mathscape Ser.). (ENG., Illus.). 66p. (gr. 6-6). per. 18.84 *(978-0-07-866796-1(8)*, 0078667968) McGraw-Hill Education.

—MathScape: Seeing & Thinking Mathematically, Course 1, Gulliver's Worlds, Student Guide' 2004. (Creative Pub: Mathscape Ser.). (ENG., Illus.). 40p. (gr. 6-6). per. 17.40 *(978-0-07-866802-9(6)*, 0078668026) McGraw-Hill Education.

—MathScape: Seeing & Thinking Mathematically, Course 1, Patterns in Numbers & Shapes, Student Guide. 2004. (Creative Pub: Mathscape Ser.). (ENG., Illus.). 42p. (gr. 6-6). per. 17.40 *(978-0-07-866804-3(2)*, 0078668042) McGraw-Hill Education.

—MathScape: Seeing & Thinking Mathematically, Course 1, the Language of Numbers, Student Guide. 2004. (Creative Pub: Mathscape Ser.). (ENG., Illus.). 38p. (gr. 6-6). per. 18.84 *(978-0-07-866794-7(1)*, 0078667941) McGraw-Hill Education.

—MathScape: Seeing & Thinking Mathematically, Course 1, What Does the Data Say?, Student Guide. 2004. (Creative Pub: Mathscape Ser.). (ENG., Illus.). 47p. (gr. 6-6). stu. ed., per. 17.40 *(978-0-07-866792-3(5)*, 0078667925) McGraw-Hill Education.

—MathScape: Seeing & Thinking Mathematically, Course 2, Buyer Beware, Student Guide. 2004. (Creative Pub: Mathscape Ser.). (ENG., Illus.). 45p. (gr. 7-7). per. 18.84 *(978-0-07-866806-7(9)*, 0078668069) McGraw-Hill Education.

—MathScape: Seeing & Thinking Mathematically, Course 2, Chance Encounters, Student Guide. 2004. (Creative Pub: Mathscape Ser.). (ENG., Illus.). 42p. (gr. 7-7). per., instr.'s gde. ed. 17.40 *(978-0-07-866808-1(5)*, 0078668085) McGraw-Hill Education.

—MathScape: Seeing & Thinking Mathematically, Course 2, from the Ground up, Student Guide. 2004. (Creative Pub: Mathscape Ser.). (ENG., Illus.). 40p. (gr. 7-7). per. 17.40 *(978-0-07-866812-8(3)*, 0078668123) McGraw-Hill Education.

—MathScape: Seeing & Thinking Mathematically, Course 2, Getting down to Business, Student Guide. 2004. (Creative Pub: Mathscape Ser.). (ENG., Illus.). 42p. (gr. 7-7). stu. ed., per. 17.40 *(978-0-07-866816-6(6)*, 0078668166) McGraw-Hill Education.

—MathScape: Seeing & Thinking Mathematically, Course 2, Making Mathematical Arguments, Student Guide. 2004. (Creative Pub: Mathscape Ser.). (ENG., Illus.). 40p. (gr. 7-7). per. 18.84 *(978-0-07-866810-4(7)*, 0078668107) McGraw-Hill Education.

—MathScape: Seeing & Thinking Mathematically, Course 2, the Language of Algebra, Student Guide. 2004. (Creative Pub: Mathscape Ser.). (ENG., Illus.). 40p. (gr. 7-7). stu. ed., per. 18.84 *(978-0-07-866814-2(X)*, 007866814X) McGraw-Hill Education.

—MathScape: Seeing & Thinking Mathematically, Course 3, Consolidated Student Guide Bk. 3. 2nd ed. 2004. (Creative Pub: Mathscape Ser.). (ENG., Illus.). 329p. (gr. 8-8). lib. bdg., stu. ed. 130.56 *(978-0-07-860468-3(0)*, 0078604680) McGraw-Hill Education.

—MathScape: Seeing & Thinking Mathematically, Course 3, Exploring the Unknown, Student Guide. 2004. (Creative Pub: Mathscape Ser.). (ENG., Illus.). 40p. (gr. 8-8). per. 17.40 *(978-0-07-866828-9(X)*, 007866828X) McGraw-Hill Education.

—MathScape: Seeing & Thinking Mathematically, Course 3, Family Portraits, Student Guide. 2004. (Creative Pub: Mathscape Ser.). (ENG., Illus.). 42p. (gr. 8-8). stu. ed., per. 17.40 *(978-0-07-866832-6(8)*, 0078668328) McGraw-Hill Education.

—MathScape: Seeing & Thinking Mathematically, Course 3, Looking Behind the Numbers, Student Guide. 2004. (Creative Pub: Mathscape Ser.). (ENG., Illus.). 45p. (gr. 8-8). per. 17.40 *(978-0-07-866820-3(4)*, 0078668204) McGraw-Hill Education.

—MathScape: Seeing & Thinking Mathematically, Course 3, Roads & Ramps, Student Guide. 2004. (Creative Pub: Mathscape Ser.). (ENG., Illus.). 42p. (gr. 8-8). per. 17.40 *(978-0-07-866830-2(1)*, 0078668301) McGraw-Hill Education.

—MathScape: Seeing & Thinking Mathematically, Course 3, Shapes & Space, Student Guide. 2004. (Creative Pub: Mathscape Ser.). (ENG., Illus.). 40p. (gr. 8-8). per. 17.40 *(978-0-07-866824-1(7)*, 0078668247) McGraw-Hill Education.

—Quick Review Math Handbook: Hot Words, Hot Topics, Book 3, Student Edition, Bk. 3. 2003. (MATH APPLIC & CONN CRSE Ser.). (ENG., Illus.). 512p. (gr. 6-8). stu. ed. 48.64 *(978-0-07-860160-6(6)*, 0078601606) McGraw-Hill Education.

—SAT 10 Test Prep, Pupil Edition. 2003. (Mmgh Mathematics Ser.). (ENG.). 64p. (gr. 2-2). spiral bd. 5.04 *(978-0-02-104077-3(X)*, 002104077X) McGraw-Hill Education.

—Skills Intervention for Pre-Algebra: Diagnosis & Remediation, Spanish Student Workbook. 2004. (Merrill Pre-Algebra Ser.). (SPA., Illus.). 176p. (gr. 6-9). per. 7.80 *(978-0-07-867809-7(9)*, 0078678099) McGraw-Hill Education.

—Skills Intervention for Pre-Algebra: Diagnosis & Remediation, Student Workbook. 2004. (Merrill Pre-Algebra Ser.). (ENG.). 176p. (gr. 8-10). pap., wbk. ed. 8.04 *(978-0-07-867808-0(0)*, 0078678080) McGraw-Hill Education.

—Timed Readings Plus Mathematics Book 1: Book 1, Bk. 1. 2005. (JT: READING RATE & FLUENCY Ser.). (ENG.). 80p. (gr. 6-12). per. 30.32 *(978-0-07-872659-0(X)*, 007872659X) McGraw-Hill Education.

McGraw-Hill - Jamestown Education Staff. Timed Readings Plus in Mathematics: Book 2, Bk. 2. 2005. (Jamestown Education Ser.). 78p. (J). per. 17.32 *(978-0-07-872660-6(3)*, 9780078726606) Glencoe/McGraw-Hill.

—Timed Readings Plus in Mathematics: Book 3, Bk. 3. 2005. (Jamestown Education Ser.). 78p. (J). per. 17.32 *(978-0-07-872661-3(1)*, 9780078726613) Glencoe/McGraw-Hill.

—Timed Readings Plus in Mathematics: Book 4, Bk. 4. 2005. (Jamestown Education Ser.). 78p. (J). per. 17.32 *(978-0-07-872662-0(X)*, 9780078726620) Glencoe/McGraw-Hill.

—Timed Readings Plus in Mathematics: Book 5, Bk. 5. 2005. (Jamestown Education Ser.). 78p. (J). per. 17.32 *(978-0-07-872663-7(8)*, 9780078726637) Glencoe/McGraw-Hill.

McGuinness, Daniel. Cool Careers Without College for People Who Are Really Good at Science & Math, 1 vol. 2nd ed. 2013. (Cool Careers Without College Ser.). (ENG., Illus.). 144p. (J). (gr. 7-7). 41.12 *(978-1-4777-1823-0(0)*, 34cdd741-e47f-4e0b-9394-f85589747e6d) Rosen Publishing Group, Inc., The.

McKell, Theresa Kane. Pre-Algebra. 2003. (Skills for Success Ser.). (ENG.). 128p. (gr. 6-8). pap. 16.99 *(978-0-88724-952-5(3)*, 4323) Carson-Dellosa Publishing, LLC.

McKellar, Danica. Do Not Open This Math Book: Addition + Subtraction. Maberry, Maranda, illus. 2018. (McKellar Math Ser.). 160p. (J). (gr. 1-4). pap. 18.99 *(978-1-101-93398-5(4)*, Crown Books For Young Readers) Random Hse. Children's Bks.

McKinney, Devon. Monuments of Washington, D. C. Use Place Value Understanding & Properties of Operations to Add & Subtract, 1 vol. 2014. (Math Masters: Number & Operations in Base Ten Ser.). (ENG., Illus.). 24p. (J). (gr. 2-2). 25.27 *(978-1-4777-6435-0(6)*, db3b93ea-a158-4534-b2b0-148adfe18673); pap. 8.25 *(978-1-4777-4771-1(0)*, ec01f885-c9d4-4a0b-ad4e-da20a79473d3) Rosen Publishing Group, Inc., The. (Rosen Classroom).

McKinney, Donna Bowen. How STEM Built the Greek Empire, 1 vol. 2019. (How STEM Built Empires Ser.). (ENG.). 80p. (gr. 7-7). pap. 16.30 *(978-1-7253-4143-2(3)*, 4b7c4e01-adb4-4aa2-9f8e-2ada50a64347) Rosen Publishing Group, Inc., The.

McManaman, Yelena & Droujkova, Maria. Moebius Noodles: Adventurous Math for the Playground Crowd. 2013. (Natural Math Ser.: 3). (ENG., Illus.). 88p. pap. 24.00 *(978-0-9776939-5-5(3))* Delta Stream Media.

McNeil, Niki, et al. HOCPP 1115 Multiplication Party. 2006. spiral bd. 21.00 *(978-1-60308-115-3(1))* In the Hands of a Child.

The MEAP Solution: Middle School Edition. 2003. 70p. (YA). (gr. 5-9). 19.95 *(978-0-9718019-1-2(6))* Twianie Roberts Consulting.

Measuring Worms Activity Cards. 2004. (J). 7.95 *(978-1-56911-529-9(X))* Learning Resources, Inc.

Meistrgopïau. 2005. (WEL., Illus.). 123p. pap. *(978-0-86174-782-5(8))* Drake Educational Assocs. Ltd.

Menotti, Andrea. How Many Jelly Beans? A Giant Book of Giant Numbers. Labat, Yancey, illus. 2012. (ENG.). 28p. (J). (gr. -1-1). 18.99 *(978-1-4521-0206-1(6))* Chronicle Bks. LLC.

Mental Math. 2004. (Help with Homework Ser.). 32p. (J). (gr. 1-4). wbk. ed. 3.99 *(978-1-904586-26-5(0))* Byeway Bks.

Meyrick, Caroline & Dwamena, Kwame. Mathematical Studies Standard Level for the IB Diploma Coursebook. 2013. (IB Diploma Ser.). (ENG., Illus.). 772p. pap. 65.20 *(978-1-107-69140-7(0))* Cambridge Univ. Pr.

Michaels, Chris. Animal Babies. 2010. (Sight Word Readers Ser.). (J). 3.49 *(978-1-60719-628-0(X))* Newmark Learning LLC.

—On My Desk. 2010. (Sight Word Readers Ser.). (J). 3.49 *(978-1-60719-625-9(5))* Newmark Learning LLC.

Middle School Math, Course 1: EEdition. 2004. (gr. 6-9). cd-rom *(978-0-618-36400-8(5)*, 2-06524) Holt McDougal.

Middle School Math, Course 1: EEdition Plus Online with print purchase - 1 Year. 2004. (gr. 6-9). *(978-0-618-39416-6(8)*, 2-05569) Holt McDougal.

Middle School Math, Course 1: EEdition Plus Online without print purchase - 6 Years. 2004. (gr. 6-9). *(978-0-618-36956-0(2)*, 2-06527) Holt McDougal.

Middle School Math, Course 1: ETutorial. 2004. (gr. 6-9). cd-rom *(978-0-618-36393-3(9)*, 2-06517); cd-rom *(978-0-618-39810-2(4)*, 2-05640); cd-rom *(978-0-618-39811-9(2)*, 2-05641) Holt McDougal.

Middle School Math, Course 1: ETutorial Plus Online. 2004. (gr. 6-9). *(978-0-618-39410-4(9)*, 2-05563) Holt McDougal.

Middle School Math, Course 1: EWorkbook Plus Online. 2004. (gr. 6-9). *(978-0-618-39413-5(3)*, 2-05566) Holt McDougal.

Middle School Math, Course 1: Exercises in Spanish. 2004. (gr. 6-9). *(978-0-618-37054-2(4)*, 2-06338) Holt McDougal.

Middle School Math, Course 1: Notetaking Guide, TE. 2004. (gr. 6-9). *(978-0-618-33453-7(X)*, 2-06212) Holt McDougal.

Middle School Math, Course 1: Practice Workbook, TE. 2004. (gr. 6-9). *(978-0-618-34360-7(1)*, 2-06229) Holt McDougal.

Middle School Math, Course 1: Pupil's Edition. 2004. (gr. 6-12). *(978-0-618-06730-5(2)*, 2-78042); *(978-0-618-08759-4(1)*, 2-06000) Holt McDougal.

Middle School Math, Course 1: Spanish Study Guide. 2004. (gr. 6-9). *(978-0-618-26962-4(2)*, 2-05798) Holt McDougal.

Middle School Math, Course 1: Test & Practice Generator. 2004. (gr. 6-9). cd-rom *(978-0-618-15838-6(3)*, 2-99755) Holt McDougal.

Middle School Math, Course 1: Worked-Out Solution Key. 2004. (gr. 6-9). *(978-0-618-28026-1(X)*, 2-06102) Holt McDougal.

Middle School Math, Course 2: EEdition. 2004. (gr. 6-12). cd-rom *(978-0-618-36401-5(3)*, 2-06525) Holt McDougal.

Middle School Math, Course 2: EEdition Plus Online with print purchase - 1 Year. 2004. (gr. 6-12). *(978-0-618-39422-7(2)*, 2-05575) Holt McDougal.

Middle School Math, Course 2: EEdition Plus Online without print purchase - 6 Years. 2004. (gr. 6-12). *(978-0-618-36957-7(0)*, 2-06528) Holt McDougal.

Middle School Math, Course 2: ETutorial. 2004. (gr. 6-12). cd-rom *(978-0-618-39812-6(0)*, 2-05642); cd-rom *(978-0-618-39813-3(9)*, 2-05643); cd-rom *(978-0-618-36396-4(3)*, 2-06520) Holt McDougal.

Middle School Math, Course 2: ETutorial Plus Online. 2004. (gr. 6-12). *(978-0-618-39411-1(7)*, 2-05564) Holt McDougal.

Middle School Math, Course 2: EWorkbook Plus Online. 2004. (gr. 6-12). *(978-0-618-39414-2(1)*, 2-05567) Holt McDougal.

Middle School Math, Course 2: Spanish Study Guide. 2004. (gr. 6-12). *(978-0-618-26882-5(0)*, 2-06083) Holt McDougal.

Middle School Math, Course 2: Worked-Out Solution Key. 2004. (gr. 6-12). *(978-0-618-28036-0(7)*, 2-06106) Holt McDougal.

Middle School Math, Course 3: EEdition. 2004. (gr. 6-12). cd-rom *(978-0-618-36402-2(1)*, 2-06526) Holt McDougal.

Middle School Math, Course 3: EEdition Plus Online with print purchase - 1 Year. 2004. (gr. 6-12). *(978-0-618-39428-9(1)*, 2-05581) Holt McDougal.

Middle School Math, Course 3: EEdition Plus Online with print purchase - 6 Years. 2004. (gr. 6-12). *(978-0-618-39433-3(8)*, 2-05586) Holt McDougal.

Middle School Math, Course 3: EEdition Plus Online without print purchase - 6 Years. 2004. (gr. 6-12). *(978-0-618-36958-4(9)*, 2-06529) Holt McDougal.

Middle School Math, Course 3: ETutorial. 2004. (gr. 6-12). cd-rom *(978-0-618-36383-4(1)*, 2-06507); cd-rom *(978-0-618-39814-0(7)*, 2-05644); cd-rom *(978-0-618-39815-7(5)*, 2-05645) Holt McDougal.

Middle School Math, Course 3: ETutorial Plus Online. 2004. (gr. 6-12). *(978-0-618-39412-8(5)*, 2-05565) Holt McDougal.

Middle School Math, Course 3: EWorkbook Plus Online. 2004. (gr. 6-12). *(978-0-618-39415-9(X)*, 2-05568) Holt McDougal.

Middle School Math, Course 3: Worked-Out Solution Key. 2004. (gr. 6-12). *(978-0-618-28040-7(5)*, 2-06110) Holt McDougal.

Mighton, John. Jump at Home: Math Worksheets for the Elementary Curriculum. 2007. (Illus.). pap. *(978-0-88784-722-6(6))*; pap. *(978-0-88784-721-9(8))*; pap. *(978-0-88784-719-6(6))* House of Anansi Pr.

—JUMP at Home — Grade 4: Math Worksheets for the Elementary Curriculum. 2007. (Illus.). pap. *(978-0-88784-720-2(X))* House of Anansi Pr.

Mihaly, Christy. Using Math in Fashion, 1 vol. 2017. (Math You Will Actually Use Ser.). (ENG.). 48p. (J). (gr. 5-5). pap. 12.75 *(978-1-4994-3860-4(5)*, 0d0c6cf7-df5f-48af-80cd-3727fbd0fb76, Rosen Central) Rosen Publishing Group, Inc., The.

Mikoley, Kate. Baseball: Stats, Facts, & Figures, 1 vol. 2017. (Do Math with Sports Stats! Ser.). (ENG.). 32p. (J). (gr. 3-4). pap. 11.50 *(978-1-5382-1125-0(4)*, 587ef37d-2444-4c1e-8e8a-21d4518536c0) Stevens, Gareth Publishing LLLP.

—Basketball: Stats, Facts, & Figures, 1 vol. 2017. (Do Math with Sports Stats! Ser.). (ENG.). 32p. (J). (gr. 3-4). pap. 11.50 *(978-1-5382-1129-8(7)*, 85609528-00f4-46c8-9fb3-d75c8698bfe1); lib. bdg. 28.27 *(978-1-5382-1131-1(9)*, 1bace44b-644e-45a5-99de-da4b0188086d) Stevens, Gareth Publishing LLLP.

—Football: Stats, Facts, & Figures, 1 vol. 2017. (Do Math with Sports Stats! Ser.). (ENG.). 32p. (J). (gr. 3-4). pap. 11.50 *(978-1-5382-1133-5(5)*, 643492e9-150d-4bc6-9774-5cbc16566afb) Stevens, Gareth Publishing LLLP.

—Soccer: Stats, Facts, & Figures, 1 vol. 2017. (Do Math with Sports Stats! Ser.). (ENG.). 32p. (J). (gr. 3-4). pap. 11.50 *(978-1-5382-1145-8(9)*, ea84b6e1-3311-44d5-853f-82e531264a9e); lib. bdg. 28.27 *(978-1-5382-1147-2(5)*, bcf517fa-673b-4d8d-afae-2e86370c1317) Stevens, Gareth Publishing LLLP.

Milanese, Celestine Marie & Peck, Carolyn. Math 8 X-treme Review: Concise Training for NYS Math Intermediate Assessment. Stich, Paul, ed. Garnsey, Wayne, illus. 2007. 160p. per. 13.95 *(978-0-935487-85-5(9)*, X-treme Reviews) N&N Publishing Co., Inc.

Miller, Derek L. Completing Tasks: Using Algorithms, 1 vol. 2017. (Everyday Coding Ser.). (ENG.). 32p. (gr. 3-3). pap. 11.58 *(978-1-5026-2983-8(6)*, f0c2e714-e0cb-410d-b6d5-df1cae9defb1) Cavendish Square Publishing LLC.

Miller, Elizabeth D. Read It! Draw It! Solve It! 2003. (Illus.). 192p. (YA). (gr. 3-18). 20.50 *(978-1-57232-436-7(8)*, 33802) Seymour, Dale Pubns.

—Read It! Draw It! Solve It! Animal Book. 2003. (Illus.). 192p. (J). 34.95 *(978-1-57232-437-4(6))* Seymour, Dale Pubns.

Miller, Nate. Sam's Soccer Game: Work with Addition & Subtraction Equations, 1 vol. 2013. (InfoMax Math Readers Ser.). (ENG.). 24p. (J). (gr. 1-1). pap. 8.25 *(978-1-4777-2189-6(4)*, c658afa3-c4d4-403c-928b-b8202454b708); pap. 49.50 *(978-1-4777-2190-2(8))* Rosen Publishing Group, Inc., The. (Rosen Classroom).

Miller, Reagan & Berry, Minta. Beginner Word Problems. 2011. (ENG., Illus.). 24p. (J). lib. bdg. *(978-0-7787-5274-5(7))* Crabtree Publishing Co.

—Beginner Word Problems, 1 vol. Crabtree Publishing Co. Staff, ed. 2011. (My Path to Math Ser.: No. 33). (ENG., Illus.). 24p. (J). (gr. k-3). pap. *(978-0-7787-5263-9(1))* Crabtree Publishing Co.

—Building Sets of Ten. 2011. (ENG.). 24p. (J). lib. bdg. *(978-0-7787-5277-6(1))* Crabtree Publishing Co.

—Patterning, 1 vol. Crabtree Publishing Staff, ed. 2011. (My Path to Math Ser.: No. 37). (ENG.). 24p. (J). (gr. k-3). pap. *(978-0-7787-5267-7(4))* Crabtree Publishing Co.

—Patterning. 2011. (ENG.). 24p. (J). lib. bdg. *(978-0-7787-5278-3(X))* Crabtree Publishing Co.

Mills, Nathan & Jefferson, Dave. Let's Do Math at the Store, 1 vol. 2012. (Rosen Readers Ser.). (ENG., Illus.). 24p. (J). (gr. 1-1). pap. 8.25 *(978-1-4488-8809-2(3)*, c673e3b0-9458-4cc2-8c15-054b6403e88c, Rosen Classroom) Rosen Publishing Group, Inc., The.

Mills, Steve & Koll, Hilary. Fast Forward Maths. 2003. (ENG., Illus.). pap., tchr. ed. 78.50 *(978-0-340-78201-9(3)*, Hodder Education) Hodder Education Group GBR. Dist: Trans-Atlantic Pubns., Inc.

—Quick Revision KS3 Maths. 2007. (ENG., Illus.). 46p. pap. 9.95 *(978-0-340-94306-9(8)*, Hodder Education) Hodder Education Group GBR. Dist: Trans-Atlantic Pubns., Inc.

Minden, Cecilia. Basketball. 2008. (21st Century Skills Library: Real World Math Ser.). (ENG., Illus.). 32p. (gr. 4-8). lib. bdg. 32.07 *(978-1-60279-245-6(3)*, 200196) Cherry Lake Publishing.

—Exercise by the Numbers. 2007. (21st Century Skills Library: Real World Math Ser.). (ENG., Illus.). 32p. (gr. 4-8). lib. bdg.

32.07 *(978-1-60279-010-0(8)*, 200063) Cherry Lake Publishing.

—Health & Wellness (Set), 8 vols., Set. Incl. Breakfast by the Numbers. (Illus.). lib. bdg. 32.07 *(978-1-60279-011-7(6)*, 200060); Cooking by the Numbers. (Illus.). lib. bdg. 32.07 *(978-1-60279-007-0(8)*, 200061); Dinner by the Numbers. (Illus.). lib. bdg. 32.07 *(978-1-60279-013-1(2)*, 200062); Exercise by the Numbers. (Illus.). lib. bdg. 32.07 *(978-1-60279-010-0(8)*, 200063); Gardening by the Numbers. (Illus.). lib. bdg. 32.07 *(978-1-60279-008-7(6)*, 200064); Grocery Shopping by the Numbers. (Illus.). lib. bdg. 32.07 *(978-1-60279-006-3(X)*, 200065); Lunch by the Numbers. (Illus.). lib. bdg. 32.07 *(978-1-60279-012-4(4)*, 200066); Restaurants by the Numbers. lib. bdg. 32.07 *(978-1-60279-009-4(4)*, 200067); (gr. 4-8). (21st Century Skills Library: Real World Math Ser.). (ENG.). 32p. 2007. 256.56 *(978-1-60279-103-9(1)*, 200059) Cherry Lake Publishing.

—Saving for the Future. 2015. (21st Century Skills Library: Real World Math Ser.). (ENG., Illus.). 32p. (J). (gr. 4-7). 32.07 *(978-1-63362-574-7(5)*, 206480) Cherry Lake Publishing.

—Smart Shopping. 2015. (21st Century Skills Library: Real World Math Ser.). (ENG., Illus.). 32p. (J). (gr. 4-7). 32.07 *(978-1-63362-575-4(3)*, 206484) Cherry Lake Publishing.

—Starting Your Own Business. (21st Century Skills Library: Real World Math Ser.). (ENG., Illus.). 32p. (gr. 4-7). 2015. (J). 32.07 *(978-1-63362-576-1(1)*, 206488) 2009. lib. bdg. 32.07 *(978-1-60279-313-2(1)*, 200209) Cherry Lake Publishing.

Misztal, Maggie. Be Creative with Beads! Use Place Value Understanding & Properties of Operations to Add & Subtract, 1 vol. 2014. (InfoMax Math Readers Ser.). (ENG.). 24p. (J). (gr. 2-2). pap. 8.25 *(978-1-4777-4797-1(4)*, 85d653c4-42c7-41d7-8039-5fbc5a634310, Rosen Classroom) Rosen Publishing Group, Inc., The.

Mitchell, Cindi. Dazzling Math Line Designs: Dozens of Reproducible Activities That Help Build Addition, Subtraction. 2003. (ENG., Illus.). 64p. pap. 9.95 *(978-0-590-00086-4(1))* Scholastic, Inc.

Modern Curriculum Press Mathematics. 2003. Level C. (J). 28.50 *(978-0-8136-3111-0(4))*Level C. pap., tchr. ed. 32.50 net. *(978-0-8136-3118-9(1))*Level D. (J). pap., wbk. ed. 28.50 *(978-0-8136-3112-7(2))*Level D. tchr. ed. 29.50 *(978-0-8136-3119-6(X))*Level A. (J). 28.50 *(978-0-8136-3109-7(2))*Level A. pap., tchr. ed. 32.50 net. *(978-0-8136-3116-5(5))*Level B. (J). 28.50 *(978-0-8136-3110-3(6))*Level B. pap., tchr. ed. 32.50 net. *(978-0-8136-3117-2(3))*Level E. pap., tchr. ed. 32.50 net. *(978-0-8136-3120-2(3))*Level F. tchr. ed. 32.50 net. *(978-0-8136-3121-9(1))*Level K. (J). 28.50 *(978-0-8136-3108-0(4))*Level K. pap., tchr. ed. 32.50 net. *(978-0-8136-3115-8(7))* Modern Curriculum Pr.

Molding Mental Mathemagicians Student Worksheets. 2005. (J). pap., wbk. ed. *(978-0-9766926-1-4(9))* JCTT, LLC.

Money Matters Series. 2005. (J). pap. *(978-1-60015-017-3(9))* Steps To Literacy, LLC.

Montague-Smith, Ann. Dividing, 8 vols. 2005. (QEB Math Club Ser.). (Illus.). 24p. (J). (gr. k-1). lib. bdg. 15.95 *(978-1-59566-115-9(8))* QEB Publishing Inc.

—Numbers. 2004. (QEB Start Math Ser.). (Illus.). 24p. (J). Vol. 1. lib. bdg. 15.95 *(978-1-59566-025-1(9))* Vol. 2. lib. bdg. 15.95 *(978-1-59566-029-9(1))* QEB Publishing Inc.

—Subtracting, 8 vols. 2005. (QEB Math Club Ser.). (Illus.). 24p. (J). (gr. k-1). lib. bdg. 15.95 *(978-1-59566-097-8(6))* QEB Publishing Inc.

—Using Numbers. 2005. (QEB Math Club Ser.). (Illus.). 24p. (J). (gr. k-1). lib. bdg. 15.95 *(978-1-59566-113-5(1))* QEB Publishing Inc.

—Using Numbers Book One, 8 vols. 2005. (QEB Math Club Ser.). (Illus.). 24p. (J). (gr. k-1). lib. bdg. 15.95 *(978-1-59566-095-4(X))* QEB Publishing Inc.

Mooney, Carla. Using Math in Sports, 1 vol. 2017. (Math You Will Actually Use Ser.). (ENG.). 48p. (J). (gr. 5-5). pap. 12.75 *(978-1-4994-3872-7(9)*, 62af4930-13cc-4070-83e1-5e7f0b40c0f6, Rosen Central) Rosen Publishing Group, Inc., The.

Moore, Gareth. Math Games for Clever Kids: More Than 100 Puzzles to Exercise Your Mind. Dickason, Chris, illus. 2018. (ENG.). 192p. (J). (gr. 2-6). pap. 7.99 *(978-1-4380-1238-4(1))* Sourcebooks, Inc.

Moreau, Nancy & Moreau, Wayne. Math A STAReview: Math Grade 9-10 Test Preparation. Stich, Paul, ed. 2003. (ENG., Illus.). 352p. (YA). per. 12.67 *(978-0-935487-78-7(6)*, STAReviews) N&N Publishing Co., Inc.

Morrison, Chloe. Laura's Lemonade Stand: Represent & Interpret Data, 1 vol. 2013. (Rosen Math Readers Ser.). (ENG.). 24p. (J). (gr. 1-1). pap. 8.25 *(978-1-4777-2079-0(0)*, e0dcb2fc-4684-4a03-8999-6db1dfd2d5dd); pap. 49.50 *(978-1-4777-2080-6(4))* Rosen Publishing Group, Inc., The. (Rosen Classroom).

Moseley, Cherri & Rees, Janet. Cambridge Primary Mathematics Stage 1 Learner's Book. 2014. (Cambridge Primary Maths Ser.). (ENG., Illus.). 90p. pap. 24.40 *(978-1-107-63131-1(9))* Cambridge Univ. Pr.

—Cambridge Primary Mathematics Stage 2 Learner's Book. 2014. (Cambridge Primary Maths Ser.). (ENG., Illus.). 78p. pap. 24.40 *(978-1-107-61582-3(8))* Cambridge Univ. Pr.

—Cambridge Primary Mathematics Stage 3 Learner's Book. 2014. (Cambridge Primary Maths Ser.). (ENG., Illus.). 138p. pap. 24.40 *(978-1-107-66767-9(4))* Cambridge Univ. Pr.

Mother Goose Cares about Math & Science: Professional Development Manual. 2004. *(978-0-9753985-2-4(0))* Mother Goose Programs.

Mother Goose Programs, prod. What's the BIG Idea? Shapes & Spaces Librarian Manual. 2008. 70p. pap. *(978-0-9753985-9-3(8))* Mother Goose Programs.

Mottershead, Lorraine. Metamorphosis. 196p. (J). (gr. 7-10). 15.95 *(978-0-86651-466-8(X)*, DS01716) Seymour, Dale Pubns.

Multiplication & Division. 2004. (Help with Homework Ser.). 32p. (J). (gr. 1-4). wbk. ed. 3.99 *(978-1-904586-21-0(X))* Byeway Bks.

Multiplication & Division. 2003. Level C. tchr. ed. 19.50 *(978-0-7652-1316-7(8))*Level C. stu. ed. 14.50 *(978-0-7652-1304-4(4))*Level D. tchr. ed. 19.50 *(978-0-7652-1320-4(6))*Level D. stu. ed. 14.50 *(978-0-7652-1308-2(7))*Level E. tchr. ed. 19.50 *(978-0-7652-1324-2(9))*Level E. stu. ed. 14.50 *(978-0-7652-1312-9(5))* Modern Curriculum Pr.

Multiplication & Division Game Board Book. 2004. (J). bds. 16.95 *(978-1-56911-161-1(8))* Learning Resources, Inc.

Mumford, Jeanette, et al. Pupil Book 3B, Bk. 3B. Evans, Steve et al, illus. 2014. (Busy Ant Maths Ser.). (ENG.). 16p. (gr. 2). pap., stu. ed. 13.99 *(978-0-00-756238-1(1))* HarperCollins Pubs. Ltd. GBR. Dist: Independent Pubs. Group.

—Pupil Book 5A, Bk. 5A. Evans, Steve et al, illus. 2014. (Busy Ant Maths Ser.). (ENG.). 128p. (gr. 4). pap. 14.95 *(978-0-00-756833-8(9))* HarperCollins Pubs. Ltd. GBR. Dist: Independent Pubs. Group.

—Pupil Book 5B, Bk. 5B. Evans, Steve et al, illus. 2014. (Busy Ant Maths Ser.). (ENG.). 128p. (gr. 4). pap. 14.95 *(978-0-00-756834-5(7))* HarperCollins Pubs. Ltd. GBR. Dist: Independent Pubs. Group.

—Pupil Book 6A, Bk. 6A. Evans, Steve et al, illus. 2014. (Busy Ant Maths Ser.). (ENG.). 128p. (gr. 4). pap. 14.95 *(978-0-00-756836-9(3))* HarperCollins Pubs. Ltd. GBR. Dist: Independent Pubs. Group.

—Pupil Book 6C, Bk. 6C. Evans, Steve et al, illus. 2014. (Busy Ant Maths Ser.). (ENG.). 128p. (gr. 4). pap. 14.99 *(978-0-00-756838-3(X))* HarperCollins Pubs. Ltd. GBR. Dist: Independent Pubs. Group.

Murphy, Patricia J. Counting with an Abacus: Learning the Place Values of Ones, Tens, & Hundreds, 1 vol. 2010. (Math for the REAL World Ser.). (ENG.). 16p. (gr. 2-3). pap. 7.05 *(978-0-8239-8880-8(5)*, a2b34c3b-5d91-4de8-83e8-908fd59fed5e, Rosen Classroom) Rosen Publishing Group, Inc., The.

—Learning Addition with Puppies & Kittens. 2017. (Math Fun with Puppies & Kittens Ser.). 32p. (J). (gr. 1-2). 63.12 *(978-0-7660-9069-9(8))* Enslow Publishing, LLC.

—Learning How to Measure with Puppies & Kittens, 1 vol. 2017. (Math Fun with Puppies & Kittens Ser.). (ENG.). 32p. (gr. 1-2). pap. 11.52 *(978-0-7660-9074-3(4)*, c4d1722a-ce4a-4742-a6c3-39983056ddcc) Enslow Publishing, LLC.

—Learning Subtraction with Puppies & Kittens, 1 vol. 2017. (Math Fun with Puppies & Kittens Ser.). (ENG.). 32p. (gr. 1-2). pap. 11.52 *(978-0-7660-9071-2(X)*, d3f20e56-7617-45d5-a3c7-f216a4c5f395) Enslow Publishing, LLC.

Murphy, Stuart J. Double the Ducks. Petrone, Valeria, illus. 2003. (MathStart Ser.). 40p. (J). 15.99 *(978-0-06-028922-5(8))* HarperCollins Pubs.

—Earth Day — Hooray! Andriani, Renée, illus. 2004. (MathStart 3 Ser.). (ENG.). 40p. (J). (gr. 2-18). 17.99 *(978-0-06-000127-8(5)*, HarperCollins) HarperCollins Pubs.

—Earth Day — Hooray! A Springtime Book for Kids, Vol. 50. Andriani, Renée, illus. 2004. (MathStart 3 Ser.). (ENG.). 40p. (J). (gr. 2-18). pap. 6.99 *(978-0-06-000129-2(1)*, HarperCollins) HarperCollins Pubs.

—Mall Mania. Andriani, Renee W., illus. 2006. (MathStart Ser.). (ENG.). 40p. (J). (gr. 1-4). 15.99 *(978-0-06-055776-8(1))* HarperCollins Pubs.

—Same Old Horse. Björkman, Steve, illus. 2005. (MathStart Ser.). 40p. (J). 15.99 *(978-0-06-055770-6(2))* HarperCollins Pubs.

—Same Old Horse. Bjorkman, Steve, illus. 2005. (MathStart 2 Ser.). (ENG.). 40p. (J). (gr. 1). pap. 6.99 *(978-0-06-055771-3(0)*, HarperCollins) HarperCollins Pubs.

Murray, Stuart A. P. Score with Baseball Math, 1 vol. 2013. (Score with Sports Math Ser.). (ENG.). 48p. (gr. 3-3). lib. bdg. 27.93 *(978-0-7660-4174-5(3)*, c9b0304e-a971-40be-8dcb-fa4c8c2718fe, Enslow Elementary) Enslow Publishing, LLC.

—Score with Race Car Math, 1 vol. 2013. (Score with Sports Math Ser.). (ENG.). 48p. (gr. 3-3). lib. bdg. 27.93 *(978-0-7660-4177-6(8)*, ec1277cc-f45f-4500-b07b-e4265b0861fb, Enslow Elementary) Enslow Publishing, LLC.

—Score with Soccer Math, 1 vol. 2013. (Score with Sports Math Ser.). (ENG.). 48p. (gr. 3-3). lib. bdg. 27.93 *(978-0-7660-4175-2(1)*, 2827d9d4-177f-463e-8eb7-0bcb0443bc43, Enslow Elementary) Enslow Publishing, LLC.

—Score with Track & Field Math, 1 vol. 2013. (Score with Sports Math Ser.). (ENG.). 48p. (gr. 3-3). lib. bdg. 27.93 *(978-0-7660-4176-9(X)*, a54f2385-784f-490a-b8da-a7ca623984be, Enslow Elementary) Enslow Publishing, LLC.

Muschla, Gary Robert. Practice Makes Perfect Multiplication & Division. 2012. (Practice Makes Perfect Ser.). (ENG., Illus.). 192p. pap. 20.00 *(978-0-07-177285-3(5)*, 0071772855) McGraw-Hill Education.

National Geographic Kids. By the Numbers 3. 14: 110. 01 Cool Infographics Packed with Stats & Figures. 2017. (Illus.). 256p. (J). (gr. 3-7). (ENG.). 19.90 *(978-1-4263-2866-4(4))*; pap. 9.99 *(978-1-4263-2865-7(6))* Disney Publishing Worldwide. (National Geographic Kids).

National Geographic Learning. Reading Expeditions (Science: Math Behind the Science): Crunching Numbers. 2007. (ENG., Illus.). 24p. (J). pap. 15.95 *(978-0-7922-4592-6(X))* CENGAGE Learning.

—Reading Expeditions (Science: Math Behind the Science): Decoding Data. 2007. (ENG., Illus.). 24p. (J). pap. 15.95 *(978-0-7922-4588-9(1))* CENGAGE Learning.

—Reading Expeditions (Science: Math Behind the Science): How Many Ants in an Anthill? 2007. (ENG., Illus.). 24p. (J). pap. 15.95 *(978-0-7922-4587-2(3))* CENGAGE Learning.

—Reading Expeditions (Science: Math Behind the Science): Number Know-How. 2007. (ENG., Illus.). 24p. (J). pap. 15.95 *(978-0-7922-4591-9(1))* CENGAGE Learning.

—Reading Expeditions (Science: Math Behind the Science): Puzzling Out Patterns. 2007. (Nonfiction Reading & Writing Workshops Ser.). (ENG., Illus.). 24p. (J). pap. 15.95 *(978-0-7922-4594-0(6))* CENGAGE Learning.

—Reading Expeditions (Science: Math Behind the Science): What's the Chance? 2007. (ENG., Illus.). 24p. (J). pap. 15.95 *(978-0-7922-4590-2(3))* CENGAGE Learning.

NCPTA Staff, et al. Better Maths. (ENG., Illus.). 32p. pap. 6.99 *(978-0-340-64668-7(3)*, Coronet) Hodder & Stoughton GBR. Dist: Trafalgar Square Publishing.

—Maths for the Brighter Child. (ENG., Illus.). 24p. pap. 6.99 *(978-0-340-71680-9(0)*, Coronet) Hodder & Stoughton GBR. Dist: Trafalgar Square Publishing.

Neuschwander, Cindy. Sir Cumference & the Fracton Faire. Geehan, Wayne, illus. 2017. (Sir Cumference Ser.). 32p. (J). (gr. 2-5). lib. bdg. 16.99 *(978-1-57091-771-4(X))* Charlesbridge Publishing, Inc.

—Sir Cumference & the Viking's Map. Geehan, Wayne, illus. 2012. (Sir Cumference Ser.). lib. bdg. 18.40 *(978-0-606-26445-7(0))* Turtleback.

New BaseTen Fries. 2004. (J). *(978-1-59242-143-5(1))* Delta Education, LLC.

New York Middle School Mathematics. 2005. (J). (gr. 7-8). pap., stu. ed. 13.95 *(978-0-13-024192-4(X))* Globe Fearon Educational Publishing.

New York Middle School Mathematics: Answer Key. 2005. (J). (gr. 7-8). pap. 1.50 *(978-0-13-023913-6(5))* Globe Fearon Educational Publishing.

Nickson, Marilyn. Teaching & Learning Mathematics: A Teacher's Guide to Recent Research & Its Application. (J). pap. *(978-0-8264-7026-3(2))* Bloomsbury Publishing Plc.

Niederman, Derrick. Mind-Stretching Math Puzzles. 2005. (Illus.). 112p. (J). *(978-1-4156-0492-2(4))* Sterling Publishing Co., Inc.

Noah, Ian & Logan, Stephanie. Mike's Math Club Presents the Monstrously Fun Fraction Book. Noah, Ian et al, eds. Milken-Noah, Joni et al, eds. 2003. (Illus.). 382p. pap. 24.95 *(978-0-9646425-1-5(4))* Milken Family Foundation.

Noble, Jonathan & Owen, Ruth. Pole Position! 2010. (Top Score Maths Ser.). (Illus.). 32p. pap. *(978-0-237-54283-2(8))* Evans Brothers, Ltd.

Nolan, Henry. Sophia Sows Seeds: Work with 11-19 to Gain Foundations for Place Value, 1 vol. 2013. (InfoMax Math Readers Ser.). (ENG.). 16p. (J). (gr. k-k). pap. 7.00 *(978-1-4777-1991-6(1)*, 6d2acc56-a337-41ce-8848-a40702b15eee); pap. 42.00 *(978-1-4777-1992-3(X))* Rosen Publishing Group, Inc., The. (Rosen Classroom).

Nowak, Jennifer. At the Flower Shop: Learning Simple Division by Forming Equal Groups, 1 vol. 2010. (Math for the REAL World Ser.). (ENG.). 16p. (gr. 2-3). pap. 7.05 *(978-0-8239-8930-0(5)*, c49a699a-8a7f-4fe8-ae1d-cc850a59e95a, Rosen Classroom) Rosen Publishing Group, Inc., The.

Numbers for 3-5 Years. Date not set. (Play & Learn Ser.). (Illus.). 192p. (J). 3.98 *(978-0-7525-6912-3(0))* Parragon, Inc.

Numbers for 5-7 Years. Date not set. (Play & Learn Ser.). 192p. (J). 3.98 *(978-0-7525-6913-0(9))* Parragon, Inc.

Numbers on the Farm. (Padded Large Learners Ser.). (Illus.). (J). bds. *(978-0-7525-9889-5(9))* Parragon, Inc.

Nunn, Daniel & Rissman, Rebecca. Patterns Outside, 1 vol. 2012. (Math Every Day Ser.). (ENG.). 24p. (gr. -1-k). pap. 9.95 *(978-1-4329-5736-0(8)*, 117385, Raintree) Capstone.

Objects in the Sky, 12 vols., Set. Incl. Exploring Comets. Way, Jennifer. lib. bdg. 26.27 *(978-1-4042-3469-7(1)*, ffbeff81-f650-4e68-b14a-1fc7e391ef90, PowerKids Pr.); Exploring Earth. Olien, Rebecca. lib. bdg. 26.27 *(978-1-4042-3465-9(9)*, 52a1b5a5-51c2-479a-b460-4096dcb62c56); Exploring Meteors. Olien, Rebecca. lib. bdg. 26.27 *(978-1-4042-3468-0(3)*, 8e585b55-a39f-4814-93fa-3ccf4f62d96d, PowerKids Pr.); Exploring the Moon. Olien, Rebecca. lib. bdg. 26.27 *(978-1-4042-3466-6(7)*, 003b77c6-da98-40f1-897b-ea98f1c4d440, PowerKids Pr.); Exploring the Planets in Our Solar System. Olien, Rebecca. lib. bdg. 26.27 *(978-1-4042-3467-3(5)*, a3e1acfe-1a80-4987-9269-aac56a1fa428, PowerKids Pr.); Exploring the Sun. Olien, Rebecca. lib. bdg. 26.27 *(978-1-4042-3464-2(0)*, b8eed2ba-a2e8-4d34-9503-ec495cb7fd65, PowerKids Pr.); (Illus.). 24p. (J). (gr. 3-3). 2007. (Objects in the Sky Ser.). (ENG.). 2006. Set lib. bdg. 157.62 *(978-1-4042-3502-1(7)*, 12b56598-5968-41e9-855a-4aceb10261a5, PowerKids Pr.) Rosen Publishing Group, Inc., The.

O'Brien, Thomas C. Off the Path Math with Tobbs, Vol. 1. Reynolds, Peter H., illus. 2003. 59p. (J). 14.50 *(978-1-891405-09-9(8))* FableVision Pr.

O'Connell, Susan, et al. Introduction to Reasoning & Proof, Grades 3-5. 2007. (ENG., Illus.). 160p. (C). (gr. 3-5). pap. 41.25 *(978-0-325-01033-5(1)*, E01033) Heinemann.

O'Dell, Angela & Carlson, Kyrsten. Math Lessons for a Living Education Level 2. 2016. (ENG.). 352p. (gr. 1-2). pap. 44.99 *(978-0-89051-924-0(2)*, Master Books) New Leaf Publishing Group.

—Math Lessons for a Living Education Level 3. 2016. (ENG.). 416p. (gr. 3). pap. 44.99 *(978-0-89051-925-7(0)*, Master Books) New Leaf Publishing Group.

—Math Lessons for a Living Education Level 4. 2016. (ENG.). 390p. (gr. 4-5). pap. 44.99 *(978-0-89051-926-4(9)*, Master Books) New Leaf Publishing Group.

—Math Lessons for a Living Education Level 5. 2016. (ENG.). 341p. (gr. 5-6). pap. 44.99 *(978-0-89051-927-1(7)*, Master Books) New Leaf Publishing Group.

O'Donnell, Kerri. The Ancient Civilizations of Greece & Rome: Solving Algebraic Equations, 1 vol. (Math for the REAL World Ser.). (ENG.). 32p. (gr. 5-6). 2009. pap. 10.00 *(978-1-4042-5123-6(5)*, 422d996d-f892-4fe2-8f28-4325fe133661, PowerKids Pr.) 2004. (Illus.). (YA). lib. bdg. 28.93 *(978-1-4042-2930-3(2)*, de64bbba-2c61-41b4-9283-e9d38fbd06c4) Rosen Publishing Group, Inc., The.

—The Ancient Civilizations of Greece & Rome: Solving Algebraic Equations Big Book. 2005. (Math for the REAL World Ser.). (J). pap. 39.95 *(978-1-4042-5292-9(4)*, Rosen Classroom) Rosen Publishing Group, Inc., The.

—The Ancient Civilizations of Greece & Rome: Solving Algebraic Equations (Big Book) 2005. (Math for the REAL World Ser.). 32p. 47.50 *(978-1-4042-5222-6(3)*, Rosen Classroom) Rosen Publishing Group, Inc., The.

—The California Gold Rush: Multiplying & Dividing Using Three- & Four-Digit Numbers. (PowerMath: Proficiency Plus Ser.). 32p. 2009. (gr. 4-5). 47.90 *(978-1-60851-419-9(6)*, PowerKids Pr.) 2005. 47.50 *(978-1-4042-5221-9(5)*, Rosen Classroom) Rosen Publishing Group, Inc., The.

Olliges, Rob. Que Viene Primero/What Comes First. Mallick, David, tr. 2006. (My First Math Discovery Ser.). (SPA., Illus.). 24p. (J). (gr. -1-3). lib. bdg. 22.79 *(978-1-60044-288-9(9))* Rourke Educational Media.

Olsen, Alana. What Do You Know about Bugs? Understand Place Value, 1 vol. 2014. (Math Masters: Number & Operations in Base Ten Ser.). (ENG., Illus.). 24p. (J). (gr. 2-2). 25.27 *(978-1-4777-6431-2(3)*, 9aa9756c-3c0b-4752-99f5-5ed8b9a8c4ad); pap. 8.25 *(978-1-4777-4663-9(3)*, 2575108a-26dd-4622-b440-3a41fb647ddd) Rosen Publishing Group, Inc., The. (Rosen Classroom).

Open Court Staff. Real Math: Level 8. (J). stu. ed. *(978-0-8126-0638-6(8)*, 60638) Open Court Publishing Co.

Opie, Brenda & McAvinn, Douglas. Masterminds Riddlemath for Elementary: Measurement, Fractions, Probability, & Logical Thinking. 2004. (Illus.). 96p. (J). per. 11.95 *(978-0-86530-611-0(7))* Incentive Pubns., Inc.

Orr, Deborah Murphy. SBAC Grade 8 Math: Smarter Balanced. 2018. (Barron's Test Prep Ser.). (ENG.). 384p. (gr. 8-8). pap. 14.99 *(978-1-4380-1090-8(7)*, Barron's Educational Series, Inc.) Kaplan Publishing.

Orr, Tamra B. Tornadoes. 2012. (21st Century Skills Library: Real World Math Ser.). (ENG., Illus.). 32p. (gr. 4-8). (J). pap. 14.21 *(978-1-61080-413-4(9)*, 201345); lib. bdg. 32.07 *(978-1-61080-326-7(4)*, 201312) Cherry Lake Publishing.

—Tsunamis. 2012. (21st Century Skills Library: Real World Math Ser.). (ENG.). 32p. (gr. 4-8). (J). pap. 14.21 *(978-1-61080-410-3(4)*, 201342); (Illus.). lib. bdg. 32.07 *(978-1-61080-327-4(2)*, 201306) Cherry Lake Publishing.

—Wildfires. 2012. (21st Century Skills Library: Real World Math Ser.). (ENG., Illus.). 32p. (gr. 4-8). (J). pap. 14.21 *(978-1-61080-412-7(0)*, 201344); lib. bdg. 32.07 *(978-1-61080-329-8(9)*, 201310) Cherry Lake Publishing.

Oswald, Nina. Saving Endangered Animals: Develop Understanding of Fractions & Numbers, 1 vol. 2014. (InfoMax Math Readers Ser.). (ENG.). 24p. (J). (gr. 3-3). pap. 8.25 *(978-1-4777-4612-7(9)*, 7f828917-00dc-4f62-b89f-f417894d1fa2, Rosen Classroom) Rosen Publishing Group, Inc., The.

Overdeck, Laura. Bedtime Math: This Time It's Personal: This Time It's Personal. Paillot, Jim, illus. 2014. (Bedtime Math Ser.). (ENG.). 96p. (J). (gr. -1-2). 17.99 *(978-1-250-04096-1(5)*, 900125483) Feiwel & Friends.

—How Many Guinea Pigs Can Fit on a Plane? Answers to Your Most Clever Math Questions. 2017. (ENG., Illus.). 144p. (J). pap. 12.99 *(978-1-250-12368-8(2)*, 900174278) Feiwel & Friends.

Pallotta, Jerry. Multiplication. Bolster, Rob, illus. 2008. 32p. (J). *(978-0-545-00686-6(4))* Scholastic, Inc.

Palmer, Stuart, et al. Cambridge Mathematics NSW Syllabus for the Australian Curriculum, Year 8. 2014. (ENG.). pap. *(978-1-107-67181-2(7))* Cambridge Univ. Pr.

—Cambridge Maths NSW Syllabus for the Australian Curriculum, Year 10. 2014. (ENG.). pap., E-Book *(978-1-107-66567-5(1))* Cambridge Univ. Pr.

Pappas, Theoni. Do the Math! Math Challenges to Exercise Your Mind. 2015. (ENG., Illus.). 224p. (gr. 5). pap. 12.95 *(978-1-884550-74-4(6))* Wide World Publishing/Tetra.

—Further Adventures of Penrose the Mathematical Cat. 2004. (ENG., Illus.). 128p. (J). pap. 12.95 *(978-1-884550-32-4(0))* Wide World Publishing/Tetra.

—More Math Adventures with Penrose the Mathematical Cat. 2017. (ENG., Illus.). 128p. (gr. 1). pap. 12.95 *(978-1-884550-76-8(2))* Wide World Publishing/Tetra.

Pardoe, Mary. Formula One Interactive Oral & Mental Starters. unabr. ed. 2005. (ENG., Illus.). cd-rom *(978-0-340-91333-8(9))* Hodder & Stoughton.

Parham, Donna. Splash of Math K-3: K-3. 2003. (Illus.). 28p. (J). (gr. k-3). tchr. ed. 5.99 *(978-1-893698-35-2(1)*, T13, SeaWorld Education Dept.) SeaWorld, Inc.

Partil, Sravan. Measuring Quilts: Understand Concepts of Area, 1 vol. 2014. (InfoMax Math Readers Ser.). (ENG.). 24p. (J). (gr. 3-3). pap. 8.25 *(978-1-4777-4591-5(2)*, a387a421-ebf0-4fca-b83b-b17bf45e67c4, Rosen Classroom) Rosen Publishing Group, Inc., The.

Payne, Ruby K. Mental Models for Math: Grades 6-12. 2006. (YA). per. 13.00 *(978-1-929229-53-6(4))* aha! Process, Inc.

Penn, M. W. Pebble Math. 2012. (Pebble Math Ser.). (ENG.). 24p. (gr. k-1). pap. 214.20 *(978-1-4296-8311-1(2)*, Pebble) Capstone.

People Together: E-Journals. (Technology: Social Studies). (SPA.). (gr. 2-18). *(978-0-02-147229-1(7))* Macmillan/McGraw-Hill Schl. Div.

Peppas, Lynn & Challen, Paul. Addition. 2009. (ENG.). 24p. (J). lib. bdg. *(978-0-7787-4345-3(4))* Crabtree Publishing Co.

Perritano, John. Building Math, 1 vol. 2009. (Math Alive! Ser.). (ENG.). 32p. (gr. 4-4). lib. bdg. 31.21 *(978-0-7614-3210-4(8)*, dc6f6038-5386-4a52-b44c-d6c2100cde10) Cavendish Square Publishing LLC.

Petersen, Jamee. Math & Nonfiction, Grades K-2. 2004. (ENG., Illus.). 144p. (gr. k-2). pap. 29.95 *(978-0-941355-61-2(6))* Math Solutions.

Pezzimenti, Grace. The Pizza Party: Learning Basic Problem-Solving Skills. 2004. (Math Big Bookstm Ser.). (ENG.). 12p. (gr. 1-2). 33.50 *(978-0-8239-7636-2(X))* Rosen Publishing Group, Inc., The.

Pfister, Marcus. The Rainbow Fish Counting. 2013. (Rainbow Fish Ser.). (ENG., Illus.). 12p. (J). (gr. -1-k). bds. 7.95 *(978-0-7358-4148-2(9))* North-South Bks., Inc.

Phillips, Vivian A. Intrique Math. Date not set. (Illus.). 16p. (Orig.). (YA). pap. *(978-1-888413-04-5(2))* Seasoning Quilting (Arts & Crafts).

Piddock, Claire. Line, Bar, & Circle Graphs. 2010. (ENG., Illus.). 24p. (J). *(978-0-7787-5247-9(X))*; pap. *(978-0-7787-5294-3(1))* Crabtree Publishing Co.

—Slides, Flips, & Turns. 2010. (ENG., Illus.). 24p. (J). *(978-0-7787-5251-6(8))*; pap. *(978-0-7787-5298-1(4))* Crabtree Publishing Co.

Pistoia, Sara. Graphs. 2016. (J). *(978-1-4896-5107-5(1))* Weigl Pubs., Inc.

—Measurements. 2016. (J). *(978-1-4896-5110-5(1))* Weigl Pubs., Inc.

—Patterns. 2016. (J). *(978-1-4896-5116-7(0))* Weigl Pubs., Inc.

Place Value Skills (Gr. 1-2) 2003. (J). *(978-1-58232-088-5(8))* ECS Learning Systems, Inc.

Place Value Skills Spanish Version. 2007. (J). per. *(978-1-58232-157-8(4))* ECS Learning Systems, Inc.

Polette, Nancy & Ebbesmeyer, Joan. Math in Fables & Myths: Solving Word Problems with Readers' Theatre. 2004. (J). pap. 14.95 *(978-1-931334-58-7(7))* Pieces of Learning.

Pomerleau, Annie. At the Arcade: Understand Place Value. 2014. (Rosen Math Readers Ser.). (ENG.). 24p. (J). (gr. 2-3). pap. 49.50 *(978-1-4777-4661-5(7))*; (illus.). 25.27 *(978-1-4777-6430-5(5),* ba21570a-b69d-4f60-8d49-f09f1aa01d52) Rosen Publishing Group, Inc., The. (Rosen Classroom).

Ponka, Katherine. Math on the Sun, 1 vol. 2016. (Solve It! Math in Space Ser.). (ENG., Illus.). 24p. (J). (gr. 2-3). 24.27 *(978-1-4824-4936-5(6),* 9edb76bc-2ee6-414b-a9cb-643c637177ba) Stevens, Gareth Publishing LLLP.

Power Math: Sets 7,8, And 9, 24 vols. 2004. (PowerMath: Proficiency Plus Ser.). (ENG., Illus.). (J). (gr. 4-5). 347.16 *(978-1-4042-2967-9(1),* 2505f44d-5968-4746-a708-3daa337dc8b0) Rosen Publishing Group, Inc., The.

PowerMath: Beginning Set 10, 12 vols. 2005. (PowerMath: Beginning Ser.). (ENG.). (J). (gr. 2-2). 133.62 *(978-1-4042-3383-6(0),* a22d75a5-4d68-4878-b94f-2abb86269382) Rosen Publishing Group, Inc., The.

PowerMath: Set 7, 8 vols. 2004. (PowerMath: Proficiency Plus Ser.). (ENG., Illus.). (J). (gr. 4-5). 115.72 *(978-1-4042-2974-7(4),* 73177b36-b378-47cc-96e9-5ad945114605) Rosen Publishing Group, Inc., The.

PowerMath: Proficiency Plus: Set 1, 8 vols. 2004. (PowerMath: Proficiency Plus Ser.). (ENG., Illus.). (J). (gr. 4-5). 115.72 *(978-1-4042-2976-1(0),* be56a2e5-4f6a-4105-9916-4bd0d9aa9dd4) Rosen Publishing Group, Inc., The.

PowerMath: Proficiency Plus: Set 2, 8 vols. 2004. (PowerMath: Proficiency Plus Ser.). (ENG., Illus.). (J). (gr. 4-5). 115.72 *(978-1-4042-2975-4(2),* dde1ecbf-2a07-4b89-98bf-351aa4b8eada) Rosen Publishing Group, Inc., The.

Practice Power School Bus Book: First Grade Mathematics. 2003. (Illus.). 24p. (J). (gr. k-1). spiral bd. *(978-1-930355-44-6(0))* Bright of America.

Pre-Algebra: EEdition. 2005. (gr. 6-12). cd-rom *(978-0-618-43339-1(2),* 2-05812) Holt McDougal.

Pre-Algebra: ETutorial. 2005. (gr. 6-12). cd-rom *(978-0-618-43355-1(4),* 2-05828); cd-rom *(978-0-618-43356-8(2),* 2-05829); cd-rom *(978-0-618-43351-3(1),* 2-05824) Holt McDougal.

Pre-Algebra: ETutorial Plus Online. 2005. (gr. 6-12). *(978-0-618-43357-5(0),* 2-05830) Holt McDougal.

Pre-Algebra: EWorkbook Plus Online. 2005. (gr. 6-12). *(978-0-618-43358-2(9),* 2-05831) Holt McDougal.

Pre-Algebra: Pupil's Edition. 2005. (McDougal Littell Math Ser.). (gr. 6-12). *(978-0-618-25003-5(4),* 2-06006) Holt McDougal.

Pre-Algebra: Worked-Out Solution Key. 2005. (gr. 6-12). *(978-0-618-28044-5(8),* 2-06114) Holt McDougal.

PRESS, Celebration. Fractals: The Art of Math. 2003. (ENG.). (J). (gr. 6-8). pap. 37.95 *(978-0-7652-3250-2(2),* Celebration Pr.) Savvas Learning Co.

Primary Mathematics Intensive Practice U. S. Edition 1A. 2004. per. 8.50 *(978-1-932906-00-4(2))* SingaporeMath.com, Inc.

Primary Mathematics Intensive Practice U. S. Edition 1B. 2004. per. 8.50 *(978-1-932906-01-1(0))* SingaporeMath.com, Inc.

Primary Mathematics Intensive Practice U. S. Edition 2A. 2004. per. 8.50 *(978-1-932906-02-8(9))* SingaporeMath.com, Inc.

Primary Mathematics Intensive Practice U. S. Edition 2B. 2004. per. 8.50 *(978-1-932906-03-5(7))* SingaporeMath.com, Inc.

Primary Mathematics Intensive Practice U. S. Edition 3A. 2004. per. 8.50 *(978-1-932906-04-2(5))* SingaporeMath.com, Inc.

Primary Mathematics Intensive Practice U. S. Edition 3B. 2004. per. 8.50 *(978-1-932906-05-9(3))* SingaporeMath.com, Inc.

Primary Mathematics Intensive Practice U. S. Edition 4A. 2004. per. 8.50 *(978-1-932906-06-6(1))* SingaporeMath.com, Inc.

Primary Mathematics Intensive Practice U. S. Edition 4B. 2004. per. 8.50 *(978-1-932906-07-3(X))* SingaporeMath.com, Inc.

Primary Mathematics Intensive Practice U. S. Edition 5A. 2004. per. 8.50 *(978-1-932906-08-0(8))* SingaporeMath.com, Inc.

Primary Mathematics Intensive Practice U. S. Edition 5B. 2004. per. 8.50 *(978-1-932906-09-7(6))* SingaporeMath.com, Inc.

Primary Mathematics Intensive Practice U. S. Edition 6A. 2004. per. 8.50 *(978-1-932906-10-3(X))* SingaporeMath.com, Inc.

Primary Mathematics Intensive Practice U. S. Edition 6B. 2004. per. 8.50 *(978-1-932906-11-0(8))* SingaporeMath.com, Inc.

Primary Mathematics Teacher's Guide 3B. 2004. spiral bd. 21.00 *(978-0-9741573-5-1(X))* SingaporeMath.com, Inc.

Primmer, Rachel. Pentomino Piazza, Vol. 1. 2006. (J). 24.99 *(978-0-9787021-0-6(7),* P001) Knowtivate, LLC.

Problem Solving. 2003. Level C. tchr. ed. 19.50 *(978-0-7652-1314-3(1))*Level C. stu. ed. 14.50 *(978-0-7652-1112-5(2))*Level D. tchr. ed. 19.50 *(978-0-7652-1318-1(4))*Level D. stu. ed. 14.50 *(978-0-7652-1306-8(0))*Level E. tchr. ed. 19.50 *(978-0-7652-1322-8(2))* Modern Curriculum Pr.

PUBLICATIONS, Dale Seymour. MCP Mathematics: Level A. 2004. (ENG.). (J). (gr. 1-1). pap., stu. ed. 25.00 net. *(978-0-7652-6056-7(5))* Seymour, Dale Pubns.

—MCP Mathematics: Level B. 2004. (ENG.). (J). (gr. 2-3). pap., stu. ed. 25.00 net. *(978-0-7652-6058-1(1))* Seymour, Dale Pubns.

—MCP Mathematics: Level C. 2004. (ENG.). (J). (gr. 3-3). pap., stu. ed. 25.00 net. *(978-0-7652-6060-4(3))* Seymour, Dale Pubns.

—MCP Mathematics: Level F. 2004. (ENG.). (J). (gr. 6-6). pap., stu. ed. 25.00 net. *(978-0-7652-6066-6(2))* Seymour, Dale Pubns.

—MCP Mathematics: Level K. 2004. (ENG.). (J). (gr. k-k). pap., stu. ed. 28.50 *(978-0-7652-6054-3(9),* Dale Seymour Publications) Savvas Learning Co.

Publications International Ltd. Staff, ed. Preschool Reading & Math Activities. 2010. 128p. 11.98 *(978-1-60553-180-9(4))* Publications International, Ltd.

QEB Maths Club National Book Stores Edition: Using Numbers Book 1. 2006. (J). per. *(978-1-59566-286-6(3))* QEB Publishing Inc.

QEB Maths Club National Book Stores Edition: Using Numbers Book 2. 2006. (J). per. *(978-1-59566-290-3(1))* QEB Publishing Inc.

Quadratische Gleichungen und Ungleichungen. (Duden-Schuelerhilfen Ser.). (GER.). 112p. (YA). (gr. 9). *(978-3-411-70102-5(1))* Bibliographisches Institut & F. A. Brockhaus AG DEU. Dist: International Bk. Import Service, Inc.

A Question of Math. 2004. (Illus.). lib. bdg. 5.95 *(978-0-8225-4440-1(7))* Lerner Publishing Group.

Rapoport, Rebecca & Yoder, J. A. Math Games Lab for Kids: 24 Fun, Hands-On Activities for Learning with Shapes, Puzzles, & Games, Volume 10. 2017. (Lab for Kids Ser.: 10). (ENG., Illus.). 144p. (J). (gr. 2-5). pap. 24.99 *(978-1-63159-252-2(1),* 220380, Quarry Bks.) Quarto Publishing Group USA.

Rauen, Amy. Getting Started with Math, 8 vols., Set. Incl. Adding & Subtracting at the Lake. lib. bdg. 21.67 *(978-0-8368-8983-3(5),* 78a46f6d-7777-4d2f-b30d-555e177ca563); Counting at the Market. lib. bdg. 21.67 *(978-0-8368-8981-9(9),* ac3553e2-1c64-4aad-800d-8e2e3acd6dc8); Finding Shortest & Longest. lib. bdg. 21.67 *(978-0-8368-8982-6(7),* 37efd4d4-1e51-4948-a434-311153a89b86); Using Math Outdoors. lib. bdg. 21.67 *(978-0-8368-8984-0(3),* 230af042-d210-4cf1-bf77-70a868d0b946); (Illus.). (gr. k-1). (Getting Started with Math Ser.). (ENG.). 16p. 2008. Set lib. bdg. 86.01 *(978-0-8368-8980-2(0),* 22dc6c91-4c07-4fba-9507-ddfa97a56d14, Weekly Reader Leveled Readers) Stevens, Gareth Publishing LLLP.

—Matemáticas para Empezar, 8 vols., Set. Incl. Vamos a Contar en el Mercado (Counting at the Market) lib. bdg. 21.67 *(978-0-8368-8991-8(6),* 3ccaec65-3d92-4258-b9cf-ec28b619d2ad); Vamos a Encontrar lo Más Corto y lo Más Largo (Finding Shortest & Longest) lib. bdg. 21.67 *(978-0-8368-8992-5(4),* 8576efdd-56dd-41f9-b23c-60a1bfa2b984); Vamos a Sumar y Restar en el Lago (Adding & Subtracting at the Lake) lib. bdg. 21.67 *(978-0-8368-8993-2(2),* c31700ed-be2d-4999-9255-06f850141487); Vamos a Usar Las Matemáticas Al Aire Libre (Using Math Outdoors) lib. bdg. 21.67 *(978-0-8368-8994-9(0),* 5eff4b9d-4c0a-4fbd-ace6-da043d90eac5); (gr. k-1). (Matemáticas para Empezar (Getting Started with Math) Ser.) (SPA., Illus.). 16p. 2008. Set lib. bdg. 86.01 *(978-0-8368-8990-1(8),* 7e410a25-9f57-40b2-898e-f46d874aa00f, Weekly Reader Leveled Readers) Stevens, Gareth Publishing LLLP.

Rawlins, Jeanne & Rainbow Bridge Publishing Staff. Math Comprehension Grade 6. 2004. (Skill Builders Ser.). 80p. (gr. 6-18). pap. 3.99 *(978-1-932210-05-7(9))* Rainbow Bridge Publishing.

Reagan, Naomi. Butterflies & Moths: Represent & Interpret Data, 1 vol. 2014. (Rosen Math Readers Ser.). (ENG., Illus.). 24p. (J). (gr. 3-3). pap. 8.25 *(978-1-4777-4901-2(2),* 54c99c90-81a3-471c-b797-cc45572303ae, Rosen Classroom) Rosen Publishing Group, Inc., The.

Recreational Mathematics, 3 vols. 2004. (Illus.). 497p. spiral bd. 45.75 *(978-1-931084-23-9(8))* Balloon Magic.

Reed, Janet. Parts of a Whole, 6 vols., Set. 2003. (Yellow Umbrella Early Level Ser.). (ENG.). 16p. (gr. k-1). pap. 35.70 *(978-0-7368-3012-6(X),* Capstone Pr.) Capstone.

Region 4 Education Service Center. Integrating Grade 11 TAKS Geometry Objectives into Algebra II Teacher Edition. 2004. (Region IV ESC Resources for Mathematics Ser.). pap. *(978-1-932797-70-1(X))* Region 4 Education Service Ctr.

—Making Connection with Measurement, TAKS Preparation Grade 6 - Student Workbook - Spanish. 2004. (Region IV ESC Resources for Mathematics Ser.). pap. *(978-1-932797-67-1(X))* Region 4 Education Service Ctr.

—Making Connections with Measurement, TAKS Preparation Grade 3 TAKS - Student Workbook - Spanish. 2004. (Region IV ESC Resources for Mathematics Ser.). pap. *(978-1-932797-64-0(5))* Region 4 Education Service Ctr.

—Making Connections with Measurement, TAKS Preparation Grade 4 TAKS - Student Workbook - Spanish. 2004. (Region IV ESC Resources for Mathematics Ser.). pap. *(978-1-932797-65-7(3))* Region 4 Education Service Ctr.

—Making Connections with Measurement, TAKS Preparation Grade 5 - Student Workbook - Spanish. 2004. (Region IV ESC Resources for Mathematics Ser.). pap. *(978-1-932797-66-4(1))* Region 4 Education Service Ctr.

—TAKS Mathematics Preparation Grade 6 - Spanish. 2004. stu. ed., per., wbk. ed. *(978-1-932524-86-4(X))* Region 4 Education Service Ctr.

Regrouping Skills (Gr. 2-3) 2003. (J). *(978-1-58232-085-4(3))* ECS Learning Systems, Inc.

Regrouping Skills Spanish Version. 2007. (J). per. *(978-1-58232-154-7(X))* ECS Learning Systems, Inc.

Renaissance Learning, Inc. Staff. Getting Started with Accelerated Math & Math Renaissance (Foundation & RP) Guide may be used by Foundaton or RP Customers. 2004. 48p. per. 12.95 *(978-1-931819-55-8(6))* Renaissance Learning, Inc.

—Math Power Lessons for Grade 4: Instruction for Accelerated Math Objectives. 2004. 164p. spiral bd. 39.95 *(978-1-931819-53-4(X))* Renaissance Learning, Inc.

—Math Power Lessons for Grade 5: Instruction for Accelerated Math Objectives. 2004. 207p. spiral bd. 39.95 *(978-1-931819-54-1(8))* Renaissance Learning, Inc.

—STAR Math Made EZ (v 3. 1) RP: Quick Guide to the Software. 2004. 27p. spiral bd. 21.95 *(978-1-931819-40-4(8))* Renaissance Learning, Inc.

Rice, Dona Herweck. The History of Listening to Music: Displaying Data. 2019. (Mathematics in the Real World Ser.). (ENG., Illus.). 32p. (gr. 5-8). pap. 11.99 *(978-1-4258-5894-0(5))* Teacher Created Materials, Inc.

—Use Your Math Mind: Group It. 2nd rev. ed. 2015. (TIME for KIDS(r): Informational Text Ser.). (ENG., Illus.). 12p. (gr. -1-k). 7.99 *(978-1-4938-2144-0(X))* Teacher Created Materials, Inc.

Richards, Steve. Hooray for Hexagons: A Colouring Book All about Shapes. Richards, Steve & Farnsworth, Lauren, illus. 2018. (ENG.). 64p. (J). (gr. 3-7). pap. 9.99 *(978-1-78055-495-2(8))* O'Mara, Michael Bks., Ltd. GBR. Dist: Independent Pubs. Group.

Richardson, Erik. Applying Functions to Everyday Life, 1 vol. 2016. (Applied Mathematics Ser.). (ENG., Illus.). 128p. (J). (gr. 9-9). 47.36 *(978-1-5026-1967-9(9),* 62da3a89-8360-4ddc-b697-83f6ae8a2e32) Cavendish Square Publishing LLC.

Ring, Susan. I See Shapes. 2005. (Emergent/Early (Prek-2) Math Package Ser.). 12p. (gr. -1-1). 25.20 *(978-0-8215-7843-8(X))* Sadlier, William H. Inc.

—Money Math, 6 vols., Set. 2003. (Yellow Umbrella Early Level Ser.). (ENG.). 16p. (gr. k-1). pap. 35.70 *(978-0-7368-3011-9(1),* Capstone Pr.) Capstone.

—One Green Frog, 6 vols., Set. 2003. (Yellow Umbrella Early Level Ser.). (ENG.). 16p. (gr. k-1). pap. 35.70 *(978-0-7368-2994-6(6),* Capstone Pr.) Capstone.

Ripley, Catherine. Great Math Ideas. 2007. (ENG., Illus.). 16p. (J). (gr. 2-2). pap. 9.47 net. *(978-0-7652-8598-0(3),* Celebration Pr.) Savvas Learning Co.

Robinson, C. L. MATH1on1 Units of Measure. 2006. (YA). per. 9.99 *(978-0-9786767-4-2(2))* Robinson, Consuelo.

Robles, D. & Minquini, Lourdes. Los 100 Mejores Acertijos Matematicos (The One Hundred Best Word Problems) (SPA., Illus.). 151p. (J). (gr. k-6). pap. 7.95 *(978-968-416-820-6(9),* FN8209) Fernandez USA Publishing.

Robson, Kirsteen. Times Tables Practice Pad. 2018. (Tear-Off Pads Ser.). (ENG.). 204p. pap. 5.99 *(978-0-7945-4128-6(3),* Usborne) EDC Publishing.

Rock, Nathaniel. Math for Everyone Combo Book: 7th Grade Math, Algebra I, Geometry I, Algebra II, Math Analysis, Calculus. 2007. 480p. per. 49.99 *(978-1-59980-009-7(8))* Nathaniel Max Rock.

Rock, Nathaniel Max. Math Is Easy So Easy, Combo Book. 2008. 540p. pap. 59.99 *(978-1-59980-050-9(0))* Nathaniel Max Rock.

Rodgers, Linda. King Joe's Garden: Unit 2: Data Analysis, Statistics & Probability, 6 vols. l.t. ed. 2003. (Illus.). 88p. per. *(978-0-9728596-1-5(6),* K22) King Joe Educational Enterprises, Inc.

Roesser, Blanche. Fast Fact Measurement, 1 vol. 2018. (Fast Fact Math Ser.). (ENG.). 24p. (gr. 2-3). 24.27 *(978-1-5382-1983-6(2),* 7cbed5f9-d0c3-4bf3-9b08-26023347dcaa) Stevens, Gareth Publishing LLLP.

Romaine, Claire. Matemáticas con Mascotas / Math with Pets, 1 vol. de la Vega, Eida, tr. 2016. (¡Matemáticas en Todas Partes! / Math Is Everywhere! Ser.). (ENG & SPA.). 24p. (gr. k-k). lib. bdg. 24.27 *(978-1-4824-5216-7(2),* 5adaf151-1e5b-44b4-afab-ead628a673aa) Stevens, Gareth Publishing LLLP.

—Matemáticas en el Parque / Math at the Park, 1 vol. de la Vega, Eida, tr. 2016. (¡Matemáticas en Todas Partes! / Math Is Everywhere! Ser.). (ENG & SPA.). 24p. (gr. k-k). lib. bdg. 24.27 *(978-1-4824-5220-4(0),* 0ff53c62-b791-41df-bbe5-8f74a1ef66fa) Stevens, Gareth Publishing LLLP.

Romanek, Trudee. Science, Medicine, & Math in the Early Islamic World. 2012. (ENG.). 48p. (J). lib. bdg. *(978-0-7787-2170-3(1))* Crabtree Publishing Co.

Rookie Read-About Math, 8 bks., Set. Incl. Grouping at the Dog Show. Ribke, Simone T. lib. bdg. 20.50 *(978-0-516-24959-9(2))*; Guess the Order. Sargent, Brian. lib. bdg. 20.50 *(978-0-516-24963-6(0))*; How Much Does It Hold? Sargent, Brian. lib. bdg. 20.50 *(978-0-516-24957-5(6))*; Look & Count. Dalton, Julie. lib. bdg. 20.50 *(978-0-516-24958-2(4))*; Making Change at the Fair. Dalton, Julie. lib. bdg. 20.50 *(978-0-516-24960-5(6))*; Math Tools. Chrismer, Melanie. lib. bdg. 20.50 *(978-0-516-24961-2(4))*; Slumber Party Problem Solving. Sargent, Brian. lib. bdg. 20.50 *(978-0-516-24962-9(2))*; (Illus.). 32p. (J). (gr. 1-2). 2006. 2006. 156.00 o.p. *(978-0-516-25416-6(2),* Children's Pr.) Scholastic Library Publishing.

Rooney, Anne. A Math Journey Through Planet Earth. 2014. (Go Figure! Ser.). (ENG., Illus.). 32p. (J). (gr. 4-4). *(978-0-7787-0728-8(8))* Crabtree Publishing Co.

—A Math Journey Through Space. 2014. (Go Figure! Ser.). (ENG., Illus.). 32p. (J). (gr. 4-4). *(978-0-7787-0730-1(X))* Crabtree Publishing Co.

—A Math Journey Through the Animal Kingdom. 2014. (Go Figure! Ser.). (ENG., Illus.). 32p. (J). (gr. 4-4). *(978-0-7787-0732-5(6))* Crabtree Publishing Co.

—A Math Journey Through the Human Body. 2014. (Go Figure! Ser.). (ENG., Illus.). 32p. (J). (gr. 4-4). *(978-0-7787-0734-9(2))* Crabtree Publishing Co.

—50 Amazing Things Kids Need to Know about Math. 2012. (ENG., Illus.). 192p. (J). (gr. 2-7). pap. 12.95 *(978-1-61608-507-0(X),* 608507, Sky Pony Pr.) Skyhorse Publishing Co., Inc.

Roper, Dawn. 30 Fun Ways to Learn about Time & Money. 2011. (30 Fun Ways to Learn Ser.). (ENG.). 80p. (gr. -1-k). pap. 12.95 *(978-0-87659-370-7(8),* Gryphon House Inc) Gryphon Hse., Inc.

Rosario, Miguel. Kitchen Math. 2015. (J). pap. *(978-1-62713-452-1(2))* Cavendish Square Publishing LLC.

Rose, Mary. Week-by-Week Homework for Building Math Skills. 2006. (Week by Week Homework Ser.). (ENG., Illus.). 96p. pap. 13.99 *(978-0-439-53134-4(9),* Teaching Resources) Scholastic, Inc.

Rosen Common Core Math Readers: Levels a - D. 2013. (Rosen Math Readers Ser.). 16p. (J). (gr. k-1). pap. 1683.00 *(978-1-4777-2214-5(9))*; pap. 280.50 *(978-1-4777-2213-8(0))* Rosen Publishing Group, Inc., The. (Rosen Classroom).

Rosen Common Core Math Readers: Levels d - I. 2013. (Rosen Math Readers Ser.). 24p. (J). (gr. 1-2). pap. 255.75 *(978-1-4777-2220-6(3))*; pap. 1534.50 *(978-1-4777-2219-0(X))* Rosen Publishing Group, Inc., The. (Rosen Classroom).

Rosen Common Core Math Readers: Levels I - L. 2014. (Rosen Math Readers Ser.). 24p. (J). (gr. 2-3). pap. 1683.00 *(978-1-4777-5170-1(X))*; pap. 280.50 *(978-1-4777-5171-8(8))* Rosen Publishing Group, Inc., The. (Rosen Classroom).

Rosen Common Core Math Readers: Levels I - O. 2014. (Rosen Math Readers Ser.). 24p. (J). (gr. 3-4). pap. 255.75 *(978-1-4777-5173-2(4))*; pap. 1534.50 *(978-1-4777-5172-5(6))* Rosen Publishing Group, Inc., The. (Rosen Classroom).

Rosen, Michael J. Mind-Boggling Numbers. Patton, Julia, illus. 2016. (ENG.). 32p. (J). (gr. 2-5). 19.99 *(978-1-4677-3489-9(6),* 4baa6444-7e37-4a76-8734-e8b558533462, Millbrook Pr.) Lerner Publishing Group.

—Mind-Boggling Numbers. Patton, Julia, illus. 2016. (ENG.). 32p. (J). (gr. 2-5). E-Book 30.65 *(978-1-5124-1108-9(6),* Millbrook Pr.) Lerner Publishing Group.

Rosen Publishing Staff. Infomax Common Core Math Readers: Levels I - L, 1 vol. 2015. (InfoMax Math Readers Ser.). (ENG.). 24p. (J). 280.50 *(978-1-4777-5175-6(0),* Rosen Classroom) Rosen Publishing Group, Inc., The.

—Infomax Common Core Math Readers: Levels I - O, 1 vol. 2015. (InfoMax Math Readers Ser.). (ENG.). 24p. (J). 255.75 *(978-1-4777-5177-0(7),* Rosen Classroom) Rosen Publishing Group, Inc., The.

Rosenberg, Mary. Math Review, Grade 3. 2003. (Practice Makes Perfect Ser.). (ENG.). 48p. (gr. 3). pap. 5.99 *(978-0-7439-3743-6(0))* Teacher Created Resources, Inc.

—Math Review, Grade 4. 2003. (Practice Makes Perfect Ser.). (ENG.). 48p. (gr. 4). pap. 5.99 *(978-0-7439-3744-3(9))* Teacher Created Resources, Inc.

—Math Review, Grade 6. 2003. (Practice Makes Perfect Ser.). (ENG.). 48p. (gr. 6). pap. 5.99 *(978-0-7439-3746-7(5))* Teacher Created Resources, Inc.

—Place Value, Grade 2. 2004. (Practice Makes Perfect Ser.). (ENG.). 48p. pap. 5.99 *(978-0-7439-8602-1(4))* Teacher Created Resources, Inc.

Rosenberg, Mary & ROSENBERG, Mary. Math Review, Grade 5. 2003. (Practice Makes Perfect Ser.). (ENG., Illus.). 48p. (gr. 5). pap. 5.99 *(978-0-7439-3745-0(7))* Teacher Created Resources, Inc.

Rosenthal, Cynthia. Matt Does Math at the Ball Game, 1 vol. 2012. (InfoMax Readers Ser.). (ENG., Illus.). 24p. (J). (gr. 1-1). pap. 8.25 *(978-1-4488-9028-6(4),* b32114d2-b49d-4716-b7b3-6555eb1e3538, Rosen Classroom) Rosen Publishing Group, Inc., The.

Royce, Ron. At the Butterfly Conservatory: Represent & Interpret Data, 1 vol. 2014. (InfoMax Math Readers Ser.). (ENG.). 24p. (J). (gr. 3-3). pap. 8.25 *(978-1-4777-4597-7(1),* 7d262df8-2b0a-4713-a75a-428eae4e89c4, Rosen Classroom) Rosen Publishing Group, Inc., The.

Roza, Greg. An Optical Artist: Exploring Patterns & Symmetry, 1 vol. 2010. (Math for the REAL World Ser.). (ENG., Illus.). 32p. (gr. 5-6). pap. 10.00 *(978-1-4042-5117-5(0),* dc80efe4-3bb6-4abe-bdfd-ee552a6b62d5) Rosen Publishing Group, Inc., The.

—Space Math. 2009. (Reading Room Collection 2 Ser.). 24p. (gr. 3-4). 42.50 *(978-1-60851-989-7(9),* PowerKids Pr.) Rosen Publishing Group, Inc., The.

Rozines Roy, Jennifer & Roy, Gregory. Holiday Fractions, 1 vol. 2007. (Math All Around Ser.). (ENG., Illus.). 32p. (gr. 2-2). lib. bdg. 32.64 *(978-0-7614-2001-9(0),* 975b06d6-faac-4684-a01d-b4d760c85c24) Cavendish Square Publishing LLC.

—Math All Around, 12 vols., Set. Incl. Addition in the Forest. lib. bdg. 32.64 *(978-0-7614-2000-2(2),* 6d4051f1-82fe-4323-85df-d3a4e7066a7a); Holiday Fractions. lib. bdg. 32.64 *(978-0-7614-2001-9(0),* 975b06d6-faac-4684-a01d-b4d760c85c24); Numbers on the Street. lib. bdg. 32.64 *(978-0-7614-2002-6(9),* cb3bfc0b-d11f-4c11-96fb-29017df3202b); Patterns in Nature. lib. bdg. 32.64 *(978-0-7614-1999-0(3),* e8be416e-1693-4604-99b4-c328a9e8e852); Sorting at the Ocean. lib. bdg. 32.64 *(978-0-7614-1998-3(5),* 54de353d-d644-4c59-92d1-520f7cfeadba); Subtraction at School. lib. bdg. 32.64 *(978-0-7614-2003-3(7),* 65d3a8b1-42c4-4699-8ffb-1d56926561a9); (Illus.). 32p. (gr. 2-2). (Math All Around Ser.). (ENG.). 2007. 195.84 *(978-0-7614-1997-6(7),* ba7088a4-eb21-47a8-b8af-a3a46981952f, Cavendish Square) Cavendish Square Publishing LLC.

—Math All Around Group 2, 12 vols., Set. Incl. Division with Toys. lib. bdg. 32.64 *(978-0-7614-2269-3(2),* 37405244-193a-4055-b8fb-6d93aa5aba4b); Graphing in the Desert. lib. bdg. 32.64 *(978-0-7614-2262-4(5),* 3b38981c-e014-4cff-8abe-33f993f138b1); Measuring at Home. lib. bdg. 32.64 *(978-0-7614-2263-1(3),* 6e4dd1cf-cb3f-4b9c-9e49-bc8683cc5f72, Cavendish Square); Money at the Store. lib. bdg. 32.64 *(978-0-7614-2264-8(1),* 862dc996-0f48-4325-82f9-b2b9d2809718); Multiplication on the Farm. lib. bdg. 32.64 *(978-0-7614-2268-6(4),* 189febc4-621f-4f52-a61b-e181f071180a); Shapes in Transportation. lib. bdg. 32.64 *(978-0-7614-2265-5(X),* 3ce6ec45-cd78-4dc2-bf97-36b786ae4847); (Illus.). 32p. (gr. 2-2). (Math All Around Ser.). (ENG.). 2007. Set lib. bdg. 195.84 *(978-0-7614-2261-7(7),* 48a70a35-d92b-48a7-818b-1f7970aa2f81, Cavendish Square) Cavendish Square Publishing LLC.

—Patterns in Nature, 1 vol. (Math All Around Ser.). (ENG., Illus.). 32p. (gr. 2-2). 2008. pap. 9.23 *(978-0-7614-3407-8(0),* d044acb2-663a-4d38-a27f-0740235eb622) 2007. lib. bdg. 32.64 *(978-0-7614-1999-0(3),* e8be416e-1693-4604-99b4-c328a9e8e852) Cavendish Square Publishing LLC.

Ruffin, Frances E. Let's Have a Bake Sale: Calculating Profit & Unit Cost, 1 vol. (Math for the REAL World Ser.). 24p. (gr. 3-4). 2010. (ENG., Illus.). pap. 8.25 *(978-0-8239-8893-8(7),* fa375125-9655-49d9-a189-2e4223c37adb, PowerKids Pr.) 2004. 43.95 *(978-0-8239-7645-4(9))* Rosen Publishing Group, Inc., The.

Rustad, Martha E. H. Je Compte 100 Flocons en Hiver. 2016. (1, 2, 3 Compte Avec Moi Ser.). (FRE., Illus.). 24p. (J). (gr. k-2). *(978-1-77092-347-8(0),* 17622) Amicus.

MNO

—Je Compte 20 Moyens de Transport. 2016. (1, 2, 3 Compte Avec Moi Ser.). (FRE., Illus.). 24p. (J). (gr. k-2). (978-1-77092-348-5(9), 17623) Amicus.

—Je Compte Par 10 Au Football. 2016. (1, 2, 3 Compte Avec Moi Ser.). (FRE., Illus.). 24p. (J). (gr. k-2). (978-1-77092-350-8(0), 17625) Amicus.

—Je Compte Par 2 les Bébés Animaux. 2016. (1, 2, 3 Compte Avec Moi Ser.). (FRE., Illus.). 24p. (J). (gr. k-2) (978-1-77092-349-2(7), 17624) Amicus.

—Je Compte Par 5 les Animaux D'Afrique. 2016. (1, 2, 3 Compte Avec Moi Ser.). (FRE., Illus.). 24p. (J). (gr. k-2). (978-1-77092-351-5(9), 17626) Amicus.

Sain, Judy L. Daily Math SKills Review Grade 4: Practice for Mastery of Math Standards. 2004. (J). spiral bd. 22.00 (978-1-929229-23-9(2)) aha! Process, Inc.

Salzmann, Mary Elizabeth. Money for Clothes, 1 vol. 2010. (Your Piggy Bank: a Guide to Spending & Saving for Kids! Ser.). (ENG.). 24p. (J). (gr. k-4). 31.36 (978-1-61641-027-8(2), 15836, Looking Glass Library) Magic Wagon.

—Money for Food, 1 vol. 2010. (Your Piggy Bank: a Guide to Spending & Saving for Kids! Ser.). (ENG.). 24p. (J). (gr. k-4). 31.36 (978-1-61641-029-2(9), 15840, Looking Glass Library) Magic Wagon.

—Money for Hobbies, 1 vol. 2010. (Your Piggy Bank: a Guide to Spending & Saving for Kids! Ser.). (ENG.). 24p. (J). (gr. k-4). 31.36 (978-1-61641-030-8(2), 15842, Looking Glass Library) Magic Wagon.

—Money for School, 1 vol. 2010. (Your Piggy Bank: a Guide to Spending & Saving for Kids! Ser.). (ENG.). 24p. (J). (gr. k-4). 31.36 (978-1-61641-031-5(0), 15844, Looking Glass Library) Magic Wagon.

—Money for Toys, 1 vol. 2010. (Your Piggy Bank: a Guide to Spending & Saving for Kids! Ser.). (ENG.). 24p. (J). (gr. k-4). 31.36 (978-1-61641-032-2(9), 15846, Looking Glass Library) Magic Wagon.

Sandviks HOP, Inc. Staff. Hooked on First Grade. 2007. 39.99 (978-1-60143-750-1(1)) HOP, LLC.

—Hooked on Kindergarten. 2007. 39.99 (978-1-60143-788-4(9)) HOP, LLC.

Sargent, Brian. Places along the Way. 2006. (Rookie Read-About Math Ser.). (ENG., Illus.). 32p. (J). (gr. 1-2). 20.50 (978-0-516-29917-4(4)) Scholastic Library Publishing.

Saunders, Hal. When Are We Ever Gonna Have to Use This? (Illus.). 14p. (J). (gr. k-6). 14.95 (978-1-57232-364-3(7)) Seymour, Dale Pubns.

Saxon Manipulatives Kit. 2004. (gr. k-3). 64.50 (978-0-01-210520-7(1)) Saxon Pubs., Inc.

Saxon Math 54 Answer Key & Test. 2004. 18.00 (978-0-01-205170-2(5)) Saxon Pubs., Inc.

Saxon Math 54 Home Study Kit. 2004. 68.50 (978-1-59141-331-8(1)) Saxon Pubs., Inc.

Saxon Math 65 Answer Key & Test. 2004. 18.00 (978-0-01-205173-3(X)) Saxon Pubs., Inc.

Saxon Math 76 Answer Key & Test. 2004. 18.00 (978-0-01-205176-4(4)) Saxon Pubs., Inc.

Saxon Math 87 Answer Key & Test. 2004. pap. 18.00 (978-0-01-210332-6(2)) Saxon Pubs., Inc.

Saxon Math 87 Home Study Kit. 2004. 57.75 (978-0-01-204723-1(6)) Saxon Pubs., Inc.

Saxon Publishers Staff & Hake, Stephen. Saxon Math 6/5 Homeschool Kit, 3 vols. rev. ed. 2004. 69.50 (978-1-59141-348-6(6), 3486) Saxon Pubs., Inc.

Schieber, Jennifer. A contar en las Olimpiadas: Fiction-to-Fact Big Book. enl. ed. 2004. (SPA.). (J). pap. 26.00 (978-1-4108-2360-1(1), 23601) Benchmark Education Co.

—Insects Measure Up! 2004. (Shared Connections Ser.). (J). instr.'s gde. ed. 34.00 net. (978-1-4108-1610-8(9)) Benchmark Education Co.

Schifter, Deborah, et al. Measuring Space in One, Two & Three Dimensions: Facilitator's Package. 2003. (Developing Mathematical Ideas Ser.). (ENG.). 81.50 (978-0-7690-2907-8(8)) Seymour, Dale Pubns.

Schmidt, Stanley F. Life of Fred — Farming. 2011. (ENG., Illus.). 128p. 16.00 (978-0-9791072-9-0(6)) Polka Dot Publishing.

—Life of Fred Calculus Expanded Edition. 2015. (ENG., Illus.). 592p. (J). 49.00 (978-1-937032-53-1(1)) Polka Dot Publishing.

Scholastic, Inc. Staff. Brain Play 1st-3rd. 2008. (J). 29.99 (978-0-545-05207-8(6)) Scholastic, Inc.

—Brain Play Preschool-1st. 2008. (J). 29.99 (978-0-439-81350-1(6)) Scholastic, Inc.

Scholastic, Inc. Staff, contrib. by. 100 Day Count up Calendar with100 Open & Peek Door. 2003. (ENG.). 4p. (J). pap. 12.95 (978-0-439-08248-8(X)) Scholastic, Inc.

School Mathematics Project. SMP Interact for Key Stage 3 Mathematics: Projectable PDFs for the T (Support) tier. 2009. (ENG.). cd-rom 189.00 (978-0-521-15861-9(3)) Cambridge Univ. Pr.

School Zone, ed. Transition Math K-1. deluxe ed. 2019. (ENG.). 64p. (J). (gr. k-1). pap., wbk. ed. 4.49 (978-1-58947-321-8(3), 89f314a4-b7c3-48cd-ae1a-eaeac5574c8a) School Zone Publishing Co.

School Zone Interactive Staff. Math Basics. rev. ed. 2004. (ENG.). 64p. (J). (gr. k-2). wbk. ed. 15.99 (978-1-58947-802-2(9)); 15.99 (978-1-58947-803-9(7)) School Zone Publishing Co.

School Zone Publishing. Math 1. 2003. (ENG.). cd-rom 19.99 (978-1-58947-908-1(4)) School Zone Publishing Co.

—Math 2. 2003. (ENG.). cd-rom 19.99 (978-1-58947-909-8(2)) School Zone Publishing Co.

—Math 3. 2003. (ENG.). cd-rom 19.99 (978-1-58947-910-4(6)) School Zone Publishing Co.

—Multiplication & Division. 2003. (ENG.). (J). (gr. 3-4). cd-rom 19.99 (978-1-58947-927-2(0)) School Zone Publishing Co.

School Zone Publishing Company Staff. Bilingual Math Basics 1. 2007. (ENG.). 64p. (J). pap. 3.99 (978-1-58947-966-1(1)) School Zone Publishing Co.

—Bilingual Math Basics 2. 2007. (ENG.). 64p. (J). pap. 3.99 (978-1-58947-967-8(X)) School Zone Publishing Co.

—Division 0-12, 56 vols. rev. ed. 2019. (ENG.). 56p. (J). (gr. 3-5). 3.49 (978-0-88743-241-5(7), b86230b2-8dc8-45ee-a72a-6273746f5046) School Zone Publishing Co.

—Matematicas Basicas Math Basics. 2007. (ENG.). 64p. (J). (gr. k-3). pap. 2.69 (978-1-58947-968-5(8)) School Zone Publishing Co.

—Math: Grades 5 & 6. (Illus.). (J). 19.99 incl. audio compact disk (978-0-88743-953-7(5)) School Zone Publishing Co.

—Math 1-2 Software. 2004. (ENG.). 64p. (J). wbk. ed. 15.99 (978-1-58947-369-0(8)) School Zone Publishing Co.

—Math 4. (Illus.). (J). 19.99 incl. audio compact disk (978-0-88743-952-0(7)) School Zone Publishing Co.

—Math Readiness. 2007. (ENG.). 64p. (J). pap. 2.69 (978-1-58947-964-7(5)) School Zone Publishing Co.

—Math War Addition & Subtraction: Addition & Subtraction, 56 vols. rev. ed. 2019. (ENG.). 52p. (J). (gr. 1-2). 3.49 (978-0-88743-273-6(5), 74587553-8ade-46aa-b8fb-61814d6c310c) School Zone Publishing Co.

—Multiplication 0-12, 56 vols. rev. ed. 2019. (ENG.). 56p. (J). (gr. 3-5). 3.49 (978-0-938256-93-9(9), 313a85f4-cfcd-4b68-85f9-73de9f01698f) School Zone Publishing Co.

—Numbers Fun! Hours of Reusable Fun! rev. ed. 2005. (ENG.). 26p. (J). (gr. k-1). pap. 3.99 (978-1-58947-786-5(3)) School Zone Publishing Co.

School Zone Publishing Company Staff & Evans, Karen. Math Basics 5: Grade 5. deluxe ed. 2019. (ENG., Illus.). 64p. (J). (gr. 5-5). pap., wbk. ed. 4.49 (978-0-88743-141-8(0), 57381c9d-7d3a-4e03-b81f-9b1fec7fee7d) School Zone Publishing Co.

Schwartz, David M. How Much Is a Million? Kellogg, Steven, illus. 20th anniv. ed. 2004. (ENG.). 40p. (J). (gr. -1-3). pap. 7.99 (978-0-688-09933-6(5), HarperCollins) HarperCollins Pubs.

—How Much Is a Million? 2004. (J). (gr. k-3). 18.40 (978-0-8085-7914-4(2)) Turtleback.

Schwartz, Linda. Math Quiz Whiz 3-5, Vol. 431. VanBlaricum, Pam, ed. Armstrong, Beverly, illus. 2004. 128p. (J). (gr. 3-5). pap. 10.99 (978-0-88160-374-3(0), LW-431) Creative Teaching Pr., Inc.

—Primary Math Quiz Whiz, Vol. 428. VanBlaricum, Pam, ed. Mason, Mark, illus. 2004. 128p. (J). (gr. 1-3). pap. 14.99 (978-0-88160-371-2(6), LW-428) Creative Teaching Pr., Inc.

Schwartz, Richard Evan. Life on the Infinite Farm. 2018. (Monograph Bks.). (ENG., Illus.). 176p. pap. 25.00 (978-1-4704-4736-6(3), P590691) American Mathematical Society.

Schweppe, Deirdre. Migrating Animals: Use Place Value Understanding & Properties of Operations to Add & Subtract, 1 vol. 2014. (Math Masters: Number & Operations in Base Ten Ser.). (ENG.). 24p. (J). (gr. 2-2). 25.27 (978-1-4777-6434-3(8), a958ca24-f1cf-4b4e-ab6c-5746c7b52591); pap. 8.25 (978-1-4777-4751-3(6), 702e298a-26de-4cf7-a346-9a21700c069d) Rosen Publishing Group, Inc., The. (Rosen Classroom).

Sciarrino, Stephanie. Multiplication at the Marina: Multiply Within 100, 1 vol. 2014. (Rosen Math Readers Ser.). (ENG., Illus.). 24p. (J). (gr. 3-3). pap. 8.25 (978-1-4777-4950-0(0), 454dda7c-0c35-4265-98eb-be1d28a387f1); lib. bdg. 25.27 (978-1-4777-6451-0(8), 3476d5a0-acb8-4313-a125-d960238e3699) Rosen Publishing Group, Inc., The. (PowerKids Pr.).

Scillian, Devin. One Kansas Farmer: A Kansas Number Book. Bowles, Doug, illus. 2009. (America by the Numbers Ser.). (ENG.). 40p. (J). (gr. 1-3). 19.99 (978-1-58536-182-3(8), 202031) Sleeping Bear Pr.

Scott Foresman - Addison Wesley Mathematics: Additional Resources. 2004. (gr. 1-18). (978-0-328-07382-5(2)); (gr. 2-18). (978-0-328-07383-2(0)); (gr. 3-18). (978-0-328-07384-9(9)); (gr. 3-4). (978-0-328-08112-7(4)); (gr. 4-18). (978-0-328-07385-6(7)); (gr. 5-18). (978-0-328-07386-3(5)); (gr. 6-18). (978-0-328-07387-0(3)) Addison-Wesley Educational Pubs., Inc. (Scott Foresman).

Scott Foresman-Addison Wesley Mathematics. 2004. (gr. k-18). stu. ed. (978-0-328-03015-6(5), Scott Foresman) Addison-Wesley Educational Pubs., Inc.

Scott Foresman-Addison Wesley Mathematics: Additional Resources. 2004. (gr. k-18). (978-0-328-04989-9(1)); (gr. k-18). (978-0-328-08559-0(6)); (gr. k-18). (978-0-328-04945-5(X)); (gr. k-18). (978-0-328-07549-2(3)); (gr. k-18). (978-0-328-03816-9(4)); (gr. k-5). (978-0-328-08797-6(1)); (gr. k-6). (978-0-328-07636-9(8)); (gr. k-6). (978-0-328-06313-0(4)); (gr. 1-18). (978-0-328-04990-5(5)); (gr. 1-18). (978-0-328-08560-6(X)); (gr. 1-18). (978-0-328-07550-8(7)); (gr. 1-18). (978-0-328-03817-6(2)); (gr. 1-18). (978-0-328-04946-2(8)); (gr. 2-18). (978-0-328-03818-3(0)); (gr. 2-18). (978-0-328-07551-5(5)); (gr. 2-18). (978-0-328-04947-9(6)); (gr. 2-18). (978-0-328-08561-3(8)); (gr. 2-18). (978-0-328-04991-2(3)); (gr. 3-18). (978-0-328-07552-2(3)); (gr. 3-18). (978-0-328-04948-6(4)); (gr. 3-18). (978-0-328-09245-1(2)); (gr. 3-18). (978-0-328-04992-9(1)); (gr. 3-18). (978-0-328-03819-0(9)); (gr. 3-18). (978-0-328-08562-0(6)); (gr. 3-4). (978-0-328-07619-2(8)); (gr. 4-18). (978-0-328-08563-7(4)); (gr. 4-18). (978-0-328-03820-6(2)); (gr. 4-18). (978-0-328-09246-8(0)); (gr. 4-18). (978-0-328-07553-9(1)); (gr. 4-18). (978-0-328-04949-3(2)); (gr. 4-18). (978-0-328-05007-9(5)); (gr. 5-18). (978-0-328-03821-3(0)); (gr. 5-18). (978-0-328-08564-4(2)); (gr. 5-18). (978-0-328-09247-5(9)); (gr. 5-18). (978-0-328-07554-6(X)); (gr. 5-18). (978-0-328-04950-9(6)); (gr. 5-18). (978-0-328-04993-6(X)); (gr. 5-6). (978-0-328-07620-8(1)); (gr. 6-18). (978-0-328-04951-6(4)); (gr. 6-18). (978-0-328-09248-2(7)); (gr. 6-18). (978-0-328-04994-3(8)); (gr. 6-18). (978-0-328-07555-3(8)); (gr. 6-18). (978-0-328-03822-0(9)); (gr. 6-18). (978-0-328-08565-1(0)) Addison-Wesley Educational Pubs., Inc. (Scott Foresman).

Scott Foresman-Addison Wesley Mathematics: Assessment, Diagnosis, & Intervention. 2004. (gr. k-18). (978-0-328-05519-7(0)); (gr. 1-18). (978-0-328-06125-9(5)); (gr. 1-18). (978-0-328-09313-7(0)); (gr. 1-18). (978-0-328-06131-0(X)); (gr. 1-18). (978-0-328-05520-3(4)); (gr. 2-18). (978-0-328-06126-6(3)); (gr. 2-18). (978-0-328-09314-4(9)); (gr. 2-18). (978-0-328-05521-0(2)); (gr. 2-18). (978-0-328-06132-7(8)); (gr. 3-18). (978-0-328-06127-3(1)); (gr. 3-18). (978-0-328-06137-2(9)); (gr. 3-18). (978-0-328-05522-7(0)); (gr. 3-18). (978-0-328-09315-1(7)); (gr. 3-18). (978-0-328-06133-4(6)); (gr. 4-18). (978-0-328-09316-8(5)); (gr. 4-18). (978-0-328-06138-9(7)); (gr. 4-18). (978-0-328-06134-1(4)); (gr. 4-18). (978-0-328-05523-4(9)); (gr. 4-18). (978-0-328-06128-0(X)); (gr. 5-18). (978-0-328-09317-5(3)); (gr. 5-18). (978-0-328-05524-1(7)); (gr. 5-18). (978-0-328-06139-6(5)); (gr. 5-18). (978-0-328-06135-8(2)); (gr. 5-18). (978-0-328-06129-7(8)); (gr. 6-18). (978-0-328-06140-2(9)); (gr. 6-18). (978-0-328-06136-5(0)); (gr. 6-18). (978-0-328-09318-2(1)); (gr. 6-18). (978-0-328-06130-3(1)); (gr. 6-18). (978-0-328-05525-8(5)) Addison-Wesley Educational Pubs., Inc. (Scott Foresman).

Scott Foresman-Addison Wesley Mathematics: Pre-K Mathematics. 2004. (gr. -1-18). (978-0-328-09228-4(2)); (978-0-328-09229-1(0)); (978-0-328-09366-3(1)); (978-0-328-08086-1(1)); (978-0-328-09244-4(4)); (978-0-328-09243-7(6)); tchr. ed. (978-0-328-08087-8(X)) Addison-Wesley Educational Pubs., Inc. (Scott Foresman).

Scott Foresman-Addison Wesley Mathematics: Pupil Edition, 4 vols. 2004. (gr. k-18). (978-0-328-07587-4(6), Scott Foresman) Addison-Wesley Educational Pubs., Inc.

Scott Foresman-Addison Wesley Mathematics: Technology. 2004. (gr. k-18). (978-0-328-08602-3(9)); (gr. k-18). E-Book incl. cd-rom (978-0-328-08566-8(9)); (gr. 1-18). (978-0-328-09350-2(5)); (gr. 1-18). (978-0-328-08603-0(7)); (gr. 1-18). E-Book incl. cd-rom (978-0-328-08567-5(7)); (gr. 1-18). cd-rom (978-0-328-07764-9(X)); (gr. 1-18). cd-rom (978-0-328-08579-8(0)); (gr. 1-18). cd-rom (978-0-328-08591-0(X)); (gr. 2-18). (978-0-328-08604-7(5)); (gr. 2-18). (978-0-328-09351-9(3)); (gr. 2-18). E-Book incl. cd-rom (978-0-328-08568-2(5)); (gr. 2-18). cd-rom (978-0-328-08592-7(8)); (gr. 2-18). cd-rom (978-0-328-07765-6(8)); (gr. 2-18). cd-rom (978-0-328-08580-4(4)); (gr. 3-18). (978-0-328-08605-4(3)); (gr. 3-18). (978-0-328-09352-6(1)); (gr. 3-18). E-Book incl. cd-rom (978-0-328-08569-9(3)); (gr. 3-18). cd-rom (978-0-328-07766-3(6)); (gr. 3-18). cd-rom (978-0-328-08593-4(6)); (gr. 3-18). cd-rom (978-0-328-08581-1(2)); (gr. 4-18). (978-0-328-09353-3(X)); (gr. 4-18). (978-0-328-08606-1(1)); (gr. 4-18). E-Book incl. cd-rom (978-0-328-08570-5(7)); (gr. 4-18). cd-rom (978-0-328-08594-1(4)); (gr. 4-18). cd-rom (978-0-328-08582-8(0)); (gr. 4-18). cd-rom (978-0-328-07767-0(4)); (gr. 4-6). (978-0-328-09311-3(4)); (gr. 4-6). (978-0-328-09312-0(2)); (gr. 5-18). (978-0-328-09354-0(8)); (gr. 5-18). (978-0-328-08607-8(X)); (gr. 5-18). E-Book incl. cd-rom (978-0-328-08571-2(5)); (gr. 5-18). cd-rom (978-0-328-07768-7(2)); (gr. 5-18). cd-rom (978-0-328-08583-5(9)); (gr. 5-18). cd-rom (978-0-328-08595-8(2)); (gr. 6-18). (978-0-328-08608-5(8)); (gr. 6-18). (978-0-328-09355-7(6)); (gr. 6-18). E-Book incl. cd-rom (978-0-328-08572-9(3)); (gr. 6-18). cd-rom (978-0-328-08584-2(7)); (gr. 6-18). cd-rom (978-0-328-08596-5(0)); (gr. 6-18). cd-rom (978-0-328-07769-4(0)) Addison-Wesley Educational Pubs., Inc. (Scott Foresman).

Scott Foresman-Addison Wesley Mathematics: Workbooks. 2004. (gr. 1-18). wbk. ed. (978-0-328-04965-3(4), Scott Foresman) Addison-Wesley Educational Pubs., Inc.

Scott Foresman Math Around the Clock. 2003. (Scott Foreman Math Around the Clock Ser.). (gr. 1-18). (978-0-328-07264-4(8)); (gr. 1-18). tchr. ed. (978-0-328-06304-8(5)); (gr. 1-2). (978-0-328-01697-6(7)); (gr. 2-18). (978-0-328-07265-1(6)); (gr. 2-18). tchr. ed. (978-0-328-06305-5(3)); (gr. 3-18). (978-0-328-07266-8(4)); (gr. 3-18). tchr. ed. (978-0-328-06306-2(1)); (gr. 3-4). (978-0-328-01698-3(5)); (gr. 4-18). (978-0-328-07267-5(2)); (gr. 4-18). tchr. ed. (978-0-328-06307-9(X)); (gr. 4-18). wbk. ed. (978-0-328-06452-6(1)); (gr. 5-18). (978-0-328-07268-2(0)); (gr. 5-18). tchr. ed. (978-0-328-06308-6(8)); (gr. 5-6). (978-0-328-01880-2(5)); (gr. 6-18). (978-0-328-07269-9(9)); (gr. 6-18). tchr. ed. (978-0-328-06309-3(6)) Addison-Wesley Educational Pubs., Inc. (Scott Foresman).

Scott, Kimberley, illus. Wipe-Clean First Math. 2014. (ENG.). (J). (gr. k-4). pap. 7.99 (978-0-7945-3354-0(X), Usborne) EDC Publishing.

Seymour, Dale. Balanced Assessment for the Mathematics Curriculum. 2003. (Illus.). 184p. (J). (gr. 3-5). 42.95 (978-0-7690-0063-3(0));Package 2. 42.95 (978-0-7690-0064-0(9)) Seymour, Dale Pubns.

—Developing Skills in Estimation, Bk. A. 55p. (J). (gr. 7-8). 14.95 net. (978-0-86651-010-3(9), DSO1161) Seymour, Dale Pubns.

Sganga, Francis. Introducing Gifted Students to the Wonders of Mathematics: Preparation for High School & Higher Mathematics, Grades 4-8. 2004. (Illus.). 75p. (978-0-910609-47-0(0)) Gifted Education Pr.

Shae, Jordan. Handy Measuring: Measure Lengths, 1 vol. 2013. (InfoMax Math Readers Ser.). (ENG.). 24p. (J). (gr. 1-1). pap. 8.25 (978-1-4777-2201-5(7), 358e9f52-0e3e-415e-b7aa-8ce845b41196); pap. 49.50 (978-1-4777-2202-2(5)) Rosen Publishing Group, Inc., The. (Rosen Classroom).

Shah, Keiran. Making Pictographs, 1 vol. 2014. (Graph It! Ser.). (ENG.). 24p. (J). (gr. 1-2). 24.27 (978-1-4824-0839-3(2), 6fa08bf4-2c1c-4315-805d-a74a8a4656f3) Stevens, Gareth Publishing LLLP.

Shakes, Suzanna, et al. Maths in Practice Year 8, Bk. 1. 2009. (ENG., Illus.). 204p. stu. ed. 39.59 (978-0-340-94858-3(2)) Hodder Education Group GBR. Dist: Trans-Atlantic Pubns., Inc.

Shakes, Suzanne, et al. Maths in Practice. 2009. (Dynamic Learning Ser.). (ENG., Illus.). Bk. 2. 244p. stu. ed. 36.50 (978-0-340-94859-0(0))Bk. 3. 284p. stu. ed. 39.50 (978-0-340-94860-6(4)) Hodder Education Group GBR. Dist: Trans-Atlantic Pubns., Inc.

—Maths in Practice Year 7, 4 vols. 2009. (ENG., Bk. 1. Illus.). 248p. stu. ed. 37.50 (978-0-340-94848-4(5))Bk. 2. stu. ed. 37.50 (978-0-340-94849-1(3))Bk. 3. (Illus.). 240p. 37.50 (978-0-340-94850-7(7)) Hodder Education Group GBR. Dist: Trans-Atlantic Pubns., Inc.

Shannon, Rosemarie, et al, adapted by. Measurement. 2003. (Kids Can Learn with Franklin Ser.). (ENG., Illus.). 32p. (J). (gr. k-1). 3.95 (978-1-55337-595-1(5)) Kids Can Pr., Ltd. CAN. Dist: Hachette Bk. Group.

Shaskan, Trisha Speed. If You Were a Divided-By Sign, 1 vol. Dillard, Sarah, illus. 2009. (Math Fun Ser.). (ENG.). 24p. (J). (gr. 2-4). pap. 7.95 (978-1-4048-5196-2(8), 95505); lib. bdg. 28.65 (978-1-4048-5195-5(X), 95504) Capstone. (Picture Window Bks.).

—If You Were a Minus Sign [LTD Commodities]. Carabelli, Francesca, illus. 2010. (Math Fun Ser.). 24p. pap. 3.50 (978-1-4048-6256-2(0), Picture Window Bks.) Capstone.

—If You Were a Minus Sign [Scholastic]. Carabelli, Francesca, illus. 2010. (Math Fun Ser.). 24p. pap. 0.52 (978-1-4048-6173-2(4), Picture Window Bks.) Capstone.

—If You Were a Plus Sign [LTD Commodities]. Carabelli, Francesca, illus. 2010. (Math Fun Ser.). 24p. pap. 3.50 (978-1-4048-6257-9(9), Picture Window Bks.) Capstone.

—If You Were a Plus Sign [Scholastic]. Carabelli, Francesca, illus. 2010. (Math Fun Ser.). 24p. pap. 0.52 (978-1-4048-6172-5(6), Picture Window Bks.) Capstone.

—If You Were a Times Sign, 1 vol. Dillard, Sarah, illus. 2009. (Math Fun Ser.). (ENG.). 24p. (J). (gr. 2-4). pap. 7.95 (978-1-4048-5211-2(5), 95515); lib. bdg. 28.65 (978-1-4048-5210-5(7), 95514) Capstone. (Picture Window Bks.).

Shea, Bobby Kennedy. Patterns with Pandas. 2013. (Animal Math Ser.). 24p. (J). (gr. 1-3). pap. 48.90 (978-1-4339-9320-6(1)) Stevens, Gareth Publishing LLLP.

Shea, Mary Molly. Making Line Graphs, 1 vol. 2014. (Graph It! Ser.). (ENG.). 24p. (J). (gr. 1-2). 24.27 (978-1-4824-0834-8(1), ccb949cc-7755-4588-972f-c4df37c21040) Stevens, Gareth Publishing LLLP.

Shea, Therese. Biosphere 2: Solving Word Problems, 1 vol. (Math for the REAL World Ser.). 32p. 2010. (ENG., Illus.). (gr. 5-6). pap. 10.00 (978-1-4042-5150-2(2), 76ddb5be-672d-47d8-a171-548c3aa362af, PowerKids Pr.) 2009. (gr. 4-5). 47.90 (978-1-60851-406-9(4), PowerKids Pr.) 2004. (ENG., Illus.). (YA). (gr. 5-6). lib. bdg. 28.93 (978-1-4042-2943-3(4), aca59918-3466-41c4-9073-309dbde80213) Rosen Publishing Group, Inc., The.

—Climbing Mount Everest: Understanding Commutative, Associative, & Distributive Properties, 1 vol. (Math for the REAL World Ser.). (ENG., Illus.). 32p. (gr. 5-6). 2010. pap. 10.00 (978-1-4042-5142-7(1), 215f7483-9459-4a81-bf7b-769d828098d7, PowerKids Pr.) 2004. (YA). lib. bdg. 28.93 (978-1-4042-2939-6(6), 960db978-e7aa-4e15-a64d-d87b693ae7a9) Rosen Publishing Group, Inc., The.

—Climbing Mount Everest: Understanding Commutative, Associative & Distributive Properties. 2009. (PowerMath: Proficiency Plus Ser.). 32p. (gr. 4-5). 47.90 (978-1-60851-408-3(0), PowerKids Pr.) Rosen Publishing Group, Inc., The.

—The Great Barrier Reef: Using Graphs & Charts to Solve Word Problems. 2009. (PowerMath: Advanced Proficiency Plus Ser.). 32p. (gr. 5-5). 47.90 (978-1-60851-367-3(X), PowerKids Pr.) Rosen Publishing Group, Inc., The.

Shea, Therese M. Werewolves Do Word Problems!, 1 vol. 2018. (Monsters Do Math! Ser.). (ENG.). 24p. (gr. 2-3). 24.27 (978-1-5382-2936-1(6), 6e9aae4f-4e11-4669-b314-4481536296df) Stevens, Gareth Publishing LLLP.

—Zombies Read Graphs!, 1 vol. 2018. (Monsters Do Math! Ser.). (ENG.). 24p. (gr. 2-3). 24.27 (978-1-5382-2938-5(2), d46d0008-bbef-4e2b-810c-e04161afca7e) Stevens, Gareth Publishing LLLP.

Sheen, Barbara. Careers If You Like Math. 2016. (ENG., Illus.). 80p. (J). (gr. 5-12). (978-1-68282-004-9(1)) ReferencePoint Pr., Inc.

Sherratt, Andrew. International Mathematics Coursebook 2, Bk. 2. 2009. (ENG., Illus.). 264p. pap. 39.50 (978-0-340-96743-0(9)) Hodder Education Group GBR. Dist: Trans-Atlantic Pubns., Inc.

Shieber, Jennifer. Insects Measure Up! Small Book. 2004. (Shared Connections Ser.). (J). pap. (978-1-4108-1634-4(6)) Benchmark Education Co.

Shiotsu, Vicky. Preschool Math: Learning Basic Concepts Through Experimenting & Play. 2006. (Early Learning Ser.). (Illus.). 128p. (J). (gr. -1-1). per. 13.99 (978-1-59198-224-1(3), 2567) Creative Teaching Pr., Inc.

Show What You Know Publishing, ed. Show What You Know on the CSAP for Grade 6, Mathematics Student Workbook. 2007. (J). per. 14.95 (978-1-59230-238-3(6)) Englefield & Assocs., Inc.

Sikkens, Crystal. Bar Graphs. 2016. (Get Graphing! Building Data Literacy Skills Ser.). (ENG., Illus.). 24p. (J). (gr. 1-3). (978-0-7787-2624-1(X)) Crabtree Publishing Co.

—Picture Graphs. 2016. (Get Graphing! Building Data Literacy Skills Ser.). (ENG., Illus.). 24p. (J). (gr. 1-3). (978-0-7787-2632-6(0)) Crabtree Publishing Co.

Silbey, Robyn. Math Hooks. 2004. (Illus.). 80p. (gr. 1). pap. 10.95 (978-0-673-58916-3(1)); (gr. 2). pap. 10.95 (978-0-673-58917-0(X)) Good Year Bks.

Simonds, Lucy. Celebrations. 2007. (Trackers-Math Ser.). (gr. 2-5). pap. 5.00 (978-1-59055-919-2(3)) Pacific Learning, Inc.

—Indoor Sports. 2007. (Trackers-Math Ser.). (gr. 2-5). pap. 5.00 (978-1-59055-921-5(5)) Pacific Learning, Inc.

—The Olympics. 2007. (Trackers-Math Ser.). (gr. 2-5). pap. 5.00 (978-1-59055-911-6(8)) Pacific Learning, Inc.

—People & Pets. 2007. (Trackers-Math Ser.). (gr. 2-5). pap. 5.00 (978-1-59055-920-8(7)) Pacific Learning, Inc.

—The Sky Is the Limit. 2007. (Trackers-Math Ser.). (gr. 2-5). pap. 5.00 (978-1-59055-922-2(3)) Pacific Learning, Inc.

—Wonders of the World. 2007. (Trackers-Math Ser.). (gr. 2-5). pap. 5.00 (978-1-59055-925-3(8)) Pacific Learning, Inc.

Simons, Lisa M. Bolt. Unusual & Awesome Jobs Using Math: Stunt Coordinator, Cryptologist, & More. 2015. (You Get Paid for THAT? Ser.). (ENG., Illus.). 32p. (J). (gr. 3-9). 28.65 (978-1-4914-2030-0(8), 127508, Capstone Pr.) Capstone.

Simons, Rae. Business Math. 2013. (Math 24/7 Ser.: 10). 48p. (J). (gr. 5-18). 19.95 (978-1-4222-2903-3(3)) Mason Crest.

Simpson, Jeff. Sharing Big Numbers, 2nd Edition, Student Edition: Count, Notice & Remember Math Intervention Volume I, MD-2. Simpson, Marilyn, ed. 2nd ed. 2007. (Count, Notice & Remember Ser.: Volume I, MD-2). ring bd. 50.00 (978-1-888976-44-1(6)) Mastery Learning Systems.

Simpson, Marilyn Bohlen, ed. Percents, Ratios, & Rates, Student Edition: Count, Notice & Remember Math

Intervention, Volume 3. 2007. ring bd. 59.95 *(978-1-888976-50-2(0))* Mastery Learning Systems.

Small, Marian, et al. Navigating Through Problem Solving & Reasoning in Grade 2. 2004. (Navigations Ser.). (ENG., Illus.). 50p. pap. 25.95 *(978-0-87353-551-9(0)*, P229405) National Council of Teachers of Mathematics.

Smith, Jodene. Cut & Paste - Math, Grades 1-3. 2003. (ENG.). 96p. pap. 12.99 *(978-0-7439-3708-5(2))* Teacher Created Resources, Inc.

Smith, Paula & Colozza Cocca, Lisa. Calendar Math. 2013. (ENG., Illus.). 24p. (J). *(978-0-7787-1075-2(0))*; pap. *(978-0-7787-1091-2(2))* Crabtree Publishing Co.

—Time Word Problems. 2013. (ENG., Illus.). 24p. (J). *(978-0-7787-1077-6(7))*; pap. *(978-0-7787-1093-6(9))* Crabtree Publishing Co.

Smith, Paula & Mason, Helen. Length Word Problems. 2013. (ENG.). 24p. (J). *(978-0-7787-1079-0(3))*; pap. *(978-0-7787-1095-0(5))* Crabtree Publishing Co.

—Word Problems: Mass & Volume. 2013. (ENG., Illus.). 24p. (J). *(978-0-7787-1081-3(5))*; pap. *(978-0-7787-1097-4(1))* Crabtree Publishing Co.

Solodar, Marisol. Bailey's Band: Develop Understanding of Fractions & Numbers, 1 vol. 2014. (InfoMax Math Readers Ser.). (ENG.). 24p. (J). (gr. 3-3). pap. 8.25 *(978-1-4777-4618-9(8)*, 8db0bc7c-a811-47f6-87d0-59b3516f2875, Rosen Classroom) Rosen Publishing Group, Inc., The.

Solve It! Math in Space, 12 vols. 2016. (Solve It! Math in Space Ser.). 24p. (ENG.). (gr. 2-3). lib. bdg. 145.62 *(978-1-4824-4602-9(2)*, b9dae529-59e3-49ff-9359-ba6d80a0ccce); (gr. 3-2). pap. 48.90 *(978-1-4824-5325-6(8))* Stevens, Gareth Publishing LLLP.

Somervill, Barbara A. Hurricanes. 2012. (21st Century Skills Library: Real World Math Ser.). (ENG.). 32p. (gr. 4-8). (J). pap. 14.21 *(978-1-61080-408-0(2)*, 201340); lib. bdg. 32.07 *(978-1-61080-325-0(6)*, 201302) Cherry Lake Publishing.

Soriano, Al. Excursions Gr 1 Sp. 2004. (Voyages Ser.). (J). (gr. 1). stu. ed., per. 10.55 *(978-1-58830-875-7(8))* Metropolitan Teaching & Learning Co.

—Excursions Gr 2 Sp. 2004. (Voyages Ser.). (J). (gr. 2). stu. ed., per. 10.55 *(978-1-58830-876-4(6))* Metropolitan Teaching & Learning Co.

—Excursions Gr 3 Sp. 2004. (Voyages Ser.). (J). (gr. 3). stu. ed., per. 10.55 *(978-1-58830-877-1(4))* Metropolitan Teaching & Learning Co.

—Excursions Grade 1. 2003. (Voyages Ser.). (J). (gr. 1). stu. ed., per. 8.95 *(978-1-58830-612-8(7))* Metropolitan Teaching & Learning Co.

—Excursions Grade 2. 2003. (Voyages Ser.). (J). (gr. 2). stu. ed., per. 8.95 *(978-1-58830-627-2(5))* Metropolitan Teaching & Learning Co.

—Excursions Grade 3. 2003. (Voyages Ser.). (J). (gr. 3). stu. ed., per. 8.95 *(978-1-58830-628-9(3))* Metropolitan Teaching & Learning Co.

—Excursions Grade 4. 2003. (Voyages Ser.). (J). (gr. 4). stu. ed., per. 8.95 *(978-1-58830-629-6(1))* Metropolitan Teaching & Learning Co.

—Excursions Grade 5. 2003. (Voyages Ser.). (J). (gr. 5). stu. ed., per. 8.95 *(978-1-58830-630-2(5))* Metropolitan Teaching & Learning Co.

—Metro Math Voyages Kindergarten Kit Sp. 2004. (Voyages Ser.). (J). (gr. k). 474.75 *(978-1-58830-977-8(0))* Metropolitan Teaching & Learning Co.

—Voyages Gr 1 Student Kit Sp. 2004. (Voyages Ser.). (J). (gr. 1). 31.37 *(978-1-58830-980-8(0))* Metropolitan Teaching & Learning Co.

—Voyages Gr 2 Student Kit Sp. 2004. (Voyages Ser.). (J). (gr. 2). 31.37 *(978-1-58830-981-5(9))* Metropolitan Teaching & Learning Co.

—Voyages Gr 3 Student Kit Sp. 2004. (Voyages Ser.). (J). (gr. 3). 31.37 *(978-1-58830-982-2(7))* Metropolitan Teaching & Learning Co.

—Voyages Grade 2 Complete Program Sp. 2005. (Voyages Ser.). (J). (gr. 2). 758.67 *(978-1-58830-868-9(5))* Metropolitan Teaching & Learning Co.

—Voyages Grade 3 Complete Program Sp. 2005. (Voyages Ser.). (J). (gr. 3). 758.67 *(978-1-58830-869-6(3))* Metropolitan Teaching & Learning Co.

—Voyages Kinder Sp Activity Cards Deck a Sp. 2004. (Voyages Ser.). (J). (gr. k). 62.85 *(978-1-58830-974-7(6))* Metropolitan Teaching & Learning Co.

—Voyages Kinder Sp Activity Cards Deck B Sp. 2004. (Voyages Ser.). (J). (gr. k). 26.45 *(978-1-58830-973-0(8))* Metropolitan Teaching & Learning Co.

—Voyages Kinder Sp Student. 2004. (Voyages Ser.). (J). (gr. k). per., act. bk. ed. 13.73 *(978-1-58830-975-4(4))* Metropolitan Teaching & Learning Co.

Sornson, Bob. Math Moms & Dads Home Program: Developing Symbolic Math Skills for Ages 5 to 8. 2004. 10.00 *(978-0-9755415-1-7(X))* Early Learning Foundation, LLC.

Sornson, Robert. The Math Moms & Dads Home Program: Preschool & Kindergarten Level, for ages 3 to 6. 2004. *(978-0-9755415-0-0(1))* Early Learning Foundation, LLC.

Sort It Out! 2015. (Sort It Out! Ser.). (ENG.). 24p. (J). (gr. k-1). pap., pap., pap. 293.40 *(978-1-4824-3493-4(8))*; pap., pap., pap. 48.90 *(978-1-4824-3494-1(6))*; lib. bdg. 145.62 *(978-1-4824-2538-3(6)*, a4e15296-a0f7-4347-8dd6-9238685d9e1f) Stevens, Gareth Publishing LLLP.

Souviney, Randall. Solving Math Problems Kids Care About. 2nd ed. 2005. (Illus.). 140p. (YA). (gr. 9-14). per. 14.95 *(978-1-59647-061-3(5))* Good Year Bks.

Souviney, Randall J., et al. Mathematical Investigations, Bk. 3. 208p. (J). 24.95 net. *(978-0-86651-585-6(2)*, DS21145) Seymour, Dale Pubns.

Spangler, David. Mathematics Explorations. 2007. 112p. (gr. 6-10). per. 9.95 *(978-1-59647-254-9(5))* Good Year Bks.

Spanish TAKS MASTER Math, Gr. 5. 2004. (J). *(978-1-57022-473-7(0))* ECS Learning Systems, Inc.

Spanish TAKS MASTER Math, Gr. 6. 2004. (J). *(978-1-57022-501-7(X))* ECS Learning Systems, Inc.

Spanish TAKS MASTER Math Grade 3. 2004. *(978-1-57022-466-9(8))* ECS Learning Systems, Inc.

Spanish TAKS MASTER Math Grade 4. 2004. *(978-1-57022-467-6(6))* ECS Learning Systems, Inc.

Spooky Math. 2015. (Spooky Math Ser.: 6). (ENG.). 32p. (J). (gr. -1-3). lib. bdg. 159.60 *(978-1-62724-329-2(1))* Bearport Publishing Co., Inc.

Sports (Set), 8 vols. Incl. Baseball. Minden, Cecilia. (Illus.). lib. bdg. 32.07 *(978-1-60279-243-2(7)*, 200194); Basketball. Minden, Cecilia. (Illus.). lib. bdg. 32.07 *(978-1-60279-245-6(3)*, 200196); Football. Marsico, Katie. (Illus.). lib. bdg. 32.07 *(978-1-60279-247-0(X)*, 200198); Running. Marsico, Katie & Minden, Cecilia. (Illus.). lib. bdg. 32.07 *(978-1-60279-249-4(6)*, 200032); Soccer. Minden, Cecilia. (Illus.). lib. bdg. 32.07 *(978-1-60279-244-9(5)*, 200195); Speed Skating. Marsico, Katie. lib. bdg. 32.07 *(978-1-60279-250-0(X)*, 200128); Swimming. Minden, Cecilia. (Illus.). lib. bdg. 32.07 *(978-1-60279-246-3(1)*, 200197); Tennis. Marsico, Katie. (Illus.). lib. bdg. 32.07 *(978-1-60279-248-7(8)*, 200127); (gr. 4-8). (21st Century Skills Library: Real World Math Ser.). (ENG.). 32p. 2008. 256.56 *(978-1-60279-289-0(5)*, 200185) Cherry Lake Publishing.

Stamper, Claire. Color by Numbers: Adding & Subtracting. 2018. (ENG.). 96p. (J). pap. 9.99 *(978-1-78828-514-8(X)*, 561a2604-4298-4e77-9c80-bac8ff0ec3e) Arcturus Publishing GBR. Dist: Baker & Taylor Publisher Services (BTPS).

Stanley, Anne, illus. Listen in Addition. 2007. (ENG.). 16p. (J). 16.99 *(978-0-9796150-0-9(3))* Jandie Jams Music LLC.

Stanley, Mandy. Arty Numbers: Early Learning Through Art. 2017. (Arty Mouse Wipe Clean with Pen Ser.). (ENG., Illus.). 24p. (J). (gr. -1-2). pap. 7.99 *(978-1-78445-865-2(1))* Top That! Publishing PLC GBR. Dist: Independent Pubs. Group.

STAR Math RP Norms Upgrade. 2004. cd-rom *(978-1-59455-183-3(9))* Renaissance Learning, Inc.

STAR Math RP Student Subscription. 2004. cd-rom 0.99 *(978-1-59455-180-2(4))* Renaissance Learning, Inc.

STAR Math RP Student Subscription Renewal. 2004. cd-rom *(978-1-59455-181-9(2))* Renaissance Learning, Inc.

STAR Math RP Subscription Package. 2004. cd-rom *(978-1-59455-178-9(2))* Renaissance Learning, Inc.

Starr, Will. Circus Math. 2008. 132p. pap. 38.95 *(978-1-4389-0836-6(9))* AuthorHouse.

Stckvagn. AC Ems Decimals & Percents. 2004. pap. *(978-0-7398-9858-1(2))* Harcourt Schl. Pubs.

—AC Ems Whole Numbers. 2004. pap. *(978-0-7398-9857-4(4))* Harcourt Schl. Pubs.

Steck-Vaughn Company, creator. Taste Like Math!, Grades K-6. 2011. (Fun Math Ser.). (ENG., Illus.). 128p. (J). (gr. k-6). pap. 16.99 *(978-0-547-62555-3(3))* Heinemann-Raintree.

Steck-Vaughn Staff. Applied Math Intermediate, 8 pack. 2004. pap. 68.00 *(978-0-7398-9930-4(9))*; pap. 8.50 *(978-0-7398-9849-9(3))* Harcourt Schl. Pubs.

—Applied Math Introductory. 2004. pap. 8.50 *(978-0-7398-9853-6(1))* Harcourt Schl. Pubs.

—Applied Math Introductory 8-Pack. 2004. pap. 68.00 *(978-0-7398-9934-2(1))* Harcourt Schl. Pubs.

—At-Home Workbooks: Division. 2004. (Illus.). pap., wbk. ed. *(978-0-7398-8532-1(4))* Steck-Vaughn.

—At-Home Workbooks: Multiplication. 2004. (Illus.). (J). pap., wbk. ed. 5.99 *(978-0-7398-8531-4(6))* Steck-Vaughn.

—At-Home Workbooks: Subtraction. 2004. (Illus.). pap., wbk. ed. *(978-0-7398-8534-5(0))* Steck-Vaughn.

—Computational & Applied Mathematics. 2004. pap. 8.50 *(978-0-7398-9846-8(9))*;8 Pack. pap. 68.00 *(978-0-7398-9927-4(9))* Harcourt Schl. Pubs.

—Early Math: 2 Digit Addition & Subtraction. 2005. pap. 2.99 *(978-1-4190-0332-5(1))* Steck-Vaughn.

—Early Math: 2 Digit Addition with Regrouping. 2005. pap. 2.99 *(978-1-4190-0333-2(X))* Steck-Vaughn.

—Early Math: Mixed Operations. 2005. pap. 2.99 *(978-1-4190-0326-4(7))* Steck-Vaughn.

—Early Math: Money I. 2005. pap. 2.99 *(978-1-4190-0328-8(3))*; pap. 29.95 *(978-1-4190-0352-3(6))* Steck-Vaughn.

—Early Math: Money II. 2005. pap. 2.99 *(978-1-4190-0338-7(0))*; pap. 29.95 *(978-1-4190-0362-2(3))* Steck-Vaughn.

—Early Math: Problem Solving I, 10 Pack. 2005. pap. 29.95 *(978-1-4190-0355-4(0))*; pap. 2.99 *(978-1-4190-0331-8(3))* Steck-Vaughn.

—Early Math: Problem Solving II. 2005. pap. 2.99 *(978-1-4190-0341-7(0))*; pap. 29.95 *(978-1-4190-0365-3(8))* Steck-Vaughn.

—Early Math: Readiness. 2005. pap. 2.99 *(978-1-4190-0318-9(6))*; pap. 29.95 *(978-1-4190-0342-4(9))* Steck-Vaughn.

—Early Math: Readiness for Problem Solving. 2005. pap. 2.99 *(978-1-4190-0321-9(6))*; pap. 29.95 *(978-1-4190-0345-5(3))* Steck-Vaughn.

—Early Math: Time I, 10 Pack. 2005. pap. 29.95 *(978-1-4190-0351-6(8))* Steck-Vaughn.

—Early Math: Time II, 10 Pack. 2005. pap. 29.95 *(978-1-4190-0361-5(5))* Steck-Vaughn.

—Focus on Math Level C: Decimals. 2005. pap. 2.99 *(978-1-4190-0268-7(6))* Harcourt Schl. Pubs.

—Focus on Math Level C: Problem Solving. 2005. pap. 2.99 *(978-1-4190-0271-7(6))* Harcourt Schl. Pubs.

—Focus on Math Level C 10-pack: Decimals. 2005. pap. 29.95 *(978-1-4190-0292-2(9))* Harcourt Schl. Pubs.

—Focus on Math Level C 10-pack: Problem Solving. 2005. pap. 29.95 *(978-1-4190-0295-3(3))* Harcourt Schl. Pubs.

—Focus on Math Level D: Decimals. 2005. pap. 2.99 *(978-1-4190-0274-8(0))* Harcourt Schl. Pubs.

—Focus on Math Level D: Measurement. 2005. pap. 2.99 *(978-1-4190-0275-5(9))* Harcourt Schl. Pubs.

—Focus on Math Level D: Mixed Operations. 2005. pap. 2.99 *(978-1-4190-0272-4(4))* Harcourt Schl. Pubs.

—Focus on Math Level D: Problem Solving. 2005. pap. 2.99 *(978-1-4190-0277-9(5))* Harcourt Schl. Pubs.

—Focus on Math Level D 10-pack: Decimals. 2005. pap. 29.95 *(978-1-4190-0298-4(8))* Harcourt Schl. Pubs.

—Focus on Math Level D 10-pack: Measurement. 2005. pap. 29.95 *(978-1-4190-0299-1(6))* Harcourt Schl. Pubs.

—Focus on Math Level D 10-pack: Problem Solving. 2005. pap. 29.95 *(978-1-4190-0301-1(1))* Harcourt Schl. Pubs.

—Focus on Math Level E: Decimals. 2005. pap. 2.99 *(978-1-4190-0279-3(1))* Harcourt Schl. Pubs.

—Focus on Math Level E: Mixed Operations. 2005. pap. 2.99 *(978-1-4190-0278-6(3))* Harcourt Schl. Pubs.

—Focus on Math Level E: Problem Solving. 2005. pap. 2.99 *(978-1-4190-0283-0(X))* Harcourt Schl. Pubs.

—Focus on Math Level E: Ratio Percent. 2005. pap. 2.99 *(978-1-4190-0282-3(1))* Harcourt Schl. Pubs.

—Focus on Math Level E 10-pack: Decimals. 2005. pap. 29.95 *(978-1-4190-0303-5(8))* Harcourt Schl. Pubs.

—Focus on Math Level E 10-pack: Problem Solving. 2005. pap. 29.95 *(978-1-4190-0307-3(0))* Harcourt Schl. Pubs.

—Focus on Math Level F: Problem Solving. 2005. pap. 2.99 *(978-1-4190-0288-5(0))* Harcourt Schl. Pubs.

—Focus on Math Level F 10-pack: Problem Solving. 2005. pap. 29.95 *(978-1-4190-0312-7(7))* Harcourt Schl. Pubs.

—Grade Level Math. 2005. (gr. 5). pap. 14.99 *(978-0-7398-9941-0(4))*; (gr. 6). pap. 14.99 *(978-0-7398-9942-7(2))* Steck-Vaughn.

—Hey Theres Math in My Literature. 2004. (Illus.). (J). pap. 12.99 *(978-0-7398-8474-4(3))* Steck-Vaughn.

—Just-a-Minute Math: Build Math Strength Through Timed Drills. 2003. (Just-A-Minute Math Ser.). (ENG.). 224p. (gr. 1-8). pap. 23.99 *(978-0-7398-7940-5(5))* Houghton Mifflin Harcourt Publishing Co.

—Looking for Patterns. 2003. pap. 4.10 *(978-0-7398-7659-6(7))* Steck-Vaughn.

—Mastering Math. 2004. (Steck-Vaughn Mastering Math Ser.). (ENG.). 160p. (gr. 4-4). pap. 25.70 *(978-0-7398-9203-9(7))*; 176p. (gr. 6-6). pap. 25.70 *(978-0-7398-9205-3(3))*; (Illus.). 48p. (gr. 1-1). pap. 11.90 *(978-0-7398-9206-0(1))*; (Illus.). 48p. (gr. 2-2). pap. 11.90 *(978-0-7398-9207-7(X))*; (Illus.). 48p. (gr. 3-3). pap. 11.90 *(978-0-7398-9208-4(8))*; (Illus.). 48p. (gr. 4-4). pap. 11.90 *(978-0-7398-9209-1(6))*; (Illus.). 48p. (gr. 5-5). pap. 11.90 *(978-0-7398-9210-7(X))*;Level C. 160p. (gr. 3-3). pap. 25.70 *(978-0-7398-9202-2(9))*;Level A. 160p. (gr. 1-1). pap., stu. ed. 25.70 *(978-0-7398-9200-8(2))*;Level B. 160p. (gr. 2-2). pap. 25.70 *(978-0-7398-9201-5(0))*;Level E. 176p. (gr. 5-5). pap. 25.70 *(978-0-7398-9204-6(5))* Houghton Mifflin Harcourt Publishing Co.

—Mastering Math, Level F. 2004. (Steck-Vaughn Mastering Math Ser.). (ENG., Illus.). 48p. (gr. 6-6). pap. 11.90 *(978-0-7398-9211-4(8))* Houghton Mifflin Harcourt Publishing Co.

—Math: Data Analysis & Statistics. 2004. pap. 5.00 *(978-0-7398-9844-4(2))* Harcourt Schl. Pubs.

—Math 10-Pack: Data, Analysis & Statistics. 2004. pap. 44.95 *(978-0-7398-9925-0(2))* Harcourt Schl. Pubs.

—Math Computation Intermediate. 2004. pap. 8.50 *(978-0-7398-9850-5(7))* Harcourt Schl. Pubs.

—Math Computation Intermediate 8-Pack. 2004. pap. 68.00 *(978-0-7398-9931-1(7))* Harcourt Schl. Pubs.

—Math Computation Introductory. 2004. pap. 8.50 *(978-0-7398-9854-3(X))* Harcourt Schl. Pubs.

—That Makes Ten! 2003. pap. 4.10 *(978-0-7398-7656-5(2))* Steck-Vaughn.

—Top Line Math: Probability. 2005. pap. 5.49 *(978-1-4190-0374-5(7))* Steck-Vaughn.

—Top Line Math: Proportions. 2005. pap. 5.49 *(978-1-4190-0369-1(0))* Harcourt Schl. Pubs.

—Top Line Math: Special Topics in Math. 2005. pap., tchr. ed. 5.95 *(978-1-4190-0385-1(2))* Harcourt Schl. Pubs.

—Top Line Math: Special Topics in Math. 2005. pap. 5.49 *(978-1-4190-0375-2(5))* Steck-Vaughn.

—Top Line Math: Tables & Maps. 2005. pap., tchr. ed. 5.95 *(978-1-4190-0381-3(X))* Harcourt Schl. Pubs.

Steck-Vaughn Staff, creator. Test Fundamentals Math Computation: Basic. 2004. (Illus.). pap. 68.00 *(978-0-7398-9935-9(X))* Harcourt Schl. Pubs.

Steffora, Tracey. Animal Math: Adding, Taking Away, & Skip Counting, 1 vol. 2014. (Animal Math Ser.). (ENG.). 32p. (J). (gr. -1-1). 29.99 *(978-1-4846-0061-0(4)*, Heinemann) Capstone.

—Math Around Us, 7 vols., Set. Incl. Counting in the City. pap. 6.29 *(978-1-4329-4929-7(2)*, 114829); Measuring in the Garden. pap. 6.29 *(978-1-4329-4934-1(9)*, 114835); Patterns at the Museum. pap. 6.29 *(978-1-4329-4931-0(4)*, 114830); Shapes in the Kitchen. pap. 6.29 *(978-1-4329-4930-3(6)*, 114832); Sorting at the Market. pap. 6.29 *(978-1-4329-4935-8(7)*, 114834); Using Addition at Home. pap. 6.29 *(978-1-4329-4932-7(2)*, 114831); Using Subtraction at the Park. pap. 6.29 *(978-1-4329-4933-4(0)*, 114833); (J). (gr. -1-1). (Math Around Us Ser.). (ENG.). 24p. 2011. pap., pap., pap. 44.03 *(978-1-4329-4936-5(5)*, 15881); 139.92 o.p. *(978-1-4329-4928-0(4)*, 15880) Capstone. (Heinemann).

—Math at the Hospital, 1 vol. 2013. (Math on the Job Ser.). (ENG., Illus.). 24p. (J). (gr. k-2). pap. 6.29 *(978-1-4329-7159-5(X)*, 121169, Heinemann) Capstone.

Stetson, Raymond. Math Mage: A Position in Addition, 1 vol. 2010. 40p. pap. 24.95 *(978-1-4489-7976-9(5))* PublishAmerica, Inc.

Stewart, Rhea A. Math in Real World Set, 10 Volumes. 2009. (Math in the Real World Ser.). (ENG.). 277p. (gr. 4-6). 280.00 *(978-1-60413-828-3(9)*, P466918, Chelsea Clubhse.) Infobase Holdings, Inc.

Stites, Ranae & Buethe, Amanda. Cooperative Mathematics. 2008. (J). per. 29.00 *(978-1-879097-36-0(2))* Kagan Publishing.

Stockland, Patricia M. Loops: Repeat, Repeat! Sanchez, Sr., illus. 2018. (Code It! Ser.). (ENG.). 24p. (C). (gr. 1-3). lib. bdg. 33.99 *(978-1-68410-390-4(8)*, 140365) Cantata Learning.

The Story of Math: Core Principles of Mathematics, 12 vols. 2014. (Story of Math Ser.). (ENG.). (YA). (gr. 8-8). lib. bdg. 205.74 *(978-1-62275-536-3(7)*, 9109e947-d308-43a9-b8b9-6421e552b204, Britannica Educational Publishing) Rosen Publishing Group, Inc., The.

Stosch, Dawn. Science Math, 1 vol. 2009. (Math Alive! Ser.). (ENG.). 32p. (gr. 4-4). lib. bdg. 31.21 *(978-0-7614-3213-5(2)*, 1bc024e4-895e-47f2-b8a6-27b25f284992) Cavendish Square Publishing LLC.

Stowasser, Peter & Burnett, James. Cupcake Capers: A Book about Take-Away Subtraction. 2012. (J). *(978-1-921959-27-1(4))* Origo Education.

Strazzabosco, John. Mathematical Thinking Reasoning & Proof, 1 vol. 2003. (BrainBuilders Ser.). (ENG.). 48p. (gr. k-4). pap. 5.25 *(978-1-4042-8522-4(9)*, cc8e4892-fa25-4b99-9fb1-4a7cb607c286) Rosen Publishing Group, Inc., The.

Stuart, Carrie. Kinds of Coins: Learning the Values of Pennies, Nickels, Dimes & Quarters, 1 vol. 2010. (Math for the REAL World Ser.). (ENG.). 12p. (gr. 1-2). pap. 5.90 *(978-0-8239-8862-4(7)*, 836dd74b-cf85-4f50-8582-6d952d0ad3a1, Rosen Classroom) Rosen Publishing Group, Inc., The.

Stuart, Colin. Fabulous Figures & Cool Calculations. 2018. (STEM Quest Ser.). lib. bdg. 22.10 *(978-0-606-41262-9(X))* Turtleback.

Stuart, Liam. The Parade: Understand Place Value, 1 vol. 2013. (Rosen Math Readers Ser.). (ENG., Illus.). 24p. (J). (gr. 1-1). pap. 8.25 *(978-1-4777-2070-7(7)*, bc1b410c-1e32-4f82-8000-f19cbb0356f9, Rosen Classroom) Rosen Publishing Group, Inc., The.

Suen, Anastasia. Top STEM Careers in Science, 1 vol. 2014. (Cutting-Edge STEM Careers Ser.). (ENG., Illus.). 128p. (J). (gr. 9-9). 38.80 *(978-1-4777-7664-3(8)*, 37125832-da8b-4594-8b87-788b3b896c8c) Rosen Publishing Group, Inc., The.

Sugiyama, Yoshishige, ed. Tokyo Shoseki's Mathematics for Elementary School (Grades 1 - 6 set, 11 vol. Set), 11 vols. 2006. Orig. Title: Atarashii Sansuu 1. (Illus.). pap. 129.55 *(978-1-934046-00-5(0))* Global Education Resources, LLC.

Sulley, Robert. First Aid in Mathematics. 2010. (ENG.). 208p. pap. 17.95 *(978-1-4441-1658-8(4))* Hodder Education Group GBR. Dist: Trans-Atlantic Pubns., Inc.

Sullivan. Test Bank to Accompany Finite Mathematics: An Appl led Approach, Ninth Edition. 9th ed. 2004. (YA). *(978-0-471-44821-1(4))* Wiley, John & Sons, Inc.

Sullivan, Erin. Mathematical Thinkers & Los Matemáticos: 6 English, 6 Spanish Adaptations, 122 vols., Vol. 2. 2011. (Navigators Ser.). (ENG & SPA.). (J). instr.'s gde. ed. 97.00 net. *(978-1-4108-1773-0(3)*, 17733) Benchmark Education Co.

—Sports Math & Matemáticas en los Deportes: 6 English, 6 Spanish Adaptations, 122 vols., Vol. 2. 2011. (Navigators Ser.). (J). instr.'s gde. ed. 97.00 net. *(978-1-4108-1774-7(1)*, 17741) Benchmark Education Co.

Sullivan, Erin Ash. The Class Election: Set Of 6. 2010. (Early Connections Ser.). (J). pap. 37.00 net. *(978-1-4108-1085-4(2))* Benchmark Education Co.

—Human Body Math: Set Of 6. 2010. (Navigators Ser.). (J). 44.00 net. *(978-1-4108-0408-2(9))* Benchmark Education Co.

—Human Body Math & Matemáticas del cuerpo Humano: 6 English, 6 Spanish Adaptations. 2011. (ENG & SPA.). (J). 89.00 net. *(978-1-4108-5682-1(8))* Benchmark Education Co.

—Math Around the Globe: Set Of 6. 2011. (Navigators Ser.). (J). pap. 48.00 net. *(978-1-4108-0417-4(8))* Benchmark Education Co.

—Math Around the Globe & Matemáticas alrededor del Mundo: 6 English, 6 Spanish Adaptations. 2011. (ENG & SPA.). (J). 97.00 net. *(978-1-4108-5689-0(5))* Benchmark Education Co.

—Math at the Olympics: Set Of 6. 2011. (Navigators Ser.). (J). 48.00 net. *(978-1-4108-0433-4(X))* Benchmark Education Co.

—Math at the Olympics & Matemáticas en las Olimpiadas: 6 English, 6 Spanish Adaptations. 2011. (ENG & SPA.). (J). 97.00 net. *(978-1-4108-5707-1(7))* Benchmark Education Co.

—Math in a Democracy: Set Of 6. 2011. (Navigators Ser.). (J). pap. 48.00 net. *(978-1-4108-0437-2(2))* Benchmark Education Co.

—Math in a Democracy & Matemáticas en una Democracia: 6 English, 6 Spanish Adaptations. 2011. (ENG & SPA.). (J). 97.00 net. *(978-1-4108-5715-6(8))* Benchmark Education Co.

—Metric Math: Set Of 6. 2011. (Navigators Ser.). (J). pap. 44.00 net. *(978-1-4108-0414-3(3))* Benchmark Education Co.

—Metric Math & Matemáticas Métricas: 6 English, 6 Spanish Adaptations. 2011. (ENG & SPA.). (J). 89.00 net. *(978-1-4108-5681-4(X))* Benchmark Education Co.

—Music Counts: Set Of 6. 2011. (Navigators Ser.). (J). 44.00 net. *(978-1-4108-0405-1(4))* Benchmark Education Co.

—Patterns in Nature: Set Of 6. 2010. (Early Connections Ser.). (J). pap. 37.00 net. *(978-1-4108-1079-3(8))* Benchmark Education Co.

Sundance/Newbridge LLC Staff. From Circles to Cubes. 2004. (Reading PowerWorks Ser.). (gr. 1-3). 37.50 *(978-0-7608-7839-2(0))*; pap. 6.10 *(978-0-7608-7840-8(4))* Sundance/Newbridge Educational Publishing.

—Make a Good Guess. 2004. (Reading PowerWorks Ser.). (gr. 1-3). 37.50 *(978-0-7608-9317-3(9))*; pap. 6.10 *(978-0-7608-9318-0(7))* Sundance/Newbridge Educational Publishing.

—Parts of a Whole. 2004. (Reading PowerWorks Ser.). (gr. 1-3). 37.50 *(978-0-7608-9293-0(8))*; pap. 6.10 *(978-0-7608-9294-7(6))* Sundance/Newbridge Educational Publishing.

Super Achievement. Math Magic Workbook. 2007. (Illus.). 88p. per. 16.99 *(978-0-9799545-1-7(7)*, Gatekeeper Pr.) Magic Works Publishing & Production.

Super Achievement, creator. Multimagic Table. 2007. (Illus.). 2p. 9.97 *(978-0-9799545-0-4(9))* Magic Works Publishing & Production.

Swain, Cynthia. Sorting at the Park. 2006. (Early Explorers Ser.). (J). pap. *(978-1-4108-6036-1(1))* Benchmark Education Co.

Swann, Kristina. Meaningful Math. 2005. (YA). ring bd. 49.95 *(978-1-58804-402-0(5))* P C I Education.

Swenson, Julie. High-Speed Trains: Use Place Value Understanding & Properties of Operations to Add & Subtract, 1 vol. 2014. (Rosen Math Readers Ser.). (ENG.). 24p. (J). (gr. 2-2). pap. 8.25 *(978-1-4777-4759-9(1)*, dd8c5e77-8118-4f86-ad5b-a5a7bb90268a, Rosen Classroom) Rosen Publishing Group, Inc., The.

Tabletop Pocket Chart Addition & Subtraction Card Set. 2004. (J). 8.95 *(978-1-56911-170-3(7))* Learning Resources, Inc.

TAKS MASTER Power Practice, Math Gr. 3. 2004. (J). *(978-1-57022-535-2(4))* ECS Learning Systems, Inc.

TAKS MASTER Power Practice, Math Gr. 4. 2004. (J). *(978-1-57022-536-9(2))* ECS Learning Systems, Inc.

TAKS MASTER Power Practice, Math Gr. 5. 2004. (J). *(978-1-57022-537-6(0))* ECS Learning Systems, Inc.

TAKS MASTER Power Practice, Math Gr. 6. 2004. (J). *(978-1-57022-538-3(9))* ECS Learning Systems, Inc.

TAKS MASTER Power Practice, Math Gr. 7. 2004. (J). *(978-1-57022-539-0(7))* ECS Learning Systems, Inc.

TAKS MASTER Power Practice, Math Gr. 8. 2004. (YA). *(978-1-57022-540-6(0))* ECS Learning Systems, Inc.

TAKS MASTER Practice Test Math, Gr. 3. 2004. (J). *(978-1-57022-474-4(9))* ECS Learning Systems, Inc.

TAKS MASTER Practice Test Math, Gr. 4. 2004. (J). *(978-1-57022-516-1(8))* ECS Learning Systems, Inc.

TAKS MASTER Practice Test Math, Gr. 5. 2004. (J). *(978-1-57022-517-8(6))* ECS Learning Systems, Inc.

TAKS MASTER Practice Test Math, Gr. 6. 2004. (J). *(978-1-57022-518-5(4))* ECS Learning Systems, Inc.

TAKS MASTER Practice Test Math, Gr. 7. 2004. (J). *(978-1-57022-519-2(2))* ECS Learning Systems, Inc.

TAKS MASTER Practice Test Math, Gr. 8. 2004. (YA). *(978-1-57022-520-8(6))* ECS Learning Systems, Inc.

TAKS Mathematics Preparation Grade 1. 2004. (Region IV ESC Resources for Mathematics Ser.). (J). (gr. 1). stu. ed., per., wbk. ed. *(978-1-932524-51-2(7))* Region 4 Education Service Ctr.

TAKS Mathematics Preparation Grade 1- Spanish. 2004. (SPA.). stu. ed., per., wbk. ed. *(978-1-932524-81-9(9))* Region 4 Education Service Ctr.

TAKS Mathematics Preparation Grade 10. 2004. (Region IV ESC Resources for Mathematics Ser.). stu. ed., per., wbk. ed. *(978-1-932524-60-4(6))* Region 4 Education Service Ctr.

TAKS Mathematics Preparation Grade 11 Exit. 2003. (Region IV ESC Resources for Mathematics Ser.). stu. ed., per., wbk. ed. *(978-1-932524-61-1(4))* Region 4 Education Service Ctr.

TAKS Mathematics Preparation Grade 2. 2004. (Region IV ESC Resources for Mathematics Ser.). (gr. 2). stu. ed., per., wbk. ed. *(978-1-932524-52-9(5))* Region 4 Education Service Ctr.

TAKS Mathematics Preparation Grade 2 - Spanish. 2004. (SPA.). stu. ed., per. *(978-1-932524-82-6(7))* Region 4 Education Service Ctr.

TAKS Mathematics Preparation Grade 3. 2004. (Region IV ESC Resources for Mathematics Ser.). (J). (gr. 3). stu. ed., per., wbk. ed. *(978-1-932524-53-6(3))* Region 4 Education Service Ctr.

TAKS Mathematics Preparation Grade 3 - Spanish. 2004. (SPA.). stu. ed., per., wbk. ed. *(978-1-932524-83-3(5))* Region 4 Education Service Ctr.

TAKS Mathematics Preparation Grade 4. 2004. (Region IV ESC Resources for Mathematics Ser.). (J). (gr. 4). stu. ed., per., wbk. ed. *(978-1-932524-54-3(1))* Region 4 Education Service Ctr.

TAKS Mathematics Preparation Grade 4 - Spanish. 2004. (SPA.). stu. ed., per., wbk. ed. *(978-1-932524-84-0(3))* Region 4 Education Service Ctr.

TAKS Mathematics Preparation Grade 5. 2003. (Region IV ESC Resources for Mathematics Ser.). (J). (gr. 5). stu. ed., per., wbk. ed. *(978-1-932524-55-0(X))* Region 4 Education Service Ctr.

TAKS Mathematics Preparation Grade 5 - Spanish. 2004. (SPA.). per., wbk. ed. *(978-1-932524-85-7(1))* Region 4 Education Service Ctr.

TAKS Mathematics Preparation Grade 6. 2004. (Region IV ESC Resources for Mathematics Ser.). (J). (gr. 6). stu. ed., per., wbk. ed. *(978-1-932524-56-7(8))* Region 4 Education Service Ctr.

TAKS Mathematics Preparation Grade 7. 2004. (Region IV ESC Resources for Mathematics Ser.). (YA). (gr. 7). stu. ed., per., wbk. ed. *(978-1-932524-57-4(6))* Region 4 Education Service Ctr.

TAKS Mathematics Preparation Grade 8. 2003. (Region IV ESC Resources for Mathematics Ser.). stu. ed., per., wbk. ed. *(978-1-932524-58-1(4))* Region 4 Education Service Ctr.

TAKS Mathematics Preparation Grade 9. 2004. (Region IV ESC Resources for Mathematics Ser.). stu. ed., per., wbk. ed. *(978-1-932524-59-8(2))* Region 4 Education Service Ctr.

TAKS Mathematics Preparation Grade K. 2004. (Region IV ESC Resources for Mathematics Ser.). stu. ed., per., wbk. ed. *(978-1-932524-50-5(9))* Region 4 Education Service Ctr.

TAKS Mathematics Preparation Grade K - Spanish. 2004. (SPA.). stu. ed., per., wbk. ed. *(978-1-932524-80-2(0))* Region 4 Education Service Ctr.

Tallinda, Theodore. Math at Henry Ford's Factory: Identify & Explain Patterns in Arithmetic, 1 vol. 2014. (InfoMax Math Readers Ser.). (ENG.). 24p. (J). (gr. 3-3). pap. 8.25 *(978-1-4777-4684-4(6),* 51101cd1-924a-43c6-a7b6-31e1a8ed2e6f, Rosen Classroom) Rosen Publishing Group, Inc., The.

Tamambang, Andrew Tangang, et al. Mastering Mathematics Form 3 Student's Book: Volume 0, Part 0. 2007. pap. 6.00 *(978-0-521-70145-7(7))* Cambridge Univ. Pr.

Tang, Greg. Math for All Seasons. Briggs, Harry, illus. 2005. (Scholastic Bookshelf Ser.). (ENG.). 40p. (J). (gr. -1-3). pap. 6.99 *(978-0-439-75537-5(9),* Scholastic Paperbacks) Scholastic, Inc.

Tangang Tamambang, Andrew, et al. Mastering Mathematics Form 1 Student's Book. 2008. pap., stu. ed. 4.00 *(978-0-521-69301-1(2))* Cambridge Univ. Pr.

—Mastering Mathematics Form 2 Student's Book. 2008. pap., stu. ed. 6.00 *(978-0-521-69300-4(4))* Cambridge Univ. Pr.

Tastes Like Math. 2003. (J). pap., stu. ed. 10.95 *(978-1-58123-341-4(8))* Larson Learning, Inc.

Tate, Kelly. Selling Popcorn: Understand Place Value. 2013. (InfoMax Math Readers Ser.). (ENG.). 24p. (J). (gr. 1-2). pap. 49.50 *(978-1-4777-2196-4(7));* (Illus.). pap. 8.25 *(978-1-4777-2195-7(9),* f94794a6-b970-4afc-8195-da3f67e56c1f) Rosen Publishing Group, Inc., The. (Rosen Classroom).

Taylor-Butler, Christine. A True Book - Information Literacy: Understanding Diagrams. 2012. (True Book: Information Literacy Ser.). (ENG.). 48p. (J). (gr. 3-5). lib. bdg. 21.19 *(978-0-531-26009-8(7),* Children's Pr.) Scholastic Library Publishing.

TestSMART Plus Math Processes, Level B-1. 2004. (J). *(978-1-57022-507-9(9))* ECS Learning Systems, Inc.

TestSMART Plus Math Processes, Level B-2. 2004. (J). *(978-1-57022-508-6(7))* ECS Learning Systems, Inc.

TestSMART Plus Math Processes, Level C. 2004. (J). *(978-1-57022-509-3(5))* ECS Learning Systems, Inc.

TestSMART Plus Math Processes, Level D. 2004. (J). *(978-1-57022-510-9(9))* ECS Learning Systems, Inc.

TestSMART Plus Math Processes, Level E. 2004. (J). *(978-1-57022-511-6(7))* ECS Learning Systems, Inc.

TestSMART Plus Math Processes, Level F. 2004. (J). *(978-1-57022-512-3(5))* ECS Learning Systems, Inc.

TestSMART Plus Math Processes, Level G. 2004. (J). *(978-1-57022-513-0(3))* ECS Learning Systems, Inc.

TestSMART Plus Math Processes, Level H. 2004. (J). *(978-1-57022-514-7(1))* ECS Learning Systems, Inc.

TestSMART Plus Math Processes, Level I. 2004. (YA). *(978-1-57022-515-4(X))* ECS Learning Systems, Inc.

TestSMART Plus Numeration, Level A-1. 2004. (J). *(978-1-57022-522-2(2))* ECS Learning Systems, Inc.

TestSMART Plus Numeration, Level A-2. 2004. (J). *(978-1-57022-523-9(0))* ECS Learning Systems, Inc.

TestSMART Plus Numeration, Level B. 2004. (J). *(978-1-57022-524-6(9))* ECS Learning Systems, Inc.

TestSmart Plus Numeration Level C/D. 2004. (J). *(978-1-57022-525-3(7))* ECS Learning Systems, Inc.

TestSmart Plus Numeration Level E/F. 2004. (J). *(978-1-57022-526-0(5))* ECS Learning Systems, Inc.

TestSmart Plus Numeration Level G/H. 2004. (J). *(978-1-57022-527-7(3))* ECS Learning Systems, Inc.

TestSMART Plus Whole Numbers, Level A. 2004. (J). *(978-1-57022-488-1(9))* ECS Learning Systems, Inc.

The Learning Company, The Learning. Learning with Curious George Pre-K Math. 2012. (Learning with Curious George Ser.). (ENG., Illus.). 64p. (J). (gr. -1-3). pap. 6.99 *(978-0-547-79055-8(4),* 1492952, Clarion Bks.) HarperCollins Pubs.

Thomas, Mary Ann. Our Train Trip: Learning to Add Times by the Half Hour, 1 vol. 2010. (Math for the REAL World Ser.). (ENG.). 12p. (gr. 1-2). pap. 5.90 *(978-0-8239-8849-5(X),* f80b45b5-a444-45e0-b417-6675e2a6d2a8, Rosen Classroom) Rosen Publishing Group, Inc., The.

Thomas, Penny M. Powwow Counting in Cree. Josie, Melinda, illus. 2013. (ENG.). 24p. (J). (gr. -1-k). 19.95 *(978-1-55379-392-2(7),* 9781553793922, HighWater Pr.) Portage & Main Pr. CAN. Dist: Orca Bk. Pubs. USA.

Thompson, Helen. Shopping Math. 2013. (Math 24/7 Ser.: 10). 48p. (J). (gr. 5-18). 19.95 *(978-1-4222-2908-8(4))* Mason Crest.

—Understanding Business Math & Budgets. Madrian, Brigitte, ed. 2013. (Young Adult Library of Small Business & Finance Ser.: 10). 64p. (J). (gr. 7-18). 22.95 *(978-1-4222-2921-7(1))* Mason Crest.

Thompson, Veronica. Earth-Friendly Math Crafts. Thompson, Veronica, photos by. 2018. (Green STEAM Ser.). (ENG., Illus.). 32p. (J). (gr. 3-5). 29.32 *(978-1-5415-2419-4(5),* 7c033490-0ebf-4b98-a7d9-8a782e01c1f1, Lerner Pubns.) Lerner Publishing Group.

Three Bear Family: Addition & Subtraction Activity Book. 2003. (J). pap. 4.95 *(978-1-56911-103-1(0))* Learning Resources, Inc.

Three Bear Family: Matching & Sorting Activity Book. 2003. (J). pap. 4.95 *(978-1-56911-101-7(4))* Learning Resources, Inc.

The TI-108 Calculator, 30. 2004. (gr. k-6). suppl. ed. 202.50 *(978-0-201-23151-9(4));* suppl. ed. 74.25 *(978-0-201-23150-2(6))* Addison-Wesley Educational Pubs., Inc. (Scott Foresman).

Time & Money Skills (Gr. 1-2) 2003. (J). *(978-1-58232-082-3(9))* ECS Learning Systems, Inc.

Tiner, John Hudson. Exploring the World of Mathematics: From Ancient Record Keeping to the Latest Advances in Computers. 2004. (Sense of Wonder Ser.). 157p. pap. 16.99 *(978-0-89051-412-2(7),* 303-050, Master Books) New Leaf Publishing Group.

To Market, to Market. 2004. cd-rom 119.00 *(978-1-889775-52-4(5))* Learning in Motion.

Top That Publishing. Writing My First Sums. 2007. (Early Days Ser.). (Illus.). 10p. bds. *(978-1-84666-338-3(5))* Top That! Publishing PLC.

Torres Moliner, Isabel & Puche, Lola Soriano. Espacio Espacial. 2005. (In-genio Ser.). (Illus.). 47p. (J). (gr. 4-7). per. 14.95 *(978-84-95895-09-7(9))* Editorial Brief ESP. Dist: Independent Pubs. Group.

Torres Moliner, Isabel & Soriano Puche, Lola. Domino Domino. 2005. (In-genio Ser.). (Illus.). 48p. (J). (gr. 4-7). pap. 14.95 *(978-84-95895-01-1(3))* Editorial Brief ESP. Dist: Independent Pubs. Group.

Trumbauer, Lisa. Let's Graph, 6 vols., Set. 2003. (Yellow Umbrella Early Level Ser.). (ENG.). 16p. (gr. k-1). pap. 35.70 *(978-0-7368-3009-6(X),* Capstone Pr.) Capstone.

Twin Sisters(r) Staff & Thompson, Kim Mitzo. Subtraction. 2011. (J). (gr. k-1). audio compact disk 4.99 *(978-1-59922-567-8(0))* Twin Sisters IP, LLC.

Tyler, Misconish Darlene. Your World: Bubblegum: Addition & Subtraction (Grade 2) 2018. (Mathematics in the Real World Ser.). (ENG., Illus.). 32p. (J). (gr. 2-3). pap. 10.99 *(978-1-4258-5746-2(9))* Teacher Created Materials, Inc.

Uhl, Xina M. How STEM Built the Roman Empire, 1 vol. 2019. (How STEM Built Empires Ser.). (ENG.). 80p. (gr. 7-7). pap. 16.30 *(978-1-7253-4152-4(2),* aea2ce53-1be1-444e-b122-08dbb30985d4) Rosen Publishing Group, Inc., The.

Unswood, Cassie. Exploring Plane Figures: Understand Concepts of Area, 1 vol. 2014. (InfoMax Math Readers Ser.). (ENG.). 24p. (J). (gr. 3-3). pap. 8.25 *(978-1-4777-4594-6(7),* 6f5c981c-8563-406b-9740-a933c38c3b51, Rosen Classroom) Rosen Publishing Group, Inc., The.

Vamos a Agrupar Por... / Sort It Out!, 12 vols. 2015. (Vamos a Agrupar Por... / Sort It Out! Ser.). (ENG & SPA.). 24p. (J). (gr. k-1). lib. bdg. 145.62 *(978-1-4824-2976-3(4),* a794da95-62f0-427e-a176-15a523d98b79) Stevens, Gareth Publishing LLLP.

Van Horn, Stephanie. Math Rapmatics: Mathematical Rhymes Right on Time. Daniel, Rick, illus. 2011. 24p. (J). 18.00 *(978-0-9814945-9-3(5))* AK Classics, LLC.

Vanderbilt, Amy & Vanderbilt, Sabrina. Negative Nine: Book 1 of the Early Math Series. Vanderbilt, Amy, illus. 2008. (Illus.). 28p. (J). 14.99 *(978-0-7639-0719-8(7))* Trend Factor Pr.

VanVoorst, Jennifer. Can You Guess?, 6 vols., Set. 2003. (Yellow Umbrella Early Level Ser.). (ENG.). 16p. (gr. k-1). pap. 35.70 *(978-0-7368-3008-9(1),* Capstone Pr.) Capstone.

—Making Shapes, 6 vols., Set. 2003. (Yellow Umbrella Early Level Ser.). (ENG.). 16p. (gr. k-1). pap. 35.70 *(978-0-7368-3010-2(3),* Capstone Pr.) Capstone.

Vaughan, Susan. Let's Eat Lunch: Learning about Picture Graphs, 1 vol. 2010. (Math for the REAL World Ser.). (ENG., Illus.). 8p. (gr. k-1). pap. 5.15 *(978-0-8239-8885-3(6),* fe902c39-27d2-4222-be19-392f1f264f8a) Rosen Publishing Group, Inc., The.

Vaughn, Sydney. At the Track Meet: Understand Place Value, 1 vol. 2013. (InfoMax Math Readers Ser.). (ENG.). 24p. (J). (gr. 1-1). pap. 8.25 *(978-1-4777-2133-9(9),* b8c4d632-7645-4f57-b8dc-39f4120acc23); pap. 49.50 *(978-1-4777-2134-6(7))* Rosen Publishing Group, Inc., The. (Rosen Classroom).

Vedic Mathematics. 2003. per. *(978-0-9727877-0-3(4))* Consciousness-Based Education Association.

Velasquez, Maria. Pet Parade. Mooney, Alyssa, illus. 2007. (J). pap. 21.00 *(978-0-15-379895-5(5))* Houghton Mifflin Harcourt School Pubs.

Viajando a traves de los Numeros - America Aponte. 2005. 32.95 *(978-1-881744-70-2(1))* Editorial Panamericana, Inc.

Vicario, Evelyn. Mathematics for Life Practice Workbook - Kindergarten. 2013. (ENG.). 118p. (J). pap. 12.99 *(978-0-9826276-2-4(9),* Bibia Publishing) Bibia, LLC.

Vilsaint, Henock. Math Pack Bilingual English, Haitian Creole: PakMat. Date not set. (Illus.). 64p. (J). (gr. 1-3). wbk. ed. 5.50 *(978-1-881839-64-4(8))* Educa Vision Inc.

Virtual Math Tutor V2. 0: CD Installable. 2005. (YA). cd-rom 60.00 *(978-1-59807-032-3(0))* American Bk. Co.

Virtual Math Tutor V2. 0: CD Playable. 2005. (YA). cd-rom 60.00 *(978-1-59807-031-6(2))* American Bk. Co.

Visto, Joy. Where Does a Graph Go? (Making Math Work Ser.). (ENG.). 48p. (J). (gr. 4-7). 2016. pap. 12.00 *(978-1-62832-176-0(8),* 20915, Creative Paperbacks) 2015. (Illus.). *(978-1-60818-575-7(3),* 20914, Creative Education) Creative Co., The.

Walch Publishing Staff. Assessment Strategies for Math. 2003. 86p. 24.99 *(978-0-8251-4492-9(2))* Walch Education.

Walch Publishing Staff, creator. Math & Science. 2007. (Daily Warm-Ups Ser.). 204p. (gr. 5-6). tchr. ed., spiral bd. 24.99 *(978-0-8251-6447-7(8))* Walch Education.

Wall, Terry & Pimental, Ric. Checkpoint Mathematics, Vol. 3. 2005. (ENG., Illus.). 192p. pap. 36.50 *(978-0-340-81293-8(1),* Hodder Education) Hodder Education Group GBR. Dist: Trans-Atlantic Pubns., Inc.

Wall, Terry & Pimentel, Ric. Checkpoint Maths, Vol. 1. 2004. (ENG., Illus.). 180p. (YA). pap. 36.50 *(978-0-340-81295-2(8),* Hodder Education) Hodder Education Group GBR. Dist: Trans-Atlantic Pubns., Inc.

Wallace, Elise. Amazing Animals: World Record Wildlife: Adding & Subtracting Fractions (Grade 5) 2018. (Mathematics in the Real World Ser.). (ENG., Illus.). 32p. (J). (gr. 4-8). pap. 11.99 *(978-1-4258-5813-1(9))* Teacher Created Materials, Inc.

Ward, Lesley. Life in Numbers: What Is Average? 2018. (TIME(r): Informational Text Ser.). (ENG., Illus.). 48p. (J). (gr. 5-8). pap. 13.99 *(978-1-4258-4997-9(0))* Teacher Created Materials, Inc.

Warren, Sandra J. Times to Remember, the Fun & Easy Way to Memorize the Multiplication Tables: Home & Classroom Resources. Vasquez, Juan Jose, illus. 2012. 246p. pap. 19.95 *(978-0-9836580-1-6(3))* Joyful Learning Publications, LLC.

Warren, Sandra Jane. Times to Remember, the Fun & Easy Way to Memorize the Multiplication Tables. Vásquez, Juan José, illus. 2012. 86p. 24.95 *(978-0-9836580-0-9(5))* Joyful Learning Publications, LLC.

Watson, Hannah. Slide & See Taking Away Subtracting. 2017. (First Math Slide & See* Ser.). (ENG.). 10p. 14.99 *(978-0-7945-3962-7(9),* Usborne) EDC Publishing.

Watt, Fiona. Big Book of Sticker Math. Wells, Rachel, illus. 2008. (Usborne Sticker Math Ser.). 151p. (J). (gr. -1-3). pap. 12.99 *(978-0-7945-1825-7(7),* Usborne) EDC Publishing.

Watt, Fiona & Wells, Rachel. Numbers. 2004. (Usborne Sticker Math Ser.). (ENG., Illus.). 1p. (J). (gr. k-1). pap., act. bk. ed. 6.95 *(978-0-7460-3731-7(7))* EDC Publishing.

—Sticker Maths: Adding. 2004. (Usborne Sticker Math Ser.). (ENG., Illus.). 1p. (J). (gr. k-1). pap., act. bk. ed. 6.95 *(978-0-7460-3728-7(7))* EDC Publishing.

—Sticker Maths: Taking Away. 2004. (Usborne Sticker Math Ser.). (ENG., Illus.). 1p. (J). (gr. k-1). pap., act. bk. ed. 6.95 *(978-0-7460-3734-8(1))* EDC Publishing.

Weiss, Ellen. Math in the Car. 2007. (Scholastic News Nonfiction Readers Ser.). (ENG., Illus.). 24p. (J). (gr. 1-2). 22.00 *(978-0-531-18530-8(3))* Scholastic Library Publishing.

—Math in the Kitchen. 2007. (Scholastic News Nonfiction Readers Ser.). (ENG., Illus.). 24p. (J). (gr. 1-2). 22.00 *(978-0-531-18531-5(1))* Scholastic Library Publishing.

—Scholastic News Nonfiction Readers: Math in the Backyard. 2007. (Scholastic News Nonfiction Readers Ser.). (ENG., Illus.). 24p. (J). (gr. 1-2). 22.00 *(978-0-531-18529-2(X))* Scholastic Library Publishing.

—Scholastic News Nonfiction Readers: Math in the Neighborhood. 2007. (Scholastic News Nonfiction Readers Ser.). (ENG., Illus.). 24p. (J). (gr. 1-2). pap. 6.95 *(978-0-531-18785-2(3))* Scholastic Library Publishing.

—Scholastic News Nonfiction Readers: Math in the Neighbourhood. 2007. (Scholastic News Nonfiction Readers Ser.). (ENG., Illus.). 24p. (J). (gr. 1-2). 22.00 *(978-0-531-18532-2(X))* Scholastic Library Publishing.

Wells, Robert E. Can You Count to a Googol? 2012. (J). *(978-1-61913-144-6(7))* Weigl Pubs., Inc.

White, Billy. Kids & Money. 2009. pap. *(978-1-61623-010-4(X))* Independent Pub.

White, Nancy. Make a Pattern: A Content Area Reader-math. 2005. (Emergent/Early (Prek-2) Math Package Ser.). 12p. (gr. k-2). 25.20 *(978-0-8215-7822-3(7))* Sadlier, William H. Inc.

Whiteford, Rhona, et al. Complete Maths, 4 bks. in 1. (ENG., Illus.). 96p. (YA). pap. 15.99 *(978-0-340-71581-9(2))* Hodder & Stoughton GBR. Dist: Trafalgar Square Publishing.

Whitmore, Andre. Math Lingo Homework Helper. 2007. (ENG.). 162p. pap. 22.50 *(978-0-615-16443-4(9))* American World Publishing.

Whyte, Elizabeth. Making Tally Charts, 1 vol. 2014. (Graph It! Ser.). (ENG.). 24p. (J). (gr. 1-2). 24.27 *(978-1-4824-0844-7(9),* 2ec78831-9dff-46b7-9374-f2bc7c0e38dd) Stevens, Gareth Publishing LLLP.

Wilkinson, Colin, contrib. by. Using Math in Construction, 1 vol. 2017. (Math You Will Actually Use Ser.). (ENG.). 48p. (J). (gr. 5-5). pap. 12.75 *(978-1-4994-3852-9(4),* 28140327-a66c-45e1-b5fa-bebfd5bbc981, Rosen Central) Rosen Publishing Group, Inc., The.

William H. Sadlier Staff. Count with Me. 2005. (Mathematics Ser.). (gr. -1-1). 24.00 net. *(978-0-8215-8928-1(8))* Sadlier, William H. Inc.

—Counting Sheep. 2005. (Emergent/Early (Prek-2) Math Package Ser.). 12p. (gr. -1-1). 25.20 *(978-0-8215-7842-1(1))* Sadlier, William H. Inc.

—New Progress in Mathematics. 2003. (New Progress in Mathematics Ser.). (gr. 7-18). stu. ed. 48.00 net. *(978-0-8215-1677-5(9));* (gr. 8-18). stu. ed. 48.00 net. *(978-0-8215-1678-2(7))* Sadlier, William H. Inc.

—Over, under, Left, Right. 2005. (Emergent/Early (Prek-2) Math Package Ser.). 12p. (gr. -1-1). 25.20 *(978-0-8215-7844-5(8))* Sadlier, William H. Inc.

—Progress in Mathematics. 2006. (Progress in Mathematics 2006 Ser.). stu. ed., wbk. ed. 8.00 net. *(978-0-8215-8222-0(4));* pap., stu. ed. 31.00 net. *(978-0-8215-8202-2(X));* (gr. k-2). stu. ed. 8.00 net. *(978-0-8215-8220-6(8));* (gr. k-2). pap., stu. ed. 23.00 net. *(978-0-8215-8200-8(3));* (gr. 1-2). stu. ed. 8.00 net. *(978-0-8215-8221-3(6));* (gr. 1-2). pap., stu. ed. 31.00 net. *(978-0-8215-8201-5(1))* Sadlier, William H. Inc.

—Yes, You Can. 2005. (Mathematics Ser.). (gr. -1-1). 24.00 net. *(978-0-8215-8918-2(0))* Sadlier, William H. Inc.

—You Can Sort. 2005. (Emergent/Early (Prek-2) Math Package Ser.). 12p. (gr. -1-1). 25.20 *(978-0-8215-7841-4(3))* Sadlier, William H. Inc.

Williams, Rozanne. Little Number Stories Addition. 2017. (Learn-To-Read Ser.). (ENG., Illus.). (J). pap. 3.49 *(978-1-68310-234-2(7))* Pacific Learning, Inc.

—Little Number Stories Subtraction. 2017. (Learn-To-Read Ser.). (ENG., Illus.). (J). pap. 3.49 *(978-1-68310-235-9(5))* Pacific Learning, Inc.

Williams, Zachary & Snyder, Jane. Cleaning up the Park: Learning to Count by Fives, 1 vol. 2010. (Math for the REAL World Ser.). (ENG.). 12p. (gr. 1-2). pap. 5.90 *(978-0-8239-8892-1(9),* 96df70c3-fcda-4835-ad6a-1ec8dc30fa74, Rosen Classroom) Rosen Publishing Group, Inc., The.

Williams, Zella & Wingard-Nelson, Rebecca. Word Problems Using Addition & Subtraction, 1 vol. 2016. (Mastering Math Word Problems Ser.). (ENG., Illus.). 48p. (gr. 3-4). pap. 12.70 *(978-0-7660-8252-6(0),* f9a329e2-a738-49e9-b154-dc6f08f0c12c) Enslow Publishing, LLC.

Williamson, Brian. Comic Maths: Sue. 2012. 116p. pap. *(978-0-9561602-1-8(2))* Captain PapadopoulosPublishing Company, The.

Willoughby, Alana. Real Math Fourth Grade. (J). (gr. 4). stu. ed. *(978-0-8126-0504-4(7),* 60504) SRA/McGraw-Hill.

Willoughby, Stephen S., et al. Real Math. 2006. (Illus.). pap., stu. ed. 107.00 *(978-0-07-603002-6(4))* Open Court Publishing Co.

Wilson, Robert B. Learn it Fast! NJ ASK4 Math. 2005. per. 34.95 *(978-0-9772020-0-3(3))* Global Institute for Maximizing Potential, Incorporated.

Wingard-Nelson, Rebecca. Algebra & Pre-Algebra: It's Easy, 1 vol. 2014. (Easy Genius Math Ser.). (ENG.). 64p. (gr. 4-6). lib. bdg. 31.93 *(978-0-7660-4251-3(0),* 66fcb2a2-cf1b-4ee6-a9e3-f1a519b32953) Enslow Publishing, LLC.

—Data, Graphing, & Statistics Smarts!, 1 vol. 2011. (Math Smarts! Ser.). (ENG., Illus.). 64p. (gr. 5-6). pap. 11.53 *(978-1-59845-323-2(8),* f5075985-42ce-432c-ba69-856619864af3); lib. bdg. 31.93 *(978-0-7660-3942-1(0),* 13fb09e0-6e14-403e-9474-c8f2967c1598) Enslow Publishing, LLC.

—Geometry Word Problems: No Problem!, 1 vol. 2010. (Math Busters Word Problems Ser.). (ENG., Illus.). 64p. (gr. 5-6). lib. bdg. 31.93 *(978-0-7660-3368-9(6),* 76d03e28-e919-41af-8a06-1af1d2aeabcd) Enslow Publishing, LLC.

—Graphing & Probability Word Problems: No Problem!, 1 vol. 2010. (Math Busters Word Problems Ser.). (ENG., Illus.). 64p. (gr. 5-6). lib. bdg. 31.93 *(978-0-7660-3372-6(4),* a8d18b1e-ff99-457d-ac8f-40cc07ee2072) Enslow Publishing, LLC.

—I Can Do Money Word Problems, 1 vol. 2010. (I Like Money Math! Ser.). (ENG., Illus.). 24p. (gr. k-2). pap. 10.35 *(978-0-7660-3659-8(6),* bf4458b3-3d77-4a3d-94e8-119404a45788, Enslow Elementary); lib. bdg. 25.27 *(978-0-7660-3145-6(4),* 497d6c6b-0eac-4c93-8ecf-9e247c114949) Enslow Publishing, LLC.

—Math Measurement Word Problems: No Problem!, 1 vol. 2010. (Math Busters Word Problems Ser.). (ENG., Illus.). 64p. (J). (gr. 5-6). lib. bdg. 31.93 *(978-0-7660-3369-6(4),* 5fa65b33-7e64-4cba-8ef9-fece2b32d460) Enslow Publishing, LLC.

—Pre-Algebra & Algebra: Ace Your Math Test, 1 vol. 2012. (Ace Your Math Test Ser.). (ENG., Illus.). 104p. (gr. 5-6). 35.93 *(978-0-7660-3782-3(7),* 2df92484-c201-4357-8ac0-a23539880632) Enslow Publishing, LLC.

—Problem Solving & Word Problem Smarts!, 1 vol. 2011. (Math Smarts! Ser.). (ENG., Illus.). 64p. (gr. 5-6). pap. 11.53 *(978-1-59845-325-6(4),* 26e73e10-9768-4399-9dbe-54d2b24cb3ba); lib. bdg. 31.93 *(978-0-7660-3943-8(9),* 746cfda1-b97e-49a7-bea3-10dfe366bfe1) Enslow Publishing, LLC.

—Ready for Addition, 1 vol. 2014. (Ready for Math Ser.). (ENG., Illus.). 48p. (gr. 3-3). 27.93 *(978-0-7660-4245-2(6),* a7696b82-f847-4b04-abb8-191a5c2a7724); pap. 11.53 *(978-1-4644-0433-7(X),* 25b07b73-28d6-45ca-94c4-889a557dec65, Enslow Elementary) Enslow Publishing, LLC.

—Ready for Word Problems & Problem Solving, 1 vol. 2014. (Ready for Math Ser.). (ENG., Illus.). 48p. (gr. 3-3). 27.93 *(978-0-7660-4250-6(2),* f5ad4897-89f8-4556-b7c5-27c80b98636a); pap. 11.53 *(978-1-4644-0443-6(7),* 20a69110-6490-46b2-be9e-fe6b8234a0c1, Enslow Elementary) Enslow Publishing, LLC.

—Space Word Problems Starring Ratios & Proportions: Math Word Problems Solved, 1 vol. 2009. (Math Word Problems Solved Ser.). (ENG., Illus.). 48p. (gr. 3-3). lib. bdg. 27.93 *(978-0-7660-2921-7(2),* 9eb62bd7-e0d3-4e60-8bf7-6eda62318895) Enslow Publishing, LLC.

—Sports Word Problems Starring Decimals & Percents: Math Word Problems Solved, 1 vol. 2009. (Math Word Problems Solved Ser.). (ENG., Illus.). 48p. (gr. 3-3). lib. bdg. 27.93 *(978-0-7660-2920-0(4),* d845e50b-92c1-481e-bf3a-28192d8e1c13) Enslow Publishing, LLC.

Wise & Paco Dog's Multiplication Books. 2003. 3.99 *(978-0-915960-35-4(4))* Ebon Research Systems Publishing, LLC.

Witt, Joe & Gallaway, Kate. Managing Your Mathematics Classroom. 2005. 88p. 19.49 *(978-1-59318-484-1(0))* Cambium Education, Inc.

Woodford, Chris. Height, 1 vol. 2012. (Measure up Math Ser.). (ENG., Illus.). 32p. (J). (gr. 4-4). pap. 11.50 *(978-1-4339-7442-7(8),* f99422b7-d3d5-45ec-bf86-02b85f5ef0ff); lib. bdg. 29.27 *(978-1-4339-7441-0(X),* 06b6eff6-1b05-4353-b3d9-02c45be25562) Stevens, Gareth Publishing LLLP.

Woods, Mark. Top Score Math, 8 vols., Set. Incl. Ace! Tennis Facts & Stats. Owen, Ruth. lib. bdg. 29.27 *(978-1-4339-4986-9(5),* 50bda16d-ab8c-4787-b50f-1e0fc32ca3ab); Goal! Soccer Facts & Stats. Owen, Ruth. lib. bdg. 29.27 *(978-1-4339-5015-5(4),* 8b988238-466a-4044-9a40-5d1ad3ae6974); Xtreme! Extreme Sports Facts & Stats. lib. bdg. 29.27 *(978-1-4339-5020-9(0),* 50cb46ae-451f-470d-bfd2-e164982d9752); (J). (gr. 4-5). (Top Score Math Ser.). (ENG., Illus.). 32p. 2011. Set lib. bdg. 117.08 *(978-1-4339-5035-3(9),* 94a2eb92-ae6b-49eb-9a90-0f72c69db8a3, Gareth Stevens Learning Library) Stevens, Gareth Publishing LLLP.

—Xtreme! Owen, Ruth, illus. 2010. (Top Score Maths Ser.). 32p. pap. *(978-0-237-54282-5(X))* Evans Brothers, Ltd.

Woods, Mark & Owen, Ruth. Ace! 2010. (Top Score Maths Ser.). (Illus.). 32p. pap. *(978-0-237-54280-1(3))* Evans Brothers, Ltd.

—Goal! 2010. (Top Score Maths Ser.). (Illus.). 32p. pap. *(978-0-237-54279-5(X))* Evans Brothers, Ltd.

—Scrum! 2010. (Top Score Maths Ser.). (Illus.). 32p. pap. *(978-0-237-54281-8(1))* Evans Brothers, Ltd.

—Slam Dunk! 2010. (Top Score Maths Ser.). (Illus.). 32p. pap. *(978-0-237-54278-8(1))* Evans Brothers, Ltd.

Woods, Michael & Woods, Mary B. Ancient Computing Technology: From Abacuses to Water Clocks. 2011. (Technology in Ancient Cultures Ser.). (ENG.). 96p. (gr. 6-12). lib. bdg. 31.93 *(978-0-7613-6528-0(1))* Lerner Publishing Group.

World Almanac Puzzler Deck for Kids: Math (BoMC) World Almanac Deck: Math, 11-13. 2007. 9.95 *(978-0-8118-6243-1(7))* Chronicle Bks. LLC.

Wren, Coretta. Counting on God. 2006. 82p. (YA). per., act. bk. ed. *(978-0-9790934-0-1(6))* Know Me Pubn. LLC.

Wright, Joe. Math's Mate Orange: Student Pad. Tutos, Joanna, ed. McKenna, Lou, illus. 2013. 72p. pap. *(978-1-921535-55-0(5))* Educational Advantage Pty, Ltd, The.

Wright, Joseph B. Math's Mate Rose: Student Pad. Tutos, Joanna, ed. McKenna, Lou, illus. 2013. 72p. pap. *(978-1-921535-56-7(3))* Educational Advantage Pty, Ltd, The.

WRITE IT! Problem Solving with Numbers & Words, Grades 1-2. 2004. (J). per. 10.95 *(978-1-58123-363-6(9))* Larson Learning, Inc.

WRITE IT! Problem Solving with Numbers & Words Grades 3-4 SE. 2004. (J). per. 10.95 *(978-1-58123-361-2(2))* Larson Learning, Inc.

WRITE IT! Problem Solving with Numbers & Words, Grades 5-6. 2004. (J). per. 10.95 *(978-1-58123-365-0(5))* Larson Learning, Inc.

WRITE IT! Problem Solving with Numbers & Words, Grades 7-8. 2004. (J). per. 10.95 *(978-1-58123-367-4(1))* Larson Learning, Inc.

Wunderlich, Richard. Math on the Job. 2016. (ENG., Illus.). 32p. (J). lib. bdg. *(978-0-7787-2360-8(7))* Crabtree Publishing Co.

Wunderlich, Rick. Math on the Job: Building a Business. 2016. (ENG., Illus.). 32p. (J). *(978-0-7787-2357-8(7))* Crabtree Publishing Co.

—Math on the Job: Caring for Marine Animals. 2016. (ENG., Illus.). 32p. (J). *(978-0-7787-2358-5(5))* Crabtree Publishing Co.

—Math on the Job: Keeping People Healthy. 2016. (ENG., Illus.). 32p. (J). *(978-0-7787-2359-2(3))* Crabtree Publishing Co.

—Math on the Job: Working in Construction. 2016. (ENG., Illus.). 32p. (J). *(978-0-7787-2361-5(5))* Crabtree Publishing Co.

—Math on the Job: Working in Sports. 2016. (ENG., Illus.). 32p. (J). *(978-0-7787-2362-2(3))* Crabtree Publishing Co.

Xingfeng, Huang & Real Shanghai Mathematics, trs. Real Shanghai Mathematics - Pupil Practice Book 5. 1, Bk. 5.1. 2018. (Real Shanghai Mathematics Ser.). (ENG.). 112p. (J). pap. 6.99 *(978-0-00-826182-5(2))* HarperCollins Pubs. Ltd. GBR. Dist: Independent Pubs. Group.

Yates, Irene. Christmas Activities for ks1 Maths. 2005. pap. *(978-1-903853-68-9(0))* Brilliant Pubns.

—Christmas Activities for Ks2 Maths. 2005. (Illus.). 64p. pap. *(978-1-903853-69-6(9))* Brilliant Pubns.

Yeatts, Karol L., et al. Navigating Through Problem Solving & Reasoning in Grade 3. 2004. (Navigations Ser.). (ENG., Illus.). 65p. pap. 30.95 *(978-0-87353-557-1(X),* P229410) National Council of Teachers of Mathematics.

Yemm, Caterhine. Maths Problem Solving: Year 1, 6 vols. Endersby, Frank, illus. 2005. 106p. pap. *(978-1-903853-74-0(5))* Brilliant Pubns.

—Maths Problem Solving: Year 2, 6 vols. Endersby, Frank, illus. 2005. 106p. pap. *(978-1-903853-75-7(3))* Brilliant Pubns.

—Maths Problem Solving: Year 3, 6 vols. Endersby, Frank, illus. 2005. 80p. pap. *(978-1-903853-76-4(1))* Brilliant Pubns.

—Maths Problem Solving: Year 4, 6 vols. Endersby, Frank, illus. 2005. 80p. pap. *(978-1-903853-77-1(X))* Brilliant Pubns.

—Maths Problem Solving: Year 5, 6 vols. Endersby, Frank, illus. 2005. 80p. pap. *(978-1-903853-78-8(8))* Brilliant Pubns.

—Maths Problem Solving: Year 6, 6 vols. Endersby, Frank, illus. 2006. 80p. pap. *(978-1-903853-79-5(6))* Brilliant Pubns.

Yoder, Eric & Yoder, Natalie. Short Mysteries You Solve with Math! / ¡Misterios Cortos Que Resuelves con Matemáticas! Geating, Karen & Villalobos, Yana Alfaro, trs. 2017. (One Minute Mysteries Ser.). (ENG & SPA., Illus.). 224p. (J). (gr. 6-9). pap. 12.95 *(978-1-938492-22-8(6))* Science, Naturally!

York, Jamie. Making Math Meaningful: A 6th Grade. 2003. stu. ed. 8.95 *(978-1-892857-05-7(7))* Whole Spirit Pr.

—Making Math Meaningful: A 7th Grade. 2004. (YA). tchr. ed., spiral bd. 18.95 *(978-1-892857-11-8(1))* Whole Spirit Pr.

—Making Math Meaningful: A 7th Grade Student's Workbook. 2004. (YA). wbk. ed. 15.95 *(978-1-892857-12-5(X))* Whole Spirit Pr.

—Making Math Meaningful: A Middle School Math Curriculum for Teachers & Parents. 2nd ed. 2003. (J). spiral bd. 17.95 *(978-1-892857-04-0(9))* 3rd ed. 2004. per. 22.95 *(978-1-892857-08-8(1))* Whole Spirit Pr.

—Making Math Meaningful: An 8th Grade. 2004. (YA). tchr. ed., spiral bd. 18.95 *(978-1-892857-09-5(X))* Whole Spirit Pr.

—Making Math Meaningful: An 8th Grade Student's Workbook. 2004. (YA). wbk. ed. 15.95 *(978-1-892857-10-1(3))* Whole Spirit Pr.

Youssef, Jagger. Fast Fact Addition, 1 vol. 2018. (Fast Fact Math Ser.). (ENG.). 24p. (gr. 2-3). 24.27 *(978-1-5382-1971-3(9),* 087317fb-356d-4f58-a3ad-308c94b82b50) Stevens, Gareth Publishing LLLP.

—Fast Fact Division, 1 vol. 2018. (Fast Fact Math Ser.). (ENG.). 24p. (gr. 2-3). 24.27 *(978-1-5382-1975-1(1),* 411ff512-863c-4167-8be1-0a20b1422ff9) Stevens, Gareth Publishing LLLP.

—Fast Fact Fractions, 1 vol. 2018. (Fast Fact Math Ser.). (ENG.). 24p. (gr. 2-3). 24.27 *(978-1-5382-1979-9(4),* 303eb04c-e545-4ce8-bf62-930dd56759bd) Stevens, Gareth Publishing LLLP.

—Making Bar Graphs, 1 vol. 2014. (Graph It! Ser.). (ENG.). 24p. (J). (gr. 1-2). 24.27 *(978-1-4824-0779-2(5),* 337b6353-a7b6-497e-8bac-a8bfb8795b14) Stevens, Gareth Publishing LLLP.

Yoyo Books, creator. Numbers. 2011. (Baby's First Library). (ENG., Illus.). 40p. (gr. -1-k). bds. *(978-94-6033-702-4(3))* YoYo Bks.

Yr Haen Fathemateg. 2005. (WEL., Illus.). 112p. pap. *(978-0-86174-781-8(X))* Drake Educational Assocs. Ltd.

Zable, Stacy. City by the Lake: Set Of 6. 2011. (Early Connections Ser.). (J). pap. 39.00 net. *(978-1-4108-1542-2(0))* Benchmark Education Co.

—Four Faces in Rock: Set Of 6. 2010. (Early Connections Ser.). (J). pap. 39.00 net. *(978-1-4108-1539-2(0))* Benchmark Education Co.

Zahn, Peter. Let's Recycle, 1 vol. 2013. (Rosen Math Readers Ser.). (ENG.). 24p. (J). (gr. 1-1). pap. 8.25 *(978-1-4777-2109-4(6),* a8582d39-3f9e-4fd8-90e8-35cb30ade5ce, Rosen Classroom) Rosen Publishing Group, Inc., The.

—Let's Recycle: Represent & Solve Addition Problems, 1 vol. 2013. (Core Math Skills: Operations & Algebraic Thinking Ser.). (ENG.). 24p. (J). (gr. 1-1). lib. bdg. 26.27 *(978-1-4777-2207-7(6),* 04483b69-e492-4310-bf73-6354d7202868, PowerKids Pr.); pap. 49.50 *(978-1-4777-2110-0(X),* Rosen Classroom) Rosen Publishing Group, Inc., The.

Zander, Alex. The School Track Meet, 1 vol. 2013. (Core Math Skills: Numbers & Operations in Base 10 Ser.). (ENG., Illus.). 24p. (J). (gr. 1-1). 26.27 *(978-1-4777-2223-7(6),* 98357026-48fc-403b-a76b-b975418b7eb7, Rosen Classroom) Rosen Publishing Group, Inc., The.

—The School Track Meet: Understand Place Value, 1 vol. 2013. (Rosen Math Readers Ser.). (ENG., Illus.). 24p. (J). (gr. 1-1). pap. 8.25 *(978-1-4777-2040-0(5),* 87f3f226-d4ab-4084-856b-877d42564daf); pap. 49.50 *(978-1-4777-2041-7(3))* Rosen Publishing Group, Inc., The. (Rosen Classroom).

Zolty, Howard. What Is Math? Answer: Math Is Everything. 2005. 28p. 14.21 *(978-1-4116-6717-4(4))* Lulu Pr., Inc.

Zuchora-Walske, Christine. Working in Math. 2018. (Career Files Ser.). (ENG., Illus.). 32p. (J). (gr. 3-6). 32.80 *(978-1-63235-446-4(2),* 13839, 12-Story Library) Bookstaves, LLC.

MATHEMATICS—DATA PROCESSING

Allen-Conn, B. J. & Rose, Kim. Powerful Ideas in the Classroom Using Squeak to Enhance Math & Science Learning. 2003. (Illus.). 86p. per. *(978-0-9743131-0-8(6))* Viewpoints Research Institute, Inc.

Drew, Jon. Matt's Field Day: Represent & Interpret Data. 2013. (InfoMax Math Readers Ser.). (ENG.). 24p. (J). (gr. 1-2). pap. 49.50 *(978-1-4777-2140-7(1));* (Illus.). pap. 8.25 *(978-1-4777-2139-1(8),* 836b3c72-bc25-424a-ab05-065856b67ddb) Rosen Publishing Group, Inc., The. (Rosen Classroom).

Harris, Patricia. Understanding Coding by Building Algorithms, 1 vol. 2016. (Spotlight on Kids Can Code Ser.). (ENG.). 24p. (J). (gr. 4-5). pap. 12.75 *(978-1-4994-2793-6(X),* 12e942b9-74a1-4941-b5ce-9b8516ad3af7, PowerKids Pr.) Rosen Publishing Group, Inc., The.

Stuart, Liam. The Parade: Understand Place Value. 2013. (Rosen Math Readers Ser.). (ENG.). 24p. (J). (gr. 1-2). pap. 49.50 *(978-1-4777-2071-4(5),* Rosen Classroom) Rosen Publishing Group, Inc., The.

MATHEMATICS—DICTIONARIES

Collins Dictionaries & Broadbent, Paul. Maths Dictionary: Illustrated Dictionary for Ages 7+ (Collins Primary Dictionaries) Herbert-Liew, Maria, illus. 2017. (ENG.). 144p. (J). (gr. k-6). pap. 15.99 *(978-0-00-821237-7(6))* HarperCollins Pubs. Ltd. GBR. Dist: Independent Pubs. Group.

De Klerk, Judith. Illustrated Maths Dictionary for Australian Schools. 2nd ed. Date not set. (Illus.). 123p. pap. 59.50 *(978-0-582-87045-1(3))* Addison-Wesley Longman, Ltd. GBR. Dist: Trans-Atlantic Pubns., Inc.

Fitzgerald, Theresa R. Math Dictionary for Kids: The #1 Guide for Helping Kids with Math. 5th rev. ed. 2021. (ENG., Illus.). 272p. (J). (gr. 4-9). pap. 14.95 *(978-1-61821-617-5(1),* Routledge) Taylor & Francis Group.

—Math Dictionary for Kids: The Essential Guide to Math Terms, Strategies, & Tables. 2005. (ENG., Illus.). 110p. (gr. 4-7). pap. 12.95 *(978-1-59363-160-4(X))* Prufrock Pr.

Large, Tori. The Usborne Illustrated Dictionary of Math. Constantine, Adam, illus. 2007. 128p. (J). (gr. 4-7). pap. 12.99 *(978-0-7945-1629-1(7),* Usborne) EDC Publishing.

—The Usborne Illustrated Dictonary of Math. Rogers, Kirsteen, ed. Constantine, Adam, illus. 2007. (Usborne Illustrated Dictionaries Ser.). 128p. (YA). (gr. 7). lib. bdg. 20.99 *(978-1-60130-013-3(1),* Usborne) EDC Publishing.

Middle School Math, Course 1: Multi-Language Visual Glossary. 2004. (gr. 6-9). *(978-0-618-26963-1(0),* 2-05799) Holt McDougal.

PRAESA & Press, Karen. The Cambridge Mathematics Dictionary for Schools Afrikaans Translation. 2008. pap. *(978-0-521-70883-8(4))* Cambridge Univ. Pr.

Rogers, Kirsteen. First Illustrated Math Dictionary IR. 2013. (Illustrated Dictionaries Ser.). 136p. (J). pap. 12.99 *(978-0-7945-3197-3(0),* Usborne) EDC Publishing.

Rogers, Kirsteen & Large, Tori. Illustrated Elementary Math Dictionary. 2010. (Illustrated Dictionaries Ser.). 135p. (YA). (gr. 3-18). pap. 12.99 *(978-0-7945-2143-1(6),* Usborne) EDC Publishing.

University of Cape Town Staff & Press, Karen. The Cambridge Mathematics Dictionary for Schools. 2008. (ENG., Illus.). 160p. pap. *(978-0-521-70882-1(6))* Cambridge Univ. Pr.

MATHEMATICS—HISTORY

Baptiste, Tracey. Mathematics: The Study of Numbers, Quantity, & Space, 1 vol. 2014. (Story of Math Ser.). (ENG.). 64p. (YA). (gr. 8-8). 34.29 *(978-1-62275-530-1(8),* 997e56f4-6db7-4810-88cb-4538fafe8c07, Britannica Educational Publishing) Rosen Publishing Group, Inc., The.

Bardoe, Cheryl. Nothing Stopped Sophie: The Story of Unshakable Mathematician Sophie Germain. McClintock, Barbara, illus. 2018. (ENG.). 40p. (J). (gr. -1-3). 18.99 *(978-0-316-27820-1(3))* Little, Brown Bks. for Young Readers.

Bendick, Jeanne. Archimedes & the Door of Science. 2018. (ENG., Illus.). 154p. (J). (gr. 5-6). pap. 9.95 *(978-1-68422-259-9(1))* Martino Fine Bks.

Colson, Rob. Masters of Math. 2018. (STEM-Gineers Ser.). (Illus.). 32p. (J). (gr. 5-5). *(978-0-7787-5737-5(4))* Crabtree Publishing Co.

Downey, Tika. How the Arabs Invented Algebra: The History of the Concept of Variables, 1 vol. 2010. (Math for the REAL World Ser.). (ENG., Illus.). 32p. (gr. 4-5). pap. 10.00 *(978-0-8239-8879-2(1),* df3e83cb-8cfd-4365-b2f7-11b4891ba432, PowerKids Pr.) Rosen Publishing Group, Inc., The.

Flynn, Mike. Infinity Explained, 1 vol. 2014. (Guide for Curious Minds Ser.). (ENG.). 149p. (J). (gr. 8-8). 42.41 *(978-1-4777-8127-2(7),* 9e00b29e-3c52-481e-9904-8eca1011e1c3, Rosen Young Adult) Rosen Publishing Group, Inc., The.

Levy, Joel. Exploring the Mysteries of Mathematics, 1 vol. 2016. (STEM Guide to the Universe Ser.). (ENG.). 192p. (gr. 9-9). lib. bdg. 47.80 *(978-1-4994-6406-1(1),* 789e9f02-3fe4-4c9c-8dde-5264c151adcb) Rosen Publishing Group, Inc., The.

World Book, Inc. Staff, contrib. by. Counting Pebbles to Writing Code: A Timeline of Mathematics & Computers. 2016. (Illus.). 40p. (J). *(978-0-7166-3541-3(0))* World Bk., Inc.

MATHEMATICS—POETRY

Franco, Betsy & Salerno, Steven. Mathematickles! 2006. (Illus.). (gr. k-5). 18.00 *(978-0-7569-6709-3(0))* Perfection Learning Corp.

Souders, Taryn. Whole-Y Cow! Fractions Are Fun. Mai-Wyss, Tatjana, illus. 2010. (ENG.). 32p. (J). (gr. 1-4). 15.95 *(978-1-58536-460-2(6),* 202182) Sleeping Bear Pr.

Vergo, Franny. Mathapalooza: A Collection of Math Poetry for Primary & Intermediate Students. 2012. 56p. pap. 11.95 *(978-1-4685-4269-1(9))* AuthorHouse.

MATHEMATICS—STUDY AND TEACHING

Anderson, Jill. Money Math with Sebastian Pig & Friends at the Farmer's Market, 1 vol. 2009. (Math Fun with Sebastian Pig & Friends! Ser.). (ENG., Illus.). 32p. (gr. k-2). lib. bdg. 26.60 *(978-0-7660-3364-1(3),* 0b2c8faa-5588-42c0-bccb-d32342709368) Enslow Publishing, LLC.

Arroyo, Sheri L. & Stewart, Rhea A. How Chefs Use Math. 2009. (Math in the Real World Ser.). (ENG.). 32p. (gr. 4-6). 28.00 *(978-1-60413-608-1(1),* P466911, Chelsea Clubhse.) Infobase Holdings, Inc.

—How Deep Sea Divers Use Math. 2009. (Math in the Real World Ser.). (ENG.). 32p. (gr. 4-6). 28.00 *(978-1-60413-611-1(1),* P466913, Chelsea Clubhse.) Infobase Holdings, Inc.

Atkinson, Sue. Supermaths: Age 4-5. 2003. (ENG., Illus.). 32p. pap. *(978-0-340-80559-6(5),* Hodder Children's Books) Hachette Children's Group.

—Supermaths 3: Age 3-6. 2003. (ENG., Illus.). 32p. pap. *(978-0-340-80561-9(7),* Hodder Children's Books) Hachette Children's Group.

Atkinson, Sue & Baxter, Cathy. Modwl 1 - Llyfr Gweithgareddau 5. 2005. (WEL., Illus.). 15p. *(978-1-86085-035-6(9))* ICA Video.

Atkinson, Sue & Canals, Sonia. A Modwl 1 - Llyfr Cyswllt Cartref. 2005. (WEL., Illus.). 15p. *(978-1-86085-045-5(6))* ICA Video.

Barron's Educational Series, Barron's Educational. Common Core Success Grade 5 Math: Preparing Students for a Brilliant Future. 2015. (Barron's Common Core Success Ser.). (ENG.). 184p. (gr. 5-5). pap. 12.99 *(978-1-4380-0678-9(0),* Barron's Educational Series, Inc.) Kaplan Publishing.

Bartch, Marian. Math & Stories, Grades K-3. Street Level Studio, illus. 2007. 173p. per. 17.95 *(978-1-59647-222-8(7))* Good Year Bks.

Bennett, Clinton. Middle School Math Course 1. 4th ed. 2004. (Holt Middle School Math Ser.). (SPA., Illus.). 60.40 *(978-0-03-070976-0(8))* Holt McDougal.

—Middle School Math Course 2. 4th ed. 2004. (Hold Middle School Math Ser.). (SPA., Illus.). 62.46 *(978-0-03-071098-8(7))* Holt McDougal.

Bingham, Chauna. A Guide to Middle School Math. 2009. 96p. pap. 15.99 *(978-1-4415-3390-6(7))* Xlibris Corp.

Boister. Exploring Mathematics. (J). pap., wbk. ed. 9.10 *(978-0-673-33130-4(X));* (gr. 1). pap., wbk. ed. 9.95 *(978-0-673-33131-1(8));* (gr. 5). pap., wbk. ed. 11.85 *(978-0-673-33135-9(0))* Addison-Wesley Educational Pubs., Inc.

Braidich, Victoria. Animals on the Farm: Learning to Compare Size, 1 vol. 2010. (Math for the REAL World Ser.). (ENG.). 12p. (gr. 1-2). pap. 5.90 *(978-0-8239-8847-1(3),* 67fd2ff5-4ab8-4f9f-be27-8997ef68d3de, Rosen Classroom) Rosen Publishing Group, Inc., The.

Brunner-Jass, Renata. Field of Play: Measuring Distance, Rate, & Time. 2013. (iMath Ser.). (ENG., Illus.). 48p. (J). (gr. 5-6). pap. 13.26 *(978-1-60357-510-2(3))* Norwood Hse. Pr.

Buckley, James, Jr. It's a Numbers Game! Basketball: The Math Behind the Perfect Bounce Pass, the Buzzer-Beating Bank Shot, & So Much More! 2020. (It's a Numbers Game! Ser.). (Illus.). 128p. (J). (gr. 3-7). (ENG.). 24.90 *(978-1-4263-3690-4(X));* 14.99 *(978-1-4263-3689-8(6))* Disney Publishing Worldwide. (National Geographic Kids).

Collins, Kathleen. A Day with the Baker: Learning to Tell Time by Quarter Hours, 1 vol. 2010. (Math for the REAL World Ser.). (ENG.). 16p. (gr. 2-3). pap. 7.05 *(978-0-8239-8854-9(6),* a79890c3-cadf-43b1-9eb3-83a8f05a6b05, Rosen Classroom) Rosen Publishing Group, Inc., The.

Cortland, D. J. A Look at Books: Learning to Count by Tens to 50, 1 vol. 2010. (Math for the REAL World Ser.). (ENG.). 12p. (gr. 1-2). pap. 5.90 *(978-0-8239-8890-7(2),* eb3ad97d-2ff9-4b07-908a-2516cb32e6ca, Rosen Classroom) Rosen Publishing Group, Inc., The.

Danielson, Christopher. How Many? 2019. (Illus.). 40p. (J). (gr. -1-3). 15.99 *(978-1-58089-943-7(9));* pap. 7.99 *(978-1-58089-945-1(5))* Charlesbridge Publishing, Inc.

—Which One Doesn't Belong? Playing with Shapes. 2019. (Illus.). 40p. (J). (gr. -1-3). lib. bdg. 15.99 *(978-1-58089-944-4(7))* Charlesbridge Publishing, Inc.

DK. DK Workbooks: Math, Pre-K: Learn & Explore. 2014. (DK Workbooks Ser.). (ENG.). 60p. (J). (gr. -1-k). pap. 6.99 *(978-1-4654-1731-2(1),* DK Children) Dorling Kindersley Publishing, Inc.

Dukes, Dorothy. Kg - 2nd Grade Basic Math Elements. 2009. 121p. pap. 10.34 *(978-0-557-16210-9(6))* Lulu Pr., Inc.

Epps, S. Emmanuel & Robateau, Lisa. Bubble Brain: Story Time Rhymes That Build the Mind. 2013. 34p. pap. 12.95 *(978-0-9911410-0-5(8))* Addi-Boo Bks.

ETA Cuisenaire Staff. Hands-On-Standards, Common Core Edition, Teacher's Resource Guide, Grade 3: Book. 2012. (ENG.). (gr. k-8). pap. 67.95 *(978-0-7406-9432-5(4),* Hands-On Standards) hand2mind.

—Hands-On-Standards, Common Core Edition, Teacher's Resource Guide, Grade 4: Book. 2012. (ENG.). (gr. k-8). pap. 67.95 *(978-0-7406-9433-2(2),* Hands-On Standards) hand2mind.

—Hands-On-Standards, Common Core Edition, Teacher's Resource Guide, Grade 5: Book. 2012. (ENG.). (gr. k-8). pap. 67.95 *(978-0-7406-9434-9(0),* Hands-On Standards) hand2mind.

—Hands-On-Standards, Common Core Edition, Teacher's Resource Guide, Grade 6: Book. 2012. (ENG.). (gr. k-8). pap. 67.95 *(978-0-7406-9444-8(8),* Hands-On Standards) hand2mind.

—Hands-On-Standards, Common Core Edition, Teacher's Resource Guide, Grade 7: Book. 2012. (ENG.). (gr. k-8). pap. 67.95 *(978-0-7406-9445-5(6),* Hands-On Standards) hand2mind.

—Hands-On-Standards, Common Core Edition, Teacher's Resource Guide, Grade 8: Book. 2012. (ENG.). (gr. k-8). pap. 67.95 *(978-0-7406-9446-2(4),* Hands-On Standards) hand2mind.

Evan-Moor Educational Publishers. At Home Tutor Math, Grade 2. 2014. (At-Home Tutor Ser.). (ENG., Illus.). 89p. (J). (gr. 2-2). pap., tchr. ed. 9.99 *(978-1-61368-982-0(9))* Evan-Moor Educational Pubs.

Everhart, Loretta Jean. Math Vitamins: Daily Dose for Students Learning How to Solve Word Problems. 2011. 164p. pap. 12.95 *(978-1-4620-3251-8(6))* iUniverse, Inc.

Exploring Mathematics. (J). (gr. 2). pap., wbk. ed. 9.95 *(978-0-673-33132-8(6));* (gr. 3). pap., wbk. ed. 11.85 *(978-0-673-33133-5(4))* Addison-Wesley Educational Pubs., Inc.

Freudentha, H. Digging Numbers: Math/Context. 3rd ed. 2003. (J). 7.86 *(978-0-03-071716-1(7))* Holt, Rinehart & Winston of Canada, Ltd. CAN. Dist: Harcourt Canada, Ltd.

—Pattern & Figures: Math/Context. 3rd ed. 2003. (Math in Context Ser.). (J). 7.86 *(978-0-03-071702-4(7))* Holt, Rinehart & Winston of Canada, Ltd. CAN. Dist: Harcourt Canada, Ltd.

—Re-Allotment: Math/Context. 3rd ed. 2003. (SPA.). (J). 7.86 *(978-0-03-072354-4(X))* Holt, Rinehart & Winston of Canada, Ltd. CAN. Dist: Harcourt Canada, Ltd.

George, Abigail. Freaky Bug Facts! Understand Place Value, 1 vol. 2014. (InfoMax Math Readers Ser.). (ENG.). 24p. (J). (gr. 2-2). pap. 8.25 *(978-1-4777-4837-4(7),* e5c0fd45-4439-4b75-a89b-aa3e6de1be0b, Rosen Classroom) Rosen Publishing Group, Inc., The.

Goodman, Jenny. Cambridge Mathematics NSW Syllabus for the Australian Curriculum Year 8 Teacher Edition. 2014. (ENG.). pap., tchr. ed. *(978-1-107-65058-9(5))* Cambridge Univ. Pr.

Gow, Mary. Archimedes: Genius Mathematician, 1 vol. 2014. (Genius Scientists & Their Genius Ideas Ser.). (ENG.). 96p. (gr. 5-5). 29.60 *(978-0-7660-6530-7(8),* 66d31456-42ef-4583-86d3-30cc12bf5526); pap. 13.88 *(978-0-7660-6531-4(6),* 17475f79-43f4-431a-b7f5-05d0d570eacd) Enslow Publishing, LLC.

MNO

Hall, Kevin. 10 Great Makerspace Projects Using Math, 1 vol. 2017. (Using Makerspaces for School Projects Ser.). (ENG., Illus.). 64p. (J). (gr. 6-6). 36.13 *(978-1-4994-3846-8(X)*, 6f6d6b7b-7efc-4cf3-af77-0b27c21fd0a7, Rosen Central) Rosen Publishing Group, Inc., The.

Hammelef, Danielle S. That Figures! A Crash Course in Math, 1 vol. 2014. (Crash Course Ser.). (ENG.). 64p. (J). (gr. 4-8). lib. bdg. 35.32 *(978-1-4914-0774-5(3)*, 126003) Capstone.

Harcourt School Publishers Staff. Harcourt Matematicas, Grade 1. 2nd ed. 2003. (Harcourt Matematicas Ser.). (SPA.). (gr. 1-18). Vol. 1. tchr. ed. 140.60 *(978-0-15-321616-9(6))* Vol. 2. tchr. ed. 140.60 *(978-0-15-321617-6(4))* Harcourt Schl. Pubs.

—Harcourt Matematicas, Grade 2. 2nd ed. 2003. (Harcourt Matematicas Ser.). (SPA.). (gr. 2-18). Vol. 1. tchr. ed. 140.60 *(978-0-15-321618-3(2))* Vol. 2. tchr. ed. 140.60 *(978-0-15-321619-0(0))* Harcourt Schl. Pubs.

—Harcourt Matematicas, Grade 3. 2nd ed. 2003. (Harcourt Matematicas Ser.). (SPA.). (gr. 3-18). Vol. 1. tchr. ed. 157.50 *(978-0-15-321620-6(4))* Vol. 2. tchr. ed. 157.50 *(978-0-15-321621-3(2))* Harcourt Schl. Pubs.

—Harcourt Matematicas, Grade 4. 2nd ed. 2003. (Harcourt Matematicas Ser.). (SPA.). (gr. 4-18). Vol. 1. tchr. ed. 158.90 *(978-0-15-321622-0(0))* Vol. 2. tchr. ed. 158.90 *(978-0-15-321623-7(9))* Harcourt Schl. Pubs.

—Harcourt Matematicas, Grade 4: Practice Workbook. 2nd ed. 2003. (Harcourt Matematicas Ser.). (SPA.). (gr. 4-18). tchr. ed., wbk. ed. 23.30 *(978-0-15-321639-8(5))* Harcourt Schl. Pubs.

—Harcourt Matematicas, Grade 5. 2nd ed. 2003. (Harcourt Matematicas Ser.). (SPA.). (gr. 5-18). Vol. 1. tchr. ed. 158.90 *(978-0-15-321624-4(7))* Vol. 2. tchr. ed. 158.90 *(978-0-15-321625-1(5))* Harcourt Schl. Pubs.

—Harcourt Matematicas, Grade 6. 2nd ed. 2003. (Harcourt Matematicas Ser.). (SPA.). (gr. 6-18). Vol. 1. tchr. ed. 158.90 *(978-0-15-321626-8(3))* Vol. 2. tchr. ed. 158.90 *(978-0-15-321627-5(1))* Harcourt Schl. Pubs.

—Harcourt Matematicas, Grade K: Teacher's Resource Book. 2nd ed. 2003. (Harcourt Matematicas Ser.). (SPA.). (gr. k-6). tchr. ed. 63.90 *(978-0-15-321680-0(8))* Harcourt Schl. Pubs.

—Harcourt Math: Practice Workbook. 2nd ed. 2003. (Harcourt School Publishers Math Ser.). (Illus.). (ENG.). 176p. (gr. 4-4). pap., wbk. ed. 13.25 *(978-0-15-320769-3(8))*; (gr. 6-18). wbk. ed. 9.80 *(978-0-15-320786-0(8))* Harcourt Schl. Pubs.

—Zoo Zillions: User's Guide. 98th ed. 2003. (Mighty Mathtm Ser.). (Illus.). (gr. k-3). pap., pupil's gde. ed. 11.00 *(978-0-15-307970-2(3))* Harcourt Schl. Pubs.

Havelka, Jacqueline. STEM in Auto Racing. 2019. (Connecting STEM & Sports Ser.). (Illus.). 80p. (J). (gr. 12). lib. bdg. 34.60 *(978-1-4222-4330-5(3))* Mason Crest.

—STEM in Extreme Sports. 2019. (Connecting STEM & Sports Ser.). (Illus.). 80p. (J). (gr. 12). lib. bdg. 34.60 *(978-1-4222-4333-6(8))* Mason Crest.

Hirakawa, Diane M. Math 101 for Busy Families: K-6 Monthly Activities. 2007. (Illus.). 48p. pap. 12.95 *(978-1-890035-63-1(7))* New Century Pr.

Holt, Rinehart and Winston Staff. Digging Numbers: Math/Context. 3rd ed. 2003. (J). tchr. ed. 31.60 *(978-0-03-071717-8(5))* Holt, Rinehart & Winston of Canada, Ltd. CAN. Dist: Harcourt Canada, Ltd.

—Holt Science & Technology: Math Skills Worksheets. 5th ed. 2004. (Illus.). pap., wbk. ed. 11.60 *(978-0-03-035198-3(7))* Holt McDougal.

—Insights & Data: Math/Context. 3rd ed. 2003. (J). tchr. ed. 31.60 *(978-0-03-071701-7(9))* Holt, Rinehart & Winston of Canada, Ltd. CAN. Dist: Harcourt Canada, Ltd.

—Number Tools: Math Context. 3rd ed. 2003. (SPA.). (J). pap. 42.66 *(978-0-03-072433-6(3))* Holt, Rinehart & Winston of Canada, Ltd. CAN. Dist: Harcourt Canada, Ltd.

—Number Tools Vol. 2: Math/Context. 3rd ed. 2003. (SPA.). (J). 42.66 *(978-0-03-072428-2(7))* Holt, Rinehart & Winston of Canada, Ltd. CAN. Dist: Harcourt Canada, Ltd.

—Number Tools Workbook Math/Contt. 3rd ed. 2003. (Math in Context Ser.). (J). pap., wbk. ed. 24.66 *(978-0-03-072582-1(8))* Holt, Rinehart & Winston of Canada, Ltd. CAN. Dist: Harcourt Canada, Ltd.

—Reflections & Numbers: Math/Context. 3rd ed. 2003. (J). tchr. ed. 31.60 *(978-0-03-071709-3(4))* Holt, Rinehart & Winston of Canada, Ltd. CAN. Dist: Harcourt Canada, Ltd.

—Teaching Math to All Students Package. 4th ed. 2004. 2266.67 *(978-0-03-037952-9(0))*; 5333.36 *(978-0-03-037953-6(9))*; 1200.00 *(978-0-03-037951-2(2))* Holt McDougal.

James, Rosemary. What Do Scientists Do? Solve Problems Involving Measurement & Estimation, 1 vol. 2014. (InfoMax Math Readers Ser.). (ENG.). 24p. (J). (gr. 3-3). pap. 8.25 *(978-1-4777-4603-5(X)*, 1b2d1f26-7b3f-40f5-af6d-56833401aee1, Rosen Classroom) Rosen Publishing Group, Inc., The.

Kaufman, Elliott, photos by. Numbers Everywhere. 2013. (ENG., Illus.). 32p. (J). (gr. -1-1). 12.95 *(978-0-7892-1157-6(2)*, 791157, Abbeville Kids) Abbeville Pr., Inc.

Layne, Steven L. Number 1 Teacher: A School Counting Book. Layne, Deborah Dover, illus. 2008. (ENG.). 40p. (J). (gr. 1-4). 17.95 *(978-1-58536-307-0(3)*, 202112) Sleeping Bear Pr.

LernerClassroom Editors, ed. Teaching Guide for Manga Math Mysteries. 2010. pap. 5.95 *(978-0-7613-6679-9(2))* Lerner Publishing Group.

Levy, Joel. Exploring the Mysteries of Mathematics, 1 vol. 2016. (STEM Guide to the Universe Ser.). (ENG.). 192p. (gr. 9-9). lib. bdg. 47.80 *(978-1-4994-6406-1(1)*, 789e9f02-3fe4-4c9c-8dde-5264c151adcb) Rosen Publishing Group, Inc., The.

Lindeen, Mary. Forest Doubles, 1 vol. 2011. (Wonder Readers Fluent Level Ser.). (ENG.). 16p. (gr. -1-2). (J). pap. 6.25 *(978-1-4296-7922-0(0)*, 118254); pap. 35.94 *(978-1-4296-8089-9(X))* Capstone. (Capstone Pr.).

Loughran, Donna & Brunner-Jass, Renata. Field of Play: Measuring Distance, Rate, & Time. 2013. (iMath Ser.). (Illus.). 48p. (J). (gr. 5-6). lib. bdg. 23.94 *(978-1-59953-571-5(8))* Norwood Hse. Pr.

Maletsky, Evan A., et al. Check What You Know: Intervention Practice Books. 2003. (Harcourt Math Ser.). (gr. 3-18). 10.70 *(978-0-15-324442-1(9))*; (gr. 4-18). 10.70 *(978-0-15-324443-8(7))*; (gr. 5-18). 11.50 *(978-0-15-324444-5(5))*; (gr. 6-18). 12.10 *(978-0-15-324445-2(3))* Harcourt Schl. Pubs.

Marie-France, Marcie & Lebuis, Peter. Additions Chansons et Activités, 2 vols. 2013. (FRE.). 64p. 19.95 *(978-1-55386-226-0(0)*, 9781553862260) Jordan, Sara Publishing.

—Divisions Chansons et Activités, 1 vol. 2013. (FRE.). 64p. 19.95 *(978-1-55386-235-2(X)*, 9781553862352) Jordan, Sara Publishing.

—Multiplications Chansons et Activités, 2 vols. 2013. (FRE.). 64p. 19.95 *(978-1-55386-229-1(5)*, 9781553862291) Jordan, Sara Publishing.

—Soustractions Chansons et Activités, 2 vols. 2013. (FRE.). 64p. 19.95 *(978-1-55386-232-1(5)*, 9781553862321) Jordan, Sara Publishing.

McCallum, Ann. A Kid's Multicultural Math Adventure: Amazing Activities to Explore Math's Global Roots! Norton, Carolyn, illus. 2004. (Williamson Multicultural Kids Can! Book Ser.). 128p. (J). pap. 14.95 *(978-1-885593-92-4(9)*, Ideals Pubns.) Worthy Publishing.

MCP Mathematics, Level E. 2003. (J). 28.50 *(978-0-8136-3113-4(0))* Modern Curriculum Pr.

MCP Mathematics. 2005. (J). (gr. k-6). tchr. ed. 29.95 *(978-0-7652-6065-9(4))*; tchr. ed. 29.95 *(978-0-7652-6063-5(8))* Seymour, Dale Pubns.

Mercer, Susan. Pathway to Pre-Algebra Proficiency. 2008. 76p. per. 14.95 *(978-1-4327-1719-3(7))* Outskirts Pr., Inc.

Miles Kelly Staff. Science & Maths. 2003. (Flip Quiz Ser.). (Illus.). 38p. (J). (gr. 10-11). spiral bd. 5.95 *(978-1-84236-032-3(9))*; (gr. 11-12). spiral bd. 5.95 *(978-1-84236-033-0(7))*; (gr. 7-9). spiral bd. 5.95 *(978-1-84236-030-9(2))*; (gr. 9-10). spiral bd. 5.95 *(978-1-84236-031-6(0))* Miles Kelly Publishing, Ltd. GBR. Dist: Independent Pubs. Group.

Murphy, Patricia J. A Frog's Life: Learning Sequential Order Using a Timeline, 1 vol. 2010. (Math for the REAL World Ser.). (ENG.). 16p. (gr. 2-3). pap. 7.05 *(978-0-8239-8905-8(4)*, 254947df-9cd1-4dd0-9d06-3c0ea766c310, Rosen Classroom) Rosen Publishing Group, Inc., The.

Nurk, Enn & Telgmaa, Aksel. Mathematics 6. Harte, Will, tr. from RUS. 2003. Orig. Title: Matematika 6. Uchebnik Dlya Obscheobrazovatel'Nykh Uchebnikh Zavedenij. (Illus.). ix, 310p. per. 38.50 *(978-0-9740234-0-3(X))* Perpendicular Pr.

Palmer, Stuart, et al. Cambridge Mathematics NSW Syllabus for the Australian Curriculum, Year 10. 2014. (ENG.). pap. *(978-1-107-69185-8(0))* Cambridge Univ. Pr.

Perritano, John. Football Numbers: Graphing Data. 2013. (iMath Ser.). 32p. (J). (gr. 3-4). lib. bdg. 22.60 *(978-1-59953-566-1(1))* Norwood Hse. Pr.

PUBLICATIONS, Dale Seymour. MCP Mathematics. 2004. (ENG.). (J). (gr. 4-4). pap., stu. ed. 25.00 net. *(978-0-7652-6062-8(X))*; (gr. 5-5). pap., stu. ed. 25.00 net. *(978-0-7652-6064-2(6))* Seymour, Dale Pubns.

Publications International Ltd. Staff, ed. Kindergarten Boot Camp. 2010. (J). 20.98 *(978-1-4508-0069-3(6))* Publications International, Ltd.

Publishing, Ferguson, creator. Mathematics & Physics. 2003. (Ferguson's Careers in Focus Ser.). (ENG., Illus.). 192p. (gr. 6-12). 29.95 *(978-0-89434-413-8(7)*, P053165, Ferguson Publishing Company) Infobase Holdings, Inc.

Rankie, Barbara. Addition Unplugged, 2 vols. 2nd ed. 2013. (ENG.). 64p. 19.95 *(978-1-55386-216-1(3)*, 1553862163) Jordan, Sara Publishing.

—Subtraction Unplugged, 2 vols. 2nd ed. 2013. (ENG.). 64p. 19.95 *(978-1-55386-217-8(1)*, 1553862171) Jordan, Sara Publishing.

Rapoport, Rebecca & Yoder, J. A. Game of Nim & Graph Theory: Fun, Hands-On Activities for Learning Math. 2018. (Math Lab for Kids Ser.). (ENG., Illus.). 32p. (J). (gr. 3-6). lib. bdg. 27.99 *(978-1-63159-453-3(2)*, c1eb6d0e-1a8d-4b26-831e-e1359ea5e460, Quarry Bks.) Quarto Publishing Group USA.

Rozines Roy, Jennifer & Roy, Gregory. Money at the Store, 1 vol. 2008. (Math All Around Ser.). (ENG.). 32p. (gr. 2-2). pap. 9.23 *(978-0-7614-3385-9(6)*, 55d54d22-45e0-4ddc-b7ca-87c1c6c663e4) Cavendish Square Publishing LLC.

Schmidt, Stanley F. Life of Fred — Edgewood. 2011. (ENG., Illus.). 128p. 16.00 *(978-0-9791072-8-3(8))* Polka Dot Publishing.

Scholastic, Inc. Staff. Scholastic Success with Addition & Subtraction. 2010. (ENG.). 48p. (gr. 3-3). pap. 5.99 *(978-0-545-20096-7(2)*, Teaching Resources) Scholastic, Inc.

—Scholastic Success with Addition & Subtraction Grade 1. 2010. (ENG.). 48p. (gr. 1-1). pap. 5.99 *(978-0-545-20098-1(9)*, Teaching Resources) Scholastic, Inc.

—Scholastic Success with Addition & Subtraction Grade 2. 2010. (ENG.). 48p. (gr. 2-2). pap. 5.99 *(978-0-545-20097-4(0)*, Teaching Resources) Scholastic, Inc.

School Specialty Publishing Staff & Carson-Dellosa Publishing Staff. 70 Must-Know Word Problems. 2009. (Singapore Math Ser.: 6). (ENG.). 160p. (gr. 1-2). pap. 12.99 *(978-0-7682-4011-5(5)*, 0768240115, Frank Schaffer Pubns.) Carson-Dellosa Publishing, LLC.

School Zone Publishing. Transition Math. 2003. (ENG.). (J). (gr. k-1). cd-rom 19.99 *(978-1-58947-911-1(4))* School Zone Publishing Co.

Sipe, Roger & Marzocchi, Alison. The Hidden World of Urban Farming: Operations with Decimals. 2019. (Mathematics in the Real World Ser.). (ENG., Illus.). 32p. (gr. 5-8). pap. 11.99 *(978-1-4258-5878-0(3))* Teacher Created Materials, Inc.

Spilsbury, Richard. I'M Good at Math... What Job Can I Get? 2012. (What's a Good Job for Me? Ser.). (ENG., Illus.). 32p. (J). (gr. 5-6). *(978-1-4488-6629-8(4)*, PowerKids Pr.) Rosen Publishing Group, Inc., The.

Steffens, Bradley. Big Data Analyst. 2017. (ENG.). 64p. (YA). (gr. 5-12). *(978-1-68282-176-3(5))* ReferencePoint Pr., Inc.

Sundance/Newbridge LLC Staff. Charts & Graphs. 2004. (Reading PowerWorks Ser.). (gr. 1-3). 37.50 *(978-0-7608-8987-9(2))*; pap. 6.10 *(978-0-7608-8988-6(0))* Sundance/Newbridge Educational Publishing.

—Dollars & Cents. 2004. (Reading PowerWorks Ser.). (gr. 1-3). 37.50 *(978-0-7608-8964-0(3))*; pap. 6.10 *(978-0-7608-8965-7(1))* Sundance/Newbridge Educational Publishing.

Taylor, Helen & Harris, Andrew J. R., eds. Learning & Teaching Mathematics 0-8. 2013. (ENG., Illus.). 280p. (C). 157.00 *(978-1-4462-5331-1(7)*, B53311C); pap. 57.00 *(978-1-4462-5332-8(5)*, B53311P) SAGE Pubns., Ltd. GBR. Dist: SAGE Pubns., Inc.

Taylor, Roger & Taylor, Robert J. Move on Maths Ages 9-11: 50+ Flexible Maths Activities, Volume 2. 2009. (ENG., Illus.). 136p. 49.95 *(978-0-415-47154-1(0)*, RX10799) Fulton, David Pubs. GBR. Dist: Taylor & Francis Group.

Velázquez Press, creator. Diario de Escritura Académica para Matemáticas. 2018. (SPA.). (YA). pap. 4.95 *(978-1-59495-717-8(7))* Velázquez Pr.

Williams, Rozanne. The Costume Parade. 2017. (Learn-To-Read Ser.). (ENG., Illus.). (J). pap. 3.49 *(978-1-68310-216-8(9))* Pacific Learning, Inc.

Workman Publishing. Everything You Need to Ace Math in One Big Fat Notebook: The Complete Middle School Study Guide. 2016. (Big Fat Notebooks Ser.). (ENG., Illus.). 528p. (J). (gr. 6-9). pap. 16.95 *(978-0-7611-6096-0(5)*, 16096) Workman Publishing Co., Inc.

Workman Publishing & Heos, Bridget. Summer Brain Quest: Between Grades Pre-K & K. Yan, Edison & Wicks, Maris, illus. 2018. (Summer Brain Quest Ser.). (ENG.). 160p. (gr. -1-k). pap. 12.95 *(978-1-5235-0299-8(1)*, 100299) Workman Publishing Co., Inc.

Year 1 Impact Intervention: Increase Pupil Progress & Attainment with Targeted Intervention Teaching Resources. 2017. (ENG., Illus.). 96p. (J). (gr. k-1). pap. 43.99 *(978-0-00-822838-5(8))* HarperCollins Pubs. Ltd. GBR. Dist: Independent Pubs. Group.

Zaccaro, Edward D. Primary Grade Challenge Math. 2003. (ENG., Illus.). 311p. (J). pap. 24.95 *(978-0-9679915-3-5(6))* Hickory Grove Pr.

MATINICUS ROCK LIGHTHOUSE (ME.)

Keep the Lights Burning. 9.95 *(978-1-59112-293-7(7))* Live Oak Media.

Roop, Connie & Roop, Peter. Keep the Lights Burning, Abbie. Hanson, Peter E., illus. 2016. (On My Own History Ser.). (ENG.). 40p. (J). (gr. 2-4). 38.65 *(978-1-5124-1862-0(5)*, Millbrook Pr.) Lerner Publishing Group.

Roop, Peter & Roop, Connie. Manten Las Luces Encendidas, Abbie. Hanson, Peter E., illus. 2005. (Yo Solo - Historia (on My Own - History) Ser.). (SPA.). 48p. (gr. 2-4). lib. bdg. 25.26 *(978-0-8225-3098-5(8))* Lerner Publishing Group.

—The Stormy Adventure of Abbie Burgess, Lighthouse Keeper. 2010. pap. 51.02 *(978-0-7613-6922-6(8))* Lerner Publishing Group.

MATISSE, HENRI, 1869-1954

Bianchi, Ms. The Swimmers: Paper Cut-Outs with Matisse. 2019. (ENG., Illus.). 32p. (J). (gr. 1-5). 15.95 *(978-1-58423-716-7(3))* Gingko Pr., Inc.

Geis, Patricia. Henri Matisse: Meet the Artist. 2014. (Meet the Artist Ser.). (ENG., Illus.). 16p. (J). (gr. 2-7). 24.95 *(978-1-61689-282-1(X))* Princeton Architectural Pr.

Hollein, Nina & Hollein, Max. Cut-Out Fun with Matisse. 2014. (ENG., Illus.). 40p. (J). (gr. 3-7). pap. 9.95 *(978-3-7913-7192-4(4))* Prestel Verlag GmbH & Co KG. DEU. Dist: Penguin Random Hse. LLC.

Le Tord, Bijou. A Bird or Two: A Story about Henri Matisse. 2004. (ENG., Illus.). 32p. (gr. 2-7). 18.00 *(978-0-8028-5184-0(3))* Eerdmans, William B. Publishing Co.

MacLachlan, Patricia. The Iridescence of Birds. Hooper, Hadley, illus. 2014. (ENG.). 40p. (J). (gr. -1-3). 19.99 *(978-1-59643-948-1(3)*, 900123811) Roaring Brook Pr.

Rubin, Susan Goldman. Matisse Dance with Joy. 2008. (Mini Masters Modern Ser.). (ENG., Illus.). 26p. (J). (gr. -1 — 1). bds. 6.99 *(978-0-8118-6288-2(7))* Chronicle Bks. LLC.

Stephens, Pamela Geiger. Dropping in on Matisse. McNeill, Jim, illus. 2004. 32p. (J). 15.95 *(978-1-56290-322-0(5))* Crystal Productions.

Winter, Jeanette. Henri's Scissors. Winter, Jeanette, illus. 2013. (ENG., Illus.). 40p. (J). (gr. k-3). 18.99 *(978-1-4424-6484-1(4)*, Beach Lane Bks.) Beach Lane Bks.

MATRIMONY

see Marriage

MATTER

Adler, David A. Solids, Liquids, Gases, & Plasma. Raff, Anna, illus. 2019. 32p. (J). (gr. 2-5). 18.99 *(978-0-8234-3962-1(3))* Holiday Hse., Inc.

Aloian, Molly. Atoms & Molecules, 1 vol. 2008. (Why Chemistry Matters Ser.). (ENG., Illus.). 32p. (J). (gr. 4-6). pap. *(978-0-7787-4247-0(4))* Crabtree Publishing Co.

Anderson, Michael. The Nature of Planets, Dwarf Planets, & Space Objects, 1 vol. 2011. (Solar System Ser.). (ENG., Illus.). 96p. (J). (gr. 8-8). lib. bdg. 35.29 *(978-1-61530-517-9(3)*, 58422bec-8a3c-42ac-8ffa-a5a83dda5ab4) Rosen Publishing Group, Inc., The.

Bell, Samantha. States of Matter. Bane, Jeff, illus. 2018. (Mi Mini Biografía (My Itty-Bitty Bio): My Early Library). (ENG.). 24p. (J). (gr. k-1). pap. 12.79 *(978-1-5341-0824-0(6)*, 210660); lib. bdg. 30.64 *(978-1-5341-0725-0(8)*, 210659) Cherry Lake Publishing.

Benchmark Education Company. Matter Is Everywhere (Teacher Guide) Solids, Liquids, & Gases. 2005. *(978-1-4108-4658-7(X))* Benchmark Education Co.

—Measuring Matter (Teacher Guide) Solids, Liquids, & Gases. 2005. *(978-1-4108-4651-8(2))* Benchmark Education Co.

—This Is Matter (Teacher Guide) Solids, Liquids, & Gases. 2005. *(978-1-4108-4644-0(X))* Benchmark Education Co.

Benchmark Education Company, LLC Staff, compiled by. Matter. 2006. spiral bd. 330.00 *(978-1-4108-7013-1(8))* 2006. (J). 148.00 *(978-1-4108-7032-2(4))* 2005. (J). spiral bd. 265.00 *(978-1-4108-5757-6(3))* Benchmark Education Co.

—Matter: Theme Set. 2006. (J). 105.00 *(978-1-4108-7060-5(X))* Benchmark Education Co.

—Science Theme: Matter. 2005. spiral bd. 115.00 *(978-1-4108-5311-0(X))* Benchmark Education Co.

Biskup, Agnieszka. The Solid Truth about States of Matter with Max Axiom, Super Scientist, 1 vol. Martin, Cynthia & Schulz, Barbara, illus. 2009. (Graphic Science Ser.). (ENG.). 32p. (J). (gr. 3-9). pap. 8.10 *(978-1-4296-3451-9(0)*, 95995) Capstone.

—The Solid Truth about States of Matter with Max Axiom, Super Scientist. Martin, Cynthia & Schulz, Barbara, illus. 2008. (Life Cycles Ser.). 24p. 289.10 *(978-1-4296-2451-0(5))* Capstone.

Bloom, Chrissa. In the Kitchen with Solids, Liquids, & Gases, 1 vol. 2008. (Real Life Readers Ser.). (ENG.). 12p. (gr. 1-2). pap. 5.90 *(978-1-4042-7897-4(4)*, e43da252-1047-465c-b8ff-11988b838565, Rosen Classroom) Rosen Publishing Group, Inc., The.

Boothroyd, Jennifer. How Big? How Heavy? How Dense? A Look at Matter. 2011. (Lightning Bolt Books Exploring Physical Science Ser.). 32p. pap. 45.32 *(978-0-7613-7649-1(6))*; (ENG., Illus.). (J). (gr. 1-3). lib. bdg. 29.32 *(978-0-7613-6095-7(6)*, 25aeb824-7ae7-45e9-9b32-94a004501fbb, Lerner Pubns.) Lerner Publishing Group.

—Many Kinds of Matter: A Look at Solids, Liquids, & Gases. 2011. (Lightning Bolt Books Exploring Physical Science Ser.). 32p. pap. 45.32 *(978-0-7613-7651-4(8))*; (ENG., Illus.). (J). (gr. 1-3). pap. 9.99 *(978-0-7613-7106-9(0)*, 0b3bdd9a-cafb-46ca-8f35-9b0f439f3579) Lerner Publishing Group.

Campbell, Margaret Christine & Goldstein, Natalie. Discovering Atoms, 1 vol. 2011. (Scientist's Guide to Physics Ser.). (ENG.). 112p. (YA). (gr. 7-7). lib. bdg. 39.80 *(978-1-4488-4700-6(1)*, 8da89c3c-3733-4cba-9641-b67be5d54bbf) Rosen Publishing Group, Inc., The.

Canavan, Thomas. Why Do Ice Cubes Float? Questions & Answers about the Science of Everyday Materials. 2013. (Science F. A. Q. Ser.). (Illus.). 32p. (gr. 3-6). 31.35 *(978-1-78212-396-5(2))* Arcturus Publishing GBR. Dist: Black Rabbit Bks.

Cardenas, Ernesto A. What Is Matter? 2009. pap. 4.95 *(978-1-60698-076-7(9))* Milo Educational Bks. & Resources.

Carr, Aaron & Siemens, Jared. Solids. 2016. (Illus.). 24p. (J). *(978-1-5105-0910-8(0))* SmartBook Media, Inc.

Clark, John O. E. The Basics of Matter, 1 vol. 2014. (Core Concepts Ser.). (ENG., Illus.). 96p. (YA). (gr. 7-7). 39.77 *(978-1-4777-7752-7(0)*, 6186e84f-63ce-478b-8d7b-590fc0cc56b0) Rosen Publishing Group, Inc., The.

Curry, Don L. What Is Matter? (Rookie Read-About Science: Physical Science: Previous Editions) 2005. (Rookie Read-About Science Ser.). (ENG., Illus.). 32p. (J). (gr. 1-2). pap. 4.95 *(978-0-516-24667-3(4)*, Children's Pr.) Scholastic Library Publishing.

Delta Education. Sci Res Bk Foss Grade 3 Next Gen Ea. 2014. (Illus.). 274p. (J). lib. bdg. *(978-1-62571-375-9(4))* Delta Education, LLC.

Dicker, Katie. Properties of Matter, 1 vol. 2010. (Sherlock Bones Looks at Physical Science Ser.). (ENG.). 32p. (YA). (gr. 5-5). lib. bdg. 29.93 *(978-1-61533-214-4(6)*, 12b245e9-266a-4972-b618-c28c68278c44, Windmill Bks.) Rosen Publishing Group, Inc., The.

Field, Andrea R. Matter, 1 vol. 2012. (Introduction to Physics Ser.). (ENG., Illus.). 80p. (YA). (gr. 8-8). 35.29 *(978-1-61530-839-2(3)*, bce4dc06-efb6-4e48-8f75-cb1150bd67cb) Rosen Publishing Group, Inc., The.

Field, Andrea R., ed. Matter, 4 vols. 2012. (Introduction to Physics Ser.). (ENG., Illus.). 80p. (YA). (gr. 8-8). 70.58 *(978-1-61530-848-4(2)*, b2658f90-ac0c-46f1-8f8b-8d66a52a1dab) Rosen Publishing Group, Inc., The.

Garcia, Karina. Karina Garcia's DIY Slime. 2017. (ENG., Illus.). 80p. (J). (gr. 4-9). pap. 7.99 *(978-1-4998-0660-1(4))* Little Bee Books Inc.

Gardner, Robert. Atoms & Molecules Experiments Using Ice, Salt, Marbles, & More: One Hour or Less Science Experiments, 1 vol. 2012. (Last-Minute Science Projects Ser.). (ENG.). 48p. (gr. 5-6). 27.93 *(978-0-7660-3961-2(7)*, be2ba508-8298-46c3-91fc-828ec175ef9a) Enslow Publishing, LLC.

Hansen, Amy S. Matter Comes in All Shapes. 2011. (My Science Library). (ENG., Illus.). 24p. (gr. 1-2). pap. 9.95 *(978-1-61741-941-6(9)*, 9781617419416) Rourke Educational Media.

Hanson-Harding, Alexandra. What Is Matter?, 1 vol. 2014. (Let's Find Out! Physical Science Ser.). (ENG.). 32p. (J). (gr. 2-3). 26.06 *(978-1-62275-487-8(5)*, 41cb61da-e4ae-4f09-9f0a-ce4398ae7cf9, Britannica Educational Publishing) Rosen Publishing Group, Inc., The.

Hibbert, Clare. Matter & Materials, 1 vol. 2018. (Science Explorers Ser.). (ENG.). 32p. (gr. 3-3). lib. bdg. 26.93 *(978-1-9785-0645-9(7)*, 51126745-b992-4093-830d-45a0a0dffb7f) Enslow Publishing, LLC.

Hirsch, Rebecca. Science Lab: Properties of Matter. 2011. (Explorer Library: Language Arts Explorer Ser.). (ENG.). 32p. (gr. 4-8). pap. 14.21 *(978-1-61080-295-6(0)*, 201217) Cherry Lake Publishing.

—Science Lab: Properties of Matter. 2011. (Explorer Library: Language Arts Explorer Ser.). (ENG., Illus.). 32p. (gr. 4-8). lib. bdg. 32.07 *(978-1-61080-206-2(3)*, 201188) Cherry Lake Publishing.

Holt, Rinehart and Winston Staff. Holt Science Spectrum Chptr. 3: States of Matter. 4th ed. Date not set. pap. 11.20 *(978-0-03-068586-6(9))* Holt McDougal.

Jennings, Terry J. Hot & Cold. 2009. (J). 28.50 *(978-1-59920-274-7(3))* Black Rabbit Bks.

Kjelle, Marylou Morano. The Properties of Metals, 1 vol. 2006. (Journeys Ser.). (ENG., Illus.). 24p. (gr. 4-4). pap. 7.05 *(978-1-4042-2164-2(6)*, a6fc3e74-3838-4545-9116-185e95ec7ade, PowerKids Pr.) Rosen Publishing Group, Inc., The.

—The Properties of Salts, 1 vol. 2006. (Library of Physical Science Ser.). (ENG., Illus.). 24p. (YA). (gr. 4-4). lib. bdg. 26.27 *(978-1-4042-3425-3(X)*, d9e97ded-9df5-449d-88b9-43761edcb601) Rosen Publishing Group, Inc., The.

—The Properties of Solids, 1 vol. 2006. (Library of Physical Science Ser.). (ENG., Illus.). 24p. (YA). (gr. 4-4). lib. bdg. 26.27 *(978-1-4042-3421-5(7)*,

3d3cd0be-2814-4c1b-a426-aa08542b11ca) Rosen Publishing Group, Inc., The.

Larson, Daniel. The Nature of Matter. 2007. (Physics in Action Ser.). (ENG., Illus.). 107p. (gr. 9-12). lib. bdg. 35.00 *(978-0-7910-8929-3(0)*, P114475, Facts On File) Infobase Holdings, Inc.

LernerClassroom Editors. First Step Nonfiction-States of Matter Teaching Guide. 2009. pap. 7.95 *(978-0-8225-6883-4(7))* Lerner Publishing Group.

Lilly, Melinda. Solid, Liquid, & Gas. Thompson, Scott M., illus. 2003. 24p. (J). 20.64 *(978-1-58952-648-8(1))* Rourke Educational Media.

MacFarlane, Katherine. The Father of the Atom: Democritus & the Nature of Matter, 1 vol. 2009. (Great Minds of Ancient Science & Math Ser.). (ENG., Illus.). 112p. (gr. 4-6). lib. bdg. 35.93 *(978-0-7660-3410-5(0)*, 7b71ef35-cafc-4b9f-9833-a968fd6b3d9b) Enslow Publishing, LLC.

Manolis, Kay. Matter. 2007. (First Science Ser.). (ENG., Illus.). 24p. (J). (gr. 2-5). lib. bdg. 26.95 *(978-1-60014-130-0(7)*, Blastoff! Readers) Bellwether Media.

Matos, Rebecca. Matter Is Everywhere: Solids, Liquids, & Gases. 2005. (J). pap. *(978-1-4108-4610-5(5))* Benchmark Education Co.

—Measuring Matter: Solids, Liquids, & Gases. 2005. (J). pap. *(978-1-4108-4603-7(2))* Benchmark Education Co.

—This Is Matter: Solids, Liquids, & Gases. 2005. (J). pap. *(978-1-4108-4596-2(6))* Benchmark Education Co.

Matter & Energy Lesson Plans & Blackline Masters (National Version) 2009. (Journeys Ser.). 20.00 *(978-1-4042-9489-9(9)*, Rosen Classroom) Rosen Publishing Group, Inc., The.

Matter & Energy Word-picture match cards, Memory game cards, Labeled picture Cards. 2008. (Journeys Ser.). 46.60 *(978-1-4042-9490-5(2)*, Rosen Classroom) Rosen Publishing Group, Inc., The.

Meredith, Susan Markowitz. The States of Matter: Set Of 6. 2010. (Early Connections Ser.). (J). pap. 37.00 net. *(978-1-4108-1083-0(6))* Benchmark Education Co.

Merrill, Amy French. Everyday Physical Science Experiments with Solids. 2009. (Science Surprises Ser.). 24p. (gr. 3-3). 42.50 *(978-1-60853-064-9(7)*, PowerKids Pr.) Rosen Publishing Group, Inc., The.

Michele, Tracey. Having Fun with Matter. 2011. (Learn-Abouts Ser.). (Illus.). 16p. (J). pap. 7.95 *(978-1-59920-628-8(5))* Black Rabbit Bks.

Moore, Elizabeth. Matter Is Everything! 2011. (Wonder Readers Early Level Ser.). (ENG.). 16p. (gr. -1-1). pap. 35.94 *(978-1-4296-8126-1(8)*, Capstone Pr.) Capstone.

Morano-Kjelle, Marylou. Gases, 1 vol., 1. 2014. (Ultimate Science: Physical Science Ser.). (ENG.). 24p. (gr. 3-3). 26.27 *(978-1-4777-6081-9(4)*, 1448d621-d2b2-418e-88b1-c21158581145, PowerKids Pr.) Rosen Publishing Group, Inc., The.

—Liquids, 1 vol., 1. 2014. (Ultimate Science: Physical Science Ser.). (ENG.). 24p. (gr. 3-3). pap. 8.05 *(978-1-4777-6078-9(4)*, 063d529a-49f3-4780-a57f-76d29650b292, PowerKids Pr.) Rosen Publishing Group, Inc., The.

—Solids, 1 vol., 1. 2014. (Ultimate Science: Physical Science Ser.). (ENG.). 24p. (gr. 3-3). pap. 8.05 *(978-1-4777-6004-8(0)*, 00637dda-b80c-4e48-9b5c-f3a6983d40bb, PowerKids Pr.) Rosen Publishing Group, Inc., The.

Mullins, Matt. States of Matter. 2009. (Explorer Library: Science Explorer Ser.). (ENG., Illus.). 32p. (gr. 4-8). lib. bdg. 32.07 *(978-1-60279-535-8(5)*, 200299) Cherry Lake Publishing.

National Geographic Learning. Language, Literacy & Vocabulary - Reading Expeditions (Physical Science): What Is Matter? 2007. (ENG., Illus.). 36p. (J). pap. 20.95 *(978-0-7922-5442-3(2))* CENGAGE Learning.

—World Windows 3 (Science): Solids, Liquids, & Gases: Content Literacy, Nonfiction Reading, Language & Literacy. 2011. (World Windows Ser.). (ENG., Illus.). 16p. (J). 10.95 *(978-1-133-49276-4(2))* Cengage Heinle.

Oxlade, Chris. Solids: An Investigation, 1 vol. 2007. (Science Investigations Ser.). (ENG., Illus.). 32p. (YA). (gr. 4-5). lib. bdg. 30.27 *(978-1-4042-4284-5(8)*, 1d8e4ccd-ba54-42dd-910e-b2454e999dc0) Rosen Publishing Group, Inc., The.

Paris, Morgaine. Composition of Matter. 2015. (Science: Informational Text Ser.). (ENG., Illus.). 32p. (gr. 4-8). pap. 11.99 *(978-1-4807-4720-3(3))* Teacher Created Materials, Inc.

Parker, Janice. The Science of Liquids & Solids. 2003. (Living Science Ser.). (Illus.). 32p. (J). (gr. 1-3). pap. 9.95 *(978-1-930954-11-3(5))* Weigl Pubs., Inc.

Peppas, Lynn. What Is a Solid? 2012. (ENG.). 24p. (J). *(978-0-7787-0771-4(7))*; (Illus.). (gr. 2-3). pap. *(978-0-7787-0778-3(4))* Crabtree Publishing Co.

Peters, Katie. Changing Water. 2019. (Science All Around Me (Pull Ahead Readers — Nonfiction) Ser.). (ENG., Illus.). 16p. (J). (gr. -1-1). pap. 8.99 *(978-1-5415-7332-1(3)*, 118cc92f-3cfa-4c1d-b740-17b5aa8cccf2); lib. bdg. 27.99 *(978-1-5415-5847-2(2)*, 3d1a77ca-d9c8-4745-b9b6-eba71b7f4550) Lerner Publishing Group. (Lerner Pubns.).

Petersen, Kristen. Understanding Kinetic Energy. 2015. (J). lib. bdg. *(978-1-62713-435-4(2))* 2014. (ENG.). 48p. (YA). (gr. 8-8). 33.07 *(978-1-5026-0144-5(3)*, a63fb8d4-8f7b-4eec-94dc-63d80ecfb319) Cavendish Square Publishing LLC.

Pettiford, Rebecca. Matter. 2018. (Science Starters Ser.). (ENG., Illus.). 24p. (J). (gr. k-3). pap. 7.99 *(978-1-61891-466-8(9)*, 12119, Blastoff! Readers) Bellwether Media.

Rector, Rebecca Kraft. Color. 2019. (Let's Learn about Matter Ser.). (ENG.). 24p. (gr. 1-2). 56.10 *(978-1-9785-0906-1(5))* Enslow Publishing, LLC.

—Texture, 1 vol. 2019. (Let's Learn about Matter Ser.). (ENG.). 24p. (gr. 1-2). 24.27 *(978-1-9785-0755-5(0)*, c809329e-e139-4114-9784-60b47756f5b2) Enslow Publishing, LLC.

Reilly, Kathleen M. Explore Solids & Liquids! With 25 Great Projects. Stone, Bryan, illus. 2014. (Explore Your World Ser.). (ENG.). 96p. (J). (gr. 1-5). 19.95 *(978-1-61930-171-9(7)*, 7f7c27af-9a1c-42b1-99ba-9ef797915109) Nomad Pr.

Riley, Peter. Matter, 1 vol. 2016. (Moving up with Science Ser.). (ENG.). 32p. (J). (gr. 3-4). pap. 11.00 *(978-1-4994-3149-0(X)*, 28b34796-e66c-41f5-8a62-aef6bcc57973, PowerKids Pr.) Rosen Publishing Group, Inc., The.

Rivera, Sheila. Dissolving. 2007. (First Step Nonfiction — Changing Matter Ser.). (ENG., Illus.). 8p. (J). (gr. k-2). pap. 5.99 *(978-0-8225-6414-0(9)*, 11d23c83-9c0a-4555-853a-fbd3ea30e999) Lerner Publishing Group.

—Heating. 2007. (First Step Nonfiction — Changing Matter Ser.). (ENG., Illus.). 8p. (J). (gr. k-2). pap. 5.99 *(978-0-8225-6415-7(7)*, f6e755d5-997c-47bd-8a5e-b591f3d38ddb) Lerner Publishing Group.

Rodriguez, Cindy & Siemens, Jared. Gas. 2016. (J). *(978-1-4896-5752-7(5))* Weigl Pubs., Inc.

—Liquid. 2016. (J). *(978-1-4896-5746-6(0))* Weigl Pubs., Inc.

Rowe, Brooke. Melting Ice. Bane, Jeff, illus. 2017. (My Early Library: My Science Fun Ser.). (ENG.). 24p. (J). (gr. k-1). lib. bdg. 30.64 *(978-1-63472-823-2(8)*, 209718) Cherry Lake Publishing.

Ryckman, Tatiana. Investigating Matter Through Modeling, 1 vol. 2019. (Science Investigators Ser.). (ENG.). 48p. (gr. 5-5). pap. 13.93 *(978-1-5026-5249-2(8)*, fc4c65d7-1fe8-4df9-b53c-875ab9fd5bae) Cavendish Square Publishing LLC.

Schaefer, Lola M. What Is Matter? 2011. (Early Connections Ser.). (J). *(978-1-61672-656-0(3))* Benchmark Education Co.

Schuh, Mari. All about Matter, 1 vol. 2011. (Science Builders Ser.). (ENG.). 24p. (J). (gr. -1-2). pap. 7.29 *(978-1-4296-7105-7(X)*, 116765); (gr. k-1). pap. 44.74 *(978-1-4296-7111-8(4)*, 16692, Capstone Pr.) Capstone.

Silverman, Buffy. State of Confusion: Solids, Liquids, & Gases. rev. ed. 2016. (Raintree Fusion: Physical Science Ser.). (ENG.). 32p. (J). (gr. 4-7). pap. 8.29 *(978-1-4109-8520-0(2)*, 134048, Raintree) Capstone.

Slade, Suzanne. Splat! Wile E. Coyote Experiments with States of Matter, 1 vol. Cornia, Christian, illus. 2014. (Wile E. Coyote, Physical Science Genius Ser.). (ENG.). 32p. (J). (gr. 3-6). 31.32 *(978-1-4765-4224-9(4)*, 124336, Capstone Pr.) Capstone.

—The Structure of Atoms. (Library of Physical Science Ser.). 24p. (gr. 4-4). 2009. 42.50 *(978-1-60853-795-2(1))* 2006. (ENG., Illus.). pap. 7.05 *(978-1-4042-2161-1(1)*, ccbf09dd-9ec1-408d-926f-2ab8bc98b454) Rosen Publishing Group, Inc., The. (PowerKids Pr.).

Slingerland, Janet. Werewolves & States of Matter. Mosquito, Angel, illus. 2011. (Monster Science Ser.). (ENG.). 32p. (J). (gr. 3-4). pap. 49.60 *(978-1-4296-7334-1(6)*, 16835); pap. 8.10 *(978-1-4296-7333-4(8)*, 116880) Capstone. (Capstone Pr.).

Solway, Andrew. Energy & Matter. 2010. (21st Century Science Ser.). (ENG.). 112p. (YA). (gr. 9-12). 42.80 *(978-1-933834-72-6(2)*, 16383) Brown Bear Bks.

Spilsbury, Louise & Spilsbury, Richard. Solids, Liquids, & Gases, 1 vol. 2013. (Essential Physical Science Ser.). (ENG., Illus.). 48p. (J). (gr. 4-6). pap. 9.95 *(978-1-4329-8160-0(9)*, 123400, Heinemann) Capstone.

Stille, Darlene R. Matter: See It, Touch It, Taste It, Smell It, 1 vol. Boyd, Sheree, illus. 2004. (Amazing Science Ser.). (ENG.). 24p. (J). (gr. k-4). per. 8.95 *(978-1-4048-0344-2(0)*, 92576, Picture Window Bks.) Capstone.

Stille, Darlene R. & Picture Window Books Staff. La Materia: Mira, Toca, Prueba, Huele, 1 vol. Robledo, Sol, tr. Boyd, Sheree, illus. 2007. (Ciencia Asombrosa Ser.). (SPA.). 24p. (J). (gr. k-4). 27.32 *(978-1-4048-3221-3(1)*, 93775, Picture Window Bks.) Capstone.

Strauss, Michael J. Investigating the Natural World of Chemistry with Kids: Experiments, Writing, & Drawing Activities for Learning Science. 2012. 226p. pap. 25.95 *(978-1-61233-155-3(6))* Universal Pubs.

Sullivan, Erin Ash. Measuring Matter: Set Of 6. 2010. (Navigators Ser.). (J). pap. 44.00 net. *(978-1-4108-5070-6(6))* Benchmark Education Co.

—Measuring Matter: Text Pairs. 2008. (Bridges/Navigators Ser.). (J). (gr. 3). 94.00 *(978-1-4108-8367-4(1))* Benchmark Education Co.

Sundance/Newbridge LLC Staff. Matter Is Everything. 2004. (Reading PowerWorks Ser.). (gr. 1-3). 37.50 *(978-0-7608-8900-8(7))*; pap. 6.10 *(978-0-7608-8901-5(5))* Sundance/Newbridge Educational Publishing.

—What Is Matter? 2007. (Early Science Ser.). (gr. k-3). 18.95 *(978-1-4007-6477-8(7))*; pap. 6.10 *(978-1-4007-6473-0(4))* Sundance/Newbridge Educational Publishing.

Troupe, Thomas Kingsley. What's the Matter with the Three Little Pigs? The Fairy-Tale Physics of Matter. Tejido, Jomike, illus. 2018. (STEM-Twisted Fairy Tales Ser.). (ENG.). 32p. (J). (gr. k-3). lib. bdg. 27.99 *(978-1-5158-2896-9(4)*, 138418, Picture Window Bks.) Capstone.

Walker, Denise. Materials. 2006. (Core Chemistry/Evans Brothers Ser.). (Illus.). 48p. (YA). (gr. 5-9). 34.25 *(978-1-58340-817-9(7))* Black Rabbit Bks.

Walker, Sally M. Investigating Matter. 2011. (Searchlight Books (tm) — How Does Energy Work? Ser.). (ENG., Illus.). (gr. 3-5). 40p. (J). pap. 9.99 *(978-0-7613-7875-4(8)*, c14848eb-749d-4a42-89aa-34d6242a337a); pap. 51.01 *(978-0-7613-8409-0(X))* Lerner Publishing Group.

—La Materia. Translations.com Staff, tr. from ENG. King, Andy, photos by. 2007. (Libros de Energía para madrugadores (Early Bird Energy) Ser.). (SPA., Illus.). 48p. (J). (gr. 2-5). lib. bdg. 26.60 *(978-0-8225-7721-8(6))* Lerner Publishing Group.

—La Materia; Matter. 2008. pap. 52.95 *(978-0-8225-9870-1(1))* Lerner Publishing Group.

—Matter. 2006. (Illus.). 48p. (J). pap. 8.95 *(978-0-8225-2844-9(4))* Lerner Publishing Group.

Weakland, Mark. The Solid Truth about Matter. Lum, Bernice, illus. 2012. (LOL Physical Science Ser.). (ENG.). 32p. (J). (gr. 3-4). pap. 49.60 *(978-1-4296-9303-5(7)*, 18534, Capstone Pr.) Capstone.

Weakland, Mark Andrew. The Solid Truth about Matter, 1 vol. Lum, Bernice, illus. 2012. (LOL Physical Science Ser.). (ENG.). 32p. (J). (gr. 3-6). pap. 8.10 *(978-1-4296-9302-8(9)*, 120363, Capstone Pr.) Capstone.

Weir, Jane. Inside the World of Matter, 1 vol. rev. ed. 2007. (Science: Informational Text Ser.). (ENG.). 32p. (gr. 3-6). pap. 12.99 *(978-0-7439-0567-1(9))* Teacher Created Materials, Inc.

—Max Planck: Uncovering the World of Matter, 1 vol. rev. ed. 2007. (Science: Informational Text Ser.). (ENG.). 32p. (gr. 3-6). pap. 12.99 *(978-0-7439-0568-8(7))* Teacher Created Materials, Inc.

Woodford, Chris & Clowes, Martin. Atoms & Molecules: Investigating the Building Blocks of Matter, 1 vol. 2012. (Scientific Pathways Ser.). (ENG., Illus.). 48p. (J). (gr. 5-5). lib. bdg. 34.47 *(978-1-4488-7196-4(4)*, 5e36ee8c-313f-414f-942c-eede505fcb37, Rosen Reference) Rosen Publishing Group, Inc., The.

World Book, Inc. Staff, contrib. by. Encyclopedia of Matter & Energy. 2013. (Illus.). 245p. (J). *(978-0-7166-7521-1(8))* World Bk., Inc.

—Matter & How It Changes. 2011. (J). *(978-0-7166-1428-9(6))* World Bk., Inc.

MATTER—PROPERTIES

Adams, Tom. Super Science: Matter Matters! Flintman, Thomas, illus. 2012. (ENG.). 18p. (J). (gr. 2-5). 18.99 *(978-0-7636-6096-3(5)*, Templar) Candlewick Pr.

Aloian, Molly. Mixtures & Solutions, 1 vol. 2008. (Why Chemistry Matters Ser.). (ENG., Illus.). 32p. (J). (gr. 3-7). pap. *(978-0-7787-4250-0(4))* Crabtree Publishing Co.

Amson-Bradshaw, Georgia. States of Matter, 1 vol. 2017. (Science in a Flash Ser.). (ENG.). 32p. (J). (gr. 5-5). pap. 11.50 *(978-1-5382-1477-0(6)*, d9046484-6282-4ada-a2c7-042b1d3c9b51); lib. bdg. 28.27 *(978-1-5382-1401-5(6)*, 906c08d0-5b95-4e6c-a67a-9e3a2e993e64) Stevens, Gareth Publishing LLLP.

Barkan, Joanne. What Is Density? 2006. (Rookie Read-About Science Ser.). (ENG., Illus.). 32p. (J). (gr. 1-2). lib. bdg. 20.50 *(978-0-516-23618-6(0))* Scholastic Library Publishing.

Bateman, Graham, ed. Atoms, Molecules, & States of Matter. 2011. (Facts at Your Fingertips: Introducing Chemistry Ser.). 64p. (YA). (gr. 7-12). lib. bdg. 35.65 *(978-1-936333-10-3(4))* Brown Bear Bks.

Baxter, Roberta. States of Matter in the Real World. 2013. (Science in the Real World Ser.). (ENG.). 48p. (J). (gr. 4-8). pap. 18.50 *(978-1-61783-795-1(4)*, 14619) ABDO Publishing Co.

Bell, Samantha. States of Matter. Bane, Jeff, illus. 2018. (Mi Mini Biografía (My Itty-Bitty Bio): My Early Library). (ENG.). 24p. (J). (gr. k-1). pap. 12.79 *(978-1-5341-0824-0(6)*, 210660); lib. bdg. 30.64 *(978-1-5341-0725-0(8)*, 210659) Cherry Lake Publishing.

Best, Arthur. Flexibility, 1 vol. 2018. (Properties of Matter Ser.). (ENG.). 24p. (J). (gr. 1-1). pap. 9.22 *(978-1-5026-4184-7(4)*, 79af2630-d976-4d04-a897-e3df57bb5bf9) Cavendish Square Publishing LLC.

—Length & Width, 1 vol. 2018. (Properties of Matter Ser.). (ENG.). 24p. (gr. 1-1). pap. 9.22 *(978-1-5026-4218-9(2)*, e86dd955-02cf-4271-b7ce-e40473ceef27) Cavendish Square Publishing LLC.

—Mass & Weight, 1 vol. 2018. (Properties of Matter Ser.). (ENG.). 24p. (J). (gr. 1-1). pap. 9.22 *(978-1-5026-4224-0(7)*, 958bc6c7-67ef-4264-9965-236e6200c1a9) Cavendish Square Publishing LLC.

Brannon, Barbara. Discover Solids. 2005. (J). pap. *(978-1-4108-5117-8(6))* Benchmark Education Co.

Braun, Eric. Curious Pearl Explains States of Matter: 4D an Augmented Reality Science Experience. Dehennin, Stephanie, illus. 2017. (Curious Pearl, Science Girl 4D Ser.). (ENG.). 24p. (J). (gr. k-2). lib. bdg. 25.99 *(978-1-5158-1342-2(8)*, 135144, Picture Window Bks.) Capstone.

—Joe-Joe the Wizard Brews up Solids, Liquids, & Gases, 1 vol. Boyden, Robin, illus. 2012. (In the Science Lab Ser.). (ENG.). 24p. (J). (gr. k-3). pap. 9.95 *(978-1-4048-7238-7(8)*, 118177, Picture Window Bks.) Capstone.

Brown Bear Books. Mechanics. 2011. (Introducing Physics Ser.). (ENG.). 64p. (J). (gr. 8-11). lib. bdg. 39.95 *(978-1-936333-09-7(0)*, 16506) Brown Bear Bks.

Cardenas, Ernesto & Saavedra, Patricia. Qué es la Materia? l.t. ed. 2006. (SPA., Illus.). 16p. pap. 4.95 *(978-1-933668-16-1(4))* Milo Educational Bks. & Resources.

Carr, Aaron. Solids. 2012. (What Is Matter? Ser.). (ENG., Illus.). 24p. (J). (gr. -1-3). lib. bdg. 27.13 *(978-1-61913-601-4(5)*, AV2 by Weigl) Weigl Pubs., Inc.

Carr, Aaron & Evans Ogden, Lesley J. Studying Properties of Matter. 2016. (Illus.). 24p. (J). *(978-1-5105-1128-6(8))* SmartBook Media, Inc.

Carr, Aaron & Siemens, Jared. Solid. 2016. (J). *(978-1-4896-5749-7(5))* Weigl Pubs., Inc.

Clark, John O. E. Matter & Materials, 1 vol. 2005. (Real World Science Ser.). (ENG., Illus.). 32p. (gr. 3-5). lib. bdg. 28.67 *(978-0-8368-6307-9(0)*, 9c78e5c2-bc82-4f99-b628-1a15deda8b17, Gareth Stevens Learning Library) Stevens, Gareth Publishing LLLP.

Claybourne, Anna. Recreate Discoveries about States of Matter. 2018. (Recreate Scientific Discoveries Ser.). (Illus.). 32p. (J). (gr. 4-5). *(978-0-7787-5062-8(0))* Crabtree Publishing Co.

—The Science of a Glass of Water, 1 vol. 2009. (Science Of... Ser.). (ENG., Illus.). 32p. (YA). (gr. 4-5). lib. bdg. 28.67 *(978-1-4339-0041-9(6)*, eb7e775e-10e9-4845-ae67-41feea29c034) Stevens, Gareth Publishing LLLP.

Cook, Trevor M. Experiments with States of Matter, 1 vol. 2009. (Science Lab Ser.). (ENG.). 32p. (J). (gr. 4-4). lib. bdg. 30.27 *(978-1-4358-2805-6(4)*, 805aa3b0-d725-4722-8de4-10bd1d8f6bdc, PowerKids Pr.) Rosen Publishing Group, Inc., The.

Cooper, Chris. The Basics of Energy & Reactions, 1 vol. 2013. (Core Concepts Ser.). (ENG.). 96p. (YA). (gr. 7-7). 39.77 *(978-1-4777-2710-2(8)*, 728705bb-701d-4e25-bd69-020704b0078e) Rosen Publishing Group, Inc., The.

Crane, Cody. Matter (Rookie Read-About Science: Physical Science) (Library Edition) 2019. (Rookie Read-About Science Ser.). (ENG., Illus.). 32p. (J). (gr. 1-2). lib. bdg. 25.00 *(978-0-531-13409-2(1)*, Children's Pr.) Scholastic Library Publishing.

Curry, Don L. What Is Mass? (Rookie Read-About Science: Physical Science: Previous Editions) Senisi, Ellen B., photos by. 2005. (Rookie Read-About Science Ser.). (ENG., Illus.). 32p. (J). (gr. 1-2). pap. 4.95 *(978-0-516-24666-6(6)*, Children's Pr.) Scholastic Library Publishing.

Diehn, Andi. Matter. Li, Hui, illus. 2018. (Picture Book Science Ser.). (ENG.). 32p. (J). (gr. k-3). 19.95 *(978-1-61930-642-4(5)*, 65b3e6fa-8009-49c5-85b7-4bcf80155600) Nomad Pr.

Does It Absorb or Repel Liquid? 2014. (What's the Matter? Ser.). (ENG., Illus.). 24p. (J). (gr. 1-2). *(978-0-7787-0537-6(4))* Crabtree Publishing Co.

Dunne, Abbie. Matter. 2016. (Physical Science Ser.). (ENG., Illus.). 24p. (J). (gr. -1-2). lib. bdg. 27.32 *(978-1-5157-0939-8(6)*, 132238, Capstone Pr.) Capstone.

Evans Ogden, Lesley J. Properties of Matter. 2011. (J). (gr. 4-6). pap. 12.95 *(978-1-61690-734-1(7)*, AV2 by Weigl); (Illus.). 24p. (gr. 3-6). 27.13 *(978-1-61690-730-3(4))* Weigl Pubs., Inc.

Fletcher, Sheila. Is It Flexible or Rigid? 2012. (ENG., Illus.). 24p. (J). *(978-0-7787-2047-8(0))*; pap. *(978-0-7787-2054-6(3))* Crabtree Publishing Co.

Flynn, James J. Air. 2003. (Matter & Materials Ser.). (J). pap. *(978-1-58417-169-0(3))*; lib. bdg. *(978-1-58417-163-8(4))* Lake Street Pubs.

Garcia, Karina. Karina Garcia's Next-Level DIY Slime. 2018. (ENG., Illus.). 80p. (J). (gr. 4). pap. 7.99 *(978-1-4998-0799-8(6))* Little Bee Books Inc.

—Karina Garcia's Next-Level DIY Slime. 2018. (Illus.). 80p. (J). pap. *(978-1-78741-373-3(X))* Templar Publishing.

Gardner, Robert. Science Fair Projects about the Properties of Matter, Using the Scientific Method, 1 vol. 2010. (Physics Science Projects Using the Scientific Method Ser.). (ENG., Illus.). 160p. (gr. 5-6). 38.60 *(978-0-7660-3417-4(8)*, af76a3b3-d47f-4afb-8acc-dd7aa224aad6) Enslow Publishing, LLC.

—Solids, Liquids, & Gases Science Projects, 1 vol. 2013. (Exploring Hands-On Science Projects Ser.). (ENG.). 128p. (gr. 5-6). lib. bdg. 30.60 *(978-0-7660-4145-5(X)*, 8b552e68-1f05-4dcc-87a5-747e774f7443) Enslow Publishing, LLC.

Gaughan, Richard. Antimatter Explained, 1 vol. 2018. (Mysteries of Space Ser.). (ENG.). 80p. (gr. 7-7). 38.93 *(978-1-9785-0453-0(5)*, b23c6896-570c-44cb-afdb-5c426251a5fd) Enslow Publishing, LLC.

Gordon, Sharon. Duro, Blando / Hard, Soft, 1 vol. 2008. (Exactamente lo Opuesto / Just the Opposite Ser.). (ENG & SPA., Illus.). 24p. (gr. k-1). lib. bdg. 25.50 *(978-0-7614-2448-2(2)*, e7a0b9fe-3b20-4d53-8a86-dbe4029fea9e) Cavendish Square Publishing LLC.

—Duro, Blando (Hard, Soft), 1 vol. 2008. (Exactamente lo Opuesto (Just the Opposite) Ser.). (SPA., Illus.). 24p. (gr. k-1). lib. bdg. 25.50 *(978-0-7614-2368-3(0)*, ee981e10-202d-411b-bd7e-97638fc06451) Cavendish Square Publishing LLC.

—Hard, Soft, 1 vol. (Just the Opposite Ser.). (ENG.). 24p. (gr. k-1). 2008. pap. 9.23 *(978-0-7614-3282-1(5)*, 95986292-9ea2-4c60-bb28-0e5fb90be301) 2003. (Illus.). lib. bdg. 25.50 *(978-0-7614-1571-8(8)*, 855fec19-0da3-4bad-93bd-7d336d70124b, Cavendish Square) Cavendish Square Publishing LLC.

Gregory, Josh. Junior Scientists: Experiment with Solids. 2010. (Explorer Junior Library: Science Explorer Junior Ser.). (ENG., Illus.). 32p. (gr. 3-6). lib. bdg. 32.07 *(978-1-60279-845-8(1)*, 200556) Cherry Lake Publishing.

Griffin, Mary. States of Matter, 1 vol. 2018. (Look at Chemistry Ser.). (ENG.). 32p. (gr. 2-2). 28.27 *(978-1-5382-3013-8(5)*, 0a25c578-da27-4005-80e0-190ac3f4993f) Stevens, Gareth Publishing LLLP.

Hewitt, Sally. Amazing Materials. 2007. (Amazing Science Ser.). (ENG.). 32p. (J). pap. *(978-0-7787-3627-1(X))* Crabtree Publishing Co.

Holland, Gini. Soft & Hard / Blando y Duro, 1 vol. 2007. (I Know Opposites / Conceptos Contrarios Ser.). (SPA & ENG., Illus.). 16p. (gr. k-2). lib. bdg. 21.67 *(978-0-8368-8306-0(3)*, 98c53770-3d41-4ba4-a91f-32be6484c785, Weekly Reader Leveled Readers) Stevens, Gareth Publishing LLLP.

Holt, Rinehart and Winston Staff. Holt Science & Technology Chapter 2: Physical Science: Properties of Matter. 5th ed. 2004. (Illus.). pap. 12.86 *(978-0-03-030361-6(3))* Holt McDougal.

Housel, Debra J. The Nature of Matter, 1 vol. rev. ed. 2014. (Science: Informational Text Ser.). (ENG., Illus.). 32p. (J). (gr. 2-3). pap. 10.99 *(978-1-4807-4603-9(7))* Teacher Created Materials, Inc.

Hughes, Susan. Does It Sink or Float? 2014. (What's the Matter? Ser.). (ENG., Illus.). 24p. (J). (gr. 1-2). lib. bdg. *(978-0-7787-0536-9(6))* Crabtree Publishing Co.

—Is It Heavy or Light? 2012. (ENG., Illus.). 24p. (J). *(978-0-7787-2048-5(9))*; pap. *(978-0-7787-2055-3(1))* Crabtree Publishing Co.

—Is It Hot or Cold? 2012. (ENG., Illus.). 24p. (J). *(978-0-7787-2049-2(7))*; pap. *(978-0-7787-2056-0(X))* Crabtree Publishing Co.

—Is It Transparent or Opaque? 2012. (ENG., Illus.). 24p. (J). *(978-0-7787-2052-2(7))*; pap. *(978-0-7787-2059-1(4))* Crabtree Publishing Co.

Is It Hard or Soft? 2014. (What's the Matter? Ser.). (ENG., Illus.). 24p. (J). (gr. 1-2). *(978-0-7787-0538-3(2))* Crabtree Publishing Co.

Is It Natural or Human-Made? 2014. (What's the Matter? Ser.). (ENG., Illus.). 24p. (J). (gr. 1-2). *(978-0-7787-0535-2(8))* Crabtree Publishing Co.

Ives, Rob. Fun Experiments with Matter: Invisible Ink, Giant Bubbles, & More. Sassin, Eva, illus. 2017. (Amazing Science Experiments Ser.). (ENG.). 32p. (J). (gr. 3-6). lib. bdg. 27.99 *(978-1-5124-3216-9(4)*, a8503d73-4445-434c-bf6d-2da4ebd9590f, Hungry Tomato (r)) Lerner Publishing Group.

Jackson, Tom. The Basics of Atoms & Molecules, 1 vol. 2013. (Core Concepts Ser.). (ENG.). 96p. (YA). (gr. 7-7). 39.77 *(978-1-4777-2715-7(9)*, 3ef6df4b-f2ba-4735-8783-0dee38507838) Rosen Publishing Group, Inc., The.

Jordan, Apple. Heavy / Light, 1 vol. 2nd rev. ed. 2012. (Opposites Ser.). (ENG.). 16p. (gr. k-1). 24.07 *(978-1-60870-408-8(4),* 061610bb-3971-4197-9552-f0f7fcf38fae) Cavendish Square Publishing LLC.

Kenney, Karen Latchana. The Science of Stars: Exploring Matter. 2015. (Science in Action Ser.). (ENG., Illus.). 32p. (J). (gr. 3-6). 32.79 *(978-1-62403-965-2(0),* 19427, Checkerboard Library) ABDO Publishing Co.

Kjelle, Marylou Morano. The Properties of Liquids. (Library of Physical Science Ser.). 24p. (gr. 4-4). 2009. 42.50 *(978-1-60853-791-4(9))* 2006. (ENG., Illus.). pap. 7.05 *(978-1-4042-2169-7(7),* dbae3dcd-a6a2-4e23-b120-c621bda98618) Rosen Publishing Group, Inc., The. (PowerKids Pr.).

—The Properties of Metals. (Library of Physical Science Ser.). 24p. (gr. 4-4). 2009. 42.50 *(978-1-60853-792-1(7),* PowerKids Pr.) 2006. (ENG., Illus.). (J). lib. bdg. 26.27 *(978-1-4042-3417-8(9),* ef24b42f-0f74-42d0-960d-9f3cb2eaf754) Rosen Publishing Group, Inc., The.

—The Properties of Salts. (Library of Physical Science Ser.). 24p. (gr. 4-4). 2009. 42.50 *(978-1-60853-793-8(5))* 2006. (ENG., Illus.). pap. 7.05 *(978-1-4042-2172-7(7),* c641e5b0-2bb9-4f50-9dc3-dfc91a10a920) Rosen Publishing Group, Inc., The. (PowerKids Pr.).

—The Properties of Solids. (Library of Physical Science Ser.). 24p. (gr. 4-4). 2009. 42.50 *(978-1-60853-794-5(3))* 2006. (ENG., Illus.). pap. 7.05 *(978-1-4042-2168-0(9),* 4ba0fd1b-336c-4cfa-abc2-a8703c925b08) Rosen Publishing Group, Inc., The. (PowerKids Pr.).

Larson, Karen. Changing Matter, 1 vol. 2015. (Science: Informational Text Ser.). (ENG., Illus.). 32p. (gr. 3-4). pap. 11.99 *(978-1-4807-4642-8(8))* Teacher Created Materials, Inc.

Leber, Nancy. Solids: Text Pairs. 2008. (Bridges/Navigators Ser.). (J). (gr. 3). 89.00 *(978-1-4108-8372-8(8))* Benchmark Education Co.

Linde, Barbara M. Atoms: It Matters, 1 vol. 2019. (Spotlight on Physical Science Ser.). (ENG.). 32p. (gr. 4-6). pap. 11.60 *(978-1-7253-1289-0(1),* b0a7ecc8-7d74-433f-9ec3-6af95059bddb, PowerKids Pr.) Rosen Publishing Group, Inc., The.

Lindeen, Mary. Color & Shape. 2017. (Beginning-To-Read Ser.). (ENG.). 32p. (J). (gr. k-2). pap. 13.26 *(978-1-68404-101-5(5));* (Illus.). 22.60 *(978-1-59953-882-2(2))* Norwood Hse. Pr.

Mason, Adrienne. Change It! Solids, Liquids, Gases & You. Dávila, Claudia, illus. 2006. (Primary Physical Science Ser.). (ENG.). 32p. (J). (gr. -1-2). 8.99 *(978-1-55337-838-9(5))* Kids Can Pr., Ltd. CAN. Dist: Hachette Bk. Group.

—Touch It! Materials, Matter & You. Dávila, Claudia, illus. 2005. (Primary Physical Science Ser.). (ENG.). 32p. (J). (gr. -1-2). 8.99 *(978-1-55337-761-0(3))* Kids Can Pr., Ltd. CAN. Dist: Hachette Bk. Group.

Maurer, Daniel D. Do You Really Want to Skate on Thin Ice? A Book about States of Matter. Alberini, Teresa, illus. 2016. (Adventures in Science Ser.). (ENG.). 24p. (J). (gr. 1-4). lib. bdg. 20.95 *(978-1-60753-958-2(6),* 15631) Amicus.

Maurer, Tracy Nelson. Changing Matter: Understanding Physical & Chemical Changes. 2012. (My Science Library). (ENG.). 24p. (gr. 4-5). pap. 8.95 *(978-1-61810-240-9(0),* 9781618102409) Rourke Educational Media.

—Mix It up! Solution or Mixture? 2012. (My Science Library). (ENG.). 24p. (gr. 3-4). pap. 8.95 *(978-1-61810-227-0(3),* 9781618102270) Rourke Educational Media.

—The Scoop about Measuring Matter. 2012. (My Science Library). (ENG.). 24p. (gr. 3-4). pap. 8.95 *(978-1-61810-226-3(5),* 9781618102263) Rourke Educational Media.

McGraw Hill. Chemistry: Matter & Change, Student Edition. 2nd ed. 2004. (Glencoe Chemistry Ser.). (ENG., Illus.). 1024p. (gr. 10-12). stu. ed. 146.00 *(978-0-07-866418-2(7),* 0078664187) McGraw-Hill Education.

Mezzanotte, Jim. Gases, 1 vol. 2006. (States of Matter Ser.). (ENG., Illus.). 24p. (gr. 2-4). pap. 9.15 *(978-0-8368-6802-9(1),* f004267e-9878-43a0-b83c-f6507aa43329); lib. bdg. 24.67 *(978-0-8368-6797-8(1),* 73daadb0-f22f-44dc-afa7-b256ca1e11d3) Stevens, Gareth Publishing LLLP. (Weekly Reader Leveled Readers).

—Sólidos (Solids), 1 vol. 2006. (Estados de la Materia (States of Matter) Ser.). (SPA.). 24p. (gr. 2-4). pap. 9.15 *(978-0-8368-7410-5(2),* a0c51127-1afa-4656-8d7a-d351cc88e072); (Illus.). lib. bdg. 24.67 *(978-0-8368-7405-1(6),* 9d5c6ace-59d9-47a1-b3a6-03bc02ab1c4c) Stevens, Gareth Publishing LLLP. (Weekly Reader Leveled Readers).

—Solids, 1 vol. 2006. (States of Matter Ser.). (ENG., Illus.). 24p. (gr. 2-4). pap. 9.15 *(978-0-8368-6805-0(6),* 899ee823-efaf-4dc4-b910-a1ad5a4f311c); lib. bdg. 24.67 *(978-0-8368-6800-5(5),* ee27bcd9-4e96-41ce-82de-f36ccb2fa1db) Stevens, Gareth Publishing LLLP. (Weekly Reader Leveled Readers).

Miller, Heather. Matter. 2009. (21st Century Skills Library: Real World Science Ser.). (ENG., Illus.). 32p. (gr. 4-8). lib. bdg. 32.07 *(978-1-60279-460-3(X),* 200235) Cherry Lake Publishing.

Monroe, Tilda. What Do You Know about States of Matter?, 1 vol. 2010. (20 Questions: Physical Science Ser.). (ENG.). 24p. (J). (gr. 2-3). pap. 9.25 *(978-1-4488-1246-2(1),* a763c23b-56d4-419c-aa1d-41c7f8d896a5, PowerKids Pr.); lib. bdg. 26.27 *(978-1-4488-0670-6(4),* c2223e01-2183-4855-8c17-c6971ebeb124) Rosen Publishing Group, Inc., The.

Montgomery, Anne. Solid or Liquid?, 1 vol. rev. ed. 2014. (Science: Informational Text Ser.). (ENG., Illus.). 24p. (J). (gr. k-1). pap. 9.99 *(978-1-4807-4527-8(8))* Teacher Created Materials, Inc.

Moore, David. National Geographic Science 1-2 (Physical Science: Properties): Explore on Your Own: Cookie Time. 2009. (C). pap. 8.95 *(978-0-7362-5543-1(5))* National Geographic School Publishing, Inc.

—National Geographic Science 1-2 (Physical Science: Properties): Explore on Your Own: Decorating a Vase. 2009. (C). pap. 8.95 *(978-0-7362-5541-7(9))* National Geographic School Publishing, Inc.

—National Geographic Science 1-2 (Physical Science: Solids, Liquids, & Gases): Explore on Your Own: Postcards from My Trip. 2009. (Illus.). 12p. (C). pap. 8.95 *(978-0-7362-5601-8(6))* National Geographic School Publishing, Inc.

Moore, Elizabeth. Matter Is Everything. 2011. (Wonder Readers Early Level Ser.). (ENG.). 16p. (J). (gr. -1-1). pap. 6.25 *(978-1-4296-8059-2(8),* 118377, Capstone Pr.) Capstone.

Murphy, John, ed. Physics: Understanding the Properties of Matter & Energy, 1 vol. 2014. (Study of Science Ser.). (ENG., Illus.). 120p. (J). (gr. 8-8). 37.82 *(978-1-62275-418-2(2),* 292cbc2c-0212-417c-97ef-643b8d615e64) Rosen Publishing Group, Inc., The.

Murray, Julie. Hard & Soft. 2018. (Opposites Ser.). (ENG., Illus.). 24p. (J). (gr. -1-2). lib. bdg. 31.36 *(978-1-5321-8179-5(5),* 29831, Abdo Kids) ABDO Publishing Co.

National Geographic Learning. World Windows 3 (Science): Solids, Liquids, & Gases: Content Literacy, Nonfiction Reading, Language & Literacy. 2011. (World Windows Ser.). (ENG., Illus.). 16p. (J). 10.95 *(978-1-133-49276-4(2))* Cengage Heinle.

O'Mara, Kennon. Atoms, 1 vol. 2018. (Look at Chemistry Ser.). (ENG.). 32p. (gr. 2-2). 28.27 *(978-1-5382-3010-7(0),* 95c89f16-b4e2-4df8-a627-213698e1fc25) Stevens, Gareth Publishing LLLP.

O'Neal, Claire. A Project Guide to Matter. 2011. (Physical Science Projects for Kids Ser.). (Illus.). 48p. (J). (gr. 3-6). lib. bdg. 29.95 *(978-1-58415-967-4(7))* Mitchell Lane Pubs.

Oxlade, Chris. Experiments with Matter & Materials, 1 vol. 2014. (Excellent Science Experiments Ser.). (ENG.). 32p. (J). (gr. 4-5). lib. bdg. 29.27 *(978-1-4777-5969-1(7),* 4f23ee91-dd3d-42e7-843a-f7f824ef9bc8, PowerKids Pr.) Rosen Publishing Group, Inc., The.

—Mixing & Separating. 2007. (ENG., Illus.). 32p. (J). (gr. -1-3). pap. *(978-0-7787-3650-9(4))* Crabtree Publishing Co.

Peterson, Megan Cooley. Scooby-Doo! a States of Matter Mystery: Revenge from a Watery Grave. Cornia, Christian, illus. 2016. (Scooby-Doo Solves It with S. T. E. M. Ser.). (ENG.). 32p. (J). (gr. 3-6). 28.65 *(978-1-5157-2592-3(8),* 132936, Capstone Pr.) Capstone.

Pettiford, Rebecca. Gravity. 2018. (Science Starters Ser.). (ENG., Illus.). 24p. (J). (gr. k-3). lib. bdg. 26.95 *(978-1-62617-807-6(0),* Blastoff! Readers) Bellwether Media.

—Matter. 2018. (Science Starters Ser.). (ENG., Illus.). 24p. (J). (gr. k-3). lib. bdg. 26.95 *(978-1-62617-810-6(0),* Blastoff! Readers) Bellwether Media.

Randolph, Joanne. Solids in My World. 2009. (My World of Science Ser.). 24p. (gr. 2-2). 37.50 *(978-1-61514-728-1(4),* PowerKids Pr.) Rosen Publishing Group, Inc., The.

—Solids in My World/Los sólidos en mi Mundo. 2009. (My World of Science/la ciencia en mi mundo Ser.). (ENG & SPA.). 48p. (gr. 2-2). 37.50 *(978-1-61514-740-3(3),* Editorial Buenas Letras) Rosen Publishing Group, Inc., The.

Rector, Rebecca Kraft. Flexibility, 1 vol. 2019. (Let's Learn about Matter Ser.). (ENG.). 24p. (gr. 1-2). pap. 10.35 *(978-1-9785-0907-8(3),* 67af7e80-0374-4243-853d-3e6824aaa678) Enslow Publishing, LLC.

—Hardness. 2019. (Let's Learn about Matter Ser.). (ENG.). 24p. (gr. 1-2). 56.10 *(978-1-9785-0911-5(1))* Enslow Publishing, LLC.

Rees, Peter. Why Does Water Freeze? Level 3 Factbook. 2010. (Cambridge Young Readers Ser.). (ENG., Illus.). 16p. pap. 6.00 *(978-0-521-13712-6(8))* Cambridge Univ. Pr.

Rising, Heather. Is It Smooth or Rough? 2012. (ENG., Illus.). 24p. (J). *(978-0-7787-2051-5(9));* pap. *(978-0-7787-2058-4(6))* Crabtree Publishing Co.

Rising, Trudy L. Is It Magnetic or Nonmagnetic? 2012. (ENG., Illus.). 24p. (J). *(978-0-7787-2050-8(0));* pap. *(978-0-7787-2057-7(8))* Crabtree Publishing Co.

Rivera, Sheila. Mixing. 2007. (First Step Nonfiction — Changing Matter Ser.). (ENG., Illus.). 8p. (J). (gr. k-2). pap. 5.99 *(978-0-8225-6411-9(4),* d2004bc0-f61e-4bc1-8489-0b5dd0e34a45) Lerner Publishing Group.

Rodriguez, Cindy. Gases. 2013. (SPA.). (J). *(978-1-62127-601-2(5))* Weigl Pubs., Inc.

—Gases, with Code. 2012. (What Is Matter? Ser.). (ENG., Illus.). 24p. (J). (gr. -1-3). pap. 12.95 *(978-1-61913-604-5(X),* AV2 by Weigl) Weigl Pubs., Inc.

—Gases with Code. 2012. (What Is Matter? Ser.). (ENG., Illus.). 24p. (J). (gr. -1-3). lib. bdg. 27.13 *(978-1-61913-602-1(3),* AV2 by Weigl) Weigl Pubs., Inc.

—Líquidos. 2013. (SPA.). (J). *(978-1-62127-603-6(1))* Weigl Pubs., Inc.

—Liquids, with Code. 2012. (What Is Matter? Ser.). (ENG., Illus.). 24p. (J). (gr. -1-3). pap. 12.95 *(978-1-61913-605-2(8),* AV2 by Weigl) Weigl Pubs., Inc.

—Liquids with Code. 2012. (What Is Matter? Ser.). (ENG., Illus.). 24p. (J). (gr. -1-3). lib. bdg. 27.13 *(978-1-61913-603-8(1),* AV2 by Weigl) Weigl Pubs., Inc.

—Sólidos. 2013. (SPA.). (J). *(978-1-62127-605-0(8))* Weigl Pubs., Inc.

Rodriguez, Cindy & Siemens, Jared. Gases. 2017. (Illus.). 24p. (J). *(978-1-5105-0904-7(6))* SmartBook Media, Inc.

Rompella, Natalie. Experiments in Material & Matter with Toys & Everyday Stuff. 2015. (Fun Science Ser.). (ENG., Illus.). 24p. (J). (gr. 1-3). lib. bdg. 27.99 *(978-1-4914-5034-5(7),* 128758, Capstone Pr.) Capstone.

Rooney, Melissa. Eddie the Electron Moves Out. Pulver, Harry, Jr., illus. 2017. (Eddie the Electron Ser.: 2). (ENG.). 27p. (J). (gr. 5-7). pap. 12.99 *(978-1-944995-14-0(5))* Amberjack Publishing Co.

Rustad, Martha E. H. What Is It Made Of? Noticing Types of Materials. Schneider, Christine M., illus. 2015. (Cloverleaf Books (tm) — Nature's Patterns Ser.). (ENG.). 24p. (J). (gr. k-2). 25.32 *(978-1-4677-8561-7(X),* ebb0e7d3-e4dc-4a76-9355-d7c5c5020e6b, Millbrook Pr.) Lerner Publishing Group.

Selwyn, Josephine. When Does Water Turn into Ice? 2012. (Level F Ser.). (ENG., Illus.). 16p. (J). (gr. k-2). pap. 7.95 *(978-1-927136-59-1(8),* 19436) RiverStream Publishing.

Silverstein, Alvin, et al. Matter. 2008. (Science Concepts, Second Ser.). (Illus.). 112p. (YA). (gr. 5-9). lib. bdg. 31.93 *(978-0-8225-7515-3(9))* Lerner Publishing Group.

Sjonger, Rebecca. Changing Matter in My Makerspace. 2018. (Matter & Materials in My Makerspace Ser.). 32p. (J). (gr. 2-3). *(978-0-7787-4606-5(2))* Crabtree Publishing Co.

—Mixing & Separating Materials in My Makerspace. 2018. (Matter & Materials in My Makerspace Ser.). 32p. (J). (gr. 2-3). *(978-0-7787-4619-5(4))* Crabtree Publishing Co.

Slade, Suzanne. Atoms, 1 vol., 1. 2014. (Ultimate Science: Physical Science Ser.). (ENG.). 24p. (gr. 3-3). 26.27 *(978-1-4777-6089-5(X),* 52a92b26-db94-4129-bb34-fda47e644abd, PowerKids Pr.) Rosen Publishing Group, Inc., The.

—Atoms & Chemical Reactions. (Library of Physical Science Ser.). 24p. (gr. 4-4). 2009. 42.50 *(978-1-60853-780-8(3),* PowerKids Pr.) 2006. (ENG., Illus.). (YA). lib. bdg. 26.27 *(978-1-4042-3415-4(2),* 0e173042-64b3-4c60-9b3b-49dfa4845b91) 2006. (ENG., Illus.). pap. 7.05 *(978-1-4042-2162-8(X),* 2db0e428-11c2-4915-bdfc-e084aa6bdff9, PowerKids Pr.) Rosen Publishing Group, Inc., The.

—Different States of Matter, 1 vol., 1. 2013. (Ultimate Science: Physical Science Ser.). (ENG.). 24p. (gr. 3-3). 26.27 *(978-1-4777-6093-2(8),* 50245f5f-2cf0-42c1-a3c2-898fc722a79d, PowerKids Pr.) Rosen Publishing Group, Inc., The.

—Scientific Instruments: Looking at Atoms & Molecules. 2009. (Library of Physical Science Ser.). 24p. (gr. 4-4). 42.50 *(978-1-60853-786-0(2),* PowerKids Pr.) Rosen Publishing Group, Inc., The.

—States of Matter. 24p. (gr. 4-4). 2009. (Library of Physical Science Ser.). 42.50 *(978-1-60853-789-1(7),* PowerKids Pr.) 2006. (Library of Physical Science Ser.: Vol. 3). (ENG., Illus.). (YA). lib. bdg. 26.27 *(978-1-4042-3416-1(0),* ffbf79fa-6766-4736-8f74-7b93a4fd1d54) 2006. (Journeys Ser.). (ENG., Illus.). pap. 7.05 *(978-1-4042-2163-5(8),* dcb2a368-d26d-48e2-a82e-181432fd83c9, PowerKids Pr.) Rosen Publishing Group, Inc., The.

Smith, Ben. Where Can You Find Hard & Soft Things? 2012. (Level E Ser.). (ENG., Illus.). 16p. (J). (gr. k-2). pap. 7.95 *(978-1-927136-49-2(0),* 19441) RiverStream Publishing.

Smith, Erica. Solid, Liquid, Gas: What Is Matter? 2009. (Reading Room Collection 2 Ser.). 24p. (gr. 3-4). 42.50 *(978-1-60851-988-0(0),* PowerKids Pr.) Rosen Publishing Group, Inc., The.

Smith, Sian. Hard & Soft, 1 vol. 2014. (Opposites Ser.). (ENG.). 24p. (J). (gr. -1-1). pap. 5.99 *(978-1-4846-0333-8(8),* 126423, Heinemann) Capstone.

Spaight, Anne J. Let's Explore Solids. 2018. (Bumba Books (r) — a First Look at Physical Science Ser.). (ENG., Illus.). 24p. (J). (gr. -1-1). 26.65 *(978-1-5124-8266-9(8),* 1c025766-a9a1-444f-8f15-63842d00b4e4, Lerner Pubns.) Lerner Publishing Group.

Squire, Ann O. Matter (a True Book: Physical Science) (Library Edition) 2019. (True Book (Relaunch) Ser.). (ENG., Illus.). 48p. (J). (gr. 3-5). lib. bdg. 31.00 *(978-0-531-13141-1(6),* Children's Pr.) Scholastic Library Publishing.

Stephens, David. A Material World: What Is Matter?, 1 vol., 1. 2014. (Discovery Education: How It Works). (ENG.). 32p. (gr. 4-5). 28.93 *(978-1-4777-6325-4(2),* 1e976569-b2fe-46b5-a112-7b62d5e59fa3, PowerKids Pr.) Rosen Publishing Group, Inc., The.

Taylor-Butler, Christine. Experiments with Solids, Liquids, & Gases. 2011. (True Book-Experiments Ser.). (ENG., Illus.). 48p. (J). lib. bdg. 29.00 *(978-0-531-26349-5(5),* Children's Pr.) Scholastic Library Publishing.

—True Book - Experiments: Experiments with Solids, Liquids, & Gases. 2011. (True Bk Ser.). (ENG., Illus.). 48p. (J). pap. 6.95 *(978-0-531-26649-6(4),* Children's Pr.) Scholastic Library Publishing.

Troupe, Thomas Kingsley. What's the Matter with the Three Little Pigs? The Fairy-Tale Physics of Matter. Tejido, Jomike, illus. 2018. (STEM-Twisted Fairy Tales Ser.). (ENG.). 32p. (J). (gr. k-3). pap. 7.95 *(978-1-5158-2900-3(6),* 138422); lib. bdg. 27.99 *(978-1-5158-2896-9(4),* 138418) Capstone. (Picture Window Bks.).

Walker, Sally M. Matter. King, Andy, illus. 2005. (Early Bird Energy Ser.). 48p. (J). (gr. 3-7). lib. bdg. 25.26 *(978-0-8225-5131-7(4),* Lerner Pubns.) Lerner Publishing Group.

Weir, Kirsten & Brent, Lynnette. States of Matter, 1 vol. 2008. (Why Chemistry Matters Ser.). (ENG., Illus.). 32p. (J). (gr. 3-7). pap. *(978-0-7787-4251-7(2))* Crabtree Publishing Co.

West, Krista. States of Matter: Gases, Liquids, & Solids. 2008. (ENG.). 128p. (gr. 7-12). 35.00 *(978-0-7910-9521-8(5),* P129238, Facts On File) Infobase Holdings, Inc.

Williams, Zella. Experiments with Solids, Liquids, & Gases. (Do-It-Yourself Science Ser.). 24p. 2009. (gr. 2-3). 47.90 *(978-1-61512-190-8(0))* 2007. (Illus.). (J). 42.30 *(978-1-4042-4013-1(6))* Rosen Publishing Group, Inc., The. (PowerKids Pr.).

World Book, Inc. Staff, contrib. by. Learning about Matter. 2011. (J). *(978-0-7166-0234-7(2))* World Bk., Inc.

—Matter & Its Properties. 2011. 32p. (J). *(978-0-7166-1429-6(4))* World Bk., Inc.

MATTHEW, SAINT, APOSTLE

Mackenzie, Carine & Gair, Cyhoeddiadau'r. Actau. Taylor, Jane, illus. 2005. (WEL.). 16p. pap. *(978-1-85994-271-0(7))* Cyhoeddiadau'r Gair.

Woodman, Ros. Bible Detectives Matthew. 2005. (Activity Ser.). (ENG.). 64p. (J). pap., act. bk. ed. 7.99 *(978-1-85792-673-6(0),* 6e96842b-e095-4e7c-849c-70ca24f6614e) Christian Focus Pubns. GBR. Dist: Baker & Taylor Publisher Services (BTPS).

MAURITANIA

Blauer, Ettagale & LeVert, Suzanne. Mauritania, 1 vol. 2009. (Cultures of the World (First Edition)(r) Ser.). (ENG., Illus.). 144p. (gr. 5-5). lib. bdg. 49.79 *(978-0-7614-3116-9(0),* 8e6fc6cf-369b-493c-a799-98f3dbe182a2) Cavendish Square Publishing LLC.

MAXI (FICTITIOUS CHARACTER)—FICTION

Bennett, Jeffrey. Max Goes to Mars: A Science Adventure with Max the Dog. Okamoto, Alan, illus. 2015. (Science Adventures with Max the Dog Ser.). (ENG.). 32p. (J). (gr. 2-4). 15.00 *(978-1-937548-44-5(9))* Big Kid Science.

MAXIMS

see Proverbs

MAY DAY—FICTION

Mora, Pat. The Rainbow Tulip. Sayles, Elizabeth, illus. 2003. 32p. (J). (gr. k-3). 7.99 *(978-0-14-250009-5(7),* Puffin Books) Penguin Young Readers Group.

—Rainbow Tulip. 2014. 17.00 *(978-1-63419-680-2(5))* Perfection Learning Corp.

MAYAS

see Indians of Mexico—Mayas

MAYFLOWER (SHIP)

Arenstam, Peter. The Mighty Mastiff of the Mayflower. Holman, Karen Busch, illus. 2012. Orig. Title: The Mighty Mastiff of the Mayflower. (ENG.). 112p. 16.99 *(978-1-60949-609-8(4),* History Pr., The) Arcadia Publishing.

Arenstam, Peter, et al. MayFlower 1620: A New Look at a Pilgrim Voyage. 2004. (Illus.). 47p. (J). (gr. k-4). 18.00 *(978-0-7567-7967-2(7))* DIANE Publishing Co.

Brindell Fradin, Dennis. The Mayflower Compact, 1 vol. 2007. (Turning Points in U. S. History Ser.). (ENG., Illus.). 48p. (gr. 4-4). lib. bdg. 34.07 *(978-0-7614-2125-2(4),* 047805e0-f50c-4cca-90d8-3562f332da95) Cavendish Square Publishing LLC.

Cook, Peter & Whelan, Kevin. You Wouldn't Want to Sail on the Mayflower! A Trip That Took Entirely Too Long. rev. ed. 2013. (ENG.). 32p. (J). 29.00 *(978-0-531-27107-0(2),* Watts, Franklin) Scholastic Library Publishing.

Emminizer, Theresa. Aboard the Mayflower. 2019. (History on the High Seas Ser.). (ENG.). 24p. (gr. 2-3). 48.90 *(978-1-5382-3795-3(4))* Stevens, Gareth Publishing LLLP.

Gunderson, Jessica. Life on the Mayflower, 1 vol. Dumm, Brian Caleb, illus. 2010. (Thanksgiving Ser.). (ENG.). 24p. (J). (gr. k-3). pap. 7.95 *(978-1-4048-6719-2(8),* 115518, Picture Window Bks.) Capstone.

Honders, Christine. Mayflower Compact, 1 vol. 2016. (Documents of American Democracy Ser.). (ENG., Illus.). 32p. (J). (gr. 5-5). pap. 11.00 *(978-1-4994-2085-2(4),* 4d5a8336-b006-4995-923b-a2b9c7947e57, PowerKids Pr.) Rosen Publishing Group, Inc., The.

Kallio, Jamie. Mayflower Compact, 1 vol. 2013. (Foundations of Our Nation Ser.). (ENG.). 48p. (J). (gr. 4-8). lib. bdg. 35.64 *(978-1-61783-711-1(3),* 7820) ABDO Publishing Co.

Lassieur, Allison. El Viaje del Mayflower. McDonnell, Peter, illus. 2006. (Historia Gráficas Ser.). (SPA.). 32p. (J). (gr. 3-9). 31.32 *(978-0-7368-6613-2(2),* 88094) Capstone.

Lusted, Marcia Amidon. The Mayflower Compact. 2019. (Shaping the United States of America Ser.). (ENG., Illus.). 24p. (J). (gr. 1-3). pap. 7.95 *(978-1-9771-1015-2(0),* 140958); lib. bdg. 25.99 *(978-1-9771-0916-3(0),* 140517) Capstone. (Pebble).

Lynch, P. J. The Boy Who Fell off the Mayflower, or John Howland's Good Fortune. Lynch, P. J., illus. (ENG., Illus.). 64p. (J). (gr. 2-5). 2018. 9.99 *(978-1-5362-0296-0(7))* 2015. 18.99 *(978-0-7636-6584-5(3))* Candlewick Pr.

National Geographic Learning. Reading Expeditions (Social Studies: Documents of Freedom): the Mayflower Compact. 2007. (ENG., Illus.). 32p. (J). pap. 18.95 *(978-0-7922-4553-7(9))* CENGAGE Learning.

Plimoth Plantation, et al. Mayflower 1620: A New Look at a Pilgrim Voyage. 2007. (Illus.). 48p. (J). (gr. 3-7). per. 6.95 *(978-0-7922-6276-3(X),* National Geographic Kids) Disney Publishing Worldwide.

Poolos, J. The Mayflower, 1 vol. 2004. (Primary Sources in American History Ser.). (ENG., Illus.). 64p. (J). (gr. 5-8). lib. bdg. 37.13 *(978-0-8239-4514-6(6),* 305b2908-454e-4a89-977c-105c73594972, Rosen Reference) Rosen Publishing Group, Inc., The.

—The Mayflower: A Primary Source History of the Pilgrims' Journey to the New World. 2009. (Primary Sources in American History Ser.). 64p. (gr. 5-8). 58.50 *(978-1-60851-499-1(4))* Rosen Publishing Group, Inc., The.

Rajczak, Michael. Life on the Mayflower, 1 vol., Vol. 1. 2013. (What You Didn't Know about History Ser.). (ENG.). 24p. (J). (gr. 2-3). 25.27 *(978-1-4824-0591-0(1),* 2e562962-9b3b-4209-98f1-f0e1f723e9f5) Stevens, Gareth Publishing LLLP.

Rajczak Nelson, Kristen. The Mayflower Compact, 1 vol. 2013. (Documents That Shaped America Ser.). (Illus.). 32p. (J). (gr. 4-5). (ENG.). pap. 11.50 *(978-1-4339-9006-9(7),* d09f0491-5854-40b8-accf-ceccd2ad1e89); (ENG., lib. bdg. 29.27 *(978-1-4339-9005-2(9),* 9fa5d6d6-0346-4074-ba27-f3727b38e89c); pap. 63.00 *(978-1-4339-9007-6(5))* Stevens, Gareth Publishing LLLP.

Raum, Elizabeth. The Mayflower Compact, 1 vol. 2012. (Documenting U. S. History Ser.). (ENG.). 48p. (J). (gr. 3-6). lib. bdg. 33.32 *(978-1-4329-6750-5(9),* 119381, Heinemann) Capstone.

Smith, Andrea P. The Journey of the Mayflower. (Illus.). 24p. (J). 2012. 63.60 *(978-1-4488-5211-6(0))* 2011. (ENG., (gr. 2-3). pap. 11.60 *(978-1-4488-5210-9(2),* ffb71748-c78c-4612-9f75-48faa5dd7d69) 2011. (ENG., (gr. 2-3). lib. bdg. 28.93 *(978-1-4488-5186-7(6),* aa04b287-2d9d-4f9d-b874-70411c20e5e6) Rosen Publishing Group, Inc., The. (PowerKids Pr.).

Son, John. If You Were a Kid on the Mayflower (If You Were a Kid) (Library Edition) Zanni, Roger, illus. 2018. (If You Were a Kid Ser.). (ENG.). 32p. (J). (gr. 2-4). lib. bdg. 26.00 *(978-0-531-23216-3(6),* Children's Pr.) Scholastic Library Publishing.

Streissguth, Tom. The Mayflower Story. 2017. (Famous Ships Ser.). (ENG., Illus.). 112p. (J). (gr. 6-12). lib. bdg. 41.36 *(978-1-5321-1320-8(X),* 27528, Essential Library) ABDO Publishing Co.

Waxman, Laura Hamilton. Why Did the Pilgrims Come to the New World? & Other Questions about the Plymouth Colony. 2010. pap. 56.72 *(978-0-7613-6951-6(1))* Lerner Publishing Group.

Whitcraft, Melissa. The Mayflower Compact. 2008. (Cornerstones of Freedom Ser.). (ENG., Illus.). 48p. (YA). (gr. 3-6). 18.69 *(978-0-516-24203-3(2))* Scholastic Library Publishing.

Whitehurst, Susan. The Mayflower. 2009. (Library of the Pilgrims Ser.). 24p. (gr. 3-4). 42.50 *(978-1-60853-914-7(8),* PowerKids Pr.) Rosen Publishing Group, Inc., The.

MAYFLOWER (SHIP)—FICTION

Klimo, Kate. Dog Diaries #5: Dash, Bk. 5. Jessell, Tim, illus. 2014. (Dog Diaries: 5). 160p. (J). (gr. 2-5). pap. 7.99

(978-0-385-37338-8(4), Random Hse. Bks. for Young Readers) Random Hse. Children's Bks.

Lawton, Wendy G. Almost Home: A Story Based on the Life of the Mayflower's Mary Chilton. 2003. (Daughters of the Faith Ser.). (ENG.). 160p. (YA). (gr. 3-3). pap. 8.99 *(978-0-8024-3637-5(4))* Moody Pubs.

Limbaugh, Rush. Rush Revere & the Brave Pilgrims: Time-Travel Adventures with Exceptional Americans. 2013. (Rush Revere Ser.: 1). (ENG., Illus.). 224p. 21.00 *(978-1-4767-5586-1(8)*, Threshold Editions) Threshold Editions.

Roy, Ron. A to Z Mysteries Super Edition 2: Mayflower Treasure Hunt. Gurney, John Steven, illus. 2nd ed. 2007. (to Z Mysteries Ser.: 2). 128p. (J). (gr. 1-4). per. 6.99 *(978-0-375-83937-5(2)*, Random Hse. Bks. for Young Readers) Random Hse. Children's Bks.

MAYORS

Bankston, John. Rudy Giuliani. Lt. ed. 2003. (Blue Banner Biography Ser.). (Illus.). 32p. (J). (gr. 3-8). lib. bdg. 25.70 *(978-1-58415-194-4(3))* Mitchell Lane Pubs.

Dawson, Emily C. Town Leaders. 2010. (My Community Ser.). (ENG.). 24p. (J). (gr. k-2). lib. bdg. 25.65 *(978-1-60753-025-1(2)*, 17151) Amicus.

Jakubiak, David J. What Does a Mayor Do? 2010. (How Our Government Works Ser.). 24p. (J). (gr. 3-6). lib. bdg., E-Book 42.50 *(978-1-4488-0026-1(9))*; (ENG., Illus.). pap. 9.25 *(978-1-4358-9814-1(1)*, 1cc0bcc2-1959-42a2-b345-b83ee70171e2, PowerKids Pr.); (ENG., Illus.). lib. bdg. 26.27 *(978-1-4358-9359-7(X)*, ea92488c-442d-4fdf-bc36-818103f8549a, PowerKids Pr.) Rosen Publishing Group, Inc., The.

Jeffries, Joyce. Meet the Mayor, 1 vol. 2013. (People Around Town Ser.). (Illus.). 24p. (J). (gr. k-k). (ENG.). pap. 9.15 *(978-1-4339-9378-7(3)*, 7294b4f3-b9d1-48cb-a7c5-31942839224f); (ENG., lib. bdg. 25.27 *(978-1-4339-9377-0(5)*, f19cff44-3a21-4ac1-bc41-deb0d5c64ea4); pap. 48.90 *(978-1-4339-9379-4(1))* Stevens, Gareth Publishing LLLP.

—Meet the Mayor / Conoce a Los Alcaldes, 1 vol. 2013. (People Around Town / Gente de Mi Ciudad Ser.). (SPA & ENG., Illus.). 24p. (J). (gr. k-k). 25.27 *(978-1-4339-9470-8(4)*, b2aa7e90-b2d6-4cc0-aadb-29ceb8786c8f) Stevens, Gareth Publishing LLLP.

Knudsen, Shannon. Mayors. 2005. (Pull Ahead Bks.). (Illus.). 32p. (J). (gr. 3-7). lib. bdg. 22.60 *(978-0-8225-2829-6(0)*, Lerner Pubns.) Lerner Publishing Group.

Laks Gorman, Jacqueline. Alcalde (Mayor), 1 vol. 2009. (Conoce Tu Gobierno (Know Your Government) Ser.). (SPA.). 24p. (J). (gr. 3-3). pap. 9.15 *(978-1-4339-0128-7(5)*, efa08395-9473-4909-90ba-b4c05a3d0e4c); lib. bdg. 24.67 *(978-1-4339-0100-3(5)*, 0d6e6ddb-74c0-4c42-9269-74da6ef30617) Stevens, Gareth Publishing LLLP. (Weekly Reader Leveled Readers).

—Mayor, 1 vol. 2009. (Know Your Government Ser.). (ENG.). 24p. (J). (gr. 3-3). pap. 9.15 *(978-1-4339-0121-8(8)*, 85dc8499-6f16-4595-a5f3-383fb716e052); lib. bdg. 24.67 *(978-1-4339-0093-8(9)*, 7f0bba5b-a99d-43e1-9352-93e7e14fd7b6) Stevens, Gareth Publishing LLLP. (Weekly Reader Leveled Readers).

Manning, Jack. The City Mayor, 1 vol. 2014. (Our Government Ser.). (ENG.). 24p. (J). (gr. 1-3). 27.99 *(978-1-4914-0336-5(5)*, 125849, Capstone Pr.) Capstone.

Marsh, Carole. Meet Shirley Franklin, Mayor of Atlanta! 2003. 32p. (gr. 3-8). 21.95 *(978-0-635-01141-1(7))* Gallopade International.

Martinez, Manuel. I Meet the Mayor! Understanding Government, 1 vol. 2018. (Civics for the Real World Ser.). (ENG.). 12p. (gr. 1-2). pap. *(978-1-5383-6421-5(2)*, a6c7cc17-8c3f-438d-a2dc-c97325b81a3e, Rosen Classroom) Rosen Publishing Group, Inc., The.

Murray, Julie. Mayor. 2017. (My Government Ser.). (ENG., Illus.). 24p. (J). (gr. -1-2). lib. bdg. 31.36 *(978-1-5321-0398-8(0)*, 26524, Abdo Kids) ABDO Publishing Co.

Shichtman, Sandra H. Michael Bloomberg. 2010. (Political Profiles Ser.). 112p. (J). 28.95 *(978-1-59935-135-3(8))* Reynolds, Morgan Inc.

Silate, Jennifer. Your Mayor: Local Government in Action. (Primary Source Library of American Citizenship Ser.). 32p. (gr. 5-5). 2009. 47.90 *(978-1-61511-237-1(5))* 2003. (ENG., Illus.). lib. bdg. 29.13 *(978-0-8239-4481-1(6)*, 85072cd8-c6b7-4740-b7b5-1bdeadb5b181) Rosen Publishing Group, Inc., The. (Rosen Reference).

MAYS, WILLIE, 1931-

Doeden, Matt. Willie Mays. 2010. (Sports Heroes & Legends Ser.). (ENG.). 120p. (gr. 5-12). lib. bdg. 30.60 *(978-0-7613-5370-6(4))* Lerner Publishing Group.

Mandel, Peter. Say Hey! A Song of Willie Mays. Tate, Don, illus. 2004. 30p. (J). (gr. k-2). reprint ed. 16.00 *(978-0-7567-8162-0(0))* DIANE Publishing Co.

Smith, Linda J. Willie Mays: The Say Hey Kid. 2005. (Illus.). 112p. (J). pap. *(978-1-59421-015-0(2))* Seacoast Publishing, Inc.

Winter, Jonah. You Never Heard of Willie Mays?! Widener, Terry, illus. 2016. 40p. (J). (gr. -1-3). 7.99 *(978-1-101-93421-0(2)*, Dragonfly Bks.) Random Hse. Children's Bks.

MAZE PUZZLES

Adam, Winky. Native American Mazes. 2003. (Dover Little Activity Bks.). (ENG., Illus.). 64p. (J). (gr. k-3). pap. 2.50 *(978-0-486-42616-7(5)*, 426165) Dover Pubns., Inc.

Altmann, Scott. Vampire Mazes. 2011. (Dover Children's Activity Bks.). (ENG., Illus.). 48p. (J). (gr. 3-4). pap. 4.99 *(978-0-486-47922-4(6)*, 479226) Dover Pubns., Inc.

Andrews McMeel Publishing, Andrews McMeel. Go Fun! Big Book of Mazes. 2014. (Go Fun! Ser.: 3). (ENG.). 144p. (J). pap. 8.99 *(978-1-4494-6485-1(8))* Andrews McMeel Publishing.

—Go Fun! Big Book of Mazes 2. 2015. (Go Fun! Ser.: 9). (ENG.). 128p. (J). pap. 8.99 *(978-1-4494-7227-6(3))* Andrews McMeel Publishing.

Artymowska, Aleksandra, illus. Amazed. 2017. (ENG.). 32p. (J). (gr. 1-4). 16.99 *(978-1-78627-051-1(X)*, King, Laurence Publishing) Orion Publishing Group, Ltd. GBR. Dist: Hachette Bk. Group.

Blair, Beth L. & Ericsson, Jennifer A. The Everything Kids' Animal Puzzles & Activity Book: Slither, Soar, & Swing Through a Jungle of Fun! 2005. (Everything(r) Kids Ser.). (ENG., Illus.). 144p. pap., act. bk. ed. 15.99 *(978-1-59337-305-4(8)*, Everything) Adams Media Corp.

Blundell, Kim & Tyler, Jenny. Treasure Mazes. rev. ed. 2003. (Illus.). 23p. (J). pap. 5.99 *(978-0-7945-0537-0(6)*, Usborne) EDC Publishing.

Brightfield, Rick. Amazing Mazes: Groovy, Graphic Games. 2012. (Dover Puzzle Bks.). (ENG.). 80p. (gr. 4). pap. 6.99 *(978-0-486-48939-1(6)*, 489396) Dover Pubns., Inc.

Carpenter, Elizabeth. MummyMaze: The Tomb Treasures Maze Book. 2nd rev. ed. 2007. (J). pap. 19.99 *(978-0-9793043-0-9(X))* Mazeology.

Donahue, Peter. Robot Mazes. 2008. (Dover Kids Activity Books: Fantasy Ser.). (ENG., Illus.). 48p. (J). (gr. k-5). pap. 4.99 *(978-0-486-46825-9(9)*, 468259) Dover Pubns., Inc.

Elder, Jeremy. Monsters Destroyed My City! Mazes. 2012. (Dover Kids Activity Books: Fantasy Ser.). (ENG.). 48p. (J). (gr. 3-5). pap. 4.99 *(978-0-486-48157-9(3)*, 481573) Dover Pubns., Inc.

—Pinball Mazes Activity Book: Can You Top the High Score? 2012. (Dover Children's Activity Bks.). (ENG.). 48p. (J). (gr. 3-8). pap. 4.99 *(978-0-486-49003-8(3))* Dover Pubns., Inc.

Goes, Peter. Follow Finn: A Search-And-Find Maze Book. Goes, Peter, illus. 2018. (ENG., Illus.). 32p. (J). (gr. k-5). 16.99 *(978-1-77657-185-7(1)*, 81ece266-25a3-4a3a-95ed-7136a8f1580d) Gecko Pr. NZL. Dist: Lerner Publishing Group.

HOP, LLC. Hooked on Learning Puzzles & Mazes. 2006. 64p. 3.79 *(978-1-933863-90-0(0))* HOP, LLC.

Kamigaki, Hiro & IC4DESIGN, illus. Pierre the Maze Detective: the Mystery of the Empire Maze Tower: (Maze Book for Kids, Adventure Puzzle Book, Seek & Find Book) 2017. (ENG.). 36p. (J). (gr. 3-7). 19.99 *(978-1-78627-059-7(5)*, King, Laurence Publishing) Orion Publishing Group, Ltd. GBR. Dist: Hachette Bk. Group.

Kumon Publishing North America, ed. Amazing Mazes. Kumon Publishing North America, . 2004. (ENG., Illus.). 80p. (J). per. 7.95 *(978-4-7743-0710-7(6))* Kumon Publishing North America, Inc.

Lamb, Stacey, illus. Wipe-Clean Mazes. 2012. (Wipe-Clean Bks). 20p. (J). pap. 7.99 *(978-0-7945-3257-4(8)*, Usborne) EDC Publishing.

Lavash, Ted & Fremont, Victoria. Spooky Mazes. 2018. (Dover Little Activity Bks.). (ENG.). 64p. (J). (gr. 1-4). pap. 2.50 *(978-0-486-82388-1(1)*, 823881) Dover Pubns., Inc.

Mazes for 1st Grade. 2003. (J). *(978-1-58232-059-5(4))* ECS Learning Systems, Inc.

Mazes for 2nd Grade. 2003. (J). *(978-1-58232-060-1(8))* ECS Learning Systems, Inc.

Mazurkiewicz, Jessica. Eco-Mania Mazes. 2010. (Dover Little Activity Bks.). (ENG., Illus.). 64p. (J). (gr. -1-5). pap. 1.50 *(978-0-486-47561-5(1))* Dover Pubns., Inc.

Munro, Roxie. Market Maze. 2015. *(978-0-8234-3358-2(7))* Holiday Hse., Inc.

My First Mazes (Gr. K-1) 2003. (J). *(978-1-58232-058-8(6))* ECS Learning Systems, Inc.

Newman-D'Amico, Fran. Alphabet Mazes. 2006. (Dover Kids Activity Bks.). (ENG., Illus.). 32p. (J). (gr. -1-2). 3.99 *(978-0-486-44894-7(0)*, 448940) Dover Pubns., Inc.

—Zoo Animal Mazes. 2004. (Dover Kids Activity Books: Animals Ser.). (ENG., Illus.). 32p. (J). (gr. -1-2). pap. 3.99 *(978-0-486-43769-9(8)*, 437698) Dover Pubns., Inc.

Phillips, Dave. Big Book of Adventure Mazes. 2003. (Dover Kids Activity Bks.). (ENG.). 128p. (J). (gr. 2-8). pap. 8.95 *(978-0-486-42900-7(8)*, 429008) Dover Pubns., Inc.

—Set Puzzles: Find Sets, Group Them, Fill the Grid. 2012. (ENG.). 48p. pap. 12.95 *(978-0-486-49055-7(6))* Dover Pubns., Inc.

Radtke, Becky. On the Go Mazes. 2005. (Dover Little Activity Bks.). (ENG., Illus.). 64p. (J). (gr. 3-5). per. 2.50 *(978-0-486-44103-0(2)*, 441032) Dover Pubns., Inc.

Robson, Kirsteen. Big Maze Book. 2013. (Doodle Bks). 64p. (J). pap. 9.99 *(978-0-7945-3345-8(0)*, Usborne) EDC Publishing.

Sallows, Lee C. F. Geometric Magic Squares: A Challenging New Twist Using Colored Shapes Instead of Numbers. 2013. (Dover Recreational Math Ser.). (ENG., Illus.). 160p. (C). pap. 19.95 *(978-0-486-48909-4(4)*, 489094) Dover Pubns., Inc.

School Zone Interactive Staff. Mazes. Simard, Remy, illus. rev. ed. 2006. (ENG.). 64p. (J). (gr. 1-2). wbk. ed. 7.99 *(978-1-58947-300-3(0))* School Zone Publishing Co.

School Zone Publishing. Mazes Animals. 2004. (ENG.). 32p. (J). pap. 2.99 *(978-1-58947-386-7(8)*, 02191) School Zone Publishing Co.

School Zone Staff, ed. Mazes Preschool. 2006. (ENG.). 32p. (J). pap. 2.99 *(978-1-58947-394-2(9)*, 02196) School Zone Publishing Co.

Sheridan, Lucie. Find Me: Play for Little Hands. Sheridan, Lucie, illus. 2019. (Play for Little Hands Ser.). (ENG., Illus.). 14p. (J). (-k). bds. 10.99 *(978-1-910552-81-0(X))* O'Mara, Michael Bks., Ltd. GBR. Dist: Independent Pubs. Group.

Smith, Sam. Around the World Mazes. 2018. (Maze Bks.). (ENG.). 64p. pap. 9.99 *(978-0-7945-4215-3(8)*, Usborne) EDC Publishing.

—Map Maze Book. 2017. (Maze Bks.). (ENG.). 64p. (J). pap. 9.99 *(978-0-7945-4028-9(7)*, Usborne) EDC Publishing.

Tallarico, Tony. Nature Trivia Mazes. 2007. (Dover Kids Activity Books: Nature Ser.). (ENG., Illus.). 48p. (J). (gr. 3-3). per. 5.99 *(978-0-486-45364-4(2)*, 453642) Dover Pubns., Inc.

Tallarico, Tony J., Jr. Bugs! Bugs! Bugs! 2012. (Dover Kids Activity Books: Animals Ser.). (ENG.). 48p. (J). (gr. 3-8). pap. 5.99 *(978-0-486-48399-3(1)*, 483991) Dover Pubns., Inc.

The Ultimate Maze Craze. 2003. (Illus.). 40p. (J). 3.95 *(978-0-9729026-0-1(0))* Midwest Cylinder Management, Inc.

University Games Staff, compiled by. i-Ballers: University Games. 2005. (i-Ballers Ser.). (ENG.). 60p. pap. 4.95 *(978-1-57528-952-6(0))* Univ. Games.

White, Graham. A Maze Adventure: Search for Pirate Treasure. 2009. (Illus.). 32p. (J). (gr. 3-7). pap. 8.95 *(978-1-4263-0459-0(5)*, National Geographic Kids) Disney Publishing Worldwide.

Woodworth, Viki. A-B-C Mazes. 2006. (Dover Little Activity Bks.). (ENG., Illus.). 64p. (J). (gr. k-3). 1.50 *(978-0-486-44726-1(X)*, 44726X) Dover Pubns., Inc.

—Little Monster Mazes. 2006. (Dover Little Activity Bks.). (ENG., Illus.). 64p. (J). (gr. 3-5). per. 1.50 *(978-0-486-45189-3(5))* Dover Pubns., Inc.

—Maze Mania. (Dover Children's Activity Bks.). (ENG.). 32p. (J). (gr. 3-5). 2017. pap. 4.99 *(978-0-486-82610-3(4))* 2005. (Illus.). per. 4.99 *(978-0-486-44604-2(2)*, 446042) Dover Pubns., Inc.

—Princess Mazes. 2012. (Dover Kids Activity Books: Fantasy Ser.). (ENG.). 48p. (J). (gr. 1-4). pap. 4.99 *(978-0-486-49058-8(0)*, 490580) Dover Pubns., Inc.

—United States Maze Craze. 2009. (Dover Kids Activity Books: U. S. A. Ser.). (ENG., Illus.). 64p. (J). (gr. 3-4). pap. 5.99 *(978-0-486-46831-0(3)*, 468313) Dover Pubns., Inc.

—World of Mazes. (Dover Children's Activity Bks.). (ENG.). (J). (gr. 3-5). 2017. 32p. pap. 4.99 *(978-0-486-82611-0(2))* 2007. (Illus.). 48p. per. 4.99 *(978-0-486-45640-9(4)*, 456404) Dover Pubns., Inc.

MEAD, MARGARET, 1901-1978

Horn, Geoffrey M. Margaret Mead, 1 vol. 2004. (Trailblazers of the Modern World Ser.). (ENG., Illus.). 48p. (gr. 5-8). pap. 15.05 *(978-0-8368-5259-2(1)*, e27a92d6-8ea4-40ea-bdf4-0b7ba376e975); lib. bdg. 33.67 *(978-0-8368-5099-4(8)*, 1d9ac75a-4672-40d6-b6c8-da2ffda80202) Stevens, Gareth Publishing LLLP. (Gareth Stevens Secondary Library).

MEAL PLANNING

see Menus; Nutrition

MEASLES

Colligan, L. H. Measles & Mumps, 1 vol. 2011. (Health Alert Ser.). (ENG., Illus.). 64p. (gr. 4-4). 35.50 *(978-0-7614-4819-8(5)*, 681b0fec-1dd6-4100-bce9-dc5d0d01f398) Cavendish Square Publishing LLC.

Hawkins, Trisha. Everything You Need to Know about Measles & Rubella. 2009. (Need to Know Library). 64p. (gr. 5-5). 58.50 *(978-1-60854-075-4(8))* Rosen Publishing Group, Inc., The.

Lewis, Mark K. Measles: How a Contagious Rash Changed History. 2019. (Infected! Ser.). (ENG., Illus.). 32p. (J). (gr. 3-9). lib. bdg. 28.65 *(978-1-5435-7240-7(5)*, 140586) Capstone.

Rosaler, Maxine. Measles. 2009. (Epidemics Ser.). 64p. (gr. 5-5). 58.50 *(978-1-61512-296-7(6))* Rosen Publishing Group, Inc., The.

Shmaefsky, Brian R. Rubella & Rubeola. 2009. (Deadly Diseases & Epidemics Ser.). (ENG., Illus.). 120p. (gr. 9-18). 34.95 *(978-1-60413-230-4(2)*, P161430, Facts On File) Infobase Holdings, Inc.

MEASUREMENT

Here are entered works on the general process of measuring. Works on the science of measurement or of weights and measures are entered under Metrology.

see also Measuring Instruments; Metrology; Surveying; Weights and Measures

Adamson, Heather & Adamson, Thomas K. How Do You Measure Length & Distance? 2010. (Measure It! Ser.). (ENG.). 32p. (J). (gr. 1-2). pap. 49.60 *(978-1-4296-6457-8(6)*, 16212, Capstone Pr.) Capstone.

—How Do You Measure Liquids? 2010. (Measure It! Ser.). (ENG.). 32p. (J). (gr. 1-2). pap. 49.60 *(978-1-4296-6458-5(4)*, 16213, Capstone Pr.) Capstone.

—How Do You Measure Time? 2010. (Measure It! Ser.). (ENG.). 32p. (J). (gr. 1-2). pap. 48.60 *(978-1-4296-6459-2(2)*, 16214, Capstone Pr.) Capstone.

Adamson, Thomas K. & Adamson, Heather. How Do You Measure Length & Distance?, 1 vol. 2010. (Measure It! Ser.). (ENG.). 32p. (J). (gr. -1-2). pap. 8.10 *(978-1-4296-6330-4(8)*, 115531) Capstone.

—How Do You Measure Liquids?, 1 vol. 2010. (Measure It! Ser.). (ENG.). 32p. (J). (gr. -1-2). pap. 8.10 *(978-1-4296-6331-1(6)*, 115532) Capstone.

—How Do You Measure Time?, 1 vol. 2010. (Measure It! Ser.). (ENG.). 32p. (J). (gr. -1-2). pap. 8.10 *(978-1-4296-6332-8(4)*, 115533, Capstone Pr.) Capstone.

Alaina, Maria. Measuring Time, 1 vol. 2011. (Wonder Readers Early Level Ser.). (ENG.). 16p. (J). (gr. -1-1). pap. 6.25 *(978-1-4296-7834-6(8)*, 118143, Capstone Pr.) Capstone.

Amstutz, Lisa J. Rulers & Tape Measures. 2019. (Science Tools Ser.). (ENG., Illus.). 24p. (J). (gr. k-2). pap. 6.95 *(978-1-9771-0062-7(7)*, 138213); lib. bdg. 27.32 *(978-1-9771-0058-0(9)*, 138209) Capstone. (Pebble).

Anderson, Jill. Measuring with Sebastian Pig & Friends on a Road Trip, 1 vol. 2009. (Math Fun with Sebastian Pig & Friends! Ser.). (ENG., Illus.). 32p. (gr. k-2). pap. 10.35 *(978-0-7660-5982-5(0)*, c6f72e0d-1e7e-4a1d-b1c3-04440e8eaafc, Enslow Elementary) Enslow Publishing, LLC.

Ayers, Amy. MEASURING at the Dog Show, 1 vol. 2007. (Math in Our World - Level 1 Ser.). (ENG.). 24p. (J). (gr. 1-1). pap. 9.15 *(978-0-8368-8483-8(3)*, ff43224b-8403-41c0-825b-4d181ac00708); (Illus.). lib. bdg. 24.67 *(978-0-8368-8474-6(4)*, f6793012-2417-4a3c-8679-212167eb30c4) Stevens, Gareth Publishing LLLP. (Weekly Reader Leveled Readers).

—MIDIENDO en la Exposición de Perros (MEASURING at the Dog Show), 1 vol. 2007. (Las Matemáticas en Nuestro Mundo - Nivel 1 (Math in Our World - Level 1) Ser.). (SPA.). 24p. (gr. 1-1). pap. 9.15 *(978-0-8368-8501-9(5)*, 72d120ce-b816-4357-a07b-3406f6ead3bf, Weekly Reader Leveled Readers) Stevens, Gareth Publishing LLLP.

Baer, T. H. Measuring Distance, 1 vol. 2015. (Measure It! Ser.). (ENG., Illus.). 24p. (J). (gr. 1-2). pap. 9.15 *(978-1-4824-3856-7(4)*, dced629e-d90e-456c-b090-d25e6efe833e) Stevens, Gareth Publishing LLLP.

—Measuring Height, 1 vol. 2015. (Measure It! Ser.). (ENG.). 24p. (J). (gr. 1-2). pap. 9.15 *(978-1-4824-3860-4(7)*, b22f7d24-2e4d-4f34-a4ef-e78b0d2a2a09) Stevens, Gareth Publishing LLLP.

—Measuring Temperature, 1 vol. 2015. (Measure It! Ser.). (ENG., Illus.). 24p. (J). (gr. 1-2). pap. 9.15 *(978-1-4824-3868-0(2)*, 87d7cf88-270a-40fa-8ebc-3f7800c971da) Stevens, Gareth Publishing LLLP.

—Measuring Volume, 1 vol. 2015. (Measure It! Ser.). (ENG., Illus.). 24p. (J). (gr. 1-2). pap. 9.15 *(978-1-4824-3872-7(0)*, aa5ed4a4-56d1-4271-9bff-1cb2a7471f59) Stevens, Gareth Publishing LLLP.

Bailer, Darice. Measuring Length. Petelinsek, Kathleen, illus. 2014. (Explorer Junior Library: Math Explorer Junior Ser.). (ENG.). 24p. (J). (gr. 1-4). 32.07 *(978-1-62431-647-0(6)*, 203100) Cherry Lake Publishing.

Baker, Maryann. My Mom Is a Carpenter: Relate Addition & Subtraction to Length, 1 vol. 2014. (Rosen Math Readers Ser.). (ENG.). 24p. (J). (gr. 2-2). pap. 8.25 *(978-1-4777-4813-8(X)*, 7bc9f936-7e74-4792-9d78-cf6747bfe7a3, Rosen Classroom) Rosen Publishing Group, Inc., The.

Barner, Bob. Ants Rule: The Long & Short of It. 2019. (Illus.). 32p. (J). (gr. -1-3). pap. 7.99 *(978-0-8234-4174-7(1))* 2017. *(978-0-8234-3790-0(6))* Holiday Hse., Inc.

Beck, Esther & Doudna, Kelly. Im on the Trail to Learn about Scale!, 1 vol. 2007. (Science Made Simple Ser.). (Illus.). 24p. (J). (gr. k-3). lib. bdg. 24.21 *(978-1-59928-592-4(4)*, SandCastle) ABDO Publishing Co.

Bellavia, Rebecca. Planting Sunflowers: Represent & Interpret Data, 1 vol. 2014. (Math Masters: Measurement & Data Ser.). (ENG.). 24p. (J). (gr. 2-2). 25.27 *(978-1-4777-6408-4(9)*, 9a9fa10b-1ade-48fc-8b47-2370205927b3); pap. 8.25 *(978-1-4777-4825-1(3)*, b353be4c-39ef-4ca3-afda-76d866d2e919) Rosen Publishing Group, Inc., The. (Rosen Classroom).

Benchmark Education Company, LLC Staff, compiled by. Measurement. 2005. spiral bd. 295.00 *(978-1-4108-3902-2(8))*; spiral bd. 295.00 *(978-1-4108-5866-5(9))*; spiral bd. 330.00 *(978-1-4108-5865-8(0))*; spiral bd. 315.00 *(978-1-4108-5455-1(8))*; spiral bd. 635.00 *(978-1-4108-5454-4(X))*; spiral bd. 305.00 *(978-1-4108-3887-2(0))*; spiral bd. 165.00 *(978-1-4108-3888-9(9))*; spiral bd. 270.00 *(978-1-4108-3895-7(1))*; spiral bd. 120.00 *(978-1-4108-3896-4(X))*; spiral bd. 110.00 *(978-1-4108-3903-9(6))*; spiral bd. 50.00 *(978-1-4108-3910-7(9))*; spiral bd. 35.00 *(978-1-4108-3914-5(1))*; spiral bd. 420.00 *(978-1-4108-4513-9(3))* Benchmark Education Co.

—Measuring: Theme Set. 2006. (J). 109.00 *(978-1-4108-7090-2(1))* Benchmark Education Co.

Best, Arthur. Length & Width, 1 vol. 2018. (Properties of Matter Ser.). (ENG.). 24p. (gr. 1-1). pap. 9.22 *(978-1-5026-4218-9(2)*, e86dd955-02cf-4271-b7ce-e40473ceef27) Cavendish Square Publishing LLC.

Bishop, Celeste. Gone Fishing!, 1 vol. 2013. (Core Math Skills: Measurement & Geometry Ser.). (ENG.). 24p. (J). (gr. 1-1). 26.27 *(978-1-4777-2227-5(0)*, 3d80ae82-5e0d-4d3f-8520-753f78c0a28a, Rosen Classroom) Rosen Publishing Group, Inc., The.

—Gone Fishing! Measure Lengths, 1 vol. 2013. (Rosen Math Readers Ser.). (ENG.). 24p. (J). (gr. 1-1). pap. 8.25 *(978-1-4777-2076-9(6)*, bb12206b-fd89-412f-957d-05df1aee14fb); pap. 49.50 *(978-1-4777-2077-6(4))* Rosen Publishing Group, Inc., The. (Rosen Classroom).

—Tall & Short: Describe & Compare Measurable Attributes. 2013. (InfoMax Math Readers Ser.). (ENG.). 16p. (J). (gr. k-1). pap. 42.00 *(978-1-4777-1923-7(7))*; (Illus.). pap. 7.00 *(978-1-4777-1922-0(9)*, 59b87d75-493a-4605-8180-ea1fdb039efe) Rosen Publishing Group, Inc., The. (Rosen Classroom).

Bodach, Vijaya Khisty. Measuring. 2008. (Discovering & Exploring Science Ser.). (Illus.). 16p. (J). (gr. -1-3). lib. bdg. 12.95 *(978-0-7569-8256-0(1))* Perfection Learning Corp.

Borden, Louise. Sea Clocks: The Story of Longitude. Blegvad, Erik, illus. 2004. (ENG.). 48p. (J). (gr. 2-5). 19.99 *(978-0-689-84216-0(3)*, McElderry, Margaret K. Bks.) McElderry, Margaret K. Bks.

Brunner- Jass, Renata. Field of Play: Measuring Distance, Rate, & Time. 2013. (iMath Ser.). (ENG., Illus.). 48p. (J). (gr. 5-6). pap. 13.26 *(978-1-60357-510-2(3))* Norwood Hse. Pr.

—A Year at the Fairgrounds: Finding Volume. 2013. (iMath Ser.). (ENG., Illus.). 48p. (J). (gr. 5-6). pap. 13.26 *(978-1-60357-514-0(6))* Norwood Hse. Pr.

Bryant-Mole, Karen. Starting to Measure. 2004. (First Learning Ser.). (ENG., Illus.). 1p. (J). (gr. -1-18). pap., act. bk. ed. 4.95 *(978-0-7460-3801-7(1))* EDC Publishing.

Burstein, John. Measuring: the Perfect Playhouse, 1 vol. 2003. (Math Monsters(tm) Ser.). (ENG., Illus.). 24p. (J). (gr. k-3). lib. bdg. 23.67 *(978-0-8368-3813-8(0)*, 6c1a556e-e974-443a-9179-5431e8939af3, Weekly Reader Leveled Readers) Stevens, Gareth Publishing LLLP.

Burton, Margie, et al. Bigger Than? Smaller Than? 2011. (Early Connections Ser.). (J). *(978-1-61672-249-4(5))* Benchmark Education Co.

—Measure Up! 2011. (Early Connections Ser.). (J). *(978-1-61672-500-6(1))* Benchmark Education Co.

—What Can You Measure with a Lollipop? & ¿Qué puedes medir con una Paleta? 6 English, 6 Spanish Adaptations. 2011. (J). spiral bd. 75.00 net. *(978-1-4108-5627-2(5))* Benchmark Education Co.

Bussiere, Desirée. Let's Measure More, 6 vols. 2013. (Let's Measure Ser.: 6). (ENG.). 24p. (J). (gr. -1-3). lib. bdg. 179.58 *(978-1-61783-594-0(3)*, 11105, SandCastle) ABDO Publishing Co.

—What in the World Is a Baker's Dozen? & Other Interesting Measurements, 1 vol. 2013. (Let's Measure Ser.). (ENG.). 24p. (J). (gr. -1-3). lib. bdg. 29.93 *(978-1-61783-595-7(1)*, 11107, SandCastle) ABDO Publishing Co.

—What in the World Is a Centimeter? & Other Metric Measurements, 1 vol. 2013. (Let's Measure Ser.). (ENG.). 24p. (J). (gr. -1-3). lib. bdg. 29.93 *(978-1-61783-596-4(X)*, 11109, SandCastle) ABDO Publishing Co.

—What in the World Is a Mile? & Other Distance Measurements, 1 vol. 2013. (Let's Measure Ser.). (ENG.). 24p. (J). (gr. -1-3). lib. bdg. 29.93 *(978-1-61783-598-8(6)*, 11113, SandCastle) ABDO Publishing Co.

—What in the World Is a Ton? & Other Weight & Volume Measurements, 1 vol. 2013. (Let's Measure Ser.). (ENG.).

24p. (J). (gr. -1-3). lib. bdg. 29.93 (978-1-61783-599-5(4), 11115, SandCastle) ABDO Publishing Co.

—What in the World Is an Acre? & Other Land & Sea Measurements, 1 vol. 2013. (Let's Measure Ser.). (ENG.). 24p. (J). (gr. -1-3). lib. bdg. 29.93 (978-1-61783-600-8(1), 11117, SandCastle) ABDO Publishing Co.

Caes, Charles J. Discovering the Speed of Light, 1 vol. 2011. (Scientist's Guide to Physics Ser.). (ENG., Illus.). 112p. (YA). (gr. 7-7). lib. bdg. 39.80 (978-1-4488-4699-3(4), 1b8657cc-8041-42be-8f09-06206583a90f) Rosen Publishing Group, Inc., The.

Cardenas, Ernesto A. Measurement. 2009. pap. 4.95 (978-1-60698-070-5(X)) Milo Educational Bks. & Resources.

—What Do You Use to Measure? 2009. 23.95 (978-1-60698-050-7(5)); pap. 4.95 (978-1-60698-048-4(3)) Milo Educational Bks. & Resources.

Chigeza, Philemon. Measurement Ideas & Possibilities. 2012. 28p. pap. 32.70 (978-1-4691-8015-1(4)) Xlibris Corp.

Cleary, Brian P. How Long or How Wide? A Measuring Guide. Gable, Brian, illus. 2009. (Math Is CATegorical (r) Ser.). (ENG.). 32p. (J). (gr. k-3). pap. 8.99 (978-1-58013-844-4(6), cc1b09dc-bd9e-4171-a70b-19cf06008f8d, Millbrook Pr.) Lerner Publishing Group.

Colson, Rob. Get the Measure: Units & Measurements (Math Everywhere) (Library Edition) 2017. (Math Everywhere Ser.). (ENG., Illus.). 32p. (J). (gr. 5-8). lib. bdg. 27.00 (978-0-531-22883-8(5), Children's Pr.) Scholastic Library Publishing.

Connelly, Luella. Let's Measure It. 2017. (Learn-To-Read Ser.). (ENG., Illus.). (J). (gr. k-2). pap. 3.49 (978-1-68310-233-5(9)) Pacific Learning, Inc.

Corcorane, Ann. Measuring, 1 vol. 2011. (Wonder Readers Emergent Level Ser.). (ENG.). 16p. (gr. -1-1). (J). pap. 6.25 (978-1-4296-7867-4(4), 118197); pap. 35.94 (978-1-4296-8128-5(4), Capstone Pr.) Capstone.

Core Math Skills: Measurement & Geometry, 12 vols. 2013. (Core Math Skills: Measurement & Geometry Ser.). (ENG.). 24p. (J). (gr. 1-1). 157.62 (978-1-4777-2236-7(X), b4e1d8a2-c44a-4e2d-8d88-776b19147d98, Rosen Classroom) Rosen Publishing Group, Inc., The.

Dase, Pam & Dugan, Christine. Hurricane Hunters. rev. ed. 2012. (Mathematics in the Real World Ser.). (ENG.). 32p. (gr. 5-8). pap. 11.99 (978-1-4333-3462-7(3)) Teacher Created Materials, Inc.

—Tornado Chasers. rev. ed. 2012. (Mathematics in the Real World Ser.). (ENG.). 32p. (gr. 5-8). pap. 11.99 (978-1-4333-3463-4(1)) Teacher Created Materials, Inc.

Davenport, Jefferson. Our Fishing Trip: Measure Lengths. 2013. (InfoMax Math Readers Ser.). (ENG.). 24p. (J). (gr. 1-2). pap. 49.50 (978-1-4777-2170-4(3)); (Illus.). pap. 8.25 (978-1-4777-2169-8(X), 5536be85-2049-428a-9632-9a0545ffbd68) Rosen Publishing Group, Inc., The. (Rosen Classroom).

Davies, Ann. Fun Size. (Illus.). 40p. (J). 19.95 (978-1-85479-230-3(X)) O'Mara, Michael Bks., Ltd. GBR. Dist: Trans-Atlantic Pubns., Inc.

Deen, Marilyn. Measure by Measure, 1 vol. 2011. (Wonder Readers Fluent Level Ser.). (ENG.). 16p. (gr. -1-2). (J). pap. 6.25 (978-1-4296-7930-5(1), 118262); pap. 35.94 (978-1-4296-8127-8(6)) Capstone. (Capstone Pr.).

Dell, Pamela. Feet & Meters. 2016. (Spring Forward Ser.). (J). (gr. 2). (978-1-4900-9416-8(4)) Benchmark Education Co.

DK. How to Measure Everything. 2018. (ENG.). 20p. (J). (gr. k-2). bds. 14.99 (978-1-4654-7030-0(1), DK Children) Dorling Kindersley Publishing, Inc.

Dreyer, Kira. My New Bedroom: Estimate Lengths in Standard Units, 1 vol. 2014. (Math Masters: Measurement & Data Ser.). (ENG.). 24p. (J). (gr. 2-2). 25.27 (978-1-4777-6438-1(0), 0c3ad933-6764-409e-a6c2-cad5b467c0bd); pap. 8.25 (978-1-4777-4801-5(6), 71287908-575c-4b55-aaf6-ea8d90f14af8) Rosen Publishing Group, Inc., The. (Rosen Classroom).

Erickson, Amelia. My First Airplane Trip: Solve Problems Involving Measurement, 1 vol. 2014. (InfoMax Math Readers Ser.). (ENG.). 24p. (J). (gr. 3-3). pap. 8.25 (978-1-4777-4606-6(4), e15c0467-0da4-4fdc-beec-30e0c41a9811, Rosen Classroom) Rosen Publishing Group, Inc., The.

Faulkner, Nicholas & Hosch, William L., eds. Numbers & Measurements, 1 vol. 2017. (Foundations of Math Ser.). (ENG., Illus.). 344p. (J). (gr. 10-10). lib. bdg. 55.59 (978-1-68048-778-7(7), ece40e52-ceb4-4c2e-8148-9f355a3a74ed, Britannica Educational Publishing) Rosen Publishing Group, Inc., The.

First, Rachel. Measure It! Fun with Length & Distance. 2015. (Math Beginnings Ser.). (ENG., Illus.). 24p. (J). (gr. -1-3). 29.93 (978-1-62403-934-8(0), 19295, SandCastle) ABDO Publishing Co.

Flatt, Lizann. Sizing up Winter. Barron, Ashley, illus. 2018. (Math in Nature Ser.: 3). (ENG.). 32p. (J). (gr. k-3). pap. 8.95 (978-1-77147-339-2(8)) Owlkids Bks. Inc. CAN. Dist: Publishers Group West (PGW).

Formichelli, Linda & Anderson, Maxine. Timekeeping: Explore the History & Science of Telling Time with 15 Projects. Carbaugh, Samuel, illus. 2012. (Build It Yourself Ser.). (ENG.). 128p. (J). (gr. 3-7). pap. 15.95 (978-1-61930-033-0(8), 9fd535cf-9dd7-435a-a4e2-9e877aa0daba) Nomad Pr.

Formichelli, Linda & Martin, W. Eric. Timekeeping: Explore the History & Science of Telling Time with 15 Projects. Carbaugh, Sam, illus. 2012. (Build It Yourself Ser.). (ENG.). 128p. (J). (gr. 3-7). 21.95 (978-1-61930-136-8(9), 2d8d6ee7-09f3-4739-b919-5da28346264c) Nomad Pr.

Freeman, Marcia S. & Gillis, Jennifer. Measuring Our World. 2003. (Readers for Writers - Fluent Ser.). (ENG.). 16p. (gr. 2-3). pap. 6.33 (978-1-59515-272-5(5), 9781595152725) Rourke Educational Media.

Furgang, Kathy. Measuring Length. 2011. (Early Connections Ser.). (J). (978-1-61672-590-7(7)) Benchmark Education Co.

Garcia, Joy. My Paper Ruler: A Garcia Hands-on Learn-about Book. 2009. (Skinny Minis Ser.). (ENG., Illus.). 44p. (J). (gr. -1-3). per. 4.99 (978-1-59092-144-9(5)) Blue Forge Pr.

Gardner, Robert. How Heavy Is Heavy? Science Projects with Weight, 1 vol. 2014. (Hot Science Experiments Ser.). (ENG.). 48p. (gr. 3-4). 26.93 (978-0-7660-6600-7(2), 6a136b12-c3ea-40af-8e30-a924c9a4b6ba) Enslow Publishing, LLC.

—How High Is High? Science Projects with Height & Depth, 1 vol. 2014. (Hot Science Experiments Ser.). (ENG.). 48p. (gr. 3-4). 26.93 (978-0-7660-6595-6(2), 3cad5a94-5695-4045-846d-a3bd3ab5b215); pap. 11.53 (978-0-7660-6596-3(0), 838c9331-738e-46a8-a4eb-3ea4d563b092, Enslow Elementary) Enslow Publishing, LLC.

Gresko, Marcia S. Fun with Measurement. 2017. pap. 3.99 (978-1-68310-308-0(4)) Creative Teaching Pr., Inc.

Gunderson, Jessica. How Long? Wacky Ways to Compare Length, 1 vol. Sinkovec, Igor, illus. 2013. (Wacky Comparisons Ser.). (ENG.). 24p. (J). (gr. -1-2). pap. 8.95 (978-1-4795-1914-9(6), 123621, Picture Window Bks.) Capstone.

Haley, Charly. Ivy Makes a Craft: A Book about Measuring. 2018. (My Day Readers Ser.). (ENG.). 24p. (J). (gr. -1-2). lib. bdg. 32.79 (978-1-5038-2492-8(6), 212355) Child's World, Inc, The.

Henn, Sophy. Lifesize. Henn, Sophy, illus. 2019. (Illus.). (J). 14.99 (978-1-61067-731-8(5)) Kane Miller.

Heos, Bridget. Measure It. Longhi, Katya, illus. 2014. (Math World Ser.). (ENG.). 24p. (J). (gr. 1-4). lib. bdg. 27.10 (978-1-60753-464-8(9), 15915) Amicus.

—What Are Measurements?, 1 vol. 2014. (Let's Find Out! Physical Science Ser.). (ENG.). 32p. (J). (gr. 2-3). 26.06 (978-1-62275-507-3(3), 0ca8f909-3f84-42de-9234-ecef827d911a) Rosen Publishing Group, Inc., The.

Hore, Rosie. Lift-The-Flap Measuring Things. 2017. (Advanced Lift-The-Flap Board Bks.). (ENG.). 16p. 14.99 (978-0-7945-4022-7(8), Usborne) EDC Publishing.

Hunt, Darleen L. Mr. Reed's Class Estimates: Estimating. Komarck, Michael, illus. 2003. (Sherman's Math Corner Ser.). (J). (gr. -1-3). (978-1-929591-06-0(3)) Reading Rock, Inc.

In Step with the Standards - Measurement. 2005. (J). spiral bd. 15.95 (978-1-58123-377-3(9)) Larson Learning, Inc.

Ipcizade, Catherine. How to Read Measurements. 2018. (Understanding the Basics Ser.). (ENG.). 24p. (J). (gr. 1-4). lib. bdg. 32.79 (978-1-5038-2332-7(6), 212207) Child's World, Inc, The.

Jacobs, Russell F. Measurement & Geometry - by Design. 2017. (ENG.). 48p. (J). pap. 19.95 (978-0-9846042-1-0(9)) Tessellations.

Jones, Tammy. What Is the Time? 2009. (Sight Word Readers Set A Ser.). (J). 3.49 net. (978-1-60719-150-6(4)) Newmark Learning LLC.

Kompelein, Tracy. I Can Measure Weight at Any Rate, 1 vol. 2007. (Math Made Fun Ser.). (Illus.). 24p. (J). (gr. k-3). lib. bdg. 24.21 (978-1-59928-519-1(3), SandCastle) ABDO Publishing Co.

Kompelien, Tracy. Lets All Assume, We Can Measure Volume!, 1 vol. 2007. (Math Made Fun Ser.). (Illus.). 24p. (J). (gr. k-3). lib. bdg. 24.21 (978-1-59928-535-1(5), SandCastle) ABDO Publishing Co.

Kompelien, Tracy & Kompelein, Tracy. I Can Measure Length, It Has No Strength!, 1 vol. 2007. (Math Made Fun Ser.). (Illus.). 24p. (J). (gr. k-3). lib. bdg. 24.21 (978-1-59928-517-7(7), SandCastle) ABDO Publishing Co.

Kralick, Evelyn. Famous Fossils: Measure Lengths in Standard Units, 1 vol. 2014. (Math Masters: Measurement & Data Ser.). (ENG.). 24p. (J). (gr. 2-2). 25.27 (978-1-4777-6437-4(2), 6dd6c5ba-7b2b-4302-be63-4b522f4d9275); pap. 8.25 (978-1-4777-4792-6(3), cd7d7411-83c6-4d03-b18f-6f41c73f9817) Rosen Publishing Group, Inc., The. (Rosen Classroom).

Krishnaswami, Uma. Learn to Estimate. 2006. (Early Explorers Ser.). (J). pap. (978-1-4108-6132-0(5)) Benchmark Education Co.

Levit, Joe. Let's Explore Math. 2018. (Bumba Books (r) — a First Look at STEM Ser.). (ENG., Illus.). 24p. (J). (gr. -1-1). pap. 8.99 (978-1-5415-2700-3(3), dc501376-92cf-4c8f-a57b-8823ffdb78e1) Lerner Publishing Group.

Levy, Janey. At Sea on a Viking Ship: Solving Problems of Length & Weight Using the Four Math Operations. 2004. (Math Big Bookstm Ser.). (ENG.). 24p. (gr. 3-4). 43.95 (978-0-8239-7642-3(4)) Rosen Publishing Group, Inc., The.

—The Great Pyramid of Giza: Measuring Length, Area, Volume, & Angles, 1 vol. (Math for the REAL World Ser.). 32p. 2010. (ENG., Illus.). (gr. 6-7). pap. 10.00 (978-1-4042-6059-7(5), 28fa8d51-1680-4de7-94fa-b8dfab85a5aa) 2009. (gr. 5-5). 47.90 (978-1-60851-368-0(8), PowerKids Pr.) Rosen Publishing Group, Inc., The.

Linde, Barbara M. Building Washington, D. C. Measuring the Area of Rectangular Spaces, 1 vol. 2010. (Math for the REAL World Ser.). (ENG., Illus.). 32p. (gr. 4-5). pap. 10.00 (978-0-8239-8867-9(8), 3daef751-1840-4cc8-945c-e5f310d4da72, PowerKids Pr.) Rosen Publishing Group, Inc., The.

—Building Washington, DC: Measuring the Area of Rectangular Shapes, 1 vol. 2003. (PowerMath: Proficiency Ser.). (ENG., Illus.). 32p. (YA). (gr. 4-5). lib. bdg. 28.93 (978-0-8239-8980-5(1), 57cac86a-0ca7-45ac-869c-d2a8177f66f3) Rosen Publishing Group, Inc., The.

Loughran, Donna. A Day at Mini-Golf: What's the Length? 2013. (IMath Ser.). (Illus.). 24p. (J). (gr. k-2). (ENG.). pap. 13.26 (978-1-60357-495-2(6)); lib. bdg. 21.27 (978-1-59953-556-2(4)) Norwood Hse. Pr.

—How Long Is It? 2005. (Rookie Read-About Math Ser.). (ENG., Illus.). 32p. (J). (gr. 1-2). pap. 5.95 (978-0-516-24671-0(2), Children's Pr.) Scholastic Library Publishing.

Loughran, Donna & Brunner-Jass, Renata. A Year at the Fairgrounds: Finding Volume. 2013. (IMath Ser.). (Illus.). 48p. (J). (gr. 5-6). lib. bdg. 23.94 (978-1-59953-575-3(0)) Norwood Hse. Pr.

Lowery, Lawrence F. How Tall Was Milton? 2012. (I Wonder Why Ser.). (ENG., Illus.). 40p. (J). (gr. k-3). pap. 11.95 (978-1-936959-43-3(7), P218556) National Science Teachers Assn.

Maloof, Torrey. Your World: Investigating Measurement: Volume & Mass (Grade 3) 2017. (Mathematics in the Real World Ser.). (ENG., Illus.). 32p. (J). (gr. 3-4). pap. 11.99 (978-1-4807-5807-0(8)) Teacher Created Materials, Inc.

Markovics, Joyce. Measure It! 2012. (Little World Math Ser.). (ENG.). 24p. (gr. -1-1). pap. 9.95 (978-1-61810-210-2(9), 9781618102102) Rourke Educational Media.

Marrewa, Jennifer. ¿a Qué Distancia? Vamos a COMPARAR Viajes (How Far Away? COMPARING Trips), 1 vol. 2008. (Las Matemáticas en Nuestro Mundo - Nivel 2 (Math in Our World - Level 2) Ser.). (SPA.). 24p. (gr. 2-2). pap. 9.15 (978-0-8368-9033-4(7), 1f6a6e01-a590-4484-9489-38619af4841a); (Illus.). lib. bdg. 24.67 (978-0-8368-9024-2(8), 15a63c75-d8e2-4cec-867e-684446a1fc71) Stevens, Gareth Publishing LLLP. (Weekly Reader Leveled Readers).

—How Far Away? COMPARING Trips, 1 vol. 2008. (Math in Our World - Level 2 Ser.). (ENG.). 24p. (gr. 2-2). pap. 9.15 (978-0-8368-9015-0(9), b0f1c192-1a36-4f19-9057-568e4cf68ede); (Illus.). lib. bdg. 24.67 (978-0-8368-9006-8(X), 91a57017-be36-4084-98fb-e55c4a8059ee) Stevens, Gareth Publishing LLLP. (Weekly Reader Leveled Readers).

—MEASURING on a Treasure Hunt, 1 vol. 2008. (Math in Our World - Level 2 Ser.). (ENG.). 24p. (gr. 2-2). pap. 9.15 (978-0-8368-9016-7(7), 9f0399c1-126b-4910-b353-65123a964dc1); (Illus.). lib. bdg. 24.67 (978-0-8368-9007-5(8), 7b6ad788-1c44-4279-b1dc-90121ac40165) Stevens, Gareth Publishing LLLP. (Weekly Reader Leveled Readers).

—MIDIENDO para una Búsqueda Del Tesoro (MEASURING on a Treasure Hunt), 1 vol. 2008. (Las Matemáticas en Nuestro Mundo - Nivel 2 (Math in Our World - Level 2) Ser.). (SPA.). 24p. (gr. 2-2). pap. 9.15 (978-0-8368-9034-1(5), e4e9c90b-974e-4ad9-8bcc-b2b0f0419a03); (Illus.). lib. bdg. 24.67 (978-0-8368-9025-9(6), 9eb6e282-9c60-4a30-9325-82dc3267bbdc) Stevens, Gareth Publishing LLLP. (Weekly Reader Leveled Readers).

Maurer, Tracy Nelson. The Scoop about Measuring Matter. 2012. (My Science Library). (ENG.). 24p. (gr. 3-4). pap. 8.95 (978-1-61810-226-3(5), 9781618102263) Rourke Educational Media.

Maxwell, Yolonda. Famous Bridges of the World: Measuring Length, Weight, & Volume, 1 vol. 2010. (Math for the REAL World Ser.). (ENG., Illus.). 32p. (gr. 5-6). pap. 10.00 (978-1-4042-5137-3(5), 7d59746f-4fb8-442c-a806-2afa2e76e375, PowerKids Pr.) Rosen Publishing Group, Inc., The.

McGraw Hill. Key to Measurement, Book 1: English Units of Length, Bk. 1. 2012. (Key To... workbooks Ser.: Bk. 1). (ENG.). 48p. (gr. 6-8). spiral bd. 6.32 (978-1-55953-021-7(9), 1559530219) McGraw-Hill Education.

—Key to Measurement, Book 2: Measuring Length & Perimeter Using English Units, 2. 2012. (Key To... workbooks Ser.: Bk. 2). (ENG.). 48p. (gr. 6-8). spiral bd. 6.32 (978-1-55953-022-4(7), 1559530227) McGraw-Hill Education.

—Key to Measurement, Book 3: Finding Area & Volume Using English Units, 3. 2012. (Key To... workbooks Ser.: Bk. 3). (ENG.). 56p. (gr. 6-8). spiral bd. 6.32 (978-1-55953-023-1(5), 1559530235) McGraw-Hill Education.

—Key to Metric Measurement, Book 2: Measuring Length & Perimeter Using Metric Units, Bk. 2. 2012. (Key To... workbooks Ser.: Bk. 2). (ENG., Illus.). 48p. (gr. 6-8). spiral bd., wbk. ed. 6.32 (978-1-55953-326-3(9), 1559533269) McGraw-Hill Education.

Measure It! 2010. (Measure It! Ser.). (ENG.). 32p. (J). (gr. 1-2). pap., pap., pap. 31.80 (978-1-4296-6334-2(0), 171188, Capstone Pr.) Capstone.

Measure It! Classroom Collection. 2010. (Measure It! Ser.). (ENG.). 32p. (J). (gr. 1-2). pap. 196.40 (978-1-4296-6461-5(4), 171227, Capstone Pr.) Capstone.

Measurement & Geometry. 2003. Level C. tchr. ed. 19.50 (978-0-7652-1317-4(6))Level C. stu. ed. 14.50 (978-0-7652-1305-1(2))Level D. tchr. ed. 19.50 (978-0-7652-1321-1(4))Level D. stu. ed. 14.50 (978-0-7652-1309-9(5))Level E. tchr. ed. 19.50 (978-0-7652-1325-9(7))Level E. stu. ed. 14.50 (978-0-7652-1313-6(3)) Modern Curriculum Pr.

Measuring. 2005. (J). Bk. 1. per. 8.95 (978-1-59566-156-2(5))Bk. 2. per. 8.95 (978-1-59566-160-9(3)) QEB Publishing Inc.

Metz, Lorijo. Using Rulers & Tape Measures, 1 vol. 2013. (Science Tools Ser.). (ENG., Illus.). 24p. (J). (gr. 2-3). 26.27 (978-1-4488-9688-2(6), 4f1ad200-82bb-47a9-9180-825e9ed5b2fd); pap. 9.25 (978-1-4488-9834-3(X), 75d0af59-54a4-4591-b9e0-29e8fd9ce221) Rosen Publishing Group, Inc., The. (PowerKids Pr.).

Mian measurement Gr4-5. 2004. (Math in A Nutshell Ser.). (gr. 4-5). (978-1-59242-185-5(7)) Delta Education, LLC.

Minden, Cecilia. How Tall? How Wide? 2010. (21st Century Basic Skills Library: Measurements Ser.). (ENG., Illus.). 24p. (gr. k-3). lib. bdg. 26.35 (978-1-60279-848-9(6), 200562) Cherry Lake Publishing.

Montague-Smith, Ann. Measuring. 2004. (QEB Start Math Ser.). (Illus.). 24p. (J). Vol. 1. lib. bdg. 15.95 (978-1-59566-027-5(5)) Vol. 2. lib. bdg. 15.95 (978-1-59566-031-2(3)) QEB Publishing Inc.

Morgan, Elizabeth. Around My Town: Describe & Compare Measurable Attributes. 2013. (InfoMax Math Readers Ser.). (ENG.). 16p. (J). (gr. k-1). pap. 42.00 (978-1-4777-1983-1(0)); (Illus.). pap. 7.00 (978-1-4777-1982-4(2), 87266b60-7a03-451d-b6be-8e4e92fe3276) Rosen Publishing Group, Inc., The. (Rosen Classroom).

Mortensen, Lori. Made to Measure. 2016. (Spring Forward Ser.). (J). (gr. 2). (978-1-4900-9442-7(3)) Benchmark Education Co.

Multiplication Dot-to-Dot Spanish Version. 2007. (J). (978-1-58232-166-0(3)) ECS Learning Systems, Inc.

Multiplication Facts Spanish Version. 2007. (J). per. (978-1-58232-155-4(8)) ECS Learning Systems, Inc.

Multiplication Skills Spanish Version. 2007. (J). per. (978-1-58232-156-1(6)) ECS Learning Systems, Inc.

Murphy, Patricia J. Learning How to Measure with Puppies & Kittens, 1 vol. 2017. (Math Fun with Puppies & Kittens Ser.). (ENG.). 32p. (gr. 1-2). pap. 11.52 (978-0-7660-9074-3(4), c4d1722a-ce4a-4742-a6c3-39983056ddcc) Enslow Publishing, LLC.

Murphy, Stuart J. Polly's Pen Pal. Simard, Remy, illus. 2005. (MathStart 3 Ser.). (ENG.). 40p. (J). (gr. 2-18). pap. 6.99 (978-0-06-053170-6(3), HarperCollins) HarperCollins Pubs.

Murray, Julie. Long & Short. 2018. (Opposites Ser.). (ENG., Illus.). 24p. (J). (gr. -1-2). lib. bdg. 31.36 (978-1-5321-8182-5(5), 29837, Abdo Kids) ABDO Publishing Co.

National Geographic Learning. Reading Expeditions (Science: Math Behind the Science): How Many Ants in an Anthill? 2007. (ENG., Illus.). 24p. (J). pap. 15.95 (978-0-7922-4587-2(3)) CENGAGE Learning.

Nielsen, Aubrie. After School. rev. ed. 2011. (Mathematics in the Real World Ser.). (ENG.). 32p. (gr. k-1). pap. 9.99 (978-1-4333-3440-5(2)) Teacher Created Materials, Inc.

—At School. rev. ed. 2011. (Mathematics in the Real World Ser.). (ENG.). 32p. (gr. k-1). pap. 9.99 (978-1-4333-3441-2(0)) Teacher Created Materials, Inc.

Nussbaum, Ben. PEEP Measuring. 2004. (ENG.). 32p. (J). (gr. -1-2). 14.95 (978-1-59249-377-7(7), 1C004) Soundprints.

Patterson, Haley. Fossils Around the World: Measure Lengths in Standard Units, 1 vol. 2014. (InfoMax Math Readers Ser.). (ENG.). 24p. (J). (gr. 2-2). pap. 8.25 (978-1-4777-4777-3(X), 4bffddfd-22c4-4214-ad60-a05b78831324, Rosen Classroom) Rosen Publishing Group, Inc., The.

Pecorella, Jane. How a Quilt Is Built: Learning to Measure an Object Using Inches, 1 vol. 2010. (Math for the REAL World Ser.). (ENG.). 16p. (gr. 2-3). pap. 7.05 (978-0-8239-8924-9(0), 1ec37b8c-74ed-4e06-bbe7-b9b1db5cf079, Rosen Classroom) Rosen Publishing Group, Inc., The.

Peppas, Lynn. How Do We Measure Matter? 2012. (ENG.). 24p. (J). (978-0-7787-0768-4(7)); (Illus.). pap. (978-0-7787-0775-2(X)) Crabtree Publishing Co.

Perritano, John. A Toy Store Summer: Finding Area. 2013. (IMath Ser.). (ENG., Illus.). 32p. (J). (gr. 3-4). pap. 13.26 (978-1-60357-504-1(9)) Norwood Hse. Pr.

Pisano, Sal. Measurement, 1 vol. 2003. (BrainBuilders Ser.). (ENG.). 48p. (gr. k-4). pap. 5.25 (978-1-4042-8543-9(1), 168db982-e613-4dcb-97fc-e69f500f47c5) Rosen Publishing Group, Inc., The.

Pistoia, Sara. Measurements. 2016. (J). (978-1-4896-5110-5(1)) Weigl Pubs., Inc.

Pluckrose, Henry. Size (Math Counts: Updated Editions) (Library Edition) 2018. (Math Counts, New & Updated Ser.). (ENG., Illus.). 32p. (J). (gr. k-3). lib. bdg. 25.00 (978-0-531-17512-5(X), Children's Pr.) Scholastic Library Publishing.

—What Size Is It? 2006. (Let's Explore, Maths Set Ser.). (Illus.). 32p. (J). (gr. -1-3). lib. bdg. 27.10 (978-1-59771-040-4(7)) Sea-To-Sea Pubns.

QEB Start Math Book Stores Edition: Measuring - Book 1. 2006. (J). per. (978-1-59566-274-3(X)) QEB Publishing Inc.

QEB Start Math Book Stores Edition: Measuring Book 2. 2006. (J). per. (978-1-59566-278-1(2)) QEB Publishing Inc.

Rauen, Amy. Finding Shortest & Longest, 1 vol. 2008. (Getting Started with Math Ser.). (ENG.). 16p. (gr. k-1). pap. 6.30 (978-0-8368-8987-1(8), 1a93b747-f868-43c6-8f18-c50c3ceff84a); (Illus.). lib. bdg. 21.67 (978-0-8368-8982-6(7), 37efd4d4-1e51-4948-a434-311153a89b86) Stevens, Gareth Publishing LLLP. (Weekly Reader Leveled Readers).

Reagan, Naomi. Butterflies & Moths: Represent & Interpret Data, 1 vol. 2014. (Rosen Math Readers Ser.). (ENG., Illus.). 24p. (J). (gr. 3-3). pap. 8.25 (978-1-4777-4901-2(2), 54c99c90-81a3-471c-b797-cc45572303ae, Rosen Classroom) Rosen Publishing Group, Inc., The.

Reinhart, Robin. Fierce Freshwater Fish: Measure Lengths in Standard Units, 1 vol. 2014. (Math Masters: Measurement & Data Ser.). (ENG., Illus.). 24p. (J). (gr. 2-2). 25.27 (978-1-4777-6404-6(6), e2408b8c-6702-4b67-aca8-a5254df8b2d0, Rosen Classroom) Rosen Publishing Group, Inc., The.

Rey, Molly. Measuring with Footsteps, 1 vol. 2013. (Rosen Math Readers Ser.). (ENG.). 24p. (J). (gr. 1-1). pap. 8.25 (978-1-4777-2100-1(2), 11c47ec2-fce4-4470-b674-00bdd5b0bf54, Rosen Classroom) Rosen Publishing Group, Inc., The.

—Measuring with Footsteps: Measure Lengths. 2013. (Rosen Math Readers Ser.). (ENG.). 24p. (J). (gr. 1-2). pap. 49.50 (978-1-4777-2101-8(0), Rosen Classroom) Rosen Publishing Group, Inc., The.

Rice, Dona Herweck. USA Las Matemáticas - Descríbelo. 2nd rev. ed. 2016. (TIME for KIDS(r): Informational Text Ser.). (SPA.). 12p. (gr. -1-k). 7.99 (978-1-4938-3023-7(6)) Teacher Created Materials, Inc.

—Use Your Math Mind: Describe It. 2nd rev. ed. 2015. (TIME for KIDS(r): Informational Text Ser.). (ENG., Illus.). 12p. (gr. -1-k). 7.99 (978-1-4938-2142-6(3)) Teacher Created Materials, Inc.

Robbins, Eliza. Which Holds More? Learning to Compare Volume, 1 vol. (Math for the REAL World Ser.). (ENG., Illus.). 8p. (gr. k-1). 2010. pap. 5.15 (978-0-8239-8845-7(7), b38b2a62-f5ac-41e5-92b1-de18b12c7112) 2004. 29.95 (978-0-8239-7631-7(9)) Rosen Publishing Group, Inc., The.

Roberts, Abigail B. Using Measuring Cups, 1 vol. 2017. (Super Science Tools Ser.). (ENG.). 24p. (gr. 1-2). pap. 9.15 (978-1-4824-6397-2(0), 777d07b1-e651-4b27-9f17-da5223d1ea1b) Stevens, Gareth Publishing LLLP.

Roman, Nora. Using a Scale, 1 vol. 2017. (Super Science Tools Ser.). (ENG.). 24p. (gr. 1-2). 24.27 (978-1-4824-6407-8(1), 17ec24a3-1939-424b-9b72-c1299c5939eb) Stevens, Gareth Publishing LLLP.

Rossiter, Brienna. High & Low. 2019. (Opposites Ser.). (ENG., Illus.). 16p. (J). (gr. k-1). 25.64 (978-1-64185-347-7(6), 1641853476, Focus Readers) North Star Editions.

Roza, Greg. Measurement, 1 vol. 2003. (BrainBuilders Ser.). (ENG.). 48p. (gr. k-4). pap. 5.25 (978-1-4042-8537-8(7), 9f3bee90-fb42-496a-b6fd-f039a7bd8758) Rosen Publishing Group, Inc., The.

—Where We Play Sports: Measuring the Perimeters of Polygons, 1 vol. 2010. (Math for the REAL World Ser.). (ENG., Illus.). 24p. (gr. 3-4). pap. 8.25

(978-0-8239-8895-2(3), 94cbddbf-bd5d-47fc-af1a-91ebc50d354d, PowerKids Pr.) Rosen Publishing Group, Inc., The.

Rozines Roy, Jennifer & Roy, Gregory. Measuring at Home, 1 vol. 2007. (Math All Around Ser.). (ENG., Illus.). 32p. (gr. 2-2). lib. bdg. 32.64 *(978-0-7614-2263-1(3),* 6e4dd1cf-cb3f-4b9c-9e49-bc8683cc5f72, Cavendish Square) Cavendish Square Publishing LLC.

Rustad, Martha E. H. Measuring Length. 2019. (Measuring Masters Ser.). (ENG., Illus.). 24p. (J). (gr. -1-2). lib. bdg. 27.32 *(978-1-9771-0371-0(5),* 139345, Capstone Pr.) Capstone.

—Measuring Volume. 2019. (Measuring Masters Ser.). (ENG., Illus.). 24p. (J). (gr. -1-2). lib. bdg. 27.32 *(978-1-9771-0368-0(5),* 139342, Capstone Pr.) Capstone.

—Measuring Weight. 2019. (Measuring Masters Ser.). (ENG., Illus.). 24p. (J). (gr. -1-2). lib. bdg. 27.32 *(978-1-9771-0370-3(7),* 139344, Capstone Pr.) Capstone.

Salzmann, Mary Elizabeth. What in the World Is an Ounce? CD & Book. 2010. (Let's Measure CD+Book Ser.). 24p. (gr. k-3). audio compact disk 42.70 *(978-1-61613-318-4(X),* SandCastle) ABDO Publishing Co.

Sargent, Brian. How Much Does It Hold? 2006. (Rookie Read-About Math Ser.). (ENG., Illus.). 32p. (J). (gr. 1-2). pap. 5.95 *(978-0-516-29812-2(7));* lib. bdg. 20.50 *(978-0-516-24957-5(6))* Scholastic Library Publishing. (Children's Pr.).

Scheff, Matt. Amazing Human Feats of Distance. 2018. (Superhuman Feats Ser.). (ENG., Illus.). 32p. (J). (gr. 4-6). lib. bdg. 28.65 *(978-1-5435-4125-0(9),* 139079, Capstone Pr.) Capstone.

Schwartz, David M. Millions to Measure. Kellogg, Steven, illus. (ENG.). 40p. (J). (gr. k-7). 2003. 17.99 *(978-0-688-12916-3(1))* 2006. reprint ed. pap. 7.99 *(978-0-06-084806-4(5))* HarperCollins Pubs. (HarperCollins).

Science Stories Foss Spanish Measurement EA CR05. 2005. (J). *(978-1-59242-586-0(0))* Delta Education, LLC.

Shae, Jordan. Handy Measuring: Measure Lengths, 1 vol. 2013. (InfoMax Math Readers Ser.). (ENG.). 24p. (J). (gr. 1-1). pap. 8.25 *(978-1-4777-2201-5(7),* 358e9f52-0e3e-415e-b7aa-8ce845b41196); pap. 49.50 *(978-1-4777-2202-2(5))* Rosen Publishing Group, Inc., The. (Rosen Classroom).

Sill, Lisa M. CTIM - Láseres: Medición de la Longitud. rev. ed. 2018. (Mathematics in the Real World Ser.). (SPA., Illus.). 32p. (J). (gr. 2-3). pap. 10.99 *(978-1-4258-2870-7(1))* Teacher Created Materials, Inc.

Simpson, Jeffrey L. Measurement & Geometry, Student Edition: Count, Notice & Remember Math Intervention, Volume 6. Simpson, Marilyn Bohlen, ed. 2007. ring bd. 59.95 *(978-1-888976-59-5(4))* Mastery Learning Systems.

Smith, Paula. Measure It!, 1 vol. 2015. (Science Sleuths Ser.). (ENG., Illus.). 24p. (J). (gr. 2-2). pap. *(978-0-7787-1544-3(2))* Crabtree Publishing Co.

Somervill, Barbara A. & Capstone Press Staff. Measure It! 2010. (Measure It! Ser.). (ENG.). 32p. lib. bdg. 103.96 *(978-1-4296-5944-4(0),* Capstone Pr.) Capstone.

Steck-Vaughn Company, creator. Measure Mints, Grades K-6. 2011. (ENG., Illus.). 200p. (J). (gr. k-6). pap. 19.99 *(978-0-547-62558-4(8))* Heinemann-Raintree.

Steck-Vaughn Staff. Early Math: Measurement I. 2005. pap. 2.99 *(978-1-4190-0329-5(1))* Steck-Vaughn.

—Early Math: Measurement II, 10 Pack. 2005. pap. 29.95 *(978-1-4190-0363-9(1));* pap. 2.99 *(978-1-4190-0339-4(9))* Steck-Vaughn.

—Early Measurement 10-pack: Measurement I. 2005. pap. 29.95 *(978-1-4190-0353-0(4))* Steck-Vaughn.

—Focus on Math Level C: Measurement. 2005. pap. 2.99 *(978-1-4190-0269-4(4))* Harcourt Schl. Pubs.

—Focus on Math Level C 10-pack: Measurement. 2005. pap. 29.95 *(978-1-4190-0293-9(7))* Harcourt Schl. Pubs.

—Measure That Tongue! 2003. pap. 4.10 *(978-0-7398-7653-4(8))* Steck-Vaughn.

—Measurement & Geometry. 2004. pap. 14.95 *(978-0-7398-9855-0(8))* Harcourt Schl. Pubs.

—Top Line Math: Measurement. 2005. pap. 5.49 *(978-1-4190-0370-7(4))* Harcourt Schl. Pubs.

Steffora, Tracey. Measuring in the Garden, 1 vol. 2011. (Math Around Us Ser.). (ENG.). 24p. (J). (gr. -1-1). pap. 6.29 *(978-1-4329-4934-1(9),* 114835, Heinemann) Capstone.

Strazzabosco, John. Measurement, 1 vol. 2003. (BrainBuilders Ser.). (ENG.). 48p. (gr. k-4). pap. 5.25 *(978-1-4042-8530-9(X),* ea6010b1-7845-4bb0-9331-3124d54fefc9) Rosen Publishing Group, Inc., The.

Sullivan, Martha. Around My City: Describe & Compare Measurable Attributes. 2013. (Rosen Math Readers Ser.). (ENG.). 16p. (J). (gr. k-1). pap. 42.00 *(978-1-4777-1597-0(5));* (Illus.). pap. 7.00 *(978-1-4777-1596-3(7),* 6c95e9e1-38bd-4e18-981c-160428f66b3a) Rosen Publishing Group, Inc., The. (Rosen Classroom).

Sullivan, Navin. Area, Distance, & Volume, 1 vol. 2007. (Measure Up! Ser.). (ENG., Illus.). 48p. (gr. 4-4). lib. bdg. 34.07 *(978-0-7614-2323-2(0),* 5d822a36-9675-4d00-861d-9c7483b060ae) Cavendish Square Publishing LLC.

—Measure Up!, 10 vols., Set. Incl. Area, Distance, & Volume. lib. bdg. 34.07 *(978-0-7614-2323-2(0),* 5d822a36-9675-4d00-861d-9c7483b060ae); Speed. lib. bdg. 34.07 *(978-0-7614-2325-6(7),* 4134ce9b-6ecf-4306-8497-746ff7ef782a); Temperature. lib. bdg. 34.07 *(978-0-7614-2322-5(2),* f5d8ab18-4ea4-486e-8a2c-d6e996d4c6bc); Time. lib. bdg. 34.07 *(978-0-7614-2321-8(4),* d4c49b00-fe7c-49f2-9885-6585e0edeb0a); Weight. lib. bdg. 34.07 *(978-0-7614-2324-9(9),* 2a69846f-af63-49fe-a21d-3b102aed822d); (Illus.). 48p. (gr. 4-4). (Measure Up! Ser.). (ENG.). 2007. Set lib. bdg. 170.35 *(978-0-7614-2320-1(6),* 9747e8fb-2310-470b-b8e2-52cd82ec15dd, Cavendish Square) Cavendish Square Publishing LLC.

—Speed, 1 vol. 2007. (Measure Up! Ser.). (ENG., Illus.). 48p. (gr. 4-4). lib. bdg. 34.07 *(978-0-7614-2325-6(7),* 4134ce9b-6ecf-4306-8497-746ff7ef782a) Cavendish Square Publishing LLC.

Sweeney, Joan. Me & the Measure of Things. Kath, Katie, illus. 2019. 32p. (J). (gr. -1-2). 12.99 *(978-1-9848-2959-7(9),* Knopf Bks. for Young Readers) Random Hse. Children's Bks.

Thanner, Eric. Leaping Lengths! Relate Addition & Subtraction to Length, 1 vol. 2014. (InfoMax Math Readers Ser.). (ENG.). 24p. (J). (gr. 2-2). pap. 8.25 *(978-1-4777-4760-5(5),* c06325e2-da84-4d05-b191-32c264881073, Rosen Classroom) Rosen Publishing Group, Inc., The.

Truran, Stacy. Troy's Tree Fort: Measure Lengths in Standard Units, 1 vol. 2014. (Rosen Math Readers Ser.). (ENG.). 24p. (J). (gr. 2-2). pap. 8.25 *(978-1-4777-4784-1(2),* 878e16d7-01e5-446a-8ce2-b894c3b66284, Rosen Classroom) Rosen Publishing Group, Inc., The.

Tuxworth, Nicola. Sizes. 2016. (Illus.). 20p. (J). (gr. -1-12). bds. 6.99 *(978-1-84322-751-9(7),* Armadillo) Anness Publishing GBR. Dist: National Bk. Network.

Tyler, Madeline. Monster Measuring. Li, Amy, illus. 2020. (Monster Math Ser.). (ENG.). 24p. (J). (gr. -1-2). pap. 7.99 *(978-1-5415-8923-0(8),* 655d2ae9-4511-4d95-b501-eea15db059b2); lib. bdg. 26.65 *(978-1-5415-7928-6(3),* 6e802131-4862-4a9d-8447-55831373f066) Lerner Publishing Group. (Lerner Pubns.).

Unswood, Cassie. Exploring Plane Figures: Understand Concepts of Area, 1 vol. 2014. (InfoMax Math Readers Ser.). (ENG.). 24p. (J). (gr. 3-3). pap. 8.25 *(978-1-4777-4594-6(7),* 6f5c981c-8563-406b-9740-a933c38c3b51, Rosen Classroom) Rosen Publishing Group, Inc., The.

Visto, Joy. Whose Foot Is a Foot? (Making Math Work Ser.). (ENG.). 48p. (J). (gr. 4-7). 2016. pap. 12.00 *(978-1-62832-177-7(6),* 20918, Creative Paperbacks) 2015. (Illus.). *(978-1-60818-576-4(1),* 20917, Creative Education) Creative Co., The.

Vogel, Julia. Length. 2018. (Illus.). 24p. (J). *(978-1-4896-5871-5(8),* AV2 by Weigl) Weigl Pubs., Inc.

—Weight. 2018. (Illus.). 24p. (J). *(978-1-4896-5886-9(6),* AV2 by Weigl) Weigl Pubs., Inc.

Watson, Hannah. Lift-The-Flap Sizes & Measuring. 2017. (Lift-The-Flap Board Bks.). (ENG.). 16p. 13.99 *(978-0-7945-4039-5(2),* Usborne) EDC Publishing.

Weakland, Mark. How Tall? Wacky Ways to Compare Height, 1 vol. Sinkovec, Igor, illus. 2013. (Wacky Comparisons Ser.). (ENG.). 24p. (J). (gr. -1-2). pap. 8.95 *(978-1-4795-1913-2(8),* 123620, Picture Window Bks.) Capstone.

Weaver, Madeline. Near & Far at the Park: Describe & Compare Measurable Attributes. 2013. (Rosen Math Readers Ser.). (ENG.). 16p. (J). (gr. k-1). pap. 42.00 *(978-1-4777-1636-6(X));* (Illus.). pap. 7.00 *(978-1-4777-1635-9(1),* 30023a08-151a-43a8-ad9a-7532c56735d8) Rosen Publishing Group, Inc., The. (Rosen Classroom).

Wingard-Nelson, Rebecca. Math Measurement Word Problems: No Problem!, 1 vol. 2010. (Math Busters Word Problems Ser.). (ENG., Illus.). 64p. (J). (gr. 5-6). lib. bdg. 31.93 *(978-0-7660-3369-6(4),* 5fa65b33-7e64-4cba-8ef9-fece2b32d460) Enslow Publishing, LLC.

Woodford, Chris. Area, 1 vol. 2012. (Measure up Math Ser.). (ENG., Illus.). 32p. (J). (gr. 4-4). pap. 11.50 *(978-1-4339-7434-2(7),* b89ac744-6627-4e8d-b00b-3779b3074217); lib. bdg. 29.27 *(978-1-4339-7433-5(9),* f64c0fab-bb61-43be-b809-c94ed8d5c688) Stevens, Gareth Publishing LLLP.

—Distance, 1 vol. 2012. (Measure up Math Ser.). (ENG., Illus.). 32p. (J). (gr. 4-4). pap. 11.50 *(978-1-4339-7438-0(X),* 8df37471-f3fe-40f9-ba89-1813e58c51dd); lib. bdg. 29.27 *(978-1-4339-7437-3(1),* 1c98d3b0-e67c-4faa-8a1e-96f82dc4aec1) Stevens, Gareth Publishing LLLP.

—Height, 1 vol. 2012. (Measure up Math Ser.). (ENG., Illus.). 32p. (J). (gr. 4-4). pap. 11.50 *(978-1-4339-7442-7(8),* f99422b7-d3d5-45ec-bf86-02b85f5ef0ff); lib. bdg. 29.27 *(978-1-4339-7441-0(X),* 06b6eff6-1b05-4353-b3d9-02c45be25562) Stevens, Gareth Publishing LLLP.

Youssef, Jagger. Which Is Taller?, 1 vol. 2020. (Time to Compare! Ser.). (ENG.). 24p. (gr. k-k). pap. 9.15 *(978-1-5382-5498-1(0),* 2c21f957-5751-4ce5-b5c4-c5d7b4649624) Stevens, Gareth Publishing LLLP.

MEASUREMENT—FICTION

Berkes, Marianne. The Tortoise & Hare's Amazing Race, 1 vol. Morrison, Cathy, illus. 2015. (ENG & SPA.). 32p. (J). (gr. k-3). 17.95 *(978-1-62855-635-3(8))* Arbordale Publishing.

Gabriel, Nat. Sam Y Sus Cuadrados de Zapatos (Sam's Sneaker Squares) 2009. (SPA.). pap. 34.95 *(978-0-7613-4790-3(9))* Lerner Publishing Group.

Hosford, Kate. Infinity & Me. Swiatkowska, Gabi, illus. 2012. (ENG.). 32p. (J). (gr. k-4). lib. bdg. 19.99 *(978-0-7613-6726-0(8),* b5831ad3-c96a-45d4-b1c4-f4aa9e049398, Carolrhoda Bks.) Lerner Publishing Group.

Kayaalp, Suzan. Inch Worm Inch Worm. Merrifield, Monarca, illus. 2013. 20p. pap. 12.95 *(978-1-62838-072-9(1))* Page Publishing Inc.

Klein, Adria F. Tia Tape Measure, 1 vol. Rowland, Andrew, illus. 2011. (Tool School Ser.). (ENG.). 32p. (J). (gr. 1-2). pap. 6.25 *(978-1-4342-3388-2(X),* 116395); lib. bdg. 22.65 *(978-1-4342-3046-1(5),* 114624) Capstone. (Stone Arch Bks.).

—Tia Tape Measure & the Move, 1 vol. Rowland, Andrew, illus. 2012. (Tool School Ser.). (ENG.). 32p. (J). (gr. 1-3). lib. bdg. 22.65 *(978-1-4342-4023-1(1),* 118404, Stone Arch Bks.) Capstone.

—Tia Tape Measure & the Move, 1 vol. Rowland, Andrew, illus. 2012. (Tool School Ser.). (ENG.). 32p. (J). (gr. 1-3). pap. 6.25 *(978-1-4342-4236-5(6),* 120293, Stone Arch Bks.) Capstone.

Law, Felicia & Way, Steve. Mirage in the Mist: Measurements in Action, 1 vol. Spoor, Mike, illus. 2009. (Mandrill Mountain Math Mysteries Ser.). (ENG.). 32p. (J). (gr. 2-3). 27.27 *(978-1-60754-818-6(6),* 3b46573c-6745-47ea-b321-23dc467821a4, Windmill Bks.) Rosen Publishing Group, Inc., The.

May, Eleanor. Let's Go, Snow! Pillo, Cary, illus. 2017. (Math Matters Ser.). 32p. (J). (gr. k-4). pap. 5.99 *(978-1-57565-807-0(0),* c10b9d6d-d8c6-494f-882f-04311f6945c8, Kane Press) Astra Publishing Hse.

—Let's Go, Snow! Temperature Measurement. Pillo, Cary, illus. 2017. (Math Matters (r) Ser.). (ENG.). 32p. (J). (gr. k-3). E-Book 23.99 *(978-1-57565-808-7(9))* Astra Publishing Hse.

Meredith, Susan Markowitz. The Royal Zookeeper. 2011. (Early Connections Ser.). (J). *(978-1-61672-678-2(4))* Benchmark Education Co.

Reynolds Naylor, Phyllis. Lovingly Alice. 2006. (Alice Ser.). (ENG., Illus.). 176p. (J). (gr. 4-7). pap. 5.99 *(978-0-689-84400-3(X),* Atheneum Bks. for Young Readers) Simon & Schuster Children's Publishing.

Spoor, Mike, illus. Desperate Measures: Units of Measurement in Action, 1 vol. 2010. (Mandrill Mountain Math Mysteries Ser.). (ENG.). 32p. (J). (gr. 2-3). pap. 11.55 *(978-1-60754-925-3(5),* 0d0a4546-a9aa-44e2-a596-6f85f71671d5); lib. bdg. 27.27 *(978-1-60754-920-8(4),* 062ce9eb-2d37-4102-905f-f0621291bce6) Rosen Publishing Group, Inc., The. (Windmill Bks.).

Thielbar, Melinda. The Secret Ghost. 3rd rev. ed. 2010. pap. 39.62 *(978-0-7613-6944-8(9))* Lerner Publishing Group.

—The Secret Ghost: A Mystery with Distance & Measurement. Ota, Yuko Geneviev, illus. 2010. (Manga Math Mysteries Ser.: 3). (ENG.). 48p. (J). (gr. 3-5). pap. 6.99 *(978-0-7613-5245-7(7),* af4534ce-d5c6-48f8-a05a-62530c2a5001, Graphic Universe™) Lerner Publishing Group.

Weston Woods Staff, creator. Inch by Inch. 2011. 38.75 *(978-0-439-90543-5(5))* Weston Woods Studios, Inc.

MEASURES

see Weights and Measures

MEASURING

see Measurement

MEASURING INSTRUMENTS

Benchmark Education Company. Measuring Matter (Teacher Guide) Solids, Liquids, & Gases. 2005. *(978-1-4108-4651-8(2))* Benchmark Education Co.

Benchmark Education Company, LLC Staff. Science Measuring Tools Teacher's Guide. 2004. *(978-1-4108-2588-9(4))* Benchmark Education Co.

Cardenas, Ernesto A. What Do You Use to Measure? 2009. 23.95 *(978-1-60698-050-7(5));* pap. 4.95 *(978-1-60698-048-4(3))* Milo Educational Bks. & Resources.

Doudna, Kelly. She'll Use a Ruler So You Won't Fool Her!, 1 vol. 2007. (Science Made Simple Ser.). (Illus.). 24p. (J). (gr. k-3). lib. bdg. 24.21 *(978-1-59928-618-1(1),* SandCastle) ABDO Publishing Co.

Furgang, Kathy. Science Measuring Tools: Set Of 6. 2011. (Navigators Ser.). (J). pap. 50.00 net. *(978-1-4108-2573-5(6))* Benchmark Education Co.

—Science Measuring Tools & Instrumentos para medir en Ciencias: 6 English, 6 Spanish Adaptations. 2011. (ENG & SPA.). (J). 101.00 net. *(978-1-4108-5727-9(1))* Benchmark Education Co.

Mangieri, Catherine. Using Measuring Tools, 1 vol. 2008. (Real Life Readers Ser.). (ENG.). 12p. (gr. 1-2). pap. 5.90 *(978-1-4042-7921-6(0),* cf38961a-2edd-450d-b5b3-f6d70ab74063, Rosen Classroom) Rosen Publishing Group, Inc., The.

Markovics, Joyce. Measure It! 2012. (Little World Math Ser.). (ENG.). 24p. (gr. -1-1). pap. 9.95 *(978-1-61810-210-2(9),* 9781618102102) Rourke Educational Media.

Marsico, Katie. Tape Measures. 2013. (21st Century Junior Library: Basic Tools Ser.). (ENG.). 24p. (J). (gr. 2-5). pap. 12.79 *(978-1-62431-305-9(1),* 203014); (Illus.). 29.21 *(978-1-62431-173-4(3),* 203012) Cherry Lake Publishing.

Matos, Rebecca. Measuring Matter: Solids, Liquids, & Gases. 2005. (J). pap. *(978-1-4108-4603-7(2))* Benchmark Education Co.

Pearson Learning Staff, creator. A Visit to the Doctor. 2007. (ENG.). (J). (gr. 2-2). pap. 10.92 *(978-0-7652-8602-4(5),* Celebration Pr.) Savvas Learning Co.

Peppas, Lynn. How Do We Measure Matter? 2012. (ENG.). 24p. (J). *(978-0-7787-0768-4(7));* (Illus.). pap. *(978-0-7787-0775-2(X))* Crabtree Publishing Co.

Rivera, Sheila. Measuring Cup. 2006. (First Step Nonfiction — Simple Tools Ser.). (ENG., Illus.). 8p. (J). (gr. k-2). pap. 5.99 *(978-0-8225-5714-2(2),* 2a475e76-67c0-4efa-a3e0-6b50f9afd19f) Lerner Publishing Group.

Rozines Roy, Jennifer & Roy, Gregory. Measuring at Home, 1 vol. (Math All Around Ser.). (ENG.). 32p. (gr. 2-2). 2008. pap. 9.23 *(978-0-7614-3384-2(8),* 637568df-c407-48e7-b5eb-88a842cb6dd2) 2007. (Illus.). lib. bdg. 32.64 *(978-0-7614-2263-1(3),* 6e4dd1cf-cb3f-4b9c-9e49-bc8683cc5f72, Cavendish Square) Cavendish Square Publishing LLC.

Rustad, Martha E. H. Measuring Distance. 2019. (Measuring Masters Ser.). (ENG., Illus.). 24p. (J). (gr. -1-2). lib. bdg. 27.32 *(978-1-9771-0367-3(7),* 139341, Capstone Pr.) Capstone.

—Measuring Length. 2019. (Measuring Masters Ser.). (ENG., Illus.). 24p. (J). (gr. -1-2). lib. bdg. 27.32 *(978-1-9771-0371-0(5),* 139345, Capstone Pr.) Capstone.

Sullivan, Erin Ash. Measuring Matter: Set Of 6. 2010. (Navigators Ser.). (J). pap. 44.00 net. *(978-1-4108-5070-6(6))* Benchmark Education Co.

Sundance/Newbridge LLC Staff. Let's Measure It! 2004. (Reading PowerWorks Ser.). (gr. 1-3). 37.50 *(978-0-7608-7831-6(5));* pap. 6.10 *(978-0-7608-7832-3(3))* Sundance/Newbridge Educational Publishing.

MEAT INDUSTRY AND TRADE

Francis, Amy, ed. Vegetarianism, 1 vol. 2015. (Current Controversies Ser.). (ENG.). 232p. (gr. 10-12). 48.03 *(978-0-7377-7227-2(1),* dd3931db-8cb8-4a28-b8a7-744798d8534e, Greenhaven Publishing) Greenhaven Publishing LLC.

Hasan, Heather. Meat: From the Farm to Your Table, 1 vol. 2012. (Truth about the Food Supply Ser.). (ENG., Illus.). 48p. (J). (gr. 5-5). lib. bdg. 34.47 *(978-1-4488-6797-4(5),* ea4e2a0f-0ed6-4066-982b-57b4c233f7a3, Rosen Reference) Rosen Publishing Group, Inc., The.

Lee, Sally. The Powerful Protein Group, 1 vol. Swift, Gary, illus. 2011. (First Graphics: Myplate & Healthy Eating Ser.). (ENG.). 24p. (J). (gr. k-3). lib. bdg. 24.65 *(978-1-4296-6091-4(0),* 115040) Capstone.

Nelson, Robin. Meats & Proteins. 2003. (First Step Nonfiction — Food Groups Ser.). (ENG., Illus.). 24p. (J). (gr. k-2). 23.99 *(978-0-8225-4630-6(2),* 2f2fb79f-e073-473e-bedc-db2c04014611, Lerner Pubns.) Lerner Publishing Group.

Singer, Jane E. Meat. 2013. (Feeding the World Ser.: 8). (Illus.). 48p. (J). (gr. 4-18). 19.95 *(978-1-4222-2746-6(4))* Mason Crest.

MECHANICAL BRAINS

see Computers

MECHANICAL DRAWING

see also Architectural Drawing; Geometrical Drawing; Graphic Methods; Lettering

Weisbacher, Anne. Earth-Friendly Design. 2008. (Saving Our Living Earth Ser.). 72p. (YA). (gr. 4-7). lib. bdg. 30.60 *(978-0-8225-7564-1(7))* Lerner Publishing Group.

MECHANICAL DRAWING—VOCATIONAL GUIDANCE

AIMS Education Foundation, et al. Machine Shop. 2007. (ENG.). 248p. (gr. 5-9). pap. 24.95 *(978-1-881431-39-8(8),* 1311) AIMS Education Foundation.

MECHANICAL ENGINEERING

see also Electric Engineering; Engines; Machinery; Power (Mechanics)

Corporate Contributor & Snedden, Robert. Mechanical Engineering & Simple Machines. 2012. (ENG.). 32p. (J). *(978-0-7787-7498-3(8))* Crabtree Publishing Co.

Crabtree Staff & Snedden, Robert. Mechanical Engineering & Simple Machines, 1 vol. 2012. (ENG., Illus.). 32p. (J). pap. *(978-0-7787-7503-4(8))* Crabtree Publishing Co.

Currie-McGhee, Leanne. A Career in Mechanical Engineering. 2018. (Careers in Engineering Ser.). (ENG.). 64p. (J). (gr. 6-12). 39.93 *(978-1-68282-353-8(9))* ReferencePoint Pr., Inc.

De Medeiros, James. All about Pulleys. 2017. (Illus.). 24p. (J). *(978-1-5105-0954-2(2))* SmartBook Media, Inc.

De Medeiros, Michael. All about Screws. 2017. (Illus.). 24p. (J). *(978-1-5105-0957-3(7))* SmartBook Media, Inc.

Dickmann, Nancy. Ramps. 2018. (Simple Machines Ser.). (ENG.). 24p. (J). (gr. 2-4). *(978-1-78121-400-8(X),* 16688) Brown Bear Bks.

Domaine, Helena. Robotics. 2005. (Cool Science Ser.). (ENG., Illus.). 48p. (gr. 4-8). lib. bdg. 27.93 *(978-0-8225-2112-9(1),* Lerner Pubns.) Lerner Publishing Group.

Eboch, Chris. Amazing Feats of Mechanical Engineering, 1 vol. 2014. (Great Achievements in Engineering Ser.). (ENG., Illus.). 112p. (YA). (gr. 6-12). lib. bdg. 41.36 *(978-1-62403-430-5(6),* 1414, Essential Library) ABDO Publishing Co.

Eboch, M. M. Mechanical Engineering in the Real World. 2016. (STEM in the Real World Set 2 Ser.). (ENG., Illus.). 48p. (J). (gr. 4-8). lib. bdg. 35.64 *(978-1-68078-481-7(1),* 23899) ABDO Publishing Co.

Enz, Tammy. Zoom It: Invent New Machines That Move. 2012. (Invent It Ser.). (ENG.). 32p. (gr. 3-4). pap. 47.70 *(978-1-4296-8458-3(5));* (J). pap. 8.10 *(978-1-4296-7984-8(0),* 118316); (J). lib. bdg. 27.99 *(978-1-4296-7634-2(5),* 117231) Capstone. (Capstone Pr.).

Gregory, Joy. Mechanical Engineer. 2020. (J). *(978-1-7911-1688-0(4),* AV2 by Weigl) Weigl Pubs., Inc.

Herweck, Don. All about Mechanical Engineering, 1 vol. rev. ed. 2007. (Science: Informational Text Ser.). (ENG.). 32p. (J). (gr. 3-6). pap. 12.99 *(978-0-7439-0577-0(6))* Teacher Created Materials, Inc.

Hinton, Kerry. A Career As an Operating & Stationary Engineer, 1 vol., 1. 2015. (Essential Careers Ser.). (ENG.). 80p. (J). (gr. 6-6). 37.47 *(978-1-4994-6223-4(9),* a68b5ca2-9e4a-4f6f-b3c8-173f644b4f95, Rosen Young Adult) Rosen Publishing Group, Inc., The.

Holland, Gini, Soft & Hard, 1 vol. 2007. (I Know Opposites Ser.). (ENG.). 16p. (gr. k-2). pap. 6.30 *(978-0-8368-8301-5(2),* 9e0e49ff-54de-4a7f-ada2-3bf2d097e35e); lib. bdg. 21.67 *(978-0-8368-8296-4(2),* 09da00ae-05fe-483b-b859-eec519b91511) Stevens, Gareth Publishing LLLP. (Weekly Reader Leveled Readers).

Howse, Jennifer. All about Levers. 2017. (Illus.). 24p. (J). *(978-1-5105-0951-1(8))* SmartBook Media, Inc.

Juarez, Christine. John Danny Olivas. 2016. (Great Hispanic & Latino Americans Ser.). (ENG., Illus.). 24p. (J). (gr. -1-2). lib. bdg. 24.65 *(978-1-5157-1890-1(5),* 132589, Pebble) Capstone.

LaMachia, Dawn. Pulleys at Work, 1 vol. 2015. (Zoom in on Simple Machines Ser.). (ENG.). 24p. (gr. 2-2). 25.60 *(978-0-7660-6736-3(X),* a344b5b8-1e3e-4878-9320-37734e609251) Enslow Publishing, LLC.

Miller, Tim. Pulleys in My Makerspace. 2017. (Simple Machines in My Makerspace Ser.). (ENG., Illus.). 32p. (J). (gr. 3-4). *(978-0-7787-3372-0(6))* Crabtree Publishing Co.

Miller, Tim & Sjonger, Rebecca. Inclined Planes in My Makerspace. 2017. (Simple Machines in My Makerspace Ser.). (ENG., Illus.). 32p. (J). (gr. 3-4). *(978-0-7787-3370-6(X))* Crabtree Publishing Co.

—Screws in My Makerspace. 2017. (Simple Machines in My Makerspace Ser.). (ENG., Illus.). 32p. (J). (gr. 3-4). *(978-0-7787-3373-7(4))* Crabtree Publishing Co.

—Wedges in My Makerspace. 2017. (Simple Machines in My Makerspace Ser.). (ENG., Illus.). 32p. (J). (gr. 3-7). *(978-0-7787-3374-4(2))* Crabtree Publishing Co.

Mooney, Carla. Becoming Invisible: From Camouflage to Cloaks. 2010. (Great Idea Ser.). 48p. (J). (gr. 4-6). lib. bdg. 26.60 *(978-1-59953-378-0(2))* Norwood Hse. Pr.

Moore Niver, Heather. Getting to Know Arduino, 1 vol. 2014. (Code Power: a Teen Programmer's Guide Ser.). (ENG., Illus.). 64p. (J). (gr. 6-6). pap. 13.95 *(978-1-4777-7501-1(3),* 872213d2-c31b-44ae-adf9-90e6234804b6, Rosen Reference) Rosen Publishing Group, Inc., The.

Randolph, Joanne. Gears in My World, 1 vol. 2005. (My World of Science Ser.). (ENG., Illus.). 24p. (J). (gr. k-2). lib. bdg. 22.27 *(978-1-4042-3311-9(3),* fc28b63b-5a91-498b-873a-babdc9ecc2f2, PowerKids Pr.) Rosen Publishing Group, Inc., The.

MNO

—Gears in My World: Engranajes en Mi Mundo, 1 vol. 2005. (My World of Science / la Ciencia en Mi Mundo Ser.). (ENG & SPA.). 24p. (J). (gr. 2-2). 22.27 *(978-1-4042-3323-2(7)*, e1588ed4-e190-4bb4-95cf-50ba64ff0365) Rosen Publishing Group, Inc., The.
—Inclined Planes in My World, 1 vol. 2005. (My World of Science Ser.). (ENG., Illus.). 24p. (J). (gr. 2-2). lib. bdg. 22.27 *(978-1-4042-3312-6(1)*, 1d3d31b0-701b-4562-bb4e-90ca57b00cd0, PowerKids Pr.) Rosen Publishing Group, Inc., The.
—Inclined Planes in My World: Planos Inclinados en Mi Mundo, 1 vol. 2005. (My World of Science / la Ciencia en Mi Mundo Ser.). (ENG & SPA.). 24p. (J). (gr. 2-2). 22.27 *(978-1-4042-3324-9(5)*, b2b4a075-3860-4899-953f-0f3c9a19d6a5) Rosen Publishing Group, Inc., The.
—Levers in My World, 1 vol. 2005. (My World of Science Ser.). (ENG., Illus.). 24p. (J). (gr. k-2). lib. bdg. 22.27 *(978-1-4042-3309-6(1)*, eba93b10-96db-4b93-bb27-8d3af0111593, PowerKids Pr.) Rosen Publishing Group, Inc., The.
—Levers in My World: Palancas en Mi Mundo, 1 vol. 2005. (My World of Science / la Ciencia en Mi Mundo Ser.). (ENG & SPA.). 24p. (J). (gr. 2-2). 22.27 *(978-1-4042-3321-8(0)*, 29c2cd6b-0ecd-4c13-b08a-499f1d5d6cda) Rosen Publishing Group, Inc., The.
—Pulleys in My World, 1 vol. 2005. (My World of Science Ser.). (ENG., Illus.). 24p. (J). (gr. k-2). lib. bdg. 22.27 *(978-1-4042-3308-9(3)*, b94eee07-9316-43a9-864d-321583e2d933, PowerKids Pr.) Rosen Publishing Group, Inc., The.
—Pulleys in My World: Poleas en Mi Mundo, 1 vol. 2005. (My World of Science / la Ciencia en Mi Mundo Ser.). (ENG & SPA., Illus.). 24p. (J). (gr. 2-2). 22.27 *(978-1-4042-3320-1(2)*, f2b7790a-9b7f-4d30-8d7a-564889c33d9e) Rosen Publishing Group, Inc., The.
—Wedges in My World, 1 vol. 2005. (My World of Science Ser.). (ENG., Illus.). 24p. (J). (gr. k-2). lib. bdg. 22.27 *(978-1-4042-3310-2(5)*, b9d6a511-abbc-447b-8cff-647bcf649577, PowerKids Pr.) Rosen Publishing Group, Inc., The.
—Wedges in My World: Cuñas en Mi Mundo, 1 vol. 2005. (My World of Science / la Ciencia en Mi Mundo Ser.). (ENG & SPA.). 24p. (J). (gr. 2-2). 22.27 *(978-1-4042-3322-5(9)*, 18433942-88c7-40fa-a1ce-d6eed07a23b2) Rosen Publishing Group, Inc., The.
Rivera, Sheila. Bending. 2007. (First Step Nonfiction — Changing Matter Ser.). (ENG., Illus.). 8p. (J). (gr. k-2). pap. 5.99 *(978-0-8225-6416-4(5)*, 5c2c66d4-163c-4b3a-87da-52bd0a761677) Lerner Publishing Group.
Rooney, Anne. Optical Engineering & the Science of Light. 2013. (ENG.). 32p. (J). *(978-0-7787-1228-2(1))*; (Illus.). pap. *(978-0-7787-1232-9(X))* Crabtree Publishing Co.
Royston, Angela. Pulleys & Gears, 1 vol. 2003. (Machines in Action Ser.). (ENG., Illus.). 32p. (gr. 3-5). pap. 7.99 *(978-1-4034-4085-3(9)*, Heinemann) Capstone.
Shea, Therese. Solving Real World Problems with Mechanical Engineering, 1 vol., 1. 2015. (Let's Find Out! Engineering Ser.). (ENG., Illus.). 32p. (J). (gr. 2-3). pap. 13.90 *(978-1-5081-0079-9(9)*, cf1f969a-98b5-489d-b10d-072e17aea73d, Britannica Educational Publishing) Rosen Publishing Group, Inc., The.
Tomljanovic, Tatiana. All about Wedges. 2017. (Illus.). 24p. (J). *(978-1-5105-0960-3(7))* SmartBook Media, Inc.
Weakland, Mark. Gears Go, Wheels Roll, 1 vol. 2010. (Science Starts Ser.). (ENG., Illus.). 32p. (J). (gr. -1-2). pap. 8.10 *(978-1-4296-6143-0(7)*, 115294, Capstone Pr.) Capstone.

MECHANICAL MODELS

see Machinery—Models

MECHANICS

see also Dynamics; Force and Energy; Hydrostatics; Liquids; Machinery; Motion; Power (Mechanics); Steam-Engines; Vibration

Brown Bear Books. Mechanics. 2011. (Introducing Physics Ser.). (ENG.). 64p. (J). (gr. 8-11). lib. bdg. 39.95 *(978-1-936333-09-7(0)*, 16506) Brown Bear Bks.
Cavell-Clarke, Steffi. Pushes & Pulls, 1 vol. 2016. (First Science Ser.). (ENG.). 24p. (J). (gr. 1-1). pap. 9.25 *(978-1-5345-2080-6(5)*, fb1bf6a9-33fa-4f11-9b1b-4fbed01112b0); lib. bdg. 26.23 *(978-1-5345-2082-0(1)*, 134aea56-031b-467f-bada-089a56c0f603) Greenhaven Publishing LLC. (KidHaven Publishing).
Clark, John O. E. The Basics of Mechanics, 1 vol. 2014. (Core Concepts Ser.). (ENG., Illus.). 96p. (YA). (gr. 7-7). 39.77 *(978-1-4777-7754-1(7)*, 971bfba0-7c3b-4315-b439-ec5cc0de79de) Rosen Publishing Group, Inc., The.
Coe, Catherine. Collins Big Cat Phonics for Letters & Sounds - Look at Them Go: Band 02B/Red B, Bd. 2B. 2018. (Collins Big Cat Phonics Ser.). (ENG.). 16p. (J). (gr. -1-k). pap. 6.99 *(978-0-00-825152-9(5))* HarperCollins Pubs. Ltd. GBR. Dist: Independent Pubs. Group.
Dangerfield, Jan. Cambridge International AS & a Level Mathematics: Mechanics Coursebook. 2018. (ENG., Illus.). 246p. pap. 32.35 *(978-1-108-40726-7(9))* Cambridge Univ. Pr.
Eason, Sarah. How Does a Car Work?, 1 vol. 2010. (How Does It Work? Ser.). (ENG., Illus.). 32p. (J). (gr. 3-4). pap. 11.50 *(978-1-4339-3463-6(9)*, f2212de5-25e7-4257-affb-1384286ffc2f); lib. bdg. 28.67 *(978-1-4339-3462-9(0)*, 15afc2c4-45f2-44d2-a672-e90a96818d70) Stevens, Gareth Publishing LLLP. (Gareth Stevens Learning Library).
Garcia, Karina. Karina Garcia's DIY Slime. 2017. (ENG., Illus.). 80p. (J). (gr. 4-9). pap. 7.99 *(978-1-4998-0660-1(4))* Little Bee Books Inc.
—Karina Garcia's Next-Level DIY Slime. 2018. (ENG., Illus.). 80p. (J). (gr. 4). pap. 7.99 *(978-1-4998-0799-8(6))* Little Bee Books Inc.
—Karina Garcia's Next-Level DIY Slime. 2018. (Illus.). 80p. (J). pap. *(978-1-78741-373-3(X))* Templar Publishing.
Gardner, Robert. How Fast Is Fast? Science Projects with Speed, 1 vol. 2014. (Hot Science Experiments Ser.). (ENG.). 48p. (gr. 3-4). 26.93 *(978-0-7660-6615-1(0)*, 29456ae8-f1b0-4655-be51-d3e2a910adb8) Enslow Publishing, LLC.
—The Physics of Toys & Games Science Projects, 1 vol. 2013. (Exploring Hands-On Science Projects Ser.). (ENG.). 128p. (gr. 5-6). pap. 13.88 *(978-1-4644-0219-7(1)*, 51857e6a-ef0b-453d-91ad-9147775c17ea); lib. bdg. 30.60 *(978-0-7660-4143-1(3)*, 06eb0f09-d618-462e-b5ba-bdb9acad4c7b) Enslow Publishing, LLC.
Hoffmann, Sara E. Rolling. 2012. (First Step Nonfiction — Balance & Motion Ser.). (ENG., Illus.). 8p. (J). (gr. k-2). pap. 5.99 *(978-1-4677-0514-1(4)*, 50c858f7-c1ee-411e-920f-64d4d792ef43) Lerner Publishing Group.
Ivancic, Linda. What Is a Wave?, 1 vol. 2015. (Unseen Science Ser.). (ENG., Illus.). 32p. (gr. 3-3). pap. 11.58 *(978-1-5026-0917-5(7)*, c9d64beb-62b9-406b-88e9-c8366f32ee77) Cavendish Square Publishing LLC.
Kawa, Katie. Loaders. 2011. (Big Machines Ser.). (Illus.). 24p. (gr. k-2). 69.20 *(978-1-4339-6890-7(6))* Stevens, Gareth Publishing LLLP.
Leaf, Christina. Mechanics. 2018. (Community Helpers Ser.). (ENG., Illus.). 24p. (J). (gr. k-3). lib. bdg. 26.95 *(978-1-62617-900-4(X)*, Blastoff! Readers) Bellwether Media.
Less, Emma. Mechanics. 2018. (Real-Life Superheroes Ser.). (ENG.). 16p. (J). (gr. k-2). pap. 7.99 *(978-1-68152-282-1(9)*, 14918) Amicus.
Mara, Wil. How Do Waves Form?, 1 vol. 2011. (Tell Me Why, Tell Me How Ser.). (ENG.). 32p. (gr. 3-3). 32.64 *(978-0-7614-4829-7(2)*, 1a822fc2-a20c-4d91-849a-d8746b360741) Cavendish Square Publishing LLC.
Mattern, Joanne. Focus on Inertia. 2017. (Hands-On STEM Ser.). (ENG., Illus.). 32p. (J). (gr. 2-3). pap. 9.95 *(978-1-63517-348-2(5)*, 1635173485); lib. bdg. 31.35 *(978-1-63517-283-6(7)*, 1635172837) North Star Editions. (Focus Readers).
Mechanik I: Bewegungslehre. (Duden Abiturhilfen Ser.). (GER.). 96p. (YA). (gr. 11). *(978-3-411-04451-1(9))* Bibliographisches Institut & F. A. Brockhaus AG DEU. Dist: International Bk. Import Service, Inc.
Mechanik II: Erhaltungssaetze. (Duden Abiturhilfen Ser.). (GER.). 96p. (YA). (gr. 11). *(978-3-411-05181-6(7))* Bibliographisches Institut & F. A. Brockhaus AG DEU. Dist: International Bk. Import Service, Inc.
Miller, Malinda. Modern Mechanics: Maintaining Tomorrow's Green Vehicles. 2010. (New Careers for the 21st Century Ser.). (Illus.). 64p. (YA). (gr. 7-18). lib. bdg. 22.95 *(978-1-4222-1818-1(X))* Mason Crest.
Randolph, Joanne. Gears in My World, 1 vol. 2006. (Journeys Ser.). (ENG.). 24p. (gr. k-2). pap. 7.05 *(978-1-4042-8423-4(0)*, fd623d93-fcd6-45a7-a99b-7319d5211970, Rosen Classroom) Rosen Publishing Group, Inc., The.
Scotin, Harry. Experiments with MacHines & Matter. Aloise, Frank, illus. 2012. 96p. 38.95 *(978-1-258-23744-8(X))*; pap. 23.95 *(978-1-258-24341-8(5))* Literary Licensing, LLC.
Walker, Sally M., et al. Work. 2005. (Early Bird Physics Ser.). (Illus.). 48p. (gr. 3-6). lib. bdg. 25.26 *(978-0-8225-2217-1(9))* Lerner Publishing Group.
Wells, Robert E. How Do You Lift a Lion? 2012. (J). 34.28 *(978-1-61913-159-0(5))* Weigl Pubs., Inc.
Wood, Matthew Brenden. Projectile Science: The Physics Behind Kicking a Field Goal & Launching a Rocket with Science Activities for Kids. 2018. (Build It Yourself Ser.). (ENG., Illus.). 128p. (J). (gr. 4-10). 22.95 *(978-1-61930-676-9(X)*, 19bcbe53-156f-49fa-aaec-7ea095e84ba4) Nomad Pr.

MECHANICS (PERSONS)

Honders, Christine. What's It Really Like to Be a Mechanic?, 1 vol. 2019. (Jobs Kids Want Ser.). (ENG.). 24p. (gr. 1-2). pap. 9.25 *(978-1-5383-4992-2(2)*, 3db34da8-01cc-4939-a04e-102e6a83e40b, PowerKids Pr.) Rosen Publishing Group, Inc., The.
Liebman, Dan & Liebman, Dan. I Want to Be a Mechanic. 2003. (I Want to Be Ser.). (ENG., Illus.). 24p. (J). (gr. -1-2). 14.95 *(978-1-55297-695-1(5)*, 2235d6df-5ceb-424a-bc29-1b5be0a3f341) Firefly Bks., Ltd.
—Quiero Ser Mecanico. 2003. (Quiero Ser.). Tr. of I Want to Be a Mechanic. (SPA., Illus.). 24p. (J). (gr. -1-2). pap. 5.99 *(978-1-55297-728-6(5)*, c1b748a1-491b-42c5-8bfe-7c4e65a4ea79) Firefly Bks., Ltd.
Marsico, Katie. Auto Technician. 2010. (21st Century Skills Library: Cool Careers Ser.). (ENG., Illus.). 32p. (gr. 4-8). lib. bdg. 32.07 *(978-1-60279-937-0(7)*, 200619) Cherry Lake Publishing.
Rogers, Kate. Mechanics, 1 vol., 1. 2015. (Hands-On Jobs Ser.). (ENG., Illus.). 24p. (J). (gr. 3-4). pap. 9.25 *(978-1-5081-4367-3(6)*, d5ee1f72-98a2-4462-857a-32b8272e9f78, PowerKids Pr.) Rosen Publishing Group, Inc., The.

MEDAL OF HONOR

Collier, Peter. Choosing Courage: Inspiring True Stories of What It Means to Be a Hero. 2016. (ENG., Illus.). 272p. (J). (gr. 4-7). pap. 8.95 *(978-1-57965-705-5(2)*, 85705) Artisan.
Marsico, Katie. John Cook's Civil War Story. Belmonte, David, illus. 2018. (Narrative Nonfiction: Kids in War Ser.). (ENG.). 32p. (J). (gr. 2-4). 27.99 *(978-1-5124-5680-6(2)*, 5f6f9e26-2fd6-4442-9c13-4ea16f171ba8, Lerner Pubns.); pap. 9.99 *(978-1-5415-1191-0(3)*, 22ac3d17-499b-4ec8-b3fc-10cf1dced47f) Lerner Publishing Group.
Mikaelian, Allen & Wallace, Mike. Medal of Honor: Profiles of America's Military Heroes from the Civil War to the Present. 2003. (ENG.). 336p. (gr. 8-17). pap. 21.99 *(978-0-7868-8576-3(9)*, Hachette Bks.) Hachette Bks.
Perritano, John. Medal of Honor. 2018. (Red Rhino Nonfiction Ser.). lib. bdg. 20.80 *(978-0-606-41253-7(0))* Turtleback.
Spradlin, Michael P. Ryan Pitts: Afghanistan: a Firefight in the Mountains of Wanat. 2019. (Medal of Honor Ser.: 2). (ENG., Illus.). 112p. (J). pap. 8.99 *(978-1-250-15710-2(2)*, 900185142, Farrar, Straus & Giroux (BYR)) Farrar, Straus & Giroux.
Stevens, Paul D., ed. The Congressional Medal of Honor: The Names, the Deeds. 2003. (Illus.). 1105p. 27.50 *(978-0-918495-01-3(6))* Sharp & Dunnigan.

MEDICAL BOTANY

see Botany, Medical

MEDICAL CENTERS

see also Hospitals

Smith, Ian. First Experiences: Going to the Doctor. 2004. (QEB Start Talking Ser.). (Illus.). 24p. (J). lib. bdg. 15.95 *(978-1-59566-003-9(8))* QEB Publishing Inc.

MEDICAL ELECTRONICS

Moe, Barbara. The Revolution in Medical Imaging. 2009. (Library of Future Medicine Ser.). 64p. (gr. 5-5). 58.50 *(978-1-60853-634-4(3))* Rosen Publishing Group, Inc., The.

MEDICAL PROFESSION

see Medicine; Physicians

MEDICAL RESEARCH

see Medicine—Research

MEDICAL TECHNOLOGY

Allen, John. How Gene Therapy Is Changing Society. 2015. (ENG., Illus.). 80p. (J). mass mkt. *(978-1-60152-898-8(1))* ReferencePoint Pr., Inc.
Allman, Toney. Cutting Edge Medical Technology. 2016. (ENG.). 80p. (YA). (gr. 5-12). lib. bdg. *(978-1-68282-042-1(4))* ReferencePoint Pr., Inc.
Bailey, Diane. Biomedical Engineers!, Vol. 10. 2015. (Scientists in Action Ser.). (Illus.). 48p. (J). (gr. 5). 20.95 *(978-1-4222-3420-4(7))* Mason Crest.
Ballen, Karen Gunnison. Seven Wonders of Medicine. 2010. (Seven Wonders Ser.). (YA). (gr. 5-9). lib. bdg. 33.26 *(978-0-7613-4239-7(7))* Twenty First Century Bks.
Bellido Schwarz, Venessa. Medical Technology Inspired by Nature. 2018. (Technology Inspired by Nature Ser.). (ENG., Illus.). 32p. (J). (gr. 3-5). lib. bdg. 31.35 *(978-1-63517-942-2(4)*, 1635179424, Focus Readers) North Star Editions.
Bickerstaff, Linda. Technology & Infertility: Assisted Reproduction & Modern Society. 2009. (Science & Society Ser.). 64p. (gr. 5-6). 58.50 *(978-1-60853-011-3(6))*; (ENG., Illus.). (YA). lib. bdg. 37.13 *(978-1-4358-5024-8(6)*, a6fe30b6-55fc-4678-9895-e897ccb84782) Rosen Publishing Group, Inc., The.
Blohm, Craig E., contrib. by. 3D Printing & Medicine. 2018. (ENG.). 80p. (YA). (gr. 5-12). *(978-1-68282-331-6(8))* ReferencePoint Pr., Inc.
Boudreau, Hélène. Miraculous Medicines. 2008. (ENG., Illus.). 32p. (J). (gr. 3-7). lib. bdg. *(978-0-7787-4168-8(0))* Crabtree Publishing Co.
Bryant, Jill. Medical Inventions: The Best of Health. 2013. (ENG., Illus.). 48p. (J). *(978-0-7787-0212-2(X))*; (gr. 4-8). pap. *(978-0-7787-0232-0(4))* Crabtree Publishing Co.
Carr, Denis. The 10 Most Significant Medical Breakthroughs. 2008. 14.99 *(978-1-55448-491-1(X))* Scholastic Library Publishing.
Colins, Luke. Medical Robots. 2020. (World of Robots Ser.). (ENG.). 24p. (J). (gr. k-3). lib. bdg. *(978-1-62310-164-0(6)*, 14426, Bolt Jr.) Black Rabbit Bks.
Dodge, Hillary. The Evolution of Medical Technology, 1 vol. 2018. (Evolving Technology Ser.). (ENG.). 64p. (gr. 6-7). lib. bdg. 34.29 *(978-1-5383-0324-5(8)*, d05046b0-7425-41e2-8ca1-3fdd3ff88eea, Britannica Educational Publishing) Rosen Publishing Group, Inc., The.
Faust, Daniel R. Medical Robots, 1 vol. 2016. (Robots & Robotics Ser.). (ENG.). 32p. (J). (gr. 5-5). pap. 12.75 *(978-1-4994-2175-0(3)*, 990599a1-e9ff-4486-bf00-81365f3a4a13, PowerKids Pr.) Rosen Publishing Group, Inc., The.
Gagne, Tammy. Exoskeletons. 2019. (Engineering the Human Body Ser.). (ENG.). 32p. (J). (gr. 3-5). pap. 9.95 *(978-1-64185-832-8(X)*, 164185832X); lib. bdg. 31.35 *(978-1-64185-763-5(3)*, 1641857633) North Star Editions. (Focus Readers).
Gardner, Jane P. Health Science, Vol. 11. Lewin, Russ, ed. 2015. (Science 24/7 Ser.). (Illus.). 48p. (J). (gr. 5). 20.95 *(978-1-4222-3411-2(8))* Mason Crest.
Greek, Joe. Working with Tech in Health Care, 1 vol. 2020. (Technology in the Workplace Ser.). (ENG.). 80p. (gr. 7-7). pap. 16.30 *(978-1-7253-4161-6(1)*, fe334155-0e28-4314-ba84-039e8c4ba7bd) Rosen Publishing Group, Inc., The.
Gutiérrez, Jolene. Bionic Beasts: Saving Animal Lives with Artificial Flippers, Legs, & Beaks. 2020. (ENG., Illus.). 48p. (J). (gr. 4-8). 31.99 *(978-1-5415-8940-7(8)*, 79ba88ea-5275-4fa2-9127-bf7dd43dc051, Millbrook Pr.) Lerner Publishing Group.
Hagler, Gina. Careers As a First Responder, 1 vol. 2012. (Essential Careers Ser.). (ENG., Illus.). 80p. (YA). (gr. 6-6). lib. bdg. 37.47 *(978-1-4488-8234-2(6)*, c4142183-ff84-4c84-b294-161c0a10266e) Rosen Publishing Group, Inc., The.
Higgins, Nadia. Medical Robots. (Robotics in Our World Ser.). (ENG., Illus.). 32p. (J). (gr. 2-5). 2018. pap. 9.99 *(978-1-68152-174-9(1)*, 14805) 2017. 20.95 *(978-1-68151-143-6(6)*, 14686) Amicus.
Hulick, Kathryn. Medical Robots. 2018. (Robot Innovations Ser.). (ENG., Illus.). 48p. (J). (gr. 4-4). pap. 11.95 *(978-1-64185-276-0(3)*, 1641852763, Core Library); lib. bdg. 35.64 *(978-1-5321-1468-7(0)*, 29128) ABDO Publishing Co.
—Robotics & Medicine. 2018. (Next-Generation Medical Technology Ser.). (ENG.). 80p. (YA). (gr. 5-12). 39.93 *(978-1-68282-329-3(6))* ReferencePoint Pr., Inc.
Kenney, Karen Latchana. What Makes Medical Technology Safer? 2015. (Engineering Keeps Us Safe Ser.). (ENG., Illus.). 32p. (J). (gr. 4-6). 26.65 *(978-1-4677-7916-6(4)*, c248be88-9b12-4db4-93ed-7077ca2d6a10); E-Book 39.99 *(978-1-4677-8651-5(9))* Lerner Publishing Group. (Lerner Pubns.).
Koontz, Robin. Biomimicry & Medicine. 2018. (Nature-Inspired Innovations Ser.). (ENG., Illus.). 48p. (gr. 4-8). pap. 10.95 *(978-1-64156-585-1(3)*, 9781641565851) Rourke Educational Media.
Kopp, Megan. Bionic Bodies. 2017. (Techno Planet Ser.). (Illus.). 32p. (J). (gr. 5-5). *(978-0-7787-3584-7(2))* Crabtree Publishing Co.
Latta, Sara L. Zoom in on Medical Robots, 1 vol. 2017. (Zoom in on Robots Ser.). (ENG.). 24p. (gr. 2-2). 25.60 *(978-0-7660-9228-0(3)*, 97670718-0f76-4e52-ab26-d67adfaa89ba) Enslow Publishing, LLC.
McFadzean, Lesley. Technology & Treatments, 1 vol. 2012. (Discovery Education: Technology Ser.). (ENG., Illus.). 32p. (J). (gr. 4-5). 28.93 *(978-1-4488-7886-4(1)*, 0b976941-d6d7-40ce-99ab-b25f05ffda7a); pap. 11.00 *(978-1-4488-7968-7(X)*, 8afa66ba-cbab-46f1-b06b-6fca3ff43a9c) Rosen Publishing Group, Inc., The. (PowerKids Pr.).
Merino, Noël, ed. Genetic Engineering, 1 vol. 2013. (Opposing Viewpoints Ser.). (ENG., Illus.). 232p. (gr. 10-12). lib. bdg. 50.43 *(978-0-7377-6424-6(4)*, 8d982c60-37ea-455a-90ce-b0c319eea1a8, Greenhaven Publishing) Greenhaven Publishing LLC.
—Genetic Engineering, 1 vol. 2013. (Opposing Viewpoints Ser.). (ENG., Illus.). 232p. (gr. 10-12). pap. 34.80 *(978-0-7377-6425-3(2)*, d5dfa993-bb37-4e6e-bf51-692ba7fac904, Greenhaven Publishing) Greenhaven Publishing LLC.
Moe, Barbara. The Revolution in Medical Imaging. 2009. (Library of Future Medicine Ser.). 64p. (gr. 5-5). 58.50 *(978-1-60853-634-4(3))* Rosen Publishing Group, Inc., The.
Mooney, Carla. Wearable Robots. 2016. (Tech Bytes Ser.). (ENG., Illus.). 48p. (J). (gr. 4-6). pap. 14.60 *(978-1-60357-868-4(4))*; lib. bdg. 26.60 *(978-1-59953-760-3(5))* Norwood Hse. Pr.
Morrison, Heather S. Inventors of Health & Medical Technology, 1 vol. 2015. (Designing Engineering Solutions Ser.). (ENG., Illus.). 144p. (YA). (gr. 8-8). 44.50 *(978-1-5026-0658-7(5)*, 13b346bc-4c2d-45b7-98dd-b5fee128c02d) Cavendish Square Publishing LLC.
Nargi, Lela. Karl's New Beak: 3-D Printing Builds a Bird a Better Life. Popham, Harriet, illus. 2019. (ENG.). 32p. (gr. -1-2). 17.95 *(978-1-68446-026-7(3)*, 139699, Capstone Editions) Capstone.
Noll, Elizabeth. Medical Robots. 2017. (World of Robots Ser.). (ENG., Illus.). 32p. (J). (gr. 3-8). lib. bdg. 27.95 *(978-1-62617-689-8(2)*, Blastoff! Discovery) Bellwether Media.
Rauf, Don. Using Computer Science in Health Care Careers, 1 vol. 2018. (Coding Your Passion Ser.). (ENG.). 80p. (gr. 7-7). pap. 16.30 *(978-1-5081-8396-9(1)*, a7100c50-7f25-4811-8224-258b76797be5, Rosen Young Adult) Rosen Publishing Group, Inc., The.
Rooney, Anne. Machines in Medicine, 1 vol. 2007. (Cutting Edge Medicine Ser.). (ENG., Illus.). 64p. (gr. 5-8). lib. bdg. 36.67 *(978-0-8368-7867-7(1)*, d0a647e0-a282-4e1f-ab87-e2ac70f67988, Gareth Stevens Secondary Library) Stevens, Gareth Publishing LLLP.
Senker, Cath. The Science of Medical Technology: from Humble Syringes to Lifesaving Robots (the Science of Engineering) (Library Edition) Affonso, Alexandre & Beach, Bryan, illus. 2019. (Science Of... Ser.). (ENG.). 32p. (J). (gr. 3-3). lib. bdg. 29.00 *(978-0-531-13193-0(9)*, Watts, Franklin) Scholastic Library Publishing.
Sheen, Barbara. Artificial Eyes. 2016. (Tech Bytes Ser.). (ENG., Illus.). 48p. (J). (gr. 4-6). lib. bdg. 26.60 *(978-1-59953-761-0(3))* Norwood Hse. Pr.
Sjonger, Rebecca. Biomedical Engineering & Human Body Systems. 2015. (Engineering in Action Ser.). (ENG., Illus.). 32p. (J). (gr. 5-5). *(978-0-7787-7505-8(4))* Crabtree Publishing Co.
Snedden, Robert. Medical Technology. 2009. (New Technology Ser.). (YA). (gr. 7-12). 34.25 *(978-1-59920-164-1(X))* Black Rabbit Bks.
Solway, Andrew. Seeing Inside the Body, 1 vol. 2007. (Cutting Edge Medicine Ser.). (ENG., Illus.). 64p. (gr. 5-8). lib. bdg. 36.67 *(978-0-8368-7869-1(8)*, 61ab6ae0-2331-479b-b04b-aca1fe7c3a15, Gareth Stevens Secondary Library) Stevens, Gareth Publishing LLLP.
Steffens, Bradley. Biomedical Engineer. 2017. (ENG.). 64p. (YA). (gr. 5-12). *(978-1-68282-178-7(1))* ReferencePoint Pr., Inc.
Strange, Cordelia. Medical Technicians: Health-Care Support for the 21st Century. 2010. (New Careers for the 21st Century Ser.). 64p. (YA). (gr. 7-18). pap. 9.95 *(978-1-4222-2038-2(9))* Mason Crest.
Thompson, Tamara, ed. Extending the Human Lifespan, 1 vol. 2013. (At Issue Ser.). (ENG.). 128p. (gr. 10-12). 41.03 *(978-0-7377-6836-7(3)*, 09160969-d0ff-489b-9614-fddcc25a5d9d, Greenhaven Publishing) Greenhaven Publishing LLC.
Troupe, Thomas Kingsley. Medical Robots. 2017. (Mighty Bots Ser.). (ENG.). 32p. (J). (gr. 4-6). pap. 9.99 *(978-1-64466-198-7(5)*, 11444); (Illus.). lib. bdg. *(978-1-68072-158-4(5)*, 10500) Black Rabbit Bks. (Bolt).
Vaughan, Jenny. Making New Life. 2010. (J). 34.25 *(978-1-59920-318-8(9))* Black Rabbit Bks.
Wittenstein, Barry. The Boo-Boos That Changed the World: A True Story about an Accidental Invention (Really!) Hsu, Chris, illus. 2018. 32p. (J). (gr. -1-3). lib. bdg. 17.99 *(978-1-58089-745-7(2))* Charlesbridge Publishing, Inc.
Wood, John. Medical Technology: Genomics, Growing Organs, & More, 1 vol. 2018. (STEM in Our World Ser.). (ENG.). 32p. (gr. 4-5). lib. bdg. 28.27 *(978-1-5382-2646-9(4)*, eddb52f7-b8b6-4dca-b3e3-683e94d6246e) Stevens, Gareth Publishing LLLP.
World Book, Inc. Staff, contrib. by. Leeches to Lasers: A Timeline of Medicine. 2016. (Illus.). 40p. (J). *(978-0-7166-3542-0(9))* World Bk.-Childcraft International.
—Medicine. 2009. *(978-0-7166-0384-9(5))* World Bk., Inc.

MEDICAL TECHNOLOGY—VOCATIONAL GUIDANCE

Greek, Joe. Working with Tech in Health Care, 1 vol. 2020. (Technology in the Workplace Ser.). (ENG.). 80p. (gr. 7-7). pap. 16.30 *(978-1-7253-4161-6(1)*, fe334155-0e28-4314-ba84-039e8c4ba7bd) Rosen Publishing Group, Inc., The.

MEDICI, LORENZO DE', 1449-1492

Greenblatt, Miriam. Lorenzo de' Medici & Renaissance Italy, 1 vol. 2003. (Rulers & Their Times Ser.). (ENG., Illus.). 80p. (gr. 6-6). lib. bdg. 36.93 *(978-0-7614-1490-2(8)*, 7c9c2d4e-da0f-463d-b40a-a44f752d3214) Cavendish Square Publishing LLC.
Hancock, Lee. Lorenzo de' Medici: Florence's Great Leader & Patron of the Arts. (Rulers, Scholars, & Artists of the

Renaissance Ser.). 112p. (gr. 5-8). 2009. 66.50 *(978-1-60852-942-1(8)*, Rosen Reference) 2004. (ENG., Illus.). (J). lib. bdg. 39.80 *(978-1-4042-0315-0(X)*, ca8076a6-2614-4397-8ac0-414e3eda79d9) Rosen Publishing Group, Inc., The.

MEDICINAL PLANTS

see Botany, Medical

MEDICINE

see also Anatomy; Bacteriology; Botany, Medical; Health; Hospitals; Hypnotism; Materia Medica; Mind and Body; Nursing; Pathology; Pharmacy; Physiology

also headings beginning with the word Medical

Abramavitz. Online Privacy & Healthcare. 2014. (Privacy in the Online World). (ENG., Illus.). 80p. (YA). lib. bdg. *(978-1-60152-652-6(0))* ReferencePoint Pr., Inc.

Anderson, Catherine Corley. John F. Kennedy. 2005. (Just the Facts Biographies Ser.). (ENG., Illus.). 112p. (gr. 5-12). lib. bdg. 27.93 *(978-0-8225-2643-8(3)*, Lerner Pubns.) Lerner Publishing Group.

Anderson, Sheila. Clinic. 2008. pap. 22.95 *(978-0-8225-9370-6(X))*; (ENG., Illus.). 8p. (J). pap. 5.99 *(978-0-8225-8840-5(4)*, 2087f154-41a0-491c-b7b6-1010cd90b314) Lerner Publishing Group.

Bayden, Maya. Medical Science, 1 vol., 1. 2016. (Study of Science Ser.). (ENG.). 144p. (J). (gr. 8-8). lib. bdg. 37.82 *(978-1-68048-229-4(7)*, 97e7d65b-6c10-48d4-a6ef-6f83b0f4f6c8, Britannica Educational Publishing) Rosen Publishing Group, Inc., The.

Bayden, Maya, ed. Medical Science, 4 vols. 2016. (Study of Science Ser.). (ENG.). 144p. (gr. 8-8). 75.64 *(978-1-68048-228-7(9)*, 54ca71bf-5a91-4136-adfe-34b58a352db4, Britannica Educational Publishing) Rosen Publishing Group, Inc., The.

Benchmark Education Company. Fighting Disease (Teacher Guide) 2005. *(978-1-4108-4657-0(1))* Benchmark Education Co.

Boring, Mel & Dendy, Leslie. Guinea Pig Scientists: Bold Self-Experimenters in Science & Medicine. Mordan, C. B., illus. 2014. (ENG.). 224p. (J). (gr. 5-12). pap. 13.99 *(978-1-250-05065-6(0)*, 900134134) Square Fish.

Boudreau, Hélène. Miraculous Medicines. 2008. (ENG., Illus.). 32p. (J). (gr. 3-7). pap. *(978-0-7787-4175-6(3))* Crabtree Publishing Co.

Bowman, Chris. Ambulances. 2018. (Mighty Machines in Action Ser.). (ENG., Illus.). 24p. (J). (gr. k-3). lib. bdg. 26.95 *(978-1-62617-756-7(2)*, Blastoff! Readers) Bellwether Media.

Bredeson, Carmen. Don't Let the Barber Pull Your Teeth: Could You Survive Medieval Medicine?, 1 vol. 2012. (Ye Yucky Middle Ages Ser.). (ENG., Illus.). 48p. (gr. 5-7). pap. 11.53 *(978-1-59845-373-7(4)*, 641b812b-29e4-4164-b1d6-601b3b9be924); lib. bdg. 27.93 *(978-0-7660-3693-2(6)*, 6662af1a-e77b-4fbd-ba9f-7d955cfa2c56) Enslow Publishing, LLC.

Brezina, Corona. Jump-Starting a Career in Ultrasound & Sonography, 1 vol. 2018. (Health Care Careers in 2 Years Ser.). (ENG.). 80p. (gr. 7-7). pap. 16.30 *(978-1-5081-8510-9(7)*, 95ae93c3-4cca-4f41-8789-db6c0fef47fd, Rosen Young Adult) Rosen Publishing Group, Inc., The.

Brill, Marlene Targ. Doctors. 2005. (Pull Ahead Bks.). (Illus.). 32p. (J). lib. bdg. 22.60 *(978-0-8225-1689-7(6))* Lerner Publishing Group.

Burgan, Michael. Medicine & Health Care, Vol. 10. 2016. (Stem in Current Events Ser.). (Illus.). 64p. (J). (gr. 7). 23.95 *(978-1-4222-3594-2(7))* Mason Crest.

Burstein, John. The Exciting Endocrine System: How Do My Glands Work? 2009. (Slim Goodbody's Body Buddies Ser.). (ENG., Illus.). 32p. (J). (gr. 3-5). pap. *(978-0-7787-4432-0(9))* Crabtree Publishing Co.

Carlson, Dale. ¿Adonde Vamos? Dentro y Fuera de tu mente. Guix, Joan Carles, tr. from ENG. Nicklaus, Carol, illus. 2004.Tr. of In & Out of your Mind. Where are we Going? (SPA.). 64p. *(978-84-9754-117-6(0)*, 88303) Ediciones Oniro S.A.

Cartlidge, Cherese. Skilled Jobs in Health Care. 2020. (Jobs for Skilled Workers Ser.). (ENG.). 80p. (YA). (gr. 6-12). 41.27 *(978-1-68282-823-6(9))* ReferencePoint Pr., Inc.

Chancellor, Deborah. Ambulance Rescue. 2013. (Emergency Vehicles Ser.). 24p. (gr. k-3). 28.50 *(978-1-59920-888-6(1))* Black Rabbit Bks.

Chandler, Alton. A Salute to African American in Medicine: Learning. Chapman, L., ed. Still, Wayne A., illus. 24p. (Orig.). (J). (gr. 3-8). pap. 1.75 *(978-1-877804-17-5(7))* Chandler/White Publishing Co.

Chilman-Blair, Kim. Superheroes on a Medical Mission: Set 1, 12 vols. Incl. "What's up with Bill?" Medikidz Explain Epilepsy. Taddeo, John. (YA). lib. bdg. 34.47 *(978-1-4358-3533-7(6)*, 05a18a0c-fb7b-4e90-b16c-e106d6fc398d); "What's up with David?" Medikidz Explain Food Allergies. Taddeo, John. (YA). lib. bdg. 34.47 *(978-1-4358-3537-5(9)*, 808c76c8-30ff-4c5a-bda6-4344516a67ef, Rosen Reference); "What's up with Ella?" Medikidz Explain Diabetes. Taddeo, John. (YA). lib. bdg. 34.47 *(978-1-4358-3538-2(7)*, 32b0f4a7-eba0-4595-acaf-d0ca5feb0438, Rosen Reference); "What's up with Max?" Medikidz Explain Asthma. Taddeo, John. (YA). lib. bdg. 34.47 *(978-1-4358-3534-4(4)*, 923c71fe-e23f-444b-afe7-bbbb248193d7, Rosen Reference); What's up with Pam? Medikidz Explain Childhood Obesity. Taddeo, John. (J). lib. bdg. 34.47 *(978-1-4358-3535-1(2)*, 588474eb-dfb5-4886-aaeb-5da1be0861f7, Rosen Reference); "What's up with Sean?" Medikidz Explain Scoliosis. Taddeo, Sean & Noordeen, Hilali. (YA). lib. bdg. 34.47 *(978-1-4358-3536-8(0)*, cd523571-9c2d-4457-a97f-40592ef90fb8, Rosen Reference); (gr. 5-5). (Superheroes on a Medical Mission Ser.). (ENG., Illus.). 40p. 2010. Set lib. bdg. 206.82 *(978-1-4358-9423-5(5)*, ada6358e-c4ab-44a6-a16d-3ed0342771e5, Rosen Reference) Rosen Publishing Group, Inc., The.

Chmielewski, Gary. The Medical Zone: Jokes, Riddles, Tongue Twisters & Daffynitions. Caputo, Jim, illus. rev. ed. 2009. (Funny Zone Ser.). (ENG.). 24p. (J). (gr. 2-4). lib. bdg. 22.60 *(978-1-59953-299-8(9))* Norwood Hse. Pr.

Clark, Rosalyn. Why We Go to the Doctor. 2018. (Bumba Books (r) — Health Matters Ser.). (ENG., Illus.). 24p. (J). (gr. -1-1). 26.65 *(978-1-5124-8290-4(0)*, dd921a60-3a90-4d13-93c0-812c6a50d5bd, Lerner Pubns.) Lerner Publishing Group.

Cobb, Allan B. First Responders. 2009. (Extreme Careers Ser.). 64p. (gr. 5-5). 58.50 *(978-1-61512-393-3(8)*, Rosen Reference) Rosen Publishing Group, Inc., The.

Cox, Judith. The Wellness Tree. Rogers, Denny, illus. 2003. (ENG.). 32p. (J). (gr. k-4). 19.95 *(978-1-878044-29-7(X))* Mayhaven Publishing, Inc.

Crabtree, Marc. Meet My Neighbor, the Doctor. 2013. (ENG., Illus.). 24p. (J). *(978-0-7787-0871-1(3))*; pap. *(978-0-7787-0875-9(6))* Crabtree Publishing Co.

Cutting Edge Medicine, 12 vols. 2007. (Cutting Edge Medicine Ser.). (ENG.). 64p. (gr. 5-8). lib. bdg. 220.02 *(978-0-8368-7863-9(9)*, 301a676d-0de4-448e-b0e3-9d5d3e4fbf4f, Gareth Stevens Secondary Library) Stevens, Gareth Publishing LLLP.

Davies, Gill. The Illustrated Timeline of Medicine, 1 vol. 2011. (History Timelines Ser.). (ENG., Illus.). 256p. (YA). (gr. 7-7). lib. bdg. 55.80 *(978-1-4488-4796-9(6)*, d2b28185-5f65-46bf-8ef2-94897363d673) Rosen Publishing Group, Inc., The.

Dawson, Ian. Prehistoric & Egyptian Medicine, 1 vol. 2006. (History of Medicine Ser.). (ENG., Illus.). 64p. (J). (gr. 5-5). 34.07 *(978-0-7614-3275-3(4)*, 4a829674-cef2-4125-b20f-36e0082db174, Cavendish Square) Cavendish Square Publishing LLC.

Dawson, Patricia A. A Doctor's Job, 1 vol. 2014. (Community Workers Ser.). (ENG.). 24p. (gr. 1-1). pap. 9.23 *(978-1-62712-991-6(X)*, 9f9e2b2a-3cb3-40de-8ac9-bb33d4a2ff58); lib. bdg. 25.93 *(978-1-62712-990-9(1)*, a26900eb-6b69-43cf-bb3b-f2a4f167d3b6) Cavendish Square Publishing LLC.

Dittmer, Lori. The Future of Medicine. 2012. (What's Next? Ser.). (Illus.). 48p. (J). (gr. 5-12). 23.95 *(978-1-60818-222-0(3)*, Creative Education) Creative Co., The.

Dowdall CLA D.Ac., Lynn. What Is Acupuncture? Greer, Gail, illus. 2004. (ENG.). 34p. pap. 17.50 *(978-1-4120-1810-4(2))* Trafford Publishing.

Edwards, Hazel & Alexander, Goldie. Talking about Illnesses, 1 vol. 2010. (Healthy Living Ser.). (ENG., Illus.). 32p. (YA). (gr. 3-4). lib. bdg. 28.67 *(978-1-4339-3657-9(7)*, d5c41ef8-5830-42c7-b7a0-67c53235bf07) Stevens, Gareth Publishing LLLP.

Elliott, Lynne. Medieval Medicine & the Plague. 2005. (Medieval World Ser.). (ENG., Illus.). 32p. (J). (gr. 5-9). lib. bdg. *(978-0-7787-1358-6(X))* Crabtree Publishing Co.

Engdahl, Sylvia, ed. Alternative Therapies, 1 vol. 2011. (Current Controversies Ser.). (ENG.). 232p. (gr. 10-12). pap. 33.00 *(978-0-7377-5611-1(X)*, 4d087fe4-b48d-48d7-b09d-129df4eae720, Greenhaven Publishing) Greenhaven Publishing LLC.

Espejo, Roman, ed. Should Vaccinations Be Mandatory?, 1 vol. 2014. (At Issue Ser.). (ENG.). 128p. (gr. 10-12). lib. bdg. 41.03 *(978-0-7377-6862-6(2)*, bf6063c9-6103-45e4-878c-e4d34c5cda5c, Greenhaven Publishing) Greenhaven Publishing LLC.

Etingoff, Kim. Women in Medicine. Karlon, Ann Lee, ed. 2013. (Major Women in Science Ser.: 10). 64p. (J). (gr. 7-18). 22.95 *(978-1-4222-2929-3(7))* Mason Crest.

Faison, Ashley Starr & Ackerman, Bettie Bennett. The Garden of Hope: A Story about the Hospice Experience. 2005. (Illus.). (J). *(978-0-9774691-0-9(7))* Hospice & Community Care Pubns.

Freedman, Jeri. Careers in Women's Health, 1 vol. 2017. (Essential Careers Ser.). (ENG., Illus.). 80p. (J). (gr. 6-6). 37.47 *(978-1-5383-8158-8(3)*, 21ede09a-4955-4fbc-8ee4-9adb6793022f); pap. 16.30 *(978-1-5081-7875-0(5)*, 9d0700c4-5d4e-4f46-b2b4-f5ff0dbbfac4) Rosen Publishing Group, Inc., The. (Rosen Young Adult).

—Professional Wrestling: Steroids in & Out of the Ring, 1 vol. 2009. (Disgraced! the Dirty History of Performance-Enhancing Drugs in Sports Ser.). (ENG., Illus.). 48p. (YA). (gr. 5-6). 34.47 *(978-1-4358-5305-8(9)*, 52b87a15-470d-4647-bf8b-be68f153dd1c) Rosen Publishing Group, Inc., The.

Gardner, Jane P. Health Science, Vol. 11. Lewin, Russ, ed. 2015. (Science 24/7 Ser.). (Illus.). 48p. (J). (gr. 5). 20.95 *(978-1-4222-3411-2(8))* Mason Crest.

Gardner, Robert & Conklin, Joshua. Experiments for Future Doctors, 1 vol. 2016. (Experiments for Future STEM Professionals Ser.). (ENG.). 128p. (gr. 6-6). 38.93 *(978-0-7660-7854-3(X)*, c6f55851-73a1-475c-88dc-399004716d1c) Enslow Publishing, LLC.

Geis, Patricia. Let's Get Well! Folch, Sergio, illus. 2009. (Good Habits with Coco & Tula Ser.). 16p. (J). (gr. -1-k). bds. 11.40 *(978-1-60754-407-4(5))* Windmill Bks.

Giddens, Sandra. Everything You Need to Know about Crohn's Disease & Ulcerative Colitis. 2009. (Need to Know Library). 64p. (gr. 5-5). 58.50 *(978-1-60854-061-7(8))* Rosen Publishing Group, Inc., The.

Given-Wilson, Rachel & Harasymiw, Therese. Your Future As a Physical Therapist, 1 vol. 2019. (High-Demand Careers Ser.). (ENG.). 80p. (gr. 7-7). pap. 16.30 *(978-1-5081-8785-1(1)*, 98a682a9-a822-404f-9e98-fba10524c32f) Rosen Publishing Group, Inc., The.

Goldish, Meish. Doctors to the Rescue. 2011. (Work of Heroes: First Responders in Action Ser.). 32p. (YA). (gr. 1-4). lib. bdg. 28.50 *(978-1-61772-285-1(5))* Bearport Publishing Co., Inc.

Gow, Mary. The Greatest Doctor of Ancient Times: Hippocrates & His Oath, 1 vol. 2009. (Great Minds of Ancient Science & Math Ser.). (ENG., Illus.). 128p. (gr. 4-6). lib. bdg. 35.93 *(978-0-7660-3118-0(7)*, 30478f77-2521-40b0-aa72-91b3d0cfb273) Enslow Publishing, LLC.

Gray, Leon. Dirty Bombs & Shell Shock: Biology Goes to War. 2017. (STEM on the Battlefield Ser.). (ENG., Illus.). 48p. (J). (gr. 4-6). 31.99 *(978-1-5124-3928-1(2)*, e3d92160-3b28-4128-b1e2-61be5de64d96, Lerner Pubns.) Lerner Publishing Group.

Gray, Susan H. Artificial Limbs. 2008. (21st Century Skills Innovation Library: Innovation in Medicine Ser.). (ENG., Illus.). 32p. (gr. 4-8). lib. bdg. 32.07 *(978-1-60279-229-6(1)*, 200160) Cherry Lake Publishing.

Gregory, Josh. What Do They Do? Doctors. 2010. (Community Connections: What Do They Do? Ser.). (ENG., Illus.). 24p. (gr. 2-5). lib. bdg. 29.21 *(978-1-60279-805-2(2)*, 200500) Cherry Lake Publishing.

Hapka, Cathy, pseud. My Little Doctor Bag Book. Sharp, Paul, illus. 2005. (J). *(978-1-57151-754-8(5))* Playhouse Publishing.

Harmon, Daniel E. Careers in Mental Health, 1 vol. 2017. (Essential Careers Ser.). (ENG., Illus.). 80p. (J). (gr. 6-6). pap. 16.30 *(978-1-5081-7885-9(2)*, 78d4d143-f119-452a-bf44-648abc31601c, Rosen Young Adult) Rosen Publishing Group, Inc., The.

HarrisNic. MEDICINE: OLD AND NEW LOW INTERMEDIATE BOOK WITH ONLINE ACCESS, 1 vol. 2014. (ENG., Illus.). 24p. (J). pap., E-Book, E-Book 9.50 *(978-1-107-65866-0(7))* Cambridge Univ. Pr.

Harrison, Lorraine. Doctors on the Job. 2017. (Jobs in Our Community Ser.). 24p. (J). (gr. k-k). pap. 49.50 *(978-1-5345-2138-4(0))* Cengage Gale.

—Doctors on the Job, 1 vol. 2016. (Jobs in Our Community Ser.). (ENG.). 24p. (J). (gr. 1-1). 26.23 *(978-1-5345-2139-1(9)*, 4af63693-ac8a-4683-83d7-63df87fdb939); pap. 9.25 *(978-1-5345-2137-7(2)*, 63d86029-c35d-427e-973c-95a428abf3d8) Greenhaven Publishing LLC. (KidHaven Publishing).

Haxton, Jason. Andrew Taylor Still: Father of Osteopathic Medicine. 2016. (ENG., Illus.). 48p. (J). 27.00 *(978-1-61248-174-6(4))* Truman State Univ. Pr.

Hersh, Iffy. Mommy Is an Histologist. (What Does Mommy Do? Ser.). (Illus.). (Orig.). (J). (gr. k-2). pap. 10.00 *(978-0-936735-04-7(X))* Grove Educational Technologies.

Hoena, Blake A. The Doctor's Office: A 4D Book. rev. ed. 2018. (Visit To... Ser.). (ENG., Illus.). 24p. (J). (gr. -1-2). lib. bdg. 29.32 *(978-1-5435-0827-7(8)*, 137590, Capstone Pr.) Capstone.

Hofer, Charles C. Snakebite! Antivenom & a Global Health Crisis. 2018. (ENG., Illus.). 104p. (YA). (gr. 6-12). 37.32 *(978-1-5124-8373-4(7)*, 355e5a84-7f5a-44b4-938d-9709d29fae6a, Twenty-First Century Bks.) Lerner Publishing Group.

Honders, Christine. Why Should I Listen to My Doctor?, 1 vol. 2019. (Listening to Leaders Ser.). (ENG.). 24p. (gr. 2-2). pap. 9.25 *(978-1-5383-4160-5(3)*, fe20115d-80c6-4a4e-bbb0-e144bc7ce536, PowerKids Pr.) Rosen Publishing Group, Inc., The.

Horn, Geoffrey M. Sports Therapist, 1 vol. 2008. (Cool Careers: Helping Careers Ser.). (ENG.). 32p. (gr. 3-3). pap. 11.50 *(978-0-8368-9329-8(8)*, 15eca04e-76c2-45d7-8de3-7ce4de80e92a); lib. bdg. 28.67 *(978-0-8368-9196-6(1)*, 6b71aba5-04fc-450e-8801-b68fe7757499) Stevens, Gareth Publishing LLLP.

Huddleston, Emma. Prosthetics. 2019. (Engineering the Human Body Ser.). (ENG., Illus.). 32p. (J). (gr. 3-5). pap. 9.95 *(978-1-64185-836-6(2)*, 1641858362); lib. bdg. 31.35 *(978-1-64185-767-3(6)*, 1641857676) North Star Editions. (Focus Readers).

Huffman, Julie. 101 Ways to Gross Out Your Friends. 2017. (101 Ser.). (ENG., Illus.). 144p. (J). (gr. 3-5). 33.32 *(978-1-942875-16-1(9)*, 1fe51a52-d2f5-4da2-ba13-15dffcad564b, Walter Foster Jr) Quarto Publishing Group USA.

Human Relations Media, prod. Clued in! on Medicines. 2005. (ENG.). (J). pap. 4.95 *(978-1-55548-149-0(3))* Human Relations Media.

Hunsaker, Jennifer. Respiratory Therapists. 2017. (Careers in Healthcare Ser.: Vol. 13). (ENG.). 64p. (YA). (gr. 7-12). 23.95 *(978-1-4222-3805-9(9))* Mason Crest.

—Ultrasound Technicians. 2017. (Careers in Healthcare Ser.: Vol. 13). (ENG., Illus.). 64p. (J). (gr. 7-12). 23.95 *(978-1-4222-3807-3(5))* Mason Crest.

Idzikowski, Lisa, ed. The Effectiveness of Alternative Medicine, 1 vol. 2018. (Introducing Issues with Opposing Viewpoints Ser.). (ENG.). 120p. (gr. 7-10). 43.63 *(978-1-5345-0421-9(4)*, 8d17e9b1-7ecc-451d-8934-e0363e78c4ea) Greenhaven Publishing LLC.

Iserson, Kenneth V. Get into Medical School! A Guide for the Perplexed. 2nd ed. 2004. (Illus.). 512p. (Orig.). pap. 36.95 *(978-1-883620-31-8(7))* Galen Pr., Ltd.

Jankowski, Connie. Hippocrates: Making the Way for Medicine, 1 vol. rev. ed. 2007. (Science: Informational Text Ser.). (ENG.). 32p. (gr. 3-6). pap. 12.99 *(978-0-7439-0596-1(2))* Teacher Created Materials, Inc.

Jones, Grace. Medicine & Illness. 2018. (Our Values - Level 3 Ser.). (Illus.). 32p. (J). (gr. 5-6). *(978-0-7787-5190-8(2))* Crabtree Publishing Co.

Kavanaugh, Beatrice. Medical Discoveries. 2017. (Illus.). 80p. (J). *(978-1-4222-3710-6(9))* Mason Crest.

Kawa, Katie. My First Trip to the Doctor / Mi Primera Visita Al Médico, 1 vol. Livingston, Jessica, illus. 2012. (My First Adventures / Mis Primeras Aventuras Ser.). (ENG & SPA.). 24p. (J). (gr. k-k). 25.27 *(978-1-4339-6629-3(8)*, 507fb27a-be38-407c-99cf-c69cf424b2dd) Stevens, Gareth Publishing LLLP.

Kelley, K. C. & Buckley, James. Paramedic, Vol. 12. 2015. (On a Mission Ser.). (Illus.). 48p. (J). (gr. 5). 20.95 *(978-1-4222-3398-6(7))* Mason Crest.

Koellhoffer, Tara. Health & Medicine. 2006. (Science News for Kids Ser.). (ENG., Illus.). 160p. (gr. 4-6). lib. bdg. 30.00 *(978-0-7910-9122-7(8)*, P159783, Chelsea Clubhse.) Infobase Holdings, Inc.

Kopp, Megan. Bionic Bodies. 2017. (Techno Planet Ser.). (Illus.). 32p. (J). (gr. 5-5). *(978-0-7787-3584-7(2))* Crabtree Publishing Co.

Kummer, Pat. Sports Medicine Doctor. 2008. (21st Century Skills Library: Cool Careers Ser.). (ENG., Illus.). 32p. (gr. 4-8). lib. bdg. 32.07 *(978-1-60279-302-6(6)*, 200141) Cherry Lake Publishing.

Labrecque, Ellen. Gertrude B. Elion & Pharmacology. 2017. (21st Century Junior Library: Women Innovators Ser.). (ENG., Illus.). 24p. (J). (gr. 2-5). pap. 12.79 *(978-1-63472-314-5(7)*, 209301) Cherry Lake Publishing.

Laks Gorman, Jacqueline. Doctors, 1 vol. 2010. (People in My Community (Second Edition) Ser.). (ENG.). 24p. (J). (gr. k-2). pap. 9.15 *(978-1-4339-3804-7(9)*, 775e6237-e96b-4d09-9720-e2099fafb242); lib. bdg. 25.27 *(978-1-4339-3803-0(0)*, c75f5605-0fdc-46cf-a6c1-b15db9d6a0c3) Stevens, Gareth Publishing LLLP.

Langwith, Jacqueline, ed. Alternative Medicine, 1 vol. 2009. (Introducing Issues with Opposing Viewpoints Ser.). (ENG.). 184p. (gr. 7-10). 43.63 *(978-0-7377-4333-3(6)*, 2beeb3ca-4d46-4898-9ee7-9896f63b1bbc, Greenhaven Publishing) Greenhaven Publishing LLC.

Lawrence, Ellen. Poop Cures. 2017. (Scoop on Poop Ser.). (ENG.). 24p. (J). (gr. -1-3). lib. bdg. 26.99 *(978-1-68402-249-6(5))* Bearport Publishing Co., Inc.

Less, Emma. Doctors. 2018. (Real-Life Superheroes Ser.). (ENG.). 16p. (J). (gr. k-2). pap. 7.99 *(978-1-68152-275-3(6)*, 14914) Amicus.

Lew, Kristi. Bat Spit, Maggots, & Other Amazing Medical Wonders. 2010. (Nasty (but Useful!) Science Ser.). (ENG.). 32p. (J). (gr. 3-4). pap. 48.60 *(978-1-4296-6470-7(3)*, 16223, Capstone Pr.); pap. 8.10 *(978-1-4296-6344-1(8)*, 115542) Capstone.

Libal, Autumn. Drug Therapy & Psychosomatic Disorders. 2003. (Psychiatric Disorders: Drugs & Psychology for the Mind & Bod Ser.). (Illus.). 124p. (YA). (gr. 4-7). pap. 14.95 *(978-1-4222-0397-2(2))* Mason Crest.

Libal, Joyce. Drug Therapy & Mental Disorders Due to a Medical Condition. 2003. (Psychiatric Disorders: Drugs & Psychology for the Mind & Body Ser.). (Illus.). 126p. (YA). (gr. 8-12). pap. 14.95 *(978-1-4222-0391-0(3))* Mason Crest.

—Mental Disorders Due to a Medical Condition. McDonnell, Mary Ann & Esherick, Donald, eds. 2013. (State of Mental Illness & Its Therapy Ser.: 19). (Illus.). 128p. (J). (gr. 7-18). 24.95 *(978-1-4222-2828-9(2))* Mason Crest.

Loh-Hagan, Virginia. Acupuncturist. 2015. (Odd Jobs Ser.). (ENG., Illus.). 32p. (J). (gr. 4-8). pap. 14.21 *(978-1-63470-057-3(0)*, 206777) Cherry Lake Publishing.

Loria, Laura. Poop Medicine, 1 vol. 2017. (Power of Poop Ser.). (ENG.). 32p. (gr. 3-4). pap. 11.52 *(978-0-7660-9111-5(2)*, 1093c991-a946-4f82-a8ec-ca7a25c1cb8a) Enslow Publishing, LLC.

Lusted, Marcia. Hippocrates. 2017. (Junior Biography From Ancient Civilization Ser.). (gr. 4-6). 29.95 *(978-1-68020-030-0(5))* Mitchell Lane Pubs.

Macdonald, Fiona. The Plague & Medicine in the Middle Ages, 1 vol. 2005. (World Almanac(r) Library of the Middle Ages Ser.). (ENG., Illus.). 48p. (gr. 5-8). pap. 15.05 *(978-0-8368-5907-2(3)*, 25481dcd-08c1-4109-b4a2-a3dc84c670aa, Gareth Stevens Secondary Library) Stevens, Gareth Publishing LLLP.

Mayo Clinic Staff, contrib. by. Alternative Medicine & Your Health. 2004. (Mayo Clinic on Health Ser.). (Illus.). 36.52p. (YA). (gr. 8-18). lib. bdg. 15.95 *(978-1-59084-248-5(0))* Mason Crest.

Meachen Rau, Dana. EMTs, 1 vol. 2008. (Tools We Use Ser.). (ENG.). 32p. (gr. k-1). pap. 9.23 *(978-0-7614-3292-0(2)*, 8550cae3-593c-44a3-871c-4b7a32941c5a); (Illus.). lib. bdg. 25.50 *(978-0-7614-2660-8(4)*, b2b35363-21d8-423b-9342-d0c73e14b4bd, Cavendish Square) Cavendish Square Publishing LLC.

—Los Paramédicos / EMTs, 1 vol. 2009. (Instrumentos de Trabajo / Tools We Use Ser.). (ENG & SPA., Illus.). 32p. (gr. k-2). lib. bdg. 25.50 *(978-0-7614-2825-1(9)*, 630d0b6d-a7ac-4596-ae00-3717a6cea554) Cavendish Square Publishing LLC.

—Los Paramédicos (EMTs), 1 vol. 2009. (Instrumentos de Trabajo (Tools We Use) Ser.). (SPA., Illus.). 32p. (gr. k-2). lib. bdg. 25.50 *(978-0-7614-2801-5(1)*, f7a96385-286d-471c-a3ff-51a4459246da) Cavendish Square Publishing LLC.

Medical Care. (YA). (gr. 6-12). pap. 10.95 *(978-0-8224-4365-0(1))* Globe Fearon Educational Publishing.

Messner, Kate. Dr. Fauci: How a Boy from Brooklyn Became America's Doctor. Bye, Alexandra, illus. 2021. (ENG.). 48p. (J). (gr. -1-3). 17.99 *(978-1-6659-0243-4(4)*, Simon & Schuster Bks. For Young Readers) Simon & Schuster Bks. For Young Readers.

Miracles of Medicine, 12 vols. 2016. (Miracles of Medicine Ser.). (ENG.). 00048p. (J). (gr. 6-6). lib. bdg. 201.60 *(978-1-4824-6122-0(6)*, c78d69f1-12ef-4f71-8be0-7c6e43918de0) Stevens, Gareth Publishing LLLP.

Montgomery, Sharon, text. Your Invisible Bodies: A Reference Book for Children & Adults about Human Energy Fields. 2011. (Illus.). *(978-0-9811069-2-6(X))* Words By Montgomery.

Morley, David. Healing Our World: Inside Doctors Without Borders, 1 vol. 2008. (ENG., Illus.). 121p. (J). (gr. 6-9). pap. 14.95 *(978-1-55455-050-0(5)*, 2f3fe390-5f24-409f-910b-39d9b527999a) Fitzhenry & Whiteside, Ltd. CAN. Dist: Firefly Bks., Ltd.

Murphy, Patricia. Everything You Need to Know about Staying in the Hospital. 2009. (Need to Know Library). 64p. (gr. 5-5). 58.50 *(978-1-60854-088-4(X))* Rosen Publishing Group, Inc., The.

Murray, Aaron R. EMTs Help Us, 1 vol. 2012. (All about Community Helpers Ser.). (ENG., Illus.). 24p. (J). (gr. -1-1). 25.27 *(978-0-7660-4050-2(X)*, 7f182c9c-4d74-43d2-869b-45809e9572e8, Enslow Publishing) Enslow Publishing, LLC.

Nardo, Don, contrib. by. Nanotechnology & Medicine. 2018. (ENG.). 80p. (YA). (gr. 5-12). *(978-1-68282-327-9(X))* ReferencePoint Pr., Inc.

National Geographic Learning. Reading Expeditions (Science: the Human Body): Fighting Disease. 2007. (Rise & Shine Ser.). (ENG., Illus.). 32p. (J). pap. 18.95 *(978-0-7922-8865-7(3))* CENGAGE Learning.

Nelson, Kristin L. EMTs. 2005. (Pull Ahead Bks.). (Illus.). (J). 22.60 *(978-0-8225-1690-3(X))* Lerner Publishing Group.

Parks, Peggy J. The Dangers of Painkillers. 2016. (ENG.). 80p. (J). (gr. 5-12). *(978-1-68282-024-7(6))* ReferencePoint Pr., Inc.

M
N
O

Parry, Ann. Doctors Without Borders. 2005. (Humanitarian Organizations Ser.). (ENG., Illus.). 32p. (gr. 5-8). lib. bdg. 25.00 *(978-0-7910-8817-3(0),* P114432, Facts On File) Infobase Holdings, Inc.
Parsons, Michelle Hyde. Fighting Disease. 2005. (J). pap. *(978-1-4108-4609-9(1))* Benchmark Education Co.
Pearson Learning Staff, creator. A Visit to the Doctor. 2007. (ENG.). (J). (gr. 2-2). pap. 10.92 *(978-0-7652-8602-4(5),* Celebration Pr.) Savvas Learning Co.
Peppas, Lynn. Plague! 2013. (ENG.). 48p. (J). *(978-0-7787-1102-5(1));* (Illus.). pap. *(978-0-7787-1122-3(6))* Crabtree Publishing Co.
Rajczak Nelson, Kristen. Freaky Stories about Our Bodies, 1 vol. 2015. (Freaky True Science Ser.). (ENG.). 32p. (J). (gr. 4-5). 28.27 *(978-1-4824-2962-6(4),* 05ce8210-d7b4-4f0f-9c96-d807af6fa567) Stevens, Gareth Publishing LLLP.
—More Freaky Stories about Our Bodies. 2019. (Freaky True Science Ser.). (ENG.). 32p. (gr. 4-5). 63.00 *(978-1-5382-4067-0(X))* Stevens, Gareth Publishing LLLP.
Ramen, Fred. Albucasis (Abu al-Qasim Al-Zahrawi) Renowned Muslim Surgeon of the Tenth Century. 2009. (Great Muslim Philosophers & Scientists of the Middle Ages Ser.). 112p. (gr. 6-6). 66.50 *(978-1-61513-178-5(7),* Rosen Reference) Rosen Publishing Group, Inc., The.
—Sleeping Sickness & Other Parasitic Tropical Diseases. 2009. (Epidemics Ser.). 64p. (gr. 5-5). 58.50 *(978-1-61512-301-8(6))* Rosen Publishing Group, Inc., The.
Randolph, Joanne. Ambulances, 1 vol. 2008. (To the Rescue! Ser.). (ENG., Illus.). 24p. (J). (gr. 1-1). lib. bdg. 26.27 *(978-1-4042-4150-3(7),* c89f3a78-fed6-4cda-9402-5c4e0788949a, PowerKids Pr.) Rosen Publishing Group, Inc., The.
—Emergency Helicopters. 2009. (To the Rescue! Ser.). 24p. (gr. 1-1). 42.50 *(978-1-60854-396-0(X),* PowerKids Pr.) Rosen Publishing Group, Inc., The.
—Emergency Helicopters/Helicopteros de Emergencia. 2009. (To the Rescue! / ¡Al rescate! Ser.). (ENG & SPA.). 24p. (gr. 1-1). 42.50 *(978-1-60854-402-8(8),* Editorial Buenas Letras) Rosen Publishing Group, Inc., The.
Reeves, Diane Lindsey. Health Sciences. 2017. (Bright Futures Press: World of Work Ser.). (ENG., Illus.). 32p. (J). (gr. 4-7). lib. bdg. 32.07 *(978-1-63472-624-5(3),* 209530) Cherry Lake Publishing.
Ricciuti, Edward R. What's Inside an Ambulance?, 1 vol. 2005. (What's Inside? Ser.). (ENG., Illus.). 32p. (gr. 1-2). lib. bdg. 25.50 *(978-0-7614-1561-9(0),* bbaf8b88-369e-4be0-9f83-71a7be9a6ec4) Cavendish Square Publishing LLC.
—What's Inside an Ambulance, 1 vol. 2008. (What's Inside? Ser.). (ENG.). 32p. (gr. 1-2). pap. 9.23 *(978-0-7614-3343-9(0),* 45df7333-572a-4295-88bb-b90f71185e49) Cavendish Square Publishing LLC.
Riggs, Kate. Ambulances. 2015. (Seedlings Ser.). (ENG., Illus.). 24p. (J). (gr. -1-k). *(978-1-60818-578-8(8),* 21010, Creative Education) Creative Co., The.
Ringstad, Arnold. Medical Myths, Busted! 2017. (Science Myths, Busted! Ser.). (ENG., Illus.). 32p. (J). (gr. 3-6). 32.80 *(978-1-63235-303-0(2),* 11808, 12-Story Library) Bookstaves, LLC.
Rivera, Sheila. Doctor. 2005. (First Step Nonfiction — Work People Do Ser.). (ENG., Illus.). 8p. (J). (gr. k-2). pap. 5.99 *(978-0-8225-5357-1(0),* e718aa0d-e8f5-4fff-883f-feb74b8911ed) Lerner Publishing Group.
Romanek, Trudee. Science, Medicine, & Math in the Early Islamic World. 2012. (ENG.). 48p. (J). lib. bdg. *(978-0-7787-2170-3(1))* Crabtree Publishing Co.
Romero, Libby. Discover Medical Chemistry. 2006. (J). pap. *(978-1-4108-6502-1(9))* Benchmark Education Co.
Rooney, Anne. Health & Medicine: The Impact of Science & Technology, 1 vol. 2009. (Pros & Cons Ser.). (ENG.). 64p. (YA). (gr. 5-8). lib. bdg. 37.67 *(978-1-4339-1988-6(5),* 5a89a95b-fbdb-4a2e-ad81-57eaf49b883c) Stevens, Gareth Publishing LLLP.
Rosario, Miguel T. A Paramedic's Job, 1 vol. 2014. (Community Workers Ser.). (ENG.). 24p. (gr. 1-1). pap. 9.23 *(978-1-62712-997-8(9),* be047948-e528-4e50-8af3-8647e79b67dd); lib. bdg. 25.93 *(978-1-62712-996-1(0),* 04b223bb-327a-4e60-9d98-762adfd9174a) Cavendish Square Publishing LLC.
Royston, Angela. Heroes of Medicine & Their Discoveries. 2010. (ENG., Illus.). 32p. (J). *(978-0-7787-9897-2(6));* pap. *(978-0-7787-9918-4(2))* Crabtree Publishing Co.
Ruffin, David C. The Duties & Responsibilities of the Secretary of Health & Human Services. (Your Government in Action Ser.). 32p. (gr. 3-3). 2009. 43.90 *(978-1-60854-917-7(8))* 2004. (ENG., Illus.). (J). lib. bdg. 27.60 *(978-1-4042-2691-3(5),* d88f0367-cc80-4111-944b-c8bd62b31318) Rosen Publishing Group, Inc., The. (PowerKids Pr.).
Sally Ride Science Editors, Sally Ride Science. What Do You Want to Be? Explore Health Sciences. 2004. (J). 6.00 *(978-0-9753920-3-4(4))* Sally Ride Science.
Sandy Creek (Firm) Staff, contrib. by. Medical Chart. 2016. (Illus.). 8p. (J). *(978-1-4351-6397-3(4))* Barnes & Noble, Inc.
Sargent, Brian. The Placebo Effect: The Power of Positive Thinking, 1 vol. 2014. (ENG., Illus.). 28p. pap., E-Book 9.50 *(978-1-107-62263-0(8))* Cambridge Univ. Pr.
Sharafeddine, Fatima. The Amazing Discoveries of Ibn Sina, 1 vol. Ali, Intelaq, illus. 2015. (ENG.). 32p. (J). (gr. 2-6). 17.95 *(978-1-55498-710-8(5))* Groundwood Bks. CAN. Dist: Publishers Group West (PGW).
Shepherd, Jodie. A Day with Paramedics. 2012. (ENG., Illus.). 32p. (J). lib. bdg. 23.00 *(978-0-531-28954-9(0))* Scholastic Library Publishing.
Sherrow, Victoria. Medical Imaging, 1 vol. 2007. (Great Inventions Ser.). (ENG., Illus.). 144p. (YA). (gr. 8-8). lib. bdg. 45.50 *(978-0-7614-2231-0(5),* 77b3a29d-2939-4f96-aca7-8c862fb59b51) Cavendish Square Publishing LLC.
Sieling, Peter. Folk Medicine. 2004. (North American Folklore Ser.). (Illus.). 112p. (J). (gr. 7-18). lib. bdg. 22.95 *(978-1-59084-341-3(X))* Mason Crest.
Silverstein, Alvin & Silverstein, Virginia. Tapeworms, Foot Fungus, Lice, & More: The Yucky Disease Book, 1 vol. 2010. (Yucky Science Ser.). (ENG., Illus.). 48p. (gr. 5-7). 27.93 *(978-0-7660-3314-6(7),* e19db042-b65d-4fbe-8b82-e777a14c2b61) Enslow Publishing, LLC.
Simon, Samantha. Emts & Paramedics. 2017. (Careers in Healthcare Ser.: Vol. 13). (ENG.). (YA). (gr. 7-12). 23.95 *(978-1-4222-3799-1(0))* Mason Crest.
—Orthotists & Prosthetists. 2017. (Careers in Healthcare Ser.: Vol. 13). (ENG., Illus.). 64p. (YA). (gr. 7-12). 23.95 *(978-1-4222-3802-8(4))* Mason Crest.
Slegers, Liesbet. Doctors & What They Do. 2018. (Illus.). 32p. (J). *(978-1-4896-6213-2(8),* AV2 by Weigl) Weigl Pubs., Inc.
Small, Cathleen. Using VR in Medicine, 1 vol. 2019. (VR on the Job: Understanding Virtual & Augmented Reality Ser.). (ENG.). 80p. (J). (gr. 8-8). lib. bdg. 37.36 *(978-1-5026-4570-8(X),* 64770452-8483-4128-95d6-66d446e5f6bd) Cavendish Square Publishing LLC.
Soloway, Cindy. Mommy, What's an MRI? Steve, Sumner, ed. Susan, Lisbin, illus. 2006. (J). mass mkt. *(978-0-9765060-2-7(5))* TouchSmart Publishing, LLC.
Solway, Andrew. Genetics in Medicine, 1 vol. 2007. (Cutting Edge Medicine Ser.). (ENG., Illus.). 64p. (gr. 5-8). lib. bdg. 36.67 *(978-0-8368-7865-3(5),* 291a3bc3-3b51-4470-a2c8-ff26067d9876, Gareth Stevens Secondary Library) Stevens, Gareth Publishing LLLP.
Spitz, Michael. Life As a Doctor in the Civil War, 1 vol. 2017. (Life As... Ser.). (ENG.). 32p. (gr. 3-3). pap. 11.58 *(978-1-5026-3035-3(4),* e11411b3-38c4-4f65-a99a-a2e86b7df7dd) Cavendish Square Publishing LLC.
Steffens, Bradley. Careers in Medical Technology. 2017. (ENG., Illus.). 80p. (YA). (gr. 5-12). *(978-1-68282-116-9(1))* ReferencePoint Pr., Inc.
Stefoff, Rebecca. Magic & Medicine, 1 vol. 2014. (Is It Science? Ser.). (ENG.). 48p. (gr. 5-5). lib. bdg. 32.64 *(978-1-62712-515-4(9),* 9ca747d8-ea07-4480-87c5-17792f02de6f) Cavendish Square Publishing LLC.
Stephens, Ronald, ed. Sports. 2014. (Safety First Ser.: 11). 48p. (J). (gr. 5-18). 20.95 *(978-1-4222-3053-4(8))* Mason Crest.
Stoltman, Joan. Weird Medical Inventions, 1 vol. 2018. (Wild & Wacky Inventions Ser.). (ENG.). 32p. (gr. 4-5). 28.27 *(978-1-5382-2083-2(0),* 9f120532-6a94-400d-ab48-c089fa54d5ee) Stevens, Gareth Publishing LLLP.
Stoyles, Pennie. The A-Z of Health. 2010. (a to Z of Health Ser.). 32p. (gr. 4-7). Vol. 1. lib. bdg. 31.35 *(978-1-59920-541-0(6))* Vol. 2. lib. bdg. 31.35 *(978-1-59920-542-7(4))* Vol. 3. lib. bdg. 31.35 *(978-1-59920-543-4(2))* Vol. 6. lib. bdg. 31.35 *(978-1-59920-546-5(7))* Black Rabbit Bks.
Stoyles, Pennie & Pentland, Peter. Medicine & Health, 1 vol. 2012. (Energy in Action Ser.). (ENG., Illus.). 32p. (gr. 6-6). 31.21 *(978-1-60870-568-9(4),* 3ab8fccb-fb9c-46d8-a36d-0655b027b485) Cavendish Square Publishing LLC.
Strange, Cordelia. Medical Technicians: Health-Care Support for the 21st Century. 2010. (New Careers for the 21st Century Ser.). 64p. (YA). (gr. 7-18). lib. bdg. 22.95 *(978-1-4222-1817-4(1))* Mason Crest.
Syrewicz, Connor. Masseur & Massage Therapist. 2013. (Earning $50,000 - $100,000 with a High School Diploma or Less Ser.: 14). 64p. (J). (gr. 7-18). 22.95 *(978-1-4222-2896-8(7))* Mason Crest.
Syrewicz, Connor & Morkes, Andrew. Massage Therapist: Providing Relief & Relaxation. 2019. (Careers with Earning Potential Ser.). (Illus.). 80p. (J). (gr. 12). lib. bdg. 34.60 *(978-1-4222-4327-5(3))* Mason Crest.
Tartakoff, Katy. Burned & Beautiful. Shields, Laurie, illus. 54p. (Orig.). (J). stu. ed. 14.95 *(978-0-9629365-1-7(0))* Children's Legacy.
—Let Me Show You My World. Shields, Laurie, illus. 54p. (Orig.). (J). stu. ed. 14.95 *(978-0-9629365-2-4(9))* Children's Legacy.
Thornton, Denise. Living with Cancer: The Ultimate Teen Guide. 2011. (It Happened to Me Ser.: 30). (ENG., Illus.). 190p. 55.00 *(978-0-8108-7277-6(3))* Scarecrow Pr., Inc.
Toriello, James. The Human Genome Project. 2009. (Library of Future Medicine Ser.). 64p. (gr. 5-5). 58.50 *(978-1-60853-632-0(7))* Rosen Publishing Group, Inc., The.
Waters, Rosa. Over-The-Counter Medications. Borus, Joshua, ed. 2014. (Downside of Drugs Ser.: 11). (Illus.). 48p. (J). (gr. 5-18). lib. bdg. 20.95 *(978-1-4222-3025-1(2))* Mason Crest.
Waters, Sophie. Seeing the Gynecologist. 2009. (Girls' Health Ser.). 48p. (gr. 5-6). 53.00 *(978-1-61512-731-3(3),* Rosen Reference) Rosen Publishing Group, Inc., The.
Watson, Stephanie. Endometriosis. 2009. (Library of Sexual Health Ser.). 64p. (gr. 6-6). 58.50 *(978-1-60853-842-3(7))* Rosen Publishing Group, Inc., The.
Waxman, Laura Hamilton. Ambulances on the Move. 2011. (Lightning Bolt Books Vroom-Vroom Ser.). 32p. pap. 45.32 *(978-0-7613-7615-6(1))* Lerner Publishing Group.
Way, Steve. Fighting Disease, 1 vol. 2011. (Planet SOS Ser.). (ENG., Illus.). 48p. (J). (gr. 4-5). pap. 15.05 *(978-1-4339-4971-5(7),* da07374c-4d53-43eb-b3d5-79c365a4b8f7); lib. bdg. 34.60 *(978-1-4339-4970-8(9),* e53ff4b0-6e68-4370-a012-259bb8cf9f5f) Stevens, Gareth Publishing LLLP. (Gareth Stevens Learning Library).
Weber, Rebecca. Science & Your Health, 1 vol. 2011. (Health & Your Body Ser.). (ENG.). 24p. (J). (gr. -1-2). pap. 7.29 *(978-1-4296-7130-9(0),* 116778); (gr. k-1). pap. 43.74 *(978-1-4296-7136-1(X),* 16709) Capstone. (Capstone Pr.).
Whiting, Jim. The Life & Times of Hippocrates. 2006. (Biography from Ancient Civilizations Ser.). (Illus.). 48p. (J). (gr. 3-7). lib. bdg. 29.95 *(978-1-58415-512-6(4),* 1259600) Mitchell Lane Pubs.
Woods, Michael & Woods, Mary B. Ancient Medical Technology: From Herbs to Scalpels. 2011. (Technology in Ancient Cultures Ser.). (ENG.). 96p. (gr. 6-12). lib. bdg. 31.93 *(978-0-7613-6522-8(2))* Lerner Publishing Group.
World Book, Inc. Staff, contrib. by. Medicine. 2009. *(978-0-7166-0384-9(5))* World Bk., Inc.
Wunderlich, Rick. Math on the Job: Keeping People Healthy. 2016. (ENG., Illus.). 32p. (J). *(978-0-7787-2359-2(3))* Crabtree Publishing Co.
Yomtov, Nelson. Medical Illustrator. 2015. (21st Century Skills Library: Cool STEAM Careers Ser.). (ENG., Illus.). 32p. (gr. 4-7). pap. 14.21 *(978-1-63362-042-1(5),* 205925) Cherry Lake Publishing.
Zott, Lynn M. & Haugen, David M., eds. Alternative Medicine, 1 vol. 2012. (Opposing Viewpoints Ser.). (ENG., Illus.). 264p. (J). (gr. 10-12). pap. 34.80 *(978-0-7377-5439-1(7),* b3958c52-774f-4574-a178-3aea06407748); lib. bdg. 50.43 *(978-0-7377-5438-4(9),* a972a1bf-2297-4285-8ac8-002148375a44) Greenhaven Publishing LLC. (Greenhaven Publishing).

MEDICINE—BIOGRAPHY

Harvey, Joanna & Crabtree, Marc. Meet My Neighbor, the Paramedic. 2010. (ENG., Illus.). 24p. (J). pap. *(978-0-7787-4585-3(6));* lib. bdg. *(978-0-7787-4575-4(9))* Crabtree Publishing Co.
Lim, Bridget & Ramen, Fred. Albucasis: The Father of Modern Surgery, 1 vol. 2016. (Physicians, Scientists, & Mathematicians of the Islamic World Ser.). (ENG.). 112p. (gr. 6-6). 38.80 *(978-1-5081-7140-9(8),* ba3e970d-391d-4ae9-979e-46d783ada49f) Rosen Publishing Group, Inc., The.
Morrison, John. Mathilde Krim & the Story of AIDS. 2004. (Women in Medicine Ser.). (ENG., Illus.). 112p. (gr. 6-12). 30.00 *(978-0-7910-8026-9(9),* P114103, Facts On File) Infobase Holdings, Inc.

MEDICINE—DATA PROCESSING

Benedict, Aaron & Gallaher, David. Using Computer Science in High-Tech Health & Wellness Careers, 1 vol. 2017. (Coding Your Passion Ser.). (ENG., Illus.). 80p. (J). (gr. 7-7). 37.47 *(978-1-5081-7515-5(2),* 3a7847a0-376b-4eaa-b949-40a275cf571c, Rosen Young Adult) Rosen Publishing Group, Inc., The.

MEDICINE, DENTAL

see Dentistry; Teeth

MEDICINE—FICTION

Accardo, Reba, told to. Surgery for Me? 2005. (J). pap. 8.00 *(978-0-8059-6697-8(8))* Dorrance Publishing Co., Inc.
Bailey, Leslie J. Jacub's Journey. DeBroeck, Sarah, illus. 2011. 28p. pap. 24.95 *(978-1-4560-9951-0(5))* America Star Bks.
Birney, Roxanne. Johannah's Lazy Eye. 2009. 28p. pap. 12.49 *(978-1-4389-3673-4(7))* AuthorHouse.
Brix-Maffei, Angela & Brix-Maffei, John. The Christmas Dinosaur. 2008. 48p. pap. 22.49 *(978-1-4389-0499-3(1))* AuthorHouse.
Bryers, Paul. Kobal. 2009. 1.00 *(978-1-4074-4320-1(8))* Recorded Bks., Inc.
Burgess, Melvin. Sara's Face. 2008. (ENG.). 288p. (YA). (gr. 9-12). pap. 7.99 *(978-1-4169-5815-4(0),* Simon Pulse) Simon Pulse.
Cowan, Charlotte. Sadie's Sore Throat. Bratun, Katy, illus. 2007. (Dr. Hippo Ser.). (ENG.). 32p. (J). (gr. 3-7). 17.95 *(978-0-9753516-4-2(8))* Hippocratic Pr., The.
Cummings, K. M. I Hate Medicine! 2007. 24p. per. 10.95 *(978-1-4327-1382-9(5))* Outskirts Pr., Inc.
Cushman, Karen. Matilda Bone. 2020. (ENG.). 192p. (J). (gr. 3-7). pap. 7.99 *(978-0-358-09752-5(5),* 1747612, Clarion Bks.) HarperCollins Pubs.
—Matilda Bone. unabr. ed. 2004. (Middle Grade Cassette Librariestm Ser.). 176p. (J). (gr. 5-9). pap. 36.00 incl. audio *(978-0-8072-1725-2(5),* S YA 252 SP, Listening Library) Random Hse. Audio Publishing Group.
Dahl, Roald. La Maravillosa Medicina de Jorge. Blake, Quentin, illus. 2005. (Alfaguara Ser.).Tr. of George's Marvellous Medicine Spanish. (SPA.). 118p. (gr. 3-5). per. 11.95 *(978-968-19-0547-7(4))* Santillana USA Publishing Co., Inc.
Danziger, Paula. The Pistachio Prescription. (J). (gr. 4-6). 160p. pap. 3.99 *(978-0-8072-1374-2(8));* 154p. pap. 3.99 *(978-0-8072-1525-8(2))* Random Hse. Audio Publishing Group. (Listening Library).
DeFelice, Cynthia. The Apprenticeship of Lucas Whitaker. 2007. (ENG.). 160p. (J). (gr. 5-9). per. 16.99 *(978-0-374-40014-9(8),* 900042005) Square Fish.
Dempsey, Tami. We Are a Champion! 2010. (ENG.). 36p. pap. 15.49 *(978-1-4490-8102-7(9))* AuthorHouse.
Dixon, Heather. Illusionarium. 2015. (ENG.). 368p. (YA). (gr. 8). 17.99 *(978-0-06-200105-4(1),* Greenwillow Bks.) HarperCollins Pubs.
Dusablon, David. Dee Dee's First Shot, 1 vol. Spoerl, Amber, illus. 2009. 17p. pap. 24.95 *(978-1-60749-113-2(3))* America Star Bks.
Ecton, Emily. The Curse of Cuddles Mcgee. 2008. (ENG.). 272p. (J). (gr. 3-7). pap. 12.99 *(978-1-4169-6450-6(9),* Simon & Schuster/Paula Wiseman Bks.) Simon & Schuster/Paula Wiseman Bks.
Gaydos, Nora. Now I'm Growing! - A Visit to the Doctor. Gutierrez, Akemi, illus. 2011. (ENG.). 30p. (J). (gr. -1-17). 8.99 *(978-1-60169-153-8(X))* Innovative Kids.
Guerra, Juan J. The Little Doctor / el Doctorcito. Castillo, Victoria, illus. 2017. (ENG & SPA.). 32p. (J). (gr. k-3). 17.95 *(978-1-55885-846-6(6),* Piñata Books) Arte Publico Pr.
Hansell, Donna. The Adventures of Kirbey the Kidney. 2012. 20p. pap. 11.59 *(978-1-4669-4527-2(3))* Trafford Publishing.
Hare, Eric B. Dr. Rabbit. Bohlmann, Siegfried, illus. fac. ed. 2010. 127p. per. 11.95 *(978-1-57258-278-1(2),* 945-6131) TEACH Services, Inc.
James, Montague Rhodes. The Five Jars. 2008. 96p. pap. *(978-1-84830-112-2(X),* Wildhern Pr.) Echo Library.
K/H (Pathways). Kindergarten Stepping Stones: Kindergarten the Bravest Dog Ever - The True Story of Balto Trade Book. rev. ed. 2010. (ENG.). 48p. pap. 9.00 *(978-0-7575-8646-0(5))* Kendall Hunt Publishing Co.
Kellerman, Faye & Kellerman, Aliza. Prism. 2009. 272p. (YA). (gr. 7-18). lib. bdg. 17.89 *(978-0-06-168722-8(7),* HarperTeen) HarperCollins Pubs.
Krossing, Karen. Pure, 1 vol. 2005. (ENG.). 248p. (YA). (gr. 7-9). per. 10.95 *(978-1-896764-96-2(7))* Second Story Pr. CAN. Dist: Orca Bk. Pubs. USA.
Krovatin, Christopher. Venomous. 2008. (ENG., Illus.). 336p. (YA). (gr. 8-18). 16.99 *(978-1-4169-2487-6(6),* Atheneum Bks. for Young Readers) Simon & Schuster Children's Publishing.
Ladd, Debbie. Nurse Robin's Hats. Nakasone, Shaun, illus. 2006. 52p. (J). 16.95 *(978-0-9727615-3-6(5))* Deb on Air Bks.
Lansdowne, Marcella. The Adventures of Patty & Annabel: Apache Lake & the Chakras. 2009. 28p. pap. 15.95 *(978-1-4389-1643-9(4))* AuthorHouse.
Milford, Kate. The Boneshaker. Offermann, Andrea, illus. 2011. (ENG.). 384p. (J). (gr. 5-7). pap. 7.99 *(978-0-547-55004-6(9),* 1450216, Clarion Bks.) HarperCollins Pubs.
Morgan, Nicola. Fleshmarket. 2003. (ENG.). 272p. (J). (gr. 7-17). pap. 9.99 *(978-0-340-85557-7(6))* Hachette Children's Group GBR. Dist: Hachette Bk. Group.
Novel Units. The Midwife's Apprentice Novel Units Teacher Guide. 2019. (ENG.). (J). pap. 12.99 *(978-1-56137-801-2(1),* Novel Units, Inc.) Classroom Library Co.
Parish, Herman. Calling Doctor Amelia Bedelia. Sweat, Lynn, illus. 2004. (I Can Read Level 2 Ser.). (ENG.). 64p. (J). (gr. k-3). pap. 4.99 *(978-0-06-008780-7(3),* Greenwillow Bks.) HarperCollins Pubs.
Patton, Katherine. Bam Bam the Bandage. 2010. 16p. pap. 10.99 *(978-1-4343-4967-5(5))* AuthorHouse.
Pelow, Lawrence. Little Larry of Lewiston Meets Bobby the Backyard Bully. 2006. 2p. 6.71 *(978-1-4116-9172-8(5))* Lulu Pr., Inc.
Powers, J. L. This Thing Called the Future, 1 vol. 2011. (ENG.). 208p. (YA). (gr. 9-12). 16.95 *(978-1-933693-95-8(9),* 23353382, Cinco Puntos Press) Lee & Low Bks., Inc.
Riner, Kendall F. The Rescue Adventures of Fireman Frank. 2006. (Illus.). 52p. (J). pap. 12.00 *(978-0-9786369-1-3(0))* Warwick Hse. Publishing.
Royster, Ka-Sandra. Cough Syrup in Mommy's Hair. 2013. 24p. pap. *(978-1-4602-2600-1(3))* FriesenPress.
Ryden, David. Andy the Ambulance: My Two Partners. 2012. 34p. 24.95 *(978-1-4626-5372-0(3))* PublishAmerica, Inc.
Samples, Suzanne. Pivot. 2011. 208p. pap. 13.00 *(978-1-257-03969-2(5))* Lulu Pr., Inc.
Stewart, Jennifer J. Close Encounters of a Third World Kind. 2004. (ENG.). 128p. (J). (gr. 4-6). tchr. ed. 16.95 *(978-0-8234-1850-3(2))* Holiday Hse., Inc.
Walsh, Ann. The Doctor's Apprentice. 2005. 160p. (YA). (gr. 3-8). pap., tchr. ed. 8.95 *(978-0-88878-389-9(2))* Beach Holme Pubs., Ltd. CAN. Dist: Literary Pr. Group of Canada.
—The Doctor's Apprentice: A Barkerville Mystery. 2007. (Barkerville Mystery Ser.: 2). (ENG.). 148p. (J). pap. 11.99 *(978-1-55002-633-7(X))* Dundurn Pr. CAN. Dist: Publishers Group West (PGW).
Wells, Dan. Partials. (ENG.). (YA). 2013. (Partials Sequence Ser.: 1). 528p. (gr. 9). pap. 11.99 *(978-0-06-207105-7(X),* Balzer & Bray) 2012. (Partials Sequence Ser.: 1). 480p. (gr. 9). 17.99 *(978-0-06-207104-0(1),* Balzer & Bray) 2012. 496p. pap. 9.99 *(978-0-06-213569-8(4))* HarperCollins Pubs.
White, Paul. Jungle Doctor Stings a Scorpion. rev. ed. 2008. (Flamingo Fiction 9-13s Ser.). (ENG., Illus.). 160p. (J). 8.99 *(978-1-84550-390-1(2),* 365d3eb7-29af-4f22-ba6a-32a6c0f815de) Christian Focus Pubns. GBR. Dist: Baker & Taylor Publisher Services (BTPS).
Yager, Jeff. Atom & Eve. 2013. (ENG.). (YA). 255p. 29.95 *(978-1-938998-36-2(7));* 262p. (gr. 8-12). pap. 16.95 *(978-1-938998-34-8(0))* Hannacroix Creek Bks., Inc.
Young, Lena. One World Healing. Tsai, Dora, illus. 2005. 26p. (J). pap. *(978-1-933554-01-3(0))* Primordia.

MEDICINE—HISTORY

Alkire, Jessie. Medicine: From Hippocrates to Jonas Salk. 2018. (STEM Stories Ser.). (ENG., Illus.). 32p. (J). (gr. 3-6). lib. bdg. 32.79 *(978-1-5321-1547-9(4),* 28948, Checkerboard Library) ABDO Publishing Co.
Allman, Toney. Medieval Medicine & Disease. 2014. (Library of Medieval Times Ser.). (ENG., Illus.). 80p. (J). lib. bdg. *(978-1-60152-656-4(3))* ReferencePoint Pr., Inc.
Anniss, Matt. Science vs. Disease, 1 vol. 2013. (Science Fights Back Ser.). (ENG., Illus.). 48p. (gr. 4-5). 34.60 *(978-1-4339-8687-1(6),* b466eb66-c0d9-42c2-b751-a62db9415e97); pap. 15.05 *(978-1-4339-8688-8(4),* 11a8306a-d519-46ef-bcdd-2bd26cad501e) Stevens, Gareth Publishing LLLP. (Gareth Stevens Learning Library).
Atkinson, Mary. Shockwave: Pills & Potions. 2007. (Shockwave: Life Science & Medicine Ser.). (ENG., Illus.). 36p. (J). (gr. 4-6). lib. bdg. 25.00 *(978-0-531-17767-9(X),* Children's Pr.) Scholastic Library Publishing.
Bankston, John. Joseph Lister & the Story of Antiseptics. 2004. (Uncharted, Unexplored, & Unexplained Ser.). (Illus.). 48p. (J). (gr. 4-8). lib. bdg. 29.95 *(978-1-58415-262-0(1))* Mitchell Lane Pubs.
Biskup, Agnieszka. Medical Marvels: The Next 100 Years of Medicine. Pota, Giovanni & Brown, Alan, illus. 2016. (Our World: the Next 100 Years Ser.). (ENG.). 32p. (J). (gr. 3-9). lib. bdg. 31.32 *(978-1-4914-8264-3(8),* 130753, Capstone Pr.) Capstone.
Brent Sandvold, Lynnette. Revolution in Medicine, 1 vol. 2010. (It Works! Ser.). (ENG.). 32p. (gr. 3-3). 31.21 *(978-0-7614-4376-6(2),* 2343ecd2-5c65-4969-bff4-13c2802ac266) Cavendish Square Publishing LLC.
Carmichael, Lindsey. Innovations in Health. 2016. (Problem Solved! Your Turn to Think Big Ser.). (ENG., Illus.). 32p. (J). (gr. 3-6). *(978-0-7787-2681-4(9))* Crabtree Publishing Co.
Clare, John D. Medicine in the Industrial World, 1 vol. 2007. (History of Medicine Ser.). (ENG., Illus.). 64p. (gr. 5-5). 34.07 *(978-1-59270-039-4(X),* 96d0461b-6435-4a6c-9099-b261205fe6b2) Cavendish Square Publishing LLC.
Claybourne, Anna. Sick at Sea? Cure It or Cut It Off! 2010. (ENG.). 32p. (J). *(978-0-7787-9901-6(8))* Crabtree Publishing Co.
Coan, Sharon. STEM Careers. 2nd rev. ed. 2017. (TIME(r): Informational Text Ser.). (ENG., Illus.). 48p. (gr. 6-8). pap. 13.99 *(978-1-4938-3621-5(8))* Teacher Created Materials, Inc.
Dawson, Ian. Greek & Roman Medicine, 1 vol. 2006. (History of Medicine Ser.). (ENG., Illus.). 64p. (J). (gr. 5-5). 34.07 *(978-1-59270-036-3(5),* 5f1e4b0c-710d-49fe-a718-1847288f29d0) Cavendish Square Publishing LLC.

—Medicine During the Renaissance, 1 vol. 2006. (History of Medicine Ser.). (ENG., Illus.). 64p. (J). (gr. 5-5). 34.07 *(978-1-59270-038-7(1),* 25a733d3-4210-47fd-a343-d35579e0ee85) Cavendish Square Publishing LLC.

Dodge, Hillary. The Evolution of Medical Technology, 1 vol. 2018. (Evolving Technology Ser.). (ENG.). 64p. (gr. 6-7). lib. bdg. 34.29 *(978-1-5383-0324-5(8),* d05046b0-7425-41e2-8ca1-3fdd3ff88eea, Britannica Educational Publishing) Rosen Publishing Group, Inc., The.

Farndon, John. Quacks & con Artists: The Dubious History of Doctors. Dean, Venitia, illus. 2017. (Sickening History of Medicine Ser.). (ENG.). 32p. (J). (gr. 3-6). E-Book 42.65 *(978-1-5124-2712-7(8));* E-Book 42.65 *(978-1-5124-3635-8(6),* 9781512436358); E-Book 4.99 *(978-1-5124-3636-5(4),* 9781512436365) Lerner Publishing Group. (Hungry Tomato (r)).

—Strange Medicine: A History of Medical Remedies. Dean, Venitia, illus. 2017. (Sickening History of Medicine Ser.). (ENG.). 32p. (J). (gr. 3-6). 27.99 *(978-1-5124-1559-9(6),* 2ba4fa64-1a68-44fa-a0ed-7f71251535b5); E-Book 4.99 *(978-1-5124-3640-2(2),* 9781512436402); E-Book 42.65 *(978-1-5124-2711-0(X));* E-Book 42.65 *(978-1-5124-3638-9(0),* 9781512436389) Lerner Publishing Group. (Hungry Tomato (r)).

—Tiny Killers: When Bacteria & Viruses Attack. Dean, Venitia, illus. 2017. (Sickening History of Medicine Ser.). (ENG.). 32p. (J). (gr. 3-6). 27.99 *(978-1-5124-1558-2(8),* 7dcf31d2-409c-4fd3-a538-7380ff4ebc9c); E-Book 42.65 *(978-1-5124-3641-9(0),* 9781512436419); E-Book 42.65 *(978-1-5124-2710-3(1));* E-Book 4.99 *(978-1-5124-3642-6(9),* 9781512436426) Lerner Publishing Group. (Hungry Tomato (r)).

Goldsmith, Connie. Cutting-Edge Medicine. 2008. pap. 52.95 *(978-0-8225-9327-0(0))* 2007. (ENG., Illus.). 48p. (gr. 4-8). lib. bdg. 27.93 *(978-0-8225-6770-7(9),* Lerner Pubns.) Lerner Publishing Group.

Green, Jen. Medicine. 2004. (Routes of Science Ser.). (Illus.). 40p. (J). (gr. 4-7). 23.70 *(978-1-4103-0168-0(0),* Blackbirch Pr., Inc.) Cengage Gale.

Haelle, Tara. Vaccination Investigation: The History & Science of Vaccines. 2018. (ENG., Illus.). 120p. (YA). (gr. 6-12). 37.32 *(978-1-5124-2530-7(3),* 38bac5f7-ccd1-41a0-ad3b-3de27c914fb5, Twenty-First Century Bks.) Lerner Publishing Group.

Hardman, Lizabeth. The History of Medicine, 1 vol. 2012. (World History Ser.). (ENG., Illus.). 120p. (gr. 7-7). 41.53 *(978-1-4205-0671-6(4),* b4ce4566-2553-468d-aa35-e7eda92abae2, Lucent Pr.) Greenhaven Publishing LLC.

Hollar, Sherman. Pioneers in Medicine: From the Classical World to Today, 1 vol. 2012. (Inventors & Innovators Ser.). (ENG., Illus.). 160p. (J). (gr. 8-8). lib. bdg. 38.82 *(978-1-61530-669-5(2),* 47eff1cd-0e20-43b2-82ec-562e949f445a) Rosen Publishing Group, Inc., The.

Hollar, Sherman, ed. Pioneers in Medicine: From the Classical World to Today, 4 vols. 2012. (Inventors & Innovators Ser.). (ENG., Illus.). 160p. (YA). (gr. 8-8). 77.64 *(978-1-61530-785-2(0),* c281e0dd-46fa-4909-b5b1-c5e1e6f9b85c) Rosen Publishing Group, Inc., The.

Isbell, Hannah. Monstrous Medicine, 1 vol. 2019. (Creepy, Kooky Science Ser.). (ENG.). 48p. (gr. 5-5). pap. 12.70 *(978-1-9785-1377-8(1),* e166138a-5340-4a16-be63-89bbbe1a83ae) Enslow Publishing, LLC.

Jeffrey, Gary. Medical Breakthroughs. (Graphic Discoveries Ser.). (ENG.). 48p. (gr. 5-5). 2009. (YA). 58.50 *(978-1-61512-932-4(4),* Rosen Reference) 2007. pap. 14.05 *(978-1-4042-9587-2(9),* a9821a4f-c8cd-4036-a6d2-64f9aa067ff4) Rosen Publishing Group, Inc., The.

—Medical Breakthroughs, 1 vol. Riley, Terry, illus. 2007. (Graphic Discoveries Ser.). (ENG.). 48p. (YA). (gr. 5-5). lib. bdg. 37.13 *(978-1-4042-1086-8(5),* fa2a6d23-8350-40e5-8294-3d410ce62189) Rosen Publishing Group, Inc., The.

Johnson, Rose. Discoveries in Medicine That Changed the World, 1 vol. 2014. (Scientific Breakthroughs Ser.). (ENG.). 48p. (YA). (gr. 6-6). 33.47 *(978-1-4777-8611-6(2),* 856b738f-c788-419b-b67f-b20c57714702, Rosen Reference) Rosen Publishing Group, Inc., The.

Krasner, Barbara. Great Medicine Fails. 2020. (Searchlight Books (tm) — Celebrating Failure Ser.). (ENG., Illus.). 32p. (J). (gr. 3-5). 30.65 *(978-1-5415-7735-0(3),* cb97735e-ac17-46a3-9967-4108ab94d8d9, Lerner Pubns.) Lerner Publishing Group.

Loh-Hagan, Virginia. Strange Medicine. 2017. (Stranger Than Fiction Ser.). (ENG., Illus.). 32p. (J). (gr. 4-8). lib. bdg. 32.07 *(978-1-63472-890-4(4),* 209986, 45th Parallel Press) Cherry Lake Publishing.

Marsico, Katie. The Doctor, 1 vol. 2012. (Colonial People Ser.). (ENG.). 48p. (gr. 4-4). 34.07 *(978-1-60870-412-5(2),* 9c3e868d-1a34-4ae0-aa47-edca7c340aed) Cavendish Square Publishing LLC.

Morrison, Heather S. Inventors of Health & Medical Technology, 1 vol. 2015. (Designing Engineering Solutions Ser.). (ENG., Illus.). 144p. (YA). (gr. 8-8). 44.50 *(978-1-5026-0658-7(5),* 13b346bc-4c2d-45b7-98dd-b5fee128c02d) Cavendish Square Publishing LLC.

Orr, Tamra B. Antibiotics (a True Book: Greatest Discoveries & Discoverers) (Library Edition) 2016. (True Book (Relaunch) Ser.). (ENG., Illus.). 48p. (J). (gr. 3-5). lib. bdg. 31.00 *(978-0-531-21860-0(0),* Children's Pr.) Scholastic Library Publishing.

Senior, Kathryn. You Wouldn't Want to Be Sick in the 16th Century! (Revised Edition) 2014. (You Wouldn't Want to... Ser.). (ENG.). 32p. (J). lib. bdg. 29.00 *(978-0-531-21176-2(2),* Watts, Franklin) Scholastic Library Publishing.

Strange, Matthew. Bleeding, Blistering, & Purging: Health & Medicine in The 1800s. 2009. (Daily Life in America in the 1800s Ser.). 64p. (YA). (gr. 7-18). pap. 9.95 *(978-1-4222-1848-8(1));* lib. bdg. 22.95 *(978-1-4222-1775-7(2))* Mason Crest.

Strom, Laura Layton. Dr. Medieval: Medicine in the Middle Ages. 2007. (Shockwave: Life Science & Medicine Ser.). (ENG., Illus.). 36p. (J). (gr. 3-5). 25.00 *(978-0-531-17765-5(3),* Children's Pr.) Scholastic Library Publishing.

Ward, Brian. The History of Medicine: Healthcare Around the World & Through the Ages. 2016. (Illus.). 64p. (J). (gr. 3-7). 12.99 *(978-1-86147-724-8(4),* Armadillo) Anness Publishing GBR. Dist: National Bk. Network.

Ward, Brian R. The Story of Medicine, 1 vol. 2011. (Journey Through History Ser.). (ENG.). 64p. (J). (gr. 5-6). lib. bdg. 37.13 *(978-1-4488-4792-1(3),* e8d0aa93-c1b9-48d2-b8a2-411d07155474, Rosen Reference) Rosen Publishing Group, Inc., The.

World Book, Inc. Staff, contrib. by. Leeches to Lasers: A Timeline of Medicine. 2016. (Illus.). 40p. (J). *(978-0-7166-3542-0(9))* World Bk.-Childcraft International.

MEDICINE, PEDIATRIC

see Children—Diseases

MEDICINE, PREVENTIVE

see Bacteriology; Health; Immunity; Public Health

MEDICINE—RESEARCH

Brocker, Susan & Furgang, Kathy. Pioneers in Medicine & Médicos Pioneros: 6 English, 6 Spanish Adaptations. 2011. (ENG & SPA.). (J). 97.00 net. *(978-1-4108-5701-9(8))* Benchmark Education Co.

Eboch, M. M. The 12 Biggest Breakthroughs in Medicine. 2014. (ENG., Illus.). 32p. (J). 32.80 *(978-1-63235-015-2(7),* 12-Story Library) Bookstaves, LLC.

Foy, Debbie. Medical Pioneers, 1 vol. 2011. (20th Century Lives Ser.). (ENG.). 32p. (YA). (gr. 5-5). lib. bdg. 30.27 *(978-1-4488-3293-4(4),* 04c6096a-be82-42cf-b07c-1a3345d29a2d) Rosen Publishing Group, Inc., The.

Kjelle, Marylou Morano. Conquering Disease. 2014. 48p. (J). (gr. 4-8). 29.95 *(978-1-61228-576-4(7))* Mitchell Lane Pubs.

Rodger, Ellen. Top Secret Science in Medicine. 2019. (Top Secret Science Ser.). 48p. (J). (gr. 5-5). *(978-0-7787-5994-2(6));* pap. *(978-0-7787-6032-0(4))* Crabtree Publishing Co.

MEDICINE—UNITED STATES

Engdahl, Sylvia, ed. Medical Rights, 1 vol. 2008. (Issues on Trial Ser.). (ENG., Illus.). 216p. (gr. 10-12). 49.93 *(978-0-7377-4179-7(1),* f02a9bda-62cb-452b-b2de-a82caedd68f1, Greenhaven Publishing) Greenhaven Publishing LLC.

Hantula, Richard. Jonas Salk, 1 vol. 2004. (Trailblazers of the Modern World Ser.). (ENG., Illus.). 48p. (J). (gr. 5-8). lib. bdg. 33.67 *(978-0-8368-5100-7(5),* 91b76e1b-e792-41ca-b702-2c41f73c8f78, Gareth Stevens Secondary Library) Stevens, Gareth Publishing LLLP.

Heing, Bridey, ed. Critical Perspectives on Health Care, 1 vol. 2019. (Analyzing the Issues Ser.). (ENG.). 232p. (gr. 8-8). 50.93 *(978-1-9785-0329-8(6),* cc4f549e-0cf5-4a1b-95e9-5a971f065d41) Enslow Publishing, LLC.

Jd, Duchess Harris & Morris, Rebecca. The Health-Care Divide. 2018. (Class in America Ser.). (ENG.). 112p. (J). (gr. 6-12). lib. bdg. 41.36 *(978-1-5321-1409-0(5),* 28800, Essential Library) ABDO Publishing Co.

McCoy, Erin L. & Naden, Corinne J. Health Care: Universal Right or Personal Responsibility?, 1 vol. 2018. (Today's Debates Ser.). (ENG.). 144p. (gr. 7-7). pap. 22.16 *(978-1-5026-4325-4(1),* 78bb0843-759e-4d9c-9715-9c675e489ff4) Cavendish Square Publishing LLC.

Naden, Corinne. Health Care: A Right or a Privilege?, 1 vol. 2010. (Controversy! Ser.). (ENG.). 112p. (YA). (gr. 8-8). lib. bdg. 39.79 *(978-0-7614-4231-8(6),* 06f66eaa-083c-4a7d-832b-a3b37b4a2810) Cavendish Square Publishing LLC.

Pearl, Melissa Sherman & Sherman, David A. Jessie Rees Foundation: Charities Started by Kids! 2017. (Community Connections: How Do They Help? Ser.). (ENG., Illus.). 24p. (J). (gr. 2-5). lib. bdg. 29.21 *(978-1-63472-844-7(0),* 209802) Cherry Lake Publishing.

Porterfield, Jason. The Law & Personal Health: Your Legal Rights, 1 vol. 2015. (Know Your Rights Ser.). (ENG., Illus.). 64p. (J). (gr. 6-6). 36.47 *(978-1-4777-8052-7(1),* c4b4093c-59bd-43e1-a4e3-dbd7eed76cf0, Rosen Young Adult) Rosen Publishing Group, Inc., The.

Raum, Elizabeth. The Cold, Hard Facts about Science & Medicine in Colonial America. 2011. (Life in the American Colonies Ser.). (ENG.). 32p. (J). (gr. 3-4). pap. 48.60 *(978-1-4296-7216-0(1),* 16775, Capstone Pr.); pap. 8.10 *(978-1-4296-7215-3(3),* 116825) Capstone.

Schroeder-Lein, Glenna R. The Encyclopedia of Civil War Medicine. 2008. (ENG., Illus.). 457p. (C). 180.00 *(978-0-7656-1171-0(6),* Y184328) Routledge.

MEDICINE, VETERINARY

see Veterinary Medicine

MEDICINE—VOCATIONAL GUIDANCE

Asher, Dana. Epidemiologists: Life Tracking Deadly Diseases, 1 vol. 2003. (Extreme Careers Ser.). (ENG., Illus.). 64p. (YA). (gr. 5-5). 37.13 *(978-0-8239-3633-5(3),* c5e41a90-a61a-4b77-83c3-6467f633a8d2) Rosen Publishing Group, Inc., The.

Bell, Samantha. Sports Medicine Doctor. 2015. (21st Century Skills Library: Cool STEAM Careers Ser.). (ENG., Illus.). 32p. (J). (gr. 4-7). pap. 14.21 *(978-1-63362-654-6(7),* 206441) Cherry Lake Publishing.

Benedict, Aaron & Gallaher, David. Using Computer Science in High-Tech Health & Wellness Careers, 1 vol. 2017. (Coding Your Passion Ser.). (ENG., Illus.). 80p. (J). (gr. 7-7). 37.47 *(978-1-5081-7515-5(2),* 3a7847a0-376b-4eaa-b949-40a275cf571c, Rosen Young Adult) Rosen Publishing Group, Inc., The.

Boyd, Nicole. A Doctor's Busy Day. 2009. (Reading Room Collection 2 Ser.). 24p. (gr. 3-4). 42.50 *(978-1-60851-952-1(X),* PowerKids Pr.) Rosen Publishing Group, Inc., The.

Bruno, Nikki. Gross Jobs in Medicine: 4D an Augmented Reading Experience. 2019. (Gross Jobs 4D Ser.). (ENG., Illus.). 32p. (J). (gr. 3-9). lib. bdg. 31.99 *(978-1-5435-5491-5(1),* 139362, Capstone Pr.) Capstone.

Careers in Focus: Geriatric Care. 3rd rev. ed. 2010. (ENG.). 208p. (gr. 6-12). 32.95 *(978-0-8160-8025-0(9),* P189784, Ferguson Publishing Company) Infobase Holdings, Inc.

Christy, Lee Louis. I Go to Work as a Doctor. 2003. (I Go to Work As Ser.). (Illus.). (J). *(978-1-58417-042-6(5));* pap. *(978-1-58417-107-2(3))* Lake Street Pubs.

Coan, Sharon. STEM Careers: Metamorphosis of Medicine. 2017. (Time for Kids Nonfiction Readers Ser.). lib. bdg. 20.85 *(978-0-606-40281-1(0))* Turtleback.

Colby, Jennifer. Hospital. 2016. (21st Century Junior Library: Explore a Workplace Ser.). (ENG., Illus.). 24p. (J). (gr. 2-5). 29.21 *(978-1-63471-074-9(6),* 208375) Cherry Lake Publishing.

Currie-McGhee, L. K. Careers in Medicine. 2017. (ENG.). 80p. (J). (gr. 5-12). *(978-1-68282-200-5(1))* ReferencePoint Pr., Inc.

Ferguson, ed. Therapists. 2nd rev. ed. 2008. (Ferguson's Careers in Focus Ser.). (ENG.). 202p. (gr. 6-12). 32.95 *(978-0-8160-7286-6(8),* P179090, Ferguson Publishing Company) Infobase Holdings, Inc.

Gitlin, Martin. Careers in Nanomedicine. 2018. (Bright Futures Press: Emerging Tech Careers Ser.). (ENG., Illus.). 32p. (J). (gr. 4-7). lib. bdg. 32.07 *(978-1-5341-2975-7(8),* 211944) Cherry Lake Publishing.

Greek, Joe. Working with Tech in Health Care, 1 vol. 2020. (Technology in the Workplace Ser.). (ENG.). 80p. (gr. 7-7). pap. 16.30 *(978-1-7253-4161-6(1),* fe334155-0e28-4314-ba84-039e8c4ba7bd) Rosen Publishing Group, Inc., The.

Henneberg, Susan. The Vo-Tech Track to Success in Health Care, 1 vol. 2014. (Learning a Trade, Preparing for a Career Ser.). (ENG., Illus.). 80p. (J). (gr. 6-6). 37.47 *(978-1-4777-7730-5(X),* b21a47c6-4e97-4e44-bb4b-905c8f701181) Rosen Publishing Group, Inc., The.

Honders, Christine. What's It Really Like to Be a Doctor?, 1 vol. 2019. (Jobs Kids Want Ser.). (ENG.). 24p. (gr. 1-2). 25.27 *(978-1-5383-4982-3(5),* 06580438-3cda-45e4-b699-68a7197bb10a, PowerKids Pr.) Rosen Publishing Group, Inc., The.

Hubbard, Rita L. What Degree Do I Need to Pursue a Career in Health Care?, 1 vol. 2014. (Right Degree for Me Ser.). (ENG., Illus.). 80p. (J). (gr. 7-7). 37.80 *(978-1-4777-7869-2(1),* 274a68df-56c7-4b7a-91c6-4496be63ef2e, Rosen Young Adult) Rosen Publishing Group, Inc., The.

Huddleston, Emma. Work in the Health Care Industry. 2019. (Career Finder Ser.). (ENG.). 80p. (YA). (gr. 6-12). 41.27 *(978-1-68282-727-7(5),* BrightPoint Pr.) ReferencePoint Pr., Inc.

Lewis, Daniel. Health Care & Science, Vol. 10. 2018. (Careers in Demand for High School Graduates Ser.). 112p. (J). (gr. 7). 34.60 *(978-1-4222-4137-0(8))* Mason Crest.

Mattern, Joanne. Tecnicos en Emergencias Medicas, 1 vol. 2003. (Trabajo en Grupo (Working Together) Ser.). (SPA., Illus.). 24p. (J). (gr. 1-2). lib. bdg. 26.27 *(978-0-8239-6839-8(1),* 7f033b28-49b6-453c-b612-892a78629fd0) Rosen Publishing Group, Inc., The.

McAlpine, Margaret. Working in Health Care, 1 vol. 2005. (My Future Career Ser.). (ENG., Illus.). 64p. (gr. 4-6). lib. bdg. 29.67 *(978-0-8368-4238-8(3),* f6fc512f-091f-4942-a0f0-8d77612865c0, Gareth Stevens Learning Library) Stevens, Gareth Publishing LLLP.

Reeves, Diane Lindsey. Career Ideas for Teens in Health Science. 2006. (Career Ideas for Teens Ser.). (Illus.). 192p. (gr. 8-12). per. 16.95 *(978-0-8160-6920-0(4),* Checkmark Bks.) Infobase Holdings, Inc.

Shaw, Jessica. Working in Health Services in Your Community, 1 vol. 2018. (Careers in Your Community Ser.). (ENG.). 80p. (gr. 7-7). 37.47 *(978-1-4994-6730-7(3),* 1d4e69f1-b97f-44a2-aabf-9b1dfb293666, Rosen Young Adult) Rosen Publishing Group, Inc., The.

Sheen, Barbara. Great Jobs in Health Care. 2019. (Great Jobs Ser.). (ENG.). 80p. (YA). (gr. 6-12). *(978-1-68282-523-5(X))* ReferencePoint Pr., Inc.

Shepherd, Jodie. A Day with Doctors. 2012. (ENG., Illus.). 32p. (J). lib. bdg. 23.00 *(978-0-531-28950-1(8))* Scholastic Library Publishing.

Silverstone, Michael. Paramedics to the Rescue: When Every Second Counts. 2004. (High Five Reading - Purple Ser.). (ENG., Illus.). 64p. (gr. 3-4). per. 9.00 *(978-0-7368-3849-8(X))* Capstone.

Wilcox, Christine. Health Care Careers. 2018. (STEM Careers Ser.). (ENG.). 80p. (YA). (gr. 6-12). 39.93 *(978-1-68282-433-7(0))* ReferencePoint Pr., Inc.

MEDIEVAL ART

see Art, Medieval

MEDIEVAL CIVILIZATION

see Civilization, Medieval

MEDITATION

Abato, Andrew. Alphabet Mandalas - Beautiful Letter-Based Mandalas for Colouring in, Learning & Meditation. 2010. 56p. pap. 14.90 *(978-3-8391-4871-6(5))* Bks. on Demand.

—Car Mandalas - Beautiful Mandalas Featuring Cars for Colouring In. 2010. 52p. pap. 15.50 *(978-3-8391-3390-3(4))* Bks. on Demand.

—Celtic Mandalas - Beautiful Mandalas & Patterns for Colouring in, Relaxation & Meditation. 2010. 52p. pap. 15.50 *(978-3-8391-3799-4(3))* Bks. on Demand.

—Christmas Mandalas - Beautiful Christmas Mandalas for Colouring In. 2010. 52p. pap. 15.50 *(978-3-8391-4000-0(5))* Bks. on Demand.

—Decorative Mandalas - Beautiful Mandalas & Patterns for Colouring in, Relaxation & Meditation. 2010. 52p. pap. 15.50 *(978-3-8391-4019-2(6))* Bks. on Demand.

—Fantasy Mandalas - Beautiful Mandalas & Ornamentation for Colouring in, Relaxation & Meditation. 2010. 54p. pap. 15.50 *(978-3-8391-4075-8(7))* Bks. on Demand.

Andrews, Linda Wasmer. Meditation. 2004. (Life Balance Ser.). (ENG.). 80p. (YA). (gr. 5-8). pap. 6.95 *(978-0-531-16609-3(0));* (J). 20.50 *(978-0-531-12219-8(0))* Scholastic Library Publishing. (Watts, Franklin).

Atlantic Publishing Group Inc. Atlantic Publishing Group Inc. The Young Adult's Guide to Meditation: Easy Techniques That Reduce Stress & Relieve Anger, Anxiety & Depression. 2016. (ENG.). (YA). lib. bdg. 34.95 *(978-1-62023-334-4(7))* Atlantic Publishing Group, Inc.

Basile, Fiona. Shhh... God Is in the Silence. 2018. (ENG., Illus.). 26p. (J). pap. 8.99 *(978-0-8294-4657-9(5))* Loyola Pr.

—Shhh... God Is in the Silence (Bilingual Edition) 2018. (ENG., Illus.). 26p. (J). pap. 8.95 *(978-0-8294-4696-8(6))* Loyola Pr.

Champeaux-Cunin, Marie-Christine & Butet, Dominique. The Magic of Meditation: Stories & Practices to Develop Gratitude & Empathy with Your Child. 2018. (Illus.). 120p. (gr. -1-2). pap. 16.95 *(978-1-61180-529-1(5))* Shambhala Pubns., Inc.

Chopra, Mallika. Just Breathe: Meditation, Mindfulness, Movement, & More. Vaughan, Brenna, illus. 2018. (Just Be Ser.). (ENG.). 128p. (J). (gr. 3-7). pap. 12.99 *(978-0-7624-9158-2(2),* Running Pr. Kids) Running Pr.

Duch, Mamen. Relaxations: Big Tools for Little Warriors. Nieto Guridi, Raúl, illus. 2018. 40p. (J). *(978-1-4338-2904-8(5),* Magination Pr.) American Psychological Assn.

Dupeyrat, Laurent & Bernard, Johanne. Meditation for Kids: How to Clear Your Head & Calm Your Mind. Gilles, Alice, illus. 2019. 96p. (J). (gr. 2-5). pap. 16.95 *(978-1-61180-620-5(8),* Bala Kids) Shambhala Pubns., Inc.

Freeman, Laurence. A Simple Way: The Path of Christian Meditation. 2004. 43p. (YA). pap. 9.95 *(978-0-9725627-6-8(1))* Medio Media Publishing.

Gates, Mariam. Meditate with Me: A Step-By-Step Mindfulness Journey. Sumaite, Margarita, illus. 2017. 40p. (J). (gr. -1-3). 18.99 *(978-0-399-18661-5(1),* Dial Bks) Penguin Young Readers Group.

Gyatso, Geshe Kelsang. What Is Meditation? Buddhism for Children Level 4. 2013. (ENG., Illus.). 32p. (J). (gr. 4-7). 8.95 *(978-1-61606-024-4(7),* 6a2581ca-621e-48ae-8e6d-0e67b3a7245a) Tharpa Pubns. USA.

Kanjuro, Carolyn. Sit with Me: Meditation for Kids in Seven Easy Steps. Lawson, Nan, illus. 2020. 32p. (J). (gr. -1-3). 17.95 *(978-1-61180-747-9(6),* Bala Kids) Shambhala Pubns., Inc.

Katz, Susan B. Meditation Station. Semirdzhyan, Anait, illus. 2020. 32p. (J). (gr. -1-3). 16.95 *(978-1-61180-791-2(3),* Bala Kids) Shambhala Pubns., Inc.

Langford, Anne. Meditation for Little People. Bethards, David, illus. 2003. 40p. (gr. k-4). reprint ed. 8.95 *(978-0-87516-211-9(8),* Devorss Pubns.) DeVorss & Co.

Levitt, Tamara. The Secret to Clara's Calm. Bondy, Jeremy, illus. 2017. (ENG.). 36p. (J). 17.95 *(978-1-61429-390-3(2))* Wisdom Pubns.

Mingyur Rinpoche, Yongey & Hayden, Torey. Ziji & the Very Scary Man. 2018. (ENG., Illus.). 50p. (J). (gr. 1-4). 16.95 *(978-1-61429-473-3(9))* Wisdom Pubns.

Mingyur, Yongey & Hayden, Torey. Ziji: The Puppy Who Learned to Meditate. Larrison, Charity, illus. 2017. (ENG.). 56p. (J). 16.95 *(978-1-61429-471-9(2))* Wisdom Pubns.

Moore, Andrew. Meditation. 2009. (Teen Mental Health Ser.). 48p. (gr. 5-6). 53.00 *(978-1-60853-296-4(8))* Rosen Publishing Group, Inc., The.

Pasricha, Neil. Awesome Is Everywhere. (ENG., Illus.). (J). (—1). 2018. 28p. bds. 7.99 *(978-0-14-319354-8(6))* 2015. 32p. 17.99 *(978-0-670-06933-0(7))* PRH Canada Young Readers CAN. (Puffin Canada). Dist: Penguin Random Hse. LLC.

Sainte Croix, Judith. Everything You Need to Know about Meditation. 2009. (Need to Know Library). 64p. (gr. 5-5). 58.50 *(978-1-60854-076-1(6))* Rosen Publishing Group, Inc., The.

Selby, John. Meditation the Cool Way to Calm: Solve Your Problems, Find Peace of Mind, & Discover the Real You. 2004. (ENG.). 1p. pap. 10.95 *(978-0-8048-3486-5(5))* Tuttle Publishing.

Simhananda, B. Jyoti for Kids: A Meditative Technique of Purification by the Light. 2011. (ENG., Illus.). 34p. (J). *(978-0-9809694-6-7(8),* 9780980969467) Orange Palm & Magnificent Magus Pubns., Inc.

Singh, Rajinder. Jyoti Meditation for Children. Schulbaum, Michael, illus. 2011. 24p. (J). (gr. -1-3). 10.00 *(978-0-918224-81-1(0))* Radiance Pubs.

Stewart, Whitney. Meditation Is an Open Sky: Mindfulness for Kids. Rippin, Sally, illus. 2015. (ENG.). 32p. (J). (gr. -1-3). 12.99 *(978-0-8075-4908-7(8),* 807549088) Whitman, Albert & Co.

—Mindful Me: Mindfulness & Meditation for Kids. Peterson, Stacy, illus. 2018. (ENG.). 160p. (J). (gr. 3-7). 16.99 *(978-0-8075-5144-8(9),* 807551449) Whitman, Albert & Co.

—Mindfulness & Meditation: Handling Life with a Calm & Focused Mind. 2019. (ENG., Illus.). 120p. (YA). (gr. 6-12). 37.32 *(978-1-5415-4021-7(2),* 9d53310f-ea44-4a6e-83f7-2961544b1745, Twenty-First Century Bks.) Lerner Publishing Group.

Viegas, Marneta. The Magic Box. 2015. (ENG., Illus.). 124p. (J). (gr. k-7). pap. 14.95 *(978-1-78279-187-4(6),* Our Street Bks.) Hunt, John Publishing Ltd. GBR. Dist: National Bk. Network.

—Relax Kids - Aladdin's Magic Carpet: Let Snow White, the Wizard of Oz & Other Fairytale Characters Show You & Your Child How to Meditate & Relax. 2015. (ENG., Illus.). 120p. (J). (gr. -1-12). pap. 14.95 *(978-1-78279-869-9(2),* Our Street Bks.) Hunt, John Publishing Ltd. GBR. Dist: National Bk. Network.

MEDITATIONS

Ayer, Jane E. Guided Meditations for Junior High: Good Judgment, Gifts, Obedience, Inner Blindness. 2003. (Quiet Place Apart Ser.). 48p. pap., tchr. ed. 9.95 *(978-0-88489-500-8(9))* Saint Mary's Press of Minnesota.

Berg, Yehuda. The 72 Names of God for Kids: A Treasury of Timeless Wisdom. 2006. (ENG., Illus.). 192p. (gr. 1-7). *(978-1-57189-543-1(4))* Klein, Richard A. scaneg Verlag.

Brost, Corey. Gospel Connections for Teens: Reflections for Sunday Mass, Cycle C. 2006. (ENG.). 132p. (YA). (gr. 8-12). per. 8.25 *(978-0-88489-641-8(2))* Saint Mary's Press of Minnesota.

Brown, Monica & Musgrave, Hilary. Be Still & know... God Is Here: Be Still. 2011. (J). pap. *(978-0-9750732-8-5(1))* Emmaus Productions.

Frazier, April. 3-Minute Devotions for Teen Girls: 180 Encouraging Readings. 2015. (3-Minute Devotions Ser.). (ENG.). 192p. pap. 5.99 *(978-1-63058-856-4(3),* Barbour Bks.) Barbour Publishing, Inc.

M N O

Friedmann, Frank. I Was Wrong, but God Made Me Right. Date not set. (Illus.). 28p. (J). (gr. k-3). pap. 4.95 *(978-0-9659319-0-8(0))* Living in Grace.

Hamilton, Amy. Indigo Dreaming: Meditations for Children. 2006. (Illus.). 141p. per. *(978-0-9757953-7-8(6))* Joshua Bks.

Hascall, Glenn. 3-Minute Devotions for Guys: 180 Encouraging Readings for Teens. 2015. (3-Minute Devotions Ser.). (ENG.). 192p. pap. 5.99 *(978-1-63058-857-1(1),* Barbour Bks.) Barbour Publishing, Inc.

Henry, Deborah, ed. My Devotions: Fifty Years. 50th anniv. ed. 2008. 368p. (J). 12.99 *(978-0-7586-1593-0(0))* Concordia Publishing Hse.

Hodgson, Joan. Our Father. Ripper, Peter, illus. 2003. 24p. (gr. k-7). 5.95 *(978-0-85487-040-0(7))* White Eagle Publishing Trust GBR. Dist: DeVorss & Co.

Paynter, Roxanne. Small Souls: Meditations for Children. 2004. 86p. (Orig.). (J). pap. *(978-0-9581891-0-1(2),* 305-004) Joshua Bks.

Reehorst, Jane. Guided Meditations for Children. 2015. 312p. pap. 38.00 *(978-1-4982-3293-7(0),* Wipf and Stock) Wipf & Stock Pubs.

Sister Susan, Sister. Each Breath a Smile. Thi Hop, Nguyen, illus. 2005. 32p. (J). (gr. -1-2). pap. 10.95 *(978-1-888375-22-0(1),* Plum Blossom Bks.) Parallax Pr.

Viegas, Mameta. Relax Kids: Little Book of Stars. 2015. (ENG., Illus.). 126p. (J). (gr. -1-12). pap. 14.95 *(978-1-78279-460-8(3),* Our Street Bks.) Hunt, John Publishing Ltd. GBR. Dist: National Bk. Network.

—Relax Kids: The Wishing Star. 2015. (ENG., Illus.). 128p. (J). (gr. -1-12). pap. 14.95 *(978-1-78279-870-5(6),* Our Street Bks.) Hunt, John Publishing Ltd. GBR. Dist: National Bk. Network.

Ytreeide, Arnold. Tabitha's Travels: A Family Story for Advent. 1 vol. 2010. (Illus.). 160p. (J). (gr. 7-18). pap. 16.99 *(978-0-8254-4172-1(2))* Kregel Pubns.

MEDITERRANEAN REGION

Behnke, Alison, et al. Cooking the Mediterranean Way. 2nd rev. ed. 2005. (Easy Menu Ethnic Cookbooks 2nd Edition Ser.). (ENG., Illus.). 72p. (gr. 5-12). 25.26 *(978-0-8225-1237-0(8),* Lerner Pubns.) Lerner Publishing Group.

Collier, Paul H. & O'Neill, Robert John. World War II: The Mediterranean 1940-1945. 1 vol. 2010. (World War II: Essential Histories Ser.). (ENG., Illus.). 96p. (YA). (gr. 10-10). lib. bdg. 38.47 *(978-1-4358-9132-6(5),* 1b1b7b2b-a34e-4801-8751-2f315236ed09) Rosen Publishing Group, Inc., The.

Greeley, August. Writing in Ancient Phoenicia. 2009. (Writing in the Ancient World Ser.). 24p. (gr. 3-3). 42.50 *(978-1-60854-908-5(9),* PowerKids Pr.) Rosen Publishing Group, Inc., The.

Green, Jen. Mediterranean Sea. 1 vol. 2005. (Oceans & Seas Ser.). (ENG., Illus.). 48p. (gr. 5-8). pap. 15.05 *(978-0-8368-6282-9(1),* 302df165-48d8-4f8f-8bb5-ea142071e5ad); lib. bdg. 33.67 *(978-0-8368-6274-4(0),* a0267d04-8e8b-464d-abe2-6e2c6c8d29ff) Stevens, Gareth Publishing LLLP. (Gareth Stevens Secondary Library).

Heing, Bridey. Phoenician Trade Routes. 1 vol. 2017. (Routes of Cross-Cultural Exchange Ser.). (ENG., Illus.). 96p. (YA). (gr. 8-8). 44.50 *(978-1-5026-2861-9(9),* 264ba440-d2ad-455c-b0fe-046afd9c221f) Cavendish Square Publishing LLC.

Jeffrey, Gary. North Africa & the Mediterranean. 2012. (ENG., Illus.). 48p. (J). *(978-0-7787-4193-0(1));* pap. *(978-0-7787-4200-5(8))* Crabtree Publishing Co.

Micklos, John & Micklos, John, Jr. Mediterranean Trade Routes. 1 vol. 2017. (Routes of Cross-Cultural Exchange Ser.). (ENG.). 96p. (J). (gr. 8-8). 44.50 *(978-1-5026-2693-6(4),* b5b3af70-611e-4d59-b26d-98dcb1770925) Cavendish Square Publishing LLC.

Stefoff, Rebecca. The Ancient Mediterranean World. 1 vol. 2006. (World Historical Atlases Ser.). (ENG., Illus.). 48p. (gr. 5-5). 34.07 *(978-0-7614-1641-8(2),* d7349a5a-a511-4315-955c-1c8ae0a3879e) Cavendish Square Publishing LLC.

—Redbeard. 2015. (J). lib. bdg. *(978-1-62713-533-7(2))* 2014. (ENG.). 48p. (gr. 4-4). 33.07 *(978-1-5026-0199-5(0),* e4b135dd-9834-4a92-bf28-59f105626332) Cavendish Square Publishing LLC.

Weintraub, Aileen. The Barbarossa Brothers: 16th-Century Pirates of the Barbary Coast. 2009. (Library of Pirates Ser.). 24p. (gr. 3-3). 42.50 *(978-1-60853-814-0(1),* PowerKids Pr.) Rosen Publishing Group, Inc., The.

MEDITERRANEAN REGION—FICTION

Fox, Robin C. & Fox, Carol White. The Traveling Adventures of the Robin & the Fox Around the World We Go! A Cruise Through the Mediterranean. 2013. 44p. pap. 20.45 *(978-1-4908-1763-7(8),* WestBow Pr.) Author Solutions, LLC.

Friesner, Esther. Nobody's Princess. 2008. (Princesses of Myth Ser.). (ENG., Illus.). 336p. (YA). (gr. 7-11). pap. 8.99 *(978-0-375-87529-8(8),* Ember) Random Hse. Children's Bks.

Greder, Armin. The Mediterranean. 2018. (ENG., Illus.). 40p. (J). (gr. 3). 25.99 *(978-1-76063-095-9(0))* Allen & Unwin AUS. Dist: Independent Pubs. Group.

Harrison, Francesca. Obus the Eucalyptus Tree Fairy. 2012. 26p. pap. *(978-1-909381-03-2(9))* Foote, Douglas.

Le Clézio, J. M. G. Lullaby. Lemoine, Georges, illus. 2007. (FRE.). 72p. (J). (gr. 5-10). pap. *(978-2-07-061258-1(9))* Gallimard, Editions.

Matthews, Andrew. Shakespeare Stories: The Tempest. Ross, Tony, illus. 2003. (ENG.). 64p. (J). (gr. 4-6). pap. 6.99 *(978-1-84121-346-0(2),* Orchard Bks.) Hachette Children's Group GBR. Dist: Hachette Bk. Group.

Moskowitz, Hannah. Salt. (Middle Grade Novel, Kids Adventure Story, Kids Book about Family) 2018. (ENG.). 268p. (YA). (gr. 7-12). 17.99 *(978-1-4521-3151-1(1))* Chronicle Bks. LLC.

Paver, Michelle. Gods & Warriors. 2013. (Gods & Warriors Ser.: 1). (ENG.). 336p. (J). (gr. 5). pap. 8.99 *(978-0-14-242284-7(3),* Puffin Books) Penguin Young Readers Group.

Saunders, Harry M. Teenagers on an Adventure: Journey of Two Boys & a Girl. 2013. 168p. pap. 19.95 *(978-1-62709-466-5(0))* America Star Bks.

MEDUSAE

Nagle, Frances. Medusa. 1 vol. 2016. (Monsters! Ser.). (ENG., Illus.). 32p. (J). (gr. 1-2). pap. 11.50 *(978-1-4824-4867-2(X),* fd05e48a-b793-4966-aa5e-ca2e81e3df8a) Stevens, Gareth Publishing LLLP.

MEIR, GOLDA, 1898-1978

Aboff, Marcie. Golda Meir Iron Lady of Israel. 2016. (Spring Forward Ser.). (J). (gr. 2). *(978-1-4900-9454-0(7))* Benchmark Education Co.

Blashfield, Jean F. Golda Meir. 1 vol. 2011. (Leading Women Ser.). (ENG.). 96p. (YA). (gr. 7-7). 42.64 *(978-0-7614-4960-7(4),* c65113b7-d6a4-4fbf-a51d-859173c00522) Cavendish Square Publishing LLC.

Krasner, Barbara. Goldie Takes a Stand!: Golda Meir's First Crusade. Garrity-Riley, Kelsey, illus. 2014. (ENG.). 32p. (J). (gr. k-4). 17.95 *(978-1-4677-1200-2(0))* Lerner Publishing Group.

—Goldie Takes a Stand: Golda Meir's First Crusade. Garrity-Riley, Kelsey, illus. 2014. (ENG.). 32p. (J). (gr. k-4). 7.95 *(978-1-4677-1201-9(9),* c426fcc0-d82b-4759-a9b0-3ae07363554b, Kar-Ben Publishing) Lerner Publishing Group.

World Book, Inc. Staff, contrib. by. Golda Meir: With Profiles of David Ben-Gurion & Yitzhak Rabin. 2006. (Biographical Connections Ser.). (Illus.). 112p. (J). *(978-0-7166-1829-4(X))* World Bk., Inc.

MEITNER, LISE, 1878-1968

Barron, Rachel Stiffler. Lise Meitner: Discoverer of Nuclear Fission. 2004. (Profiles in Science Ser.). (Illus.). 112p. (YA). (gr. 6-12). lib. bdg. 23.95 *(978-1-883846-52-7(8),* First Biographies) Reynolds, Morgan Inc.

Spiller, Sara. Lise Meitner. Bane, Jeff, illus. 2018. (My Early Library: My Itty-Bitty Bio Ser.). (ENG.). 24p. (J). (gr. k-1). lib. bdg. 30.64 *(978-1-5341-2883-5(2),* 211576) Cherry Lake Publishing.

Venezia, Mike. Getting to Know the World's Greatest Inventors & Scientists: Lise Meitner. Venezia, Mike, illus. 2010. (Getting to Know the World's Greatest Inventors & Scientists Ser.). (ENG., Illus.). 32p. (J). (gr. 3-4). pap. 6.95 *(978-0-531-20776-5(5),* Children's Pr.) Scholastic Library Publishing.

MELVILLE, HERMAN, 1819-1891

Faiella, Graham. Moby Dick & the Whaling Industry of the 19th Century. 2009. (Looking at Literature Through Primary Sources Ser.). 64p. (gr. 5-8). 58.50 *(978-1-61514-305-4(X))* Rosen Publishing Group, Inc., The.

Gibson, Karen Bush. Herman Melville. 2006. (J). lib. bdg. *(978-1-58415-453-2(5))* Mitchell Lane Pubs.

Meltzer, Milton. Herman Melville: A Biography. 2005. (Literary Greats Ser.). (ENG., Illus.). 128p. (gr. 7-12). 33.26 *(978-0-7613-2749-3(5),* Twenty-First Century Bks.) Lerner Publishing Group.

MEMOIRS

see Autobiographies; Biography

MEMORY

Berry, Joy. Help Me Be Good about Being Forgetful. 2009. (Help Me Be Good Ser.). 32p. pap. 7.95 *(978-1-60577-102-1(3))* Berry, Joy Enterprises.

Berry, Joy Wilt. A Book about Being Forgetful. 2005. (Illus.). (J). *(978-0-7172-8589-1(8))* Scholastic, Inc.

Brown Bear Books. Intellectual Development. 2011. (Psychology Ser.). (ENG., Illus.). 112p. (J). (gr. 9-12). lib. bdg. 42.80 *(978-1-936333-18-9(X),* 16776) Brown Bear Bks.

Coirault, Christine, illus. My First Book of Learning. 2009. (J). *(978-1-74089-930-7(X))* Fog City Pr.

Cusimano/Achieve Publications Staff. Achieve Levels I-IV: A Visual Memory Program Levels I-IV. 4 vols., Set. 2003. (ENG.). 412p. tchr. ed., ring bd. 79.95 *(978-0-9727762-0-2(6),* 206) Achieve Pubns.

—Achieve Levels V & VI: A Visual Memory Program Levels V & VI. 2 vols., Set. 2003. 242p. tchr. ed., ring bd. 43.95 *(978-0-9727762-1-9(4))* Achieve Pubns.

Fry, Ron. Surefire Tips to Improve Your Memory Skills. 1 vol., 1. 2015. (Surefire Study Success Ser.). (ENG.). 144p. (YA). (gr. 7-8). 38.80 *(978-1-5081-7089-1(4),* e6a7ce85-aa68-4893-8d97-02a5116b0159, Rosen Young Adult) Rosen Publishing Group, Inc., The.

Hardyman, Robyn. Memory & Your Brain. 1 vol. 2018. (What Goes on Inside Your Brain? Ser.). (ENG.). 48p. (gr. 4-5). pap. 15.05 *(978-1-5382-3563-8(3),* a96b6ebd-8e4b-42d8-86da-fdc6d179fc97) Stevens, Gareth Publishing LLLP.

Martin, Steve. Miss Pell Never Misspells: More Cool Ways to Remember Stuff. Remphry, Martin, illus. 2013. (ENG.). 128p. (J). (gr. 4-7). 12.99 *(978-0-545-49477-9(X),* Scholastic Reference) Scholastic, Inc.

Murphy, Patricia J. Never Eat Soggy Waffles: Fun Mnemonic Memory Tricks. 1 vol. LaBaff, Tom, illus. 2009. (Prime (Elementary) Ser.). (ENG.). 48p. (gr. 3-3). lib. bdg. 27.93 *(978-0-7660-2710-7(4),* 574fd096-94bb-4664-bc48-39ac806bf466) Enslow Publishing, LLC.

O'Brien, Cynthia. Amazing Brain Mysteries. 2015. (Mystery Files Ser.). (ENG., Illus.). 32p. (J). (gr. 4-4). *(978-0-7787-8070-0(8))* Crabtree Publishing Co.

Packiam Alloway, Tracy Packiam. How Can I Remember All That? Simple Stuff to Improve Your Working Memory. O'Connell, David, illus. 2019. 64p. 17.95 *(978-1-78592-633-4(0),* 697019) Kingsley, Jessica Pubs. GBR. Dist: Hachette UK Distribution.

Randol, Susan. I Before e (Except after C): the Young Readers Edition: Easy, Cool Ways to Remember Facts. 2011. (ENG.). 144p. (YA). (gr. 4-6). 9.99 *(978-1-60652-348-3(1))* Reader's Digest Assn., Inc., The.

Weinstein, Jacob Sager & Odd Dot. How to Remember Everything: Tips & Tricks to Become a Memory Master! Malley, Barbara, illus. 2020. (ENG.). 144p. (J). pap. 12.99 *(978-1-250-23526-8(X),* 900210264, Odd Dot) St. Martin's Pr.

Wells, Marcia. Eddie Red Undercover: Mystery on Museum Mile. Calo, Marcos, illus. 2015. (Eddie Red Undercover Ser.). (ENG.). 256p. (J). (gr. 5-7). pap. 7.99 *(978-0-544-43940-5(6),* 1596839, Clarion Bks.) HarperCollins Pubs.

MEN

see also Human Beings

Brooks, Ben. Stories for Boys Who Dare to Be Different: True Tales of Amazing Boys Who Changed the World Without Killing Dragons. Winter, Quinton, illus. 2018. (Dare to Be Different Ser.). (ENG.). 160p. (J). (gr. 3-7). 16.99 *(978-0-7624-6592-7(1),* Running Pr. Kids) Running Pr.

Carlinsky, Dan. Do You Know Your Boyfriend? 2nd ed. 2013. (Do You Know? Ser.: 0). 48p. (YA). (gr. 9-12). pap. 5.99 *(978-1-4022-8539-4(6))* Sourcebooks, Inc.

Chin-Lee, Cynthia. Akira to Zoltan: Twenty-Six Men Who Changed the World. Halsey, Megan & Addy, Sean, illus. 32p. (J). (gr. 3-7). 2008. pap. 7.95 *(978-1-57091-580-2(6))* 2006. lib. bdg. 15.95 *(978-1-57091-579-6(2))* Charlesbridge Publishing, Inc.

Eboch, M. M., ed. Masculinity in the Twenty-First Century. 1 vol. 2018. (Introducing Issues with Opposing Viewpoints Ser.). (ENG.). 120p. (gr. 7-10). 43.63 *(978-1-5345-0361-8(7),* 8fcf224e-b227-4be4-88a2-31553bf2d09e) Greenhaven Publishing LLC.

High Five to the Boys: A Celebration of Ace Australian Men. 2018. 224p. (J). (gr. 2-5). 29.99 *(978-0-14-379178-2(8))* Random Hse. Australia AUS. Dist: Independent Pubs. Group.

Kelly, Bill. Guys' Guides, 6 bks. Incl. You Ought to Know: A Guy's Guide to Sex. (Illus.). 48p. (J). (gr. 5-8). 1999. lib. bdg. 34.47 *(978-0-8239-3084-5(X),* 55304f57-eb72-494c-8f9c-42710374192a); (Illus.). Set lib. bdg. 107.70 o.p. *(978-0-8239-9088-7(5),* GUGUID, Rosen Reference) Rosen Publishing Group, Inc., The.

Krasner, Barbara, ed. Toxic Masculinity. 1 vol. 2019. (Opposing Viewpoints Ser.). (ENG.). 176p. (gr. 10-12). pap. 34.80 *(978-1-5345-0505-6(9),* c224c417-4d90-4f06-96c7-2136defb983b) Greenhaven Publishing LLC.

Kyi, Tanya Lloyd. Canadian Boys Who Rocked the World. 1 vol. Bagley, Tom, illus. 2007. (ENG.). 126p. (J). (gr. 3-2). pap. 12.95 *(978-1-55285-799-1(9),* cdd5bd07-9efa-44a5-b2bd-f3a752998b15) Whitecap Bks., Ltd. CAN. Dist: Firefly Bks., Ltd.

Mccann, Michelle Roehm. Boys Who Rocked the World: Heroes from King Tut to Shaun White. 2012. lib. bdg. 22.10 *(978-0-606-26897-4(9))* Turtleback.

McCarthy, Meghan. Strong Man: The Story of Charles Atlas. 2015. (Illus.). 40p. (J). (gr. k-3). 7.99 *(978-0-553-11354-9(2),* Dragonfly Bks.) Random Hse. Children's Bks.

Morkes, Andrew & McKenna, Amy. Nontraditional Careers for Women & Men: More Than 30 Great Jobs for Women & Men with Apprenticeships Through Phds. 2011. (ENG., Illus.). vii, 280p. (J). pap. 19.95 *(978-0-9745251-9-8(7))* College & Career Pr., LLC.

Roehm McCann, Michelle. Boys Who Rocked the World: Heroes from King Tut to Bruce Lee. Hahn, David, illus. 2012. (ENG.). 256p. (J). (gr. 3-7). pap. 11.99 *(978-1-58270-331-2(0))* Aladdin/Beyond Words.

—Boys Who Rocked the World: Heroes from King Tut to Bruce Lee. Hahn, David, illus. 2012. (ENG.). 256p. (J). (gr. 3-7). 21.99 *(978-1-58270-362-6(0))* Simon & Schuster, Inc.

Shone, Rob. Bigfoot & Other Strange Beasts. 2009. (Graphic Mysteries Ser.). (ENG.). 48p. (YA). (gr. 5-5). 58.50 *(978-1-61512-961-4(8),* Rosen Reference) Rosen Publishing Group, Inc., The.

MENAGERIES—FICTION

MacDonald, George. A Rough Shaking. 2017. (ENG., Illus.). (J). pap. 16.95 *(978-1-374-88365-9(4))* Capital Communications, Inc.

MENDEL, GREGOR, 1822-1884

Bankston, John. Gregor Mendel & the Discovery of the Gene. 2004. (Uncharted, Unexplored, & Unexplained Ser.). (Illus.). 48p. (J). (gr. 4-8). lib. bdg. 29.95 *(978-1-58415-266-8(4))* Mitchell Lane Pubs.

Bardoe, Cheryl. Gregor Mendel: The Friar Who Grew Peas. 2015. (ENG., Illus.). 32p. (J). (gr. k-4). pap. 10.99 *(978-1-4197-1840-3(1),* 591503, Abrams Bks. for Young Readers) Abrams, Inc.

—Gregor Mendel: The Friar Who Grew Peas. Smith, Jos. A., illus. 2006. (ENG.). 40p. (J). (gr. k-4). 21.95 *(978-0-8109-5475-5(3),* Abrams Bks. for Young Readers) Abrams, Inc.

Bortz, Fred. The Laws of Genetics & Gregor Mendel. 1 vol. 2013. (Revolutionary Discoveries of Scientific Pioneers Ser.). (ENG., Illus.). 80p. (J). (gr. 6-6). 38.41 *(978-1-4777-1806-3(0),* 0f692ffb-d9d7-4d54-bcee-2cbec240cc9d) Rosen Publishing Group, Inc., The.

Klare, Roger. Gregor Mendel: Genius of Genetics. 2015. (J). *(978-0-7660-6565-9(0))* Enslow Publishing, LLC.

Leech, Bonnie. Gregor Mendel's Genetic Theory: Understanding & Applying Concepts of Probability. (PowerMath: Advanced Proficiency Plus Ser.). 32p. (gr. 5-5). 2009. 47.90 *(978-1-60851-356-7(4))* 2006. (ENG.). pap. 56.25 *(978-1-4358-3820-8(3),* 56a53214-f6be-45c7-8207-a98dfff3a1d6) Rosen Publishing Group, Inc., The. (PowerKids Pr.).

Leech, Bonnie Coulter. Gregor Mendel's Genetic Theory: Understanding & Applying Concepts of Probability. 1 vol. (Math for the REAL World Ser.). (ENG., Illus.). 32p. (gr. 5-5). 2009. pap. 10.00 *(978-1-4042-6063-4(3),* 896c90f3-be13-4df4-a40a-404ebde7ee3f) 2006. (YA). lib. bdg. 28.93 *(978-1-4042-3355-3(5),* 8204e305-b024-42ed-9c4b-308b9367f93d) Rosen Publishing Group, Inc., The.

Van Gorp, Lynn. Gregor Mendel: Genetics Pioneer. 1 vol. rev. ed. 2007. (Science: Informational Text Ser.). (ENG.). 32p. (J). (gr. 3-6). pap. 12.99 *(978-0-7439-0598-5(9))* Teacher Created Materials, Inc.

Wilmer, George. Gregor Mendel, Vol. 11. 2018. (Scientists & Their Discoveries Ser.). (Illus.). 96p. (J). (gr. 7). lib. bdg. 34.60 *(978-1-4222-4030-4(4))* Mason Crest.

MENDELEYEV, DMITRY IVANOVICH, 1834-1907

Zannos, Susan. Dmitri Mendeleyev & the Periodic Table. 2004. (Uncharted, Unexplored, & Unexplained Ser.). (Illus.). 48p. (J). (gr. 4-8). lib. bdg. 29.95 *(978-1-58415-267-5(2))* Mitchell Lane Pubs.

MENDEL'S LAW

Leech, Bonnie. Gregor Mendel's Genetic Theory: Understanding & Applying Concepts of Probability. 2009. (PowerMath: Advanced Proficiency Plus Ser.). 32p. (gr. 5-5). 47.90 *(978-1-60851-356-7(4),* PowerKids Pr.) Rosen Publishing Group, Inc., The.

MENNONITES

see also Amish

Fleming, Thomas. The King of Prussia & a Peanut Butter Sandwich. 2009. (ENG.). 48p. (J). (gr. 2-4). pap. 6.99 *(978-1-4424-1215-6(1),* Atheneum Bks. for Young Readers) Simon & Schuster Children's Publishing.

Null, David. Introduction to Mennonite Doctrine & Practice. 2004. 90p. 3.25 *(978-0-7399-2316-0(1),* 2356) Rod & Staff Pubs., Inc.

Therrien, Patricia. Amish & Mennonite Cooking. (American Regional Cooking Library). (Illus.). 72p. 2006. (YA). lib. bdg. 19.95 *(978-1-59084-612-4(5))* 2005. (J). lib. bdg. 299.25 *(978-1-59084-609-4(5))* Mason Crest.

MENNONITES—FICTION

Barry, Rick. Gunner's Run: A World War II Novel. 2007. 215p. (YA). (gr. 8-12). per. 8.99 *(978-1-59166-761-2(5))* BJU Pr.

Boll, Darlene. Olive & Her Lost Friend. Hoover, Charity, illus. 2013. 176p. (J). *(978-0-7399-2463-1(X))* Rod & Staff Pubs., Inc.

—Olive & Macy. Hoover, Charity, illus. 2015. (ENG.). 182p. (J). (gr. -1). 9.50 *(978-0-7399-2506-5(7))* Rod & Staff Pubs., Inc.

Brenneman, Lynette Leaman, photos by. Susanna's Surprise: A Day at the Hans Herr House. 2012. (Illus.). 32p. (J). *(978-0-9859737-0-4(6))* Brenneman, Lynette.

Byers, Arlene. Rainbows for Rosa. Halverson, Randal, illus. 2016. (ENG.). 172p. 9.50 *(978-0-7399-2521-8(0))* Rod & Staff Pubs., Inc.

Gerber, Mary Lichty. Mary's Family Stories. Whitehead, Victoria E. & Shirk, Linda, illus. 2015. (ENG.). 124p. (J). (gr. -1). 8.50 *(978-0-7399-2512-6(1))* Rod & Staff Pubs., Inc.

Gugler, Laurel Dee. Catching Forever. 1 vol. 2007. (Lorimer Streetlights Ser.). (ENG.). 104p. (J). (gr. 2-5). 7.95 *(978-1-55028-954-1(3),* 954) James Lorimer & Co. Ltd., Pubs. CAN. Dist: Formac Lorimer Bks. Ltd.

—A Piece of Forever. 1 vol. 2008. (Lorimer Streetlights Ser.). (ENG.). 168p. (J). (gr. 2-4). 8.95 *(978-1-55277-026-9(5),* 026) James Lorimer & Co. Ltd., Pubs. CAN. Dist: Formac Lorimer Bks. Ltd.

Hege, Lynnita. The Little Black Hen. Keyes, Tina Misrasi, illus. 2013. 208p. (J). *(978-0-7399-2465-5(6))* Rod & Staff Pubs., Inc.

Hege, Lynnita Rae. Mother Hen & Her Ten. Myers, Shirley, illus. 2015. (ENG.). 164p. (J). (gr. -1). 13.50 *(978-0-7399-2499-0(0))* Rod & Staff Pubs., Inc.

Horrocks, Anita. Almost Eden. 2006. 288p. (J). (gr. 5-9). pap. 9.95 *(978-0-88776-742-5(7),* Tundra Bks.) Tundra Bks. CAN. Dist: Penguin Random Hse. LLC.

Hurst, Elva. The Pony Cart Adventure. 2014. (Farm Life Ser.). 64p. pap. 6.99 *(978-0-7369-6089-2(9))* Harvest Hse. Pubs.

—Summer on the Farm. 2014. (Farm Life Ser.). 80p. pap. 6.99 *(978-0-7369-6091-5(0))* Harvest Hse. Pubs.

Klassen, Kirsten L. Katelyn's Affection. 2004. (ENG.). 280p. pap. 11.99 *(978-0-8361-9281-0(8))* Herald Pr.

Krahn, Maria. Charity Prays for Rain. Eshbach, Ariel, illus. 2014. 32p. (J). *(978-0-7399-2475-4(3))* Rod & Staff Pubs., Inc.

Kuepfer, Sharon (Durksen) Schnupp. Little Prairie Girl: Are We Rich ... or Poor? 2009. (ENG., Illus.). 115p. pap. 7.95 *(978-1-60126-187-8(X))* Masthof Pr.

Martin, Elaine S. Bowman. The Rooster's Fate: And Other Stories. Hackman, Evelyn, illus. 2014. 184p. (J). *(978-0-7399-2481-5(8))* Rod & Staff Pubs., Inc.

Martin, Joanna F. Betsey's Wishes. 2010. (Illus.). 255p. (J). (gr. 3-6). 9.80 *(978-0-7399-2424-2(9))* Rod & Staff Pubs., Inc.

Martin, Mabel. Days with Mary. Hoover, Charity, illus. 2015. (ENG.). 159p. (J). (gr. -1). 9.25 *(978-0-7399-2515-7(6))* Rod & Staff Pubs., Inc.

Martin, Mary. God Made Nuts. Derstine, Charlene, illus. 2012. 53p. (J). *(978-0-7399-2501-0(6))* Rod & Staff Pubs., Inc.

—Grandma's Goose. Hoover, Charity, illus. 2012. 188p. *(978-0-7399-2452-5(4))* Rod & Staff Pubs., Inc.

Martin, Mildred A. Growing with the Millers. Burkholder, Edith, illus. 2012. 144p. (J). *(978-1-884377-23-5(8))* Green Pastures Pr.

Martin, Rebecca. Blossoms on the Roof. 2015. (Amish Frontier Ser.). (ENG.). 160p. (J). (gr. 2-6). pap. 10.99 *(978-0-7369-6367-1(7),* 6963671) Harvest Hse. Pubs.

—Joanna's Journey. Yoder, Laura & Weaver, Lisa, illus. 2006. 168p. (YA). pap. 9.99 *(978-1-933753-01-0(3))* Carlisle Pr.-Walnut Creek.

Mast, Dorcas R. Andy's Pocketknife. Balhoim, Peter, illus. 2018. (J). pap. *(978-0-7399-2581-2(4))* Rod & Staff Pubs., Inc.

—The Cranberry House. 2015. (ENG.). 249p. (YA). 11.50 *(978-0-7399-2507-2(5))* Rod & Staff Pubs., Inc.

—The Gold Carnival Pitcher. 2017. (ENG., Illus.). 116p. (J). pap. 5.50 *(978-0-7399-2562-1(8))* Rod & Staff Pubs., Inc.

Sawyer, Kim Vogel. Katy's New World. 1 vol., 1. 2010. (Katy Lambright Ser.: No. 1). (ENG.). 208p. (YA). (gr. 9-12). pap. 9.99 *(978-0-310-71924-3(0))* Zondervan.

Seyfert, Ella Maie. Amish Moving Day. Jones, Henrietta, illus. 2011. 132p. 40.95 *(978-1-258-01315-8(0))* Literary Licensing, LLC.

Smith, Eunice Geil. Treasure Hunt. 2006. 119p. (J). (gr. 3-7). per. 9.99 *(978-0-8361-9332-9(6))* Herald Pr.

Snider, Cindy Gay. Finding Anna Bee. Chambers, Mary, illus. 2007. 163p. (J). (gr. 3-7). per. 9.99 *(978-0-8361-9392-3(X))* Herald Pr.

Stoltzfus, Donna J. Captive. 1 vol. 2018. (ENG.). 128p. (gr. 3-6). 12.99 *(978-0-7643-5551-6(1),* 9859) Schiffer Publishing, Ltd.

Trottier, Maxine. Migrant. 1 vol. Arsenault, Isabelle, illus. 2011. (ENG.). 40p. (J). (gr. -1-2). 18.95 *(978-0-88899-975-7(5))* Groundwood Bks. CAN. Dist: Publishers Group West (PGW).

Weaver, Anna E. Stories From Grandma's Day. 2011. (Illus.). 285p. (YA). (gr. 4-9). pap. 8.90 *(978-0-7399-2426-6(5))* Rod & Staff Pubs., Inc.

MENSTRUATION

Bonnice, Sherry. Premenstrual Disorders. McDonnell, Mary Ann & Esherick, Donald, eds. 2013. (State of Mental Illness & Its Therapy Ser.: 19). 128p. (J). (gr. 7-18). 24.95 *(978-1-4222-2833-3(9))* Mason Crest.

Byers, Ann. Menstruation. 2009. (Girls' Health Ser.). 48p. (gr. 5-6). 53.00 *(978-1-61512-730-6(5)*, Rosen Reference) Rosen Publishing Group, Inc., The.

Feinmann, Jane. Everything a Girl Needs to Know about Her PeriodS. 2003. (Illus.). 144p. pap. 14.95 *(978-1-56906-555-6(1)*, BTM-555) Sellers Publishing, Inc.

Morais, Joan. A Time to Celebrate: A Celebration of a Girl's First Menstrual Period. 2004. (Illus.). 112p. (YA). per. 16.95 *(978-0-9746304-5-8(4)*, 1196060) Lua Publishing.

Movsessian, Shushann. Puberty Girl. 2005. (ENG., Illus.). 128p. (J). (gr. 4-7). pap. 19.95 *(978-1-74114-104-7(4))* Allen & Unwin AUS. Dist: Independent Pubs. Group.

Okamoto, Nadya. Period Power: A Manifesto for the Menstrual Movement. Elfast, Rebecca, illus. 2018. (ENG.). 368p. (YA). (gr. 7). 19.99 *(978-1-5344-3021-1(0))*; pap. 12.99 *(978-1-5344-3020-4(2))* Simon & Schuster Bks. For Young Readers. (Simon & Schuster Bks. For Young Readers).

Orr, Tamra. Amenorrhea: Why Your Period Stops. 2009. (Library of Sexual Health Ser.). 64p. (gr. 6-6). 58.50 *(978-1-60853-838-6(9))* Rosen Publishing Group, Inc., The.

Parker, Victoria. Little Book of Growing Up. 2007. (ENG., Illus.). 128p. (J). (gr. 7-17). pap. 6.99 *(978-0-340-93099-1(3))* Hachette Children's Group GBR. Dist: Hachette Bk. Group.

Seckin, Tamer. EndoMEtriosis: A Guide for Girls. 2020. 208p. (YA). pap. 21.99 *(978-1-68442-365-1(1))* Turner Publishing Co.

Waters, Sophie. Dealing with PMS. (Girls' Health Ser.). 48p. (gr. 5-6). 2009. 53.00 *(978-1-61512-729-0(1)*, Rosen Reference) 2007. (ENG., Illus.). (YA). lib. bdg. 34.47 *(978-1-4042-1949-6(8)*, 2242a8a4-ff06-4b04-893e-9a66d2b170d8) Rosen Publishing Group, Inc., The.

MENSTRUATION—FICTION

Gaudet, Cindy. Moon Time Prayer. Dorion, Leah, illus. 2nd ed. 2018. (ENG.). 80p. (J). pap. *(978-1-7752231-4-6(0))* MotherButterfly Bks.

Gordon, Lorell Cynthia. Tilly's Birthday: A Young Girl's Introduction to Menstruation. 2005. (Illus.). 64p. (J). per. 6.99 *(978-0-9763961-0-9(6))* Learning All About Me, LLC.

Reynolds Naylor, Phyllis. Lovingly Alice. 2004. (Alice Bks.). 166p. (J). (gr. 4-6). 13.65 *(978-0-7569-6604-1(3))* Perfection Learning Corp.

MENSURATION

see Measurement

MENTAL DEFICIENCY

see People with Mental Disabilities

MENTAL DEPRESSION

see Depression, Mental

MENTAL DISEASES

see Mental Illness; Psychology, Pathological

MENTAL HEALTH

see also Mental Illness; Mind and Body; Psychology, Pathological

Belfield, Annie. Stressed-Out Girl? Girls Dealing with Feelings, 1 vol. 2014. (Girls Dealing with Feelings Ser.). (ENG.). 64p. (gr. 5-6). 19.61 *(978-1-62293-040-1(1)*, 2221dedd-9e6c-4210-bedb-acefb4d62498) Enslow Publishing, LLC.

Bonnice, Sherry. Drug Therapy & Adjustment Disorders. 2003. (Psychiatric Disorders: Drugs & Psychology for the Mind & Bod Ser.). (Illus.). 126p. (YA). (gr. 4-7). pap. 14.95 *(978-1-4222-0384-2(0))* Mason Crest.

—Drug Therapy for Adjustment Disorders. 2004. (Encyclopedia of Psychiatric Drugs & Their Disorders Ser.). (Illus.). 128p. (YA). lib. bdg. 24.95 *(978-1-59084-560-8(9))* Mason Crest.

Brinkerhoff, Shirley. Drug Therapy & Anxiety Disorders. (Encyclopedia of Psychiatric Drugs & Their Disorders Ser.). (Illus.). 2004. 128p. (J). lib. bdg. 24.95 *(978-1-59084-561-5(7))* 2003. 124p. (YA). (gr. 7). pap. 14.95 *(978-1-4222-0385-9(9))* Mason Crest.

—Drug Therapy & Childhood & Adolescent Disorders. 2003. (Psychiatric Disorders: Drugs & Psychology for the Mind & Bod Ser.). (Illus.). 125p. (YA). (gr. 4-7). pap. 14.95 *(978-1-4222-0386-6(7))* Mason Crest.

Clark, Travis. A Stressed-Out Guy's Guide: How to Deal, 1 vol. 2014. (Guy's Guide Ser.). (ENG.). 64p. (gr. 5-7). 19.61 *(978-1-62293-010-4(X)*, 3bb2e1de-29cb-4e5d-b29f-a72ab6d8c6f6) Enslow Publishing, LLC.

Conte, Paola, et al. Someone to Talk To: Getting Good at Feeling Better. Keay, Claire, illus. 2017. 64p. (J). pap. *(978-1-4338-2672-6(0)*, Magination Pr.) American Psychological Assn.

Dawson, Juno & Hewitt, Olivia. Mind Your Head. Correll, Gemma, illus. 2016. (ENG.). 208p. (YA). (gr. 7). pap. 12.99 *(978-1-4714-0531-0(1))* Bonnier Publishing GBR. Dist: Independent Pubs. Group.

Engdahl, Sylvia, ed. Mental Health, 1 vol. 2010. (Issues on Trial Ser.). (ENG.). 200p. (gr. 10-12). 49.93 *(978-0-7377-4738-6(2)*, 56edd58d-94da-4138-97e4-153e0a9ca868, Greenhaven Publishing) Greenhaven Publishing LLC.

Fisher, Beverly. Mental Toughness for Personal Fitness: Workbook for Life 2004. (Illus.). 64p. pap. 10.99 *(978-0-9745066-0-9(5))* Sports In Mind.

—Mental Toughness for Weight Management: Workbook for Life. 2004. (Illus.). 60p. pap. 10.99 *(978-0-9745066-1-6(3))* Sports In Mind.

Harmon, Daniel E. Careers in Mental Health, 1 vol. 2017. (Essential Careers Ser.). (ENG., Illus.). 80p. (J). (gr. 6-6). 37.47 *(978-1-5383-8154-0(0)*, 2c484112-d139-4e22-a03f-47499a552722, Rosen Young Adult) Rosen Publishing Group, Inc., The.

Kawa, Katie. What Happens When Someone Has Depression?, 1 vol. 2019. (KidHaven Health Library). (ENG.). 32p. (gr. 4-4). 28.88 *(978-1-5345-3243-4(9)*, f53f5b34-3db8-4e9a-a559-c08073f24290, KidHaven Publishing) Greenhaven Publishing LLC.

Lambillion, Paul. Staying Cool. 2004. (Illus.). 196p. pap. 13.95 *(978-0-7171-3598-1(5))* M.H. Gill & Co. U. C. IRL. Dist: Hushion Hse. Publishing, Ltd.

Libal, Autumn. Drug Therapy & Postpartum Disorders. 2003. (Psychiatric Disorders: Drugs & Psychology for the Mind & Bod Ser.). (Illus.). 124p. (YA). (gr. 4-7). pap. 14.95 *(978-1-4222-0395-8(6))* Mason Crest.

Mcpherson, Stephanie Sammartino. Stressed Out in School? Learning to Deal with Academic Pressure, 1 vol. 2010. (Issues in Focus Today Ser.). (ENG., Illus.). 112p. (gr. 6-7). lib. bdg. 35.93 *(978-0-7660-3069-5(5)*, b8b74d97-b350-4df4-9058-a7ba12f3f96b) Enslow Publishing, LLC.

Meyer, Joyce. Battlefield of the Mind for Kids. rev. ed. 2018. (ENG., Illus.). 192p. (J). (gr. 3-7). pap. 15.99 *(978-1-5460-3321-9(1)*, Faithwords) FaithWords.

Miller, Susan B. When Parents Have Problems: A Book for Teens & Older Children Who Have a Disturbed or Difficult Parent. 2nd ed. 2012. xiv, 105p. (J). pap. 19.95 *(978-0-398-08713-5(X))* Thomas, Charles C. Pub., Ltd.

Morse, Philip C. Kick Out Stress - Teen Stress Reduction Program: Improving Self-Esteem, Optimizing Performance in School & Sports & Improving Physical & Emotional Health. 2004. (YA). (gr. 8-12). pap. *(978-0-9748548-0-9(8))* Mind/Body Workshops.

Nardo, Don. Teen Guide to Mental Health. 2019. (ENG.). 80p. (J). (gr. 6-12). 41.27 *(978-1-68282-753-6(4))* ReferencePoint Pr., Inc.

Nittle, Nadra, ed. America's Mental Health Crisis, 1 vol. 2019. (Current Controversies Ser.). (ENG.). 200p. (gr. 10-12). pap. 33.00 *(978-1-5345-0613-8(6)*, 92223951-df19-4d11-942d-6de025953d2a) Greenhaven Publishing LLC.

Parks, Peggy J. Teens & Stress. 2015. (ENG., Illus.). 96p. (J). lib. bdg. *(978-1-60152-768-4(3))* ReferencePoint Pr., Inc.

Rauf, Don. Personality. 2017. (Freaky Phenomena Ser.: Vol. 8). (ENG., Illus.). 48p. (J). (gr. 5-8). 20.95 *(978-1-4222-3778-6(8))* Mason Crest.

Reber, Deborah. Chill: Stress-Reducing Techniques for a More Balanced, Peaceful You. 2008. 208p. (YA). (gr. 7-12). pap. 9.99 *(978-1-4169-6555-8(6)*, Simon Pulse) Simon Pulse.

Spalding, Maddie. 12 Tips to Maintain Brain Health. 2017. (Healthy Living Ser.). (ENG., Illus.). 32p. (J). (gr. 3-6). 32.80 *(978-1-63235-368-9(7)*, 11846); pap. 9.95 *(978-1-63235-386-3(5)*, 11854) Bookstaves, LLC. (12-Story Library).

Teen Mental Health, 10 vols., Set. Incl. Addictive Personality. Juzwiak, Richard. lib. bdg. 34.47 *(978-1-4042-1802-4(5)*, 38d603c5-5160-43e4-87b6-a4b63c7c74ad); Anxiety & Panic Attacks. Levin, Judith. lib. bdg. 34.47 *(978-1-4042-1797-3(5)*, 90c85477-8a2e-43de-8061-1bb0c027f8e5); Depression & Mood Disorders. Levin, Judith. lib. bdg. 34.47 *(978-1-4042-1798-0(3)*, 9c40e589-e64e-4404-b343-55eb231f226a); Meditation. Moore, Andrew. lib. bdg. 34.47 *(978-1-4042-1799-7(1)*, 09f7d881-47e4-49fc-a994-bcb5ecbad3f2); (Illus.). 48p. (YA). (gr. 5-6). 2008. (Teen Mental Health Ser.). (ENG.). 2008. Set lib. bdg. 172.35 *(978-1-4042-1888-8(2)*, 54036480-a68c-4627-bdf3-e012a25e8456) Rosen Publishing Group, Inc., The.

Teen Mental Health: Set 4, 12 vols. 2013. (Teen Mental Health Ser.). (ENG.). 48p. (YA). (gr. 5-6). 206.82 *(978-1-4777-1761-5(7)*, f23c20a6-fddc-4b9b-ac32-fffc3a1486b6) Rosen Publishing Group, Inc., The.

Tousey, Ben. Acting Your Dreams: Using Acting Techniques to Interpret Your Dreams, 1. 2003. (C). per. 14.95 *(978-0-9724292-0-7(4))* Yhabbut Publishing.

Ward, James. Asylum Light: Stories from the George A. Zeller Era & Beyond, Peoria State Hospital, Galesburg Mental Health Center, & George A. Zeller Mental Health Center. 2005. (Illus.). 298p. pap. 19.95 *(978-0-9748742-0-3(5)*, 1210408) Mental Health Historic Preservation Society Of Central Illinois.

Williams, Dinah. Abandoned Insane Asylums. 2008. (Scary Places Ser.). (Illus.). 32p. (YA). (gr. 4-7). lib. bdg. 28.50 *(978-1-59716-575-4(1))* Bearport Publishing Co., Inc.

Wroble, Lisa A. Dealing with Stress: A How-To Guide, 1 vol. 2011. (Life: a How-To Guide Ser.). (ENG., Illus.). 128p. (gr. 6-7). pap. 13.88 *(978-1-59845-309-6(2)*, 63e7ab87-ee86-43c4-9146-1a5cda9c93c1) Enslow Publishing, LLC.

MENTAL HYGIENE

see Mental Health

MENTAL ILLNESS

see also Mental Health

Abramovitz, Melissa. Dealing with Bipolar Disorder. 2020. (ENG.). 80p. (J). (gr. 6-12). 41.27 *(978-1-68282-787-1(9))* ReferencePoint Pr., Inc.

—Mental Retardation, 1 vol. 2007. (Diseases & Disorders Ser.). (ENG., Illus.). 104p. (gr. 7-7). lib. bdg. 41.53 *(978-1-59018-412-7(2)*, d0aaa44b-fa11-4821-a704-b90cb542bbc5, Lucent Pr.) Greenhaven Publishing LLC.

Anana, Christy Lynn. I Can Feel Better: a Tapping Story: Emotional Freedom Technique (EFT): Effective Step by Step Mind & Body Relaxation for Kids, Teens & Adults. 2021. pap. 15.00 *(978-1-957400-00-6(5))* Anana Pr.

Andersen, Michelle Garcia. Living with OCD. 2018. (Living with Disorders & Disabilities Ser.). (ENG.). 80p. (YA). (gr. 6-12). 39.93 *(978-1-68282-483-2(7))* ReferencePoint Pr., Inc.

Bjorklund, Ruth. Tourette Syndrome, 1 vol. 2010. (Health Alert Ser.). (ENG.). 64p. (gr. 4-4). 35.50 *(978-0-7614-3985-1(4)*, b1a12a4a-cce5-4fce-afeb-089be49d9df1) Cavendish Square Publishing LLC.

Bleuel, Amy. Project Semicolon: Your Story Isn't Over. 2017. (ENG., Illus.). 352p. (YA). (gr. 9). pap. 9.99 *(978-0-06-246652-5(6)*, HarperCollins) HarperCollins Pubs.

Bonnice, Sherry. Drug Therapy & Adjustment Disorders. 2003. (Psychiatric Disorders: Drugs & Psychology for the Mind & Bod Ser.). (Illus.). 126p. (YA). (gr. 4-7). pap. 14.95 *(978-1-4222-0384-2(0))* Mason Crest.

—Drug Therapy & Premenstrual Disorders. 2003. (Psychiatric Disorders: Drugs & Psychology for the Mind & Bod Ser.). (Illus.). 124p. (YA). (gr. 4-7). pap. 14.95 *(978-1-4222-0396-5(4))* Mason Crest.

Bonnice, Sherry & Hoard, Carolyn. Drug Therapy & Cognitive Disorders. (Encyclopedia of Psychiatric Drugs & Their Disorders Ser.). (Illus.). (YA). 2004. 128p. lib. bdg. 24.95 *(978-1-59084-562-2(5))* 2003. 126p. (gr. 7). pap. 14.95 *(978-1-4222-0387-3(5))* Mason Crest.

Brinkerhoff, Shirley. Drug Therapy & Obsessive-Compulsive Disorders. 2003. (Psychiatric Disorders: Drugs & Psychology for the Mind & Bod Ser.). (Illus.). 124p. (YA). (gr. 7). pap. 14.95 *(978-1-4222-0393-4(X))* Mason Crest.

—Drug Therapy & Personality Disorders. (Encyclopedia of Psychiatric Drugs & Their Disorders Ser.). (Illus.). (YA). 2004. 128p. lib. bdg. 24.95 *(978-1-59084-571-4(4))* 2003. 126p. (gr. 4-7). pap. 14.95 *(978-1-4222-0394-1(8))* Mason Crest.

—Drug Therapy & Schizophrenia. 2003. (Psychiatric Disorders: Drugs & Psychology for the Mind & Bod Ser.). (Illus.). 124p. (YA). (gr. 4-7). pap. 14.95 *(978-1-4222-0398-9(0))* Mason Crest.

—Schizophrenia. McDonnell, Mary Ann & Esherick, Donald, eds. 2013. (State of Mental Illness & Its Therapy Ser.: 19). (Illus.). 128p. (J). (gr. 7-18). 24.95 *(978-1-4222-2835-7(5))* Mason Crest.

Bryfonski, Dedria, ed. Depression in J. D. Salinger's the Catcher in the Rye, 1 vol. 2008. (Social Issues in Literature Ser.). (ENG., Illus.). 224p. (J). (gr. 10-12). lib. bdg. 48.03 *(978-0-7377-4256-5(9)*, c4525e06-4525-4e96-a218-8feb3b2ed580, Greenhaven Publishing) Greenhaven Publishing LLC.

Burkhart, Jessica, et al. Life Inside My Mind: 31 Authors Share Their Personal Struggles. Burkhart, Jessica, ed. 2018. (ENG., Illus.). 320p. (YA). (gr. 9). 17.99 *(978-1-4814-9464-9(3)*, Simon Pulse) Simon Pulse.

Burnett, Betty. Coping with Multiple Sclerosis. 2009. (Coping Ser.). 192p. (gr. 7-12). 63.90 *(978-1-61512-005-5(X))* Rosen Publishing Group, Inc., The.

Centore, Michael. Drug Use & Mental Health, Vol. 13. Becker, Sara, ed. 2016. (Drug Addiction & Recovery Ser.). (Illus.). 64p. (J). (gr. 7). 23.95 *(978-1-4222-3601-7(3))* Mason Crest.

Chastain, Zachary. Sick All the Time: Kids with Chronic Illness. 2009. (Kids with Special Needs Ser.). 48p. (YA). (gr. 5-18). pap. 7.95 *(978-1-4222-1922-5(4))* Mason Crest.

Chou, Joey. Crazy by the Letters. Chou, Joey, illus. 2006. (Illus.). 15.99 *(978-0-9788670-0-3(9))* Choo Choo Clan.

Clarke, Lisa A. Wishing Wellness: A Workbook for Children of Parents with Mental Illness. Matthews, Bonnie, illus. 2006. (ENG.). 128p. (J). (gr. 1-7). per. 14.95 *(978-1-59147-313-8(6)*, Magination Pr.) American Psychological Assn.

Dawson, Juno & Hewitt, Olivia. Mind Your Head. Correll, Gemma, illus. 2016. (ENG.). 208p. (YA). (gr. 7). pap. 12.99 *(978-1-4714-0531-0(1))* Bonnier Publishing GBR. Dist: Independent Pubs. Group.

de Sosa, Linda. I'm Not Crazy: A Workbook for Teens with Depression & Bipolar Disorder. 2010. 128p. pap. 13.95 *(978-0-595-52118-0(5))* iUniverse, Inc.

Engdahl, Sylvia, ed. Mental Health, 1 vol. 2010. (Issues on Trial Ser.). (ENG.). 200p. (gr. 10-12). 49.93 *(978-0-7377-4738-6(2)*, 56edd58d-94da-4138-97e4-153e0a9ca868, Greenhaven Publishing) Greenhaven Publishing LLC.

Esherick, Joan. The FDA & Psychiatric Drugs: How a Drug Is Approved. McDonnell, Mary Ann & Esherick, Donald, eds. 2013. (State of Mental Illness & Its Therapy Ser.: 19). 128p. (J). (gr. 7-18). 24.95 *(978-1-4222-2826-5(6))* Mason Crest.

Goldstein, Natalie. Parkinson's Disease. 2009. (Genes & Disease Ser.). (ENG., Illus.). 128p. (gr. 7-12). 35.00 *(978-0-7910-9584-3(3)*, P159113, Facts On File) Infobase Holdings, Inc.

Hall, Kirk. Carina & Her Care Partner Gramma. Paolini, Alison, illus. 2013. 26p. 19.95 *(978-1-61314-158-8(0))*; pap. 15.95 *(978-1-61314-171-7(8))* Innovo Publishing, LLC.

Hardman, Lizabeth. Dementia, 1 vol. 2009. (Diseases & Disorders Ser.). (ENG., Illus.). 112p. (gr. 7-7). lib. bdg. 41.53 *(978-1-4205-0042-4(2)*, eb9acab7-ec9b-44bb-982d-4c8962e6caf5, Lucent Pr.) Greenhaven Publishing LLC.

Hyman, Bruce M. & Pedrick, Cherry. Obsessive-Compulsive Disorder. 2008. (Twenty-First Century Medical Library). (YA). (gr. 7-12). lib. bdg. 33.26 *(978-0-8225-8579-4(0))* Twenty First Century Bks.

Iorizzo, Carrie. Schizophrenia & Other Psychotic Disorders. 2013. (ENG., Illus.). 48p. (J). *(978-0-7787-0085-2(2))* Crabtree Publishing Co.

—Schizophrenia & Psychotic Disorders, 1 vol. 2013. (ENG., Illus.). 48p. (J). pap. *(978-0-7787-0091-3(7))* Crabtree Publishing Co.

Jovinelly, Joann. Coping with Bipolar Disorder & Manic-Depressive Illness. 2009. (Coping Ser.). 192p. (gr. 7-12). 63.90 *(978-1-61511-992-9(2))* Rosen Publishing Group, Inc., The.

Kelly, Evelyn. Coping with Schizophrenia. 2009. (Coping Ser.). 192p. (gr. 7-12). 63.90 *(978-1-61512-011-6(4))* Rosen Publishing Group, Inc., The.

Kent, Deborah. Snake Pits, Talking Cures, & Magic Bullets: A History of Mental Illness. 2003. (Single Titles Ser.). (ENG., Illus.). 160p. (gr. 7-12). lib. bdg. 26.60 *(978-0-7613-2704-2(5)*, Twenty-First Century Bks.) Lerner Publishing Group.

Larson, Elaine Marie. The Kaleidoscope Kid: Focusing on the Strengths of Children with Asperger Syndrome & High-Functioning Autism. Strand, Vivian, illus. 2007. 35p. 17.95 *(978-1-931282-41-3(2))* Autism Asperger Publishing Co.

Leicester, Mal. Can I Tell You about Tourette Syndrome? A Guide for Friends, Family & Professionals. Apsley, illus. 2013. (Can I Tell You About...? Ser.). 56p. (C). pap. 15.95 *(978-1-84905-407-2(X)*, 694427) Kingsley, Jessica Pubs. GBR. Dist: Hachette UK Distribution.

Libal, Autumn. Drug Therapy & Dissociative Disorders. 2003. (Psychiatric Disorders: Drugs & Psychology for the Mind & Bod Ser.). (Illus.). 124p. (YA). (gr. 7). pap. 14.95 *(978-1-4222-0388-0(3))* Mason Crest.

—Drug Therapy & Impulse Control Disorders. 2003. (Psychiatric Disorders: Drugs & Psychology for the Mind & Bod Ser.). (Illus.). 124p. (YA). (gr. 4-7). pap. 14.95 *(978-1-4222-0390-3(5))* Mason Crest.

—Drug Therapy & Psychosomatic Disorders. (Encyclopedia of Psychiatric Drugs & Their Disorders Ser.). (Illus.). 2004. 128p. (J). lib. bdg. 24.95 *(978-1-59084-573-8(0))* 2003. 124p. (YA). (gr. 4-7). pap. 14.95 *(978-1-4222-0397-2(2))* Mason Crest.

—The FDA & Psychiatric Drugs: Drugs & Psychology for the Mind & Body, 19 vols., Set. 2004. (Psychiatric Disorders Ser.). (Illus.). 128p. (J). lib. bdg. *(978-1-59084-559-2(5))* Mason Crest.

Libal, Joyce. Drug Therapy & Mental Disorders Due to a Medical Condition. 2003. (Psychiatric Disorders: Drugs & Psychology for the Mind & Bod Ser.). (Illus.). 126p. (YA). (gr. 8-12). pap. 14.95 *(978-1-4222-0391-0(3))* Mason Crest.

Marcovitz, Hal. Bipolar Disorder. 2009. (Compact Research Ser.). 112p. (YA). (gr. 7-12). 43.93 *(978-1-60152-066-1(2))* ReferencePoint Pr., Inc.

Marcus, Mary Brophy. Sleep Disorders. 2009. (Psychological Disorders Ser.). (ENG., Illus.). 128p. (gr. 7-12). 37.50 *(978-1-60413-085-0(7)*, P159431, Facts On File) Infobase Holdings, Inc.

McIntosh, Kenneth & Livingston, Phyllis. Youth with Juvenile Schizophrenia: The Search for Reality. 2009. (Helping Youth with Mental, Physical, & Social Challenges Ser.). (Illus.). 128p. (YA). (gr. 7-18). lib. bdg. 24.95 *(978-1-4222-0148-0(1))* Mason Crest.

Meisel, Abigail. Depression & Bipolar Disorder: Examining Chemical Imbalances & Mood Disorders, 1 vol. 2014. (Diseases, Disorders, Symptoms Ser.). (ENG., Illus.). 96p. (gr. 9-10). 31.61 *(978-1-62293-060-9(6)*, 360256a5-d82e-4df7-9ba9-c1b3fb38961c) Enslow Publishing, LLC.

Moe, Barbara. Coping with Mental Illness. 2009. (Coping Ser.). 192p. (gr. 7-12). 63.90 *(978-1-61512-004-8(1))* Rosen Publishing Group, Inc., The.

mooney, carla. Mental Illness Research. 2011. (Inside Science Ser.). 96p. (YA). (gr. 7-12). lib. bdg. 43.93 *(978-1-60152-234-4(7))* ReferencePoint Pr., Inc.

Murphy, Tara & Millar, Damon. Tourette Syndrome: A Survival Kit. Enoki, Hiro, illus. 2019. 208p. (J). 19.95 *(978-1-78592-359-3(5)*, 696612) Kingsley, Jessica Pubs. GBR. Dist: Hachette UK Distribution.

Palmer, Libbi. The PTSD Workbook for Teens: Simple, Effective Skills for Healing Trauma. 2012. (ENG.). 160p. (YA). (gr. 6-12). pap. 21.95 *(978-1-60882-321-5(0)*, 23215, Instant Help Books) New Harbinger Pubns.

Parks, Peggy J. Kids & Mental Illness. 2018. (Diseases & Disorders of Youth Ser.). (ENG.). 80p. (YA). (gr. 6-12). 39.93 *(978-1-68282-401-6(2))* ReferencePoint Pr., Inc.

parks, peggy j. Schizophrenia. 2011. (YA). lib. bdg. 41.27 *(978-1-60152-140-8(5))* ReferencePoint Pr., Inc.

Rice, Donna. The Magic Is Me. Rice, Doug, illus. 2012. 34p. (J). mass mkt. 15.99 *(978-1-936497-16-4(6))* Searchlight Pr.

Rose, Deborah. Joshua Wears A Red Cape. 2007. 44p. 25.45 *(978-1-4357-0006-2(6))* Lulu Pr., Inc.

Rykken, Cheryl. My Shaky Grandma. 2008. 32p. pap. 11.50 *(978-1-4357-3496-8(3))* Lulu Pr., Inc.

Sabin, Ellen & Driscoll, Patricia. The Healing Heroes Book: Braving the Changes When Someone You Love Is Wounded in Service. 2012. (ENG., Illus.). 64p. (J). spiral bd. 19.95 *(978-0-9826416-0-6(5))* Watering Can.

Service, The National and Specialist OCD, B. D. D. and Related Disorders. Appearance Anxiety: A Guide to Understanding Body Dysmorphic Disorder for Young People, Families & Professionals. 2019. (Illus.). 88p. (J). 17.95 *(978-1-78592-456-9(7)*, 696667) Kingsley, Jessica Pubs. GBR. Dist: Hachette UK Distribution.

Sharpe, Tanja. CBT Doodling for Kids: 50 Illustrated Handouts to Help Build Confidence & Emotional Resilience in Children Aged 6-11. 2018. (Illus.). 112p. pap. 26.95 *(978-1-78592-537-5(7)*, 696875) Kingsley, Jessica Pubs. GBR. Dist: Hachette UK Distribution.

Shea, Therese. Dementia, 1 vol. 2011. (Understanding Brain Diseases & Disorders Ser.). (ENG.). 64p. (YA). (gr. 6-6). lib. bdg. 37.13 *(978-1-4488-5545-2(4)*, 1b5945a0-1621-4fdd-b2e7-92d05aa2b9a5) Rosen Publishing Group, Inc., The.

Simpson, Carolyn. Coping with Post-Traumatic Stress Disorder (PTSD) Dealing with Tragedy. 2009. (Coping Ser.). 192p. (gr. 7-12). 63.90 *(978-1-61512-008-6(4))* Rosen Publishing Group, Inc., The.

Smith, Paula. Schizophrenia & Other Psychotic Disorders. 2013. 48p. (J). *(978-0-7787-0834-6(9))*; (Illus.). pap. *(978-0-7787-0861-2(6))* Crabtree Publishing Co.

Sommers, Michael A. Everything You Need to Know about Bipolar Disorder & Manic Depressive Illness. 2009. (Need to Know Library). 64p. (gr. 5-5). 58.50 *(978-1-60854-055-6(3))* Rosen Publishing Group, Inc., The.

Spilsbury, Richard. Bipolar Disorder, 1 vol. 2018. (Genetic Diseases & Gene Therapies Ser.). (ENG., Illus.). 48p. (J). (gr. 5-5). 33.47 *(978-1-5081-8268-9(X)*, 507c3ed7-d70b-46ee-ae12-03b7c125ac44, Rosen Central) Rosen Publishing Group, Inc., The.

MENTAL ILLNESS—FICTION

Adams, Mark. Bucky's Best Friend, Vol. 1. Dolan, Amy, illus. 2006. 15p. (J). pap. 5.00 *(978-0-9670245-4-7(4))* Enthusi Adams, Inc.

Alkaf, Hanna. The Weight of Our Sky. 2019. (ENG., Illus.). 288p. (YA). (gr. 7). 19.99 *(978-1-5344-2608-5(6)*, Salaam Reads) Simon & Schuster Bks. For Young Readers.

Anderson, Jessica Lee. Border Crossing. 2009. (ENG.). 160p. (J). (gr. 5-10). pap. 8.00 *(978-1-57131-691-2(4))* Milkweed Editions.

Anderson, Laurie Halse. The Impossible Knife of Memory. 2015. (ENG.). 432p. (YA). (gr. 7). pap. 10.99 *(978-0-14-751072-3(4)*, Penguin Books) Penguin Young Readers Group.

Andrews, Emily. The Finer Points of Becoming Machine. 2008. (Cutting Edge Ser.). (ENG.). 200p. pap. *(978-1-84167-714-9(0))* Ransom Publishing Ltd.

Armstrong, Kelley. The Summoning. 2009. (Darkest Powers Ser.: 1). (ENG.). 416p. (YA). (gr. 8). pap. 10.99 *(978-0-06-145054-9(5)*, HarperCollins) HarperCollins Pubs.

—The Summoning, 7 vols. 2009. (Darkest Powers Ser.: 1). (J). 81.75 *(978-1-4361-9717-5(1))*; 243.75 *(978-1-4361-9718-2(X))* Recorded Bks., Inc.

Atwater-Rhodes, Amelia. Persistence of Memory. 2010. (Den of Shadows Ser.: 5). (ENG.). 224p. (YA). (gr. 7). pap. 8.99 *(978-0-440-24004-4(2)*, Delacorte Pr.) Random Hse. Children's Bks.

Bailey, Em. Shift. 2016. (ENG.). 320p. (YA). (gr. 9). pap. 18.99 *(978-1-76012-698-8(5))* Hardie Grant Children?s Publishing AUS. Dist: Independent Pubs. Group.

Baker, Rhiannon. My Mummy's Brain Is Sick. 2019. (ENG.). 26p. 37.94 *(978-1-7960-0156-3(2))*; (Illus.). pap. 24.14 *(978-1-7960-0155-6(4))* Xlibris Corp.

Baldwin, Cindy. Where the Watermelons Grow. (ENG.). (J). (gr. 3-7). 2020. 272p. pap. 9.99 *(978-0-06-266587-4(1))* 2018. 256p. 16.99 *(978-0-06-266586-7(3))* HarperCollins Pubs. (Quill Tree Bks.).

Brewer, Zac. Madness. 2017. (ENG.). 304p. (YA). (gr. 9). 17.99 *(978-0-06-245785-1(3)*, HarperTeen) HarperCollins Pubs.

Caletti, Deb. Love Is All You Need: Wild Roses; the Nature of Jade. 2013. (ENG.). 608p. (YA). (gr. 7-7). pap. 11.99 *(978-1-4424-6636-4(7)*, Simon Pulse) Simon Pulse.

—Wild Roses. 2008. (ENG.). 320p. (YA). (gr. 7-12). pap. 8.99 *(978-1-4169-5782-9(0)*, Simon Pulse) Simon Pulse.

Carey, Becky. 47 Strings: Tessa's Special Code. Stidwell O'Boyle, Carrie, ed. Leick, Bonnie, illus. 2012. (ENG.). 36p. 22.95 *(978-0-9849245-6-1(6))* Little Creek Press.

Carter, Alden R. Walkaway. 2008. (ENG.). 192p. (YA). (gr. 7-18). 16.95 *(978-0-8234-2106-0(6))* Holiday Hse., Inc.

Chand, Emlyn. Farsighted. 2012. 260p. 19.95 *(978-0-9839308-2-2(1))* Blue Crown Pr.

Christiansen, Rebecca. Maybe in Paris. 2017. (ENG.). 224p. (YA). (gr. 6-6). 16.99 *(978-1-5107-0880-8(4)*, Sky Pony Pr.) Skyhorse Publishing Co., Inc.

Clark, Clara Gillow. Hattie on Her Way. Thompson, John, illus. 2005. (Trials of Hattie Belle Basket Ser.). (ENG.). 208p. (J). (gr. 5-18). 15.99 *(978-0-7636-2286-2(9))* Candlewick Pr.

Cleaver, Vera & Cleaver, Bill. Donde Florecen los Lirios. (SPA.). 168p. (YA). (gr. 5-8). *(978-84-204-3648-7(8)*, AF0285) Ediciones Alfaguara ESP. Dist: Lectorum Pubns., Inc.

Colfer, Eoin. The Atlantis Complex. 2012. (Artemis Fowl Ser.: 7). (J). lib. bdg. 19.65 *(978-0-606-23614-0(7))* Turtleback.

de la Peña, Matt. I Will Save You. 2011. (ENG.). 336p. (YA). (gr. 9). pap. 11.99 *(978-0-385-73828-6(5)*, Ember) Random Hse. Children's Bks.

Durmush, F. Ayshe, an Anatolian Tale. 2007. (ENG.). 84p. per. *(978-1-84747-171-0(4))* Chipmunkapublishing.

Easton, Kelly. To Be Mona. (ENG.). 224p. (YA). (gr. 7). 2009. pap. 7.99 *(978-1-4169-0055-9(1))* 2008. 16.99 *(978-1-4169-0054-2(3))* McElderry, Margaret K. Bks. (McElderry, Margaret K. Bks.).

Eden, Alexandra. Holy Smoke: A Bones & the Duchess Mystery. 2004. (ENG., Illus.). 117p. (J). 16.00 *(978-1-888310-46-7(4))* Knoll, Allen A. Pubs.

Ella, Sara. Coral, 1 vol. 2019. (ENG.). 384p. (YA). 18.99 *(978-0-7852-2445-7(9))* Nelson, Thomas Inc.

Evangelista, Kate. No Love Allowed. 2016. (Dodge Cove Trilogy Ser.: 1). (ENG.). 256p. (YA). pap. 15.99 *(978-1-250-07390-7(1)*, 900150895) Feiwel & Friends.

Firmston, Kim. Schizo, 1 vol. 2011. (Lorimer SideStreets Ser.). (ENG.). 152p. (YA). (gr. 9-12). pap. 8.99 *(978-1-55277-871-5(1)*, 8741e7ad-019c-40e4-831c-e95be7ded3a5) James Lorimer & Co. Ltd., Pubs. CAN. Dist: Lerner Publishing Group.

Fortunati, Karen. The Weight of Zero. 2018. (ENG.). 400p. (YA). (gr. 9). 11.99 *(978-1-101-93892-8(7)*, Ember) Random Hse. Children's Bks.

Fox, Helena. How It Feels to Float. 2019. (ENG.). 384p. (YA). (gr. 9). 18.99 *(978-0-525-55429-5(7)*, Dial Bks) Penguin Young Readers Group.

Franklin, Kristine L. Dove Song. 2006. (ENG.). 192p. (J). (gr. 5-9). per. 5.99 *(978-0-7636-3219-9(8))* Candlewick Pr.

Friedman, Robin. Nothing. 2008. (ENG.). 240p. (YA). (gr. 9-12). pap. 9.95 *(978-0-7387-1304-5(X)*, 073871304X, Flux) North Star Editions.

Friend, Natasha. Where You'll Find Me. 2017. (YA). lib. bdg. 20.85 *(978-0-606-39591-5(1))* Turtleback.

Gale, Emily. Girl Out Loud. 2012. 274p. (YA). *(978-0-545-30439-9(3)*, Chicken Hse., The) Scholastic, Inc.

Geiger, A. V. Tell Me No Lies. 2018. (Follow Me Back Ser.: 2). 336p. (YA). (gr. 8-12). pap. 10.99 *(978-1-4926-4825-3(6))* Sourcebooks, Inc.

Gephart, Donna. Lily & Dunkin. (ENG.). 352p. (J). (gr. 5). 2018. 8.99 *(978-0-553-53677-5(X)*, Yearling) 2016. 16.99 *(978-0-553-53674-4(5)*, Delacorte Bks. for Young Readers) Random Hse. Children's Bks.

Ghislain, Gary. How I Stole Johnny Depp's Alien Girlfriend. 2011. (ENG., Illus.). 208p. (YA). (gr. 7-17). 16.99 *(978-0-8118-7460-1(5))* Chronicle Bks. LLC.

Goldberg Sloan, Holly. I'll Be There. 2012. (ENG.). 416p. (YA). (gr. 7-17). pap. 11.99 *(978-0-316-12276-4(9))* Little, Brown Bks. for Young Readers.

Green, John. Turtles All the Way Down. (ENG.). (YA). (gr. 9). 2019. 320p. pap. 14.99 *(978-0-525-55537-7(4)*, Penguin Books) 2017. 304p. 19.99 *(978-0-525-55536-0(6)*, Dutton Books for Young Readers) Penguin Young Readers Group.

—Turtles All the Way Down. 2017. lib. bdg. 33.05 *(978-0-606-40748-9(0))* Turtleback.

Greenberg, Joanne. I Never Promised You a Rose Garden. 256p. (YA). (gr. 7-18). pap. 5.99 *(978-0-8072-1362-9(4)*, Listening Library) Random Hse. Audio Publishing Group.

Griffin, Adele. Tighter. 2012. (ENG.). 224p. (J). (gr. 8-12). lib. bdg. 24.94 *(978-0-375-96645-3(5))* Random House Publishing Group.

—Tighter. 2012. (ENG.). 240p. (YA). (gr. 7). pap. 8.99 *(978-0-375-85933-5(0)*, Ember) Random Hse. Children's Bks.

—Where I Want to Be. (ENG.). (YA). (gr. 7-12). 2011. 150p. 22.44 *(978-0-399-23783-6(6))* 2007. 176p. 8.99 *(978-0-14-240948-0(0)*, Speak) Penguin Young Readers Group.

Griffin, Paul. The Orange Houses. 2011. (ENG.). 160p. (YA). (gr. 9-12). 22.44 *(978-0-8037-3346-6(1)*, Dial) Penguin Publishing Group.

—The Orange Houses. 2011. 176p. (YA). (gr. 9-18). 8.99 *(978-0-14-241982-3(6)*, Speak) Penguin Young Readers Group.

Guest, Jacqueline. Racing Fear, 1 vol. 2004. (Lorimer SideStreets Ser.). (ENG.). 160p. (YA). (gr. 9-12). 16.95 *(978-1-55028-839-1(3)*, 839) James Lorimer & Co. Ltd., Pubs. CAN. Dist: Formac Lorimer Bks. Ltd.

Halliday, John. Shooting Monarchs. 2007. (ENG.). 144p. (YA). (gr. 8). pap. 8.95 *(978-1-4169-5559-7(3)*, McElderry, Margaret K. Bks.) McElderry, Margaret K. Bks.

Halpern, Julie. Get Well Soon. 2009. (ENG.). 224p. (YA). (gr. 7-12). pap. 18.99 *(978-0-312-58148-0(3)*, 900062005) Square Fish.

Halse Anderson, Laurie. The Impossible Knife of Memory. 2015. (ENG.). (YA). (gr. 7). lib. bdg. 20.60 *(978-1-68065-510-0(8))* Perfection Learning Corp.

—The Impossible Knife of Memory. 2015. lib. bdg. 20.85 *(978-0-606-36798-1(5))* Turtleback.

Harrington, Karen. Sure Signs of Crazy. 2014. (ENG.). 304p. (J). (gr. 5-17). pap. 7.00 *(978-0-316-21049-2(8))* Little, Brown Bks. for Young Readers.

Hautman, Pete. Invisible. Hautman, Pete, illus. 2006. (ENG., Illus.). 160p. (YA). (gr. 7-12). reprint ed. pap. 10.99 *(978-0-689-86903-7(7)*, Simon & Schuster Bks. For Young Readers) Simon & Schuster Bks. For Young Readers.

Heilig, Heidi. For a Muse of Fire. (ENG.). (YA). (gr. 8). 2019. 528p. pap. 10.99 *(978-0-06-238082-1(6))* 2018. (Illus.). 512p. 17.99 *(978-0-06-238081-4(8))* HarperCollins Pubs. (Greenwillow Bks.).

Henry, April. The Lonely Dead. 2020. (ENG.). 240p. (YA). pap. 14.99 *(978-1-250-23376-9(3)*, 900185223) Square Fish.

Hopkins, Ellen. Impulse. (ENG.). (YA). (gr. 9-12). 2008. 688p. pap. 14.99 *(978-1-4169-0357-4(7))* 2007. 672p. 24.99 *(978-1-4169-0356-7(9))* McElderry, Margaret K. Bks. (McElderry, Margaret K. Bks.).

Howard, A. G. Splintered. 2013. (Splintered Ser.). (ENG.). 384p. (YA). (gr. 8-17). pap. 8.95 *(978-1-4197-0627-1(6))* Abrams, Inc.

—Splintered. 2014. (Splintered Ser.: 1). (J). lib. bdg. 19.60 *(978-0-606-35235-2(X))* Turtleback.

—Unhinged. 2014. (Splintered Ser.). (ENG.). 384p. (YA). (gr. 8-17). pap. 8.95 *(978-1-4197-1047-6(8))* Abrams, Inc.

—Unhinged. 2015. (Splintered Ser.: 2). (J). lib. bdg. 19.60 *(978-0-606-36565-9(6))* Turtleback.

—Unhinged (Splintered Series #2) 2015. (Splintered Ser.). (ENG.). 416p. (YA). (gr. 8-17). pap. 10.99 *(978-1-4197-1373-6(6)*, 1036403) Abrams, Inc.

Huston, Donna. Inch by Inch. 2006. (J). spiral bd. 19.95 *(978-0-9771192-3-3(8))* Shayne Publishing.

Hyde, Spencer. Waiting for Fitz. 2019. (ENG.). 256p. (YA). (gr. 9). 17.99 *(978-1-62972-527-7(7)*, 5211772, Shadow Mountain) Shadow Mountain Publishing.

Ireland, Justina. Vengeance Bound. 2013. (ENG.). 320p. (YA). (gr. 9). 17.99 *(978-1-4424-4462-1(2)*, Simon & Schuster Bks. For Young Readers) Simon & Schuster Bks. For Young Readers.

Ius, Dawn. Lizzie. 2018. (ENG., Illus.). 336p. (YA). (gr. 7). 18.99 *(978-1-4814-9076-4(1)*, Simon Pulse) Simon Pulse.

James, Caleb. Haffling. 2nd ed. 2016. (Haffling Ser.: 1). (ENG., Illus.). 250p. pap. 16.99 *(978-1-63476-795-8(0)*, DSP Pubns.) Dreamspinner Pr.

Kehret, Peg. Deadly Stranger. 2012. (ENG.). 176p. (J). (gr. 3-7). pap. 9.99 *(978-1-4424-6044-7(X)*, Simon & Schuster/Paula Wiseman Bks.) Simon & Schuster/Paula Wiseman Bks.

King, Wesley. OCDaniel. (ENG., Illus.). 304p. (J). (gr. 3-7). 2017. pap. 8.99 *(978-1-4814-5532-9(X))* 2016. 18.99 *(978-1-4814-5531-2(1))* Simon & Schuster/Paula Wiseman Bks. (Simon & Schuster/Paula Wiseman Bks.).

—OCDaniel. 2017. lib. bdg. 18.40 *(978-0-606-39743-8(4))* Turtleback.

Lahey, Sandra. Let's Talk. 2016. (ENG., Illus.). 26p. (J). pap. 28.22 *(978-1-5245-1995-7(2))* Xlibris Corp.

Levithan, David. Every You, Every Me. Farmer, Jonathan, photos by. 2012. (Illus.). 256p. (YA). (gr. 7). pap. 9.99 *(978-0-375-85451-4(7)*, Ember) Random Hse. Children's Bks.

—Every You, Every Me. Farmer, Jonathan, photos by. 2012. (Illus.). lib. bdg. 20.85 *(978-0-606-26816-5(2))* Turtleback.

Levoy, Myron. Alan & Naomi. 2011. 14.12 *(978-0-7848-3566-1(7)*, Everbind) Marco Bk. Co.

Littman, Sarah Darer. Anything but Okay. 2019. (ENG.). 352p. (YA). (gr. 7-7). pap. 9.99 *(978-1-338-17758-9(3)*, Scholastic Paperbacks) Scholastic, Inc.

Lord, Emery. When We Collided. 2016. (ENG.). 352p. (YA). 17.99 *(978-1-61963-845-7(2)*, 900150257, Bloomsbury USA Childrens) Bloomsbury Publishing USA.

Lowenstein, Sallie Claire. Waiting for Eugene. 2006. (Illus.). 201p. (J). *(978-1-4156-6166-6(9))* Book Wholesalers, Inc.

Masciola, Carol. The Yearbook. 2015. (ENG.). 224p. (YA). 17.99 *(978-1-4405-8897-6(X)*, Simon Pulse) Simon Pulse.

McCombs, A. Lisa. Abby. 2011. 184p. *(978-1-77067-327-4(X))* FriesenPress.

McCombs, Lisa A. Abby. 2011. 184p. pap. *(978-1-77067-328-1(8))* FriesenPress.

McGinnis, Mindy. This Darkness Mine. (ENG.). (YA). (gr. 9). 2019. 400p. pap. 9.99 *(978-0-06-256160-2(X))* 2017. 384p. 17.99 *(978-0-06-256159-6(6))* HarperCollins Pubs. (Tegen, Katherine Bks).

McNish, Cliff. Angel. 2008. (Exceptional Reading & Language Arts Titles for Intermediate Grades Ser.). 311p. (YA). (gr. 8-12). 16.95 *(978-0-8225-8900-6(1))* Lerner Publishing Group.

Meadows, Jodi. Before She Ignites. (Fallen Isles Ser.: 1). (ENG.). 496p. (YA). (gr. 8). 2018. 10.99 *(978-0-06-246941-0(X))* 2017. 17.99 *(978-0-06-246940-3(1))* HarperCollins Pubs. (Tegen, Katherine Bks).

Melmed, Raun & Abramson, S. E. Harriet's Monster Diary: Awfully Anxious (but I Squish It, Big Time), Volume 3. Kriembonga, Arief, illus. 2019. (Monster Diaries: 3). (ENG.). 116p. (J). (gr. 2-6). pap. 12.99 *(978-1-64170-127-3(7)*, 550127) Familius LLC.

Michaels, Rune. Nobel Genes. (ENG., (YA). (gr. 7). 2011. Illus.). 208p. pap. 8.99 *(978-1-4424-2401-2(X))* 2010. 192p. 16.99 *(978-1-4169-1259-0(2))* Simon & Schuster Children's Publishing. (Atheneum Bks. for Young Readers).

Miller, Barnabas. The Girl with the Wrong Name. 2016. (Illus.). 272p. (YA). (gr. 9). pap. 10.99 *(978-1-61695-704-9(2)*, Soho Teen) Soho Pr., Inc.

Neale, Jonathan. Lost at Sea. 2004. (ENG.). 112p. (J). (gr. 5-7). reprint ed. pap. 8.95 *(978-0-618-43236-3(1)*, 491905, Clarion Bks.) HarperCollins Pubs.

Neufeld, John. Lisa, Bright & Dark: A Novel. 2007. 152p. per. 12.95 *(978-0-595-45048-0(2)*, Backinprint.com) iUniverse, Inc.

Nijkamp, Marieke. Before I Let Go. 2019. 384p. (YA). (gr. 8-12). pap. 10.99 *(978-1-4926-6807-7(9))* Sourcebooks, Inc.

Olson, Norah. Twisted Fate. 2016. (ENG.). 288p. (YA). (gr. 8). pap. 9.99 *(978-0-06-227206-5(3)*, Tegen, Katherine Bks) HarperCollins Pubs.

Phillips, Linda Vigen. Crazy. 2014. (ENG.). 320p. (YA). pap. 9.00 *(978-0-8028-5437-7(0)*, Eerdmans Bks For Young Readers) Eerdmans, William B. Publishing Co.

Pickering, Amanda. Alfred the Alien: Number Adventure. 2011. 18p. pap. 15.95 *(978-1-4327-7522-3(7))* Outskirts Pr., Inc.

The Place Between Breaths. (ENG., Illus.). (YA). (gr. 7). 2019. 208p. pap. 10.99 *(978-1-4814-2226-0(X)*, Atheneum Bks. for Young Readers) 2018. 192p. 17.99 *(978-1-4814-2225-3(1)*, Atheneum/Caitlyn Dlouhy Books) Simon & Schuster Children's Publishing.

Plitt, Kay. Why Isn't Bobby Like Me, Mom? 2010. 32p. 14.75 *(978-1-4269-4038-5(6))* Trafford Publishing.

Polsky, Sara. This Is How I Find Her. 2015. (ENG.). 272p. (YA). (gr. 8-12). pap. 9.99 *(978-0-8075-7880-3(0)*, 807578800) Whitman, Albert & Co.

Ransom, Marty. Our Father, Our Soldier, Our Hero. 2011. 36p. pap. 24.95 *(978-1-4626-1377-9(2))* America Star Bks.

Redford, Alison. The Boy Who Built a Wall Around Himself. Simpson, Kara, illus. 2015. 32p. (J). 17.95 *(978-1-84905-683-0(8)*, 693905) Kingsley, Jessica Pubs. GBR. Dist: Hachette UK Distribution.

Reed, Amy. Crazy. (ENG., (YA). (gr. 9). 2013. Illus.). 416p. pap. 9.99 *(978-1-4424-1348-1(4))* 2012. 384p. 16.99 *(978-1-4424-1347-4(6))* Simon Pulse. (Simon Pulse).

Reeves, Dia. Bleeding Violet. 2010. (ENG.). 480p. (YA). (gr. 9). pap. 20.99 *(978-1-4169-8619-5(7)*, Simon Pulse) Simon Pulse.

Richards, Natalie D. We All Fall Down. 2017. (ENG.). 368p. (YA). (gr. 8-12). pap. 10.99 *(978-1-4926-5438-4(8))* Sourcebooks, Inc.

Rinaldi, Ann. Or Give Me Death. 2004. (Great Episodes Ser.). 226p. (gr. 5-9). 17.00 *(978-0-7569-3462-0(1))* Perfection Learning Corp.

Roux, Madeleine. Asylum. (Asylum Ser.: 1). (ENG.). (YA). (gr. 9). 2014. 336p. pap. 15.99 *(978-0-06-222097-4(7))* 2013. (Illus.). 320p. 17.99 *(978-0-06-222096-7(9))* HarperCollins Pubs. (HarperCollins).

—Asylum. 2015. (SPA.). 320p. (YA). (gr. 9-12). pap. 20.99 *(978-987-612-778-3(0))* V&R Editoras.

Russell, Anna. What If, 1 vol. 2018. (YA Verse Ser.). (ENG.). 200p. (YA). (gr. 3-4). 25.80 *(978-1-5383-8258-5(X)*, 1ca3d90c-eec5-4577-a1cb-b3995b9459d3); pap. 16.35 *(978-1-5383-8257-8(1)*, 794c8adc-1bfb-4fbb-90f7-4712d2b3916d) Enslow Publishing, LLC.

Scelsa, Kate. Fans of the Impossible Life. 2015. (ENG.). 368p. (YA). (gr. 9). 17.99 *(978-0-06-233175-5(2)*, Balzer & Bray) HarperCollins Pubs.

Schantz, Sarah Elizabeth. Fig. 2016. (ENG.). 352p. (YA). (gr. 9). pap. 11.99 *(978-1-4814-2359-5(2)*, McElderry, Margaret K. Bks.) McElderry, Margaret K. Bks.

Schraff, Anne. The Vandal. 2008. 132p. (J). (gr. 4-7). 13.95 *(978-0-7569-8388-8(6))* Perfection Learning Corp.

Shaw, Susan. Black-Eyed Suzie. 2007. (ENG.). 176p. (J). (gr. 1-4). pap. 9.95 *(978-1-59078-533-1(9)*, Astra Young Readers) Astra Publishing Hse.

Shusterman, Neal. Challenger Deep. Shusterman, Brendan, illus. (ENG.). 320p. (YA). (gr. 9). 2016. pap. 15.99 *(978-0-06-113414-2(7))* 2015. 17.99 *(978-0-06-113411-1(2))* HarperCollins Pubs. (Quill Tree Bks.).

Singleton, Paul. Sometimes Mama's Just Like That. 2013. 30p. pap. 17.99 *(978-0-578-13425-3(X))* Drinking Gourd Pr.

Sirowy, Alexandra. The Creeping. 2015. (ENG., Illus.). 400p. (YA). (gr. 7). 17.99 *(978-1-4814-1886-7(6))* Simon & Schuster Children's Publishing.

Stahler, David, Jr. Spinning Out. 2011. (ENG.). 288p. (YA). (gr. 7-17). 16.99 *(978-0-8118-7780-0(9))* Chronicle Bks. LLC.

Strasser, Todd. Price of Duty. 2018. (ENG., Illus.). 192p. (YA). (gr. 9). 17.99 *(978-1-4814-9709-1(X)*, Simon & Schuster Bks. For Young Readers) Simon & Schuster Bks. For Young Readers.

—The Wave. 2013. lib. bdg. 20.85 *(978-0-606-27009-0(4))* Turtleback.

Taree, Aerie. Molly's Mental Health: Love Me Too. 2008. 36p. pap. 24.95 *(978-1-60441-064-8(7))* PublishAmerica, Inc.

Taylor, Whitney. Definitions of Indefinable Things. 2019. (ENG.). 336p. (YA). (gr. 9). pap. 9.99 *(978-1-328-49801-4(8)*, 1717859, Clarion Bks.) HarperCollins Pubs.

Toten, Teresa. Beware That Girl. 2018. (ENG.). 336p. (YA). (gr. 9). pap. 9.99 *(978-0-553-50793-5(1)*, Ember) Random Hse. Children's Bks.

Trueman, Terry. Inside Out. 128p. 2003. (J). lib. bdg. 16.89 *(978-0-06-623963-7(X))* 2004. (ENG.). (YA). (gr. 9). reprint ed. pap. 9.99 *(978-0-06-447376-7(7)*, HarperTeen) HarperCollins Pubs.

Truly Blessed Ink. I Know You Won't Forget. Jordan, Carol, illus. 2007. (ENG.). 40p. (J). 16.95 *(978-0-9789066-1-0(6))* Square Circle Pr. LLC.

Vaught, Susan. Footer Davis Probably Is Crazy. Reinhardt, Jennifer Black, illus. 2015. (ENG.). 240p. (J). (gr. 5-9). 16.99 *(978-1-4814-2276-5(6)*, Simon & Schuster Bks. For Young Readers) Simon & Schuster Bks. For Young Readers.

Ventresca, Yvonne. Black Flowers, White Lies. (ENG.). (J). 2018. 280p. (gr. 8-8). pap. 9.99 *(978-1-5107-2596-6(2))* 2016. 272p. (gr. 6-6). 16.99 *(978-1-5107-0988-1(6))* Skyhorse Publishing Co., Inc. (Sky Pony Pr.).

Vizzini, Ned. It's Kind of a Funny Story. 2007. (ENG.). 464p. (J). (gr. 7-12). per. 10.99 *(978-0-7868-5197-3(X)*, Disney-Hyperion) Disney Publishing Worldwide.

—It's Kind of a Funny Story. 2011. 11.04 *(978-0-7848-3383-4(4)*, Everbind) Marco Bk. Co.

—It's Kind of a Funny Story. 2007. (YA). lib. bdg. 20.85 *(978-1-4178-1818-1(2))* Turtleback.

Walton, Julia. Words on Bathroom Walls. 304p. (YA). (gr. 7). 2018. pap. 9.99 *(978-0-399-55091-1(7)*, Ember) 2017. 17.99 *(978-0-399-55088-1(7)*, Random Hse. Bks. for Young Readers) Random Hse. Children's Bks.

Weeks, Sarah. So B. It. (ENG.). (J). (gr. 5). 2005. 288p. pap. 9.99 *(978-0-06-441047-2(1))* 2004. 256p. 16.99 *(978-0-06-623622-3(3))* HarperCollins Pubs. (HarperCollins).

—So B. It. 2009. 9.00 *(978-0-7848-3326-1(5)*, Everbind) Marco Bk. Co.

—So B. It. 2005. 17.00 *(978-0-7569-5112-2(7))* Perfection Learning Corp.

—So B. It. 2007. (J). 1.25 *(978-1-4193-7988-8(7))* Recorded Bks., Inc.

Williams, Carol Lynch. Miles from Ordinary: A Novel. 2012. (ENG.). 208p. (YA). (gr. 8-12). 26.19 *(978-0-312-55512-2(1))* St. Martin's Pr.

Winfrey, Kerry. Love & Other Alien Experiences. 2017. (ENG.). 272p. (YA). pap. 19.99 *(978-1-250-11952-0(9)*, 900172820) Feiwel & Friends.

Woods, Elizabeth. Choker. 2012. (ENG.). 240p. (YA). (gr. 9). pap. 12.99 *(978-1-4424-1234-7(8)*, Simon & Schuster Bks. For Young Readers) Simon & Schuster Bks. For Young Readers.

Young, Janet Ruth. My Beautiful Failure. (ENG., Illus.). 320p. (YA). (gr. 7). 2013. pap. 9.99 *(978-1-4424-8269-2(9))* 2012. 16.99 *(978-1-4169-5489-7(9))* Simon & Schuster Children's Publishing. (Atheneum Bks. for Young Readers).

—Things I Shouldn't Think. 2012. (ENG., Illus.). 352p. (YA). (gr. 9). pap. 8.99 *(978-1-4424-5107-0(6)*, Atheneum Bks. for Young Readers) Simon & Schuster Children's Publishing.

Zappia, Francesca. Made You Up. 2017. (ENG.). 464p. (YA). (gr. 9). pap. 11.99 *(978-0-06-229011-3(8)*, Greenwillow Bks.) HarperCollins Pubs.

MENTAL PHILOSOPHY

see Philosophy; Psychology

MENTAL TELEPATHY

see Thought Transference

MENTALLY DISABLED PERSONS

see People with Mental Disabilities

MENTALLY HANDICAPPED

see People with Mental Disabilities

MENTALLY ILL

see also People with Mental Disabilities

Abramovitz, Melissa. What Is Schizophrenia? 2015. (ENG., Illus.). 80p. (J). lib. bdg. *(978-1-60152-926-8(0))* ReferencePoint Pr., Inc.

Brinkerhoff, Shirley. Childhood & Adolescent Disorders. McDonnell, Mary Ann & Esherick, Donald, eds. 2013. (State of Mental Illness & Its Therapy Ser.: 19). 128p. (J). (gr. 7-18). 24.95 *(978-1-4222-2822-7(3))* Mason Crest.

Burkhart, Jessica, et al. Life Inside My Mind: 31 Authors Share Their Personal Struggles. Burkhart, Jessica, ed. 2018. (ENG., Illus.). 320p. (YA). (gr. 9). 17.99 *(978-1-4814-9464-9(3)*, Simon Pulse) Simon Pulse.

Champion, Gina. Anna & Her Mommy. Mitchell, Nanci, illus. 2005. 36p. (J). (gr. k-6). pap. 10.00 *(978-1-884363-20-7(2))* Odenwald Pr.

Clarke, Lisa A. Wishing Wellness: A Workbook for Children of Parents with Mental Illness. Matthews, Bonnie, illus. 2006. (ENG.). 128p. (J). (gr. 1-7). per. 14.95 *(978-1-59147-313-8(6)*, Magination Pr.) American Psychological Assn.

Evans, Jan. Repetitive Rhonda: A Coloring Book. 2007. (Illus.). 16p. (J). *(978-0-9720176-8-8(2))* Breath & Shadows Productions.

Goldman, Stan. CPCS Mental Health Proceedings in Massachusetts. 2014. (ENG.). pap. 125.00 *(978-1-57589-853-7(5))* Massachusetts Continuing Legal Education, Inc.

Knight, S. Black Magic. 2007. (ENG.). 156p. per. *(978-1-84747-007-2(6))* Chipmunkapublishing.

Landau, Elaine. Schizophrenia. 2004. (Life Balance Ser.). (ENG.). 80p. (J). 20.50 *(978-0-531-12215-0(8)*, Watts, Franklin) Scholastic Library Publishing.

Nakaya, Andrea C. What Is Bipolar Disorder? 2015. (ENG., Illus.). 80p. (J). lib. bdg. *(978-1-60152-922-0(8))* ReferencePoint Pr., Inc.

Netzley, Patricia D. What Impact Does Mental Illness Have on Crime? 2014. (In Controversy Ser.). (ENG., Illus.). 96p. (J). lib. bdg. *(978-1-60152-660-1(1))* ReferencePoint Pr., Inc.

Ross, Allison J. Coping When a Parent Is Mentally Ill. 2009. (Coping Ser.). 192p. (gr. 7-12). 63.90 *(978-1-61511-987-5(6))* Rosen Publishing Group, Inc., The.

Rustad, Martha E. H. Some Kids Have Autism, 1 vol. 2008. (Understanding Differences Ser.). (ENG., Illus.). 24p. (J). (gr. -1-2). pap. 6.29 *(978-1-4296-1772-7(1)*, 94819, Pebble) Capstone.

Stewart, Sheila. Something's Wrong! Kids with Emotional Disturbance. 2009. (Kids with Special Needs Ser.). 48p. (YA). (gr. 5-18). pap. 7.95 *(978-1-4222-1923-2(2))* Mason Crest.

Turner, Amanda. Helping Those with Mental Illnesses. 2019. (Careers Making a Difference Ser.). (Illus.). 80p. (J). (gr. 12). lib. bdg. 34.60 *(978-1-4222-4260-5(9))* Mason Crest.

Wood, Kelly & Fletcher, Douglas. Stand up to OCD! A CBT Self-Help Guide & Workbook for Teens. 2019. (Illus.). 164p. 21.95 *(978-1-78592-835-2(X)*, 696911) Kingsley, Jessica Pubs. GBR. Dist: Hachette UK Distribution.

MENTALLY ILL—FICTION

Anderson, R. J. Ultraviolet. 2013. (ENG.). 312p. (YA). (gr. 7-12). pap. 9.95 *(978-1-4677-0914-9(X)*, 49905a67-b3d3-4207-afce-401434fab3bd, Carolrhoda Lab™) Lerner Publishing Group.

Bacigalupi, Paolo, et al. Diverse Energies, 1 vol. Buckell, Tobias S. & Monti, Joe, eds. 2012. (ENG., Illus.). 368p. (YA). (gr. 8-12). pap. 13.95 *(978-1-62014-011-6(X)*, leelowtu) Lee & Low Bks., Inc.

Bérubé, Amelinda. The Dark Beneath the Ice. 2019. (ENG.). 336p. (YA). (gr. 8-12). pap. 10.99 *(978-1-4926-7878-6(3))* Sourcebooks, Inc.

Bodeen, S. A. The Compound. 2009. (Compound Ser.: 1). (ENG.). 272p. (YA). (gr. 7-12). pap. 10.99 *(978-0-312-57860-2(1)*, 900061807) Square Fish.

Brown, Jahla. Nathan Is Nathan. 2009. (ENG., Illus.). 20p. (J). pap. 19.95 *(978-0-9778083-8-0(6))* Everlasting Publishing.

Dorfman, Joaquin. The Long Wait for Tomorrow. 2009. (YA). *(978-0-375-84696-0(4))* Random Hse., Inc.

Elizabeth Arkward Newton. The Little Boy Who Wished God Had Not Given Him a Brain: Big Momma Books. 2009. 36p. pap. 18.99 *(978-1-4389-0133-6(X))* AuthorHouse.

Firmston, Kim. Schizo, 1 vol. 2011. (Lorimer SideStreets Ser.). (ENG.). 152p. (YA). (gr. 9-12). 16.95 *(978-1-55277-872-2(X),* 872) James Lorimer & Co. Ltd., Pubs. CAN. Dist: Formac Lorimer Bks. Ltd.

Ford, J. One in Four. 2007. pap. *(978-1-84747-173-4(0))* Chipmunkapublishing.

Greenberg, Joanne. I Never Promised You a Rose Garden. 256p. (YA). (gr. 7-18). pap. 5.99 *(978-0-8072-1362-9(4),* Listening Library) Random Hse. Audio Publishing Group.

Heiman, Herb. Running on Dreams. 2007. 293p. (YA). (gr. 8-14). per. 22.95 *(978-1-931282-28-4(5))* Autism Asperger Publishing Co.

Hills, Curt. Hannah's Legalized Kidnapping: A Rush to React Took Her Away for 207 Days. 2007. 68p. per. 12.95 *(978-1-4327-0668-5(3))* Outskirts Pr., Inc.

Jayne, Hannah. The Escape. 2015. (ENG., Illus.). 256p. (YA). (gr. 8-12). pap. 10.99 *(978-1-4926-1654-2(0),* 9781492616542) Sourcebooks, Inc.

Ketchen, Susan. Made That Way. 2010. (ENG.). 160p. (J). pap. 12.95 *(978-0-88982-270-2(0))* Oolichan Bks. CAN. Dist: Univ. of Toronto Pr.

Lambert, Mary E. Family Game Night & Other Catastrophes. 2018. (ENG.). 256p. (J). (gr. 3-7). pap. 7.99 *(978-0-545-93199-1(1),* Scholastic Pr.) Scholastic, Inc.

Lorenz, Nancy. The Strength of Ballerinas. 2014. 249p. (YA). pap. 15.99 *(978-1-4621-1452-8(0))* Cedar Fort, Inc./CFI Distribution.

Lupica, Mike. No Slam Dunk. (ENG.). (J). (gr. 5-9). 2019. 256p. 8.99 *(978-0-525-51487-9(2),* Puffin Books) 2018. 240p. 17.99 *(978-0-525-51485-5(6),* Philomel Bks.) Penguin Young Readers Group.

Mayfield, Jamie. A Broken Kind of Life. 2016. (ENG., Illus.). (YA). (gr. 9-12). 24.99 *(978-1-63477-926-5(6),* Harmony Ink Pr.) Dreamspinner Pr.

McAnulty, Stacy. The Miscalculations of Lightning Girl. 2018. (Illus.). 304p. (J). (gr. 3-7). 17.99 *(978-1-5247-6757-0(3),* Random Hse. Bks. for Young Readers) Random Hse. Children's Bks.

Moskowitz, Hannah. Break. 2009. (ENG.). 272p. (YA). (gr. 9-18). pap. 12.99 *(978-1-4169-8275-3(2),* Simon Pulse) Simon Pulse.

Oliver, Lauren. Vanishing Girls. (ENG.). (YA). (gr. 9). 2016. 384p. pap. 11.99 *(978-0-06-222411-8(5))* 2015. 368p. 18.99 *(978-0-06-222410-1(7))* HarperCollins Pubs. (HarperCollins).

—Vanishing Girls. 2016. (YA). lib. bdg. 20.85 *(978-0-606-38171-0(6))* Turtleback.

Peterson, Lois. Three Good Things, 1 vol. 2015. (Orca Currents Ser.). (ENG.). 144p. (J). (gr. 4-7). pap. 9.95 *(978-1-4598-0985-7(8))* Orca Bk. Pubs. USA.

Porter, Pamela. The Crazy Man. 2013. 164p. pap. *(978-1-4596-6446-3(9))* ReadHowYouWant.com, Ltd.

Rice, Luanne. Pretend She's Here. 2019. (ENG.). 352p. (YA). (gr. 7-7). 18.99 *(978-1-338-29850-5(X),* Scholastic Pr.) Scholastic, Inc.

Roorda, Julie. Wings of a Bee, 1 vol. 2008. (ENG., Illus.). 224p. (YA). (gr. 7-11). pap. *(978-1-894549-68-4(6),* Sumach Pr.) Canadian Scholars.

Sheinmel, Alyssa. A Danger to Herself & Others. 2019. (ENG.). 352p. (YA). (gr. 9-12). 17.99 *(978-1-4926-6724-7(2))* Sourcebooks, Inc.

Stauffacher, Sue. Donuthead. 2005. (Donuthead Ser.). 176p. (J). (gr. 3-7). reprint ed. per. 7.99 *(978-0-440-41934-1(4),* Yearling) Random Hse. Children's Bks.

Strasser, Todd. Price of Duty. 2019. (ENG.). 192p. (YA). (gr. 9). pap. 11.99 *(978-1-4814-9710-7(3))* Simon & Schuster, Inc.

Sunderland, Margot. Willy & the Wobbly House: A Story for Children Who Are Anxious or Obsessional. 2017. (ENG.). 28p. (C). 215.00 *(978-1-138-43414-1(0),* Y370330) Routledge.

Winegar, Tracy. Keeping Keller. 2008. 207p. pap. 14.99 *(978-1-59955-115-9(2))* Cedar Fort, Inc./CFI Distribution.

MENTALLY RETARDED PERSONS

see People with Mental Disabilities

MENUS

Silate, Jennifer. Planning & Preparing Healthy Meals & Snacks: A Day-to-Day Guide to a Healthier Diet. (Library of Nutrition Ser.). 48p. 2009. (gr. 5-8). 53.00 *(978-1-60853-776-1(5),* Rosen Reference) 2007. (ENG., Illus.). (gr. 5-8). per. 12.75 *(978-1-4042-1634-1(0),* 0ef2d217-9d00-4fa8-b55f-5f29767e2608) 2004. (Illus.). (J). lib. bdg. 26.50 *(978-1-4042-0302-0(8))* Rosen Publishing Group, Inc., The.

Tuminelly, Nancy. Super Simple Dinners: Easy No-Bake Recipes for Kids, 1 vol. 2010. (Super Simple Cooking Ser.). (ENG.). 32p. (J). (gr. -1-4). 34.21 *(978-1-61613-385-6(6),* 13916, Super SandCastle) ABDO Publishing Co.

MERCHANDISE

see Commercial Products

MERCHANDISING

see Marketing; Retail Trade

MERCHANTS

Behnke, Alison. Grocers. 2005. (Pull Ahead Bks.). (Illus.). 32p. (J). (gr. 3-7). lib. bdg. 22.60 *(978-0-8225-2801-2(0),* Lerner Pubns.) Lerner Publishing Group.

Bennett, Eric G. Pull up the Ladder Jack: Seamen Behaving Badly. 2012. 182p. 29.99 *(978-1-4797-3476-4(4));* pap. 19.99 *(978-1-4797-3475-7(6))* Xlibris Corp.

Bow, James. Your Guide to Trade in the Middle Ages. 2017. (Destination: Middle Ages Ser.). (ENG., Illus.). 32p. (J). (gr. 5-5). *(978-0-7787-2996-9(6));* pap. *(978-0-7787-3052-1(2))* Crabtree Publishing Co.

Dyan, Penelope. The Place of Tales — a Kid's Guide to Canterbury, Kent, England. Weigand, John, photos by. 2011. (Illus.). 40p. pap. 12.95 *(978-1-935630-66-1(0))* Bellissima Publishing, LLC.

Hull, Robert. Merchant. 2009. (Medieval Lives Ser.). (J). 32.80 *(978-1-59920-170-2(4))* Black Rabbit Bks.

Mead, Wendy. The Merchant, 1 vol. 2013. (Colonial People Ser.). (ENG.). 48p. (gr. 4-4). 34.07 *(978-1-60870-415-6(7),* f18c8cad-bf17-4dc2-972b-b264fb47ea42); pap. 13.93 *(978-1-62712-047-0(5),* 6a3babb9-af96-4e31-a45f-9ce34247d589) Cavendish Square Publishing LLC.

O'Brien, Cynthia. Go West with Merchants & Traders. 2016. (ENG.). 32p. (J). *(978-0-7787-2326-4(7))* Crabtree Publishing Co.

MERCURY (PLANET)

Adamson, Thomas K. Do You Really Want to Visit Mercury? Fabbri, Daniele, illus. 2013. (Do You Really Want to Visit the Solar System? Ser.). (ENG.). 24p. (J). (gr. 1-4). 27.10 *(978-1-60753-195-1(X),* 16263) Amicus.

—Mercury [Scholastic]: Revised Edition. 2010. (Exploring the Galaxy Ser.). (ENG.). 24p. pap. 0.49 *(978-1-4296-5812-6(6),* Capstone Pr.) Capstone.

Bernay, Emma & Berne, Emma Carlson. The Secrets of Mercury. 2015. (Planets Ser.). (ENG., Illus.). 32p. (J). (gr. 2-4). lib. bdg. 32.65 *(978-1-4914-5866-2(6),* 128829) Capstone.

Beth, Georgia. Discover Mercury. 2018. (Searchlight Books (tm) — Discover Planets Ser.). (ENG., Illus.). 32p. (J). (gr. 3-5). 30.65 *(978-1-5415-2336-4(9),* 2c98872f-abae-45b1-a1d5-853932de3ce4, Lerner Pubns.) Lerner Publishing Group.

Bloom, J. P. Mercurio (Mercury), 1 vol. 2016. (Planetas (Planets) Ser.). (SPA., Illus.). 24p. (J). (gr. -1-2). lib. bdg. 32.79 *(978-1-68080-755-4(2),* 22672, Abdo Kids) ABDO Publishing Co.

—Mercury, 1 vol. 2015. (Planets Ser.). (ENG.). 24p. (J). (gr. -1-2). lib. bdg. 32.79 *(978-1-62970-718-1(X),* 17235, Abdo Kids) ABDO Publishing Co.

—Mercury. 2017. (Planets Ser.). (ENG.). 24p. (J). (gr. -1-2). pap. 7.95 *(978-1-4966-1283-0(3),* 135015, Capstone Classroom) Capstone.

Carson, Mary Kay. Far-Out Guide to Mercury, 1 vol. 2010. (Far-Out Guide to the Solar System Ser.). (ENG.). 48p. (gr. 4-6). 27.93 *(978-0-7660-3180-7(2),* 75115966-2db2-45ef-b2d9-5b206ba9ef2f); (Illus.). pap. 11.53 *(978-1-59845-181-8(2),* 8ef5e73a-5a47-461e-a11c-1ee8f2535537, Enslow Elementary) Enslow Publishing, LLC.

Colligan, L. H. Mercury, 1 vol. 2010. (Space! Ser.). (ENG.). 64p. (gr. 5-5). lib. bdg. 35.50 *(978-0-7614-4239-4(1),* 6e76b094-35fa-4eb1-8b7a-515ba181678e) Cavendish Square Publishing LLC.

Croce, Carlo P. Mercury. (Library of Planets Ser.). 48p. (gr. 5-8). 2009. 55.90 *(978-1-60853-818-8(4),* Rosen Reference) 2008. (ENG., Illus.). (YA). lib. bdg. 34.47 *(978-1-4042-1427-9(5),* 2a77101b-f4dd-4e67-ab49-af250612f2de) Rosen Publishing Group, Inc., The.

Dickmann, Nancy. Exploring the Inner Planets, 1 vol. 2015. (Spectacular Space Science Ser.). (ENG., Illus.). 48p. (J). (gr. 5-6). 33.47 *(978-1-4994-3629-7(7),* ab513eb5-c984-4eb0-b82d-98012308a5f4, Rosen Central) Rosen Publishing Group, Inc., The.

Dittmer, Lori. Mercure. 2018. (Graines de Savoir Ser.). (FRE., Illus.). 24p. (J). *(978-1-77092-408-6(6),* 19697) Creative Co., The.

—Mercury. 2018. (Seedlings Ser.). (ENG., Illus.). 24p. (J). (gr. -1-1). pap. 7.99 *(978-1-62832-532-4(1),* 19614, Creative Paperbacks); *(978-1-60818-916-8(3),* 19616, Creative Education) Creative Co., The.

Dunn, Mary R. A Look at Mercury. 2009. (Astronomy Now! Ser.). 24p. (gr. 2-3). 42.50 *(978-1-61511-470-2(X),* PowerKids Pr.) Rosen Publishing Group, Inc., The.

Glaser, Chaya. Mercurio: El MÁS PequeÑo de Todos. 2015. (Fuera de Este Mundo Ser.). (SPA., Illus.). 24p. (J). (gr. -1-3). lib. bdg. 26.99 *(978-1-62724-592-0(8))* Bearport Publishing Co., Inc.

—Mercury: The Smallest of All. 2015. (Out of This World Ser.). (ENG.). 24p. (J). (gr. -1-3). lib. bdg. 23.93 *(978-1-62724-561-6(8))* Bearport Publishing Co., Inc.

Goldstein, Margaret J. Mercury. 2005. (Pull Ahead Bks.). (Illus.). 32p. (J). (gr. 2-4). lib. bdg. 22.60 *(978-0-8225-4648-1(5))* Lerner Publishing Group.

Hamilton, Robert M. Exploring Mercury. 2017. (Journey Through Our Solar System Ser.). 24p. (gr. 1-2). 49.50 *(978-1-5345-2256-5(5),* KidHaven Publishing) Greenhaven Publishing LLC.

Hantula, Richard & Asimov, Isaac. Mercurio (Mercury), 1 vol. 2003. (Isaac Asimov's Biblioteca Del Universo Del Siglo XXI (Isaac Asimov's 21st Century Library of the Universe) Ser.).Tr. of Mercury: The Quick Planet. (SPA., Illus.). 32p. (gr. 3-5). lib. bdg. 28.67 *(978-0-8368-3857-2(2),* 08ce5c1c-4855-4a1b-a429-f6b6072454a7, Gareth Stevens Learning Library) Stevens, Gareth Publishing LLLP.

Hollar, Sherman. The Inner Planets: Mercury, Venus, & Mars, 1 vol. 2011. (Solar System Ser.). (ENG., Illus.). 96p. (J). (gr. 8-8). 35.29 *(978-1-61530-512-4(2),* d524e35f-a616-40a6-a97b-953a5b929220) Rosen Publishing Group, Inc., The.

James, Lincoln. Mercury, 1 vol. 2010. (Our Solar System Ser.). (ENG.). 24p. (J). (gr. k-2). pap. 9.15 *(978-1-4339-3828-3(6),* 27a39344-5a6a-4732-b3fe-a3888126760e); (Illus.). lib. bdg. 25.27 *(978-1-4339-3827-6(8),* b82059b0-ef6a-4fcb-87e0-da1802ceedd1) Stevens, Gareth Publishing LLLP.

Jefferis, David. Hot Planets: Mercury & Venus. 2008. (ENG., Illus.). 32p. (J). (gr. 3-7). pap. *(978-0-7787-3751-3(9))* Crabtree Publishing Co.

Kazunas, Ariel. Mercury. 2011. (21st Century Junior Library: Solar System Ser.). (ENG., Illus.). 24p. (gr. 2-5). lib. bdg. 29.21 *(978-1-61080-088-4(5),* 201086) Cherry Lake Publishing.

Lew, Kristi. Mercury. 2009. (Understanding the Elements of the Periodic Table Ser.). 48p. (gr. 6-6). 53.00 *(978-1-60854-666-4(7),* Rosen Reference) Rosen Publishing Group, Inc., The.

Loewen, Nancy. Nearest to the Sun: The Planet Mercury, 1 vol. Yesh, Jeffrey, illus. 2008. (Amazing Science: Planets Ser.). (ENG.). 24p. (J). (gr. k-4). lib. bdg. 27.32 *(978-1-4048-3954-0(2),* 94526, Picture Window Bks.) Capstone.

Miller, Ron. Mercury & Pluto. 2003. (Worlds Beyond Ser.). (Illus.). 80p. (J). (gr. 7-18). lib. bdg. 27.93 *(978-0-7613-2361-7(9),* Twenty-First Century Bks.) Lerner Publishing Group.

Murray, Julie. Mercury. 2018. (Planets (Dash!) Ser.). (ENG., Illus.). 24p. (J). (gr. k-4). lib. bdg. 31.36 *(978-1-5321-2529-4(1),* 30067, Abdo Zoom-Dash) ABDO Publishing Co.

Owen, Ruth. Mercury, 1 vol. 2013. (Explore Outer Space Ser.). (ENG.). 32p. (J). (gr. 2-3). pap. 11.00 *(978-1-61533-761-3(X),* 20bd8ffc-7dbb-4af3-8e82-845be7c362be); lib. bdg. 29.93 *(978-1-61533-722-4(9),* 56e29fb0-300b-4a33-a9e7-473b7f500c5b) Rosen Publishing Group, Inc., The. (Windmill Bks.).

—Mercury. 2013. (Explore Outer Space Ser.). 32p. (J). (gr. 3-6). pap. 60.00 *(978-1-61533-762-0(8))* Windmill Bks.

Oxlade, Chris. Mercury, Mars, & Other Inner Planets, 1 vol. 2007. (Earth & Space Ser.). (ENG., Illus.). 48p. (YA). (gr. 6-6). lib. bdg. 34.47 *(978-1-4042-3735-3(6),* 69b00a7b-f6f7-4e68-a243-b4d1bb8e955a) Rosen Publishing Group, Inc., The.

Rhodes, Mary Wilson. Journey to Mercury, 1 vol. 2014. (Spotlight on Space Science Ser.). (ENG.). 32p. (J). (gr. 5-5). pap. 12.75 *(978-1-4994-0372-5(0),* bd74e974-8e60-4551-b4ee-eb3f3b437035, PowerKids Pr.) Rosen Publishing Group, Inc., The.

Ring, Susan. Mercury. (J). 2013. 27.13 *(978-1-62127-266-3(4))* 2013. pap. 12.95 *(978-1-62127-275-5(3))* 2004. (Illus.). pap. 8.95 *(978-1-59036-225-9(X))* 2004. (Illus.). 24p. (gr. 4-7). lib. bdg. 24.45 *(978-1-59036-098-9(2))* Weigl Pubs., Inc.

Ring, Susan & Roumanis, Alexis. Mercury. 2016. (Illus.). 24p. (J). *(978-1-5105-0980-1(1))* SmartBook Media, Inc.

Roumanis, Alexis. Mercury. 2016. (J). *(978-1-5105-2051-6(1))* SmartBook Media, Inc.

—Mercury. 2015. (Illus.). 24p. (J). *(978-1-4896-3292-0(1))* Weigl Pubs., Inc.

Sommer, Nathan. Mercury. 2019. (Space Science Ser.). (ENG., Illus.). 24p. (J). (gr. 3-7). lib. bdg. 26.95 *(978-1-62617-974-5(3),* Torque Bks.) Bellwether Media.

Sparrow, Giles. Destination Mercury, 1 vol. 2009. (Destination Solar System Ser.). (ENG.). 32p. (J). (gr. 3-4). lib. bdg. 28.93 *(978-1-4358-3441-5(0),* d02370b7-5a8c-46b0-acb1-669ebad14c24); (Illus.). pap. 11.00 *(978-1-4358-3455-2(0),* 9dbf2a09-30ef-4a3e-a76c-e17e114079c4) Rosen Publishing Group, Inc., The. (PowerKids Pr.).

Squire, Ann O. Planet Mercury. 2014. (True Book — Space (Revised Edition) Ser.). (ENG.). 48p. (J). lib. bdg. 29.00 *(978-0-531-21153-3(3))* Scholastic Library Publishing.

Steinkraus, Kyla. Planetas Rocosos - Mercurio, Venus, la Tierra y Marte. 2017. (Inside Outer Space Ser.).Tr. of Rocky Planets - Mercury, Venus, Earth, & Mars. (SPA.). 24p. (gr. k-3). pap. 9.95 *(978-1-68342-262-4(7),* 9781683422624) Rourke Educational Media.

Stone, Tanya Lee. Mercury, 1 vol. 2003. (Blastoff! Ser.). (ENG., Illus.). 64p. (gr. 5-5). 34.07 *(978-0-7614-1403-2(7),* 55b133bf-ce16-476e-8948-6f371fb14a47) Cavendish Square Publishing LLC.

Taylor-Butler, Christine. Mercury. 2007. (Scholastic News Nonfiction Readers Ser.). (ENG., Illus.). 24p. (J). (gr. 1-2). 22.00 *(978-0-531-14698-9(7))* Scholastic Library Publishing.

Tocci, Salvatore. Mercury. 2005. (True Bks.). (ENG., Illus.). 48p. (J). (gr. 3-7). lib. bdg. 25.00 *(978-0-516-23700-8(4),* Children's Pr.) Scholastic Library Publishing.

Vogt, Gregory. Mercury. 2009. (Early Bird Astronomy Ser.). (ENG.). 48p. (gr. 2-5). lib. bdg. 26.60 *(978-0-7613-4150-5(1))* Lerner Publishing Group.

Wimmer, Teresa. Mercury. 2007. (My First Look at: Planets Ser.). (Illus.). 24p. (J). (gr. -1-3). lib. bdg. 24.25 *(978-1-58341-519-1(X),* Creative Education) Creative Co., The.

World Book, Inc. Staff, contrib. by. Mercury & Venus. (J). 2010. *(978-0-7166-9534-9(0))* 2006. (Illus.). 63p. *(978-0-7166-9502-8(2))* 2nd ed. 2006. (Illus.). 64p. *(978-0-7166-9517-2(0))* World Bk., Inc.

Zobel, Derek. Mercury. 2010. (Exploring Space Ser.). (ENG., Illus.). 24p. (J). (gr. k-3). lib. bdg. 26.95 *(978-1-60014-402-8(0),* Blastoff! Readers) Bellwether Media.

MERCURY PROJECT

see Project Mercury (U.S.)

MERCY DEATH

see Euthanasia

MERCY KILLING

see Euthanasia

MEREDITH, JAMES, 1933-

Bausum, Ann. The March Against Fear: The Last Great Walk of the Civil Rights Movement & the Emergence of Black Power. 2017. (Illus.). 144p. (YA). (gr. 7-12). 18.99 *(978-1-4263-2665-3(3),* National Geographic Kids) Disney Publishing Worldwide.

MERLIN (LEGENDARY CHARACTER)—FICTION

Barron, T. A. Doomraga's Revenge: Book 7, 7 vols., Bk. 7. 2011. (Merlin Saga Ser.: 7). (ENG.). 272p. (J). (gr. 5-18). 8.99 *(978-0-14-241925-0(7),* Puffin Books) Penguin Young Readers Group.

—The Dragon of Avalon: Book 6, Bk. 6. 2011. (Merlin Saga Ser.: 6). (ENG.). 336p. (J). (gr. 5-18). 8.99 *(978-0-14-241924-3(9),* Puffin Books) Penguin Young Readers Group.

—The Lost Years: Book 1, Bk. 1. 2011. (Merlin Saga Ser.: 1). (ENG.). 352p. (J). (gr. 5-18). 9.99 *(978-0-14-241889-5(7),* Puffin Books) Penguin Young Readers Group.

—The Raging Fires: Book 3, Bk. 3. 2011. (Merlin Saga Ser.: 3). (ENG.). 288p. (J). (gr. 5-18). 8.99 *(978-0-14-241921-2(4),* Puffin Books) Penguin Young Readers Group.

—The Seven Songs: Book 2, Bk. 2. 2011. (Merlin Saga Ser.: 2). (ENG.). 336p. (J). (gr. 5-18). 9.99 *(978-0-14-241920-5(6),* Puffin Books) Penguin Young Readers Group.

—The Wizard's Wings: Book 5, Bk. 5. 2011. (Merlin Saga Ser.: 5). (ENG.). 384p. (J). (gr. 5-18). 8.99 *(978-0-14-241923-6(0),* Puffin Books) Penguin Young Readers Group.

Côté, Denis. La Forêt aux Mille et un Périls. Tome 2. Poulin, Stephane, illus. 2004. (Roman Jeunesse Ser.). (FRE.). 96p. (J). (gr. 4-7). pap. *(978-2-89021-696-9(9))* Diffusion du livre Mirabel (DLM).

Epstein, Alex. The Circle Cast: The Lost Years of Morgan le Fey, 1 vol. 2011. (ENG., Illus.). 240p. (YA). (gr. 8-12). pap. 12.95 *(978-1-896580-63-0(7))* Tradewind Bks. CAN. Dist: Orca Bk. Pubs. USA.

Gale, Eric Kahn. The Wizard's Dog Fetches the Grail. 2018. (ENG., Illus.). 288p. (J). (gr. 3-7). 16.99 *(978-0-553-53740-6(7),* Crown Books For Young Readers) Random Hse. Children's Bks.

Gamble, Paul. The Knight's Armor: Book 3 of the Ministry of SUITs. 2018. (Ministry of SUITs Ser.: 3). (ENG., Illus.). 368p. (J). 25.99 *(978-1-250-07684-7(6),* 900152371) Feiwel & Friends.

Liess, Claudia Schmidt. Henry the Magical, Mythical Dragon. 2008. 74p. pap. 19.95 *(978-1-60672-956-4(X))* America Star Bks.

Mass, Wendy. Stealing the Sword: a Branches Book (Time Jumpers #1) Vidal, Oriol, illus. 2018. (Time Jumpers Ser.: 1). (ENG.). 96p. (J). (gr. 1-3). pap. 5.99 *(978-1-338-21736-0(4))* Scholastic, Inc.

Memling, Carl. The Sword in the Stone (Disney) RH Disney, illus. 2015. (Little Golden Book Ser.). (ENG.). 24p. (J). (-k). 5.99 *(978-0-7364-3374-7(0),* Golden/Disney) Random Hse. Children's Bks.

Phelan, Matt. Knights vs. Dinosaurs. Phelan, Matt, illus. (ENG., Illus.). (J). (gr. 3-7). 2019. 176p. pap. 7.99 *(978-0-06-268624-4(0))* 2018. 160p. 16.99 *(978-0-06-268623-7(2))* HarperCollins Pubs. (Greenwillow Bks.).

Pilkington, Linda Rash. Arthur Collins & the Three Wishes: Arthur the Brave! 322p. (gr. 4-18). 2009. (YA). pap. 13.95 *(978-0-615-26743-2(2))* 2008. (J). 20.95 *(978-0-615-22213-4(7))* City Castles Publishing.

Salerni, Dianne K. The Inquisitor's Mark. 2015. (Eighth Day Ser.: 2). (ENG.). 352p. (J). (gr. 3-7). 16.99 *(978-0-06-227218-8(7),* HarperCollins) HarperCollins Pubs.

Spinner, Stephanie. The Magic of Merlin. Sokolova, Valerie, illus. 2004. (Stepping Stones: A Chapter Book: Fantasy Ser.). 42p. (J). 11.65 *(978-0-7569-0905-5(8))* Perfection Learning Corp.

Treskillard, Robert. Merlin's Nightmare, 1 vol. 2014. (Merlin Spiral Ser.). (ENG.). 432p. (YA). pap. 12.99 *(978-0-310-73509-0(2))* Blink.

Yolen, Jane. The Young Merlin Trilogy: Passager, Hobby, & Merlin. 2004. (ENG., Illus.). 276p. (J). (gr. 3-7). pap. 16.95 *(978-0-15-205211-9(9),* 1195715, Clarion Bks.) HarperCollins Pubs.

MERMAIDS

Alberti, Theresa Jarosz. Mermaids. 2018. (Illus.). 32p. (J). *(978-1-4896-9846-9(9),* AV2 by Weigl) Weigl Pubs., Inc.

Altmann, Scott. Mermaids — Sirens of the Sea. 2009. (Dover Fantasy Coloring Bks.). (ENG., Illus.). 32p. (J). (gr. 1-5). pap. 3.99 *(978-0-486-46990-4(5),* 469905) Dover Pubns., Inc.

Carlson-Berne, Emma. A First Look at Mermaids. 2020. (Bumba Books (r) — Fantastic Creatures Ser.). (ENG., Illus.). 24p. (J). (gr. -1-1). 26.65 *(978-1-5415-9685-6(4),* 36e837f5-12c1-499d-9257-f72d5a519723, Lerner Pubns.) Lerner Publishing Group.

Gish, Ashley. Mermaids. (Amazing Mysteries Ser.). (J). 2020. 24p. (gr. 1-3). pap. 9.99 *(978-1-62832-782-3(0),* 18178, Creative Paperbacks) 2019. (ENG.). 32p. (gr. 3-6). *(978-1-64026-197-6(4),* 19244, Creative Education) Creative Co., The.

Hile, Lori. Mermaids: Myth or Reality? 2018. (Investigating Unsolved Mysteries Ser.). (ENG., Illus.). 32p. (J). (gr. 3-9). lib. bdg. 28.65 *(978-1-5435-3567-9(4),* 138908, Capstone Pr.) Capstone.

Hinds, Kathryn. Mermaids, 1 vol. 2013. (Creatures of Fantasy Ser.). (ENG.). 64p. (gr. 6-6). pap. 16.28 *(978-1-62712-053-1(X),* 2ba0a824-3602-4257-aa29-f65f75a31465); (Illus.). 36.93 *(978-0-7614-4924-9(8),* 04dc1bde-4b50-4789-aede-b0df5b5c8032) Cavendish Square Publishing LLC.

Jarosz Alberti, Theresa. Mermaids. 2018. (Mythical Creatures Ser.). (ENG., Illus.). 32p. (J). (gr. 2-3). pap. 9.95 *(978-1-64185-004-9(3),* 1641850043); lib. bdg. 31.35 *(978-1-63517-902-6(5),* 1635179025) North Star Editions. (Focus Readers).

Jeffrey, Gary. Mermaids, 1 vol. Boccanfuso, Emanuele, illus. 2012. (Graphic Mythical Creatures Ser.). (ENG.). 24p. (J). (gr. 3-3). pap. 9.15 *(978-1-4339-6765-8(0),* fa6ec4da-819d-49b6-a95c-311c40d23eed); lib. bdg. 26.60 *(978-1-4339-6763-4(4),* dbcacff9-5719-402e-9182-3f02f1d3916d) Stevens, Gareth Publishing LLLP. (Gareth Stevens Learning Library).

Knudsen, Shannon. Mermaids & Mermen. 2009. (Fantasy Chronicles Ser.). (ENG.). 48p. (gr. 4-7). lib. bdg. 27.93 *(978-0-8225-9981-4(3))* Lerner Publishing Group.

Loh-Hagan, Virginia. Mermaids. 2017. (Magic, Myth, & Mystery Ser.). (ENG., Illus.). 32p. (J). (gr. 4-8). lib. bdg. 32.07 *(978-1-63472-149-3(7),* 209168, 45th Parallel Press) Cherry Lake Publishing.

Mahoney, Emily. Learn Collective Nouns with Mermaids, 1 vol. 2020. (Grammar Magic! Ser.). (ENG.). 24p. (gr. 2-3). pap. 9.15 *(978-1-5382-4731-0(3),* d8dc980d-848b-4d8b-ab44-3c7b713f0228) Stevens, Gareth Publishing LLLP.

Meachen Rau, Dana. Mermaids, 1 vol. 2011. (For Real? Ser.). (ENG.). 24p. (gr. 3-3). 25.50 *(978-0-7614-4862-4(4),* afd7023e-83d4-41b5-8647-fb371e68dc3b) Cavendish Square Publishing LLC.

O'Brien, Cynthia. Mermaid Myths, 1 vol. 2017. (Myths Across the Map Ser.). (ENG.). 48p. (J). (gr. 5-6). pap. 15.05 *(978-1-5382-1445-9(8),* 8d0a2973-d960-4442-85fc-2baed294d20d); lib. bdg. 33.60 *(978-1-5382-1372-8(9),* e514faf7-da37-476f-8f8d-809ccb8dcf74) Stevens, Gareth Publishing LLLP.

Pratt, Leonie. Mermaid things to make & Do. 2005. 32p. (J). pap. 6.95 *(978-0-7945-1062-6(0),* Usborne) EDC Publishing.

Preston, Lizzie. I Heart Mermaids. 2018. (I Heart Ser.: 3). (ENG., Illus.). 128p. (J). (gr. 1-3). pap. 9.95 *(978-1-4549-3167-6(1))* Sterling Publishing Co., Inc.

Publications International Ltd. Staff, creator. Look & Find: Disney Princess: the Little Mermaid. 2013. 24p. (J). (gr. 1-3). 7.98 *(978-1-4508-6996-6(3),* 23104826-4b2a-459d-8edc-2f0362eaf16d) Phoenix International Publications, Inc.

Redmond, Shirley Raye. Mermaids, 1 vol. 2007. (Monsters Ser.). (ENG., Illus.). 48p. (gr. 4-8). lib. bdg. 36.83 *(978-0-7377-3634-2(8),* 0998ffbf-c1e7-4fd3-8ec2-cebed4f5dcd8, KidHaven Publishing) Greenhaven Publishing LLC.

The Summer Mermaid: R-Controlled e, i, u: Level B, 6 vols. (Wright Skills Ser.). 16p. (gr. k-3). 26.50 *(978-0-322-01488-6(3))* Wright Group/McGraw-Hill.

M N O

Summers, Portia & Meachen Rau, Dana. Are Mermaids Real?, 1 vol. 2016. (I Want to Know Ser.). (ENG., Illus.). 32p. (gr. 3-3). pap. 11.52 (978-0-7660-8240-3(7), af0389ad-4338-49f5-94fe-296558d17640) Enslow Publishing, LLC.

Watt, Fiona. Mermaids. Cartwright, Stephen, illus. 2004. 10p. (J). 15.95 (978-0-7945-0727-5(1), Usborne) EDC Publishing.

MERMAIDS—FICTION

Aaron, Chester. Home to the Sea 2004. (Illus.). 125p. (YA). (gr. 8-12). per. 10.95 (978-0-9746481-2-5(4)) Brown Barn Bks.

Andersen, Hans Christian. & Kusama, Yayoi. The Little Mermaid: A Fairy Tale of Infinity & Love Forever. 2016. (ENG., Illus.). 96p. 45.00 (978-87-92877-59-8(1)) Louisana Museum of Modern Art DNK. Dist: D.A.P./Distributed Art Pubs.

Anderson, Hans Christian. Ariel & the Secret Grotto. (Read-Along Ser.). (J). 7.99 incl. audio (978-0-7634-0287-7(7)) Walt Disney Records.

—Little Mermaid: The Classic Edition. 2013. (Charles Santore Children's Classics Ser.).Tr. of Den Lille Havfrue. (ENG., Illus.). 48p. (J). (gr. -1). 19.95 (978-1-60433-377-0(4), Applesauce Pr.) Cider Mill Pr. Bk. Pubs., LLC.

—The Little Mermaid Retold. Charlotte, J. M., illus. 2013. 48p. 18.00 (978-0-9895422-0-3(3)) MHC Ministries.

Ann Scott, Lisa. Goodnight Lagoon. Sordo, Paco, illus. 2019. (ENG.). 40p. (J). (gr. -1-3). 17.99 (978-1-4998-0845-2(3)) Little Bee Books Inc.

Appelt, Kathi. Keeper. Hall, August, illus. (ENG.). (J). (gr. 3-7). 2012. 432p. pap. 9.99 (978-1-4169-5061-5(3)) 2010. 416p. 17.99 (978-1-4169-5060-8(5)) Simon & Schuster Children's Publishing. (Atheneum Bks. for Young Readers).

Ariel Make Believe Bride. 2008. (Disney 8*8 Ser.). 24p. pap. (978-1-4075-1620-2(5)) Parragon, Inc.

Arnell, Patricia. Forget Us Not Castle. 2007. (ENG.). 42p. pap. 17.99 (978-1-4257-4568-4(7)) Xlibris Corp.

Artful Doodlers Limited Staff. Dora Salva a las Sirenas. 2007. (Dora la Exploradora Ser.). (SPA., Illus.). 24p. (J). (gr. -1-2). pap. 3.99 (978-1-4169-4725-7(6), Libros Para Ninos) Libros Para Ninos.

Artful Doodlers Ltd Staff. Dora Saves Mermaid Kingdom! 2007. (Dora the Explorer Ser.: 24). (ENG., Illus.). 24p. (J). (gr. -1-2). pap. 3.99 (978-1-4169-3841-5(9), Simon Spotlight/Nickelodeon) Simon Spotlight/Nickelodeon.

Asher, Sally. The Mermaids' Night Before Christmas. Vandiver, Melissa, illus. 2019. (J). (978-1-946160-55-3(5)) Univ. of Louisiana at Lafayette Pr.

—Mermaids of New Orleans. Vandiver, Melissa, illus. 2018. (J). (978-1-946160-28-7(8)) Univ. of Louisiana at Lafayette Pr.

Balletta, Janet. The Legend of the Colombian Mermaid. Mejía, Estella, illus. 2013. 36p. (J). pap. 14.95 (978-0-9856762-9-2(9)) WRB Pub.

Banks, Rosie. Mermaid Reef. 2014. (Secret Kingdom Ser.: 4). lib. bdg. 14.75 (978-0-606-35842-2(0)) Turtleback.

Bar-el, Dan. That One Spooky Night. Huyck, David, illus. 2012. (ENG.). 80p. (J). (gr. 2-5). 8.95 (978-1-55453-752-5(5)) Kids Can Pr., Ltd. CAN. Dist: Hachette Bk. Group.

Bardhan-Quallen, Sudipta. Purrmaids #1: the Scaredy Cat. Wu, Vivien, illus. 2017. (Purrmaids Ser.: 1). (ENG.). 96p. (J). (gr. 1-4). 6.99 (978-1-5247-0161-1(0), Random Hse. Bks. for Young Readers) Random Hse. Children's Bks.

—Purrmaids #2: the Catfish Club. Wu, Vivien, illus. 2017. (Purrmaids Ser.: 2). (ENG.). 96p. (J). (gr. 1-4). 6.99 (978-1-5247-0164-2(5), Random Hse. Bks. for Young Readers) Random Hse. Children's Bks.

—Purrmaids #3: Seasick Sea Horse. Wu, Vivien, illus. 2018. (Purrmaids Ser.: 3). (ENG.). 96p. (J). (gr. 1-4). 5.99 (978-1-5247-0167-3(X), Random Hse. Bks. for Young Readers) Random Hse. Children's Bks.

—Purrmaids #4: Search for the Mermicorn. Wu, Vivien, illus. 2018. (Purrmaids Ser.: 4). (ENG.). 96p. (J). (gr. 1-4). pap. 5.99 (978-1-5247-0170-3(X), Random Hse. Bks. for Young Readers) Random Hse. Children's Bks.

—Purrmaids #5: a Star Purr-Formance. Wu, Vivien, illus. 2019. (Purrmaids Ser.: 5). (ENG.). 96p. (J). (gr. 1-4). 6.99 (978-0-525-64634-1(5), Random Hse. Bks. for Young Readers) Random Hse. Children's Bks.

—Purrmaids #6: Quest for Clean Water. Wu, Vivien, illus. 2019. (Purrmaids Ser.: 6). (ENG.). 96p. (J). (gr. 1-4). pap. 6.99 (978-0-525-64637-2(X), Random Hse. Bks. for Young Readers) Random Hse. Children's Bks.

—Purrmaids #7: Kittens in the Kitchen. Wu, Vivien, illus. 2020. (Purrmaids Ser.: 7). (ENG.). 96p. (J). (gr. 1-4). 6.99 (978-1-9848-9607-0(5), Random Hse. Bks. for Young Readers) Random Hse. Children's Bks.

Baxter, Nicola. The Mermaid & the Star. Rigby, Deborah, illus. 2025. 14p. (J). bds. (978-1-84322-907-0(2), Armadillo) Anness Publishing.

Beinstein, Phoebe. ¡A nadar, Boots! (Swim, Boots, Swim!) Roper, Robert, illus. 2009. (Dora la Exploradora Ser.). (SPA.). 24p. (J). pap. 3.99 (978-1-4169-7939-5(5), Libros Para Ninos) Libros Para Ninos.

—Swim, Boots, Swim! Roper, Robert, illus. 2009. (Dora the Explorer Ser.: 29). (ENG.). 24p. (J). (gr. -1-2). pap. 3.99 (978-1-4169-7195-5(5), Simon Spotlight/Nickelodeon) Simon Spotlight/Nickelodeon.

Berg, Deva Jean. A Tail of Two Sisters. Berg, Deva Jean, illus. 2013. (Illus.). 26p. pap. 9.95 (978-1-939790-07-1(7)) Lorian Assn., The.

Berk, Ari. The Secret History of Mermaids & Creatures of the Deep. 2009. (ENG., Illus.). 48p. (J). (gr. 3-7). 22.99 (978-0-7636-4515-1(X)) Candlewick Pr.

Bernstein, Danielle V. The Magic in a Mermaid's Tear. 2013. 28p. pap. 24.95 (978-1-62709-604-1(3)) America Star Bks.

Booker, Dwayne. Mia the Mermaid: Looking at Data, 1 vol. 2017. (Computer Science for the Real World Ser.). (ENG.). 12p. (gr. 1-2). pap. (978-1-5383-5122-2(6), 0340a020-b157-4358-95c0-60de6eb4f513, Rosen Classroom) Rosen Publishing Group, Inc., The.

Borgia, Mary. Tales of the Texas Mermaid: The Charro. 2007. (J). 17.95 (978-0-9778451-1-8(7)) Goretti Publishing.

Boudreau, Helene. Real Mermaids Don't Hold Their Breath. 2012. (ENG.). 240p. (J). (gr. 4-8). pap. 9.99 (978-1-4022-6446-7(1)) Sourcebooks, Inc.

—Real Mermaids Don't Need High Heels. 2013. (ENG.). 240p. (J). (gr. 4-8). pap. 10.99 (978-1-4022-6458-0(5)) Sourcebooks, Inc.

Braswell, Liz. Part of Your World (a Twisted Tale) A Twisted Tale. 2018. (Twisted Tale Ser.). (ENG., Illus.). 480p. (YA). (gr. 7-12). 18.99 (978-1-368-01381-9(3), Disney-Hyperion) Disney Publishing Worldwide.

Brennan-Nelson, Denise. Tallulah: Mermaid of the Great Lakes. Hartung, Susan Kathleen, illus. 2015. (ENG.). 40p. (J). (gr. 1-4). 16.99 (978-1-58536-909-6(8), 203812) Sleeping Bear Pr.

Brett, Jan. The Mermaid. Brett, Jan, illus. 2017. (Illus.). 32p. (J). (gr. -1 — 1). 19.99 (978-0-399-17072-0(3), G.P. Putnam's Sons Books for Young Readers) Penguin Young Readers Group.

Brown, Carron, ed. The Little Mermaid & the Princess & the Pea: Two Tales & Their Histories, 1 vol. 2009. (World of Fairy Tales Ser.). (ENG., Illus.). 32p. (J). (gr. 1-2). pap. 11.55 (978-1-60754-638-2(8), a3d137ff-acb1-4389-bda1-d37f43fac53f); lib. bdg. 27.27 (978-1-60754-637-5(X), dca8f046-f575-474d-a9b9-fdc02afe63f7) Rosen Publishing Group, Inc., The. (Windmill Bks.).

Bryan, Barbara. Starfish, Seashells, Coral & Gems. 2010. 47p. (J). pap. 27.95 (978-1-4327-6265-0(6)); pap. 21.95 (978-1-4327-6009-0(2)) Outskirts Pr., Inc.

Burns, Laura J. Magic Below. 2016. (Bewitched in Oz Ser.). (ENG.). 240p. (J). (gr. 4-8). lib. bdg. 30.65 (978-1-4965-2603-8(1), 130909, Stone Arch Bks.) Capstone.

Cabell, Robert W. The Mermaid Adventures of Princess Miranda: Volume One. Cabell, Robert W., illus. 2013. (Illus.). 128p. pap. 7.95 (978-0-9890974-3-7(9), Oceanus Bks.) Warrington Pubns.

Childs, Tera Lynn. Fins Are Forever. 2012. (Forgive My Fins Ser.: 2). (ENG.). 288p. (YA). (gr. 8). pap. 8.99 (978-0-06-191470-6(3), Tegen, Katherine Bks) HarperCollins Pubs.

—Forgive My Fins. 2011. (Forgive My Fins Ser.: 1). (ENG.). 336p. (YA). (gr. 8). pap. 8.99 (978-0-06-191467-6(3), Tegen, Katherine Bks) HarperCollins Pubs.

—Just for Fins. 2013. (Forgive My Fins Ser.: 3). (ENG.). 256p. (YA). (gr. 8). pap. 9.99 (978-0-06-219208-0(6), Tegen, Katherine Bks) HarperCollins Pubs.

Christo, Alexandra. To Kill a Kingdom. 2018. (Hundred Kingdoms Ser.). (ENG.). 352p. (YA). 19.99 (978-1-250-11268-2(0), 900170524) Feiwel & Friends.

—To Kill a Kingdom. 2019. (Hundred Kingdoms Ser.). (ENG.). 368p. (YA). pap. 10.99 (978-1-250-11270-5(2), 900170525) Square Fish.

Clibbon, Meg. Shimmering Mermaids. Clibbon, Lucy, illus. 2011. (My World Of Ser.). (ENG.). 32p. (J). (gr. k-2). pap. 9.99 (978-1-84089-594-0(2)) Meg and Lucy Bks. GBR. Dist: Independent Pubs. Group.

Collins, Michael. Anu & the Blue. 2009. 166p. pap. 16.68 (978-0-557-20316-1(3)) Lulu Pr., Inc.

Cordova, Zoraida. The Vicious Deep. 2012. (Vicious Deep Ser.: 1). (ENG.). 384p. (YA). (gr. 7-12). pap. 13.99 (978-1-4022-7441-1(6)) Sourcebooks, Inc.

Crump, Fred, Jr., illus. & retold by. The Little Mermaid. Crump, Fred, Jr., retold by. 2007. 32p. (J). 12.95 (978-1-934056-72-1(3)); pap. 9.95 (978-1-60352-063-8(5)) UMI (Urban Ministries, Inc.).

Dadey, Debbie. Battle of the Best Friends. Avakyan, Tatevik, illus. 2012. (Mermaid Tales Ser.: 2). (ENG.). 112p. (J). (gr. 1-4). 18.99 (978-1-4424-4979-4(9)); pap. 6.99 (978-1-4424-2982-6(8)) Simon & Schuster Children's Publishing. (Aladdin).

—Books vs. Looks. Avakyan, Tatevik, illus. 2016. (Mermaid Tales Ser.: 15). (ENG.). 128p. (J). (gr. 1-4). pap. 6.99 (978-1-4814-4081-3(0), Aladdin) Simon & Schuster Children's Publishing.

—Books vs. Looks. Avakyan, Tatevik, illus. 2016. (Mermaid Tales Ser.: 15). (ENG.). 128p. (J). (gr. 1-4). 17.99 (978-1-4814-4082-0(9), Simon & Schuster/Paula Wiseman Bks.) Simon & Schuster/Paula Wiseman Bks.

—The Crook & the Crown. Avakyan, Tatevik, illus. 2015. (Mermaid Tales Ser.: 13). (ENG.). 128p. (J). (gr. 1-4). pap. 6.99 (978-1-4814-4075-2(6), Aladdin) Simon & Schuster Children's Publishing.

—Danger in the Deep Blue Sea. Avakyan, Tatevik, illus. 2013. (Mermaid Tales Ser.: 4). (ENG.). 112p. (J). (gr. 1-4). 17.99 (978-1-4424-5319-7(2)); pap. 6.99 (978-1-4424-2986-4(0)) Simon & Schuster Children's Publishing. (Aladdin).

—Dream of the Blue Turtle. Avakyan, Tatevik, illus. 2014. (Mermaid Tales Ser.: 7). (ENG.). 128p. (J). (gr. 1-4). 17.99 (978-1-4424-8264-7(8)); pap. 6.99 (978-1-4424-8263-0(X)) Simon & Schuster Children's Publishing. (Aladdin).

—Fairy Chase. Avakyan, Tatevik, illus. 2018. (Mermaid Tales Ser.: 18). (ENG.). 112p. (J). (gr. 1-4). 17.99 (978-1-4814-8712-2(4)); pap. 5.99 (978-1-4814-8711-5(6)) Simon & Schuster Children's Publishing. (Aladdin).

—Flower Girl Dreams. Avakyan, Tatevik, illus. 2017. (Mermaid Tales Ser.: 16). (ENG.). 128p. (J). (gr. 1-4). pap. 5.99 (978-1-4814-4084-4(5), Simon & Schuster/Paula Wiseman Bks.) Simon & Schuster/Paula Wiseman Bks.

—The Lost Princess. Avakyan, Tatevik, illus. 2013. (Mermaid Tales Ser.: 5). (ENG.). 128p. (J). (gr. 1-4). 17.99 (978-1-4424-8258-6(3)); pap. 6.99 (978-1-4424-8257-9(5)) Simon & Schuster Children's Publishing. (Aladdin).

—Mermaid Tales, 8 vols., Set. Avakyan, Tatevik, illus. 2015. (Mermaid Tales Ser.: Vol. 8). (ENG.). 96p. (J). (gr. 1-4). 250.88 (978-1-61479-321-2(2), 17143, Chapter Bks.) Spotlight.

—Mermaid Tales 3-Books-In-1! Trouble at Trident Academy; Battle of the Best Friends; a Whale of a Tale. Avakyan, Tatevik, illus. 2016. (Mermaid Tales Ser.). (ENG.). 320p. (J). (gr. 1-4). pap. 8.99 (978-1-4814-8555-5(5), Aladdin) Simon & Schuster Children's Publishing.

—A Mermaid Tales Sparkling Collection (Boxed Set) Trouble at Trident Academy; Battle of the Best Friends; a Whale of a Tale; Danger in the Deep Blue Sea; the Lost Princess. Avakyan, Tatevik, illus. 2013. (Mermaid Tales Ser.). (ENG.). 592p. (J). (gr. 1-4). pap. 29.99 (978-1-4814-0055-8(X), Aladdin) Simon & Schuster Children's Publishing.

—The Narwhal Problem. Avakyan, Tatevik, illus. 2019. (Mermaid Tales Ser.: 19). (ENG.). 112p. (J). (gr. 1-4). 18.99 (978-1-4814-8715-3(9)); pap. 6.99 (978-1-4814-8714-6(0)) Simon & Schuster Children's Publishing. (Aladdin).

—The Polar Bear Express. Avakyan, Tatevik, illus. 2015. (Mermaid Tales Ser.: 11). (ENG.). 128p. (J). (gr. 1-4). pap. 6.99 (978-1-4814-0260-6(9), Aladdin) Simon & Schuster Children's Publishing.

—Ready, Set, Goal! Avakyan, Tatevik, illus. 2017. (Mermaid Tales Ser.: 17). (ENG.). 112p. (J). (gr. 1-4). 17.99 (978-1-4814-8709-2(4)); pap. 5.99 (978-1-4814-8708-5(6)) Simon & Schuster Children's Publishing. (Aladdin).

—A Tale of Two Sisters. Avakyan, Tatevik, illus. 2015. (Mermaid Tales Ser.: 10). (ENG.). 128p. (J). (gr. 1-4). 17.99 (978-1-4814-0258-3(7)); pap. 6.99 (978-1-4814-0257-6(9)) Simon & Schuster Children's Publishing. (Aladdin).

—Treasure in Trident City. Avakyan, Tatevik, illus. 2014. (Mermaid Tales Ser.: 8). (ENG.). 128p. (J). (gr. 1-4). pap. 6.99 (978-1-4424-8266-1(4), Aladdin) Simon & Schuster Children's Publishing.

—Trouble at Trident Academy. Avakyan, Tatevik, illus. 2012. (Mermaid Tales Ser.: 1). (ENG.). 112p. (J). (gr. 1-4). 17.99 (978-1-4424-4978-7(0)); pap. 6.99 (978-1-4424-2980-2(1)) Simon & Schuster Children's Publishing. (Aladdin).

—Twist & Shout. Avakyan, Tatevik, illus. 2016. (Mermaid Tales Ser.: 14). (ENG.). 112p. (J). (gr. 1-4). pap. 6.99 (978-1-4814-4078-3(0), Aladdin) Simon & Schuster Children's Publishing.

—A Whale of a Tale. Avakyan, Tatevik, illus. 2012. (Mermaid Tales Ser.: 3). (ENG.). 128p. (J). (gr. 1-4). 17.99 (978-1-4424-5318-0(4)); pap. 6.99 (978-1-4424-2984-0(4)) Simon & Schuster Children's Publishing. (Aladdin).

—Wish upon a Starfish. Avakyan, Tatevik, illus. 2015. (Mermaid Tales Ser.: 12). (ENG.). 128p. (J). (gr. 1-4). pap. 6.99 (978-1-4814-0263-7(3), Aladdin) Simon & Schuster Children's Publishing.

Dadey, Debby & Dadey, Debbie. Battle of the Best Friends, Bk. 2. Avakyan, Tatevik, illus. 2015. (Mermaid Tales Ser.). (ENG.). 104p. (J). (gr. 1-4). 31.36 (978-1-61479-323-6(9), 17145, Chapter Bks.) Spotlight.

—Danger in the Deep Blue Sea, Bk. 4. Avakyan, Tatevik, illus. 2015. (Mermaid Tales Ser.). (ENG.). 104p. (J). (gr. 1-4). 31.36 (978-1-61479-325-0(5), 17147, Chapter Bks.) Spotlight.

—Dream of the Blue Turtle, Bk. 7. Avakyan, Tatevik, illus. 2015. (Mermaid Tales Ser.). (ENG.). 112p. (J). (gr. 1-4). 31.36 (978-1-61479-328-1(X), 17150, Chapter Bks.) Spotlight.

—Secret Sea Horse, Bk. 6. Avakyan, Tatevik, illus. 2015. (Mermaid Tales Ser.). (ENG.). 96p. (J). (gr. 1-4). 31.36 (978-1-61479-327-4(1), 17149, Chapter Bks.) Spotlight.

—Treasure in Trident City, Bk. 8. Avakyan, Tatevik, illus. 2015. (Mermaid Tales Ser.). (ENG.). 120p. (J). (gr. 1-4). 31.36 (978-1-61479-329-8(8), 17151, Chapter Bks.) Spotlight.

—Trouble at Trident Academy, Bk. 1. Avakyan, Tatevik, illus. 2015. (Mermaid Tales Ser.). (ENG.). 104p. (J). (gr. 1-4). 31.36 (978-1-61479-322-9(0), 17144, Chapter Bks.) Spotlight.

—Whale of a Tale, Bk. 3. Avakyan, Tatevik, illus. 2015. (Mermaid Tales Ser.). (ENG.). 120p. (J). (gr. 1-4). 31.36 (978-1-61479-324-3(7), 17146, Chapter Bks.) Spotlight.

Dahl, Michael. The Marshmallow Mermaid. Crowther, Jeff, illus. 2010. (Princess Candy Ser.). (ENG.). 40p. (J). (gr. 2-5). pap. 5.95 (978-1-4342-2802-4(9), 114069, Stone Arch Bks.) Capstone.

Davidson, Susanna. Stories of Mermaids. 2009. (Young Reading 1 Ser.). 48p. (J). (gr. 2). 6.99 (978-0-7945-2589-7(X), Usborne) EDC Publishing.

De Brunhoff, Jean. Babar & Zephir. De Brunhoff, Jean., illus. 2005. (Illus.). 38p. (J). (gr. k-4). reprint ed. 16.00 (978-0-7567-8935-0(4)) DIANE Publishing Co.

Deep Trouble (Book 5) 2017. (Secret Mermaid Ser.). (ENG.). (J). pap. 4.99 (978-0-7945-3685-5(9), Usborne) EDC Publishing.

Dipinto, Michael J. The Princess Mermaid & the Missing Sea Shells. Marsh, Bobbie, illus. 2013. 36p. pap. 15.95 (978-1-61493-151-5(8)) Peppertree Pr., The.

Disney & Disney / LeapFrog. Disney Princess: Les aventures D'Ariel. 2008. (J). 20.79 (978-1-59319-944-9(9)) LeapFrog Enterprises, Inc.

Disney Books. The Little Mermaid ReadAlong Storybook & CD. 2013. (Read-Along Storybook & CD Ser.). (ENG., Illus.). 32p. (J). (gr. -1-k). pap. 6.99 (978-1-4231-6889-8(5), Disney Press Books) Disney Publishing Worldwide.

Disney Storybook Artists Staff & Thammavongsa, Christine, illus. The Little Mermaid. 2007. (Play-A-Sound Bks.). 18p. (J). (gr. -1-3). bds. 16.98 (978-1-4127-8775-8(0)) Publications International, Ltd.

Donaldson, Julia. The Mermaid & the Octopus: Band 04/Blue (Collins Big Cat) 2006. (Collins Big Cat Ser.). (ENG., Illus.). 16p. (J). (gr. 1-1). pap. 7.99 (978-0-00-718684-6(3)) HarperCollins Pubs. Ltd. GBR. Dist: Independent Pubs. Group.

Donnelly, Jennifer. Waterfire Saga, Book Four: Sea Spell. 2017. (Waterfire Saga Ser.). (ENG.). 368p. (J). (gr. 7-12). pap. 9.99 (978-1-4847-1303-7(6), Disney-Hyperion) Disney Publishing Worldwide.

Dougherty, Brandi. Wild Fairies #2: Lily's Water Woes. Kurilla, Renée, illus. 2018. (Wild Fairies Ser.: 2). 96p. (J). (gr. 1-4). 10.99 (978-1-63565-135-5(2), 9781635651355, Rodale Kids) Random Hse. Children's Bks.

Dunmore, Helen. Ingo. 2008. (Ingo Ser.: 1). (ENG.). 336p. (YA). (gr. 5). per. 15.99 (978-0-06-081854-8(9), HarperTeen) HarperCollins Pubs.

—The Tide Knot. 2008. 330p. (J). 5.99 (978-0-06-081857-9(3)) HarperCollins Pubs.

Ealy, Gerald & Ealy, Gerald. I Made a Wish to Be a Fish. 2012. 32p. pap. 9.95 (978-0-9843837-5-7(1)) G340 Publishing.

Eberly, Chelsea. Surf Princess. 2012. (Barbie Step into Reading Level 2 Ser.). lib. bdg. 13.55 (978-0-606-23718-5(6)) Turtleback.

Editors of Klutz. The Marvelous Book of Magical Mermaids: Dress up Paper Mermaids & Their Seahorse Friends. 2014. (ENG.). 50p. (J). (gr. 1). 19.99 (978-0-545-69214-4(8)) Klutz.

Ella, Sara. Coral, 1 vol. 2019. (ENG.). 384p. (YA). 18.99 (978-0-7852-2445-7(9)) Nelson, Thomas Inc.

Epperson, Kathy. Mermaids. 2013. 28p. pap. 24.95 (978-1-4626-9631-4(7)) America Star Bks.

Fama, Elizabeth. Monstrous Beauty. 2013. (ENG.). 352p. (YA). (gr. 7-12). pap. 17.99 (978-1-250-03425-0(6), 900120598) Square Fish.

Farmer, Nancy. The Islands of the Blessed. (ENG., Illus.). 496p. (YA). (gr. 7). 2012. pap. 13.99 (978-1-4169-0738-1(6), Atheneum Bks. for Young Readers) 2009. 18.99 (978-1-4169-0737-4(8), Atheneum/Richard Jackson Bks.) Simon & Schuster Children's Publishing.

—The Islands of the Blessed. l.t. ed. 2010. (Sequel to the Land of the Silver Apples Ser.). (ENG.). 607p. (J). 23.95 (978-1-4104-2253-8(4)) Thorndike Pr.

Felix, Rebecca. The Little Mermaid. Petelinsek, Kathleen, illus. 2013. (Fairy Tale Collection). (ENG.). 24p. (J). (gr. k-3). 32.79 (978-1-62323-612-0(6), 206379) Child's World, Inc, The.

Filakosky, Sandra. Star the Mermaid. Anderson, Susan, illus. 2010. 20p. pap. 10.49 (978-1-4389-8626-5(2)) AuthorHouse.

Gallemore, M. H. Annie & the Mermaid. 2005. 9.00 (978-0-8059-9787-3(3)) Dorrance Publishing Co., Inc.

Gamble, Adam & Jasper, Mark. Good Night Mermaids. Chan, Suwin, illus. 2015. (Good Night Our World Ser.). (ENG.). 20p. (J). (— 1). bds. 9.95 (978-1-60219-226-3(X)) Good Night Bks.

George, Kallie. The Melancholic Mermaid. Halpin, Abigail, illus. 2011. (ENG.). 64p. (J). (gr. k-4). 16.95 (978-1-897476-53-6(1)) Simply Read Bks. CAN. Dist: Ingram Publisher Services.

Gilbert, Julie. Fire & Ice: A Mermaid's Journey. Fagan, Kirbi, illus. 2017. (Dark Waters Ser.). (ENG.). 160p. (J). (gr. 5-9). lib. bdg. 26.65 (978-1-4965-4168-0(5), 133766, Stone Arch Bks.) Capstone.

—Into the Storm: A Mermaid's Journey. Fagan, Kirbi, illus. 2017. (Dark Waters Ser.). (ENG.). 160p. (J). (gr. 5-9). lib. bdg. 26.65 (978-1-4965-4171-0(5), 133769, Stone Arch Bks.) Capstone.

—Neptune's Trident: A Mermaid's Journey. Fagan, Kirbi, illus. 2017. (Dark Waters Ser.). (ENG.). 160p. (J). (gr. 5-9). lib. bdg. 26.65 (978-1-4965-4169-7(3), 133767, Stone Arch Bks.) Capstone.

—The Sighting: A Mermaid's Journey. Fagan, Kirbi, illus. 2017. (Dark Waters Ser.). (ENG.). 160p. (J). (gr. 5-9). lib. bdg. 26.65 (978-1-4965-4170-3(7), 133768, Stone Arch Bks.) Capstone.

Greening, Rosie. Mermaid Mia & the Royal Visit. Ede, Lara, illus. 2018. (ENG.). 32p. (J). (gr. 1-5). pap. 8.99 (978-1-78692-908-2(2)) Make Believe Ideas GBR. Dist: Scholastic, Inc.

Guettier, Nancy. Mermaids on Mars. 2013. (ENG.). 36p. (-3). pap. 9.95 (978-1-61448-670-1(0)); (Illus.). (gr. 1-3). 19.95 (978-1-61448-640-4(9)) Morgan James Publishing.

Gurtler, Janet. Shyanna's Wish. Wood, Katie, illus. 2015. (Mermaid Kingdom Ser.). (ENG.). 96p. (J). (gr. 3-5). 23.99 (978-1-4342-9696-2(2), 127009, Stone Arch Bks.) Capstone.

Hanes, Tracey. The Adventures of Kung Foo Poo. 2009. 84p. pap. 15.99 (978-1-4415-4045-4(8)) Xlibris Corp.

Hargreaves, Roger. Little Miss Trouble & the Mermaid. 2008. (Mr. Men & Little Miss Ser.). (ENG., Illus.). 32p. (J). (gr. -1-2). mass mkt. 4.99 (978-0-8431-3277-9(9), Grosset & Dunlap) Penguin Young Readers Group.

Hecker, Vera, illus. A Home for Rainbow. 2007. 32p. (J). (978-0-9799729-0-4(6)) Banta, Sandra.

Herman, Gail & Studio Iboix Staff. Ariel: The Birthday Surprise. 2011. (Disney Princess Ser.). (ENG., Illus.). 96p. (J). (gr. 2-6). 31.36 (978-1-59961-877-7(X), 5177, Chapter Bks.) Spotlight.

Hicks, Angie, illus. Moonlight & the Mermaid. 2012. (ENG.). 24p. (J). 9.95 (978-1-84135-833-8(9)) Award Pubns. Ltd. GBR. Dist: Parkwest Pubns., Inc.

Hinkler Books Staff. CD Storybook: Beauty & the Beast; The Little Mermaid; Cinderella; Snow White. rev. ed. 2004. (Illus.). 128p. (J). (gr. 4-12). 14.95 incl. cd-rom (978-1-86515-754-2(6)) Hinkler Bks. Pty, Ltd. AUS. Dist: Penton Overseas, Inc.

Holub, Joan & Williams, Suzanne. Amphitrite the Bubbly. 2015. (Goddess Girls Ser.: 17). (ENG., Illus.). 288p. (J). (gr. 3-7). pap. 8.99 (978-1-4424-8832-8(8), Aladdin) Simon & Schuster Children's Publishing.

Homberg, Ruth. The Little Mermaid. 2013. (Disney Princess Step into Reading Ser.). lib. bdg. 13.55 (978-0-606-32202-7(7)) Turtleback.

—The Little Mermaid Step into Reading (Disney Princess) RH Disney, illus. 2013. (Step into Reading Ser.). (ENG.). 32p. (J). (gr. -1-1). 5.99 (978-0-7364-8128-1(1), RH/Disney) Random Hse. Children's Bks.

Hunter, Mollie. The Mermaid Summer. 2003. 118p. (J). (978-1-4131-4688-2(0), Harper Trophy) HarperCollins Pubs.

Hutchinson, Kerrian. The Fish People. 2011. 18p. pap. 16.95 (978-1-4626-2692-2(0)) PublishAmerica, Inc.

Idle, Molly. Pearl. 2018. (ENG., Illus.). 48p. (J). (gr. -1-3). 18.99 (978-0-316-46567-0(4)) Little, Brown Bks. for Young Readers.

Jackson, Susan. The Secret of Mermaid Island. 2004. (J). per. 9.95 (978-0-9748087-1-0(7)) Journey Pubns., LLC.

Jarek, Janice. Mya & the Mermaid. 2012. 28p. 24.95 (978-1-4626-3277-0(7)) America Star Bks.

Johnson, Gillian. Thora. Johnson, Gillian, illus. 2003. (Illus.). 128p. (978-0-207-19815-1(2)) HarperCollins Pubs. Australia.

—Thora & the Green Sea-Unicorn. Johnson, Gillian, illus. 2005. (Illus.). 272p. (978-0-207-20016-8(5)) HarperCollins Pubs. Australia.

—Thora & the Incredible Crystals. 2007. (Illus.). 272p. (978-0-207-20017-5(3)) HarperCollins Pubs. Australia.

Jones, Cheri. The Adventures of a Mermaid Princess. 2013. 76p. (gr. -1). pap. 10.84 (978-1-4907-0598-9(8)) Trafford Publishing.

Kann, Victoria. Aqualicious. Kann, Victoria, illus. 2015. (ENG., Illus.). 40p. (J). (gr. -1-3). 18.99 (978-0-06-233016-1(0), HarperCollins) HarperCollins Pubs.

—Pinkalicious & Aqua, the Mini-Mermaid. Kann, Victoria, illus. 2016. (Pinkalicious Ser.). (ENG., Illus.). 24p. (J). (gr. -1-3). pap. 5.99 (978-0-06-241075-7(X), HarperFestival) HarperCollins Pubs.

—Pinkalicious & Aqua, the Mini-Mermaid. 2016. (Pinkalicious Ser.). (J). lib. bdg. 14.75 (978-0-606-38773-6(0)) Turtleback.

—Pinkalicious & the Pirates. Kann, Victoria, illus. 2018. (I Can Read Level 1 Ser.). (ENG., Illus.). 32p. (J). (gr. -1-3). 16.99 (978-0-06-256699-7(7)); pap. 4.99 (978-0-06-256698-0(9)) HarperCollins Pubs. (HarperCollins).

Kato, Haruhi, illus. Disney Manga: Fairies - Rani & the Mermaid Lagoon: Rani & the Mermaid Lagoon. 2018.

(Disney Manga: Fairies - Rani & the Mermaid Lagoon Ser.). 208p. (J). (gr. 3-1). pap. 10.99 *(978-1-4278-5801-6(2),* 65fb80d5-b38f-4bb8-9fdb-6dceb533ac60, TOKYOPOP Manga) TOKYOPOP, Inc.

Kessler, Liz. Emily Windsnap & the Castle in the Mist. Ledwidge, Natacha, illus. 2012. (Emily Windsnap Ser.: 3). (ENG.). 208p. (J). (gr. 3-7). pap. 6.99 *(978-0-7636-6017-8(5))* Candlewick Pr.

—Emily Windsnap & the Castle in the Mist. 2012. (Emily Windsnap Ser.: Bk. 3). lib. bdg. 16.00 *(978-0-606-25596-7(6))* Turtleback.

—Emily Windsnap & the Land of the Midnight Sun. 2014. (Emily Windsnap Ser.: Bk. 5). lib. bdg. 16.00 *(978-0-606-35165-2(5))* Turtleback.

—Emily Windsnap & the Monster from the Deep. Gibb, Sarah, illus. 2012. (Emily Windsnap Ser.: 2). (ENG.). 240p. (J). (gr. 3-7). pap. 6.99 *(978-0-7636-6018-5(3))* Candlewick Pr.

—Emily Windsnap & the Monster from the Deep. 2012. (Emily Windsnap Ser.: Bk. 2). lib. bdg. 16.00 *(978-0-606-25573-8(7))* Turtleback.

—Emily Windsnap & the Siren's Secret. (Emily Windsnap Ser.: 4). (ENG., Illus.). 304p. (J). (gr. 3-7). 2012. pap. 6.99 *(978-0-7636-6019-2(1))* 2010. 15.99 *(978-0-7636-4374-4(2))* Candlewick Pr.

—Emily Windsnap & the Siren's Secret. 2012. (Emily Windsnap Ser.: Bk. 4). lib. bdg. 16.00 *(978-0-606-25601-8(6))* Turtleback.

—Emily Windsnap: Two Magical Mermaid Tales. Gibb, Sarah, illus. 2014. (Emily Windsnap Ser.). (ENG.). 464p. (J). (gr. 3-7). pap. 11.99 *(978-0-7636-7452-6(4))* Candlewick Pr.

—The Tail of Emily Windsnap. Gibb, Sarah, illus. 2012. (Emily Windsnap Ser.: 1). (ENG.). 224p. (J). (gr. 3-7). pap. 6.99 *(978-0-7636-6020-8(5))* Candlewick Pr.

—The Tail of Emily Windsnap. 2012. (Emily Windsnap Ser.: Bk. 1). lib. bdg. 16.00 *(978-0-606-25544-8(3))* Turtleback.

King-Smith, Dick. The Merman. unabr. ed. 2004. 102p. (J). (gr. 3-7). pap. 29.00 incl. audio *(978-0-8072-8132-1(8),* Listening Library) Random Hse. Audio Publishing Group.

Klimo, Kate. The Dragon in the Sea, 5. Shroades, John, illus. 2012. (Dragon Keepers Ser.). 224p. (J). (gr. 4-6). lib. bdg. 22.44 *(978-0-375-97065-8(7))* Random Hse. Bks. for Young Readers.

—Dragon Keepers #4: the Dragon in the Volcano. Shroades, John, illus. 2012. (Dragon Keepers Ser.: 4). (ENG.). 256p. (J). (gr. 3-7). 7.99 *(978-0-375-86688-3(4),* Yearling) Random Hse. Children's Bks.

—Dragon Keepers #5: the Dragon in the Sea. Shroades, John, illus. 2013. (Dragon Keepers Ser.: 5). 224p. (J). (gr. 3-7). 7.99 *(978-0-375-87116-0(0),* Yearling) Random Hse. Children's Bks.

Koster, Amy Sky. Ariel & the Big Baby: Rapunzel Finds a Friend. Batson, Alan et al, illus. 2017. (J). *(978-1-5379-1732-0(3))* Random Hse., Inc.

Koster, Amy Sky & Patrick, Ella. Ariel & the Big Baby / Rapunzel Finds a Friend. 2017. (Disney Princess 8x8 Ser.). (Illus.). (J). lib. bdg. 16.00 *(978-0-606-40249-1(7))* Turtleback.

La Rose, Melinda & Ward, Kelly. Treasure of the Tides. 2014. (Jake & the Never Land Pirates Ser.). (ENG., Illus.). 32p. (J). (gr. k-2). 16.19 *(978-1-4844-3449-9(8))* Disney Pr.

Lagonegro, Melissa. Sealed with a Kiss (Disney Princess) Marrucchi, Elisa, illus. 2005. (Step into Reading Ser.). (ENG.). 32p. (J). (gr. k-3). per. 4.99 *(978-0-7364-2363-2(X),* RH/Disney) Random Hse. Children's Bks.

Larkin, Rochelle, ed. The Little Mermaid & Other Stories. (Illus.). 239p. (J). 9.95 *(978-0-86611-676-3(1))* Waldman Publishing Corp.

Larose, Melinda. Treasure of the Tides. 2014. (Jake & the Never Land Pirates Ser.). (J). lib. bdg. 13.55 *(978-0-606-35269-7(4))* Turtleback.

Lasaracina, Barbara. Mermaid Tears: A Magical Sea Tale. Peer, Nancy, illus. 2010. 28p. pap. 11.99 *(978-1-60844-451-9(1))* Dog Ear Publishing, LLC.

Lasky, Kathryn. Lucy (Daughters of the Sea #3) 2012. (Daughters of the Sea Ser.: 3). (ENG.). 320p. (J). (gr. 7). 17.99 *(978-0-439-78312-5(7),* Scholastic Pr.) Scholastic, Inc.

Levine, Gail Carson. Fairy Haven & the Quest for the Wand. Christiana, David, illus. 2007. 191p. (J). *(978-1-4287-6391-3(0))* Disney Pr.

Little Mermaid. 2009. (Disney Glitter Board Book Ser.). 5p. *(978-1-4054-9825-8(0))* Parragon, Inc.

Little Reader Digital Storybook: The Little Mermaid. 2005. (J). cd-rom 11.99 *(978-0-9767657-0-7(5))* Mullings Media.

Little Sticker Dolly Dressing Mermaids. 2017. (Little Sticker Dolly Dressing Ser.). (ENG.). (J). pap. 8.99 *(978-0-7945-3809-5(6),* Usborne) EDC Publishing.

Lovric, Michelle. The Undrowned Child, 1. 2012. (Undrowned Child Ser.). (ENG.). 464p. (J). (gr. 6-8). lib. bdg. 22.44 *(978-0-385-90814-6(8),* Delacorte Pr.) Random Hse. Children's Bks.

Madigan, L. K. The Mermaid's Mirror. 2011. (ENG.). 320p. (YA). (gr. 7). pap. 8.99 *(978-0-547-57735-7(4),* 1458544, Clarion Bks.) HarperCollins Pubs.

Man-Kong, Mary. A Fairy-Tail Adventure. 2012. (Barbie 8X8 Ser.). lib. bdg. 13.55 *(978-0-606-23850-2(6))* Turtleback.

Marks, Alan, illus. The Little Mermaid. 2005. 48p. (J). (gr. 4-7). 8.95 *(978-0-7945-1122-7(8),* Usborne) EDC Publishing.

Marroquin, Melissa. Tide Day, 1000 vols. 2016. (ENG., Illus.). (J). (gr. -1-3). 16.95 *(978-1-59298-684-2(6))* Beaver's Pond Pr., Inc.

Massenot, Véronique. The Mermaid & the Parakeet: A Children's Book Inspired by Henri Matisse. Hié, Vanessa, illus. 2016. (Children's Books Inspired by Famous Artworks Ser.). (ENG.). 32p. (J). (gr. -1-3). 14.95 *(978-3-7913-7265-5(3))* Prestel Verlag GmbH & Co KG. DEU. Dist: Penguin Random Hse. LLC.

McDermott, Noel. Kiviuq & the Mermaids, 1 vol. Feizo Gas, Toma, illus. 2016. (Kiviuq Ser.: 1). (ENG.). 40p. (J). (gr. 4-8). 16.95 *(978-1-77227-082-2(2))* Inhabit Media Inc. CAN. Dist: Consortium Bk. Sales & Distribution.

McGann, Oisín. Mad Grandad & the Mutant River. 2005. (Flyers Ser.: 14). (ENG., Illus.). 64p. (J). pap. 9.95 *(978-0-86278-939-8(7))* O'Brien Pr., Ltd., The IRL. Dist: Dufour Editions, Inc.

McKenzie, J. Lee. Vampires Don't Believe in Mermaids. 2011. 54p. pap. 16.95 *(978-1-4560-1157-4(X))* America Star Bks.

McLaren, Heather. Mythos. 2013. (ENG.). 260p. pap. 17.95 *(978-1-60619-093-7(8))* Twilight Times Bks.

McLeod, Kris Aro. Hush-a-Bye Counting: A Bedtime Book. Allyn, Virginia, illus. 2008. (ENG.). 20p. (J). (gr. -1). 14.95 *(978-1-58117-785-5(2),* Intervisual/Piggy Toes) Bendon, Inc.

Mlynowski, Sarah. Sink or Swim. 2013. (Whatever After Ser.: No. 3). 165p. (J). *(978-0-545-53316-4(3),* Scholastic Pr.) Scholastic, Inc.

—Sink or Swim (Whatever After #3) 2014. (Whatever After Ser.: 3). (ENG.). 176p. (J). (gr. 3-7). pap. 6.99 *(978-0-545-41570-5(5),* Scholastic Pr.) Scholastic, Inc.

Moffitt, Sara. Merlin & the Frog Meet Chatty & Noble. 2011. 25p. (J). pap. 18.95 *(978-1-4327-5921-6(3))* Outskirts Pr., Inc.

Morpurgo, Michael. Mairi's Mermaid. 2006. (Blue Bananas Ser.). (ENG., Illus.). 48p. (J). (gr. -1-3). lib. bdg. *(978-0-7787-0851-3(9))* Crabtree Publishing Co.

Munro, Moira. The Mermaid Who Came to School. 2012. 64p. pap. *(978-0-9571099-0-2(3))* Paperchard Bks.

Nail, Eric. The Wave Wranglers & the New Order of the Pyramid. 2007. 268p. (YA). pap. 18.95 *(978-1-4303-2254-2(3))* Lulu Pr., Inc.

Napoli, Donna Jo. Fish Girl. 2017. (ENG.). (J). (gr. 5-7). lib. bdg. 30.60 *(978-0-606-39824-4(4))* Turtleback.

Napoli, Donna Jo & Wiesner, David. Fish Girl. Wiesner, David, illus. 2017. (ENG., Illus.). 192p. (J). (gr. 5-7). pap. 17.99 *(978-0-547-48393-1(7),* 1439924, Clarion Bks.) HarperCollins Pubs.

Nesbit, E. Wet Magic. 2006. 188p. (gr. -1-7). 26.95 *(978-1-59818-174-6(2))* Aegypan.

—Wet Magic. 2006. 200p. (gr. -1-7). per. *(978-1-84350-095-7(7))* Soft Editions Ltd.

Nickelodeon. Swim, Boots, Swim! 2013. (Dora the Explorer 8X8 Ser.). lib. bdg. 13.55 *(978-0-606-31933-1(6))* Turtleback.

Noble, Trinka Hakes. Legend of Sea Glass. Ettlinger, Doris, illus. 2016. (Myths, Legends, Fairy & Folktales Ser.). (ENG.). 32p. (J). (gr. 1-4). 18.99 *(978-1-58536-611-8(0),* 204027) Sleeping Bear Pr.

Owen, Sarah. The Enchanted Tales. 2009. 39p. pap. 26.50 *(978-1-4452-5948-2(6))* Lulu Pr., Inc.

Papademetriou, Lisa & Morris, Kimberly. Rani: Two Friendship Tales. Disney Storybook Artists Staff, illus. 2010. (Disney Fairies Ser.). (ENG.). 240p. (J). (gr. 1-4). 24.94 *(978-0-7364-2730-2(9))* Random House Publishing Group.

Paquette, Ammi-Joan. The Tiptoe Guide to Tracking Mermaids. LeTourneau, Marie, illus. 2012. (ENG.). 32p. (J). (gr. k-5). 16.95 *(978-1-933718-59-0(5))* Tanglewood Pr.

Parker, Emma. The Lucky Pearl. 2010. (Illus.). 20p. pap. *(978-1-877561-18-4(5))* First Edition Ltd.

Parker, Vic, ed. The Little Mermaid & Other Stories, 1 vol. 2015. (Scary Fairy Tales Ser.). (ENG.). 40p. (J). (gr. 3-4). pap. 15.05 *(978-1-4824-3085-1(1),* c9de130e-bb9f-45d8-a7f0-12317744645a) Stevens, Gareth Publishing LLLP.

PC Treasures Staff, prod. The Little Mermaid. 2007. (J). *(978-1-60072-020-8(X))* PC Treasures, Inc.

Pearl, Paige. ARTLANTICA: the Secret Kingdom Beneath Galveston Island. 2008. 38p. 18.95 *(978-1-4357-0389-6(8))* Lulu Pr., Inc.

Peetoom, Laura. Mermaid in the Bathtub, 1 vol. Fernandes, Eugenie, illus. 2006. (First Flight: Level 4 Ser.). (ENG.). 104p. (J). (gr. 4-7). pap. 4.95 *(978-1-55041-362-5(7))* Fitzhenry & Whiteside, Ltd. CAN. Dist: F&W Media, Inc.

Perrault, Charles, contrib. by. The Little Mermaid. 2012. (Musical Fairy Tales Ser.). (ENG., Illus.). 12p. (J). (gr. -1-3). bds. 15.95 *(978-1-61889-066-5(2))* AZ Bks. LLC.

La Petite Sirene.Tr. of Little Mermaid. (FRE.). 48p. (J). pap. 12.95 incl. audio compact disk *(978-2-89558-071-3(5))* Coffragants CAN. Dist: Penton Overseas, Inc.

Philips, A. If You Believe in Mermaids Don't Tell. 2007. 160p. per. 12.95 *(978-1-59858-359-5(X))* Dog Ear Publishing, LLC.

Phillips, Beth Ann. Crystal Kingdom, 1 vol. 2009. 63p. pap. 19.95 *(978-1-60813-003-0(7))* America Star Bks.

Pinkney, Jerry. The Little Mermaid. 2020. (ENG., Illus.). 48p. (J). (gr. -1-3). 18.99 *(978-0-316-44031-8(0))* Little, Brown Bks. for Young Readers.

Playmore Publishers Staff. Sirenita. 2011. pap. 4.95 *(978-0-86611-653-4(2))* Waldman Publishing Corp.

Porter, Sarah. The Twice Lost. 2014. (Lost Voices Trilogy Ser.: 3). (ENG.). 480p. (YA). (gr. 7). pap. 9.99 *(978-0-547-48255-2(8),* 1439698, Clarion Bks.) HarperCollins Pubs.

—Waking Storms. 2013. (Lost Voices Trilogy Ser.: 2). (ENG.). 416p. (YA). (gr. 7). pap. 8.99 *(978-0-547-48254-5(X),* 1439697, Clarion Bks.) HarperCollins Pubs.

Pounder, Sibéal. Bad Mermaids Make Waves. Cockcroft, Jason, illus. 2018. (Bad Mermaids Ser.). (ENG.). 256p. (J). 13.99 *(978-1-68119-792-0(8),* 900187211, Bloomsbury Children's Bks.) Bloomsbury Publishing USA.

Publications International Ltd. Staff, ed. Disney Princess Ariel. 2011. 14p. (J). bds. 16.98 *(978-1-4127-9206-6(1))* Publications International, Ltd.

Quinn, Jordan. The Secret World of Mermaids. McPhillips, Robert, illus. 2015. (Kingdom of Wrenly Ser.: 8). (ENG.). 128p. (J). (gr. k-4). pap. 6.99 *(978-1-4814-3122-4(6),* Little Simon) Little Simon.

Rakos, Lynnda, et al. Princesses, Mermaids & Fairies Coloring Book. 2012. (Dover Fantasy Coloring Bks.). (ENG.). 32p. (J). (gr. -1-2). pap. 3.99 *(978-0-486-48664-2(8),* 486648) Dover Pubns., Inc.

Random House. Magical Mermaids! (Shimmer & Shine) Aikins, Dave, illus. 2017. (Step into Reading Ser.). (ENG.). 24p. (J). (gr. -1-1). pap. 4.99 *(978-0-399-55886-3(1),* Random Hse. Bks. for Young Readers) Random Hse. Children's Bks.

—Nickelodeon 5-Minute Christmas Stories (Nickelodeon) Random House, illus. 2017. (ENG., Illus.). 160p. (J). (gr. -1-2). 12.99 *(978-1-5247-6398-5(5),* Random Hse. Bks. for Young Readers) Random Hse. Children's Bks.

—Swim, Boots, Swim! (Dora the Explorer) Random House, illus. 2013. (Pictureback(R) Ser.). (ENG., Illus.). 24p. (J). (gr. -1-2). 3.99 *(978-0-449-81850-3(0),* Random Hse. Bks. for Young Readers) Random Hse. Children's Bks.

Ray, Jane. Can You Catch a Mermaid? 2003. (ENG., Illus.). 32p. (J). (gr. -1-12). pap. 9.99 *(978-1-84121-296-8(2))* Hodder & Stoughton GBR. Dist: Hachette Bk. Group.

Raymundo, Peter. Third Grade Mermaid. 2017. (ENG., Illus.). 208p. (J). (gr. 1-3). 14.99 *(978-0-545-91816-9(2),* Scholastic Pr.) Scholastic, Inc.

—Third Grade Mermaid & the Unicorns of the Sea. 2018. (ENG., Illus.). 208p. (J). (gr. 1-3). 13.99 *(978-0-545-94034-4(6),* Scholastic Pr.) Scholastic, Inc.

Reef Rescue (Book 4) 2017. (Secret Mermaid Ser.). (ENG.). (J). pap. 4.99 *(978-0-7945-3686-2(7),* Usborne) EDC Publishing.

Reeve, Philip. Oliver & the Sea Monkeys. McIntyre, Sarah, illus. 2016. (Not-So-Impossible Tale Ser.). (ENG.). 224p. (J). (gr. 2-5). pap. 7.99 *(978-0-385-38789-7(X),* Yearling) Random Hse. Children's Bks.

Reilly, Antoinette. Mr. Lobster & the Mermaid. 2011. 24p. pap. 14.93 *(978-1-4269-5683-6(5))* Trafford Publishing.

Return of the Dark Queen (Book 6) 2017. (Secret Mermaid Ser.). (ENG.). (J). pap. 4.99 *(978-0-7945-3684-8(0),* Usborne) EDC Publishing.

Riding, Robin. Mermaids Fast Asleep. Persico, Zoe, illus. 2019. (ENG.). 32p. (J). 17.99 *(978-1-250-07635-9(8),* 900152143) Feiwel & Friends.

Roberts, Roxanne. Angel Wings, Faery Dust & Other Magical Things: A Story about Merpeople. 2011. 24p. pap. 11.50 *(978-1-61204-588-7(X),* Strategic Bk. Publishing) Strategic Book Publishing & Rights Agency (SBPRA).

Robleda, Margarita. Suenos. Suarez, Maribel, illus. (Rana, Rema, Rimas Ser.). (SPA.). 16p. (J). (gr. k-3). 7.95 *(978-1-59437-821-8(5))* Santillana USA Publishing Co., Inc.

Rodriguez, Ashley. A Mermaid Tale. 2010. (ENG.). 60p. pap. 10.50 *(978-0-557-65601-1(X))* Lulu Pr., Inc.

Rossi, Francesca., illus. The Little Mermaid. 2015. (Fairy Tale Adventures Ser.). (ENG.). 64p. (J). (gr. 2-6). 7.95 *(978-1-4549-1509-6(9))* Sterling Publishing Co., Inc.

A Royal Tea. 2014. (Mermaid Tales Ser.: 9). (ENG., Illus.). 112p. (J). (gr. 1-4). pap. 6.99 *(978-1-4814-0254-5(4),* Aladdin) Simon & Schuster Children's Publishing.

Sabuda, Robert. The Little Mermaid. Sabuda, Robert, illus. 2013. (ENG., Illus.). 12p. (J). (gr. 1). 39.99 *(978-1-4169-6080-5(5),* Little Simon) Little Simon.

Saxton, Patricia. The Book of Mermaids. Saxton, Patricia, illus. 2006. (ENG., Illus.). 32p. (J). (gr. 1-5). 14.95 *(978-0-9726614-6-1(8))* Shenanigan Bks.

Schlegl, Stacey Lynn & Schlegl, Abigail. MerMountain. 2012. 84p. (J). pap. 11.95 *(978-0-9850272-2-3(3))* Jan-Carol Publishing, INC.

Schreiber, Ellen. Teenage Mermaid. 2003. 160p. (J). (gr. 4-18). lib. bdg. 16.89 *(978-0-06-008205-5(4))* HarperCollins Pubs.

Selfors, Suzanne. To Catch a Mermaid. 2009. (ENG.). 272p. (J). (gr. 3-7). pap. 15.99 *(978-0-316-01817-3(1))* Little, Brown Bks. for Young Readers.

Shin, Yujin, illus. My Magical Mermaid. 2019. (My Magical Friends Ser.). (ENG.). 8p. (J). (gr. -1 — 1). bds. 8.99 *(978-1-4197-3730-5(9),* 1278010, Abrams Appleseed) Abrams, Inc.

Steele, Michael Anthony. Attack of the Zombie Mermaids: A 4D Book. Reeves, Pauline, illus. 2018. (Nearly Fearless Monkey Pirates Ser.). (ENG.). 48p. (J). (gr. k-2). lib. bdg. 23.99 *(978-1-5158-2677-4(5),* 137832, Picture Window Bks.) Capstone.

Stine, R. L. Deep Trouble (Classic Goosebumps #2) 2008. (Classic Goosebumps Ser.: 2). (ENG.). 144p. (J). (gr. 3-7). 7.99 *(978-0-545-03519-4(8),* Scholastic Paperbacks) Scholastic, Inc.

Studio Mouse Editorial. Ariel: The Brave Little Mermaid. 2008. (ENG., Illus.). 36p. (gr. -1-k). 7.99 *(978-1-59069-434-3(1))* Studio Mouse LLC.

Swenlin, Brian & Bardekoff, Jennifer. Magical Mermaids! Aikins, Dave, illus. 2017. 24p. (J). *(978-1-5182-3609-9(X))* Random Hse., Inc.

Taylor, C. J. Spirits, Fairies, & Merpeople: Native Stories of Other Worlds. 2009. (Illus.). 40p. (J). (gr. 2-4). 19.95 *(978-0-88776-872-9(5),* Tundra Bks.) Tundra Bks. CAN. Dist: Penguin Random Hse. LLC.

Tea, Michelle. Girl at the Bottom of the Sea. Verwey, Amanda, illus. 2015. 240p. (J). (gr. 6). 19.95 *(978-1-940450-00-1(4),* 3f4b9717-9960-4c67-8ef0-24515f98345f) McSweeney's Publishing.

—Mermaid in Chelsea Creek. Polan, Jason, illus. 2013. 240p. (J). (gr. 5-11). 19.95 *(978-1-938073-36-6(3),* ea44eacc-0b51-4a46-b778-cae153d08009) McSweeney's Publishing.

Teitelbaum, Michael. The Little Mermaid (Disney Princess) DiCicco, Sue, illus. 2003. (Little Golden Book Ser.). (ENG.). 24p. (J). (gr. -1-2). 5.99 *(978-0-7364-2177-5(7),* Golden/Disney) Random Hse. Children's Bks.

Thorpe, Kiki. Never Girls #13: under the Lagoon (Disney: the Never Girls) Christy, Jana, illus. 2016. (Never Girls Ser.: 13). (ENG.). 128p. (J). (gr. 1-4). 6.99 *(978-0-7364-3529-1(8),* RH/Disney) Random Hse. Children's Bks.

Tillworth, Mary. Mermaid Treasure Hunt. 2015. (Dora the Explorer 8X8 Ser.). lib. bdg. 13.55 *(978-0-606-36395-2(5))* Turtleback.

ToyBox Innovations, creator. Disney's the Little Mermaid. abr. ed. 2006. (Disney's Read along Collection). (ENG.). (J). (gr. -1-3). pap. *(978-0-7634-2184-7(7))* Walt Disney Records.

—Disney's the Little Mermaid: Read-along. 2006. (Disney's Read Along Ser.). (ENG., Illus.). 24p. (J). pap. *(978-0-7634-2174-8(X))* Walt Disney Records.

Toybox Innovations Staff & Toybox Innovations, creators. Disney Read along Little Mermaid Collection, 3 vols. 2009. (ENG., Illus.). (J). (gr. -1-1). *(978-0-7634-1202-9(3))* Walt Disney Records.

Trowell, Michelle. Magical Mermaids. Top That Publishing Staff, ed. Richards, Kirsten, illus. 2008. (Magnetic Story & Play Scene Ser.). 9p. (J). (gr. -1). *(978-1-84666-442-7(X),* Tide Mill Pr.) Top That! Publishing PLC.

Ungaro, Marley. Darling Dozen of the Deep. 2012. (ENG.). (J). pap. 24.99 *(978-1-4675-4418-4(3))* Independent Pub.

Valencia, O. R. Savior in the Blue Mermaid. 2008. 180p. pap. 14.35 *(978-1-4251-2824-1(6))* Trafford Publishing.

Valentino, Serena. Poor Unfortunate Soul-Villains, Book 3. 2016. (Villains Ser.: 3). (ENG., Illus.). 224p. (YA). (gr. 7-12). 17.99 *(978-1-4847-2405-7(4),* Disney Press Books) Disney Publishing Worldwide.

Van Fleet, Mara. Three Little Mermaids. Van Fleet, Mara, illus. 2011. (ENG., Illus.). 16p. (J). (gr. -1-k). 17.99 *(978-1-4424-1286-6(0),* Simon & Schuster/Paula Wiseman Bks.) Simon & Schuster/Paula Wiseman Bks.

Wade, Judith. Mermaid Dreams. 2005. (J). per. 5.99 *(978-0-9728958-3-5(3))* Riley Pr.

—The Mermaid's Gift. 2004. 140p. (J). per. 5.99 *(978-0-9728958-1-1(7),* 750) Riley Pr.

—The Secret of Mermaid Island. 2003. 136p. (J). mass mkt. 5.99 *(978-0-9728958-0-4(9))* Riley Pr.

Wallace, Adam. How to Catch a Mermaid. Elkerton, Andy, illus. 2018. (How to Catch Ser.: 0). (ENG.). 40p. (J). (gr. k-5). 10.99 *(978-1-4926-6247-1(X))* Sourcebooks, Inc.

Watt, Fiona. That's Not My Mermaid. rev. ed. 2012. (Touchy-Feely Board Bks). 10p. (J). bds. 9.99 *(978-0-7945-3307-6(8),* Usborne) EDC Publishing.

Webster, Christy. Barbie in a Mermaid Tale. 2010. (Barbie Step into Reading Level 2 Ser.). lib. bdg. 13.55 *(978-0-606-07031-7(1))* Turtleback.

—Barbie in a Mermaid Tale (Barbie) Random House, illus. 2010. (Step into Reading Ser.). (ENG.). 32p. (J). (gr. -1-1). pap. 5.99 *(978-0-375-86450-6(4),* Random Hse. Bks. for Young Readers) Random Hse. Children's Bks.

Wetzel, JoAnne Stewart. Mermaid School. Swaney, Julianna, illus. 2018. (ENG.). 32p. (J). (gr. -1-2). 18.99 *(978-0-399-55716-3(4),* Knopf Bks. for Young Readers) Random Hse. Children's Bks.

Whelon, Chuck. Where's the Mermaid: A Mermazing Search-And-Find Adventure. 2018. (Illus.). 48p. (J). (gr. k-3). pap. 14.99 *(978-1-78503-988-1(1))* Penguin Random Hse. AUS. Dist: Independent Pubs. Group.

Wiese, Fritz H. & Wiese, Erika J. Erika & the Mermaids. 2011. 180p. 29.99 *(978-1-4568-6364-7(9));* pap. 19.99 *(978-1-4568-6363-0(0))* Xlibris Corp.

Williams, Becky. Ten Little Mermaids. East, Jacqueline, illus. 2007. (Story Book Ser.). 22p. (J). (gr. -1). bds. *(978-1-84666-375-8(X),* Tide Mill Pr.) Top That! Publishing PLC.

Witcher, Lillie. Ican & the Little Mermaid. 2006. (Illus.). (J). 8.95 *(978-1-56167-945-4(3),* Shooting Star Edition) American Literary Pr.

Young, Sarah. Gasparilla's Key & the Revenge of the Purple Mermaid. 2013. 254p. pap. 15.99 *(978-1-935986-58-4(9))* Liberty University Press.

MERRIMACK (FRIGATE)

Abnett, Dan. The Monitor Versus the Merrimac: Ironclads at War, 1 vol. Verma, Dheeraj, illus. 2006. (Graphic Battles of the Civil War Ser.). (ENG.). 48p. (J). (gr. 4-5). lib. bdg. 37.13 *(978-1-4042-0778-3(3),* c1104d37-0229-4941-a9a3-6bd0f959a40e) Rosen Publishing Group, Inc., The.

Brager, Bruce. The Monitor Versus the Merrimack. 2003. (Great Battles Thru the Ages Ser.). (ENG., Illus.). 112p. (gr. 6-12). 30.00 *(978-0-7910-7439-8(0),* P113829, Facts On File) Infobase Holdings, Inc.

O'Brien, Patrick. Duel of the Ironclads: The Monitor vs. the Virginia. 2003. (Illus.). 40p. (J). (gr. 1-5). 18.85 *(978-0-8027-8843-6(2))* Walker & Co.

MERRY-GO-ROUND

Bodden, Valerie. Carousels. 2012. (Thrill Rides Ser.). (ENG., Illus.). 24p. (J). (gr. 1-4). 25.65 *(978-1-60818-112-4(X),* 22310, Creative Education) Creative Co., The.

Langley, Sharon & Nathan, Amy. A Ride to Remember: A Civil Rights Story. Cooper, Floyd, illus. 2020. (ENG.). 40p. (J). (gr. 1-4). 19.99 *(978-1-4197-3685-8(X),* 1149701) Abrams, Inc.

MERRY-GO-ROUND—FICTION

Branson, Terri & Wilks, Jackie. Mirror of the Carousel. I.t. ed. 2006. (Illus.). 24p. (J). per. 14.99 *(978-0-9765786-8-0(9))* Dragonfly Publishing, Inc.

Carousel Writers' Group Staff, contrib. by. Every Pony Has a Tale. 2003. (Illus.). 88p. (J). pap. *(978-0-89802-787-7(X))* Beautiful America Publishing Co.

Demeritt, Mary Anne. The Twilight Ride of the Pink Fairy. Daniel, Ellen, illus. 2006. 36p. (J). pap. 17.95 *(978-1-58597-410-8(2))* Leathers Publishing.

Fiddick, Calay. The Fortieth Horse. Levy, Shaun & Jamieson, Eden, illus. 2006. 32p. (J). *(978-1-55306-876-1(9),* Epic Pr.) Essence Publishing.

Graves, Sue. Harry & the Horse. 2011. (Tadpoles Ser.). (ENG., Illus.). 24p. (J). (gr. k-2). *(978-0-7787-0579-6(X));* pap. *(978-0-7787-0590-1(0))* Crabtree Publishing Co.

Hyde, Heidi Smith. Feivel's Flying Horses. van der Sterre, Johanna, illus. 2010. (ENG.). 32p. (J). (gr. k-4). lib. bdg. 17.95 *(978-0-7613-3957-1(4),* Kar-Ben Publishing) Lerner Publishing Group.

Parker, Emma. The Carousel. 2010. (Illus.). 16p. pap. *(978-1-877561-73-3(8))* First Edition Ltd.

Rodda, Emily. The Best-Kept Secret. 2020. 128p. 7.99 *(978-1-4607-5372-9(0),* HarperCollins) HarperCollins Pubs.

Schiller, Pamela Byrne. Merry-Go-Round: El Carrusel. Workman, Lisa, illus. 2015. (SPA & ENG.). 11p. (J). *(978-1-63237-039-6(5))* Frog Street Pr.

Shire, Poppy. Magic Pony Carousel #4: Jewel the Midnight Pony. Berg, Ron, illus. 2008. (Magic Pony Carousel Ser.: 4). (ENG.). 96p. (J). (gr. 2-5). pap. 4.99 *(978-0-06-083788-4(8),* HarperCollins) HarperCollins Pubs.

—Magic Pony Carousel #5: Flame the Desert Pony. Berg, Ron, illus. 2008. (Magic Pony Carousel Ser.: 5). (ENG.). 96p. (J). (gr. 2-5). pap. 3.99 *(978-0-06-083794-5(2),* HarperCollins) HarperCollins Pubs.

Towell, Katy. Skary Childrin & the Carousel of Sorrow. 2013. 272p. (J). (ENG.). (gr. 8-12). lib. bdg. 24.94 *(978-0-375-96860-0(1));* (gr. 3-7). pap. 8.99 *(978-0-375-87240-2(X))* Random Hse. Children's Bks. (Knopf Bks. for Young Readers).

Wing, Carol. Lio the Carousel Horse. Moen, Ruth, illus. 2010. (ENG.). 32p. (J). (gr. -1-2). 14.95 *(978-1-933067-37-7(3))* Beachhouse Publishing, LLC.

MERTON, THOMAS, 1915-1968

Crompton, Samuel Willard. Thomas Merton. 2004. (Spiritual Leaders & Thinkers Ser.). (ENG., Illus.). 120p. (gr. 9-13). 30.00 *(978-0-7910-7862-4(0),* P114030, Facts On File) Infobase Holdings, Inc.

MESA VERDE NATIONAL PARK (COLO.)

Blake, Kevin & Yates, Martha. Cliff Dwellings: Empty Windows. 2015. (Abandoned: Towns Without People Ser.). (ENG.). 32p. (J). (gr. 2-7). lib. bdg. 28.50 *(978-1-62724-522-7(7))* Bearport Publishing Co., Inc.

MNO

Brannon, Barbara. Discover Mesa Verde. 2005. (J). pap. *(978-1-4108-5143-7(5))* Benchmark Education Co.

Collins, Terry. The Mesa Verde Cliff Dwellers: An Isabel Soto Archaeology Adventure, 1 vol. 2010. (Graphic Expeditions Ser.). (ENG., Illus.). 32p. (J). (gr. 3-9). lib. bdg. 31.32 *(978-1-4296-3971-2(7)*, 102581, Capstone Pr.) Capstone.

MESA VERDE NATIONAL PARK (COLO.)—FICTION

Skurzynski, Gloria. Mysteries in Our National Parks: Cliffhanger: A Mystery in Mesa Verde National Park. 2007. (Mysteries in Our National Park Ser.). (Illus.). 160p. (J). (gr. 3-7). per. 4.99 *(978-1-4263-0092-9(1)*, National Geographic Kids) Disney Publishing Worldwide.

MESMERISM

see Hypnotism

MESOPOTAMIA

see Iraq—History—To 634

METABOLISM

see also Nutrition

Barchers, Suzanne I. Energy in Action, 1 vol. 2015. (Science: Informational Text Ser.). (ENG., Illus.). 32p. (gr. 3-4). pap. 11.99 *(978-1-4807-4643-5(6))* Teacher Created Materials, Inc.

Cole, Joanna. The Magic School Bus Inside the Human Body, 1 vol. Degen, Bruce, illus. 2011. (Magic School Bus Ser.). (ENG.). (J). (gr. 2-5). audio compact disk 10.99 *(978-0-545-24083-3(2))* Scholastic, Inc.

Curran, Christine Perdan, ed. Metabolic Processes & Energy Transfers: An Anthology of Current Thought. (Contemporary Discourse in the Field of Biology Ser.). (gr. 10-12). 2009. 224p. 63.90 *(978-1-61511-911-0(6))* 2005. (ENG., Illus.). 158p. (YA). lib. bdg. 41.13 *(978-1-4042-0399-0(0)*, 49fd039d-122e-4192-9e2c-7e7274da530f) Rosen Publishing Group, Inc., The.

Eaton, Louise & Rogers, Kara, eds. Examining Biochemical Reactions, 1 vol. 2017. (Building Blocks of Life Ser.). (ENG., Illus.). 328p. (J). (gr. 10-10). lib. bdg. 47.59 *(978-1-5383-0006-0(0)*, 8761c321-c200-4a63-8ef2-996ec1fa0fc9) Rosen Publishing Group, Inc., The.

Fishman, Seth. Power Up. Greenberg, Isabel, illus. 2019. (ENG.). 40p. (J). (gr. -1-3). 17.99 *(978-0-06-245579-6(6)*, Greenwillow Bks.) HarperCollins Pubs.

McLaughlin, Marc, et al. How Cells Send, Receive, & Process Information, 1 vol. 2014. (Britannica Guide to Cell Biology Ser.). (ENG.). 64p. (YA). (gr. 8-8). 34.29 *(978-1-62275-800-5(5)*, 6cf5a565-6a74-4bbe-8477-720a99718413, Britannica Educational Publishing) Rosen Publishing Group, Inc., The.

Morgan, Philip & Turnbull, Stephanie. Generating Energy. 2011. (Secrets of Magic Ser.). 32p. (gr. 4-7). lib. bdg. 31.35 *(978-1-59920-495-6(9))* Black Rabbit Bks.

Shryer, Donna. Body Fuel: A Guide to Good Nutrition, 1 vol. 2008. (Food & Fitness Ser.). (ENG., Illus.). 128p. (YA). (gr. 7-7). lib. bdg. 41.21 *(978-0-7614-2552-6(7)*, 4576a223-73c6-46b3-9fe2-6bc73b005989) Cavendish Square Publishing LLC.

Stewart, Melissa. Summertime Sleepers: Animals That Estivate. Brannen, Sarah S., illus. 2021. 40p. (J). (gr. 1-4). lib. bdg. 16.99 *(978-1-58089-716-7(9))* Charlesbridge Publishing, Inc.

Stoffwechsel und Energieumsatz: Fachliche Inhalte und Uebungsaufgaben. 2nd ed. (Duden Abiturhilfen Ser.). (GER.). 112p. (YA). (gr. 12-13). *(978-3-411-04282-1(6))* Bibliographisches Institut & F. A. Brockhaus AG DEU. Dist: International Bk. Import Service, Inc.

Williams, Mary E., ed. Growth Disorders, 1 vol. 2011. (Perspectives on Diseases & Disorders Ser.). (ENG., Illus.). 168p. (gr. 10-12). 45.93 *(978-0-7377-5774-3(4)*, fccaf2b8-029d-4c68-8532-cd56910ea011, Greenhaven Publishing) Greenhaven Publishing LLC.

METAL-WORK

see also Jewelry; Silversmithing; Steel; Welding

Meister, Cari. From Metal to Bicycles. Pinilla, Albert, illus. 2019. (Who Made My Stuff? Ser.). (ENG.). 24p. (J). (gr. 1-4). lib. bdg. *(978-1-68151-695-0(0)*, 10847) Amicus.

Nelson, David Erik. Soldering. 2014. (21st Century Skills Innovation Library: Makers As Innovators Ser.). (ENG., Illus.). 32p. (J). (gr. 4-8). 32.07 *(978-1-63137-774-7(4)*, 205339) Cherry Lake Publishing.

Orr, Tamra. Careers in Sheet Metal & Ironwork, 1 vol., 1. 2015. (Essential Careers Ser.). (ENG.). 80p. (J). (gr. 6-6). 37.47 *(978-1-4994-6221-0(2)*, 07fd478f-ce4d-48f8-8c59-7b163e486349, Rosen Young Adult) Rosen Publishing Group, Inc., The.

Petersen, Christine. The Blacksmith, 1 vol. 2011. (Colonial People Ser.). (ENG.). 48p. (gr. 4-4). 34.07 *(978-0-7614-4799-3(7)*, 5550975a-2157-40e4-956e-eb1c4cc25d4a) Cavendish Square Publishing LLC.

Staff, Gareth Editorial Staff. Metal, 1 vol. 2004. (Let's Create! Ser.). (ENG., Illus.). 32p. (gr. 2-4). lib. bdg. 28.67 *(978-0-8368-4016-2(X)*, d519c336-9f2f-4f05-a2a4-9513d65826c2, Gareth Stevens Learning Library) Stevens, Gareth Publishing LLLP.

METALS

Adair, Rick. Beryllium. 2009. (Understanding the Elements of the Periodic Table Ser.). 48p. (gr. 6-6). 53.00 *(978-1-60854-634-3(9)*, Rosen Reference) Rosen Publishing Group, Inc., The.

Beatty, Richard W. The Lanthanides, 1 vol. 2008. (Elements Ser.). (ENG., Illus.). 32p. (gr. 4-4). lib. bdg. 31.21 *(978-0-7614-2687-5(6)*, 82648b8e-7a04-46b9-a5eb-afe53af8c6d7) Cavendish Square Publishing LLC.

—Manganese, 1 vol. 2006. (Elements Ser.). (ENG.). 32p. (gr. 4-4). 31.21 *(978-0-7614-1813-9(X)*, ac698b0a-6e17-40b5-97fe-a26e00dac4d4) Cavendish Square Publishing LLC.

Colich, Abby. Metal, 1 vol. 2013. (Exploring Materials Ser.). (ENG.). 24p. (J). (gr. -1-1). pap. 6.95 *(978-1-4329-8023-8(8)*, 123179, Heinemann) Capstone.

Crabtree Publishing Company Staff & Montgomerie, Adrienne. Metals. 2012. (ENG., Illus.). 32p. (J). *(978-0-7787-4231-9(8))*; pap. *(978-0-7787-4235-7(0))* Crabtree Publishing Co.

Jennings, Terry. Metal. 2006. (Illus.). 32p. (YA). (gr. 1-18). lib. bdg. 27.10 *(978-1-932333-01-5(0))* Chrysalis Education.

Johanson, Paula. Cobalt. 2009. (Understanding the Elements of the Periodic Table Ser.). 48p. (gr. 6-6). 53.00 *(978-1-60854-645-9(4)*, Rosen Reference) Rosen Publishing Group, Inc., The.

—Lithium. 2009. (Understanding the Elements of the Periodic Table Ser.). 48p. (gr. 6-6). 53.00 *(978-1-60854-661-9(6)*, Rosen Reference) Rosen Publishing Group, Inc., The.

Kjelle, Marylou Morano. The Properties of Metals. 24p. (gr. 4-4). 2009. (Library of Physical Science Ser.). 42.50 *(978-1-60853-792-1(7)*, PowerKids Pr.) 2006. (Library of Physical Science Ser.: Vol. 3). (ENG., Illus.). (J). lib. bdg. 26.27 *(978-1-4042-3417-8(9)*, ef24b42f-0f74-42d0-960d-9f3cb2eaf754) 2006. (Journeys Ser.). (ENG., Illus.). pap. 7.05 *(978-1-4042-2164-2(6)*, a6fc3e74-3838-4545-9116-185e95ec7ade, PowerKids Pr.) Rosen Publishing Group, Inc., The.

Langley, Andrew. Metal. 2008. (ENG., Illus.). 24p. (J). (gr. k-3). pap. *(978-0-7787-4134-3(6))* Crabtree Publishing Co.

Llewellyn, Claire. Metal. 2005. (I Know That! Ser.). (Illus.). 24p. (J). (gr. 1-4). lib. bdg. 22.80 *(978-1-932889-52-9(3))* Sea-To-Sea Pubns.

MacCarald, Clara. Silicon, 1 vol. 2018. (Exploring the Elements Ser.). (ENG.). 48p. (gr. 6-6). 29.60 *(978-1-9785-0370-0(9)*, 8ce9df93-414d-431f-8d38-b7a225ae7125) Enslow Publishing, LLC.

Meachen Rau, Dana. Metal, 1 vol. 2012. (Use It! Reuse It! Ser.). (ENG.). 24p. (gr. 3-3). 25.50 *(978-1-60870-516-0(1)*, 3bdc4fcf-2b21-4187-a1ce-9b68ceb68647) Cavendish Square Publishing LLC.

Mitchell, Melanie S. Metal. 2003. (First Step Nonfiction - Materials Ser.). (ENG., Illus.). 24p. (gr. k-2). lib. bdg. 23.93 *(978-0-8225-4622-1(1))* Lerner Publishing Group.

Morris, Neil. Metals. 2010. (Materials That Matter Ser.). (ENG.). 32p. (J). (gr. 4-6). lib. bdg. 28.50 *(978-1-60753-066-4(X)*, 17218) Amicus.

Morris, Neil & Johnson, Jinny. Metals. 2011. (Watery Worlds Ser.). 32p. (gr. 3-6). lib. bdg. 31.35 *(978-1-59920-506-9(8))* Black Rabbit Bks.

National Geographic Learning. World Windows 3 (Science): Magnets: Content Literacy, Nonfiction Reading, Language & Literacy. 2011. (World Windows Ser.). (ENG., Illus.). 16p. (J). stu. ed. 10.95 *(978-1-133-49266-5(5))* Cengage Heinle.

Rivera, Andrea. Metal. 2017. (Materials Ser.). (ENG., Illus.). 24p. (J). (gr. -1-2). lib. bdg. 31.36 *(978-1-5321-2031-2(1)*, 25298, Abdo Zoom-Launch) ABDO Publishing Co.

Royston, Angela. Metal: Let's Look at a Knife & Fork. 2005. (J). *(978-1-4109-1822-2(X))*; (ENG.). 24p. pap. *(978-1-4109-1831-4(9))* Steck-Vaughn.

Roza, Greg. Chromium. 2009. (Understanding the Elements of the Periodic Table Ser.). 48p. (gr. 6-6). 53.00 *(978-1-60854-644-2(6)*, Rosen Reference) Rosen Publishing Group, Inc., The.

—Titanium, 1 vol., Vol. 1. 2013. (Rare & Precious Metals Ser.). (ENG.). 24p. (J). (gr. 2-3). 25.27 *(978-1-4824-0518-7(0)*, 85331ae3-94ef-43a4-98c2-227639abba62) Stevens, Gareth Publishing LLLP.

—Zirconium. 2009. (Understanding the Elements of the Periodic Table Ser.). 48p. (gr. 6-6). 53.00 *(978-1-60854-690-9(X)*, Rosen Reference) Rosen Publishing Group, Inc., The.

Sherman, Jill. Minerals & Heavy Metals, 1 vol. 2017. (Let's Learn about Natural Resources Ser.). (ENG.). 24p. (gr. 1-2). pap. 10.35 *(978-0-7660-9147-4(3)*, cd31c3b0-b55f-43e7-b0a7-2b932257c069) Enslow Publishing, LLC.

Sparrow, Giles. Nickel, 1 vol. 2006. (Elements Ser.). (ENG.). 32p. (gr. 4-4). 31.21 *(978-0-7614-1811-5(3)*, c9d34196-a2c2-4700-94e4-a925ed3b2aaa) Cavendish Square Publishing LLC.

Staff, Gareth Editorial Staff. Metal, 1 vol. 2004. (Let's Create! Ser.). (ENG., Illus.). 32p. (gr. 2-4). lib. bdg. 28.67 *(978-0-8368-4016-2(X)*, d519c336-9f2f-4f05-a2a4-9513d65826c2, Gareth Stevens Learning Library) Stevens, Gareth Publishing LLLP.

Storey, Rita. Metal. 2007. (How We Use Materials/Watts Ser.). (Illus.). 30p. (J). (gr. 4-7). lib. bdg. 28.50 *(978-1-59920-003-3(1))* Black Rabbit Bks.

Taylor-Butler, Christine. Experiments with Magnets & Metals, 1 vol. 2011. (My Science Investigations Ser.). (ENG.). 32p. (J). (gr. 1-3). pap. 8.29 *(978-1-4329-5365-2(6)*, 116078, Heinemann) Capstone.

Thomas, Michele. Sodium. 2009. (Understanding the Elements of the Periodic Table Ser.). 48p. (gr. 6-6). 53.00 *(978-1-60854-685-5(3)*, Rosen Reference) Rosen Publishing Group, Inc., The.

Tocci, Salvatore. Lead. 2005. (True Bks.). (ENG., Illus.). 48p. (J). (gr. 3-7). lib. bdg. 25.00 *(978-0-516-23699-5(7)*, Children's Pr.) Scholastic Library Publishing.

—True Books: Zinc. 2005. (True Bks.). (ENG., Illus.). 48p. (J). (gr. 3-7). lib. bdg. 25.00 *(978-0-516-23703-9(9)*, Children's Pr.) Scholastic Library Publishing.

Turrell, Kerry. Tungsten, 1 vol. 2005. (Elements Ser.). (ENG., Illus.). 32p. (gr. 4-4). lib. bdg. 31.21 *(978-0-7614-1548-0(3)*, c57c0da8-f8a0-428e-9ffd-bdad131437cd) Cavendish Square Publishing LLC.

West, Krista. The Basics of Metals & Metalloids, 1 vol. 2013. (Core Concepts Ser.). (ENG.). 96p. (YA). (gr. 7-7). 39.77 *(978-1-4777-2713-3(2)*, d06314b7-8b83-4c10-9313-1a3fca704954) Rosen Publishing Group, Inc., The.

Wood, Ian. Platinum, 1 vol. 2005. (Elements Ser.). (ENG., Illus.). 32p. (gr. 4-4). lib. bdg. 31.21 *(978-0-7614-1550-3(5)*, c2385546-9a43-416a-a057-a65508747769) Cavendish Square Publishing LLC.

Woodford, Chris. Titanium, 1 vol. 2003. (Elements Ser.). (ENG., Illus.). 32p. (gr. 4-4). lib. bdg. 31.21 *(978-0-7614-1461-2(4)*, e4887687-1e71-4972-a753-a815d219d04d) Cavendish Square Publishing LLC.

Zronik, John Paul & Zronik, John. Metals. 2004. (Rocks, Minerals, & Resources Ser.). (ENG., Illus.). 32p. (J). lib. bdg. *(978-0-7787-1418-7(7))* Crabtree Publishing Co.

—Metals - Shaping Our World. 2004. (Rocks, Minerals, & Resources Ser.). (ENG., Illus.). 32p. (J). pap. *(978-0-7787-1450-7(0))* Crabtree Publishing Co.

METALWORK

see Metal-Work

METAMORPHIC ROCKS

see Rocks

METEORITES

Gallagher, Brigid. Exploring Meteor Showers. 2017. (Discover the Night Sky Ser.). (ENG., Illus.). 32p. (J). (gr. 3-6). lib. bdg. 27.99 *(978-1-5157-8737-2(0)*, 136313, Capstone Pr.) Capstone.

Hansen, Grace. Asteroids & Meteoroids. 2017. (Our Galaxy Ser.). (ENG., Illus.). 24p. (J). (gr. -1-2). lib. bdg. 32.79 *(978-1-5321-0049-9(3)*, 25172, Abdo Kids) ABDO Publishing Co.

Nicolson, Cynthia. Discover Space Rocks. Slavin, Bill, illus. 2006. 32p. (J). lib. bdg. 15.38 *(978-1-4242-1195-1(6))* Fitzgerald Bks.

Orme, David. Comets. 2009. (Fact to Fiction Ser.). (Illus.). 36p. (J). pap. 6.95 *(978-0-7891-7899-2(0))* Perfection Learning Corp.

Orr, Tamra B. I See Falling Stars. 2015. (Tell Me Why Library). (ENG., Illus.). 24p. (gr. 2-5). pap. 12.79 *(978-1-63362-035-3(2)*, 205897) Cherry Lake Publishing.

—Searching the Sky. 2014. (Explorer Library: Science Explorer Ser.). (ENG., Illus.). 32p. (J). (gr. 4-8). 32.07 *(978-1-62431-782-8(0)*, 203324) Cherry Lake Publishing.

Parker, Steve. Space Objects: Comets, Asteroids & Meteors, 1 vol. 2007. (Earth & Space Ser.). (ENG., Illus.). 48p. (YA). (gr. 6-6). lib. bdg. 34.47 *(978-1-4042-3738-4(0)*, dd53e722-21c3-4c67-9000-8d3d5302deaf) Rosen Publishing Group, Inc., The.

Rose, Simon. Meteors. 2016. (Illus.). 32p. (J). *(978-1-4896-5818-0(1)*, AV2 by Weigl) Weigl Pubs., Inc.

Rusch, Elizabeth. Impact! Asteroids & the Science of Saving the World. Anderson, Karin, illus. 2017. (Scientists in the Field Ser.). (ENG.). 80p. (J). (gr. 3-7). 18.99 *(978-0-544-67159-1(7)*, 1625794, Clarion Bks.) HarperCollins Pubs.

Rustad, Martha E. H. Shooting Stars. 2017. (Amazing Sights of the Sky Ser.). (ENG., Illus.). 24p. (J). (gr. -1-2). lib. bdg. 27.32 *(978-1-5157-6752-7(3)*, 135290, Capstone Pr.) Capstone.

Wilberforce, Bert. Comets, Asteroids, & Meteoroids, 1 vol. 2020. (Look at Space Science Ser.). (ENG.). 32p. (gr. 2-2). pap. 11.50 *(978-1-5382-5930-6(3)*, 99ec6150-d4c3-4ed1-98ad-f6c1913dda6f) Stevens, Gareth Publishing LLLP.

METEOROLOGICAL INSTRUMENTS

see also Thermometers

Kampff, Joseph. What Are Weather Instruments?, 1 vol. 2014. (Let's Find Out! Weather Ser.). (ENG.). 32p. (J). (gr. 2-3). 26.06 *(978-1-62275-791-6(2)*, 4f1d1ad2-b0b6-41cf-963e-34946339f375, Britannica Educational Publishing) Rosen Publishing Group, Inc., The.

Wills, Susan & Wills, Steven R. Meteorology: Predicting the Weather. 2003. (Innovators Ser.: Vol. 12). (Illus.). 144p. (gr. 5-18). lib. bdg. 21.95 *(978-1-881508-61-8(7))* Oliver Pr., Inc.

METEOROLOGICAL SATELLITES

Baker, David & Kissock, Heather. Satellites. 2016. (Illus.). 32p. (J). *(978-1-4896-5830-2(0)*, AV2 by Weigl) Weigl Pubs., Inc.

Cobb, Allan. Weather Observation Satellites. 2003. 68p. pap. 29.25 *(978-1-4358-3643-3(X))* Rosen Publishing Group, Inc., The.

Hansen, Jim & Burns, John. How to Draw Dragons, 1 vol. 2007. (Drawing Fantasy Art Ser.: Vol. 4). (ENG., Illus.). 32p. (J). (gr. 4-5). lib. bdg. 30.27 *(978-1-4042-3856-5(5)*, c578ba72-973a-4635-abf6-a97500d88d1b) Rosen Publishing Group, Inc., The.

Orr, Tamra B. Selfies from Space: How Satellites Help Science on Earth. 2019. (Future Space Ser.). (ENG., Illus.). 32p. (J). (gr. 3-9). pap. 7.95 *(978-1-5435-7517-0(X)*, 141048); lib. bdg. 28.65 *(978-1-5435-7272-8(3)*, 140603) Capstone.

METEOROLOGISTS

Brezina, Corona. Careers in Meteorology, 1 vol. 2012. (Essential Careers Ser.). (ENG., Illus.). 80p. (YA). (gr. 6-6). lib. bdg. 37.47 *(978-1-4488-8241-0(9)*, be546461-fca1-4edb-a871-7bfe62e29c86) Rosen Publishing Group, Inc., The.

Demarest, Chris L. Hurricane Hunters! Riders on the Storm. Demarest, Chris L., illus. 2006. (ENG., Illus.). 40p. (J). (gr. -1-5). 19.99 *(978-0-689-86168-0(0)*, McElderry, Margaret K. Bks.) McElderry, Margaret K. Bks.

Dreier, David. Be a Storm Chaser. 2008. (Scienceworks! Ser.). (Illus.). 32p. (gr. 3-5). lib. bdg. 26.00 *(978-0-8368-8929-1(0))* Stevens, Gareth Publishing LLLP.

Dreier, David Louis. Be a Storm Chaser. 2008. (Scienceworks! Ser.). 32p. pap. 8.95 *(978-0-8368-8936-9(3))* Stevens, Gareth Publishing LLLP.

Gaffney, Timothy R. Storm Scientist: Careers Chasing Severe Weather, 1 vol. 2010. (Wild Science Careers Ser.). (ENG., Illus.). 112p. (gr. 5-6). lib. bdg. 35.93 *(978-0-7660-3050-3(4)*, 583909e9-419d-4dba-a2d3-dad1bde33be4) Enslow Publishing, LLC.

Hollar, Sherman. Pioneers in the World of Weather & Climatology, 4 vols. 2012. (Inventors & Innovators Ser.). (ENG., Illus.). 128p. (YA). (gr. 8-8). 77.64 *(978-1-61530-787-6(7)*, 59308aeb-233c-4105-9106-c350e56bf8c7); 38.82 *(978-1-61530-702-9(8)*, 46791175-1e17-4c49-b474-33afa200fbe6) Rosen Publishing Group, Inc., The.

Horn, Geoffrey M. Meteorologist, 1 vol. 2008. (Cool Careers: Helping Careers Ser.). (ENG.). 32p. (gr. 3-3). pap. 11.50 *(978-0-8368-9327-4(1)*, ad93c7b3-e2b8-4dac-88c0-862ce1e4f32f); (YA). lib. bdg. 28.67 *(978-0-8368-9194-2(5)*, acabdd96-240b-4229-9936-6ae589f7cf88) Stevens, Gareth Publishing LLLP.

Jeffrey, Gary. Hurricane Hunters & Tornado Chasers. 2009. (Graphic Careers Ser.). (ENG.). 48p. (YA). (gr. 5-5). 58.50 *(978-1-61512-885-3(9)*, Rosen Reference) Rosen Publishing Group, Inc., The.

Lindop, Laurie. Chasing Tornadoes. 2003. (Science on the Edge Ser.). (Illus.). 80p. (gr. 5-18). lib. bdg. 26.90 *(978-0-7613-2703-5(7)*, Twenty-First Century Bks.) Lerner Publishing Group.

Martin, Jacqueline Briggs. Snowflake Bentley. 2004. (Illus.). (J). (gr. -1-3). spiral bd. *(978-0-616-01714-2(6))* Canadian National Institute for the Blind/Institut National Canadien pour les Aveugles.

—Snowflake Bentley: A Caldecott Award Winner. Azarian, Mary, illus. 2009. (ENG.). 32p. (J). (gr. -1-3). pap. 8.99 *(978-0-547-24829-5(6)*, 1100744, Clarion Bks.) HarperCollins Pubs.

Owen, Ruth. Climatologists & Meteorologists. 2013. (Out of the Lab: Extreme Jobs in Science Ser.). 32p. (J). (gr. 3-6). pap. 60.00 *(978-1-4777-1377-8(8))*; (ENG.). (gr. 4-5). 28.93 *(978-1-4777-1288-7(7)*, d2e45f97-fd01-4e2d-8c42-d301243a44f6); (ENG.). (gr. 4-5). pap. 11.00 *(978-1-4777-1376-1(X)*, a5f99d64-c6c1-4bd4-93a1-1cbb706e50a4) Rosen Publishing Group, Inc., The. (PowerKids Pr.).

Peterson, Judy Monroe. Weather Watchers: Climate Scientists. (Extreme Scientists Ser.). 24p. (gr. 2-3). 2009. 42.50 *(978-1-61512-454-1(3)*, PowerKids Pr.) 2008. (ENG., Illus.). (YA). lib. bdg. 26.27 *(978-1-4042-4527-3(8)*, 963410c5-33a5-4c49-9f8c-5478f5e904f0) Rosen Publishing Group, Inc., The.

Rajczak, Kristen. Be a Meteorologist. 2014. (Be a Scientist! Ser.). (Illus.). 32p. (J). (gr. 3-6). pap. 63.00 *(978-1-4824-1197-3(0))* Stevens, Gareth Publishing LLLP.

Rajczak Nelson, Kristen. Be a Meteorologist, 1 vol. 2014. (Be a Scientist! Ser.). (ENG., Illus.). 32p. (J). (gr. 3-4). pap. 11.50 *(978-1-4824-1210-9(1)*, e1ead41c-ca49-4bb8-9ac6-8a4646875299) Stevens, Gareth Publishing LLLP.

Weston Woods Staff, creator. Snowflake Bentley. 2011. 18.95 *(978-0-545-31414-5(3))*; 38.75 *(978-0-545-31415-2(1))* Weston Woods Studios, Inc.

Wills, Susan & Wills, Steven R. Meteorology: Predicting the Weather. 2003. (Innovators Ser.: Vol. 12). (Illus.). 144p. (gr. 5-18). lib. bdg. 21.95 *(978-1-881508-61-8(7))* Oliver Pr., Inc.

METEOROLOGY

see also Air; Atmosphere; Climate; Clouds; Floods; Fog; Hurricanes; Lightning; Rain and Rainfall; Seasons; Snow; Storms; Thunderstorms; Tornadoes; Weather; Weather Forecasting; Winds

Alkire, Jessie. Super Simple Weather Projects: Science Activities for Future Meteorologists. 2017. (Super Simple Earth Investigations Ser.). (ENG., Illus.). 32p. (J). (gr. k-4). lib. bdg. 34.21 *(978-1-5321-1241-6(6)*, 27628, Super SandCastle) ABDO Publishing Co.

Allaby, Michael. The World's Weather. 2012. (ENG., Illus.). 48p. (J). 15.00 *(978-1-899762-81-1(7))* Award Pubns. Ltd. GBR. Dist: Parkwest Pubns., Inc.

Anaxos Inc. Staff, contrib. by. UXL Encyclopedia of Weather & Natural Disasters. 2007. (J). *(978-1-4144-1882-7(5))*; *(978-1-4144-1883-4(3))*; *(978-1-4144-1884-1(1))*; *(978-1-4144-1880-3(9))*; *(978-1-4144-1881-0(7))* Cengage Gale.

Bang, Molly & Chisholm, Penny. Buried Sunlight: How Fossil Fuels Have Changed the Earth. Bang, Molly, illus. 2014. (ENG., Illus.). 48p. (J). (gr. -1-3). 19.99 *(978-0-545-57785-4(3)*, Blue Sky Pr., The) Scholastic, Inc.

—Ocean Sunlight: How Tiny Plants Feed the Seas. Bang, Molly, illus. 2012. (ENG., Illus.). 48p. (J). (gr. -1-3). 19.99 *(978-0-545-27322-0(6)*, Blue Sky Pr., The) Scholastic, Inc.

Bell, Samantha. Weather. Bane, Jeff, illus. 2018. (Mi Mini Biografía (My Itty-Bitty Bio): My Early Library). (ENG.). 24p. (J). (gr. k-1). pap. 12.79 *(978-1-5341-0822-6(X)*, 210652); lib. bdg. 30.64 *(978-1-5341-0723-6(1)*, 210651) Cherry Lake Publishing.

Berger, Melvin & Berger, Gilda. Hurricanes Have Eyes but Can't See: And Other Amazing Facts about Wild Weather. 2003. (Illus.). 48p. (J). *(978-0-439-54980-6(9))* Scholastic, Inc.

Birch, Robin. How Weather Works, 1 vol. 2010. (Weather & Climate Ser.). (ENG.). 32p. (gr. 3-3). 31.21 *(978-0-7614-4466-4(1)*, 05521072-c53e-403d-b7c5-69cd9253ac4d) Cavendish Square Publishing LLC.

Blackwell, Amy Hackney, ed. U-X-L Encyclopedia of Weather & Natural Disasters, 5 vols. 2nd ed. 2016. (U-X-L Encyclopedia of Weather & Natural Disasters Ser.). (ENG., Illus.). 1200p. (gr. 6-8). 557.00 *(978-1-4103-3290-5(X)*, UXL) Cengage Gale.

Borngraber, Elizabeth & Bard, Mariel. Air Masses & Fronts, 1 vol. 2018. (Spotlight on Weather & Natural Disasters Ser.). (ENG.). 24p. (gr. 4-6). 27.93 *(978-1-5081-6866-9(0)*, 1e90ddb0-f083-420f-ae36-8a9072cf9203, PowerKids Pr.) Rosen Publishing Group, Inc., The.

Brezina, Corona. Careers in Meteorology, 1 vol. 2012. (Essential Careers Ser.). (ENG., Illus.). 80p. (YA). (gr. 6-6). lib. bdg. 37.47 *(978-1-4488-8241-0(9)*, be546461-fca1-4edb-a871-7bfe62e29c86) Rosen Publishing Group, Inc., The.

Bright, Michael. Weather Explained, 1 vol. 2014. (Guide for Curious Minds Ser.). (ENG.). 152p. (YA). (gr. 8-8). 42.41 *(978-1-4777-8129-6(3)*, 7d9dd675-bcf1-49cf-9076-a50a1ce99ecc, Rosen Young Adult) Rosen Publishing Group, Inc., The.

Brinker, Spencer. An Icy Day. 2018. (Weather Watch Ser.). (ENG.). 16p. (J). (gr. -1-1). 6.99 *(978-1-64280-139-2(9))*; (Illus.). 16.96 *(978-1-68402-998-3(8))* Bearport Publishing Co., Inc.

Brodfuehrer, Marc. Measuring the Weather, 1 vol. 2008. (Real Life Readers Ser.). (ENG.). 16p. (gr. 2-3). pap. 7.05 *(978-1-4358-0105-9(9)*, 2c6b1e08-7516-4915-9d12-b008b2802ff2, Rosen Classroom) Rosen Publishing Group, Inc., The.

Brown, Don. Up & Down: The Adventures of John Jeffries, First American to Fly. Brown, Don, illus. 2018. (Illus.). 40p. (J). (gr. 1-4). 16.99 *(978-1-58089-812-6(2))* Charlesbridge Publishing, Inc.

Bush Gibson, Karen. Meteorology: Cool Women Who Weather Storms. Chandhok, Lena, illus. 2017. (Girls in Science Ser.). (ENG.). 112p. (J). (gr. 4-6). 19.95 *(978-1-61930-537-3(2)*, 73eea755-affc-4910-9825-76d749fa2ad4); pap. 9.95 *(978-1-61930-541-0(0)*, d9d2c598-d66b-42f5-b65f-8f167b748485) Nomad Pr.

Challen, Paul C. & Challen, Paul. Drought & Heat Wave Alert!, 1 vol. 2004. (Disaster Alert! Ser.). (ENG., Illus.). 32p. (J). pap

(978-0-7787-1610-5(4)); lib. bdg. *(978-0-7787-1578-8(7))* Crabtree Publishing Co.

Clarke, Catriona. Weather: Level 7. Chen, Kuo Kang, illus. 2006. (Usborne Beginners Ser.). 32p. (J). (gr. 4-7). lib. bdg. 12.99 *(978-1-58086-892-1(4)*, Usborne) EDC Publishing.

Cobb, Allan. Weather Observation Satellites. 2003. 68p. pap. 29.25 *(978-1-4358-3643-3(X))* Rosen Publishing Group, Inc., The.

Como Ser un Experto en Clima. (Coleccion Ciencia y Proyectos). (SPA., Illus.). (YA). (gr. 5-8). pap. *(978-950-724-283-0(X)*, LMA8238) Lumen ARG. Dist: Lectorum Pubns., Inc.

Corbett, Sean. Heat Waves. 2015. (Illus.). 32p. (J). *(978-1-5105-0078-5(2))* SmartBook Media, Inc.

—Heat Waves. 2014. (J). *(978-1-4896-3272-2(7))* Weigl Pubs., Inc.

El Cuerpo Humano, 6 vols. (Explorers. Exploradores Nonfiction Sets Ser.). (SPA.). 32p. (gr. 3-6). 44.95 *(978-0-7699-0635-5(4))* Shortland Pubns. (U. S. A.) Inc.

El Cuerpo Humano. (Coleccion Estrella del Saber). (SPA., Illus.). (J). 14.95 *(978-950-11-0035-8(9)*, SGM035) Sigmar ARG. Dist: Continental Bk. Co., Inc.

D'Aubuisson, Elisabeth. Rainy Days, 1 vol. 2006. (What's the Weather? Ser.). (ENG., Illus.). 24p. (J). (gr. 2-3). lib. bdg. 26.27 *(978-1-4042-3682-0(1)*, c8e12711-da4b-4ca1-90d4-9b3bc4ab2dfe, PowerKids Pr.) Rosen Publishing Group, Inc., The.

d'Aubuisson, Elisabeth. Rainy Days. 2009. (What's the Weather? Ser.). 24p. (gr. 2-3). 42.50 *(978-1-60854-775-3(2)*, PowerKids Pr.) Rosen Publishing Group, Inc., The.

DeLallo, Laura. Hammered by a Heat Wave! 2010. (Disaster Survivors Ser.). (Illus.). 32p. (YA). (gr. 4-7). lib. bdg. 28.50 *(978-1-936087-51-8(0))* Bearport Publishing Co., Inc.

Delta Education. Sci Res Bk Foss Grade 1 Next Gen Ea. 2015. (Illus.). 244p. (J). lib. bdg. *(978-1-62571-445-9(9))* Delta Education, LLC.

DiSiena, Laura Lyn & Eliot, Hannah. Rainbows Never End: And Other Fun Facts. Oswald, Pete, illus. 2014. (Did You Know? Ser.). (ENG.). 32p. (J). (gr. -1-3). 17.99 *(978-1-4814-0277-4(3))*; pap. 7.99 *(978-1-4814-0275-0(7))* Little Simon. (Little Simon).

Duling, Kaitlyn. It's Raining Fish & Other Cool Weather Facts. 2019. (Mind-Blowing Science Facts Ser.). (ENG., Illus.). 32p. (J). (gr. 4-6). lib. bdg. 28.65 *(978-1-5435-5770-1(8)*, 139726) Capstone.

Extreme Threats, 4 vols., Set. Incl. Asteroids & Comets. Nardo, Don. (YA). lib. bdg. 28.95 *(978-1-59935-121-6(8))*; Climate Change. Nardo, Don. (Illus.). (J). lib. bdg. 28.95 *(978-1-59935-119-3(6))*; Wildfires. Cunningham, Kevin. (YA). lib. bdg. 28.95 *(978-1-59935-120-9(X))*; 112p. 2009. 2009. Set lib. bdg. 115.80 *(978-1-59935-128-5(5))* Reynolds, Morgan Inc.

Fleisher, Paul. Gases, Pressure, & Wind: The Science of the Atmosphere. 2010. (Weatherwise Ser.). (ENG., Illus.). 48p. (gr. 4-8). lib. bdg. 29.27 *(978-0-8225-7537-5(X))* Lerner Publishing Group.

—Vapor, Rain, & Snow: The Science of Clouds & Precipitation. 2010. (Weatherwise Ser.). (ENG.). 48p. (gr. 4-8). lib. bdg. 29.27 *(978-0-8225-7534-4(5))* Lerner Publishing Group.

Gaffney, Timothy R. Storm Scientist: Careers Chasing Severe Weather, 1 vol. 2010. (Wild Science Careers Ser.). (ENG., Illus.). 112p. (gr. 5-6). lib. bdg. 35.93 *(978-0-7660-3050-3(4)*, 583909e9-419d-4dba-a2d3-dad1bde33be4) Enslow Publishing, LLC.

Gallant, Roy A. Atmosphere, 1 vol. 2003. (EarthWorks Ser.). (ENG., Illus.). 80p. (gr. 6-6). 36.93 *(978-0-7614-1366-0(9)*, a19524b1-50dd-4209-8a05-fd374d6a4843) Cavendish Square Publishing LLC.

Ganeri, Anita. El Sol (Sunshine), 1 vol. 2004. (Tiempo de Aqui (Weather Around You) Ser.). (SPA.). 24p. (gr. 2-4). lib. bdg. 24.67 *(978-0-8368-4365-1(7)*, 0c7c6f7d-a1b3-4571-ba2d-48f106006821, Weekly Reader Leveled Readers) Stevens, Gareth Publishing LLLP.

Gardner, Robert. Meteorology Experiments in Your Own Weather Station, 1 vol. 2015. (Design, Build, Experiment Ser.). (ENG.). 128p. (gr. 7-7). lib. bdg. 38.93 *(978-0-7660-6957-2(5)*, 6243ae0e-7471-4293-b968-7e4c654d9685) Enslow Publishing, LLC.

—Meteorology Projects with a Weather Station You Can Build, 1 vol. 2008. (Build-A-Lab! Science Experiments Ser.). (ENG., Illus.). 128p. (gr. 5-6). lib. bdg. 35.93 *(978-0-7660-2807-4(0)*, 618a523a-009c-4ed9-af2b-7fbdb4c1e576) Enslow Publishing, LLC.

Gardner, Robert & Conklin, Joshua. Experiments for Future Meteorologists, 1 vol. 2016. (Experiments for Future STEM Professionals Ser.). (ENG., Illus.). 128p. (gr. 6-6). 38.93 *(978-0-7660-8196-3(6)*, 8700b661-02ae-4cce-84f3-de012a7f4261) Enslow Publishing, LLC.

Gibbons, Gail. It's Raining! 2014. (ENG., Illus.). 32p. (J). (gr. -1-3). 17.95 *(978-0-8234-2924-0(5))* Holiday Hse., Inc.

Goldstein, Natalie. Drought & Heat Waves: A Practical Survival Guide. 2009. (Library of Emergency Preparedness Ser.). 64p. (gr. 6-6). 29.25 *(978-1-60853-592-7(4)*, Rosen Reference) Rosen Publishing Group, Inc., The.

Graham, Ian. The Science of Weather: the Changing Truth about Earth's Climate (the Science of the Earth) (Library Edition) Romanet, Caroline, illus. 2018. (Science Of... Ser.). (ENG.). 32p. (J). (gr. 3-7). lib. bdg. 29.00 *(978-0-531-22769-5(3)*, Watts, Franklin) Scholastic Library Publishing.

Gregory, Josh. Climate Scientist. 2013. (21st Century Skills Library: Cool STEM Careers Ser.). (ENG.). 32p. (gr. 4-8). (J). pap. 14.21 *(978-1-62431-026-3(5)*, 202461); (Illus.). 32.07 *(978-1-62431-002-7(8)*, 202459) Cherry Lake Publishing.

Hackney Blackwell, Amy & Manar, Elizabeth P. U-X-L Encyclopedia of Weather & Natural Disasters. 2016. (Illus.). (J). *(978-1-4103-3291-2(8))*; *(978-1-4103-3292-9(6))* Cengage Gale. (Blackbirch Pr., Inc.).

Hand, Carol. Science Lab: Weather Patterns. 2011. (Explorer Library: Language Arts Explorer Ser.). (ENG.). 32p. (gr. 4-8). pap. 14.21 *(978-1-61080-299-4(3)*, 201221) Cherry Lake Publishing.

—Science Lab: Weather Patterns. 2011. (Explorer Library: Language Arts Explorer Ser.). (ENG., Illus.). 32p. (gr. 4-8). lib. bdg. 32.07 *(978-1-61080-210-9(1)*, 201196) Cherry Lake Publishing.

—Weather Myths, Busted! 2017. (Science Myths, Busted! Ser.). (ENG., Illus.). 32p. (J). (gr. 3-6). pap. 9.95 *(978-1-63235-357-3(1)*, 11820); lib. bdg. 32.80 *(978-1-63235-307-8(5)*, 11812) Bookstaves, LLC. (12-Story Library).

Hansen, Jim & Burns, John. How to Draw Dragons, 1 vol. 2007. (Drawing Fantasy Art Ser.: Vol. 4). (ENG., Illus.). 32p. (J). (gr. 4-5). lib. bdg. 30.27 *(978-1-4042-3856-5(5)*, c578ba72-973a-4635-abf6-a97500d88d1b) Rosen Publishing Group, Inc., The.

Hayes, Amy & Lyman, Geraldine. Meteorology & Forecasting the Weather, 1 vol. 2018. (Spotlight on Weather & Natural Disasters Ser.). (ENG.). 24p. (gr. 4-6). 27.93 *(978-1-5081-6906-2(3)*, 3736b68f-52cd-4442-a0d2-0fab19f34695, PowerKids Pr.) Rosen Publishing Group, Inc., The.

Hollar, Sherman. Pioneers in the World of Weather & Climatology, 4 vols. 2012. (Inventors & Innovators Ser.). (ENG., Illus.). 128p. (YA). (gr. 8-8). 77.64 *(978-1-61530-787-6(7)*, 59308aeb-233c-4105-9106-c350e56bf8c7); 38.82 *(978-1-61530-702-9(8)*, 46791175-1e17-4c49-b474-33afa200fbe6) Rosen Publishing Group, Inc., The.

Hunter, Nick. Science vs. Climate Change, 1 vol. 2013. (Science Fights Back Ser.). (ENG., Illus.). 48p. (gr. 4-5). 34.60 *(978-1-4339-8678-9(7)*, 91e2a7c0-d8e3-4c14-8dbf-c9b21c0fdfd0); pap. 15.05 *(978-1-4339-8679-6(5)*, 6de42026-1470-4fd8-8ba2-779436426ead) Stevens, Gareth Publishing LLLP. (Gareth Stevens Learning Library).

Jacobs, Marian B. Why Does It Rain?, 1 vol. 2003. (Library of Why Ser.). (ENG., Illus.). 24p. (J). (gr. 3-4). lib. bdg. 25.27 *(978-0-8239-5273-1(8)*, df8e6c12-ab40-4221-b8b7-bffa4708f492, PowerKids Pr.) Rosen Publishing Group, Inc., The.

Johnson, Robin. What Is a Heat Wave? 2016. (ENG., Illus.). 24p. (J). *(978-0-7787-2397-4(6))* Crabtree Publishing Co.

—What Is Precipitation? 2012. (ENG.). 24p. (J). *(978-0-7787-0754-7(7))*; (Illus.). pap. *(978-0-7787-0761-5(X))* Crabtree Publishing Co.

Kerrod, Robin. Exploring Science: Weather an Amazing Fact File & Hands-On Project Book. 2014. (ENG., Illus.). 64p. (J). (gr. 3-7). 12.99 *(978-1-86147-307-3(9)*, Armadillo) Anness Publishing GBR. Dist: National Bk. Network.

Kizer Whitt, Kelly. Solar System Forecast, 1 vol. Allen Klein, Laurie, illus. 2012. 32p. (J). (ENG.). (gr. -1-4). 17.95 *(978-1-60718-523-9(7))*; (SPA.). (gr. -1-4). 17.95 *(978-1-60718-678-6(0))*; (ENG.). (gr. -1-4). pap. 9.95 *(978-1-60718-532-1(6))*; (SPA.). (gr. 4-5). pap. 11.95 *(978-1-62855-425-0(8)*, 37d710b2-fba7-4415-9f35-5e65258eecc7) Arbordale Publishing.

Kjelle, Marylou Morano. A Project Guide to Wind, Weather, & the Atmosphere. 2010. (Earth Science Projects for Kids Ser.). (Illus.). 48p. (J). (gr. 4-7). lib. bdg. 29.95 *(978-1-58415-869-1(7))* Mitchell Lane Pubs.

Krajnik, Elizabeth. Clouds & Precipitation, 1 vol. 2018. (Spotlight on Weather & Natural Disasters Ser.). (ENG.). 24p. (gr. 4-6). 27.93 *(978-1-5081-6886-7(5)*, 1c1c38a9-e9f6-484e-9104-c5b221ce6723, PowerKids Pr.) Rosen Publishing Group, Inc., The.

Lawrence, Ellen. How Are Rain, Snow, & Hail Alike? 2012. (Weather Wise Ser.). 24p. (J). (gr. -1-3). lib. bdg. 26.99 *(978-1-61772-403-9(3))* Bearport Publishing Co., Inc.

—What Is Weather? 2018. (Weather Wise Ser.). (ENG.). 24p. (J). (gr. -1-3). 7.99 *(978-1-64280-093-7(7))* Bearport Publishing Co., Inc.

Levine, Shar & Johnstone, Leslie. Wonderful Weather. Harpster, Steve, illus. 2005. (First Science Experiments Ser.). (ENG.). 48p. (J). (gr. 2-4). 17.44 *(978-0-8069-7249-7(1))* Sterling Publishing Co., Inc.

Lunis, Natalie. Making a Weather Station. 2011. (Early Connections Ser.). (J). *(978-1-61672-613-3(X))* Benchmark Education Co.

Machajewski, Sarah. Weather & Climate Around the World, 1 vol. 2018. (Spotlight on Weather & Natural Disasters Ser.). (ENG.). 24p. (gr. 4-6). 27.93 *(978-1-5081-6920-8(9)*, 393c23a4-ab85-4e6e-9a6e-62901d41aef0, PowerKids Pr.) Rosen Publishing Group, Inc., The.

Mara, Wil. Why Does It Rain?, 1 vol. 2010. (Tell Me Why, Tell Me How Ser.). (ENG.). 32p. (gr. 3-3). 32.64 *(978-0-7614-3991-2(9)*, c05579b7-5861-4743-92a1-872870ab1603) Cavendish Square Publishing LLC.

—Why Is the Sky Blue?, 1 vol. 2008. (Tell Me Why, Tell Me How Ser.). (ENG., Illus.). 32p. (gr. 3-3). pap. 9.23 *(978-0-7614-3368-2(6)*, f704997e-a0d3-4b3c-8079-fb06a839d7d2) Cavendish Square Publishing LLC.

Marsico, Katie. Scholastic News Nonfiction Readers: Wild Weather Days. 2006. (Scholastic News Nonfiction Readers Ser.). (ENG., Illus.). 24p. (J). (gr. 1-2). lib. bdg. 22.00 *(978-0-531-16771-7(2))* Scholastic Library Publishing.

Martin, Bobi. What Are Air Masses & Weather Fronts?, 1 vol. 2014. (Let's Find Out! Weather Ser.). (ENG.). 32p. (J). (gr. 2-3). 26.06 *(978-1-62275-787-9(4)*, 6bfb12d1-e61b-4bbd-a6e2-67a983c3b537, Britannica Educational Publishing) Rosen Publishing Group, Inc., The.

Martin, Emmett. Exploring the Weather, 1 vol. 2018. (So into Science! Ser.). (ENG.). 24p. (gr. k-k). 24.27 *(978-1-5382-2889-0(0)*, 46bc1b8b-5015-47e8-9076-9063e1135ba5) Stevens, Gareth Publishing LLLP.

Mattern, Joanne. What Are Weather & Climate?, 1 vol. 2014. (Let's Find Out! Weather Ser.). (ENG.). 32p. (J). (gr. 2-3). 26.06 *(978-1-62275-779-4(3)*, cb6e0160-cc8e-4374-8411-2169bf2dc9b5, Britannica Educational Publishing) Rosen Publishing Group, Inc., The.

McAneney, Caitie. Precipitation, 1 vol. 2016. (Where's the Water? Ser.). (ENG., Illus.). 24p. (J). (gr. 2-3). pap. 9.15 *(978-1-4824-4684-5(7)*, 66e210d4-eb3d-4435-aef4-00076d9214c8); lib. bdg. 24.27 *(978-1-4824-4686-9(3)*, cd38b477-9d2c-4857-aea9-a25f63db3ed2) Stevens, Gareth Publishing LLLP.

Morgan, Emily. Next Time You See a Cloud. 2017. (Next Time You See Ser.). (ENG., Illus.). 32p. (J). (gr. -1-k). pap. 13.99 *(978-1-938946-36-3(7)*, P531928) National Science Teachers Assn.

Mullins, Matt. Think Like a Scientist in the Backyard. 2011. (Explorer Junior Library: Science Explorer Junior Ser.). (ENG., Illus.). 32p. (gr. 4-8). lib. bdg. 32.07 *(978-1-61080-167-6(9)*, 201104) Cherry Lake Publishing.

El Mundo de la Meteorologia, 6 vols., Vol. 3. (Explorers. Exploradores Nonfiction Sets Ser.). (SPA.). (gr. 3-6). *(978-0-7699-0654-6(0))* Shortland Pubns. (U. S. A.) Inc.

Oard, Michael. The New Weather Book. 2015. (Illus.). 96p. (J). (gr. 9-12). 18.99 *(978-0-89051-861-8(0)*, Master Books) New Leaf Publishing Group.

Olson, Elsie. Exploring Weather: Meteorologists at Work! 2017. (Earth Detectives Ser.). (ENG., Illus.). 24p. (J). (gr. k-4). lib. bdg. 32.79 *(978-1-5321-1234-8(3)*, 27621, Super SandCastle) ABDO Publishing Co.

Orr, Tamra B. Junior Scientists: Experiment with Weather. 2010. (Explorer Junior Library: Science Explorer Junior Ser.). (ENG., Illus.). 32p. (gr. 3-6). lib. bdg. 32.07 *(978-1-60279-841-0(9)*, 200548) Cherry Lake Publishing.

Parker, Janice. Weather. 2016. (Illus.). 48p. (J). *(978-1-5105-2243-5(3))* SmartBook Media, Inc.

Peterson, Judy Monroe. Weather Watchers: Climate Scientists. (Extreme Scientists Ser.). 24p. (gr. 2-3). 2009. 42.50 *(978-1-61512-454-1(3)*, PowerKids Pr.) 2008. (ENG., Illus.). (YA). lib. bdg. 26.27 *(978-1-4042-4527-3(8)*, 963410c5-33a5-4c49-9f8c-5478f5e904f0) Rosen Publishing Group, Inc., The.

Poolos, Christine. What Is an Object in the Sky?, 1 vol. 2014. (Let's Find Out! Space Science Ser.). (ENG.). 32p. (J). (gr. 2-3). 26.06 *(978-1-62275-471-7(9)*, a2002684-d044-4905-9f84-daf1bf1ed8ca) Rosen Publishing Group, Inc., The.

Purdie, Kate. Sunshine & Drought, 1 vol. 2010. (Weatherwise Ser.). (ENG.). 32p. (gr. 4-4). (J). pap. 11.60 *(978-1-61532-278-7(7)*, c3a6e697-fb3b-48d5-b174-35946350cac0, PowerKids Pr.); (Illus.). (YA). lib. bdg. 30.27 *(978-1-61532-266-4(3)*, 785fa62e-ff1f-4efc-9d6b-9d894d8ef4e7) Rosen Publishing Group, Inc., The.

Purslow, Frances. Precipitation. 2015. (Illus.). 24p. (J). *(978-1-5105-0054-9(5))* SmartBook Media, Inc.

—Precipitation. (Illus.). 24p. 2016. (J). *(978-1-4896-5797-8(5))* 2010. (J). (gr. 3-5). pap. 11.95 *(978-1-61690-008-3(3))* 2010. (YA). (gr. 3-6). lib. bdg. 25.70 *(978-1-61690-002-1(4))* 2005. (J). (gr. 3-7). pap. 8.95 *(978-1-59036-311-9(6))* 2005. (J). (gr. 3-7). lib. bdg. 24.45 *(978-1-59036-305-8(1))* Weigl Pubs., Inc.

Richards, Jon. Light & Sight. 2009. (Science Factory Ser.). 32p. (gr. 4-5). 50.50 *(978-1-60853-022-9(1)*, PowerKids Pr.) Rosen Publishing Group, Inc., The.

Roker, Al. Al Roker's Extreme Weather: Tornadoes, Typhoons, & Other Weather Phenomena. 2017. (ENG., Illus.). 48p. (J). (gr. 3-7). 16.99 *(978-0-06-248499-4(0)*, HarperCollins) HarperCollins Pubs.

Rowe, Brooke. Creating Rain. Bane, Jeff, illus. 2016. (My Early Library: My Science Fun Ser.). (ENG.). 24p. (J). (gr. k-1). 30.64 *(978-1-63471-027-5(4)*, 208188) Cherry Lake Publishing.

Schuetz, Kristin. Precipitation. 2015. (Understanding Weather Ser.). (ENG., Illus.). 24p. (J). (gr. k-3). lib. bdg. 26.95 *(978-1-62617-253-1(6)*, Blastoff! Readers) Bellwether Media.

Shea, Therese. Droughts & Heat Waves, 1 vol. 2018. (Spotlight on Weather & Natural Disasters Ser.). (ENG.). 24p. (gr. 4-6). 27.93 *(978-1-5081-6891-1(1)*, 0a0dda2a-d58c-48a2-9c3e-b310dbb6854f, PowerKids Pr.) Rosen Publishing Group, Inc., The.

Silverstein, Alvin, et al. Weather & Climate. 2007. (Science Concepts, Second Ser.). (Illus.). 96p. (J). (gr. 6-8). lib. bdg. 31.93 *(978-0-8225-6796-7(2)*, Twenty-First Century Bks.) Lerner Publishing Group.

Smith, Alastair & Clarke, Phillip. Weather: With Internet Links. 2006. (Usborne Spotter's Guides). (Illus.). 64p. (J). (gr. 2). lib. bdg. 13.99 *(978-1-58086-915-7(7)*, Usborne) EDC Publishing.

Spalding, Maddie & Willis, John. Weather. 2018. (Illus.). 24p. (J). pap. *(978-1-4896-9686-1(5)*, AV2 by Weigl) Weigl Pubs., Inc.

Spilsbury, Louise & Claybourne, Anna. The Complete Guide to Extreme Weather. 2016. (Illus.). 144p. (J). *(978-1-4351-6354-6(0))* Barnes & Noble, Inc.

Spilsbury, Richard & Spilsbury, Louise. Weather & Seasons, 1 vol. 2018. (Flowchart Smart Ser.). (ENG.). 48p. (gr. 4-5). pap. 15.05 *(978-1-5382-3482-2(3)*, 47e5a693-74a0-4796-a037-bcdc2e31bef0) Stevens, Gareth Publishing LLLP.

Taylor-Butler, Christine. Meteorology: The Study of Weather. 2012. (True Book Ser.). (ENG., Illus.). 48p. (J). lib. bdg. 29.00 *(978-0-531-24678-8(7)*, Children's Pr.) Scholastic Library Publishing.

—Meteorology (a True Book: Earth Science) 2012. (True Book (Relaunch) Ser.). (ENG., Illus.). 48p. (J). (gr. 3-5). pap. 6.95 *(978-0-531-28272-4(4)*, Children's Pr.) Scholastic Library Publishing.

Thompson, Jean M. Water Wonders Every Child Should Know: L. 2005. reprint ed. pap. 26.95 *(978-1-4179-3339-6(9))* Kessinger Publishing, LLC.

USA Today Staff, contrib. by. USA Today Weather Wonders: Discover What's up & What's Coming Down. 2009. (Illus.). 80p. (J). *(978-1-4027-6534-6(7)*, Sterling Innovation) Sterling Publishing Co., Inc.

Vogt, Gregory. Meteorology in the Real World. 2016. (STEM in the Real World Set 2 Ser.). (ENG., Illus.). 48p. (J). (gr. 4-8). lib. bdg. 35.64 *(978-1-68078-482-4(X)*, 23901) ABDO Publishing Co.

Way, Jennifer & Gaffney, Timothy R. Severe-Storm Scientists: Chasing Tornadoes & Hurricanes, 1 vol. 2015. (Extreme Science Careers Ser.). (ENG., Illus.). 128p. (gr. 7-7). 38.93 *(978-0-7660-6968-8(0)*, 2133208f-6fb7-4dce-9047-f1a91154d0b7) Enslow Publishing, LLC.

Williams, Judith. ¿Cómo el Sol Afecta el Clima? / How Does the Sun Make Weather?, 1 vol. 2010. (Me Gusta el Clima / I Like Weather! Ser.). (SPA & ENG.). 24p. (gr. k-2). 26.60 *(978-0-7660-3237-8(X)*, a5804d2a-7141-4c80-82e1-0756de08fa84, Enslow Elementary) Enslow Publishing, LLC.

Wood, Alix. Backyard Meteorology Experiments, 1 vol. 2018. (Backyard Scientist Ser.). (ENG.). 32p. (gr. 3-3). 27.93 *(978-1-5383-3741-7(X)*, eac72318-29f9-4bae-b7e0-4df7e70cd940, PowerKids Pr.) Rosen Publishing Group, Inc., The.

World Book, Inc. Staff, contrib. by. Heat Waves. (J). 2007. *(978-0-7166-9807-4(2))* 2nd ed. 2009. (Illus.). 47p. *(978-0-7166-9823-4(4))* 3rd ed. 2018. *(978-0-7166-9934-7(6))* World Bk., Inc.

—Learning about Weather. 2011. (J). *(978-0-7166-0235-4(0))* World Bk., Inc.

Yasuda, Anita. Explore Comets & Asteroids! With 25 Great Projects. Stone, Bryan, illus. 2017. (Explore Your World Ser.). (ENG.). 96p. (J). (gr. 1-5). 19.95 *(978-1-61930-511-3(9)*, ec25ec5e-4d22-45e7-ada3-139f498c0a13) Nomad Pr.

METEOROLOGY—VOCATIONAL GUIDANCE

Cortinas, John. On the Job with a Meteorologist. 2003. (Adventures in Science Professions Ser.). (J). *(978-1-58417-061-7(1))*; pap. *(978-1-58417-124-9(3))* Lake Street Pubs.

Horn, Geoffrey M. Meteorologist, 1 vol. 2008. (Cool Careers: Helping Careers Ser.). (ENG.). 32p. (gr. 3-3). pap. 11.50 *(978-0-8368-9327-4(1)*, ad93c7b3-e2b8-4dac-88c0-862ce1e4f32f); (YA). lib. bdg. 28.67 *(978-0-8368-9194-2(5)*, acabdd96-240b-4229-9936-6ae589f7cf88) Stevens, Gareth Publishing LLLP.

Mullins, Matt. Meteorologist. 2011. (21st Century Skills Library: Cool Science Careers Ser.). (ENG., Illus.). 32p. (gr. 4-8). lib. bdg. 32.07 *(978-1-61080-034-1(6)*, 200994) Cherry Lake Publishing.

Rajczak Nelson, Kristen. Be a Meteorologist, 1 vol. 2014. (Be a Scientist! Ser.). (ENG., Illus.). 32p. (J). (gr. 3-4). pap. 11.50 *(978-1-4824-1210-9(1)*, e1ead41c-ca49-4bb8-9ac6-8a4646875299) Stevens, Gareth Publishing LLLP.

METEORS

see also Meteorites

Cutting, Robert. Falling Star. Ng, Drew, illus. 2007. 48p. (J). lib. bdg. 23.08 *(978-1-4242-1625-3(7))* Fitzgerald Bks.

Dickmann, Nancy. Asteroids, Meteors, & Comets, 1 vol. 2018. (Space Facts & Figures Ser.). (ENG.). 32p. (gr. 2-3). 28.93 *(978-1-5081-9506-1(4)*, 7ffa8c75-86fc-4766-850b-dceb7f44ec8b, Windmill Bks.) Rosen Publishing Group, Inc., The.

—Exploring Comets, Asteroids, & Other Objects in Space, 1 vol. 2015. (Spectacular Space Science Ser.). (ENG., Illus.). 48p. (J). (gr. 5-6). 33.47 *(978-1-4994-3637-2(8)*, 670562d8-c46b-4c18-a44e-6c803f2766d7, Rosen Central) Rosen Publishing Group, Inc., The.

Dybvik, Tina. Space Cowboy Caleb & the Night Sky Round-Up: Learning about the Night Sky, 1 vol. Record, Adam, illus. 2013. (Take It Outside Ser.). (ENG.). 24p. (J). (gr. -1-2). pap. 8.95 *(978-1-4795-1938-5(3)*, 123639, Picture Window Bks.) Capstone.

Faulkner, Nicholas & Gregersen, Erik. Asteroids, Meteors, Meteorites, & Comets, 1 vol. 2018. (Universe & Our Place in It Ser.). (ENG., Illus.). 128p. (J). (gr. 10-10). pap. 20.95 *(978-1-68048-873-9(2)*, 67187ff7-81d9-4d3a-ac23-a13cb74a1a7d, Britannica Educational Publishing) Rosen Publishing Group, Inc., The.

Gifford, Clive. The Solar System, Meteors, & Comets. 2015. (Watch This Space! Ser.). (ENG., Illus.). 32p. (J). (gr. 4-5). lib. bdg. *(978-0-7787-2023-2(3))* Crabtree Publishing Co.

Hantula, Richard & Asimov, Isaac. Comets & Meteors, 1 vol. 2004. (Isaac Asimov's 21st Century Library of the Universe: near & Far Ser.). (ENG., Illus.). 32p. (gr. 3-5). lib. bdg. 28.67 *(978-0-8368-3966-1(8)*, 7801ec97-7d4e-47df-9315-ed0562359c70) Stevens, Gareth Publishing LLLP.

Mason Crest. Comets & Meteors, Vol. 7. 2016. (Solar System Ser.: Vol. 7). (ENG., Illus.). 48p. (J). (gr. 5-8). 20.95 *(978-1-4222-3548-5(3))* Mason Crest.

Mason Crest Publishers Staff, contrib. by. The Sun. 2017. (Illus.). 40p. (J). *(978-1-4222-3547-8(5))* Mason Crest.

Miller, Ron. Asteroids, Comets, & Meteors. 2006. (Worlds Beyond Ser.). (Illus.). 80p. (J). (gr. 5-9). 27.93 *(978-0-7613-2363-1(5)*, Twenty-First Century Bks.) Lerner Publishing Group.

Ollen, Rebecca. Exploring Meteors. (Objects in the Sky Ser.). 24p. (gr. 3-3). 2009. 42.50 *(978-1-60851-139-6(1))* 2007. (ENG., Illus.). (J). lib. bdg. 26.27 *(978-1-4042-3468-0(3)*, 8e585b55-a39f-4814-93fa-3ccf4f62d96d) Rosen Publishing Group, Inc., The. (PowerKids Pr.).

Orr, Tamra B. I See Falling Stars. 2015. (Tell Me Why Library). (ENG., Illus.). 24p. (gr. 2-5). pap. 12.79 *(978-1-63362-035-3(2)*, 205897) Cherry Lake Publishing.

—Searching the Sky. 2014. (Explorer Library: Science Explorer Ser.). (ENG., Illus.). 32p. (J). (gr. 4-8). 32.07 *(978-1-62431-782-8(0)*, 203324) Cherry Lake Publishing.

Rajczak Nelson, Kristen. Shooting Stars, 1 vol. 2012. (Nature's Light Show Ser.). (ENG., Illus.). 24p. (J). (gr. 2-3). pap. 9.15 *(978-1-4339-7036-8(8)*, c224754d-fcb1-4faf-8c6f-584d43db1d5f); lib. bdg. 25.27 *(978-1-4339-7035-1(X)*, 08b81ea7-b540-4764-b5f1-7d160f2e79a8) Stevens, Gareth Publishing LLLP.

Rose, Simon. Meteors. 2016. (Illus.). 32p. (J). *(978-1-4896-5818-0(1)*, AV2 by Weigl) 2011. (J). (gr. 4-6). pap. 13.95 *(978-1-61690-638-2(3)*, AV2 by Weigl) 2011. (Illus.). 32p. (YA). (gr. 2-5). 28.55 *(978-1-61690-634-4(0))* Weigl Pubs., Inc.

Sherman, Josepha. Asteroids, Meteors, & Comets, 1 vol. 2010. (Space! Ser.). (ENG.). 64p. (gr. 5-5). lib. bdg. 35.50 *(978-0-7614-4252-3(9)*, cc1d488f-8aac-4101-980d-527efb6bf637) Cavendish Square Publishing LLC.

Sparrow, Giles. Destination Asteroids, Comets, & Meteors, 1 vol. 2009. (Destination Solar System Ser.). (ENG., Illus.). 32p. (J). (gr. 3-4). 28.93 *(978-1-4358-3449-1(6)*, 2c8c0ba9-b825-4430-875a-9e5821e56f6d); pap. 11.00 *(978-1-4358-3469-9(0)*,

M
N
O

76f52369-b13b-4db2-bc41-04a122032829) Rosen Publishing Group, Inc., The. (PowerKids Pr.).

Stewart, Melissa. National Geographic Readers: Meteors. 2015. (Readers Ser.). (Illus.). 48p. (J). (gr. 1-3). pap. 4.99 *(978-1-4263-1943-3(6)*, National Geographic Kids) Disney Publishing Worldwide.

Vogt, Gregory. Meteors & Comets. 2010. (Early Bird Astronomy Ser.). (ENG.). 48p. (gr. 2-5). lib. bdg. 26.60 *(978-0-7613-3876-5(4))* Lerner Publishing Group.

Wilkins, Mary-Jane. Asteroids, Comets, & Meteors. 2017. (Fast Track: Our Solar System Ser.). 24p. (J). (gr. k-3). 28.50 *(978-1-78121-368-1(2))* Brown Bear Bks.

METER

see Versification

METER (UNIT)

see Metric System

METHOD OF STUDY

see Study Skills

METHODIST CHURCH

Benge, Janet & Benge, Geoff. Christian Heroes - Then & Now - John Wesley: The World, His Parish. 2007. (Christian Heroes Ser.). (ENG.). 190p. (YA). (gr. 3-7). pap. 11.99 *(978-1-57658-382-1(1))* YWAM Publishing.

Weatherford, Carole Boston. By & By: Charles Albert Tindley, the Father of Gospel Music. Collier, Bryan, illus. 2020. (ENG.). 48p. (J). (gr. -1-3). 17.99 *(978-1-5344-2636-8(1))* Simon & Schuster Children's Publishing.

METRIC SYSTEM

Adler, David A. The Metric System. Miller, Edward, illus. 2020. 32p. (J). (gr. 2-5). 18.99 *(978-0-8234-4096-2(6))* Holiday Hse., Inc.

Benjamin, Lindsay. Measurement Action! 2005. (Yellow Umbrella Fluent Level Ser.). (ENG., Illus.). 16p. (gr. k-1). pap. 35.70 *(978-0-7368-5322-4(7)*, Capstone Pr.) Capstone.

Bussell, Linda. MEASURING at the Pond, 1 vol. 2008. (Math in Our World - Level 3 Ser.). (ENG.). 24p. (gr. 3-3). (J). lib. bdg. 24.67 *(978-0-8368-9291-8(7)*, bb1ceb8d-2254-4043-9dd0-9f35cea088e1); pap. 9.15 *(978-0-8368-9390-8(5)*, 20cf248f-b6e7-4ce6-a2e4-7de41ffae8b0) Stevens, Gareth Publishing LLLP. (Weekly Reader Leveled Readers).

—Vamos a MEDIR en el Estanque (MEASURING at the Pond), 1 vol. 2008. (Las Matemáticas en Nuestro Mundo - Nivel 3 (Math in Our World - Level 3) Ser.). (SPA.). 24p. (gr. 3-3). (J). lib. bdg. 24.67 *(978-0-8368-9299-4(2)*, 22257668-c140-48b0-a6a5-00d45e66050e); pap. 9.15 *(978-0-8368-9398-4(0)*, 7d5e1084-f6c4-45df-9bf8-67a23c275b88) Stevens, Gareth Publishing LLLP. (Weekly Reader Leveled Readers).

Bussiere, Desirée. What in the World Is a Centimeter? & Other Metric Measurements, 1 vol. 2013. (Let's Measure Ser.). (ENG.). 24p. (J). (gr. -1-3). lib. bdg. 29.93 *(978-1-61783-596-4(X)*, 11109, SandCastle) ABDO Publishing Co.

Challen, Paul. The Metric System. 2009. (ENG.). 24p. (J). lib. bdg. *(978-0-7787-4352-1(7))*; pap. *(978-0-7787-4313-2(6))* Crabtree Publishing Co.

Fandel, Jennifer. The Metric System. 2006. (What in the World? Ser.). (Illus.). 48p. (J). (gr. 4-7). lib. bdg. 21.95 *(978-1-58341-430-9(4)*, Creative Education) Creative Co., The.

Mattern, Joanne. Let's Visit Canada: The Metric System, 1 vol. (Math for the REAL World Ser.). (ENG., Illus.). 24p. (gr. 3-4). 2010. pap. 8.25 *(978-0-8239-8872-3(4)*, f9be11d4-924a-4fdb-997d-c99cee4f5851) 2003. (J). lib. bdg. 26.27 *(978-0-8239-8967-6(4)*, 9bf4cca3-fae9-4499-902c-688170c1dfd3) Rosen Publishing Group, Inc., The. (PowerKids Pr.).

Murphy, Stuart J. Polly's Pen Pal. Simard, Remy, illus. 2005. (MathStart 3 Ser.). (ENG.). 40p. (J). (gr. 2-18). pap. 6.99 *(978-0-06-053170-6(3)*, HarperCollins) HarperCollins Pubs.

O'Donnell, Kerri. Natural Wonders of the World: Converting Distance Measurements to Metric Units. 2009. (PowerMath: Proficiency Plus Ser.). 32p. (gr. 4-5). 47.90 *(978-1-60851-414-4(5)*, PowerKids Pr.) Rosen Publishing Group, Inc., The.

—Natural Wonders of the World: Converting Measurements to Metric Units, 1 vol. 2004. (PowerMath: Proficiency Plus Ser.). (ENG., Illus.). 32p. (J). (gr. 5-6). lib. bdg. 28.93 *(978-1-4042-2928-0(0)*, 5c2ea680-9b31-45fd-bb0d-ac54c677dd07, PowerKids Pr.) Rosen Publishing Group, Inc., The.

—Natural Wonders of the World: Understanding & Representing Numbers in the Billions, 1 vol. 2010. (Math for the REAL World Ser.). (ENG., Illus.). 32p. (gr. 5-6). pap. 10.00 *(978-1-4042-5119-9(7)*, 933a3be5-d151-44b2-bc03-c234e2f49077) Rosen Publishing Group, Inc., The.

Schwartz, David M. Millions to Measure. Kellogg, Steven, illus. (ENG.). 40p. (J). (gr. k-7). 2003. 17.99 *(978-0-688-12916-3(1))* 2006. reprint ed. pap. 7.99 *(978-0-06-084806-4(5))* HarperCollins Pubs. (HarperCollins).

Sullivan, Erin Ash. Metric Math & Matemáticas Métricas: 6 English, 6 Spanish Adaptations. 2011. (ENG & SPA.). (J). 89.00 net. *(978-1-4108-5681-4(X))* Benchmark Education Co.

Sullivan, Navin. Area, Distance, & Volume, 1 vol. 2007. (Measure Up! Ser.). (ENG., Illus.). 48p. (gr. 4-4). lib. bdg. 34.07 *(978-0-7614-2323-2(0)*, 5d822a36-9675-4d00-861d-9c7483b060ae) Cavendish Square Publishing LLC.

METROLOGY

Here are entered works on the science of measurement or of weights and measures. Works on the general process of measuring are entered under Measurement. Works on a system of standard units of measure are entered under Weights and Measures.

see also Measurement; Weights and Measures

Branson, Sam. Let's Measure the Weather, 1 vol. 2012. (InfoMax Readers Ser.). (ENG., Illus.). 24p. (J). (gr. 1-1). pap. 8.25 *(978-1-4488-9019-4(5)*, f489e9d2-876c-4746-9278-0dfe9e0e73d3, Rosen Classroom) Rosen Publishing Group, Inc., The.

Gardner, Robert. Ace Your Math & Measuring Science Project: Great Science Fair Ideas, 1 vol. 2009. (Ace Your Physics Science Project Ser.). (ENG., Illus.). 128p. (gr. 5-6). lib. bdg. 35.93 *(978-0-7660-3224-8(8)*, 3e2f0053-4afa-4ce7-ae09-8351cd47fc5e) Enslow Publishing, LLC.

METROPOLITAN MUSEUM OF ART (NEW YORK, N.Y.)

Gregory, Joy. The Metropolitan Museum of Art. 2014. (Illus.). 24p. (J). *(978-1-4896-1194-9(0))* Weigl Pubs., Inc.

Metropolitan Museum of Art Staff, contrib. by. Museum Colors: The Metropolitan Museum of Art. 2006. (J). 16.99 *(978-1-58839-183-4(3))* Metropolitan Museum of Art, The.

MEXICAN AMERICANS

see also Mexicans—United States

Alaniz, Valeria & García, Sarah Rafael. Barrio Writers: Empowering Teens Through Creative Writing —: A Collection of Works by Teens for Teens, Teachers & Our Communities. 2012. (SPA & ENG.). 147p. (YA). pap. *(978-1-890701-32-1(7))* La Mancha Publishing Group.

Alter, Judy. Martin de Leon: Tejano Empresario. 2007. (Stars of Texas Ser.: 4). (ENG., Illus.). 72p. (J). (gr. 4-7). 14.95 *(978-1-933337-08-1(7)*, P121287) State Hse. Pr.

Ancona, George. Mi Casa: My House. 2005. (Somos Latinos (We Are Latinos) Ser.). (SPA & ENG., Illus.). 32p. (J). (gr. 1-3). pap. 8.95 *(978-0-516-25065-6(5)*, Children's Pr.) Scholastic Library Publishing.

—Mis Juegos/My Games. 2005. (Somos Latinos (We Are Latinos) Ser.). (SPA., Illus.). 32p. (J). (gr. 1-3). lib. bdg. 21.00 *(978-0-516-25293-3(3)*, Children's Pr.) Scholastic Library Publishing.

Angel, Ann. A Reader's Guide to Sandra Cisneros's the House on Mango Street, 1 vol. 2010. (Multicultural Literature Ser.). (ENG., Illus.). 128p. (gr. 9-10). 35.93 *(978-0-7660-3167-8(5)*, c2d817ad-497e-4312-afa5-cdacedc5e77b) Enslow Publishing, LLC.

Anza, Ana Luisa. Amigos del Otro Lado. Gomez, Eddie Martinez, illus. rev. ed. 2004. (Castillo de la Lectura Naranja Ser.). (SPA & ENG.). 136p. (J). pap. 7.95 *(978-970-20-0130-0(7))* Castillo, Ediciones, S. A. de C. V. MEX. Dist: Macmillan.

Apte, Sunita. Cesar Chavez: We Can Do It! 2005. (Defining Moments Ser.). (Illus.). 32p. (J). (gr. 2-5). lib. bdg. 28.50 *(978-1-59716-073-5(3))* Bearport Publishing Co., Inc.

Arce, Julissa. Someone Like Me: How One Undocumented Girl Fought for Her American Dream. (ENG., Illus.). 240p. (J). (gr. 5-17). 2019. pap. 9.99 *(978-0-316-48170-0(X))* 2018. 30.99 *(978-0-316-48174-8(2))* Little, Brown Bks. for Young Readers.

Baughan, Brian. Cesar Chavez. 2009. (Sharing the American Dream Ser.). (Illus.). 64p. (YA). (gr. 7-12). 22.95 *(978-1-4222-0582-2(7))* Mason Crest.

Behnke, Alison. Mexicans in America. 2004. (In America Ser.). (ENG., Illus.). 80p. (gr. 5-8). lib. bdg. 27.93 *(978-0-8225-3955-1(1))* Lerner Publishing Group.

Bernay, Emma & Berne, Emma Carlson. Cinco de Mayo. Rodriguez, Geraldine, illus. 2018. (Holidays in Rhythm & Rhyme Ser.). (ENG.). 24p. (J). (gr. k-2). lib. bdg. 33.99 *(978-1-68410-397-3(5)*, 140360) Cantata Learning.

Bloom, Barbara Lee. The Mexican Americans. 2005. (Immigrants in America Ser.). (ENG., Illus.). 112p. (J). 30.85 *(978-1-56006-753-5(5)*, Lucent Bks.) Cengage Gale.

Boyer Binns, Tristan. Mexican Americans. 2003. (We Are America Ser.). (Illus.). 32p. (J). (gr. 2-4). lib. bdg. 24.22 *(978-1-4034-0163-2(2))* Heinemann-Raintree.

Brimner, Larry Dane. Strike! The Farm Workers' Fight for Their Rights. 2014. (ENG., Illus.). 172p. (J). (gr. 5). 16.99 *(978-1-59078-997-1(0)*, Calkins Creek) Highlights Pr., c/o Highlights for Children, Inc.

Brown, Jonatha A. César Chávez, 1 vol. (Gente Que Hay Que Conocer (People We Should Know) Ser.). 2005. (SPA.). 24p. (gr. 2-4). pap. 9.15 *(978-0-8368-4766-6(0)*, b98ea793-6731-49c5-adf5-131db8ecbb55, Weekly Reader Leveled Readers) 2005. (ENG., Illus.). 24p. (gr. 2-4). lib. bdg. 24.67 *(978-0-8368-4745-1(8)*, b08a0da5-bcb9-4d07-916b-08fbc9b54ab5, Weekly Reader Leveled Readers) 2005. (SPA., Illus.). 24p. (gr. 2-4). lib. bdg. 24.67 *(978-0-8368-4759-8(8)*, 47c9aecc-dbd0-4961-9b94-8813dc904c2a, Weekly Reader Leveled Readers) 2004. (ENG., Illus.). 48p. (gr. 5-8). lib. bdg. 33.67 *(978-0-8368-5097-0(1)*, 90a1df70-6160-4ee6-9805-349b20666679, Gareth Stevens Secondary Library) Stevens, Gareth Publishing LLLP.

Brown, Jonatha A., et al. César Chávez, 1 vol. 2007. (Biografías Gráficas (Graphic Biographies) Ser.). (SPA., Illus.). 32p. (gr. 3-3). lib. bdg. 29.67 *(978-0-8368-7879-0(5)*, 08774358-75bd-4346-a4e3-766b518a332f) Stevens, Gareth Publishing LLLP.

Bryan, Nichol. Mexican Americans, 1 vol. 2004. (One Nation Set 1 Ser.). (ENG.). 32p. (gr. k-6). 27.07 *(978-1-57765-987-7(2)*, Checkerboard Library) ABDO Publishing Co.

Carlson-Berne, Emma. What's Your Story, Cesar Chavez? 2015. (Cub Reporter Meets Famous Americans Ser.). (ENG., Illus.). 32p. (J). (gr. k-3). 26.65 *(978-1-4677-7967-8(9)*, db58c6a0-49c5-47af-9800-e04e45de723c, Lerner Pubns.) Lerner Publishing Group.

Cesar Chavez, Lider Laboral. 2003. pap. 48.95 *(978-0-8136-9205-0(9))* Modern Curriculum Pr.

Clemens Warrick, Karen. Sandra Cisneros: Inspiring Latina Author, 1 vol. 2010. (Latino Biography Library). (ENG., Illus.). 128p. (gr. 6-7). lib. bdg. 35.93 *(978-0-7660-3162-3(4)*, 158666f4-fa40-4f8e-8c71-69baa23ec462) Enslow Publishing, LLC.

Collard, Sneed B., III. Cesar Chavez, 1 vol. 2010. (American Heroes Ser.). (ENG.). 48p. (gr. 3-3). 32.64 *(978-0-7614-4055-0(0)*, abfe4b16-e58b-4817-8708-b7bdbc77951d) Cavendish Square Publishing LLC.

Collins, David R. Cesar Chavez. 2005. (Just the Facts Biographies Ser.). (Illus.). 112p. (J). (gr. 6-12). 27.93 *(978-0-8225-2248-5(9))* Lerner Publishing Group.

Cruz, Bárbara C. César Chávez: Civil Rights Activist, 1 vol. 2015. (Influential Latinos Ser.). (ENG.). 128p. (gr. 7-8). lib. bdg. 38.93 *(978-0-7660-7179-7(0)*, 67488698-384c-48fc-b6f0-63bc38040d7e) Enslow Publishing, LLC.

Cuesta, Vivian. It Can Be Done: The Life & Legacy of César Chávez. 2003. (ENG., Illus.). 32p. (J). (gr. 6-8). pap. 9.00 net. *(978-0-7652-3271-7(5))* Celebration Pr.

Deiters, Erika & Deiters, Jim. The Mexican Community in America. 2003. (J). *(978-1-58417-030-3(1))*; pap. *(978-1-58417-092-1(1))* Lake Street Pubs.

DePietro, Frank. Mexican Americans. 2013. (Illus.). 64p. (J). pap. *(978-1-4222-2345-1(0))* Mason Crest.

—Mexican Americans. Limón, José E., ed. 2012. (Hispanic Americans: Major Minority Ser.). (Illus.). 64p. (J). (gr. 4). 22.95 *(978-1-4222-2328-4(0))* Mason Crest.

Ebon Research Systems Staff. Dare to Be... A Hero Vol. 3: Cesar Chavez. l.t. ed. 2003.Tr. of Atrevete Ser.. Un Heroe Cesar Chavez. (ENG & SPA., Illus.). 16p. (J). 3.99 *(978-0-9648313-6-0(8))* Ebon Research Systems Publishing, LLC.

Finley, Toiya Kristen. Russell Simmons. 2007. (Sharing the American Dream Ser.). 64p. (YA). (gr. 7-18). pap. 9.95 *(978-1-4222-0762-8(5))* Mason Crest.

Flynn, Jean. Henry B. Gonzalez: Rebel with a Cause. 2003. (Illus.). v, 140p. (J). 16.95 *(978-1-57168-780-7(7)*, Eakin Pr.) Eakin Pr.

Freedman, Russell. In the Days of the Vaqueros. 2008. (ENG., Illus.). 80p. (YA). (gr. 7). pap. 9.99 *(978-0-547-13365-2(0)*, 1048765, Clarion Bks.) HarperCollins Pubs.

Frey, Wendy. Citizen Heroes. 2007. (Illus.). 68p. (J). *(978-1-4105-0887-4(0))*; *(978-1-4105-0888-1(9))* Building Wings LLC.

Gallegos, Yuliana. Mi Sueno de America/My American Dream. Baeza, Georgina, tr. 2009. (ENG & SPA., Illus.). 55p. (J). (gr. 4-7). pap. 9.95 *(978-1-55885-534-2(3)*, Piñata Books) Arte Publico Pr.

Gelletly, LeeAnne. Mexican Immigration. 2005. (Changing Face of North America Ser.). (Illus.). 112p. (YA). lib. bdg. 24.95 *(978-1-59084-680-3(X))* Mason Crest.

Gitlin, Martin, ed. The Border Wall with Mexico, 1 vol. 2017. (Current Controversies Ser.). (ENG.). 144p. (J). (gr. 10-12). pap. 33.00 *(978-1-5345-0090-7(1)*, 401111fd-516f-4e7e-b978-8802fb4b0645); lib. bdg. 48.03 *(978-1-5345-0085-3(5)*, 73c9cd1f-24fe-49d4-8804-70f4d202ce1b) Greenhaven Publishing LLC.

Gnojewski, Carol. Celebrating Cinco de Mayo, 1 vol. 2012. (Celebrating Holidays Ser.). (ENG., Illus.). 48p. (gr. 3-3). pap. 11.53 *(978-1-59845-399-7(8)*, 51c22a17-4523-4ee0-a6d8-0fc1bffb9258, Enslow Elementary) Enslow Publishing, LLC.

Gotsch, Patrice. Cesar Chavez: Changing Lives. Arreola, Gil, illus. 2006. 19p. pap. 6.30 *(978-1-55501-780-4(0))* Ballard & Tighe Pubs.

Grande, Reyna. The Distance Between Us: Young Readers Edition. 2017. (ENG., Illus.). 336p. (J). (gr. 5-9). pap. 8.99 *(978-1-4814-6370-6(5)*, Aladdin) Simon & Schuster Children's Publishing.

—The Distance Between Us: Young Readers Edition. 2016. (ENG., Illus.). 336p. (J). (gr. 5-9). 19.99 *(978-1-4814-6371-3(3)*, Simon & Schuster/Paula Wiseman Bks.) Simon & Schuster/Paula Wiseman Bks.

Hale, Christy. Todos Iguales/All Equal: Un Corrido de Lemon Grove/a Ballad of Lemon Grove, 1 vol. 2019. (SPA., Illus.). 40p. (J). (gr. 3-7). 20.95 *(978-0-89239-427-2(7)*, leelowcbp, Children's Book Press) Lee & Low Bks., Inc.

Hanel, Rachael. When Cesar Chavez Climbed the Umbrella Tree. Herrerias, Alex, illus. 2019. (Leaders Doing Headstands Ser.). (ENG.). 32p. (J). (gr. 1-4). lib. bdg. 28.65 *(978-1-5158-3042-9(X)*, 138682, Picture Window Bks.) Capstone.

Henzel, Cynthia Kennedy. Mexican Immigrants: In Their Shoes. 2017. (Immigrant Experiences Ser.). (ENG.). 32p. (J). (gr. 3-6). lib. bdg. 35.64 *(978-1-5038-2030-2(0)*, 211850) Child's World, Inc, The.

Hernández, Roger E. & Hernández, Roger E. 1898 to World War II, 1 vol. 2010. (Hispanic America Ser.). (ENG.). 80p. (gr. 5-5). 36.93 *(978-0-7614-4176-2(X)*, cd22c781-913c-43d9-a0ab-9cc0282583ea) Cavendish Square Publishing LLC.

Herrera, Juan Felipe. El Canto de las Palomas/Calling the Doves. 2004. (Illus.). (J). (gr. 3-6). spiral bd. *(978-0-616-14607-1(8))* Canadian National Institute for the Blind/Institut National Canadien pour les Aveugles.

—Upside down Boy/el Nino de Cabeza, 1 vol. 2013.Tr. of Nino de Cabeza. (ENG., Illus.). 32p. (J). (gr. 1-5). per. 11.95 *(978-0-89239-217-9(7)*, leelowcbp, Children's Book Press) Lee & Low Bks., Inc.

Honders, Christine. Mexican American Rights Movement, 1 vol. 2016. (Civic Participation: Working for Civil Rights Ser.). (ENG., Illus.). 32p. (J). (gr. 5-5). pap. 11.00 *(978-1-4994-2684-7(4)*, 7d056249-1a63-41dd-bea6-5a72cc18ca10, PowerKids Pr.) Rosen Publishing Group, Inc., The.

Imery-Garcia, Ash. How Mexican Immigrants Made America Home, 1 vol. 2018. (Coming to America: the History of Immigration to the United States Ser.). (ENG., Illus.). 80p. (gr. 6-6). 38.80 *(978-1-5081-8132-3(2)*, c9dcf589-ac41-4b34-b47d-9465179c9906, Rosen Reference) Rosen Publishing Group, Inc., The.

Ingram, Scott. Mexican Americans, 1 vol. 2006. (World Almanac(r) Library of American Immigration Ser.). (ENG., Illus.). 48p. (gr. 5-8). lib. bdg. 33.67 *(978-0-8368-7316-0(5)*, 0f6605b8-5111-41ba-b996-6c08c8917a7e, Gareth Stevens Secondary Library) Stevens, Gareth Publishing LLLP.

Jourdane, Maurice & Glick, Marty. The Soledad Children: The Fight to End Discriminatory IQ Tests. 2019. (ENG., Illus.). 262p. pap. 19.95 *(978-1-55885-888-6(1))* Arte Publico Pr.

Juarez, Christine. Hector P. Garcia. 2016. (Great Hispanic & Latino Americans Ser.). (ENG., Illus.). 24p. (J). (gr. -1-2). lib. bdg. 24.65 *(978-1-5157-1891-8(3)*, 132590, Capstone Pr.) Capstone.

—José Antonio Navarro. 2016. (Great Hispanic & Latino Americans Ser.). (ENG., Illus.). 24p. (J). (gr. -1-2). lib. bdg. 24.65 *(978-1-5157-1889-5(1)*, 132588, Pebble) Capstone.

Keedle, Jayne. Mexican Americans, 1 vol. 2010. (New Americans Ser.). (ENG.). 80p. (gr. 5-5). 38.36 *(978-0-7614-4307-0(X)*, a5443211-e45e-4f4d-8c27-304d59f620a0) Cavendish Square Publishing LLC.

Kirkpatrick, Rob. Oscar de la Hoya: Boxeador de Medalla de Oro (Gold-Medal Boxer) 2009. (Grandes Idolos (Hot Shots) Ser.). (SPA.). 24p. (gr. 1-1). 42.50 *(978-1-61512-738-2(0)*, Editorial Buenas Letras) Rosen Publishing Group, Inc., The.

—Oscar de la Hoya: Gold-Medal Boxer / Boxeador de Medalla de Oro. 2009. (Hot Shots/Grandes idolos Ser.). (ENG & SPA.). 24p. (gr. 1-1). 42.50 *(978-1-61513-416-8(6)*, Editorial Buenas Letras) Rosen Publishing Group, Inc., The.

Krull, Kathleen. Cosechando Esperanza: La Historia de César Chávez (Harvesting Hope Spanish Edition) Ada, Alma Flor & Campoy, F. Isabel, trs. Morales, Yuyi, illus. 2004. (SPA.). 48p. (J). (gr. -1-3). pap. 7.99 *(978-0-15-205169-3(4)*, 1195591, Clarion Bks.) HarperCollins Pubs.

—Harvesting Hope: The Story of Cesar Chavez. Morales, Yuyi, illus. 2003. (ENG.). 48p. (J). (gr. -1-3). 17.99 *(978-0-15-201437-7(3)*, 1189864, Clarion Bks.) HarperCollins Pubs.

Langston-George, Rebecca. Cesar Chavez: Get to Know the Leader Who Won Rights for Workers. 2019. (People You Should Know Ser.). (ENG., Illus.). 32p. (J). (gr. 3-6). lib. bdg. 27.99 *(978-1-5435-5522-6(5)*, 139384, Capstone Pr.) Capstone.

Magoon, Kekla. Cesar Chavez: Crusader for Labor Rights, 1 vol. 2010. (Essential Lives Set 5 Ser.). (ENG., Illus.). 112p. (YA). (gr. 6-12). lib. bdg. 41.36 *(978-1-61613-512-6(3)*, 6707, Essential Library) ABDO Publishing Co.

Marcovitz, Hal. Mexican Americans. (Successful Americans Ser.). 64p. (YA). 2009. (gr. 9-12). 22.95 *(978-1-4222-0515-0(0))* 2007. (gr. 7-18). pap. 9.95 *(978-1-4222-0865-6(6))* Mason Crest.

Martinez, Diana Davila. A School Named for Someone Like Me (Una Escuela Con un Nombre Como ell Mio) (Illus.). 48p. (YA). (gr. 3-8). pap. 7.95 *(978-1-55885-334-8(0)*, Piñata Books) Arte Publico Pr.

Marvis, Barbara J. Selena. 2003. (Blue Banner Biography Ser.). (Illus.). 32p. (J). (gr. 3-8). lib. bdg. 25.70 *(978-1-58415-226-2(5))* Mitchell Lane Pubs.

Medina, Jane. Tomás Rivera. Martinez, Edward, illus. 2004. (ENG.). 24p. (J). (gr. -1-3). pap. 4.99 *(978-0-15-205145-7(7)*, 1195527, Clarion Bks.) HarperCollins Pubs.

—Tomás Rivera. Martinez, Edward, illus. 2004. (Green Light Reader Level 2 Ser.). (ENG.). 24p. (J). (gr. k-2). 16.19 *(978-0-15-205146-4(5))* Houghton Mifflin Harcourt Publishing Co.

Miklowitz, Gloria. Cesar Chavez. 2009. pap. 13.25 *(978-1-60559-056-1(8))* Hameray Publishing Group, Inc.

Miklowitz, Gloria D. César Chávez. 2004. (ENG., Illus.). 29p. (J). (gr. 2-5). pap. 5.97 net. *(978-0-7685-1215-1(8)*, Dominie Elementary) Savvas Learning Co.

Moening, Kate. Dolores Huerta. 2019. (Women Leading the Way Ser.). (ENG., Illus.). 24p. (J). (gr. k-3). lib. bdg. 26.95 *(978-1-64487-099-0(1)*, Blastoff! Readers) Bellwether Media.

—Dolores Huerta: Labor Activist: Labor Activist. 2019. (Women Leading the Way Ser.). (ENG., Illus.). 24p. (J). (gr. k-3). pap. 7.99 *(978-1-61891-722-5(6)*, 12303, Blastoff! Readers) Bellwether Media.

Morales, Yuyi. Dreamers. 2018. (Illus.). 40p. (J). (gr. -1-3). 18.99 *(978-0-8234-4055-9(9)*, Neal Porter Bks) Holiday Hse., Inc.

—Soñadores. 2018. (SPA.). 40p. (J). (gr. -1-3). 18.99 *(978-0-8234-4258-4(6)*, Neal Porter Bks) Holiday Hse., Inc.

Moreno, Barry. The Mexican Americans. (Major American Immigration Ser.). (YA). 2010. (Illus.). 64p. (gr. 9-12). 22.95 *(978-1-4222-0614-0(9))* 2007. pap. 9.95 *(978-1-4222-0681-2(5))* Mason Crest.

Nelson, Robin. Crayola (r) Cinco de Mayo Colors. 2018. (Crayola (r) Holiday Colors Ser.). (ENG., Illus.). 32p. (J). (gr. -1-3). pap. 6.99 *(978-1-5415-2746-1(1)*, d5154a2a-0912-41dd-bdc0-4ce50cee9ca7); lib. bdg. 29.32 *(978-1-5415-1095-1(X)*, f9c317bd-ed6c-40ec-987d-791c7423b1fe) Lerner Publishing Group. (Lerner Pubns.).

Parker, Lewis K. Why Mexican Immigrants Came to America. 2009. (Coming to America Ser.). 24p. (gr. 2-3). 42.50 *(978-1-61511-887-8(X)*, PowerKids Pr.) Rosen Publishing Group, Inc., The.

Peppas, Lynn. Why Martín de Léon Matters to Texas, 1 vol. 2013. (Texas Perspectives Ser.). (ENG., Illus.). 32p. (J). (gr. 4-4). lib. bdg. 28.93 *(978-1-4777-0916-0(9)*, 137bd19a-875c-40dd-9aa4-4267a46f79a9) Rosen Publishing Group, Inc., The.

Prather, Michelle. Crossing Oceans: Immigrating to California (California) rev. ed. 2017. (Social Studies: Informational Text Ser.). (ENG., Illus.). 32p. (J). (gr. 3-5). pap. 11.99 *(978-1-4258-3242-1(3))* Teacher Created Materials, Inc.

Randolph, Joanne. The Angel of Goliad: Francisca Alvarez & the Texas War for Independence. 2009. (Great Moments in American History Ser.). 32p. (gr. 3-3). 47.90 *(978-1-61513-151-8(5))* Rosen Publishing Group, Inc., The.

Rice, Liz. Bill Richardson. (Sharing the American Dream Ser.). (Illus.). 64p. (J). (gr. 7-12). 2009. 22.95 *(978-1-4222-0589-1(4))* 2007. pap. 9.95 *(978-1-4222-0761-1(7))* Mason Crest.

Rinaldo, Denise. Cesar Chavez: With a Discussion of Compassion. 2003. (Values in Action Ser.). (J). *(978-1-59203-064-4(5))* Learning Challenge, Inc.

Ruiz, José. Mexican Immigrants. 2017. (Illus.). 112p. (J). *(978-1-4222-3679-6(X))* Mason Crest.

Sanna, Ellyn. Mexican Americans' Role in the United States: A History of Pride, a Future of Hope. 2007. (Hispanic Heritage Ser.). (Illus.). 112p. (YA). (gr. 4-7). lib. bdg. 22.95 *(978-1-59084-926-2(4))* Mason Crest.

Schroeder, Michael J. Mexican Americans. Johnston, Robert D., ed. 2006. (ENG., Illus.). 150p. (gr. 6-12). lib. bdg. 30.00 *(978-0-7910-8785-5(9)*, P114408, Facts On File) Infobase Holdings, Inc.

Seidman, David. Cesar Chavez: Labor Leader. 2004. (Great Life Stories Ser.). (ENG., Illus.). 128p. (J). 30.50 *(978-0-531-12319-5(7)*, Watts, Franklin) Scholastic Library Publishing.

Seymour, Isobel. I am Mexican American. 2009. (Our American Family Ser.). 24p. (gr. 2-3). 42.50 *(978-1-60851-149-5(9)*, PowerKids Pr.) Rosen Publishing Group, Inc., The.

Shane, C. J. The Mexicans. 2005. pap. 22.45 *(978-0-7377-2157-7(X)*, Greenhaven Pr., Inc.) Cengage Gale.

Side by Side/Lado a Lado. 2010.Tr. of Side by Side - The Story of Dolores Huerta & Cesar Chavez. (ENG., Illus.). 32p. (J). (gr. -1-3). 17.99 *(978-0-06-122781-3(1))* HarperCollins Español.

Soto, Gary. Cesar Chavez: A Hero for Everyone. Lohstoeter, Lori, illus. 2003. (Milestone Ser.). (ENG.). 80p. (J). (gr. 2-5). pap. 6.99 *(978-0-689-85922-9(8)*, Simon & Schuster/Paula Wiseman Bks.) Simon & Schuster/Paula Wiseman Bks.

Stoltman, Joan. Cesar Chavez, 1 vol. 2017. (Little Biographies of Big People Ser.). (ENG.). 24p. (J). (gr. 1-2). pap. 9.15 *(978-1-5382-0919-6(5)*, a98adc72-6756-45de-8966-b5f3f57f927a); lib. bdg. 24.27 *(978-1-5382-0921-9(7)*, 2e81a573-8a97-4a3f-83e4-2e9ff53d32de) Stevens, Gareth Publishing LLLP.

Tait, Leia. Cinco de Mayo. (American Celebrations Ser.). (Illus.). 24p. (J). (gr. 3-5). 2010. pap. 11.95 *(978-1-60596-934-3(6))* 2010. lib. bdg. 25.70 *(978-1-60596-776-9(9))* 2006. lib. bdg. 24.45 *(978-1-59036-460-4(0))* 2006. per. 8.95 *(978-1-59036-463-5(5))* Weigl Pubs., Inc.

Thompson, E. L. Cesar Chavez, with Profiles of Terence V. Powderly & Dolores Huerta. 2006. (Biographical Connections Ser.). (Illus.). 112p. (J). *(978-0-7166-1827-0(3))* World Bk., Inc.

Tol, Alex Van & National Geographic Learning Staff. Dolores Huerta: Voice for the Working Poor. 2010. (ENG., Illus.). 112p. (J). pap. *(978-0-7787-2545-9(6))* Crabtree Publishing Co.

Tonatiuh, Duncan. Soldier for Equality: José de la Luz Sáenz & the Great War. 2019. (ENG., Illus.). 40p. (J). (gr. 1-3). 19.99 *(978-1-4197-3682-7(5)*, 1193001, Abrams Bks. for Young Readers) Abrams, Inc.

Van Tol, Alex. Dolores Huerta: Voice for the Working Poor. 2010. (Crabtree Groundbreaker Biographies Ser.). (ENG., Illus.). 112p. (J). (gr. 5-8). lib. bdg. *(978-0-7787-2536-7(7))* Crabtree Publishing Co.

Wadsworth, Ginger. Cesar Chavez. Schroeder, Mark, illus. 2005. (Yo Solo - Biografias (on My Own - Biographies) Ser.). (SPA.). 48p. (J). (gr. 2-4). per. 6.95 *(978-0-8225-3125-8(9))* Lerner Publishing Group.

—Cesar Chavez. 2005. (On My Own Biography Ser.). (Illus.). 48p. (J). 25.26 *(978-1-57505-652-4(6)*, Carolrhoda Bks.) Lerner Publishing Group.

—Cesar Chavez. Schroder, Mark, illus. 2005. (On My Own Biography Ser.). (ENG.). 48p. (J). (gr. 2-4). pap. 7.99 *(978-1-57505-826-9(X)*, 3096e92a-3c32-4501-b3d1-51b70163fef7, First Avenue Editions) Lerner Publishing Group.

—César Chávez. Schroder, Mark, illus. 2005. (Yo Solo: Biografías (on My Own Biographies) Ser.). (SPA.). 48p. (J). (gr. 2-4). lib. bdg. 25.32 *(978-0-8225-3124-1(0)*, 76116012-0cf6-4ba4-9705-0a63dc62bf1c, Ediciones Lerner) Lerner Publishing Group.

Warren, Sarah. Dolores Huerta: A Hero to Migrant Workers, 0 vols. Casilla, Robert, illus. 2012. (ENG.). 32p. (J). (gr. 1-4). 17.99 *(978-0-7614-6107-4(8)*, 9780761461074, Two Lions) Amazon Publishing.

Webster, Christine. Sandra Cisneros: My Favorite Writer. 2008. (J). 29.05 *(978-1-59036-933-3(5))* Weigl Pubs., Inc.

Wheeler, Jill C. Cesar Chavez. 2003. (Breaking Barriers Ser.). 64p. (gr. 3-8). 27.07 *(978-1-57765-905-1(8)*, Abdo & Daughters) ABDO Publishing Co.

World Book, Inc. Staff, contrib. by. !Feliz Navidad¡: Celebrating a Mexican Christmas. 2015. 80p. (J). *(978-0-7166-0830-1(8))* World Bk., Inc.

Worth, Richard. The Texas War of Independence: The 1800s, 1 vol. 2009. (Hispanic America Ser.). (ENG.). 80p. (gr. 5-5). lib. bdg. 36.93 *(978-0-7614-2934-0(4)*, 15e26fa2-4c55-418b-9cdd-d43ad323078b) Cavendish Square Publishing LLC.

Young, Jeff C. Cesar Chavez. 2007. (American Workers Ser.). (Illus.). 160p. (J). (gr. 3-7). lib. bdg. 27.95 *(978-1-59935-036-3(X))* Reynolds, Morgan Inc.

Zilka, Rose. Larry Itliong Leads the Way for Farmworkers' Rights. 2019. (Taking a Stand Ser.). (ENG., Illus.). 48p. (J). (gr. 5-6). pap. 11.95 *(978-1-64185-414-6(6)*, 1641854146); lib. bdg. 34.21 *(978-1-64185-356-9(5)*, 1641853565) North Star Editions. (Focus Readers).

MEXICAN AMERICANS—FICTION

Acosta, Daniel. Iron River, 1 vol. 2018. (ENG.). 224p. (YA). (gr. 9-12). 19.95 *(978-1-941026-93-9(1)*, 23353382); pap. 13.95 *(978-1-941026-94-6(X)*, 23353382) Lee & Low Bks., Inc. (Cinco Puntos Press).

Ada, Alma Flor. I Love Saturdays y Domingos. Savadier, Elivia, illus. 2004. (ENG.). 32p. (J). (gr. -1-3). reprint ed. 7.99 *(978-0-689-87409-3(X)*, Atheneum Bks. for Young Readers) Simon & Schuster Children's Publishing.

Ada, Alma Flor & Zubizarreta, Gabriel M. Con Cariño, Amalia (Love, Amalia) (SPA., Illus.). (J). (gr. 3-7). 2013. 160p. pap. 7.99 *(978-1-4424-2406-7(0))* 2012. 144p. 18.99 *(978-1-4424-2405-0(2)*, Atheneum Bks. for Young Readers) Simon & Schuster Children's Publishing.

—Dancing Home. (ENG., (J). (gr. 3-7). 2013. Illus.). 176p. pap. 7.99 *(978-1-4424-8175-6(7))* 2011. 160p. 17.99 *(978-1-4169-0088-7(8))* Simon & Schuster Children's Publishing. (Atheneum Bks. for Young Readers).

—Love, Amalia. 2012. (ENG., Illus.). 144p. (J). (gr. 3-7). 18.99 *(978-1-4424-2402-9(8)*, Atheneum Bks. for Young Readers) Simon & Schuster Children's Publishing.

—Nacer Bailando (Dancing Home) 2011. (SPA.). 160p. (J). (gr. 3-7). lib. bdg. 17.99 *(978-1-4424-2061-8(8)*, Atheneum Bks. for Young Readers) Simon & Schuster Children's Publishing.

Alegria, Malin. Cruzar el Limite (Crossing the Boundary) 2012. (Border Town (Spanish) Ser.: 1). (SPA.). lib. bdg. 16.00 *(978-0-606-26239-2(3))* Turtleback.

—Estrella's Quinceañera. (ENG.). (gr. 7-18). 2007. 288p. (YA). pap. 11.99 *(978-0-689-87810-7(9))* 2006. (Illus.). 272p. (J). 15.99 *(978-0-689-87809-1(5))* Simon & Schuster Bks. For Young Readers. (Simon & Schuster Bks. For Young Readers).

—Guerra de Quinceaneras (Quince Clash) 2013. (Border Town (Spanish) Ser.: 2). (SPA.). lib. bdg. 16.00 *(978-0-606-32401-4(1))* Turtleback.

—Sofi Mendoza's Guide to Getting Lost in Mexico. 2008. (ENG.). 304p. (YA). (gr. 7). pap. 11.99 *(978-0-689-87812-1(5)*, Simon & Schuster Bks. For Young Readers) Simon & Schuster Bks. For Young Readers.

Alexander, William. Ambassador. 2015. (ENG.). 256p. (J). (gr. 3-7). pap. 7.99 *(978-1-4424-9765-8(3)*, McElderry, Margaret K. Bks.) McElderry, Margaret K. Bks.

—Nomad. 2015. (ENG., Illus.). 272p. (J). (gr. 3-7). 16.99 *(978-1-4424-9767-2(X)*, McElderry, Margaret K. Bks.) McElderry, Margaret K. Bks.

Alvarez, Julia. Devolver Al Remitente (Return to Sender Spanish Edition) 2010. (SPA.). 368p. (J). (gr. 3-7). 8.99 *(978-0-375-85124-7(0)*, Yearling) Random Hse. Children's Bks.

—How Tia Lola Ended up Starting Over. 2012. (Tia Lola Stories Ser.: 4). (ENG.). 160p. (J). (gr. 3-7). pap. 6.99 *(978-0-375-87320-1(1)*, Yearling) Random Hse. Children's Bks.

Anaya, Rudolfo. Santero's Miracle: A Bilingual Story. Lamadrid, Enrique R., tr. Córdova, Amy, illus. 2004. (ENG.). 32p. (J). 19.95 *(978-0-8263-2847-2(4)*, P123068) Univ. of New Mexico Pr.

Aragón, Carla, et al. Dance of the Eggshells: Baile de Los Cascarones. Aragon, Socorro, tr. Saville, Kathy Dee, illus. 2010. (ENG.). 32p. (J). (gr. 1). 18.95 *(978-0-8263-4770-1(3)*, P174638) Univ. of New Mexico Pr.

Armas, Teresa. Remembering Grandma / Recordando a Abuela. Ventura, Gabriela Baeza, tr. from ENG. Rodriguez Howard, Pauline, illus. 2003. (ENG & SPA.). 32p. (J). 16.95 *(978-1-55885-344-7(8)*, Piñata Books) Arte Publico Pr.

Baca, Ana. Benito's Sopaipillas/Las Sopaipillas de Benito. Villarroel, Carolina, tr. Accardo, Anthony, illus. 2007. (ENG & SPA.). 32p. (J). (gr. -1-2). 16.95 *(978-1-55885-370-6(7)*, Piñata Books) Arte Publico Pr.

—Chiles for Benito (Chiles para Benito) Colin, Jose Juan, tr. Accardo, Anthony, illus. (ENG & SPA.). 32p. (J). 16.95 *(978-1-55885-389-8(8)*, Piñata Books) Arte Publico Pr.

—Tía's Tamales. Chilton, Noël, illus. 2012. (ENG & SPA.). 32p. (J). pap. 16.95 *(978-0-8263-5027-5(5)*, P225697) Univ. of New Mexico Pr.

Belford, Bibi. Canned & Crushed. 2015. (ENG.). 192p. (J). (gr. 2-7). 14.99 *(978-1-63220-435-6(5)*, Sky Pony Pr.) Skyhorse Publishing Co., Inc.

Bertrand, Diane Gonzales. Cecilia & Miguel Are Best Friends. Ventura, Gabriela Baeza, tr. Muraida, Thelma, illus. 2014.Tr. of Cecilia y Miguel Son Mejores Amigos. (SPA & ENG.). 32p. (J). 17.95 *(978-1-55885-794-0(X))* Arte Publico Pr.

—The Empanadas That Abuela Made/Las Empandas Que Hacia la Abuela. Ventura, Gabriela Baeza, tr. DeLange, Alex Pardo, illus. (ENG & SPA.). 32p. (J). 16.95 *(978-1-55885-388-1(X)*, Piñata Books) Arte Publico Pr.

—El Momento de Trino. Sanmiguel, Rosario, tr. from ENG. 2006. (SPA.). 181p. (J). (gr. 3-7). per. 9.95 *(978-1-55885-473-4(8)*, Piñata Books) Arte Publico Pr.

—Sip, Slurp, Soup, Soup/Caldo, Caldo, Caldo. Castilla, Julia Mercedes, tr. Delange, Alex Pardo, illus. 2008. (SPA & ENG.). 32p. (J). (gr. -1-2). pap. 7.95 *(978-1-55885-241-9(7)*, Piñata Books) Arte Publico Pr.

—Sip, Slurp, Soup Soup/Caldo Caldo Caldo: CD & Book Set. DeLange, Alex Pardo, illus. 2008. 32p. (J). pap. 19.95 *(978-0-9815686-1-4(0))* Lorito Bks., Inc.

Billingsley, ReShonda Tate. Friends 'til the End. 2009. (Good Girlz Ser.: 6). (ENG., Illus.). 174p. pap. 14.99 *(978-1-4165-5877-4(2)*, Gallery Bks.) Gallery Bks.

Blos, Joan W. Letters from the Corrugated Castle: A Novel of Gold Rush California, 1850-1852. 2008. (ENG.). 320p. (J). (gr. 5-9). pap. 5.99 *(978-0-689-87078-1(7)*, Atheneum Bks. for Young Readers) Simon & Schuster Children's Publishing.

Brammer, Ethriam Cash. My Tata's Guitar / la guitarra de mi Tata. Lechon, Daniel, illus. (ENG & SPA.). 32p. (J). 16.95 *(978-1-55885-369-0(3)*, Piñata Books) Arte Publico Pr.

—The Rowdy, Rowdy Ranch / Alla en el Rancho Grande. Cruz, D. Nina, illus. 2003. (ENG & SPA.). 32p. (J). 16.95 *(978-1-55885-409-3(6)*, Piñata Books) Arte Publico Pr.

Brightwood, Laura, illus. Growing up in East L. A. Brightwood, Laura, . 2006. (J). *(978-0-9779290-8-5(6))* 3-C Institute for Social Development.

Brooks, Melanie & Spenser and Mom Staff. Spenser Goes to el Paso. Jacobsen, Amie, illus. 2010. (ENG.). 32p. (J). 14.95 *(978-0-9817598-3-8(1)*, cbc0cc91-0341-4e1a-a28e-405962e8c495) Simple Fish Bk. Co., LLC.

Brown, Monica. Butterflies on Carmen Street/Mariposas en la Calle Carmen. Ward, April, illus. 2007. (SPA & ENG.). 32p. (J). (gr. -1-2). 16.95 *(978-1-55885-484-0(3)*, Piñata Books) Arte Publico Pr.

Camper, Cathy. Lowriders Blast from the Past. Raul the Third, illus. 2018. (Lowriders Ser.: 3). (ENG.). 128p. (J). (gr. 3-7). pap. 9.99 *(978-1-4521-6316-1(2))* Chronicle Bks. LLC.

—Lowriders in Space, 1 vol. the Third, Raul, illus. 2014. (Lowriders Ser.). (ENG.). 112p. (J). (gr. 3-7). pap. 9.99 *(978-1-4521-2869-6(3)*, da9edee5-f1ff-4bfb-91f6-5ca5cf0178dd) Chronicle Bks. LLC.

Campos, Tito. Muffler Man el Hombre Mofle. Alvarez, Lamberto, illus. 2009. 32p. (J). pap. 7.95 *(978-1-55885-557-1(2)*, Piñata Books) Arte Publico Pr.

Canales, Viola. The Tequila Worm. 2007. (ENG., Illus.). 208p. (YA). (gr. 7-11). pap. 7.99 *(978-0-375-84089-0(3)*, Lamb, Wendy Bks.) Random Hse. Children's Bks.

Castilla, Julia Mercedes. Strange Parents. 2009. 144p. (J). (gr. 6-18). pap. 9.95 *(978-1-55885-590-8(4)*, Piñata Books) Arte Publico Pr.

Center for Learning Network Staff. The House on Mango Street: Curriculum Unit. 2005. (Novel Ser.). (YA). tchr. ed., spiral bd. 19.95 *(978-1-56077-783-0(4))* Center for Learning, The.

Cervantes, Jennifer. Tortilla Sun. 2014. (ENG.). 224p. (J). (gr. 3-7). pap. 8.99 *(978-1-4521-3150-4(3))* Chronicle Bks. LLC.

Conkling, Winifred. Sylvia & Aki. 2013. 160p. (J). (gr. 4-7). 7.99 *(978-1-58246-345-2(X)*, Yearling) Random Hse. Children's Bks.

Contreras, Kathleen & Lindmark, Margaret. Sweet Memories/Dulces Recuerdos. Lindmark, Margaret, illus. 2014. (SPA & ENG., Illus.). 32p. (J). (gr. 2-4). pap. 14.99 *(978-1-933032-91-7(X))* Lectorum Pubns., Inc.

Costales, Amy. Sundays on Fourth Street/Los Domingos en la Calle Cuatro. Jerome, Elaine, illus. 2009. (SPA & ENG.). 32p. (J). (gr. -1-3). 16.95 *(978-1-55885-520-5(3))* Arte Publico Pr.

Cox, Judy. Carmen Learns English. Dominguez, Angela N., illus. 2010. (ENG.). 32p. (J). (gr. -1-3). 16.95 *(978-0-8234-2174-9(0))* Holiday Hse., Inc.

Cruz, Maria Colleen. Border Crossing. 2003. 128p. (J). pap. 9.95 *(978-1-55885-405-5(3)*, Piñata Books) Arte Publico Pr.

—Border Crossing. 2006. 122p. (gr. 8-12). 19.95 *(978-0-7569-6587-7(X))* Perfection Learning Corp.

De Anda, Diane. Kikirikí / Quiquiriquí. Hernández, Karina, tr. from ENG. Lechón, Daniel, illus. 2004. (ENG & SPA.). 32p. 16.95 *(978-1-55885-382-9(0)*, Piñata Books) Arte Publico Pr.

de la Peña, Matt. The Living. 2015. (Living Ser.). (ENG.). 336p. (YA). (gr. 9). pap. 10.99 *(978-0-385-74121-7(9)*, Ember) Random Hse. Children's Bks.

Diamond, Jill. Lou Lou & Pea & the Bicentennial Bonanza. Vamos, Lesley, illus. 2018. (Lou Lou & Pea Ser.). (ENG.). 272p. (J). 16.99 *(978-0-374-30298-6(7)*, 900152885, Farrar, Straus & Giroux (BYR)) Farrar, Straus & Giroux.

—Lou Lou & Pea & the Mural Mystery. Vamos, Lesley, illus. 2018. (Lou Lou & Pea Ser.). (ENG.). 288p. (J). pap. 10.99 *(978-1-250-14373-0(X)*, 900180548) Square Fish.

Dix, Catherine R. Rosetta Stones. 2009. (ENG.). 213p. (J). pap. 14.95 *(978-0-9798452-2-2(X)*, 9780979845222) Central Ave. Pr.

Dumas Lachtman, Ofelia. Looking for la Unica. 2004. (ENG & SPA., Illus.). 190p. (J). pap. 9.95 *(978-1-55885-412-3(6)*, Piñata Books) Arte Publico Pr.

Edwards, Michelle. A Hat for Mrs. Goldman: A Story about Knitting & Love. Karas, G. Brian, illus. 2016. 40p. (J). (gr. -1-3). 18.99 *(978-0-553-49710-6(3)*, Schwartz & Wade Bks.) Random Hse. Children's Bks.

Elkeles, Simone. Chain Reaction. 2015. (Perfect Chemistry Novel Ser.). (ENG.). 336p. (YA). (gr. 9). pap. 10.99 *(978-1-61963-703-0(0)*, 900146044, Bloomsbury USA Childrens) Bloomsbury Publishing USA.

—Rules of Attraction. 2015. (Perfect Chemistry Novel Ser.). (ENG.). 352p. (YA). (gr. 9). pap. 10.99 *(978-1-61963-702-3(2)*, 900146045, Bloomsbury USA Childrens) Bloomsbury Publishing USA.

Elya, Susan Middleton. Al Fin en Casa, 1 vol. Davalos, Felipe, illus. 2011.Tr. of Home at Last. (SPA.). 32p. (J). (gr. 1-5). pap. 12.95 *(978-1-60060-654-0(7)*, leelowbooks) Lee & Low Bks., Inc.

Engle, Margarita. Jazz Owls: A Novel of the Zoot Suit Riots. Gutierrez, Rudy, illus. 2018. (ENG.). 192p. (YA). (gr. 7). 17.99 *(978-1-5344-0943-9(2))* Simon & Schuster Children's Publishing.

Estevis, Anne. Chicken Foot Farm. 2008. 154p. (J). (gr. 6-18). pap. 10.95 *(978-1-55885-505-2(X)*, Piñata Books) Arte Publico Pr.

—Down Garrapata Road. 2003. 128p. (J). pap. 12.95 *(978-1-55885-397-3(9))* Arte Publico Pr.

Finnegan, Marco. Lizard in a Zoot Suit. Finnegan, Marco, illus. 2020. (ENG., Illus.). 144p. (YA). (gr. 7-12). 31.99 *(978-1-5415-2365-4(2)*, a6f85d3f-7999-47b7-b6d3-96fccb4d533f, Graphic Universe™) Lerner Publishing Group.

Flor Ada, Alma. Celebrate Thanksgiving Day with Beto & Gaby. Hayes, Joe & Franco, Sharon, trs. from SPA. Rueda, Claudia, illus. 2006. (Cuentos para Celebrar / Stories to Celebrate Ser.). 30p. (J). (gr. k-6). per. 11.95 *(978-1-59820-133-8(6))* Santillana USA Publishing Co., Inc.

—El Vuelo de los Colibries. Jacobson, Judith, illus. 32p. (J). (gr. 3-6). pap. 9.95 *(978-1-56492-211-3(1))* Laredo Publishing Co., Inc.

Flores, Carlos Nicolas. Our House on Hueco. 2006. (ENG.). 234p. (gr. 8-12). per. 17.95 *(978-0-89672-573-7(1)*, P171748) Texas Tech Univ. Pr.

Flores-Scott, Patrick. American Road Trip. 2019. (ENG.). 336p. (YA). pap. 10.99 *(978-1-250-21165-1(4)*, 900158804) Square Fish.

—Jumped In. 2014. (ENG., Illus.). 304p. (YA). (gr. 7). pap. 15.99 *(978-1-250-05398-5(6)*, 900137223) Square Fish.

Fontes, Justine. Deadly Drive. 2013. (Surviving Southside Ser.). (ENG.). 104p. (YA). (gr. 6-12). pap. 7.95 *(978-1-4677-0704-6(X)*, 5c48578d-899a-4c8e-8346-cd1eb212b284); lib. bdg. 27.99 *(978-1-4677-0310-9(9)*, c9a0bca8-bd5f-4333-a2d8-4acb9e86b077) Lerner Publishing Group. (Darby Creek).

Freschet, Gina. Beto & the Bone Dance. Freschet, Gina, illus. 2005. (Illus.). 30p. (J). (gr. 4-8). reprint ed. 16.00 *(978-0-7567-8933-6(8))* DIANE Publishing Co.

Galindo, Mary Sue. Icy Watermelon/Sandia Fria. Rodriguez Howard, Pauline & Howard, Pauline Rodriguez, illus. 2008. (J). (gr. -1-2). pap. 7.95 *(978-1-55885-307-2(3)*, Piñata Books) Arte Publico Pr.

Garcia McCall, Guadalupe. Summer of the Mariposas. 2012. (ENG.). 352p. (YA). 19.95 *(978-1-60060-900-8(7)*, Tu Bks.) Lee & Low Bks., Inc.

García, Nasario. Grandma Lale's Magic Adobe Oven: El Horno Magico de Abuelita Lale. Aragon, Dolores, illus. 2018. (SPA & ENG.). (J). pap. *(978-1-943681-64-8(3)*, Rio Grande Bks.) LPD Pr.

—Grandpa Lolo & Trampa: A Story of Surprise & Mystery = Abuelito Lolo y Trampa: Un Cuento de Sorpresa y Misterio. Montoya, Jeremy, illus. 2014. (SPA & ENG.). 41p. (J). 9.99 *(978-1-936744-30-5(9))* LPD Pr.

—Grandpa Lolo's Navajo Saddle Blanket: La Tilma de Abuelito Lolo. Moeller, Richard, illus. Moeller, Richard, photos by. 2012. (J). *(978-0-8263-5078-7(X))* Univ. of New Mexico Pr.

—Grandpa Lolo's Navajo Saddle Blanket: La Tilma de Abuelito Lolo. 2012. (ENG., Illus.). 72p. (J). E-Book *(978-0-8263-5080-0(1))* Univ. of New Mexico Pr.

García, Nasario & Aragon, Dolores, illus. Grandpa Lolo's Matanza: A New Mexican Tradition = la Matanza de Abuelito Lolo: Una Tradición Nuevo Mexicana. 2015. (SPA & ENG.). 70p. (J). *(978-1-936744-47-3(3)*, Rio Grande Bks.) LPD Pr.

García, Nasario & Moeller, Richard. Grandpa Lolo's Navajo Saddle Blanket: La Tilma de Abuelito Lolo. 2012. (ENG & SPA., Illus.). 72p. (J). pap. 19.95 *(978-0-8263-5079-4(8)*, P203507) Univ. of New Mexico Pr.

Garza, Xavier. Charro Claus & the Tejas Kid, 1 vol. 2008. (ENG., Illus.). 40p. (J). (gr. k-7). 17.95 *(978-1-933693-24-8(X)*, 16d199ce-82b8-4fe3-be9f-43115f4edae3, Cinco Puntos Press) Lee & Low Bks., Inc.

—Maximilian - The Bingo Rematch: A Bilingual Lucha Libre Thriller, 1 vol. Garza, Xavier, illus. 2013. (Max's Lucha Libre Adventures Ser.: 2).Tr. of (Max's Lucha Libre Adventures #2). (ENG., Illus.). 224p. (J). (gr. 3-7). pap. 18.95 *(978-1-935955-46-7(2)*, 23353382, Cinco Puntos Press) Lee & Low Bks., Inc.

—Maximilian & the Mystery of the Guardian Angel, 1 vol. Garza, Xavier, illus. 2011. (Max's Lucha Libre Adventures Ser.: 1). (ENG., Illus.). 208p. (J). (gr. 3-7). pap. 18.95 *(978-1-933693-98-9(3)*, 23353382, Cinco Puntos Press) Lee & Low Bks., Inc.

Garza, Xavier & Villarroel, Carolina. Zulema & the Witch Owl/Zulema y la Bruja Lechuza. Garza, Xavier, illus. 2009. (SPA & ENG., Illus.). 32p. (J). (gr. -1-4). 16.95 *(978-1-55885-515-1(7)*, Piñata Books) Arte Publico Pr.

Gates, J. Gabriel & Keel, Charlene. Ghost Crown. 2012. (Tracks Ser.). (ENG.). 456p. (YA). (gr. 6-12). pap. 9.95 *(978-0-7573-1594-7(1)*, HCI Teens) Health Communications, Inc.

Gilliland, Raquel Vasquez. Sia Martinez & the Moonlit Beginning of Everything. 2020. (ENG., Illus.). 432p. (YA). (gr. 7). 19.99 *(978-1-5344-4863-6(2)*, Simon Pulse) Simon Pulse.

Gonzalez, Genaro. A So-Called Vacation. 2009. 192p. (YA). (gr. 9-18). pap. 10.95 *(978-1-55885-545-8(9)*, Piñata Books) Arte Publico Pr.

Griffith, Gretchen. When Christmas Feels Like Home. Farias, Carolina, illus. 2014. (AV2 Fiction Readalong Ser.: Vol. 119). (ENG.). 32p. (J). (gr. k-3). lib. bdg. 34.28 *(978-1-4896-2392-8(2)*, AV2 by Weigl) Weigl Pubs., Inc.

Harvey, Gwen. Esperanza Means Hope. Porfirio, Guy, illus. 2010. ix, 256p. (J). *(978-0-910037-51-8(5))*; pap. *(978-0-910037-52-5(3))* Arizona Historical Society.

Hayes, Joe. Ghost Fever: Mal de Fantasma, 1 vol. Pennypacker, Mona, illus. 2006. (ENG.). 96p. (J). (gr. 4-6). pap. 14.95 *(978-1-933693-03-3(7)*, 23353382, Cinco Puntos Press) Lee & Low Bks., Inc.

Herrera, Juan Felipe. Featherless: Desplumado (English & Spanish Edition), 1 vol. Cuevas, Ernesto, Jr., illus. 2013.Tr. of Desplumado. (ENG.). 32p. (J). (gr. k-3). pap. 11.95 *(978-0-89239-303-9(3)*, leelowcbp) Lee & Low Bks., Inc.

—Grandma & Me at the Flea: Los Meros Meros Remateros, 1 vol. De Lucio-Brock, Anita, illus. 2013. (ENG.). 32p. (J). (gr. 2-5). pap. 11.95 *(978-0-89239-279-7(7)*, leelowcbp, Children's Book Press) Lee & Low Bks., Inc.

Herrera, Juan Felipe & Herrera, Juan. La Superníña del Cilantro. Robledo Tapia, Honorio, illus. 2003.Tr. of Super Cilantro Girl. (ENG & SPA.). 32p. (J). 16.95 *(978-0-89239-187-5(1))* Lee & Low Bks., Inc.

Hobbs, Will. Crossing the Wire. 2007. (ENG.). 224p. (J). (gr. 5-8). pap. 7.99 *(978-0-06-074140-2(6)*, HarperCollins) HarperCollins Pubs.

Irma Perez, Amada. My Diary from Here/Mi Diario de Aqui Has, 1 vol. 2013.Tr. of My Diary from Here to There. (ENG., Illus.). 32p. (J). (gr. 2-5). pap. 11.95 *(978-0-89239-230-8(4)*, leelowcbp) Lee & Low Bks., Inc.

Iyengar, Malathi Michelle. Romina's Rangoli. 2007. (Romina's Rangoli Ser.). (ENG., Illus.). 32p. (J). (gr. -1-3). 16.95 *(978-1-885008-32-9(5)*, Shen's Bks.) Lee & Low Bks., Inc.

James, Brian. The Heights. 2009. (ENG.). 272p. (YA). (gr. 7-12). 22.44 *(978-0-312-60736-4(9))* Square Fish.

Jiménez, Francisco. La Mariposa. Silva, Simon, illus. 2004. 38p. (J). (gr. k-4). reprint ed. pap. 14.00 *(978-0-7567-8433-1(6))* DIANE Publishing Co.

Jiménez, Francisco. Taking Hold: From Migrant Childhood to Columbia University. 2017. (Circuit Ser.: 4). (ENG.). 208p. (J). (gr. 3-7). pap. 9.99 *(978-1-328-74209-4(1)*, 1677326, Clarion Bks.) HarperCollins Pubs.

Johnson, LouAnne. Muchacho: a Novel. 2011. (ENG.). 208p. (YA). (gr. 7). pap. 9.99 *(978-0-375-85903-8(9)*, Ember) Random Hse. Children's Bks.

Johnston, Tony. Any Small Goodness: a Novel of the Barrio. ón, Raúl, illus. 2003. (ENG.). 128p. (J). (gr. 2-5). pap. 6.99 *(978-0-439-23384-2(4))* Scholastic, Inc.

—My Abuelita. Morales, Yuyi, illus. 2009. (ENG.). 32p. (J). (gr. -1-3). 17.99 *(978-0-15-216330-3(1)*, 1200683, Clarion Bks.) HarperCollins Pubs.

Jones, Patrick. Always Faithful. 2015. (Support & Defend Ser.). (ENG.). 112p. (YA). (gr. 6-12). E-Book 6.99 *(978-1-4677-9014-7(1)*, 9781467790147, Darby Creek) Lerner Publishing Group.

Juan, Felipe Herrera. Coralito's Bay: Bahia de Coralito. 2004. (SPA & ENG.). 41p. 14.95 *(978-0-9742810-0-1(X))* Monterey Bay Sanctuary Foundation.

Keil, Michelle Ruiz. All of Us with Wings. 2019. (ENG., Illus.). 360p. (YA). (gr. 11). 18.99 *(978-1-64129-034-0(X)*, Soho Teen) Soho Pr., Inc.

Korman, Susan J. Overexposed. 2013. (Surviving Southside Ser.). (ENG.). 104p. (YA). (gr. 6-12). pap. 7.95 *(978-1-4677-0706-0(6)*, 091b163c-8f58-4068-b967-aef626809667, Darby Creek) Lerner Publishing Group.

Laínez, René Colato. From North to South/Del Norte Al Sur. Cepeda, Joe, illus. 2010.Tr. of Del norte al Sur. (ENG & SPA.). 32p. (J). (gr. k-3). 17.95 *(978-0-89239-231-5(2))* Lee & Low Bks., Inc.

Lamadrid, Enrique R. Amadito & the Hero Children: Amadito y Los Niños Héroes. Córdova, Amy, illus. 2011. (SPA & ENG.). (J). *(978-0-8263-4978-1(1))* Univ. of New Mexico Pr.

—Amadito & the Hero Children: Amadito y Los niños Héroes. Córdova, Amy & Córdova, Amy, illus. 2011. (ENG.). 60p. (J). E-Book *(978-0-8263-4980-4(3))* Univ. of New Mexico Pr.

Luenn, Nancy. A Gift for Abuelita: Celebrating the Day of the Dead. Chapman, Robert, illus. 2004. (ENG.). 32p. (J). (gr. k-3). 15.95 *(978-0-87358-688-7(3))* Cooper Square Publishing Llc.

Lupita Manana. 3rd ed. (J). pap., stu. ed. *(978-0-13-772500-7(0))* Prentice Hall (Schl. Div.).

Lynch, Janet Nichols. Addicted to Her. 2010. (ENG.). 256p. (YA). (gr. 7-18). pap. 17.95 *(978-0-8234-2186-2(4))* Holiday Hse., Inc.

The Magic Paper (Mexicans) 76p. (YA). (gr. 6-12). pap. 9.95 *(978-0-8224-3686-7(8))* Globe Fearon Educational Publishing.

Marquardt, Marie. Dream Things True: A Novel. 2018. (ENG.). 352p. (YA). pap. 25.99 *(978-1-250-13536-0(2)*, 900160838, Wednesday Bks.) St. Martin's Pr.

M
N
O

Martínez, Arturo O. & Martínez, Arturo O. Pedrito's World. 2007. (ENG., Illus.). 160p. (J). (gr. 4-6). pap. 16.95 *(978-0-89672-600-0(2)*, P171756) Texas Tech Univ. Pr.
Martinez, Victor. Parrot in the Oven: Mi Vida. Scott, Steve, illus. rev. ed. 2004. (ENG.). 240p. (YA). (gr. 8-18). pap. 10.99 *(978-0-06-447186-2(1))* HarperCollins Español.
May, Eleanor. The Best Mother's Day Ever. Pilz, M. H., illus. 2010. (Social Studies Connects Ser.). 32p. (J). (gr. 1-4). pap. 6.99 *(978-1-57565-299-3(4)*, 10a30778-f71f-4dc6-9aae-05d93685d79f, Kane Press) Astra Publishing Hse.
McCall, Guadalupe Garcia. Under the Mesquite, 1 vol. 2013. (ENG., Illus.). 240p. (J). (gr. 6-12). 21.95 *(978-1-60060-429-4(3)*, leelowbooks) Lee & Low Bks., Inc.
McCall, Guadalupe García. El Verano de Las Mariposas, 1 vol. Bowles, David, tr. 2018. Orig. Title: Summer of the Mariposas. (SPA.). 384p. (YA). (gr. 6-12). pap. 16.95 *(978-1-62014-786-3(6)*, leelowtu, Tu Bks.) Lee & Low Bks., Inc.
Meister, Cari. Airplane Adventure. Janovitz, Marilyn, illus. 2010. (My First Graphic Novel Ser.). 32p. pap. 4.95 *(978-1-4342-3602-9(1)*, Stone Arch Bks.) Capstone.
Mendez, Matt. Barely Missing Everything. (ENG.). 320p. (YA). (gr. 9). 2020. pap. 11.99 *(978-1-5344-0446-5(5))* 2019. (Illus.). 18.99 *(978-1-5344-0445-8(7))* Simon & Schuster Children's Publishing.
Middleton Elya, Susan. Home at Last. 2013. (ENG., Illus.). 32p. (J). 16.95 *(978-1-58430-020-5(5))* Lee & Low Bks., Inc.
Mora, Pat. Una Cesta de Cumpleanos para Tia Abuela. Lang, Cecily, illus. (SPA.). (J). (gr. k-2). pap. 3.16 net. *(978-0-395-78817-2(X)*, HMS088) Houghton Mifflin Harcourt Publishing Co.
—The Rainbow Tulip. Sayles, Elizabeth, illus. 2003. 32p. (J). (gr. k-3). 7.99 *(978-0-14-250009-5(7)*, Puffin Books) Penguin Young Readers Group.
—Rainbow Tulip. 2014. 17.00 *(978-1-63419-680-2(5))* Perfection Learning Corp.
—Tomas & the Library Lady. Colón, Raúl, illus. 2007. (gr. k-3). 18.00 *(978-0-7569-7935-5(8))* Perfection Learning Corp.
—Tomas y la Senora de la Biblioteca. 2004. (SPA., Illus.). (J). (gr. k-3). spiral bd. *(978-0-616-03092-9(4))* Canadian National Institute for the Blind/Institut National Canadien pour les Aveugles.
Naylor, Phyllis Reynolds. Eating Enchiladas. 0 vols. Ramsey, Marcy, illus. 2013. (Simply Sarah Ser.: 4). (ENG.). 80p. (J). (gr. 1-4). pap. 9.99 *(978-0-7614-5885-2(9)*, 9780761458852, Two Lions) Amazon Publishing.
Noble, Diana J. Evangelina Takes Flight. 2017. (ENG.). 152p. (J). (gr. 5-8). pap. 10.95 *(978-1-55885-848-0(2)*, Piñata Books) Arte Publico Pr.
Ofelia, Dumas Lachtman. Big Enough Bastante Grande. Enrique, Sanchez, illus. 2008. 32p. (J). pap. 7.95 *(978-1-55885-239-6(5))* Arte Publico Pr.
O'Neill, Alexis. Estela en el Mercado de Pulgas (Spanish Edition), 1 vol. 2005. (Illus.). 32p. (J). (SPA.). (gr. 1-4). pap. 12.95 *(978-1-58430-246-9(1)*, leelowbooks); (ENG., (gr. -1-k). 16.95 *(978-1-58430-245-2(3))* Lee & Low Bks., Inc.
—Estela's Swap, 1 vol. 2005. (ENG., Illus.). 32p. (J). (gr. 1-4). pap. 11.95 *(978-1-60060-253-5(3)*, leelowbooks) Lee & Low Bks., Inc.
Ortega, Cristina. Eyes of the Weaver: Los Ojos Del Tejedor. Garcia, Patricio E., illus. 2006. (ENG.). 64p. (J). 19.95 *(978-0-8263-3990-4(5)*, P123378) Univ. of New Mexico Pr.
Parra, Kelly. Graffiti Girl. 2007. (ENG.). 256p. (YA). (gr. 8-12). pap. 16.99 *(978-1-4165-3461-7(X)*, MTV Bks.) MTV Books.
Perales, Alonso M. Brujas, Lechuzas y Espantos/Witches, Owls & Spooks. Pluecker, John, tr. from SPA. 2008. (ENG & SPA., Illus.). 96p. (J). (gr. 3-7). pap. 9.95 *(978-1-55885-512-0(2)*, Piñata Books) Arte Publico Pr.
Perez, Amada. My Very Own Room/Mi Propio Cuartito, 1 vol. 2013. (ENG., Illus.). 32p. (J). (gr. 2-5). pap. 11.95 *(978-0-89239-223-0(1)*, leelowcbp) Lee & Low Bks., Inc.
Perez, Amada Irma. Mi Propio Cuartito. 2004. (SPA & ENG., Illus.). (J). (gr. k-3). spiral bd. *(978-0-616-14609-5(4))* Canadian National Institute for the Blind/Institut National Canadien pour les Aveugles.
Perez, Amada Irma & Children's Book Press Staff. Nana, Que Sorpresa! Gonzalez, Maya Christina, illus. 2007.Tr. of Nana's Big Surprise. (ENG & SPA.). 32p. (J). (gr. k-2). lib. bdg. 16.95 *(978-0-89239-190-5(1))* Lee & Low Bks., Inc.
Pérez, Amada Irma & Perez, Amada Irma. Nana's Big Surprise, 1 vol. Gonzalez, Maya Christina, illus. 2014.Tr. of Nana, ¡Qué Sorpresa! (ENG.). 32p. (J). (gr. 3-5). pap. 11.95 *(978-0-89239-307-7(6)*, leelowcbp, Children's Book Press) Lee & Low Bks., Inc.
Pérez, Ashley Hope. Out of Darkness. 2019. 400p. (YA). (gr. 9). pap. 12.99 *(978-0-8234-4503-5(8))* Holiday Hse., Inc.
—Out of Darkness. 2015. (ENG., Illus.). 408p. (YA). (gr. 8-12). 20.99 *(978-1-4677-4202-3(3)*, ba661708-6e62-4586-8cfb-a9177c8dc6e3, Carolrhoda Lab™) Lerner Publishing Group.
—What Can't Wait. 2011. (Carolrhoda YA Ser.). (ENG.). 240p. (YA). (gr. 9-12). 17.95 *(978-0-7613-6155-8(3)*, Carolrhoda Bks.) Lerner Publishing Group.
Pérez, Celia C. The First Rule of Punk. (Illus.). 336p. (J). (gr. 4-7). 2018. 8.99 *(978-0-425-29042-2(5)*, Puffin Books) 2017. 17.99 *(978-0-425-29040-8(9)*, Viking Books for Young Readers) Penguin Young Readers Group.
Perez, L. King. First Day in Grapes, 1 vol. Casilla, Robert, illus. 2004. (ENG.). 32p. (J). pap. 9.95 *(978-1-55041-340-3(6)*, a920fac5-51e0-4465-9963-9c60eb31b190) Fitzhenry & Whiteside, Ltd. CAN. Dist: Firefly Bks., Ltd.
Perkins, Mitali. Between Us & Abuela: A Family Story from the Border. Palacios, Sara, illus. 2019. (ENG.). 40p. (J). 18.99 *(978-0-374-30373-0(8)*, 900157191, Farrar, Straus & Giroux (BYR)) Farrar, Straus & Giroux.
Pohl, Laura. The Last 8. (Last 8 Ser.: 1). (YA). (gr. 8-12). 2020. 384p. pap. 10.99 *(978-1-4926-9156-3(9))* 2019. (ENG.). 368p. 17.99 *(978-1-4926-6989-0(X))* Sourcebooks, Inc.
Price, Mara & Ventura, Gabriela Baeza. Grandma's Chocolate/El Chocolate de Abuelita. Fields, Lisa, illus. 2010. (SPA.). 32p. (J). (gr. -1-3). 16.95 *(978-1-55885-587-8(4)*, Piñata Books) Arte Publico Pr.
Quintero, Isabel. Gabi, a Girl in Pieces, 1 vol. 2014. (ENG.). 208p. (YA). (gr. 9-12). pap. 16.95 *(978-1-935955-95-5(0)*, 23353382, Cinco Puntos Press) Lee & Low Bks., Inc.
—Ugly Cat & Pablo. Knight, Tom, illus. 2017. 88p. (J). *(978-1-338-05396-8(5))* Scholastic, Inc.
Raúl the Third, Raúl the, III. ¡Vamos! Let's Go to the Market. Raúl the Third, Raúl the, III, illus. 2019. (World Of ¡Vamos! Ser.). (ENG., Illus.). 48p. (J). (gr. k-3). 14.99 *(978-1-328-55726-1(X)*, 1725405, Versify) HarperCollins Pubs.
Resau, Laura. Estrella en el Bosque (Star in the Forest) 2016. (ENG & SPA.). 160p. (J). (gr. 2-5). 18.40 *(978-0-606-39132-0(0))* Turtleback.
—Star in the Forest. 2012. (ENG., Illus.). 160p. (J). (gr. 2-5). 7.99 *(978-0-375-85410-1(X)*, Yearling) Random Hse. Children's Bks.
Rice, David. Crazy Loco. 2008. 135p. 16.00 *(978-0-7569-8951-4(5))* Perfection Learning Corp.
Rice, David & Garcia, Mike D. Heart-Shaped Cookies. 2011. (YA). pap. *(978-1-931010-79-5(X))* Bilingual Pr./Editorial Bilingue.
Rivera-Ashford, Roni Capin & Johnson, Richard. Hip Hip Hooray, It's Monsoon Day! 2007. (ENG & SPA.). (YA). pap. 15.95 *(978-1-886679-36-8(3))* Arizona Sonora Desert Museum Pr.
Rodriguez, Emma Vera & Scogin, Connie. Blanca Rosa's Quinceaner. 2011. 34p. pap. 13.50 *(978-1-60911-444-2(2)*, Eloquent Bks.) Strategic Book Publishing & Rights Agency (SBPRA).
Romeyn, Debra. Passage to Monterey. May, Dan, tr. May, Dan, illus. 2003. (Adventures of Juan & Mariano Ser.: No. 1). 39p. (J). pap. 9.95 *(978-0-9729016-0-4(4))* Gossamer Bks.
Ruiz, Joseph J. Angel on Daniel's Shoulder. 2004. (SPA & ENG., Illus.). 108p. (J). pap. 12.95 *(978-0-86534-402-0(7))* Sunstone Pr.
—Manuel & the Magic Ring. 2003. (SPA & ENG., Illus.). 108p. (J). pap. 12.95 *(978-0-86534-399-3(3))* Sunstone Pr.
Ryan, Pam Muñoz. Becoming Naomi león (Scholastic Gold) 2005. (ENG.). 272p. (J). (gr. 4-7). reprint ed. per. 8.99 *(978-0-439-26997-1(0)*, Scholastic Paperbacks) Scholastic, Inc.
—Esperanza Rising. l.t. ed. 2019. (ENG.). 260p. (J). (gr. 6-10). pap. 12.99 *(978-1-4328-6388-3(6)*, Large Print Pr.) Thorndike Pr.
Sáenz, Benjamin Alire. A Gift from Papá Diego, 1 vol. Garcia, Gerónimo, illus. 2022. (Little Diego Book Ser.). (ENG.). 40p. (J). (gr. k-3). pap. 12.95 *(978-0-938317-33-3(4)*, 23353382, Cinco Puntos Press) Lee & Low Bks., Inc.
Saenz, Benjamin Alire. The Inexplicable Logic of My Life. 2017. (ENG.). 464p. (YA). (gr. 7). 17.99 *(978-0-544-58650-5(6)*, 1614143, Clarion Bks.) HarperCollins Pubs.
Sáenz, Benjamin Alire & Sáenz, Benjamin Alire. Aristotle & Dante Discover the Secrets of the Universe. (Aristotle & Dante Ser.). (ENG., Illus.). (YA). (gr. 7). 2014. 384p. pap. 14.99 *(978-1-4424-0893-7(6))* 2012. 368p. 24.99 *(978-1-4424-0892-0(8))* Simon & Schuster Bks. For Young Readers. (Simon & Schuster Bks. For Young Readers).
Saldaña, Jr. A Good Long Way. 2010. 128p. (J). (gr. 6-18). pap. 10.95 *(978-1-55885-607-3(2)*, Piñata Books) Arte Publico Pr.
Saldaña, René. Dancing with the Devil & Other Tales from Beyond / Bailando con el Diablo y Otros Cuentos del Más Allá. Baeza Ventura, Gabriela, tr. from ENG. 2012. (SPA & ENG.). (YA). pap. 9.95 *(978-1-55885-744-5(3)*, Piñata Books) Arte Publico Pr.
Saldana, Rene, Jr. The Jumping Tree. 2008. 181p. (gr. 5-7). 16.50 *(978-0-7569-8950-7(7))* Perfection Learning Corp.
—A Mystery Bigger Than Big / un Misterio Mas Grande Que Grandisimo: A Mickey Rangel Mystery / Colección Mickey Rangel, Detective Privado. 2016. (Mickey Rangel Mystery / Coleccion Mickey Rangel, Detective P Ser.). (MUL, ENG & SPA., Illus.). 64p. (J). (gr. 3-6). pap. 9.95 *(978-1-55885-824-4(5)*, Piñata Books) Arte Publico Pr.
Sanchez, Alex. Bait. 2010. (ENG.). 256p. (YA). (gr. 7). pap. 12.99 *(978-1-4169-3774-6(9)*, Simon & Schuster Bks. For Young Readers) Simon & Schuster Bks. For Young Readers.
—Bait. 2009. (ENG.). 256p. (YA). (gr. 7-12). 17.99 *(978-1-4169-3772-2(2))* Simon & Schuster, Inc.
—Getting It. 2007. (ENG., Illus.). 232p. (YA). (gr. 7-12). pap. 8.99 *(978-1-4169-0898-2(6)*, Simon & Schuster Bks. For Young Readers) Simon & Schuster Bks. For Young Readers.
—So Hard to Say. 2006. (ENG., Illus.). 232p. (YA). (gr. 7-12). reprint ed. pap. 12.99 *(978-1-4169-1189-0(8)*, Simon & Schuster Bks. For Young Readers) Simon & Schuster Bks. For Young Readers.
Sánchez, Erika L. I Am Not Your Perfect Mexican Daughter. 2019. (ENG.). lib. bdg. 22.80 *(978-1-6636-2193-1(4))* Perfection Learning Corp.
—I Am Not Your Perfect Mexican Daughter. (ENG.). (YA). (gr. 9). 2019. 368p. pap. 12.99 *(978-1-5247-0051-5(7)*, Ember) 2017. 352p. 19.99 *(978-1-5247-0048-5(7)*, Knopf Bks. for Young Readers) Random Hse. Children's Bks.
Sandoval, Victor. Roll over, Big Toben. 2003. 128p. (J). pap. 9.95 *(978-1-55885-401-7(0)*, Piñata Books) Arte Publico Pr.
Schraff, Anne. The Lost, 1 vol. unabr. ed. 2011. (Urban Underground Ser.). (ENG.). 198p. (YA). (gr. 9-12). pap. 11.95 *(978-1-61651-585-0(6))* Saddleback Educational Publishing, Inc.
Serros, Michele. ¡Scandalosa! A Honey Blonde Chica Novel. 2008. (ENG.). 320p. (YA). (gr. 9). pap. 14.99 *(978-1-4169-1594-2(X)*, Simon Pulse) Simon Pulse.
Sitomer, Alan Lawrence. The Secret Story of Sonia Rodriguez. 2010. (ENG.). 320p. (J). (gr. 5-9). pap. 17.99 *(978-1-4231-3027-7(8)*, Jump at the Sun) Hyperion Bks. for Children.
Soto, Gary. Buried Onions. 2006. (ENG., Illus.). 176p. (YA). (gr. 7-12). pap. 10.99 *(978-0-15-206265-1(3)*, 1063436, Clarion Bks.) HarperCollins Pubs.
—Buried Onions. 2006. 149p. 16.95 *(978-0-7569-7218-9(3))* Perfection Learning Corp.
—Chato & the Party Animals. Guevara, Susan, illus. (Chato Ser.). 28.95 incl. audio compact disk *(978-1-59112-920-2(6))*; 25.95 incl. audio *(978-1-59112-460-3(3))*; 28.95 incl. audio compact disk *(978-1-59112-920-2(6))*; pap. 39.95 incl. audio compact disk *(978-1-59112-921-9(4))*; pap. 37.95 incl. audio *(978-1-59112-461-0(1))* Live Oak Media.
—Chato & the Party Animals. Guevara, Susan, illus. 2004. 32p. (J). (gr. -1-3). reprint ed. pap. 8.99 *(978-0-14-240032-6(7)*, Puffin Books) Penguin Young Readers Group.
—Chato & the Party Animals. Guevara, Susan, illus. 2004. (Chato Ser.). (gr. -1-3). 17.00 *(978-0-7569-2921-3(0))* Perfection Learning Corp.
—Chato Goes Cruisin' Guevara, Susan, illus. 2008. (Chato Ser.). (J). 25.95 incl. audio *(978-1-59519-906-5(3))* Live Oak Media.
—Chato Goes Cruisin' Guevara, Susan, illus. 2007. (Chato Ser.). (J). (gr. -1-3). 14.65 *(978-0-7569-8147-1(6))* Perfection Learning Corp.
—Chato's Kitchen. Guevara, Susan, illus. 2003. (Chato Ser.). (J). (gr. -1-2). pap. 39.95 *(978-1-59112-527-3(8))* Live Oak Media.
—Facts of Life: Stories. 2012. (ENG.). 192p. (YA). (gr. 7-7). pap. 7.99 *(978-0-547-57734-0(6)*, 1458543, Clarion Bks.) HarperCollins Pubs.
—Help Wanted: Stories. 2007. (ENG., Illus.). 240p. (YA). (gr. 7-12). pap. 8.99 *(978-0-15-205663-6(7)*, 1197028, Clarion Bks.) HarperCollins Pubs.
—Jesse. 2006. (ENG., Illus.). 192p. (YA). (gr. 7-12). pap. 7.99 *(978-0-15-205425-0(1)*, 253005, Clarion Bks.) HarperCollins Pubs.
—Jesse. 2006. 166p. (gr. 7-12). 16.95 *(978-0-7569-6688-1(4))* Perfection Learning Corp.
—Petty Crimes. 2006. (ENG., Illus.). 176p. (J). (gr. 5-7). pap. 7.99 *(978-0-15-205437-3(5)*, 1196362, Clarion Bks.) HarperCollins Pubs.
Spenser & Brooks, Melanie. Spenser Via a el Paso. Jacobsen, Amie, illus. 2010. (ENG.). 32p. (J). 14.95 *(978-0-9817598-5-2(8)*, e87219c4-b810-49f7-81c2-eb35fd1a4e0b) Simple Fish Bk. Co., LLC.
Stewart, Sarah. The Quiet Place, 1 vol. Small, David, illus. 2012. (ENG.). 44p. (J). (gr. k-4). 19.99 *(978-0-374-32565-7(0)*, 900065971, Farrar, Straus & Giroux (BYR)) Farrar, Straus & Giroux.
Stork, Francisco X. The Last Summer of the Death Warriors. 2012. (ENG.). 352p. (J). (gr. 9-12). 26.19 *(978-0-545-15134-4(1)*, Levine, Arthur A. Bks.) Scholastic, Inc.
Tafolla, Carmen. ¿Qué Puedes Hacer con una Paleta? (What Can You Do with a Paleta Spanish Edition) Morales, Magaly, illus. 32p. (J). (gr. -1-2). 2014. 8.99 *(978-0-385-75537-5(6)*, Dragonfly Bks.) 2009. (SPA.). 17.99 *(978-1-58246-289-9(5)*, Tricycle Pr.) Random Hse. Children's Bks.
—What Can You Do with a Paleta? Morales, Magaly, illus. 2009. 32p. (J). (gr. -1-2). 18.99 *(978-1-58246-221-9(6)*, Tricycle Pr.) Random Hse. Children's Bks.
—What Can You Do with a Rebozo? / ¿Qué Puedes Hacer con un Rebozo? Cordova, Amy, illus. 2009. 32p. (J). (gr. -1-2). pap. 8.99 *(978-1-58246-271-4(2)*, Tricycle Pr.) Random Hse. Children's Bks.
Temblador, Alex. Secrets of the Casa Rosada. 2018. (ENG.). 160p. (YA). (gr. 6-10). pap. 12.95 *(978-1-55885-870-1(9)*, Piñata Books) Arte Publico Pr.
Tonatiuh, Duncan. Dear Primo: A Letter to My Cousin. 2010. (ENG., Illus.). 32p. (J). (gr. k-2). 18.99 *(978-0-8109-3872-4(3)*, 661901, Abrams Bks. for Young Readers) Abrams, Inc.
Torres, Jennifer. Stef Soto, Taco Queen. 2018. (ENG.). 192p. (J). (gr. 3-7). pap. 7.99 *(978-0-316-30684-3(3))* Little, Brown Bks. for Young Readers.
—Stef Soto, Taco Queen. 2019. (Penworthy Picks Middle School Ser.). (ENG.). 166p. (J). (gr. 4-5). 18.49 *(978-1-64310-901-5(4))* Penworthy Co., LLC, The.
—Stef Soto, Taco Queen. 2018. (J). lib. bdg. 17.20 *(978-0-606-40991-9(2))* Turtleback.
Tripp, Valerie. Josefina Story Collection. Tibbles, Jean-Paul, illus. 2008. 420p. pap. 29.95 *(978-1-59369-453-1(9))* American Girl Publishing, Inc.
Velásquez, Gloria. Forgiving Moses. 2018. (Roosevelt High School Ser.). (ENG.). 160p. (YA). (gr. 8-12). pap. 10.95 *(978-1-55885-864-0(4)*, Piñata Books) Arte Publico Pr.
Velasquez, Gloria. Teen Angel. 2003. (Roosevelt High School Ser.). 160p. (J). pap. 9.95 *(978-1-55885-391-1(X)*, Piñata Books) Arte Publico Pr.
Villareal, Ray. Alamo Wars. 2008. 187p. (J). (gr. 6-18). pap. 10.95 *(978-1-55885-513-7(0)*, Piñata Books) Arte Publico Pr.
—Body Slammed! 2012. (YA). pap. 11.95 *(978-1-55885-749-0(4)*, Piñata Books) Arte Publico Pr.
—Who's Buried in the Garden? 2009. 160p. (YA). (gr. 6-18). pap. 10.95 *(978-1-55885-546-5(7)*, Piñata Books) Arte Publico Pr.
Weston Woods Staff, creator. Chato & the Party Animals. 2011. 18.95 *(978-0-439-73984-9(5))* 2011. 38.75 *(978-0-439-84581-6(5))* 2004. 29.95 *(978-1-55592-703-5(3))* Weston Woods Studios, Inc.
—Chato's Kitchen. 2004. (J). 18.95 *(978-1-55592-386-0(0))*; 38.75 *(978-1-55592-388-4(7))* Weston Woods Studios, Inc.
—Too Many Tamales. 2011. 18.95 *(978-0-439-87361-1(4))*; 38.75 *(978-0-439-84580-9(7))* Weston Woods Studios, Inc.
Yardi, Robin. The Midnight War of Mateo Martinez. 2018. (ENG.). 184p. (J). (gr. 3-6). pap. 9.99 *(978-1-5415-1483-6(1)*, db266dd5-e965-4980-9ce2-73d5fa151b04, Carolrhoda Bks.) Lerner Publishing Group.
Zenk, Molly. United to Strike: A Story of the Delano Grape Workers. Freeberg, Eric, illus. 2019. (I Am America Set 2 Ser.). (ENG.). 160p. (J). (gr. 3-4). pap. 8.99 *(978-1-63163-284-6(1)*, 1631632841); lib. bdg. 28.50 *(978-1-63163-283-9(3)*, 1631632833) North Star Editions. (Jolly Fish Pr.).

MEXICAN WAR, 1846-1848

Carnagie, Julie L. & Howes, Kelly King, eds. Mexican-American War. 2003. (Mexican-American War Ser.). (ENG., Illus.). 288p. (J). lib. bdg. 129.00 *(978-0-7876-6537-1(1)*, GML00502-182439, UXL) Cengage Gale.
Deibel, Zachary. Manifest Destiny & the Mexican-American War, 1 vol. 2017. (Primary Sources of Westward Expansion Ser.). (ENG.). 64p. (gr. 6-6). lib. bdg. 35.93 *(978-1-5026-2643-1(8)*, a4378558-bf98-40fa-baa8-802b89a94b03) Cavendish Square Publishing LLC.
DiConsiglio, John. The Mexican-American War, 1 vol. 2012. (Living Through... Ser.). (ENG.). 80p. (J). (gr. 6-10). pap. 11.95 *(978-1-4329-6007-0(5)*, 117798); lib. bdg. 39.99 *(978-1-4329-5998-2(0)*, 117790) Capstone. (Heinemann).
Feldman, Ruth Tenzer. The Mexican-American War. 2004. (Chronicle of America's Wars Ser.). (Illus.). 96p. (J). (gr. 5-12). 27.93 *(978-0-8225-0831-1(1))* Lerner Publishing Group.
Gaddi, Rosalie. The U.S.-Mexican War & Its Impact on the United States, 1 vol. 2016. (Spotlight on American History Ser.). (ENG., Illus.). 24p. (J). (gr. 4-6). 27.93 *(978-1-5081-4946-0(1)*, ce549958-ed08-47c3-8ef3-849447115c40, PowerKids Pr.) Rosen Publishing Group, Inc., The.
Loria, Laura. The Mexican-American War. 2017. (Westward Expansion: America's Push to the Pacific Ser.). 48p. (J). (gr. 10-14). 84.30 *(978-1-5383-0014-5(1)*, Britannica Educational Publishing) Rosen Publishing Group, Inc., The.
Mills, Bronwyn. U. S. -Mexican War. Revised Edition. Bowman, John S., ed. 3rd rev. ed. 2010. (ENG.). 192p. (gr. 6-12). 45.00 *(978-0-8160-8195-0(6)*, P197777, Facts On File) Infobase Holdings, Inc.
Porterfield, Jason. The Treaty of Guadalupe Hidalgo 1848: A Primary Source Examination of the Treaty That Ended the Mexican-American War. (Primary Sources of American Treaties Ser.). 64p. (gr. 5-8). 2009. 58.50 *(978-1-60851-516-5(8))* 2005. (ENG., Illus.). (J). lib. bdg. 37.13 *(978-1-4042-0440-9(7)*, 3c7b2db0-2451-4ea5-8075-db09305b9572) Rosen Publishing Group, Inc., The.
Poulakidas, Georgene. The Mexican-American War. (Primary Sources of American Wars Ser.). 24p. (gr. 3-4). 2009. 42.50 *(978-1-60851-527-1(3)*, PowerKids Pr.) 2005. (ENG., Illus.). (YA). lib. bdg. 26.27 *(978-1-4042-2683-8(4)*, 48146290-5454-42a5-a38c-89cde89295ba) Rosen Publishing Group, Inc., The.
Raabe, Emily. The Mexican-American War. 2009. (Westward Ho! Ser.). 24p. (gr. 2-3). 42.50 *(978-1-60854-760-9(4)*, PowerKids Pr.) Rosen Publishing Group, Inc., The.
Rauf, Don. The Mexican-American War, 1 vol. 2018. (Redrawing the Map Ser.). (ENG.). 112p. (YA). (gr. 9-9). lib. bdg. 45.93 *(978-1-5026-3574-7(7)*, c12a25e0-6f08-4e77-bf96-c00b181b1d31) Cavendish Square Publishing LLC.
Rebman, Nick. The Mexican-American War. 2018. (Expansion of Our Nation Ser.). (ENG., Illus.). 32p. (J). (gr. 3-5). pap. 9.95 *(978-1-63517-986-6(6)*, 1635179866); lib. bdg. 31.35 *(978-1-63517-885-2(1)*, 1635178851) North Star Editions. (Focus Readers).
—The Mexican-American War. 2020. (Illus.). 32p. (J). pap. *(978-1-4896-9883-4(3)*, AV2 by Weigl) Weigl Pubs., Inc.
Rice, Earle. Causes of the Mexican-American War. 2010. (J). lib. bdg. *(978-1-59556-033-9(5))* OTTN Publishing.
Rose, Simon. Mexican-American War. 2014. (J). pap. *(978-1-4896-0509-2(6))* Weigl Pubs., Inc.
Shoup, Kate. Texas & the Mexican War, 1 vol. 2015. (Expanding America Ser.). (ENG., Illus.). 96p. (YA). (gr. 8-8). 44.50 *(978-1-5026-0964-9(9)*, 13856eb5-390f-40da-8db6-c8e09c49ab01) Cavendish Square Publishing LLC.
Sonneborn, Liz. The Mexican-American War, 1 vol. 2004. (Primary Sources in American History Ser.). (ENG., Illus.). 64p. (J). (gr. 5-8). lib. bdg. 37.13 *(978-1-4042-0180-4(7)*, ee4d5b66-bcd3-45dc-9062-2c9f686333b4) Rosen Publishing Group, Inc., The.
—The Mexican-American War: A Primary Source History of the Expansion of the Western Lands of the United States. 2009. (Primary Sources in American History Ser.). 64p. (gr. 5-8). 58.50 *(978-1-60851-500-4(1))* Rosen Publishing Group, Inc., The.
Stein, R. Conrad. Mexican-American War. 2011. (Story of Mexico Ser.). 144p. (gr. 7-12). 28.95 *(978-1-59935-160-5(9))* Reynolds, Morgan Inc.
Sterngass, Jon & Kachur, Matthew. The Mexican-American War, 1 vol. 2006. (Wars That Changed American History Ser.). (ENG., Illus.). 48p. (gr. 5-8). pap. 15.05 *(978-0-8368-7299-6(1)*, ccc79954-9be9-4ab9-a76a-73137a6f2c55, Gareth Stevens Secondary Library) Stevens, Gareth Publishing LLLP.
Worth, Richard. The Texas War of Independence: The 1800s, 1 vol. 2009. (Hispanic America Ser.). (ENG.). 80p. (gr. 5-5). lib. bdg. 36.93 *(978-0-7614-2934-0(4)*, 15e26fa2-4c55-418b-9cdd-d43ad323078b) Cavendish Square Publishing LLC.

MEXICAN WAR, 1846-1848—FICTION

Fleischman, Sid. The Giant Rat of Sumatra. Hendrix, John, illus. 2005. 208p. (J). (gr. 5-18). 15.99 *(978-0-06-074238-6(0))* HarperCollins Pubs.
—The Giant Rat of Sumatra: Or Pirates Galore. Hendrix, John, illus. 2006. (ENG.). 208p. (J). (gr. 5-9). reprint ed. pap. 7.99 *(978-0-06-074240-9(2)*, Greenwillow Bks.) HarperCollins Pubs.

MEXICANS—UNITED STATES

Alva, Alfredo & Mills, Deborah. La Frontera. Navarro, Claudia, illus. 2018. (ENG.). 48p. (J). (gr. k-3). pap. 10.99 *(978-1-78285-392-3(8))*; 17.99 *(978-1-78285-388-6(X))* Barefoot Bks., Inc.
Bernay, Emma & Berne, Emma Carlson. Immigrants from Mexico & Central America. 2018. (Immigration Today Ser.). (ENG., Illus.). 32p. (J). (gr. 3-6). pap. 7.95 *(978-1-5435-1387-5(5)*, 137792, Capstone Pr.) Capstone.
Egan, Tracie. Francisca Alvarez: El ángel de Goliad (Francisca Alvarez: the Angel of Goliad) 2009. (Grandes personajes en la historia de los Estados Unidos (Famous People in American History) Ser.). (SPA.). 32p. (gr. 2-3). 47.90 *(978-1-61512-798-6(4)*, Editorial Buenas Letras) Rosen Publishing Group, Inc., The.
—Francisca Alvarez: The Angel of Goliad. (Primary Sources of Famous People in American History Ser.). 32p. (gr. 2-3). 2009. 47.90 *(978-1-60851-675-9(X))* 2003. (ENG & SPA., Illus.). lib. bdg. 29.13 *(978-0-8239-4157-5(4)*, 8d646879-3215-45e0-97ba-5af78ef58304, Editorial Buenas Letras) Rosen Publishing Group, Inc., The.
—Francisca Alvarez: The Angel of Goliad / el ángel de Goliad. 2009. (Famous People in American History/Grandes

personajes en la historia de los Estados Unidos Ser.). (ENG & SPA.). 32p. (gr. 2-3). 47.90 *(978-1-61512-544-9(2),* Editorial Buenas Letras) Rosen Publishing Group, Inc., The.

Hurt, Avery Elizabeth. Joaquín Murrieta: Robin Hood of the California Gold Rush, 1 vol. 2019. (Our Voices: Spanish & Latino Figures of American History Ser.). (ENG.). 48p. (gr. 6-6). pap. 12.75 *(978-1-5081-8483-6(6),* 248299b8-6e5f-409b-a46a-f17623bb55ec) Rosen Publishing Group, Inc., The.

Taylor, Theodore. The Maldonado Miracle. 2003. (ENG.). 176p. (J). (gr. 3-7). pap. 6.95 *(978-0-15-205036-8(1),* 1195211, Clarion Bks.) HarperCollins Pubs.

MEXICO

Alaníz, Eduardo Martínez. Hugo Sanchez. 2012. (Superstars of Soccer SPANISH Ser.). (SPA.). 32p. (J). (gr. 4). 19.95 *(978-1-4222-2615-5(8))* Mason Crest.

—Hugo Sanchez. 2012. (Superstars of Soccer ENGLISH Ser.). (Illus.). 32p. (J). (gr. 4). 19.95 *(978-1-4222-2668-1(9))* Mason Crest.

Alva, Alfredo & Mills, Deborah. La Frontera. Navarro, Claudia, illus. 2018. (ENG.). 48p. (J). (gr. k-3). pap. 10.99 *(978-1-78285-392-3(8))*; 17.99 *(978-1-78285-388-6(X))* Barefoot Bks., Inc.

Alvarez, Mateo. Diego Rivera: Famous Mexican Painter, 1 vol. 2015. (Exceptional Latinos Ser.). (ENG., Illus.). 24p. (J). (gr. 3-4). pap. 10.35 *(978-0-7660-6702-8(5),* 3596e525-8f1c-40ac-8bd9-b2d6f4e062e4) Enslow Publishing, LLC.

Arturo Miranda Bravo, Jorge. Andres Guardado. 2012. (Superstars of Soccer ENGLISH Ser.). 32p. (J). (gr. 4). 19.95 *(978-1-4222-2666-7(2))*; (SPA., Illus.). 19.95 *(978-1-4222-2613-1(1))* Mason Crest.

Asher, Sandy. Mexico, 1 vol. 2003. (Discovering Cultures Ser.). (ENG., Illus.). 48p. (gr. 3-4). 31.21 *(978-0-7614-1175-8(5),* c90d4c93-b6cf-4d75-9672-4268b48e1da6) Cavendish Square Publishing LLC.

Aykroyd, Clarissa. The Government of Mexico. (Mexico: Beautiful Land, Diverse People Ser.). 64p. (YA). (gr. 7-12). 2009. (Illus.). 21.95 *(978-1-4222-0662-1(9))* 2007. pap. 9.95 *(978-1-4222-0729-1(3))* Mason Crest.

Blaxland, Wendy. Mexican Food. 2011. (I Can Cook ! Ser.). 32p. (YA). (gr. 2-5). 28.50 *(978-1-59920-668-4(4))* Black Rabbit Bks.

Blevins, Wiley. Mexico (Follow Me Around) (Library Edition) 2017. (Follow Me Around... Ser.). (ENG., Illus.). 32p. (J). (gr. 3-4). 27.00 *(978-0-531-23706-9(0),* Children's Pr.) Scholastic Library Publishing.

Burt, Janet. The Pacific North States of Mexico. (Mexico: Beautiful Land, Diverse People Ser.). 64p. (YA). (gr. 7-12). 2009. (Illus.). 21.95 *(978-1-4222-0667-6(X))* 2007. pap. 9.95 *(978-1-4222-0734-5(X))* Mason Crest.

Cobb, Allan B. Mexico: A Primary Source Cultural Guide, 1 vol. 2003. (Primary Sources of World Cultures Ser.). (ENG., Illus.). 128p. (gr. 4-5). lib. bdg. 43.60 *(978-0-8239-3840-7(9),* 9d301f75-939c-41f2-80e0-22437e5818f9) Rosen Publishing Group, Inc., The.

Day-MacLeod, Deirdre. The States of Central Mexico. (Mexico: Beautiful Land, Diverse People Ser.). 64p. (YA). (gr. 7-12). 2009. (Illus.). 21.95 *(978-1-4222-0664-5(5))* 2007. pap. 9.95 *(978-1-4222-0731-4(5))* Mason Crest.

—The States of Northern Mexico. (Mexico: Beautiful Land, Diverse People Ser.). 64p. (YA). (gr. 7-12). 2009. (Illus.). 21.95 *(978-1-4222-0665-2(3))* 2007. pap. 9.95 *(978-1-4222-0732-1(3))* Mason Crest.

Elzaurdia, Paco. Cuauhtemoc Blanco. 2012. (Superstars of Soccer ENGLISH Ser.). (Illus.). 32p. (J). (gr. 4). 19.95 *(978-1-4222-2667-4(0))*; (SPA., 19.95 *(978-1-4222-2614-8(X))* Mason Crest.

—Rafael Marquez. 32p. (J). 2013. (Illus.). *(978-1-4222-2594-3(1))* 2012. (SPA.). (gr. 4). 19.95 *(978-1-4222-2598-1(4))* Mason Crest.

Gall, Timothy L. & Gall, Susan B. Junior Worldmark Encyclopedia of the Mexican States. 2nd rev. ed. 2007. (ENG., Illus.). 456p. (J). 106.00 *(978-1-4144-1112-5(X),* UXL) Cengage Gale.

George, Lynn. Teotihuacan: Designing an Ancient Mexican City: Calculating Perimeters & Areas of Squares & Rectangles, 1 vol. (Math for the REAL World Ser.). (ENG., Illus.). 32p. (gr. 4-5). 2010. pap. 10.00 *(978-0-8239-8876-1(7),* c4d8bb9f-6ff0-4abb-90d3-d5baaac35f6e) 2003. (J). lib. bdg. 28.93 *(978-0-8239-8983-6(6),* 50feef82-c5c9-48b0-81bd-1cb7ed4e0350) Rosen Publishing Group, Inc., The. (PowerKids Pr.).

Gitlin, Marty. Mexico. 2017. (Country Profiles Ser.). (ENG., Illus.). 32p. (J). (gr. 3-8). lib. bdg. 27.95 *(978-1-62617-685-0(X),* Blastoff! Discovery) Bellwether Media.

Golden, Nancy. Exploring Mexico with the Five Themes of Geography, 1 vol. (Library of the Western Hemisphere Ser.). 24p. 2005. (ENG., Illus.). (J). (gr. 3-4). lib. bdg. 26.27 *(978-1-4042-2668-5(0),* 32520023-1206-41e2-95ff-d73c003d20b7, PowerKids Pr.) 2009. (gr. 4-4). 42.50 *(978-1-60853-928-4(8),* PowerKids Pr.) 2004. (ENG., Illus.). (gr. 3-4). pap. 8.25 *(978-0-8239-4628-0(2),* 9b5c94e3-845c-4249-8357-c3006e4e7a93) Rosen Publishing Group, Inc., The.

Green, Jen. Caribbean Sea & Gulf of Mexico, 1 vol. 2005. (Oceans & Seas Ser.). (ENG., Illus.). 48p. (gr. 5-8). lib. bdg. 33.67 *(978-0-8368-6272-0(4),* 0e62af6f-2d2e-400a-b617-dbed7354b822, Gareth Stevens Secondary Library) Stevens, Gareth Publishing LLLP.

Green, Yuko. Let's Learn about MEXICO: Activity & Coloring Book. 2013. (Dover Kids Activity Bks.). (ENG.). 48p. (J). (gr. 1-5). pap. 5.99 *(978-0-486-48994-0(9),* 489949) Dover Pubns., Inc.

Group/McGraw-Hill, Wright. Mexico: Land of Old & New, 6 vols. (Book2WebTM Ser.). (gr. 4-8). 36.50 *(978-0-322-04445-6(6))* Wright Group/McGraw-Hill.

Gruber, Beth. National Geographic Countries of the World: Mexico. 2009. (Countries of the World Ser.). (Illus.). 64p. (J). (gr. 5-9). pap. 12.95 *(978-1-4263-0566-5(4),* National Geographic Kids) Disney Publishing Worldwide.

Hardwick, Susan, ed. Mexico. 2004. (World-Wise Kids Project Guides). (Illus.). 96p. *(978-1-59258-079-8(3))* Hylas Publishing.

Johnston, Tony. P Is for Pinata: A Mexico Alphabet. Parra, John, illus. 2008. (Discover the World Ser.). (ENG.). 40p. (J). (gr. 1-3). 17.95 *(978-1-58536-144-1(5),* 202004) Sleeping Bear Pr.

Juarez, Christine. Mexico, 1 vol. 2013. (Countries Ser.). (ENG.). 24p. (J). (gr. -1-2). 27.32 *(978-1-4765-3076-5(9),* 123050, Capstone Pr.) Capstone.

Kalman, Bobbie. Mexico: The Culture. 3rd rev. ed. 2008. (Lands, Peoples, & Cultures Ser.). (ENG., Illus.). 32p. (J). (gr. 3-9). lib. bdg. *(978-0-7787-9295-6(1))* Crabtree Publishing Co.

—Mexico - The Land, 1 vol. 3rd rev. ed. 2008. (Lands, Peoples, & Cultures Ser.). (ENG., Illus.). 32p. (J). (gr. 3-9). pap. *(978-0-7787-9661-9(2))* Crabtree Publishing Co.

Landau, Elaine. Mexico. 2008. (True Book: Geography — Countries Revised Ser.). (ENG., Illus.). 48p. (J). (gr. 3-5). 21.19 *(978-0-531-16853-0(0),* Children's Pr.) Scholastic Library Publishing.

—True Books: Mexico. 2008. (True Bks.). (ENG.). 48p. (J). pap. 6.95 *(978-0-531-20727-7(7),* Children's Pr.) Scholastic Library Publishing.

Lindeen, Mary. Welcome to Mexico. 2011. (Wonder Readers Fluent Level Ser.). (ENG.). 16p. (J). (gr. -1-2). pap. 6.25 *(978-1-4296-7973-2(5),* 118305, Capstone Pr.) Capstone.

—Welcome to North America, 1 vol. 2011. (Wonder Readers Fluent Level Ser.). (ENG.). 16p. (J). (gr. -1-2). pap. 6.25 *(978-1-4296-7974-9(3),* 118306, Capstone Pr.) Capstone.

El maravilloso maiz de Mexico: 6 Small Books. (Saludos Ser.: Vol. 2). (SPA.). (gr. 3-5). 31.00 *(978-0-7635-1815-8(8))* Rigby Education.

Marsh, Carole. Mexico: A Colorful Land of Exotic Culture! 2009. (It's Your World Ser.). 48p. (J). (gr. 2-9). pap. 7.99 *(978-0-635-06821-7(4))* Gallopade International.

Martínez Alaníz, Eduardo. Hugo Sanchez. 2013. (Illus.). 32p. (J). *(978-1-4222-2647-6(6))* Mason Crest.

McCartney Lewis, Pat. The Colors of the Coloni: Los Colores de la Colonia. 2009. 36p. pap. 16.99 *(978-1-4389-2306-2(6))* AuthorHouse.

McDonnell, Ginger. Next Stop - Mexico, 1 vol. 2nd rev. ed. 2011. (TIME for KIDS(r): Informational Text Ser.). (ENG.). 24p. (gr. 2-3). pap. 9.99 *(978-1-4333-3610-2(3))* Teacher Created Materials, Inc.

McNamara, Margaret. Mexico. 2006. (J). pap. *(978-1-4108-6456-7(1))* Benchmark Education Co.

Moon, Walt K. Exploremos Cuba (Let's Explore Cuba) 2017. (Bumba Books (r) en Español — Exploremos Países (Let's Explore Countries) Ser.). (SPA., Illus.). 24p. (J). (gr. -1-1). lib. bdg. 26.65 *(978-1-5124-4123-9(6),* f4d6a0f1-e5d3-49bd-a542-6bcc49c9c2ef, Ediciones Lerner) Lerner Publishing Group.

—Let's Explore Mexico. 2017. (Bumba Books (r) — Let's Explore Countries Ser.). (ENG., Illus.). 24p. (J). (gr. -1-1). 26.65 *(978-1-5124-3005-9(6),* 5817aa56-9c2f-43c9-8669-534fc62c1eaf); E-Book 39.99 *(978-1-5124-3740-9(9),* 9781512437409); E-Book 4.99 *(978-1-5124-3741-6(7),* 9781512437416); E-Book 39.99 *(978-1-5124-3023-3(4))* Lerner Publishing Group. (Lerner Pubns.).

Nantus, Sheryl. The Pacific South States of Mexico. (Mexico: Beautiful Land, Diverse People Ser.). 64p. (YA). (gr. 7-12). 2009. (Illus.). 21.95 *(978-1-4222-0666-9(1))* 2007. pap. 9.95 *(978-1-4222-0733-8(1))* Mason Crest.

Obregón, José María. Mexico - México, Vol. 1. 2009. (Great National Soccer Teams / Grandes Selecciones Del Fútbol Mundial Ser.). (SPA & ENG.). 24p. (J). (gr. 2-3). pap. 8.25 *(978-1-4358-2498-0(9),* 22c8536d-35c9-444e-8682-bd1e2228ae3b, PowerKids Pr.) Rosen Publishing Group, Inc., The.

—Mexico/México, 1 vol. Benson, Megan, tr. 2009. (Great National Soccer Teams / Grandes Selecciones Del Fútbol Mundial Ser.). (SPA & ENG., Illus.). 24p. (J). (gr. 2-3). lib. bdg. 26.27 *(978-1-4358-2497-3(0),* 11495e57-a0c4-426b-a369-376960f13c41) Rosen Publishing Group, Inc., The.

—Mexico/México. 2009. (SPA & ENG.). (J). 49.50 *(978-1-4358-3234-3(5),* PowerKids Pr.) Rosen Publishing Group, Inc., The.

Orr, Tamra. Meet Our New Student from Mexico. 2008. (Meet Our New Student Ser.). (Illus.). 48p. (YA). (gr. 2-5). lib. bdg. 29.95 *(978-1-58415-646-8(5))* Mitchell Lane Pubs.

Pohl, Kathleen. Looking at Mexico, 1 vol. 2007. (Looking at Countries Ser.). (ENG.). 32p. (gr. 2-4). pap. 11.50 *(978-0-8368-8179-0(6),* 3af59e58-aef7-494c-8960-8352f96a062e); (Illus.). lib. bdg. 28.67 *(978-0-8368-8172-1(9),* e92d071d-4761-46c6-978b-2684617b265e) Stevens, Gareth Publishing LLLP. (Gareth Stevens Learning Library).

Reilly, Mary-Jo, et al. Mexico, 1 vol. 3rd rev. ed. 2012. (Cultures of the World (Third Edition)(r) Ser.). (ENG., Illus.). 144p. (gr. 5-5). 48.79 *(978-1-60870-802-4(0),* 5efb30cd-e64a-4f7d-8531-a353b2ee2b1f) Cavendish Square Publishing LLC.

Richardson, Adele. Mexico. 2006. (My First Look at Countries Ser.). (Illus.). 24p. (J). (gr. -1-3). lib. bdg. 15.95 *(978-1-58341-448-4(7),* Creative Education) Creative Co., The.

Ring, Susan. Come to Mexico. 2005. (Yellow Umbrella Fluent Level Ser.). (ENG.). 16p. (gr. k-1). pap. 35.70 *(978-0-7368-5310-1(3),* Capstone Pr.) Capstone.

Rose, Elizabeth. A Primary Source Guide to Mexico. 2009. (Countries of the World). 24p. (gr. 2-3). 42.50 *(978-1-61512-039-0(4),* PowerKids Pr.) Rosen Publishing Group, Inc., The.

Rudolph, Jessica. México. 2019. (Los Países de Donde Venimos/Countries We Come From Ser.). (SPA., Illus.). 32p. (J). (gr. k-3). 19.95 *(978-1-64280-231-3(X))* Bearport Publishing Co., Inc.

Sabeca International Investment Staff. Enciclopedia de Mexico. 2004. (SPA., Illus.). (YA). cd-rom *(978-1-56409-069-0(8))* EBP Latin America Group, Inc.

Sanna, Ellyn. Mexico: Facts & Figures. 2009. (Mexico: Beautiful Land, Diverse People Ser.). (Illus.). 64p. (YA). (gr. 7-12). 21.95 *(978-1-4222-0660-7(2))* Mason Crest.

Simpson, Kathleen. Geography of Mexico: Set Of 6. 2011. (Navigators Ser.). (J). pap. 50.00 net. *(978-1-4108-6263-1(1))* Benchmark Education Co.

Somervill, Barbara A. It's Cool to Learn about Countries: Mexico. 2010. (Explorer Library: Social Studies Explorer Ser.). (ENG., Illus.). 48p. (gr. 4-8). lib. bdg. 34.93 *(978-1-60279-833-5(8),* 200532) Cherry Lake Publishing.

Stein, R. Conrad. Mexico. rev. ed. 2006. (Enchantment of the World Ser.). (ENG., Illus.). 144p. (J). (gr. 5-9). 39.00 *(978-0-516-24868-4(5),* Children's Pr.) Scholastic Library Publishing.

Stokes, Erica M. The Economy of Mexico. (Mexico: Beautiful Land, Diverse People Ser.). 64p. (YA). (gr. 7-12). 2009. (Illus.). 21.95 *(978-1-4222-0658-4(0))* 2007. pap. 9.95 *(978-1-4222-0725-3(0))* Mason Crest.

Streissguth, Thomas. Mexico. 2007. (Country Explorers Ser.). (Illus.). 48p. (J). (gr. k-2). lib. bdg. 27.93 *(978-0-8225-7130-8(7),* Lerner Pubns.) Lerner Publishing Group.

Streissguth, Tom. Mexico. 2008. pap. 40.95 *(978-0-8225-9305-8(X))* Lerner Publishing Group.

Tidmarsh, Celia. Focus on Mexico, 1 vol. 2005. (World in Focus Ser.). (ENG., Illus.). 64p. (gr. 5-8). pap. 15.05 *(978-0-8368-6238-6(4),* 01d79587-1be0-4c71-9763-5b9430aaafce); lib. bdg. 36.67 *(978-0-8368-6219-5(8),* a8a4a089-9fbf-4cb0-a2fe-acd8a4d9f5f6) Stevens, Gareth Publishing LLLP. (Gareth Stevens Secondary Library).

Urrutia, Maria Cristina & Orozco, Rebeca. Cinco de Mayo. 2nd ed. 2008. (ENG., Illus.). 32p. (J). (gr. 4). pap. 7.95 *(978-0-88899-877-4(5))* Groundwood Bks. CAN. Dist: Publishers Group West (PGW).

Williams, Colleen Madonna Flood. The Geography of Mexico. (Mexico: Beautiful Land, Diverse People Ser.). (Illus.). 64p. (J). (gr. 7-12). 2009. 21.95 *(978-1-4222-0661-4(0))* 2007. pap. 9.95 *(978-1-4222-0728-4(5))* Mason Crest.

World Book, Inc. Staff, contrib. by. !Feliz Navidad¡: Celebrating a Mexican Christmas. 2015. 80p. (J). *(978-0-7166-0830-1(8))* World Bk., Inc.

Zocchi, Judy. In Mexico. Brodie, Neale, illus. 2005. (Global Adventures II Ser.). 32p. (J). per. 10.95 *(978-1-59646-136-9(5))* Dingles & Co.

—In Mexico/en México. Brodie, Neale, illus. 2005. (Global Adventures II Ser.).Tr. of En México. (ENG & SPA.). 32p. (J). per. 10.95 *(978-1-59646-138-3(1))* Dingles & Co.

MEXICO—ANTIQUITIES

Croy, Anita. What Became of the Aztec Cities?, 1 vol. 2017. (Mysteries in History: Solving the Mysteries of the Past Ser.). (ENG.). 48p. (gr. 5-5). lib. bdg. 33.07 *(978-1-5026-2800-8(7),* baa3db49-e29b-42cd-aac3-60d0c94298bb) Cavendish Square Publishing LLC.

Hofer, Charles. Ancient Maya Technology, 1 vol. 2016. (Spotlight on the Maya, Aztec, & Inca Civilizations Ser.). (ENG., Illus.). 32p. (J). (gr. 4-6). 27.93 *(978-1-4994-1983-2(X),* 345530b4-49be-48b9-ada2-5c1718e100c4, PowerKids Pr.) Rosen Publishing Group, Inc., The.

Mahoney, Emily Jankowski. Ancient Aztec Technology, 1 vol. 2016. (Spotlight on the Maya, Aztec, & Inca Civilizations Ser.). (ENG., Illus.). 32p. (J). (gr. 4-6). pap. 12.75 *(978-1-4994-1923-8(6),* 64c7714e-3c60-4376-b40f-1c89ed65e7c2, PowerKids Pr.) Rosen Publishing Group, Inc., The.

Woods, Mary B. & Woods, Michael. Seven Wonders of Ancient North America. 2008. (Seven Wonders Ser.). (ENG., Illus.). 80p. (gr. 5-8). lib. bdg. 33.26 *(978-0-8225-7572-6(8))* Lerner Publishing Group.

MEXICO—BIOGRAPHY

Antonio Lopez de Santa Anna. 2010. (ENG., Illus.). 104p. (gr. 6-12). 35.00 *(978-1-60413-734-7(7),* P179359, Facts On File) Infobase Holdings, Inc.

Brown, Monica. Frida Kahlo & Her Animalitos. Parra, John, illus. 2017. (ENG.). 40p. (J). (gr. -1-3). 18.95 *(978-0-7358-4269-4(8))* North-South Bks., Inc.

Carew-Miller, Anna. Famous People of Mexico. (Mexico: Beautiful Land, Diverse People Ser.). 64p. (YA). (gr. 7-12). 2009. (Illus.). 21.95 *(978-1-4222-0659-1(9))* 2007. pap. 9.95 *(978-1-4222-0726-0(9))* Mason Crest.

Contro, Arturo. Rafael Marquez, 1 vol. Benson, Megan, tr. 2008. (World Soccer Stars / Estrellas Del Fútbol Mundial Ser.). (SPA & ENG., Illus.). 24p. (J). (gr. 2-2). lib. bdg. 26.27 *(978-1-4042-7667-3(X),* 532df3a4-41c1-41d6-a62e-5a6aa686ccbc) Rosen Publishing Group, Inc., The.

Dickens, Lydia. The Little Donkey Nico / el Burrito Nico. 2012. 32p. pap. 19.99 *(978-1-4772-7026-4(4))* AuthorHouse.

Dougherty, Terri. Salma Hayek, 1 vol. 2008. (People in the News Ser.). (ENG., Illus.). 104p. (J). (gr. 7-7). lib. bdg. 41.03 *(978-1-4205-0096-7(1),* 9184cb81-e27d-424a-9abb-4e94f5fc833f, Lucent Pr.) Greenhaven Publishing LLC.

Elzaurdia, Paco. Rafael Marquez. 2012. (Superstars of Soccer ENGLISH Ser.). (Illus.). 32p. (J). (gr. 4). 19.95 *(978-1-4222-2651-3(4))* Mason Crest.

Fabiny, Sarah & Who HQ. Who Was Frida Kahlo? Hoare, Jerry, illus. 2013. (Who Was? Ser.). 112p. (J). (gr. 3-7). 6.99 *(978-0-448-47938-5(9),* Penguin Workshop) Penguin Young Readers Group.

Foard, Sheila Wood. Diego Rivera. 2nd rev. ed. 2010. (Great Hispanic Heritage Ser.). (Illus.). 120p. (gr. 6-12). 35.00 *(978-1-60413-845-0(9),* Facts On File) Infobase Holdings, Inc.

Gordon, Nick. Alberto Del Rio. 2012. (Pro Wrestling Champions Ser.). (ENG., Illus.). 24p. (J). (gr. 3-7). lib. bdg. 26.95 *(978-1-60014-782-1(8),* Torque Bks.) Bellwether Media.

Hart, Paul. Emiliano Zapata: Mexico's Social Revolutionary. 2017. (World in a Life Ser.). (ENG., Illus.). 352p. (C). pap. 39.99 *(978-0-19-068808-0(4))* Oxford Univ. Pr., Inc.

Hillstrom, Kevin. Diego Rivera: Muralist, 1 vol. 2008. (Twentieth Century's Most Influential Hispanics Ser.). (ENG., Illus.). 104p. (gr. 7-10). 41.03 *(978-1-4205-0018-9(X),* 212725d4-e359-4aa5-ae66-34b29c40bd52, Lucent Pr.) Greenhaven Publishing LLC.

Jauregui, Diego. Libros de Arte para Ninos: Diego Rivera.Tr. of Art Books for Children: Diego Rivera. (SPA., Illus.). 73p. (YA). (gr. 5-8). pap. *(978-968-494-026-0(2))* Centro de Informacion y Desarrollo de la Comunicacion y la Literatura.

Lazaro, Georgina. Juana Ines. Preza, Bruno Gonzalez, illus. 2007. (SPA.). 32p. (J). (gr. 3-5). 14.99 *(978-1-930332-57-7(2))* Lectorum Pubns., Inc.

Loria, Laura. Malinche: Indigenous Translator for Hernán Cortés in Mexico, 1 vol. 2017. (Women Who Changed History Ser.). (ENG., Illus.). 48p. (J). (gr. 6-7). pap. 15.05 *(978-1-68048-649-0(7),* 3b67bd0f-a6fb-4595-8081-5ff479f11cf6, Britannica Educational Publishing) Rosen Publishing Group, Inc., The.

Marín, Guadalupe Rivera. My Papá Diego & Me (Mi Papa Diego y Yo) Memories of My Father & His Art (Recuerdos de Mi Padre y Su Arte) Rivera, Diego, illus. 2013. (SPA & ENG.). 32p. (J). (gr. k-5). 18.95 *(978-0-89239-228-5(2))* Lee & Low Bks., Inc.

Marsh, Carole. Diego Rivera: Acclaimed Mural Painter: Acclaimed Mural Painter. 2003. 12p. (gr. k-4). 2.95 *(978-0-635-02137-3(4))* Gallopade International.

Mora, Pat. Una Biblioteca para Juana: El Mundo de Sor Juana inésThe World of Sor Juana Inés, 1 vol. Vidal, Beatriz, illus. 2019. Orig. Title: A Library for Juana. (SPA.). 32p. (J). (gr. k-3). pap. 12.95 *(978-1-64379-059-6(5),* leelowcbp) Lee & Low Bks., Inc.

Morales, Yuyi. Viva Frida. Morales, Yuyi & O'Meara, Tim, illus. 2014. (ENG.). 40p. (J). (gr. -1-3). 19.99 *(978-1-59643-603-9(4),* 900065746) Roaring Brook Pr.

Nardo, Don. Frida Kahlo, 1 vol. 2012. (Eye on Art Ser.). (ENG., Illus.). 104p. (gr. 7-7). lib. bdg. 41.03 *(978-1-4205-0850-5(4),* 0d29b11b-0d31-429f-894d-3e5dbb106df0, Lucent Pr.) Greenhaven Publishing LLC.

Obregón, José María. Cuauhtémoc Blanco, 1 vol. 2009. (World Soccer Stars / Estrellas Del Fútbol Mundial Ser.). (SPA & ENG., Illus.). 24p. (J). (gr. 2-2). lib. bdg. 26.27 *(978-1-4358-2731-8(7),* f122bf04-473b-4bed-8ba2-a529eaf32dbb) Rosen Publishing Group, Inc., The.

Owens, Lisa L. A Journey with Hernán Cortés. 2017. (Primary Source Explorers Ser.). (ENG., Illus.). 40p. (J). (gr. 3-5). 30.65 *(978-1-5124-0777-8(1),* 1a7f988c-a4ce-4b11-a824-160a4148d5c3, Lerner Pubns.) Lerner Publishing Group.

Quintero, Isabel. Photographic: The Life of Graciela Iturbide. Peña, Zeke, illus. 2018. (ENG.). 96p. (YA). (gr. 7-17). 19.95 *(978-1-947440-00-5(4),* 1317401) Getty Pubns.

Ramen, Fred. Hernán Cortés: The Conquest of Mexico & the Aztec Empire. 2009. (Library of Explorers & Exploration Ser.). 112p. (gr. 5-8). 66.50 *(978-1-60853-606-1(8),* Rosen Reference) Rosen Publishing Group, Inc., The.

Reef, Catherine. Frida & Diego: Art, Love, Life. 2014. (ENG., Illus.). 176p. (YA). (gr. 7-12). 18.99 *(978-0-547-82184-9(0),* 1497178, Clarion Bks.) HarperCollins Pubs.

Richards, Virginia Helen & Halpin, D. Thomas, illus. Blessed Miguel Pro. 2011. (J). pap. 2.95 *(978-0-8198-1192-9(0))* Pauline Bks. & Media.

Rubin, Susan Goldman. Diego Rivera: An Artist for the People. 2013. (ENG., Illus.). 56p. (J). (gr. 3-7). 22.95 *(978-0-8109-8411-0(3),* 666701, Abrams Bks. for Young Readers) Abrams, Inc.

Sapet, Kerrily. Salma Hayek. (Transcending Race in America Ser.). 64p. (YA). (gr. 5-18). 2010. (Illus.). lib. bdg. 22.95 *(978-1-4222-1616-3(0))* 2009. pap. 9.95 *(978-1-4222-1630-9(6))* Mason Crest.

Stein, R. Conrad. Emiliano Zapata & the Mexican Revolution. 2011. (Story of Mexico Ser.). (Illus.). 144p. (gr. 7-12). 28.95 *(978-1-59935-163-6(3))* Reynolds, Morgan Inc.

Tonatiuh, Duncan. Danza! Amalia Hernández & el Ballet Folklórico de México. 2017. (ENG., Illus.). 32p. (J). (gr. 1-5). 19.99 *(978-1-4197-2532-6(7),* 1103201) Abrams, Inc.

—Diego Rivera: His World & Ours. 2011. (ENG., Illus.). 40p. (J). (gr. 1-4). 18.99 *(978-0-8109-9731-8(2),* 692401) Abrams, Inc.

—Funny Bones: Posada & His Day of the Dead Calaveras. 2015. (ENG., Illus.). 40p. (J). (gr. 1-5). 19.99 *(978-1-4197-1647-8(6),* 1103301, Abrams Bks. for Young Readers) Abrams, Inc.

Valay, Ana Patricia. Giovani Dos Santos. 2012. (Superstars of Soccer SPANISH Ser.). (SPA.). 32p. (J). (gr. 4). 19.95 *(978-1-4222-2597-4(6))* Mason Crest.

Wagner, Heather Lehr. Hernan Cortes. 2009. (Great Explorers Ser.). (ENG., Illus.). 120p. (gr. 6-12). 30.00 *(978-1-60413-424-7(0),* P173420, Facts On File) Infobase Holdings, Inc.

West, David. Hernán Cortés: The Life of a Spanish Conquistador. 2009. (Graphic Nonfiction Biographies Ser.). (ENG.). 48p. (YA). (gr. 4-5). 58.50 *(978-1-61513-019-1(5),* Rosen Reference) Rosen Publishing Group, Inc., The.

Wine, Bill. Salma Hayek. (Sharing the American Dream Ser.). 64p. (YA). (gr. 7-12). 2009. (Illus.). 22.95 *(978-1-4222-0585-3(1))* 2007. pap. 9.95 *(978-1-4222-0748-2(X))* Mason Crest.

MEXICO CITY (MEXICO)

Bingham, Jane. Aztec Empire (Freestyle Express) 2014. 22.50 *(978-1-63419-686-4(4))* Perfection Learning Corp.

Croy, Anita. Solving the Mysteries of Aztec Cities, 1 vol. 2009. (Digging into History Ser.). (ENG.). 32p. (gr. 3-3). lib. bdg. 32.64 *(978-0-7614-3102-2(0),* 577dc9ca-f0bb-40e9-bf5b-00822eb4bbfa) Cavendish Square Publishing LLC.

Mahoney, Emily. 20 Fun Facts about Tenochtitlán, 1 vol. 2019. (Fun Fact File: World Wonders! Ser.). (ENG., Illus.). 32p. (gr. 2-3). pap. 11.50 *(978-1-5382-3762-5(8),* 44069a7d-5e02-446a-af2b-daa85359f46e) Stevens, Gareth Publishing LLLP.

Markovics, Joyce. Mexico City. 2017. (Citified! Ser.). (ENG., Illus.). 24p. (J). (gr. k-3). lib. bdg. 17.95 *(978-1-68402-236-6(3))* Bearport Publishing Co., Inc.

Pugliano-Martin, Carol. Discover Mexico City. 2006. (J). pap. *(978-1-4108-6423-9(5))* Benchmark Education Co.

—Mexico City, Mexico. 2006. (J). pap. *(978-1-4108-6420-8(0))* Benchmark Education Co.

MEXICO—FICTION

Agustin, Jose. La Panza del Tepozteco. Tino, illus. 2003. (SPA.). 118p. (J). (gr. 8-12). pap. 12.95 *(978-968-19-0187-5(8))* Santillana USA Publishing Co., Inc.

Ahern, Carolyn L. Tino Turtle Travels to Mexico City, Mexico. Burt Sullivan, Neallia, illus. 2008. (ENG & SPA.). 32p. (J). (gr. -1-4). 19.95 incl. audio compact disk *(978-0-9793158-2-4(4))* Tino Turtle Travels, LLC.

Alegria, Malin. Sofi Mendoza's Guide to Getting Lost in Mexico. 2008. (ENG.). 304p. (YA). (gr. 7). pap. 11.99 *(978-0-689-87812-1(5)*, Simon & Schuster Bks. For Young Readers) Simon & Schuster Bks. For Young Readers.

Alsaid, Adi. North of Happy. 2019. (ENG.). 320p. (YA). pap. 10.99 *(978-1-335-65999-6(4))* Harlequin Enterprises ULC CAN. Dist: HarperCollins Pubs.

Anaya, Rudolfo. Curse of the ChupaCabra. 2013. (ENG.). 176p. (YA). pap. 19.95 *(978-0-8263-4115-0(2)*, P225261) Univ. of New Mexico Pr.

—The First Tortilla: A Bilingual Story. Lamadrid, Enrique R., tr. Córdova, Amy, illus. 2012. (ENG & SPA.). 32p. (J). pap. 16.95 *(978-0-8263-4215-7(9)*, P208966) Univ. of New Mexico Pr.

And Then it was Sugar, 6 vols. (Multicultural Programs Ser.). 16p. (gr. 1-6). 31.95 *(978-0-7802-8324-4(4))* Wright Group/McGraw-Hill.

Angel, Ido. Vipo in Mexico: The Maya Treasure Mystery. 2015. (AV2 Animated Storytime Ser.). (ENG.). (J). lib. bdg. 29.99 *(978-1-4896-3908-0(X)*, AV2 by Weigl) Weigl Pubs., Inc.

Anza, Ana Luisa. El Misterio de la Casa Chueca (y el Bulto Color Mugre) The Mystery of the Crooked House. Escobar, Antonio Rocha, illus. rev. ed. 2006. (Castillo de la Lectura Naranja Ser.). (SPA & ENG.). 120p. (J). (gr. 4-7). pap. 7.95 *(978-970-20-0200-0(1))* Castillo, Ediciones, S. A. de C. V. MEX. Dist: Macmillan.

Appleton, Victor. Tom Swift in the City of Gold. 2005. 27.95 *(978-1-4218-1510-7(9))*; 204p. pap. 12.95 *(978-1-4218-1610-4(5))* 1st World Publishing, Inc. (1st World Library - Literary Society).

—Tom Swift in the City of Gold or Marvelo. 2006. pap. *(978-1-4065-0916-8(7))* Dodo Pr.

Archbold, David M. The Amazing Adventures of Chumley, Robin, Snickers & Mac. 2011. 48p. (gr. 4-6). pap. 19.26 *(978-1-4634-1518-1(4))* AuthorHouse.

Avalon-Pai, Phyllis. Children's Stories from Around the World. Arrott, Nancy, illus. 2008. 70p. pap. 9.95 *(978-0-9788283-8-7(0))* Acacia Publishing, Inc.

Bennett, Marilyn J. The Poinsettia Adventure. 2010. 60p. pap. 21.99 *(978-1-4490-7108-0(2))* AuthorHouse.

Blair, Kathryn S. Diario de Lucia (1939) 2003. (Mexican Diaries). (SPA., Illus.). 132p. (J). pap. *(978-970-690-039-5(X)*, SOM7943) Planeta Mexicana Editorial S. A. de C. V. MEX. Dist: Lectorum Pubns., Inc.

Bowles, David. Rise of the Halfling King, 1 vol. Bowles, Charlene, illus. 2020. (Tales of the Feathered Serpent Ser.: 1). (ENG.). 64p. (J). (gr. 4-8). pap. 14.95 *(978-1-947627-37-6(6)*, 23353382, Cinco Puntos Press) Lee & Low Bks., Inc.

Bowles, David & Bowles, Charlene, illus. The Rise of the Halfling King. 2021. 63p. (J). *(978-1-947627-36-9(8)*, Cinco Puntos Press) Lee & Low Bks., Inc.

Brammer, Ethriam Cash. The Rowdy, Rowdy Ranch / Alla en el Rancho Grande. Cruz, D. Nina, illus. 2003. (ENG & SPA.). 32p. (J). 16.95 *(978-1-55885-409-3(6)*, Piñata Books) Arte Publico Pr.

Brandeis, Madeline. The Little Mexican Donkey Boy. 2011. 226p. 44.95 *(978-1-258-09794-3(X))* Literary Licensing, LLC.

Bray, Diane E. B. First Generation: The Story of Annie. 2008. 53p. pap. 16.95 *(978-1-60563-516-3(2))* America Star Bks.

Brooks, Melanie & Spenser and Mom Staff. Spenser Goes to el Paso. Jacobsen, Amie, illus. 2010. (ENG.). 32p. (J). 14.95 *(978-0-9817598-3-8(1)*, cbc0cc91-0341-4e1a-a28e-405962e8c495) Simple Fish Bk. Co., LLC.

Brown, Jeff. Flat Stanley's Worldwide Adventures #5: the Amazing Mexican Secret. Pamintuan, Macky, illus. 2010. (Flat Stanley's Worldwide Adventures Ser.: 5). (ENG.). 112p. (J). (gr. 2-5). pap. 4.99 *(978-0-06-142998-9(8))*;No. 5. 15.99 *(978-0-06-142999-6(6))* HarperCollins Pubs. (HarperCollins).

Cantwell, Michael. The Rising of the Fifth Sun. 2012. 120p. (gr. 4-6). 20.95 *(978-1-4620-7203-3(8))*; pap. 10.95 *(978-1-4620-7201-9(1))* iUniverse, Inc.

Capucilli, Alyssa Satin. Pedro's Burro. 2008. (My First I Can Read Ser.). (ENG., Illus.). 32p. (J). (gr. -1 — 1). pap. 4.99 *(978-0-06-056033-1(9)*, HarperCollins) HarperCollins Pubs.

Carter, Aubrey Smith. The Enchanted Lizard: La Lagartijita Mágica. Nelson, Esther Whitt, ed. Branton, Molly, illus. 2006. (ENG & SPA.). 96p. (J). 18.95 *(978-1-893271-38-8(2)*, Maverick Bks.) Trinity Univ. Pr.

Coburn, Jewell Reinhart & McLennan, Connie. Domítila: A Cinderella Tale from the Mexican Tradition, 1 vol. 2014. (Cinderella Ser.). (ENG., Illus.). 32p. (J). (gr. 2-5). pap. 11.95 *(978-1-885008-43-5(0)*, leelowshens, Shen's Bks.) Lee & Low Bks., Inc.

Cohn. Dream Carver Pb. 2009. (Illus.). 40p. pap. 6.99 *(978-0-8118-7050-4(2))* Chronicle Bks. LLC.

Corpi, Lucha. & National Geographic Learning Staff. Where Fireflies Dance: Ahi, Donde Bailan Las Luciernagas, 1 vol. Reisberg, Mira, illus. 2013. (ENG.). 32p. (J). (gr. k-2). pap. 12.95 *(978-0-89239-177-6(4)*, leelowcbp, Children's Book Press) Lee & Low Bks., Inc.

Cruz, Maria Colleen. Border Crossing. 2003. 128p. (J). pap. 9.95 *(978-1-55885-405-5(3)*, Piñata Books) Arte Publico Pr.

—Border Crossing. 2006. 122p. (gr. 8-12). 19.95 *(978-0-7569-6587-7(X))* Perfection Learning Corp.

Cuesy, Silvia. Diario de Mercedes (1844-48) 2003. (Mexican Diaries). (SPA., Illus.). 161p. (J). pap. *(978-970-690-037-1(3)*, SOM7983) Planeta Mexicana Editorial S. A. de C. V. MEX. Dist: Lectorum Pubns., Inc.

DaColl, Ivar. El Dia de Muertos. 2004.Tr. of Day of the Dead. (SPA., Illus.). (J). 14.95 *(978-1-930332-44-7(0))* Lectorum Pubns., Inc.

Damitz, Charlie. Diving for el Corazon. Diefendorf, Cathy, illus. 2007. (ENG.). 101p. (J). pap. 10.95 *(978-0-9744446-3-5(4))* All About Kids Publishing.

Dear Abuelita, 6, Pack. (Greetings Ser.: Vol. 2). (gr. 3-5). 31.00 *(978-0-7635-1765-6(8))* Rigby Education.

Death at the Border. 64p. (YA). (gr. 6-12). pap. *(978-0-8224-2361-4(8))* Globe Fearon Educational Publishing.

Desisti, Sam F. The Paco & Angelina Stories, 1 vol. 2009. 48p. pap. 16.95 *(978-1-61582-604-9(1))* America Star Bks.

Duncklee, John. Manchado & His Friends Manchado Y Sus Amigos. 2009. 52p. pap. 9.95 *(978-1-4401-2496-9(5))* iUniverse, Inc.

Estrada Michel, Rafael, tr. Diario de Lupita. 2003. (Mexican Diaries). (SPA., Illus.). 179p. (J). pap. *(978-970-690-114-9(0))* Planeta Mexicana Editorial S. A. de C. V.

Estrada, Pau. Pedro's Burro. Estrada, Pau, illus. 2007. (My First I Can Read Bks.). (Illus.). 32p. (J). (gr. -1-k). lib. bdg. 16.89 *(978-0-06-056032-4(0))* HarperCollins Pubs.

Ets, Marie Hall & Labastida, Aurora. Nine Days to Christmas: A Story of Mexico. 2017. (ENG., Illus.). 48p. 15.95 *(978-0-486-81532-9(3)*, 815323) Dover Pubns., Inc.

Ezirim, E. C. Jet Black & the Ebony Knights. 2010. 40p. 16.99 *(978-1-4520-7567-9(0))* AuthorHouse.

Feliciano, Maria Inez. Meximan. 2012. 28p. pap. 24.95 *(978-1-4626-9248-4(6))* America Star Bks.

Fine, Edith. Armando & the Blue Tarp School, 1 vol. 2007. (ENG., Illus.). 32p. (J). (gr. -1-3). lib. bdg. 17.95 *(978-1-58430-278-0(X))* Lee & Low Bks., Inc.

Fine, Edith H. Bajo la Luna de Limon. 2004. (SPA., Illus.). (J). (gr. k-3). spiral bd. *(978-0-616-03089-9(4))* Canadian National Institute for the Blind/Institut National Canadien pour les Aveugles.

Fine, Edith Hope & Pinkerton Josephson, Judith. Armando y la Escuela de Lona Azul: Armando & the Blue Tarp School, 1 vol. Sosa, Hernán, illus. 2014.Tr. of Armando & the Blue Tarp School. (SPA.). 32p. (J). (gr. 3-5). pap. 12.95 *(978-1-60060-449-2(8)*, leelowbooks) Lee & Low Bks., Inc.

Fleischman, Sid. The Dream Stealer. Sis, Peter, illus. 2011. (ENG.). 128p. (J). pap. 6.99 *(978-0-06-178729-4(9)*, Greenwillow Bks.) HarperCollins Pubs.

Flor Ada, Alma. Celebra el Cinco de Mayo con un Jarabe Tapatio. Gomez, Marcela & Silva, David, illus. 2006. (Cuentos para Celebrar / Stories to Celebrate Ser.). 30p. (gr. k-6). per. 11.95 *(978-1-59820-118-5(2))* Ediciones Alfaguara ESP. Dist: Santillana USA Publishing Co., Inc.

Flowers, J. J. Juan Pablo & the Butterflies. 2017. (ENG., Illus.). 224p. (YA). (gr. 9-12). 17.99 *(978-1-5072-0214-2(8)*, Simon Pulse) Simon Pulse.

Fowler, Frank. The Broncho Rider Boys with Funston at Vera Cruz: Or, Upholding the Honor of the Stars & Stripes. 2017. (ENG., Illus.). (J). pap. 13.95 *(978-1-374-84495-7(0))* Capital Communications, Inc.

Garza, Fabiola, illus. Coco. 2017. (J). *(978-1-5379-5892-7(5)*, Golden Bks.) Random Hse. Children's Bks.

Garza, Xavier. Lucha Libre: The Man in the Silver Mask - A Bilingual Cuento, 1 vol. 2007. (SPA., Illus.). 40p. (J). (gr. 2-7). pap. 12.95 *(978-1-933693-10-1(X)*, 23353382, Cinco Puntos Press) Lee & Low Bks., Inc.

Geeslin, Campbell. Elena's Serenade. Juan, Ana, illus. 2004. (ENG.). 40p. (J). (gr. -1-2). 19.99 *(978-0-689-84908-4(7)*, Atheneum Bks. for Young Readers) Simon & Schuster Children's Publishing.

Gibbs, Stuart. Spy School Goes South. 2018. (Spy School Ser.). (ENG., Illus.). 352p. (J). (gr. 3-7). 17.99 *(978-1-4814-7785-7(4)*, Simon & Schuster Bks. For Young Readers) Simon & Schuster Bks. For Young Readers.

Gill, Heidi & Carter, Kris. 2 Kurious Kids: Mexico. 2012. (Illus.). 38p. (J). 14.95 *(978-1-936319-91-6(8))* Amplify Publishing Group.

Gollub, Matthew. The Twenty-Five Mixtec Cats. Martinez, Leovigildo, illus. 2004. (J). *(978-1-889910-30-7(9))* Tortuga Pr.

Guillain, Adam. Bella Balistica & the Izta Warriors, 1 vol. 2012. (Bella Balistica Ser.). (ENG., Illus.). 192p. (J). (gr. 4-7). pap. 9.95 *(978-1-84059-771-4(2))* Milet Publishing.

Hancock, H. Irving. Dave Darrin at Vera Cruz. rev. ed. 2006. 216p. 27.95 *(978-1-4218-1745-3(4))*; pap. 12.95 *(978-1-4218-1845-0(0))* 1st World Publishing, Inc. (1st World Library - Literary Society).

—Dave Darrin at Vera Cruz. 2018. (ENG., Illus.). 170p. (YA). (gr. 7-12). pap. *(978-93-5297-333-0(X))* Alpha Editions.

—Dave Darrin at Vera Cruz. 2007. 180p. per. *(978-1-4065-1973-0(1))* Dodo Pr.

—The Young Engineers in Mexico. rev. ed. 2006. 208p. 27.95 *(978-1-4218-1738-5(1))*; pap. 12.95 *(978-1-4218-1838-2(8))* 1st World Publishing, Inc. (1st World Library - Literary Society).

—The Young Engineers in Mexico. 2007. 176p. per. *(978-1-4065-1994-5(4))* Dodo Pr.

—The Young Engineers in Mexico: Or, Fighting the Mine Swindlers. 2017. (ENG., Illus.). (J). 23.95 *(978-1-374-93146-6(2))*; pap. 13.95 *(978-1-374-93145-9(4))* Capital Communications, Inc.

—The Young Engineers in Mexico: Or, Fighting the Mine Swindlers. 2017. (ENG., Illus.). (J). pap. *(978-0-649-20896-8(X))* Trieste Publishing Pty Ltd.

Herman-O'Neal, Jackie. Moctezuma's Zoo: A Tale from an Enchanted City. 2013. 28p. pap. 24.95 *(978-1-62709-271-5(4))* America Star Bks.

Hope Fine, Edith. Under the Lemon Moon, 1 vol. King Moreno, René, illus. 2013.Tr. of Bajo la Luna de Limon. (ENG.). 32p. (J). (gr. 1-3). pap. 11.95 *(978-1-58430-051-9(5)*, leelowbooks) Lee & Low Bks., Inc.

Hunt, Elizabeth Singer. Secret Agent Jack Stalwart: Book 10: the Quest for Aztec Gold: Mexico, Bk. 10. 2009. (Secret Agent Jack Stalwart Ser.: 10). (ENG.). 128p. (J). (gr. 1-4). pap. 5.99 *(978-1-60286-079-7(3))* Hachette Bk. Group.

Irwin, Bindi & Black, Jess. Surfing with Turtles: Bindi Wildlife Adventures, 8. 2013. (Bindi's Wildlife Adventures Ser.: 8). (ENG.). 112p. (J). (gr. 3-6). pap. 8.99 *(978-1-4022-8094-8(7)*, Sourcebooks Jabberwocky) Sourcebooks, Inc.

Isabel, Delgado Maria. Chave's Memories / Los Recuerdos de Chave. Yvonne, Symank, illus. 2008. 32p. (J). pap. 7.95 *(978-1-55885-244-0(1)*, Piñata Books) Arte Publico Pr.

Jaramillo, Ann. La Linea: A Novel. 2008. (ENG.). 144p. (J). (gr. 5-9). pap. 8.99 *(978-0-312-37354-2(6)*, 900045403) Square Fish.

Johnson, Terry Lynn. Dust Storm! Orban, Jani, illus. 2018. (Survivor Diaries). (ENG.). 128p. (J). (gr. 1-5). 9.99 *(978-0-544-97098-4(5)*, 1662531, Clarion Bks.) HarperCollins Pubs.

Johnston, Tony. Isabel's House of Butterflies. Guevara, Susan, illus. 2005. 32p. pap. 6.95 *(978-1-58685-844-5(0))* Gibbs Smith, Publisher.

Johnston, Tony & de Rhoads, María Elena Fontanot. Beast Rider. 2019. (ENG., Illus.). 176p. (J). (gr. 7-17). 18.99 *(978-1-4197-3363-5(X)*, 1251301, Amulet Bks.) Abrams, Inc.

Jungle Crossing. 2011. (ENG.). 228p. (J). (gr. 5-7). pap. 13.99 *(978-0-547-55009-1(X)*, 1450218, Clarion Bks.) HarperCollins Pubs.

Kerr, Cora. Love Lessons on Bird Beach. 2010. 88p. pap. 26.50 *(978-1-60860-713-6(5)*, Strategic Bk. Publishing) Strategic Book Publishing & Rights Agency (SBPRA).

Key, Watt. Deep Water. 2019. (ENG.). 288p. (J). pap. 7.99 *(978-1-250-29439-5(8)*, 900177053) Square Fish.

King, Dedie. I See the Sun in Mexico, 1 vol. Inglese, Judith, illus. 2012. (I See the Sun Ser.: 5). (ENG & SPA.). 40p. (J). (gr. 1-7). pap. 12.95 *(978-1-935874-14-0(4))* Satya Hse. Pubns.

Krensky, Stephen. The Tale of la Llorona: A Mexican Folktale. 2009. pap. 40.95 *(978-0-7613-4819-1(0))* Lerner Publishing Group.

Lainez, Rene. From North to South, 1 vol. Cepeda, Joe, illus. 2014.Tr. of Del Norte Al Sur. (ENG.). 32p. (J). (gr. k-3). pap. 11.95 *(978-0-89239-304-6(1)*, leelowcbp, Children's Book Press) Lee & Low Bks., Inc.

Laínez, René Colato. From North to South/Del Norte Al Sur. Cepeda, Joe, illus. 2010.Tr. of Del norte al Sur. (ENG & SPA.). 32p. (J). (gr. k-3). 17.95 *(978-0-89239-231-5(2))* Lee & Low Bks., Inc.

Laínez, René Colato & Arena, Jill. Playing Loteria: El Juego de la Loteria. 2005. (ENG, MUL & SPA., Illus.). 32p. (J). (gr. -1-3). 15.95 *(978-0-87358-881-2(9))* Cooper Square Publishing Llc.

Leal, Luis, compiled by. Cuentos Mexicanos - de los origenes a la Revolucion. 2007. (SPA.). 184p. (J). per. 23.90 *(978-1-934768-04-4(9))* Stockcero, Inc.

LeBlanc, Margaret Ann. The Mexico Adventure: Book Three of Ms. Maddy Series, 1 vol. 2010. 72p. pap. 19.95 *(978-1-4489-8090-1(9))* America Star Bks.

Levy, Janice & Arisa, Miguel. I Remember Abuelito: A Day of the Dead Story. Lopez, Loretta, illus. 2012.Tr. of Yo Recuerdo a Abuelito - Un Cuento del Dia de los Muertos. (SPA & ENG.). (J). *(978-1-61913-114-9(5))* Weigl Pubs., Inc.

Long, Eula. Pirate's Doll: The Story of the China Poblana. 2011. 82p. 37.95 *(978-1-258-08444-8(9))* Literary Licensing, LLC.

Lorraine, Nancy. Tatty, the Lonely Monarch. Herron, Dorothy, illus. 2013. 48p. pap. 17.50 *(978-0-9893063-8-6(0))* ProsePress.

Lowery, Linda. The Tale of la Llorona: A Mexican Folktale. 2008. 48p. (J). pap. 6.95 *(978-0-8225-6743-1(1)*, First Avenue Editions) Lerner Publishing Group.

—Truth & Salsa, 1 vol. 2009. 176p. (J). (gr. 3-7). pap. 7.95 *(978-1-56145-498-3(2))* Peachtree Publishing Co. Inc.

Luedtke, Courtney. Baby Boo: The Happy Beginning. 2009. (Illus.). 72p. pap. 27.49 *(978-1-4389-2696-4(0))* AuthorHouse.

Maclachlan, Patricia. More Perfect Than the Moon. 2005. 16.00 *(978-0-7569-5437-6(1))* Perfection Learning Corp.

Madrigal, Antonio Hernandez. Erandi's Braids. dePaola, Tomie, illus. 2015. 32p. pap. 7.00 *(978-1-61003-530-9(5))* Center for the Collaborative Classroom.

Marquez, Sofia. Pepe Perez Mexican Mouse: Pepe Perez Comes to the United States: Book 1, 1 vol. Marquez, Sofia, illus. 2009. (Illus.). 20p. pap. 24.95 *(978-1-61546-496-8(4))* America Star Bks.

—Pepe Perez Mexican Mouse: Pepe Perez Comes to the United States: Book 1, 1 vol. 2010. 20p. 24.95 *(978-1-4489-6600-4(0))* PublishAmerica, Inc.

Marsden, Carolyn. Starfields. 2011. (ENG., Illus.). 224p. (J). (gr. 5). 15.99 *(978-0-7636-4820-6(5))* Candlewick Pr.

Matthews. Death in the Desert. (Thumbprint Mysteries Ser.). 32.86 *(978-0-8092-0416-8(9))* McGraw-Hill/Contemporary.

May, Eleanor. The Best Mother's Day Ever. Pilz, M. H., illus. 2010. (Social Studies Connects Ser.). 32p. (J). (gr. 1-4). pap. 6.99 *(978-1-57565-299-3(4)*, 10a30778-f71f-4dc6-9aae-05d93685d79f, Kane Press) Astra Publishing Hse.

McAlister, Caroline. Holy Mole! A Folktale from Mexico. Czernecki, Stefan, illus. 2006. (ENG.). 32p. (J). (gr. k-3). 16.95 *(978-0-87483-775-9(8))* August Hse. Pubs., Inc.

McDougal-Littell Publishing Staff. Literature Connections English: A Place Where the Sea Remembers. 2004. (McDougal Littell Literature Connections Ser.). (ENG.). 208p. (gr. 10-10). 16.25 *(978-0-395-83361-2(2)*, 2-70784) Great Source Education Group, Inc.

McKenzie, Precious. A Vacation in Ruins. 2015. (Rourke's World Adventure Chapter Bks.). (ENG.). 96p. (gr. 3-5). 29.93 *(978-1-63430-393-4(8)*, 9781634303934) Rourke Educational Media.

Medina, Meg. The Girl Who Could Silence the Wind. (ENG.). 256p. (YA). (gr. 9). 2013. pap. 8.99 *(978-0-7636-6419-0(7))* 2012. (Illus.). 17.99 *(978-0-7636-4602-8(4))* Candlewick Pr.

Meek, S. P. Pagan: A Border Patrol Horse. 2011. 254p. 46.95 *(978-1-258-08439-4(2))* Literary Licensing, LLC.

Meister, Cari. Airplane Adventure, 1 vol. Janovitz, Marilyn, illus. 2010. (My First Graphic Novel Ser.). (ENG.). 32p. (J). (gr. k-2). pap. 6.25 *(978-1-4342-2286-2(1)*, 103154, Stone Arch Bks.) Capstone.

Mervis (Yudith Pantoja), Judith. Yuyi & la Rama: Yuyi y la Rama. 2012. (ENG.). 24p. pap. 17.99 *(978-1-4685-7600-9(3))* AuthorHouse.

Molina, Silvia & Silvia, Molina. Le Comieron la Lengua los Ratones. Rodriguez, Mari, illus. 2005. (Montana Encantada Ser.). (SPA.). 96p. (YA). (gr. 3-5). pap. 9.50 *(978-84-241-8557-2(9))* Everest Editora ESP. Dist: Lectorum Pubns., Inc.

Mora, Pat & Ventura, Gabriela Baeza. The Remembering Day / el Día de Los Muertos. Casilla, Robert, illus. 2015. (SPA & ENG.). 32p. (J). (gr. k-3). 17.95 *(978-1-55885-805-3(9)*, Piñata Books) Arte Publico Pr.

Nail, Eric. The Wave Wranglers & the New Order of the Pyramid. 2007. 268p. (YA). pap. 18.95 *(978-1-4303-2254-2(3))* Lulu Pr., Inc.

Naylor, Phyllis Reynolds. Eating Enchiladas, 0 vols. Ramsey, Marcy, illus. 2013. (Simply Sarah Ser.: 4). (ENG.). 80p. (J). (gr. 1-4). pap. 9.99 *(978-0-7614-5885-2(9)*, 9780761458852, Two Lions) Amazon Publishing.

Nelson, Suzanne. Heart & Salsa. 2006. (S. A. S. S. Ser.). (Illus.). 224p. (YA). (gr. 7-18). 6.99 *(978-0-14-240647-2(3)*, Speak) Penguin Young Readers Group.

Noble, Diana J. Evangelina Takes Flight. 2017. (ENG.). 152p. (J). (gr. 5-8). pap. 10.95 *(978-1-55885-848-0(2)*, Piñata Books) Arte Publico Pr.

O'Dell, Scott. The Black Pearl: A Newbery Honor Award Winner. 2010. (ENG.). 144p. (J). (gr. 5-7). pap. 9.99 *(978-0-547-33400-4(1)*, 1417753, Clarion Bks.) HarperCollins Pubs.

—The King's Fifth: A Newbery Honor Award Winner. 2006. (ENG., Illus.). 272p. (YA). (gr. 7). pap. 15.99 *(978-0-618-74783-2(4)*, 492357, Clarion Bks.) HarperCollins Pubs.

Olberg, Henry, illus. The Magical Tooth Fairies: A Surprise in Mexico. 2012. (J). *(978-0-86715-568-6(X))* Edition Q, Inc.

Oliver, Juanbjuan, illus. The Prince & the Three Oranges a Fairy Tale from Mexico. 2017. (Text Connections Guided Close Reading Ser.). (J). (gr. 1). *(978-1-4900-1822-5(0))* Benchmark Education Co.

Oppenheim, Joanne F. El Milagro de la Primera Flora de Nochebuena: Un Cuento Mexicano Sobre la Navidad. Negrin, Fabian, illus. 2003. (SPA & ENG.). 32p. (J). 16.99 *(978-1-84148-308-5(7))* Barefoot Bks., Inc.

—The Miracle of the First Poinsettia: a Mexican Christmas Story. Negrin, Fabian, illus. 2003. (ENG.). 32p. (J). 16.99 *(978-1-84148-245-3(5))* Barefoot Bks., Inc.

Orozco, Rebeca & Muro, Claudia Burr. Dona Josefa y sus Conspiraciones. 2005. (Ya Veras Ser.). (SPA., Illus.). (J). (gr. 3-5). pap. 9.95 *(978-968-7381-29-9(9))* Tecolote, Ediciones, S.A. de C.V. MEX. Dist: Iaconi, Mariuccia Bk. Imports.

Osborne, Mary Pope. Shadow of the Shark. Murdocca, Sal, illus. 2017. (Magic Tree House (R) Merlin Mission Ser.: 25). 144p. (J). (gr. 2-5). 5.99 *(978-0-553-51084-3(3)*, Random Hse. Bks. for Young Readers) Random Hse. Children's Bks.

—Soccer on Sunday. Murdocca, Sal, illus. 2016. (Magic Tree House (R) Merlin Mission Ser.: 24). 144p. (J). (gr. 2-5). 6.99 *(978-0-307-98056-4(1)*, Random Hse. Bks. for Young Readers) Random Hse. Children's Bks.

Paulsen, Gary. The Crossing. 2005. (ENG.). 128p. (J). (gr. 2-5). per. 7.99 *(978-0-439-78661-4(4)*, Scholastic Paperbacks) Scholastic, Inc.

Pedraza, M. Eugenia Rueda. Nico's Voyage. 2013. 32p. pap. *(978-1-4602-2360-4(8))* FriesenPress.

Pequeña the Burro: Evaluation Guide. 2006. (J). *(978-1-55942-420-2(6))* Witcher Productions.

Petretti, Silvia I. Rachel's Easter Vacation in Mexico. James, Elizabeth, ed. 2011. (Illus.). 50p. (J). pap. 14.99 *(978-1-931671-37-8(0))* Ma"at American Aborigine Tribal Nation.

Pidutti, Nancy L. José the Donkey. 2013. 36p. pap. 16.99 *(978-1-4497-9213-8(8)*, WestBow Pr.) Author Solutions, LLC.

Pugliano-Martin, Carol. Quetzacoatl Brings Corn to His People: A Legend from Mexico. 2006. (J). pap. *(978-1-4108-7168-8(1))* Benchmark Education Co.

Ralphson, G. Harvey. Boy Scouts in Mexico. 2007. 112p. (gr. 4-7). per. *(978-1-4068-3728-5(8))* Echo Library.

—Boy Scouts in Mexico or on Guard with un. 2005. pap. 27.95 *(978-1-885529-52-7(X))* Stevens Publishing.

—Boy Scouts in Mexico,Or on Guard with Uncle Sam. 2003. 136p. pap. 14.99 *(978-1-59224-085-2(2))* Wildside Pr., LLC.

Ralphson, George Harvey. Boy Scouts in Mexico: Or, on Guard with Uncle Sam. 2017. (ENG., Illus.). (J). 23.95 *(978-1-374-83158-2(1))*; pap. 13.95 *(978-1-374-83157-5(3))* Capital Communications, Inc.

Resau, Laura. Red Glass. (ENG.). 2009. 304p. (YA). (gr. 7). pap. 9.99 *(978-0-440-24025-9(5)*, Delacorte Bks. for Young Readers) 2007. 275p. (J). (gr. 6-8). lib. bdg. 24.94 *(978-0-385-90464-3(9)*, Delacorte Pr.) Random Hse. Children's Bks.

Rice, Dona Herwick & Isecke, Harriet. Remember the Alamo, 1 vol. rev. ed. 2009. (Reader's Theater Ser.). (ENG., Illus.). 32p. (gr. 3-8). pap. 11.99 *(978-1-4333-0541-2(0))* Teacher Created Materials, Inc.

Richardson, Arleta. Across the Border. 2016. (Beyond the Orphan Train Ser.: 4). (ENG.). 192p. (J). (gr. 3-6). pap. 7.99 *(978-0-7814-1358-9(3)*, 136205) Cook, David C.

Romeu, Emma. Gregorio Vuelve a Mexico. 2003. (SPA., Illus.). 148p. (J). (gr. 5-8). pap. 9.95 *(978-968-19-0367-1(6))* Santillana USA Publishing Co., Inc.

Rosas, Alejandro. Diario de Aurora. 2003. (Mexican Diaries). (SPA.). 164p. (J). pap. *(978-968-406-990-9(1)*, SOM7961) Planeta Mexicana Editorial S. A. de C. V. MEX. Dist: Lectorum Pubns., Inc.

Rosenthal, S. L. Mama, Where Do Our Butterflies Go in the Winter? 2011. 40p. pap. 24.95 *(978-1-4560-7498-2(9))* America Star Bks.

Rothshank, Brooke, illus. Cups Held Out. 2006. 40p. (J). (gr. -1-3). per. 12.99 *(978-0-8361-9316-9(4))* Herald Pr.

Ryan, Pam Muñoz. Becoming Naomi león (Scholastic Gold) 2005. (ENG.). 272p. (J). (gr. 4-7). reprint ed. per. 8.99 *(978-0-439-26997-1(0)*, Scholastic Paperbacks) Scholastic, Inc.

—Esperanza Rising. 2016. (gr. 5-8). lib. bdg. 17.20 *(978-0-613-53807-7(2))* Turtleback.

—Mice & Beans. Cepeda, Joe, illus. 2005. (gr. -1-3). lib. bdg. 17.00 *(978-0-7569-5089-7(9))* Perfection Learning Corp.

Sanchez, Juanita L. Pancho the Green Parrot Lays an Egg, 1 vol. Ramirez, Samuel, illus. 2009. 24p. pap. 24.95 *(978-1-61546-150-9(7))* America Star Bks.

Sanderson, Nancy. Horse of the Four Winds. 2011. 152p. (gr. 10-12). pap. 14.50 *(978-1-4634-4802-8(3))* AuthorHouse.

Schafer, Steve. The Border. (ENG.). (YA). (gr. 8-12). 2018. 368p. pap. 10.99 *(978-1-4926-6088-0(4))* 2017. 360p. 17.99 *(978-1-4926-4683-9(0))* Sourcebooks, Inc.

Scieszka, Jon. Me Oh Maya. McCauley, Adam, illus. 2005. (Time Warp Trio Ser.: No. 13). 69p. (gr. 2-6). 15.00 *(978-0-7569-5060-6(0))* Perfection Learning Corp.

—Me Oh Maya #13. McCauley, Adam, illus. 2005. (Time Warp Trio Ser.: 13). 96p. (J). (gr. 2-4). 5.99 *(978-0-14-240300-6(8)*, Puffin Books) Penguin Young Readers Group.

Sclafani, Terry. The Thompson Twins Western Adventure. 2009. 114p. pap. 11.95 *(978-1-4327-3783-2(X))* Outskirts Pr., Inc.

Silva, Carlos. Diario de Fernando. 2003. (Mexican Diaries). (SPA., Illus.). 172p. (J). pap. *(978-970-690-244-3(9))* Planeta Mexicana Editorial S. A. de C. V.

Smith, Emilie & Tejada, Margarita Kenefic. Viva Zapata, 1 vol. Czernecki, Stefan, illus. 2009. (ENG.). 32p. (J). (gr. -1-k).

14.95 *(978-1-896580-55-5(6))* Tradewind Bks. CAN. Dist: Orca Bk. Pubs. USA.
Spenser & Brooks, Melanie. Spenser Via a el Paso. Jacobsen, Amie, illus. 2010. (ENG.). 32p. (J). 14.95 *(978-0-9817598-5-2(8),* e87219c4-b810-49f7-81c2-eb35fd1a4e0b) Simple Fish Bk. Co., LLC.
Stalcup. La Loncheria. Arroyo, illus. 2008. (SPA & ENG.). 28p. (J). pap. 8.95 *(978-1-60448-006-1(8))* Lectura Bks.
—La Loncheria. Arroyo, illus. 2008. (SPA & ENG.). 28p. (J). 15.95 *(978-1-60448-005-4(X))* Lectura Bks.
Stavans, Ilan. Golemito. Villegas, Teresa, illus. 2013. (ENG.). 32p. (J). 16.95 *(978-1-58838-292-4(3),* 8804, NewSouth Bks.) NewSouth, Inc.
Stokes, Erica M. Sports of Mexico. 2009. (Mexico: Beautiful Land, Diverse People Ser.). (Illus.). 64p. (YA). (gr. 7-12). 21.95 *(978-1-4222-0654-6(8))* Mason Crest.
Stork, Francisco X. Disappeared. 2017. (ENG.). 336p. (YA). (gr. 7-7). 17.99 *(978-0-545-94447-2(3),* Scholastic Pr.) Scholastic, Inc.
Sutton, Laurie S. The Mystery of the Aztec Tomb. 1 vol. Neely, Scott, illus. 2014. (You Choose Stories: Scooby-Doo Ser.). (ENG.). 112p. (J). (gr. 2-6). 32.65 *(978-1-4342-9127-1(8),* 125572, Stone Arch Bks.) Capstone.
Titus, Eve. Basil in Mexico. Galdone, Paul, illus. 2016. (Great Mouse Detective Ser.: 3). (ENG.). 112p. (J). (gr. 1-4). pap. 6.99 *(978-1-4814-6407-9(8),* Aladdin) Simon & Schuster Children's Publishing.
Tonatiuh, Duncan. Dear Primo: A Letter to My Cousin. 2010. (ENG., Illus.). 32p. (J). (gr. k-2). 18.99 *(978-0-8109-3872-4(3),* 661901, Abrams Bks. for Young Readers) Abrams, Inc.
Toretto, Jordana. The Runaway Children. 2013. 30p. pap. 16.95 *(978-1-63004-706-1(6))* America Star Bks.
Torres, Eliseo & Sawyer, Timothy L. Stories of Mexico's Independence Days & Other Bilingual Children's Fables. Ramirez, Herman, illus. 2005. (ENG.). 70p. (J). (gr. 3-7). pap. 16.95 *(978-0-8263-3886-0(0),* P123362) Univ. of New Mexico Pr.
Trottier, Maxine. Migrant. 1 vol. Arsenault, Isabelle, illus. 2011. (ENG.). 40p. (J). (gr. -1-2). 18.95 *(978-0-88899-975-7(5))* Groundwood Bks. CAN. Dist: Publishers Group West (PGW).
Unrau, Adela. A Big Change. 1 vol. Friesen, Anni, illus. 2010. 16p. pap. 24.95 *(978-1-4489-7672-0(3))* PublishAmerica, Inc.
Vernon, Ursula. Dani Bocafuego. la Cueva Del Murcielago Gigante. 2012. (SPA.). 204p. (J). (gr. 4-6). pap. 20.99 *(978-84-246-3599-2(X))* La Galera, S.A. Editorial ESP. Dist: Lectorum Pubns., Inc.
—Dragonbreath #4: Lair of the Bat Monster. 4th ed. (Dragonbreath Ser.: 4). 208p. (J). (gr. 3-7). 2014. pap. 8.99 *(978-0-14-751320-5(0),* Puffin Books) 2011. 14.99 *(978-0-8037-3525-5(1),* Dial Bks) Penguin Young Readers Group.
—Lair of the Bat Monster. 2014. (Dragonbreath Ser.: 4). lib. bdg. 17.20 *(978-0-606-35711-1(4))* Turtleback.
Villalpando, Jose Manuel. Diario de Clara Eugenia (1864-67) 2003. (Diarios Mexicanos Coleccion). (SPA., Illus.). 174p. (J). (gr. 5-8). pap. *(978-968-406-900-8(6),* SOM7940) Planeta Mexicana Editorial S. A. de C. V.
Villanueva, Pedro. Chronicle of a New Kid. 2017. (Text Connections Guided Close Reading Ser.). (J). (gr. 1). *(978-1-4900-1825-6(5))* Benchmark Education Co.
Walker, Kathryn. Unsolved! 2008. (J). (gr. 4-7). *(978-0-7787-4140-4(0))* Crabtree Publishing Co.
Wells, Marcia. Eddie Red Undercover: Mystery in Mayan Mexico. Calo, Marcos, illus. 2016. (Eddie Red Undercover Ser.: 2). (ENG.). 224p. (J). (gr. 5-7). pap. 7.99 *(978-0-544-66850-8(2),* 1625472, Clarion Bks.) HarperCollins Pubs.
—Mystery in Mayan Mexico. 2016. (Eddie Red Undercover Ser.: 2). lib. bdg. 18.40 *(978-0-606-39664-6(0))* Turtleback.
Williams, Geoffrey T. The Devil Fish. Artful Doodlers, illus. Campbell, Tom, photos by. 2008. (Save Our Seas Adventure Bks.). (ENG.). 64p. (J). (gr. 4-7). 8.95 *(978-0-9800444-1-6(3))* Save Our Seas, Ltd.
Zeleny, Sylvia. The Everything I Have Lost. 1 vol. 2020. (ENG.). 256p. (YA). (gr. 9-12). 15.95 *(978-1-947627-17-8(1),* 23353382, Cinco Puntos Press) Lee & Low Bks., Inc.
Zepeda, Monique. Las Pinatas. Graullera, Fabiola, illus.Tr. of Pinatas. (SPA.). 26p. (J). (gr. 3-5). pap. 6.95 *(978-968-19-0612-2(8))* Santillana USA Publishing Co., Inc.
Zevin, Gabrielle. Because It Is My Blood: A Novel. 2013. (Birthright Ser.: 2). (ENG.). 384p. (YA). (gr. 7). pap. 19.99 *(978-1-250-03422-9(1),* 900120595) Square Fish.

MEXICO—FOREIGN RELATIONS

Porterfield, Jason. The Treaty of Guadalupe Hidalgo 1848: A Primary Source Examination of the Treaty That Ended the Mexican-American War. 2009. (Primary Sources of American Treaties Ser.). 64p. (gr. 5-8). 58.50 *(978-1-60851-516-5(8))* Rosen Publishing Group, Inc., The.
Yomtov, Nelson. The United States & Mexico. 2013. (Cornerstones of Freedom™, Third Ser.). (ENG., Illus.). 64p. (J). pap. 8.95 *(978-0-531-21963-8(1))* Scholastic Library Publishing.

MEXICO—HISTORY

Abnett, Dan. Hernán Cortés y la Caída Del Imperio Azteca. 1 vol. 2009. (Historietas Juveniles: Biografías (Jr. Graphic Biographies) Ser.). (SPA., Illus.). 24p. (gr. 2-3). pap. 10.60 *(978-1-4358-3314-2(7),* 7d898923-96ae-408d-bbf0-3829d841840c) Rosen Publishing Group, Inc., The.
—Hernán Cortés y la Caída Del Imperio Azteca. 1 vol. Abregón, José María, tr. 2009. (Historietas Juveniles: Biografías (Jr. Graphic Biographies) Ser.). (SPA., Illus.). 24p. (J). (gr. 2-3). 28.93 *(978-1-4358-8560-8(0),* 6cab2766-f1ef-4163-b64a-cf3e2abf23f5) Rosen Publishing Group, Inc., The.
Avery, Logan. El Parque Nacional Tulum: Suma. rev. ed. 2019. (Mathematics in the Real World Ser.). (SPA., Illus.). 24p. (J). (gr. 1-2). pap. 9.99 *(978-1-4258-2848-6(5))* Teacher Created Materials, Inc.
—Travel Adventures: Tulum National Park: Addition (Grade 1) 2018. (Mathematics in the Real World Ser.). (ENG., Illus.). 24p. (J). (gr. 1-2). pap. 9.99 *(978-1-4258-5686-1(1))* Teacher Created Materials, Inc.
Aykroyd, Clarissa. Meeting Future Challenges: The Government of Mexico. 2014. (Mexico: Leading the Southern Hemisphere Ser.: 16). 64p. (J). (gr. 7-18). lib. bdg. 22.95 *(978-1-4222-3223-1(9))* Mason Crest.
Bernay, Emma & Berne, Emma Carlson. Immigrants from Mexico & Central America. 2018. (Immigration Today Ser.). (ENG., Illus.). 32p. (J). (gr. 3-6). lib. bdg. 27.99 *(978-1-5435-1383-7(2),* 137788, Capstone Pr.) Capstone.
Bull, Mary P. It's Cool! Early Inhabitants of Santa Cruz Valley. 2003. (ENG., Illus.). 54p. pap. 28.50 *(978-1-4120-0178-6(1))* Trafford Publishing.
Burt, Janet. Mexico's Pacific North States. 2014. (Mexico: Leading the Southern Hemisphere Ser.: 16). 64p. (J). (gr. 7-18). lib. bdg. 22.95 *(978-1-4222-3225-5(5))* Mason Crest.
Cain, Marie Mowery. George Takes a Road Trip, Mexico. 2013. (Big Books, Red Ser.). (ENG & SPA., Illus.). 16p. pap. 33.00 *(978-1-59246-206-3(5))* Big Books, by George!
Carew-Miller, Anna. Famous People of Mexican History. 2014. (Mexico: Leading the Southern Hemisphere Ser.: 16). 64p. (J). (gr. 7-18). lib. bdg. 22.95 *(978-1-4222-3215-6(8))* Mason Crest.
—Vital & Creative: The Art & Architecture of Mexico. 2014. (Mexico: Leading the Southern Hemisphere Ser.: 16). 64p. (J). (gr. 7-18). lib. bdg. 22.95 *(978-1-4222-3219-4(0))* Mason Crest.
Celebrate! Mexico. 2009. (Celebrate! (Chelsea Clubhouse) Ser.). (ENG.). 32p. (gr. 4-6). 28.00 *(978-1-60413-267-0(1),* P169970, Chelsea Clubhse.) Infobase Holdings, Inc.
Cobb, Allan B. Mexico: A Primary Source Cultural Guide. 2009. (Primary Sources of World Cultures Ser.). 128p. (gr. 4-5). 79.90 *(978-1-60851-927-9(9))* Rosen Publishing Group, Inc., The.
Conklin, Wendy. Moctezuma: Aztec Ruler. 1 vol. rev. ed. 2007. (Social Studies: Informational Text Ser.). (ENG.). 32p. (J). (gr. 4-8). pap. 11.99 *(978-0-7439-0457-5(5))* Teacher Created Materials, Inc.
Dawson, Imogen. Food & Feasts with the Aztecs. 2004. (Illus.). 32p. (J). (gr. 4-8). reprint ed. 14.00 *(978-0-7567-7143-0(9))* DIANE Publishing Co.
Field, Randi. Mexico's Gulf States. 2014. (Mexico: Leading the Southern Hemisphere Ser.: 16). 64p. (J). (gr. 7-18). lib. bdg. 22.95 *(978-1-4222-3224-8(7))* Mason Crest.
Gagne, Tammy. We Visit Mexico. 2010. (Your Land & My Land Ser.). (Illus.). 64p. (J). (gr. 3-6). lib. bdg. 33.95 *(978-1-58415-889-9(1))* Mitchell Lane Pubs.
Garbus, Julia, ed. Mexico. 1 vol. 2015. (Introducing Issues with Opposing Viewpoints Ser.). (ENG., Illus.). 144p. (gr. 7-10). lib. bdg. 43.63 *(978-0-7377-7237-1(9),* abe6c54d-8908-4ab0-a5e0-2f183d9169c3, Greenhaven Publishing) Greenhaven Publishing LLC.
García Dávila, Sandra. Los Antepasados Para Ninos. 2018. (SPA.). 142p. (J). (gr. 4-8). pap. 6.95 *(978-970-643-359-6(7))* Selector, S.A. de C.V. MEX. Dist: Spanish Pubs., LLC.
George, Lynn. Teotihuacan: Designing an Ancient Mexican City: Calculating Perimeters & Areas of Squares & Rectangles. 2009. (PowerMath: Proficiency Ser.). 32p. (gr. 4-5). 47.90 *(978-1-60851-400-7(5),* PowerKids Pr.) Rosen Publishing Group, Inc., The.
Goddard, Phyllis M. Sprating Silver: Recognizing a Sprating Silver Treasure: a Field Guide. 2003. (Illus.). 152p. per. 39.95 *(978-0-9740907-3-3(5))* Keenan Tyler Paine.
Hart, Paul. Emiliano Zapata: Mexico's Social Revolutionary. 2017. (World in a Life Ser.). (ENG., Illus.). 352p. (C). pap. 39.99 *(978-0-19-068808-0(4))* Oxford Univ. Pr., Inc.
Higgins, Nadia. Spanish Missions of the Old West. 2006. (Events in American History Ser.). (Illus.). 48p. (YA). (gr. 3-6). lib. bdg. 31.36 *(978-1-60044-128-8(9))* Rourke Educational Media.
Hudak, Heather C. A Refugee's Journey from Guatemala. 2017. (Leaving My Homeland Ser.). (Illus.). 32p. (J). (gr. 4-4). *(978-0-7787-3673-8(3))* Crabtree Publishing Co.
Hunter, Amy N. Ancient Land with a Fascinating Past: The History of Mexico. 2014. (Mexico: Leading the Southern Hemisphere Ser.: 16). 64p. (J). (gr. 7-18). lib. bdg. 22.95 *(978-1-4222-3218-7(2))* Mason Crest.
—The History of Mexico. 2009. (Mexico: Beautiful Land, Diverse People Ser.). (Illus.). 64p. (YA). (gr. 7-12). 21.95 *(978-1-4222-0653-9(X))* Mason Crest.
Hutchison, Patricia. Explore Mexico: 12 Key Facts. 2019. (Country Profiles Ser.). (ENG., Illus.). 32p. (J). (gr. 3-6). 9.95 *(978-1-63235-613-0(9),* 13962); lib. bdg. 32.80 *(978-1-63235-557-7(4),* 13952) Bookstaves, LLC. (12-Story Library).
Imery-Garcia, Ash. How Mexican Immigrants Made America Home. 1 vol. 2018. (Coming to America: the History of Immigration to the United States Ser.). (ENG., Illus.). 80p. (gr. 6-6). 38.80 *(978-1-5081-8132-3(2),* c9dcf589-ac41-4b34-b47d-9465179c9906, Rosen Reference) Rosen Publishing Group, Inc., The.
Ingram, Scott. Mexican Americans. 1 vol. 2006. (World Almanac(r) Library of American Immigration Ser.). (ENG., Illus.). 48p. (gr. 5-8). pap. 15.05 *(978-0-8368-7329-0(7),* d40b2e85-ab11-4281-aa0d-a22c10ac7b7a); lib. bdg. 33.67 *(978-0-8368-7316-0(5),* 0f6605b8-5111-41ba-b996-6c08c8917a7e) Stevens, Gareth Publishing LLLP. (Gareth Stevens Secondary Library).
Jermyn, Leslie & Conboy, Fiona. Welcome to Mexico. 1 vol. 2011. (Welcome to My Country Ser.). (ENG.). 48p. (gr. 3-3). 31.21 *(978-1-60870-157-5(3),* 3d72de39-0863-4df0-b354-40e499691fb1) Cavendish Square Publishing LLC.
Jordan, Elisa. Art & Culture: Exploring Mexican Artifacts: Measurement (Grade 5) 2018. (Mathematics in the Real World Ser.). (ENG., Illus.). 32p. (J). (gr. 4-8). pap. 11.99 *(978-1-4258-5811-7(2))* Teacher Created Materials, Inc.
Jovinelly, Joann. The Crafts & Culture of the Aztecs. 2009. (Crafts of the Ancient World Ser.). 48p. (gr. 5-8). 58.50 *(978-1-61512-064-2(5),* Rosen Reference) Rosen Publishing Group, Inc., The.
Juarez, Christine. Mexico. 1 vol. 2013. (Countries Ser.). (ENG.). 24p. (J). (gr. -1-2). pap. 6.95 *(978-1-4765-3516-6(7),* 123567, Pebble) Capstone.
Kalman, Bobbie & Walker, Niki. Conoce México. 2009. (Conoce Mi País Ser.). (SPA.). 32p. (J). (gr. 2-5). pap. *(978-0-7787-8215-5(8))* Crabtree Publishing Co.
—Spotlight on Mexico. 2007. (Spotlight on My Country Ser.). (ENG., Illus.). 32p. (J). (gr. 4-7). pap. *(978-0-7787-3477-2(3))* Crabtree Publishing Co.
Kaminski, Leah. Hola, Mexico. 2019. (Countries of the World Ser.). (ENG., Illus.). 48p. (J). (gr. 4-8). pap. 17.07 *(978-1-5341-5090-4(0),* 213667); lib. bdg. 39.21 *(978-1-5341-4804-8(3),* 213666) Cherry Lake Publishing.
Kent, Deborah. Mexico. 2011. (Enchantment of the World Ser.). (ENG.). 144p. (J). (gr. 5-9). lib. bdg. 40.00 *(978-0-531-25355-7(4))* Scholastic Library Publishing.
King, David C. Projects about the Ancient Aztecs. 1 vol. 2007. (Hands-On History Ser.). (ENG., Illus.). 48p. (gr. 3-3). lib. bdg. 34.07 *(978-0-7614-2256-3(0),* b0e5e12c-d7d3-4713-95cd-6922d265908a) Cavendish Square Publishing LLC.
Kopp, Megan. Mexico. 2017. (Illus.). 32p. (J). *(978-1-5105-0835-4(X))* SmartBook Media, Inc.
—Mexico. 2014. (J). *(978-1-4896-1022-5(7))* Weigl Pubs., Inc.
Lassieur, Allison. Maya Civilization. 2019. (Civilizations of the World Ser.). (ENG., Illus.). 32p. (J). (gr. 3-5). pap. 9.95 *(978-1-64185-828-1(1),* 1641858281); lib. bdg. 31.35 *(978-1-64185-759-8(5),* 1641857595) North Star Editions. (Focus Readers).
Levy, Janey. Mexico. 1 vol. 2005. (Content-Area Literacy Collections). (ENG.). 24p. (gr. 3-4). pap. 8.85 *(978-1-4042-5669-9(5),* 46793680-730c-40ef-a826-790c8858006e) Rosen Publishing Group, Inc., The.
Lindeen, Mary. Welcome to Mexico! 2011. (Wonder Readers Fluent Level Ser.). (ENG.). 16p. (gr. -1-2). pap. 35.94 *(978-1-4296-8202-2(7),* Capstone Pr.) Capstone.
—Welcome to North America. 1 vol. (Wonder Readers: Social Studies). (ENG.). (gr. -1-2). 2012. 20p. (J). lib. bdg. 25.32 *(978-1-4296-9617-3(6),* 120533) 2011. 16p. pap. 35.94 *(978-1-4296-8204-6(3))* Capstone. (Capstone Pr.).
MacLeod, Deirdre Day. Mexico's Central States. 2014. (Mexico: Leading the Southern Hemisphere Ser.: 16). 64p. (J). (gr. 7-18). lib. bdg. 22.95 *(978-1-4222-3228-6(X))* Mason Crest.
—Mexico's Northern States. 2014. (Mexico: Leading the Southern Hemisphere Ser.: 16). 64p. (J). (gr. 7-18). lib. bdg. 22.95 *(978-1-4222-3227-9(1))* Mason Crest.
Madonna, Colleen & Williams, Flood. Beautiful Diversity: The Geography of Mexico. 2014. (Mexico: Leading the Southern Hemisphere Ser.: 16). 64p. (J). (gr. 7-18). lib. bdg. 22.95 *(978-1-4222-3214-9(X))* Mason Crest.
—Fiesta! the Festivals of Mexico. 2014. (Mexico: Leading the Southern Hemisphere Ser.: 16). 64p. (J). (gr. 7-18). lib. bdg. 22.95 *(978-1-4222-3217-0(4))* Mason Crest.
—Spirit of a Nation: The People of Mexico. 2014. (Mexico: Leading the Southern Hemisphere Ser.: 16). 64p. (J). (gr. 7-18). lib. bdg. 22.95 *(978-1-4222-3216-3(6))* Mason Crest.
Maloy, Jackie. The Ancient Maya. 2009. (True Book(tm), a — Ancient Civilizations Ser.). (ENG.). 48p. (J). (gr. 2-5). 31.00 *(978-0-531-25229-1(9))* Scholastic Library Publishing.
—The Ancient Maya (a True Book: Ancient Civilizations) 2010. (True Book (Relaunch) Ser.). (ENG., Illus.). 48p. (J). (gr. 3-5). pap. 6.95 *(978-0-531-24110-3(6),* Children's Pr.) Scholastic Library Publishing.
Marcovitz, Hal. Pancho Villa. 2003. (Great Hispanic Heritage Ser.). (ENG., Illus.). 112p. (gr. 6-12). 30.00 *(978-0-7910-7257-8(6),* P113774, Facts On File) Infobase Holdings, Inc.
Marsico, Katie. The Colorado River. 2013. (Explorer Library: Social Studies Explorer Ser.). (ENG.). 32p. (gr. 4-8). (J). pap. 14.21 *(978-1-62431-038-6(9),* 202509); (Illus.). 32.07 *(978-1-62431-014-0(1),* 202507) Cherry Lake Publishing.
—The Rio Grande. 2013. (Explorer Library: Social Studies Explorer Ser.). (ENG.). 32p. (gr. 4-8). (J). pap. 14.21 *(978-1-62431-036-2(2),* 202501); (Illus.). 32.07 *(978-1-62431-012-6(5),* 202499) Cherry Lake Publishing.
McCullough, Naomi V. The Technology of the Aztecs. 1 vol. 2016. (Ancient Innovations Ser.). (ENG., Illus.). 64p. (J). (gr. 6-6). 35.93 *(978-1-5026-2239-6(4),* 39cf373b-1888-49fa-8286-ebf8416c517a) Cavendish Square Publishing LLC.
McDaniel, Jan. Zesty & Colorful Cuisine: The Food of Mexico. 2014. (Mexico: Leading the Southern Hemisphere Ser.: 16). 64p. (J). (gr. 7-18). lib. bdg. 22.95 *(978-1-4222-3222-4(0))* Mason Crest.
McNamara, Margaret. Discover Mexico. 2006. (J). pap. *(978-1-4108-6459-8(6))* Benchmark Education Co.
The Mexican Revolution. 2011. (ENG., Illus.). 128p. (gr. 9). 35.00 *(978-1-60413-459-9(3),* P189849, Facts On File) Infobase Holdings, Inc.
Mexican Revolution 2003. (Illus.). (YA). spiral bd. *(978-0-9759194-6-0(6))* Publicaciones Papelandia.
Mexico: Leading the Southern Hemisphere. 2015. (Illus.). (J). *(978-1-4222-3213-2(1))* Mason Crest.
Mexico's Desert Country 2003. (Illus.). (YA). spiral bd. *(978-0-9759194-7-7(4))* Publicaciones Papelandia.
Morris, Ting. Arts & Crafts of the Aztecs & Maya. Young, Emma, illus. 2006. (Arts & Crafts of the Ancient World Ser.). 32p. (J). lib. bdg. 28.50 *(978-1-58340-915-2(7),* 1262694) Black Rabbit Bks.
Nantus, Sheryl. Mexico's Pacific South States. 2014. (Mexico: Leading the Southern Hemisphere Ser.: 16). 64p. (J). (gr. 7-18). lib. bdg. 22.95 *(978-1-4222-3226-2(3))* Mason Crest.
Nicholson, Dorinda Makanaonalani. The School the Aztec Eagle Built. 1 vol. 2016. (ENG., Illus.). 40p. (J). (gr. 3-7). 18.95 *(978-1-60060-440-9(4),* leelowbooks) Lee & Low Bks., Inc.
Noticias de Fin de Siglo. 2005. (SPA.). (J). pap. *(978-968-7381-10-7(8))* Tecolote, Ediciones, S.A. de C.V.
Oachs, Emily Rose. Ancient Aztecs. 2020. (Ancient Civilizations Ser.). (ENG., Illus.). 32p. (J). (gr. 3-8). pap. 8.99 *(978-1-61891-857-4(5),* 12586, Blastoff! Discovery) Bellwether Media.
Ortiz, Lars. Explore Mexico: A Coco Discovery Book. 2019. (Disney Learning Discovery Bks.). (ENG., Illus.). 48p. (J). (gr. 2-5). pap. 8.99 *(978-1-5415-7828-9(7),* 9781541578289); lib. bdg. 31.99 *(978-1-5415-7827-2(9),* 9781541578272) Lerner Publishing Group. (Lerner Pubns.).
Palos, Lilia. Acercate a la Historia 3 de las Raices Indigenas al Mexico Contemprineo Actores Sociales, Vida Cotidiana, Mentalidades y Cultura. 2003. (SPA.). 350p. (YA). *(978-968-7903-42-2(2))* Edere, S. A. de C. V.
Parker, Lewis K. Why Mexican Immigrants Came to America. 2009. (Coming to America Ser.). 24p. (gr. 2-3). 42.50 *(978-1-61511-887-8(X),* PowerKids Pr.) Rosen Publishing Group, Inc., The.
Perkins, Chloe. Living in ... Mexico: Ready-To-Read Level 2. Woolley, Tom, illus. 2016. (Living in... Ser.). (ENG.). 32p. (J). (gr. k-2). pap. 4.99 *(978-1-4814-6050-7(1),* Simon Spotlight) Simon Spotlight.
Pliego, Jane. La Reforma para Ninos. (SPA.). (J). 8.98 *(978-970-643-394-7(5))* Selector, S.A. de C.V. MEX. Dist: Spanish Pubs., LLC.
Pohl, Kathleen. Descubramos México (Looking at Mexico). 1 vol. 2007. (Descubramos Países Del Mundo (Looking at Countries) Ser.). (SPA.). 32p. (gr. 2-4). pap. 11.50 *(978-0-8368-8193-6(1),* c64fd735-10c5-419a-b79d-afdece31d358); (Illus.). lib. bdg. 28.67 *(978-0-8368-8186-8(9),* 1d8df9d2-285f-4f42-9bee-83b6a857a501) Stevens, Gareth Publishing LLLP. (Gareth Stevens Learning Library).
Ponto, Joanna & Gnojewski, Carol. Day of the Dead. 1 vol. 2016. (Story of Our Holidays Ser.). (ENG., Illus.). 32p. (gr. 3-3). pap. 11.52 *(978-0-7660-7642-6(3),* 9b173964-0d8c-4bf9-b2c3-ece67e9b3bf9f) Enslow Publishing, LLC.
Reed, Ellis M. Roswell. 2019. (Aliens Ser.). (ENG., Illus.). 32p. (J). (gr. 4-6). 28.65 *(978-1-5435-7107-3(7),* 140399) Capstone.
Revolucion a Todo Vapor (Rev. Full Stream Ahead) 2005. (SPA.). (J). pap. *(978-968-7381-08-4(6))* Tecolote, Ediciones, S.A. de C.V.
Rosenthal, Cynthia. A Day in Mexico. 2013. (InfoMax Readers Ser.). (ENG.). 24p. (J). (gr. 2-3). pap. 49.50 *(978-1-4777-2316-6(1));* (Illus.). pap. 8.25 *(978-1-4777-2315-9(3),* a3e5efd2-32c9-42c1-b26c-a1c9c47245d6) Rosen Publishing Group, Inc., The. (Rosen Classroom).
Rudolph, Jessica. Mexico. 2015. (Countries We Come From Ser.). (ENG., Illus.). 32p. (J). (gr. k-3). lib. bdg. 28.50 *(978-1-62724-853-2(6))* Bearport Publishing Co., Inc.
Sanna, Ellyn. Mexican Americans' Role in the United States: A History of Pride, a Future of Hope. 2007. (Hispanic Heritage Ser.). (Illus.). 112p. (YA). (gr. 4-7). lib. bdg. 22.95 *(978-1-59084-926-2(4))* Mason Crest.
—Mexican Facts & Figures. 2014. (Mexico: Leading the Southern Hemisphere Ser.: 16). 64p. (J). (gr. 7-18). lib. bdg. 22.95 *(978-1-4222-3229-3(8))* Mason Crest.
Savery, Annabel. Mexico. 2011. (ENG., Illus.). 32p. (J). pap. 10.95 *(978-1-77092-026-2(9))* Saunders Bk. Co. CAN. Dist: RiverStream Publishing.
Scholl, Elizabeth J. The Mayan Civilization. 2009. (How'd They Do That? Ser.). (Illus.). 64p. (J). (gr. 4-8). lib. bdg. 33.95 *(978-1-58415-822-6(0))* Mitchell Lane Pubs.
Schuh, Mari. Crayola (r) Colors of Mexico. 2020. (Crayola (r) Country Colors Ser.). (ENG., Illus.). 24p. (J). (gr. k-3). pap. 6.99 *(978-1-5415-8717-5(0),* 4921bbf2-dc5c-4e21-824c-1b9863dba583); lib. bdg. 29.32 *(978-1-5415-7264-5(5),* 304f6a28-2004-4634-9f72-2a8db11f78a6) Lerner Publishing Group. (Lerner Pubns.).
Senker, Cath. Mexico. 1 vol. 2016. (Land & the People Ser.). (ENG.). 48p. (gr. 5-5). pap. 15.05 *(978-1-4824-5099-6(2),* 48dc4c21-392e-41bf-bf65-9db6ef6cd02a) Stevens, Gareth Publishing LLLP.
Serrano, Francisco. The Poet King of Tezcoco: A Great Leader of Ancient Mexico. 1 vol. Serrano, Pablo, illus. 2007. (ENG.). 48p. (J). (gr. 3-6). 18.95 *(978-0-88899-787-6(6))* Groundwood Bks. CAN. Dist: Publishers Group West (PGW).
Sexton, Colleen. Mexico. 2010. (Exploring Countries Ser.). (ENG., Illus.). 32p. (J). (gr. 3-7). lib. bdg. 27.95 *(978-1-60014-487-5(X),* Blastoff! Readers) Bellwether Media.
Simpson, Kathleen. Geography of Mexico: Text Pairs. 2008. (Bridges/Navigators Ser.). (J). (gr. 6). 94.00 *(978-1-4108-8439-8(2))* Benchmark Education Co.
Snedden, Robert. Aztec, Inca & Maya. 2009. (Technology in Times Past Ser.). (J). 32.80 *(978-1-59920-299-0(9))* Black Rabbit Bks.
Stein, R. Conrad. Ancient Mexico. 2011. (Story of Mexico Ser.). (Illus.). 144p. (gr. 7-12). 28.95 *(978-1-59935-161-2(7))* Reynolds, Morgan Inc.
—Emiliano Zapata & the Mexican Revolution. 2011. (Story of Mexico Ser.). (Illus.). 144p. (gr. 7-12). 28.95 *(978-1-59935-163-6(3))* Reynolds, Morgan Inc.
—Modern Mexico. 2011. (Story of Mexico Ser.). (Illus.). 144p. (gr. 7-12). 28.95 *(978-1-59935-162-9(5))* Reynolds, Morgan Inc.
—The Story of Mexico Set, vols. 8, vol. 8. Incl. Ancient Mexico. (Illus.). 144p. (gr. 7-12). 2011. 28.95 *(978-1-59935-161-2(7));* Benito Juarez & the French Intervention. (Illus.). 160p. (YA). (gr. 8-12). 2007. lib. bdg. 27.95 *(978-1-59935-052-3(1));* Cortes & the Spanish Conquest. (Illus.). 160p. (J). (gr. 3-7). 2007. lib. bdg. 27.95 *(978-1-59935-053-0(X));* Emiliano Zapata & the Mexican Revolution. (Illus.). 144p. (gr. 7-12). 2011. 28.95 *(978-1-59935-163-6(3));* Mexican-American War. 144p. (gr. 7-12). 2011. 28.95 *(978-1-59935-160-5(9));* Mexican Revolution. (Illus.). 160p. (YA). (gr. 7-18). 2007. lib. bdg. 27.95 *(978-1-59935-051-6(3));* Mexican War of Independence. (Illus.). 144p. (J). (gr. 3-7). 2007. lib. bdg. 27.95 *(978-1-59935-054-7(8));* Modern Mexico. (Illus.). 144p. (gr. 7-12). 2011. 28.95 *(978-1-59935-162-9(5));* 2007. Set lib. bdg. 231.60 *(978-1-59935-074-5(2))* Reynolds, Morgan Inc.
Stokes, Erica M. Finding a Financial Balance: The Economy of Mexico. 2014. (Mexico: Leading the Southern Hemisphere Ser.: 16). 64p. (J). (gr. 7-18). lib. bdg. 22.95 *(978-1-4222-3221-7(2))* Mason Crest.
—Sports of Mexico. 2007. (Mexico: Beautiful Land, Diverse People Ser.). 64p. (YA). (gr. 7-18). pap. 9.95 *(978-1-4222-0721-5(8))* Mason Crest.
—Victoria! the Sports of Mexico. 2014. (Mexico: Leading the Southern Hemisphere Ser.: 16). 64p. (J). (gr. 7-18). lib. bdg. 22.95 *(978-1-4222-3220-0(4))* Mason Crest.
Taylor, Trace. Mexico. 2010. pap. 39.62 *(978-1-61541-127-6(5))* American Reading Co.
Taylor, Trace & SáNchez, LucíA M. Mexico. 2010. pap. 39.62 *(978-1-61541-150-4(X))* American Reading Co.

Taylor, Trace & Sánchez, Lucía M. Mexico. 2015. (1Y Nuestro Mundo Ser.). (SPA.). 16p. (J). (gr. k-1). pap. 8.00 (978-1-61541-149-8(6)) American Reading Co.

Tieck, Sarah. Mexico, 1 vol. 2013. (Explore the Countries Ser.). (ENG.). 40p. (J). (gr. 2-5). lib. bdg. 35.64 (978-1-61783-816-3(0), 6937, Big Buddy Bks.) ABDO Publishing Co.

Trueba, Jose Luis. Descubre... Las Raices de Mexico. Cortes, Osvaldo, illus. 2004. (Ser. Descubre). (SPA.). 96p. (J). (gr. 3-5). pap. 18.95 (978-970-29-0508-0(7)) Santillana USA Publishing Co., Inc.

Trujillo, Francisco. Conquista para Ninos. (SPA.). (J). 7.98 (978-970-643-360-2(0)) Selector, S.A. de C.V. MEX. Dist: Spanish Pubs., LLC.

Wagner, Heather Lehr. Hernan Cortes. 2009. (Great Explorers Ser.). (ENG., Illus.). 120p. (gr. 6-12). 30.00 (978-1-60413-424-7(0), P173420, Facts On File) Infobase Holdings, Inc.

Zocchi, Judy. In Mexico. Brodie, Neale, illus. 2005. (Global Adventures I Ser.). 32p. (J). pap. 10.95 (978-1-59646-135-2(7)); lib. bdg. 21.65 (978-1-59646-002-7(4)) Dingles & Co.

—In Mexico/en México. Brodie, Neale, illus. 2005. (Global Adventures I Ser.).Tr. of En México. (ENG & SPA.). 32p. (J). pap. 10.95 (978-1-59646-137-6(3)); lib. bdg. 21.65 (978-1-59646-003-4(2)) Dingles & Co.

MEXICO—HISTORY—CONQUEST, 1519-1540

Abnett, Dan. Hernan Cortes & the Fall of the Aztec Empire. (Jr. Graphic Biographies Ser.). (ENG.). 24p. (gr. 2-3). 2009. (J). 47.90 (978-1-61513-819-7(6), PowerKids Pr.) 2006. (Illus.). (J). lib. bdg. 28.93 (978-1-4042-3391-1(1), 8dd7d5ac-b879-43a8-962f-3015d0941234) 2006. (Illus.). pap. 10.60 (978-1-4042-2144-4(1), 291fdcbf-63dd-4f3e-9328-6a9a06ba1f39, PowerKids Pr.) Rosen Publishing Group, Inc., The.

Anderson, Zachary. Hernán Cortés: Conquering the Aztec Empire, 1 vol. 2014. (Incredible Explorers Ser.). (ENG., Illus.). 64p. (YA). (gr. 7-7). 35.93 (978-1-5026-0129-2(X), 068e8eb1-db7a-401e-863a-205fd9309ce8) Cavendish Square Publishing LLC.

Calvert, Patricia. Hernando Cortés: Fortune Favored the Bold, 1 vol. 2003. (Great Explorations Ser.). (ENG., Illus.). 80p. (gr. 6-6). 36.93 (978-0-7614-1482-7(7), 23b38e04-f239-4fc7-8cf9-46020846fad4) Cavendish Square Publishing LLC.

Gaff, Jackie. Hernan Cortes: The Life of a Spanish Conquistador, 1 vol. 2005. (Graphic Nonfiction Biographies Ser.). (ENG., Illus.). 48p. (YA). (gr. 4-6). lib. bdg. 37.13 (978-1-4042-0244-3(7), 20aae60a-afcd-45a6-966f-d71cfc9486d4) Rosen Publishing Group, Inc., The.

Green, Carl R. Cortés: Conquering the Powerful Aztec Empire, 1 vol. 2009. (Great Explorers of the World Ser.). (ENG., Illus.). 112p. (gr. 6-7). 35.93 (978-1-59845-099-6(9), 5d911ead-c3fc-4a96-8038-2ff81f92b380) Enslow Publishing, LLC.

Johnson, Sylvia A. The Spanish Conquest of Mexico. 2009. (Pivotal Moments in History Ser.). (ENG.). 160p. (gr. 9-12). 38.60 (978-0-8225-9079-8(4)) Lerner Publishing Group.

Ramen, Fred. Hernan Cortes: The Conquest of Mexico & the Aztec Empire, 1 vol. 2003. (Library of Explorers & Exploration Ser.). (ENG., Illus.). 112p. (gr. 5-8). lib. bdg. 39.80 (978-0-8239-3622-9(8), de6f2735-acf7-4ede-8106-eb0d82485333, Rosen Reference) Rosen Publishing Group, Inc., The.

—Hernán Cortés: The Conquest of Mexico & the Aztec Empire. 2009. (Library of Explorers & Exploration Ser.). 112p. (gr. 5-8). 66.50 (978-1-60853-606-1(8), Rosen Reference) Rosen Publishing Group, Inc., The.

Schulz, Elizabeth. Montezuma II, 1 vol. 2017. (Great Military Leaders Ser.). (ENG.). 128p. (YA). (gr. 9-9). 47.36 (978-1-5026-2789-6(2), 922400b8-71f4-4451-b223-951ff9855275) Cavendish Square Publishing LLC.

Serrano, Francisco. La Malinche: The Princess Who Helped Cortés Conquer the Aztec Empire, 1 vol. Ouriou, Susan, tr. Serrano, Pablo, illus. 2012. (ENG.). 40p. (J). (gr. 4-7). 18.95 (978-1-55498-111-3(5)) Groundwood Bks. CAN. Dist: Publishers Group West (PGW).

Stein, R. Conrad. Cortes & the Spanish Conquest. 2007. (Story of Mexico Ser.). (Illus.). 160p. (J). (gr. 3-7). lib. bdg. 27.95 (978-1-59935-053-0(X)) Reynolds, Morgan Inc.

West, David. Hernán Cortés: The Life of a Spanish Conquistador. 2009. (Graphic Nonfiction Biographies Ser.). (ENG.). 48p. (YA). (gr. 4-5). 58.50 (978-1-61513-019-1(5), Rosen Reference) Rosen Publishing Group, Inc., The.

Whiting, Jim. The Life & Times of Hernando Cortes. 2006. (Profiles in American History Ser.). (Illus.). 48p. (J). (gr. 3-7). lib. bdg. 29.95 (978-1-58415-449-5(7)) Mitchell Lane Pubs.

MEXICO—HISTORY—CONQUEST, 1519-1540—FICTION

Bronson, Wilfrid S., illus. Stooping Hawk & Stranded Whale, Sons of Liberty. 2009. 236p. (J). pap. 22.95 (978-0-86534-715-1(8)) Sunstone Pr.

MEXICO—HISTORY—SPANISH COLONY, 1540-1810

Burr, Claudia, et al. When the Viceroy Came. 2006. (Illus.). 29p. (J). (gr. 4-8). reprint ed. 16.00 (978-1-4223-5465-0(2)) DIANE Publishing Co.

MEXICO—HISTORY—SPANISH COLONY, 1540-1810—FICTION

Barrera, Norma. Diario de Tlauhquechol (1518) 2003. (Mexican Diaries). (SPA., Illus.). 146p. (J). pap. (978-970-690-042-5(X), SOM7948) Planeta Mexicana Editorial S. A. de C. V. MEX. Dist: Lectorum Pubns., Inc.

Zarco, Carmen Saucedo. Diario de Mariana (1695-95) 2003. (Mexican Diaries). (SPA., Illus.). 164p. (J). pap. (978-970-690-113-2(2), SOM7943) Planeta Mexicana Editorial S. A. de C. V. MEX. Dist: Lectorum Pubns., Inc.

MEXICO—SOCIAL LIFE AND CUSTOMS

Aloian, Molly & Peppas, Lynn. Cultural Traditions in Mexico. 2012. (ENG.). 32p. (J). lib. bdg. (978-0-7787-7587-4(9)) Crabtree Publishing Co.

Aloian, Molly & Peppas, Lynne. Cultural Traditions in Mexico, 1 vol. 2012. (ENG.). 32p. (J). pap. (978-0-7787-7594-2(1)) Crabtree Publishing Co.

Andrade, Mary J., photos by. Day of the Dead A Passion for Life: Día de los Muertos Pasión por la Vida. Andrade, Mary J., . 2nd ed. 2007. (SPA & ENG., Illus.). 200p. lib. bdg., stu. ed., tchr.'s training gde. ed. 29.95 (978-0-9791624-0-4(8)) La Oferta Publishing Co.

Augustin, Byron. The Food of Mexico, 1 vol. 2012. (Flavors of the World Ser.). (ENG.). 64p. (gr. 5-5). 34.07 (978-1-60870-237-4(5), 8bb93611-fd56-41e8-aace-44a9a798c27f) Cavendish Square Publishing LLC.

Barker, Geoff. The World of Food - Mexico. 2010. (World of Food Ser.). 32p. (YA). (gr. 4-7). lib. bdg. 24.95 (978-1-934545-13-3(9)) Oliver Pr., Inc.

Berg, Elizabeth. Festivals of the World: Mexico, 1 vol. 2011. (Festivals of the World Ser.). (ENG.). 32p. (gr. 4-4). 31.21 (978-1-60870-104-9(2), 0695727c-55fc-4d4d-a1e6-8558ae0485fa) Cavendish Square Publishing LLC.

Bernay, Emma & Berne, Emma Carlson. Cinco de Mayo. Rodriguez, Geraldine, illus. 2018. (Holidays in Rhythm & Rhyme Ser.). (ENG.). 24p. (J). (gr. k-2). lib. bdg. 33.99 (978-1-68410-397-3(5), 140360) Cantata Learning.

Bingham, Jane. Costume Around the World: Mexico. 2008. (Costume Around the World Ser.). (ENG., Illus.). 32p. (gr. 4-6). 28.00 (978-0-7910-9771-7(4), P227073, Chelsea Clubhse.) Infobase Holdings, Inc.

Bullard, Lisa. Marco's Cinco de Mayo. Conger, Hollil, illus. 2012. (Holidays & Special Days Ser.). 24p. (J). (gr. k-2). pap. 39.62 (978-0-7613-9249-1(1), Millbrook Pr.) Lerner Publishing Group.

—Marco's Cinco de Mayo. Conger, Holli, illus. 2012. (Cloverleaf Books (tm) — Holidays & Special Days Ser.). (ENG.). 24p. (J). (gr. k-2). pap. 8.99 (978-0-7613-8580-6(0), c9f9f8f5-4ff4-406d-b33c-7e8854965344, Millbrook Pr.) Lerner Publishing Group.

—My Family Celebrates Day of the Dead. Conger, Holli, illus. 2018. (Holiday Time (Early Bird Stories (tm)) Ser.). (ENG.). 24p. (J). (gr. k-2). pap. 9.99 (978-1-5415-2739-3(9), 61afe369-db7d-4af0-9ca9-17bc1f2b540c) Lerner Publishing Group.

Cassriel, Betsy. My Teenage Life in Mexico. 2017. (Customs & Cultures of the World Ser.). (ENG., Illus.). 64p. (J). (gr. 7-12). 23.95 (978-1-4222-3907-0(1)) Mason Crest.

Celebrate! Mexico. 2009. (Celebrate! (Chelsea Clubhouse) Ser.). (ENG.). 32p. (gr. 4-6). 28.00 (978-1-60413-267-0(1), P169970, Chelsea Clubhse.) Infobase Holdings, Inc.

Centore, Michael. Mexico, Vol. 12. 2015. (Major Nations in a Global World: Tradition, Culture, & Daily Life Ser.). (Illus.). 64p. (J). (gr. 7). 23.95 (978-1-4222-3348-1(0)) Mason Crest.

Coleman, Miriam. The Culture & Crafts of Mexico, 1 vol. 2015. (Cultural Crafts Ser.). (ENG., Illus.). 32p. (J). (gr. 4-6). pap. 12.75 (978-1-4994-1126-3(X), 2fb8ca6a-4dac-44f9-97c4-758695332f3a, PowerKids Pr.) Rosen Publishing Group, Inc., The.

Cunningham, Patrick. Mexico. 2010. (Letters from Around the World Ser.). (Illus.). 32p. pap. (978-1-84234-614-3(8)) Cherrytree Bks.

Enderlein, Cheryl L. Christmas in Mexico, 1 vol. 2013. (Christmas Around the World Ser.). (ENG.). 24p. (J). (gr. 1-3). lib. bdg. 27.99 (978-1-62065-138-4(6), 120828, Capstone Pr.) Capstone.

Flood Williams, Colleen Madonna, et al. The Festivals of Mexico. 2009. (Mexico: Beautiful Land, Diverse People Ser.). (Illus.). 64p. (YA). (gr. 7-12). 21.95 (978-1-4222-0657-7(2)) Mason Crest.

Freedman, Russell. In the Days of the Vaqueros. 2008. (ENG., Illus.). 80p. (YA). (gr. 7). pap. 9.99 (978-0-547-13365-2(0), 1048765, Clarion Bks.) HarperCollins Pubs.

Fretland VanVoorst, Jennifer. The Ancient Maya, 1 vol. 2012. (Exploring the Ancient World Ser.). (ENG., Illus.). 48p. (J). (gr. 5-9). pap. 9.10 (978-0-7565-4584-0(6), 120433, Compass Point Bks.) Capstone.

Gnojewski, Carol. Celebrating Cinco de Mayo, 1 vol. 2012. (Celebrating Holidays Ser.). (ENG.). 48p. (gr. 3-3). 27.93 (978-0-7660-4032-8(1), 6dcb0e59-a75a-41be-8311-60046131b2af); (Illus.). pap. 11.53 (978-1-59845-399-7(8), 51c22a17-4523-4ee0-a6d8-0fc1bffb9258) Enslow Publishing, LLC. (Enslow Elementary).

Gnojewski, Carol & Ponto, Joanna. Cinco de Mayo, 1 vol. 2016. (Story of Our Holidays Ser.). (ENG., Illus.). 32p. (gr. 3-3). pap. 11.52 (978-0-7660-8328-8(4), 8fc1e87a-a030-4687-8be3-323f7331f4d7) Enslow Publishing, LLC.

Grack, Rachel. Cinco de Mayo. 2017. (Celebrating Holidays Ser.). (ENG.). 24p. (J). (gr. k-3). lib. bdg. 26.95 (978-1-62617-617-1(5), Blastoff! Readers) Bellwether Media.

—Day of the Dead. 2017. (Celebrating Holidays Ser.). (ENG., Illus.). 24p. (J). (gr. k-3). lib. bdg. 26.95 (978-1-62617-618-8(3), Blastoff! Readers) Bellwether Media.

Green, Sara. Ancient Maya. 2020. (Ancient Civilizations Ser.). (ENG., Illus.). 32p. (J). (gr. 3-8). pap. 8.99 (978-1-61891-862-8(1), 12591, Blastoff! Discovery) Bellwether Media.

Hawker, Frances & Paz, Noemi. Christianity in Mexico. Campbell, Bruce, photos by. 2009. (ENG., Illus.). 32p. (J). (gr. 3-6). (978-0-7787-5007-9(8)); pap. (978-0-7787-5024-6(8)) Crabtree Publishing Co.

Holm, Kirsten C. Everyday Life in the Maya Civilization, 1 vol. 2012. (Jr. Graphic Ancient Civilizations Ser.). (ENG.). 24p. (J). (gr. 2-3). pap. 11.60 (978-1-4488-6393-8(7), 813f2f0f-e4e2-4960-b046-e31769739b66); lib. bdg. 28.93 (978-1-4488-6217-7(5), 7acb4b4d-fc46-4b0a-bd11-0a590ff314e8) Rosen Publishing Group, Inc., The.

Jones, Theodore. Celebrating Day of the Dead, 1 vol. 2015. (History of Our Holidays Ser.). (ENG., Illus.). 24p. (J). (gr. 1-2). pap. 9.15 (978-1-4824-3886-4(0), 98097418-d6fa-4c4b-a6e7-c0864e072b48) Stevens, Gareth Publishing LLLP.

Kalman, Bobbie. Mexico: The Culture. 3rd rev. ed. 2008. (Lands, Peoples, & Cultures Ser.). (ENG., Illus.). 32p. (J). (gr. 3-9). pap. (978-0-7787-9663-3(9)) Crabtree Publishing Co.

—Mexico: The People. 3rd rev. ed. 2008. (Lands, Peoples, & Cultures Ser.). (ENG., Illus.). 32p. (J). (gr. 3-9). lib. bdg. (978-0-7787-9294-9(3)) Crabtree Publishing Co.

—Mexico - The People, 1 vol. 3rd rev. ed. 2008. (Lands, Peoples, & Cultures Ser.). (ENG., Illus.). 32p. (J). (gr. 3-9). pap. (978-0-7787-9662-6(0)) Crabtree Publishing Co.

Kaplan, Leslie. Cinco de Mayo, 1 vol. 2003. (Library of Holidays Ser.). (ENG., Illus.). 24p. (J). (gr. 2-3). lib. bdg. 26.27 (978-0-8239-6662-2(3), 3d73d6db-9a36-4471-b5c1-02020fca16fc, PowerKids Pr.) Rosen Publishing Group, Inc., The.

Kaplan, Leslie C. Cinco de Mayo. 2009. (Library of Holidays Ser.). 24p. (gr. 2-3). 42.50 (978-1-60853-708-2(0), PowerKids Pr.) Rosen Publishing Group, Inc., The.

King, Aven. My Mexican Heritage, 1 vol. 2013. (Rosen Readers Ser.). (ENG.). 24p. (J). (gr. 2-2). pap. 8.25 (978-1-4777-2331-9(5), 2951c78f-4d21-409b-a494-c16d26953eec); pap. 49.50 (978-1-4777-2332-6(3)) Rosen Publishing Group, Inc., The. (Rosen Classroom).

Krebs, Laurie. ¡Nos Vamos a Mexico! Corr, Christopher, illus. 2006. (SPA.). 32p. (J). (gr. k-5). pap. 9.99 (978-1-84686-014-0(8)) Barefoot Bks., Inc.

—Off We Go to Mexico. Corr, Christopher, illus. (ENG.). 32p. (J). (gr. k-5). 2008. pap. 9.99 (978-1-84686-159-8(4)) 2006. 16.99 (978-1-905236-40-4(9)) Barefoot Bks., Inc.

Lowery, Linda. Cinco de Mayo. Knutson, Barbara, illus. 2005. (On My Own Holidays Ser.). 48p. (J). (gr. k-3). per. 6.95 (978-1-57505-764-4(6)); (gr. 2-4). 25.26 (978-1-57505-654-8(2)) Lerner Publishing Group.

—Day of the Dead. Knutson, Barbara, illus. 2003. (On My Own Holidays Ser.). (ENG.). 48p. (gr. 2-4). lib. bdg. 25.26 (978-0-87614-914-0(X)) Lerner Publishing Group.

McGill, Jordan, ed. Cinco de Mayo. 2011. (J). (gr. 3-5). pap. 12.95 (978-1-61690-688-7(X), AV2 by Weigl); (Illus.). 24p. (gr. 2-5). 27.13 (978-1-61690-682-5(0)) Weigl Pubs., Inc.

Morlock, Rachael. The People & Culture of Mexico, 1 vol. 2017. (Celebrating Hispanic Diversity Ser.). (ENG., Illus.). 32p. (J). (gr. 4-5). 27.93 (978-1-5081-6310-7(3), 54f8fbf5-4e37-4691-ab21-decf402dbc89, PowerKids Pr.) Rosen Publishing Group, Inc., The.

Murray, Julie. Cinco de Mayo. 2018. (Holidays (Abdo Kids Junior) Ser.). (ENG., Illus.). 24p. (J). (gr. -1-2). lib. bdg. 31.36 (978-1-5321-8172-6(8), 29817, Abdo Kids) ABDO Publishing Co.

Murray, Laura K. Exploring the Aztec Empire. 2018. (Exploring Ancient Civilizations Ser.). (ENG., Illus.). 32p. (J). (gr. 3-6). 32.80 (978-1-63235-467-9(5), 13890, 12-Story Library) Bookstaves, LLC.

Nelson, Robin. Crayola (r) Cinco de Mayo Colors. 2018. (Crayola (r) Holiday Colors Ser.). (ENG., Illus.). 32p. (J). (gr. -1-3). pap. 6.99 (978-1-5415-2746-1(1), d5154a2a-0912-41dd-bdc0-4ce50cee9ca7); lib. bdg. 29.32 (978-1-5415-1095-1(X), f9c317bd-ed6c-40ec-987d-791c7423b1fe) Lerner Publishing Group. (Lerner Pubns.).

Orr, Tamra. Mexican Heritage. 2018. (21st Century Junior Library: Celebrating Diversity in My Classroom Ser.). (ENG., Illus.). 24p. (J). (gr. 2-4). pap. 12.79 (978-1-5341-0832-5(7), 210692); lib. bdg. 30.64 (978-1-5341-0733-5(9), 210691) Cherry Lake Publishing.

Pearce, Kevin. Foods of Mexico, 1 vol. 2011. (Culture in the Kitchen Ser.). (ENG.). 24p. (J). (gr. 2-3). pap. 9.15 (978-1-4339-5716-1(7), ed21998c-9044-4297-a872-9cac17dceda4); lib. bdg. 25.27 (978-1-4339-5714-7(0), 06128386-f8e2-4bc2-8442-cd316d649608) Stevens, Gareth Publishing LLLP. (Gareth Stevens Learning Library).

Poole, Hilary W. The Mexican Family Table, Vol. 11. 2018. (Connecting Cultures Through Family & Food Ser.). (Illus.). 64p. (J). (gr. 7). 31.93 (978-1-4222-4048-9(7)) Mason Crest.

Roholt, Christine VeLure. Foods of Mexico. 2014. (Cook with Me Ser.). (ENG., Illus.). 24p. (J). (gr. 3-8). 26.95 (978-1-62617-121-3(1), Express Bks.) Bellwether Media.

Sheen, Barbara. Growing up in Mexico. 2017. (Growing up Around the World Ser.). (ENG.). 80p. (YA). (gr. 5-12). (978-1-68282-221-0(4)) ReferencePoint Pr., Inc.

Shofner, Melissa Raé. The Story Behind Day of the Dead, 1 vol. 2019. (Holiday Histories Ser.). (ENG.). 24p. (gr. 1-2). 25.27 (978-1-7253-0042-2(7), 30e7c1e0-c29e-4374-943d-57cb6a162706, PowerKids Pr.) Rosen Publishing Group, Inc., The.

Somervill, Barbara A. Ancient Maya. 2012. (ENG.). 112p. (J). (gr. 6-9). lib. bdg. 34.00 (978-0-531-25181-2(0)) Scholastic Library Publishing.

Stevenson, Mónica. Tradiciones Mexicanas Para Ninos. 2006. (SPA.). 136p. (YA). (gr. 4-7). pap. (978-968-403-934-6(4)) Selector, S.A. de C.V.

Stuckey, Rachel. Ancient Maya Inside Out. 2017. (Ancient Worlds Inside Out Ser.). (ENG., Illus.). 32p. (J). (gr. 4-5). (978-0-7787-2878-8(1)); pap. (978-0-7787-2892-4(7)) Crabtree Publishing Co.

Tabor, Nancy Maria Grande. Celebraciones / Celebrations: Dias Feriados de Los Estados Unidos y Mexico. Tabor, Nancy Maria Grande, illus. 2004. (Charlesbridge Bilingual Bks.).Tr. of Celebrations (Bilingual). (Illus.). 32p. (J). (gr. -1-2). pap. 7.95 (978-1-57091-550-5(4)) Charlesbridge Publishing, Inc.

Tait, Leia. Cinco de Mayo. (American Celebrations Ser.). (Illus.). 24p. (J). (gr. 3-5). 2010. pap. 11.95 (978-1-60596-934-3(6)) 2010. lib. bdg. 25.70 (978-1-60596-776-9(9)) 2006. lib. bdg. 24.45 (978-1-59036-460-4(0)) 2006. per. 8.95 (978-1-59036-463-5(5)) Weigl Pubs., Inc.

Taylor, Trace. Mexico. 2013. (ICP Our World Ser.). (ENG.). 16p. (J). (gr. k-1). pap. 8.00 (978-1-61541-126-9(7)) American Reading Co.

Taylor, Trace & Sánchez, Lucía M. Mexico. 2015. (1Y Nuestro Mundo Ser.). (SPA.). 16p. (J). (gr. k-1). pap. 8.00 (978-1-61541-149-8(6)) American Reading Co.

Torpie, Kate. Cinco de Mayo. 2008. (Celebrations in My World Ser.). (ENG., Illus.). 32p. (J). (gr. k-3). pap. (978-0-7787-4299-9(7)) Crabtree Publishing Co.

Urrutia, Maria Cristina & Orozco, Rebeca. Cinco de Mayo: Yesterday & Today. 2006. (SPA., Illus.). 29p. (J). (gr. 4-8). reprint ed. 16.00 (978-1-4223-5464-3(4)) DIANE Publishing Co.

Wade, Mary Dodson. Cinco de Mayo (Rookie Read-About Holidays: Previous Editions) 2003. (Rookie Read-About Holidays Ser.). (ENG., Illus.). 32p. (J). (gr. 1-2). pap. 5.95 (978-0-516-27489-8(9), Children's Pr.) Scholastic Library Publishing.

Weston Woods Staff, creator. The Day of the Dead / el DÍa de Los Muertos. 2011. (ENG & SPA.). 18.95 (978-0-545-42606-0(5)); 29.95 (978-0-545-37417-0(0)); 38.75 (978-0-545-42607-7(3)) Weston Woods Studios, Inc.

Wiseman, Blaine & Kissock, Heather. Aztecs. 2016. (Illus.). 32p. (J). (978-1-5105-1094-4(X)) SmartBook Media, Inc.

Wood, Ira. A Mexican Feast: The Foods & Recipes of Mexico. 2009. (Reading Room Collection 2 Ser.). 24p. (gr. 3-4). 42.50 (978-1-60851-953-8(8), PowerKids Pr.) Rosen Publishing Group, Inc., The.

Zocchi, Judy. In Mexico. Brodie, Neale, illus. 2005. (Global Adventures I Ser.). 32p. (J). lib. bdg. 21.65 (978-1-59646-002-7(4)) Dingles & Co.

—In Mexico/en México. Brodie, Neale, illus. 2005. (Global Adventures I Ser.).Tr. of En México. (ENG & SPA.). 32p. (J). pap. 10.95 (978-1-59646-137-6(3)); lib. bdg. 21.65 (978-1-59646-003-4(2)) Dingles & Co.

MEXICO, GULF OF

Benoit, Peter. The BP Oil Spill. 2011. (J). pap. (978-0-531-29029-3(8)) Children's Pr., Ltd.

—The BP Oil Spill. 2011. (True Bks.). 48p. (J). (gr. 3-5). lib. bdg. 29.00 (978-0-531-20630-0(0), Children's Pr.) Scholastic Library Publishing.

Bodden, Valerie. The Deepwater Horizon Oil Spill. 2018. (Disasters for All Time Ser.). (ENG.). 48p. (J). (gr. 4-7). pap. 12.00 (978-1-62832-548-5(8), 19725, Creative Paperbacks) Creative Co., The.

Brennan, Linda Crotta. Gulf Oil Spill, 1 vol. 2013. (History's Greatest Disasters Ser.). (ENG.). 48p. (J). (gr. 4-8). lib. bdg. 35.64 (978-1-61783-957-3(4), 9485) ABDO Publishing Co.

—Gulf Oil Spill Paperback. 2013. (History's Greatest Disasters Ser.). (ENG.). (J). (gr. 4-8). pap. 18.50 (978-1-62403-022-2(X), 10771) ABDO Publishing Co.

Field, Randi. The Gulf States of Mexico. (Mexico: Beautiful Land, Diverse People Ser.). 64p. (YA). (gr. 7-12). 2009. (Illus.). 21.95 (978-1-4222-0668-3(8)) 2007. pap. 9.95 (978-1-4222-0735-2(8)) Mason Crest.

Friedman, Lauri S., ed. The B. P. Oil Spill, 1 vol. 2011. (Writing the Critical Essay: an Opposing Viewpoints Guide Ser.). (ENG., Illus.). 128p. (gr. 7-12). 39.93 (978-0-7377-5833-7(3), 5a741e56-329f-47b8-92de-e9b3a9e50581, Greenhaven Publishing) Greenhaven Publishing LLC.

Goldish, Meish. Oil Spill: Deepwater Horizon. 2017. (Eco-Disasters Ser.). (ENG.). 32p. (J). (gr. 2-7). 19.95 (978-1-68402-226-7(6)) Bearport Publishing Co., Inc.

Green, Jen. Caribbean Sea & Gulf of Mexico, 1 vol. 2005. (Oceans & Seas Ser.). (ENG., Illus.). 48p. (gr. 5-8). pap. 15.05 (978-0-8368-6280-5(5), d29c92a0-4320-433a-91da-3e84c3a45a9b, Gareth Stevens Secondary Library) Stevens, Gareth Publishing LLLP.

Haugen, David M., ed. The B. P. Oil Spill, 1 vol. 2011. (At Issue Ser.). (ENG.). 112p. (gr. 10-12). 41.03 (978-0-7377-5568-8(7), b39fe2f5-3de5-4f21-8e33-2b07156ca183); pap. 28.80 (978-0-7377-5569-5(5), 6d1a6d21-c7c8-4a54-a75a-5409c71f3a64) Greenhaven Publishing LLC. (Greenhaven Publishing).

Marsico, Katie. The Gulf of Mexico. 2013. (Explorer Library: Social Studies Explorer Ser.). (ENG.). 32p. (gr. 4-8). pap. 14.21 (978-1-62431-040-9(0), 202517); (Illus.). lib. bdg. 32.07 (978-1-62431-016-4(8), 202515) Cherry Lake Publishing.

Mitchell, Mark. Raising la Belle. Mitchell, Mark, illus. (Professor Wigglestix & the Weather Ser.). (Illus.). 112p. 10.95 (978-1-57168-703-6(3)) Eakin Pr.

Orr, Tamra B. BP Oil Spill & Energy Policy. 2017. (Perspectives Library: Modern Perspectives Ser.). (ENG., Illus.). 32p. (J). (gr. 4-7). lib. bdg. 32.07 (978-1-63472-864-5(5), 209882) Cherry Lake Publishing.

Peppas, Lynn. Gulf Oil Spill. 2011. (ENG., Illus.). 32p. (J). (978-0-7787-1592-4(2), 1325405); (Disaster Alert! Ser.: No. 20). (gr. 3-6). pap. (978-0-7787-1625-9(2), 1325405) Crabtree Publishing Co.

Stone, Adam. The Deepwater Horizon Oil Spill. 2014. (Disaster Stories Ser.). (ENG., Illus.). 24p. (J). (gr. 3-8). 29.95 (978-1-62617-152-7(1), Black Sheep) Bellwether Media.

MIAMI DOLPHINS (FOOTBALL TEAM)

Adamson, Thomas K. The Miami Dolphins Story. 2016. (NFL Teams Ser.). (ENG., Illus.). 32p. (J). (gr. 3-7). lib. bdg. 26.95 (978-1-62617-371-2(0), Torque Bks.) Bellwether Media.

Burgess, Zack. Meet the Miami Dolphins. 2016. (Big Picture Sports Ser.). (ENG., Illus.). 24p. (J). (gr. k-3). lib. bdg. 22.60 (978-1-59953-733-7(8)) Norwood Hse. Pr.

Caffrey, Scott. The Story of the Miami Dolphins. 2009. (NFL Today Ser.). 48p. (YA). (gr. 5-9). 22.95 (978-1-58341-761-4(3)) Creative Co., The.

Cohn, Nate. Miami Dolphins. 2018. (Illus.). 24p. (J). (978-1-4896-5561-5(1), AV2 by Weigl) Weigl Pubs., Inc.

Frisch, Aaron. Miami Dolphins. 2011. (Super Bowl Champions Ser.). (J). (gr. 1-3). 24.25 (978-1-60818-021-9(2)) Creative Co., The.

—Miami Dolphins. 2014. (Super Bowl Champions Ser.). (ENG., Illus.). 24p. (J). (gr. 1-4). (978-1-60818-379-1(3), 21562, Creative Education) Creative Co., The.

Leboutillier, Nate. Miami Dolphins. 2005. (Super Bowl Champions Ser.). (Illus.). 24p. (J). (gr. 1-4). lib. bdg. 16.95 (978-1-58341-385-2(5), Creative Education) Creative Co., The.

MacRae, Sloan. The Miami Dolphins, 1 vol. 2011. (America's Greatest Teams Ser.). (ENG., Illus.). 24p. (J). (gr. 2-3). pap. 9.25 (978-1-4488-3172-2(5), 9a4c7eb2-db66-4cdc-9ba8-5a17802d6d5c); lib. bdg. 26.27 (978-1-4488-3167-8(9), d17e5833-f4f6-4304-b79e-6620ddef1855) Rosen Publishing Group, Inc., The. (PowerKids Pr.).

Miami Dolphins, 1 vol. 2014. (NFL's Greatest Teams Ser.). (ENG.). 32p. (J). (gr. 2-5). 34.21 (978-1-62403-362-9(8), 1578, Big Buddy Bks.) ABDO Publishing Co.

Schmalzbauer, Adam. The History of the Miami Dolphins. 2004. (NFL Today Ser.). (Illus.). 32p. (YA). (gr. 5-9). 18.95 (978-1-58341-302-9(2)) Creative Co., The.

Storm, Marysa. Highlights of the Miami Dolphins. 2018. (Team Stats — Football Edition Ser.). (ENG.). 32p. (J). (gr. 4-6). pap. 9.99 (978-1-64466-281-6(7), 12377); (Illus.). lib. bdg. (978-1-68072-434-9(7), 12376) Black Rabbit Bks. (Bolt).

Whiting, Jim. Miami Dolphins. rev. ed. 2019. (NFL Today Ser.). (ENG.). 48p. (J). (gr. 4-7). pap. 12.00 *(978-1-62832-711-3(1)*, 19052, Creative Paperbacks) Creative Co., The.
—The Story of the Miami Dolphins. (NFL Today Ser.). 48p. (J). 2019. (ENG.). (gr. 3-6). *(978-1-64026-148-6(6)*, 19054) 2013. (Illus.). 35.65 *(978-1-60818-308-1(4))* Creative Co., The. (Creative Education).
Wyner, Zach. Miami Dolphins. (Illus.). 32p. 2015. pap. *(978-1-4896-0847-5(8))* 2014. (ENG., (J). (gr. 4-7). lib. bdg. 28.55 *(978-1-4896-0846-8(X)*, AV2 by Weigl) Weigl Pubs., Inc.

MICE

Allegra, Mike. Scampers Thinks Like a Scientist. Zechel, Elizabeth, illus. 2019. 32p. (J). (gr. k-3). 16.95 *(978-1-58469-642-1(7)*, Dawn Pubns.) Sourcebooks, Inc.
Coppendale, Jean. Mice. 2004. (QEB You & Your Pet Ser.). (Illus.). 32p. (J). lib. bdg. 18.95 *(978-1-59566-056-5(9))* QEB Publishing Inc.
Dittmer, Lori. Mice. 2018. (Seedlings: Backyard Animals Ser.). (ENG.). 24p. (J). (gr. k-2). pap. 8.99 *(978-1-62832-599-7(2)*, 19928, Creative Paperbacks); (gr. -1-k). *(978-1-60818-972-4(4)*, 19919, Creative Education) Creative Co., The.
Jackson, Tom. Mice. 2008. (Nature's Children Ser.). (Illus.). 52p. (J). *(978-0-7172-6239-7(1))* Grolier, Ltd.
Johnson, Jinny. Rats & Mice. 2009. (Get to Know Your Pet Ser.). (J). 28.50 *(978-1-59920-091-0(0))* Black Rabbit Bks.
—Rats & Mice. 2009. (Get to Know Your Pet Ser.). (ENG., Illus.). 32p. (J). (gr. 4-7). pap. *(978-1-897563-33-5(7))* Saunders Bk. Co.
Leavitt, Amie Jane. Care for a Pet Mouse. 2007. (How to Convince Your Parents You Can ... Ser.). (Illus.). 32p. (J). (gr. 1-4). lib. bdg. 25.70 *(978-1-58415-606-2(6))* Mitchell Lane Pubs.
Lupo, Tamar. Caring for Your Mouse. 2006. (Caring for Your Pet Ser.). (Illus.). 32p. (J). (gr. 3-7). lib. bdg. 26.00 *(978-1-59036-472-7(4))* Weigl Pubs., Inc.
McLellan, Joe. Nikik & Wapus Save the People, 1 vol. Traverse, Jackie, illus. 2015. (ENG.). 32p. (J). mass mkt. 10.95 *(978-1-894717-70-0(8)*, baddc49e-5bc9-4569-a55f-6ed5d2b298d0) Pemmican Pubns., Inc. CAN. Dist: Firefly Bks., Ltd.
Mice at School: Individual Title Six-Packs. (Story Steps Ser.). (gr. k-2). 32.00 *(978-0-7635-9825-9(9))* Rigby Education.
Moose, Jay. Ratoncitos Pequeñitos / Itty Bitty Mice, 1 vol., Vol. 1. 2013. (Animales Pequeñitos / Itty Bitty Animals Ser.). (SPA & ENG.). 24p. (J). (gr. k-2). 25.27 *(978-1-4339-9912-3(9)*, 460f535d-8f0d-432f-8430-3ac7acf763b1) Stevens, Gareth Publishing LLLP.
Morgan, Sally. Rats & Mice. 2012. (Pets Plus Ser.). (Illus.). 32p. (gr. 3-6). lib. bdg. 31.35 *(978-1-59920-703-2(6))* Black Rabbit Bks.
Morris Mouse: Individual Title Six-Pack. (Story Steps Ser.). (gr. k-2). 23.00 *(978-0-7635-9827-3(5))* Rigby Education.
Nardi, James. In Mouse's Backyard, 1 vol. 2011. (ENG., Illus.). 40p. (gr. 3-6). 16.99 *(978-0-7643-3833-5(1)*, 4269, Schiffer Publishing Ltd) Schiffer Publishing, Ltd.
Nice Mice! Long Vowel i, CVCe Pattern: Level B, 6 vols. (Wright Skills Ser.). 16p. (gr. k-3). 17.95 *(978-0-322-03102-9(8))* Wright Group/McGraw-Hill.
Owen, Karen. As Quiet As a Mouse. Golubeva, Evgenia, illus. 2019. (Early Bird Readers — Purple (Early Bird Stories (tm)) Ser.). (ENG.). 32p. (J). (gr. k-3). 30.65 *(978-1-5415-4224-2(X)*, b86f0cb2-2d79-445c-8403-245c1b6207f6); pap. 9.99 *(978-1-5415-7421-2(4)*, 7ab98954-7f51-43e1-8346-0c7f37861472) Lerner Publishing Group. (Lerner Pubns.).
Owen, Ruth. Harvest Mouse. 2018. (Wildlife Watchers Ser.). (ENG., Illus.). 24p. (J). (gr. k-2). 8.99 *(978-1-78856-072-6(8)*, 36f4bdc6-a63f-4c67-bfaa-3598378c3d29) Ruby Tuesday Books Limited GBR. Dist: Lerner Publishing Group.
Perkins, Wendy. Mouse. 2011. (Amicus Readers. Animal Life Cycles (Level 2) Ser.). (ENG.). 24p. (J). (gr. 1-4). lib. bdg. 25.65 *(978-1-60753-157-9(7)*, 17065) Amicus.
El Ratón. 2017. (Animales Del Patio Ser.). (Illus.). 16p. (J). (gr. -1-2). lib. bdg. 17.95 *(978-1-68151-273-0(4)*, 14714) Amicus.
Riggs, Kate. Mice. 2016. (In My Backyard Ser.). (ENG., Illus.). 24p. (J). (gr. 1-3). *(978-1-60818-699-0(7)*, 20593, Creative Education); pap. 8.99 *(978-1-62832-295-8(0)*, 20591, Creative Paperbacks) Creative Co., The.
Roza, Greg. Your Neighbor the Mouse, 1 vol. 2011. (City Critters Ser.). (ENG., Illus.). 24p. (J). (gr. 2-3). pap. 9.25 *(978-1-4488-5125-6(4)*, c104c6da-c3de-4f30-90c4-150df79cfd5c); lib. bdg. 27.27 *(978-1-4488-4998-7(5)*, bda96e0e-1137-4d4b-a9fd-8b1fcabefc4b) Rosen Publishing Group, Inc., The. (Windmill Bks.).
Rustad, Martha E. H. Mice. 2013. (ENG., Illus.). 24p. (J). lib. bdg. 25.65 *(978-1-62031-070-0(8))* Jump! Inc.
Savage, Stephen. Mouse, 1 vol. 2008. (Animal Neighbors Ser.). (ENG.). 32p. (gr. 3-3). pap. 11.60 *(978-1-4042-4567-9(7)*, 61b97313-d499-4b38-9b86-f6626fa0ab44, Rosen Classroom); (Illus.). (J). lib. bdg. 28.93 *(978-1-4358-4990-7(6)*, ca23a7f4-eaeb-4357-a9d8-5205635f19dc, PowerKids Pr.) Rosen Publishing Group, Inc., The.
Schuetz, Kari. Mice. 2014. (Backyard Wildlife Ser.). (ENG., Illus.). 24p. (J). (gr. k-3). lib. bdg. 26.95 *(978-1-62617-060-5(6)*, Blastoff! Readers) Bellwether Media.
Shusterman, Danielle. Here I Come, Mouse! 2012. (1G Predator Animals Ser.). (ENG., Illus.). 28p. (J). pap. 9.60 *(978-1-63437-570-2(X))* American Reading Co.
—A Mouse Is a Mouse. 2012. (1-3Y Animals Ser.). (ENG., Illus.). 16p. (J). pap. 9.60 *(978-1-63437-573-3(4))* American Reading Co.
Sjonger, Rebecca & Kalman, Bobbie. Mice, 1 vol. Crabtree, Marc, illus. Crabtree, Marc, photos by. 2003. (Pet Care Ser.). (ENG.). 32p. (J). pap. *(978-0-7787-1786-7(0))*; lib. bdg. *(978-0-7787-1754-6(2))* Crabtree Publishing Co.
Sjonger, Rebecca, et al. Les Souris. 2011. (Petit Monde Vivant (Small Living World) Ser.: No. 77). (FRE., Illus.). 32p. (J). pap. 9.95 *(978-2-89579-371-7(9))* Bayard Canada Livres CAN. Dist: Crabtree Publishing Co.
Storm, Marysa. Mice. (Spot Backyard Animals Ser.). (ENG., Illus.). 16p. (J). (gr. -1-2). 2018. pap. 7.99 *(978-1-68152-218-0(7)*, 14749) 2017. 17.95 *(978-1-68151-093-4(6)*, 14630) Amicus.
Tait, Leia. Mice. 2009. (Backyard Animals Ser.). (Illus.). 24p. (J). (gr. 3-5). pap. 8.95 *(978-1-60596-081-4(0))*; lib. bdg. 24.45 *(978-1-60596-080-7(2))* Weigl Pubs., Inc.
Watts, Barrie. Mouse. 2004. (Illus.). 32p. (J). (gr. -1-17). lib. bdg. 24.25 *(978-1-58340-231-3(4))* Black Rabbit Bks.

MICE—FICTION

Adam, Sally. The Cats of Ellis Island. 2009. 28p. pap. 12.50 *(978-1-4389-6012-8(3))* AuthorHouse.
Adams, Tina. Chris Mouse & the Promise. 2012. 24p. (-18). pap. 9.99 *(978-1-939217-01-1(6))* 5 Prince Publishing.
Aesop. The Lion & the Mouse. 2007. (ENG., Illus.). 32p. (J). (gr. -1-1). pap. 9.95 *(978-0-7358-2129-3(1))* North-South Bks., Inc.
Aesop, Aesop. The Country Mouse & the City Mouse. 2012. (J). 29.99 *(978-1-61913-100-2(5))* Weigl Pubs., Inc.
—The Lion & the Mouse. 2016. (ENG.). 79.82 *(978-1-367-86708-6(8))* Blurb, Inc.
—The Lion & the Mouse, 1 vol. 2017. (Let's Learn Aesop's Fables Ser.). (ENG.). 24p. (gr. 2-2). 26.27 *(978-1-4994-8369-7(4)*, 671d2cb3-f561-416e-b63d-842bf50098cd); pap. 9.25 *(978-1-4994-8374-1(0)*, a893e800-3002-4315-81fc-fa50b67aca2f) Rosen Publishing Group, Inc., The. (Windmill Bks.).
Alfred Oscar Valentine: Tales from Spoon Creek: New Beginnings. 2006. (J). 12.00 *(978-0-9766894-5-4(6))* Stanley, Donna Lacy.
Allen, Eleanor. Mouse Monk in a Christmas Adventure. 2009. 36p. pap. 15.49 *(978-1-4490-2197-9(2))* AuthorHouse.
Allepuz, Anuska. That Fruit Is Mine! 2018. (Illus.). 32p. (J). *(978-1-4063-7548-0(9))* Whitman, Albert & Co.
Alrawi, Karim. The Mouse Who Saved Egypt. Willey, Bee, illus. 2011. (ENG.). 32p. (J). (gr. -1-2). 16.95 *(978-1-56656-856-2(0)*, Crocodile Bks.) Interlink Publishing Group, Inc.
Ammirato, Lidia. Why Does the Dog Chase the Cat & the Cat Chase the Mouse? 2012. 24p. pap. 15.99 *(978-1-4771-0651-8(0))* Xlibris Corp.
Anderson, Sorrel. The CLUMSIES MAKE a MESS of the BIG SHOW (the Clumsies, Book 3), Book 3. 2011. (ENG., Illus.). 112p. (J). (gr. 2-4). 6.99 *(978-0-00-733936-5(4))* HarperCollins Pubs. Ltd. GBR. Dist: Independent Pubs. Group.
—The Clumsies Make a Mess of the Seaside (the Clumsies, Book 2), Book 2. 2010. (Clumsies Ser.: 2). (ENG., Illus.). 112p. (J). pap. 5.99 *(978-0-00-733935-8(6)*, HarperCollins Children's Bks.) HarperCollins Pubs. Ltd. GBR. Dist: HarperCollins Pubs.
—The Clumsies Make a Mess (the Clumsies, Book 1), Book 1. 2010. (Clumsies Ser.: 1). (ENG., Illus.). 112p. (J). pap. 5.99 *(978-0-00-733090-4(1)*, HarperCollins Children's Bks.) HarperCollins Pubs. Ltd. GBR. Dist: HarperCollins Pubs.
Andrews, Julie & Hamilton, Emma Walton. The Great American Mousical. Walton, Tony, illus. 2006. (Julie Andrews Collection). (J). (gr. k-4). 160p. 15.99 *(978-0-06-057918-0(8)*, Julie Andrews Collection); 147p. lib. bdg. 16.89 *(978-0-06-057919-7(6))* HarperCollins Pubs.
Anfousse, Ginette. Polo et L'anniversaire. Sarrazin, Marisol, tr. 2003. (Polo Baby Board Bks.). (FRE., Illus.). 16p. (J). (— 1). bds. *(978-2-89021-656-3(X))* Diffusion du livre Mirabel (DLM).
Archambault, Marc. Mommy Is Too Tired to Play. 2010. 32p. 18.97 *(978-0-557-23350-2(X))* Lulu Pr., Inc.
Arends, Donald L. Norm the Ninja River Mouse. 2006. (J). *(978-0-9768880-1-7(7))* Mission Manuscripts, Inc.
Arenstam, Peter. Nicholas, a New Hampshire Tale. Holman, Karen Busch, illus. 2015. (Nicholas Northeastern Ser.: 3). 158p. (J). (gr. k-7). pap. 8.95 *(978-1-938170-68-3(7)*, Mitten Pr.) Ann Arbor Editions LLC.
—Nicholas: a New Hampshire Tale. Holman, Karen Busch, illus. 2009. (Nicholas Northeastern Ser.: 3). 144p. (J). (gr. k-7). 14.95 *(978-1-58726-521-1(4)*, Mitten Pr.) Ann Arbor Editions LLC.
—Nicholas: a Vermont Tale. Holman, Karen Busch, illus. 2010. (Nicholas Northeastern Ser.: 4). 144p. (J). (gr. k-7). 14.95 *(978-1-58726-522-8(2)*, Mitten Pr.) Ann Arbor Editions LLC.
Asch, Frank. Battle in a Bottle. Kanzler, John, illus. 2014. (Class Pets Ser.). (ENG.). 96p. (J). (gr. 2-6). pap. 13.99 *(978-1-4814-3625-0(2)*, Simon & Schuster/Paula Wiseman Bks.) Simon & Schuster/Paula Wiseman Bks.
—The Ghost of P. S. 42. Kanzler, John, illus. 2014. (Class Pets Ser.). (ENG.). 96p. (J). (gr. 2-5). pap. 13.99 *(978-1-4814-3624-3(4)*, Simon & Schuster/Paula Wiseman Bks.) Simon & Schuster/Paula Wiseman Bks.
—Here Comes the Cat! Vagin, Vladimir, illus. 25th ed. 2011. (ENG.). 32p. (J). (gr. -1-3). 12.95 *(978-1-936365-41-8(3)*, 4d525d0f-b9b3-48c5-84df-1f07a194b197) McSweeney's Publishing.
—Mr. Maxwell's Mouse, 0 vols. Asch, Devin, illus. 2014. (ENG.). 32p. (J). (gr. k-4). pap. 8.95 *(978-1-77138-117-8(5))* Kids Can Pr., Ltd. CAN. Dist: Hachette Bk. Group.
Avi. Poppy. Floca, Brian, illus. 2020. (Poppy Ser.: 3). (ENG.). 192p. (J). (gr. 3-7). pap. 9.99 *(978-0-380-72769-8(2)*, HarperCollins) HarperCollins Pubs.
—Poppy. 2006. (Poppy Stories Ser.: 2). (J). (gr. 3-6). lib. bdg. 17.20 *(978-0-613-03338-1(8))* Turtleback.
—Poppy & Ereth. Floca, Brian, illus. 2020. (Poppy Ser.: 7). (ENG.). 240p. (J). (gr. 3-7). pap. 7.99 *(978-0-06-111971-2(7)*, HarperCollins) HarperCollins Pubs.
—Poppy & Rye. Floca, Brian, illus. 2020. (Poppy Ser.: 4). (ENG.). 240p. (J). (gr. 3-7). pap. 9.99 *(978-0-380-79717-2(8)*, HarperCollins) HarperCollins Pubs.
—Poppy & Rye. Floca, Brian, illus. 2006. (Poppy Stories Ser.: 3). 182p. (J). (gr. 3-7). lib. bdg. 17.20 *(978-0-613-17447-3(X))* Turtleback.
—Ragweed. Floca, Brian, illus. 2020. (Poppy Ser.: 1). (ENG.). 224p. (J). (gr. 3-7). pap. 9.99 *(978-0-380-80167-1(1)*, HarperCollins) HarperCollins Pubs.
Aviation Book Company Staff. Ragweed. 2006. (Poppy Stories Ser.: 1). (J). (gr. 3-6). lib. bdg. 17.20 *(978-0-613-26699-4(4))* Turtleback.
Award, Anna & Aesop, Aesop. The Donkey & the Lapdog with the Lion & the Mouse. Biro, Val, illus. 2014. (ENG.). 24p. (J). pap. 6.95 *(978-1-84135-953-3(X))* Award Pubns. Ltd. GBR. Dist: Parkwest Pubns., Inc.
Award, Anna, et al. The Eagle & the Man with the Town Mouse & the Country Mouse. 2014. (ENG.). 24p. (J). pap. 6.95 *(978-1-84135-958-8(0))* Award Pubns. Ltd. GBR. Dist: Parkwest Pubns., Inc.
Baglio, Ben M. The Midnight Mouse. Ellis, Andy, illus. 2003. 59p. (J). *(978-0-439-41916-1(6))* Scholastic, Inc.
Baker, Alan, illus. Two Tiny Mice: A Mouse-Eye Exploration of Nature. rev. ed. 2014. (ENG.). 40p. (J). (gr. -1-3). 16.95 *(978-1-62914-627-0(7)*, Sky Pony Pr.) Skyhorse Publishing Co., Inc.
Baker, Keith. Hickory Dickory Dock. Baker, Keith, illus. 2007. (ENG., Illus.). 32p. (J). (gr. -1-3). 17.99 *(978-0-15-205818-0(4)*, 1197481, Clarion Bks.) HarperCollins Pubs.
Balian, Lorna. Mother's Mother's Day, 1 vol. 2004. (ENG., Illus.). 32p. (J). 8.95 *(978-1-932065-39-8(3))* Star Bright Bks., Inc.
Bardhan-Quallen, Sudipta. Snoring Beauty. Manning, Jane, illus. 2014. (J). *(978-0-06-087405-6(8))* Harper & Row Ltd.
—Snoring Beauty. Manning, Jane, illus. 2014. (ENG.). 32p. (J). (gr. -1-3). 17.99 *(978-0-06-087403-2(1)*, HarperCollins) HarperCollins Pubs.
Barklem, Jill. Autumn Story. Barklem, Jill, illus. 2011. (Brambly Hedge Ser.). (ENG., Illus.). 32p. (J). 9.99 *(978-0-00-183739-3(7)*, HarperCollins Children's Bks.) HarperCollins Pubs. Ltd. GBR. Dist: HarperCollins Pubs.
—Los Bebes de Amapola.Tr. of Poppy's Babies. (SPA., Illus.). 30p. (J). 8.95 *(978-84-233-2769-0(8))* Ediciones Destino ESP. Dist: Planeta Publishing Corp.
—Brambly Hedge: the Classic Collection. 2018. (ENG.). 248p. (J). 34.99 *(978-0-00-828282-0(X)*, HarperCollins Children's Bks.) HarperCollins Pubs. Ltd. GBR. Dist: HarperCollins Pubs.
—Poppy's Babies (Brambly Hedge) Barklem, Jill, illus. 2018. (Brambly Hedge Ser.). (ENG., Illus.). 32p. (J). 9.99 *(978-0-00-828281-3(1)*, HarperCollins Children's Bks.) HarperCollins Pubs. Ltd. GBR. Dist: HarperCollins Pubs.
—Spring Story. Barklem, Jill, illus. 2011. (Brambly Hedge Ser.). (ENG., Illus.). 32p. (J). 9.99 *(978-0-00-183922-9(5)*, HarperCollins Children's Bks.) HarperCollins Pubs. Ltd. GBR. Dist: HarperCollins Pubs.
—Summer Story. Barklem, Jill, illus. 2011. (Brambly Hedge Ser.). (ENG., Illus.). 32p. (J). 9.99 *(978-0-00-183923-6(3)*, HarperCollins Children's Bks.) HarperCollins Pubs. Ltd. GBR. Dist: HarperCollins Pubs.
Barlone, M. J. A Mouse & Rabbits Tale. 2010. (Illus.). 40p. pap. 16.99 *(978-1-4490-7771-6(4))* AuthorHouse.
Barnes, Peter W. House Mouse, Senate Mouse. Barnes, Cheryl Shaw, illus. 2012. (ENG.). 40p. (J). (gr. k-3). 17.99 *(978-1-59698-790-6(1)*, Little Patriot Pr.) Regnery Publishing.
—Liberty Lee's Tail of Independence. Barnes, Cheryl Shaw, illus. 2012. (ENG.). 36p. (J). (gr. k-3). 16.95 *(978-1-59698-792-0(8)*, Little Patriot Pr.) Regnery Publishing.
—Maestro Mouse: And the Mystery of the Missing Baton. Barnes, Cheryl Shaw, illus. 2013. (ENG.). 40p. (J). (gr. k-5). 16.95 *(978-1-62157-036-3(3)*, Little Patriot Pr.) Regnery Publishing.
—Maestro Mouse: And the Mystery of the Missing Baton. Barnes, Cheryl Shaw, illus. 2005. 32p. (J). 16.95 *(978-1-893622-17-3(7)*, VSP Bks.) Vacation Spot Publishing.
—Marshall, the Courthouse Mouse: A Tail of the U. S. Supreme Court. Barnes, Cheryl Shaw, illus. 2012. (ENG.). 40p. (J). (gr. k). 18.99 *(978-1-59698-789-0(8)*, Little Patriot Pr.) Regnery Publishing.
—Woodrow, the White House Mouse. Barnes, Cheryl Shaw, illus. 2012. (ENG.). 40p. (J). (gr. k-3). 17.99 *(978-1-59698-788-3(X)*, Little Patriot Pr.) Regnery Publishing.
Barnett, Mac. The Wolf, the Duck, & the Mouse. Klassen, Jon, illus. 2017. (ENG.). 40p. (J). (gr. -1-3). 18.99 *(978-0-7636-7754-1(X))* Candlewick Pr.
Basil of Baker Street, 1 vol. 2016. (Your Reading Path Ser.: 1). (Illus.). 112p. (J). (gr. 4-4). pap. *(978-1-4814-6401-7(9)*, c557f760-fd35-4d9b-81b4-60e49570d332, Rosen Classroom) Rosen Publishing Group, Inc., The.
Bassett, Madge A. At Bumblebee Farm. Bassett, Madge A., illus. 2009. (Illus.). 20p. pap. 13.46 *(978-1-4251-9230-3(0))* Trafford Publishing.
Beander, Lillian. Mylah's Bedtime Stories, 1 vol. 2009. 48p. pap. 16.95 *(978-1-61546-981-9(8))* America Star Bks.
Beam, Emily. Tumtum & Nutmeg: Adventures Beyond Nutmouse Hall. 2011. (Tumtum & Nutmeg Ser.: 1). (ENG., Illus.). 512p. (J). (gr. 3-7). pap. 14.99 *(978-0-316-07574-9(4))* Little, Brown Bks. for Young Readers.
Becker, Bonny. A Bedtime for Bear. Denton, Kady MacDonald, illus. 2010. (J). *(978-0-7636-5364-4(0))* Candlewick Pr.
—A Birthday for Bear. Candlewick Sparks. Denton, Kady MacDonald, illus. 2013. (Candlewick Sparks Ser.). (ENG.). 56p. (J). (gr. k-4). pap. 5.99 *(978-0-7636-6861-7(3))* Candlewick Pr.
—A Visitor for Bear. Denton, Kady MacDonald, illus. (Bear & Mouse Ser.). (ENG.). 56p. (J). (gr. -1-2). 2012. pap. 7.99 *(978-0-7636-4611-0(3))* 2008. 18.99 *(978-0-7636-2807-9(7))* Candlewick Pr.
—A Visitor for Bear. Denton, Kady MacDonald, illus. 2012. lib. bdg. 17.20 *(978-0-606-26930-8(4))* Turtleback.
Beckler, Bruce. The Secrets of the Green Mansion. l.t. ed. 2004. (Illus.). 240p. (J). per. 13.99 *(978-0-9745210-1-5(9))* Myers Publishing Co.
Beiser, Tim. Miss Mousie's Blind Date. Berman, Rachel, illus. 2012. 24p. (J). (gr. -1-2). 17.95 *(978-1-77049-251-6(8)*, Tundra Bks.) Tundra Bks. CAN. Dist: Penguin Random Hse. LLC.
Bellón, Teresa, illus. Speak up, Mouse! 2018. (J). bds. 7.99 *(978-1-61067-779-0(X))* Kane Miller.
Bennett, Diane. Put a Smile on Your Face. 2008. 24p. per. 24.95 *(978-1-4241-9895-5(X))* America Star Bks.
Benson, Jeffrey. The Adventures of Avortt & Rooney. 2005. pap. *(978-1-84401-490-3(8))* Athena Pr.
Bently, Peter. The Cat, the Mouse, & the Runaway Train. Cox, Steve, illus. 2013. (J). *(978-1-4351-4968-7(8))* Barnes & Noble, Inc.
Beraducci, Deborah. Tyler's Halloween Horror, 1 vol. Eyre, Jane, illus. 2009. 22p. pap. 24.95 *(978-1-4489-2133-1(3))* America Star Bks.
Berkowitz, Barbara. A Mouse in the House. 2009. 32p. pap. 14.49 *(978-1-4490-4258-5(9))* AuthorHouse.
Bernheimer, Kate. The Girl Who Wouldn't Brush Her Hair. Parker, Jake, illus. 2013. 40p. (J). (gr. -1-3). 17.99 *(978-0-375-86878-8(X)*, Schwartz & Wade Bks.) Random Hse. Children's Bks.
Bertouille, Ariane. Otis & Alice, 1 vol. Favreau, Marie-Claude, illus. 2013. (ENG.). 32p. (J). (gr. -1-k). 18.95 *(978-1-55455-294-8(X)*, ee91b326-3b75-46b6-b640-7e73fcb25770) Trifolium Bks., Inc. CAN. Dist: Firefly Bks., Ltd.
Best, Jessica Gabrielle. The Wish Giver's Promise. 2011. 16p. 16.95 *(978-1-4567-1385-0(X))* AuthorHouse.
Beverly-Barrier, Essie. Ouse the Mouse. Allen, Joshua, illus. 2009. 20p. pap. 12.99 *(978-1-4389-4518-7(3))* AuthorHouse.
Beverly, Cleary. The Mouse & the Motorcycle. 2014. (Mouse & the Motorcycle Ser.). (ENG.). 208p. (J). (gr. 2-5). 11.24 *(978-1-63245-245-0(6))* Lectorum Pubns., Inc.
Billingsley, Franny. Big Bad Bunny. Karas, G. Brian, illus. 2008. (ENG.). 40p. (J). (gr. k-3). 19.99 *(978-1-4169-0601-8(0)*, Atheneum/Richard Jackson Bks.) Simon & Schuster Children's Publishing.
Bird, Benjamin. A Cat Is Chasing Me Through This Book!, 1 vol. Pérez, Carmen & Pérez, Carmen, illus. 2014. (Tom & Jerry Ser.). (ENG.). 32p. (J). (gr. -1-2). 22.65 *(978-1-4795-5229-0(1)*, 125701, Picture Window Bks.) Capstone.
—Don't Give This Book a Bowl of Milk!, 1 vol. Pérez, Carmen & Pérez, Carmen, illus. 2014. (Tom & Jerry Ser.). (ENG.). 32p. (J). (gr. -1-2). 22.65 *(978-1-4795-5230-6(5)*, 125702, Picture Window Bks.) Capstone.
—This Book Is Not a Piece of Cheese!, 1 vol. Pérez, Carmen & Pérez, Carmen, illus. 2014. (Tom & Jerry Ser.). (ENG.). 32p. (J). (gr. -1-2). 22.65 *(978-1-4795-5231-3(3)*, 125703, Picture Window Bks.) Capstone.
Bishop, Anne. Anne Bishop's Christmas Dram: The Gift of Three. 2013. 28p. pap. 24.95 *(978-1-4626-8276-8(6))* America Star Bks.
Bishop, Brandy. The Christmas Mice, 1 vol. 2010. 30p. 24.95 *(978-1-4489-4438-5(4))* PublishAmerica, Inc.
Björkman, Steve. Look Out, Mouse! 2015. (I Like to Read Ser.). (ENG., Illus.). 24p. (J). (gr. -1-3). 7.99 *(978-0-8234-3397-1(8))* Holiday Hse., Inc.
Blair, Eric. The Country Mouse & the City Mouse: A Retelling of Aesop's Fable, 1 vol. Silverman, Dianne, illus. 2013. (My First Classic Story Ser.). (ENG.). 24p. (J). (gr. k-3). pap. 7.10 *(978-1-4795-1858-6(1)*, 123447, Picture Window Bks.) Capstone.
Blanchard, Patricia & Suhr, Joanne. There Was a Mouse. Gorbachev, Valeri, illus. 2003. (ENG.). 16p. (J). pap. 15.00 *(978-1-57274-702-9(1)*, BB2210, Bks. for Young Learners) Owen, Richard C. Pubs., Inc.
Bloser, Cheryl. Little Mouse & the Muddy Feet. 2012. 28p. pap. 9.99 *(978-0-9836771-1-6(5))* Mindstir Media.
Bloumis, Joy. An Adventure in Fairyland. 2013. 84p. pap. 10.50 *(978-1-62212-835-8(4)*, Strategic Bk. Publishing) Strategic Book Publishing & Rights Agency (SBPRA).
Bogart, Jo Ellen & Bogart, Jill. Out & about with the Big Tree Gang, 1 vol. Griffiths, Dean, illus. 2006. (Orca Echoes Ser.). (ENG.). 64p. (J). (gr. 2-4). 17.44 *(978-1-55143-603-6(5))* Orca Bk. Pubs. USA.
Bolander, Sharon Miller. At the Stroke of Midnight. 2012. 40p. pap. 24.95 *(978-1-4626-8905-7(1))* America Star Bks.
Bond, Felicia. The Halloween Play. Bond, Felicia, illus. 2008. Orig. Title: The Halloween Performance. (ENG., Illus.). 32p. (J). (gr. -1-1). pap. 7.99 *(978-0-06-135796-1(0)*, HarperCollins) HarperCollins Pubs.
Bonnell, Kris. Mmm, Apples. 2006. (J). pap. 3.95 *(978-1-933727-22-6(5))* Reading Reading Bks., LLC.
Botha, Ingrid. Chikin & Scrub. 2011. 108p. pap. 10.50 *(978-1-60976-295-7(9)*, Strategic Bk. Publishing) Strategic Book Publishing & Rights Agency (SBPRA).
Bottner, Barbara & Kruglik, Gerald. Wallace's Lists. Landstrom, Olof, illus. 2004. (ENG.). 40p. (J). (gr. -1-2). 17.99 *(978-0-06-000224-4(7)*, Tegen, Katherine Bks) HarperCollins Pubs.
—Wallace's Lists. Landstrom, Olof, illus. 2011. (J). (gr. 1-3). 29.95 *(978-0-545-04275-8(5))* Weston Woods Studios, Inc.
Bowen, Marvin. Adventures of the Fluffytail Mouse. 2011. 52p. (gr. -1). pap. 12.99 *(978-1-4670-3879-9(2))* AuthorHouse.
Bowman, Crystal. Little David & His Best Friend, 1 vol. Hartung, Susan Kathleen & Endersly, Frank, illus. 2010. (I Can Read! / Little David Ser.). (ENG.). 32p. (J). pap. 4.99 *(978-0-310-71710-2(8))* Zonderkidz.
—Little David Sings for the King, 1 vol. Hartung, Susan Kathleen, illus. 2010. (I Can Read! / Little David Ser.). (ENG.). 32p. (J). pap. 4.99 *(978-0-310-71711-9(6))* Zonderkidz.
—Little David's Big Heart, 1 vol. Hartung, Susan Kathleen & Endersby, Frank, illus. 2010. (I Can Read! Ser.). (ENG.). 32p. (J). pap. 4.99 *(978-0-310-71708-9(6))* Zonderkidz.
—Little David's Brave Day, 1 vol. Hartung, Susan Kathleen & Endersly, Frank, illus. 2010. (I Can Read! / Little David Ser.). (ENG.). 32p. (J). pap. 4.99 *(978-0-310-71709-6(4))* Zonderkidz.
Boyd, Ken. Tinsel Tail Mouse. 2009. 48p. pap. 16.25 *(978-1-60860-403-6(9)*, Eloquent Bks.) Strategic Book Publishing & Rights Agency (SBPRA).
Bradford James Nolan. The Mouse Who Lived in Fenway Park. Jim Connelly, illus. 2009. 36p. pap. 19.99 *(978-1-4389-4491-3(8))* AuthorHouse.
Bratun, Katy. Gingerbread Mouse. Bratun, Katy, illus. 2003. (Illus.). 32p. (J). (gr. -1-2). lib. bdg. 13.89 *(978-0-06-009081-4(2))* HarperCollins Pubs.
—Gingerbread Mouse: A Christmas Holiday Book for Kids. Bratun, Katy, illus. 2007. (ENG., Illus.). 32p. (J). (gr. -1-3). per. 7.99 *(978-0-06-009082-1(0)*, HarperCollins) HarperCollins Pubs.
Braun, Sebastien. Back to Bed, Ed!, 1 vol. (ENG., Illus.). 32p. (J). (gr. -1-k). 2014. pap. 7.95 *(978-1-56145-775-5(2))* 2010. 16.95 *(978-1-56145-518-8(0))* Peachtree Publishing Co. Inc.
—Mayday Mouse. Braun, Sebastien, illus. 2017. (Child's Play Library). (Illus.). 32p. (J). pap. *(978-1-84643-758-8(X))*; (ENG., *(978-1-84643-759-5(8))* Child's Play International Ltd.
Brave Little Mouse: Individual Title Six-Packs. (Story Steps Ser.). (gr. k-2). 32.00 *(978-0-7635-9831-0(3))* Rigby Education.

M N O

Brightwood, Laura, illus. Lion & Mousie. Brightwood, Laura, . 2007. (J). DVD *(978-1-934409-00-8(6))* 3-C Institute for Social Development.

Brown, Dan. Wild Symphony. Batori, Susan, illus. 2020. (ENG.). 44p. (J). (gr. -1-2). 19.99 *(978-0-593-12384-3(0)*, Rodale Kids) Random Hse. Children's Bks.

Brown, Dan. Wild Symphony. Batori, Susan, illus. 2023. (ENG.). 44p. (J). (gr. -1-2). pap. 8.99 ***(978-0-593-70423-3(1)***, Dragonfly Bks.) Random Hse. Children's Bks.

Brown, Michael. Santa Mouse. De Witt, Elfrieda, illus. 2019. (Santa Mouse Book Ser.). (ENG.). 32p. (J). (gr. -1-1). 17.99 *(978-1-5344-3793-7(2)*, Little Simon) Little Simon.

Brown, Palmer. Cheerful. 2012. (ENG., Illus.). 72p. (J). (gr. -1-2). 14.95 *(978-1-59017-501-9(8)*, NYR Children's Collection) New York Review of Bks., Inc., The.

—Hickory. Brown, Palmer, illus. 2013. (ENG., Illus.). 56p. (J). (gr. -1-2). 16.95 *(978-1-59017-627-6(8)*, NYR Children's Collection) New York Review of Bks., Inc., The.

—Something for Christmas. Brown, Palmer, illus. 2011. (ENG., Illus.). 40p. (J). (gr. -1-2). 14.95 *(978-1-59017-462-3(3)*, NYR Children's Collection) New York Review of Bks., Inc., The.

Brown, Ruth, illus. The Christmas Mouse. 2013. (J). *(978-1-4351-5021-8(X))* Barnes & Noble, Inc.

Bucklaschuk, Angela. My Doggy the Big Helper. 2012. 30p. pap. 11.95 *(978-1-61286-124-1(5))* Avid Readers Publishing Group.

Buehner, Caralyn. Merry Christmas, Mr. Mouse. Buehner, Mark, illus. 2015. 40p. (J). (gr. -1-k). 17.99 *(978-0-8037-4010-5(7)*, Dial Bks) Penguin Young Readers Group.

Bunting, Eve. The Mother's Day Mice Gift Edition. Brett, Jan, illus. 2017. (Holiday Classics Ser.). (ENG.). 40p. (J). (gr. -1-3). 8.99 *(978-0-544-88033-7(1)*, 1651181, Clarion Bks.) HarperCollins Pubs.

—Whose Shoe? Ruzzier, Sergio, illus. 2015. (ENG.). 32p. (J). (gr. -1-3). 16.99 *(978-0-544-30210-5(9)*, 1575895, Clarion Bks.) HarperCollins Pubs.

Burgess, Thornton W. The Adventures of Danny Meadow Mouse. (J). 18.95 *(978-0-8488-0377-3(9))* Amereon Ltd.

—Tommy & the Wishing-Stone. Cady, Harrison, illus. 2012. (Dover Children's Thrift Classics Ser.). (ENG.). 240p. (J). (gr. k-3). pap. 4.00 *(978-0-486-48105-0(0))* Dover Pubns., Inc.

—Whitefoot the Wood Mouse. (J). 18.95 *(978-0-8488-0395-7(7))* Amereon Ltd.

—Whitefoot the Wood Mouse. Cady, Harrison, illus. 2006. (Dover Children's Thrift Classics Ser.). (ENG.). 112p. (J). (gr. 3-8). per. 5.00 *(978-0-486-44944-9(0)*, 449440) Dover Pubns., Inc.

—Whitefoot the Woodmouse. 2007. 120p. per. 10.95 *(978-1-60312-258-0(3))*; 22.95 *(978-1-60312-756-1(9))* Aegypan.

—Whitefoot the Woodmouse. 2011. 118p. 23.95 *(978-1-4638-9567-9(4))* Rodgers, Alan Bks.

Burke, Christina. Melvin et le Grand Match de Hockey. Minguet, Anne, tr. Franfou, illus. 2013. 52p. *(978-0-9918561-3-8(9))*; pap. *(978-0-9918561-2-1(0))* Stars Aligned Publishing.

Burkert, Rand. Mouse & Lion. Burkert, Nancy Ekholm, illus. 2011. (ENG.). 32p. (J). (gr. -1-3). 18.99 *(978-0-545-10147-9(6)*, Di Capua, Michael) Scholastic, Inc.

Burningham, John. Mouse House. Burningham, John, illus. 2018. (ENG., Illus.). 32p. (J). (gr. -1-2). 16.99 *(978-1-5362-0039-3(5))* Candlewick Pr.

Burton, Jeffrey. The Itsy Bitsy Pilgrim. Rescek, Sanja, illus. 2016. (Itsy Bitsy Ser.). (ENG.). 16p. (J). (gr. -1 — 1). bds. 5.99 *(978-1-4814-6852-7(9)*, Little Simon) Little Simon.

Burton, Katherine. Une Souris Grise. Fernandes, Kim, illus.Tr. of Souris Grise. (FRE.). 24p. (J). pap. 6.99 *(978-0-590-16023-0(0))* Scholastic, Inc.

Bush, Robert Quacken. The Return of Pete Pack Rat. Bush, Robert Quacken, ed. rev. deluxe ed. 2005. (Illus.). 64p. (J). (gr. 2-4). reprint ed. 12.95 *(978-0-9712757-1-3(8))*; pap. 6.95 *(978-0-9712757-2-0(6))* Quackenbush, Robert Studios.

Bushnell, Steven G. The Big Adventures of Little Church Mouse: The Parables of Jesus. 2009. 96p. pap. 31.99 *(978-1-4490-0620-4(5))* AuthorHouse.

Butterworth, Nick. Jingle Bells. 2014. (ENG.). 32p. (J). 9.99 *(978-0-00-758399-7(0)*, HarperCollins Children's Bks.) HarperCollins Pubs. Ltd. GBR. Dist: HarperCollins Pubs.

Byers, Marcella. Mitsy & Marty Mouse Visit Grandpa. Grant, Cheryl, illus. 2014. (ENG.). 32p. (gr. -1-2). pap. 8.95 *(978-1-61448-740-1(5)*, 9781614487401) Morgan James Publishing.

Cabral, Noel. Rachel's Four-Legged Friend. 2012. 24p. 24.95 *(978-1-4626-6089-6(4))* America Star Bks.

Calmenson, Stephanie. Birthday at the Panda Palace. Cushman, Doug, illus. 2007. 32p. (J). (gr. -1-3). 15.99 *(978-0-06-052663-4(7))* HarperCollins Pubs.

Camp, V. Ray. The Little Mouse on the Prairie. Baker, David, illus. 2011. 28p. pap. 24.95 *(978-1-4560-1028-7(X))* America Star Bks.

Carlson, Nancy. First Grade, Here I Come! 2006. (Illus.). (J). *(978-1-4156-8114-5(7)*, Viking Adult) Penguin Publishing Group.

—Henry & the Bully. 2012. (ENG., Illus.). 32p. (J). (gr. -1-1). 21.19 *(978-0-670-01148-3(7)*, Viking) Penguin Publishing Group.

—Henry's Show & Tell. Carlson, Nancy, illus. 2012. (Nancy Carlson Picture Bks). (Illus.). 32p. (J). (gr. k-2). 56.72 *(978-0-7613-9308-5(0)*, Carolrhoda Bks.) Lerner Publishing Group.

—I Don't Like to Read! Carlson, Nancy, illus. 2007. (ENG., Illus.). 32p. (J). (gr. -1-1). 21.19 *(978-0-670-06191-4(3))* Penguin Young Readers Group.

Carman, Debby. I'm Maximum Cat, That's a Fact! 2007. (Illus.). 28p. (J). 14.99 *(978-0-9777340-2-3(1))* Faux Paw Media Group.

Carpenter, Joyce M. An Unexpected Friend. Hall, Bobby, illus. 2010. (ENG.). 24p. pap. 11.49 *(978-1-4520-0758-8(6))* AuthorHouse.

Carroll, Claudia. Missy Mouse & the Rocket Ship. 2008. (ENG.). 39p. pap. 9.95 *(978-0-557-01769-0(6))* Lulu Pr., Inc.

Carroll, Harlisha. Miracle Mouse & Jesus - Book: (Short Stories 1) 2012. 36p. pap. 24.95 *(978-1-4626-6615-7(9))* America Star Bks.

—Miracle Mouse & Jesus Book #3: Short Stories 2. 2013. 32p. pap. 24.95 *(978-1-4626-6647-8(7))* America Star Bks.

Carter, David A. & Carter, Noelle. Little Mouse & Daddy. Carter, David A. & Carter, Noelle, illus. 2005. (Little Mouse Ser.). (Illus.). 12p. (J). 7.95 *(978-1-58117-223-2(0)*, Intervisual/Piggy Toes) Bendon, Inc.

—Little Mouse & Mommy. Carter, David A. & Carter, Noelle, illus. 2005. (Little Mouse Ser.). (Illus.). 12p. (J). 7.95 *(978-1-58117-224-9(9)*, Intervisual/Piggy Toes) Bendon, Inc.

—Little Mouse Plays Peek-a-Boo. Carter, David A. & Carter, Noelle, illus. 2005. (Little Mouse Ser.). (Illus.). 12p. (J). 7.95 *(978-1-58117-225-6(7)*, Intervisual/Piggy Toes) Bendon, Inc.

—Little Mouse's Christmas. Carter, David A. & Carter, Noelle, illus. 2005. (Illus.). 12p. (J). 7.95 *(978-1-58117-226-3(5)*, Intervisual/Piggy Toes) Bendon, Inc.

Cartlidge, Michelle. The Mouse Christmas House: A Press-Out Model Book. (Illus.). 32p. (J). *(978-1-904613-67-1(5)*, Buster Bks.) O'Mara, Michael Bks., Ltd.

Casey, Grandpa. Meet the Müsh-Mice. 2008. 32p. per. 24.95 *(978-1-60441-061-7(2))* America Star Bks.

—The Trilogy: Three adventures of the Müsh-Mice. Brennan, Lisa, illus. 2011. 48p. pap. 24.95 *(978-1-4626-2095-1(7))* America Star Bks.

Chandler, Paul. Mouse of Commons - Mouse of Lords. 2006. 186p. pap. 14.99 *(978-1-4116-8447-8(8))* Lulu Pr., Inc.

Charles, Faustin & Terry, Michael. The Selfish Crocodile Book of Nursery Rhymes. Terry, Michael, illus. 2008. (Illus.). (J). (gr. -1-k). audio compact disk 25.95 *(978-0-7475-9523-6(2))* Bloomsbury Publishing Plc GBR. Dist: Independent Pubs. Group.

Charlie Church Mouse Bible Adventures! Early Elementary. 2003. (J). cd-rom 19.98 *(978-0-9714753-1-1(8))* LifeLine Studios, Inc.

Chinnery, Karen. Secret Agent Squirrel. 2006. (ENG.). 48p. per. 16.95 *(978-1-4241-5459-3(6))* America Star Bks.

Christian, Norma. A Christmas Mouse. 2012. 32p. pap. 13.99 *(978-1-4624-0328-8(X)*, Inspiring Voices) Author Solutions, LLC.

Christie, R. Gregory. Mousetropolis. 2016. (ENG., Illus.). 32p. (J). (gr. -1-3). 6.99 *(978-0-8234-3692-7(6))* Holiday Hse., Inc.

Chronicle Books, Chronicle & ImageBooks. Little Mouse: Finger Puppet Book: (Finger Puppet Book for Toddlers & Babies, Baby Books for First Year, Animal Finger Puppets) 2007. (Little Finger Puppet Board Bks.: FING). (ENG., Illus.). 12p. (J). (gr. -1 — 1). bds. 6.99 *(978-0-8118-6110-6(4))* Chronicle Bks. LLC.

Clairmont, Patsy. 5 Cheesy Stories: About Friendship, Bravery, Bullying, & More, 1 vol. Oeltjenbruns, Joni, illus. 2007. (Tails from the Pantry Ser.). (ENG.). 144p. (J). (gr. -1-2). 15.99 *(978-1-4003-1042-5(3)*, Tommy Nelson) Nelson, Thomas Inc.

Clark, Ruth. Airport Mouse Explores on Opening Day. 2008. (ENG.). 32p. (J). 15.95 *(978-0-9792963-4-5(X))* Hibiscus Publishing.

—Airport Mouse Works the Nightshift. 2008. (ENG.). 32p. (J). 15.95 *(978-0-9792963-3-8(1))* Hibiscus Publishing.

Clark, Ruth E. Airport Mouse. Jones, Phil, illus. 2008. (ENG.). 32p. (J). (gr. -1-3). 15.95 *(978-0-9792963-2-1(3))* Hibiscus Publishing.

—Airport Mouse Activity Fun Book 1. Jones, Phil, illus. 2010. 16p. (J). pap. 5.99 *(978-0-9792963-6-9(6))* Hibiscus Publishing.

—Airport Mouse Becomes a VIP/VIM World Traveler. Jones, Phil, illus. 2009. 32p. (J). 15.95 *(978-0-9792963-5-2(8))* Hibiscus Publishing.

—Airport Mouse Becomes a VIP/VIM World Traveler Activity Fun Book 4. Jones, Phil, illus. 2010. 16p. (J). pap. 5.99 *(978-0-9792963-9-0(0))* Hibiscus Publishing.

—Airport Mouse Explores on Opening Day Activity Fun Book 3. Jones, Phil, illus. 2010. 16p. (J). pap. 5.99 *(978-0-9792963-8-3(2))* Hibiscus Publishing.

—Airport Mouse Works the Night Shift Activity Fun Book 2. Jones, Phil, illus. 2010. 16p. (J). pap. 5.99 *(978-0-9792963-7-6(4))* Hibiscus Publishing.

Clark, Seneca & Giardi, Sandy. Frankie Goes to Fenway: The Tale of the Faithful, Red Sox-Loving Mouse. Decedue, Julie, illus. 2008. 56p. (J). 18.95 *(978-0-9767276-3-7(3))* Three Bean Pr.

Cleary, Beverly. The Mouse & the Motorcycle. Rogers, Jacqueline, illus. 2021. (Ralph S. Mouse Ser.: 1). (ENG.). 208p. (J). (gr. 3-7). 18.99 *(978-0-688-21698-6(6))*; reprint ed. pap. 9.99 *(978-0-380-70924-3(4))* HarperCollins Pubs. (HarperCollins).

—The Mouse & the Motorcycle: a Harper Classic. Rogers, Jacqueline, illus. 2017. (Harper Classic Ser.). (ENG.). 224p. (J). (gr. 3-7). 16.99 *(978-0-06-265798-5(4)*, HarperCollins) HarperCollins Pubs.

—The Ralph Mouse 3-Book Collection: The Mouse & the Motorcycle, Runaway Ralph, Ralph S. Mouse. 2023. (Ralph S. Mouse Ser.). (ENG.). 624p. (J). (gr. 3-7). pap. 23.97 *(978-0-06-441004-5(8)*, HarperCollins) HarperCollins Pubs.

—Ralph S. Mouse. Rogers, Jacqueline, illus. 2021. (Ralph S. Mouse Ser.: 3). (ENG.). 192p. (J). (gr. 3-7). 16.99 *(978-0-688-01452-0(6))*; pap. 9.99 *(978-0-380-70957-1(0))* HarperCollins Pubs. (HarperCollins).

—Ralph S. Mouse. (Mouse & the Motorcycle Ser.). 160p. (J). (gr. 3-5). pap. 4.95 *(978-0-8072-1476-3(0)*, Listening Library) Random Hse. Audio Publishing Group.

—El Ratoncito de la Moto. 2006.Tr. of Mouse & the Motorcycle. (SPA.). (J). (gr. 3-6). 16.00 *(978-0-613-67220-7(8))* Turtleback.

—El Ratoncito de la Moto: The Mouse & the Motorcycle (Spanish Edition), 1 vol. Darling, Louis, illus. 2006. (Ralph S. Mouse Ser.: 1).Tr. of Mouse & the Motorcycle. (SPA.). 160p. (J). (gr. 3-7). pap. 9.99 *(978-0-06-000057-8(0))* HarperCollins Español.

—Runaway Ralph. Rogers, Jacqueline, illus. 2021. (Ralph S. Mouse Ser.: 2). (ENG.). 224p. (J). (gr. 3-7). pap. 7.99 *(978-0-380-70953-3(8)*, HarperCollins) HarperCollins Pubs.

Clement, Emily. Thea Stilton & the Hollywood Hoax. Pellizzari, Barbara & Balleello, Chiara, illus. 2015. 159p. (J). *(978-1-5182-1175-1(5))* Scholastic, Inc.

—Thea Stilton & the Tropical Treasure. Cairoli, Valeria et al, illus. 2015. 157p. (J). *(978-1-4806-9889-5(X))* Scholastic, Inc.

Cochran, Kate & Benchmark Education Co., LLC Staff. Why Mice Hide. 2015. (BuildUp Ser.). (J). (gr. 1). *(978-1-4900-0728-1(8))* Benchmark Education Co.

Cole, Henry. A Nest for Celeste: A Story about Art, Inspiration, & the Meaning of Home. 2012. (Nest for Celeste Ser.: 1). (ENG., Illus.). 352p. (J). (gr. 3-7). pap. 9.99 *(978-0-06-170412-3(1)*, Tegen, Katherine Bks) HarperCollins Pubs.

—A Nest for Celeste: A Story about Art, Inspiration, & the Meaning of Home. Cole, Henry, illus. 2010. (Nest for Celeste Ser.: 1). (ENG., Illus.). 352p. (J). (gr. 3-7). 16.99 *(978-0-06-170410-9(5)*, Tegen, Katherine Bks) HarperCollins Pubs.

—The Somewhat True Adventures of Sammy Shine, 1 vol. 2018. (Illus.). 272p. (J). (gr. 3-7). pap. 7.95 *(978-1-56145-778-6(7))* Peachtree Publishing Co. Inc.

Cole, Rachael. Mousie, I Will Read to You. Crowton, Melissa, illus. 2018. 40p. (J). (gr. -1-2). 17.99 *(978-1-5247-1536-6(0)*, Schwartz & Wade Bks.) Random Hse. Children's Bks.

Collicott, Sharleen. Mildred & Sam. Collicott, Sharleen, illus. (I Can Read Bks.). (Illus.). (J). 2008. 64p. (gr. -1-2). lib. bdg. 17.89 *(978-0-06-058115-2(8)*, Geringer, Laura Book) 2004. (ENG., 48p. (gr. k-3). pap. 4.99 *(978-0-06-000200-8(X)*, HarperCollins) 2003. 48p. (gr. -1-18). 15.99 *(978-0-06-026681-3(3))* HarperCollins Pubs.

—Mildred & Sam & Their Babies. Collicott, Sharleen, illus. 2005. (I Can Read Bks.). (Illus.). 48p. (J). (gr. -1-2). 15.99 *(978-0-06-058111-4(5)*, Geringer, Laura Book) HarperCollins Pubs.

Condenzio, Mary. The Mouse & the Star. Long, Paulette Rich, illus. 2008. 13p. pap. 24.95 *(978-1-60441-449-3(9))* America Star Bks.

Cook, Sherry & Johnson, Terri. Mary Motion, 26 vols. Kuhn, Jesse, illus. l.t. ed. 2006. (Quirkles — Exploring Phonics through Science Ser.: 13). 32p. (J). 7.99 *(978-1-933815-12-1(4)*, Quirkles, The) Creative 3, LLC.

Coons, Susan. The Lighthouse Mouse. 2006. 19.99 *(978-0-9721410-1-7(4))* Vinland Pr.

Coons, Susan Anderson. Lighthouse Mouse Meets Simon the Cat. Sanne, Don, illus. 2012. 52p. pap. 10.03 *(978-1-4669-1223-6(5))* Trafford Publishing.

Corderoy, Tracey. Squish Squash Squeeze! Chapman, Jane, illus. 2016. (ENG.). 32p. (J). (gr. -1-2). 16.99 *(978-1-68010-011-2(4))* Tiger Tales.

Cosson, Kip. Ned Visits New York. 2006. (ENG., Illus.). 40p. (J). 16.95 *(978-0-9789384-0-6(2))* Kip Kids of New York.

Cote, Nancy, illus. Watch the Birdie! 2016. (ENG.). 32p. (J). (gr. -1-k). 16.99 *(978-1-63450-202-3(7)*, Sky Pony Pr.) Skyhorse Publishing Co., Inc.

—Watch the Cookie! 2014. (ENG.). 32p. (J). (gr. -1-k). 16.95 *(978-1-62914-630-0(7)*, Sky Pony Pr.) Skyhorse Publishing Co., Inc.

Cousins, Lucy. Maisy Goes Camping. 2009. (Maisy First Experiences Ser.). lib. bdg. 17.20 *(978-0-606-06667-9(5))* Turtleback.

—Maisy Goes Camping: A Maisy First Experience Book. Cousins, Lucy, illus. 2009. (Maisy Ser.). (ENG., Illus.). 32p. (J). (gr. k-k). pap. 7.99 *(978-0-7636-4368-3(8))* Candlewick Pr.

—Maisy Goes on Vacation: A Maisy First Experiences Book. Cousins, Lucy, illus. 2012. (Maisy Ser.). (ENG., Illus.). 32p. (J). (gr. -1-2). pap. 7.99 *(978-0-7636-6039-0(6))* Candlewick Pr.

—Maisy Goes to Preschool: A Maisy First Experiences Book. Cousins, Lucy, illus. 2010. (Maisy Ser.). (ENG., Illus.). 32p. (J). (gr. k-k). pap. 7.99 *(978-0-7636-5086-5(2))* Candlewick Pr.

—Maisy Goes to the City. 2014. (Maisy First Experiences Ser.). lib. bdg. 17.20 *(978-0-606-35157-7(4))* Turtleback.

—Maisy Goes to the City: A Maisy First Experiences Book. Cousins, Lucy, illus. 2014. (Maisy Ser.). (ENG., Illus.). 32p. (J). (gr. -1-2). 7.99 *(978-0-7636-6834-1(6))* Candlewick Pr.

—Maisy Goes to the Hospital: A Maisy First Experience Book. Cousins, Lucy, illus. 2009. (Maisy Ser.). (ENG., Illus.). 32p. (J). (gr. k-k). pap. 7.99 *(978-0-7636-4372-0(6))* Candlewick Pr.

—Maisy Goes to the Library. 2009. (Maisy First Experiences Ser.). lib. bdg. 17.20 *(978-0-606-06687-7(X))* Turtleback.

—Maisy Goes to the Library: A Maisy First Experience Book. Cousins, Lucy, illus. 2009. (Maisy Ser.). (ENG., Illus.). 32p. (J). (gr. k-k). pap. 6.99 *(978-0-7636-4371-3(8))* Candlewick Pr.

—Maisy Goes to the Local Bookstore. 2018. (Maisy First Experiences Pic Bks). (ENG.). 26p. (J). (gr. -1-k). 17.36 *(978-1-64310-238-2(9))* Penworthy Co., LLC, The.

—Maisy Goes to the Local Bookstore. 2018. (Maisy First Experiences Ser.). lib. bdg. 17.20 *(978-0-606-40914-8(9))* Turtleback.

—Maisy Goes to the Local Bookstore: A Maisy First Experiences Book. Cousins, Lucy, illus. (Maisy Ser.). (ENG., Illus.). 32p. (J). (-k). 2018. 6.99 *(978-1-5362-0085-0(9))* 2017. 12.99 *(978-0-7636-9255-1(7))* Candlewick Pr.

—Maisy Goes to the Museum: A Maisy First Experience Book. Cousins, Lucy, illus. 2009. (Maisy Ser.). (ENG., Illus.). 32p. (J). (gr. k-k). pap. 6.99 *(978-0-7636-4370-6(X))* Candlewick Pr.

—Maisy Learns to Swim: A Maisy First Experience Book. Cousins, Lucy, illus. 2015. (Maisy Ser.). (ENG., Illus.). 32p. (J). (-k). 7.99 *(978-0-7636-7749-7(3))* Candlewick Pr.

—Maisy's Animals Los Animales de Maisy: A Maisy Dual Language Book. Cousins, Lucy, illus. 2009. (Maisy Ser.). (Illus.). 16p. (J). (gr. -1-2). bds. 6.99 *(978-0-7636-4517-5(6))* Candlewick Pr.

—Maisy's Clothes la Ropa de Maisy: A Maisy Dual Language Book. Cousins, Lucy, illus. 2009. (Maisy Ser.). (Illus.). 16p. (J). (gr. -1-2). bds. 6.99 *(978-0-7636-4518-2(4))* Candlewick Pr.

—Maisy's Field Day. 2019. (Maisy First Experiences Pic Bks). (ENG.). 26p. (J). (gr. k-1). 17.36 *(978-0-87617-299-5(0))* Penworthy Co., LLC, The.

—Maisy's Field Day: A Maisy First Experiences Book. Cousins, Lucy, illus. 2016. (Maisy Ser.). (ENG., Illus.). 32p. (J). (-k). 12.99 *(978-0-7636-8441-9(4))* Candlewick Pr.

—Maisy's Fire Engine: A Maisy Shaped Board Book. Cousins, Lucy, illus. 2009. (Maisy Ser.). (ENG., Illus.). 16p. (J). (gr. k-k). bds. 7.99 *(978-0-7636-4252-5(5))* Candlewick Pr.

—Maisy's First Clock: A Maisy Fun-To-Learn Book. Cousins, Lucy, illus. 2011. (Maisy Ser.). (ENG., Illus.). 16p. (J). (gr. k-k). bds. 14.99 *(978-0-7636-5095-7(1))* Candlewick Pr.

—Maisy's Food Los Alimentos de Maisy: A Maisy Dual Language Book. Cousins, Lucy, illus. 2009. (Maisy Ser.). (SPA., Illus.). 16p. (J). (gr. -1-2). bds. 5.99 *(978-0-7636-4519-9(2))* Candlewick Pr.

—Maisy's Pool. 2015. 24p. pap. 4.00 *(978-1-61003-408-1(2))* Center for the Collaborative Classroom.

—Maisy's Train: A Maisy Shaped Board Book. Cousins, Lucy, illus. 2009. (Maisy Ser.). (ENG., Illus.). 16p. (J). (gr. k-k). bds. 7.99 *(978-0-7636-4251-8(7))* Candlewick Pr.

—Sweet Dreams, Maisy. Cousins, Lucy, illus. 2009. (Maisy Ser.). (ENG., Illus.). 32p. (J). (gr. -1-2). bds. 6.99 *(978-0-7636-4532-8(X))* Candlewick Pr.

—El Tren de Maisy. 2006.Tr. of Maisy's Train. (CAT & SPA., Illus.). 28p. (J). (gr. -1-k). 18.50 *(978-84-8488-043-1(5))* Serres, Ediciones, S. L. ESP. Dist: Lectorum Pubns., Inc.

—Where Are Maisy's Friends? A Maisy Lift-The-Flap Book. Cousins, Lucy, illus. 2010. (Maisy Ser.). (ENG., Illus.). 12p. (J). (-k). bds. 6.99 *(978-0-7636-4669-1(5))* Candlewick Pr.

—Where Does Maisy Live? 2010. 12p. bds. 4.99 *(978-976-3-64668-7(5))* Candlewick Pr.

—Where Does Maisy Live? A Maisy Lift-The-Flap Book. Cousins, Lucy, illus. 2010. (Maisy Ser.). (ENG., Illus.). 12p. (J). (-k). bds. 6.99 *(978-0-7636-4668-4(7))* Candlewick Pr.

—Where Is Maisy? A Maisy Lift-The-Flap Book. Cousins, Lucy, illus. 2010. (Maisy Ser.). (ENG., Illus.). 14p. (J). (gr. k-k). bds. 6.99 *(978-0-7636-4673-8(3))* Candlewick Pr.

Covey, Sean. When I Grow Up: Habit 2. Curtis, Stacy, illus. 2018. (7 Habits of Happy Kids Ser.: 2). (ENG.). 32p. (J). (gr. -1-1). 6.99 *(978-1-5344-1579-9(3)*, Simon & Schuster Bks. For Young Readers) Simon & Schuster Bks. For Young Readers.

—When I Grow Up: Habit 2 (Ready-To-Read Level 2) Curtis, Stacy, illus. 2019. (7 Habits of Happy Kids Ser.: 2). (ENG.). 32p. (J). (gr. k-2). 17.99 *(978-1-5344-4448-5(3))*; pap. 4.99 *(978-1-5344-4447-8(5))* Simon Spotlight. (Simon Spotlight).

Cowhard, Patricia Ann. B J 's Underground Adventure. 2011. 28p. pap. 15.99 *(978-1-4628-5577-3(6))* Xlibris Corp.

Cox, Judy. Cinco de Mouse-O! Ebbeler, Jeffrey, illus. 2011. (Adventures of Mouse Ser.: 2). (ENG.). 32p. (J). (gr. -1-3). pap. 7.99 *(978-0-8234-2328-6(X))* Holiday Hse., Inc.

—One Is a Feast for Mouse: A Thanksgiving Tale. Ebbeler, Jeffrey, illus. 2009. (Adventures of Mouse Ser.: 1). (ENG.). 32p. (J). (gr. -1-3). pap. 7.99 *(978-0-8234-2231-9(3))* Holiday Hse., Inc.

Cox, Phil Roxbee. Mouse Moves House. Tyler, Jenny, ed. Cartwright, Stephen, illus. rev. ed. 2006. (Phonic Readers Ser.). 16p. (J). (gr. -1-3). pap. 6.99 *(978-0-7945-1507-2(X)*, Usborne) EDC Publishing.

Cox, Phil Roxbee & Cartwright, Stephen. Mouse Moves House. 2004. (Easy Words to Read Ser.). (Illus.). 16p. (J). (gr. 1-18). pap. 6.95 *(978-0-7945-0367-3(5)*, Usborne) EDC Publishing.

Coxe, Molly. Princess Pig. 2018. (Bright Owl Bks.). (Illus.). 40p. (J). (gr. -1-2). pap. 6.99 *(978-1-57565-979-4(4)*, 1349fd5e-e9d9-4c7a-b8c9-e9f69e3c4360); lib. bdg. 17.99 *(978-1-57565-978-7(6)*, 95fbd3b3-968c-4313-9d96-307237a342f5) Astra Publishing Hse. (Kane Press).

—Rat Attack. 2018. (Bright Owl Bks.). (Illus.). 40p. (J). (gr. -1-2). pap. 6.99 *(978-1-57565-973-2(5)*, 34bdb775-fddd-4009-b783-5c0e1b6665d2); lib. bdg. 17.99 *(978-1-57565-972-5(7)*, b1838b00-5a75-4e2b-b0f5-3c67b44a1465) Astra Publishing Hse. (Kane Press).

Crane, Walter, illus. Mr Michael Mouse Unfolds His Tale. 2011. 36p. pap. 35.95 *(978-1-258-07891-1(0))* Literary Licensing, LLC.

Creed, Elizabeth. Millie's Merry Christmas. 2011. 26p. (J). pap. 12.95 *(978-1-4327-0580-0(6))* Outskirts Pr., Inc.

Creighton, B. L. Max's Seaworthy Adventure. 2009. 28p. pap. 13.99 *(978-1-4389-7329-6(2))* AuthorHouse.

Crespeno, John. Toby: The Mouse Who Lived in a Pumpkin. 2011. 84p. pap. 28.68 *(978-1-4634-1632-4(6))* AuthorHouse.

Crofoot, Nancy. Christmas in the Barn, 1 vol. Rawat, Tania, illus. 2009. 37p. pap. 24.95 *(978-1-61582-585-1(1))* America Star Bks.

—Sandy & Mitzi: Their First Adventure, 1 vol. Rawat, Tania, illus. 2009. 31p. pap. 24.95 *(978-1-60836-707-8(X))* America Star Bks.

Crouch, Kathryn L. Nibbly Noshers. 2010. (Illus.). 44p. pap. 16.99 *(978-1-4490-9448-5(1))* AuthorHouse.

Curato, Mike. Little Elliot, Big City. Curato, Mike, illus. 2014. (Little Elliot Ser.: 1). (ENG., Illus.). 40p. (J). (gr. -1-3). 18.99 *(978-0-8050-9825-9(9)*, 900121237, Holt, Henry & Co. Bks. For Young Readers) Holt, Henry & Co.

—Little Elliot, Big Family. Curato, Mike, illus. 2015. (Little Elliot Ser.: 2). (ENG., Illus.). 40p. (J). (gr. -1-3). 18.99 *(978-0-8050-9826-6(7)*, 900121238, Holt, Henry & Co. Bks. For Young Readers) Holt, Henry & Co.

—Little Elliot, Big Fun. Curato, Mike, illus. 2016. (Little Elliot Ser.: 3). (ENG., Illus.). 40p. (J). 18.99 *(978-0-8050-9827-3(5)*, 900121239, Holt, Henry & Co. Bks. For Young Readers) Holt, Henry & Co.

—Little Elliot, Fall Friends. Curato, Mike, illus. 2017. (Little Elliot Ser.: 4). (ENG., Illus.). 40p. (J). 18.99 *(978-1-62779-640-8(1)*, 900157312, Holt, Henry & Co. Bks. For Young Readers) Holt, Henry & Co.

Currey, Anna. Truffle Goes to Town. Currey, Anna, illus. 2003. (Illus.). 32p. (YA). *(978-1-85602-429-7(6)*, Pavilion Children's Books) Pavilion Bks.

Curtis, Shelly. Shellbear's Adventures. 2012. 56p. pap. *(978-1-4602-0601-0(0))* FriesenPress.

Cushman, Doug. Halloween Mice! Board Book. Cushman, Doug, illus. 2011. (ENG., Illus.). 28p. (J). (gr. -1-k). bds. 5.99 *(978-0-547-57573-5(4)*, 1457868, Clarion Bks.) HarperCollins Pubs.

D. Carlo the Mouse/ Book 1: Too Many Rules for One Little Mouse. 2013. 40p. pap. 19.99 *(978-1-4575-1917-8(8))* Dog Ear Publishing, LLC.

Dachman, Adam. The Player Piano Mouse. Julich, Jenniffer, illus. 2008. 32p. (J). 14.99 *(978-0-9797794-0-4(5))* Player Piano Mouse Productions (PPMP).

Dahl, Michael. Mouse Says Sorry, 1 vol. Vidal, Oriol, illus. 2012. (Hello Genius Ser.). (ENG.). 20p. (J). (gr. -1 — 1). bds. 7.99 *(978-1-4048-6789-5(9)*, 116227, Picture Window Bks.) Capstone.

Dahl, Roald. The Witches. Blake, Quentin, illus. 2007. (ENG.). 224p. (J). (gr. 3-7). 8.99 (978-0-14-241011-0(X), Puffin Books) Penguin Young Readers Group.

Danby, Aaron. Jazzmin's Jamboree. Martin, M. J., illus. 2005. 40p. 13.95 (978-0-9730583-3-8(1)) Lion & Mouse Tales, Inc. CAN. Dist: Hushion Hse. Publishing, Ltd.

Daniel, Martha Ann. Mimi Mouse Meets Roger Rat: A Tail of Bullying. 2012. 32p. (-18). pap. 19.99 (978-1-4772-8295-3(5)) AuthorHouse.

Danielson, Diane K. There Is a Mouse That Is Haunting Our House. 2012. (ENG.). 28p. (J). pap. 14.99 (978-0-9885157-0-3(9)) SDP Publishing.

Das, Christina. Munchy Mouse. l.t. ed. 2005. (Illus.). 32p. (J). 15.95 (978-0-9763082-0-1(7), A JuneOne Production) JuneOne Publishing Hub.

Dashney, John. The Adventures of Walter the Weremouse; the Adventures of Mishka the Mousewere. Somerville, Sheila, illus. 2005. 202p. (J). pap. (978-0-9633236-7-5(9)) Storm Peak Pr.

Davey, Keith Peter. Squeaks Narrow Squeaks. Frost, Justine, illus. 2009. 32p. pap. 14.62 (978-1-4120-4402-8(2)) Trafford Publishing.

Davies, Kate, illus. Little Squeak School. 2014. (J). (978-1-4351-5582-4(3)) Barnes & Noble, Inc.

—Welcome to the Mouse House. 2014. (J). (978-1-4351-5583-1(1)) Barnes & Noble, Inc.

De Boer, Joan. THE SULTAN AND THE MICE. 2007. (ENG., Illus.). 36p. (J). 18.95 (978-84-96788-84-8(9)) OQO, Editora ESP. Dist: Baker & Taylor Bks.

de Las Casas, Dianne. The House That Santa Built, 1 vol. Stone-Barker, Holly, illus. 2013. (ENG.). 32p. (J). (gr. -1-k). 16.99 (978-1-4556-1750-0(4), Pelican Publishing) Arcadia Publishing.

De Long, Robert & De Long, Janice. Redwall Study Guide. 2003. ring bd. 14.99 (978-1-58609-196-5(4)) Progeny Pr.

De Sena, Joseph. Mrs. Mouse & the Golden Flower. 2007. 56p. per. 19.95 (978-1-4327-1525-0(9)) Outskirts Pr., Inc.

Dean, Barbara. Rattalia's Birthday Stories. 2nd ed. 2013. 132p. (978-0-9572470-4-8(4)); pap. (978-0-9572470-5-5(2)) Newpole Bks.

Deedy, Carmen Agra & Wright, Randall. The Cheshire Cheese Cat: A Dickens of a Tale, 1 vol. Moser, Barry, illus. 256p. (J). (gr. 3-7). 2014. pap. 9.95 (978-1-56145-810-3(4)) 2011. 16.95 (978-1-56145-595-9(4)) Peachtree Publishing Co. Inc.

Deem, Saitofi Anne. Myrtle Teachable Moments Series, 16 vols. Incl. Myrtle Learns about Asthma. 8p. (gr. -1-3). pap. 7.95 (978-1-930694-00-2(8)); Myrtle Learns about Dangerous Situations. 8p. (gr. -1-3). pap. 7.95 (978-1-930694-03-3(2)); Myrtle Learns about Diabetes. 12p. (gr. -1-3). pap. 7.95 (978-1-930694-04-0(0)); Myrtle Learns about Hygiene. 8p. (gr. -1-3). pap. 7.95 (978-1-930694-09-5(1)); Myrtle Learns about Lice. 12p. (gr. -1-3). pap. 7.95 (978-1-930694-11-8(3)); Myrtle Learns about Medicine. 8p. (gr. -1-3). pap. 7.95 (978-1-930694-12-5(1)); Myrtle Learns about Safety. 8p. (gr. -1-3). pap. 7.95 (978-1-930694-13-2(X)); Myrtle Learns about Seizures. 8p. (gr. -1-3). pap. 7.95 (978-1-930694-14-9(8)); Myrtle Learns How You Catch an Illness. 8p. (gr. -1-3). pap. 7.95 (978-1-930694-10-1(5)); Myrtle Learns to Eat Well. 12p. (gr. -1-3). pap. 7.95 (978-1-930694-05-7(9)); Myrtle Learns to Get Along. 8p. (gr. -1-3). pap. 7.95 (978-1-930694-08-8(3)); Myrtle Learns to Make Friends. 8p. (gr. -1-3). pap. 7.95 (978-1-930694-07-1(5)); Myrtle Learns to Take Care of Boo Boos. 12p. (gr. -1-3). pap. 7.95 (978-1-930694-01-9(6)); Myrtle Learns Why Exercise Is Important. 8p. pap. 7.95 (978-1-930694-06-4(7)); Myrtle Makes a Choice. 8p. (gr. -1-3). pap. 7.95 (978-1-930694-02-6(4)); Myrtle's Friend Is Very Sick. 8p. (gr. -1-3). pap. 7.95 (978-1-930694-15-6(6)); (J). 1998. (Illus.). Set pap. 114.48 (978-1-930694-16-3(4)) Myrtle Learns.

Del Moral, Susana. La Casa de Violet. Zaidi, Nadeem, illus. 2005. (Baby Einstein: Libros de Carton Ser.). (SPA.). 10p. (J). (gr. -1). bds. (978-970-718-305-6(5), Silver Dolphin en Español) Advanced Marketing, S. de R. L. de C. V.

Delaney, Ned. Two Strikes, Four Eyes. Date not set. (J). pap. (978-0-679-84172-2(5)); lib. bdg. (978-0-679-94172-9(X)) Random Hse. Children's Bks. (Random Hse. Bks. for Young Readers).

DeLuise, Dom & Brown, Tim. No Place Like Home. 2007. 240p. pap. 9.95 (978-0-9769369-1-6(7)) Bacchus Bks.

Dennis, Chantal. Sammy the Mouse. 2011. 36p. pap. 32.70 (978-1-4568-2773-1(1)) Xlibris Corp.

Dennis, Kathryn. Too Many Questions. Dennis, Kathryn, illus. 2016. (ENG., Illus.). 32p. (J). 10.99 (978-1-61067-460-7(X)) Kane Miller.

DePrisco, Dorothea. Country Mouse & City Mouse. 2006. (ENG.). 12p. 10.95 (978-1-58117-479-3(9), Intervisual/Piggy Toes) Bendon, Inc.

Diaz, S. Jemmy & the Little Spider of Hope. 2012. 40p. pap. 20.99 (978-1-4772-7032-5(9)) AuthorHouse.

Dicamillo, Kate. The Tale of Despereaux: Being the Story of a Mouse, a Princess, Some Soup & a Spool of Thread. Ering, Timothy Basil, illus. 2013. 296p. (J). (978-0-7636-7205-8(X)) Candlewick Pr.

—The Tale of Despereaux: Being the Story of a Mouse, a Princess, Some Soup & a Spool of Thread. 2008. (J). 34.99 (978-0-7393-7105-3(3)) Findaway World, LLC.

—The Tale of Despereaux: Being the Story of a Mouse, a Princess, Some Soup & a Spool of Thread. 2006. 272p. (gr. 4-6). 18.00 (978-0-7569-6580-8(2)) Perfection Learning Corp.

—The Tale of Despereaux: Being the Story of a Mouse, a Princess, Some Soup & a Spool of Thread, 3 vols. 2006. 42.75 (978-1-4193-7734-1(5)) Recorded Bks., Inc.

—The Tale of Despereaux: Being the Story of a Mouse, a Princess, Some Soup & a Spool of Thread. Ering, Timothy Basil, illus. 2003. pap. (978-0-439-70167-9(8), Scholastic) Scholastic, Inc.

—The Tale of Despereaux: Being the Story of a Mouse, a Princess, Some Soup & a Spool of Thread. 2015. lib. bdg. 18.40 (978-0-606-37888-8(X)) Turtleback.

DiCamillo, Kate. The Tale of Despereaux: Being the Story of a Mouse, a Princess, Some Soup, & a Spool of Thread. Ering, Timothy Basil, illus. 2015. (ENG.). 272p. (J). (gr. 2-5). pap. 8.99 (978-0-7636-8089-3(3)) Candlewick Pr.

Dicamillo, Kate. The Tale of Despereaux: Being the Story of a Mouse, a Princess, Some Soup & a Spool of Thread. 2009. 9.84 (978-0-7848-3043-7(6), Everbind) Marco Bk. Co.

—The Tale of Despereaux: Being the Story of a Mouse, a Princess, Some Soup & a Spool of Thread. Ering, Timothy Basil, illus. l.t. ed. 2004. (Thorndike Literacy Bridge Ser.). (ENG.). 247p. (J). pap. 11.95 (978-1-4104-1527-1(9)) Thorndike Pr.

DiCamillo, Kate. The Tale of Despereaux Deluxe Anniversary Edition: Being the Story of a Mouse, a Princess, Some Soup, & a Spool of Thread. Ering, Timothy Basil, illus. 2023. (ENG.). 288p. (J). (gr. 2-5). 24.99 **(978-1-5362-2867-0(2))** Candlewick Pr.

Dicamillo, Kate & Ering, Timothy Basil. The Tale of Despereaux: Being the Story of a Mouse, a Princess, Some Soup & a Spool of Thread. 2005. (CHI.). (J). pap. 12.95 (978-7-5307-3545-9(4)) New Buds Publishing Hse. CHN. Dist: Chinasprout, Inc.

Dickson, Robert. Sam Ferret Mysteries. 2010. 88p. pap. 14.95 (978-1-4259-2741-7(6)) AuthorHouse.

Dillard, Sarah. Mouse Scouts: Make Friends. 2018. (Mouse Scouts Ser.: 4). (Illus.). 160p. (J). (gr. 2-5). pap. 7.99 (978-0-385-75612-9(7), Yearling) Random Hse. Children's Bks.

Disney Books. Mickey Mouse Clubhouse: Minnie's Valentine. rev. ed. 2007. (ENG., Illus.). 24p. (J). (gr. -1-k). pap. 4.99 (978-1-4231-0746-0(2), Disney Press Books) Disney Publishing Worldwide.

—5-Minute Mickey Mouse Stories. 2018. (5-Minute Stories Ser.). (ENG., Illus.). 192p. (J). (gr. 1-3). 12.99 (978-1-368-02235-4(9), Disney Press Books) Disney Publishing Worldwide.

Dixon, Amy. Marathon Mouse. Denlinger, Sam, illus. 2012. (ENG.). 32p. (J). (gr. -1-k). 16.95 (978-1-61608-966-5(0), 608966, Sky Pony Pr.) Skyhorse Publishing Co., Inc.

Doerrfeld, Cori. Little Bunny Foo Foo: The Real Story. 2016. (Illus.). 32p. (J). (-k). pap. 8.99 (978-1-101-99774-1(5), Puffin Books) Penguin Young Readers Group.

Dogzilla (Digest) 2003. (ENG., Illus.). 32p. (J). (gr. -1-3). pap. 8.99 (978-0-15-204949-2(5), 1194945, Clarion Bks.) HarperCollins Pubs.

Donaldson, Julia. El Grufalo. Scheffler, Axel, illus. 2003. (SPA.). 32p. (J). (gr. k-2). 7.96 (978-84-233-3145-1(8), DS4478) Ediciones Destino ESP. Dist: Lectorum Pubns., Inc.

—The Gruffalo. 2006. (ENG., Illus.). 32p. (J). (gr. -1-2). pap. 7.99 (978-0-14-240387-7(3), Puffin Books) Penguin Young Readers Group.

—The Gruffalo. Scheffler, Axel, illus. 2005. (ENG.). (J). (gr. -1-2). 32p. 18.99 (978-0-8037-3109-7(4)); 26p. bds. 8.99 (978-0-8037-3047-2(0)) Penguin Young Readers Group. (Dial Bks).

—The Gruffalo. 2006. lib. bdg. 18.40 (978-0-606-23141-1(2)) Turtleback.

—Gruffalo in Scots. Robertson, James, tr. Scheffler, Axel, illus. 2012. (SCO.). 32p. (J). (-k). pap. 10.99 (978-1-84502-503-8(2)) Black and White Publishing Ltd. GBR. Dist: Independent Pubs. Group.

—The Gruffalo's Child. Scheffler, Axel, illus. 2007. (ENG.). 32p. (J). (gr. -1-2). pap. 7.99 (978-0-14-240754-7(2), Puffin Books) Penguin Young Readers Group.

Donovan, Michelle O. Joshua, Helmut, & Bethlehem. 2011. 56p. pap. 8.95 (978-1-4620-5867-9(1)) iUniverse, Inc.

Douglas, Babette. Miss Evonne: And the Mice of Nice! Johnson, John, illus. 2006. (Kiss a Me Teacher Creature Stories Ser.). (J). (gr. -1-3). 9.99 (978-1-890343-19-4(6)) Kiss A Me Productions, Inc.

Driscoll, Laura. Count off, Squeak Scouts! Melmon, Deborah, illus. 2013. (Mouse Math Ser.). 32p. (J). (gr. -1-1). 22.60 (978-1-57565-524-6(1)); pap. 7.99 (978-1-57565-525-3(X), 277c03f0-6275-4a53-8910-63eb90361d8d, Kane Press) Astra Publishing Hse.

—Count off, Squeak Scouts! 2018. (Mouse Math Ser.). (ENG.). 32p. (J). (gr. -1-1). lib. bdg. 34.28 (978-1-4896-8289-5(9), AV2 by Weigl) Weigl Pubs., Inc.

—A Mousy Mess. Melmon, Deborah, illus. 2014. (Mouse Math (r) Ser.). 32p. (J). (gr. -1-1). 22.60 (978-1-57565-646-5(9)) Astra Publishing Hse.

—A Mousy Mess. 2018. (Mouse Math Ser.). (ENG.). 32p. (J). (gr. -1-1). lib. bdg. 34.28 (978-1-4896-8295-6(3), AV2 by Weigl) Weigl Pubs., Inc.

Dubuc, Marianne. Mr. Postmouse's Rounds. Dubuc, Marianne, illus. 2015. (ENG., Illus.). 24p. (J). (gr. -1-2). 17.95 (978-1-77138-572-5(3)) Kids Can Pr., Ltd. CAN. Dist: Hachette Bk. Group.

Dufresne, Michèle. Town Mouse & Country Mouse. 2005. (Folk Tales Set 2 Ser.). (J). pap. 7.67 (978-1-58453-303-0(X)) Pioneer Valley Bks.

Duncan, Sharyn. The Mouse House & other Stories: You Are the Artist. 2004. 40p. (J). 9.95 (978-1-933002-04-0(2)) PublishingWorks.

Duskey Rinker, Sherri. It's So Quiet: A Not-Quite-Going-To-Bed Book. Fucile, Tony, illus. 2021. (ENG.). 56p. (J). (gr. -1-k). 17.99 (978-1-4521-4544-0(X)) Chronicle Bks. LLC.

Dyan, Penelope. The Day an Elephant Flies! Dyan, Penelope, illus. 2013. (Illus.). 34p. pap. 11.95 (978-1-61477-113-5(8)) Bellissima Publishing, LLC.

—The Warrior Mouse of Forest Hollow. Quinn, Courtney, illus. 2008. 108p. 17.95 (978-1-935118-00-8(5)) Bellissima Publishing, LLC.

—The Warrior Mouse of Forest Hollow. 2005. (J). per. 5.95 (978-0-9771916-5-9(6)) Bellissima Publishing, LLC.

Earhart, Kristin. Roscoe & the Pony Parade. Gurney, John, illus. 2008. (Little Apple Ser.). 88p. (J). (978-0-545-08094-1(0)) Scholastic, Inc.

East, Jacqueline, illus. The Town Mouse & the Country Mouse. 2007. (Picture Book Classics Ser.). (J). (gr. -1-3). 24p. 9.99 (978-0-7945-1877-6(X)); 48p. 8.99 (978-0-7945-1613-0(0)) EDC Publishing. (Usborne).

Eaton, Gordon J. Piebald & the Parade of Small Animals. 2009. 184p. pap. 14.99 (978-1-60791-991-9(5)) Salem Author Services.

Eberle, Dina P. The Mice Next Door, 1 vol. 2010. 18p. 24.95 (978-1-4512-1206-8(2)) PublishAmerica, Inc.

Ebie, Mora. Little Mouse's Hawaiian Christmas Present. Braffet, Holly, illus. 2011. 28p. (J). (978-1-56647-956-1(8)) Mutual Publishing LLC.

Egan, Tim. Dodsworth in Paris (Reader) Egan, Tim, illus. 2010. (Dodsworth Book Ser.). (ENG., Illus.). 48p. (J). (gr. 1-4). pap. 4.99 (978-0-547-33192-8(4), 1417441, Clarion Bks.) HarperCollins Pubs.

Eggleton, Jill. Brave Mouse, 3 vols., Pack. Taylor, Clive, illus. (Sails Literacy Ser.). 24p. (gr. 1-18). 57.00 (978-0-7578-3205-5(9)) Rigby Education.

Egielski, Richard. Slim & Jim. Egielski, Richard, illus. 2005. (Illus.). 37p. (J). (gr. k-4). reprint ed. 16.00 (978-0-7567-8936-7(2)) DIANE Publishing Co.

Ehlert, Lois. Boo to You! Ehlert, Lois, illus. 2009. (ENG., Illus.). 42p. (J). (gr. -1-2). 19.99 (978-1-4169-8625-6(1), Beach Lane Bks.) Beach Lane Bks.

—The Scraps Book: Notes from a Colorful Life. Ehlert, Lois, illus. 2014. (ENG., Illus.). 72p. (J). (gr. k-5). 17.99 (978-1-4424-3571-1(2)) Simon & Schuster Children's Publishing.

Emberley, Rebecca. The Lion & the Mice. Emberley, Ed, illus. 2012. (I Like to Read Ser.). (ENG.). 24p. (J). (gr. -1-3). pap. 7.99 (978-0-8234-2641-6(6)) Holiday Hse., Inc.

—Mice on Ice. Emberley, Ed, illus. 2013. (I Like to Read Ser.). (ENG.). 24p. (J). (gr. -1-3). pap. 7.99 (978-0-8234-2908-0(3)) Holiday Hse., Inc.

Engelbreit, Mary. Mary Engelbreit's A Merry Little Christmas: Celebrate from A to Z. Engelbreit, Mary, illus. 2006. (Illus.). 40p. (J). (gr. -1-3). lib. bdg. 17.89 (978-0-06-074159-4(7)) HarperCollins Pubs.

—Mary Engelbreit's a Merry Little Christmas: Celebrate from a to Z: a Christmas Holiday Book for Kids. Engelbreit, Mary, illus. 2010. (ENG., Illus.). 40p. (J). (gr. -1-3). pap. 7.99 (978-0-06-074160-0(0), HarperCollins) HarperCollins Pubs.

Epstein, Diane & Sullivan, Abigail. Three Nearsighted Mice. 2009. 32p. pap. 14.49 (978-1-4343-8822-3(0)) AuthorHouse.

Evelyn. Lucy the Elephant & Sami the Mouse: A Bedtime Story. Conforti, John W., tr. Conforti, John W., illus. 2003. (J). (978-0-9740115-0-9(9)) WeBeANS Corp.

—Lucy the Elephant & Sami the Mouse: The Birthday Party. Conforti, John W., illus. 2004. (J). (978-0-9740115-1-6(7)) WeBeANS Corp.

Ewert, Marcus. Mr. Pack Rat Really Wants That. Stark, Kayla, illus. 2018. 40p. (J). (gr. -1-3). 14.95 (978-1-946764-25-6(6), Plum Blossom Bks.) Parallax Pr.

Fagan, Cary. Ten Old Men & a Mouse. Clement, Gary, illus. 2007. 32p. (J). (gr. 3-7). 18.95 (978-0-88776-716-6(8), Tundra Bks.) Tundra Bks. CAN. Dist: Penguin Random Hse. LLC.

Falla, Lynne. World of the Weeples: Sophie & the Weeples. 2012. 24p. pap. 15.99 (978-1-4771-2078-1(5)) Xlibris Corp.

Farley, Jan. Fleur, a Lonely Pocket Mouse. 2011. 32p. pap. 16.95 (978-1-4560-4073-4(1)) America Star Bks.

Feldman, Thea, et al. Harry Cat & Tucker Mouse: Harry to the Rescue! 2011. (My Readers: Level 2 Ser.). (ENG., Illus.). 48p. (J). (gr. k-2). 16.19 (978-0-312-62507-8(3)) Square Fish.

Félix, Monique. The Alphabet. 2015. (J). pap. (978-1-62832-262-0(4), Creative Paperbacks) Creative Co., The.

Felix, Monique. Mouse Book: the Colors. Felix, Monique, illus. 2013. (ENG., Illus.). 32p. (J). (gr. -1-k). 12.99 (978-1-56846-234-9(4), 21757, Creative Editions) Creative Co., The.

Felix, Monique, illus. The Alphabet. 2012. (Mouse Book Ser.). 32p. (J). (gr. -1-k). 12.99 (978-1-56846-226-4(3), 22054, Creative Editions) Creative Co., The.

—Mouse Book: the Numbers. 2013. 32p. (J). (gr. -1-k). 12.99 (978-1-56846-235-6(2), 21759, Creative Editions) Creative Co., The.

—Mouse Books: the Boat. 2014. 32p. (J). (gr. -1-k). 12.99 (978-1-56846-252-3(2), 21603, Creative Editions) Creative Co., The.

—Mouse Books: the Opposites. 2014. 32p. (J). (gr. -1-k). 12.99 (978-1-56846-251-6(4), 21605, Creative Editions) Creative Co., The.

—The Wind. 2012. (Mouse Book Ser.). (ENG.). 32p. (J). (gr. -1-k). 12.99 (978-1-56846-227-1(1), 22055, Creative Editions) Creative Co., The.

Fiedler, Lisa. Hopper's Destiny. To, Vivienne, illus. 2016. (Mouseheart Ser.: 2). (ENG.). 368p. (J). (gr. 3-7). pap. 8.99 (978-1-4814-2090-7(9), McElderry, Margaret K. Bks.) McElderry, Margaret K. Bks.

—Mouseheart. To, Vivienne, illus. (Mouseheart Ser.: 1). (ENG.). (J). (gr. 3-7). 2015. 336p. pap. 8.99 (978-1-4424-8783-3(6)) 2014. 320p. 18.99 (978-1-4424-8781-9(X)) McElderry, Margaret K. Bks. (McElderry, Margaret K. Bks.).

—Return of the Forgotten. To, Vivienne, illus. 2015. (Mouseheart Ser.: 3). (ENG.). 320p. (J). (gr. 3-7). 16.99 (978-1-4814-2092-1(5), McElderry, Margaret K. Bks.) McElderry, Margaret K. Bks.

Filoche, Eric. Hey ! We're Talking about Ourselves ! 2013. 68p. pap. (978-2-9538737-4-0(0)) Koshkindom.

Finch, Mary. The Little Red Hen. Slater, Kate, illus. 2018. (ENG.). 32p. (J). (gr. k-5). pap. 9.99 (978-1-78285-041-0(4)) Barefoot Bks., Inc.

Finch, Mary & Messing, Debra. The Little Red Hen. Slater, Kate, illus. 2013. 32p. (J). (gr. -1-2). 9.99 (978-1-84686-751-4(7)); 16.99 (978-1-84686-575-6(1)) Barefoot Bks., Inc.

Finkelstein, Ruth. Mendel the Mouse, Bk. 1. (Illus.). (J). 10.00 (978-0-914131-43-4(5), D350) Torah Umesorah Pubns.

Fisher, Meaghan. Mousekabitz. Dunnier, Tina, illus. 2013. (ENG.). 32p. (J). pap. 8.99 (978-1-938768-31-6(0)) Gypsy Pubns.

Fitch, Sheree. There's a Mouse in My House! braille ed. 2004. (Illus.). (J). (gr. k-3). spiral bd. (978-0-616-07235-6(X)); spiral bd. (978-0-616-07234-9(1)) Canadian National Institute for the Blind/Institut National Canadien pour les Aveugles.

Fitzgerald, June. Squeaky: The Little Mouse Who Didn't Listen. 2013. (ENG.). 20p. (J). pap. 14.95 (978-1-4787-1559-7(6)) Outskirts Pr., Inc.

Fitzpatrick-Hale-Herself, Donna Marie. Snake & Mouse: Ryan's birthday Tea. 2011. (Illus.). 44p. pap. 17.04 (978-1-4567-8590-1(7)) AuthorHouse.

Fleming, Denise. Alphabet under Construction. Fleming, Denise, illus. 2006. (ENG., Illus.). 32p. (J). (gr. -1-k). reprint ed. pap. 8.99 (978-0-8050-8112-1(7), 900039580) Square Fish.

—Go, Shapes, Go! Fleming, Denise, illus. 2014. (ENG., Illus.). 40p. (J). (gr. -1-3). 18.99 (978-1-4424-8240-1(0), Beach Lane Bks.) Beach Lane Bks.

—Lunch. 2014. 32p. pap. 8.00 (978-1-61003-225-4(X)) Center for the Collaborative Classroom.

Floen, Douglas. Knowing Noah: The Adventures of a Mouse Who Could Read. 2012. 88p. pap. 13.95 (978-1-4772-4506-4(5)) AuthorHouse.

Fogle, Christina Melato, illus. Museum Mouse. 2017. (J). pap. (978-1-5393-7488-6(2)) CreateSpace Independent Publishing Platform.

Fors, Judi & Elizabeth, Megan. Twitch. 2017. (ENG.). 48p. (J). 17.99 (978-1-68198-246-5(3)) Rocky Nook.

Fox, Mem. This & That. Horacek, Judy, illus. 2017. (ENG.). 32p. (J). (gr. -1-k). 17.99 (978-1-338-03780-7(3), Scholastic Pr.) Scholastic, Inc.

Fraggalosch, Audrey. Let's Explore, Moose! Forest, Crista, illus. 2003. (Soundprints' Read-and-Discover Ser.). (ENG.). 32p. (J). (gr. -1-1). 12.95 (978-1-59249-152-0(9), PS2017) Soundprints.

Frederick, Heather Vogel. The Black Paw, 1. 2013. (Spy Mice Ser.: 1). (ENG., Illus.). 224p. (J). (gr. 3-6). pap. 7.99 (978-1-4424-6701-9(0)) Simon & Schuster, Inc.

—For Your Paws Only. 2013. (Spy Mice Ser.: 2). (ENG., Illus.). 240p. (J). (gr. 3-6). pap. 6.99 (978-1-4424-6703-3(7), Simon & Schuster Bks. For Young Readers) Simon & Schuster Bks. For Young Readers.

—For Your Paws Only. Comport, Sally Wern, illus. 2006. (Spy Mice Ser.: 2). (ENG.). 272p. (J). (gr. 3-6). pap. 5.99 (978-1-4169-4025-8(1), Simon & Schuster Bks. For Young Readers) Simon & Schuster Bks. For Young Readers.

—For Your Paws Only. Comport, Sally Wern, illus. 2005. (Spy Mice Ser.). (ENG.). 272p. (J). (gr. 4-6). 9.95 (978-1-4169-0573-8(1)) Simon & Schuster Children's Publishing.

—Hide-And-Squeak. Payne, C. F., illus. 2011. (ENG.). 32p. (J). (gr. -1-1). 16.99 (978-0-689-85570-2(2), Simon & Schuster Bks. For Young Readers) Simon & Schuster Bks. For Young Readers.

Freedman, Claire. The Monster of the Woods! Julian, Russell, illus. 2013. (ENG.). 32p. (J). pap. (978-0-545-51571-9(8), Cartwheel Bks.) Scholastic, Inc.

Friedman, J. S. Casablanca. Beatrice, Chris, illus. 2013. (Maurice's Valises Ser.: Vol. 3). (ENG.). 53p. (J). (gr. k-4). 16.95 (978-94-91613-09-8(X)) Mouse Prints Pr. NLD. Dist: Ingram Publisher Services.

—In the Beginning. Beatrice, Chris, illus. 2013. (Maurice's Valises Ser.: Vol. 1). (ENG.). 45p. (J). (gr. k-4). 16.95 (978-94-91613-03-6(0)) Mouse Prints Pr. NLD. Dist: Ingram Publisher Services.

—The Micetro of Moscow. Beatrice, Chris, illus. 2013. (Maurice's Valises Ser.: Vol. 2). (ENG.). 44p. (J). (gr. k-4). 16.95 (978-94-91613-06-7(5)) Mouse Prints Pr. NLD. Dist: Ingram Publisher Services.

Fuerst, Jeffrey B. Three Blind Mice. Walker, Sholto, illus. 2010. (Rising Readers Ser.). (J). 3.49 (978-1-60719-707-2(3)) Newmark Learning LLC.

Fujikawa, Brian. The Adventures of Bibole, Rivol & Michelle: The French Fry Caper. 2013. 72p. pap. 24.27 (978-1-4907-0954-3(1)) Trafford Publishing.

Furie, Matt. The Night Riders. 2012. (Illus.). 48p. (J). 17.95 (978-1-936365-56-2(1), 2454ed7d-2dca-42de-ba36-428c14a0a599) McSweeney's Publishing.

Fyleman, Rose. Mice. Ehlert, Lois, illus. 2012. (ENG.). 40p. (J). (gr. -1-k). 16.99 (978-1-4424-5684-6(1), Beach Lane Bks.) Beach Lane Bks.

Gall, Allan R. Of Mouse & Magic. 2011. (ENG., Illus.). 269p. (J). (gr. 3-7). pap. 12.95 (978-1-936401-78-9(9)) Salem Author Services.

Gallagher, Diana G. Mice Capades, 1 vol. Puglisi, Adriana & Puglisi, Adriana, illus. 2013. (Pet Friends Forever Ser.). (ENG.). 88p. (J). (gr. 1-3). pap. 5.95 (978-1-4795-1863-0(8), 123501, Picture Window Bks.) Capstone.

Galvin, Laura Gates. Deer Mouse at Old Farm Road. 2005. (Smithsonian's Backyard Ser.). (ENG., Illus.). 32p. (J). (gr. -1-2). 8.95 (978-1-59249-223-7(1), SC5015); pap. 6.95 (978-1-59249-195-7(2), S5015) Soundprints.

Gandy, Deborah A. A Squeaky Little Mouse Named Rainbow. 2011. 44p. pap. 21.99 (978-1-4568-7546-6(9)) Xlibris Corp.

Gannon, Patty. Desdemona & the Eggs. 2011. 52p. pap. 23.00 (978-1-4567-1581-6(X)) AuthorHouse.

Garfein, Stanley Joe. Tales of the Temple Mice. 2006. (Illus.). 92p. (J). 14.95 (978-0-9787422-0-1(6)) Garfein, Stanley.

Garland, Michael. Hooray José!, 1 vol. Garland, Michael, illus. 2007. (ENG., Illus.). 32p. (J). (gr. -1-3). 16.99 (978-0-7614-5345-1(8)) Marshall Cavendish Corp.

—Pizza Mouse. 2017. (I Like to Read Ser.). (ENG.). 32p. (J). (gr. -1-3). 7.99 (978-0-8234-3853-2(8)) Holiday Hse., Inc.

Gauthier, Lance C., text. The One-Eared Mouse of Pasture Hill. 2003. 55p. (J). per. 6.95 (978-1-884540-70-7(8)) Haley's.

George, Joshua. Fame Mouse. 2017. (ENG., Illus.). 32p. (J). (gr. -1-k). pap. 10.99 (978-1-78445-704-4(3)) Top That! Publishing PLC GBR. Dist: Independent Pubs. Group.

George, Kallie. The Greatest Gift. Graegin, Stephanie, illus. 2017. (Heartwood Hotel Ser.: 2). (ENG.). 176p. (J). (gr. 2-5). 14.99 (978-1-4847-3234-2(0)) Hyperion Bks. for Children.

—The Greatest Gift. 2017. (Heartwood Hotel Ser.: 2). (J). lib. bdg. 16.00 (978-0-606-39967-8(4)) Turtleback.

—A True Home. Graegin, Stephanie, illus. 2017. (Heartwood Hotel Ser.: 1). (ENG.). 176p. (J). (gr. 2-5). 14.99 (978-1-4847-3161-1(1)) Disney Pr.

—A True Home. 2017. (Heartwood Hotel Ser.: 1). (J). lib. bdg. 16.00 (978-0-606-39968-5(2)) Turtleback.

George, Lindsay Barrett. Inside Mouse, Outside Mouse. George, Lindsay Barrett, illus. (ENG., Illus.). 40p. (J). (gr. -1-3). 2004. 17.99 (978-0-06-000466-8(5)) 2006. reprint ed. pap. 8.99 (978-0-06-000468-2(1)) HarperCollins Pubs. (Greenwillow Bks.).

Geronimo Stilton Staff. Dinosaur Danger. 2016. (Illus.). 128p. (J). pap. (978-1-338-05288-6(8)) Scholastic, Inc.

Getsinger, Mary. A Dream Come True. 2009. 20p. pap. 9.50 (978-1-4251-8885-6(0)) Trafford Publishing.

M
N
O

Gibbs, Lynne. Molly Mouse Is Shy: A Story of Shyness, 1 vol. Mitchell, Missy, illus. 2009. (Let's Grow Together Ser.). (ENG.). 32p. (J). (gr. k-1). pap. 11.55 *(978-1-60754-761-7(9),* 6aac5f9c-dab3-409a-95c2-a45eaeb14dcd); lib. bdg. 27.27 *(978-1-60754-756-3(2),* 2e202d76-3c52-42a4-b9bb-002ce24a3c6d) Rosen Publishing Group, Inc., The. (Windmill Bks.).

Gifford, Dorinda. Harriet the Ferret, 1 vol. Luevano, Raul, illus. 2009. 20p. pap. 24.95 *(978-1-59129-405-4(3))* America Star Bks.

Gillis, Jennifer Blizin. Two Nice Mice. Krejca, Gary, illus. 2006. (Barron's Reader's Clubhouse Level 2 Ser.). (ENG.). 24p. (J). (gr. k-3). 16.19 *(978-0-7641-3295-7(4),* B.E.S. Publishing) Peterson's.

Godden, Rumer. Mouse House. Adams, Adrienne, illus. 2016. (ENG.). 72p. (J). (gr. -1-2). 18.95 *(978-1-59017-998-7(6),* NYR Children's Collection) New York Review of Bks., Inc., The.

Godwin, Jane. Red House, Tree House, Little Bitty Brown Mouse. Gómez, Blanca, illus. 2019. (ENG.). 40p. (J). (-k). 18.99 *(978-0-525-55381-6(9),* Dial Bks) Penguin Young Readers Group.

Goodhart, Pippa. Big Cat. 2011. (Tadpoles Ser.: No. 28). (ENG., Illus.). 24p. (J). (gr. k-3). pap. *(978-0-7787-0585-7(4))* Crabtree Publishing Co.

Gore, Emily. And Nick. Gore, Leonid, illus. 2015. (ENG.). 40p. (J). (gr. -1-3). 17.99 *(978-1-4169-5506-1(2))* Simon & Schuster Children's Publishing.

Gore, Leonid. Mommy, Where Are You? Gore, Leonid, illus. 2009. (ENG., Illus.). 32p. (J). (gr. -1-2). 18.99 *(978-1-4169-5505-4(4),* Atheneum Bks. for Young Readers) Simon & Schuster Children's Publishing.

Gott, Barry. Honk! Splat! Vroom! Gott, Barry, illus. 2018. (ENG., Illus.). 32p. (J). (gr. -1-k). lib. bdg. 17.99 *(978-1-5124-4140-6(6),* ebdc41f3-e48d-40e3-8fac-8e165507d02d, Carolrhoda Bks.) Lerner Publishing Group.

Grammy Sunshine. The Adventures of Mouse: The Mouse Who Wanted to Be A Pig. 2009. 20p. pap. 12.49 *(978-1-4389-9268-6(8))* AuthorHouse.

Grandpa Casey. Another Müsh-Mice Adventure. Brennan, Lisa, illus. 2012. 48p. 24.95 *(978-1-4626-9379-5(2))* America Star Bks.

—Another Müsh-Mice Adventure: Florida Vacation, 1 vol. Brennan, Lisa, illus. 2009. 45p. pap. 24.95 *(978-1-60813-329-1(X))* America Star Bks.

—Going Green: Another Mush-Mice Adventure, 1 vol. Brennan, Lisa, illus. 2010. 34p. pap. 24.95 *(978-1-4489-7375-0(9))* America Star Bks.

—Meet the Müsh-Mice. Brennan, Lisa, illus. 2012. 28p. 24.95 *(978-1-4626-9380-1(6))* America Star Bks.

—The Trilogy: Three Adventures of the Müsh-Mice. Brenn, Lisa, illus. 2012. 46p. 24.95 *(978-1-4626-9378-8(4))* America Star Bks.

Grandpa Dennis, as told by. George Washington's Smallest Army: The Miracle Before Trenton. 2009. 216p. (J). pap. 17.49 *(978-1-4389-3147-0(6))* AuthorHouse.

Grant, Rose. Right Where You Need Me. Bryant, Julie, illus. 2012. 16p. pap. 15.99 *(978-1-4685-6856-1(6))* AuthorHouse.

Grant, V. F. Stories from Grimley Forest. 2011. 48p. (gr. 1-2). pap. 19.50 *(978-1-4567-4709-1(6))* AuthorHouse.

Graves, Damien. The Deadly Catch. 2006. (Midnight Library: 8). (ENG., Illus.). 170p. (J). (gr. 6-8). 18.69 *(978-0-439-89395-4(X))* Scholastic, Inc.

Gravett, Emily. Little Mouse's Big Book of Fears. Gravett, Emily, illus. 2008. (ENG., Illus.). 32p. (J). (gr. -1-3). 24.99 *(978-1-4169-5930-4(0),* Simon & Schuster Bks. For Young Readers) Simon & Schuster Bks. For Young Readers.

Greathouse, Cindy. Wilbur Learns to Forgive, 1 vol. 2010. 18p. 24.95 *(978-1-4489-7374-3(0))* PublishAmerica, Inc.

Green, Poppy. The Clover Curse. Bell, Jennifer A., illus. 2016. (Adventures of Sophie Mouse Ser.: 7). (ENG.). 128p. (J). (gr. k-4). 17.99 *(978-1-4814-5184-0(7),* Little Simon) Little Simon.

—The Emerald Berries. Bell, Jennifer A., illus. 2015. (Adventures of Sophie Mouse Ser.: 2). (ENG.). 128p. (J). (gr. k-4). pap. 6.99 *(978-1-4814-2835-4(7),* Little Simon) Little Simon.

—Forget-Me-Not Lake. Bell, Jennifer A., illus. 2015. (Adventures of Sophie Mouse Ser.: 3). (ENG.). 128p. (J). (gr. k-4). 17.99 *(978-1-4814-3000-5(9),* Little Simon) Little Simon.

—Forget-Me-Not Lake. Bell, Jennifer A., illus. 2017. (Adventures of Sophie Mouse Ser.). (ENG.). 128p. (J). (gr. k-4). lib. bdg. 31.36 *(978-1-5321-4112-6(2),* 26985, Chapter Bks.) Spotlight.

—The Great Big Paw Print. Bell, Jennifer A., illus. 2016. (Adventures of Sophie Mouse Ser.: 9). (ENG.). 128p. (J). (gr. k-4). 17.99 *(978-1-4814-7149-7(X),* Little Simon) Little Simon.

—It's Raining, It's Pouring. Bell, Jennifer A., illus. 2017. (Adventures of Sophie Mouse Ser.: 10). (ENG.). 128p. (J). (gr. k-4). 17.99 *(978-1-4814-8590-6(3),* Little Simon) Little Simon.

—Journey to the Crystal Cave. Bell, Jennifer A., illus. 2017. (Adventures of Sophie Mouse Ser.: 12). (ENG.). 128p. (J). (gr. k-4). 17.99 *(978-1-4814-9986-6(6));* pap. 6.99 *(978-1-4814-9985-9(8))* Little Simon. (Little Simon).

—Looking for Winston. Bell, Jennifer A., illus. 2017. (Adventures of Sophie Mouse Ser.). (ENG.). 128p. (J). (gr. k-4). lib. bdg. 31.36 *(978-1-5321-4113-3(0),* 26986, Chapter Bks.) Spotlight.

—The Maple Festival. Bell, Jennifer A., illus. 2015. (Adventures of Sophie Mouse Ser.: 5). (ENG.). 128p. (J). (gr. k-4). pap. 6.99 *(978-1-4814-4196-4(5),* Little Simon) Little Simon.

—The Maple Festival. Bell, Jennifer A., illus. 2017. (Adventures of Sophie Mouse Ser.). (ENG.). 128p. (J). (gr. k-4). lib. bdg. 31.36 *(978-1-5321-4114-0(9),* 26987, Chapter Bks.) Spotlight.

—The Mouse House. Bell, Jennifer A., illus. 2017. (Adventures of Sophie Mouse Ser.: 11). (ENG.). 128p. (J). (gr. k-4). pap. 6.99 *(978-1-4814-9435-9(X),* Little Simon) Little Simon.

—A New Friend. Bell, Jennifer A., illus. 2015. (Adventures of Sophie Mouse Ser.: 1). (ENG.). 128p. (J). (gr. k-4). pap. 6.99 *(978-1-4814-2832-3(2),* Little Simon) Little Simon.

—Silverlake Art Show. Bell, Jennifer A., illus. 2018. (Adventures of Sophie Mouse Ser.: 13). (ENG.). 128p. (J). (gr. k-4). 17.99 *(978-1-5344-1725-0(7));* pap. 6.99 *(978-1-5344-1724-3(9))* Little Simon. (Little Simon).

—A Surprise Visitor. Bell, Jennifer A., illus. 2016. (Adventures of Sophie Mouse Ser.: 8). (ENG.). 128p. (J). (gr. k-4). pap. 6.99 *(978-1-4814-6698-1(4),* Little Simon) Little Simon.

—Winter's No Time to Sleep! Bell, Jennifer A., illus. 2015. (Adventures of Sophie Mouse Ser.: 6). (ENG.). 128p. (J). (gr. k-4). pap. 6.99 *(978-1-4814-4199-5(X),* Little Simon) Little Simon.

—Winter's No Time to Sleep! Bell, Jennifer A., illus. 2017. (Adventures of Sophie Mouse Ser.). (ENG.). 128p. (J). (gr. k-4). lib. bdg. 31.36 *(978-1-5321-4115-7(7),* 26988, Chapter Bks.) Spotlight.

Greene, Stephanie. Christmas at Stony Creek. Sheban, Chris, illus. 2007. 96p. (gr. -1-3). lib. bdg. 15.89 *(978-0-06-121487-5(6))* HarperCollins Pubs.

—The Show-Off, 0 vols. Mathieu, Joe, illus. 2013. (Moose & Hildy Ser.: 4). (ENG.). 64p. (J). (gr. 1-3). pap. 9.99 *(978-1-4778-1686-8(0),* 9781477816868, Two Lions) Amazon Publishing.

Griffin, Daniel. The Adventures of Merlin the Mouse 2005. (Illus.). 44p. (J). *(978-0-9768348-0-9(4))* DiGuiseppi, Joseph.

Grubman, Bonnie. How Do You Get a Mouse to Smile?, 1 vol. Van Wright, Cornelius, illus. 2009. (ENG.). 32p. (J). (gr. -1-3). pap. 6.50 *(978-1-59572-167-9(3))* Star Bright Bks., Inc.

Guibert, Emmanuel. The Little Rats of the Opera. 2017. (Ariol Ser.: 10). (J). lib. bdg. 24.50 *(978-0-606-39879-4(1))* Turtleback.

Gump, Granny. The Giraffe Who Went to School. 2011. 48p. pap. 21.99 *(978-1-4568-5805-6(X))* Xlibris Corp.

Gutman, Anne. Gaspard et Lisa au Musee. (FRE.). pap. 19.95 *(978-2-01-224132-9(8))* Hachette Groupe Livre FRA. Dist: Distribooks, Inc.

Hall, Shirley. The Adventure of Molly the Mouse. 2012. (ENG.). (J). pap. 14.95 *(978-1-4675-1717-1(8))* Independent Pub.

Haller, Reese. The Adventures Begin. Lynn, Galsterer, illus. 2005. (Fred the Mouse Ser.). 108p. (J). (gr. -1-3). per. 4.97 *(978-0-9616046-8-4(9))* Personal Power Pr.

—Making Friends, 2. Galsterer, Lynne, illus. 2nd ed. 2006. (Fred the Mouse Ser.). 112p. (J). per. 4.97 *(978-0-9772321-0-9(7))* Personal Power Pr.

—Rescuing Freedom. Haller, Thomas, illus. 3rd ed. 2006. (Fred the Mouse Ser.). 112p. (J). (gr. k-4). per. 4.97 *(978-0-9772321-3-0(1))* Personal Power Pr.

Halliday-King, Michaela. The Pennine Mouse. 2012. (Illus.). 40p. pap. 27.99 *(978-1-4678-8709-0(9))* AuthorHouse.

Hallinan, Annie. Brinkley Boyd of Weymouth. Preveza, Amy, illus. 2017. 46p. (J). *(978-0-9971477-4-2(1))* Turnberry Pr.

Hamilton, Laura, reader. Sheila Rae, the Brave. 2003. (Illus.). (J). (gr. -1-2). 28.95 incl. audio compact disk *(978-1-59112-550-1(2))* Live Oak Media.

Harff, David. Mouse Mayhem, 1 vol. 2009. 24p. pap. 24.95 *(978-1-60749-610-6(0))* America Star Bks.

Harms, Jeanine, illus. Boss Mouse Coloring Book & Theme Song. 2006. (J). 4.00 *(978-1-4276-0118-6(6))* Aardvark Global Publishing.

Harper, Benjamin. The Lion & the Mouse & the Invaders from Zurg: A Graphic Novel. Rodriguez, Pedro, illus. 2017. (Far Out Fables Ser.). (ENG.). 40p. (J). (gr. 3-6). pap. 4.95 *(978-1-4965-5426-0(4),* 136359); lib. bdg. 25.32 *(978-1-4965-5422-2(1),* 136355) Capstone. (Stone Arch Bks.).

Harris, Christine. Four Tails: An Anthology of Four Tales for Children. 2011. (Illus.). 92p. (gr. -1). pap. 12.10 *(978-1-4520-7643-0(X))* AuthorHouse.

Harris, Robie H. Adios, Ratoncito. Rioja, Alberto Jimenez, tr. Ormerod, Jan, illus. (SPA.). (J). (gr. k-2). 16.00 *(978-1-930332-34-8(3),* LC8567) Lectorum Pubns., Inc.

—Goodbye Mousie. Ormerod, Jan, illus. 2004. (ENG.). 32p. (J). (gr. -1-3). reprint ed. 9.99 *(978-0-689-87134-4(1),* Aladdin) Simon & Schuster Children's Publishing.

Harrison, Paul. Three Blind Mice Team up with the Three Little Pigs. Epelbaum, Mariano, illus. 2016. (Fairy Tale Mix-Ups Ser.). (ENG.). 24p. (J). (gr. k-2). lib. bdg. 23.99 *(978-1-4109-8301-5(3),* 132996, Raintree) Capstone.

Hart, Caryl. One Shoe Two Shoes. Underwood, Edward, illus. 2019. (ENG.). 32p. (J). 17.99 *(978-1-5476-0094-6(2),* 900198463, Bloomsbury Children's Bks.) Bloomsbury Publishing USA.

Hart, Melissa. A Guide for Using the Tale of Despereaux in the Classroom. 2005. (ENG.). 48p. pap. 9.99 *(978-1-4206-3164-7(0))* Teacher Created Resources, Inc.

Hart, Owen. I Can't Sleep! Pedler, Caroline, illus. 2017. (ENG.). 32p. (J). (gr. -1-2). 16.99 *(978-1-68010-066-2(1))* Tiger Tales.

Harvey, Kate. Tiberius & the Chocolate Cake, 1 vol. Kirk, Heather, illus. 2009. (Tiberius Tales Ser.). (ENG.). 24p. (J). (gr. 1-1). pap. 9.15 *(978-1-60754-836-2(4),* 6aef6e4d-5789-47ad-83e2-b9ccfc8425ac); lib. bdg. 27.27 *(978-1-60754-832-4(1),* abb2dd2a-7817-43d7-982c-5272b1b0f72d) Rosen Publishing Group, Inc., The. (Windmill Bks.).

—Tiberius & the Friendly Dragon, 1 vol. Kirk, Heather, illus. 2009. (Tiberius Tales Ser.). (ENG.). 24p. (J). (gr. 1-1). pap. 9.15 *(978-1-60754-834-8(8),* a62b4e0e-a004-4478-9902-9004c7cca82f); lib. bdg. 27.27 *(978-1-60754-830-0(5),* eee8dc7b-150a-44ca-96db-a6514f0e4411) Rosen Publishing Group, Inc., The. (Windmill Bks.).

—Tiberius Goes to School, 1 vol. Brown, Kelli, illus. 2009. (Tiberius Tales Ser.). (ENG.). 24p. (J). (gr. 1-1). pap. 9.15 *(978-1-60754-837-9(2),* 537bd707-9b7a-45c4-94fb-3635a32c62ee); lib. bdg. 27.27 *(978-1-60754-833-1(X),* 32c9f65e-77ca-462e-a74f-80baf37214e2) Rosen Publishing Group, Inc., The. (Windmill Bks.).

—Tiberius Meets Sneaky Cat, 1 vol. Hickman, Paula, illus. 2009. (Tiberius Tales Ser.). (ENG.). 24p. (J). (gr. 1-1). pap. 9.15 *(978-1-60754-835-5(6),* b6c0c671-9324-4910-a4fe-c6c166a71b66); lib. bdg. 27.27 *(978-1-60754-831-7(3),* 0516c677-88d2-487b-905e-90f61ac15806) Rosen Publishing Group, Inc., The. (Windmill Bks.).

Harvey, Keith. Tiberius Goes to School. Brown, Kate & Hickman, Paula, illus. 2014. (ENG.). 24p. pap. 8.95 *(978-1-84135-919-9(X))* Award Pubns. Ltd. GBR. Dist: Parkwest Pubns., Inc.

Harvey, Keith & Kirk, Heather. Tiberius & the Friendly Dragon. 2014. (ENG., Illus.). 24p. pap. 8.95 *(978-1-84135-917-5(3))* Award Pubns. Ltd. GBR. Dist: Parkwest Pubns., Inc.

Harvey, Tom. Rat in the Red Truck. Proulx, Denis, illus. 2011. (ENG.). 44p. pap. 17.99 *(978-1-4269-6236-3(3))* Trafford Publishing.

Hash, Stella. The Christmas Caravan. 2011. 32p. pap. 24.95 *(978-1-4626-0533-0(8))* America Star Bks.

Hayes, Geoffrey. Benny & Penny in How to Say Goodbye: TOON Level 2. 2016. (Benny & Penny Ser.). (Illus.). 32p. (J). (gr. -1-3). 12.99 *(978-1-935179-99-3(3),* TOON Books) Astra Publishing Hse.

—Benny & Penny in Just Pretend, 1 vol. Hayes, Geoffrey, illus. 2013. (Toon Bks.). (ENG., Illus.). 36p. (J). (gr. 1-2). lib. bdg. 32.79 *(978-1-61479-148-5(1),* 14840) Spotlight.

—Benny & Penny in Just Pretend. 2013. (Toon Books Level 2 Ser.). lib. bdg. 14.75 *(978-0-606-31597-5(7))* Turtleback.

—Benny & Penny in Lights Out: Toon Books Level 2. Hayes, Geoffrey, illus. 2012. (Toon Ser.). (ENG., Illus.). 32p. (J). (gr. -1-3). 12.99 *(978-1-935179-20-7(9),* Toon Books) Astra Publishing Hse.

—Benny & Penny in Lost & Found: Toon Books Level 2. Hayes, Geoffrey, illus. 2014. (Toon Ser.). (ENG., Illus.). 40p. (J). (gr. -1-3). 12.99 *(978-1-935179-64-1(0),* TOON Books) Astra Publishing Hse.

—Benny & Penny in the Big No-No! Toon Books Level 2. Hayes, Geoffrey, illus. 2009. (Toon Ser.). (ENG., Illus.). 32p. (J). (gr. -1-3). 12.99 *(978-0-9799238-9-0(1),* TOON Books) Astra Publishing Hse.

—Benny & Penny in the Toy Breaker. 2013. (Toon Books Level 2 Ser.). lib. bdg. 14.75 *(978-0-606-31598-2(5))* Turtleback.

—Benny & Penny in the Toy Breaker: Toon Books Level 2. Hayes, Geoffrey, illus. 2010. (Toon Ser.). (ENG., Illus.). 32p. (J). (gr. -1-3). 12.95 *(978-1-935179-07-8(1),* Toon Books) Astra Publishing Hse.

Hazel, Jan. Marshall Meets the Little Dragons. 2013. 38p. pap. 9.99 *(978-1-62509-396-7(9))* Salem Author Services.

Hazlewood, Leyland. Chester Goes to Afric. 2011. 32p. pap. 21.99 *(978-1-4568-6466-8(1))* Xlibris Corp.

Heim, Julia & Dami, Elisabetta. The Little Book of Happiness. Bluecheese, Wally, illus. 2013. 42p. (J). pap. *(978-0-545-48255-4(0))* Scholastic, Inc.

Hellberg, Joanne S. Thomas S Tucker & the Silver Buckle. 2009. 32p. pap. 12.99 *(978-1-4389-8723-1(4))* AuthorHouse.

Henderson, Virginia. Zippy the Dreamer. 2010. 20p. 13.77 *(978-1-4269-3448-3(3))* Trafford Publishing.

Hendry, Diana. Que Noche Mas Ruidosa! Chapman, Jane, illus. 2003. (SPA.). 28p. (J). (gr. k-2). 16.95 *(978-84-488-0865-5(7),* BS3550) Beascoa, Ediciones S.A. ESP. Dist: Lectorum Pubns., Inc.

—The Very Snowy Christmas. Chapman, Jane, illus. (J). 2013. (ENG.). 16p. (gr. -1-k). bds. 8.95 *(978-1-58925-617-0(4))* 2007. 32p. pap. 6.95 *(978-1-58925-406-0(6))* 2005. 32p. (gr. -1-2). 15.95 *(978-1-58925-051-2(6))* Tiger Tales.

Henkes, Kevin. Chester's Way. (Illus.). 28.95 incl. audio compact disk *(978-1-59112-972-1(9));* 25.95 incl. audio *(978-1-59112-968-4(0));* pap. 35.95 incl. audio compact disk *(978-1-59112-973-8(7));* pap. 33.95 incl. audio *(978-1-59112-969-1(9))* Live Oak Media.

—El Gran día de Lily: Lily's Big Day (Spanish Edition), 1 vol. Henkes, Kevin, illus. 2008. (SPA., Illus.). 40p. (J). (gr. -1-3). 17.99 *(978-0-06-136316-0(2))* HarperCollins Español.

—Julius, el Rey de la Casa. 2017.Tr. of Julius, the Baby of the World. (SPA., Illus.). 31p. (J). pap. 9.99 *(978-1-63245-668-7(0))* Lectorum Pubns., Inc.

—Lilly's Big Day. Henkes, Kevin, illus. 2006. (ENG., Illus.). 40p. (J). (gr. -1-3). 18.99 *(978-0-06-074236-2(4));* lib. bdg. 18.89 *(978-0-06-074237-9(2))* HarperCollins Pubs. (Greenwillow Bks.).

—Lilly's Big Day. 2014. (J). lib. bdg. 17.20 *(978-0-606-35472-1(7))* Turtleback.

—Lilly's Purple Plastic Purse. Henkes, Kevin, illus. 10th anniv. ed. 2006. (ENG., Illus.). 40p. (J). (gr. -1-4). 19.99 *(978-0-688-12897-5(1),* Greenwillow Bks.) HarperCollins Pubs.

—Lilly's Purple Plastic Purse. Henkes, Kevin, illus. (Illus.). pap. 16.95 incl. audio *(978-0-87499-686-9(4));* pap. incl. audio *(978-0-87499-688-3(0));* pap. incl. audio compact disk *(978-1-59112-557-0(X));* pap. 18.95 incl. audio compact disk *(978-1-59112-347-7(X))* Live Oak Media.

—Lilly's Purple Plastic Purse 20th Anniversary Edition. Henkes, Kevin, illus. 20th ed. 2016. (ENG., Illus.). 40p. (J). (gr. -1-3). 17.99 *(978-0-06-242419-8(X),* Greenwillow Bks.) HarperCollins Pubs.

—Lily y Su Bolso de Plastico Morado. 2017.Tr. of Lilly's Purple Plastic Purse. (SPA.). (J). pap. 9.99 *(978-1-63245-667-0(2))* Lectorum Pubns., Inc.

—Owen. 2017. (SPA., Illus.). 24p. (J). pap. 9.99 *(978-1-63245-665-6(6))* Lectorum Pubns., Inc.

—Penny & Her Doll. Henkes, Kevin, illus. 2012. (ENG., Illus.). 32p. (J). (gr. -1-3). 14.99 *(978-0-06-208199-5(3));* lib. bdg. 15.89 *(978-0-06-208200-8(0))* HarperCollins Pubs. (Greenwillow Bks.).

—Penny & Her Doll. 2013. (I Can Read! Level 1 Ser.). (J). lib. bdg. 13.55 *(978-0-606-27147-9(3))* Turtleback.

—Penny & Her Marble. Henkes, Kevin, illus. 2013. (I Can Read Level 1 Ser.). (ENG., Illus.). 48p. (J). (gr. -1-3). pap. 4.99 *(978-0-06-208205-3(1));* 14.89 *(978-0-06-208204-6(3));* 12.99 *(978-0-06-208203-9(5))* HarperCollins Pubs. (Greenwillow Bks.).

—Penny & Her Marble. 2013. (J). lib. bdg. 13.55 *(978-0-606-32151-8(9))* Turtleback.

—Penny & Her Song. Henkes, Kevin, illus. 2012. (I Can Read Level 1 Ser.). (ENG., Illus.). 32p. (J). (gr. -1-3). pap. 4.99 *(978-0-06-208197-1(7));* 12.99 *(978-0-06-208195-7(0));* lib. bdg. 14.89 *(978-0-06-208196-4(9))* HarperCollins Pubs. (Greenwillow Bks.).

—Penny & Her Song. 2012. (J). lib. bdg. 13.55 *(978-0-606-26847-9(2))* Turtleback.

—Prudencia Se Preocupa. 2017.Tr. of Wemberly Worried. (SPA.). (J). pap. 9.99 *(978-1-63245-666-3(4))* Lectorum Pubns., Inc.

—Prudencia Se Preocupa (Wemberly Worried) 2018. lib. bdg. 20.85 *(978-0-606-41285-8(9))* Turtleback.

—Sheila Rae, the Brave. Henkes, Kevin, illus. (Illus.). 9.95 *(978-1-59112-865-6(X))* Live Oak Media.

—Wemberly Worried. Henkes, Kevin, illus. 2010. (ENG., Illus.). 32p. (J). (gr. -1-4). pap. 9.99 *(978-0-06-185776-8(9),* Greenwillow Bks.) HarperCollins Pubs.

—Wemberly Worried. Henkes, Kevin, illus. (Illus.). pap. 18.95 incl. audio compact disk *(978-1-59112-359-0(3));* pap. incl. audio *(978-0-87499-808-5(5));* pap. 16.95 incl. audio *(978-0-87499-806-1(9));* pap. 39.95 incl. audio compact disk *(978-1-59112-561-7(8))* Live Oak Media.

—Wemberly Worried. 2010. (J). lib. bdg. 17.20 *(978-0-606-14757-6(8))* Turtleback.

Henry, Jed. Good Night, Mouse! Henry, Jed, illus. 2013. (ENG., Illus.). 32p. (J). (gr. -1-3). 16.99 *(978-0-547-98156-7(2),* 1523510, Clarion Bks.) HarperCollins Pubs.

Hess, Megan. Claris Vol. 2: The Chicest Mouse in Paris, Volume 1. 2018. (Claris Ser.: Bk. 1). (ENG., Illus.). 48p. (J). (gr. -1-3). 17.99 *(978-1-76050-259-1(6))* Hardie Grant Bks. AUS. Dist: Hachette Bk. Group.

Hickman, B. Jo. Old Cat, Fat Rat, & Boo. 2011. 28p. pap. 15.99 *(978-1-4653-3615-6(X))* Xlibris Corp.

Higgins, Ryan T. Bruce's Big Fun Day. 2019. (World of Reading Ser.). (ENG.). 28p. (J). (gr. k-1). 13.96 *(978-0-87617-903-1(0))* Penworthy Co., LLC, The.

—Hey, Bruce! An Interactive Book. 2022. (Mother Bruce Ser.). (Illus.). 48p. (J). (gr. -1-k). 17.99 *(978-1-368-08411-6(7),* Disney-Hyperion) Disney Publishing Worldwide.

Hines, D. H. L. College Mouse. 2009. 24p. pap. 16.49 *(978-1-4490-2976-0(0))* AuthorHouse.

Hinkelman, Carole & Rebik, Nan. The Herman Chronicles: *Herman the Horrible Trailer Mouse *Herman & the Donkeys * Herman's Midnight Trek * Herman's Vacation. 2012. 84p. (gr. 2-4). pap. 11.50 *(978-1-4669-5202-7(4))* Trafford Publishing.

Hobbs, Brice Edward. Beth's Woodpecker. 2004. 108p. 26.45 *(978-1-4208-0135-4(X))* AuthorHouse.

Hockerman, Dennis, illus. The Country Mouse & the City Mouse: A Tale of Tolerance. 2006. (J). 6.99 *(978-1-59939-003-1(5))* Cornerstone Pr.

—The Lion & the Mouse: A Tale about Being Helpful. 2006. (J). 6.99 *(978-1-59939-007-9(8))* Cornerstone Pr.

Hockinson, Liz. Marcello the Movie Mouse: The Movie Mouse. Otoshi, Kathryn, illus. 2005. (ENG.). 40p. (J). (gr. k). 16.95 *(978-0-9723946-2-8(1))* KO Kids Bks.

Hodgkinson, Jo. A Big Day for Migs. Hodgkinson, Jo, illus. 2014. (ENG., Illus.). 32p. (J). (gr. -1-3). 16.95 *(978-1-4677-5014-1(X),* 0b824eb0-70bb-4274-8930-93d90269e2c6) Lerner Publishing Group.

Hodgkinson, Leigh. Boris & the Wrong Shadow. 2012. (ENG.). 32p. (J). pap. *(978-1-58925-434-3(1))* Tiger Tales.

Hoefler, Kate. Great Big Things. Klocek, Noah, illus. 2017. (ENG.). 40p. (J). (gr. -1-3). 17.99 *(978-0-544-77477-3(9),* 1637144, Clarion Bks.) HarperCollins Pubs.

Hoenecke, Karen. Little Mouse. Gedeon, Gloria, illus. I.t. ed. 2005. (ENG.). 12p. (J). (gr. k-2). pap. 7.95 *(978-1-57874-023-9(1),* Kaeden Bks.) Kaeden Corp.

Hoeye, Michael. Una Cuestion de Tiempo. (SPA.). 304p. (J). (gr. 6-8). 17.56 *(978-84-8441-167-3(2),* MO1007) Grijalbo Mondadori, S.A.-Montena ESP. Dist: Lectorum Pubns., Inc.

—The Sands of Time. 2007. (ENG.). 288p. (J). (gr. 3-7). pap. 8.99 *(978-0-14-240983-1(9),* Puffin Books) Penguin Young Readers Group.

—The Sands of Time: A Hermux Tantamoq AdventureTM. 2004. 288p. (J). (gr. 5-9). pap. 40.00 incl. audio *(978-1-4000-9016-7(4),* Listening Library) Random Hse. Audio Publishing Group.

—Time Stops for No Mouse. 2003. (Hermux Tantamoq Adventure Ser.). (Illus.). 250p. (J). (gr. 4-7). 18.40 *(978-0-613-62122-9(0))* Turtleback.

—Time Stops for No Mouse: A Hermux Tantamoq AdventureTM. 2004. 272p. (J). (gr. 5-9). pap. 40.00 incl. audio *(978-0-8072-2280-5(1),* Listening Library) Random Hse. Audio Publishing Group.

Hoffman, Karen Burkinshaw. The Story about Tee Low: A Mouse with a Knot in His Tail. 2013. 36p. pap. 18.41 *(978-1-4669-9715-8(X))* Trafford Publishing.

Holabird, Katharine. Angelina Ballerina. Craig, Helen, illus. 2019. (Angelina Ballerina Ser.). (ENG.). 32p. (J). (gr. -1-3). 18.99 *(978-1-5344-5151-3(X),* Little Simon) Little Simon.

—A Dance of Friendship. Craig, Helen, illus. 2006. (Angelina Ballerina Ser.). (ENG.). 23p. (J). (gr. -1-1). 16.19 *(978-0-448-44115-3(2))* Penguin Young Readers Group.

Holabird, Katharine & Craig, Helen, creators. Angelina & the Tummy Butterflies. 2013. (Angelina Ballerina Ser.). (ENG., Illus.). 24p. (J). (gr. -1-1). 17.44 *(978-0-448-46281-3(8))* Penguin Young Readers Group.

Holm, Jennifer L. Babymouse #1: Queen of the World! Holm, Matthew, illus. 2005. (Babymouse Ser.: 1). (ENG.). 96p. (J). (gr. 2-5). pap. 6.99 *(978-0-375-83229-1(7));* lib. bdg. 12.99 *(978-0-375-93229-8(1))* Penguin Random Hse. LLC.

—Little Babymouse & the Christmas Cupcakes. Holm, Matthew, illus. 2016. (ENG.). 40p. (J). (gr. -1-2). 17.99 *(978-1-101-93743-3(2),* Random Hse. Bks. for Young Readers) Random Hse. Children's Bks.

—Miss Communication. Holm, Matthew, illus. 2018. (Babymouse Tales from the Locker Ser.: 2). (ENG.). 208p. (J). (gr. 3-7). 13.99 *(978-0-399-55441-4(6),* Random Hse. Bks. for Young Readers) Random Hse. Children's Bks.

Holm, Jennifer L. & Holm, Matthew. Babymouse #10: the Musical. Holm, Jennifer L. & Holm, Matthew, illus. 2009. (Babymouse Ser.: 10). (ENG., Illus.). 96p. (J). (gr. 2-5). pap. 6.99 *(978-0-375-84388-4(4));* lib. bdg. 12.99 *(978-0-375-93791-0(9))* Penguin Random Hse. LLC.

—Babymouse #11: Dragonslayer. Holm, Jennifer L. & Holm, Matthew, illus. 2009. (Babymouse Ser.: 11). (ENG., Illus.). 96p. (J). (gr. 2-5). pap. 6.99 *(978-0-375-85712-6(5))* Penguin Random Hse. LLC.

—Babymouse #14: Mad Scientist. Holm, Jennifer L. & Holm, Matthew, illus. 2011. (Babymouse Ser.: 14). (ENG., Illus.). 96p. (J). (gr. 2-5). pap. 7.99 *(978-0-375-86574-9(8));* lib. bdg. 12.99 *(978-0-375-96574-6(2))* Penguin Random Hse. LLC.

—Babymouse #15: a Very Babymouse Christmas. Holm, Jennifer L. & Holm, Matthew, illus. 2011. (Babymouse Ser.: 15). (ENG., Illus.). 96p. (J). (gr. 2-5). 12.99 *(978-0-375-96779-5(6));* pap. 6.99 *(978-0-375-86779-8(1))* Penguin Random Hse. LLC.

—Babymouse #16: Babymouse for President. Holm, Jennifer L. & Holm, Matthew, illus. 2012. (Babymouse Ser.: 16). (ENG., Illus.). 96p. (J). (gr. 2-5). pap. 7.99 (978-0-375-86780-4(5)) Penguin Random Hse. LLC.
—Babymouse #17: Extreme Babymouse. Holm, Jennifer L. & Holm, Matthew, illus. 2013. (Babymouse Ser.: 17). (ENG., Illus.). 96p. (J). (gr. 2-5). pap. 6.99 (978-0-307-93160-3(9)) Penguin Random Hse. LLC.
—Babymouse #18: Happy Birthday, Babymouse. Holm, Jennifer L. & Holm, Matthew, illus. 2014. (Babymouse Ser.: 18). (ENG., Illus.). 96p. (J). (gr. 2-5). pap. 6.99 (978-0-307-93161-0(7)) Penguin Random Hse. LLC.
—Babymouse #19: Bad Babysitter. Holm, Jennifer L. & Holm, Matthew, illus. 2015. (Babymouse Ser.: 19). (ENG., Illus.). 96p. (J). (gr. 2-5). pap. 6.99 (978-0-307-93162-7(5)) Penguin Random Hse. LLC.
—Babymouse #2: Our Hero. 2005. (Babymouse Ser.: 2). (ENG., Illus.). 96p. (J). (gr. 2-5). pap. 6.99 (978-0-375-83230-7(0)) Penguin Random Hse. LLC.
—Babymouse #20: Babymouse Goes for the Gold. Holm, Jennifer L. & Holm, Matthew, illus. 2016. (Babymouse Ser.: 20). (ENG., Illus.). 96p. (J). (gr. 2-5). pap. 6.99 (978-0-307-93163-4(3)) Penguin Random Hse. LLC.
—Babymouse #3: Beach Babe. 2006. (Babymouse Ser.: 3). (ENG., Illus.). 96p. (J). (gr. 2-5). pap. 6.99 (978-0-375-83231-4(9)) Penguin Random Hse. LLC.
—Babymouse #4: Rock Star. 2006. (Babymouse Ser.: 4). (ENG., Illus.). 96p. (J). (gr. 2-5). pap. 6.99 (978-0-375-83232-1(7)) Penguin Random Hse. LLC.
—Babymouse #6: Camp Babymouse. 2007. (Babymouse Ser.: 6). (ENG., Illus.). 96p. (J). (gr. 2-5). lib. bdg. 12.99 (978-0-375-93988-4(1)) Penguin Random Hse. LLC.
—Babymouse #6: Camp Babymouse. 2007. (Babymouse Ser.: 6). (ENG., Illus.). 96p. (J). (gr. 2-5). pap. 6.99 (978-0-375-83988-7(7), Random Hse. Bks. for Young Readers) Random Hse. Children's Bks.
—Babymouse #9: Monster Mash. Holm, Jennifer L. & Holm, Matthew, illus. 2008. (Babymouse Ser.: 9). (ENG., Illus.). 96p. (J). (gr. 2-5). pap. 6.99 (978-0-375-84387-7(6)) Penguin Random Hse. LLC.
—Babymouse for President. 2012. (Babymouse Ser.: 16). lib. bdg. 17.20 (978-0-606-26404-4(3)) Turtleback.
—Burns Rubber. 2010. (Babymouse Ser.: 12). lib. bdg. 17.20 (978-0-606-07025-6(7)) Turtleback.
—Camp Babymouse. 2007. (Babymouse Ser.: No. 6). (Illus.). 91p. (J). (gr. 2-5). 13.65 (978-0-7569-8344-4(4)) Perfection Learning Corp.
—Camp Babymouse. 2007. (Babymouse Ser.: 6). lib. bdg. 17.20 (978-1-4177-8070-9(3)) Turtleback.
—Extreme Babymouse. 2013. (Babymouse Ser.: 17). lib. bdg. 17.20 (978-0-606-26999-5(1)) Turtleback.
—Happy Birthday, Babymouse. 2014. (Babymouse Ser.: 18). lib. bdg. 17.20 (978-0-606-35567-4(7)) Turtleback.
Hood, Susan. The Tooth Mouse. Nadeau, Janice, illus. 2012. (ENG.). 32p. (J). (gr. -1-2). 16.95 (978-1-55453-565-1(4)) Kids Can Pr., Ltd. CAN. Dist: Hachette Bk. Group.
Hope-Simpson, Lila. Fiddles & Spoons (pb) Journey of an Acadian Mouse, 1 vol. 2017. (ENG., Illus.). 32p. (J). (gr. 1-3). pap. 14.95 (978-1-77108-562-5(2), 0111bba3-b60b-4751-968b-82be0680d6b3) Nimbus Publishing, Ltd. CAN. Dist: Baker & Taylor Publisher Services (BTPS).
Horácek, Petr. A Surprise for Tiny Mouse. Horácek, Petr, illus. 2015. (ENG., Illus.). 16p. (J). (— 1). bds. 8.99 (978-0-7636-7967-5(4)) Candlewick Pr.
Horacek, Petr & Horacek, Petr. The Mouse Who Wasn't Scared. Horacek, Petr & Horacek, Petr, illus. 2018. (ENG., Illus.). 32p. (J). (-k). 15.99 (978-0-7636-9881-2(4)) Candlewick Pr.
Houdek, Andi. Mice in My Tummy. 2006. (J). per. 16.95 (978-0-9771939-9-8(3), 012) New World Publishing.
Houdek, Andrea. Mice in My Tummy. Collier, Kevin Scott, illus. 2012. 16p. pap. 9.95 (978-1-61633-219-8(0)) Guardian Angel Publishing, Inc.
Houran, Lori Haskins. Bravo, Albert! Melmon, Deborah, illus. 2017. (Mouse Math Ser.). 32p. (J). (gr. -1-1). 7.99 (978-1-57565-859-9(3), 26fe98e5-df49-4b39-bc55-ae1d229d393b, Kane Press) Astra Publishing Hse.
—Space Mice. Alpaugh, Priscilla, illus. 2020. (ENG.). 32p. (J). (gr. -1-3). 16.99 (978-0-8075-7553-6(4), 807575534) Whitman, Albert & Co.
Howe, James. Horace & Morris, but Mostly Dolores. Waldrod, Amy, illus. 2003. pap. 39.95 incl. audio compact disk (978-1-59112-538-9(3)); pap. 37.95 incl. audio (978-1-59112-243-2(0)) Live Oak Media.
—Horace & Morris but Mostly Dolores. Walrod, Amy, illus. 2003. 30p. (J). (gr. -1-3). 15.65 (978-0-7569-2936-7(9)) Perfection Learning Corp.
—Horace & Morris Join the Chorus (but What about Dolores?) Walrod, Amy, illus. 2006. (J). pap. 44.95 incl. audio compact disk (978-1-59112-909-7(5)); pap. incl. audio (978-1-59112-449-8(2)) Live Oak Media.
—Horace & Morris Join the Chorus (but What about Dolores?) Walrod, Amy, illus. 2005. (ENG.). 32p. (J). (gr. -1-3). 7.99 (978-1-4169-0616-2(9), Atheneum Bks. for Young Readers) Simon & Schuster Children's Publishing.
—Horace & Morris Say Cheese (Which Makes Dolores Sneeze!) Walrod, Amy, illus. 2010. (ENG.). 32p. (J). (gr. -1-3). 7.99 (978-0-689-87177-1(5), Atheneum Bks. for Young Readers) Simon & Schuster Children's Publishing.
—Horace & Morris Say Cheese (Which Makes Dolores Sneeze!) Walrod, Amy, illus. 2009. (ENG.). 32p. (J). (gr. -1-3). 16.99 (978-0-689-83940-5(5)) Simon & Schuster, Inc.
Howie, Vicki. Silent Night. Kallai, Kriszta Nagy, illus. 2009. 32p. (J). (gr. -1). pap. 13.49 (978-0-7586-1779-8(8)) Concordia Publishing Hse.
Huck, Jeremy. Charlie, the Christmas Caterpillar, & Marvin Mouse. 2013. 16p. pap. 24.95 (978-1-62709-632-4(9)) America Star Bks.
Hughes, Mónica. Little Mouse Deer & the Crocodile. Moricuchi, Mique, illus. 2004. 24p. (J). lib. bdg. 23.65 (978-1-59646-684-5(7)) Dingles & Co.
Hurrell, Dianne. Tom Burrows & Friends: Short Stories, Rhymes & Poems. 2010. (ENG., Illus.). 50p. pap. (978-1-84748-782-7(3)) Athena Pr.
Husar, Stephane. Cat & Mouse Come to My House! Mehee, Loic, illus. 2015. (Av2 Fiction Readalong 2016 Ser.). (ENG.). (J). lib. bdg. 34.28 (978-1-4896-3804-5(0), AV2 by Weigl) Weigl Pubs., Inc.
—Cat & Mouse Eat Good Food! Mehee, Loic, illus. 2015. (Av2 Fiction Readalong 2016 Ser.). (ENG.). (J). lib. bdg. 34.28 (978-1-4896-3807-6(5), AV2 by Weigl) Weigl Pubs., Inc.
—Cat & Mouse Feelings. Mehee, Loic, illus. 2015. (Av2 Fiction Readalong 2016 Ser.). (ENG.). (J). lib. bdg. 34.28 (978-1-4896-3810-6(5), AV2 by Weigl) Weigl Pubs., Inc.
—Cat & Mouse Let's Go Shopping! Mehee, Loic, illus. 2015. (Av2 Fiction Readalong 2016 Ser.). (ENG.). (J). lib. bdg. 34.28 (978-1-4896-3816-8(4), AV2 by Weigl) Weigl Pubs., Inc.
—Cat & Mouse Meet the Animals! Mehee, Loic, illus. 2015. (Av2 Fiction Readalong 2016 Ser.). (ENG.). (J). lib. bdg. 34.28 (978-1-4896-3819-9(9), AV2 by Weigl) Weigl Pubs., Inc.
Hutton, John. Flowers for Mr. President. 2012. (Illus.). (J). (978-0-9789608-3-4(1)) Salem Academy & College.
—Sister Maus: A Small Tale of Sisters House in Salem. 2006. (Illus.). 32p. (J). 20.00 (978-0-9789608-0-3(7)) Salem Academy & College.
Huusmann, Thomas-Bo & Fables, Aesops. The Lion & the Mouse. 2013. 26p. pap. (978-87-995724-4-1(3)) Huusmann, Thomas-Bo.
I Am a Painter: Individual Title, 6 Packs. (Sails Literacy Ser.). 16p. (gr. k-18). 27.00 (978-0-7635-4410-2(8)) Rigby Education.
I Can: Individual Title Six-Packs. (Sails Literacy Ser.). 16p. (gr. k-18). 27.00 (978-0-7635-4396-9(9)) Rigby Education.
I Like Boxes: Individual Title, 6 Packs. (Sails Literacy Ser.). 16p. (gr. k-18). 27.00 (978-0-7635-4442-3(6)) Rigby Education.
I Like Riding: Individual Title, 6 Packs. (Sails Literacy Ser.). 16p. (gr. k-18). 27.00 (978-0-7635-4400-3(0)) Rigby Education.
Isbell, Shaun. The Mouse & the Witch, 1 vol. 2009. 56p. pap. 16.95 (978-1-61546-892-8(7)) PublishAmerica, Inc.
Jacques, Brian. The Legend of Luke: A Tale from Redwall. 2005. (Redwall Ser.: 12). (ENG., Illus.). 384p. (J). (gr. 5-7). pap. 9.99 (978-0-14-250109-2(3), Firebird) Penguin Young Readers Group.
—Mariel of Redwall. 2004. (Redwall Ser.). 1.00 (978-1-4175-6449-1(0)) Recorded Bks., Inc.
—Mariel of Redwall: A Tale from Redwall. Chalk, Gary, illus. 2003. (Redwall Ser.: 4). (ENG.). 400p. (J). (gr. 5-5). pap. 10.99 (978-0-14-230239-2(2), Firebird) Penguin Young Readers Group.
—Martin the Warrior: A Tale from Redwall. 2004. (Redwall Ser.: 6). (ENG., Illus.). 384p. (J). (gr. 5-18). pap. 9.99 (978-0-14-240055-5(6), Firebird) Penguin Young Readers Group.
—Mattimeo. 2003. (Redwall Ser.). 1.00 (978-1-4175-5316-7(2)) Recorded Bks., Inc.
—Mattimeo: A Tale from Redwall. Chalk, Gary, illus. 2003. (Redwall Ser.: 3). (ENG.). 448p. (J). (gr. 5-7). pap. 9.99 (978-0-14-230240-8(6), Firebird) Penguin Young Readers Group.
—Die Mauer. pap. 19.95 (978-3-570-26021-0(6)) Bertelsman, Verlagsgruppe C. GmbH DEU. Dist: Distribooks, Inc.
—Redwall. 20th anniv. ed. 2007. (Redwall Ser.: 1). (ENG., Illus.). 352p. (J). (gr. 5-18). 23.99 (978-0-399-24794-1(7), Philomel Bks.) Penguin Young Readers Group.
James, Rosalind. Bertie Rides Again. 2012. (Illus.). 126p. 29.99 (978-1-4771-2272-3(9)) Xlibris Corp.
Jaskiewicz, A. E. Hickory & the Big Clock. 2006. (ENG.). 56p. per. 16.95 (978-1-4241-6024-2(3)) America Star Bks.
Jasnoch, Dorothy. Adventure of Little Mouse Maggie. Kern, Kimberly, ed. Jasnoch, Dorothy, illus. 2012. (ENG., Illus.). 36p. (J). pap. 14.99 (978-1-937752-06-4(2)) Owl About Bks. Pubs.
Jeffs, Stephanie. Llygoden y Nadolig. Wyn, Delyth, tr. Thorne, Jenny, illus. 2005. (WEL.). 28p. (978-1-85994-497-4(3)) Cyhoeddiadau'r Gair.
Jenkins, Amanda. The Lion & the Mouse Shoot Hoops. 2006. (J). pap. (978-1-4108-7173-2(8)) Benchmark Education Co.
Jeong, SoYun. Lulu the Shy Piglet. Orsolini, Laura, illus. rev. ed. 2014. (MySELF Bookshelf Ser.). (ENG.). 32p. (J). (gr. k-2). pap. 11.94 (978-1-60357-654-3(1)); lib. bdg. 25.27 (978-1-59953-645-3(5)) Norwood Hse. Pr.
Jepsen, D. R. Fabulous Fred Gets the Cheese. 2007. 16p. per. 24.95 (978-1-4241-8456-9(8)) America Star Bks.
Jeram, Anita. Bunny My Honey. Jeram, Anita, illus. 2009. (ENG., Illus.). 22p. (J). (gr. k-k). bds. 7.99 (978-0-7636-4645-5(8)) Candlewick Pr.
Jerome, Kate Boehm. Miniature Golf Madness. 2005. (Illus.). 32p. (J). 15.95 (978-0-9769087-3-9(5)) Vertical Connect Pr.
Jeswald, Mary J. The Crazy Adventure of Nicholas Mouse. Trimble, Anne M., illus. 2004. 32p. (J). 14.99 (978-0-9760651-0-4(X)) OrangeFoot Publishing Co.
Jewell, Teresa. How Charlie Mouse Learned about Cystic Fibrosis. 2011. 48p. pap. 21.66 (978-1-4567-2557-0(2)) AuthorHouse.
Johnson, Gerald J. J. Bessie's Little Mouse Day Care. Miltenberger, Dave & Miltenberger, Jeri, illus. 2012. 32p. pap. 24.95 (978-1-62709-430-6(X)) America Star Bks.
—The Mouse Family Christmas, 1 vol. Bousum, Julie, illus. 2009. 26p. pap. 24.95 (978-1-61546-536-1(7)) America Star Bks.
Johnson, Joanna. Phoebe's Sweater. Johnson, Eric, illus. 2010. (ENG.). 38p. (J). 18.95 (978-0-578-04697-6(0)) Slate Falls Pr., LLC.
Johnson, Spencer. WHO MOVED MY CHEESE? for Kids. Pileggi, Steve, illus. 2003. (ENG.). 64p. (J). (gr. -1-3). 20.99 (978-0-399-24016-4(0), G.P. Putnam's Sons Books for Young Readers) Penguin Young Readers Group.
Johnston-Brown, A. M. The Chronicles of Pleasant Grove. 2006. (J). pap. 12.95 (978-0-9760718-5-3(1)) Retriever Pr.
—The Chronicles of Pleasant Grove (Glossary of Terms) 2006. (J). pap. 1.95 (978-0-9760718-6-0(X)) Retriever Pr.
Jones, Brenda. The Adventures of Murphy the Mouse. Moore, Dwain, illus. 2007. (J). per. 12.99 (978-1-59712-069-2(3)) Catawba Publishing Co.
Jones, Carroll. Grandma Battles the Mouse. Giovannini, Jody, illus. 2007. 52p. pap. 16.95 (978-0-9774260-1-0(7)) Omdee Omnimedia, Inc.
Jones, Rosemary. The Mouse House. 2010. (ENG., Illus.). 52p. pap. (978-1-84748-818-3(8)) Athena Pr.
Jules, Jacqueline. The Missing Mouse. Smith, Kim, illus. 2015. (Sofia Martinez Ser.). (ENG.). 32p. (J). (gr. k-2). lib. bdg. 21.32 (978-1-4795-5774-5(9), 126806, Picture Window Bks.) Capstone.
Kabir, Shohag. Mice & Squirrel. 2009. 24p. pap. 13.99 (978-1-4389-9164-1(9)) AuthorHouse.
Kakugawa, Frances. Wordsworth Dances the Waltz. DeSica, Melissa, illus. 2007. 32p. (J). 10.95 (978-0-9790647-3-9(2)) Watermark Publishing, LLC.
Kakugawa, Francis. Wordsworth the Poet. Goto, Scott, illus. 2003. 32p. (J). (gr. -1-3). 10.95 (978-0-9742672-0-3(1)) Watermark Publishing, LLC.
Kawai, Ritsuko. Hamtaro Gets Lost & Other Stories. Kawai, Ritsuko, illus. 2003. (Adventures of Hamtaro Ser.: Vol. 2). (ENG., Illus.). 92p. (J). (gr. 1-3). 9.95 (978-1-56931-817-1(4)) Viz Media.
—Hamtaro, Vol. 3. Kawai, Ritsuko, illus. 2003. (ENG., Illus.). 16p. (J). pap. 7.95 (978-1-56931-816-4(6)) Viz Media.
—Let's Play! Vol. 4: A Playground for Ham-Ham. 2003. (Hamtaro Ser.). (ENG., Illus.). 16p. (J). (gr. 1-3). bds. 7.95 (978-1-56931-821-8(2)) Viz Media.
Keane, Sarah. The Town Mouse & the Country Mouse: An Aesop Fable Retold by Sarah Keane, 1 vol. rev. ed. 2013. (Literary Text Ser.). (ENG., Illus.). 24p. (J). (gr. 1-3). pap. 8.99 (978-1-4333-5525-7(6)) Teacher Created Materials, Inc.
Kellingley, Krystina. Mistflower - the Loneliest Mouse. 2013. (ENG., Illus.). 112p. (J). (gr. -1-12). pap. 9.95 (978-1-78099-468-0(0), Our Street Bks.) Hunt, John Publishing Ltd. GBR. Dist: National Bk. Network.
Kelly, Mark. Mousetronaut: Based on a (Partially) True Story. Payne, C. F., illus. 2012. (Mousetronaut Ser.). (ENG.). 40p. (J). (gr. -1-3). 19.99 (978-1-4424-5824-6(0), Simon & Schuster/Paula Wiseman Bks.) Simon & Schuster/Paula Wiseman Bks.
—Mousetronaut Goes to Mars. Payne, C. F., illus. 2013. (Mousetronaut Ser.). (ENG.). 40p. (J). (gr. -1-3). 19.99 (978-1-4424-8426-9(8), Simon & Schuster/Paula Wiseman Bks.) Simon & Schuster/Paula Wiseman Bks.
Kelso, Mary Jean & Snider, K. C. Rv Mouse. 2013. 24p. 19.95 (978-1-61633-399-7(5)) Guardian Angel Publishing, Inc.
Kennedy, Kim & Kennedy, Doug. Hee-Haw-Dini & the Great Zambini. 2009. (ENG., Illus.). 32p. (J). (gr. k-2). 15.95 (978-0-8109-7025-0(2), 586001, Abrams Bks. for Young Readers) Abrams, Inc.
Kernahan, J. C. & Kernahan, C. Tom, Dot & Talking Mouse & Other Bedtime Stories. 2007. (Illus.). 48p. per. (978-1-4065-1897-9(2)) Dodo Pr.
Kevin, Henkes. Owen. 2006. (Coleccion Rascacielos Ser.). (SPA., Illus.). 32p. (gr. k-1). pap. 9.99 (978-84-241-1519-7(8)) Everest Editora ESP. Dist: Lectorum Pubns., Inc.
Kilgore, Lee. The Mr. Munch Adventures: Six Short Stories, 1 vol. 2010. 73p. pap. 19.95 (978-1-4489-2876-7(1)) America Star Bks.
Kilner, Dorothy. The Life & Perambulations of a Mouse. 2005. 26.95 (978-1-4218-0923-6(0), 1st World Library - Literary Society) 1st World Publishing, Inc.
—Life & Perambulations of a Mouse. 2005. 96p. pap. 10.95 (978-1-59540-623-1(9), 1st World Library - Literary Society) 1st World Publishing, Inc.
—The Life & Perambulations of a Mouse. 2004. reprint ed. pap. 15.95 (978-1-4191-6941-0(6)) Kessinger Publishing, LLC.
—The Life & Perambulations of A Mouse. 2004. reprint ed. pap. 1.99 (978-1-4192-6941-7(0)) Kessinger Publishing, LLC.
King-Smith, Dick. Three Terrible Trins. 105p. (J). pap. 4.99 (978-0-8072-1482-4(5), Listening Library) Random Hse. Audio Publishing Group.
Kirby, Karen. Mr Magic Mouse. 2017. (ENG., Illus.). 20p. pap. 13.95 (978-1-78612-764-8(4), 898e121c-172a-4e06-83c8-802d0188df4b) Austin Macauley Pubs. Ltd. GBR. Dist: Baker & Taylor Publisher Services (BTPS).
—MR Magic Mouse. 2018. (ENG., Illus.). 20p. (J). (978-1-5289-2506-8(8)); pap. (978-1-5289-2507-5(6)) Austin Macauley Pubs. Ltd.
Kirk, Daniel. Library Mouse, No. 1. 2007. (ENG., Illus.). 32p. (J). (gr. 1-4). 18.99 (978-0-8109-9346-4(5), 5735, Abrams Bks. for Young Readers) Abrams, Inc.
—Library Mouse: A World to Explore. 2010. (ENG., Illus.). 30p. (J). (gr. 1-4). 18.99 (978-0-8109-8968-9(9), 647401, Abrams Bks. for Young Readers) Abrams, Inc.
—Library Mouse: Home Sweet Home. 2013. (ENG., Illus.). 40p. (J). (gr. k-4). 18.99 (978-1-4197-0544-1(X), 1007601, Abrams Bks. for Young Readers) Abrams, Inc.
—Library Mouse #2: a Friend's Tale Bk. 2. 2009. (ENG., Illus.). 32p. (J). (gr. 1-4). 18.99 (978-0-8109-8927-6(1), 647301, Abrams Bks. for Young Readers) Abrams, Inc.
Kirkwood, Jeff. The Adventures of Little Mouse. 2008. (ENG.). 24p. pap. 12.99 (978-1-4389-2874-6(2)) AuthorHouse.
Klimpton, Diana. Amy Wild, Animal Talker - the Musical Mouse. 2013. pap. 4.99 (978-0-7945-3145-4(8), Usborne) EDC Publishing.
Kline, Trish & Donev, Mary. Don't Frown, Clown! KA Reader 9. 2007. (Illus.). 32p. (J). per. 20.00 (978-1-934307-02-1(5)) Ghost Hunter Productions.
Knight, Hilary. A Firefly in a Fir Tree: A Carol for Mice. Knight, Hilary, illus. 2004. (Illus.). 32p. (J). (gr. -1-3). lib. bdg. 15.89 (978-0-06-000992-2(6), Tegen, Katherine Bks) HarperCollins Pubs.
Knowles, Daniel S. Mouse. 2011. 710p. pap. 23.99 (978-1-4535-9629-6(1)) Xlibris Corp.
Koch, Theresa F. The Gift of Laughter. 2007. 16p. per. 24.95 (978-1-4241-8343-2(X)) America Star Bks.
Krause, J. R. & Chua, Maria. Poco Loco, 0 vols. Krause, J. R., illus. 2013. (ENG.). 32p. (J). (gr. -1-3). 15.99 (978-1-4778-1649-3(6), 9781477816493, Two Lions) Amazon Publishing.
Krensky, Stephen. Case of the Missing Mice: A Simon Mystery. 2003. (Illus.). 14.95 (978-1-59319-022-4(0)) LeapFrog Enterprises, Inc.
—Malarkey & the Big Trap. Shortley, Michele, illus. 2011. 29p. (J). pap. (978-0-7680-3487-5(6)) SAE Intl.
Kroll, Steven. The Biggest Christmas Tree Ever, 1 vol. Bassett, Jeni, illus. 2009. (ENG.). 32p. (J). (gr. -1-3). pap. 4.99 (978-0-545-12119-4(1), Cartwheel Bks.) Scholastic, Inc.
—The Biggest Snowman Ever. Bassett, Jeni, illus. 2005. (ENG.). 32p. (J). (gr. -1-3). 5.99 (978-0-439-62768-9(0), Cartwheel Bks.) Scholastic, Inc.
—The Biggest Valentine Ever. Bassett, Jeni, illus. 2005. (ENG.). 32p. (J). (gr. -1-k). pap. 3.99 (978-0-439-76419-3(X)) Scholastic, Inc.
—The Hanukkah Mice, 0 vols. Shapiro, Michelle, illus. 2012. (ENG.). 42p. (J). (gr. -1-2). pap. 7.99 (978-0-7614-5988-0(X), 9780761459880, Two Lions) Amazon Publishing.
Kroupa, Robert J. Just Like You. 2011. (J). (978-0-9825503-4-2(0)) IGI Pr.
Kuhlmann, Torben. Armstrong: The Adventurous Journey of a Mouse to the Moon. Kuhlmann, Torben, illus. 2016. (Mouse Adventures Ser.). (ENG., Illus.). 128p. (J). (gr. 2-6). 19.95 (978-0-7358-4262-5(0)) North-South Bks., Inc.
—Armstrong Special Edition: The Adventurous Journey of a Mouse to the Moon. 2019. (Mouse Adventures Ser.). (ENG.). 128p. (J). (gr. 2-6). 19.95 (978-0-7358-4378-3(3)) North-South Bks., Inc.
—Lindbergh: The Tale of a Flying Mouse. 2014. (Mouse Adventures Ser.). (ENG., Illus.). 96p. (J). (gr. 2-6). 19.95 (978-0-7358-4167-3(5)) North-South Bks., Inc.
Labadie, Sally Zolkosky. The Schoolhouse Mouse. 2013. 32p. pap. (978-1-4602-3128-9(7)) FriesenPress.
Lamb, Lenny. Facing Your Fears: Greener Grass Volume 4. 2012. 48p. pap. 24.95 (978-1-4626-5398-0(7)) America Star Bks.
Lambert, Jonny. The Great Aaa-Ooo! 2016. (ENG., Illus.). 32p. (J). pap. (978-1-84869-276-3(5)) Tiger Tales.
Lang, Andrew. The Queen & the Mouse: A Story about Friendship. Lohmann, Renate, illus. 2006. (J). (978-1-59939-081-9(7), Reader's Digest Young Families, Inc.) Studio Fun International.
Lange, Willem. The White-Footed Mouse. Dodson, Bert, illus. 2012. (ENG.). 32p. (J). (gr. 1-3). 17.95 (978-1-59373-109-0(4)) Bunker Hill Publishing, Inc.
Langford, Virginia. Monty Says Mice Are Nice. 2009. 20p. pap. 12.95 (978-1-4389-3429-7(7)) AuthorHouse.
Langley, Noel. Desbarolida, the Waltzing Mouse. Ardizzone, Edward, illus. 2008. 80p. pap. (978-1-905946-01-3(5)) Durrant Publishing.
Larson, Angela. Anthony Smoochiano: First Loves. 2012. pap. (978-1-4507-7998-2(0)) Independent Pub.
Le Gall, Frank. Freedom! Balthazar, Flore, illus. 2012. (Miss Annie Ser.). 48p. (J). (gr. 2-4). pap. 39.62 (978-0-7613-9281-1(5)); (ENG.). lib. bdg. 29.27 (978-0-7613-7884-6(7)) Lerner Publishing Group. (Graphic Universe™).
—Miss Annie. Balthazar, Flore, illus. 2012. (Miss Annie Ser.). 48p. (J). (gr. 2-4). lib. bdg. 58.54 (978-0-7613-8902-6(4), Graphic Universe™) Lerner Publishing Group.
—Miss Annie: 6Pack Set. Balthazar, Flore, illus. 2012. (Miss Annie Ser.). 48p. (J). (gr. 2-4). pap. 79.23 (978-0-7613-9284-2(X), Graphic Universe™) Lerner Publishing Group.
—Miss Annie: Single Copy Set. Balthazar, Flore, illus. 2012. (Miss Annie Ser.). 48p. (J). (gr. 2-4). pap. 13.21 (978-0-7613-9283-5(1), Graphic Universe™) Lerner Publishing Group.
—Rooftop Cat. Balthazar, Flore, illus. 2012. (Miss Annie Ser.). 48p. (J). (gr. 2-4). pap. 39.62 (978-0-7613-9282-8(3), Graphic Universe™) Lerner Publishing Group.
Le Guin, Úrsula K. Tom Mouse. 2004. (Illus.). (J). (gr. k-3). spiral bd. (978-0-616-14584-5(5)) Canadian National Institute for the Blind/Institut National Canadien pour les Aveugles.
Leavitt, Lindsey. Commander in Cheese Super Special #1: Mouse Rushmore. Ford, A. G., illus. 2017. (Commander in Cheese Ser.: 1). 128p. (J). (gr. 2-5). 5.99 (978-1-5247-2047-6(X), Random Hse. Bks. for Young Readers) Random Hse. Children's Bks.
LeBaron, Cecilia. Nat & Tab. 2007. (Illus.). 16p. (J). 5.95 (978-0-9798869-0-4(2)) Crush Publishing.
Lecaye, Olga. El Ratoncito Perez. (SPA.). 40p. 18.95 (978-84-95150-03-5(4)); 2005. 24p. (J). 9.95 (978-84-8470-051-7(8)) Corimbo, Editorial S.L. ESP. Dist: Distribooks, Inc., Iaconi, Mariuccia Bk. Imports.
Lee, P. Janet. Ella Elephant: And Her Fear of Mice. 2007. (ENG., Illus.). 36p. (J). per. 15.95 (978-1-59800-713-8(0)) Outskirts Pr., Inc.
Leeson, Christine. Just for You! Ellis, Andy, illus. (Tiger Tales Ser.). (J). 2008. 24p. (gr. -1-2). pap. 6.95 (978-1-58925-408-4(2)) 2004. 32p. tchr. ed. 15.95 (978-1-58925-042-0(7)) Tiger Tales.
—Molly & the Storm. Hansen, Gaby, illus. 2003. 32p. (J). (gr. k-2). tchr. ed. 15.95 (978-1-58925-027-7(3)) Tiger Tales.
Leeuwen, Jean. The Great Cheese Conspiracy, 0 vols. 2012. (ENG.). 96p. (J). (gr. 1-3). 15.99 (978-0-7614-5972-9(3), 9780761459729, Two Lions) Amazon Publishing.
Leonard, Nellie M. Grand Daddy Whiskers, M. D. 2004. reprint ed. pap. 1.99 (978-1-4192-2227-6(9)); pap. 15.95 (978-1-4191-2227-9(4)) Kessinger Publishing, LLC.
Lestelle, Wende. Science Mouse. 2004. pap. (978-1-930493-65-0(7)) Athena Pr.
Leung, Julie. Mice of the Round Table #1: a Tail of Camelot. Carr, Lindsey, illus. 2016. (Mice of the Round Table Ser.: 1). (ENG.). 304p. (J). (gr. 3-7). 16.99 (978-0-06-240399-5(0), HarperCollins) HarperCollins Pubs.
—Mice of the Round Table #2: Voyage to Avalon. Carr, Lindsey, illus. 2018. (Mice of the Round Table Ser.: 2). (ENG.). 352p. (J). (gr. 3-7). pap. 6.99 (978-0-06-240403-9(2), HarperCollins) HarperCollins Pubs.
Lias, Joe. The Wood Rats Dragging Their Long Tales. 2005. 183p. pap. 24.95 (978-1-4137-5900-6(9)) America Star Bks.
Lieberman, Sylvia. Archibald's Swiss Cheese Mountain. Wendell, Jeremy, illus. 2007. 44p. (J). (gr. k-2). 17.95 (978-0-9795852-5-8(2)) Seven Locks Pr.
Linehan, Jess Golden. Martin Mixed-Up at the Beach. 2011. (ENG., Illus.). 32p. (J). 15.95 (978-0-615-45705-5(3)) Salty Pond Pubs.
Liniers. Buenas Noches, Planeta: TOON Level 2. 2017. (SPA., Illus.). 36p. (J). (gr. k-1). 12.99 (978-1-943145-21-8(0), 9781943145218, TOON Books) Astra Publishing Hse.

—Buenas Noches, Planeta: TOON Level 2. 2017. (SPA., Illus.). 36p. (J). (gr. k-1). pap. 7.99 (978-1-943145-19-5(9), 9781943145195, Toon Books) Candlewick Pr.

—Good Night, Planet: TOON Level 2. 2017. (ENG., Illus.). 36p. (J). (gr. k-2). 12.99 (978-1-943145-20-1(2), 9781943145201, TOON Books) Astra Publishing Hse.

Lionni, Leo. Alexander & the Wind-Up Mouse (Step into Reading, Step 3) 2014. (Step into Reading Ser.). (Illus.). 40p. (J). (gr. 1-4). 4.99 (978-0-385-75551-1(1), Random Hse. Bks. for Young Readers) Random Hse. Children's Bks.

—Frederic. (FRE.). (J). pap. 14.95 (978-2-211-06589-4(9)) Archimede Editions FRA. Dist: Distribooks, Inc.

—Frederick. 2017. (ENG., Illus.). 40p. (J). (gr. -1-2). 8.99 (978-0-399-55552-7(8), Dragonfly Bks.) Random Hse. Children's Bks.

—Geraldine, the Music Mouse. (Illus.). 32p. (J). (gr. -1-2). 2016. (ENG.). 20.99 (978-0-394-94238-4(8), Knopf Bks. for Young Readers) 2009. 8.99 (978-0-375-85514-6(9), Dragonfly Bks.) Random Hse. Children's Bks.

—The Greentail Mouse. 2003. (Illus.). 32p. (J). (gr. -1-2). 15.95 (978-0-375-82399-2(9), Knopf Bks. for Young Readers) Random Hse. Children's Bks.

—Let's Play. 2003. (Illus.). 28p. (J). (— 1). 6.99 (978-0-375-82528-6(2), Knopf Bks. for Young Readers) Random Hse. Children's Bks.

—Nicolas, Where Have You Been? 2010. (Illus.). 32p. (J). (gr. -1-2). pap. 8.99 (978-0-375-85549-8(1), Dragonfly Bks.) Random Hse. Children's Bks.

—El Sueno de Matias. (SPA.). 32p. (J). (gr. 1-3). 13.56 (978-84-264-3675-7(7), LM4689) Editorial Lumen ESP. Dist: Lectorum Pubns., Inc.

Listening with Zachary. (J). pap. 13.75 (978-0-8136-4655-8(3)) Modern Curriculum Pr.

Litchmore, Michael. The MB Force: Heroes at the Best! 2007. 56p. pap. 9.00 (978-0-8059-7399-0(0)) Dorrance Publishing Co., Inc.

Lithgow, John. Mahalia Mouse Goes to College: Book & CD. Oleynikov, Igor, illus. 2007. (ENG.). 40p. (J). (gr. -1-3). 19.99 (978-1-4169-2715-0(8), Simon & Schuster Bks. For Young Readers) Simon & Schuster Bks. For Young Readers.

Litton, Jonathan. Mouse in the Haunted House. Anderson, Nicola, illus. 2015. (Planet Pop-Up Ser.). (ENG.). 12p. (J). (gr. -1). 12.95 (978-1-62686-485-6(3), Silver Dolphin Bks.) Readerlink Distribution Services, LLC.

Lloyd, Megan Wagner. Paper Mice. Wahl, Phoebe, illus. 2019. (ENG.). 40p. (J). (gr. -1-3). 17.99 (978-1-4814-8166-3(5), Simon & Schuster Bks. For Young Readers) Simon & Schuster Bks. For Young Readers.

Lobel, Arnold. Historias de Ratones. 2003. (SPA.). 64p. (978-84-95123-95-4(9), KA7695) Kalandraka Editora, S.L. ESP. Dist: Lectorum Pubns., Inc.

—Sopa de Ratón. 2003. (SPA., Illus.). 62p. (gr. 1-3). pap. 10.99 (978-980-257-286-1(1)) Ekare, Ediciones VEN. Dist: Lectorum Pubns., Inc.

Lobo, Julia. Will You Be My Sunshine. Cottage Door Press, ed. Slater, Nicola, illus. 2015. (ENG.). 18p. (J). (gr. -1-1). bds. 9.99 (978-1-68052-027-9(X), 1000280) Cottage Door Pr.

Loewen, Nancy. The Lion & the Mouse, Narrated by the Timid but Truthful Mouse. Bernardini, Cristian, illus. 2018. (Other Side of the Fable Ser.). (ENG.). 24p. (J). (gr. -1-3). lib. bdg. 27.99 (978-1-5158-2866-2(2), 138404, Picture Window Bks.) Capstone.

Long, Ethan. Me & My Big Mouse, 0 vols. 2014. (ENG.). 32p. (J). (gr. -1-2). 16.99 (978-1-4778-4728-2(6), 9781477847282, Two Lions) Amazon Publishing.

Long, Julie Anne. A Notorious Countess Confesses: Pennyroyal Green Series. 2012. (Pennyroyal Green Ser.: 7). (ENG.). 384p. mass mkt. 8.99 (978-0-06-211802-8(1), Avon Bks.) HarperCollins Pubs.

Lord, Cynthia. Hot Rod Hamster. Anderson, Derek, illus. 2010. (ENG.). 40p. (J). (gr. -1-1). 18.99 (978-0-545-03530-9(9), Scholastic Pr.) Scholastic, Inc.

—Hot Rod Hamster Meets His Match! Anderson, Derek & Paprocki, Greg, illus. 2016. (J). (978-1-5182-0993-2(9), Scholastic Pr.) Scholastic, Inc.

Lord, Pia. The Adventures of M M , Music Mouse. 2011. 50p. pap. 16.95 (978-1-4626-3755-3(8)) America Star Bks.

Louthain, J. A. Arne the Elephant: Terrorized by Evil Mice. Eberbach, Andrea, illus. 2nd l.t. ed. 2003. 48p. (J). 12.97 (978-0-9679416-2-2(8), 0-9679416-2-8) Alexie Bks.

Low, Alice. Blueberry Mouse. Friend, David Michael, tr. Friend, David Michael, illus. 2004. (J). 15.95 (978-1-59336-111-2(4)); pap. (978-1-59336-112-9(2)) Mondo Publishing.

Lowe, Nakesha. It's All about Me. 2010. 12p. 17.50 (978-1-4490-8464-6(8)) AuthorHouse.

Loyd, Mark. Big Ben: A Little Known Story. Loyd, Mark, illus. 2005. (Illus.). (J). (978-0-9773317-1-0(7)) Too Fun Publshing.

Lucado, Max. Itsy Bitsy Christmas: A Reimagined Nativity Story for Advent & Christmas, 1 vol. 2013. (ENG., Illus.). 32p. (J). 14.99 (978-1-4003-2262-6(6), Tommy Nelson) Nelson, Thomas Inc.

—Itsy Bitsy Christmas: You're Never Too Little for His Love, 1 vol. 2013. (ENG., Illus.). 32p. (J). pap. 9.99 (978-1-4003-2404-0(1)) Nelson, Thomas Inc.

Lucy, Cousins. Nochebuena de maisy. 2004. (SPA., Illus.). 32p. (J). 16.99 (978-84-8488-106-3(7)) Serres, Ediciones, S. L. ESP. Dist: Lectorum Pubns., Inc.

—Sueños de colores. 2004. (SPA., Illus.). 32p. (J). 18.99 (978-84-8488-108-7(3)) Serres, Ediciones, S. L. ESP. Dist: Lectorum Pubns., Inc.

Lynne, Kimberlee, illus. The Frog & the Mouse. 2011. (First Steps in Music Ser.). (ENG.). 32p. (J). (gr. k-2). 17.95 (978-1-57999-802-8(X)) G I A Pubns., Inc.

Lyon, Tammie Speer, illus. Hickory Dickory Dock! gif. ed. 2006. 10p. (J). (gr. -1-k). bds. 10.95 (978-1-57791-213-2(6)) Brighter Minds Children's Publishing.

MacDonald, Alan. Scaredy Mouse. Warnes, Tim, illus. 2007. (Storytime Board Bks.). 16p. (J). (gr. -1-k). bds. 6.95 (978-1-58925-827-3(4)) Tiger Tales.

Macho, Geri. A Beautiful Mouse, 1 vol. 2009. 44p. pap. 24.95 (978-1-60703-004-1(7)) America Star Bks.

Mack, Jeff. Good News, Bad News. 2012. (ENG., Illus.). 40p. (J). (gr. -1-1). 16.99 (978-1-4521-0110-1(8)) Chronicle Bks. LLC.

—Mine! (Read Aloud Books for Kids, Funny Children's Books) 2017. (ENG., Illus.). 40p. (J). 16.99 (978-1-4521-5234-9(9)) Chronicle Bks. LLC.

Madonna, Lenae. Lost & Found. Conde, Manuel, illus. 2012. 38p. (J). 16.95 (978-1-60131-115-3(X), Castlebridge Bks.) Big Tent Bks.

Make Believe Ideas, creator. Twinkle Book & Mouse Plush. 2007. (Illus.). (J). (gr. -1-3). (978-1-84610-694-1(X)) Make Believe Ideas.

Malaspina, Ann. The Mouse & the Wizard: A Hindu Folktale. Sylvaine, Jenny, illus. 2013. (Folktales from Around the World Ser.). (ENG.). 24p. (J). (gr. k-3). 32.79 (978-1-62323-633-5(9), 206384) Child's World, Inc, The.

Mangum, Ariana. Carlos, the Mouse Who Discovered Americ. 2008. 272p. pap. 17.99 (978-1-4343-6344-2(9)) AuthorHouse.

Mariconda, Barbara. Sort It Out! Spanish. Rogers, Sherry, illus. 2008.Tr. of Sort It Out! (SPA.). 32p. (J). (gr. k-4). 17.95 (978-1-60718-695-3(0)) Arbordale Publishing.

Marinaro, Stacy. The Cat who rules the Star Mice. 2009. 32p. pap. 15.95 (978-0-557-08180-6(7)) Lulu Pr., Inc.

Marquez, Sofia. Pepe Perez Mexican Mouse: Pepe Perez Comes to the United States: Book 1, 1 vol. Marquez, Sofia, illus. 2009. (Illus.). 20p. pap. 24.95 (978-1-61546-496-8(4)) America Star Bks.

Martin, David. All for Pie, Pie for All. Gorbachev, Valeri, illus. 2008. (ENG.). 32p. (J). (gr. -1-2). pap. 7.99 (978-0-7636-3891-7(9)) Candlewick Pr.

Martin, Rosemary. Rosie's Story. 2011. (ENG., Illus.). 32p. pap. (978-1-84876-699-0(8)) Troubador Publishing Ltd.

Martin, Yvonne. A Mouse in the House. 2012. 28p. pap. 18.65 (978-1-4691-3819-0(0)) Xlibris Corp.

Marwood, Diane. The Lion & the Mouse. 2012. (ENG., Illus.). 24p. (J). (978-0-7787-7893-6(2)); pap. (978-0-7787-7905-6(X)) Crabtree Publishing Co.

Matsutani, Miyoko. Peek-A-Boo. Segawa, Yasuo, illus. 2006. 20p. (J). (gr. -1). 10.95 (978-1-74126-047-2(7)) R.I.C. Pubns. AUS. Dist: SCB Distributors.

May, Eleanor. Albert Adds Up! Melmon, Deborah, illus. 2014. (Mouse Math (r) Ser.). 32p. (J). (gr. -1-1). 22.60 (978-1-57565-744-8(9)) Astra Publishing Hse.

—Albert Adds Up! 2018. (Mouse Math Ser.). (ENG.). 32p. (J). (gr. -1-1). lib. bdg. 34.28 (978-1-4896-8297-0(X), AV2 by Weigl) Weigl Pubs., Inc.

—Albert Doubles the Fun. 2018. (Mouse Math Ser.). (ENG.). 32p. (J). (gr. -1-1). lib. bdg. 34.28 (978-1-4896-8299-4(6), AV2 by Weigl) Weigl Pubs., Inc.

—Albert Helps Out. Melmon, Deborah, illus. 2017. (Mouse Math Ser.). 32p. (J). (gr. -1-1). 7.99 (978-1-57565-860-5(7), 559a9afd-0705-4b1b-960c-61cc23cdd3ca, Kane Press) Astra Publishing Hse.

—Albert Is Not Scared. Melmon, Deborah, illus. 2013. (Mouse Math Ser.). (ENG.). 32p. (J). (gr. -1-1). lib. bdg. 22.60 (978-1-57565-628-1(0)) Astra Publishing Hse.

—Albert Is Not Scared. 2018. (Mouse Math Ser.). (ENG.). 32p. (J). (gr. -1-1). lib. bdg. 34.28 (978-1-4896-8303-8(8), AV2 by Weigl) Weigl Pubs., Inc.

—Albert Is NOT Scared. Melmon, Deborah, illus. 2013. (Mouse Math Ser.). 32p. (J). (gr. -1-1). pap. 7.99 (978-1-57565-629-8(9), f39281cb-4eaa-4711-bad8-263dc6b559f4, Kane Press) Astra Publishing Hse.

—Albert Is NOT Scared: Direction Words. Melmon, Deborah, illus. 2013. (Mouse Math (r) Ser.). (ENG.). 32p. (J). (gr. -1-1). E-Book 34.65 (978-1-57565-630-4(2)) Astra Publishing Hse.

—Albert Starts School. 2018. (Mouse Math Ser.). (ENG.). 32p. (J). (gr. -1-1). lib. bdg. 34.28 (978-1-4896-8311-3(9), AV2 by Weigl) Weigl Pubs., Inc.

—Albert the Muffin-Maker. Melmon, Deborah, illus. 2014. (Mouse Math Ser.). 32p. (J). (gr. -1-1). lib. bdg. 22.60 (978-1-57565-631-1(0)) Astra Publishing Hse.

—Albert the Muffin-Maker. 2018. (Mouse Math Ser.). (ENG.). 32p. (J). (gr. -1-1). lib. bdg. 34.28 (978-1-4896-8313-7(5), AV2 by Weigl) Weigl Pubs., Inc.

—Albert's Amazing Snail. Melmon, Deborah, illus. 2012. (Mouse Math Ser.). 32p. (J). (gr. -1-1). (ENG.). 22.60 (978-1-57565-448-5(2)); pap. 7.99 (978-1-57565-442-3(3), 66896184-54ad-4084-ae2c-c88e04a215c0, Kane Press) Astra Publishing Hse.

—Albert's Amazing Snail. 2018. (Mouse Math Ser.). (ENG.). 32p. (J). (gr. -1-1). lib. bdg. 34.28 (978-1-4896-8307-6(0), AV2 by Weigl) Weigl Pubs., Inc.

—Albert's Bigger Than Big Idea. 2018. (Mouse Math Ser.). (ENG.). 32p. (J). (gr. -1-1). lib. bdg. 34.28 (978-1-4896-8309-0(7), AV2 by Weigl) Weigl Pubs., Inc.

—Albert's BIGGER Than Big Idea. Melmon, Deborah, illus. 2013. (Mouse Math Ser.). 32p. (J). (gr. -1-1). pap. 7.99 (978-1-57565-522-2(5), d6fbf856-4964-472b-bcd8-64f9d26d0cbd, Kane Press) Astra Publishing Hse.

—A Beach for Albert. Melmon, Deborah, illus. 2013. (Mouse Math Ser.). 32p. (gr. -1-1). lib. bdg. 22.60 (978-1-57565-530-7(6)); (J). pap. 7.99 (978-1-57565-531-4(4), b38f0cb2-7040-4d3e-87c6-7c42db43b2cb, Kane Press) Astra Publishing Hse.

—A Beach for Albert. 2018. (Mouse Math Ser.). (ENG.). 32p. (J). (gr. -1-1). lib. bdg. 34.28 (978-1-4896-8285-7(6), AV2 by Weigl) Weigl Pubs., Inc.

—Lost in the Mouseum. 2018. (Mouse Math Ser.). (ENG.). 32p. (J). (gr. -1-1). lib. bdg. 34.28 (978-1-4896-8291-8(0), AV2 by Weigl) Weigl Pubs., Inc.

—Mice on Ice. Melmon, Deborah, illus. 2013. (Mouse Math Ser.). 32p. (J). (gr. -1-1). 22.60 (978-1-57565-527-7(6)); pap. 7.99 (978-1-57565-528-4(4), 2a9ca53b-ef64-4466-beb6-a3300c56f275, Kane Press) Astra Publishing Hse.

—The Mousier the Merrier. Melmon, Deborah, illus. 2012. (Mouse Math Ser.). (ENG.). 32p. (J). (gr. -1-1). 22.60 (978-1-57565-447-8(4)) Astra Publishing Hse.

—The Mousier the Merrier! 2018. (Mouse Math Ser.). (ENG.). 32p. (J). (gr. -1-1). lib. bdg. 34.28 (978-1-4896-8293-2(7), AV2 by Weigl) Weigl Pubs., Inc.

—Where's Albert? Melmon, Deborah, illus. 2017. (Mouse Math Ser.). 32p. (J). (gr. -1-1). 7.95 (978-1-57565-858-2(5), cff7b1e7-6c1b-4a39-a35b-105d9ef4bf37, Kane Press) Astra Publishing Hse.

Maya Z And Nadajia R. Hall. The New-Fangled Adventures of Alexia & Z: The Case of Grams' Missing Teeth. 2009. 36p. pap. 15.95 (978-1-4389-4508-8(6)) AuthorHouse.

Mayerhofer, Felix. Horace the Great Harmonica King. MacFarlane, John, illus. 2006. 31p. (J). (gr. -1-7). per. 16.95 (978-1-60002-255-5(3), 4313) Mountain Valley Publishing, LLC.

Mayhew, James. Bubble & Squeak. Vulliamy, Clara, illus. 2013. (J). (978-1-4351-4770-6(7)) Barnes & Noble, Inc.

Mazula, Derek. A Drifen's Tale. 2009. 48p. pap. 24.99 (978-1-4490-2782-7(2)) AuthorHouse.

Mcadams, Kate. Flynn the Post Office Mouse. 2010. 28p. pap. 12.49 (978-1-4520-0816-5(7)) AuthorHouse.

Mcaleney, Kimberly. The Mouse & the Music Box: A Bedtime Story. 2008. 16p. pap. 8.49 (978-1-4389-3134-0(4)) AuthorHouse.

McClintock, Barbara. Three Little Kittens. McClintock, Barbara, illus. 2020. (ENG., Illus.). 32p. (J). (gr. -1-k). 18.99 (978-1-338-12587-0(7), Scholastic Pr.) Scholastic, Inc.

McCully, Emily Arnold. First Snow. McCully, Emily Arnold, illus. 2003. (ENG., Illus.). 32p. (J). (gr. -1-3). 17.99 (978-0-06-623852-4(8), HarperCollins) HarperCollins Pubs.

—Late Nate in a Race. 2013. (I Like to Read Ser.). (ENG., Illus.). 24p. (J). (gr. -1-3). pap. 7.99 (978-0-8234-2755-0(2)) Holiday Hse., Inc.

—Picnic. McCully, Emily Arnold, illus. 2003. (Illus.). 32p. (J). (gr. -1-k). 16.89 (978-0-06-623855-5(2)) HarperCollins Pubs.

—Picnic. 2003. (ENG., Illus.). 32p. (J). (gr. -1-k). 17.99 (978-0-06-623854-8(4), HarperCollins) HarperCollins Pubs.

—School. McCully, Emily Arnold, illus. 2005. (Illus.). 32p. (J). lib. bdg. 16.89 (978-0-06-623857-9(9)) HarperCollins Pubs.

McElreath, Kim. Mikey the Schoolhouse Mouse. 2006. (J). 13.95 (978-0-9769271-1-2(X)) McElreath, K.M.

McGann, James, illus. The Tailor & the Mouse. 2012. (First Steps in Music Ser.). 32p. (J). (gr. -1-k). 17.95 (978-1-57999-903-2(4)) G I A Pubns., Inc.

McGowan, Steve. The Adventures of Keke & the Golden Coconut. 2012. 48p. pap. 21.92 (978-1-4251-4407-4(1)) Trafford Publishing.

McGregor, Suzy. The Garden Fairy & Mrs. Mouse. 2013. 58p. pap. 14.95 (978-0-9824926-6-6(9)) Lollipop Media Productions, LP.

McHeffey, Adam. Rudy & Claude Splash into Art, 0 vols. 2014. (ENG., Illus.). 32p. (J). (gr. -1-2). 16.99 (978-1-4778-4777-0(4), 9781477847770, Two Lions) Amazon Publishing.

McIntyre, Mel & Mcintyre, Mel. Flutter Bunnies Fossil of Fortune. Grady, Kit, illus. 2011. 20p. pap. 9.95 (978-1-61633-170-2(4)) Guardian Angel Publishing, Inc.

McKissack, Patricia C. Who Will Bell the Cat? 2018. (978-0-8234-4078-8(8)) Holiday Hse., Inc.

McMillan, Bruce. Mouse Views. 2014. 32p. pap. 7.00 (978-1-61003-308-4(6)) Center for the Collaborative Classroom.

McMullan, Kate. One Funny Day. Alley, R. W., illus. 2012. (Pearl & Wagner Ser.: 1). 48p. (J). (gr. 1-3). pap. 4.99 (978-0-448-45866-3(7), Penguin Young Readers) Penguin Young Readers Group.

—Pearl & Wagner: Three Secrets. 2013. (Penguin Young Readers: Level 3 Ser.). lib. bdg. 13.55 (978-0-606-31708-5(2)) Turtleback.

—Pearl & Wagner: Three Secrets. Alley, R. W., illus. 2013. (Pearl & Wagner Ser.: 3). 48p. (J). (gr. 1-3). pap. 4.99 (978-0-448-46472-5(1), Penguin Young Readers) Penguin Young Readers Group.

—Pearl & Wagner: Two Good Friends. Alley, R. W., illus. 2011. (Pearl & Wagner Ser.: 2). 48p. (J). (gr. 1-3). pap. 4.99 (978-0-448-45690-4(7), Penguin Young Readers) Penguin Young Readers Group.

Meachen Rau, Dana. Sweet Pea: Escape in the Garden. Hannon, Holly, illus. 2006. (J). (978-1-58987-200-4(2)) Kindermusik International.

The Meadow Mouse Treasury: Stories, Poems, Pictures from Canada's Finest Authors & Illustrators. (Illus.). (J). 9.99 (978-0-88899-249-9(1)) Groundwood Bks. CAN. Dist: Publishers Group West (PGW).

Meadows, Michelle. Itsy-Bitsy Baby Mouse. Cordell, Matthew, illus. 2012. (ENG.). 40p. (J). (gr. -1-2). 15.99 (978-1-4169-3786-9(2), Simon & Schuster Bks. For Young Readers) Simon & Schuster Bks. For Young Readers.

Medina, Carol-Ann. The Adventures of Gustav Peter Larson Mouse: A Little Mouse in Trouble. 2006. (ENG.). 64p. pap. 28.49 (978-1-4259-0656-6(7)) AuthorHouse.

Meek, Jeffrey/K. Nimble the Thimble Mouse, 1. Dungey, Thomas, illus. 2007. 21p. (J). 9.95 (978-0-9794522-0-8(1)) Thimble Mouse Publishing, Inc.

Messimer, Wanda Fay. Tiny Teacup & Pot Belly Pig Go to Africa to Meet the 'Great Lion' 2013. 24p. pap. 24.95 (978-1-4626-8736-7(9)) America Star Bks.

Messner, Kate. Fergus & Zeke. Ross, Heather, illus. 2018. (Candlewick Sparks Ser.). (ENG.). 56p. (J). (gr. k-4). pap. 5.99 (978-0-7636-9953-6(5)) Candlewick Pr.

—Fergus & Zeke. 2018. (Fergus & Zeke Ser.). lib. bdg. 14.75 (978-0-606-40912-4(2)) Turtleback.

Mice & Other Stories: Individual Title Six-Pack. (Story Steps Ser.). (gr. k-2). 48.00 (978-0-7635-9823-5(2)) Rigby Education.

Mice on Ice: KinderReaders Individual Title Six-Packs. (Kinderstarters Ser.). 8p. (gr. -1-1). 21.00 (978-0-7635-8664-5(1)) Rigby Education.

Miceli, Mary Anne. Boston North Shore's... Mouse Tales of Early Salem. 2013. 44p. pap. 20.00 (978-0-9888654-1-9(6)) Miceli, Mary Anne.

Milbourne, A. & Wells, R. Mouse on the Moon. 2004. (Touchy-Feely Board Bks.). (Illus.). 10p. (J). (gr. -1-18). 4.95 (978-0-7945-0163-1(X), Usborne) EDC Publishing.

Milgrim, David. See Pip Flap. 2019. (Ready-To-Read Ser.). (ENG.). 32p. (J). (gr. k-1). 13.89 (978-1-64310-885-8(9)) Penworthy Co., LLC, The.

—See Pip Flap: Ready-To-Read Pre-Level 1. Milgrim, David, illus. 2018. (Adventures of Otto Ser.). (ENG., Illus.). 32p. (J). (gr. -1-k). 17.99 (978-1-5344-1636-9(6)); pap. 4.99 (978-1-5344-1635-2(8)) Simon Spotlight. (Simon Spotlight).

—See Pip Point: Ready-To-Read Pre-Level 1. Milgrim, David, illus. 2016. (Adventures of Otto Ser.). (ENG., Illus.). 32p. (J). (gr. -1-k). pap. 4.99 (978-1-4814-6784-1(0), Simon Spotlight) Simon Spotlight.

Miller, Dorothy North. How Mr Foxy Fox Was Outfoxed. 2009. 32p. pap. 14.95 (978-0-9825086-1-9(1)) Fiction Publishing, Inc.

Miller, Linda K. Ronald the Church Mouse. 2008. 96p. pap. 12.00 (978-1-60693-063-2(X), Eloquent Bks.) Strategic Book Publishing & Rights Agency (SBPRA).

Milway, Alex. The Mousehunter, 1. 2011. (Mousehunter Ser.). (ENG.). 448p. (J). (gr. 4-6). 18.69 (978-0-316-02455-6(4)) Little Brown & Co.

Miracle Mouse Cranky's Miracle. 2006. (J). lib. bdg. 19.95 (978-1-934017-00-5(0)) Hignites, Tom Miracle Studio.

Mitchard, Jacquelyn. Starring Prima! The Mouse of the Ballet Jolie. Tusa, Tricia, illus. 2004. 160p. (J). (gr. 3-18). 16.89 (978-0-06-057357-7(0)); (ENG.). 15.99 (978-0-06-057356-0(2)) HarperCollins Pubs.

Mitchell, Carolyn. The Tale of the Pumpkin Seed Squad. 2006. (ENG.). 40p. per. 16.99 (978-1-4259-7004-8(4)) AuthorHouse.

Mitchell, Gloria. The Mouse That Went to Find Christmas. Johnson, Jerome A., illus. (J). pap. (978-0-9706186-0-3(3)) Fourth Generation Pubs.

Mitchell, Sheena. Out of the Ark. 2012. 48p. pap. 18.41 (978-1-4669-1489-6(0)) Trafford Publishing.

Mitton, Tony & Parker, Ant. Super Submarines. 2014. (Amazing Machines Ser.). (ENG., Illus.). 24p. (J). (gr. -1-k). 5.99 (978-0-7534-7208-8(2), 900143121, Kingfisher) Roaring Brook Pr.

—Super Submarines. 2014. (Amazing Machines Ser.). (J). lib. bdg. 16.00 (978-0-606-36133-0(2)) Turtleback.

Molloy, Tom. Everything but the Beach: A Slice of Manchester Life. 2012. (ENG., Illus.). 192p. (J). pap. 9.60 (978-1-291-15817-5(0)) Lulu Pr., Inc.

Moore, Clement Clarke & Goodrich, Carter. A Creature Was Stirring. Goodrich, Carter, illus. 2006. (ENG., Illus.). 40p. (J). (gr. -1-3). 18.99 (978-0-689-86399-8(3), Simon & Schuster Bks. For Young Readers) Simon & Schuster Bks. For Young Readers.

Moore, Suzi. Whoops! Ayto, Russell, illus. 2016. (ENG.). 32p. (J). (gr. -1-2). 16.99 (978-0-7636-8180-7(6), Templar) Candlewick Pr.

Moore, Thomas. Zoe & the Back Yard Boys: The Magic Garden Haunted House Adventure. 2012. 24p. pap. 17.99 (978-1-4772-9086-6(9)) AuthorHouse.

Mora, Pat & Martinez, Libby. Bravo, Chico Canta! Bravo! Spanish Edition, 1 vol. Iribarren, Elena, tr. Carling, Amelia Lau, illus. 2014. (SPA.). 32p. (J). (gr. -1-2). 8.95 (978-1-55498-344-5(4)) Groundwood Bks. CAN. Dist: Publishers Group West (PGW).

Morgan, Michaela. Dear Bunny: A Bunny Love Story. Church, Caroline Jayne, illus. 2006. (Scholastic Bookshelf Ser.). (ENG.). 32p. (J). (gr. k-2). 18.69 (978-0-439-74834-6(8)) Scholastic, Inc.

—Mouse with No Name. Mikhail, Jess, illus. 2004. (ENG.). 24p. (J). lib. bdg. 23.65 (978-1-59646-682-1(0)) Dingles & Co.

Morrissey, Dean & Krensky, Stephen. The Wizard Mouse. Morrissey, Dean, illus. 2011. (ENG., Illus.). 32p. (J). (gr. k-4). 16.99 (978-0-06-008066-2(3)) HarperCollins Pubs.

Morse, William A. Bip & the Bulb. 2009. 64p. pap. 23.49 (978-1-4490-2498-7(X)) AuthorHouse.

Mortimer, Anne. Christmas Mouse: A Christmas Holiday Book for Kids. Mortimer, Anne, illus. 2013. (ENG., Illus.). 24p. (J). (gr. -1-3). 12.99 (978-0-06-208928-1(5), Tegen, Katherine Bks) HarperCollins Pubs.

—Pumpkin Cat. Mortimer, Anne, illus. 2011. (ENG., Illus.). 24p. (J). (gr. -1-2). 14.99 (978-0-06-187485-7(X), Tegen, Katherine Bks) HarperCollins Pubs.

Moser, Erwin, et al. Manuel y Didi y el Coche de Maiz. (Manuel & Didi Ser.).Tr. of Manuel & Didi & the Corn Car. (SPA., Illus.). 48p. (J). (978-84-392-8721-6(6)) Gaviota Ediciones ESP. Dist: Lectorum Pubns., Inc.

Mould, Chris. The Great Cheese Robbery. Mould, Chris, illus. 2018. (Pocket Pirates Ser.: 1). (ENG., Illus.). 160p. (J). (gr. 1-4). 17.99 (978-1-4814-9115-0(6)); pap. 6.99 (978-1-4814-9114-3(8)) Simon & Schuster Children's Publishing. (Aladdin).

Moulton, Bob. Rosey & Josey Meet Big Feet. 2010. 20p. 10.49 (978-1-4490-9151-4(2)) AuthorHouse.

Moulton, Mark K. A Royal Wedding. Good, Karen H., illus. 2007. (ENG.). 32p. (J). (gr. k-3). 14.99 (978-0-8249-8677-3(6), Ideals Pubns.) Worthy Publishing.

Moulton, Mark Kimball. One Enchanted Evening. Crouch, Karen Hillard, illus. 2003. 32p. (J). 14.95 (978-0-8249-5480-2(7), Ideals Pubns.) Worthy Publishing.

The Mouse & the Grouse. 2006. (J). lib. bdg. (978-0-9787826-0-3(7)) Happy Bks. Pr.

The Mouse in the House. (J). (gr. 1). (978-0-669-17653-7(2)) Houghton Mifflin Harcourt School Pubs.

A Mouse on the Moon. Date not set. 5.95 (978-0-89868-347-9(5)) ARO Publishing Co.

Mr. Cheesehead Goes for a Ride... 2nd rev. ed. 2005. (Illus.). 32p. (J). 12.99 (978-0-9764463-1-6(6)) Vertigo Publishing.

Nakagawa, Masafumi. Dr. Mouse's Mission. Perry, Mia Lynn, tr. Yamawaki, Yuriko, illus. 2007. (R. I. C. Story Chest Ser.). 27p. (J). (gr. -1-1). 14.95 incl. audio compact disk (978-1-74126-051-9(5)) R.I.C. Pubns. AUS. Dist: SCB Distributors.

Nastanlieva, Vanya. Mo & Beau. 2015. (Illus.). 36p. (J). (gr. -1-3). 15.95 (978-1-927018-63-7(3)) Simply Read Bks. CAN. Dist: Ingram Publisher Services.

Needham, T. L. Kitty Claus. 2012. (ENG.). 27p. (J). (-18). pap. 19.95 (978-1-4787-1788-1(2)) Outskirts Pr., Inc.

Nelkin Wieder, Joy. The Passover Mouse. Kober, Shahar, illus. 2020. (ENG.). 32p. (J). (gr. -1-2). 20.99 (978-1-9848-9552-3(4), Doubleday Bks. for Young Readers) Random Hse. Children's Bks.

Newell, Jeff. Skimper-Scamper. Hranilovich, Barbara, illus. 2005. (Green Light Readers Level 2 Ser.). (J). (gr. k-2). 11.60 (978-0-7569-5244-0(1)) Perfection Learning Corp.

Newman, Robin. The Case of the Poached Egg: A Wilcox & Griswold Mystery. Zemke, Deborah, illus. 2017. (Wilcox & Griswold Mysteries Ser.). (ENG.). 48p. (J). (gr. k-5). 15.95 (978-1-939547-30-9(X), cbab25a3-2b05-4789-9d4c-891ebca2b9b7) Creston Bks.

Newman, Vivian Bonnie. Moti the Mitzvah Mouse. Knopp-Kilpert, Inga, illus. 2017. (ENG.). 24p. (J). (gr. -1-k). 17.99 (978-1-5124-2647-2(4),

11b75fab-3f40-4b46-b9b9-50eea00768f6, Kar-Ben Publishing) Lerner Publishing Group.
Newton, Lesley. Ralphie's Christmas Story, 1 vol. 2010. 16p. pap. 24.95 *(978-1-4489-2674-9(2))* PublishAmerica, Inc.
Nibble, Nibble, Nibble: KinderConcepts Individual Title Six-Packs. (Kinderstarters Ser.). 8p. (gr. -1-1). 21.00 *(978-0-7635-8716-1(8))* Rigby Education.
Nimmo, Jenny. Matty Mouse. 2006. (Blue Bananas Ser.). (ENG., illus.). 48p. (J). (gr. -1-3). *(978-0-7787-0898-8(5))*; lib. bdg. *(978-0-7787-0852-0(7))* Crabtree Publishing Co.
Norton, Miriam. The Kitten Who Thought He Was a Mouse. Williams, Garth, illus. 2008. (Little Golden Book Ser.). 24p. (J). (gr. -1-2). 5.99 *(978-0-375-84822-3(3)*, Golden Bks.) Random Hse. Children's Bks.
Novel Units. The Mouse & the Motorcycle Novel Units Teacher Guide. 2019. (ENG.). (J). pap. 12.99 *(978-1-56137-274-4(9)*, Novel Units, Inc.) Classroom Library Co.
—Ralph S. Mouse Novel Units Teacher Guide. 2019. (ENG.). (J). pap., tchr. ed. 12.99 *(978-1-56137-173-0(4)*, Novel Units, Inc.) Classroom Library Co.
—The Tale of Despereaux Novel Units Student Packet. 2019. (ENG.). (J). (gr. 3-4). pap., stu. ed. 13.99 *(978-1-58130-524-1(9)*, Novel Units, Inc.) Classroom Library Co.
Numeroff, Laura. The Best Mouse Cookie. Bond, Felicia, illus. 2006. (If You Give... Ser.). (ENG.). 32p. (J). (gr. -1-2). 9.99 *(978-0-06-113760-0(X)*, HarperCollins) HarperCollins Pubs.
—The Best Mouse Cookie Board Book. Bond, Felicia, illus. 2019. (If You Give... Ser.). (ENG.). 24p. (J). (gr. -1 — 1). bds. 7.99 *(978-0-694-01270-1(X)*, HarperFestival) HarperCollins Pubs.
—Happy Birthday, Mouse! Bond, Felicia, illus. 2020. (If You Give... Ser.). (ENG.). 24p. (J). (gr. -1 — 1). bds. 7.99 *(978-0-694-01425-5(7)*, HarperFestival) HarperCollins Pubs.
—Happy Valentine's Day, Mouse! Bond, Felicia, illus. 2019. (If You Give... Ser.). (ENG.). 24p. (J). (gr. -1 — 1). bds. 7.99 *(978-0-06-180432-8(0)*, HarperFestival) HarperCollins Pubs.
—Happy Valentine's Day, Mouse! Lap Edition. Bond, Felicia, illus. 2015. (If You Give... Ser.). (ENG.). 24p. (J). (gr. -1-3). bds. 12.99 *(978-0-06-242740-3(7)*, HarperFestival) HarperCollins Pubs.
—If You Give a Mouse a Brownie. Bond, Felicia, illus. 2016. (If You Give... Ser.). (ENG.). 32p. (J). (gr. -1-3). 18.99 *(978-0-06-027571-6(5)*, HarperCollins) HarperCollins Pubs.
—If You Take a Mouse to the Movies: a Special Christmas Edition: A Christmas Holiday Book for Kids. Bond, Felicia, illus. 2009. (If You Give... Ser.). (ENG.). 72p. (J). (gr. -1-3). 18.99 *(978-0-06-176280-2(6)*, HarperCollins) HarperCollins Pubs.
—It's Pumpkin Day, Mouse! Bond, Felicia, illus. 2019. (If You Give... Ser.). (ENG.). 24p. (J). (gr. -1 — 1). 9.99 *(978-0-694-01429-3(X)*, HarperFestival) HarperCollins Pubs.
—Merry Christmas, Mouse! A Christmas Holiday Book for Kids. Bond, Felicia, illus. 2019. (If You Give... Ser.). (ENG.). 24p. (J). (gr. -1 — 1). bds. 9.99 *(978-0-06-134499-2(0)*, HarperFestival) HarperCollins Pubs.
—Mouse Cookies & More: A Treasury. Bond, Felicia, illus. 2015. (If You Give... Ser.). (ENG.). 224p. (J). (gr. -1-3). 24.99 *(978-0-06-113763-1(4)*, HarperCollins) HarperCollins Pubs.
—Si Llevas un Ratón a la Escuela: If You Take a Mouse to School (Spanish Edition), 1 vol. Bond, Felicia, illus. 2003. (If You Give... Ser.).Tr. of If You Take a Mouse to School. (SPA.). 32p. (J). (gr. -1-3). 17.99 *(978-0-06-052340-4(9)*, HarperCollins) HarperCollins Pubs.
—Time for School, Mouse! Bond, Felicia, illus. 2019. (If You Give... Ser.). (ENG.). 24p. (J). (gr. -1 — 1). bds. 7.99 *(978-0-06-143307-8(1)*, HarperFestival) HarperCollins Pubs.
Numeroff, Laura J. A Mouse Cookie First Library. 2007. (If You Give... Ser.). (ENG., Illus.). 100p. (J). (gr. -1-2). bds. 15.99 *(978-0-06-117479-7(3)*, HarperFestival) HarperCollins Pubs.
Numeroff, Laura Joffe. If You Give a Mouse a Cookie. 2004. (Illus.). (J). (gr. k-3). spiral bd. *(978-0-616-01751-7(0))*; spiral bd. *(978-0-616-01752-4(9))* Canadian National Institute for the Blind/Institut National Canadien pour les Aveugles.
—If You Give a Mouse a Cookie. Bond, Felicia, illus. (J). (gr. -1-2). Date not set. 32p. 4.95 *(978-0-06-443166-8(5))* 25th anniv. ed. 2015. (ENG.). 40p. 19.99 *(978-0-06-024586-3(7)*, HarperCollins) HarperCollins Pubs.
—If You Take a Mouse to School. 2004. (Illus.). (J). (gr. k-3). spiral bd. *(978-0-616-14593-7(4))*; spiral bd. *(978-0-616-14594-4(2))* Canadian National Institute for the Blind/Institut National Canadien pour les Aveugles.
—If You Take a Mouse to the Movies. 2004. (Illus.). (J). (gr. k-3). spiral bd. *(978-0-616-11128-4(2))*; spiral bd. *(978-0-616-11129-1(0))* Canadian National Institute for the Blind/Institut National Canadien pour les Aveugles.
—Mouse's Family Album. Date not set. 32p. (J). 10.99 *(978-0-06-028561-6(3)*, Geringer, Laura Book) HarperCollins Pubs.
Oakley, Graham. Church Mice Take a Break. (ENG., Illus.). 25p. (J). 17.99 *(978-0-340-73254-0(7))* Hodder & Stoughton GBR. Dist: Trafalgar Square Publishing.
O'Brien, Robert C. Mrs. Frisby & the Rats of NIMH. 2006. (KOR.). 280p. (J). (gr. 4-7). *(978-89-90794-37-6(4))* Green Bks. Co., Ltd.
—Mrs. Frisby & the Rats of NIMH. (J). 2009. 73.75 *(978-1-4618-3748-0(0))* 2003. 81.75 *(978-1-4025-6007-1(9))* Recorded Bks., Inc.
Ocker, Christ Holder. A Mouse Without a House. 2006. (J). per. *(978-1-59872-711-1(7))* Instant Pub.
Oe, Patricia Daly. Blue Mouse, Yellow Mouse. Oe, Patricia Daly, illus. 2007. (R. I. C. Story Chest Ser.). (Illus.). 20p. (J). (gr. -1-k). 11.95 incl. audio compact disk *(978-1-74126-439-5(1))* R.I.C. Pubns. AUS. Dist: SCB Distributors.
Oeming, Michael Avon & Glass, Bryan J. L. Legend. 2013. (ENG., Illus.). 248p. (YA). 29.99 *(978-1-60706-822-8(2)*, ae6a4f93-2537-4b24-80b2-ca153ed967a4) Image Comics.
Ofoche, Uzo. Monte & Me. 2012. 20p. pap. 10.95 *(978-1-60911-511-1(2)*, Eloquent Bks.) Strategic Book Publishing & Rights Agency (SBPRA).
Oh, Jiwon. Mr. Monkey's Classroom. Oh, Jiwon, illus. 2005. (Illus.). 32p. (J). (gr. -1-2). lib. bdg. 15.89 *(978-0-06-055722-5(2))* HarperCollins Pubs.
Olien, Jessica. When a Tiger Comes to Dinner. Olien, Jessica, illus. 2019. (ENG., Illus.). 32p. (J). (gr. -1-3). 17.99 *(978-0-06-256829-8(9)*, Balzer & Bray) HarperCollins Pubs.
O'Malley, Kevin. Herbert Fieldmouse, Secret Agent. 2003. (Illus.). 32p. (J). pap. *(978-1-59336-043-6(6))*; (gr. 1-6). 15.95 *(978-1-59336-042-9(8))* Mondo Publishing.
Oram, Hiawyn. The Giant Surprise: A Narnia Story. Humphries, Tudor, illus. 2005. (Step into Narnia Ser.). 40p. (J). (gr. -1-2). lib. bdg. 16.89 *(978-0-06-001360-8(5))* HarperCollins Pubs.
—Mr Strongmouse & the Baby. Chapman, Lynne, illus. 2006. (ENG.). 32p. (J). pap. *(978-1-84362-588-9(1)*, Orchard Bks.) Scholastic, Inc.
Orshoski, Paul. We Both Read Bilingual Edition-The Mouse in My House/un Raton en Mi Casa. Canetti, Yanitzia, tr. from ENG. Ebbeler, Jeffrey, illus. 2014. (We Both Read - Level 1 (Quality) Ser.). (ENG & SPA.). 44p. (J). (gr. 1). pap. 5.99 *(978-1-60115-056-1(3))* Treasure Bay, Inc.
—We Both Read-The Mouse in My House. Ebbeler, Jeffrey, illus. 2012. 44p. (J). pap. 5.99 *(978-1-60115-258-9(2))* Treasure Bay, Inc.
Orshoski, Paul & Max, Dave. We Both Read-The Ant & the Pancake. 2015. (ENG., Illus.). 44p. (J). (gr. k-1). pap. 5.99 *(978-1-60115-272-5(8))* Treasure Bay, Inc.
O'Ryan, Ellie. Cinderella: The Great Mouse Mistake. Studio IBOIX Staff, illus. 2011. (Disney Princess Ser.). (ENG.). 96p. (J). (gr. 2-6). 31.36 *(978-1-59961-879-1(6)*, 5179, Chapter Bks.) Spotlight.
—George & the Dragon. 2009. (All Aboard Reading: Station Stop 2 Ser.). (ENG.). 48p. (J). (gr. 1-3). 16.19 *(978-0-448-45242-5(1))* Penguin Young Readers Group.
Otten, Charlotte. The Flying Mouse. Crawford, Greg, illus. 2014. (ENG.). 32p. (J). (gr. -1-3). 17.95 *(978-1-59373-152-6(3))* Bunker Hill Publishing, Inc.
Packard, Albert. Cavern of Babel. Boyles, Shawn, illus. 2006. (J). per. 14.95 *(978-0-9790652-0-0(8))* Diamond Triple C Ranch.
Page, J. & Rainier, S. T. Curiosity Strikes: Ben & Elvis Adventures. Rainier, S. T., illus. 2011. (Illus.). 28p. (J). pap. 8.99 *(978-0-9829669-3-8(8))* Elv Enterprises.
Pankiw, Dr Mary & Pankiw, Mary. Misilla Mouse. 2011. 32p. pap. *(978-1-4269-5476-4(X))* Trafford Publishing (UK) Ltd.
Parker, Emma & Aesop, Aesop. The Lion & the Mouse. 2010. (Illus.). 32p. pap. *(978-1-877547-45-4(X))* First Edition Ltd.
Parker, Jake. Rescue on Tankium3. 2011. (Missile Mouse Ser.: 2). (ENG., Illus.). 160p. (J). (gr. 3-7). 21.99 *(978-0-545-11716-6(X)*, Graphix) Scholastic, Inc.
Parker, Vic, ed. The Mice & the Weasels & Other Fables. 2014. (Aesop's Fables Ser.). 40p. (J). (gr. 2-5). pap. 84.95 *(978-1-4824-1259-8(4))* Stevens, Gareth Publishing LLLP.
—The Town Mouse & the Country Mouse & Other Fables. 2014. (Aesop's Fables Ser.). 40p. (J). (gr. 2-5). pap. 84.95 *(978-1-4824-1260-4(8))* Stevens, Gareth Publishing LLLP.
Parr, Garnet A. Mosey. 2012. 60p. pap. 31.99 *(978-1-4691-7928-5(8))* Xlibris Corp.
Patrick, Jim. The Adventures of Artemous Bk. 1: Mouse in the Museum. 2015. (ENG., Illus.). 52p. (J). pap. 12.95 *(978-1-62287-915-1(5))* First Edition Design Publishing.
Patterson, James. Word of Mouse. Sutphin, Joe, illus. (ENG.). (J). (gr. 3-7). 2018. 320p. pap. 7.99 *(978-0-316-41401-2(8))* 2016. 304p. 13.99 *(978-0-316-34956-7(9))* Little Brown & Co. (Jimmy Patterson).
Paty, Miss. The Mystery of the Tree Stump Ghost: Book 2. 2018. (Whiskers Sisters Ser.). (ENG., Illus.). (J). (gr. k-3). Bk. 2. 48p. pap. 9.99 *(978-1-5415-1045-6(3)*, fd30a799-5e30-44ba-94f8-87e9549a58bf)No. 2. 40p. 26.65 *(978-1-5124-2528-4(1)*, 0e4f01e7-88e0-4f26-b068-a65d6dca2270) Lerner Publishing Group. (Graphic Universe™).
Pearson, Judith Frank. Chester the Christmas Church Mouse. 2013. 18p. pap. 9.95 *(978-1-61493-176-8(3))* Peppertree Pr., The.
Peck, Richard. The Mouse with the Question Mark Tail. 2014. (ENG.). 256p. (J). (gr. 3-7). pap. 8.99 *(978-0-14-242530-5(3)*, Puffin Books) Penguin Young Readers Group.
—Secrets at Sea. 2012. (ENG.). 272p. (J). (gr. 3-7). pap. 8.99 *(978-0-14-242183-3(9)*, Puffin Books) Penguin Young Readers Group.
Pellegata, Donna, illus. The Harp Mouse Chooses Her Home: The Adventure Begins. 2008. 24p. (J). pap. 6.95 *(978-0-9742174-1-3(7))* Heart & Harp LLC.
Perry, Phyllis J. The Secrets of the Rock. Lipking, Ron, illus. 2004. (Fribble Mouse Library Mystery Ser.). 96p. (J). 16.95 *(978-1-932146-22-6(9)*, 1237661) Highsmith Inc.
Peters, Suzanne. Misee Mouse. 2011. 36p. pap. 15.49 *(978-1-4269-5738-3(6))* Trafford Publishing.
Pfanner, Louise. Little Lucies Diary. 2006. (Illus.). 24p. pap. *(978-1-877003-98-1(0))* Little Hare Bks. AUS. Dist: HarperCollins Pubs. Australia.
Pfister, Marcus. Milo & the Magical Stones. 2010. (Milo Ser.). (ENG., Illus.). 32p. (J). (gr. k-2). 17.95 *(978-0-7358-2253-5(0))* North-South Bks., Inc.
Pham, LeUyen. A Piece of Cake. Pham, LeUyen, illus. 2014. (ENG., Illus.). 40p. (J). (gr. -1-3). 16.99 *(978-0-06-199264-3(X)*, Balzer & Bray) HarperCollins Pubs.
Pierre, Dana. Mousey, Mousey Finds Cheese? Illustrated by Wellon Pierre. 2006. 17.00 *(978-0-8059-9867-2(5))* Dorrance Publishing Co., Inc.
Pilkey, Dav. Dogzilla. Pilkey, Dav, illus. 2014. (Illus.). 32p. pap. 7.00 *(978-1-61003-187-5(3))* Center for the Collaborative Classroom.
—Kat Kong. Pilkey, Dav, illus. 2003. (ENG., Illus.). 32p. (J). pap. 9.99 *(978-0-15-204950-8(9)*, 1194948, Clarion Bks.) HarperCollins Pubs.
—Kat Kong. 2003. (gr. k-3). lib. bdg. 15.95 *(978-0-613-71635-2(3))* Turtleback.
—Ricky Ricotta's Mighty Robot. 2014. (Ricky Ricotta's Mighty Robot Ser.: 1). lib. bdg. 16.00 *(978-0-606-35799-9(8))* Turtleback.
—Ricky Ricotta's Mighty Robot (Ricky Ricotta's Mighty Robot #1) Santat, Dan, illus. 2014. (Ricky Ricotta's Mighty Robot Ser.: 1). (ENG.). 112p. (J). (gr. -1-3). pap. 5.99 *(978-0-545-63009-2(6))* Scholastic, Inc.
—Ricky Ricotta's Mighty Robot (Ricky Ricotta's Mighty Robot #1) (Library Edition) Santat, Dan, illus. 2014. (Ricky Ricotta's Mighty Robot Ser.: 1). (ENG.). 112p. (J). (gr. -1-3). lib. bdg. 15.99 *(978-0-545-63106-8(8))* Scholastic, Inc.
—Ricky Ricotta's Mighty Robot vs. the Jurassic Jackrabbits from Jupiter (Ricky Ricotta's Mighty Robot #5), Vol. 5. Santat, Dan, illus. 2014. (Ricky Ricotta's Mighty Robot Ser.: 5). (ENG.). 128p. (J). (gr. -1-3). pap. 5.99 *(978-0-545-63013-9(4))* Scholastic, Inc.
—Ricky Ricotta's Mighty Robot vs. the Mecha-Monkeys from Mars (Ricky Ricotta's Mighty Robot #4) Santat, Dan, illus. 2014. (Ricky Ricotta's Mighty Robot Ser.: 4). (ENG.). 144p. (J). (gr. -1-3). pap. 5.99 *(978-0-545-63012-2(6))* Scholastic, Inc.
—Ricky Ricotta's Mighty Robot vs. the Mutant Mosquitoes from Mercury (Ricky Ricotta's Mighty Robot #2) Santat, Dan, illus. 2014. (Ricky Ricotta's Mighty Robot Ser.: 2). (ENG.). 128p. (J). (gr. -1-3). pap. 5.99 *(978-0-545-63010-8(X))* Scholastic, Inc.
—Ricky Ricotta's Mighty Robot vs. the Naughty Nightcrawlers from Neptune (Ricky Ricotta's Mighty Robot #8) Santat, Dan, illus. 2016. (Ricky Ricotta's Mighty Robot Ser.: 8). (ENG.). 128p. (J). (gr. -1-3). pap. 5.99 *(978-0-439-37709-6(9))* Scholastic, Inc.
—Ricky Ricotta's Mighty Robot vs. the Uranium Unicorns from Uranus (Ricky Ricotta's Mighty Robot #7), Bk. 7. 2015. (Ricky Ricotta's Mighty Robot Ser.: 7). (ENG., Illus.). 128p. (J). (gr. -1-3). pap. 5.99 *(978-0-545-63015-3(0))* Scholastic, Inc.
—Ricky Ricotta's Mighty Robot vs. the Video Vultures from Venus (Ricky Ricotta's Mighty Robot #3) Santat, Dan, illus. 2014. (Ricky Ricotta's Mighty Robot Ser.: 3). (ENG.). 128p. (J). (gr. -1-3). pap. 5.99 *(978-0-545-63011-5(8))* Scholastic, Inc.
Pinkwater, Daniel M. Mrs. Noodlekugel & Four Blind Mice. Stower, Adam, illus. (Mrs. Noodlekugel Ser.: 2). (ENG.). 96p. (J). (gr. k-4). 2015. pap. 7.99 *(978-0-7636-7658-2(6))* 2013. 14.99 *(978-0-7636-5054-4(4))* Candlewick Pr.
Pistinier, Caroline. La Noche Del Ratoncito Perez. 2004. (SPA.). 40p. (J). 19.99 *(978-84-8470-055-5(0))* Corimbo, Editorial S.L. ESP. Dist: Lectorum Pubns., Inc.
Platt, Cynthia. Little Bit of Love. Whitty, Hannah, illus. 2011. (ENG.). 32p. (J). (gr. -1-2). pap. 7.95 *(978-1-58925-426-8(0))* Tiger Tales.
Pogo the Clown. A Little Gray Mouse: Harley's Great Adventures. Miller, Richard D., illus. 2005. (J). 12.95 *(978-0-9755253-7-1(9))* Chilirio Pubns.
Posner-Sanchez, Andrea. Shop with Minnie (Disney Junior: Mickey Mouse Clubhouse) RH Disney, illus. 2012. (Little Golden Book Ser.). (ENG.). 24p. (J). (gr. k-k). 4.99 *(978-0-7364-3031-9(8)*, Golden/Disney) Random Hse. Children's Bks.
Powell, Richard. Quiet as a Mouse: A Moving Picture Storybook. Hendra, Sue, illus. 2003. 16p. (J). 7.95 *(978-1-58925-678-1(6))* Tiger Tales.
Powell, Richard & Davis, Caroline. Mouse's Tail. 2003. (Animal Tails Ser.). (Illus.). 10p. (J). 3.95 *(978-1-58925-675-0(1))* Tiger Tales.
Prentice-Hall Staff. Of Mice & Men. 2nd ed. (J). stu. ed. *(978-0-13-717018-0(1))* Prentice Hall (Schl. Div.).
Priebe, Gigi. The Adventures of Henry Whiskers. Duncan, Daniel, illus. 2017. (Adventures of Henry Whiskers Ser.: 1). (ENG.). 160p. (J). (gr. 2-5). pap. 5.99 *(978-1-4814-6574-8(0)*, Simon & Schuster/Paula Wiseman Bks.) Simon & Schuster/Paula Wiseman Bks.
—The Long Way Home. Duncan, Daniel, illus. 2017. (Adventures of Henry Whiskers Ser.: 2). (ENG.). 160p. (J). (gr. 2-5). 17.99 *(978-1-4814-6578-6(3))*; pap. 5.99 *(978-1-4814-6577-9(5))* Simon & Schuster Children's Publishing. (Aladdin).
The Pumpkin House, 6 Packs. (Literatura 2000 Ser.). (gr. 2-3). 33.00 *(978-0-7635-0182-2(4))* Rigby Education.
Pursglove, Sheila. Mouse Ate the House. 2008. pap. 16.95 *(978-1-932399-19-6(4))* Huron River Pr.
Puttock, Simon. Mouse's First Night at Moonlight School. Pye, Ali, illus. 2015. (ENG.). 32p. (J). (gr. -1-2). 16.99 *(978-0-7636-7607-0(1))* Candlewick Pr.
Pym, Christine. Little Mouse's Big Breakfast. Pym, Christine, illus. 2018. (ENG., Illus.). 32p. (J). (gr. -1-2). 15.99 *(978-0-7636-9626-9(9))* Candlewick Pr.
Quayle, Susan. Mouse & the Storm. Muldoon, Melissa, illus. 2017. 56p. 15.95 *(978-1-84819-344-4(0)*, 696462, Singing Dragon) Kingsley, Jessica Pubs. GBR. Dist: Hachette UK Distribution.
Quintanilla, Billie. The Greatest Mousemas Ever! Barnum, Tabatha, illus. 2012. 36p. 24.95 *(978-1-4626-9725-0(9))*; pap. 24.95 *(978-1-4626-5236-5(0))* America Star Bks.
Quintero, Isabel. Ugly Cat & Pablo. Knight, Tom, illus. 2017. 88p. (J). *(978-1-338-05396-8(5))* Scholastic, Inc.
—Ugly Cat & Pablo & the Missing Brother. Knight, Tom, illus. 2018. (ENG.). 144p. (J). (gr. 2-5). pap. 6.99 *(978-0-545-94095-5(8)*, Scholastic Paperbacks) Scholastic, Inc.
—Ugly Cat & Pablo & the Missing Brother (Library Edition) Knight, Tom, illus. 2018. (ENG.). 144p. (J). (gr. 2-5). lib. bdg. 14.99 *(978-0-545-94096-2(6)*, Scholastic Pr.) Scholastic, Inc.
Quinton, Sasha. Eek-A-Squeak: A Phonics Reader. 2009. (Illus.). pap. *(978-1-936199-05-1(X))* Book Shop, Ltd., The.
Rabei, Carolina. Crunch! Rabei, Carolina, illus. 2016. (Child's Play Library). (ENG., Illus.). 36p. (J). *(978-1-84643-733-5(4))* Child's Play International Ltd.
Rabley, Stephen. Easystart: Marcel & the Mona Lisa. 2nd ed. 2008. (Pearson English Graded Readers Ser.). (ENG., Illus.). 20p. pap. 11.99 *(978-1-4058-6955-3(0)*, Pearson ELT) Pearson Education.
Ramsay, Kim Heaton. Will You Be My Friend? 2012. 16p. pap. 15.99 *(978-1-4772-9503-8(8))* AuthorHouse.
Ramsay, Mark. The Good Neighbors' Cheese Feast: A Cheesy Mouse Tale of Subtraction with Regrouping. Robinson, Susan G., illus. 2010. (ENG.). 32p. (J). pap. 9.95 *(978-0-9842863-1-7(4))* Strategic Educational Tools.
—The Good Neighbors Store an Award: A Cheesy Mouse Tale of Addition with Regrouping. Robinson, Susan G., illus. 2010. (ENG.). 32p. (J). pap. 9.95 *(978-0-9842863-0-0(6))* Strategic Educational Tools.
Rath, Tom H. Donkey Oatie's Field Trip. Gaudet, Christine, illus. 2013. 26p. pap. *(978-0-9918033-4-7(5))* Wood Islands Prints.
Ratnayake, Kumari/Keiko. Monsieur Bagel's War. Ratnayake, Kumari/Keiko, illus. 2007. (Illus.). 25p. (J). spiral bd. 15.00 net. *(978-0-9797015-1-1(1))* Augustana College Geology Dept. Pr.
Ray, Christie Jones & Ray, Christie Jones. Eliz. 2012. (Illus.). 28p. pap. 15.00 *(978-0-9853223-1-1(4))* Rose Water Cottage Pr.
—Eliza & a Cottage Door. 2012. (Illus.). 40p. pap. 15.00 *(978-0-9853223-0-4(6))* Rose Water Cottage Pr.
—Eliza Celebrates a Royal Wedding. 2012. (Illus.). 48p. pap. 15.00 *(978-0-9853223-6-6(5))* Rose Water Cottage Pr.
—Eliza Has a Cousin. 2012. (Illus.). 32p. pap. 15.00 *(978-0-9853223-5-9(7))* Rose Water Cottage Pr.
—Eliza Will Not Be Afraid. 2012. (Illus.). 24p. pap. 12.00 *(978-0-9853223-7-3(3))* Rose Water Cottage Pr.
—Pick-A-Pick-a-Pumpkin. 2012. (Illus.). 36p. pap. 12.00 *(978-0-9853223-4-2(9))* Rose Water Cottage Pr.
Read, Miss. The Christmas Mouse. Goodall, John, illus. (J). lib. bdg. 14.95 *(978-0-8488-1452-6(5))* Amereon Ltd.
Reasoner, Charles. Inside Jolly Rodger's Pirate Ship. 2014. (Illus.). (J). *(978-1-4351-5466-7(5))* Barnes & Noble, Inc.
—The 3 Blind Mice Inside the Spooky Scary & Creepy Haunted House. Reasoner, Charles, illus. 2007. (Story Book Ser.). (Illus.). 10p. (J). (gr. -1-3). bds. *(978-1-84666-381-9(4)*, Tide Mill Pr.) Top That! Publishing PLC.
Reed, Patricia. Mousetrap. 2005. pap. 15.99 *(978-1-4196-0540-6(2))* CreateSpace Independent Publishing Platform.
Reid, Barbara. The Subway Mouse. Reid, Barbara, illus. (Illus.). 2017. 40p. (gr. 1-2). pap. 7.95 *(978-0-439-78917-2(6))* 2005. (J). *(978-0-439-77430-7(6))* Scholastic, Inc.
Remsburg, Rebecca. The Camping Trip, 1 vol. 2010. 22p. pap. 24.95 *(978-1-4489-2508-7(8))* PublishAmerica, Inc.
Resnick, Jacqueline, text. Splat the Cat: Twice the Mice. 2015. (Illus.). 31p. (J). *(978-1-4898-9823-4(9))* Harper & Row Ltd.
Reyes, Analisse. It Wasn't Me! 2011. (Illus.). 25p. (J). pap. 14.95 *(978-1-4327-6851-5(4))* Outskirts Pr., Inc.
Reynolds, Paul A. Sydney & Simon: Go Green! Reynolds, Peter H., illus. 2015. (Sydney & Simon Ser.: 2). 48p. (J). (gr. 1-4). lib. bdg. 12.95 *(978-1-58089-677-1(4))* Charlesbridge Publishing, Inc.
—Sydney & Simon: to the Moon! Reynolds, Peter H., illus. 2017. (Sydney & Simon Ser.: 3). 48p. (J). (gr. 1-4). lib. bdg. 12.99 *(978-1-58089-679-5(0))* Charlesbridge Publishing, Inc.
Rice, Dona Herwick. The Lion & the Mouse, 1 vol. rev. ed. 2008. (Reader's Theater Ser.). (ENG.). 24p. (gr. 1-3). pap. 8.99 *(978-1-4333-0293-0(4))* Teacher Created Materials, Inc.
Rice, Dona Herwick & Housel, Debra. The Town Mouse & the Country Mouse, 1 vol. rev. ed. 2008. (Reader's Theater Ser.). (ENG., Illus.). 24p. (gr. 1-3). pap. 8.99 *(978-1-4333-0294-7(2))* Teacher Created Materials, Inc.
Rigby, Ed & Dooley, Angela. Mouse of the Match. 2009. 41p. pap. 10.50 *(978-1-4452-2692-7(8))* Lulu Pr., Inc.
Rigby Education Staff. A Mouse Manual. (Sails Literacy Ser.). (Illus.). 16p. (gr. 2-3). 27.00 *(978-0-7635-9942-3(5)*, 699425C99) Rigby Education.
Risom, Ole. I Am a Mouse. Miller, J. P., illus. 2018. (Golden Sturdy Book Ser.). 26p. (J). (gr. -1 — 1). bds. 7.99 *(978-0-375-87491-8(7)*, Golden Bks.) Random Hse. Children's Bks.
Robaard, Jedda. The Little Mouse Who Lost Her Squeak. 2015. (ENG., Illus.). 12p. (J). (gr. -1-k). 7.99 *(978-1-4998-0002-9(9))* Little Bee Books Inc.
Robbins, Maria Polushkin. Mother, Mother, I Want Another. Goodell, Jon, illus. 2005. (ENG.). 32p. (J). (gr. -1-1). lib. bdg. 21.19 *(978-0-375-92588-7(0))* Random House Publishing Group.
Roberts, Bethany. Fourth of July Mice ! 2004. (ENG., Illus.). 32p. (J). (gr. -1-1). tchr. ed. 13.00 *(978-0-618-31367-9(2)*, Clarion Bks.) HarperCollins Pubs.
—Thanksgiving Mice! Cushman, Doug, illus. 2005. (ENG.). 32p. (J). (gr. -1 — 1). 5.95 *(978-0-618-60486-9(3))* Houghton Mifflin Harcourt Publishing Co.
—Valentine Mice! Cushman, Doug, illus. 2016. (Green Light Readers Level 1 Ser.). (ENG.). 32p. (J). (gr. -1-3). 12.99 *(978-0-544-80897-3(5)*, 1641296, Clarion Bks.) HarperCollins Pubs.
—Valentine Mice! Board Book. Cushman, Doug, illus. 2011. (Green Light Readers Level 1 Ser.). (ENG.). 28p. (J). (gr. k — 1). bds. 5.99 *(978-0-547-37144-3(6)*, 1423785, Clarion Bks.) HarperCollins Pubs.
Roberts, Daniel. Mouse & His Balloon. 2011. 32p. pap. 14.95 *(978-1-4634-2090-1(0))* AuthorHouse.
Roberts, Smith. A House for a Mouse. Roberts, Smith, illus. 2003. (Illus.). 56p. (J). per. 16.00 *(978-0-9727315-3-9(9))* Prospero's Pr.
Robinson Ed. D., Shannon R. The Adventures of Katie Koala: Oops! My Momma Is Lost!, 1 vol. Swope, Brenda, illus. 2009. 23p. pap. 24.95 *(978-1-60749-733-2(6))* America Star Bks.
Robleda, Margarita. Ramon y Su Raton. Suarez, Maribel, illus. (Rana, Rema, Rimas Ser.). (SPA.). 16p. (J). (gr. k-3). 7.95 *(978-1-59437-818-8(5))* Santillana USA Publishing Co., Inc.
Rockas, Leo. Mice Make War. 2007. 53p. 16.95 *(978-1-4241-5708-2(0))* America Star Bks.
Roddie, Shen. You're Too Small! Lavis, Steve, illus. 2004. 32p. (J). 6.95 *(978-1-58925-385-8(X))*; tchr. ed. 15.95 *(978-1-58925-038-3(9))* Tiger Tales.
Rodrigues, Naomi. Molly Mouse & the Christmas Mystery. 2013. 24p. pap. 15.99 *(978-1-4797-6511-9(2))* Xlibris Corp.
Rogers, Anne. Sooty Wooty Is a Cat. 2008. (ENG.). 32p. pap. 23.95 *(978-1-4092-2565-2(8))* Lulu Pr., Inc.
Rohmann, Eric. My Friend Rabbit: A Picture Book. Rohmann, Eric, illus. 2007. (ENG., Illus.). 32p. (J). (gr. -1-1). pap. 8.99 *(978-0-312-36752-7(X)*, 900042356) Square Fish.
Rose, Chloe Gayle & Rose, Tammy Marie. The Snake That Eats Cake. 2012. 28p. pap. 24.95 *(978-1-4626-9882-0(4))* America Star Bks.
Ross, Dev. We Both Read-Frank & the Tiger. Reinhart, Larry, illus. 2012. 44p. (J). pap. 5.99 *(978-1-60115-260-2(4))* Treasure Bay, Inc.
Roth, Susan L. Mi Amor Por Ti/My Love for You. 2003. (Illus.). 26p. (J). (gr. -1 — 1). bds. 6.99 *(978-0-8037-2944-5(8)*, Dial Bks) Penguin Young Readers Group.
Rourke, Janet W. The New Baby: Featuring Marta the Mouse. 2004. (Illus.). 20p. (J). 7.99 *(978-0-9729583-1-8(2))* Hale Publishing.
Rowland, Patty. Marvelous Max, the Mansion Mouse. Rasmussen, Wendy, tr. Rasmussen, Wendy, illus. 2003. 32p. (J). 17.95 *(978-0-9649934-4-0(9))* Norfleet Pr., Inc.

M N O

Roy, Philip. Mouse Tales. Torrey Balsara, Andrea, illus. 2014. (ENG.). 32p. pap. 9.95 *(978-1-55380-262-4(4))* Ronsdale Pr. CAN. Dist: SPD-Small Pr. Distribution.

Rubin, Bruce Joel & Michaels, Julie. Stuart Little 2 Vol. 2: El Libro de la Película. 2003. (SPA., Illus.). 60p. (J). (gr. 3-5). 14.95 *(978-84-204-6503-6(8))* Santillana USA Publishing Co., Inc.

Rudy, Maggie. City Mouse, Country Mouse. 2017. (ENG., Illus.). 40p. (J). 18.99 *(978-1-62779-616-3(9)*, 900156976, Holt, Henry & Co. Bks. For Young Readers) Holt, Henry & Co.

Rudy, Maggie & Abrams, Pam. The House That Mouse Built. Wolf, Bruce, photos by. 2011. (ENG., Illus.). 32p. (J). (gr. -1). 14.99 *(978-1-935703-25-9(0))* Downtown Bookworks.

Russell, Allyson. The Lizard Who Wanted to Be a Mouse. Bubp, Jennifer, illus. 2009. 28p. pap. 12.95 *(978-1-59858-938-2(5))* Dog Ear Publishing, LLC.

Russell, John. Sam & Socrates. 2012. 60p. (gr. 4-6). pap. 8.95 *(978-1-4620-6830-2(8))* iUniverse, Inc.

Ryan, Mary C., illus. & text. Twitcher Mcgee & the Wonderful Tree. Ryan, Mary C., text. 2008. 12p. (J). 4.95 *(978-0-9678115-3-6(8))* Dragonseed Pr.

Ryan, Pam Muñoz. Mice & Beans. Cepeda, Joe, illus. 2005. (gr. -1-3). lib. bdg. 17.00 *(978-0-7569-5089-7(9))* Perfection Learning Corp.

Rylant, Cynthia. The Eagle. McDaniels, Preston, illus. (Lighthouse Family Ser.: 3). (ENG.). 64p. (J). (gr. 1-5). 2005. pap. 5.99 *(978-0-689-86311-0(X))* 2004. 17.99 *(978-0-689-86243-4(1))* Simon & Schuster Bks. For Young Readers. (Simon & Schuster Bks. For Young Readers).

—Motor Mouse. Howard, Arthur, illus. 2019. (Motor Mouse Bks.). (ENG.). 64p. (J). (gr. -1-3). 17.99 *(978-1-4814-9126-6(1)*, Beach Lane Bks.) Beach Lane Bks.

—The Octopus. McDaniels, Preston, illus. 2005. (Lighthouse Family Ser.: 5). (ENG.). 64p. (J). (gr. 1-5). 17.99 *(978-0-689-86246-5(6)*, Simon & Schuster Bks. For Young Readers) Simon & Schuster Bks. For Young Readers.

Said Mouse to Mole. 2005. (J). per. 8.95 *(978-1-59566-139-5(5))* QEB Publishing Inc.

Sales, Kyle M. On Our Way to Fontinasi. 2011. 60p. pap. 23.88 *(978-1-4634-2739-9(5))* AuthorHouse.

Sally, Zak. Sammy the Mouse #1 (Ignatz) 2007. (ENG., Illus.). 32p. pap. 7.95 *(978-1-56097-865-7(1)*, 9781560978657) Fantagraphics Bks.

Salmassian, Jennifer. Sally Saves the Mice. 2007. (J). per. 0.01 net. *(978-1-60402-115-8(2))* Independent Pub.

Sammel, Rochelle. Tales of Two Mouse Brothers. 2008. 45p. pap. 24.95 *(978-1-4241-9798-9(8))* America Star Bks.

San Souci, Robert D. Zigzag. Czernecki, Stefan, illus. 2005. (ENG.). 32p. (J). (gr. -1-2). 16.95 *(978-0-87483-764-3(2))* August Hse. Pubs., Inc.

Sanders, Jeane F. Ramón. 2008. 100p. pap. 19.95 *(978-1-60610-768-3(2))* America Star Bks.

Sandifer, Audie Cavett. The Exciting Adventures of Eekie & Squeeky. 2011. 52p. (gr. -1). pap. 12.95 *(978-1-4567-4289-8(2))* AuthorHouse.

Sanna, Charles A. There's a Mouse in the House. Hill, Dave, illus. 2006. (J). 10.00 *(978-0-9762839-1-1(3))* Elizabooks.

Santat, Dan, illus. Ricky Ricotta's Mighty Robot vs. the Stupid Stinkbugs from Saturn (Ricky Ricotta's Mighty Robot #6) 2015. (Ricky Ricotta's Mighty Robot Ser.: 6). (ENG.). 128p. (J). (gr. -1-3). pap. 5.99 *(978-0-545-63014-6(2))* Scholastic, Inc.

Santore, Charles. Stowaway on Noah's Ark Oversized Padded Board Book: The Classic Edition. 2018. (Oversized Padded Board Bks.). (ENG., Illus.). 24p. (J). (gr. -1). bds. 12.95 *(978-1-60433-801-0(6)*, Applesauce Pr.) Cider Mill Pr. Bk. Pubs., LLC.

Sargent, Dave & Sargent, Pat. Big Jake: I'm Very Curious. 56 vols., Vol. 12. Huff, Jeane, illus. 2nd rev. ed. 2003. (Animal Pride Ser.: 12). 42p. (J). lib. bdg. 20.95 *(978-1-56763-781-6(7))* Ozark Publishing.

Scam, Busta. The Kingdom of Nome. 2006. (Illus.). 44p. pap. 12.95 *(978-1-59663-516-6(9)*, Castle Keep Pr.) Rock, James A. & Co. Pubs.

Scarry, Patricia. Richard Scarry's the Country Mouse & the City Mouse. Scarry, Richard, illus. 2018. (Little Golden Book Ser.). 24p. (J). (-k). 5.99 *(978-1-5247-7145-4(7)*, Golden Bks.) Random Hse. Children's Bks.

Scarry, Patsy, et al. Richard Scarry's Best Little Golden Books Ever! Scarry, Richard, illus. 2014. 224p. (J). (-k). 12.99 *(978-0-385-37912-0(9)*, Golden Bks.) Random Hse. Children's Bks.

Scarry, Richard. Richard Scarry's Christmas Mice. Scarry, Richard, illus. 2014. (Little Golden Book Ser.). (Illus.). 24p. (J). (-k). 5.99 *(978-0-385-38421-6(1)*, Golden Bks.) Random Hse. Children's Bks.

Schade, Susan. Riff Raff Sails the High Cheese. Kennedy, Anne, illus. 2014. (I Can Read Level 2 Ser.). (ENG.). 24p. (J). (gr. -1-3). pap. 3.99 *(978-0-06-230509-1(3)*, HarperCollins) HarperCollins Pubs.

—Riff Raff the Mouse Pirate. 2014. (I Can Read Level 2 Ser.). (ENG., Illus.). 24p. (J). (gr. -1-3). pap. 3.99 *(978-0-06-230507-7(7)*, HarperCollins) HarperCollins Pubs.

Scheer, Ruth D. The Mouse & the Angel. 2003. (J). lib. bdg. 15.95 *(978-0-9671761-3-0(1))* Scheer Delight Publishing.

Scheffler, Axel, illus. Pip & Posy: the New Friend. 2017. (Pip & Posy Ser.). (ENG.). 32p. (J). (-k). 12.99 *(978-0-7636-9339-8(1))* Candlewick Pr.

Schertle, Alice. Such a Little Mouse. Yue, Stephanie, illus. 2015. (ENG.). 32p. (J). (gr. -1-k). 16.99 *(978-0-545-64929-2(3))* Scholastic, Inc.

Schmidt, Hans-Christian & Bieber, Hartmut. The Wondrous Day. 2004. (Illus.). 18p. (J). 10.99 *(978-1-59384-047-1(0))* Parklane Publishing.

Schoenherr, Ian. Cat & Mouse. Schoenherr, Ian, illus. 2008. (Illus.). 40p. (J). (gr. -1). lib. bdg. 17.89 *(978-0-06-136314-6(6)*, Greenwillow Bks.) HarperCollins Pubs.

—Pip & Squeak. Schoenherr, Ian, illus. 2007. (Illus.). 32p. (J). (gr. -1-k). 18.89 *(978-0-06-087254-0(3))* HarperCollins Pubs.

Schomberger, Mary. The Adventures of Goldy the Mouse. 2013. 36p. pap. 16.95 *(978-1-4908-0375-3(0)*, WestBow Pr.) Author Solutions, LLC.

Schories, Pat. Squeak the Mouse Likes His House. 2018. (I Like to Read Ser.). (Illus.). 32p. (J). (gr. -1-3). 15.99 *(978-0-8234-3943-0(7))* Holiday Hse., Inc.

Schreck, Tabatha M. Welcome to God's Big Backyard: Little Mouse's Adventure. 2012. 28p. pap. 14.95 *(978-1-4520-5524-4(6))* AuthorHouse.

Schue, Lori Vankirk. Peapod. 2009. (ENG.). 42p. pap. 16.99 *(978-1-4415-2356-3(1))* Xlibris Corp.

Schwabauer, Daniel. Runt the Hunted. 2007. (ENG., Illus.). 304p. (J). (gr. 4-7). 17.99 *(978-0-9742972-3-1(2))* Clear Water Pr.

Scott, Cathy. Lily Mouse. 2011. (Illus.). 32p. pap. 12.95 *(978-1-4575-0305-4(0))* Dog Ear Publishing, LLC.

Scott, Janine. Mars Mouse, 1 vol. Wood, Hannah, illus. 2009. (Treasure Chest Readers Ser.). (ENG.). 24p. (J). (gr. 1-1). pap. 9.15 *(978-1-60754-677-1(9)*, 91ae73ab-a879-4fb8-9c38-fd87648aaf30); lib. bdg. 27.27 *(978-1-60754-676-4(0)*, c87bb159-35dd-4473-a072-85a046b4d8b0) Rosen Publishing Group, Inc., The. (Windmill Bks.).

Scotton, Rob. On with the Snow. 2013. (Splat the Cat 8X8 Ser.). (J). lib. bdg. 13.55 *(978-0-606-27152-3(X))* Turtleback.

—Splat the Cat. 2011. (J). (gr. -1-2). 29.95 *(978-0-545-23794-9(7))* Weston Woods Studios, Inc.

—Splat the Cat: The Name of the Game. 2012. (I Can Read Level 1 Ser.). (ENG., Illus.). 32p. (J). (gr. -1-3). 16.99 *(978-0-06-209015-7(1)*, HarperCollins) HarperCollins Pubs.

—Splat the Cat: Big Reading Collection. Scotton, Rob, illus. 2012. (I Can Read Level 1 Ser.). (ENG., Illus.). 100p. (J). (gr. k-3). pap. 19.99 *(978-0-06-209029-4(1)*, HarperCollins) HarperCollins Pubs.

—Twice the Mice. 2015. (Splat the Cat: I Can Read Ser.). (Illus.). 31p. (J). lib. bdg. 13.55 *(978-0-606-37633-4(X))* Turtleback.

—Up in the Air at the Fair. 2014. (Splat the Cat: I Can Read Ser.). (J). lib. bdg. 13.55 *(978-0-606-35059-4(4))* Turtleback.

Scriber, Christian. The Adventures of Almighty Mouse: And Tales of His Friends. 2009. 112p. pap. 10.99 *(978-1-4389-4313-8(X))* AuthorHouse.

Seaman, Lucy. Mr Mouse Morgan. Swope, Brenda, illus. 2011. 28p. pap. 24.95 *(978-1-4560-0916-8(8))* America Star Bks.

Seddon, Jane. Tales of Bermy Wood, 1 vol. 2010. 64p. pap. 19.95 *(978-1-4489-2195-9(3))* America Star Bks.

Segal, Andrew. Clarissa the Clown. Scott, Peter & JessT, Grant, illus. 2007. 32p. per. *(978-1-905823-20-8(7))* Panoma Pr. Ltd.

Seigel, Jonathan & Rother, Beverly S. Myrtle the Turtle & Popeye the Mouse: Learning about Our Solar System. 2012. 40p. pap. 24.95 *(978-1-4626-6587-7(X))* America Star Bks.

Selden, George. Harry Kitten & Tucker Mouse / Chester Cricket's Pigeon Ride: Two Books in One. Williams, Garth, illus. 2009. (Chester Cricket & His Friends Ser.). (ENG.). 144p. (J). (gr. 1-4). pap. 8.99 *(978-0-312-58248-7(X)*, 900062061) Square Fish.

—Tucker's Countryside. Williams, Garth, illus. 2012. (Chester Cricket & His Friends Ser.: 2). (ENG.). 192p. (J). (gr. 3-7). pap. 7.99 *(978-1-250-00256-3(7)*, 900079480) Square Fish.

Seltzer, Eric. Bake, Mice, Bake! Rosenberg, Natascha, illus. 2012. (Penguin Young Readers, Level 1 Ser.). 32p. (J). (gr. k-1). mass mkt. 4.99 *(978-0-448-45763-5(6)*, Penguin Young Readers) Penguin Young Readers Group.

—Bake, Mice, Bake! 2012. (Penguin Young Readers: Level 1 Ser.). lib. bdg. 13.55 *(978-0-606-23625-6(2))* Turtleback.

Shea, Therese. A House for Mouse, 1 vol. 2006. (Neighborhood Readers Ser.). (ENG.). 8p. (gr. k-1). pap. 5.15 *(978-1-4042-5672-9(5)*, 4a3af609-6796-44e3-b9df-adb3e8d380db, Rosen Classroom) Rosen Publishing Group, Inc., The.

Shelton, Crystal G. Theodore's Rings. 2013. 24p. pap. 24.95 *(978-1-62709-378-1(8))* America Star Bks.

Shepard, Aaron. The Adventures of Mouse Deer. Gamble, Kim, illus. 2005. 48p. (J). (gr. -1-4). pap. 10.00 *(978-0-938497-32-5(4)*, Skyhook Pr.) Shepard Pubns.

Shields, Christine. The Tiny Little Scary Mouse. 2012. 20p. pap. 12.68 *(978-1-4669-2147-4(1))* Trafford Publishing.

Shimberg, Elaine Fantle. Helga, the Hippopotamouse. Walling, Sandy Seeley, illus. 2008. (ENG.). 36p. (J). 7.95 *(978-0-9741940-4-2(2))* Abernathy Hse. Publishing.

Shin, Ami & Harris, Jamie. Mice in the City: Around the World. 2018. (Mice in the City Ser.: 0). (Illus.). 40p. (J). (gr. k-3). 19.95 *(978-0-500-65152-0(3)*, 565152) Thames & Hudson.

Shock, Tanya & Thomson, Roger. Walking in Courage: Stories of Virtue's Forest. 2012. 24p. pap. 12.95 *(978-1-4497-3443-5(X)*, WestBow Pr.) Author Solutions, LLC.

Shope, Ray & Shope, Lois. Sandy Claws & Chris Mouse. White, Michael, illus. 2003. 32p. (J). 13.95 *(978-0-9714734-0-9(4))* Flutter-By Productions.

Siivola, Liz. Little Mouse Finds a New Home. DuPont, Brittany, illus. 2013. 24p. pap. 9.99 *(978-1-937165-42-0(6))* Orange Hat Publishing.

Silvestro, Annie. Mice Skating. White, Teagan, illus. 2017. (Mice Skating Ser.: 1). 32p. (J). (gr. -1). 17.99 *(978-1-4549-1632-1(X))* Sterling Publishing Co., Inc.

Singh, Jay. Once upon a Time in a Forest Far Away. 2009. 394p. pap. 33.12 *(978-1-4251-9122-1(3))* Trafford Publishing.

Skinner, Daphne. Albert Keeps Score. Melmon, Deborah, illus. 2012. (Mouse Math Ser.). (ENG.). 32p. (J). (gr. -1-1). lib. bdg. 22.60 *(978-1-57565-449-2(0))* Astra Publishing Hse.

—Albert Keeps Score. 2018. (Mouse Math Ser.). (ENG.). 32p. (J). (gr. -1-1). lib. bdg. 34.28 *(978-1-4896-8305-2(4)*, AV2 by Weigl) Weigl Pubs., Inc.

—The Right Place for Albert. Melmon, Deborah, illus. 2012. (Mouse Math Ser.). 32p. (J). (gr. -1-1). (ENG.). lib. bdg. 22.60 *(978-1-57565-446-1(6))*; 7.99 *(978-1-57565-438-6(5)*, c08e4b27-bd35-44c1-83e4-20dace060a22, Kane Press) Astra Publishing Hse.

Skrbina, Daniel William. A Knight to Remember: Gulliver's Journey Continues, 1 vol. 2009. 74p. pap. 19.95 *(978-1-60836-737-5(1))* America Star Bks.

Slanina, Anne M. Baby Brother Goes to the Hospital. Agnew, Alicia, illus. 2007. (Adventures of Annie Mouse Ser.: Bk. 2). 28p. (J). 18.99 *(978-0-9793379-1-8(7))*; per. 9.99 *(978-0-9793379-0-1(9))* Annie Mouse Bks.

Slanina, Anne Maro. Annie Mouse's Route 66 Adventure: A Photo Journal, vols. 6, vol. 5. Collins, Kelsey, illus. 2011. (ENG.). 48p. (J). pap. 14.99 *(978-0-9793379-6-3(8))* Annie Mouse Bks.

Small, Lily. Chloe the Kitten: Fairy Animals of Misty Wood. 2015. (Fairy Animals of Misty Wood Ser.: 1). (ENG., Illus.). 144p. (J). (gr. k-3). pap. 6.99 *(978-1-62779-141-0(8)*, 900137174, Holt, Henry & Co. Bks. For Young Readers) Holt, Henry & Co.

—Mia the Mouse: Fairy Animals of Misty Wood. 2015. (Fairy Animals of Misty Wood Ser.: 4). (ENG., Illus.). 144p. (J). (gr. k-3). pap. 6.99 *(978-1-62779-144-1(2)*, 900137177, Holt, Henry & Co. Bks. For Young Readers) Holt, Henry & Co.

Smiley, Jeremy. Mice City. 2007. 48p. per. 24.95 *(978-1-4241-8835-2(0))* America Star Bks.

Smith, Charmaine. The Bookhouse. 2006. (ENG.). 360p. pap. 19.95 *(978-0-615-13989-0(2))* Smith, Charmain.

Smith, Gloria. Annie Elf Meets Mitty Mouse. Smith, Claire, illus. 2012. 24p. 29.95 *(978-1-62709-398-9(2))*; pap. 24.95 *(978-1-4626-8151-8(4))* America Star Bks.

Smith, Holly C. Tyler the Monkey & Andy the Mouse. 2012. 28p. (-18). pap. 24.95 *(978-1-4626-9501-0(9))* America Star Bks.

Smith, Jeff. Little Mouse Gets Ready. 2013. (Toon Books Level 1 Ser.). lib. bdg. 14.75 *(978-0-606-31593-7(4))* Turtleback.

—Little Mouse Gets Ready: Toon Books Level 1. (Toon Ser.). (ENG., Illus.). 32p. (J). (gr. -1-3). 2013. pap. 7.99 *(978-1-935179-24-5(1)*, TOON Books) 2009. 12.99 *(978-1-935179-01-6(2)*, Toon Books) Astra Publishing Hse.

Smith, Sindy. Ervin & Alma's Little Mouse House. 2013. 38p. 24.95 *(978-1-63004-209-7(9))*; 40p. pap. 24.95 *(978-1-62709-189-3(0))* America Star Bks.

Snively, Carolyn. Zippo's First Christmas. 2012. 19.95 *(978-0-7414-7383-7(6))*; pap. 11.95 *(978-0-7414-7382-0(8))* Infinity Publishing.

Sobol, John. Friend or Foe?, 1 vol. Tolstikova, Dasha, illus. 2016. (ENG.). 32p. (J). (gr. -1-2). 18.95 *(978-1-55498-407-7(6))* Groundwood Bks. CAN. Dist: Publishers Group West (PGW).

Solomon, Martha. Christmas in Da Hood. 2012. 28p. pap. 12.50 *(978-0-9883126-3-0(8))* iScribe Pubns. LLC.

Sommer, Carl. If Only I Were. . . 2003. (Another Sommer-Time Story Ser.). (Illus.). 48p. (J). (gr. 1-4). 16.95 incl. audio *(978-1-57537-551-9(6))* Advance Publishing, Inc.

—If Only I Were. . . James, Kennon, illus. 2003. (Another Sommer-Time Story Ser.). (ENG.). 48p. (J). 16.95 incl. audio compact disk *(978-1-57537-502-1(8))* Advance Publishing, Inc.

—If Only I Were- James, Kennon, illus. 2014. (J). pap. *(978-1-57537-954-8(6))* Advance Publishing, Inc.

—If Only I Were...(Si Yo Fuese...) James, Kennon, illus. 2009. (Another Sommer-Time Story Bilingual Ser.). (SPA & ENG.). 48p. (J). lib. bdg. 16.95 *(978-1-57537-154-2(5))* Advance Publishing, Inc.

—The Lion & the Mouse. Mercado, Jorge, illus. 2014. (Sommer-Time Story Classics Ser.). (ENG.). 32p. (J). (gr. k-4). 16.95 *(978-1-57537-082-8(4))* Advance Publishing, Inc.

—Noise! Noise! Noise! James, Kennon, illus. (J). 2014. pap. *(978-1-57537-963-0(5))* 2003. (ENG.). 48p. 9.95 *(978-1-57537-020-0(4))* 2003. (ENG.). 48p. lib. bdg. 16.95 *(978-1-57537-069-9(7))* 2003. (ENG.). 48p. (gr. 1-4). 16.95 incl. audio compact disk *(978-1-57537-519-9(2))* Advance Publishing, Inc.

—Noise! Noise! Noise! 2003. (Another Sommer-Time Story Ser.). (Illus.). 48p. (J). (gr. 1-4). 16.95 incl. audio *(978-1-57537-568-7(0))* Advance Publishing, Inc.

—Noise! Noise! Noise! Read-along 2003. (Another Sommer-Time Story Ser.). (Illus.). 48p. (J). lib. bdg. 23.95 incl. audio *(978-1-57537-769-8(1))* Advance Publishing, Inc.

—Noise! Noise! Noise!(Ruido! Ruido! Ruido!) James, Kennon, illus. 2009. (Another Sommer-Time Story Bilingual Ser.). (SPA & ENG.). 48p. (J). lib. bdg. 16.95 *(978-1-57537-161-0(8))* Advance Publishing, Inc.

Sorenson, Margo. Ambrose & the Cathedral Dream. Szegedi, Katalin, illus. 2006. (ENG.). 32p. (J). (gr. -1-3). pap. 4.24 *(978-0-8146-3004-4(9))* Liturgical Pr.

—Ambrose & the Princess. Szegedi, Katalin, illus. 2005. (ENG.). 32p. (J). (gr. -1-3). 16.95 *(978-0-8146-3043-3(X))* Liturgical Pr.

Soto, Gary. Chato's Kitchen. Guevara, Susan, illus. 2003. (Chato Ser.). (J). (gr. -1-2). pap. 39.95 *(978-1-59112-527-3(8))* Live Oak Media.

Spangenberg, Greg. A Christmas Eve Victory. Lodwick, Sarah, illus. Lt. ed. 2006. 32p. (J). 16.99 *(978-1-59879-140-2(0))* Lifevest Publishing, Inc.

—Churchy & the Light on Christmas Eve. Lodwick, Sarah, illus. Lt. ed. 2006. 40p. (J). (gr. -1-7). 14.99 *(978-1-59879-017-7(X))* Lifevest Publishing, Inc.

Spellmeyer, William. Ick-N-Pog: The Encounter Book 2. 2012. 104p. (gr. 2-4). pap. 12.81 *(978-1-4251-9237-2(8))* Trafford Publishing.

Spin & Match - Tell Me a Story: The Grasshopper & the Ants, the Fox & the Grapes, the Turtle & the Rabbit. 2006. (ENG.). 66p. (J). 9.99 *(978-1-59204-202-9(3))* Learning Wrap-Ups, Inc.

Spinelli, Eileen. Now It Is Summer. DePalma, Mary, illus. 2011. (ENG.). 36p. (YA). (gr. -1-3). 16.00 *(978-0-8028-5340-0(4)*, Eerdmans Bks For Young Readers) Eerdmans, William B. Publishing Co.

—Now It Is Winter. DePalma, Mary Newell, illus. 2004. 32p. (J). 16.00 *(978-0-8028-5244-1(0))* Eerdmans, William B. Publishing Co.

Springman, I. C. More. Lies, Brian, illus. 2019. (ENG.). 40p. (J). (gr. -1-3). pap. 7.99 *(978-0-358-11790-2(9)*, 1750732, Clarion Bks.) HarperCollins Pubs.

Square Cat ABC. 2014. (ENG., Illus.). 32p. (J). (gr. -1-3). 15.99 *(978-1-4424-9895-2(1)*, Aladdin) Simon & Schuster Children's Publishing.

St. Pierre, Todd-Michael. Chicory & Roux: The Creole Mouse & the Cajun Mouse, 1 vol. Randall, Lee Brandt, illus. 2017. (ENG.). 32p. (J). (gr. k-3). 17.99 *(978-1-4556-2237-5(0)*, Pelican Publishing) Arcadia Publishing.

Staehli, Melissa. Charlie's Gingerbread House. Rottinger, Amy, illus. 2012. 24p. pap. 11.95 *(978-1-61244-063-7(0))* Halo Publishing International.

Stahl, Stephanie. The Best Snowman Ever. Vasylenko, Veronica, illus. 2013. (ENG.). 16p. (J). (gr. -1-k). bds. 8.95 *(978-1-58925-605-7(0))* Tiger Tales.

Stave, Mel. How Harry Found the Meaning of Friendship. 2010. (Illus.). 40p. pap. 14.95 *(978-1-60911-147-2(8)*, Eloquent Bks.) Strategic Book Publishing & Rights Agency (SBPRA).

Steig, William. Abel's Island. 2007. (Newbery Award & Honor Bks.). (Illus.). 117p. (gr. 3-7). 17.00 *(978-0-7569-8290-4(1))* Perfection Learning Corp.

—Abel's Island. Steig, William, illus. 2007. (ENG., Illus.). 128p. (J). (gr. 3-7). per. 7.99 *(978-0-312-37143-2(8)*, 900044681) Square Fish.

—Amos & Boris. 2011. 8.30 *(978-0-7848-3427-5(X)*, Everbind) Marco Bk. Co.

—Amos & Boris. Steig, William, illus. 2009. (ENG., Illus.). 32p. (J). (gr. k-3). pap. 8.99 *(978-0-312-53566-7(X)*, 900054745) Square Fish.

—Amos & Boris. 2009. (J). (gr. -1-2). lib. bdg. 18.40 *(978-0-8085-2709-1(6))* Turtleback.

—Doctor de Soto. 2003. (Picture Books Collection). (SPA.). 32p. (J). (gr. k-3). 16.95 *(978-84-372-6616-9(5))* Altea, Ediciones, S.A. - Grupo Santillana ESP. Dist: Santillana USA Publishing Co., Inc.

—Doctor de Soto. 2004. (J). (gr. k-3). spiral bd. *(978-0-616-01785-2(5))*; spiral bd. *(978-0-616-01784-5(7))* Canadian National Institute for the Blind/Institut National Canadien pour les Aveugles.

—Doctor de Soto. Steig, William, illus. 2010. (ENG., Illus.). 32p. (J). (gr. -1-3). pap. 8.99 *(978-0-312-61189-7(7)*, 900065535) Square Fish.

—Doctor de Soto. 2010. (J). lib. bdg. 18.40 *(978-0-606-14606-7(7))* Turtleback.

Stengel, Joyce. St. Patrick & the Three Brave Mice, 1 vol. Leonhard, Herb, illus. 2009. (ENG.). 32p. (J). (gr. k-3). 16.99 *(978-1-58980-663-4(8)*, Pelican Publishing) Arcadia Publishing.

Stewart, Shawna. Amazing Tails of Zomber Doodles & Buttons, 1 vol. 2010. 30p. pap. 24.95 *(978-1-4489-7913-4(7))* PublishAmerica, Inc.

Stilton, Geronimo. All Because of a Cup of Coffee (Geronimo Stilton #10), Volume 10. 2004. (Geronimo Stilton Ser.: 10). (ENG., Illus.). 128p. (J). (gr. 2-5). pap. 7.99 *(978-0-439-55972-0(3)*, Scholastic Paperbacks) Scholastic, Inc.

—The Amazing Voyage (Geronimo Stilton & the Kingdom of Fantasy #3) The Third Adventure in the Kingdom of Fantasy. 2011. (Geronimo Stilton & the Kingdom of Fantasy Ser.: 3). (ENG., Illus.). 320p. (J). (gr. 2-5). 16.99 *(978-0-545-30771-0(6))* Scholastic, Inc.

—Attack of the Dragons (Geronimo Stilton Micekings #1), 1 vol. 2016. (Geronimo Stilton Micekings Ser.: 1). (ENG., Illus.). 128p. (J). (gr. 2-5). pap. 6.99 *(978-0-545-87238-6(3)*, ed8d17cb-263f-4dae-9a4a-0151fde04bd9, Scholastic Paperbacks) Scholastic, Inc.

Stilton, Gerónimo. Cat & Mouse in a Haunted House. 2004. (Geronimo Stilton Ser.: 3). (gr. 3-6). lib. bdg. 18.40 *(978-0-613-72224-7(8))* Turtleback.

Stilton, Geronimo. Cat & Mouse in a Haunted House (Geronimo Stilton #3) Keys, Larry, illus. 2004. (Geronimo Stilton Ser.: 3). (ENG.). 128p. (J). (gr. 2-5). pap. 7.99 *(978-0-439-55965-2(0)*, Scholastic Paperbacks) Scholastic, Inc.

Stilton, Gerónimo. Christmas Catastrophe. 2007. (Geronimo Stilton Ser.). (Illus.). 93p. (J). (gr. 2-5). 14.65 *(978-0-7569-8804-3(7))* Perfection Learning Corp.

Stilton, Geronimo. Christmas Catastrophe (Geronimo Stilton Special Edition) 2007. (Geronimo Stilton Ser.). (ENG., Illus.). 128p. (J). (gr. 2-5). pap. 7.99 *(978-0-545-00902-7(2)*, Scholastic Paperbacks) Scholastic, Inc.

—The Christmas Toy Factory (Geronimo Stilton #27) 2006. (Geronimo Stilton Ser.: 27). (ENG., Illus.). 128p. (J). (gr. 2-5). pap. 7.99 *(978-0-439-84118-4(6)*, Scholastic Paperbacks) Scholastic, Inc.

—The Curse of the Cheese Pyramid (Geronimo Stilton #2), Volume 2. Keys, Larry, illus. 2004. (Geronimo Stilton Ser.: No. 2). (ENG.). 128p. (J). (gr. 2-5). pap. 7.99 *(978-0-439-55964-5(2)*, Scholastic Paperbacks) Scholastic, Inc.

Stilton, Gerónimo. Don't Wake the Dinosaur! 2014. (Geronimo Stilton Cavemice Ser.: 6). lib. bdg. 18.40 *(978-0-606-36057-9(3))* Turtleback.

—Down & Out down Under. 2007. (Geronimo Stilton Ser.: 29). lib. bdg. 18.40 *(978-1-4177-7837-9(7))* Turtleback.

Stilton, Geronimo. The Dragon of Fortune (Geronimo Stilton & the Kingdom of Fantasy: Special Edition #2) An Epic Kingdom of Fantasy Adventure. 2017. (Geronimo Stilton & the Kingdom of Fantasy Ser.: 2). (ENG., Illus.). 592p. (J). (gr. 2-5). 19.99 *(978-1-338-15939-4(9)*, Scholastic Paperbacks) Scholastic, Inc.

—The Enchanted Charms (Geronimo Stilton & the Kingdom of Fantasy #7) 2015. (Geronimo Stilton & the Kingdom of Fantasy Ser.: 7). (ENG., Illus.). 320p. (J). (gr. 2-5). 16.99 *(978-0-545-74615-1(9)*, Scholastic Paperbacks) Scholastic, Inc.

Stilton, Gerónimo. The Enormouse Pearl Heist. 2012. (Geronimo Stilton Ser.: 51). lib. bdg. 18.40 *(978-0-606-26756-4(5))* Turtleback.

—A Fabumouse School Adventure. 2009. (Geronimo Stilton Ser.: 38). lib. bdg. 18.40 *(978-0-606-00229-5(4))* Turtleback.

Stilton, Geronimo. A Fabumouse Vacation for Geronimo (Geronimo Stilton #9), Vol. 9. 2004. (Geronimo Stilton Ser.: 9). (ENG., Illus.). 128p. (J). (gr. 2-5). pap. 7.99 *(978-0-439-55971-3(5)*, Scholastic Paperbacks) Scholastic, Inc.

—Flight of the Red Bandit (Geronimo Stilton #56), Volume 56. 2014. (Geronimo Stilton Ser.: 56). (ENG., Illus.). 128p. (J). (gr. 2-5). pap. 7.99 *(978-0-545-55630-9(9)*, Scholastic Paperbacks) Scholastic, Inc.

Stilton, Gerónimo. Flood Mission. 2015. (Illus.). 117p. (J). *(978-0-545-92010-0(8))* Scholastic, Inc.

Stilton, Geronimo. Four Mice Deep in the Jungle (Geronimo Stilton #5), Volume 5. 2004. (Geronimo Stilton Ser.: No. 5). (ENG., Illus.). 128p. (J). (gr. 2-5). pap. 7.99 *(978-0-439-55967-6(7)*, Scholastic Paperbacks) Scholastic, Inc.

Stilton, Gerónimo. Fright Night. 2013. (Geronimo Stilton — Creepella Von Cacklefur Ser.: 5). lib. bdg. 18.40 *(978-0-606-26181-4(8))* Turtleback.

—Geronimo & the Gold Medal Mystery. 2008. (Geronimo Stilton Ser.). (Illus.). 87p. (J). (gr. 2-5). lib. bdg. 14.65 *(978-0-7569-8803-6(9))* Perfection Learning Corp.

—Geronimo Stilton Bks. 7-9: Red Pizzas for a Blue Count, Attack of the Bandit Cats, a Fabumouse Vacation for Gernimo. 2005. (J). *(978-0-439-79161-8(8))* Scholastic, Inc.

Stilton, Geronimo. Geronimo Stilton Boxed Set Vol. #4-6, Set. 2011. (Geronimo Stilton Graphic Novels Ser.). (ENG., Illus.). 168p. (J). (gr. 2-6). 29.99 *(978-1-59707-271-7(0),* 900078888, Papercutz) Mad Cave Studios.

—Geronimo Stilton Boxed Set Vol. #7-9. 2012. (Geronimo Stilton Graphic Novels Ser.). (ENG., Illus.). 168p. (J). (gr. 2-6). 29.99 *(978-1-59707-344-8(X),* 900098166, Papercutz) Mad Cave Studios.

—Geronimo Stilton Graphic Novels #11: We'll Always Have Paris, Vol. 11. 2012. (Geronimo Stilton Graphic Novels Ser.: 11). (ENG., Illus.). 56p. (J). (gr. 2-6). 9.99 *(978-1-59707-347-9(4),* 900087551, Papercutz) Mad Cave Studios.

—Geronimo Stilton Graphic Novels #4: Following the Trail of Marco Polo, Vol. 4. 2010. (Geronimo Stilton Graphic Novels Ser.: 4). (ENG., Illus.). 56p. (J). (gr. 2-6). 9.99 *(978-1-59707-188-8(9),* 900065778, Papercutz) Mad Cave Studios.

—Geronimo Stilton Graphic Novels #5: The Great Ice Age, Vol. 5. 2010. (Geronimo Stilton Graphic Novels Ser.: 5). (ENG., Illus.). 56p. (J). (gr. 2-6). 9.99 *(978-1-59707-202-1(8),* 900068264, Papercutz) Mad Cave Studios.

Stilton, Gerónimo. Geronimo Stilton Heromice Bk. 3: Flood Mission. 2015. (Illus.). 128p. (J). pap. *(978-0-545-66814-9(X))* Scholastic, Inc.

—Geronimo Stilton Heromice #11: Revenge of the Mini-Mice. 2017. (Illus.). 128p. (J). *(978-1-338-18273-6(0))* Scholastic, Inc.

—Geronimo's Valentine. 2009. (Geronimo Stilton Ser.: 36). (Illus.). 103p. (J). 18.40 *(978-1-4364-5051-5(9))* Turtleback.

—Get the Scoop, Geronimo! 2015. (Geronimo Stilton Cavemice Ser.: 9). 128p. (J). lib. bdg. 17.20 *(978-0-606-37779-9(4))* Turtleback.

—Ghost Pirate Treasure. 2012. (Geronimo Stilton — Creepella Von Cacklefur Ser.: 3). lib. bdg. 18.40 *(978-0-606-23931-8(6))* Turtleback.

—The Golden Statue Plot. 2013. (Geronimo Stilton Ser.: 55). (Illus.). 106p. lib. bdg. 18.40 *(978-0-606-32380-2(5))* Turtleback.

Stilton, Geronimo. The Golden Statue Plot (Geronimo Stilton #55) 2018. (True Book (Relaunch) Ser.: 55). (ENG.). 128p. (J). (gr. 3-5). E-Book 31.00 *(978-0-545-55681-1(3),* Scholastic Paperbacks) Scholastic, Inc.

—The Helmet Holdup (Geronimo Stilton Micekings #6) 2017. (Geronimo Stilton Micekings Ser.: 6). (ENG., Illus.). 128p. (J). (gr. 2-5). pap. 7.99 *(978-1-338-15921-9(6),* Scholastic Paperbacks) Scholastic, Inc.

Stilton, Gerónimo. Help, I'm in Hot Lava! 2013. (Geronimo Stilton Cavemice Ser.: 3). lib. bdg. 17.20 *(978-0-606-32407-6(0))* Turtleback.

Stilton, Geronimo. The Hour of Magic (Geronimo Stilton & the Kingdom of Fantasy #8) 2016. (Geronimo Stilton & the Kingdom of Fantasy Ser.: 8). (ENG., Illus.). 320p. (J). (gr. 2-5). 16.99 *(978-0-545-82336-4(6))* Scholastic, Inc.

—I'm a Scaredy-Mouse! (Geronimo Stilton Cavemice #7) Bk. 7. 2015. (Geronimo Stilton Cavemice Ser.: 7). (ENG., Illus.). 128p. (J). (gr. 2-5). pap. 7.99 *(978-0-545-74616-8(7),* Scholastic Paperbacks) Scholastic, Inc.

Stilton, Gerónimo. I'm Too Fond of My Fur! Wolf, Matt, illus. 2004. (Geronimo Stilton Ser.: No. 4). 116p. (J). lib. bdg. 10.00 *(978-1-4242-0698-8(7))* Fitzgerald Bks.

—I'm Too Fond of My Fur! 2004. (Geronimo Stilton Ser.: 4). (Illus.). 116p. (gr. 3-6). lib. bdg. 18.40 *(978-0-613-72225-4(6))* Turtleback.

Stilton, Geronimo. I'm Too Fond of My Fur! (Geronimo Stilton #4) Keys, Larry, illus. 2004. (Geronimo Stilton Ser.: No. 4). (ENG.). 128p. (J). (gr. 2-5). pap. 7.99 *(978-0-439-55966-9(9),* Scholastic Paperbacks) Scholastic, Inc.

Stilton, Gerónimo. It's Halloween, You 'Fraidy Mouse! Wolf, Matt, illus. 2004. 113p. (J). lib. bdg. 10.00 *(978-1-4242-0280-5(9))* Fitzgerald Bks.

Stilton, Geronimo. The Journey Through Time (Geronimo Stilton Special Edition) 2014. (Geronimo Stilton Journey Through Time Ser.). (ENG., Illus.). 320p. (J). (gr. 2-5). 16.99 *(978-0-545-55623-1(6),* Scholastic Paperbacks) Scholastic, Inc.

Stilton, Gerónimo. The Karate Mouse. 2010. (Geronimo Stilton Ser.: 40). lib. bdg. 18.40 *(978-0-606-06847-5(3))* Turtleback.

—Lost Treasure of the Emerald Eye. Wolf, Matt, illus. 2004. (Geronimo Stilton Ser.: No. 1). 116p. (J). lib. bdg. 10.00 *(978-1-4242-0695-7(2))* Fitzgerald Bks.

Stilton, Geronimo. Lost Treasure of the Emerald Eye. 2004. (Geronimo Stilton Ser.: 2). (gr. 3-6). lib. bdg. 18.40 *(978-0-613-72223-0(X))* Turtleback.

—Lost Treasure of the Emerald Eye (Geronimo Stilton #1), Volume 1. 2004. (Geronimo Stilton Ser.: 1). (ENG., Illus.). 128p. (J). (gr. 2-5). pap. 7.99 *(978-0-439-55963-8(4),* Scholastic Paperbacks) Scholastic, Inc.

Stilton, Gerónimo. Meet Me in Horrorwood. 2011. (Geronimo Stilton — Creepella Von Cacklefur Ser.: 2). (Illus.). 112p. (J). lib. bdg. 18.40 *(978-0-606-22947-0(7))* Turtleback.

—The Mona Mousa Code. Wolf, Matt, illus. 2005. (Geronimo Stilton Ser.: No. 15). 113p. (J). lib. bdg. 10.00 *(978-1-4242-0284-3(1))* Fitzgerald Bks.

—Mouse House Hunter. 2015. (Geronimo Stilton Ser.: 61). lib. bdg. 18.40 *(978-0-606-37780-5(8))* Turtleback.

—The Mouse Island Marathon. 2007. (Geronimo Stilton Ser.: 30). lib. bdg. 18.40 *(978-1-4177-7839-3(3))* Turtleback.

Stilton, Geronimo. My Name Is Stilton, Geronimo Stilton (Geronimo Stilton #19), Volume 19. 2005. (Geronimo Stilton Ser.: 19). (ENG., Illus.). 128p. (J). (gr. 2-5). pap. 7.99 *(978-0-439-69142-0(7),* Scholastic Paperbacks) Scholastic, Inc.

Stilton, Gerónimo. The Mysterious Cheese Thief. 2007. (Geronimo Stilton Ser.). (Illus.). 111p. (J). (gr. 2-5). 14.65 *(978-0-7569-8303-1(7))* Perfection Learning Corp.

—The Mysterious Cheese Thief. 2007. (Geronimo Stilton Ser.: 31). (Illus.). 111p. (gr. 4-7). 18.40 *(978-1-4177-9646-5(4))* Turtleback.

—The Mystery in Venice. 2012. (Geronimo Stilton Ser.: 48). lib. bdg. 18.40 *(978-0-606-23729-1(1))* Turtleback.

—The Phantom of the Subway. Wolf, Matt, illus. 2004. (Geronimo Stilton Ser.: No. 13). 112p. (J). lib. bdg. 10.00 *(978-1-4242-0282-9(5))* Fitzgerald Bks.

Stilton, Geronimo. The Phoenix of Destiny (Geronimo Stilton & the Kingdom of Fantasy: Special Edition) An Epic Kingdom of Fantasy Adventure. 2015. (Geronimo Stilton & the Kingdom of Fantasy Ser.). (ENG., Illus.). 592p. (J). (gr. 2-5). 19.99 *(978-0-545-82907-6(0),* Scholastic Paperbacks) Scholastic, Inc.

Stilton, Gerónimo. The Race Across America. 2009. (Geronimo Stilton Ser.: 37). lib. bdg. 18.40 *(978-0-606-00228-6(8))* Turtleback.

Stilton, Geronimo. The Race Against Time (Geronimo Stilton Journey Through Time #3) 2018. (ENG.). 320p. (J). (gr. -1-3). E-Book 4.99 *(978-0-545-87298-0(7),* Scholastic Paperbacks) Scholastic, Inc.

Stilton, Gerónimo. Rescue Rebellion. 2015. (Geronimo Stilton Spacemice Ser.: 5). lib. bdg. 17.20 *(978-0-606-37775-1(1))* Turtleback.

—Return of the Vampire. 2012. (Geronimo Stilton — Creepella Von Cacklefur Ser.: 4). lib. bdg. 18.40 *(978-0-606-26180-7(X))* Turtleback.

—Ride for Your Life! 2014. (Geronimo Stilton — Creepella Von Cacklefur Ser.: 6). lib. bdg. 18.40 *(978-0-606-35847-7(1))* Turtleback.

—Rumble in the Jungle. 2013. (Geronimo Stilton Ser.: 53). lib. bdg. 18.40 *(978-0-606-31527-2(6))* Turtleback.

—The Search for Sunken Treasure. Wolf, Matt, illus. 2006. (Geronimo Stilton Ser.: No. 25). 111p. (J). lib. bdg. 10.00 *(978-1-4242-1519-5(6))* Fitzgerald Bks.

Stilton, Geronimo. The Search for Treasure (Geronimo Stilton & the Kingdom of Fantasy #6) (ENG.). 320p. (J). 2017. (gr. -1-k). E-Book 12.99 *(978-0-545-65895-9(0))*Volume 6. 2014. (Geronimo Stilton & the Kingdom of Fantasy Ser.: 6). (Illus.). (gr. 2-5). 16.99 *(978-0-545-65604-7(4))* Scholastic, Inc. (Scholastic Paperbacks).

Stilton, Gerónimo. Singing Sensation. 2009. (Geronimo Stilton Ser.: 39). lib. bdg. 18.40 *(978-0-606-00230-1(8))* Turtleback.

—The Stinky Cheese Vacation. 2014. (Geronimo Stilton Ser.: 57). lib. bdg. 18.40 *(978-0-606-35843-9(9))* Turtleback.

—The Stone of Fire. 2013. (Geronimo Stilton Cavemice Ser.: 1). lib. bdg. 18.40 *(978-0-606-31526-5(8))* Turtleback.

Stilton, Geronimo. The Stone of Fire (Geronimo Stilton Cavemice #1) 2004. (Geronimo Stilton Ser.: 1). (ENG.). 128p. (J). (gr. 2-5). E-Book 7.99 *(978-0-545-52048-5(7),* Scholastic Paperbacks) Scholastic, Inc.

—A Suitcase Full of Ghosts (Creepella Von Cacklefur #7) A Geronimo Stilton Adventure. 2015. (Creepella Von Cacklefur Ser.: 7). (ENG.). 128p. (J). (gr. 2-5). pap. 7.99 *(978-0-545-74611-3(6),* Scholastic Paperbacks) Scholastic, Inc.

Stilton, Gerónimo. The Super Chef Contest. 2014. (Geronimo Stilton Ser.: 58). lib. bdg. 18.40 *(978-0-606-36056-2(5))* Turtleback.

—The Temple of the Ruby of Fire. Wolf, Matt, illus. 2004. (Geronimo Stilton Ser.: No. 14). 109p. (J). lib. bdg. 10.00 *(978-1-4242-0283-6(3))* Fitzgerald Bks.

—Thea Stilton & the Dragon's Code. 2009. (Geronimo Stilton Special Edition Ser.: No. 1). (Illus.). 158p. 18.00 *(978-1-60686-420-3(3))* Perfection Learning Corp.

—Thea Stilton & the Dragon's Code. 2009. (Thea Stilton Ser.: 1). lib. bdg. 19.65 *(978-0-606-00231-8(6))* Turtleback.

—Thea Stilton & the Niagara Splash, 27. 2019. (Geronimo Stilton Ser.). (ENG.). 164p. (J). (gr. 2-3). 18.36 *(978-1-64310-997-8(9))* Penworthy Co., LLC, The.

—This Hotel Is Haunted! 2012. (Geronimo Stilton Ser.: 50). lib. bdg. 18.40 *(978-0-606-26182-1(6))* Turtleback.

—Valentine's Day Disaster. Keys, Larry et al, illus. 2006. (Geronimo Stilton Ser.: No. 23). 122p. (J). lib. bdg. 18.46 *(978-1-4242-0292-8(2))* Fitzgerald Bks.

—Valley of the Giant Skeletons. 2008. (Illus.). 111p. (J). lib. bdg. 15.38 *(978-1-4242-4303-7(3))* Fitzgerald Bks.

—Valley of the Giant Skeletons. 2008. (Geronimo Stilton Ser.). (Illus.). 110p. (gr. 2-5). 17.00 *(978-0-7569-8805-0(5))* Perfection Learning Corp.

—Valley of the Giant Skeletons. 2008. (Geronimo Stilton Ser.: 32). lib. bdg. 18.40 *(978-1-4364-2713-5(4))* Turtleback.

Stilton, Geronimo. A Very Merry Christmas (Geronimo Stilton #35), Vol. 35. 2008. (Geronimo Stilton Ser.: 35). (ENG.). 128p. (J). (gr. 2-5). 7.99 *(978-0-545-02135-7(9),* Scholastic Paperbacks) Scholastic, Inc.

—The Volcano of Fire (Geronimo Stilton & the Kingdom of Fantasy #5) 2013. (Geronimo Stilton & the Kingdom of Fantasy Ser.: 5). (ENG., Illus.). 320p. (J). (gr. 2-5). 16.99 *(978-0-545-55625-5(2),* Scholastic Paperbacks) Scholastic, Inc.

Stilton, Gerónimo. Watch Your Tail! 2013. (Geronimo Stilton Cavemice Ser.: 2). lib. bdg. 18.40 *(978-0-606-31998-0(0))* Turtleback.

—The Way of the Samurai. 2012. (Geronimo Stilton Ser.: 49). lib. bdg. 18.40 *(978-0-606-26094-7(3))* Turtleback.

—Welcome to Moldy Manor. 2014. (Geronimo Stilton Ser.: 59). lib. bdg. 18.40 *(978-0-606-36351-8(3))* Turtleback.

Stilton, Geronimo. The Wizard's Wand (Geronimo Stilton & the Kingdom of Fantasy #9) 2016. (Geronimo Stilton & the Kingdom of Fantasy Ser.: 9). (ENG., Illus.). 320p. (J). (gr. 2-5). 16.99 *(978-1-338-03291-8(7),* Scholastic Paperbacks) Scholastic, Inc.

Stilton, Gerónimo. You're Mine, Captain! 2014. (Geronimo Stilton Spacemice Ser.: 2). lib. bdg. 18.40 *(978-0-606-35845-3(5))* Turtleback.

Stilton, Gerónimo & Clement, Emily. Attack of the Dragons. Facciotto, Giuseppe & Costa, Alessandro, illus. 2016. 115p. (J). *(978-0-605-93525-9(4))* Scholastic, Inc.

Stilton, Gerónimo & Heim, Julia. My Autosaurus Will Win! Facciotto, Giuseppe et al, illus. 2016. 113p. (J). *(978-1-5182-0304-6(3))* Scholastic, Inc.

—Operation: Secret Recipe. Loizedda, Danilo et al, illus. 2017. 107p. (J). *(978-1-5379-1881-5(8))* Scholastic, Inc.

—The Perilous Plants. Usai, Luca et al, illus. 2016. 117p. (J). *(978-0-545-93092-5(8))* Scholastic, Inc.

Stilton, Gerónimo & Pizzelli, Anna. Cyber-Thief Showdown. Ferrario, Giuseppe et al, illus. 2018. 107p. (J). *(978-1-5490-0240-3(6))* Scholastic, Inc.

—The Underwater Planet. Facciotto, Giuseppe & Verzini, Daniele, illus. 2016. 113p. (J). *(978-1-5182-0303-9(5))* Scholastic, Inc.

Stilton, Gerónimo & Schaffer, Andrea. The Helmet Holdup. Facciotto, Giuseppe & Costa, Alessandro, illus. 2017. 112p. (J). *(978-1-5379-5611-4(6))* Scholastic, Inc.

—The Invisible Thief. Usai, Luca et al, illus. 2015. 114p. (J). pap. *(978-0-545-92755-0(2))* Scholastic, Inc.

—Mice to the Rescue! Usai, Luca & Verzini, Daniele, illus. 2014. 116p. (J). pap. *(978-0-545-86795-5(9))* Scholastic, Inc.

Stilton, Gerónimo & Stilton, Thea. Thea Stilton & the Ghost of the Shipwreck. 2010. (Thea Stilton Ser.: 3). lib. bdg. 19.65 *(978-0-606-06843-7(0))* Turtleback.

—Thea Stilton & the Mountain of Fire. 2009. (Thea Stilton Ser.: 2). lib. bdg. 19.65 *(978-0-606-00232-5(4))* Turtleback.

Stilton, Gerónimo & Tramontozzi, Lidia Morson. The Cheese Experiment. De Negri, Andrea, illus. 2016. 103p. (J). *(978-1-5182-1588-9(2))* Scholastic, Inc.

Stilton, Gerónimo & Wolf, Matt. All Because of a Cup of Coffee. 2004. (Geronimo Stilton Ser.: No. 10). (Illus.). 112p. (J). lib. bdg. 10.00 *(978-1-4242-0279-9(5))* Fitzgerald Bks.

Stilton, Gerónimo, et al. Get the Scoop, Geronimo! Facciotto, Giuseppe & Costa, Alessandro, illus. 2015. 113p. (J). *(978-1-5182-0417-3(1))* Scholastic, Inc.

—The Journey Through Time. 2014. (Illus.). 94p. (J). *(978-0-545-61129-9(6))* Scholastic, Inc.

—Robot Attack. Usai, Luca & Verzini, Daniele, illus. 2015. 117p. (J). *(978-0-545-86796-2(7))* Scholastic, Inc.

Stilton, Thea. The Cloud Castle (Thea Stilton: Special Edition #4) A Geronimo Stilton Adventure. 2016. (ENG.). 320p. (J). (gr. -1-3). E-Book 3.99 *(978-0-545-83537-4(2),* Scholastic Paperbacks) Scholastic, Inc.

—A Fashionable Mystery (Thea Stilton Mouseford Academy #8) Stilton, Thea, illus. 2019. (Thea Stilton Mouseford Academy Ser.: 8). (ENG., Illus.). 128p. (J). (gr. 2-5). pap. 7.99 *(978-0-545-87096-2(8),* Scholastic Paperbacks) Scholastic, Inc.

—The Secret of the Crystal Fairies (Thea Stilton: Special Edition #7) A Geronimo Stilton Adventure. 2018. (Thea Stilton Ser.: 7). (ENG., Illus.). 320p. (J). (gr. 2-5). 14.99 *(978-1-338-26859-1(7),* Scholastic Paperbacks) Scholastic, Inc.

—The Secret of the Snow (Thea Stilton: Special Edition #3) A Geronimo Stilton Adventure. (ENG.). 320p. (J). 2016. (gr. -1-k). E-Book 4.99 *(978-0-545-65902-4(7))* 2014. (gr. 2-5). 16.99 *(978-0-545-65605-4(2))* Scholastic, Inc. (Scholastic Paperbacks).

—Thea Stilton & the Blue Scarab Hunt. 2012. (Thea Stilton Ser.: 11). lib. bdg. 19.65 *(978-0-606-26183-8(4))* Turtleback.

—Thea Stilton & the Dancing Shadows. 2013. (Thea Stilton Ser.: 14). lib. bdg. 19.65 *(978-0-606-31528-9(4))* Turtleback.

—Thea Stilton & the Dancing Shadows (Thea Stilton #14) A Geronimo Stilton Adventure. 2017. (True Book (Relaunch) Ser.: 14). (ENG.). 176p. (J). (gr. 3-5). E-Book 31.00 *(978-0-545-52053-9(3),* Scholastic Paperbacks) Scholastic, Inc.

—Thea Stilton & the Frozen Fiasco. 2017. (Thea Stilton Ser.: 25). lib. bdg. 19.65 *(978-0-606-40181-4(4))* Turtleback.

—Thea Stilton & the Frozen Fiasco (Thea Stilton #25) A Geronimo Stilton Adventure. (Thea Stilton Ser.: 25). (ENG., 176p. (J). (gr. 2-5). 2017. Illus.). pap. 8.99 *(978-1-338-08786-4(X))* 2016. E-Book 5.99 *(978-1-338-08787-1(8))* Scholastic, Inc. (Scholastic Paperbacks).

—Thea Stilton & the Great Tulip Heist. 2014. (Thea Stilton Ser.: 18). lib. bdg. 19.65 *(978-0-606-35386-1(0))* Turtleback.

—Thea Stilton & the Hollywood Hoax. 2016. (Thea Stilton Ser.: 23). lib. bdg. 18.40 *(978-0-606-38799-6(4))* Turtleback.

—Thea Stilton & the Lost Letters. 2015. (Thea Stilton Ser.: 21). (Illus.). 159p. (J). lib. bdg. 18.40 *(978-0-606-37061-5(7))* Turtleback.

—Thea Stilton & the Missing Myth. 2014. (Thea Stilton Ser.: 20). lib. bdg. 19.65 *(978-0-606-36058-6(1))* Turtleback.

—Thea Stilton & the Prince's Emerald. 2012. (Thea Stilton Ser.: 12). lib. bdg. 19.65 *(978-0-606-26534-8(1))* Turtleback.

—Thea Stilton & the Secret of the Old Castle. 2012. (Thea Stilton Ser.: 10). lib. bdg. 19.65 *(978-0-606-23930-1(8))* Turtleback.

—Thea Stilton Mouseford Academy #10: A Dream on Ice. 2016. (Illus.). 128p. (J). *(978-0-545-91797-1(2))* Scholastic, Inc.

—Thea Stilton Mouseford Academy #9: The Mysterious Love Letter. 2016. (Illus.). 128p. (J). *(978-0-545-91796-4(4))* Scholastic, Inc.

Stilton, Thea & Dami, Elisabetta. The Secret Invention. 2015. (Illus.). 112p. (J). *(978-0-545-80899-6(5))* Scholastic, Inc.

Stilton, Thea & Pizzelli, Anna. The Friendship Recipe. Pellizzari, Barbara & Castelli, Francesco, illus. 2017. 128p. (J). *(978-1-338-18274-3(9))* Scholastic, Inc.

Stilton, Thea & Schaffer, Andrea. The Royal Ball. Pellizzari, Barbara et al, illus. 2017. 108p. (J). *(978-1-338-18275-0(7))* Scholastic, Inc.

Stompin' Boots. 2013. (Illus.). 24p. pap. *(978-1-4602-2767-1(0))* FriesenPress.

Stone, Kate. Happy Birthday, Mouse! 2014. (ENG.). 16p. (J). bds. 5.99 *(978-1-4494-4387-0(7))* Andrews McMeel Publishing.

—Mouse Goes to School. 2012. (ENG.). 16p. (J). bds. 10.99 *(978-1-4494-1788-8(4))* Andrews McMeel Publishing.

Stone, Sara Elizabeth. Colors. 2018. (God's Creation Ser.: Vol. 1). (ENG., Illus.). 46p. (J). pap. 11.95 *(978-1-64003-100-5(6))* Covenant Bks.

Stoner, Sherri. Mickey's Perfecto Day! 2018. (World of Reading Ser.). (ENG.). 31p. (J). (gr. -1-1). 13.89 *(978-1-64310-620-5(1))* Penworthy Co., LLC, The.

Suarez, Maribel, illus. Ramon & His Mouse. (Rowing Frog's Rhymes Ser.). 16p. (J). (gr. k-3). 7.95 *(978-1-59437-839-3(8))* Santillana USA Publishing Co., Inc.

Susan, Paradis. Edna. Susan, Paradis, illus. 2013. (Illus.). 32p. pap. 11.95 *(978-1-60898-153-3(3))* namelos llc.

Swanson, Maggie. illus. The Tale of Two Bad Mice. 2006. (J). 6.99 *(978-1-59939-030-7(2))* Cornerstone Pr.

Swarbrick, David E. Peggy's Play House. 2011. 24p. pap. 24.95 *(978-1-4626-1989-4(4))* America Star Bks.

Sweeney, Kimberly A. Tippy Meets the Easter Bunny! 2012. 24p. pap. 17.99 *(978-1-4685-8460-8(X))* AuthorHouse.

Talbot, Amy. Deer & His Dear Friends: A Tale from India. 2006. (J). pap. *(978-1-4108-6173-3(2))* Benchmark Education Co.

Tara, Stephanie Lisa. Little Library Mouse. Walton, Alex, illus. 2006. 32p. (J). (gr. k). lib. bdg. 16.95 *(978-1-933285-39-9(7))* Brown Books Publishing Group.

Tashiro, Chisato. Five Nice Mice & the Great Car Race. Tashiro, Chisato, illus. 2014. (Five Nice Mice Ser.). (Illus.). 40p. (J). (gr. k-2). 17.99 *(978-988-8240-73-9(0),* Minedition) Penguin Young Readers Group.

Taylor, Thomas. Little Mouse & the Big Cupcake. Barton, Jill, illus. 2017. (ENG.). 24p. (J). (— 1). bds. 6.95 *(978-1-910716-32-8(4))* Boxer Bks., Ltd. GBR. Dist: Sterling Publishing Co., Inc.

Teague, Patricia. Gilda the Gluten Free Mouse: A Story about Living Gloriously with Celiac Sprue Disease. 2013. 24p. pap. 10.95 *(978-1-4908-1276-2(8),* WestBow Pr.) Author Solutions, LLC.

Terada, Junzo. A Good Home for Max. 2014. (ENG., Illus.). 40p. (J). (gr. -1-k). 16.99 *(978-1-4521-2702-6(6))* Chronicle Bks. LLC.

Terrian, Michael W. Chalie's Brand New Coat. 2011. 24p. pap. 12.50 *(978-1-4670-3858-4(X))* AuthorHouse.

Tetirick, Jack E. Joey the Motor Home Mouse. 2012. 110p. 20.95 *(978-1-4759-3702-2(4));* pap. 10.95 *(978-1-4759-3703-9(2))* iUniverse, Inc.

Thayer, Jane. Gus & the Baby Ghost. Fleishman, Seymour, illus. 2018. (Gus the Ghost Ser.). (ENG.). 32p. (J). 17.95 *(978-1-948959-05-6(4))* Purple Hse. Pr.

Thomas, Jan. Pumpkin Trouble. Thomas, Jan, illus. 2011. (ENG., Illus.). 40p. (J). (gr. -1-3). 9.99 *(978-0-06-169284-0(0),* HarperCollins) HarperCollins Pubs.

Thomas, Mikey. The Mouse & the House. 2012. 24p. pap. 24.95 *(978-1-4626-7854-9(8))* America Star Bks.

Thomas, Patricia. Mouse's Christmas Cookie, 0 vols. Nez, Jon, illus. 2013. (ENG.). 24p. (J). (gr. -1-2). 14.99 *(978-1-4778-4704-6(9),* 9781477847046, Two Lions) Amazon Publishing.

Thomas, Shelley Moore. This Book Is Not about Dragons. Koehler, Fred, illus. 2016. (ENG., Illus.). 32p. (J). (gr. -1-2). 16.95 *(978-1-62979-168-5(7),* Astra Young Readers) Astra Publishing Hse.

Thompson, Lauren. Little Lamb. Butler, John, illus. 2014. (J). *(978-1-4351-5352-3(9),* Simon & Schuster Bks. For Young Readers) Simon & Schuster Bks. For Young Readers.

—Mouse Loves Fall: Ready-To-Read Pre-Level 1. Erdogan, Buket, illus. 2018. (Mouse Ser.). (ENG.). 32p. (J). (gr. -1-k). 17.99 *(978-1-5344-2147-9(5));* pap. 4.99 *(978-1-5344-2146-2(7))* Simon Spotlight. (Simon Spotlight).

—Mouse Loves Love: Ready-To-Read Pre-Level 1. Erdogan, Buket, illus. 2018. (Mouse Ser.). (ENG.). 32p. (J). (gr. -1-k). 17.99 *(978-1-5344-2150-9(5));* pap. 4.99 *(978-1-5344-2149-3(1))* Simon Spotlight. (Simon Spotlight).

—Mouse Loves School: Ready-To-Read Pre-Level 1. Erdogan, Buket, illus. 2011. (Mouse Ser.). (ENG.). 24p. (J). (gr. -1-k). pap. 4.99 *(978-1-4424-2898-0(8));* lib. bdg. 17.99 *(978-1-4424-2899-7(6))* Simon Spotlight. (Simon Spotlight).

—Mouse Loves Spring. 2018. (Simon & Schuster Ready-To-Read Level 1 Ser.). lib. bdg. 13.55 *(978-0-606-40862-2(2))* Turtleback.

—Mouse Loves Spring: Ready-To-Read Pre-Level 1. Erdogan, Buket, illus. 2018. (Mouse Ser.). (ENG.). 32p. (J). (gr. -1-k). 17.99 *(978-1-5344-0185-3(7));* pap. 4.99 *(978-1-5344-0184-6(9))* Simon Spotlight. (Simon Spotlight).

—Mouse Loves Summer: Ready-To-Read Pre-Level 1. Erdogan, Buket, illus. 2018. (Mouse Ser.). (ENG.). 32p. (J). (gr. -1-k). 17.99 *(978-1-5344-2057-1(6));* pap. 4.99 *(978-1-5344-2056-4(8))* Simon Spotlight. (Simon Spotlight).

—Mouse's First Christmas. Erdogan, Buket, illus. 2003. (ENG.). 32p. (J). (gr. -1-3). 8.99 *(978-0-689-86348-6(9),* Simon & Schuster Bks. For Young Readers) Simon & Schuster Bks. For Young Readers.

—Mouse's First Christmas. Erdogan, Buket, illus. 2003. (gr. -1-1). lib. bdg. 18.40 *(978-0-613-91039-2(7))* Turtleback.

—Mouse's First Day of School. Erdogan, Buket, illus. 2010. (Mouse Ser.). (ENG.). 34p. (J). (gr. -1 — 1). bds. 8.99 *(978-1-4169-9476-3(9),* Little Simon) Little Simon.

—Mouse's First Day of School. Erdogan, Buket, illus. 2003. (Mouse Ser.). (ENG.). 32p. (J). (gr. -1-3). 19.99 *(978-0-689-84727-1(0),* Simon & Schuster Bks. For Young Readers) Simon & Schuster Bks. For Young Readers.

—Mouse's First Fall. Erdogan, Buket, illus. 2010. (Classic Board Bks.). (ENG.). 34p. (J). (gr. -1 — 1). bds. 8.99 *(978-1-4169-9477-0(7),* Little Simon) Little Simon.

—Mouse's First Fall. 2006. (ENG., Illus.). 32p. (J). (gr. -1-1). 18.99 *(978-0-689-85837-6(X),* Simon & Schuster Bks. For Young Readers) Simon & Schuster Bks. For Young Readers.

—Mouse's First Halloween. Erdogan, Buket, illus. 2003. (Classic Board Bks.). (ENG.). 34p. (J). (gr. -1 — 1). bds., bds. 7.99 *(978-0-689-85584-9(2),* Little Simon) Little Simon.

—Mouse's First Snow. Erdogan, Buket, illus. 2011. (Classic Board Bks.). (ENG.). 34p. (J). (gr. -1 — 1). bds. 7.99 *(978-1-4424-2651-1(9),* Little Simon) Little Simon.

—Mouse's First Snow. Erdogan, Buket, illus. 2005. (ENG.). 32p. (J). (gr. -1-3). 19.99 *(978-0-689-85836-9(1),* Simon & Schuster Bks. For Young Readers) Simon & Schuster Bks. For Young Readers.

—Mouse's First Spring. Erdogan, Buket, illus. 2012. (Classic Board Bks.). (ENG.). 34p. (J). (gr. -1-3). bds. 8.99 *(978-1-4424-3431-8(7),* Little Simon) Little Simon.

—Mouse's First Spring. Erdogan, Buket, illus. 2005. (ENG.). 32p. (J). (gr. -1-3). 19.99 *(978-0-689-85838-3(8),* Simon & Schuster Bks. For Young Readers) Simon & Schuster Bks. For Young Readers.

—Mouse's First Summer. Erdogan, Buket, illus. 2013. (Classic Board Bks.). (ENG.). 34p. (J). (gr. -1 — 1). bds. 8.99 *(978-1-4424-5842-0(9),* Little Simon) Little Simon.

—Mouse's First Summer. Erdogan, Buket, illus. 2014. (J). *(978-1-4351-5506-0(8))* Simon & Schuster.

—Mouse's First Summer. Erdogan, Buket, illus. 2004. (ENG.). 32p. (J). (gr. -1-3). 19.99 *(978-0-689-85835-2(3),* Simon & Schuster Bks. For Young Readers) Simon & Schuster Bks. For Young Readers.

—Mouse's First Valentine. Erdogan, Buket, illus. 2013. (J). *(978-1-4351-5014-0(7))* Barnes & Noble, Inc.

—Mouse's First Valentine. Erdogan, Buket, illus. 2004. (Classic Board Bks.). (ENG.). 34p. (J). (gr. -1 — 1). bds. 8.99 *(978-0-689-85585-6(0),* Little Simon) Little Simon.

—Wee Little Lamb. Butler, John, illus. 2009. (Wee Little Ser.). (ENG.). 32p. (J). (gr. -1-3). 19.99 *(978-1-4169-3469-1(3),* Simon & Schuster Bks. For Young Readers) Simon & Schuster Bks. For Young Readers.

Tibbs, Ely. The Mouse under My House - Ingle & the Cats Meow. 2010. (ENG.). 73p. pap. 27.81 *(978-0-557-39421-0(X))* Lulu Pr., Inc.

Tirado, Raquel. That Sticky Cat. 2012. 20p. pap. 17.99 *(978-1-4685-8857-6(5))* AuthorHouse.

Titus, Eve. Anatole. (Anatole Ser.). (Illus.). (J). (gr. k-3). 2010. 32p. pap. 8.99 *(978-0-375-85546-7(7),* Dragonfly Bks.) 50th ed. 2006. (ENG., 40p. 16.99 *(978-0-375-83901-6(1),* Knopf Bks. for Young Readers) Random Hse. Children's Bks.

—Anatole & the Cat. 2010. (Anatole Ser.). (Illus.). 32p. (J). (gr. k-3). pap. 7.99 *(978-0-375-85547-4(5),* Dragonfly Bks.) Random Hse. Children's Bks.

—Basil & the Cave of Cats. Galdone, Paul, illus. 2016. (Great Mouse Detective Ser.: 2). (ENG.). 112p. (J). (gr. 1-4). pap. 6.99 *(978-1-4814-6404-8(3),* Aladdin) Simon & Schuster Children's Publishing.

—Basil & the Lost Colony. Galdone, Paul, illus. 2017. (Great Mouse Detective Ser.: 5). (ENG.). 96p. (J). (gr. 1-4). pap. 6.99 *(978-1-4814-6413-0(2),* Aladdin) Simon & Schuster Children's Publishing.

—Basil in Mexico. Galdone, Paul, illus. 2016. (Great Mouse Detective Ser.: 3). (ENG.). 112p. (J). (gr. 1-4). pap. 6.99 *(978-1-4814-6407-9(8),* Aladdin) Simon & Schuster Children's Publishing.

—Basil in Mexico. Galdone, Paul, illus. 2016. (Great Mouse Detective Ser.: 3). (ENG.). 112p. (J). (gr. 1-4). 16.99 *(978-1-4814-6408-6(6),* Simon & Schuster/Paula Wiseman Bks.) Simon & Schuster/Paula Wiseman Bks.

—Basil of Baker Street. Galdone, Paul, illus. 2016. (Great Mouse Detective Ser.: 1). (ENG.). 112p. (J). (gr. 1-4). 16.99 *(978-1-4814-6402-4(7),* Aladdin) Simon & Schuster Children's Publishing.

Tolan, Stephanie S. Bartholomew's Blessing. Moore, Margie, illus. 2004. 32p. (J). (gr. -1-3). lib. bdg. 16.89 *(978-0-06-001198-7(X))* HarperCollins Pubs.

Tolstoy, Aleksei, et al. The Gigantic Turnip. 2009. (Illus.). (J). 16.99 *(978-1-84686-298-4(1))* Barefoot Bks., Inc.

Tomos, Angharad. Cosyn. 2005. (WEL., Illus.). 24p. pap. *(978-0-86243-566-0(8))* Y Lolfa.

Toon Books, 6 vols., Set. 2013. (Toon Bks.: 10). (ENG.). 36p. (J). (gr. k-3). lib. bdg. 196.74 *(978-1-61479-147-8(3),* 14839) Spotlight.

Top That Publishing Staff, ed. Mr. Mouse Needs House. 2005. (Illus.). 8p. *(978-1-84510-128-2(6))* Top That! Publishing PLC.

Touma, Patricia. Happy Times, Book: Ish & Mish Go to the Carnival. 2007. 56p. per. 9.95 *(978-1-59899-093-5(4))* Long Dash Publishing.

Town Mouse & Country Mouse: Individual Title Six-Packs. (Story Steps Ser.). (gr. k-2). 32.00 *(978-0-7635-9826-6(7))* Rigby Education.

Townsend, Stephanie Z. Not Too Small at All: A Mouse Tale. Looney, Bill, illus. 2008. (ENG.). 30p. (J). (gr. -1). 13.99 *(978-0-89051-524-2(7),* Master Books) New Leaf Publishing Group.

Toybox Innovations, creator. Pixar's Ratatouille. 2007. (Ratatouille Ser.). (ENG.). (J). (gr. -1-3). pap. *(978-0-7634-2185-4(5))* Walt Disney Records.

Travis, Lucille. The Far Journey. 2009. 160p. (J). (gr. 4-7). 8.99 *(978-1-60682-023-0(0))* BJU Pr.

Trimble, Gina. The Little Tiny Mouse, 1 vol. 2009. 17p. pap. 24.95 *(978-1-61546-540-8(5))* America Star Bks.

Tupera, Tupera. Polar Bear's Underwear. 2015. (ENG., Illus.). 32p. (J). (gr. -1-k). 16.99 *(978-1-4521-4199-2(1))* Chronicle Bks. LLC.

Turley, Sandy. The Clock & the Mouse: A Teaching Rhyme about Time. Peterson, Sara & Lindstrom, Brita, illus. 2006. 32p. (J). lib. bdg. 26.95 *(978-0-9778548-0-6(9))* Helps4Teachers.

Tuttle, Lucia. There's a Mouse in the House. 2008. 36p. pap. 19.99 *(978-1-4363-4000-7(4))* Xlibris Corp.

Twigger, J. Nicci & Her Amazing Adventure. 2008. (Illus.). 40p. pap. 18.49 *(978-1-4389-1295-0(1))* AuthorHouse.

Twohy, Mike. Mouse & Hippo. Twohy, Mike, illus. 2017. (ENG., Illus.). 32p. (J). (gr. -1-3). 17.99 *(978-1-4814-5124-6(3),* Simon & Schuster/Paula Wiseman Bks.) Simon & Schuster/Paula Wiseman Bks.

Ugarte, Ane Miren De Rotaeche. A Very Special Tea Party. 2010. 24p. (J). 25.99 *(978-1-4500-5378-5(5))* Xlibris Corp.

Underwood, Deborah. Here Comes the Tooth Fairy Cat. Rueda, Claudia, illus. 2015. 96p. (J). (gr. -1-k). 17.99 *(978-0-525-42774-2(0),* Dial Bks) Penguin Young Readers Group.

—Monster & Mouse Go Camping. Chapman, Jared, illus. 2018. (ENG.). 32p. (J). (gr. -1-3). 17.99 *(978-0-544-64832-6(3),* 1621605, Clarion Bks.) HarperCollins Pubs.

Unger-Pengilly, Elaine. Rat. Trockstad, Marcy, illus. 2013. 120p. *(978-1-4602-2262-1(8))* FriesenPress.

Urban, Linda. Mouse Was Mad. Cole, Henry, illus. 2012. (ENG.). 40p. (J). (gr. -1-3). pap. 7.99 *(978-0-547-72750-9(X),* 1483175, Clarion Bks.) HarperCollins Pubs.

Urbanek Reese, Dorothy. When Mice Sing — the Story of Mei & Yu. 2008. 138p. pap. 13.95 *(978-1-4357-6104-9(9))* Lulu Pr., Inc.

Vaniko, K. L. Why the Dog Chases the Cat & the Cat Chases the Mouse. 2006. 189p. 30.99 *(978-1-59926-863-7(9))* Xlibris Corp.

Vaswani, Navina. A Wonderful Christmas. 2004. (YA). per. *(978-0-9754818-5-1(1))* Creative Bk. Pubs.

Vasylenko, Veronica. Deck the Halls. Tiger Tales Staff, ed. 2011. (ENG., Illus.). 20p. bds. 8.95 *(978-1-58925-868-6(1))* Tiger Tales.

Vere, Ed. Max el Valiente. 2014. (SPA.). 36p. (gr. k-2). 20.99 *(978-84-261-4071-5(8))* Juventud, Editorial ESP. Dist: Lectorum Pubns., Inc.

—Max the Brave. (ENG.). (J). 2017. 30p. bds. 8.99 *(978-1-4926-5706-4(9))* 2015. (Max Ser.: 1). 32p. (gr. -1-2). 16.99 *(978-1-4926-1651-1(6),* 9781492616511) Sourcebooks, Inc. (Sourcebooks Jabberwocky).

Verrett, Michael. Galid's Christmas Wish. 2010. 44p. pap. 22.90 *(978-0-557-29109-0(7))* Lulu Pr., Inc.

Vidal, Séverine. Mega Mouse. Barroux, Stephane, illus. 2015. (Mega Hero Bks.). (ENG.). 28p. (J). (gr. k-2). 12.95 *(978-1-77085-639-4(0),* c6f360d6-18f7-46de-991e-6c79286c54ec) Firefly Bks., Ltd.

Villarreal, Tanya E. Izzie's First Christmas, 1 vol. Villarreal, Tanya E., illus. 2009. (Illus.). 28p. pap. 24.95 *(978-1-61546-093-9(4))* America Star Bks.

Villeneuve, Marie-Paule & Audet, Patrice. Qui a Enleve Polka? 2004. (FRE., Illus.). 122p. (J). 8.95 *(978-2-922565-81-2(5))* Editions de la Paix CAN. Dist: World of Reading, Ltd.

Vincent, Karen. Robbie Learns a Lesson on Truth. 2010. (ENG.). 24p. pap. 12.49 *(978-1-4490-5772-5(1))* AuthorHouse.

Viva, Frank. A Trip to the Bottom of the World with Mouse. 2018. (Toon Books Level 1 Ser.). lib. bdg. 17.20 *(978-0-606-41222-3(0))* Turtleback.

—A Trip to the Bottom of the World with Mouse: Toon Books Level 1. Viva, Frank, illus. 2012. (Toon Ser.). (ENG., Illus.). 32p. (J). (gr. -1-1). 12.99 *(978-1-935179-19-1(5),* TOON Books) Astra Publishing Hse.

—A Trip to the Top of the Volcano with Mouse: TOON Level 1. 2019. (Trips with Mouse Ser.). (Illus.). 36p. (J). (gr. -1-k). 12.99 *(978-1-943145-36-2(9),* TOON Books) Astra Publishing Hse.

Vize, Bonnie. The Mystery of the Park Pavilion. 2009. pap. 14.22 *(978-1-61584-491-3(0))* Independent Pub.

Vizzi, Maria. Morely: The Mouse in the Bakery. 2011. 24p. (gr. 1-2). pap. 13.33 *(978-1-4567-4621-6(9))* AuthorHouse.

Wahl, Jan. Pleasant Fieldmouse. Sendak, Maurice, illus. 2007. (Sendak Reissues Ser.). (ENG.). 72p. (J). 15.95 *(978-0-06-029725-1(5))* HarperCollins Pubs.

Waites, Joan, illus. An Artist's Night Before Christmas, 1 vol. 2017. (Night Before Christmas Ser.). (ENG.). 32p. (J). (gr. -1-3). 16.99 *(978-1-4556-2205-4(2),* Pelican Publishing) Arcadia Publishing.

Wall, Pauline & Smith, Shelley. What the Mouse Saw: An Easter Story. 2013. 20p. pap. 16.82 *(978-1-4669-3503-7(0))* Trafford Publishing.

Wallace, Chad. The Mouse & the Meadow, 1 vol. 2014. (Illus.). 32p. (J). (gr. k-4). 16.95 *(978-1-58469-481-6(5),* Dawn Pubns.) Sourcebooks, Inc.

Wallace, Karen. Ghost Mouse, 1 vol. Blake, Beccy, illus. 2009. (Go! Readers Ser.). (ENG.). 48p. (J). (gr. 1-2). pap. 13.85 *(978-1-60754-273-5(0),* da732a0a-eb3d-467f-831b-730eace83de4); lib. bdg. 33.93 *(978-1-60754-272-8(2),* 262ae7a1-40fd-4d35-848a-305e37704684) Rosen Publishing Group, Inc., The. (Windmill Bks.).

Walsh, Ellen Stoll. Dot & Jabber & the Big Bug Mystery. 2017. (Green Light Readers Level 2 Ser.: Vol. 3). (ENG.). (J). (gr. -1-3). lib. bdg. 13.55 *(978-0-606-39827-5(9))* Turtleback.

—Mouse Paint Lap-Size Board Book. 2006. (ENG., Illus.). 15p. (J). (gr. -1-k). bds. 11.99 *(978-0-15-205533-2(9),* 1196639, Clarion Bks.) HarperCollins Pubs.

—Mouse Paint/Pintura de Raton Board Book: Bilingual English-Spanish. 2010. (ENG., Illus.). 30p. (J). (gr. -1-k). bds. 5.99 *(978-0-547-33332-8(3),* 1417608, Clarion Bks.) HarperCollins Pubs.

—Mouse Shapes. (ENG., Illus.). 40p. (J). (gr. -1-3). 2017. pap. 8.99 *(978-1-328-74053-3(6),* 1677023) 2007. 16.99 *(978-0-15-206091-6(X),* 1198296) HarperCollins Pubs. (Clarion Bks.).

—Where Is Jumper? Walsh, Ellen Stoll, illus. 2015. (ENG., Illus.). 32p. (J). (gr. -1-3). 18.99 *(978-1-4814-4508-5(1),* Beach Lane Bks.) Beach Lane Bks.

Wargin, Kathy-jo. Minn from Minnesota. Holman, Karen Busch, illus. 2006. (Mitt Midwest Ser.: 2). 144p. (J). (gr. k-7). 14.95 *(978-1-58726-304-0(1),* Mitten Pr.) Ann Arbor Editions LLC.

—Mitt & Minn at the Wisconsin Cheese Jamboree. Holman, Karen Busch, illus. 2007. (Mitt Midwest Ser.: 3). 144p. (J). (gr. k-7). 14.95 *(978-1-58726-305-7(X),* Mitten Pr.) Ann Arbor Editions LLC.

—Mitt & Minn's Illinois Adventure. Holman, Karen Busch, illus. 2007. (Mitt Midwest Ser.: 4). 144p. (J). (gr. k-7). 14.95 *(978-1-58726-306-4(8),* Mitten Pr.) Ann Arbor Editions LLC.

Warner, Jeremy. Hidden Mickeys: A Mouse in the Land. Warner, Danielle, illus. 2012. 68p. pap. 5.95 *(978-0-9853555-2-4(2))* Portrait Health Publishing.

Warnes, Tim. Chalk & Cheese. Warnes, Tim, illus. 2008. (ENG., Illus.). 32p. (J). (gr. -1-3). 19.99 *(978-1-4169-1378-8(5),* Simon & Schuster Bks. For Young Readers) Simon & Schuster Bks. For Young Readers.

Waters, Tony. Cinnamon's Busy Year. Waters, Tony, illus. 2003. (Illus.). 32p. (J). (gr. -1-3). pap. 5.95 *(978-0-9710278-2-4(X))* All About Kids Publishing.

Watkins, Greg. Brendon Mouse's Big Idea to Save the Bad Bird Bunch. 2006. (Illus.). 29p. (J). 14.95 *(978-0-9761318-0-9(3))* Cute & Cuddly Productions, Inc.

Watson, Jane Werner. Walt Disney's Cinderella's Friends. 2017. (Illus.). (J). *(978-1-5182-4598-5(6),* Golden Bks.) Random Hse. Children's Bks.

Watson, Louise. The Mouse in Our House. 2005. (J). pap. 8.00 *(978-0-8059-6719-7(2))* Dorrance Publishing Co., Inc.

Watt, Fiona. Christmas Eve. Wells, Rachel, illus. 2007. (Luxury Touchy-Feely Board Bks). 10p. (J). (gr. -1-k). bds. 11.99 *(978-0-7945-1478-5(2),* Usborne) EDC Publishing.

—Christmas Mice. 2004. (Big Touchy Feely Board Bks.). (Illus.). 10p. (J). 11.95 *(978-0-7945-0482-3(5),* Usborne) EDC Publishing.

—That's Not My Kitten. Wells, Rachel, illus. rev. ed. 2006. (Touchy-Feely Board Bks.). 10p. (J). (gr. -1-k). bds. 7.99 *(978-0-7945-1266-8(6),* Usborne) EDC Publishing.

Watts, Frances. Goodnight, Mice! Watson, Judy, illus. 2017. (ENG.). 24p. bds. 6.99 *(978-0-7333-3530-3(6))* ABC Bks. AUS. Dist: HarperCollins Pubs.

—The Song of the Winns: the Spies of Gerander. 2013. (ENG., Illus.). 320p. (J). (gr. -1-2). 28.00 *(978-0-7624-4658-2(7),* Running Pr. Kids) Running Pr.

Waugh, Peter. Cannon Beach Mouse Caper. 2007. 128p. per. 13.95 *(978-0-944638-68-2(6))* Educare Pr.

Weaver, Verity. Lab Mice Heist. Huddleston, Courtney, illus. 2019. (What Happened? Ser.). (ENG.). 120p. (J). (gr. 3-4). pap. 7.99 *(978-1-63163-308-9(2),* 1631633082); lib. bdg. 27.13 *(978-1-63163-307-2(4),* 1631633074) North Star Editions. (Jolly Fish Pr.).

The Wedding of the Mouse: An Asian Folktale. 2006. (J). 17.95 *(978-0-9790033-0-1(X))* Playground Pr.

Weeks, Sarah. Pip Squeak. Manning, Jane, illus. 2008. (I Can Read Level 1 Ser.). (ENG.). 32p. (J). (gr. k-3). pap. 4.99 *(978-0-06-075638-3(1),* HarperCollins) HarperCollins Pubs.

—Pip Squeak. Manning, Jane K., illus. 2007. (I Can Read Bks.). 32p. (J). (gr. -1-3). lib. bdg. 16.89 *(978-0-06-075637-6(3),* Geringer, Laura Book) HarperCollins Pubs.

Weigl Publishers, creator. The Lion & the Mouse: Can Little Friends Be Great Friends? 2013. (AV2 Animated Storytime Ser.: Vol. 15). (ENG., Illus.). 32p. (J). (gr. -1-3). lib. bdg. 29.99 *(978-1-62127-919-8(7),* AV2 by Weigl) Weigl Pubs., Inc.

Welling, Peter J. Darlene Halloween & the Great Chicago Fire, 1 vol. Welling, Peter J., illus. 2007. (ENG., Illus.). 32p. (J). (gr. k-3). 16.99 *(978-1-58980-479-1(1),* Pelican Publishing) Arcadia Publishing.

Wellington-Johnson, Sharon. A Mouse in My House. 2008. 28p. pap. 15.99 *(978-1-4363-3113-5(7))* Xlibris Corp.

Wells, Rosemary. Julieta, Estate Quieta! (SPA.). 43p. (J). 5.50 *(978-84-372-1523-5(4))* Santillana USA Publishing Co., Inc.

Westerlund, Kate. A Whisper in the Snow. Oral, Feridun, illus. 2018. 32p. (J). (gr. k-2). 17.99 *(978-988-8341-52-8(9),* Minedition) Penguin Young Readers Group.

Westling, Vicki Diane. Hannibal Goes to the Hospital: A Sam & Friends Book. 2011. 32p. pap. 15.99 *(978-1-4634-0997-5(4))* AuthorHouse.

Weston Woods Staff, creator. Chato's Kitchen. 2004. (J). 18.95 *(978-1-55592-386-0(0));* 38.75 *(978-1-55592-388-4(7))* Weston Woods Studios, Inc.

—Chrysanthemum. 2004. (SPA.). (J). 18.95 *(978-1-55592-395-2(X));* 38.75 *(978-1-55592-397-6(6))* Weston Woods Studios, Inc.

—A Dark, Dark Tale. 2004. (J). 18.95 *(978-1-55592-804-9(8));* 38.75 *(978-1-55592-821-6(8))* Weston Woods Studios, Inc.

—Doctor de Soto. 2011. (SPA.). 38.75 *(978-0-439-78365-1(8));* 29.95 *(978-0-439-73624-4(2))* Weston Woods Studios, Inc.

—Doctor Desoto. 2004. (SPA.). (J). 18.95 *(978-0-7882-0950-5(7))* Weston Woods Studios, Inc.

—The Island of the Skog. 2011. 29.95 *(978-0-545-23365-1(8));* 18.95 *(978-0-545-23366-8(6));* 38.75 *(978-0-545-23367-5(4))* Weston Woods Studios, Inc.

—Norman the Doorman. 2011. 29.95 *(978-0-439-78648-5(7))* Weston Woods Studios, Inc.

—Owen. 2011. (SPA.). 38.75 *(978-0-439-02178-4(2));* 18.95 *(978-0-439-02177-7(4));* 29.95 *(978-0-439-02310-8(6))* Weston Woods Studios, Inc.

—Seven Blind Mice. 2011. 38.75 *(978-0-439-02777-9(2))* Weston Woods Studios, Inc.

—A Weeekend with Wendell. 2004. 29.95 *(978-1-55592-129-3(9));* (J). 18.95 *(978-1-55592-116-3(7))* Weston Woods Studios, Inc.

—A Weekend with Wendell. 2004. (J). 38.75 *(978-1-55592-647-2(9))* Weston Woods Studios, Inc.

Westover, Gail. Mrs Mouse's Garden Party in Giggleswick Village. Daly, Karen Anne, illus. 2012. 26p. pap. 9.95 *(978-0-9821507-9-5(2))* Thistlewood Publishing.

Wheatley, Sandra. Marmaduke the Mighty. 2010. (Illus.). 28p. (gr. -1). 13.99 *(978-1-4490-4290-5(2))* AuthorHouse.

Wherry, Alwyn. The Hungry Little Mouse. 2006. 17p. (J). 12.08 *(978-1-4116-8056-2(1))* Lulu Pr., Inc.

White, E. B. Le Avventure di Stuart Little.Tr. of Stuart Little. (ITA.). pap. 17.95 *(978-88-451-2736-6(2))* Fabbri Editori - RCS Libri ITA. Dist: Distribooks, Inc.

—Stuart Little. Date not set. 141p. 18.95 *(978-0-8488-2602-4(7))* Amereon Ltd.

—Stuart Little. 2008. (J). 34.99 *(978-0-7393-7101-5(0))* Findaway World, LLC.

—Stuart Little. Williams, Garth, illus. 60th anniv. ed. 2005. (ENG.). 144p. (J). (gr. 3-7). 18.99 *(978-0-06-026395-9(4),* HarperCollins) HarperCollins Pubs.

—Stuart Little. 131p. (J). pap. 5.95 *(978-0-8072-8333-2(9));* 2004. (gr. 3-7). pap. 29.00 incl. audio *(978-0-8072-8332-5(0),* YA165SP) Random Hse. Audio Publishing Group. (Listening Library).

—Stuart Little. Williams, Garth, illus. 2004. (SPA.). 144p. (gr. 3-5). pap. 10.95 *(978-1-59437-554-5(2))* Santillana USA Publishing Co., Inc.

—Stuart Little 75th Anniversary Edition. Williams, Garth, illus. 60th anniv. ed. 2020. (ENG.). 144p. (J). (gr. 3-7). pap. 9.99 *(978-0-06-440056-5(5),* HarperCollins) HarperCollins Pubs.

—Stuart Little Book & Charm. Williams, Garth, illus. 2006. (Charming Classics). 144p. (J). (gr. 3-7). 6.99 *(978-0-06-082334-4(8),* HarperFestival) HarperCollins Pubs.

—Stuart Little: Full Color Edition. Williams, Garth & Wells, Rosemary, illus. 60th anniv. ed. 2005. (ENG.). 144p. (J). (gr. 3-7). pap. 9.99 *(978-0-06-441092-2(7),* HarperCollins) HarperCollins Pubs.

White, E. B. & White, E. Stuart Little. 2005. (J). (gr. 3-6). lib. bdg. 17.20 *(978-0-8085-3806-6(3))* Turtleback.

White, Kathryn. The Tickle Test. Reynolds, Adrian, illus. 2017. (ENG.). 32p. (J). (gr. -1-3). 17.99 *(978-1-5124-8126-6(2),* d1c8fd07-3e9a-42d4-951c-c5b526566cbe) Lerner Publishing Group.

White, Loricia. Little Tail's Rhyming Roots. 2012. 74p. pap. 19.95 *(978-1-4626-6885-4(2))* America Star Bks.

White, Mark. The Lion & the Mouse: A Retelling of Aesop's Fable, 1 vol. Rojo Pérez, Sara, illus. 2011. (My First Classic Story Ser.). (ENG.). 24p. (J). (gr. k-3). pap. 7.10 *(978-1-4048-7365-0(1),* 118580, Picture Window Bks.) Capstone.

Whybrow, Ian. Miss Wire's Christmas Surprise. Chichester Clark, Emma, illus. 2007. 45p. (J). (gr. -1-3). pap. 3.95 *(978-0-7534-6136-5(6),* Kingfisher) Roaring Brook Pr.

Wight, Al. Do Mice Eat Rice? Clarke, Roger, illus. 2005. (ENG.). 32p. (J). (gr. -1-3). 12.95 *(978-0-8048-3643-2(4))* Tuttle Publishing.

Wilbur, Richard. Loudmouse. 2015. (ENG., Illus.). 64p. (J). pap. 9.99 *(978-0-486-79807-3(0),* 798070) Dover Pubns., Inc.

William H. Sadlier Staff. The Lion & the Mouse, Vol. 2. 2005. (Fluent Library). (gr. 1-3). 29.34 *(978-0-8215-8968-7(7))* Sadlier, William H. Inc.

Williams, Brenda May. The Shop of Magical Things. 2013. (ENG., Illus.). 44p. pap. 13.50 *(978-1-78035-526-9(2),* Fastprint Publishing) Upfront Publishing Ltd. GBR. Dist: Printondemand-worldwide.com.

—The Unusual Pet Shop. Williams, Raymond, illus. 2012. 24p. pap. 11.50 *(978-1-61897-798-4(9),* Strategic Bk. Publishing) Strategic Book Publishing & Rights Agency (SBPRA).

Williams, Rozanne. City Mouse & Country Mouse. 2017. (Learn-To-Read Ser.). (ENG., Illus.). (J). pap. 3.49 *(978-1-68310-202-1(9))* Pacific Learning, Inc.

Williams, Sherri. The Adventures of Little Mouse: (Life Outside the Mouse Hole) 2012. 48p. pap. 21.99 *(978-1-4772-2937-8(X))* AuthorHouse.

Willis, Jeanne. Cottonball Colin. Ross, Tony, illus. 2008. 26p. (J). (gr. -1-4). 16.00 *(978-0-8028-5331-8(5),* Eerdmans Bks For Young Readers) Eerdmans, William B. Publishing Co.

—Never Too Little to Love. Fearnley, Jan, illus. 2013. (ENG.). 32p. (J). (gr. -1-2). 9.99 *(978-0-7636-6656-9(4))* Candlewick Pr.

Wilsdon, Christina. An Alligator Adventure in Florida. Mayo, Frank, illus. 2006. 26p. (J). 7.99 *(978-1-59939-010-9(8))* Cornerstone Pr.

—An Amusement Park Mystery in Ohio. Ebert, Len, illus. 2006. 26p. (J). 7.99 *(978-1-59939-013-0(2))* Cornerstone Pr.

—Lights! Action! California! Hockerman, Dennis, illus. 2006. 26p. (J). 7.99 *(978-1-59939-009-3(4))* Cornerstone Pr.

—A New York Sailing Adventure. Hockerman, Dennis, illus. 2006. 26p. (J). 7.99 *(978-1-59939-014-7(0))* Cornerstone Pr.

—On the Trail of Bigfoot in Washington. McCreary, Jane, illus. 2006. 26p. (J). 7.99 *(978-1-59939-012-3(4))* Cornerstone Pr.

—A Wild Ride in Texas. Jaekel, Susan, illus. 2006. 26p. (J). 7.99 *(978-1-59939-011-6(6))* Cornerstone Pr.

Wilson, Karma. Bear Counts. Chapman, Jane, illus. 2015. (Bear Bks.). (ENG.). 32p. (J). (gr. -1-2). 18.99 *(978-1-4424-8092-6(0),* McElderry, Margaret K. Bks.) McElderry, Margaret K. Bks.

—Big Bear, Small Mouse. Chapman, Jane, illus. 2016. (Bear Bks.). (ENG.). 32p. (J). (gr. -1-3). 18.99 *(978-1-4814-5971-6(6),* McElderry, Margaret K. Bks.) McElderry, Margaret K. Bks.

—Mortimer's First Garden. Andreasen, Dan, illus. 2009. (ENG.). 32p. (J). (gr. -1-3). 19.99 *(978-1-4169-4203-0(3),* McElderry, Margaret K. Bks.) McElderry, Margaret K. Bks.

—Who Goes There? Currey, Anna, illus. 2013. (ENG.). 40p. (J). (gr. -1-3). 19.99 *(978-1-4169-8002-5(4),* McElderry, Margaret K. Bks.) McElderry, Margaret K. Bks.

Wilson, Rosalee. A Mushy Mouse Tale. 2009. (ENG.). 69p. pap. 24.58 *(978-0-557-10084-2(4))* Lulu Pr., Inc.

Wilton, Briar. The Strongest Mouse (Big Book Edition) A Tale from East Africa. Corke, Estelle, illus. 2016. 24p. (J). pap. *(978-1-927244-69-2(2))* Flying Start Bks.

Winter, Rosalind. The Mice of St Goran. 2010. 70p. pap. *(978-1-84923-461-0(2))* YouWriteOn.

Wise, William. Christopher Mouse. 2004. (J). *(978-1-58234-961-9(4))* Bloomsbury Publishing USA.

—Christopher Mouse: The Tale of a Small Traveler. Benson, Patrick, illus. 2006. (ENG.). 160p. (YA). (gr. 2-5). per. 8.99 *(978-1-58234-708-0(5),* 900039046, Bloomsbury USA Childrens) Bloomsbury Publishing USA.

Wood, Audrey & Wood, Don. The Little Mouse, the Red Ripe Strawberry & the Big Hungry Bear. Wood, Don, illus. 2007. (Child's Play Library). (ENG., Illus.). 32p. (J). audio compact disk *(978-1-84643-050-3(X))* Child's Play International Ltd.

Wood, David & Wood, Aimee. The Beautiful Swan. 2008. 24p. pap. 14.95 *(978-1-59858-624-4(6))* Dog Ear Publishing, LLC.

Wood, Kathryn J. Morty Mouse: I Wish I Could Fly. 2012. 24p. pap. 15.99 *(978-1-4771-1116-1(6))* Xlibris Corp.

Wright, Mary H. & Frontiera, Deborah K. Sloan & Company: Flea Market Mice. Scott, Korey, illus. l.t. ed. 2016. (ENG.). 110p. (J). (gr. 2). pap. 11.99 *(978-1-940591-04-9(X))* By Grace Enterprises.

Wright, Sky'asia. The Big, Blue Raspberry. 2012. 30p. pap. 5.99 *(978-0-9857095-1-8(0))* RRJ Publishing, Inc.

Wright, Unasue Sellers. Dr. Chubby. 2013. 32p. pap. 13.95 *(978-1-4497-8931-2(5),* WestBow Pr.) Author Solutions, LLC.

Wyman, Susan. Pipsqueak's Puny Peepholes. 2013. 40p. pap. 15.99 *(978-1-4908-0412-5(9),* WestBow Pr.) Author Solutions, LLC.

Wyneken, Cherise. Spaceship Lands in Africa, 1 vol. 2010. 50p. pap. 16.95 *(978-1-4489-5417-9(7))* America Star Bks.

Yamashita, Haruo. Seven Little Mice Go to School. Iwamura, Kazuo, illus. 2011. (ENG.). 32p. (J). (gr. -1-k). 17.95 *(978-0-7358-4012-6(1))* North-South Bks., Inc.

Yang, Stella, illus. My Family: Individual Title Six-Packs. (Sails Literacy Ser.). 16p. (gr. k-18). 27.00 *(978-0-7635-4393-8(4))* Rigby Education.

Yee, Wong Herbert. Abracadabra! Magic with Mouse & Mole (Reader) 2010. (Mouse & Mole Story Ser.). (ENG., Illus.). 48p. (J). (gr. -1-3). pap. 4.99 *(978-0-547-40621-3(5),* 1428499, Clarion Bks.) HarperCollins Pubs.

—A Brand-New Day with Mouse & Mole. 2012. (Green Light Readers Level 3 Ser.). lib. bdg. 13.55 *(978-0-606-24437-4(9))* Turtleback.

—A Brand-New Day with Mouse & Mole (Reader) 2012. (Mouse & Mole Story Ser.). (ENG., Illus.). 48p. (J). (gr. 1-4). pap. 4.99 *(978-0-547-72209-2(5),* 1482465, Clarion Bks.) HarperCollins Pubs.

—Mouse & Mole: a Perfect Halloween. Yee, Wong Herbert, illus. 2011. (Mouse & Mole Story Ser.). (ENG., Illus.). 48p. (J). (gr. 1-4). 14.99 *(978-0-547-55152-4(5),* 1450576, Clarion Bks.) HarperCollins Pubs.

—Mouse & Mole, a Winter Wonderland: A Winter & Holiday Book for Kids. Yee, Wong Herbert, illus. 2011. (Mouse & Mole Story Ser.). (ENG., Illus.). 48p. (J). (gr. 1-4). pap. 4.99 *(978-0-547-57697-8(8),* 1458451, Clarion Bks.) HarperCollins Pubs.

—Mouse & Mole: Fine Feathered Friends. Yee, Wong Herbert, illus. 2011. (Mouse & Mole Story Ser.). (ENG., Illus.). 48p. (J). (gr. 1-4). pap. 4.99 *(978-0-547-51977-7(X),* 1445276, Clarion Bks.) HarperCollins Pubs.

—Mouse & Mole: Secret Valentine. Yee, Wong Herbert, illus. (Mouse & Mole Story Ser.). (ENG., Illus.). 48p. (J). 2017. (gr. -1-3). 12.99 *(978-1-328-97533-1(9),* 1708707) 2017. (gr. -1-3). pap. 4.99 *(978-1-328-74059-5(5),* 1677035) 2013. (gr. 1-4). 15.99 *(978-0-547-88719-7(1),* 1507662) HarperCollins Pubs. (Clarion Bks.).

—Upstairs Mouse, Downstairs Mole (Reader) 12th ed. 2007. (Mouse & Mole Story Ser.). (ENG., Illus.). 48p. (J). (gr. -1-3).

4.99 *(978-0-618-91586-6(9)*, 1014891, Clarion Bks.) HarperCollins Pubs.

Yeoman, John. Mouse Trouble. Blake, Quentin, illus. 2011. (ENG.). 32p. (J). (gr. -1-k). pap. 12.99 *(978-1-84939-201-3(3))* Andersen Pr. GBR. Dist: Independent Pubs. Group.

Young, Ed. Seven Blind Mice. Young, Ed, illus. 2007. (Illus.). pap. 14.95 incl. audio *(978-0-439-02784-7(5))*; (J). 24.95 incl. audio *(978-0-439-02782-3(9))* Scholastic, Inc.

—Seven Blind Mice. Young, Ed, illus. 2011. (Illus.). 18.95 *(978-0-439-02785-4(3))*; (J). 29.95 *(978-0-439-02783-0(7))* Weston Woods Studios, Inc.

Young, Ed, ed. Siete Ratones Ciegos. Uribe, Verónica, tr. 2009. (SPA., Illus.). 40p. (gr. k-2). pap. 9.99 *(978-980-257-255-7(1))* Ekare, Ediciones VEN. Dist: Lectorum Pubns., Inc.

Younger, David. Spanky, the Brave Space Mouse, 1 vol. 2010. 18p. 24.95 *(978-1-4489-4661-7(1))* PublishAmerica, Inc.

Yu, Brenna Burns. Hazel & Twig: the Birthday Fortune. Yu, Brenna Burns, illus. 2018. (Hazel & Twig Ser.). (ENG., Illus.). 40p. (J). (gr. -1-2). 15.99 *(978-0-7636-8970-4(X))* Candlewick Pr.

Ziefert, Harriet. The Best Smelling Christmas Book Ever: 9 Scents to Scratch & Sniff! Rader, Laura, illus. 2004. 18p. (J). (gr. k-4). reprint ed. 13.00 *(978-0-7567-7600-8(7))* DIANE Publishing Co.

Zimmerman, Michael. The Mouse & the Acorn. 2007. 32p. per. 11.95 *(978-1-4327-0462-9(1))* Outskirts Pr., Inc.

Zinner, Gennieve. The UFB's of Bugsville, Florida USA, 1 vol. Ballinger, Carolyn, illus. 2010. 48p. pap. 24.95 *(978-1-4489-7977-6(3))* PublishAmerica, Inc.

Zoboli, Giovanna. A Most Mysterious Mouse. D'Andrea, Lisa, illus. 2016. 40p. (J). (gr. -1-4). 17.95 *(978-1-59270-213-8(9))* Enchanted Lion Bks., LLC.

MICE—POETRY

Akister, Finola, et al, selected by. Sports Poems & Mouse Poems. 2008. (Illus.). 32p. (J). pap. 10.95 *(978-1-59646-619-7(7))* Dingles & Co.

Akister, Finola, et al. Sports Poems & Mouse Poems. 2008. (Illus.). 32p. (J). lib. bdg. 23.65 *(978-1-59646-618-0(9))* Dingles & Co.

MICHELANGELO BUONARROTI, 1475-1564

Carr, Simonetta. Michelangelo for Kids: His Life & Ideas, with 21 Activities. 2016. (For Kids Ser.: 63). (ENG., Illus.). 144p. (J). (gr. 4). pap. 18.99 *(978-1-61373-193-2(0))* Chicago Review Pr., Inc.

Carvalho de Magalhaes, Roberto. Michelangelo. 2005. (Great Artists Ser.). (Illus.). 40p. (J). (gr. 4-7). per. 7.95 *(978-1-59270-049-3(7))* Enchanted Lion Bks., LLC.

Cook, Diane. Michelangelo: Renaissance Artist. (Illus.). 32p. (J). 2013. (People of Importance Ser.: 21). (gr. 4-18). 19.95 *(978-1-4222-2851-7(7))* 2004. (Great Names Ser.). (gr. 3-18). lib. bdg. 19.95 *(978-1-59084-156-3(5))* Mason Crest.

Di Cagno, Gabriella. Michelangelo. 2008. (Art Masters Ser.). 64p. (YA). (gr. 6-18). lib. bdg. 24.95 net. *(978-1-934545-01-0(5))* Oliver Pr., Inc.

Howse, Jennifer. Michelangelo. 2016. (Illus.). 32p. (J). *(978-1-4896-4623-1(X))* Weigl Pubs., Inc.

Nichols, Catherine. Michelangelo Buonarroti. (Primary Source Library of Famous Artists Ser.). 32p. (gr. 3-4). 2009. 42.50 *(978-1-60854-102-7(9))* 2005. (ENG., Illus.). (J). lib. bdg. 27.60 *(978-1-4042-2763-7(6)*, 670fa8f9-ab12-4269-808f-1fc937aa1c38) Rosen Publishing Group, Inc., The. (PowerKids Pr.).

Orr, Tamra B. Michelangelo: Master of the Renaissance, 1 vol. 2018. (Eye on Art Ser.). (ENG.). 104p. (gr. 7-7). 41.03 *(978-1-5345-6534-0(5)*, ef9321bf-a200-4872-96e5-99fed26ca089, Lucent Pr.) Greenhaven Publishing LLC.

Quill, Charlie. Michelangelo: His Life & Art. 2009. (Reading Room Collection 2 Ser.). 24p. (gr. 3-4). 42.50 *(978-1-60851-980-4(5)*, PowerKids Pr.) Rosen Publishing Group, Inc., The.

Raybin Emert, Phyllis. Michelangelo, 1 vol. 2012. (Eye on Art Ser.). (ENG., Illus.). 120p. (gr. 7-7). lib. bdg. 41.03 *(978-1-4205-0696-9(X)*, 7b430297-2d0f-4a1f-8d91-e3e8ea15a9f0, Lucent Pr.) Greenhaven Publishing LLC.

Richardson, Adele. Michelangelo. 2016. (Odysseys in Artistry Ser.). (ENG., Illus.). 80p. (J). (gr. 7-10). *(978-1-60818-719-5(5)*, 20659, Creative Education); pap. 14.99 *(978-1-62832-315-3(9)*, 20657, Creative Paperbacks) Creative Co., The.

Sherrow, Victoria & Buonarroti, Michelangelo. Michelangelo, 1 vol. 2005. (Great Artists Ser.). (ENG., Illus.). 40p. (gr. 4-6). 28.36 *(978-1-59270-008-0(X)*, b982752a-6e45-485a-a0e8-0f3128e76fb8) Cavendish Square Publishing LLC.

Stanley, Diane. Michelangelo. Stanley, Diane, illus. 2003. (ENG., Illus.). 48p. (J). (gr. 2-18). pap. 9.99 *(978-0-06-052113-4(9)*, HarperCollins) HarperCollins Pubs.

Sutcliffe, Jane. Stone Giant: Michelangelo's David & How He Came to Be. Shelley, John, illus. 2014. (J). 32p. pap. 16.95 *(978-1-60734-614-2(1))*; (ENG.). 32p. (gr. 1-4). lib. bdg. 17.99 *(978-1-58089-295-7(7))*; pap. *(978-1-58089-296-4(5))* Charlesbridge Publishing, Inc.

Venezia, Mike. Michelangelo (Revised Edition) (Getting to Know the World's Greatest Artists) Venezia, Mike, illus. 2014. (Getting to Know the World's Greatest Artists Ser.). (ENG.). 40p. (J). (gr. 3-4). pap. 7.95 *(978-0-531-22538-7(0)*, Children's Pr.) Scholastic Library Publishing.

Whiting, Jim. Michelangelo. 2007. (Art Profiles for Kids Ser.). (Illus.). 48p. (YA). (gr. 4-7). lib. bdg. 29.95 *(978-1-58415-562-1(0))* Mitchell Lane Pubs.

Wilkinson, Philip. World History Biographies: Michelangelo: The Young Artist Who Dreamed of Perfection. 2006. (National Geographic World History Biographies Ser.). (ENG., Illus.). 64p. (J). (gr. 3-7). 17.95 *(978-0-7922-5533-8(X)*, National Geographic Children's Bks.) National Geographic Society.

MICHELANGELO BUONARROTI, 1475-1564—FICTION

Brezina. Who Can Open Michelangelo's Seven Seals? (Illus.). 112p. *(978-3-7913-3555-1(3))* Prestel Verlag GmbH & Co KG.

Hi-stories presents Michelangelo Bunnyrroti. 2006. (J). bds. 14.99 *(978-0-9763233-2-7(X))* Little Germ That Could...Creations, Inc., The.

Murdock, Catherine Gilbert. Da Vinci's Cat. 2021. (ENG., Illus.). 288p. (J). (gr. 3-7). 17.99 *(978-0-06-301525-8(0)*, Greenwillow Bks.) HarperCollins Pubs.

MICHIGAN

Abramowski, Christina. Something Special. (Illus.). 32p. (J). (gr. 2-4). 9.95 *(978-0-9634927-0-8(5))* Junior League of Grand Rapids Michigan, Inc.

Arrathoon, Leigh A. & Davio, John. Jody's Travelbooks for Kids Vol. I: Frankenmuth, Michigan. Morris, Jeanne L., illus. 48p. (J). (gr. 2-6). pap. 4.95 *(978-0-9648564-7-9(6))* Archus Pr., LLC.

—Jody's Travelbooks for Kids Vol. II: Holland, Michigan. Morris, Jeanne L., illus. 48p. (J). (gr. 2-6). pap. 4.95 *(978-0-9648564-8-6(4))* Archus Pr., LLC.

—Jody's Travelbooks for Kids Vol. III: Mackinaw, Michigan. Morris, Jeanne L., illus. 48p. (J). (gr. 2-6). pap. 4.95 *(978-0-9648564-9-3(2))* Archus Pr., LLC.

Bower, Gary. I'm a Michigan Kid! Bower, Jan, illus. 2005. 48p. (J). 17.99 *(978-0-9704621-6-9(6))* Storybook Meadow Publishing.

Brenner, C. M. The Petoskey & Me: Look & Find. 2016. (Illus.). 24p. (J). 16.95 *(978-0-9980042-0-4(0))* SimplyCMB,LLC.

Cooper, Candy J. & Aronson, Marc. Poisoned Water: How the Citizens of Flint, Michigan, Fought for Their Lives & Warned the Nation. 2020. (ENG., Illus.). 256p. (J). 18.99 *(978-1-5476-0232-2(5)*, 900204200, Bloomsbury Children's Bks.) Bloomsbury Publishing USA.

Craats, Rennay. Michigan. 2011. (Guide to American States Ser.). (Illus.). 48p. (YA). (gr. 3-6). 29.99 *(978-1-61690-794-5(0))*; (J). *(978-1-61690-470-8(4))* Weigl Pubs., Inc.

Deinard, Jenny. How to Draw Michigan's Sights & Symbols. 2009. (Kid's Guide to Drawing America Ser.). 32p. (gr. k-k). 50.50 *(978-1-61511-071-1(2)*, PowerKids Pr.) Rosen Publishing Group, Inc., The.

Dubois, Muriel L. Michigan, 1 vol. 2005. (Portraits of the States Ser.). (ENG., Illus.). 32p. (gr. 3-5). pap. 11.50 *(978-0-8368-4646-1(X)*, 604c92d5-9ef8-47db-a4ec-1b2307068951); lib. bdg. 28.67 *(978-0-8368-4627-0(3)*, 8834cddd-81aa-4af0-96d2-96ccae303115) Stevens, Gareth Publishing LLLP. (Gareth Stevens Learning Library).

Dupuis, Karina, illus. Michigan Monsters: A Search & Find Book. 2018. (ENG.). 22p. (J). (gr. -1). bds. 9.99 *(978-2-924734-10-0(X))* City Monsters Bks. CAN. Dist: Publishers Group West (PGW).

Eisbruch, Emily. Curious Kids Activity Guide to Michigan. 2007. pap. 9.95 *(978-0-9789140-0-4(7))* Curious Kids Guides.

Haney, Johannah. Michigan, 1 vol. Santoro, Christopher, illus. 2005. (It's My State! (First Edition)(r) Ser.). (ENG.). 80p. (gr. 4-4). lib. bdg. 34.07 *(978-0-7614-1861-0(X)*, 2d007384-5db7-456e-915f-6a3d00fdca6d) Cavendish Square Publishing LLC.

Heidtke, John. Family Golf Adventures on Michigan Links. 2010. 242p. (J). pap. 12.95 *(978-1-60920-000-8(4))* Ajoyin Publishing, Inc.

Jerome, Kate B. The Wise Animal Handbook Michigan. 2017. (Arcadia Kids Ser.). (ENG., Illus.). 32p. (J). 16.99 *(978-0-7385-2826-7(9))* Arcadia Publishing.

Kammeraad, Kevin & Kammeraad, Stephanie. A Curious Glimpse of Michigan. Kammeraad, Kevin & Hipp, Ryan, illus. 32p. (J). 2006. (gr. 4-7). pap. 9.95 *(978-0-9749412-9-5(8))* 2004. (gr. 3-7). 19.95 *(978-0-9712692-9-3(7))* EDCO Publishing, Inc.

L is for Ludington: An alphabet book about Ludington, MI created by Children. 2006. (J). pap. 10.00 *(978-0-9786128-0-1(9))* Bosse, Andre Ctr.

Lewis, Anne Margaret & Campbell, Janis. Hidden Michigan. Popko, Wendy, illus. 2006. 40p. (J). (gr. 1-4). 12.95 *(978-1-934133-01-9(9)*, Mackinac Island Press, Inc.) Charlesbridge Publishing, Inc.

Mader, Jan. Michigan. 2003. (Rookie Read-About Geography Ser.). (ENG., Illus.). 32p. (J). (gr. 1-2). 20.50 *(978-0-516-22736-8(X)*, Children's Pr.) Scholastic Library Publishing.

Marsh, Carole. The Magnificent Michigan Coloring Book. 2004. (Michigan Experience! Ser.). (Illus.). 32p. (J). (gr. k-2). pap. 3.95 *(978-0-7933-9567-5(4))* Gallopade International.

—Michigan Current Events Projects: 30 Cool, Activities, Crafts, Experiments & More for Kids to Do to Learn about Your State! 2003. (Michigan Experience Ser.). 32p. (gr. k-8). pap. 5.95 *(978-0-635-02041-3(6)*, Marsh, Carole Bks.) Gallopade International.

—The Michigan Experience Pocket Guide. 2004. (Michigan Experience! Ser.). (Illus.). 96p. (J). (gr. 3-8). pap. 6.95 *(978-0-7933-9562-0(3))* Gallopade International.

—Michigan Geography Projects: 30 Cool, Activities, Crafts, Experiments & More for Kids to Do to Learn about Your State! 2003. (Michigan Experience Ser.). 32p. (gr. k-5). pap. 5.95 *(978-0-635-01841-0(1)*, Marsh, Carole Bks.) Gallopade International.

—Michigan Government Projects: 30 Cool, Activities, Crafts, Experiments & More for Kids to Do to Learn about Your State! 2003. (Michigan Experience Ser.). 32p. (gr. k-5). pap. 5.95 *(978-0-635-01941-7(8)*, Marsh, Carole Bks.) Gallopade International.

—Michigan Jeopardy! Answers & Questions about Our State! 2004. (Michigan Experience! Ser.). (Illus.). 32p. (J). (gr. 3-8). pap. 7.95 *(978-0-7933-9564-4(X))* Gallopade International.

—Michigan "Jography" A Fun Run Thru Our State! 2004. (Michigan Experience! Ser.). (Illus.). 32p. (J). (gr. 3-8). pap. 7.95 *(978-0-7933-9565-1(8))* Gallopade International.

—Michigan People Projects: 30 Cool, Activities, Crafts, Experiments & More for Kids to Do to Learn about Your State! 2003. (Michigan Experience Ser.). 32p. (gr. k-5). pap. 5.95 *(978-0-635-01991-2(4)*, Marsh, Carole Bks.) Gallopade International.

—Michigan Symbols & Facts Projects: 30 Cool, Activities, Crafts, Experiments & More for Kids to Do to Learn about Your State! 2003. (Michigan Experience Ser.). 32p. (gr. k-5). pap. 5.95 *(978-0-635-01891-5(8)*, Marsh, Carole Bks.) Gallopade International.

—My First Book about Michigan. 2004. (Michigan Experience! Ser.). (Illus.). 32p. (J). (gr. k-4). pap. 7.95 *(978-0-7933-9563-7(1))* Gallopade International.

—Texas's Big Activity Book. 2004. (Texas Experience! Ser.). (Illus.). 96p. (J). (gr. 2-6). pap. 9.95 *(978-0-7933-9465-4(1))* Gallopade International.

McNamara, Connie. My First Michigan Words. 2004. (J). bds. 11.95 *(978-0-9743244-6-3(9))* Shamrock Publishing, Inc.

Murray, Julie. Michigan, 1 vol. 2006. (Buddy Book Ser.). (ENG., Illus.). 32p. (gr. 2-4). 27.07 *(978-1-59197-681-3(2)*, Buddy Bks.) ABDO Publishing Co.

Obregon, Jose Maria. Michigan, 1 vol. Brusca, Maria Cristina, tr. 2005. (Bilingual Library of the United States of America Ser.: Set 1). (ENG & SPA., Illus.). 32p. (J). (gr. 2-2). lib. bdg. 28.93 *(978-1-4042-3087-3(4)*, cbdf930b-a72f-4cd5-9f7b-5be381565afe) Rosen Publishing Group, Inc., The.

Raatma, Lucia. America the Beautiful, Third Series: Michigan (Revised Edition) 2014. (America the Beautiful Ser.: 3). (ENG.). 144p. (J). lib. bdg. 40.00 *(978-0-531-24890-4(9))* Scholastic Library Publishing.

Riggs, Kate. Michigan. 2008. (This Land Called America Ser.). (Illus.). 32p. (YA). (gr. 3-6). 22.95 *(978-1-58341-647-1(1))* Creative Co., The.

Sirvaitis, Karen. Michigan. 2012. (J). lib. bdg. 25.26 *(978-0-7613-4539-8(6)*, Lerner Pubns.) Lerner Publishing Group.

Targ Brill, Marlene. Michigan, 1 vol. 2nd rev. ed. 2007. (Celebrate the States (Second Edition) Ser.). (ENG., Illus.). 144p. (gr. 6-6). lib. bdg. 39.79 *(978-0-7614-2351-5(6)*, d7634b0a-ead6-456c-836c-fdc4df8c9986) Cavendish Square Publishing LLC.

MICHIGAN—FICTION

Andrews, Randall. The Last Guardian of Magic. 2008. 448p. (YA). per. 23.95 *(978-0-595-47345-8(8))* iUniverse, Inc.

Anthony, David & David, Charles. Heroes A2Z #1: (Heroes a to Z): Alien Ice Cream. Blakeslee, Lys, illus. 2007. 128p. (J). pap. 4.99 *(978-0-9728461-8-9(2))* Sigil Publishing.

—Heroes A2Z #2: (Heroes a to Z): Bowling over Halloween: Bowling over Halloween. Blakeslee, Lys, illus. 2007. (Heroes A2Z Ser.). 128p. (J). pap. 4.99 *(978-0-9728461-9-6(0))* Sigil Publishing.

Arrathoon, Leigh A. Summer of the Bear: An Historical Novel about the Anishinabeg & the Fur Traders in Michigan. 2005. (Journals of Kevin Murphy Ser.: Bk. 1). (J). *(978-1-893047-07-5(5))* Archus Pr., LLC.

Arrathoon, Leigh A. Magical Adventures in Michigan. 2003. (Illus.). viii, 349p. *(978-1-893047-10-5(5))* Archus Pr., LLC.

Ashford, Rachel. My First Santa's Coming to Michigan. Dunn, Robert, illus. 2015. (Santa Claus Is on His Way Ser.). (ENG.). 18p. (J). (gr. -1-k). bds. 9.99 *(978-1-4926-2873-6(5)*, Hometown World) Sourcebooks, Inc.

Balash, Sue Beth. Mimi the Inchworm. 2009. (ENG.). 32p. pap. 10.95 *(978-1-933916-44-6(3)*, Ferne Pr.) Nelson Publishing & Marketing.

Balliett, Blue. The Danger Box. 2012. (ENG.). 320p. (J). (gr. 4-7). pap. 7.99 *(978-0-439-85210-4(2)*, Scholastic Paperbacks) Scholastic, Inc.

Baumer, Dawn McVay, creator. Dune Daze: Silver Lake. 2004. (Illus.). (J). *(978-0-9754960-0-8(X))* Butters Pr.

Bellairs, John. The House with a Clock in Its Walls. Gorey, Edward, illus. 2004. (Lewis Barnavelt Ser.: Bk. 1). (ENG.). 192p. (J). (gr. 3-7). pap. 7.99 *(978-0-14-240257-3(5)*, Puffin Books) Penguin Young Readers Group.

—The House with a Clock in Its Walls. Gorey, Edward, illus. 2004. (John Bellairs Mysteries Ser.). 179p. (J). (gr. 3-7). 13.65 *(978-0-7569-5257-0(3))* Perfection Learning Corp.

—The House with a Clock in Its Walls. (Lewis Barnavelt Ser.: Bk. 1). 179p. (J). (gr. 4-6). pap. 4.50 *(978-0-8072-1423-7(X)*, Listening Library) Random Hse. Audio Publishing Group.

—The House with a Clock in Its Walls. 2004. 17.20 *(978-1-4176-3513-9(4))* Turtleback.

Birkholz, Gay Lyn. Veneti: Lake Michigan's Treasure. Williamson, Linda K., illus. 2010. 52p. pap. 17.00 *(978-1-60860-129-5(3)*, Strategic Bk. Publishing) Strategic Book Publishing & Rights Agency (SBPRA).

Blos, Joan W. Brothers of the Heart: A Story of the Old Northwest, 1837-1838. 2008. (ENG.). 176p. (J). (gr. 3-7). pap. 5.99 *(978-1-4169-7561-8(6)*, Simon & Schuster/Paula Wiseman Bks.) Simon & Schuster/Paula Wiseman Bks.

Bower, Gary. I'm a Michigan Kid Coloring & Activity Book. Bower, Jan & Bower, Brittany, illus. 2006. 48p. (J). pap. 7.95 *(978-0-9704621-5-2(8)*, Bower Bks.) Storybook Meadow Publishing.

Brewer, Heather. The Cemetery Boys. 2016. (ENG.). 304p. (YA). (gr. 8). pap. 9.99 *(978-0-06-230789-7(4)*, HarperTeen) HarperCollins Pubs.

—The Cemetery Boys. 2016. (YA). lib. bdg. 20.85 *(978-0-606-38741-5(2))* Turtleback.

Carney-Coston, Barbara. To the Copper Country: Mihaela's Journey. 2018. (Great Lakes Books Ser.). (ENG., Illus.). 128p. pap. 14.99 *(978-0-8143-4363-0(5)*, P551024) Wayne State Univ. Pr.

Carr, Annie Roe. Nan Sherwoods Winter Holidays or Rescuin. 2007. pap. *(978-1-4065-1296-0(6))* Dodo Pr.

Carter, Aimée. The Goddess Test. 2011. (Goddess Test Ser.: 1). lib. bdg. 20.85 *(978-0-606-26943-8(6))* Turtleback.

Carter, Aimée & Carter, Aimée. The Goddess Test. 2011. (Goddess Test Novel Ser.: 1). (ENG.). 304p. (YA). (gr. 9-18). pap. 11.99 *(978-0-373-21026-8(4)*, Harlequin Teen) Harlequin Enterprises ULC CAN. Dist: HarperCollins Pubs.

Chevoya, Dawn. Trapper's Grounding. 2019. 204p. (gr. 4-7). pap. 14.95 *(978-1-64279-134-1(2))* Morgan James Publishing.

Cory, Kim Delmar. Home to Mackinac: The Tale of Young Jack Murphy's Discovery of Loyalty, Family, & Forgiveness. Evans, Laura, illus. 2007. (ENG.). 175p. (J). (gr. 3-7). per. 9.95 *(978-0-911872-87-3(6))* Mackinac State Historic Parks.

—Tending Ben's Garden. 2009. 121p. (J). pap. *(978-0-88092-778-9(X))* Royal Fireworks Publishing Co.

Curtis, Christopher Paul. Bucking the Sarge. 2006. (ENG.). 288p. (YA). (gr. 7-7). reprint ed. mass mkt. 8.99 *(978-0-440-41331-8(1)*, Laurel Leaf) Random Hse. Children's Bks.

—Bud, Not Buddy. unabr. ed. 2004. 256p. (J). (gr. 4-7). pap. 36.00 incl. audio *(978-0-8072-8210-6(3)*, LYA 140 S{, Listening Library) Random Hse. Audio Publishing Group.

—Bud, Not Buddy: (Newbery Medal Winner) 2004. (ENG., Illus.). 288p. (J). (gr. 5-7). mass mkt. 8.99 *(978-0-553-49410-5(4)*, Laurel Leaf) Random Hse. Children's Bks.

—The Mighty Miss Malone. 320p. (J). (gr. 4-7). 2013. pap. 8.99 *(978-0-440-42214-3(0)*, Yearling) 2012. 15.99 *(978-0-385-73491-2(3)*, Lamb, Wendy Bks.) Random Hse. Children's Bks.

—The Mighty Miss Malone. 2013. lib. bdg. 18.40 *(978-0-606-27007-6(8))* Turtleback.

—Mr. Chickee's Funny Money. 2007. (Mr. Chickee's Ser.: 1). (ENG.). 160p. (J). (gr. 3-7). 6.99 *(978-0-440-22919-3(7)*, Yearling) Random Hse. Children's Bks.

—Mr. Chickee's Messy Mission. 2008. (Mr. Chickee's Ser.: 2). (ENG., Illus.). 240p. (J). (gr. 3-7). 6.99 *(978-0-440-22922-3(7)*, Yearling) Random Hse. Children's Bks.

—The Watsons Go to Birmingham — 1963. 2013. (ENG., Illus.). 224p. (J). (gr. 3-7). 8.99 *(978-0-385-38294-6(4)*, Yearling) Random Hse. Children's Bks.

—The Watsons Go to Birmingham 1963. 210p. (YA). (gr. 5-18). pap. 5.50 *(978-0-8072-8336-3(3))*; 2004. (J). (gr. 4-18). pap. 38.00 incl. audio *(978-0-8072-8335-6(5)*, YA166SP) Random Hse. Audio Publishing Group. (Listening Library).

Curtis, Christopher Paul & Vega, Eida de la. Los Watson Van a Birmingham - 1963. 2016. (SPA.). 200p. (J). (gr. 5-12). pap. 12.99 *(978-1-63245-640-3(0))* Lectorum Pubns., Inc.

Dalton, Michelle. Fifteenth Summer. 2013. (ENG.). 272p. (YA). (gr. 7). 17.99 *(978-1-4424-7267-9(7))*; (Illus.). pap. 11.99 *(978-1-4424-7266-2(9))* Simon Pulse. (Simon Pulse).

Damerau, Diane Deci. The Petoskey Stones, 1 vol. 2009. 135p. pap. 24.95 *(978-1-60749-903-9(7))* America Star Bks.

Day, Karen. No Cream Puffs. 224p. (J). 2010. (gr. 3-7). 8.99 *(978-0-375-83776-0(0)*, Yearling) 2008. (ENG.). (gr. 6-8). lib. bdg. 21.19 *(978-0-375-93775-0(7)*, Lamb, Wendy Bks.) Random Hse. Children's Bks.

Delco, Bobby. Lil Mack Jr. 2009. 108p. pap. 11.99 *(978-1-4389-0473-3(8))* AuthorHouse.

Derby, Sally. Kyle's Island. 2014. 192p. (J). (gr. 5). pap. 7.95 *(978-1-58089-317-6(1))* Charlesbridge Publishing, Inc.

Deshone, Jerry Michael. Bear in Mind. 2011. 24p. pap. 24.95 *(978-1-4626-2973-2(3))* America Star Bks.

Elster, Jean Alicia. Who's Jim Hines? 2008. (ENG., Illus.). 146p. pap. 12.95 *(978-0-8143-3402-7(4)*, P158269) Wayne State Univ. Pr.

Frankenhuyzen, Robbyn Smith van. Kelly of Hazel Ridge. Frankenhuyzen, Gijsbert van, illus. 3rd rev. ed. 2006. (Hazel Ridge Farm Stories Ser.). (ENG.). 48p. (J). (gr. 1-4). 17.95 *(978-1-58536-268-4(9)*, 202082) Sleeping Bear Pr.

Frost, Helen. Crossing Stones. 2009. (ENG., Illus.). 192p. (YA). (gr. 7-18). 19.99 *(978-0-374-31653-2(8)*, 900050356, Farrar, Straus & Giroux (BYR)) Farrar, Straus & Giroux.

—Hidden. 2015. (ENG.). (J). (gr. 5-9). lib. bdg. 17.60 *(978-1-62765-725-9(8))* Perfection Learning Corp.

Gaertner, Connie. Wake-Up Calls. 2013. 154p. (gr. 10-12). pap. 12.95 *(978-1-4759-6646-6(6))* iUniverse, Inc.

Gamble, Adam. Good Night Michigan. Rosen, Anne, illus. 2011. (Good Night Our World Ser.). (ENG.). 20p. (J). (gr. k — 1). bds. 9.95 *(978-1-60219-054-2(2))* Good Night Bks.

Giff, Patricia Reilly. Willow Run. 2007. 149p. (J). 13.65 *(978-0-7569-7769-6(X))* Perfection Learning Corp.

—Willow Run. 2007. (ENG.). 160p. (J). (gr. 3-7). per. 6.99 *(978-0-440-23801-0(3)*, Yearling) Random Hse. Children's Bks.

Grund, Carol A. Anna Mei, Blessing in Disguise. 2011. 181p. (J). pap. *(978-0-8198-0796-0(6))* Pauline Bks. & Media.

—Anna Mei, Escape Artist. 2011. 168p. (J). (gr. 4-7). pap. 8.95 *(978-0-8198-0794-6(X))* Pauline Bks. & Media.

Guarneri, Cristina. The Invincible, 1 vol. 2010. 48p. pap. 16.95 *(978-1-4489-4086-8(9))* America Star Bks.

Haynes, Marilee. Pictures of Me. 2016. 149p. (J). pap. *(978-0-8198-6019-4(0))* Pauline Bks. & Media.

Henry, Emily. A Million Junes. 2018. 400p. (YA). (gr. 7). pap. 12.99 *(978-0-448-49397-8(7)*, Razorbill) Penguin Young Readers Group.

Holbrook, Sara E. The Enemy: Detroit 1954. 2017. (ENG., Illus.). 224p. (J). (gr. 5-9). 17.99 *(978-1-62979-498-3(8)*, Calkins Creek) Highlights Pr., c/o Highlights for Children, Inc.

Howard, Ellen. The Log Cabin Wedding. Himler, Ronald, illus. 2006. (ENG.). 64p. (J). (gr. -1-3). 15.95 *(978-0-8234-1989-0(4))* Holiday Hse., Inc.

Jacobs, Lily. The Littlest Bunny in Michigan: An Easter Adventure. Dunn, Robert, illus. 2015. (Littlest Bunny Ser.). (ENG.). 32p. (J). (gr. -1-3). 9.99 *(978-1-4926-1117-2(4)*, Hometown World) Sourcebooks, Inc.

James, Eric. Santa's Sleigh Is on Its Way to Michigan: A Christmas Adventure. Dunn, Robert, illus. 2015. (Santa's Sleigh Is on Its Way Ser.). (ENG.). 32p. (J). (gr. k-2). 12.99 *(978-1-4926-2741-8(0)*, Hometown World) Sourcebooks, Inc.

—The Spooky Express Michigan. Piwowarski, Marcin, illus. 2017. (Spooky Express Ser.). (ENG.). 32p. (J). (gr. k-6). 9.99 *(978-1-4926-5370-7(5)*, Hometown World) Sourcebooks, Inc.

—Tiny the Michigan Easter Bunny. 2018. (Tiny the Easter Bunny Ser.). (ENG.). 40p. (J). (gr. k-3). 9.99 *(978-1-4926-5937-2(1)*, Hometown World) Sourcebooks, Inc.

Johnson, Lois Walfrid. Mystery of the Missing Map. 2009. (J). 8.99 *(978-0-88062-283-7(0))* Mott Media.

Langley, Jan. Captain & Harry Haunting Tail. 2004. pap. *(978-0-9724777-0-3(5))* Captain & Harry LLC, The.

Lewis, Anne Margaret. The Runaway Mitten: A Michigan Adventure Story. Zenz, Aaron, illus. 2015. (ENG.). 40p. (J). (gr. -1-k). 15.99 *(978-1-63450-213-9(2)*, Sky Pony Pr.) Skyhorse Publishing Co., Inc.

MacPherson, M. j. The Magic Thread: Overcoming challenges during World War II, a young girl discovers secrets that change adversity into Adventure. 2009. 208p. pap. 17.95 *(978-0-595-52812-7(0))* iUniverse, Inc.

Magsamen, Sandra. I Love Michigan (an ABC Adventure) 2015. (ABC Adventure Ser.). (ENG.). 40p. (J). (gr. -1-5). 12.99 *(978-1-4926-2844-6(1)*, Hometown World) Sourcebooks, Inc.

Marsh, Barry. Good Harbor Bay. 2009. (J). 14.95 *(978-0-9767268-1-4(5))* Crofton Creek Pr.

MNO

McCahan, Erin. I Now Pronounce You Someone Else. 2010. (ENG.). 272p. (J). (gr. 7-18). 16.99 *(978-0-545-08818-3(6))*, Levine, Arthur A. Bks.) Scholastic, Inc.
Merkel, Ruth Vitrano. Hannah's Girls: Elaine. 2008. (Hannah's Girls Ser.: 5). (Illus.). 176p. (J). pap. 9.99 *(978-0-8280-1955-2(X))* Review & Herald Publishing Assn.
Noble, Trinka Hakes. The Legend of Michigan. Frankenhuyzen, Gijsbert van, illus. 2006. (Myths, Legends, Fairy & Folktales Ser.). (ENG.). 48p. (J). (gr. 2-5). 17.95 *(978-1-58536-278-3(6)*, 202089) Sleeping Bear Pr.
Nye, Naomi Shihab. The Turtle of Oman: A Novel. 2014. (ENG.). 304p. (J). (gr. 3-7). 16.99 *(978-0-06-201972-1(4)*, Greenwillow Bks.) HarperCollins Pubs.
O'Neill, Elizabeth. Alfred Visits Michigan. 2006. (Illus.). 24p. pap. 12.00 *(978-0-9771836-6-1(1))* Funny Bone Bks.
Otten, Charlotte F. Home in a Wilderness Fort: Copper Harbor 1844. 2006. (Illus.). 232p. (J). (gr. 2-7). per. 14.95 *(978-0-9766104-5-8(0))* Arbutus Pr.
Panagopoulos, Janie Lynn. A Castle at the Straits. Evans, Laura, illus. 2003. 48p. (J). (gr. 1-6). *(978-0-911872-83-5(3))* Mackinac State Historic Parks.
—Mark of the Bear Claw. 2007. 224p. (J). pap. 8.95 *(978-0-938682-83-7(0))* River Road Pubns., Inc.
Paul, Curtis Christopher. Bud, Not Buddy. 2014. (ENG.). 256p. (J). (gr. 12-12). 11.24 *(978-1-63245-063-0(1))* Lectorum Pubns., Inc.
—The Watsons Go to Birmingham 1963. 2014. (ENG.). 224p. (J). (gr. 12-12). 11.24 *(978-1-63245-108-8(5))* Lectorum Pubns., Inc.
Phelan, Matt. Bluffton: My Summers with Buster. Phelan, Matt, illus. 2017. (ENG., Illus.). (J). (gr. 4-7). lib. bdg. 24.50 *(978-0-606-39837-4(6))* Turtleback.
—Bluffton: My Summers with Buster Keaton. Phelan, Matt, illus. 2017. (ENG., Illus.). 232p. (J). (gr. 4-7). pap. 14.99 *(978-0-7636-8706-9(5))* Candlewick Pr.
Pirzada, Nefes & Simeone, Angelique. Young Equestrian: Something in Common. 2012. 386p. (gr. 4-18). pap. 21.14 *(978-1-4669-5242-3(3))* Trafford Publishing.
Pyke, Helen Godfrey. Pinch River: Growing up Hard & Fast on the Michigan Frontier. 2008. (J). pap. 7.97 *(978-0-8163-2250-3(3))* Pacific Pr. Publishing Assn.
Quackenbush-Douglas, Diane. That's Just the Way it Was! (Not a Fairy Tale) 2010. 28p. 15.49 *(978-1-4520-2941-2(5))* AuthorHouse.
Rand, Jonathan. Michigan Chillers #14 Bionic Bats Bay City. 2007. 208p. (J). pap. 5.99 *(978-1-893699-65-6(X))* AudioCraft Publishing, Inc.
Richards, Sonja. Comet Kid. 2007. 31p. pap. 8.95 *(978-0-9794935-0-8(1))* Olde Towne Publishing.
—My Maize & Blue Day. Viall, Pauline, illus. 2008. 32p. (J). 19.95 *(978-0-9794935-1-5(X))* Olde Towne Publishing.
Robinson, A. M. Vampire Crush. 2010. (ENG.). 416p. (YA). (gr. 8-18). pap. 8.99 *(978-0-06-198971-1(1)*, HarperTeen) HarperCollins Pubs.
Schröder, Monika & Schröder, Monika. Be Light Like a Bird. 2016. (ENG.). 240p. (J). (gr. 3-7). lib. bdg. 14.95 *(978-1-62370-749-1(8)*, 132439, Capstone Young Readers) Capstone.
Shabazz, Ilyasah & Magoon, Kekla. X: a Novel. 2016. (ENG.). 384p. (J). (gr. 9). pap. 9.99 *(978-0-7636-9092-2(9))* Candlewick Pr.
Shaw, J. D. Leave No Footprints. 2011. (ENG.). 276p. (J). (gr. 7). pap. 14.95 *(978-0-9845318-6-8(6))* Tiny Stachel Pr.
Smallman, Steve. Santa Is Coming to Michigan. Dunn, Robert, illus. (ENG.). (J). 2012. 32p. (-3). 9.99 *(978-1-4022-7539-5(0)*, Sourcebooks Jabberwocky) 2nd ed. 2019. 40p. (gr. -1-3). 12.99 *(978-1-7282-0071-2(7)*, Hometown World) Sourcebooks, Inc.
Smith, Ruth. Buddy Bear: Visits Michigan Lighthouses. 2010. 28p. pap. 13.99 *(978-1-4490-8363-2(3))* AuthorHouse.
Smucker, Anna Egan. To Keep the South Manitou Light. (Great Lakes Books Ser.). (ENG., Illus.). 2006. 130p. (gr. 3-7). per. 14.95 *(978-0-8143-3236-8(6)*, P120417) 2004. 140p. 23.95 *(978-0-8143-3235-1(8)*, P029609) Wayne State Univ. Pr.
Stinson, Aimee & Somson, Kathy. The Bearless City, 1 vol. 2009. 22p. pap. 24.95 *(978-1-60749-406-5(X))* America Star Bks.
Sully, Katherine. Night-Night Michigan. Poole, Helen, illus. 2016. (Night-Night Ser.). (ENG.). 20p. (J). (gr. -1-1). bds. 9.99 *(978-1-4926-3934-3(6)*, 9781492639343, Hometown World) Sourcebooks, Inc.
Tamara Devitre Lueders. A Weekend with Tuk. 2006. (ENG.). 40p. pap. 16.99 *(978-1-4257-3028-4(0))* Xlibris Corp.
Thorne, K. C. The Troll of MacKinac. Johnson, Vickie, illus. 2010. 32p. pap. 13.00 *(978-1-60911-178-6(8)*, Eloquent Bks.) Strategic Book Publishing & Rights Agency (SBPRA).
Tillson, M. C. Secret of Bete Grise Bay: A Michigan Lighthouse Adventure. Bailey, Lisa, illus. 2008. (ENG.). (J). (gr. 1-5). pap. 9.95 *(978-0-9764824-2-0(8))* A & M Writing and Publishing.
Tracy, Kristen. Crimes of the Sarahs. 2014. (ENG., Illus.). 384p. (YA). (gr. 9). pap. 9.99 *(978-1-4424-8100-8(5)*, Simon Pulse) Simon Pulse.
Walter, Debbie. Introducing Russell. Walter, Debbie, illus. 2007. (Illus.). 68p. (J). per. 6.95 *(978-0-9766315-2-1(0))* Moose Run Productions.
Wargin, Kathy-jo. Mitt, the Michigan Mouse. Holman, Karen Busch, illus. 2015. (Mitt Midwest Ser.: 1). 160p. (J). (gr. k-7). pap. 8.95 *(978-1-938170-65-2(2)*, Mitten Pr.) Ann Arbor Editions LLC.
Whelan, Gloria. Forgive the River, Forgive the Sky. 2004. 96p. (J). pap. 8.00 *(978-0-8028-5256-4(4))* Eerdmans, William B. Publishing Co.
—Mackinac Bridge: The Story of the Five Mile Poem. Frankenhuyzen, Gijsbert van, illus. 2006. (Tales of Young Americans Ser.). (ENG.). 40p. (J). (gr. 1-4). 17.95 *(978-1-58536-283-7(2)*, 202094) Sleeping Bear Pr.
Winfield, Arthur M. The Rover Boys on the Great Lakes. 2004. reprint ed. pap. 22.95 *(978-1-4191-8119-1(X))* Kessinger Publishing, LLC.
—The Rover Boys on the Great Lakes. 2004. reprint ed. pap. 1.99 *(978-1-4192-8119-8(4))* Kessinger Publishing, LLC.
Wood, David. The Little House on Buchanan Street. 2007. 24p. per. 12.95 *(978-1-934246-64-1(6))* Peppertree Pr., The.
Zee, Ginger. Chasing Helicity: First She Has to Face the Storm. 2018. *(978-1-368-02030-5(5))* Disney Publishing Worldwide.

MICHIGAN—HISTORY

Bernard-Nollins, Sonya M. Here I Stand: A Musical History of African Americans in Battle Creek, Michigan. 2003. (Illus.). (YA). pap. 15.00 *(978-0-9741611-0-5(1))* Fortitude Graphic Design & Printing.
Brennan-Nelson, Denise. Little Michigan. Monroe, Michael Glenn, illus. 2010. (Little State Ser.). (ENG.). 20p. (J). (gr. -1-1). bds. 9.95 *(978-1-58536-479-4(7)*, 202243) Sleeping Bear Pr.
Connery-Boyd, Peg. Totally Michigan! 2016. (Hawk's Nest Activity Bks.: 0). (ENG.). 64p. (J). (gr. k-3). pap. 8.99 *(978-1-4926-4191-9(X)*, 9781492641919) Sourcebooks, Inc.
Craats, Rennay. Michigan: The Wolverine State. 2016. (J). *(978-1-4896-4881-5(X))* Weigl Pubs., Inc.
Foster, Tracy, et al. Benson's Adventures in Michigan. 2016. (Illus.). 32p. (J). 17.95 *(978-0-9980066-0-4(2))* Britton & Case Prs.
Frank, David. The Kids & Sites of Kalamazoo. 2004. 80p. *(978-0-9758971-0-2(1))* Artstreet LLC.
Gamble, Adam & Jasper, Mark. Count to Sleep Michigan. Veno, Joe, illus. 2014. (Count to Sleep Ser.). (ENG.). 20p. (J). (— 1). bds. 9.95 *(978-1-60219-327-7(4))* Good Night Bks.
Glupker, Dianne. Great Tastes of Michigan. Delsi, Dawna, illus. 2006. (J). per. 9.95 *(978-0-9769846-1-0(X))* Harambee Pr.
Hamilton, John. Michigan, 1 vol. 2016. (United States of America Ser.). (ENG., Illus.). 48p. (J). (gr. 5-9). 34.21 *(978-1-68078-324-7(6)*, 21633, Abdo & Daughters) ABDO Publishing Co.
Haney, Johannah & Hantula, Richard. Michigan, 1 vol. 2nd rev. ed. 2012. (It's My State! (Second Edition)(r) Ser.). (ENG.). 80p. (gr. 4-4). 34.07 *(978-1-60870-523-8(4)*, c3bfb6c3-4c23-431f-90b3-a064ac9bd821) Cavendish Square Publishing LLC.
Haney, Johannah, et al. Michigan: The Great Lakes State, 1 vol. 3rd rev. ed. 2016. (It's My State! (Third Edition)(r) Ser.). (ENG., Illus.). 80p. (gr. 4-4). 35.93 *(978-1-62713-163-6(9)*, da3888ff-c998-4fc7-b9c6-ae953afe3955) Cavendish Square Publishing LLC.
Harmon, Daniel E. Minnesota: Past & Present, 1 vol. 2010. (United States: Past & Present Ser.). (ENG., Illus.). 48p. (J). (gr. 5-5). lib. bdg. 34.47 *(978-1-4358-3524-5(7)*, 648922d0-ff64-4255-9ead-74b765f86cb9, Rosen Reference) Rosen Publishing Group, Inc., The.
Heinrichs, Ann. Michigan. Kania, Matt, illus. 2017. (U. S. A. Travel Guides). (ENG.). 40p. (J). (gr. 2-5). lib. bdg. 38.50 *(978-1-5038-1962-7(0)*, 211599) Child's World, Inc, The.
Helweg, Laura. Eastern Great Lakes: Indiana, Michigan, Ohio, Vol. 19. 2015. (Let's Explore the States Ser.). 64p. (J). (gr. 5). 23.95 *(978-1-4222-3323-8(5))* Mason Crest.
Hoffman, Mary Hramiec. Elizabeth Whitney Williams & the Little Traverse Light. 2004. (Illus.). 38p. (J). 17.95 *(978-0-9746901-0-0(4))* Hramiec Hoffman Publishing.
Jerome, Kate B. Lucky to Live in Michigan. 2017. (Arcadia Kids Ser.). (ENG., Illus.). 32p. (J). 16.99 *(978-0-7385-2777-2(7))* Arcadia Publishing.
Killingbeck, Dale. Michigan Triumphs & Tragedies 2005. (Illus.). 160p. per. 9.95 *(978-0-9762758-0-0(5))* Killingbeck, Dale.
Levy, Janey. Michigan: Past & Present, 1 vol. 2010. (United States: Past & Present Ser.). (ENG., Illus.). 48p. (J). (gr. 5-5). pap. 12.75 *(978-1-4358-8496-0(5)*, 76501f99-ca5a-47d4-b669-d7046ce7d5a3); lib. bdg. 34.47 *(978-1-4358-3523-8(9)*, 61241ced-e574-4e96-92f1-80ea0ee442c6) Rosen Publishing Group, Inc., The. (Rosen Reference).
Marsh, Carole. Exploring Michigan Through Project-Based Learning: Geography, History, Government, Economics & More. 2016. (Michigan Experience Ser.). (ENG.). (J). pap. 9.99 *(978-0-635-12346-6(0))* Gallopade International.
—I'm Reading about Michigan. 2014. (Michigan Experience Ser.). (ENG., Illus.). (J). pap. 8.99 *(978-0-635-11297-2(3))* Gallopade International.
—Michigan History Projects: 30 Cool, Activities, Crafts, Experiments & More for Kids to Do to Learn about Your State! 2003. (Michigan Experience Ser.). 32p. (gr. k-5). pap. 5.95 *(978-0-635-01791-8(1)*, Marsh, Carole Bks.) Gallopade International.
McDowell, Pamela. Michigan: The Wolverine State. 2012. (J). *(978-1-61913-363-1(6))*; pap. *(978-1-61913-364-8(4))* Weigl Pubs., Inc.
McDowell, Pamela & Craats, Rennay. Michigan. 2018. (Illus.). 24p. (J). *(978-1-4896-7445-6(4)*, AV2 by Weigl) Weigl Pubs., Inc.
McGraw-Hill Education Editors. Michigan 2009 Gr 3 Practice & Activity Workbook. 2009. (ENG.). (gr. 3). pap. 5.48 *(978-0-02-153646-7(5)*, 0021536465) Macmillan/McGraw-Hill Schl. Div.
Newman, Mark. Sooper Yooper: Environmental Defender. Heckman, Mark, illus. 2010. 48p. (J). 17.95 *(978-1-933272-26-9(0))* Thunder Bay Pr.
Obregón, José María. Michigan. 2009. (Bilingual Library of the United States of America Ser.). (ENG & SPA.). 32p. (gr. 2-2). 47.90 *(978-1-60853-367-1(0)*, Editorial Buenas Letras) Rosen Publishing Group, Inc., The.
Powell, Jennifer. The Colors of Mackinac Island. Powell, Jennifer, photos by. 2015. (ENG., Illus.). 30p. (J). (gr. 1-2). 10.95 *(978-1-933272-49-8(X))* Thunder Bay Pr.
Smucker, Anna Egan. To Keep the South Manitou Light. 2006. (Great Lakes Books Ser.). (ENG., Illus.). 130p. (gr. 3-7). per. 14.95 *(978-0-8143-3236-8(6)*, P120417) Wayne State Univ. Pr.
Vernick, Shirley. I Love You, Michigan Baby. Bergin, Molly, illus. 2018. (ENG.). 22p. (J). (gr. -1-k). bds. 8.99 *(978-1-946064-96-7(3)*, 806496) Duo Pr. LLC.
Wargin, Kathy-jo. S Is for Sleeping Bear Dunes: A National Lakeshore Alphabet. Frankenhuyzen, Gijsbert van, illus. 2015. (ENG.). 32p. (J). (gr. 2-4). 16.99 *(978-1-58536-917-1(9)*, 203818) Sleeping Bear Pr.
Wells, Sherry A. Father, Ford, $5 a Day: The Mullers from Missouri. Bulla, Randy, illus. 2003. 128p. lib. bdg. 14.00 *(978-0-934981-11-8(6))* Lawells Publishing.

MICHIGAN, LAKE

Crane, Carol. The Christmas Tree Ship. Ellison, Chris, illus. 2011. (ENG.). 32p. (J). (gr. 1-4). 15.95 *(978-1-58536-285-1(9)*, 202096) Sleeping Bear Pr.

MICHIGAN, LAKE—FICTION

Chellis, Marie. The Hayburner, 1 vol. 2010. 60p. pap. 19.95 *(978-1-4512-9053-0(5))* America Star Bks.
Darke, J. A. & Terrell, Brandon. Sasquatch Island. Evans, Neil, illus. 2018. (Spine Shivers Ser.). (ENG.). 128p. (J). (gr. 4-6). lib. bdg. 26.65 *(978-1-4965-6432-0(4)*, 138272, Stone Arch Bks.) Capstone.
Jean. Jean's Story. 2009. 40p. pap. 18.49 *(978-1-4389-4531-6(0))* AuthorHouse.
Prestwood, Donna. Center World. 2006. 120p. per. 10.95 *(978-1-59824-206-5(7))* E-BookTime LLC.

MICKEY MOUSE (FICTITIOUS CHARACTER)—FICTION

Acampora, Courtney. Disney Mickey & Friends: Scaredy-Mouse. Loter, Inc., illus. 2018. (ENG.). 8p. (J). (gr. -1-k). bds. 9.99 *(978-0-7944-4162-3(9)*, Studio Fun International) Printers Row Publishing Group.
Ambrosio, Stefano. Mouse Magic. Pastrovicchio, Lorenzo, illus. 2010. (ENG.). 112p. (J). 24.99 *(978-1-60886-550-5(9))*; Vol. 1. pap. 9.99 *(978-1-60886-541-3(X))* BOOM! Studios.
—Wizards of Mickey - Grand Tournament, Vol. 2. Pastrovicchio, Lorenzo & Magic Eye Studios, illus. 2010. (Wizards of Mickey Ser.). (ENG.). 128p. (J). (gr. 3-6). pap. 9.99 *(978-1-60886-564-2(9))* BOOM! Studios.
Barks, Carl, et al. Walt Disney's Christmas Parade #5. 2008. (Illus.). 80p. pap. 9.50 *(978-1-60360-005-7(1))* Gemstone Publishing, Inc.
—Walt Disney's Comics & Stories #702. 2009. 64p. pap. 7.99 *(978-1-60360-092-7(2))* Gemstone Publishing, Inc.
—Walt Disney's Comics & Stories #704. 2009. 64p. pap. 7.99 *(978-1-60360-094-1(9))* Gemstone Publishing, Inc.
Casolaro, Nancy & Green, Joanna. Meeska Mooska Tales. 2015. (Illus.). (J). *(978-1-4847-2565-8(4))* Disney Publishing Worldwide.
Castellan, Andrea. Mickey Mouse & the Orbiting Nightmare. 2011. (ENG., Illus.). 128p. (J). pap. *(978-1-60886-630-4(0))* BOOM! Studios.
Castellan, Andrea "Casty". Mickey Mouse & the World to Come. Castellan, Andrea "Casty" & Mazzon, Michelle, illus. 2010. (ENG.). 112p. (J). (gr. 3-6). pap. 9.99 *(978-1-60886-562-8(2))* BOOM! Studios.
Clark, John, ed. Mickey Mouse Adventures, Vol. 5. 2005. (ENG., Illus.). 128p. (YA). pap. 7.95 *(978-0-911903-70-6(4)*, 9780911903706) Gemstone Publishing, Inc.
—Mystery of the Old Mansion, Vol. 6. 2005. (ENG., Illus.). 128p. (YA). pap. 7.95 *(978-0-911903-71-3(2)*, 9780911903713) Gemstone Publishing, Inc.
De Maris, Merrill, et al. Mickey Mouse: The Greatest Adventures. 2018. (Walt Disney's Mickey Mouse Ser.: 0). (ENG., Illus.). 304p. 49.99 *(978-1-68396-122-2(6)*, 683122) Fantagraphics Bks.
Disney Book Group Staff & Higginson, Sheila Sweeny. Minnie: Minnie's Valentine. Disney Storybook Artists Staff, illus. 2013. 10p. 5.99 *(978-1-4231-8811-7(X))* Disney Pr.
Disney Books. Haunted Clubhouse. 2010. (ENG., Illus.). 12p. (J). (gr. -1-k). bds. 6.99 *(978-1-4231-2832-8(X)*, Disney Press Books) Disney Publishing Worldwide.
—Mickey Mouse Clubhouse: Mickey's Halloween. 2015. (ENG., Illus.). 10p. (J). (gr. -1-k). bds. 8.99 *(978-1-4847-2096-7(2)*, Disney Press Books) Disney Publishing Worldwide.
—Mickey Saves Santa. 2009. (ENG., Illus.). 24p. (J). (gr. -1-k). pap. 5.99 *(978-1-4231-1846-6(4)*, Disney Press Books) Disney Publishing Worldwide.
—Mickey's Halloween Treat. 2008. (ENG., Illus.). 16p. (J). (gr. -1-k). pap. 4.99 *(978-1-4231-0983-9(X)*, Disney Press Books) Disney Publishing Worldwide.
Disney Classic Story Collection: 3 Movie Storybooks. 2017. *(978-1-368-00723-8(6))* Disney Publishing Worldwide.
Disney Mickey Mouse Clubhouse, ed. Clubhouse ABCs: Mickey Mouse Clubhouse. 2009. (ENG.). 24p. 7.99 *(978-1-59069-771-9(5))* Studio Mouse LLC.
Disney Press Staff, ed. Mickey's New Friend. 2011. (Illus.). 32p. (J). *(978-1-4231-4585-1(2))* Disney Pr.
Flood, Heather. Mousey Mousey & the Witches' Revenge. 2012. 220p. pap. *(978-1-909359-03-1(3))* My Voice Publishing.
Galvin, Laura Gates. Mickey Mouse Clubhouse Fun with Numbers & Shapes. 2008. (ENG.). 20p. (J). (gr. -1-3). 9.99 *(978-1-59069-655-2(7))* Studio Mouse LLC.
—Mickey Mouse Clubhouse Teamwork: Let's Do It Together. 2008. (ENG.). 40p. (J). (gr. -1). 12.99 *(978-1-59069-738-2(3))* Studio Mouse LLC.
—Musical Fun: Colors & Patterns. Williams, Tracee, ed. 2011. (Carry a Tune Ser.). (ENG., Illus.). 24p. (J). (gr. -1-1). 4.99 *(978-1-60727-305-9(5))* Studio Mouse LLC.
Gilbert, Michael T., et al. Mickey Mouse Adventures, Vol. 8. Clark, John, ed. 2006. (ENG., Illus.). 128p. (YA). pap. 7.95 *(978-1-888472-09-7(X)*, 9781888472097) Gemstone Publishing, Inc.
—Walt Disney's Comics & Stories #693. Clark, John, ed. 2008. (ENG., Illus.). 64p. pap. 7.99 *(978-1-60360-038-5(8)*, 9781603600385) Gemstone Publishing, Inc.
Gottfredson, Floyd. Race to Death Valley, Vol. 1. Gerstein, David & Groth, Gary, eds. 2011. (Walt Disney's Mickey Mouse Ser.: 0). (ENG., Illus.). 320p. 29.99 *(978-1-60699-441-2(7)*, 699441) Fantagraphics Bks.
Gottfredson, Floyd, et al. Walt Disney's Comics & Stories #700. 2008. 80p. pap. 9.99 *(978-1-60360-057-6(4))* Gemstone Publishing, Inc.
Hinkler Studios Staff., ed. Mickey Mouse Clubhouse: Preschool Skills. 2011. 12p. 9.99 *(978-1-74183-869-5(X))* Hinkler Bks. Pty, Ltd. AUS. Dist: Ideals Pubns.
Jippes, Daan, et al. Walt Disney's Comics & Stories #703. 2009. 64p. pap. 7.99 *(978-1-60360-093-4(0))* Gemstone Publishing, Inc.
Keast, Jennifer H. Mickey Mouse Clubhouse (Giant First Play-a-Sound) 2010. 10p. (J). bds. 17.98 *(978-1-60553-545-6(1))* Phoenix International Publications, Inc.
Korhonen, Kari, et al. Walt Disney's Comics & Stories #705. 2009. 64p. pap. 7.99 *(978-1-60360-095-8(7))* Gemstone Publishing, Inc.
Kruse, Jan, et al. Walt Disney's Spring Fever Volume 3. 2009. 80p. pap. 9.99 *(978-1-60360-097-2(3))* Gemstone Publishing, Inc.
Kurchinski, Alessandra. Disney Story. 2010. 36p. pap. 17.30 *(978-0-557-25447-7(7))* Lulu Pr., Inc.
Marsoli, Lisa Ann. Minnierella. 2013. (Mickey & Friends World of Reading Ser.). (J). lib. bdg. 13.55 *(978-0-606-34103-5(X))* Turtleback.
Marsoli, Lisa Ann & Mendoza, Ashley. Mickey Mouse Clubhouse: Minnie-Rella. Loter, Inc., illus. 2018. (World of Reading Level 1 Ser.). (ENG.). 32p. (J). (gr. -1-3). lib. bdg. 31.36 *(978-1-5321-4191-1(2)*, 28533) Spotlight.
McGreal, Pat, et al. Walt Disney's Comics & Stories #701. 2009. 64p. pap. 7.99 *(978-1-60360-091-0(4))* Gemstone Publishing, Inc.
Parragon Staff. Mickey Mouse: Adventure Tales & Stories. 2010. (Disney Diecut Classics). (Illus.). 72p. (J). (gr. -1-1). *(978-1-4075-8937-4(7))* Parragon, Inc.
PI Kids. Disney: Mickey Mouse Clubhouse Ask a Silly Question Sound Book. 2010. (ENG.). 6p. (J). bds. 7.99 *(978-1-60553-037-6(9)*, 3954, PI Kids) Phoenix International Publications, Inc.
PI, Kids. Mickey Mouse Flashlight Adventure O/P. 2011. (ENG.). 14p. (J). 8.45 net. *(978-1-4508-0564-3(7))* Phoenix International Publications, Inc.
Posner-Sanchez, Andrea. Shop with Minnie (Disney Junior: Mickey Mouse Clubhouse) RH Disney, illus. 2012. (Little Golden Book Ser.). (ENG.). 24p. (J). (gr. k-k). 4.99 *(978-0-7364-3031-9(8)*, Golden/Disney) Random Hse. Children's Bks.
Publications International Ltd. Staff. Little Sound Mickey Mouse Club. 2007. 10p. (J). 10.98 *(978-1-4127-6711-8(3))* Phoenix International Publications, Inc.
—Mickey Mouse Club First Look & Find. 2008. 18p. (J). bds. 9.98 *(978-1-4127-7455-0(1))* Phoenix International Publications, Inc.
—Mickey Mouse Club House Little Pop up Sd. 2008. 8p. (J). 10.50 *(978-1-4127-8869-4(2))* Phoenix International Publications, Inc.
Publications International Ltd. Staff, ed. Disney Mickey Mouse Clubhouse: Mickey's Adventure. 2010. (ENG.). 14p. (J). bds. 21.99 *(978-1-4127-4599-4(3)*, 13903) Phoenix International Publications, Inc.
—Disney(r) Mickey Mouse ClubhouseCalling All Pals. 2015. 14p. (J). bds. *(978-1-4508-9352-7(X)*, 145089352X) Publications International, Ltd.
—Goof's Adventure. 2010. 24p. (J). 19.98 *(978-1-4127-5367-8(8)*, PIL Kids) Publications International, Ltd.
—Little Lift & Listen Sound Mickey Mouse Clubhouse. 2007. (J). 10.98 *(978-1-4127-8457-3(3))* Phoenix International Publications, Inc.
—Look & Find Activity Pad Mickey Mouse. 2011. 64p. (J). 10.98 *(978-1-4508-0733-3(X))* Publications International, Ltd.
—Mickey Mouse Clubhouse. 2010. 128p. (J). pap. 12.98 *(978-1-60553-129-8(4)*, PIL Kids) Publications International, Ltd.
—Mickey Mouse Clubhouse: Hot Dog! Sing Along! 2010. 10p. (J). bds. 14.98 *(978-1-60553-047-5(6))* Publications International, Ltd.
—Mickey Mouse Clubhouse: Las canciones de piano de Mickey. 2011. 24p. (J). 17.98 *(978-1-4508-1616-8(9))* Publications International, Ltd.
—Mickey Mouse Clubhouse: Lights on, Lights Off! 2011. 12p. (J). (gr. k-3). bds. 10.99 *(978-1-4508-0763-0(1)*, 1450807631) Phoenix International Publications, Inc.
—Mickey Mouse Clubhouse: Mickey & Friends (Look & Find) 2010. 24p. (J). 7.98 *(978-1-60553-747-4(0))* Publications International, Ltd.
—Mickey Mouse Clubhouse: Telling Time with Mickey. 2011. 12p. (J). bds. 13.98 *(978-1-4508-0914-6(6))* Publications International, Ltd.
—Mickey Mouse Clubhouse - Who's Not Sleepy? 2011. 12p. (J). bds. *(978-1-4508-0398-4(9))* Publications International, Ltd.
—Mickey Mouse Clubhouse (book Block) 2010. (J). 10.98 *(978-1-4508-0673-2(2))* Publications International, Ltd.
—Mickey Mouse Clubhouse: Colors: Sing & Learn. 2010. 12p. (J). bds. 10.98 *(978-1-4127-1729-8(9))* Publications International, Ltd.
—Mickey Mouse Clubhouse: Mickey's Surprise! 2013. 14p. (J). (gr. k-3). bds. 16.99 *(978-1-4508-2188-9(X)*, 87b7723a-b11c-4ce1-8b21-522e3e8ff7e2) Phoenix International Publications, Inc.
—Mickey Mouse Clubhouse: Sing-along Christmas Songs: Holiday Play-a-Song Book. 2010. 10p. (J). bds. 12.98 *(978-1-4127-7862-6(X))* Publications International, Ltd.
—Mickey Mouse Clubhouse Super Look & Find Activity Pad with Stickers. 2010. 64p. (J). *(978-1-4508-0732-6(1)*, 1450807321) Phoenix International Publications, Inc.
—Mickey Mouse Clubhouse Super Look & Find Activity Pad with Stickers. 2011. 64p. (J). 10.98 *(978-1-4508-1887-2(0))* Publications International, Ltd.
—Mickey's Piano Songs Play & Learn. 2010. 24p. (J). 12.98 *(978-1-4508-0114-0(5))* Phoenix International Publications, Inc.
—Who's Not Sleepy? 2010. 18p. (J). bds. 10.98 *(978-1-60553-463-3(3)*, PIL Kids) Publications International, Ltd.
Reader's Digest Staff. Mickey Mouse Clubhouse Gift Set. 2012. (ENG.). 64p. (J). 39.98 *(978-0-7944-2669-9(7))* Reader's Digest Assn., Inc., The.
Ring, Susan. Pete's Surprise. 2009. (ENG.). 24p. (J). pap. 3.99 *(978-1-4231-1827-5(8))* Disney Pr.
Ritchey, Kate. A Perfect Picnic. 2013. (Mickey & Friends World of Reading Ser.). (J). lib. bdg. 13.55 *(978-0-606-31753-5(8))* Turtleback.
Silver Dolphin en Español Editors, creator. Mickey Mouse: Tesoros para Llevar: Una Coleccion de Cuentos Adaptada de los Dibujos Animados Clasicos de Mickey. 2006. (Tesoros para Llevar Ser.). (Illus.). 24p. (J). (gr. -1-k). bds. *(978-970-718-357-5(8)*, Silver Dolphin en Español) Advanced Marketing, S. de R. L. de C. V.
Stoner, Sherri. Gone Fishing! (Disney Junior: Mickey & the Roadster Racers) Golden Books, illus. 2018. (Little Golden Book Ser.). (ENG.). 24p. (J). (-k). 4.99 *(978-0-7364-3844-5(0)*, Golden/Disney) Random Hse. Children's Bks.
Werner, Jane. Mickey Mouse & His Spaceship (Disney: Mickey Mouse) RH Disney, illus. 2016. (Little Golden Book Ser.).

(ENG.). 24p. (J). (-k). 5.99 (978-0-7364-3633-5(2), Golden/Disney) Random Hse. Children's Bks.

MICROBES

see Bacteriology; Microorganisms; Viruses

MICROBIOLOGY

see also Bacteriology; Microorganisms; Microscopes

Alexander, Lori. All in a Drop: How Antony Van Leeuwenhoek Discovered an Invisible World. Mildenberger, Vivien, illus. 2019. (ENG.). 96p. (J). (gr. 3-7). 17.99 (978-1-328-88420-6(1), 1698170, Clarion Bks.) HarperCollins Pubs.

Alphin, Elaine Marie. Germ Hunter: A Story about Louis Pasteur. Verstraete, Elaine, illus. 2003. (Creative Minds Biographies Ser.). (ENG.). 64p. (J). (gr. 4-8). per. 9.99 (978-0-87614-929-4(8), 136cda8a-5a1e-4dc9-9e0b-6b7431df4759) Lerner Publishing Group.

Bacteria up Close. 2013. (Under the Microscope Ser.). 32p. (J). (gr. 4-6). pap. 70.20 (978-1-4339-8336-8(2)) Stevens, Gareth Publishing LLLP.

Basher, Simon & Green, Dan. Basher Science: Microbiology. Basher, Simon, illus. 2015. (Basher Science Ser.). (ENG., Illus.). 128p. (J). (gr. 5-9). pap. 9.99 (978-0-7534-7194-4(9), 900146975, Kingfisher) Roaring Brook Pr.

Ben-Barak, Idan. Do Not Lick This Book. Frost, Julian, illus. 2018. (ENG.). 40p. (J). 18.99 (978-1-250-17536-6(4), 900189389) Roaring Brook Pr.

Bozzone, Donna M. Understanding Microbes, 1 vol. 2018. (Heredity & Genetics Ser.). (ENG.). 80p. (gr. 8-8). 37.60 (978-0-7660-9944-9(X), e4c46767-d273-4a8d-bdac-65b256f94f5d) Enslow Publishing, LLC.

Crewe, Sabrina. In Rivers, Lakes, & Ponds. 2010. (Under the Microscope Ser.). 32p. (gr. 2-4). 30.00 (978-1-60413-826-9(2), Chelsea Clubhse.) Infobase Holdings, Inc.

Davies, Nicola. Tiny Creatures: The World of Microbes. Sutton, Emily, illus. 2016. (Our Natural World Ser.). (ENG.). 40p. (J). (gr. k-3). pap. 7.99 (978-0-7636-8904-9(1)) Candlewick Pr.

de la Bedoyere, Camille. Micro Monsters: Activate Augmented Reality Minibeasts! 2018. (Y Ser.). (ENG., Illus.). 32p. (J). (gr. 3-7). 14.95 (978-1-78312-256-1(0)) Carlton Kids GBR. Dist: Two Rivers Distribution.

D'yans, Masha. A Garden in Your Belly: Meet the Microbes in Your Gut. D'yans, Masha, illus. 2020. (ENG., Illus.). 32p. (J). (gr. 2-5). 19.99 (978-1-5415-7840-1(6), e1662b1e-07ea-4c25-8740-dc168a90bdca, Millbrook Pr.) Lerner Publishing Group.

Eamer, Claire. Inside Your Insides: A Guide to the Microbes That Call You Home. Tremblay, Marie-Ève & Tremblay, Marie-Ève, illus. 2016. (ENG.). 36p. (J). (gr. 3-7). 17.95 (978-1-77138-332-5(1)) Kids Can Pr., Ltd. CAN. Dist: Hachette Bk. Group.

EBOLA & MARBURG VIRUS, 2ND EDITION. 2nd rev. ed. 2010. (ENG., Illus.). 104p. (gr. 9). 34.95 (978-1-60413-252-6(3), P179257, Facts On File) Infobase Holdings, Inc.

Hirsch, Rebecca E. The Human Microbiome: The Germs That Keep You Healthy. 2016. (ENG., Illus.). 112p. (YA). (gr. 6-12). 34.65 (978-1-4677-8568-6(7), d9bd6f34-f380-488f-8035-02d32ea9980f); E-Book 51.99 (978-1-5124-1140-9(X)) Lerner Publishing Group. (Twenty-First Century Bks.).

Holewa, Lisa. Using Marine Microbes. rev. ed. 2018. (Smithsonian: Informational Text Ser.). (ENG., Illus.). 32p. (J). (gr. 4-8). pap. 11.99 (978-1-4938-6720-2(2)) Teacher Created Materials, Inc.

Hollar, Sherman. A Closer Look at Biology, Microbiology, & the Cell, 1 vol. 2011. (Introduction to Biology Ser.). (ENG.). 96p. (J). (gr. 8-8). lib. bdg. 35.29 (978-1-61530-514-8(9), 42f82a53-7f89-4793-9ed8-52e5dc589da3) Rosen Publishing Group, Inc., The.

Kornberg, Arthur. Germ Stories. Alaniz, Adam, illus. Kolter, Roberto, photos by. 2007. (ENG.). 84p. (J). (gr. 3-7). 36.00 (978-1-891389-51-1(3)) Univ. Science Bks.

Levy, Janey. Tiny Bugs up Close, 1 vol. 2013. (Under the Microscope Ser.). (ENG.). 32p. (J). (gr. 4-5). pap. 12.70 (978-1-4339-8351-1(6), 39872d3f-4789-4ee7-a378-138c5042876d); lib. bdg. 29.27 (978-1-4339-8350-4(8), f42c7b73-9c1c-4e6d-b0a2-864358533929) Stevens, Gareth Publishing LLLP.

Lew, Kristi. The Exterminator: Stopping the World's Most Infectious Diseases, 1 vol. 2009. (Current Science Ser.). (ENG.). 48p. (YA). (gr. 4-6). lib. bdg. 33.67 (978-1-4339-2061-5(1), 556ed92a-d417-45bf-aa84-2e3d5b3d47df) Stevens, Gareth Publishing LLLP.

Marsico, Katie. Look Out for Germs! Bane, Jeff, illus. 2019. (My Early Library: My Healthy Habits Ser.). (ENG.). 24p. (J). (gr. k-1). lib. bdg. 30.64 (978-1-5341-4281-7(9), 212576) Cherry Lake Publishing.

—Lookout for Germs! Bane, Jeff, illus. 2019. (My Early Library: My Healthy Habits Ser.). (ENG.). 24p. (J). (gr. k-1). pap. 12.79 (978-1-5341-3937-4(0), 212577) Cherry Lake Publishing.

Mitchell, Melanie. Killing Germs. 2005. (Pull Ahead Bks.). (Illus.). 32p. (J). (gr. -1-3). lib. bdg. 22.60 (978-0-8225-2450-2(3), Lerner Pubns.) Lerner Publishing Group.

—Matar los Gérmenes. Aguirre, Barbara & Fitzpatrick, Julia, trs. 2005. (Libros para Avanzar-La Salud (Pull Ahead Books-Health) Ser.). (SPA., Illus.). 32p. (gr. k-3). lib. bdg. 22.60 (978-0-8225-3144-9(5), Ediciones Lerner) Lerner Publishing Group.

Orr, Tamra. Public Health Microbiologist. 2007. (21st Century Skills Library: Cool Science Careers Ser.). (ENG.). 32p. (gr. 4-8). pap. 14.21 (978-1-60279-082-7(5), 200643) Cherry Lake Publishing.

Orr, Tamra B. Public Health Microbiologist. 2007. (21st Century Skills Library: Cool Science Careers Ser.). (ENG., Illus.). 32p. (gr. 4-8). lib. bdg. 32.07 (978-1-60279-053-7(1), 200015) Cherry Lake Publishing.

Owen, Ruth. Creepy Backyard Invaders. 2011. (Up Close & Gross Ser.). 24p. (YA). (gr. 2-5). lib. bdg. 26.99 (978-1-61772-125-0(5)) Bearport Publishing Co., Inc.

—Icky House Invaders. 2011. (Up Close & Gross Ser.). 24p. (YA). (gr. 2-5). lib. bdg. 26.99 (978-1-61772-124-3(7)) Bearport Publishing Co., Inc.

Rainis, Kenneth G. Cell & Microbe Science Fair Projects, Using the Scientific Method, 1 vol. rev. exp. ed. 2010. (Biology Science Projects Using the Scientific Method Ser.). (ENG., Illus.). 160p. (gr. 5-6). 38.60 (978-0-7660-3420-4(8), e757c3ee-9023-4b9c-a039-a9b382e225c9) Enslow Publishing, LLC.

Roza, Greg. Bacteria up Close, 1 vol. 2013. (Under the Microscope Ser.). (ENG.). 32p. (J). (gr. 4-5). 29.27 (978-1-4339-8334-4(6), bc32d779-dbe7-494e-b355-389facda22c6); pap. 12.70 (978-1-4339-8335-1(4), f33a0052-bf96-42ab-874c-1851f1e5df4c) Stevens, Gareth Publishing LLLP.

—Deadly Bacteria, 1 vol. 2011. (Small but Deadly Ser.). (ENG., Illus.). 24p. (J). (gr. 2-3). pap. 9.15 (978-1-4339-5728-4(0), 11261e57-1367-4592-a840-c434145a7423); lib. bdg. 25.27 (978-1-4339-5726-0(4), 8dd7c5d9-c4c1-43be-a4a7-90853f8403df) Stevens, Gareth Publishing LLLP. (Gareth Stevens Learning Library).

Salt, Zelda. Be a Microbiologist, 1 vol. 2018. (Be a Scientist! Ser.). (ENG.). 32p. (gr. 3-4). 28.27 (978-1-5382-2998-9(6), ea9c305a-b697-49e4-9819-dace66b7239f) Stevens, Gareth Publishing LLLP.

Sherman, Josepha. The War Against Germs. 2009. (Germs: the Library of Disease-Causing Organisms Ser.). 48p. (gr. 5-5). 53.00 (978-1-61512-718-4(6)) Rosen Publishing Group, Inc., The.

Stefoff, Rebecca. The Moneran Kingdom, 1 vol. 2009. (Family Trees Ser.). (ENG.). 96p. (gr. 6-6). lib. bdg. 36.93 (978-0-7614-3076-6(8), 94de301b-b05a-49ee-bb1c-62a6f43f03d0) Cavendish Square Publishing LLC.

Swanson, Jennifer. Uninvited Guests: Invisible Creatures Lurking in Your Home. 2011. (Tiny Creepy Creatures Ser.). (ENG.). 32p. (gr. 3-4). pap. 47.70 (978-1-4296-7276-4(5), Capstone Pr.) Capstone.

Taylor-Butler, Christine. Tiny Life in the Air. 2005. (Rookie Read-About Science Ser.). (ENG., Illus.). 32p. (J). (gr. 1-2). lib. bdg. 20.50 (978-0-516-25273-5(9), Children's Pr.) Scholastic Library Publishing.

Tiny Bugs up Close. 2013. (Under the Microscope Ser.). 32p. (J). (gr. 4-6). pap. 70.20 (978-1-4339-8352-8(4)) Stevens, Gareth Publishing LLLP.

Trumbauer, Lisa. Tiny Life in Your Home. 2005. (Rookie Read-About Science Ser.). (ENG., Illus.). 32p. (J). (gr. 1-2). lib. bdg. 20.50 (978-0-516-25274-2(7), Children's Pr.) Scholastic Library Publishing.

Wanjie, Anne, ed. The Basics of Microbes, 1 vol. 2013. (Core Concepts Ser.). (ENG., Illus.). 96p. (YA). (gr. 7-7). lib. bdg. 39.77 (978-1-4777-0550-6(3), 420ff027-0a94-4d23-9e33-a43a0db4e4c3) Rosen Publishing Group, Inc., The.

MICROCOMPUTERS

Graham, Ian. Great Electronic Gadget Designs 1900 - Today. 2015. (Iconic Designs Ser.). (ENG., Illus.). 48p. (J). (gr. 4-6). pap. 8.99 (978-1-4846-2623-8(0), 130092, Heinemann) Capstone.

Liukas, Linda. Hello Ruby: Journey Inside the Computer. 2017. (Hello Ruby Ser.: 2). (ENG., Illus.). 96p. (J). 18.99 (978-1-250-06532-2(1), 900144682) Feiwel & Friends.

Martin, Bobi. What Tasks Can Computers Perform? 2017. (Let's Find Out! Computer Science Ser.). (Illus.). 32p. (J). (gr. 6-10). 77.40 (978-1-5383-0037-4(0), Britannica Educational Publishing) Rosen Publishing Group, Inc., The.

Rooney, Anne. Communicate Online. 2004. (QEB Learn Computing Ser.). (Illus.). 32p. (J). lib. bdg. 18.95 (978-1-59566-043-5(7)) QEB Publishing Inc.

—Fact Factory. 2004. (QEB Learn Computing Ser.). (Illus.). 32p. (J). lib. bdg. 18.95 (978-1-59566-042-8(9)) QEB Publishing Inc.

Scrivano, Álvaro. Coding with Hopscotch. Downing, Sue, illus. 2019. (Ready, Set, Code! Ser.). (ENG.). 32p. (J). (gr. 2-5). 29.32 (978-1-5415-3874-0(9), 4a16a014-3581-4b1b-90bf-769e4ba6d7e2, Lerner Pubns.) Lerner Publishing Group.

Severance, Charles R. & Fontichiaro, Kristin. Raspberry Pi. 2013. (21st Century Skills Innovation Library: Makers As Innovators Ser.). (ENG., Illus.). 32p. (J). (gr. 4-8). 32.07 (978-1-62431-139-0(3), 202876); pap. 14.21 (978-1-62431-271-7(3), 202878) Cherry Lake Publishing.

Weber, Sandra. The Personal Computer. 2003. (Transforming Power of Technology Ser.). (ENG., Illus.). 112p. (gr. 9-13). 30.00 (978-0-7910-7450-3(1), P113839, Facts On File) Infobase Holdings, Inc.

Wentk, Richard. Getting Started with Raspberry Pi. 2016. (Illus.). iv, 124p. (J). (978-1-5182-3424-8(0)) Wiley, John & Sons, Inc.

MICROCOMPUTERS—MAINTENANCE AND REPAIR

Machajewski, David. Handling Hardware Problems, 1 vol. 2018. (Tech Troubleshooters Ser.). (ENG.). 24p. (gr. 3-3). 25.27 (978-1-5383-2959-7(X), 278c0ae0-223d-4846-ac5c-16d06b55105d, PowerKids Pr.) Rosen Publishing Group, Inc., The.

MICROCOMPUTERS—PROGRAMMING

Grant, Rachel. Coding Games from Scratch: 4D an Augmented Reading Experience. 2018. (Code It Yourself 4D Ser.). (ENG., Illus.). 48p. (J). (gr. 3-5). lib. bdg. 33.99 (978-1-5157-6658-2(6), 135227, Capstone Pr.) Capstone.

Harris, Patricia. Understanding Coding with Hopscotch, 1 vol., 1. 2015. (Spotlight on Kids Can Code Ser.). (ENG., Illus.). 24p. (J). (gr. 4-5). pap. 12.75 (978-1-5081-4459-5(1), b596a44e-e949-4c6f-bdcd-29982262aea2, PowerKids Pr.) Rosen Publishing Group, Inc., The.

—Understanding Coding with Raspberry Pi(tm), 1 vol., 1. 2015. (Spotlight on Kids Can Code Ser.). (ENG., Illus.). 24p. (J). (gr. 4-5). pap. 12.75 (978-1-5081-4478-6(8), 3b972968-cb5c-4fa1-856f-83efddd1c517, PowerKids Pr.) Rosen Publishing Group, Inc., The.

—Understanding Coding with Scratch, 1 vol., 1. 2015. (Spotlight on Kids Can Code Ser.). (ENG., Illus.). 24p. (J). (gr. 4-5). pap. 12.75 (978-1-5081-4482-3(6), ed87fb13-2bc4-43a6-a699-478a8e7b0c85, PowerKids Pr.) Rosen Publishing Group, Inc., The.

Sweigart, Al. Scratch Programming Playground: Learn to Program by Making Cool Games. 2016. (Illus.). 288p. (J). (gr. 5). pap. 24.95 (978-1-59327-762-8(8)) No Starch Pr., Inc.

Woodcock, Jon & Setford, Steve. DK Workbooks: Coding in Scratch: Projects Workbook: Make Cool Art, Interactive Images, & Zany Music. 2016. (DK Workbooks Ser.). (ENG.). 40p. (J). (gr. 1-4). pap. 6.99 (978-1-4654-4402-8(5), DK Children) Dorling Kindersley Publishing, Inc.

MICROGRAPHIC ANALYSIS

see Microscopes

MICRONESIA

Department of Chamorro Affairs, Division of Research, Publication and Training Staff. I Manfayi Vol. I: Who's Who in Chamorro History. (Hale'-ta Ser.). (Illus.). 250p. (J). (gr. 6-7). pap. 30.00 (978-1-883488-04-8(4)) Dept. of Chamorro Affairs.

—I Manfayi Vol. II: Who's Who in Chamorro History. Date not set. (Illus.). 250p. (J). (gr. 6-7). pap. 25.00 (978-1-883488-06-2(0)) Dept. of Chamorro Affairs.

Millhoff, Brian L. The Micronesian Coloring Book. 2nd l.t. ed. 2006. (Illus.). 68p. (J). per. 6.50 net. (978-0-9790111-0-8(8)) M-m-mauleg Publishing.

MICROORGANISMS

see also Bacteriology; Microbiology; Microscopes; Protozoa; Viruses

Alkire, Jessie. Super Gross Germ Projects. 2018. (Super Simple Super Gross Science Ser.). (ENG., Illus.). 32p. (J). (gr. k-4). lib. bdg. 34.21 (978-1-5321-1731-2(0), 30750, Super SandCastle) ABDO Publishing Co.

Anderson, Rodney P. The Invisible ABCs: Exploring the World of Microbes, 1 vol. 2006. (ASM Bks.). (ENG., Illus.). 64p. (gr. 3-7). 20.95 (978-1-55581-386-4(0), 5b4e9371-e808-4484-9399-b0eef56651c5) ASM Pr.

Ben-Barak, Idan. Do Not Lick This Book. Frost, Julian, illus. 2018. (ENG.). 40p. (J). 18.99 (978-1-250-17536-6(4), 900189389) Roaring Brook Pr.

Benchmark Education Company, LLC Staff, compiled by. Organisms: Past & Present. 2005. (English Explorers Ser.). (J). spiral bd. 265.00 (978-1-4108-5758-3(1)) Benchmark Education Co.

—Organisms: Theme Set. 2006. (J). 303.00 (978-1-4108-7122-0(3)) Benchmark Education Co.

—Organisms Past & Present. 2006. spiral bd. 330.00 (978-1-4108-7016-2(2)) Benchmark Education Co.

Bozzone, Donna M. Understanding Microbes, 1 vol. 2018. (Heredity & Genetics Ser.). (ENG.). 80p. (gr. 8-8). 37.60 (978-0-7660-9944-9(X), e4c46767-d273-4a8d-bdac-65b256f94f5d) Enslow Publishing, LLC.

Brown Bear Books. Plants & Microorganisms. 2011. (Introducing Biology Ser.). (ENG.). 64p. (J). (gr. 8-11). lib. bdg. 39.95 (978-1-936333-02-8(3), 16513) Brown Bear Bks.

Burillo-Kirch, Christine. Microbes: Discover an Unseen World. Casteel, Tom, illus. 2015. (Build It Yourself Ser.). (ENG.). 128p. (J). (gr. 3-7). 22.95 (978-1-61930-306-5(X), 2427b64f-6386-403c-8337-946ac4c0f864) Nomad Pr.

Crewe, Sabrina. In the Backyard. 2010. (Under the Microscope Ser.). 32p. (gr. 2-4). 30.00 (978-1-60413-822-1(X), Chelsea Clubhse.) Infobase Holdings, Inc.

—In the Home. 2010. (Under the Microscope Ser.). 32p. (gr. 2-4). 30.00 (978-1-60413-823-8(8), Chelsea Clubhse.) Infobase Holdings, Inc.

—In Your Body. 2010. (Under the Microscope Ser.). 32p. (gr. 2-4). 30.00 (978-1-60413-825-2(4), Chelsea Clubhse.) Infobase Holdings, Inc.

Davies, Nicola. Tiny Creatures: The World of Microbes. Sutton, Emily, illus. 2016. (Our Natural World Ser.). (ENG.). 40p. (J). (gr. k-3). pap. 7.99 (978-0-7636-8904-9(1)) Candlewick Pr.

Day, Trevor. Body Bugs! [Scholastic]: Uninvited Guests on Your Body. 2010. (Extreme! Ser.). 32p. pap. 0.65 (978-1-4296-4993-3(3), Capstone Pr.) Capstone.

de la Bedoyere, Camille. Micro Monsters: Activate Augmented Reality Minibeasts! 2018. (Y Ser.). (ENG., Illus.). 32p. (J). (gr. 3-7). 14.95 (978-1-78312-256-1(0)) Carlton Kids GBR. Dist: Two Rivers Distribution.

Eamer, Claire. Inside Your Insides: A Guide to the Microbes That Call You Home. Tremblay, Marie-Ève & Tremblay, Marie-Ève, illus. 2016. (ENG.). 36p. (J). (gr. 3-7). 17.95 (978-1-77138-332-5(1)) Kids Can Pr., Ltd. CAN. Dist: Hachette Bk. Group.

Favor, Lesli J. Eukaryotic & Prokaryotic Cell Structures: Understanding Cells with & Without a Nucleus. 2009. (Library of Cells Ser.). 48p. (gr. 5-5). 53.00 (978-1-60853-571-2(1)) Rosen Publishing Group, Inc., The.

Gardy, Jennifer. It's Catching: The Infectious World of Germs & Microbes. Holinaty, Josh, illus. 2014. (ENG.). 64p. (J). (gr. 3-7). pap. 13.95 (978-1-77147-053-7(4), Owlkids) Owlkids Bks. Inc. CAN. Dist: Publishers Group West (PGW).

Germ Warfare: Individual Title Six-Packs. (Bookweb Ser.). 32p. (gr. 5-18). 34.00 (978-0-7635-3798-2(5)) Rigby Education.

Germs: Disease Causing Organisms, 12 vols. 2016. (Germs: Disease-Causing Organisms Ser.). 48p. (gr. 5-5). (ENG.). 200.82 (978-1-4994-3839-0(7), 5d8f5483-04d5-47de-87b3-9893f621d06f); pap. 70.50 (978-1-4777-8982-7(0)) Rosen Publishing Group, Inc., The. (Rosen Central).

Germs: The Library of Disease-Causing Organisms, 8 vols., Vol. 4. 2003. (Germs: the Library of Disease-Causing Organisms Ser.). (ENG., Illus.). 48p. (gr. 5-5). lib. bdg. 137.88 (978-1-4042-0143-9(2), 09c94a24-2497-4e5f-8b36-b0aa6530a889) Rosen Publishing Group, Inc., The.

Gibson, Brylee. Unseen by the Eye. 2007. (Connectors Ser.). (gr. 2-5). pap. (978-1-877453-00-7(5)) Global Education Systems Ltd.

Graham, Ian. Microscopic Scary Creatures. 2009. (Scary Creatures Ser.). (ENG., Illus.). 32p. (J). (gr. 3-5). 27.00 (978-0-531-21673-6(X), Children's Pr.) Scholastic Library Publishing.

Green, Jen. Inside Animals, 1 vol. 2011. (Invisible Worlds Ser.). (ENG.). 48p. (gr. 4-4). 31.21 (978-0-7614-4195-3(6), b441287e-76af-48d8-82ac-6501f1bfad70) Cavendish Square Publishing LLC.

Hand, Carol. The Gross Science of Germs All Around You, 1 vol. 2018. (Way Gross Science Ser.). (ENG.). 48p. (gr. 5-5). 33.47 (978-1-5081-8168-2(3), ac8952df-5b68-4a53-aacb-a3245233163a, Rosen Reference) Rosen Publishing Group, Inc., The.

Harrison, Paul. Micro Bugs. (Up Close Ser.). 24p. (gr. 3-3). 2009. 47.90 (978-1-60854-696-1(9)) 2006. (ENG., Illus.). (J). lib. bdg. 28.93 (978-1-4042-3760-5(7), 64d83584-7064-42ec-8555-8bf189856047) Rosen Publishing Group, Inc., The. (PowerKids Pr.).

Holt, Rinehart and Winston Staff. Holt Science & Technology Chapter 11: Life Science: Protists & Fungi. 5th ed. 2004. (Illus.). pap. 12.86 (978-0-03-030211-4(0)) Holt McDougal.

—Microorganisms, Fungi, & Plants. 5th ed. 2003. (Holt Science & Technology [Short Course] Ser.: Vol. A). (ENG.). 192p. (gr. 6-8). stu. ed. 28.60 (978-0-03-025533-5(3)) Houghton Mifflin Harcourt Publishing Co.

Hyde, Natalie. Micro Life in Soil. 2010. (Everybody Digs Soil Ser.). (ENG., Illus.). 32p. (J). (gr. 3-4). pap. (978-0-7787-5415-2(4)); lib. bdg. (978-0-7787-5402-2(2)) Crabtree Publishing Co.

Kroll, Jennifer. Mighty Macros: Little Things, Big Results, 1 vol. 2nd rev. ed. 2013. (TIME for KIDS(r): Informational Text Ser.). (ENG.). 64p. (gr. 4-8). pap. 14.99 (978-1-4333-4948-5(5)) Teacher Created Materials, Inc.

Levy, Janey. The World of Microbes: Bacteria, Viruses, & Other Microorganisms, 1 vol. 2010. (Understanding Genetics Ser.). (ENG.). 80p. (YA). (gr. 7-8). lib. bdg. 38.47 (978-1-4358-9536-2(3), d1ef1f5f-7e9e-40c5-a0a0-0bfab7d8ea8a) Rosen Publishing Group, Inc., The.

Lew, Kristi. The Exterminator: Wiping Out the World's Most Infectious Diseases. 2009. (Current Science Ser.). (ENG.). 48p. (J). (gr. 4-6). pap. 8.95 (978-1-4339-2132-2(4), Gareth Stevens Learning Library) Stevens, Gareth Publishing LLLP.

—The Exterminator: Stopping the World's Most Infectious Diseases, 1 vol. 2009. (Current Science Ser.). (ENG.). 48p. (YA). (gr. 4-6). lib. bdg. 33.67 (978-1-4339-2061-5(1), 556ed92a-d417-45bf-aa84-2e3d5b3d47df) Stevens, Gareth Publishing LLLP.

Lindström, Karin. Tiny Life on Plants. (Rookie Read-About Science Ser.). (ENG., Illus.). 32p. (J). (gr. 1-2). 2006. per. 4.95 (978-0-516-25478-4(2)) 2005. lib. bdg. 20.50 (978-0-516-25297-1(6)) Scholastic Library Publishing. (Children's Pr.).

Markovics, Joyce L. Tiny Invaders! Deadly Microorganisms, 1 vol. 2013. (Nature's Invaders Ser.). (ENG.). 32p. (J). (gr. 3-9). lib. bdg. 28.65 (978-1-4765-0142-0(4), 122219, Capstone Pr.) Capstone.

May, Suellen. Invasive Microbes. 2007. (Invasive Species Ser.). (ENG., Illus.). 100p. (gr. 6-12). lib. bdg. 30.00 (978-0-7910-9131-9(7), P114536, Facts On File) Infobase Holdings, Inc.

Merchant, Raina G. & Favor, Lesli J. How Eukaryotic & Prokaryotic Cells Differ, 1 vol. 2014. (Britannica Guide to Cell Biology Ser.). (ENG.). 64p. (YA). (gr. 8-8). 34.29 (978-1-62275-806-7(4), 21f572c9-5aed-4e68-b02a-489c42f4d3fb, Britannica Educational Publishing) Rosen Publishing Group, Inc., The.

Micromonsters: Microscopic Life up Close, 8 vols. 2016. (Micromonsters: Microscopic Life up Close Ser.). 32p. (gr. 4-4). (ENG.). 111.72 (978-1-4994-2251-1(2), f51803b8-8f76-48b8-a1de-592dbdf3ac4a); pap. 40.00 (978-1-4994-2450-8(7)) Rosen Publishing Group, Inc., The. (PowerKids Pr.).

Mikoley, Kate. What Are Protists?, 1 vol. 2019. (Look at Life Science Ser.). (ENG.). 32p. (gr. 2-2). pap. 11.50 (978-1-5382-4863-8(8), 6b44cfa5-7d2e-4d18-aba1-7867b3d5c02a) Stevens, Gareth Publishing LLLP.

Minden, Cecilia. Keep It Clean: Germ Free. 2010. (21st Century Basic Skills Library: Keep It Clean Ser.). (ENG., Illus.). 24p. (gr. k-3). lib. bdg. 26.35 (978-1-60279-857-1(5), 200580) Cherry Lake Publishing.

Oetting, Judy. Germs. Herr, Tad, illus. 2006. (Rookie Reader Skill Set Ser.). (ENG.). 32p. (J). (gr. k-2). pap. 4.95 (978-0-516-24995-7(9)) Scholastic Library Publishing.

Owen, Ruth. Creepy Backyard Invaders. 2011. (Up Close & Gross Ser.). 24p. (YA). (gr. 2-5). lib. bdg. 26.99 (978-1-61772-125-0(5)) Bearport Publishing Co., Inc.

—Up Close & Gross: Microscopic Creatures, 4 vols., Set. Incl. Creepy Backyard Invaders. lib. bdg. 26.99 (978-1-61772-125-0(5)); Disgusting Food Invaders. lib. bdg. 26.99 (978-1-61772-127-4(1)); Gross Body Invaders. lib. bdg. 26.99 (978-1-61772-126-7(3)); Icky House Invaders. lib. bdg. 26.99 (978-1-61772-124-3(7)); (YA). (gr. 2-5). 24p. 2011. Set lib. bdg. 90.44 (978-1-61772-123-6(9)) Bearport Publishing Co., Inc.

Porter, Esther. What's Sprouting in My Trash? A Book about Composting. 2013. (Earth Matters Ser.). (ENG.). 32p. (J). (gr. 1-2). pap. 48.60 (978-1-62065-746-1(5), 19326, Capstone Pr.) Capstone.

Rake, Jody Sullivan. Why Feet Smell & Other Gross Facts about Your Body. 2012. (Gross Me Out Ser.). (ENG.). 24p. (gr. 1-2). pap. 41.70 (978-1-4296-8377-7(5)); (J). pap. 7.29 (978-1-4296-7955-8(7), 118287); (J). lib. bdg. 25.99 (978-1-4296-7610-6(8), 117207) Capstone. (Capstone Pr.).

Romano, Amy. Germ Warfare, 1 vol. 2003. (Germs: the Library of Disease-Causing Organisms Ser.). (ENG., Illus.). 48p. (gr. 5-5). lib. bdg. 34.47 (978-0-8239-4493-4(X), 2a1bc2b5-4059-4f96-acf8-41849963d8a7) Rosen Publishing Group, Inc., The.

Schlitt, Christine. Journey into the Invisible: The World from under the Microscope. 2013. (ENG., Illus.). 80p. (J). (gr. -1-k). 16.95 (978-1-62087-116-4(5), 620116, Sky Pony Pr.) Skyhorse Publishing Co., Inc.

Sherman, Josepha. The War Against Germs. 2009. (Germs: the Library of Disease-Causing Organisms Ser.). 48p. (gr. 5-5). 53.00 (978-1-61512-718-4(6)) Rosen Publishing Group, Inc., The.

Sian revision Microworlds. 2004. (J). (978-1-59242-045-2(1)) Delta Education, LLC.

Sian revision sm Wonders. 2004. (J). (978-1-59242-067-4(2)) Delta Education, LLC.

Spilsbury, Richard. Cave: Look Inside. Hanna, Gary, illus. 2013. (Look Inside Ser.). (ENG.). 32p. (J). (gr. 1-3). pap. 8.29 (978-1-4329-7201-1(4), 121255, Heinemann) Capstone.

Swanson, Jennifer. Body Bugs: Invisible Creatures Lurking Inside You. 2011. (Tiny Creepy Creatures Ser.). (ENG.). 32p. (J). (gr. 3-4). pap. 50.74 (978-1-4296-7272-6(2), 16801);

pap. 8.29 (978-1-4296-7271-9(4), 116854) Capstone. (Capstone Pr.).
—Uninvited Guests: Invisible Creatures Lurking in Your Home. 2011. (Tiny Creepy Creatures Ser.). (ENG.). 32p. (gr. 3-4). pap. 47.70 (978-1-4296-7276-4(5), Capstone Pr.) Capstone.
Wanjie, Anne, ed. The Basics of Microbes, 1 vol. 2013. (Core Concepts Ser.). (ENG., Illus.). 96p. (YA). (gr. 7-7). lib. bdg. 39.77 (978-1-4777-0550-6(3), 420ff027-0a94-4d23-9e33-a43a0db4e4c3) Rosen Publishing Group, Inc., The.
Watson, Stephanie. Superbugs: The Rise of Drug-Resistant Germs, 1 vol. 2010. (In the News Ser.). (ENG.). 64p. (YA). (gr. 6-6). pap. 13.95 (978-1-4358-8553-0(8), d6486bf6-fbb6-41d5-9ca3-18007e5f7498); (Illus.). lib. bdg. 37.13 (978-1-4358-3585-6(9), 4059a9ef-83f8-4ce4-b01c-fc1d1cd0133f) Rosen Publishing Group, Inc., The.
Weakland, Mark. Gut Bugs, Dust Mites, & Other Microorganisms You Can't Live Without. 2010. (Nasty (but Useful!) Science Ser.). (ENG.). 32p. (J). (gr. 3-4). pap. 49.60 (978-1-4296-6472-1(X), 16225); pap. 8.10 (978-1-4296-6346-5(4), 115544) Capstone. (Capstone Pr.).
Wilker, Ian & Ambrose, Marylou. Investigating Tuberculosis & Superbugs: Real Facts for Real Lives, 1 vol. 2010. (Investigating Diseases Ser.). (ENG.). 160p. (gr. 9-10). 38.60 (978-0-7660-3343-6(0), f9b32aa2-7f34-48fe-aea5-653a33dde41c) Enslow Publishing, LLC.
Yount, Lisa. Antoni Van Leeuwenhoek: Genius Discoverer of Microscopic Life, 1 vol. 2014. (Genius Scientists & Their Genius Ideas Ser.). (ENG.). 96p. (gr. 5-5). pap. 13.88 (978-0-7660-6526-0(X), db072058-a2a3-416c-a7e1-619e9409190f) Enslow Publishing, LLC.
Zamosky, Lisa. Investigating Simple Organisms, 1 vol. rev. ed. 2007. (Science: Informational Text Ser.). (ENG., Illus.). 32p. (gr. 3-6). pap. 12.99 (978-0-7439-0587-9(3)) Teacher Created Materials, Inc.

MICROPROCESSORS

High-Tech DIY Projects with Microcontrollers. 2014. (Maker Kids Ser.). (Illus.). 32p. (J). (gr. 3-6). pap. 70.50 (978-1-4777-6658-3(8), PowerKids Pr.) Rosen Publishing Group, Inc., The.

MICROSCOPE AND MICROSCOPY

see Microscopes; Microscopy

MICROSCOPES

Here are entered works on microscopes in general as well as works specifically on light or optical microscopes.

Alexander, Lori. All in a Drop: How Antony Van Leeuwenhoek Discovered an Invisible World. Mildenberger, Vivien, illus. 2019. (ENG.). 96p. (J). (gr. 3-7). 17.99 (978-1-328-88420-6(1), 1698170, Clarion Bks.) HarperCollins Pubs.
Amstutz, Lisa J. Microscopes & Hand Lenses. 2019. (Science Tools Ser.). (ENG., Illus.). 24p. (J). (gr. k-2). pap. 6.95 (978-1-9771-0064-1(3), 138215); lib. bdg. 27.32 (978-1-9771-0060-3(0), 138211) Capstone. (Pebble).
Beckett, Leslie. Miguel Uses a Microscope, 1 vol. 2013. (Rosen Readers Ser.). (ENG.). 24p. (J). (gr. 3-3). pap. 8.25 (978-1-4777-2498-9(2), d9485807-692d-4a4e-876e-64011aabe5bc); pap. 49.50 (978-1-4777-2499-6(0)) Rosen Publishing Group, Inc., The. (Rosen Classroom).
Bullock, Linda. Looking Through a Microscope (Rookie Read-About Science: Physical Science: Previous Editions) 2004. (Rookie Read-About Science Ser.). (ENG., Illus.). 32p. (J). (gr. 1-2). pap. 4.95 (978-0-516-27972-1(2), Children's Pr.) Scholastic Library Publishing.
Crewe, Sabrina. In Your Body. 2010. (Under the Microscope Ser.). 32p. (gr. 2-4). 30.00 (978-1-60413-825-2(4), Chelsea Clubhse.) Infobase Holdings, Inc.
Crewe, Sabrina & Camper, Anne K. Under the Microscope, 6 vols., Set. 2010. (Under the Microscope Ser.). (gr. 2-4). 180.00 (978-1-60413-965-5(X), Chelsea Clubhse.) Infobase Holdings, Inc.
Gikow, Louise. Science. 2004. (True Tales Ser.). (ENG., Illus.). 48p. (J). 22.50 (978-0-516-23729-9(2), Children's Pr.) Scholastic Library Publishing.
Greg's Microscope. 2003. 22.95 (978-0-673-75918-4(0)) Celebration Pr.
Hall, Kirsten. Up Close & Gross. Jankowski, Dan, illus. 2009. 64p. (J). (978-0-545-13583-2(4)) Scholastic, Inc.
Kramer, Stephen. Hidden Worlds: Looking Through a Scientist's Microscope. 2003. (Scientists in the Field Ser.). (ENG., Illus.). 64p. (J). (gr. 5-7). pap. 9.99 (978-0-618-35405-4(0), 489120, Clarion Bks.) HarperCollins Pubs.
—Hidden Worlds: Looking Through a Scientist's Microscope. Kunkel, Dennis, photos by. 2005. (Illus.). 57p. (gr. 4-7). 20.00 (978-0-7569-5188-7(7)) Perfection Learning Corp.
—Hidden Worlds: Looking Through a Scientist's Microscope. 2003. (gr. k-3). lib. bdg. 20.85 (978-0-613-88665-9(8)) Turtleback.
Lang, Sheri. What's Wrong with the Microscope? Fixing the Problem, 1 vol. 2017. (Computer Kids: Powered by Computational Thinking Ser.). (ENG.). 24p. (J). (gr. 3-4). 25.27 (978-1-5383-2447-9(4), c6b7ca1e-2752-4454-bffa-8c1492f89bd4, PowerKids Pr.); pap. (978-1-5383-5317-2(2), 74223e6e-f69f-4b89-9d05-7937c032c558, Rosen Classroom) Rosen Publishing Group, Inc., The.
Levine, Shar & Johnstone, Leslie. The Ultimate Guide to Your Microscope. 2008. (Illus.). 144p. (J). (gr. 6-8). pap. 26.19 (978-1-4027-4329-0(7)) Sterling Publishing Co., Inc.
Lopez, Max. How Do Microscopes Work?, 1 vol. 2013. (InfoMax Readers Ser.). (ENG.). 24p. (J). (gr. 3-3). pap. 8.25 (978-1-4777-2504-7(0), 5f1b0ce8-f070-4248-a5e7-ac48571f0196); pap. 49.50 (978-1-4777-2505-4(9)) Rosen Publishing Group, Inc., The. (Rosen Classroom).
Melendez, Alicia & Benchmark Education Co. Staff. Behind the Microscope: Solving Scientific Mysteries. 2014. (Text Connections Ser.). (J). (gr. 6). (978-1-4900-1532-3(9)) Benchmark Education Co.
Oxlade, C. & Stockley, C. Micro Kit (Box) rev. ed. 2008. (Kid Kits Ser.). 48p. (J). pap. 29.99 (978-1-60130-108-6(1), Usborne) EDC Publishing.
Oxlade, Chris & Stockley, Corinne. The World of the Microscope. Chen, Kuo Kang et al, illus. 2008. (Usborne Science & Experiments Ser.). 48p. (J). (gr. 5-11). pap. 8.99 (978-0-7945-1524-9(X), Usborne) EDC Publishing.
Rodgers, Kirsteen. El Gran Libro del Microscopio. 2004. (Complete Bks.).Tr. of Complete Book of the Microscope. (SPA., Illus.). 96p. (J). (gr. 3-18). lib. bdg. 22.95 (978-1-58086-317-9(5), EU31324) EDC Publishing.
Rogers, K. Complete Book of the Microscope. 2004. (Complete Bks.). (SPA., Illus.). 96p. (J). lib. bdg. 22.95 (978-1-58086-384-1(1)) EDC Publishing.
Rogers, Kirsteen. The Complete Book of the Microscope. Dowswell, Paul, ed. Lane, Kim, illus. rev. ed. 2005. (Complete Bks.). 96p. (J). pap. 14.99 (978-0-7945-1558-4(4), Usborne) EDC Publishing.
Schlitt, Christine. Journey into the Invisible: The World from under the Microscope. 2013. (ENG., Illus.). 80p. (J). (gr. -1-k). 16.95 (978-1-62087-116-4(5), 620116, Sky Pony Pr.) Skyhorse Publishing Co., Inc.
See & Learn Science: A Curriculum Guide for Using Your Digital Microscope. 2007. (J). (978-1-933229-69-0(1)) APTE, Inc.
Slade, Suzanne. Scientific Instruments for Studying Atoms & Molecules, 1 vol. 2006. (Physical Science Ser.). (ENG., Illus.). 24p. (gr. 4-4). pap. 7.05 (978-1-4042-2166-6(2), 2bae84fe-53e0-452e-a5cd-789628855913, PowerKids Pr.) Rosen Publishing Group, Inc., The.
Stefoff, Rebecca. Microscopes & Telescopes, 1 vol. 2007. (Great Inventions Ser.). (ENG., Illus.). 144p. (YA). (gr. 8-8). lib. bdg. 45.50 (978-0-7614-2230-3(7), 11dc8094-4cd3-42ab-964c-4d6b85996783) Cavendish Square Publishing LLC.
Under the Microscope, 12 vols. 2013. (Under the Microscope Ser.). 32p. (J). (gr. 4-5). (ENG.). 175.62 (978-1-4339-8358-0(3), fbd3dcf5-3621-4032-84ca-baf1b85f4de6); pap. 70.20 (978-1-4339-9735-8(5)); pap. 421.20 (978-1-4339-9736-5(3)) Stevens, Gareth Publishing LLLP.
Yount, Lisa. Antoni Van Leeuwenhoek: First to See Microscopic Life, 1 vol. rev. ed. 2009. (Great Minds of Science Ser.). (ENG., Illus.). 128p. (gr. 5-6). lib. bdg. 35.93 (978-0-7660-3012-1(1), dac680c1-ca1a-41f8-af72-aaeff98dce53) Enslow Publishing, LLC.
—Antoni Van Leeuwenhoek: Genius Discoverer of Microscopic Life, 1 vol. 2014. (Genius Scientists & Their Genius Ideas Ser.). (ENG.). 96p. (gr. 5-5). 29.60 (978-0-7660-6525-3(1), e5734917-5b05-43e7-9909-c0835f58d414); pap. 13.88 (978-0-7660-6526-0(X), db072058-a2a3-416c-a7e1-619e9409190f) Enslow Publishing, LLC.

MICROSCOPIC ANALYSIS

see Microscopy

MICROSCOPIC ORGANISMS

see Microorganisms

MICROSCOPY

Here are entered works on microscopy in general as well as works specifically on light or optical microscopy.

Bacteria up Close. 2013. (Under the Microscope Ser.). 32p. (J). (gr. 4-6). pap. 70.20 (978-1-4339-8336-8(2)) Stevens, Gareth Publishing LLLP.
Crewe, Sabrina. In Rivers, Lakes, & Ponds. 2010. (Under the Microscope Ser.). 32p. (gr. 2-4). 30.00 (978-1-60413-826-9(2), Chelsea Clubhse.) Infobase Holdings, Inc.
—In the Backyard. 2010. (Under the Microscope Ser.). 32p. (gr. 2-4). 30.00 (978-1-60413-822-1(X), Chelsea Clubhse.) Infobase Holdings, Inc.
—In the Home. 2010. (Under the Microscope Ser.). 32p. (gr. 2-4). 30.00 (978-1-60413-823-8(8), Chelsea Clubhse.) Infobase Holdings, Inc.
—In Your Body. 2010. (Under the Microscope Ser.). 32p. (gr. 2-4). 30.00 (978-1-60413-825-2(4), Chelsea Clubhse.) Infobase Holdings, Inc.
Early, Bobbi. Tiny Life in a Puddle. 2005. (Rookie Read-About Science Ser.). (ENG., Illus.). 32p. (J). (gr. 1-2). lib. bdg. 20.50 (978-0-516-25272-8(0), Children's Pr.) Scholastic Library Publishing.
Kramer, Stephen. Hidden Worlds: Looking Through a Scientist's Microscope. 2003. (Scientists in the Field Ser.). (ENG., Illus.). 64p. (J). (gr. 5-7). pap. 9.99 (978-0-618-35405-4(0), 489120, Clarion Bks.) HarperCollins Pubs.
—Hidden Worlds: Looking Through a Scientist's Microscope. Kunkel, Dennis, photos by. 2005. (Illus.). 57p. (gr. 4-7). 20.00 (978-0-7569-5188-7(7)) Perfection Learning Corp.
—Hidden Worlds: Looking Through a Scientist's Microscope. 2003. (gr. k-3). lib. bdg. 20.85 (978-0-613-88665-9(8)) Turtleback.
Levine, Shar & Johnstone, Leslie. The Ultimate Guide to Your Microscope. 2008. (Illus.). 144p. (J). (gr. 6-8). pap. 26.19 (978-1-4027-4329-0(7)) Sterling Publishing Co., Inc.
Levy, Janey. Tiny Bugs up Close, 1 vol. 2013. (Under the Microscope Ser.). (ENG.). 32p. (J). (gr. 4-5). pap. 12.70 (978-1-4339-8351-1(6), 39872d3f-4789-4ee7-a378-138c5042876d); lib. bdg. 29.27 (978-1-4339-8350-4(8), f42c7b73-9c1c-4e6d-b0a2-864358533929) Stevens, Gareth Publishing LLLP.
Metz, Lorijo. Using Hand Lenses & Microscopes, 1 vol. 2013. (Science Tools Ser.). (ENG., Illus.). 24p. (J). (gr. 2-3). 26.27 (978-1-4488-9687-5(8), ede44812-220b-4de7-b596-f57143386bb6); pap. 9.25 (978-1-4488-9832-9(3), 2c62d945-369b-4135-94ea-72cc082b97fa) Rosen Publishing Group, Inc., The. (PowerKids Pr.).
Nelson, Maria. Cells up Close. 2013. (Under the Microscope Ser.). 32p. (J). (gr. 4-6). pap. 70.20 (978-1-4339-8340-5(0)); (ENG., Illus.). 29.27 (978-1-4339-8338-2(9), d382681a-3972-4733-af6f-ddb539bf0029); (ENG., Illus.). pap. 12.70 (978-1-4339-8339-9(7), e5726a4e-cf11-4cab-9523-c017800582e7) Stevens, Gareth Publishing LLLP.
Rogers, Kirsteen. The Complete Book of the Microscope. Dowswell, Paul, ed. Lane, Kim, illus. rev. ed. 2005. (Complete Bks.). 96p. (J). pap. 14.99 (978-0-7945-1558-4(4), Usborne) EDC Publishing.
Roza, Greg. Bacteria up Close, 1 vol. 2013. (Under the Microscope Ser.). (ENG.). 32p. (J). (gr. 4-5). 29.27 (978-1-4339-8334-4(6), bc32d779-dbe7-494e-b355-389facda22c6); pap. 12.70 (978-1-4339-8335-1(4), f33a0052-bf96-42ab-874c-1851f1e5df4c) Stevens, Gareth Publishing LLLP.
Schlitt, Christine. Journey into the Invisible: The World from under the Microscope. 2013. (ENG., Illus.). 80p. (J). (gr. -1-k). 16.95 (978-1-62087-116-4(5), 620116, Sky Pony Pr.) Skyhorse Publishing Co., Inc.
Tiny Bugs up Close. 2013. (Under the Microscope Ser.). 32p. (J). (gr. 4-6). pap. 70.20 (978-1-4339-8352-8(4)) Stevens, Gareth Publishing LLLP.

MICROSOFT SOFTWARE

Goff, Terry. 44 Fast & Fun Microsoft Word Activities. 2008. 130p. (J). per. 34.95 (978-0-9774748-5-1(2)) Brewer Technologies.
Gregory, Josh. Bill & Melinda Gates. 2013. (True Book(tm), A — Biographies Ser.). (ENG., Illus.). 48p. (J). lib. bdg. 31.00 (978-0-531-21905-8(4)); pap. 6.95 (978-0-531-23876-9(8)) Scholastic Library Publishing.
Lane, Laura. Microsoft. 2018. (Tech Titans Ser.). (ENG., Illus.). 112p. (J). (gr. 6-12). lib. bdg. 41.36 (978-1-5321-1689-6(6), 30630, Essential Library) ABDO Publishing Co.
Lesinski, Jeanne M. Bill Gates. rev. ed. 2007. (Biography Ser.). (Illus.). 112p. (J). (gr. 6-9). lib. bdg. 29.27 (978-0-8225-7363-0(6), Twenty-First Century Bks.) Lerner Publishing Group.
McGraw Hill. ICheck Series: Microsoft Office 2007, Real World Applications, PowerPoint, Student Edition. 2008. (Achieve Microsoft Office 2003 Ser.). (ENG., Illus.). 288p. (gr. 9-12). stu. ed. 102.48 (978-0-07-880267-6(9), 0078802679) McGraw-Hill Education.
Wanniarachchi, Ruwan. Early Childhood Computer Learning Workbook - Level 1. 2007. (ENG.). 79p. pap. 18.50 (978-0-615-17026-8(9)) Wanniarachchige, Somiruwan.

MIDDLE AGES

see also Art, Medieval; Chivalry; Civilization, Medieval; Knights and Knighthood; Renaissance

Allen, Kathy. The Horrible, Miserable Middle Ages: The Disgusting Details about Life During Medieval. 2010. (Disgusting History Ser.). (ENG.). 32p. (J). (gr. 3-4). pap. 48.60 (978-1-4296-6479-0(7), 16231, Capstone Pr.) Capstone.
—The Horrible, Miserable Middle Ages: The Disgusting Details about Life During Medieval Times. 2010. (Disgusting History Ser.). (ENG., Illus.). 32p. (J). (gr. 3-6). pap. 8.10 (978-1-4296-6350-2(2), 1308636); lib. bdg. 27.99 (978-1-4296-3958-3(X), 1308636) Capstone. (Capstone Pr.).
Bauer, Susan Wise. The Middle Ages Vol. 2: From the Fall of Rome to the Rise of the Renaissance. 2003. (Story of the World: Vol. 2). (ENG., Illus.). 1p. 21.95 (978-0-9714129-8-9(7)) Well-Trained Mind Pr.
Baum, Margaux & Bhote, Tehmina. Foods, Feasts, & Celebrations, 1 vol. 2016. (Life in the Middle Ages Ser.). (ENG., Illus.). 64p. (J). (gr. 5-5). 36.13 (978-1-4994-6470-2(3), 72b4a4fd-a3ba-418c-a237-5464d4d4265d, Rosen Central) Rosen Publishing Group, Inc., The.
Baum, Margaux & Hopkins, Andrea. The Lives of Women, 1 vol. 2016. (Life in the Middle Ages Ser.). (ENG.). 64p. (J). (gr. 5-5). E-Book 36.13 (978-1-4994-6467-2(3), a36b64b6-1644-4a2f-8051-fc2036dc7847) Rosen Publishing Group, Inc., The.
Benduhn, Tea. La Edad Media (the Middle Ages), 1 vol. 2007. (Vida en el Pasado (Life Long Ago) Ser.). (SPA., Illus.). 24p. (gr. 2-4). pap. 9.15 (978-0-8368-8040-3(4), 759b2af1-2a7e-48fe-8095-0a09f01544ac); lib. bdg. 24.67 (978-0-8368-8035-9(8), 461ca903-0f5c-4c6f-9c50-025d1a14ecf9) Stevens, Gareth Publishing LLLP. (Weekly Reader Leveled Readers).
—The Middle Ages, 1 vol. 2007. (Life Long Ago Ser.). (ENG., Illus.). 24p. (gr. 2-4). pap. 9.15 (978-0-8368-7789-2(6), d8f220b5-7bd7-4787-ab9a-d4d3ea269361); lib. bdg. 24.67 (978-0-8368-7784-7(5), fe343ccd-94a8-476a-8cff-06097944f491) Stevens, Gareth Publishing LLLP. (Weekly Reader Leveled Readers).
Bingham, Jane. Medieval world - internet Linked. Firenze, Inklink, illus. rev. ed. 2004. 96p. (J). pap. 14.95 (978-0-7945-0815-9(4), Usborne) EDC Publishing.
Bingham, Marjorie. An Age of Empires, 1200-1750. 2006. 32.95 (978-0-19-522268-5(7)) Oxford Univ. Pr., Inc.
Bingham, Marjorie Wall. An Age of Empires, 1200-1750. 2005. (Medieval & Early Modern World Ser.: 4). (ENG., Illus.). 160p. (YA). 44.99 (978-0-19-517839-5(4)) Oxford Univ. Pr., Inc.
Bodden, Valerie. Barbarians. (X-Books: Fighters Ser.). 2017. (ENG., Illus.). 32p. (J). (gr. 3-6). (978-1-60818-811-6(6), 20366, Creative Education) 2013. 24p. pap. (978-1-60818-466-8(8)) Creative Co., The.
—X-Books: Barbarians. 2017. (X-Bks.). (Illus.). 32p. (J). (gr. 3-7). pap. 9.99 (978-1-62832-414-3(7), 20367, Creative Paperbacks) Creative Co., The.
Bow, James. Your Guide to Trade in the Middle Ages. 2017. (Destination: Middle Ages Ser.). (ENG., Illus.). 32p. (J). (gr. 5-5). (978-0-7787-2996-9(6)); pap. (978-0-7787-3052-1(2)) Crabtree Publishing Co.
Bower, Bert. History Alive! The Medieval World & Beyond. 2011. (Illus.). xiv, 505p. (J). (978-1-58371-916-9(4)) Teachers' Curriculum Institute.
Brown Bear Books. The Middle Ages 600-1492. 2010. (Atlas of World History Ser.). (ENG.). 112p. (J). (gr. 9-12). 42.80 (978-1-933834-67-2(6), 16452) Brown Bear Bks.
Chambers, Catherine. A King's Guide. Pentney, Ryan, illus. 2017. (How-To Guides for Fiendish Rulers Ser.). (ENG.). 32p. (J). (gr. 3-6). pap. 27.99 (978-1-5124-1550-6(2), afacdecf-cdb4-484c-a5f4-1d2a06ba988e); E-Book 42.65 (978-1-5124-3623-5(2), 9781512436235); E-Book 42.65 (978-1-5124-2706-6(3)); E-Book 4.99 (978-1-5124-3624-2(0), 9781512436242) Lerner Publishing Group. (Hungry Tomato (r)).
—Why Why Why... Did Knights Wear Heavy Armor? 2010. (Why Why Why Ser.). (Illus.). 32p. (J). (gr. 1-3). lib. bdg. 18.95 (978-1-4222-1575-3(X)) Mason Crest.
Corrick, James A. The Early Middle Ages. 2005. (World History Ser.). (ENG., Illus.). 112p. (J). (gr. 5-8). lib. bdg. 34.95 (978-1-59018-652-7(4), Lucent Bks.) Cengage Gale.
Delaware, Steven S. Art & Culture of the Medieval World. 2010. (Ancient Art & Cultures Ser.). 40p. (YA). (gr. 5-8). lib. bdg., E-Book 53.00 (978-1-61532-966-3(8)) Rosen Publishing Group, Inc., The.
Delaware, Steven S., et al. Art & Culture of the Medieval World, 1 vol. 2010. (Ancient Art & Cultures Ser.). (ENG., Illus.). 40p. (gr. 6-6). (J). pap. 12.75 (978-1-61532-887-1(4), d260f0a5-59cf-4b51-a36e-0461a029246a); (YA). lib. bdg. 31.80 (978-1-4358-3592-4(1), 8b7706c8-6e7f-4216-bcaa-a690d52f0ce4) Rosen Publishing Group, Inc., The. (Rosen Reference).
Dorling Kindersley Publishing Staff. Vikings: DKFindOut! 2018. (Illus.). 64p. (J). (978-0-241-32302-1(9)) Dorling Kindersley Publishing, Inc.
Eastwood, Kay. Medieval Society, 1 vol. 2003. (Medieval World Ser.). (ENG., Illus.). 32p. (J). (gr. 5). pap. (978-0-7787-1377-7(6)) Crabtree Publishing Co.
—Women & Girls in the Middle Ages, 1 vol. 2003. (Medieval World Ser.). (ENG., Illus.). 32p. (J). (gr. 5). pap. (978-0-7787-1378-4(4)) Crabtree Publishing Co.
English Heritage Staff. My Life as a Knight. 2005. (Illus.). 32p. pap. 19.95 (978-1-85074-985-1(X)) Historic England Publishing GBR. Dist: Casemate Academic.
—My Life as a Princess. 2005. (Illus.). 32p. pap. 19.95 (978-1-85074-984-4(1)) Historic England Publishing GBR. Dist: Casemate Academic.
Exploring the Ancient & Medieval Worlds, 20 vols. 2015. (Exploring the Ancient & Medieval Worlds Ser.). (ENG.). 160p. (YA). (gr. 8-8). lib. bdg. 473.60 (978-1-5026-0374-6(8), c1eabc21-89a7-484f-819c-6ada90a860e4, Cavendish Square) Cavendish Square Publishing LLC.
Farndon, John. The Middle Ages: New Conquests & Dynasties. Cornia, Christian, illus. 2018. (Human History Timeline Ser.). (ENG.). 32p. (J). (gr. 3-6). 27.99 (978-1-5124-5972-2(0), 52325bb3-4917-423a-a7b3-64d7af67ae3d, Hungry Tomato (r)) Lerner Publishing Group.
George, Enzo. The Middle Ages, 1 vol. 2016. (Primary Sources in World History Ser.). (ENG.). 48p. (gr. 6-6). 33.07 (978-1-5026-1800-9(1), f1c7b749-a8d9-45a8-96d8-8dad408c55f5) Cavendish Square Publishing LLC.
George, Linda S. 800, 1 vol. 2003. (Around the World In... Ser.). (ENG., Illus.). 96p. (gr. 6-6). 36.93 (978-0-7614-1085-0(6), 1d2b8e69-68ea-41b9-afec-bc145d2cf1c2) Cavendish Square Publishing LLC.
Gitlin, Marty. The Totally Gross History of Medieval Europe, 1 vol., 1. 2015. (Totally Gross History Ser.). (ENG.). 48p. (J). (gr. 5-5). pap. 12.75 (978-1-4994-3764-5(1), 084ac054-5059-4f3b-9d7a-ca083e87366d, Rosen Central) Rosen Publishing Group, Inc., The.
Grant, Neil. Medieval Europe. 2003. (Uncovering History Ser.). 46p. (J). lib. bdg. 28.50 (978-1-58340-254-2(3)) Black Rabbit Bks.
Hanawalt, Barbara. The European World, 400-1450. 2006. (Illus.). 189p. 32.95 (978-0-19-522267-8(9)) Oxford Univ. Pr., Inc.
Hanawalt, Barbara A. The European World, 400-1450. 2005. (Medieval & Early Modern World Ser.). (Illus.). 192p. (YA). 39.99 (978-0-19-517844-9(0)) Oxford Univ. Pr., Inc.
Harding, Samuel. The Story of the Middle Ages. 2008. 116p. pap. 9.45 (978-1-60459-530-7(2)) Wilder Pubns., Corp.
Harding, Samuel Bannister. The Story of the Middle Ages (Yesterday's Classics) 2006. (Illus.). 228p. (YA). per. 10.95 (978-1-59915-157-1(X)) Yesterday's Classics.
Hartson, Tamara. Castles & Knights, 1 vol. 2019. (Super Explorers Ser.). (ENG., Illus.). 64p. (J). pap. 6.99 (978-1-926700-98-4(8), 3ece1447-c74b-4987-b954-428830e9150b) Blue Bike Bks. CAN. Dist: Lone Pine Publishing USA.
Hattstein, Markus & Udelhoven, Hermann-Josef. The Middle Ages & the Early Modern Period: From the 5th Century to the 18th Century, 1 vol. 2012. (Witness to History: a Visual Chronicle of the World Ser.). (ENG., Illus.). 208p. (J). (gr. 7-7). 51.80 (978-1-4488-7223-7(5), 52b59ccf-0526-45fc-a5eb-2e04497032d6) Rosen Publishing Group, Inc., The.
Hazen, Walter. Middle Ages. 2005. (Everyday Life (Good Year Books) Ser.). (Illus.). 92p. (J). (gr. 6-9). per. 12.95 (978-1-59647-059-0(3)) Good Year Bks.
Helget, Nicole Lea. Barbarians. 2012. (Fearsome Fighters Ser.). 48p. (gr. 5-12). 23.95 (978-1-60818-182-7(0), Creative Education) Creative Co., The.
Hindley, Judy, et al. Time Traveler: Visit Medieval Times, the Viking Age, the Roman World & Ancient Egypt. rev. ed. 2004. (Time Travelers Bks.). (Illus.). 130p. (J). (gr. 3-6). 22.95 (978-0-7460-3365-4(6)) EDC Publishing.
Hinds, Kathryn. Everyday Life in Medieval Europe, 1 vol. 2009. (Everyday Life Ser.). (ENG.). 288p. (gr. 6-7). lib. bdg. 45.50 (978-0-7614-3927-1(7), ba897e71-848a-402f-846c-70ee440ef233) Cavendish Square Publishing LLC.
Hoena, Blake. Medieval Knights: Europe's Fearsome Armored Soldiers. Orban, Janos, illus. 2019. (Graphic History: Warriors Ser.). (ENG.). 32p. (J). (gr. 3-9). pap. 7.95 (978-1-5435-5928-6(X), 139906); lib. bdg. 33.32 (978-1-5435-5501-1(2), 139374) Capstone.
Hopkins, Andrea. Damsels Not in Distress: The True Story of Women in Medieval Times. 2009. (Library of the Middle Ages Ser.). 64p. (gr. 5-8). 58.50 (978-1-60853-898-0(2), Rosen Reference) Rosen Publishing Group, Inc., The.
Jovinelly, Joann. The Crafts & Culture of a Medieval Cathedral. 2009. (Crafts & Cultures of the Middle Ages Ser.). 48p. (gr. 5-5). 58.50 (978-1-61512-054-3(8), Rosen Reference) Rosen Publishing Group, Inc., The.
—The Crafts & Culture of a Medieval Guild. 2009. (Crafts & Cultures of the Middle Ages Ser.). 48p. (gr. 5-5). 58.50

(978-1-61512-055-0(6), Rosen Reference) Rosen Publishing Group, Inc., The.
—The Crafts & Culture of a Medieval Manor. 2009. (Crafts & Cultures of the Middle Ages Ser.). 48p. (gr. 5-5). 58.50 (978-1-61512-053-6(X), Rosen Reference) Rosen Publishing Group, Inc., The.
Jovinelly, Joann & Netelkos, Jason. The Crafts & Culture of a Medieval Cathedral. 1 vol. 2006. (Crafts & Cultures of the Middle Ages Ser.). (ENG., Illus.). 48p. (J). (gr. 5-5). lib. bdg. 34.47 (978-1-4042-0758-5(9), 58491446-fd56-4ac7-85a7-46c6ad630cc0) Rosen Publishing Group, Inc., The.
—The Crafts & Culture of a Medieval Guild. 1 vol. 2006. (Crafts & Cultures of the Middle Ages Ser.). (ENG., Illus.). 48p. (J). (gr. 5-5). lib. bdg. 34.47 (978-1-4042-0757-8(0), c2ecdf58-48d5-40dc-9d84-fe750abe436c) Rosen Publishing Group, Inc., The.
—The Crafts & Culture of a Medieval Manor. 1 vol. 2006. (Crafts & Cultures of the Middle Ages Ser.). (ENG., Illus.). 48p. (J). (gr. 5-5). lib. bdg. 34.47 (978-1-4042-0756-1(2), 2ffc22f5-d1bf-4765-be4e-2e39c4193cbc) Rosen Publishing Group, Inc., The.
Kenney, Karen Latchana. Shockwave: Harsh or Heroic? 2007. (Shockwave: History & Politics Ser.). (ENG., Illus.). 36p. (J). (gr. 3-5). 25.00 (978-0-531-17754-9(8), Children's Pr.) Scholastic Library Publishing.
Keppeler, Jill. A Modern Nerd's Guide to Renaissance Fairs. 1 vol. 2019. (Geek Out! Ser.). (ENG.). 32p. (gr. 3-4). pap. 11.50 (978-1-5382-4022-9(X), 79ce5921-4c9e-4463-adc3-d9fa041c3b71) Stevens, Gareth Publishing LLLP.
Lassieur, Allison. The Middle Ages: An Interactive History Adventure. rev. ed. 2016. (You Choose: Historical Eras Ser.). (ENG.). 112p. (J). (gr. 3-7). pap. 6.95 (978-1-5157-4250-0(4), 134007, Capstone Pr.) Capstone.
Levy, Janey. 20 Fun Facts about Women of the Middle Ages. 1 vol. 2015. (Fun Fact File: Women in History Ser.). (ENG., Illus.). 32p. (J). (gr. 2-3). pap. 11.50 (978-1-4824-2824-7(5), 79ef435d-dc51-4e5b-8c2a-66b65f95d03f) Stevens, Gareth Publishing LLLP.
Life in the Middle Ages. 12 vols. 2016. (Life in the Middle Ages Ser.). (ENG.). 00064p. (J). (gr. 5-5). 216.78 (978-1-5081-7364-9(8), 479dbe61-21cd-4e19-a676-479165006841, Rosen Central) Rosen Publishing Group, Inc., The.
Macdonald, Fiona. The Medieval Chronicles: Vikings, Knights, & Castles. Antram, David, illus. 2013. 92p. (J). (978-1-4351-5067-6(8)) Barnes & Noble, Inc.
—Monarchs in the Middle Ages. 1 vol. 2005. (World Almanac(r) Library of the Middle Ages Ser.). (ENG., Illus.). 48p. (gr. 5-8). pap. 15.05 (978-0-8368-5905-8(7), 11f90bae-547f-4dbf-ab2d-bba358592d42); lib. bdg. 33.67 (978-0-8368-5896-9(4), 7fda729c-d319-42ad-a855-c1a852db9174) Stevens, Gareth Publishing LLLP. (Gareth Stevens Secondary Library).
—You Wouldn't Want to Be in a Medieval Dungeon! Prisoners You'd Rather Not Meet. Antram, David, illus. rev. ed. 2013. (You Wouldn't Want to... Ser.). (ENG.). 32p. (J). 29.00 (978-0-531-25948-1(X), Watts, Franklin) Scholastic Library Publishing.
—You Wouldn't Want to Be in a Medieval Dungeon! Prisoners You'd Rather Not Meet. 2013. (You Wouldn't Want To Ser.). lib. bdg. 20.80 (978-0-606-31629-3(9)) Turtleback.
—You Wouldn't Want to Work on a Medieval Cathedral! A Difficult Job That Never Ends. 2010. (You Wouldn't Want to... Ser.). 32p. (J). 29.00 (978-0-531-20504-4(5), Watts, Franklin) Scholastic Library Publishing.
Mayer, Cassie. Knights & Castles. 2012. (Illus.). 64p. (J). pap. 12.99 (978-1-62267-007-9(8)) Bright Connections Media.
McNab, Chris. Famous Battles of the Medieval Period. 1 vol. 2017. (Classic Warfare Ser.). (ENG.). 104p. (YA). (gr. 8-8). lib. bdg. 37.36 (978-1-5026-3248-7(9), 9d27e13f-f099-4135-b067-0a0790611c6a) Cavendish Square Publishing LLC.
McNeil, Niki, et al. HOCPP 1054 Middle Ages. 2006. spiral bd. 21.00 (978-1-60308-054-5(6)) In the Hands of a Child.
Medieval Africa DBA. 2003. spiral bd. 16.95 (978-1-56004-170-2(6)) Social Studies Schl. Service.
Middle Ages: Fun Projects for World History. 2006. cd-rom 29.95 net. (978-1-56004-252-5(4)) Social Studies Schl. Service.
Miles, Liz. Meet the Medievals. 1 vol. 2014. (Encounters with the Past Ser.). (ENG.). 32p. (J). (gr. 3-4). 28.27 (978-1-4824-0889-8(9), 96e407b7-ce61-4dcb-a8f7-f15eee68bd68) Stevens, Gareth Publishing LLLP.
O'Brian, Pliny. Empires, Crusaders, & Invasions Through the Middle Ages. 1 vol. 2015. (Exploring the Ancient & Medieval Worlds Ser.). (ENG., Illus.). 160p. (YA). (gr. 8-8). lib. bdg. 47.36 (978-1-5026-0679-2(8), 26bae633-3dfd-4983-893b-6397f6420177) Cavendish Square Publishing LLC.
O'Brien, Cynthia. Your Guide to Knights & the Age of Chivalry. 2017. (Destination: Middle Ages Ser.). (ENG., Illus.). 32p. (J). (gr. 5-5). (978-0-7787-2992-1(3)); pap. (978-0-7787-2998-3(2)) Crabtree Publishing Co.
—Your Guide to the Arts in the Middle Ages. 2017. (Destination: Middle Ages Ser.). (ENG., Illus.). 32p. (J). (gr. 5-5). (978-0-7787-2995-2(8)); pap. (978-0-7787-3002-6(6)) Crabtree Publishing Co.
Paprocki, Greg, illus. C Is for Castle: A Medieval Alphabet. 1 vol. 2016. (BabyLit Ser.). (ENG.). 32p. (J). (— 1). bds. 9.99 (978-1-4236-4281-7(3)) Gibbs Smith, Publisher.
Park, Louise. Life in the Middle Ages. 1 vol. 2013. (Discovery Education: Ancient Civilizations Ser.). (ENG., Illus.). 32p. (J). (gr. 4-5). pap. 11.00 (978-1-4777-0095-2(1), ff3bb7cc-7565-47d6-86e3-a7555205baee); lib. bdg. 28.93 (978-1-4777-0055-6(2), 79cc28db-cdeb-433e-a762-8dfab19d0363) Rosen Publishing Group, Inc., The. (PowerKids Pr.).
Plain, Nancy. Eleanor of Aquitaine & the High Middle Ages. 1 vol. 2007. (Rulers & Their Times Ser.). (ENG., Illus.). 80p. (gr. 6-6). lib. bdg. 36.93 (978-0-7614-1834-4(2), 047cd939-e7d7-4819-9889-f0ec13ebce85) Cavendish Square Publishing LLC.
Powell, Jillian. The Middle Ages. 1 vol. 2010. (Gruesome Truth About Ser.). (ENG.). 32p. (J). (gr. 5-5). lib. bdg. 29.93 (978-1-61533-219-9(7), 8f05825e-dca9-446d-8686-f1cceda95ce2, Windmill Bks.) Rosen Publishing Group, Inc., The.
Roesser, Marie. The Middle Ages. 1 vol. 2019. (Look at World History Ser.). (ENG.). 32p. (gr. 2-2). pap. 11.50 (978-1-5382-4138-7(2), 3119c64d-2fb2-436e-89d8-4b29d46de34f) Stevens, Gareth Publishing LLLP.
Roscoe, Kelly, ed. The End of the Middle Ages. 1 vol. 2017. (Power & Religion in Medieval & Renaissance Times Ser.). (ENG., Illus.). 112p. (gr. 10-10). 37.82 (978-1-68048-623-0(3), 33215f07-3ad7-4514-821c-d3b1ec52c0d5, Britannica Educational Publishing) Rosen Publishing Group, Inc., The.
Samuels, Charlie. Timeline of the Middle Ages. 1 vol. 2010. (History Highlights: a Gareth Stevens Timeline Ser.). (ENG., Illus.). 48p. (gr. 6-8). (J). pap. 15.05 (978-1-4339-3484-1(1), aade1df6-4131-4bf8-bde9-d250043a292d); (YA). lib. bdg. 34.60 (978-1-4339-3483-4(3), 4e49a067-3edc-441c-b677-2e50c9a7c80a) Stevens, Gareth Publishing LLLP. (Gareth Stevens Secondary Library).
Smith, Bonnie G. & Kelley, Donald R. The Medieval & Early Modern World: Primary Sources & Reference Volume. 2006. 32.95 (978-0-19-522300-2(4)) Oxford Univ. Pr., Inc.
Steele, Philip & Losland, Ragnhild. Vikings. 2018. (Illus.). 64p. (J). (978-1-5444-1093-7(X)) Dorling Kindersley Publishing, Inc.
Steloff, Rebecca. The Medieval World. 1 vol. 2006. (World Historical Atlases Ser.). (ENG., Illus.). 48p. (gr. 5-5). 34.07 (978-0-7614-1642-5(0), c305c035-8e42-4726-9717-97f8d919f6b8) Cavendish Square Publishing LLC.
Stevens, Catrin, et al. Yr Oesoedd Canol Cythryblus. 2005. (WEL., Illus.). 144p. pap. 4.99 (978-1-84323-423-4(8)) Gomer Pr. GBR. Dist: Gomer Pr.
Stewart, David. You Wouldn't Want to Be in a Medieval Dungeon! Antram, David, illus. rev. ed. 2013. (You Wouldn't Want to... Ser.). (ENG.). 32p. (J). 29.00 (978-0-531-25949-8(8), Watts, Franklin) Scholastic Library Publishing.
Stiefel, Chana. Ye Castle Stinketh: Could You Survive Living in a Castle?. 1 vol. 2012. (Ye Yucky Middle Ages Ser.). (ENG., Illus.). 48p. (gr. 5-7). pap. 11.53 (978-1-59845-374-4(2), 686b4634-44c0-476a-88e3-626b79c204a2); lib. bdg. 27.93 (978-0-7660-3786-1(X), 14d651f4-c7d1-47ee-a62e-d0e6b0baf75a) Enslow Publishing, LLC.
Stokes, Jonathan W. The Thrifty Guide to Medieval Times: A Handbook for Time Travelers. Bonet, Xavier, illus. 2019. (Thrifty Guides). (ENG.). 176p. (J). (gr. 3-7). pap. 8.99 (978-0-451-48028-6(7), Puffin Books) Penguin Young Readers Group.
Stuckey, Rachel. Your Guide to Medieval Society. 2017. (Destination: Middle Ages Ser.). (ENG., Illus.). 32p. (J). (gr. 5-5). (978-0-7787-2991-4(5)); pap. (978-0-7787-2997-6(4)) Crabtree Publishing Co.
Taylor, Barbara. The Amazing History of Castles & Knights. 2016. (Illus.). 64p. (J). (gr. -1-12). 12.99 (978-1-86147-717-0(1), Armadillo) Anness Publishing GBR. Dist: National Bk. Network.
Trembinski, Donna. Famous People of the Middle Ages. 2005. (Medieval World Ser.). (ENG., Illus.). 32p. (J). (gr. 5-9). lib. bdg. (978-0-7787-1356-2(3)) Crabtree Publishing Co.
Walker, Jane. Knights & Castles. 2013. (Illus.). 48p. (J). (978-1-4351-5093-5(7)) Barnes & Noble, Inc.
—Knights & Castles. 2015. (100 Facts Ser.). (Illus.). (J). (978-1-78209-374-9(5)) Miles Kelly Publishing, Ltd.
—100 Things You Should Know about Knights & Castles. 2008. (Illus.). 64p. (J). (978-1-84236-002-6(7)) Miles Kelly Publishing, Ltd.
Whitfield, Cathy. History Odyssey, Middle Ages - Level One. 2006. (J). ring bd. 31.00 (978-0-9766057-7-5(5)) Pandia Pr.
Wiesner-Hanks, Merry E. An Age of Voyages, 1350-1600. 2005. (Medieval & Early Modern World Ser.: 5). (ENG., Illus.). 192p. (YA). (gr. 7-18). lib. bdg. 35.99 (978-0-19-517672-8(3)) Oxford Univ. Pr., Inc.
Wiesner, Merry E. An Age of Voyages, 1450-1600. 2006. (Illus.). 189p. 32.95 (978-0-19-522264-7(4)) Oxford Univ. Pr., Inc.
Wilkinson, Carole. How to Live in the Dark Ages. 2007. 96p. (J). pap. (978-1-4207-0725-0(6)) Sundance/Newbridge Educational Publishing.
Woog, Adam. The Early Middle Ages. 2011. (Understanding World History Ser.). (ENG., Illus.). 96p. (YA). (gr. 7-12). lib. bdg. 43.93 (978-1-60152-151-4(0)) ReferencePoint Pr., Inc.
—A Medieval Knight. 2003. (Daily Life Ser.). (ENG., Illus.). 48p. (J). (gr. 4-6). pap. 27.00 (978-0-7377-0992-6(8), Kidhaven) Cengage Gale.
World Almanac Library of the Middle Ages. 4 vols., 8. 2005. (World Almanac(r) Library of the Middle Ages Ser.). (ENG.). 48p. (gr. 5-8). lib. bdg. 67.34 (978-0-8368-5891-4(3), 4be97f28-64e5-49ce-b5eb-cb1e95d43e9d, Gareth Stevens Secondary Library) Stevens, Gareth Publishing LLLP.

MIDDLE AGES—BIOGRAPHY

Dixon, Darla, illus. What Really Happened During the Middle Ages: A Collection of Historical Biographies. 4. 2007. (What Really Happened Ser.). 222p. per. 15.95 (978-1-932786-22-4(8)) Knowledge Quest.
Haaren, John H. Famous Men of the Middle Ages. 2017. (ENG., Illus.). (YA). (gr. 7-12). pap. (978-93-86423-13-9(8)) Alpha Editions.
—Famous Men of the Middle Ages. 2017. (ENG., Illus.). (YA). (gr. 7-12). pap. (978-0-649-58147-4(4)) Trieste Publishing Pty Ltd.
Trembinski, Donna. Famous People of the Middle Ages. 1 vol. 2005. (Medieval World Ser.). (ENG., Illus.). 32p. (J). (gr. 5-9). pap. (978-0-7787-1388-3(1)) Crabtree Publishing Co.

MIDDLE AGES—FICTION

Avi. Crispin: La Cruz de Plomo. 2004. Tr. of Crispin: The Cross of Lead. (SPA., Illus.). (YA). pap. 7.99 (978-84-348-9601-7(X)) SM Ediciones ESP. Dist: Lectorum Pubns., Inc.
—Crispin: the Cross of Lead (Newbery Medal Winner) 2004. (Crispin Ser.). (ENG.). 320p. (J). (gr. 3-7). reprint ed. pap. 8.99 (978-0-7868-1658-3(9)) Little, Brown Bks. for Young Readers.
—Crispin: the End of Time. 2011. (ENG.). 240p. (J). (gr. 5). pap. 7.99 (978-0-06-174083-1(7), Balzer & Bray) HarperCollins Pubs.
Aviation Book Company Staff. Crispin: The Cross of Lead. 2004. (J). (gr. 3-6). 18.40 (978-0-613-74965-7(0)) Turtleback.
Banks, Steven. Lost in Time. The Artifact Group, illus. 2006. 22p. (J). lib. bdg. 15.00 (978-1-4242-0977-4(3)) Fitzgerald Bks.
Barnhouse, Rebecca. The Book of the Maidservant. 2011. (ENG., Illus.). 240p. (J). (gr. 3-7). pap. 7.99 (978-0-375-85857-4(1), Yearling) Random Hse. Children's Bks.
Biggs, Stephen. The Time Barrel. 2009. 152p. pap. (978-1-84923-434-4(5)) YouWriteOn.
Bilgrey, Marc. And Don't Forget to Rescue the Other Princess. 2009. 252p. 25.95 (978-1-59414-744-9(2), Five Star) Cengage Gale.
Black, Kat. A Templar's Apprentice. 2009. (Book of Tormod Ser.: 1). (ENG.). 288p. (J). (gr. 7-18). 17.99 (978-0-545-05654-0(3)) Scholastic, Inc.
—Templar's Apprentice. 1. 2010. (Book of Tormod Ser.: 1). (ENG.). 288p. (J). (gr. 7-12). 24.94 (978-0-545-23411-5(5)) Scholastic, Inc.
—The Book of Tormod: A Templar's Gifts. 2011. (Book of Tormod Ser.: 2). (ENG.). 272p. (YA). (gr. 7-7). 17.99 (978-0-545-05675-5(6), Scholastic Pr.) Scholastic, Inc.
Chaucer, Geoffrey. The Canterbury Tales. (ENG.). (J). 2018. 394p. 46.95 (978-0-344-40404-7(8)) 2018. 394p. pap. 29.95 (978-0-344-40403-0(X)) 2018. (Illus.). 394p. 27.95 (978-0-342-43319-3(9)) 2018. (Illus.). 394p. pap. 17.95 (978-0-342-43318-6(0)) 2017. (Illus.). pap. 22.95 (978-1-375-53090-3(9)) Creative Media Partners, LLC.
Chaucer, Geoffrey & Trywhitt, Thomas. The Canterbury Tales. 2019. (ENG.). 598p. (J). 30.95 (978-1-01-113380-2(6)); pap. 21.95 (978-1-01-113379-6(2)) Creative Media Partners, LLC. (Wentworth Pr.).
Chaucer, Geoffrey & Tyrwhitt, Thomas. The Canterbury Tales. (ENG.). (J). 2018. 624p. 52.95 (978-0-343-91099-0(3)) 2018. 624p. pap. 37.95 (978-0-343-91098-3(5)) 2018. (Illus.). 624p. 31.95 (978-0-341-95514-6(0)) 2018. (Illus.). 624p. pap. 22.95 (978-0-341-95513-9(2)) 2015. (Illus.). 31.95 (978-1-296-67113-6(5)) Creative Media Partners, LLC.
Clayton, Colleen. What Happens Next. 2013. (ENG.). 320p. (YA). (gr. 10-17). pap. 17.99 (978-0-316-19869-1(2), Poppy) Little, Brown Bks. for Young Readers.
Coats, J. Anderson. The Wicked & the Just. 2013. (ENG.). 352p. (YA). (gr. 7). pap. 9.99 (978-0-544-02221-8(1), 1528479, Clarion Bks.) HarperCollins Pubs.
Collins, Tim. The Long-Lost Secret Diary of the World's Worst Knight. Horne, Sarah, illus. 2018. (Long-Lost Secret Diary Ser.). (ENG.). 216p. (J). (gr. 4-5). lib. bdg. 28.50 (978-1-63163-136-8(5), 1631631365, Jolly Fish Pr.) North Star Editions.
—World's Worst Knight. Horne, Sarah, illus. 2017. (Long-Lost Secret Diary Ser.). (ENG.). 216p. (J). (gr. 4-5). pap. 9.99 (978-1-63163-137-5(3), 1631631373, Jolly Fish Pr.) North Star Editions.
Comrie, Margaret S. The Heroes of Castle Bretten. 2003. (Illus.). 229p. (J). (978-1-894666-65-7(8)) Inheritance Pubns.
Cornwell, Betsy. The Forest Queen. (ENG.). (YA). (gr. 7). 2020. 320p. pap. 9.99 (978-0-358-13361-2(0), 1749855) 2018. 304p. 17.99 (978-0-544-88819-7(7), 1653253) HarperCollins Pubs. (Clarion Bks.).
Costanza, Stephen, illus. Smudge & the Book of Mistakes: A Christmas Story. 2012. (ENG.). 48p. (J). (gr. 1-4). 17.95 (978-1-58536-483-1(5), 202314) Sleeping Bear Pr.
Cremer, Andrea. Rift. 2013. (Nightshade Novels Ser.). (ENG.). 464p. (YA). (gr. 8-12). 26.19 (978-0-399-25613-4(X)) Penguin Young Readers Group.
Crossley-Holland, Kevin. At the Crossing-Places. 2004. (Arthur Trilogy). (Illus.). 394p. (YA). (gr. 7-12). 15.65 (978-0-7569-3182-7(7)) Perfection Learning Corp.
—Crossing to Paradise. 2008. (Illus.). 339p. (J). pap. (978-0-545-05868-1(6), Levine, Arthur A. Bks.) Scholastic, Inc.
Cushman, Karen. Catherine, Called Birdy. 2012. lib. bdg. 18.40 (978-0-606-24712-2(2)) Turtleback.
—Catherine, Called Birdy: A Newbery Honor Award Winner. 2019. (ENG.). 192p. (J). (gr. 3-7). pap. 9.99 (978-1-328-63111-4(7), 1734955, Clarion Bks.) HarperCollins Pubs.
—Grayling's Song. 2020. (ENG.). 240p. (J). (gr. 3-7). pap. 7.99 (978-0-358-09748-8(7), 1747604, Clarion Bks.) HarperCollins Pubs.
—Matilda Bone. 2020. (ENG.). 192p. (J). (gr. 3-7). pap. 7.99 (978-0-358-09752-5(5), 1747612, Clarion Bks.) HarperCollins Pubs.
—Matilda Bone. unabr. ed. 2004. (Middle Grade Cassette Librariestm Ser.). 176p. (J). (gr. 5-9). pap. 36.00 incl. audio (978-0-8072-1725-2(5), S YA 252 SP, Listening Library) Random Hse. Audio Publishing Group.
—The Midwife's Apprentice. 2012. lib. bdg. 18.40 (978-0-606-24696-5(7)) Turtleback.
—The Midwife's Apprentice: A Newbery Award Winner. 2019. (ENG.). 144p. (J). (gr. 3-7). pap. 7.99 (978-1-328-63112-1(5), 1734957, Clarion Bks.) HarperCollins Pubs.
Davis, Tony. Brand New Page, 2. Rogers, Gregory, illus. 2012. (Roland Wright Ser.). (ENG.). 144p. (J). (gr. 1-4). lib. bdg. 18.69 (978-0-385-90707-1(9), Yearling) Random Hse. Children's Bks.
—Roland Wright: at the Joust. Rogers, Gregory, illus. 2011. (Roland Wright Ser.: 3). (ENG.). 144p. (J). (gr. 1-4). 6.99 (978-0-375-87328-7(7), Yearling) Random Hse. Children's Bks.
de Bonneval, Gwen. William & the Lost Spirit. Bonhomme, Matthieu, illus. 2013. (ENG.). 160p. (YA). (gr. 8-12). lib. bdg. 30.65 (978-0-7613-8567-7(3), 38866c96-abfc-4e7f-9449-c6a5f12f8f1a, Graphic Universe™) Lerner Publishing Group.
Dickerson, Melanie. The Huntress of Thornbeck Forest. 1 vol. 2015. (Medieval Fairy Tale Ser.: 1). (ENG.). 320p. pap. 15.99 (978-0-7180-2624-0(1)) Nelson, Thomas Inc.
—The Noble Servant. 1 vol. 2017. (Medieval Fairy Tale Ser.: 3). (ENG.). 336p. (YA). 14.99 (978-0-7180-2660-8(8)) Nelson, Thomas Inc.
—The Orphan's Wish. 1 vol. 2018. (ENG.). 352p. (YA). 16.99 (978-0-7180-7483-8(1)) Nelson, Thomas Inc.
—The Piper's Pursuit. 1 vol. 2019. (ENG.). 320p. (YA). 18.99 (978-0-7852-2814-1(4)) Nelson, Thomas Inc.
French, Allen. The Story of Rolf & the Viking Bow. 2008. 148p. (gr. 7-12). pap. 8.15 (978-1-60459-522-2(1)) Wilder Pubns., Corp.
French, Jackie. My Dad the Dragon. King, Stephen Michael, illus. 2018. (Wacky Families Ser.: 03). (ENG.). 128p. 5.99 (978-0-207-19950-9(7), HarperCollins) HarperCollins Pubs.
Gashler, Stephen. The Bent Sword. 2010. (YA). pap. 15.99 (978-1-59955-401-3(1)) Cedar Fort, Inc./CFI Distribution.
Gidwitz, Adam. The Inquisitor's Tale: Or, the Three Magical Children & Their Holy Dog. Aly, Hatem, illus. (ENG.). (J). (gr. 5). 2018. 400p. 9.99 (978-0-14-242737-8(3), Puffin Books) 2016. 384p. 18.99 (978-0-525-42616-5(7), Dutton Books for Young Readers) Penguin Young Readers Group.
—The Inquisitor's Tale: Or, the Three Magical Children & Their Holy Dog. 2018. lib. bdg. 20.85 (978-0-606-40873-8(8)) Turtleback.
Gilman, Laura Anne. The Camelot Spell. 2006. (Grail Quest Ser.: No. 1). 291p. (J). (gr. 5-9). 10.99 (978-0-06-077279-6(4)) HarperCollins Pubs.
Grant, K. M. Blood Red Horse. 2006. (DeGranville Trilogy Ser.: 1). (ENG.). 320p. (YA). (gr. 5-9). per. 10.99 (978-0-8027-7734-8(1), 900039395, Bloomsbury USA Childrens) Bloomsbury Publishing USA.
Gray, Elizabeth Janet. Adam of the Road (Puffin Modern Classics) Lawson, Robert, illus. 2006. (Puffin Modern Classics Ser.). (ENG.). 320p. (J). (gr. 3-7). 8.99 (978-0-14-240659-5(7), Puffin Books) Penguin Young Readers Group.
Hardinge, Frances. Fly by Night. 2006. 487p. (J). (gr. 5-9). 16.99 (978-0-06-087627-2(1)) HarperCollins Pubs.
Hedlund, Jody. A Daring Sacrifice. 1 vol. 2016. (ENG.). 224p. (YA). pap. 12.99 (978-0-310-74937-0(9)) Zondervan.
Herz, Henry, et al. When You Give an Imp a Penny. 1 vol. Larson, Abigail, illus. 2016. (ENG.). 32p. (J). (gr. k-3). 16.99 (978-1-4556-2144-6(7), Pelican Publishing) Arcadia Publishing.
Hidden. 2014. (ENG., Illus.). 384p. (YA). (gr. 7). 17.99 (978-1-4424-8300-2(8), Simon & Schuster/Paula Wiseman Bks.) Simon & Schuster/Paula Wiseman Bks.
Howard, Eva. The Stolen Crown. 2017. (League of Archers Ser.: 2). (ENG., Illus.). 304p. (J). (gr. 4-8). 16.99 (978-1-4814-6040-8(4), Aladdin) Simon & Schuster Children's Publishing.
Hulme-Cross, Benjamin. The Knight's Enemies. Rinaldi, Angelo, illus. 2015. (Warrior Heroes Ser.). (ENG.). 160p. (J). (gr. 6-6). (978-0-7787-1765-2(8)) Crabtree Publishing Co.
Jackson, Marilee. Midnight Runner. 2015. 261p. (YA). pap. 17.99 (978-1-4621-1615-7(9)) Cedar Fort, Inc./CFI Distribution.
Jinks, Catherine. Babylonne. 2008. (ENG., Illus.). 400p. (YA). (gr. 7). 18.99 (978-0-7636-3650-0(9)) Candlewick Pr.
Jones, Rob Lloyd. The Story of Robin Hood. Marks, Alan, illus. 2010. (Picture Book Classics Ser.). 24p. (J). 9.99 (978-0-7945-2859-1(7), Usborne) EDC Publishing.
Keller, John E. The Emperor's Elephant. 2006. 127p. (YA). per. 12.95 (978-0-942566-45-1(9)) LinguaText, LLC.
Lamprey, L. Masters of the Guild. I.t. ed. 2006. 168p. pap. 21.99 (978-1-4264-2076-4(5)) Creative Media Partners, LLC.
Love, D. Anne. The Puppeteer's Apprentice. 2004. (ENG., Illus.). 192p. (J). (gr. 3-7). reprint ed. pap. 9.99 (978-0-689-84425-6(5), McElderry, Margaret K. Bks.) McElderry, Margaret K. Bks.
—The Puppeteer's Apprentice. 2004. (Aladdin Historical Fiction Ser.). 185p. (gr. 3-7). 17.00 (978-0-7569-4323-3(X)) Perfection Learning Corp.
McMullan, Kate. Countdown to the Year 1000 #8. Basso, Bill, illus. 2003. (Dragon Slayers' Academy Ser.: 8). 112p. (J). (gr. 2-5). pap. 6.99 (978-0-448-43508-4(X), Grosset & Dunlap) Penguin Young Readers Group.
Millen, C. M. The Ink Garden of Brother Theophane. Wisnewski, Andrea, illus. 2010. (ENG.). 32p. (J). (gr. k-3). 18.99 (978-1-58089-179-0(9)) Charlesbridge Publishing, Inc.
Morris, Gerald. The Adventures of Sir Balin the Ill-Fated. Renier, Aaron, illus. 2013. (Knights' Tales Ser.: 4). (ENG.). 112p. (J). (gr. 1-4). pap. 6.99 (978-0-544-10488-4(9), 1540796, Clarion Bks.) HarperCollins Pubs.
—The Legend of the King. 2010. (Squire's Tales Ser.: 10). (ENG.). 304p. (YA). (gr. 5-7). 16.99 (978-0-547-14420-7(2), 1050377, Clarion Bks.) HarperCollins Pubs.
—The Lioness & Her Knight. 2008. (Squire's Tales Ser.: 7). (ENG.). 352p. (J). (gr. 5-7). pap. 19.99 (978-0-547-01485-2(6), 1031103, Clarion Bks.) HarperCollins Pubs.
Moss, Barbara E. The Adventures of Sir Goblin, the Feline Knight. Houx, Emily Marie Cornell du, illus. 2009. 336p. pap. 15.95 (978-1-882190-03-4(3)) Solon Ctr. for Research & Publishing.
Muir, Suzanne. The Magic Tile. 2007. (Illus.). 48p. (J). lib. bdg. 15.00 (978-1-4242-1619-2(2)) Dingles & Co.
Murdock, Catherine Gilbert. The Book of Boy: A Newbery Honor Award Winner. 2018. (ENG., Illus.). 288p. (J). (gr. 3-7). 16.99 (978-0-06-268620-6(8), Greenwillow Bks.) HarperCollins Pubs.
Murphy, Shirley Rousseau. Silver Woven in My Hair. 2015. (ENG., Illus.). 128p. (J). (gr. 3-7). pap. 13.99 (978-1-4814-5865-8(5), Atheneum Bks. for Young Readers) Simon & Schuster Children's Publishing.
Napoli, Donna Jo. Hush: An Irish Princess' Tale. 2007. (ENG., Illus.). 340p. (YA). (gr. 7-12). 18.69 (978-0-689-86176-5(1)) Simon & Schuster, Inc.
Nunes, Rachel Ann. The Secret of the King. Ward, Jay Bryant, illus. 2005. 32p. (J). (gr. -1-3). 17.95 (978-1-59038-241-7(2), Shadow Mountain) Shadow Mountain Publishing.
Osborne, Mary Pope. The Knight at Dawn. unabr. ed. 2004. (Magic Tree House Ser.: No. 2). 66p. (J). (gr. k-3). pap. 17.00 incl. audio (978-0-8072-0331-6(9), Listening Library) Random Hse. Audio Publishing Group.
Peirce, Lincoln. Max & the Midknights: Battle of the Bodkins. 2020. (Max & the Midknights Ser.: 2). (ENG., Illus.). 272p. (J). (gr. 3-7). 13.99 (978-0-593-12590-8(8)); E-Book (978-0-593-12592-2(4)) Random Hse. Children's Bks. (Crown Books For Young Readers).

—Max & the Midknights: the Tower of Time. 2022. (Illus.). 262p. (J). *(978-0-593-37792-5(3))* Bantam Doubleday Dell Large Print Group, Inc.
—Max & the Midknights: the Tower of Time. 2022. (Max & the Midknights Ser.: 3). (Illus.). 272p. (J). (gr. 3-7). 13.99 *(978-0-593-37789-5(3),* Crown Books For Young Readers) Random Hse. Children's Bks.
Picard, Barbara Leonie. Ransom for a Knight. 2008. (Nautilus Ser.). (ENG.). 314p. (J). (gr. 6). pap. 14.95 *(978-1-58988-043-6(9))* Dry, Paul Bks., Inc.
Platt, Richard. Castle Diary: The Journal of Tobias Burgess. Riddell, Chris, illus. 2003. (ENG.). 128p. (J). (gr. 4-7). 7.99 *(978-0-7636-2164-3(1))* Candlewick Pr.
Pringle, Eric. Big George & the Winter King. Paine, Colin, illus. 2004. 208p. (J). pap. 12.99 *(978-0-7475-6341-9(1))* Bloomsbury Publishing Plc GBR. Dist: Independent Pubs. Group.
Pyle, Howard. Otto of the Silver Hand. 2020. (ENG.). 96p. (J). pap. 8.95 *(978-1-715-11038-3(2))* Blurb, Inc.
—Otto of the Silver Hand. (ENG., Illus.). (J). (gr. 4-7). 2018. 202p. 39.95 *(978-0-344-84701-1(2))* 2015. 204p. 24.95 *(978-1-297-56711-7(0))* Creative Media Partners, LLC.
—Otto of the Silver Hand. (J). 2019. (ENG.). 172p. (gr. 4-7). pap. 9.99 *(978-1-7019-6627-7(1))* 2019. (ENG.). 66p. (gr. 4-7). pap. 5.99 *(978-1-6968-9017-5(9))* 2019. (ENG.). 176p. (gr. 4-7). pap. 12.99 *(978-1-6911-6301-4(5))* 2019. (ENG.). 176p. (gr. 4-7). pap. 12.99 *(978-1-6951-1669-6(0))* 2019. (ENG.). 176p. (gr. 4-7). pap. 12.99 *(978-1-6965-7633-8(4))* 2019. (ENG.). 130p. (gr. 4-7). pap. 12.99 *(978-1-0865-6695-6(5))* 2019. (ENG.). 274p. (gr. 4-7). pap. 19.99 *(978-1-6888-4076-8(1))* 2019. (ENG.). 88p. (gr. 4-7). pap. 9.99 *(978-1-0804-0240-3(3))* 2019. (ENG.). 274p. (gr. 4-7). pap. 16.99 *(978-1-0816-9365-7(7))* 2019. (ENG.). 274p. (gr. 4-7). pap. 16.99 *(978-1-0828-3194-2(8))* 2019. (ENG.). 174p. (gr. 4-7). pap. 13.99 *(978-1-0781-0599-6(5))* 2019. (ENG.). 130p. (gr. 4-7). pap. 9.99 *(978-1-0730-1164-3(X))* 2019. (ENG.). 176p. (gr. 4-7). pap. 14.99 *(978-1-0753-6853-0(7))* 2019. (ENG.). 130p. (gr. 4-7). pap. 9.99 *(978-1-0756-9135-5(4))* 2019. (ENG.). 274p. (gr. 4-7). pap. 16.99 *(978-1-0772-0217-7(2))* 2019. (ENG.). 116p. (gr. 4-7). pap. 8.99 *(978-1-0969-8662-1(0))* 2019. (ENG.). 186p. (gr. 4-7). pap. 12.99 *(978-1-0986-1885-8(8))* 2019. (ENG.). 176p. (gr. 4-7). pap. 12.99 *(978-1-0998-6544-2(1))* 2019. (ENG.). 88p. (gr. 4-7). pap. 9.99 *(978-1-0706-1174-7(3))* 2019. (ENG.). 116p. (gr. 4-7). pap. 7.99 *(978-1-0961-2408-5(4))* 2019. (ENG.). 88p. (gr. 4-7). pap. 7.99 *(978-1-0955-5327-5(5))* 2019. (FRE.). 170p. pap. 29.99 *(978-1-0902-3470-4(8))* 2019. (ENG.). 176p. (gr. 4-7). pap. 12.99 *(978-1-0916-3477-0(7))* 2019. (ENG.). 176p. (gr. 4-7). pap. 11.99 *(978-1-7969-1992-9(6))* 2018. (ENG., Illus.). 112p. (gr. 4-7). pap. 6.99 *(978-1-7903-0678-7(7))* Independently Published.
—Otto of the Silver Hand. 2008. 72p. pap. 8.15 *(978-1-60459-556-7(6))* Wilder Pubns., Corp.
Rallison, Janette. My Fair Godmother. 2009. (ENG.). 384p. (J). (gr. 6-8). 21.19 *(978-0-8027-9780-3(6),* 900051897) Walker & Co.
—My Unfair Godmother. 2012. (ENG.). 352p. (YA). (gr. 7-12). 26.19 *(978-0-8027-2236-2(9),* 9780802722362) Bloomsbury Publishing USA.
Rautenberg, Karen Rita. Lady Lucy's Gallant Knight. 2007. (ENG.). 156p. (J). (gr. 4-7). per. *(978-1-933255-22-4(6))* DNA Pr.
Santillo, LuAnn. Medieval Magic, 6 vols. Santillo, LuAnn, ed. 2003. (Half-Pint Kids Readers Ser.). (Illus.). 42p. (J). (gr. -1-1). pap. 6.95 *(978-1-59256-049-3(0))* Half-Pint Kids, Inc.
Service, Pamela F. The Wizards of Wyrd World. Gorman, Mike, illus. 2015. (Way-Too-Real Aliens Ser.: 3). (ENG.). 112p. (J). (gr. 4-6). E-Book 53.32 *(978-1-4677-5962-5(7),* 9781467759625, Lerner Digital) Lerner Publishing Group.
Sleiman, Dina L. Chivalrous. 2015. (Valiant Hearts Ser.: 2). (ENG.). 360p. (YA). pap. 16.00 *(978-0-7642-1313-7(X))* Bethany Hse. Pubs.
—Courageous. 2016. (Valiant Hearts Ser.: 3). (ENG.). 362p. (YA). pap. 16.00 *(978-0-7642-1314-4(8))* Bethany Hse. Pubs.
—Dauntless. 2015. (Valiant Hearts Ser.: 1). (ENG.). 368p. (YA). pap. 16.00 *(978-0-7642-1312-0(1))* Bethany Hse. Pubs.
Smith, Danna. The Hawk of the Castle: A Story of Medieval Falconry. Ibatoulline, Bagram, illus. 2017. (ENG.). 40p. (J). (gr. -1-3). 19.99 *(978-0-7636-7992-7(5))* Candlewick Pr.
Spradlin, Michael. Keeper of the Grail: Book 1, Bk. 1. 2009. (Youngest Templar Ser.: 1). (ENG.). 272p. (J). (gr. 5-6). 7.99 *(978-0-14-241461-3(1),* Puffin Books) Penguin Young Readers Group.
—Orphan of Destiny, 3 vols. 2011. (Youngest Templar Ser.: 3). (ENG.). 272p. (J). (gr. 5-18). 7.99 *(978-0-14-241959-5(1),* Puffin Books) Penguin Young Readers Group.
—Trail of Fate: Book 2, 2 vols., Bk. 2. 2010. (Youngest Templar Ser.: 2). (ENG.). 256p. (J). (gr. 5-7). 7.99 *(978-0-14-241707-2(6),* Puffin Books) Penguin Young Readers Group.
Spradlin, Michael P. Orphan of Destiny. 2012. (Youngest Templar Ser.: 3). (ENG., Illus.). 256p. (J). (gr. 6-8). 22.44 *(978-0-399-24765-1(3))* Penguin Young Readers Group.
Springer, Nancy. Wild Boy. 2005. (Tales of Rowan Hood Ser.). 115p. (J). (gr. 3). 13.65 *(978-0-7569-5490-1(8))* Perfection Learning Corp.
Stine, Faye. The Golden Goblet: 200 Years in a Medieval Castle. 2013. (ENG.). 169p. (YA). pap. 12.95 *(978-1-4787-1063-9(2))* Outskirts Pr., Inc.
Weatherill, Cat. Wild Magic. 2008. (ENG., Illus.). 288p. (YA). (gr. 4-6). 21.19 *(978-0-8027-9799-5(7),* 9780802797995) Walker & Co.
Williams, Laura E. The Executioner's Daughter. 2007. (ENG.). 144p. (YA). (gr. 5-9). pap. 10.99 *(978-0-8050-8186-2(0),* 900040615, Holt, Henry & Co. Bks. For Young Readers) Holt, Henry & Co.

MIDDLE ATLANTIC STATES

see Atlantic States

MIDDLE CLASS

Jd, Duchess Harris & Herschbach, Elisabeth. Class Mobility. 2018. (Class in America Ser.). (ENG., Illus.). 112p. (J). (gr. 6-12). lib. bdg. 41.36 *(978-1-5321-1407-6(9),* 28796, Essential Library) ABDO Publishing Co.
Jd, Duchess Harris & Rowell, Rebecca. The American Middle Class. 2018. (Class in America Ser.). (ENG., Illus.). 112p. (J). (gr. 6-12). lib. bdg. 41.36 *(978-1-5321-1403-8(6),* 28788, Essential Library) ABDO Publishing Co.

MIDDLE EARTH (IMAGINARY PLACE)—FICTION

Novel Units. The Hobbit Novel Units Teacher Guide. 2019. (ENG.). (YA). pap. 12.99 *(978-1-56137-253-9(6),* Novel Units, Inc.) Classroom Library Co.
Tolkien, J. R. R. El Hobbit. 2003. (Lord of the Rings Ser.). (SPA.). 320p. (YA). 17.95 *(978-84-450-7141-0(6),* MQ9001) Minotauro Ediciones ESP. Dist: Distribooks, Inc.
—The Hobbit. 70th anniv. ed. 2011. (ENG., Illus.). 400p. mass mkt. *(978-0-261-10221-7(4))* HarperCollins Pubs. Ltd.
—The Hobbit. movie tie-in ed. 2012. lib. bdg. 19.65 *(978-0-606-26240-8(7))* Turtleback.
—Senhor dos Aneis. pap. 36.95 *(978-85-336-1337-9(7))* Livraria Martins Editora BRA. Dist: Distribooks, Inc.

MIDDLE EAST

Here are entered works on the region consisting of Asia west of Pakistan, northeastern Africa, and occasionally Greece and Pakistan. Works treating collectively the Arabic-speaking countries of Asia and Africa, or of Asia only, are entered under Arab Countries.

Alcraft, Rob. Dubai from the Sky: Band 08/Purple. 2015. (Collins Big Cat Ser.). (ENG., Illus.). 24p. (J). (gr. 2-2). pap. 9.99 *(978-0-00-759115-2(2))* HarperCollins Pubs. Ltd. GBR. Dist: Independent Pubs. Group.
Conklin, Blane. Modern Middle East, 1 vol. rev. ed. 2007. (Social Studies: Informational Text Ser.). (ENG.). 32p. (gr. 4-8). pap. 11.99 *(978-0-7439-0674-5(8))* Teacher Created Materials, Inc.
Downing, David. Geography & Resources of the Middle East, 1 vol. 2006. (World Almanac(r) Library of the Middle East Ser.). (ENG., Illus.). 48p. (gr. 5-8). pap. 15.05 *(978-0-8368-7341-2(6),* c35660ba-d711-42b1-bd2b-ea313d3f56f7); lib. bdg. 33.67 *(978-0-8368-7334-4(3),* 6015ec5a-10cb-469b-94db-ce6ade0fec4a) Stevens, Gareth Publishing LLLP. (Gareth Stevens Secondary Library).
—Governments & Leaders of the Middle East, 1 vol. 2006. (World Almanac(r) Library of the Middle East Ser.). (ENG., Illus.). 48p. (gr. 5-8). pap. 15.05 *(978-0-8368-7342-9(4),* 7a94275d-fdd2-472a-a640-779df34b3a57); lib. bdg. 33.67 *(978-0-8368-7335-1(1),* 649fe476-eea0-4504-89e8-a110512adb9c) Stevens, Gareth Publishing LLLP. (Gareth Stevens Secondary Library).
Gelletly, LeeAnne. The Kurds. 2010. (Major Muslim Nations Ser.). (Illus.). 120p. (J). (gr. 5-18). lib. bdg. 25.95 *(978-1-4222-1407-7(9))* Mason Crest.
Gunderson, Cory Gideon. Religions of the Middle East. 2003. (World in Conflict-the Middle East Ser.). 32p. (gr. 4-8). 27.07 *(978-1-59197-412-3(7),* Abdo & Daughters) ABDO Publishing Co.
Heing, Bridey. The Children Soldiers of ISIS, 1 vol. 2017. (Crimes of ISIS Ser.). (ENG.). 104p. (gr. 8-8). 38.93 *(978-0-7660-9211-2(9),* b02bce7e-1f6e-4774-a4f3-8c9d65714a04) Enslow Publishing, LLC.
King, David C. The United Arab Emirates, 1 vol. 2008. (Cultures of the World (First Edition)(r) Ser.). (ENG.). 144p. (gr. 5-5). lib. bdg. 49.79 *(978-0-7614-2565-6(9),* c8721dc9-e02c-41a1-9d85-e5763367b73b) Cavendish Square Publishing LLC.
Kort, Michael G. The Handbook of the Middle East. 2007. (Handbook Of... Ser.). (Illus.). 320p. (YA). (gr. 7-12). lib. bdg. 39.93 *(978-0-8225-7143-8(9))* Twenty First Century Bks.
The Making of the Middle East, 10 vols., Set. Incl. Arab-Israeli Relations, 1950-1979. Baughan, Brian. 80p. (YA). (gr. 3-7). 2009. lib. bdg. 22.95 *(978-1-4222-0171-8(6));* Arabian Peninsula in the Age of Oil. Calvert, John. 88p. (YA). (gr. 3-7). 2009. lib. bdg. 22.95 *(978-1-4222-0172-5(4));* Cold War in the Middle East, 1950-1991. Sasley, Brent. 80p. (YA). (gr. 7-18). 2009. lib. bdg. 22.95 *(978-1-4222-0173-2(2));* First World War & the End of the Ottoman Order. Brennan, Kristine. 80p. (YA). (gr. 7-18). 2009. lib. bdg. 22.95 *(978-1-4222-0168-8(6));* Iranian Revolution & the Resurgence of Islam. Rubin, Barry A. 88p. (YA). (gr. 7-18). 2009. lib. bdg. 22.95 *(978-1-4222-0174-9(0));* Middle East in the Age of Uncertainty, 1991-Present. Rubin, Barry A. 78p. (YA). (gr. 3-7). 2009. lib. bdg. 22.95 *(978-1-4222-0176-3(7));* Ottoman & Qajar Empires in the Age of Reform. Robbins, Gerald. 80p. (YA). (gr. 7-18). 2009. lib. bdg. 22.95 *(978-1-4222-0167-1(8));* Palestine Mandate & the Creation of Israel, 1920-1949. Luxenberg, Alan. 80p. (J). (gr. 3-7). 2007. lib. bdg. 22.95 *(978-1-4222-0170-1(8));* Rise of Nationalism: The Arab World, Turkey, & Iran. Spyer, Jonathan & Brown, Cameron. 80p. (YA). (gr. 7-18). 2007. lib. bdg. 22.95 *(978-1-4222-0169-5(4));* Tensions in the Gulf, 1978-1991. Peterson, J. E. 88p. (J). (gr. 3-7). 2007. lib. bdg. 22.95 *(978-1-4222-0175-6(9));* (Illus.). (Making of the Middle East Ser.). 2009. Set lib. bdg. 229.95 *(978-1-4222-0166-4(X))* Mason Crest.
Marsh, Carole. Middle East: Ancient Countries of Current Events Headlines! 2009. (It's Your World Ser.). 48p. (J). (gr. 2-9). pap. 7.99 *(978-0-635-06808-8(7))* Gallopade International.
McCoy, Lisa. Middle East: Facts & Figures. 2010. (Major Muslim Nations Ser.). (Illus.). 112p. (J). (gr. 5-18). lib. bdg. 25.95 *(978-1-4222-1400-8(1))* Mason Crest.
—United Arab Emirates. 2010. (Major Muslim Nations Ser.). (Illus.). 112p. (YA). (gr. 5-18). lib. bdg. 25.95 *(978-1-4222-1390-2(0),* 1306268) Mason Crest.
Miller, Debra A., ed. The Middle East, 1 vol. 2007. (Current Controversies Ser.). (ENG., Illus.). 224p. (gr. 10-12). 48.03 *(978-0-7377-3960-2(6),* 13f34d39-21af-498c-ab31-6d7fc422b132); pap. 33.00 *(978-0-7377-3961-9(4),* 3b9a55d8-44f1-4244-89b8-6efbffc75fd8) Greenhaven Publishing LLC. (Greenhaven Publishing).
Stacey, Gill. Religions of the Middle East, 1 vol. 2006. (World Almanac(r) Library of the Middle East Ser.). (ENG., Illus.). 48p. (gr. 5-8). pap. 15.05 *(978-0-8368-7345-0(9),* 4f136c28-9f0e-4d9b-bcda-097c624415a0); lib. bdg. 33.67 *(978-0-8368-7338-2(6),* d1cd55a9-e8fa-4188-84f9-7934a6661712) Stevens, Gareth Publishing LLLP. (Gareth Stevens Secondary Library).
Steele, Philip. Middle East. 2009. (Kingfisher Knowledge Ser.). (ENG., Illus.). 64p. (J). (gr. 3-8). pap. 22.44 *(978-0-7534-6313-0(X),* 9780753463130) Roaring Brook Pr.
Townsend, Chris. The Violent Rise of ISIS, 1 vol. 2017. (Crimes of ISIS Ser.). (ENG.). 104p. (gr. 8-8). 38.93 *(978-0-7660-9210-5(0),* f22ec1a9-c044-419a-a5a2-d36f7f546231) Enslow Publishing, LLC.
Wimmer, Teresa. Causes. 2011. (War on Terror Ser.). (ENG., Illus.). 48p. (J). (gr. 5-8). 34.25 *(978-1-60818-097-4(2),* 22302) Creative Co., The.
Woods, Michael & Woods, Mary B. Seven Natural Wonders of Asia & the Middle East. 2009. (Seven Wonders Ser.). (ENG., Illus.). 80p. (gr. 5-8). 33.26 *(978-0-8225-9073-6(5))* Lerner Publishing Group.
Yomtov, Nel. Immigrants from Afghanistan & the Middle East. 2018. (Immigration Today Ser.). (ENG., Illus.). 32p. (J). (gr. 3-6). lib. bdg. 27.99 *(978-1-5435-1384-4(0),* 137789, Capstone Pr.) Capstone.

MIDDLE EAST—ANTIQUITIES

Down, David. Archaeology Book. 2009. 96p. (YA). (gr. 7-12). 18.99 *(978-0-89051-573-0(5),* Master Books) New Leaf Publishing Group.
Heing, Bridey. Cultural Destruction by ISIS, 1 vol. 2017. (Crimes of ISIS Ser.). (ENG.). 104p. (gr. 8-8). 38.93 *(978-0-7660-9215-0(1),* 2c01d7a3-0a00-4986-bda5-67597ae48ae7) Enslow Publishing, LLC.
Robinson Jr., Charles Alexander. The First Book of Ancient Mesopotamia & Persi. 2011. 70p. 36.95 *(978-1-258-10112-1(2))* Literary Licensing, LLC.
Tubb, Jonathan. Eyewitness Bible Lands: Discover the Story of the Holy Land. 2016. (DK Eyewitness Ser.). (ENG., Illus.). 64p. (J). (gr. 3-7). pap. 9.99 *(978-1-4654-4010-5(0),* 1405880, DK Children) Dorling Kindersley Publishing, Inc.

MIDDLE EAST—DESCRIPTION AND TRAVEL

Cooke, Tim. Explore with Gertrude Bell. 2017. (Travel with the Great Explorers Ser.). (Illus.). 32p. (J). (gr. 4-5). *(978-0-7787-3910-4(4));* pap. *(978-0-7787-3925-8(2))* Crabtree Publishing Co.
Feiler, Bruce. Walking the Bible: An Illustrated Journey for Kids Through the Greatest Stories Ever Told. Meret, Sasha, tr. Meret, Sasha, illus. 2004. 112p. (J). (gr. 2-7). 16.99 *(978-0-06-051117-3(6))* HarperCollins Pubs.
Goldsworthy, Kaite. Burj Khalifa. (Structural Wonders of the World Ser.). (J). 2018. (ENG.). 24p. (gr. 2-5). lib. bdg. 28.55 *(978-1-4896-8178-2(7),* AV2 by Weigl) 2012. 27.13 *(978-1-61913-252-8(4))* 2012. pap. 12.95 *(978-1-61913-258-0(3))* Weigl Pubs., Inc.
Groner, Judye & Wikler, Madeline. Let's Visit Israel. Nathan, Cheryl, illus. 2004. (ENG.). 12p. (J). (gr. -1 — 1). 5.95 *(978-1-58013-087-5(9),* Kar-Ben Publishing) Lerner Publishing Group.
Kallen, Stuart. Burj Khalifa: The Tallest Tower in the World. 2014. (Great Idea Ser.). (ENG.). 48p. (J). (gr. 4-6). pap. 13.26 *(978-1-60357-578-2(2))* Norwood Hse. Pr.
Kallen, Stuart A. Burj Khalifa: The Tallest Tower in the World. 2014. (Great Idea Ser.). (ENG.). 48p. (J). (gr. 4-6). lib. bdg. 26.60 *(978-1-59953-598-2(X))* Norwood Hse. Pr.

MIDDLE EAST—FICTION

Abawi, Atia. A Land of Permanent Goodbyes. 2019. 304p. (YA). (gr. 7). pap. 11.99 *(978-0-399-54685-3(5),* Penguin Books) Penguin Young Readers Group.
Addison, George R. Iii. When Mom Came Home. 2012. 32p. pap. 21.99 *(978-1-4691-6406-9(X))* Xlibris Corp.
Ali, S. K. Love from a to Z. 2019. (ENG., Illus.). 352p. (YA). (gr. 9). 19.99 *(978-1-5344-4272-6(3),* Salaam Reads) Simon & Schuster Bks. For Young Readers.
Anthony, Horowitz. Scorpia Rising, 9 vols. (J). 2012. 90.75 *(978-1-4561-3363-4(2))* 2012. 256.75 *(978-1-4561-3362-7(4))* 2012. 1.25 *(978-1-4640-0577-0(X))* 2011. 122.75 *(978-1-4561-3365-8(9))* 2011. 120.75 *(978-1-4561-3367-2(5))* Recorded Bks., Inc.
—Scorpia Rising. 2012. (Alex Rider Ser.: 9). lib. bdg. 19.65 *(978-0-606-23638-6(4))* Turtleback.
Appelt, Kathi. Keeper. Hall, August, illus. 2010. (ENG.). 416p. (J). (gr. 3-7). 17.99 *(978-1-4169-5060-8(5),* Atheneum Bks. for Young Readers) Simon & Schuster Children's Publishing.
Bhoola, Prisha. Hashay Says Goodbye & Hello. 2013. 24p. pap. 22.68 *(978-1-4669-9209-2(3))* Trafford Publishing.
Bowen, Carl. Shadow Squadron: Rogue Agent. Tortosa, Wilson, illus. 2015. (Shadow Squadron Ser.). (ENG.). 224p. (J). (gr. 4-8). pap., pap., pap. 8.95 *(978-1-62370-296-0(8),* 128369, Capstone Young Readers) Capstone.
Carleson, J. C. The Tyrant's Daughter. 2015. (ENG.). 304p. (YA). (gr. 7). pap. 10.99 *(978-0-449-80999-0(4),* Ember) Random Hse. Children's Bks.
Center for Learning Staff. Habibi/Seven Daughters & Seven Sons: Novel Curriculum Unit. 2004. (Novel Ser.). 73p. (YA). tchr. ed., spiral bd. 19.95 *(978-1-56077-770-0(2))* Center for Learning, The.
Clinton, Cathryn. A Stone in My Hand. 2010. (ENG., Illus.). 208p. (J). (gr. 5). pap. 7.99 *(978-0-7636-4772-8(1))* Candlewick Pr.
Collingwood, Harry. The Cruise of The 'Esmeralda' 2009. 220p. pap. 15.95 *(978-1-60664-391-4(6))* Rodgers, Alan Bks.
Cowley, Marjorie. The Golden Bull: A Mesopotamian Adventure. 2012. 224p. (J). (gr. 4-7). pap. 8.95 *(978-1-58089-182-0(9))* Charlesbridge Publishing, Inc.
E. O., Monalisa. Dan & Derrick's Prayer to the Troops. 2007. 36p. per. 16.95 *(978-1-4327-0753-8(1))* Outskirts Pr., Inc.
Edwards, Wayne. Ali & the Magic Ball. Golden, Rayna, illus. 2009. 24p. pap. 12.50 *(978-1-60860-367-1(9),* Eloquent Bks.) Strategic Book Publishing & Rights Agency (SBPRA).
Ellis, Deborah. The Breadwinner Trilogy, 1 vol. 2009. (Breadwinner Ser.: 1 - 3). (ENG.). 440p. (J). (gr. 5-9). pap. 19.99 *(978-0-88899-959-7(3))* Groundwood Bks. CAN. Dist: Publishers Group West (PGW).
Etheridge, Judy. Olivia's Wish. 2009. 32p. pap. 21.99 *(978-1-4415-3915-1(8))* Xlibris Corp.
Faizal, Hafsah. We Hunt the Flame. 2019. (Sands of Arawiya Ser.: 1). (ENG., Illus.). 480p. (YA). 18.99 *(978-0-374-31154-4(4),* 900195159, Farrar, Straus & Giroux (BYR)) Farrar, Straus & Giroux.
—We Hunt the Flame. 2020. (Sands of Arawiya Ser.: 1). (ENG., Illus.). 480p. (YA). pap. 12.99 *(978-1-250-25079-7(X),* 900195160) Square Fish.
Formento, Alison Ashley. Twigs. 2013. (ENG.). 272p. (YA). 17.99 *(978-1-4405-6565-6(1),* Simon Pulse) Simon Pulse.
Gormally, Eleanor. St Paul: The Man with the Letters. 2010. (ENG., Illus.). 32p. (J). pap. 16.95 *(978-1-84730-177-2(0))* Veritas Pubns. IRL. Dist: Casemate Pubs. & Bk. Distributors, LLC.
Goscinny, René. The Caliph's Vacation. 2009. (Iznogoud Ser.: 2). (Illus.). 48p. (J). (gr. 4-7). pap. 11.95 *(978-1-905460-61-8(9))* CineBook GBR. Dist: National Bk. Network.
—The Grand Vizier Iznogoud, Vol. 9. Tabary, illus. 2012. (Iznogoud Ser.: 9). 52p. (J). (gr. 3-12). pap. 13.95 *(978-1-84918-131-0(4))* CineBook GBR. Dist: National Bk. Network.
—Iznogoud - The Infamous, Vol. 7. Tabary, illus. 2011. (Iznogoud Ser.: 7). 48p. (J). (gr. -1-12). pap. 11.95 *(978-1-84918-074-0(1))* CineBook GBR. Dist: National Bk. Network.
—Iznogoud Vol. 10: Iznogoud the Relentless. Tabary, Jean, illus. 2013. (Iznogoud Ser.: 10). 48p. (J). (gr. 3-12). pap. 11.95 *(978-1-84918-181-5(0))* CineBook GBR. Dist: National Bk. Network.
—Rockets to Stardom - Iznogoud, Vol. 8. Tabary, illus. 2011. (Iznogoud Ser.: 8). 48p. (J). (gr. -1-12). pap. 11.95 *(978-1-84918-092-4(X))* CineBook GBR. Dist: National Bk. Network.
—The Wicked Wiles of Iznogoud, Vol. 1. Tabary, Armelle, illus. 2008. (Iznogoud Ser.: 1). 48p. (J). (gr. -1-12). pap. 13.95 *(978-1-905460-46-5(5))* CineBook GBR. Dist: National Bk. Network.
Goscinny, René & Tabary, Jean. A Carrot for Iznogoud, Vol. 5. 2010. (Iznogoud Ser.: 5). (Illus.). 48p. (J). (gr. 4-7). pap. 11.95 *(978-1-84918-021-4(0))* CineBook GBR. Dist: National Bk. Network.
Hamid, Yasmin. Swimming on the Lawn. 2018. 144p. (YA). (gr. 7). pap. 12.99 *(978-1-925164-85-5(3))* Fremantle Pr. AUS. Dist: Independent Pubs. Group.
Hancock, H. Irving. The Young Engineers on the Gulf. rev. ed. 2006. 216p. 27.95 *(978-1-4218-1752-1(7));* pap. 12.95 *(978-1-4218-1852-8(3))* 1st World Publishing, Inc. (1st World Library - Literary Society).
—Young Engineers on the Gulf: Or, the Dread Mystery of the Million Dollar Breakwater. 2017. (ENG., Illus.). (J). 23.95 *(978-1-374-93150-3(0));* pap. 13.95 *(978-1-374-93149-7(7))* Capital Communications, Inc.
Hapka, Catherine, pseud. Horse Diaries #6: Yatimah. Sanderson, Ruth, illus. 2011. (Horse Diaries: 6). 176p. (J). (gr. 3-7). pap. 7.99 *(978-0-375-86719-4(8),* Random Hse. Bks. for Young Readers) Random Hse. Children's Bks.
Hathorn, Sarah Alexandra. Teenagents: World Challenge. 2012. 240p. pap. 12.99 *(978-2-9700738-2-6(X))* Simon & Schuster, Inc.
Higgins, Jack & Richards, Justin. Sharp Shot. 2010. (ENG.). 240p. (YA). (gr. 7-18). 8.99 *(978-0-14-241730-0(0),* Speak) Penguin Young Readers Group.
Hillman, John E. Ancient Stories of the Hodj. 2012. (Illus.). 52p. pap. 27.45 *(978-1-4685-8215-4(1))* AuthorHouse.
Horowitz, Anthony. Scorpia Rising. 2012. (Alex Rider Ser.: 9). (ENG.). 432p. (J). (gr. 5-18). 9.99 *(978-0-14-241985-4(0),* Puffin Books) Penguin Young Readers Group.
Islam, M. N. Hamza's Journey of a Lifetime. 2012. 124p. pap. *(978-1-909395-70-1(6))* Legend Pr.
Jolin, Paula. In the Name of God. 2008. (ENG.). 224p. (YA). (gr. 9-12). pap. 18.99 *(978-0-312-38455-5(6),* 900053460) Square Fish.
Kullab, Samya. Escape from Syria. Roche, Jackie, illus. 2017. (ENG.). 96p. (gr. 7-12). 19.95 *(978-1-77085-982-1(9),* d1b74160-dd04-46de-bb91-929f73e88949) Firefly Bks., Ltd.
LaFevers, R. L. Flight of the Phoenix Bk. 1. Murphy, Kelly, illus. 2010. (Nathaniel Fludd, Beastologist Ser.: 1). (ENG.). 144p. (J). (gr. 1-4). pap. 6.99 *(978-0-547-40845-3(5),* 1428742, Clarion Bks.) HarperCollins Pubs.
Litrel, Suzanne. Jackie Tempo & the House of Wisdom. 2012. 150p. (gr. 10-12). 21.95 *(978-1-4620-5887-7(6));* pap. 11.95 *(978-1-4620-5886-0(8))* iUniverse, Inc.
Lough, Amber. The Blind Wish. 2015. (Jinni Wars Ser.: 2). (ENG.). 320p. (YA). (gr. 7). 17.99 *(978-0-385-36980-0(8),* Random Hse. Bks. for Young Readers) Random Hse. Children's Bks.
Luedke, Robert James. Eye Witness: A Fictional Tale of Absolute Truth. 2005. (Eye Witness Ser.). (ENG., Illus.). 96p. pap. 13.99 *(978-0-9758924-0-4(1));* lib. bdg. 24.99 *(978-0-9758924-1-1(X))* Head Pr. Publishing.
Marsden, Carolyn. The White Zone. 2012. (Exceptional Reading & Language Arts Titles for Intermediate Grades Ser.). (ENG.). 192p. (J). (gr. 4-8). 17.95 *(978-0-7613-7383-4(7),* Carolrhoda Bks.) Lerner Publishing Group.
Marston, Elsa. Figs & Fate: Stories about Growing up in the Arab World Today. 2005. (ENG.). 146p. (J). 22.50 *(978-0-8076-1551-5(X));* pap. 15.95 *(978-0-8076-1554-6(4))* Braziller, George Inc.
—Santa Claus in Baghdad & Other Stories about Teens in the Arab World. 2008. (ENG.). 216p. (gr. 3-7). pap. 15.95 *(978-0-253-22004-2(1),* 978-0-253-22004-2) Indiana Univ. Pr.
Mason, Prue. Camel Rider. 2011. 9.49 *(978-0-7848-3618-7(3),* Everbind) Marco Bk. Co.
Mazer, Harry & Lerangis, Peter. Somebody, Please Tell Me Who I Am. 2013. (ENG.). 160p. (YA). (gr. 7). pap. 9.99 *(978-1-4169-3896-5(6),* Simon & Schuster Bks. For Young Readers) Simon & Schuster Bks. For Young Readers.
McCormick, Patricia. Purple Heart. 2009. (ENG.). 208p. (YA). (gr. 8-18). 16.99 *(978-0-06-173090-0(4),* Balzer & Bray) HarperCollins Pubs.
Montgomery, R. A. Trouble on Planet Earth. 2007. 144p. (J). pap. *(978-1-86504-933-5(6))* Chooseco LLC.
—Trouble on Planet Earth. Trod, Mariano et al, illus. 2006. (ENG.). 144p. (J). (gr. 4-8). per. 6.99 *(978-1-933390-11-6(5),* CHCL11) Chooseco LLC.
—Trouble on Planet Earth. 2005. (Illus.). 113p. (J). pap. *(978-0-7608-9699-0(2))* Sundance/Newbridge Educational Publishing.

Myers, Walter Dean. Sunrise over Fallujah. 2009. (ENG.). 320p. (J). (gr. 7-12). 10.99 *(978-0-439-91625-7(9)*, Scholastic Pr.) Scholastic, Inc.
—Sunrise over Fallujah. l.t. ed. 2008. 468p. (YA). 23.95 *(978-1-4104-1019-1(6))* Thorndike Pr.
Nawrocki, Mike. Squirreled Away. Séguin-Magee, Luke, illus. 2019. (Dead Sea Squirrels Ser.: 1). (ENG.). 128p. (J). pap. 6.99 *(978-1-4964-3498-2(6)*, 20_31671, Tyndale Kids) Tyndale Hse. Pubs.
Nye, Naomi Shihab. The Turtle of Oman: A Novel. 2014. (ENG.). 304p. (J). (gr. 3-7). 16.99 *(978-0-06-201972-1(4)*, Greenwillow Bks.) HarperCollins Pubs.
Osborne, Mary Pope. Season of the Sandstorms. 2014. (Magic Tree House Merlin Missions Ser.: No. 6). 15.00 *(978-1-63419-681-9(3))* Perfection Learning Corp.
—Season of the Sandstorms, Bk. 6. Murdocca, Sal, illus. 2006. (Magic Tree House (R) Merlin Mission Ser.: 6). 144p. (J). (gr. 2-5). 6.99 *(978-0-375-83032-7(4)*, Random Hse. Bks. for Young Readers) Random Hse. Children's Bks.
Osborne, Mary Pope, et al. La Estación de Las Tormentas de Arena. Murdocca, Sal, illus. 2016. (SPA.). 107p. (J). (gr. 2-4). pap. 5.99 *(978-1-63245-644-1(3))* Lectorum Pubns., Inc.
Parry, Rosanne. Heart of a Shepherd. 2010. (ENG.). 176p. (J). (gr. 4-6). lib. bdg. 22.44 *(978-0-375-94802-2(3))* Random House Publishing Group.
—Heart of a Shepherd. 2010. 176p. (J). (gr. 3-7). pap. 7.99 *(978-0-375-84803-2(7)*, Yearling) Random Hse. Children's Bks.
Raether, Erin F. When Auntie Angie Left for Iraq & Remi Came to Stay. 2008. 15p. pap. 24.95 *(978-1-4241-8735-5(4))* America Star Bks.
Romagnoli, L. M. The Worn-Out Backpack. Campbell, Lisa, illus. 2008. 15p. pap. 24.95 *(978-1-60563-934-5(6))* America Star Bks.
Rumford, James. Silent Music: A Story of Bagdad. Rumford, James, illus. 2008. (ENG., Illus.). 32p. (J). (gr. -1-3). 19.99 *(978-1-59643-276-5(4)*, 900044099) Roaring Brook Pr.
Schami, Rafik. The Storyteller of Damascus. Knorr, Peter, illus. 2018. (ENG.). 48p. (J). 18.95 *(978-1-62371-971-5(2)*, Crocodile Bks.) Interlink Publishing Group, Inc.
Senzai, N. H. Escape from Aleppo. 2018. (ENG., Illus.). 336p. (J). (gr. 3-7). 17.99 *(978-1-4814-7217-3(8)*, Simon & Schuster/Paula Wiseman Bks.) Simon & Schuster/Paula Wiseman Bks.
Serafin, Mike. 7 Stories from Baghdad. 2005. 50p. pap. 16.95 *(978-1-4137-8808-2(4))* PublishAmerica, Inc.
Shah, Idries. The Silly Chicken. Jackson, Jeff, illus. 2005. 32p. (J). pap., pap. 6.99 *(978-1-883536-50-3(2)*, Hoopoe Bks.) I S H K.
—The Silly Chicken/el Pollo Bobo. Wirkala, Rita, tr. Jackson, Jeff, illus. 2005. 32p. (J). (gr. -1-3). 18.00 *(978-1-883536-37-4(5)*, Hoopoe Bks.) I S H K.
Smith, Chris. One City, Two Brothers. Fronty, Aurélia, illus. 2007. (ENG.). 32p. (J). (gr. -1-3). 16.99 *(978-1-84686-042-3(3))* Barefoot Bks., Inc.
Sovago-Royal, Sandra. Magimus. 2009. 33p. (J). pap. 19.95 *(978-1-4327-4375-8(9))* Outskirts Pr., Inc.
Summers, Susan. The Greatest Gift: The Story of the Other Wise Man. Morris, Jackie, illus. 2011. 30p. (J). 16.99 *(978-1-84686-578-7(6))* Barefoot Bks., Inc.
Townsend, S. P. The Star of Persia. 2008. 120p. pap. 12.50 *(978-1-84799-532-2(2))* Lulu Pr., Inc.
Weulersse, Odile. Nasreddine. Dautremer, Rébecca, illus. 2013. (ENG.). 34p. (J). 17.00 *(978-0-8028-5416-2(8)*, Eerdmans Bks For Young Readers) Eerdmans, William B. Publishing Co.
Whelan, Gloria. Parade of Shadows. 2007. 304p. (J). (gr. 5-18). lib. bdg. 16.89 *(978-0-06-089029-2(0))* HarperCollins Pubs.
Williams, Emma. The Story of Hurry. Quraishi, Ibrahim, illus. 2014. 36p. (J). (gr. -1-2). 16.95 *(978-1-60980-589-0(5)*, Triangle Square) Seven Stories Pr.

MIDDLE EAST—HISTORY

ABDO Publishing Company Staff. World in Conflict-the Middle East. 2003. (World in Conflict-the Middle East Ser.). (gr. 4-8). 324.84 *(978-1-59197-409-3(7)*, Abdo & Daughters) ABDO Publishing Co.
Abery, Julie. Yusra Swims. Deng, Sally, illus. 2020. 32p. (J). (gr. 1-3). 19.99 *(978-1-56846-329-2(4)*, 18373, Creative Editions) Creative Co., The.
Adamson, Heather. United Arab Emirates. 2016. (Exploring Countries Ser.). (ENG., Illus.). 32p. (J). (gr. 3-7). lib. bdg. 27.95 *(978-1-62617-346-0(X)*, Blastoff! Readers) Bellwether Media.
Bryan, Antonia D. United Arab Emirates. 2009. (True Book Ser.). (ENG.). 48p. (J). pap. 6.95 *(978-0-531-21361-2(7)*, Children's Pr.) Scholastic Library Publishing.
Coletti, Sharon. Everything You Need to Teach the Middle East. 2005. (YA). ring bd. 149.95 *(978-1-933558-04-2(0))* InspirEd Educators.
Cooper, Robert, et al. Bahrain, 1 vol. 3rd ed. 2019. (Cultures of the World (Third Edition)(r) Ser.). (ENG.). 144p. (gr. 5-5). 48.79 *(978-1-5026-5074-0(6)*, c6ec26fd-f05f-49b4-b851-1bc5f669fc24) Cavendish Square Publishing LLC.
Crisp, Peter. Mesopotamia: Iraq in Ancient Times. 2004. (Picturing the Past Ser.). (Illus.). 32p. (J). 15.95 *(978-1-59270-024-0(1))* Enchanted Lion Bks., LLC.
Darraj, Susan Muaddi & Puller, Meredyth. United Arab Emirates. 2009. (Creation of the Modern Middle East Ser.). (ENG., Illus.). 120p. (gr. 6-12). 35.00 *(978-1-60413-071-3(7)*, P159429, Facts On File) Infobase Holdings, Inc.
Davenport, John. A Brief Political & Geographic History of the Middle East: Where Are... Persia, Babylon, & the Ottoman Empire. 2007. (Places in Time Ser.). (Illus.). 112p. (YA). (gr. 5-9). lib. bdg. 37.10 *(978-1-58415-622-2(8))* Mitchell Lane Pubs.
DeCarlo, Carolyn, ed. The Islamic Caliphate, 1 vol. 2017. (Empires in the Middle Ages Ser.). (ENG., Illus.). 48p. (J). (gr. 6-7). 28.41 *(978-1-68048-783-1(3)*, 8888d3b5-e536-4114-af1d-c0eb77ba4109, Britannica Educational Publishing) Rosen Publishing Group, Inc., The.
Dell, Pamela. Queen Noor, 1 vol. 2013. (Leading Women Ser.). (ENG.). 128p. (YA). (gr. 7-7). 42.64 *(978-0-7614-4958-4(2)*, 552592c1-3555-489d-9243-53b4e3eafb6a); pap. 20.99 *(978-1-62712-116-3(1)*, 506d66d2-3481-4700-981b-44403f2703aa) Cavendish Square Publishing LLC.
Don, Katherine. Nujood Ali & the Fight Against Child Marriage. 2014. (J). *(978-1-59935-466-8(7))* Reynolds, Morgan Inc.
Downing, David. Conflicts of the Middle East, 1 vol. 2006. (World Almanac(r) Library of the Middle East Ser.). (ENG., Illus.). 48p. (gr. 5-8). pap. 15.05 *(978-0-8368-7340-5(8)*, a3d2f15e-0c43-4628-af16-3bf72a40d0df); lib. bdg. 33.67 *(978-0-8368-7333-7(5)*, e710a20c-6eb1-4acb-a3da-f452e1115a1e) Stevens, Gareth Publishing LLLP. (Gareth Stevens Secondary Library).
—History of the Middle East, 1 vol. 2006. (World Almanac(r) Library of the Middle East Ser.). (ENG., Illus.). 48p. (gr. 5-8). pap. 15.05 *(978-0-8368-7343-6(2)*, 7cf777f1-69d7-436a-8cbe-4327092314cc); lib. bdg. 33.67 *(978-0-8368-7336-8(X)*, 9508b1bc-9426-44c4-a4fd-39393c51e481) Stevens, Gareth Publishing LLLP. (Gareth Stevens Secondary Library).
Doyle, Bill H. Behind Enemy Lines: Under Fire in the Middle East. 2011. 136p. (J). pap. *(978-0-545-33463-1(2))* Scholastic, Inc.
Duhig, Holly. Cultural Contributions from the Middle East: Hospitals, Algebra, & More, 1 vol. 2018. (Great Cultures, Great Ideas Ser.). (ENG.). 32p. (gr. 3-4). 27.93 *(978-1-5383-3833-9(5)*, 49b2896f-a44d-43ae-a6aa-4658232ff9e3, PowerKids Pr.) Rosen Publishing Group, Inc., The.
Eugster, Rachel & Whiting, Jim. The Role of Religion in the Early Islamic World. 2012. (ENG., Illus.). 48p. (J). lib. bdg. *(978-0-7787-2169-7(8))* Crabtree Publishing Co.
Flatt, Lizann. Early Islamic Empires. 2013. (ENG., Illus.). 48p. (J). lib. bdg. *(978-0-7787-2171-0(X))* Crabtree Publishing Co.
Gale. Middle East Conflict: Almanac. 2nd ed. 2012. (Middle East Conflict Reference Library). (ENG.). 464p. 129.00 *(978-1-4144-8608-6(1)*, UXL) Cengage Gale.
—Middle East Conflict: Biographies. 2nd ed. 2012. (Middle East Conflict Reference Library). (ENG.). 480p. 129.00 *(978-1-4144-8609-3(X)*, UXL) Cengage Gale.
—Middle East Conflict: Primary Sources. 2nd ed. 2012. (Middle East Conflict Reference Library). (ENG.). 408p. 129.00 *(978-1-4144-8610-9(3)*, UXL) Cengage Gale.
—Middle East Conflict Reference Library, 4 vols. 2nd ed. 2012. (Middle East Conflict Reference Library). (ENG.). 1412p. 348.00 *(978-1-4144-8607-9(3))*; (Illus.). 400p. 5.00 *(978-1-4144-8612-3(X))* Cengage Gale. (UXL).
Gelletly, LeeAnne. The Kurds, Vol. 13. 2015. (Major Nations of the Modern Middle East Ser.). (Illus.). 120p. (J). (gr. 7). lib. bdg. 25.95 *(978-1-4222-3454-9(1))* Mason Crest.
Gillespie, Frances & Al-Naimi, Faisal. Hidden in the Sands - Arabic: Uncovering Qatar's Past. 2013. (ENG., Illus.). 48p. pap. 12.99 *(978-1-909339-03-3(2))* Medina Publishing, Ltd. GBR. Dist: Casemate Pubs. & Bk. Distributors, LLC.
Hampton, Wilborn. War in the Middle East: A Reporter's Story: Black September & the Yom Kippur War. (ENG., Illus.). 128p. (J). (gr. 5). 2009. pap. 9.99 *(978-0-7636-4376-8(9))* 2007. 19.99 *(978-0-7636-2493-4(4))* Candlewick Pr.
Heing, Bridey. The Children Soldiers of ISIS, 1 vol. 2017. (Crimes of ISIS Ser.). (ENG.). 104p. (gr. 8-8). pap. 20.95 *(978-0-7660-9580-9(0)*, a0925f5f-024d-4e7d-90ec-860cd03151a9) Enslow Publishing, LLC.
—The Persecution of Christians & Religious Minorities by ISIS, 1 vol. 2017. (Crimes of ISIS Ser.). (ENG.). 104p. (gr. 8-8). 38.93 *(978-0-7660-9216-7(X)*, 9b809955-9b80-4aec-8640-44247674f520); pap. 20.95 *(978-0-7660-9584-7(3)*, 32c73849-47b1-46fc-b5c4-d73d8257cc86) Enslow Publishing, LLC.
Hestler, Anna, et al. Yemen. 3rd ed. 2018. (J). *(978-1-5026-4161-8(5))* Cavendish Square Publishing LLC.
Hudak, Heather C. A Refugee's Journey from Yemen. 2017. (Leaving My Homeland Ser.). (Illus.). 32p. (J). (gr. 4-4). *(978-0-7787-3677-6(6))* Crabtree Publishing Co.
January, Brendan. Isis: The Global Face of Terrorism. 2017. (ENG., Illus.). 104p. (YA). (gr. 8-12). 37.32 *(978-1-5124-2998-5(8)*, 42e58d57-c5ab-47ec-b577-346d107e9285, Twenty-First Century Bks.) Lerner Publishing Group.
Kerrigan, Michael, et al. Exploring the Life, Myth, & Art of the Ancient near East, 1 vol. 2016. (Civilizations of the World Ser.). (ENG., Illus.). 144p. (J). (gr. 8-8). lib. bdg. 47.80 *(978-1-4994-6397-2(9)*, ee7ecfe9-a717-4268-a7b6-89f663b70dd7) Rosen Publishing Group, Inc., The.
Krasner, Barbara. Ancient Mesopotamian Daily Life, 1 vol. 2016. (Spotlight on the Rise & Fall of Ancient Civilizations Ser.). (ENG., Illus.). 48p. (J). (gr. 6-6). pap. 12.75 *(978-1-4777-8905-6(7)*, 2e906b56-a014-493b-9649-3edfdc7fec1a) Rosen Publishing Group, Inc., The.
Liberman, Sherri. A Historical Atlas of Azerbaijan. 2009. (Historical Atlases of South Asia, Central Asia, & the Middle East Ser.). 64p. (gr. 6-6). 61.20 *(978-1-61513-316-1(X))* Rosen Publishing Group, Inc., The.
LoBaido, Anthony C., et al. The Kurds of Asia. 2005. (First Peoples Ser.). (Illus.). 48p. (gr. 4-8). lib. bdg. 23.95 *(978-0-8225-0664-5(5))* Lerner Publishing Group.
Lowery, Zoe & Levy, Janey. The Darfur Genocide, 1 vol. 2016. (Bearing Witness: Genocide & Ethnic Cleansing Ser.). (ENG., Illus.). 64p. (J). (gr. 6-6). 36.13 *(978-1-4994-6306-4(5)*, db9c0ff8-9416-47e3-a60c-18cd4e78d117) Rosen Publishing Group, Inc., The.
Macaulay, David. Mosque. 2008. (ENG., Illus.). 96p. (J). (gr. 5-7). pap. 12.99 *(978-0-547-01547-7(X)*, 1031263, Clarion Bks.) HarperCollins Pubs.
Maury, Rob. Immigration from the Middle East. 2005. (Changing Face of North America Ser.). (Illus.). 112p. (YA). lib. bdg. 24.95 *(978-1-59084-695-7(8))* Mason Crest.
Maxim, Bailey, ed. The Colonial & Postcolonial Middle East, 1 vol. 2016. (Colonial & Postcolonial Experience Ser.). (ENG., Illus.). 280p. (J). (gr. 10-10). 55.59 *(978-1-5081-0437-7(9)*, d4bb2694-8c84-43a6-bfbf-a0a4ee5e3090, Britannica Educational Publishing) Rosen Publishing Group, Inc., The.
O'Neal, Claire. We Visit Yemen. 2011. (Your Land & My Land Ser.). (Illus.). 64p. (J). (gr. 4-7). lib. bdg. 33.95 *(978-1-58415-961-2(8))* Mitchell Lane Pubs.
Podany, Amanda H. & McGee, Marni. The Ancient near Eastern World. 2005. (World in Ancient Times Ser.). (ENG., Illus.). 176p. (YA). (gr. 7-12). 39.99 *(978-0-19-516159-5(9))* Oxford Univ. Pr., Inc.
Rauf, Don. Near East, Vol. 10. 2016. (Social Progress & Sustainability Ser.). (Illus.). 80p. (J). (gr. 7). 24.95 *(978-1-4222-3497-6(5))* Mason Crest.
Rechner, Amy. South Sudan. 2019. (Country Profiles Ser.). (ENG., Illus.). 32p. (J). (gr. 3-8). lib. bdg. 27.95 *(978-1-62617-963-9(8)*, Blastoff! Discovery) Bellwether Media.
Rice Jr., Earle. Islamic State. 2017. (J). lib. bdg. 29.95 *(978-1-68020-055-3(0))* Mitchell Lane Pubs.
Robinson, Peg, et al. Yemen, 1 vol. 3rd ed. 2018. (Cultures of the World (Third Edition)(r) Ser.). (ENG.). 144p. (J). (gr. 5-5). lib. bdg. 48.79 *(978-1-5026-4162-5(3)*, 062933c7-d647-4fec-acf0-8b64d54f6383) Cavendish Square Publishing LLC.
Rodger, Ellen. A Refugee's Journey from South Sudan. 2017. (Leaving My Homeland Ser.). (Illus.). 32p. (J). (gr. 4-4). *(978-0-7787-3676-9(8))* Crabtree Publishing Co.
Romanek, Trudee. Science, Medicine, & Math in the Early Islamic World. 2012. (ENG.). 48p. (J). lib. bdg. *(978-0-7787-2170-3(1))* Crabtree Publishing Co.
Romano, Amy. A Historical Atlas of United Arab Emirates, 1 vol. 2003. (Historical Atlases of South Asia, Central Asia, & the Middle East Ser.). (ENG., Illus.). 64p. (gr. 6-6). lib. bdg. 37.13 *(978-0-8239-4501-6(4)*, 677dd16e-8a40-4185-a985-de0774323371) Rosen Publishing Group, Inc., The.
—A Historical Atlas of Yemen, 1 vol. 2003. (Historical Atlases of South Asia, Central Asia, & the Middle East Ser.). (ENG., Illus.). 64p. (gr. 6-6). lib. bdg. 37.13 *(978-0-8239-4502-3(2)*, f2d25b7c-5545-474c-adbd-d64f749a0a64) Rosen Publishing Group, Inc., The.
Rubin, Barry A. The Middle East in the Age of Uncertainty, 1991-Present. 2009. (Making of the Middle East Ser.). (Illus.). 78p. (YA). (gr. 3-7). lib. bdg. 22.95 *(978-1-4222-0176-3(7))* Mason Crest.
Scheppler, Bill. Al-Biruni: Master Astronomer & Muslim Scholar of the Eleventh Century. 2009. (Great Muslim Philosophers & Scientists of the Middle Ages Ser.). 112p. (gr. 6-6). 66.50 *(978-1-61513-177-8(9)*, Rosen Reference) Rosen Publishing Group, Inc., The.
Senker, Cath. Israel & the Middle East. 2011. (Our World Divided Ser.). (ENG.). 48p. (YA). (gr. 5-8). 27.95 *(978-1-4488-6032-6(6)*, Rosen Reference) Rosen Publishing Group, Inc., The.
Stefoff, Rebecca. The Ancient near East, 1 vol. 2006. (World Historical Atlases Ser.). (ENG.). 48p. (gr. 5-5). 34.07 *(978-0-7614-1639-5(0)*, 321d5b71-b403-48fd-9495-2d162f2a125f) Cavendish Square Publishing LLC.
Townsend, Chris. The Violent Rise of ISIS, 1 vol. 2017. (Crimes of ISIS Ser.). (ENG.). 104p. (gr. 8-8). pap. 20.95 *(978-0-7660-9579-3(7)*, 51df27e7-92f3-42cf-a90e-8d18e0e3bce0) Enslow Publishing, LLC.
Understanding the Cultures of the Middle East, 8 vols. 2016. (Understanding the Cultures of the Middle East Ser.). (ENG.). 112p. (YA). (gr. 9-9). lib. bdg. 178.00 *(978-1-5026-2372-0(2)*, c085b049-bdd8-41c2-b8c4-a5aa00ea1b92, Cavendish Square) Cavendish Square Publishing LLC.
War & Conflict in the Middle East, 12 vols. 2003. (War & Conflict in the Middle East Ser.). (ENG., Illus.). 64p. (gr. 5-5). lib. bdg. 222.78 *(978-1-4042-0146-0(7)*, ceb82535-199b-43c8-b24f-5f1595f5e4c9) Rosen Publishing Group, Inc., The.
Warms, Ed. Immigration to North America: Middle Eastern Immigrants, Vol. 11. Anderson, Stuart, ed. 2016. (Immigration to North America Ser.: Vol. 11). (ENG., Illus.). 112p. (J). (gr. 7-12). 25.95 *(978-1-4222-3689-5(7))* Mason Crest.
Young Voices from the Arab World: The Lives & Times of Five Teenagers. 2004. 139p. (YA). (gr. 5-18). tchr. ed. 35.00 incl. VHS *(978-0-913957-15-8(1))* AMIDEAST.

MIDDLE EAST—POLITICS AND GOVERNMENT

Conklin, Blane. Leaders of the Middle East, 1 vol. rev. ed. 2007. (Social Studies: Informational Text Ser.). (ENG.). 32p. (gr. 4-8). pap. 11.99 *(978-0-7439-0675-3(6))* Teacher Created Materials, Inc.
Einfeld, Jann, ed. Can Democracy Succeed in the Middle East?, 1 vol. 2006. (At Issue Ser.). (ENG., Illus.). 128p. (gr. 10-12). 41.03 *(978-0-7377-3393-8(4)*, 48042521-6dcb-45f0-b43b-52d518155ee2, Greenhaven Publishing) Greenhaven Publishing LLC.
Elish, Dan. Inside the Situation Room: How a Photograph Showed America Defeating Osama Bin Laden. 2018. (Captured History Ser.). (ENG., Illus.). 64p. (J). (gr. 5-9). pap. 8.95 *(978-0-7565-5881-9(6)*, 138649, Compass Point Bks.) Capstone.
Foreign Policy Research Institute Staff, ed. Modern Middle East Nations & Their Strategic Places in the World, 25 vols., Set. 2003. (Illus.). 112,128p. (YA). (gr. 7-18). lib. bdg. *(978-1-59084-504-2(8))* Mason Crest.
Gunderson, Cory Gideon. The Need for Oil. 2003. (World in Conflict-the Middle East Ser.). 32p. (gr. 4-8). 27.07 *(978-1-59197-417-8(8)*, Abdo & Daughters) ABDO Publishing Co.
Haugen, David M., et al, eds. Iraq, 1 vol. 2009. (Opposing Viewpoints Ser.). (ENG., Illus.). 192p. (gr. 10-12). pap. 34.80 *(978-0-7377-4525-2(8)*, 722b2966-c9c2-49cb-b811-f845bdbe4269);No. 9. lib. bdg. 50.43 *(978-0-7377-4524-5(X)*, c2c737cd-a425-40a8-8f6f-150e90beb9e4) Greenhaven Publishing LLC. (Greenhaven Publishing).
Heing, Bridey. Geography, Government, & Conflict Across the Middle East, 1 vol. 2016. (Understanding the Cultures of the Middle East Ser.). (ENG., Illus.). 112p. (YA). (gr. 9-9). lib. bdg. 44.50 *(978-1-5026-2367-6(6)*, b02357c0-5893-4caf-b744-19b0a9c4a01d) Cavendish Square Publishing LLC.
Hunnicutt, Susan C., ed. The Middle East Peace Process, 1 vol. 2010. (Opposing Viewpoints Ser.). (ENG.). 192p. (gr. 10-12). 50.43 *(978-0-7377-4976-2(8)*, 75f77f41-b059-4fda-b109-6af2d8b6a7ca); pap. 34.80 *(978-0-7377-4977-9(6)*, ed8ec9cb-986f-402c-9dc8-8d75ce3da60f) Greenhaven Publishing LLC. (Greenhaven Publishing).
Rich, Mari. The Middle Eastern Family Table, Vol. 11. 2018. (Connecting Cultures Through Family & Food Ser.). (Illus.). 64p. (J). (gr. 7). lib. bdg. 31.93 *(978-1-4222-4049-6(5))* Mason Crest.
Romanek, Trudee. Government & Law in the Early Islamic World. 2013. (ENG.). 48p. (J). lib. bdg. *(978-0-7787-2168-0(X))* Crabtree Publishing Co.
Sasley, Brent. The Cold War in the Middle East, 1950-1991. 2009. (Making of the Middle East Ser.). (Illus.). 80p. (YA). (gr. 7-18). lib. bdg. 22.95 *(978-1-4222-0173-2(2))* Mason Crest.
Steele, Philip. Uprisings in the Middle East & North Africa. 2016. (Behind the News Ser.). (Illus.). 48p. (J). (gr. 6-9). *(978-0-7787-2589-3(8))* Crabtree Publishing Co.
Wagner, Heather Lehr. Anwar Sadat & Menachem Begin. 2007. (Modern Peacemakers Ser.). (ENG., Illus.). 122p. (gr. 9-12). lib. bdg. 30.00 *(978-0-7910-9000-8(0)*, P114507, Facts On File) Infobase Holdings, Inc.
Witte, Sam. Gamal Abdel Nasser. 2009. (Middle East Leaders Ser.). 112p. (gr. 5-8). 66.50 *(978-1-61514-646-8(6)*, Rosen Reference) Rosen Publishing Group, Inc., The.

MIDDLE STATES

see Atlantic States

MIDDLE WEST

Here are entered works on the region of the United States between the Rocky Mountains and the Allegheny Mountains and north of the Ohio River and the southern border of Missouri and Kansas, generally including the states of Ohio, Indiana, Michigan, Illinois, Wisconsin, Minnesota, Iowa, Missouri, Kansas, Nebraska, South Dakota and North Dakota.

Benchmark Education Company. The Midwest Region (Teacher Guide) 2005. *(978-1-4108-4653-2(9))* Benchmark Education Co.
Chandler, Matt. El Cementerio de Bachelor's Grove y Otros Lugares Embrujados Del Medio Oeste. Aparicio Publishing LLC, Aparicio Publishing, tr. 2020. (América Embrujada Ser.).Tr. of Bachelor's Grove Cemetery & Other Haunted Places of the Midwest. (SPA., Illus.). 32p. (J). (gr. 3-9). lib. bdg. 30.65 *(978-1-4966-8510-0(5)*, 200616, Capstone Pr.) Capstone.
Codell, Esmé Raji. Seed by Seed: The Legend & Legacy of John Appleseed Anniversary. Perkins, Lynne Rae, illus. 2012. (ENG.). 32p. (J). (gr. -1-3). 17.89 *(978-0-06-145516-2(4)*, Greenwillow Bks.) HarperCollins Pubs.
—Seed by Seed: The Legend & Legacy of John Appleseed Chapman. Perkins, Lynne Rae, illus. 2012. (ENG.). 32p. (J). (gr. -1-3). 16.99 *(978-0-06-145515-5(6)*, Greenwillow Bks.) HarperCollins Pubs.
Houran, Lori Haskins. My Little Golden Book about Johnny Appleseed. Godbout, Geneviève, illus. 2017. (Little Golden Book Ser.). 24p. (J). (gr. -1-3). 5.99 *(978-0-399-55590-9(0)*, Golden Bks.) Random Hse. Children's Bks.
Leonardo, Victoria. The Midwest Region. 2005. (J). pap. *(978-1-4108-4605-1(9))* Benchmark Education Co.
Miller, Reagan & Johnson, Robin. What's in the Midwest? Crabtree Publishing Staff, ed. 2011. (All Around the U.S. Ser.). (ENG.). 32p. (J). (gr. 3-6). pap. *(978-0-7787-1829-1(8))* Crabtree Publishing Co.
—What's in the Midwest? 2011. (ENG.). 32p. (J). lib. bdg. *(978-0-7787-1823-9(9))* Crabtree Publishing Co.
National Geographic Learning. Language, Literacy & Vocabulary - Reading Expeditions (U. S. Regions): Explore the Midwest. 2007. (ENG., Illus.). 36p. (J). pap. 20.95 *(978-0-7922-5458-4(9))* CENGAGE Learning.
—Reading Expeditions (Social Studies: Readings about America): the Midwest Today. 2007. (ENG., Illus.). 32p. (J). pap. 18.95 *(978-0-7922-4534-6(2))* CENGAGE Learning.
Orr, Tamra B. It's Cool to Learn about the United States Midwest. 2011. (Explorer Library: Social Studies Explorer Ser.). (ENG.). 48p. (gr. 4-8). pap. 15.64 *(978-1-61080-302-1(7)*, 201198) Cherry Lake Publishing.
Radomski, Kassandra. People & Places of the Midwest. 2016. (United States by Region Ser.). (ENG., Illus.). 32p. (J). (gr. 3-6). lib. bdg. 27.99 *(978-1-5157-2440-7(9)*, 132820, Capstone Pr.) Capstone.
Schaeffer, Julia. The Midwest States: Set Of 6. 2011. (Navigators Ser.). (J). pap. 48.00 net. *(978-1-4108-6253-2(4))* Benchmark Education Co.
Schaffer, Julia. The Midwest States: Text Pairs. 2008. (BridgesNavigators Ser.). (J). (gr. 4). 89.00 *(978-1-4108-8390-2(6))* Benchmark Education Co.
Wiseman, Blaine. The Midwest. 2016. (Illus.). 48p. (J). *(978-1-5105-1136-1(9))* SmartBook Media, Inc.
Yomtov, Nel. The Children's Blizzard Of 1888: A Cause-And-Effect Investigation. 2016. (Cause-And-Effect Disasters Ser.). (ENG., Illus.). 40p. (J). (gr. 4-6). lib. bdg. 30.65 *(978-1-5124-1118-8(3)*, af5bc601-6032-4d4b-9f15-d9c74ebbb667, Lerner Pubns.) Lerner Publishing Group.

MIDDLE WEST—FICTION

Anderson, Peggy King. Two-Moon Journey: The Potawatomi Trail of Death. 2018. 356p. (J). *(978-0-87195-424-4(9))* Indiana Historical Society.
Bean, Margo Cronbaugh. Brutus the Bull. Perry, Aumi Kauffman, illus. 2013. 24p. 19.95 *(978-1-61633-373-7(1))*; pap. 11.95 *(978-1-61633-374-4(X))* Guardian Angel Publishing, Inc.
Chand, Emlyn. Farsighted. 2012. 260p. pap. 12.95 *(978-0-9839308-3-9(X))* Blue Crown Pr.
Damron, Dugan. Further Adventures of Old Shorty: Tales of a Midwest Country Boy, 1 vol. 2010. 112p. pap. 19.95 *(978-1-4489-5838-2(5))* America Star Bks.
Geisert, Arthur, creator. Thunderstorm. 2015. (ENG., Illus.). 34p. (J). (gr. k). 60.00 *(978-1-59270-170-4(1))* Enchanted Lion Bks., LLC.
Hammond, John, as told by. Lucky in Life. 2003. 150p. (YA). per. 13.95 *(978-1-885631-76-3(6))* Hutchison, G.F. Pr.
Kegerreis, Carl. Tibby & His Friend's Big Secret. 2010. 96p. pap. 13.95 *(978-1-4327-4449-6(6))* Outskirts Pr., Inc.
Kraus, Daniel. Rotters. 2012. (ENG.). 464p. (YA). (gr. 9). pap. 10.99 *(978-0-385-73858-3(7)*, Ember) Random Hse. Children's Bks.

M
N
O

L'Allier, Peter Wesley Thomas. Rotten Robbie & the Legend of Wanabinoo. 2006. (Illus.). 215p. 18.95 *(978-0-9724022-8-6(4))* TangleTown Media Inc.

Lewis, Richard. The Demon Queen. 2012. (ENG.). 240p. (YA). (gr. 7). pap. 11.99 *(978-1-4169-3590-2(8))*, Simon & Schuster Bks. For Young Readers) Simon & Schuster Bks. For Young Readers.

Lillehaug-Collins, Yvonne. Little Dragon. 2009. 70p. pap. 21.00 *(978-1-60693-344-2(2))*, Eloquent Bks.) Strategic Book Publishing & Rights Agency (SBPRA).

Macaraeg, Diane. Last Meal. 2008. 132p. pap. *(978-3-639-03548-3(8))* AV Akademikerverlag GmbH & Co. KG.

Peck, Richard. The Ghost Belonged to Me. 2005. 176p. (YA). 21.00 *(978-0-8446-7275-5(0))*, 3590) Smith, Peter Pub., Inc.

Tilson, Gina L. Patches: Adventures of a Country Cavalier. 2011. 48p. pap. 9.99 *(978-1-4567-6386-2(5))* AuthorHouse.

Wargin, Kathy-jo. Mitt & Minn at the Wisconsin Cheese Jamboree. Holman, Karen Busch, illus. 2007. (Mitt Midwest Ser.: 3). 144p. (J). (gr. k-7). 14.95 *(978-1-58726-305-7(X))*, Mitten Pr.) Ann Arbor Editions LLC.

—Mitt & Minn's Illinois Adventure. Holman, Karen Busch, illus. 2007. (Mitt Midwest Ser.: 4). 144p. (J). (gr. k-7). 14.95 *(978-1-58726-306-4(8))*, Mitten Pr.) Ann Arbor Editions LLC.

Weaver, Will. Checkered Flag Cheater: A Motor Novel. 2010. (Motor Novels Ser.: 3). (ENG.). 208p. (YA). (gr. 7-12). 19.99 *(978-0-374-35062-8(0))*, 900042718, Farrar, Straus & Giroux (BYR)) Farrar, Straus & Giroux.

Weber, Richard D. Elvis & Me. 2004. 511p. (YA). per. 17.41 *(978-1-4116-0549-7(7))* Lulu Pr., Inc.

Wilder, Laura Ingalls. Pioneer Sisters. 2017. (Little House Chapter Book Ser.: 2). (ENG., Illus.). 112p. (J). (gr. 1-5). pap. 6.99 *(978-0-06-237710-4(8))*, HarperCollins) HarperCollins Pubs.

MIDDLE WEST—HISTORY

Brannon, Barbara. Discover the Midwest Region. 2005. (J). pap. *(978-1-4108-5151-2(6))* Benchmark Education Co.

Burkes-Larrañaga, Dustin, illus. Johnny Appleseed Plants Trees Across the Land, 1 vol. 2014. (American Folk Legends Ser.). (ENG.). 32p. (J). (gr. k-2). lib. bdg. 27.99 *(978-1-4795-5428-7(6))*, 126076, Picture Window Bks.) Capstone.

Chandler, Matt. Bachelor's Grove Cemetery & Other Haunted Places of the Midwest, 1 vol. 2014. (Haunted America Ser.). (ENG., Illus.). 32p. (J). (gr. 3-9). lib. bdg. 28.65 *(978-1-4765-3913-3(8))*, 123912, Capstone Pr.) Capstone.

Connors, Kathleen. Let's Explore the Midwest, 1 vol. 2013. (Road Trip: Exploring America's Regions Ser.). (ENG.). 24p. (J). (gr. 2-3). pap. 9.15 *(978-1-4339-9130-1(6))*, 1f175db0-77dd-4a4a-a4a8-8edaefbae0f9); (Illus.). lib. bdg. 25.27 *(978-1-4339-9129-5(2))*, 8fdc6bd8-b5e6-43c6-9ab3-776224d4acba) Stevens, Gareth Publishing LLLP.

Doherty, Kieran. Voyageurs, Lumberjacks & Farmers: Pioneers of the Midwest. 2003. (Shaping America Ser.: Vol. 5). (Illus.). 176p. (gr. 7-18). lib. bdg. 22.95 *(978-1-881508-54-0(4))* Oliver Pr., Inc.

Gagne, Tammy. Exploring the Midwest. 2017. (Exploring America's Regions Ser.). (ENG., Illus.). 48p. (J). (gr. 4-8). lib. bdg. 35.64 *(978-1-5321-1382-6(X))*, 27680) ABDO Publishing Co.

Garland, Sherry. Voices of the Dust Bowl, 1 vol. Hierstein, Judith, illus. 2012. (Voices of History Ser.). (ENG.). 40p. (J). (gr. 3-3). 19.99 *(978-1-58980-964-2(5))*, Pelican Publishing) Arcadia Publishing.

Henley, Margaret. Johnny Appleseed: the Grand Old Man of the Forest, 1 vol. 2014. (American Legends & Folktales Ser.). (ENG., Illus.). 32p. (gr. 3-3). 31.21 *(978-1-62712-277-1(X))*, 1c5ce59e-05fc-4d74-a485-4b52f7e5494a); pap. 11.58 *(978-1-62712-278-8(8))*, aef33383-cf04-4a9f-843c-662daefcc3e6) Cavendish Square Publishing LLC.

Herschbach, Elisabeth. Lower Plains: Kansas, Nebraska, Vol. 19. 2015. (Let's Explore the States Ser.). (Illus.). 64p. (J). (gr. 5). 23.95 *(978-1-4222-3326-9(X))* Mason Crest.

Hook, Sue Vander. Southern Atlantic Coast Region. 2014. (United States Regions Ser.). (ENG.). 32p. (gr. 4-8). 32.79 *(978-1-62717-676-7(4))*, 9781627176767) Rourke Educational Media.

Let's Explore the Midwest. 2013. (Road Trip: Exploring America's Regions Ser.). 24p. (J). (gr. 2-5). pap. 48.90 *(978-1-4339-9131-8(4))* Stevens, Gareth Publishing LLLP.

The Midwest. 2014. (Land That I Love: Regions of the United States Ser.). (Illus.). 32p. (J). (gr. 3-6). pap. 60.00 *(978-1-4777-6637-8(5))*, PowerKids Pr.) Rosen Publishing Group, Inc., The.

Orr, Tamra B. It's Cool to Learn about the United States: Midwest. 2011. (Explorer Library: Social Studies Explorer Ser.). (ENG., Illus.). 48p. (gr. 4-8). lib. bdg. 34.93 *(978-1-61080-179-9(2))*, 201152) Cherry Lake Publishing.

Rau, Dana Meachen. The Midwest (a True Book: the U. S. Regions) 2012. (True Book (Relaunch) Ser.). (ENG., Illus.). 48p. (J). (gr. 3-5). pap. 6.95 *(978-0-531-28325-7(9))*, Children's Pr.) Scholastic Library Publishing.

—A True Book: the Midwest. 2012. (True Book: U. S. Regions Ser.). (ENG., Illus.). 48p. (J). (gr. 3-5). 21.19 *(978-0-531-24850-8(X))*, Children's Pr.) Scholastic Library Publishing.

Westcott, Jim. Upper Plains: Montana, North Dakota, South Dakota, Vol. 19. 2015. (Let's Explore the States Ser.). (Illus.). 64p. (J). (gr. 5). 23.95 *(978-1-4222-3336-8(7))* Mason Crest.

Wiseman, Blaine. The Midwest. 2014. (Illus.). 32p. (J). *(978-1-4896-1226-7(2))* Weigl Pubs., Inc.

Yomtov, Nel. The Children's Blizzard Of 1888: A Cause-And-Effect Investigation. 2016. (Cause-And-Effect Disasters Ser.). (ENG., Illus.). 40p. (J). (gr. 4-6). E-Book 46.65 *(978-1-5124-1129-4(9))*, Lerner Pubns.) Lerner Publishing Group.

MIDGETS

see Dwarfs

MIDWAY, BATTLE OF, 1942

Abnett, Dan. The Battle of Midway: The Destruction of the Japanese Fleet, 1 vol. Elson, Richard, illus. 2007. (Graphic Battles of World War II Ser.). (ENG.). 48p. (YA). (gr. 5-5). lib. bdg. 37.13 *(978-1-4042-0783-7(X))*, 504f9af2-4160-40ae-8de9-6d3ee0f78eca) Rosen Publishing Group, Inc., The.

Mara, Wil. The Battle of Midway: Turning the Tide of World War II. 2017. (Major Battles in US History Ser.). (ENG., Illus.). 32p. (J). (gr. 3-5). pap. 9.95 *(978-1-63517-077-1(X))*, 163517077X, Focus Readers) North Star Editions.

White, Steve. The Battle of Midway: The Destruction of the Japanese Fleet, 1 vol. 2006. (Graphic Battles of World War II Ser.). (ENG., Illus.). 48p. (gr. 5-5). pap. 14.05 *(978-1-4042-7424-2(3))*, f00a846a-54a8-4216-ad09-d4e489d4a5e8) Rosen Publishing Group, Inc., The.

MIDWEST

see Middle West

MIDWIFERY

see Childbirth

MIGRANT LABOR

Here are entered works dealing with casual or seasonal workers who move from place to place in search of employment. Works on the movement of population within a country for permanent settlement are entered under Migration, Internal.

Cooper, Michael L. Dust to Eat: Drought & Depression in The 1930s. 2004. (ENG., Illus.). 96p. (YA). (gr. 7-9). tchr. ed. 17.00 *(978-0-618-15449-4(3))*, 111116, Clarion Bks.) HarperCollins Pubs.

Cruz, Bárbara C. César Chávez: Civil Rights Activist, 1 vol. 2015. (Influential Latinos Ser.). (ENG.). 128p. (gr. 7-8). lib. bdg. 38.93 *(978-0-7660-7179-7(0))*, 67488698-384c-48fc-b6f0-63bc38040d7e) Enslow Publishing, LLC.

Herrera, Juan Felipe. El Canto de las Palomas/Calling the Doves. 2004. (Illus.). (J). (gr. 3-6). spiral bd. *(978-0-616-14607-1(8))* Canadian National Institute for the Blind/Institut National Canadien pour les Aveugles.

Zuchora-Walske, Christine. The Dust Bowl: A History Perspectives Book. 2013. (Perspectives Library). (ENG., Illus.). 32p. (J). (gr. 4-8). 32.07 *(978-1-62431-417-9(1))*, 202788); pap. 14.21 *(978-1-62431-493-3(7))*, 202790) Cherry Lake Publishing.

MIGRANT LABOR—FICTION

Altman, Linda Jacobs. El Camino de Amelia. 2004. (SPA., Illus.). (J). (gr. k-3). spiral bd. *(978-0-616-14603-3(5))* Canadian National Institute for the Blind/Institut National Canadien pour les Aveugles.

Alvarez, Julia. Devolver Al Remitente (Return to Sender Spanish Edition) 2010. (SPA.). 368p. (J). (gr. 3-7). 8.99 *(978-0-375-85124-7(0))*, Yearling) Random Hse. Children's Bks.

—Return to Sender. 2010. (ENG.). 352p. (J). (gr. 3-7). 8.99 *(978-0-375-85123-0(2))*, Yearling) Random Hse. Children's Bks.

Castillo, Gary D. Quesadilla Moon. 2007. 100p. (J). (gr. 3-7). per. 9.95 *(978-1-55885-433-8(9))*, Piñata Books) Arte Publico Pr.

Gonzalez, Genaro. A So-Called Vacation. 2009. 192p. (YA). (gr. 9-18). pap. 10.95 *(978-1-55885-545-8(9))*, Piñata Books) Arte Publico Pr.

Literature Connections English: ... & the Earth Did Not Devour Him. 2004. (gr. 6-12). *(978-0-395-77139-6(0))*, 2-70217) Holt McDougal.

Lowery, Linda. Truth & Saisa, 1 vol. 2009. 176p. (J). (gr. 3-7). pap. 7.95 *(978-1-56145-498-3(2))* Peachtree Publishing Co. Inc.

Mora, Pat. Tomas & the Library Lady. Colón, Raúl, illus. 2007. (gr. k-3). 18.00 *(978-0-7569-7935-5(8))* Perfection Learning Corp.

—Tomas y la Senora de la Biblioteca. 2004. (SPA., Illus.). (J). (gr. k-3). spiral bd. *(978-0-616-03092-9(4))* Canadian National Institute for the Blind/Institut National Canadien pour les Aveugles.

Paulsen, Gary. The Beet Fields. 2011. (ENG.). 176p. (YA). (gr. 9). pap. 7.99 *(978-0-375-87305-8(8))*, Delacorte Bks. for Young Readers) Random Hse. Children's Bks.

Perez, L. King. First Day in Grapes, 1 vol. Casilla, Robert, illus. 2004. (ENG.). 32p. (J). pap. 9.95 *(978-1-55041-340-3(6))*, a920fac5-51e0-4465-9963-9c60eb81b190) Fitzhenry & Whiteside, Ltd. CAN. Dist: Firefly Bks., Ltd.

Prinz, Yvonne. All You Get Is Me. 2010. (ENG.). 288p. (YA). (gr. 9-18). 16.99 *(978-0-06-171580-8(8))* HarperCollins Pubs.

Rio, Adam del & Arroyo, David. Vines of the Earth. Rio, Adam del & Arroyo, David, illus. 2006. (SPA & ENG., Illus.). 27p. *(978-0-9772852-7-3(8))*; pap. *(978-0-9772852-6-6(X))* Lectura Bks.

Smothers, Ethel Footman. The Hard-Times Jar. Holyfield, John, illus. 2003. (ENG.). 32p. (J). (gr. k-3). 19.99 *(978-0-374-32852-8(8))*, 900021204, Farrar, Straus & Giroux (BYR)) Farrar, Straus & Giroux.

Tonatiuh, Duncan. Pancho Rabbit & the Coyote: A Migrant's Tale. 2013. (ENG., Illus.). 32p. (J). (gr. 1-4). 18.99 *(978-1-4197-0583-0(0))*, 692601, Abrams Bks. for Young Readers) Abrams, Inc.

MIGRANT LABOR—UNITED STATES

Brown, Jonatha A. César Chávez, 1 vol. (Gente Que Hay Que Conocer (People We Should Know) Ser.). 2005. (SPA.). 24p. (gr. 2-4). pap. 9.15 *(978-0-8368-4766-6(0))*, b98ea793-6731-49c5-adf5-131db8ecbb55, Weekly Reader Leveled Readers) 2005. (ENG., Illus.). 24p. (gr. 2-4). lib. bdg. 24.67 *(978-0-8368-4745-1(8))*, b08a0da5-bcb9-4d07-916b-08fbc9b54ab5, Weekly Reader Leveled Readers) 2005. (SPA., Illus.). 24p. (gr. 2-4). lib. bdg. 24.67 *(978-0-8368-4759-8(8))*, 47c9aecc-dbd0-4961-9b94-8813dc904c2a, Weekly Reader Leveled Readers) 2004. (ENG., Illus.). 48p. (gr. 5-8). lib. bdg. 33.67 *(978-0-8368-5097-0(1))*, 90a1df70-6160-4ee6-9805-349b20666679, Gareth Stevens Secondary Library) Stevens, Gareth Publishing LLLP.

DePietro, Frank. Latino Migrant Workers. 2013. (Illus.). 64p. (J). pap. *(978-1-4222-2343-7(4))* Mason Crest.

—Latino Migrant Workers. Limón, José E., ed. 2012. (Hispanic Americans: Major Minority Ser.). (Illus.). 64p. (J). (gr. 4). 22.95 *(978-1-4222-2326-0(4))* Mason Crest.

Krull, Kathleen. Cosechando Esperanza: La Historia de César Chávez (Harvesting Hope Spanish Edition) Ada, Alma Flor & Campoy, F. Isabel, trs. Morales, Yuyi, illus. 2004. (SPA.). 48p. (J). (gr. -1-3). pap. 7.99 *(978-0-15-205169-3(4))*, 1195591, Clarion Bks.) HarperCollins Pubs.

—Harvesting Hope: The Story of Cesar Chavez. Morales, Yuyi, illus. 2003. (ENG.). 48p. (J). (gr. -1-3). 17.99 *(978-0-15-201437-7(3))*, 1189864, Clarion Bks.) HarperCollins Pubs.

Mattern, Joanne. Cesar Chavez: Labor Rights Activist, 1 vol. 2019. (Barrier-Breaker Bios Ser.). (ENG.). 32p. (gr. 2-2). pap. 11.58 *(978-1-5026-4952-2(7))*, ff86fa33-8ac1-4442-8faf-3a7210156900) Cavendish Square Publishing LLC.

Rinaldo, Denise. Cesar Chavez: With a Discussion of Compassion. 2003. (Values in Action Ser.). (J). *(978-1-59203-064-4(5))* Learning Challenge, Inc.

Seidman, David. Cesar Chavez: Labor Leader. 2004. (Great Life Stories Ser.). (ENG., Illus.). 128p. (J). 30.50 *(978-0-531-12319-5(7))*, Watts, Franklin) Scholastic Library Publishing.

Soto, Gary. Cesar Chavez: A Hero for Everyone. Lohstoeter, Lori, illus. 2003. (Milestone Ser.). (ENG.). 80p. (J). (gr. 2-5). pap. 6.99 *(978-0-689-85922-9(8))*, Simon & Schuster/Paula Wiseman Bks.) Simon & Schuster/Paula Wiseman Bks.

Thompson, E. L. Cesar Chavez, with Profiles of Terence V. Powderly & Dolores Huerta. 2006. (Biographical Connections Ser.). (Illus.). 112p. (J). *(978-0-7166-1827-0(3))* World Bk., Inc.

Wheeler, Jill C. Cesar Chavez. 2003. (Breaking Barriers Ser.). 64p. (gr. 3-8). 27.07 *(978-1-57765-905-1(8))*, Abdo & Daughters) ABDO Publishing Co.

MIGRANTS

see Immigrants; Migrant Labor

MIGRATION

see Emigration and Immigration

MIGRATION, INTERNAL

De Medeiros, James. The Migration North. (J). 2013. 29.99 *(978-1-62127-193-2(5))* 2013. pap. 14.95 *(978-1-62127-199-4(4))* 2008. (Illus.). 48p. (gr. 5-8). pap. 10.95 *(978-1-59036-881-7(9))* 2008. (Illus.). 48p. (gr. 5-8). lib. bdg. 29.05 *(978-1-59036-880-0(0))* Weigl Pubs., Inc.

Griffin, Brett. American Migration & Settlement, 1 vol. 2018. (Discovering America: an Exceptional Nation Ser.). (ENG.). 112p. (gr. 7-7). lib. bdg. 44.50 *(978-1-5026-4265-3(4))*, 12165498-85f1-4377-9ff8-b318aa021305) Cavendish Square Publishing LLC.

Harris, Irene. African American Migrations in North America, 1 vol., 1. 2015. (Spotlight on Immigration & Migration (Special Edition) Ser.). (ENG., Illus.). 24p. (J). (gr. 4-5). pap. 11.00 *(978-1-5081-4046-7(4))*, dc586c28-afd7-463e-8f3c-f6e846658007, PowerKids Pr.) Rosen Publishing Group, Inc., The.

Naidoo, Beverley. Making It Home: Real-Life Stories from Children Forced to Flee. 2005. (Illus.). 117p. (gr. 3-7). 17.00 *(978-0-7569-5823-7(7))* Perfection Learning Corp.

Obadina, Tunde. Population & Overcrowding. Ojakorotu, Victor & Rotberg, Robert I., eds. 2013. (Africa: Progress & Problems Ser.: 13). (Illus.). 112p. (J). (gr. 7-18). 24.95 *(978-1-4222-2945-3(9))* Mason Crest.

Rosen Classroom, creator. Map Activities for Primary Sources of Immigration & Migration in America: Reproducible Blackline Masters. 2011. (Illus.). 15p. (J). pap. 15.99 *(978-0-8239-4597-9(9))*, Rosen Classroom) Rosen Publishing Group, Inc., The.

Sioux, Tracee. Immigrants, Migration, & the Growth of the American City, 1 vol. 2003. (Primary Sources of Immigration & Migration in America Ser.). (ENG., Illus.). 24p. (J). (gr. 3-4). lib. bdg. 26.27 *(978-0-8239-6828-2(6))*, 12be3da0-f355-4506-bdaf-bf68bdaee002, PowerKids Pr.) Rosen Publishing Group, Inc., The.

—Immigration, Migration, & the Growth of the American City, 1 vol. 2003. (Primary Sources of Immigration & Migration in America Ser.). (ENG., Illus.). 24p. (gr. 3-4). pap. 9.40 *(978-0-8239-8954-6(2))*, 0303e238-ed02-4de0-8169-f108b5d977d3, PowerKids Pr.) Rosen Publishing Group, Inc., The.

—Immigration, Migration, & the Industrial Revolution, 1 vol. 2003. (Primary Sources of Immigration & Migration in America Ser.). (ENG., Illus.). 24p. (gr. 3-4). pap. 9.40 *(978-0-8239-8998-0(4))*, 7136c3ff-b4ea-41db-a705-449a93f6e243, PowerKids Pr.) Rosen Publishing Group, Inc., The.

Walker, Robert. Pushes & Pulls: Why Do People Migrate?, 1 vol. 2010. (Investigating Human Migration & Settlement Ser.). (ENG., Illus.). 48p. (J). (gr. 5-8). *(978-0-7787-5183-0(X))*; pap. *(978-0-7787-5198-4(8))* Crabtree Publishing Co.

MIGRATION OF ANIMALS

see Animals—Migration

MIGRATION OF BIRDS

see Birds—Migration

MIGRATORY WORKERS

see Migrant Labor

MILITARY AERONAUTICS

see Aeronautics, Military

MILITARY AIR BASES

see Air Bases

MILITARY AIRPLANES

see Airplanes, Military

MILITARY ART AND SCIENCE

see also Aeronautics, Military; Armies; Battles; Disarmament; Fortification; Guerrilla Warfare; Ordnance; Signals and Signaling; Soldiers; Spies; War; Weapons

also headings beginning with the word Military

Adams, Simon. DK Eyewitness Books: Soldier: Discover the World of Soldiers — Their Training, Tactics, Vehicles, & Weapons. 2009. (DK Eyewitness Ser.). (ENG., Illus.). 72p. (J). (gr. 3-7). 16.99 *(978-0-7566-4539-7(5))*, DK Children) Dorling Kindersley Publishing, Inc.

AZ Books Staff. Great Warriors. Aksinovich, Natalia & Yaroshevich, Angelica, eds. 2012. (Sounds Around Us Ser.). (ENG.). 16p. (J). (gr. 1-3). bds. 17.95 *(978-1-61889-033-7(6))* AZ Bks. LLC.

Bailey, Diane. Rescue from an ISIS Prison! Delta Force in Iraq During the War on Terror, Vol. 8. 2018. (Special Forces Stories Ser.). 64p. (J). (gr. 7). lib. bdg. 31.93 *(978-1-4222-4080-9(0))* Mason Crest.

Barnham, Kay. The Fact or Fiction Behind Battles & Wars, 1 vol. 2015. (Fact or Phony? Ser.). (ENG.). 96p. (J). (gr. 5-6). lib. bdg. 34.93 *(978-1-4824-4268-7(X))*, 1304b0b1-00b6-4ce4-94be-15152c58d1b3) Stevens, Gareth Publishing LLLP.

Baum, Margaux & Hilliam, Paul. Weapons & Warcraft, 1 vol. 2016. (Life in the Middle Ages Ser.). (ENG., Illus.). 64p. (J). (gr. 5-5). 36.13 *(978-1-4994-6472-6(X))*, 93883e1a-169a-41d7-b447-31af09c5d7fc) Rosen Publishing Group, Inc., The.

Bodden, Valerie. Barbarians. 2017. (X-Books: Fighters Ser.). (ENG., Illus.). 32p. (J). (gr. 3-6). *(978-1-60818-811-6(6))*, 20366, Creative Education) Creative Co., The.

Bow, James. Top Secret Science in the Military. 2019. (Top Secret Science Ser.). (Illus.). 48p. (J). (gr. 5-5). *(978-0-7787-5995-9(4))*; pap. *(978-0-7787-6033-7(2))* Crabtree Publishing Co.

—Your Guide to Castles & Medieval Warfare. 2017. (Destination: Middle Ages Ser.). (ENG., Illus.). 32p. (J). (gr. 5-5). *(978-0-7787-2994-5(X))*; pap. *(978-0-7787-3000-2(X))* Crabtree Publishing Co.

Bozzo, Linda. Marine Expeditionary Units. 2014. (Serving in the Military Ser.). (ENG., Illus.). 32p. (J). (gr. 2-5). lib. bdg. 28.50 *(978-1-60753-493-8(2))*, 16033) Amicus.

—U. S. Special Forces. 2013. (Serving in the Military Ser.). (ENG., Illus.). 32p. (J). (gr. 2-5). lib. bdg. 28.50 *(978-1-60753-394-8(4))*, 14526) Amicus.

Browne, G. Waldo. With Rogers' Rangers: Woodranger Tales. 2011. 296p. 48.95 *(978-1-258-06137-1(6))* Literary Licensing, LLC.

Burgan, Michael. Chronology of U.S. Special Ops. 2016. (U. S. Special Ops Ser.). (ENG., Illus.). 48p. (J). (gr. 3-6). lib. bdg. 29.99 *(978-1-5157-1850-5(6))*, 132573, Stone Arch Bks.) Capstone.

Calkhoven, Laurie. Flash, Boom, Blast! Amazing Inventions from the War Front. 2004. (Illus.). 72p. (J). pap. *(978-0-439-68357-9(2))* Scholastic, Inc.

Caraccilo, Dominic J. Military Intelligence Technology of the Future, 1 vol. 2006. (Library of Future Weaponry Ser.). (ENG., Illus.). 64p. (YA). (gr. 6-6). lib. bdg. 37.13 *(978-1-4042-0528-4(4))*, 35b7bde3-3894-4a86-939d-a75240d708af) Rosen Publishing Group, Inc., The.

Cassell, John. The Marching Book / Marchar. 2009. (Let's Get Moving / Diviértete en movimiento Ser.). (SPA.). 24p. (gr. k-1). 42.50 *(978-1-61514-235-4(5))*, Editorial Buenas Letras) Rosen Publishing Group, Inc., The.

Chapman, Caroline. Battles & Weapons: Exploring History Through Art. 2007. (Picture That Ser.). (ENG., Illus.). 64p. (J). (gr. 3-5). 19.95 *(978-1-58728-588-2(6))* Cooper Square Publishing Llc.

Christian, Mary Blount. Special Ops: Tactical Training, 1 vol. 2014. (Inside Special Forces Ser.). (ENG.). 64p. (YA). (gr. 6-6). 36.13 *(978-1-4777-7547-9(1))*, 26286a01-e9a5-4c90-918d-7725873ef473, Rosen Reference) Rosen Publishing Group, Inc., The.

Classic Warfare, 8 vols. 2017. (Classic Warfare Ser.). (ENG.). (J). (gr. 8-8). lib. bdg. 149.44 *(978-1-5026-3269-2(1))*, 857f8e39-0c8b-422c-a171-a16483e30310) Cavendish Square Publishing LLC.

Coleman, Miriam. Mujeres en Las Fuerzas Armadas (Women in the Military), 1 vol. 2015. (Ellas Abrieron Camino (Women Groundbreakers) Ser.). (SPA.). 32p. (J). (gr. 4-5). 27.93 *(978-1-4994-0522-4(7))*, ea5a8470-0b06-403c-bf05-af71c4b1462f, PowerKids Pr.) Rosen Publishing Group, Inc., The.

Collins, Luke. Military Robots. 2020. (World of Robots Ser.). (ENG.). 24p. (J). (gr. k-3). pap. 8.99 *(978-1-64466-109-3(8))*, 14431, Bolt Jr.) Black Rabbit Bks.

Collier, James Lincoln. Gunpowder & Weaponry, 1 vol. 2005. (Great Inventions Ser.). (ENG., Illus.). 144p. (YA). (gr. 8-8). lib. bdg. 45.50 *(978-0-7614-1540-4(8))*, ae1eccc5-77ee-494f-9cc6-858cbfad3deb) Cavendish Square Publishing LLC.

Dell, Pamela & Raatma, Lucia. The Science of Soldiers, 1 vol. 2012. (Science of War Ser.). (ENG.). 48p. (J). (gr. 6-9). lib. bdg. 34.65 *(978-0-7565-4460-7(2))*, 115723, Compass Point Bks.) Capstone.

Doeden, Matt. Can You Survive in the Special Forces? An Interactive Survival Adventure, 1 vol. 2012. (You Choose: Survival Ser.). (ENG., Illus.). 112p. (J). (gr. 3-7). pap. 6.95 *(978-1-4296-9480-3(7))*, 120429); lib. bdg. 32.65 *(978-1-4296-8582-5(4))*, 118587) Capstone. (Capstone Pr.).

—Cutting-Edge Military Tech. 2020. (Searchlight Books (tm) — Cutting-Edge STEM Ser.). (ENG., Illus.). 32p. (J). (gr. 3-5). 30.65 *(978-1-5415-7683-4(7))*, 28498637-4164-42c1-9bb5-0f04d7cd3ac4, Lerner Pubns.) Lerner Publishing Group.

Donovan, Sandy. U. S. Naval Special Warfare Forces. 2004. (U. S. Armed Forces Ser.). (ENG., Illus.). 64p. (gr. 4-8). lib. bdg. 26.60 *(978-0-8225-1650-7(0))* Lerner Publishing Group.

Dougherty, Martin. The Most Amazing Weapons of War. 2010. (Extreme! Ser.). (ENG.). 32p. (gr. 3-4). pap. 47.70 *(978-1-4296-5133-2(4))*, Capstone Pr.) Capstone.

Dougherty, Martin J. Land Warfare, 1 vol. 2010. (Modern Warfare Ser.). (ENG., Illus.). 32p. (YA). (gr. 3-5). lib. bdg. 28.67 *(978-1-4339-2727-0(6))*, d634ac7a-beb5-42ab-b550-34d9a3eef86c) Stevens, Gareth Publishing LLLP.

—Modern Warfare, 8 vols., Set. Incl. Air Warfare. (YA). lib. bdg. 28.67 *(978-1-4339-2720-1(9))*, c61a8608-6393-475a-a093-ec2060aa1814); Land Warfare. (Illus.). (YA). lib. bdg. 28.67 *(978-1-4339-2727-0(6))*, d634ac7a-beb5-42ab-b550-34d9a3eef86c); Sea Warfare. (Illus.). (J). lib. bdg. 28.67 *(978-1-4339-2734-8(9))*, 45af19c0-ebb4-47bd-acbf-dcc391772edf); Weapons & Technology. (YA). lib. bdg. 28.67 *(978-1-4339-2741-6(1))*, 211a8154-2cf5-4e65-b0dd-bc7a97d5b2ba); (gr. 3-5). (Modern Warfare Ser.). (ENG.). 32p. 2010. Set lib. bdg. 114.68 *(978-1-4339-3582-4(1))*, c4682182-1be2-4189-b169-f183db9b56d6, Gareth Stevens Learning Library) Stevens, Gareth Publishing LLLP.

Earl, C. F. World's Best Soldiers. 2010. (Special Forces Ser.). 64p. (YA). (gr. 7-18). lib. bdg. 22.95 *(978-1-4222-1846-4(5))* Mason Crest.

Earl, C. F. & Vanderhoof, Gabrielle. Army Rangers. 2010. (Special Forces Ser.). (Illus.). 64p. (YA). (gr. 7-18). lib. bdg. 22.95 *(978-1-4222-1838-9(4))* Mason Crest.

Ellis, Catherine. Helicopters/Helicopteros, 1 vol. Brusca, Maria Cristina, tr. 2007. (Mega Military Machines / Megamaquinas Militares Ser.). (ENG & SPA., Illus.). 24p. (J). (gr. 1-1). lib. bdg. 26.27 *(978-1-4042-7621-5(1),* 921786ac-e46f-49c0-b168-5ac692cd13c9) Rosen Publishing Group, Inc., The.

Farndon, John. Special Forces. 2010. (Remarkable Man & Beast Ser.). (Illus.). 48p. (J). (gr. 3-18). lib. bdg. 19.95 *(978-1-4222-1976-8(3))* Mason Crest.

Farndon, John & Kelly, Miles. Special Forces. Kelly, Richard, ed. 2017. (Illus.). 48p. (J). pap. 9.95 *(978-1-84810-283-5(6))* Miles Kelly Publishing, Ltd. GBR. Dist: Parkwest Pubns., Inc.

Fowler, Will. The Story of Modern Weapons & Warfare, 1 vol. 2011. (Journey Through History Ser.). (ENG.). 64p. (J). (gr. 5-6). lib. bdg. 37.13 *(978-1-4488-4793-8(1),* f339e89b-6e8a-4873-a241-f7feca6f668d) Rosen Publishing Group, Inc., The.

Freedman, Jeri. Special Ops: Air Commandos, 1 vol. 2014. (Inside Special Forces Ser.). (ENG.). 64p. (YA). (gr. 6-6). 36.13 *(978-1-4777-7993-4(0),* f75a4f6d-0103-47cd-821d-15ae13e0c2e6, Rosen Reference) Rosen Publishing Group, Inc., The.

Fremont-Barnes, Gregory. Rescue at the Iranian Embassy: The Most Daring SAS Raid, 1 vol. 2011. (Most Daring Raids in History Ser.). (ENG., Illus.). 64p. (YA). (gr. 7-7). lib. bdg. 37.13 *(978-1-4488-1869-3(9),* 248d6de7-a710-41a2-a2d0-36238874c537) Rosen Publishing Group, Inc., The.

Frontline Families, 12 vols. 2015. (Frontline Families Ser.). (ENG.). 48p. (J). (gr. 5-6). lib. bdg. 201.60 *(978-1-4824-2558-1(0),* 647f7e26-21c6-4678-899a-a7103850656e) Stevens, Gareth Publishing LLLP.

Fusek Peters, Andrew. Free Running: Band 11 Lime/Band 14 Ruby (Collins Big Cat Progress) 2014. (Collins Big Cat Progress Ser.). (ENG., Illus.). 32p. (J). (gr. 3-4). pap. 9.99 *(978-0-00-751934-7(6))* HarperCollins Pubs. Ltd. GBR. Dist: Independent Pubs. Group.

Gaertner, Meg. Make a Catapult. 2018. (Make Your Own Ser.). (ENG.). 32p. (J). (gr. 2-4). 26.60 *(978-1-59953-926-3(8))* Norwood Hse. Pr.

Garstecki, Julia. Equipos y Suministros Militares. 2017. (Tecnologia Militar Ser.). (SPA., Illus.). 32p. (J). (gr. 4-6). lib. bdg. *(978-1-68072-581-0(5),* 10587, Bolt) Black Rabbit Bks.

—Military Gear & Supplies. 2017. (Military Tech Ser.). (ENG., Illus.). 32p. (J). (gr. 4-6). lib. bdg. *(978-1-68072-164-5(X),* 10512, Bolt) Black Rabbit Bks.

Gitlin, Martin. Green Berets. 2013. (Great Warriors Ser.). (ENG., Illus.). 48p. (J). (gr. 4-8). pap. 18.50 *(978-1-61783-773-9(3),* 10805) ABDO Publishing Co.

Gitlin, Marty. Military Dogs. 2018. (Illus.). 24p. (J). pap. *(978-1-4896-9911-4(2),* AV2 by Weigl) Weigl Pubs., Inc.

Glass, Maya. The Marching Book. 2009. (Let's Get Moving Ser.). 24p. (gr. k-k). 42.50 *(978-1-61514-229-3(0),* PowerKids Pr.) Rosen Publishing Group, Inc., The.

Gonzalez, Lissette. Bomb Squads in Action, 1 vol. 2007. (Dangerous Jobs Ser.). (ENG., Illus.). 24p. (J). (gr. 2-3). lib. bdg. 26.27 *(978-1-4042-3781-0(X),* dd280082-9564-40df-80f4-9c3b6145dc98, PowerKids Pr.) Rosen Publishing Group, Inc., The.

Graham, Ian. Military Technology. 2010. (New Technology Ser.). (ENG., Illus.). 48p. (J). 23.99 *(978-0-237-53428-8(2))* Evans Brothers, Ltd. GBR. Dist: Independent Pubs. Group.

Gregory, Josh. Special Ops. 2012. (21st Century Skills Library: Cool Military Careers Ser.). (ENG.). 32p. (gr. 4-8). pap. 14.21 *(978-1-61080-620-6(4),* 202230); (Illus.). 32.07 *(978-1-61080-446-2(5),* 202056) Cherry Lake Publishing.

Guinta, Peter & Cribbs, Randy. Illumination Rounds. 2004. (Illus.). 192p. (YA). per. *(978-0-9725796-4-3(8),* 9051945) River Pr.

Hamilton, John, contrib. by. Weapons of World War I. 2017. (World War I Ser.). (ENG.). 48p. (J). (gr. 5-9). lib. bdg. 34.21 *(978-1-5321-1290-4(4),* 27498, Abdo & Daughters) ABDO Publishing Co.

Hand, Carol. Special Ops: Search & Rescue Operations, 1 vol. 2014. (Inside Special Forces Ser.). (ENG.). 64p. (J). (gr. 6-6). 36.13 *(978-1-4777-7997-2(3),* 085e888f-272d-49fa-b873-346ac8277a48, Rosen Reference) Rosen Publishing Group, Inc., The.

Harasymiw, Mark J. Pararescuemen, 1 vol. 2012. (U. S. Special Forces Ser.). (ENG., Illus.). 32p. (J). (gr. 3-4). pap. 11.50 *(978-1-4339-6571-5(2),* e1caeac4-d4b7-4ac0-b69e-ac86616c0ec9); lib. bdg. 29.27 *(978-1-4339-6569-2(0),* 09b57886-b9e9-4d81-b6b8-a87747d34428) Stevens, Gareth Publishing LLLP. (Gareth Stevens Learning Library).

Heppermann, Christine. Samurai. 2013. (Great Warriors Ser.). (ENG., Illus.). 48p. (J). (gr. 4-8). pap. 18.50 *(978-1-61783-777-7(6),* 10809) ABDO Publishing Co.

History's Greatest Warriors, 10 vols. 2014. (History's Greatest Warriors Ser.). (ENG.). 48p. (J). (gr. 4-4). lib. bdg. 165.35 *(978-1-5026-0296-1(2),* e7490a5f-f088-4aec-8e15-a5ce082977d8, Cavendish Square) Cavendish Square Publishing LLC.

Hubbard, Ben. Samurai Warriors, 1 vol. 2016. (Conquerors & Combatants Ser.). (ENG.). 224p. (YA). (gr. 9-9). lib. bdg. 56.71 *(978-1-5026-2459-8(1),* e50fe6b7-017b-4eea-accc-69c43318804b) Cavendish Square Publishing LLC.

Hudak, Heather. Military Entrepreneurs. 2018. (Science & Technology Start-Up Stars Ser.). (ENG., Illus.). 32p. (J). (gr. 5-5). *(978-0-7787-4422-1(1))* Crabtree Publishing Co.

Incentive Publications by World Book (Firm) Staff, contrib. by. CRISPR & Other Biotech. 2019. (Illus.). 48p. (J). *(978-0-7166-2429-5(X))* World Bk., Inc.

Ives, Rob. Ready, Aim, Launch! Make Your Own Small Launchers. Paul de Quay, John, illus. 2016. (Tabletop Wars Ser.). (ENG.). 32p. (J). (gr. 3-6). lib. bdg. 27.99 *(978-1-5124-0636-8(8),* 96405206-b643-4dfc-86e2-461253d95971, Hungry Tomato (r)) Lerner Publishing Group.

—Surprise the Enemy: Make Your Own Traps & Triggers. Paul de Quay, John, illus. 2016. (Tabletop Wars Ser.). (ENG.). 32p. (J). (gr. 3-6). lib. bdg. 27.99 *(978-1-5124-0637-5(6),* f63cb0ca-af47-48c7-9b12-95a800ff3094, Hungry Tomato (r)) Lerner Publishing Group.

Janeczko, Paul B. Double Cross: Deception Techniques in War. 2017. (ENG., Illus.). 256p. (J). (gr. 5-9). 16.99 *(978-0-7636-6042-0(6))* Candlewick Pr.

Kamberg, Mary-Lane. Special Ops: Snipers, 1 vol. 2014. (Inside Special Forces Ser.). (ENG., Illus.). 64p. (J). (gr. 6-6). 36.13 *(978-1-4777-7989-7(2),* b9b09e28-3f3f-46a3-bc1a-16ec9901a8a2, Rosen Reference) Rosen Publishing Group, Inc., The.

Kassnoff, David. Special Ops: Weapons & Gear, 1 vol. 2014. (Inside Special Forces Ser.). (ENG.). 64p. (J). (gr. 6-6). 36.13 *(978-1-4777-7567-7(6),* b1604221-4812-4b59-8452-f5b81966b78e, Rosen Reference) Rosen Publishing Group, Inc., The.

Leavitt, Amie Jane. Stories from Those Who Fought in America's Special Ops. 2016. (U. S. Special Ops Ser.). (ENG., Illus.). 48p. (J). (gr. 3-6). lib. bdg. 29.99 *(978-1-5157-1851-2(4),* 132572, Stone Arch Bks.) Capstone.

Levete, Sarah. The Army, 1 vol. 2015. (Defend & Protect Ser.). (ENG.). 48p. (J). (gr. 4-5). pap. 15.05 *(978-1-4824-4119-2(5),* 14bd9108-2d4e-4e5d-a0e0-94c5df9689cc) Stevens, Gareth Publishing LLLP.

—Special Forces, 1 vol. 2015. (Defend & Protect Ser.). (ENG.). 48p. (J). (gr. 4-5). pap. 15.05 *(978-1-4824-4115-4(2),* d3d19342-08db-462e-a5dc-b9d6549bbaf3) Stevens, Gareth Publishing LLLP.

—Undercover Operations, 1 vol. 2015. (Defend & Protect Ser.). (ENG.). 48p. (J). (gr. 4-5). pap. 15.05 *(978-1-4824-4127-7(6),* 112bfda6-842e-450f-b640-a313f0faa90d) Stevens, Gareth Publishing LLLP.

Lewis, Mark L. Combat Rescues. 2019. (Rescues in Focus Ser.). (ENG., Illus.). 32p. (J). (gr. 2-3). pap. 9.95 *(978-1-64185-840-3(0),* 1641858400, Focus Readers) North Star Editions.

Linde, Barbara M. Military Courts, 1 vol. 2019. (Court is in Session Ser.). (ENG.). 32p. (gr. 4-5). pap. 11.00 *(978-1-5383-4324-1(X),* b024217b-920d-4e52-8da4-b3a7a4172df8, PowerKids Pr.) Rosen Publishing Group, Inc., The.

Lusted, Marcia Amidon. Ninja Science: Camouflage, Weapons, & Stealthy Attacks. 2016. (Warrior Science Ser.). (ENG., Illus.). 32p. (J). (gr. 3-9). lib. bdg. 28.65 *(978-1-4914-8115-8(3),* 130606, Capstone Pr.) Capstone.

Marciniak, Kristin. Navy SEALs. 2013. (Great Warriors Ser.). (ENG., Illus.). 48p. (J). (gr. 4-8). pap. 18.50 *(978-1-61783-775-3(X),* 10807) ABDO Publishing Co.

Marcovitz, Dan. Critical World Issues: The Arms Trade, Vol. 16. 2016. (Critical World Issues Ser.: Vol. 16). (ENG., Illus.). 112p. (J). (gr. 7-12). 25.95 *(978-1-4222-3648-2(X))* Mason Crest.

Margulies, Phillip. Strategic Defense Systems of the Future. 2009. (Library of Future Weaponry Ser.). 64p. (gr. 6-6). 58.50 *(978-1-60853-641-2(6))* Rosen Publishing Group, Inc., The.

Martin, Martha. D-Day. 2012. (ENG., Illus.). 48p. (J). *(978-0-7787-7924-7(6));* pap. *(978-0-7787-7933-9(5))* Crabtree Publishing Co.

Marx, Christy. Battlefield Command Systems of the Future. (Library of Future Weaponry Ser.). 64p. (gr. 6-6). 2009. 58.50 *(978-1-60853-636-8(X))* 2006. (ENG., Illus.). (J). lib. bdg. 37.13 *(978-1-4042-0521-5(7),* 017a41a9-86de-4377-907e-e434043c2bf3) Rosen Publishing Group, Inc., The.

Marx, Mandy R. Amazing Military Facts. 2016. (Amazing Military Facts Ser.). (ENG., Illus.). 24p. (J). (gr. -1-2). 117.28 *(978-1-5157-1362-3(8),* 24867, Capstone Pr.) Capstone.

Maybury, Richard J. World War II: The Rest of the Story & How It Affects You Today, 1930 to September 11 2001. Williams, Jane A., ed. rev. ed. 2003. ("Uncle Eric" Bk.: 11). (ENG., Illus.). 349p. pap. 19.95 *(978-0-942617-43-6(6))* Bluestocking Pr.

McIntosh, J. S. Elite Forces Selection. 2010. (Special Forces Ser.). 64p. (YA). (gr. 7-18). lib. bdg. 22.95 *(978-1-4222-1839-6(2))* Mason Crest.

Montana, Jack. Urban Warfare. 2010. (Special Forces Ser.). 64p. (YA). (gr. 7-18). lib. bdg. 22.95 *(978-1-4222-1844-0(9))* Mason Crest.

Mooney, Carla. Becoming Invisible: From Camouflage to Cloaks. 2010. (Great Idea Ser.). 48p. (J). (gr. 4-6). lib. bdg. 26.60 *(978-1-59953-378-0(2))* Norwood Hse. Pr.

Murrell, Deborah Jane & Dennis, Peter. Samurai. 2012. (ENG., Illus.). 32p. (gr. 3-5). pap. 8.95 *(978-1-926853-55-0(5))* Saunders Bk. Co. CAN. Dist: RiverStream Publishing.

Newman, Lauren. Drones. 2017. (21st Century Skills Innovation Library: Emerging Tech Ser.). (ENG., Illus.). 32p. (J). (gr. 4-8). lib. bdg. 32.07 *(978-1-63472-699-3(5),* 210122) Cherry Lake Publishing.

Noll, Elizabeth. Special Ops Forces. 2016. (Rank It! Ser.). (ENG.). 32p. (J). (gr. 4-6). pap. 9.99 *(978-1-64466-135-2(7),* 10243); (Illus.). 31.35 *(978-1-68072-063-1(5),* 11392) Black Rabbit Bks. (Bolt).

O'Brian, Pliny. Knights: Warriors of the Middle Ages, 1 vol. 2014. (History's Greatest Warriors Ser.). (ENG., Illus.). 48p. (gr. 4-4). 33.07 *(978-1-5026-0120-9(6),* 5367d25b-50fd-4353-8b6a-f566cf53e240) Cavendish Square Publishing LLC.

Orr, Tamra B. USMC Special Reaction Teams, 1 vol. 2008. (Inside Special Operations Ser.). (ENG., Illus.). 64p. (gr. 6-6). pap. 12.95 *(978-1-4358-5130-6(7),* a38b48b0-f178-4f01-848c-75afaebc9cce, Rosen Classroom) Rosen Publishing Group, Inc., The.

Osborne, Mary Pope & Boyce, Natalie Pope. Warriors: A Nonfiction Companion to Magic Tree House #31: Warriors in Winter. Mones, Isidre, illus. 2019. (Magic Tree House (R) Fact Tracker Ser.: 40). 128p. (J). (gr. 2-5). 6.99 *(978-1-101-93651-1(7),* Random Hse. Bks. for Young Readers) Random Hse. Children's Bks.

Oxlade, Chris. Inside Tanks & Heavy Artillery. 2017. (Inside Military Machines Ser.). (ENG., Illus.). 32p. (J). (gr. 3-6). lib. bdg. 27.99 *(978-1-5124-3226-8(1),* 5b03bbc1-aa54-4c2c-9909-b88b7e2be301, Hungry Tomato (r)) Lerner Publishing Group.

Park, Louise & Love, Timothy. Japanese Samurai, 1 vol. 2010. (Ancient & Medieval People Ser.). (ENG.). 32p. (gr. 5-5). 31.21 *(978-0-7614-4448-0(3),* 1a1a6f84-5d32-4503-9bb2-f91e7d521053) Cavendish Square Publishing LLC.

Parker, Steve. A Brief Illustrated History of Warfare. 2017. (ENG., Illus.). 32p. (J). pap. *(978-1-4747-2708-2(5))* Capstone.

Perritano, John. War & the Military, Vol. 10. 2016. (Stem in Current Events Ser.). (ENG., Illus.). 64p. (J). (gr. 7). 23.95 *(978-1-4222-3597-3(1))* Mason Crest.

Poolos, J. Army Rangers: Surveillance & Reconnaissance for the U. S. Army. 2009. (Inside Special Operations Ser.). 64p. (gr. 6-6). 58.50 *(978-1-61513-549-3(9),* Rosen Reference) Rosen Publishing Group, Inc., The.

Porterfield, Jason. USAF Special Tactics Teams, 1 vol. 2008. (Inside Special Operations Ser.). (ENG., Illus.). 64p. (gr. 6-6). (J). lib. bdg. 37.13 *(978-1-4042-1753-9(3),* e1f18262-3c27-4679-a508-869870dac242); pap. 12.95 *(978-1-4358-5131-3(5),* 708d7262-fc75-4a00-ba6a-823c5f7aaf4e, Rosen Classroom) Rosen Publishing Group, Inc., The.

Protecting Our Country, 10 vols. 2013. (Protecting Our Country Ser.). 32p. (J). (gr. 3-4). (ENG.). 144.65 *(978-1-4777-1543-7(6),* 9e62d217-129c-49af-a960-5d5a5a959358); pap. 300.00 *(978-1-4777-2686-0(1));* pap. 50.00 *(978-1-4777-2685-3(3))* Rosen Publishing Group, Inc., The. (PowerKids Pr.).

Rice, Rob S. Ancient Greek Warfare, 1 vol. 2009. (Ancient Warfare Ser.). (ENG., Illus.). 32p. (J). (gr. 5-6). lib. bdg. 28.67 *(978-1-4339-1972-5(9),* e36fd023-1420-4f2e-910f-c246ad4c5c25, Gareth Stevens Learning Library) Stevens, Gareth Publishing LLLP.

Ripley, Tim. Torpedoes, Missiles, & Cannons: Physics Goes to War. 2017. (STEM on the Battlefield Ser.). (ENG., Illus.). 48p. (J). (gr. 4-6). 31.99 *(978-1-5124-3926-7(6),* 4886172c-1774-4b59-99e0-1607c2641e75, Lerner Pubns.) Lerner Publishing Group.

Roberts, Jeremy. U. S. Air Force Special Operations. 2004. (U. S. Armed Forces Ser.). (ENG., Illus.). 64p. (gr. 4-8). lib. bdg. 26.60 *(978-0-8225-1644-6(6))* Lerner Publishing Group.

Rose, Simon. Air Force Special Operations. 2014. (Illus.). 24p. (J). *(978-1-62127-448-3(9))* Weigl Pubs., Inc.

—Marine Corps Special Operations. 2013. (J). 27.13 *(978-1-62127-452-0(7));* pap. *(978-1-62127-458-2(6))* Weigl Pubs., Inc.

Rudolph, Jessica. CIA Paramilitary Operatives in Action. 2013. (Special Ops II Ser.). 32p. (J). (gr. 2-7). lib. bdg. 28.50 *(978-1-61772-892-1(6))* Bearport Publishing Co., Inc.

Sandler, Michael. Marine Force Recon in Action. 2008. (Special Ops Ser.). (Illus.). 32p. (J). (gr. 3-6). lib. bdg. 28.50 *(978-1-59716-634-8(0))* Bearport Publishing Co., Inc.

—Pararescuemen in Action. 2008. (Special Ops Ser.). (Illus.). 32p. (J). (gr. 3-6). lib. bdg. 28.50 *(978-1-59716-633-1(2))* Bearport Publishing Co., Inc.

Scheff, Matt. Humvees: A 4D Book. 2018. (Mighty Military Machines Ser.). (ENG., Illus.). 24p. (J). (gr. -1-2). lib. bdg. 24.65 *(978-1-9771-0109-9(7),* 138300, Pebble) Capstone.

Schmidt, Roderic D. Infantry of the Future. (Library of Future Weaponry Ser.). 64p. (gr. 6-6). 2009. 58.50 *(978-1-60853-637-5(8))* 2006. (ENG., Illus.). (J). lib. bdg. 37.13 *(978-1-4042-0525-3(X),* 57729a88-1666-44b5-9782-9da09ef7ac4b) Rosen Publishing Group, Inc., The.

—Land Warfare of the Future. (Library of Future Weaponry Ser.). 64p. (gr. 6-6). 2009. 58.50 *(978-1-60853-638-2(6))* 2006. (ENG., Illus.). (J). lib. bdg. 37.13 *(978-1-4042-0524-6(1),* 0fb32f24-b525-47c6-b12e-06915e0b5ab1) Rosen Publishing Group, Inc., The.

Shea, Therese. Black Ops & Other Special Missions of the U. S. Army Green Berets, 1 vol. 2012. (Inside Special Forces Ser.). (ENG., Illus.). 64p. (YA). (gr. 6-6). pap. 13.95 *(978-1-4488-8387-5(3),* 719ab3d4-2751-4199-9b5b-4e5271c0a19f); lib. bdg. 37.13 *(978-1-4488-8381-3(4),* e71b2aac-e7d6-427b-8ffa-4c8647af1c38) Rosen Publishing Group, Inc., The.

Silverstein Gray, Judy & Kiland, Taylor Baldwin. Cyber Technology: Using Computers to Fight Terrorism, 1 vol. 2016. (Military Engineering in Action Ser.). (ENG.). 48p. (gr. 5-6). pap. 12.70 *(978-0-7660-7535-1(4),* bd37435d-2be7-4cb1-bc14-20a58822c23c) Enslow Publishing, LLC.

Sodaro, Craig. The U. S. Marines Special Operations Regiment: The Missions. 2012. (American Special Ops Ser.). (ENG., Illus.). 48p. (J). (gr. 5-9). 32.65 *(978-1-4296-8658-7(8),* 118995) Capstone.

Somervill, Barbara A. Samurai, Shoguns, & Soldiers: The Rise of the Japanese Military, 1 vol. 2007. (Lucent Library of Historical Eras Ser.). (ENG., Illus.). 104p. (gr. 7-10). lib. bdg. 36.43 *(978-1-4205-0030-1(9),* fb05be30-2642-475c-a91c-413eb2f59647, Lucent Pr.) Greenhaven Publishing LLC.

Special Forces: Protecting, Building, Teaching & Fighting, 10 vols., Set. Incl. Air Force. Vanderhoof, Gabrielle. lib. bdg. 22.95 *(978-1-4222-1837-2(6));* Army Rangers. Earl, C. F. & Vanderhoof, Gabrielle. (Illus.). lib. bdg. 22.95 *(978-1-4222-1838-9(4));* Elite Forces Selection. McIntosh, J. S. lib. bdg. 22.95 *(978-1-4222-1839-6(2));* Green Berets. Earl, C. F. lib. bdg. 22.95 *(978-1-4222-1841-9(4));* Marines. Montana, Jack. lib. bdg. 22.95 *(978-1-4222-1842-6(2));* Navy SEALs. Montana, Jack. lib. bdg. 22.95 *(978-1-4222-1843-3(0));* Parachute Regiment. Montana, Jack. lib. bdg. 22.95 *(978-1-4222-1845-7(7));* Urban Warfare. Montana, Jack. lib. bdg. 22.95 *(978-1-4222-1844-0(9));* World's Best Soldiers. Earl, C. F. lib. bdg. 22.95 *(978-1-4222-1846-4(5));* 64p. (YA). (gr. 7-18). 2010. 2011. Set lib. bdg. 229.50 *(978-1-4222-1836-5(8))* Mason Crest.

Special OPS: Search & Rescue Operations: Set 2, 12 vols. 2014. (Inside Special Forces Ser.). (ENG.). 64p. (YA). (gr. 6-6). lib. bdg. 222.78 *(978-1-4777-8001-5(7),* 315ef99e-1761-4524-8e1f-a49c4d8f215a, Rosen Central) Rosen Publishing Group, Inc., The.

Steele, Tara. Medieval Warfare, 1 vol. 2003. (Medieval World Ser.). (ENG., Illus.). 32p. (J). (gr. 5). pap. *(978-0-7787-1376-0(8))* Crabtree Publishing Co.

Stewart, Alex. Greek Soldiers. 2013. (Greatest Warriors Ser.). 32p. (gr. 3-7). 28.50 *(978-1-78212-399-6(7))* Arcturus Publishing GBR. Dist: Black Rabbit Bks.

Sutherland, Adam. Armed Services. 2012. (On the Radar: Defend & Protect Ser.). (ENG., Illus.). 32p. (gr. 4-8). lib. bdg. 26.60 *(978-0-7613-7771-9(9),* Lerner Pubns.) Lerner Publishing Group.

Terrell, Brandon. Guarding Area 51. 2016. (Highly Guarded Places Ser.). (ENG.). 24p. (J). (gr. 2-5). 32.79 *(978-1-5038-0809-6(2),* 210644) Child's World, Inc, The.

Tools of War. (Illus.). 192p. (J). *(978-0-7835-0154-3(4))* Time-Life Education, Inc.

Tougas, Shelley. The Science of Weapons, 1 vol. 2012. (Science of War Ser.). (ENG.). 48p. (J). (gr. 6-9). lib. bdg. 34.65 *(978-0-7565-4461-4(0),* 115724, Compass Point Bks.) Capstone.

Troupe, Thomas Kingsley. Battle Zone: The Inspiring Truth Behind Popular Combat Video Games. 2018. (Video Games vs. Reality Ser.). (ENG., Illus.). 32p. (J). (gr. 3-9). lib. bdg. 28.65 *(978-1-5435-2570-0(9),* 138052, Capstone Pr.) Capstone.

U. S. Special Forces. 2019. (Serving Our Country Ser.). (ENG.). 24p. (J). (gr. 1-4). lib. bdg. *(978-1-68151-565-6(2),* 17597) Amicus.

Weapons & Warfare. 2003. (Illus.). 32p. (YA). pap. *(978-1-904516-31-6(9),* Pavilion Children's Books) Pavilion Bks.

Whiting, Jim. Air Force Special Operations Command. 2014. (U. S. Special Forces Ser.). (ENG.). 48p. (J). (gr. 5-8). *(978-1-60818-460-6(9),* 21424, Creative Education) Creative Co., The.

—Marine Force Recon. 2018. (U. S. Special Forces Ser.). (ENG.). 48p. (J). (gr. 3-6). *(978-1-60818-984-7(8),* 19984, Creative Education) Creative Co., The.

Wilson, Patrick. Survival Equipment. Carney, John, ed. 2014. (Extreme Survival in the Military Ser.: 12). 64p. (J). (gr. 7-18). lib. bdg. 23.95 *(978-1-4222-3085-5(6))* Mason Crest.

Wolny, Philip. Weapons Satellites. 2009. (Library of Satellites Ser.). 64p. (gr. 5-8). 58.50 *(978-1-60853-834-8(6),* Rosen Reference) Rosen Publishing Group, Inc., The.

Woog, Adam. Careers in Homeland Security. 2013. (J). 34.21 *(978-1-60870-959-5(0))* Marshall Cavendish Corp.

World Book, Inc. Staff, contrib. by. Robot Soldiers & Other Military Tech. 2019. (Illus.). 48p. (J). *(978-0-7166-2431-8(1))* World Bk., Inc.

—Wooden Spears to Military Drones: A Timeline of Warfare. 2016. (Illus.). 40p. (J). *(978-0-7166-3544-4(5))* World Bk.-Childcraft International.

Yomtov, Nel. Special Ops. 2016. (Military Missions Ser.). (ENG., Illus.). 24p. (J). (gr. 3-7). 26.95 *(978-1-62617-439-9(3),* Epic Bks.) Bellwether Media.

—U. S. Ghost Army: The Master Illusionists of World War II. Valdrighi, Alessandro, illus. 2019. (Amazing World War II Stories Ser.). (ENG.). 32p. (J). (gr. 3-9). pap. 7.95 *(978-1-5435-7551-4(X),* 141083); lib. bdg. 34.65 *(978-1-5435-7316-9(9),* 140621) Capstone.

Zaloga, Steven J. The Most Daring Raid of World War II: D-Day — Pointe-Du-Hoc, 1 vol. 2011. (Most Daring Raids in History Ser.). (ENG., Illus.). 64p. (YA). (gr. 7-7). lib. bdg. 37.13 *(978-1-4488-1867-9(2),* 3ef3ba30-ecb1-412b-bdd2-8540d49e07d0) Rosen Publishing Group, Inc., The.

MILITARY ART AND SCIENCE—HISTORY

Baum, Margaux & Hopkins, Andrea. Jousts, Tournaments, & War Training, 1 vol. 2016. (Life in the Middle Ages Ser.). (ENG., Illus.). 64p. (J). (gr. 5-5). 36.13 *(978-1-4994-6474-0(6),* ec601171-e572-426b-b6dc-05dcff48d913) Rosen Publishing Group, Inc., The.

Bergin, Mark. Warfare in the 16th to 19th Centuries. 2015. (Warriors Ser.). (Illus.). 48p. (gr. 4-7). 37.10 *(978-1-62588-357-5(9))* Black Rabbit Bks.

—Warfare in the Ancient World. 2015. (Warriors Ser.). (Illus.). 48p. (gr. 4-7). 37.10 *(978-1-62588-355-1(2))* Black Rabbit Bks.

Bodden, Valerie. Barbarians. 2013. 24p. pap. *(978-1-60818-466-8(8))* Creative Co., The.

—X-Books: Barbarians. 2017. (X-Bks.). (Illus.). 32p. (J). (gr. 3-7). pap. 9.99 *(978-1-62832-414-3(7),* 20367, Creative Paperbacks) Creative Co., The.

Bougie, Matt. Strategic Inventions of the Cold War, 1 vol. 2015. (Tech in the Trenches Ser.). (ENG., Illus.). 112p. (YA). (gr. 9-9). 44.50 *(978-1-5026-1022-5(1),* ade1ae44-2ff8-4dfe-9a9e-61a6b84a0bca) Cavendish Square Publishing LLC.

Brian, Dittmar. Mongol Warriors. 2012. (History's Greatest Warriors Ser.). (ENG., Illus.). 24p. (J). (gr. 3-7). lib. bdg. 26.95 *(978-1-60014-746-3(1),* Torque Bks.) Bellwether Media.

Brown Bear Books. Air & Space. 2012. (Invention & Technology Ser.). (ENG.). 64p. (J). (gr. 8-11). lib. bdg. 39.95 *(978-1-936333-40-0(6),* 16520) Brown Bear Bks.

—Weapons, Tactics, & Strategy. 2011. (Civil War Ser.). (ENG.). 112p. (J). (gr. 9-12). 42.80 *(978-1-936333-46-2(5),* 16459) Brown Bear Bks.

Burrows, Terry. Hovercrafts & Humvees: Engineering Goes to War. 2017. (STEM on the Battlefield Ser.). (ENG., Illus.). 48p. (J). (gr. 4-6). 31.99 *(978-1-5124-3929-8(0),* 0f902c5c-a4ce-415c-aaad-d99cfb90675f, Lerner Pubns.) Lerner Publishing Group.

Cooper, Meghan. Sun Tzu, 1 vol. 2017. (Great Military Leaders Ser.). (ENG., Illus.). 128p. (YA). (gr. 9-9). 47.36 *(978-1-5026-2867-1(8),* 069f2f6c-dec4-48bb-a898-a978596e4fa6) Cavendish Square Publishing LLC.

Fowler, Will. The Story of Ancient Weapons, 1 vol. 2010. (Journey Through History Ser.). (ENG.). 64p. (YA). (gr. 5-6). lib. bdg. 37.13 *(978-1-4488-0623-2(2),* 6c53eee1-ccaa-46c3-aa3a-f2d958a54521, Rosen Reference) Rosen Publishing Group, Inc., The.

Gunderson, Jessica. Conquistadors. 2012. (Fearsome Fighters Ser.). (ENG.). 48p. (J). (gr. 5-9). 23.95 *(978-1-60818-183-4(9),* 21885, Creative Education) Creative Co., The.

Helget, Nicole Lea. Mongols. 2012. (Fearsome Fighters Ser.). (ENG., Illus.). 48p. (J). (gr. 5-9). 23.95 *(978-1-60818-184-1(7),* 21886, Creative Education) Creative Co., The.

Jestice, Phyllis G. Ancient Egyptian Warfare, 1 vol. 2009. (Ancient Warfare Ser.). (ENG., Illus.). 32p. (J). (gr. 5-6). lib. bdg. 28.67 *(978-1-4339-1971-8(0),*

M
N
O

d99bc651-6cf7-4601-9b6e-517fd3aacf8a, Gareth Stevens Learning Library) Stevens, Gareth Publishing LLLP.

—Ancient Persian Warfare, 1 vol. 2009. (Ancient Warfare Ser.). (ENG., Illus.). 32p. (J). (gr. 5-6). lib. bdg. 28.67 *(978-1-4339-1973-2(7),* 9b02b6f1-9ec7-480f-84df-5c7b257e0494, Gareth Stevens Learning Library) Stevens, Gareth Publishing LLLP.

Larson, Kirsten W. Statistics about U. S. Special Ops - Past & Present. 2016. (U. S. Special Ops Ser.). (ENG., Illus.). 48p. (J). (gr. 3-6). lib. bdg. 29.99 *(978-1-5157-1852-9(2),* 132574, Stone Arch Bks.) Capstone.

MacDonald, Fiona. Knights & Castles. 2009. (History Explorers Ser.). (ENG.). 24p. (J). (gr. k-2). pap. 5.95 *(978-1-84696-215-8(3),* TickTock Books) Octopus Publishing Group GBR. Dist: Independent Pubs. Group.

Macdonald, Fiona. Knights, Castles, & Warfare in the Middle Ages, 1 vol. 2005. (World Almanac(r) Library of the Middle Ages Ser.). (ENG., Illus.). 48p. (gr. 5-8). pap. 15.05 *(978-0-8368-5904-1(9),* 8bfc5058-6c7c-4392-8caf-ad75e92215cb); lib. bdg. 33.67 *(978-0-8368-5895-2(6),* 058d95bb-6e8e-46b3-95fd-f94a3829197d) Stevens, Gareth Publishing LLLP. (Gareth Stevens Secondary Library).

—Top 10 Worst Ruthless Warriors, 1 vol. Antram, David, illus. 2012. (Top 10 Worst Ser.). (ENG.). 32p. (J). (gr. 3-5). pap. 11.50 *(978-1-4339-6686-6(7),* 61436c43-ce49-4ece-b5e8-9a1d479bf1b6); lib. bdg. 29.27 *(978-1-4339-6685-9(9),* b8b7cc54-3972-4678-8765-14c346f65f35) Stevens, Gareth Publishing LLLP. (Gareth Stevens Learning Library).

—Warfare in the Middle Ages. 2015. (Warriors Ser.). (Illus.). 48p. (gr. 4-7). 37.10 *(978-1-62588-356-8(0))* Black Rabbit Bks.

Malam, John. Warriors. 2010. (Remarkable Man & Beast Ser.). (Illus.). 48p. (J). (gr. 3-18). lib. bdg. 19.95 *(978-1-4222-1979-9(8))* Mason Crest.

Matthews, Rupert. Weapons & Armor, 1 vol. 2014. (100 Facts You Should Know Ser.). (ENG., Illus.). 48p. (J). (gr. 4-5). lib. bdg. 33.60 *(978-1-4824-2193-4(3),* 72bf708d-d7ca-409c-9cb5-3aadffc4e502) Stevens, Gareth Publishing LLLP.

Moments in History, 12 vols., Set. Incl. Why Did Hiroshima Happen? Grant, R. G. lib. bdg. 34.60 *(978-1-4339-4163-4(5),* 2b6ea7b6-a641-4b5e-86c9-252c57d25795); Why Did the Cold War Happen? Harrison, Paul. lib. bdg. 34.60 *(978-1-4339-4166-5(X),* eae20eee-654b-480c-9bb2-4b4e7dcf1173); Why Did the Great Depression Happen? Grant, R. G. lib. bdg. 34.60 *(978-1-4339-4169-6(4),* 2cef96c8-83ef-49c1-9b92-65399e65e0dc); Why Did the Holocaust Happen? Sheehan, Sean. lib. bdg. 34.60 *(978-1-4339-4172-6(4),* c48c81b5-7fe6-4406-90ae-f694e53f11c8); Why Did the Rise of the Nazis Happen? Freeman, Charles. lib. bdg. 34.60 *(978-1-4339-4175-7(9),* 325cb1a1-640f-4027-a952-3ea9ec96c7d3); Why Did the Vietnam War Happen? Gifford, Clive. lib. bdg. 34.60 *(978-1-4339-4178-8(3),* 49a09c6a-e207-45a7-83ee-602b45d6bad5); Why Did World War I Happen? Grant, R. G. lib. bdg. 34.60 *(978-1-4339-4181-8(3),* dbc68180-7d50-4924-bbf4-621b4712124b); Why Did World War II Happen? Senker, Cath. lib. bdg. 34.60 *(978-1-4339-4184-9(8),* 8cebe7d6-0af0-46bd-ab47-a1890c7ffe55); (YA). (gr. 6-8). (Moments in History Ser.). (ENG., Illus.). 48p. 2010. Set lib. bdg. 207.66 *(978-1-4339-4195-5(3),* d1f5d570-c32f-4b02-8aca-1b000b3a4f21, Gareth Stevens Secondary Library) Stevens, Gareth Publishing LLLP.

Murrell, Deborah. Fighting a Battle, 1 vol. 2008. (Medieval Warfare Ser.). (ENG., Illus.). 32p. (J). (gr. 3-3). lib. bdg. 28.67 *(978-0-8368-9209-3(7),* a1a06110-b849-4c73-b7d0-a78db2ae352c, Gareth Stevens Secondary Library) Stevens, Gareth Publishing LLLP.

Murrell, Deborah Jane & Dennis, Peter. Greek Warrior. 2012. (ENG., Illus.). 32p. (gr. 3-5). pap. 8.95 *(978-1-926853-53-6(9))* Saunders Bk. Co. CAN. Dist: RiverStream Publishing.

Nardo, Don. In the Water: Strategies & Tactics. 2014. (J). *(978-1-59935-464-4(0))* Reynolds, Morgan Inc.

O'Brian, Pliny. Knights: Warriors of the Middle Ages. 2015. (J). lib. bdg. *(978-1-62713-407-1(7))* Cavendish Square Publishing LLC.

Park, Louise & Love, Timothy. Pharaohs' Armies, 1 vol. 2010. (Ancient & Medieval People Ser.). (ENG.). 32p. (gr. 5-5). 31.21 *(978-0-7614-4451-0(3),* 9d83c8e9-5cbe-4154-b163-bcdaf68d2615) Cavendish Square Publishing LLC.

Rice, Rob S. Ancient Roman Warfare, 1 vol. 2009. (Ancient Warfare Ser.). (ENG., Illus.). 32p. (J). (gr. 5-6). lib. bdg. 28.67 *(978-1-4339-1974-9(5),* 32884157-b843-45aa-a55c-57d6205af466, Gareth Stevens Learning Library) Stevens, Gareth Publishing LLLP.

Ripley, Tim. Smoke Screens & Gas Masks: Chemistry Goes to War. 2017. (STEM on the Battlefield Ser.). (ENG., Illus.). 48p. (J). (gr. 4-6). 31.99 *(978-1-5124-3925-0(8),* 0134e1f8-717d-49a9-b2e4-14b44726a46c, Lerner Pubns.) Lerner Publishing Group.

Robertshaw, Andrew. Warfare in the 20th Century. 2015. (Warriors Ser.). (Illus.). 48p. (gr. 4-7). 37.10 *(978-1-62588-358-2(7))* Black Rabbit Bks.

Scheppler, Bill. British Royal Marines: Amphibious Division of the United Kingdom's Royal Navy. 2009. (Inside Special Operations Ser.). 64p. (gr. 6-6). 58.50 *(978-1-61513-550-9(2),* Rosen Reference) Rosen Publishing Group, Inc., The.

Soriano, Joan & Malizia, Diana, eds. A Visual History of Soldiers & Armies Around the World, 1 vol. 2016. (Visual History of the World Ser.). (ENG., Illus.). 96p. (J). (gr. 8-8). 38.80 *(978-1-4994-6592-1(0),* ece7bd18-1bd9-4d15-86d0-1b3ea7277c4f, Rosen Young Adult) Rosen Publishing Group, Inc., The.

Steele, Tara. Medieval Warfare. 2003. (Medieval World Ser.). (ENG., Illus.). 32p. (J). (gr. 5). lib. bdg. *(978-0-7787-1344-9(X))* Crabtree Publishing Co.

Troupe, Thomas Kingsley. Fantastic Worlds: The Inspiring Truth Behind Popular Role-Playing Video Games. 2018. (Video Games vs. Reality Ser.). (ENG., Illus.). 32p. (J). (gr. 3-9). lib. bdg. 28.65 *(978-1-5435-2569-4(5),* 138051, Capstone Pr.) Capstone.

Woods, Mary B. & Woods, Michael. Ancient Warfare: From Clubs to Catapults. 2005. (Ancient Technology Ser.). (Illus.). 96p. (gr. 6-12). 25.26 *(978-0-8225-2999-6(8))* Lerner Publishing Group.

—Ancient Warfare Technology: From Javelins to Chariots. 2011. (Technology in Ancient Cultures Ser.). (ENG., Illus.). 96p. (J). (gr. 6-12). lib. bdg. 31.93 *(978-0-7613-6525-9(7))* Lerner Publishing Group.

World Book, Inc. Staff, contrib. by. Warfare. 2009. (J). *(978-0-7166-0388-7(8))* World Bk., Inc.

MILITARY ART AND SCIENCE—STUDY AND TEACHING

see Military Education

MILITARY ART AND SCIENCE—VOCATIONAL GUIDANCE

see Armed Forces—Vocational Guidance

MILITARY EDUCATION

see also names of military schools, e.g. United States Military Academy, West Point; etc.

Goldish, Meish. Army: Civilian to Soldier. 2010. (Becoming a Soldier Ser.). 24p. (YA). (gr. 3-6). lib. bdg. 26.99 *(978-1-936088-11-9(8))* Bearport Publishing Co., Inc.

—Navy: Civilian to Sailor. 2010. (Becoming a Soldier Ser.). 24p. (YA). (gr. 3-6). lib. bdg. 26.99 *(978-1-936088-14-0(2))* Bearport Publishing Co., Inc.

Wehrertuchtigungslager der Hitler-Jugend, 1942-1945. (GER.). *(978-3-928379-00-7(3))* Verein zur Fordenrung der Umweltforschung.

MILITARY ENGINEERING

see also Fortification

Military Engineering in Action. 2015. (Military Engineering in Action Ser.). (ENG.). 48p. (J). (gr. 6-6). pap., pap., pap. 70.20 *(978-0-7660-7071-4(9));* pap., pap., pap. 421.20 *(978-0-7660-7072-1(7))* Enslow Publishing, LLC.

Military Engineering in Action: Set 2, 12 vols. 2016. (Military Engineering in Action Ser.). 48p. (ENG.). (gr. 5-6). lib. bdg. 177.60 *(978-0-7660-7499-6(4),* 691b621a-17a5-4f03-9649-8a09a41ad7ae); (gr. 6-5). pap. 70.20 *(978-0-7660-7970-0(8))* Enslow Publishing, LLC.

Military Engineering in Action: Set 1, 12 vols. 2015. (Military Engineering in Action Ser.). (ENG.). 48p. (J). (gr. 6-6). lib. bdg. 177.60 *(978-0-7660-6692-2(4),* 9c320586-1aa4-44de-9d8d-ac8fe2d559a2) Enslow Publishing, LLC.

MILITARY FORCES

see Armies

MILITARY HISTORY

see also Battles; Naval History

also names of countries with the subdivision Army or History, Military

Baum, Margaux & Hilliam, Paul. Weapons & Warcraft, 1 vol. 2016. (Life in the Middle Ages Ser.). (ENG., Illus.). 64p. (J). (gr. 5-5). 36.13 *(978-1-4994-6472-6(X),* 93883e1a-169a-41d7-b447-31af09c5d7fc) Rosen Publishing Group, Inc., The.

Bow, James. Your Guide to Castles & Medieval Warfare. 2017. (Destination: Middle Ages Ser.). (ENG., Illus.). 32p. (J). (gr. 5-5). *(978-0-7787-2994-5(X));* pap. *(978-0-7787-3000-2(X))* Crabtree Publishing Co.

Cawthorne, Nigel. Military Commanders: The 100 Greatest Throughout History. 2004. (Illus.). 208p. 18.95 *(978-1-59270-029-5(2))* Enchanted Lion Bks., LLC.

—Victory: 100 Great Military Commanders. 2012. (Illus.). 208p. (J). *(978-1-4351-4242-8(X))* Metro Bks.

Dargie, Richard. Castles under Siege, 1 vol. 2007. (Age of Castles Ser.). (ENG., Illus.). 48p. (J). (gr. 4-5). lib. bdg. 32.93 *(978-1-4042-4294-4(5),* 1c7346c4-6868-4a5f-a92a-32a2dfbad9f6, PowerKids Pr.) Rosen Publishing Group, Inc., The.

Dougherty, Martin J. Land Warfare, 1 vol. 2010. (Modern Warfare Ser.). (ENG., Illus.). 32p. (YA). (gr. 3-5). lib. bdg. 28.67 *(978-1-4339-2727-0(6),* d634ac7a-beb5-42ab-b550-34d9a3eef86c) Stevens, Gareth Publishing LLLP.

Frontline Families. 2015. (Frontline Families Ser.). (ENG.). 48p. (J). (gr. 5-6). pap., pap., pap. 84.30 *(978-1-4824-3472-9(5))* Stevens, Gareth Publishing LLLP.

Gale Editors, ed. Worldmark Conflict & Diplomacy: 2 Volume Set, 2 vols. 2014. (Worldmark Conflict & Diplomacy Ser.). (ENG.). 1000p. 399.00 *(978-1-57302-726-7(X))* Cengage Gale.

Great Military Leaders, 16 vols. 2017. (Great Military Leaders Ser.). (ENG.). 128p. (gr. 9-9). lib. bdg. 378.88 *(978-1-5026-2686-8(1),* a5fae9b3-a623-466e-afa0-d9ae4500cf93, Cavendish Square) Cavendish Square Publishing LLC.

Hargrove, Julia. Tomb of the Unknowns. 2003. (Historic Monuments Ser.). (Illus.). 48p. (J). pap. 6.95 *(978-1-57310-405-0(1))* Teaching & Learning Co.

Henry, Claire. The World's Deadliest Wars, 1 vol., 1. 2014. (World's Deadliest Ser.). (ENG.). 32p. (J). (gr. 4-5). 28.93 *(978-1-4777-6153-3(5),* 5a755f5e-6d12-49e3-8933-7d0a9b51136a, PowerKids Pr.) Rosen Publishing Group, Inc., The.

Hull, Robert. Trade & Warfare. 2007. (World of Ancient Greece Ser.). (Illus.). 32p. (YA). (gr. 3-6). lib. bdg. 27.10 *(978-1-59771-062-6(8))* Sea-To-Sea Pubns.

Jestice, Phyllis G. Ancient Egyptian Warfare, 1 vol. 2009. (Ancient Warfare Ser.). (ENG., Illus.). 32p. (J). (gr. 5-6). lib. bdg. 28.67 *(978-1-4339-1971-8(0),* d99bc651-6cf7-4601-9b6e-517fd3aacf8a, Gareth Stevens Learning Library) Stevens, Gareth Publishing LLLP.

—Ancient Persian Warfare, 1 vol. 2009. (Ancient Warfare Ser.). (ENG., Illus.). 32p. (J). (gr. 5-6). lib. bdg. 28.67 *(978-1-4339-1973-2(7),* 9b02b6f1-9ec7-480f-84df-5c7b257e0494, Gareth Stevens Learning Library) Stevens, Gareth Publishing LLLP.

Johnson, Cynthia. Worldmark Conflict & Diplomacy. 2014. (J). *(978-1-57302-727-4(8))* Cengage Gale.

Krasner, Barbara, ed. Civilian Casualties in War, 1 vol. 2018. (Global Viewpoints Ser.). (ENG.). 200p. (gr. 10-12). 47.83 *(978-1-5345-0337-3(4),* 0a4013e6-2770-4431-99c7-816202833a91) Greenhaven Publishing LLC.

Macdonald, Fiona. Top 10 Worst Ruthless Warriors, 1 vol. Antram, David, illus. 2012. (Top 10 Worst Ser.). (ENG.). 32p. (J). (gr. 3-5). pap. 11.50 *(978-1-4339-6686-6(7),* 61436c43-ce49-4ece-b5e8-9a1d479bf1b6); lib. bdg. 29.27 *(978-1-4339-6685-9(9),* b8b7cc54-3972-4678-8765-14c346f65f35) Stevens, Gareth Publishing LLLP. (Gareth Stevens Learning Library).

Malam, John. Warriors. 2013. (Illus.). 48p. (J). *(978-1-4351-5100-0(3))* Barnes & Noble, Inc.

—Warriors. 2010. (Remarkable Man & Beast Ser.). (Illus.). 48p. (J). (gr. 3-18). lib. bdg. 19.95 *(978-1-4222-1979-9(8))* Mason Crest.

—You Wouldn't Want to Be a Ninja Warrior! A Secret Job That's Your Destiny. Antram, David, illus. 2012. (ENG.). 32p. (J). (gr. 3-12). lib. bdg. 29.00 *(978-0-531-20873-1(7))* Scholastic Library Publishing.

McNab, Chris. Famous Battles of the Age of Revolution, 1 vol. 2017. (Classic Warfare Ser.). (ENG.). 72p. (YA). (gr. 8-8). lib. bdg. 37.36 *(978-1-5026-3252-4(7),* cda2c722-c80a-466a-ae3b-757873daefea) Cavendish Square Publishing LLC.

—Famous Battles of the Ancient World, 1 vol. 2017. (Classic Warfare Ser.). (ENG.). 88p. (YA). (gr. 8-8). lib. bdg. 37.36 *(978-1-5026-3246-3(2),* 948053ca-9d5d-43df-aa05-b241c797b1c8) Cavendish Square Publishing LLC.

—Famous Battles of the Early Modern Period, 1 vol. 2017. (Classic Warfare Ser.). (ENG.). 72p. (YA). (gr. 8-8). lib. bdg. 37.36 *(978-1-5026-3250-0(0),* b4eb2b53-c957-40ba-b103-a8f5f1b19ec8) Cavendish Square Publishing LLC.

—Famous Battles of the Medieval Period, 1 vol. 2017. (Classic Warfare Ser.). (ENG.). 104p. (YA). (gr. 8-8). lib. bdg. 37.36 *(978-1-5026-3248-7(9),* 9d27e13f-f099-4135-b067-0a0790611c6a) Cavendish Square Publishing LLC.

Miller, Connie Colwell. The Biggest Military Battles. 2018. (History's Biggest Disasters Ser.). (ENG., Illus.). 32p. (J). (gr. 3-9). lib. bdg. 27.32 *(978-1-5157-9989-4(1),* 136978, Capstone Pr.) Capstone.

Miller, Shannon & Hoena, B. A. A Low-Tech Mission. 2018. (J). *(978-1-68410-227-3(8))* Cantata Learning.

Moments in History, 12 vols., Set. Incl. Why Did Hiroshima Happen? Grant, R. G. lib. bdg. 34.60 *(978-1-4339-4163-4(5),* 2b6ea7b6-a641-4b5e-86c9-252c57d25795); Why Did the Cold War Happen? Harrison, Paul. lib. bdg. 34.60 *(978-1-4339-4166-5(X),* eae20eee-654b-480c-9bb2-4b4e7dcf1173); Why Did the Great Depression Happen? Grant, R. G. lib. bdg. 34.60 *(978-1-4339-4169-6(4),* 2cef96c8-83ef-49c1-9b92-65399e65e0dc); Why Did the Holocaust Happen? Sheehan, Sean. lib. bdg. 34.60 *(978-1-4339-4172-6(4),* c48c81b5-7fe6-4406-90ae-f694e53f11c8); Why Did the Rise of the Nazis Happen? Freeman, Charles. lib. bdg. 34.60 *(978-1-4339-4175-7(9),* 325cb1a1-640f-4027-a952-3ea9ec96c7d3); Why Did the Vietnam War Happen? Gifford, Clive. lib. bdg. 34.60 *(978-1-4339-4178-8(3),* 49a09c6a-e207-45a7-83ee-602b45d6bad5); Why Did World War I Happen? Grant, R. G. lib. bdg. 34.60 *(978-1-4339-4181-8(3),* dbc68180-7d50-4924-bbf4-621b4712124b); Why Did World War II Happen? Senker, Cath. lib. bdg. 34.60 *(978-1-4339-4184-9(8),* 8cebe7d6-0af0-46bd-ab47-a1890c7ffe55); (YA). (gr. 6-8). (Moments in History Ser.). (ENG., Illus.). 48p. 2010. Set lib. bdg. 207.66 *(978-1-4339-4195-5(3),* d1f5d570-c32f-4b02-8aca-1b000b3a4f21, Gareth Stevens Secondary Library) Stevens, Gareth Publishing LLLP.

The Most Daring Raids in History, 12 vols., Set. Incl. Counterterrorism in West Africa: The Most Dangerous SAS Assault. Fowler, Will. lib. bdg. 37.13 *(978-1-4488-1871-6(0),* 22f33d10-ef04-408d-a5c0-1c6cf42079c8); Entebbe: The Most Daring Raid of Israel's Special Forces. Dunstan, Simon. 37.13 *(978-1-4488-1868-6(0),* bd8a47e5-10de-494b-81a2-a4b07b1abfff); Most Daring Raid of the Civil War: The Great Locomotive Chase. Rottman, Gordon L. 37.13 *(978-1-4488-1870-9(2),* 39516277-a6d8-4cc8-a833-62e9509030a5); Most Daring Raid of the Samurai. Turnbull, Stephen R. lib. bdg. 37.13 *(978-1-4488-1872-3(9),* b7b3e90d-ba10-464d-925e-df4a877d580b); Most Daring Raid of World War II: D-Day — Pointe-Du-Hoc. Zaloga, Steven J. lib. bdg. 37.13 *(978-1-4488-1867-9(2),* 3ef3ba30-ecb1-412b-bdd2-8540d49e07d0); Rescue at the Iranian Embassy: The Most Daring SAS Raid. Fremont-Barnes, Gregory. lib. bdg. 37.13 *(978-1-4488-1869-3(9),* 248d6de7-a710-41a2-a2d0-36238874c537); (YA). (gr. 7-7). (Most Daring Raids in History Ser.). (ENG., Illus.). 64p. 2011. Set lib. bdg. 222.78 *(978-1-4488-1956-0(3),* d57e7594-1b97-4c4a-971c-7b4275223dba) Rosen Publishing Group, Inc., The.

Murrell, Deborah. Medieval Warfare, 6 vols., Set. Incl. Castles. lib. bdg. 28.67 *(978-0-8368-9208-6(9),* 5f3c4530-97a9-408f-9f22-a59f4fd3ae8a); Fighting a Battle. (Illus.). lib. bdg. 28.67 *(978-0-8368-9209-3(7),* a1a06110-b849-4c73-b7d0-a78db2ae352c); Knights & Armor. lib. bdg. 28.67 *(978-0-8368-9210-9(0),* 70d52ad7-e696-42e3-a36b-adcd12a89f22); (J). (gr. 3-3). (Medieval Warfare Ser.). (ENG.). 32p. 2008. Set lib. bdg. 86.01 *(978-0-8368-9305-2(0),* 4985cdca-73f3-4d35-8844-3accdfe0522f, Gareth Stevens Secondary Library) Stevens, Gareth Publishing LLLP.

Nardo, Don. Bad Days in Battle. 2017. (Whoops! a History of Bad Days Ser.). (ENG., Illus.). 48p. (J). (gr. 5-8). lib. bdg. 35.99 *(978-1-4109-8562-0(8),* 134312, Raintree) Capstone.

Nelson, Sheila & Zoldak, Joyce. In Defense of Our Country: Survivors of Military Conflict. 2009. (J). pap. 24.95 *(978-1-4222-1465-7(6))* Mason Crest.

Nelson, Sheila, et al. In Defense of Our Country: Survivors of Military Conflict. 2010. (Survivors Ser.). 128p. (YA). (gr. 7-12). 24.95 *(978-1-4222-0452-8(9))* Mason Crest.

Osborne, Mary Pope & Boyce, Natalie Pope. Warriors: A Nonfiction Companion to Magic Tree House #31: Warriors in Winter. Mones, Isidre, illus. 2019. (Magic Tree House (R) Fact Tracker Ser.: 40). 128p. (J). (gr. 2-5). 6.99 *(978-1-101-93651-1(7),* Random Hse. Bks. for Young Readers) Random Hse. Children's Bks.

Oxlade, Chris. The Top Ten Battles That Changed the World. 2009. (J). 60.00 *(978-1-4358-9178-4(3),* PowerKids Pr.); (ENG.). 32p. (J). (gr. 4-5). pap. 11.00 *(978-1-4358-9177-7(5),* 8efc1fec-641e-4190-b74d-5fa0083d19ea, PowerKids Pr.); (ENG., Illus.). 32p. (YA). (gr. 4-5). 30.27 *(978-1-4358-9176-0(7),* 0901ec84-9346-4820-82bb-1ee6b4fa4156) Rosen Publishing Group, Inc., The.

Raum, Elizabeth, et al. Military by the Numbers, 1 vol. 2014. (Military by the Numbers Ser.). (ENG.). 32p. (J). (gr. 3-9). 122.60 *(978-1-4765-7837-8(0),* 20773, Capstone Pr.) Capstone.

Rice, Rob S. Ancient Greek Warfare, 1 vol. 2009. (Ancient Warfare Ser.). (ENG., Illus.). 32p. (J). (gr. 5-6). lib. bdg. 28.67 *(978-1-4339-1972-5(9),* e36fd023-1420-4f2e-910f-c246ad4c5c25, Gareth Stevens Learning Library) Stevens, Gareth Publishing LLLP.

—Ancient Roman Warfare, 1 vol. 2009. (Ancient Warfare Ser.). (ENG., Illus.). 32p. (J). (gr. 5-6). lib. bdg. 28.67 *(978-1-4339-1974-9(5),* 32884157-b843-45aa-a55c-57d6205af466, Gareth Stevens Learning Library) Stevens, Gareth Publishing LLLP.

Steele, Tara. Medieval Warfare, 1 vol. 2003. (Medieval World Ser.). (ENG., Illus.). 32p. (J). (gr. 5). pap. *(978-0-7787-1376-0(8))* Crabtree Publishing Co.

Turner, Tracey. Hard as Nails Warriors. Lenman, Jamie, illus. 2015. (Hard As Nails in History Ser.). (ENG.). 64p. (J). (gr. 4-5). pap. *(978-0-7787-1517-7(5))* Crabtree Publishing Co.

Turner, Tracey & Lenman, Jamie. Hard As Nails in Wars & Battles. 2015. (Hard As Nails in History Ser.). (ENG., Illus.). 64p. (J). (gr. 4-5). pap. *(978-0-7787-1526-9(4))* Crabtree Publishing Co.

Woods, Mary B. & Woods, Michael. Ancient Warfare Technology: From Javelins to Chariots. 2011. (Technology in Ancient Cultures Ser.). (ENG., Illus.). 96p. (J). (gr. 6-12). lib. bdg. 31.93 *(978-0-7613-6525-9(7))* Lerner Publishing Group.

Zuchora-Walske, Christine. Tuskegee Airmen, 1 vol. 2015. (Essential Library of World War II Ser.). (ENG., Illus.). 112p. (YA). (gr. 6-12). 41.36 *(978-1-62403-795-5(X),* 17788, Essential Library) ABDO Publishing Co.

MILITARY LIFE

see Soldiers; United States—Army—Military Life

MILITARY POWER

see Armies; Disarmament; Military Art and Science; Sea Power

MILITARY SCHOOLS

see Military Education

MILITARY SCIENCE

see Military Art and Science

MILITARY SERVICE, COMPULSORY

see Draft

MILITARY SIGNALING

see Signals and Signaling

MILITARY TRAINING

see Military Education

MILITARY UNIFORMS

Carman, William Y. The Ackermann Military Prints: Uniforms of the British & Indian Armies 1840-1855, 1 vol. 2003. (ENG., Illus.). 176p. (gr. 10-13). 59.95 *(978-0-7643-1671-5(0),* 3146, Schiffer Military History) Schiffer Publishing, Ltd.

Harris, Carol & Brown, Mike. Ceremonial Costumes. 2004. (Twentieth-Century Developments in Fashion & Costume Ser.). (Illus.). 64p. (YA). (gr. 7-18). lib. bdg. 19.95 *(978-1-59084-424-3(6))* Mason Crest.

—Military Uniforms. 2004. (Twentieth-Century Developments in Fashion & Costume Ser.). (Illus.). 64p. (YA). (gr. 7-18). lib. bdg. 19.95 *(978-1-59084-418-2(1))* Mason Crest.

Mingo, Norman. Navy Scouts Paper Dolls. Taliadoros, Jenny, ed. Mingo, Norman & Ernst, Clara, illus. 2007. (ENG.). 16p. pap. 12.00 *(978-0-9790668-3-2(2))* Paper Studio Pr.

Stowell, Louie. Sticker Dressing Second World War. 2012. (Sticker Dressing Ser.). 24p. (J). pap. 8.99 *(978-0-7945-3314-4(0),* Usborne) EDC Publishing.

Tucker, Louise, ed. The Visual Dictionary of Military Uniforms: Eyewitness Visual Dictionaries. 2004. (Illus.). 64p. (J). (gr. 4-8). reprint ed. 18.00 *(978-0-7567-7820-0(4))* DIANE Publishing Co.

MILITARY VEHICLES

see Vehicles, Military

MILITARY WEAPONS

see also Disarmament; Ordnance

Bergin, Mark. Warfare in the Ancient World. 2015. (Warriors Ser.). (Illus.). 48p. (gr. 4-7). 37.10 *(978-1-62588-355-1(2))* Black Rabbit Bks.

Blackford, Cheryl. This Book Is Top Secret: A Collection of Awesome Military Trivia, 1 vol. 2012. (Super Trivia Collection). (ENG., Illus.). 32p. (J). (gr. 3-9). lib. bdg. 28.65 *(978-1-4296-8591-7(3),* 118603, Capstone Pr.) Capstone.

Bow, James. Tech to Protect. 2017. (Techno Planet Ser.). (Illus.). 32p. (J). (gr. 5-5). *(978-0-7787-3606-6(7))* Crabtree Publishing Co.

Brezina, Corona. Weapons of Mass Destruction: Proliferation & Control, 1 vol. 2004. (Library of Weapons of Mass Destruction Ser.). (ENG., Illus.). 64p. (J). (gr. 5-5). lib. bdg. 37.13 *(978-1-4042-0298-6(6),* 27822255-dd3f-417d-9c70-b10836760dd4) Rosen Publishing Group, Inc., The.

Burrows, Terry. Hovercrafts & Humvees: Engineering Goes to War. 2017. (STEM on the Battlefield Ser.). (ENG., Illus.). 48p. (J). (gr. 4-6). 31.99 *(978-1-5124-3929-8(0),* 0f902c5c-a4ce-415c-aaad-d99cfb90675f, Lerner Pubns.) Lerner Publishing Group.

Campbell, Geoffrey A. Weapons of War. 2004. (American War Library). (Illus.). 112p. (J). (gr. 7-10). 30.85 *(978-1-59018-544-5(7),* Lucent Bks.) Cengage Gale.

Cohn, Jessica. Military Machines, 1 vol. 2013. (Machines in Motion Ser.). 48p. (J). (gr. 3-3). (ENG.). pap. 15.05 *(978-1-4339-9605-4(7),* be9e9466-a0fb-4133-90ce-0e6fa7147cdd); pap. 84.30

(978-1-4339-9606-1(5)); (ENG., Illus.). lib. bdg. 34.61 *(978-1-4339-9604-7(9)*, 5d11d558-1934-40ca-a0e1-e03398e71ffc) Stevens, Gareth Publishing LLLP.

Doeden, Matt. The Manhattan Project. 2018. (Heroes of World War II (Alternator Books (r)) Ser.). (ENG., Illus.). 32p. (J). (gr. 3-6). 30.65 *(978-1-5415-2150-6(1)*, e2e6a5d2-827b-4c5a-80ad-3897eb71e2bc, Lerner Pubns.) Lerner Publishing Group.

—Weapons of the Civil War. rev. ed. 2017. (Weapons of War Ser.). (ENG., Illus.). 32p. (J). (gr. 3-9). lib. bdg. 27.32 *(978-1-5157-7909-4(2)*, 136024, Capstone Pr.) Capstone.

—Weapons of the Revolutionary War. rev. ed. 2017. (Weapons of War Ser.). (ENG., Illus.). 32p. (J). (gr. 3-9). lib. bdg. 27.32 *(978-1-5157-7908-7(4)*, 136023, Capstone Pr.) Capstone.

—Weapons of War. rev. ed. 2017. (Weapons of War Ser.). (ENG.). 32p. (J). (gr. 3-9). 117.28 *(978-1-5157-7936-0(X)*, 26953, Capstone Pr.) Capstone.

—Weapons of World War I. rev. ed. 2017. (Weapons of War Ser.). (ENG., Illus.). 32p. (J). (gr. 3-9). lib. bdg. 27.32 *(978-1-5157-7907-0(6)*, 136022, Capstone Pr.) Capstone.

—Weapons of World War II. rev. ed. 2017. (Weapons of War Ser.). (ENG., Illus.). 32p. (J). (gr. 3-9). lib. bdg. 27.32 *(978-1-5157-7906-3(8)*, 136021, Capstone Pr.) Capstone.

Dougherty, Martin J. Weapons & Technology, 1 vol. 2010. (Modern Warfare Ser.). (ENG.). 32p. (YA). (gr. 3-5). lib. bdg. 28.67 *(978-1-4339-2741-6(1)*, 211a8154-2cf5-4e65-b0dd-bc7a97d5b2ba) Stevens, Gareth Publishing LLLP.

Garstecki, Julia. Armas Militares. 2017. (Tecnología Militar Ser.). (SPA., Illus.). 32p. (J). (gr. 4-6). lib. bdg. *(978-1-68072-584-1(X)*, 10593, Bolt) Black Rabbit Bks.

—Military Weapons. 2017. (Military Tech Ser.). (ENG., Illus.). 32p. (J). (gr. 4-6). lib. bdg. *(978-1-68072-167-6(4)*, 10518, Bolt) Black Rabbit Bks.

Hagler, Gina & Baker, Linda R. The Evolution of Military Technology, 1 vol. 2018. (Evolving Technology Ser.). (ENG.). 64p. (gr. 6-7). lib. bdg. 34.29 *(978-1-5383-0285-9(3)*, fef67db4-8d32-467e-a6dc-446995e1dbf2, Britannica Educational Publishing) Rosen Publishing Group, Inc., The.

Hudak, Heather. Military Entrepreneurs. 2018. (Science & Technology Start-Up Stars Ser.). (ENG., Illus.). 32p. (J). (gr. 5-5). *(978-0-7787-4422-1(1))* Crabtree Publishing Co.

Incentive Publications by World Book (Firm) Staff, contrib. by. CRISPR & Other Biotech. 2019. (Illus.). 48p. (J). *(978-0-7166-2429-5(X))* World Bk., Inc.

Kassnoff, David. Special Ops: Weapons & Gear, 1 vol. 2014. (Inside Special Forces Ser.). (ENG.). 64p. (J). (gr. 6-6). 36.13 *(978-1-4777-7567-7(6)*, b1604221-4812-4b59-8452-f5b81966b78e, Rosen Reference) Rosen Publishing Group, Inc., The.

Macdonald, Fiona. Warfare in the Middle Ages. 2015. (Warriors Ser.). (Illus.). 48p. (gr. 4-7). 37.10 *(978-1-62588-356-8(0))* Black Rabbit Bks.

Mapua, Jeff. Weaponizing Poop, 1 vol. 2017. (Power of Poop Ser.). (ENG.). 32p. (gr. 3-4). pap. 11.52 *(978-0-7660-9093-4(0)*, e438156d-0d04-4bea-90f1-32437ae65716) Enslow Publishing, LLC.

Matthews, Rupert. Weapons & Armor, 1 vol. 2014. (100 Facts You Should Know Ser.). (ENG., Illus.). 48p. (J). (gr. 4-5). lib. bdg. 33.60 *(978-1-4824-2193-4(3)*, 72bf708d-d7ca-409c-9cb5-3aadffc4e502) Stevens, Gareth Publishing LLLP.

Mighty Military Machines, 12 vols. 2014. (Mighty Military Machines Ser.). (ENG.). 32p. (J). (gr. 1-1). lib. bdg. 161.58 *(978-1-4824-1649-7(2)*, 3b196470-0e28-407f-9aa8-79f6d010a63e) Stevens, Gareth Publishing LLLP.

Nardo, Don. The Civil War, 1 vol. 2008. (American History Ser.). (ENG.). 104p. (gr. 7-7). pap. 29.30 *(978-1-4205-0302-9(2)*, c76d53a8-1719-4d90-9a47-3a5eb761f337, Lucent Pr.) Greenhaven Publishing LLC.

Parker, Steve. Military Machines. 2010. (How It Works Ser.). 40p. (J). (gr. 3-18). lib. bdg. 19.95 *(978-1-4222-1797-9(3))* Mason Crest.

Perritano, John. War & the Military, Vol. 10. 2016. (Stem in Current Events Ser.). (Illus.). 64p. (J). (gr. 7). 23.95 *(978-1-4222-3597-3(1))* Mason Crest.

Ripley, Tim. Smoke Screens & Gas Masks: Chemistry Goes to War. 2017. (STEM on the Battlefield Ser.). (ENG., Illus.). 48p. (J). (gr. 4-6). 31.99 *(978-1-5124-3925-0(8)*, 0134e1f8-717d-49a9-b2e4-14b44726a46c, Lerner Pubns.) Lerner Publishing Group.

Robertshaw, Andrew. Warfare in the 20th Century. 2015. (Warriors Ser.). (Illus.). 48p. (gr. 4-7). 37.10 *(978-1-62588-358-2(7))* Black Rabbit Bks.

Samuels, Charlie. Machines & Weaponry of the Vietnam War, 1 vol. 2013. (Machines That Won the War Ser.). (ENG., Illus.). 48p. (J). (gr. 5-6). pap. 15.05 *(978-1-4339-8600-0(0)*, c3075805-43c1-4b7a-b55a-9f3f345a9677); lib. bdg. 34.60 *(978-1-4339-8599-7(3)*, ff35beae-f162-4186-bb61-f60b8e596527) Stevens, Gareth Publishing LLLP.

—Machines & Weaponry of World War I, 1 vol. 2013. (Machines That Won the War Ser.). (ENG., Illus.). 48p. (J). (gr. 5-6). pap. 15.05 *(978-1-4339-8604-8(3)*, def5d1aa-6819-4514-ae97-a3ec6ee02951); lib. bdg. 34.60 *(978-1-4339-8603-1(5)*, 1622fcc1-73e4-4789-9d45-744b4ace99a4) Stevens, Gareth Publishing LLLP.

—Machines & Weaponry of World War II, 1 vol. 2013. (Machines That Won the War Ser.). (ENG., Illus.). 48p. (J). (gr. 5-6). pap. 15.05 *(978-1-4339-8608-6(6)*, 97164ac8-6562-4407-aacd-bcf84d741d8d); lib. bdg. 34.60 *(978-1-4339-8607-9(8)*, 08005b31-3a63-49db-93b2-5c260d4ab83f) Stevens, Gareth Publishing LLLP.

Schmidt, Roderic D. Infantry of the Future, 1 vol. 2006. (Library of Future Weaponry Ser.). (ENG., Illus.). 64p. (J). (gr. 6-6). lib. bdg. 37.13 *(978-1-4042-0525-3(X)*, 57729a88-1666-44b5-9782-9da09ef7ac4b) Rosen Publishing Group, Inc., The.

Sheen, Barbara. Cutting Edge Military Technology. 2016. (ENG.). 80p. (J). (gr. 5-12). *(978-1-68282-044-5(0))* ReferencePoint Pr., Inc.

Sherman, Jill. Guarding Nuclear Weapons Facilities. 2016. (Highly Guarded Places Ser.). (ENG.). 24p. (J). (gr. 2-5). 32.79 *(978-1-5038-0813-3(0)*, 210647) Child's World, Inc., The.

Small, Cathleen. Strategic Inventions of the Korean War, 1 vol. 2016. (Tech in the Trenches Ser.). (ENG., Illus.). 112p. (YA). (gr. 9-9). 44.50 *(978-1-5026-2345-4(5)*, 12a6e201-fa7a-481d-b720-d560c44d31ed) Cavendish Square Publishing LLC.

Swanson, Jennifer. Top Secret Science: Projects You Aren't Supposed to Know About, 1 vol. 2014. (Scary Science Ser.). (ENG., Illus.). 32p. (J). (gr. 3-6). lib. bdg. 27.99 *(978-1-4765-3926-3(X)*, 123924, Capstone Pr.) Capstone.

Tougas, Shelley. The Science of Weapons, 1 vol. 2012. (Science of War Ser.). (ENG.). 48p. (J). (gr. 6-9). lib. bdg. 34.65 *(978-0-7565-4461-4(0)*, 115724, Compass Point Bks.) Capstone.

—Weapons, Gear, & Uniforms of the Iraq War, 1 vol. 2012. (Equipped for Battle Ser.). (ENG.). 32p. (J). (gr. 3-9). lib. bdg. 28.65 *(978-1-4296-7652-6(3)*, 117249, Capstone Pr.) Capstone.

Woods, Mary B. & Woods, Michael. Ancient Warfare Technology: From Javelins to Chariots. 2011. (Technology in Ancient Cultures Ser.). (ENG., Illus.). 96p. (J). (gr. 6-12). lib. bdg. 31.93 *(978-0-7613-6525-9(7))* Lerner Publishing Group.

World Book, Inc. Staff, contrib. by. Robot Soldiers & Other Military Tech. 2019. (Illus.). 48p. (J). *(978-0-7166-2431-8(1))* World Bk., Inc.

—Robots in Action. 2019. (Illus.). 48p. (J). *(978-0-7166-4135-3(6))* World Bk., Inc.

—Robots on the Move. 2019. (Illus.). 48p. (J). *(978-0-7166-4132-2(1))* World Bk., Inc.

Yomtov, Nel. Civil War Weapons. 2016. (Essential Library of the Civil War Ser.). (ENG., Illus.). 112p. (J). (gr. 8-12). 59.93 *(978-1-68077-467-2(0)*, 22358, Essential Library) ABDO Publishing Co.

MILK

Benduhn, Tea. Milk & Cheese, 1 vol. 2007. (Find Out about Food Ser.). (ENG.). 24p. (gr. k-2). pap. 9.15 *(978-0-8368-8260-5(1)*, c7dba598-12c0-47e5-a23c-0ad65a36de50); (Illus.). lib. bdg. 24.67 *(978-0-8368-8253-7(9)*, af90f223-e3f2-4284-8879-3a50b586b499) Stevens, Gareth Publishing LLLP. (Weekly Reader Leveled Readers).

—Milk & Cheese / Leche y Queso, 1 vol. 2007. (Find Out about Food / Conoce la Comida Ser.). (SPA & ENG., Illus.). 24p. (gr. k-2). lib. bdg. 24.67 *(978-0-8368-8457-9(4)*, 62847ee5-c490-4cc1-86cf-8cc45c737733, Weekly Reader Leveled Readers) Stevens, Gareth Publishing LLLP.

The Book Carton, 6 vols. (Let's Read about... Ser.). (Illus.). 10p. (J). *(978-2-7643-0028-2(X))* Phidal Publishing, Inc./Editions Phidal, Inc.

Dilkes, D. H. Milk & Dairy, 1 vol. 2011. (All about Good Foods We Eat Ser.). (ENG., Illus.). 24p. (gr. -1-1). pap. 10.35 *(978-1-59845-253-2(3)*, 8eb86e59-9f47-40dc-98bf-c5ac2bedf08c); lib. bdg. 25.27 *(978-0-7660-3924-7(2)*, cf6961b5-b21b-4512-b521-75a7f76ebbf5) Enslow Publishing, LLC. (Enslow Publishing).

Donlon, Bridget. Got Milk? How? Chelsey, Emily, illus. 2012. 26p. (-18). 29.95 *(978-1-62709-613-3(2))* America Star Bks.

Fox, Phoebe. Babies Nurse: Así Se Alimentan los Bebés. Geating, Karen Rivera, tr. Fox, Jim, illus. 2018. (ENG.). 32p. (J). (gr. -1-2). 14.95 *(978-1-930775-73-2(3))* Platypus Media, L.L.C.

—Babies Nurse / Así Se Alimentan Los Bebés. Geating, Karen Rivera, tr. Fox, Jim, illus. 2018. (ENG.). 32p. (J). (gr. -1-2). pap. 9.95 *(978-1-930775-72-5(5))* Platypus Media, L.L.C.

Grack, Rachel. Grass to Milk. 2020. (Beginning to End Ser.). (ENG., Illus.). 24p. (J). (gr. k-3). lib. bdg. 26.95 *(978-1-64487-140-9(8)*, Blastoff! Readers) Bellwether Media.

Hewitt, Sally. Milk & Cheese, 1 vol. 2007. (Good for Me Ser.). (ENG., Illus.). 24p. (J). (gr. 1-2). lib. bdg. 26.27 *(978-1-4042-4268-5(6)*, ba72ef9b-5954-4761-b82f-27fe87574ef0, PowerKids Pr.) Rosen Publishing Group, Inc., The.

Kalz, Jill. Dairy Products. 2003. 24p. (J). lib. bdg. 21.35 *(978-1-58340-297-9(7))* Black Rabbit Bks.

Lee, Sally. The Delicious Dairy Group, 1 vol. Poling, Kyle, illus. 2011. (First Graphics: Myplate & Healthy Eating Ser.). (ENG.). 24p. (J). (gr. k-3). lib. bdg. 24.65 *(978-1-4296-6092-1(9)*, 115041) Capstone.

Martineau, Susan & James, Hel. Milk, Butter, & Cheese. 2012. (Healthy Eating Ser.). (Illus.). 32p. (gr. 2-6). pap. 8.95 *(978-1-59920-245-7(X))* Black Rabbit Bks.

Nelson, Maria. I'm Allergic to Milk, 1 vol. 2014. (I'm Allergic Ser.). (ENG.). 24p. (J). (gr. 1-2). 24.27 *(978-1-4824-0968-0(2)*, 08001da1-f5cf-4619-a3aa-5b29b90141fc) Stevens, Gareth Publishing LLLP.

Owen, Ruth. Milk! Life on a Dairy Farm, 1 vol. 2012. (Food from Farmers Ser.). (ENG.). 32p. (J). (gr. 1-2). pap. 12.75 *(978-1-61533-534-3(X)*, bc992fa1-ebd5-4425-92ca-2bc36b63fe07); lib. bdg. 29.93 *(978-1-61533-528-2(5)*, c4efde62-8ee4-44f2-83a2-59a7b9ee5d72) Rosen Publishing Group, Inc., The. (Windmill Bks.).

Shores, Erika L. How Food Gets from Farms to Store Shelves. 2016. (Here to There Ser.). (ENG., Illus.). 24p. (J). (gr. -1-2). lib. bdg. 27.32 *(978-1-4914-8428-9(4)*, 130857, Capstone Pr.) Capstone.

Taus-Bolstad, Stacy. From Grass to Milk. (ENG., Illus.). 24p. (gr. k-3). 2012. (Start to Finish, Second Ser.: No. 2). (J). pap. 7.99 *(978-1-58013-966-3(3)*, 484246f7-def7-45c7-91e4-73402137394c) 2003. (Start to Finish Ser.). 19.93 *(978-0-8225-4664-1(7)*, Lerner Pubns.) Lerner Publishing Group.

—The Story of Milk: It Starts with Grass. 2021. (Step by Step Ser.). (ENG., Illus.). 24p. (J). (gr. -1-2). 26.65 *(978-1-5415-9728-0(1)*, f7081661-a61f-449d-af38-6b9ace4adb08, Lerner Pubns.) Lerner Publishing Group.

Wasmer Smith, Linda. Louis Pasteur: Genius Disease Fighter, 1 vol. 2014. (Genius Scientists & Their Genius Ideas Ser.). (ENG.). 96p. (gr. 5-5). 29.60 *(978-0-7660-6575-8(8)*, 1caafcef-6933-4d89-a0a7-dfa51ab0bfd5); pap. 13.88 *(978-0-7660-6576-5(6)*, 1d5493be-8ec4-4f56-9eed-c81e0d260546) Enslow Publishing, LLC.

Will Mayo, Gretchen. Milk, 1 vol. 2004. (Where Does Our Food Come From? Ser.). (ENG., Illus.). 24p. (gr. 2-4). pap. 9.15 *(978-0-8368-4074-2(7)*, 1073b164-ae6f-48a2-b531-f1ed8be0ffd2, Weekly Reader Leveled Readers) Stevens, Gareth Publishing LLLP.

MILKWEED

Holland, Mary. Milkweed Visitors. Holland, Mary, photos by. 2006. (Illus.). 32p. (J). per. 10.95 *(978-0-9657472-4-0(7))* Bas Relief, LLC.

Perish, Patrick. Milkweed Bugs. 2018. (Insects up Close Ser.). (ENG., Illus.). 24p. (J). (gr. k-3). lib. bdg. 26.95 *(978-1-62617-716-1(3)*, Blastoff! Readers) Bellwether Media.

MILL AND FACTORY BUILDINGS

see Factories

MILLAY, EDNA ST. VINCENT, 1892-1950

Goddu, Krystyna Poray. A Girl Called Vincent: The Life of Poet Edna St. Vincent Millay. 2018. (ENG.). 224p. (J). (gr. 4). pap. 12.99 *(978-0-912777-85-6(0))* Chicago Review Pr., Inc.

MILLIPEDES

Clapper, Nikki Bruno. Millipedes. 2015. (Creepy Crawlers Ser.). (ENG., Illus.). 24p. (J). (gr. -1-2). lib. bdg. 27.32 *(978-1-4914-6214-0(0)*, 129008, Capstone Pr.) Capstone.

Clark, Willow & Rockwood, Leigh. Centipedes & Millipedes Are Gross!, 1 vol. 2010. (Creepy Crawlers Ser.). (ENG.). 24p. (J). (gr. 2-3). pap. 9.25 *(978-1-4488-1363-6(8)*, 66b9f784-6249-469e-bb12-163fec673a6f, PowerKids Pr.); (Illus.). lib. bdg. 26.27 *(978-1-4488-0701-7(8)*, 5964f441-a1ce-40cc-bc21-0fb1e0de0e28) Rosen Publishing Group, Inc., The.

Radley, Gail. Los Milpiés. 2019. (Criaturas Rastreras Ser.). (SPA., Illus.). 32p. (J). (gr. 4-6). lib. bdg. *(978-1-62310-200-5(6)*, 12846, Bolt) Black Rabbit Bks.

—Millipedes. 2019. (Crawly Creatures Ser.). (ENG.). 32p. (J). (gr. 4-6). pap. 9.99 *(978-1-64466-022-5(9)*, 12677); (Illus.). lib. bdg. *(978-1-68072-811-8(3)*, 12676) Black Rabbit Bks. (Bolt).

Rhodes, Wendell. Millipedes, 1 vol. 2016. (Dig Deep! Bugs That Live Underground Ser.). (ENG.). 24p. (J). (gr. 3-3). pap. 9.25 *(978-1-4994-2058-6(7)*, 30153d1b-a734-49be-b154-953a154e9704, PowerKids Pr.) Rosen Publishing Group, Inc., The.

Ross, Michael Elsohn. Millipedeology. Erickson, Darren, illus. Grogan, Brian, photos by. 2005. (Backyard Buddies Ser.). 48p. (gr. 3-6). lib. bdg. 19.93 *(978-1-57505-398-1(5))* Lerner Publishing Group.

Schuetz, Kari. Millipedes. 2015. (Creepy Crawlies Ser.). (ENG., Illus.). 24p. (J). (gr. k-3). lib. bdg. 26.95 *(978-1-62617-225-8(0)*, Blastoff! Readers) Bellwether Media.

Williams, Susie. Centipedes & Millipedes. Tolson, Hannah, illus. 2020. 32p. (J). *(978-0-7787-7387-0(6))* Crabtree Publishing Co.

MILNE, A. A. (ALAN ALEXANDER), 1882-1956

Ellison, Virginia. The Winnie-The-Pooh Cookbook. Shepard, Ernest H., illus. 2010. (Winnie-The-Pooh Ser.). 112p. (J). (gr. 3-7). 19.99 *(978-0-525-42359-1(1)*, Dutton Books for Young Readers) Penguin Young Readers Group.

Rubiano, Brittany & Disney Books. Christopher Robin: the Little Book of Poohisms: With Help from Piglet, Eeyore, Rabbit, Owl, & Tigger, Too! 2018. (ENG., Illus.). 216p. (gr. 3-7). pap. 9.99 *(978-1-368-02589-8(7)*, Disney Press Books) Disney Publishing Worldwide.

Ward, S. Meet A. A. Milne. 2009. (About the Author Ser.). 24p. (gr. 4-4). 42.50 *(978-1-61511-243-2(X)*, PowerKids Pr.) Rosen Publishing Group, Inc., The.

MILWAUKEE (WIS.)

Joosse, Barbara. Lulu & Rocky in Milwaukee. Graef, Renée, illus. 2018. (Lulu & Rocky Adventures Ser.). (ENG.). 32p. (J). (gr. k-3). 16.99 *(978-1-5341-1017-5(8)*, 204642) Sleeping Bear Pr.

Ruebartsch, John, photos by. All about Wisconsin: Todo Acerca de Wisconsin. 2007. Tr. of Todo Acerca de Wisconsin. (ENG & SPA., Illus.). 84p. (J). pap. 16.00 *(978-0-9770816-3-9(X))* SHARP Literacy, Inc.

MILWAUKEE (WIS.)—FICTION

Calford, Farley. The Complete Disaster, Rhonda's Birthday Party. 2009. 86p. pap. 9.95 *(978-1-60860-210-0(9)*, Eloquent Bks.) Strategic Book Publishing & Rights Agency (SBPRA).

Cline-Ransome, Lesa. Leaving Lymon. 2020. (Finding Langston Trilogy Ser.: 2). 208p. (J). (gr. 3-7). 17.99 *(978-0-8234-4442-7(2))* Holiday Hse., Inc.

MILWAUKEE (WIS.)—HISTORY

Stotts, Stuart. Father Groppi: Marching for Civil Rights. 2013. (Badger Biographies Ser.). (ENG., Illus.). 160p. (J). pap. 12.95 *(978-0-87020-575-0(7))* Wisconsin Historical Society.

MILWAUKEE BREWERS (BASEBALL TEAM)

Epstein, Brad M. Milwaukee Brewers 101: My First Team-Board-Book. l.t. ed. 2007. (101 — My First Text-Board Books). (Illus.). 22p. (J). *(978-1-932530-75-9(4)*, 101 Bk.) Michaelson Entertainment.

Fishman, Jon M. Christian Yelich. 2020. (Sports All-Stars (Lerner (tm) Sports) Ser.). (ENG., Illus.). 32p. (J). (gr. 2-5). pap. 9.99 *(978-1-5415-9791-4(5)*, 3398aa2f-334d-4d30-95f6-413d23f88b46); lib. bdg. 29.32 *(978-1-5415-9790-7(7)*, f2876e76-b558-47c3-90ee-58cb59979ef3) Lerner Publishing Group. (Lerner Pubns.).

Gilbert, Sara. The Story of the Milwaukee Brewers. (Illus.). 48p. 2011. (J). 35.65 *(978-1-60818-046-2(8)*, Creative Education) 2007. (YA). (gr. 4-7). lib. bdg. 32.80 *(978-1-58341-492-7(4))* Creative Co., The.

Stewart, Mark. The Milwaukee Brewers. 2012. (Team Spirit Ser.). 48p. (J). (gr. 3-6). lib. bdg. 29.27 *(978-1-59953-487-9(8))* Norwood Hse. Pr.

MIND

see Intellect; Psychology

MIND AND BODY

see also Dreams; Hypnotism; Nervous System; Psychoanalysis; Psychology, Pathological; Sleep

Andrus, Aubre & Bluth, Karen. Happiness Hacks: How to Find Energy & Inspiration. Collignon, Veronica, illus. 2017. (Stress-Busting Survival Guides). (ENG.). 48p. (J). (gr. 4-8). lib. bdg. 31.99 *(978-1-5157-6820-3(1)*, 135349, Capstone Pr.) Capstone.

Be Your Best Self, 10 vols. 2017. (Be Your Best Self Ser.). (ENG.). 158p. (gr. 9-9). 231.35 *(978-1-4994-6658-4(7)*, 110e22be-c4fa-48a6-8b7a-38ee6738f01c, Rosen Young Adult) Rosen Publishing Group, Inc., The.

Chopra, Deepak. Teens Ask Deepak: All the Right Questions. Barchowsky, Damien, illus. 2006. (ENG.). 208p. (YA). (gr. 7). pap. 17.99 *(978-0-689-86218-2(0)*, Simon Pulse) Simon Pulse.

Cook, David Fuller, compiled by. A Balanced Approach to Long Life & Vitality, Signature Edition: As Used in Fitness, Wellness, Clinical Weight Loss, & Cardiac Rehabilitation Programs. 2003. (Illus.). 80p. spiral bd. 31.95 *(978-0-9741629-0-4(6))* Cook, David.

Dahn Healer School. Home Massage Therapy Book 1: Heal Yourself & Your Loved Ones, 2 vols. 2004. (Dahnhak, the Way to Perfect Health Ser.: Vol. 2). (Illus.). 142p. per. 17.95 *(978-0-9720282-9-5(3))* Healing Society, Inc.

Engel, Christiane. ABC for Me: ABC Mindful Me, Volume 4. 2018. (ABC for Me Ser.: 4). (ENG., Illus.). 36p. (J). (gr. -1-1). bds. 16.95 *(978-1-63322-510-7(0)*, 301672, Walter Foster Jr) Quarto Publishing Group USA.

Esherick, Joan. Diet & Your Emotions: The Comfort Food Falsehood. 2004. (Obesity Ser.). (Illus.). 104p. (J). (gr. 4-7). lib. bdg. 23.95 *(978-1-59084-950-7(7))* Mason Crest.

Fisher, Beverly. Level One Workbook: Getting Started 2004. (Illus.). pap. 9.99 *(978-0-9745066-2-3(1))* Sports In Mind.

Leavitt, Amy. Yoga Fitness. 2014. (ENG.). 48p. (gr. 4-8). 29.95 *(978-1-61228-551-1(1))* Mitchell Lane Pubs.

Lite, Lori. Affirmation Weaver: A Believe in Yourself Story Designed to Help Children Increase Self-Esteem While Decreasing Stress & Anxiety. 2nd ed. 2011. 24p. pap. 14.95 *(978-0-9836256-9-8(7))* Stress Free Kids.

—Angry Octopus: An Anger Management Story Introducing Active Progressive Muscular Relaxation & Deep Breathing. 2011. (Illus.). 30p. (gr. -1-3). pap. 14.95 *(978-0-9836256-8-1(9))* Stress Free Kids.

—A Boy & a Turtle: A Relaxation Story Teaching Young Children Visualization Techniques to Increase Creativity While Lowering Stress & Anxiety Lev. 3rd ed. 2012. Tr. of niño y una Tortuga. (ENG.). 16p. (J). pap. 12.95 *(978-1-937985-13-4(X))* Stress Free Kids.

—Bubble Riding: A Relaxation Story Designed to Teach Children Visualization Techniques to Increase Creativity While Lowering Stress & Anxiety. 2012. Tr. of Montando Burbujas. (ENG.). (J). pap. 14.95 *(978-1-937985-03-5(2))* Stress Free Kids.

—Buenas Noches Oruga: Una Historia para la Relajación Que Ayuda a Los Niños a Controlar la Ira y el Estrés para Que Se Queden Dormidos Sosegadamente. 2012. Tr. of Goodnight Caterpillar. (SPA., Illus.). 16p. (J). pap. 12.95 *(978-1-937985-16-5(4))* Stress Free Kids.

—Caleta de la Nutria Marina: Un Cuento para la Ansiedad Infantil, Enseña la Relajación, la Respiración Profunda para Reducir la Ansiedad, el Estrés y la Ira, a la Vez Que Fomenta el Sueño Sosegado. 2011. Tr. of Sea Otter Cove. (SPA., Illus.). 28p. (J). pap. 14.95 *(978-1-937985-11-0(3))* Stress Free Kids.

—The Goodnight Caterpillar: A Children's Relaxation Story to Improve Sleep, Manage Stress, Anxiety, Anger. 3rd abr. ed. 2011. Tr. of Buenas Noches, Oruga. (ENG.). 18p. (J). pap. 12.95 *(978-1-937985-00-4(8))* Stress Free Kids.

—Montando Burbujas: Un Cuento con Ejercicios de Relajación para Niños, Diseñada para Enseñar a Los Niños Técnicas de Visualización para Aumentar la Creatividad Mientras Disminuyen Sus Niveles de Ansiedad y de Estrés. 2012. Tr. of Bubble Riding. (SPA., Illus.). 32p. (J). pap. 14.95 *(978-1-937985-12-7(1))* Stress Free Kids.

—El Niño y la Tortuga: Un Cuento para Promover la Relajación. 2012. Tr. of Boy & a Turtle. (SPA., Illus.). 16p. (J). pap. 12.95 *(978-1-937985-17-2(2))* Stress Free Kids.

—El Pulpo Enojado: Un Cuento Sobre Cómo Controlar la Ira Que Enseña la Relajación Muscular Activa y Progresiva, y la Respiración: un Cuento Sobre Cómo Controlar la Ira Que Enseña la Relajación Muscular Activa y Progresiva, y la Respiración. 2012. Tr. of Angry Octopus. (SPA., Illus.). 30p. (J). pap. 14.95 *(978-1-937985-01-1(6))* Stress Free Kids.

—Sea Otter Cove: A Relaxation Story, Introducing Deep Breathing to Decrease Anxiety, Stress & Anger While Promoting Peaceful Sleep. 2nd ed. 2012. Tr. of Caleta de la Nutria Marina. (SPA & ENG., Illus.). 24p. (J). 14.95 *(978-1-937985-08-0(3))* Stress Free Kids.

—Tejedor de Afirmaciones: Un Cuento Que Aumenta la Autoestima en Los Niños, Creer en Ellos Mismos, Mientras Que Reducen Su Estrés y Su Ansiedad. 2012. Tr. of Affirmation Weaver. (SPA., Illus.). 24p. (J). pap. 14.95 *(978-1-937985-02-8(4))* Stress Free Kids.

Mather, Kelly. The Five Keys to Wellness. Schneller, Lisa, illus. 2006. 46p. *(978-0-9787179-8-8(8))* Harmony Healing Hse.

Mattern, Joanne. Famous Mystics & Psychics. 2004. (gr. 7-10). 27.45 *(978-1-59018-558-2(7))* Cengage Gale.

Ripley Entertainment Staff, contrib. by. Body & Mind. 2010. (Ripley's Believe It or Not Ser.). (Illus.). 36p. (J). (gr. 3-18). lib. bdg. 19.95 *(978-1-4222-1532-6(6))* Mason Crest.

Rosemary, Wells. El mundo que nos rodea. 2004. (SPA., Illus.). 32p. (J). (gr. -1-1). 14.99 *(978-84-241-8711-8(3))* Everest Editora ESP. Dist: Lectorum Pubns., Inc.

Sargent, Brian. The Placebo Effect: The Power of Positive Thinking, 1 vol. 2014. (ENG., Illus.). 28p. pap., E-Book 9.50 *(978-1-107-62263-0(8))* Cambridge Univ. Pr.

Steps to Healthy Touching: Activities to Help Kids Understand & Control Their Problems with Touching. 2nd ed. 2003. (Illus.). 128p. (J). per., wbk. ed. 14.95 *(978-1-55864-138-9(6))* JIST Publishing.

MIND CURE

see Christian Science; Mind and Body

MINERAL INDUSTRIES

see Mines and Mineral Resources

M
N
O

MINERAL LANDS
see Mines and Mineral Resources
MINERAL OIL
see Petroleum
MINERAL RESOURCES
see Mines and Mineral Resources
MINERALOGY
see also Gems; Precious Stones

Alkire, Jessie. Super Simple Mineral Projects: Science Activities for Future Mineralogists. 2017. (Super Simple Earth Investigations Ser.). (ENG.). 32p. (J). (gr. k-4). lib. bdg. 34.21 *(978-1-5321-1238-6(6)*, 27625, Super SandCastle) ABDO Publishing Co.

Allen, Nancy Kelly. Minerals & Rocks. 2009. (Rock It! Ser.). 24p. (gr. 3-4). 42.50 *(978-1-60852-492-1(2)*, PowerKids Pr.); (ENG.). (J). pap. 9.25 *(978-1-4358-3184-1(5)*, 366286da-4df6-49cc-9d8b-1583f24cbdbd); (ENG.). (YA). lib. bdg. 26.27 *(978-1-4358-2761-5(9)*, cb48fa66-1f83-46a1-b75e-555eadcaad16) Rosen Publishing Group, Inc., The.

Anderson, Michael. Investigating Minerals, Rocks, & Fossils, 1 vol. 2011. (Introduction to Earth Science Ser.). (ENG., Illus.). 88p. (J). (gr. 8-8). lib. bdg. 35.29 *(978-1-61530-500-1(9)*, c9677133-40d9-4292-ab20-1c7626071522) Rosen Publishing Group, Inc., The.

Aston, Dianna Hutts. A Rock Is Lively. 2015. (J). lib. bdg. 18.40 *(978-0-606-37444-6(2))* Turtleback.

Atwood, Frederick D. Rocks & Minerals - Pb: A Portrait of the Natural World. 2013. (Portrait of the Natural World Ser.). (Illus.). 72p. pap. 9.95 *(978-1-59764-332-0(7))* New Line Bks.

Basher, Simon & Green, Dan. Basher Science: Rocks & Minerals: A Gem of a Book. Basher, Simon, illus. 2009. (Basher Science Ser.). (ENG., Illus.). 128p. (J). (gr. 5-9). pap. 9.99 *(978-0-7534-6314-7(8)*, 900059036, Kingfisher) Roaring Brook Pr.

Benchmark Education Company, LLC Staff, compiled by. Rocks & Minerals: Theme Set. 2006. (J). 215.00 *(978-1-4108-7135-0(5))* Benchmark Education Co.

—Rocky Tales & Earth Systems. 2005. spiral bd. 225.00 *(978-1-4108-5819-1(7))* Benchmark Education Co.

Bingham, Caroline & Dorling Kindersley Publishing Staff. Rocks & Minerals. 2004. (DK Eye Wonder Ser.). (ENG., Illus.). 48p. (J). (gr. 3-6). lib. bdg. 22.44 *(978-0-7894-9894-6(4))* Dorling Kindersley Publishing, Inc.

Bowman, Chris. Minerals. (Illus.). 24p. (J). 2015. lib. bdg. *(978-0-531-20588-4(6))* 2014. (ENG., lib. bdg. 26.95 *(978-1-60014-980-1(4)*, Blastoff! Readers) Bellwether Media.

Brandt, Daniel & Brandt, Deanna. Rock Log Kids. 2018. (Nature Journals). (ENG., Illus.). 80p. (J). (gr. 1-7). spiral bd. 11.95 *(978-1-59193-777-7(9)*, Adventure Pubns.) AdventureKEEN.

Brannon, Cecelia H. A Look at Minerals, 1 vol. 2015. (Rock Cycle Ser.). (ENG.). 32p. (gr. 3-4). pap. 11.52 *(978-0-7660-7307-4(6)*, 3ab6b1bb-d4f8-467e-a689-f21a7faedfbd); (Illus.). 26.93 *(978-0-7660-7309-8(2)*, 301628d5-eefb-4195-935a-1533ca8fca42) Enslow Publishing, LLC.

Brezina, Corona. What Are Minerals?, 1 vol. 2018. (Let's Find Out! Good Health Ser.). (ENG.). 32p. (gr. 2-3). 26.06 *(978-1-5383-0302-3(7)*, 6bd32c1c-d3ff-434b-9c61-741ecf772524, Britannica Educational Publishing) Rosen Publishing Group, Inc., The.

Brinkman, Patricia. Discover Minerals. 2006. (J). pap. *(978-1-4108-6495-6(2))* Benchmark Education Co.

—Minerals. 2006. (J). pap. *(978-1-4108-6492-5(8))* Benchmark Education Co.

Centore, Michael, contrib. by. Vitamins & Minerals. 2017. (Illus.). 64p. (J). *(978-1-4222-3745-8(1))* Mason Crest.

Challoner, Jack. Find Out about Rocks & Minerals: With 23 Projects & More Than 350 Pictures. 2013. (Illus.). 64p. (J). (gr. k-8). 9.99 *(978-1-84322-747-2(9)*, Armadillo) Anness Publishing GBR. Dist: National Bk. Network.

Challoner, Jack & Walshaw, Rodney. Rocks & Minerals: Crystals, Erosion, Geology, Fossils: With 19 Easy-To-Do Experiments & 400 Exciting Pictures. 2015. (Illus.). 64p. (J). (gr. -1-12). 12.99 *(978-1-86147-465-0(2)*, Armadillo) Anness Publishing GBR. Dist: National Bk. Network.

Clarke, Phillip & Tudhope, Simon, eds. 100 Rocks & Minerals to Spot. 2009. (Spotter's Cards Ser.). 52p. (J). 9.99 *(978-0-7945-2255-1(6)*, Usborne) EDC Publishing.

Close, Edward. Earth's Treasures: Rocks & Minerals: Rocks & Minerals, 1 vol., 1. 2014. (Discovery Education: Earth & Space Science Ser.). (ENG.). 32p. (gr. 4-5). 28.93 *(978-1-4777-6170-0(5)*, c4a4e26d-c7eb-449e-8841-13163d6cb1e9, PowerKids Pr.) Rosen Publishing Group, Inc., The.

Corriel, Michele. Weird Rocks, 1 vol. Bilyeu, Dan, illus. 2013. (ENG.). 36p. (J). 12.00 *(978-0-87842-597-6(7))* Mountain Pr. Publishing Co., Inc.

Cull, Selby. Rocks & Minerals. 2009. (Restless Earth Ser.). (ENG., Illus.). 112p. (gr. 5-9). 35.00 *(978-0-7910-9702-1(1)*, P159123, Facts On File) Infobase Holdings, Inc.

Davidson, Rose. The Big Book of Bling: Ritzy Rocks, Extravagant Animals, Sparkling Science, & More! 2019. (ENG., Illus.). 192p. (J). (gr. 3-7). 19.99 *(978-1-4263-3531-0(8)*, National Geographic Kids) Disney Publishing Worldwide.

Dayton, Connor. Crystals. (Rocks & Minerals Ser.). 24p. (gr. 2-3). 2009. 42.50 *(978-1-60852-498-3(1)*, PowerKids Pr.) 2007. (ENG., Illus.). (YA). lib. bdg. 26.27 *(978-1-4042-3687-5(2)*, 2dae38e0-8527-4208-8824-3f91b3cf2f5a) Rosen Publishing Group, Inc., The.

—Minerals. (Rocks & Minerals Ser.). 24p. (gr. 2-3). 2009. 42.50 *(978-1-60852-501-0(5)*, PowerKids Pr.) 2007. (ENG., Illus.). (YA). lib. bdg. 26.27 *(978-1-4042-3691-2(0)*, 52a1b0ec-8b2d-4684-9dc0-98772414aaca) Rosen Publishing Group, Inc., The.

—Rocks & Minerals, 6 vols., Set. Incl. Crystals. lib. bdg. 26.27 *(978-1-4042-3687-5(2)*, 2dae38e0-8527-4208-8824-3f91b3cf2f5a); Fossils. lib. bdg. 26.27 *(978-1-4042-3689-9(9)*, 80eb0549-38cd-4a93-8ee3-cc6212497920); Gemstones. lib. bdg. 26.27 *(978-1-4042-3686-8(4)*, c20b98f2-57c6-4139-9647-fa661c9e94e6); Minerals. lib. bdg. 26.27 *(978-1-4042-3691-2(0)*, 52a1b0ec-8b2d-4684-9dc0-98772414aaca); Volcanic Rocks. lib. bdg. 26.27 *(978-1-4042-3688-2(0)*, b601e067-75a8-47e3-bb40-10171ded1102); (Illus.). 24p. (YA). (gr. 2-3). 2007. (Rocks & Minerals Ser.). (ENG.). 2006. Set lib. bdg. 78.81 *(978-1-4042-3610-3(4)*, ffbe7174-b5e4-4ab6-a667-cc1ca707c00c, PowerKids Pr.) Rosen Publishing Group, Inc., The.

Dee, Willa. Earth's Rock Cycle, 1 vol., 1. 2014. (Rocks: the Hard Facts Ser.). (ENG.). 24p. (J). (gr 3-3). 26.27 *(978-1-4777-2903-8(8)*, 087c1be5-1643-4d4a-92ec-ce38499fbb8f, PowerKids Pr.) Rosen Publishing Group, Inc., The.

—Minerals, 1 vol., 1. 2014. (Rocks: the Hard Facts Ser.). (ENG.). 24p. (J). (gr. 3-3). 26.27 *(978-1-4777-2905-2(4)*, 4b63e16c-ad95-4a65-805c-11e8cdbb3eef, PowerKids Pr.) Rosen Publishing Group, Inc., The.

Dennie, Devin. My Book of Rocks & Minerals: Things to Find, Collect, & Treasure. 2017. (My Book Of Ser.). (ENG., Illus.). 96p. (J). (gr. k-4). 14.99 *(978-1-4654-6190-2(6)*, DK Children) Dorling Kindersley Publishing, Inc.

DK. Eye Wonder: Rocks & Minerals: Open Your Eyes to a World of Discovery. 2014. (Eye Wonder Ser.). (ENG.). 56p. (J). (gr. k-4). 10.99 *(978-1-4654-1559-2(9)*, DK Children) Dorling Kindersley Publishing, Inc.

—Pocket Genius: Rocks & Minerals: Facts at Your Fingertips. 2016. (Pocket Genius Ser.: 13). (ENG., Illus.). 160p. (J). (gr. 3-7). pap. 6.99 *(978-1-4654-4590-2(0)*, DK Children) Dorling Kindersley Publishing, Inc.

Dunlop, Jenna & Morganelli, Adrianna. Minerals. 2004. (Rocks, Minerals, & Resources Ser.). (ENG., Illus.). 32p. (J). lib. bdg. *(978-0-7787-1415-6(2))* Crabtree Publishing Co.

Encyclopaedia Britannica, Inc. Staff, compiled by. Britannica Illustrated Science Library: Rocks & Minerals, 16 vols. 2008. (Illus.). (J). 29.95 *(978-1-59339-396-0(2))* Encyclopaedia Britannica, Inc.

Ethan, Eric. Diamonds, 1 vol. 2011. (Gems: Nature's Jewels Ser.). (ENG., Illus.). 24p. (gr. 2-3). 25.27 *(978-1-4339-4715-5(3)*, 9d08a1cc-4aed-4432-9d8f-7b959f2faef4); pap. 9.15 *(978-1-4339-4716-2(1)*, bc89139d-4064-4021-b6b3-6738e37d0959) Stevens, Gareth Publishing LLLP. (Gareth Stevens Learning Library).

—Emeralds, 1 vol. 2011. (Gems: Nature's Jewels Ser.). (ENG., Illus.). 24p. (J). (gr. 2-3). pap. 9.15 *(978-1-4339-4720-9(X)*, b67619da-fc82-414a-98eb-1876c66ea075); lib. bdg. 25.27 *(978-1-4339-4719-3(6)*, 7fae6e8a-7e6f-42d0-a993-ffcb62f8b1cd) Stevens, Gareth Publishing LLLP. (Gareth Stevens Learning Library).

—Opals, 1 vol. 2011. (Gems: Nature's Jewels Ser.). (ENG., Illus.). 24p. (gr. 2-3). 25.27 *(978-1-4339-4723-0(4)*, 8d454d14-6ca4-4808-a103-d8f27ac40a4a); pap. 9.15 *(978-1-4339-4724-7(2)*, 6906940a-4773-46d1-b33a-379f17c63aa8) Stevens, Gareth Publishing LLLP. (Gareth Stevens Learning Library).

—Rubies, 1 vol. 2011. (Gems: Nature's Jewels Ser.). (ENG., Illus.). 24p. (gr. 2-3). 25.27 *(978-1-4339-4727-8(7)*, 90673cf4-b01f-4ea1-a9dc-e030984f9c65); pap. 9.15 *(978-1-4339-4728-5(5)*, 8b1cfe95-d520-4ed2-8983-cdafd1589e71) Stevens, Gareth Publishing LLLP. (Gareth Stevens Learning Library).

—Sapphires, 1 vol. 2011. (Gems: Nature's Jewels Ser.). (ENG., Illus.). 24p. (gr. 2-3). 25.27 *(978-1-4339-4731-5(5)*, 731345c2-86d1-4d96-bd91-1e492df73487); pap. 9.15 *(978-1-4339-4732-2(3)*, b847e5b6-4a0a-4fe8-a159-2db8ef4c920a) Stevens, Gareth Publishing LLLP. (Gareth Stevens Learning Library).

—Turquoise, 1 vol. 2011. (Gems: Nature's Jewels Ser.). (ENG., Illus.). 24p. (J). (gr. 2-3). pap. 9.15 *(978-1-4339-4712-4(9)*, fe8f150c-dc6a-4737-bac8-2a26291be1af); lib. bdg. 25.27 *(978-1-4339-4711-7(0)*, b2d63051-318b-487e-8bd0-8ed25b94f109) Stevens, Gareth Publishing LLLP. (Gareth Stevens Learning Library).

Farndon, John. Rocks, Minerals & Gems. 2016. (ENG., Illus.). 120p. (J). (gr. 6-10). 24.95 *(978-1-77085-740-7(0)*, d39e1c49-14c0-4156-aa08-850d0f207958); pap. 12.95 *(978-1-77085-868-8(7)*, 2458ce02-8895-4dc3-bb4b-42e8a999fa1c) Firefly Bks., Ltd.

Gallagher, Belinda, et al. Rocks & Minerals: Identify & Record Your Sightings. 2017. (Illus.). 96p. (J). pap. 9.95 *(978-1-78209-572-9(1))* Miles Kelly Publishing, Ltd. GBR. Dist: Parkwest Pubns., Inc.

Glaser, Jason. Minerals up Close, 1 vol. 2013. (Under the Microscope Ser.). 32p. (J). (gr. 4-5). (ENG.). pap. 12.70 *(978-1-4339-8347-4(8)*, d55ef910-c329-4eba-b95f-98cae50863fd); (ENG.). lib. bdg. 29.27 *(978-1-4339-8346-7(X)*, dbec8e71-ce41-4d1e-95af-330f730343dc); pap. 70.20 *(978-1-4339-8348-1(6))* Stevens, Gareth Publishing LLLP.

Goldman, Phyllis B., ed. Monkeyshines on Rocks & Minerals. (Illus.). 148p. (J). (gr. -1-7). reprint ed. pap. 26.95 *(978-1-888325-14-0(3))* Allosaurus Pubs.

Gregorovna, Anna. Inside Earth: Rocks & Minerals, 1 vol. 2012. (InfoMax Readers Ser.). (ENG., Illus.). 24p. (J). (gr. 1-1). pap. 8.25 *(978-1-4488-9043-9(8)*, 266801ae-a168-4c98-a64d-1604f41cef5d, Rosen Classroom) Rosen Publishing Group, Inc., The.

Group/McGraw-Hill, Wright. Materials Que Hay en la Tierra, 6 vols. (First Explorers. Primeros Exploradores Nonfiction Sets Ser.). (SPA.). (gr. 1-2). 29.95 *(978-0-7699-1468-8(3))* Shortland Pubns. (U. S. A.) Inc.

Guide to Rocks & Minerals, 8 vols. 2007. (Guide to Rocks & Minerals Ser.). (ENG.). 32p. (gr. 3-5). lib. bdg. 114.68 *(978-0-8368-7905-6(8)*, 58071aeb-f6ca-4aba-a00b-dab04fa5b830, Gareth Stevens Learning Library) Stevens, Gareth Publishing LLLP.

Hand, Carol. Experiments with Rocks & Minerals. 2011. (True Bk Ser.). (ENG., Illus.). 48p. (J). pap. 6.95 *(978-0-531-26648-9(6))*; lib. bdg. 29.00 *(978-0-531-26348-8(7))* Scholastic Library Publishing. (Children's Pr.).

Hansen, Grace. Menas. 2016. (¡Súper Geología! Ser.). (SPA.). 24p. (J). (gr. -1-2). pap. 7.95 *(978-1-4966-0681-5(7)*, 131733, Capstone Classroom) Capstone.

—Minerales. 2016. (¡Súper Geología! Ser.). (SPA.). 24p. (J). (gr. -1-2). pap. 7.95 *(978-1-4966-0680-8(9)*, 131732, Capstone Classroom) Capstone.

—Minerals, 1 vol. 2015. (Geology Rocks! (Abdo Kids Jumbo) Ser.). (ENG., Illus.). 24p. (J). (gr. -1-2). 32.79 *(978-1-62970-907-9(7)*, 18272, Abdo Kids) ABDO Publishing Co.

—Ores, 1 vol. 2015. (Geology Rocks! (Abdo Kids Jumbo) Ser.). (ENG., Illus.). 24p. (J). (gr. -1-2). 32.79 *(978-1-62970-908-6(5)*, 18274, Abdo Kids) ABDO Publishing Co.

—Rocks, 1 vol. 2015. (Geology Rocks! (Abdo Kids Jumbo) Ser.). (ENG., Illus.). 24p. (J). (gr. -1-2). 32.79 *(978-1-62970-909-3(3)*, 18276, Abdo Kids) ABDO Publishing Co.

Hantula, Richard. Rocks & Fossils, 1 vol. 2007. (Gareth Stevens Vital Science Library: Earth Science Ser.). (ENG., Illus.). 48p. (gr. 5-8). pap. 15.05 *(978-0-8368-7876-9(0)*, 683f0af3-8c5c-401c-ab7f-adcf0f6b3f7a, Gareth Stevens Secondary Library) Stevens, Gareth Publishing LLLP.

Harrison, Lorraine. All Kinds of Rocks. 2013. (InfoMax Readers Ser.). (ENG.). 24p. (J). (gr. 2-3). pap. 49.50 *(978-1-4777-2408-8(7))*; (Illus.). pap. 8.25 *(978-1-4777-2407-1(9)*, cfcc71ed-5946-406e-80ad-0ec9a1a0088e) Rosen Publishing Group, Inc., The. (Rosen Classroom).

Hirschmann, Kris. Rocks & Minerals. 2004. (World Discovery Science Readers Ser.). (Illus.). 31p. (J). pap. 4.95 *(978-0-439-56630-8(4))* Scholastic, Inc.

Hodge, Judith. Riches from Earth & Las riquezas de la Tierra: 6 English, 6 Spanish Adaptations. 2011. (ENG & SPA.). (J). 97.00 net. *(978-1-4108-5716-3(6))* Benchmark Education Co.

Hoffman, Steven M. Rock Study: A Guide to Looking at Rocks, 1 vol. 2011. (Rock It! Ser.). (ENG., Illus.). 24p. (J). (gr. 3-4). pap. 9.25 *(978-1-4488-2713-8(2)*, 6bb46636-3110-4b00-b789-201eef284cef); lib. bdg. 26.27 *(978-1-4488-2562-2(8)*, 5d93d3a4-2b28-4f48-88cb-d8a7037bde18) Rosen Publishing Group, Inc., The. (PowerKids Pr.).

Honovich, Nancy. Ultimate Explorer Field Guide: Rocks & Minerals. 2016. (ENG., Illus.). 160p. (J). (gr. 3-7). lib. bdg. 22.90 *(978-1-4263-2302-7(6)*, National Geographic Kids) Disney Publishing Worldwide.

—Ultimate Explorer Field Guide: Rocks & Minerals. 2016. (Illus.). 160p. (J). (gr. 3-7). pap. 12.99 *(978-1-4263-2301-0(8)*, National Geographic Kids) Disney Publishing Worldwide.

Hyde, Natalie. How to Be a Rock Collector. 2012. (Let's Rock! Ser.). (ENG., Illus.). 32p. (J). (gr. 3-6). lib. bdg. *(978-0-7787-7212-5(8))* Crabtree Publishing Co.

—What Are Minerals?, 1 vol. 2012. (ENG., Illus.). 32p. (J). pap. *(978-0-7787-7220-0(9))*; (gr. 3-6). lib. bdg. *(978-0-7787-7215-6(2))* Crabtree Publishing Co.

Hyler, Nelson W. The How & Why Wonder Book of Rocks & Minerals. Blackwood, Paul E., ed. Shannon, Kenyon, illus. 2011. 52p. 36.95 *(978-1-258-10482-5(2))* Literary Licensing, LLC.

Ivancic, Linda. Soil for Tools & Art, 1 vol. 2016. (Science of Soil Ser.). (ENG., Illus.). 48p. (J). (gr. 4-4). 33.07 *(978-1-5026-2166-5(5)*, 0c13b27c-cab6-49f7-a6d7-0ed59dab694d) Cavendish Square Publishing LLC.

Lawrence, Ellen. How Do People Use Rocks? 2014. (Science Slam!: Rock-Ology Ser.). (ENG.). 24p. (J). (gr. -1-3). lib. bdg. 26.99 *(978-1-62724-303-2(8))* Bearport Publishing Co., Inc.

—Rocks & Minerals. 2015. (FUN-Damental Experiments Ser.). (ENG.). 24p. (J). (gr. -1-3). lib. bdg. 26.99 *(978-1-62724-540-1(5))* Bearport Publishing Co., Inc.

Lockwood, Sophie. Minerals. 2009. (Explorer Library: Science Explorer Ser.). (ENG., Illus.). 32p. (gr. 4-8). lib. bdg. 32.07 *(978-1-60279-524-2(X)*, 200291) Cherry Lake Publishing.

Lynch, Dan R. Rock Collecting for Kids: An Introduction to Geology. 2018. (Simple Introductions to Science Ser.). (Illus.). 144p. (J). (gr. 1-7). pap. 12.95 *(978-1-59193-773-9(6)*, Adventure Pubns.) AdventureKEEN.

Lynch, Dan R. & Lynch, Bob. Rocks & Minerals of the Pacific Coast: Your Way to Easily Identify Rocks & Minerals. 2018. (Adventure Quick Guides). (ENG., Illus.). 22p. spiral bd. 9.95 *(978-1-59193-775-3(2)*, Adventure Pubns.) AdventureKEEN.

MacAulay, Kelley. Why Do We Need Rocks & Minerals? 2014. (Natural Resources Close-Up Ser.). (ENG., Illus.). 24p. (J). (gr. 1-1). *(978-0-7787-0492-8(0))*; pap. *(978-0-7787-0496-6(3))* Crabtree Publishing Co.

Malizia, Diana. A Visual Guide to Rocks & Minerals, 1 vol. 2017. (Visual Exploration of Science Ser.). (ENG.). 104p. (YA). (gr. 8-8). 38.80 *(978-1-5081-7710-4(4)*, 5137ab09-e79c-4934-88e8-e22d50f2276d); pap. 18.65 *(978-1-5081-7886-6(0)*, 4e42db98-1c6f-4537-94b1-4b6ccfa3d72c) Rosen Publishing Group, Inc., The. (Rosen Young Adult).

Maloof, Torrey. Rocks & Minerals, 1 vol. rev. ed. 2014. (Science: Informational Text Ser.). (ENG.). 32p. (gr. 2-3). pap. 10.99 *(978-1-4807-4610-7(X))* Teacher Created Materials, Inc.

Mattern, Joanne. Minerals & the Rock Cycle. (Shaping & Reshaping of Earth's Surface Ser.). 24p. (gr. 4-4). 2009. 42.50 *(978-1-60854-218-5(1)*, PowerKids Pr.) 2005. (ENG., Illus.). (YA). lib. bdg. 26.27 *(978-1-4042-3199-3(4)*, 1a5c5be0-113a-4da5-b8b7-25c6cbaa5616) Rosen Publishing Group, Inc., The.

McQueen, David. The Mineral Book. 2014. (ENG.). 96p. (gr. 9-12). 18.99 *(978-0-89051-802-1(5)*, Master Books) New Leaf Publishing Group.

Meredith, Susan. Las Rocas, los Minerales y el Suelo. 2012. (Let's Explore Science Ser.). (SPA.). 48p. (gr. 4-8). pap. 10.95 *(978-1-61810-470-0(5)*, 9781618104700) Rourke Educational Media.

—Rocks, Minerals, & Soil. 2009. (Let's Explore Science Ser.). (Illus.). 48p. (J). (gr. 4-8). lib. bdg. 32.79 *(978-1-60694-411-0(8))* Rourke Educational Media.

Miles, Lisa. Usborne Rocks & Minerals Sticker Book. Khan, Sarah & Armstrong, Carrie, eds. Freeman, Mike & Julings, Emma, photos by. rev. ed. 2006. (Spotter's Guides Sticker Books - New Format Ser.). (Illus.). 16p. (J). (gr. 2-5). pap. 8.99 *(978-0-7945-1413-6(8)*, Usborne) EDC Publishing.

Miller-Schroeder, Patricia. Minerals. (Focus on Earth Science Ser.). (gr. 3-7). 2015. (ENG.). (J). lib. bdg. 27.13 *(978-1-4896-4085-7(1)*, AV2 by Weigl) 2010. (Illus.). 24p. (J). pap. 11.95 *(978-1-60596-977-0(X))* 2010. (Illus.). 24p. (YA). lib. bdg. 25.70 *(978-1-60596-976-3(1))* 2006. (Illus.). 24p. (J). lib. bdg. 24.45 *(978-1-59036-214-3(4))* Weigl Pubs., Inc.

Mills, Nathan & Roza, Greg. Exploring Rocks & Minerals. 2012. (Rosen Readers Ser.). (ENG., Illus.). 24p. (J). (gr. 1-2). pap. 49.50 *(978-1-4488-8831-3(X)*, 1348003); pap. 8.25 *(978-1-4488-8830-6(1)*, cea7c3c6-1c6b-445c-a127-bd820e828bb3) Rosen Publishing Group, Inc., The. (Rosen Classroom).

Mooney, Carla. What Are Minerals?, 1 vol., 1. 2015. (Junior Geologist Ser.). (ENG., Illus.). 32p. (J). (gr. 2-3). pap. 13.90 *(978-1-5081-0049-2(7)*, a038fb7c-ca96-4833-91d6-18b3bbb62f7a, Britannica Educational Publishing) Rosen Publishing Group, Inc., The.

National Geographic Learning. Reading Expeditions (Science: Earth Science): Rocks & Minerals. 2007. (Nonfiction Reading & Writing Workshops Ser.). (ENG., Illus.). 32p. (J). pap. 18.95 *(978-0-7922-4571-1(7))* CENGAGE Learning.

Natural History Museum Collection Staff. Rocks & Minerals Sticker Book. 2013. (ENG.). 14p. (J). (gr. -1-1). pap. 9.99 *(978-0-565-09300-6(2))* Natural History Museum Pubns. GBR. Dist: Independent Pubs. Group.

Nelson, Maria. Earth's Minerals. 2013. (That Rocks! Ser.). 24p. (J). (gr. 2-5). pap. 48.90 *(978-1-4339-8311-5(7))*; (ENG., Illus.). pap. 9.15 *(978-1-4339-8310-8(9)*, 31471e60-1674-44f3-840c-f8fb53693133); (ENG., Illus.). lib. bdg. 25.27 *(978-1-4339-8309-2(5)*, 3f239176-0c85-4b5c-82f2-7adbd09761ad) Stevens, Gareth Publishing LLLP.

Nsrc, prod. Science & Technology for Children BOOKS: Rocks & Minerals. 2007. (J). *(978-1-933008-40-0(7)*, Science and Technology Concepts (STC)) Smithsonian Science Education Ctr. (SSEC).

O'Donoghue, Michael. Rocks & Minerals of the World. 2004. (World Book's Science & Nature Guides Ser.). (Illus.). 80p. (J). *(978-0-7166-4217-6(4))* World Bk., Inc.

Olson, Elsie. Exploring Minerals: Mineralogists at Work! 2017. (Earth Detectives Ser.). (ENG., Illus.). 24p. (J). (gr. k-4). lib. bdg. 32.79 *(978-1-5321-1231-7(9)*, 27618, Super SandCastle) ABDO Publishing Co.

Ostopowich, Melanie. Rocks. 2010. (Earth Science Ser.). (Illus.). 24p. (gr. 3-5). (J). pap. 11.95 *(978-1-60596-962-6(1))*; (YA). lib. bdg. 25.70 *(978-1-60596-961-9(3))* Weigl Pubs., Inc.

Pellant, Chris & Pellant, Helen. Quartz & Other Minerals, 1 vol. 2007. (Guide to Rocks & Minerals Ser.). (ENG., Illus.). 32p. (gr. 3-5). lib. bdg. 28.67 *(978-0-8368-7908-7(2)*, f98294f7-80a9-4418-9765-709a80d0553e, Gareth Stevens Learning Library) Stevens, Gareth Publishing LLLP.

Pinet, Michele. Be Your Own Rock & Mineral Expert. Greenbaum, Fay, tr. from FRE. Korkos, Alain, illus. 2003. 40p. (J). (gr. 5-7). 14.95 *(978-0-8069-9580-9(7))* Sterling Publishing Co., Inc.

Rajczak Nelson, Kristen. What Are Minerals?, 1 vol. 2017. (Look at Earth's Rocks Ser.). (ENG., Illus.). 32p. (J). (gr. 2-2). 28.27 *(978-1-4824-6244-9(3)*, ac65a3f1-4b19-4d5c-9d70-42ee738f7949) Stevens, Gareth Publishing LLLP.

Rau, Dana Meachen. Rocks & Minerals. 2009. (21st Century Skills Library: Real World Science Ser.). (ENG., Illus.). 32p. (gr. 4-8). lib. bdg. 32.07 *(978-1-60279-463-4(4)*, 200233) Cherry Lake Publishing.

Reynolds, Shaye. Volcanoes, 1 vol. 2016. (Spotlight on Earth Science Ser.). (ENG.). 24p. (J). (gr. 4-6). pap. 11.00 *(978-1-4994-2537-6(6)*, f8ca81ff-e7e7-439b-ae9a-0d270f3d1cf8, PowerKids Pr.) Rosen Publishing Group, Inc., The.

Rivera, Andrea. Minerals. 2017. (Rocks & Minerals (Launch!) Ser.). (ENG., Illus.). 24p. (J). (gr. -1-2). lib. bdg. 31.36 *(978-1-5321-2045-9(1)*, 25340, Abdo Zoom-Launch) ABDO Publishing Co.

—Ores. 2017. (Rocks & Minerals (Launch!) Ser.). (ENG., Illus.). 24p. (J). (gr. -1-2). lib. bdg. 31.36 *(978-1-5321-2046-6(X)*, 25342, Abdo Zoom-Launch) ABDO Publishing Co.

Rocks & Minerals, 5 vols. 2014. (Rocks & Minerals Ser.: 8). (ENG.). 48p. (J). (gr. 4-8). lib. bdg. 213.84 *(978-1-62403-383-4(0)*, 1616) ABDO Publishing Co.

Rocks & Minerals. 2005. 48p. (J). per. 6.99 *(978-1-59441-202-8(2)*, CD-104110) Carson-Dellosa Publishing, LLC.

Rocks & Minerals. 2009. (Hammond Undercover Ser.). 72p. (J). (gr. 3-7). 15.95 *(978-0-8437-1932-1(X))* Hammond World Atlas Corp.

Roza, Greg. Exploring Rocks & Minerals, 1 vol. 2012. (Exploring Earth & Space Ser.). (ENG., Illus.). 24p. (J). (gr. 1-2). 26.27 *(978-1-4488-8576-3(0)*, 21abb025-21f7-4501-b80e-eb3e9c214cbd, PowerKids Pr.) Rosen Publishing Group, Inc., The.

Salzano, Tammi J. Rocks, Minerals, & Gemstones. Jankowski, Daniel, illus. 2009. 24p. (J). pap. *(978-0-545-19868-4(2))* Scholastic, Inc.

Schuh, Mari. Learning about Rocks. 2011. (Science Builders Ser.). (ENG.). 24p. (J). (gr. k-1). pap. 44.74 *(978-1-4296-7114-9(9)*, 16695, Capstone Pr.) Capstone.

Schuh, Mari C. Learning about Rocks, 1 vol. 2011. (Science Builders Ser.). (ENG.). 24p. (J). (gr. -1-2). lib. bdg. 27.32 *(978-1-4296-6072-3(4)*, 115006); pap. 7.29 *(978-1-4296-7108-8(4)*, 116768) Capstone.

Science stories foss spanish earth materials ea Cr05. 2005. (J). *(978-1-59242-590-7(9))* Delta Education, LLC.

Sherman, Jill. Minerals & Heavy Metals, 1 vol. 2017. (Let's Learn about Natural Resources Ser.). (ENG.). 24p. (gr. 1-2). pap. 10.35 *(978-0-7660-9147-4(3)*, cd31c3b0-b55f-43e7-b0a7-2b932257c069) Enslow Publishing, LLC.

Simon, Seymour. Rocks & Minerals. 2017. (ENG., Illus.). 48p. (J). (gr. 1-5). 17.99 *(978-0-06-228918-6(7))*; pap. 7.99 *(978-0-06-228917-9(9))* HarperCollins Pubs. (HarperCollins).

Smith, Miranda & Callery, Sean. Rocks, Minerals & Gems. 2016. (ENG., Illus.). 224p. (J). (gr. 3-7). 19.99

(978-0-545-94719-0(7), Scholastic Nonfiction) Scholastic, Inc.

Spilsbury, Louise. Minerales. 2011. (Las Rocas Ser.). (SPA.). 32p. (gr. 3-6). pap. 8.29 *(978-1-4329-5661-5(2)*, 117357, Heinemann) Capstone.

Squire, Ann O. Minerals. 2012. (True Book(tm), a — Earth Science Ser.). (ENG.). 48p. (J). lib. bdg. 31.00 *(978-0-531-26144-6(1))*; pap. 6.95 *(978-0-531-26252-8(9))* Scholastic Library Publishing.

—Rocks. 2012. (True Book(tm), a — Earth Science Ser.). (ENG.). 48p. (J). lib. bdg. 31.00 *(978-0-531-26145-3(X))*; pap. 6.95 *(978-0-531-26253-5(7))* Scholastic Library Publishing.

Stamper, Judith Bauer. Rocks & Minerals. 2010. (Illus.). 32p. (J). pap. *(978-0-545-28544-5(5))* Scholastic, Inc.

Strother, Ruth. Absolute Expert: Rocks & Minerals. 2019. (Absolute Expert Ser.). (Illus.). 112p. (J). (gr. 3-7). 14.99 *(978-1-4263-3279-1(3)*, National Geographic Kids) Disney Publishing Worldwide.

Tomecek, Steve. Jump into Science: Rocks & Minerals. 2010. (Jump into Science Ser.). (Illus.). 32p. (J). (gr. -1-k). 16.95 *(978-1-4263-0538-2(9)*, National Geographic Kids) Disney Publishing Worldwide.

—National Geographic Kids Everything Rocks & Minerals: Dazzling Gems of Photos & Info That Will Rock Your World. 2011. (National Geographic Kids Everything Ser.). (ENG., Illus.). 64p. (J). (gr. 3-7). 25.90 *(978-1-4263-0801-7(9)*, National Geographic Kids) Disney Publishing Worldwide.

—National Geographic Kids Everything Rocks & Minerals: Dazzling Gems of Photos & Info That Will Rock Your World! 2011. (National Geographic Kids Everything Ser.). (Illus.). 64p. (J). (gr. 3-7). pap. 12.95 *(978-1-4263-0768-3(3)*, National Geographic Kids) Disney Publishing Worldwide.

Trueit, Trudi Strain. Rocks, Gems, & Minerals. 2003. (Watts Library). (ENG.). 64p. (gr. 5-7). pap. 8.95 *(978-0-531-16241-5(9)*, Watts, Franklin) Scholastic Library Publishing.

Tuchman, Gail. Rocks & Minerals. 2015. (Scholastic Reader Level 2 Ser.). lib. bdg. 13.55 *(978-0-606-37757-7(3))* Turtleback.

Walker, Sally M. Marveling at Minerals. 2013. (Searchlight Books (tm) — Do You Dig Earth Science? Ser.). (ENG., Illus.). 40p. (J). (gr. 3-5). pap. 9.99 *(978-1-4677-0792-3(9)*, 2ce3eac5-2b46-4572-a938-9aa8b1de52d6) Lerner Publishing Group.

—Minerals. (Early Bird Earth Science Ser.). (Illus.). 48p. (J). 2007. pap. 8.95 *(978-0-8225-6620-5(6))* 2006. (gr. 3-7). lib. bdg. 25.26 *(978-0-8225-5946-7(3))* Lerner Publishing Group. (Lerner Pubns.).

Watson, Stephanie. Vitamins & Minerals: Getting the Nutrients Your Body Needs, 1 vol. 2010. (Healthy Habits Ser.). (ENG., Illus.). 64p. (YA). (gr. 5-5). pap. 13.95 *(978-1-4488-0613-3(5)*, 83d6025c-1098-4ccd-9ff7-0cff792fc7a2); lib. bdg. 37.13 *(978-1-4358-9443-3(X)*, f005eb6c-f697-40e7-9759-741c28d4e6b1) Rosen Publishing Group, Inc., The. (Rosen Reference).

West, Krista. Hands-On Projects about Rocks, Minerals & Fossils, 1 vol. 2004. (Great Earth Science Projects Ser.). (ENG., Illus.). 24p. (J). (gr. 3-4). lib. bdg. 26.27 *(978-0-8239-5842-9(6)*, c9db3f00-971e-458d-be3b-09eb1599b156, PowerKids Pr.) Rosen Publishing Group, Inc., The.

Woolley, A. Rocks & Minerals. 2004. (Spotter's Guides). (Illus.). 64p. (J). lib. bdg. 13.95 *(978-1-58086-309-4(4))* EDC Publishing.

Woolley, Alan. Rocks & Minerals Spotter's Guide: With Internet Links. Freeman, Mike, photos by. rev. ed. 2007. (Spotter's Guides). (Illus.). 64p. (J). pap. 5.99 *(978-0-7945-1304-7(2)*, Usborne) EDC Publishing.

Zoehfeld, Kathleen. National Geographic Readers: Rocks & Minerals. 2012. (Readers Ser.). (Illus.). 32p. (J). (gr. 1-3). pap. 5.99 *(978-1-4263-1038-6(2)*, National Geographic Kids); (ENG., lib. bdg. 14.90 *(978-1-4263-1039-3(0)*, National Geographic Children's Bks.) Disney Publishing Worldwide.

MINERALS

see Mineralogy

MINERS

Gordon, Nick. Coal Miner. 2013. (Dangerous Jobs Ser.). (ENG., Illus.). 24p. (J). (gr. 3-7). lib. bdg. 26.95 *(978-1-60014-893-4(X)*, Torque Bks.) Bellwether Media.

Hyde, Natalie. Life in a Mining Community. 2009. (Learn about Rural Life Ser.). (ENG., Illus.). 32p. (J). (gr. 3-6). pap. *(978-0-7787-5087-1(6))*; lib. bdg. *(978-0-7787-5074-1(4))* Crabtree Publishing Co.

Landau, Elaine. The California Gold Rush: Would You Go for the Gold?, 1 vol. 2009. (What Would You Do? Ser.). (ENG., Illus.). 48p. (gr. 3-3). pap. 11.53 *(978-1-59845-193-1(6)*, 2e64983a-5b64-44a6-b3ef-b5463dcc9b4c, Enslow Elementary) Enslow Publishing, LLC.

O'Brien, Cynthia. Go West with Miners, Prospectors, & Loggers. 2016. (ENG.). 32p. (J). *(978-0-7787-2328-8(3))* Crabtree Publishing Co.

Savage, Jeff. Rugged Gold Miners: True Tales of the Wild West, 1 vol. 2012. (True Tales of the Wild West Ser.). (ENG., Illus.). 48p. (gr. 5-7). 25.27 *(978-0-7660-4020-5(8)*, 2766b14f-bc91-4fc8-b99c-fe5ac886c13b) Enslow Publishing, LLC.

Stanbridge, Joanne. Maurice Ruddick: Un Survivant. 2004. (FRE., Illus.). (J). *(978-2-7650-0744-9(6))* Les Editions de la Cheneliere, Inc.

MINERS—FICTION

Blackwater Mine, 6 Pack. (Bookweb Ser.). 32p. (gr. 6-18). 34.00 *(978-0-7578-0893-7(X))* Rigby Education.

Croker, Verity. May Day Mine. (ENG., Illus.). 2016. (J). 24.99 *(978-1-63533-048-9(3))* 2015. 180p. (YA). pap. 14.99 *(978-1-63216-717-0(4))* Dreamspinner Pr. (Harmony Ink Pr.).

Gregory, Kristiana. My Darlin' Clementine. 2009. (ENG.). 192p. (J). (gr. 5-18). 16.95 *(978-0-8234-2196-5(8))* Holiday Hse., Inc.

Hancock, H. Irving. The Young Engineers in Mexico. 2007. 176p. per. *(978-1-4065-1994-5(4))* Dodo Pr.

Hutton, Keely. Secret Soldiers: A Novel of World War I. 2019. (ENG.). 320p. (J). 17.99 *(978-0-374-30903-9(5)*, 900188381, Farrar, Straus & Giroux (BYR)) Farrar, Straus & Giroux.

John, Patricia St. A Home for Virginia. rev. ed. 2005. (ENG., Illus.). 24p. (J). (gr. 4-7). 9.99 *(978-1-85792-961-4(6)*, f2bb3bee-fda9-4bf2-9f94-d8ee85188548) Christian Focus Pubns. GBR. Dist: Baker & Taylor Publisher Services (BTPS).

Marsh, Carole. The Gosh Awful! Gold Rush Mystery. (Real Kids, Real Places Ser.). (Illus.). 146p. (J). 2009. lib. bdg. 18.99 *(978-0-635-07026-5(X)*, Marsh, Carole Mysteries) 2007. (gr. 2-8). 14.95 *(978-0-635-06390-8(5))* Gallopade International.

Steele, Michael Anthony & Scholastic Editors. Look Out Below! Kiernan, Kenny, illus. 2012. (LEGO City Scholastic Readers Level 1 Ser.). lib. bdg. 13.55 *(978-0-606-26236-1(9))* Turtleback.

Varonka, Steve. Hard Coal Times: Pennsylvania Anthracite Stories, Vol. 1. 2003. (Illus.). 40p. (J). 4.72 *(978-0-9709630-2-4(5))* Coal Hole Productions.

Whale Watch, 6 Packs. (Bookweb Ser.). 32p. (gr. 6-18). 34.00 *(978-0-7578-0895-1(6))* Rigby Education.

Wiseman, David. Jeremy Visick. 2005. 176p. (YA). (gr. 5-18). 21.25 *(978-0-8446-7271-7(8)*, 3594) Smith, Peter Pub., Inc.

MINES AND MINERAL RESOURCES

see also Mineralogy; Mining Engineering; Precious Metals also specific types of mines and mining, e.g. Coal Mines and Mining; etc.

Blake, Kevin. Deadly Mine: Libby, Montana. 2017. (Eco-Disasters Ser.). (ENG., Illus.). 32p. (J). (gr. 2-7). 19.95 *(978-1-68402-222-9(3))* Bearport Publishing Co., Inc.

Crowther, Robert. Deep down under Ground: A Pop-up Book of Amazing Facts & Feats. Crowther, Robert, illus. 2004. (Illus.). 18p. (J). (gr. 3-8). reprint ed. pap. 22.00 *(978-0-7567-7179-9(X))* DIANE Publishing Co.

Hayhurst, Chris. John Sutter: California Pioneer. 2009. (Primary Sources of Famous People in American History Ser.). 32p. (gr. 2-3). 47.90 *(978-1-60851-696-4(2))* Rosen Publishing Group, Inc., The.

Holt, Rinehart and Winston Staff. Environmental Science Chptr. 16: Mining & Mineral Resources. 4th ed. 2004. pap. 11.20 *(978-0-03-068077-9(8))* Holt McDougal.

Hyde, Natalie. Life in a Mining Community. 2009. (Learn about Rural Life Ser.). (ENG., Illus.). 32p. (J). (gr. 3-6). pap. *(978-0-7787-5087-1(6))*; lib. bdg. *(978-0-7787-5074-1(4))* Crabtree Publishing Co.

Krajnik, Elizabeth. Mining for Emeralds, 1 vol. 2017. (Gemstones of the World Ser.). (ENG.). 24p. (J). (gr. 3-3). 25.27 *(978-1-5081-6421-0(5)*, 14798a8e-ea00-46fd-9b1a-7547c5b0eca6); pap. 9.25 *(978-1-5383-2828-6(3)*, 4ed72d19-dc7f-4917-be46-5a09fb086fbe) Rosen Publishing Group, Inc., The. (PowerKids Pr.).

Leaf, Christina. Kolmanskop: The Diamond Mine Ghost Town. 2020. (Abandoned Places Ser.). (ENG., Illus.). 24p. (J). (gr. 3-7). lib. bdg. 26.95 *(978-1-64487-161-4(0)*, Torque Bks.) Bellwether Media.

Lewis, Mark L. Underground Rescues. 2019. (Rescues in Focus Ser.). (ENG., Illus.). 32p. (J). (gr. 2-3). pap. 9.95 *(978-1-64185-844-1(3)*, 1641858443); lib. bdg. 31.35 *(978-1-64185-775-8(7)*, 1641857757) North Star Editions. (Focus Readers).

MacAulay, Kelley. Why Do We Need Rocks & Minerals? 2014. (Natural Resources Close-Up Ser.). (ENG., Illus.). 24p. (J). (gr. 1-1). *(978-0-7787-0492-8(0))*; pap. *(978-0-7787-0496-6(3))* Crabtree Publishing Co.

Marsico, Katie. What's It Like to Live Here? Mining Town. 2014. (Community Connections: What's It Like to Live Here? Ser.). (ENG., Illus.). 24p. (J). (gr. 2-5). pap. 12.79 *(978-1-62431-582-4(8)*, 203253) Cherry Lake Publishing.

McDonnell, Julia. How Precious Metals Form, 1 vol. 2016. (From the Earth: How Resources Are Made Ser.). (ENG., Illus.). 32p. (J). (gr. 3-4). pap. 11.50 *(978-1-4824-4727-9(4)*, 19178746-c5de-4e77-9270-e3045d306209) Stevens, Gareth Publishing LLLP.

Miles, Lisa. Rocks & Minerals. 2003. (Usborne Hotshots Ser.). (ENG., Illus.). 1p. (YA). (gr. 2-18). pap. 2.95 *(978-0-7460-2790-5(7))* EDC Publishing.

O'Neal, Claire. A Project Guide to Rocks & Minerals. 2010. (Earth Science Projects for Kids Ser.). (Illus.). 48p. (J). (gr. 4-7). lib. bdg. 29.95 *(978-1-58415-866-0(2))* Mitchell Lane Pubs.

Stanbridge, Joanne. Maurice Ruddick: Un Survivant. 2004. (FRE., Illus.). (J). *(978-2-7650-0744-9(6))* Les Editions de la Cheneliere, Inc.

Tower, Eric J. The Unofficial Guide to Mining in Minecraft, 1 vol. 2018. (STEM Projects in Minecraft(r) Ser.). (ENG.). 24p. (gr. 3-3). pap. 9.25 *(978-1-5383-4248-0(0)*, 45a4853e-313f-416e-b61a-0031e1116ba2, PowerKids Pr.) Rosen Publishing Group, Inc., The.

Zronik, John Paul & Zronik, John. Metals. 2004. (Rocks, Minerals, & Resources Ser.). (ENG., Illus.). 32p. (J). lib. bdg. *(978-0-7787-1418-7(7))* Crabtree Publishing Co.

—Metals - Shaping Our World. 2004. (Rocks, Minerals, & Resources Ser.). (ENG., Illus.). 32p. (J). pap. *(978-0-7787-1450-7(0))* Crabtree Publishing Co.

MINES AND MINERAL RESOURCES—FICTION

Blaine, John. The Blue Ghost Mystery: A Rick Brant Science Adventure Story. 2011. 188p. 42.95 *(978-1-258-09526-0(2))* Literary Licensing, LLC.

Collins, A. L. Outcry: Defenders of Mars. Tikulin, Tomislav, illus. 2018. (Redworld Ser.). (ENG.). 128p. (J). (gr. 3-8). lib. bdg. 25.99 *(978-1-4965-5887-9(1)*, 137025, Stone Arch Bks.) Capstone.

Cushman, Karen. The Ballad of Lucy Whipple. 2019. (ENG.). 208p. (J). (gr. 5-7). pap. 7.99 *(978-1-328-63113-8(3)*, 1734959, Clarion Bks.) HarperCollins Pubs.

Harlow, Joan Hiatt. Breaker Boy. 2017. (ENG., Illus.). 288p. (J). (gr. 3-7). 16.99 *(978-1-4814-6537-3(6)*, McElderry, Margaret K. Bks.) McElderry, Margaret K. Bks.

Hopeless, Dennis. Disney Kingdoms: Big Thunder Mountain Railroad #1. Walker, Tigh & Beaulieu, Jean-François, illus. 2016. (Disney Kingdoms: Big Thunder Mountain Railroad Ser.). (ENG.). 24p. (J). (gr. k-5). lib. bdg. 31.36 *(978-1-61479-575-9(4)*, 24356, Graphic Novels) Spotlight.

—Disney Kingdoms: Big Thunder Mountain Railroad #2. Walker, Tigh & Beaulieu, Jean-François, illus. 2016. (Disney Kingdoms: Big Thunder Mountain Railroad Ser.). (ENG.). 24p. (J). (gr. k-5). lib. bdg. 31.36 *(978-1-61479-576-6(2)*, 24357, Graphic Novels) Spotlight.

—Disney Kingdoms: Big Thunder Mountain Railroad #3. Ruiz, Felix & Beaulieu, Jean-François, illus. 2016. (Disney Kingdoms: Big Thunder Mountain Railroad Ser.). (ENG.). 24p. (J). (gr. k-5). lib. bdg. 31.36 *(978-1-61479-577-3(0)*, 24358, Graphic Novels) Spotlight.

—Disney Kingdoms: Big Thunder Mountain Railroad #4. Walker, Tigh & Beaulieu, Jean-François, illus. 2016. (Disney Kingdoms: Big Thunder Mountain Railroad Ser.). (ENG.). 24p. (J). (gr. k-5). lib. bdg. 31.36 *(978-1-61479-578-0(9)*, 24359, Graphic Novels) Spotlight.

—Disney Kingdoms: Big Thunder Mountain Railroad #5. Walker, Tigh et al, illus. 2016. (Disney Kingdoms: Big Thunder Mountain Railroad Ser.). (ENG.). 24p. (J). (gr. k-5). lib. bdg. 31.36 *(978-1-61479-579-7(7)*, 24360, Graphic Novels) Spotlight.

Kay, Ross. The Go Ahead Boys & Simon's Mine. Owen, R. Emmett, illus. 2007. 184p. per. *(978-1-4065-1857-3(3))* Dodo Pr.

—The Go Ahead Boys & Simon's Mine. 2007. 112p. per. *(978-1-4068-1924-3(7))* Echo Library.

Moyer, Jenny. Flashfall. 2016. (Flashfall Ser.: 1). (ENG., Illus.). 352p. (YA). 29.99 *(978-1-62779-481-7(6)*, 900152138, Holt, Henry & Co. Bks. For Young Readers) Holt, Henry & Co.

Reintgen, Scott. Nyxia Unleashed. (Nyxia Triad Ser.: 2). (ENG.). (YA). (gr. 7). 2019. 416p. pap. 10.99 *(978-0-399-55686-9(9)*, Ember) 2018. 400p. 17.99 *(978-0-399-55683-8(4)*, Crown Books For Young Readers) Random Hse. Children's Bks.

—Nyxia Uprising. 2019. (Nyxia Triad Ser.: 3). (ENG.). 368p. (YA). (gr. 7). 17.99 *(978-0-399-55687-6(7)*, Crown Books For Young Readers) Random Hse. Children's Bks.

Stamper, Judith Bauer. Rocky Road Trip. Gangloff, Hope, illus. 2004. (Magic School Bus Science Chapter Bks.). 89p. (gr. 2-5). lib. bdg. 15.00 *(978-0-7569-3093-6(6))* Perfection Learning Corp.

Steele, Michael Anthony & Scholastic Editors. Look Out Below! Kiernan, Kenny, illus. 2012. (LEGO City Scholastic Readers Level 1 Ser.). lib. bdg. 13.55 *(978-0-606-26236-1(9))* Turtleback.

Sutton, Laurie S. Invisible Enemy. Nathan, James, illus. 2017. (Bug Team Alpha Ser.). (ENG.). 112p. (J). (gr. 3-6). lib. bdg. 26.65 *(978-1-4965-5184-9(2)*, 136187, Stone Arch Bks.) Capstone.

Sylvester, Kevin. MiNRS. (MiNRS Ser.: 1). (ENG., Illus.). (J). (gr. 3-7). 2016. 352p. pap. 8.99 *(978-1-4814-4040-0(3))* 2015. 336p. 18.99 *(978-1-4814-4039-4(X))* McElderry, Margaret K. Bks. (McElderry, Margaret K. Bks.).

—MiNRS 2. 2016. (MiNRS Ser.: 2). (ENG., Illus.). 352p. (J). (gr. 3-7). 17.99 *(978-1-4814-4042-4(X)*, McElderry, Margaret K. Bks.) McElderry, Margaret K. Bks.

Wells, Helen. Cherry Ames, Island Nurse. 2007. (Cherry Ames Nurse Stories Ser.). 200p. (J). (gr. 3-7). 14.95 *(978-0-8261-0423-6(1))* Springer Publishing Co., Inc.

Wiechman, Kathy Cannon. Empty Places. 2016. (ENG., Illus.). 240p. (J). (gr. 4-7). 17.95 *(978-1-62979-451-8(1)*, Calkins Creek) Highlights Pr., c/o Highlights for Children, Inc.

Winfield, Arthur M. The Rover Boys Out West. 2007. 228p. 26.95 *(978-1-4218-4140-3(1))*; per. 11.95 *(978-1-4218-4238-7(6))* 1st World Publishing, Inc. (1st World Library - Literary Society).

MINIATURE CAMERAS

see Cameras

MINIATURE GARDENS

see Gardens, Miniature

MINIATURE OBJECTS

see Dollhouses; Models and Modelmaking; Toys

see names of objects with the subdivision Models, e.g. Airplanes—Models

MINING

see Mines and Mineral Resources; Mining Engineering

MINING ENGINEERING

Linde, Barbara M. Strip Mining, 1 vol. 2013. (Habitat Havoc Ser.). (ENG., Illus.). 32p. (J). (gr. 3-4). 29.27 *(978-1-4339-9862-1(9)*, b95febf8-f657-487a-ba7a-f027e12f1950) Stevens, Gareth Publishing LLLP.

Nagle, Jeanne. A Career in Mining & Logging, 1 vol. 2018. (Jobs for Rebuilding America Ser.). (ENG.). 80p. (gr. 6-6). 38.80 *(978-1-5081-7999-3(9)*, 43187897-4a54-4c22-8525-37e4cea72418) Rosen Publishing Group, Inc., The.

Thomas, Mark. Discoverer Enterprise: La plataforma de perforación más grande del mundo (the Discoverer Enterprise: World's Largest Offshore Drilling Rig) 2009. (Estructuras extraordinarias (Record-Breaking Structures) Ser.). (SPA.). 24p. (gr. 1-2). 42.50 *(978-1-61512-310-0(5)*, Editorial Buenas Letras) Rosen Publishing Group, Inc., The.

—The Discoverer Enterprise: World's Largest Offshore Drilling Rig. 2009. (Record-Breaking Structures Ser.). 24p. (gr. 1-2). 42.50 *(978-1-60852-454-9(X)*, PowerKids Pr.) Rosen Publishing Group, Inc., The.

Tower, Eric J. The Unofficial Guide to Mining in Minecraft, 1 vol. 2018. (STEM Projects in Minecraft(r) Ser.). (ENG.). 24p. (gr. 3-3). pap. 9.25 *(978-1-5383-4248-0(0)*, 45a4853e-313f-416e-b61a-0031e1116ba2, PowerKids Pr.) Rosen Publishing Group, Inc., The.

MINISTERS (DIPLOMATIC AGENTS)

see Diplomats

MINISTERS OF THE GOSPEL

see Clergy

MINKS

Gray, Susan H. American Mink. 2008. (21st Century Skills Library: Animal Invaders Ser.). (ENG., Illus.). 32p. (gr. 4-8). lib. bdg. 32.07 *(978-1-60279-114-5(7)*, 200092) Cherry Lake Publishing.

MINKS—FICTION

Burgess, Thornton W. Billy Mink. (J). 18.95 *(978-0-8488-0397-1(3))* Amereon Ltd.

—Billy Mink. Cady, Harrison, illus. 2012. (Dover Children's Thrift Classics Ser.). (ENG.). 128p. (J). (gr. k-3). pap. 5.00 *(978-0-486-48107-4(7)*, 481077) Dover Pubns., Inc.

—Tommy & the Wishing-Stone. Cady, Harrison, illus. 2012. (Dover Children's Thrift Classics Ser.). (ENG.). 240p. (J). (gr. k-3). pap. 4.00 *(978-0-486-48105-0(0))* Dover Pubns., Inc.

Kink the Mink: KinderReaders Individual Title Six-Packs. (Kinderstarters Ser.). 8p. (gr. -1-1). 21.00 *(978-0-7635-8652-2(8))* Rigby Education.

Sargent, Dave & Sargent, Pat. Mad Jack: I Throw Fits, 15 vols., Vol. 16. Huff, Jeane, illus. 2nd rev. ed. 2003. (Animal Pride Ser.: 16). 42p. (J). pap. 10.95 *(978-1-56763-790-8(6))*; lib. bdg. 20.95 *(978-1-56763-789-2(2))* Ozark Publishing.

MINNESOTA

Brown, Vanessa. Minnesota. 2009. (Bilingual Library of the United States of America Ser.). (ENG & SPA.). 32p. (gr. 2-2). 47.90 *(978-1-60853-368-8(9)*, Editorial Buenas Letras) Rosen Publishing Group, Inc., The.

—Minnesota, 1 vol. Brusca, María Cristina, tr. 2005. (Bilingual Library of the United States of America Ser.: Set 1). (ENG & SPA., Illus.). 32p. (J). (gr. 2-2). lib. bdg. 28.93 *(978-1-4042-3088-0(2)*, ad501a84-a2b3-4327-b296-d14de2ea6f81) Rosen Publishing Group, Inc., The.

Dolan, Sean. Minnesota. 2005. (Rookie Read-About Geography Ser.). (ENG., Illus.). 32p. (J). (gr. 1-2). lib. bdg. 20.50 *(978-0-516-25257-5(7)*, Children's Pr.) Scholastic Library Publishing.

Gedatus, Gus. Minnesota, 1 vol. 2005. (Portraits of the States Ser.). (ENG., Illus.). 32p. (gr. 3-5). pap. 11.50 *(978-0-8368-4688-1(5)*, c33385ff-c28f-4f28-92a4-b675e86b0e4e); lib. bdg. 28.67 *(978-0-8368-4669-0(9)*, d22a4117-6017-4b26-81e8-56fed5c6510a) Stevens, Gareth Publishing LLLP. (Gareth Stevens Learning Library).

Greenberg, Keith Elliot. Jesse Ventura. 2003. (Biography Ser.). (Illus.). 112p. (YA). (gr. 6-12). pap. 7.95 *(978-0-8225-9680-6(6)*, Carolrhoda Bks.) Lerner Publishing Group.

Keranen, Rachel, et al. Minnesota: Land of 10,000 Lakes, 1 vol. 2018. (It's My State! (Fourth Edition)(r) Ser.). (ENG.). 80p. (gr. 4-4). pap. 18.64 *(978-1-5026-4445-9(2)*, 6b868b85-c365-4c74-a420-1d5109f89003) Cavendish Square Publishing LLC.

Kuedee, Jayce. How to Draw Minnesota's Sights & Symbols. 2009. (Kid's Guide to Drawing America Ser.). 32p. (gr. k-k). 50.50 *(978-1-61511-072-8(0)*, PowerKids Pr.) Rosen Publishing Group, Inc., The.

Lowrie, Paul. Hooray for Minnesota Lakes. 2008. 19.95 *(978-0-9755801-8-9(3))* Questmarc Publishing.

—Hooray for Minnesota Winters. 2008. 19.95 *(978-0-9755801-9-6(1))* Questmarc Publishing.

Marsh, Carole. Minnesota Current Events Projects: 30 Cool, Activities, Crafts, Experiments & More for Kids to Do to Learn about Your State! 2003. (Minnesota Experience Ser.). 32p. (gr. k-8). pap. 5.95 *(978-0-635-02042-0(4)*, Marsh, Carole Bks.) Gallopade International.

—Minnesota Geography Projects: 30 Cool, Activities, Crafts, Experiments & More for Kids to Do to Learn about Your State! 2003. (Minnesota Experience Ser.). 32p. (gr. k-5). pap. 5.95 *(978-0-635-01842-7(X)*, Marsh, Carole Bks.) Gallopade International.

—Minnesota Government Projects: 30 Cool, Activities, Crafts, Experiments & More for Kids to Do to Learn about Your State! 2003. (Minnesota Experience Ser.). 32p. (gr. k-5). pap. 5.95 *(978-0-635-01942-4(6)*, Marsh, Carole Bks.) Gallopade International.

—Minnesota People Projects: 30 Cool, Activities, Crafts, Experiments & More for Kids to Do to Learn about Your State! 2003. (Minnesota Experience Ser.). 32p. (gr. k-5). pap. 5.95 *(978-0-635-01992-9(2)*, Marsh, Carole Bks.) Gallopade International.

—Minnesota Symbols & Facts Projects: 30 Cool, Activities, Crafts, Experiments & More for Kids to Do to Learn about Your State! 2003. (Minnesota Experience Ser.). 32p. (gr. k-5). pap. 5.95 *(978-0-635-01892-2(6)*, Marsh, Carole Bks.) Gallopade International.

Moore, Dave, compiled by. A Free People: Tracing Our Hmong Roots. 2nd ed. 2003. (ENG., Illus.). 144p. (J). per. 19.95 *(978-1-888194-42-5(1))* Master Communications, Inc.

Murray, Julie. Minnesota, 1 vol. 2006. (United States Ser.). (ENG., Illus.). 32p. (gr. 2-4). 27.07 *(978-1-59197-682-0(0)*, Buddy Bks.) ABDO Publishing Co.

Paplow, Paula. Hands upon the Rock. 2013. 48p. 19.99 *(978-0-9884268-0-1(3))* Little Cottonwood River Bks.

Paulsen, Gary. Woodsong. unabr. ed. 2004. 132p. (J). (gr. 6-18). pap. 29.00 incl. audio *(978-0-8072-0460-3(9)*, Listening Library) Random Hse. Audio Publishing Group.

—Woodsong. 2007. (ENG., Illus.). 144p. (J). (gr. 5-9). pap. 7.99 *(978-1-4169-3939-9(3)*, Simon & Schuster Bks. For Young Readers) Simon & Schuster Bks. For Young Readers.

Peterson, Sheryl. Minnesota. 2008. (This Land Called America Ser.). 32p. (YA). (gr. 3-6). 22.95 *(978-1-58341-648-8(X))* Creative Co., The.

Porter, A. P. Minnesota. (J). 2012. lib. bdg. 25.26 *(978-0-7613-4188-8(9)*, Lerner Pubns.) 2nd rev. exp. ed. 2003. (Illus.). 84p. (gr. 3-6). pap. 6.95 *(978-0-8225-4149-3(1))* Lerner Publishing Group.

Purslow, Neil. Minnesota. 2011. (Guide to American States Ser.). (Illus.). 48p. (YA). (gr. 3-6). 29.99 *(978-1-61690-795-2(9))* Weigl Pubs., Inc.

River Lake Press. An Osprey Summer. 2010. (Illus.). 32p. (J). 17.95 *(978-0-615-36951-8(0))* River Lake Pr.

Scheff, Matt & Campbell, Dave. Minnesota Vikings, 1 vol. 2016. (NFL up Close Ser.). (ENG., Illus.). 32p. (J). (gr. 3-9). lib. bdg. 32.79 *(978-1-68078-223-3(1)*, 22049, SportsZone) ABDO Publishing Co.

Schwabacher, Martin & Kummer, Patricia K. Minnesota, 1 vol. 2nd rev. ed. 2008. (Celebrate the States (Second Edition) Ser.). (ENG.). 144p. (gr. 6-6). lib. bdg. 39.79 *(978-0-7614-2716-2(3)*, 9daa6308-da8b-4f23-a60a-de71b989ce87) Cavendish Square Publishing LLC.

Sleeping Bear Press. Diary of a Minnesota Kid. Moore, Cyd, illus. 2010. (State Journal Ser.). (ENG.). 128p. (J). (gr. 4-8). pap. 9.95 *(978-1-58536-539-5(4)*, 202217) Sleeping Bear Pr.

Targ Brill, Marlene. Minnesota, 1 vol. Santoro, Christopher, illus. 2005. (It's My State! (First Edition)(r) Ser.). (ENG.). 80p. (gr. 4-4). lib. bdg. 34.07 *(978-0-7614-1534-3(3)*, 97098d44-4f6d-4125-9c1a-98b2eb875f1d) Cavendish Square Publishing LLC.

Thompson, Gabrielle. The ABCs of Childhood Cancer. 2008. (Illus.). (J). *(978-1-59298-247-9(6))* Beaver's Pond Pr., Inc.

Wargin, Kathy-jo. I Spy with My Little Eye Minnesota: Minnesota. 2008. (I Spy with My Little Eye Ser.). (ENG., Illus.). 32p. (J). (gr. 1-4). 15.99 *(978-1-58536-359-9(6),* 202144) Sleeping Bear Pr.

—North Star Numbers: A Minnesota Number Book. Caple, Laurie, illus. 2008. (America by the Numbers Ser.). (ENG.). 40p. (J). (gr. 1-3). 17.95 *(978-1-58536-187-8(9),* 202033) Sleeping Bear Pr.

—V Is for Viking: A Minnesota Alphabet. Latham, Rebecca & Latham, Karen, illus. 2003. (Discover America State by State Ser.). (ENG.). 40p. (J). (gr. 1-3). 18.99 *(978-1-58536-125-0(9),* 201988) Sleeping Bear Pr.

MINNESOTA—FICTION

Applegate, Katherine. Home of the Brave. 2008. (ENG.). 272p. (J). (gr. 5-9). pap. 8.99 *(978-0-312-53563-6(5),* 900054740) Square Fish.

Ashford, Rachel. My First Santa's Coming to Minnesota. Dunn, Robert, illus. 2015. (Santa Claus Is on His Way Ser.). (ENG.). 18p. (J). (gr. -1-k). bds. 9.99 *(978-1-4926-2879-8(4),* Hometown World) Sourcebooks, Inc.

Atwood, Megan. Molly Gets a Goat (and Wants to Give It Back) Llewhellin, Gareth, illus. 2018. (Dear Molly, Dear Olive Ser.). (ENG.). 96p. (J). (gr. 1-3). lib. bdg. 21.99 *(978-1-5158-2921-8(9),* 138457, Picture Window Bks.) Capstone.

Baum, Diane Ganzer & Olson, Dan. Dakota's Trail. 2011. 48p. pap. 11.99 *(978-1-61286-029-9(X))* Avid Readers Publishing Group.

Bird, James. The Brave. 2022. (ENG., Illus.). 320p. (J). pap. 7.99 *(978-1-250-79174-0(X),* 900214708) Square Fish.

Bissonette, Aimee. North Woods Girl. McGehee, Claudia, illus. 2015. (ENG.). 32p. (J). 17.95 *(978-0-87351-966-3(3))* Minnesota Historical Society Pr.

Blejwas, Emily. Like Nothing Amazing Ever Happened. 2020. (ENG.). 224p. (J). (gr. 4-7). 19.99 *(978-1-9848-4849-9(6),* Delacorte Bks. for Young Readers) Random Hse. Children's Bks.

Blume, Lesley M. M. The Rising Star of Rusty Nail. 2009. (ENG.). 288p. (J). (gr. 3-7). 7.99 *(978-0-440-42111-5(X),* Yearling) Random Hse. Children's Bks.

Bredeson, Michelle. Legends. 2012. 220p. pap. *(978-1-61706-158-5(1))* Roxby Media Ltd.

Brezenoff, Steve. Dolls of Doom: A Tale of Terror. Epelbaum, Mariano, illus. 2018. (Michael Dahl Presents: Phobia Ser.). (ENG.). 72p. (J). (gr. 4-6). lib. bdg. 25.32 *(978-1-4965-7342-1(0),* 138929, Stone Arch Bks.) Capstone.

—Guy in Real Life. 2015. (ENG.). 400p. (YA). (gr. 9). pap. 9.99 *(978-0-06-226684-2(5),* Balzer & Bray) HarperCollins Pubs.

Brost, Diane. Courage at Crow Wing River. 1 vol. 2010. 36p. 24.95 *(978-1-4512-1254-9(2))* PublishAmerica, Inc.

Carlson-Voiles, Polly. Summer of the Wolves. 2013. (ENG.). 352p. (J). (gr. 5-7). pap. 7.99 *(978-0-544-02276-8(9),* 1528497, Clarion Bks.) HarperCollins Pubs.

Carson, John & Carson, Marlene. Ramblin' Rose: The Chinese Fortune Cookie. 2008. 291p. pap. 8.99 *(978-0-9800034-1-3(5))* Aspirations Media, Inc.

Casanova, Mary. Frozen. 2013. (Fesler-Lampert Minnesota Heritage Ser.). (ENG.). 256p. pap. 11.95 *(978-0-8166-8057-3(4))* Univ. of Minnesota Pr.

—Ice-Out. (ENG., Illus.). 264p. 2017. pap. 11.95 *(978-1-5179-0211-7(8))* 2016. (YA). 16.95 *(978-0-8166-9417-4(6))* Univ. of Minnesota Pr.

—When Eagles Fall. 2014. (Fesler-Lampert Minnesota Heritage Ser.). (ENG.). 160p. pap. 9.95 *(978-0-8166-9211-8(4))* Univ. of Minnesota Pr.

Clark, Marshunna & Jones, Patrick. Duty or Desire. 2016. (Unbarred Ser.). (ENG.). 112p. (YA). (gr. 6-12). pap. 7.99 *(978-1-5124-0089-2(0),* 7e7f910c-b924-41c6-8a5b-472ea3801b0f); E-Book 42.65 *(978-1-5124-0090-8(4))* Lerner Publishing Group. (Darby Creek).

Cochrane, Mick. Fitz. 2013. (ENG.). 192p. (YA). (gr. 7). pap. 8.99 *(978-0-375-84611-3(5),* Ember) Random Hse. Children's Bks.

Cronn-Mills, Kirstin. Beautiful Music for Ugly Children. 2012. (ENG.). 288p. (YA). (gr. 9-12). pap. 14.99 *(978-0-7387-3251-0(6),* 0738732516, Flux) North Star Editions.

Debruzzi, Jeremy. A Minnesota Fish Tail. 2012. 48p. 24.99 *(978-1-4628-8580-0(2));* pap. 15.99 *(978-1-4628-8579-4(9))* Xlibris Corp.

Delsol, Wendy. Stork. (ENG., Illus.). 368p. (YA). (gr. 7). 2011. pap. 8.99 *(978-0-7636-5687-4(9))* 2010. 15.99 *(978-0-7636-4844-2(2))* Candlewick Pr.

Downing, Erin. Kiss It. 2010. (ENG.). 288p. (YA). (gr. 9-18). pap. 9.99 *(978-1-4169-9700-9(8),* Simon Pulse) Simon Pulse.

Durbin, William. Blackwater Ben. 2014. (Fesler-Lampert Minnesota Heritage Ser.). (ENG., Illus.). 216p. (J). pap. 9.95 *(978-0-8166-9192-0(4))* Univ. of Minnesota Pr.

Durbin, William & Durbin, Barbara. Dead Man's Rapids. 2018. (ENG.). 200p. (J). (gr. 4-8). pap. 9.95 *(978-1-5179-0224-7(X))* Univ. of Minnesota Pr.

Ellsworth, Loretta. The Shrouding Woman. 2007. (ENG., Illus.). 160p. (YA). (gr. 4-9). pap. 18.99 *(978-0-8050-8185-5(2),* 900040614, Holt, Henry & Co. Bks. For Young Readers) Holt, Henry & Co.

Gamble, Adam. Good Night Minnesota. Veno, Joe, illus. 2009. (Good Night Our World Ser.). (ENG.). 20p. (J). (gr. -1-k). bds. 9.95 *(978-1-60219-034-4(8))* Good Night Bks.

Ganser, Sara. The Weekend Getaway. 2009. 24p. pap. 15.59 *(978-1-4490-2423-9(8))* AuthorHouse.

Gibney, Shannon. Dream Country. 2019. (ENG., Illus.). 368p. (YA). (gr. 9). pap. 10.99 *(978-0-7352-3168-9(0),* Penguin Books) Penguin Young Readers Group.

Glaser, Linda. Hannah's Way. Gustavson, Adam, illus. 2012. (ENG.). 32p. (J). (gr. k-3). pap. 7.95 *(978-0-7613-5138-2(8),* 59392402-0f00-41e2-b7cf-f8230b7c8ebc, Kar-Ben Publishing) Lerner Publishing Group.

Goode, Laura. Sister Mischief. (ENG.). 384p. (YA). (gr. 9). 2013. pap. 8.99 *(978-0-7636-6456-5(1))* 2011. (Illus.). 16.99 *(978-0-7636-4640-0(7))* Candlewick Pr.

Griffin, Molly Beth. Silhouette of a Sparrow. 2013. (Milkweed Prize for Children's Literature Ser.). (Illus.). 208p. pap. 12.00 *(978-1-57131-704-9(X))* Milkweed Editions.

Groethe, Kd. The Virtual Adventures of Megan & Timmy. 2012. 230p. (gr. 4-6). 27.99 *(978-1-4685-5050-4(0));* pap. 16.95 *(978-1-4685-5049-8(7))* AuthorHouse.

Harbo, Gary. The Northern Woods Adventure: Advanced Reader, 6 vols. Harbo, Gary, illus. I.t. ed. 2004. (If You Want to Succeed, You Need to Read! Ser.: 6). (ENG., Illus.). 33p. (J). 10.95 *(978-1-884149-15-3(4))* Kutie Kari Bks., Inc.

Hautman, Pete. The Big Crunch. 2011. (ENG.). 288p. (J). (gr. 9-8). 17.99 *(978-0-545-24075-8(1),* Scholastic Pr.) Scholastic, Inc.

Havill, Juanita. Grow: A Novel in Verse, 1 vol. Kodman, Stanislawa, illus. 160p. (J). (gr. 3-7). 2011. pap. 7.99 *(978-1-56145-575-1(X))* 2008. 14.95 *(978-1-56145-441-9(9))* Peachtree Publishing Co. Inc.

Hayles, Marsha. Breathing Room. 2013. (ENG., Illus.). 272p. (J). (gr. 5-9). pap. 13.99 *(978-1-250-03411-3(6),* 900120581) Square Fish.

Herbach, Geoff. Fat Boy vs. the Cheerleaders. 2014. 320p. (YA). (gr. 7-12). 16.99 *(978-1-4022-9141-8(8),* 9781402291418) Sourcebooks, Inc.

—Gabe Johnson Takes Over. 2015. 352p. (YA). (gr. 6-12). pap. 13.99 *(978-1-4926-0865-3(3))* Sourcebooks, Inc.

Holmes, Katherine L. The Wide Awake Loons. 2013. 188p. pap. 9.95 *(978-1-938083-18-1(0))* Black Forge.

Ireland, Justina. Tiffany Donovan vs. the Cookie Elves of Destruction. Champion, Tyler, illus. 2017. (Devils' Pass Ser.). (ENG.). 128p. (J). (gr. 4-8). lib. bdg. 25.99 *(978-1-4965-4987-7(2),* 135879, Stone Arch Bks.) Capstone.

Ivy, Maggie, illus. Ghostly Reunion. 2018. (Haunted States of America Ser.). (ENG.). 136p. (J). (gr. 3-4). lib. bdg. 27.13 *(978-1-63163-207-5(8),* 1631632078, Jolly Fish Pr.) North Star Editions.

Jacobs, Lily. The Littlest Bunny in Minnesota: An Easter Adventure. Dunn, Robert, illus. 2015. (Littlest Bunny Ser.). (ENG.). 32p. (J). (gr. -1-3). 9.99 *(978-1-4926-1120-2(4),* Hometown World) Sourcebooks, Inc.

James, Eric. Santa's Sleigh Is on Its Way to Minnesota: A Christmas Adventure. Dunn, Robert, illus. 2015. (Santa's Sleigh Is on Its Way Ser.). (ENG.). 32p. (J). (gr. k-2). 12.99 *(978-1-4926-2748-7(8),* Hometown World) Sourcebooks, Inc.

—The Spooky Express Minnesota. Piwowarski, Marcin, illus. 2017. (Spooky Express Ser.). (ENG.). 32p. (J). (gr. k-6). 9.99 *(978-1-4926-5371-4(3),* Hometown World) Sourcebooks, Inc.

—Tiny the Minnesota Easter Bunny. 2018. (Tiny the Easter Bunny Ser.). (ENG.). 40p. (J). (gr. k-3). 9.99 *(978-1-4926-5938-9(X),* Hometown World) Sourcebooks, Inc.

Johnson, Kristin. Deep Freeze. 2017. (Day of Disaster Ser.). (ENG.). 104p. (YA). (gr. 6-12). 26.65 *(978-1-5124-2776-9(4),* 3aba1100-6d46-4bf9-bdd4-e096edba4172); E-Book 39.99 *(978-1-5124-2783-7(7));* E-Book 39.99 *(978-1-5124-3509-2(0),* 9781512435092) Lerner Publishing Group. (Darby Creek).

Johnson, Kristin F. Deep Freeze. 2017. (Day of Disaster Ser.). (ENG.). 104p. (YA). (gr. 6-12). E-Book 6.99 *(978-1-5124-3510-8(4),* 9781512435108, Darby Creek) Lerner Publishing Group.

Jones, Patrick. Doing Right. 2015. (Locked Out Ser.). (ENG.). 104p. (YA). (gr. 6-12). E-Book 42.65 *(978-1-4677-7691-2(2),* 9781467776912, Darby Creek) Lerner Publishing Group.

—Taking Sides. 2015. (Locked Out Ser.). (ENG.). 104p. (YA). (gr. 6-12). lib. bdg. 27.99 *(978-1-4677-5800-0(0),* 666c07ab-a572-44f0-a456-5017c9fe1267, Darby Creek) Lerner Publishing Group.

—Taking Sides. 2015. (Locked Out Ser.). (ENG.). 104p. (J). (gr. 6-12). E-Book 6.99 *(978-1-4677-7703-2(X),* 9781467777032, Darby Creek) Lerner Publishing Group.

Kadence, Sam. On the Right Track. 2016. (ENG., Illus.). (YA). (gr. 9-12). 24.99 *(978-1-63533-057-1(2))* 2013. 184p. pap. 14.99 *(978-1-62798-069-2(5))* Dreamspinner Pr. (Harmony Ink Pr.).

Kallander, Susan & Boomgaarden, Larry. Up in Smoke. 2010. (Illus.). 24p. pap. 11.50 *(978-1-60860-934-5(0),* Eloquent Bks.) Strategic Book Publishing & Rights Agency (SBPRA).

Kantar, Andrew. Game Face. Keleher, Fran, illus. 2013. 160p. pap. 12.95 *(978-1-61160-566-2(0))* Whiskey Creek Restorations.

Kingsley Troupe, Thomas. Ghostly Reunion. Ivy, Maggie, illus. 2018. (Haunted States of America Ser.). (ENG.). 136p. (J). (gr. 3-4). pap. 7.99 *(978-1-63163-208-2(6),* 1631632086, Jolly Fish Pr.) North Star Editions.

Long, Loren & Bildner, Phil. Water, Water Everywhere. Long, Loren, illus. (Sluggers Ser.: 4). (ENG., Illus.). (J). (gr. 3-7). 2010. 288p. pap. 9.99 *(978-1-4169-1890-5(6))* 2009. 272p. 14.99 *(978-1-4169-1866-0(3))* Simon & Schuster Bks. For Young Readers. (Simon & Schuster Bks. For Young Readers).

Lovelace, Maud Hart. The Betsy-Tacy Treasury: The First Four Betsy-Tacy Books. 2011. (ENG.). 736p. pap. 18.99 *(978-0-06-209587-9(0),* William Morrow Paperbacks) HarperCollins Pubs.

Maddox, Jake. Home Safe Home. 2018. (Jake Maddox JV Ser.). (ENG., Illus.). 96p. (J). (gr. 4-6). lib. bdg. 26.65 *(978-1-4965-5931-9(2),* 137133, Stone Arch Bks.) Capstone.

—Slap-Shot Slump. 2015. (Jake Maddox JV Ser.). (ENG., Illus.). 96p. (J). (gr. 4-6). lib. bdg. 26.65 *(978-1-4342-9635-1(0),* 126914, Stone Arch Bks.) Capstone.

Marsh, Carole. The Mystery in the Twin Cities. Baker, Janice, ed. 2011. (Carole Marsh Mysteries Ser.). (Illus.). (J). pap. 7.99 *(978-0-635-07960-2(7),* Marsh, Carole Mysteries) Gallopade International.

—The Mystery on the Mighty Mississippi. 2009. (Real Kids, Real Places Ser.). (Illus.). 146p. (J). lib. bdg. 18.99 *(978-0-635-07001-2(4),* Marsh, Carole Mysteries) Gallopade International.

Marvin, Isabel R. A Bride for Anna's Papa. 2004. (Historical Fiction for Young Readers Ser.). (ENG., Illus.). 144p. (J). pap. 6.95 *(978-1-57131-650-9(7))* Milkweed Editions.

—The Tenth Rifle. Costner, Howard, illus. Date not set. 128p. (Orig.). (J). (gr. 3-8). pap. 9.95 *(978-0-89896-109-6(2))* Larksdale.

McGhee, Alison. Julia Gillian 3. 2010. *(978-0-545-10467-8(X))* Scholastic, Inc.

McMann, Lisa. Dead to You. 2012. (ENG.). (YA). (gr. 9). 272p. pap. 11.99 *(978-1-4424-0389-5(6));* 256p. 16.99 *(978-1-4424-0388-8(8))* Simon Pulse. (Simon Pulse).

Mercier, Deborah. The Captain's Hat. Mills, Faythe, illus. 2007. 32p. (J). 17.99 *(978-0-9799410-0-9(8))* Minnewaska Pr.

Miller-Burke, Jude. Snowball, Come Home! 2005. (Illus.). 32p. (J). bds. 16.95 *(978-1-59298-093-2(7))* Beaver's Pond Pr., Inc.

Minnema, Cheryl. Johnny's Pheasant. Flett, Julie, illus. 2019. (ENG.). 32p. (J). (gr. -1-3). 16.95 *(978-1-5179-0501-9(X))* Univ. of Minnesota Pr.

Oceanak, Karla. Cahoots. Spanjer, Kendra, illus. 2011. (Aldo Zelnick Comic Novel Ser.: 3). (ENG.). 151p. (J). (gr. 3-7). 12.95 *(978-1-934649-08-4(2))* Bailiwick Pr.

Olson, Norah. Before Now. 2017. (ENG.). 208p. (YA). (gr. 9). 17.99 *(978-0-06-234707-7(1),* Tegen, Katherine Bks) HarperCollins Pubs.

O'Neill, Elizabeth. Alfred Visits Minnesota. 2007. (Illus.). 24p. (J). pap. 12.00 *(978-0-9799121-2-2(1))* Funny Bone Bks.

Paulsen, Gary. Dancing Carl. 2007. (ENG.). 112p. (J). (gr. 5-9). pap. 8.99 *(978-1-4169-3938-2(5),* Simon & Schuster Bks. For Young Readers) Simon & Schuster Bks. For Young Readers.

—Foxman. I.t. ed. 2004. (YA). (gr. 6-12). 27.95 *(978-1-58118-112-8(4))* LRS.

Perry, Marie. A Gift for Sadia. Perry, Marie, illus. I.t. ed. 2005. (Illus.). 32p. (J). lib. bdg. 15.95 *(978-0-9755675-1-7(9))* Buttonweed Pr., L.L.C.

Peterson, Jay D. & Morgan, Collette A., eds. Sky Blue Water: Great Stories for Young Readers. 2016. (ENG.). 240p. 19.95 *(978-0-8166-9876-9(7))* Univ. of Minnesota Pr.

Pietron, Barbara. Thunderstone. 2013. (Legacy in Legend Ser.: 1). (ENG.). 262p. (YA). (gr. 7). pap. 12.99 *(978-1-940368-91-7(X))* Scribe Publishing Co.

Polinski, Jo. Minnesota Moon. Webber, Carol, illus. 2007. 20p. per. 12.95 *(978-1-933482-60-6(5))* White Turtle Bks.

Preus, Margi. Enchantment Lake: A Northwoods Mystery. 2017. 200p. pap. 11.95 *(978-1-5179-0419-7(6))* Univ. of Minnesota Pr.

Qualey, Marsha. Come in from the Cold. 2008. (ENG.). 224p. (YA). (gr. 7). pap. 14.95 *(978-0-547-01439-5(2),* 1030986, Clarion Bks.) HarperCollins Pubs.

Rempel, Leah. Hey, Hmong Girl, Whassup? The Journal of Choua Vang. 2004. (Illus.). v, 138p. (YA). pap. *(978-0-9723721-5-2(6))* Hamline Univ. Pr.

Rich, Juliann. Caught in the Crossfire. 2014. (ENG.). 264p. (J). (gr. 7). pap. 11.95 *(978-1-62639-070-6(3))* Bold Strokes Bks.

Root, Phyllis. One North Star: A Counting Book. Prange, Beckie & Bowen, Betsy, illus. 2016. (ENG.). 36p. 16.95 *(978-0-8166-5063-7(2))* Univ. of Minnesota Pr.

Rubens, Michael. Sons of The 613. 2012. (ENG.). 320p. (YA). (gr. 7). 16.99 *(978-0-547-61216-4(8),* 1464621, Clarion Bks.) HarperCollins Pubs.

Rylant, Cynthia. Old Town in the Green Groves. 2007. (Little House Ser.). (ENG.). 192p. (J). (gr. 3-7). pap. 9.99 *(978-0-06-088546-5(7),* HarperCollins) HarperCollins Pubs.

Scaletta, Kurtis. Mudville. 272p. (J). 2010. (gr. 3-7). 8.99 *(978-0-375-84472-0(4),* Yearling) 2009. (ENG.). (gr. 4-6). lib. bdg. 22.44 *(978-0-375-95579-2(8),* Knopf Bks. for Young Readers) Random Hse. Children's Bks.

Schultz, Jan Neubert. Firestorm. 2003. (Adventures in Time Ser.). 204p. (YA). (gr. 4-7). 15.95 *(978-0-87614-276-9(5),* Carolrhoda Bks.) Lerner Publishing Group.

—Horse Sense: The Story of Will Sasse, His Horse Star & the Outlaw Jesse James. 2005. (Adventures in Time Ser.). (Illus.). 180p. (J). (gr. 4-8). 15.95 *(978-1-57505-998-3(3))* Lerner Publishing Group.

Schultz, Leslie & Braulick, J. J. M. And Sometimes Y. Newman, Heather, illus. 2013. 302p. pap. 12.99 *(978-1-937848-07-1(8))* Do Life Right, Inc.

Scott, Luke. Through a Crystal Doorknob. 2012. 88p. 24.95 *(978-1-4626-9420-4(9));* pap. 19.95 *(978-1-4626-7361-2(9))* America Star Bks.

Shaw, Janet. Kirsten Story Collection. Graef, Renee, illus. 2008. 380p. 29.95 *(978-1-59369-454-8(7))* American Girl Publishing, Inc.

—Kirsten's Short Story Collection. Lewis, Kim & Graef, Renee, illus. 2006. (American Girls Collection). 213p. (J). (gr. 3-8). 12.95 *(978-1-59369-323-7(0))* American Girl Publishing, Inc.

Siemsen, Nancy. The Girl Who Loved Jupiter. 2005. 151p. pap. 24.95 *(978-1-4137-9004-7(6))* America Star Bks.

Sims, Lori. Starvin' Marvin & Skinny Minnie Melt Minnesota. 2010. 115p. pap. 11.95 *(978-1-4327-5628-4(1))* Outskirts Pr., Inc.

Smallman, Steve. Santa Is Coming to Minnesota. Dunn, Robert, illus. (ENG.). (J). 2012. 32p. (-3). 9.99 *(978-1-4022-7530-2(7),* Sourcebooks Jabberwocky) 2nd ed. 2019. 40p. (gr. -1-3). 12.99 *(978-1-7282-0072-9(5),* Hometown World) Sourcebooks, Inc.

Sommerdorf, Norma. Red River Girl. 2006. (ENG., Illus.). 192p. (J). (gr. 3-7). 16.95 *(978-0-8234-1903-6(7))* Holiday Hse., Inc.

Sommers, Jackie Lea. Truest. 2015. (ENG.). 384p. (YA). (gr. 8). 17.99 *(978-0-06-234825-8(6),* HarperCollins) HarperCollins Pubs.

Springer, Michael. The Bootlegger's Secret. 2010. (Illus.). 164p. pap. 15.95 *(978-1-4327-5792-2(X))* Outskirts Pr., Inc.

St. Anthony, Jane. Isabelle Day Refuses to Die of a Broken Heart. 2018. (ENG.). 152p. (YA). pap. 9.95 *(978-0-8166-9922-3(4))* Univ. of Minnesota Pr.

—Whatever Normal Is. 2019. 160p. (YA). (gr. 8-10). 14.95 *(978-1-5179-0677-1(6))* Univ. of Minnesota Pr.

St. Antoine, Sara. Three Bird Summer. 2018. (ENG.). 256p. (J). (gr. 5). pap. 6.99 *(978-1-5362-0045-4(X))* Candlewick Pr.

Sully, Katherine. Night-Night Minnesota. Poole, Helen, illus. 2016. (Night-Night Ser.). (ENG.). 20p. (J). (gr. -1-1). bds. 9.99 *(978-1-4926-3940-4(0),* 9781492639404, Hometown World) Sourcebooks, Inc.

Tagged. 2015. 208p. (YA). (gr. 7). lib. bdg. 16.95 *(978-1-58089-583-5(2))* Charlesbridge Publishing, Inc.

Tetzlaff, Wendy Jo. Summertime: A Girl Named Frannie, 1 vol. 2010. 38p. pap. 24.95 *(978-1-4489-2598-8(3))* PublishAmerica, Inc.

Treacy, Ann. The Search for the Homestead Treasure: A Mystery. 2016. (ENG., Illus.). 160p. 16.95 *(978-0-8166-9956-8(9))* Univ. of Minnesota Pr.

Wargin, Kathy-jo. The Legend of Minnesota. Geister, David, illus. 2006. (Myths, Legends, Fairy & Folktales Ser.). (ENG.). 40p. (J). (gr. 2-5). 17.95 *(978-1-58536-262-2(X),* 202077) Sleeping Bear Pr.

—Minn from Minnesota. Holman, Karen Busch, illus. 2006. (Mitt Midwest Ser.: 2). 144p. (J). (gr. k-7). 14.95 *(978-1-58726-304-0(1),* Mitten Pr.) Ann Arbor Editions LLC.

Weaver, Will. Clay. 2004. 232p. (YA). (gr. 8-12). 14.65 *(978-0-7569-4594-7(1))* Perfection Learning Corp.

—Saturday Night Dirt: A MOTOR Novel. 2009. (Motor Novels Ser.: 1). (ENG.). 192p. (YA). (gr. 7-12). pap. 14.99 *(978-0-312-56131-4(8),* 900058866) Square Fish.

Wedgeworth, Anthony G. Nums of Shoreview: Baka's Curse. 2009. (ENG.). 68p. pap. 9.97 *(978-0-578-04710-2(1))* Wedgeworth, Anthony G.

Westlund, Emmaline. Fatim. 2012. 42p. pap. 16.95 *(978-1-4626-9660-4(0))* America Star Bks.

Wilder, Laura Ingalls. On the Banks of Plum Creek: A Newbery Honor Award Winner. Williams, Garth, illus. 2008. (Little House Ser.: 4). (ENG.). 352p. (J). (gr. 3-7). pap. 9.99 *(978-0-06-440004-6(2),* HarperCollins) HarperCollins Pubs.

—On the Banks of Plum Creek: Full Color Edition: A Newbery Honor Award Winner. Williams, Garth, illus. 2004. (Little House Ser.: 4). (ENG.). 352p. (J). (gr. 3-7). pap. 9.99 *(978-0-06-058183-1(2),* HarperCollins) HarperCollins Pubs.

Williams, Heather. Farmer Boy Goes West. 2012. (Little House Sequel Ser.). (ENG.). 320p. (J). (gr. 3-7). 16.99 *(978-0-06-124251-9(9),* HarperCollins) HarperCollins Pubs.

Wood, Gail. Lizzie & the Big Lake Mystery. 2015. (Illus.). ix, 93p. (J). pap. *(978-1-57249-416-9(6),* White Mane Kids) White Mane Publishing Co., Inc.

—Lizzie, Light Feather & the Quarry Bluff Storm. 2015. (Illus.). viii, 88p. (J). pap. *(978-1-57249-415-2(8),* White Mane Kids) White Mane Publishing Co., Inc.

Zielin, Lara. Donut Days. 2010. (ENG.). 256p. (YA). (gr. 6-8). 22.44 *(978-0-399-25066-8(2))* Penguin Young Readers Group.

MINNESOTA—HISTORY

Anderson, Debby L. Minnesota for Mini-Sotans. 2004. (Illus.). spiral bd. 24.95 *(978-0-9759281-0-3(4))* Busy Bee Bks.

Carlson, Nancy & Wilbur, Helen L. T Is for Twin Cities: A Minneapolis/St. Paul Alphabet. Geister, David, illus. 2012. (City Alphabet Ser.). (ENG.). 32p. (J). (gr. 1-3). 16.95 *(978-1-58536-583-8(1),* 202325) Sleeping Bear Pr.

Coleman, Karlyn. Where Are All the Minnesotans? Hartman, Carrie, illus. 2017. (ENG.). 32p. (J). 16.95 *(978-1-68134-040-1(2))* Minnesota Historical Society Pr.

Coy, John. My Mighty Journey: A Waterfall's Story. Schanilec, Gaylord, illus. 2019. (ENG.). 40p. (J). 18.95 *(978-1-68134-008-1(9))* Minnesota Historical Society Pr.

Davis, W. Harry. Changemaker: W. Harry Davis. Sturdevant, Lori, ed. 2004. (Illus.). 136p. (J). pap. 17.95 *(978-1-890434-60-1(4))* Afton Historical Society Pr.

Dudley Gold, Susan. Protecting Hate Speech: R. A. V. V. St. Paul, 1 vol. 2014. (First Amendment Cases Ser.). (ENG.). 144p. (YA). (gr. 9-9). lib. bdg. 45.50 *(978-1-62712-393-8(8),* 474fb2d4-89d8-46b5-a5f2-895e36c29604) Cavendish Square Publishing LLC.

Eggerling, Kristin J. Breath of Wilderness: The Life of Sigurd Olson. 2014. (ENG., Illus.). 112p. (J). (gr. 4-7). pap. 12.95 *(978-1-938486-10-4(2))* Fulcrum Publishing.

Ellis, Paula. Minnesota Activity Book, 1 vol. Nitzsche, Shane, illus. 2013. (Color & Learn Ser.). (ENG.). 64p. (J). (gr. k-5). pap. 6.95 *(978-1-59193-377-9(3),* Adventure Pubns.) AdventureKEEN.

Freshman, Wendy & Jansson, Kristin. Making History: Have a Blast with 15 Crafts. 2014. (ENG., Illus.). 216p. (J). (gr. 2-6). pap. 17.95 *(978-0-87351-919-9(1))* Minnesota Historical Society Pr.

Gove-Berg, Christie. Minnesota Must-See for Families: An A-Z List. 2015. (ENG., Illus.). 64p. pap. 12.95 *(978-1-59193-525-4(3),* Adventure Pubns.) AdventureKEEN.

Graham, Joan Claire. Minnesota Memories 3. 2003. (Illus.). 192p. per. 13.95 *(978-0-9711971-2-1(1))* Megyeri, Graham Bks.

Graham, JoanClaire, compiled by. Minnesota Memories 4. 2004. 208p. per. 13.95 *(978-0-9711971-3-8(X))* Megyeri, Graham Bks.

Green, Sara. Target. 2015. (Brands We Know Ser.). (ENG., Illus.). 24p. (J). (gr. 3-8). lib. bdg. 27.95 *(978-1-62617-289-0(7),* Pilot Bks.) Bellwether Media.

Hamilton, John. Minnesota, 1 vol. 2016. (United States of America Ser.). (ENG., Illus.). 48p. (J). (gr. 5-9). 34.21 *(978-1-68078-325-4(4),* 21635, Abdo & Daughters) ABDO Publishing Co.

Harmon, Daniel E. Minnesota: Past & Present, 1 vol. 2010. (United States: Past & Present Ser.). (ENG., Illus.). 48p. (J). (gr. 5-5). pap. 12.75 *(978-1-4358-8498-4(1),* 84f19596-b359-4056-8300-3666ff0c4df9, Rosen Reference) Rosen Publishing Group, Inc., The.

Heinrichs, Ann. America the Beautiful: Minnesota (Revised Edition) 2014. (America the Beautiful, Third Ser. (Revised Edition) Ser.). (ENG.). 144p. (J). lib. bdg. 40.00 *(978-0-531-28281-6(3))* Scholastic Library Publishing.

—Minnesota. Kania, Matt, illus. 2017. (U. S. A. Travel Guides). (ENG.). 40p. (J). (gr. 2-5). lib. bdg. 38.50 *(978-1-5038-1963-4(9),* 211600) Child's World, Inc, The.

Jerome, Kate B. Lucky to Live in Minnesota. Radtke, Roger, illus. 2017. (Arcadia Kids Ser.). (ENG.). 32p. (J). 16.99 *(978-0-7385-2786-4(6))* Arcadia Publishing.

—The Wise Animal Handbook Minnesota. 2017. (Arcadia Kids Ser.). (ENG., Illus.). 32p. (J). 16.99 *(978-0-7385-2827-4(7))* Arcadia Publishing.

Kallas, Randi & Dougherty, Mike, eds. Rochester, Minnesota: A Visual & Historic Journey. 2003. (Illus.). 136p. pap. 24.95 *(978-0-9659875-3-0(1))* Riggott, Dean Photography.

Kenney, Dave. Northern Lights Revised Second Edition: The Stories of Minnesota's Past. 2nd rev. ed. 2013. (ENG.). 508p. (J). (gr. 5-6). 62.50 *(978-0-87351-885-7(3))* Minnesota Historical Society Pr.

Keranen, Rachel, et al. Minnesota: Land of 10,000 Lakes, 1 vol. 2018. (It's My State! (Fourth Edition)(r) Ser.). (ENG.). 80p. (gr. 4-4). 35.93 *(978-1-5026-2629-5(2),* 03879c1b-44c4-4e73-805d-84fdb4889a3a) Cavendish Square Publishing LLC.

Marling, Karal Ann. Minnesota Hail to Thee! A Sesquicentennial History. 2008. (Illus.). 163p. (J). (gr. 3-7). 28.00 *(978-1-890434-78-6(7))* Afton Historical Society Pr.

Marsh, Carole. Exploring Minnesota Through Project-Based Learning: Geography, History, Government, Economics & More. 2016. (Minnesota Experience Ser.). (ENG.). (J). pap. 9.99 *(978-0-635-12347-3(9))* Gallopade International.

—I'm Reading about Minnesota. 2014. (Minnesota Experience Ser.). (ENG., Illus.). (J). pap., pap. 8.99 *(978-0-635-11298-9(1))* Gallopade International.

—Minnesota History Projects: 30 Cool, Activities, Crafts, Experiments & More for Kids to Do to Learn about Your State! 2003. (Minnesota Experience Ser.). 32p. (gr. k-5). pap. 5.95 *(978-0-635-01792-5(X),* Marsh, Carole Bks.) Gallopade International.

McCabe, Matthew. It's Great to Be a Fan in Minnesota. 2018. (Sports Nation Ser.). (ENG., Illus.). 48p. (J). (gr. 5-6). pap. 11.95 *(978-1-64185-034-6(5),* 1641850345); lib. bdg. 34.21 *(978-1-63517-932-3(7),* 1635179327) North Star Editions. (Focus Readers).

McDowell, Pamela. Minnesota: The North Star State. 2012. (J). *(978-1-61913-365-5(2))*; pap. *(978-1-61913-366-2(0))* Weigl Pubs., Inc.

Mills, Jordan & Parker, Bridget. Minnesota. 2016. (States Ser.). (ENG., Illus.). 32p. (J). (gr. 3-6). lib. bdg. 27.99 *(978-1-5157-0410-2(6),* 132021, Capstone Pr.) Capstone.

Purslow, Neil. Minnesota: The North Star State. 2016. (J). *(978-1-4896-4884-6(4))* Weigl Pubs., Inc.

Root, Phyllis. The Lost Forest. Bowen, Betsy, illus. 2019. (ENG.). 40p. (J). 17.95 *(978-0-8166-9796-0(5))* Univ. of Minnesota Pr.

Rossi, Joe, photos by. Minnesota's Hidden Alphabet. 2010. (ENG., Illus.). 48p. (J). (gr. -1-1). 16.95 *(978-0-87351-808-6(X))* Minnesota Historical Society Pr.

Ruff, Carolyn. Keystones of the Stone Arch Bridge. 2014. (ENG., Illus.). 80p. (J). (gr. 2-3). pap. 9.95 *(978-0-87351-923-6(X))* Minnesota Historical Society Pr.

Schwabacher, Martin. Minnesota (a True Book: My United States) (Library Edition) 2018. (True Book (Relaunch) Ser.). (ENG., Illus.). 48p. (J). (gr. 3-5). lib. bdg. 31.00 *(978-0-531-23561-4(0),* Children's Pr.) Scholastic Library Publishing.

Targ Brill, Marlene & Kaplan, Elizabeth. Minnesota, 1 vol. (It's My State! (Second Edition)(r) Ser.). (ENG.). 80p. (gr. 4-4). 2nd rev. ed. 2011. lib. bdg. 34.07 *(978-1-60870-054-7(2),* 8ad030f8-87fd-42ed-9ab2-a05d8c3ecfe5) 3rd rev. ed. 2014. lib. bdg. 35.93 *(978-1-62712-748-6(8),* ae6f7eef-9590-4942-aea3-f9b1ea7e3809) Cavendish Square Publishing LLC.

Wargin, Kathy-jo. Little Minnesota. Urban, Helle, illus. 2011. (Little State Ser.). (ENG.). 20p. (J). (gr. -1-1). bds. 9.95 *(978-1-58536-174-8(7),* 202263) Sleeping Bear Pr.

Ziff, John. Western Great Lakes: Illinois, Minnesota, Wisconsin, Vol. 19. 2015. (Let's Explore the States Ser.). (Illus.). 64p. (J). (gr. 5). 23.95 *(978-1-4222-3338-2(3))* Mason Crest.

MINNESOTA TWINS (BASEBALL TEAM)

Epstein, Brad. Minnesota Twins 101: My First Team-Board-book. 2008. (Illus.). 22p. (J). pap. *(978-1-932530-97-1(5),* 101 Bk.) Michaelson Entertainment.

Frisch, Aaron. Minnesota Twins. 2009. (World Series Champions Ser.). (Illus.). 23p. (J). (gr. 2-3). 24.25 *(978-1-58341-695-2(1),* Creative Education) Creative Co., The.

Gilbert, Sara. Minnesota Twins. 2013. (World Series Champions Ser.). (ENG.). 24p. (J). (gr. 1-4). pap. 7.99 *(978-0-89812-818-5(8),* 21849, Creative Paperbacks); (Illus.). 25.65 *(978-1-60818-267-1(3),* 21848, Creative Education) Creative Co., The.

Kelley, K. C. Minnesota Twins. 2019. (Major League Baseball Teams Ser.). (ENG.). 32p. (J). (gr. 2-5). lib. bdg. 35.64 *(978-1-5038-2830-8(1),* 212637) Child's World, Inc, The.

LeBoutillier, Nate. The Story of the Minnesota Twins. 2011. (J). 35.65 *(978-1-60818-047-9(6),* Creative Education) Creative Co., The.

Leboutillier, Nate. The Story of the Minnesota Twins. 2007. (Baseball, the Great American Game Ser.). (Illus.). 48p. (YA). (gr. 4-7). lib. bdg. 32.80 *(978-1-58341-493-4(2))* Creative Co., The.

MacRae, Sloan. The Minnesota Twins. 24p. (J). 2012. 49.50 *(978-1-4488-5158-4(0))* 2011. (ENG.). (gr. 2-3). pap. 9.25 *(978-1-4488-5157-7(2),* 02374921-22f5-4493-b1e2-761fb633fb6d) 2011. (ENG.). (gr. 2-3). lib. bdg. 26.27 *(978-1-4488-5012-9(6),* 56ea13c4-fc20-4a8c-bd54-9979036fa8b0) Rosen Publishing Group, Inc., The. (PowerKids Pr.).

Stewart, Mark. The Minnesota Twins. 2012. (Team Spirit Ser.). 48p. (J). (gr. 3-6). lib. bdg. 29.27 *(978-1-59953-488-6(6))* Norwood Hse. Pr.

Wesley, Caroline. Minnesota Twins. 2018. (MLB's Greatest Teams Ser.). (ENG., Illus.). 32p. (J). (gr. 2-5). lib. bdg. 34.21 *(978-1-5321-1810-4(4),* 30666, Big Buddy Bks.) ABDO Publishing Co.

Zuehlke, Jeffrey. Joe Mauer. 2008. pap. 40.95 *(978-0-8225-9490-1(0))* Lerner Publishing Group.

—Joe Mauer, 2nd Edition. rev. ed. 2011. (ENG., Illus.). 32p. E-Book 25.26 *(978-0-7613-7204-2(0))* Lerner Publishing Group.

—Joe Mauer (Revised Edition) 2011. (Amazing Athletes Ser.). 32p. (J). pap. 45.32 *(978-0-7613-7653-8(4))* Lerner Publishing Group.

MINNESOTA VIKINGS (FOOTBALL TEAM)

Adamson, Thomas K. The Minnesota Vikings Story. 2016. (NFL Teams Ser.). (ENG., Illus.). 32p. (J). (gr. 3-7). lib. bdg. 26.95 *(978-1-62617-372-9(9),* Torque Bks.) Bellwether Media.

Burgess, Zack. Meet the Minnesota Vikings. 2016. (Big Picture Sports Ser.). (ENG., Illus.). 24p. (J). (gr. k-3). lib. bdg. 22.60 *(978-1-59953-752-8(4))* Norwood Hse. Pr.

Epstein, Brad M. Minnesota Vikings 101. 2010. (ENG., Illus.). 24p. (J). bds. *(978-1-60730-117-2(2),* 101 Bk.) Michaelson Entertainment.

Frisch, Aaron. Adrian Peterson. 2014. (Big Time Ser.). (ENG.). 24p. (J). (gr. 1-4). pap. 9.99 *(978-1-62832-060-2(5),* 21800, Creative Paperbacks) Creative Co., The.

—The History of the Minnesota Vikings. 2004. (NFL Today Ser.). (Illus.). 32p. (YA). (gr. 5-9). 18.95 *(978-1-58341-303-6(0))* Creative Co., The.

Gilbert, Sara. The Story of the Minnesota Vikings. 2013. (Illus.). 48p. (J). 35.65 *(978-1-60818-309-8(2),* Creative Education) Creative Co., The.

Grabowski, John F. The Minnesota Vikings. 2003. (Great Sports Teams in History Ser.). (ENG., Illus.). 112p. (J). 30.85 *(978-1-56006-943-0(0),* Lucent Bks.) Cengage Gale.

LeBoutillier, Nate. The Story of the Minnesota Vikings. 2009. (NFL Today Ser.). 48p. (YA). (gr. 5-9). 22.95 *(978-1-58341-762-1(1))* Creative Co., The.

MacRae, Sloan. The Minnesota Vikings, 1 vol. 2011. (America's Greatest Teams Ser.). (ENG., Illus.). 24p. (J). (gr. 2-3). pap. 9.25 *(978-1-4488-3174-6(1),* a8f766db-a11f-4fdb-80e6-1c272c820f03); lib. bdg. 26.27 *(978-1-4488-3168-5(7),* 72f13e10-315c-4fdc-8f1d-31d2b8dae401) Rosen Publishing Group, Inc., The. (PowerKids Pr.).

Sandler, Michael. Adrian Peterson. 2010. (Football Heroes Making a Difference Ser.). (Illus.). 24p. (YA). (gr. 2-5). lib. bdg. 26.99 *(978-1-936087-59-4(6))* Bearport Publishing Co., Inc.

Scarpati, Kevin. Minnesota Vikings. 2014. (Inside the NFL Ser.). (ENG., Illus.). 32p. (J). (gr. 4-7). lib. bdg. 28.55 *(978-1-4896-0850-5(8),* AV2 by Weigl) Weigl Pubs., Inc.

Stewart, Mark. The Minnesota Vikings. rev. ed. 2012. (Team Spirit Ser.). (ENG.). 48p. (J). (gr. 3-6). lib. bdg. 29.27 *(978-1-59953-529-6(7))* Norwood Hse. Pr.

Storm, Marysa. Highlights of the Minnesota Vikings. 2019. (Team Stats — Football Edition Ser.). (ENG., Illus.). 32p. (J). (gr. 4-6). pap. 9.99 *(978-1-64466-085-0(7),* 12829, Bolt) Black Rabbit Bks.

Whiting, Jim. Minnesota Vikings. rev. ed. 2019. (NFL Today Ser.). (ENG.). 48p. (J). (gr. 4-7). pap. 12.00 *(978-1-62832-712-0(X),* 19055, Creative Paperbacks) Creative Co., The.

—The Story of the Minnesota Vikings. 2019. (NFL Today Ser.). (ENG.). 48p. (J). (gr. 3-6). *(978-1-64026-149-5(4),* 19057, Creative Education) Creative Co., The.

Wyner, Zach. Minnesota Vikings. 2015. (Illus.). 32p. pap. *(978-1-4896-0851-2(6))* Weigl Pubs., Inc.

Zappa, Marcia. Minnesota Vikings, 1 vol. 2015. (NFL's Greatest Teams Ser.). (ENG.). 32p. (J). (gr. 2-5). 34.21 *(978-1-62403-587-6(6),* 17201, Big Buddy Bks.) ABDO Publishing Co.

MINORITIES

see also Assimilation (Sociology); Discrimination; Race Relations

African American Eras. 2010. *(978-1-4144-3600-5(9)); (978-1-4144-3599-2(1)); (978-1-4144-3598-5(3)); (978-1-4144-3597-8(5))* Cengage Gale. (UXL).

Anderson, Sonya, et al, eds. Facing Racism in Education. 3rd ed. 2004. (HER Reprint Ser.: No. 39). (ENG., Illus.). 324p. pap. 28.00 *(978-0-916690-42-7(3),* P185264, Harvard Educational Review Reprint Series) Harvard Education Publishing Group (HEPG).

Bauchner, Elizabeth. Teen Minorities in Rural North America: Growing up Different. 2009. (Youth in Rural North America Ser.). (Illus.). 96p. (YA). (gr. 3-7). lib. bdg. 22.95 *(978-1-4222-0014-8(0))* Mason Crest.

Berlatsky, Noah, ed. Interracial America, 1 vol. 2011. (Opposing Viewpoints Ser.). (ENG., Illus.). 224p. (gr. 10-12). pap. 34.80 *(978-0-7377-5728-6(0),* c2cc9548-14f2-49f8-9a00-0f12bd54c9fb, Greenhaven Publishing) Greenhaven Publishing LLC.

Brezina, Corona. Standing up to Bullying at School, 1 vol. 2017. (LGBTQ+ Guide to Beating Bullying Ser.). (ENG., Illus.). 64p. (J). (gr. 6-6). pap. 13.95 *(978-1-5081-7429-5(6),* e46c582d-4b7d-4c7c-8ccd-ed2e53367afb, Rosen Young Adult) Rosen Publishing Group, Inc., The.

Burgan, Michael. The Voting Rights Act Of 1965: An Interactive History Adventure. 2015. (You Choose: History Ser.). (ENG., Illus.). 112p. (J). (gr. 3-7). pap. 6.95 *(978-1-4914-1805-5(2),* 127252, Capstone Pr.) Capstone.

Cronn-Mills, Kirstin. Transgender Lives: Complex Stories, Complex Voices. 2014. (ENG., Illus.). 88p. (YA). (gr. 6-12). lib. bdg. 34.65 *(978-0-7613-9022-0(7),* 04314bff-0e7e-42f6-96a2-88e66b806d3f, Twenty-First Century Bks.) Lerner Publishing Group.

Currie-McGhee, Leanne. LGBT Families. 2018. (Changing Families Ser.). (ENG.). 64p. (J). (gr. 6-12). 39.93 *(978-1-68282-359-0(8))* ReferencePoint Pr., Inc.

Descola, Philippe. Diversité des Natures, Diversité des Cultures. 2010. (FRE.). 84p. *(978-2-227-48207-4(9))* Bayard Editions.

Dorr, Christina & Deskins, Liz. LGBTQAI+ Books for Children & Teens: Providing a Window for All. 2018. (ENG., Illus.). 168p. pap. 45.00 *(978-0-8389-1649-0(X))* American Library Assn.

Gayle-Evans, Guda. An Annotated Bibliography of Multi-Cultural Literature for Children Three to Ten Years. 2004. (Mellen Studies in Children's Literature: Vol. 6). (Illus.). 204p. 109.95 *(978-0-7734-6474-2(3))* Mellen, Edwin Pr., The.

Grinapal, Corinne. Racial Profiling & Discrimination: Your Legal Rights, 1 vol. 2015. (Know Your Rights Ser.). (ENG., Illus.). 64p. (J). (gr. 7-7). pap. 13.95 *(978-1-4777-8619-2(8),* 0127463f-6ab4-425f-8f00-e2b733732cd2, Rosen Young Adult) Rosen Publishing Group, Inc., The.

Grinapol, Corinne. Racial Profiling & Discrimination: Your Legal Rights, 1 vol. 2015. (Know Your Rights Ser.). (ENG., Illus.). 64p. (J). (gr. 7-7). 36.47 *(978-1-4777-8020-6(3),* 5ceacb72-a9ca-4d3b-a623-3cccceb4ac46, Rosen Young Adult) Rosen Publishing Group, Inc., The.

Hansen-Krening, Nancy, et al, eds. Kaleidoscope: A Multicultural Booklist for Grades K-8. 4th ed. 2003. (NCTE Bibliography Ser.). (Illus.). 118p. (J). pap. 30.95 *(978-0-8141-2539-7(5),* 25395) National Council of Teachers of English.

Hearn, Emily. Our New Home: Immigrant Children Speak, 1 vol. Milne, Marywinn, ed. 2007. (ENG., Illus.). 130p. (J). (gr. 4-8). pap. 13.95 *(978-1-897187-32-6(7))* Second Story Pr. CAN. Dist: Orca Bk. Pubs. USA.

Heredia, David. Little Heroes of Color: 50 Who Made a BIG Difference. Heredia, David, illus. 2019. (ENG., Illus.). 24p. (J). (gr. -1 — 1). bds. 10.99 *(978-1-338-32642-0(2),* Scholastic Pr.) Scholastic, Inc.

Hernandez, Daniel. They Call Me a Hero: A Memoir of My Youth. 2013. (ENG., Illus.). 240p. (YA). (gr. 7). 17.99 *(978-1-4424-6228-1(0),* Simon & Schuster Bks. For Young Readers) Simon & Schuster Bks. For Young Readers.

Hiber, Amanda, ed. Is the United States Ready for a Minority President?, 1 vol. 2007. (At Issue Ser.). (ENG., Illus.). 112p. (gr. 10-12). 41.03 *(978-0-7377-3878-0(2),* 33436de7-e1be-4d9e-a059-2a6fc759e904); pap. 28.80 *(978-0-7377-3879-7(0),* 7fec2bde-69d8-47e6-af30-2de2909c8f3d) Greenhaven Publishing LLC. (Greenhaven Publishing).

Higgins, Melissa. We All Come from Different Cultures, 1 vol. 2012. (Celebrating Differences Ser.). (ENG.). 24p. (J). (gr. -1-2). pap. 7.29 *(978-1-4296-7887-2(9),* 118219); (gr. k-1). pap. 41.70 *(978-1-4296-8320-3(1),* Capstone Pr.) Capstone.

Hirschmann, Kris. Understanding Sexual Identity & Orientation. 2017. (Understanding Psychology Ser.). (ENG.). 80p. (YA). (gr. 5-12). *(978-1-68282-281-4(8))* ReferencePoint Pr., Inc.

Holt, David H. Religious, Cultural, & Minority Rights, Vol. 8. Lansford, Tom, ed. 2016. (Foundations of Democracy Ser.). (Illus.). 64p. (J). (gr. 7). 23.95 *(978-1-4222-3632-1(3))* Mason Crest.

Howse, Jennifer. Reconstruction. 2013. (Illus.). 48p. (J). *(978-1-62127-194-9(3))*; pap. *(978-1-62127-200-7(1))* Weigl Pubs., Inc.

Hudson, Wade & Hudson, Cheryl Willis, eds. The Talk: Conversations about Race, Love & Truth. (Illus.). 160p. (J). (gr. 5). 2021. 7.99 *(978-0-593-12164-1(3),* Yearling) 2020. 16.99 *(978-0-593-12161-0(9),* Crown Books For Young Readers) 2020. (ENG., lib. bdg. 19.99 *(978-0-593-12162-7(7),* Crown Books For Young Readers) Random Hse. Children's Bks.

Hunter, Miranda. Story of Latino Civil Rights: Fighting for Justice. 2007. (Hispanic Heritage Ser.). (Illus.). 112p. (YA). lib. bdg. 22.95 *(978-1-59084-934-7(5))* Mason Crest.

Hurt, Avery Elizabeth. Confronting LGBTQ+ Discrimination, 1 vol. 2017. (Speak up! Confronting Discrimination in Your Daily Life Ser.). (ENG., Illus.). 64p. (J). (gr. 7-7). pap. 13.95 *(978-1-5383-8172-4(9),* a76e9c71-9670-4aff-82a8-1ebb3a1c6e38) Rosen Publishing Group, Inc., The.

Hyde, Natalie. LGBTQ Rights. 2017. (Uncovering the Past: Analyzing Primary Sources Ser.). (Illus.). 48p. (J). (gr. 5-6). *(978-0-7787-3942-5(2))* Crabtree Publishing Co.

Jones, Patrick. Teen Incarceration: From Cell Bars to Ankle Bracelets. 2016. (ENG., Illus.). 120p. (YA). (gr. 6-12). lib. bdg. 37.32 *(978-1-4677-7572-4(X),* 58d0d81c-d5b0-474f-ad5f-8de2d5a24ba5, Twenty-First Century Bks.) Lerner Publishing Group.

—Teen Incarceration: From Cell Bars to Ankle Bracelets. 2016. (ENG., Illus.). 120p. (YA). (gr. 6-12). E-Book 55.99 *(978-1-5124-1138-6(8),* Twenty-First Century Bks.) Lerner Publishing Group.

Karson, Damon. Human Rights in Focus: The LGBT Community. 2017. (Human Rights in Focus Ser.). (ENG.). 80p. (YA). (gr. 5-12). *(978-1-68282-231-9(1))* ReferencePoint Pr., Inc.

Kootz, Russell & Seidman, David. Understanding Civil Rights, 1 vol. 2011. (Personal Freedom & Civic Duty Ser.). (ENG., Illus.). 184p. (J). (gr. 7-7). lib. bdg. 39.80 *(978-1-4488-4666-5(8),* 0c23dd49-f0eb-426b-9653-1b11e9e21b83) Rosen Publishing Group, Inc., The.

Kortemeier, Todd. Unsung Heroes of Social Justice. 2017. (Unsung Heroes Ser.). (ENG., Illus.). 32p. (J). (gr. 3-6). 32.80 *(978-1-63235-310-8(5),* 11830, 12-Story Library) Bookstaves, LLC.

Lombardo, Jennifer. Inside the LGBTQ+ Movement, 1 vol. 2017. (Eyewitness to History Ser.). (ENG.). 32p. (J). (gr. 4-5). lib. bdg. 29.27 *(978-1-5382-1167-0(X),* ad325068-2eba-40b6-bbd6-147628979cda) Stevens, Gareth Publishing LLLP.

Marcovitz, Hal. Race Relations. 2008. (Gallup Major Trends & Events Ser.). (Illus.). 127p. (YA). (gr. 7-18). lib. bdg. 22.95 *(978-1-59084-968-2(X))* Mason Crest.

Nagle, Jeanne. Are You LGBTQ?, 1 vol. 2015. (Got Issues? Ser.). (ENG.). 112p. (gr. 7-8). lib. bdg. 38.93 *(978-0-7660-7139-1(1),* d3d9468d-31e4-4f71-bfbf-548074243dee) Enslow Publishing, LLC.

Naidoo, Jamie Campbell. Rainbow Family Collections: Selecting & Using Children's Books with Lesbian, Gay, Bisexual, Transgender, & Queer Content, 1 vol. 2012. (Children's & Young Adult Literature Reference Ser.). (ENG., Illus.). 280p. 70.00 *(978-1-59884-960-8(3),* 800429, Libraries Unlimited) Bloomsbury Publishing USA.

Perrin, Pat. Getting Started-America's Melting Pot. 2004. (Illus.). (J). *(978-1-932663-04-4(5))* History Compass, LLC.

—Getting Started-Our 50 United States. 2004. (Illus.). (J). *(978-1-932663-03-7(7))* History Compass, LLC.

—Getting Started-Our Government. 2004. (Illus.). (J). *(978-1-932663-02-0(9))* History Compass, LLC.

Prager, Sarah. Queer, There, & Everywhere: 23 People Who Changed the World. O'Ferrall, Zoe More, illus. (ENG.). 272p. (YA). (gr. 8). 2018. pap. 10.99 *(978-0-06-247432-2(4))* 2017. 17.99 *(978-0-06-247431-5(6))* HarperCollins Pubs. (HarperCollins).

Remarkable LGBTQ Lives, 12 vols. 2014. (Remarkable LGBTQ Lives Ser.). (ENG.). 112p. (YA). (gr. 7-7). lib. bdg. 232.80 *(978-1-4777-7903-3(5),* 3dce7864-b47f-435a-bb36-e57e4ba2f598, Rosen Young Adult) Rosen Publishing Group, Inc., The.

Robins, Maureen Picard. One Land, Many Cultures. 2012. (Little World Social Studies). (ENG.). 24p. (gr. k-2). pap. 9.95 *(978-1-61810-276-8(1),* 9781618102768) Rourke Educational Media.

Santos, Rita. Beyond Gender Binaries: The History of Trans, Intersex, & Third-Gender Individuals, 1 vol. 2018. (History of the LGBTQ+ Rights Movement Ser.). (ENG., Illus.). 112p. (J). (gr. 7-7). 38.80 *(978-1-5383-8126-7(5),* 809c132f-2735-4900-a71f-3cdab587b924) Rosen Publishing Group, Inc., The.

Seba, Jaime. Gay People of Color: Facing Prejudices, Forging Identities. 2009. (Gallup's Guide to Modern Gay, Lesbian, & Transgender Lifestyle Ser.). 64p. (YA). (gr. 7-18). pap. 9.95 *(978-1-4222-1877-8(5))*; (Illus.). lib. bdg. 22.95 *(978-1-4222-1748-1(5))* Mason Crest.

Smith, Devlin. The Fight for LGBTQ+ Rights, 1 vol. 2019. (Activism in Action: a History Ser.). (ENG.). 112p. (gr. 8-8). pap. 18.65 *(978-1-5081-8546-8(8),* ccd5fdd8-2e82-4e91-b30a-2f55e3cf4405) Rosen Publishing Group, Inc., The.

Steele, Philip. Race & Crime. 2016. (Behind the News Ser.). (Illus.). 48p. (J). (gr. 6-9). *(978-0-7787-2588-6(X))* Crabtree Publishing Co.

Takaki, Ronald. A Different Mirror for Young People: A History of Multicultural America. 2012. (For Young People Ser.). (Illus.). 384p. (J). (gr. 5). pap. 22.95 *(978-1-60980-416-9(3),* Triangle Square) Seven Stories Pr.

Thomas, Zachary & Wilson, Natashya. The Melting Pot: The People & Cultures of New York. (Illus.). 24p. (J). 2012. 60.00 *(978-1-4488-5768-5(6))* 2011. (ENG., (gr. 3-4). lib. bdg. 26.27 *(978-1-4488-5747-0(3),* 25a1b07b-b474-4a01-aca9-a0a7371381f7) Rosen Publishing Group, Inc., The. (PowerKids Pr.).

Thomas, Zachary, et al. The Melting Pot: The People & Cultures of New York, 1 vol. 2011. (Spotlight on New York Ser.). (ENG., Illus.). 24p. (J). (gr. 3-4). pap. 10.00 *(978-1-4488-5767-8(8),* 49e46d01-80be-4899-a626-e696ca9d48be, PowerKids Pr.) Rosen Publishing Group, Inc., The.

Turner, Joshua. What Are Minority Rights?, 1 vol. 2019. (Principles of Democracy Ser.). (ENG.). 24p. (gr. 3-3). pap. 9.25 *(978-1-5383-4260-2(X),* f3497dcb-5ace-4ffb-aff1-48c225256813, PowerKids Pr.) Rosen Publishing Group, Inc., The.

Wiener, Gary, ed. Microaggressions, Safe Spaces, & Trigger Warnings, 1 vol. 2017. (Current Controversies Ser.). (ENG.). 168p. (YA). (gr. 10-12). 48.03 *(978-1-5345-0236-9(X),* 58fbb69e-9b02-41c5-ad43-4123654231f5) Greenhaven Publishing LLC.

Wright, John D. Race & Crime. 2004. (Crime & Detection Ser.). (Illus.). 96p. (YA). (gr. 7-18). lib. bdg. 22.95 *(978-1-59084-378-9(9))* Mason Crest.

—Race & Crime, Vol. 20. Gomez, Manny, ed. 2016. (Crime & Detection Ser.). (Illus.). 96p. (J). (gr. 7). 24.95 *(978-1-4222-3485-3(1))* Mason Crest.

MINTS

Morrison, Taylor. The Buffalo Nickel. Morrison, Taylor, illus. 2006. (Illus.). 32p. (J). (gr. 4-8). reprint ed. 16.00 *(978-1-4223-5858-0(5))* DIANE Publishing Co.

Vox, Everett. The U. S. Mint: The History of U. S. Money, 1 vol. 2017. (Landmarks of Democracy: American Institutions Ser.). (ENG.). 24p. (J). (gr. 3-3). pap. 9.25 *(978-1-5081-6101-1(1),* 966702f8-0bbd-466e-8e44-d334201245a1, PowerKids Pr.) Rosen Publishing Group, Inc., The.

MIRACLE PLAYS

see Bible Plays

MIRRORS

Edom, H. Science Activities, Vol. 1. 2010. (Science Activities Ser.). 72p. (J). 13.99 *(978-0-7945-2752-5(3),* Usborne) EDC Publishing.

Holden, Pam. Look in the Mirror, 1 vol. 2015. (ENG., Illus.). 16p. (-1). pap. *(978-1-77654-082-2(4),* Red Rocket Readers) Flying Start Bks.

Strom, Laura Layton. Mirror Power. 2007. (Shockwave: Technology & Manufacturing Ser.). (ENG., Illus.). 36p. (J). (gr. 3-5). 25.00 *(978-0-531-17588-0(X),* Children's Pr.) Scholastic Library Publishing.

MISDEMEANORS

see Crime

MISS SPIDER (FICTITIOUS CHARACTER)—FICTION

Kirk, David. Little Miss Spider. 2018. (ENG., Illus.). 32p. (J). (gr. -1-k). 14.95 *(978-0-935112-14-6(6))* Callaway Editions, Inc.

—Miss Spider's Tea Party. 2018. (ENG., Illus.). 32p. (J). (gr. -1-3). 19.95 *(978-0-935112-13-9(8))* Callaway Editions, Inc.

—Miss Spider's Tea Party. unabr. ed. 2008. (Scholastic Bookshelf Ser.). (ENG., Illus.). (J). (gr. -1-3). 18.95 *(978-0-545-02979-7(1))* Scholastic, Inc.

Kirk, David & Scholastic / LeapFrog. Miss Spider's Tea Party. 2008. (J). 13.99 *(978-1-59319-934-0(1))* LeapFrog Enterprises, Inc.

MISSILES, GUIDED

see Guided Missiles

MISSING PERSONS

Herbst, Judith. Vanished. 2004. (Unexplained Ser.). (Illus.). 48p. (J). pap. 8.95 *(978-0-8225-2404-5(X),* Lerner Pubns.); (ENG., (gr. 5-12). lib. bdg. 26.60 *(978-0-8225-1631-6(4))* Lerner Publishing Group.

McCarthy, Tom. Weird Disappearances: Real Tales of Missing People. 2017. (Mystery & Mayhem Ser.). (ENG., Illus.). 128p. (J). (gr. 4-7). 19.95 *(978-1-61930-526-7(7),* 15fb5cff-6f0d-4ad5-8e92-f1f81e58621d) Nomad Pr.

Rollason, Jane. Killer Bees Level 2 Elementary/Lower-intermediate American English. 2010. (Cambridge Experience Readers Ser.). (ENG., Illus.). 64p. pap. 14.75 *(978-0-521-14896-2(0))* Cambridge Univ. Pr.

Stewart, Gail B. Missing Persons, 1 vol. 2011. (Crime Scene Investigations Ser.). (ENG.). 96p. (gr. 7-7). lib. bdg. 42.03 *(978-1-4205-0534-4(3),* 7c5d8685-46bf-4c2b-81f0-e1fb4a9ba04c, Lucent Pr.) Greenhaven Publishing LLC.

Townsend, John. Gone Missing. 2009. (Amazing Mysteries Ser.). (ENG.). 32p. (J). (gr. 3-6). 28.50 *(978-1-59920-364-5(2),* 19253); (Illus.). pap. *(978-1-897563-96-0(5),* 23876) Black Rabbit Bks. (Smart Apple Media).

Troupe, Thomas Kingsley. Extreme Stories about Disappearances. 2018. (That's Just Spooky! Ser.). (ENG., Illus.). 24p. (J). (gr. 4-6). lib. bdg. 28.50 *(978-1-68072-637-4(4),* 12574, Hi Jinx) Black Rabbit Bks.

MISSING PERSONS—FICTION

Abbott, Tony. The Battle Begins. 2012. (Underworlds Ser.: 1). lib. bdg. 14.75 *(978-0-606-23928-8(6))* Turtleback.

Acton, Vanessa. Tracks. 2018. (Mason Falls Mysteries Ser.). (ENG.). 104p. (YA). (gr. 6-12). pap. 7.99

MNO

(978-1-5415-0121-8(7), 013e8880-d624-43f4-9f49-8dbf6563ea4a); lib. bdg. 25.32 (978-1-5415-0112-6(8), e7831c22-3231-4acf-adf6-c7fd5c57a480) Lerner Publishing Group. (Darby Creek).

Adam, Paul. Escape from Shadow Island. (ENG.). 304p. (J). (gr. 5). 2011. (Max Cassidy Ser.: Bk. 1). pap. 5.99 (978-0-06-186325-7(4)) 2010. 16.99 (978-0-06-186323-3(8)) HarperCollins Pubs. (Waldon Pond Pr.).

Adler, David A. Bones & the Football Mystery. 2013. (Bones Ser.: 9). (ENG.). 32p. (J). (gr. 1-3). pap. 4.99 (978-0-448-47942-2(7), Penguin Young Readers) Penguin Young Readers Group.

—Cam Jansen & the Spaghetti Max Mystery. Allen, Joy, illus. 2014. (Cam Jansen Ser.: 33). (ENG.). 64p. (J). (gr. 2-5). pap. 4.99 (978-0-14-751232-1(8), Puffin Books) Penguin Young Readers Group.

—Young Cam Jansen & the Circus Mystery. Natti, Susanna, illus. 2013. (Young Cam Jansen Ser.: 17). (ENG.). 32p. (J). (gr. 1-3). pap. 4.99 (978-0-448-46614-9(7), Penguin Young Readers) Penguin Young Readers Group.

—Young Cam Jansen & the Magic Bird Mystery. Natti, Susanna, illus. 2013. (Young Cam Jansen Ser.: 18). (ENG.). 32p. (J). (gr. 1-3). pap. 4.99 (978-0-448-46613-2(9), Penguin Young Readers) Penguin Young Readers Group.

Aiken, Joan. Black Hearts in Battersea, No. 2. 2004. (Illus.). 256p. (J). pap. 10.95 (978-0-09-945639-1(7), Red Fox) Random House Children's Books GBR. Dist: Random Hse. of Canada.

Alexander, K. R. The Collector. 2019. (Penworthy Picks YA Fiction Ser.). (ENG.). 217p. (J). (gr. 4-5). 17.59 (978-0-87617-662-7(7)) Penworthy Co., LLC, The.

—The Collector. 2018. (ENG.). 224p. (J). (gr. 4-7). pap. 7.99 (978-1-338-21224-2(9), Scholastic Pr.) Scholastic, Inc.

Alexander, William. Goblin Secrets. (ENG., Illus.). (J). (gr. 3-7). 2013. 256p. pap. 7.99 (978-1-4424-2727-3(2)) 2012. 240p. 19.99 (978-1-4424-2726-6(4)) McElderry, Margaret K. Bks. (McElderry, Margaret K. Bks.).

Alphin, Elaine Marie. Picture Perfect. 2003. (ENG., Illus.). 256p. (YA). (gr. 5-12). 15.95 (978-0-8225-0535-8(5), c127bed3-b5f7-4f26-be27-1bd20d565a98, Carolrhoda Bks.) Lerner Publishing Group.

Alpine, Rachele. A Void the Size of the World. 2017. (ENG., Illus.). 368p. (YA). (gr. 9). 17.99 (978-1-4814-8571-5(7), Simon Pulse) Simon Pulse.

Alston, B. B. Amari & the Great Game. (Supernatural Investigations Ser.). (ENG.). 432p. 2023. (gr. 4-7). 28.69 **(978-1-5364-8191-4(2))** 2023. (J). (gr. 3-7). pap. 10.99 **(978-0-06-297520-1(X))** 2022. (Illus.). (J). (gr. 3-7). 18.99 (978-0-06-297519-5(6)) HarperCollins Pubs. (Balzer & Bray).

—Amari & the Night Brothers. (Supernatural Investigations Ser.: 1). (ENG.). 2022. 432p. (J). (gr. 3-7). pap. 11.99 (978-0-06-297517-1(X)) 2021. (Illus.). 416p. (J). (gr. 3-7). 17.99 (978-0-06-297516-4(1))1. 2022. 432p. (gr. 4-7). 29.94 (978-1-5364-7242-4(5)) HarperCollins Pubs. (Balzer & Bray).

Alston, B. B. Amari y Los Hermanos de la Noche / Amari & the Night Brothers. 2023. (Amari Ser.). (SPA.). 448p. (J). (gr. 4-7). pap. 14.95 **(978-1-64473-875-7(9))** Penguin Random House Grupo Editorial ESP. Dist: Penguin Random Hse. LLC.

Altebrando, Tara. The Leaving. 2016. (ENG.). 432p. (YA). 18.99 (978-1-61963-803-7(7), 900149146, Bloomsbury USA Childrens) Bloomsbury Publishing USA.

Anastasiu, Heather & Brown, Anne Greenwood. Girl Last Seen. 2016. (ENG.). 272p. (YA). (gr. 8-12). 16.99 (978-0-8075-8140-7(2), 807581402); pap. 9.99 (978-0-8075-8141-4(0), 807581410) Whitman, Albert & Co.

Anderson, E. V. The Many Lives of Lilith Lane, 0 vols. unabr. ed. 2012. (ENG.). 162p. (J). (gr. 7-12). pap. 14.95 (978-1-61109-792-4(4), 9781611097924, Skyscape) Amazon Publishing.

Ansari, Rebecca K. S. The Missing Piece of Charlie O'Reilly. (ENG.). (J). (gr. 3-7). 2020. 416p. pap. 9.99 (978-0-06-267967-3(8)) 2019. 400p. 16.99 (978-0-06-267966-6(X)) HarperCollins Pubs. (Waldon Pond Pr.).

Arsenault, Emily. The Leaf Reader. 2018. 256p. (YA). (gr. 9). pap. 10.99 (978-1-61695-907-4(X), Soho Teen) Soho Pr., Inc.

Ashley, Bernard. A Present for Paul. Mitchell, David, illus. 2004. 28p. (J). (978-1-85269-360-2(6)); (978-1-85269-359-6(2)) Mantra Lingua.

Atlas, Lilly. Journey to the Deep Woods. 2008. 36p. pap. 16.99 (978-1-4389-2596-7(4)) AuthorHouse.

Austin, Jamie Lea-Elizabeth. Reverie. 2012. 312p. 29.95 (978-1-4626-6734-5(1)) PublishAmerica, Inc.

Bachmann, Stefan. The Whatnot. 2014. (Peculiar Ser.: 2). (ENG.). 432p. (J). (gr. 3-7). pap. 8.99 (978-0-06-219522-7(0), Greenwillow Bks.) HarperCollins Pubs.

Bacon, C. G. Mean Mandy. 2009. 103p. pap. 11.00 (978-0-557-05740-5(X)) Lulu Pr., Inc.

Baggott, Julianna. The Ever Breath. 2011. (ENG.). 240p. (J). (gr. 4-6). lib. bdg. 21.19 (978-0-385-90676-0(5), Delacorte Pr.) Random Hse. Children's Bks.

Baguley, Elizabeth. Just Like Brothers. Blanz, Aurélie, illus. 2018. (ENG.). 32p. (J). (gr. -1-2). 16.99 (978-1-78285-345-9(6)) Barefoot Bks., Inc.

Bailey, Margaret A. Dragonworld & the Room of Strange Hangings. 2009. 172p. pap. 11.99 (978-1-4389-8252-6(6)) AuthorHouse.

Ballantyne, R. M. Silver Lake. 2004. reprint ed. pap. 19.95 (978-1-4191-4729-6(3)); pap. 1.99 (978-1-4192-4729-3(8)) Kessinger Publishing, LLC.

Balliett, Blue. The Calder Game. Helquist, Brett, illus. 2010. (ENG.). 416p. (J). (gr. 4-7). 7.99 (978-0-439-85208-1(0), Scholastic Paperbacks) Scholastic, Inc.

—Hold Fast. 2015. (ENG.). 288p. (J). (gr. 3-7). pap. 8.99 (978-0-545-29989-3(6), Scholastic Paperbacks) Scholastic, Inc.

Balmer, Fred. Festus & the Stranger. Miller, Callie, ed. Newcomb, Kristene, illus. 2007. 30p. (J). per. 7.00 (978-0-9760790-4-0(6)) Folsom Fallies Pr.

Banim, Lisa. Case of the Missing She-Geek. 2004. 125p. (J). lib. bdg. 16.92 (978-1-4242-0683-4(9)) Fitzgerald Bks.

Baptiste, Tracey. Rise of the Jumbies. 2017. (Jumbies Ser.). (ENG.). 272p. (J). (gr. 3-7). 17.99 (978-1-61620-665-9(9), 73665) Algonquin Young Readers.

Barker, Michelle. The House of One Thousand Eyes. 2018. (ENG., Illus.). 354p. (YA). (gr. 9). 18.95 (978-1-77321-071-1(8)) Annick Pr., Ltd. CAN. Dist: Publishers Group West (PGW).

Barnhill, Kelly. The Ogress & the Orphans. (ENG.). 2023. 416p. (gr. 6-8). 28.69 **(978-1-5364-8190-7(4))** 2022. 400p. (J). (gr. 5-13). 19.95 (978-1-64375-074-3(7), 74074) Algonquin Young Readers.

—The Ogress & the Orphans. Lt. ed. 2022. (ENG.). lib. bdg. 22.99 Cengage Gale.

Barrett, Tracy. The Missing Heir. 2012. (Sherlock Files Ser.: 4). (J). lib. bdg. 19.65 (978-0-606-26131-9(1)) Turtleback.

Bashe, Kayla. Kitty Cadawell & the Shadowslayers of Fym. 2008. (ENG.). 290p. pap. 16.50 (978-0-557-01916-8(8)) Lulu Pr., Inc.

Baum, L. Frank. L Frank Baum's Book of Santa Claus. 2007. 84p. per. 7.99 (978-1-60459-118-7(6)) Wilder Pubns., Corp.

Baumgartner, John Robert. Like Losing Your Left Hand. 2011. 244p. pap. 24.95 (978-1-4560-4043-7(X)) America Star Bks.

Beaudoin, Sean. Fade to Blue. 2011. (ENG., Illus.). 208p. (YA). (gr. 6-8). 24.94 (978-0-316-01417-5(5)) Little Brown & Co.

Beaumier, Randy P. Snapshot Billy: I Remember. 2012. 36p. pap. 24.95 (978-1-4626-1787-6(5)) America Star Bks.

Beckham, David. Charlie Barker & the Secret of the Deep Dark Woods. 2006. 570p. pap. 33.20 (978-1-4120-9264-7(7)) Trafford Publishing.

Behrens, Kathryn J. Breakdown. 2016. (Atlas of Cursed Places Ser.). (ENG.). 96p. (YA). (gr. 6-12). lib. bdg. 26.65 (978-1-5124-1323-6(2), db301279-6588-4513-88e6-fa63ae4be1cc, Darby Creek) Lerner Publishing Group.

Bennett, Jenn. The Lady Rogue. 2019. (ENG., Illus.). 384p. (YA). (gr. 9). 18.99 (978-1-5344-3199-7(3), Simon Pulse) Simon Pulse.

Berenstain, Jan & Berenstain, Mike. The Berenstain Bears & the Little Lost Cub, 1 vol. 2011. (I Can Read! / Berenstain Bears / Good Deed Scouts / Living Lights: a Faith Story Ser.). (ENG.). 32p. (J). pap. 4.99 (978-0-310-72100-0(8)) Zonderkidz.

Berube, Amelinda. Here There Are Monsters. 2019. (ENG., Illus.). 352p. (YA). (gr. 8-12). pap. 10.99 (978-1-4926-7101-5(0)) Sourcebooks, Inc.

Bessen, Luc. Arthur & the Minimoys. Sowchek, Ellen, tr. from FRE. 2005. (ENG.). 240p. (J). 15.99 (978-0-06-059623-1(6)) HarperCollins Pubs.

Besson, Luc. Arthur & the Minimoys. 2005. (Illus.). 240p. (J). lib. bdg. 16.89 (978-0-06-059624-8(4)) HarperCollins Pubs.

Bilen, Tracy. What She Left Behind. 2012. (ENG.). 256p. (YA). (gr. 9-12). pap. 9.99 (978-1-4424-3951-1(3), Simon Pulse) Simon Pulse.

Binding, Tim. Sylvie & the Songman. 2011. (ENG.). 352p. (J). (gr. 4-6). lib. bdg. 22.44 (978-0-385-75159-9(1), Yearling) Random Hse. Children's Bks.

Black, Yelena. Dance of Shadows. 2014. (Dance of Shadows Ser.). (ENG., Illus.). 384p. (YA). (gr. 7). pap. 9.99 (978-1-61963-185-4(7), 900125810, Bloomsbury USA Childrens) Bloomsbury Publishing USA.

Blackstock, Terri. Southern Storm, 1 vol. 2014. (Cape Refuge Ser.: 2). (ENG.). 400p. pap. 17.99 (978-0-310-34280-9(5)) Zondervan.

Blakemore, Megan Frazer. The Story Web. 2019. (ENG.). 336p. (J). 16.99 (978-1-68119-525-4(9), 900176198, Bloomsbury Children's Bks.) Bloomsbury Publishing USA.

Blevins, Wiley. Ten Missing Princesses. Cox, Steve, illus. 2017. (Scary Tales Retold Ser.). (ENG.). 24p. (J). (gr. k-3). pap. 6.99 (978-1-63440-172-2(7), 97967ed0-13a8-4453-839f-022d2bc5b970); lib. bdg. 27.99 (978-1-63440-168-5(9), 1aaeb31e-b7b1-4f1d-805e-10da6b4e6aaf) Red Chair Pr.

Bliss, Harry. Luke on the Loose. 2014. (Toon Books Level 2 Ser.). lib. bdg. 14.75 (978-0-606-32101-3(2)) Turtleback.

—Luke on the Loose: Toon Books Level 2. Bliss, Harry, illus. 2009. (ENG., Illus.). 32p. (J). (gr. -1-3). 12.99 (978-1-935179-00-9(4), TOON Books) Astra Publishing Hse.

Bobulski, Chelsea. The Wood. 2017. (ENG.). 320p. (YA). 27.99 (978-1-250-09426-1(7), 900160379) Feiwel & Friends.

Bond, Gwenda. Strange Alchemy. 2017. (ENG., Illus.). 336p. (YA). (gr. 9-12). 17.95 (978-1-63079-076-9(1), 134212, Switch Pr.) Capstone.

Bosch, Pseudonymous. This Book Is Not Good for You. 2009. (Secret Ser.: 3). (ENG.). 400p. (J). (gr. 3-7). 18.99 (978-0-316-04086-0(X)) Little, Brown Bks. for Young Readers.

Bowler, Tim. Frozen Fire. 2010. (ENG.). 352p. (YA). (gr. 7-18). 8.99 (978-0-14-241465-1(4), Speak) Penguin Young Readers Group.

Bracegirdle, P. J. Sinister Scenes. (Joy of Spooking Ser.). (ENG.). 320p. (J). (gr. 3-7). 2012. pap. 6.99 (978-1-4169-3421-9(9)) 2011. 15.99 (978-1-4169-3420-2(0)) McElderry, Margaret K. Bks. (McElderry, Margaret K. Bks.).

Bradbury, Jennifer. Shift. (ENG., Illus.). (YA). (gr. 7). 2012. 272p. pap. 12.99 (978-1-4424-0852-4(9)) 2008. 256p. 17.99 (978-1-4169-4732-5(9)) Simon & Schuster Children's Publishing. (Atheneum Bks. for Young Readers).

Branning, Debe. The Adventures of Chickolet Pigolet: The Bribe of Frankenbeans. Knold, Nijlon, illus. 2008. 48p. pap. 7.95 (978-1-935137-40-5(9)) Guardian Angel Publishing, Inc.

Brezenoff, Steven. The Missing Bully: An Interactive Mystery Adventure. Calo, Marcos, illus. 2017. (You Choose Stories: Field Trip Mysteries Ser.). (ENG.). 112p. (J). (gr. 3-7). lib. bdg. 32.65 (978-1-4965-2642-7(2), 131205, Stone Arch Bks.) Capstone.

Brian, Kate, pseud. Ominous. 2011. (Private Ser.). (ENG.). 224p. (YA). (gr. 9-18). pap. 9.99 (978-1-4169-8472-6(0), Simon & Schuster Bks. For Young Readers) Simon & Schuster Bks. For Young Readers.

Briggs, Andy. Tarzan: The Greystoke Legacy. 2011. (ENG.). 304p. pap. (978-0-571-27238-9(X)) Faber & Faber, Ltd.

Briley, Randy. Mr Underneath. 2013. 134p. pap. 12.99 (978-0-9896269-0-3(3)) Raven Mad Studios.

Brown, Jo. Where's My Mommy? Brown, Jo, illus. 2006. (Storytime Board Bks.). (Illus.). 18p. (J). (gr. -1-3). bds. 6.95 (978-1-58925-795-5(2)) Tiger Tales.

Brummit, Ariyana. A Soldier's Way Home. 2013. 124p. pap. 11.97 (978-0-9801060-7-7(9)) Heard Word Publishing, LLC.

Bullock, Rob. Noah Ramsbottom & the Cave Elves. 2009. 48p. pap. 12.25 (978-1-60860-335-0(0), Strategic Bk. Publishing) Strategic Book Publishing & Rights Agency (SBPRA).

Bumgarner, Sam. Little Sami's Silly Again, 1 vol. 2009. 32p. pap. 24.95 (978-1-60813-863-0(1)) America Star Bks.

Bunzl, Peter. Cogheart. 2019. (Cogheart Adventures Ser.). (ENG.). 368p. (J). (gr. 3-7). pap. 12.99 (978-1-63163-287-7(6), 1631632876, Jolly Fish Pr.) North Star Editions.

Bursztyn, Dina. The Land of Lost Things: El País de las Cosas Perdidas. Bursztyn, Dina, illus. 2011. (SPA & ENG., Illus.). 32p. (J). (gr. -1-3). 16.95 (978-1-55885-690-5(0), Piñata Books) Arte Publico Pr.

Busby, Cylin. The Stranger Game. (ENG.). 288p. (YA). (gr. 8). 2018. pap. 9.99 (978-0-06-235461-7(2)) 2016. 17.99 (978-0-06-235460-0(4)) HarperCollins Pubs. (Balzer & Bray).

Butler, Dori Hillestad. The Case of the Missing Family, 1 vol., Bk. 3. Tugeau, Jeremy, illus. 2010. (Buddy Files Ser.: 3). (ENG.). 144p. (J). (gr. 1-5). pap. 5.99 (978-0-8075-0934-0(5), 807509345) Whitman, Albert & Co.

Cabot, Meg. Code Name Cassandra. 2007. (1-800-Where-R-You Ser.: No. 2). (ENG., Illus.). 272p. (YA). (gr. 9-12). mass mkt. 6.99 (978-1-4169-2704-4(2), Simon Pulse) Simon Pulse.

—Safe House. 2011. (1-800-Where-R-You Ser.: 3). (ENG.). 272p. (YA). (gr. 9). pap. 12.99 (978-1-4424-3084-6(2), Simon Pulse) Simon Pulse.

—Vanished Books One & Two: When Lightning Strikes; Code Name Cassandra. 2010. (Vanished Ser.: Bks. 1 & 2). (ENG., Illus.). 560p. (YA). (gr. 7). pap. 15.99 (978-1-4424-0629-2(1), Simon Pulse) Simon Pulse.

—Vanished Books Three & Four: Safe House; Sanctuary. 2011. (Vanished Ser.: Bks. 3 & 4). (ENG.). 512p. (YA). (gr. 7-12). pap. 15.99 (978-1-4424-0631-5(3), Simon Pulse) Simon Pulse.

Cain, Janan. Roonie B. Moonie: Lost & Alone. 2007. (Illus.). 32p. (J). (gr. -1-3). 15.95 (978-0-9740190-8-6(9)) Illumination Arts Publishing Co., Inc.

Caine, Rachel, pseud. Kiss of Death: The Morganville Vampires, 8 vols. 2010. (Morganville Vampires Ser.: 8). (ENG.). 256p. (YA). (gr. 9-18). 6.99 (978-0-451-22973-1(8), Berkley) Penguin Publishing Group.

—The Morganville Vampires, Volume 4, Vol. 4. 2011. (Morganville Vampires Ser.: Bks. 7-8). (ENG.). 464p. (YA). (gr. 9-18). 12.99 (978-0-451-23426-1(X), Berkley) Penguin Publishing Group.

Calejo, Ryan. Charlie Hernández & the League of Shadows. (Charlie Hernández Ser.: 1). (ENG.). (J). (gr. 5-9). 2019. 352p. pap. 8.99 (978-1-5344-2659-7(0)) 2018. (Illus.). 336p. 18.99 (978-1-5344-2658-0(2)) Simon & Schuster Children's Publishing. (Aladdin).

Callender, Kacen. Hurricane Child (Scholastic Gold) (ENG.). (J). (gr. 3-7). 2019. 240p. pap. 8.99 (978-1-338-12931-1(7)) 2018. 224p. 17.99 (978-1-338-12930-4(9)) Scholastic, Inc. (Scholastic Pr.).

Cannon, Sarah. Oddity. 2019. (ENG.). 320p. (J). pap. 7.99 (978-1-250-17906-7(8), 900174055) Square Fish.

Cantini, Barbara. Ghoulia & the Mysterious Visitor (Book #2) 2019. (Ghoulia Ser.). (ENG., Illus.). 64p. (YA). (gr. 1-3). 9.99 (978-1-4197-3690-2(6), 1254601) Abrams, Inc.

Cantor, Jillian. The September Sisters. 2009. (ENG.). 368p. (YA). (gr. 8-18). 16.99 (978-0-06-168648-1(4), HarperTeen) HarperCollins Pubs.

Carlson, Caroline. The Terror of the Southlands. Phillips, Dave, illus. 2014. (ENG.). 336p. (J). pap. (978-0-06-236178-3(3)) Harper & Row Ltd.

Carlson, Melody. Bad Connection. 2006. (Secret Life of Samantha Mcgregor Ser.: 1). (ENG.). 256p. (J). (gr. 7-12). per. 12.99 (978-1-59052-692-7(9), Multnomah) Crown Publishing Group, The.

Caron, Eleonore. Gizmo & Ellen Mysteries: The Case of the Missing Boy. 2012. 24p. pap. 24.95 (978-1-4626-6747-5(3)) America Star Bks.

Carr, Debra. Misty Is Missing. Carr, Stephen, illus. 2008. 52p. pap. 8.95 (978-0-9816172-7-5(1)) Westview Publishing Co., Inc.

Carson, Jack. Battle Champions: Swampland Slam. 2013. (ENG., Illus.). 128p. (J). pap. 7.99 (978-0-85707-563-5(2), Simon & Schuster Children's) Simon & Schuster, Ltd. GBR. Dist: Simon & Schuster, Inc.

Carter, Rachel. This Strange & Familiar Place. 2013. (ENG.). 272p. (YA). (gr. 9). 17.99 (978-0-06-208108-7(X), HarperTeen) HarperCollins Pubs.

Cartwright, Ran. The Adventures of Billy Space Boy, 1 vol. 2010. 208p. pap. 24.95 (978-1-4489-3901-5(1)) America Star Bks.

Casey, Jane. Hide & Seek. 2015. (Jess Tennant Mysteries Ser.: 3). (ENG.). 288p. (YA). (gr. 8). 36.99 (978-1-250-04067-1(1), 900123900, St. Martin's Griffin) St. Martin's Pr.

Cassidy, Cathy. Love from Lexie (the Lost & Found) 2019. (Lost & Found Ser.: 1). (Illus.). 336p. (J). (gr. 4-6). pap. 9.99 (978-0-14-138512-9(X)) Penguin Random Hse. AUS. Dist: Independent Pubs. Group.

Cate, Annette LeBlanc. The Magic Rabbit. Cate, Annette LeBlanc, illus. 2013. (ENG., Illus.). 32p. (J). (gr. -1-1). 21.19 (978-0-7636-2672-3(4)) Candlewick Pr.

Chan, Queenie. The Dreaming Collection. 2010. (ENG., Illus.). 576p. pap. 19.99 (978-1-4278-1871-3(1)) TOKYOPOP, Inc.

Chappell, Crissa. Snowbirds. 2017. (ENG.). 272p. (YA). 17.99 (978-1-5072-0069-8(2), Simon Pulse) Simon Pulse.

Charbonneau, Joelle. The Testing. 2015. (Testing Ser.: 1). (ENG.). 352p. (YA). (gr. 7). pap. 15.99 (978-0-544-33623-0(2), 1584169, Clarion Bks.) HarperCollins Pubs.

Childress, Jamie. Galactic Treasure Hunt 5: Lost Fortress of Light. Braun, Chris, illus. 2010. (Galactic Treasure Hunt Ser.). (ENG.). 230p. (J). pap. 6.99 (978-1-935487-06-7(X)) Adventures Unlimited Pr.

Clarke, Cat. The Lost & the Found. 2016. (ENG.). 368p. (YA). (gr. 9). 17.99 (978-1-101-93204-9(X), Crown Books For Young Readers) Random Hse. Children's Bks.

Clarke, E. J. Oakwing: A Fairy's Tale. 2017. (Oakwing Ser.: 1). (ENG., Illus.). 192p. (J). (gr. 2-6). 16.99 (978-1-4814-8191-5(6), Aladdin) Simon & Schuster Children's Publishing.

—Oakwing: A Fairy's Tale. 2018. (Oakwing Ser.: 1). (ENG.). 208p. (J). (gr. 2-6). pap. 6.99 (978-1-4814-8190-8(8), Simon & Schuster/Paula Wiseman Bks.) Simon & Schuster/Paula Wiseman Bks.

Clugston-Flores, Chynna. Lumberjanes/Gotham Academy. 2017. lib. bdg. 33.05 (978-0-606-39766-7(3)) Turtleback.

Coben, Harlan. Shelter. Lt. ed. 2011. (Mickey Bolitar Ser.: Bk. 1). (ENG.). 354p. (J). (gr. 9-12). 23.99 (978-1-4104-4365-6(5)) Thorndike Pr.

—Shelter. 2012. (Mickey Bolitar Ser.: 1). lib. bdg. 20.85 (978-0-606-26669-7(0)) Turtleback.

—Shelter (Book One) A Mickey Bolitar Novel, Bk. 1. 2012. (Mickey Bolitar Novel Ser.: 1). (ENG.). 336p. (YA). (gr. 7). pap. 11.99 (978-0-14-242203-8(7), Speak) Penguin Young Readers Group.

Coburn, Ann. Glint. 2007. 423p. (YA). (gr. 4-7). 17.99 (978-0-06-084723-4(9)) HarperCollins Pubs.

Coleman, K. R. Truth or Dare. 2017. (Midnight Ser.). (ENG.). (YA). 108p. (gr. 4-4). E-Book (978-1-5124-3495-8(7), 9781512434958); 104p. (gr. 6-12). E-Book 39.99 (978-1-5124-3494-1(9), 9781512434941); 104p. (gr. 6-12). E-Book 39.99 (978-1-5124-2788-2(8)) Lerner Publishing Group. (Darby Creek).

Coley, Liz. Pretty Girl-13. 2013. (ENG.). 352p. (YA). (gr. 9). 17.99 (978-0-06-212737-2(3), Tegen, Katherine Bks) HarperCollins Pubs.

Cook, Eileen. The Almost Truth. 2013. (ENG., Illus.). 272p. (YA). (gr. 9). pap. 9.99 (978-1-4424-4020-3(1), Simon Pulse) Simon Pulse.

Cook, Philip. Erden: Flame of the Creator. 2014. xiii, 259p. (YA). (978-1-4908-2033-0(7), WestBow Pr.) Author Solutions, LLC.

Cooney, Caroline B. Janie Face to Face. 2014. (Face on the Milk Carton Ser.). 352p. (YA). (gr. 7). pap. 11.99 (978-0-385-74207-8(X), Ember) Random Hse. Children's Bks.

Cooper, E. E. Vanished. 2015. (Vanished Ser.: 1). (ENG.). 320p. (YA). (gr. 9). 17.99 (978-0-06-229390-9(7), Tegen, Katherine Bks) HarperCollins Pubs.

Cordell, Matthew. Wolf in the Snow. 2017. (ENG., Illus.). 48p. (J). 18.99 (978-1-250-07636-6(6), 900152144) Feiwel & Friends.

—Wolf in the Snow. 2018. (CHI.). (gr. -1-1). (978-986-189-861-2(1)) Grimm Cultural Ent., Co., Ltd.

Cray, Jordan. Stalker. 2009. (Danger. com Ser.: 5). (ENG.). 224p. (YA). (gr. 7). pap. 10.99 (978-1-4169-9850-1(0), Simon Pulse) Simon Pulse.

Creech, Sharon. The Boy on the Porch. 2014. (ENG.). 176p. (J). (gr. 3-7). pap. 7.99 (978-0-06-189238-7(6), HarperCollins) HarperCollins Pubs.

Crockett, S. D. After the Snow. 2013. (After the Snow Ser.: 1). (ENG.). 320p. (YA). (gr. 7-12). pap. 13.99 (978-1-250-01676-8(2), 900087090) Square Fish.

Cronin, Doreen. Bear Country: Bearly a Misadventure. Gilpin, Stephen, illus. (Chicken Squad Ser.: 6). (ENG.). 112p. (J). (gr. 2-5). 2019. pap. 7.99 (978-1-5344-0575-2(5)) 2018. 12.99 (978-1-5344-0574-5(7), Atheneum/Caitlyn Dlouhy Books) Simon & Schuster Children's Publishing.

Crow, Matthew. Another Place. 2017. (ENG.). 288p. (YA). 11.99 (978-1-4721-1420-4(5), Atom Books) Little, Brown Book Group Ltd. GBR. Dist: Hachette Bk. Group.

Crowl, Janice. Kili & the Singing Snails. Orme, Harinani, illus. 2011. (J). 16.95 (978-1-58178-104-5(0)) Bishop Museum Pr.

Crowley, James. Monsterland. 2018. lib. bdg. 19.65 (978-0-606-41311-4(1)) Turtleback.

Cruz, Marie Miranda. Everlasting Nora. 2018. 287p. (YA). (978-1-250-31468-0(2), Starscape) Doherty, Tom Assocs., LLC.

Culwell, Lori. The Dirt. 2011. (ENG.). 208p. (YA). pap. 11.95 (978-1-935961-36-9(5), Booktrope Editions) Booktrope.

Dahl, Lisa. Gorm the Viking: The Lost Voyage. 2013. 282p. (gr. 4-6). 26.95 (978-1-4759-5809-6(9)); pap. 16.95 (978-1-4759-5807-2(2)) iUniverse, Inc.

Danziger, Paula. Es Dia de Feria, Ambar Dorado. Ross, Tony, illus. 2007. (de Ámbar / a Is for Amber Easy-To-Read Ser.).Tr. of It's a Fair Day, Amber Brown. (SPA.). 48p. (gr. k-3). pap. 8.95 (978-1-59820-596-1(X)) Santillana USA Publishing Co., Inc.

—It's a Fair Day, Amber Brown. Ross, Tony, illus. 2003. pap. 31.95 incl. audio compact disk (978-1-59112-564-8(2)); (J). (gr. -1-2). audio compact disk 28.95 (978-1-59112-565-5(0)); (J). (gr. -1-2). audio compact disk 28.95 (978-1-59112-565-5(0)) Live Oak Media.

DasGupta, Sayantani. The Serpent's Secret (Kiranmala & the Kingdom Beyond #1) (Kiranmala & the Kingdom Beyond Ser.: 1). (ENG.). 368p. (J). (gr. 3-7). 2019. pap. 8.99 (978-1-338-18571-3(3)) 2018. 18.99 (978-1-338-18570-6(5)) Scholastic, Inc. (Scholastic Pr.).

Dauber, J. A. Mayhem & Madness: Chronicles of a Teenaged Supervillain. 2019. 304p. (J). (gr. 7). 18.99 (978-0-8234-4255-3(1)) Holiday Hse., Inc.

David, Jamie. Johann Sebastian Humpbach. David, Jamie, illus. 2009. (Illus.). 167p. pap. 14.95 (978-0-615-31840-0(1)) Chai Yo Maui Pr.

Davis, Harold. The Starrigans of Little Brook Bottom, 1 vol. Carter, Dana, illus. 2007. (ENG.). 150p. (J). (gr. 3-7). per. (978-1-894294-85-0(8)) Breakwater Bks., Ltd.

Dawn, Sasha. Blink. 2018. (ENG.). 344p. (YA). (gr. 8-12). 17.99 (978-1-5124-3977-9(0), df9a5d50-6f73-45f3-8467-9620d5e1b05f, Carolrhoda Lab™) Lerner Publishing Group.

—Splinter. 2018. (ENG.). 304p. (YA). (gr. 8-12). pap. 9.99 (978-1-5415-3845-0(5), e570372a-60e4-45dc-8e51-088b983b546f, Carolrhoda Lab™) Lerner Publishing Group.

de Beer, Hans. Little Polar Bear. 2016. (ENG., Illus.). 32p. (J). 16.95 (978-0-7358-4264-9(7)) North-South Bks., Inc.

De la Cruz, Melissa. Angels on Sunset Boulevard. 2008. (Angels on Sunset Boulevard Ser.: Bk. 1). (ENG.). 240p. (YA). (gr. 9-18). pap. 8.99 (978-1-4169-3991-7(1), Simon & Schuster Bks. For Young Readers) Simon & Schuster Bks. For Young Readers.

Decker, Wendy. The Bedazzling Bowl. 2006. pap. 13.99 (978-1-60034-468-8(2)) Salem Author Services.

Deen, Natasha. Terminate, 1 vol. 2017. (Orca Soundings Ser.: 4). (ENG.). 192p. (YA). (gr. 8-12). pap. 9.95 (978-1-4598-1462-2(2)) Orca Bk. Pubs. USA.

DefoeDaniel. Robinson Crusoe: Paperback Student Book Without Answers. 2009. (Cambridge Experience Readers Ser.). (ENG.). 96p. pap. 14.75 (978-84-8323-553-9(6)) Cambridge Univ. Pr.

Dicamillo, Kate. The Magician's Elephant. 2015. lib. bdg. 17.20 (978-0-606-37891-8(X)) Turtleback.

DiCamillo, Kate. The Magician's Elephant. Tanaka, Yoko, illus. (ENG.). (J). (gr. 3-7). 2015. 224p. pap. 8.99 (978-0-7636-8088-6(5)) 2009. 208p. 18.99 (978-0-7636-4410-9(2)) Candlewick Pr.

Dicamillo, Kate. The Magician's Elephant. l.t. ed. 2010. (ENG.). 242p. 23.95 (978-1-4104-2493-8(6)) Thorndike Pr.

—The Magician's Elephant. 2011. lib. bdg. 17.20 (978-0-606-15375-1(6)) Turtleback.

Dickerson, Melanie. The Piper's Pursuit, 1 vol. 2019. (ENG.). 320p. (YA). 18.99 (978-0-7852-2814-1(4)) Nelson, Thomas Inc.

Dillon, Elena. Crushing. 2013. 368p. (YA). pap. 13.99 (978-0-9886353-4-0(8)) Dillon, Elena.

Ding, Yuhui Andrew. Warrior Soul. 2009. 28p. pap. 15.99 (978-1-4415-6734-5(8)) Xlibris Corp.

Disney Books. Finding Nemo ReadAlong Storybook & CD. 2012. (Read-Along Storybook & CD Ser.). (ENG.). 32p. (J). (gr. -1 — 1). pap. 6.99 (978-1-4231-6028-1(2), Disney Press Books) Disney Publishing Worldwide.

Dixon, Franklin. Hardy Boys Adventures 3-Books-In-1! Secret of the Red Arrow; Mystery of the Phantom Heist; the Vanishing Game. 2016. (Hardy Boys Adventures Ser.). (ENG., Illus.). 448p. (J). (gr. 3-7). pap. 8.99 (978-1-4814-8553-1(9), Aladdin) Simon & Schuster Children's Publishing.

Dixon, Franklin W. The Children of the Lost: Book One in the Lost Mystery Trilogy, Bk. 1. 2010. (Hardy Boys (All New) Undercover Brothers Ser.: 34). (ENG.). 192p. (J). (gr. 3-7). pap. 5.99 (978-1-4424-0262-1(8), Aladdin) Simon & Schuster Children's Publishing.

—The Disappearance. 2019. (Hardy Boys Adventures Ser.: 18). (ENG.). 160p. (J). (gr. 3-7). 17.99 (978-1-5344-1489-1(4)); (Illus.). pap. 7.99 (978-1-5344-1488-4(6)) Simon & Schuster Children's Publishing. (Aladdin).

—Double Deception: Book Three in the Double Danger Trilogy, 27. 2009. (Hardy Boys (All New) Undercover Brothers Ser.: 27). (ENG.). 176p. (J). (gr. 3-7). pap. 6.99 (978-1-4169-6766-8(4)) Simon & Schuster, Inc.

—Double Down: Book Two in the Double Danger Trilogy, 26. 26th ed. 2008. (Hardy Boys (All New) Undercover Brothers Ser.: 26). (ENG.). 172p. (J). (gr. 3-7). pap. 7.99 (978-1-4169-7446-8(6)) Simon & Schuster, Inc.

—Forever Lost: Book Three in the Lost Mystery Trilogy. 2011. (Hardy Boys (All New) Undercover Brothers Ser.: 36). (ENG.). 160p. (J). (gr. 3-7). pap. 6.99 (978-1-4424-0264-5(4), Aladdin) Simon & Schuster Children's Publishing.

—Into Thin Air. 2013. (Hardy Boys Adventures Ser.: 4). (ENG., Illus.). 128p. (J). (gr. 3-7). 17.99 (978-1-4424-7345-4(2)); pap. 7.99 (978-1-4424-5983-0(2)) Simon & Schuster Children's Publishing. (Aladdin).

—The Madman of Black Bear Mountain. 2016. (Hardy Boys Adventures Ser.: 12). (ENG., Illus.). 144p. (J). (gr. 3-7). pap. 6.99 (978-1-4814-3880-3(8), Aladdin) Simon & Schuster Children's Publishing.

—The Missing Chums #4. 2016. (Hardy Boys Ser.: 4). (Illus.). 192p. (J). (gr. 3-7). 8.99 (978-0-448-48955-1(4), Grosset & Dunlap) Penguin Young Readers Group.

—Pushed. 18th ed. 2007. (Hardy Boys (All New) Undercover Brothers Ser.: 18). (ENG., Illus.). 160p. (J). (gr. 3-7). pap. 7.99 (978-1-4169-4802-5(3), Aladdin) Simon & Schuster Children's Publishing.

—The Secret of the Caves #7, Bk. 7. 2017. (Hardy Boys Ser.: 7). 192p. (J). (gr. 3-7). 8.99 (978-0-515-15909-7(3), Grosset & Dunlap) Penguin Young Readers Group.

—The Vanishing Game. 2013. (Hardy Boys Adventures Ser.: 3). (ENG.). 144p. (J). (gr. 3-7). 17.99 (978-1-4424-7344-7(4)); (Illus.). pap. 7.99 (978-1-4424-5981-6(6)) Simon & Schuster Children's Publishing. (Aladdin).

Doane, Pelagie. Clue in the Patchwork Quilt #14, No. 14. Doane, Pelagie, illus. 2008. (Judy Bolton Ser.). (ENG., Illus.). 228p. (J). (gr. 4-7). pap. 14.95 (978-1-4290-9034-6(0)) Applewood Bks.

—Riddle of the Double Ring #10, No. 10. Doane, Pelagie, illus. 2008. (Judy Bolton Ser.). (ENG., Illus.). 236p. (J). (gr. 4-7). pap. 14.95 (978-1-4290-9030-8(8)) Applewood Bks.

Dormer, Frank W. The Sword in the Stove. Dormer, Frank W., illus. 2016. (ENG., Illus.). 40p. (J). (gr. -1-3). 17.99 (978-1-4814-3167-5(6)) Simon & Schuster, Inc.

Doro, Ann. The Missing Canary. l.t. ed. 2005. 93p. 12.95 (978-0-9745052-2-0(6), Peeper & Friends) Tree Of Life Publishing.

Dotlich, Rebecca. Peanut & Pearl's Picnic Adventure. Alley, R. W., illus. 2008. (My First I Can Read Ser.). (ENG.). 32p. (J). (gr. -1 — 1). pap. 4.99 (978-0-06-054922-0(X), HarperCollins) HarperCollins Pubs.

Dowd, Siobhan. The London Eye Mystery. 2009. (ENG.). 336p. (J). (gr. 3-7). 8.99 (978-0-385-75184-1(2), Yearling) Random Hse. Children's Bks.

—The London Eye Mystery. 2009. (London Eye Mystery Ser.: 1). lib. bdg. 18.40 (978-0-606-14413-1(7)) Turtleback.

Doyle, Marissa. Bewitching Season. 2009. (ENG.). 368p. (YA). (gr. 9-12). 24.94 (978-0-312-59695-8(2), 9780312596958) Square Fish.

Duey, Kathleen & Bale, Karen A. Swamp: Louisiana 1851. 2016. (Survivors Ser.). (ENG., Illus.). 160p. (J). (gr. 3-7). pap. 6.99 (978-1-4814-2783-8(0), Aladdin) Simon & Schuster Children's Publishing.

—Swamp: Louisiana 1851. 2016. (Survivors Ser.). (ENG., Illus.). 160p. (J). (gr. 3-7). 17.99 (978-1-4814-2784-5(9), Simon & Schuster/Paula Wiseman Bks.) Simon & Schuster/Paula Wiseman Bks.

Duff, Hilary. Elixir. 2011. (Playaway Young Adult Ser.). (YA). 59.99 (978-1-4417-7416-3(5)) Findaway World, LLC.

—Elixir. 2011. (Elixir Ser.). (ENG.). 336p. (YA). (gr. 9). pap. 12.99 (978-1-4424-0854-8(5), Simon & Schuster Bks. For Young Readers) Simon & Schuster Bks. For Young Readers.

Dunham, Wendy. My Name Is River. 2015. (ENG.). 144p. (J). (gr. 2-6). pap. 8.99 (978-0-7369-6461-6(4), 6964616) Harvest Hse. Pubs.

Dunker, Kristina. Summer Storm, 0 vols. Dembo, Margot Bettauer, tr. unabr. ed. 2011. (ENG.). 146p. (J). (gr. 3-6). pap. 9.95 (978-1-61109-030-7(X), 9781611090307, AmazonCrossing) Amazon Publishing.

Durant, Alan. Little Miss Muffet's Big Scare. Heming, Leah-Ellen, illus. 2012. (ENG.). 32p. (J). (978-0-7787-8030-4(9)); pap. (978-0-7787-8041-0(4)) Crabtree Publishing Co.

Durrant, Geraldine. Twinbane: an Appalling True History. 2010. 142p. pap. 16.95 (978-1-4457-7998-0(6)) Lulu Pr., Inc.

Dver, Alyssa. When Whizzly Wanders. 2005. 15p. 6.78 (978-1-4116-4667-4(3)) Lulu Pr., Inc.

Dyer, Hadley. Johnny Kellock Died Today. 2007. (ENG.). 192p. (J). (gr. 5-9). mass mkt. 8.99 (978-0-00-639534-8(1), Harper Trophy) HarperCollins Pubs.

Easley, Sean. The Hotel Between. 2018. (ENG., Illus.). 352p. (J). (gr. 4-7). 19.99 (978-1-5344-1697-0(8), Simon & Schuster Bks. For Young Readers) Simon & Schuster Bks. For Young Readers.

—The Key of Lost Things. 2020. (ENG.). 400p. (J). (gr. 4-7). pap. 8.99 (978-1-5344-3788-3(6), Simon & Schuster Bks. For Young Readers) Simon & Schuster Bks. For Young Readers.

Eastman, Brock D. & Eastman, Brock. Taken. 2011. (Illus.). 315p. (J). pap. (978-1-59638-245-9(7)) P & R Publishing.

Eichler, Ken. Swift Eagle's Wagon Train Adventure, 1 vol. 2010. 80p. pap. 19.95 (978-1-4489-4364-7(7)) America Star Bks.

Eldridge, Courtney. Ghost Time. 2016. (ENG.). 418p. (YA). (gr. 7-12). pap. 9.99 (978-1-4778-1697-4(6), 9781477816974, Skyscape) Amazon Publishing.

Elgert, C. J. The Elder Brothers & the Padstow Crystals. 2013. 208p. (978-1-4602-1788-7(8)); pap. (978-1-4602-1789-4(6)) FriesenPress.

Elish, Dan. The School for the Insanely Gifted. 2011. (ENG.). 304p. (J). (gr. 3-7). 15.99 (978-0-06-113873-7(8), Balzer & Bray) HarperCollins Pubs.

Elizabeth's Story 1848. 2014. (Secrets of the Manor Ser.: 3). (ENG., Illus.). 160p. (J). (gr. 3-7). pap. 7.99 (978-1-4814-1840-9(8), Simon Spotlight) Simon Spotlight.

Ellis, Deborah. Parvana's Journey, 1 vol. 2015. (Breadwinner Ser.: 2). (ENG., Illus.). 200p. (J). (gr. 5-9). pap. 10.99 (978-1-55498-770-2(9)) Groundwood Bks. CAN. Dist: Publishers Group West (PGW).

Emerson, Alice B. Ruth Fielding at Snow Camp: Or, Lost in the Backwoods. 2017. (ENG., Illus.). (J). pap. 12.95 (978-1-374-90179-7(2)) Capital Communications, Inc.

Emerson, Scott. The Case of the Cat with the Missing Ear: From the Notebooks of Edward R. Smithfield D. V. M. Mullett, Viv, illus. 2011. (Adventures of Samuel Blackthorne Ser.: 1). (ENG.). 240p. (J). (gr. 3-7). pap. 11.99 (978-0-689-87615-8(7), Simon & Schuster Bks. For Young Readers) Simon & Schuster Bks. For Young Readers.

Evans, Ann. Cry Danger. 2006. 184p. per. (978-1-904529-31-6(3), Back to Front) Solidus.

Evans, Richard Paul. Michael Vey 5: Storm of Lightning. 2015. (Michael Vey Ser.: 5). (ENG., Illus.). 288p. (YA). (gr. 7). 19.99 (978-1-4814-4410-1(7), Simon Pulse/Mercury Ink) Simon Pulse/Mercury Ink.

Everheart, Chris. Concrete Gallery. 2015. (Tartan House Ser.). (ENG.). 96p. (J). (gr. 3-6). (978-1-63235-053-4(X), 11680, 12-Story Library) Bookstaves, LLC.

Fantich, Susanna. A Cat's Tale. 2012. 210p. 33.99 (978-1-4582-0527-8(4)); pap. 15.99 (978-1-4582-0525-4(8)) Author Solutions, LLC. (Abbott Pr.).

Feehan-Vileria, Elaine. The Legend of Old Mr. Clarke. 2004. 58p. per. 17.95 (978-1-4116-1523-6(9)) Lulu Pr., Inc.

Feiffer, Kate. Signed by Zelda. (ENG.). 240p. (J). (gr. 3-7). 2013. pap. 6.99 (978-1-4424-3332-8(9)) 2012. (Illus.). 16.99 (978-1-4424-3331-1(0)) Simon & Schuster/Paula Wiseman Bks. (Simon & Schuster/Paula Wiseman Bks.).

Fiani, M. A Cat Named Monkey. 2008. 24p. pap. 14.99 (978-1-4389-1966-9(2)) AuthorHouse.

Fickey, Brenda. Whispering Darkness. 2007. (ENG.). 136p. per. 24.95 (978-1-4241-6932-0(1)) America Star Bks.

Fields, Jan. Ghost Light Burning: An Up2U Mystery Adventure, 1 vol. Fabbretti, Valerio, illus. 2015. (Up2U Adventures Ser.). (ENG.). 80p. (J). (gr. 2-5). 35.64 (978-1-62402-092-6(5), 17353, Calico Chapter Bks.) ABDO Publishing Co.

Fishbone, Greg. The Penguins of Doom. 2007. (From the Desk of Septina Nash Ser.). (ENG., Illus.). 182p. (J). (gr. 2-7). 13.95 (978-1-933831-03-9(0)) Blooming Tree Pr.

Fletcher, Christopher. The Guardian Angel. 2008. 212p. pap. (978-1-84923-031-5(5)) YouWriteOn.

Fletcher, J. S. Scarhaven Keep. 2011. (YA). (978-1-60682-173-2(3)) BJU Pr.

Flinn, Alex. Cloaked. 2011. 341p. (YA). lib. bdg. 17.89 (978-0-06-087423-0(6), HarperTeen) HarperCollins Pubs.

—Towering. 2013. 296p. (YA). (978-0-06-227632-2(8)) HarperCollins Pubs.

Fogg, K. L. Diamondback Cave: A Novel. 2008. 377p. (J). (978-1-59811-512-3(X)) Covenant Communications.

Forde, Patricia. The List. 2018. lib. bdg. 18.40 (978-0-606-41230-8(1)) Turtleback.

Foreman, Michael. Tufty. Foreman, Michael, illus. 2016. (ENG., Illus.). 32p. (J). (gr. -1-3). E-Book 27.99 (978-1-5124-0448-7(9)) Lerner Publishing Group.

Formento, Alison Ashley. Twigs. 2013. (ENG.). 272p. (YA). 17.99 (978-1-4405-6565-6(1), Simon Pulse) Simon Pulse.

Frade, B. A. & Deutsch, Stacia. Haunted Sleepover. 2017. (Tales from the Scaremaster Ser.: 6). (ENG.). 160p. (J). (gr. 3-7). pap. 5.99 (978-0-316-43802-5(2)) Little, Brown Bks. for Young Readers.

—Haunted Sleepover. 2017. (Tales of the Scaremaster Ser.). (J). lib. bdg. 16.00 (978-0-606-40631-4(X)) Turtleback.

France, Emily. Zen & Gone. 2019. (ENG.). 1p. (YA). (gr. 9). pap. 10.99 (978-1-64129-031-9(5), Soho Teen) Soho Pr., Inc.

French, Gillian. The Missing Season. 2019. (ENG.). 304p. (YA). (gr. 8). 17.99 (978-0-06-280333-7(6), HarperTeen) HarperCollins Pubs.

Friedman, Stanley. Quantum Outlaws. 2010. 210p. pap. 11.95 (978-1-935630-09-8(1)) Bellissima Publishing, LLC.

Friedmann, Patty. Taken Away. 2010. (ENG.). 427p. (J). (gr. 6). pap. 18.95 (978-0-9845318-2-0(3)) Tiny Stachel Pr.

Galvin, Laura Gates. Baby Duck Gets Lost. 2007. (Baby Animals Ser.). (ENG., Illus.). 16p. (gr. -1-k). 6.95 (978-1-59249-747-8(0)) Soundprints.

Garis, Howard Roger. Larry Dexter's Great Search or, the Hunt for the Missing Millionaire. 2007. 196p. per. (978-1-4065-2768-1(8)) Dodo Pr.

Garrick, Veda. The Place: Jello. 2012. 302p. pap. 19.99 (978-1-4525-5081-7(6)) Balboa Pr.

Gershator, David. Where Did the Baby Go? Gershator, Phillis, illus. 2016. (J). pap. (978-1-934370-57-5(6)) Editorial Campana.

Gibbons, Alan. The Dying Photo. 2012. (Stoke Books Titles Ser.). 64p. (J). (gr. 5-8). pap. 7.95 (978-1-78112-020-0(X)); pap. 45.32 (978-0-7613-9217-0(3)); lib. bdg. 22.60 (978-1-78112-019-4(6)) Stoke Bks.

Gilbert, David D. Feodor Fitz: Journey to Harmony Ville. 2012. 40p. pap. 17.57 (978-1-4772-1983-6(8)); pap. 20.99 (978-1-4685-8122-5(8)) AuthorHouse.

Gilliland, Raquel Vasquez. Sia Martinez & the Moonlit Beginning of Everything. 2020. (ENG., Illus.). 432p. (YA). (gr. 7). 19.99 (978-1-5344-4863-6(2), Simon Pulse) Simon Pulse.

Ginns, Russell. Samantha Spinner & the Spectacular Specs. 2019. (Samantha Spinner Ser.: 2). (Illus.). 416p. (J). (gr. 3-7). 16.99 (978-1-5247-2004-9(6), Delacorte Bks. for Young Readers) Random Hse. Children's Bks.

—Samantha Spinner & the Super-Secret Plans. Fisinger, Barbara, illus. 2018. (Samantha Spinner Ser.: 1). 208p. (J). (gr. 3-7). 16.99 (978-1-5247-2000-1(3), Delacorte Bks. for Young Readers) Random Hse. Children's Bks.

Godwin, Jane. Falling from Grace. 2007. (ENG.). 204p. (J). (gr. 6-12). 16.95 (978-0-8234-2105-3(8)) Holiday Hse., Inc.

Goodman, Nancy. The Camping Kids Adventures. 2010. 74p. pap. 10.99 (978-1-60957-474-1(5)) Salem Author Services.

Goodrich, Carter. We Forgot Brock! Goodrich, Carter, illus. (ENG., Illus.). 48p. (J). (gr. -1-3). 2017. 7.99 (978-1-5344-1433-4(9)) 2015. 17.99 (978-1-4424-8090-2(4)) Simon & Schuster Bks. For Young Readers. (Simon & Schuster Bks. For Young Readers).

Gordon, Roderick. Deeper, 15 vols. 2009. (J). 128.75 (978-1-4361-3717-1(9)); 134.75 (978-1-4361-3721-8(7)); 132.75 (978-1-4361-3723-2(3)); 126.75 (978-1-4361-3719-5(5)); 301.75 (978-1-4361-3718-8(7)); 1.25 (978-1-4361-3714-0(4)) Recorded Bks., Inc.

Gosling, Cherie & Disney Storybook Artists Staff. Mulan Is Loyal: Merida Is Brave. 2017. (Illus.). 24p. (J). (978-1-5379-5745-6(7)) Random Hse., Inc.

Grant, Holly. The Witch's Glass. Portillo, Josie, illus. 2017. (League of Beastly Dreadfuls Ser.: Bk. 3). 305p. (J). pap. (978-1-101-93369-5(0)) Random Hse., Inc.

Graphman, Wm. Matthew. Chel & Riley Adventures: The K9 Kidnapping Adventure. 2011. 80p. (gr. 4-6). pap. 9.99 (978-1-4567-9574-0(0)) AuthorHouse.

Gratton, Tessa. The Apple Throne. 2015. (YA). (978-0-307-97756-4(0)) Random Hse., Inc.

Gray, Grandpa. The Land of the Three Elves Vol. 1: Beginnings. 2012. (ENG.). 317p. pap. 14.95 (978-1-4327-9551-1(1)) Outskirts Pr., Inc.

Green, John. Paper Towns. 2018. (RUS., Illus.). 338p. (978-5-519-56613-1(5)); 322p. (978-5-519-56615-5(1)); 322p. pap. (978-5-519-52005-8(4)); 338p. pap. (978-5-519-52003-4(8)) Books on Demand.

—Paper Towns. 2011. 11.04 (978-0-7848-3497-8(0), Everbind) Marco Bk. Co.

—Paper Towns. (ENG.). (YA). (gr. 9-18). 2009. 336p. 12.99 (978-0-14-241493-4(X), Penguin Books) 2008. 320p. 18.99 (978-0-525-47818-8(3), Dutton Books for Young Readers) Penguin Young Readers Group.

—Paper Towns. 2010. (ENG., Illus.). 305p. (gr. 9-12). 20.00 (978-1-60686-913-0(2)) Perfection Learning Corp.

—Paper Towns. 2009. lib. bdg. 20.85 (978-0-606-10658-0(8)) Turtleback.

—Penguin Minis: Paper Towns. 2018. (ENG.). 648p. (YA). (gr. 9). pap. 12.00 (978-0-525-55573-5(0), Dutton Books for Young Readers) Penguin Young Readers Group.

—Turtles All the Way Down. (ENG.). (YA). (gr. 9). 2019. 320p. pap. 14.99 (978-0-525-55537-7(4), Penguin Books) 2017. 304p. 19.99 (978-0-525-55536-0(6), Dutton Books for Young Readers) Penguin Young Readers Group.

—Turtles All the Way Down. 2017. lib. bdg. 33.05 (978-0-606-40748-9(0)) Turtleback.

Green, Judith. A Family Secret. Hammah, Aisha, illus. 2013. 32p. pap. (978-0-9810759-7-6(5)) WTL International.

Green, Poppy. Looking for Winston. Bell, Jennifer A., illus. 2015. (Adventures of Sophie Mouse Ser.: 4). (ENG.). 128p. (J). (gr. k-4). pap. 6.99 (978-1-4814-3003-6(3), Little Simon) Little Simon.

—Looking for Winston. Bell, Jennifer A., illus. 2017. (Adventures of Sophie Mouse Ser.). (ENG.). 128p. (J). (gr. k-4). lib. bdg. 31.36 (978-1-5321-4113-3(0), 26986, Chapter Bks.) Spotlight.

Greenwood, Arin. Your Robot Dog Will Die. 2019. 192p. (YA). (gr. 9). pap. 10.99 (978-1-61695-852-7(9), Soho Teen) Soho Pr., Inc.

Griffiths, Andy. The 52-Story Treehouse. 2017. (Treehouse Adventures Ser.: 4). (J). lib. bdg. 17.20 (978-0-606-40350-4(7)) Turtleback.

—The 52-Story Treehouse: Vegetable Villains! Denton, Terry, illus. 2016. (Treehouse Bks.: 4). (ENG.). 336p. (J). (gr. 2-5). 17.99 (978-1-250-02693-4(8), 900098158) Feiwel & Friends.

—The 52-Story Treehouse: Vegetable Villains! Denton, Terry, illus. 2017. (Treehouse Bks.: 4). (ENG.). 352p. (J). pap. 8.99 (978-1-250-10379-6(7), 900163638) Square Fish.

Griggs, Terry. Nieve. Griggs-Burr, Alexander, illus. 2010. 264p. (J). (gr. 4-10). pap. 14.95 (978-1-897231-87-6(3)) Biblioasis CAN. Dist: Consortium Bk. Sales & Distribution.

Grinti, Mike & Grinti, Rachel. Claws. 2012. (J). (978-0-545-43314-3(2), Chicken Hse., The) Scholastic, Inc.

Grove, S. E. The Golden Specific. 2016. (Mapmakers Ser.: 2). lib. bdg. 19.65 (978-0-606-38836-8(2)) Turtleback.

Guest, Elissa Haden. Iris & Walter & the Field Trip. Davenier, Christine, illus. 2013. (Iris & Walter Ser.). (ENG.). 44p. (J). (gr. 1-4). pap. 4.99 (978-0-544-10665-9(2), 1540873, Clarion Bks.) HarperCollins Pubs.

—Iris & Walter & the Field Trip. Davenier, Christine, illus. 2007. (Iris & Walter Ser.). 44p. (J). (gr. 1-4). 13.60 (978-0-7569-8041-2(0)) Perfection Learning Corp.

—Iris & Walter & the Field Trip. 2013. (Iris & Walter — Green Light Reader Ser.). lib. bdg. 13.55 (978-0-606-33987-2(6)) Turtleback.

Haddix, Margaret Peterson. Greystone Secrets #1: the Strangers. Lambelet, Anne, illus. (Greystone Secrets Ser.: 1). (ENG.). (J). (gr. 3-7). 2020. 432p. pap. 9.99 (978-0-06-283838-4(5)) 2019. 416p. 17.99 (978-0-06-283837-7(7)) 2019. 432p. E-Book (978-0-06-283839-1(3), 9780062838391) HarperCollins Pubs. (Tegen, Katherine Bks).

—Greystone Secrets #2: the Deceivers. (Greystone Secrets Ser.: 2). (ENG.). (J). (gr. 3-7). 2021. 464p. pap. 10.99 (978-0-06-283841-4(5)) 2020. (Illus.). 448p. 17.99 (978-0-06-283840-7(7)) HarperCollins Pubs. (Tegen, Katherine Bks).

Hagen, George. Gabriel Finley & the Lord of Air & Darkness. 2017. 288p. (J). (gr. 4-7). 16.99 (978-0-399-55347-9(9), Schwartz & Wade Bks.) Random Hse. Children's Bks.

Haig, Matt. To Be a Cat. Curtis, Stacy, illus. (ENG.). 304p. (J). (gr. 3-7). 2014. pap. 8.99 (978-1-4424-5406-4(7)) 2013. 16.99 (978-1-4424-5405-7(9)) Simon & Schuster Children's Publishing.

Halbrook, K. D. Smoke & Mirrors. 2018. (ENG., Illus.). 240p. (J). (gr. 3-7). 16.99 (978-1-5344-0504-2(6), Simon & Schuster/Paula Wiseman Bks.) Simon & Schuster/Paula Wiseman Bks.

Hannibal, James R. The Lost Property Office. 2016. (Section 13 Ser.: 1). (ENG., Illus.). 400p. (J). (gr. 3-7). 18.99 (978-1-4814-6709-4(3), Simon & Schuster Bks. For Young Readers) Simon & Schuster Bks. For Young Readers.

Hargrave, Kiran Millwood. The Way Past Winter. 2020. (ENG., Illus.). 284p. (J). (gr. 5-10). 17.99 (978-1-4521-8155-4(1)) Chronicle Bks. LLC.

Harper, Ken. Mystery in Mansfield. 2008. 60p. pap. 19.95 (978-1-60441-055-6(8)) America Star Bks.

Harris, Lewis. A Taste for Red. 2010. (ENG.). 180p. (J). (gr. 5-7). pap. 12.95 (978-0-547-39851-8(4), 1427650, Clarion Bks.) HarperCollins Pubs.

—A Taste for Red. 2010. (ENG.). 176p. (J). (gr. 4-6). 18.69 (978-0-547-14462-7(8)) Houghton Mifflin Harcourt Publishing Co.

Harrison, Michelle. The Thirteen Treasures. 2014. (ENG., Illus.). 352p. pap. 8.99 (978-1-4711-2167-8(4), Simon & Schuster Children's) Simon & Schuster, Ltd. GBR. Dist: Simon & Schuster, Inc.

Hartnett, Sonya. What the Birds See. 2007. (ENG., Illus.). 208p. (YA). (gr. 9). pap. 7.99 (978-0-7636-3680-7(0)) Candlewick Pr.

—What the Birds See. 2019. (ENG.). 208p. (YA). (gr. 9). pap. 7.99 (978-1-5362-0881-8(7)) Candlewick Pr.

Hathorn, Sarah Alexandra. Teenagents: World Challenge. 2012. 240p. pap. 12.99 (978-2-9700738-2-6(X)) Simon & Schuster, Inc.

Hautman, Pete. The Cydonian Pyramid. (Klaatu Diskos Ser.: 2). (ENG.). 368p. (YA). (gr. 7). 2014. pap. 8.99 (978-0-7636-6933-1(4)) 2013. 16.99 (978-0-7636-5404-7(3)) Candlewick Pr.

Hayes, Juliana. Ari Sylph Valley. 2012. 84p. 19.95 (978-1-4626-6912-7(3)) America Star Bks.

Heimbuch, Carol. Shadow Stallion. 2011. 170p. pap. 11.50 (978-1-59330-693-9(8)) Aventine Pr.

Heltzel, Anne. Charlie, Presumed Dead. 2016. (ENG.). 272p. (YA). (gr. 9). pap. 8.99 (978-0-544-66869-0(3), 1625496, Clarion Bks.) HarperCollins Pubs.

Henninger, Robert. The Rangers of the Forest. Higgins, Beatrice, illus. 2003. (ENG.). 82p. pap. 12.95 (978-1-4120-0368-1(7)) Trafford Publishing.

Henry, April. The Night She Disappeared. 2013. (ENG.). 256p. (YA). (gr. 7-12). pap. 10.99 (978-1-250-01674-4(6), 900087088) Square Fish.

Henseleit, Jack. The Troll Heart, Volume 2. 2018. (Witching Hours Ser.: 2). (ENG., Illus.). 264p. (J). (gr. 2-4). pap. 15.99 (978-1-76012-926-2(7)) Hardie Grant Children?s Publishing AUS. Dist: Independent Pubs. Group.

Hertz, Kellen. Tenney Shares the Stage. 2017. 189p. (J). (978-1-338-16722-1(7)) Scholastic, Inc.

Hesse, Monica. Girl in the Blue Coat. (ENG.). 320p. (YA). (gr. 7-17). 2017. pap. 11.99 (978-0-316-26063-3(0)) 2016. E-Book 45.00 (978-0-316-26064-0(9)) Little, Brown Bks. for Young Readers.

—Girl in the Blue Coat. 2017. (YA). lib. bdg. 20.85 (978-0-606-39918-0(6)) Turtleback.

Hiaasen, Carl. Chomp. (ENG.). 320p. (J). (gr. 5). 2020. 8.99 (978-0-593-17766-2(5), Yearling) 2013. pap. 9.99 (978-0-375-86827-6(5), Ember) Random Hse. Children's Bks.

—Scat. 2011. 10.54 (978-0-7848-3574-6(8), Everbind) Marco Bk. Co.

—Scat. 2010. 19.00 (978-1-60686-585-9(4)) Perfection Learning Corp.

—Scat. (ENG.). 400p. (J). (gr. 5). 2012. 8.99 (978-0-440-42104-7(7), Yearling) 2010. pap. 9.99 (978-0-375-83487-5(7), Ember) Random Hse. Children's Bks.

—Scat. 2012. lib. bdg. 18.40 (978-0-606-26532-4(5)) Turtleback.

—Skink — No Surrender. (ENG.). (YA). (gr. 7). 2015. 304p. pap. 10.99 (978-0-307-93059-0(9), Ember) 2014. 288p. 18.99 (978-0-375-87051-4(2), Knopf Bks. for Young Readers) Random Hse. Children's Bks.

Hiassen, Carl. Chomp. l.t. ed. 2012. (ENG.). 364p. 23.99 (978-1-4104-5101-9(1)) Thorndike Pr.

—Chomp. 2013. lib. bdg. 19.65 (978-0-606-27006-9(X)) Turtleback.

Hill, Michelle M. Stanley. 2012. 12p. pap. 15.99 (978-1-4772-2923-1(X)) AuthorHouse.

Hobbs, Leigh. Mr Badger & the Missing Ape. l.t. ed. 2012. 120p. (J). pap. (978-1-4596-3344-5(X)) ReadHowYouWant.com, Ltd.

Holland, Sara. Havenfall. 2020. (Havenfall Ser.: 1). (ENG.). 320p. (YA). 18.99 (978-1-5476-0379-4(8), 900215313, Bloomsbury Young Adult) Bloomsbury Publishing USA.

Holt, K. A. Gnome-A-geddon. Jack, Colin, illus. (ENG.). 304p. (J). (gr. 3-7). 2018. pap. 7.99 *(978-1-4814-7846-5(X))* 2017. 16.99 *(978-1-4814-7845-8(1))* McElderry, Margaret K. Bks. (McElderry, Margaret K. Bks.).

Horowitz, Nancy Ellis. Nicely Dunn & the Lost Little Sister. 2009. 88p. pap. 30.49 *(978-1-4389-3011-4(9))* AuthorHouse.

Horwitz, Sarah Jean. Carmer & Grit, Book One: the Wingsnatchers, Volume 1. 2018. (Carmer & Grit Ser.). (ENG.). 368p. (gr. 5-9). pap. 8.99 *(978-1-61620-802-8(3),* 73802) Algonquin Young Readers.

Hughes, Alison. Lost in the Backyard, 1 vol. 2015. (ENG.). 144p. (J). (gr. 4-7). pap. 10.95 *(978-1-4598-0794-5(4))* Orca Bk. Pubs. USA.

Hulst, W. G. van de & Hulst, Willem G. van de, illus. The Rockity Rowboat. 2014. (J). *(978-1-928136-18-7(4))* Inheritance Pubns.

Hunt, Elizabeth Singer. Secret Agent Jack Stalwart: Book 2: the Search for the Sunken Treasure: Australia. 2007. (Secret Agent Jack Stalwart Ser.: 2). (ENG., Illus.). 128p. (J). (gr. 1-4). per. 5.99 *(978-1-60286-002-5(5),* Running Pr. Kids) Running Pr.

—Secret Agent Jack Stalwart: Book 3: the Mystery of the Mona Lisa: France, Bk. 3. 2007. (Secret Agent Jack Stalwart Ser.: 3). (ENG., Illus.). 128p. (J). (gr. 1-4). per. 5.99 *(978-1-60286-001-8(7),* Running Pr. Kids) Running Pr.

Hutchinson, Shaun David. The Apocalypse of Elena Mendoza. 2019. (ENG., Illus.). 464p. (YA). (gr. 9). pap. 12.99 *(978-1-4814-9855-5(X),* Simon Pulse) Simon Pulse.

—At the Edge of the Universe. (ENG.). (YA). (gr. 9). 2018. 512p. pap. 13.99 *(978-1-4814-4967-0(2))* 2017. (Illus.). 496p. 17.99 *(978-1-4814-4966-3(4))* Simon Pulse. (Simon Pulse).

Imfeld, Robert. Baylor's Guide to Dreadful Dreams. 2017. (ENG., Illus.). 320p. (J). (gr. 5-9). 16.99 *(978-1-4814-6639-4(9),* Aladdin) Simon & Schuster Children's Publishing.

Ireland, Justina. Scream Site. 2018. (ENG.). 264p. (YA). (gr. 7-12). 15.95 *(978-1-63079-102-5(4),* 138468, Capstone Editions) Capstone.

Irwin, Chris. Nightmare of Shadows. 2007. 140p. pap. 18.95 *(978-0-615-15008-6(X))* Irwin, Christine.

Jackson, Tiffany D. Monday's Not Coming. (ENG.). (YA). (gr. 8). 2019. 464p. pap. 12.99 *(978-0-06-242268-2(5))* 2018. 448p. 18.99 *(978-0-06-242267-5(7))* HarperCollins Pubs. (Tegen, Katherine Bks).

Jacobson, Jennifer Richard. Andy Shane & the Barn Sale Mystery. Carter, Abby, illus. 2010. (Andy Shane Ser.: 5). (ENG.). 64p. (J). (gr. k-3). 5.99 *(978-0-7636-4827-5(2))* Candlewick Pr.

Jacques, Karen. Monsters Have My Brother. Cahanes, Erin, illus. 2015. (ENG.). (J). 16.95 *(978-1-59298-863-1(6))* Beaver's Pond Pr., Inc.

James, Caleb. Haffling. 2nd ed. 2016. (Haffling Ser.: 1). (ENG., Illus.). 250p. pap. 16.99 *(978-1-63476-795-8(0),* DSP Pubns.) Dreamspinner Pr.

James, Ellie. Broken Illusions: A Midnight Dragonfly Novel. 2012. (Midnight Dragonfly Novel Ser.: 2). (ENG.). 352p. (YA). (gr. 7-12). 26.19 *(978-0-312-64703-2(4))* St. Martin's Pr.

Jean, Sagine. Darkness. 2017. (Survive Ser.). (ENG.). 192p. (YA). (gr. 5-12). lib. bdg. 31.42 *(978-1-68076-731-5(3),* 25396, Epic Escape) EPIC Pr.

Jenisch, Betty. Rennie. 2007. 9.00 *(978-0-8059-8947-2(1))* Dorrance Publishing Co., Inc.

Jenkins, Carla LaVern. The Disappearance of Mrs. Brown: A Jenkins Girl Mystery. 2010. 72p. 23.55 *(978-1-4269-4537-3(X))*; pap. 13.55 *(978-1-4251-6659-5(8))* Trafford Publishing.

Johnson, Elana. Possession. 2012. (Possession Novel Ser.). (ENG.). 416p. (YA). (gr. 7-12). 26.19 *(978-1-4424-2125-7(8))* Simon & Schuster, Inc.

—Possession. 2012. (ENG.). 432p. (YA). (gr. 9). pap. 11.99 *(978-1-4424-2126-4(6),* Simon Pulse) Simon Pulse.

Johnson, Terry Lynn. Falcon Wild. 2017. 176p. (J). (gr. 5). lib. bdg. 16.99 *(978-1-58089-788-4(6))* Charlesbridge Publishing, Inc.

—Overboard! Orban, Jani, illus. 2018. (Survivor Diaries). (ENG.). 112p. (J). (gr. 1-5). pap. 8.99 *(978-1-328-51905-4(8),* 1720631, Clarion Bks.) HarperCollins Pubs.

—Overboard! 2018. (Survivor Diaries). lib. bdg. 16.00 *(978-0-606-41208-7(5))* Turtleback.

Jones, Cath. The Magic Helmet. Gray, Dean, illus. 2021. (Early Bird Readers — Gold (Early Bird Stories (tm)) Ser.). (ENG.). 32p. (J). (gr. k-3). 30.65 *(978-1-5415-9009-0(0),* 2cb67c0e-c1b9-458b-ab34-b7f29347e3a4, Lerner Pubns.) Lerner Publishing Group.

Joyce, William. The Sandman & the War of Dreams. Joyce, William, illus. 2013. (Guardians Ser.: 4). (ENG., Illus.). 240p. (J). (gr. 2-6). 18.99 *(978-1-4424-3054-9(0),* Atheneum Bks. for Young Readers) Simon & Schuster Children's Publishing.

Jules, Jacqueline. Un Paseo de Compras Problemático. Smith, Kim, illus. 2018. (Sofia Martinez en Español Ser.). (SPA.). 32p. (J). (gr. k-2). lib. bdg. 21.32 *(978-1-5158-2451-0(9),* 137554, Picture Window Bks.) Capstone.

—Shopping Trip Trouble. Smith, Kim, illus. 2017. (Sofia Martinez Ser.). (ENG.). 32p. (J). (gr. k-2). lib. bdg. 21.32 *(978-1-5158-0729-2(0),* 133611, Picture Window Bks.) Capstone.

—Shopping Trip Trouble Smith, Kim, illus. 2018. (Sofia Martinez Ser.). (ENG.). 32p. (J). (gr. k-2). pap. 5.95 *(978-1-5158-0731-5(2),* 133613, Picture Window Bks.) Capstone.

Justis, Jon. Pumpkin & the Great Dragon Caper. 2012. 32p. pap. 24.95 *(978-1-4626-9733-5(X))* America Star Bks.

Kaaberbøl, Lene. Heartbreak Island. 2005. (W. I. T. C. H. Adventures Ser.: Bk. 3). (Illus.). 105p. (J). lib. bdg. 11.00 *(978-1-4242-0786-2(X))* Fitzgerald Bks.

Kantor, Melissa. The Amanda Project. 2011. 287p. (J). 8.99 *(978-0-06-202706-1(9),* HarperTeen) HarperCollins Pubs.

Kanu, Rosslyn. The Little Girl Called Princess: Princess Where Are You? 2012. 32p. pap. 19.99 *(978-1-4685-2375-1(9))* AuthorHouse.

Keene, Carolyn. Hidden Pictures. 2020. (Nancy Drew Diaries: 19). (ENG.). 192p. (J). (gr. 3-7). pap. 6.99 *(978-1-5344-2102-8(5),* Simon & Schuster/Paula Wiseman Bks.) Simon & Schuster/Paula Wiseman Bks.

Kelly, Erin Entrada. Hello, Universe. Roxas, Isabel, illus. 2018. (ENG.). 320p. (J). (gr. 3-7). 8.99 *(978-0-06-287750-5(X),* Greenwillow Bks.) HarperCollins Pubs.

—Hello, Universe. 2018. lib. bdg. 17.20 *(978-0-606-41021-2(X))* Turtleback.

—Hello, Universe: A Newbery Award Winner. Roxas, Isabel, illus. (ENG.). (J). (gr. 3-7). 2020. 352p. pap. 9.99 *(978-0-06-241416-8(X))* 2017. 320p. 16.99 *(978-0-06-241415-1(1))* HarperCollins Pubs. (Greenwillow Bks.).

Kenah, Katharine. The Best Seat in Second Grade. Carter, Abby, illus. 2006. (I Can Read Bks.). 48p. (J). (gr. -1-3). 11.65 *(978-0-7569-6979-0(4))* Perfection Learning Corp.

Kennedy, Kelly & Burroughs, Scott, illus. Juliet Saves the Day! Ready-To-Read Level 2. 2018. (Sherlock Gnomes Ser.). (ENG.). 32p. (J). (gr. k-2). pap. 3.99 *(978-1-5344-1094-7(5),* Simon Spotlight) Simon Spotlight.

Kephart, Beth. Wild Blues. Sulit, William, illus. (ENG.). (J). (gr. 5-9). 2019. 352p. pap. 9.99 *(978-1-4814-9154-9(7))* 2018. 336p. 17.99 *(978-1-4814-9153-2(9),* Atheneum/Caitlyn Dlouhy Books) Simon & Schuster Children's Publishing.

Kessler, Liz. North of Nowhere. (ENG.). 272p. (J). (gr. 4-7). 2015. pap. 8.99 *(978-0-7636-7672-8(1))* 2013. (Illus.). 15.99 *(978-0-7636-6727-6(7))* Candlewick Pr.

Kilgras, Heidi. Peanut. Reed, Mike, illus. 2003. (Step into Reading Ser.). 32p. (J). (gr. -1-1). pap. 5.99 *(978-0-375-80618-6(0),* Random Hse. Bks. for Young Readers) Random Hse. Children's Bks.

King, A. S. Everybody Sees the Ants. 2012. (ENG.). 320p. (YA). (gr. 10-17). pap. 11.99 *(978-0-316-12927-5(5))* Little, Brown Bks. for Young Readers.

King, Caro. Seven Sorcerers. 2012. (ENG.). 352p. (J). (gr. 3-7). pap. 6.99 *(978-1-4424-2043-4(X),* Aladdin) Simon & Schuster Children's Publishing.

—Shadow Spell. 2012. (ENG.). 320p. (J). (gr. 3-7). pap. 6.99 *(978-1-4423-3908-8(X),* Aladdin) Simon & Schuster Children's Publishing.

—Shadow Spell. 2012. (ENG.). 320p. (J). (gr. 3-7). 15.99 *(978-1-4424-2045-8(6),* Simon & Schuster/Paula Wiseman Bks.) Simon & Schuster/Paula Wiseman Bks.

Klim, Christopher. Firecracker Jones Is on the Case. 2006. (Illus.). 116p. (J). lib. bdg. 19.95 *(978-1-933435-11-4(9))* Hopewell Pubns., LLC.

Klingele, Lindsey. The Truth Lies Here. 2018. (ENG.). 416p. (YA). (gr. 8). 17.99 *(978-0-06-238039-5(7),* HarperTeen) HarperCollins Pubs.

Knight, Barbara. The Lost Boy. 2008. (Illus.). 32p. (J). 14.95 *(978-0-9766270-3-6(5))* Mustang BKS.

Knight, Christopher. World Is Black & White. 2008. 459p. (YA). pap. 14.95 *(978-1-893699-97-7(8))* AudioCraft Publishing, Inc.

Kress, Adrienne. The Explorers: the Reckless Rescue. 2019. (Explorers Ser.: 2). (ENG.). 400p. (J). (gr. 3-7). 7.99 *(978-1-101-94012-9(3),* Yearling) Random Hse. Children's Bks.

Krokos, Dan. The Black Stars. 2015. (Planet Thieves Ser.: 2). (ENG., Illus.). 304p. (J). (gr. 3-8). pap. 17.99 *(978-0-7653-7668-8(7),* 900134306, Starscape) Doherty, Tom Assocs., LLC.

Kropp, Paul. The Kid Is Lost. Melanson, Matt, illus. 2004. (HIP Sr Ser.). (ENG.). 88p. (J). (gr. 7-12). 26.19 *(978-1-897039-04-5(2))* High Interest Publishing (HIP) CAN. Dist: Children's Plus, Inc.

Krosoczka, Jarrett J. Lunch Lady & the Author Visit Vendetta: Lunch Lady #3. 2009. (Lunch Lady Ser.: 3). (ENG.). 96p. (J). (gr. 2-5). pap. 6.99 *(978-0-375-86094-2(0),* Knopf Bks. for Young Readers) Random Hse. Children's Bks.

Krulik, Nancy. Get Lost! #6, 6 vols. John and Wendy, illus. 6th ed. 2006. (Katie Kazoo, Switcheroo Ser.: 6). 80p. (J). (gr. 2-4). 6.99 *(978-0-448-43101-7(7),* Grosset & Dunlap) Penguin Young Readers Group.

Laird, Chynna. Dark Water. 2012. 166p. pap. *(978-1-926997-76-6(X))* Imajin Bks.

Lane, Andrew. Fire Storm. 2014. (Sherlock Holmes: the Legend Begins Ser.: 4). (ENG.). 368p. (YA). (gr. 7-12). pap. 16.99 *(978-1-250-05072-4(3),* 900134143) Square Fish.

LaReau, Kara. The Jolly Regina (the Unintentional Adventures of the Bland Sisters Book 1) Hill, Jen, illus. 2018. (Unintentional Adventures of the Bland Sisters Ser.). (ENG.). 184p. (J). (gr. 3-7). pap. 7.99 *(978-1-4197-2605-7(6),* 1138303, Amulet Bks.) Abrams, Inc.

—The Uncanny Express (the Unintentional Adventures of the Bland Sisters Book 2) Hill, Jen, illus. 2018. (Unintentional Adventures of the Bland Sisters Ser.). (ENG.). (J). (gr. 3-7). 184p. pap. 7.99 *(978-1-4197-3204-1(8),* 1139403); 176p. 14.99 *(978-1-4197-2568-5(8),* 1139401) Abrams, Inc. (Amulet Bks.).

—Unintentional Adventures of the Bland Sisters: The Jolly Regina. Hill, Jen, illus. 2017. (ENG.). 176p. (J). (gr. 3-7). 14.95 *(978-1-4197-2136-6(4),* 1138301, Amulet Bks.) Abrams, Inc.

Larson, Hope. Compass South. 2017. (Four Points Ser.: 1). (J). lib. bdg. 24.50 *(978-0-606-39953-1(4))* Turtleback.

Latimer, Alex. Am I Yours?, 1 vol. 2018. (ENG., Illus.). 32p. (J). (gr. -1-3). 16.95 *(978-1-68263-044-0(7))* Peachtree Publishing Co. Inc.

Lawrence, Caroline. The Secrets of Vesuvius. 2004. (Roman Mysteries Ser.). (Illus.). 173p. (J). (gr. 3-7). 13.65 *(978-0-7569-5947-0(0))* Perfection Learning Corp.

Legrand, Claire. The Cavendish Home for Boys & Girls. Watts, Sarah, illus. (ENG.). (J). (gr. 5). 2013. 368p. pap. 8.99 *(978-1-4424-4292-4(1))* 2012. 352p. 17.99 *(978-1-4424-4291-7(3))* Simon & Schuster Bks. For Young Readers. (Simon & Schuster Bks. For Young Readers).

Leighton-Porter, Wendy. The Shadow of Camelot. 2013. 262p. pap. *(978-1-909411-06-7(X))* Mauve Square Publishing.

Leonard, Connie King. Sleeping in My Jeans. 2018. (ENG.). 240p. (YA). pap. 16.00 *(978-1-947845-00-8(4))* Ooligan Pr.

Leveen, Tom. Hellworld. (ENG.). (YA). (gr. 9). 2018. 320p. pap. 11.99 *(978-1-4814-6634-9(8))* 2017. (Illus.). 304p. 17.99 *(978-1-4814-6633-2(X))* Simon Pulse. (Simon Pulse).

Levithan, David. The Mysterious Disappearance of Aidan S. (as Told to His Brother) 2021. (ENG.). 224p. (J). (gr. 3-7). 16.99 *(978-1-9848-4859-8(3),* Knopf Bks. for Young Readers) Random Hse. Children's Bks.

Littman, Sarah Darer. Want to Go Private? (ENG.). 336p. (YA). (gr. 9-9). 2019. pap. 10.99 *(978-0-545-15147-4(3))* 2011. 17.99 *(978-0-545-15146-7(5),* Scholastic Pr.) Scholastic, Inc.

Lord, Gabrielle. Black Ops Missing: Conspiracy 365. 2014. 192p. (J). 10.99 *(978-1-61067-168-2(6))* Kane Miller.

The Lost Boy. 2008. (Illus.). 32p. (Orig.). (J). per. 14.95 *(978-0-9766720-3-6(0))* Mustang BKS.

Lucier, Makiia. Isle of Blood & Stone. (Tower of Winds Ser.). (ENG.). (YA). (gr. 7). 2019. 416p. pap. 9.99 *(978-1-328-60429-3(2),* 1731502) 2018. 400p. 17.99 *(978-0-544-96857-8(3),* 1662274) HarperCollins Pubs. (Clarion Bks.).

Lück, Stefanie. Carla's Worlds. 2010. 222p. pap. 20.90 *(978-3-8391-4857-0(X))* Bks. on Demand.

Lynn, Jenna. Hoodnapped: Book 3. Cruz, Abigail Dela, illus. 2018. (Robyn Hood Ser.). (ENG.). 48p. (J). (gr. 3-7). lib. bdg. 34.21 *(978-1-5321-3378-7(2),* 31179, Spellbound) Magic Wagon.

MacDonald, George. A Rough Shaking. 2017. (ENG., Illus.). (J). pap. 16.95 *(978-1-374-88365-9(4))* Capital Communications, Inc.

MacGregor, Roy. The Secret of the Deep Woods (#17), No. 17. 2003. (Screech Owls Ser.: 17). (ENG.). 128p. (J). (gr. 3-7). mass mkt. 4.95 *(978-0-7710-5646-8(X),* Screech Owls) McClelland & Stewart CAN. Dist: Penguin Random Hse. LLC.

MacIntyre, R. P. Revved. 2006. (ENG.). 220p. pap. 12.95 *(978-1-894345-46-0(0))* Thistledown Pr., Ltd. CAN. Dist: Univ. of Toronto Pr.

MacPhail, Cathy. Hide & Seek. 2012. (Stoke Books Titles Ser.). 72p. (J). (gr. 5-8). pap. 7.95 *(978-1-78112-024-8(2))*; lib. bdg. 22.60 *(978-1-78112-023-1(4))* Stoke Bks.

Madonia, Kristen-Paige. Invisible Fault Lines. 2016. (ENG.). 320p. (YA). (gr. 7). 17.99 *(978-1-4814-3071-5(8),* Simon & Schuster Bks. For Young Readers) Simon & Schuster Bks. For Young Readers.

Mafi, Tahereh. Furthermore. 2017. (ENG.). 432p. (J). (gr. 4-7). 9.99 *(978-1-101-99477-1(0),* Puffin Books) Penguin Young Readers Group.

—Furthermore. 2017. (Furthermore Ser.: 1). lib. bdg. 19.65 *(978-0-606-40493-8(7))* Turtleback.

Magoon, Kekla. Shadows of Sherwood. (Robyn Hoodlum Adventure Ser.). (ENG.). 368p. 2016. (J). pap. 8.99 *(978-1-68119-023-5(0),* 900156154) 2015. (YA). (gr. 3-6). 16.99 *(978-1-61963-634-7(4),* 900143012) Bloomsbury Publishing USA. (Bloomsbury USA Childrens).

—Shadows of Sherwood. 2016. (Robyn Hoodlum Ser.: 1). (ENG.). 355p. (J). (gr. 3-6). 18.40 *(978-0-606-39281-5(5))* Turtleback.

Makechnie, Amy. The Unforgettable Guinevere St. Clair. (ENG.). 336p. (J). (gr. 3-7). 2019. pap. 8.99 *(978-1-5344-1447-1(9))* 2018. (Illus.). 18.99 *(978-1-5344-1446-4(0))* Simon & Schuster Children's Publishing. (Atheneum Bks. for Young Readers).

Malkin, Nina. Swear. (ENG.). 480p. (YA). (gr. 11). 2012. pap. 9.99 *(978-1-4424-2111-0(8))* 2011. 17.99 *(978-1-4424-2110-3(X))* Simon Pulse. (Simon Pulse).

Mammina, David. The Circle Stone Group: Book 1: the Beginning. 2009. 112p. pap. 13.35 *(978-1-4269-1478-2(4))* Trafford Publishing.

Manushkin, Fran. Katie Woo, Where Are You?, 1 vol. Lyon, Tammie, illus. 2011. (Katie Woo Ser.). (ENG.). 32p. (J). (gr. k-2). pap. 5.95 *(978-1-4048-6853-3(4),* 116434, Picture Window Bks.) Capstone.

Margaret I. Pascuzzo. Anton Finds a Treasure. Bicking, Judith, illus. 2008. (ENG.). 18p. pap. 12.00 *(978-1-4251-8683-8(1))* Trafford Publishing.

Margolis, Leslie. Vanishing Acts. 2013. (Maggie Brooklyn Mystery Ser.). (ENG.). 256p. (J). (gr. 3-6). pap. 7.99 *(978-1-59990-981-3(2),* 900096404, Bloomsbury USA Childrens) Bloomsbury Publishing USA.

MariNaomi. Gravity's Pull: Book 2. MariNaomi, illus. 2019. (Life on Earth Ser.). (ENG., Illus.). 224p. (YA). (gr. 9-12). 29.32 *(978-1-5124-4911-2(3),* 548a8fb2-504e-4895-9420-fca6c9b02ba8, Graphic Universe™) Lerner Publishing Group.

—Losing the Girl: Book 1. MariNaomi, illus. 2018. (Life on Earth Ser.). (ENG., Illus.). 280p. (YA). (gr. 9-12). 29.32 *(978-1-5124-4910-5(5),* 2099d044-5e92-416d-809c-e5c159524808, Graphic Universe™) Lerner Publishing Group.

—Losing the Girl: Book 1, Bk. 1. MariNaomi, illus. 2018. (Life on Earth Ser.). (ENG., Illus.). 280p. (YA). (gr. 9-12). pap. 15.99 *(978-1-5415-1044-9(5),* d3711532-bab9-4c12-a95c-d701ee92bbc9, Graphic Universe™) Lerner Publishing Group.

Marsh, Carole. The Mystery at Fort Sumter. Friedlander, Randolyn, illus. 2010. (Real Kids, Real Places Ser.). 32p. (J). pap. 7.99 *(978-0-635-07432-4(X),* Marsh, Carole Mysteries) Gallopade International.

—The Mystery at Fort Sumter: First Shot Fired in the Civil War! 2010. (Real Kids, Real Places Ser.). (Illus.). 158p. (J). 18.99 *(978-0-635-07430-0(3),* Marsh, Carole Mysteries) Gallopade International.

Marsh, Sarah Glenn. Fear the Drowning Deep. (ENG.). 312p. (gr. 6-12). 2018. (YA). pap. 8.99 *(978-1-5107-2658-1(6))* 2016. (J). 16.99 *(978-1-5107-0348-3(9))* Skyhorse Publishing Co., Inc. (Sky Pony Pr.).

Marsham, Liz. Wonder Woman: Maze of Magic. 2017. (I Can Read! Level 2 Ser.). (Illus.). 32p. (J). lib. bdg. 13.55 *(978-0-606-40057-2(5))* Turtleback.

Martin, Amy. Symphony City. 2011. (ENG., Illus.). 48p. (J). (gr. -1-4). 17.95 *(978-1-936365-39-5(1),* 4506c646-7825-42ba-9674-8978332756b5) McSweeney's Publishing.

Martin, Emily Winfield. Snow & Rose. (Illus.). 224p. (J). (gr. 3-7). 2019. pap. 9.99 *(978-0-553-53821-2(7),* Yearling) 2017. 17.99 *(978-0-553-53818-2(7),* Random Hse. Bks. for Young Readers) Random Hse. Children's Bks.

Martin, Laura. The Ark Plan. DesChamps, Eric, illus. 2017. (Edge of Extinction Ser.: 1). (ENG.). (J). (gr. 3-7). lib. bdg. 17.20 *(978-0-606-40046-6(X))* Turtleback.

Martin, R. T. Dark Star. 2017. (Midnight Ser.). (ENG.). 96p. (YA). (gr. 6-12). 26.65 *(978-1-5124-2769-1(1),* 8eeb8a61-2d0b-4e89-bb5c-bc1bee46c19d); E-Book 39.99 *(978-1-5124-3485-9(X),* 9781512434859) Lerner Publishing Group. (Darby Creek).

Maselli, Christopher P. N. The Runaway Mission. 2004. 104p. 5.99 *(978-1-57562-805-9(8))* Copeland, Kenneth Pubns.

Mathieu, Jennifer. Afterward. 2017. (YA). lib. bdg. 20.85 *(978-0-606-40590-4(9))* Turtleback.

May, Eleanor. Lost in the Mouseum. 2018. (Mouse Math Ser.). (ENG.). 32p. (J). (gr. -1-1). lib. bdg. 34.28 *(978-1-4896-8291-8(0),* AV2 by Weigl) Weigl Pubs., Inc.

McBride, Anthony & McBride, Autumn. The Lost Cat. 2007. (Illus.). pap. 11.00 *(978-1-56411-540-9(2),* CB Publishing & Design) UBUS Communications Systems.

McClintock, Norah. About That Night, 1 vol. 2014. (ENG.). 248p. (YA). (gr. 8-12). pap. 12.95 *(978-1-4598-0594-1(1))* Orca Bk. Pubs. USA.

McCracken, Connie. Indigo Boy & Crystalline Girl. Craig, Chris, illus. 2009. 24p. pap. 10.95 *(978-1-4269-0423-3(1))* Trafford Publishing.

McCreight, Kimberly. The Outliers. (Outliers Ser.: 1). (ENG.). (YA). (gr. 9). 2017. 368p. pap. 10.99 *(978-0-06-235910-0(X))* 2016. 352p. 18.99 *(978-0-06-235909-4(6))* HarperCollins Pubs. (HarperCollins).

McCullough, Victoria. Charlotte's Hummock: a Young Adult Woman's Mystery Detective Novel. 2007. 124p. per. 19.95 *(978-1-4241-6703-6(5))* America Star Bks.

McDonald, Megan. When the Library Lights Go Out. Tillotson, Katherine, illus. 2009. (ENG.). 40p. (J). (gr. -1-1). 9.99 *(978-1-4169-8028-5(8),* Atheneum Bks. for Young Readers) Simon & Schuster Children's Publishing.

McDougall, Sophia. Mars Evacuees. (ENG.). (J). (gr. 3-7). 2016. 432p. pap. 7.99 *(978-0-06-229400-5(8))* 2015. 416p. 16.99 *(978-0-06-229399-2(0))* HarperCollins Pubs. (HarperCollins).

McMann, Lisa. Cryer's Cross. 2011. (ENG.). (YA). (gr. 9). 256p. pap. 9.99 *(978-1-4169-9482-4(3))*; (Illus.). 240p. 16.99 *(978-1-4169-9481-7(5))* Simon Pulse. (Simon Pulse).

McManus, Karen M. Two Can Keep a Secret. 2019. (ENG.). 352p. lib. bdg. 21.80 *(978-1-6636-2970-8(6))* Perfection Learning Corp.

—Two Can Keep a Secret. (ENG.). 352p. (YA). (gr. 9). 2021. pap. 12.99 *(978-1-5247-1471-0(2),* Ember) 2019. 19.99 *(978-1-5247-1472-7(0),* Delacorte Pr.) Random Hse. Children's Bks.

McMillan, Frank. Cezanne Is Missing. 2006. (ENG.). 323p. (YA). (gr. 7). per. 14.95 *(978-0-9711359-4-9(0))* Cambridge Hse. Publishing Co., LLC.

McMullan, Kate. I'm Big! McMullan, Jim, illus. 2010. (ENG.). 40p. (J). (gr. -1-3). 17.99 *(978-0-06-122974-9(1),* Balzer & Bray) HarperCollins Pubs.

McNeal, Tom. Far Far Away. 2014. (ENG.). 400p. (YA). (gr. 7). pap. 10.99 *(978-0-375-84329-7(9),* Ember) Random Hse. Children's Bks.

McNeece, Alexander. Sam Iver: Imminent Threat. 2009. 138p. pap. 10.95 *(978-1-935278-02-3(9),* iUniverse Star) iUniverse, Inc.

McNeill, Malcolm. The Beginning Woods. 2018. (ENG.). 528p. (J). (gr. 5-5). 17.99 *(978-1-5107-2290-3(4),* Sky Pony Pr.) Skyhorse Publishing Co., Inc.

McSorley, Paul J. & Bearss, Patricia. The Adventures of Forealdo: Finding Millie. 2012. 34p. 24.95 *(978-1-4626-6721-5(X))* America Star Bks.

Meadows, Michelle. Itsy-Bitsy Baby Mouse. Cordell, Matthew, illus. 2012. (ENG.). 40p. (J). (gr. -1-2). 15.99 *(978-1-4169-3786-9(2),* Simon & Schuster Bks. For Young Readers) Simon & Schuster Bks. For Young Readers.

Meehl, Brian. Blowback '07: When the Only Way Forward Is Back. 2016. (Illus.). 346p. (J). pap. 12.95 *(978-1-63505-185-8(1))* Salem Author Services.

Melki-Wegner, Skye. The Hush. 2017. (ENG.). 386p. (J). (gr. 6-6). 16.99 *(978-1-5107-1248-5(8),* Sky Pony Pr.) Skyhorse Publishing Co., Inc.

Meloy, Colin. Wildwood. Ellis, Carson, illus. 2011. (Wildwood Chronicles Ser.: 1). (ENG.). 560p. (J). (gr. 3-7). 19.99 *(978-0-06-202468-8(X),* Balzer & Bray) HarperCollins Pubs.

—Wildwood. Ellis, Carson, illus. 2012. (Wildwood Chronicles Ser.: 1). (J). lib. bdg. 20.85 *(978-0-606-26864-6(2))* Turtleback.

Merritt, Kory. No Place for Monsters. Merritt, Kory, illus. 2020. (No Place for Monsters Ser.). (ENG., Illus.). 384p. (J). (gr. 3-7). 14.99 *(978-0-358-12853-3(6),* 1752984, Clarion Bks.) HarperCollins Pubs.

Messner, Kate. Escape from the Twin Towers (Ranger in Time #11) McMorris, Kelley, illus. 2020. (Ranger in Time Ser.: 11). (ENG.). 144p. (J). (gr. 2-5). pap. 5.99 *(978-1-338-53794-9(6),* Scholastic Pr.) Scholastic, Inc.

Meyer, Deanna. Buffalo on the Ridge. 2010. pap. 12.95 *(978-0-7414-6103-2(X))* Infinity Publishing.

Meyer, Marissa. Scarlet. 2013. (Lunar Chronicles Ser.: 2). (ENG.). 464p. (YA). (gr. 7). 19.99 *(978-0-312-64296-9(2),* 900078309) Feiwel & Friends.

—Scarlet. l.t. ed. 2013. (Lunar Chronicles: Bk. 2). (ENG.). 572p. 23.99 *(978-1-4104-5623-6(4))* Thorndike Pr.

—Scarlet. 2014. (Lunar Chronicles Ser.: 2). (YA). lib. bdg. 20.85 *(978-0-606-35097-6(7))* Turtleback.

—Scarlet. 2016. (SPA.). 430p. (YA). (gr. 9-12). pap. 20.99 *(978-987-612-990-9(2))* V&R Editoras.

Michael Batdorf. Pair of Jacks: A Novel. 2009. 332p. 29.95 *(978-1-4401-4482-0(6))*; pap. 19.95 *(978-1-4401-4479-0(6))* iUniverse, Inc.

Michaelis, Antonia. The Secret of the Twelfth Continent. 2013. (ENG., Illus.). 288p. (J). (gr. 2-7). 14.95 *(978-1-62087-539-1(X),* 620539, Sky Pony Pr.) Skyhorse Publishing Co., Inc.

Miklowitz, Gloria D. The Enemy Has a Face. 2004. (ENG.). 143p. (YA). pap. 8.00 *(978-0-8028-5261-8(0))* Eerdmans, William B. Publishing Co.

Miller, Stefne & Madison, Bailee. Losing Brave, 1 vol. 2018. (ENG.). 352p. (YA). 17.99 *(978-0-310-76054-2(2))* Blink.

Millet, Lydia. The Fires Beneath the Sea. 2012. (Dissenters Ser.). (ENG.). 256p. (J). (gr. 3-7). pap. 12.00 *(978-1-931520-47-8(X),* Big Mouth Hse.) Small Beer Pr.

—The Shimmers in the Night: A Novel. 2012. (Dissenters Ser.). (ENG.). 256p. (J). (gr. 3-7). 16.95 *(978-1-931520-78-2(X),* Big Mouth Hse.) Small Beer Pr.

Milway, Alex. Operation Robot Storm: The Mythical 9th Division. 2013. (ENG., Illus.). 224p. (J). pap. 5.99 *(978-1-61067-074-6(4))* Kane Miller.

Mishica, Clare. Samantha Stays Safe. Dubin, Jill, illus. 2012. 32p. (J). pap. 8.00 (978-1-935014-40-9(4)) Hutchings, John Pubs.

The Missing Man & the Twenty Dragons. 2nd ed. 2005. (ENG., Illus.). 204p. (J). reprint ed. per. 11.99 (978-0-9760045-1-6(8), Reluctant Reader Bks.) Cronus College.

Morgan, Winter. Beneath the Blocks. 2018. (Unofficial Minecrafter Mysteries Ser.: 2). lib. bdg. 18.40 (978-0-606-41297-1(2)) Turtleback.

Moriarty, Jaclyn. A Corner of White (the Colors of Madeleine, Book 1) 2013. (Colors of Madeleine Ser.: 1). (ENG.). 384p. (YA). (gr. 7-7). 18.99 (978-0-545-39736-0(7), Levine, Arthur A. Bks.) Scholastic, Inc.

—A Tangle of Gold (the Colors of Madeleine, Book 3) 2016. (Colors of Madeleine Ser.: 3). (ENG.). 480p. (YA). (gr. 7-7). 18.99 (978-0-545-39740-7(5), Levine, Arthur A. Bks.) Scholastic, Inc.

Morrill, Stephanie. The Lost Girl of Astor Street, 1 vol. 2018. (ENG.). 352p. (YA). pap. 10.99 (978-0-310-75840-2(8)) Blink.

Mowry, Jess. Tyger Tales. 2007. 227p. per. 14.99 (978-1-59092-358-0(8)) Blue Forge Pr.

Mrozek, Elizabeth. The Fifth Chair. Mrozek, Elizabeth, illus. 2013. (Illus.). 38p. 19.95 (978-1-935766-80-3(5)) Windy City Pubs.

Mull, Brandon. Master of the Phantom Isle. 2019. (Dragonwatch Ser.: 3). (ENG., Illus.). 496p. (J). (gr. 5). 18.99 (978-1-62972-604-5(4), 5222032, Shadow Mountain) Deseret Bk. Co.

—Master of the Phantom Isle: A Fablehaven Adventure. 2020. (Dragonwatch Ser.: 3). (ENG., Illus.). 496p. (J). (gr. 3-8). pap. 9.99 (978-1-4814-8506-7(7), Aladdin) Simon & Schuster Children's Publishing.

Munday, Dj. The Secret Dummy of Joshua Bean. 2008. 84p. pap. (978-1-84923-029-2(3)) YouWriteOn.

Murphy, Stuart J. En Busca de Freda. 2012. (I See I Learn Ser.: 23). (Illus.). 32p. (J). (-k). 14.95 (978-1-58089-494-4(1)) Charlesbridge Publishing, Inc.

—Freda Is Found. 2011. (I See I Learn Ser.: 7). (Illus.). 32p. (J). (-k). 14.95 (978-1-58089-462-3(3)); pap. 6.95 (978-1-58089-463-0(1)) Charlesbridge Publishing, Inc.

Naffziger, Lisa. Minus. 2019. (ENG., Illus.). 178p. (YA). pap. 15.00 (978-1-945820-32-8(2)) Iron Circus Comics.

Narsimhan, Mahtab. The Third Eye: Tara Trilogy. 2007. (Tara Trilogy Ser.: 1). (ENG.). 240p. (YA). (gr. 5-7). pap. 12.99 (978-1-55002-750-1(6), Boardwalk Bks.) Dundurn Pr. CAN. Dist: Ingram Publisher Services.

Neil, Deanna. The Land of Curiosities (Book 2)) Lost in Yellowstone, 1872-1873. 2009. 320p. (J). pap. 12.95 (978-0-9798800-2-5(5)) EcoSeekers, The.

Ness, Patrick & Goss, James. Class: What She Does Next Will Astound You. 2018. (Class Ser.: 3). (ENG.). 320p. (YA). (gr. 8). 17.99 (978-0-06-266623-9(1), Quill Tree Bks.) HarperCollins Pubs.

Nilsson, Ulf. Detective Gordon: a Case for Buffy. Spee, Gitte, illus. 2018. (Detective Gordon Ser.). (ENG.). 108p. (J). (gr. k-5). 16.99 (978-1-77657-178-9(9), c920efa5-2f2a-4261-a17f-c17d9ea10668) Gecko Pr. NZL. Dist: Lerner Publishing Group.

Nix, Garth. The Fall. 2004. (Seventh Tower Ser.). 195p. (gr. 4-7). 18.00 (978-0-7569-3516-0(4)) Perfection Learning Corp.

Nobel, Julia. The Mystery of Black Hollow Lane. 2020. (Black Hollow Lane Ser.: 1). 320p. (J). (gr. 3-7). pap. 8.99 (978-1-4926-9154-9(2)) Sourcebooks, Inc.

Noël, Alyson. Unrivaled. 2017. (Beautiful Idols Ser.: 1). (YA). lib. bdg. 20.85 (978-0-606-39609-7(8)) Turtleback.

Northrop, Michael. Surrounded by Sharks. 2014. (ENG.). 224p. (YA). (gr. 4-7). 18.99 (978-0-545-61545-7(3), Scholastic Pr.) Scholastic, Inc.

Ocean, Davy. Fishin' Impossible, 8. Blecha, Aaron, illus. 2017. (Shark School Ser.). (ENG.). 144p. (J). (gr. 1-3). 21.19 (978-1-5364-1675-6(4), Aladdin) Simon & Schuster Children's Publishing.

—Fishin': Impossible. Blecha, Aaron, illus. 2017. (Shark School Ser.: 8). (ENG.). 144p. (J). (gr. 1-4). pap. 6.99 (978-1-4814-6549-6(X), Aladdin) Simon & Schuster Children's Publishing.

Oliver, Lauren. Vanishing Girls. (ENG.). (YA). (gr. 9). 2016. 384p. pap. 11.99 (978-0-06-222411-8(5)) 2015. 368p. 18.99 (978-0-06-222410-1(7)) HarperCollins Pubs. (HarperCollins).

—Vanishing Girls. 2016. (YA). lib. bdg. 20.85 (978-0-606-38171-0(6)) Turtleback.

O'Neil-Andrews, Milly. Bandolines & Bubbles. 2011. 88p. pap. 11.25 (978-1-4269-3089-8(5)) Trafford Publishing.

Ostlere, Cathy. Karma: First Edition. 2012. (ENG.). 544p. (YA). (gr. 7-18). 9.99 (978-1-59514-384-6(X), Razorbill) Penguin Young Readers Group.

Panckridge, Michael & Harvey, Pam. Into the Fire. 2008. (ENG.). 194p. (J). (978-0-207-20061-8(0)) HarperCollins Pubs. Australia.

Parks, Kathy. Notes from My Captivity. (ENG.). (YA). (gr. 8). 2019. 368p. pap. 10.99 (978-0-06-239401-9(0)) 2018. 352p. 17.99 (978-0-06-239400-2(2)) HarperCollins Pubs. (Tegen, Katherine Bks).

Parrish, Harry. Kate & Alice. 2009. 28p. pap. 13.40 (978-1-4389-3120-3(4)) AuthorHouse.

Patterson, James. Ali Cross. (Ali Cross Ser.: 1). (ENG.). (J). (gr. 5-9). 2020. 336p. pap. 8.99 (978-0-316-70568-4(3)) 2019. 320p. 16.99 (978-0-316-53041-5(7)) Little Brown & Co. (Jimmy Patterson).

—Not So Normal Norbert. Aly, Hatem, illus. 2018. (ENG.). 368p. (J). (gr. 3-9). 13.99 (978-0-316-46541-0(0), Jimmy Patterson) Little Brown & Co.

Patterson, James & Grabenstein, Chris. Treasure Hunters. Neufeld, Juliana, illus. (Treasure Hunters Ser.: 1). (ENG.). 480p. (J). (gr. 3-7). 2015. pap. 9.99 (978-0-316-20757-7(8)) 2013. 14.99 (978-0-316-20756-0(X)) Little Brown & Co. (Jimmy Patterson).

—Treasure Hunters. 2015. (Treasure Hunters Ser.: 1). (J). lib. bdg. 18.45 (978-0-606-37305-0(5)) Turtleback.

—Treasure Hunters: Danger down the Nile. Neufeld, Juliana, illus. (Treasure Hunters Ser.: 2). (ENG.). 480p. (J). (gr. 3-7). 2018. pap. 8.99 (978-0-316-51510-8(8)) 2014. 14.99 (978-0-316-37086-8(X)) Little Brown & Co. (Jimmy Patterson).

—Treasure Hunters: Secret of the Forbidden City. Neufeld, Juliana, illus. 2015. (Treasure Hunters Ser.: 3). (ENG.). 448p. (J). (gr. 3-7). 14.99 (978-0-316-28480-6(7), Jimmy Patterson) Little Brown & Co.

Patterson, James, et al. Treasure Hunters. Neufeld, Juliana, illus. 2013. 451p. (J). (978-0-316-24262-2(4)) Little Brown & Co.

Pattison, Darcy. The Journey of Oliver K. Woodman. Cepeda, Joe, illus. 2009. (ENG.). 52p. (J). (gr. -1-3). pap. 8.99 (978-0-15-206118-0(5), 1099013, Clarion Bks.) HarperCollins Pubs.

Paulsen, Gary. Mudshark. 2010. (ENG.). 96p. (J). (gr. 3-7). 6.99 (978-0-553-49464-8(3), Yearling) Random Hse. Children's Bks.

Peacock, Shane. Vanishing Girl: The Boy Sherlock Holmes, His Third Case. 2010. (Boy Sherlock Holmes Ser.: 3). (Illus.). 336p. (YA). (gr. 7-9). pap. 11.99 (978-1-77049-234-9(8), Tundra Bks.) Tundra Bks. CAN. Dist: Penguin Random Hse. LLC.

Pearce, Jackson. The Doublecross: (And Other Skills I Learned As a Superspy) 2015. (ENG.). 304p. (YA). (gr. 3-6). 16.99 (978-1-61963-414-5(7), 9781619634145, Bloomsbury USA Childrens) Bloomsbury Publishing USA.

Pearce, Margaret. A Belinda Robinson Novel Book 2: Belinda & the Holidays It Rained. 2013. 78p. pap. (978-1-922233-22-6(6)) Writers Exchange E-Publishing.

Pedraza, M. Eugenia Rueda. Nico's Voyage. 2013. 32p. pap. (978-1-4602-2360-4(8)) FriesenPress.

Peet, Mal. The Penalty. (ENG.). 272p. 2016. (J). (gr. 7). pap. 8.99 (978-0-7636-8747-2(2)) 2007. (Illus.). (YA). (gr. 9-12). 16.99 (978-0-7636-3399-8(2)) Candlewick Pr.

Pennypacker, Sara. Clementine Friend of the Week. Frazee, Marla, illus. 2010. (Clementine Ser.: 4). (ENG.). 176p. (J). (gr. 1-3). 14.99 (978-1-4231-1355-3(1)) Little, Brown Bks. for Young Readers.

Perry, Michael. The Scavengers. (ENG.). 336p. (J). (gr. 3-7). 2015. pap. 9.99 (978-0-06-202617-0(8)) 2014. 16.99 (978-0-06-202616-3(X)) HarperCollins Pubs. (HarperCollins).

Perry, Naresha S. Zora's Valentine. Marx, Jessy, illus. 2005. (ENG.). (J). (gr. -1-3). per. 13.00 (978-0-9767189-0-1(1)) Better Day Publishing.

Pett, Mark. The Boy & the Airplane. Pett, Mark, illus. 2013. (ENG., Illus.). 40p. (J). (gr. -1). 18.99 (978-1-4424-5123-0(8), Simon & Schuster Bks. For Young Readers) Simon & Schuster Bks. For Young Readers.

Pfoutz, Sally. Missing Person. 2009. 192p. (gr. 7-18). pap. 12.95 (978-1-4401-5108-8(3)) iUniverse, Inc.

Phillips, Helen. Here Where the Sunbeams Are Green. 2013. (ENG.). 304p. (J). (gr. 5). 7.99 (978-0-307-93145-0(5), Yearling) Random Hse. Children's Bks.

Phumiruk, Dow. Mela & the Elephant. Chen, Ziyue, illus. 2018. (ENG.). 32p. (J). (gr. k-3). 18.99 (978-1-58536-998-0(5), 204407) Sleeping Bear Pr.

The Place Between Breaths. (ENG., Illus.). (YA). (gr. 7). 2019. 208p. pap. 10.99 (978-1-4814-2226-0(X), Atheneum Bks. for Young Readers) 2018. 192p. 17.99 (978-1-4814-2225-3(1), Atheneum/Caitlyn Dlouhy Books) Simon & Schuster Children's Publishing.

Plozza, Shivaun. Frankie: A Novel. 2018. (ENG.). 352p. (YA). pap. 19.99 (978-1-250-14300-6(4), 900180438) Flatiron Bks.

Plum-Ucci, Carol. The Body of Christopher Creed: A Printz Honor Winner. 2008. (ENG., Illus.). 272p. (YA). (gr. 7). pap. 7.99 (978-0-15-206386-3(2), 1199120, Clarion Bks.) HarperCollins Pubs.

—The Night My Sister Went Missing. 2008. (ENG., Illus.). 228p. (YA). (gr. 7). pap. 6.95 (978-0-15-206191-3(6), 1198582, Clarion Bks.) HarperCollins Pubs.

Podos, Rebecca. The Mystery of Hollow Places. 2016. (ENG.). 304p. (YA). (gr. 9). 17.99 (978-0-06-237334-2(X), Balzer & Bray) HarperCollins Pubs.

Polak, Monique. Flip Turn, 1 vol. 2004. (Lorimer Sports Stories Ser.: 67). (ENG.). 104p. (J). (gr. 4-8). 16.95 (978-1-55028-819-3(9), 819) James Lorimer & Co. Ltd., Pubs. CAN. Dist: Formac Lorimer Bks. Ltd.

Pollock, Tom. This Story Is a Lie. 2019. (ENG.). 336p. (YA). (gr. 9). pap. 10.99 (978-1-64129-032-6(3), Soho Teen) Soho Pr., Inc.

Porter, Kevin Don. Missing. 2013. 166p. pap. 11.99 (978-0-9857014-7-5(1)) Artists' Orchard, LLC, The.

Poth, Karen. Sheerluck Holmes & the Case of the Missing Friend, 1 vol. 2014. (I Can Read! / Big Idea Books / VeggieTales Ser.). (ENG.). 32p. (J). pap. 4.99 (978-0-310-74171-8(8)) Zonderkidz.

Powell, Laura. Witch Fire. 2013. (ENG.). 336p. (YA). (gr. 7). 17.99 (978-1-61963-006-2(0), 900098189, Bloomsbury USA Childrens) Bloomsbury Publishing USA.

Prevost, Guillaume. The Gate of Days, 2. 2009. (Book of Time Ser.: 2). (ENG.). 272p. (J). (gr. 6-8). 18.69 (978-0-439-88380-1(6)) Scholastic, Inc.

Priddy, Roger. Giraffe Is Lost: An Animal Search-And-find Book. 2019. (Search & Find Ser.). (ENG., Illus.). 10p. (J). bds. 9.99 (978-0-312-52789-1(6), 900194735) St. Martin's Pr.

Redwine, C. J. Defiance. 2013. (Defiance Trilogy Ser.: 1). (ENG.). 432p. (YA). (gr. 8). pap. 9.99 (978-0-06-211717-5(3), Balzer & Bray) HarperCollins Pubs.

Reeve, Philip. Oliver & the Sea Monkeys. McIntyre, Sarah, illus. 2016. (Not-So-Impossible Tale Ser.). (ENG.). 224p. (J). (gr. 2-5). pap. 7.99 (978-0-385-38789-7(X), Yearling) Random Hse. Children's Bks.

Reid, F. J. The Midwinter Child. 2009. 224p. pap. (978-1-84923-496-2(5)) YouWriteOn.

Rewalt, Nancy E. Lost & Found: Goldilocks & the Three Bears Revisited. Cranford, Darren, illus. 2012. 64p. (J). pap. 6.95 (978-0-9821110-2-4(9)) Ronan Enterprises, Inc.

Rex, Adam. The True Meaning of Smekday, 1. Rex, Adam, illus. 2009. (Smek Smeries Ser.: 1). (ENG., Illus.). 432p. (J). (gr. 3-7). pap. 8.99 (978-0-7868-4901-7(0)) Little, Brown Bks. for Young Readers.

—The True Meaning of Smekday. 2009. (Illus.). 423p. 18.00 (978-1-60686-525-5(0)) Perfection Learning Corp.

Richard Richtmyer. A Bit of Magic: A Novel. 2009. 116p. pap. 10.95 (978-1-4401-5565-9(8)) iUniverse, Inc.

Roach, Joyce Gibson, tr. Cowgirl of the Rocking R. 2003. (J). (978-0-9726573-0-3(4)) Crosswinds Bks.

Roberts, Kelly Hughes. The Road to Chianti. 2012. 214p. (gr. 4-6). 33.99 (978-1-4525-5963-6(5)); pap. 15.99 (978-1-4525-5961-2(9)) Balboa Pr.

Robins, Eleanor. Where Is Mr. Zane?, 1 vol. unabr. ed. 2011. (Carter High Mysteries Ser.). (ENG.). 48p. (YA). (gr. 9-12). 9.75 (978-1-61651-569-0(4)) Saddleback Educational Publishing, Inc.

Roehrig, Caleb. Last Seen Leaving. 2018. (ENG.). 352p. (YA). pap. 14.99 (978-1-250-12967-3(2), 900176105) Square Fish.

RollasonJane. Killer Bees Level 2 Elementary/Lower-intermediate. 2009. (Cambridge Experience Readers Ser.). (ENG.). 64p. pap. 14.75 (978-84-8323-503-4(X)) Cambridge Univ. Pr.

Rollins, James. Jake Ransom & the Skull King's Shadow. 2010. (Jake Ransom Ser.: 1). (ENG.). 432p. (J). (gr. 5). pap. 7.99 (978-0-06-147381-4(2), HarperCollins) HarperCollins Pubs.

Rooftoppers. 2014. (ENG., Illus.). 304p. (J). (gr. 3-7). pap. 8.99 (978-1-4424-9059-8(4), Simon & Schuster Bks. For Young Readers) Simon & Schuster Bks. For Young Readers.

Root, Phyllis. Lilly & the Pirates. Shepperson, Rob, illus. 2013. (ENG.). 180p. (J). (gr. 3-7). pap. 8.95 (978-1-62091-027-6(6), Astra Young Readers) Astra Publishing Hse.

Rosenthal, Eileen. Bobo the Sailor Man! Rosenthal, Marc, illus. 2013. (ENG.). 40p. (J). (gr. -1-1). 15.99 (978-1-4424-4443-0(6)) Simon & Schuster Children's Publishing.

Ross, Jeff. Dawn Patrol, 1 vol. 2012. (Orca Sports Ser.). (ENG.). 160p. (J). (gr. 4-7). pap. 9.95 (978-1-4598-0062-5(1)) Orca Bk. Pubs. USA.

—Set You Free, 1 vol. 2015. (ENG.). 256p. (YA). (gr. 8-12). pap. 14.95 (978-1-4598-0797-6(9)) Orca Bk. Pubs. USA.

Roy, Ron. A to Z Mysteries: Collection #1, No. 1. Gurney, John Steven, illus. 2010. (to Z Mysteries Ser.: Nos. 1-4). (ENG.). 384p. (J). (gr. 1-4). 9.99 (978-0-375-85946-5(2), Random Hse. Bks. for Young Readers) Random Hse. Children's Bks.

Rubin, Sarah. The Impossible Clue. 2017. 293p. (J). pap. (978-0-545-94272-0(1), Chicken Hse., The) Scholastic, Inc.

Rundell, Katherine. Rooftoppers. Fan, Terry, illus. 2013. (ENG.). 288p. (J). (gr. 3-7). 19.99 (978-1-4424-9058-1(6), Simon & Schuster Bks. For Young Readers) Simon & Schuster Bks. For Young Readers.

Rush, Jennifer. Devils & Thieves. 2017. (Devils & Thieves Ser.: 1). (ENG.). 336p. (YA). (gr. 9-17). 17.99 (978-0-316-39089-7(5)) Little, Brown Bks. for Young Readers.

Rushford, Patricia H. Secrets of Ghost Island. 2007. (J). (978-88-02-46255-4(0)) Moody Pubs.

Rykken, John. Bloodwood: The Chronicles of Max Mayhem. 2011. 264p. (gr. 10-12). 26.95 (978-1-4620-0656-4(6)); pap. 16.95 (978-1-4620-0657-1(4)) iUniverse, Inc.

Sage, Angie. TodHunter Moon, Book One: PathFinder. Zug, Mark, illus. 2015. (World of Septimus Heap Ser.: 1). (ENG.). 496p. (J). (gr. 3-7). pap. 7.99 (978-0-06-227246-1(2), Tegen, Katherine Bks) HarperCollins Pubs.

Sanderson, Nancy. Horse of the Four Winds. 2011. 152p. (gr. 10-12). pap. 14.50 (978-1-4634-4802-8(3)) AuthorHouse.

Sands, Kevin. Call of the Wraith. (Blackthorn Key Ser.: 4). (ENG.). 512p. (J). (gr. 5-9). 2019. pap. 9.99 (978-1-5344-2848-5(8)) 2018. (Illus.). 19.99 (978-1-5344-2847-8(X)) Simon & Schuster Children's Publishing. (Aladdin).

Santiago, Brianna A. Why Is the Moon Following Us? 2008. 16p. pap. 24.95 (978-1-60474-944-1(X)) America Star Bks.

Santopolo, Jill. Nina, the Pinta, & the Vanishing Treasure (an Alec Flint Mystery #1), 1. 2009. (ENG.). 192p. (J). (gr. 2-5). mass mkt. 6.99 (978-0-439-90353-0(X), Scholastic Paperbacks) Scholastic, Inc.

Sargent, Dave & Sargent, Pat. Young Dike: Teamwork! Woodward, Elaine, illus. 2003. (Young Animal Pride Ser.: 5). 24p. (J). 5. pap. 6.95 (978-1-56763-872-1(4)) Vol. 5. lib. bdg. 20.95 (978-1-56763-871-4(6)) Ozark Publishing.

Sazaklis, John. Return of the Dinobot. 2014. (Transformers 8x8 Ser.). (J). lib. bdg. 13.55 (978-0-606-35296-3(1)) Turtleback.

Schmidt, Werner. The Forests of Adventure. 2005. 137p. pap. 12.50 (978-1-4116-4721-3(1)) Lulu Pr., Inc.

Schoon, Christian. Under Nameless Stars. 2014. (ENG.). 368p. (J). (gr. 9). pap. 9.99 (978-1-908844-87-3(6), Strange Chemistry) Watkins Media Limited GBR. Dist: Penguin Random Hse. LLC.

Schraff, Anne. Lost & Found. Langan, Paul, ed. 2007. (Bluford High Ser.). 133p. (gr. 8-12). 16.00 (978-0-7569-8076-4(3)) Perfection Learning Corp.

—Lost & Found. 2007. (Bluford High — Scholastic Ser.: 1). lib. bdg. 16.00 (978-1-4177-7141-7(0)) Turtleback.

—Something Dreadful down Below, 1 vol. unabr. ed. 2010. (Q Reads Ser.). (ENG.). 32p. (YA). (gr. 9-12). pap. 8.50 (978-1-61651-205-7(9)) Saddleback Educational Publishing, Inc.

Scott, Kieran. Pretty Fierce. 2017. (ENG.). 304p. (YA). (gr. 6-12). pap. 10.99 (978-1-4926-3798-1(X), 9781492637981) Sourcebooks, Inc.

Seaman, Kathleen. Annycole, 1 vol. 2009. 49p. pap. 16.95 (978-1-4489-1970-3(3)) America Star Bks.

Sedgwick, Marcus. She Is Not Invisible. 2015. (ENG.). 240p. (YA). (gr. 7). pap. 11.99 (978-1-250-05698-6(5), 900139107) Square Fish.

Sedoti, Chelsea. Hundred Lies of Lizzie Lovett. 2017. (ENG.). 400p. (YA). (gr. 8-12). 17.99 (978-1-4926-3608-3(8), 9781492636083) Sourcebooks, Inc.

Shaw, J. D. The Secrets of Loon Lake. 2010. (ENG.). 338p. (J). (gr. 5). pap. 16.95 (978-0-9845318-0-6(7)) Tiny Stachel Pr.

Shelton, C. M. Cosmic Chaos. 2015. (ENG., Illus.). 226p. (J). pap. 8.99 (978-1-941720-25-7(0)) Ashberry Lane.

Sheninger, Rick. Buddy the Duck Gets Lost. 2012. 20p. pap. 15.99 (978-1-4685-8371-7(9)) AuthorHouse.

Shepard, Sara. Pretty Little Liars Bind-Up #1: Pretty Little Liars & Flawless. 2014. (Pretty Little Liars Ser.). (ENG.). 656p. (YA). (gr. 9). pap. 10.99 (978-0-06-232292-0(3), HarperTeen) HarperCollins Pubs.

Sherrard, Valerie. Chasing Shadows: A Shelby Belgarden Mystery. 2004. (ENG.). 216p. (YA). pap. 9.99 (978-1-55002-502-6(3)) Dundurn Pr. CAN. Dist: Publishers Group West (PGW).

—Searching for Yesterday: A Shelby Belgarden Mystery. 2008. (ENG.). 224p. (YA). (gr. 6-10). pap. 12.99 (978-1-55002-788-4(3)) Dundurn Pr. CAN. Dist: Publishers Group West (PGW).

Sheth, Kashmira. Boys Without Names. 2010. (ENG.). 320p. (J). (gr. 4-7). 16.99 (978-0-06-185760-7(2), Balzer & Bray) HarperCollins Pubs.

Silvey, Diane. Time of the Thunderbird. Mantha, John, illus. 2008. (ENG.). 88p. (J). (gr. 6-5). pap. 11.99 (978-1-55002-792-1(1)) Dundurn Pr. CAN. Dist: Publishers Group West (PGW).

Siobhan, Dowd. The London Eye Mystery. 2014. (ENG.). 336p. (J). (gr. 3-7). 12.24 (978-1-63245-320-4(7)) Lectorum Pubns., Inc.

Sirowy, Alexandra. The Creeping. 2015. (ENG., Illus.). 400p. (YA). (gr. 7). 17.99 (978-1-4814-1886-7(6)) Simon & Schuster Children's Publishing.

Skurzynski, Gloria. Running Scared: A Mystery in Carlsbad Caverns National Park. 2008. (Mysteries in Our National Park Ser.). (Illus.). 160p. (J). (gr. 3-7). mass mkt. 4.99 (978-1-4263-0182-7(0), National Geographic Kids) Disney Publishing Worldwide.

Skye, Obert. Wizard for Hire. 2018. (Wizard for Hire Ser.: 1). (ENG.). 416p. (J). (gr. 5-9). 17.99 (978-1-62972-412-6(2), 5194480, Shadow Mountain) Shadow Mountain Publishing.

Sloane, Roxy. Missing: The Heather Harding Mysteries. 2011. 100p. pap. 15.99 (978-1-4628-9061-3(X)) Xlibris Corp.

Small, Lily. Chloe the Kitten: Fairy Animals of Misty Wood. 2015. (Fairy Animals of Misty Wood Ser.: 1). (ENG., Illus.). 144p. (J). (gr. k-3). pap. 6.99 (978-1-62779-141-0(8), 900137174, Holt, Henry & Co. Bks. For Young Readers) Holt, Henry & Co.

Smith, Andrew. Exile from Eden: Or, after the Hole. Smith, Andrew, illus. 2019. (ENG., Illus.). 368p. (YA). (gr. 9). 18.99 (978-1-5344-2223-0(4), Simon & Schuster Bks. For Young Readers) Simon & Schuster Bks. For Young Readers.

Smith, Holly C. Tyler the Monkey & Andy the Mouse. 2012. 28p. (-18). pap. 24.95 (978-1-4626-9501-0(9)) America Star Bks.

Smith, R. L. The Journals of Underwich: Book One. 2007. 253p. pap. 27.95 (978-1-60441-490-5(1)) America Star Bks.

Smith-Ready, Jeri. This Side of Salvation. 2014. (ENG., Illus.). 384p. (YA). (gr. 9). 17.99 (978-1-4424-3948-1(3), Simon Pulse) Simon Pulse.

Smith, Roland. Chupacabra. (J). 2015. (ENG.). 304p. (gr. 3-7). pap. 7.99 (978-0-545-17818-1(5), Scholastic Paperbacks) 2013. (Illus.). xv, 285p. pap. (978-0-545-62984-3(5), Scholastic Pr.) Scholastic, Inc.

—Mutation (Cryptid Hunters #4) 2016. (Cryptid Hunters Ser.: 4). (ENG.). 352p. (J). (gr. 3-7). pap. 7.99 (978-0-545-08181-8(5), Scholastic Pr.) Scholastic, Inc.

Snicket, Lemony, pseud. "When Did You See Her Last?" Seth, illus. (All the Wrong Questions Ser.: 2). (ENG.). 304p. (J). (gr. 3-17). 2014. pap. 8.99 (978-0-316-33684-0(X)) 2013. 33.99 (978-0-316-23993-6(3)) Little, Brown Bks. for Young Readers.

Soontornvat, Christina. The Changelings. 2017. (Changelings Ser.: 1). (ENG.). 304p. (J). (gr. 5-8). pap. 8.99 (978-1-4926-4795-9(0)) Sourcebooks, Inc.

Sparkes, Ali. Alligator Action, No. 14. Collins, Ross, illus. 2014. (S. W. I. T. C. H. Ser.: 14). (ENG.). 112p. (J). (gr. 2-5). lib. bdg. 27.99 (978-1-4677-2117-2(4), a29ee350-23b8-409b-9c6f-f08687ada878, Darby Creek) Lerner Publishing Group.

Specter, Baron. To Werewolf or Not to Werewolf, 1 vol. Kneupper, Setch, illus. 2012. (Graveyard Diaries). (ENG.). 128p. (J). (gr. 2-5). 38.50 (978-1-61641-901-1(6), 9180, Calico Chapter Bks.) ABDO Publishing Co.

Spoor, Mike, illus. Desperate Measures: Units of Measurement in Action, 1 vol. 2010. (Mandrill Mountain Math Mysteries Ser.). (ENG.). 32p. (J). (gr. 2-3). pap. 11.55 (978-1-60754-925-3(5), 0d0a4546-a9aa-44e2-a596-6f85f71671d5); lib. bdg. 27.27 (978-1-60754-920-8(4), 062ce9eb-2d37-4102-905f-f0621291bce6) Rosen Publishing Group, Inc., The. (Windmill Bks.).

—The Emperor's Guards: Concepts of Time, 1 vol. 2010. (Mandrill Mountain Math Mysteries Ser.). (ENG.). 32p. (J). (gr. 2-3). lib. bdg. 27.27 (978-1-60754-922-2(0), 85dd0127-799d-49a7-b02c-a55c0fa8b8a4, Windmill Bks.) Rosen Publishing Group, Inc., The.

—The Hidden Valley: Reasoning in Action, 1 vol. 2010. (Mandrill Mountain Math Mysteries Ser.). (ENG.). 32p. (J). (gr. 2-3). lib. bdg. 27.27 (978-1-60754-919-2(0), aad83b41-3bb8-4a8c-be7f-3ca4a5a6da9c, Windmill Bks.) Rosen Publishing Group, Inc., The.

Springer, Nancy. The Case of the Bizarre Bouquets, 3. 2008. (Enola Holmes Mystery Ser.: 3). (ENG.). 176p. (J). (gr. 6-8). 21.19 (978-0-399-24518-3(9)) Penguin Young Readers Group.

—Enola Holmes: the Case of the Bizarre Bouquets. 2009. (Enola Holmes Mystery Ser.: 3). (ENG.). 192p. (J). (gr. 3-7). pap. 8.99 (978-0-14-241390-6(9), Puffin Books) Penguin Young Readers Group.

—Enola Holmes: the Case of the Cryptic Crinoline. 2011. (Enola Holmes Mystery Ser.: 5). (ENG., Illus.). 176p. (J). (gr. 3-7). 8.99 (978-0-14-241690-7(8), Puffin Books) Penguin Young Readers Group.

—Enola Holmes: the Case of the Missing Marquess. 2007. (Enola Holmes Mystery Ser.: 1). (ENG.). 240p. (J). (gr. 3-7). 7.99 (978-0-14-240933-6(2), Puffin Books) Penguin Young Readers Group.

Stanfield, Michael. Bucky & Becky - the Magic of Wigglepoo Mountain. 2009. 144p. pap. 14.96 (978-0-557-02614-2(8)) Lulu Pr., Inc.

Starmer, Aaron. The Riverman. 2015. (Riverman Trilogy Ser.: 1). (ENG.). 336p. (YA). (gr. 5-9). pap. 12.99 (978-1-250-05685-6(3), 900139058) Square Fish.

Stauffacher, Sue. The Space Between Before & After. 2019. 288p. (J). (gr. 4-7). 17.99 (978-0-8234-4148-8(2), Margaret Ferguson Books) Holiday Hse., Inc.

Steig, William. Sylvester & the Magic Pebble. Steig, William, illus. 2006. (Stories to Go! Ser.). (Illus.). 32p. (J). (gr. -1-3). 4.99 (978-1-4169-1857-8(4), Simon & Schuster/Paula Wiseman Bks.) Simon & Schuster/Paula Wiseman Bks.

—Sylvester & the Magic Pebble: Book & CD. Steig, William, illus. 2012. (ENG., Illus.). 32p. (J). (gr. -1-2). pap. 10.99 (978-1-4424-3560-5(7), Little Simon) Little Simon.

Stevenson, S. Roy. The Magic Act: A Mystery by S. Roy Stevenson. 2008. 108p. 20.95 (978-0-595-51841-8(9)); pap. 10.95 (978-0-595-53062-5(1)) iUniverse, Inc.

Stewart, Trenton Lee. The Mysterious Benedict Society & the Perilous Journey. Sudyka, Diana, illus. (Mysterious Benedict Society Ser.: 2). (ENG.). (J). (gr. 3-7). 2009. 464p. pap. 9.99 (978-0-316-03673-3(0)) 2008. 448p. 19.99 (978-0-316-05780-6(0)) Little, Brown Bks. for Young Readers.

—The Mysterious Benedict Society & the Perilous Journey. 2009. (Mysterious Benedict Society Ser.: 2). (J). lib. bdg. 19.65 (978-0-606-07462-9(7)) Turtleback.

Stilton, Gerónimo. Ride for Your Life! 2014. (Geronimo Stilton — Creepella Von Cacklefur Ser.: 6). lib. bdg. 18.40 (978-0-606-35847-7(1)) Turtleback.

—Thea Stilton & the Dragon's Code. 2009. (Geronimo Stilton Special Edition Ser.: No. 1). (Illus.). 158p. 18.00 (978-1-60686-420-3(3)) Perfection Learning Corp.

—Thea Stilton & the Dragon's Code. 2009. (Thea Stilton Ser.: 1). lib. bdg. 19.65 (978-0-606-00231-8(6)) Turtleback.

Stilton, Gerónimo & Stilton, Thea. Thea Stilton & the Ghost of the Shipwreck. 2010. (Thea Stilton Ser.: 3). lib. bdg. 19.65 (978-0-606-06843-7(0)) Turtleback.

Stilton, Thea. Thea Stilton & the Dragon's Code (Thea Stilton #1) A Geronimo Stilton Adventure. 2009. (Thea Stilton Ser.: 1). (ENG., Illus.). 176p. (J). (gr. 2-5). pap. 8.99 (978-0-545-10367-1(3), Scholastic Paperbacks) Scholastic, Inc.

—Thea Stilton & the Frozen Fiasco. 2017. (Thea Stilton Ser.: 25). lib. bdg. 19.65 (978-0-606-40181-4(4)) Turtleback.

—Thea Stilton & the Ghost of the Shipwreck (Thea Stilton #3) A Geronimo Stilton Adventure. 2010. (Thea Stilton Ser.: 3). Orig. Title: Il Vascello Fantasma. (ENG., Illus.). 176p. (J). (gr. 2-5). pap. 8.99 (978-0-545-15059-0(0), Scholastic Paperbacks) Scholastic, Inc.

—Thea Stilton & the Missing Myth. 2014. (Thea Stilton Ser.: 20). lib. bdg. 19.65 (978-0-606-36058-6(1)) Turtleback.

—Thea Stilton & the Secret of the Old Castle. 2012. (Thea Stilton Ser.: 10). lib. bdg. 19.65 (978-0-606-23930-1(8)) Turtleback.

Stokes, Paula. Liars, Inc. 2015. (ENG.). 368p. (YA). (gr. 8). 17.99 (978-0-06-232328-6(8), HarperTeen) HarperCollins Pubs.

Strasnick, Lauren. Then You Were Gone. (ENG., 272p. (YA). (gr. 9). 2014. Illus.). pap. 9.99 (978-1-4424-2716-7(7)) 2013. 16.99 (978-1-4424-2715-0(9)) Simon Pulse. (Simon Pulse).

Strasser, Todd. Wish You Were Dead. (ENG.). 240p. (gr. 9-12). 2010. (YA). pap. 9.99 (978-1-60684-138-9(6), 83351663-102d-409d-ba04-349ec33baab2) 2009. 16.99 (978-1-60684-007-8(X)) Lerner Publishing Group. (Carolrhoda Lab™).

Summers, Courtney. All the Rage: A Novel. 2016. (ENG.). 336p. (YA). pap. 12.99 (978-1-250-06915-3(7), 900096244, St. Martin's Griffin) St. Martin's Pr.

Sutliff, Jamie. The Elves of Owl's Head Mountain. Blumberg, Christine A., ed. Evens, Kevin C., illus. 2007. 276p. pap. 10.95 (978-0-9712867-8-8(7)) Cold River Pubns.

—The Elves of Owl's Head Mountain. Blumberg, Christine A., ed. Evans, Kevin, illus. 2007. 280p. (gr. 8-12). 26.95 (978-0-9712867-7-1(9)) Cold River Pubns.

Swindells, Robert. The Strange Tale of Ragger Bill. Hartas, Leo, illus. 2021. (Outfit Ser.). (ENG.). 104p. (J). (gr. 5-8). 26.65 (978-1-5415-7910-1(0), 07dc9564-47d9-4ebc-8d25-7305e12ec24b, Darby Creek) Lerner Publishing Group.

Taddonio, Lea. The Curse of Deadwood Hill: Book 2. Trunfio, Alessia, illus. 2017. (Lucky 8 Ser.). (ENG.). 48p. (J). (gr. 3-7). lib. bdg. 34.21 (978-1-5321-3054-0(6), 27061, Spellbound) Magic Wagon.

—Deadwood Hill Strikes Back: Book 3. Trunfio, Alessia, illus. 2017. (Lucky 8 Ser.). (ENG.). 48p. (J). (gr. 3-7). lib. bdg. 34.21 (978-1-5321-3055-7(4), 27062, Spellbound) Magic Wagon.

Tafuri, Nancy. Have You Seen My Duckling? Tafuri, Nancy, illus. 2007. (Illus.). (gr. -1-k). 17.00 (978-0-7569-7869-3(6)) Perfection Learning Corp.

Terry, Teri. Contagion. 2019. (Dark Matter Trilogy Ser.). (ENG.). 416p. (YA). (gr. 7). lib. bdg. 18.99 (978-1-58089-989-5(7), Charlesbridge Teen) Charlesbridge Publishing, Inc.

Tharp, Tim. Mojo. 2014. (ENG.). 288p. (YA). (gr. 7). pap. 8.99 (978-0-375-86402-5(4), Ember) Random Hse. Children's Bks.

Theo. Oscar & Hoo. Dudok de Wit, Michael, illus. 2003. 32p. (J). (gr. -1-2). 17.99 (978-0-00-710793-3(5), HarperCollins Children's Bks.) HarperCollins Pubs. Ltd. GBR. Dist: Trafalgar Square Publishing.

Thiel Annie. The Playdate Kids Dakota Gets Lost. 2007. 32p. 12.95 (978-1-933721-08-8(1)) Playdate Kids Publishing.

Thiel, Annie & Fanning, Tena. Dakota Gets Lost. Edwards, William M., illus. 2007. (Playdate Kids: Let's Be Friends! Ser.). 27p. (J). (gr. -1-3). per. 6.95 (978-1-933721-20-0(0)) Playdate Kids Publishing.

Thomas, Kara. Little Monsters. 2018. (ENG.). 368p. (YA). (gr. 9). pap. 10.99 (978-0-553-52152-8(7), Ember) Random Hse. Children's Bks.

Thompson, Lisa. The Goldfish Boy. 2018. (ENG.). 320p. (J). (gr. 3-7). pap. 7.99 (978-1-338-05393-7(0)) Scholastic, Inc.

Thorpe, Kiki. A Dandelion Wish. Christy, Jana, illus. 2013. (Never Girls Ser.: 3). lib. bdg. 16.00 (978-0-606-32199-0(3)) Turtleback.

—Never Girls #3: a Dandelion Wish (Disney: the Never Girls) Christy, Jana, illus. 2013. (Never Girls Ser.: 3). (ENG.). 128p. (J). (gr. 1-4). 6.99 (978-0-7364-2796-8(1), RH/Disney) Random Hse. Children's Bks.

Tillworth, Mary, adapted by. Sherlock Gnomes the Deluxe Movie Novelization. 2018. (Sherlock Gnomes Ser.). (ENG., Illus.). 144p. (J). (gr. 3-7). 9.99 (978-1-5344-2940-6(9), Simon Spotlight) Simon Spotlight.

Torres, Jennifer. The Disappearing: The Briny Deep Mysteries Book 1, 1 vol. 2014. (Briny Deep Mysteries Ser.: Bk. 1). (ENG., Illus.). 96p. (J). (gr. 4-6). pap. 13.88 (978-1-62285-173-7(0), 585ba180-2450-4cac-a487-b9bd7d4e81a9) Enslow Publishing, LLC.

—The Return: The Briny Deep Mysteries Book 2, 1 vol. 2014. (Briny Deep Mysteries Ser.: Bk. 2). (ENG., Illus.). 96p. (J). (gr. 4-6). pap. 13.88 (978-1-62285-182-9(X), 469249a8-6de1-4339-a610-4d64bcb9e170) Enslow Publishing, LLC.

Tromly, Stephanie. Trouble Never Sleeps. 2019. (ENG.). 304p. (YA). (gr. 7). pap. 10.99 (978-0-14-751545-2(9), Penguin Books) Penguin Young Readers Group.

Trope, Nicole. Forgotten: A Completely Gripping Domestic Noir Thriller. 2018. (ENG.). 400p. pap. 19.95 (978-1-76029-677-3(5)) Allen & Unwin AUS. Dist: Independent Pubs. Group.

Tucker, Mark. Super Phil & the Missing Mom. Patete, Christine, illus. 2003. 24p. (J). 4.50 (978-1-882440-01-6(3)) God's World Pubns. Inc.

Umansky, Kaye. Clover Twig & the Perilous Path. Wright, Johanna, illus. 2013. (ENG.). 272p. (J). (gr. 3-7). pap. 15.99 (978-1-250-02727-6(6), 900098299) Square Fish.

Ure, Jean. Is Anybody There? 2004. (ENG., Illus.). 192p. (J). (gr. 4-7). pap. 9.95 (978-0-00-716136-2(0), HarperCollins Children's Bks.) HarperCollins Pubs. Ltd. GBR. Dist: HarperCollins Pubs.

Valentine, Nicole. A Time Traveler's Theory of Relativity. 2019. (ENG., Illus.). 352p. (J). (gr. 4-8). 17.99 (978-1-5415-5538-9(4), 2b60b16e-6e91-4b27-b7dd-76c86cce49dc, Carolrhoda Bks.) Lerner Publishing Group.

Valverde, Mikel. Paula en Nueva York. 2006. (SPA., Illus.). 32p. (J). (gr. 6-8). 14.99 (978-1-933032-15-3(4)) Lectorum Pubns., Inc.

Van Draanen, Wendelin. Sammy Keyes & the Night of Skulls. 2012. (Sammy Keyes Ser.: 14). (ENG.). 336p. (J). (gr. 5-7). 10.99 (978-0-375-85457-6(6), Yearling) Random Hse. Children's Bks.

—Sammy Keyes & the Power of Justice Jack. 2012. (Sammy Keyes Ser.: 15). (ENG.). 320p. (J). (gr. 5-7). 7.99 (978-0-307-93060-6(2), Yearling) Random Hse. Children's Bks.

Vandepeer, Helen. Gifts. 2008. 76p. pap. 35.80 (978-0-557-03191-7(5)) Lulu Pr., Inc.

Varley, Dax. Book 5: Stained. Proctor, Jon, illus. 2017. (Demon Slayer Set 2 Ser.). (ENG.). 48p. (J). (gr. 3-7). lib. bdg. 34.21 (978-1-5321-3006-9(6), 25558, Spellbound) Magic Wagon.

Vaught, Susan. Footer Davis Probably Is Crazy. Reinhardt, Jennifer Black, illus. 2015. (ENG.). 240p. (J). (gr. 5-9). 16.99 (978-1-4814-2276-5(6), Simon & Schuster Bks. For Young Readers) Simon & Schuster Bks. For Young Readers.

Vegas, Peter. Bones of the Sun God. (Pyramid Hunters Ser.: 2). (ENG.). 416p. (J). (gr. 5-9). 2018. pap. 8.99 (978-1-4814-4583-2(9)) 2017. (Illus.). 17.99 (978-1-4814-4582-5(0)) Simon & Schuster Children's Publishing. (Aladdin).

—The Iron Tomb. 2016. (Pyramid Hunters Ser.: 1). (ENG., Illus.). 304p. (J). (gr. 5-9). 16.99 (978-1-4814-4578-8(2), Aladdin) Simon & Schuster Children's Publishing.

Via, Jennifer Welsh. The Foggy Meadow Discovery. 2007. 216p. per. 14.95 (978-0-595-44680-3(9)) iUniverse, Inc.

Voake, Steve. Daisy Dawson & the Big Freeze. Meserve, Jessica, illus. 2011. (Daisy Dawson Ser.). (ENG.). 96p. (J). (gr. 1-4). pap. 5.99 (978-0-7636-5627-0(5)) Candlewick Pr.

Voigt, Cynthia. Mister Max: the Book of Kings: Mister Max 3. Bruno, Iacopo, illus. 2016. (Mister Max Ser.: 3). (ENG.). 352p. (J). (gr. 3-7). 8.99 (978-0-307-97688-8(2), Yearling) Random Hse. Children's Bks.

—Mister Max: the Book of Lost Things: Mister Max 1. Bruno, Iacopo, illus. 2014. (Mister Max Ser.: 1). (ENG.). 400p. (J). (gr. 3-7). 10.99 (978-0-307-97682-6(3), Yearling) Random Hse. Children's Bks.

—Mister Max: the Book of Secrets: Mister Max 2. Bruno, Iacopo, illus. 2015. (Mister Max Ser.: 2). (ENG.). 384p. (J). (gr. 3-7). 8.99 (978-0-307-97685-7(8), Yearling) Random Hse. Children's Bks.

Vrettos, Adrienne Maria. Sight. 2008. (ENG.). 272p. (YA). (gr. 7). pap. 8.99 (978-1-4169-0658-2(4), McElderry, Margaret K. Bks.) McElderry, Margaret K. Bks.

—Sight. 2007. (ENG., Illus.). 254p. (YA). (gr. 7-12). 21.19 (978-1-4169-0657-5(6)) Simon & Schuster, Inc.

Wallach, Diana Rodriguez. Proof of Lies. 2017. (ENG., Illus.). (YA). (gr. 7-12). pap. 18.99 (978-1-68281-469-7(6)) Entangled Publishing, LLC.

Walsh, Sara. The Dark Light. 2013. (ENG., Illus.). 512p. (YA). (gr. 9). pap. 9.99 (978-1-4424-3458-5(9), Simon Pulse) Simon Pulse.

Walter, Lee. The Gifts That Are Forgotten. 2006. 60p. pap. 16.95 (978-1-4137-9070-2(4)) PublishAmerica, Inc.

Warden, John. The Chronicles of Zabaduk. 2009. 116p. pap. 13.53 (978-1-4251-6488-1(9)) Trafford Publishing.

Warner, Gertrude Chandler, creator. The Mystery of the Missing Pop Idol. 2015. (Boxcar Children Mysteries Ser.: 138). (ENG., Illus.). 128p. (J). (gr. 2-5). 15.99 (978-0-8075-5605-4(X), 080755605X, Random Hse. Bks. for Young Readers) Random Hse. Children's Bks.

—The Vanishing Passenger. 2006. (Boxcar Children Mysteries Ser.: 106). (ENG., Illus.). 112p. (J). (gr. 2-5). per. 7.99 (978-0-8075-1067-4(X), 080751067X, Random Hse. Bks. for Young Readers) Random Hse. Children's Bks.

Warner, Penny. The Hunt for the Missing Spy. 2016. (Code Busters Club Ser.: 5). (ENG.). 168p. (J). (gr. 3-6). E-Book 26.65 (978-1-5124-0305-3(9), Darby Creek) Lerner Publishing Group.

Watson, Michael. Search, Secrets, & Spies. 2011. 32p. pap. 13.00 (978-1-61204-357-9(7), Strategic Bk. Publishing) Strategic Book Publishing & Rights Agency (SBPRA).

Weingarten, Lynn. Wherever Nina Lies (Point Paperbacks) 2018. (ENG.). 272p. (YA). (gr. 7-7). pap. 9.99 (978-1-338-29178-0(5)) Scholastic, Inc.

Welch, J. D. The Einstein Code. 2016. (ENG.). 304p. (J). pap. 13.95 (978-1-78612-987-1(6), 92fe78e9-f95c-4bb1-9363-5914295786c3) Austin Macauley Pubs. Ltd. GBR. Dist: Baker & Taylor Publisher Services (BTPS).

Welvaert, Scott R. The Alabaster Ring. 2015. (Tartan House Ser.). (ENG.). 96p. (J). (gr. 3-6). (978-1-63235-052-7(1), 11679, 12-Story Library) Bookstaves, LLC.

West, Carly Anne. The Bargaining. 2015. (ENG., Illus.). 416p. (YA). (gr. 9). 17.99 (978-1-4424-4182-8(8), Simon Pulse) Simon Pulse.

West, Madeleine. Lily d V. A. P: Lost Dorothy, Volume 2. 2020. (Lily d, V. A. P Ser.: 2). (ENG.). 112p. (J). (gr. k-2). pap. 9.99 (978-1-76068-301-6(9)) Little Hare Bks. AUS. Dist: Independent Pubs. Group.

Westerfeld, Scott. So Yesterday. 2005. (ENG.). 256p. (YA). (gr. 7-12). reprint ed. 8.99 (978-1-59514-032-6(8), Razorbill) Penguin Young Readers Group.

Weston Woods Staff, creator. Children Make Terrible Pets. 2011. 29.95 (978-0-545-40221-7(2)) Weston Woods Studios, Inc.

—Sylvester & the Magic Pebble. 2011. 38.75 (978-0-439-72898-0(3)); 29.95 (978-0-439-73522-3(X)) Weston Woods Studios, Inc.

Weymouth, Laura E. The Light Between Worlds. (ENG.). (YA). (gr. 8). 2019. 384p. pap. 10.99 (978-0-06-269688-5(2)) 2018. 368p. 17.99 (978-0-06-269687-8(4)) HarperCollins Pubs. (HarperTeen).

Whaley, John Corey. Where Things Come Back. 2012. (ENG., Illus.). 272p. (YA). (gr. 9). pap. 12.99 (978-1-4424-1334-4(4), Atheneum Bks. for Young Readers) Simon & Schuster Children's Publishing.

—Where Things Come Back. 2011. (ENG., Illus.). 240p. (YA). (gr. 9-12). 19.99 (978-1-4424-1333-7(6)) Simon & Schuster, Inc.

Whelan, Gloria. The Disappeared. 2010. 144p. (YA). (gr. 7-18). 6.99 (978-0-14-241540-5(5), Speak) Penguin Young Readers Group.

Wiggin, Kate Douglas. A Summer in a Canyon. 2007. 140p. 24.95 (978-1-60312-626-7(0)) Aegypan.

Willey, Margaret. Four Secrets. Hauser, Bill, illus. 2014. (ENG.). 288p. (YA). (gr. 7-12). pap. 9.95 (978-1-4677-1626-0(X), 319967e1-284e-4939-a26f-d2c8cf3cd8a4, Carolrhoda Lab™) Lerner Publishing Group.

Williams, Geoffrey T. The Hammerheads of Treasure Island. 2010. (ENG., Illus.). 64p. (J). (gr. 3-7). 8.95 (978-0-9800444-2-3(1)) Save Our Seas, Ltd.

Willis, Jeanne. Shamanka. 2009. (J). pap. (978-0-7636-3767-5(X)) Candlewick Pr.

Wilson, Karma. Bear Feels Scared. Chapman, Jane, illus. 2011. (Bear Bks.). (ENG.). 34p. (J). (gr. -1 — 1). bds. 7.99 (978-1-4424-2755-6(8), Little Simon) Little Simon.

—Bear Feels Scared. Chapman, Jane, illus. 2008. (Bear Bks.). (ENG.). 40p. (J). (gr. -1-3). 18.99 (978-0-689-85986-1(4), McElderry, Margaret K. Bks.) McElderry, Margaret K. Bks.

Wilson, N. D. Leepike Ridge. 2007. (ENG., Illus.). 224p. (J). (gr. 4-6). lib. bdg. 22.44 (978-0-375-93873-3(7)) Random House Publishing Group.

—Leepike Ridge. 2008. (ENG., Illus.). 256p. (J). (gr. 3-7). 8.99 (978-0-375-83874-3(0), Yearling) Random Hse. Children's Bks.

Winston, Sherri. Jada Sly, Artist & Spy. 2019. (ENG., Illus.). 272p. (J). (gr. 3-7). 32.99 (978-0-316-50536-9(6)) Little, Brown Bks. for Young Readers.

Wirt, Mildred A. Whispering Walls. 2011. 174p. pap. 9.99 (978-1-935774-83-9(2), Resurrected Pr.) Intrepid Ink, LLC.

Wittlinger, Ellen. Someone Else's Shoes. 304p. (J). (gr. 5). 2019. pap. 9.99 (978-1-62354-113-2(1)) 2018. 16.99 (978-1-58089-749-5(5)) Charlesbridge Publishing, Inc.

Wright, Peter M. The Stone Prince, 1 vol. 2009. 48p. pap. 16.95 (978-1-4489-2591-9(6)) America Star Bks.

Wundram, Bill. Finnius: The Tale of a Lost Little Elephant. Tucker, Eric, illus. 2003. (J). (978-1-59152-011-5(8), Sweetgrass Bks.) Farcountry Pr.

Yelchin, Eugene. Spy Runner. Yelchin, Eugene, illus. 2019. (ENG., Illus.). 352p. (J). 21.99 (978-1-250-12081-6(0), 900173090, Holt, Henry & Co. Bks. For Young Readers) Holt, Henry & Co.

Young, Brigit. Worth a Thousand Words. 2020. (ENG.). 304p. (J). pap. 7.99 (978-1-250-30875-7(5), 900177859) Square Fish.

Yovanoff, Brenna. The Replacement. 2011. (ENG.). 368p. (YA). (gr. 7-18). 8.99 (978-1-59514-381-5(5), Razorbill) Penguin Young Readers Group.

Yusuf. Butterfly & Bumble Bee: Adventure in Yellow Stone National Park. 2010. 16p. 8.49 (978-1-4520-4022-6(2)) AuthorHouse.

Zadoff, Allen. I Am the Weapon. 2014. (Unknown Assassin Ser.: 1). (ENG.). 368p. (YA). (gr. 10-17). pap. 11.99 (978-0-316-19967-4(2)) Little, Brown Bks. for Young Readers.

Zahler, Diane. A True Princess. (ENG.). (J). (gr. 3-7). 2012. 208p. pap. 6.99 (978-0-06-182503-3(4)) 2011. 192p. 15.99 (978-0-06-182501-9(8)) HarperCollins Pubs. (HarperCollins).

Zhang, Kat. The Emperor's Riddle. (ENG.). (J). (gr. 3-7). 2018. 272p. pap. 8.99 (978-1-4814-7863-2(X)) 2017. (Illus.). 256p. 16.99 (978-1-4814-7862-5(1)) Simon & Schuster Children's Publishing. (Aladdin).

Zucker, Jonny. Mission 6: Short Circuit. Woodman, Ned, illus. 2013. (Max Flash Ser.: 6). (ENG.). 144p. (J). (gr. 2-5). pap. 7.95 (978-1-4677-1480-8(1), c61e92f5-c442-45a0-a1a5-43191834b8d6, Darby Creek) Lerner Publishing Group.

4RV Publishing LLC Staff. Case of the Missing Coach. 2007. (Illus.). 144p. (J). per. 18.99 (978-0-9797513-1-8(4)) 4RV Pub.

MISSIONARIES

Anderson, Dick. African Adventures. 2006. (Adventure Ser.). (ENG., Illus.). 96p. (J). pap. 8.99 (978-1-85792-807-5(5), d3cdf6b5-7dbe-41d1-ac2a-53743d91f508) Christian Focus Pubns. GBR. Dist: Baker & Taylor Publisher Services (BTPS).

Andrew, et al. God's Smuggler. Foley, Tim, illus. 2017. (ENG.). 224p. (J). pap. 10.99 (978-0-8007-9805-5(8)) Chosen Bks.

Benge, Janet & Benge, Geoff. Christian Heroes - Then & Now - C. T. Studd: No Retreat. 2005. (Christian Heroes Ser.). (ENG., Illus.). 192p. (YA). (gr. 4-7). pap. 11.99 (978-1-57658-288-6(4)) YWAM Publishing.

—Christian Heroes - Then & Now - Florence Young: Mission Accomplished. 2005. (Christian Heroes Ser.). (ENG.). 183p. (YA). (gr. 4-7). pap. 11.99 (978-1-57658-313-5(9)) YWAM Publishing.

—Christian Heroes - Then & Now - Ida Scudder: Healing Bodies, Touching Hearts. 2003. (Christian Heroes Ser.). (ENG.). 189p. (YA). pap. 11.99 (978-1-57658-285-5(X)) YWAM Publishing.

—Christian Heroes - Then & Now - Lillian Trasher: The Greatest Wonder in Egypt. 2003. (Christian Heroes Ser.). (ENG.). 189p. (YA). pap. 11.99 (978-1-57658-305-0(8)) YWAM Publishing.

—Christian Heroes - Then & Now - Rowland Bingham: Into Africa's Interior. 2003. (Christian Heroes Ser.). (Illus.). 192p. pap. 11.99 (978-1-57658-282-4(5)) YWAM Publishing.

—Heroes Cristianos de Ayer y de Hoy - la Intrepida Rescatadora: La Vida de Amy Carmichael. 2003.Tr. of Christian Heroes: Then & Now - Amy Carmichael. (SPA.). 205p. (YA). pap. 7.99 (978-1-57658-309-8(0)) YWAM Publishing.

—Jacob Deshazer: Forgive Your Enemies. 2009. (ENG.). 224p. (YA). pap. 11.99 (978-1-57658-475-0(5)) YWAM Publishing.

—Klaus-Dieter John: Hope in the Land of the Incas. 2014. (Illus.). 224p. (J). pap. 11.99 (978-1-57658-755-3(X)) YWAM Publishing.

—Peripecia en la China: La Vida de Hudson Taylor. 2004.Tr. of Christian Heroes - Then & Now - Hudson Taylor. (SPA.). 196p. (YA). pap. 7.99 (978-1-57658-260-2(4)) YWAM Publishing.

Bodden, Valerie. To the Heart of Africa. 2011. (Great Expeditions Ser.). (ENG., Illus.). 48p. (J). (gr. 5-8). 35.65 (978-1-60818-066-0(2), 22152, Creative Education) Creative Co., The.

Caughey, Ellen. Eric Liddell: Gold Medal Missionary. 2006. (Heros of the Faith Ser.). 206p. (YA). (gr. 8-12). per. 2.97 (978-1-59789-115-8(0)) Barbour Publishing, Inc.

Edwards, Andrew & Thornton, Fleur. William Carey: The Story of a Country Boy & Shoe Mender Whose Big Dreams Took Him to India. 2005. (Footsteps of the Past Ser.). (Illus.). 32p. pap. 5.00 (978-1-84625-012-5(9)) DayOne Pubns. GBR. Dist: Send The Light Distribution LLC.

Fitzpatrick, Anne. Mother Teresa. 2005. (Genius Ser.). (Illus.). 48p. (J). (gr. 5-9). lib. bdg. 21.95 (978-1-58341-330-2(8), Creative Education) Creative Co., The.

Gigliotti, Jim & Who HQ. Who Was Mother Teresa? Groff, David, illus. 2015. (Who Was? Ser.). 112p. (J). (gr. 3-7). 5.99 (978-0-448-48299-6(1), Penguin Workshop) Penguin Young Readers Group.

Glavich, Mary Kathleen. Blessed Teresa of Calcutta: Missionary of Charity. Kiwak, Barbara, tr. Kiwak, Barbara, illus. 2003. (Encounter the Saints Ser.: Vol. 17). 136p. (J). pap. 7.95 (978-0-8198-1160-8(2), 332-024) Pauline Bks. & Media.

Haluska, David. Jesus Loves Trucks. Ford, Emily, illus. 2014. 32p. (J). 7.99 (978-0-8280-2719-9(6)) Review & Herald Publishing Assn.

Harkins, Susan Sales & Harkins, William H. The Life & Times of Father Jacques Marquette. 2008. (Profiles in American History Ser.). (Illus.). 48p. (J). (gr. 4-8). lib. bdg. 29.95 (978-1-58415-528-7(0)) Mitchell Lane Pubs.

Harness, Cheryl. The Tragic Tale of Narcissa Whitman & a Faithful History of the Oregon Trail (Direct Mail Edition) 2006. (Cheryl Harness Histories Ser.). (Illus.). 144p. (J). (gr. 5-9). 16.95 (978-0-7922-5920-6(3), National Geographic Kids) Disney Publishing Worldwide.

Howat, Irene. James Chalmers: The Rainmaker's Friend. 2006. (Torchbearers Ser.). (ENG., Illus.). 160p. (J). (gr. 4-7). per. 8.99 (978-1-84550-154-9(3), ca748eb6-f8da-4c18-9d63-c5d56a171e2f) Christian Focus Pubns. GBR. Dist: Baker & Taylor Publisher Services (BTPS).

Ishkanian, Charlotte. Best Ever Mission Stories: Kids in Action Around the World. 2008. (J). 5.97 (978-0-8163-2263-3(5)) Pacific Pr. Publishing Assn.

Jay, Ruth Johnson. Mary Slessor: Missionary to Calabar. 2006. (Illus.). 143p. (J). (978-1-56265-077-3(7)) Accelerated Christian Education, Inc.

Kelly, Terri B. Mary Slessor: Missionary Mother. 2014. (Illus.). 164p. (J). (978-1-60682-630-0(1)) BJU Pr.

Kidder, Tracy. Mountains Beyond Mountains (Adapted for Young People) The Quest of Dr. Paul Farmer, a Man Who Would Cure the World. 2014. (ENG.). (YA). (gr. 7). lib. bdg. 19.60 (978-1-68065-029-7(7)) Perfection Learning Corp.

Kidder, Tracy & French, Michael. Mountains Beyond Mountains (Adapted for Young People) The Quest of Dr. Paul Farmer, a Man Who Would Cure the World. 2014. (ENG.). 288p. (YA). (gr. 7). pap. 9.99 (978-0-385-74319-8(X), Ember) Random Hse. Children's Bks.

Klaus, Sandra. Surrounded by Headhunters. Date not set. (ARA.). (J). (gr. 2-7). pap. (978-1-890940-03-4(8)) Gospel Missionary Union.

Langley, Judy. God's World & Me from A to Z. Coker, Carla, illus. 2004. 32p. (gr. -1). 8.99 (978-1-56309-367-8(7), New Hope Pubs.) Iron Stream Media.

Leidenfrost, Lisa. At the Edge of the Village: Musings of a Missionary Wife. 2004. Orig. Title: African Sketches. (ENG., Illus.). 212p. (YA). pap. 17.00 (978-1-59128-017-0(6)) Canon Pr.

MacKenzie, Catherine. Amy Carmichael: Can Brown Eyes Be Made Blue? rev. ed. 2011. (Little Lights Ser.). (ENG., Illus.). 24p. (J). (gr. -1-2). 7.99 (978-1-84550-108-2(X), 8c326d94-40e1-4e7f-b26f-e02c92531c8f) Christian Focus Pubns. GBR. Dist: Baker & Taylor Publisher Services (BTPS).

—Hudson Taylor: Could Somebody Pass the Salt? rev. ed. 2012. (Little Lights Ser.). (ENG., Illus.). 24p. (J). (gr. 4-7). 7.99 (978-1-84550-111-2(X), d9f93b7b-f6f4-475f-bc0e-3ff11e568f9d) Christian Focus Pubns. GBR. Dist: Baker & Taylor Publisher Services (BTPS).

Martin, Mildred A. Missionary Stories with the Millers. Burkholder, Edith, illus. 2009. 208p. (J). (978-1-884377-17-4(3)); pap. (978-1-884377-16-7(5)) Green Pastures Pr.

Mattews, Basil. Livingstone: The Pathfinder. 2003. (ENG.). 112p. (YA). pap. 9.95 (978-0-923309-86-2(1)) Hartland Pubns.

McElhaney, Dolly. Pilot Bennie's Amazing Amazon Adventures. 2018. (Illus.). 132p. (J). (978-0-7577-4610-9(1)) Word Aflame Pr.

McNeil, Niki, et al. HOCPP 1096 Missionaries to Know. 2006. spiral bd. 21.00 (978-1-60308-096-5(1)) In the Hands of a Child.

Meloche, Renee. Heroes for Young Readers - Hudson Taylor: Friend of China. Pollard, Bryan, illus. 2004. (ENG.). 32p. (J). 8.99 *(978-1-57658-234-3(5))* YWAM Publishing.

Miller, William. Tales of Persia: Missionary Stories from Islamic Iran. Van Patten, Bruce, illus. 2005. 163p. per. 9.99 *(978-0-87552-615-7(2))* P & R Publishing.

Nelson, Robin. Mother Teresa: A Life of Caring. (Pull Ahead Books — Biographies Ser.). (Illus.). 32p. (J). 2007. (ENG.). (gr. k-3). pap. 7.99 *(978-0-8225-6433-1(5),* d3ca9c7a-8cce-4f0e-ba3c-b256c4dc2ba9) 2006. (gr. 3-7). lib. bdg. 22.60 *(978-0-8225-6384-6(3),* Lerner Pubns.) Lerner Publishing Group.

Otfinoski, Steven. David Livingstone: Deep in the Heart of Africa, 1 vol. 2007. (Great Explorations Ser.). (ENG., Illus.). 80p. (gr. 6-6). lib. bdg. 36.93 *(978-0-7614-2226-6(9),* 7a28dbce-109c-476e-99fa-e3fac1da0bdd) Cavendish Square Publishing LLC.

Robinson, Virgil E. Curse of the Cannibals. 2011. (Illus.). 126p. per. 11.95 *(978-1-57258-355-9(X))* TEACH Services, Inc.

Slavicek, Louise Chipley. Mother Teresa. 2007. (Modern Peacemakers Ser.). (ENG., Illus.). 113p. (gr. 9-12). lib. bdg. 30.00 *(978-0-7910-9433-4(2),* P124650, Facts On File) Infobase Holdings, Inc.

Sullivan, Anne Marie. Mother Teresa: Religious Humanitarian. 2013. (People of Importance Ser.: 21). (Illus.). 32p. (J). (gr. 4-18). 19.95 *(978-1-4222-2853-1(3))* Mason Crest.

—Mother Theresa: Religious Humanitarian. 2004. (Great Names Ser.). (Illus.). 32p. (J). (gr. 3-18). lib. bdg. 19.95 *(978-1-59084-142-6(5))* Mason Crest.

Tan, Joyce. Finding the Lord's ELect: How Missionaries can Tract Fruitfully. 2004. per. 12.95 *(978-0-9746016-0-1(8))* Eclectic Dragon Pr.

Toliver, Gwen. Seed Sowers: Gospel-Planting Adventures. 2012. 180p. (gr. -1). 30.95 *(978-1-4497-7132-4(7))*; pap. 13.95 *(978-1-4497-7130-0(0))* Author Solutions, LLC. (WestBow Pr.).

Valentine, Emily. Mother Teresa: With a Discussion of Compassion. 2004. (Values in Action Ser.). (J). *(978-1-59203-070-5(X))* Learning Challenge, Inc.

Vogel, Cara Lynn. The Lottie & Annie Upside-down Book. Adkins, Loretta B., illus. 2003. 16p. (J). 8.99 *(978-1-56309-627-3(7))* Woman's Missionary Union.

Walsh, Kay. John G. Paton: South Sea Island Rescue. rev. ed. 2005. (Trail Blazers Ser.). (ENG.). 160p. (J). mass mkt. 8.99 *(978-1-85792-852-5(0),* 9d15d6a0-3b10-4a50-b6bb-a625a28e7687) Christian Focus Pubns. GBR. Dist: Baker & Taylor Publisher Services (BTPS).

Wilder, M. L. Missionary Annuls: Memoir of Robert Moffat. 2003. (ENG.). 64p. (YA). pap. 8.95 *(978-0-923309-88-6(8))* Hartland Pubns.

Williams, Laura E. Father Damien. Kofsky, Kristen, illus. 2009. (ENG.). 60p. (J). (gr. 4). pap. *(978-1-59700-757-3(9))* Island Heritage Publishing.

Winder, Michael Kent. Called to Serve: Celebrating Missionary Work Around the World. 2014. (Illus.). 112p. (J). pap. 15.99 *(978-1-62108-667-3(4))* Covenant Communications, Inc.

MISSIONARIES—FICTION

Allison, Carol. Missionary Adventures: Stories for Boys & Girls. 2011. 94p. 38.95 *(978-1-258-08225-3(X))* Literary Licensing, LLC.

The Captain, His Daughter, & Their Discovery. 2007. 48p. pap. 6.50 *(978-0-8341-2296-3(0),* 083-412-2960) Beacon Hill Pr. of Kansas City.

The Case of the Secret Box. 2007. 56p. pap. 7.75 *(978-0-8341-2288-8(X),* 083-412-288X) Beacon Hill Pr. of Kansas City.

Eby, Wes. Jungle Jeopardy. 2006. 56p. 7.75 *(978-0-8341-2228-4(6))* Beacon Hill Pr. of Kansas City.

Forbes, Dillon. Careful Enough? 2008. (YA). 8.99 *(978-1-59166-835-0(2))* BJU Pr.

Haislip, Phyllis Hall. Lottie's Courage: A Contraband Slave's Story. 2003. (Illus.). 120p. (J). pap. 7.95 *(978-1-57249-311-7(9),* White Mane Kids) White Mane Publishing Co., Inc.

Hardy, LeAnne. Between Two Worlds: A Novel. 2003. 160p. (J). pap. 7.99 *(978-0-8254-2793-0(2))* Kregel Pubns.

Hering, Marianne. In Fear of the Spear. 2016. (AIO Imagination Station Bks.: 17). (ENG., Illus.). 144p. (J). pap. 5.99 *(978-1-58997-804-1(8),* 4622356) Focus on the Family Publishing.

Howat, Irene. Helen Roseveare: On His Majesty's Service. rev. ed. 2008. (Trail Blazers Ser.). (ENG.). 176p. (J). (gr. 4-9). per. 8.99 *(978-1-84550-259-1(0),* e13685db-3248-44b9-bde0-24f841ba2e10) Christian Focus Pubns. GBR. Dist: Baker & Taylor Publisher Services (BTPS).

Hudson, Bonnie Rose. The Hidden Village. 2017. (J). *(978-1-62856-311-5(7))* BJU Pr.

MacKenzie, Catherine. Gladys Aylward: Are You Going to Stop? rev. ed. 2013. (Little Lights Ser.). (ENG., Illus.). 24p. (J). 7.99 *(978-1-78191-161-7(4),* 08b31318-b6d2-461c-a2d2-b2fea960edd6) Christian Focus Pubns. GBR. Dist: Baker & Taylor Publisher Services (BTPS).

McHugh, Michael. Giant of the Western Trail: Father Peter de Smet. Dougherty, Charles L., illus. 2011. 186p. 42.95 *(978-1-258-05887-6(1))* Literary Licensing, LLC.

Moffett, Slyvia. The Missionary Kids Adventure Series: Bo. 2006. 48p. pap. 16.95 *(978-1-4241-2854-9(4))* PublishAmerica, Inc.

Nogar, Anna M. & Lamadrid, Enrique R. Sisters in Blue/Hermanas de Azul: Sor María de Ágreda Comes to New Mexico/Sor María de Ágreda Viene a Nuevo México. 2017. (Querencias Ser.). (ENG., Illus.). 88p. (J). 19.95 *(978-0-8263-5821-9(7),* P532838) Univ. of New Mexico Pr.

Palmer, Viola. The Man in the Green Jeep. 2006. (ENG.). 144p. pap. *(978-0-929292-61-8(8),* 800-747-0738) Creative Properties LLC.

Riordan, Robert. Medicine for Wildcat: A Story of the Friendship between a Menominee Indian & Frontier Priest Samuel Mazzuchelli. 2006. (Illus.). 132p. (YA). per. 14.95 *(978-0-9774934-0-1(7))* Sinsinawa Dominicans, Inc.

Singleton, Linda Joy. Melissa's Mission Impossible/Mail Order Monster: Twin Spins. 2005. (Twin Spins Ser.: 10). (ENG.). 168p. (YA). per. 10.95 *(978-0-7599-1009-6(X))* Hard Shell Word Factory.

Smith, Robert F. Bitten: A Romantic Comedy. 2008. 510p. (YA). pap. *(978-1-59038-904-1(2))* Deseret Bk. Co.

Snowballs & Coconuts. 2006. 56p. pap. 7.75 *(978-0-8341-2295-6(2),* 083-412-2952) Beacon Hill Pr. of Kansas City.

St. John, Patricia. Secret of the Fourth Candle. rev. ed. 2003. (Illus.). 94p. 6.49 *(978-1-85999-511-2(X))* Scripture Union GBR. Dist: Gabriel Resources.

Stewart, Jennifer J. Close Encounters of a Third World Kind. 2004. (ENG.). 128p. (J). (gr. 4-6). tchr. ed. 16.95 *(978-0-8234-1850-3(2))* Holiday Hse., Inc.

—Close Encounters of a Third-World Kind. 2008. (ENG., Illus.). 181p. (J). (gr. 3-7). 6.95 *(978-0-8234-2161-9(9))* Holiday Hse., Inc.

Tada, Joni Eareckson & Jensen, Steve. The Mission Adventure. 2005. (Darcy & Friends Ser.). 143p. (gr. 3-6). pap. 5.99 *(978-1-58134-257-4(8),* Crossway Bibles) Crossway.

Williamson, Denise J. River of Danger. 2008. (J). 8.99 *(978-1-59166-854-1(9))* BJU Pr.

—Silent Road to Rescue. 2008. (J). 8.99 *(978-1-59166-852-7(2))* BJU Pr.

Wilson, Heather Gemmen. Lydia Barnes & the Blood Diamond Treasure. 2007. (Global Warning Ser.). 159p. (J). (gr. 3-7). per. 7.99 *(978-0-89827-350-2(1))* Wesleyan Publishing Hse.

—Lydia Barnes & the Escape from Shark Bay. 2008. 160p. (J). 9.99 *(978-0-89827-352-6(8))* Wesleyan Publishing Hse.

Youngberg, Norma R. Jungle Thorn. 2010. (Illus.). 132p. reprint ed. per. 11.95 *(978-1-57258-157-9(3),* 945-6024) TEACH Services, Inc.

Zaugg, Sandra L. Hidden Notes & High Seas. 2005. (Illus.). 95p. (J). *(978-0-8163-2052-3(7))* Pacific Pr. Pubns.

—The Man in the Blue Skirt. 2005. (Illus.). 95p. (J). pap. *(978-0-8163-2055-4(1))* Pacific Pr. Pubns.

—A Prayer for Mother. 2005. (Illus.). 95p. (J). *(978-0-8163-2056-1(X))* Pacific Pr. Pubns.

MISSIONS

see also Missionaries

also names of churches, denominations, religious orders, etc. with the subdivision Missions, e.g. Catholic Church—Missions; etc.

Abbink, Emily. Monterey Bay Area Missions. 2007. (Exploring California Missions Ser.). (ENG., Illus.). 64p. (gr. 4-7). lib. bdg. 27.93 *(978-0-8225-0887-8(7),* Lerner Pubns.) Lerner Publishing Group.

Anderson, Zachary. Discovering Mission Nuestra Señora de la Soledad, 1 vol. 2014. (California Missions Ser.). (ENG.). 48p. (gr. 4-4). 33.07 *(978-1-62713-079-0(9),* 05733073-aaf3-4234-83ba-586f03f4a103) Cavendish Square Publishing LLC.

Andrew, et al. God's Smuggler. Foley, Tim, illus. 2017. (ENG.). 224p. (J). pap. 10.99 *(978-0-8007-9805-5(8))* Chosen Bks.

Arnéz, Lynda & Arnéz, Lynda. Father Junipero Serra: Founder of the California Missions, 1 vol. 2015. (Exceptional Latinos Ser.). (ENG.). 24p. (gr. 3-4). pap. 10.35 *(978-0-7660-6710-3(6),* 0f4490d7-4307-473c-90b9-d935e8b061b1) Enslow Publishing, LLC.

Behrens, June. Central Coast Missions in California. 2007. (Exploring California Missions Ser.). (Illus.). 64p. (J). lib. bdg. 27.93 *(978-0-8225-0897-7(4),* Lerner Pubns.) Lerner Publishing Group.

Benge, Janet & Benge, Geoff. Christian Heroes - Then & Now - Rowland Bingham: Into Africa's Interior. 2003. (Christian Heroes Ser.). (Illus.). 192p. pap. 11.99 *(978-1-57658-282-4(5))* YWAM Publishing.

Bert, Ruth J. Everyone Called Her Sister Sarah. Westbeld, Kristine, illus. 2004. (ENG.). 32p. (J). (gr. -1-3). pap. 4.99 *(978-1-928915-62-1(0))* Evangel Publishing Hse.

Blackwell, Jodi. Fundamentals: Secret Mission Children's Pack. (J). (gr. 1-6). *(978-0-633-05795-4(9))* Lifeway Christian Resources.

Brower, Pauline. Inland Valleys Missions in California. 2007. (Exploring California Missions Ser.). (ENG., Illus.). 64p. (gr. 4-7). lib. bdg. 27.93 *(978-0-8225-0899-1(0),* Lerner Pubns.) Lerner Publishing Group.

Ching, Jacqueline. Mission San Fernando Rey de Espana, 1 vol. 2003. (Missions of California Ser.). (ENG.). 64p. (J). (gr. 4-4). lib. bdg. 32.93 *(978-0-8239-5893-1(0),* fa0bff59-5cc5-43b5-9dfe-17e6dc9b3465, PowerKids Pr.) Rosen Publishing Group, Inc., The.

—Mission San Rafael Arcangel, 1 vol. 2003. (Missions of California Ser.). (ENG.). 64p. (J). (gr. 4-4). 32.93 *(978-0-8239-5886-3(8),* 43b9b517-56e2-4e7b-87eb-375f371294d0, PowerKids Pr.) Rosen Publishing Group, Inc., The.

—Mission Santa Ines. (Missions of California Ser.). 64p. (gr. 4-4). 2009. 58.50 *(978-1-60854-042-6(1))* 2003. (ENG.). (J). lib. bdg. 32.93 *(978-0-8239-5894-8(9),* 6efe94fa-eadd-45da-aef2-6d15723aa114) Rosen Publishing Group, Inc., The. (PowerKids Pr.).

Crouch, Cheryl. Trouble in East Timor. 2010. (Illus.). 56p. (J). *(978-0-8341-2488-2(2))* Beacon Hill Pr. of Kansas City.

Draper, Allison Stark. Mission San Fransisco de Solano, 1 vol. 2003. (Missions of California Ser.). (ENG., Illus.). 64p. (J). (gr. 4-4). 32.93 *(978-0-8239-5884-9(1),* d512b236-86c9-4fda-883c-c91812ec900d) Rosen Publishing Group, Inc., The.

—Mission San Juan Bautista, 1 vol. 2003. (Missions of California Ser.). (ENG.). 64p. (J). (gr. 4-4). lib. bdg. 32.93 *(978-0-8239-5879-5(5),* c8e0ff8f-9166-4615-9a2d-5f02db08b4b7, PowerKids Pr.) Rosen Publishing Group, Inc., The.

Eby, Wes. Coban Treasure Hunt. 2010. (Illus.). 56p. (J). *(978-0-8341-2489-9(0))* Beacon Hill Pr. of Kansas City.

Edgar, Kathleen J. Mission San Juan Capistrano, 1 vol. 2003. (Missions of California Ser.). (ENG.). 64p. (YA). (gr. 4-4). 32.93 *(978-0-8239-5889-4(2),* a0145ab6-9623-4dcf-9d70-b2efb7d627be) Rosen Publishing Group, Inc., The.

Edgar, Kathleen J. & Edgar, Susan E. Mission San Carlos Borromeo Del Rio Carmelo, 1 vol. 2003. (Missions of California Ser.). (ENG., Illus.). 64p. (YA). (gr. 4-4). 32.93 *(978-0-8239-5890-0(6),* 96255969-843d-4221-a621-db40541b63e8) Rosen Publishing Group, Inc., The.

—Mission San Diego de Alcala, 1 vol. 2003. (Missions of California Ser.). (ENG.). 64p. (J). (gr. 4-4). lib. bdg. 32.93 *(978-0-8239-5885-6(X),* ce809b44-a366-4f17-922a-0873f8045116, PowerKids Pr.) Rosen Publishing Group, Inc., The.

—Mission San Francisco de Asis, 1 vol. 2003. (Missions of California Ser.). (ENG., Illus.). 64p. (J). (gr. 4-4). 32.93 *(978-0-8239-5887-0(6),* b5aaff74-f0b3-485b-a284-2349295d81f4) Rosen Publishing Group, Inc., The.

—Mission San Luis Obispo de Tolosa, 1 vol. 2003. (Missions of California Ser.). (ENG., Illus.). 64p. (J). (gr. 4-4). lib. bdg. 32.93 *(978-0-8239-5898-6(1),* c80d0d3c-d30a-46e8-a284-ee8fa0b98b72) Rosen Publishing Group, Inc., The.

—Mission San Miguel Arcangel, 1 vol. 2003. (Missions of California Ser.). (ENG.). 64p. (J). (gr. 4-4). lib. bdg. 32.93 *(978-0-8239-5896-2(5),* 14255257-e070-4343-9b21-1cadaa56e62e, PowerKids Pr.) Rosen Publishing Group, Inc., The.

Gendell, Megan. Spanish Missions of California. 2010. (True Book(tm), a — Spanish Missions Ser.). (Illus.). 48p. (J). (gr. 2-5). 31.00 *(978-0-531-20577-8(0))* Scholastic Library Publishing.

—A True Book: Spanish Missions of Texas. 2010. (True Book Ser.). (ENG., Illus.). 48p. (J). pap. 6.95 *(978-0-531-21243-1(2))* Scholastic Library Publishing.

—True Books: the Spanish Missions of Texas. 2010. (True Book(tm), a — Spanish Missions Ser.). (ENG.). 48p. (J). (gr. 2-5). 31.00 *(978-0-531-20580-8(0))* Scholastic Library Publishing.

Grate, Gina. Project Noah. 2006. 32p. 4.50 *(978-0-8341-2231-4(6))* The Foundry Publishing.

Haluska, David. Jesus Loves Trucks. Ford, Emily, illus. 2014. 32p. (J). 7.99 *(978-0-8280-2719-9(6))* Review & Herald Publishing Assn.

Hare, Eric B. Jungle Heroes & Other Stories. 2005. (Illus.). 106p. (J). 9.99 *(978-0-8163-2063-9(2))* Pacific Pr. Publishing Assn.

Herrera, Matthew D. History Guide to Old Mission San Luis Obispo de Tolosa. 2003. (Illus.). 77p. 9.95 *(978-0-9723720-1-5(6))* Tixlini Scriptorium, Inc.

Jingling, Kathy, ed. Bernabe y su Gran Mision por Cristo. Oyola, Milta, tr. from ENG. Tobar, Malena, illus. 2011.Tr. of Barnabas & his Great Mission for Christ. (SPA.). 191p. (J). spiral bd. 7.00 *(978-1-931984-41-6(7),* 2002-00S1) Faith & Action Team.

Langley, Judy. God's World & Me from A to Z. Coker, Carla, illus. 2004. 32p. (gr. -1). 8.99 *(978-1-56309-367-8(7),* New Hope Pubs.) Iron Stream Media.

Lemke, Nancy. Southern Coast Missions in California. 2007. (Exploring California Missions Ser.). (ENG., Illus.). 64p. (gr. 4-7). lib. bdg. 27.93 *(978-0-8225-1935-5(6),* Lerner Pubns.) Lerner Publishing Group.

Lilly, Melinda. Misiones Espanolas (Spanish Missions) Capaldi, Gina, illus. 2005. (Lecturas Historicas Norteamericanas (Reading American Histor Ser.). 24p. (J). (gr. 3-7). lib. bdg. 22.79 *(978-1-59515-638-9(0))* Rourke Educational Media.

Lyon, Robin. The Spanish Missions of Arizona. 2010. (True Book(tm), a — Spanish Missions Ser.). 48p. (J). (gr. 2-5). 31.00 *(978-0-531-20576-1(2))* Scholastic Library Publishing.

—A True Book: Spanish Missions of Arizona. 2010. (True Book Ser.). (ENG.). 48p. (J). pap. 6.95 *(978-0-531-21239-4(4))* Scholastic Library Publishing.

—A True Book: Spanish Missions of New Mexico. 2010. (True Book Ser.). (ENG.). 48p. (J). pap. 6.95 *(978-0-531-21242-4(4),* Children's Pr.) Scholastic Library Publishing.

—True Books: the Spanish Missions of New Mexico. 2010. (True Book: Spanish Missions Ser.). (ENG.). 48p. (J). (gr. 3-5). 21.19 *(978-0-531-20579-2(7),* Children's Pr.) Scholastic Library Publishing.

MacMillan, Dianne M. Los Angeles Area Missions. 2007. (Exploring California Missions Ser.). (Illus.). 64p. (J). lib. bdg. 27.93 *(978-0-8225-0898-4(2),* Lerner Pubns.) Lerner Publishing Group.

Margaret, Amy. Mission San Buenaventura, 1 vol. 2003. (Missions of California Ser.). (ENG., Illus.). 64p. (J). (gr. 4-4). 32.93 *(978-0-8239-5888-7(4),* a8e2962e-edf8-4970-b0ae-63359f88e7c0) Rosen Publishing Group, Inc., The.

—Mission San Jose de Guadalupe, 1 vol. 2003. (Missions of California Ser.). (ENG.). 64p. (J). (gr. 4-4). lib. bdg. 32.93 *(978-0-8239-5897-9(3),* 15b1dd57-38f3-4231-9710-5c00892faebd, PowerKids Pr.) Rosen Publishing Group, Inc., The.

—Mission Santa Barbara. (Missions of California Ser.). 64p. (gr. 4-4). 2009. 58.50 *(978-1-60854-037-2(5),* PowerKids Pr.) 2003. (ENG., Illus.). (J). 32.93 *(978-0-8239-5880-1(9),* 10aa196e-9880-47e4-bdc9-6bebf8ac5092) Rosen Publishing Group, Inc., The.

—Mission Santa Clara de Asis. (Missions of California Ser.). 64p. (gr. 4-4). 2009. 58.50 *(978-1-60854-038-9(3),* PowerKids Pr.) 2003. (ENG., Illus.). (J). 32.93 *(978-0-8239-5883-2(3),* d511685b-0e42-4f35-9e27-7a04e0d90fdd) Rosen Publishing Group, Inc., The.

Mcginty, Alice B. Mission San Gabriel Arcangel, 1 vol. 2003. (Missions of California Ser.). (ENG., Illus.). 64p. (J). (gr. 4-4). 32.93 *(978-0-8239-5892-4(2),* 96fa2684-20d0-463c-8de5-9855d5776664) Rosen Publishing Group, Inc., The.

La Mision (The Mission) Quarter 2, Level 3. (Caminando con Jesus (Walking with Jesus) Series A). (SPA.). (J). stu. ed. 3.50 *(978-0-570-05150-3(9))* Concordia Publishing Hse.

Munson, Jared. Courageous Witness: A Teenager Shares Jesus. 2003. (ENG., Illus.). 88p. pap. 8.95 *(978-0-8309-1069-4(7))* Herald Publishing Hse.

National Geographic Learning. Reading Expeditions (Social Studies: Voices from America's Past): Missions & Ranchos. 2007. (ENG., Illus.). 40p. (J). pap. 21.95 *(978-0-7922-4548-3(2))* CENGAGE Learning.

Nelson, Libby. California Missions Projects & Layouts. 2007. (Exploring California Missions Ser.). (Illus.). 112p. (J). lib. bdg. 27.93 *(978-0-8225-7950-2(2),* Lerner Pubns.) Lerner Publishing Group.

Nunes, Sofia. Discovering Mission Santa Clara de Asís, 1 vol. 2014. (California Missions Ser.). (ENG., Illus.). 48p. (gr. 4-4). lib. bdg. 33.07 *(978-1-62713-067-7(5),* 12939286-ba5d-4ba2-b407-cc72d596d4fb) Cavendish Square Publishing LLC.

—Discovering Mission Santa Cruz, 1 vol. 2014. (California Missions Ser.). (ENG., Illus.). 48p. (gr. 4-4). lib. bdg. 33.07 *(978-1-62713-070-7(5),* 43efb26d-0d33-46b7-a24e-668ce85de5b8) Cavendish Square Publishing LLC.

Nussbaum, Ben. Junipero Serra: A Spanish Missionary. rev. ed. 2017. (Social Studies: Informational Text Ser.). (ENG., Illus.). 32p. (J). (gr. 3-5). pap. 11.99 *(978-1-4258-3235-3(0))* Teacher Created Materials, Inc.

Ostrow, Kim. Mission Nuestra Senora de la Soledad, 1 vol. 2003. (Missions of California Ser.). (ENG., Illus.). 64p. (J). (gr. 4-4). 32.93 *(978-0-8239-5882-5(5),* 43d1b423-072f-4efb-a6df-3ee966841829) Rosen Publishing Group, Inc., The.

—Mission Santa Cruz. (Missions of California Ser.). 64p. (gr. 4-4). 2009. 58.50 *(978-1-60854-041-9(3))* 2003. (ENG.). (J). lib. bdg. 32.93 *(978-0-8239-5878-8(7),* 36445898-78eb-4d59-9d14-a04636675ca9) Rosen Publishing Group, Inc., The. (PowerKids Pr.).

Peckham, Lori. Guide's Greatest Mission Stories. 2009. 158p. (J). *(978-0-8280-2501-0(0))* Review & Herald Publishing Assn.

People of the California Missions, 12 vols. 2003. (People of the California Missions Ser.). (ENG., Illus.). (J). (gr. 4-4). 197.58 *(978-0-8239-7263-0(1),* 00dd023b-f243-4039-b97c-8027543b9175) Rosen Publishing Group, Inc., The.

Perritano, John. Spanish Missions. 2010. (True Book Ser.). (Illus.). 48p. (J). pap. 6.95 *(978-0-531-21238-7(6))*; (ENG., (gr. 3-5). 21.19 *(978-0-531-20575-4(4),* Children's Pr.) Scholastic Library Publishing.

Price, Matt. The Mystery of the Ancient Anchor. Ettinger, Dorris, illus. 2010. 56p. (J). *(978-0-8341-2490-5(4))* Beacon Hill Pr. of Kansas City.

Primeros pasitos misioneros (First Steps, Spanish) 2004. pap. 12.99 *(978-1-56309-930-4(6))* Woman's Missionary Union.

Quantrell, Angie. I Can Do It! Lollar, Cathy, illus. 2003. 9.99 *(978-1-56309-626-6(9))* Woman's Missionary Union.

Quasha, Jennifer. Mission San Luis Rey de Francia, 1 vol. 2003. (Missions of California Ser.). (ENG.). 64p. (J). (gr. 4-4). lib. bdg. 32.93 *(978-0-8239-5895-5(7),* c7243d82-0e9e-4c2a-a2f5-e08a436c9a96, PowerKids Pr.) Rosen Publishing Group, Inc., The.

Roberts, Helen M. Miguel & the Pirates: A Tale of Mission Santa Cruz. Lawrence, Muriel, illus. 2011. 28p. 35.95 *(978-1-258-02882-4(4))* Literary Licensing, LLC.

Serafin, Kim. Mission San Antonio de Padua, 1 vol. 2003. (Missions of California Ser.). (ENG., Illus.). 64p. (J). (gr. 4-4). 32.93 *(978-0-8239-5891-7(4),* aecce6b0-3d13-462c-af3b-457ca33d0adb) Rosen Publishing Group, Inc., The.

Suben, Eric. The Spanish Missions of Florida. 2010. (True Book: Spanish Missions Ser.). 48p. (J). (gr. 3-5). (ENG.). 21.19 *(978-0-531-20578-5(9),* Children's Pr.); pap. 6.95 *(978-0-531-21241-7(6))* Scholastic Library Publishing.

Swinford, Betty. Missionary Stories from Around the World. 2005. (ENG., Illus.). 187p. (J). (gr. 4-7). per. 9.99 *(978-1-84550-042-9(3),* Christian Focus) Christian Focus Pubns. GBR. Dist: Send The Light Distribution LLC.

White, Tekla. San Francisco Bay Area Missions. 2007. (Exploring California Missions Ser.). (ENG., Illus.). 64p. (gr. 4-7). lib. bdg. 27.93 *(978-0-8225-0900-4(8),* Lerner Pubns.) Lerner Publishing Group.

Williams, Jack S. Indians of the California Mission Frontier. 2009. (People of the California Missions Ser.). 64p. (gr. 4-4). 58.50 *(978-1-60851-157-0(X),* PowerKids Pr.) Rosen Publishing Group, Inc., The.

—Padres of the California Mission Frontier. 2009. (People of the California Missions Ser.). 64p. (gr. 4-4). 58.50 *(978-1-60851-158-7(8),* PowerKids Pr.) Rosen Publishing Group, Inc., The.

—Sailors, Merchants, & Muleteers of the California Mission Frontier. 2009. (People of the California Missions Ser.). 64p. (gr. 4-4). 58.50 *(978-1-60851-159-4(6),* PowerKids Pr.) Rosen Publishing Group, Inc., The.

—Soldiers & Their Families of the California Mission Frontier. 2009. (People of the California Missions Ser.). 64p. (gr. 4-4). 58.50 *(978-1-60851-160-0(X),* PowerKids Pr.) Rosen Publishing Group, Inc., The.

—Townspeople & Ranchers of the California Mission Frontier. 2009. (People of the California Missions Ser.). 64p. (gr. 4-4). 58.50 *(978-1-60851-161-7(8),* PowerKids Pr.) Rosen Publishing Group, Inc., The.

Williams, Jack S. & Davis, Thomas L. Padres of the California Mission Frontier, 1 vol. 2003. (People of the California Missions Ser.). (ENG., Illus.). 64p. (J). (gr. 4-4). lib. bdg. 32.93 *(978-0-8239-6283-9(0),* 46a03ef1-64a1-4b15-a758-fb643866ebd6, PowerKids Pr.) Rosen Publishing Group, Inc., The.

—Soldiers & Their Families of the California Mission Frontier, 1 vol. 2003. (People of the California Missions Ser.). (ENG., Illus.). 64p. (J). (gr. 4-4). lib. bdg. 32.93 *(978-0-8239-6285-3(7),* 086e78d2-099a-4db3-abd3-9f67a8f32e61) Rosen Publishing Group, Inc., The.

—Townspeople & Ranchers of the California Mission Frontier, 1 vol. 2003. (People of the California Missions Ser.). (ENG., Illus.). 64p. (J). (gr. 4-4). lib. bdg. 32.93 *(978-0-8239-6284-6(9),* 79594bde-d148-4066-8ee5-6683face926f, PowerKids Pr.) Rosen Publishing Group, Inc., The.

Williamson, Nancy. 52 Ways to Teach Missions. 2004. (Fifty-Two Ways Ser.). (Illus.). 64p. (J). (gr. -1-7). pap. 9.95 *(978-0-937282-67-0(7),* RB36169) Rainbow Pubs. & Legacy Pr.

WorldVenture 1 Activity Book for Girls in Action Grade 1. 2004. pap. 4.99 *(978-1-56309-628-0(5))* Woman's Missionary Union.

WorldVenture 2 Activity Book for Girls in Action Grade 2. 2003. pap. 4.99 *(978-1-56309-629-7(3))* Woman's Missionary Union.

WorldVenture 3 Activity Book for Girls in Action Grade 3. 2003. pap. 4.99 *(978-1-56309-630-3(7))* Woman's Missionary Union.

WorldVenture 4 Activity Book for Girls in Action Grade 4. 2003. pap. 4.99 *(978-1-56309-631-0(5))* Woman's Missionary Union.

WorldVenture 5 Activity Book for Girls in Action Grade 5. 2003. pap. 4.99 *(978-1-56309-632-7(3))* Woman's Missionary Union.

WorldVenture 6 Activity Book for Girls in Action Grade 6. 2003. pap. 4.99 *(978-1-56309-633-4(1))* Woman's Missionary Union.

WorldVenture Guide for Leaders of Grades 1-6. 2003. pap. 8.99 *(978-1-56309-634-1(X))* Woman's Missionary Union.

MISSISSIPPI

Brown, Vanessa. Mississippi. 2009. (Bilingual Library of the United States of America Ser.). (ENG & SPA.). 32p. (gr. 2-2). 47.90 *(978-1-60853-369-5(7)*, Editorial Buenas Letras) Rosen Publishing Group, Inc., The.

—Mississippi, 1 vol. Brusca, Maria Cristina, tr. 2005. (Bilingual Library of the United States of America Ser.: Set 2). (ENG & SPA., Illus.). 32p. (J). (gr. 2-2). lib. bdg. 28.93 *(978-1-4042-3089-7(0)*, 7303f8be-aea9-40e2-84ae-9749c64ecf45) Rosen Publishing Group, Inc., The.

Dell, Pamela. America the Beautiful, Third Series: Mississippi (Revised Edition) 2014. (America the Beautiful Ser.: 3). (ENG.). 144p. (J). lib. bdg. 40.00 *(978-0-531-24891-1(7))* Scholastic Library Publishing.

Dill, Pamela Wescovich. Katrina's Rainbow: The Miracle of the Storm Crosses. 2006. (Illus.). 42p. (J). 17.99 *(978-1-59879-302-4(0))* Lifevest Publishing, Inc.

Figueroa, Acton. Mississippi, 1 vol. 2003. (World Almanac(r) Library of the States Ser.). (ENG., Illus.). 48p. (gr. 4-6). pap. 15.05 *(978-0-8368-5323-0(7)*, fb8b95f1-961d-4472-89b2-672180974538); lib. bdg. 33.67 *(978-0-8368-5152-6(8)*, 7f2dbb57-b617-43ae-8d54-9f857d30eca5) Stevens, Gareth Publishing LLLP. (Gareth Stevens Learning Library).

Foran, Jill. Mississippi. 2011. (Guide to American States Ser.). (Illus.). 48p. (YA). (gr. 3-6). 29.99 *(978-1-61690-796-9(7))* Weigl Pubs., Inc.

Graham Gaines, Ann. Mississippi, 1 vol. Santoro, Christopher, illus. 2007. (It's My State! (First Edition)(r) Ser.). (ENG.). 80p. (gr. 4-4). lib. bdg. 34.07 *(978-0-7614-2214-3(5)*, 70fa6744-99a6-45d8-8531-52022b7e2857) Cavendish Square Publishing LLC.

Heinrichs, Ann. Mississippi. Kania, Matt, illus. 2017. (U. S. A. Travel Guides). (ENG.). 40p. (J). (gr. 2-5). lib. bdg. 38.50 *(978-1-5038-1964-1(7)*, 211601) Child's World, Inc, The.

Hoena, Blake. Mississippi. 2013. (Exploring the States Ser.). (ENG., Illus.). 32p. (J). (gr. 3-7). lib. bdg. 27.95 *(978-1-62617-023-0(1)*, Blastoff! Readers) Bellwether Media.

Kuedee, Jaycee. How to Draw Mississippi's Sights & Symbols. 2009. (Kid's Guide to Drawing America Ser.). 32p. (gr. k-k). 50.50 *(978-1-61511-073-5(9)*, PowerKids Pr.) Rosen Publishing Group, Inc., The.

Marsh, Carole. The Magnificent Mississippi Coloring Book. 2004. (Mississippi Experience! Ser.). (Illus.). 32p. (J). (gr. k-2). pap. 3.95 *(978-0-7933-9559-0(3))* Gallopade International.

—Mississippi Big Activity Book. 2004. (Mississippi Experience! Ser.). (Illus.). 96p. (J). (gr. 2-6). pap. 9.95 *(978-0-7933-9558-3(5))* Gallopade International.

—Mississippi Current Events Projects: 30 Cool, Activities, Crafts, Experiments & More for Kids to Do to Learn about Your State! 2003. (Mississippi Experience Ser.). 32p. (gr. k-8). pap. 5.95 *(978-0-635-02043-7(2)*, Marsh, Carole Bks.) Gallopade International.

—The Mississippi Experience Pocket Guide. 2004. (Mississippi Experience! Ser.). (Illus.). 96p. (J). (gr. 3-8). pap. 6.95 *(978-0-7933-9554-5(2))* Gallopade International.

—Mississippi Geography Projects: 30 Cool, Activities, Crafts, Experiments & More for Kids to Do to Learn about Your State! 2003. (Mississippi Experience Ser.). 32p. (gr. k-5). pap. 5.95 *(978-0-635-01843-4(8)*, Marsh, Carole Bks.) Gallopade International.

—Mississippi Government Projects: 30 Cool, Activities, Crafts, Experiments & More for Kids to Do to Learn about Your State! 2003. (Mississippi Experience Ser.). 32p. (gr. k-5). pap. 5.95 *(978-0-635-01943-1(4)*, Marsh, Carole Bks.) Gallopade International.

—Mississippi Jeopardy. 2004. (Mississippi Experience! Ser.). (Illus.). 32p. (J). (gr. 3-8). pap. 7.95 *(978-0-7933-9556-9(9))* Gallopade International.

—Mississippi "Jography" A Fun Run Thru Our State! 2004. (Mississippi Experience! Ser.). (Illus.). 32p. (J). (gr. 3-8). pap. 7.95 *(978-0-7933-9557-6(7))* Gallopade International.

—Mississippi People Projects: 30 Cool, Activities, Crafts, Experiments & More for Kids to Do to Learn about Your State! 2003. (Mississippi Experience Ser.). 32p. (gr. k-5). pap. 5.95 *(978-0-635-01993-6(0)*, Marsh, Carole Bks.) Gallopade International.

—Mississippi Symbols & Facts Projects: 30 Cool, Activities, Crafts, Experiments & More for Kids to Do to Learn about Your State! 2003. (Mississippi Experience Ser.). 32p. (gr. k-5). pap. 5.95 *(978-0-635-01893-9(4)*, Marsh, Carole Bks.) Gallopade International.

—My First Book about Mississippi. 2004. (Mississippi Experience! Ser.). (Illus.). 32p. (J). (gr. k-4). pap. 7.95 *(978-0-7933-9555-2(0))* Gallopade International.

The Mississippi. 2011. (River Journey Ser.). (ENG.). 48p. (YA). (gr. 5-8). 27.95 *(978-1-4488-6015-9(6)*, Rosen Reference) Rosen Publishing Group, Inc., The.

Murray, Julie. Mississippi, 1 vol. 2006. (United States Ser.). (ENG., Illus.). 32p. (gr. 2-4). 27.07 *(978-1-59197-683-7(9)*, Buddy Bks.) ABDO Publishing Co.

Putnam, Richelle & Aycock, John. The Inspiring Life of Eudora Welty. 2014. Orig. Title: The Inspiring Life of Eudora Welty. (ENG., Illus.). 144p. (gr. 4-7). pap. 16.99 *(978-1-62619-000-9(3)*, History Pr., The) Arcadia Publishing.

Ready, Anna. Mississippi. 2nd exp. rev. ed. 2003. (Hello U. S. A. Ser.). (Illus.). 84p. (J). (gr. 3-6). 25.26 *(978-0-8225-4109-7(2)*, Lerner Pubns.) Lerner Publishing Group.

Ruffin, Frances E. & Brown, Jonatha A. Mississippi, 1 vol. 2005. (Portraits of the States Ser.). (ENG., Illus.). 32p. (gr. 3-5). pap. 11.50 *(978-0-8368-4689-8(3)*, b55837be-28d8-41b5-b848-81dafd7ad098); lib. bdg. 28.67 *(978-0-8368-4670-6(2)*, 64846d63-7f03-413a-a734-bf2a23641409) Stevens, Gareth Publishing LLLP. (Gareth Stevens Learning Library).

Shirley, David & Kummer, Patricia K. Mississippi, 1 vol. 2nd rev. ed. 2008. (Celebrate the States (Second Edition) Ser.). (ENG.). 144p. (gr. 6-6). lib. bdg. 39.79 *(978-0-7614-2717-9(1)*, 90a00d0c-5b41-4180-b968-7fbeef5d17f0) Cavendish Square Publishing LLC.

Shofner, Shawndra. Mississippi. 2008. (This Land Called America Ser.). 32p. (YA). (gr. 3-6). 22.95 *(978-1-58341-649-5(8))* Creative Co., The.

Shoulders, Michael. Little Mississippi. Urban, Helle, illus. 2016. (Little State Ser.). (ENG.). 20p. (J). (gr. -1-k). bds. 9.95 *(978-1-58536-974-4(8)*, 204111) Sleeping Bear Pr.

Trueit, Trudi Strain. Mississippi. 2007. (Rookie Read-About Geography Ser.). (Illus.). 31p. (J). (gr. 1-2). 20.50 *(978-0-531-12572-4(6)*, Children's Pr.) Scholastic Library Publishing.

Wilson, Cristi. Just Because. Wilson, Cristi, illus. l.t. ed. 2006. (Illus.). 24p. (J). (gr. -1-3). per. 10.99 *(978-1-59879-251-5(2))* Lifevest Publishing, Inc.

Zeiger, Jennifer. Mississippi (a True Book: My United States) (Library Edition) 2018. (True Book (Relaunch) Ser.). (ENG., Illus.). 48p. (J). (gr. 3-5). 31.00 *(978-0-531-23167-8(4)*, Children's Pr.) Scholastic Library Publishing.

MISSISSIPPI—FICTION

Armistead, John. The Return of Gabriel. Gregory, Fran, illus. 2004. 218p. (gr. 3-8). 17.45 *(978-0-7569-3460-6(5))* Perfection Learning Corp.

Bomgaars, Sharon. The Best Clubhouse Ever. 2009. 232p. pap. 14.49 *(978-1-4259-9306-1(0))* AuthorHouse.

Brook, Henry, retold by. Tom Sawyer. 2008. (Usborne Classics Retold Ser.). 160p. (J). pap. 4.99 *(978-0-7945-2063-2(4)*, Usborne) EDC Publishing.

Buckey, Sarah M. The Hidden Gold. Bernstein, Galia & Giovine, Sergio, illus. 2012. (American Girl Mysteries Ser.). (ENG.). 150p. (J). (gr. 4-6). pap. 21.19 *(978-1-59369-902-4(6))* American Girl Publishing, Inc.

Chris, Crowe. Mississippi Trial 1955. 2014. (ENG.). 240p. (YA). (gr. 7-12). 10.24 *(978-1-63245-211-5(1))* Lectorum Pubns., Inc.

Cook, Kristi. Magnolia. 2014. (ENG., Illus.). 336p. (YA). (gr. 9). 17.99 *(978-1-4424-8535-8(3))*; pap. 10.99 *(978-1-4424-8534-1(5))* Simon Pulse. (Simon Pulse).

Crowe, Chris. Mississippi Trial 1955. 2003. 240p. (YA). (gr. 7-18). 8.99 *(978-0-14-250192-4(1)*, Speak) Penguin Young Readers Group.

—The Mississippi Trial 1955. 2003. (gr. 7-12). lib. bdg. 16.00 *(978-0-613-86522-7(7))* Turtleback.

Curry, Kenneth. The Legend of the Dancing Trees: An African American Folk Tale. 2007. 111p. (J). per. 14.95 *(978-0-9798364-0-4(9))* Curry Brothers Publishing Group.

Curry, Kenneth, et al. The Legend of the Dancing Tees Teachers Resource: The Legend of the Dancing Trees. 2007.Tr. of Teachers Resource. per. 19.95 *(978-0-9798364-1-1(7))* Curry Brothers Publishing Group.

Darlington, Edgar. The Circus Boys on the Mississippi. 2007. 116p. per. *(978-1-4068-4235-7(4))* Echo Library.

Darlington, Edgar B. P. The Circus Boys on the Mississippi. 2005. 27.95 *(978-1-4218-1023-2(9))*; 220p. pap. 12.95 *(978-1-4218-1123-9(5))* 1st World Publishing, Inc. (1st World Library - Literary Society).

Delashmit, Margaret V. Thief! 2012. 148p. (gr. 4-6). pap. 12.99 *(978-1-4624-0348-6(4)*, Inspiring Voices) Author Solutions, LLC.

Dill, Margo L. Finding My Place: One Girl's Strength at Vicksburg. 2012. (ENG.). 202p. (J). pap. 8.95 *(978-1-57249-408-4(5)*, White Mane Kids) White Mane Publishing Co., Inc.

Downing, Johnette. Down in Mississippi, 1 vol. Zecca, Katherine, illus. 2016. (ENG.). 32p. (J). 16.99 *(978-1-4556-2098-2(X)*, Pelican Publishing) Arcadia Publishing.

Edgin, Brenda. Little Winston & His Big Adventures in Natchez: New Home near the Woods. 2011. 16p. 12.99 *(978-1-4567-3639-2(6))* AuthorHouse.

Ernst, Kathleen. Ghosts of Vicksburg. 2003. (White Main Kids Ser.: 13). (Illus.). 180p. (J). pap. 8.95 *(978-1-57249-322-3(4)*, White Mane Kids) White Mane Publishing Co., Inc.

Gamble, Adam & Jasper, Mark. Good Night Mississippi. Veno, Joe, illus. 2015. (Good Night Our World Ser.). (ENG.). 20p. (J). (— 1). bds. 9.95 *(978-1-60219-221-8(9))* Good Night Bks.

Gibson, B. W. Extra Innings: The Diamond Thieves. 2014. 152p. pap. 14.95 *(978-1-4918-5663-5(7))* AuthorHouse.

Herwick Rice, Dona & Paris, Stephanie. Sal Fink, 1 vol. rev. ed. 2009. (Reader's Theater Ser.). (ENG.). 24p. (gr. 2-4). pap. 8.99 *(978-1-4333-0995-3(5))* Teacher Created Materials, Inc.

Higgins, M. G. Finding Apeman. 2015. (Gravel Road Ser.). (YA). lib. bdg. 20.80 *(978-0-606-37210-7(5))* Turtleback.

Horn, Shannon. Pirates of the Mississippian: The Adventures of Jerry & Draco. 2012. 24p. pap. 17.99 *(978-1-4772-6991-6(6))* AuthorHouse.

Jackson, Linda Williams. Midnight Without a Moon. 2017. (ENG.). 320p. (J). (gr. 5-7). pap. 7.99 *(978-1-328-75363-2(8)*, 1678711, Clarion Bks.) HarperCollins Pubs.

Jacobs, Lily. The Littlest Bunny in Mississippi: An Easter Adventure. Dunn, Robert, illus. 2015. (Littlest Bunny Ser.). (ENG.). 32p. (J). (gr. -1-3). 9.99 *(978-1-4926-1123-3(9)*, Hometown World) Sourcebooks, Inc.

James, Eric. Santa's Sleigh Is on Its Way to Mississippi: A Christmas Adventure. Dunn, Robert, illus. 2016. (Santa's Sleigh Is on Its Way Ser.). (ENG.). 32p. (J). (gr. k-2). 12.99 *(978-1-4926-4337-1(8)*, 9781492643371, Hometown World) Sourcebooks, Inc.

—The Spooky Express Mississippi. Piwowarski, Marcin, illus. 2017. (Spooky Express Ser.). (ENG.). 32p. (J). (gr. k-6). 9.99 *(978-1-4926-5372-1(1)*, Hometown World) Sourcebooks, Inc.

—Tiny the Mississippi Easter Bunny. 2018. (Tiny the Easter Bunny Ser.). (ENG.). 40p. (J). (gr. k-3). 9.99 *(978-1-4926-5939-6(8)*, Hometown World) Sourcebooks, Inc.

Johnson, Angela. I Dream of Trains. Long, Loren, illus. 2003. (ENG.). 32p. (J). (gr. k-2). 19.99 *(978-0-689-82609-2(5)*, Simon & Schuster Bks. For Young Readers) Simon & Schuster Bks. For Young Readers.

Key, Watt. Hideout. 2018. (ENG.). 336p. (J). pap. 9.99 *(978-1-250-14397-6(7)*, 900160565) Square Fish.

Masters, Susan Rowan. Night Journey to Vicksburg. Killcoyne, Hope L., ed. Smith, Duane A., illus. 2003. (Adventures in America Ser.). 74p. (J). (gr. 4). 14.95 *(978-1-893110-30-4(3))* Silver Moon Pr.

McDougal-Littell Publishing Staff. Literature Connections English: Roll of Thunder, Hear My Cry. 2004. (McDougal Littell Literature Connections Ser.). (ENG.). 288p. (gr. 8-8). stu. ed. 16.90 *(978-0-395-77530-1(2)*, 2-80099) Great Source Education Group, Inc.

McMullan, Margaret. How I Found the Strong. 2006. (ENG.). 144p. (YA). (gr. 7-12). reprint ed. mass mkt. 6.99 *(978-0-553-49492-1(9)*, Laurel Leaf) Random Hse. Children's Bks.

—When I Crossed No-Bob. 2008. (ENG.). 224p. (J). (gr. 6-8). 22.44 *(978-0-618-71715-6(3))* Houghton Mifflin Harcourt Publishing Co.

Mellor, Colleen Kelly. Grandpa & the Truck Book 2. Irwin, Dana M., illus. 2012. 34p. pap. 9.99 *(978-0-9856770-2-2(3))* truckerkidzPr.

Murphy, Julie. Ramona Blue. (ENG.). (YA). (gr. 8). 2018. 448p. pap. 11.99 *(978-0-06-241836-4(X))* 2017. 432p. 17.99 *(978-0-06-241835-7(1))* HarperCollins Pubs. (Balzer & Bray).

—Ramona Blue. 2018. (YA). lib. bdg. 20.85 *(978-0-606-41364-0(2))* Turtleback.

P.A.W. My Summer Road Trip. 2012. 28p. pap. 15.99 *(978-1-4691-5077-2(8))* Xlibris Corp.

Rand, Johnathan. American Chillers #25 Mississippi Megalodon. 2008. 208p. (J). pap. 5.99 *(978-1-893699-33-5(1))* AudioCraft Publishing, Inc.

Rees, Douglas. Elektra's Adventures in Tragedy. 2018. (ENG.). 288p. (YA). (gr. 8-17). 33.99 *(978-0-7624-6303-9(1)*, Running Pr. Kids) Running Pr.

Rinaldi, Ann. My Vicksburg. 2011. (ENG.). 160p. (YA). (gr. 7). pap. 11.95 *(978-0-547-55000-8(6)*, 1450172, Clarion Bks.) HarperCollins Pubs.

Robinson, Gary. Little Brother of War. 2013. (PathFinders Ser.). (ENG.). 120p. (YA). (gr. 8-12). pap. 9.95 *(978-1-939053-02-2(1)*, 7th Generation) BPC.

Rodman, Mary Ann. Yankee Girl. 2008. (ENG.). 240p. (J). (gr. 4-6). pap. 19.99 *(978-0-312-53576-6(7)*, 900054756) Square Fish.

Rubright, Lynn. Mama's Window. Smith, Duane, illus. 2005. 89p. (J). 16.95 *(978-1-57480-160-6(0))* Lee & Low Bks., Inc.

Scattergood, Augusta. Glory Be. 2014. (ENG.). 208p. (J). (gr. 4-7). pap. 7.99 *(978-0-545-33181-4(1)*, Scholastic Pr.) Scholastic, Inc.

Sully, Katherine. Night-Night Mississippi. Poole, Helen, illus. 2017. (Night-Night Ser.). (ENG.). 20p. (J). (gr. -1-1). bds. 9.99 *(978-1-4926-5477-3(9)*, Hometown World) Sourcebooks, Inc.

Taylor, Mildred D. Roll of Thunder, Hear My Cry. 2004. 276p. (gr. 4-8). reprint ed. pap. 10.00 *(978-0-7567-7955-9(3))* DIANE Publishing Co.

—Roll of Thunder, Hear My Cry: 40th Anniversary Special Edition. 40th anniv. ed. 2016. (ENG., Illus.). 304p. (J). (gr. 3-7). 19.99 *(978-1-101-99388-0(X)*, Dial Bks) Penguin Young Readers Group.

Telgemeier, Raina. Drama: a Graphic Novel. Telgemeier, Raina, illus. 2012. (ENG., Illus.). 240p. (J). (gr. 5-9). pap. 10.99 *(978-0-545-32699-5(0)*, Graphix) Scholastic, Inc.

—Drama: a Graphic Novel. Telgemeier, Raina, illus. 2012. (ENG., Illus.). 240p. (J). (gr. 5-9). 24.99 *(978-0-545-32698-8(2)*, Graphix) Scholastic, Inc.

Tingle, Tim. Crossing Bok Chitto: A Choctaw Tale of Friendship & Freedom, 1 vol. Bridges, Jeanne Rorex, illus. 2008. (ENG.). 40p. (J). (gr. 1-7). pap. 12.95 *(978-1-933693-20-0(7)*, 23353382, Cinco Puntos Press) Lee & Low Bks., Inc.

—Stone River Crossing, 1 vol. 2019. (ENG., Illus.). 336p. (J). (gr. 3-7). 20.95 *(978-1-62014-823-5(4)*, leelowtu, Tu Bks.) Lee & Low Bks., Inc.

Twain, Mark, pseud. Classic Starts(r): the Adventures of Tom Sawyer: Retold from the Mark Twain Original. Corvino, Lucy, illus. 2005. (Classic Starts(r) Ser.). 160p. (J). (gr. 2-4). 7.99 *(978-1-4027-1216-6(2))* Sterling Publishing Co., Inc.

—Tom Sawyer, 1 vol. Mullarkey, Lisa & McWilliam, Howard, illus. 2010. (Calico Illustrated Classics Ser.: No. 1). (ENG.). 112p. (J). (gr. 2-5). 38.50 *(978-1-60270-704-7(9)*, 3961, Calico Chapter Bks.) ABDO Publishing Co.

—Tom Sawyer. 2009. 196p. (gr. 4-7). pap. 12.99 *(978-1-934941-63-8(8))* Red & Black Pubs.

Vander Zee, Ruth. Mississippi Morning. Cooper, Floyd, illus. 2004. 32p. (J). 16.00 *(978-0-8028-5211-3(4))* Eerdmans, William B. Publishing Co.

Vaught, Susan. Footer Davis Probably Is Crazy. Reinhardt, Jennifer Black, illus. 2015. (ENG.). 240p. (J). (gr. 5-9). 16.99 *(978-1-4814-2276-5(6)*, Simon & Schuster Bks. For Young Readers) Simon & Schuster Bks. For Young Readers.

—Things Too Huge to Fix by Saying Sorry. 2016. (ENG., Illus.). 352p. (J). (gr. 5-9). 16.99 *(978-1-4814-2279-6(0)*, Simon & Schuster Bks. For Young Readers) Simon & Schuster Bks. For Young Readers.

—Things Too Huge to Fix by Saying Sorry. 2017. (ENG.). 368p. (J). (gr. 5-9). pap. 8.99 *(978-1-4814-2280-2(4)*, Simon & Schuster/Paula Wiseman Bks.) Simon & Schuster/Paula Wiseman Bks.

Waller, Linda. Hard Road to Manhood: I Ain't No Snitch. 2010. 128p. pap. 10.99 *(978-1-4490-6892-9(8))* AuthorHouse.

Wiles, Deborah. The Aurora County All-Stars. 2009. (ENG., Illus.). 256p. (J). (gr. 2-5). pap. 7.99 *(978-0-15-206626-0(8)*, 1063363, Clarion Bks.) HarperCollins Pubs.

—Love, Ruby Lavender. 2005. (ENG., Illus.). 240p. (J). (gr. 3-7). reprint ed. pap. 9.99 *(978-0-15-205478-6(2)*, 1196483, Clarion Bks.) HarperCollins Pubs.

—Love, Ruby Lavender. 2004. 216p. (J). (gr. 3-7). pap. 36.00 incl. audio *(978-0-8072-2096-2(5)*, Listening Library) Random Hse. Audio Publishing Group.

—Revolution (the Sixties Trilogy #2) (Sixties Trilogy Ser.: 2). (ENG.). 544p. 2017. (J). (gr. 3-7). pap. 12.99 *(978-0-545-10608-5(7))* 2014. (Illus.). (YA). (gr. 5-7). 21.99 *(978-0-545-10607-8(9)*, Scholastic Pr.) Scholastic, Inc.

Woodson, Jacqueline. Beneath a Meth Moon. 2013. (ENG.). 240p. (YA). (gr. 7). pap. 9.99 *(978-0-14-242392-9(0)*, Penguin Books) Penguin Young Readers Group.

MISSISSIPPI—HISTORY

Aretha, David. Freedom Summer. 2007. (Civil Rights Movement Ser.). (Illus.). 128p. (J). (gr. 3-7). lib. bdg. 27.95 *(978-1-59935-059-2(9))* Reynolds, Morgan Inc.

—The Murder of Emmett Till. 2007. (Civil Rights Movement Ser.). (Illus.). 160p. (J). (gr. 3-7). lib. bdg. 27.95 *(978-1-59935-057-8(2))* Reynolds, Morgan Inc.

Barton, Chris. The Amazing Age of John Roy Lynch. Tate, Don, illus. 2015. (ENG.). 50p. (J). 17.00 *(978-0-8028-5379-0(X)*, Eerdmans Bks For Young Readers) Eerdmans, William B. Publishing Co.

Casil, Amy Sterling. Mississippi: Past & Present, 1 vol. 2010. (United States: Past & Present Ser.). (ENG.). 48p. (YA). (gr. 5-5). pap. 12.75 *(978-1-4358-9512-6(6)*, a0249c66-64ea-4c3a-9f01-d2515a2bcf08); lib. bdg. 34.47 *(978-1-4358-9485-3(5)*, e85fcd46-4b25-4b05-a5b7-b60aaa0709f9) Rosen Publishing Group, Inc., The. (Rosen Reference).

Coleman, Miriam. Mississippi: The Magnolia State, 1 vol. 2010. (Our Amazing States Ser.). (ENG.). 24p. (J). (gr. 3-3). pap. 9.25 *(978-1-4488-0738-3(7)*, b197486b-d40e-45f4-9dff-9a81193e3e74); lib. bdg. 26.27 *(978-1-4488-0653-9(4)*, 9cfafd2c-16b5-4dc9-9258-28c0fd0460ca) Rosen Publishing Group, Inc., The. (PowerKids Pr.).

Fiorelli, June Estep. Fannie Lou Hamer: A Voice for Freedom. 2004. (Avisson Young Adult Ser.). (Illus.). 117p. (J). pap. 19.95 *(978-1-888105-62-9(3))* Avisson Pr., Inc.

Foran, Jill. Mississippi: The Magnolia State. 2016. (J). *(978-1-4896-4887-7(9))* Weigl Pubs., Inc.

Graham Gaines, Ann. Mississippi, 1 vol. 2nd rev. ed. 2014. (It's My State! (Second Edition)(r) Ser.). (ENG.). 80p. (gr. 4-4). lib. bdg. 35.93 *(978-1-62712-239-9(7)*, 58673caf-2ad3-44c4-8bd8-285f3290c4e0) Cavendish Square Publishing LLC.

Graham Gaines, Ann & Jones Waring, Kerry. Mississippi: The Magnolia State, 1 vol. 3rd rev. ed. 2015. (It's My State! (Third Edition)(r) Ser.). (ENG., Illus.). 80p. (gr. 4-4). 35.93 *(978-1-62713-241-1(4)*, 2afd5fb7-4ec8-4064-be60-ac69ad586379) Cavendish Square Publishing LLC.

Hamilton, John. Mississippi, 1 vol. 2016. (United States of America Ser.). (ENG., Illus.). 48p. (J). (gr. 5-9). 34.21 *(978-1-68078-326-1(2)*, 21637, Abdo & Daughters) ABDO Publishing Co.

Lichter, Nick. The Road of Souls: Reflections on the Mississippi. 2004. (Illus.). 150p. per. 14.95 *(978-0-9758615-0-9(6))* Wing Dam Pr.

Marsh, Carole. Exploring Mississippi Through Project-Based Learning: Geography, History, Government, Economics & More. 2016. (Mississippi Experience Ser.). (ENG.). (J). pap. 9.99 *(978-0-635-12348-0(7))* Gallopade International.

—I'm Reading about Mississippi. 2014. (Mississippi Experience Ser.). (ENG., Illus.). (J). pap., pap. 8.99 *(978-0-635-11299-6(X))* Gallopade International.

—Mississippi History Projects: 30 Cool, Activities, Crafts, Experiments & More for Kids to Do to Learn about Your State! 2003. (Mississippi Experience Ser.). 32p. (gr. k-5). pap. 5.95 *(978-0-635-01793-2(8)*, Marsh, Carole Bks.) Gallopade International.

McDowell, Pamela. Mississippi: The Magnolia State. 2012. (J). *(978-1-61913-367-9(9))*; pap. *(978-1-61913-368-6(7))* Weigl Pubs., Inc.

Mills, Jordan & Parker, Bridget. Mississippi. 2016. (States Ser.). (ENG., Illus.). 32p. (J). (gr. 3-6). lib. bdg. 27.99 *(978-1-5157-0411-9(4)*, 132022, Capstone Pr.) Capstone.

Mooney, Carla. Freedom Summer 1964, 1 vol. 2015. (Stories of the Civil Rights Movement Ser.). (ENG., Illus.). 48p. (J). (gr. 4-8). 35.64 *(978-1-62403-878-5(6)*, 18126) ABDO Publishing Co.

Ready, Anna. Mississippi. 2013. (J). lib. bdg. 25.26 *(978-0-7613-4540-4(X)*, Lerner Pubns.) Lerner Publishing Group.

Shoulders, Michael. 1 Mississippi, 2 Mississippi: A Mississippi Numbers Book. Anderson, Rick, illus. 2004. (America by the Numbers Ser.). (ENG.). 40p. (J). (gr. 1-3). 19.99 *(978-1-58536-188-5(7)*, 202034) Sleeping Bear Pr.

Somervill, Barbara A. From Sea to Shining Sea: Mississippi. 2009. (From Sea to Shining Sea, Second Ser.). (ENG.). 80p. (J). pap. 7.95 *(978-0-531-21134-2(7)*, Children's Pr.) Scholastic Library Publishing.

Spilsbury, Louise. The Mississippian Culture: the Mound Builders, 1 vol. 2018. (Analyze the Ancients Ser.). (ENG.). 48p. (gr. 5-6). lib. bdg. 33.60 *(978-1-5382-2566-0(2)*, 10890d22-137b-4e15-bb0f-e6f351a55114) Stevens, Gareth Publishing LLLP.

Taylor, Mildred D. Roll of Thunder, Hear My Cry (Puffin Modern Classics) 25th rev. ed. 2014. (Puffin Modern Classics Ser.). (ENG.). 288p. (J). 12.24 *(978-1-63245-097-5(6))* Lectorum Pubns., Inc.

Wright, Simeon & Boyd, Herb. Simeon's Story: An Eyewitness Account of the Kidnapping of Emmett Till. 2011. (ENG., Illus.). 160p. (J). (gr. 7). pap. 14.99 *(978-1-56976-819-8(6)*, Hill, Lawrence Bks.) Chicago Review Pr., Inc.

Zeiger, Jennifer. Mississippi (a True Book: My United States) 2018. (True Book (Relaunch) Ser.). (ENG., Illus.). 48p. (J). (gr. 3-5). pap. 7.95 *(978-0-531-24718-1(X)*, Children's Pr.) Scholastic Library Publishing.

Ziff, John. Gulf States: Alabama, Louisiana, Mississippi, Vol. 19. 2015. (Let's Explore the States Ser.). (Illus.). 64p. (J). (gr. 5). 23.95 *(978-1-4222-3324-5(3))* Mason Crest.

MISSISSIPPI RIVER

Adil, Janeen R. Mississippi River. 2013. (J). *(978-1-62127-475-9(6))*; pap. *(978-1-62127-481-0(0))* Weigl Pubs., Inc.

—The Mississippi River: The Largest River in the United States. 2004. (Natural Wonders of the U. S. A. Ser.). (Illus.). 32p. (J). (gr. 3-6). per. 9.95 *(978-1-59036-163-4(6))*; lib. bdg. 26.00 *(978-1-59036-041-5(9))* Weigl Pubs., Inc.

Anastasio, Dina & Who HQ. Where Is the Mississippi River? Hammond, Ted, illus. 2017. (Where Is? Ser.). 112p. (J). (gr. 3-7). 7.99 *(978-0-515-15824-3(0)*, Penguin Workshop) Penguin Young Readers Group.

Bauer, Marion Dane. The Mighty Mississippi. Wallace, John, illus. 2007. (Ready-To-Read Level 1 Ser.). (ENG.). 32p. (J). (gr. -1-1). lib. bdg. 16.19 *(978-0-689-86951-8(7))* Simon & Schuster, Inc.

—The Mighty Mississippi: Ready-To-Read Level 1. Wallace, John, illus. 2007. (Wonders of America Ser.). (ENG.). 32p. (J). (gr. -1-1). pap. 4.99 *(978-0-689-86950-1(9))*, Simon Spotlight) Simon Spotlight.

Bechtold, Phyliss. Seymour Bluffs & the Legend of the Piasa Bird. 2007. 26p. 9.95 *(978-0-9728532-8-6(6))* New Horizons Christian Ctr.

Crompton, Samuel Willard. Robert de la Salle. 2009. (Great Explorers Ser.). (ENG., Illus.). 112p. (gr. 6-12). 30.00 *(978-1-60413-419-3(4))*, P173417, Facts On File) Infobase Holdings, Inc.

Donaldson-Forbes, Jeff. La Salle. 2009. (Primary Source Library of Famous Explorers Ser.). 24p. (gr. 4-4). 42.50 *(978-1-60854-129-4(0))*, PowerKids Pr.) Rosen Publishing Group, Inc., The.

Green, Jen. The Mississippi River, 1 vol. 2003. (Rivers of North America Ser.). (ENG., Illus.). 32p. (gr. 3-5). lib. bdg. 28.67 *(978-0-8368-3757-5(6))*, a37c4e39-d8d7-4725-89ee-2f0ef17d0341, Gareth Stevens Learning Library) Stevens, Gareth Publishing LLLP.

Harkins, Susan Sales & Harkins, William H. The Life & Times of Father Jacques Marquette. 2008. (Profiles in American History Ser.). (Illus.). 48p. (J). (gr. 4-8). lib. bdg. 29.95 *(978-1-58415-528-7(0))* Mitchell Lane Pubs.

Johnson, Robin. The Mississippi: America's Mighty River, 1 vol. 2010. (Rivers Around the World Ser.). (ENG., Illus.). 32p. (J). (gr. 5-8). pap. *(978-0-7787-7467-9(8))*; lib. bdg. *(978-0-7787-7444-0(9))* Crabtree Publishing Co.

Jordan, Shirley. Benjamin Brown & the Great Steamboat Race. Kemly, Kathleen, illus. 2011. (History Speaks: Picture Books Plus Reader's Theater Ser.). 48p. pap. 56.72 *(978-0-7613-7630-9(5))*; (ENG.). (gr. 2-4). pap. 9.95 *(978-0-7613-6133-6(2))* Lerner Publishing Group.

Larson, Paul Cliff & Larson, Pamela All. Mississippi Escapade: Reliving the Grand Excursion Of 1854. 2004. (Illus.). 128p. (J). (gr. 3-7). pap. 17.95 *(978-1-890434-64-9(7))* Afton Historical Society Pr.

Manning, Paul. The Mississippi. 2014. (River Adventures Ser.). (J). lib. bdg. 31.35 *(978-1-59920-916-6(0))* Black Rabbit Bks.

Marsico, Katie. The Mississippi River. 2013. (Explorer Library: Social Studies Explorer Ser.). (ENG.). 32p. (gr. 4-8). (J). pap. 14.21 *(978-1-62431-035-5(4))*, 202497); (Illus.). 32.07 *(978-1-62431-011-9(7))*, 202495) Cherry Lake Publishing.

McNeese, Tim. The Mississippi River. 2004. (Rivers in American Life & Times Ser.). (ENG., Illus.). 120p. (gr. 9-13). 32.50 *(978-0-7910-7723-8(3))*, P113988, Facts On File) Infobase Holdings, Inc.

O'Neal, Claire. The Mississippi River. 2012. (J). lib. bdg. 29.95 *(978-1-61228-296-1(2))* Mitchell Lane Pubs.

Payment, Simone. La Salle: Claiming the Mississippi River for France. 2009. (Library of Explorers & Exploration Ser.). 112p. (gr. 5-8). 66.50 *(978-1-60853-610-8(6))*, Rosen Reference) Rosen Publishing Group, Inc., The.

Rodger, Ellen. Mississippi River Research Journal. 2018. (Ecosystems Research Journal Ser.). (Illus.). 32p. (J). (gr. 4-5). *(978-0-7787-4659-1(3))* Crabtree Publishing Co.

Sullivan, Laura. Life As a Mississippi Riverboat Captain, 1 vol. 2017. (Life As... Ser.). (ENG.). 32p. (gr. 3-3). pap. 11.58 *(978-1-5026-3039-1(7))*, 29b6c611-a9c9-46b7-a0c1-e64d525d0dcf) Cavendish Square Publishing LLC.

Vaughn, Royce, illus. Seymour Bluffs & the Legend of the Piasa Bird. 2006. 24p. (J). pap. 9.95 *(978-0-9728538-2-8(0))* Amica Publishing.

Vieira, Linda. The Mighty Mississippi: The Life & Times of America's Greatest River. Bond, Higgins, illus. 2005. (J). *(978-7-80802-789-7(8))* Walker & Co.

Young, Jeff C. Hernando de Soto: Spanish Conquistador in the Americas, 1 vol. 2009. (Great Explorers of the World Ser.). (ENG., Illus.). 112p. (gr. 6-7). lib. bdg. 35.93 *(978-1-59845-104-7(9))*, 7fbdf9e0-91cc-47ae-9b32-2d3838629a61) Enslow Publishing, LLC.

Youngblood, Wayne. Mark Twain along the Mississippi, 1 vol. 2005. (In the Footsteps of American Heroes Ser.). (ENG., Illus.). 64p. (gr. 5-8). pap. 15.05 *(978-0-8368-6435-9(2))*, fc650921-fafb-4dde-ae34-50f8069dd1ae); lib. bdg. 36.67 *(978-0-8368-6430-4(1))*, 075f253e-b58f-4ce9-9e41-a0fcee83e823) Stevens, Gareth Publishing LLLP. (Gareth Stevens Secondary Library).

Zelenyi, Alexander & Zelenyj, Alexander. Marquette & Jolliet: Quest for the Mississippi. 2006. (In the Footsteps of Explorers Ser.). (ENG., Illus.). 32p. (J). (gr. 4-7). pap. *(978-0-7787-2467-4(0))*; lib. bdg. *(978-0-7787-2431-5(X))* Crabtree Publishing Co.

Zronik, John Paul. Sieur de la Salle: New World Adventurer. 2005. (In the Footsteps of Explorers Ser.). (ENG., Illus.). 32p. (J). (gr. 4-5). pap. *(978-0-7787-2449-0(2))* Crabtree Publishing Co.

MISSISSIPPI RIVER—FICTION

Aaron, Chester. An American Ghost. 2011. (YA). pap. *(978-1-936144-28-0(X))* Zumaya Pubns. LLC.

Altsheler, Joseph A. The Free Rangers. 2007. (Young Trailers Ser.: Vol. 5). 244p. reprint ed. per. 14.45 *(978-1-60424-038-2(5))*, Bk. Jungle) Standard Publications, Inc.

—The Free Rangers: A Story of the Early Days along the Mississippi. 2005. (Young Trailers Ser.: Vol. 5). (J). reprint ed. 29.95 *(978-1-4218-1477-3(3))*; 312p. pap. 14.95 *(978-1-4218-1577-0(X))* 1st World Publishing, Inc. (1st World Library - Literary Society).

—The Free Rangers: A Story of the Early Days along the Mississippi. 2009. (Young Trailers Ser.: Vol. 4). 294p. (J). reprint ed. 27.99 *(978-1-60512-311-0(0))*; pap. 14.99 *(978-1-60512-411-7(7))* Akasha Publishing, LLC. (Akasha Classics).

—The Free Rangers: A Story of the Early Days along the Mississippi. (Young Trailers Ser.: Vol. 5). (J). reprint ed. 26.95 *(978-0-8488-1237-9(9))* Amereon Ltd.

—The Free Rangers: A Story of the Early Days along the Mississippi. 2010. (Young Trailers Ser.: Vol. 5). (ENG.). 382p. (J). (gr. 4-7). reprint ed. pap. 33.75 *(978-1-176-61076-7(7))* Creative Media Partners, LLC.

—The Free Rangers: A Story of the Early Days along the Mississippi. 2006. (Young Trailers Ser.: Vol. 5). (J). reprint ed. pap. *(978-1-4065-0811-6(X))* Dodo Pr.

—The Free Rangers: A Story of the Early Days along the Mississippi. 2006. (Young Trailers Ser.: Vol. 5). reprint ed. pap. *(978-1-4068-0743-1(5))* Echo Library.

—The Free Rangers: A Story of the Early Days along the Mississippi. 2010. (Young Trailers Ser.: Vol. 5). (J). 170p. pap. 13.87 *(978-1-152-24703-1(4))*; 162p. (gr. 4-7). reprint ed. pap. 19.99 *(978-1-4432-1506-0(6))* General Bks. LLC.

—The Free Rangers: A Story of the Early Days along the Mississippi. (Young Trailers Ser.: Vol. 5). (J). 2010. 232p. pap. *(978-1-4076-1356-7(1))* 2012. 388p. (gr. 4-7). reprint ed. pap. *(978-1-290-66522-3(2))* HardPr.

—The Free Rangers: A Story of the Early Days along the Mississippi. 2012. (Young Trailers Ser.: Vol. 5). 220p. (J). (gr. 4-7). pap. 14.95 *(978-1-60444-735-4(4))* IndoEuropeanPublishing.com.

—The Free Rangers: A Story of the Early Days along the Mississippi. (Young Trailers Ser.: Vol. 5). (J). reprint ed. 2010. 248p. (gr. 4-7). 33.56 *(978-1-169-30153-5(3))* 2010. 248p. (gr. 4-7). pap. 21.56 *(978-1-162-69513-6(7))* 2010. 41.95 *(978-1-161-46378-1(X))* 2004. pap. 1.99 *(978-1-4192-6302-6(1))* 2004. pap. 26.95 *(978-1-4191-6302-9(7))* Kessinger Publishing, LLC.

—The Free Rangers: A Story of the Early Days along the Mississippi. 2012. (Young Trailers Ser.: Vol. 5). 256p. (J). (gr. 4-7). reprint ed. *(978-3-8491-6283-2(4))*; pap. *(978-3-8491-5398-4(3))* tredition Verlag.

Cockrum, James L. Short Boat on a Long River. Sansevero, Tony, illus. 2013. 180p. (YA). pap. 14.95 *(978-0-9768586-1-4(4))* Pangloss Publishing.

Ely, Scott. The Elephant Mountains, 1 vol. 2011. (ENG.). 216p. (YA). (gr. 8-12). lib. bdg. 19.95 *(978-1-55469-406-8(X))* Orca Bk. Pubs. USA.

Helgerson, Joseph. Horns & Wrinkles. Ceccoli, Nicoletta, illus. 2008. (ENG.). 240p. (J). (gr. 5-7). pap. 7.99 *(978-0-618-98178-6(0))*, 1025446, Clarion Bks.) HarperCollins Pubs.

Howard, Annabelle. Keelboat Annie: An American Tall Tale. 2006. (J). pap. *(978-1-4108-6169-6(4))* Benchmark Education Co.

Hugger, M. A. Danny Malloy & His Mississippi River Samurai. 2008. 132p. 21.95 *(978-0-595-49382-1(3))*; pap. 11.95 *(978-0-595-48462-1(X))* iUniverse, Inc.

Marsh, Carole. The Mystery on the Mighty Mississippi. 2009. (Real Kids, Real Places Ser.). (Illus.). 146p. (J). lib. bdg. 18.99 *(978-0-635-07001-2(4))*, Marsh, Carole Mysteries) Gallopade International.

Meigs, Cornelia. Swift Rivers. 2004. (Newbery Honor Book Ser.). (ENG., Illus.). 288p. (J). (gr. 5). pap. 8.99 *(978-0-8027-7703-4(1))*, 900032885, Bloomsbury USA Childrens) Bloomsbury Publishing USA.

Meyer, L. A. Mississippi Jack: Being an Account of the Further Waterborne Adventures of Jacky Faber, Midshipman, Fine Lady, & Lily of the West. (Bloody Jack Adventures Ser.: 5). (ENG., Illus.). 624p. (YA). (gr. 7-12). 2007. 17.00 *(978-0-15-206003-9(0))*, 1198027) 2nd ed. 2010. pap. 8.99 *(978-0-15-206632-1(2))*, 1099015) HarperCollins Pubs. (Clarion Bks.).

Novel Units. The Adventures of Tom Sawyer Novel Units Student Packet. 2019. (ENG.). (YA). pap., stu. ed. 13.99 *(978-1-56137-528-8(4))*, NU5284SP, Novel Units, Inc.) Classroom Library Co.

Racehorse Publishing & Twain, Mark. Classics to Color: the Adventures of Huckleberry Finn. 2016. (ENG., Illus.). 80p. (J). (gr. 1-6). pap. 8.99 *(978-1-944686-99-4(1))*, Racehorse Publishing) Skyhorse Publishing Co., Inc.

Rathborne, St. George. The House Boat Boys; or, Drifting down to the Sunny South. 2007. 108p. per. *(978-1-4068-3747-6(4))* Echo Library.

Ross, Patrick. Runt River Rat's Wild Ride, 1 vol. Burcham, David, illus. 2010. 24p. 24.95 *(978-1-4512-0067-6(6))* PublishAmerica, Inc.

Rouzer, Walter. Rebel Stone & the Ghost Whisperers. 2009. 304p. 28.95 *(978-0-595-51192-1(9))* iUniverse, Inc.

Stevermer, Caroline & Collin, Francesca. River Rats. 2005. (ENG., Illus.). 320p. (YA). (gr. 7-12). pap. 19.95 *(978-0-15-205554-7(1))*, 1196703) Houghton Mifflin Harcourt Publishing Co.

Twain, Mark, pseud. The Adventures of Huckleberry Finn. 96p. (J). pap. 4.95 *(978-0-7910-4108-6(5))*, Facts On File) Infobase Holdings, Inc.

—The Adventures of Huckleberry Finn. abr. ed. 2011. (Go Reader Audiobooks Ser.). (ENG.). (YA). (gr. 7-12). 49.93 *(978-1-61641-434-4(0))* Magic Wagon.

—The Adventures of Huckleberry Finn: With a Discussion of Friendship. Lauter, Richard, tr. Lauter, Richard, illus. 2003. (Values in Action Illustrated Classics Ser.). (J). *(978-1-59203-042-2(4))* Learning Challenge, Inc.

—The Adventures of Tom Sawyer: With a Discussion of Imagination. Butterfield, Ned, illus. 2003. (Values in Action Illustrated Classics Ser.). 190p. (J). *(978-1-59203-027-9(0))* Learning Challenge, Inc.

—Las Aventuras de Huckleberry Finn. de Atauri, Ines & de Atauri, Juan Diaz, eds. 2006. (Clasicos Juveniles Ser.).Tr. of Adventures of Huckleberry Finn. (SPA., Illus.). 359p. pap. 17.95 *(978-84-263-5252-1(9))* Vives, Luis Editorial (Edelvives) ESP. Dist: Lectorum Pubns., Inc.

—Classic Starts(r): the Adventures of Huckleberry Finn: Retold from the Mark Twain Original. Andreasen, Dan, illus. 2006. (Classic Starts(r) Ser.). 160p. (J). (gr. 2-4). 7.99 *(978-1-4027-2499-2(3))* Sterling Publishing Co., Inc.

—Tom Sawyer. 2005. 264p. 28.95 *(978-1-4218-0768-3(8))*, 1st World Library - Literary Society) 1st World Publishing, Inc.

—Tom Sawyer. 2006. (Classic Retelling Ser.). (Illus.). 224p. (YA). (gr. 8-12). *(978-0-618-12053-6(X))*, 2-00218) Holt McDougal.

—Tom Sawyer. 2004. reprint ed. pap. 1.99 *(978-1-4192-5166-5(X))* Kessinger Publishing, LLC.

—Tom Sawyer. (Young Collector's Illustrated Classics Ser.). (Illus.). 192p. (J). (gr. 3-7). 9.95 *(978-1-56156-453-8(2))* Kidsbooks, LLC.

—Tom Sawyer. (Coleccion Clasicos de la Juventud). (SPA., Illus.). 220p. (J). 12.95 *(978-84-7189-029-0(1))*, ORT310) Ortells, Alfredo Editorial S.L. ESP. Dist: Continental Bk. Co., Inc.

Vaughn, Royce, illus. Seymour Bluffs & Robert Wadlow, the Tallest Man in the World: A Story about Diversity & Tolerance. 2007. 28p. (J). 12.95 *(978-0-9728538-4-2(7))* Amica Publishing.

Warner, Gertrude Chandler. The Haunted Cabin Mystery, 1 vol. Bloodworth, Mark, illus. 2010. (Boxcar Children Graphic Novels Ser.). (ENG.). 32p. (J). (gr. 3-8). 32.79 *(978-1-60270-717-7(0))*, 3678, Graphic Planet - Fiction) Magic Wagon.

MISSISSIPPI RIVER VALLEY

see also Middle West

Aretha, David. La Salle: French Explorer of the Mississippi, 1 vol. 2009. (Great Explorers of the World Ser.). (ENG., Illus.). 112p. (gr. 6-7). lib. bdg. 35.93 *(978-1-59845-098-9(0))*, 2b91d3c2-fd41-4889-a6f1-505cb03714e4) Enslow Publishing, LLC.

Cefrey, Holly. The Pinckney Treaty: America Wins the Right to Travel the Mississippi River. 2009. (Life in the New American Nation Ser.). 32p. (gr. 4-4). 47.90 *(978-1-61514-286-6(X))* Rosen Publishing Group, Inc., The.

Donaldson-Forbes, Jeff. Jacques Marquette & Louis Jolliet. 2009. (Primary Source Library of Famous Explorers Ser.). 24p. (gr. 4-4). 42.50 *(978-1-60854-127-0(4))*, PowerKids Pr.) Rosen Publishing Group, Inc., The.

Dougherty, Terri. Admiral David Farragut: "Full Speed Ahead!" 2011. (J). *(978-1-59556-041-4(6))*; pap. *(978-1-59556-047-6(5))* OTTN Publishing.

Hazleton, Amie. Sieur de la Salle: An Explorer of the Great West. 2017. (World Explorers Ser.). (ENG., Illus.). 32p. (J). (gr. 3-6). lib. bdg. 27.99 *(978-1-5157-4206-7(7))*, 133973, Capstone Pr.) Capstone.

Larkin, Tanya. Jacques Marquette & Louis Jolliet: Explorers of the Mississippi. 2009. (Library of Explorers & Exploration Ser.). 112p. (gr. 5-8). 66.50 *(978-1-60853-608-5(4))*, Rosen Reference) Rosen Publishing Group, Inc., The.

Manning, Paul. The Mississippi. 2014. (River Adventures Ser.). (J). lib. bdg. 31.35 *(978-1-59920-916-6(0))* Black Rabbit Bks.

Owens, Lisa L. A Journey with Sieur de la Salle. 2017. (Primary Source Explorers Ser.). (ENG., Illus.). 40p. (J). (gr. 3-5). 30.65 *(978-1-5124-0775-4(5))*, 6ffa2a44-c9c5-4023-aa81-e9e9b293546f, Lerner Pubns.) Lerner Publishing Group.

River Lake Press. An Osprey Summer. 2010. (Illus.). 32p. (J). 17.95 *(978-0-615-36951-8(0))* River Lake Pr.

MISSISSIPPI RIVER VALLEY—HISTORY

Felsing, Dean E. New Orleans or Sunk! 2011. (Illus.). 64p. (gr. -1). pap. 13.95 *(978-1-4582-0092-1(2))*, Abbott Pr.) Author Solutions, LLC.

Larson, Paul Cliff & Larson, Pamela All. Mississippi Escapade: Reliving the Grand Excursion Of 1854. 2004. (Illus.). 128p. (J). (gr. 3-7). pap. 17.95 *(978-1-890434-64-9(7))* Afton Historical Society Pr.

Peppas, Lynn. Why Sieur de La Salle Matters to Texas, 1 vol. 2013. (Texas Perspectives Ser.). (ENG., Illus.). 32p. (J). (gr. 4-4). lib. bdg. 28.93 *(978-1-4777-0917-7(7))*, 0b3a3eaf-af71-420f-acc9-7bcff56efa29) Rosen Publishing Group, Inc., The.

MISSOURI

Barile, Mary Collins. J. Milton Turner; an American Hero. Guest, Peggy, illus. 2013. 52p. 24.95 *(978-0-9889643-0-3(9))* MathisJones Communications, LLC.

Boekhoff, P. M. Missouri, 1 vol. 2005. (Portraits of the States Ser.). (ENG., Illus.). 32p. (gr. 3-5). pap. 11.50 *(978-0-8368-4647-8(8))*, 434e7e2a-7682-4a61-86d6-704ed731782c); lib. bdg. 28.67 *(978-0-8368-4628-7(1))*, d5d5bf4f-88d2-4ba8-a179-f306d1fe85bf) Stevens, Gareth Publishing LLLP. (Gareth Stevens Learning Library).

Discover the Missouri River KIDS Activity Booklet. 2003. (J). pap. *(978-1-888631-20-3(1))* Project WET Foundation.

Evdokimoff, Natasha. Missouri. 2011. (Guide to American States Ser.). (Illus.). 48p. (YA). (gr. 3-6). 29.99 *(978-1-61690-797-6(5))*; (J). *(978-1-61690-473-9(9))* Weigl Pubs., Inc.

Haxton, Jason. Andrew Taylor Still: Father of Osteopathic Medicine. 2016. (ENG., Illus.). 48p. (J). 27.00 *(978-1-61248-174-6(4))* Truman State Univ. Pr.

Heinrichs, Ann. Missouri. Kania, Matt, illus. 2017. (U. S. A. Travel Guides). (ENG.). 40p. (J). (gr. 2-5). lib. bdg. 38.50 *(978-1-5038-1965-8(5))*, 211602) Child's World, Inc, The.

Kavanaugh, Dorothy. Central Mississippi River Basin: Arkansas, Iowa, Missouri, Vol. 19. 2015. (Let's Explore the States Ser.). (Illus.). 64p. (J). (gr. 5). lib. bdg. 23.95 *(978-1-4222-3321-4(9))* Mason Crest.

Kuedee, Jaycee. How to Draw Missouri's Sights & Symbols. 2009. (Kid's Guide to Drawing America Ser.). 32p. (gr. k-k). 50.50 *(978-1-61511-074-2(7))*, PowerKids Pr.) Rosen Publishing Group, Inc., The.

Lago, Mary Ellen & Karnovsky, Susan. Missouri. 2003. (From Sea to Shining Sea Ser.: 2). (ENG., Illus.). 80p. (J). 30.50 *(978-0-516-22390-2(9))*, Children's Pr.) Scholastic Library Publishing.

Lowe, Pamela Fleming. Missouri Then & Now. 2004. (ENG., Illus.). (gr. 4-k). 240p. (J). pap., stu. ed., act. bk. ed. 18.00 *(978-0-8262-1540-6(8))*; 184p. pap., tchr. ed., act. bk. ed. 25.00 *(978-0-8262-1539-0(4))* Univ. of Missouri Pr.

Marsh, Carole. The Big Missouri Reproducible Big Activity Book. 2004. (Missouri Experience! Ser.). (Illus.). 128p. (J). (gr. 2-6). per. 9.95 *(978-0-7933-9574-3(7))* Gallopade International.

—The Magnificant Missouri Coloring Book. 2004. (Missouri Experience! Ser.). (Illus.). 32p. (J). (gr. k-2). pap. 3.95 *(978-0-7933-9575-0(5))* Gallopade International.

—Missouri Current Events Projects: 30 Cool, Activities, Crafts, Experiments & More for Kids to Do to Learn about Your State! 2003. (Missouri Experience Ser.). 32p. (gr. k-8). pap. 5.95 *(978-0-635-02044-4(0))*, Marsh, Carole Bks.) Gallopade International.

—Missouri Geography Projects: 30 Cool, Activities, Crafts, Experiments & More for Kids to Do to Learn about Your State! 2003. (Missouri Experience Ser.). 32p. (gr. k-5). pap. 5.95 *(978-0-635-01844-1(6))*, Marsh, Carole Bks.) Gallopade International.

—Missouri Government Projects: 30 Cool, Activities, Crafts, Experiments & More for Kids to Do to Learn about Your State! 2003. (Missouri Experience Ser.). 32p. (gr. k-5). pap. 5.95 *(978-0-635-01944-8(2))*, Marsh, Carole Bks.) Gallopade International.

—Missouri Jeopardy! Answers & Questions about Our State! 2004. (Missouri Experience! Ser.). (Illus.). 32p. (J). (gr. 3-8). pap. 7.95 *(978-0-7933-9572-9(0))* Gallopade International.

—Missouri "Jography" A Fun Run Thru Our State! 2004. (Missouri Experience! Ser.). (Illus.). 32p. (J). (gr. 3-8). pap. 7.95 *(978-0-7933-9573-6(9))* Gallopade International.

—Missouri People Projects: 30 Cool, Activities, Crafts, Experiments & More for Kids to Do to Learn about Your State! 2003. (Missouri Experience Ser.). 32p. (gr. k-5). pap. 5.95 *(978-0-635-01994-3(9))*, Marsh, Carole Bks.) Gallopade International.

—Missouri Symbols & Facts Projects: 30 Cool, Activities, Crafts, Experiments & More for Kids to Do to Learn about Your State! 2003. (Missouri Experience Ser.). 32p. (gr. k-5). pap. 5.95 *(978-0-635-01894-6(2))*, Marsh, Carole Bks.) Gallopade International.

—My First Book about Missouri. 2004. (Missouri Experience! Ser.). (Illus.). 32p. (J). (gr. k-4). pap. 7.95 *(978-0-7933-9571-2(2))* Gallopade International.

Mills, Jordan & Parker, Bridget. Missouri. 2016. (States Ser.). (ENG., Illus.). 32p. (J). (gr. 3-6). lib. bdg. 27.99 *(978-1-5157-0412-6(2))*, 132023, Capstone Pr.) Capstone.

Murray, Julie. Missouri, 1 vol. 2006. (Buddy Book Ser.). (ENG., Illus.). 32p. (gr. 2-4). 27.07 *(978-1-59197-684-4(7))*, Buddy Bks.) ABDO Publishing Co.

Obregon, Jose Maria. Missouri, 1 vol. Brusca, Maria Cristina, tr. 2005. (Bilingual Library of the United States of America Ser.: Set 2). (ENG & SPA., Illus.). 32p. (J). (gr. 2-2). lib. bdg. 28.93 *(978-1-4042-3090-3(4))*, 619ebf12-9836-4cc6-aa08-19f84c887a6f) Rosen Publishing Group, Inc., The.

Obregón, José María. Missouri. 2009. (Bilingual Library of the United States of America Ser.). (SPA.). 32p. (gr. 2-2). 47.90 *(978-1-60853-370-1(0))*, Editorial Buenas Letras) Rosen Publishing Group, Inc., The.

Sanders, Doug. Missouri, 1 vol. Santoro, Christopher, illus. 2006. (It's My State! (First Edition)(r) Ser.). (ENG.). 80p. (gr. 4-4). lib. bdg. 34.07 *(978-0-7614-1822-1(9))*, f04eb1f6-5661-4050-84af-b2b7bea4917e) Cavendish Square Publishing LLC.

Taylor-Butler, Christine. Missouri. 2005. (Rookie Read-About Geography Ser.). (ENG., Illus.). 32p. (J). (gr. 1-2). lib. bdg. 20.50 *(978-0-516-25258-2(5))*, Children's Pr.) Scholastic Library Publishing.

—The Missouri River. 2006. (Rookie Read-About Geography Ser.). (ENG., Illus.). 32p. (J). (gr. 1-2). lib. bdg. 20.50 *(978-0-516-25037-3(X))*, Children's Pr.) Scholastic Library Publishing.

Wimmer, Teresa. Missouri. 2008. (This Land Called America Ser.). 32p. (YA). (gr. 3-6). 22.95 *(978-1-58341-650-1(1))* Creative Co., The.

Young, Judy. Show Me the Number: A Missouri Number Book. Young, Ross B., illus. rev. ed. 2007. (America by the Numbers Ser.). (ENG.). 40p. (J). (gr. 1-3). 17.95 *(978-1-58536-156-4(9))*, 202016) Sleeping Bear Pr.

Zeiger, Jennifer. Missouri (a True Book: My United States) (Library Edition) 2018. (True Book (Relaunch) Ser.). (ENG., Illus.). 48p. (J). (gr. 3-5). 31.00 *(978-0-531-23562-1(9))*, Children's Pr.) Scholastic Library Publishing.

MISSOURI—FICTION

Champlin, Tim. Tom Sawyer's Dark Plot. 2018. (Adventures in Time - 1849 Ser.: 2). (ENG.). 234p. (J). 25.95 *(978-1-4328-4475-2(X))*, Five Star) Cengage Gale.

Ciocca, Donna. Tavern Tales. 2005. 136p. per. 14.95 *(978-0-9747361-3-6(9))* Oak Manor Publishing, Inc.

Coleman, Roger. The Pope & the Snowman: A Christmas Tale. Becker, Richard, illus. 2009. (ENG.). 108p. 23.99 *(978-1-4490-1128-4(4))*; pap. 12.49 *(978-1-4490-1127-7(6))* AuthorHouse.

Crofford, Emily. When the River Ran Backward. (Adventures in Time Ser.). (gr. 4-8). 2005. (Illus.). 84p. 15.95 *(978-1-57505-305-9(5))* 2003. 80p. (J). pap. 6.95 *(978-1-57505-488-9(4))* Lerner Publishing Group.

Cutler, Jane. Susie Q Fights Back. 2018. (ENG.). 112p. (J). (gr. 3-7). pap. 6.99 *(978-0-8234-3993-5(3))* Holiday Hse., Inc.

Dalton, Sherry A. Do Indians Eat Soup? 2011. 32p. pap. 24.95 *(978-1-4560-7463-0(6))* America Star Bks.

Doty, Kathryn Adams. Wild Orphan. 2006. (ENG.). 144p. (gr. 3-7). per. 14.95 *(978-1-889020-20-4(6))* Edinborough Pr.

Doweiko, Melanie. The Rapids. 2017. (Summer Road Trip Ser.). (ENG.). 184p. (YA). (gr. 5-12). 31.42 *(978-1-68076-723-0(2))*, 27438, Epic Escape) EPIC Pr.

Figley, Marthy Rhodes & Figley, Marty Rhodes. The Night the Chimneys Fell. Marschall, Felicia, illus. 2011. 48p. (J). pap. 6.95 *(978-0-7613-3939-7(6))*, First Avenue Editions) Lerner Publishing Group.

Figley, Marty Rhodes. The Night the Chimneys Fell. Marschall, Felicia, illus. 2011. (On My Own History Ser.). 48p. (J). pap. 39.62 *(978-0-7613-7622-4(4))*, First Avenue Editions) Lerner Publishing Group.

—The Night the Chimneys Fell. Marshall, Felicia, illus. 2009. (On My Own History Ser.). (ENG.). 48p. (gr. 2-4). 25.26 *(978-0-8225-7894-9(8))* Lerner Publishing Group.

Fleischner, Jennifer. Nobody's Boy. 2006. (ENG., Illus.). 112p. (gr. 4). per. 12.95 *(978-1-883982-58-4(8))* Missouri Historical Society Pr.

Ford, Laura. Buster Brown & Tige in Misfit Heroes. 2004. (Illus.). 320p. (J). 19.95 *(978-1-881554-28-8(7))* Skyward Publishing Co.

Gilfert, Shirley Tankersley. The Other Side of Jordan: A Story of the Underground Railroad. 2007. 140p. 21.95 *(978-0-595-70289-3(9))*; per. 11.95 *(978-0-595-46274-2(X))* iUniverse, Inc.

Gratton, Tessa. Blood Magic. 2012. (Blood Journals). (ENG.). 416p. (YA). (gr. 8-12). lib. bdg. 26.19 *(978-0-375-96733-7(8))* Random House Publishing Group.

—Blood Magic. 2011. 408p. (YA). pap. *(978-0-375-86486-5(5))* Random Hse. Children's Bks.

H., Yves & Hermann. Manhattan Beach 1957. 2003. (Illus.). 56p. (YA). (gr. 11-18). 12.95 *(978-1-931724-23-4(7))* Diamond Select Toys & Collectibles.

Helgerson, Joseph. Crows & Cards. 2010. (ENG.). 352p. (J). (gr. 3-7). pap. 19.99 *(978-0-547-33909-2(7))*, 1418456, Clarion Bks.) HarperCollins Pubs.

M
N
O

Hubbard, Crystal. Alive & Unharmed. 2013. 164p. (J). pap. 12.95 *(978-1-60043-144-9(5))* Parker Publishing Inc.

Hughes, Dean. As Wide As the River. 2005. 156p. (J). pap. *(978-1-59038-450-3(4))* Deseret Bk. Co.

—Facing the Enemy. 2005. (Illus.). 153p. (J). pap. *(978-1-59038-449-7(0))* Deseret Bk. Co.

—Under the Same Stars. 2005. viii, 152p. (J). pap. *(978-1-59038-448-0(2))* Deseret Bk. Co.

Jackson, Louise A. Exiled! From Tragedy to Triumph on the Missouri Frontier. 2007. (Illus.). 235p. (YA). (gr. 7-9). per. 16.95 *(978-1-57168-948-1(6),* Eakin Pr.) Eakin Pr.

Jacobs, Lily. The Littlest Bunny in Missouri: An Easter Adventure. Dunn, Robert, illus. 2015. (Littlest Bunny Ser.). (ENG.). 32p. (J). (gr. -1-3). 9.99 *(978-1-4926-1126-4(3),* Hometown World) Sourcebooks, Inc.

James, Eric. Santa's Sleigh Is on Its Way to Missouri: A Christmas Adventure. Dunn, Robert, illus. 2015. (Santa's Sleigh Is on Its Way Ser.). (ENG.). 32p. (J). (gr. k-2). 12.99 *(978-1-4926-2759-3(3),* Hometown World) Sourcebooks, Inc.

—The Spooky Express Missouri. Piwowarski, Marcin, illus. 2017. (Spooky Express Ser.). (ENG.). 32p. (J). (gr. k-6). 9.99 *(978-1-4926-5373-8(X),* Hometown World) Sourcebooks, Inc.

—Tiny the Missouri Easter Bunny. 2018. (Tiny the Easter Bunny Ser.). (ENG.). 40p. (J). (gr. k-3). 9.99 *(978-1-4926-5940-2(1),* Hometown World) Sourcebooks, Inc.

Johnson, Annabel. A Rock Candy Dream. 2009. 140p. 22.49 *(978-1-4389-4233-9(8));* pap. 11.99 *(978-1-4389-4234-6(6))* AuthorHouse.

Johnson, DeAnna. Blarron Creek Chronicles. 2009. 108p. 23.49 *(978-1-4389-5580-3(4))* AuthorHouse.

Jones, Kristy. The Adventures of Ziggy the Trucker Dog. 2010. (ENG.). 24p. pap. 15.99 *(978-1-4500-8751-3(5))* Xlibris Corp.

Jude, Sarah. The May Queen Murders. 2017. (ENG.). 304p. (YA). (gr. 9). pap. 9.99 *(978-0-544-93725-3(2),* 1658701, Clarion Bks.) HarperCollins Pubs.

Katcher, Brian. Almost Perfect. 2010. 368p. (YA). (gr. 9). pap. 10.99 *(978-0-385-73665-7(7),* Delacorte Bks. for Young Readers) Random Hse. Children's Bks.

—Playing with Matches. 2009. 304p. (YA). (gr. 9). mass mkt. 8.99 *(978-0-385-73545-2(6),* Laurel Leaf) Random Hse. Children's Bks.

Klise, Kate. Grounded. 2013. (ENG.). 224p. (J). (gr. 4-8). pap. 18.99 *(978-0-312-55591-7(1),* 900074608) Square Fish.

Lane, M. j. & Lane, M. J. Where in the World Is Snickers? 2010. (ENG.). 42p. pap. 19.99 *(978-0-557-81843-3(5))* Lulu Pr., Inc.

MacBride, Roger Lea. Little Farm in the Ozarks. 2007. (Little House Ser.). 157p. (J). (gr. 2-5). per. 5.99 *(978-0-06-114810-1(5),* Harper Trophy) HarperCollins Pubs.

Mackall, Dandi Daley. A Girl Named Dan. Graef, Renée, illus. 2008. (ENG.). 32p. (J). (gr. 1-4). 16.95 *(978-1-58536-351-3(0),* 202138) Sleeping Bear Pr.

May, Gary L. The Wilkins Family Farm, 1 vol. Monks, Christian, illus. 2009. 75p. pap. 19.95 *(978-1-4489-2605-3(X))* America Star Bks.

McKissack, Patricia C. A Friendship for Today. 2008. 172p. (J). pap. *(978-0-545-06563-4(1))* Scholastic, Inc.

Meyer, Franklyn. More Me & Caleb Again. 2008. (Illus.). 191p. (J). 16.95 *(978-0-9789388-2-6(8))* Hester Publishing.

Meyer, Franklyn E. Me & Caleb. fac. ed. 2015. 162p. reprint ed. 22.95 *(978-1-62654-362-1(3));* (ENG.). pap. 16.95 *(978-1-62654-361-4(5))* Echo Point Bks. & Media, LLC.

—Me & Caleb. Smith, Lawrence Beall, illus. 2006. (J). kivar 16.95 *(978-0-9789388-0-2(1))* Hester Publishing.

—Me & Caleb Again. Liese, Charles, illus. 2006. (J). kivar 16.95 *(978-0-9789388-1-9(X))* Hester Publishing.

Milford, Kate. The Boneshaker. Offermann, Andrea, illus. 2011. (ENG.). 384p. (J). (gr. 5-7). pap. 7.99 *(978-0-547-55004-6(9),* 1450216, Clarion Bks.) HarperCollins Pubs.

Moonshower, Candie. The Legend of Zoey. 2007. (ENG.). 224p. (J). (gr. 3-7). 6.99 *(978-0-440-23924-6(9),* Yearling) Random Hse. Children's Bks.

Moriarty, Laura. American Heart. 2019. (ENG.). 416p. (YA). (gr. 8). pap. 9.99 *(978-0-06-269411-9(1),* HarperTeen) HarperCollins Pubs.

Moss, Helen. Time Dogs: Seaman & the Great Northern Adventure. Saburi, Misa, illus. 2020. (Time Dogs Ser.: 2). (ENG.). 160p. (J). pap. 20.99 *(978-1-250-25023-0(4),* 900191583) Square Fish.

Mulford, Carolyn. The Feedsack Dress. 2007. 227p. (J). per. 7.95 *(978-0-9713497-4-2(6))* Cave Hollow Pr.

Neighbors, Jolene. Nobody's Dog. 2010. 107p. pap. 14.95 *(978-1-4327-5957-5(4))* Outskirts Pr., Inc.

Nelson, Karen, creator. Crystal Brave: Literature Theme Unit. 2012. (Illus.). 48p. spiral bd. 19.99 *(978-1-930584-02-0(4))* Progreso Publishing Group , LLC.

Novel Units. The Adventures of Tom Sawyer Novel Units Student Packet. 2019. (ENG.). (YA). pap., stu. ed. 13.99 *(978-1-56137-528-8(4),* NU5284SP, Novel Units, Inc.) Classroom Library Co.

O'Neill, Elizabeth. Alfred Visits Missouri. 2008. 24p. (J). pap. 12.00 *(978-0-9799121-4-6(8))* Funny Bone Bks.

Papa's Gold. 2013. 196p. pap. 11.97 *(978-0-9851274-4-2(9))* Pen-L Publishing.

Racehorse Publishing & Twain, Mark. Classics to Color: the Adventures of Huckleberry Finn. 2016. (ENG., Illus.). 80p. (J). (gr. 1-6). pap. 8.99 *(978-1-944685-99-4(1),* Racehorse Publishing) Skyhorse Publishing Co., Inc.

Sargent, Daina. Missouri: Teamwork. Lenoir, Jane, illus. l.t. ed. 2004. (Double Trouble Ser.). 48p. (J). pap. 10.95 *(978-1-59381-127-3(6));* lib. bdg. 23.60 *(978-1-59381-126-6(8))* Ozark Publishing.

Stuber, Barbara. Crossing the Tracks. (ENG.). 272p. (YA). (gr. 7). 2011. pap. 11.99 *(978-1-4169-9704-7(0))* 2010. 16.99 *(978-1-4169-9703-0(2))* McElderry, Margaret K. Bks. (McElderry, Margaret K. Bks.).

Sully, Katherine. Night-Night Missouri. Poole, Helen, illus. 2017. (Night-Night Ser.). (ENG.). 20p. (J). (gr. -1-1). bds. 9.99 *(978-1-4926-4780-5(2),* 9781492647805, Hometown World) Sourcebooks, Inc.

Tarshis, Lauren. I Survived the Joplin Tornado, 2011 (I Survived #12) Dawson, Scott, illus. 2015. (I Survived Ser.: 12). (ENG.). 112p. (J). (gr. 2-5). pap. 5.99 *(978-0-545-65848-5(9),* Scholastic Paperbacks) Scholastic, Inc.

Twain, Mark, pseud. The Adventures of Huckleberry Finn. abr. ed. 2011. (Go Reader Audiobooks Ser.). (ENG.). (YA). (gr. 7-12). 49.93 *(978-1-61641-434-0(9))* Magic Wagon.

—The Adventures of Huckleberry Finn: With a Discussion of Friendship. Lauter, Richard, tr. Lauter, Richard, illus. 2003. (Values in Action Illustrated Classics Ser.). (J). *(978-1-59203-042-2(4))* Learning Challenge, Inc.

—The Adventures of Tom Sawyer: With a Discussion of Imagination. Butterfield, Ned, illus. 2003. (Values in Action Illustrated Classics Ser.). 190p. (J). *(978-1-59203-027-9(0))* Learning Challenge, Inc.

—Las Aventuras de Huckleberry Finn. de Atauri, Ines & de Atauri, Juan Diaz, eds. 2006. (Clasicos Juveniles Ser.).Tr. of Adventures of Huckleberry Finn. (SPA., Illus.). 359p. pap. 17.95 *(978-84-263-5252-1(9))* Vives, Luis Editorial (Edelvives) ESP. Dist: Lectorum Pubns., Inc.

—Classic Starts(r): the Adventures of Tom Sawyer: Retold from the Mark Twain Original. Corvino, Lucy, illus. 2005. (Classic Starts(r) Ser.). 160p. (J). (gr. 2-4). 7.99 *(978-1-4027-1216-6(2))* Sterling Publishing Co., Inc.

—Tom Sawyer. 2005. 264p. 28.95 *(978-1-4218-0768-3(8),* 1st World Library - Literary Society) 1st World Publishing, Inc.

—Tom Sawyer, 1 vol. Mullarkey, Lisa & McWilliam, Howard, illus. 2010. (Calico Illustrated Classics Ser.: No. 1). (ENG.). 112p. (J). (gr. 2-5). 38.50 *(978-1-60270-704-7(9),* 3961, Calico Chapter Bks.) ABDO Publishing Co.

—Tom Sawyer. 2008. (Bring the Classics to Life Ser.). (Illus.). 72p. (gr. 2-12). pap., act. bk. ed. 10.95 *(978-0-931334-29-0(2),* EDCTR-202B) EDCON Publishing Group.

—Tom Sawyer. 2006. (Classic Retelling Ser.). (Illus.). 224p. (YA). (gr. 8-12). *(978-0-618-12053-6(X),* 2-00218) Holt McDougal.

—Tom Sawyer. 2004. reprint ed. pap. 1.99 *(978-1-4192-5166-5(X))* Kessinger Publishing, LLC.

—Tom Sawyer. (Young Collector's Illustrated Classics Ser.). (Illus.). 192p. (J). (gr. 3-7). 9.95 *(978-1-56156-453-8(2))* Kidsbooks, LLC.

—Tom Sawyer. (Coleccion Clasicos de la Juventud). (SPA., Illus.). 220p. (J). 12.95 *(978-84-7189-029-0(1),* ORT310) Ortells, Alfredo Editorial S.L. ESP. Dist: Continental Bk. Co., Inc.

—Tom Sawyer. 2009. 196p. (gr. 4-7). pap. 12.99 *(978-1-934941-63-8(8))* Red & Black Pubs.

—Tom Sawyer. 2003. (Timeless Classics Ser.). (SPA., Illus.). 95p. (J). (gr. 5-8). pap. 12.95 *(978-84-372-2235-6(4))* Santillana USA Publishing Co., Inc.

Webster, Amye. Shell's Journey. 2013. 162p. pap. 9.99 *(978-0-9891510-2-3(6))* Zebra Ginkgo.

Whaley, John Corey. Noggin. 2015. (ENG., Illus.). 368p. (YA). (gr. 9). pap. 12.99 *(978-1-4424-5873-4(9),* Atheneum Bks. for Young Readers) Simon & Schuster Children's Publishing.

The Year We Sailed the Sun. 2015. (ENG., Illus.). 432p. (J). (gr. 3-7). 17.99 *(978-0-689-85827-7(2),* Atheneum/Richard Jackson Bks.) Simon & Schuster Children's Publishing.

MISSOURI—HISTORY

Bennett, Michelle & Hart, Joyce. Missouri, 1 vol. 2nd rev. ed. 2010. (Celebrate the States (Second Edition) Ser.). (ENG.). 144p. (gr. 6-6). 39.79 *(978-0-7614-4727-6(X),* 7d8bcba1-2b26-4d0a-9464-237a779dc6de) Cavendish Square Publishing LLC.

Blashfield, Jean F. America the Beautiful: Missouri (Revised Edition) 2014. (America the Beautiful, Third Ser. (Revised Edition) Ser.). (ENG.). 144p. (J). lib. bdg. 40.00 *(978-0-531-28282-3(1))* Scholastic Library Publishing.

Cruz, Ginny Wilson. E Is for Ellisville. 2011. (Illus.). (J). pap. *(978-0-615-55095-4(9))* Pioneer Poet Publishing.

Evdokimoff, Natasha. Missouri: The Show Me State. 2016. (J). *(978-1-4896-4890-7(9))* Weigl Pubs., Inc.

Gamble, Adam & Jasper, Mark. Good Night Missouri. Veno, Joe, illus. 2013. (Good Night Our World Ser.). (ENG.). 20p. (J). (— 1). bds. 9.95 *(978-1-60219-077-1(1))* Good Night Bks.

Hamilton, John. Missouri, 1 vol. 2016. (United States of America Ser.). (ENG., Illus.). 48p. (J). (gr. 5-9). 34.21 *(978-1-68078-327-8(0),* 21639, Abdo & Daughters) ABDO Publishing Co.

Huddleston, Emma. Exploring the Gateway Arch. 2019. (Travel America's Landmarks Ser.). (ENG., Illus.). 32p. (J). (gr. 2-3). pap. 9.95 *(978-1-64185-855-7(9),* 1641858559); lib. bdg. 31.35 *(978-1-64185-786-4(2),* 1641857862) North Star Editions. (Focus Readers).

Jackson, Robert. Meet Me in St. Louis: A Trip to the 1904 World's Fair. 2004. (ENG., Illus.). 144p. (J). (gr. 3-18). 17.99 *(978-0-06-009267-2(X))* HarperCollins Pubs.

Jerome, Kate B. Lucky to Live in Missouri. 2017. (Arcadia Kids Ser.). (ENG., Illus.). 32p. (J). 16.99 *(978-0-7385-2788-8(2))* Arcadia Publishing.

—The Wise Animal Handbook Missouri. 2017. (Arcadia Kids Ser.). (ENG., Illus.). 32p. (J). 16.99 *(978-0-7385-2828-1(5))* Arcadia Publishing.

Lago, Mary Ellen. From Sea to Shining Sea: Missouri. 2008. (ENG.). 80p. (J). pap. 7.95 *(978-0-531-20809-0(5),* Children's Pr.) Scholastic Library Publishing.

Lusted, Marcia Amidon. Missouri: The Show-Me State, 1 vol. 2010. (Our Amazing States Ser.). (ENG., Illus.). 24p. (J). (gr. 3-3). pap. 9.25 *(978-1-4358-9796-0(X),* 3f8e91f3-cda3-4bc0-baf2-4291e9afc363); lib. bdg. 26.27 *(978-1-4358-9351-1(4),* b5bc4381-9eda-458e-a101-06d08499d74a) Rosen Publishing Group, Inc., The. (PowerKids Pr.).

Marsh, Carole. Exploring Missouri Through Project-Based Learning: Geography, History, Government, Economics & More. 2016. (Missouri Experience Ser.). (ENG.). (J). pap. 9.99 *(978-0-635-12349-7(5))* Gallopade International.

—Missouri History Projects: 30 Cool, Activities, Crafts, Experiments & More for Kids to Do to Learn about Your State! 2003. (Missouri Experience Ser.). 32p. (gr. k-5). pap. 5.95 *(978-0-635-01794-9(6),* Marsh, Carole Bks.) Gallopade International.

McDowell, Pamela. Missouri: The Show Me State. 2012. (J). *(978-1-61913-369-3(5));* pap. *(978-1-61913-370-9(9))* Weigl Pubs., Inc.

McManus, Donald. Emmett Kelly: The Greatest Clown on Earth. 2014. (ENG., Illus.). 48p. (J). lib. bdg. 24.00 *(978-1-61248-120-3(5))* Truman State Univ. Pr.

McVicker, Maryellen. Joseph Kinney: Steamboat Captain. Hare, John, illus. 2014. (ENG.). 48p. (J). lib. bdg. 24.00 *(978-1-61248-116-6(7))* Truman State Univ. Pr.

Missouri, Our Home Program Kit: All program components for Missouri, Our Home, 1 vol. 2009. 129.95 *(978-1-4236-0721-2(X))* Gibbs Smith, Publisher.

Montgomery, Christine. George Washington Carver: Teacher & Environmentalist. 2017. (ENG., Illus.). 48p. (J). lib. bdg. 27.00 *(978-1-61248-214-9(7))* Truman State Univ. Pr.

Randolph, Joanne, ed. Slave States, Free States, & the Missouri Compromise, 1 vol. 2018. (Civil War & Reconstruction: Rebellion & Rebuilding Ser.). (ENG.). 32p. (gr. 4-5). 27.93 *(978-1-5383-4101-8(8),* a2949855-2a38-48fb-913d-fce43b2ce925, PowerKids Pr.) Rosen Publishing Group, Inc., The.

Ripley County Historical Society (Ripley County, Mo.) Staff, contrib. by. Ripley County, Missouri: History & Heritage. 2007. (Illus.). 176p. *(978-0-9773198-5-5(7))* Acclaim Pr., Inc.

Roza, Greg. Missouri: Past & Present, 1 vol. 2010. (United States: Past & Present Ser.). (ENG., Illus.). 48p. (J). (gr. 5-5). pap. 12.75 *(978-1-4358-8490-8(6),* ee314650-e2e2-4a40-a426-1488bb55b5a8); lib. bdg. 34.47 *(978-1-4358-3520-7(4),* d726a4ee-cd3d-4b8f-b85f-0446b10f6d04) Rosen Publishing Group, Inc., The. (Rosen Reference).

Sanders, Doug. Missouri, 1 vol. 2nd rev. ed. 2014. (It's My State! (Second Edition)(r) Ser.). (ENG.). 80p. (gr. 4-4). lib. bdg. 35.93 *(978-1-62712-240-5(0),* 1e9a7c85-e6cd-4587-a670-de54417f9a6e) Cavendish Square Publishing LLC.

Sanders, Doug & Boehme, Gerry. Missouri, 1 vol. 3rd rev. ed. 2015. (It's My State! (Third Edition)(r) Ser.). (ENG., Illus.). 80p. (gr. 4-4). 35.93 *(978-1-62713-244-2(9),* fde9fef9-853f-4051-8ea9-4d0bf6216dba) Cavendish Square Publishing LLC.

Schultz, James Willard. Floating on the Missouri: 100 Years after Lewis & Clark. 2003. (ENG., Illus.). 152p. per. 19.95 *(978-1-931832-15-1(3),* 18667872363) Riverbend Publishing.

St. Louis Union Station: A City Within a City. 2003. 19.95 *(978-0-9748109-0-4(8))* Market 1 Group Inc.

Young, Judy. Little Missouri. Urban, Helle, illus. 2012. (Little State Ser.). (ENG.). 20p. (J). (gr. -1-1). bds. 9.95 *(978-1-58536-206-6(9),* 202348) Sleeping Bear Pr.

—The Missouri Reader. Darnell, K. L., illus. 2010. (State/Country Readers Ser.). (ENG.). 96p. (J). (gr. 1-4). 12.95 *(978-1-58536-437-4(1),* 202165) Sleeping Bear Pr.

MITCHELL, MARIA, 1818-1889

Anderson, Dale. Maria Mitchell. 2003. (Women in Science Ser.). (ENG., Illus.). 112p. (gr. 6-12). 30.00 *(978-0-7910-7249-3(5),* P113768, Facts On File) Infobase Holdings, Inc.

Barrett, Hayley. What Miss Mitchell Saw. Sudyka, Diana, illus. 2019. (ENG.). 40p. (J). (gr. -1-3). 17.99 *(978-1-4814-8759-7(0),* Beach Lane Bks.) Beach Lane Bks.

Butzer, Anna. Maria Mitchell, 1 vol. 2014. (Great Women in History Ser.). (ENG., Illus.). 24p. (J). (gr. -1-2). pap. 6.29 *(978-1-4914-0542-0(2),* 125894, Pebble) Capstone.

Gormley, Beatrice. Maria Mitchell: The Soul of an Astronomer. 2004. (Illus.). 166p. (J). pap. 12.00 *(978-0-8028-5264-9(5))* Eerdmans, William B. Publishing Co.

MITCHELL, WILLIAM, 1879-1936

Miller, Roger G. Billy Mitchell: Evangelist of Airpower. 2007. (Illus.). 152p. (J). (gr. 10-18). lib. bdg. 25.95 *(978-1-59556-025-4(4))* OTTN Publishing.

MIXED MARRIAGE

see Intermarriage

MOBILES (SCULPTURE)

French, Cathy. Make an Animal Mobile & Haz un móvil de Animales: 6 English, 6 Spanish Adaptations. 2011. (SPA & ENG.). (J). 75.00 net. *(978-1-4108-5619-7(4))* Benchmark Education Co.

MOBS

see Riots

MOCKINGBIRDS

Amim, Aife. A Bird Watcher's Guide to Mockingbirds, 1 vol. 2017. (Backyard Bird Watchers Ser.). (ENG.). 32p. (J). (gr. 2-3). pap. 11.50 *(978-1-5382-0319-4(7),* 28f6bfee-215c-4c53-b16a-654cd4e4f4f7) Stevens, Gareth Publishing LLLP.

Lunis, Natalie. Mockingbird: Noisy Mimic. 2011. (Animal Loudmouths: Noisy Animals Ser.). 24p. (YA). (gr. k-3). lib. bdg. 26.99 *(978-1-61772-277-6(4))* Bearport Publishing Co., Inc.

Swisher, Dianne. To Save a Mockingbird. 2013. 32p. pap. *(978-1-77097-049-6(5))* FriesenPress.

MODEL CAR RACING

Mercer, Bobby. The Racecar Book: Build & Race Mousetrap Cars, Dragsters, Tri-Can Haulers & More. 2013. (Science in Motion Ser.). (ENG., Illus.). 216p. (J). (gr. 4). pap. 14.95 *(978-1-61374-714-8(4))* Chicago Review Pr., Inc.

Olson, Elsie. Make a Race Car Your Way! 2018. (Super Simple DIY Ser.). (ENG., Illus.). 32p. (J). (gr. k-4). lib. bdg. 34.21 *(978-1-5321-1718-3(3),* 30724, Super SandCastle) ABDO Publishing Co.

Thorne, Troy. Getting Started in Pinewood Derby: Step-By-Step Workbook to Building Your First Car. 2011. (ENG., Illus.). 96p. pap. 12.95 *(978-1-56523-617-2(3),* 6172) Fox Chapel Publishing Co., Inc.

—Pinewood Derby Designs & Patterns: The Ultimate Guide to Creating the Coolest Car. 2007. (ENG., Illus.). 118p. (gr. 3-6). 29.94 *(978-0-7566-3262-5(5))* Dorling Kindersley Publishing, Inc.

MODELING

see also Sculpture—Technique; Soap Sculpture

Bienik, Stella. Sculpting with Clay: Reason with Shapes & Their Attributes, 1 vol. 2014. (Math Masters: Geometry Ser.). (ENG.). 24p. (J). (gr. 2-2). 25.27 *(978-1-4777-6444-2(5),* f73197c7-b598-4bb2-a986-fe9f997baa26); pap. 8.25 *(978-1-4777-4906-7(3),* ac5ccb34-644b-4532-acef-b1883fe2aea4) Rosen Publishing Group, Inc., The. (Rosen Classroom).

Diamond, Cheryl. Model: A Memoir. 2008. (ENG., Illus.). 368p. (YA). (gr. 9-18). pap. 11.99 *(978-1-4169-5904-5(1),* Simon Pulse) Simon Pulse.

Fernandes, Kim. Gifts to Make with Crayola Model Magic, Incl. modelling material.Tr. of Surprises a Modeler avec Model Magic de Crayola. (FRE., Illus.). 32p. (J). 12.99 *(978-0-590-24760-3(3))* Scholastic, Inc.

Fontichiaro, Kristin & Thomas, AnnMarie P. Squishy Circuits. 2014. (21st Century Skills Innovation Library: Makers As Innovators Ser.). (ENG., Illus.). 32p. (J). (gr. 4-8). 32.07 *(978-1-63137-775-4(2),* 205343) Cherry Lake Publishing.

Frankish, Lorraine. 30 Fun Ways to Learn with Clay & Squishy Stuff. 2011. (30 Fun Ways to Learn Ser.). (ENG.). 80p. (gr. -1-k). pap. 12.95 *(978-0-87659-371-4(6),* Gryphon House Inc) Gryphon Hse., Inc.

Hammonds, Heather. Modellieren MIT Knete. 2005. (GER., Illus.). 64p. (J). *(978-3-937495-94-1(0))* Mud Puddle, Inc.

Henry, Sally. Clay Modeling, 1 vol. 2008. (Make Your Own Art Ser.). (ENG., Illus.). 32p. (gr. 3-4). pap. 12.75 *(978-1-4358-2641-0(8),* 9f01a4a8-681e-4815-9205-484f226149e9, PowerKids Pr.) Rosen Publishing Group, Inc., The.

Llimós, Anna. Earth-Friendly Clay Crafts in 5 Easy Steps, 1 vol. 2013. (Earth-Friendly Crafts in 5 Easy Steps Ser.). (ENG., Illus.). 32p. (gr. 3-3). lib. bdg. 26.61 *(978-0-7660-4189-9(1),* fd819273-a020-400c-98e6-2413e166ae30) Enslow Publishing, LLC.

Llimós, Anna & Llimós, Anna. Earth-Friendly Clay Crafts in 5 Easy Steps, 1 vol. 2013. (Earth-Friendly Crafts in 5 Easy Steps Ser.). (ENG.). 32p. (gr. 3-3). pap. 10.35 *(978-1-4644-0309-5(0),* d9620225-8b43-4925-9c1b-f8a90dc8b4ef, Enslow Elementary) Enslow Publishing, LLC.

Morris, Ting & Morris, Neil. Dinosaurs. Levy, Ruth & Cowne, Joanne, illus. 2006. (Sticky Fingers Ser.). 32p. (J). lib. bdg. 28.50 *(978-1-59771-029-9(6))* Sea-To-Sea Pubns.

Newell, Keith. Models. 2005. (Art & Craft Skills (Sea-to-Sea) Ser.). (Illus.). 32p. (J). (gr. 3-6). lib. bdg. 27.10 *(978-1-932889-85-7(X),* 1247657) Sea-To-Sea Pubns.

Petelinsek, Kathleen. Modeling Clay Creations. Petelinsek, Kathleen, illus. 2014. (How-To Library). (ENG., Illus.). 32p. (J). (gr. 3-6). 32.07 *(978-1-63137-783-9(3),* 205375) Cherry Lake Publishing.

Ryall, Jeanette. Clay Art, 1 vol. 2012. (Awesome Art Ser.). (ENG., Illus.). 32p. (J). (gr. 3-3). 31.27 *(978-1-4488-8085-0(8),* 404fe2f7-893f-415b-bbfd-fc371b09f179); pap. 12.75 *(978-1-4488-8138-3(2),* 1a63b8c5-2a3d-4680-b92c-261dce3630de) Rosen Publishing Group, Inc., The. (Windmill Bks.).

Speechley, Greta. Step-by-Step Clay Modelling. 2004. (Step-by-Step Children's Crafts Ser.). (Illus.). 32p. pap. 7.95 *(978-0-85532-914-3(9),* 9149) Midpoint Trade Bks., Inc.

Stacia, Ann. Make Your Own Squishies: 15 Slow-Rise & Smooshy Projects for You to Create. 2018. (ENG., Illus.). 96p. (J). (gr. 3-9). pap. 12.99 *(978-1-63158-451-0(0),* Racehorse Publishing) Skyhorse Publishing Co., Inc.

MODELS (PERSONS)

Abdo, Kenny. Millie Bobby Brown. 2018. (Star Biographies Ser.). (ENG., Illus.). 24p. (J). (gr. 2-8). lib. bdg. 31.36 *(978-1-5321-2547-8(X),* 30103, Abdo Zoom-Fly) ABDO Publishing Co.

Beker, Jeanne. Strutting it! The Grit Behind the Glamour. 2011. (Illus.). 88p. (J). (gr. 5-18). pap. 17.95 *(978-1-77049-224-0(0),* Tundra Bks.) Tundra Bks. CAN. Dist: Penguin Random Hse. LLC.

Bell, Samantha S. Karlie Kloss. 2019. (Influential People Ser.). (ENG., Illus.). 32p. (J). (gr. 4-6). pap. 7.95 *(978-1-5435-6041-1(5),* 140087); lib. bdg. 28.65 *(978-1-5435-5796-1(1),* 139752) Capstone.

Berne, Emma Carlson. Paris & Nicky Hilton. (Pop Culture Ser.). (Illus.). 64p. (gr. 3-7). 2008. (J). lib. bdg. 22.95 *(978-1-4222-0204-3(6))* 2007. (YA). pap. 7.95 *(978-1-4222-0358-3(1))* Mason Crest.

Davidson, Avelyn. Elle Fanning, 1 vol. 2012. (Rising Stars Ser.). (ENG., Illus.). 32p. (J). (gr. 1-1). 27.93 *(978-1-4339-7280-5(8),* ec5971a8-0b58-4991-a0fe-56e884c3d313); pap. 11.50 *(978-1-4339-7281-2(6),* b503aa61-1717-4f05-9e35-cece1ce99aea) Stevens, Gareth Publishing LLLP.

—Kendall Jenner, 1 vol. 2012. (Rising Stars Ser.). (ENG., Illus.). 32p. (J). (gr. 1-1). 27.93 *(978-1-4339-7288-1(3),* 95aa59c2-e838-4614-aff3-e23bb1e1020c); pap. 11.50 *(978-1-4339-7289-8(1),* 536846d5-bee8-4195-a84d-c5e6574eedbd) Stevens, Gareth Publishing LLLP.

Diamond, Cheryl. Model: A Memoir. 2008. (ENG., Illus.). 368p. (YA). (gr. 9-18). pap. 11.99 *(978-1-4169-5904-5(1),* Simon Pulse) Simon Pulse.

Dougherty, Terri. Tyra Banks, 1 vol. 2009. (People in the News Ser.). (ENG., Illus.). 112p. (gr. 7-7). 41.03 *(978-1-4205-0161-2(5),* 3b763cdd-2fa0-4afd-af21-641b03845535, Lucent Pr.) Greenhaven Publishing LLC.

Essential Lives Set 7, 7 vols. 2011. (Essential Lives Set 7 Ser.: 8). (ENG., Illus.). 112p. (YA). (gr. 6-12). lib. bdg. 289.52 *(978-1-61783-000-6(3),* 6739, Essential Library) ABDO Publishing Co.

Franks, Katie. I Want to Be a Supermodel. 2007. 28p. (gr. 3-7). pap. 21.25 *(978-1-4358-3834-5(3),* PowerKids Pr.) Rosen Publishing Group, Inc., The.

Hibbert, Clare & Hachette Children's Group. Fashion Model: Find Out How the Top Fashion Models Made It! 2012. (Celeb Ser.). (ENG., Illus.). 32p. (gr. 4-6). lib. bdg. 28.50 *(978-1-59771-331-3(7))* Sea-To-Sea Pubns.

Hill, Anne E. Tyra Banks: From Supermodel to Role Model. 2009. (Gateway Biographies Ser.). (ENG.). 48p. (gr. 4-8). 26.60 *(978-1-57505-949-5(5))* Lerner Publishing Group.

James, Kelle. Smile for the Camera: A Memoir. 2011. (ENG.). 400p. (YA). (gr. 9). pap. 9.99 *(978-1-4424-0624-7(0),* Simon & Schuster Bks. For Young Readers) Simon & Schuster Bks. For Young Readers.

Johnson, Robin. Zendaya. 2018. (Superstars! Ser.). (ENG., Illus.). 32p. (J). (gr. 4-4). *(978-0-7787-4843-4(X));* pap. *(978-0-7787-4872-4(3))* Crabtree Publishing Co.

Sauver, Dennis St. Elle Fanning. 2018. (Big Buddy Pop Biographies Ser.). (ENG., Illus.). 32p. (J). (gr. 2-5). lib. bdg. 34.21 *(978-1-5321-1799-2(X)*, 30644, Big Buddy Bks.) ABDO Publishing Co.

—Millie Bobby Brown. 2018. (Big Buddy Pop Biographies Ser.). (ENG.). 32p. (J). (gr. 2-5). lib. bdg. 34.21 *(978-1-5321-1797-8(3)*, 30640, Big Buddy Bks.) ABDO Publishing Co.

Shea, Therese M. Zendaya: Actress & Singer, 1 vol. 2018. (Junior Biographies Ser.). (ENG.). 24p. (gr. 3-4). 24.27 *(978-1-9785-0209-3(5)*, 49cc4396-c320-481f-9a23-ad342efb211d) Enslow Publishing, LLC.

Superwomen Role Models, 12 vols. 2016. (Superwomen Role Models Ser.). 32p. (ENG.). (gr. 3-4). 167.58 *(978-1-4994-1888-0(4)*, d5b67c22-c5d3-40e6-ab26-e5bb906490fc); (gr. 4-3). pap. 70.50 *(978-1-4994-2461-4(2))* Rosen Publishing Group, Inc., The. (PowerKids Pr.).

Tobey, Cheryl. Choosing a Career as a Model. 2009. (World of Work Ser.). 64p. (gr. 5-5). 58.50 *(978-1-60854-322-9(6))* Rosen Publishing Group, Inc., The.

Torres, Jennifer. Paris Hilton. 2005. (Blue Banner Biography Ser.). (Illus.). 32p. (J). (gr. 4-8). lib. bdg. 25.70 *(978-1-58415-382-5(2))* Mitchell Lane Pubs.

Woodcock, Sandra, et al. Being a Model. 2005. (ENG., Illus.). 32p. pap. *(978-0-340-74716-2(1))* Cambridge Univ. Pr.

Zakarin, Debra Mostow. Who's Your Superstar BFF? 2010. 112p. pap. 4.95 *(978-1-60747-775-4(0)*, Pickwick Pr.) Phoenix Bks., Inc.

—Who's Your Superstar Soul Mate? 2010. 112p. pap. 4.95 *(978-1-60747-776-1(9)*, Pickwick Pr.) Phoenix Bks., Inc.

MODELS (PERSONS)—FICTION

Axelsson, Carina. Model Undercover: London. 2016. (Model Undercover Ser.: 3). (ENG.). 368p. (J). (gr. 5-8). pap. 6.99 *(978-1-4926-2088-4(2))* Sourcebooks, Inc.

—Model Undercover: New York. 2015. (Model Undercover Ser.: 2). (ENG.). 320p. (J). (gr. 4-8). pap. 10.99 *(978-1-4926-0785-4(1))* Sourcebooks, Inc.

Banks, Tyra. Modelland. 2011. 569p. (YA). (gr. 7). 17.99 *(978-0-375-97259-1(5)*, Delacorte Pr) Random House Publishing Group.

Bell, Taryn. In the Spotlight. 2010. (ENG.). 256p. pap. 8.99 *(978-0-545-21444-5(0))* Scholastic, Inc.

Bennett, Sophia. The Look. 2013. (ENG.). 336p. (YA). (gr. 7). 17.99 *(978-0-545-46438-3(2))*; (J). *(978-0-545-46439-0(0))* Scholastic, Inc. (Chicken Hse., The).

Berk, Sheryl & Berk, Carrie. Fashion Academy: Model Madness. 2017. (Fashion Academy Ser.: 4). 192p. (J). (gr. 5-8). pap. 10.99 *(978-1-4926-4496-5(X)*, 9781492644965) Sourcebooks, Inc.

Berry, Joy. Tattling. 2018. (Help Me Be Good Ser.). (ENG.). 34p. (J). pap. 8.99 *(978-0-7396-0332-1(9))* Inspired Studios Inc.

Carlson, Melody. New York Debut, 1 vol. 2014. (Carter House Girls Ser.: 6). (ENG.). 224p. (YA). pap. 9.99 *(978-0-310-74779-6(1))* Zondervan.

Cross, Julie & Perini, Mark. Halfway Perfect. 2015. 384p. (YA). (gr. 8-12). pap. 9.99 *(978-1-4022-9719-9(X)*, 9781402297199) Sourcebooks, Inc.

—You Before Anyone Else. 2016. 400p. (YA). (gr. 8-12). pap. 10.99 *(978-1-4926-0492-1(5)*, 9781492604921) Sourcebooks, Inc.

Dessen, Sarah. Just Listen. 2008. (ENG.). 400p. (YA). (gr. 7-18). 12.99 *(978-0-14-241097-4(7)*, Speak) Penguin Young Readers Group.

—Just Listen. 2007. 20.00 *(978-0-7569-8270-6(7))* Perfection Learning Corp.

—Just Listen. 2008. 22.10 *(978-1-4178-2016-0(0))* Turtleback.

Hyde, Lara. Mosquito Bites. 2009. 132p. 21.95 *(978-0-595-51697-1(1))*; pap. 11.95 *(978-0-595-52079-4(0))* iUniverse, Inc.

Keene, Carolyn. Model Suspect: Book Three in the Model Mystery Trilogy. 2009. (Nancy Drew (All New) Girl Detective Ser.: 38). (ENG.). 160p. (J). (gr. 3-7). pap. 6.99 *(978-1-4169-7841-1(0)*, Aladdin) Simon & Schuster Children's Publishing.

Macaraeg, Diane. Last Meal. 2008. 132p. pap. *(978-3-639-03548-3(8))* AV Akademikerverlag GmbH & Co. KG.

The Model, 6 vols., Pack. (Chiquilibros Ser.). (gr. k-1). 23.00 *(978-0-7635-0426-7(2))* Rigby Education.

Morgan, Alex. Switching Goals. (Kicks Ser.). (ENG.). (J). (gr. 3-7). 2020. 144p. pap. 7.99 *(978-1-5344-2796-9(1))* 2019. 128p. 17.99 *(978-1-5344-2795-2(3))* Simon & Schuster Bks. For Young Readers. (Simon & Schuster Bks. For Young Readers).

Osborne, Jill. Riley Mae & the Sole Fire Safari, 1 vol. 2014. (Faithgirlz / the Good News Shoes Ser.: 3). (ENG.). 256p. (J). pap. 7.99 *(978-0-310-74283-8(8))* Zonderkidz.

Paige, D. M. Size 0. 2015. (Opportunity Ser.). (ENG.). 120p. (YA). (gr. 6-12). E-Book 53.32 *(978-1-4677-6017-1(X)*, 9781467760171, Lerner Digital) Lerner Publishing Group.

Philbin, Joanna. The Daughters. 2010. (Daughters Ser.: 1). (ENG.). 304p. (YA). (gr. 7-17). pap. 16.99 *(978-0-316-04901-6(8)*, Poppy) Little, Brown Bks. for Young Readers.

Rayban, Chloe. Models Move on to Starring Roles. (ENG.). 137p. pap. *(978-0-340-71428-7(X))* Hodder & Stoughton.

—Skin Deep, Vol. 2. (ENG.). 138p. pap. *(978-0-340-71429-4(8))* Hodder & Stoughton.

Simon, Coco. Emma Catwalks & Cupcakes! 2018. (Cupcake Diaries: 31). (ENG.). 160p. (J). (gr. 3-7). 17.99 *(978-1-5344-1736-6(2))*; (Illus.). pap. 6.99 *(978-1-5344-1735-9(4))* Simon Spotlight. (Simon Spotlight).

—Emma, Smile & Say "Cupcake!" (Cupcake Diaries: 11). (ENG.). 160p. (J). (gr. 3-7). 2014. Illus.). 17.99 *(978-1-4424-9611-8(8))* 2012. pap. 6.99 *(978-1-4424-5398-2(2))* Simon Spotlight. (Simon Spotlight).

—Emma's Not-So-Sweet Dilemma. 2014. (Cupcake Diaries: 23). lib. bdg. 17.20 *(978-0-606-36102-6(2))* Turtleback.

Smale, Holly. Geek Girl. 2015. (Geek Girl Ser.: 1). (ENG.). 384p. (YA). (gr. 8). 17.99 *(978-0-06-233357-5(7)*, HarperTeen) HarperCollins Pubs.

—Geek Girl: Model Misfit. 2016. (Geek Girl Ser.: 2). (ENG.). 416p. (YA). (gr. 8). pap. 11.99 *(978-0-06-233361-2(5)*, HarperTeen) HarperCollins Pubs.

—Geek Girl: Picture Perfect. 2016. (Geek Girl Ser.: 3). (ENG.). 416p. (YA). (gr. 8). 17.99 *(978-0-06-233363-6(1)*, HarperTeen) HarperCollins Pubs.

Vail, Rachel. Gorgeous. 2009. (Avery Sisters Trilogy Ser.: 2). (ENG.). 288p. (YA). (gr. 8-18). 16.99 *(978-0-06-089046-9(0)*, HarperTeen) HarperCollins Pubs.

Wagstaff, Janiel M. Stella Writes Set, 1 vol. 2018. (ENG.). (gr. k-3). pap., pap., pap. 24.99 *(978-1-338-25519-5(3))* Scholastic, Inc.

MODELS (PERSONS)—VOCATIONAL GUIDANCE

Franks, Katie. I Want to Be a Supermodel. 2009. (Dream Jobs Ser.). 24p. (gr. 2-3). 42.50 *(978-1-61512-212-7(5)*, PowerKids Pr.) Rosen Publishing Group, Inc., The.

O'Donnell, Kerri. Careers in Modeling. 2009. (Career Resource Library). 192p. (gr. 7-12). 63.90 *(978-1-60853-400-5(6))* Rosen Publishing Group, Inc., The.

Prescott, Sheri. How to Be a Super Model: A Guide to Inner Beauty. 2004. 237p. (YA). per. 14.99 *(978-1-58930-129-0(3))* Selah Publishing Group, LLC.

MODELS, FASHION

see Models (Persons)

MODELS, MECHANICAL

see Machinery—Models

MODELS AND MODELMAKING

see also subdivision Models under types of objects, e.g. Automobiles—Models; Machinery—Models; and phrase headings for types of models

Ashman, Iain. Egyptian Mummy. 2004. (Cut-Out Models Ser.). (Illus.). 32p. (J). pap. 9.95 *(978-0-7945-0255-3(5)*, Usborne) EDC Publishing.

Beck, Esther & Doudna, Kelly. Im on the Trail to Learn about Scale!, 1 vol. 2007. (Science Made Simple Ser.). (Illus.). 24p. (J). (gr. k-3). lib. bdg. 24.21 *(978-1-59928-592-4(4)*, SandCastle) ABDO Publishing Co.

Campodonica, Carol A. How Congress Works. Miller, Bondell, ed. Anderson, Bill, illus. Uni Photo Picture Agency Staff, photos by. Date not set. (J). (gr. 4-5). pap. *(978-0-9648488-9-4(9))* Buzzard Pr. International.

—How to Build a California Mission: Santa Barbara, 20 vols. Wardup, Shirley et al, eds. Sousa, Jay, photos by. Date not set. (How to Build a California Mission Ser.). (Illus.). (J). (gr. 4-5). pap. *(978-0-9648488-3-2(X))* Buzzard Pr. International.

—How to Build a California Mission: Santa Cruz, 20 vols. Weber, Francis J. et al, eds. Anderson, Bill, illus. Anderson, Jay, photos by. Date not set. (How to Build a California Mission Ser.). (J). (gr. 4-5). pap. *(978-0-9648488-5-6(6))* Buzzard Pr. International.

Dees, Sarah. Epic LEGO Adventures with Bricks You Already Have: Build Crazy Worlds Where Aliens Live on the Moon, Dinosaurs Walk among Us, Scientists Battle Mutant Bugs & You Bring Their Hilarious Tales to Life. 2017. (ENG., Illus.). 192p. (J). pap. 19.99 *(978-1-62414-386-1(5)*, 900177087) Page Street Publishing Co.

—Genius LEGO Inventions with Bricks You Already Have: 40+ New Robots, Vehicles, Contraptions, Gadgets, Games & Other STEM Projects with Real Moving Parts. 2018. (ENG., Illus.). 192p. (J). pap. 20.99 *(978-1-62414-678-7(3)*, 900197369) Page Street Publishing Co.

DK. LEGO Star Wars Visual Dictionary, New Edition: With Exclusive Finn Minifigure. 2019. (ENG., Illus.). 160p. (J). (gr. 2-4). 21.99 *(978-1-4654-7888-7(4)*, DK Children) Dorling Kindersley Publishing, Inc.

Dyer, Janice. Get into Dioramas & Models. 2016. (Get-Into-It Guides). (ENG.). 32p. (J). (gr. 3-6). *(978-0-7787-2640-1(1))* Crabtree Publishing Co.

Elsmore, Warren. Brick by Brick Dinosaurs: More Than 15 Awesome LEGO Brick Projects. 2018. (ENG., Illus.). 224p. (J). (gr. 3-7). pap. 19.99 *(978-0-7624-9147-6(7)*, Running Pr. Kids) Running Pr.

Felix, Rebecca. Cool Construction & Building Blocks: Crafting Creative Toys & Amazing Games. 2015. (Cool Toys & Games Ser.). (ENG., Illus.). 32p. (J). (gr. 3-6). lib. bdg. 34.21 *(978-1-68078-047-5(6)*, 19099, Checkerboard Library) ABDO Publishing Co.

French, Cathy. Make an Island & Haz una Isla: 6 English, 6 Spanish Adaptations. 2011. (ENG & SPA.). (J). 75.00 net. *(978-1-4108-5632-6(1))* Benchmark Education Co.

Garstecki, Julia & Derkovitz, Stephanie. Make Your Own Mini Rocket Car. 2020. (J). pap. *(978-1-62310-128-2(X))* Black Rabbit Bks.

Henry, Sally. Clay Modeling, 1 vol. 2008. (Make Your Own Art Ser.). (ENG., Illus.). 32p. (J). (gr. 3-4). lib. bdg. 30.27 *(978-1-4358-2508-6(X)*, 89020edc-cf7d-44e6-b170-245ed1de5a49, PowerKids Pr.) Rosen Publishing Group, Inc., The.

Hugo, Simon. 365 Things to Do with LEGO Bricks: Lego Fun Every Day of the Year. 2016. (ENG., Illus.). 256p. (J). (gr. 2-6). 24.99 *(978-1-4654-5302-0(4)*, DK Children) Dorling Kindersley Publishing, Inc.

Ives, Rob. Castle Attack: Make Your Own Medieval Battlefield. Paul de Quay, John, illus. 2016. (Tabletop Wars Ser.). (ENG.). 32p. (J). (gr. 3-6). 27.99 *(978-1-5124-0639-9(2)*, 81a92a1a-b0f0-4473-af08-b8b8d667cdd7, Hungry Tomato (r)) Lerner Publishing Group.

Jefferis, David. Flying Models: From Soaring Flight to Real Rockets. 2018. (Model-Making Mindset Ser.). 32p. (J). (gr. 5-5). *(978-0-7787-5015-4(9))* Crabtree Publishing Co.

—Miniature Figures: From Model Soldiers to Fantasy Gaming. 2018. (Model-Making Mindset Ser.). (Illus.). 32p. (J). (gr. 5-5). *(978-0-7787-5016-1(7))* Crabtree Publishing Co.

—Model Trains: Creating Tabletop Railroads. 2018. (Model-Making Mindset Ser.). 32p. (J). (gr. 5-5). *(978-0-7787-5017-8(5))* Crabtree Publishing Co.

—Scale Models: Making a Miniature Masterpiece. 2018. (Model-Making Mindset Ser.). 32p. (J). (gr. 5-5). *(978-0-7787-5018-5(3))* Crabtree Publishing Co.

Kemmeter, Jennifer. Build It! Make Supercool Models with Your LEGO(r) Classic Set. 3. 2016. (Brick Bks.: 3). (ENG., Illus.). 86p. (J). (gr. k-3). pap. 16.99 *(978-1-943328-82-6(X)*, Graphic Arts Bks.) West Margin Pr.

—Build It! Farm Animals: Make Supercool Models with Your Favorite LEGO(r) Parts. 2017. (Brick Bks.: 8). (ENG., Illus.). 86p. (J). (gr. -1-2). 32.99 *(978-1-5132-6085-3(5))*; pap. 16.99 *(978-1-5132-6082-2(0))* West Margin Pr. (Graphic Arts Bks.).

—Build It! Robots: Make Supercool Models with Your Favorite LEGO(r) Parts. 2017. (Brick Bks.: 9). (ENG., Illus.). 86p. (J). (gr. -1-2). pap. 16.99 *(978-1-5132-6083-9(9)*, Graphic Arts Bks.) West Margin Pr.

—Build It! Trains: Make Supercool Models with Your Favorite LEGO(r) Parts. 2018. (Brick Bks.: 12). (ENG., Illus.). 102p. (J). (gr. k-3). 32.99 *(978-1-5132-6114-0(2))*; pap. 17.99 *(978-1-5132-6113-3(4))* West Margin Pr. (Graphic Arts Bks.).

—Build It! Volume 3: Make Supercool Models with Your LEGO(r) Classic Set. 2016. (Brick Bks.: 3). (ENG., Illus.). 86p. (J). 32.99 *(978-1-5132-6044-0(8)*, Graphic Arts Bks.) West Margin Pr.

—Build It! World Landmarks: Make Supercool Models with Your Favorite LEGO(r) Parts. 2016. (Brick Bks.: 4). (ENG., Illus.). 70p. (J). 32.99 *(978-1-5132-6045-7(6))*; pap. 16.99 *(978-1-943328-83-3(8))* West Margin Pr. (Graphic Arts Bks.).

Kerley, Barbara. The Dinosaurs of Waterhouse Hawkins: An Illuminating History of Mr. Warehouse Hawkins, Artist & Lecturer. Selznick, Brian, illus. 2011. (J). (gr. 2-5). 29.95 *(978-0-545-19697-0(3))*; 18.95 *(978-0-545-19703-8(1))* Weston Woods Studios, Inc.

Lipkowitz, Daniel. The LEGO Ideas Book: Unlock Your Imagination. 2011. (Lego Ideas Ser.). (ENG., Illus.). 200p. (J). (gr. 2-5). 24.99 *(978-0-7566-8606-2(7)*, DK Children) Dorling Kindersley Publishing, Inc.

Lipkowitz, Daniel & Dorling Kindersley Publishing Staff. The Lego Ideas Book: You Can Build Anything! 2011. (Illus.). 200p. *(978-1-4053-5067-9(9))* Dorling Kindersley.

Marrewa, Jennifer. Making a Model with SOLID FIGURES, 1 vol. 2008. (Math in Our World - Level 2 Ser.). (ENG.). 24p. (gr. 2-2). pap. 9.15 *(978-0-8368-9014-3(0)*, 4b6e9b39-2756-48d0-a90a-de1df9162655); (Illus.). lib. bdg. 24.67 *(978-0-8368-9005-1(1)*, b8144a98-4e78-4067-a199-4a6b88b3c655) Stevens, Gareth Publishing LLLP. (Weekly Reader Leveled Readers).

—Vamos a Hacer una Maqueta con FIGURAS SÓLIDAS (Making a Model with SOLID FIGURES), 1 vol. 2008. (Las Matemáticas en Nuestro Mundo - Nivel 2 (Math in Our World - Level 2) Ser.). (SPA.). 24p. (gr. 2-2). pap. 9.15 *(978-0-8368-9032-7(9)*, 0e15bf56-9192-4d23-9324-a232e78f482a); (Illus.). lib. bdg. 24.67 *(978-0-8368-9023-5(X)*, 32b42e0e-d27d-436f-982b-25ce673ad623) Stevens, Gareth Publishing LLLP. (Weekly Reader Leveled Readers).

Miller, Reagan. Engineers Build Models. 2013. (ENG., Illus.). 24p. (J). *(978-0-7787-0093-7(3))*; pap. *(978-0-7787-0100-2(X))* Crabtree Publishing Co.

Models. (Jump Ser.). (Illus.). 36p. (J). (gr. 2-6). pap. *(978-1-882210-36-7(0))* Action Publishing, Inc.

Nelson, Libby. California Missions Projects & Layouts. 2007. (Exploring California Missions Ser.). (Illus.). 112p. (J). lib. bdg. 27.93 *(978-0-8225-7950-2(2)*, Lerner Pubns.) Lerner Publishing Group.

Radford, Tracey. Make Your Own Zoo: 35 Projects for Kids Using Everyday Cardboard Packaging. Turn Your Recycling into a Zoo! 2015. (ENG., Illus.). 128p. (J). (gr. 3-11). pap. 19.95 *(978-1-78249-256-6(9)*, 1782492569, CICO Books) Ryland Peters & Small GBR. Dist: WIPRO.

Rothrock, Megan H. The LEGO Adventure Book, Vol. 2 Vol. 2: Spaceships, Pirates, Dragons & More! 2013. (Illus.). 196p. (J). (gr. 5). 24.95 *(978-1-59327-512-9(9)*, 9781593275129) No Starch Pr., Inc.

—The LEGO Adventure Book, Vol. 3: Robots, Planes, Cities & More!, Vol. 3. 2015. (Illus.). 192p. (J). (gr. 5). 24.95 *(978-1-59327-610-2(9))* No Starch Pr., Inc.

Smith, A. G. Cut & Make a Human Skeleton. 2011. (Dover Kids Activity Bks.). (ENG., Illus.). 16p. (J). (gr. 4-8). pap. 7.99 *(978-0-486-26124-9(7)*, 261247) Dover Pubns., Inc.

Sohn, Emily. Models & Designs. 2019. (iScience Ser.). (ENG., Illus.). 48p. (J). (gr. 5-6). 23.94 *(978-1-68450-946-1(7))*; pap. 13.26 *(978-1-68404-406-1(5))* Norwood Hse. Pr.

Stadler, Charlotte. Making Patterns. Adams, Alison, ed. 2011. (Early Connections Ser.). (ENG.). (J). (gr. 2). 8.00 net. *(978-1-61672-640-9(7))* Benchmark Education Co.

Stark, Kristy. Fun & Games: Building Miniature Models: Multiplying Decimals (Grade 5) 2018. (Mathematics in the Real World Ser.). (ENG., Illus.). 32p. (J). (gr. 4-8). pap. 11.99 *(978-1-4258-5821-6(X))* Teacher Created Materials, Inc.

Vink, Amanda. A Modern Nerd's Guide to Miniatures, 1 vol. 2019. (Geek Out! Ser.). (ENG.). 32p. (gr. 3-4). 28.27 *(978-1-5382-4020-5(3)*, 45a342b4-2581-465e-a94f-530a75c72476) Stevens, Gareth Publishing LLLP.

Zuravicky, Orli. Exploring Pyramids Around the World: Making Models of Geometric Solids, 1 vol. (Math for the REAL World Ser.). (ENG., Illus.). 32p. (gr. 4-5). 2010. pap. 10.00 *(978-0-8239-8908-9(9)*, d7fc3d15-9034-42b9-97cb-a8c77767ee97) 2003. (J). lib. bdg. 28.93 *(978-0-8239-8992-8(5)*, 5b92d1b2-80fa-4330-b2d9-d9049261cd92) 2003. (J). lib. bdg. 28.93 *(978-0-8239-8992-8(5)*, 5b92d1b2-80fa-4330-b2d9-d9049261cd92) Rosen Publishing Group, Inc., The. (PowerKids Pr.).

MODERN CIVILIZATION

see Civilization, Modern

MODERN HISTORY

see History, Modern

MODERNISM (ART)

Fitzpatrick, Anne. Late Modernism. 2006. (Movements in Art Ser.). (ENG., Illus.). 48p. (J). (gr. 5-8). lib. bdg. 21.95 *(978-1-58341-348-7(0)*, 22253) Creative Co., The.

—Late Modernism: Movements in Art. 2015. (Odysseys in Art Ser.). (ENG., Illus.). 80p. (J). (gr. 7-10). *(978-1-60818-534-4(6)*, 20935, Creative Education) Creative Co., The.

Gunderson, Jessica. Realism: Movements in Art. 2015. (Odysseys in Art Ser.). (ENG., Illus.). 80p. (J). (gr. 7-10). *(978-1-60818-535-1(4)*, 20938, Creative Education) Creative Co., The.

Hardy, Rachael. Cézanne, Vol. 7. 2015. (Great Artists Collection). (Illus.). 64p. (J). (gr. 7). lib. bdg. 23.95 *(978-1-4222-3257-6(3))* Mason Crest.

Kallen, Stuart A. Postmodern Art, 1 vol. 2008. (Eye on Art Ser.). (ENG., Illus.). 112p. (gr. 7-7). lib. bdg. 41.03 *(978-1-4205-0075-2(9)*, 78598d88-93f4-499e-9327-13ae38f8ec66, Lucent Pr.) Greenhaven Publishing LLC.

Minond, Edgardo. Drac, Tell Us about Modernism. (SPA.). 80p. *(978-84-96137-13-4(9))* A. Asppan, S.L. Distribuidora Internacional de Libros y Revistas.

Orme, Helen. Body Art. 2011. (Fact to Fiction Grafx Ser.). (ENG., Illus.). 36p. (J). (gr. 4-7). lib. bdg. 17.45 *(978-1-61384-017-7(9))* Perfection Learning Corp.

Riggs, Kate. What Is Modernism? 2016. (Art World Ser.). (ENG.). 24p. (J). (gr. 1-4). pap. 9.99 *(978-1-62832-225-5(X)*, 20457, Creative Paperbacks); (Illus.). *(978-1-60818-627-3(X)*, 20459, Creative Education) Creative Co., The.

Robinson, Shannon. Cubism: Movements in Art. 2015. (Odysseys in Art Ser.). (ENG., Illus.). 80p. (J). (gr. 7-10). *(978-1-60818-531-3(1)*, 20926, Creative Education) Creative Co., The.

MOGUL EMPIRE

Shirodkar, Suhag. Captured in Miniature. 2010. (ENG., Illus.). 56p. 16.95 *(978-0-944142-61-5(3))* Mapin Publishing Pvt. Ltd IND. Dist: National Bk. Network.

MOHAMMED, PROPHET, -632

see Muhammad, Prophet, -632

MOHAMMEDAN ART

see Islamic Art

MOLDS (BOTANY)

Kittinger, Jo S., et al. Un Aliento de Esperanza. Galey, Chuck, illus. 2013. (SPA.). (J). *(978-1-61438-868-5(7))* American Bar Assn.

Viegas, Jennifer & Baum, Margaux. Fungi & Molds, 1 vol. 2016. (Germs: Disease-Causing Organisms Ser.). (ENG., Illus.). 48p. (J). (gr. 5-5). pap. 12.75 *(978-1-4777-8840-0(9)*, 86901077-3fa5-4219-8d4f-3b876ae2a016, Rosen Reference) Rosen Publishing Group, Inc., The.

MOLECULAR BIOCHEMISTRY

see Molecular Biology

MOLECULAR BIOLOGY

Olsen, Alana. A Day at Work with a Molecular Biologist, 1 vol., 1. 2015. (Super STEM Careers Ser.). (ENG., Illus.). 24p. (J). (gr. 3-4). pap. 9.25 *(978-1-5081-4410-6(9)*, 667bb165-e2be-4ffd-b517-0562e7c691fa, PowerKids Pr.) Rosen Publishing Group, Inc., The.

MOLECULAR BIOPHYSICS

see Molecular Biology

MOLECULES

Aloian, Molly. Atoms & Molecules, 1 vol. 2008. (Why Chemistry Matters Ser.). (ENG., Illus.). 32p. (J). (gr. 4-6). pap. *(978-0-7787-4247-0(4))* Crabtree Publishing Co.

Bodden, Valerie. Proteins. 2015. (Healthy Plates Ser.). (ENG.). 24p. (J). (gr. 1-4). *(978-1-60818-511-5(7)*, 21215, Creative Education) Creative Co., The.

Gardner, Robert. Atoms & Molecules Experiments Using Ice, Salt, Marbles, & More: One Hour or Less Science Experiments, 1 vol. 2012. (Last-Minute Science Projects Ser.). (ENG.). 48p. (J). (gr. 5-6). 27.93 *(978-0-7660-3961-2(7)*, be2ba508-8298-46c3-91fc-828ec175ef9a) Enslow Publishing, LLC.

Gish, Melissa. Temperature. 2005. (My First Look at Science Ser.). (Illus.). 24p. (J). (gr. k-3). lib. bdg. 15.95 *(978-1-58341-375-3(8)*, Creative Education) Creative Co., The.

Gratzer, Walter. Giant Molecules: From Nylon to Nanotubes. 2009. (ENG., Illus.). 176p. (J). 24.95 *(978-0-19-955002-9(6))* Oxford Univ. Pr., Inc.

Hall, Linley Erin. DNA & RNA, 1 vol. 2010. (Understanding Genetics Ser.). (ENG.). 80p. (YA). (gr. 7-8). lib. bdg. 38.47 *(978-1-4358-9532-4(0)*, 233d9343-1818-4303-9e5e-3517c0ca8d79) Rosen Publishing Group, Inc., The.

Jackson, Tom. The Basics of Atoms & Molecules, 1 vol. 2013. (Core Concepts Ser.). (ENG.). 96p. (YA). (gr. 7-7). 39.77 *(978-1-4777-2715-7(9)*, 3ef6df4b-f2ba-4735-8783-0dee38507838) Rosen Publishing Group, Inc., The.

Juettner, Bonnie. Molecules. 2004. (Kidhaven Science Library). (ENG., Illus.). 48p. (J). (gr. 4-7). 27.50 *(978-0-7377-2076-1(X))* Cengage Gale.

Lepora, Nathan. Atoms & Molecules, 1 vol. 2011. (Invisible Worlds Ser.). (ENG.). 48p. (gr. 4-4). 31.21 *(978-0-7614-4192-2(1)*, b2d9d614-dfe4-49b0-bbc6-22e01138ca4c) Cavendish Square Publishing LLC.

Manning, Phillip. Atoms, Molecules, & Compounds. 2008. (Essential Chemistry Ser.). (ENG., Illus.). 137p. (gr. 7-12). lib. bdg. 35.00 *(978-0-7910-9534-8(7)*, P142935, Facts On File) Infobase Holdings, Inc.

Monroe, Tilda. What Do You Know about Atoms & Molecules?, 1 vol. 2010. (20 Questions: Physical Science Ser.). (ENG.). 24p. (gr. 2-3). (J). pap. 9.25 *(978-1-4488-1223-3(2)*, 909b7c4f-ab01-41a5-b244-41b858a0c43f, PowerKids Pr.); (YA). lib. bdg. 26.27 *(978-1-4488-0669-0(0)*, fd49115b-8619-475f-922a-487444b46c37) Rosen Publishing Group, Inc., The.

O'Mara, Kennon. Molecules, 1 vol. 2018. (Look at Chemistry Ser.). (ENG.). 32p. (gr. 2-2). 28.27 *(978-1-5382-3012-1(7)*, 0241038c-0afe-4f02-a054-93f8bd320c1f) Stevens, Gareth Publishing LLLP.

Slade, Suzanne. Scientific Instruments for Studying Atoms & Molecules, 1 vol. 2006. (Physical Science Ser.). (ENG., Illus.). 24p. (gr. 4-4). pap. 7.05 *(978-1-4042-2166-6(2)*, 2bae84fe-53e0-452e-a5cd-789628855913, PowerKids Pr.) Rosen Publishing Group, Inc., The.

—States of Matter, 1 vol. 2006. (Journeys Ser.). (ENG., Illus.). 24p. (gr. 4-4). pap. 7.05 *(978-1-4042-2163-5(8)*, dcb2a368-d26d-48e2-a82e-181432fd83c9, PowerKids Pr.) Rosen Publishing Group, Inc., The.

Slingerland, Janet. Explore Atoms & Molecules! With 25 Great Projects. Aucoin, Matt, illus. 2017. (Explore Your World Ser.). (ENG.). 96p. (J). (gr. 1-5). 19.95 *(978-1-61930-491-8(0)*, a7e44c8b-b69c-4b00-b090-a383ba907565) Nomad Pr.

Woodford, Chris & Clowes, Martin. Atoms & Molecules: Investigating the Building Blocks of Matter, 1 vol. 2012. (Scientific Pathways Ser.). (ENG., Illus.). 48p. (J). (gr. 5-5). lib. bdg. 34.47 *(978-1-4488-7196-4(4)*, 5e36ee8c-313f-414f-942c-eede505fcb37, Rosen Reference) Rosen Publishing Group, Inc., The.

MNO

MOLES (ANIMALS)

Dittmer, Lori. Moles. 2018. (Seedlings: Backyard Animals Ser.). (ENG.). 24p. (J). (gr. k-2). pap. 8.99 (978-1-62832-600-0(X), 19929, Creative Paperbacks); (gr. -1-k). (978-1-60818-973-1(2), 19920, Creative Education) Creative Co., The.

George, Jean Craighead. Winter Moon. 2003. (J). (gr. 3-7). 20.75 (978-0-8446-7244-1(0)) Smith, Peter Pub., Inc.

Owen, Ruth. Mole. 2018. (Wildlife Watchers Ser.). (ENG., Illus.). 24p. (J). (gr. k-2). 8.99 (978-1-78856-073-3(6), c24be2fb-4935-4529-950b-a64337de3ee1) Ruby Tuesday Books Limited GBR. Dist: Lerner Publishing Group.

Owings, Lisa. Star-Nosed Mole. 2014. (Extremely Weird Animals Ser.). (ENG., Illus.). 24p. (J). (gr. 3-8). lib. bdg. 27.95 (978-1-62617-078-0(9), Pilot Bks.) Bellwether Media.

Perkins, Wendy. Star-Nosed Moles. (Weird & Unusual Animals Ser.). (ENG., Illus.). 24p. (J). (gr. 1-4). 2018. pap. 8.99 (978-1-68152-192-3(X), 16104) 2017. 20.95 (978-1-68151-161-0(4), 14704) Amicus.

Poliquin, Rachel. Moles. Frith, Nicholas John, illus. 2019. (Superpower Field Guide Ser.). (ENG.). 96p. (J). (gr. 3-7). 18.99 (978-0-544-95107-5(7), 1659965, Clarion Bks.) HarperCollins Pubs.

Riggs, Kate. Moles. 2016. (In My Backyard Ser.). (ENG., Illus.). 24p. (J). (gr. 1-3). (978-1-60818-700-3(4), 20596, Creative Education); pap. 8.99 (978-1-62832-296-5(9), 20594, Creative Paperbacks) Creative Co., The.

Savage, Stephen. Mole, 1 vol. 2008. (Animal Neighbors Ser.). (ENG.). 32p. (gr. 3-3). pap. 11.60 (978-1-4042-4566-2(9), e6f56445-b7dc-4d08-8680-782a3f4aa808, Rosen Classroom); (Illus.). (J). lib. bdg. 28.93 (978-1-4358-4989-1(2), 58c119ed-5393-44d4-bbcb-f24f50702eba, PowerKids Pr.) Rosen Publishing Group, Inc., The.

Webster, Christine. Les Condylures étoilés: Les Animaux du Canada. Karvonen, Tanjah, tr. from ENG. 2011. (FRE.). 24p. (gr. 3-6). (978-1-77071-416-8(2)) Weigl Educational Pubs. Ltd.

—Star-Nosed Mole. 2010. (Illus.). 24p. (978-1-55388-665-5(8)); pap. (978-1-55388-666-2(6)) Weigl Educational Pubs. Ltd.

Zappa, Marcia. Star-Nosed Moles, 1 vol. 2015. (World's Weirdest Animals Ser.). (ENG., Illus.). 32p. (J). (gr. 2-5). 34.21 (978-1-62403-778-8(X), 17858, Big Buddy Bks.) ABDO Publishing Co.

MOLES (ANIMALS)—FICTION

Bailey, Arthur Scott. The Tale of Grandfather Mole. 2005. reprint ed. pap. 20.95 (978-0-7661-9549-3(X)) Kessinger Publishing, LLC.

Bedford, David. Mole's Babies. Beardshaw, Rosalind, illus. 2012. (ENG.). 32p. (J). (978-1-58925-108-3(3)); pap. (978-1-58925-435-0(X)) Tiger Tales.

Caballero, Erica. Mount Mole. 2006. pap. 10.00 (978-1-4257-2301-9(2)) Xlibris Corp.

Conchie, Kathryn. I Am a Mole, & I Live in a Hole. Top That Publishing Staff, ed. Howarth, Daniel, illus. 2008. (Story Book Ser.). 12p. (J). (gr. -1). (978-1-84666-575-2(2), Tide Mill Pr.) Top That! Publishing PLC.

Delessert, Etienne. Alert! 2007. (ENG., Illus.). 32p. (J). (gr. -1-3). 17.00 (978-0-618-73474-0(0), 584451, Clarion Bks.) HarperCollins Pubs.

Duckers, John. The Amazing Adventures of the Silly Six. 2013. (Illus.). 188p. pap. (978-1-78148-626-9(3)) Grosvenor Hse. Publishing Ltd.

Eaton, Maxwell, III. The Flying Beaver Brothers & the Mud-Slinging Moles. 2013. (Flying Beaver Brothers Ser.: 3). lib. bdg. 17.20 (978-0-606-32233-1(7)) Turtleback.

Eaton, Maxwell, III & Eaton, Maxwell. The Flying Beaver Brothers & the Mud-Slinging Moles: (a Graphic Novel) 2013. (Flying Beaver Brothers Ser.: 3). (Illus.). 96p. (J). (gr. 1-4). pap. 7.99 (978-0-449-81019-4(4), Knopf Bks. for Young Readers) Random Hse. Children's Bks.

Ehlert, Lois. Holey Moley. Ehlert, Lois, illus. 2015. (ENG., Illus.). 40p. (J). (gr. -1-3). 17.99 (978-1-4424-9301-8(1), Beach Lane Bks.) Beach Lane Bks.

Erlbruch, Wolf & Holzwarth, Werner. The Story of the Little Mole Who Knew It was None of His Business: Plop Up Edition. 2007. (978-0-7322-8697-2(2)) HarperCollins Pubs. Australia.

Fagan, Cary. Danny, Who Fell in a Hole. 1 vol. 2013. (ENG., Illus.). 96p. (J). 14.95 (978-1-55498-311-7(8)) Groundwood Bks. CAN. Dist: Publishers Group West (PGW).

—Danny, Who Fell in a Hole. 2013. 84p. pap. (978-1-4596-6456-2(6)) ReadHowYouWant.com, Ltd.

Gates, Susan. Mole Who was Scared of the Dark. Breakespeare, Andrew, illus. 2005. (ENG.). 24p. (J). lib. bdg. 23.65 (978-1-59646-710-1(X)) Dingles & Co.

Grahame, Kenneth. The Wind in the Willows. Ingpen, Robert R., illus. 2012. (Union Square Kids Illustrated Classics Ser.). (ENG.). 224p. (J). (gr. 2-8). 24.99 (978-1-4027-8283-1(7)) Sterling Publishing Co., Inc.

—The Wind in the Willows. Iosa, Ann, illus. 2003. 32p. (J). (978-0-7607-3214-4(0)) Barnes & Noble, Inc.

Hahnl, John. Pocket & Toast, 1 vol. Hahnl, Olivia, illus. 2010. 40p. 24.95 (978-1-4489-8425-1(4)) PublishAmerica, Inc.

Haile, Matthew. Worms Is Fool. 2010. (Illus.). 88p. pap. 10.49 (978-1-4520-1956-7(8)) AuthorHouse.

Hart, Owen. I Can't Sleep! Pedler, Caroline, illus. 2017. (ENG.). 32p. (J). (gr. -1-2). 16.99 (978-1-68010-066-2(1)) Tiger Tales.

Hillenbrand, Jane. What a Treasure! Hillenbrand, Will, illus. 2018. (I Like to Read Ser.). (ENG.). 32p. (J). (gr. -1-3). 7.99 (978-0-8234-3987-4(9)) Holiday Hse., Inc.

Hillenbrand, Will. All for a Dime! A Bear & Mole Story. (Bear & Mole Ser.: 4). (ENG.). 32p. (J). (gr. -1-k). 2016. 7.99 (978-0-8234-3684-2(5)) 2015. (Illus.). 16.95 (978-0-8234-2946-2(6)) Holiday Hse., Inc.

—Kite Day: A Bear & Mole Story. (Bear & Mole Ser.: 2). (ENG., Illus.). 32p. (J). (-k). 2013. pap. 7.99 (978-0-8234-2758-1(7)) 2012. 17.99 (978-0-8234-1603-5(8)) Holiday Hse., Inc.

—Spring Is Here: A Bear & Mole Story. 2012. (Bear & Mole Ser.: 1). (ENG., Illus.). 32p. (J). (-k). pap. 7.99 (978-0-8234-2431-3(6)) Holiday Hse., Inc.

Holzwarth, Werner & Erlbruch, Wolf. The Story of the Little Mole Who Went in Search of Whodunit Mini Edition. 2007. (ENG., Illus.). 22p. (J). (gr. -1-17). 11.99 (978-0-8109-4457-2(X), Abrams Image) Abrams, Inc.

Honigsberg, Peter Jan. Armful of Memories. Morse, Tony, illus. 2004. 32p. 17.95 (978-1-57143-089-2(X)) RDR Bks.

—Pillow of Dreams. Morse, Tony, illus. 2004. 32p. (gr. k-4). 17.95 (978-1-57143-076-2(8)) RDR Bks.

Jenkins, Amanda. Why Mole Lives Underground: A Folktale from Peru. 2006. (J). pap. (978-1-4108-7160-2(6)) Benchmark Education Co.

Jonell, Lynne. Bravemole. 2004. (Illus.). (J). (gr. k-3). spiral bd. (978-0-616-14579-1(9)) Canadian National Institute for the Blind/Institut National Canadien pour les Aveugles.

Kim, Sang-Keun. Little Mole's Wish. 2019. (Illus.). 40p. (J). (gr. -1-2). 17.99 (978-0-525-58134-5(0), Schwartz & Wade Bks.) Random Hse. Children's Bks.

Maloney, Peter. A Bump on the Head. 2003. (Just Schoolin' Around Ser.). (Illus.). 32p. (J). pap. (978-0-439-39520-5(8)) Scholastic, Inc.

Niner, Holly L. No More Noisy Nights. 2017. (ENG., Illus.). (J). (gr. k-2). 7.99 (978-1-936261-96-3(0)) Flashlight Pr.

—No More Noisy Nights. Wolek, Guy, illus. 2017. (ENG.). 32p. (J). (gr. k-2). 17.95 (978-1-936261-93-2(6)) Flashlight Pr.

Owen, Chris. Hairy Mole the Pirate 1. 2007. (Hairy Mole the Pirate Ser.). (ENG., Illus.). 82p. pap. (978-1-84167-562-6(8)) Ransom Publishing Ltd.

Pearce, Philippa. The Little Gentleman. Pohrt, Tom, illus. 2004. 208p. (J). (gr. 3-18). lib. bdg. 16.89 (978-0-06-073161-8(3)) HarperCollins Pubs.

Pearce, Philippa & Pearl, Matthew. The Little Gentleman, 3 vols. unabr. ed. 2005. (J). 55.75 (978-1-4193-3601-0(0), 42047) Recorded Bks., Inc.

Pochocki, Ethel. The Mushroom Man, 1 vol. Moser, Barry, illus. 2006. (ENG.). 32p. (J). (gr. 2-6). reprint ed. 7.95 (978-0-88448-278-9(2), 884278) Tilbury Hse. Pubs.

Said Mouse to Mole. 2005. (J). per. 8.95 (978-1-59566-139-5(5)) QEB Publishing Inc.

Santillo, LuAnn. Mole. Santillo, LuAnn, ed. 2003. (Half-Pint Kids Readers Ser.). (Illus.). 7p. (J). (gr. -1-1). pap. (978-1-59256-111-7(X)) Half-Pint Kids, Inc.

—Rose. Santillo, LuAnn, ed. 2003. (Half-Pint Kids Readers Ser.). (Illus.). 7p. (J). (gr. -1-1). pap. 1.00 (978-1-59256-101-8(2)) Half-Pint Kids, Inc.

Sargent, Dave & Sargent, Pat. Molly's Journey: I'm Getting Older, 15 vols., Vol. 19. Huff, Jeane, illus. 2nd rev. ed. 2003. (Animal Pride Ser.: 19). 42p. (J). pap. 10.95 (978-1-56763-796-0(5)); lib. bdg. 20.95 (978-1-56763-795-3(7)) Ozark Publishing.

Schwartz, Roslyn. The Mole Sisters & the Way Home. 2003. (Mole Sisters Ser.). (ENG., Illus.). 32p. (J). (gr. -1-k). 14.95 (978-1-55037-821-4(X), 9781550378214) Annick Pr., Ltd. CAN. Dist: Publishers Group West (PGW).

Yaccarino, Dan. Morris Mole. Yaccarino, Dan, illus. 2017. (ENG., Illus.). 40p. (J). (gr. -1-3). 17.99 (978-0-06-241107-5(1), HarperCollins) HarperCollins Pubs.

Yee, Wong Herbert. Abracadabra! Magic with Mouse & Mole (Reader) 2010. (Mouse & Mole Story Ser.). (ENG., Illus.). 48p. (J). (gr. -1-3). pap. 4.99 (978-0-547-40621-3(5), 1428499, Clarion Bks.) HarperCollins Pubs.

—A Brand-New Day with Mouse & Mole. 2012. (Green Light Readers Level 3 Ser.). lib. bdg. 13.55 (978-0-606-24437-4(9)) Turtleback.

—A Brand-New Day with Mouse & Mole (Reader) 2012. (Mouse & Mole Story Ser.). (ENG., Illus.). 48p. (J). (gr. 1-4). pap. 4.99 (978-0-547-72209-2(5), 1482465, Clarion Bks.) HarperCollins Pubs.

—Mouse & Mole: a Perfect Halloween. Yee, Wong Herbert, illus. 2011. (Mouse & Mole Story Ser.). (ENG., Illus.). 48p. (J). (gr. 1-4). 14.99 (978-0-547-55152-4(5), 1450576, Clarion Bks.) HarperCollins Pubs.

—Mouse & Mole, a Winter Wonderland: A Winter & Holiday Book for Kids. Yee, Wong Herbert, illus. 2011. (Mouse & Mole Story Ser.). (ENG., Illus.). 48p. (J). (gr. 1-4). pap. 4.99 (978-0-547-57697-8(8), 1458451, Clarion Bks.) HarperCollins Pubs.

—Mouse & Mole: Fine Feathered Friends. Yee, Wong Herbert, illus. 2011. (Mouse & Mole Story Ser.). (ENG., Illus.). 48p. (J). (gr. 1-4). pap. 4.99 (978-0-547-51977-7(X), 1445276, Clarion Bks.) HarperCollins Pubs.

—Mouse & Mole: Secret Valentine. Yee, Wong Herbert, illus. (Mouse & Mole Story Ser.). (ENG., Illus.). 48p. (J). 2017. (gr. -1-3). 12.99 (978-1-328-97533-1(9), 1708707) 2017. (gr. -1-3). pap. 4.99 (978-1-328-74059-5(5), 1677035) 2013. (gr. 1-4). 15.99 (978-0-547-88719-7(1), 1507662) HarperCollins Pubs. (Clarion Bks.).

—Upstairs Mouse, Downstairs Mole (Reader) 12th ed. 2007. (Mouse & Mole Story Ser.). (ENG., Illus.). 48p. (J). (gr. -1-3). 4.99 (978-0-618-91586-6(9), 1014891, Clarion Bks.) HarperCollins Pubs.

MOLLUSKS

see also Shells

Berger, Melvin & Berger, Gilda. Shellfish. 2013. (Illus.). 16p. (J). pap. (978-0-545-35172-0(3)) Scholastic, Inc.

Bishop, Celeste. Slimy Slugs, 1 vol. 2015. (Icky Animals! Small & Gross Ser.). (ENG., Illus.). 24p. (J). (gr. 1-1). pap. 9.25 (978-1-4994-0713-6(0), 7c3d8586-fb50-42ff-b99b-ac3c3ffbd9ab, PowerKids Pr.) Rosen Publishing Group, Inc., The.

Bodden, Valerie. Slugs. 2013. (Creepy Creatures Ser.). (ENG., Illus.). 24p. (J). (gr. 1-4). pap. 8.99 (978-0-89812-796-6(3), 21741, Creative Paperbacks); 25.65 (978-1-60818-233-6(9), 21740, Creative Education) Creative Co., The.

Boothroyd, Jennifer. Shells. 2011. (First Step Nonfiction — Body Coverings Ser.). (gr. k-2). (ENG., Illus.). 24p. (J). pap. 6.99 (978-0-7613-7830-3(8), cd062e6f-906d-457c-8a42-d66b6571ce41); pap. 33.92 (978-0-7613-8610-0(6)); (ENG., Illus.). 24p. lib. bdg. 23.93 (978-0-7613-5788-9(2)) Lerner Publishing Group.

Borgert-Spaniol, Megan. Slugs. 2016. (Creepy Crawlies Ser.). (ENG., Illus.). 24p. (J). (gr. k-3). lib. bdg. 26.95 (978-1-62617-301-9(X), Blastoff! Readers) Bellwether Media.

Cerullo, Mary. Giant Squid: Searching for a Sea Monster, 1 vol. 2012. (Smithsonian Ser.). (ENG., Illus.). 48p. (J). (gr. 2-6). pap. 8.95 (978-1-4296-8023-3(7), 118355, Capstone Pr.) Capstone.

Cerullo, Mary M. Giant Squid: Searching for a Sea Monster. 2012. (Smithsonian Ser.). (ENG.). 48p. (gr. 4-5). pap. 53.70 (978-1-4296-8523-8(9)) Capstone.

—Giant Squid: Searching for a Sea Monster, 1 vol. Roper, Clyde F. E., photos by. 2012. (Smithsonian Ser.). (ENG., Illus.). 48p. (J). (gr. 2-6). lib. bdg. 29.99 (978-1-4296-7541-3(1), 117118, Capstone Pr.) Capstone.

Drimmer, Stephanie Warren. National Geographic Readers: Ink! (L3) 100 Fun Facts about Octopuses, Squid, & More. 2019. (Readers Ser.). (Illus.). 48p. (J). (gr. 3-7). pap. 4.99 (978-1-4263-3501-3(6)); (ENG., lib. bdg. 14.90 (978-1-4263-3502-0(4)) Disney Publishing Worldwide. (National Geographic Kids).

Emminizer, Theresa. What If Sea Urchins Disappeared? 2019. (Life Without Animals Ser.). (ENG.). 24p. (gr. 1-2). 48.90 (978-1-5382-3827-1(6)) Stevens, Gareth Publishing LLLP.

Gravel, Elise. The Slug: The Disgusting Critters Series. (Disgusting Critters Ser.). (ENG., Illus.). 32p. (J). (gr. 1-4). 2016. pap. 5.99 (978-1-77049-656-9(4)) 2014. 10.99 (978-1-77049-655-2(6)) Tundra Bks. CAN. (Tundra Bks.). Dist: Penguin Random Hse. LLC.

Gray, Susan H. Nudibranch. 2014. (21st Century Skills Library: Exploring Our Oceans Ser.). (ENG., Illus.). 32p. (J). (gr. 3-6). 32.07 (978-1-63188-021-6(7), 205491) Cherry Lake Publishing.

Gross, Miriam J. The Sea Slug: Nudibranchs. 2009. (Weird Sea Creatures Ser.). 24p. (gr. 3-3). 42.50 (978-1-60854-757-9(4), PowerKids Pr.) Rosen Publishing Group, Inc., The.

Himmelman, John. Basic Illustrated Guide to Frogs, Snakes, Bugs, & Slugs. 2013. (Basic Illustrated Ser.). (ENG., Illus.). 104p. (J). (gr. k-5). pap. 12.95 (978-0-7627-8259-8(5), Falcon Guides) Globe Pequot Pr., The.

Hopkins, Therese. Shells, 1 vol. 2009. (Home Sweet Home Ser.). (ENG.). 24p. (J). (gr. 1-1). pap. 9.25 (978-1-4358-3070-7(9), d48a888e-e899-4e59-a000-ae6dfeb58a45, PowerKids Pr.); lib. bdg. 26.27 (978-1-4358-2696-0(5), 0959ecd2-3b2f-4bd3-9c65-662b936778fc) Rosen Publishing Group, Inc., The.

Jones, Tammy. At the Shore. 2009. (Sight Word Readers Set A Ser.). (J). 3.49 net. (978-1-60719-137-7(7)) Newmark Learning LLC.

Kelly, Joni. 500-Year-Old Clams!, 1 vol. 2018. (World's Longest-Living Animals Ser.). (ENG.). 24p. (gr. 1-2). 24.27 (978-1-5382-1682-8(5), f9d03e7d-657d-4aa5-af6e-3bda1f542de2) Stevens, Gareth Publishing LLLP.

Lake, Kirsten. Clams in the Sand, 1 vol. 2017. (Critters by the Sea Ser.). (ENG.). 24p. (J). (gr. 3-3). pap. 9.25 (978-1-5081-6297-1(2), 9d97d8f3-eedd-4f88-9b6c-2779f9e977e1, PowerKids Pr.) Rosen Publishing Group, Inc., The.

LaPlante, Walter. I'm Allergic to Shellfish, 1 vol. 2018. (I'm Allergic Ser.). (ENG.). 24p. (gr. 1-2). 24.27 (978-1-5382-2906-4(4), c09a63f5-4625-4dc1-9c03-9696de4a00f1) Stevens, Gareth Publishing LLLP.

Lunis, Natalie. Slimy Sea Slugs. 2016. (No Backbone! Marine Invertebrates Ser.). (ENG.). 24p. (J). (gr. k-3). pap. 7.99 (978-1-944998-78-3(0)) Bearport Publishing Co., Inc.

McNeil, Niki, et al. HOCPP 1103 Mollusks. 2006. spiral bd. 19.00 (978-1-60308-103-0(8)) In the Hands of a Child.

Metz, Lorijo. Discovering Clams, 1 vol. 2011. (Along the Shore Ser.). (ENG., Illus.). 24p. (J). (gr. 2-3). lib. bdg. 26.27 (978-1-4488-4994-9(2), 93b8e26e-6980-4610-be14-840ac52bda41) Rosen Publishing Group, Inc., The.

Morgan, Emily. Next Time You See a Seashell. 2012. (Next Time You See Ser.). (ENG., Illus.). 32p. (J). (gr. -1-k). pap. 13.99 (978-1-936959-15-0(1), P218554) National Science Teachers Assn.

Newman, Mark. Sooper Yooper: Environmental Defender. Heckman, Mark, illus. 2010. 48p. (J). 17.95 (978-1-933272-26-9(0)) Thunder Bay Pr.

Prezant, Fran Pollock & Marshak, Laura E. Dr. Vermeij's Conch Quest. 2010. (ENG.). 34p. pap. 15.99 (978-1-4490-9199-6(7)) AuthorHouse.

Rajczak, Michael. Attack of the Zebra Mussels, 1 vol. 2016. (Animal Invaders: Destroying Native Habitats Ser.). (ENG., Illus.). 24p. (J). (gr. 2-3). pap. 9.15 (978-1-4824-5683-7(4), 71d7c15d-32b2-4f3e-96d8-20d09dcfc2f9) Stevens, Gareth Publishing LLLP.

Ralph Lewis, Brenda. Crabs & Mollusks, 1 vol. 2005. (Nature's Monsters: Water Creatures Ser.). (ENG., Illus.). 32p. (J). (gr. 3-5). lib. bdg. 28.67 (978-0-8368-6176-1(0), 64baf8ac-c210-453a-93db-f4a04106a377, Gareth Stevens Learning Library) Stevens, Gareth Publishing LLLP.

Rice, Dona Herweck. Color-Changing Cephalopods. rev. ed. 2018. (Smithsonian: Informational Text Ser.). (ENG., Illus.). 32p. (J). (gr. 4-8). pap. 11.99 (978-1-4938-6714-1(8)) Teacher Created Materials, Inc.

Richardson, Joy. Mollusks, 1 vol. 2004. (Variety of Life Ser.). (ENG., Illus.). 32p. (gr. 2-4). lib. bdg. 28.67 (978-0-8368-4507-5(2), 5502fe2e-8c4a-4f84-87a2-159e35923e21, Gareth Stevens Learning Library) Stevens, Gareth Publishing LLLP.

Robb, Jackie & Stringle, Berny. The Story of Slug. Duncan, Karen & Stringle, Sam, illus. 2004. (Bang on the Door Ser.). 32p. (YA). pap. (978-1-85602-317-7(6), Pavilion Children's Books) Pavilion Bks.

Rockwood, Leigh. Slugs Are Gross!, 1 vol. 2010. (Creepy Crawlies Ser.). (ENG., Illus.). 24p. (gr. 2-3). (J). pap. 9.25 (978-1-4488-1369-8(7), 6d2eebf5-c075-4898-8ad1-236a99b8005d, PowerKids Pr.); (YA). 26.27 (978-1-4488-0704-8(2), b7c85d2e-72f2-4dd3-bfd0-e867bd8a244f) Rosen Publishing Group, Inc., The.

Smalley, Carol. A Project Guide to Sponges, Worms, & Mollusks. 2010. (Life Science Projects for Kids Ser.). (Illus.). 48p. (J). (gr. 4-8). lib. bdg. 29.95 (978-1-58415-876-9(X)) Mitchell Lane Pubs.

Stewart, Melissa. Seashells: More Than a Home. Brannen, Sarah S., illus. 2019. 32p. (J). (gr. 1-4). lib. bdg. 16.99 (978-1-58089-810-2(6)) Charlesbridge Publishing, Inc.

Strain Trueit, Trudi. Slugs, Snails, & Worms, 1 vol. 2013. (Backyard Safari Ser.). (ENG.). 32p. (gr. 3-3). 31.21 (978-1-60870-247-3(2), 8efd9e6f-7a42-4131-8c18-b405c5b18cd2); pap. 11.58 (978-1-62712-030-2(0), 19a27dfb-191e-4634-a652-c7279b71561f) Cavendish Square Publishing LLC.

Swan Miller, Sara. Secret Lives of Seashell Dwellers, 1 vol. 2011. (Secret Lives Ser.). (ENG.). 48p. (gr. 4-4). 32.64 (978-0-7614-4228-8(6), e12159c2-1087-4da5-b773-958c6d3f0cfc) Cavendish Square Publishing LLC.

White, Nancy. Creeping Land Snails. 2009. (No Backbone! Ser.). (Illus.). 24p. (J). (gr. k-3). lib. bdg. 26.99 (978-1-59716-753-6(3)) Bearport Publishing Co., Inc.

World Book, Inc. Staff, contrib. by. Mollusks & Similar Sea Creatures. 2009. (J). (978-0-7166-0407-5(8)) World Bk., Inc.

Zoehfeld, Kathleen Weidner. What Lives in a Shell? Davie, Helen K., illus. 2015. (Let's-Read-And-Find-Out Science 1 Ser.). (ENG.). 32p. (J). (gr. -1-3). pap. 6.99 (978-0-06-238196-5(2), HarperCollins) HarperCollins Pubs.

MONACO

Hintz, Martin. Monaco. 2004. (Enchantment of the World Ser.). (ENG., Illus.). 144p. (YA). (gr. 5-9). 39.00 (978-0-516-24251-4(2)) Scholastic Library Publishing.

King, David C. Monaco, 1 vol. 2008. (Cultures of the World (First Edition)(r) Ser.). (ENG.). 144p. (gr. 5-5). lib. bdg. 49.79 (978-0-7614-2567-0(5), 14787a5a-9235-454c-8bf1-255e113c3208) Cavendish Square Publishing LLC.

MONARCHS

see Kings, Queens, Rulers, etc.

MONASTERIES

see also Monasticism and Religious Orders

Anderson, Dale. Monks & Monasteries in the Middle Ages, 1 vol. 2005. (World Almanac(r) Library of the Middle Ages Ser.). (ENG.). 48p. (gr. 5-8). pap. 15.05 (978-0-8368-5906-5(5), 74889f0e-51d0-4ad9-877d-6c4856e75baa); (Illus.). lib. bdg. 33.67 (978-0-8368-5897-6(2), f6ae3e3c-d3d7-4c9d-b680-b99932de766a) Stevens, Gareth Publishing LLLP. (Gareth Stevens Secondary Library).

Jovinelly, Joann. The Crafts & Culture of a Medieval Monastery. 2009. (Crafts & Cultures of the Middle Ages Ser.). 48p. (gr. 5-5). 58.50 (978-1-61512-056-7(4), Rosen Reference) Rosen Publishing Group, Inc., The.

Jovinelly, Joann & Netelkos, Jason. The Crafts & Culture of a Medieval Monastery, 1 vol. 2006. (Crafts & Cultures of the Middle Ages Ser.). (ENG., Illus.). 48p. (J). (gr. 5-5). lib. bdg. 34.47 (978-1-4042-0759-2(7), 5ab52817-2f62-4042-af01-c1eed52fd7e6) Rosen Publishing Group, Inc., The.

MONASTIC ORDERS

see Monasticism and Religious Orders

MONASTICISM AND RELIGIOUS ORDERS

see also Monasteries

Anderson, Dale. Monks & Monasteries in the Middle Ages, 1 vol. 2005. (World Almanac(r) Library of the Middle Ages Ser.). (ENG.). 48p. (gr. 5-8). pap. 15.05 (978-0-8368-5906-5(5), 74889f0e-51d0-4ad9-877d-6c4856e75baa); (Illus.). lib. bdg. 33.67 (978-0-8368-5897-6(2), f6ae3e3c-d3d7-4c9d-b680-b99932de766a) Stevens, Gareth Publishing LLLP. (Gareth Stevens Secondary Library).

Crompton, Samuel Willard. Thomas Merton. 2004. (Spiritual Leaders & Thinkers Ser.). (ENG., Illus.). 120p. (gr. 9-13). 30.00 (978-0-7910-7862-4(0), P114030, Facts On File) Infobase Holdings, Inc.

Ficocelli, Elizabeth. Where Do Priests Come From? Wirrenga, Shannon, illus. 2010. (J). pap. 7.99 (978-0-9844864-0-3(2)) Bezalel Bks.

Grube, Edward C. Martin Luther. White, Deborah J., illus. 2012. (Hero of Faith Ser.). (ENG.). 58p. (J). pap. 7.99 (978-0-7586-3075-9(1)) Concordia Publishing Hse.

Jain, Manoj. Mahavira: The Hero of Nonviolence. Demi, illus. 2014. 28p. (J). (gr. k-4). 17.95 (978-1-937786-21-2(8), Wisdom Tales) World Wisdom, Inc.

Lee, Puck Hee. The Wizard Monk of Kamayut & Six Other True Stories. 2005. 48p. per. 10.00 (978-1-4134-8216-4(3)) Xlibris Corp.

Rau, Dana Meachen & Who HQ. Who Is the Dalai Lama? Putra, Dede, illus. 2018. (Who Was? Ser.). 112p. (J). (gr. 3-7). 5.99 (978-1-101-99554-9(8), Penguin Workshop) Penguin Young Readers Group.

Rivera, Sheila. The Dalai Lama: A Life of Compassion. 2007. (Pull Ahead Books — Biographies Ser.). (ENG., Illus.). 32p. (J). (gr. k-3). pap. 7.99 (978-0-8225-6435-5(1), 7e1c0035-ea92-4ce4-b4a8-9d104ed7c420) Lerner Publishing Group.

Young, Patricia A. The Holy Monks of Mt. Athos. Young, Patricia A., illus. l.t. ed. 2005. (Illus.). 28p. (J). 10.00 (978-0-913026-49-6(2)); 20.00 (978-0-913026-24-3(7)) St. Nectarios Pr.

MONASTICISM AND RELIGIOUS ORDERS—FICTION

Bogart, Jo Ellen. The White Cat & the Monk: A Retelling of the Poem Pangur Bán, 1 vol. Smith, Sydney, illus. 2016. (ENG.). 36p. (J). (gr. -1-3). 18.95 (978-1-55498-780-1(6)) Groundwood Bks. CAN. Dist: Publishers Group West (PGW).

Costanza, Stephen, illus. Smudge & the Book of Mistakes: A Christmas Story. 2012. (ENG.). 48p. (J). (gr. 1-4). 17.95 (978-1-58536-483-1(5), 202314) Sleeping Bear Pr.

DiCamillo, Kate. The Beatryce Prophecy. Blackall, Sophie, illus. (ENG.). 256p. (J). (gr. 3-7). 2023. pap. 14.99 (978-1-5362-2645-4(9)) 2021. 19.99 (978-1-5362-1361-4(6)) Candlewick Pr.

—The Beatryce Prophecy: Gift Edition. Blackall, Sophie, illus. gif. ed. 2021. (ENG.). 256p. (J). (gr. 3-7). 50.00 (978-1-5362-1867-1(7)) Candlewick Pr.

Leslie, Emma. The Martyr's Victory: A Story of Danish England. Stacey, W., illus. 2007. 300p. 24.95 (978-1-934671-08-5(8)); per. 14.95 (978-1-934671-09-2(6)) Salem Ridge Press LLC.

Maguire, Gregory. Egg & Spoon. 2014. (ENG., Illus.). 496p. (YA). (gr. 7). 17.99 (978-0-7636-7220-1(3)) Candlewick Pr.

Millen, C. M. The Ink Garden of Brother Theophane. Wisnewski, Andrea, illus. 2010. (ENG.). 32p. (J). (gr. k-3). 18.99 (978-1-58089-179-0(9)) Charlesbridge Publishing, Inc.

Nelson, Marilyn. Snook Alone. Ering, Timothy Basil, illus. 2010. (ENG.). 48p. (J). (gr. -1-3). 16.99 (978-0-7636-2667-9(8)) Candlewick Pr.

Novel Units. The Canterbury Tales Novel Units Teacher Guide. 2019. (ENG.). (YA). pap. 12.99 *(978-1-56137-919-4(0)*, Novel Units, Inc.) Classroom Library Co.

Padma, T. V. The Cleverest Thief. 2008. (Story Cove Ser.). (ENG., Illus.). 32p. (J). (gr. -1-3). pap. 4.95 *(978-0-87483-882-4(7))* August Hse. Pubs., Inc.

Smucker, Anna Egan. Brother Giovanni's Little Reward: How the Pretzel Was Born. Hall, Amanda, illus. 2015. (ENG.). 34p. (J). 17.00 *(978-0-8028-5420-9(6)*, Eerdmans Bks For Young Readers) Eerdmans, William B. Publishing Co.

Smyth, Bethinna & Winkelmann, Rachele. The Sleepy Monk. 2012. 34p. pap. 16.95 *(978-1-105-43625-3(X))* Lulu.com GBR. Dist: Lulu Pr., Inc.

MONET, CLAUDE, 1840-1926

Björk, Christina. Linnea in Monet's Garden. Sandin, Joan, tr. Anderson, Lena, illus. 2012. 48p. (J). (gr. k-3). 16.99 *(978-1-4022-7729-0(6))* Sourcebooks, Inc.

Bober, Suzanne & Merberg, Julie. A Picnic with Monet. 2003. (Mini Masters Ser.: 3). (ENG., Illus.). 22p. (J). (gr. -1-7). bds. 7.99 *(978-0-8118-4046-0(8))* Chronicle Bks. LLC.

Carvalho de Magalhaes, Roberto. Claude Monet. 2005. (Great Artists Ser.). (Illus.). 40p. (J). (gr. 5). per. 7.95 *(978-1-59270-050-9(0))* Enchanted Lion Bks., LLC.

Connolly, Sean. Claude Monet. 1 vol. 2004. (Lives of the Artists Ser.). (ENG., Illus.). 48p. (gr. 5-8). pap. 15.05 *(978-0-8368-5655-2(4)*, 4a0a3de8-c2f3-4847-ad47-7b72fc925ec7, Gareth Stevens Secondary Library) Stevens, Gareth Publishing LLLP.

Danneberg, Julie. Monet Paints a Day. Heimerl, Caitlin, illus. 2012. 32p. (J). (gr. 1-4). 16.99 *(978-1-58089-240-7(X))* Charlesbridge Publishing, Inc.

Danneberg, Julie & Monet, Claude. Monet Paints a Day. Heimerl, Caitlin, illus. 2012. (J). pap. 15.95 *(978-1-58089-241-4(8))* Charlesbridge Publishing, Inc.

Girel, Stephane, illus. Where Is the Frog? A Children's Book Inspired by Claude Monet. 2013. (Children's Books Inspired by Famous Artworks Ser.). (ENG.). 32p. (J). (gr. -1-3). 14.95 *(978-3-7913-7139-9(8))* Prestel Verlag GmbH & Co KG. DEU. Dist: Penguin Random Hse. LLC.

Kallen, Stuart A. Claude Monet. 1 vol. 2008. (Eye on Art Ser.). (ENG., Illus.). 112p. (gr. 7-7). lib. bdg. 41.03 *(978-1-4205-0074-5(0)*, 903ee674-0b0f-4a3d-b42d-5b994a5d0a9a, Lucent Pr.) Greenhaven Publishing LLC.

Kutschbach, Doris. Coloring Book Monet. 2006. (Coloring Bks.). (ENG., Illus.). 32p. (J). (gr. 1-4). 8.95 *(978-3-7913-3713-5(0))* Prestel Verlag GmbH & Co KG. DEU. Dist: Penguin Random Hse. LLC.

Lomberg, Michelle. Claude Monet. 2016. (Illus.). 32p. (J). *(978-1-4896-4619-4(1))* Weigl Pubs., Inc.

Nichols, Catherine. Claude Monet. (Primary Source Library of Famous Artists Ser.). 32p. (gr. 3-4). 2009. 42.50 *(978-1-60854-100-3(2))* 2005. (ENG., Illus.). (J). lib. bdg. 27.60 *(978-1-4042-2761-3(X)*, d98df970-1792-480c-87b1-27f64d46cc85) Rosen Publishing Group, Inc., The. (PowerKids Pr.).

Pappworth, Sara. The Life & Art of Claude Monet. 1 vol. Ryn, Aude van, illus. 2016. (Lives of Great Artists Ser.). (ENG.). 80p. (J). (gr. 8-8). 37.47 *(978-1-4994-6584-6(X)*, cc5ec9d4-f3a0-4790-b94e-7dc3291d80d2) Rosen Publishing Group, Inc., The.

Rodriguez, Susan & Monet, Claude. Travels with Monet: Travel in the Artist's Footsteps. 2010. (ENG.). 32p. (J). 15.95 *(978-1-56290-664-1(X))* Crystal Productions.

Sánchez, Consuelo. Claudet Monet. 2005. (SPA.). 132p. (YA). *(978-958-30-1869-5(4))* Panamericana Editorial.

Sherrow, Victoria & Buonarroti, Michelangelo. Claude Monet. 1 vol. 2005. (Great Artists Ser.). (ENG., Illus.). 40p. (gr. 4-6). 28.36 *(978-1-59270-009-7(8)*, 55f6e21e-a7fe-4df8-8e36-df4da5d8aecc) Cavendish Square Publishing LLC.

Spence, David. The Impressionists: Monet, Cezanne, Renoir, Degas. 2010. (ENG.). 128p. (J). (gr. 4-7). pap. 12.95 *(978-1-84696-217-2(X)*, TickTock Books) Octopus Publishing Group GBR. Dist: Independent Pubs. Group.

Venezia, Mike. Claude Monet. Venezia, Mike, illus. rev. ed. 2014. (Getting to Know the World's Greatest Artists Ser.). (ENG., Illus.). 40p. (J). lib. bdg. 29.00 *(978-0-531-21979-9(8))* Scholastic Library Publishing.

—Claude Monet (Revised Edition) (Getting to Know the World's Greatest Artists) Venezia, Mike, illus. 2014. (Getting to Know the World's Greatest Artists Ser.). (ENG., Illus.). 40p. (J). (gr. 3-4). pap. 7.95 *(978-0-531-22540-0(2)*, Children's Pr.) Scholastic Library Publishing.

Waldron, Ann. Who Was Claude Monet? 2009. (Who Was...? Ser.). lib. bdg. 16.00 *(978-0-606-04028-0(5))* Turtleback.

Waldron, Ann & Who HQ. Who Was Claude Monet? Marchesi, Stephen, illus. 2009. (Who Was? Ser.). 112p. (J). (gr. 3-7). pap. 5.99 *(978-0-448-44985-2(4)*, Penguin Workshop) Penguin Young Readers Group.

Whiting, Jim. Claude Monet. 2007. (Art Profiles for Kids Ser.). (Illus.). 48p. (YA). (gr. 4-7). lib. bdg. 29.95 *(978-1-58415-563-8(9))* Mitchell Lane Pubs.

Wood, Alix. Claude Monet. 1 vol. 2013. (Artists Through the Ages Ser.). (ENG., Illus.). 32p. (J). (gr. 2-3). pap. 11.00 *(978-1-61533-627-2(3)*, c668e58e-49ae-4910-8c6d-9f3d705b571d); lib. bdg. 29.93 *(978-1-61533-620-3(6)*, 0181c944-67ee-4fed-be4a-4e6e2f2a3d75) Rosen Publishing Group, Inc., The. (Windmill Bks.).

MONET, CLAUDE, 1840-1926—FICTION

Anholt, Laurence. The Magical Garden of Claude Monet. 2007. (Anholt's Artists Books for Children Ser.). (ENG., Illus.). 32p. (J). (gr. k-3). pap. 9.99 *(978-0-7641-3855-3(3))* Sourcebooks, Inc.

Mayhew, James & McQuillan, Mary. Katie & the Waterlily Pond. 2015. (Katie Ser.). (ENG., Illus.). 32p. (J). (gr. -1-k). pap. 10.99 *(978-1-4083-3245-0(0))* Hodder & Stoughton GBR. Dist: Hachette Bk. Group.

MONETARY QUESTION

see Money

MONEY

see also Banks and Banking; Coins; Credit; Gold; Mints; Paper Money

ABDO Publishing Company Staff & Doudna, Kelly. Dollars & Cents, Set. 2003. (Dollars & Cents Set 3 Ser.: 4). (ENG.). 24p. (J). (gr. k-3). lib. bdg. 96.84 *(978-1-57765-910-5(4)*, SandCastle) ABDO Publishing Co.

ABDO Publishing Company Staff & Molter, Carey. Dollars & Cents, Set. 2003. (Dollars & Cents Set 2 Ser.: 6). (ENG.). 24p. (J). (gr. k-3). lib. bdg. 145.26 *(978-1-57765-909-9(0)*, SandCastle) ABDO Publishing Co.

—Dollars & Cents Set 1, 1 vol. 2003. (Dollars & Cents Set 1 Ser.: 6). (ENG.). 24p. (J). (gr. k-3). lib. bdg. 145.26 *(978-1-57765-883-2(3)*, SandCastle) ABDO Publishing Co.

Adler, David A. Money Madness. Miller, Edward, illus. 2009. (ENG.). 32p. (J). (gr. -1-3). pap. 7.99 *(978-0-8234-2272-2(0))* Holiday Hse., Inc.

—Money Math: Addition & Subtraction. Miller, Edward, illus. 32p. (J). (gr. 1-4). 2019. pap. 7.99 *(978-0-8234-4182-2(2))* 2017. (ENG.). 17.95 *(978-0-8234-3698-9(5))* Holiday Hse., Inc.

—Prices! Prices! Prices! Why They Go up & Down. Miller, Edward, illus. 2016. (ENG.). 32p. (J). (gr. 1-4). 7.99 *(978-0-8234-3574-6(1))* Holiday Hse., Inc.

Alaina, Maria. Counting Money. 1 vol. 2011. (Wonder Readers Early Level Ser.). (ENG.). 16p. (gr. -1-1). (J). pap. 6.25 *(978-1-4296-7801-8(1)*, 117973); pap. 35.94 *(978-1-4296-8081-3(4))* Capstone. (Capstone Pr.).

Anderson, Jill. Money Math with Sebastian Pig & Friends at the Farmer's Market. 1 vol. 2009. (Math Fun with Sebastian Pig & Friends! Ser.). (ENG., Illus.). 32p. (gr. k-2). pap. 10.35 *(978-0-7660-5983-2(9)*, 139ccee4-053f-41d8-b2cb-6bd6bc39da94, Enslow Elementary); lib. bdg. 26.60 *(978-0-7660-3364-1(3)*, 0b2c8faa-5588-42c0-bccb-d32342709368) Enslow Publishing, LLC.

Ayers, Amy. USAMOS DINERO en el Puesto de Limonada (USING MONEY at the Lemonade Stand). 1 vol. 2007. (Las Matemáticas en Nuestro Mundo - Nivel 1 (Math in Our World - Level 1) Ser.). (SPA.). 24p. (gr. 1-1). pap. 9.15 *(978-0-8368-8499-9(X)*, e6a34462-4c36-429f-ac58-c9c97dd0ab3c); (Illus.). lib. bdg. 24.67 *(978-0-8368-8490-6(6)*, f6a87e3c-8614-4163-b692-901b020e725b) Stevens, Gareth Publishing LLLP. (Weekly Reader Leveled Readers).

—USING MONEY at the Lemonade Stand. 1 vol. 2007. (Math in Our World - Level 1 Ser.). (ENG.). 24p. (gr. 1-1). pap. 9.15 *(978-0-8368-8481-4(7)*, 4386a2d0-345f-43ea-aff4-b665ea56e8b7); (Illus.). lib. bdg. 24.67 *(978-0-8368-8472-2(8)*, 6f742241-06fa-4018-8f8b-da23ce255790) Stevens, Gareth Publishing LLLP. (Weekly Reader Leveled Readers).

Bailey, Diane. Top 10 Secrets for Creating & Sticking to a Budget Successfully. 2013. (Student's Guide to Financial Empowerment Ser.). (Illus.). 64p. (YA). (gr. 7-12). pap. 77.70 *(978-1-4488-9370-6(4))*; (ENG.). 37.12 *(978-1-4488-9360-7(7)*, 605b3666-fa7c-49b8-ab5b-a6919466f6f93); (ENG., pap. 13.95 *(978-1-4488-9369-0(0)*, 49a7afa2-92d6-4507-b560-1b0e3340a7ac) Rosen Publishing Group, Inc., The.

Bailey, Gerry. World Money. Beech, Mark, illus. 2015. (How Money Works). (ENG.). 64p. (J). (gr. 4-6). pap. 15.93 *(978-1-68404-071-1(X))* Norwood Hse. Pr.

—Your Money. Beech, Mark, illus. 2015. (How Money Works). (ENG.). 64p. (J). (gr. 4-6). pap. 15.93 *(978-1-68404-072-8(8))* Norwood Hse. Pr.

Bailey, Gerry & Law, Felicia. World Money. Beech, Mark, illus. 2015. (How Money Works). (ENG.). 64p. (J). (gr. 4-6). lib. bdg. 29.27 *(978-1-59953-720-7(6))* Norwood Hse. Pr.

—Your Money. Beech, Mark, illus. 2015. (How Money Works). (ENG.). 64p. (J). (gr. 4-6). lib. bdg. 29.27 *(978-1-59953-718-4(4))* Norwood Hse. Pr.

Bateman, Katherine R. The Young Investor: Projects & Activities for Making Your Money Grow. 2nd ed. 2010. (ENG., Illus.). 144p. (J). (gr. 4). pap. 14.95 *(978-1-56976-546-3(4))* Chicago Review Pr., Inc.

Benchmark Education Company, LLC Staff, compiled by. Money: Theme Set. 2006. (J). 105.00 *(978-1-4108-7077-3(4))* Benchmark Education Co.

Berger, Melvin. Round & Round the Money Goes. (Discovery Readers Ser.). (ENG.). 48p. (J). pap. 3.95 *(978-0-8249-5310-2(X)*, Ideals Pubns.) Worthy Publishing.

Berne, Stanley. Legal Tender - Or - It's All About Money! 2003. 160p. (YA). pap. 40.00 *(978-0-913844-27-4(6))* Rising Tide Pr.

Berry, Rob & Duey, Kathleen. The Smart Kids Allowance System: Step-by-Step Money Management Guidebook. Bartholomew, illus. Date not set. (Family Skill Builders Ser.). (J). (gr. k-6). pap. 9.95 *(978-1-883761-34-9(4))* Family Life Productions.

Bolon, Janine. Cash, Cars & College. 2006. (ENG.). 102p. pap. 22.75 *(978-0-615-13730-8(X))* SmartCents, Inc.

Boritzer, Etan. What Is Money? West, Jennifer, illus. 2006. 40p. (J). pap. 6.95 *(978-0-9762743-3-9(7))* Lane, Veronica Bks.

—What Is Money? 2006. (What Is? Ser.). (Illus.). 40p. (J). 14.95 *(978-0-9762743-2-2(9))* Lane, Veronica Bks.

Brighter Child, compiled by. Time & Money. 2006. (ENG., Illus.). 54p. (gr. k-3). 2.99 *(978-0-7696-6480-4(6)*, 0769664806, Brighter Child) Carson-Dellosa Publishing, LLC.

Brindell Fradin, Dennis & Bloom Fradin, Judith. Spending. 1 vol. 2011. (Money Smart Ser.). (ENG.). 64p. (gr. 5-5). 35.50 *(978-1-60870-126-1(3)*, c4a5d335-b433-4950-8bee-30053534f0fb) Cavendish Square Publishing LLC.

Bullard, Lisa. Kyle Keeps Track of Cash. Byrne, Mike, illus. 2013. (Cloverleaf Books (tm) — Money Basics Ser.). (ENG.). 24p. (J). (gr. k-2). pap. 8.99 *(978-1-4677-1510-2(7)*, 19d12429-1526-4f57-aeb7-3594888b65f3, Millbrook Pr.) Lerner Publishing Group.

Burstein, John. Dollars & Sense: Developing Good Money Habits. 2010. (ENG., Illus.). 32p. (J). pap. *(978-0-7787-4810-6(3))*; lib. bdg. *(978-0-7787-4794-9(8))* Crabtree Publishing Co.

Burton, Margie, et al. Our Money. 2011. (Early Connections Ser.). (J). *(978-1-61672-502-0(8))* Benchmark Education Co.

—Sorting My Money. 2011. (Early Connections Ser.). (J). *(978-1-61672-538-9(9))* Benchmark Education Co.

—Sorting My Money & Clasificar mi Dinero: 6 English, 6 Spanish Adaptations. 2011. (J). spiral bd. 75.00 net. *(978-1-4108-5630-2(5))* Benchmark Education Co.

Byrd, Josiah. Makayla's Birthday Money! Work with Money. 1 vol. 2014. (Math Masters: Measurement & Data Ser.). (ENG.). 24p. (J). (gr. 2-2). 25.27 *(978-1-4777-6407-7(0)*, 75fd9611-f80b-4aff-a1c3-1f0315c739db); pap. 8.25 *(978-1-4777-4822-0(9)*, 9489dfb3-2f67-4cf0-87cd-b4a8500eb9ab) Rosen Publishing Group, Inc., The. (Rosen Classroom).

Cartogna, Eileen. Fun at the Fair: Learning Subtraction Facts To 10. 1 vol. 2010. (Math for the REAL World Ser.). (ENG.). 12p. (gr. 1-2). pap. 5.90 *(978-0-8239-8846-4(5)*, b682f24f-f727-477d-8905-8cbccebae848, Rosen Classroom) Rosen Publishing Group, Inc., The.

Catel, Patrick. Money & Trade. 1 vol. 2011. (Understanding Money Ser.). (ENG.). 48p. (J). (gr. 3-6). 35.99 *(978-1-4329-4635-7(8)*, 114308); pap. 9.95 *(978-1-4329-4642-5(0)*, 114314) Capstone. (Heinemann).

Cavell-Clarke, Steffi. Spending & Saving Money. 2018. (Our Values - Level 2 Ser.). (Illus.). 24p. (J). (gr. 2-3). *(978-0-7787-5432-9(4))* Crabtree Publishing Co.

Cernek, Kim. Build-a-Skill Instant Books Time & Money. Faulkner, Stacey, ed. Campbell, Jenny & Tom, Darcy, illus. 2007. (J). 4.99 *(978-1-59198-417-7(3))* Creative Teaching Pr., Inc.

Chatzky, Jean. Not Your Parents' Money Book: Making, Saving, & Spending Your Own Money. Haya, Erwin, illus. 2010. (ENG.). 176p. (J). (gr. 5-9). pap. 12.99 *(978-1-4169-9472-5(6)*, Simon & Schuster Bks. For Young Readers) Simon & Schuster Bks. For Young Readers.

Claire, Linda. Cuestion de Dinero: Conocimientos Financieros. rev. ed. 2019. (Mathematics in the Real World Ser.). (SPA.). 20p. (J). (gr. k-1). 8.99 *(978-1-4258-2825-7(6))* Teacher Created Materials, Inc.

—Money Matters: Find the Money. 2018. (Mathematics in the Real World Ser.). (ENG., Illus.). 20p. (gr. k-1). 8.99 *(978-1-4258-5618-2(7))* Teacher Created Materials, Inc.

Cleary, Brian P. A Dollar, a Penny, How Much & How Many? Gable, Brian, illus. (Math Is CATegorical (r) Ser.). (ENG.). 32p. (gr. k-3). 2014. (J). pap. 8.99 *(978-1-4677-2629-0(X)*, 3f1cc80a-88c5-4d71-8abc-999e332bcd6f) 2012. lib. bdg. 16.95 *(978-0-8225-7882-6(4))* Lerner Publishing Group. (Millbrook Pr.).

Clifford, Tim. American Coins & Bills. 2008. (Study of Money Ser.). (Illus.). 32p. (YA). (gr. 3-6). 28.50 *(978-1-60472-402-8(1))* Rourke Educational Media.

—Paying Without Money. 2008. (Illus.). 32p. (J). 28.50 *(978-1-60472-407-3(2))* Rourke Educational Media.

Cohen, Marina. Money Problems. 2010. (ENG.). 24p. (J). *(978-0-7787-6782-4(5))*; pap. *(978-0-7787-6791-6(4))* Crabtree Publishing Co.

Coins & Money. 2015. (Coins & Money Ser.). (ENG.). 24p. (J). (gr. 1-1). pap., pap., pap. 297.00 *(978-1-4994-1276-5(2)*, PowerKids Pr.) Rosen Publishing Group, Inc., The.

Colby, Jennifer. Borrowing & Returning. Bane, Jeff, illus. 2018. (My Early Library: My Guide to Money Ser.). (ENG.). 24p. (J). (gr. k-1). lib. bdg. 30.64 *(978-1-5341-2898-9(0)*, 211636) Cherry Lake Publishing.

—Jobs & Money. Bane, Jeff, illus. 2018. (My Early Library: My Guide to Money Ser.). (ENG.). 24p. (J). (gr. k-1). lib. bdg. 30.64 *(978-1-5341-2897-2(2)*, 211632) Cherry Lake Publishing.

—Managing Money. Bane, Jeff, illus. 2018. (My Early Library: My Guide to Money Ser.). (ENG.). 24p. (J). (gr. k-1). lib. bdg. 30.64 *(978-1-5341-2895-8(6)*, 211624) Cherry Lake Publishing.

—Money & Value. Bane, Jeff, illus. 2018. (My Early Library: My Guide to Money Ser.). (ENG.). 24p. (J). (gr. k-1). lib. bdg. 30.64 *(978-1-5341-2900-9(6)*, 211644) Cherry Lake Publishing.

—Spending & Saving. Bane, Jeff, illus. 2018. (My Early Library: My Guide to Money Ser.). (ENG.). 24p. (J). (gr. k-1). lib. bdg. 30.64 *(978-1-5341-2896-5(4)*, 211628) Cherry Lake Publishing.

Connolly, Sean. Money & Credit. 2010. (World Economy Explained Ser.). (ENG.). 48p. (J). (gr. 6-10). lib. bdg. 35.65 *(978-1-60753-081-7(3)*, 17236) Amicus.

—Money & Credit. 2012. (ENG., Illus.). 48p. (gr. 6-10). pap. 9.95 *(978-1-926722-79-5(5))* Saunders Bk. Co. CAN. Dist: RiverStream Publishing.

Cooke, Tim. Money & Trade. 1 vol. 2017. (What's the Big Idea? a History of the Ideas That Shape Our World Ser.). (ENG.). 48p. (gr. 6-6). lib. bdg. 33.07 *(978-1-5026-2816-9(3)*, bfa8c049-eb80-4af8-8f9d-8bb17808dc39) Cavendish Square Publishing LLC.

Cooper, Jason. Department of the Treasury. 2007. (ENG., Illus.). 24p. (gr. 2-5). 28.50 *(978-1-60472-123-2(5))* Rourke Educational Media.

Coss, Lauren. Let's Sort Money. 2014. (21st Century Basic Skills Library: Sorting Ser.). (ENG., Illus.). 24p. (J). (gr. k-3). 26.35 *(978-1-63137-633-7(0)*, 205315) Cherry Lake Publishing.

Cribb, Joe. Eyewitness Money: Discover the Fascinating Story of Money — From Silver Ingots to Smart Cards. 2016. (DK Eyewitness Ser.). (ENG., Illus.). 72p. (J). (gr. 3-7). pap. 9.99 *(978-1-4654-5178-1(1)*, 1405885, DK Children) Dorling Kindersley Publishing, Inc.

Croke, Liam & Naik, Anita. I'm Broke! The Money Handbook. 2009. (Really Useful Handbooks Ser.). (ENG., Illus.). 48p. (J). (gr. 5-11). pap. *(978-0-7787-4402-3(7))*; lib. bdg. *(978-0-7787-4389-7(6))* Crabtree Publishing Co.

Dalton, Julie. Counting Money. 2006. (Rookie Read-About Math Ser.). (ENG., Illus.). 32p. (J). (gr. 1-2). per. 5.95 *(978-0-516-25361-9(1)*, Children's Pr.) Scholastic Library Publishing.

—Making Change at the Fair. 2006. (Rookie Read-About Math Ser.). (ENG., Illus.). 32p. (J). (gr. 1-2). lib. bdg. 20.50 *(978-0-516-24960-5(6)*, Children's Pr.) Scholastic Library Publishing.

Daniels, Kathryn. A Bluestocking Guide - the Money Mystery: Based on Richard J. Maybury's book the Money Mystery. Williams, Jane A., ed. 2004. (Bluestocking Guide Ser.). (ENG.). 31p. (YA). pap. 8.95 *(978-0-942617-49-8(5))* Bluestocking Pr.

DaSilva-Gordon, Maria. Top 10 Secrets for Making Money & Even More Money. 2013. (Student's Guide to Financial Empowerment Ser.). 64p. (YA). (gr. 7-12). pap. 77.70 *(978-1-4488-9374-4(7))*; (ENG.). 37.12 *(978-1-4488-9359-1(3)*, 53adb910-64ce-4385-85bc-efeea7a738a0); (ENG.). pap. 13.95 *(978-1-4488-9373-7(9)*, a2f3d23c-b685-4259-876c-d3b60086817c) Rosen Publishing Group, Inc., The.

Deen, Marilyn. Dollars & Cents. 1 vol. 2011. (Wonder Readers Fluent Level Ser.). (ENG.). 16p. (gr. -1-2). (J). pap. 6.25 *(978-1-4296-7915-2(8)*, 118247); pap. 35.94 *(978-1-4296-8084-4(9))* Capstone. (Capstone Pr.).

DK. Heads up Money. 2017. (DK Heads Up Ser.). (ENG., Illus.). 160p. (YA). (gr. 5-12). pap. 15.99 *(978-1-4654-5626-7(0)*, DK Children) Dorling Kindersley Publishing, Inc.

Donovan, Sandy. Budgeting. 2005. (How Economics Works). (ENG., Illus.). 48p. (gr. 4-6). lib. bdg. 25.26 *(978-0-8225-2665-0(4)*, Lerner Pubns.) Lerner Publishing Group.

Doudna, Kelly. Let's Add Bills. 2003. (Dollars & Cents Set 3 Ser.). (Illus.). 24p. (J). (gr. k-3). lib. bdg. 24.21 *(978-1-57765-898-6(1)*, SandCastle) ABDO Publishing Co.

—Let's Add Coins. 2003. (Dollars & Cents Set 3 Ser.). (Illus.). 24p. (J). (gr. k-3). lib. bdg. 24.21 *(978-1-57765-896-2(5)*, SandCastle) ABDO Publishing Co.

—Let's Add Money. 2003. (Dollars & Cents Set 3 Ser.). (ENG., Illus.). 24p. (J). (gr. k-3). lib. bdg. 24.21 *(978-1-57765-900-6(7)*, SandCastle) ABDO Publishing Co.

—Let's Subtract Bills. 2003. (Dollars & Cents Set 3 Ser.). (ENG., Illus.). 24p. (J). (gr. k-3). lib. bdg. 24.21 *(978-1-57765-899-3(X)*, SandCastle) ABDO Publishing Co.

—Let's Subtract Coins. 2003. (Dollars & Cents Set 3 Ser.). (Illus.). 24p. (J). (gr. k-3). lib. bdg. 24.21 *(978-1-57765-897-9(3)*, SandCastle) ABDO Publishing Co.

—Let's Subtract Money. 2003. (Dollars & Cents Set 3 Ser.). (Illus.). 24p. (J). (gr. k-3). lib. bdg. 24.21 *(978-1-57765-901-3(5)*, SandCastle) ABDO Publishing Co.

Douglas, Vincent & Blevins, Wiley. Money, 6, Set. 2004. (Phonics Readers Books 37-72 Ser.). (ENG.). 8p. (gr. k-1). pap. 35.70 *(978-0-7368-4052-1(4))* Capstone.

Dowdy, Penny. Money. 1 vol. 2008. (My Path to Math Ser.). (ENG., Illus.). 24p. (J). (gr. k-3). pap. *(978-0-7787-4360-6(8))*; lib. bdg. *(978-0-7787-4342-2(X))* Crabtree Publishing Co.

Einspruch, Andrew. The Money System. 2012. (Money Sense Ser.). (Illus.). 32p. (gr. 4-6). lib. bdg. 28.50 *(978-1-59920-429-1(0))* Black Rabbit Bks.

Endres, Hollie J. How Much Money? 2005. (Yellow Umbrella Fluent Level Ser.). (ENG.). 16p. (gr. k-1). pap. 35.70 *(978-0-7368-5325-5(1)*, Capstone Pr.) Capstone.

Fan, Daphne. Money Champ: Teaching Kids about Money Management. 2010. 144p. pap. 57.95 *(978-1-4327-4990-3(0))* Outskirts Pr., Inc.

Fay, Gail. Using Money. 1 vol. 2011. (Understanding Money Ser.). (ENG.). 48p. (J). (gr. 3-6). pap. 9.95 *(978-1-4329-4641-8(2)*, 114313, Heinemann) Capstone.

First, Rachel. What's It Worth? Fun with Coins & Bills. 2015. (Math Beginnings Ser.). (ENG., Illus.). 24p. (J). (gr. -1-3). 29.93 *(978-1-62403-937-9(5)*, 19301, SandCastle) ABDO Publishing Co.

Fitzgerald, Lee. Pennies!. 1 vol. 2015. (Coins & Money Ser.). (ENG., Illus.). 24p. (J). (gr. 1-1). 25.27 *(978-1-4994-0502-6(2)*, dfa08465-68db-4ba1-ba92-174060ba95dc, PowerKids Pr.) Rosen Publishing Group, Inc., The.

Flash Kids Editors, ed. Time & Money: Grade 1 (Flash Skills) 2010. (Flash Skills Ser.). (ENG.). 64p. (J). pap. 4.95 *(978-1-4114-3450-9(1)*, Spark Publishing Group) Sterling Publishing Co., Inc.

Godfrey, Neale S. A Money Adventure: Earning, Saving, Spending, Sharing: Primary Home-School Kit. 2003. (One & Only Common Sense/cents Ser.). 44.50 *(978-0-7652-2451-4(8))* Modern Curriculum Pr.

Graham, Roland. Making Money. 1 vol. 2003. (Rosen REAL Readers Ser.). (ENG., Illus.). 12p. (gr. 1-2). pap. 5.90 *(978-0-8239-6358-4(6)*, 908dadd1-e211-4f32-9d4b-1b550563bde9) Rosen Publishing Group, Inc., The.

Greenes, Carol, et al. Time & Money. 2003. (Illus.). 60p. (J). (gr. -1-3). 16.95 *(978-0-7690-0004-6(5))* Seymour, Dale Pubns.

Gregoire, Maryellen. Ganar Dinero. 2012. (Wonder Readers Spanish Emergent Ser.). (SPA.). 16p. (J). (gr. -1-1). pap. 37.50 *(978-1-62065-572-6(1)*, 19237) Capstone.

—Making Money. 2012. (Wonder Readers Emergent Level Ser.). (ENG.). 16p. (J). (gr. -1-1). pap. 37.50 *(978-1-4296-9206-9(5)*, 18495); pap. 6.25 *(978-1-4296-9196-3(4)*, 120181) Capstone. (Capstone Pr.).

Guy, Pauline. Let's Count. 2004. 24p. (J). (gr. -1). 15.99 *(978-0-9744205-6-1(5))* Golden Eagle Publishing Hse., Inc.

Hamilton, Robert M. Dimes!. 1 vol. 2015. (Coins & Money Ser.). (ENG., Illus.). 24p. (J). (gr. 1-1). 25.27 *(978-1-4994-0498-2(0)*, 7442c2e6-a2d1-4db1-bd9e-fe8b8259716b, PowerKids Pr.) Rosen Publishing Group, Inc., The.

Harman, Hollis Page. Money Sense for Kids! 2nd ed. 2004. (ENG., Illus.). 192p. (J). (gr. 3-6). pap. 14.99 *(978-0-7641-2894-3(9))* Sourcebooks, Inc.

Heos, Bridget. Counting Change. Longhi, Katya, illus. 2014. (Math World Ser.). (ENG.). 24p. (J). (gr. 1-4). lib. bdg. 27.10 *(978-1-60753-462-4(2)*, 14872) Amicus.

Hicer, Nancy. Pennies, Nickles, & Dimes. 1 vol. 2015. (Rosen REAL Readers: STEM & STEAM Collection). (ENG.). 8p. (gr. k-1). pap. 5.46 *(978-1-4994-9723-6(7)*, effd0bd7-a443-41e7-8177-2e477331c1b7, Rosen Classroom) Rosen Publishing Group, Inc., The.

The History of Money. pap. 12.95 *(978-89-314-3702-7(1))* Youngjin.com Publishing Co., Ltd. KOR. Dist: Transition Vendor.

Hollander, Barbara. Money Matters. 2010. (Global Marketplace Ser.). (ENG., Illus.). 56p. (J). (gr. 6-9). 37.32 *(978-1-4329-3929-8(7)*, 113049, Heinemann) Capstone.

—Top 10 Secrets for Spending Your Money Wisely. 2013. (Student's Guide to Financial Empowerment Ser.). (Illus.). 64p. (YA). (gr. 7-12). pap. 77.70 *(978-1-4488-9381-2(X))*; (ENG., pap. 13.95 *(978-1-4488-9380-5(1)*, b5942685-ed9a-4981-84c0-abafd5295692) Rosen Publishing Group, Inc., The.

—What Are Saving & Spending?. 1 vol. 2016. (Let's Find Out! Community Economics Ser.). (ENG.). 32p. (J). (gr. 2-3). lib. bdg. 26.06 *(978-1-68048-405-2(2)*,

M N O

64a5e472-908b-49f3-bfae-f56891a47fd6) Rosen Publishing Group, Inc., The.

Hollander, Barbara & Gottfried Hollander, Barbara. Top 10 Secrets for Spending Your Money Wisely, 1 vol. 2013. (Student's Guide to Financial Empowerment Ser.). (ENG., Illus.). 64p. (YA). (gr. 7-7). 37.12 (978-1-4488-9361-4(5), 0c0c126a-b0fe-42b4-a6e6-d24729f92092) Rosen Publishing Group, Inc., The.

Hollander, Barbara Gottfried. Bitcoins: Navigating Open Source Currency, 1 vol. 2014. (Digital & Information Literacy Ser.). (ENG.). 48p. (YA). (gr. 5-5). 33.47 (978-1-4777-7930-9(2), fd16ba19-b660-4f43-a85a-bedc5ef2c89b, Rosen Reference) Rosen Publishing Group, Inc., The.

Holyoke, Nancy. A Smart Girl's Guide: Money: How to Make It, Save It, & Spend It. Barrager, Brigette, illus. 2014. (American Girl(r) Wellbeing Ser.). (ENG.). 96p. (J). pap. 12.99 (978-1-60958-407-8(4)) American Girl Publishing, Inc.

Houghton, Gillian. Cash & ATMs. 2009. (Invest Kids Ser.). 24p. (gr. 2-3). 42.50 (978-1-61513-611-7(8)); (ENG.). (J). lib. bdg. 26.27 (978-1-4358-2771-4(6), d5bc14c1-14da-40fb-b4e2-53e52cd58c13); (ENG., Illus.). (J). pap. 9.25 (978-1-4358-3206-0(X), 202fb691-d3fd-4160-9691-9b0d2fbff1bd) Rosen Publishing Group, Inc., The. (PowerKids Pr.).

—How Credit Cards Work, 1 vol. 2009. (Invest Kids Ser.). (ENG., Illus.). 24p. (J). (gr. 2-3). pap. 9.25 (978-1-4358-3208-4(6), 3b8969c6-68d2-4dcf-91e8-1e9146358a06); lib. bdg. 26.27 (978-1-4358-2773-8(2), 54de8348-456e-4220-a0dd-b85f7a929bb2) Rosen Publishing Group, Inc., The. (PowerKids Pr.).

Hubbard, Ben. Earning Money. Castro, Beatriz, illus. 2020. 32p. (J). (978-0-7787-7371-9(X)) Crabtree Publishing Co.

—Saving Money. Castro, Beatriz, illus. 2020. 32p. (J). (978-0-7787-7372-6(8)) Crabtree Publishing Co.

—Spending Money. Castro, Beatriz, illus. 2020. 32p. (J). (978-0-7787-7373-3(6)) Crabtree Publishing Co.

—What Is Money? Castro, Beatriz, illus. 2020. 32p. (J). (978-0-7787-7381-8(7)) Crabtree Publishing Co.

Hunt, Darleen L. Dog's Dollars: Patterns. Komarck, Michael, illus. 2003. (Sherman's Math Corner Ser.). (J). (gr. -1-3). (978-1-929591-08-4(X)) Reading Rock, Inc.

James, Jack. How to Let Your Parents Raise a Millionaire: A Kid-To-Kid View on How to Make Money Make a Difference & Have Fun Doing Both. 2012. (ENG.). 115p. pap. 14.95 (978-1-61448-248-2(9)) Morgan James Publishing.

John, Daymond. Little Daymond Learns to Earn. Miles, Nicole, illus. 2023. 40p. (J). (gr. -1-3). 19.99 (978-0-593-56727-2(7)); (ENG.). 22.99 (978-0-593-56728-9(5)) Random Hse. Children's Bks. (Random Hse. Bks. for Young Readers).

Jones, Patrick. My Dog-Walking Business: Work with Money, 1 vol. 2014. (InfoMax Math Readers Ser.). (ENG.). 24p. (J). (gr. 2-2). pap. 8.25 (978-1-4777-4750-6(8), 61bf77cc-1dc3-43bc-80f0-be67d05665a0, Rosen Classroom) Rosen Publishing Group, Inc., The.

Jovin, Michelle. Contemos Monedas: Conocimientos Financieros. rev. ed. 2019. (Mathematics in the Real World Ser.). (SPA., Illus.). 24p. (J). (gr. 1-2). pap. 9.99 (978-1-4258-2852-3(3)) Teacher Created Materials, Inc.

—Money Matters: Counting Coins. rev. ed. 2018. (Mathematics in the Real World Ser.). (ENG., Illus.). 24p. (J). (gr. 1-2). pap. 9.99 (978-1-4258-5690-8(X)) Teacher Created Materials, Inc.

Joy, Berry. Help Me Good about Being Greedy. 2009. 32p. 7.95 (978-1-60577-109-0(0)) Berry, Joy Enterprises.

Junior Library of Money, 14 vols., Set. Incl. Earning Money: Jobs. Fischer, James. pap. 9.95 (978-1-4222-1882-2(1)); Entrepreneurship. Simons, Rae. pap. 9.95 (978-1-4222-1883-9(X)); Guide to Teaching Young Adults about Money. Simons, Rae. pap. 9.95 (978-1-4222-1884-6(8)); Investing Money. Thompson, Helen. pap. 9.95 (978-1-4222-1885-3(6)); Money & Relationships. Simons, Rae. pap. 9.95 (978-1-4222-1886-0(4)); Planning for Your Education. Fischer, James. pap. 9.95 (978-1-4222-1887-7(2)); Power to Do Good: Money & Charity. Fischer, James. pap. 9.95 (978-1-4222-1888-4(0)); Sustainable Lifestyles in a Changing Economy. Simons, Rae. pap. 9.95 (978-1-4222-1890-7(2)); 64p. (YA). (gr. 7-18). 2010. 2011. Set pap. 139.30 (978-1-4222-1878-5(3)) Mason Crest.

Karpan, Andrew, ed. Cryptocurrencies & Blockchain Technology, 1 vol. 2019. (Current Controversies Ser.). (ENG.). 176p. (gr. 10-12). 48.03 (978-1-5345-0533-9(4), 332bf6f7-3d36-4787-96b1-16d5f6328d74) Greenhaven Publishing LLC.

Kemper, Bitsy. Budgeting, Spending, & Saving. 2015. (Searchlight Books (tm) — How Do We Use Money? Ser.). (ENG., Illus.). 40p. (gr. 3-5). 39.99 (978-1-4677-8914-1(3), Lerner Digital); (J). pap. 9.99 (978-1-4677-6105-5(2), c10af1ec-a3f4-4046-ac94-5acd7735710d); (J). lib. bdg. 30.65 (978-1-4677-5228-2(2), 2eb33ba7-b393-49bf-a5ab-b2b2df1c1062, Lerner Pubns.) Lerner Publishing Group.

—Earning Income. 2015. (Searchlight Books (tm) — How Do We Use Money? Ser.). (ENG., Illus.). 40p. (gr. 3-5). 39.99 (978-1-4677-8915-8(1), Lerner Digital) Lerner Publishing Group.

—Growing Your Money. 2015. (Searchlight Books (tm) — How Do We Use Money? Ser.). (ENG., Illus.). 40p. (gr. 3-5). 39.99 (978-1-4677-8916-5(X), Lerner Digital) Lerner Publishing Group.

Knowles, Amy. Working in a School Store, 1 vol. 2013. (Rosen Readers Ser.). (ENG.). 24p. (J). (gr. 3-3). pap. 8.25 (978-1-4777-2539-9(3), ab5caed4-81ba-4f9a-8ed5-fa23ca2a6109); pap. 49.50 (978-1-4777-2540-5(7)) Rosen Publishing Group, Inc., The. (Rosen Classroom).

Kompelien, Tracy. I Know about Money, It Is So Funny!, 1 vol. 2007. (Math Made Fun Ser.). (Illus.). 24p. (J). (gr. k-3). lib. bdg. 24.21 (978-1-59928-527-6(4), SandCastle) ABDO Publishing Co.

Kravitz, Robert J. A Collector's Guide to Fractional Currency: The Pocket Change of the Union Soldier. collector's ed. 2003. (Illus.). 262p. pap. 29.95 (978-0-918501-46-2(6), RK-2003, Archives Pr.) Media Assocs.

Kulp, Donald. Money Puppies: America's #1 Money Management Book for Kids. 2010. 36p. pap. 14.99 (978-1-4490-8977-1(1)) AuthorHouse.

Kummer, Patricia K. Currency. 2006. (Inventions That Shaped the World Ser.). (Illus.). 80p. (gr. 5-8). 19.95 (978-0-7569-6856-4(9)) Perfection Learning Corp.

Kumon Publishing North America, creator. My Book of Money Counting Dollars & Cents. Kumon Publishing North America, . 2007. (ENG., Illus.). 80p. (J). (gr. -1-3). per. 7.95 (978-1-933241-43-2(8)) Kumon Publishing North America, Inc.

—My First Book of Money Counting Coins. Kumon Publishing North America, . 2007. (ENG., Illus.). 80p. (J). (gr. -1-3). per. 7.95 (978-1-933241-42-5(X)) Kumon Publishing North America, Inc.

Larson, Jennifer S. What Is Money, Anyway? Why Dollars & Coins Have Value. 2010. (Lightning Bolt Books (r) — Exploring Economics Ser.). (ENG., Illus.). 32p. (J). (gr. 1-3). pap. 9.99 (978-0-7613-5668-4(1), c993a1df-f742-4d1a-b473-eaece3637f67) Lerner Publishing Group.

Lawrence, Lane & Ridgway, Tom. Buying Goods & Services. 2011. (J). 77.70 (978-1-4488-4751-8(6), Rosen Reference); (ENG.). 64p. (J). (gr. 5-5). pap. 13.95 (978-1-4488-4719-8(2), 56df5705-788a-41f4-8f88-c7aad8a5f83d, Rosen Reference); (ENG.). 64p. (YA). (gr. 5-5). lib. bdg. 37.13 (978-1-4488-4715-0(X), 404ac74e-36ce-4e10-8610-7737df73e1eb) Rosen Publishing Group, Inc., The.

Linde, Barbara M. A Shopping Trip: Learning to Add Dollars & Cents up to $10. 00 Without Regrouping, 1 vol. 2010. (Math for the REAL World Ser.). (ENG.). 16p. (gr. 2-3). pap. 7.05 (978-0-8239-8900-3(3), bd150635-7edf-4382-b9b6-c435b7e17e9e, Rosen Classroom) Rosen Publishing Group, Inc., The.

Lindeen, Mary. Earning Money. 2019. (BeginningtoRead Ser.). (ENG., Illus.). 32p. (J). (gr. -1-2). 22.60 (978-1-68450-934-8(3)); (gr. k-2). pap. 13.26 (978-1-68404-434-4(0)) Norwood Hse. Pr.

—Spending & Saving. 2019. (Beginning-To-Read Ser.). (ENG.). 32p. (J). (gr. k-2). pap. 13.26 (978-1-68404-435-1(9)) Norwood Hse. Pr.

Llewellyn, Claire. My Money Choices, 1 vol. Gordon, Mike, illus. 2016. (Your Money Ser.). (ENG.). 24p. (J). (gr. 1-1). pap. 9.25 (978-1-4994-8191-4(8), f2034267-dca0-4591-811d-e4c6a3423a71, Windmill Bks.) Rosen Publishing Group, Inc., The.

—Saving My Money. Gordon, Mike, illus. 2017. (Your Money Ser.). (ENG.). 24p. (J). (gr. -1-2). 19.05 (978-1-5311-8629-6(7)) Perfection Learning Corp.

—Saving My Money, 1 vol. Gordon, Mike, illus. 2016. (Your Money Ser.). (ENG.). 24p. (J). (gr. 1-1). pap. 9.25 (978-1-4994-8194-5(2), 9329c56a-7166-4aed-bf56-98417962895e, Windmill Bks.) Rosen Publishing Group, Inc., The.

—Spending My Money. Gordon, Mike, illus. 2017. (Your Money Ser.). (ENG.). 24p. (J). (gr. -1-2). 19.05 (978-1-5311-8652-4(1)) Perfection Learning Corp.

—Spending My Money, 1 vol. Gordon, Mike, illus. 2016. (Your Money Ser.). (ENG.). 24p. (J). (gr. 1-1). pap. 9.25 (978-1-4994-8197-6(7), 64369c28-a467-4b1f-982f-6bf0fc5df08b, Windmill Bks.) Rosen Publishing Group, Inc., The.

—What Is Money? Gordon, Mike, illus. 2017. (Your Money Ser.). (ENG.). 24p. (J). (gr. -1-2). 19.05 (978-1-5311-8697-5(1)) Perfection Learning Corp.

—What Is Money?, 1 vol. Gordon, Mike, illus. 2016. (Your Money Ser.). (ENG.). 24p. (J). (gr. 1-1). pap. 9.25 (978-1-4994-8200-3(0), 3d3a4791-b422-42b1-beca-78205b70b18c, Windmill Bks.) Rosen Publishing Group, Inc., The.

Loughran, Donna. Carnival Coins: How Will We Count Our Money? 2013. (IMath Ser.). (Illus.). 24p. (J). (gr. k-2). (ENG.). pap. 13.26 (978-1-60357-491-4(3)); lib. bdg. 21.27 (978-1-59953-552-4(1)) Norwood Hse. Pr.

Make Money Now!, 14 vols. 2013. (Make Money Now! Ser.). (ENG.). 80p. (YA). (gr. 7-7). 268.87 (978-1-4488-9396-6(8), 48ffa609-cd04-4c27-92eb-7961493c028f) Rosen Publishing Group, Inc., The.

Maloof, Torrey. Money Matters: What's It Worth? Financial Literacy (Grade 3) 2017. (Mathematics in the Real World Ser.). (ENG., Illus.). 32p. (J). (gr. 3-4). pap. 11.99 (978-1-4807-5806-3(X)) Teacher Created Materials, Inc.

Marrewa, Jennifer. USING MONEY on a Shopping Trip, 1 vol. 2008. (Math in Our World - Level 2 Ser.). (ENG., Illus.). 24p. (gr. 2-2). lib. bdg. 24.67 (978-0-8368-9004-4(3), d98ca260-9cc2-457e-a0fc-87cf69862017, Weekly Reader Leveled Readers) Stevens, Gareth Publishing LLLP.

—Vamos a USAR DINERO en un Viaje de Compras (USING MONEY on a Shopping Trip), 1 vol. 2008. (Las Matemáticas en Nuestro Mundo - Nivel 2 (Math in Our World - Level 2) Ser.). (SPA.). 24p. (gr. 2-2). pap. 9.15 (978-0-8368-9031-0(0), a2a3d2cf-9d52-47fc-be46-a907ab91cff3); (Illus.). lib. bdg. 24.67 (978-0-8368-9022-8(1), 469afe3a-36ad-4e49-895f-3c97fe96c86a) Stevens, Gareth Publishing LLLP. (Weekly Reader Leveled Readers).

Marsico, Katie. What Is Money? 2015. (21st Century Skills Library: Real World Math Ser.). (ENG., Illus.). 32p. (J). (gr. 4-7). 32.07 (978-1-63362-579-2(6), 206500) Cherry Lake Publishing.

Mason, Paul. Frauds & Counterfeits. 2010. (Solve It with Science Ser.). (YA). (gr. 5-9). 34.25 (978-1-59920-329-4(4)) Black Rabbit Bks.

Matheson, Murdoch H. Building Wealth for Teens: Answers to Questions Teens Care About. 2007. 116p. 24.65 (978-1-4251-2358-1(9)) Trafford Publishing.

Mathews, Janice. Happy Jack: How Much Stuff Is Enough? 2014. (Stewardship Jack Ser.: Vol. 4). (ENG., Illus.). 30p. (J). (gr. 3-7). 7.99 (978-0-8280-2786-1(2)) Review & Herald Publishing Assn.

McGillian, Jamie Kyle. The Kids' Money Book. Phillips, Ian, illus. 2006. 96p. (J). (gr. 4-8). reprint ed. 18.00 (978-0-7567-9900-7(7)) DIANE Publishing Co.

Mckenna, James & Glista, Jeannine. How to Turn $100 Into $1,000,000: Earn! Invest! Save! 2016. lib. bdg. 24.45 (978-0-606-37953-3(3)) Turtleback.

McKenna, James, et al. How to Turn $100 Into $1,000,000: Earn! Invest! Save! 2016. (ENG., Illus.). 144p. (J). (gr. 5-9). pap. 12.95 (978-0-7611-8080-7(X), 18080) Workman Publishing Co., Inc.

McManus, Lori. Money Through History, 1 vol. 2011. (Understanding Money Ser.). (ENG., Illus.). 48p. (J). (gr. 3-6). pap. 9.95 (978-1-4329-4643-2(9), 114315, Heinemann) Capstone.

Meachen Rau, Dana. Gastar el Dinero (Spending Money), 1 vol. 2010. (Dinero y Los Bancos (Money & Banks) Ser.). (SPA., Illus.). 24p. (gr. 2-4). pap. 9.15 (978-1-4339-3724-8(7), 326b3b59-c629-4642-be84-acb418cac782); (J). lib. bdg. 24.67 (978-1-4339-3723-1(9), 6b006798-8328-47aa-ba7e-1d03de2a6cc0) Stevens, Gareth Publishing LLLP.

—Spending Money, 1 vol. 2010. (Money & Banks (New Edition) Ser.). (ENG., Illus.). 24p. (gr. 2-4). pap. 9.15 (978-1-4339-3390-5(X), 8ce28bf2-af7f-43f1-8fe5-8e197fe1dda6); (J). lib. bdg. 24.67 (978-1-4339-3389-9(6), f0a195e2-90fd-4dae-9e03-f860a3d04797) Stevens, Gareth Publishing LLLP.

Miller, Derek. Money in Politics, 1 vol. 2019. (Dilemmas in Democracy Ser.). (ENG.). 80p. (gr. 7-7). lib. bdg. 37.36 (978-1-5026-4493-0(2), 34caaa1a-ed6a-4396-a62a-f5fcb6ad6b39) Cavendish Square Publishing LLC.

Minden, Cecilia. What Is Money? 2009. (21st Century Skills Library: Real World Math Ser.). (ENG.). 32p. (gr. 4-8). lib. bdg. 32.07 (978-1-60279-312-5(3), 200208) Cherry Lake Publishing.

Molter, Carey. A Dime = 10 Cents. 2003. (Dollars & Cents Set 1 Ser.). (Illus.). 24p. (J). (gr. k-3). lib. bdg. 24.21 (978-1-57765-884-9(1)) ABDO Publishing Co.

—A Dollar = $1.00. 2003. (Dollars & Cents Set 1 Ser.). (Illus.). 24p. (J). (gr. k-3). lib. bdg. 24.21 (978-1-57765-885-6(X)) ABDO Publishing Co.

—A Half-Dollar = 50 Cents. 2003. (Dollars & Cents Set 1 Ser.). (Illus.). 24p. (J). (gr. k-3). lib. bdg. 24.21 (978-1-57765-886-3(8), SandCastle) ABDO Publishing Co.

—How Much Is $10. 00?, 1 vol. 2003. (Dollars & Cents Set 2 Ser.: Level Ii). (Illus.). 24p. (J). (gr. k-3). lib. bdg. 24.21 (978-1-57765-894-8(9), SandCastle) ABDO Publishing Co.

—How Much Is $1.00? 2003. (Dollars & Cents Set 2 Ser.). (Illus.). 24p. (J). (gr. k-3). lib. bdg. 24.21 (978-1-57765-892-4(2), SandCastle) ABDO Publishing Co.

—How Much Is $100. 00?, 1 vol. 2003. (Dollars & Cents Set 2 Ser.). (Illus.). 24p. (J). (gr. k-3). lib. bdg. 24.21 (978-1-57765-893-1(0), SandCastle) ABDO Publishing Co.

—How Much Is $20. 00?, 1 vol. 2003. (Dollars & Cents Set 2 Ser.). (Illus.). 24p. (J). (gr. k-3). lib. bdg. 24.21 (978-1-57765-895-5(7), SandCastle) ABDO Publishing Co.

—How Much Is $5. 00?, 1 vol. 2003. (Dollars & Cents Set 2 Ser.). (Illus.). 24p. (J). (gr. k-3). lib. bdg. 24.21 (978-1-57765-891-7(4), SandCastle) ABDO Publishing Co.

—How Much Is $50.00? 2003. (Dollars & Cents Set 2 Ser.). (Illus.). 24p. (J). (gr. k-3). lib. bdg. 24.21 (978-1-57765-890-0(6), SandCastle) ABDO Publishing Co.

—A Nickel = 5 Cents. 2003. (Dollars & Cents Set 1 Ser.). (Illus.). 24p. (J). (gr. k-3). lib. bdg. 24.21 (978-1-57765-887-0(6), SandCastle) ABDO Publishing Co.

—A Penny = 1 Cent. 2003. (Dollars & Cents Set 1 Ser.). (Illus.). 24p. (J). (gr. k-3). lib. bdg. 24.21 (978-1-57765-888-7(4), SandCastle) ABDO Publishing Co.

—A Quarter= 25 Cents. 2003. (Dollars & Cents Set 1 Ser.: Level I). 24p. (J). (gr. k-3). lib. bdg. 24.21 (978-1-57765-889-4(2), SandCastle) ABDO Publishing Co.

Moneta. The Journey to the Money Tree. 2009. (Illus.). 28p. pap. 12.49 (978-1-4389-1499-2(7)) AuthorHouse.

Money. 2004. (Illus.). lib. bdg. 7.95 (978-0-8225-5257-4(4)) Lerner Publishing Group.

Money - Set 2: Dollars that Add Up. 2005. (J). spiral bd. 19.90 (978-0-9770248-5-8(7)) Sidedoor Publishing LLC.

Money Skills for Kids. 2017. (Money Skills for Kids Ser.). 32p. (gr. 10-10). pap. 50.00 (978-1-5081-5431-0(7)); (ENG.). (gr. 5-5). 139.65 (978-1-4994-3402-6(2), 4ce65b2c-ea20-404f-944f-850079f4f0f1) Rosen Publishing Group, Inc., The. (PowerKids Pr.).

Morey, Allan. A Dime. Bower, Jennifer, illus. 2018. (Money Values Ser.). (ENG.). 24p. (J). (gr. 1-3). 33.99 (978-1-68410-126-9(3), 31845) Cantata Learning.

—A Nickel. Bower, Jennifer, illus. 2018. (Money Values Ser.). (ENG.). 24p. (J). (gr. 1-3). 33.99 (978-1-68410-133-7(6), 31846) Cantata Learning.

—A Penny. Bower, Jennifer, illus. 2018. (Money Values Ser.). (ENG.). 24p. (J). (gr. 1-3). 33.99 (978-1-68410-120-7(4), 31844) Cantata Learning.

—A Quarter. Bower, Jennifer, illus. 2018. (Money Values Ser.). (ENG.). 24p. (J). (gr. 1-3). 33.99 (978-1-68410-138-2(7), 31847) Cantata Learning.

Morgan, Elizabeth. Nickels!, 1 vol. 2015. (Coins & Money Ser.). (ENG., Illus.). 24p. (J). (gr. 1-1). 25.27 (978-1-4994-0501-9(4), fe339085-47f3-476a-8f17-77c5a4012ab7, PowerKids Pr.) Rosen Publishing Group, Inc., The.

Morgan, Sally. Earth's Energy Sources. 2011. (Earth Cycles Ser.). 32p. (YA). (gr. 3-6). lib. bdg. 28.50 (978-1-59920-522-9(X)) Black Rabbit Bks.

Moriarty, J. T. The Birth of American Capitalism: The Growth of American Banks, 1 vol. 2003. (Primary Sources of America's Industrial Society in the 19th Century Ser.). (ENG., Illus.). 32p. (gr. 4-5). pap. 10.00 (978-0-8239-4280-0(5), 43f37bb4-5f32-4b2c-a10b-e6ac1b66becc) Rosen Publishing Group, Inc., The.

—The Rise of American Capitalism: The Growth of American Banks, 1 vol. 2003. (America's Industrial Society in the 19th Century Ser.). (ENG., Illus.). 32p. (gr. 4-5). lib. bdg. 29.13 (978-0-8239-4022-6(5), 67146d07-e35e-42b0-82b4-657f394a2c3b, Rosen Reference) Rosen Publishing Group, Inc., The.

Morrison, Jessica. Saving. 2017. (J). (978-1-5105-1947-3(5)) SmartBook Media, Inc.

Mototsune, Kat. Money: Deal with It or Pay the Price, 1 vol. Geoffroi, Remie, illus. 2007. (Lorimer Deal with It Ser.). (ENG.). 32p. (J). (gr. 4-9). pap. 12.95 (978-1-55028-958-9(6), 26c9254f-4d3b-4c68-badb-53a9c47bb281) James Lorimer & Co. Ltd., Pubs. CAN. Dist: Lerner Publishing Group.

Murphy, Patricia J. Earning Money. 2005. (How Economics Works). (Illus.). 48p. (J). (gr. 3-7). lib. bdg. 25.26 (978-0-8225-2149-5(0), Lerner Pubns.) Lerner Publishing Group.

Nagle, Jeanne. Money, Banking, & Finance, 1 vol. 2018. (Understanding Economics Ser.). (ENG.). 48p. (gr. 6-7). lib. bdg. 28.41 (978-1-5383-0270-5(5), 0120e9bf-b104-4665-ba7e-8c2b6622f432, Britannica Educational Publishing) Rosen Publishing Group, Inc., The.

—What Are Money & Banks? 2016. (Let's Find Out! Ser.). (ENG.). 32p. (J). (gr. 3-7). 23.70 (978-1-5311-8662-3(9)) Perfection Learning Corp.

Nelson, Sandi. A Fly on the Wall Street. Beckstrand, Jared, illus. 2013. 23p. (J). 19.99 (978-1-938690-29-7(X)) Salem Author Services.

Nourigat, Paul. Why Is There Money? A Facinating Journey Through the Evolution of Money. Schofield, Angela, illus. 2011. (ENG.). 36p. (J). pap. 11.29 (978-1-936872-00-8(5)) FarBeyond Publishing LLC.

Orr, Tamra. Money Matters: A Kid's Guide to Money, 5 vols., Set. Incl. Budgeting Tips for Kids. lib. bdg. 29.95 (978-1-58415-644-4(9)); Coins & Other Currency. lib. bdg. 29.95 (978-1-58415-640-6(6)); Kid's Guide to Earning Money. lib. bdg. 29.95 (978-1-58415-643-7(0)); Kid's Guide to Stock Market Investing. lib. bdg. 29.95 (978-1-58415-642-0(2)); Savings Tips for Kids. lib. bdg. 29.95 (978-1-58415-641-3(4)); (Illus.). 48p. (YA). (gr. 3-6). 2008. 2008. Set lib. bdg. 149.75 (978-1-58415-645-1(7)) Mitchell Lane Pubs.

Osburn, Mary Rose. Using Money at the Zoo, 1 vol. 2017. (Animal Math Ser.). (ENG.). 24p. (J). (gr. 1-2). pap. 9.15 (978-1-5382-0864-9(4), 3594b480-5db0-4a15-9494-6dd282d7776e) Stevens, Gareth Publishing LLLP.

Outram, Richard. The Adventures of Exokid & the Teachings of Money. Kapatos, Elizabeth, illus. 2009. 36p. pap. 12.95 (978-1-59858-898-9(2)) Dog Ear Publishing, LLC.

Pellittiere II, Michael. GROW MONEY - A Kid's Guide to Saving & Investing. 2007. (ENG.). 60p. (YA). pap. 10.40 (978-0-615-14589-1(2)) Dakota Assocs., Inc.

—GROW MONEY II - A Teenager's Guide to Saving & Investing. 2007. (ENG.). 118p. (YA). pap. 11.42 (978-0-615-18343-5(3)) Dakota Assocs., Inc.

Penn, M. W. Counting Money!, 1 vol. 2012. (Pebble Math Ser.). (ENG.). 24p. (J). (gr. -1-2). pap. 6.29 (978-1-4296-7875-9(5), 118207); (J). (gr. -1-2). lib. bdg. 24.65 (978-1-4296-7562-8(4), 117159); (gr. k-1). pap. 35.70 (978-1-4296-8308-1(2)) Capstone. (Pebble).

Phillips Mba, Nancy. The Zela Wela Kid: Build a Bank. 2010. 36p. pap. 15.75 (978-1-4490-7413-5(8)) AuthorHouse.

Pistoia, Sara. Money. 2016. (J). (978-1-4896-5113-6(6)) Weigl Pubs., Inc.

Quin, Caroline. Shopping. 2004. (Activities for 3-5 Year Olds Ser.). (Illus.). 32p. pap. 11.00 (978-1-897675-58-8(5)) Brilliant Pubns. GBR. Dist: Parkwest Pubns., Inc.

Raij, Emily. Donate Money. 2019. (Earn It, Save It, Spend It! Ser.). (ENG., Illus.). 24p. (J). (gr. 1-3). pap. 7.95 (978-1-9771-1005-3(3), 140948); lib. bdg. 25.99 (978-1-9771-0834-0(2), 140455) Capstone. (Pebble).

—Earn Money. 2019. (Earn It, Save It, Spend It! Ser.). (ENG., Illus.). 24p. (J). (gr. 1-3). pap. 7.95 (978-1-9771-1002-2(9), 140945); lib. bdg. 25.99 (978-1-9771-0831-9(8), 140452) Capstone. (Pebble).

Reina, Mary. Learn about Money. 2015. (Money & You Ser.). (ENG., Illus.). 24p. (J). (gr. -1-2). lib. bdg. 24.65 (978-1-4914-2084-3(7), 127562) Capstone.

—Make Money Choices. 2015. (Money & You Ser.). (ENG., Illus.). 24p. (J). (gr. -1-2). pap. 5.95 (978-1-4914-2300-4(5), 127762) Capstone.

—Money & You. 2015. (Money & You Ser.). (ENG.). 24p. (J). (gr. -1-2). 98.60 (978-1-4914-2569-5(5), 22561, Pebble) Capstone.

—Save Money. 2019. (Earn It, Save It, Spend It! Ser.). (ENG., Illus.). 24p. (J). (gr. 1-3). pap. 7.95 (978-1-9771-1003-9(7), 140946); lib. bdg. 25.99 (978-1-9771-0832-6(6), 140453) Capstone. (Pebble).

—Spend Money. 2019. (Earn It, Save It, Spend It! Ser.). (ENG., Illus.). 24p. (J). (gr. 1-3). pap. 7.95 (978-1-9771-1004-6(5), 140947); lib. bdg. 25.99 (978-1-9771-0833-3(4), 140454) Capstone. (Pebble).

Rice, Dona Herweck. Money Matters: A Classroom Economy: Adding & Subtracting Decimals (Grade 5) rev. ed. 2018. (Mathematics in the Real World Ser.). (ENG., Illus.). 32p. (J). (gr. 4-8). pap. 11.99 (978-1-4258-5820-9(1)) Teacher Created Materials, Inc.

Roberson, Erin. All about Money. 2005. (Rookie Read-About Math Ser.). (ENG., Illus.). 32p. (J). (gr. 1-2). pap. 5.95 (978-0-516-24672-7(0), Children's Pr.) Scholastic Library Publishing.

Roper, Dawn. 30 Fun Ways to Learn about Time & Money. 2011. (30 Fun Ways to Learn Ser.). (ENG.). 80p. (gr. -1-k). pap. 12.95 (978-0-87659-370-7(8), Gryphon House Inc) Gryphon Hse., Inc.

Rose, Simon. Loonies: Canadian Icons. 2010. (Illus.). 24p. (978-1-77071-579-0(7)); pap. (978-1-77071-586-8(X)) Weigl Educational Pubs. Ltd.

Rowe, Brooke. What Kind of Spender Are You? 2015. (Best Quiz Ever Ser.). (ENG., Illus.). 32p. (J). (gr. 4-8). 32.07 (978-1-63470-040-5(6), 206800) Cherry Lake Publishing.

Rozines Roy, Jennifer & Roy, Gregory. Money at the Store, 1 vol. (Math All Around Ser.). (ENG.). 32p. (gr. 2-2). 2008. pap. 9.23 (978-0-7614-3385-9(6), 55d54d22-45e0-4ddc-b7ca-87c1c6c663e4) 2007. (Illus.). lib. bdg. 32.64 (978-0-7614-2264-8(1), 862dc996-0f48-4325-82f9-b2b9d2809718) Cavendish Square Publishing LLC.

Russell, Solveig Paulson. From Barter to Gold: The Story of Money. Cary, illus. 2011. 66p. 36.95 (978-1-258-01865-8(9)) Literary Licensing, LLC.

Salzmann, Mary Elizabeth. Money for Clothes, 1 vol. 2010. (Your Piggy Bank: a Guide to Spending & Saving for Kids!

Ser.). (ENG.). 24p. (J). (gr. k-4). 31.36 (978-1-61641-027-8(2), 15836, Looking Glass Library) Magic Wagon.

—Money for Food, 1 vol. 2010. (Your Piggy Bank: a Guide to Spending & Saving for Kids! Ser.). (ENG.). 24p. (J). (gr. k-4). 31.36 (978-1-61641-029-2(9), 15840, Looking Glass Library) Magic Wagon.

—Money for Hobbies, 1 vol. 2010. (Your Piggy Bank: a Guide to Spending & Saving for Kids! Ser.). (ENG.). 24p. (J). (gr. k-4). 31.36 (978-1-61641-030-8(2), 15842, Looking Glass Library) Magic Wagon.

—Money for School, 1 vol. 2010. (Your Piggy Bank: a Guide to Spending & Saving for Kids! Ser.). (ENG.). 24p. (J). (gr. k-4). 31.36 (978-1-61641-031-5(0), 15844, Looking Glass Library) Magic Wagon.

—Money for Toys, 1 vol. 2010. (Your Piggy Bank: a Guide to Spending & Saving for Kids! Ser.). (ENG.). 24p. (J). (gr. k-4). 31.36 (978-1-61641-032-2(9), 15846, Looking Glass Library) Magic Wagon.

School Zone Interactive Staff. Time, Money & Fractions. rev. ed. 2004. (ENG.). 64p. (J). (gr. k-2). 15.99 (978-1-58947-832-9(0)) School Zone Publishing Co.

School Zone Staff. Time & Money. 2004. (ENG.). 56p. (J). 2.79 (978-1-58947-990-6(4)) School Zone Publishing Co.

School Zone Staff, ed. Time & Money. 2005. (ENG.). 26p. (J). (gr. 1-2). pap. 3.79 (978-1-58947-788-9(X)) School Zone Publishing Co.

—Time, Money & Fractions. 2003. (ENG.). (J). (gr. 1-2). cd-rom 19.99 (978-1-58947-930-2(0)) School Zone Publishing Co.

Schuh, Mari. Counting Money. 2015. (Money Matters Ser.). (ENG., Illus.). 24p. (J). (gr. k-3). lib. bdg. 26.95 (978-1-62617-245-6(5), Blastoff! Readers) Bellwether Media.

—Earning Money. 2015. (Money Matters Ser.). (ENG., Illus.). 24p. (J). (gr. k-3). lib. bdg. 26.95 (978-1-62617-246-3(3), Blastoff! Readers) Bellwether Media.

—How Money Is Made. 2018. (Money & Me Ser.). (ENG., Illus.). 24p. (gr. -1-2). lib. bdg. 28.50 (978-1-64156-400-7(8), 9781641564007) Rourke Educational Media.

—Money Around the World. 2018. (Money & Me Ser.). (ENG., Illus.). 24p. (gr. -1-2). lib. bdg. 28.50 (978-1-64156-403-8(2), 9781641564038) Rourke Educational Media.

—Save, Spend, or Share. 2018. (Money & Me Ser.). (ENG., Illus.). 24p. (gr. -1-2). lib. bdg. 28.50 (978-1-64156-399-4(0), 9781641563994) Rourke Educational Media.

—Spending Money. 2015. (Money Matters Ser.). (ENG., Illus.). 24p. (J). (gr. k-3). lib. bdg. 26.95 (978-1-62617-248-7(X), Blastoff! Readers) Bellwether Media.

—Types of Money. 2015. (Money Matters Ser.). (ENG., Illus.). 24p. (J). (gr. k-3). lib. bdg. 26.95 (978-1-62617-249-4(8), Blastoff! Readers) Bellwether Media.

—Wants & Needs. 2018. (Money & Me Ser.). (ENG., Illus.). 24p. (gr. -1-2). pap. 9.95 (978-1-64156-528-8(4), 9781641565288) Rourke Educational Media.

Schwartz, Heather E. Save Wisely. 2015. (Money Smarts Ser.). (ENG., Illus.). 32p. (J). (gr. 2-5). lib. bdg. 19.95 (978-1-60753-794-6(X), 15310) Amicus.

Seba, Jaime A. Smashing the Stereotypes: What Does It Mean to Be Gay, Lesbian, Bisexual, or Transgender? 2009. (Gallup's Guide to Modern Gay, Lesbian, & Transgender Lifestyle Ser.). 64p. (YA). (gr. 7-18). pap. 9.95 (978-1-4222-1874-7(0)) Mason Crest.

Sember, Brette. The Everything Kids' Money Book: Earn It, Save It, & Watch It Grow! 2nd ed. 2008. (Everything(r) Kids Ser.). (ENG., Illus.). 160p. pap. 9.99 (978-1-59869-784-1(6)) Adams Media Corp.

Seuling, Barbara. There Are Millions of Millionaires: And Other Freaky Facts About Earning, Saving, & Spending. Haugen, Ryan, illus. 2010. (Freaky Facts Ser.). 40p. pap. 0.35 (978-1-4048-6550-1(0), Picture Window Bks.) Capstone.

Sherman, Jill. Money: What You Need to Know. 2017. (Fact Files Ser.). (ENG., Illus.). 24p. (J). (gr. 1-3). lib. bdg. 27.99 (978-1-5157-8120-2(8), 136129, Capstone Pr.) Capstone.

Sieplinga, Drew. Paint Your Own Piggy Bank. 2007. (Illus.). 32p. (J). (978-0-545-02112-8(X)) Scholastic, Inc.

Silbert, Jack. Honest Abe's Funny Money Book. 2012. (Illus.). 32p. (978-0-545-36740-0(9)) Scholastic, Inc.

Simons, Rae. All about Money: The History, Culture, & Meaning of Modern Finance. 2010. (Junior Library of Money). 64p. (YA). (gr. 7-18). lib. bdg. 22.95 (978-1-4222-1760-3(4)) Mason Crest.

—Money & Relationships. 2010. (Junior Library of Money). 64p. (YA). (gr. 7-18). pap. 9.95 (978-1-4222-1886-0(4)); lib. bdg. 22.95 (978-1-4222-1767-2(1)) Mason Crest.

—Spending Money. 2010. (Junior Library of Money). 64p. (YA). (gr. 7-18). lib. bdg. 22.95 (978-1-4222-1770-2(1)) Mason Crest.

St. Germain, Mark. Three Cups: Teaching Children How to Save, Spend & Be Charitable with Money Is As Easy As 1, 2, 3. Willy, April, illus. 2007. (ENG.). 28p. (J). pap. 10.00 (978-0-9794563-0-5(4)) IRONSTREAM Pr.

Stanley, Joseph. Half-Dollars!, 1 vol. 2015. (Coins & Money Ser.). (ENG., Illus.). 24p. (J). (gr. 1-1). 25.27 (978-1-4994-0500-2(6), d849d7b7-807f-4e74-bd4d-c21e6c9d58cd, PowerKids Pr.) Rosen Publishing Group, Inc., The.

Steck-Vaughn Staff. At-Home Workbooks: Money. 2004. (Illus.). pap., wbk. ed. 5.99 (978-0-7398-8537-6(5)) Steck-Vaughn.

Sterling, Kristin. Money. 2008. pap. 22.95 (978-0-8225-9361-4(0)); (ENG., Illus.). 8p. (J). pap. 5.99 (978-0-8225-8848-1(X), 825a91dc-50e1-4eaa-b26e-a8742a494c4a) Lerner Publishing Group.

Stuart, Carrie. Kinds of Coins: Learning the Values of Pennies, Nickels, Dimes & Quarters, 1 vol. 2010. (Math for the REAL World Ser.). (ENG.). 12p. (gr. 1-2). pap. 5.90 (978-0-8239-8862-4(7), 836dd74b-cf85-4f50-8582-6d952d0ad3a1, Rosen Classroom) Rosen Publishing Group, Inc., The.

Studio 2B Focus - On the Money. 2004. (YA). (978-0-88441-687-6(9)) Girl Scouts of the USA.

Suen, Anastasia. Downloading & Online Shopping Safety & Privacy. 2013. (21st Century Safety & Privacy Ser.). (Illus.). 64p. (J). (gr. 5-8). pap. 77.70 (978-1-4488-9583-0(9)); (ENG., (gr. 6-6). 37.12 (978-1-4488-9571-7(5), dbd494a4-7f90-4b34-bfd1-ea363afce0d4); (ENG., (gr. 6-6). pap. 13.95 (978-1-4488-9582-3(0), e614a906-fa2e-4d7e-9970-3de002d45588) Rosen Publishing Group, Inc., The.

Summers, Portia. Adding Coins & Bills, 1 vol. 2016. (Value of Money Ser.). (ENG.). 24p. (gr. 1-2). pap. 10.35 (978-0-7660-7693-8(8), e2088aa8-476d-48b0-93d1-d4704dfbefd0) Enslow Publishing, LLC.

—Counting Coins & Bills, 1 vol. 2016. (Value of Money Ser.). (ENG., Illus.). 24p. (gr. 1-2). pap. 10.35 (978-0-7660-7700-3(4), e84300ad-f712-4b7b-9c8e-54c6e58c55e0) Enslow Publishing, LLC.

—One Dollar: How Many Pennies?, 1 vol. 2016. (Value of Money Ser.). (ENG., Illus.). 24p. (gr. 1-2). pap. 10.35 (978-0-7660-7685-3(7), 5f37c8de-26cb-4d07-8ff1-f7cc8611c094) Enslow Publishing, LLC.

—Subtracting Coins & Bills, 1 vol. 2016. (Value of Money Ser.). (ENG.). 24p. (gr. 1-2). pap. 10.35 (978-0-7660-7720-1(9), 45dac0d8-7c1b-406e-92a3-3a01486617dc) Enslow Publishing, LLC.

—What Is Money?, 1 vol. 2016. (Value of Money Ser.). (ENG., Illus.). 24p. (gr. 1-2). pap. 10.35 (978-0-7660-7715-7(2), 8bd92cb9-3f73-4c32-83ae-4627b0b9772f) Enslow Publishing, LLC.

—Word Problems with Money, 1 vol. 2016. (Value of Money Ser.). (ENG., Illus.). 24p. (gr. 1-2). pap. 10.35 (978-0-7660-7707-2(1), 56a3c5db-01d9-4748-a124-81dd0f672758) Enslow Publishing, LLC.

Sundance/Newbridge LLC Staff. Dollars & Cents. 2004. (Reading PowerWorks Ser.). (gr. 1-3). 37.50 (978-0-7608-8964-0(3)); pap. 6.10 (978-0-7608-8965-7(1)) Sundance/Newbridge Educational Publishing.

Swain, Cynthia. I Have a Coin. 2006. (Early Explorers Ser.). (J). pap. (978-1-4108-6040-8(X)) Benchmark Education Co.

Sylvester, Kevin & Hlinka, Michael. Follow Your Money: Who Gets It, Who Spends It, Where Does It Go? 2nd ed. 2013. (ENG., Illus.). 60p. (J). (gr. 5-12). pap. 14.95 (978-1-55451-480-9(0), 9781554514809) Annick Pr., Ltd. CAN. Dist: Publishers Group West (PGW).

—Follow Your Money: Who Gets It, Who Spends It, Where Does It Go? Beck, Julia, tr. 2nd ed. 2013. (ENG., Illus.). 60p. (J). (gr. 5-12). 24.95 (978-1-55451-481-6(9), 9781554514816) Annick Pr., Ltd. CAN. Dist: Publishers Group West (PGW).

Thayer, Tanya. Counting Money. 2005. (First Step Nonfiction Ser.). (Illus.). 24p. (gr. k-2). lib. bdg. 17.27 (978-0-8225-1258-5(0)) Lerner Publishing Group.

Thomas, Keltie. The Kids Guide to Money Cent$ MacEachern, Stephen, tr. MacEachern, Stephen, illus. 2004. (ENG.). 56p. (J). 8.95 (978-1-55337-391-9(X)); (gr. 4-6). 8.95 (978-1-55337-390-2(1)) Kids Can Pr., Ltd. CAN. Dist: Hachette Bk. Group.

Thompson, Helen. Investing Money. 2010. (Junior Library of Money). 64p. (YA). (gr. 7-18). pap. 9.95 (978-1-4222-1885-3(6)); lib. bdg. 22.95 (978-1-4222-1766-5(3)) Mason Crest.

—Understanding Credit. 2010. (Junior Library of Money). 64p. (YA). (gr. 7-18). lib. bdg. 22.95 (978-1-4222-1772-6(8)) Mason Crest.

Thouin, Juanita. Get Your Wallet On: The Money Quiz for High School Grads. 2003. 97p. (YA). per. 6.49 (978-0-9740641-0-9(6)) Daisy Publishing.

The Value of Money, 12 vols. 2016. (Value of Money Ser.). 24p. (ENG.). (gr. 1-2). lib. bdg. 145.62 (978-0-7660-7491-0(9), 6b51a1f0-b414-4312-bee6-6f2befa7379e); (gr. 2-1). pap. 56.10 (978-0-7660-7988-5(0)) Enslow Publishing, LLC.

Vickers, Rebecca. 101 Ways to Be Smart about Money. 2011. (101 Ser.). (ENG.). 56p. (gr. 5-9). pap. 9.95 (978-1-4109-4382-8(8), 117340, Raintree) Capstone.

Wallach, Jonah M. & Tattersall, Clare. Money & Banking. 2011. (J). 77.70 (978-1-4488-4752-5(4), Rosen Reference); (ENG.). 64p. (J). (gr. 5-5). pap. 13.95 (978-1-4488-4720-4(6), 3f948e9f-86b3-41f0-813a-592f7042d372, Rosen Reference); (ENG.). 64p. (YA). (gr. 5-5). lib. bdg. 37.13 (978-1-4488-4713-6(3), 3d13be3a-c23e-4494-b2f2-765fed6848bd) Rosen Publishing Group, Inc., The.

Waxman, Laura Hamilton. Let's Explore Needs & Wants. 2019. (Bumba Books (r) — a First Look at Money Ser.). (ENG., Illus.). 24p. (J). (gr. -1-1). 26.65 (978-1-5415-3852-8(8), 7ea0ae0c-826f-4489-97d1-7e3bf01eecb3, Lerner Pubns.); pap. 8.99 (978-1-5415-4572-4(9), ce99ae5e-103f-4c8d-b396-1163182d3e92) Lerner Publishing Group.

Weston Woods Staff, creator. If You Made a Million. 2011. 38.75 (978-0-439-84579-3(3)) 2004. (J). 29.95 (978-1-55592-134-7(5)) Weston Woods Studios, Inc.

White, Billy. Kids & Money. 2009. pap. (978-1-61623-010-4(X)) Independent Pub.

Whitehead, William. Country Money. Beech, Mark, illus. 2015. (How Money Works). (ENG.). 64p. (J). (gr. 4-6). pap. 15.93 (978-1-68404-069-8(8)) Norwood Hse. Pr.

—Family Money. Beech, Mark, illus. 2015. (How Money Works). (ENG.). 64p. (J). (gr. 4-6). pap. 15.93 (978-1-68404-070-4(1)); lib. bdg. 29.27 (978-1-59953-717-7(6)) Norwood Hse. Pr.

Whitehead, William, et al. Country Money. Beech, Mark, illus. 2015. (How Money Works). (ENG.). 64p. (J). (gr. 4-6). lib. bdg. 29.27 (978-1-59953-719-1(2)) Norwood Hse. Pr.

Williams, Deborah. Nickels & Pennies. Gedeon, Gloria, illus. l.t. ed. 2005. (ENG.). 12p. (gr. k-1). pap. 7.95 (978-1-879835-87-0(8), Kaeden Bks.) Kaeden Corp.

Wingard-Nelson, Rebecca. How Many Pennies Make a Dollar?, 1 vol. 2010. (I Like Money Math! Ser.). (ENG., Illus.). 24p. (gr. k-2). pap. 10.35 (978-0-7660-3656-7(1), 63313a50-9e7b-43b0-a0cb-ba39508a71da, Enslow Elementary); lib. bdg. 25.27 (978-0-7660-3141-8(1), ebd8f4ca-9f54-47dd-9023-137001b49fcd) Enslow Publishing, LLC.

—I Can Add Bills & Coins, 1 vol. 2010. (I Like Money Math! Ser.). (ENG., Illus.). 24p. (gr. k-2). pap. 10.35 (978-0-7660-3657-4(X), d1d1fb21-170f-4c93-9d98-8cc87c1aa031, Enslow Elementary); lib. bdg. 25.27 (978-0-7660-3143-2(8), a71592dd-7009-49a7-bc49-7dd61c5cdc0f) Enslow Publishing, LLC.

—I Can Count Money, 1 vol. 2010. (I Like Money Math! Ser.). (ENG., Illus.). 24p. (gr. k-2). pap. 10.35 (978-0-7660-3658-1(8), b166a432-104a-4c01-8c2b-a69fff1cdc5e, Enslow Elementary); lib. bdg. 25.27 (978-0-7660-3142-5(X), 1469c200-6bc5-4c33-9ef9-10ba18eeafef) Enslow Publishing, LLC.

—I Can Do Money Word Problems, 1 vol. 2010. (I Like Money Math! Ser.). (ENG., Illus.). 24p. (gr. k-2). pap. 10.35 (978-0-7660-3659-8(6), bf4458b3-3d77-4a3d-94e8-119404a45788, Enslow Elementary); lib. bdg. 25.27 (978-0-7660-3145-6(4), 497d6c6b-0eac-4c93-8ecf-9e247c114949) Enslow Publishing, LLC.

—I Can Name Bills & Coins, 1 vol. 2010. (I Like Money Math! Ser.). (ENG., Illus.). 24p. (gr. k-2). pap. 10.35 (978-0-7660-3660-4(X), d1652fd0-b429-47a3-948e-af3e51391448, Enslow Elementary); lib. bdg. 25.27 (978-0-7660-3140-1(3), d327bac2-6207-4c5e-93e4-3b5209d3fa48) Enslow Publishing, LLC.

—I Can Subtract Bills & Coins, 1 vol. 2010. (I Like Money Math! Ser.). (ENG., Illus.). 24p. (gr. k-2). pap. 10.35 (978-0-7660-3661-1(8), 0b86b8c6-203c-411d-afa8-dc5df4397740, Enslow Elementary); lib. bdg. 25.27 (978-0-7660-3144-9(6), 48531658-8f6a-4943-ad5c-da64e8d8dfcd) Enslow Publishing, LLC.

Woolf, Alex. You Wouldn't Want to Live Without Money! Antram, David, illus. 2015. (You Wouldn't Want to Live Without Ser.). (ENG.). 12p. (J). (gr. 3-6). 20.75 (978-1-5311-8766-8(8)) Perfection Learning Corp.

Worth, Bonnie. One Cent, Two Cents, Old Cent, New Cent: All about Money. Ruiz, Aristides, illus. 2008. (Cat in the Hat's Learning Library). (ENG.). 48p. (J). (gr. -1-3). 9.99 (978-0-375-82881-2(8), Random Hse. Bks. for Young Readers) Random Hse. Children's Bks.

Your Money, 8 vols. 2016. (Your Money Ser.). (ENG.). 00024p. (J). (gr. 1-1). 105.08 (978-1-4994-8137-2(3), 4391f421-152f-45e3-9346-e99614fc17b5, Windmill Bks.) Rosen Publishing Group, Inc., The.

Zediker, Rose Ross. Wealth in Biblical Times. 2009. (Money at its Best: Millionaires of the Old Testament Ser.). 112p. (YA). (gr. 7-12). 24.95 (978-1-4222-0477-1(4)) Mason Crest.

MONEY—FICTION

Amoore, Nat. Secrets of a Schoolyard Millionaire. 2019. (Illus.). 288p. (J). (gr. 4-6). 14.99 (978-0-14-379637-4(2), Puffin) Penguin Random Hse. AUS. Dist: Independent Pubs. Group.

Anna. The Magic Money Tree. 2009. (Illus.). 20p. pap. 15.49 (978-1-4389-0472-6(X)) AuthorHouse.

Atchley, Dalton. If I Had a Million Dollars. 2012. 20p. pap. 17.99 (978-1-4772-7934-2(2)) AuthorHouse.

Auseon, Andrew. Funny Little Monkey. 2006. (ENG., Illus.). 312p. (YA). (gr. 9-12). pap. 17.99 (978-0-15-205413-7(8), 1196293, Clarion Bks.) HarperCollins Pubs.

Barks, Carl, et al. Uncle Scrooge #389. 2009. 64p. pap. 7.99 (978-1-60360-089-7(2)) Gemstone Publishing, Inc.

Bhakta, Sanjini. My Life as a Dollar Bill. 2010. 28p. pap. 12.95 (978-1-4520-6152-8(1)) AuthorHouse.

Blume, Judy. Double Fudge. 2007. (ENG.). 240p. (J). (gr. 3-7). 8.99 (978-0-14-240878-0(6), Puffin Books) Penguin Young Readers Group.

—Double Fudge. 2004. (Fudge Ser.). 160p. (J). (gr. 3-7). pap. 36.00 incl. audio (978-0-8072-2036-8(1), Listening Library) Random Hse. Audio Publishing Group.

—Double Fudge. 2013. pap. (978-0-439-58549-1(X), Scholastic) Scholastic, Inc.

—Double Fudge. 2007. (Fudge Bks.: 5). lib. bdg. 18.40 (978-1-4177-8371-7(0)) Turtleback.

Bohrer, Maddie. Penny's Penny Puzzle. 2010. 24p. pap. 11.49 (978-1-4490-6477-8(9)) AuthorHouse.

Boyce, Frank Cottrell. Millions. 2005. 247p. (gr. 3-7). 19.00 (978-0-7569-5439-0(8)) Perfection Learning Corp.

Brandeis, Batsheva. Faiga Finds the Way. Levitas, Alexander, illus. 2005. (Fun to Read Book Ser.). (ENG.). 120p. (J). pap. 10.95 (978-1-929628-28-5(5)) Hachai Publishing.

Brian, Kate, pseud. Invitation Only. 2009. (Private Ser.: No. 2). (ENG.). 272p. (YA). pap. 9.99 (978-1-4169-9947-8(7), Simon & Schuster Bks. For Young Readers) Simon & Schuster Bks. For Young Readers.

Bricker, Chris. The Leaping Frogs of Calameris County. 2006. 48p. pap. 16.95 (978-1-4241-2408-4(5)) PublishAmerica, Inc.

Brisson, Pat. Benny's Pennies. 2014. 17.00 (978-1-63419-688-8(0)) Perfection Learning Corp.

Burke, Patrick J. Getting Your First Allowance. Severino, Philip, illus. 2008. 28p. pap. 24.95 (978-1-60441-882-8(6)) America Star Bks.

Caletti, Deb. The Fortunes of Indigo Skye. 2009. (ENG.). 320p. (YA). (gr. 7). pap. 9.99 (978-1-4169-1008-4(5), Simon Pulse) Simon Pulse.

Callaghan, Cindy. Lost in Hollywood. 2016. (Mix Ser.). (ENG., Illus.). 240p. (J). (gr. 4-8). pap. 8.99 (978-1-4814-6571-7(6), Aladdin) Simon & Schuster Children's Publishing.

—Lost in Hollywood. 2016. (Mix Ser.). (ENG., Illus.). 240p. (J). (gr. 4-8). 17.99 (978-1-4814-6572-4(4), Simon & Schuster/Paula Wiseman Bks.) Simon & Schuster/Paula Wiseman Bks.

Chad Borrows Money. l.t. ed. 2003. (Illus.). 16p. (J). ring bd. 15.95 (978-0-9722829-6-3(3)) Red Carpet Publishing.

Chinn, Karen. Sam & the Lucky Money, 1 vol. Hu, Ying-Hwa & Van Wright, Cornelius, illus. 2013. (ENG.). 32p. (J). (gr. k-3). reprint ed. pap. 11.95 (978-1-880000-53-3(9), leelowbooks) Lee & Low Bks., Inc.

Choyce, Lesley. Dumb Luck, 1 vol. 2011. (ENG.). 232p. (YA). (gr. 4-6). pap. 12.95 (978-0-88995-465-6(8), 7307c493-9fe7-42e9-ad67-b26766c11636) Trifolium Bks., Inc. CAN. Dist: Firefly Bks., Ltd.

Christelow, Eileen. Five Little Monkeys Play Hide & Seek. Christelow, Eileen, illus. 2010. (Five Little Monkeys Story Ser.). (ENG., Illus.). 40p. (J). (gr. -1-3). pap. 9.99 (978-0-547-33787-6(6), 1418278, Clarion Bks.) HarperCollins Pubs.

Clark, Clara Gillow. Secrets of Greymoor. 2009. (Trials of Hattie Belle Basket Ser.). (Illus.). 176p. (J). (gr. 5). 15.99 (978-0-7636-3249-6(X)) Candlewick Pr.

Cleave, Brenda. The Money Tree. 2010. 40p. pap. 18.99 (978-1-4490-7468-5(5)) AuthorHouse.

Coe, Mary E. Willy: the Best Christmas Gift Ever. 2008. 127p. 25.95 (978-0-557-02890-0(6)); pap. 10.95 (978-1-4357-1627-8(2)) Lulu Pr., Inc.

—Willy: the Best Christmas Gift Ever a Children's Book. 2009. 95p. pap. 9.95 (978-0-557-09420-2(8)) Lulu Pr., Inc.

—Willy: the Best Christmas Gift Ever A Children's Book. 2009. 55p. pap. 9.95 (978-0-557-08687-0(6)) Lulu Pr., Inc.

Collins, Nancy A. Vamps. 2008. (Vamps Ser.: 1). (ENG.). 256p. (YA). (gr. 9-18). pap. 8.99 (978-0-06-134917-1(8), HarperTeen) HarperCollins Pubs.

Corbett, Sue. The Last Newspaper Boy in America. 2010. (ENG.). 176p. (J). (gr. 6-8). 21.19 (978-0-525-42205-1(6)) Penguin Young Readers Group.

Costain, Meredith. Kids for Hire. Dale, Rae, illus. 2004. iv, 36p. (J). pap. (978-0-7608-6748-8(8)) Sundance/Newbridge Educational Publishing.

Curtis, Christopher Paul. Mr. Chickee's Funny Money. 2007. (Mr. Chickee's Ser.: 1). (ENG.). 160p. (J). (gr. 3-7). 6.99 (978-0-440-22919-3(7), Yearling) Random Hse. Children's Bks.

Daniels, Dominique. Mike & the Bike: Money Doesn't Grow on Trees. 2010. (Illus.). 20p. pap. 13.50 (978-1-4490-1768-2(1)) AuthorHouse.

The Darling of Wall Street. 2005. (J). pap. (978-0-9744863-1-4(0)) Paulus Publishing.

D'Arruda, Kim. A Day to Play. 2007. (Illus.). 32p. (J). 14.95 (978-0-9777993-2-9(8)) Financial Safari Pr.

deRubertis, Barbara. Deena Y Su Centavo de la Suerte; Deena's Lucky Penny. 2008. pap. 34.95 (978-1-58013-756-0(3)) Astra Publishing Hse.

Deutsch, Tehilla. Dollars & Sense. Zimmer, Glenn, illus. 2012. 36p. (J). (978-1-929628-65-0(X)) Hachai Publishing.

Dufresne, Michèle. The Lost Money. 2005. (Georgie Giraffe Set 1 Ser.). (ENG.). (J). pap. 7.33 (978-1-932570-37-3(3)) Pioneer Valley Bks.

Dussling, Jennifer. Fair Is Fair! Palmisciano, Diane, illus. 2003. (Math Matters Ser.). (ENG.). 32p. (J). (gr. 1-3). pap. 5.95 (978-1-57565-131-6(9), edcf2df2-a7f6-45bf-897b-c57ce5eb8088, Kane Press) Astra Publishing Hse.

—Lo Justo Es Justo; Fair Is Fair. 2008. pap. 34.95 (978-1-58013-785-0(7)) Astra Publishing Hse.

Earnest Took It with Him. 2005. (J). 12.95 (978-0-9762679-0-4(X)) Birdsall, Bonnie Thomas.

Espinoza, Vicki. Donnie Dollar. 2008. 38p. pap. 16.78 (978-0-557-01616-7(9)) Lulu Pr., Inc.

Ferguson, Gloria. Fair Money. 2012. 62p. 19.95 (978-1-4626-3037-0(5)) America Star Bks.

Fox, Jeannine. Feeding Penny Pig. 2009. 32p. (J). 14.95 (978-0-9841589-1-1(X)) Mimi's Funhouse, LLC.

Friedman, Laurie. In Business with Mallory. Pollak, Barbara, illus. 2007. (Mallory Ser.: 5). (ENG.). 160p. (J). (gr. 2-5). per. 6.99 (978-0-8225-6561-1(7), d7f9be85-65cb-4625-b159-d0f6c72cf370, Darby Creek) Lerner Publishing Group.

Gallagher, Diana G. Advice about Work & Play: Claudia Cristina Cortez Uncomplicates Your Life. Garvey, Brann, illus. 2010. (Claudia Cristina Cortez Ser.). (ENG.). 80p. (J). (gr. 4-8). pap. 6.10 (978-1-4342-2253-4(5), 103116, Stone Arch Bks.) Capstone.

Gilmore, Grace. The Lucky Wheel. Brown, Petra, illus. 2015. (Tales from Maple Ridge Ser.: 2). (ENG.). 128p. (J). (gr. k-4). pap. 5.99 (978-1-4814-2627-5(3), Little Simon) Little Simon.

Grandpa. The Beginning of Meet the Müsh-Mice: (a Visit to the North Pole) 2012. 34p. 29.95 (978-1-4626-9377-1(6)) America Star Bks.

Greene, Stephanie. Owen Foote, Money Man. Weston, Martha, illus. 2003. (ENG.). 96p. (J). (gr. -1-3). pap. 7.99 (978-0-618-37837-1(5), 100325, Clarion Bks.) HarperCollins Pubs.

Hargreaves, Roger. Mr. Stingy. 2011. (Mr. Men & Little Miss Ser.). (ENG.). 32p. (J). (gr. -1-2). mass mkt. 4.99 (978-0-8431-9959-8(8), Price Stern Sloan) Penguin Young Readers Group.

Harris, Ted. Catney Reid Who Needs Money? (978-0-9744597-5-2(5)) Brown Books Publishing Group.

Haskins, Lori. No Money? No Problem! Smath, Jerry, illus. 2004. (Social Studies Connects Ser.). 32p. (J). (gr. k-2). pap. 5.95 (978-1-57565-141-5(6), 5234bd1d-be5d-415f-b2c2-a5dac458bb0d, Kane Press) Astra Publishing Hse.

Hill, Joyce. A Penny in My Pocket. 2007. 220p. 27.95 (978-0-9795818-0-9(X)); pap. 14.95 (978-0-9795818-1-6(8)) Mushgush Pr.

Holland, Sara. Everless. 2018. (SPA.). 352p. (YA). (gr. 8). 15.95 (978-84-96886-88-9(3)) Ediciones Urano S. A. ESP. Dist: Spanish Pubs., LLC.

—Everless. 2018. (ENG.). (YA). (gr. 8). 384p. pap. 11.99 (978-0-06-265367-3(9)); 368p. 17.99 (978-0-06-265365-9(2)) HarperCollins Pubs. (HarperTeen).

Holub, Joan & Williams, Suzanne. Medusa the Rich. 2015. (Goddess Girls Ser.: 16). lib. bdg. 18.40 (978-0-606-36309-9(2)) Turtleback.

Horowitz, Anthony. The Switch. 2010. (ENG.). 192p. (J). (gr. 5-18). 7.99 (978-0-14-241547-4(2), Puffin Books) Penguin Young Readers Group.

Houran, Lori Haskins. Money Doesn't Grow on Mars (Book 8) Warrick, Jessica, illus. 2017. (How to Be an Earthling Ser.: 8). 64p. (J). (gr. 1-4). 6.99 (978-1-57565-850-6(X), 6203e0f5-a1e1-42f0-9d7c-72467d932644, Kane Press) Astra Publishing Hse.

—Money Doesn't Grow on Mars (Book 8) Self-Control. Warrick, Jessica, illus. 2017. (How to Be an Earthling (r) Ser.: 8). (ENG.). 64p. (J). (gr. 1-3). E-Book 34.65 (978-1-57565-854-4(2)) Astra Publishing Hse.

Jackson, Keith. I Forgot My Lunch Money. 2009. 32p. pap. 12.99 (978-1-4389-9008-8(1)) AuthorHouse.

Jacobs, Sheila. Jake Earns A Treat: A Life & Money Book. 2011. 24p. 11.99 (978-1-4567-3001-7(0)) AuthorHouse.

—Jake Saves the Day: A Life & Money Book. 2011. 24p. 11.99 *(978-1-4520-9929-3(4))* AuthorHouse.

Julie Marie. The Adventures of Fred the Five Pound Note. 2009. (Illus.). 52p. pap. 10.49 *(978-1-4389-4921-5(9))* AuthorHouse.

Karapetkova, Holly & Picou, Lin. Ouch! Stitches. Reese, Bob, illus. 2011. (Little Birdie Readers Ser.). (ENG.). 24p. (gr. 1-2). pap. 9.95 *(978-1-61236-023-2(8),* 9781612360232) Rourke Educational Media.

Lee, Kathy. Phoebe's Fortune. 2003. 128p. 6.49 *(978-1-85999-700-0(7))* Scripture Union GBR. Dist: Gabriel Resources.

Little, Robert. Jamaal's Lucky Day. Fitzpatrick, Audrey, illus. 2003. 32p. (J). (gr. 2-6). 15.95 *(978-0-9701863-4-8(7))* Relde Publishing.

Locurto, Ian N. The Christmas Penny. 2010. 20p. 11.99 *(978-1-4490-7100-4(7))* AuthorHouse.

Lorimer, Janet. Look to the Light, 1 vol. unabr. ed. 2010. (Q Reads Ser.). (ENG.). 32p. (YA). (gr. 9-12). pap. 8.50 *(978-1-61651-193-7(1))* Saddleback Educational Publishing, Inc.

Mackey, Lori. Money Mama & the Three Little Pigs. 2004. (Illus.). 48p. (J). 19.95 *(978-0-9744570-2-4(7))* P4K Publishing.

Mallon, Lynn & Marshall, Jennifer. It Pays to Be Honest. 2010. 28p. pap. 11.95 *(978-1-60594-440-1(8),* Llumina Pr.) Aeon Publishing Inc.

Manushkin, Fran. Piggy Bank Problems, 1 vol. Lyon, Tammie, illus. 2013. (Katie Woo Ser.). (ENG.). 32p. (J). (gr. k-2). pap. 5.95 *(978-1-4048-8048-1(8),* 121723); lib. bdg. 21.32 *(978-1-4048-7654-5(5),* 120171) Capstone. (Picture Window Bks.).

Manzo, Christopher. Oliver Brightside: You Don't Want That Penny. Adams, Lisa, illus. 2016. (ENG.). 36p. (J). 16.95 *(978-0-9963756-4-1(3))* All About Kids Publishing.

Marie, Tina. Isabella Learns the Value of Money. 2011. 24p. pap. 12.95 *(978-1-4567-4537-0(9))* AuthorHouse.

May, Eleanor. Albert Helps Out. Melmon, Deborah, illus. 2017. (Mouse Math Ser.). 32p. (J). (gr. -1-1). 7.99 *(978-1-57565-860-5(7),* 559a9afd-0705-4b1b-960c-61cc23cdd3ca, Kane Press) Astra Publishing Hse.

Mayer, Mercer. Just a Little Luck. Mayer, Mercer, illus. 2011. (Little Critter Ser.). (ENG., Illus.). 24p. (J). (gr. -1-2). pap. 3.99 *(978-0-06-147800-0(8),* HarperFestival) HarperCollins Pubs.

—Little Critter: Just Saving My Money. Mayer, Mercer, illus. 2010. (My First I Can Read Ser.). (ENG., Illus.). 32p. (J). (gr. -1-3). pap. 4.99 *(978-0-06-083557-6(5),* HarperCollins) HarperCollins Pubs.

Mazer, Anne. That's the Way the Cookie Crumbles. 2005. (Amazing Days of Abby Hayes Ser.: Bk. 16). (Illus.). 119p. (J). (gr. 3-7). 12.65 *(978-0-7569-6480-1(6))* Perfection Learning Corp.

McDougall, Jill. Jinxed! 2008. (Lightning Strikes Ser.). (ENG.). 112p. (J). pap. *(978-1-921150-59-3(9))* Walker Bks. Australia Pty. Ltd.

McGreal, Pat & McGreal, Carol. Uncle Scrooge #385. 2008. 64p. pap. 7.99 *(978-1-60360-062-0(0))* Gemstone Publishing, Inc.

McGreal, Pat, et al. Uncle Scrooge #390. 2009. 64p. pap. 7.99 *(978-1-60360-090-3(6))* Gemstone Publishing, Inc.

McKay, Hilary. Binny Bewitched. Ross, Tony, illus. 2017. (ENG.). 240p. (J). (gr. 3-7). 17.99 *(978-1-4814-9102-0(4),* McElderry, Margaret K. Bks.) McElderry, Margaret K. Bks.

McLeod, Cinders. Earn It! McLeod, Cinders, illus. 2017. (Moneybunny Book Ser.). (ENG., Illus.). 32p. (J). (-k). 16.99 *(978-0-399-54444-6(5),* Nancy Paulsen Books) Penguin Young Readers Group.

—Save It! McLeod, Cinders, illus. 2019. (Moneybunny Book Ser.). (ENG., Illus.). 32p. (J). (-k). 16.99 *(978-1-9848-1240-7(8),* Nancy Paulsen Books) Penguin Young Readers Group.

—Spend It! McLeod, Cinders, illus. 2019. (Moneybunny Book Ser.). (ENG., Illus.). 32p. (J). (-k). 16.99 *(978-0-399-54446-0(1),* Nancy Paulsen Books) Penguin Young Readers Group.

McQueen, Amelia. A Penny for Your Thoughts. 2010. 56p. pap. 23.99 *(978-1-4490-8046-4(4))* AuthorHouse.

Medina, Meg. Tia Isa Quiere un Carro. Munoz, Claudio, illus. 2012.Tr. of Tia Isa Wants a Car. (SPA.). 32p. (J). (gr. -1-2). pap. 7.99 *(978-0-7636-5751-2(4))* Candlewick Pr.

—Tia Isa Quiere un Carro. 2012.Tr. of Tia Isa Wants a Car. (SPA.). lib. bdg. 17.20 *(978-0-606-23801-4(8))* Turtleback.

—Tia Isa Wants a Car. Munoz, Claudio, illus. (ENG.). 32p. (J). (gr. -1-2). 2016. 7.99 *(978-0-7636-5752-9(2))* 2011. 17.99 *(978-0-7636-4156-6(1))* Candlewick Pr.

Milway, Katie Smith. One Hen: How One Small Loan Made a Big Difference. Fernandes, Eugenie, illus. 2008. (CitizenKid Ser.). (ENG.). 32p. (J). (gr. 3-7). 18.99 *(978-1-55453-028-1(8))* Kids Can Pr., Ltd. CAN. Dist: Hachette Bk. Group.

Mollel, Tololwa M. My Rows & Piles of Coins. Lewis, E. B., illus. 2019. (ENG.). 32p. (J). (gr. -1-3). pap. 8.99 *(978-0-358-12447-4(6),* 1753728, Clarion Bks.) HarperCollins Pubs.

El Mono Azul. (Fantasmas de Fear Street Coleccion). (SPA.). (YA). (gr. 5-8). pap. 7.95 *(978-950-04-2022-8(8),* EM10965) Emecé Editores S.A. ARG. Dist: Lectorum Pubns., Inc., Planeta Publishing Corp.

Moonjar, ed. Conversations to Go - Money. 2005. 36p. 9.95 *(978-0-9724282-5-5(9))* Moonjar, LLC.

—Noom & Raj Start Business. 2005. 36p. 19.95 *(978-0-9724282-2-4(4))* Moonjar, LLC.

Paige, D. M. Chart Topper. 2013. (Opportunity Ser.). (ENG.). 112p. (YA). (gr. 6-12). pap. 7.95 *(978-1-4677-1493-8(3),* 3e683878-42ab-4c6c-bf78-9d047cd1dd48); lib. bdg. 27.99 *(978-1-4677-1370-2(8),* 805d86f3-15a4-45a2-a20a-b9fe52e31213) Lerner Publishing Group. (Darby Creek).

Parker, John. Sucked In. 2008. (Lightning Strikes Ser.). (ENG.). 96p. (J). pap. *(978-1-921150-62-3(9))* Walker Bks. Australia Pty. Ltd.

Pascal, Francine. Dinero Desaparecido. Orig. Title: Jessica & the Money Mix-Up. (SPA.). (J). 6.95 *(978-84-272-3600-4(X))* Molino, Editorial ESP. Dist: AIMS International Bks., Inc.

Paulsen, Gary. The Tent. 2006. (ENG., Illus.). 96p. (YA). (gr. 7-12). pap. 7.95 *(978-0-15-205833-3(8),* 1197523, Clarion Bks.) HarperCollins Pubs.

—The Tent: A Parable in One Sitting. 2006. 86p. (gr. 7-12). 15.95 *(978-0-7569-6891-5(7))* Perfection Learning Corp.

Pujol, Miquel, et al. Uncle Scrooge #388. 2009. 64p. pap. 7.99 *(978-1-60360-088-0(4))* Gemstone Publishing, Inc.

Ramsey, Dave. Careless at the Carnival: Junior Discovers Spending. Ramsey, Marshall, illus. 2003. 26p. (J). 7.95 *(978-0-9726323-1-7(X))* Ramsey Pr.

—Dave Ramsey's 6 Kids Books Boxed Set. 2005. (J). 39.95 *(978-0-9774895-8-9(2))* Ramsey Pr.

—My Fantastic Fieldtrip: Junior Discovers Saving. Ramsey, Marshall, illus. 2003. 26p. (J). 7.95 *(978-0-9726323-3-1(6))* Ramsey Pr.

Reitz, Theresa, et al. The Money Tree: A Financial Book for Children. 2009. (Illus.). 52p. pap. 22.95 *(978-1-4327-3653-8(1))* Outskirts Pr., Inc.

RIGBY. The Moneybag: a Tale from Korea: Third Grade Big Books. 2003. (Rigby on Our Way to English Ser.). (ENG.). 24p. (gr. 3-3). pap. 50.70 *(978-0-7578-4214-6(3))* Rigby Education.

Rochester, Mary Frances. The Turquoise Monkey. 2010. 48p. pap. 17.99 *(978-1-4490-7260-5(7))* AuthorHouse.

Rogers, Ramona. Buck & Penny. 2013. 26p. pap. 9.99 *(978-0-9894748-9-4(5))* Mindstir Media.

Rose, Simon. Les Loonies: Les Emblèmes Canadiens. McMann, Julie, tr. from ENG. 2011. (FRE.). 24p. (YA). (gr. 2-4). *(978-1-77071-409-0(X))* Weigl Educational Pubs. Ltd.

Roy, Ron. Capital Mysteries #7: Trouble at the Treasury. Bush, Timothy, illus. 2006. (Capital Mysteries Ser.: 7). 96p. (J). (gr. 1-4). per. 6.99 *(978-0-375-83969-6(0),* Random Hse. Bks. for Young Readers) Random Hse. Children's Bks.

—The Talking T. Rex. Gurney, John, illus. 2003. (to Z Mysteries Ser.: 20). (gr. 3-6). lib. bdg. 14.75 *(978-0-613-85127-5(7))* Turtleback.

Roza, Greg. A Piggy Bank for Pedro, 1 vol. 2006. (Neighborhood Readers Ser.). (ENG.). 8p. (gr. k-1). pap. 5.15 *(978-1-4042-5714-6(4),* a44543a8-a638-4a94-9d39-44dac6499a0e, Rosen Classroom) Rosen Publishing Group, Inc., The.

Sabo-Western, Deborah. Peter Penny: Discovers the Gift. 2007. (ENG.). 46p. pap. 15.99 *(978-1-4196-8115-8(X))* CreateSpace Independent Publishing Platform.

Sadler, Marilyn & Bollen, Roger. Money, Money, Honey Bunny! 2006. (Bright & Early Books(R) Ser.). (ENG., Illus.). 36p. (J). (gr. -1-k). 9.99 *(978-0-375-83370-0(6),* Random Hse. Bks. for Young Readers) Random Hse. Children's Bks.

Santillo, LuAnn. Digging for Clams. Santillo, LuAnn, ed. 2003. (Half-Pint Kids Readers Ser.). (Illus.). 7p. (J). (gr. -1-1). pap. *(978-1-59256-092-9(X))* Half-Pint Kids, Inc.

Schraff, Anne E. Second Chances. 2013. (Urban Underground — Harriet Tubman High School Ser.). (YA). lib. bdg. 20.80 *(978-0-606-31584-5(5))* Turtleback.

Scraper, Katherine. Tag Sale Today. 2005. (J). pap. *(978-1-4108-4210-7(X))* Benchmark Education Co.

Shannon Simmons. The Community Club: #1 Aubrey & the Fight for Life. 2009. 112p. pap. 10.95 *(978-1-4401-7616-6(7))* iUniverse, Inc.

Siems, Thomas F. The Dangerous Pet. Blye, Steven G., illus. 2009. (ENG.). 46p. pap. 21.99 *(978-1-4415-3454-5(7))* Xlibris Corp.

Simmons, Michael. Pool Boy. 2005. 164p. (gr. 7). 17.95 *(978-0-7569-5064-4(3))* Perfection Learning Corp.

Singleton, Linda Joy. Cash Kat, 1 vol. Wald, Christina, illus. 2016. 39p. (J). (gr. k-1). (SPA.). pap. 11.95 *(978-1-62855-742-8(7),* 6feabda1-c792-415b-93f3-672f5c32d488); (ENG.). 17.95 *(978-1-62855-728-2(1))* Arbordale Publishing.

Slater, Jean M. Monkey Business: At the Market. Slater, Jean M., illus. 2003. (Illus.). 10p. (J). bds. 16.00 *(978-0-9743149-4-5(3))* Slater Software, Inc.

Sparks, Candi. Max Gets It!, 4 vols. William, Graf, illus. 2008. (Can I Have Some Money? Ser.: Vol. 3). (ENG.). 32p. (J). pap. *(978-0-9789445-1-3(8))* Sparks Fly.

—Of Course You Can! Educating Children about Money. Graf, William, illus. 2006. (Can I Have Some Money? Ser.). pap. 11.99 *(978-0-9789445-0-6(X))* Sparks Fly.

Sparks, Candi & Sparks, Kelvin. Lemonade Sold Out: Can I Have Some Money? (No. 5) 2015. (Can I Have Some Money? Ser.: 5). (ENG., Illus.). 34p. (J). (gr. 1-8). pap. 12.98 *(978-0-9789445-9-9(3))* Sparks Fly.

Sparks, Candi, et al. Nacho Money. Bill, Graf, illus. 2012. (Can I Have Some Money? Ser.). 36p. pap. 11.99 *(978-0-9789445-6-8(9))* Sparks Fly.

Standish, Burt L. Dick Merriwell's Marked Money. Rudman, Jack, ed. 2003. (Frank Merriwell Ser.). pap. 9.95 *(978-0-8373-9100-7(8))* Merriwell, Frank Inc.

Strasser, Todd. For Money & Love. 2007. (Mob Princess Ser.: 1). (ENG.). 208p. (YA). (gr. 9-18). pap. 10.99 *(978-1-4169-3533-9(9),* Simon Pulse) Simon Pulse.

Suddard, Lisa. Money Grows with Bees. Cabrillo, Cinthya, illus. 2009. 24p. pap. 14.95 *(978-1-4251-8673-9(4))* Trafford Publishing.

Sundaram, Siddhartha & Raghuraman, Renuka S. Horace Leclaire & His Bottles of Air. Raghuraman, Savitri, illus. 2008. 36p. pap. 9.99 *(978-1-935105-03-9(5))* Avid Readers Publishing Group.

Thompson, David. The Nine Clues of Christmas, 1 vol. 2009. 172p. pap. 24.95 *(978-1-60813-410-6(5))* America Star Bks.

Toole, Spencer. Selena Saves Money: Checking Your Work, 1 vol. 2017. (Computer Science for the Real World Ser.). (ENG.). 16p. (gr. 2-3). pap. *(978-1-5383-5214-4(1),* 9086dab0-86c6-47d5-8f2b-fcf033b515d5, Rosen Classroom) Rosen Publishing Group, Inc., The.

Tyrrell, Helen. Nora & the Dancing Horse. 2003. 231p. (J). pap. 14.95 *(978-0-7414-1349-9(3))* Infinity Publishing.

Van Draanen, Wendelin. Sammy Keyes & the Cold Hard Cash. 2010. (Sammy Keyes Ser.: 12). (ENG.). 320p. (J). (gr. 5-7). 7.99 *(978-0-440-42113-9(6),* Yearling) Random Hse. Children's Bks.

Watson Dubisch, Carolyn. The Horribles. 2011. (ENG.). 73p. pap. 16.96 *(978-0-557-35938-7(4))* Lulu Pr., Inc.

Whitby, Adele. Kay's Story 1934. 2015. (Secrets of the Manor Ser.: 6). (ENG., Illus.). 160p. (J). (gr. 3-7). pap. 6.99 *(978-1-4814-2755-5(5),* Simon Spotlight) Simon Spotlight.

Williams, Shannon. Where Does Money Come From? Book One of Money Matters for Children. 2013. (Illus.). 20p. pap. 13.77 *(978-1-4907-0551-4(1))* Trafford Publishing.

Williams, Vera B. A Chair for My Mother: A Caldecott Honor Award Winner. Williams, Vera B., illus. 25th anniv. ed. 2007. (ENG., Illus.). 32p. (J). (gr. -1-3). pap. 8.99 *(978-0-688-04074-1(8),* Greenwillow Bks.) HarperCollins Pubs.

Williams, Zachary. The Lost Nickel, 1 vol. 2006. (Neighborhood Readers Ser.). (ENG.). 8p. (gr. k-1). pap. 5.15 *(978-1-4042-5786-3(1),* 8da9b16b-c31f-4375-8494-fba9372d20a9, Rosen Classroom) Rosen Publishing Group, Inc., The.

Zajac, Kristen K. El Primo de Ebeneezer. Houdeshell, Jennifer Thomas, illus. 2011. 20p. pap. 10.95 *(978-1-61633-164-1(X))* Guardian Angel Publishing, Inc.

MONEY—HISTORY

Brasch, Nicolas. The Invention of Money. 2013. (Discovery Education: Discoveries & Inventions Ser.). 32p. (J). (gr. 3-6). pap. 60.00 *(978-1-4777-1509-3(6));* (ENG.). (gr. 4-5). pap. 11.00 *(978-1-4777-1508-6(8),* cf056bc0-81e6-4e32-a283-3a544e35f323); (ENG.). (gr. 4-5). lib. bdg. 28.93 *(978-1-4777-1333-4(6),* ebdcc480-0fcd-4657-8681-26434ac78c3f) Rosen Publishing Group, Inc., The. (PowerKids Pr.).

Furgang, Kathy. National Geographic Kids Everything Money: A Wealth of Facts, Photos, & Fun! 2013. (National Geographic Kids Everything Ser.). (Illus.). 64p. (J). (gr. 3-7). pap. 12.95 *(978-1-4263-1026-3(9));* (ENG., lib. bdg. 21.90 *(978-1-4263-1027-0(7))* Disney Publishing Worldwide. (National Geographic Kids).

Gregory, Helen. We Need Money, 1 vol. 2011. (Wonder Readers Early Level Ser.). (ENG.). 16p. (gr. -1-1). (J). pap. 6.25 *(978-1-4296-7808-7(9),* 117980); pap. 35.94 *(978-1-4296-8201-5(9))* Capstone. (Capstone Pr.).

Housel, Debra J. & Rice, Dona Herwick. Buy It! History of Money, 1 vol. 2nd rev. ed. 2012. (TIME for KIDS(r): Informational Text Ser.). (ENG.). 32p. (gr. 3-5). pap. 12.99 *(978-1-4333-3681-2(2))* Teacher Created Materials, Inc.

Jenkins, Martin. The History of Money: From Bartering to Banking. Kitamura, Satoshi, illus. 2014. (ENG.). 64p. (J). (gr. 4-7). 16.99 *(978-0-7636-6763-4(3))* Candlewick Pr.

Meachen Rau, Dana. The History of Money, 1 vol. (Money & Banks (New Edition) Ser.). (ENG., Illus.). 24p. (gr. 2-4). 2010. pap. 9.15 *(978-1-4339-3381-3(0),* 45a8fd3f-0796-4713-b87f-6375049643d9) 2010. (J). lib. bdg. 24.67 *(978-1-4339-3380-6(2),* 0e0ab191-ab63-4ae0-a55e-4812fa325ef4) 2005. lib. bdg. 23.67 *(978-0-8368-4869-4(1),* ba7132ed-471c-4f29-865c-5f7d70a1be85, Weekly Reader Leveled Readers) Stevens, Gareth Publishing LLLP.

Resnick, Abraham. Money. 2009. 136p. pap. 18.95 *(978-1-4401-1318-5(1))* iUniverse, Inc.

Tiner, John. The Story of in God We Trust: Discovering Our Nations Heritage. 2003. (Discovering Our Nation's Heritage Ser.). (Illus.). 48p. (J). 6.99 *(978-0-89051-392-7(9),* 303-090, Master Books) New Leaf Publishing Group.

Vox, Everett. The U. S. Mint: The History of U. S. Money, 1 vol. 2017. (Landmarks of Democracy: American Institutions Ser.). (ENG.). 24p. (J). (gr. 3-3). pap. 9.25 *(978-1-5081-6101-1(1),* 966702f8-0bbd-466e-8e44-d334201245a1, PowerKids Pr.) Rosen Publishing Group, Inc., The.

MONEY-MAKING PROJECTS FOR CHILDREN

see Moneymaking Projects

MONEY, PAPER

see Paper Money

MONEY RAISING

see Fund Raising

MONEYMAKING PROJECTS

Antill, Sara. 10 Ways I Can Earn Money, 1 vol. 2012. (I Can Make a Difference Ser.). (ENG., Illus.). 24p. (J). (gr. 2-3). pap. 9.25 *(978-1-4488-6371-6(6),* f4195fa7-d826-4f6d-a209-f2c9349e7d5a); lib. bdg. 26.27 *(978-1-4488-6206-1(X),* 63e13ef8-dbd8-4413-ba35-ac07b800d0b4) Rosen Publishing Group, Inc., The. (PowerKids Pr.).

Bea Is for Business: The Party Planning Venture. 2014. (ENG., Illus.). 35p. (J). 9.99 *(978-0-9893403-2-8(5))* Bea is for Business.

Bochner, Arthur, et al. New Totally Awesome Business Book for Kids: Revised Edition. 3rd rev. ed. 2007. (New Totally Awesome Ser.: 2). (ENG., Illus.). 192p. (gr. 7-9). per. 15.99 *(978-1-55704-757-1(X),* William Morrow Paperbacks) HarperCollins Pubs.

Bradley, Kathleen E. Making Money Grow, 1 vol. 2nd rev. ed. 2013. (TIME for KIDS(r): Informational Text Ser.). (ENG.). 64p. (gr. 4-8). pap. 14.99 *(978-1-4333-4908-9(6))* Teacher Created Materials, Inc.

Bullard, Lisa. Ella Earns Her Own Money. Moran, Mike, illus. 2013. (Cloverleaf Books (tm) — Money Basics Ser.). (ENG.). 24p. (J). (gr. k-2). pap. 8.99 *(978-1-4677-1511-9(5),* b168e408-3e49-4a15-844f-da1cd1a4830f, Millbrook Pr.) Lerner Publishing Group.

—Kyle Keeps Track of Cash. Byrne, Mike, illus. 2013. (Cloverleaf Books (tm) — Money Basics Ser.). (ENG.). 24p. (J). (gr. k-2). pap. 8.99 *(978-1-4677-1510-2(7),* 19d12429-1526-4f57-aeb7-3594888b65f3, Millbrook Pr.) Lerner Publishing Group.

Carlson Berne, Emma. Run Your Own Babysitting Business, 1 vol., 1. 2013. (Young Entrepreneurs Ser.). (ENG., Illus.). 32p. (J). (gr. 4-5). 28.93 *(978-1-4777-2922-9(4),* 51eb31f4-6ba4-4d81-ae05-b55141626d55, PowerKids Pr.) Rosen Publishing Group, Inc., The.

—Run Your Own Bake Sale, 1 vol. 2013. (Young Entrepreneurs Ser.). (ENG., Illus.). 32p. (J). (gr. 4-5). pap. 11.00 *(978-1-4777-3007-2(9),* 973a2ce6-8470-4738-8575-15212c7a9454);1. 28.93 *(978-1-4777-2918-2(6),* b4c8f2d1-aace-4b36-8164-4ce2d94b8083) Rosen Publishing Group, Inc., The. (PowerKids Pr.).

—Run Your Own Car Wash, 1 vol. 2014. (Young Entrepreneurs Ser.). (ENG., Illus.). 32p. (J). (gr. 4-5). pap. 11.00 *(978-1-4777-3009-6(5),* 5adb9280-3976-4a91-bb56-8d454addf4c0);1. 28.93 *(978-1-4777-2920-5(8),* 268ac1d1-f6c7-4844-a823-487459c5780a) Rosen Publishing Group, Inc., The. (PowerKids Pr.).

—Run Your Own Yard-Work Business, 1 vol. 2013. (Young Entrepreneurs Ser.). (ENG., Illus.). 32p. (J). (gr. 4-5). pap. 11.00 *(978-1-4777-3010-2(9),* f8fbf2f4-0f9f-45ed-beb6-e1fb12b0418e);1. 28.93 *(978-1-4777-6125-0(X),* 0e89da16-6c83-4ddd-b20b-38c14e7553d0) Rosen Publishing Group, Inc., The. (PowerKids Pr.).

Daly, Ruth. Dog Walker. 2017. (Illus.). 24p. (J). *(978-1-4896-6086-2(0),* AV2 by Weigl) Weigl Pubs., Inc.

Gagne, Tammy. Start Your Petsitting Service. 2017. (Build Your Business Ser.). (ENG., Illus.). 32p. (J). (gr. 3-9). lib. bdg. 28.65 *(978-1-5157-6689-6(6),* 135251, Capstone Pr.) Capstone.

Hagler, Gina. Money-Making Opportunities for Teens Who Are Artistic, 1 vol. 2013. (Make Money Now! Ser.). (ENG., Illus.). 80p. (YA). (gr. 7-7). lib. bdg. 38.41 *(978-1-4488-9387-4(9),* c4f51914-1559-4110-b282-9142951b13c5) Rosen Publishing Group, Inc., The.

Hansen, Mark Victor. The Richest Kids in America: How They Earn It, How They Spend It, How You Can Too. 2009. (ENG.). 168p. pap. 14.99 *(978-0-9819709-0-5(7))* Hay Hse., Inc.

Henneberg, Susan. Money-Making Opportunities for Teens Who Like Working with Kids, 1 vol. 2013. (Make Money Now! Ser.). (ENG., Illus.). 80p. (YA). (gr. 7-7). lib. bdg. 38.41 *(978-1-4488-9385-0(2),* c76f2e72-638b-4924-91fd-5ee4d977b4e9) Rosen Publishing Group, Inc., The.

Holyoke, Nancy. A Smart Girl's Guide: Money: How to Make It, Save It, & Spend It. Barrager, Brigette, illus. 2014. (American Girl(r) Wellbeing Ser.). (ENG.). 96p. (J). pap. 12.99 *(978-1-60958-407-8(4))* American Girl Publishing, Inc.

John, Daymond. Little Daymond Learns to Earn. Miles, Nicole, illus. 2023. 40p. (J). (gr. -1-3). (ENG.). 22.99 *(978-0-593-56728-9(5));* 19.99 *(978-0-593-56727-2(7))* Random Hse. Children's Bks. (Random Hse. Bks. for Young Readers).

Kiefer, Jeanne. Jobs for Kids: A Smart Kid's Q & A Guide. Green, Anne Canevari, illus. 2003. (Single Titles Ser.). 112p. (gr. 5-8). lib. bdg. 25.90 *(978-0-7613-2611-3(1),* Millbrook Pr.) Lerner Publishing Group.

Leavitt, Amie Jane. How to Create Digital Portfolios for Collaborative Projects, 1 vol. 2017. (Project Learning Using Digital Portfolios Ser.). (ENG.). 64p. (gr. 7-7). 36.13 *(978-1-5081-7524-7(1),* c9ada486-9f6d-490a-8e71-6d4a0dc18d37, Rosen Young Adult) Rosen Publishing Group, Inc., The.

—Start Your Yard Work Business. 2017. (Build Your Business Ser.). (ENG., Illus.). 32p. (J). (gr. 3-9). lib. bdg. 28.65 *(978-1-5157-6692-6(6),* 135253, Capstone Pr.) Capstone.

Martin, Steve. Entrepeneur Academy. Robertson, Maisie, illus. 2019. (ENG.). 64p. (J). pap. 12.99 *(978-1-61067-716-5(1))* Kane Miller.

Money Matters: A Kid's Guide to Money, 6 vols., Set. 2010. (J). (gr. 3-6). lib. bdg. 179.70 *(978-1-58415-835-6(2))* Mitchell Lane Pubs.

Murphy, Patricia J. Earning Money. 2005. (How Economics Works). (Illus.). 48p. (J). (gr. 3-7). lib. bdg. 25.26 *(978-0-8225-2149-5(0),* Lerner Pubns.) Lerner Publishing Group.

Orr, Tamra. A Kid's Guide to Earning Money. 2008. (Money Matters Ser.). (Illus.). 48p. (YA). (gr. 3-6). lib. bdg. 29.95 *(978-1-58415-643-7(0))* Mitchell Lane Pubs.

Saidian, Siyavush. Ways to Make Money Working with Animals, 1 vol. 2019. (Cash in on Your Skills Ser.). (ENG.). 80p. (gr. 7-7). pap. 18.60 *(978-1-9785-1551-2(0),* 1bef07a1-fbbb-42c3-8c5d-313694534afb) Enslow Publishing, LLC.

Swanson, Jennifer A. Smart Strategies for Turning an Idea into a Product or Service, 1 vol. 2014. (Financial Security & Life Success for Teens Ser.). (ENG.). 80p. (YA). (gr. 7-7). 37.47 *(978-1-4777-7634-6(6),* 156213e9-4850-4b5e-9cae-72a24c170306) Rosen Publishing Group, Inc., The.

Tangerine Press Staff & Scholastic, Inc. Staff, contrib. by. Kid Biz. 2004. (Illus.). 62p. (J). *(978-0-439-69986-0(X))* Scholastic, Inc.

Thornton, J. D. How to Make Money. 2006. (Illus.). 92p. (J). pap. *(978-0-545-07195-6(X))* Scholastic, Inc.

Waxman, Laura Hamilton. Let's Explore Earning Money. 2019. (Bumba Books (r) — a First Look at Money Ser.). (ENG., Illus.). 24p. (J). (gr. -1-1). 26.65 *(978-1-5415-3855-9(2),* e69ee47e-2f23-4cba-b63d-5a7ad086d5dc, Lerner Pubns.) Lerner Publishing Group.

MONEYMAKING PROJECTS—FICTION

Bair, Sheila. Isabel's Car Wash. Stead, Judy, illus. 2012. (J). 34.28 *(978-1-61913-118-7(8))* Weigl Pubs., Inc.

—Isabel's Car Wash. Stead, Judy, illus. 2011. (Money Tales Ser.). (ENG.). 32p. (J). (gr. 1-5). 9.99 *(978-0-8075-3653-7(9),* 807536539) Whitman, Albert & Co.

Banim, Lisa. In the Doghouse. 2005. 124p. (J). lib. bdg. 16.92 *(978-1-4242-0685-8(5))* Fitzgerald Bks.

Barrows, Annie. Ivy & Bean No News Is Good News (Book 8) Blackall, Sophie, illus. 2011. (Ivy & Bean Ser.: IVYB). (ENG.). 128p. (J). (gr. 1-5). 14.99 *(978-0-8118-6693-4(9))* Chronicle Bks. LLC.

—Ivy & Bean No News Is Good News (Book 8) (Best Friends Books for Kids, Elementary School Books, Early Chapter Books), Volume 8. Blackall, Sophie, illus. 2012. (Ivy & Bean Ser.). (ENG.). 144p. (J). (gr. 1-5). pap. 5.99 *(978-1-4521-0781-3(5))* Chronicle Bks. LLC.

Barrows, Annie & Blackall, Sophie. Ivy + Bean. 2011. (Ivy & Bean Ser.). (ENG., Illus.). 120p. (J). (gr. 2-5). 31.36 *(978-1-59961-928-6(8),* 10108, Chapter Bks.) Spotlight.

Belford, Bibi. Canned & Crushed. 2015. (ENG.). 192p. (J). (gr. 2-7). 14.99 *(978-1-63220-435-6(5),* Sky Pony Pr.) Skyhorse Publishing Co., Inc.

Benton, Jim. Dumbness Is a Dish Best Served Cold (Dear Dumb Diary: Deluxe) Benton, Jim, illus. 2016. (Dear Dumb Diary Ser.). (ENG., Illus.). 224p. (J). (gr. 3-7). 12.99 *(978-0-545-93228-8(9),* Scholastic Pr.) Scholastic, Inc.

Birdsall, Jeanne. The Penderwicks in Spring. 2015. (Penderwicks Ser.: 4). (ENG.). 352p. (J). (gr. 3-7). 16.99 *(978-0-375-87077-4(6),* Knopf Bks. for Young Readers) Random Hse. Children's Bks.

Bloom, Steve. The Stand-In. (ENG.). 360p. (YA). (gr. 8-12). 2018. pap. 9.99 *(978-1-5415-1484-3(X),* ef16da22-6bda-4a9a-b3cc-fb51cb52fdb1) 2016. 18.99 *(978-1-5124-1023-5(3),* ad1a2cb5-3967-4d9a-95c9-732e41848b05) 2016. E-Book 29.32 *(978-1-5124-1121-8(3))* Lerner Publishing Group. (Carolrhoda Lab™).

Bowe, Julie. Dance Fever. 2017. (Victoria Torres, Unfortunately Average Ser.). (ENG.). 160p. (J). (gr. 4-8). lib. bdg. 27.99 *(978-1-4965-3819-2(6),* 133118, Stone Arch Bks.) Capstone.

Bradman, Tony. Jack & the Bean Snacks, 1 vol. Warburton, Sarah, illus. (After Happily Ever After Ser.). (ENG.). 56p. (J). (gr. 3-6). 2014. pap. 4.95 *(978-1-4342-7964-4(2),* 124713) 2009. 25.99 *(978-1-4342-1305-1(6),* 95630) Capstone. (Stone Arch Bks.).

Branford, Anna. Violet Mackerel's Brilliant Plot. Allen, Elanna, illus. 2012. (Violet Mackerel Ser.). (ENG.). 112p. (J). (gr. 1-5). 15.99 *(978-1-4424-3585-8(2));* pap. 5.99 *(978-1-4424-3586-5(0))* Simon & Schuster Children's Publishing. (Atheneum Bks. for Young Readers).

Carlson, Melody. Raising Faith, 1 vol. 2016. (Faithgirlz / Girls of Harbor View Ser.). (ENG.). 272p. (J). pap. 9.99 *(978-0-310-75375-9(9))* Zonderkidz.

Clements, Andrew. Lunch Money. Selznick, Brian, illus. 2007. (ENG.). 240p. (J). (gr. 3-7). pap. 7.99 *(978-0-689-86685-2(2),* Atheneum Bks. for Young Readers) Simon & Schuster Children's Publishing.

—Lunch Money. 2007. 17.20 *(978-1-4177-8116-4(5))* Turtleback.

Conford, Ellen. A Job for Jenny Archer. 2006. (ENG., Illus.). 80p. (J). (gr. 1-4). per. 8.99 *(978-0-316-01484-7(2))* Little, Brown Bks. for Young Readers.

—What's Cooking, Jenny Archer? 2006. (ENG., Illus.). 80p. (J). (gr. 1-4). per. 8.99 *(978-0-316-01488-5(5))* Little, Brown Bks. for Young Readers.

conrad, catherine. The Lemonade Stand. 2008. (Illus.). 32p. (J). lib. bdg. 16.99 *(978-0-9799065-0-3(4))* Banana Pr.

Cossanteli, Veronica. The Extincts. Muradov, Roman, illus. 2016. (ENG.). 240p. (J). 27.99 *(978-1-62779-403-9(4),* 900149181, Holt, Henry & Co. Bks. For Young Readers) Holt, Henry & Co.

Davies, Jacqueline. The Lemonade War. (Lemonade War Ser.: 1). (ENG.). 192p. (J). (gr. 3-7). 2022. pap. 9.99 *(978-0-547-23765-7(0),* 1083876) 2007. (Illus.). 18.99 *(978-0-618-75043-6(6),* 511891) HarperCollins Pubs. (Clarion Bks.).

Deriso, C. H. Elisabeth & the Unwanted Advice. 2016. (Babysitter Chronicles Ser.). (ENG., Illus.). 160p. (J). (gr. 4-7). lib. bdg. 26.65 *(978-1-4965-2757-8(7),* 131485, Stone Arch Bks.) Capstone.

deRubertis, Barbara & DeRubertis, Barbara. Walter Warthog's Wonderful Wagon. Alley, R. W., illus. 2012. (Animal Antics A to Z Ser.). 32p. (J). (gr. 2 — 1). cd-rom 7.95 *(978-1-57565-416-4(4))* Astra Publishing Hse.

Dowell, Frances O'Roark. Phineas L. MacGuire ... Blasts Off! McDaniels, Preston, illus. 2011. (From the Highly Scientific Notebooks of Phineas L. MacGuire Ser.). (ENG.). 224p. (J). (gr. 3-7). pap. 7.99 *(978-1-4424-2204-9(1),* Atheneum Bks. for Young Readers) Simon & Schuster Children's Publishing.

—Sam the Man & the Chicken Plan. Bates, Amy June, illus. (Sam the Man Ser.: 1). (ENG.). (J). (gr. 1-4). 2017. 144p. pap. 8.99 *(978-1-4814-4067-7(5))* 2016. 128p. 16.99 *(978-1-4814-4066-0(7))* Simon & Schuster Children's Publishing.

Doyle, Bill. Attack of the Shark-Headed Zombie. Altman, Scott, illus. 2011. (Stepping Stone Book(TM) Ser.). (ENG.). 112p. (J). (gr. 1-4). 5.99 *(978-0-375-86675-3(2),* Random Hse. Bks. for Young Readers) Random Hse. Children's Bks.

Draper, Sharon M. The Backyard Animal Show. Watson, Jesse Joshua, illus. 2012. (Clubhouse Mysteries Ser.: 5). (ENG.). 128p. (J). (gr. 3-7). pap. 6.99 *(978-1-4424-5022-6(3),* Aladdin) Simon & Schuster Children's Publishing.

—The Backyard Animal Show. Watson, Jesse Joshua, illus. 2012. (Clubhouse Mysteries Ser.: 5). (ENG.). 128p. (J). (gr. 3-7). 17.99 *(978-1-4424-5023-3(1),* Simon & Schuster/Paula Wiseman Bks.) Simon & Schuster/Paula Wiseman Bks.

—Stars & Sparks on Stage. Watson, Jesse Joshua, illus. 2012. (Clubhouse Mysteries Ser.: 6). (ENG.). 144p. (J). (gr. 3-7). pap. 6.99 *(978-1-4424-5457-6(1),* Aladdin) Simon & Schuster Children's Publishing.

—Stars & Sparks on Stage. Watson, Jesse Joshua, illus. 2012. (Clubhouse Mysteries Ser.: 6). (ENG.). 144p. (J). (gr. 3-7). 17.99 *(978-1-4424-5459-0(8),* Simon & Schuster/Paula Wiseman Bks.) Simon & Schuster/Paula Wiseman Bks.

Eggleton, Jill. The Ice-Cream Machine. Pye, Trevor, illus. 2003. (Rigby Sails Early Ser.). (ENG.). 16p. (gr. 1-2). pap. 6.95 *(978-0-7578-8728-4(7))* Houghton Mifflin Harcourt Publishing Co.

Elliott, Rebecca. The Wildwood Bakery. 2017. (Owl Diaries — Branches Ser.: 7). lib. bdg. 14.75 *(978-0-606-40660-4(3))* Turtleback.

—The Wildwood Bakery: a Branches Book (Owl Diaries #7) Elliott, Rebecca, illus. 2017. (Owl Diaries: 7). (ENG., Illus.). 80p. (J). (gr. k-2). pap. 4.99 *(978-1-338-16300-1(0))* Scholastic, Inc.

—The Wildwood Bakery: a Branches Book (Owl Diaries #7) (Library Edition) Elliott, Rebecca, illus. 2017. (Owl Diaries: 7). (ENG., Illus.). 80p. (J). (gr. k-2). lib. bdg. 15.99 *(978-1-338-16301-8(9))* Scholastic, Inc.

Fix, Philippe. Seraphin. Nicholson-Smith, Donald, tr. Fix, Philippe, illus. 2019. (ENG., Illus.). 28p. (J). (gr. k-3). pap. 18.00 *(978-1-939810-25-0(6),* Elsewhere Editions) Steerforth Pr.

Friedman, Laurie. In Business with Mallory. Pollak, Barbara, illus. 2007. (Mallory Ser.: 5). (ENG.). 160p. (J). (gr. 2-5). per. 6.99 *(978-0-8225-6561-1(7),* d7f9be85-65cb-4625-b159-d0f6c72cf370, Darby Creek) Lerner Publishing Group.

Graff, Lisa. The Life & Crimes of Bernetta Wallflower. 2015. (ENG.). 288p. (J). (gr. 3-7). 9.99 *(978-0-14-751675-6(7),* Puffin Books) Penguin Young Readers Group.

Graves, Emma T. Total FREAK-Out. Boo, Binny, illus. 2018. (My Undead Life Ser.). (ENG.). 112p. (J). (gr. 3-6). pap. 7.95 *(978-1-4965-6450-4(2),* 138362); lib. bdg. 25.99 *(978-1-4965-6446-7(4),* 138358) Capstone. (Stone Arch Bks.).

Green, D. L. Kaitlyn & the Competition. 2016. (Babysitter Chronicles Ser.). (ENG.). 160p. (J). (gr. 4-7). pap. 6.95 *(978-1-4914-8861-4(1),* 131486, Stone Arch Bks.) Capstone.

—Zeke Meeks vs the No-Fun Fund-Raiser, 1 vol. Alves, Josh, illus. 2013. (Zeke Meeks Ser.). (ENG.). 128p. (J). (gr. 2-4). lib. bdg. 22.65 *(978-1-4048-7640-8(5),* 120159, Picture Window Bks.) Capstone.

Greene, Stephanie. Owen Foote, Money Man. Weston, Martha, illus. 2003. 88p. (gr. 2-4). 14.95 *(978-0-7569-1559-9(7))* Perfection Learning Corp.

Gutman, Dan. The Get Rich Quick Club. (ENG.). 128p. (J). 2006. (gr. 3-7). pap. 6.99 *(978-0-06-053442-4(7),* HarperCollins) 2004. 15.99 *(978-0-06-053440-0(0))* HarperCollins Pubs.

—Mrs. Master Is a Disaster! 2017. (My Weirdest School Ser.: 8). (Illus.). 105p. (J). lib. bdg. 14.75 *(978-0-606-40078-7(8))* Turtleback.

—My Weirdest School #8: Mrs. Master Is a Disaster! Paillot, Jim, illus. 2017. (My Weirdest School Ser.: 8). (ENG.). 112p. (J). (gr. 1-5). pap. 5.99 *(978-0-06-242933-9(7),* HarperCollins) HarperCollins Pubs.

Hambrick, Sharon. Tommy's Race. Manning, Maurie J., illus. 2004. (Fig Street Kids Ser.). 95p. (J). (gr. 1-2). 7.49 *(978-1-59166-286-0(9))* BJU Pr.

Hartinger, Brent. Project Sweet Life. 2009. (J). lib. bdg. 17.89 *(978-0-06-082412-9(3),* HarperTeen) HarperCollins Pubs.

Haugaard, Kay. No Place. 2nd ed. 2007. (ENG., Illus.). 140p. (J). (gr. 2-8). per. 6.95 *(978-1-57131-675-2(2))* Milkweed Editions.

Heine, Theresa & Barefoot Books Staff. Chandra's Magic Light. Gueyfier, Judith, illus. 2013. (J). 16.99 *(978-1-84686-493-3(3))* Barefoot Bks., Inc.

Holm, Jennifer L. Full of Beans. 2018. 224p. (J). (gr. 3-7). 8.99 *(978-0-553-51038-6(X),* Yearling) Random Hse. Children's Bks.

Holm, Jennifer L. & Holm, Matthew. Babymouse #19: Bad Babysitter. Holm, Jennifer L. & Holm, Matthew, illus. 2015. (Babymouse Ser.: 19). (ENG., Illus.). 96p. (J). (gr. 2-5). pap. 6.99 *(978-0-307-93162-7(5))* Penguin Random Hse. LLC.

Hooks, Gwendolyn. The Pet Wash: A Pet Club Story, 1 vol. Byrne, Mike, illus. 2011. (Pet Club Ser.). (ENG.). 32p. (J). (gr. 1-2). pap. 6.25 *(978-1-4342-3054-6(6),* 114654); lib. bdg. 22.65 *(978-1-4342-2514-6(3),* 113347) Capstone. (Stone Arch Bks.).

Jakubowski, Michele. Big Dog Decisions, 1 vol. Montalto, Luisa, illus. 2014. (Sidney & Sydney Ser.). (ENG.). 128p. (J). (gr. 1-3). 25.32 *(978-1-4795-5226-9(7),* 125699, Picture Window Bks.) Capstone.

Jenkins, Emily. Lemonade in Winter: A Book about Two Kids Counting Money. Karas, G. Brian, illus. 2012. 40p. (J). (gr. -1-2). 18.99 *(978-0-375-85883-3(0),* Schwartz & Wade Bks.) Random Hse. Children's Bks.

Johnson, Peter. The Amazing Adventures of John Smith, Jr. AKA Houdini. 2014. (ENG.). 192p. (J). (gr. 3-7). pap. 6.99 *(978-0-06-198891-2(X),* HarperCollins) HarperCollins Pubs.

Jones, Jen. Lissa & the Fund-Raising Funk: #3, 1 vol. 2012. (Team Cheer Ser.). (ENG.). 112p. (J). (gr. 4-6). pap. 7.19 *(978-1-4342-4251-8(X),* 120309, Stone Arch Bks.) Capstone.

Kelly, Katy. Melonhead & the We-Fix-It Company. Johnson, Gillian, illus. 2014. (Melonhead Ser.: 5). 240p. (J). (gr. 3-7). 7.99 *(978-0-307-92970-9(1),* Yearling) Random Hse. Children's Bks.

Kennedy, Marlane. The Dog Days of Charlotte Hayes. 2009. (ENG., Illus.). 240p. (J). (gr. 3-7). 16.99 *(978-0-06-145241-3(6),* Greenwillow Bks.) HarperCollins Pubs.

Kim, Patti. I'm Ok. 2018. (ENG., Illus.). 288p. (J). (gr. 5). 16.99 *(978-1-5344-1929-2(2),* Atheneum Bks. for Young Readers) Simon & Schuster Children's Publishing.

Klein, Abby. Ready, Freddy! #9: Shark Tooth Tale. McKinley, John, illus. 2006. (Ready, Freddy! Ser.: 9). (ENG.). 96p. (J). (gr. -1-3). 5.99 *(978-0-439-78458-0(1),* Blue Sky Pr., The) Scholastic, Inc.

Krulik, Nancy. World's Worst Wedgie #3. 3. Blecha, Aaron, illus. 2010. (George Brown, Class Clown Ser.: 3). 128p. (J). (gr. 2-4). 6.99 *(978-0-448-45369-9(X),* Grosset & Dunlap) Penguin Young Readers Group.

Krulik, Nancy & Burwasser, Amanda. Give a 'Bot a Bone. Moran, Mike, illus. 2018. (Project Droid Ser.: 5). (ENG.). 112p. (J). (gr. 1-3). 13.99 *(978-1-5107-2663-5(2));* pap. 4.99 *(978-1-5107-2655-0(1))* Skyhorse Publishing Co., Inc. (Sky Pony Pr.).

Lindman. Flicka, Ricka, Dicka Go to Market. Lindman, illus. 2012. (Flicka, Ricka, Dicka Ser.). (ENG., Illus.). 32p. (J). (gr. -1-3). 9.99 *(978-0-8075-2478-7(6),* 807524786) Whitman, Albert & Co.

London, Jonathan. Froggy's Lemonade Stand. Remkiewicz, Frank, illus. 2018. (Froggy Ser.). 32p. (J). (-k). 16.99 *(978-1-101-99967-7(5),* Viking Books for Young Readers) Penguin Young Readers Group.

Lubar, David. Meltdown Madness: a Branches Book (Looniverse #2) Loveridge, Matt, illus. 2013. (Looniverse Ser.: 2). (ENG.). 96p. (J). (gr. 1-3). pap. 4.99 *(978-0-545-49604-9(7))* Scholastic, Inc.

Luper, Eric. Jeremy Bender vs. the Cupcake Cadets. 2011. (ENG.). 240p. (J). (gr. 3-7). 16.99 *(978-0-06-201512-9(5),* Balzer & Bray) HarperCollins Pubs.

Margolis, Leslie. Monkey Business. 2014. (Annabelle Unleashed Ser.: 5). (ENG.). 224p. (YA). (gr. 3-6). 16.99 *(978-1-61963-393-3(0),* 900135698, Bloomsbury USA Childrens) Bloomsbury Publishing USA.

May, Eleanor. Albert Helps Out. Melmon, Deborah, illus. 2017. (Mouse Math Ser.). 32p. (J). (gr. -1-1). 7.99 *(978-1-57565-860-5(7),* 559a9afd-0705-4b1b-960c-61cc23cdd3ca, Kane Press) Astra Publishing Hse.

Mcdonald, Megan. Stink & the Midnight Zombie Walk. Reynolds, Peter H., illus. 2019. (Stink Ser.). (ENG.). 152p. (J). (gr. 1-5). lib. bdg. 31.36 *(978-1-5321-4332-8(X),* 31862, Chapter Bks.) Spotlight.

McDonald, Megan. Stink & the Midnight Zombie Walk. Reynolds, Peter H., illus. 2013. (Stink Ser.: 7). (ENG.). 160p. (J). (gr. 1-4). 14.99 *(978-0-7636-6394-0(8))* Candlewick Pr.

Mcdonald, Megan. Stink & the Midnight Zombie Walk. 2013. (Stink Ser.: 7). lib. bdg. 14.75 *(978-0-606-31586-9(1))* Turtleback.

McKay, Hilary. The Exiles at Home. 2007. (ENG.). 208p. (J). (gr. 3-7). pap. 12.95 *(978-1-4169-6729-3(X),* McElderry, Margaret K. Bks.) McElderry, Margaret K. Bks.

Metz, Melinda. Bri's Big Crush. 2016. (Babysitter Chronicles Ser.). (ENG.). 160p. (J). (gr. 4-7). lib. bdg. 26.65 *(978-1-4965-2756-1(9),* 1400591, Stone Arch Bks.) Capstone.

Morgan, Alex. Hat Trick. 2015. (Kicks Ser.). (ENG., Illus.). 128p. (J). (gr. 3-7). 17.99 *(978-1-4814-5096-6(4),* Simon & Schuster Bks. For Young Readers) Simon & Schuster Bks. For Young Readers.

Nesbit, E. Story of the Treasure Seekers. 2006. pap. *(978-1-4068-3507-6(2))* Echo Library.

—The Story of the Treasure Seekers: Being the Adventures of the Bastable Children in Search of A Fortune. l.t. ed. 2005. 288p. pap. *(978-1-84637-207-0(0))* Echo Library.

O'Connor, Jane. Fancy Nancy & the Fabulous Fashion Boutique. Glasser, Robin Preiss, illus. 2010. (Fancy Nancy Ser.). (ENG.). 32p. (J). (gr. -1-3). 17.99 *(978-0-06-123592-4(X));* lib. bdg. 18.89 *(978-0-06-123593-1(8))* HarperCollins Pubs. (HarperCollins).

Olson, Gretchen. Call Me Hope. 2008. (ENG.). 288p. (J). (gr. 3-7). pap. 15.99 *(978-0-316-01239-3(4))* Little, Brown Bks. for Young Readers.

O'Neal, Shaquille. Little Shaq. Taylor, Theodore, illus. 2015. 73p. (J). *(978-1-68119-119-5(9))* Bloomsbury Pr.

—Little Shaq. Taylor, Theodore, III, illus. 2015. (ENG.). 80p. (J). (gr. k-2). 9.99 *(978-1-61963-721-4(9),* 900146374, Bloomsbury USA Childrens) Bloomsbury Publishing USA.

O'Neill, Alexis. Estela's Swap, 1 vol. 2005. (ENG., Illus.). 32p. (J). (gr. k-4). pap. 11.95 *(978-1-60060-253-5(3),* leelowbooks) Lee & Low Bks., Inc.

Orme, Helen. Who's Who?, 2 vols., Set. 2008. (Siti's Sisters Ser.). (ENG., Illus.). 36p. pap. *(978-1-84167-687-6(X))* Ransom Publishing Ltd.

Parish, Herman. Amelia Bedelia Bind-Up: Books 1 & 2: Amelia Bedelia Means Business; Amelia Bedelia Unleashed. Avril, Lynne, illus. 2015. (Amelia Bedelia Ser.). (ENG.). 320p. (J). (gr. 1-5). 12.99 *(978-0-06-240367-4(2),* Greenwillow Bks.) HarperCollins Pubs.

—Amelia Bedelia Chapter Book #1: Amelia Bedelia Means Business. Avril, Lynne, illus. 2013. (Amelia Bedelia Ser.: No. 1). (ENG.). 160p. (J). (gr. 1-5). 15.99 *(978-0-06-209497-1(1));* pap. 5.99 *(978-0-06-209496-4(3))* HarperCollins Pubs. (Greenwillow Bks.).

—Amelia Bedelia Means Business. Avril, Lynne. illus. 2013. (Amelia Bedelia Chapter Book Ser.: 1). (J). lib. bdg. 14.75 *(978-0-606-27137-0(6))* Turtleback.

Patterson, James & Tebbetts, Chris. Middle School: Dog's Best Friend. Tejido, Jomike, illus. 2016. (Middle School Ser.: 8). (ENG.). 256p. (J). (gr. 3-7). 13.99 *(978-0-316-34954-3(2),* Jimmy Patterson) Little Brown & Co.

Paulsen, Gary. Flat Broke: The Theory, Practice & Destructive Properties of Greed. 2012. (Liar Liar Ser.). (ENG.). 128p. (J). (gr. 3-7). pap. 6.99 *(978-0-375-86612-8(4),* Yearling) Random Hse. Children's Bks.

—Lawn Boy. 2009. (Lawn Boy Ser.). (ENG.). 96p. (J). (gr. 3-7). 7.99 *(978-0-553-49465-5(1),* Yearling) Random Hse. Children's Bks.

Peschke, Marci. Cupcake Queen, 1 vol. Mourning, Tuesday, illus. 2013. (Kylie Jean Ser.). (ENG.). 112p. (J). (gr. 1-3). lib. bdg. 22.65 *(978-1-4048-7580-7(8),* 119872, Picture Window Bks.) Capstone.

Pett, Mark. The Girl & the Bicycle. Pett, Mark, illus. 2014. (ENG., Illus.). 40p. (J). (gr. -1). 18.99 *(978-1-4424-8319-4(9),* Simon & Schuster Bks. For Young Readers) Simon & Schuster Bks. For Young Readers.

Reichert, Paul. The Lemonade Ripple: A Sweet Story of Kindness & Charity. 2012. (ENG., Illus.). 40p. (J). (gr. -1-k). 12.95 *(978-1-61608-701-2(3),* 608701, Sky Pony Pr.) Skyhorse Publishing Co., Inc.

Rey, H. A. Lemonade Stand. 2016. (Curious George TV Tie-In Early Reader Ser.). lib. bdg. 13.55 *(978-0-606-37993-9(2))* Turtleback.

Salisbury, Graham. Calvin Coconut: the Zippy Fix. 2010. (Calvin Coconut Ser.: 2). (ENG., Illus.). 176p. (J). (gr. 3-7). pap. 6.99 *(978-0-375-84601-4(8),* Yearling) Random Hse. Children's Bks.

Scraper, Katherine. The Yard Sale. 2006. (Early Explorers Ser.). (J). pap. *(978-1-4108-6043-9(4))* Benchmark Education Co.

Simon, Coco. Emma: Lights! Camera! Cupcakes! 2014. (Cupcake Diaries: 19). lib. bdg. 17.20 *(978-0-606-35437-0(9))* Turtleback.

—Emma on Thin Icing. 2013. (Cupcake Diaries: 3). (ENG., Illus.). 160p. (J). (gr. 3-7). 17.99 *(978-1-4424-7492-5(0),* Simon Spotlight) Simon Spotlight.

—Emma on Thin Icing. 2011. (Cupcake Diaries: 3). lib. bdg. 17.20 *(978-0-606-23734-5(8))* Turtleback.

Spinelli, Eileen. Miss Fox's Class Earns a Field Trip. Kennedy, Anne, illus. 2012. (J). *(978-1-61913-122-4(6))* Weigl Pubs., Inc.

Terrell, Brandon. Above. Cano, Fernando, illus. 2013. (Tony Hawk: Live2Skate Ser.). (ENG.). 72p. (gr. 3-4). pap. 35.70 *(978-1-4342-6266-0(9),* Stone Arch Bks.) Capstone.

Viorst, Judith. Lulu Walks the Dogs. Smith, Lane, illus. 2012. (Lulu Ser.). (ENG.). 160p. (J). (gr. 1-5). 19.99 *(978-1-4424-3579-7(8),* Atheneum Bks. for Young Readers) Simon & Schuster Children's Publishing.

—Lulu Walks the Dogs. 2014. (Lulu Ser.: 2). lib. bdg. 18.40 *(978-0-606-35438-7(7))* Turtleback.

Watson, J. A. Nocturnal Symphony: A Bat Detector's Journal. Olbey, Arpad, illus. 2019. (Science Squad Set 2 Ser.). (ENG.). 192p. (J). (gr. 3-4). 28.50 *(978-1-63163-299-0(X),* 163163299X, Jolly Fish Pr.) North Star Editions.

Willson, Sarah. Pet Peeves. 2005. (Social Studies Connects Ser.). (Illus.). 32p. (J). (gr. 1-3). pap. 5.99 *(978-1-57565-149-1(1),* b2e53ab7-d45f-4ca7-b743-35182adb4c08, Kane Press) Astra Publishing Hse.

Wilson, Troy. Liam Takes a Stand. Holinaty, Josh, illus. 2017. (ENG.). 32p. (J). (gr. k-4). 16.95 *(978-1-77147-161-9(1))* Owlkids Bks. Inc. CAN. Dist: Publishers Group West (PGW).

Wisler, Joelle. Ariana Gold. 2016. (What's Your Dream? Ser.). (ENG., Illus.). 96p. (J). (gr. 4-6). lib. bdg. 25.99 *(978-1-4965-3442-2(5),* 132564, Stone Arch Bks.) Capstone.

Witherspoon, Reese. Busy Betty. Yan, Xindi, illus. 2022. (ENG.). 40p. (J). (gr. -1-2). 19.99 *(978-0-593-46588-2(1))* Flamingo Bks.

Yang, Kelly. New from Here. (ENG.). (J). (gr. 3-7). 2023. 384p. pap. 8.99 *(978-1-5344-8831-5(6))* 2022. (Illus.). 368p. 18.99 *(978-1-5344-8830-4(8))* Simon & Schuster Bks. For Young Readers. (Simon & Schuster Bks. For Young Readers).

MONGOLIA

Adamson, Heather. Mongolia. 2016. (Exploring Countries Ser.). (ENG., Illus.). 32p. (J). (gr. 3-7). lib. bdg. 27.95 *(978-1-62617-344-6(3),* Blastoff! Readers) Bellwether Media.

Aloian, Molly. The Gobi Desert. 2012. (ENG.). 32p. (J). *(978-0-7787-0710-3(5));* (Illus.). pap. *(978-0-7787-0718-9(0))* Crabtree Publishing Co.

Graves, Sue. Meet Erdene. 2004. (ENG.). 24p. (J). (gr. 2-2). pap. 10.92 *(978-0-7652-5189-3(2),* Celebration Pr.) Savvas Learning Co.

Harper, Judith E. Unique Places. 2005. (Real Deal Ser.). (Illus.). 32p. (J). pap. *(978-0-7608-9635-8(6))* Sundance/Newbridge Educational Publishing.

Joo, Mi-hwa. Where the Winds Meet: Mongolia. Cowley, Joy, ed. Oh, Lee, illus. 2015. (Global Kids Storybooks Ser.). (ENG.). 32p. (gr. 1-4). 26.65 *(978-1-925246-03-2(5));* 26.65 *(978-1-925246-29-2(9));* 7.99 *(978-1-925246-55-1(8))* ChoiceMaker Pty. Ltd., The AUS. (Big and SMALL). Dist: Lerner Publishing Group.

—Where the Winds Meet: Mongolia. Lee, Oh, illus. 2015. (Global Kids Storybooks Ser.). (ENG.). 32p. (J). (gr. 1-4). pap. 8.99 *(978-1-925233-49-0(9),* 6c4e8304-2bd4-4d42-8173-fbbc5a0b7239, Big and SMALL) ChoiceMaker Pty. Ltd., The AUS. Dist: Lerner Publishing Group.

Montgomery, Sy. Saving the Ghost of the Mountain: An Expedition among Snow Leopards in Mongolia. Bishop, Nic, photos by. 2012. (Scientists in the Field Ser.). (ENG., Illus.). 80p. (J). (gr. 5-7). pap. 10.99 *(978-0-547-72734-9(8),* 1483153, Clarion Bks.) HarperCollins Pubs.

Pang, Guek-Cheng. Mongolia, 1 vol. 2nd rev. ed. 2010. (Cultures of the World (Second Edition)(r) Ser.). (ENG.). 144p. (gr. 5-5). 49.79 *(978-0-7614-4849-5(7),* 93064e71-88d8-44d5-b70c-20bc7ceef43f) Cavendish Square Publishing LLC.

Toth, Henrietta & Pang, Guek Cheng. Mongolia. 2018. (J). pap. *(978-1-5026-4128-1(3))* Musa Publishing.

MONGOLIA—FICTION

Dahl, Michael. Dragonblood: Dragon in the Desert. Vue, Tou, illus. 2010. (Dragonblood Ser.). (ENG.). 40p. (J). (gr. 4-8). pap. 6.25 *(978-1-4342-2309-8(4),* 103178, Stone Arch Bks.) Capstone.

Jamba, Dashdondog & Pellowski, Anne. Story of the Mongolian Tent House. Vidal, Beatriz, illus. 2020. 40p. (J). (gr. k-3). 16.95 *(978-1-937786-81-6(1),* Wisdom Tales) World Wisdom, Inc.

Service, Pamela F. Alien Expedition. 2010. pap. 33.92 *(978-0-7613-6958-5(9))* Lerner Publishing Group.

Stilton, Gerónimo. Valley of the Giant Skeletons. 2008. (Illus.). 111p. (J). lib. bdg. 15.38 *(978-1-4242-4303-7(3))* Fitzgerald Bks.

—Valley of the Giant Skeletons. 2008. (Geronimo Stilton Ser.). (Illus.). 110p. (gr. 2-5). 17.00 *(978-0-7569-8805-0(5))* Perfection Learning Corp.

—Valley of the Giant Skeletons. 2008. (Geronimo Stilton Ser.: 32). lib. bdg. 18.40 *(978-1-4364-2713-5(4))* Turtleback.

Wilson, Diane. I Rode a Horse of Milk White Jade. 2010. 272p. (J). (gr. 4-10). pap. 10.99 *(978-1-4022-4027-0(9))* Sourcebooks, Inc.

MONGOLIA—HISTORY—FICTION

Hotchkiss, Gerald G. Emily in Kara Koto: A Young Girl's Adventure in Mongolia. 2014. (J). pap. *(978-1-63293-013-2(7))* Sunstone Pr.

MONGOLISM

see Down Syndrome

MONGOLS

Harrison, Kathryn. Mongols on the Silk Road: Trade, Transportation, & Cross-Cultural Exchange in the Mongol Empire, 1 vol. 2016. (Mongols Ser.). (ENG., Illus.). 64p. (J). (gr. 6-6). pap. 14.95 *(978-1-4994-6370-5(7),* 8badaac5-a340-4d1d-b3cc-be3c9ce52916) Rosen Publishing Group, Inc., The.

Knight, P. V. Genghis Khan: Fierce Mongolian Conqueror, 1 vol. 2016. (History's Most Murderous Villains Ser.). (ENG., Illus.). 32p. (J). (gr. 4-5). pap. 11.50 *(978-1-4824-4790-3(8),* 64a0f98e-b558-4729-a2a5-eae4df02c321) Stevens, Gareth Publishing LLLP.

Krull, Kathleen. Kubla Khan: The Emperor of Everything. Byrd, Robert, illus. 2010. 48p. (J). (gr. 3-7). 18.99 *(978-0-670-01114-8(2),* Viking Books for Young Readers) Penguin Young Readers Group.

Linde, Barbara M. Genghis Khan: Creating the Mongol Empire, 1 vol. 2017. (World History Ser.). (ENG.). 104p. (YA). (gr. 7-7). pap. 20.99 *(978-1-5345-6307-0(5),* 11a42843-f7b9-402b-9e16-55b255e5bddd); lib. bdg. 41.53 *(978-1-5345-6248-6(6),* 4cdeece1-a83d-42b6-bf31-10c256ef4fed) Greenhaven Publishing LLC. (Lucent Pr.).

Matthews, Rupert. Mongols, 1 vol. 2015. (History's Fearless Fighters Ser.). (ENG., Illus.). 48p. (J). (gr. 5-6). pap. 15.05 *(978-1-4824-3169-8(6),* 6cfbf5e8-1a34-45e8-a58c-6713f4eb12bd) Stevens, Gareth Publishing LLLP.

Radomski, Kassi. Genghis Khan, 1 vol. 2017. (Great Military Leaders Ser.). (ENG.). 128p. (YA). (gr. 9-9). 47.36 *(978-1-5026-2787-2(6),* 0e8e5080-d964-4669-8263-ecf33291eaae) Cavendish Square Publishing LLC.

Reynolds, Jan. Mongolia, 1 vol. 2007. (Vanishing Cultures Ser.). (ENG., Illus.). 32p. (J). (gr. 4-7). 16.95 *(978-1-60060-145-3(6));* (gr. k-6). 10.95 *(978-1-60060-130-9(8);* leelowbooks) Lee & Low Bks., Inc.

Rice, Earle, Jr. Empire in the East: The Story of Genghis Khan. 2005. (World Leaders Ser.). (Illus.). 160p. (J). (gr. 3-7). 28.95 *(978-1-931798-62-4(1))* Reynolds, Morgan Inc.

MNO

Watson, Galadriel Findlay. Mongols. 2013. (J). (978-1-62127-509-1(4)) 2013. (J). pap. (978-1-62127-513-8(2)) 2005. 32p. pap. 9.95 (978-1-59036-257-0(8)) 2004. (Illus.). 32p. (J). lib. bdg. 26.00 (978-1-59036-220-4(9)) Weigl Pubs., Inc.

Zelenyj, Alexander. Marco Polo: Overland to China, 1 vol. 2005. (In the Footsteps of Explorers Ser.). (ENG., Illus.). 32p. (J). (gr. 4-5). pap. (978-0-7787-2453-7(0)) Crabtree Publishing Co.

MONGOLS—FICTION

Boyce, Frank Cottrell. The Unforgotten Coat. 2011. (ENG., Illus.). 112p. (J). (gr. 3-7). 16.99 (978-0-7636-5729-1(8)) Candlewick Pr.

—The Unforgotten Coat. 2011. (Playaway Children Ser.). (ENG.). (J). (gr. 4-7). 39.99 (978-1-4558-4539-2(6)) Findaway World, LLC.

Jones Yang, Dori. Daughter of Xanadu. 2012. (ENG.). 352p. (YA). (gr. 7). pap. 9.99 (978-0-385-73924-5(9), Ember) Random Hse. Children's Bks.

McCaughrean, Geraldine. The Kite Rider. 2003. (ENG., Illus.). 320p. (YA). (gr. 8-18). pap. 15.99 (978-0-06-441091-5(9), HarperTeen) HarperCollins Pubs.

MONGOLS—HISTORY

Behnke, Alison. The Conquests of Genghis Khan. 2008. (Pivotal Moments in History Ser.). (ENG., Illus.). 160p. (gr. 9-12). lib. bdg. 38.60 (978-0-8225-7519-1(1)) Lerner Publishing Group.

Bodden, Valerie. Mongols (Great Warriors) 2013. 24p. pap. (978-1-60818-468-2(4)) Creative Co., The.

Brian, Dittmar. Mongol Warriors. 2012. (History's Greatest Warriors Ser.). (ENG., Illus.). 24p. (J). (gr. 3-7). lib. bdg. 26.95 (978-1-60014-746-3(1), Torque Bks.) Bellwether Media.

Burgan, Michael. Empire of the Mongols. 2nd rev. ed. 2009. (Great Empires of the Past Ser.). (ENG., Illus.). 160p. (gr. 6-12). 35.00 (978-1-60413-163-5(2), P173430, Facts On File) Infobase Holdings, Inc.

Helget, Nicole Lea. Mongols. 2012. (Fearsome Fighters Ser.). (ENG., Illus.). 48p. (J). (gr. 5-9). 23.95 (978-1-60818-184-1(7), 21886, Creative Education) Creative Co., The.

Loh-Hagan, Virginia. The Real Genghis Khan. 2018. (History Uncut Ser.). (ENG., Illus.). 32p. (J). (gr. 4-8). lib. bdg. 32.07 (978-1-5341-2950-4(2), 211844, 45th Parallel Press) Cherry Lake Publishing.

Medina, Nico & Who HQ. Who Was Genghis Khan? Thomson, Andrew, illus. 2014. (Who Was? Ser.). 112p. (J). (gr. 3-7). pap. 6.99 (978-0-448-48260-6(6), Penguin Workshop) Penguin Young Readers Group.

The Mongols, 14 vols. 2016. (Mongols Ser.). 64p. (gr. 6-6). (ENG.). 252.91 (978-1-4777-8554-6(X), af5fb3ea-b47f-4e6a-bfc5-fa4de11034b0); pap. 90.65 (978-1-4994-6425-2(8)) Rosen Publishing Group, Inc., The. (Rosen Young Adult).

Nardo, Don. Genghis Khan & the Mongol Empire, 1 vol. 2010. (World History Ser.). (ENG.). 96p. (gr. 7-7). 41.53 (978-1-4205-0326-5(X), 7fb96b72-32c2-4475-a279-2c85413ed3a6, Lucent Pr.) Greenhaven Publishing LLC.

Whiting, Jim. The Life & Times of Genghis Khan. 2005. (Biography from Ancient Civilizations Ser.). (Illus.). 48p. (J). (gr. 4-8). lib. bdg. 29.95 (978-1-58415-348-1(2)) Mitchell Lane Pubs.

MONGOOSES

Bodden, Valerie. Amazing Animals: Meerkats. 2017. (Amazing Animals Ser.). (ENG., Illus.). 24p. (J). (gr. 1-3). pap. 9.99 (978-1-62832-364-1(7), 20042, Creative Paperbacks) Creative Co., The.

—Meerkats. 2017. (Amazing Animals Ser.). (ENG., Illus.). 24p. (J). (gr. 1-4). (978-1-60818-756-0(X), 20044, Creative Education) Creative Co., The.

Borgert-Spaniol, Megan. Mongooses. 2013. (Animal Safari Ser.). (ENG., Illus.). 24p. (J). (gr. k-3). lib. bdg. 26.95 (978-1-60014-912-2(X), Blastoff! Readers) Bellwether Media.

Gish, Melissa. Meerkats. 2016. (Living Wild Ser.). (ENG.). 48p. (J). (gr. 5-9). pap. 12.00 (978-1-62832-170-8(9), 20894, Creative Paperbacks) Creative Co., The.

Gregory, Josh. Meerkats. 2016. (Nature's Children Ser.). (ENG., Illus.). 48p. (J). pap. 6.95 (978-0-531-22519-6(4), Children's Pr.) Scholastic Library Publishing.

Halfmann, Janet. Mongoose. 2004. (Nature's Predators Ser.). (ENG., Illus.). 48p. (J). 27.50 (978-0-7377-2622-0(9), Greenhaven Pr., Inc.) Cengage Gale.

Hansen, Grace. Meerkat. 2017. (African Animals (Abdo Kids Jumbo) Ser.). (ENG., Illus.). 24p. (J). (gr. -1-2). lib. bdg. 32.79 (978-1-5321-0420-6(0), 26546, Abdo Kids) ABDO Publishing Co.

Meerkat Chat, 6 vols., Pack. (Story Steps Ser.). (gr. k-2). 32.00 (978-0-7635-9850-1(X)) Rigby Education.

Schuetz, Kari. Warthogs & Banded Mongooses. 2019. (Animal Tag Teams Ser.). (ENG., Illus.). 24p. (J). (gr. k-3). lib. bdg. 26.95 (978-1-62617-958-5(1), Blastoff! Readers) Bellwether Media.

Somervill, Barbara A. Small Indian Mongoose. 2010. (21st Century Skills Library: Animal Invaders Ser.). (ENG., Illus.). 32p. (gr. 4-8). lib. bdg. 32.07 (978-1-60279-630-0(0), 200336) Cherry Lake Publishing.

MONGOOSES—FICTION

Bannerman, Helen. The Story of Little Black Mingo (Illustr. 2006. pap. (978-1-4065-0770-6(9)) Dodo Pr.

Cameron, Wade. Melvin the Mischievous Mongoose First Day of School. 2012. 28p. pap. 18.65 (978-1-4797-0270-1(6)) Xlibris Corp.

Facey, Paulet. Tom-Tom & the Punch Bowl of Irish Moss. 2012. 24p. pap. 15.99 (978-1-4797-3908-0(1)) Xlibris Corp.

Gill, Patricia. Pabi, Beega & the Mongoose Monster. 2009. 28p. pap. 14.99 (978-1-4490-2566-3(8)) AuthorHouse.

Holzwarth, Werner. I Wish I Were A ... Jeschke, Stefanie, illus. 2013. (ENG.). 40p. (J). (gr. -1-k). 16.95 (978-1-62087-993-1(X), 620993, Sky Pony Pr.) Skyhorse Publishing Co., Inc.

Jones, Gareth P. Ninja Meerkats (#7) the Ultimate Dragon Warrior. Finlayson, Luke, illus. 2014. (Ninja Meerkats Ser.: 7). (ENG.). 128p. (J). (gr. 2-4). pap. 16.99 (978-1-250-04665-9(3), 900131694) Square Fish.

Kipling, Rudyard. Rikki-Tikki-Tavi & Toomai of the Elephants. 2008. (Unabridged Classics (in Audio) Ser.). (J). pap. 36.00 incl. audio compact disk (978-1-58472-431-5(5), In Audio) Sound Room Pubs., Inc.

Kipling, Rudyard & Pinkney, Jerry. Rikki-Tikki-Tavi. Pinkney, Jerry, illus. 2004. (ENG., Illus.). 48p. (J). (gr. -1-3). reprint ed. pap. 7.99 (978-0-06-058785-7(7), HarperCollins) HarperCollins Pubs.

—Rikki-Tikki-Tavi. 2004. (Illus.). (gr. -1-3). 17.00 (978-0-7569-3250-3(5)) Perfection Learning Corp.

Miller, Mark. Meerkats Don't Fly. Butterfield, Cathy, illus. 2007. (J). (978-0-9794393-0-8(2)) Good Turn Publishing.

Mongoose, Mongoose, Stop! Don't Run. 2004. (J). 11.95 (978-0-931548-65-9(9)) Island Heritage Publishing.

Smithey, Donna. Nichisan & the Ancient Ones. 2012. 36p. pap. 24.99 (978-1-62419-240-1(8)) Salem Author Services.

Tyler, William H. Who Let the Mongoose Loose? 2011. 48p. pap. 18.41 (978-1-4269-5694-2(0)) Trafford Publishing.

Watt, Fiona. That's Not My Meerkat. 2015. (Touchy-Feely Board Bks.). (ENG.). 10p. (J). 9.99 (978-0-7945-3599-5(2), Usborne) EDC Publishing.

Weston Woods Staff, creator. Rikki-Tikki-Tavi. 2011. 18.95 (978-0-439-72977-2(7)); 38.75 (978-0-439-72979-6(3)) Weston Woods Studios, Inc.

MONITOR (IRONCLAD)

Abnett, Dan. The Monitor Versus the Merrimac: Ironclads at War, 1 vol. Verma, Dheeraj, illus. 2006. (Graphic Battles of the Civil War Ser.). (ENG.). 48p. (J). (gr. 4-5). lib. bdg. 37.13 (978-1-4042-0778-3(3), c1104d37-0229-4941-a9a3-6bd0f959a40e) Rosen Publishing Group, Inc., The.

Brager, Bruce. The Monitor Versus the Merrimack. 2003. (Great Battles Thru the Ages Ser.). (ENG., Illus.). 112p. (gr. 6-12). 30.00 (978-0-7910-7439-8(0), P113829, Facts On File) Infobase Holdings, Inc.

Doeden, Matt. At the Battle of the Ironclads: An Interactive Battlefield Adventure. 2018. (You Choose: American Battles Ser.). (ENG., Illus.). 112p. (J). (gr. 3-7). pap. 6.95 (978-1-5435-0294-7(6), 137163); lib. bdg. 32.65 (978-1-5435-0290-9(3), 137159) Capstone. (Capstone Pr.).

O'Brien, Patrick. Duel of the Ironclads: The Monitor vs. the Virginia. 2003. (Illus.). 40p. (J). (gr. 1-5). 18.85 (978-0-8027-8843-6(2)) Walker & Co.

Thompson, Gare. The Monitor: The Iron Warship That Changed the World. Day, Larry, illus. 2003. (All Aboard Reading: Station Stop 3 Ser.). (ENG.). 48p. (J). (gr. 2-4). 16.19 (978-0-448-43283-0(8)) Penguin Young Readers Group.

MONKEYS

see also Baboons

Aloian, Molly & Kalman, Bobbie. Endangered Monkeys, 1 vol. rev. ed. 2007. (Earth's Endangered Animals Ser.). (ENG., Illus.). 32p. (J). (gr. 1-5). pap. (978-0-7787-1908-3(1)) Crabtree Publishing Co.

—Les Singes. 2010. (FRE., illus.). 32p. (J). pap. 9.95 (978-2-89579-288-8(7)) Bayard Canada Livres CAN. Dist: Crabtree Publishing Co.

Avery, Logan. Amazing Animals: Spider Monkeys: Place Value. 2018. (Mathematics in the Real World Ser.). (ENG., Illus.). 24p. (J). (gr. 1-2). pap. 9.99 (978-1-4258-5678-6(0)) Teacher Created Materials, Inc.

—Monos Araña: Valor Posicional. rev. ed. 2019. (Mathematics in the Real World Ser.). (SPA., Illus.). 24p. (J). (gr. 1-2). pap. 9.99 (978-1-4258-2840-0(X)) Teacher Created Materials, Inc.

Banks, Rosie. Vicious Monkeys, 1 vol. 2017. (Cutest Animals... That Could Kill You! Ser.). (ENG.). 24p. (J). (gr. 2-3). pap. 9.15 (978-1-5382-1097-0(5), 0414b57f-ddd8-45c9-960c-d979bf48e8eb) Stevens, Gareth Publishing LLLP.

Bodden, Valerie. Monkeys. 2010. (Amazing Animals Ser.). 24p. (J). (gr. -1-3). 16.95 (978-1-58341-808-6(3), Creative Education) Creative Co., The.

Borgert-Spaniol, Megan. Spider Monkeys. 2014. (Animal Safari Ser.). (ENG., Illus.). 24p. (J). (gr. k-3). lib. bdg. 26.95 (978-1-62617-064-3(9), Blastoff! Readers) Bellwether Media.

Bowman, Lucy. Monkeys. Cooper, Jenny & King, Sue, illus. 2011. (Beginner's Nature Ser.). 32p. (J). ring bd. 4.99 (978-0-7945-2978-9(X), Usborne) EDC Publishing.

Brownlee, Christen. Beware of (Prairie) Dog! A Pet Swap Goes Viral. 2011. (J). pap. (978-0-545-32805-0(5)) Scholastic, Inc.

Daly, Ruth. Mandrills. 2014. (J). (978-1-4896-2882-4(7)) Weigl Pubs., Inc.

De La Bédoyère, Camilla. Monkeys & Apes, 1 vol. 2014. (Animal Q & A Ser.). (ENG., Illus.). 24p. (J). (gr. 2-2). lib. bdg. 26.27 (978-1-4777-9190-5(6), 40781a2d-f132-48c8-b1cc-6c0b401cabbe, Windmill Bks.) Rosen Publishing Group, Inc., The.

Dunn, Joeming & Dunn, Ben. Albert II: The 1st Monkey in Space, 1 vol. 2011. (Famous Firsts: Animals Making History Ser.). (ENG., Illus.). 32p. (J). (gr. 3-8). 32.79 (978-1-61641-637-9(8), 7204, Graphic Planet - Fiction) Magic Wagon.

Dyan, Penelope. The Comeback Kids — Book 9 — the Barbary Macaques of Gibraltar. Weigand, John D., photos by. 2012. (Illus.). 36p. pap. 14.95 (978-1-61477-036-7(0)) Bellissima Publishing, LLC.

Early Macken, JoAnn. Monkeys / Los Monos, 1 vol. 2004. (Animals I See at the Zoo / Animales Que Veo en el Zoológico Ser.). (SPA & ENG., Illus.). 24p. (gr. k-2). pap. 9.15 (978-0-8368-4388-0(6), 587ba187-efee-4c04-8038-7a341b6c3e63); lib. bdg. 24.67 (978-0-8368-4383-5(5), 71140c8e-67d7-41b2-b060-7530fa6b1ef5) Stevens, Gareth Publishing LLLP. (Weekly Reader Leveled Readers).

Franchino, Vicky. Spider Monkeys. 2014. (Nature's Children Ser.). (ENG., Illus.). 48p. (J). lib. bdg. 28.00 (978-0-531-21229-5(7)) Scholastic Library Publishing.

Gish, Melissa. Monkeys. 2009. (Living Wild Ser.). (ENG., Illus.). 48p. (J). (gr. 5-8). 22.95 (978-1-58341-740-9(0), 22189, Creative Education) Creative Co., The.

Glaser, Rebecca. Monkeys Swing. 2016. (ENG., Illus.). 16p. (J). (gr. -1 — 1). bds. 7.99 (978-1-68152-072-8(9), 15818) Amicus.

Gosman, Gillian. Howler Monkeys. (Illus.). 24p. (J). 2012. 49.50 (978-1-4488-5172-0(6), PowerKids Pr.) 2011. (ENG., (gr. 2-3). pap. 9.25 (978-1-4488-5171-3(8), 4d1e5ef6-2a48-40b7-b5aa-dfeab44e0991, PowerKids Pr.) 2011. (ENG., (gr. 2-3). lib. bdg. 26.27 (978-1-4488-5019-8(3), 753e0165-5b8f-4d13-a8d0-e810dbc0d04b) Rosen Publishing Group, Inc., The.

—Proboscis Monkeys. (Illus.). 24p. 2012. (J). 49.50 (978-1-4488-5184-3(X), PowerKids Pr.) 2011. (ENG., (J). (gr. 2-3). pap. 9.25 (978-1-4488-5183-6(1), 03e9a882-e19f-4378-99be-a306b933ca61, PowerKids Pr.) 2011. (ENG., (YA). (gr. 2-3). lib. bdg. 26.27 (978-1-4488-5024-2(X), ec9f9b11-31f2-4714-b62e-0639a8c8a5de) Rosen Publishing Group, Inc., The.

—Rhesus Monkeys. (Illus.). 24p. 2012. (J). 49.50 (978-1-4488-5182-9(3), PowerKids Pr.) 2011. (ENG., (J). (gr. 2-3). pap. 9.25 (978-1-4488-5181-2(5), 0580ae0f-1948-451b-bbf9-98c18e26c769, PowerKids Pr.) 2011. (ENG., (YA). (gr. 2-3). lib. bdg. 26.27 (978-1-4488-5023-5(1), 5ae62e38-0884-4033-9415-0eec1581ac5c) Rosen Publishing Group, Inc., The.

—Spider Monkeys. 2012. (J). 49.50 (978-1-4488-5174-4(2), PowerKids Pr.) 2011. (ENG., Illus.). 24p. (J). (gr. 2-3). pap. 9.25 (978-1-4488-5173-7(4), 07dcdaf7-78e6-4bf9-9eed-7ba58f4e7e94, PowerKids Pr.) 2011. (ENG., Illus.). 24p. (YA). (gr. 2-3). lib. bdg. 26.27 (978-1-4488-5020-4(7), 7e89e3ca-931f-4553-a891-daf1cf9dcd70) Rosen Publishing Group, Inc., The.

—Tamarins. (Illus.). 24p. (J). 2012. 49.50 (978-1-4488-5176-8(9), 1329354, PowerKids Pr.) 2011. (ENG., (gr. 2-3). pap. 9.25 (978-1-4488-5175-1(0), 961032aa-b2c5-4443-8d21-4e71addc922e, PowerKids Pr.) 2011. (ENG., (gr. 2-3). lib. bdg. 26.27 (978-1-4488-5021-1(5), 07bdafdf-f95b-4719-ad1f-9dd6a8fcbf70) Rosen Publishing Group, Inc., The.

Gray, Susan H. Spider Monkey. 2015. (21st Century Skills Library: Exploring Our Rainforests Ser.). (ENG., Illus.). 32p. (gr. 3-6). 32.07 (978-1-63188-980-6(X), 205832) Cherry Lake Publishing.

Green, John. Monkeys & Apes Coloring Book. 2013. (Dover Animal Coloring Bks.). (ENG., Illus.). 48p. (J). (gr. 3-12). pap. 4.99 (978-0-486-25798-3(3), 257983) Dover Pubns., Inc.

Greenwall, Jessica & Brooks, Felicity. First Sticker Book Monkeys. 2013. (First Sticker Bks). 16p. (J). pap. 6.99 (978-0-7945-3288-8(8), Usborne) EDC Publishing.

Gregory, Josh. Monkeys. 2012. (J). pap. (978-0-531-21079-6(0)); lib. bdg. (978-0-531-20904-2(0)) Children's Pr., Ltd.

Guidone, Julie. Monkeys, 1 vol. 2009. (Animals That Live in the Rain Forest Ser.). (ENG.). 24p. (gr. 1-1). (J). lib. bdg. 25.27 (978-1-4339-0024-2(6), abf1a056-ff4c-4311-b792-7b0e1c26d974); pap. 9.15 (978-1-4339-0106-5(4), 1da4a598-1102-4292-ab87-12cb1adc63b8) Stevens, Gareth Publishing LLLP. (Weekly Reader Leveled Readers).

—Monkeys / Monos, 1 vol. 2009. (Animals That Live in the Rain Forest / Animales de la Selva Ser.). (SPA & ENG.). 24p. (J). (gr. 1-1). pap. 9.15 (978-1-4339-0113-3(7), ccd0c891-e7ee-423c-8583-7da061829954); lib. bdg. 25.27 (978-1-4339-0063-1(7), 4a030314-7160-42cd-8b52-2a90364ac110) Stevens, Gareth Publishing LLLP. (Weekly Reader Leveled Readers).

Gunn, Shadonna. What Do Monkeys Eat? 2016. (1-3Y Mammals Ser.). (ENG., Illus.). 16p. (J). pap. 9.60 (978-1-64053-138-3(6), ARC Pr. Bks.) American Reading Co.

Hardyman, Robyn. Apes & Monkeys. 2008. (World of Animals Ser.). (ENG.). 32p. (J). (gr. 2-4). 31.35 (978-1-933834-37-5(4), 16822) Brown Bear Bks.

Hewett, Richard, illus. & photos by. A Monkey Baby Grows Up. Hewett, Richard, photos by. Hewett, Joan, photos by. 2004. (Baby Animals Ser.). 32p. (J). (gr. k-3). lib. bdg. 21.27 (978-1-57505-199-4(0)) Lerner Publishing Group.

Hoff, Mary King. Monkeys. 2005. (Wild World of Animals (Creative Education) Ser.). (Illus.). 32p. (J). (gr. 2-5). lib. bdg. 18.95 (978-1-58341-352-4(9), Creative Education) Creative Co., The.

Howell, Laura. Monkeys Sticker Book. 2011. (Spotter's Guides Sticker Book Ser.). 24p. (J). pap. 6.99 (978-0-7945-3004-4(4), Usborne) EDC Publishing.

Ikids Staff. 10 Little Monkeys. King, Travis, illus. 2009. (ENG.). 20p. (J). (gr. -1-k). 14.99 (978-1-58476-938-5(6)) Innovative Kids.

Jackson, Tom. Monkeys: Baboons, Macaques, Mandrills, Lemurs & Other Primates, All Shown in More Than 180 Enticing Pictures. 2016. (Illus.). 64p. (J). (gr. -1-12). 15.00 (978-1-86147-497-1(0), Armadillo) Anness Publishing GBR. Dist: National Bk. Network.

Jones, Teresa Chin. Tales of the Monkey King. Harris, Miki, illus. 2008. (J). (978-1-881896-30-2(7)) Pacific View Pr.

Jordan, Apple. Guess Who Grabs, 1 vol. 2nd rev. ed. 2012. (Guess Who? Ser.). (ENG., Illus.). 32p. (gr. k-1). 24.07 (978-1-60870-426-2(2), a69564e1-5d7b-4082-8875-4f660dc3c12e) Cavendish Square Publishing LLC.

Kalman, Bobbie. Les Singes et Autres Primates. Sjonger, Rebecca, illus. 2012. (FRE.). 32p. (J). pap. 9.95 (978-2-89579-440-0(5)) Bayard Canada CAN. Dist: Crabtree Publishing Co.

Klutz Editors, ed. Fuzzy Little Monkeys. 2009. (ENG.). 12p. (J). (gr. -1). 9.95 (978-1-59174-646-1(9), Chicken Socks) Klutz.

Levy, Janey. The Frightful Proboscis Monkey, 1 vol. 2019. (Nature's Freak Show: Ugly Beasts Ser.). (ENG.). 24p. (gr. 2-3). pap. 9.15 (978-1-5382-4610-8(4), 6857828a-ac7a-4f8a-a95c-58343907a10f) Stevens, Gareth Publishing LLLP.

Lindeen, Mary. Monkeys. 2013. (ENG., Illus.). 24p. (J). lib. bdg. 25.65 (978-1-62031-065-6(1)) Jump! Inc.

Lunde, Darrin. Monkey Colors. Wynne, Patricia J., illus. 2012. (ENG.). 32p. (J). (gr. -1-2). pap. 7.99 (978-1-57091-742-4(6)) Charlesbridge Publishing, Inc.

Lunis, Natalie. Howler Monkey: Super Loud. 2011. (Animal Loudmouths: Noisy Animals Ser.). 24p. (J). (gr. k-3). lib. bdg. 26.99 (978-1-61772-276-9(6)) Bearport Publishing Co., Inc.

Lynch, Seth. Monkeys at the Zoo, 1 vol. 2019. (Zoo Animals Ser.). (ENG.). 24p. (gr. k-k). pap. 9.15 (978-1-5382-3934-6(5), ec789337-943e-41e7-a823-e49e40a35c41) Stevens, Gareth Publishing LLLP.

Lynette, Rachel. Squirrel Monkeys. 2013. (Jungle Babies of the Amazon Rain Forest Ser.). 24p. (J). (gr. -1-3). lib. bdg. 25.65 (978-1-61772-757-3(1)) Bearport Publishing Co., Inc.

Markle, Sandra. The Great Monkey Rescue: Saving the Golden Lion Tamarins. 2015. (Sandra Markle's Science Discoveries Ser.). (ENG., Illus.). 40p. (J). (gr. 4-6). E-Book 47.99 (978-1-4677-8850-2(3), Millbrook Pr.) Lerner Publishing Group.

—The Woolly Monkey Mysteries: The Quest to Save a Rain Forest Species. 2019. (Sandra Markle's Science Discoveries Ser.). (ENG., Illus.). 40p. (J). (gr. 4-6). 33.32 (978-1-5124-5868-8(6), 4cca8fc1-9617-4780-86b6-63370b9b987d, Millbrook Pr.) Lerner Publishing Group.

Marsh, Laura. National Geographic Readers: Cutest Animals Collection. 2014. (Readers Ser.). (Illus.). 128p. (J). (gr. 1-3). pap. 7.99 (978-1-4263-1522-0(8), National Geographic Kids) Disney Publishing Worldwide.

Marsh, Sarah Glenn. Ninita's Big World: The True Story of a Deaf Pygmy Marmoset. Coleman, Stephanie Fizer, illus. 2019. (ENG.). 32p. (J). (gr. -1-3). 17.99 (978-1-328-77001-1(X), 1680998, Clarion Bks.) HarperCollins Pubs.

Marshall, Deb. Orangutans. 2014. (J). (978-1-4896-2886-2(X)) Weigl Pubs., Inc.

Mcdaniel, Melissa. Monkeys, 1 vol. 2005. (Animals, Animals Ser.). (ENG., Illus.). 48p. (gr. 5-5). lib. bdg. 32.64 (978-0-7614-1615-9(3), d57663eb-bca2-4a14-843f-fcdb1ceefe1e) Cavendish Square Publishing LLC.

Meister, Cari. Do You Really Want to Meet a Monkey? Fabbri, Daniele, illus. 2014. (Do You Really Want to Meet ... ? Ser.). (ENG.). 24p. (J). (gr. 1-4). 27.10 (978-1-60753-456-3(8), 15897) Amicus.

Moldovo, Eustacia. Baby Monkeys at the Zoo. 2015. (J). (978-0-7660-6597-0(9)); (ENG., Illus.). 24p. (gr. -1-1). pap. 10.35 (978-0-7660-7073-8(5), 3495e041-ffce-45a2-bd51-720b3822052e) Enslow Publishing, LLC.

Monkey. 2004. (Peek-A-Boo Coloring Pads Ser.). 48p. (J). act. bk. ed. 3.99 (978-1-85997-393-6(0)) Byeway Bks.

Monkey. (Buggy Buddies Ser.). (Illus.). (J). (gr. -1). bds. (978-1-56021-353-6(1), 204) W.J. Fantasy, Inc.

Moore Niver, Heather. When Monkeys Laugh, 1 vol. 2017. (Animal Emotions Ser.). (ENG.). 32p. (gr. 3-3). pap. 11.52 (978-0-7660-8861-0(8), 16f64aed-7da5-4a95-b3ed-60a30e445ec6); lib. bdg. 26.93 (978-0-7660-8619-7(4), 8ecdea96-3873-4382-ae24-d22cb42a0357) Enslow Publishing, LLC.

Murray, Julie. Monkeys. (Animal Kingdom Ser.). (ENG., Illus.). (J). 2019. 32p. (gr. 2-5). lib. bdg. 34.21 (978-1-5321-1644-5(6), 32399, Big Buddy Bks.) 2016. 24p. (gr. -1-2). lib. bdg. 31.36 (978-1-68080-533-8(9), 21346, Abdo Kids) ABDO Publishing Co.

Neme, Laurel. Orangutan Houdini. Kelleher, Kathie, illus. 2014. (ENG.). 32p. (J). (gr. 1-7). 17.95 (978-1-59373-153-3(1)) Bunker Hill Publishing, Inc.

Neuman, Susan B. Hang on, Monkey! (1 Hardcover/1 CD) 2017. (National Geographic Kids Ser.). (ENG.). (J). 29.95 (978-1-4301-2641-6(8)) Live Oak Media.

—Hang on, Monkey! (1 Paperback/1 CD) 2017. (National Geographic Kids Ser.). (ENG.). (J). pap. 19.95 (978-1-4301-2640-9(X)) Live Oak Media.

—Hang on, Monkey! (4 Paperbacks/1 CD), 4 vols. 2017. (National Geographic Kids Ser.). (ENG.). (J). pap. 31.95 (978-1-4301-2642-3(6)) Live Oak Media.

—National Geographic Readers: Hang on Monkey! 2014. (Readers Ser.). 24p. (J). (gr. -1-k). pap. 4.99 (978-1-4263-1755-2(7), National Geographic Kids) Disney Publishing Worldwide.

Nickel, Bonnie. Those Mischievous Monkeys. Weaver, Steve, illus. 2012. (Those Amazing Animals Ser.). (ENG.). 56p. (J). (gr. -1-12). pap. 9.95 (978-1-56164-509-1(5)); lib. bdg. 14.95 (978-1-56164-510-7(9)) Pineapple Pr., Inc.

Owen, Ruth. Mischievous Monkeys, 1 vol. 2012. (Eye to Eye with Animals Ser.). (ENG., Illus.). 32p. (J). (gr. 2-2). 29.93 (978-1-4488-8071-3(8), 1899b317-1c9d-4cb7-88c6-f035f23fea17); pap. 11.00 (978-1-4488-8107-9(2), 88b657af-8b9c-4e82-a095-bec60f9e46b5) Rosen Publishing Group, Inc., The. (Windmill Bks.).

Owings, Lisa. Proboscis Monkey. 2014. (Extremely Weird Animals Ser.). (ENG., Illus.). 24p. (J). (gr. 3-8). lib. bdg. 27.95 (978-1-62617-077-3(0), Pilot Bks.) Bellwether Media.

Parramon Staff & Costa-Pau, Rosa. Gorilas. 2006. (SPA.). 32p. (J). (gr. 2-3). 10.40 (978-84-342-2733-0(9), PR33932) Parramon Ediciones S.A. ESP. Dist: Lectorum Pubns., Inc.

Pelusey, Michael & Pelusey, Jane. Apes & Monkeys, 1 vol. 2009. (Zoo Animals Ser.). (ENG.). 32p. (gr. 2-2). lib. bdg. 21.27 (978-0-7614-3144-2(6), 8eac7eab-e7d7-4293-ab33-2f7fe1c3fe18) Cavendish Square Publishing LLC.

Phillips, Dee. Spider Monkey. 2013. (Science Slam: Treed-Animal Life in the Trees Ser.). 24p. (J). (gr. -1-3). lib. bdg. 26.99 (978-1-61772-912-6(4)) Bearport Publishing Co., Inc.

Pyers. Sail Main5 Monkeys, Diverse Animals. 2003. (Rigby Sails Ser.). (ENG.). 32p. (gr. 5-5). pap. 10.20 (978-0-7578-8019-3(3)) Rigby Education.

Rebman, Nick. Monkeys. 2018. (Animals Ser.). (ENG., Illus.). 16p. (J). (gr. k-1). pap. 7.95 (978-1-63517-953-8(X), 163517953X); lib. bdg. 25.64 (978-1-63517-852-4(5), 1635178525) North Star Editions. (Focus Readers).

Redmond, Ian. Gorilas. Anderson, Peter & Brightling, Geoff, illus. 2003. (SPA.). 64p. 14.95 (978-84-372-2323-0(7)) Altea, Ediciones, S.A. - Grupo Santillana ESP. Dist: Santillana USA Publishing Co., Inc.

Riggs, Kate. Monkeys. 2012. (Seedlings Ser.). (ENG.). 24p. (J). (gr. -1-k). 15.95 (978-1-60818-278-7(9), 21996, Creative Education) Creative Co., The.

—Seedlings: Monkeys. 2013. (Seedlings Ser.). (ENG.). 24p. (J). (gr. -1-k). pap. 9.99 (978-0-89812-785-0(8), 22002, Creative Paperbacks) Creative Co., The.

Ryndak, Rob. Monkeys, 1 vol. 2014. (Jungle Animals Ser.). (ENG., Illus.). 24p. (J). (gr. k-k). 24.27 (978-1-4824-1752-4(9), ba7e23f7-d70e-448c-9270-677d6756b2e4) Stevens, Gareth Publishing LLLP.

Schreiber, Anne. National Geographic Readers: Monkeys. 2013. (Readers Ser.). 32p. (J). (gr. 1-3). pap. 4.99 (978-1-4263-1106-2(0), National Geographic Kids); (ENG.). lib. bdg. 14.90 (978-1-4263-1107-9(9), National Geographic Children's Bks.) Disney Publishing Worldwide.

Schuetz, Kari. Baby Monkeys. 2013. (Super Cute! Ser.). (ENG., Illus.). 24p. (J). (gr. k-3). lib. bdg. 26.95 (978-1-60014-929-0(4), Blastoff! Readers) Bellwether Media.

Sebe, Masayuki. 100 Hungry Monkeys!, 0 vols. Sebe, Masayuki, illus. 2014. (ENG., Illus.). 24p. (J). (gr. -1-2). 16.95 (978-1-77138-045-4(4)) Kids Can Pr., Ltd. CAN. Dist: Hachette Bk. Group.

Sterry, Paul. Monkeys & Apes, Vol. 12. 2018. (Animals in the Wild Ser.). (Illus.). 80p. (J). (gr. 7). 33.27 (978-1-4222-4172-1(6)) Mason Crest.

Stewart, Melissa. New World Monkeys. 2007. (Nature Watch Ser.). (ENG., Illus.). 48p. (J). (gr. 4-8). lib. bdg. 27.93 (978-0-8225-6765-3(2), Lerner Pubns.) Lerner Publishing Group.

Thatcher, Henry. Mandrills & Marmosets, 1 vol., 1. 2014. (Big Animals, Small Animals Ser.). (ENG.). 32p. (J). (gr. 2-3). 28.93 (978-1-4777-6118-2(7), e73b1c71-efcf-4d9e-828a-db6afeb7dc8c, PowerKids Pr.) Rosen Publishing Group, Inc., The.

Turner, Sarah E. The Littlest Monkey, 1 vol. 2010. (ENG., Illus.). 32p. (J). (gr. 1-3). pap. 9.95 (978-1-55039-174-9(7)) Sono Nis Pr. CAN. Dist: Orca Bk. Pubs. USA.

Twine, Alice. Monkeys. (Baby Animals Ser.). 24p. (gr. 1-1). 2009. 42.50 (978-1-61511-493-1(9), PowerKids Pr.) 2007. (ENG., Illus.). (J). lib. bdg. 26.27 (978-1-4042-3775-9(5), 503b3bac-9acd-4bee-a5ed-ccb5056a2bbc) Rosen Publishing Group, Inc., The.

—Monkeys/Monos. 2009. (Baby Animals/Animales bebé Ser.). (SPA.). 24p. (gr. 1-1). 42.50 (978-1-61511-505-1(6), Editorial Buenas Letras) Rosen Publishing Group, Inc., The.

—Monkeys/Monos, 1 vol. Obregon, Jose Maria, tr. 2007. (Baby Animals / Animales Bebé Ser.). (ENG & SPA., Illus.). 24p. (J). (gr. 1-1). lib. bdg. 26.27 (978-1-4042-7635-2(1), 2792ccc2-90ea-4940-a353-2e2be93da3a5) Rosen Publishing Group, Inc., The.

Wildlife Education, Ltd Staff, contrib. by. Monkeys. 2006. (Critters Up Close Ser.). (Illus.). (J). bds. 5.95 (978-1-932396-15-7(2)) National Wildlife Federation.

Williams, Zella. Howler Monkeys & Other Latin America Monkeys: Monos Aulladores y Otros Monos de Latino América, 1 vol. 2009. (Animals of Latin America / Animales de Latinoamérica Ser.). (SPA & ENG., Illus.). 24p. (J). (gr. 2-2). pap. 8.25 (978-1-4358-3384-5(8), 87aa4f8f-c411-4a52-bb8d-97a6e20b3852, PowerKids Pr.) Rosen Publishing Group, Inc., The.

Wilsdon, Christina. Monkeys, 1 vol. 2009. (Amazing Animals Ser.). (ENG.). 48p. (gr. 3-5). (J). pap. 11.50 (978-1-4339-2026-4(3), 9a1c1ccd-f8f3-4c7d-83c4-e07860611fc6, Gareth Stevens Learning Library); (YA). lib. bdg. 30.67 (978-0-8368-9109-6(0), 833d10e8-c596-414a-b887-66af9ca088b8) Stevens, Gareth Publishing LLLP.

—Monkeys. 2007. (J). (978-1-59939-134-2(1), Reader's Digest Young Families, Inc.) Studio Fun International.

Yasuda, Anita. Gibbons. 2014. (J). (978-1-4896-2874-9(6)) Weigl Pubs., Inc.

Zabludoff, Marc. Monkeys, 1 vol. 2008. (Animal Ways Ser.). (ENG., Illus.). 112p. (gr. 6-6). lib. bdg. 38.36 (978-0-7614-2535-9(7), 6f46f84f-b6c4-4052-a7d3-1abe6841e139) Cavendish Square Publishing LLC.

Zappa, Marcia. Proboscis Monkeys, 1 vol. 2015. (World's Weirdest Animals Ser.). (ENG., Illus.). 32p. (J). (gr. 2-5). 34.21 (978-1-62403-777-1(1), 17856, Big Buddy Bks.) ABDO Publishing Co.

MONKEYS—FICTION

Ackerman, Arlene. Glimmer de Gloop de Monkey Face: The Elf Named Pee-U & What He Knew. 2003. pap. 8.00 (978-0-8059-6031-0(7)) Dorrance Publishing Co., Inc.

Adams, Ben. Chico Plays Hide & Seek. Cameron, Craig, illus. 2013. (Googly Eyes Ser.). (ENG.). 12p. (J). (gr. -1-k). bds. 6.99 (978-1-84322-280-4(9), Armadillo) Anness Publishing GBR. Dist: National Bk. Network.

Alderfer, Lauren. Mindful Monkey, Happy Panda. MacLean, Kerry Lee, illus. 2011. (ENG.). 32p. (J). (gr. -1-3). 18.95 (978-0-86171-683-8(3)) Wisdom Pubns.

Allen, Jonathan. Banana! Allen, Jonathan, illus. 2006. (Illus.). 32p. (J). pap. (978-1-905417-02-5(0)) Boxer Bks., Ltd.

Amato, Mary. Missing Monkey! Jenkins, Ward, illus. 2014. (Good Crooks Ser.: Bk. 1). (ENG.). 128p. (J). (gr. 2-4). 9.99 (978-1-60684-509-7(8), 7b9b0307-7e15-4dbc-8be4-66e30decb56e, Darby Creek) Lerner Publishing Group.

and Film Studio, Shanghai Animation & Tang, Sanmu. An Attempt to Scoop up the Moon. Ying, Wu, tr. 2010. (Favorite Childrens Cartoons from China Ser.). (ENG., Illus.). 32p. (gr. -1-3). pap. 5.95 (978-1-60220-971-8(5)) Shanghai Pr.

—Monkey Makes Havoc in Heaven. Xiaozhen, Wu, tr. from CHI. 2010. (Favorite Childrens Cartoons from China Ser.). (ENG., Illus.). 32p. (gr. -1-3). pap. 5.95 (978-1-60220-974-9(X)) Shanghai Pr.

Anderson, Airlie. Momo & Snap. 2013. (Child's Play Library). (ENG., Illus.). 32p. (J). (978-1-84643-603-1(6)) Child's Play International Ltd.

Anthony, David & Clasman, Charles David. Heroes A2Z #13: (Heroes a to Z): Monkey Monster Truck. Blakeslee, Lys, illus. 2012. 128p. (J). mass mkt. 4.99 (978-0-9846528-1-5(7)) Sigil Publishing.

Ariel, A. D. The Tricky Monkey. 2016. (Spring Forward Ser.). (J). (gr. 2). (978-1-4900-9441-0(5)) Benchmark Education Co.

Arnold, Audrey. Elkin's Tail. 2012. (Illus.). 52p. pap. 27.45 (978-1-4772-2180-8(8)) AuthorHouse.

Award, Anna, et al. Monkey & the Fishermen & the Donkey in the Pond. 2014. (ENG.). 24p. (J). pap. 6.95 (978-1-84135-956-4(4)) Award Pubns. Ltd. GBR. Dist: Parkwest Pubns., Inc.

Aylesworth, Jim. Naughty Little Monkeys. Cole, Henry, illus. 2006. (ENG.). 32p. (J). (gr. -1-2). reprint ed. 7.99 (978-0-14-240562-8(0), Puffin Books) Penguin Young Readers Group.

AZ Books, creator. Fidget Monkey. 2012. (Curious Eyes Ser.). (ENG., Illus.). 12p. (J). (gr. -1 — 1). bds. 12.95 (978-1-61889-103-7(0)) AZ Bks. LLC.

Banana-Tail. 2003. lib. bdg. 13.95 (978-0-9727681-0-8(6)) Active Media Publishing, LLC.

Barnett, Mac. Hi, Jack! Pizzoli, Greg, illus. 2019. (Jack Book Ser.: 1). 80p. (J). (gr. -1-3). 9.99 (978-0-593-11379-0(9), Viking Books for Young Readers) Penguin Young Readers Group.

—Jack at Bat. Pizzoli, Greg, illus. 2020. (Jack Book Ser.: 3). 80p. (J). (gr. -1-3). 9.99 (978-0-593-11382-0(9), Viking Books for Young Readers) Penguin Young Readers Group.

Barragan, Sophia & Barragan, Ivy. Susana Banana the Fantastic Figure Skater. 2008. 32p. pap. 12.99 (978-1-4389-0169-5(0)) AuthorHouse.

Barton, John. The Monkey Boy That Stood Up. 2012. (Illus.). 24p. pap. 19.82 (978-1-4685-8581-0(9)) AuthorHouse.

Bell, Cece. Sock Monkey Boogie Woogie: A Friend Is Made. Bell, Cece, illus. 2015. (Cece Bell's Sock Monkey Ser.). (ENG., Illus.). 32p. (J). (gr. -1-3). 14.00 (978-0-7636-7758-9(2)) Candlewick Pr.

—Sock Monkey Rides Again. Bell, Cece, illus. 2015. (Cece Bell's Sock Monkey Ser.). (ENG., Illus.). 32p. (J). (gr. -1-3). 14.00 (978-0-7636-7760-2(4)) Candlewick Pr.

—Sock Monkey Takes a Bath. Bell, Cece, illus. 2015. (Cece Bell's Sock Monkey Ser.). (ENG., Illus.). 32p. (J). (gr. -1-3). 14.00 (978-0-7636-7759-6(0)) Candlewick Pr.

Bentley, Douglas W. What Will It Take for a Toad to Kiss a Monkey: The Adventures of Princess Gracie & Prince Wallaby. Bentley, Julia Faye, illus. 2008. 52p. per. 24.95 (978-1-4137-8849-5(1)) America Star Bks.

Benton, Lynne. The Sad Princess. Catling, Andy, illus. 2009. (Tadpoles Ser.). (ENG.). 24p. (J). (gr. k-2). pap. (978-0-7787-3903-6(1)) Crabtree Publishing Co.

Beobi & the Magic Coloring Book A Visit to the Doctor. 2005. (J). 3.99 (978-0-9743847-3-3(9)) Cohn, Tricia.

Beobi & the Magic Coloring Book Funland. 2006. (Illus.). 24p. (J). 3.99 (978-0-9743847-7-1(1)) Cohn, Tricia.

Berenstain, Jan & Berenstain, Mike. Lift & Flap the Berenstain Bears' Baby Easter Bunny. 2008. (Berenstain Bears Ser.). (ENG., Illus.). 16p. (J). (gr. -1-1). pap. 6.99 (978-0-06-057420-8(8), HarperFestival) HarperCollins Pubs.

Bernstein, Ariel. I Have a Balloon. Magoon, Scott, illus. 2017. (ENG.). 40p. (J). (gr. -1-3). 19.99 (978-1-4814-7250-0(X), Simon & Schuster/Paula Wiseman Bks.) Simon & Schuster/Paula Wiseman Bks.

—Where Is My Balloon? Magoon, Scott, illus. 2019. (ENG.). 40p. (J). (gr. -1-3). 17.99 (978-1-5344-1451-8(7), Simon & Schuster Bks. For Young Readers) Simon & Schuster Bks. For Young Readers.

Bernstein, Galia. Leyla. 2019. (ENG., Illus.). 32p. (J). (gr. -1-3). 16.99 (978-1-4197-3543-1(8), 1268901, Abrams Bks. for Young Readers) Abrams, Inc.

Beth, Libby. There's a Rainbow in the Mud. 2013. 52p. pap. 23.04 (978-1-4669-9641-0(2)) Trafford Publishing.

Blackford, Andy. The Hungry Little Monkey. 2011. (Tadpoles Ser.). (ENG., Illus.). 24p. (J). (gr. k-2). lib. bdg. (978-0-7787-0581-9(1)); pap. (978-0-7787-0592-5(7)) Crabtree Publishing Co.

Blanks, Morgan Georgia. The Desert Island. 2008. 52p. pap. 20.49 (978-1-4343-9006-6(3)) AuthorHouse.

Bloom, C. P. The Monkey Goes Bananas. Raymundo, Peter, illus. 2014. (Monkey Goes Bananas Ser.). (ENG.). 40p. (J). (gr. k-2). 14.95 (978-1-4197-0885-5(6), 1060301, Abrams Bks. for Young Readers) Abrams, Inc.

Boldt, Claudia. Melvin the Luckiest Monkey. 2013. (ENG., Illus.). 32p. (J). (gr. -1-k). 14.95 (978-1-84976-086-7(1)) Tate Publishing, Ltd. GBR. Dist: Hachette Bk. Group.

Boon, Emilie. Ella & Monkey at Sea. Boon, Emilie, illus. 2018. (Illus.). 32p. (J). (gr. -1-2). 16.99 (978-0-7636-9233-9(6)) Candlewick Pr.

Brenner, Norm. The Leopard Who Lost His Spots. 2010. (ENG.). 28p. pap. 21.99 (978-1-4535-2436-7(3)) Xlibris Corp.

Brian, Janeen. Maya Monkey, 1 vol. rev. ed. 2013. (Literary Text Ser.). (ENG., Illus.). 20p. (gr. k-2). 7.99 (978-1-4333-5486-1(1)) Teacher Created Materials, Inc.

Briley, Jennifer Lenore. Justin's Journey. 2008. 48p. pap. 16.95 (978-1-60672-150-6(X)) America Star Bks.

Brimner, Larry Dane. Monkey Math. Kulka, Joe, illus. 2007. (Rookie Reader Skill Set Ser.). (ENG.). 32p. (J). (gr. k-2). pap. 4.95 (978-0-531-13850-2(X)) Scholastic Library Publishing.

Brooks, Susie. 5 Cheeky Monkeys. Tarbett, Debbie, illus. 2016. (J). (978-1-84857-539-4(4)) Little Tiger Pr. Group.

Brown, Alan James. Michael & the Monkey King. 2008. (ENG.). 177p. pap. 16.95 (978-1-4092-0241-7(0)) Lulu Pr., Inc.

Brown, Marc, illus. Monkey: Not Ready for Bedtime. 2017. (J). pap. (978-0-399-55782-8(2)) Knopf, Alfred A. Inc.

Browne, Paula. El Cumpleanos de la Mona. Isabel, Isaias, tr. Browne, Paula, illus. 2004. (Paca, la Macaca Ser.). (SPA., Illus.). 20p. pap. 4.95 (978-85-7416-214-0(0)) Callis Editora Ltda BRA. Dist: Independent Pubs. Group.

—Paca, la macaca en la Cocina. Isabel, Isaias, tr. Browne, Paula, illus. 2004. (Paca, la Macaca Ser.). (SPA., Illus.). 20p. pap. 4.95 (978-85-7416-210-2(8)) Callis Editora Ltda BRA. Dist: Independent Pubs. Group.

—Paca, la Macaca va al Mercado. Isabel, Isaias, tr. Browne, Paula, illus. 2004. (Paca, la Macaca Ser.). (Illus.). 20p. pap. 4.95 (978-85-7416-215-7(9)) Callis Editora Ltda BRA. Dist: Independent Pubs. Group.

—Que Desbarajuste, Paca. Isabel, Isaias, tr. Browne, Paula, illus. 2004. (Paca, la Macaca Ser.). (Illus.). 20p. pap. 6.95 (978-85-7416-211-9(6)) Callis Editora Ltda BRA. Dist: Independent Pubs. Group.

Burson, Ronda Pfohl. Monk-Monk the Monkey. 2010. 20p. 10.49 (978-1-4520-0351-1(3)) AuthorHouse.

Campbell, Shirlene. Ook Ook the Monkey. 2013. 24p. pap. 24.95 (978-1-63004-355-1(9)) America Star Bks.

Capucilli, Alyssa Satin. Monkey Play. 2012. (Step into Reading Ser.). (Illus.). 32p. (J). (gr. -1-1). pap. 5.99 (978-0-375-86993-8(X), Random Hse. Bks. for Young Readers) Random Hse. Children's Bks.

Catalanotto, Peter. Monkey & Robot. Catalanotto, Peter, illus. 2014. (ENG., Illus.). 64p. (J). (gr. 1-4). pap. 8.99 (978-1-4424-2979-6(8), Atheneum Bks. for Young Readers) Simon & Schuster Children's Publishing.

—More of Monkey & Robot. Catalanotto, Peter, illus. 2014. (ENG., Illus.). 64p. (J). (gr. 1-4). 15.99 (978-1-4424-5251-0(X), Atheneum/Richard Jackson Bks.) Simon & Schuster Children's Publishing.

Chamberlain, Nick. The Adventures of Papillon. 2008. 176p. pap. 15.95 (978-1-60290-092-9(2)) Nassau-Street.com.

Chen, Wei Dong. The Expulsion of Sun Wu Kong. Peng, Chao, illus. 2013. (Monkey King Ser.: 7). 176p. (YA). (gr. 6-12). lib. bdg. 29.27 (978-89-94208-75-6(5)) Lerner Publishing Group.

—Fight to the Death. Peng, Chao, illus. 2013. (Monkey King Ser.: 11). 176p. (YA). (gr. 6-12). lib. bdg. 29.27 (978-89-94208-79-4(8)) Lerner Publishing Group.

—The Lost Children. Peng, Chao, illus. 2013. (Monkey King Ser.: 12). 176p. (YA). (gr. 6-12). lib. bdg. 29.27 (978-89-94208-80-0(1)) Lerner Publishing Group.

—Monkey King: Birth of the Stone Monkey. Peng, Chao, illus. 2012. (Monkey King Ser.: 1). (ENG.). 176p. (gr. 5-8). lib. bdg. 29.27 (978-89-94208-69-5(0)) JR Comics KOR. Dist: Lerner Publishing Group.

—Monkey King: Enemies & a New Friend. Peng, Chao, illus. 2012. (Monkey King Ser.: 4). (ENG.). 176p. (gr. 5-8). lib. bdg. 29.27 (978-89-94208-72-5(0)) JR Comics KOR. Dist: Lerner Publishing Group.

—Monkey King: Journey to the West. Peng, Chao, illus. 2012. (Monkey King Ser.: 3). (ENG.). 176p. (gr. 5-8). lib. bdg. 29.27 (978-89-94208-71-8(2)) JR Comics KOR. Dist: Lerner Publishing Group.

—Monkey King: The Bane of Heaven. Peng, Chao, illus. 2012. (Monkey King Ser.: 2). (ENG.). 176p. (gr. 5-8). lib. bdg. 29.27 (978-89-94208-70-1(4)) JR Comics KOR. Dist: Lerner Publishing Group.

—Monkey King: The Sacred Tree. Peng, Chao, illus. 2012. (Monkey King Ser.: 6). (ENG.). 176p. (gr. 5-8). lib. bdg. 29.27 (978-89-94208-74-9(7)) JR Comics KOR. Dist: Lerner Publishing Group.

—Monkey King: Three Trials. Peng, Chao, illus. 2012. (Monkey King Ser.: 5). (ENG.). 176p. (gr. 5-8). lib. bdg. 29.27 (978-89-94208-73-2(9)) JR Comics KOR. Dist: Lerner Publishing Group.

—The Realm of the Infant King. Peng, Chao, illus. 2013. (Monkey King Ser.: 10). 176p. (YA). (gr. 6-12). lib. bdg. 29.27 (978-89-94208-78-7(X)) Lerner Publishing Group.

—The Stolen Kingdom. Peng, Chao, illus. 2013. (Monkey King Ser.: 9). 176p. (YA). (gr. 6-12). lib. bdg. 29.27 (978-89-94208-77-0(1)) Lerner Publishing Group.

—Treasures of the Mountain Kings. Peng, Chao, illus. 2013. (Monkey King Ser.: 8). 176p. (YA). (gr. 6-12). lib. bdg. 29.27 (978-89-94208-76-3(3)) Lerner Publishing Group.

Cheng'en, Wu. Journey to the West. Chiang, Shirley, illus. 2013. (Chinese Classics Ser.). (ENG.). 64p. pap. 7.95 (978-1-906230-34-0(X)) Real Reads Ltd. GBR. Dist: Casemate Pubs. & Bk. Distributors, LLC.

Chichester Clark, Emma. No More Kissing! 2018. (Mimi & Momo Ser.). (ENG., Illus.). 32p. (J). (-k). pap. 10.99 (978-1-78344-585-1(8)) Andersen Pr. GBR. Dist: Independent Pubs. Group.

Chin, Oliver. The Year of the Monkey: Tales from the Chinese Zodiac. Ono, Kenji, illus. 2015. (Tales from the Chinese Zodiac Ser.: 11). (ENG.). 36p. (J). (gr. -1). 15.95 (978-1-59702-118-0(0)) Immedium.

Chojnowski, Bryan. Muffin Time: Origins. 2005. 98p. pap. 25.01 (978-1-4116-4440-3(9)) Lulu Pr., Inc.

Christelow, Eileen. Five Little Monkeys 5-Minute Stories. Christelow, Eileen, illus. 2018. (Five Little Monkeys Story Ser.). (ENG., Illus.). 256p. (J). (gr. -1-3). 14.99 (978-1-328-45359-4(6), 1711798, Clarion Bks.) HarperCollins Pubs.

—Five Little Monkeys Bake a Birthday Cake. Christelow, Eileen, illus. 2005. (Five Little Monkeys Story Ser.). (ENG., Illus.). 32p. (J). (gr. -1-3). pap. 7.99 (978-0-618-49648-8(3), 100403, Clarion Bks.) HarperCollins Pubs.

—Five Little Monkeys Go Shopping. 2012. (Five Little Monkeys Story Ser.). lib. bdg. 17.20 (978-0-606-23990-5(1)) Turtleback.

—Five Little Monkeys Jump in the Bath. Christelow, Eileen, illus. 2012. (Five Little Monkeys Story Ser.). (ENG., Illus.). 20p. (J). (gr. k — 1). bds. 7.99 (978-0-547-87527-9(4), 1505756, Clarion Bks.) HarperCollins Pubs.

—Five Little Monkeys Jumping on the Bed Big Book. Christelow, Eileen, illus. 2006. (Five Little Monkeys Story Ser.). (ENG., Illus.). 32p. (J). (gr. -1-3). pap. 26.99 (978-0-618-83682-6(9), 491894, Clarion Bks.) HarperCollins Pubs.

—Five Little Monkeys Jumping on the Bed Lap Board Book. Christelow, Eileen, illus. 2008. (Five Little Monkeys Story Ser.). (ENG., Illus.). 30p. (J). (gr. -1 — 1). bds. 12.99 (978-0-547-13176-4(3), 1048452, Clarion Bks.) HarperCollins Pubs.

—Five Little Monkeys Jumping on the Bed Padded Board Book. Christelow, Eileen, illus. 2017. (Five Little Monkeys Story Ser.). (ENG., Illus.). 30p. (J). (gr. -1 — 1). bds. 11.99 (978-0-547-51075-0(6), 1443772, Clarion Bks.) HarperCollins Pubs.

—Five Little Monkeys Play Hide & Seek. 2010. (Five Little Monkeys Story Ser.). lib. bdg. 17.20 (978-0-606-14479-7(X)) Turtleback.

—Five Little Monkeys Set for Costco 2005. 2006. (J). bds. 0.01 (978-0-618-73326-2(4), Clarion Bks.) HarperCollins Pubs.

—Five Little Monkeys Sitting in a Tree/Cinco Monitos Subidos a un árbol Board Bk: Bilingual English-Spanish. Christelow, Eileen, illus. 2014. (Five Little Monkeys Story Ser.). (ENG., Illus.). 28p. (J). (gr. -1 — 1). bds. 7.99 (978-0-544-30218-1(4), 1577854, Clarion Bks.) HarperCollins Pubs.

—Five Little Monkeys Storybook Treasury. Christelow, Eileen, illus. 2009. (Five Little Monkeys Story Ser.). (ENG., Illus.). 192p. (J). (gr. -1-3). 12.99 (978-0-547-23873-9(8), 1084232, Clarion Bks.) HarperCollins Pubs.

—Five Little Monkeys Storybook Treasury/Cinco Monitos Coleccion de Oro: Bilingual English-Spanish. Christelow, Eileen, illus. 2012. (Five Little Monkeys Story Ser.). (ENG., Illus.). 192p. (J). (gr. -1-3). 12.99 (978-0-547-74593-0(1), 1486369, Clarion Bks.) HarperCollins Pubs.

—Five Little Monkeys Trick-Or-Treat. Christelow, Eileen, illus. 2013. (Five Little Monkeys Story Ser.). (ENG., Illus.). 40p. (J). (gr. -1-3). 16.99 (978-0-547-85893-7(0), 1502434, Clarion Bks.) HarperCollins Pubs.

—Five Little Monkeys Trick-Or-Treat. 2018. (Five Little Monkeys Story Ser.). lib. bdg. 18.40 (978-0-606-41003-8(1)) Turtleback.

—Five Little Monkeys Wash the Car. Christelow, Eileen, illus. 2004. (Five Little Monkeys Story Ser.). (ENG., Illus.). 40p. (J). (gr. -1-3). 7.99 (978-0-618-48602-1(X), 100389, Clarion Bks.) HarperCollins Pubs.

—5 Little Monkeys Bake Birthday Cake/Cinco Monitos Hacen un Pastel de Cumpleanos: Bilingual English-Spanish. Christelow, Eileen, illus. 2014. (Five Little Monkeys Story Ser.).Tr. of Five Little Monkeys Bake a Birthday Cake. (ENG., Illus.). 30p. (J). (— 1). bds. 7.99 (978-0-544-08899-3(9), 1537637, Clarion Bks.) HarperCollins Pubs.

Chronicle Books & ImageBooks. Little Monkey: Finger Puppet Book: (Finger Puppet Book for Toddlers & Babies, Baby Books for First Year, Animal Finger Puppets) 2013. (Little Finger Puppet Board Bks.). (ENG., Illus.). 12p. (J). (gr. -1 — 1). 7.99 (978-1-4521-1250-3(9)) Chronicle Bks. LLC.

Chuslo-Shur, Lauren, ed. The Golden Friendship. 2012. (ENG.). (J). pap. (978-1-4675-4581-5(3)) Independent Pub.

Claiborn, Trevor M. The Monkey & the Forbidden Fruit. 2012. 112p. pap. 34.99 (978-1-4772-0987-5(5)) AuthorHouse.

Clarke, Jane. How to Feed Your Cheeky Monkey. Birkett, Georgie, illus. 2017. 16p. (J). bds. 8.99 (978-1-61067-497-3(9)) Kane Miller.

Cleveland, Rob. The Clever Monkey: A Folktale from West Africa. Hoffmire, Baird, illus. 2006. (Story Cove Ser.). (ENG.). 32p. (J). (gr. -1-3). pap. 4.95 (978-0-87483-801-5(0)) August Hse. Pubs., Inc.

Cohn, Tricia L. Beobi & the Magic Coloring Book ABC First Words. 2003. (J). (978-0-9743847-0-2(4)) Cohn, Tricia.

conrad, catherine. The Lemonade Stand. 2008. (Illus.). 32p. (J). lib. bdg. 16.99 (978-0-9799065-0-3(4)) Banana Pr.

Cornell, Kevin. Mojo the Sock Monkey. 2005. 48p. (YA). pap. 15.99 (978-1-4116-5713-7(6)) Lulu Pr., Inc.

Courtauld, Sarah. Monkeys Internet-Referenced. 2009. (First Reading Level 3 Ser.). 48p. (J). 6.99 (978-0-7945-2290-2(4), Usborne) EDC Publishing.

Crenshaw, Glenda. Friends of the Enchanted Forest: How they Save Christmas. 2011. 28p. pap. 15.47 (978-1-4520-0512-6(5)) AuthorHouse.

Curious George: A Halloween Boo Fest. 2018. (Curious George Ser.). (ENG., Illus.). 12p. (J). (— 1). bds. 9.99 (978-1-328-54832-0(5), 1724314, Clarion Bks.) HarperCollins Pubs.

Curious George: Sweet Dreams, Curious George. 2016. (Curious George Ser.). (ENG., Illus.). 24p. (J). (gr. -1-3). 4.99 (978-0-544-50321-2(X), 1604665, Clarion Bks.) HarperCollins Pubs.

Curious George & the Dump Truck (8x8 with Stickers) Curiou. 2010. (Curious George Ser.). (ENG., Illus.). 24p. (J). (gr. -1-3). pap. 4.99 (978-0-547-50425-4(X), 1442863, Clarion Bks.) HarperCollins Pubs.

Curious George & the Ice Cream Surprise. 2011. (Curious George Ser.). (ENG., Illus.). 24p. (J). (gr. -1-3). pap. 4.99 (978-0-547-24285-9(9), 1099394, Clarion Bks.) HarperCollins Pubs.

Curious George & the Pizza Party with Downloadable Audio. 2013. (Curious George Ser.). (ENG., Illus.). 24p. (J). (gr. -1-3). pap. 4.99 (978-0-544-10988-9(0), 1541242, Clarion Bks.) HarperCollins Pubs.

Curious George Apple Harvest. 2012. (Curious George Ser.). (ENG., Illus.). 24p. (J). (gr. -1-3). pap. 4.99 (978-0-547-51705-6(X), 1444784, Clarion Bks.) HarperCollins Pubs.

Curious George at the Park Touch-And-Feel (Cgtv Board Book) 2010. (Curious George Ser.). (ENG., Illus.). 10p. (J). (gr. -1 — 1). bds. 6.99 (978-0-547-24300-9(6), 1099424, Clarion Bks.) HarperCollins Pubs.

Curious George Builds a Home. 2006. (Curious George Ser.). (ENG., Illus.). 24p. (J). (gr. -1-3). 4.99 (978-0-618-72395-9(1), 416298, Clarion Bks.) HarperCollins Pubs.

Curious George Builds a Tree House (Reader Level 2) 2017. (Curious George Ser.). (ENG., Illus.). 24p. (J). (gr. -1-3). pap. 4.99 (978-0-544-86704-8(1), 1648560, Clarion Bks.) HarperCollins Pubs.

Curious George Builds an Igloo (Reader Level 2), 1 vol. 2013. (Curious George TV Ser.). (ENG., Illus.). 24p. (J). (gr. -1-3). pap. 4.99 (978-0-544-09666-0(5), 0a90920f-82c9-45bd-9f3e-96cc49159a36, Clarion Bks.) HarperCollins Pubs.

Curious George Car Wash. 2013. (Curious George Ser.). (ENG., Illus.). 24p. (J). (gr. -1-3). pap. 5.99 (978-0-547-94086-1(6), 1516996, Clarion Bks.) HarperCollins Pubs.

Curious George Dinosaur Tracks (Reader Level 1) 2011. (Curious George TV Ser.). (ENG., Illus.). 24p. (J). (gr. -1-3). pap. 4.99 (978-0-547-43888-7(5), 1433465, Clarion Bks.) HarperCollins Pubs.

Curious George Discovers Germs. 2015. (Curious George Ser.). (ENG., Illus.). 32p. (J). (gr. -1-3). 6.99 (978-0-544-43066-2(2), 1595741, Clarion Bks.) HarperCollins Pubs.

Curious George Discovers the Ocean. 2015. (Curious George Ser.). (ENG., Illus.). 32p. (J). (gr. -1-3). 6.99 (978-0-544-43065-5(4), 1595740, Clarion Bks.) HarperCollins Pubs.

Curious George Discovers the Rainbow. 2015. (Curious George Ser.). (ENG., Illus.). 32p. (J). (gr. -1-3). 6.99 (978-0-544-43068-6(9), 1595743, Clarion Bks.) HarperCollins Pubs.

Curious George Discovers the Senses. 2015. (Curious George Ser.). (ENG., Illus.). 32p. (J). (gr. -1-3). 6.99 (978-0-544-50023-5(7), 1604222, Clarion Bks.) HarperCollins Pubs.

Curious George Discovery Day. 2007. (Curious George Ser.). (ENG., Illus.). 14p. (J). (gr. k — 1). bds. 13.95 *(978-0-618-73761-1(8)*, 529819, Clarion Bks.) HarperCollins Pubs.

Curious George Goes to the Beach. 2014. (Curious George Ser.). (ENG., Illus.). 24p. (J). (gr. -1-3). pap. 5.99 *(978-0-544-25001-7(X)*, 1566524, Clarion Bks.) HarperCollins Pubs.

Curious George Goes to the Hospital Book & Cd, 1 vol. 2008. (Curious George Ser.). (ENG., Illus.). 48p. (J). (gr. -1-3). audio compact disk 10.95 *(978-0-618-80063-6(8)*, 429489, Clarion Bks.) HarperCollins Pubs.

Curious George Goes to the Zoo. 2014. (Curious George Ser.). (ENG., Illus.). 24p. (J). (gr. -1-3). 4.99 *(978-0-544-11000-7(5)*, 1541240, Clarion Bks.) HarperCollins Pubs.

Curious George Grows a Garden (2 Books In 1) 2012. (Curious George TV Ser.). (ENG., Illus.). 48p. (J). (gr. -1-3). pap. 5.99 *(978-0-547-64304-5(7)*, 1469833, Clarion Bks.) HarperCollins Pubs.

Curious George Haunted Halloween (Cgtv Reader) 2014. (Curious George TV Ser.). (ENG., Illus.). 24p. (J). (gr. -1-3). pap. 4.99 *(978-0-544-32079-6(4)*, 1582517, Clarion Bks.) HarperCollins Pubs.

Curious George Learns to Count from 1 To 100. 2011. (Curious George Ser.). (ENG., Illus.). 80p. (J). (gr. -1-3). pap. 8.99 *(978-0-547-13841-1(5)*, 1049584, Clarion Bks.) HarperCollins Pubs.

Curious George Makes a Valentine (Gtr Level 2) 2017. (Curious George Ser.). (ENG., Illus.). 24p. (J). (gr. -1-3). pap. 4.99 *(978-1-328-69556-7(5)*, 1671217, Clarion Bks.) HarperCollins Pubs.

Curious George Makes Pancakes. 2018. (Curious George Ser.). (ENG., Illus.). 24p. (J). (— 1). bds. 12.99 *(978-1-328-76461-4(3)*, 1681069, Clarion Bks.) HarperCollins Pubs.

Curious George Plants a Tree. 2010. (Curious George Ser.). (ENG., Illus.). 24p. (J). (gr. -1-3). pap. 5.99 *(978-0-547-29776-7(9)*, 1413169, Clarion Bks.) HarperCollins Pubs.

Curious George Plays Mini Golf (Reader Level 1) 2008. (Curious George Ser.). (ENG., Illus.). 24p. (J). (gr. -1-3). pap. 4.99 *(978-0-618-99986-6(8)*, 1027755, Clarion Bks.) HarperCollins Pubs.

Curious George Ready for School. 2017. (Curious George Ser.). (ENG., Illus.). 14p. (J). (— 1). bds. 7.99 *(978-0-544-93120-6(3)*, 1657523, Clarion Bks.) HarperCollins Pubs.

Curious George Saves His Pennies. 2014. (Curious George Ser.). (ENG., Illus.). 24p. (J). (gr. -1-3). pap. 5.99 *(978-0-547-81853-5(X)*, 1496643, Clarion Bks.) HarperCollins Pubs.

Curious George Says Thank You. 2012. (Curious George Ser.). (ENG., Illus.). 24p. (J). (gr. -1-3). pap. 5.99 *(978-0-547-81852-8(1)*, 1496582, Clarion Bks.) HarperCollins Pubs.

Curious George Super Sticker Coloring Book. 2008. (Curious George Ser.). (ENG., Illus.). 64p. (J). (gr. -1-3). 12.99 *(978-0-618-99877-7(2)*, 1027757, Clarion Bks.) HarperCollins Pubs.

Curious George Takes a Job Book & CD. 2007. (Curious George Ser.). (ENG., Illus.). 48p. (J). (gr. -1-3). audio 10.99 *(978-0-618-72406-2(0)*, 462918, Clarion Bks.) HarperCollins Pubs.

Curious George the Boat Show (Reader Level 1) 2008. (Curious George TV Ser.). (ENG., Illus.). 24p. (J). (gr. -1-3). pap. 4.99 *(978-0-618-89196-2(X)*, 491961, Clarion Bks.) HarperCollins Pubs.

Curious George the Donut Delivery. 2007. (Curious George Ser.). (ENG., Illus.). 24p. (J). (gr. -1-3). 4.99 *(978-0-618-73757-4(X)*, 489189, Clarion Bks.) HarperCollins Pubs.

Curious George the Perfect Carrot (Reader Level 1) 2010. (Curious George TV Ser.). (ENG., Illus.). 24p. (J). (gr. -1-3). pap. 4.99 *(978-0-547-24299-6(9)*, 1099423, Clarion Bks.) HarperCollins Pubs.

Curious George Tool Time (Cgtv Board Book) 2013. (Curious George Ser.). (ENG., Illus.). 12p. (J). (gr. -1 — 1). bds. 6.99 *(978-0-547-96818-6(3)*, 1521230, Clarion Bks.) HarperCollins Pubs.

Curious George Visits the Library. 2013. (Curious George Ser.). (ENG., Illus.). 24p. (J). (gr. -1-3). pap. 4.99 *(978-0-544-11450-0(7)*, 1541812, Clarion Bks.) HarperCollins Pubs.

Curious George Windy Delivery. 2014. (Curious George Ser.). (ENG., Illus.). 24p. (J). (gr. -1-3). pap. 4.99 *(978-0-544-32076-5(X)*, 1582515, Clarion Bks.) HarperCollins Pubs.

Curious George's Dinosaur Discovery. 2006. (Curious George Ser.). (ENG., Illus.). 24p. (J). (gr. -1-3). pap. 4.99 *(978-0-618-66377-4(0)*, 446458, Clarion Bks.) HarperCollins Pubs.

Curry, Kenneth. Priscilla & the Talking Monkey. 2007. (Illus.). 22p. (J). 10.95 *(978-0-9798364-6-6(8))* Curry Brothers Publishing Group.

Dahl, Roald. Eejits. Fitt, Matthew, tr. 2006. (SCO., Illus.). 96p. (J). (gr. 1-7). pap. 9.99 *(978-1-84502-097-2(9))* Black and White Publishing Ltd. GBR. Dist: Independent Pubs. Group.

—The Giraffe, the Pelly & Me. 2009. (Orig.). (gr. 3-6). 18.40 *(978-0-8085-9436-9(2))* Turtleback.

Dale, Jay. Big Green Crocodile, 1 vol. Hancock, Anna, illus. 2012. (Engage Literacy Blue Ser.). (ENG.). 16p. (J). (gr. k-2). pap. 6.99 *(978-1-4296-8984-7(6)*, 119997, Capstone Pr.) Capstone.

—Min Monkey. Hancock, Anna, illus. 2012. (Engage Literacy Red Ser.). (ENG.). 16p. (J). (gr. k-2). pap. 36.94 *(978-1-4296-8945-8(5)*, 18369); pap. 6.99 *(978-1-4296-8944-1(7)*, 119976) Capstone. (Capstone Pr.).

—Up Here, 1 vol. Hancock, Anna, illus. 2012. (Engage Literacy Magenta Ser.). (ENG.). 16p. (J). (gr. k-2). pap. 6.99 *(978-1-4296-8862-8(9)*, 119935, Capstone Pr.) Capstone.

Daywalt, Drew. This Is MY Fort! (Monkey & Cake) Tallec, Olivier, illus. 2019. (Monkey & Cake Ser.: 2). (ENG.). 56p. (J). (gr. -1-3). 9.99 *(978-1-338-14390-4(5)*, Orchard Bks.) Scholastic, Inc.

De Brunhoff, Jean. Babar & Zephir. De Brunhoff, Jean., illus. 2005. (Illus.). 38p. (J). (gr. k-4). reprint ed. 16.00 *(978-0-7567-8935-0(4))* DIANE Publishing Co.

de la Mare, Walter. The Three Mulla-Mulgars. 2011. 196p. pap. 14.95 *(978-1-60664-560-4(9))* Rodgers, Alan Bks.

—The Three Mulla-Mulgars (the Three Royal Monkeys) Lathrop, Dorothy P., illus. 2013. (ENG.). 288p. (J). (gr. 3-6). pap. 12.95 *(978-0-486-49380-0(6)*, 493806) Dover Pubns., Inc.

Deacon, Melissa. I Have a Monkey in My Tub! 2011. 32p. pap. 24.95 *(978-1-4626-2001-2(9))* America Star Bks.

Dean, James & Dean, Kimberly. Pete the Cat & the Bad Banana. Dean, James, illus. 2014. (My First I Can Read Ser.). (ENG., Illus.). 32p. (J). (gr. -1-3). pap. 4.99 *(978-0-06-230382-0(1)*, HarperCollins) HarperCollins Pubs.

DelaHaye, Rachel. The Mean Monkey Blue Band. Mosedale, Julian, illus. 2017. (Cambridge Reading Adventures Ser.). (ENG.). 16p. pap. 6.15 *(978-1-108-43971-8(3))* Cambridge Univ. Pr.

Derdowski, Chad. All Robots Must Die: Nacho-Geddon. 2013. 187p. (J). pap. 7.99 *(978-1-933925-50-9(7)*, Agent of Danger) Komikwerks, LLC.

Deutsch, David. In Search of the Little People. l.t. ed. 2005. (Illus.). 60p. (J). per. 13.95 *(978-1-59879-013-9(7))* Lifevest Publishing, Inc.

Dharma Publishing Staff. The Monkey King: A Story about Compassion & Leadership. 2nd ed. 2013. (Jataka Tales Ser.). (Illus.). 36p. (gr. -1-7). pap. 8.95 *(978-0-89800-495-3(0))* Dharma Publishing.

DiCamillo, Kate. Great Joy (midi Edition) Ibatoulline, Bagram, illus. 2010. (ENG.). 32p. (J). (gr. -1-3). 12.00 *(978-0-7636-4996-8(1))* Candlewick Pr.

Dixon, Chuck. Way of the Rat Traveler, Vol. 1. 2003. (Way of the Rat Traveler Ser.). (Illus.). 160p. (YA). pap. 9.95 *(978-1-59314-032-8(0))* CrossGeneration Comics, Inc.

Do, Kim-Thu, tr. from ENG. Tang Monk Disciples Monkey King: English/Vietnamese. Ma, Wenhai, illus. 2005. (Adventures of Monkey King Ser.: No. 3). (ENG & VIE.). 32p. (J). 16.95 *(978-1-57227-087-9(X))* Pan Asia Pubns. (USA), Inc.

Dockery, L. D. Michael Monkey Saves the Day. 2012. (ENG.). 30p. pap. 19.99 *(978-1-4772-6893-8(7))* AuthorHouse.

Dodd, Emma. More & More. Dodd, Emma, illus. 2014. (Emma Dodd's Love You Bks.). (ENG., Illus.). 24p. (J). (-k). 12.99 *(978-0-7636-7543-1(1)*, Templar) Candlewick Pr.

Donaldson, Julia. Where's My Mom? Scheffler, Axel, illus. 2008. (ENG.). 32p. (J). (gr. -1-2). 18.99 *(978-0-8037-3228-5(7)*, Dial Bks) Penguin Young Readers Group.

Dong Chen, Wei. Monkey King Volume 04: Enemies & a New Friend. 2012. (Monkey King Ser.: 4). (ENG., Illus.). 176p. (gr. 5-8). pap. 9.99 *(978-89-94208-43-0(8))* JR Comics KOR. Dist: Lerner Publishing Group.

—Monkey King Volume 05: Three Trials. 2012. (Monkey King Ser.: 5). (ENG., Illus.). 176p. (gr. 5-8). pap. 9.99 *(978-89-94208-49-7(6))* JR Comics KOR. Dist: Lerner Publishing Group.

—Monkey King Volume 06: The Sacred Tree. 2012. (Monkey King Ser.: 6). (ENG., Illus.). 176p. (gr. 5-8). pap. 9.99 *(978-89-94208-50-3(X))* JR Comics KOR. Dist: Lerner Publishing Group.

—Monkey King Volume 07: The Expulsion of Sun Wu Kong. 2013. (Monkey King Ser.: 7). (ENG., Illus.). 176p. (YA). (gr. 6-12). pap. 9.99 *(978-89-94208-51-0(8))* Lerner Publishing Group.

—Monkey King Volume 08: Treasures of the Mountain Kings. 2013. (Monkey King Ser.: 8). (ENG., Illus.). 176p. (YA). (gr. 6-12). pap. 9.99 *(978-89-94208-52-7(6))* Lerner Publishing Group.

—Monkey King Volume 09: The Stolen Kingdom. 2013. (Monkey King Ser.: 9). (ENG., Illus.). 176p. (YA). (gr. 6-12). pap. 9.99 *(978-89-94208-53-4(4))* Lerner Publishing Group.

—Monkey King Volume 10: The Realm of the Infant King. 2013. (Monkey King Ser.: 10). (ENG., Illus.). 176p. (YA). (gr. 6-12). pap. 9.99 *(978-89-94208-54-1(2))* Lerner Publishing Group.

—Monkey King Volume 11: Fight to the Death. 2013. (Monkey King Ser.: 11). (ENG., Illus.). 176p. (YA). (gr. 6-12). pap. 9.99 *(978-89-94208-56-5(9))* Lerner Publishing Group.

—Monkey King Volume 12: The Lost Children. 2013. (Monkey King Ser.: 12). (ENG., Illus.). 176p. (YA). (gr. 6-12). pap. 9.99 *(978-89-94208-57-2(7))* Lerner Publishing Group.

—Monkey King Volume 13: Trust & Temptation. 2013. (Monkey King Ser.: 13). (ENG., Illus.). 176p. (gr. 6-12). pap. 9.99 *(978-89-94208-58-9(5))* JR Comics KOR. Dist: Lerner Publishing Group.

—Monkey King Volume 14: The Dual. 2013. (Monkey King Ser.: 14). (ENG., Illus.). 176p. (gr. 6-12). pap. 9.99 *(978-89-94208-59-6(3))* JR Comics KOR. Dist: Lerner Publishing Group.

—Monkey King Volume 15: Fanning the Flames. 2013. (Monkey King Ser.: 15). (ENG., Illus.). 176p. (gr. 6-12). pap. 9.99 *(978-89-94208-60-2(7))* JR Comics KOR. Dist: Lerner Publishing Group.

—Monkey King Volume 16: The Golden Temple. 2013. (Monkey King Ser.: 16). (ENG., Illus.). 176p. (gr. 6-12). pap. 9.99 *(978-89-94208-61-9(5))* JR Comics KOR. Dist: Lerner Publishing Group.

—Monkey King Volume 18: Bands of Brothers. 2013. (Monkey King Ser.: 18). (ENG., Illus.). 176p. (gr. 6-12). pap. 9.99 *(978-89-94208-63-3(1))* JR Comics KOR. Dist: Lerner Publishing Group.

—Monkey King Volume 19: Masters & Disciples. 2013. (Monkey King Ser.: 19). (ENG., Illus.). 176p. (gr. 6-12). pap. 9.99 *(978-89-94208-64-0(X))* JR Comics KOR. Dist: Lerner Publishing Group.

—Monkey King Volume 20: The Journey Ends. 2013. (Monkey King Ser.: 20). (ENG., Illus.). 176p. (gr. 6-12). pap. 9.99 *(978-89-94208-65-7(8))* JR Comics KOR. Dist: Lerner Publishing Group.

—The Seven Sisters. Peng, Chao, illus. 2013. (Monkey King Ser.: 17). (ENG.). 176p. (gr. 6-12). pap. 9.99 *(978-89-94208-62-6(3))* JR Comics KOR. Dist: Lerner Publishing Group.

Dong Chen, Wei & Peng, Chao. Bane of Heaven. 2012. (Monkey King Ser.: 2). (ENG., Illus.). 176p. (gr. 5-8). pap. 9.99 *(978-89-94208-46-6(1))* JR Comics KOR. Dist: Lerner Publishing Group.

—Birth of Stone Monkey. 2012. (Monkey King Ser.: 1). (ENG., Illus.). 176p. (gr. 5-8). pap. 9.99 *(978-89-94208-45-9(3))* JR Comics KOR. Dist: Lerner Publishing Group.

—Journey to the West. 2012. (Monkey King Ser.: 3). (ENG., Illus.). 176p. (gr. 5-8). pap. 9.99 *(978-89-94208-47-3(X))* JR Comics KOR. Dist: Lerner Publishing Group.

Don't Let the Monkey Drive! 2004. (J). 10.95 *(978-0-9761350-1-2(9))* Murphey, Hiromi.

Drake, Christina M. Milo the Monkey. 2013. 88p. *(978-1-4602-2323-9(3))* FriesenPress.

Duckett, Brenda. Jeffrey & the blue Monkey. 2005. 32p. (J). spiral bd. 14.99 *(978-1-4116-5504-1(4))* Lulu Pr., Inc.

Durango, Julia. Cha-Cha Chimps. Taylor, Eleanor, illus. 2006. (ENG.). 32p. (J). (gr. -1-3). 19.99 *(978-0-689-86456-8(6)*, Simon & Schuster Bks. For Young Readers) Simon & Schuster Bks. For Young Readers.

Durant, Alan. I Love You Little Monkey. 2003. 32p. (J). *(978-0-7534-5555-5(2))* Kingfisher Publications, plc.

Elliot, Rachel. Monkey. East, Jacqueline, illus. 2009. (Wiggle-Waggles Bks.). (ENG.). 8p. (J). (gr. -1). bds. 4.99 *(978-0-7641-6238-1(1))* Sourcebooks, Inc.

Elliott, George. The Boy Who Loved Bananas. Krystoforski, Andrej, illus. 2005. 32p. (J). (gr. -1-2). 15.95 *(978-1-55337-744-3(3))* Kids Can Pr., Ltd. CAN. Dist: Hachette Bk. Group.

Elliott, Stacey "Sissy". What Kind of Bread Does a Monkey Eat ? 2011. 28p. pap. 15.99 *(978-1-4628-5921-4(6))* Xlibris Corp.

Erickson, John. The Case of the Monkey Burglar. Holmes, Gerald L., illus. 2011. (Hank the Cowdog Ser.: No. 48). (ENG.). 129p. (J). (gr. 3-6). pap. 5.99 *(978-1-59188-148-3(X))* Maverick Bks., Inc.

—Hank the Cowdog & Monkey Business. Holmes, Gerald L., illus. 2011. (Hank the Cowdog Ser.). (ENG.). 110p. (J). (gr. 3-6). pap. 5.99 *(978-1-59188-114-8(5))* Maverick Bks., Inc.

Esphyr, Slobodkina & Slobodkina. Caps for Sale: A Tale of a Peddler, Some Monkeys & Their Monkey Business. 2014. (Reading Rainbow Bks). (ENG.). 48p. (J). 11.24 *(978-1-63245-155-2(7))* Lectorum Pubns., Inc.

Evans, Leah Beth. A Different Kind of Hero. Gedrich, Colleen, illus. 2007. 40p. (J). per. 14.95 *(978-0-9795045-2-5(X))* Tribute Bks.

Faruqi, Saadia. Yasmin, la Guardiana Del Zoo. Aparicio Publishing LLC, Aparicio Publishing, tr. from ENG. Aly, Hatem, illus. 2020. (Yasmin en Español Ser.).Tr. of Yasmin the Zookeeper. (SPA.). 32p. (J). (gr. k-2). pap. 5.95 *(978-1-5158-5735-8(2)*, 142100); lib. bdg. 20.65 *(978-1-5158-5731-0(X)*, 142096) Capstone. (Picture Window Bks.).

—Yasmin the Zookeeper. Aly, Hatem, illus. 2019. (Yasmin Ser.). (ENG.). 32p. (J). (gr. k-2). pap. 5.95 *(978-1-5158-4581-2(8)*, 141181); lib. bdg. 22.65 *(978-1-5158-3785-5(8)*, 139367) Capstone. (Picture Window Bks.).

Fiani, M. A Cat Named Monkey. 2008. 24p. pap. 14.99 *(978-1-4389-1966-9(2))* AuthorHouse.

Find the Monkey. 2005. (J). *(978-0-9767179-2-8(1))* ABC Development, Inc.

Fitch, Sheree. There Were Monkeys in My Kitchen. braille ed. 2004. (Illus.). (J). (gr. k-3). spiral bd. *(978-0-616-01639-8(5))* Canadian National Institute for the Blind/Institut National Canadien pour les Aveugles.

Five Monkeys. 8p. (J). *(978-0-8136-3516-3(0))* Modern Curriculum Pr.

Foreman, Michael. Can't Catch Me! 2013. (Silver Tales Ser.). (ENG., Illus.). 28p. (J). (gr. -1-1). pap. *(978-1-74352-442-8(0))* Hinkler Bks. Pty, Ltd.

Fournier, Elizabeth. Sailboat Dreams: Monkey Island. 2012. 16p. pap. 15.99 *(978-1-4772-7670-9(X))* AuthorHouse.

Fox, Alex. Windsock Wesley & His Wild & Wonderful Weather MacHine, Living in Cloud. Bazzoni, Lainie M. A., illus. 2010. 48p. pap. 16.50 *(978-1-60911-873-0(1)*, Eloquent Bks.) Strategic Book Publishing & Rights Agency (SBPRA).

Fox, Mem. Two Little Monkeys. Barton, Jill, illus. 2012. (ENG.). 32p. (J). (gr. -1-3). 16.99 *(978-1-4169-8687-4(1)*, Beach Lane Bks.) Beach Lane Bks.

Freeman, Tina, illus. Ten Little Monkeys Jumping on the Bed. (Classic Books with Holes 8x8 with CD Ser.). (ENG.). 16p. (J). 2007. (gr. -1-1). *(978-1-904550-67-9(3))* 2004. bds. *(978-0-85953-450-5(2))* Child's Play International Ltd.

Gail, Becky. How the Little White Monkey Became a Woman. 2008. 19p. pap. 24.95 *(978-1-60563-471-5(9))* America Star Bks.

Galloway, Ginger. Jasper. Zemke, Deborah, illus. 2003. (Books for Young Learners). (ENG.). 16p. (J). 5.75 net. *(978-1-57274-539-1(8)*, 2457, Bks. for Young Learners) Owen, Richard C. Pubs., Inc.

Garis, Howard Roger. Curly & Floppy Twistytail. 2005. 26.95 *(978-1-4218-1461-2(7))*; 164p. pap. 11.95 *(978-1-4218-1561-9(3))* 1st World Publishing, Inc. (1st World Library - Literary Society).

—Curly & Floppy Twistytail. 2004. reprint ed. pap. 19.95 *(978-1-4191-1479-3(4))*; pap. 1.99 *(978-1-4192-1479-0(9))* Kessinger Publishing, LLC.

—Umboo, the Elephant. 2005. 26.95 *(978-1-4218-0956-4(7))*; 132p. pap. 10.95 *(978-1-59540-656-9(5))* 1st World Publishing, Inc. (1st World Library - Literary Society).

Gates, Josephine Scribner. Nannette & the baby Monkey. 2007. (Illus.). 50p. (J). lib. bdg. 59.00 *(978-1-60304-020-4(X))* Dollworks.

Gates, Margo. Up the Tree. Engell, Mette, illus. 2019. (Let's Look at Animal Habitats (Pull Ahead Readers — Fiction) Ser.). (ENG.). 16p. (J). (gr. -1-1). 27.99 *(978-1-5415-5868-7(5)*, ba1fd997-0137-45a8-becb-2d919231ac89, Lerner Pubns.) Lerner Publishing Group.

Gill, Raj. A Monkey Ate My Pancakes. 2013. (ENG.). 34p. pap. 10.95 *(978-1-927005-28-6(0))* Burman Books, Inc. CAN. Dist: Innovative Logistics.

Gold, Gina, et al. Harvest Hoedown. 2017. (Illus.). (J). *(978-1-5182-5126-9(9))* Harcourt.

Good Night, Curious George. 2017. (ENG., Illus.). 12p. (J). (— 1). bds. 9.99 *(978-1-328-79591-5(8)*, 1685558, Clarion Bks.) HarperCollins Pubs.

Gravett, Emily. Monkey & Me. Gravett, Emily, illus. 2008. (ENG., Illus.). 32p. (J). (gr. -1-3). 18.99 *(978-1-4169-5457-6(0)*, Simon & Schuster Bks. For Young Readers) Simon & Schuster Bks. For Young Readers.

Greco, Francesca. Cyril the Mandrill, 1 vol. Greco, Francesca., illus. 2004. (ENG., Illus.). 32p. (J). (gr. -1 — 1). 16.95 *(978-1-932065-92-3(X))* Star Bright Bks., Inc.

Greene, Rhonda Gowler. Mail Monkeys. Bender, Robert, illus. 2006. (J). pap. *(978-1-58669-217-9(8))* Childcraft Education Corp.

Hager, Mickey. Clarence Duntz & the Monkey Spell. 2009. (ENG.). 62p. pap. 11.33 *(978-0-557-14381-8(0))* Lulu Pr., Inc.

Haidar, Hanna. Earl's Big Adventure in Costa Rica. Newton, Kimberly, illus. 2nd ed. 2012. 22p. (J). *(978-0-9800975-2-8(5))* Old Silver Pr.

—Earl's Big Adventure in Japan. Newton, Kimberly, illus. 2012. 26p. (J). *(978-0-9800975-1-1(7))* Old Silver Pr.

Hall, Bureda Ann Greathouse. Stories of My Little Blue Monkey. 2007. (Illus.). 32p. (J). pap. 15.00 *(978-0-8059-7397-6(4))* Dorrance Publishing Co., Inc.

Hall, Jennifer. Reginald's Broken Arm. 2008. 28p. pap. 16.95 *(978-1-4343-7532-2(3))* AuthorHouse.

Hall, Michael. Monkey Time. Hall, Michael, illus. 2019. (ENG., Illus.). 48p. (J). (gr. -1-3). 17.99 *(978-0-06-238302-0(7)*, Greenwillow Bks.) HarperCollins Pubs.

Hamiduddin, Rabab, et al. Arabic Club Readers: Blue Band: the Monkey & the Crocodile, Bk. 9. 2014. (ENG.). 16p. pap. 4.99 *(978-1-4085-2497-8(X))* Oxford Univ. Pr., Inc.

Hamilton, Linda. The Big-Hearted Monkey & the Crocodile. 2005. (J). *(978-1-933248-01-7(7))* World Quest Learning.

Hammerslough, Jane. Langur Monkey's Day. Buelt, Laura, illus. 2005. (Wild Reading Adventures! Ser.). (ENG.). 36p. (J). (gr. -1-2). 9.95 *(978-1-59249-144-5(8)*, PS7156); 2.95 *(978-1-59249-143-8(X)*, S7156) Soundprints.

—Langur Monkey's Day. Buelt, Laura, tr. Buelt, Laura, illus. 2005. (Wild Reading Adventures! Ser.). (ENG.). 36p. (J). (gr. -1-2). 15.95 *(978-1-59249-141-4(3)*, B7106); pap. 6.95 *(978-1-59249-142-1(1)*, S7106) Soundprints.

—Langur Monkey's Day. Buelt, Laura, illus. 2005. (Wild Reading Adventures! Ser.). (ENG.). 32p. (J). (gr. -1-2). 19.95 *(978-1-59249-221-3(5)*, BC7106); 8.95 *(978-1-59249-222-0(3)*, SC7106) Soundprints.

Hammerslough, Jane & Smithsonian Institution Staff. Langur Monkey's Day. Buelt, Laura, illus. rev. ed. 2008. (ENG.). 24p. (J). (gr. -1-3). 4.99 *(978-1-59249-706-5(3)*, Little Soundprints) Soundprints.

Hana's Year: Evaluation Guide. 2006. (J). *(978-1-55942-408-0(7))* Witcher Productions.

Hansell, Robin. Mason & Monkey's Big Adventure. 2013. 52p. pap. 23.99 *(978-1-4808-0254-4(9))* Archway Publishing.

Hanson, Anders. Monkey Business. Chawla, Neena, illus. 2006. (Fact & Fiction Ser.). 24p. (J). pap. 48.42 *(978-1-59679-952-3(8))* ABDO Publishing Co.

Happy Easter, Curious George: Gift Book with Egg-Decorating Stickers! 2010. (Curious George Ser.). (ENG., Illus.). 24p. (J). (gr. -1-3). 9.99 *(978-0-547-04825-3(4)*, 1035143, Clarion Bks.) HarperCollins Pubs.

Happy Halloween, Curious George Tabbed Board Book. 2008. (Curious George Ser.). (ENG., Illus.). 14p. (J). (gr. -1 — 1). bds. 7.99 *(978-0-618-91952-9(X)*, 1015625, Clarion Bks.) HarperCollins Pubs.

Happy Hanukkah, Curious George: Curious George. 2012. (Curious George Ser.). (ENG., Illus.). 14p. (J). (gr. -1-k). bds. 8.99 *(978-0-547-75731-5(X)*, 1488174, Clarion Bks.) HarperCollins Pubs.

Happy St. Patrick's Day, Curious George: Tabbed Board Book. 2014. (Curious George Ser.). (ENG., Illus.). 14p. (J). (— 1). bds. 7.99 *(978-0-544-08888-7(3)*, 1537662, Clarion Bks.) HarperCollins Pubs.

Happy Valentine's Day Curious George. 2011. (Curious George Ser.). (ENG., Illus.). 14p. (J). (gr. -1-3). 8.99 *(978-0-547-13107-8(0)*, 1048361, Clarion Bks.) HarperCollins Pubs.

Harris, Stephanie C. The Wonders of Monkey Mac! 2009. 302p. pap. 15.95 *(978-1-60693-257-5(8)*, Eloquent Bks.) Strategic Book Publishing & Rights Agency (SBPRA).

Hasany, Syed M. Stop the Train, Monkey! 2013. 28p. pap. 16.09 *(978-1-4669-7792-1(2))* Trafford Publishing.

Hascamp, Steve, illus. Eight Silly Monkeys. 2006. (ENG.). 18p. (J). 9.95 *(978-1-58117-186-0(2)*, Intervisual/Piggy Toes) Bendon, Inc.

Haskamp, Steve, illus. Five Silly Monkeys. 2006. (ENG.). 12p. (J). bds. 14.95 *(978-1-58117-264-5(8)*, Intervisual/Piggy Toes) Bendon, Inc.

—Ocho Monitos. 2005.Tr. of Eight Silly Monkeys. (SPA & ENG.). 18p. (J). 9.95 *(978-1-58117-334-5(2)*, Intervisual/Piggy Toes) Bendon, Inc.

Haskamp, Steven, illus. Eight Silly Monkeys. 2007. (ENG.). 18p. (J). (gr. -1-3). bds. 15.95 *(978-1-58117-577-6(9)*, Intervisual/Piggy Toes) Bendon, Inc.

—Five Silly Monkeys. 2006. (ENG.). 12p. (J). (gr. -1-k). 12.95 *(978-1-58117-460-1(8)*, Intervisual/Piggy Toes) Bendon, Inc.

Heck, Ed. Monkey Lost. 2005. (Illus.). 32p. (J). 15.95 *(978-0-689-04633-9(2)*, Milk & Cookies) ibooks, Inc.

Hellman, Blake Liliane. Cuddle Monkey. Otis, Chad, illus. 2020. (ENG.). 40p. (J). (gr. -1-3). 18.99 *(978-1-5344-3117-1(9)*, Atheneum Bks. for Young Readers) Simon & Schuster Children's Publishing.

Hevesi, Rachel. I Am a Monkey. Tyson, Liz, illus. 2008. 44p. pap. *(978-1-906210-75-5(6))* Grosvenor Hse. Publishing Ltd.

—Peppy - a Long Way from Home. Parathian, Hannah, illus. 2008. 48p. pap. *(978-1-906210-76-2(4))* Grosvenor Hse. Publishing Ltd.

Holden, Pam. The Flying Monkey, 1 vol. East, Jacqueline, illus. 2009. (Red Rocket Readers Ser.). (ENG.). 16p. (gr. -1-1). pap. *(978-1-877363-29-0(4)*, Red Rocket Readers) Flying Start Bks.

—Max Monkey, 1 vol. East, Jacqueline, illus. 2009. (Red Rocket Readers Ser.). (ENG.). 16p. (gr. -1-1). pap. *(978-1-877363-24-5(3)*, Red Rocket Readers) Flying Start Bks.

Holsey, Ron. The Great Monkey Show! Cassity, Don, illus. 2018. 24p. (J). *(978-1-5490-4051-1(0))* Random Hse., Inc.

Hood, Sue. Monkey Business. Chapman, Susan, illus. 2005. (J). bds. *(978-1-890647-17-9(9))* TOMY International, Inc.

Hooray for Halloween. 2016. (Curious George Ser.). (ENG., Illus.). 24p. (J). (gr. -1-3). 9.99 *(978-0-544-69956-4(4)*, 1627726, Clarion Bks.) HarperCollins Pubs.

Horn, Neithard. Evi, My Little Monkey: A Good Night Book for You & for Grown-Ups, Too, 1 vol. 2011. (ENG., Illus.). 32p.

(J). 16.99 *(978-0-7643-3827-4(7)*, 4275, Schiffer Publishing Ltd) Schiffer Publishing, Ltd.
Horne, Constance. Emily Carr's Woo. 2005. (ENG., Illus.). 72p. (J). pap. 9.95 *(978-0-88982-149-1(6))* Oolichan Bks. CAN. Dist: Univ. of Toronto Pr.
Horowitz, Dave. A Monkey among Us. Horowitz, Dave, illus. 2004. (Illus.). 40p. (J). (gr. -1-1). 14.99 *(978-0-06-054335-8(3)*, HarperFestival) HarperCollins Pubs.
Howell, Gill. Tortoise & the Baboon. Woody, illus. 2004. (ENG.). 16p. (J). lib. bdg. 23.65 *(978-1-59646-686-9(3))* Dingles & Co.
Hunter, Erin. Bravelands #1: Broken Pride. Richardson, Owen, illus. 2018. (Bravelands Ser.: 1). (ENG.). 352p. (J). (gr. 3-7). pap. 7.99 *(978-0-06-264204-2(9)*, HarperCollins) HarperCollins Pubs.
—Bravelands #2: Code of Honor. 2018. (Bravelands Ser.: 2). (ENG.). 400p. (J). (gr. 3-7). pap. 7.99 *(978-0-06-264208-0(1)*, HarperCollins) HarperCollins Pubs.
—Bravelands #3: Blood & Bone. (Bravelands Ser.: 3). (ENG.). (J). (gr. 3-7). 2019. 320p. pap. 9.99 *(978-0-06-264212-7(X))* 2018. (Illus.). 304p. 16.99 *(978-0-06-264210-3(3))* 2018. (Illus.). 304p. lib. bdg. 17.89 *(978-0-06-264211-0(1))* HarperCollins Pubs. (HarperCollins).
Hutcheson, John C. Tom Finch's Monkey. 2004. reprint ed. pap. 1.99 *(978-1-4192-9041-1(X))*; pap. 15.95 *(978-1-4191-9041-4(5))* Kessinger Publishing, LLC.
Idiaghe, Efosa Francis. A Day of a Monkey: Tricky the Monkey. 2012. 20p. pap. 13.77 *(978-1-4669-4158-8(8))* Trafford Publishing.
Inches, Alison. Súper Bebés! Miller, Victoria, illus. 2006. (Dora la Exploradora Ser.). (SPA.). 24p. (J). (gr. -1-3). pap. 3.99 *(978-1-4169-2461-6(2)*, Libros Para Ninos) Libros Para Ninos.
Jarvis. Fred Forgets. 2016. (ENG., Illus.). 32p. (J). (gr. -1-3). 17.99 *(978-0-06-234916-3(3)*, HarperCollins) HarperCollins Pubs.
Jenkins, Henry A. The Adventures of Monkey Squirrel & Frogman: Sand Trap. 2009. 16p. pap. 8.49 *(978-1-4343-7827-9(6))* AuthorHouse.
Jian, Li. The Little Monkey King's Journey: Retold in English & Chinese (Stories of the Chinese Zodiac) Wert, Yijin, tr. Li, Jian, illus. 2012. (Stories of the Chinese Zodiac Ser.). 48p. (gr. -1-3). 16.95 *(978-1-60220-981-7(2))* Shanghai Pr.
Jin, Susie Lee. It's Bedtime for Little Monkeys. 2010. (ENG., Illus.). 10p. (J). (-k). bds. 5.99 *(978-0-7369-2832-8(4)*, 6928328) Harvest Hse. Pubs.
Johnson, Myrna. Let's Take a Hike. 2013. (ENG., Illus.). 32p. (gr. -1-1). pap. 13.95 *(978-1-936205-79-0(3)*, P223206) Austin, Stephen F. State Univ. Pr.
Jones, David. Baboon. 4th ed. 2007. (ENG.). 176p. (J). (gr. 5-9). pap. 11.95 *(978-1-55451-053-5(8)*, 9781554510535) Annick Pr., Ltd. CAN. Dist: Publishers Group West (PGW).
Jordan, Mark. Courage the Monkey. 2006. (Illus.). 40p. (J). 13.95 *(978-0-9717013-7-3(7))* Decere Publishing.
Joy, Eliza. The Blue Monkey. 2012. (Illus.). 12p. pap. 18.30 *(978-1-4685-8265-9(8))* AuthorHouse.
Juhasz, Mike. Posey & Mosey Go Camping. Juhasz, Brenda, illus. 2008. 16p. pap. 24.95 *(978-1-60610-258-9(3))* America Star Bks.
Juliette, the Modern Art Monkey: Individual Title Six-Packs. (Bookweb Ser.). 32p. (gr. 5-18). 34.00 *(978-0-7635-3776-0(4))* Rigby Education.
Kamau, G. How Porcupine Got His Spines. 2004. (Illus.). 26p. pap. *(978-9966-25-168-8(5))* Heinemann Kenya, Limited (East African Educational Publishers Ltd E.A.E.P.) KEN. Dist: Michigan State Univ. Pr.
Kann, Victoria. Pinkalicious & the Pinkatastic Zoo Day. 2012. (Pinkalicious I Can Read Ser.). (J). lib. bdg. 13.55 *(978-0-606-26527-0(9))* Turtleback.
Kelsey-Livin, Barbara. The Monkey & the Frog. 2012. 30p. 24.95 *(978-1-4626-6161-9(0))* America Star Bks.
Kienzle, Jackie. It's a Monkey's Life. 2011. (J). 32p. 31.99 *(978-1-4568-4353-3(2))*; 36p. pap. 21.99 *(978-1-4568-4352-6(4))* Xlibris Corp.
Kitunga, Demere. Lupompo & the Baby Monkey. 2004. (ENG., Illus.). 36p. pap. *(978-9987-411-21-4(5))* E & D Ltd TZA. Dist: Michigan State Univ. Pr.
Kramer, Adam. Monkey of the Month, 1 vol. 2012. (ENG., Illus.). 40p. (J). (gr. -1-3). 16.99 *(978-0-7643-4156-4(1)*, 4633) Schiffer Publishing, Ltd.
Kravetz, Nathan. A Monkey's Tale. 2012. 64p. (gr. 4-6). pap. 8.95 *(978-1-4759-5825-6(0))* iUniverse, Inc.
Kulling, Monica. When Emily Carr Met Woo, 1 vol. Griffiths, Dean, illus. 2014. (ENG.). 32p. (J). (gr. k-4). 19.95 *(978-1-927485-40-8(1))* Pajama Pr. CAN. Dist: Publishers Group West (PGW).
Ladybird. Anansi Helps a Friend Activity Book - Ladybird Readers Level 1. 2016. (Ladybird Readers Ser.). (ENG.). 16p. (J). (gr. 2-4). pap., act. bk. ed. 5.99 *(978-0-241-25420-2(5))* Penguin Bks., Ltd. GBR. Dist: Independent Pubs. Group.
Laird, Elizabeth & Davison, Roz. Jungle School. Sim, David, illus. 2006. (Green Bananas Ser.). (ENG.). 48p. (J). (gr. -1-3). *(978-0-7787-1042-4(4))*; lib. bdg. *(978-0-7787-1026-4(2))* Crabtree Publishing Co.
Landstrom, Lena. A Hippo's Tale. Sandin, Joan, tr. from SWE. 2007. (Illus.). 32p. (J). (gr. -1-1). 15.00 *(978-91-29-66603-8(1))* R & S Bks. SWE. Dist: Macmillan.
Lang, Suzanne. Grumpy Monkey Don't Be Scared. Lang, Max, illus. 2023. (Grumpy Monkey Ser.). (ENG.). 32p. (J). (gr. -1-3). 10.99 ***(978-0-593-48695-5(1))***; lib. bdg. 13.99 ***(978-0-593-48696-2(X))*** Random Hse. Children's Bks.
Lansky, Bruce. Monkey See, Monkey Do at the Zoo. Wummer, Amy, illus. 2010. 10p. (J). bds. 6.99 *(978-1-4169-9317-9(7))* Meadowbrook Pr.
LaReau, Kara. Rocko & Spanky Call It Quits. LaReau, Jenna, illus. 2008. (Rocko & Spanky Ser.). 40p. (J). 16.00 *(978-0-15-216611-3(4))* Harcourt Children's Bks.
Latimer, Alex. Wild Violet! Latimer, Patrick, illus. 2018. (ENG.). 32p. (J). (gr. -1-k). pap. 9.99 *(978-1-84365-382-0(6)*, Pavilion) Pavilion Bks. GBR. Dist: Independent Pubs. Group.
Law, Felicia & Way, Steve. Castaway Code: Sequencing in Action, 1 vol. Spoor, Mike, illus. 2009. (Mandrill Mountain Math Mysteries Ser.). (ENG.). 32p. (J). (gr. 2-3). 27.27 *(978-1-60754-817-1(8)*, 320e8775-ea88-4765-9f6f-3f39bcf63269); pap. 11.55 *(978-1-60754-822-5(4)*, 45ca3189-6d1a-4aba-bc1e-313695ab5542) Rosen Publishing Group, Inc., The. (Windmill Bks.).
—Crocodile Teeth: Geometric Shapes in Action, 1 vol. Spoor, Mike, illus. 2009. (Mandrill Mountain Math Mysteries Ser.). (ENG.). 32p. (J). (gr. 2-3). 27.27 *(978-1-60754-816-4(X)*, f316fc20-91e6-4a71-a59a-55448d4523ab); pap. 11.55 *(978-1-60754-821-8(6)*, d64648f7-9081-4d51-9365-af6071b54489) Rosen Publishing Group, Inc., The. (Windmill Bks.).
—Mirage in the Mist: Measurements in Action, 1 vol. Spoor, Mike, illus. 2009. (Mandrill Mountain Math Mysteries Ser.). (ENG.). 32p. (J). (gr. 2-3). 27.27 *(978-1-60754-818-8(6)*, 3b46573c-6745-47ea-b321-23dc467821a4, Windmill Bks.) Rosen Publishing Group, Inc., The.
—The Mystery of Nine: Number Place & Value in Action, 1 vol. Spoor, Mike, illus. 2009. (Mandrill Mountain Math Mysteries Ser.). (ENG.). 32p. (J). (gr. 2-3). 27.27 *(978-1-60754-819-5(4)*, eb540fd4-8485-47c7-9a25-12d4c647ff10); pap. 11.55 *(978-1-60754-824-9(0)*, 3d506973-6103-4b56-aa0a-977d78cbb7d1) Rosen Publishing Group, Inc., The. (Windmill Bks.).
—A Storm at Sea: Sorting, Mapping, & Grids in Action, 1 vol. Spoor, Mike, illus. 2009. (Mandrill Mountain Math Mysteries Ser.). (ENG.). 32p. (J). (gr. 2-3). 27.27 *(978-1-60754-815-7(1)*, 8ef36f64-756f-4e9e-ba11-50de241ce395); pap. 11.55 *(978-1-60754-820-1(8)*, 97b78dc7-e6a6-4efd-9acc-1d62e87eeaf2) Rosen Publishing Group, Inc., The. (Windmill Bks.).
Lawati, A. The Jungle Adventure of Chimpoo. 2011. 40p. pap. 21.99 *(978-1-4634-2921-8(5))* AuthorHouse.
Leatham, Alan D. Four Cats, Five Monkeys, Absurd Birds & Other Fanciful Stuff. 2006. 108p. pap. 19.95 *(978-1-4241-0692-9(3))* America Star Bks.
Lee, Karen. Mushy Mashed Bananas. Lee, Karen, illus. 2012. (Illus.). 24p. pap. *(978-1-4602-0136-7(1))* FriesenPress.
Lehrhaupt, Adam. Warning: Do Not Open This Book! Forsythe, Matthew, illus. 2013. (ENG.). 40p. (J). (gr. -1-3). 18.99 *(978-1-4424-3582-7(8)*, Simon & Schuster Bks. For Young Readers) Simon & Schuster Bks. For Young Readers.
Lemonade Zoo Monkeys. 2006. (Illus.). 33p. (YA). 10.95 *(978-0-9765321-2-5(3))* Taven Hill Studio.
Lewis, J. Patrick. Jungle Surprises, Bk. 2. Denise, Christopher, illus. 2011. (I AM a READER!: Tugg & Teeny Ser.). (ENG.). 40p. (J). (gr. 2-3). pap. 3.99 *(978-1-58536-686-6(2)*, 202374); lib. bdg. 9.95 *(978-1-58536-515-9(7)*, 202205) Sleeping Bear Pr.
—That's What Friends Are For. Denise, Christopher, illus. 2012. (I AM a READER!: Tugg & Teeny Ser.). (ENG.). 40p. (J). (gr. 2-3). pap. 3.99 *(978-1-58536-687-3(0)*, 202376); lib. bdg. 9.95 *(978-1-58536-516-6(5)*, 202206) Sleeping Bear Pr.
—Tugg & Teeny. Denise, Christopher, illus. 2011. (I AM a READER!: Tugg & Teeny Ser.). (ENG.). 40p. (J). (gr. 2-3). pap. 3.99 *(978-1-58536-685-9(4)*, 202329);Bk. 1. lib. bdg. 9.95 *(978-1-58536-514-2(9)*, 202204) Sleeping Bear Pr.
Lindgren, Astrid. Do You Know Pippi Longstocking? Dyssegaard, Elisabeth Kallick, tr. Nyman, Ingrid, illus. 2005. 32p. (J). pap. 4.95 *(978-91-29-66203-0(6))* R & S Bks. SWE. Dist: Macmillan.
Lloyd, Sam R. Yummy Yummy! Food for My Tummy. Tickle, Jack, illus. 2004. 32p. (J). tchr. ed. 15.95 *(978-1-58925-035-2(4))* Tiger Tales.
Lonczak, Heather. Mookey the Monkey Gets over Being Teased. Ramsey, Marcy, illus. 2006. 32p. (J). (gr. -1-3). 14.95 *(978-1-59147-479-1(5)*, Magination Pr.) American Psychological Assn.
Lonczak, Heather Suzanne. Mookey the Monkey Gets over Being Teased. Ramsey, Marcy Dunn, illus. 2006. 32p. (J). (gr. -1-3). 9.95 *(978-1-59147-480-7(9)*, Magination Pr.) American Psychological Assn.
Lopez, Maria Lorena. The Bird's Party, Birds in the Tropical Dry Forest. 2009. 28p. pap. 13.00 *(978-1-60860-156-1(0)*, Eloquent Bks.) Strategic Book Publishing & Rights Agency (SBPRA).
Lucas, David. Peanut. Lucas, David, illus. 2008. (ENG., Illus.). 32p. (J). (gr. k-k). 15.99 *(978-0-7636-3925-9(7))* Candlewick Pr.
Lumry, Amanda & Hurwitz, Laura. Operation Orangutan. 2007. (Adventures of Riley (Unnumbered) Ser.). (Illus.). 36p. (J). (gr. -1-3). 18.95 *(978-0-9748411-7-5(X))* Eaglemont Pr.
Ma, Wenhai, illus. Tang Monk Disciples Monkey King. 2005. (Adventures of Monkey King Ser.: No. 3). 32p. (J). 16.95 *(978-1-57227-084-8(5))* Pan Asia Pubns. (USA), Inc.
—Tang Monk Disciples Monkey King: English/Chinese. 2005. (Adventures of Monkey King Ser.: No. 3). (ENG & CHI.). 32p. (J). 16.95 *(978-1-57227-086-2(1))* Pan Asia Pubns. (USA), Inc.
Mack, Jeff. Mr. Monkey Bakes a Cake. Mack, Jeff, illus. 2018. (Mr. Monkey Ser.: 1). (ENG., Illus.). 64p. (J). (gr. -1-3). 9.99 *(978-1-5344-0431-1(7)*, Simon & Schuster Bks. For Young Readers) Simon & Schuster Bks. For Young Readers.
—Mr. Monkey Takes a Hike. Mack, Jeff, illus. 2019. (Mr. Monkey Ser.: 3). (ENG., Illus.). 64p. (J). (gr. -1-3). 9.99 *(978-1-5344-0433-5(3)*, Simon & Schuster Bks. For Young Readers) Simon & Schuster Bks. For Young Readers.
—Mr. Monkey Visits a School. Mack, Jeff, illus. 2018. (Mr. Monkey Ser.: 2). (ENG., Illus.). 64p. (J). (gr. -1-3). 9.99 *(978-1-5344-0429-8(5)*, Simon & Schuster Bks. For Young Readers) Simon & Schuster Bks. For Young Readers.
MacLeod, Jennifer Tzivia. Yossi & the Monkeys: A Shavuot Story. Waisman, Shirley, illus. 2017. (ENG.). 32p. (J). (gr. -1-3). 17.99 *(978-1-4677-8932-5(1)*, 56456978-1d54-4322-b8a3-6987dd47787f, Kar-Ben Publishing) Lerner Publishing Group.
Madison, Paul. The Purple Monkey. 2012. (Illus.). 32p. pap. 17.25 *(978-1-4669-3909-7(5))* Trafford Publishing.
Make Believe Ideas. Five Little Monkeys & Other Counting Rhymes. Machell, Dawn, illus. 2017. (ENG.). 12p. (J). (gr. -1 — 1). 6.99 *(978-1-78598-946-9(4))* Make Believe Ideas GBR. Dist: Scholastic, Inc.
Malone, D. L. 52 Purple Monkeys. 2009. 24p. pap. 24.95 *(978-1-60749-085-2(4))* America Star Bks.
Margaret. Curious George im Schokolade. 20.95 *(978-3-8157-2329-6(9))* Coppenrath, F. Verlag KG DEU. Dist: Distribooks, Inc.
—Curious George und der Lastwa. 20.95 *(978-3-8157-2327-2(2))* Coppenrath, F. Verlag KG DEU. Dist: Distribooks, Inc.
—Curious George und der Seiltsa. 20.95 *(978-3-8157-2330-2(2))* Coppenrath, F. Verlag KG DEU. Dist: Distribooks, Inc.
—Curious George und die Hundelb. 20.95 *(978-3-8157-2328-9(0))* Coppenrath, F. Verlag KG DEU. Dist: Distribooks, Inc.
Marinaro, Stacy. Treasure Monkey. 2008. 32p. pap. 15.95 *(978-1-4357-2840-0(8))* Lulu Pr., Inc.
Maroulis, Danielle. Monk in the Trunk. 2011. 24p. (gr. 1-2). pap. 13.99 *(978-1-4634-0598-4(7))* AuthorHouse.
Martin, Alison J. Charlie, the Brave Monkey. Martin, Alison J., illus. 2013. (Illus.). 24p. pap. 13.97 *(978-1-62516-155-0(7)*, Strategic Bk. Publishing) Strategic Book Publishing & Rights Agency (SBPRA).
Mason, Albert. Ooshu the Monkey Escapes from the Zoo. 2009. 40p. pap. 16.99 *(978-1-4389-0974-5(8))* AuthorHouse.
Mason, Albert D. Ooshu & Dorothy's Cricket. 2011. 36p. pap. 15.99 *(978-1-4567-1667-7(0))* AuthorHouse.
McBrayer, Cassidy. You Can, Toucan! You Can. 2008. 20p. pap. 15.95 *(978-1-4327-1132-0(6))* Outskirts Pr., Inc.
McCarroll, Barbara. Tongue Turning Tales for the Classroom. Godfrey, Arthur Dwayne, illus. 2008. 36p. pap. 24.95 *(978-1-60703-254-0(6))* America Star Bks.
McDermott, Gerald. Monkey: A Trickster Tale from India. (ENG., Illus.). 32p. (J). (gr. -1-3). 2014. pap. 9.99 *(978-0-544-33918-7(5)*, 1584489) 2011. 16.99 *(978-0-15-216596-3(7)*, 1201443) HarperCollins Pubs. (Clarion Bks.).
Mcevoy, Ariane. Little Monkey Learns to Share. 2012. 28p. pap. 15.99 *(978-1-4691-5830-3(2))* Xlibris Corp.
McKenna, Mark, creator. Banana Tail's Tales & Activities. 2006. (Illus.). (J). 4.95 *(978-0-9727681-1-5(4))* McKenna, Mark.
McKenna, Mark, et al, illus. Banana Tail. 2003. 32p. (J). 12.95 *(978-0-9727681-3-9(0))* Active Media Publishing, LLC.
McNeil, Niki, et al. HOCPP 1069 Curious George Rides a Bike. 2006. spiral bd. 15.50 *(978-1-60308-069-9(4))* In the Hands of a Child.
Meek, Nora. Sniffing for Democracy. 2004. (J). per. *(978-0-9753852-0-3(8))* PM, INK.
Menard, Michele R. The Canopy House - Lost among the Stars. 2013. 38p. pap. 13.95 *(978-0-9887969-4-2(5))* Four Menards, The.
—The Canopy House - Vol 2- Gus & Ester Meet the Neighbors. 2013. 34p. pap. 12.50 *(978-0-9891734-1-4(0))* Four Menards, The.
Merry Christmas, Curious George. 2017. (Curious George Ser.). (ENG., Illus.). 24p. (J). (gr. -1-3). pap. 5.99 *(978-1-328-69558-1(1)*, 1671221, Clarion Bks.) HarperCollins Pubs.
Merry Christmas, Curious George: Curious George. 2012. (Curious George Ser.). (ENG., Illus.). 32p. (J). (gr. -1-3). 12.99 *(978-0-547-76054-4(X)*, 1488729, Clarion Bks.) HarperCollins Pubs.
Metzger, Steve. Dancing Clock. Nez, John Abbott, illus. 2011. (ENG.). 32p. 12.95 *(978-1-58925-100-7(8))*; (J). pap. 7.95 *(978-1-58925-429-9(5))* Tiger Tales.
Milgrim, David. Look Out! a Storm! Ready-To-Read Pre-Level 1. Milgrim, David, illus. 2019. (Adventures of Otto Ser.). (ENG., Illus.). 32p. (J). (gr. -1-k). 17.99 *(978-1-5344-4197-2(2))*; pap. 4.99 *(978-1-5344-4196-5(4))* Simon Spotlight. (Simon Spotlight).
—See Otto: Ready-To-Read Pre-Level 1. Milgrim, David, illus. 2016. (Adventures of Otto Ser.). (ENG., Illus.). 32p. (J). (gr. -1-k). pap. 4.99 *(978-1-4814-6796-4(4)*, Simon Spotlight) Simon Spotlight.
—Swing Otto Swing! Milgrim, David, illus. 2005. (Ready-to-Read Ser.). (Illus.). (J). (gr. -1-k). 11.65 *(978-0-7569-6497-9(0))* Perfection Learning Corp.
Mitchell, Stan R. Oskar & Myer at the Lake. 2013. 24p. pap. 24.95 *(978-1-63000-414-9(6))* America Star Bks.
Mommy, Tell Me a Story about What Daddy Does. 2nd ed. 2013. 32p. pap. 13.99 *(978-0-9855699-6-9(4))* Richer Life, LLC.
A Monkey Ate My Homework. 2007. 32p. pap. 4.50 *(978-0-8341-2287-1(1)*, 083-412-2871) Beacon Hill Pr. of Kansas City.
Monkey Business. 2005. (J). 4.95 *(978-1-59792-015-5(0))* F.A.S.T. Learning LLC.
Monkey Girl Staff. Jay Travels to the U S A. 2012. 20p. pap. 17.99 *(978-1-4685-4778-8(X))* AuthorHouse.
Monkeys: Individual Title, 6 packs. (Sails Literacy Ser.). 16p. (gr. k-18). 27.00 *(978-0-7635-4405-8(1))* Rigby Education.
Monkeys Can't Cook! 2004. (J). 10.95 *(978-0-9761350-3-6(5))* Murphey, Hiromi.
Monkeys Can't Fly! 2004. (J). 10.95 *(978-0-9761350-2-9(7))* Murphey, Hiromi.
Monkey's Friends: Individual Title Six-Packs. (Literatura 2000 Ser.). (gr. 1-2). 28.00 *(978-0-7635-0098-6(4))* Rigby Education.
Monkey's Shoes: 3-in-1 Package. (Sails Literacy Ser.). 24p. (gr. k-18). 57.00 *(978-0-7578-3201-7(6))* Rigby Education.
Monkey's Shoes: Big Book Only. (Sails Literacy Ser.). 24p. (gr. k-18). 27.00 *(978-0-7635-6987-7(9))* Rigby Education.
Monroe, Chris. Monkey with a Tool Belt. Monroe, Chris, illus. 2008. (Monkey with a Tool Belt Ser.). (ENG., Illus.). 32p. (J). (gr. -1-2). 17.99 *(978-0-8225-7631-0(7)*, 1a4939c4-35a1-48ef-bfc0-2a63bac96957, Carolrhoda Bks.) Lerner Publishing Group.
—Monkey with a Tool Belt & the Maniac Muffins. Monroe, Chris, illus. 2016. (Monkey with a Tool Belt Ser.). (ENG., Illus.). 32p. (J). (gr. -1-2). 17.99 *(978-1-4677-2155-4(7)*, 72e58124-43b0-441a-ba6a-44699c291b1a); E-Book 35.99 *(978-1-4677-9562-3(3))* Lerner Publishing Group. (Carolrhoda Bks.).
—Monkey with a Tool Belt & the Noisy Problem. Monroe, Chris, illus. 2009. (Monkey with a Tool Belt Ser.). (ENG., Illus.). 32p. (J). (gr. -1-2). 17.99 *(978-0-8225-9247-1(9)*, 9324df12-db0d-4e72-a01a-673555bee853, Carolrhoda Bks.) Lerner Publishing Group.
—Monkey with a Tool Belt Blasts Off! Monroe, Chris, illus. 2020. (Monkey with a Tool Belt Ser.). (ENG., Illus.). 32p. (J). (gr. -1-2). 17.99 *(978-1-5415-7757-2(4)*, eed07eba-23fa-4179-a41f-6af4139dabb2, Carolrhoda Bks.) Lerner Publishing Group.
Moorthy, Anita. Monkey's Drum. Sarkar, Soumitro, illus. 2003. (ENG.). 24p. pap. 3.99 *(978-81-86211-15-1(2))* Penguin Publishing Group.
Morimoto, Diana. Max, He Likes it that Way, 1 vol. 2010. 24p. pap. 24.95 *(978-1-4489-6851-0(8))* PublishAmerica, Inc.
Morrel Disbrow, Corlyss. Ran's Upside-Down Day. 2012. 20p. pap. 24.95 *(978-1-4626-8368-0(1))* America Star Bks.
Morris, Dudley. Mike the Monk. 2011. 58p. 36.95 *(978-1-258-02967-8(7))* Literary Licensing, LLC.
Morrow, Tara Jaye. Just Mommy & Me. Bratun, Katy, illus. 2004. 32p. (J). 13.89 *(978-0-06-000725-6(7))* HarperCollins Pubs.
Muldrow, Diane. How Do Penguins Play? Walker, David M., illus. 2011. (Little Golden Book Ser.). 24p. (J). (gr. -1-k). 5.99 *(978-0-375-86501-5(2)*, Golden Bks.) Random Hse. Children's Bks.
Munro, Rosemary. The Adventures of Fidget the Monkey. 2017. (ENG., Illus.). (gr. 1-2). pap. *(978-1-78222-509-6(9))* Paragon Publishing, Rothersthorpe.
Myers, Martha. Nibbles, the Mostly Mischievous Monkey. 2003. (Julius & Friends Ser.: Vol. 10). (Illus.). 91p. (J). 6.99 *(978-0-8163-1947-3(2))* Pacific Pr. Publishing Assn.
Myers, Walter Dean. Looking for the Easy Life. Harper, Lee, illus. 2011. (ENG.). 40p. (J). (gr. -1-3). 16.99 *(978-0-06-054375-4(2)*, HarperCollins) HarperCollins Pubs.
Namjoshi, Suniti. The One-Eyed Monkey, 1 vol. Jain, Shefalee, illus. 2022. (Aditi Adventures Ser.: 1). (ENG.). 80p. (J). (gr. 3-5). pap. 9.99 *(978-81-86896-13-6(9))* Tulika Pubs. IND. Dist: Independent Pubs. Group.
Napoli, Donna Jo & Johnston, Shelagh. Hotel Jungle. Spengler, Kenneth, tr. Spengler, Kenneth, illus. 2004. 33p. (J). 15.95 *(978-1-59336-002-3(9))*; pap. *(978-1-59336-003-0(7))* Mondo Publishing.
Neff, Ethel Maxine. Sally: The Runaway Monkey. 2004. (Illus.). 42p. (J). 5.99 *(978-0-8163-2062-2(4))* Pacific Pr. Publishing Assn.
Nyirenda, Vukani G. The Wise Old Tortoise & the Monkey. 2011. 24p. pap. 15.99 *(978-1-4568-9133-6(2))* Xlibris Corp.
Olshan, Matthew. The Flown Sky, 1. 2007. (Illus.). 352p. 19.95 *(978-0-9789391-0-6(7))* Chacmool Pr.
Opie, David, illus. Monkey & the Engineer. 2007. 24p. (J). 14.95 *(978-0-9793972-6-4(X))* JD Publishing.
Ovani, Germano, illus. The Monkey King. 2007. (Young Reading Series 1 Gift Bks). 47p. (J). (gr. -1-3). 8.99 *(978-0-7945-1593-5(2)*, Usborne) EDC Publishing.
Pankratz, Justin, illus. Blue Monkey. 2003. (J). 5.95 *(978-0-9742637-0-0(2))* Pankratz Creations.
Papp, Robert, illus. Monkey Trouble. 2011. (Boxcar Children Mysteries Ser.: 127). (ENG.). 128p. (J). (gr. 2-5). pap. 7.99 *(978-0-8075-5240-7(2)*, 807552402); lib. bdg. 14.99 *(978-0-8075-5239-1(9)*, 807552399) Random Hse. Children's Bks. (Random Hse. Bks. for Young Readers).
Parker, Emma. The Monkey in the Tree. 2010. (Illus.). pap. *(978-1-877547-91-1(3))* First Edition Ltd.
—What a Hullabaloo. 2010. 20p. pap. *(978-1-877561-32-0(0))* First Edition Ltd.
Passen, Lisa. Monkey Mountain. 2013. 234p. pap. 14.99 *(978-1-60820-880-7(X))* MLR Pr., LLC.
Paul & Lady Jan. Mako in My Backyard. Beeson, Jan, illus. 2013. 34p. pap. 12.99 *(978-0-9890482-3-1(3))* Beeson, Jan.
Pepper, Lily. Bananas. 2012. (Illus.). 20p. pap. 19.82 *(978-1-4772-1964-5(1))* AuthorHouse.
Percival, Tom. The Genie's Curse. 2017. (Little Legends Ser.: 3). (ENG., Illus.). 208p. (J). (gr. 2-5). pap. 8.99 *(978-1-4926-4256-5(8)*, 9781492642565, Sourcebooks Jabberwocky) Sourcebooks, Inc.
Phillips, Clifton. Ten Spunky Monkeys. Jung, Shirley, illus. 2007. 32p. (J). 8.99 *(978-0-9797106-4-3(2))* Avid Readers Publishing Group.
Phillips, Dee & Ticktock Media, Ltd. Staff. What Do Monkeys Do? 2009. (What Do Animals Do? Ser.). (ENG.). 5p. (J). (gr. k — 1). bds. 4.95 *(978-1-84696-960-7(3)*, TickTock Books) Octopus Publishing Group GBR. Dist: Independent Pubs. Group.
Pilkey, Dav. Ricky Ricotta's Mighty Robot vs. the Mecha-Monkeys from Mars (Ricky Ricotta's Mighty Robot #4) Santat, Dan, illus. 2014. (Ricky Ricotta's Mighty Robot Ser.: 4). (ENG.). 144p. (J). (gr. -1-3). pap. 5.99 *(978-0-545-63012-2(6))* Scholastic, Inc.
Popper, Garry. Scary Monkeys: Going Ape. Forshaw, John, illus. 2004. 48p. 9.00 *(978-1-84161-014-6(3))* Ravette Publishing, Ltd. GBR. Dist: Parkwest Pubns., Inc.
Porter, Matthew. Monkey World ABC. 2012. (ENG., Illus.). 26p. (J). 8.95 *(978-1-927018-07-1(2))* Simply Read Bks. CAN. Dist: Ingram Publisher Services.
Posner-Sanchez, Andrea. Bubble-Rific! (Disney Junior: Doc Mcstuffins) RH Disney, illus. 2014. (Little Golden Book Ser.). (ENG.). 24p. (J). (-k). 5.99 *(978-0-7364-3236-8(1)*, Golden/Disney) Random Hse. Children's Bks.
Poulin, Andrée. Monkey in the Mud, 1 vol. Eudes-Pascal, Élisabeth, illus. 2009. (Rainy Day Readers Ser.). (ENG.). 32p. (J). (gr. 1-2). 27.27 *(978-1-60754-370-1(2)*, 5131cf14-a2fd-4f18-8757-ace21e9c9915); pap. 11.55 *(978-1-60754-371-8(0)*, a3c27341-a9ae-467b-82ea-0094df091457) Rosen Publishing Group, Inc., The. (Windmill Bks.).
Powell, Richard. Mandy Monkey. Rhodes, Katie, illus. 2004. (Fuzzy Friends Ser.). 10p. (J). 7.95 *(978-1-58925-720-7(0))* Tiger Tales.
Prouty, Krista. George Monkeys Around, 1 vol. 2010. 42p. 24.95 *(978-1-4489-4936-6(X))* PublishAmerica, Inc.
Pulford, Elizabeth. Finding Monkey Moon. Wilkinson, Kate, illus. 2015. (ENG.). 32p. (J). (gr. -1-2). 15.99 *(978-0-7636-6777-1(3))* Candlewick Pr.
Quigley, Michael. A Monkey's Riddle. 2013. 24p. pap. 24.95 *(978-1-63000-506-1(1))* America Star Bks.
Rabelo-Beacroft, Katia. The Grumpy Monkey Who Only Eats Bananas. 2012. 28p. pap. 16.10 *(978-1-4669-3957-8(5))* Trafford Publishing.
Ramoutar, Tagore. Brownie the Monkey Visits the Zoo. Cline, Ian, photos by. 2012. (Illus.). 38p. pap. *(978-1-907837-48-7(5))* Longshot Ventures, Ltd.
Rathmann, Peggy. Buenas Noches, Gorila. 2004. (SPA., Illus.). 36p. (J). (gr. k-k). pap. 16.99 *(978-980-257-265-6(9))* Ekare, Ediciones VEN. Dist: Lectorum Pubns., Inc.

MNO

Redlich, Ben. Who Flung Dung? 2013. (ENG., Illus.). 28p. (J). (gr. -1-k). 16.95 *(978-1-62087-543-8(8)*, 620543, Sky Pony Pr.) Skyhorse Publishing Co., Inc.

Renier Nash, Oliver. The Primate Puzzle: A tale of two friends & the missing long-nosed Monkeys. 2009. 272p. pap. 15.49 *(978-1-4490-3099-5(8))* AuthorHouse.

Rey and others, Rey and. Start Your Engines 5-Minute Stories. 2014. (5-Minute Stories Ser.). (ENG., Illus.). 224p. (J). (gr. -1-3). 12.99 *(978-0-544-15881-8(4)*, 1550258, Clarion Bks.) HarperCollins Pubs.

Rey, H. A. Apple Harvest: Curious about Harvest Time. 2012. (Curious George TV Tie-In 8x8 Ser.). lib. bdg. 13.55 *(978-0-606-23984-4(7))* Turtleback.

—Busy Days with Curious George. 2017. (Curious George Ser.). (ENG., Illus.). 208p. (J). (gr. -1-3). 11.99 *(978-1-328-69598-7(0)*, 1671312, Clarion Bks.) HarperCollins Pubs.

—C. G. Fish, Rides. (ENG., Illus.). bds., bds., bds. 95.20 *(978-0-618-13189-1(2))* Houghton Mifflin Harcourt Publishing Co.

—Curious Baby: Curious about Christmas Touch-And-Feel Board Book: A Christmas Holiday Book for Kids. 2011. (Curious Baby Curious George Ser.). (ENG., Illus.). 12p. (J). (gr. k — 1). bds. 8.99 *(978-0-547-58841-4(0)*, 1461240, Clarion Bks.) HarperCollins Pubs.

—Curious Baby: My Favorite Things Padded Board Book. 2011. (Curious Baby Curious George Ser.). (ENG., Illus.). 14p. (J). (gr. -1 — 1). bds. 8.99 *(978-0-547-42893-2(6)*, 1432083, Clarion Bks.) HarperCollins Pubs.

—Curious George & the Kite. 2007. (Curious George TV Ser.). (ENG., Illus.). 24p. (J). (gr. -1-3). 4.99 *(978-0-618-72396-6(X)*, 419819, Clarion Bks.) HarperCollins Pubs.

—Curious George at the Aquarium/Jorge el Curioso Visita el Acuario: Bilingual English-Spanish. 2010. (Curious George Ser.).Tr. of Curious George at the Aquarium. (ENG., Illus.). 24p. (J). (gr. -1-3). pap. 6.99 *(978-0-547-29963-1(X)*, 1413256, Clarion Bks.) HarperCollins Pubs.

—Curious George at the Baseball Game. Hines, Anna Grossnickle, illus. 2006. (Curious George Ser.). (ENG.). 24p. (J). (gr. -1-3). pap. 4.99 *(978-0-618-66375-0(4)*, 461984, Clarion Bks.) HarperCollins Pubs.

—Curious George at the Baseball Game/Jorge el Curioso en el Partido de Béisbol: Bilingual English-Spanish. 2011. (Curious George Ser.). (ENG., Illus.). 24p. (J). (gr. -1-3). pap. 4.99 *(978-0-547-51500-7(6)*, 1444364, Clarion Bks.) HarperCollins Pubs.

—Curious George Big Book of Adventures (CGTV) 2013. (Curious George Ser.). (ENG., Illus.). 296p. (J). (gr. -1-3). 16.99 *(978-0-544-08463-6(2)*, 1537931, Clarion Bks.) HarperCollins Pubs.

—Curious George Builds Tree House/Jorge el Curioso Construye una Casa en Un árbol: Bilingual English-Spanish. 2017. (Curious George TV Ser.). (ENG., Illus.). 24p. (J). (gr. -1-3). 12.99 *(978-0-544-97461-6(1)*, 1663440, Clarion Bks.) HarperCollins Pubs.

—Curious George Classic Collection. 2015. (Curious George Ser.). (ENG., Illus.). 416p. (J). (gr. -1-3). pap. 39.99 *(978-0-544-56239-4(9)*, 1611507, Clarion Bks.) HarperCollins Pubs.

—Curious George Cleans up/Jorge el Curioso Limpia el Reguero: Bilingual English-Spanish. 2007. (Curious George TV Ser.). (ENG., Illus.). 24p. (J). (gr. -1-3). mass mkt. 4.99 *(978-0-618-89687-5(2)*, 416169, Clarion Bks.) HarperCollins Pubs.

—Curious George Costume Party/Jorge el Curioso Va a una Fiesta de Disfraces: Bilingual English-Spanish. 2012. (Curious George Ser.). (ENG., Illus.). 24p. (J). (gr. -1-3). pap. 4.99 *(978-0-547-86575-1(9)*, 1503625, Clarion Bks.) HarperCollins Pubs.

—Curious George Curious You: on Your Way!/¡Eres Curioso Todo el Tiempo! Bilingual English-Spanish. 2012. (Curious George Ser.). (ENG.). 32p. (J). (gr. -1-3). 9.99 *(978-0-547-79368-9(5)*, 1493387, Clarion Bks.) HarperCollins Pubs.

—Curious George: Dinosaur Tracks/Jorge el Curioso Huellas de Dinosaurio: Bilingual English-Spanish. 2011. (Curious George TV Ser.). (ENG., Illus.). 24p. (J). (gr. -1-3). pap. 4.99 *(978-0-547-55798-4(1)*, 1453316, Clarion Bks.) HarperCollins Pubs.

—Curious George Discovers the Sun. 2015. (Curious George Ser.). (ENG., Illus.). 32p. (J). (gr. -1-3). pap. 6.99 *(978-0-544-43067-9(0)*, 1595742, Clarion Bks.) HarperCollins Pubs.

—Curious George Flies a Kite. 2004. (J). (gr. k-3). spiral bd. *(978-0-616-01770-8(7))*; spiral bd. *(978-0-616-01771-5(5))* Canadian National Institute for the Blind/Institut National Canadien pour les Aveugles.

—Curious George Harvest Hoedown (CGTV 8 X 8) 2017. (Curious George Ser.). (ENG., Illus.). 24p. (J). (gr. -1-3). pap. 4.99 *(978-1-328-69597-0(2)*, 1671310, Clarion Bks.) HarperCollins Pubs.

—Curious George Home Run. 2012. (Curious George TV Ser.). (ENG., Illus.). 24p. (J). (gr. -1-3). pap. 5.99 *(978-0-547-69118-3(1)*, 1478654, Clarion Bks.) HarperCollins Pubs.

—Curious George Home Run/Jorge el Curioso el Jonrón: Bilingual English-Spanish. 2012. (Curious George TV Ser.). (ENG., Illus.). 24p. (J). (gr. -1-3). pap. 4.99 *(978-0-547-69114-5(9)*, 1478547, Clarion Bks.) HarperCollins Pubs.

—Curious George Magnetic Maze Book. 2012. (Curious George Ser.). (ENG., Illus.). 10p. (J). (gr. -1-3). 12.99 *(978-0-547-64302-1(0)*, 1469820, Clarion Bks.) HarperCollins Pubs.

—Curious George Makes a Valentine (CGTV Reader) 2017. (Curious George Ser.). (ENG., Illus.). 24p. (J). (gr. -1-3). 12.99 *(978-1-328-69557-4(3)*, 1671219, Clarion Bks.) HarperCollins Pubs.

—Curious George Makes Maple Syrup (CGTV 8x8) A Winter & Holiday Book for Kids. 2014. (Curious George Ser.). (ENG., Illus.). 24p. (J). (gr. -1-3). pap. 5.99 *(978-0-544-03252-1(7)*, 1530242, Clarion Bks.) HarperCollins Pubs.

—Curious George Parade Day Tabbed Board Book. 2011. (Curious George Ser.). (ENG., Illus.). 14p. (J). (gr. -1 — 1). bds. 8.99 *(978-0-547-47282-9(X)*, 1438167, Clarion Bks.) HarperCollins Pubs.

—Curious George Pat-A-Cake. 2011. (Curious George Ser.). (ENG., Illus.). 8p. (J). (gr. k — 1). bds. 12.99 *(978-0-547-51689-9(4)*, 1444706, Clarion Bks.) HarperCollins Pubs.

—Curious George Plants a Seed/Jorge el Curioso Siembra una Semilla: Bilingual English-Spanish. 2007. (Curious George TV Ser.). (ENG., Illus.). 24p. (J). (gr. -1-3). mass mkt. 5.99 *(978-0-618-89688-2(0)*, 498198, Clarion Bks.) HarperCollins Pubs.

—Curious George Plants a Tree. 2009. (Curious George Ser.). (ENG., Illus.). 32p. (J). (gr. -1-3). 14.99 *(978-0-547-15087-1(3)*, 1051758, Clarion Bks.) HarperCollins Pubs.

—Curious George Roller Coaster. 2007. (Curious George TV Ser.). (ENG., Illus.). 24p. (J). (gr. -1-3). pap. 4.99 *(978-0-618-80040-7(9)*, 463219, Clarion Bks.) HarperCollins Pubs.

—Curious George the Dog Show. 2007. (Curious George TV Ser.). (ENG., Illus.). 24p. (J). (gr. -1-3). 4.99 *(978-0-618-72397-3(8)*, 419820, Clarion Bks.) HarperCollins Pubs.

—Curious George: Time for School Lift-The-Flaps (CGTV) 2011. (Curious George Ser.). (ENG., Illus.). 16p. (J). (gr. -1-3). 6.99 *(978-0-547-42230-5(X)*, 1431226, Clarion Bks.) HarperCollins Pubs.

—Curious George Visits the Library/Jorge el Curioso Va a la Biblioteca: Bilingual English-Spanish. 2011. (Curious George Ser.). (ENG., Illus.). 24p. (J). (gr. -1-3). pap. 4.99 *(978-0-547-55075-6(8)*, 1450249, Clarion Bks.) HarperCollins Pubs.

—Curious George's 5-Minute Stories. 2013. (Curious George Ser.). (ENG., Illus.). 192p. (J). (gr. -1-3). 16.99 *(978-0-544-10793-9(4)*, 1541117, Clarion Bks.) HarperCollins Pubs.

—Curious George's Box of Books. 2018. (Curious George Ser.). (ENG., Illus.). 80p. (J). (— 1). pap. 18.99 *(978-1-328-79895-4(X)*, 1685686, Clarion Bks.) HarperCollins Pubs.

—Curious George's Dump Truck (Mini Movers Shaped Board Books) 2014. (Curious George Ser.). (ENG., Illus.). 12p. (J). (— 1). bds. 8.99 *(978-0-544-14686-0(7)*, 1547360, Clarion Bks.) HarperCollins Pubs.

—Curious George's Fire Truck (Mini Movers Shaped Board Books) 2014. (Curious George Ser.). (ENG., Illus.). 12p. (J). (— 1). bds. 8.99 *(978-0-544-14709-6(X)*, 1547361, Clarion Bks.) HarperCollins Pubs.

—Curious George's First Day of School. 2005. (Curious George Ser.). (ENG., Illus.). 24p. (J). (gr. -1-3). pap. 5.99 *(978-0-618-60564-4(9)*, 448941, Clarion Bks.) HarperCollins Pubs.

—Curious George's First Day of School Book & Cd. 2005. (Curious George Ser.). (ENG., Illus.). 24p. (J). (gr. -1-3). audio compact disk 10.99 *(978-0-618-60565-1(7)*, 448943, Clarion Bks.) HarperCollins Pubs.

—Curious George's Train (Mini Movers Shaped Board Books) 2014. (Curious George Ser.). (ENG., Illus.). 12p. (J). (— 1). bds. 8.99 *(978-0-544-32074-1(3)*, 1582513, Clarion Bks.) HarperCollins Pubs.

—Get Well, Curious George. 2017. (Curious George Ser.). (ENG., Illus.). 24p. (J). (gr. -1-3). 14.99 *(978-0-544-97750-1(5)*, 1663693, Clarion Bks.) HarperCollins Pubs.

—Happy Thanksgiving, Curious George Tabbed Board Book. 2010. (Curious George Ser.). (ENG., Illus.). 14p. (J). (gr. -1 — 1). bds. 8.99 *(978-0-547-13106-1(2)*, 1048360, Clarion Bks.) HarperCollins Pubs.

—Jorge el Curioso Encuentra Trabajo: Curious George Takes a Job (Spanish Edition) 2003. (Curious George Ser.).Tr. of Curious George Takes a Job. (SPA., Illus.). 48p. (J). (gr. -1-3). pap. 7.99 *(978-0-618-33600-5(1)*, 494387, Clarion Bks.) HarperCollins Pubs.

—Merry Christmas, Curious George/Feliz Navidad, Jorge el Curioso: A Christmas Holiday Book for Kids (Bilingual English-Spanish) Young, Mary O'Keefe, illus. 2012. (Curious George Ser.).Tr. of Merry Christmas, Curious George. (ENG.). 32p. (J). (gr. -1-3). 10.99 *(978-0-547-74503-9(6)*, 1486266, Clarion Bks.) HarperCollins Pubs.

Rey, H. A. & Berger, Sholem. [Dzshordzsh der Naygeriker/Fun H. A. Rey; Yidish, Sholem Berger] George der Naygeriker. 2005. (YID., Illus.). 57p. (J). *(978-0-9726939-2-9(0))* Twenty-fourth Street Bks, LLC.

Rey, H. A. & Hines, Anna Grossnickle. Curious George & the Firefighters Board Book: Lap Edition. 2007. (Curious George Ser.). (ENG., Illus.). 24p. (J). (gr. -1-3). bds. 11.99 *(978-0-618-89194-8(3)*, 569981, Clarion Bks.) HarperCollins Pubs.

Rey, H. A. & Rey, Margret. The Complete Adventures of Curious George. 2005. (J). (gr. -1-k). 30.00 *(978-0-618-64550-3(0))* Houghton Mifflin Harcourt Trade & Reference Pubs.

—The Complete Adventures of Curious George: 7 Classic Books in 1 Giftable Hardcover. 75th ed. 2016. (Curious George Ser.). (ENG., Illus.). 432p. (J). (gr. -1-3). 34.99 *(978-0-544-64448-9(4)*, 1621548, Clarion Bks.) HarperCollins Pubs.

—Curious George & the Pizza Party. 2010. (Curious George Ser.). (ENG., Illus.). 24p. (J). (gr. -1-3). 14.99 *(978-0-547-23211-9(X)*, 1082701, Clarion Bks.) HarperCollins Pubs.

—Curious George & the Puppies Lap Edition. Rey, H. A., illus. 2006. (Curious George Ser.). (ENG., Illus.). 24p. (J). (gr. -1 — 1). bds. 11.99 *(978-0-618-77241-4(3)*, 594895, Clarion Bks.) HarperCollins Pubs.

—Curious George at the Aquarium. 2014. (Curious George Ser.). (ENG., Illus.). 24p. (J). (gr. -1-3). pap. 4.99 *(978-0-544-17674-4(X)*, 1556495, Clarion Bks.) HarperCollins Pubs.

—Curious George Feeds the Animals Book & Cd, 1 vol. 2005. (Curious George Ser.). (ENG., Illus.). 24p. (J). (gr. -1-3). audio compact disk 10.99 *(978-0-618-60387-9(5)*, 495928, Clarion Bks.) HarperCollins Pubs.

—Curious George Goes Camping Book & Cd, 1 vol. Shalleck, Alan J., illus. 2007. (Curious George Ser.). (ENG.). 24p. (J). (gr. -1-3). audio compact disk 10.99 *(978-0-618-73764-2(2)*, 414165, Clarion Bks.) HarperCollins Pubs.

—Curious George in Follow That Hat! 2018. (Curious George's Funny Readers Ser.). (ENG., Illus.). 40p. (J). (gr. -1-3). 9.99 *(978-1-328-73718-2(7)*, 1676354, Clarion Bks.) HarperCollins Pubs.

—Curious George in Super George! Artful Doodlers Ltd, Artful Doodlers, illus. 2018. (Curious George's Funny Readers Ser.). (ENG.). 40p. (J). (gr. -1-3). 9.99 *(978-1-328-73623-9(7)*, 1676620, Clarion Bks.) HarperCollins Pubs.

—Curious George Learns the Alphabet Book & CD, 1 vol. 2009. (Curious George Ser.). (ENG., Illus.). 80p. (J). (gr. -1-3). audio 10.99 *(978-0-618-95966-2(1)*, 1021901, Clarion Bks.) HarperCollins Pubs.

—Curious George Says Thank You. 2012. (Curious George 8x8 Ser.). lib. bdg. 14.75 *(978-0-606-26601-7(1))* Turtleback.

—Curious George Stories to Share. 2011. (Curious George Ser.). (ENG., Illus.). 208p. (J). (gr. -1-3). 12.99 *(978-0-547-59529-0(8)*, 1462559, Clarion Bks.) HarperCollins Pubs.

—Curious George Takes a Train with Stickers. Weston, Martha, illus. 2010. (Curious George Ser.). (ENG.). 24p. (J). (gr. -1-3). pap. 5.99 *(978-0-547-50424-7(1)*, 1442842, Clarion Bks.) HarperCollins Pubs.

—George O Curioso. pap. 23.95 *(978-85-336-0916-7(7))* Livraria Martins Editora BRA. Dist: Distribooks, Inc.

—Home Run. 2012. (Curious George TV Tie-In Early Reader Ser.). lib. bdg. 13.55 *(978-0-606-23985-1(5))* Turtleback.

—Librarian for a Day. 2012. (Curious George TV Tie-In Early Reader Ser.). lib. bdg. 13.55 *(978-0-606-26602-4(X))* Turtleback.

—The New Adventures of Curious George. 2006. (Curious George Ser.). (ENG., Illus.). 208p. (J). (gr. -1-3). 12.99 *(978-0-618-66373-6(8)*, 589198, Clarion Bks.) HarperCollins Pubs.

—Three Tales for a Winter's Night. 2012. (Curious George TV Tie-In 8x8 Ser.). lib. bdg. 18.40 *(978-0-606-26603-1(8))* Turtleback.

Rey, H. A. & Rey, Margret, illus. Curious George's ABCs. 2003. (J). bds. 9.95 *(978-0-618-27708-7(0))* Houghton Mifflin Harcourt Trade & Reference Pubs.

—Curious George's Are You Curious? 2003. (J). bds. 9.95 *(978-0-618-27710-0(2))* Houghton Mifflin Harcourt Trade & Reference Pubs.

—Curious George's Opposites. 2003. (J). bds. 9.95 *(978-0-618-27709-4(9))* Houghton Mifflin Harcourt Trade & Reference Pubs.

Rey, Margret. Margret & H. A. Rey's Curious George Goes Camping. Vipah Interactive, illus. 2015. 24p. pap. 4.00 *(978-1-61003-550-7(X))* Center for the Collaborative Classroom.

Rey, Margret & Rey, H. A. Curious George at the Aquarium. 2014. (Curious George 8x8 Ser.). lib. bdg. 14.75 *(978-1-4177-9792-9(4))* Turtleback.

—Curious George Goes to an Ice Cream Shop. Rey, Margret, ed. 2011. (Curious George 8x8 Ser.). (gr. -1-2). lib. bdg. 14.75 *(978-0-8335-3957-1(4))* Turtleback.

—Curious George Goes to the Beach. 2014. (Curious George 8x8 Ser.). (gr. k-3). lib. bdg. 13.55 *(978-0-613-21392-9(0))* Turtleback.

Riccio, Nina M. Five Kids & a Monkey, 3 vols., Set. Blair, Beth L., illus. (J). (gr. 2-6). 23.85 *(978-0-9653955-3-3(7))* Creative Attic, Inc., The.

Rickett, Sally. Minky the Shoebox Monkey - a Little Monkey with a Long Way to Go. 2010. 54p. pap. 17.95 *(978-1-60860-625-2(2)*, Strategic Bk. Publishing) Strategic Book Publishing & Rights Agency (SBPRA).

Rigo, Laura, illus. Little Chimp. 2011. (Mini Look at Me Bks.). 10p. (J). (gr. -1). bds. 7.99 *(978-0-7641-6428-6(7))* Sourcebooks, Inc.

Risco, Elle D. Dora Had a Little Lamb. Savitsky, Steve, illus. 2007. (Dora the Explorer Ser.). (J). (gr. -1-2). 11.65 *(978-0-7569-8294-2(4))* Perfection Learning Corp.

Roberts, Daniel. Three Funky Monkeys. 2011. 36p. pap. 16.99 *(978-1-4634-4732-8(9))* AuthorHouse.

Roberts, In Pursuit of the Curious Bangle J. In Pursuit of the Curious Bangle. 2010. 170p. pap. 14.50 *(978-1-4457-7210-3(8))* Lulu Pr., Inc.

Rohrer, Kim. The Adventures of Little Dooey: The Doctor. 2012. 24p. pap. 9.95 *(978-0-9848050-7-5(9)*, Little Creek Bks.) Jan-Carol Publishing, INC.

Roland, Timothy. Monkey Me & the New Neighbor. 2014. (Monkey Me Ser.: 3). lib. bdg. 14.75 *(978-0-606-35360-1(7))* Turtleback.

—Monkey Me & the Pet Show. 2014. (Monkey Me Ser.: 2). lib. bdg. 14.75 *(978-0-606-35359-5(3))* Turtleback.

—Monkey Me & the Pet Show: a Branches Book (Monkey Me #2) Roland, Timothy, illus. 2014. (Monkey Me Ser.: 2). (ENG., Illus.). 96p. (J). (gr. 1-3). pap. 4.99 *(978-0-545-55980-5(4))* Scholastic, Inc.

—Monkey Me & the School Ghost. 2014. (Monkey Me Ser.: 4). lib. bdg. 14.75 *(978-0-606-36053-1(0))* Turtleback.

Rosano, John. Molly Monkey. 2008. (Illus.). (J). 14.95 *(978-1-60131-013-2(7))* Big Tent Bks.

Rosario, Joann. Bitty Witty Witty Witty Witty Monkey! Rosario, Joann, illus. 2004. (Illus.). 10p. (J). pap. 10.00 *(978-0-9758746-9-1(1)*, 1246169) J.G.R. Enterprises.

Ross, Patrick. Oliver: The Great Escape. Burcham, David, illus. 2009. 34p. pap. 24.95 *(978-1-60749-151-4(6))* America Star Bks.

Rothstein, Arminio & Brixler, Andreas. TOBY & TOBIAS: Die Abenteuer aus dem ZIRKUS HABAKUK. 2010. 134p. pap. 14.90 *(978-3-8391-0292-3(8))* Bks. on Demand.

Roy, Ron. Capital Mysteries #8: Mystery at the Washington Monument. Bush, Timothy, illus. 2007. (Capital Mysteries Ser.: 8). (ENG.). 96p. (J). (gr. 1-4). per. 5.99 *(978-0-375-83970-2(4)*, Random Hse. Bks. for Young Readers) Random Hse. Children's Bks.

—Mystery at the Washington Monument. Bush, Timothy, illus. 2007. (Capital Mysteries Ser.: No. 8). 87p. (gr. 1-4). 15.00 *(978-0-7569-7845-7(9))* Perfection Learning Corp.

—Mystery at the Washington Monument, 8. Bush, Timothy, illus. 2007. (Capital Mysteries Ser.: No. 8). (ENG.). 87p. (J). (gr. 3-6). lib. bdg. 17.44 *(978-0-375-93970-9(9))* Random House Publishing Group.

Ruiz, Rachel. The Wild Field Trip. May, Steve, illus. 2017. (Superhero Harry Ser.). (ENG.). 48p. (J). (gr. k-2). pap. 8.95 *(978-1-4795-9861-8(5)*, 135318); lib. bdg. 23.32 *(978-1-4795-9857-1(7)*, 135310) Capstone. (Picture Window Bks.).

Rylant, Cynthia. The Case of the Missing Monkey. Karas, G. Brian, illus. 2003. (High-Rise Private Eyes Ser.: No. 1). (J). 25.95 incl. audio *(978-1-59112-194-7(9))*; pap. 29.95 incl. audio *(978-1-59112-195-4(7))* Live Oak Media.

—The Case of the Missing Monkey. Karas, G. Brian, illus. 2003. (High-Rise Private Eyes Ser.: 1). 46p. (J). (gr. 1-17). 14.75 *(978-0-613-44194-0(X))* Turtleback.

—The High-Rise Private Eyes #1: the Case of the Missing Monkey. Karas, G. Brian, illus. 2003. (I Can Read Level 2 Ser.: No. 1). (ENG.). 48p. (J). (gr. k-3). pap. 4.99 *(978-0-06-444306-7(X)*, Greenwillow Bks.) HarperCollins Pubs.

Sandusky, Thomas & Hill, Kathy. Spidy the Spider Monkey. Johnson, Gretchen, illus. 2009. 32p. pap. 12.95 *(978-0-9823002-5-1(5))* Peppertree Pr., The.

Santat, Dan. The Guild of Geniuses. Santat, Dan, illus. 2015. (ENG., Illus.). 40p. (J). (gr. -1-3). 17.99 *(978-0-439-43096-8(8)*, Levine, Arthur A. Bks.) Scholastic, Inc.

Saunders, Len. Spunky the Monkey: An Adventure in Exercise. 2010. 32p. pap. 14.95 *(978-1-4389-3991-9(4))* AuthorHouse.

Sayles, Kristi. Jacob's Monkey-the Trouble with Lying. 2005. 38p. (J). pap. 10.29 *(978-1-4116-6429-6(9))* Lulu Pr., Inc.

Schaefer, Carole Lexa. Monkey & Elephant: Candlewick Sparks. Bernstein, Galia, illus. 2013. (Candlewick Sparks Ser.). (ENG.). 48p. (J). (gr. k-4). pap. 5.99 *(978-0-7636-6261-5(5))* Candlewick Pr.

—Monkey & Elephant & a Secret Birthday Surprise. Bernstein, Galia, illus. (Candlewick Sparks Ser.). (ENG.). 48p. (J). (gr. k-4). 2016. pap. 5.99 *(978-0-7636-8744-1(8))* 2015. 14.99 *(978-0-7636-6131-1(7))* Candlewick Pr.

—Monkey & Elephant & the Babysitting Adventure. Bernstein, Galia, illus. (Candlewick Sparks Ser.). (ENG.). 48p. (J). (gr. k-4). 2017. pap. 5.99 *(978-0-7636-9781-5(8))* 2016. 14.99 *(978-0-7636-6535-7(5))* Candlewick Pr.

—Monkey & Elephant Get Better: Candlewick Sparks. Bernstein, Galia, illus. 2013. (ENG.). 48p. (J). (gr. k-4). 14.99 *(978-0-7636-4841-1(8))* Candlewick Pr.

—Monkey & Elephant Go Gadding. Bernstein, Galia, illus. 2015. (Candlewick Sparks Ser.). (ENG.). 48p. (J). (gr. k-4). pap. 5.99 *(978-0-7636-8030-5(3))* Candlewick Pr.

Schrefer, Eliot. The Lost Rainforest #2: Gogi's Gambit. Dziubak, Emilia, illus. 2019. (ENG.). (J). (gr. 3-7). 368p. pap. 6.99 *(978-0-06-249115-2(6))*; 352p. 16.99 *(978-0-06-249111-4(3))* HarperCollins Pubs. (Tegen, Katherine Bks).

Schweizer, Chris. Tricky Monkey Tales. Thomas, Chad, illus. 2011. (Tricky Journeys Ser.: 6). (ENG.). (J). (gr. 2-4). pap. 39.62 *(978-0-7613-8630-8(0))* Lerner Publishing Group.

Sehgal, Kabir & Sehgal, Surishtha. A Bucket of Blessings. Tsong, Jing Jing, illus. 2014. (ENG.). 32p. (J). (gr. -1-3). 19.99 *(978-1-4424-5870-3(4)*, Beach Lane Bks.) Beach Lane Bks.

Selznick, Brian. Baby Monkey, Private Eye. 2018. (CHI.). (J). (gr. -1-3). *(978-957-08-5160-1(0))* Linking Publishing Co., Ltd.

Selznick, Brian & Serlin, David. Baby Monkey, Private Eye. Selznick, Brian, illus. 2018. (ENG., Illus.). 192p. (J). (gr. -1-3). 16.99 *(978-1-338-18061-9(4)*, Scholastic Pr.) Scholastic, Inc.

Seow, David. The Monkey King: A Classic Chinese Tale for Children. Tay-Audouard, L. K., illus. 2017. 32p. (J). (gr. -1-3). 9.95 *(978-0-8048-4840-4(8))* Tuttle Publishing.

Sexton, Jessa R. Mobert's Irish Experience. Sexton, Jessa R., photos by. 2012. (Illus.). 34p. pap. 10.00 *(978-0-9860150-3-8(2))* O'More Publishing.

Shannon, Carol. Dusky Langurs at the Zoo. 2013. 40p. pap. 16.95 *(978-1-4525-1014-9(8)*, Balboa Pr.) Author Solutions, LLC.

Shepard, Aaron. The Monkey King: A Superhero Tale of China, Retold from the Journey to the West. (Ancient Fantasy Ser.: Vol. 4). (J). 2017. (ENG., Illus.). (gr. 4-6). pap. 6.00 *(978-1-62035-544-2(2))* 2008. 50p. lib. bdg. 15.00 *(978-0-938497-40-0(5))* 2008. 44p. lib. bdg. 6.00 *(978-0-938497-41-7(3))* Shepard Pubns. (Skyhook Pr.).

Shipton, Paul. Get the Fruit: Band 00/Lilac (Collins Big Cat) Dunton, Trevor, illus. 2004. (Collins Big Cat Ser.). (ENG.). 24p. (J). (gr. -1-k). pap. 6.99 *(978-0-00-718529-0(4))* HarperCollins Pubs. Ltd. GBR. Dist: Independent Pubs. Group.

Shoopman, Jim. Cowboy Zack & the Monkey from the Muggletown Zoo. 2013. 50p. pap. 13.98 *(978-0-9887836-2-1(2))* Taylor and Seale Publishing.

Shreve, Steve. Monkey Island: Or the Advantage of Opposable Thumbs. Shreve, Steve, illus. 2010. (Adventures of Charlie Ser.). (Illus.). 32p. pap. *(978-0-237-54288-7(9))* Evans Brothers, Ltd.

Sierra, Judy. What Time Is It, Mr. Crocodile? Cushman, Doug, illus. 2007. (ENG.). 32p. (J). (gr. -1-3). pap. 7.99 *(978-0-15-205850-0(8)*, 1197570, Clarion Bks.) HarperCollins Pubs.

Silberman, Dani. The Three Monkey Brothers. 2009. 28p. pap. 14.50 *(978-1-60860-366-4(0)*, Eloquent Bks.) Strategic Book Publishing & Rights Agency (SBPRA).

Sithole, Thelma. The Little Monkey & the Crocodile. Montague, Christine, illus. 2007. 32p. per. 12.00 *(978-1-59858-204-8(6))* Dog Ear Publishing, LLC.

—Little Shoko & the Crocodile. Holmes, Rebecca, illus. 2007. 36p. per. 12.00 *(978-1-59858-330-4(1))* Dog Ear Publishing, LLC.

Skinner, J. C. Ringo & the Fruit Tree. 2008. 24p. pap. 24.95 *(978-1-60441-028-0(0))* America Star Bks.

Slater III, John D. The Monkey & the Dragon Meet. 2009. (ENG.). 28p. pap. 12.99 *(978-1-4389-4353-4(9))* AuthorHouse.

Slobodkina, Esphyr. Caps for Sale: A Tale of a Peddler, Some Monkeys & Their Monkey Business. Slobodkina, Esphyr, illus. 2015. (ENG., Illus.). 48p. (J). (gr. -1-3). 17.99 *(978-0-201-09147-2(X))*; 75th ed. pap. 8.99 *(978-0-06-443143-9(6))* HarperCollins Pubs. (HarperCollins).

—Caps for Sale: A Tale of a Peddler, Some Monkeys & Their Monkey Businesss. Slobodkina, Esphyr, illus. 2008. (ENG.,

Illus.). 48p. (J). (gr. -1-3). lib. bdg. 17.89 *(978-0-06-025778-1(4)*, HarperCollins) HarperCollins Pubs.

—Caps for Sale Board Book: A Tale of a Peddler, Some Monkeys & Their Monkey Business. Slobodkina, Esphyr, illus. 75th ed. 2015. (ENG., Illus.). 32p. (J). (gr. -1-3). bds. 8.99 *(978-0-06-147453-8(3)*, HarperFestival) HarperCollins Pubs.

—More Caps for Sale: Another Tale of Mischievous Monkeys Board Book. 2018. (ENG., Illus.). 32p. (J). (gr. -1-3). bds. 8.99 *(978-0-06-240560-9(8)*, HarperFestival) HarperCollins Pubs.

Slobodkina, Esphyr & Sayer, Ann Marie Mulhearn. Caps for Sale & the Mindful Monkeys. Slobodkina, Esphyr, illus. 2017. (ENG., Illus.). 48p. (J). (gr. -1-3). 17.99 *(978-0-06-249988-2(2)*, HarperCollins) HarperCollins Pubs.

—More Caps for Sale: Another Tale of Mischievous Monkeys. Slobodkina, Esphyr, illus. (ENG., Illus.). 40p. (J). (gr. -1-3). 2017. pap. 8.99 *(978-0-06-249957-8(2))* 2015. 18.99 *(978-0-06-240545-6(4))* HarperCollins Pubs. (HarperCollins).

Slobodkina, Esphyr & Slobodkina, E. Caps for Sale. 2015. (J). (gr. k-3). 17.20 *(978-0-8085-2604-9(9))* Turtleback.

Smalley, Roger, adapted by. The Big-Hearted Monkey & the Lion. 2005. (J). *(978-1-933248-02-8(5))* World Quest Learning.

Smart, Jamie. Bunny vs. Monkey: a Graphic Novel. Smart, Jamie, illus. 2016. (Bunny vs. Monkey Ser.: 1). (ENG., Illus.). 64p. (J). (gr. 2-5). pap. 7.99 *(978-0-545-86184-7(5)*, Graphix) Scholastic, Inc.

—Bunny vs. Monkey Book 3. 2018. (Bunny vs. Monkey Ser.: 3). lib. bdg. 18.40 *(978-0-606-41145-5(3))* Turtleback.

—Bunny vs. Monkey: Book Three. 2018. (Bunny vs. Monkey Ser.: 3). (ENG.). 64p. (J). (gr. 2-5). pap. 7.99 *(978-1-338-17686-5(2))* Scholastic, Inc.

Smart, Kimberly. A New Home for Gabril. 2008. 32p. 15.95 *(978-1-4357-0762-7(1))* Lulu Pr., Inc.

Smith, Carrie. Jumping Monkeys: Lap Book Edition. Daubney, Kate, illus. 2016. (My First Reader's Theater Tales Ser.). (J). (gr. k). *(978-1-5021-5507-8(9))* Benchmark Education Co.

—Jumping Monkeys: Small Book Edition. Daubney, Kate, illus. 2016. (My First Reader's Theater Tales Ser.). (J). (gr. k). *(978-1-5021-5512-2(5))* Benchmark Education Co.

Smith, Holly C. Tyler the Monkey & Andy the Mouse. 2012. 28p. (-18). pap. 24.95 *(978-1-4626-9501-0(9))* America Star Bks.

Smith, Leone. Jasmine Finds a Doctor. Smith, Marcelle, illus. 2011. 30p. pap. 12.50 *(978-1-61204-042-4(X)*, Strategic Bk. Publishing) Strategic Book Publishing & Rights Agency (SBPRA).

Smith, Todd Aaron. The Average Monkey. Smith, Todd Aaron, illus. 2003. (Higby the Monkey Ser.). (Illus.). 32p. (J). pap. 4.97 *(978-1-58660-857-6(6))* Barbour Publishing, Inc.

—Higby Throws a Fit. Smith, Todd Aaron, illus. 2003. (Higby the Monkey Ser.). (Illus.). 32p. (J). pap. 4.97 *(978-1-58660-858-3(4))* Barbour Publishing, Inc.

Snyder, Vicki & West, Lois. Lighten up Lenny. Kam, Mike, illus. 2005. (J). *(978-0-9773187-0-4(2))* Snyder, Vicki.

Sonneborn, Scott. The Good, the Bad, & the Monkeys, 1 vol. Bradley, Jess, illus. 2013. (Comics Land Ser.). (ENG.). 32p. (J). (gr. k-2). lib. bdg. 25.32 *(978-1-4342-4945-6(X)*, 122226, Stone Arch Bks.) Capstone.

Southard, Patricia. Captain André's Adventure in the Sky. 2008. 27p. pap. 24.95 *(978-1-4241-8613-6(7))* America Star Bks.

Spoor, Mike, illus. Desperate Measures: Units of Measurement in Action, 1 vol. 2010. (Mandrill Mountain Math Mysteries Ser.). (ENG.). 32p. (J). (gr. 2-3). pap. 11.55 *(978-1-60754-925-3(5)*, 0d0a4546-a9aa-44e2-a596-6f85f71671d5); lib. bdg. 27.27 *(978-1-60754-920-8(4)*, 062ce9eb-2d37-4102-905f-f0621291bce6) Rosen Publishing Group, Inc., The. (Windmill Bks.).

—The Emperor's Guards: Concepts of Time, 1 vol. 2010. (Mandrill Mountain Math Mysteries Ser.). (ENG.). 32p. (J). (gr. 2-3). lib. bdg. 27.27 *(978-1-60754-922-2(0)*, 85dd0127-799d-49a7-b02c-a55c0fa8b8a4, Windmill Bks.) Rosen Publishing Group, Inc., The.

—The Emperor's Last Command: Problem-Solving in Action, 1 vol. 2010. (Mandrill Mountain Math Mysteries Ser.). (ENG.). 32p. (J). (gr. 2-3). lib. bdg. 27.27 *(978-1-60754-923-9(9)*, 6cfa914f-78f4-4422-84b7-89ec55697406, Windmill Bks.) Rosen Publishing Group, Inc., The.

—The Hidden Valley: Reasoning in Action, 1 vol. 2010. (Mandrill Mountain Math Mysteries Ser.). (ENG.). 32p. (J). (gr. 2-3). lib. bdg. 27.27 *(978-1-60754-919-2(0)*, aad83b41-3bb8-4a8c-be7f-3ca4a5a6da9c, Windmill Bks.) Rosen Publishing Group, Inc., The.

—Lightning Flash: Probability in Action, 1 vol. 2010. (Mandrill Mountain Math Mysteries Ser.). (ENG.). 32p. (J). (gr. 2-3). pap. 11.55 *(978-1-60754-926-0(3)*, dd74b064-99ba-4c5a-8f94-699cc3a14a7f); lib. bdg. 27.27 *(978-1-60754-921-5(2)*, de03c233-9c49-4baf-a9f9-69cb03855381) Rosen Publishing Group, Inc., The. (Windmill Bks.).

Staniszewski, Anna. The Magic Mirror: a Branches Book (Once upon a Fairy Tale #1) Pamintuan, Macky, illus. 2019. (Once upon a Fairy Tale Ser.: 1). (ENG.). 96p. (J). (gr. 1-3). pap. 4.99 *(978-1-338-34971-9(6))* Scholastic, Inc.

Steele, Michael Anthony. Attack of the Zombie Mermaids: A 4D Book. Reeves, Pauline, illus. 2018. (Nearly Fearless Monkey Pirates Ser.). (ENG.). 48p. (J). (gr. k-2). lib. bdg. 23.99 *(978-1-5158-2677-4(5)*, 137832, Picture Window Bks.) Capstone.

—Battle of the Pirate Bands: A 4D Book. Reeves, Pauline, illus. 2018. (Nearly Fearless Monkey Pirates Ser.). (ENG.). 48p. (J). (gr. k-2). pap. 7.95 *(978-1-5158-2687-3(2)*, 137838); lib. bdg. 23.99 *(978-1-5158-2679-8(1)*, 137834) Capstone. (Picture Window Bks.).

—Escape from Haunted Treasure Island: A 4D Book. Reeves, Pauline, illus. 2018. (Nearly Fearless Monkey Pirates Ser.). (ENG.). 48p. (J). (gr. k-2). lib. bdg. 23.99 *(978-1-5158-2678-1(3)*, 137833, Picture Window Bks.) Capstone.

—Hunt for the Octo-Shark: A 4D Book. Reeves, Pauline, illus. 2018. (Nearly Fearless Monkey Pirates Ser.). (ENG.). 48p. (J). (gr. k-2). lib. bdg. 23.99 *(978-1-5158-2680-4(5)*, 137835, Picture Window Bks.) Capstone.

Stiles, Erinn. The Monkey & the Rainbow. 2012. 36p. pap. 20.99 *(978-1-4772-6918-3(5))* AuthorHouse.

Stilton, Thea. Thea Stilton & the Prince's Emerald. 2012. (Thea Stilton Ser.: 12). lib. bdg. 19.65 *(978-0-606-26534-8(1))* Turtleback.

Strasser, Stephanie. Blue Bananas. 2010. 28p. pap. 12.49 *(978-1-4490-5327-7(0))* AuthorHouse.

Studio Mouse Staff. Five Little Monkeys: And Other Counting Rhymes. Elliott, Rebecca et al, illus. rev. ed. 2007. (ENG.). 24p. (J). (gr. -1-k). 4.99 *(978-1-59069-608-8(5))* Studio Mouse LLC.

Sturm, James. Birdsong: A Story in Pictures. 2016. (Illus.). 60p. (J). (gr. k-1). 12.95 *(978-1-935179-94-8(2)*, TOON Books) Astra Publishing Hse.

Styczynski, Gary. The Animals of Greenback Valley: The Magic Card. 2009. 32p. pap. 24.95 *(978-1-59858-930-6(X))* Dog Ear Publishing, LLC.

Subrina. Jacko the Monkey. 2013. 16p. pap. 24.95 *(978-1-63000-145-2(7))* America Star Bks.

Sweet Dreams, Curious George. 2013. (Curious George Ser.). (ENG., Illus.). 24p. (J). (gr. -1-3). 9.99 *(978-0-544-03860-6(0)*, 1531375, Clarion Bks.) HarperCollins Pubs.

Tabares, Veronica. Monkeys on an Island. Tabares, Bridgitt, illus. 2012. 32p. (J). pap. 14.50 *(978-1-60916-005-0(3))* Sun Break Publishing.

Tagge, Mark. The Coma & Convulsion Club: The Retreat. 2008. 112p. pap. 13.99 *(978-1-4259-7221-9(7))* AuthorHouse.

Tang, Youshan, illus. The Magical Monkey King: Mischief in Heaven. 2004. (J). (gr. 2-5). 113p. 14.95 *(978-1-885008-24-4(4))*; (ENG.). 128p. per. 16.95 *(978-1-885008-25-1(2)*, leelowshens) Lee & Low Bks., Inc. (Shen's Bks.).

Tao, Ted. The Monkey King & the Book of Death. 2008. (ENG., Illus.). 200p. (YA). pap. 7.99 *(978-1-930655-01-0(0))* Golden Peach Publishing.

Tashjian, Janet. My Life As a Youtuber. Tashjian, Jake, illus. 2018. (My Life Ser.: 7). (ENG.). 272p. (J). 13.99 *(978-1-62779-892-1(7)*, 900161978, Holt, Henry & Co. Bks. For Young Readers) Holt, Henry & Co.

—My Life As a Youtuber. Tashjian, Jake, illus. 2020. (My Life Ser.: 7). (ENG.). 288p. (J). pap. 7.99 *(978-1-250-23367-7(4)*, 900161979) Square Fish.

Taylor, Sean. Mojo & Weeza & the New Hat: Band 04/Blue (Collins Big Cat) Mosedale, Julian, illus. 2007. (Collins Big Cat Ser.). (ENG.). 16p. (J). (gr. -1-1). pap. 7.99 *(978-0-00-718662-4(2))* HarperCollins Pubs. Ltd. GBR. Dist: Independent Pubs. Group.

Tekavec, Heather. Manners Are Not for Monkeys. Huyck, David, illus. 2016. (ENG.). 32p. (J). (gr. -1-2). 16.95 *(978-1-77138-051-5(9))* Kids Can Pr., Ltd. CAN. Dist: Hachette Bk. Group.

Terada, Junzo. Animal Friends: Swimming Hole Party! (Animal Books for Toddlers, Jungle Animal Board Book) 2017. (Animal Friends Ser.). (ENG., Illus.). 10p. (J). bds. 9.99 *(978-1-4521-4983-7(6))* Chronicle Bks. LLC.

Thompson, Kim Mitzo. Five Little Monkeys Jumping on the Bed. Girouard, Patrick, illus. 2010. (Padded Board Book W/CD Ser.). 8p. (J). (gr. k-2). bds. 10.99 incl. audio compact disk *(978-1-59922-581-4(6))* Twin Sisters IP, LLC.

Thomson, Sarah L. Quick, Little Monkey! Judge, Lita, illus. 2016. (ENG.). 32p. (J). (gr. -1-2). 16.95 *(978-1-62979-100-5(8)*, Astra Young Readers) Astra Publishing Hse.

Thottam, Meena, adapted by. Monkey Do as Monkey Does. 2006. (J). 3.95 *(978-0-9776917-0-8(5)*, Curcumin Bks.) Davlaw Press.

Tidwell, Mae B. & Hancock, Vicki. Kyle Wants to Be a Monkey, 1 vol. 2009. 24p. pap. 24.95 *(978-1-60749-751-6(4))* America Star Bks.

Timmers, Leo. Monkey on the Run. Timmers, Leo, illus. 2019. (ENG., Illus.). 32p. (J). (gr. -1-k). 17.99 *(978-1-77657-250-2(5)*, e8b6aeda-6b84-4a21-8ff1-5de56aa08dfb) Gecko Pr. NZL. Dist: Lerner Publishing Group.

Top That! Playtime Shapes (large Version) Parry, Jo, illus. 2007. 10p. (J). (gr. -1). *(978-1-84666-555-4(8)*, Tide Mill Pr.) Top That! Publishing PLC.

Top That!, creator. Animals with Martha the Monkey. 2012. (Learn with Magnets Ser.). (ENG., Illus.). 10p. (gr. -1-k). *(978-1-84956-670-4(4))* Top That! Publishing PLC.

Toral, Miguel A. Babu Goes Back to the Zoo. 2009. 32p. pap. 15.70 *(978-1-4389-6330-3(0))* AuthorHouse.

Towe, H.P. Mr. Monkey Sees & Mr. Monkey Do. 2013. 24p. pap. 14.93 *(978-1-4669-8760-9(X))* Trafford Publishing.

Ufer, David A. The Giraffe Who Was Afraid of Heights, 1 vol. Carlson, Kirsten., illus. 2006. (ENG.). 32p. (J). (gr. -1-3). 15.95 *(978-0-9768823-0-5(2))* Arbordale Publishing.

Uncle Chuck. The Monkey Puzzle Tree. 2011. 32p. pap. 24.95 *(978-1-4560-6992-6(6))* America Star Bks.

Valentine, Victoria. The Cutest Little Duckie. Tucker, Amanda, illus. 2007. 80p. (J). per. 15.00 *(978-0-9723493-4-5(0)*, Water Forest Pr.) Skyline Pubn.

Vickery-Bharadwaj, Janice. Valentino & His Friends: It's Magic! 2012. 28p. pap. 12.99 *(978-1-4691-7709-0(9))* Xlibris Corp.

Viselman, Kenn. I Love You Bunches. 2004. (Illus.). 28p. 14.98 *(978-0-9722361-0-2(4))* Viselman, Kenn Presents...

Vorster, Nicola. A Monkeys' Wedding. 2012. (Illus.). 24p. pap. 21.35 *(978-1-4772-3126-5(9))* AuthorHouse.

Wang, Margaret. Monkey Tumbles. Elliott, Rebecca, illus. 2007. (ENG.). 10p. (gr. -1-k). bds. 9.95 *(978-1-58117-501-1(9)*, Intervisual/Piggy Toes) Bendon, Inc.

Watt, Fiona. That's Not My Monkey. 2008. (Touchy-Feely Board Bks). 10p. (J). bds. 7.99 *(978-0-7945-2178-3(9)*, Usborne) EDC Publishing.

Weaver, Greg & Weaver, Allie. Mickey the Monkey Makes a Friend. 2013. 24p. pap. 24.95 *(978-1-63000-802-4(8))* America Star Bks.

Weiss, Fred G. Mag-Nan-I-Mous Monkey & Gerald Giraffe. 2013. 28p. 18.99 *(978-0-9898820-5-7(5))* Mindstir Media.

Weston Woods Staff, creator. Curious George Rides a Bike. 2004. (J). 18.95 *(978-1-55592-802-5(1))*; 38.75 *(978-1-55592-819-3(6))* Weston Woods Studios, Inc.

Whitfield, Peter. Zen Tails up & Down. Bevington, Nancy, illus. 2005. (ENG.). 28p. (J). (gr. -1-3). 15.95 *(978-1-894965-22-4(1))* Simply Read Bks. CAN. Dist: Ingram Publisher Services.

Wiley. The Extraordinary Adventures of Ordinary Basil: Island of the Volcano Monkeys. 2007. (Ordinary Basil Ser.). (J). pap. *(978-0-439-86133-5(0))* Blue Sky Pr.

Wilkerson, Dawn. Katie & Katoa Travel down the River. 2009. 48p. pap. 16.95 *(978-1-61582-862-3(1))* America Star Bks.

Williams, Emma Louise. What's That Smell Monkey? williams, Emma Louise, illus. 2012. 12p. pap. 7.99 *(978-1-939076-07-6(2))* Wiggies, Piggy.

Williams, Rozanne Lanczak. Monkey in the Story Tree. Hanke, Karen, illus. 2006. (Learn to Write Ser.). 8p. (J). (gr. k-2). pap. 3.49 *(978-1-59198-282-1(0)*, 6176) Creative Teaching Pr., Inc.

—Monkey in the Story Tree. Maio, Barbara & Faulkner, Stacey, eds. Hanke, Karen, illus. 2006. (J). per. 6.99 *(978-1-59198-333-0(9))* Creative Teaching Pr., Inc.

Williams, Suzanne. Ten Naughty Little Monkeys. Watts, Suzanne, illus. 2007. 32p. (J). lib. bdg. 17.89 *(978-0-06-059905-8(7))* HarperCollins Pubs.

Wilson, Keely, Ivy, & Me. 2009. 28p. pap. 14.99 *(978-1-4389-7219-0(9))* AuthorHouse.

Wissman, Celeste Farris. When I Teach My Monkey How to Dance. 2012. 24p. pap. 17.99 *(978-1-4772-6035-7(8))* AuthorHouse.

Wolf, Justin. The Adventures of Silly Monkey & Jack. 2011. 20p. (gr. 1-2). pap. 12.99 *(978-1-4567-6452-4(7))* AuthorHouse.

Wood, Deanna Plummer. Whenever Monkeys Move Next Door, 1 volume. 2005. (Illus.). 24p. (J). pap. 8.50 *(978-0-9762935-1-4(X))* Perkins Crawford.

Woodward, Joanie. Seven Little Monkeys. Woodward, Joanie, illus. 2005. (Illus.). 40p. (J). per. *(978-0-9754676-4-0(6))* Yeoman Hse.

Wurge, B. B. Squiggle. 2009. (LeapKids Ser.). (ENG., Illus.). 152p. (J). (gr. 2-7). pap. 9.95 *(978-0-9815148-9-5(8))* Leapfrog Pr.

Yerrid, Gable. Marley's Treasure. Fitzgerald, Jennifer, illus. 2007. 28p. (J). (gr. -1-3). 15.95 *(978-0-9767442-6-9(0))* Yorkville Pr.

Yunger, Joshua. Hippo & Monkey. 2012. (Adventures of Hippo & Monkey Ser.: 1). (ENG., Illus.). 48p. (J). (gr. -1-2). 19.95 *(978-1-59373-107-6(8))* Bunker Hill Publishing, Inc.

Zajac, Kristen J. Ebeneezer's Cousin. Houdeshell, Jennifer T., illus. 2010. 20p. pap. 10.95 *(978-1-61633-045-3(7))* Guardian Angel Publishing, Inc.

Zajac, Kristen K. Ebeneezer's Cousin. Houdeshell, Jennifer Thomas, illus. 2013. 24p. 19.95 *(978-1-61633-440-6(1))* Guardian Angel Publishing, Inc.

Zana, Brian. Maurice Tries New Foods. 2012. 24p. pap. 15.99 *(978-1-4797-1430-8(5))* Xlibris Corp.

Ziefert, Harriet. Monkey's Noisy Jungle. Newton, Jill, illus. 2007. bds. 7.95 *(978-1-59354-598-7(3))* Blue Apple Bks.

Zur Muehlen, Nersel. Monkey in the Mirror. Sanchez, Sara, illus. 2012. 56p. pap. 14.95 *(978-0-9829224-2-2(6))* BPM Research LLC.

Zvetkoff, Kathleen Charnes. The Adventures of Willy the Monkey. 2008. 40p. pap. *(978-0-9784909-5-9(9))* Soul Asylum Poetry.

MONKS

see Monasticism and Religious Orders

MONOLOGUES

Here are entered collections of monologues.

Bauman, Elizabeth. Private Stories: Monologues for Young Actors Ages 8 to 16 & the Seven Key Questions to Unlock Your Imagination. 2007. (Limelight Ser.). (ENG.). 152p. per. 10.95 *(978-0-87910-341-5(8)*, 0879103418, Limelight Editions) Leonard, Hal Corp.

Bolton, Martha. Humorous Monologues. Behr, Joyce, illus. 2003. 128p. (J). (gr. 2-7). 19.00 *(978-0-8069-6750-9(1))* Sterling Publishing Co., Inc.

Dabrowski, Kristen. My Second Monologue Book: Famous & Historical People: 100 Monologues for Young Children. 2008. (My First Acting Ser.). (Illus.). 112p. (J). (gr. 1-8). pap. 11.95 *(978-1-57525-601-6(0))* Smith & Kraus Pubs., Inc.

—My Third Monologue Book: 100 Monologues about Places near & Far. 2008. 112p. (J). (gr. 1-8). pap. 11.95 *(978-1-57525-602-3(9))* Smith & Kraus Pubs., Inc.

—Teens Speak, Girls Ages 13 to 15: Sixty Original Character Monologues. 2005. (Kids Speak Ser.). 80p. pap. 11.95 *(978-1-57525-412-8(3))* Smith & Kraus Pubs., Inc.

—The Ultimate Audition Book for Middle School Actors Volume IV: 111 One-Minute Monologues: the Rich, the Famous, the Historical, Vol. 4. 2008. (Young Actors Ser.: Vol. IV). 160p. (J). pap. 11.95 *(978-1-57525-579-8(0))* Smith & Kraus Pubs., Inc.

—111 One-Minute Monologues: The Ultimate Monologue Book for Middle School Actors, Vol. 3. 2004. (Ultimate Monologue Book for Middle School Actors Ser.: Vol. 1). 136p. (J). pap. 11.95 *(978-1-57525-419-7(0))* Smith & Kraus Pubs., Inc.

Depner, Mary. Smart Monologues: Vocabulary Building Monologues for Teens & Young Adults. 2012. (ENG.). (YA). pap. 9.95 *(978-1-4675-3844-2(2))* Independent Pub.

Fife, Stephen, et al, eds. One on One: Playing with a Purpose - Monologues for Kids, Ages 7-14. 2013. (Applause Acting Ser.). (ENG., Illus.). 248p. pap. 16.99 *(978-1-55783-841-4(0)*, 1557838410, Applause Theatre & Cinema) Leonard, Hal Corp.

Gaddis, Alisha. Kids' Comedic Monologues That Are Actually Funny. 2016. (Applause Acting Ser.). 208p. pap. 14.99 *(978-1-4950-1176-4(3)*, 1495011763, Applause Theatre & Cinema) Leonard, Hal Corp.

—Teen Boys' Comedic Monologues That Are Actually Funny. 2015. (Applause Acting Ser.). 216p. pap. 14.99 *(978-1-4803-9679-1(6)*, 1480396796, Applause Theatre & Cinema) Leonard, Hal Corp.

—Teen Girls' Comedic Monologues That Are Actually Funny. 2015. (Applause Acting Ser.). 208p. pap. 14.99 *(978-1-4803-9680-7(X)*, 148039680X) Leonard, Hal Corp.

Haehnel, Alan. Remotely Related: Comedy Monologue. 2003. (YA). pap. 4.50 *(978-1-932404-05-0(8)*, 273) Brooklyn Pubs.

Harvey, Anne, ed. The Methuen Book of Monologues for Young Actors. 2009. (Audition Speeches Ser.). (ENG.). 192p. pap. 21.95 *(978-0-413-77279-4(9)*, 900072536, Methuen Drama) Bloomsbury Publishing Plc GBR. Dist: Macmillan.

Howard, Vernon. Monologues for Teens. Landes, William-Allan, ed. unabr. ed. 2003. (Illus.). 120p. (J). pap. 15.00 *(978-0-88734-666-8(9))* Players Pr., Inc.

Jelliroll. Echo Booming Monologues. 2007. per. 11.95 net. *(978-1-60402-529-3(8))* Independent Pub.

Johansen, Mila. 50 Scenes to Go: And 20 Monologues to Show. 2003. (Illus.). 160p. (YA). (gr. 4-12). pap. 25.00 *(978-0-88734-933-1(1))* Players Pr., Inc.

Lamedman, Debbie. The Ultimate Audition Book for Teens Vol. II: 111 Monologues from Classical Theater, 2 Minutes & Under. 2006. 11.95 *(978-1-57525-458-6(1))* Smith & Kraus Pubs., Inc.

—The Ultimate Audition Book for Teens Vol. III: 111 Monologues from Classical Literature, 2 Minutes & Under, VIII. 2006. (ENG.). (J). 11.95 *(978-1-57525-459-3(X))* Smith & Kraus Pubs., Inc.

—The Ultimate Audition Book for Teens IV: 111 One Minute Monologues. 2003. (Ultimate Audition Book for Teens Ser.: Vol. 4). viii, 117p. (J). 11.95 *(978-1-57525-353-4(4))* Smith & Kraus Pubs., Inc.

McCormick, Kimberly A. Hey, Girlfriend: Seventy-five monologues for Girls, 1 vol. 2009. (ENG.). 160p. (YA). (gr. 9-18). pap. 15.95 *(978-1-56608-162-7(9))* Meriwether Publishing, Ltd.

Meadows, Kelly. The Dating Game: Comedy Monologue. 2003. (YA). pap. 4.50 *(978-1-932404-06-7(6)*, 274) Brooklyn Pubs.

Mercanti, J. V. In Performance: Contemporary Monologues for Teens. 2015. (Applause Acting Ser.). 200p. pap. 16.99 *(978-1-4803-9661-6(3)*, 1480396613, Applause Theatre & Cinema) Leonard, Hal Corp.

Milstein, Janet. Winners Competition Series: Award-Winning, Custom-Made, 90-Second Comic Monologues Ages 13-18, Vol. 3. 2008. 96p. (YA). pap. 14.95 *(978-1-57525-614-6(2))* Smith & Kraus Pubs., Inc.

—Winners Competition Series Volume I: Award-winning, Custom-made, 60-Second Comic Monologues Ages 4-12. 2008. 96p. (J). pap. *(978-1-57525-612-2(6))* Smith & Kraus Pubs., Inc.

Muir, Kerry. Childsplay: A Collection of Scenes & Monologues for Children, 1 vol. Johnson, Kris, photos by. 2004. (Limelight Ser.). (Illus.). 260p. (Orig.). (gr. -1-18). pap. 16.99 *(978-0-87910-188-6(1)*, 0879101881, Limelight Editions) Leonard, Hal Corp.

Roddy, Ruth Mae. More Minute Monologues for Kids: Contemporary Scene-Study Pieces for Kids. 2005. 57p. (J). pap. 9.95 *(978-0-940669-57-4(9))* Dramaline Pubns.

Stevens, Chambers. Magnificent Monologues for Kids 2: More Kids' Monologues for Every Occasion! 2008. (Hollywood 101 Ser.). 79p. (J). (gr. k-7). pap. 14.95 *(978-1-883995-14-0(0))* Sandcastle Publishing.

Surface, Mary Hall. More Short Scenes & Monologues for Middle School Students: Inspired by Literature, Social Studies, & Real Life. 2007. (Young Actors Ser.). 207p. (J). (gr. 3-7). pap. 11.95 *(978-1-57525-560-6(X))* Smith & Kraus Pubs., Inc.

Young, Rebecca. 102 Great Monologues: A versatile collection of monologues & duologues for student Actors, 1 vol. 2010. (ENG.). 154p. (J). pap. 16.95 *(978-1-56608-171-9(8))* Meriwether Publishing, Ltd.

MONOPLANES

see Airplanes

MONROE, JAMES, 1758-1831

Gross, Miriam. How to Draw the Life & Times of James Monroe. 2009. (Kid's Guide to Drawing the Presidents of the United States of America Ser.). 32p. (gr. 4-4). 50.50 *(978-1-61511-149-7(2)*, PowerKids Pr.) Rosen Publishing Group, Inc., The.

Gunderson, Megan M. James Monroe, 1 vol. 2016. (United States Presidents *2017 Ser.). (ENG., Illus.). 40p. (J). (gr. 2-5). lib. bdg. 35.64 *(978-1-68078-109-0(X)*, 21835, Big Buddy Bks.) ABDO Publishing Co.

Kelley, K. C. James Monroe: The 5th President. 2016. (First Look at America's Presidents Ser.). (ENG., Illus.). 24p. (J). (gr. -1-3). 26.99 *(978-1-944102-64-7(7))* Bearport Publishing Co., Inc.

Levy, Debbie. James Monroe. 2005. (Presidential Leaders Ser.). (Illus.). 112p. (J). 29.27 *(978-0-8225-0824-3(9)*, Lerner Pubns.) Lerner Publishing Group.

Lusted, Marcia Amidon. Revolution & the New Nation: 1750-Early 1800s. 2007. (Presidents of the United States Ser.). (Illus.). 48p. (J). (gr. 4-7). lib. bdg. 29.05 *(978-1-59036-739-1(1))*; per. 10.95 *(978-1-59036-740-7(5))* Weigl Pubs., Inc.

Marcovitz, Hal. James Monroe. 2004. (Childhoods of the Presidents Ser.). (Illus.). 48p. (J). (gr. 4-18). lib. bdg. 17.95 *(978-1-59084-283-6(9))* Mason Crest.

Naden, Corinne J. & Blue, Rose. James Monroe, 1 vol. 2009. (Presidents & Their Times Ser.). (ENG.). 96p. (gr. 6-6). lib. bdg. 36.93 *(978-0-7614-2838-1(0)*, e4f2cacd-fce0-428c-9759-526bc3220fdb) Cavendish Square Publishing LLC.

Venezia, Mike. Getting to Know the U. S. Presidents: James Monroe. Venezia, Mike, illus. 2005. (Getting to Know the U. S. Presidents Ser.). (ENG., Illus.). 32p. (J). (gr. 3-4). pap. 7.95 *(978-0-516-27479-9(1)*, Children's Pr.) Scholastic Library Publishing.

MONROE DOCTRINE

Alagna, Magdalena. The Monroe Doctrine: An End to European Colonies in America. (Life in the New American Nation Ser.). 32p. (gr. 4-4). 2009. 47.90 *(978-1-61514-285-9(1))* 2003. (ENG., Illus.). pap. 10.00 *(978-0-8239-4258-9(9)*, 535cb124-e574-4a58-801d-68b74cb78869) 2003. (ENG., Illus.). lib. bdg. 29.13 *(978-0-8239-4040-0(3)*, 32f11f4a-81eb-4781-80aa-51b11ca1edb2, Rosen Reference) Rosen Publishing Group, Inc., The.

Renehan, Edward J., Jr. & Renehan, Edward J. The Monroe Doctrine: The Cornerstone of American Foreign Policy. 2007. (Milestones in American History Ser.). (ENG., Illus.). 128p. (gr. 7-12). 35.00 *(978-0-7910-9353-5(0)*, P125502, Facts On File) Infobase Holdings, Inc.

MONSTERS

see also Dragons; Dwarfs; Giants

Abbott, Simon, illus. Learn to Draw: Monsters. 2011. (Learn to Draw Ser.). (ENG.). 24p. (J). (gr. k-2). pap. 6.95

M N O

(978-1-84898-200-0(3), TickTock Books) Octopus Publishing Group GBR. Dist: Independent Pubs. Group.

Abdo, Kenny. Frankenstein. 2018. (Hollywood Monsters Ser.). (ENG., Illus.). 24p. (J). (gr. 2-8). lib. bdg. 31.36 *(978-1-5321-2318-4(3)*, 28403, Abdo Zoom-Fly) ABDO Publishing Co.

—Freddy Krueger. 2019. (Hollywood Monsters Ser.). (ENG., Illus.). 24p. (J). (gr. 2-8). lib. bdg. 31.36 *(978-1-5321-2745-8(6)*, 31697, Abdo Zoom-Fly) ABDO Publishing Co.

—The Invisible Man. 2018. (Hollywood Monsters Ser.). (ENG., Illus.). 24p. (J). (gr. 2-8). lib. bdg. 31.36 *(978-1-5321-2319-1(1)*, 28405, Abdo Zoom-Fly) ABDO Publishing Co.

—Jason Voorhees. 2019. (Hollywood Monsters Ser.). (ENG., Illus.). 24p. (J). (gr. 2-8). lib. bdg. 31.36 *(978-1-5321-2746-5(4)*, 31699, Abdo Zoom-Fly) ABDO Publishing Co.

—Leatherface. 2019. (Hollywood Monsters Ser.). (ENG., Illus.). 24p. (J). (gr. 2-8). lib. bdg. 31.36 *(978-1-5321-2747-2(2)*, 31701, Abdo Zoom-Fly) ABDO Publishing Co.

—The Mummy. 2018. (Hollywood Monsters Ser.). (ENG.). 24p. (J). (gr. 2-8). lib. bdg. 31.36 *(978-1-5321-2320-7(5)*, 28407, Abdo Zoom-Fly) ABDO Publishing Co.

—The Wolf Man. 2018. (Hollywood Monsters Ser.). (ENG., Illus.). 24p. (J). (gr. 2-8). lib. bdg. 31.36 *(978-1-5321-2321-4(3)*, 28409, Abdo Zoom-Fly) ABDO Publishing Co.

Altmann, Scott. Vampire Mazes. 2011. (Dover Children's Activity Bks.). (ENG., Illus.). 48p. (J). (gr. 3-4). pap. 4.99 *(978-0-486-47922-4(6)*, 479226) Dover Pubns., Inc.

Anderson, Holly Lynn. Unexplained Monsters & Cryptids. 2015. (J). *(978-1-61900-071-1(7))* Eldorado Ink.

Ard, Catherine. Origami Monsters, 1 vol. 2014. (Amazing Origami Ser.). (ENG., Illus.). 32p. (J). (gr. 2-3). 29.27 *(978-1-4824-2201-6(8)*, da7d56a7-09c5-4274-b401-3ba51266f131) Stevens, Gareth Publishing LLLP.

Aunt Darla. There's a Monster under the Captain's Bed!!! Erik's Monster. Petersen, Darla & Shields, Erik P., illus. Date not set. 32p. 16.00 *(978-0-9658926-1-2(1))* Poet Tree Pubns.

Bardhan-Quallen, Sudipta. The Real Monsters. Cochran, Josh, illus. 2008. (Mysteries Unwrapped Ser.). (ENG.). 88p. (J). (gr. 5-8). 18.69 *(978-1-4027-3776-3(9))* Sterling Publishing Co., Inc.

Bearport Publishing. The Busy Monsters. 2018. (ENG.). 24p. (J). (gr. -1-2). 31.80 *(978-1-78856-076-4(0))* Bearport Publishing Co., Inc.

Beaumont, Steve. Drawing Legendary Monsters, 12 vols., Set. Incl. Drawing Dragons: And Other Cold-Blooded Creatures. lib. bdg. 30.27 *(978-1-4488-3324-5(8)*, 149c16db-2674-430a-8cda-cca7cace3f4e); Drawing Griffins & Other Winged Wonders. lib. bdg. 30.27 *(978-1-4488-3253-8(5)*, d3a938bb-1b49-4efe-9867-a4e9e0a9a8e7); Drawing the Kraken & Other Sea Monsters. lib. bdg. 30.27 *(978-1-4488-3252-1(7)*, 23ad63e2-a907-4899-b536-e961cfda7b75); Drawing the Minotaur & Other Demihumans. lib. bdg. 30.27 *(978-1-4488-3250-7(0)*, 29fcab51-cef4-42b3-bd1a-b6a2ab3c9714); Drawing Unicorns & Other Mythical Beasts. lib. bdg. 30.27 *(978-1-4488-3251-4(9)*, 7fdbc74d-fe4f-4f40-ad2a-2022c6a18a30); Drawing Werewolves & Other Gothic Ghouls. 30.27 *(978-1-4488-3254-5(3)*, b198716e-8499-413e-b6ea-3faf8c5b3776); (J). (gr. 4-4). (Drawing Legendary Monsters Ser.). (ENG., Illus.). 32p. 2011. Set lib. bdg. 181.62 *(978-1-4488-3267-5(5)*, a36ff2a1-4ca3-444e-85cb-91b9d4c9410d, PowerKids Pr.) Rosen Publishing Group, Inc., The.

BeaverSimon. Fantastic Creatures: Monsters, Mermaids, & Wild Men Beginning Book with Online Access, 1 vol. 2014. (ENG., Illus.). 24p. (J). pap., E-Book, E-Book 9.50 *(978-1-107-69637-2(2))* Cambridge Univ. Pr.

Beccia, Carlyn. Monstrous: The Lore, Gore, & Science Behind Your Favorite Monsters. Beccia, Carlyn, illus. 2019. (ENG., Illus.). 148p. (J). (gr. 4-8). lib. bdg. 24.99 *(978-1-5124-4916-7(4)*, 1c9e5fb1-af4a-4f21-bff0-9f7f6f19a85d, Carolrhoda Bks.) Lerner Publishing Group.

Becker, Helaine. Monster Science: Could Monsters Survive (and Thrive!) in the Real World? McAndrew, Phil, illus. 2016. (ENG.). 96p. (J). (gr. 3-7). 18.95 *(978-1-77138-054-6(3))* Kids Can Pr., Ltd. CAN. Dist: Hachette Bk. Group.

Bergin, Mark. Ghosts & Ghouls, 1 vol. 2012. (It's Fun to Draw Ser.). (ENG., Illus.). 32p. (J). (gr. 2-2). lib. bdg. 31.27 *(978-1-61533-600-5(1)*, 25d5a033-e3ef-438d-81ef-1b0f6ca98b32, Windmill Bks.) Rosen Publishing Group, Inc., The.

—Monsters, 1 vol. 2012. (It's Fun to Draw Ser.). (ENG., Illus.). 32p. (J). (gr. 2-2). lib. bdg. 31.27 *(978-1-61533-601-2(X)*, 65f5be4d-a726-4d93-b3b5-6691caba7bf7, Windmill Bks.) Rosen Publishing Group, Inc., The.

Bernhardt, Carolyn. Gila Monster: Venomous Desert Dweller. 2017. (Real Monsters Ser.). (ENG., Illus.). 32p. (J). (gr. 3-6). 51.35 *(978-1-68079-773-2(5)*, 24005, Checkerboard Library) ABDO Publishing Co.

Blade, Adam. Beast Quest: a to Z of Beasts: New Edition over 150 Beasts. 2020. (Beast Quest Ser.). (ENG., Illus.). 272p. (J). (gr. 2-4). 16.99 *(978-1-4083-6073-6(X)*, Orchard Bks.) Hachette Children's Group GBR. Dist: Hachette Bk. Group.

Bowman, Chris. The Mothman Sightings. 2019. (Paranormal Mysteries Ser.). (ENG., Illus.). 24p. (J). (gr. 3-8). pap. 8.99 *(978-1-61891-733-1(1)*, 12335, Black Sheep) Bellwether Media.

Bradley, Timothy. The Science of Monsters (Grade 6) 2nd rev. ed. 2016. (TIME(r): Informational Text Ser.). (ENG., Illus.). 64p. (gr. 5-8). pap. 13.99 *(978-1-4938-3607-9(2))* Teacher Created Materials, Inc.

Bradley, Timothy J. The Science of Monsters. 2016. (Time for Kids Nonfiction Readers Ser.). (ENG.). (J). (gr. 5-8). lib. bdg. 22.10 *(978-0-606-39543-4(1))* Turtleback.

—Strange but True: Bizarre Animals, 1 vol. 2nd rev. ed. 2012. (TIME for KIDS(r): Informational Text Ser.). (ENG.). 48p. (gr. 4-5). pap. 13.99 *(978-1-4333-4861-7(6))* Teacher Created Materials, Inc.

Brassey, Richard. Nessie the Loch Ness Monster. 2010. (ENG., Illus.). 24p. (gr. k-2). pap. 9.99 *(978-1-4440-0056-6(X)*, Orion Children's Bks.) Hachette Children's Group GBR. Dist: Hachette Bk. Group.

Brett, Flora. Get to Know Gila Monsters. 2015. (Get to Know Reptiles Ser.). (ENG., Illus.). 24p. (J). (gr. 1-3). lib. bdg. 27.99 *(978-1-4914-2061-4(8)*, 127539, Capstone Pr.) Capstone.

Brinker, Spencer. Odd or Even in a Monstrous Season. 2015. (Illus.). 32p. (J). lib. bdg. 28.50 *(978-1-62724-331-5(3))* Bearport Publishing Co., Inc.

Brown, Marcy & Haley, Dennis. We Both Read Bilingual Edition-The Well-Mannered Monster/el Monstruo Debuenos Modales. Raglin, Tim, illus. 2011. (ENG & SPA.). 44p. (J). pap. 5.99 *(978-1-60115-044-8(X))* Treasure Bay, Inc.

Calcium Staff, contrib. by. The Monsters & Creatures of Greek Mythology, 1 vol. 2011. (Ancient Greek Mythology Ser.). (ENG.). 64p. (J). (gr. 5-9). lib. bdg. 34.65 *(978-0-7565-4481-2(5)*, 115728, Compass Point Bks.) Capstone.

Carlson-Berne, Emma. A First Look at Monsters. 2020. (Bumba Books (r) — Fantastic Creatures Ser.). (ENG., Illus.). 24p. (J). (gr. -1-1). 26.65 *(978-1-5415-9683-2(8)*, dc32c716-0e75-4ebc-ae4f-39301117a0f8, Lerner Pubns.) Lerner Publishing Group.

Cheatham, Mark. Gremlins!, 1 vol., 1. 2013. (Jr. Graphic Monster Stories Ser.). (ENG.). 24p. (J). (gr. 2-3). 28.93 *(978-1-4777-6215-8(9)*, 9ad66673-9fbb-43d3-97f5-4d98072137af, PowerKids Pr.) Rosen Publishing Group, Inc., The.

Chmielewski, Gary. The Ghost Zone: Jokes, Riddles, Tongue Twisters & Daffynitions. Caputo, Jim, illus. rev. ed. 2009. (Funny Zone Ser.). (ENG.). 24p. (J). (gr. 2-4). lib. bdg. 22.60 *(978-1-59953-297-4(2))* Norwood Hse. Pr.

Christopher, Neil. Those That Cause Fear, 1 vol. Amattaujuq (Arnaktauyok), Germaine, illus. 2016. (ENG.). 48p. (J). (gr. 1-3). 16.95 *(978-1-77227-085-3(7))* Inhabit Media Inc. CAN. Dist: Consortium Bk. Sales & Distribution.

Clark, Willow. Gila Monster!, 1 vol. 2010. (Animal Danger Zone Ser.). (ENG.). 24p. (J). (gr. 2-3). lib. bdg. 27.27 *(978-1-60754-960-4(3)*, ceb8ecaf-e3e3-4846-8df9-0b467866294a); (Illus.). pap. 9.15 *(978-1-60754-966-6(2)*, 2bd929c7-e6a9-4c7c-ae69-a304d148c80f) Rosen Publishing Group, Inc., The. (Windmill Bks.).

Collins, Terry Lee & Weakland, Mark Andrew. Scooby-Doo! & the Truth Behind Zombies. 2016. (ENG., Illus.). 24p. (J). pap. *(978-1-4062-8894-0(2))* Capstone.

—The Truth Behind Sea Monsters. 2016. (ENG., Illus.). 24p. (J). pap. *(978-1-4062-8898-8(5))* Capstone.

Cox, Barbara & Forbes, Scott. Beyond the Grave, 1 vol., Vol. 1. 2014. (Creepy Chronicles Ser.). (ENG., Illus.). 32p. (J). (gr. 5-6). 29.27 *(978-1-4824-0226-1(2)*, b31805b5-ea17-4efe-9dc3-194774bd20bc) Stevens, Gareth Publishing LLLP.

—Maniacal Monsters & Bizarre Beasts, 1 vol., Vol. 1. 2014. (Creepy Chronicles Ser.). (ENG., Illus.). 32p. (J). (gr. 5-6). 29.27 *(978-1-4824-0236-0(X)*, d0e0d8b8-243d-4e51-844b-6ac5f6038fbe) Stevens, Gareth Publishing LLLP.

—Spooky Spirits & Creepy Creatures, 1 vol., Vol. 1. 2014. (Creepy Chronicles Ser.). (ENG., Illus.). 32p. (J). (gr. 5-6). 29.27 *(978-1-4824-0243-8(2)*, 6cc5b9f5-3189-4879-974b-4339c8ee5299) Stevens, Gareth Publishing LLLP.

—Wicked Waters, 1 vol., Vol. 1. 2014. (Creepy Chronicles Ser.). (ENG.). 32p. (J). (gr. 5-6). 29.27 *(978-1-4824-0262-9(9)*, c3351447-e36a-443c-9bdb-0915778f4ce2) Stevens, Gareth Publishing LLLP.

Creatures of Legend, 5 vols. 2014. (Creatures of Legend Ser.: 6). (ENG.). 48p. (J). (gr. 4-8). lib. bdg. 178.20 *(978-1-62403-149-6(8)*, 4932) ABDO Publishing Co.

Curran, Bob. Frankenstein & Other Man-Made Monsters, 1 vol. 2013. (Haunted: Ghosts & the Paranormal Ser.). (ENG., Illus.). 208p. (YA). (gr. 8-8). 42.47 *(978-1-4777-0679-4(8)*, 94fe23c9-dadb-4882-9ecc-20a6516f7a57) Rosen Publishing Group, Inc., The.

Dakota, Heather, et al. Monster: Survival Guide. Castro, Ali, illus. 2015. 128p. (J). *(978-0-545-85166-4(1)*, Tangerine Pr.) Scholastic, Inc.

The Dangerous Book of Monsters. 2015. (ENG., Illus.). 176p. (J). 16.99 *(978-1-4059-2003-2(3)*, 831f00b4-5e7d-4d4d-8604-56d796214fc8) Penguin Bks., Ltd. GBR. Dist: Diamond Comic Distributors, Inc.

Dennett, Preston. Bigfoot, Yeti, & Other Ape-Men. 2008. (Mysteries, Legends, & Unexplained Phenomena Ser.). (ENG., Illus.). 152p. (gr. 7-12). 29.95 *(978-0-7910-9386-3(7)*, P159098, Facts On File) Infobase Holdings, Inc.

Devadasan, Rashmi Ruth. Kumari Loves a Monster. Kumariyin Ratcaca Katalan. Shyam, illus. 2010. (TAM & ENG.). 52p. pap. 17.95 *(978-93-80636-01-6(6))* Blaft Pubns.

Dicker, Katie. Mysterious Creatures. 2015. (Mystery! Ser.). (ENG.). 24p. (J). (gr. 2-5). 28.50 *(978-1-62588-202-8(5)*, 17359) Black Rabbit Bks.

Diker, Katie. Mysterious Creatures. 2015. (ENG., Illus.). 24p. (J). pap. 8.95 *(978-1-77092-233-4(4))* RiverStream Publishing.

Dinosaurs & Monsters. Date not set. (Illus.). 64p. (J). 2.98 *(978-1-4054-0448-8(5))* Parragon, Inc.

DK. Children's Book of Mythical Beasts & Magical Monsters. 2018. (DK Children's Book Of Ser.). (ENG.). 144p. (J). (gr. 2-5). pap. 16.99 *(978-1-4654-7462-9(5)*, DK Children) Dorling Kindersley Publishing, Inc.

Doeden, Matt. Real-World Dragons, 1 vol. Pellegrino, Rich, illus. 2013. (World of Dragons Ser.). (ENG.). 32p. (J). (gr. 3-9). lib. bdg. 27.32 *(978-1-62065-146-9(7)*, 120835, Capstone Pr.) Capstone.

Early Macken, JoAnn. Gila Monsters, 1 vol. 2nd rev. ed. 2009. (Animals That Live in the Desert (Second Edition) Ser.). (ENG.). 24p. (J). (gr. 1-1). pap. 9.15 *(978-1-4339-2449-1(8)*, 5ad4996f-c820-4e49-a5a8-53cddf9302e8); lib. bdg. 25.27 *(978-1-4339-1951-0(6)*, b6e3bc3c-cbdd-4cc7-ae1e-52f4f9b803ae) Stevens, Gareth Publishing LLLP. (Weekly Reader Leveled Readers).

—Gila Monsters / Monstruos de Gila, 1 vol. (Animals That Live in the Desert / Animales Del Desierto (First Edition) Ser.). (ENG & SPA., 24p. (gr. 1-1). 2005. Illus.). pap. 9.15 *(978-0-8368-4848-9(9)*, fd85b3eb-e824-4465-a1f8-8ecb4c5db293, Weekly Reader Leveled Readers) 2nd rev. ed. 2009. (J). pap. 9.15 *(978-1-4339-2457-6(9)*, 136108a7-350f-45bf-bbd7-579ce3d72436, Weekly Reader Leveled Readers) 2nd rev. ed. 2009. (J). lib. bdg. 25.27 *(978-1-4339-2062-2(X)*, 752deb7a-10ef-4257-9d50-d18e6a223726) Stevens, Gareth Publishing LLLP.

Edwards, Katie. Myths & Monsters: Secrets Revealed. Mendez, Simon, illus. 2004. 29p. (J). pap. 6.95 *(978-1-57091-582-6(2))* Charlesbridge Publishing, Inc.

Elder, Jeremy. Monsters Destroyed My City! Stained Glass Coloring Book. 2011. (Dover Fantasy Coloring Bks.). (ENG., Illus.). 32p. (J). (gr. 2-5). pap. 6.99 *(978-0-486-47910-1(2)*, 479102) Dover Pubns., Inc.

Eliot, Hannah. Monsters Are Real! And Other Fun Facts. Spurgeon, Aaron, illus. 2016. (Did You Know? Ser.). (ENG.). 32p. (J). (gr. -1-3). pap. 6.99 *(978-1-4814-6781-0(6)*, Little Simon) Little Simon.

Famous Movie Monsters, 16 vols., Set. 2004. (Famous Movie Monsters Ser.). (ENG.). (YA). (gr. 6-6). 275.76 *(978-1-4042-0377-8(X)*, 1844ac00-127e-4c41-a0e3-405c7b6eef65) Rosen Publishing Group, Inc., The.

Feldman, Thea. Monsters: Myth or Fact? 2015. (Discover More Readers Level 2 Ser.). lib. bdg. 13.55 *(978-0-606-37758-4(1))* Turtleback.

Flowerpot Press, creator. Monsters Coloring Book. 2013. (Sockheadz Ser.). (ENG., Illus.). 72p. (J). (gr. -1-3). 4.99 *(978-1-77093-545-7(2))* Flowerpot Pr.

Freedman, Claire. Monstersaurus. Cort, Ben, illus. 2013. (J). *(978-1-4351-4952-6(1))* Barnes & Noble, Inc.

Fullman, Joe. Sea Monsters & Flying Monsters, 1 vol. 2018. (Amazing Origami Ser.). (ENG.). 32p. (J). (gr. 2-3). pap. 11.50 *(978-1-5382-3468-6(8)*, f8d7e5d3-d319-4f31-9e32-2cd4a58e6d36); lib. bdg. 29.27 *(978-1-5382-3470-9(X)*, ee9d8265-209c-4319-ad83-b76d3d7dfebe) Stevens, Gareth Publishing LLLP.

Ganeri, Anita & West, David. Creatures of Myths & Legends. (J). 2012. 70.50 *(978-1-4488-5235-2(8))* 2011. (ENG.). 32p. (gr. 4-5). pap. 12.75 *(978-1-4488-5234-5(X)*, 93065ec9-8b7f-4e77-8c2a-06ef39072cbb) 2011. (ENG.). 32p. (gr. 4-5). lib. bdg. 30.27 *(978-1-4488-5198-0(X)*, f4704ba5-fc8f-4e0c-8a08-93c776319aa7) Rosen Publishing Group, Inc., The. (PowerKids Pr.).

—Supernatural Creatures. (Illus.). 32p. 2012. 70.50 *(978-1-4488-5233-8(1))* 2011. (ENG., (gr. 4-5). pap. 12.75 *(978-1-4488-5232-1(3)*, 56c4a09f-9807-4ecc-af96-e879d984970f) 2011. (ENG., (gr. 4-5). lib. bdg. 30.27 *(978-1-4488-5197-3(1)*, 3a308f88-80f8-434b-a57b-5a38ef5cac64) Rosen Publishing Group, Inc., The. (PowerKids Pr.).

Gilpin, Rebecca. Monster Things to Make & Do. Harrison, Erica et al, illus. Allman, Howard, photos by. 2006. (Usborne Activities Ser.). 32p. (J). (gr. -1-3). pap. 6.99 *(978-0-7945-1354-2(9)*, Usborne) EDC Publishing.

Goddu, Krystyna Poray. Movie Monsters: From Godzilla to Frankenstein. 2017. (Monster Mania Ser.). (ENG., Illus.). 32p. (J). (gr. 2-5). E-Book 39.99 *(978-1-5124-3825-3(1)*, 9781512438253); E-Book 39.99 *(978-1-5124-2816-2(7))*; E-Book 4.99 *(978-1-5124-3824-6(3)*, 9781512438246) Lerner Publishing Group. (Lerner Pubns.).

—Sea Monsters: From Kraken to Nessie. 2017. (Monster Mania Ser.). (ENG., Illus.). 32p. (J). (gr. 2-5). E-Book 39.99 *(978-1-5124-2817-9(5))*; E-Book 4.99 *(978-1-5124-3827-7(8)*, 9781512438277); E-Book 39.99 *(978-1-5124-3828-4(6)*, 9781512438284) Lerner Publishing Group. (Lerner Pubns.).

Gray, Peter. Monsters. (Drawing Manga Ser.). 32p. (gr. 4-4). 2009. 50.50 *(978-1-61512-200-4(1))* 2005. (ENG., Illus.). (YA). lib. bdg. 30.27 *(978-1-4042-3331-7(8)*, c8889d80-ca7d-4dd1-baf7-d337c2b78c20) Rosen Publishing Group, Inc., The.

Greatest Movie Monsters. 2015. (Greatest Movie Monsters Ser.). (ENG.). 48p. (J). (gr. 5-6). pap., pap., pap. 82.25 *(978-1-4994-3679-2(3)*, Rosen Central) Rosen Publishing Group, Inc., The.

Green, Barry. How to Draw 101 Monsters. Green, Dan, illus. 2003. (How to Draw 101 Ser.: 2). (ENG.). 48p. (J). (gr. k). pap. 4.99 *(978-1-84229-742-1(2))* Top That! Publishing PLC GBR. Dist: Independent Pubs. Group.

Guess McKerley, Jennifer. The Kraken, 1 vol. 2007. (Monsters Ser.). (ENG., Illus.). 48p. (gr. 4-8). lib. bdg. 36.83 *(978-0-7377-3531-4(7)*, ed9724af-a4e3-420d-ba02-6d4270c02cd0, KidHaven Publishing) Greenhaven Publishing LLC.

Halls, Kelly Milner. Cryptid Creatures: A Field Guide to 50 Fascinating Beasts. Spears, Rick, illus. 2019. 224p. (J). (gr. 2). pap. 16.99 *(978-1-63217-210-5(0)*, Little Bigfoot) Sasquatch Bks.

Halls, Kelly Milner, et al. Tales of the Cryptids: Mysterious Creatures That May or May Not Exist. Spears, Rick C., illus. 2006. (ENG.). 72p. (J). (gr. 5-12). 19.99 *(978-1-58196-049-5(2)*, 64e0a3c9-b9fb-4eec-931e-925eb94fa268, Millbrook Pr.) Lerner Publishing Group.

Harris, John. My Monster Notebook. Todd, Mark, illus. 2011. (ENG.). 48p. (J). (gr. 3-18). 16.95 *(978-1-60606-050-6(3)*, J. Paul Getty Museum) Getty Pubns.

Harrison, Paul. Sea Monsters, 1 vol. 2007. (Up Close Ser.). (ENG., Illus.). 24p. (J). (gr. 3-3). lib. bdg. 28.93 *(978-1-4042-4224-1(4)*, 2812d95a-b355-4ba1-857f-1cfa3f97309e, PowerKids Pr.) Rosen Publishing Group, Inc., The.

Hawkins, John. Bigfoot & Other Monsters, 1 vol. 2012. (Mystery Hunters Ser.). (ENG., Illus.). 32p. (J). (gr. 4-5). pap. 11.60 *(978-1-4488-6445-4(3)*, 9a364bfb-b38e-4821-9ae4-2afe083f65e6); lib. bdg. 28.93 *(978-1-4488-6431-7(3)*, 476bb760-6f11-41d1-85b3-d021e27f9b8c) Rosen Publishing Group, Inc., The. (PowerKids Pr.).

Herbst, Judith. Monsters. (Unexplained Ser.). (ENG., Illus.). 48p. (gr. 5-12). 2005. pap. 8.95 *(978-0-8225-2408-3(2)*, Lerner Pubns.) 2004. lib. bdg. 26.60 *(978-0-8225-1626-2(8))* Lerner Publishing Group.

Hile, Kevin. Centaurs, 1 vol. 2008. (Monsters Ser.). (ENG., Illus.). 48p. (gr. 4-8). lib. bdg. 36.83 *(978-0-7377-4042-4(6)*, c45ffb54-f681-4202-a2c0-1eb300c93fe1, KidHaven Publishing) Greenhaven Publishing LLC.

Holland, Simon. Magnificent Magical Beasts: Inside Their Secret World. Wyatt, David & Walker, Kev, illus. 2016. (ENG.). 48p. (J). 17.99 *(978-1-68119-430-1(9)*, 9781681194301, Bloomsbury USA Childrens) Bloomsbury Publishing USA.

Horowitz, Anthony. Beasts & Monsters. 2011. (Legends Ser.). (ENG., Illus.). 128p. (YA). (gr. 4-6). pap. 21.19 *(978-0-7534-6631-5(7)*, 9780753466315) Kingfisher Publications, plc GBR. Dist: Children's Plus, Inc.

Hunter, Llyn. A Little Book of Monsters. Hunter, Llyn, illus. 2007. (Illus.). 32p. (J). 7.95 *(978-0-9776419-0-1(2)*, 0-9776419-0-2) Bobcat Publishing.

Jango-Cohen, Judith. Real-Life Sea Monsters. 2009. pap. 40.95 *(978-0-7613-4820-7(4))* Lerner Publishing Group.

Jeffrey, Gary. Ogres, 1 vol. 2011. (Graphic Mythical Creatures Ser.). (ENG.). 24p. (J). (gr. 3-3). pap. 9.15 *(978-1-4339-6039-0(7)*, 48236fee-46b3-4787-87e0-4ab9fc9c1cf5, Gareth Stevens Learning Library); lib. bdg. 26.60 *(978-1-4339-6037-6(0)*, a9047d30-38c9-441b-936f-4e621e3ed73a) Stevens, Gareth Publishing LLLP.

—Sea Monsters, 1 vol. 2011. (Graphic Mythical Creatures Ser.). (ENG., Illus.). 24p. (J). (gr. 3-3). pap. 9.15 *(978-1-4339-6043-7(5)*, c528da0a-903d-42bf-aecc-d15041b9cbee, Gareth Stevens Learning Library); lib. bdg. 26.60 *(978-1-4339-6041-3(9)*, cab2e344-dc59-4bf8-b112-31bc49c68ee9) Stevens, Gareth Publishing LLLP.

Keenan, Sheila & Who HQ. What Is the Story of Frankenstein? Malan, David, illus. 2019. (What Is the Story Of? Ser.). (ENG.). 112p. (J). (gr. 3-7). 7.99 *(978-1-5247-8842-1(2)*, Penguin Workshop) Penguin Young Readers Group.

Kingsley, Imogen. Gila Monsters. 2019. (Lizards in the Wild Ser.). (ENG.). 24p. (J). (gr. 1-4). lib. bdg. *(978-1-68151-557-1(1)*, 14518) Amicus.

Kington, Emily. Monster Mâché Art. 2019. (Wild Art Projects Ser.). (ENG., Illus.). 32p. (J). (gr. 3-6). 27.99 *(978-1-5415-0127-0(6)*, 37892cc6-e85c-42cb-93a5-4e2d8d0c46e8, Hungry Tomato (r)) Lerner Publishing Group.

Klutz Editors. Monsters. Date not set. (Illus.). 40p. (J). 3.98 *(978-1-4054-0175-3(3))* Parragon, Inc.

Krensky, Stephen. The Bogeyman. 2008. pap. 52.95 *(978-0-8225-9891-6(4))* 2007. (ENG., Illus.). 48p. (gr. 4-7). lib. bdg. 26.60 *(978-0-8225-6760-8(1)*, Lerner Pubns.) Lerner Publishing Group.

—Creatures from the Deep. 2007. (Monster Chronicles Ser.). (ENG., Illus.). 48p. (gr. 4-7). lib. bdg. 26.60 *(978-0-8225-6761-5(X)*, Lerner Pubns.) Lerner Publishing Group.

—Frankenstein. 2005. (Monster Chronicles Ser.). (Illus.). 48p. (J). (gr. 3-7). lib. bdg. 26.60 *(978-0-8225-5923-8(4))* Lerner Publishing Group.

—Monster Chronicles Set II: Complete Library. 2008. pap. 263.95 *(978-1-58013-617-4(6))* Lerner Publishing Group.

—Monster Chronicles Set II Classroom Library. 2008. pap. 43.95 *(978-0-8225-8981-5(8))* Lerner Publishing Group.

Lake, G. G. Take Your Pick of Monster Encounters. 2017. (Take Your (Equally Horrible) Pick! Ser.). (ENG., Illus.). 32p. (J). (gr. 3-9). pap. 7.95 *(978-1-5157-4476-4(0)*, 134178); lib. bdg. 27.32 *(978-1-5157-4472-6(8)*, 134174) Capstone. (Capstone Pr.).

Leblanc, Catherine. How to Mash Monsters. Garrigue, Roland, illus. 2013. (ENG.). 32p. (J). (gr. -1). 14.99 *(978-1-60887-190-2(8))* Insight Editions.

—My Monster-Mashing Activity Book. Garrigue, Roland, illus. 2016. (ENG.). 80p. (J). (gr. -1). pap., act. bk. ed. 14.99 *(978-1-60887-710-2(8))* Insight Editions.

Lew, Kristi. Monsters, Beasts, & Demons in America, 1 vol. 2011. (America's Supernatural Secrets Ser.). (ENG.). 48p. (YA). (gr. 5-5). pap. 12.75 *(978-1-4488-5584-1(5)*, dbc3b1bf-c890-49d3-96f3-826570dc19b9); lib. bdg. 34.47 *(978-1-4488-5532-2(2)*, 7d1c080d-bed8-4bd6-8ede-54b22fd3bdef) Rosen Publishing Group, Inc., The. (Rosen Reference).

Lewis, J. Patrick. M Is for Monster: A Fantastic Creatures Alphabet. Kelley, Gerald, illus. 2014. (ENG.). 32p. (J). (gr. 2-5). 16.99 *(978-1-58536-818-1(0)*, 203669) Sleeping Bear Pr.

Linde, Barbara M. & Benchmark Education Co. Staff. Monsters among Us? 2014. (Text Connections Ser.). (J). (gr. 6). *(978-1-4900-1519-4(1))* Benchmark Education Co.

Llenas, Anna. The Color Monster: A Pop-Up Book of Feelings. 2015. (ENG., Illus.). 20p. (J). (gr. -1-2). 24.99 *(978-1-4549-1729-8(6))* Sterling Publishing Co., Inc.

Loh-Hagan, Virginia. Mothman. 2018. (Urban Legends: Don't Read Alone! Ser.). (ENG., Illus.). 32p. (J). (gr. 4-8). pap. 14.21 *(978-1-5341-0860-8(2)*, 210804); lib. bdg. 32.07 *(978-1-5341-0761-8(4)*, 210803) Cherry Lake Publishing. (45th Parallel Press).

Lusted, Marcia Amidon. Tasmanian Devil: Savage Island Scavenger. 2016. (Real Monsters Ser.). (ENG., Illus.). 32p. (J). (gr. 3-6). lib. bdg. 32.79 *(978-1-68078-423-7(4)*, 23705, Checkerboard Library) ABDO Publishing Co.

Lynette, Rachel. The Abominable Snowman, 1 vol. 2007. (Monsters Ser.). (ENG., Illus.). 48p. (gr. 4-8). lib. bdg. 36.83 *(978-0-7377-3448-5(5)*, f79d1bfd-1b1a-4575-a178-a6516084c105, KidHaven Publishing) Greenhaven Publishing LLC.

Macdonald, Fiona. The Amazing History of Monsters: Discover Creatures Beyond Your Wildest Imagination in over 300 Exciting Pictures. 2016. (Illus.). 64p. (J). (gr. -1-12). 12.99 *(978-1-86147-744-6(9)*, Armadillo) Anness Publishing GBR. Dist: National Bk. Network.

—Murderous Mythical Creatures, 1 vol. Antram, David, illus. 2010. (Top 10 Worst Ser.). (ENG.). 32p. (J). (gr. 3-5). pap. 11.50 *(978-1-4339-4083-5(3)*, 07b36513-a47e-4d75-a72a-07c04d9ba1c2); lib. bdg. 29.27 *(978-1-4339-4082-8(5)*, 0ec860eb-23db-41a2-8d69-733c682cf51e) Stevens, Gareth Publishing LLLP. (Gareth Stevens Learning Library).

The Making of a Monster: Vampires & Werewolves, 9 vols., Set. Incl. Ancient Werewolves & Vampires: The Roots of the

Teeth. Bennett, Adelaide. (Illus.). pap. 9.95 *(978-1-4222-1955-3(0))*; Dracula & Beyond: Famous Vampires & Werewolves in Literature & Film. Indovino, Shaina Carmel. (Illus.). pap. 9.95 *(978-1-4222-1956-0(9))*; Fighting the Fangs: A Guide to Vampires & Werewolves. Martin, Nicholas. (Illus.). pap. 9.95 *(978-1-4222-1957-7(7))*; Global Legends & Lore: Vampires & Werewolves Around the World. Bennett, Adelaide. pap. 9.95 *(978-1-4222-1963-8(1))*; Howling at the Moon: Vampires & Werewolves in the New World. Etingoff, Kim. (Illus.). pap. 9.95 *(978-1-4222-1958-4(5))*; Pop Monsters: The Modern-Day Craze for Vampires & Werewolves. Sanna, Emily. pap. 9.95 *(978-1-4222-1959-1(3))*; Psychology of Our Dark Side: Humans' Love Affair with Vampires & Werewolves. Stewart, Sheila. (Illus.). pap. 9.95 *(978-1-4222-1960-7(7))*; Science of the Beast: The Facts Behind the Fangs. Etingoff, Kim. (Illus.). pap. 9.95 *(978-1-4222-1961-4(5))*; Transylvania & Beyond: Vampires & Werewolves in Old Europe. Indovino, Shaina Carmel. pap. 9.95 *(978-1-4222-1962-1(3))*; 64p. (YA). (gr. 7-18). 2010. 2011. Set pap. 89.55 *(978-1-4222-1954-6(2))*; Set lib. bdg. 206.55 *(978-1-4222-1801-3(5))* Mason Crest.

March, Julia. Monster Battles. 2016. (DK Reader Level 3 Ser.). lib. bdg. 13.55 *(978-0-606-38228-1(3))* Turtleback.

Marsico, Katie. Undead Monsters: From Mummies to Zombies. 2017. (Monster Mania Ser.). (ENG., Illus.). 32p. (J). (gr. 2-5). 26.65 *(978-1-5124-2594-9(X)*, 9cd855c1-9bdb-43d5-9817-74a96f4b7653); E-Book 39.99 *(978-1-5124-2818-6(3))*; E-Book 4.99 *(978-1-5124-3830-7(8)*, 9781512438307); E-Book 39.99 *(978-1-5124-3831-4(6)*, 9781512438314) Lerner Publishing Group. (Lerner Pubns.).

McNab, Chris. Mythical Monsters: The Scariest Creatures from Legends, Books, & Movies. 2006. (Illus.). 95p. (J). *(978-0-439-85479-5(2))* Scholastic, Inc.

Meachen Rau, Dana. Monsters, 1 vol. 2011. (For Real? Ser.). (ENG.). 24p. (gr. 3-3). 25.50 *(978-0-7614-4863-1(2)*, 7f1fa02e-cc35-4958-9d10-248a73e4fecd) Cavendish Square Publishing LLC.

Miles, Liz. Sea Monsters, 1 vol. 2015. (Danger! Dinosaurs Ser.). (ENG.). 32p. (J). (gr. 4-5). pap. 11.50 *(978-1-4824-3045-5(2)*, bfb57fc8-0806-41b8-b9a9-6436b1cc3dcf) Stevens, Gareth Publishing LLLP.

Mokele-Mbembe. 2010. (ENG., Illus.). 104p. (gr. 5-8). 32.95 *(978-0-7910-9781-6(1)*, P179189, Facts On File) Infobase Holdings, Inc.

Monster Hunting, 8 vols. 2016. (Monster Hunting Ser.). (ENG.). 00088p. (YA). (gr. 8-8). 155.20 *(978-1-4994-6570-9(X)*, 5981f53a-9aba-4f28-9e65-033a255df827, Rosen Young Adult) Rosen Publishing Group, Inc., The.

Monsters! Set 2, 12 vols. 2016. (Monsters! Ser.). 32p. (ENG.). (gr. 1-2). lib. bdg. 169.62 *(978-1-4824-4609-8(X)*, ea5dcea0-dc5f-4019-896e-bc4e61cd4fcd); (gr. 2-1). pap. 63.00 *(978-1-4824-5292-1(8))* Stevens, Gareth Publishing LLLP.

Morey, Allan. 12 Terrifying Monsters. 2017. (Scary & Spooky Ser.). (ENG., Illus.). 32p. (J). (gr. 3-6). 32.80 *(978-1-63235-297-2(4)*, 11781, 12-Story Library) Bookstaves, LLC.

Morpurgo, Michael. Beowulf. Foreman, Michael, illus. 2015. (ENG.). 160p. (J). (gr. 3-7). pap. 8.99 *(978-0-7636-7297-3(1))* Candlewick Pr.

Mortensen, Lori. Sphinx, 1 vol. 2007. (Monsters Ser.). (ENG., Illus.). 48p. (gr. 4-8). lib. bdg. 29.13 *(978-0-7377-3633-5(X)*, 52fc50b0-c8cc-4a2d-90b9-c6abed476701, KidHaven Publishing) Greenhaven Publishing LLC.

Murray, Laura K. Chupacabra. 2017. (Are They Real? Ser.). (ENG., Illus.). 24p. (J). (gr. 1-4). pap. 8.99 *(978-1-62832-370-2(1)*, 20060, Creative Paperbacks); *(978-1-60818-762-1(4)*, 20062, Creative Education) Creative Co., The.

—Loch Ness Monster. 2017. (Are They Real? Ser.). (ENG., Illus.). 24p. (J). (gr. 1-4). pap. 8.99 *(978-1-62832-372-6(8)*, 20066, Creative Paperbacks) Creative Co., The.

My Big Creepy Sticker. 2003. (Illus.). 48p. (J). 5.98 *(978-1-4054-1218-6(6))* Parragon, Inc.

Mysterious Monsters. 2014. (Mysterious Monsters Ser.). 32p. (J). (gr. 3-6). pap. 60.00 *(978-1-4777-7234-8(0))*; (ENG.). (gr. 4-5). 167.58 *(978-1-4777-7094-8(1)*, 95219a17-13c8-47ad-bb6c-9c4b5cae584d) Rosen Publishing Group, Inc., The. (PowerKids Pr.).

Namm, Diane. Monsters! Chambliss, Maxie, illus. 2003. (My First Reader Ser.). (ENG.). 32p. (J). 18.50 *(978-0-516-22933-1(8)*, Children's Pr.) Scholastic Library Publishing.

Nardo, Don. Martians, 1 vol. 2007. (Monsters Ser.). (ENG., Illus.). 48p. (gr. 4-8). lib. bdg. 36.83 *(978-0-7377-3639-7(9)*, ab7ffb1b-0b7b-4fef-aa7d-9eec07ff14e6, KidHaven Publishing) Greenhaven Publishing LLC.

Nichols, Catherine. True Books: Periodic Table. 2005. (True Tales Ser.). (ENG., Illus.). 48p. (J). (gr. 2-4). lib. bdg. 22.50 *(978-0-516-25182-0(1)*, Children's Pr.) Scholastic Library Publishing.

O'Hearn, Michael. Monster Wars. Moffet, Patricia et al, illus. 2011. (Monster Wars Ser.). (ENG.). 32p. (gr. 3-4). pap. 190.80 *(978-1-4296-7270-2(6)*, Capstone Pr.) Capstone.

—Sea Monsters vs. Dragons: Showdown of the Legends. Altmann, Scott, illus. 2011. (Monster Wars Ser.). (ENG.). 32p. (gr. 3-4). pap. 47.70 *(978-1-4296-7264-1(1)*, Capstone Pr.) Capstone.

Olson, Elsie. Make a Mini Monster Your Way! 2018. (Super Simple DIY Ser.). (ENG., Illus.). 32p. (J). (gr. k-4). lib. bdg. 34.21 *(978-1-5321-1717-6(5)*, 30722, Super SandCastle) ABDO Publishing Co.

Omoth, Tyler. Handbook to Bigfoot, Nessie, & Other Unexplained Creatures. 2016. (Paranormal Handbooks Ser.). (ENG., Illus.). 32p. (J). (gr. 3-9). lib. bdg. 28.65 *(978-1-5157-1311-1(3)*, 132358, Capstone Pr.) Capstone.

Onn, Aidan. A - Z of Monsters & Magical Beings. Hodgson, Rob, illus. 2017. (Magma for Laurence King Ser.). (ENG.). 56p. (J). (gr. 1-4). 17.99 *(978-1-78627-067-2(6)*, King, Laurence Publishing) Orion Publishing Group, Ltd. GBR. Dist: Hachette Bk. Group.

Owen, Ruth. Becoming a Zombie. 2018. (Zombie Zone Ser.). (ENG.). 24p. (J). (gr. 2-7). lib. bdg. 26.99 *(978-1-68402-441-4(2))*; E-Book 18.95 *(978-1-68402-499-5(4))* Bearport Publishing Co., Inc.

—Half-Human Monsters & Other Fiends. 2013. (Not near Normal: the Paranormal Ser.). 32p. (J). (gr. 3-8). lib. bdg. 28.50 *(978-1-61772-725-2(3))* Bearport Publishing Co., Inc.

Peabody, Erin. Bigfoot. Rivas, Victor, illus. 2017. (Behind the Legend Ser.: 2). (ENG.). 128p. (J). (gr. 2-5). pap. 9.99 *(978-1-4998-0425-6(3))* Little Bee Books Inc.

—The Loch Ness Monster. Rivas, Victor, illus. 2017. (Behind the Legend Ser.: 1). (ENG.). 128p. (J). (gr. 2-5). pap. 9.99 *(978-1-4998-0423-2(7))* Little Bee Books Inc.

Pearce, Q. L. Mothman, 1 vol. 2010. (Mysterious Encounters Ser.). (ENG., Illus.). 48p. (gr. 4-8). 35.23 *(978-0-7377-5037-9(5)*, 4132dd4a-dc6f-455b-bac4-3aa400890b5a, KidHaven Publishing) Greenhaven Publishing LLC.

Pearson, Marie. Frankenstein's Monster. 2019. (Monster Histories Ser.). (ENG., Illus.). 32p. (J). (gr. 4-6). pap. 7.95 *(978-1-5435-7499-9(8)*, 141029); lib. bdg. 30.65 *(978-1-5435-7122-6(0)*, 140404) Capstone.

—Loch Ness Monster. 2019. (Monster Histories Ser.). (ENG., Illus.). 32p. (J). (gr. 4-6). pap. 7.95 *(978-1-5435-7500-2(5)*, 141030); lib. bdg. 30.65 *(978-1-5435-7123-3(9)*, 140405) Capstone.

Peterson, Megan Cooley. Super Scary Monsters. 2016. (Super Scary Stuff Ser.). (ENG., Illus.). 24p. (J). (gr. 3-5). lib. bdg. 27.99 *(978-1-5157-0277-1(4)*, 131922, Capstone Pr.) Capstone.

Pipe, Jim. Monsters, 1 vol. 2013. (Twilight Realm Ser.). (ENG., Illus.). 32p. (J). (gr. 4-5). 29.27 *(978-1-4339-8755-7(4)*, 63cffb07-9a29-4960-ad54-424d1a2a7065); pap. 11.50 *(978-1-4339-8756-4(2)*, 1f8083c4-226a-4d6b-bda6-b38095528d48) Stevens, Gareth Publishing LLLP. (Gareth Stevens Learning Library).

Raum, Elizabeth. Gila Monsters. 2014. (Lizards Ser.). (ENG., Illus.). 32p. (J). (gr. 2-5). lib. bdg. 28.50 *(978-1-60753-486-0(X)*, 15989) Amicus.

Redmond, Shirley Raye. Bunyips, 1 vol. 2011. (Monsters Ser.). (ENG., Illus.). 48p. (gr. 4-8). lib. bdg. 36.83 *(978-0-7377-5919-8(4)*, 1c6aa751-d5db-4ccd-b994-c96220533bf5, KidHaven Publishing) Greenhaven Publishing LLC.

—Golem, 1 vol. 2011. (Monsters Ser.). (ENG., Illus.). 48p. (gr. 4-8). lib. bdg. 36.83 *(978-0-7377-5866-5(X)*, dc381994-d1b2-4c4f-93bb-2f3309cceda5, KidHaven Publishing) Greenhaven Publishing LLC.

—The Jersey Devil, 1 vol. 2009. (Monsters Ser.). (ENG., Illus.). 48p. (gr. 4-8). lib. bdg. 36.83 *(978-0-7377-4407-1(3)*, 1e251748-232c-4978-89d1-26ed7371251b, KidHaven Publishing) Greenhaven Publishing LLC.

Reid, Dee. Monster Max's BIG Breakfast: Have Fun with Numbers. 2018. (Busy Monsters Ser.). (ENG., Illus.). 24p. (J). (gr. k-2). 8.99 *(978-1-78856-068-9(X)*, 18891b3c-bd4a-40c8-ae43-4fda28072f5b) Ruby Tuesday Books Limited GBR. Dist: Lerner Publishing Group.

—Monster Megan's BIG Clean Up: Have Fun with Shapes. 2018. (Busy Monsters Ser.). (ENG., Illus.). 24p. (J). (gr. k-2). 8.99 *(978-1-78856-069-6(8)*, eb5f6fb9-82b5-4862-a5f0-fda14c0d30bb) Ruby Tuesday Books Limited GBR. Dist: Lerner Publishing Group.

—Monster Molly's BIG Day Out: Have Fun with Opposites. 2018. (Busy Monsters Ser.). (ENG., Illus.). 24p. (J). (gr. k-2). 8.99 *(978-1-78856-071-9(X)*, c2bd3966-d45f-43e1-b14f-4affe61aa2e4) Ruby Tuesday Books Limited GBR. Dist: Lerner Publishing Group.

—Monster Mo's BIG Party: Have Fun with Colors. 2018. (Busy Monsters Ser.). (ENG., Illus.). 24p. (J). (gr. k-2). 8.99 *(978-1-78856-070-2(1)*, 9eb16fcc-cfda-4f6c-b181-83894efa5dc0) Ruby Tuesday Books Limited GBR. Dist: Lerner Publishing Group.

Riggs, Kate. Magical Creatures. 2013. (Happily Ever After Ser.). (ENG., Illus.). 24p. (J). (gr. 1-4). 25.65 *(978-1-60818-242-8(8)*, 21780, Creative Education) Creative Co., The.

Rivkin, Jennifer. Searching for el Chupacabra, 1 vol. 2014. (Mysterious Monsters Ser.). (ENG., Illus.). 32p. (J). (gr. 4-5). 27.93 *(978-1-4777-7113-6(1)*, 6180c2e7-ad1a-4e63-a97d-707ffe868685, PowerKids Pr.) Rosen Publishing Group, Inc., The.

—Searching for the Wendigo, 1 vol. 2014. (Mysterious Monsters Ser.). (ENG., Illus.). 32p. (J). (gr. 4-5). lib. bdg. 27.93 *(978-1-4777-7117-4(4)*, ce536101-0d38-4ab2-9c01-40364249206a, PowerKids Pr.) Rosen Publishing Group, Inc., The.

Roberts, Steven. Chupacabras!, 1 vol. 2012. (Jr. Graphic Monster Stories Ser.). (ENG., Illus.). 24p. (J). (gr. 2-3). 28.93 *(978-1-4488-7902-1(7)*, 6788bfdf-673f-4c9f-b476-87761a862eeb); pap. 11.60 *(978-1-4488-8002-7(5)*, 4c69fe4e-2cbf-415b-95d2-7896217c1608) Rosen Publishing Group, Inc., The. (PowerKids Pr.).

Ross, Dave. The Not-so-Scary Monster Handbook: Halloween. Ross, Dave, illus. 2003. (Illus.). (J). 135.44 *(978-0-06-055492-7(4))* HarperCollins Pubs.

Rowe, Brooke. What Monster Are You Most Like? 2016. (Best Quiz Ever Ser.). (ENG., Illus.). 32p. (J). (gr. 4-8). 32.07 *(978-1-63470-511-0(4)*, 207775) Cherry Lake Publishing.

Russ, John Paul. The Monster Hunters' Survival Guide. Brusha, Joe, ed. 2011. (ENG., Illus.). 176p. (YA). pap. 12.99 *(978-0-9827507-8-0(1)*, 4b762811-f1f4-40c9-9c0d-a9ed2a8ceb4f) Zenescope Entertainment.

Sabelko, Rebecca. Gila Monsters. 2018. (North American Animals Ser.). (ENG., Illus.). 24p. (J). (gr. k-3). lib. bdg. 26.95 *(978-1-62617-797-0(X)*, Blastoff! Readers) Bellwether Media.

Satyr. 2008. (Monsters Ser.). (Illus.). 48p. (gr. 4-8). 26.20 *(978-0-7377-4083-7(3)*, Kidhaven) Cengage Gale.

Sautter, A. J. Discover Dragons, Giants, & Other Deadly Fantasy Monsters. 2017. (All about Fantasy Creatures Ser.). (ENG., Illus.). 32p. (J). (gr. 3-9). lib. bdg. 27.32 *(978-1-5157-6839-5(2)*, 135366, Capstone Pr.) Capstone.

—Discover Orcs, Boggarts, & Other Nasty Fantasy Creatures. 2017. (All about Fantasy Creatures Ser.). (ENG., Illus.). 32p. (J). (gr. 3-9). lib. bdg. 27.32 *(978-1-5157-6837-1(6)*, 135364, Capstone Pr.) Capstone.

—A Field Guide to Dragons, Trolls, & Other Dangerous Monsters, 1 vol. Ashcroft, Colin et al, illus. 2014. (Fantasy Field Guides). (ENG.). 32p. (J). (gr. 3-9). lib. bdg. 28.65 *(978-1-4914-0691-5(7)*, 125960, Capstone Pr.) Capstone.

—A Field Guide to Goblins, Gremlins, & Other Wicked Creatures, 1 vol. Ashcroft, Colin et al, illus. 2014. (Fantasy Field Guides). (ENG.). 32p. (J). (gr. 3-9). lib. bdg. 28.65 *(978-1-4914-0689-2(5)*, 125958, Capstone Pr.) Capstone.

Savery, Annabel. Monsters. 2012. (It's Amazing Ser.). (Illus.). 32p. (gr. 3-6). lib. bdg. 31.35 *(978-1-59920-689-9(7))* Black Rabbit Bks.

Schulte, Mary. The Dover Demon, 1 vol. 2009. (Mysterious Encounters Ser.). (ENG., Illus.). 48p. (gr. 4-8). 35.23 *(978-0-7377-4570-2(3)*, 662c62b6-291d-489d-861b-7a8c091f651f, KidHaven Publishing) Greenhaven Publishing LLC.

—Sirens, 1 vol. 2007. (Monsters Ser.). (ENG., Illus.). 48p. (gr. 4-8). lib. bdg. 36.83 *(978-0-7377-3451-5(5)*, 2ebb0ad2-c20e-4c61-b2f9-94bd74870459, KidHaven Publishing) Greenhaven Publishing LLC.

Scrace, Carolyn. Drawing Monsters. 2016. (Art Works). 32p. (gr. 2-6). 31.35 *(978-1-62588-346-9(3)*, Smart Apple Media) Black Rabbit Bks.

Sertori, J. M. Monsters, 1 vol. 2005. (Unexplained Ser.). (ENG., Illus.). 36p. (gr. 4-6). lib. bdg. 28.67 *(978-0-8368-6266-9(X)*, 524b105b-3b61-4163-805c-6ccddcc7b427, Gareth Stevens Learning Library) Stevens, Gareth Publishing LLLP.

Shea, Therese M. Real-Life Monsters?, 1 vol. 2014. (History's Mysteries Ser.). (ENG., Illus.). 32p. (J). (gr. 4-5). pap. 11.50 *(978-1-4824-2094-4(5)*, 6140d2ef-75c3-4048-9e13-d758fb5d8e0c) Stevens, Gareth Publishing LLLP.

—Was Dr. Frankenstein Real?, 1 vol. 2017. (I Want to Know Ser.). (ENG.). 32p. (gr. 3-3). 26.93 *(978-0-7660-9198-6(8)*, 8a16cf5f-8585-48e4-92f3-5bdd17598621) Enslow Publishing, LLC.

Stowell, Louie. The Usborne Big Book of Big Monsters. Fiorin, Fabiano, illus. 2013. (Usborne Big Book Of... Ser.). (ENG.). 16p. (J). (gr. -1-3). 14.99 *(978-0-7945-3025-9(7)*, Usborne) EDC Publishing.

Sullivan, Kyle. Monster ABC. Sullivan, Derek, illus. 2018. (Hazy Dell Press Monster Ser.). 30p. (J). (gr. k-1). bds. 13.95 *(978-0-9965787-0-7(6))* Hazy Dell Pr.

Summers, Portia & Meachen Rau, Dana. Are Monsters Real?, 1 vol. 2016. (I Want to Know Ser.). (ENG., Illus.). 32p. (gr. 3-3). pap. 11.52 *(978-0-7660-8244-1(X)*, 471e5aac-972d-4c53-a4d1-278e6813860f) Enslow Publishing, LLC.

Tallarico, Tony, Sr. & Drawing Staff. Drawing & Cartooning Monsters: A Step-by-Step Guide for the Aspiring Monster-Maker. 2010. (Dover How to Draw Ser.). (ENG., Illus.). 96p. (J). (gr. 3-6). pap. 6.99 *(978-0-486-47278-2(7)*, 472787) Dover Pubns., Inc.

Taylor, Trace. Wheels. Taylor, Trace, illus. 2009. (1-3Y Getting Around Ser.). (ENG., Illus.). 16p. (J). pap. 8.00 *(978-1-61406-201-1(3))* American Reading Co.

Tobler, Elise. Gila Monsters Have a Deadly Bite!, 1 vol. 2020. (Reptiles Rock! Ser.). (ENG.). 32p. (gr. 2-3). pap. 11.53 *(978-1-9785-1820-9(X)*, 0aa7d983-48a4-44a2-bd3e-da4bea08929c) Enslow Publishing, LLC.

Top That Publishing, ed. Mixed up Monsters. 2007. 144p. pap. *(978-1-84666-405-2(5))* Top That! Publishing PLC.

Top That Publishing Staff, ed. Funny Monsters. 2005. 12p. *(978-1-84510-734-5(9))* Top That! Publishing PLC.

Townsend, John. Strange Creatures. 2010. (Amazing Mysteries Ser.). (Illus.). 32p. (J). (gr. 3-6). 28.50 *(978-1-59920-365-2(0)*, 1299767) Black Rabbit Bks.

Trantham, Cary. The Monster of Lake Champlain. 2012. 24p. pap. 17.99 *(978-1-4772-4907-9(9))* AuthorHouse.

Troupe, Thomas Kingsley. Extreme Monster Stories. (J). 2019. pap. *(978-1-68072-765-4(6))* 2018. (ENG.). 24p. (gr. 4-6). pap. 8.99 *(978-1-64466-318-9(X)*, 12567, Hi Jinx) 2018. (ENG.). 24p. (gr. 4-6). lib. bdg. 28.50 *(978-1-68072-635-0(8)*, 12566, Hi Jinx) Black Rabbit Bks.

Turner, Tracy. Beasts & Monsters. 2015. (Head-To-Head Ser.). (ENG., Illus.). 24p. (gr. 3-8). 28.50 *(978-1-62588-153-3(3))* Black Rabbit Bks.

Tyler, Madeline. Monster Counting. Li, Amy, illus. 2020. (Monster Math Ser.). (ENG.). 24p. (J). (gr. -1-2). pap. 7.99 *(978-1-5415-8920-9(3)*, b7722f5f-7e1a-48d8-8600-85b209380dba); lib. bdg. 26.65 *(978-1-5415-7927-9(5)*, fa2580e1-e23d-413c-82bd-a48a432d9c18) Lerner Publishing Group. (Lerner Pubns.).

—Monster Measuring. Li, Amy, illus. 2020. (Monster Math Ser.). (ENG.). 24p. (J). (gr. -1-2). pap. 7.99 *(978-1-5415-8923-0(8)*, 655d2ae9-4511-4d95-b501-eea15db059b2); lib. bdg. 26.65 *(978-1-5415-7928-6(3)*, 6e802131-4862-4a9d-8447-55831373f066) Lerner Publishing Group. (Lerner Pubns.).

—Monster Patterns. Li, Amy, illus. 2020. (Monster Math Ser.). (ENG.). 24p. (J). (gr. -1-2). pap. 7.99 *(978-1-5415-8921-6(1)*, 23c9a3ae-08b6-46a4-b87a-3bbc8b8a2062); lib. bdg. 26.65 *(978-1-5415-7929-3(1)*, 83c9bb97-b340-449a-9d97-abbebb659144) Lerner Publishing Group. (Lerner Pubns.).

—Monster Shapes. Li, Amy, illus. 2020. (Monster Math Ser.). (ENG.). 24p. (J). (gr. -1-2). pap. 7.99 *(978-1-5415-8922-3(X)*, 55b1a377-1fa8-48eb-9ddb-23b493d06833); lib. bdg. 26.65 *(978-1-5415-7930-9(5)*, 3093a34c-8570-404b-bd7c-ec814354854e) Lerner Publishing Group. (Lerner Pubns.).

Vallejo-Nagera, Alejandra. Los Cazadores de Monstruos. Guerrero, Andres, illus.Tr. of Monsters Hunters. (SPA.). 31p. (J). (gr. k-1). 8.95 *(978-1-58986-549-5(9))* Santillana USA Publishing Co., Inc.

Watt, Fiona. Monster Doodles. 2010. (Doodle Cards Ser.). 50p. (J). 9.99 *(978-0-7945-2550-7(4)*, Usborne) EDC Publishing.

—Spooky Things to Make & Do. 2012. (Activity Bks). 34p. (J). pap. 6.99 *(978-0-7945-1863-9(X)*, Usborne) EDC Publishing.

Weakland, Mark & Collins, Terry. Scooby-Doo! Unmasks Monsters: The Truth Behind Zombies, Werewolves, & Other Spooky Creatures. Cornia, Christian et al, illus. 2015. (ENG.). 144p. (J). (gr. k-2). pap., pap., pap. 9.95 *(978-1-62370-216-8(X)*, 127283) Capstone.

Weakland, Mark Andrew & Collins, Terry Lee. The Truth Behind Mummies. 2016. (ENG., Illus.). 24p. (J). pap. *(978-1-4062-8897-1(7))* Capstone.

—Truth Behind Vampires. 2016. (ENG., Illus.). 24p. (J). pap. *(978-1-4062-8895-7(0))* Capstone.

—Truth Behind Werewolves. 2016. (ENG., Illus.). 24p. (J). pap. *(978-1-4062-8896-4(9))* Capstone.

West, David & Ganeri, Anita. Giants & Ogres, 1 vol. West, David & Ganeri, Anita, illus. 2010. (Dark Side Ser.). (ENG., Illus.). 32p. (J). (gr. 4-5). pap. 11.50 *(978-1-4488-1568-5(1)*, 1313997); lib. bdg. 30.27 *(978-1-61531-898-8(4)*, 1313997) Rosen Publishing Group, Inc., The. (PowerKids Pr.).

Whatmore, Candace. Monsters Coloring Book. 2012. (Coloring Bks). 32p. (J). pap. 5.99 *(978-0-7945-3195-9(4)*, Usborne) EDC Publishing.

Whelon, Chuck. Alien Invasion! Stickers. 2010. (Dover Little Activity Books Stickers Ser.). (ENG., Illus.). 4p. (J). (gr. k-3). 2.50 *(978-0-486-47234-8(5)*, 472345) Dover Pubns., Inc.

—Create Your Own Monsters Sticker Activity Book. 2010. (Dover Little Activity Books Stickers Ser.). (ENG., Illus.). 4p. (J). (gr. 1-4). 2.50 *(978-0-486-47515-8(8)*, 475158) Dover Pubns., Inc.

Whitmore, Andrew. How to Build a Monster. 2007. 96p. (J). *(978-1-4207-0727-4(2))* Sundance/Newbridge Educational Publishing.

World Book, Inc. Staff, contrib. by. Monsters All Around: A Supplement to Childcraft — The How & Why Library. 2018. (Illus.). 160p. (J). *(978-0-7166-0636-9(4))* World Bk., Inc.

Wright, Shannon. Dinosaurs & Monsters Coloring Book. 2013. (ENG.). 38p. 13.00 *(978-1-62884-683-6(6)*, Baby Professor (Education Kids)) Speedy Publishing LLC.

Wyborny, Sheila. The Headless Horseman, 1 vol. 2009. (Monsters Ser.). (ENG., Illus.). 48p. (gr. 4-8). lib. bdg. 35.08 *(978-0-7377-4583-2(5)*, 44cd1672-e70d-4d95-b0c4-04b8b5771dc9, KidHaven Publishing) Greenhaven Publishing LLC.

Young, Judy. The Hidden Bestiary of Marvelous, Mysterious, & (Maybe Even) Magical Creatures. Filippucci, Laura Francesca, illus. 2009. (ENG.). 32p. (J). (gr. 1-4). 16.95 *(978-1-58536-433-6(9)*, 202163) Sleeping Bear Pr.

Zenko, Darren. Field Guide to Monsters, 1 vol. 2009. (ENG.). 208p. (J). pap. 14.95 *(978-1-896124-38-4(0)*, 1c1eb4eb-2481-4152-9fc0-da7fe629a799) Dragon Hill Publishing CAN. Dist: Lone Pine Publishing USA.

MONSTERS—FICTION

Abbott, Tony. In the Ice Caves of Krog. Adams, Gil & Jessell, Tim, illus. 2003. (Secrets of Droon Ser.: No. 20). 114p. (J). (gr. 2-5). 12.65 *(978-0-7569-3940-3(2))* Perfection Learning Corp.

ABDO Publishing Company Staff. Story Time for Little Monsters, 4 vols. 2014. (Story Time for Little Monsters Ser.: 4). (ENG.). 24p. (J). (gr. -1-4). lib. bdg. 125.44 *(978-1-62402-019-3(4)*, 624, Looking Glass Library) Magic Wagon.

Accord Publishing Staff. Trucks: A Mini Animotion Book. 2013. (ENG.). 12p. (J). bds. 5.99 *(978-1-4494-3558-5(0))* Andrews McMeel Publishing.

Adams, Leonard. Two Girls & Two Monsters. 2008. (ENG.). 48p. pap. 7.95 *(978-0-557-01456-9(5))* Lulu Pr., Inc.

Al Mehairi, Maitha. Sally Ride's Adventure: The Dangerous Sea Monster Zelurius. 2013. 24p. pap. 20.21 *(978-1-4669-3538-9(3))* Trafford Publishing.

Albee, Sarah & Stone, Jon. Sesame Street Little Golden Book Library 5-Book Boxed Set: My Name Is Elmo; Elmo Loves You; Elmo's Tricky Tongue Twisters; the Monster on the Bus; the Monster at the End of This Book, 5 vols. Smollin, Michael & Swanson, Maggie, illus. 2017. (Little Golden Book Ser.). (ENG.). 120p. (J). (-k). 24.95 *(978-1-5247-2077-3(1)*, Golden Bks.) Random Hse. Children's Bks.

Alexander, Maria. Snowed. 2016. (ENG., Illus.). 211p. (YA). pap. 14.95 *(978-1-935738-89-3(5))*; (gr. 7-12). 29.95 *(978-1-935738-91-6(7))* Raw Dog Screaming Pr.

Alfau, Georgette. Alfred & Alex & the Toy Eating Monster. 2009. 16p. 18.95 *(978-0-557-15276-6(3))* Lulu Pr., Inc.

Anaya, Rudolfo. ChupaCabra & the Roswell UFO. 2008. (ENG.). 144p. (YA). (gr. 9-18). 9.95 *(978-0-8263-4469-4(0)*, P154251) Univ. of New Mexico Pr.

—Curse of the ChupaCabra. 2013. (ENG.). 176p. (YA). pap. 19.95 *(978-0-8263-4115-0(2)*, P225261) Univ. of New Mexico Pr.

Anderson, Al. Adventures with Bingo Borden. Agora Publications Staff, tr. Kurzyca, Krystyna Emilia, illus. 2010. 77p. (J). pap. 9.50 *(978-1-887250-46-7(8))* Agora Pubns., Inc.

Anderson, Shel. Spoofaloof's Adventures: Rainy Day Fun. Anderson, Shauna, illus. 2008. 52p. pap. 22.50 *(978-1-4389-1689-7(2))* AuthorHouse.

Andreae, Giles. Morris the Mankiest Monster. McIntyre, Sarah, illus. 2011. 32p. (J). (gr. -1-k). pap. 14.95 *(978-0-552-55935-5(0))* Transworld Publishers Ltd. GBR. Dist: Independent Pubs. Group.

Anthony, David & David, Charles. Heroes A2Z #2: (Heroes a to Z): Bowling over Halloween: Bowling over Halloween. Blakeslee, Lys, illus. 2007. (Heroes A2Z Ser.). 128p. (J). pap. 4.99 *(978-0-9728461-9-6(0))* Sigil Publishing.

Arabadjis, Heather. Monster Mas. 2013. 34p. pap. 11.95 *(978-1-4575-2493-6(7))* Dog Ear Publishing, LLC.

Armenteros, Sarah. Emma & the Mashed Potato Monster. 2009. (ENG., Illus.). 44p. (J). 18.99 *(978-1-59092-384-9(7))* Blue Forge Pr.

Armstrong-Ellis, Carey F. I Love You More Than Moldy Ham. 2015. (ENG., Illus.). 32p. (J). (gr. -1-3). 14.95 *(978-1-4197-1646-1(8)*, 1102101, Abrams Bks. for Young Readers) Abrams, Inc.

Armstrong, K. L. & Marr, Melissa. Loki's Wolves. 2014. (Blackwell Pages Ser.: 1). (ENG.). 374p. (J). (gr. 3-7). pap. 8.99 *(978-0-316-20497-2(8))* Little, Brown Bks. for Young Readers.

Arnold, Tedd. Fly Guy & the Frankenfly. 2013. (Fly Guy Ser.: 13). lib. bdg. 17.20 *(978-0-606-32440-3(2))* Turtleback.

—Fly Guy & the Frankenfly (Fly Guy #13) Arnold, Tedd, illus. 2013. (Fly Guy Ser.: 13). (ENG., Illus.). 32p. (J). (gr. -1-3). 6.99 *(978-0-545-49328-4(5)*, Cartwheel Bks.) Scholastic, Inc.

M
N
O

Atteberry, Kevan. Bunnies!!! 2015. (ENG., Illus.). 32p. (J). (gr. -1-3). 12.99 (978-0-06-230783-5(5), HarperCollins) HarperCollins Pubs.

—I Love You More Than the Smell of Swamp Gas. Atteberry, Kevan, illus. 2017. (ENG., Illus.). 40p. (J). (gr. -1-3). 17.99 (978-0-06-240871-6(2), HarperCollins) HarperCollins Pubs.

Auerbach, Annie. Scooby-Doo in the Coolsville Contraption Contest, 1 vol. 2015. (Scooby-Doo! Ser.). (ENG., Illus.). 32p. (J). (gr. k-4). lib. bdg. 31.36 (978-1-61479-409-7(X), 19448, Picture Bk.) Spotlight.

Austin, Mike. Monsters Love Colors. Austin, Mike, illus. 2013. (ENG., Illus.). 40p. (J). (gr. -1-3). 19.99 (978-0-06-212594-1(X), HarperCollins) HarperCollins Pubs.

Avila, Kat. Hanako Loves Monsters. 2008. 32p. 14.98 (978-1-4357-0188-5(7)) Lulu Pr., Inc.

AZ Books Staff. Terribly Funny Monsters. Shumovich, Nadezhda, ed. 2012. (Terribly Funny Monsters Ser.). (ENG.). 10p. (J). (gr. -1-1). bds. 15.95 (978-1-61889-133-4(2)) AZ Bks. LLC.

AZ Books Staff & Evans, Olivia. Haunted Castle. Shumovich, Nadezhda, ed. 2012. (Terribly Funny Monsters Ser.). (ENG., Illus.). 10p. (J). bds. 15.95 (978-1-61889-134-1(0)) AZ Bks. LLC.

Babbitt, Natalie. El Cerro del Abismo. 2003.Tr. of Knee-Knock Rise. (SPA., Illus.). 128p. (J). (gr. 3-5). (978-84-236-3420-0(5), ED0964) Edebé ESP. Dist: Lectorum Pubns., Inc.

Bader, Bonnie. 100 Monsters in My School. Hendrix, Bryan, illus. 2003. (All Aboard Math Reader Ser.). 48p. (gr. -1-3). 14.00 (978-0-7569-1648-0(8)) Perfection Learning Corp.

Baghdasaryan, Rouzanna. The Dark. Morchiladze, Manana, illus. 2007. 32p. (J). (POL & ENG.). pap. 12.95 (978-1-60195-096-3(9)); (ARA & ENG.). pap. 12.95 (978-1-60195-086-4(1)) International Step by Step Assn.

Bailey City Monsters. 2005. (J). (978-1-59564-798-6(8)) Steps To Literacy, LLC.

Balian, Lorna. The Aminal, 1 vol. Balian, Lorna & Balian, Lecia, illus. 2005. (ENG.). 48p. (J). 17.95 (978-1-59572-006-1(5)) Star Bright Bks., Inc.

—Leprechauns Never Lie, 1 vol. Balian, Lorna, illus. 2004. (ENG., Illus.). 32p. (J). 16.99 (978-1-932065-37-4(7)) Star Bright Bks., Inc.

Ballarini, Joe. A Babysitter's Guide to Monster Hunting #1. To, Vivienne, illus. (Babysitter's Guide to Monsters Ser.: 1). (ENG.). 352p. (J). (gr. 3-7). 2019. pap. 9.99 (978-0-06-243784-6(4)) 2017. 13.99 (978-0-06-243783-9(6)) HarperCollins Pubs. (Tegen, Katherine Bks).

—A Babysitter's Guide to Monster Hunting #2: Beasts & Geeks. To, Vivienne, illus. 2018. (Babysitter's Guide to Monsters Ser.: 2). (ENG.). 320p. (J). (gr. 3-7). 13.99 (978-0-06-243787-7(9), Tegen, Katherine Bks) HarperCollins Pubs.

—A Babysitter's Guide to Monster Hunting #3: Mission to Monster Island. 2019. (Babysitter's Guide to Monsters Ser.: 3). (ENG., Illus.). 320p. (J). (gr. 3-7). 13.99 (978-0-06-243790-7(9), Tegen, Katherine Bks) HarperCollins Pubs.

Balmer, Fred. Festus & the Monster. Newcomb, Kristene, illus. 2004. 27p. (J). per. 6.95 (978-0-9760790-2-6(X)) Folsom Fallies Pr.

Balsley, Tilda & Fischer, Ellen. Shalom Everybodeee! Grover's Adventures in Israel. Leigh, Tom, illus. 2016. (ENG.). 24p. (J). (gr. -1-2). 16.99 (978-0-7613-7558-6(9), 85965fa2-0b9e-4ecb-be71-ebb705e8225a, Kar-Ben Publishing) Lerner Publishing Group.

Bardugo, Leigh. Ruin & Rising. 2014. (Shadow & Bone Trilogy Ser.: 3). (ENG., Illus.). 432p. (YA). (gr. 7-12). 19.99 (978-0-8050-9461-9(X), 900078589, Holt, Henry & Co. Bks. For Young Readers) Holt, Henry & Co.

—Shadow & Bone. 2012. (Shadow & Bone Trilogy Ser.: 1). (ENG.). 368p. (YA). (gr. 7-12). 19.99 (978-0-8050-9459-6(8), 900078585, Holt, Henry & Co. Bks. For Young Readers) Holt, Henry & Co.

—Shadow & Bone. 2013. (Shadow & Bone Trilogy Ser.: 1). (ENG.). 416p. (YA). (gr. 7-12). pap. 10.99 (978-1-250-02743-6(8), 900098315) Square Fish.

—Shadow & Bone. 2013. (Grisha Trilogy Ser.: 1). (YA). lib. bdg. 22.10 (978-0-606-31903-4(4)) Turtleback.

—Siege & Storm. 2013. (Shadow & Bone Trilogy Ser.: 2). (ENG., Illus.). 448p. (YA). (gr. 7). 19.99 (978-0-8050-9460-2(1), 900078587, Holt, Henry & Co. Bks. For Young Readers) Holt, Henry & Co.

—Siege & Storm. 2014. (Shadow & Bone Trilogy Ser.: 2). (ENG.). 496p. (YA). (gr. 7). pap. 10.99 (978-1-250-04443-3(X), 900128342) Square Fish.

Bargiel, Nina G. & Amsterdam, Shane. Fintastic Friends Forever. 2016. (Illus.). 32p. (J). (978-1-5182-1661-9(7)) Little Brown & Co.

Barnard, Sarah. The Map & the Stone. 2nd ed. 2010. (Illus.). 142p. pap. 16.95 (978-0-9556887-2-0(8)) Ethics Trading GBR. Dist: Lulu Pr., Inc.

Barnett, Susanne. Pink & the Mystery of the Stable Room Monster. 2012. 34p. pap. 19.99 (978-1-4772-0921-9(2)) AuthorHouse.

Bass, Guy. Dinkin Dings & the Double from Dimension 9. Williamson, Pete, illus. 2011. (Dinkin Dings Ser.). (ENG.). 128p. (J). (gr. 3-6). 17.44 (978-0-448-45434-4(3)) Penguin Young Readers Group.

—The Pirate's Eye, 1 vol. Williamson, Pete, illus. 2013. (Stitch Head Ser.). (ENG.). 208p. (J). (gr. 3-6). 10.95 (978-1-62370-008-9(6), 123265, Capstone Young Readers) Capstone.

Bataille Lange, Nikki. Extreme Monsters Joke Book. Stuby, Tim, illus. gif. ed. 2005. 95p. (J). (gr. 2-5). per. 3.99 (978-1-57791-181-4(4)) Brighter Minds Children's Publishing.

Batchelor, Love. Mean Mo & the Christmas Star. 2013. (ENG., Illus.). (J). (gr. -1-3). pap. 9.95 (978-1-62086-461-6(4)) Amplify Publishing Group.

Baumgarten, Josephine & Baumgarten, Michael. My Baby Monsters & I went to the Park. 2005. 32p. pap. 14.99 (978-1-4116-6348-0(9)) Lulu Pr., Inc.

Bayham, Dalan J. The Loch Ness Monster Incident - Junior Explorers Society Episode 2. 2007. 160p. pap. 12.95 (978-1-4303-2291-7(8)) Lulu Pr., Inc.

Beacham, Travis. Pacific Rim: Tales from Year Zero. 2013. (ENG., Illus.). 128p. (gr. 8-17). 24.99 (978-0-7851-5394-8(2)) Legendary Comics.

Beakman, Onk. Lightning Rod Faces the Cyclops Queen. Geremia, Daniela, illus. 2014. 155p. (J). (978-1-4242-6276-2(3), Grosset & Dunlap) Penguin Publishing Group.

—The Mask of Power, 1. Santanach, Tino, illus. 2013. (Skylanders Universe: Mask of Power Ser.). (ENG.). 160p. (J). (gr. 4-6). 18.69 (978-0-448-46355-1(5)) Penguin Young Readers Group.

Beaty, Andrea. Hush, Baby Ghostling. Lemaitre, Pascal, illus. 2009. (ENG.). 32p. (J). (gr. -1-3). 14.99 (978-1-4169-2545-3(7), McElderry, Margaret K. Bks.) McElderry, Margaret K. Bks.

Beck, Scott. Monster Sleepover! 2009. (ENG., Illus.). 32p. (J). (gr. k-2). 15.95 (978-0-8109-4059-8(0), 601001, Abrams Bks. for Young Readers) Abrams, Inc.

Bee, William. Worst in Show. Hindley, Kate, illus. 2015. (ENG.). 40p. (J). (gr. -1-2). 15.99 (978-0-7636-7318-5(8)) Candlewick Pr.

Bell, Braden. Penumbras. 2013. (Middle School Magic Ser.). (ENG.). 305p. (J). (gr. 3-7). 14.99 (978-1-4621-1220-3(X), Sweetwater Bks.) Cedar Fort, Inc./CFI Distribution.

Bellin, Joshua David. Scavenger of Souls. 2016. (ENG., Illus.). 368p. (YA). (gr. 9). 18.99 (978-1-4814-6244-0(X), McElderry, Margaret K. Bks.) McElderry, Margaret K. Bks.

—Survival Colony 9. 2015. (ENG., Illus.). 336p. (YA). (gr. 9). pap. 12.99 (978-1-4814-0355-9(9), McElderry, Margaret K. Bks.) McElderry, Margaret K. Bks.

Bemis, John Claude. Lord of Monsters. 2017. (Out of Abaton Ser.: 2). (ENG.). 320p. (J). (gr. 3-7). 16.99 (978-1-4847-0741-8(9)) Hyperion Bks. for Children.

Benjamin, Paul. Monsters, Inc: Laugh Factory. Mebberson, Amy, illus. 2011. (Kaboom! Graphic Novels Ser.). (ENG.). 112p. (J). (gr. 4-7). 26.19 (978-1-60886-508-6(8)) BOOM! Studios.

Benjamin, Paul & Rosa, Don. Monsters, Inc: Laugh Factory. Mebberson, Amy & Rosa, Don, illus. 2010. (ENG.). 112p. (J). 24.99 (978-1-60886-533-8(9)) BOOM! Studios.

Bennett, Veronica. Angelmonster. 2006. (ENG.). 240p. (YA). (gr. 9-12). 15.99 (978-0-7636-2994-6(4)) Candlewick Pr.

Benton, Jim. Lunch Walks among Us. Benton, Jim, illus. (Franny K. Stein, Mad Scientist Ser.: 1). (ENG., Illus.). 112p. (J). (gr. 2-5). 2004. mass mkt. 6.99 (978-0-689-86295-3(4)) 2003. 17.99 (978-0-689-86291-5(1)) Simon & Schuster Bks. For Young Readers. (Simon & Schuster Bks. For Young Readers).

—Lunch Walks among Us. Benton, Jim, illus. 2011. (Franny K. Stein, Mad Scientist Ser.). (ENG., Illus.). 112p. (J). (gr. 2-6). 31.36 (978-1-59961-817-3(6), 7827, Chapter Bks.) Spotlight.

—Lunch Walks among Us. Benton, Jim, illus. 2004. (Franny K. Stein, Mad Scientist Ser.: 1). (Illus.). 102p. (gr. 2-5). lib. bdg. 16.00 (978-1-4176-4054-6(5)) Turtleback.

Berger, Samantha. Monster's New Undies. Carpenter, Tad, illus. 2017. (ENG.). 40p. (J). (gr. -1-k). 18.99 (978-0-545-87973-6(6), Orchard Bks.) Scholastic, Inc.

Berglin, Ruth Marie & DiRocco, Carl. Dear Big, Mean, Ugly, Monster. 2006. (ENG., Illus.). 40p. (gr. -1-7). pap. 14.95 (978-1-58760-072-2(2), P544213, Child & Family Pr.) Child Welfare League of America, Inc.

Bernoudy, Jasmine L. The Horrible Monster. 2012. 38p. pap. 9.99 (978-0-9858378-0-8(2)) Blu Phi'er Publishing, LLC.

Berrios, Frank. Rootin' Tootin' Racetrack! (Blaze & the Monster Machines) Foley, Niki, illus. 2017. (Little Golden Book Ser.). (ENG.). 24p. (J). (-k). 5.99 (978-1-5247-1668-4(5), Golden Bks.) Random Hse. Children's Bks.

Berry, Julie & Gardner, Sally Faye. The Rat Brain Fiasco. 2010. (Splurch Academy for Disruptive Boys Ser.: 1). (ENG.). 187p. (J). (gr. 4-6). 21.19 (978-0-448-45359-0(2)) Penguin Young Readers Group.

Berube, Amelinda. Here There Are Monsters. 2019. (ENG., Illus.). 352p. (YA). (gr. 8-12). pap. 10.99 (978-1-4926-7101-5(0)) Sourcebooks, Inc.

Billings, Tirrea. The Monster in the Basement. 2010. 12p. pap. 10.99 (978-1-4490-2817-6(9)) AuthorHouse.

Biro, Val. Gumdrop & the Monster. (ENG., Illus.). 32p. (J). (978-0-340-71446-1(8)) Hodder & Stoughton.

—Gumdrop & the Monster. (ENG., Illus.). 32p. (J). pap. 11.99 (978-0-340-71447-8(6)) Hodder & Stoughton GBR. Dist: Trafalgar Square Publishing.

Bissett, Josie. Boogie Monster. Atteberry, Kevan, illus. 2011. 36p. (J). (gr. -1-3). 16.95 (978-1-935414-10-0(0)) Compendium, Inc., Publishing & Communications.

Blabey, Aaron. The Bad Guys in Alien vs Bad Guys (the Bad Guys #6), 1 vol. 2018. (Bad Guys Ser.: 6). (ENG., Illus.). 144p. (J). (gr. 2-5). pap. 5.99 (978-1-338-18959-9(X), Scholastic Paperbacks) Scholastic, Inc.

Black, Holly. Valiant: A Modern Faerie Tale. 2020. (Modern Faerie Tales Ser.). (ENG.). 256p. (YA). (gr. 9). 19.99 (978-1-5344-8453-5(1)); pap. 11.99 (978-1-5344-8452-8(3)) McElderry, Margaret K. Bks. (McElderry, Margaret K. Bks.).

Black, Tara. That's Not the Monster We Ordered. Fairgray, Richard & Jones, Terry, illus. 2016. (ENG.). 32p. (J). (gr. -1-k). 16.99 (978-1-5107-1136-5(8), Sky Pony Pr.) Skyhorse Publishing Co., Inc.

Blade, Adam. Beast Quest: 100: Korvax the Sea Dragon. 2017. (Beast Quest Ser.). (ENG., Illus.). 144p. (J). (gr. 2-4). 7.99 (978-1-4083-4313-5(4), Orchard Bks.) Hachette Children's Group GBR. Dist: Hachette Bk. Group.

—Beast Quest: 101: Vetrix the Poison Dragon. 2017. (Beast Quest Ser.). (ENG., Illus.). 144p. (J). (gr. 2-4). 5.99 (978-1-4083-4315-9(0), Orchard Bks.) Hachette Children's Group GBR. Dist: Hachette Bk. Group.

—Beast Quest: 102: Strytor the Skeleton Dragon. 2017. (Beast Quest Ser.). (ENG., Illus.). 144p. (J). (gr. 2-4). 5.99 (978-1-4083-4317-3(7), Orchard Bks.) Hachette Children's Group GBR. Dist: Hachette Bk. Group.

—Beast Quest: 83: Wardok the Sky Terror. 2016. (Beast Quest Ser.). (ENG., Illus.). 144p. (J). (gr. 2-4). pap. 5.99 (978-1-4083-3487-4(9), Orchard Bks.) Hachette Children's Group GBR. Dist: Hachette Bk. Group.

—Beast Quest: 84: Xerik the Bone Cruncher. 2016. (Beast Quest Ser.). (ENG., Illus.). 144p. (J). (gr. 2-4). pap. 7.99 (978-1-4083-3489-8(5), Orchard Bks.) Hachette Children's Group GBR. Dist: Hachette Bk. Group.

—Beast Quest: 85: Plexor the Raging Reptile. 2016. (Beast Quest Ser.). (ENG., Illus.). 144p. (J). (gr. 2-4). pap. 5.99 (978-1-4083-3491-1(7), Orchard Bks.) Hachette Children's Group GBR. Dist: Hachette Bk. Group.

—Beast Quest: 91: Gryph the Feathered Fiend. 2016. (Beast Quest Ser.). (ENG., Illus.). 144p. (J). (gr. 2-17). pap. 7.99 (978-1-4083-4076-9(3), Orchard Bks.) Hachette Children's Group GBR. Dist: Hachette Bk. Group.

—Beast Quest: 92: Thoron the Living Storm. 2016. (Beast Quest Ser.). (ENG., Illus.). 144p. (J). (gr. 2-17). pap. 6.99 (978-1-4083-4080-6(1), Orchard Bks.) Hachette Children's Group GBR. Dist: Hachette Bk. Group.

—Beast Quest: 93: Okko the Sand Monster. 2016. (Beast Quest Ser.). (ENG., Illus.). 144p. (J). (gr. 2-17). pap. 7.99 (978-1-4083-4082-0(8), Orchard Bks.) Hachette Children's Group GBR. Dist: Hachette Bk. Group.

—Beast Quest: 94: Saurex the Silent Creeper. 2016. (Beast Quest Ser.). (ENG., Illus.). 144p. (J). (gr. 2-17). pap. 5.99 (978-1-4083-4084-4(4), Orchard Bks.) Hachette Children's Group GBR. Dist: Hachette Bk. Group.

—Beast Quest: 95: Krytor the Blood Bat. 2016. (Beast Quest Ser.). (ENG., Illus.). 144p. (J). (gr. 2-4). pap. 5.99 (978-1-4083-4086-8(0), Orchard Bks.) Hachette Children's Group GBR. Dist: Hachette Bk. Group.

—Beast Quest: 98: Karixa the Diamond Warrior. 2016. (Beast Quest Ser.). (ENG., Illus.). 144p. (J). (gr. 2-4). pap. 5.99 (978-1-4083-4309-8(6), Orchard Bks.) Hachette Children's Group GBR. Dist: Hachette Bk. Group.

—Beast Quest: Battle of the Beasts 1: Ferno vs Epos. 2014. (Beast Quest Ser.: 1). (ENG., Illus.). 192p. (J). (gr. 2-4). pap. 9.99 (978-1-4083-1867-6(9), Orchard Bks.) Hachette Children's Group GBR. Dist: Hachette Bk. Group.

—Beast Quest: Early Reader Mortaxe the Skeleton Warrior. 2016. (Beast Quest Ser.). (ENG., Illus.). 80p. (J). (gr. k-17). pap. 5.99 (978-1-4083-4182-7(4), Orchard Bks.) Hachette Children's Group GBR. Dist: Hachette Bk. Group.

—Beast Quest: Grymon the Biting Horror: Series 21 Book 1. 2018. (Beast Quest Ser.). (ENG., Illus.). 144p. (J). (gr. 2-4). 5.99 (978-1-4083-4327-2(4), Orchard Bks.) Hachette Children's Group GBR. Dist: Hachette Bk. Group.

—Beast Quest: Lypida the Shadow Fiend: Series 21 Book 4. 2018. (Beast Quest Ser.). (ENG., Illus.). 144p. (J). (gr. 2-4). 5.99 (978-1-4083-4333-3(9), Orchard Bks.) Hachette Children's Group GBR. Dist: Hachette Bk. Group.

—Beast Quest: Master Your Destiny 1: the Dark Cauldron. 2014. (Beast Quest Ser.). (ENG., Illus.). 112p. (J). (gr. 2-4). pap. 5.99 (978-1-4083-0943-8(2), Orchard Bks.) Hachette Children's Group GBR. Dist: Hachette Bk. Group.

—Beast Quest: Master Your Destiny 2: the Dagger of Doom. 2014. (Beast Quest Ser.). (ENG., Illus.). 128p. (J). (gr. 2-4). 5.99 (978-1-4083-1406-7(1), Orchard Bks.) Hachette Children's Group GBR. Dist: Hachette Bk. Group.

—Beast Quest: Master Your Destiny 3: the Pirate's Curse. 2016. (Beast Quest Ser.). (ENG., Illus.). 144p. (J). (gr. 2-4). pap. 5.99 (978-1-4083-1840-9(7), Orchard Bks.) Hachette Children's Group GBR. Dist: Hachette Bk. Group.

—Beast Quest: Okira the Crusher: Series 20 Book 3. 2017. (Beast Quest Ser.). (ENG., Illus.). 144p. (J). (gr. 1-6). 5.99 (978-1-4083-4323-4(1), Orchard Bks.) Hachette Children's Group GBR. Dist: Hachette Bk. Group.

—Beast Quest: Quarg the Stone Dragon: Series 19 Book 1. 2017. (Beast Quest Ser.). (ENG., Illus.). 144p. (J). (gr. 2-4). 7.99 (978-1-4083-4311-1(8), Orchard Bks.) Hachette Children's Group GBR. Dist: Hachette Bk. Group.

—Beast Quest: Rykar the Fire Hound: Series 20 Book 4. 2017. (Beast Quest Ser.). (ENG., Illus.). 144p. (J). (gr. 1-6). 5.99 (978-1-4083-4325-8(8), Orchard Bks.) Hachette Children's Group GBR. Dist: Hachette Bk. Group.

—Beast Quest: Skalix the Snapping Horror: Series 20 Book 2. 2017. (Beast Quest Ser.). (ENG., Illus.). 144p. (J). (gr. 1-6). 5.99 (978-1-4083-4321-0(5), Orchard Bks.) Hachette Children's Group GBR. Dist: Hachette Bk. Group.

—Beast Quest: Skrar the Night Scavenger: Series 21 Book 2. 2018. (Beast Quest Ser.). (ENG., Illus.). 144p. (J). (gr. 2-4). 5.99 (978-1-4083-4329-6(0), Orchard Bks.) Hachette Children's Group GBR. Dist: Hachette Bk. Group.

—Beast Quest: Special 12: Anoret the First Beast. 2014. (Beast Quest Ser.: 12). (ENG., Illus.). 192p. (J). (gr. 2-4). pap. 6.99 (978-1-4083-2410-3(5), Orchard Bks.) Hachette Children's Group GBR. Dist: Hachette Bk. Group.

—Beast Quest: Special 17: Tempra the Time Stealer. 2016. (Beast Quest Ser.). (ENG., Illus.). 192p. (J). (gr. 2-4). pap. 5.99 (978-1-4083-4078-3(X), Orchard Bks.) Hachette Children's Group GBR. Dist: Hachette Bk. Group.

—Beast Quest: Special 18: Falkor the Coiled Terror. 2017. (Beast Quest Ser.). (ENG., Illus.). 192p. (J). (gr. 2-4). pap. 5.99 (978-1-4083-4297-8(9), Orchard Bks.) Hachette Children's Group GBR. Dist: Hachette Bk. Group.

—Beast Quest: Special 19: Kyrax the Metal Warrior. 2017. (Beast Quest Ser.). (ENG., Illus.). 192p. (J). (gr. 2-17). 5.99 (978-1-4083-4299-2(5), Orchard Bks.) Hachette Children's Group GBR. Dist: Hachette Bk. Group.

—Beast Quest: Tarantix the Bone Spider: Series 21 Book 3. 2018. (Beast Quest Ser.). (ENG., Illus.). 144p. (J). (gr. 2-4). 5.99 (978-1-4083-4331-9(2), Orchard Bks.) Hachette Children's Group GBR. Dist: Hachette Bk. Group.

—Beast Quest: Ultimate Collection. 2016. (Beast Quest Ser.). (ENG., Illus.). 384p. (J). (gr. 2-4). 17.99 (978-1-4083-4547-4(1), Orchard Bks.) Hachette Children's Group GBR. Dist: Hachette Bk. Group.

—Beast Quest: Verak the Storm King: Special 21. 2018. (Beast Quest Ser.). (ENG., Illus.). 192p. (J). (gr. 2-4). 5.99 (978-1-4083-4303-6(7), Orchard Bks.) Hachette Children's Group GBR. Dist: Hachette Bk. Group.

Blance, Ellen. Monstruo, 12 bks., Set. Incl. Monstruo Compre un Animalito. Cook, Ann. 1.98 (978-0-8372-3482-3(4)); Monstruo Encuentra Trabajo. Cook, Tony. 1.98 (978-0-8372-3485-4(9)); Monstruo, la Senorita Monstruo y el Paseo en Bicicleta. Cook, Tony. 1.98 (978-0-8372-3488-5(3)); Monstruo Recorre la Ciudad. Cook, Tony. 1.98 (978-0-8372-3490-8(5)); Monstruo Va a la Playa. Cook, Tony. 1.98 (978-0-8372-3479-3(4)); Monstruo Va Al Circo. Cook, Tony. 1.98 (978-0-8372-3483-0(2)); Monstruo Va Al Hospital. Cook, Tony. 1.98 (978-0-8372-3489-2(1)); Monstruo y el Muro. Cook, Tony. 1.98 (978-0-8372-3487-8(5)); Monstruo y la Galleta de Sorpresa. Cook, Tony. 1.98 (978-0-8372-3486-1(7)); Monstruo y la Liquidacion de Juguetes. Cook, Tony. 1.98 (978-0-8372-3480-9(8)); Plan de la Senorita Monstruo. Cook, Tony. 1.98 (978-0-8372-3481-6(6)); Senorita Monstruo Ayuda. Cook, Tony. 1.98 (978-0-8372-3484-7(0)); (J). (Illus.). Set pap. 215.00 (978-0-8372-3493-9(X)) Bowmar/Noble Pubs.

Blance, Ellen & Cook, Ann. Monstruo Compre un Animalito. (J). 1.98 (978-0-8372-3482-3(4)) Bowmar/Noble Pubs.

Blance, Ellen & Cook, Tony. Lady Monster Has a Plan. Date not set. (Illus.). 40p. pap. 129.15 (978-0-582-19312-3(5)) Addison-Wesley Longman, Ltd. GBR. Dist: Trans-Atlantic Pubns., Inc.

—Lady Monster Helps Out. Date not set. (Illus.). 32p. pap. 129.15 (978-0-582-19302-4(8)) Addison-Wesley Longman, Ltd. GBR. Dist: Trans-Atlantic Pubns., Inc.

—Monster & Magic Umbrella. Date not set. (Illus.). 16p. pap. 129.15 (978-0-582-18593-7(9)) Addison-Wesley Longman, Ltd. GBR. Dist: Trans-Atlantic Pubns., Inc.

—Monster & Surprise Cookie. Date not set. (Illus.). 38p. pap. 129.15 (978-0-582-19308-6(7)) Addison-Wesley Longman, Ltd. GBR. Dist: Trans-Atlantic Pubns., Inc.

—Monster at School. Date not set. (Illus.). 24p. pap. 129.15 (978-0-582-18597-5(1)) Addison-Wesley Longman, Ltd. GBR. Dist: Trans-Atlantic Pubns., Inc.

—Monster Buys a Pet. Date not set. (Illus.). 40p. pap. 129.15 (978-0-582-19311-6(7)) Addison-Wesley Longman, Ltd. GBR. Dist: Trans-Atlantic Pubns., Inc.

—Monster Cleans His House. Date not set. (Illus.). 16p. pap. 129.15 (978-0-582-18590-6(4)) Addison-Wesley Longman, Ltd. GBR. Dist: Trans-Atlantic Pubns., Inc.

—Monster Comes to the City. Date not set. (Illus.). 16p. pap. 129.15 (978-0-582-18588-3(2)) Addison-Wesley Longman, Ltd. GBR. Dist: Trans-Atlantic Pubns., Inc.

—Monster Gets a Job. Date not set. (Illus.). 40p. pap. 129.15 (978-0-582-19307-9(9)) Addison-Wesley Longman, Ltd. GBR. Dist: Trans-Atlantic Pubns., Inc.

—Monster Goes Around Town. Date not set. (Illus.). 38p. pap. 129.15 (978-0-582-19309-3(5)) Addison-Wesley Longman, Ltd. GBR. Dist: Trans-Atlantic Pubns., Inc.

—Monster Goes to Circus. Date not set. (Illus.). 32p. pap. 129.15 (978-0-582-19304-8(4)) Addison-Wesley Longman, Ltd. GBR. Dist: Trans-Atlantic Pubns., Inc.

—Monster Goes to School. Date not set. (Illus.). 24p. pap. 129.15 (978-0-582-18596-8(3)) Addison-Wesley Longman, Ltd. GBR. Dist: Trans-Atlantic Pubns., Inc.

—Monster Goes to the Beach. Date not set. (Illus.). 40p. pap. 129.15 (978-0-582-19306-2(0)) Addison-Wesley Longman, Ltd. GBR. Dist: Trans-Atlantic Pubns., Inc.

—Monster Goes to the Hospital. Date not set. (Illus.). 40p. pap. 129.15 (978-0-582-19305-5(2)) Addison-Wesley Longman, Ltd. GBR. Dist: Trans-Atlantic Pubns., Inc.

—Monster Goes to the Zoo. Date not set. (Illus.). 24p. pap. 129.15 (978-0-582-18599-9(8)) Addison-Wesley Longman, Ltd. GBR. Dist: Trans-Atlantic Pubns., Inc.

—Monster Looks for a House. Date not set. (Illus.). 16p. pap. 129.15 (978-0-582-18589-0(0)) Addison-Wesley Longman, Ltd. GBR. Dist: Trans-Atlantic Pubns., Inc.

—Monster Looks for Friend. Date not set. (Illus.). 16p. pap. 129.15 (978-0-582-18591-3(2)) Addison-Wesley Longman, Ltd. GBR. Dist: Trans-Atlantic Pubns., Inc.

—Monster Meets Lady Monster. Date not set. (Illus.). 16p. pap. 129.15 (978-0-582-18592-0(0)) Addison-Wesley Longman, Ltd. GBR. Dist: Trans-Atlantic Pubns., Inc.

—Monster on the Bus. Date not set. (Illus.). 24p. pap. 129.15 (978-0-582-18595-1(5)) Addison-Wesley Longman, Ltd. GBR. Dist: Trans-Atlantic Pubns., Inc.

—Monstruo Encuentra Trabajo. (J). 1.98 (978-0-8372-3485-4(9)) Bowmar/Noble Pubs.

—Monstruo, la Senorita Monstruo y el Paseo en Bicicleta. (J). 1.98 (978-0-8372-3488-5(3)) Bowmar/Noble Pubs.

—Monstruo Recorre la Ciudad. (J). 1.98 (978-0-8372-3490-8(5)) Bowmar/Noble Pubs.

—Monstruo Va a la Playa. (J). 1.98 (978-0-8372-3479-3(4)) Bowmar/Noble Pubs.

—Monstruo Va Al Circo. (J). 1.98 (978-0-8372-3483-0(2)) Bowmar/Noble Pubs.

—Monstruo Va Al Hospital. (J). 1.98 (978-0-8372-3489-2(1)) Bowmar/Noble Pubs.

—Monstruo y el Muro. (J). 1.98 (978-0-8372-3487-8(5)) Bowmar/Noble Pubs.

—Monstruo y la Galleta de Sorpresa. (J). 1.98 (978-0-8372-3486-1(7)) Bowmar/Noble Pubs.

—Monstruo y la Liquidacion de Juguetes. (J). 1.98 (978-0-8372-3480-9(8)) Bowmar/Noble Pubs.

—El Plan de la Senorita Monstruo. (J). 1.98 (978-0-8372-3481-6(6)) Bowmar/Noble Pubs.

—La Senorita Monstruo Ayuda. (J). 1.98 (978-0-8372-3484-7(0)) Bowmar/Noble Pubs.

Bledsoe, C. L. The Necro-Files. 2013. 174p. pap. 10.99 (978-1-939194-93-0(8)) Etopia Pr.

Blume, Rebecca. A Really, Really, Scary Monster Story! Koji, Jeanette, illus. l.t. ed. 2006. 32p. (J). 24.95 (978-0-9785427-0-2(3)) Liberty Artists Management.

Bogel, Rachel Anne. A Ride on the Monster's Back. Greenfelder, Jill, illus. 2008. 28p. pap. 15.99 (978-1-59858-752-4(8)) Dog Ear Publishing, LLC.

Bolger, Kevin. Zombiekins 2. Blecha, Aaron, illus. 2011. (J). 10.99 (978-1-59514-432-4(3), Razorbill) Penguin Publishing Group.

Bond, Gwenda & Rowe, Christopher. The Supernormal Sleuthing Service #1: the Lost Legacy. Thomas, Glenn, illus. 2018. (Supernormal Sleuthing Service Ser.: 1). (ENG.). 432p. (J). (gr. 3-7). pap. 6.99 (978-0-06-245995-4(3), Greenwillow Bks.) HarperCollins Pubs.

—The Supernormal Sleuthing Service #2: the Sphinx's Secret. 2019. (Supernormal Sleuthing Service Ser.: 2). (ENG.). 352p. (J). (gr. 3-7). pap. 6.99 (978-0-06-245998-5(8), Greenwillow Bks.) HarperCollins Pubs.

Bondestam, Linda, illus. My Little Small. 2018. (ENG.). 52p. (J). (gr. -1-3). 15.95 (978-1-59270-209-1(0)) Enchanted Lion Bks., LLC.

Bonniol, Magali. El Ogro De Mariuchi. 2003. (SPA.). 40p. (978-84-8470-112-5(3)) Corimbo, Editorial S.L.

Bottner, Barbara & Kruglik, Gerald. Pish & Posh Wish for Fairy Wings. Bottner, Barbara, illus. 2007. (I Can Read Level 2 Ser.). (ENG., Illus.). 48p. (J). (gr. k-3). pap. 4.99

(978-0-06-051421-1(3), Tegen, Katherine Bks) HarperCollins Pubs.

Boucher, Sarah E. Becoming Beauty: A Retelling of Beauty & the Beast. 2014. 249p. (YA). pap. 15.99 *(978-1-4621-1455-9(5))* Cedar Fort, Inc./CFI Distribution.

Boutte, Brock. Gris-Gris & the Cypress Tree: Louisiana. 2012. (ENG.). (J). pap. 17.95 *(978-1-4675-4497-9(3))* Independent Pub.

Bowen, Carl. Jak & the Magic Nano-Beans: A Graphic Novel. Lozano, Omar, illus. 2016. (Far Out Fairy Tales Ser.). (ENG.). 40p. (J). (gr. 3-6). lib. bdg. 26.65 *(978-1-4965-2510-9(8)*, 130480, Stone Arch Bks.) Capstone.

Bowman, Erin. Contagion. (Contagion Ser.: 1). (ENG.). (YA). (gr. 8). 2019. 448p. pap. 11.99 *(978-0-06-257416-9(7))* 2018. (Illus.). 432p. 17.99 *(978-0-06-257414-5(0))* HarperCollins Pubs. (HarperTeen).

Boyd, Colin. The Bath Monster. Ross, Tony, illus. 2016. (ENG.). 32p. (J). (gr. -1-3). 17.99 *(978-1-5124-0426-5(8)*, 3ef4f4ac-9d75-45b3-80f9-9db52df2b281) Lerner Publishing Group.

Boynton-Hughes, Brooke. Brave Molly: (Empowering Books for Kids, Overcoming Fear Kids Books, Bravery Books for Kids) 2019. (ENG., Illus.). 48p. (J). (gr. k-3). 16.99 *(978-1-4521-6100-6(3))* Chronicle Bks. LLC.

Bradford, Arthur & Webster, Chuck. 43 Monsters. 2015. (ENG., Illus.). 88p. 18.95 *(978-1-933149-92-9(2))* Manic D Pr.

Brallier, Max. Galactic Hot Dogs 2: The Wiener Strikes Back. Maguire, Rachel & Kelley, Nichole, illus. 2016. (Galactic Hot Dogs Ser.: 2). (ENG.). 288p. (J). (gr. 3-7). 13.99 *(978-1-4814-2496-7(3)*, Aladdin) Simon & Schuster Children's Publishing.

—The Last Kids on Earth. Holgate, Douglas, illus. 2015. (Last Kids on Earth Ser.: 1). (ENG.). 256p. (J). (gr. 3-7). 13.99 *(978-0-670-01661-7(6)*, Viking Books for Young Readers) Penguin Young Readers Group.

—The Last Kids on Earth & the Cosmic Beyond. Holgate, Douglas, illus. 2017. 257p. (J). pap. *(978-0-425-28872-6(2)*, Viking Books for Young Readers) Penguin Young Readers Group.

—The Last Kids on Earth & the Cosmic Beyond. 2015. *(978-1-338-03913-9(X))* Scholastic, Inc.

—The Last Kids on Earth & the Nightmare King. Holgate, Douglas, illus. 2017. (Last Kids on Earth Ser.: 3). (ENG.). 272p. (J). (gr. 3-7). 13.99 *(978-0-425-28871-9(4)*, Viking Books for Young Readers) Penguin Young Readers Group.

—The Last Kids on Earth & the Zombie Parade. Holgate, Douglas, illus. 2016. (Last Kids on Earth Ser.: 2). (ENG.). 320p. (J). (gr. 3-7). 13.99 *(978-0-670-01662-4(4)*, Viking Books for Young Readers) Penguin Young Readers Group.

—The Last Kids on Earth: the Monster Box (books 1-3). 3 vols., Set. Holgate, Douglas, illus. 2018. (Last Kids on Earth Ser.). (ENG.). 816p. (J). (gr. 3-7). 41.97 *(978-0-451-48108-5(9)*, Viking Books for Young Readers) Penguin Young Readers Group.

Brallier, Max & Holgate, Douglas. The Last Kids on Earth & the Cosmic Beyond. 2018. (Last Kids on Earth Ser.: 4). (ENG., Illus.). 288p. (J). (gr. 3-7). 13.99 *(978-0-425-29208-2(8)*, Viking Books for Young Readers) Penguin Young Readers Group.

Braun, Eric. Taking Care of Your Sea Monster. 2019. (Caring for Your Magical Pets Ser.). (ENG., Illus.). 24p. (J). (gr. 2-4). pap. 8.99 *(978-1-64466-093-5(8)*, 12945); (gr. 4-6). lib. bdg. *(978-1-68072-914-6(4)*, 12944) Black Rabbit Bks. (Hi Jinx).

Brege, K. B. All Isn't Well in Roswell! 2005. (Mick Morris Myth Solver Ser.: No. 1). (Illus.). 188p. (J). pap. 6.99 *(978-0-9774119-0-0(7))* Team B Creative LLC.

—Bigfoot... Big Trouble! 2006. (Mick Morris Myth Solver Ser.: No. 2). (J). pap. 6.99 *(978-0-9774119-1-7(5))* Team B Creative LLC.

Brennan-Nelson, Denise. He's Been a Monster All Day. Moore, Cyd, illus. 2013. (ENG.). 32p. (J). (gr. -1-1). 14.99 *(978-1-58536-827-3(X)*, 202363) Sleeping Bear Pr.

Bridgman, Rae. Kingdom of Trolls: A Middlegate Book. 2010. (Illus.). 287p. (J). pap. 15.00 *(978-0-9864974-1-4(X))* Sybertooth, Inc. CAN. Dist: Ingram Content Group.

Bright, Rachel. Love Monster. (Love Monster Ser.). (ENG., Illus.). 32p. (J). (gr. -1 — 1). 2014. bds. 8.99 *(978-0-374-30186-6(7)*, 900141200) 2013. 18.99 *(978-0-374-34646-1(1)*, 900121826) Farrar, Straus & Giroux. (Farrar, Straus & Giroux (BYR)).

—Love Monster & the Last Chocolate. 2015. (Love Monster Ser.). (ENG., Illus.). 32p. (J). (gr. -1-k). 21.99 *(978-0-374-34690-4(9)*, 900149206, Farrar, Straus & Giroux (BYR)) Farrar, Straus & Giroux.

—Love Monster & the Perfect Present. 2014. (Love Monster Ser.). (ENG., Illus.). 32p. (J). (gr. -1-k). 21.99 *(978-0-374-34648-5(8)*, 900121827, Farrar, Straus & Giroux (BYR)) Farrar, Straus & Giroux.

—Love Monster & the Scary Something. 2016. (Love Monster Ser.). (ENG., Illus.). 32p. (J). 21.99 *(978-0-374-34691-1(7)*, 900149207, Farrar, Straus & Giroux (BYR)) Farrar, Straus & Giroux.

Briley, Randy. Mr Underneath. 2013. 134p. pap. 12.99 *(978-0-9896269-0-3(3))* Raven Mad Studios.

Brittain, Bill. The Wizards & the Monster. Date not set. 96p. (J). (gr. 2-5). pap. 4.25 *(978-0-06-442003-7(5))* HarperCollins Pubs.

Brockington, Drew. Hangry. 2019. (ENG., Illus.). 40p. (J). (gr. -1-3). 17.99 *(978-0-316-55932-4(6))* Little, Brown Bks. for Young Readers.

Bronson, Bill. Bill Bronson's Guide to Monsters, 1 vol. 2010. 24p. pap. 24.95 *(978-1-4489-6111-5(4))* PublishAmerica, Inc.

Brooks, Felicity. Jason & the Argonauts. Humphreys, Graham, illus. 2005. 144p. (J). pap. 4.95 *(978-0-7945-0275-1(X)*, Usborne) EDC Publishing.

Brown, Bruce. Mwumba. O'Reilly, Sean Patrick, ed. 2011. (Illus.). 48p. (J). pap. 7.95 *(978-1-897548-03-5(6))* Arcana Studio, Inc.

Brown, Marcy & Haley, Dennis. We Both Read-the Well-Mannered Monster. Raglin, Tim, illus. 2006. (We Both Read Ser.). 40p. (J). (gr. -1-4). 7.99 *(978-1-891327-65-0(8))* Treasure Bay, Inc.

—We Both Read-The Well-Mannered Monster. Raglin, Tim, illus. 2006. (We Both Read Ser.). 44p. (J). (gr. -1-4). pap. 5.99 *(978-1-891327-66-7(6))* Treasure Bay, Inc.

Brown, Mick. From Round about Midnight until about Five! 2012. 60p. pap. 27.45 *(978-1-4772-2701-5(6))* AuthorHouse.

Brown, Peter. My Teacher Is a Monster! (No, I Am Not.) 2014. (ENG., Illus.). 40p. (J). (gr. -1-3). 18.99 *(978-0-316-07029-4(7))* Little, Brown Bks. for Young Readers.

Brownlow, Michael. Ten Little Monsters. Rickerty, Simon, illus. 2016. 30p. (J). *(978-1-4351-6405-5(9))* Barnes & Noble, Inc.

Bruchac, Joseph. The Dark Pond. Comport, Sally Wern, illus. 2005. (ENG.). 160p. (J). (gr. 5-18). pap. 7.99 *(978-0-06-052998-7(9)*, HarperCollins) HarperCollins Pubs.

—The Dark Pond. Comport, Sally Wern, illus. 2005. 142p. (gr. 5-9). 17.00 *(978-0-7569-5436-9(3))* Perfection Learning Corp.

—Night Wings. Comport, Sally Wern, illus. 2018. (ENG.). 224p. (J). (gr. 3-7). pap. 7.99 *(978-0-06-112321-4(8)*, HarperCollins) HarperCollins Pubs.

Bryan, Ashley. Can't Scare Me! Bryan, Ashley, illus. 2013. (ENG., Illus.). 40p. (J). (gr. -1-3). 16.99 *(978-1-4424-7657-8(5)*, Atheneum Bks. for Young Readers) Simon & Schuster Children's Publishing.

Buchanan, Nelda. The Hall Closet Light. 2009. 36p. (J). pap. 13.95 *(978-1-4327-4584-4(0))* Outskirts Pr., Inc.

Buckley, Michael. The Fairy-Tale Detectives. (Sisters Grimm Ser.: 1). (J). 2008. 81.45 *(978-1-4361-0398-5(3))* 2007. 214.75 *(978-1-4193-6197-5(X))* 2007. 1.25 *(978-1-4193-6193-7(7))* 2006. 71.75 *(978-1-4193-6198-2(8))* 2006. 74.75 *(978-1-4193-6196-8(1))* 2006. 86.75 *(978-1-4193-8749-4(9))* 2006. 89.75 *(978-1-4193-8747-0(2))* Recorded Bks., Inc.

—The Fairy-Tale Detectives: And the Unusual Suspects. Ferguson, Peter, illus. 2012. 580p. (J). *(978-1-4351-4487-3(2)*, Amulet Bks.) Abrams, Inc.

—The Fairy-Tale Detectives (the Sisters Grimm #1) 10th Anniversary Edition. 10th anniv. ed. 2017. (Sisters Grimm Ser.). (ENG., Illus.). 288p. (J). (gr. 3-7). pap. 9.99 *(978-1-4197-2005-5(8)*, 580406) Abrams, Inc.

Burfoot, Ella. Louie & the Monsters. Burfoot, Ella, illus. 2005. (Illus.). 32p. (J). (gr. -1-2). 6.95 *(978-1-58925-395-7(7))* Tiger Tales.

Butterworth, MyLinda. The Monster Run. Day, Linda S., ed. Mercer, Matthew, illus. l.t. ed. 2004. 32p. (J). (gr. -1-3). 14.95 *(978-1-890905-23-1(2)*, Day to Day Bks.) Day to Day Enterprises.

Byng, Georgia. Molly Moon & the Monster Music. 2013. (Molly Moon Ser.: 6). (ENG.). 320p. (J). (gr. 3-7). 16.99 *(978-0-06-166163-1(5)*, HarperCollins) HarperCollins Pubs.

Carmen, Martin Anguita. Cuando llega la noche. 2008. (SPA., Illus.). 32p. (J). 10.99 *(978-84-241-5400-4(2))* Everest Editora ESP. Dist: Lectorum Pubns., Inc.

Carter, Jimmy & Carter, Amy. The Little Baby Snoogle- Fleejer. 2014. (ENG., Illus.). 24p. 19.95 *(978-1-55728-671-0(X)*, P240466) Univ. of Arkansas Pr.

Cavaliere, Katrina. Mom! There's a Monster under My Bed! 2008. 24p. per. 24.95 *(978-1-60441-066-2(3))* America Star Bks.

Cazet, Denys. Minnie & Moo Meet Frankenswine. Cazet, Denys, illus. 2004. (Readalongs for Beginning Readers Ser.). (Illus.). 28.95 incl. audio compact disk *(978-1-59112-876-2(5))*; (J). 25.95 incl. audio *(978-1-59112-262-3(7))*; (J). pap. 29.95 incl. audio *(978-1-59112-263-0(5))* Live Oak Media.

—Minnie & Moo Meet Frankenswine, 4 bks. 2004. (Readalongs for Beginning Readers Ser.). (Illus.). 48p. (J). (gr. -1-2). pap. 31.95 incl. audio compact disk *(978-1-59112-877-9(3))* Live Oak Media.

Cerasini, Marc. Godzilla Saves America: A Monster Showdown In 3-D! Morgan, Tom & Mounts, Paul, illus. 2006. 20p. (J). (gr. k-4). reprint ed. 12.00 *(978-1-4223-5409-4(1))* DIANE Publishing Co.

Chalifoux, Lisa M. Bravery Is like Love. Perras, Marielle, illus. 2009. 24p. pap. 10.99 *(978-1-4269-0942-9(X))* Trafford Publishing.

Chandler, Elizabeth. Monsters Are We. 2011. 28p. pap. 15.99 *(978-1-4628-8485-8(7))* Xlibris Corp.

Chartrand, Lili. Taming Horrible Harry. Ouriou, Susan, tr. from FRE. Roge, illus. 2006. (ENG.). 32p. (J). (gr. -1-3). 16.95 *(978-0-88776-772-2(9)*, Tundra Bks.) Tundra Bks. CAN. Dist: Penguin Random Hse. LLC.

Chase, L. P. Elliot Stone & the Mystery of the Summer Vacation Sea Monster. DiRocco, Carl, illus. 2011. (ENG.). 165p. (J). pap. 8.99 *(978-0-9792918-7-6(9))* Blue Marlin Pubns.

Cheverton, Mark. Monsters in the Mist. 2017. (Mystery of Entity303 Ser.: 2). lib. bdg. 20.85 *(978-0-606-40313-9(2))* Turtleback.

Child, Lauren. Ruby Redfort Take Your Last Breath. Child, Lauren, illus. (Ruby Redfort Ser.: 2). (ENG., Illus.). 432p. (J). (gr. 5-9). 2018. pap. 7.99 *(978-1-5362-0048-5(4))* 2013. 16.99 *(978-0-7636-5468-9(X))* Candlewick Pr.

Childs, Tera Lynn. Sweet Legacy. 2013. (Sweet Venom Ser.: 3). (ENG.). 384p. (YA). (gr. 8). 17.99 *(978-0-06-200185-6(X)*, Tegen, Katherine Bks) HarperCollins Pubs.

—Sweet Shadows. (Sweet Venom Ser.: 2). (ENG.). (YA). (gr. 8). 2013. 352p. pap. 9.99 *(978-0-06-200184-9(1))* 2012. 336p. 17.99 *(978-0-06-200183-2(3))* HarperCollins Pubs. (Tegen, Katherine Bks).

—Sweet Venom. 2012. (Sweet Venom Ser.: 1). (ENG.). 384p. (YA). (gr. 8). pap. 9.99 *(978-0-06-200182-5(5)*, Tegen, Katherine Bks) HarperCollins Pubs.

Chin, Oliver. Welcome to Monster Isle. Miracola, Jeff, illus. 2008. (ENG.). 36p. (J). (gr. -1-3). 15.95 *(978-1-59702-016-9(8))* Immedium.

Chouteau, Jordan. No More Monsters under Your Bed! Even Or, Anat, illus. 2019. (ENG.). 32p. (J). (gr. -1-1). 16.99 *(978-0-316-45388-2(9)*, Jimmy Patterson) Little Brown & Co.

Christensen, Gerda. Troll Peter Discovers the Bog-Woman's Secret & Other Stories. 2010. 40p. pap. 18.27 *(978-1-4251-8822-1(2))* Trafford Publishing.

Christian, Mary Blount. Swamp Monsters. Brown, Marc, illus. 48p. (J). (gr. 1-2). pap. 3.99 *(978-0-8072-1355-1(1)*, Listening Library) Random Hse. Audio Publishing Group.

Chupeco, Rin. The Heart Forger: Bone Witch #2. (Bone Witch Ser.: 2). (YA). (gr. 8-12). 2019. 544p. pap. 10.99 *(978-1-4926-6808-4(7))* 2018. (ENG., Illus.). 528p. 17.99 *(978-1-4926-3585-7(5))* Sourcebooks, Inc.

—The Shadowglass: Bone Witch #3. (Bone Witch Ser.: 3). 480p. (YA). (gr. 8-12). 2020. pap. 12.99 *(978-1-4926-9332-1(4))* 2019. (ENG., Illus.). 17.99 *(978-1-4926-6060-6(4))* Sourcebooks, Inc.

Cimorelli, Amber. There Are Monsters Here! Galante, Ashley, illus. 2013. 40p. pap. 24.95 *(978-1-62709-064-3(9))* America Star Bks.

Cioffi, Dom, illus. Digby & the Lake Monster. l.t. ed. 2006. 36p. (J). per. *(978-0-9745931-0-4(9))* Vermont Bookworks.

Clark, Platte F. Good Ogre. 2015. (Bad Unicorn Trilogy Ser.: 3). (ENG., Illus.). 384p. (J). (gr. 3-7). 17.99 *(978-1-4424-5018-9(5)*, Aladdin) Simon & Schuster Children's Publishing.

Clarke, Justine & Baysting, Arthur. The Gobbledygook Is Eating a Book. Jellett, Tom, illus. 2016. 32p. (J). (gr. -1-2). 13.99 *(978-0-14-350693-5(5))* Random Hse. Australia AUS. Dist: Independent Pubs. Group.

Class P3 in Scoil Chiarain Staff. 10 Scary Monsters. 2007. (ENG., Illus.). 32p. (J). pap. 12.95 *(978-1-84717-002-6(1))* O'Brien Pr., Ltd., The IRL. Dist: Dufour Editions, Inc.

Claybourne, Anna. Adventures of Ulysses. 2005. 144p. (J). pap. 4.95 *(978-0-7945-0322-2(5)*, Usborne) EDC Publishing.

Clayton, Coo. Maggie's Monsters. Soye, Alison, illus. 2018. (Maggie Ser.). (ENG.). 36p. (J). (gr. -1-k). pap. 12.99 *(978-1-78530-177-3(2))* Black and White Publishing Ltd. GBR. Dist: Independent Pubs. Group.

Clocktowerhill Research & Publishing Group. Loyd & Boyd & the Slug Monster of Webster County. 2011. (ENG., Illus.). 104p. (J). 12.99 *(978-0-9832130-0-0(3)*, Lucas Violet) Clocktower Hill Research & Publishing Group, LLC.

Cohen, Caron Lee. Broom, Zoom! Ruzzier, Sergio, illus. 2010. (ENG.). 32p. (J). (gr. -1-3). 17.99 *(978-1-4169-9113-7(1)*, Simon & Schuster Bks. For Young Readers) Simon & Schuster Bks. For Young Readers.

Cole, Lisa. Chessie of the Chesapeake Bay. Cole, Lisa, illus. 2011. (Illus.). 110p. pap. 9.95 *(978-1-936343-94-2(0))* Peppertree Pr., The.

Cole, Quinn. Alphabet Puke: Monsters' Medicine A-Z. Eubanks, Charles, illus. 2013. 32p. pap. 6.99 *(978-1-936214-94-5(6))* Wyatt-MacKenzie Publishing.

Collier, Kevin Scott. Professor Horace, Cryptozoologist. Collier, Kevin Scott, illus. 2008. (Illus.). 20p. pap. 9.95 *(978-1-935137-14-6(X))* Guardian Angel Publishing, Inc.

Condie, Ally & Reichs, Brendan. The Beast. 2019. (Darkdeep Ser.). (ENG.). 336p. (J). 16.99 *(978-1-5476-0203-2(1)*, 900203288, Bloomsbury Children's Bks.) Bloomsbury Publishing USA.

Conley, Jennise M. I Think There's a Monster under My Bed! 2013. 28p. 9.99 *(978-1-61061-972-1(2))* My Three Sisters Publishing.

Connolly, MarcyKate. Monstrous. 2016. (J). lib. bdg. 18.40 *(978-0-606-38136-9(8))* Turtleback.

Connor, David. Archie & Billy in Monster Cave. 2011. (Illus.). 40p. 18.68 *(978-1-4567-7308-3(9))* AuthorHouse.

Cooper, Susan. The Boggart & the Monster. 2018. (Boggart Ser.). (ENG.). 224p. (J). (gr. 3-7). pap. 7.99 *(978-1-5344-2012-0(6)*, McElderry, Margaret K. Bks.) McElderry, Margaret K. Bks.

Corentin, Philippe. Papa! (SPA.). 32p. *(978-84-95150-38-7(7))* Corimbo, Editorial S.L.

—Papa. 2003. (SPA.). (J). (gr. -1-k). 19.99 *(978-84-8470-094-4(1))* Corimbo, Editorial S.L. ESP. Dist: Lectorum Pubns., Inc.

Corey, Shana. Monster Parade. Terry, Will, illus. 2009. (Step into Reading: Step 2 Ser.). (ENG.). 24p. (J). (gr. -1-1). lib. bdg. 16.19 *(978-0-375-95638-6(7))* Random House Publishing Group.

—Monster Parade. Terry, Will, illus. 2009. (Step into Reading Ser.). 24p. (J). (gr. -1-1). 5.99 *(978-0-375-85638-9(2)*, Random Hse. Bks. for Young Readers) Random Hse. Children's Bks.

corjanjamnic. Angels on Earth, 1 vol. 2010. 48p. pap. 16.95 *(978-1-4512-0050-8(1))* America Star Bks.

Cornelia, Funke. Ghosthunters & the Muddy Monster of Doom! Cornelia, Funke, illus. 2007. (Ghosthunters Ser.: 4). (ENG., Illus.). 165p. (J). (gr. 3-6). 17.44 *(978-0-439-86269-1(8))* Scholastic, Inc.

Cornell, Kevin. Go to Sleep, Monster! Cornell, Kevin, illus. 2016. (ENG., Illus.). 32p. (J). (gr. -1-3). 17.99 *(978-0-06-234915-6(5)*, Balzer & Bray) HarperCollins Pubs.

Cornish, D. M. Foundling. Cornish, D. M., illus. 2007. (Monster Blood Tattoo Ser.). (Illus.). 434p. (gr. 7-12). 20.00 *(978-0-7569-7957-7(9))* Perfection Learning Corp.

Cosgrove, Stephen. Snugg N. Flitter: Facing Your Fears. Arroyo, Fian, illus. 2004. (J). *(978-1-58804-377-1(0))* P C I Education.

Côté, Geneviève & Côté, Geneviève. Mr. King's Things. Côté, Geneviève & Côté, Geneviève, illus. 2012. (Mr. King Ser.). (ENG., Illus.). 32p. (J). (gr. -1-2). 16.95 *(978-1-55453-700-6(2))* Kids Can Pr., Ltd. CAN. Dist: Hachette Bk. Group.

Cotter, Bill. Don't Push the Button! 2013. (Illus.). 32p. (J). (gr. -1-3). 16.99 *(978-1-4022-8746-6(1)*, Sourcebooks Jabberwocky) Sourcebooks, Inc.

—Don't Touch This Book! 2016. (Illus.). (J). (gr. -1-k). 28p. bds. 6.99 *(978-1-4926-4804-8(3)*, 9781492648048); 32p. 16.99 *(978-1-4926-3224-5(4)*, 9781492632245) Sourcebooks, Inc. (Sourcebooks Jabberwocky).

Coville, Bruce. Always October. 2012. (ENG.). 384p. (J). (gr. 3-7). 16.99 *(978-0-06-089095-7(9)*, HarperCollins) HarperCollins Pubs.

—The Mischief Monster. Coville, Katherine, illus. 2008. (Moongobble & Me Ser.: Bk. 4). (ENG.). 80p. (J). (gr. 1-5). pap. 6.99 *(978-1-4169-0808-1(0)*, Aladdin) Simon & Schuster Children's Publishing.

—The Mischief Monster. Coville, Katherine, illus. 2007. (Moongobble & Me Ser.: Bk. 4). (ENG.). 80p. (J). (gr. 3-6). 16.19 *(978-1-4169-0807-4(2))* Simon & Schuster, Inc.

—The Monster's Ring: A Magic Shop Book. Coville, Katherine, illus. 2008. (Magic Shop Book Ser.: 1). (ENG.). 128p. (J). (gr. 5-7). pap. 7.99 *(978-0-15-206442-6(7)*, 1199254, Clarion Bks.) HarperCollins Pubs.

—The Naughty Nork. Coville, Katherine, illus. 2009. (Moongobble & Me Ser.). (ENG.). 128p. (J). (gr. 1-5). pap. 6.99 *(978-1-4169-0810-4(2)*, Aladdin) Simon & Schuster Children's Publishing.

Cowley, Joy. Meanies in the House Big Book. 2010. 48.25 *(978-1-60559-251-0(X))* Hameray Publishing Group, Inc.

Cranch, Christopher. The Last of the Huggermuggers. 2004. reprint ed. pap. 15.95 *(978-1-4191-6876-5(2))* Kessinger Publishing, LLC.

Cranch, Christopher Pierce. The Last of the Huggermuggers. 2004. reprint ed. pap. 1.99 *(978-1-4192-6876-2(7))* Kessinger Publishing, LLC.

Crayon, Paula. Mittens in the Attic. 2010. 40p. pap. 18.99 *(978-1-4520-9218-8(4))* AuthorHouse.

Crimi, Carolyn. Boris & Bella. Grimly, Gris, illus. 2006. (ENG.). 32p. (J). (gr. -1-3). reprint ed. pap. 7.99 *(978-0-15-205900-2(8)*, 1197714, Clarion Bks.) HarperCollins Pubs.

—Where's My Mummy? Manders, John, illus. 2008. 32p. (J). (gr. -1-3). 15.99 *(978-0-7636-3196-3(5))* Candlewick Pr.

Crosby, June. A Monster in the Attic. Chapman, Michelle, illus. 2011. 16p. pap. 24.95 *(978-1-4560-6959-9(4))* America Star Bks.

Crow, Kristyn. Bedtime at the Swamp. 2008. (ENG., Illus.). 32p. (J). (gr. -1-1). 16.99 *(978-0-06-083951-2(1)*, HarperCollins) HarperCollins Pubs.

Crow, Marilee & Foster, Jack. Once There Was a Monster. 2012. 20p. pap. 9.95 *(978-1-61633-331-7(6))* Guardian Angel Publishing, Inc.

Crowe, Caroline. Tiny Tantrum. Okstad, Ella, illus. 2017. (ENG.). 32p. (J). (gr. -1-2). 16.99 *(978-1-68010-072-3(6))* Tiger Tales.

Crowley, James. Monsterland. 2018. lib. bdg. 19.65 *(978-0-606-41311-4(1))* Turtleback.

Crownberry, Ethan. The Willies. 2012. 80p. pap. 8.95 *(978-1-300-00798-2(2))* Lulu Pr., Inc.

—The Willies. 2012. 80p. pap. 10.95 *(978-0-557-96056-9(8))* Lulu.com GBR. Dist: Lulu Pr., Inc.

Cua, Marcus Loo. How the Hungry T-Rex Got Fixed. 2012. 24p. pap. 28.03 *(978-1-4653-9643-3(8))* Xlibris Corp.

Cuccia, Ronni. Maria & the Monster. 2010. 16p. 10.99 *(978-1-4520-8966-9(3))* AuthorHouse.

Culpepper, Karen. The Homework Monster. 2011. 32p. (J). 23.95 *(978-0-9765641-2-6(2))* Rai Publishing.

Cummings, Pat. Ananse & the Monster. (Illus.). (YA). 16.99 *(978-0-8050-7782-7(0))* Holt, Henry & Co.

Cummings, Troy. Attack of the Shadow Smashers. 2013. (Notebook of Doom Ser.: 3). lib. bdg. 14.75 *(978-0-606-32369-7(4))* Turtleback.

—Attack of the Shadow Smashers: a Branches Book (the Notebook of Doom #3) Cummings, Troy, illus. 2013. (Notebook of Doom Ser.: 3). (ENG.). 96p. (J). (gr. 1-3). pap. 5.99 *(978-0-545-55297-4(4))* Scholastic, Inc.

—Battle of the Boss-Monster. Cummings, Troy, illus. 2017. (Notebook of Doom Ser.: 13). (ENG.). 96p. (J). (gr. 1-3). lib. bdg. 15.99 *(978-1-338-03457-8(X))* Scholastic, Inc.

—Battle of the Boss-Monster. 2018. (Notebook of Doom — Branches Ser.: 14). lib. bdg. 14.75 *(978-0-606-41147-9(X))* Turtleback.

—Battle of the Boss-Monster: a Branches Book (the Notebook of Doom #13) Cummings, Troy, illus. 2017. (Notebook of Doom Ser.: 13). (ENG., Illus.). 96p. (J). (gr. 1-3). pap. 5.99 *(978-1-338-03456-1(1))* Scholastic, Inc.

—Boa Constructor: a Branches Book (the Binder of Doom #2) Cummings, Troy, illus. 2019. (Binder of Doom Ser.: 2). (ENG., Illus.). 96p. (J). (gr. 1-3). pap. 5.99 *(978-1-338-31469-4(6))* Scholastic, Inc.

—Boa Constructor: a Branches Book (the Binder of Doom #2) (Library Edition) Cummings, Troy, illus. 2019. (Binder of Doom Ser.: 2). (ENG., Illus.). 96p. (J). (gr. 1-3). 24.99 *(978-1-338-31470-0(X))* Scholastic, Inc.

—Brute-Cake: a Branches Book (the Binder of Doom #1) Cummings, Troy, illus. 2019. (Binder of Doom Ser.: 1). (ENG., Illus.). 96p. (J). (gr. 1-3). pap. 5.99 *(978-1-338-31466-3(1))* Scholastic, Inc.

—Charge of the Lightning Bugs: a Branches Book (the Notebook of Doom #8) Cummings, Troy, illus. 2015. (Notebook of Doom Ser.: 8). (ENG., Illus.). 96p. (J). (gr. 1-3). pap. 5.99 *(978-0-545-79555-5(9))*; 8th ed. 15.99 *(978-0-545-79554-8(0))* Scholastic, Inc.

—Chomp of the Meat-Eating Vegetables. 2014. (Notebook of Doom Ser.: 4). lib. bdg. 14.75 *(978-0-606-35362-5(3))* Turtleback.

—Chomp of the Meat-Eating Vegetables: a Branches Book (the Notebook of Doom #4) Cummings, Troy, illus. 2014. (Notebook of Doom Ser.: 4). (ENG., Illus.). 96p. (J). (gr. 1-3). pap. 5.99 *(978-0-545-55299-8(0))* Scholastic, Inc.

—Day of the Night Crawlers. 2013. (Notebook of Doom Ser.: 2). (ENG.). 96p. (J). (gr. 1-3). 15.99 *(978-0-545-49324-6(2))* Scholastic, Inc.

—Day of the Night Crawlers. 2013. (Notebook of Doom Ser.: 2). lib. bdg. 14.75 *(978-0-606-32368-0(6))* Turtleback.

—Day of the Night Crawlers: a Branches Book (the Notebook of Doom #2) Cummings, Troy, illus. 2013. (Notebook of Doom Ser.: 2). (ENG.). 96p. (J). (gr. 1-3). pap. 6.99 *(978-0-545-49325-3(0))* Scholastic, Inc.

—Day of the Night Crawlers: a Branches Book (the Notebook of Doom #2) A Branches Book. Cummings, Troy, illus. 2013. (Notebook of Doom Ser.: 2). (ENG.). 96p. (J). (gr. 1-3). E-Book *(978-0-545-49327-7(7))* Scholastic, Inc.

—Flurry of the Snombies. 2015. (Notebook of Doom Ser.: 7). (ENG., Illus.). 96p. (J). (gr. 1-3). 15.99 *(978-0-545-79551-7(6))* Scholastic, Inc.

—Flurry of the Snombies: a Branches Book (the Notebook of Doom #7) Cummings, Troy, illus. 2015. (Notebook of Doom Ser.: 7). (ENG., Illus.). 96p. (J). (gr. 1-3). pap. 5.99 *(978-0-545-79550-0(8))* Scholastic, Inc.

—March of the Vanderpants. 2017. (Notebook of Doom — Branches Ser.: 12). lib. bdg. 14.75 *(978-0-606-40192-0(X))* Turtleback.

—March of the Vanderpants: a Branches Book (the Notebook of Doom #12) Cummings, Troy, illus. 2017. (Notebook of Doom Ser.: 12). (ENG., Illus.). 96p. (J). (gr. 1-3). pap. 5.99 *(978-1-338-03452-3(9))* Scholastic, Inc.

—Monster Notebook: a Branches Special Edition (the Notebook of Doom) Cummings, Troy, illus. 2017. (Notebook of Doom Ser.). (ENG., Illus.). 144p. (J). (gr. 1-3). pap. 6.99 *(978-1-338-15742-0(6))* Scholastic, Inc.

—The Notebook of Doom #6: Pop of the Bumpy Mummy (a Branches Book) - Library Edition. 2014. (Notebook of Doom

MNO

Ser.: 6). (ENG.). 96p. (J). (gr. 1-3). 15.99 *(978-0-545-69899-3(5))* Scholastic, Inc.

—The Notebook of Doom (Books 1-3): a Branches Box Set, 1 vol. Cummings, Troy, illus. 2016. (Notebook of Doom Ser.). (ENG., Illus.). 288p. (J). (gr. 1-3). pap., pap., pap. 9.99 *(978-1-338-10199-7(4))* Scholastic, Inc.

—Pop of the Bumpy Mummy. 2014. (Notebook of Doom Ser.: 6). lib. bdg. 14.75 *(978-0-606-36339-6(4))* Turtleback.

—Pop of the Bumpy Mummy: a Branches Book (the Notebook of Doom #6) Cummings, Troy, illus. 2014. (Notebook of Doom Ser.: 6). (ENG., Illus.). 96p. (J). (gr. 1-3). pap. 5.99 *(978-0-545-69898-6(7))* Scholastic, Inc.

—Rise of the Balloon Goons: a Branches Book (the Notebook of Doom #1) Cummings, Troy, illus. 2013. (Notebook of Doom Ser.: 1). (ENG., Illus.). 96p. (J). (gr. 1-3). pap. 5.99 *(978-0-545-49323-9(4))* Scholastic, Inc.

—Rumble of the Coaster Ghost: a Branches Book (the Notebook of Doom #9) Cummings, Troy, illus. 2016. (Notebook of Doom Ser.: 9). (ENG., Illus.). 96p. (J). (gr. 1-3). pap. 5.99 *(978-0-545-86497-8(6))* Scholastic, Inc.

—Snap of the Super-Goop: A Branches Book , Vol. 10. Cummings, Troy, illus. 2016. (Notebook of Doom Ser.: 10). (ENG., Illus.). 96p. (J). (gr. 1-3). 24.99 *(978-0-545-86500-5(X))* Scholastic, Inc.

—Snap of the Super-Goop: a Branches Book (the Notebook of Doom #10) Cummings, Troy, illus. 2016. (Notebook of Doom Ser.: 1). (ENG., Illus.). 96p. (J). (gr. 1-3). pap. 5.99 *(978-0-545-86499-2(2))* Scholastic, Inc.

—Sneeze of the Octo-Schnozz: a Branches Book (the Notebook of Doom #11) Cummings, Troy, illus. 2016. (Notebook of Doom Ser.: 11). (ENG.). 96p. (J). (gr. 1-3). pap. 5.99 *(978-1-338-03448-6(0))* Scholastic, Inc.

—The Notebook of Doom: Rise of the Balloon Goons, Vol. 1. Cummings, Troy, illus. 2013. (Notebook of Doom Ser.: 1). (ENG., Illus.). 96p. (J). (gr. 1-3). 15.99 *(978-0-545-49322-2(6))* Scholastic, Inc.

—Whack of the P-Rex: a Branches Book (the Notebook of Doom #5) Cummings, Troy, illus. 2014. (Notebook of Doom Ser.: 5). (ENG.). 96p. (J). (gr. 1-3). pap. 5.99 *(978-0-545-69895-5(2))* Scholastic, Inc.

Cunliffe, John. Postman Pat & the Beast of Greendale, Bk. 12. (ENG., Illus.). 32p. (J). *(978-0-340-67816-9(X))* Hodder & Stoughton.

Cusack, Dale. Grace & the Drawl. 2008. (Illus.). 169p. pap. 11.95 *(978-1-4357-0926-3(8))* Lulu Pr., Inc.

Cuyler, Margery. Bonaparte Falls Apart. Terry, Will, illus. 2020. 40p. (J). (gr. -1-2). 8.99 *(978-1-101-93772-3(6)*, Dragonfly Bks.) Random Hse. Children's Bks.

—Monster Mess! Schindler, S. D., illus. 2008. (ENG.). 32p. (J). (gr. -1-1). 19.99 *(978-0-689-86405-6(1)*, McElderry, Margaret K. Bks.) McElderry, Margaret K. Bks.

Cuyler, Margery & Terry, Will. Bonaparte Falls Apart. 2017. (Illus.). 40p. (J). (gr. -1-2). 17.99 *(978-1-101-93768-6(8)*, Crown Books For Young Readers) Random Hse. Children's Bks.

Czajak, Paul. Monster Needs a Christmas Tree. Grieb, Wendy, illus. 2014. (Monster & Me Ser.). (ENG.). 32p. (J). (-k). 16.95 *(978-1-938063-46-6(5)*, Mighty Media Kids) Mighty Media Pr.

—Monster Needs a Costume. Grieb, Wendy, illus. (Monster & Me Ser.). (ENG.). 32p. (J). (-k). 2014. 6.99 *(978-1-938063-38-1(4))* 2013. 16.95 *(978-1-938063-09-1(0))* Mighty Media Pr. (Mighty Media Kids).

—Monster Needs a Party. Grieb, Wendy, illus. 2015. (Monster & Me Ser.). (ENG.). 32p. (J). (-k). 16.95 *(978-1-938063-55-8(4)*, Mighty Media Kids) Mighty Media Pr.

—Monster Needs His Sleep. Grieb, Wendy, illus. 2014. (Monster & Me Ser.). (ENG.). 32p. (J). (-k). 16.95 *(978-1-938063-26-8(0)*, Mighty Media Kids) Mighty Media Pr.

—Monster Needs Your Vote. Grieb, Wendy, illus. 2015. (Monster & Me Ser.). (ENG.). 32p. (J). (gr. -1-3). 16.95 *(978-1-938063-63-3(5)*, Mighty Media Kids) Mighty Media Pr.

Dadey, Debbie. Great Green Gator Graduation. Lucas, Margeaux, illus. 2006. (Swamp Monster in Third Grade Ser.). 58p. (J). pap. *(978-0-439-79401-5(3))* Scholastic, Inc.

Dadey, Debbie & Jones, Marcia. Monsters Don't Scuba Dive. (Adventures of the Bailey School Kids Ser.: No. 14). (FRE., Illus.). 80p. (J). (gr. 2-4). pap. 5.99 *(978-0-590-24550-0(3))* Scholastic, Inc.

Dahl, Michael. The Beast Beneath the Stairs: 10th Anniversary Edition. Moffett, Patricia, illus. 10th ed. 2017. (Library of Doom Ser.). (ENG.). 48p. (J). (gr. 4-8). pap. 6.25 *(978-1-4965-5536-6(8)*, 136560); lib. bdg. 23.99 *(978-1-4965-5530-4(9)*, 136554) Capstone. (Stone Arch Bks.).

—Dark Tower Rising, 1 vol. Kovar, Ben, illus. 2012. (Troll Hunters Ser.). (ENG.). 112p. (J). (gr. 5-9). lib. bdg. 25.32 *(978-1-4342-3308-0(1)*, 116272, Stone Arch Bks.) Capstone.

—Dungeon of Seven Dooms, 1 vol. 2011. (Good vs Evil Ser.). (ENG.). 48p. (J). (gr. 5-9). lib. bdg. 23.99 *(978-1-4342-2091-2(5)*, 102837, Stone Arch Bks.) Capstone.

—Fallen Star, 1 vol. Kovar, Ben, illus. 2012. (Troll Hunters Ser.). (ENG.). 112p. (J). (gr. 5-9). lib. bdg. 25.32 *(978-1-4342-3310-3(3)*, 116274, Stone Arch Bks.) Capstone.

—The Library Claw: And Other Scary Tales. Bonet, Xavier, illus. 2017. (Michael Dahl's Really Scary Stories Ser.). (ENG.). 72p. (J). (gr. 1-3). lib. bdg. 25.32 *(978-1-4965-4902-0(3)*, 135654, Stone Arch Bks.) Capstone.

—Maze Monster. Catling, Andy, illus. 2016. (Igor's Lab of Fear Ser.). (ENG.). 40p. (J). (gr. 4-8). lib. bdg. 23.99 *(978-1-4965-3528-3(6)*, 132642, Stone Arch Bks.) Capstone.

—The Monster in the Mailbox: And Other Scary Tales. Bonet, Xavier, illus. 2016. (Michael Dahl's Really Scary Stories Ser.). (ENG.). 72p. (J). (gr. 1-3). lib. bdg. 25.32 *(978-1-4965-3771-3(8)*, 133102, Stone Arch Bks.) Capstone.

—Monster Street Complete Set, Set. Omia-Blanco, Miguel, illus. Incl. Two Heads Are Better Than One. (ENG., Illus.). 32p. (J). (gr. 1-3). 2010. lib. bdg. 23.99 *(978-1-4048-6067-4(3)*, 103251, Picture Window Bks.); (Monster Street Ser.). (ENG.). Illus.). 32p. 2010. 71.97 o.p. *(978-1-4048-6352-1(4)*, 15360, Picture Window Bks.) Capstone.

—Skyfall, 1 vol. Kovar, Ben, illus. 2012. (Troll Hunters Ser.). (ENG.). 112p. (J). (gr. 5-9). lib. bdg. 25.32 *(978-1-4342-3307-3(3)*, 116271, Stone Arch Bks.) Capstone.

—The Spine Tingler. Evergreen, Nelson, illus. 2015. (Library of Doom: the Final Chapters Ser.). (ENG.). 40p. (J). (gr. 4-8). 23.99 *(978-1-4342-9680-1(6)*, 126987, Stone Arch Bks.) Capstone.

—Troll Hunters, 1 vol. Kovar, Ben, illus. 2012. (Troll Hunters Ser.). (ENG.). 320p. (J). (gr. 4-6). 12.95 *(978-1-4342-4590-8(X)*, 120539, Stone Arch Bks.) Capstone.

—Two Heads Are Better Than One, 1 vol. Omia-Blanco, Miguel, illus. 2010. (Monster Street Ser.). (ENG.). 32p. (J). (gr. 1-3). lib. bdg. 23.99 *(978-1-4048-6067-4(3)*, 103251, Picture Window Bks.) Capstone.

—Under the Hood: A 4D Book. Cook, Euan, illus. 2018. (School Bus of Horrors Ser.). (ENG.). 40p. (J). (gr. 4-8). pap. 4.95 *(978-1-4965-6276-0(3)*, 138007); lib. bdg. 24.65 *(978-1-4965-6270-8(4)*, 137997) Capstone. (Stone Arch Bks.).

Dahl, Roald. The Minpins. 2009. (ENG.). 32p. (J). (gr. 1-3). pap. 8.99 *(978-0-14-241474-3(3)*, Puffin Books) Penguin Young Readers Group.

Daisy, April. The Monster's in My Room. Daisy, April, illus. 2005. (Illus.). (J). per. 7.95 *(978-1-59466-048-1(4)*, Little Ones) Port Town Publishing.

d'Allancé, Mireille. Vaya Rabieta.Tr. of What A Tantrum! (SPA.). 32p. (J). *(978-84-95150-89-9(1))* Corimbo, Editorial S.L. ESP. Dist: Lectorum Pubns., Inc.

Dambrot, Marc. The Destined: A Hero's Calling. 2008. 116p. pap. 19.95 *(978-1-60474-792-8(7))* America Star Bks.

Daniels, Donna. What Do Monsters Do Tonight? 2009. (Illus.). 24p. pap. 11.49 *(978-1-4389-2650-6(2))* AuthorHouse.

Darke, J. A. Do Not Watch. Evans, Neil, illus. 2016. (Spine Shivers Ser.). (ENG.). 128p. (J). (gr. 4-6). lib. bdg. 27.32 *(978-1-4965-3071-4(3)*, 131947, Stone Arch Bks.) Capstone.

David, Lawrence. The Invasion of the Shag Carpet Creature. Gott, Barry, illus. 2004. (Horace Splattly Ser.). 151p. (J). (gr. 4-7). 12.65 *(978-0-7569-2818-6(4))* Perfection Learning Corp.

—To Catch a Clownosaurus. Gott, Barry, tr. Gott, Barry, illus. 2003. (Horace Splattly: Cupcaked Crusader Ser.). (ENG.). 150p. (J). (gr. 3-6). 17.44 *(978-0-525-47154-7(5))* Penguin Young Readers Group.

Davidson, Danica. The Armies of Herobrine: An Unofficial Overworld Adventure, Book Five. 2016. (Unofficial Overworld Adventure Ser.). (ENG.). 112p. (J). (gr. 1-7). pap. 7.99 *(978-1-5107-1620-9(3)*, Sky Pony Pr.) Skyhorse Publishing Co., Inc.

—Escape from the Overworld: An Unofficial Overworld Adventure, Book One. 2015. (Unofficial Overworld Adventure Ser.). (ENG.). 112p. (J). (gr. 1-7). pap. 7.99 *(978-1-63450-103-3(9)*, Sky Pony Pr.) Skyhorse Publishing Co., Inc.

Davis, Daniel M. & Davis, Dawna Jo. Klawberry: Good Girl. Bad World. McClellan, Sara, ed. ltd. ed. 2007. (Illus.). per. 20.00 *(978-0-9774173-3-9(6))* Steam Crow Pr.

Davis, Eleanor. Stinky: Toon Books Level 2. 2008. (ENG., Illus.). 40p. (J). (gr. -1-3). 12.99 *(978-0-9799238-4-5(0)*, Toon Books) Astra Publishing Hse.

Dayan, Linda Marcos. El Monstruo Graciopeo. Nepomniachi, Leonid, illus. (Barril Sin Fondo Ser.). (SPA.). (J). (gr. 3-5). pap. *(978-968-6465-60-0(X))* Casa de Estudios de Literatura y Talleres Artisticos Amaquemecan A.C. MEX. Dist: Lectorum Pubns., Inc.

Dean, Denise. Under Tommy's Bed: A Tommy Maloney Book. 2011. 40p. pap. 24.95 *(978-1-4560-7293-3(5))* America Star Bks.

Dean, James, illus. Pete the Cat & the Treasure Map. 2017. (J). *(978-1-5182-3828-4(9))* HarperCollins Pubs. Ltd.

Delaney, Joseph. The Last Apprentice: Slither (Book 11), Bk. 11. (Last Apprentice Ser.). (ENG.). (YA). (gr. 8). 2014. 432p. pap. 11.99 *(978-0-06-219235-6(3))* 2013. 416p. 17.99 *(978-0-06-219234-9(5))* HarperCollins Pubs. (Greenwillow Bks.).

—A New Darkness. 2014. (ENG.). 352p. (YA). (gr. 8). 17.99 *(978-0-06-233453-4(0)*, Greenwillow Bks.) HarperCollins Pubs.

Denise, Anika. Monster Trucks. Wragg, Nate, illus. 2016. (ENG.). 32p. (J). (gr. -1-3). 17.99 *(978-0-06-234522-6(2)*, HarperCollins) HarperCollins Pubs.

—Monster Trucks Board Book. Wragg, Nate, illus. 2018. (ENG.). 32p. (J). (gr. -1 — 1). bds. 7.99 *(978-0-06-274162-2(4)*, HarperFestival) HarperCollins Pubs.

DePrisco, Dorothea. Maximus the Monster Roars NO! 2009. (ENG.). 12p. 7.95 *(978-1-58117-915-6(4)*, Intervisual/Piggy Toes) Bendon, Inc.

Derejko-Viinikka, Jennifer. Marko & the Monster. 2008. 28p. pap. 12.49 *(978-1-4389-2898-2(X))* AuthorHouse.

Dezago, Todd. Fantastic Four: The Menace of Monster Isle! Davis, Shane, illus. 2006. (Spider-Man Team Up Ser.). (ENG.). 24p. (J). (gr. 2-6). lib. bdg. 31.36 *(978-1-59961-006-1(X)*, 13646, Marvel Age) Spotlight.

—Kitty Pryde: Down with the Monsters! 2006. (Spider-Man Team Up Ser.). (ENG., Illus.). 24p. (J). (gr. 2-6). lib. bdg. 31.36 *(978-1-59961-002-3(7)*, 13642, Marvel Age) Spotlight.

Dhami, Narinder. Monster under the Stairs. Spoor, Mike, illus. 2005. (ENG.). 24p. (J). lib. bdg. 23.65 *(978-1-59646-718-7(5))* Dingles & Co.

Di Stiso, Robin Rountree. Cyber Monsters. 2008. 16p. pap. 19.00 *(978-1-4389-1354-4(0))* AuthorHouse.

Dickerson, Sharon. Jessica & the Tangle Monster. 2003. (J). pap. 9.00 *(978-0-8059-5991-8(2))* Dorrance Publishing Co., Inc.

Dillon, Elena. Breathe. 2013. 190p. pap. 9.99 *(978-0-9886353-2-6(1))* Dillon, Elena.

Dimpel, Matt. The War of the Serpent Swords. 2011. 230p. pap. 24.95 *(978-1-4626-3169-8(X))* PublishAmerica, Inc.

DiPucchio, Kelly. Monster Makeovers. Pham, LeUyen, illus. 2006. (J). *(978-0-7868-5181-2(3))* Hyperion Bks. for Children.

Disney Books. Moana ReadAlong Storybook & CD. 2016. (Read-Along Storybook & CD Ser.). (ENG., Illus.). 32p. (J). (gr. 1-3). pap. 6.99 *(978-1-4847-4361-4(X)*, Disney Press Books) Disney Publishing Worldwide.

Disney Editors. Scaring Lessons. 2013. (Step into Reading Level 2 Ser.). lib. bdg. 13.55 *(978-0-606-31923-2(9))* Turtleback.

Dixon, Andy. Star Quest. Brooks, Felicity, ed. Harris, Nick, illus. 2006. (Usborne Fantasy Puzzle Bks.). 32p. (YA). (gr. 7). lib. bdg. 15.99 *(978-1-58086-906-5(8)*, Usborne) EDC Publishing.

Dixon, Franklin W. Attack of the Bayport Beast. 2017. (Hardy Boys Adventures Ser.: 14). (ENG., Illus.). 112p. (J). (gr. 3-7). pap. 7.99 *(978-1-4814-6834-3(0)*, Simon & Schuster/Paula Wiseman Bks.) Simon & Schuster/Paula Wiseman Bks.

Dixon, Jackie R. Gilroy the Fairy Collector. 2015. (ENG.). 369p. (J). (gr. 4-6). mass mkt. 11.95 *(978-1-78455-407-1(3)*, e421f58a-af8c-418f-9457-2b3115f29a1c) Austin Macauley Pubs. Ltd. GBR. Dist: Baker & Taylor Publisher Services (BTPS).

Doan, Janet Mailan. A Monster Stole My Chickens! 2012. 28p. pap. 16.09 *(978-1-4669-6468-6(5))* Trafford Publishing.

Doeden, Matt. Beauty & the Beast: An Interactive Fairy Tale Adventure. Miramon, Sabrina, illus. 2018. (You Choose: Fractured Fairy Tales Ser.). (ENG.). 112p. (J). (gr. 3-7). lib. bdg. 32.65 *(978-1-5435-3007-0(9)*, 138604, Capstone Pr.) Capstone.

Dogzilla (Digest) 2003. (ENG., Illus.). 32p. (J). (gr. -1-3). pap. 8.99 *(978-0-15-204949-2(5)*, 1194945, Clarion Bks.) HarperCollins Pubs.

Doherty, Gillian. 1001 MonsterThings to Spot. 2008. (1001 Things to Spot Ser.). 32p. (J). 9.99 *(978-0-7945-2091-5(X)*, Usborne) EDC Publishing.

Don, Lari. The Treasure of the Loch Ness Monster, 30 vols. Ilincic, Natasa, illus. 2023. (Traditional Scottish Tales Ser.). 32p. (J). 14.95 **(978-1-78250-480-1(X)**, Kelpies) Floris Bks. GBR. Dist: Consortium Bk. Sales & Distribution.

—The Treasure of the Loch Ness Monster, 30 vols. Ilincic, Nataea, illus. 2018. (Traditional Scottish Tales Ser.). (ENG.). 32p. (J). (gr. -1-2). 17.95 *(978-1-78250-485-6(0)*, Kelpies) Floris Bks. GBR. Dist: Consortium Bk. Sales & Distribution.

Donaldson, Connie & Polinko, Les. The Ganorch under the Porch. Polinko, Les, illus. 2013. (Illus.). 36p. pap. 9.95 *(978-0-9836682-3-7(X))* Hearthstone Rose.

Donaldson, Julia. The Gruffalo. 2006. (ENG., Illus.). 32p. (J). (gr. -1-2). pap. 7.99 *(978-0-14-240387-7(3)*, Puffin Books) Penguin Young Readers Group.

—The Gruffalo. Scheffler, Axel, illus. 2005. (ENG.). (J). (gr. -1-2). 32p. 18.99 *(978-0-8037-3109-7(4))*; 26p. bds. 8.99 *(978-0-8037-3047-2(0))* Penguin Young Readers Group. (Dial Bks).

—The Gruffalo. 2006. lib. bdg. 18.40 *(978-0-606-23141-1(2))* Turtleback.

Donato, Cindy. Monsters! Monsters! 2004. 33p. pap. 24.95 *(978-1-4137-3221-4(6))* PublishAmerica, Inc.

Donnanna. Jamie & the Cheesy Foot Monster. 2010. (Illus.). 44p. pap. 16.99 *(978-1-4490-9785-1(5))* AuthorHouse.

Dooley, Larry. A Peanut Butter & Monster Sandwich. Grzelak, Kyle, illus. 2013. 24p. pap. 12.95 *(978-1-61493-206-2(9))* Peppertree Pr., The.

Dorling Kindersley Publishing Staff & Murray, Helen. Stop the Stone Monsters! 2017. (DK Reader Level 1 Ser.). lib. bdg. 13.55 *(978-0-606-39896-1(1))* Turtleback.

Dowding, Philippa. The Gargoyle in My Yard. 2009. (Lost Gargoyle Ser.: 1). (ENG.). 128p. (J). (gr. 4-7). pap. 9.99 *(978-1-894917-82-7(0)*, Napoleon & Co.) Dundurn Pr. CAN. Dist: Publishers Group West (PGW).

—Myles & the Monster Outside: Weird Stories Gone Wrong. 2015. (Weird Stories Gone Wrong Ser.: 2). (ENG., Illus.). 136p. (J). pap. 8.99 *(978-1-4597-2943-8(9))* Dundurn Pr. CAN. Dist: Publishers Group West (PGW).

Dower, Laura. The Beast with 1000 Eyes #3. Schlafman, Dave, illus. 2009. (Monster Squad Ser.: 3). 144p. (J). (gr. 3-7). pap. 5.99 *(978-0-448-44914-2(5)*, Grosset & Dunlap) Penguin Young Readers Group.

—The Slime That Would Not Die, 1. Schlafman, Dave, illus. 2009. (Monster Squad Ser.: 1). (ENG.). 144p. (J). (gr. 4-6). 17.44 *(978-0-448-44912-8(9))* Penguin Young Readers Group.

Doyle, Bill. The Zombie at the Finish Line, 4. Lee, Jared, illus. 2013. (Scream Team Ser.). (ENG.). 96p. (J). (gr. 2-4). 17.44 *(978-0-545-47978-3(9))* Scholastic, Inc.

Dozier, Kamilah. The Monster Named Fear. 2012. (ENG.). 68p. pap. 26.00 *(978-1-4772-9148-1(2))* AuthorHouse.

Dracula. (J). 9.95 *(978-1-56156-373-9(0))* Kidsbooks, LLC.

Drago, Ty. The Undertakers: Queen of the Dead. Williams, Eric, illus. 2012. 432p. (J). (gr. 5-8). pap. 12.99 *(978-1-4022-7557-9(9))* Sourcebooks, Inc.

Drescher, Henrik. Simon's Book. 2006. (ENG., Illus.). 32p. (J). (gr. -1-1). *(978-1-59692-135-1(8))* MacAdam/Cage Publishing, Inc.

Du Lac, Leo J. Dogfish on the Moon: Santa Claus & the Flying Carpet 2. Baker, David, illus. 2012. 26p. 24.95 *(978-1-4560-1036-2(0))* America Star Bks.

Dube, Tory. A Trixi, a Shmoop & a Monster. Vasilevsky, Marina, illus. 2013. 32p. 19.99 *(978-0-9886193-1-9(8))* Dube, Tory.

Dube, Tory Lee. A Trixi, a Shmoop & a Monster. 2013. 32p. pap. 9.99 *(978-0-9886193-0-2(X))* Dube, Tory.

Duerr, Doug. The Adventures of Jazz & Elliott: The Love Ness Monster. 2012. (ENG.). 37p. (J). pap. 14.95 *(978-1-4327-7746-3(7))* Outskirts Pr., Inc.

Dufresne, Michèle. Look Out for Space Monster: Spaceboy Set 1. 2003. (Spaceboy Set 1 Ser.). (J). pap. 7.33 *(978-1-932570-04-5(7))* Pioneer Valley Bks.

—Space Monster Saves the Day. 2007. (Spaceboy Chapter Ser.). (ENG.). (J). per. 7.67 *(978-1-932570-61-8(6))* Pioneer Valley Bks.

Durant, Alan. Billy Monster's Daymare. Collins, Ross, illus. 2008. 32p. (J). (gr. -1-2). pap. 6.95 *(978-1-58925-412-1(0))* Tiger Tales.

Dussling, Jennifer. In a Dark, Dark House. Jones, Davy, illus. Date not set. (All Aboard Reading Ser.). 32p. (J). (gr. -1-k). pap. *(978-0-448-40974-0(7)*, Grosset & Dunlap) Penguin Publishing Group.

Dwight, Revena. The Together Book (Sesame Street) Bradfield, Roger, illus. 2017. (Little Golden Book Ser.). (ENG.). 24p. (J). (-k). 4.99 *(978-1-5247-1978-4(1)*, Golden Bks.) Random Hse. Children's Bks.

Dye, Troy & Kelesides, Tom. Goblin Chronicles 01A. 2008. (YA). 3.50 *(978-0-9801314-0-6(5))* Ape Entertainment.

—Goblin Chronicles #1B. 2008. (YA). 3.50 *(978-0-9801314-1-3(3))* Ape Entertainment.

—Goblin Chronicles #2A. 2008. (Illus.). 32p. (J). 3.50 *(978-0-9801314-2-0(1))* Ape Entertainment.

—Goblin Chronicles #2B. 2008. (Illus.). 32p. (J). 3.50 *(978-0-9801314-3-7(X))* Ape Entertainment.

Eagar, Lindsay. The Bigfoot Files. 2018. (ENG.). 384p. (J). (gr. 5-9). 16.99 *(978-0-7636-9234-6(4))* Candlewick Pr.

Eaton, Deborah. Canciones de Monstruos. Translations.com Staff, tr. from ENG. Handelman, Dorothy, photos by. 2007. (Lecturas para niños de verdad - Nivel 2 (Real Kids Readers - Level 2) Ser.).Tr. of Monster Songs. (SPA., Illus.). 32p. (gr. k-3). per. 5.95 *(978-0-8225-7803-1(4))* Lerner Publishing Group.

Ecton, Emily. Night of the Living Lawn Ornaments. 2009. (ENG.). 240p. (J). (gr. 3-7). pap. 5.99 *(978-1-4169-6451-3(7)*, Aladdin) Simon & Schuster Children's Publishing.

Edwards, Elizabeth Marshall. How Parker James Got the Monsters Out from under His Bed. 2012. 20p. pap. 24.95 *(978-1-4626-6796-3(1))* America Star Bks.

Eggers, Dave. The Lifters. (ENG., Illus.). 352p. (J). (gr. 3-7). 2019. pap. 9.99 *(978-1-5247-6419-7(1)*, Yearling) 2018. lib. bdg. 20.99 *(978-1-5247-6417-3(5)*, Knopf Bks. for Young Readers) Random Hse. Children's Bks.

Eifrig, Kate. Scary Monster. Graves, Dennis, illus. 2003. (ENG.). 8p. (gr. k-1). pap. 7.95 *(978-1-879835-29-0(0)*, Kaeden Bks.) Kaeden Corp.

Emberley, Ed. Bye-Bye, Big Bad Bullybug! Emberley, Ed, illus. 2007. (ENG., Illus.). 32p. (J). (gr. -1-3). 16.99 *(978-0-316-01762-6(0))* Little, Brown Bks. for Young Readers.

—Nighty Night, Little Green Monster. 2013. (ENG.). 32p. (J). (gr. -1-1). 11.99 *(978-0-316-21041-6(2))* Little, Brown Bks. for Young Readers.

Enderle, Dotti & McWilliam, Howard. Ghost Detectors Book 12: Monsters!, 1 vol. 2011. (Ghost Detectors Ser.). (ENG., Illus.). 80p. (J). (gr. 2-5). 35.64 *(978-1-61641-628-7(9)*, 8824, Calico Chapter Bks.) ABDO Publishing Co.

Ering, Timothy Basil. The Story of Frog Belly Rat Bone. Ering, Timothy Basil, illus. 2013. (ENG., Illus.). 48p. (J). (gr. -1-3). 18.99 *(978-0-7636-6661-3(0))* Candlewick Pr.

Escondete y Grita, Vol. II. (Fantasmas de Fear Street Coleccion: No. 1). (SPA.). (J). (gr. 4-7). pap. 7.95 *(978-950-04-1999-4(8)*, EM4474) Emecé Editores S.A. ARG. Dist: Lectorum Pubns., Inc., Planeta Publishing Corp.

Etherington, Robin. Freaky & Fearless: Bazookas for Beginners. Bielecki, Jan, illus. 2017. (Freaky & Fearless Ser.: 3). (ENG.). 304p. (J). (gr. 4-7). pap. 8.99 *(978-1-84812-584-1(4))* Bonnier Publishing GBR. Dist: Independent Pubs. Group.

—Freaky & Fearless: the Art of Being a Freak. Bielecki, Jan, illus. 2017. (Freaky & Fearless Ser.: 2). (ENG.). 288p. (J). (gr. 4-7). pap. 8.99 *(978-1-84812-512-4(7))* Bonnier Publishing GBR. Dist: Independent Pubs. Group.

Eugenio, Johnny. Lil' Jordan's 9 Holes of Fear. 2009. (ENG., Illus.). 50p. (J). (gr. k-3). 16.95 *(978-1-60747-703-7(3))* Phoenix Bks., Inc.

—Lil Jordan's 9 Holes of Fear. 2009. 48p. (J). 11.95 *(978-1-60747-706-8(8))* Phoenix Bks., Inc.

Evans, Angela. A Monster Can Be Friendly. 2012. 28p. pap. 32.70 *(978-1-4797-3645-4(7))* Xlibris Corp.

Fantastik, B. Save the Sleepless Slumbernots! Valentine, M. K., illus. 2013. 32p. *(978-1-4602-2777-0(8))* FriesenPress.

Farber, Erica, et al. The Swamp Thing, 1. 2006. (Mercer Mayer's Critter Kids Adventures Ser.). (ENG., Illus.). 32p. (J). (gr. k-3). 17.44 *(978-0-7696-4762-3(6))* School Specialty, Incorporated.

Farrey, Brian. The Vengekeep Prophecies. Helquist, Brett, illus. 2013. (Vengekeep Prophecies Ser.: 1). (ENG.). 416p. (J). (gr. 3-7). pap. 7.99 *(978-0-06-204929-2(1)*, HarperCollins) HarperCollins Pubs.

Feaster, Raven Joye Raye. Merrileggs of Macon County. 2011. 72p. (gr. -1). pap. 10.75 *(978-1-4567-6971-0(5))* AuthorHouse.

Ferrari, Antongionata, illus. Hercules, 1 vol. 2009. (Hotel Olympus Ser.). (ENG.). 128p. (J). (gr. 2-3). 36.60 *(978-1-60754-708-2(2)*, e2f56b82-ddb6-45bd-8206-9278ae26dbce, Windmill Bks.) Rosen Publishing Group, Inc., The.

Fields, Jan. Chase the Chupacabra, 1 vol. Brundage, Scott, illus. 2014. (Monster Hunters Ser.). (ENG.). 80p. (J). (gr. 2-5). 35.64 *(978-1-62402-044-5(5)*, 1523, Calico Chapter Bks.) ABDO Publishing Co.

—Search for Bigfoot, 1 vol. Brundage, Scott, illus. 2014. (Monster Hunters Ser.). (ENG.). 80p. (J). (gr. 2-5). 35.64 *(978-1-62402-046-9(1)*, 1527, Calico Chapter Bks.) ABDO Publishing Co.

—Tame Tahoe Tessie, 1 vol. Brundage, Scott, illus. 2014. (Monster Hunters Ser.). (ENG.). 80p. (J). (gr. 2-5). 35.64 *(978-1-62402-047-6(X)*, 1529, Calico Chapter Bks.) ABDO Publishing Co.

Fienberg, Anna. Monsters. Gamble, Kim & Axelsen, Stephen, illus. 2018. (ENG.). 32p. (J). (gr. k-3). 20.99 *(978-1-76029-336-9(9))* Allen & Unwin AUS. Dist: Independent Pubs. Group.

La Fiesta Monstruosa, 6 Pks. (Chiquilibros Ser.). (SPA.). (gr. k-1). 23.00 *(978-0-7635-8600-3(5))* Rigby Education.

Filliozat, Isabelle. Fear: A Monsters, Inc. Story. 2020. (J). *(978-1-5415-9858-4(X))* Lerner Publishing Group.

Fletcher, Tom. There's a Monster in Your Book. Abbott, Greg, illus. (Who's in Your Book? Ser.). (ENG.). (J). 2018. 34p. (— 1). bds. 8.99 *(978-0-525-64578-8(0))* 2017. 32p. (gr. -1-2). 18.99 *(978-1-5247-6456-2(6))* Random Hse. Children's Bks. (Random Hse. Bks. for Young Readers).

Flitcroft, Jean. The Pacific Giants. 2014. (Cryptid Files Ser.: No. 3). (ENG.). 240p. (J). (gr. 4-8). lib. bdg. 27.99 *(978-1-4677-3266-6(4)*, d3ba07f4-111c-4622-b3c7-98963d252a64);No. 3. pap. 7.95 *(978-1-4677-3485-1(3)*, e22f0480-1a44-447f-9d39-6484db0f2c33) Lerner Publishing Group. (Darby Creek).

Födi, Lee Edward. Kendra Kandlestar & the Crack in Kazah. 2011. (ENG., Illus.). 294p. (J). pap. 8.95 *(978-1-61254-019-1(8))* Brown Books Publishing Group.

—Kendra Kandlestar & the Crack in Kazah. Födi, Lee Edward, illus. 2011. (ENG., Illus.). 282p. (J). (gr. 4-7). 16.95 (978-1-61254-018-4(X)) Brown Books Publishing Group.

Fontes, Justine & Fontes, Ron. Casebook: The Loch Ness Monster, 1 vol. 2009. (Top Secret Graphica Mysteries Ser.). (ENG., Illus.). 48p. (YA). (gr. 4-4). 33.93 (978-1-60754-602-3(7), 52c0a569-8ac9-4d7e-8216-cb02fc86f91b); pap. 12.75 (978-1-60754-600-9(0), 99260723-11e8-4db1-8517-0804e8a05bba) Rosen Publishing Group, Inc., The. (Windmill Bks.).

Fourniea, Stephanie. Are You a Monster When You Eat. 2011. 24p. pap. 12.29 (978-1-4634-2958-4(4)) AuthorHouse.

Fox-Smith, Angela. The Clock-Mess Monster. 2011. 32p. pap. 24.95 (978-1-4560-5723-7(5)) America Star Bks.

Fred, Anthony. Fred & Anthony Meet the Heinie Goblins from the Black Lagoon. Primavera, Elise, illus. rev. ed. 2008. 128p. 14.99 (978-0-7868-3681-9(4)) Hyperion Bks. for Children.

Fredrickson, Lane. Monster Trouble! Robertson, Michael, illus. 2015. 32p. (J). (gr. -1-2). 16.95 (978-1-4549-1345-0(2)) Sterling Publishing Co., Inc.

Freedman, Claire. Don't Wake the Yeti! Ranucci, Claudia, illus. 2017. (ENG.). 32p. (J). (gr. -1-3). 17.99 (978-0-8075-1690-4(2), 807516902) Whitman, Albert & Co.

—Dragon Jelly. Hendra, Sue, illus. 2015. (ENG.). 32p. (J). (gr. k-3). 14.99 (978-1-61963-682-8(4), 900145471, Bloomsbury USA Childrens) Bloomsbury Publishing USA.

—The Monster of the Woods! Julian, Russell, illus. 2013. (ENG.). 32p. (J). pap. (978-0-545-51571-9(8), Cartwheel Bks.) Scholastic, Inc.

—The Monster of the Woods!/By Claire Freedman & Russell Julian. Julian, Russell, illus. 2013. (J). (978-0-545-56837-1(4), Cartwheel Bks.) Scholastic, Inc.

—Scary Hairy Party. Hendra, Sue, illus. 2017. (ENG.). 32p. (J). pap. (978-1-4088-6717-4(6), 281266, Bloomsbury Children's Bks.) Bloomsbury Publishing Plc.

—Spider Sandwiches. Hendra, Sue, illus. 2014. (ENG.). 32p. (J). (gr. k-3). 15.99 (978-1-61963-364-3(7), 900134246, Bloomsbury USA Childrens) Bloomsbury Publishing USA.

Freese, Thomas. Halloween Sleepwalker, 1 vol. 2013. (ENG., Illus.). 64p. (J). (gr. -1-3). 16.99 (978-0-7643-4399-5(8), 4866) Schiffer Publishing, Ltd.

Freidman, Mel. The Blue Moon Effect. Smith, Eric, illus. gif. ed. 2005. (Extreme Monsters Ser.). 96p. (J). (gr. 2-5). per. 3.99 (978-1-57791-178-4(4)) Brighter Minds Children's Publishing.

French, Vivian. The Snow Dragon. Fisher, Chris, illus. 2003. 32p. (J). pap. 11.99 (978-0-552-54595-2(3)) Transworld Publishers Ltd. GBR. Dist: Trafalgar Square Publishing.

Froman, Annabelle. Beezeur. 2013. 34p. pap. 9.95 (978-0-9842053-1-8(4)) Breathless Vintage Enterprises.

Fujikawa, Brian. The Adventures of Bibole, Ri: The CURSE of the WEREMOUSE. 2012. 52p. pap. 18.41 (978-1-4669-3547-1(2)) Trafford Publishing.

Funari-Willever, Lisa. Theres A Kid under My Bed (Cj) 2008. 40p. 12.95 (978-0-9760469-4-3(6)) Franklin Mason Pr.

Gaiman, Neil. The Dangerous Alphabet. Grimly, Gris, illus. (ENG.). 32p. (J). (gr. -1-3). 2010. pap. 7.99 (978-0-06-078335-8(4)) 2008. 17.99 (978-0-06-078333-4(8)) HarperCollins Pubs. (HarperCollins).

Galindo, Claudia. It's Bedtime, Cucuy!/A la Cama, Cucuy. Pluecker, John, tr. Coombs, Jonathan, illus. 2008. (SPA & ENG.). 32p. (J). (gr. -1-2). 16.95 (978-1-55885-491-8(6), Piñata Books) Arte Publico Pr.

Galindo, Claudia & Pluecker, John. Do You Know the Cucuy? Conoces Al Cucuy? Coombs, Jonathan, illus. 2008. (SPA & ENG.). 32p. (J). (gr. -1-2). 16.95 (978-1-55885-492-5(4), Piñata Books) Arte Publico Pr.

Gall, Chris. Substitute Creacher. 2011. (ENG., Illus.). 40p. (J). (gr. -1-3). 18.99 (978-0-316-08915-9(X)) Little, Brown Bks. for Young Readers.

Gamble, Adam & Jasper, Mark. Good Night Little Monsters. Kelly, Cooper, illus. 2017. (Good Night Our World Ser.). 20p. (J). (gr. -1 — 1). bds. 9.95 (978-1-60219-489-2(0)) Good Night Bks.

Gamble, Marion. Jack & the Boody Monster. 2018. (ENG., Illus.). 38p. (J). (978-1-5289-2449-8(5)); pap. (978-1-5289-2450-4(9)) Austin Macauley Pubs. Ltd.

—Jack & the Boody Monster. 2018. (ENG., Illus.). 38p. (J). pap. 14.95 (978-1-78629-874-4(0), cd46df8c-a858-4ee3-baff-887bae3968d1) Austin Macauley Pubs. Ltd. GBR. Dist: Baker & Taylor Publisher Services (BTPS).

Garza, Xavier. Juan & the Chupacabras/Juan y el Chupacabras. Ward, April, illus. 2006. (ENG & SPA.). 32p. (J). (gr. -1-2). 16.95 (978-1-55885-454-3(1), Piñata Books) Arte Publico Pr.

Gates, Susan. The Pumpkin Monster Blue Band. Sua, Laura, illus. 2016. (Cambridge Reading Adventures Ser.). (ENG.). 16p. pap. 7.95 (978-1-316-60576-9(0)) Cambridge Univ. Pr.

Geoghegan, Adrienne. There's a Wardrobe in My Monster! Johnson, Adrian, illus. 2003. (Picture Bks.). 32p. (J). (gr. -1-3). 15.95 (978-1-57505-414-8(0), Carolrhoda Bks.) Lerner Publishing Group.

Ghost, Derek The. Scary School #2: Monsters on the March. Fischer, Scott M., illus. 2012. (Scary School Ser.: 2). (ENG.). 256p. (J). (gr. 3-7). 15.99 (978-0-06-196095-6(0), HarperCollins) HarperCollins Pubs.

Giangregorio, Kimberly A. The Smelly Shoe. O'Toole, Julianne, illus. 2012. 24p. pap. 24.95 (978-1-4626-9387-0(3)) America Star Bks.

Gibala-Broxholm, Scott. Maddie's Monster Dad, 0 vols. Gibala-Broxholm, Scott, illus. 2012. (ENG., Illus.). 40p. (J). (gr. -1-3). 16.99 (978-0-7614-5846-3(8), 9780761458463, Two Lions) Amazon Publishing.

Gibson, James E. & Gibson, Sylvia Scott. Treetoe the Space Monster, 1 vol. Gibson, Gregory V., illus. 2010. 28p. 24.95 (978-1-4489-4896-3(7)) PublishAmerica, Inc.

Gilchrist, J. Into the Land of Nede. 2010. 108p. (gr. 4-6). 20.95 (978-1-4502-5433-5(0)); pap. 10.95 (978-1-4502-5432-8(2)) iUniverse, Inc.

Gilden, Mel. M Is for Monster. Pierard, John & Fastner, Steve, illus. 2018. (ENG.). 104p. (J). (gr. 4-7). pap. 11.95 (978-1-59687-778-8(2)) ibooks, Inc.

Gill, Jacqueline Paske. The Monster in the Basement. Gill, Jacqueline Paske, illus. 2011. (Illus.). 32p. pap. 12.95 (978-1-61493-003-7(1)) Peppertree Pr., The.

Gilligan, Shannon. The Lake Monster Mystery. Newton, Keith, illus. 2009. (ENG.). 80p. (J). (gr. 2-2). pap. 8.99 (978-1-933390-60-4(3)) Chooseco LLC.

Glasser, Frederick. Monsters Come Out Tonight! Miller, Edward, illus. 2019. (Festive Flaps Ser.). (ENG.). 18p. (J). (gr. -1-k). bds. 9.99 (978-1-4197-3722-0(8), 1277110, Abrams Appleseed) Abrams, Inc.

Glenn Marsh, Sarah. Reign of the Fallen. 2019. (Reign of the Fallen Ser.: 1). 400p. (YA). (gr. 7). pap. 10.99 (978-0-448-49440-1(X), Razorbill) Penguin Young Readers Group.

Golden Books. Oscar's Book (Sesame Street) Golden Books, illus. 2018. (Little Golden Book Ser.). (ENG., Illus.). 24p. (J). (-k). 5.99 (978-0-525-57840-6(4), Golden Bks.) Random Hse. Children's Bks.

Goldthorpe, Jake. Mommy! Daddy! Help! There's a Monster in My Room! 2008. 28p. pap. 15.99 (978-1-4363-7114-8(7)) Xlibris Corp.

Gollub, Matthew. Ten Oni Drummers. Stone, Kazuko G., illus. 2018. (Ten Oni Drummers Ser.). (ENG.). 32p. (J). (gr. -1-k). 17.95 (978-1-889910-51-2(1)) Tortuga Pr.

—Ten Oni Drummers / Diez Tamborileros Oni. Stone, Kazuko, illus. 2019. (Ten Oni Drummers Ser.). (SPA & ENG.). 32p. (J). (gr. -1-k). 17.95 (978-1-889910-53-6(8)) Tortuga Pr.

Gollub, Matthew & Stone, Kazuko G. Ten Oni Drummers. 2013. (ENG., Illus.). 32p. (J). (gr. -1-3). 16.95 (978-1-58430-011-3(6)) Lee & Low Bks., Inc.

Gomes, Alexandre de Castro. Folclore de Chuteiras. Visca, illus. 2014. (POR.). 67p. (J). (978-85-7596-341-8(4)) Editora Peiropolis Ltda.

Gómez Cerdá, Alfredo. El Monstruo y la Bibliotecaria. 4th ed. (SPA., Illus.). 62p. (J). (gr. 3-5). (978-84-279-3456-6(4), NG1580) Noguer y Caralt Editores, S. A. ESP. Dist: Lectorum Pubns., Inc.

Gong, Chloe. These Violent Delights. 2023. (ENG.). 496p. (These Violent Delights Ser.). (gr. 8-13). 33.69 **(978-1-5364-8037-5(1))**; (These Violent Delights Duet Ser.: 1). (YA). (gr. 9). pap. 13.99 **(978-1-6659-2176-3(5))** McElderry, Margaret K. Bks. (McElderry, Margaret K. Bks.).

—These Violent Delights. 2020. (These Violent Delights Duet Ser.: 1). (ENG., Illus.). 464p. (YA). (gr. 9). 19.99 (978-1-5344-5769-0(0), Simon Pulse) Simon Pulse.

Gonyea, Mark. One Little Monster. Gonyea, Mark, illus. 2018. (ENG., Illus.). 40p. (J). (gr. -1-3). 17.99 (978-1-5344-0674-2(3), Aladdin) Simon & Schuster Children's Publishing.

Gonzalez, L. M. R. Gifts Lucy. The Terrible Monster. 2008. 52p. pap. 24.93 (978-1-4357-5500-0(6)) Lulu Pr., Inc.

Goodner, David & Thomas, Louis. Ginny Goblin Cannot Have a Monster for a Pet. 2019. (ENG., Illus.). 40p. (J). (gr. -1-3). 17.99 (978-0-544-76416-3(1), 1635201, Clarion Bks.) HarperCollins Pubs.

Goodwin, Vincent. Call of Cthulhu, 1 vol. 2014. (Graphic Horror Ser.). (ENG., Illus.). 32p. (J). (gr. 5-8). lib. bdg. 32.79 (978-1-62402-014-8(3), 9098, Graphic Planet - Fiction) Magic Wagon.

—Wendigo, 1 vol. 2014. (Graphic Horror Ser.). (ENG.). 32p. (J). (gr. 5-8). lib. bdg. 32.79 (978-1-62402-018-6(6), 9106, Graphic Planet - Fiction) Magic Wagon.

Gorey, Edward. The Wuggly Ump. Gorey, Edward, illus. 2007. (Illus.). 32p. 12.95 (978-0-7649-4192-4(5), A142) Pomegranate Communications, Inc.

Gorman, Zac. Thisby Thestoop & the Wretched Scrattle. Bosma, Sam, illus. 2019. (ENG.). 384p. (J). (gr. 3-7). 16.99 (978-0-06-249574-7(7), HarperCollins) HarperCollins Pubs.

Gos. The Smurfs #7: The Astrosmurf. 2011. (Smurfs Graphic Novels Ser.: 7). (ENG., Illus.). 56p. (J). (gr. 2-5). pap. 5.99 (978-1-59707-250-2(8), 900075394, Papercutz) Mad Cave Studios.

Gos & Delporte, Yvan. The Smurfs #6: Smurfs & the Howlibird: The Smurfs & the Howlibird, Vol. 6. 2011. (Smurfs Graphic Novels Ser.: 6). (ENG., Illus.). 56p. (J). (gr. 2-5). pap. 5.99 (978-1-59707-260-1(5), 900075410, Papercutz) Mad Cave Studios.

—The Smurfs #6: Smurfs & the Howlibird: The Smurfs & the Howlibird, Vol. 6. 2011. (Smurfs Graphic Novels Ser.: 6). (ENG., Illus.). 56p. (J). (gr. 2-5). 10.99 (978-1-59707-261-8(3), 900075411, Papercutz) Mad Cave Studios.

Gosier, Phil. Snow Beast Comes to Play. Gosier, Phil, illus. 2017. (ENG., Illus.). 32p. (J). 17.99 (978-1-62672-519-5(5), 9781626725195) Roaring Brook Pr.

Graham, Alastair. Full Moon Soup. 2007. (Illus.). 32p. (J). (gr. k-3). 12.95 (978-1-905417-54-4(3)) Boxer Bks., Ltd. GBR. Dist: Sterling Publishing Co., Inc.

Graham, Richard. Jack y el Monstruo. Varley, Susan, illus. (Cotton Cloud Ser.). (SPA.). 32p. (J). (gr. 1-3). (978-84-7722-680-2(6)) Timun Mas, Editorial S.A. ESP. Dist: Lectorum Pubns., Inc.

Grandma. There Is a Vampire in Our Cellar: Adventures of Butterfly Nectar Meadows. 2008. 20p. pap. 24.95 (978-1-60813-128-0(9)) America Star Bks.

Grant, Michael. Monster. (Gone Ser.: 7). (ENG.). (YA). (gr. 9). 2018. 448p. pap. 11.99 (978-0-06-246785-0(9)) 2017. 432p. 18.99 (978-0-06-246784-3(0)) HarperCollins Pubs. (Tegen, Katherine Bks).

Gratz, Alan. The League of Seven. Helquist, Brett, illus. 2015. (League of Seven Ser.: 1). (ENG.). 352p. (J). (gr. 5-9). pap. 10.99 (978-0-7653-3825-9(4), 900126212, Starscape) Doherty, Tom Assocs., LLC.

Grau, Sheila. Dr. Critchlore's School for Minions: Book One. Sutphin, Joe, illus. 2016. (Dr. Critchlore's School for Minions Ser.). (ENG.). 304p. (J). (gr. 3-7). pap. 7.95 (978-1-4197-2029-1(5), 1091603, Amulet Bks.) Abrams, Inc.

—Polar Distress: Dr. Critchlore's School for Minions #3. Sutphin, Joe, illus. 2017. (Dr. Critchlore's School for Minions Ser.). (ENG.). 288p. (J). (gr. 3-7). 14.95 (978-1-4197-2294-3(8), 1132101) Abrams, Inc.

Grau, Sheila & Sutphin, Joe. Dr. Critchlore's School for Minions: Book Two: Gorilla Tactics. 2016. (Dr. Critchlore's School for Minions Ser.). (ENG., Illus.). 304p. (J). (gr. 3-7). 14.95 (978-1-4197-1371-2(X), 1091701, Amulet Bks.) Abrams, Inc.

Gravel, Elise. I Want a Monster! Gravel, Elise, illus. 2016. (ENG., Illus.). 40p. (J). (gr. -1-3). 17.99 (978-0-06-241533-2(6), HarperCollins) HarperCollins Pubs.

Graves, Emma T. OMG, Zombie! Boo, Binny, illus. 2018. (My Undead Life Ser.). (ENG.). 112p. (J). (gr. 3-6). lib. bdg. 25.99 (978-1-4965-6444-3(8), 138356, Stone Arch Bks.) Capstone.

Graves, Judith. Second Skin. 2011. 280p. (J). pap. 16.99 (978-1-61603-006-3(2)) Leap Bks.

—Under My Skin. Cox, Val, illus. 2010. 328p. (YA). (gr. 8-18). pap. 16.99 (978-1-61603-000-1(3)) Leap Bks.

Gray, Kes. Nelly, the Monster Sitter. 2009. (ENG., Illus.). 272p. (J). (gr. 3-7). 8.99 (978-1-59514-259-7(2), Razorbill) Penguin Young Readers Group.

Green, Andi. The Lonely Little Monster. 2007. (WorryWoo Monsters Ser.). (Illus.). 68p. (J). 14.99 (978-0-9792860-0-1(X)) Monsters in My Head, LLC, The.

—The Monster in the Bubble. 2009. (WorryWoo Monsters Ser.). (Illus.). 68p. (J). 14.99 (978-0-9792860-2-5(6)) Monsters in My Head, LLC, The.

—The Monster Who Couldn't Decide. 2010. (WorryWoo Monsters Ser.). 98p. (J). 14.99 (978-0-9792860-3-2(4)) Monsters in My Head, LLC, The.

Green, K. C. Regular Show Vol. 1. 2014. lib. bdg. 26.95 (978-0-606-35467-7(0)) Turtleback.

Greenwell, Jessica. Noisy Monsters. Wildish, Lee, illus. 2010. (Busy Sounds Board Bks). 10p. (J). bds. 18.99 (978-0-7945-2769-3(8), Usborne) EDC Publishing.

Gresko, Marcia S. Monster Stew. 2017. (Learn-To-Read Ser.). (ENG., Illus.). (J). pap. 3.49 (978-1-68310-280-9(0)) Pacific Learning, Inc.

Gross, Kimberley & Gross, Kaiya. The Multiplication Monster. Gross, Sanai, illus. 2013. 84p. pap. 10.95 (978-0-9886402-3-8(6)) Vision Bks. LLC.

Groves. Pond Monster, Bk. 5A. Date not set. (Illus.). 16p. (J). pap. 129.15 (978-0-582-18796-2(6)) Addison-Wesley Longman, Ltd. GBR. Dist: Trans-Atlantic Pubns., Inc.

Gunhus, Jeff. Jack Templar & the Monster Hunter Academy. 2013. 330p. pap. 12.95 (978-0-9884259-4-1(7)) Seven Guns Pr.

—Jack Templar Monster Hunter. 2012. 196p. pap. 10.95 (978-0-9884259-0-3(4)) Seven Guns Pr.

Gutierrez, Rochelle. Dear Monster. 2010. 16p. pap. 8.95 (978-1-4490-7281-0(X)) AuthorHouse.

Haesche, Richard Paul, Sr. The Magic of the Leprechaun. 2007. (ENG.). 182p. (YA). (978-0-9798536-3-0(X)) Kreative X-Pressions Pubns.

Haggarty, Holly. Summer Dragons. 2007. (ENG.). 176p. (J). (gr. 3-18). per. 9.95 (978-1-894917-52-0(9), Napoleon & Co.) Dundurn Pr. CAN. Dist: Publishers Group West (PGW).

Hahn, Molly. Under the Sneep Tree: The Wamboozling of a Village. 2009. pap. (978-1-61623-907-7(7)) Independent Pub.

Hale, Shannon & Hale, Dean. The Princess in Black. Pham, LeUyen, illus. (Princess in Black Ser.: 1). (ENG.). 96p. (J). (gr. k-3). 2015. pap. 6.99 (978-0-7636-7888-3(0)) 2014. 15.99 (978-0-7636-6510-4(X)) Candlewick Pr.

—The Princess in Black. 2015. (Princess in Black Ser.: 1). lib. bdg. 17.20 (978-0-606-36863-6(9)) Turtleback.

—The Princess in Black & the Hungry Bunny Horde. Pham, LeUyen, illus. 2016. (Princess in Black Ser.: 3). (ENG.). 96p. (J). (gr. k-3). pap. 6.99 (978-0-7636-9089-2(9)); 15.99 (978-0-7636-6513-5(4)) Candlewick Pr.

—The Princess in Black & the Hungry Bunny Horde. Pham, LeUyen, illus. 2016. (Princess in Black Ser.: 3). (ENG.). 85p. (J). (gr. k-3). 17.20 (978-0-606-39109-2(6)) Turtleback.

—The Princess in Black & the Mysterious Playdate. Pham, LeUyen, illus. (Princess in Black Ser.: 5). (ENG.). 96p. (J). (gr. k-3). 2018. pap. 6.99 (978-1-5362-0051-5(4)) 2017. 15.99 (978-0-7636-8826-4(6)) Candlewick Pr.

—The Princess in Black & the Mysterious Playdate. Pham, LeUyen, illus. 2018. (Princess in Black Ser.). (ENG.). 96p. (J). (gr. k-3). lib. bdg. 31.36 (978-1-5321-4223-9(4), 28560, Chapter Bks.) Spotlight.

—The Princess in Black & the Mysterious Playdate. 2018. (Princess in Black Ser.: 5). (J). lib. bdg. 17.20 (978-0-606-40910-0(6)) Turtleback.

—The Princess in Black & the Perfect Princess Party. Pham, LeUyen, illus. (J). (gr. k-3). 2016. (Princess in Black Ser.: 2). (ENG.). 96p. pap. 6.99 (978-0-7636-8758-8(8)) 2015. (Princess in Black Ser.: 2). (ENG.). 96p. 15.99 (978-0-7636-6511-1(8)) 2015. 87p. (978-1-338-11281-8(3)) Candlewick Pr.

—The Princess in Black & the Perfect Princess Party, 2. 2016. (Princess in Black Ser.). (ENG.). 96p. (gr. k-3). 21.19 (978-1-4844-7927-8(0)) Candlewick Pr.

—The Princess in Black & the Perfect Princess Party. Pham, LeUyen, illus. 2018. (Princess in Black Ser.). (ENG.). 96p. (J). (gr. k-3). lib. bdg. 31.36 (978-1-5321-4220-8(X), 28557, Chapter Bks.) Spotlight.

—The Princess in Black & the Perfect Princess Party. 2016. (Princess in Black Ser.: 2). (Illus.). 87p. (J). lib. bdg. 17.20 (978-0-606-37945-8(2)) Turtleback.

Hall, Jacque. Boo! Oertel, Jennifer, illus. 2018. (ENG.). 26p. (J). (gr. k-3). 18.99 (978-1-63132-054-5(8)) Advanced Publishing LLC.

Hall, Michael. Frankencrayon. 2016. (ENG., Illus.). 40p. (J). (gr. -1-3). 17.99 (978-0-06-225211-1(9), Greenwillow Bks.) HarperCollins Pubs.

—Frankencrayon. Hall, Michael, illus. 2016. (ENG., Illus.). 40p. (J). (gr. -1-3). lib. bdg. 18.89 (978-0-06-225212-8(7), Greenwillow Bks.) HarperCollins Pubs.

Hamilton, John. Mission To Mars, 6 bks. Incl. Mariner Missions to Mars. 32p. (gr. 5). 1998. 27.07 (978-1-56239-828-6(8), Abdo & Daughters); (Illus.). Set lib. bdg. 136.68 o.p. (978-1-57765-258-8(4), Abdo & Daughters) ABDO Publishing Co.

Hansen, Justin LaRocca. Monster Hunter. 2012. (ENG., Illus.). 32p. (J). (gr. -1-k). 16.95 (978-1-61608-968-9(7), 608968, Sky Pony Pr.) Skyhorse Publishing Co., Inc.

Hardin, J. R. Kalvin the Kudzu Monster. 2010. 76p. (J). pap. 8.95 (978-1-4502-5764-0(X)) iUniverse, Inc.

Harrington, Kim. Attack of the Not-So-Virtual Monsters (Gamer Squad 1) Gamer Squad #1. 2017. (Gamer Squad Ser.). 208p. (J). (gr. 3-7). pap. 6.95 (978-1-4549-2612-2(0)) Sterling Publishing Co., Inc.

Harris, Christine. Undercover Girl #5: Twisted. 2007. (ENG.). 136p. (J). per. 10.95 (978-1-59594-151-0(7), Wingspan Pr.) WingSpan Publishing.

Harris, M. S. Ed Rebecca a. & Harris, M. S. Ed. Megan's Monster. Lee, Joe, illus. 2009. 28p. pap. 15.00 (978-1-4490-2822-0(5)) AuthorHouse.

Harrison, Lisi. Monster High. 2011. (Monster High Ser.: 1). (YA). lib. bdg. 19.65 (978-0-606-23459-7(4)) Turtleback.

Hartley Bellows, Carol. Icey. 2009. 32p. pap. 14.99 (978-1-4389-4475-3(6)) AuthorHouse.

Harvey, Keith & Beard, Lauren. Say Please, Louise! A Story of a Little Girl With Monstrous Manners. 2015. (ENG., Illus.). 24p. pap. 8.99 (978-1-84135-921-2(1)) Award Pubns. Ltd. GBR. Dist: Parkwest Pubns., Inc.

Hawkins, Jacqui. Snap! Snap! 2005. (ENG., Illus.). 32p. (J). pap. 7.99 (978-1-4052-1099-7(0)) Farshore GBR. Dist: Trafalgar Square Publishing.

Hawley, Kelvin, illus. My Things, 6 Packs. (Sails Literacy Ser.). 16p. (gr. k-18). 27.00 (978-0-7635-4395-2(0)) Rigby Education.

—The Vacation: Individual Title Six-Packs. (Sails Literacy Ser.). 16p. (gr. k-18). 27.00 (978-0-7635-4434-8(5)) Rigby Education.

Hawthorn, Phillip & Tyler, Jenny. There's A Monster in My House. 2007. 16p. (J). 9.99 (978-0-7945-1567-6(3), Usborne) EDC Publishing.

Hayes, Terri. The Day the Blue Puff Trees Bloomed. 2011. 36p. pap. 24.95 (978-1-4560-6096-1(1)) America Star Bks.

Hegarty, Shane. Darkmouth #4: Hero Rising. 2018. (Darkmouth Ser.: 4). (ENG., Illus.). 400p. (J). (gr. 3-7). 17.99 (978-0-06-231138-2(7), HarperCollins) HarperCollins Pubs.

Heidicker, Christian McKay. Attack of the 50 Foot Wallflower. Bosma, Sam, illus. (ENG.). 320p. (YA). (gr. 9). 2019. pap. 11.99 (978-1-4814-9914-9(9)) 2018. 18.99 (978-1-4814-9913-2(0)) Simon & Schuster Bks. For Young Readers. (Simon & Schuster Bks. For Young Readers).

Helm, Julie G. The Lost Monster Tales. Cary, Debbi, illus. 2010. 212p. pap. 14.49 (978-1-4490-3823-6(9)) AuthorHouse.

Henning, Sarah. Sea Witch. (ENG.). 2019. 384p. (YA). (gr. 8). pap. 10.99 (978-0-06-243880-5(8)) 2018. 368p. (YA). (gr. 8). 17.99 (978-0-06-243877-5(8)) 2018. 368p. (J). (978-0-00-830084-5(4)) HarperCollins Pubs. (Tegen, Katherine Bks).

—Sea Witch Rising. 2019. (ENG.). 416p. (YA). (gr. 8). 17.99 (978-0-06-293147-4(4), Tegen, Katherine Bks) HarperCollins Pubs.

Herman, Gail. Boo on the Loose (Disney/Pixar Monsters, Inc.) Tilley, Scott & Norman, Floyd, illus. 2022. (Step into Reading Ser.). (ENG.). 32p. (J). (gr. -1-1). pap. 5.99 (978-0-7364-2860-6(7), RH/Disney) Random Hse. Children's Bks.

—Scooby-Doo in the Lighthouse Mystery, 1 vol. 2015. (Scooby-Doo! Ser.). (ENG., Illus.). 32p. (J). (gr. k-4). lib. bdg. 31.36 (978-1-61479-410-3(3), 19449, Picture Bk.) Spotlight.

Hernández, Gabriel, et al. Slappy's Tales of Horror. Roman, Dave et al, illus. 2015. 171p. (J). (978-0-545-87203-4(0), Graphix) Scholastic, Inc.

Heshka, Ryan. Welcome to Monster Town. Heshka, Ryan, illus. 2012. (ENG., Illus.). 32p. (J). (gr. -1-1). 18.69 (978-1-250-00405-5(5)) Square Fish.

Hewitt, Franz. Monster Doctor, M. D. 2010. 40p. pap. 18.49 (978-0-557-53188-2(8)) Lulu Pr., Inc.

Hibbs, Sasha. Black Amaranth. 2013. 286p. pap. (978-1-77130-526-6(6)) Evernight Publishing.

Hickey, Laura L. What's in the Woods. 2012. 84p. pap. 19.95 (978-1-4626-9025-1(4)) America Star Bks.

Higesanbon. Mo Mo Mo Mo Monster: Mon Monster. 2011. 56p. pap. 34.95 (978-1-4327-4149-5(7)) Outskirts Pr., Inc.

Higgins, F. E. The Lunatic's Curse. 2011. (ENG.). 352p. (J). (gr. 5-9). 31.99 (978-0-312-56682-1(4), 900059221) Feiwel & Friends.

Higgins, Jim. The Enchanted Nursery: Nessie's Friends. 2008. 24p. pap. 11.49 (978-1-4343-8993-0(6)) AuthorHouse.

Higginson, Sheila Sweeny. Henry Loves Beckett. 2014. (J). lib. bdg. 14.75 (978-0-606-35907-8(9)) Turtleback.

Hill, Andrew G. The Song of the Seraphim. 2009. 196p. pap. 13.95 (978-1-60860-194-3(3), Strategic Bk. Publishing) Strategic Book Publishing & Rights Agency (SBPRA).

Hirst, Daisy. I Do Not Like Books Anymore! Hirst, Daisy, illus. 2018. (ENG., Illus.). 40p. (J). (gr. -1-2). 17.99 (978-1-5362-0334-9(3)) Candlewick Pr.

Hodgkinson, Leigh. The Big Monster Snorey Book. Hodgkinson, Leigh, illus. 2016. (ENG., Illus.). 32p. (J). (gr. -1-2). 16.99 (978-0-7636-8660-4(3)) Candlewick Pr.

Hodgman, Ann. Monsters Dance. Wood, Hannah, illus. 2013. (ENG.). 16p. (J). (gr. -1). bds. 8.95 (978-1-58925-627-9(1)) Tiger Tales.

Hoena, Blake. Beet Juice Buddies. Bardin, Dave, illus. 2018. (Monster Heroes Ser.). (ENG.). 32p. (J). (gr. k-2). lib. bdg. 21.32 (978-1-4965-6416-0(2), 138263, Stone Arch Bks.) Capstone.

—Boy under the Bed. Bardin, Dave, illus. 2018. (Monster Heroes Ser.). (ENG.). 32p. (J). (gr. k-2). lib. bdg. 21.32 (978-1-4965-6414-6(6), 138261, Stone Arch Bks.) Capstone.

—The Horrible Hex. Bardin, Dave, illus. 2018. (Monster Heroes Ser.). (ENG.). 32p. (J). (gr. k-2). lib. bdg. 21.32 (978-1-4965-6413-9(8), 138260, Stone Arch Bks.) Capstone.

—Monster Heroes. 2018. (Monster Heroes Ser.). (ENG.). 32p. (J). (gr. k-2). 181.20 (978-1-4965-6425-2(1), 28280, Stone Arch Bks.) Capstone.

—Monster Heroes. Bardin, Dave, illus. 2017. (ENG.). 96p. (J). (gr. k-2). pap., pap., pap. 5.95 (978-1-62370-783-5(8), 133089, Capstone Young Readers) Capstone.

—The Not-So-Helpless Princess. Cunyat, Pol, illus. 2016. (Thud & Blunder Ser.). (ENG.). 56p. (J). (gr. 1-3). lib. bdg. 23.99 (978-1-4965-3218-3(X), 132413, Stone Arch Bks.) Capstone.

—The Werewolf Bully. Bardin, Dave, illus. 2018. (Monster Heroes Ser.). (ENG.). 32p. (J). (gr. k-2). lib. bdg. 21.32 (978-1-4965-6415-3(4), 138262, Stone Arch Bks.) Capstone.

—Witch's Brew. Bardin, Dave, illus. 2016. (Monster Heroes Ser.). (ENG.). 32p. (J). (gr. k-2). lib. bdg. 21.32

(978-1-4965-3756-0(4), 133082, Stone Arch Bks.) Capstone.

Hoena, Blake & Hoena, Blake A. The Ghost Trap. Bardin, Dave, illus. 2016. (Monster Heroes Ser.). (ENG.). 32p. (J). (gr. k-2). lib. bdg. 21.32 *(978-1-4965-3757-7(2)*, 133084, Stone Arch Bks.) Capstone.

—Vampires & Veggies. Bardin, Dave, illus. 2016. (Monster Heroes Ser.). (ENG.). 32p. (J). (gr. k-2). lib. bdg. 21.32 *(978-1-4965-3755-3(6)*, 133083, Stone Arch Bks.) Capstone.

—Zombies & Meatballs. Bardin, Dave, illus. 2016. (Monster Heroes Ser.). (ENG.). 32p. (J). (gr. k-2). lib. bdg. 21.32 *(978-1-4965-3754-6(8)*, 133081, Stone Arch Bks.) Capstone.

Holcomb, Carrie E., ed. Monster Nation JR. 2004. (Discovery Channel Bks.). (ENG., Illus.). 32p. (J). (gr. 3-6). 18.69 *(978-0-696-23688-4(5))* Meredith Bks.

Holmqvist, Carin. African Tales. 2009. (ENG.). 64p. pap. 28.70 *(978-0-557-18184-1(4))* Lulu Pr., Inc.

Hook. Wrinkled Crinkled Grapes: A Purple Monster. 2007. 52p. per. 8.95 *(978-0-595-42310-1(8))* iUniverse, Inc.

Hopper, Karyn. There's a Monster in My Opu. 2006. (Illus.). 24p. (J). 11.95 *(978-1-57306-244-2(8))* Bess Pr., Inc.

Howland, Ashley. Ghostnapped. 2009. 64p. pap. 9.99 *(978-1-60860-145-5(5)*, Strategic Bk. Publishing) Strategic Book Publishing & Rights Agency (SBPRA).

Huber, Randolph. Monsters from the ID. 2007. 48p. per. 16.95 *(978-1-4241-4682-6(8))* PublishAmerica, Inc.

Huehner, Mariah. Love in the the Time of Assumption. 2018. (Stitched Ser.: 2). (J). lib. bdg. 20.85 *(978-0-606-40831-8(2))* Turtleback.

Hull, Claudia. Procrastimonsters! They're Everywhere. Mikle, Toby, illus. 2012. 44p. pap. 15.95 *(978-1-257-64007-2(0))* Shalako Pr.

Hulme-Cross, Benjamin. The Marsh Demon. Evergreen, Nelson, illus. 2015. (Dark Hunter Ser.). (ENG.). 64p. (J). (gr. 4-8). E-Book 34.65 *(978-1-4677-8658-4(6)*, Darby Creek) Lerner Publishing Group.

Hunter, Erin. Warriors Manga: Warrior's Return, 3 vols. Barry, James L., illus. 2008. (Warriors Manga Ser.: No. 3). (ENG.). 112p. (J). (gr. 3-7). pap. 9.99 *(978-0-06-125233-4(6)*, HarperCollins) HarperCollins Pubs.

Hutchins, M. K. Drift, 1 vol. 2014. (ENG.). 398p. (YA). (gr. 6-12). 19.95 *(978-1-62014-145-8(0)*, leelowtu) Lee & Low Bks., Inc.

Huws, Emily. Anghenfil O Joc. 2005. (WEL., Illus.). 24p. pap. *(978-0-86174-164-9(1))* Drake Educational Assocs. Ltd.

Hyman, Jack G. Breakfast with the Birds. 2013. 216p. pap. 15.99 *(978-1-4525-8453-9(2)*, Balboa Pr.) Author Solutions, LLC.

I Am Working, 6 Packs. (Sails Literacy Ser.). 16p. (gr. k-18). 27.00 *(978-0-7635-4407-2(8))* Rigby Education.

I Like Jam: Individual Title, 6 Packs. (Sails Literacy Ser.). 16p. (gr. k-18). 27.00 *(978-0-7635-4440-9(X))* Rigby Education.

If You're Gonna be a Monster do it Right. 2005. (YA). per. *(978-1-59872-088-4(0))* Instant Pub.

In the Mud, Pk. 6. (Sails Literacy Ser.). 16p. (gr. k-18). 27.00 *(978-0-7635-4428-7(0))* Rigby Education.

Inches, Alison. I Can Save the Earth! One Little Monster Learns to Reduce, Reuse, & Recycle. Garofoli, Viviana, illus. 2008. (Little Green Bks.). (ENG.). 24p. (J). (gr. -1-1). pap. 5.99 *(978-1-4169-6789-7(3)*, Little Simon) Little Simon.

—I'm Not Little! Thomas, Glenn, illus. 2017. (ENG.). 32p. (J). (gr. -1-3). 16.99 *(978-1-4998-0377-8(X))* Little Bee Books Inc.

Ireland, Justina. Evie Allen vs. the Quiz Bowl Zombies. Champion, Tyler, illus. 2017. (Devils' Pass Ser.). (ENG.). 128p. (J). (gr. 4-8). lib. bdg. 25.99 *(978-1-4965-4988-4(0)*, 135880, Stone Arch Bks.) Capstone.

—Jeff Allen vs. the Time Suck Vampire. Champion, Tyler, illus. 2017. (Devils' Pass Ser.). (ENG.). 128p. (J). (gr. 4-8). lib. bdg. 25.99 *(978-1-4965-4986-0(4)*, 135878, Stone Arch Bks.) Capstone.

—Tiffany Donovan vs. the Cookie Elves of Destruction. Champion, Tyler, illus. 2017. (Devils' Pass Ser.). (ENG.). 128p. (J). (gr. 4-8). lib. bdg. 25.99 *(978-1-4965-4987-7(2)*, 135879, Stone Arch Bks.) Capstone.

—Tiffany Donovan vs. the Poison Werewolves. Champion, Tyler, illus. 2018. (Devils' Pass Ser.). (ENG.). 128p. (J). (gr. 4-8). lib. bdg. 25.99 *(978-1-4965-6525-9(8)*, 138528, Stone Arch Bks.) Capstone.

—Zach Lopez vs. the Shadow Cats. Champion, Tyler, illus. 2018. (Devils' Pass Ser.). (ENG.). 128p. (J). (gr. 4-8). lib. bdg. 25.99 *(978-1-4965-6524-2(X)*, 138524, Stone Arch Bks.) Capstone.

—Zach Lopez vs. the Unicorns of Doom. Champion, Tyler, illus. 2017. (Devils' Pass Ser.). (ENG.). 128p. (J). (gr. 4-8). lib. bdg. 25.99 *(978-1-4965-4989-1(9)*, 135881, Stone Arch Bks.) Capstone.

Jacks, C. S. The Adventures of Pisten Billy: Pisten Billy Makes the Grade! 2010. 32p. pap. 12.99 *(978-1-4520-6624-0(8))* AuthorHouse.

Jahangiri, Holly. Trockle. 2008. (Illus.). 32p. (J). 18.99 *(978-0-9797513-2-5(2))* 4RV Pub.

James, Hollis. Mikey's Monster (Teenage Mutant Ninja Turtles) Spaziante, Patrick, illus. 2013. (Step into Reading Ser.). (ENG.). 48p. (J). (gr. k-3). 5.99 *(978-0-449-81826-8(8)*, Random Hse. Bks. for Young Readers) Random Hse. Children's Bks.

Jane, Pamela. Little Goblins Ten. Manning, Jane, illus. 2011. (ENG.). 32p. (J). (gr. -1-3). 16.99 *(978-0-06-176798-2(0)*, HarperCollins) HarperCollins Pubs.

Janese, Julie. The Little Booger Book. 2009. 24p. pap. 11.49 *(978-1-4490-0310-4(9))* AuthorHouse.

Jay, Stacey. Of Beast & Beauty. 2014. (ENG.). 400p. (YA). (gr. 9). pap. 9.99 *(978-0-385-74321-1(1)*, Ember) Random Hse. Children's Bks.

Jaycox, Jaclyn. Attack of the Cute. Cotroneo, Marilisa, illus. 2019. (Boo Bks.). (ENG.). 32p. (J). (gr. k-2). lib. bdg. 21.32 *(978-1-5158-4483-9(8)*, 140579, Picture Window Bks.) Capstone.

Jennings, Sharon. No Monsters Here, 1 vol. Ohi, Ruth, illus. 2006. (ENG.). 24p. (J). (gr. -1-k). pap. 7.95 *(978-1-55041-789-0(4)*, d353d85b-81e0-45ff-841d-064ed711334e) éditeur, Annika Parance CAN. Dist: Firefly Bks., Ltd.

Jensen, Lisa. Beast: a Tale of Love & Revenge. 2018. (ENG.). 352p. (YA). (gr. 11). 18.99 *(978-0-7636-8880-6(0))* Candlewick Pr.

Jinks, Catherine. The Last Bogler. 2017. (How to Catch a Bogle Ser.: 3). (ENG.). 336p. (J). (gr. 5-7). pap. 7.99 *(978-0-544-81309-0(X)*, 1641901, Clarion Bks.) HarperCollins Pubs.

—A Plague of Bogles. 2015. (How to Catch a Bogle Ser.: 2). (ENG.). 336p. (J). (gr. 5-7). pap. 6.99 *(978-0-544-54067-5(0)*, 1608871); (Illus.). 16.99 *(978-0-544-08747-7(X)*, 1538140) HarperCollins Pubs. (Clarion Bks.).

JJ Rabbit & the Monster: Level K, 6 vols. 128p. (gr. 2-3). 49.95 *(978-0-7699-0981-3(7))* Shortland Pubns. (U. S. A.) Inc.

John, Jory. Quit Calling Me a Monster! Shea, Bob, illus. 2016. 40p. (J). (gr. -1-2). 18.99 *(978-0-385-38990-7(6))* Random Hse. Children's Bks.

Johnson, James A. The Beast & the Backpack. 2009. 64p. pap. 8.95 *(978-1-4401-5390-7(6))* iUniverse, Inc.

Johnson, Vickey L. The Monster Mix-Up. 2003. (Illus.). (J). pap. 9.00 *(978-0-8059-6125-6(9))* Dorrance Publishing Co., Inc.

Jones, Pip. The Chocolate Monster. Hughes, Laura, illus. 2019. (Ruby Roo Ser.: 2). (ENG.). 32p. pap. 9.95 *(978-0-571-32751-5(6)*, Faber & Faber Children's Bks.) Faber & Faber, Inc.

Judge, Chris. The Snow Beast. Judge, Chris, illus. 2015. (ENG., Illus.). 32p. (J). (gr. -1-3). 17.99 *(978-1-4677-9313-1(2)*, a711d3a5-9c18-4a5e-a4f5-dd8ef98bb756) Lerner Publishing Group.

Juncar, Nicola. The Legend of Thornton Wood. 2012. 238p. pap. *(978-1-78176-184-7(1))* FeedARead.com.

Jungman, Ann. Vlad the Drac Returns. 2006. (Vlad the Drac Ser.). (Illus.). 123p. (J). pap. 6.95 *(978-1-903015-34-6(0))* Barn Owl Bks, London GBR. Dist: Independent Pubs. Group.

—Vlad the Drac Superstar. Thompson, George, illus. 2006. (Vlad the Drac Ser.). 122p. (J). (gr. 2-4). pap. 6.95 *(978-1-903015-45-2(6))* Barn Owl Bks, London GBR. Dist: Independent Pubs. Group.

Juster, Norton. The Odious Ogre. Feiffer, Jules, illus. 2010. (ENG.). 32p. (J). (gr. -1-2). 17.95 *(978-0-545-16202-9(5)*, Di Capua, Michael) Scholastic, Inc.

Kang, A. N. My Big Bad Monster. Kang, A. N., illus. 2019. (ENG., Illus.). 40p. (J). (gr. -1-3). 16.99 *(978-1-4847-2882-6(3))* Disney Pr.

Kaplan, Bruce Eric. Monsters Eat Whiny Children. Kaplan, Bruce Eric, illus. 2010. (ENG., Illus.). 40p. (J). (gr. -1-3). 18.99 *(978-1-4169-8689-8(8)*, Simon & Schuster Bks. For Young Readers) Simon & Schuster Bks. For Young Readers.

Kasza, Keiko. Los Secretos de Abuelo Sapo. (SPA., Illus.). (J). (gr. 1-3). *(978-958-04-3624-9(X)*. NR7688) Norma S.A.

Katschke, Judy. Monster Power: Exploring Renewable Energy. 2018. (Magic School Bus Rides Again — Branches Ser.: 2). lib. bdg. 14.75 *(978-0-606-41054-0(6))* Turtleback.

Kaufman, Kathleen. The Lairdbalor. 2017. (ENG.). 288p. (YA). 29.99 *(978-1-68336-588-4(7))*; pap. 15.99 *(978-1-68336-587-7(9))* Turner Publishing Co.

Keane, Dave. Monster School: First Day Frights. Keane, Dave, illus. 2012. (I Can Read Level 2 Ser.). (ENG., Illus.). 32p. (J). (gr. -1-3). 16.99 *(978-0-06-085476-8(6))*; pap. 4.99 *(978-0-06-085475-1(8))* HarperCollins Pubs. (HarperCollins).

—Monster School: the Spooky Sleepover. Keane, Dave, illus. 2014. (I Can Read Level 2 Ser.). (ENG., Illus.). 32p. (J). (gr. -1-3). pap. 4.99 *(978-0-06-085477-5(4)*, HarperCollins) HarperCollins Pubs.

Keaton, Kelly. A Beautiful Evil. (ENG.). (YA). (gr. 9). 2013. 320p. pap. 11.99 *(978-1-4424-0928-6(2))*2. 2012. 304p. 17.99 *(978-1-4424-0927-9(4))* Simon Pulse. (Simon Pulse).

—Darkness Becomes Her. (ENG.). (YA). (gr. 9). 2012. 320p. pap. 12.99 *(978-1-4424-0925-5(8))* 2011. 288p. 16.99 *(978-1-4424-0924-8(X))* Simon Pulse. (Simon Pulse).

Kelley, Jane. Octo-Man & the Headless Monster. 2017. (Escapades of Clint Mccool Ser.: 1). lib. bdg. 16.00 *(978-0-606-40109-8(1))* Turtleback.

Kenner, Crystal R. The King of All Tickle Bugs & Other Stories. 2011. (Illus.). 124p. (gr. -1). pap. 10.95 *(978-1-4502-9466-9(9))* iUniverse, Inc.

Kennis, Don. Monsters Have Big Feet. Gowens, Kyle & Richmond, Bob, illus. 2006. (J). per. 8.95 *(978-0-9788553-0-7(2))* Guppy Publishing LLC.

Kent, Jaden. Ella & Owen 2: Attack of the Stinky Fish Monster! Bodnaruk, Iryna, illus. 2017. (Ella & Owen Ser.: 2). (ENG.). 112p. (J). (gr. k-3). pap. 5.99 *(978-1-4998-0369-3(9))* Little Bee Books Inc.

Kessler, Liz. Emily Windsnap & the Monster from the Deep. Gibb, Sarah, illus. 2012. (Emily Windsnap Ser.: 2). (ENG.). 240p. (J). (gr. 3-7). pap. 6.99 *(978-0-7636-6018-5(3))* Candlewick Pr.

—Emily Windsnap & the Monster from the Deep. 2012. (Emily Windsnap Ser.: Bk. 2). lib. bdg. 16.00 *(978-0-606-25573-8(7))* Turtleback.

—Emily Windsnap: Two Magical Mermaid Tales. Gibb, Sarah, illus. 2014. (Emily Windsnap Ser.). (ENG.). 464p. (J). (gr. 3-7). pap. 11.99 *(978-0-7636-7452-6(4))* Candlewick Pr.

Ketteman, Helen. Goodnight, Little Monster, 0 vols. Leick, Bonnie, illus. 2012. (Little Monster Ser.: 1). (ENG.). 32p. (J). (gr. k-2). 16.99 *(978-0-7614-5683-4(X)*, 9780761456834, Two Lions) Amazon Publishing.

Kettle, Jenny. Monster Hunting. 2011. 24p. pap. 15.99 *(978-1-4568-2857-8(6))* Xlibris Corp.

Kibuishi, Kazu. The Stonekeeper, 1. 2018. (Amulet Ser.). (ENG.). 185p. (J). (gr. 4-5). 23.96 *(978-1-64310-255-9(9))* Penworthy Co., LLC, The.

—The Stonekeeper. 2008. (Amulet Ser.: 1). (Illus.). 185p. lib. bdg. 24.50 *(978-1-4177-9712-7(6))* Turtleback.

—The Stonekeeper: a Graphic Novel (Amulet #1) Kibuishi, Kazu, illus. (Amulet Ser.: 1). (ENG., Illus.). 192p. (J). (gr. 3-7). 2015. 24.99 *(978-0-439-84680-6(3))* Vol. 1. 2008. pap. 12.99 *(978-0-439-84681-3(1))* Scholastic, Inc. (Graphix).

Kilgore, Lee. The Mr. Munch Adventures: Six Short Stories, 1 vol. 2010. 73p. pap. 19.95 *(978-1-4489-2876-7(1))* America Star Bks.

Kimmelman, Leslie. A Valentine for Frankenstein. Banks, Timothy, illus. 2018. (ENG.). 32p. (J). (gr. k-3). 17.99 *(978-1-5124-3129-2(X)*, 167d90ab-668e-49b7-9865-a741925f37aa, Carolrhoda Bks.) Lerner Publishing Group.

King, Jane. The Monster Bash. 2013. (Ghoul School Ser.: 3). (ENG., Illus.). 80p. (J). (gr. 1-4). pap. 13.99 *(978-1-4814-2164-5(6)*, Simon & Schuster/Paula Wiseman Bks.) Simon & Schuster/Paula Wiseman Bks.

King, Jeremy Jordan. In Stone: A Grotesque Faerie Tale. 2012. (ENG.). 264p. (gr. 7). pap. 11.95 *(978-1-60282-761-5(3))* Bold Strokes Bks.

Kingsley, Ron D. Stories from the Life of Ronnie Kaye: Monsters. 2013. (ENG.). 125p. (YA). pap. 8.95 *(978-1-4787-1121-6(3))* Outskirts Pr., Inc.

Kirkland, Justin B. Jb Pumpernikel vs the Sock Monster. 2013. 74p. pap. 5.50 *(978-0-615-81456-8(5))* KIRKLAND, JUSTIN B.

Kishimoto, Masashi. Naruto: Chapter Book, Vol. 12: Coward. 2010. (Naruto: Chapter Bks.: 12). (ENG., Illus.). 80p. (J). pap. 4.99 *(978-1-4215-3042-0(2))* Viz Media.

—Naruto: Chapter Book, Vol. 13: Beauty Is the Beast. 2010. (Naruto: Chapter Bks.: 13). (ENG., Illus.). 80p. (J). pap. 4.99 *(978-1-4215-3043-7(0))* Viz Media.

Klemer, Amy Wade. The Scary Snake Monster. 2003. (Illus.). 16p. (J). pap. 8.00 *(978-0-9729216-1-9(3))* ABCDMoon Publishing.

Kleven, Elisa. A Monster in the House. 2013. 34p. 16.99 *(978-1-62352-036-6(3))*; pap. 9.99 *(978-1-62352-041-0(X))* IntoPrint Publishing LLC.

Kline, Spencer. The Adventures of Fujimori-San. Brown, E. Jackie, illus. 2010. 20p. 12.99 *(978-1-4520-6275-4(7))* AuthorHouse.

Kloepfer, John. Monsters Unleashed. 2018. (Monsters Unleashed Ser.: 1). (ENG., Illus.). 224p. (J). (gr. 3-7). pap. 6.99 *(978-0-06-229031-1(2)*, HarperCollins) HarperCollins Pubs.

—Monsters Unleashed #2: Bugging Out. Oliver, Mark, illus. 2018. (Monsters Unleashed Ser.: 2). (ENG.). 192p. (J). (gr. 3-7). pap. 6.99 *(978-0-06-242754-0(7)*, HarperCollins) HarperCollins Pubs.

Klug, Eric. The Monster in My Closet. Klug, Eric, illus. 2007. (Illus.). 32p. (J). (gr. -1-3). 15.95 *(978-1-60108-007-3(7))* Red Cygnet Pr.

Klutz Editors & Rose, Amber. Monsters. 2009. (Hammond Undercover Ser.). 72p. (J). (gr. 3-7). pap. 13.99 *(978-0-8416-1497-0(0))* Hammond World Atlas Corp.

Knight, Andrew. The Monster in the Loch. (Thumbprint Mysteries Ser.). 32.86 *(978-0-8092-0411-3(8))* McGraw-Hill/Contemporary.

Knudsen, Michelle. Marilyn's Monster. Phelan, Matt, illus. 2017. (ENG.). 40p. (J). (gr. -1-3). 8.99 *(978-0-7636-9301-5(4))* Candlewick Pr.

—Marilyn's Monster. Phelan, Matt, illus. 2017. (ENG.). (J). (gr. -1-3). lib. bdg. 17.20 *(978-0-606-39844-2(9))* Turtleback.

Kochalka, James. Johnny Boo & the Happy Apples (Johnny Boo Book 3), Bk. 3. 2009. (Johnny Boo Ser.: 3). (Illus.). 40p. (J). (gr. -1-3). 9.95 *(978-1-60309-041-4(X)*, 9781603090414) Top Shelf Productions.

Korté, Steve. Myth Monster Mayhem. Lozano, Omar, illus. 2019. (You Choose Stories: Wonder Woman Ser.). (ENG.). 112p. (J). (gr. 2-6). pap. 6.95 *(978-1-4965-8439-7(2)*, 140964); lib. bdg. 32.65 *(978-1-4965-8349-9(3)*, 140643) Capstone. (Stone Arch Bks.).

Kretzer, Joyce B. Shane & the Jackadoo: A Butcher Hollow Fantasy. 2008. 24p. pap. 11.49 *(978-1-4389-1894-5(1))* AuthorHouse.

Kropp, Joseph P. Nathan Meets His Monsters. Johnston, Phillip, illus. 2012. 34p. 16.95 *(978-1-890905-59-0(3))*; pap. 9.95 *(978-1-890905-58-3(5))* Day to Day Enterprises.

Kropp, Paul. Behind the Door. 2007. (HIP Edge Ser.). (Illus.). 112p. (YA). (gr. 7-12). pap. *(978-1-897039-26-7(3))* High Interest Publishing (HIP).

Kubler, Annie. Wheels on the Bus, 15 vols. Kubler, Annie, illus. 2005. (Illus.). 14p. (J). (ENG, HIN, MUL & GUJ.). bds. *(978-1-84444-975-0(0))*; (ARA, ENG & MUL., bds. *(978-1-84444-970-5(X))*; (BEN, ENG & MUL., bds. *(978-1-84444-971-2(8))*; (ENG, CHI & MUL., bds. *(978-1-84444-972-9(6))*; (CHI, ENG & MUL., bds. *(978-1-84444-973-6(4))*; (ENG, FRE & MUL., bds. *(978-1-84444-974-3(2))* Mantra Lingua.

—Wheels on the Bus, 15 vols. 2005. (Illus.). 14p. (J). (PAN, ENG & MUL.). bds. *(978-1-84444-976-7(9))*; (POR, ENG & MUL., bds. *(978-1-84444-977-4(7))* Mantra Lingua.

—Wheels on the Bus, 15 vols. Kubler, Annie, illus. 2005. (ENG, SOM & MUL., Illus.). 14p. (J). bds. *(978-1-84444-978-1(5))* Mantra Lingua.

—Wheels on the Bus, 15 vols. 2005. (ENG, SPA & MUL., Illus.). 14p. (J). bds. *(978-1-84444-979-8(3))* Mantra Lingua.

—Wheels on the Bus, 15 vols. Kubler, Annie, illus. 2005. (Illus.). 14p. (J). (ENG, TUR & MUL.). bds. *(978-1-84444-980-4(7))*; (URD, ENG & MUL., bds. *(978-1-84444-981-1(5))* Mantra Lingua.

Kutner, Merrily. The Zombie Nite Cafe. Long, Ethan, illus. 2007. (ENG.). 32p. (J). (gr. -1-3). 16.95 *(978-0-8234-1963-0(0))* Holiday Hse., Inc.

Labatt, Mary. Lake Monster Mix-Up, 2. Rioux, Jo-Anne, illus. 2009. (Sam & Friends Mysteries Ser.). 96p. (J). (gr. 2-4). 21.19 *(978-1-55337-822-8(9))* Kids Can Pr., Ltd. CAN. Dist: Children's Plus, Inc.

Ladybird. The Monster Next Door: Ladybird Readers Level 2, Vol. 2. 2016. (Ladybird Readers Ser.). (Illus.). 48p. (J). (gr. 2-4). pap. 9.99 *(978-0-241-25444-8(2))* Penguin Bks., Ltd. GBR. Dist: Independent Pubs. Group.

Lagonegro, Melissa. Beauty & the Beast. 2017. (Illus.). 24p. (J). *(978-1-5182-3646-4(4))* Random Hse., Inc.

—Monster Games. 2013. (Step into Reading - Level 1 Ser.). lib. bdg. 13.55 *(978-0-606-32208-9(6))* Turtleback.

L'Allier, Peter Wesley Thomas. Rotten Robbie & the Legend of Wanabinoo. 2006. (Illus.). 215p. 18.95 *(978-0-9724022-8-6(4))* TangleTown Media Inc.

Lam, Thao. Wallpaper. 2018. (ENG., Illus.). 32p. (J). (gr. -1-3). 18.95 *(978-1-77147-283-8(9))* Owlkids Bks. Inc. CAN. Dist: Publishers Group West (PGW).

Landgraf, James, Jr. Monsters Monsters Go Away. Warrick, Jessica, illus. 2008. 40p. (J). 8.99 *(978-0-9819283-0-2(7))* Makdan Publishing.

Langridge, Roger. The Muppet Show Comic Book - Muppet Mash. Langridge, Roger, illus. 2011. (Muppet Show Ser.). (Illus.). 128p. pap. 9.99 *(978-1-60886-611-3(4))* BOOM! Studios.

Langrish, Katherine. Troll Fell. 2004. (Illus.). 272p. (J). (gr. 5-18). lib. bdg. 16.89 *(978-0-06-058305-7(3))* HarperCollins Pubs.

Lara, Sahai. My Loveable Little Monster. Hunt, Jim, illus. 2011. 22p. (J). pap. 5.99 *(978-0-615-48221-7(X))* SNL Publishing.

Latimer, Alex. Lula & the Sea Monster, 1 vol. 2019. (ENG., Illus.). 32p. (J). (gr. -1-3). 16.95 *(978-1-68263-122-5(2))* Peachtree Publishing Co. Inc.

Lawler, Janet. Fright School. Galletti, Chiara, illus. 2018. (ENG.). 32p. (J). (gr. -1-3). 16.99 *(978-0-8075-2553-1(7)*, 807525537) Whitman, Albert & Co.

Lawrence, Dionne L. The Story of Her?! 2012. 28p. (-18). pap. 16.95 *(978-1-62709-253-1(6))* America Star Bks.

Layne, Steven L. My Brother Dan's Delicious, 1 vol. Galey, Chuck, illus. 2003. (ENG.). 32p. (J). (gr. k-3). 16.99 *(978-1-58980-071-7(0)*, Pelican Publishing) Arcadia Publishing.

Lazar, Tara. The Monstore. Burks, James, illus. 2013. (ENG.). 32p. (J). (gr. -1-2). 19.99 *(978-1-4424-2017-5(0)*, Aladdin) Simon & Schuster Children's Publishing.

Lcg. The Pencil Monster! 2011. 28p. pap. 14.95 *(978-0-557-94993-9(9))* Lulu Pr., Inc.

LeBow, Michael. Sally Salli & the Case of the Tic Monster: A Book for Kids Who Tic. Barnett, Thora, illus. 2013. 75p. (J). pap. 18.95 *(978-1-59630-060-6(4))* Science & Humanities Pr.

Lemmens, Riske. A Box Full of Monsters. 2004. (Illus.). 26p. (J). *(978-1-85269-852-2(7))*; *(978-1-85269-847-8(0))*; *(978-1-85269-842-3(X))*; *(978-1-85269-837-9(3))*; (ARA., *(978-1-85269-827-0(6))* Mantra Lingua.

Lemmens, Riske & Dutta, Kunal, texts. A Box Full of Monsters: Kutia Plot Me Monstra. 2004. (ALB., Illus.). 25p. (J). *(978-1-85269-822-5(5))* Mantra Lingua.

Leuck, Laura. Goodnight, Baby Monster. Date not set. 32p. (J). (gr. -1-1). pap. 4.99 *(978-0-06-443723-3(X))* HarperCollins Pubs.

—My Creature Teacher. Nash, Scott, illus. 2004. (ENG.). 32p. (J). (gr. -1-1). 15.99 *(978-0-06-029694-0(1))* HarperCollins Pubs.

Light, Steven. Have You Seen My Monster? Light, Steve, illus. 2015. (ENG.). 48p. (J). (-k). 16.99 *(978-0-7636-7513-4(X))* Candlewick Pr.

Lijewski, Christy. Next Exit, Vol. 1. 2006. (ENG., Illus.). 168p. (YA). pap. 12.95 *(978-1-59362-037-0(3)*, 5ed0fc34-53fd-494c-99b7-6102d1d840d0) Slave Labor Bks.

Lindquist, K. Margaret. Tyler Poncho's Amalgamated Menagerie. 2010. 62p. pap. 24.00 *(978-0-557-31419-5(4))* Lulu Pr., Inc.

Lindquist, Kaeti. Tyler Poncho's Amalgamated Menagerie. 2010. (ENG.). 56p. pap. 25.00 *(978-0-557-99490-8(X))* Lulu Pr., Inc.

Link, Kelly. Pretty Monsters. 2010. (ENG., Illus.). 416p. (YA). (gr. 7-12). pap. 11.99 *(978-0-14-241672-3(X)*, Speak) Penguin Young Readers Group.

Little, Awen. Sid y Bwystfil Bwyta Sanau. 2009. (WEL., Illus.). 32p. pap. 14.49 *(978-1-4389-2711-4(8))* AuthorHouse.

Llanes, Adrian & Llanes, Christi. There's a Monster in My Closet. 2011. 28p. pap. 12.03 *(978-1-4634-4054-1(5))* AuthorHouse.

Llenas, Anna. The Color Monster: A Story about Emotions. 2018. (Color Monster Ser.). (ENG., Illus.). 40p. (J). (gr. -1-3). 18.99 *(978-0-316-45001-0(4))* Little, Brown Bks. for Young Readers.

Lloyd, A. Wallis. Das Monster-Musical. 2013. 32p. pap. *(978-3-944704-02-9(9))* Nothnagle, Alan. Edition Graugans.

Lloyd, Alicia. When the Monsters Are Quiet. Rottinger, Amy, illus. 2013. 26p. pap. 11.95 *(978-1-61244-219-8(6))* Halo Publishing International.

Lonely Sea Monster. 2007. per. *(978-1-59916-155-6(9))* Printing Systems.

Long, Ethan. Fangsgiving. 2018. (ENG., Illus.). 32p. (J). 18.99 *(978-1-68119-825-5(8)*, 900188260, Bloomsbury Children's Bks.) Bloomsbury Publishing USA.

—Fright Club. 2015. (ENG., Illus.). 32p. (J). (gr. -1-2). 17.99 *(978-1-61963-337-7(X)*, 900132758, Bloomsbury USA Childrens) Bloomsbury Publishing USA.

—Valensteins. (ENG., Illus.). (J). 2018. 30p. bds. 7.99 *(978-1-68119-894-1(0)*, 900191673, Bloomsbury Children's Bks.) 2017. 32p. 17.99 *(978-1-61963-433-6(3)*, 900135962, Bloomsbury USA Childrens) Bloomsbury Publishing USA.

Longson, D. M. The Scunner. 2009. 32p. pap. 21.50 *(978-1-4092-6995-3(7))* Lulu Pr., Inc.

Lorey, Dean. Monster Law. 2009. 304p. 10.99 *(978-0-06-134048-2(0))* HarperCollins Pubs.

Loma, Balian. The Aminal, 1 vol. Loma, Balian & Lecia, Balian, illus. 2012. (ENG.). 48p. (J). pap. 7.95 *(978-1-59572-363-5(3))* Star Bright Bks., Inc.

Louis, Robb. Monster in the Moat. 2011. (Illus.). 44p. (gr. -1). pap. 18.46 *(978-1-4567-4053-5(9))* AuthorHouse.

Lubar, David. The Bully Bug: A Monsterrific Tale. 2014. (Monsterrific Tales Ser.). (ENG., Illus.). 144p. (J). (gr. 3-7). 24.99 *(978-0-7653-3082-6(2)*, 900078525, Starscape) Doherty, Tom Assocs., LLC.

Lund, Deb. Monsters on Machines. Neubecker, Robert, illus. 2017. (ENG.). 40p. (J). (gr. -1-3). pap. 6.99 *(978-0-544-92783-4(4)*, 1657204, Clarion Bks.) HarperCollins Pubs.

—Monsters on Machines. Neubecker, Robert, illus. 2017. (ENG.). (J). (gr. -1-3). lib. bdg. 17.20 *(978-0-606-39815-2(5))* Turtleback.

Maberry, Jonathan. The Orphan Army. 2015. (Nightsiders Ser.: 1). (ENG., Illus.). 400p. (J). (gr. 3-7). 16.99 *(978-1-4814-1575-0(1)*, Simon & Schuster Bks. For Young Readers) Simon & Schuster Bks. For Young Readers.

—The Orphan Army. 2016. (Nightsiders Ser.: 1). lib. bdg. 18.40 *(978-0-606-38959-4(8))* Turtleback.

—Vault of Shadows. (Nightsiders Ser.: 2). (ENG.). 464p. (J). (gr. 3-7). 2017. pap. 8.99 *(978-1-4814-1579-8(4))* 2016. (Illus.). 16.99 *(978-1-4814-1578-1(6))* Simon & Schuster Bks. For Young Readers. (Simon & Schuster Bks. For Young Readers).

MacHale, D. J. The Monster Princess. Boiger, Alexandra, illus. 2010. (ENG.). 40p. (J). (gr. -1-1). 17.99 *(978-1-4169-4809-4(0)*, Aladdin) Simon & Schuster Children's Publishing.

—Surrender the Key (the Library Book 1) 2017. (Library: 1). 272p. (J). (gr. 3-7). 7.99 (978-1-101-93256-8(2), Yearling) Random Hse. Children's Bks.

Mae, Jamie. Isle of Misfits 1: First Class. Hartas, Freya, illus. 2019. (Isle of Misfits Ser.: 1). (ENG.). 112p. (J). (gr. k-3). 16.99 (978-1-4998-0822-3(4)); pap. 5.99 (978-1-4998-0821-6(6)) Little Bee Books Inc.

Maggiore, Lisa. Ava the Monster Slayer. Felten, Ross, illus. 2015. (Ava the Monster Slayer Ser.: 1). (ENG.). 36p. (J). (gr. -1-k). 16.99 (978-1-63450-151-4(9), Sky Pony Pr.) Skyhorse Publishing Co., Inc.

Magoon, Scott. The Boy Who Cried Bigfoot! Magoon, Scott, illus. 2013. (ENG., Illus.). 48p. (J). (gr. -1-3). 18.99 (978-1-4424-1257-6(7), Simon & Schuster Bks. For Young Readers) Simon & Schuster/Paula Wiseman Bks.

Mahoney, Daniel J., illus. I See a Monster. 2008. (ENG.). 12p. (J). bds. 5.95 (978-1-58117-729-9(1), Intervisual/Piggy Toes) Bendon, Inc.

Mangum, James A. & Spires, Sidney. The Fairy the Chupacabra & Those Marfa Lights: A West Texas Fable. Mangum, James A., illus. 2008. (Illus.). 32p. (J). 17.95 (978-0-9798391-5-3(7)) Texas Bk. Pubs. Assn.

Manning, Matthew K. Mystery of the Mist Monster. Neely, Scott, illus. 2016. (Scooby-Doo Comic Chapter Bks.). (ENG.). 88p. (J). (gr. 3-7). lib. bdg. 27.32 (978-1-4965-3586-3(3), 132732, Stone Arch Bks.) Capstone.

Manushkin, Fran. Pedro's Monster. Lyon, Tammie, illus. 2018. (Pedro Ser.). (ENG.). 32p. (J). (gr. k-2). lib. bdg. 21.32 (978-1-5158-2821-1(2), 137986, Picture Window Bks.) Capstone.

March, Julia. Monster Battles. 2016. (Illus.). 63p. (J). (978-1-5182-1852-1(0)) Dorling Kindersley Publishing, Inc.

Mardani, Parisa. Nathan Sees a Monster But... . 2012. 16p. pap. 15.99 (978-1-4685-9405-8(2)) AuthorHouse.

Markell, Denis. Hush, Little Monster. Iwai, Melissa, illus. 2012. (ENG.). 32p. (J). (gr. -1-1). 9.99 (978-1-4424-4195-8(X), Little Simon) Little Simon.

Marriott, Zoë. The Name of the Blade. 2014. (Name of the Blade Ser.: 1). (ENG.). 368p. (YA). (gr. 7). 16.99 (978-0-7636-6957-7(1)) Candlewick Pr.

Marsh, Mike. The Grumblies Set a Trap. Jain, Priti, illus. 2012. 24p. pap. (978-0-9878019-2-0(9)) Yellow Toadstool Pr.

Marsh, Robert. Monster & Me, Set. Percival, Tom, illus. Incl. Monster Moneymaker. (ENG., Illus.). 40p. (J). (gr. 2-5). 2010. lib. bdg. 23.99 (978-1-4342-1891-9(0), 102350, Stone Arch Bks.); (Monster & Me Ser.). (ENG.). Illus.). 40p. 2010. 71.97 o.p. (978-1-4342-2671-6(9), 15368, Stone Arch Bks.) Capstone.

—Monster Moneymaker, 1 vol. Percival, Tom, illus. 2010. (Monster & Me Ser.). (ENG.). 40p. (J). (gr. 2-5). lib. bdg. 23.99 (978-1-4342-1891-9(0), 102350, Stone Arch Bks.) Capstone.

Marsh, Sarah Glenn. Fear the Drowning Deep. (ENG.). 312p. (gr. 6-12). 2018. (YA). pap. 8.99 (978-1-5107-2658-1(6)) 2016. (J). 16.99 (978-1-5107-0348-3(9)) Skyhorse Publishing Co., Inc. (Sky Pony Pr.).

Martin, Nicole. The Werewolf. 2006. 146p. pap. 14.99 (978-1-4120-8802-2(X)) Trafford Publishing.

Matharu, Taran. The Battlemage. 2018. (Summoner Ser.: 3). (YA). lib. bdg. 22.10 (978-0-606-41115-8(1)) Turtleback.

—The Battlemage: Summoner, Book Three. 2018. (Summoner Trilogy Ser.: 3). (ENG.). 384p. (YA). pap. 11.99 (978-1-250-15863-5(X), 900185524) Square Fish.

Mathis, Kate. Moon over Monsters. 2013. 318p. pap. 12.95 (978-0-9819789-9-4(1)) PowWow Publishing.

Matthews, John. Henry Hunter & the Beast of Snagov: Henry Hunter Series #1. 2016. (Henry Hunter Ser.). (ENG., Illus.). 240p. (J). (gr. 2-7). 15.99 (978-1-5107-1038-2(8), Sky Pony Pr.) Skyhorse Publishing Co., Inc.

May, R. B. Charlie Finds a Friend. 2010. 32p. pap. 12.99 (978-1-4490-6913-1(4)) AuthorHouse.

Mayer, Mercer. Mercer Mayer's Little Monster Fun & Learn Book. 2011. (Classic Collectible Ser.: 2). (ENG.). 96p. (J). (gr. -1-3). 12.95 (978-1-60746-419-8(5), Premiere) FastPrncil, Inc.

—Mercer Mayer's Little Monster Home School & Work Book. 2012. (Classic Collectible Ser.: 3). (ENG.). 96p. (J). 12.95 (978-1-60746-945-2(6), Premiere) FastPrncil, Inc.

—Mercer Mayer's Little Monster Word Book with Mother Goose. 2012. (Classic Collectible Ser.: 4). (ENG.). 96p. (J). 12.95 (978-1-60746-688-8(0), Premiere) FastPrncil, Inc.

Mayer, Meyer. Il y a un cauchemar dans Mon. pap. 16.95 (978-2-07-054814-9(7)) Gallimard, Editions FRA. Dist: Distribooks, Inc.

Mbalia, Kwame. Rick Riordan Presents Tristan Strong Destroys the World (a Tristan Strong Novel, Book 2) (Tristan Strong Ser.: 2). (J). (gr. 3-7). 2021. 48p. pap. 8.99 (978-1-368-04240-6(6)) 2020. (Illus.). 12p. 17.99 (978-1-368-04238-3(4)) Disney Publishing Worldwide. (Riordan, Rick).

McBain, Chani. No Such Thing As Nessie! A Loch Ness Monster Adventure, 30 vols. Harris-Jones, Kirsteen, illus. 2013. (ENG.). 32p. (J). pap. 11.95 (978-0-86315-953-4(2), Kelpies) Floris Bks. GBR. Dist: Consortium Bk. Sales & Distribution.

McCann, Emma. Munch. 2015. (ENG., Illus.). 24p. (J). (gr. k-4). 7.99 (978-1-85733-731-0(X)); 19.99 (978-1-85733-732-7(8)) Lerner Publishing Group.

McCann, Jesse Leon. Scooby-Doo & the Fishy Phantom, 1 vol. Sur, Duendes Del, illus. 2011. (Scooby-Doo! Ser.: No. 2). (ENG.). 24p. (J). (gr. k-4). lib. bdg. 31.36 (978-1-59961-866-1(4), 13244, Picture Bk.) Spotlight.

McCurry, Meryl. The Seamonster's Back. 2005. (J). per. 8.99 (978-0-9764690-4-9(9)) Professional Publishing Hse. LLC.

McDermott, Tom. Otis Steele & the Taileebone: A Southern Tall Tale, 1 vol. Crosby, Jeff, illus. 2013. (ENG.). 32p. (J). (gr. k-2). 16.99 (978-1-4556-1736-4(9), Pelican Publishing) Arcadia Publishing.

McDonald, Ann-Eve. There are No Such Thing as Monsters. 2004. (J). (978-0-9770158-4-9(X)) BeachWalk Bks. Inc.

McDonnell, Patrick. The Monsters' Monster. 2012. (ENG., Illus.). 40p. (J). (gr. -1-3). 18.99 (978-0-316-04547-6(0)) Little, Brown Bks. for Young Readers.

McElligott, Matthew. Even Monsters Need Haircuts. McElligott, Matthew, illus. 2012. (ENG., Illus.). 40p. (J). (gr. k-8). pap. 8.99 (978-0-8027-2801-2(4), 900081563, Bloomsbury USA Childrens) Bloomsbury Publishing USA.

McGee, Warner, illus. Monster Halloween Party. 2007. (Backyardigans Ser.). (ENG.). 14p. (J). (gr. -1-k). bds. 6.99 (978-1-4169-3435-6(9), Simon Spotlight/Nickelodeon) Simon Spotlight/Nickelodeon.

McGrath, Raymond, illus. The Moon: Individual Title Six-Packs. (Sails Literacy Ser.). 16p. (gr. k-18). 27.00 (978-0-7635-4426-3(4)) Rigby Education.

McHale, Remme. No Place for Niappy. 2010. 28p. pap. 12.85 (978-1-4490-6900-1(2)) AuthorHouse.

Mcintyre, Mel. The Legend of Lumpus & Ogols. McQuillan, David, illus. 2009. 28p. pap. 10.95 (978-1-935137-96-2(4)) Guardian Angel Publishing, Inc.

McKee. Two Monsters. Date not set. 25p. (J). pap. (978-0-05-004546-6(6)) Addison-Wesley Longman, Inc.

McKee, David. Not Now, Bernard. 35th ed. 2015. (ENG., Illus.). 32p. (J). (gr. -1-k). 24.99 (978-1-78344-298-0(0)) Andersen Pr. GBR. Dist: Independent Pubs. Group.

—Three Monsters. 2007. (ENG., Illus.). 32p. (J). (gr. -1-7). 14.95 (978-1-59354-121-7(X)) Chronicle Bks. LLC.

McKee, David & Mckee, David. Tres Monstruos. 2006. (SPA., Illus.). 24p. (J). (gr. -1-2). (978-980-257-317-2(5)) Ekare, Ediciones.

McKenna, James. The Mind Traveller. 2013. 212p. pap. (978-0-9569723-8-5(1)) Lone Cloud Publishing.

McKinnon, Heidi. I Just Ate My Friend. McKinnon, Heidi, illus. 2018. (ENG., Illus.). 40p. (J). (gr. -1-3). 17.99 (978-1-5344-1032-9(5), Simon & Schuster Bks. For Young Readers) Simon & Schuster Bks. For Young Readers.

McKissack, Patricia C. & Moss, Onawumi Jean. Precious & the Boo Hag. Brooker, Kyrsten, illus. 2005. (ENG.). 40p. (J). (gr. -1-3). 19.99 (978-0-689-85194-0(4), Atheneum Bks. for Young Readers) Simon & Schuster Children's Publishing.

McKown, Martha. The Adventures of Zingway, the Monster. 2011. 28p. 12.03 (978-1-4567-1087-3(7)) AuthorHouse.

McNamee, Graham. Bonechiller. 2012. (ENG.). 304p. (YA). (gr. 7). pap. 11.99 (978-0-307-97593-5(2), Ember) Random Hse. Children's Bks.

McShane, Pol. Return to Animal Land: The Adventures of Johnny & Joey. 2007. 132p. (J). per. 10.95 (978-0-595-45804-2(1)) iUniverse, Inc.

Meister, Cari. Moopy the Underground Monster, 1 vol. Messner, Dennis, illus. 2009. (Monster Friends Ser.). (ENG.). 32p. (J). (gr. 2-3). 22.65 (978-1-4342-1630-4(6), 95804); pap. 6.25 (978-1-4342-1745-5(0), 102217) Capstone. (Stone Arch Bks.).

—Ora - The Sea Monster. Messner, Dennis, illus. 2009. (Monster Friends Ser.). (ENG.). 32p. (J). (gr. 2-3). pap. 6.25 (978-1-4342-1746-2(9), 102218, Stone Arch Bks.) Capstone.

—Ora at the Monster Contest, 1 vol. Messner, Dennis, illus. 2010. (Monster Friends Ser.). (ENG.). 32p. (J). (gr. 2-3). lib. bdg. 22.65 (978-1-4342-1875-9(9), 102334, Stone Arch Bks.) Capstone.

—Snorp on the Slopes, 1 vol. Messner, Dennis, illus. 2010. (Monster Friends Ser.). (ENG.). 32p. (J). (gr. 2-3). lib. bdg. 22.65 (978-1-4342-1873-5(2), 102333, Stone Arch Bks.) Capstone.

—Snorp the City Monster. Messner, Dennis, illus. 2009. (Monster Friends Ser.). (ENG.). 32p. (J). (gr. 2-3). 22.65 (978-1-4342-1632-8(2), 95806); pap. 6.25 (978-1-4342-1747-9(7), 102219) Capstone. (Stone Arch Bks.).

—Three Claws the Mountain Monster. Messner, Dennis, illus. 2009. (Monster Friends Ser.). (ENG.). 32p. (J). (gr. 2-3). 22.65 (978-1-4342-1633-5(0), 95807, Stone Arch Bks.) Capstone.

Meomi. The Octonauts & the Only Lonely Monster. 2006. (Octonauts Ser.). (ENG., Illus.). 36p. (J). (gr. -1-3). 15.95 (978-1-59702-005-3(2)) Immedium.

Merritt, Kory. The Dreadful Fate of Jonathan York: A Yarn for the Strange at Heart. 2015. (ENG., Illus.). 128p. (J). pap. 9.99 (978-1-4494-7100-2(5)) Andrews McMeel Publishing.

—No Place for Monsters. Merritt, Kory, illus. 2020. (No Place for Monsters Ser.). (ENG., Illus.). 384p. (J). (gr. 3-7). 14.99 (978-0-358-12853-3(6), 1752984, Clarion Bks.) HarperCollins Pubs.

Meyer, Linda. The Kid in My Closet. Roberts, Miranda, illus. 2008. (ENG.). 32p. (J). pap. 12.95 (978-1-887542-94-4(9)) Bk. Pubs. Network.

Michalczewski, Raime. Monsters of a Different Color: Being Different Is Beautiful. 2011. 36p. pap. 18.99 (978-1-4567-2769-7(9)) AuthorHouse.

Michelle, Nelson-Schmidt. Jonathan James & the Whatif Monster. 2013. (ENG., Illus.). 32p. (J). pap. 6.99 (978-1-61067-118-7(X)) Kane Miller.

—Jonathan James & Whatif Monster. 2012. (ENG., Illus.). (J). 12.99 (978-1-61067-131-6(7)) Kane Miller.

Miedoso, Andres. Surf's up, Creepy Stuff! Rivas, Victor, illus. 2018. (Desmond Cole Ghost Patrol Ser.: 3). (ENG.). 128p. (J). (gr. k-4). 17.99 (978-1-5344-1802-8(4)); pap. 6.99 (978-1-5344-1801-1(6)) Little Simon. (Little Simon).

Miller, Kelly Hufnagle. The Monster in the Washer. 2012. 48p. pap. 21.99 (978-1-4772-5187-4(1)) AuthorHouse.

Milway, Alex. Terror of the Deep: Armed, Dangerous & Covered in Fur! Milway, Alex, illus. 2013. (ENG., Illus.). 256p. (J). pap. 5.99 (978-1-61067-075-3(2)) Kane Miller.

Monica Brown. Marisol Mcdonald & the Monster: Marisol Mcdonald y el Monstruo (English & Spanish Edition), 1 vol. 2016. (Marisol Mcdonald Ser.). (ENG., Illus.). 32p. (J). (gr. k-3). 19.95 (978-0-89239-326-8(2), leelowcbp) Lee & Low Bks., Inc.

Monster at the End of This Book. 2009. (ENG.). 24p. 14.99 (978-1-74181-222-0(4), Ideals Pubns.) Worthy Publishing.

A Monster House: Individual Title Six-Packs. (Sails Literacy Ser.). 16p. (gr. k-18). 27.00 (978-0-7635-4385-3(3)) Rigby Education.

The Monster of Mirror Mountain: Individual Title Six-Packs. (Literatura 2000 Ser.). (gr. 2-3). 33.00 (978-0-7635-0231-7(6)) Rigby Education.

Monster Party: Individual Title Six-Packs. (Chiquilibros Ser.). (gr. k-1). 23.00 (978-0-7635-0422-9(X)) Rigby Education.

Monster Stories. 2003. 256p. (J). 5.98 (978-1-4054-1008-3(6)) Parragon, Inc.

El monstruo de Montespejo: Individual Title Six-Packs. (Literatura 2000 Ser.). (SPA.). (gr. 2-3). 33.00 (978-0-7635-1265-1(6)) Rigby Education.

Montgomery, R. A. The Abominable Snowman: (Choose Your Own Adventure #1) Peguy, Laurence, illus. 2006. (ENG.). 144p. (J). (gr. 4-8). per. 7.99 (978-1-933390-01-7(8), CHCL01) Chooseco LLC.

Montoya, Martha, creator. Cenando con el Monstruo: Take-Home. 2005. (Los Kitos Ser.). (SPA.). (YA). (gr. 1-3). 15.00 (978-0-8215-8813-0(3)) Sadlier, William H. Inc.

Moore, Ashley L. The Story of Princess K. 2012. 20p. pap. 24.95 (978-1-4626-6800-7(3)) America Star Bks.

Moore, Nicholas & Murton, Gareth. Princess Lydia & the wailing Monster. 2008. (ENG.). 32p. pap. 18.95 (978-1-4092-4993-1(X)) Lulu Pr., Inc.

Morales, Yuyi. Niño Wrestles the World. Morales, Yuyi, illus. 2013. (ENG., Illus.). 40p. (J). (gr. -1-3). 19.99 (978-1-59643-604-6(2), 900065749) Roaring Brook Pr.

Morpurgo, Michael. Gentle Giant. Foreman, Michael, illus. 2006. 28p. (J). (gr. k-4). reprint ed. pap. 12.00 (978-1-4223-5667-8(1)) DIANE Publishing Co.

Morris, Garvin. Dump Dog. Morris, Garvin, illus. (Illus.). (J). 2008. 32p. pap. 6.95 (978-1-60108-022-6(0)) 2007. 40p. (gr. -1-2). 15.95 (978-1-60108-012-7(3)) Red Cygnet Pr.

Morris, Jennifer E. The Sea Monster. 2014. (Scholastic Reader Level 1 Ser.). (Illus.). (J). lib. bdg. 13.55 (978-0-606-36046-3(8)) Turtleback.

Morrissey, Dean & Krensky, Stephen. The Monster Trap. Morrissey, Dean, illus. 2004. (Illus.). 40p. (J). lib. bdg. 17.89 (978-0-06-052499-9(5)) HarperCollins Pubs.

Mortensen, Lori. The Missing Monster Card, 1 vol. Simard, Rémy, illus. 2010. (My First Graphic Novel Ser.). (ENG.). 32p. (J). (gr. k-2). pap. 6.25 (978-1-4342-2284-8(5), 103153); lib. bdg. 24.65 (978-1-4342-1888-9(0), 102347) Capstone. (Stone Arch Bks.).

Moser, Lisa. The Monster in the Backpack: Candlewick Sparks. Jones, Noah Z., illus. 2013. (Candlewick Sparks Ser.). (ENG.). 40p. (J). (gr. k-4). pap. 5.99 (978-0-7636-6643-9(2)) Candlewick Pr.

Murphy, Jill. All for One. 2004. (Illus.). (J). (gr. -1-2). spiral bd. (978-0-616-14591-3(8)); spiral bd. (978-0-616-14592-0(6)) Canadian National Institute for the Blind/Institut National Canadien pour les Aveugles.

Murphy, Rose. Monster Mayhem. Arthur, Jenny, illus. 2011. (Pat & Sound Stories Ser.). (ENG.). 12p. (gr. -1). 14.95 (978-1-61524-497-3(2), Intervisual/Piggy Toes) Bendon, Inc.

Murphy, Stuart J. Percy Plays It Safe. 2010. (I See I Learn Ser.: 4). (Illus.). 32p. (J). (gr. -1-k). pap. 6.95 (978-1-58089-453-1(4)) Charlesbridge Publishing, Inc.

Murray, Helen. Stop the Stone Monsters! 2017. (Illus.). 24p. (J). (978-1-5182-3635-8(9)) Dorling Kindersley Publishing, Inc.

My Monster Friends, 6 Packs. (Literatura 2000 Ser.). (gr. 1-2). 28.00 (978-0-7635-0102-0(6)) Rigby Education.

Myers, Walter Dean. Monster. l.t. ed. 2005. 231p. pap. 10.95 (978-0-7862-7363-8(1), Large Print Pr.) Thorndike Pr.

Nagler, Michelle H. Scooby-Doo & the Monster in the Woods, 1 vol. Sur, Duendes del, illus. 2016. (Scooby-Doo Early Reading Adventures Ser.). (ENG.). 24p. (J). (gr. -1-2). lib. bdg. 31.36 (978-1-61479-468-4(5), 21381) Spotlight.

Naifeh, Ted. Courtney Crumrin Vol. 4: Monstrous Holiday. 2013. (Courtney Crumrin Ser.: 4). (ENG., Illus.). 136p. (J). 24.99 (978-1-934964-92-7(1), 9781934964927, Lion Forge) Oni Pr., Inc.

Namm, Diane. Monsters! 2004. (My First Reader Ser.). (ENG.). 32p. (J). (gr. k-1). pap. 3.95 (978-0-516-24635-2(6), Children's Pr.) Scholastic Library Publishing.

Nelson-Schmidt, Michelle. Jonathan James & the Whatif Monster. 2013. (ENG., Illus.). (J). 26.99 (978-1-61067-194-1(5)) Kane Miller.

—José Juan y el Monstruo Ysi. Nelson-Schmidt, Michelle, illus. 2019. Tr. of Jonathan James & the Whatif Monster. (SPA., Illus.). (J). pap. 6.99 (978-1-61067-924-4(5)) Kane Miller.

Nemmers, Lee. No Monsters Here! A Bedtime Shadow Book. Zschock, Martha Day, illus. 2015. (Bedtime Shadow Bks.). (ENG.). 7p. (J). spiral bd. 12.99 (978-1-4413-1833-6(X), d103ab20-5bba-44d4-b577-c73cea14dd14) Peter Pauper Pr. Inc.

Ness, Patrick. A Monster Calls: Inspired by an Idea from Siobhan Dowd. Kay, Jim, illus. (ENG.). 224p. (YA). (gr. 7). 2013. pap. 12.00 (978-0-7636-6065-9(5)) 2011. 22.99 (978-0-7636-5559-4(7)) Candlewick Pr.

—A Monster Calls: Inspired by an Idea from Siobhan Dowd. 2011. (Playaway Children Ser.). (YA). (gr. 7-12). 54.99 (978-1-4558-4499-9(3)) Findaway World, LLC.

—A Monster Calls: Inspired by an Idea from Siobhan Dowd. 2013. lib. bdg. 23.30 (978-0-606-31603-3(5)) Turtleback.

—A Monster Calls: a Novel (Movie Tie-In) Inspired by an Idea from Siobhan Dowd. 2016. (ENG.). 240p. (YA). (gr. 7). pap. 9.99 (978-0-7636-9215-5(8)) Candlewick Pr.

Neubecker, Robert. Too Many Monsters! A Halloween Counting Book. Neubecker, Robert, illus. 2010. (ENG., Illus.). 26p. (J). (gr. -1-k). bds. 7.99 (978-1-4424-0172-3(9), Little Simon) Little Simon.

Neuman, M. Robert. Clawing & Scratching & Thumping About. 2013. 30p. pap. 9.99 (978-0-9898820-0-2(4)) Mindstir Media.

Newmann, Ed, illus. Marvin Monster's Big Date. 2007. (ENG.). 32p. (J). (gr. -1-3). 6.95 (978-0-9792371-4-0(9)) Keene Publishing.

—Marvin Monster's Teacher Jitters. 2006. (ENG.). 48p. (J). (gr. 4-7). per. 6.95 (978-0-9766805-3-6(X)) Keene Publishing.

Newton, Naiya. Thomas the Monster. 2007. (ENG.). 24p. (J). pap. 15.99 (978-1-4257-6596-5(3)) Xlibris Corp.

Ngo, Lap. The Teaser Monster. 2012. (Illus.). 24p. (J). 11.99 (978-0-9838321-9-5(6)) Higher Ground Pr.

Nickel, Scott. Attack of the Mutant Lunch Lady: A Buzz Beaker Brainstorm, 1 vol. Smith, Andy, illus. 2008. (Buzz Beaker Brainstorm Ser.). (ENG.). 40p. (J). (gr. 2-5). lib. bdg. 23.99 (978-1-4342-0451-6(0), 94400); per. 5.95 (978-1-4342-0501-8(0), 94449) Capstone. (Stone Arch Bks.).

Nicolle, Ethan, illus. Ollie Possum. 2018. (J). pap. (978-1-947644-48-9(3)) Canon Pr.

Night, P. J. The Terror Behind the Mask. 2014. (You're Invited to a Creepover Ser.: 19). (ENG., Illus.). 160p. (J). (gr. 3-7). pap. 6.99 (978-1-4814-0460-0(1), Simon Spotlight) Simon Spotlight.

—The Terror Behind the Mask. 2014. (Creepover Ser.: 19). lib. bdg. 17.20 (978-0-606-35797-5(1)) Turtleback.

—There's Something Out There. (You're Invited to a Creepover Ser.: 5). (ENG.). 160p. (J). (gr. 3-7). 2018. 17.99 (978-1-5344-3168-3(3)) 2011. pap. 6.99 (978-1-4424-4148-4(8)) Simon Spotlight. (Simon Spotlight).

Niner, Holly L. No More Noisy Nights. 2017. (ENG., Illus.). (J). (gr. k-2). 7.99 (978-1-936261-96-3(0)) Flashlight Pr.

—No More Noisy Nights. Wolek, Guy, illus. 2017. (ENG.). 32p. (J). (gr. k-2). 17.95 (978-1-936261-93-2(6)) Flashlight Pr.

Noble, Ron. Letter Beasties. 2013. 34p. 19.95 (978-1-4575-1931-4(3)); pap. 12.95 (978-1-4575-1893-5(7)) Dog Ear Publishing, LLC.

Noble, Trinka Hakes. The Legend of the Jersey Devil. Kelley, Gerald, illus. 2013. (ENG.). 32p. (J). (gr. 2-5). 16.99 (978-1-58536-837-2(7), 202886) Sleeping Bear Pr.

Nolan, Lucy. The Lizard Man of Crabtree County, 1 vol. Kastner, Jill, illus. 2003. (ENG.). 32p. (J). (gr. 1-4). pap. 5.95 (978-0-7614-5144-0(7)) Marshall Cavendish Corp.

Noll, Amanda. Are You My Monster? McWilliam, Howard, illus. 2019. (I Need My Monster Ser.). 26p. (J). bds. 8.99 (978-1-947277-32-8(4)) Flashlight Pr.

—Hey, That's MY Monster! McWilliam, Howard, illus. 2016. (I Need My Monster Ser.). 32p. (J). (gr. k-2). 17.95 (978-1-936261-37-6(5)) Flashlight Pr.

—I Need My Monster. McWilliam, Howard, illus. 2009. (I Need My Monster Ser.). 32p. (J). (gr. k-3). 17.95 (978-0-9799746-2-5(3)) Flashlight Pr.

Nordling, Lee. Andrew the Seeker. Roberts, Scott, illus. 2017. (Game for Adventure Ser.). (ENG.). 32p. (J). (gr. k-3). 25.32 (978-1-5124-1330-4(5), 4f77d2e5-2cdc-4d1d-823e-a3c0a48f5399, Graphic Universe™) Lerner Publishing Group.

Norton, Andre. The Monster's Legacy. Lee, Jody A., illus. 2017. (ENG.). 160p. (YA). (gr. 7). pap. 13.99 (978-1-5344-1247-7(6), Atheneum Bks. for Young Readers) Simon & Schuster Children's Publishing.

Novel Units. Donde Viven Los Monstruos (Where the Wild Things Are) Novel Units Teacher Guide. 2019. (ENG.). (J). pap. 12.99 (978-1-56137-544-8(6), NU5725, Novel Units, Inc.) Classroom Library Co.

—Where the Wild Things Are Novel Units Teacher Guide. 2019. (ENG.). (J). pap. 12.99 (978-1-56137-022-1(3), Novel Units, Inc.) Classroom Library Co.

Novotny-Hunter, Jana. My Tail's Not Tired. Bowles, Paula, illus. 2017. (Child's Play Library). 32p. (J). (ENG.). (978-1-84643-985-8(X)); pap. (978-1-84643-986-5(8)) Child's Play International Ltd.

O'Donnell, Liam. Tank & Fizz: the Case of Firebane's Folly, 1 vol. Deas, Mike, illus. 2018. (Tank & Fizz Ser.: 4). (ENG.). 256p. (J). (gr. 4-7). pap. 9.95 (978-1-4598-1261-1(1)) Orca Bk. Pubs. USA.

O'Hearn, Kate. The Flame of Olympus. 2012. (Pegasus Ser.: 1). (ENG.). 400p. (J). (gr. 3-7). 19.99 (978-1-4424-4409-6(6), Simon & Schuster/Paula Wiseman Bks.) Simon & Schuster/Paula Wiseman Bks.

OHora, Zachariah. The Not So Quiet Library. 2016. (Illus.). 40p. (J). (-k). 17.99 (978-0-8037-4140-9(5), Dial Bks) Penguin Young Readers Group.

Olander, Johan. A Field Guide to Monsters: Googly-Eyed Wart Floppers, Shadow-Casters, Toe-Eaters, & Other Creatures, 0 vols. Olander, Johan, illus. 2012. (ENG.). 64p. (J). (gr. 2-6). pap. 9.99 (978-0-7614-5728-2(3), 9780761457282, Two Lions) Amazon Publishing.

Onion Head Monster Attacks. 2007. (YA). per. 12.95 (978-0-9793676-0-1(3)) Friedrich, Paul.

Onion Head Monster Attacks (XL) 2006. per. 19.99 (978-0-9793676-3-2(8)) Friedrich, Paul.

Onion Head Monster Bombastic. 2007. (YA). per. 12.95 (978-0-9793676-1-8(1)) Friedrich, Paul.

Onion Head Monster Catastrophic. 2007. per. 11.99 (978-0-9793676-2-5(X)) Friedrich, Paul.

Onyebuchi, Tochi. Beasts Made of Night. (YA). (gr. 7). 2018. 320p. pap. 9.99 (978-0-448-49391-6(8)) 2017. 304p. 17.99 (978-0-448-49390-9(X)) Penguin Young Readers Group. (Razorbill).

O'Reilly, Sean. The Missing Mummy, 1 vol. 2011. (Mighty Mighty Monsters Ser.). (ENG., Illus.). 48p. (J). (gr. 2-4). lib. bdg. 23.99 (978-1-4342-3218-2(2), 116190, Stone Arch Bks.) Capstone.

—Monster Beach, 1 vol. 2011. (Mighty Mighty Monsters Ser.). (ENG., Illus.). 48p. (J). (gr. 2-4). lib. bdg. 23.99 (978-1-4342-3217-5(4), 116189, Stone Arch Bks.) Capstone.

—Monster Beach, 1 vol. Arcana Studio Staff, illus. 2012. (Mighty Mighty Monsters Ser.). (ENG.). 48p. (J). (gr. 2-4). pap. 6.10 (978-1-4342-4608-0(6), 120596, Stone Arch Bks.) Capstone.

—The Monster Crooks, 1 vol. Arcana Studio Staff, illus. 2012. (Mighty Mighty Monsters Ser.). (ENG.). 48p. (J). (gr. 2-4). pap. 6.10 (978-1-4342-4610-3(8), 120598, Stone Arch Bks.) Capstone.

—The Scare Fair, 1 vol. 2011. (Mighty Mighty Monsters Ser.). (ENG., Illus.). 48p. (J). (gr. 2-4). lib. bdg. 23.99 (978-1-4342-3220-5(4), 116192, Stone Arch Bks.) Capstone.

Orsi, Tea. Tinker Bell & the Legend of the NeverBeast. 2015. (Disney Fairies Graphic Novels Ser.: 17). (J). lib. bdg. 18.40 (978-0-606-37295-4(4)) Turtleback.

Ortas, Rachel. The Messy Monster Book. 2014. (ENG., Illus.). 96p. (J). (gr. k-17). 19.95 (978-1-84976-105-5(1)) Tate Publishing, Ltd. GBR. Dist: Abrams, Inc.

Ortega, Claribel A. The Golden Frog Games (Witchlings 2) 2023. (Witchlings Ser.). (ENG.). 384p. (J). (gr. 3-7). 17.99 (978-1-338-74579-5(4), Scholastic Pr.) Scholastic, Inc.

O'Ryan, Ray. Monsters in Space! Jack, Colin, illus. 2013. (Galaxy Zack Ser.: 4). (ENG.). 128p. (J). (gr. k-2). 16.99 (978-1-4424-6721-7(5)); pap. 6.99 (978-1-4424-6718-7(5)) Little Simon. (Little Simon).

—Monsters in Space! 2013. (Galaxy Zack Ser.: 4). lib. bdg. 16.00 (978-0-606-32460-1(7)) Turtleback.

Otoshi, Kathryn. Simon & the Sock Monster. 2004. (ENG., Illus.). 36p. (J). 16.95 (978-0-9723946-1-1(3)) KO Kids Bks.

Owen, Rena. Moana: Read-Along Storybook & CD. 2016. (Illus.). (J). (978-1-5182-2280-1(3)) Disney Publishing Worldwide.

Pace, Anne Marie. Vampirina in the Snow-A Vampirina Ballerina Book. 2018. (Vampirina Ser.: 4). (ENG., Illus.). 40p. (J). (gr. -1-k). 17.99 (978-1-368-02318-4(5), Disney-Hyperion) Disney Publishing Worldwide.

Page, Terry. The Saddest Centaur. Page, Terry, illus. (Illus.). 24p. (J). (gr. 2-6). pap. 4.00 (978-1-887864-68-8(7)); lib. bdg. 7.00 (978-1-887864-36-7(9)) Boo Bks., Inc.

Paiva, Johannah Gilman. Is There a Monster in My Closet? Read with Me. Grey, James, ed. Long, Paulette Rich, illus. 2014. (ENG.). 32p. (J). (gr. -1-3). 7.99 (978-1-4867-0002-8(0)) Flowerpot Children's Pr. Inc. CAN. Dist: Cardinal Pubs. Group.

Paquette, Ammi-Joan. Ghost in the House. Record, Adam, illus. 2019. (ENG.). 32p. (J). (gr. -1-2). 5.99 (978-0-7636-9892-8(X)) Candlewick Pr.

Parish, Alex. Peter & the Flying Sergeant. 2009. 30p. 21.50 (978-0-9561613-0-7(8)) Parish, Alex GBR. Dist: Lulu Pr., Inc.

Parish, Peggy. No More Monsters for Me! 2003. 22.95 (978-0-673-75926-9(1)) Celebration Pr.

Park, Barbara. Junie B. Jones Has a Monster under Her Bed. unabr. ed. 2004. (Junie B. Jones Ser.: No. 8). 69p. (J). (gr. k-3). pap. 17.00 incl. audio (978-0-8072-0644-7(X), Listening Library) Random Hse. Audio Publishing Group.

Parnell, Fran. The Barefoot Book of Monsters! Fatus, Sophie, illus. 2003. (ENG.). 64p. (J). 19.99 (978-1-84148-178-4(5), 1187407) Barefoot Bks., Inc.

Parnell, Fran & Fatus, Sophie. Grim, Grunt & Grizzle-Tail: A Story from Chile. Fatus, Sophie, illus. 2013. (Monster Stories Ser.: 6). (Illus.). 48p. (J). (gr. 1-4). pap. 8.99 (978-1-84686-910-5(2)) Barefoot Bks., Inc.

—Rona Long-Teeth: A Story from Tahiti. Fatus, Sophie, illus. 2013. (Monster Stories Ser.: 5). (Illus.). 48p. (J). (gr. 1-5). pap. 8.99 (978-1-84686-908-2(0)) Barefoot Bks., Inc.

Parton, Matthew R. My Closet Monster Ate My Homework, 1 vol. 2009. (ENG.). 30p. 24.95 (978-1-60836-184-7(5)) America Star Bks.

The Party, 6 Packs. (Sails Literacy Ser.). 16p. (gr. k-18). 27.00 (978-0-7635-4414-0(0)) Rigby Education.

Paschkis, Julie. Kalinka & Grakkle, 1 vol. 2018. (Illus.). 32p. (J). (gr. -1-3). 17.95 (978-1-68263-030-3(7)) Peachtree Publishing Co. Inc.

Patiño, Carlos. Dave Loves Chickens, 1 vol. 2013. (ENG., Illus.). 36p. (J). 16.95 (978-1-940184-01-2(0)) Vegan Pubs.

Patricelli, Leslie. The Patterson Puppies & the Midnight Monster Party. Patricelli, Leslie, illus. 2010. (Patterson Puppies Ser.). (ENG., Illus.). 32p. (J). (gr. -1-k). 14.99 (978-0-7636-3243-4(0)) Candlewick Pr.

Patten, E. J. The Legend Thief. Rocco, John, illus. (Hunter Chronicles Ser.: 2). (ENG.). 384p. (J). (gr. 3-7). 2014. pap. 9.99 (978-1-4424-2036-6(7)) 2013. 16.99 (978-1-4424-2035-9(9)) Simon & Schuster Bks. For Young Readers. (Simon & Schuster Bks. For Young Readers).

—Return to Exile. Rocco, John, illus. (Hunter Chronicles Ser.: 1). (ENG.). 512p. (J). (gr. 3-7). 2013. pap. 7.99 (978-1-4424-2033-5(2)) 2011. 16.99 (978-1-4424-2032-8(4)) Simon & Schuster Bks. For Young Readers. (Simon & Schuster Bks. For Young Readers).

Patterson, Rebecca. The Pirate House. 2013. (Illus.). (J). (978-1-4351-4762-1(6)) Barnes & Noble, Inc.

Peacock, Shane. The Dark Missions of Edgar Brim: Monster. 2019. (Dark Missions of Edgar Brim Ser.: 2). 288p. (YA). (gr. 7). pap. 9.99 (978-0-7352-6273-7(X), Penguin Teen) PRH Canada Young Readers CAN. Dist: Penguin Random Hse. LLC.

—The Dark Missions of Edgar Brim: Monster. 2018. (Dark Missions of Edgar Brim Ser.: 2). 288p. (YA). (gr. 7). 16.99 (978-1-77049-701-6(3), Tundra Bks.) Tundra Bks. CAN. Dist: Penguin Random Hse. LLC.

Pearce, Jackson. Fathomless. 2013. (Fairy Tale Retelling Ser.). (ENG.). 320p. (YA). (gr. 10-17). pap. 8.99 (978-0-316-20777-5(2)) Little, Brown Bks. for Young Readers.

Pell, Jason. Woody & the Noble. O'Reilly, Sean Patrick, ed. 2011. (Illus.). 80p. (YA). pap. 14.95 (978-1-926914-33-6(3)) Arcana Studio, Inc.

Peretti, Frank E. The Cooper Kids Adventure Series. 2004. (Cooper Kids Adventure Ser.). (gr. 5-7). 23.96 (978-0-89107-901-9(7)) Crossway.

Pérez Anton, Pablo. THE GLUTTON. 2007. (ENG., Illus.). 48p. (J). 18.95 (978-84-96788-91-6(1)) OQO, Editora ESP. Dist: Baker & Taylor Bks.

Perro Monstruoso. (Fantasmas de Fear Street Coleccion). (SPA.). (YA). (gr. 5-8). pap. 7.95 (978-950-04-1930-7(0), EM0316) Emecé Editores S.A. ARG. Dist: Lectorum Pubns., Inc., Planeta Publishing Corp.

Peter Pauper Press, Inc., creator. Teddy the Terrible. 2017. (ENG., Illus.). 34p. (J). 16.99 (978-1-4413-2318-7(X), d865ed2d-9b3f-40b1-b5a3-ebca79759a97) Peter Pauper Pr. Inc.

Peters, Anna. The Friendly Rubbish Monsters. 2011. 92p. pap. 10.00 (978-1-60911-878-5(2), Eloquent Bks.) Strategic Book Publishing & Rights Agency (SBPRA).

Peters, Stephanie True. Johnny Slimeseed & the Freaky Forest: A Graphic Novel. Muñiz, Berenice, illus. 2019. (Far Out Folktales Ser.). (ENG.). 40p. (J). (gr. 3-6). lib. bdg. 26.65 (978-1-4965-7843-3(0), 139309, Stone Arch Bks.) Capstone.

Petracca, C. A. B. The Chronicles of Petr The. 2005. 208p. per. 14.95 (978-1-59858-012-9(4)) Dog Ear Publishing, LLC.

Petty, J. T. & Pope, Paul. The Fall of the House of West. Rubín, David, illus. 2015. 157p. (J). (978-1-5182-0095-3(8), First Second Bks.) Roaring Brook Pr.

Pfister, Marcus. The Rainbow Fish & the Sea Monsters' Cave. 2015. (Rainbow Fish Ser.). (ENG., Illus.). 32p. (J). pap. 9.95 (978-3-314-01733-9(2)) North-South Bks., Inc.

Phelan, Matt. Knights vs. Monsters. Phelan, Matt, illus. 2019. (ENG., Illus.). 176p. (J). (gr. 3-7). 16.99 (978-0-06-268626-8(7), Greenwillow Bks.) HarperCollins Pubs.

PI Kids. Disney Pixar: Friends & Heroes First Look & Find. 2007. (ENG.). 16p. (J). bds. 12.99 (978-1-4127-6848-1(9), 4155, PIL Kids) Phoenix International Publications, Inc.

Pike, Christopher, pseud. Monstre de l'Armoire.Tr. of Spooksville. (FRE.). (J). pap. 12.95 (978-2-266-08418-5(6)) Presses Pocket FRA. Dist: Distribooks, Inc.

—The Secret of Ka. 2011. (ENG.). 416p. (YA). (gr. 7). pap. 8.99 (978-0-547-57729-6(X), 1458529, Clarion Bks.) HarperCollins Pubs.

Pilkey, Dav. Dogzilla. Pilkey, Dav, illus. 2014. (Illus.). 32p. pap. 7.00 (978-1-61003-187-5(3)) Center for the Collaborative Classroom.

Pixar, told to. Monsters University Look & Find. 2013. 24p. (J). (gr. 1-3). 7.99 (978-1-4127-9649-1(0), ce47602a-38de-4bb7-82b3-69fb3502ef5d) Phoenix International Publications, Inc.

—Monsters University Play a Sound. 2013. (Illus.). 24p. (J). (gr. 1-3). 12.98 (978-1-4508-1607-6(X), 0e9ec920-3cca-43ee-9d08-a87cc2047168) Phoenix International Publications, Inc.

Poblocki, Dan. The Stone Child. 2010. 288p. (J). (gr. 3-7). pap. 8.99 (978-0-375-84255-9(1), Yearling) Random Hse. Children's Bks.

Pollock, Hal. Meet the Brittles: In Monstermania. 2009. (ENG., Illus.). 32p. (J). (gr. -1-3). 15.95 (978-1-59687-858-7(4)) IBks., Inc.

—Monster at the Bat. 2009. (ENG., Illus.). 28p. (J). (gr. 4-7). pap. 15.95 (978-1-59687-884-6(3)) IBks., Inc.

—Monster for President. Parisi, Anthony, illus. 2008. 28p. 14.95 (978-0-9816554-1-3(6)) Esquire Publishing, Inc.

Posner-Sanchez, Andrea. I Am Belle (Disney Beauty & the Beast) Batson, Alan, illus. 2017. (Little Golden Book Ser.). (ENG.). 24p. (J). (-k). 5.99 (978-0-7364-3905-3(6), Golden/Disney) Random Hse. Children's Bks.

—I Am the Beast (Disney Beauty & the Beast) Batson, Alan, illus. 2017. (Little Golden Book Ser.). (ENG.). 24p. (J). (-k). 4.99 (978-0-7364-3907-7(2), Golden/Disney) Random Hse. Children's Bks.

Potter, Ellen. The Monster Detector (Big Foot & Little Foot #2) Sala, Felicita, illus. 2018. (Big Foot & Little Foot Ser.). (ENG.). 128p. (J). (gr. 1-4). 13.99 (978-1-4197-3122-8(X), 1201501, Amulet Bks.) Abrams, Inc.

—The Monster Detector (Big Foot & Little Foot #2), Vol. 2. Sala, Felicita, illus. 2019. (ENG.). 144p. (J). (gr. 1-4). pap. 6.99 (978-1-4197-3386-4(9), 1201503, Amulet Bks.) Abrams, Inc.

Powell, Martin. Rapunzel vs. Frankenstein: A Graphic Novel. Lozano, Omar, illus. 2019. (Far Out Fairy Tales Ser.). (ENG.). 40p. (J). (gr. 3-6). pap. 5.95 (978-1-4965-8444-1(9), 140969); lib. bdg. 26.65 (978-1-4965-8395-6(7), 140686) Capstone. (Stone Arch Bks.).

Pratchett, Terry. A Hat Full of Sky. 2015. (Tiffany Aching Ser.: 2). (ENG.). 400p. (YA). (gr. 8). pap. 10.99 (978-0-06-243527-9(2), Clarion Bks.) HarperCollins Pubs.

—A Hat Full of Sky. 2005. 407p. (gr. 7). 19.00 (978-0-7569-5126-9(7)) Perfection Learning Corp.

—A Hat Full of Sky. 2005. (Discworld Ser.: 32). 407p. (YA). 19.65 (978-1-4177-2658-5(X)) Turtleback.

Primavera, Elise. Fred & Anthony Meet the Heinie Goblins from the Black Lagoon. Primavera, Elise, illus. rev. ed. 2008. (ENG., Illus.). 128p. (J). (gr. 2-4). pap. 4.99 (978-0-7868-3682-6(2)) Hyperion Bks. for Children.

Primavera, Elise & Arevamirp, Esile. Fred & Anthony Escape from the Netherworld. Primavera, Elise, illus. 2007. (Fred & Anthony Ser.). (ENG., Illus.). 122p. (J). (gr. 3-6). 17.44 (978-0-7868-3678-9(4)) Hyperion Bks. for Children.

Proctor, Darrell. The Cigarette Monster. 2006. (J). pap. 8.00 (978-0-8059-6790-6(7)) Dorrance Publishing Co., Inc.

Publications International Ltd. Staff, ed. Busy Little Monster. 2010. 14p. (J). bds. 10.98 (978-1-60553-125-0(1), PIL Kids) Publications International, Ltd.

—Elmo Goes to the Doctor. 2010. 14p. (J). bds. 16.98 (978-1-4127-4609-0(4)) Phoenix International Publications, Inc.

—Full Moon Monster Madness (Look & Find) 2010. (Illus.). 24p. (J). 7.98 (978-1-4508-0154-6(4)) Publications International, Ltd.

—Monsters Can Share. 2010. 20p. bds. 10.98 (978-1-60553-464-0(1), PIL Kids) Publications International, Ltd.

—Potty Time for Monsters. 2011. 14p. (J). bds. 17.98 (978-1-4508-0572-8(8)) Phoenix International Publications, Inc.

—Sesame Street: Monsters in the Bathroom. 2009. 18p. (J). bds. 10.98 (978-1-4127-1734-2(5), PIL Kids) Publications International, Ltd.

—Sesame Street Happy Birthday to You. 2013. 12p. (J). bds. 9.98 (978-1-4508-6159-5(8), 0fc64c9f-9454-4eb3-b56f-9c42ccb72c61) Phoenix International Publications, Inc.

Punter, Russell. Monsters, Stories Of. 2004. (Young Reading Series One Ser.). 48p. (J). (gr. 2-18). pap. 5.95 (978-0-7945-0757-2(3), Usborne) EDC Publishing.

Quinn, David. Go to Sleep, Little Creep. Spires, Ashley, illus. 2018. 32p. (J). (-k). 17.99 (978-1-101-93944-4(3), Crown Books For Young Readers) Random Hse. Children's Bks.

Quinn, Jordan. Sea Monster! McPhillips, Robert, illus. 2014. (Kingdom of Wrenly Ser.: 3). (ENG.). 128p. (J). (gr. k-4). pap. 6.99 (978-1-4814-0072-5(X), Little Simon) Little Simon.

The Race Car: Individual Title Six-Packs. (Sails Literacy Ser.). 16p. (gr. k-18). 27.00 (978-0-7635-4438-6(8)) Rigby Education.

Ralph, Brian. Cave In. 2013. (ENG., Illus.). 96p. (J). (gr. 7-12). pap. 14.95 (978-1-77046-094-2(2), 900087207) Drawn & Quarterly Pubns. CAN. Dist: Macmillan.

Ramos, Mario. A La Cama, Monstruito! (SPA.). 32p. (J). 16.95 (978-84-8470-007-4(0)) Corimbo, Editorial S.L. ESP. Dist: Lectorum Pubns., Inc., Distribooks, Inc.

Rand, Johnathan. Amer Ch Double Thrillers. 2010. 256p. pap. 6.99 (978-1-893699-26-7(9)) AudioCraft Publishing, Inc.

Rand, Jonathan. Michigan Chillers #14 Bionic Bats Bay City. 2007. 208p. (J). pap. 5.99 (978-1-893699-65-6(X)) AudioCraft Publishing, Inc.

Rasheed, M. Monsters 101, Book One. 2007. 152p. pap. 15.00 (978-1-4303-2946-6(7)) Lulu Pr., Inc.

Raughley, Sarah. Legacy of Light. (Effigies Ser.: 3). (ENG.). 512p. (YA). (gr. 9). 2019. pap. 14.99 (978-1-4814-6684-4(4)) 2018. (Illus.). 21.99 (978-1-4814-6683-7(6)) Simon Pulse. (Simon Pulse).

—Siege of Shadows. (Effigies Ser.: 2). (ENG.). (YA). (gr. 9). 2018. 464p. pap. 12.99 (978-1-4814-6681-3(X)) 2017. (Illus.). 448p. 18.99 (978-1-4814-6680-6(1)) Simon Pulse. (Simon Pulse).

Really Scary Stuff [Capstone Sole Source]. 2010. (Really Scary Stuff Ser.). 24p. lib. bdg. 95.96 (978-1-4296-5877-5(0), Capstone Pr.) Capstone.

Reed, Len. Monsters at My Bed. 2011. 16p. (gr. 1-2). pap. 8.49 (978-1-4567-6786-0(0)) AuthorHouse.

Regan, Dian Curtis. Space Boy & the Snow Monster. Neubecker, Robert, illus. 2017. (Space Boy Ser.). (ENG.). 32p. (J). (gr. -1-2). 17.95 (978-1-59078-957-5(1), Astra Young Readers) Astra Publishing Hse.

Regan, Lisa. Monsters & Myths, 16 vols., Set. Incl. Ancient Legends. McCall, Gerrie. lib. bdg. 34.60 (978-1-4339-4988-3(1), eb130233-a7a4-479d-9776-12b360936557); Bloodsucking Beasts. lib. bdg. 34.60 (978-1-4339-4991-3(1), 6ed66bf8-bb1c-4a04-9da7-82c68e92cc83); Classical Myths. McCall, Gerrie. lib. bdg. 34.60 (978-1-4339-4994-4(6), e4b2726a-e986-43c4-ade9-7e645c2f265e); Dragons & Serpents. McCall, Gerrie. lib. bdg. 34.60 (978-1-4339-4997-5(0), 5e44e9fb-4309-4cf4-8439-25fc4f051ca3); Movie Monsters. McCall, Gerrie. lib. bdg. 34.60 (978-1-4339-5006-3(5), cdd2fe63-241e-441d-9ca6-09c98f38de1d); Urban Myths & Legendary Creatures. McNab, Chris. lib. bdg. 34.60 (978-1-4339-5009-4(X), 52145f49-55fd-4312-9d13-4f6f844a8bc5); (J). (gr. 4-5). (Monsters & Myths Ser.). (ENG., Illus.). 48p. 2011. Set lib. bdg. 276.80 (978-1-4339-5012-4(X), 19326b06-33a7-4536-bf7c-d06cf61049fb, Gareth Stevens Learning Library) Stevens, Gareth Publishing LLLP.

Regan, Patrick. The Marvelous Monsters Talent Show. Bonson, Tom, illus. 2014. (J). (978-1-4351-5617-3(X), Blackbirch Pr., Inc.) Barnes & Noble, Inc.

Reida, Sarah S. Monsterville: a Lissa Black Production. 2016. (ENG.). 368p. (J). (gr. 2-7). 16.99 (978-1-5107-0733-7(6), Sky Pony Pr.) Skyhorse Publishing Co., Inc.

Reilly, Michael. Monster Sandwich. 2009. 50p. (J). pap. 31.99 (978-1-4415-0056-4(1)) Xlibris Corp.

Reiner, Carl. Tell Me A Scary Story... but Not Too Scary. 2009. (ENG.). (J). (gr. 1-3). 18.95 incl. lp (978-1-59687-926-3(2)) IBks., Inc.

Reschke, Kathleen. Monsters in My Basement. 2009. 72p. pap. 24.99 (978-1-4389-5793-7(9)) AuthorHouse.

Rex, Adam. Frankenstein Takes the Cake. 2012. (ENG., Illus.). 48p. (J). (gr. 1-4). pap. 8.99 (978-0-547-85062-7(X), 1501046, Clarion Bks.) HarperCollins Pubs.

Rex, Michael. Eat Pete. Rex, Michael, illus. 2018. (Illus.). 32p. (J). (-k). 17.99 (978-1-5247-3880-8(8), Nancy Paulsen Books) Penguin Young Readers Group.

—Goodnight Goon: a Petrifying Parody. Rex, Michael, illus. 2012. (Illus.). 30p. (J). (gr. -1 — 1). bds. 6.99 (978-0-399-26011-7(0), G.P. Putnam's Sons Books for Young Readers) Penguin Young Readers Group.

Rex, Michael, illus. Goodnight Goon: a Petrifying Parody. 2008. 32p. (J). (gr. -1-k). 17.99 (978-0-399-24534-3(0), G.P. Putnam's Sons Books for Young Readers) Penguin Young Readers Group.

Rey and others, Rey and. Start Your Engines 5-Minute Stories. 2014. (5-Minute Stories Ser.). (ENG., Illus.). 224p. (J). (gr. -1-3). 12.99 (978-0-544-15881-8(4), 1550258, Clarion Bks.) HarperCollins Pubs.

RH Disney. M Is for Monster (Disney/Pixar Monsters, Inc.) RH Disney, illus. 2014. (Little Golden Book Ser.). (ENG., Illus.). 24p. (J). (-k). 5.99 (978-0-7364-3170-5(5), Golden/Disney) Random Hse. Children's Bks.

—Monsters, Inc. Little Golden Book (Disney/Pixar Monsters, Inc.) RH Disney, illus. 2012. (Little Golden Book Ser.). (ENG., Illus.). 24p. (J). (-k). 5.99 (978-0-7364-2799-9(6), Golden/Disney) Random Hse. Children's Bks.

Rhoden, Chris J. B. How Niseag Became a Legend in Scoti. 2008. 48p. pap. 23.99 (978-1-4343-5461-7(X)) AuthorHouse.

Ricci, Christine. Legend Hunters! McGee, Warner, illus. 2007. (Backyardigans Ser.: 9). (ENG.). 24p. (J). (gr. -1-1). 16.19 (978-1-4169-4058-6(8)) Simon & Schuster, Inc.

Rice, Morgan. A Charge of Valor. 2013. (Sorcerer's Ring Ser.: 6). 250p. (YA). pap. 14.99 (978-1-939416-18-6(3), Morgan Rice) Morgan Rice Bks.

Richards, Dan. The Problem with Not Being Scared of Monsters. Neubecker, Robert, illus. 2014. (ENG.). 32p. (J). (gr. -1-3). 15.95 (978-1-62091-024-5(1), Astra Young Readers) Astra Publishing Hse.

Riddle, Mark. Margarash. Miller, Tim, illus. 2016. (ENG.). 48p. (J). (gr. -1-3). 17.95 (978-1-59270-216-9(3)) Enchanted Lion Bks., LLC.

Rideau, Nicole. What Is a Pookalaka? 2009. 28p. pap. 13.99 (978-1-4389-2275-1(2)) AuthorHouse.

Ridley, R. W. Dèlon City: Book Two of the Oz Chronicles. 2006. (YA). per. 9.99 (978-0-9792067-0-2(7)) Middleburry Hse. Publishing.

Riley, James. The Last Dragon. 2020. (Revenge of Magic Ser.: 2). (ENG.). 400p. (J). (gr. 3-7). pap. 8.99 (978-1-5344-2573-6(X), Aladdin) Simon & Schuster Children's Publishing.

—The Last Dragon. 2019. (Revenge of Magic Ser.: 2). (ENG., Illus.). 384p. (J). (gr. 3-7). 18.99 (978-1-5344-2572-9(1), Simon & Schuster/Paula Wiseman Bks.) Simon & Schuster/Paula Wiseman Bks.

—The Revenge of Magic. 2019. (Revenge of Magic Ser.: 1). (ENG., Illus.). 416p. (J). (gr. 3-7). 18.99 (978-1-4814-8577-7(6), Simon & Schuster/Paula Wiseman Bks.) Simon & Schuster/Paula Wiseman Bks.

Riordan, Rick. The Battle of the Labyrinth. 2011. 9.68 (978-0-7848-3442-8(3), Everbind) Marco Bk. Co.

—The Battle of the Labyrinth. l.t. ed. 2008. (Percy Jackson & the Olympians Ser.: Bk. 4). (ENG.). 462p. (J). (gr. 4-7). 23.95 (978-1-4104-1018-4(8)) Thorndike Pr.

—The Battle of the Labyrinth. 2009. (Percy Jackson & the Olympians Ser.: 4). (J). lib. bdg. 18.40 (978-0-606-02158-6(2)) Turtleback.

—Demigods & Magicians: Percy & Annabeth Meet the Kanes. 2016. (ENG.). 224p. (J). (gr. 3-7). 14.99 (978-1-4847-3278-6(2), Disney-Hyperion) Disney Publishing Worldwide.

—Heroes of Olympus, the, Book One: Lost Hero, the-Heroes of Olympus, the, Book One. (Heroes of Olympus Ser.: 1). (ENG.). (J). (gr. 5-9). 2012. 592p. pap. 9.99 (978-1-4231-1346-1(2)) 2010. 576p. 19.99 (978-1-4231-1339-3(X)) Disney Publishing Worldwide. (Disney-Hyperion).

—Heroes of Olympus, the, Book Two: the Son of Neptune-Heroes of Olympus, the, Book Two. (Heroes of Olympus Ser.: 2). (ENG.). (J). (gr. 5-9). 2013. 560p. pap. 10.99 (978-1-4231-4199-0(7)) 2011. (Illus.). 544p. 19.99 (978-1-4231-4059-7(1)) Disney Publishing Worldwide. (Disney-Hyperion).

—The Heroes of Olympus: the Demigod Diaries-The Heroes of Olympus, Book 2. 2012. (Heroes of Olympus Ser.: 2). (ENG.). 256p. (J). (gr. 5-9). 12.99 (978-1-4231-6300-8(1), Disney-Hyperion) Disney Publishing Worldwide.

—The Lost Hero. 2011. (Heroes of Olympus Ser.: Bk. 1). (ENG.). 576p. pap. 9.99 (978-1-4231-5537-9(8)) Disney Pr.

—The Lost Hero. 2010. (Heroes of Olympus Ser.). (ENG.). 576p. (YA). (gr. 5-9). pap. 12.00 (978-1-4231-4265-2(9)) Hyperion Bks. for Children.

—The Lost Hero. 2011. (CHI.). 380p. (J). (gr. 5-9). pap. (978-7-5448-2046-2(7)) Jieli Publishing Hse.

—The Lost Hero. l.t. ed. 2010. (Heroes of Olympus Ser.: Bk. 1). (ENG.). 708p. 23.99 (978-1-4104-3359-6(5)) Thorndike Pr.

—The Lost Hero. 2012. (Heroes of Olympus Ser.: 1). (J). lib. bdg. 20.85 (978-0-606-23615-7(5)) Turtleback.

—The Lost Hero. 2011. (Heroes of Olympus Ser.: Vol. 1). (CHI & ENG.). 528p. (J). (gr. 5-8). pap. (978-957-32-6804-8(3)) Yuan-liou Publishing Co., Ltd.

—Percy Jackson & the Olympians. l.t. ed. 2009. (Percy Jackson & the Olympians Ser.: 5). (ENG.). 485p. (J). 22.99 (978-1-4104-1678-0(X)) Cengage Gale.

—Percy Jackson & the Olympians. 2011. (Percy Jackson & the Olympians Ser.: 5). (J). lib. bdg. 18.40 (978-0-606-10567-5(0)) Turtleback.

—Percy Jackson & the Olympians: Battle of the Labyrinth: the Graphic Novel, the-Percy Jackson & the Olympians. 2018. (Percy Jackson & the Olympians Ser.: 4). (ENG., Illus.). 128p. (J). (gr. 5-9). 21.99 (978-1-4847-8235-4(6)); pap. 12.99 (978-1-4847-8639-0(4)) Disney Publishing Worldwide. (Disney-Hyperion).

—Percy Jackson & the Olympians, Book Five: Last Olympian, the-Percy Jackson & the Olympians, Book Five, Bk. 5. 5th ed. 2009. (Percy Jackson & the Olympians Ser.: 5). (ENG.). 400p. (J). (gr. 5-9). 17.99 (978-1-4231-0147-5(2), Disney-Hyperion) Disney Publishing Worldwide.

—Percy Jackson & the Olympians, Book Five: the Last Olympian, Bk. 5. 2011. (Percy Jackson & the Olympians Ser.: 5). (ENG.). 432p. (J). (gr. 5-9). pap. 7.99 (978-1-4231-0150-5(2), Disney-Hyperion) Disney Publishing Worldwide.

—Percy Jackson & the Olympians, Book Four: Battle of the Labyrinth, the-Percy Jackson & the Olympians, Book Four, Bk. 4. 2008. (Percy Jackson & the Olympians Ser.: 4). (ENG.). 384p. (J). (gr. 5-9). 17.99 (978-1-4231-0146-8(4), Hyperion Books for Children) Disney Publishing Worldwide.

—Percy Jackson & the Olympians, Book Four the Battle of the Labyrinth (Percy Jackson & the Olympians, Book Four), Bk. 4. 2009. (Percy Jackson & the Olympians Ser.: 4). (ENG.). 400p. (J). (gr. 5-9). pap. 7.99 (978-1-4231-0149-9(9), Disney-Hyperion) Disney Publishing Worldwide.

—Percy Jackson & the Olympians, Book Three: the Titan's Curse, Bk. 3. 2008. (Percy Jackson & the Olympians Ser.: 3). (ENG.). 352p. (J). (gr. 5-9). pap. 7.99 (978-1-4231-0148-2(0), Disney-Hyperion) Disney Publishing Worldwide.

—Percy Jackson & the Olympians, Book Three: Titan's Curse, the-Percy Jackson & the Olympians, Book Three, Bk. 3. rev. ed. 2007. (Percy Jackson & the Olympians Ser.: 3). (ENG.). 320p. (J). (gr. 5-9). 17.99 (978-1-4231-0145-1(6), Disney-Hyperion) Disney Publishing Worldwide.

—Percy Jackson & the Olympians, Book Two: Sea of Monsters, the-Percy Jackson & the Olympians, Book Two, Bk. 2. 2nd rev. ed. 2006. (Percy Jackson & the Olympians Ser.: 2). (ENG.). 288p. (J). (gr. 5-9). 17.99 (978-0-7868-5686-2(6), Disney-Hyperion) Disney Publishing Worldwide.

—Percy Jackson & the Olympians Hardcover Boxed Set, Set. 2010. (Percy Jackson & the Olympians Ser.). (ENG.). 1744p. (J). (gr. 5-9). 89.99 (978-1-4231-4189-1(X), Disney-Hyperion) Disney Publishing Worldwide.

—The Percy Jackson & the Olympians: Last Olympian: the Graphic Novel. 2019. (Percy Jackson & the Olympians Ser.). (ENG., Illus.). 128p. (J). (gr. 5-9). 21.99 (978-1-4847-8233-0(X)); pap. 14.99 (978-1-4847-8638-3(6)) Disney Publishing Worldwide. (Disney-Hyperion).

—The Percy Jackson & the Olympians: Titan's Curse: the Graphic Novel. 2013. (Percy Jackson & the Olympians Ser.). (ENG., Illus.). 128p. (J). (gr. 5-9). pap. 14.99 (978-1-4231-4551-6(8), Disney-Hyperion) Disney Publishing Worldwide.

—Percy Jackson & the Olympians: Titan's Curse: the Graphic Novel, the-Percy Jackson & the Olympians. 2013. (Percy Jackson & the Olympians Ser.: 3). (ENG., Illus.). 128p. (J). (gr. 5-9). 19.99 (978-1-4231-4530-1(5), Disney-Hyperion) Disney Publishing Worldwide.

—Percy Jackson: the Demigod Files. 2009. (Percy Jackson & the Olympians Ser.). (ENG., Illus.). 160p. (J). (gr. 5-9). 12.99 (978-1-4231-2166-4(X), Disney-Hyperion) Disney Publishing Worldwide.

—The Sea of Monsters. 2011. 9.68 (978-0-7848-3440-4(7), Everbind) Marco Bk. Co.

—The Son of Neptune. l.t. ed. 2011. (Heroes of Olympus Ser.: Bk. 2). (ENG.). 616p. 23.99 (978-1-4104-4122-5(9)) Thorndike Pr.

—The Son of Neptune. 2013. (Heroes of Olympus Ser.: 2). (J). lib. bdg. 20.85 (978-0-606-31759-7(7)) Turtleback.

—The Titan's Curse. 2008. (Percy Jackson & the Olympians Ser.: No. 3). 312p. (J). lib. bdg. 20.00 (978-1-4242-4710-3(1)) Fitzgerald Bks.

—The Titan's Curse. 2011. 9.68 (978-0-7848-3441-1(5), Everbind) Marco Bk. Co.

—The Titan's Curse. l.t. rev. ed. 2007. (Percy Jackson & the Olympians Ser.: 3). (ENG.). 402p. (gr. 5-9). 23.99 (978-0-7862-9701-6(8)) Thorndike Pr.

Riordan, Rick & Venditti, Robert. Percy Jackson & the Olympians: Sea of Monsters, the: the Graphic Novel. 2013. (Percy Jackson & the Olympians Ser.). (ENG., Illus.). 128p.

(J). (gr. 5-9). pap. 12.99 *(978-1-4231-4550-9(X),* Disney-Hyperion) Disney Publishing Worldwide.
—The Titan's Curse. 2013. (Percy Jackson & the Olympians Graphic Novels Ser.: 3). (J). lib. bdg. 26.95 *(978-0-606-32286-7(8))* Turtleback.
Rippin, Sally. Billie's Outer Space Adventure. Coburn, Alisa, illus. 2017. (ENG.). 24p. (J). 10.99 *(978-1-61067-608-3(4))* Kane Miller.
Ritter, William. Beastly Bones. 2016. (Jackaby Ser.: 2). lib. bdg. 20.80 *(978-0-606-39017-0(0))* Turtleback.
Rivas, Spelile & Plascencia, Amira. No Time for Monsters/No Hay Tiempo para Monstruos. Cervantes, Valeria, illus. 2010. (SPA & ENG.). 32p. (J). (gr. -1-3). 16.95 *(978-1-55885-445-1(2))* Arte Publico Pr.
Roach. Frogosaurus vs. the Bog Monster. 2013. (Monstrous Stories Ser.: 3). lib. bdg. 14.75 *(978-0-606-32002-3(4))* Turtleback.
—Monstrous Stories #3: Frogosaurus vs. the Bog Monster, 3. 2013. (Dr. Roach's Monstrous Stories Ser.: 3). (ENG.). 64p. (J). (gr. 2-4). 17.44 *(978-0-545-42556-8(5))* Scholastic, Inc.
—Night of the Zombie Goldfish. 2013. (Monstrous Stories Ser.: 1). lib. bdg. 14.75 *(978-0-606-31523-4(3))* Turtleback.
Roanhorse, Rebecca. Race to the Sun. 2021. (ENG.). 256p. (gr. 3-6). 22.44 *(978-1-5364-6679-9(4),* Riordan, Rick) Disney Pr.
—Race to the Sun. 2021. (Penworthy Picks YA Fiction Ser.). (ENG., Illus.). 298p. (J). (gr. 4-5). 19.46 *(978-1-68505-027-6(1))* Penworthy Co., LLC, The.
—Rick Riordan Presents Race to the Sun. (J). (gr. 3-7). 2021. 48p. pap. 7.99 *(978-1-368-02482-2(3))* 2020. 12p. 16.99 *(978-1-368-02466-2(1))* Disney Publishing Worldwide. (Riordan, Rick).
Robberecht, Thierry. Superhero School. Goossens, Philippe, illus. 2012. (ENG.). 30p. (J). (gr. -1-k). 16.95 *(978-1-60537-140-5(8))* Clavis Publishing.
Roberts, Chris. A Mcspooky Halloween. 2006. (J). pap. 9.00 *(978-0-8059-7196-5(3))* Dorrance Publishing Co., Inc.
Roberts, Daniel. Harrison & His Dinosaur Robot & the Purple Spotted Sea Monster. 2012. 36p. pap. 20.99 *(978-1-4772-6979-4(7))* AuthorHouse.
Roberts, Jeyn. Dark Inside. (ENG.). (YA). (gr. 9). 2012. 352p. pap. 12.99 *(978-1-4424-2352-7(8))* 2011. 336p. 17.99 *(978-1-4424-2351-0(X))* Simon & Schuster Bks. For Young Readers. (Simon & Schuster Bks. For Young Readers).
—Rage Within. (ENG., 368p. (YA). (gr. 9). 2013. Illus.). pap. 11.99 *(978-1-4424-2355-8(2))* 2012. 17.99 *(978-1-4424-2354-1(4))* Simon & Schuster Bks. For Young Readers. (Simon & Schuster Bks. For Young Readers).
Robico. My Little Monster 2. 2014. (My Little Monster Ser.: 2). (Illus.). 168p. (gr. 8-12). pap. 10.99 *(978-1-61262-598-0(3))* Kodansha America, Inc.
Robinson, Brenda. A Monster Came to Our House. 2013. 40p. pap. 16.46 *(978-1-4669-9569-7(6))* Trafford Publishing.
Robinson, Gary. Billy Buckhorn Paranormal. 2015. (Billy Buckhorn Ser.: 2). (ENG.). 120p. (YA). (gr. 8-12). pap. 9.95 *(978-1-939053-08-4(0),* 7th Generation) BPC.
Robinson, Keith. Valley of Monsters. 2013. 212p. pap. *(978-0-9843906-6-3(9))* Roxby Media Ltd.
Rockwood, Roy. The Wizard of the Se. 2008. 124p. 23.95 *(978-1-60664-931-2(0));* pap. 10.95 *(978-1-60664-051-7(8))* Aegypan.
Rodda, Emily. The Silver Door. 2013. (Illus.). 278p. (J). pap. *(978-0-545-42993-1(5),* Scholastic Pr.) Scholastic, Inc.
—The Third Door. 2013. (J). pap. *(978-0-545-42995-5(1),* Scholastic Pr.) Scholastic, Inc.
Rodriguez, Lourdes. Mandy, Princess of la la Land: The Green Monster. 2013. 52p. pap. 24.99 *(978-1-4817-0077-1(4))* AuthorHouse.
Rogalski, Mark. Make Me a Monster: (Juvenile Fiction, Kids Novelty Book, Children's Monster Book, Children's Lift the Flaps Book) 2019. (ENG., Illus.). 16p. (J). (gr. -1-k). bds. 14.99 *(978-1-4521-6715-2(X))* Chronicle Bks. LLC.
Rogers, Kirsteen. Monsters Sticker Book. 2012. (Sticker Activity Book Ser.). 34p. (J). pap. 8.99 *(978-0-7945-3325-0(6),* Usborne) EDC Publishing.
Rogers, Michelle Elizabeth. The Adventures of Brutus & Baby: A Haunted Halloween. Collier, Kevin Scott, illus. 2010. 50p. pap. 16.50 *(978-1-60860-592-7(2),* Eloquent Bks.) Strategic Book Publishing & Rights Agency (SBPRA).
Rotellar, Carlos. Little Red Monster: Tales of Monica. 2009. 24p. pap. 11.49 *(978-1-4490-2812-1(8))* AuthorHouse.
Rowling, J. K. The Ickabog. 1 vol. 2020. (ENG.). 304p. (J). (gr. 3-3). 26.99 *(978-1-338-73287-0(0))* Scholastic, Inc.
Rozum, John & Pope, Robert. Scooby-Doo & the Monster of a Thousand Faces!, 1 vol. 2011. (Scooby-Doo Graphic Novels Ser.: No. 2). (ENG., Illus.). 24p. (J). (gr. 2-6). 31.36 *(978-1-59961-916-3(4),* 570, Graphic Novels) Spotlight.
Rubin, Adam. Big Bad Bubble. Salmieri, Daniel, illus. (ENG.). 40p. (J). (gr. -1-3). 2017. pap. 9.99 *(978-0-544-92782-7(6),* 1657202) 2014. 17.99 *(978-0-544-04549-1(1),* 1532278) HarperCollins Pubs. (Clarion Bks.).
Rudden, Dave. The Endless King. 2018. (J). *(978-0-553-52305-8(8))* Random Hse., Inc.
Ruiz, Rachel. When Penny Met POTUS. Manwill, Melissa & Manwill, Melissa, illus. 2016. (Fiction Picture Bks.). (ENG.). 32p. (J). (gr. -1-3). lib. bdg. 27.99 *(978-1-5158-0218-1(3),* 132451, Picture Window Bks.) Capstone.
Russell, Shane. Phloomp! 2010. (ENG.). 158p. pap. *(978-1-84748-759-9(9))* Athena Pr.
Saddlewick, A. B. Monstrous Maud: Big Fright. 2017. (ENG., Illus.). 128p. (J). (gr. 1-5). pap. 7.99 *(978-1-5107-1698-8(X),* Sky Pony Pr.) Skyhorse Publishing Co., Inc.
Saracino, Luciano & Bernatene, Poly. The Monster Diaries. Bernatene, Poly, illus. 2009. (Illus.). 32p. (J). 15.99 *(978-1-60010-502-9(5),* Worthwhile Bks.) Idea & Design Works, LLC.
Sargent, Dave, et al. Grubby: (Smutty Olive Grullo) Have a Good Disposition, 30 vols., Vol. 31. 2003. (Saddle up Ser.: Vol. 31). (Illus.). 42p. (J). lib. bdg. 23.60 *(978-1-56763-691-8(8))* Ozark Publishing.
Sauer, Tammi. Mostly Monsterly. Magoon, Scott, illus. 2010. (ENG.). 40p. (J). (gr. -1-3). 18.99 *(978-1-4169-6110-9(0),* Simon & Schuster/Paula Wiseman Bks.) Simon & Schuster/Paula Wiseman Bks.
Savage, J. Scott. Case File 13 #3: Evil Twins. Holgate, Doug, illus. (Case File 13 Ser.: 3). (ENG.). (J). (gr. 3-7). 2015. 288p. pap. 7.99 *(978-0-06-213338-0(1))* 2014. 272p. 14.99 *(978-0-06-213337-3(3))* HarperCollins Pubs. (HarperCollins).
Sazaklis, John. Goat on a Boat, 1 vol. Bradley, Jess, illus. 2013. (Comics Land Ser.). (ENG.). 32p. (J). (gr. k-2). 7.95 *(978-1-4342-6282-0(0),* 123726, Stone Arch Bks.) Capstone.
Schaefer, Lola M. Frankie Stein, 0 vols. Atteberry, Kevan J., illus. 2012. (ENG.). 34p. (J). (gr. -1-3). pap. 7.99 *(978-0-7614-5608-7(2),* 9780761456087, Two Lions) Amazon Publishing.
—Frankie Stein Starts School. Atteberry, Kevan J., illus. (ENG.). (J). (gr. -1-3). 2018. 34p. pap. 7.99 *(978-1-4778-1049-1(8),* 9781477810491) 2012. 32p. 15.99 *(978-0-7614-5656-8(2),* 9780761456568) Amazon Publishing. (Two Lions).
Schaeffer, Rebecca. Not Even Bones. (Market of Monsters Ser.: 1). (ENG.). (YA). (gr. 9). 2019. 384p. pap. 9.99 *(978-0-358-10825-2(X),* 1748891) 2018. 368p. 17.99 *(978-1-328-86354-6(9),* 1694449) HarperCollins Pubs. (Clarion Bks.).
—Only Ashes Remain. 2019. (Market of Monsters Ser.: 2). (ENG.). 432p. (YA). (gr. 9). 17.99 *(978-1-328-86355-3(7),* 1694451, Clarion Bks.) HarperCollins Pubs.
Schauer, M., et al. Rip, M. D. 2010. (ENG., Illus.). 88p. pap. 12.99 *(978-1-60699-369-9(0),* 699369) Fantagraphics Bks.
Schmitz, James H. The Other Likeness. 2011. 30p. 14.95 *(978-1-4638-9904-2(1))* Rodgers, Alan Bks.
Schnitzlein, Danny. The Monster Who Ate My Peas, 1 vol. Faulkner, Matt, illus. 2010. 32p. (J). (gr. -1-3). pap. 7.95 *(978-1-56145-533-1(4))* Peachtree Publishing Co. Inc.
—The Monster Who Did My Math, 1 vol. Mayer, Bill, illus. 32p. (J). (gr. -1-3). 2012. pap. 8.99 *(978-1-56145-668-0(3))* 2007. 16.95 *(978-1-56145-420-4(6))* Peachtree Publishing Co. Inc.
—Trick or Treat on Monster Street, 1 vol. Faulkner, Matt, illus. 2008. 32p. (J). (gr. -1-3). 16.95 *(978-1-56145-465-5(6))* Peachtree Publishing Co. Inc.
Scholastic, Inc. Staff. Scooby-Doo: Frankencreepy Movie Reader. 2014. (Scooby Doo Reader Ser.). lib. bdg. 13.55 *(978-0-606-36270-2(3))* Turtleback.
Scholastic, Inc. Staff & Stine, R. L. Write Your Fright. 2011. (Goosebumps Horrorland Ser.). (ENG.). 64p. 12.99 *(978-0-545-33295-8(8),* Scholastic Paperbacks) Scholastic, Inc.
Schopp, Bernice Frances. The Legend of Moon-Goblin Town. 2012. 32p. pap. 21.99 *(978-1-4771-4475-6(7))* Xlibris Corp.
Schwab, V. E. Our Dark Duet. (Monsters of Verity Ser.: 2). (ENG.). (YA). (gr. 9). 2020. 544p. pap. 15.99 *(978-0-06-298340-4(7))* 2017. 528p. 17.99 *(978-0-06-238088-3(5))* HarperCollins Pubs. (Greenwillow Bks.).
Schwab, Victoria. Our Dark Duet. 2018. (Monsters of Verity Ser.: 2). (ENG.). 544p. (YA). (gr. 9). pap. 9.99 *(978-0-06-238089-0(3))* 2017. 528p. pap. *(978-0-06-267203-2(7))* HarperCollins Pubs. (Greenwillow Bks.).
—Our Dark Duet. 2018. (Monsters of Verity Ser.: 02). (YA). lib. bdg. 20.85 *(978-0-606-41367-1(7))* Turtleback.
Seagle, Steven T. Camp Midnight. 2016. lib. bdg. 29.40 *(978-0-606-37808-6(1))* Turtleback.
The Secret of the Monster Book, 6 vols., Vol. 2. (Woodland Mysteriestm Ser.). 133p. (gr. 3-7). 42.50 *(978-0-7802-7933-9(6))* Wright Group/McGraw-Hill.
Sendak, Maurice. Donde Viven los Monstruos. 2003. (SPA., Illus.). 40p. (J). (gr. k-3). 12.95 *(978-84-372-2185-4(4))* Altea, Ediciones, S.A. - Grupo Santillana ESP. Dist: Santillana USA Publishing Co., Inc.
—Where the Wild Things Are. 2010. (HEB., Illus.). 38p. (J). *(978-965-07-1793-3(5))* Keter Publishing Hse.
—Where the Wild Things Are. (J). pap. 12.95 incl. audio Weston Woods Studios, Inc.
—Where the Wild Things Are: A Caldecott Award Winner. Sendak, Maurice, illus. 25th anniv. ed. 2012. (ENG., Illus.). 48p. (J). (gr. -1-3). 21.99 *(978-0-06-025492-6(0));* pap. 8.95 *(978-0-06-443178-1(9))* HarperCollins Pubs. (HarperCollins).
Sendak, Maurice & LaFleur, Richard A. Ubi Fera Sunt: Fabula Ed Picturae. 2015. (ENG., Illus.). (J). pap. 24.00 *(978-0-86516-831-2(8))* Bolchazy-Carducci Pubs.
Sensel, Joni. The Garbage Monster. Bivins, Christopher, illus. 2003. 24p. (J). (gr. -1-18). 14.95 *(978-0-9701195-2-0(6))* Dream Factory Bks.
Seroney, Kibny'aanko Arap. Cheebtabuut, Blue Berries & the Monsters Den. 2013. 36p. pap. *(978-1-909204-28-7(5))* BookPublishingWorld.
SFX Fantasy. Tween Tales - Robots, Dragons & the Interworld Machine. 2007. (ENG.). 131p. pap. 12.99 *(978-1-4303-2546-8(1))* Lulu Pr., Inc.
Shankman, Ed. Champ & Me by the Maple Tree: A Vermont Tale. O'Neill, Dave, illus. 2010. (Shankman & O'Neill Ser.). (ENG.). 32p. (J). (gr. -1-3). 14.95 *(978-0-9819430-5-3(5),* Commonwealth Editions) Applewood Bks.
Shapiro D., Brian. Plaquetooth. 2008. 28p. pap. 13.99 *(978-1-4343-8913-8(8))* AuthorHouse.
Sharp, Michael. Vayda Jayne Bean - Vanilla. Van Tine, Laura, illus. 2007. 20p. (J). (gr. -1-3). pap. *(978-0-9780969-5-3(9))* Avatar Pubns., Inc.
Shealy, Dennis R. T. Rex Trouble! (DC Super Friends) Doescher, Erik et al, illus. 2011. (Step into Reading Ser.). (ENG.). 32p. (J). (gr. -1-1). pap. 5.99 *(978-0-375-86777-4(5),* Random Hse. Bks. for Young Readers) Random Hse. Children's Bks.
Shelley, Mary. Frankenstein, 1 vol. 2009. (Foundation Classics Ser.). (ENG., Illus.). 56p. (J). (gr. 5-5). lib. bdg. 32.60 *(978-1-60754-848-5(8),* e68c3398-340f-47ac-9fab-81f353f47c53, Windmill Bks.) Rosen Publishing Group, Inc., The.
—Frankenstein, 1 vol. Ho, Jason, illus. 2007. (Graphic Horror Ser.). (ENG.). 32p. (J). (gr. 3-6). 32.79 *(978-1-60270-059-8(1),* 9072, Graphic Planet - Fiction) Magic Wagon.
—Frankenstein. 2013. (Differentiated Timeless Classics Ser.). (ENG.). 80p. (YA). (gr. 4-12). 14.95 *(978-1-62250-717-7(7))* Saddleback Educational Publishing, Inc.
—Frankenstein. abr. ed. 2010. (Dover Horror Coloring Bks.). (ENG.). 48p. (J). (gr. 3-8). pap. 4.99 *(978-0-486-47415-1(1),* 474151) Dover Pubns., Inc.
—Frankenstein: With a Discussion of Tolerance. Clift, Eva, tr. Clift, Eva, illus. 2003. (Values in Action Illustrated Classics Ser.). (J). *(978-1-59203-048-4(3))* Learning Challenge, Inc.
—Gris Grimly's Frankenstein. Grimly, Gris, illus. (ENG.). 208p. (J). (gr. 8). 2015. pap. 17.99 *(978-0-06-186298-4(3))* 2013. 24.99 *(978-0-06-186297-7(5))* HarperCollins Pubs. (Balzer & Bray).
—YNA2 Frankenstein Everything You Need to Catch up, Study & Prepare for & 2023 & 2024 Exams & Assessments. 2004. (ENG.). 112p. pap. 20.00 *(978-0-582-82301-3(3))* Pearson Education, Ltd. GBR. Dist: Trans-Atlantic Pubns., Inc.
Shelley, Mary Wollstonecraft & Shelley, Mary Wollstonecraft. Classic Starts(r): Frankenstein: Retold from the Mary Shelley Original. Akib, Jamel, illus. 2006. (Classic Starts(r) Ser.). 160p. (J). (gr. 2-4). 7.99 *(978-1-4027-2666-8(X))* Sterling Publishing Co., Inc.
Sherrill, Rusty & Miers, Doug. Kid Nitro & the Sinister Slorp. Sherrill, Cathy, ed. Sherrill, Rusty, illus. 2007. (Illus.). 273p. (YA). per. 14.95 *(978-0-9787729-0-1(3))* RS Art Studio.
Shiels, Tony "Doc". Monstrum! a Wizard's Tale. 2011. 148p. pap. *(978-1-905723-55-3(5))* CFZ Pr.
Shook, Karl. The Family Thing. 2004. 166p. (YA). pap. 12.95 *(978-0-595-31121-7(0))* iUniverse, Inc.
Shopping, 6 Packs. (Sails Literacy Ser.). 16p. (gr. k-18). 27.00 *(978-0-7635-4422-5(1))* Rigby Education.
Shoshan, Beth. Mess Monsters at Christmas. 2009. 24p. (J). pap. 6.99 *(978-1-60010-560-9(2),* Worthwhile Bks.) Idea & Design Works, LLC.
Shreve, Steve. The Bogey Man: Or a Good Argument for Not Picking Your Nose. Shreve, Steve, illus. 2010. (Adventures of Charlie Ser.). (Illus.). 32p. pap. *(978-0-237-54287-0(0))* Evans Brothers, Ltd.
Siclari, Theresa. The Pond Behind Grandmother's House. 2007. 32p. per. 24.95 *(978-1-4137-8597-5(2))* America Star Bks.
Sidong, Li, illus. Beowulf. 2010. (Graphic Classics Ser.). (ENG.). 48p. (J). (gr. 5-8). 19.95 *(978-0-7641-6301-2(9),* B.E.S. Publishing) Peterson's.
Sierra, Sergio A. Frankenstein by Mary Shelley: A Dark Graphic Novel, 1 vol. 2013. (Dark Graphic Novels Ser.). (ENG., Illus.). 96p. (J). (gr. 5-6). 33.60 *(978-0-7660-4084-7(4),* ecdc803c-f69e-4ad7-baaa-c940cb7415a0) Enslow Publishing, LLC.
Sill, Cathryn. About Mollusks: A Guide for Children, 1 vol. Sill, John, illus. 2008. (About... Ser.: 9). 40p. (J). (gr. -1-2). pap. 7.95 *(978-1-56145-406-8(0))* Peachtree Publishing Co. Inc.
Simon, Francesca. Horrid Henry & the Abominable Snowman. 2010. (Horrid Henry Ser.). (Illus.). 87p. (J). lib. bdg. 17.20 *(978-0-606-14063-8(8))* Turtleback.
Simonson, Louise. Battling Bigfoot. Elston, James W., illus. 2007. (Extreme Monsters Ser.). 94p. (J). (gr. 2-5). per. 3.99 *(978-1-57791-275-0(6),* Penny Candy Pr.) Brighter Minds Children's Publishing.
—Meet Mr. Hydeous, Vol. 3. Elston, James W., illus. gif. ed. 2006. (Extreme Monsters Ser.). 96p. (J). per. 3.99 *(978-1-57791-255-2(1))* Brighter Minds Children's Publishing.
—What's with Wulf? Elston, James W., illus. gif. ed. 2005. (Extreme Monsters Ser.). 96p. (J). (gr. 2-5). per. 3.99 *(978-1-57791-179-1(2))* Brighter Minds Children's Publishing.
—Wonder Woman: Monster Magic. Schoening, Dan, illus. 2010. (Wonder Woman Ser.). (ENG.). 56p. (J). (gr. 3-6). pap. 4.95 *(978-1-4342-2260-2(8),* 103123, Stone Arch Bks.) Capstone.
Sirowy, Alexandra. The Creeping. 2015. (ENG., Illus.). 400p. (YA). (gr. 7). 17.99 *(978-1-4814-1886-7(6))* Simon & Schuster Children's Publishing.
Sisler, Stephanie. Matthews Monsters, a Creative Comprehensive Exercise. Grzelak, Kyle, illus. 2011. 32p. pap. 12.95 *(978-1-61493-015-0(5))* Peppertree Pr., The.
—One Bright Monster. Holcomb, Nicholas, illus. 2012. 36p. pap. 12.95 *(978-1-61493-124-9(0))* Peppertree Pr., The.
Skrutskie, Emily. The Abyss Surrounds Us. 2016. (Abyss Ser.). (ENG., Illus.). 288p. (YA). (gr. 9-12). pap. 11.99 *(978-0-7387-4691-3(6),* 0738746916, Flux) North Star Editions.
—The Abyss Surrounds Us. 2016. lib. bdg. 23.30 *(978-0-606-38499-5(5))* Turtleback.
Skye, Obert. The Lord of the Hat. Skye, Obert, illus. 2015. (Creature from My Closet Ser.: 5). (ENG., Illus.). 256p. (J). (gr. 4-7). 13.99 *(978-1-62779-162-5(0),* 900138586, Holt, Henry & Co. Bks. For Young Readers) Holt, Henry & Co.
—The Lord of the Hat. Skye, Obert, illus. 2018. (Creature from My Closet Ser.: 5). (ENG., Illus.). 272p. (J). pap. 11.99 *(978-1-250-15836-9(2),* 900185488) Square Fish.
—Wonkenstein. Skye, Obert, illus. 2015. (Creature from My Closet Ser.: 1). (ENG., Illus.). 256p. (J). (gr. 4-7). pap. 9.99 *(978-1-250-01022-3(5),* 900084759) Square Fish.
Slade, Arthur. Monsterology: Fabulous Lives of the Creepy, the Revolting, & the Undead. Mah, Derek, illus. 2005. 96p. (J). (gr. 4-7). pap. 8.95 *(978-0-88776-714-2(1),* Tundra Bks.) Tundra Bks. CAN. Dist: Penguin Random Hse. LLC.
Slonim, David. I Loathe You. Slonim, David, illus. (ENG., Illus.). 24p. (J). (gr. -1-3). 2018. 7.99 *(978-1-5344-3311-3(2))* 2012. 15.99 *(978-1-4424-2244-5(0))* Simon & Schuster Children's Publishing. (Aladdin).
Smiley, Jess Smart. 10 Little Monsters Visit New York City, Volume 5. Hardyman, Nathan, illus. 2016. (10 Little Monsters Ser.: 5). (ENG.). 32p. (J). (gr. k-3). 16.95 *(978-1-942934-67-7(X),* 553467) Familius LLC.
Smith, Alexander Gordon. The Devil's Engine: Hellfighters: (Book 2) 2016. (Devil's Engine Ser.: 2). (ENG.). 320p. (YA). 29.99 *(978-0-374-30172-9(7),* 900140532, Farrar, Straus & Giroux (BYR)) Farrar, Straus & Giroux.
—The Devil's Engine: Hellfighters: (Book 2) 2017. (Devil's Engine Ser.: 2). (ENG.). 336p. (YA). pap. 10.99 *(978-1-250-12965-9(6),* 900176103) Square Fish.
—The Devil's Engine: Hellraisers: (Book 1) 2015. (Devil's Engine Ser.: 1). (ENG.). 352p. (YA). (gr. 7). 29.99 *(978-0-374-30169-9(7),* 900140530, Farrar, Straus & Giroux (BYR)) Farrar, Straus & Giroux.
—The Devil's Engine: Hellwalkers: (Book 3) 2017. (Devil's Engine Ser.: 3). (ENG.). 320p. (YA). 29.99 *(978-0-374-30174-3(3),* 900140534, Farrar, Straus & Giroux (BYR)) Farrar, Straus & Giroux.
—Hellfighters. 2017. (Devil's Engine Ser.: 2). (YA). lib. bdg. 22.10 *(978-0-606-40588-1(7))* Turtleback.
Smith, Caighlan. Children of Icarus. 2016. (ENG.). 312p. (YA). (gr. 9-12). 16.95 *(978-1-63079-057-8(5),* 132186, Switch Pr.) Capstone.
Smith, Gloria. Tommy's Monster. 2009. (ENG.). 28p. pap. 21.99 *(978-1-4415-6366-8(0))* Xlibris Corp.
Smith, James J. Mikey's Monster. 2013. (Step into Reading Level 4 Ser.). lib. bdg. 13.55 *(978-0-606-32223-2(X))* Turtleback.
Smith, Lisa R. There's a Monster in My Washing MacHine. 2011. (ENG.). 16p. 13.00 *(978-1-4357-6497-2(8))* Lulu Pr., Inc.
Snider, Brandon T. The Attack of the Movie Monsters. 2015. (Transformers 8x8 Ser.). (J). lib. bdg. 14.75 *(978-0-606-37514-6(7))* Turtleback.
Snider, Brandon T., adapted by. Meet Quickshadow. 2017. (Illus.). 31p. (J). *(978-1-5182-4447-6(5))* Little Brown & Co.
Snow, Alan. Here Be Monsters! Snow, Alan, illus. (Ratbridge Chronicles Ser.: 1). (ENG., Illus.). 544p. (J). (gr. 3-9). 2007. per. 9.99 *(978-0-689-87048-4(5))* 2006. 17.95 *(978-0-689-87047-7(7))* Simon & Schuster Children's Publishing. (Atheneum Bks. for Young Readers).
Snow, Jeff. Beasts in the Closet. Snow, Jeff, illus. 2006. (Illus.). 32p. (J). 17.95 *(978-1-932362-11-4(8))* Snowbound Pr., Inc.
Soderberg, Erin. Puppy Pirates #5: Search for the Sea Monster. 2016. (Puppy Pirates Ser.: 5). (Illus.). 96p. (J). (gr. 1-4). 5.99 *(978-1-101-93776-1(9),* Random Hse. Bks. for Young Readers) Random Hse. Children's Bks.
Something Is There & Other Stories: Individual Title Six-Pack. (Story Steps Ser.). (gr. k-2). 48.00 *(978-0-7635-9828-0(3))* Rigby Education.
Sonneborn, Scott. The Frankenstein Journals, 1 vol. Banks, Timothy, illus. 2014. (Frankenstein Journals). (ENG.). 160p. (J). (gr. 2-4). 9.95 *(978-1-4342-9130-1(8),* 125575, Stone Arch Bks.) Capstone.
—The Frankenstein Journals: Guts or Bust. Banks, Timothy, illus. 2015. (Frankenstein Journals). (ENG.). 160p. (J). (gr. 2-4). 9.95 *(978-1-4965-0223-0(X),* 128037, Stone Arch Bks.) Capstone.
—A Pain in the Butt. Banks, Timothy, illus. 2015. (Frankenstein Journals). (ENG.). 80p. (J). (gr. 2-4). 22.65 *(978-1-4965-0222-3(1),* 128036, Stone Arch Bks.) Capstone.
Soo, Kean. Jellaby: Monster in the City. 2014. (Jellaby Ser.). (ENG., Illus.). 184p. (J). (gr. 4-6). pap. 12.95 *(978-1-4342-6421-3(1),* 123939, Stone Arch Bks.) Capstone.
Sowder, G. Wesley & Sowder, Joseph, told to. Hunter-Lee & the Toy Monster: Book One. 2008. 48p. pap. 16.95 *(978-1-60703-137-6(X))* America Star Bks.
Spaht-Gill, Janie. Monster Stew. Reese, Bob, illus. (J). 5.95 *(978-0-89868-307-3(6))* ARO Publishing Co.
Sparkes, Amy. Collins Big Cat Phonics for Letters & Sounds - Monster Treat: Band 05/Green, Bd. 5. Brown, Steve, illus. 2018. (Collins Big Cat Phonics Ser.). (ENG.). 24p. (J). (gr. k-1). pap. 8.99 *(978-0-00-825167-3(3))* HarperCollins Pubs. Ltd. GBR. Dist: Independent Pubs. Group.
Sparrow, Katherine. Little Apocalypse. 2019. (ENG.). 336p. (J). (gr. 3-7). 16.99 *(978-0-06-284976-2(X),* HarperCollins) HarperCollins Pubs.
Spiliotopoulos, Evan, et al. Beauty & the Beast. 2017. 275p. (J). *(978-1-368-00765-8(1))* Disney Publishing Worldwide.
Spinale, Wendy. Umberland (the Everland Trilogy, Book 2) (Everland Ser.: 2). (ENG.). (YA). (gr. 7). 2018. 304p. pap. 9.99 *(978-0-545-95319-1(7),* Scholastic Paperbacks) 2017. 288p. 17.99 *(978-0-545-95318-4(9),* Scholastic Pr.) Scholastic, Inc.
Spotswood, Jessica, ed. A Tyranny of Petticoats: 15 Stories of Belles, Bank Robbers & Other Badass Girls. (ENG.). 368p. (YA). (gr. 9). 2018. pap. 9.99 *(978-1-5362-0025-6(5))* 2016. 17.99 *(978-0-7636-7848-7(1))* Candlewick Pr.
Spradlin, Michael P. Feeding Frenzy. 2013. (Illus.). 167p. (J). *(978-0-545-62200-4(X))* Scholastic, Inc.
—Menace from the Deep. 2013. (Illus.). 225p. (J). *(978-0-545-56366-6(6))* Scholastic, Inc.
—Out for Blood. 2014. 168p. (J). pap. *(978-0-545-67523-9(5))* Scholastic, Inc.
—Out for Blood. 2014. (Killer Species Ser.: 3). lib. bdg. 16.00 *(978-0-606-35398-4(4))* Turtleback.
—Ultimate Attack. 2014. (Killer Species Ser.: 4). lib. bdg. 16.00 *(978-0-606-35853-8(6))* Turtleback.
Spurr, Elizabeth. Monsters, Mind Your Manners! Scales, Simon, illus. 2012. (J). 34.28 *(978-1-61913-124-8(2))* Weigl Pubs., Inc.
Stahl, Jon. The Dragons Eat Noodles on Tuesdays. Bentley, Tadgh, illus. 2019. (ENG.). 40p. (J). (gr. -1-3). 17.99 *(978-1-338-12551-1(6),* Scholastic Pr.) Scholastic, Inc.
Stanford, Cody L. Sinews of the Heart. 2013. 186p. pap. 10.99 *(978-1-62757-059-6(4))* Storm Moon Pr., LLC.
Stanley, John. Melvin Monster: More Maniacial Monster Meltdowns!, 3 vols., Vol. 2. 2010. (John Stanley Library). (ENG., Illus.). 112p. 24.95 *(978-1-77046-003-4(9),* 900064372) Drawn & Quarterly Pubns. CAN. Dist: Macmillan.
Stanton, Elizabeth Rose. Bub. Stanton, Elizabeth Rose, illus. 2018. (ENG., Illus.). 40p. (J). (gr. -1-3). 17.99 *(978-1-4814-8757-3(4),* Simon & Schuster/Paula Wiseman Bks.) Simon & Schuster/Paula Wiseman Bks.
Staunton, Ted. Morgan & the Dune Racer. Slavin, Bill, illus. 2011. (Formac First Novels Ser.). (ENG.). 64p. (J). (gr. 2-3). 14.95 *(978-0-88780-966-8(9),* 966) Formac Publishing Co., Ltd. CAN. Dist: Formac Lorimer Bks. Ltd.
—Morgan on Ice, 1 vol. Slavin, Bill, illus. 2013. (Formac First Novels Ser.). (ENG.). 56p. (J). (gr. 2-3). 14.95 *(978-1-4595-0289-5(2),* 0289) Formac Publishing Co., Ltd. CAN. Dist: Formac Lorimer Bks. Ltd.
Steele, Michael Anthony. Monster Mutt Madness. Jeralds, Scott, illus. 2017. (Scooby-Doo! Beginner Mysteries Ser.). (ENG.). 112p. (J). (gr. 1-3). lib. bdg. 22.65 *(978-1-4965-4767-5(5),* 135304, Stone Arch Bks.) Capstone.
Steer, Dugald A. Snappy Little Halloween. Matthews, Derek, illus. 2004. 20p. (J). (gr. k-4). reprint ed. 13.00 *(978-0-7567-7403-5(9))* DIANE Publishing Co.

MNO

Steig, William. Shrek! Steig, William, illus. 20th anniv. ed. 2010. (ENG., Illus.). 40p. (J). (gr. -1-3). 21.99 (978-0-374-36879-1(1), 900065703, Farrar, Straus & Giroux (BYR)) Farrar, Straus & Giroux.

—Shrek! Steig, William, illus. 2003. (Illus.). (J). (gr. -1-2). pap. 35.95 incl. audio compact disk (978-1-59112-551-8(0)) Live Oak Media.

—Shrek! 2008. (Illus.). (gr. -1-3). 17.00 (978-1-60686-207-0(3)) Perfection Learning Corp.

—Shrek! Steig, William, illus. 2008. (ENG., Illus.). 32p. (J). (gr. -1-3). pap. 8.99 (978-0-312-38449-4(1), 900053435) Square Fish.

—Shrek! 2008. (J). (gr. -1-2). 18.40 (978-0-7857-2221-2(1)) Turtleback.

Stephens, John. The Emerald Atlas. 2012. (Books of Beginning Ser.: 1). (ENG.). 464p. (J). (gr. 3-7). 10.99 (978-0-375-87271-6(X), Yearling) Random Hse. Children's Bks.

—The Emerald Atlas. Lt. ed. 2012. (Books of Beginning Ser.). (ENG.). 547p. (J). (gr. 4-7). 23.99 (978-1-4104-4234-5(9)) Thorndike Pr.

—The Fire Chronicle. 2012. (Illus.). 437p. (J). (978-0-449-81015-6(1)) Knopf, Alfred A. Inc.

—The Fire Chronicle. 2013. (Books of Beginning Ser.: 2). (ENG., Illus.). 464p. (J). (gr. 3-7). 9.99 (978-0-375-87272-3(8), Yearling) Random Hse. Children's Bks.

Stephenson, Susan. Monster Maddie. Snider, K. C., illus. 2010. 20p. pap. 10.95 (978-1-61633-027-9(9)) Guardian Angel Publishing, Inc.

Steps To Literacy Staff, compiled by. Beast Quest Collection Grades 2-5: Class Pack (6 Titles, 6 Each) 2010. (ENG.). (J). pap. 170.75 (978-1-60923-616-8(5)) Steps To Literacy, LLC.

—Beast Quest Collection Grades 2-5: Variety Pack (6 Titles, 1 Each) 2010. (ENG.). (J). pap. 29.90 (978-1-60923-615-1(7)) Steps To Literacy, LLC.

—Percy Jackson & the Olympians Series: Variety Pack (5 Titles, 1 Each) 2010. (J). pap. 39.95 (978-1-60923-745-5(5)) Steps To Literacy, LLC.

Sterner, Wendy L. Seymore Monster. 2008. 32p. pap. 24.95 (978-1-60441-748-7(X)) America Star Bks.

Stevens, Lynda. The Lawn Monster: A Book to Help Kids Learn to Be Brave. 2012. 44p. pap. 21.99 (978-1-4771-0291-6(4)) Xlibris Corp.

Stilton, Gerónimo. Meet Me in Horrorwood. 2011. (Geronimo Stilton — Creepella Von Cacklefur Ser.: 2). (Illus.). 112p. (J). lib. bdg. 18.40 (978-0-606-22947-0(7)) Turtleback.

—Return of the Vampire. 2012. (Geronimo Stilton — Creepella Von Cacklefur Ser.: 4). lib. bdg. 18.40 (978-0-606-26180-7(X)) Turtleback.

Stine, R. L. Creep from the Deep. 2008. (Goosebumps HorrorLand Ser.: No. 2). 137p. (gr. 4-7). 17.00 (978-0-7569-8815-9(2)) Perfection Learning Corp.

—Dr. Maniac vs. Robby Schwartz (Goosebumps HorrorLand #5) 2008. (Goosebumps Horrorland Ser.: 5). (ENG., Illus.). 160p. (J). (gr. 3-7). pap. 7.99 (978-0-439-91873-2(1), Scholastic Paperbacks) Scholastic, Inc.

—Escape from Shudder Mansion (Goosebumps SlappyWorld #5) 2018. (Goosebumps SlappyWorld Ser.: 5). (ENG.). 160p. (J). (gr. 3-7). pap. 6.99 (978-1-338-22299-9(6), Scholastic Paperbacks) Scholastic, Inc.

—Fear Street Super Thriller. 2015. (Fear Street Ser.). (ENG.). 592p. (YA). (gr. 7-12). pap. 12.99 (978-1-250-07693-9(5), 900152585, St. Martin's Griffin) St. Martin's Pr.

—Here Comes the Shaggedy. 2016. (Goosebumps Most Wanted Ser.: 9). (Illus.). 140p. (J). lib. bdg. 17.20 (978-0-606-38587-9(8)) Turtleback.

—Here Comes the Shaggedy (Goosebumps Most Wanted #9), Vol. 9. 2016. (Goosebumps Most Wanted Ser.: 9). (ENG., Illus.). 160p. (J). (gr. 3-7). pap. 6.99 (978-0-545-82547-4(4), Scholastic Paperbacks) Scholastic, Inc.

—The Horror at Chiller House (Goosebumps HorrorLand #19) 2011. (Goosebumps Horrorland Ser.: 19). (ENG., Illus.). 160p. (J). (gr. 3-7). pap. 6.99 (978-0-545-16200-5(9), Scholastic Paperbacks) Scholastic, Inc.

—How to Be a Vampire. 2011. (R. L. Stine's Ghosts of Fear Street Ser.). (ENG.). 128p. (J). (gr. 3-7). pap. 7.99 (978-1-4424-2760-0(4), Aladdin) Simon & Schuster Children's Publishing.

—Little Shop of Hamsters. 2010. 160p. (J). pap. 2.99 (978-1-4071-1635-8(5)) Scholastic, Inc.

—Little Shop of Hamsters. 2010. (Goosebumps HorrorLand Ser.: 14). lib. bdg. 17.20 (978-0-606-10559-0(X)) Turtleback.

—The Little Shop of Monsters. Brown, Marc, illus. 2015. (ENG.). 40p. (J). (gr. -1-3). 18.99 (978-0-316-36983-1(7)) Little, Brown Bks. for Young Readers.

—Monster Blood (Classic Goosebumps #3) 2008. (Classic Goosebumps Ser.: 3). (ENG.). 144p. (J). (gr. 3-7). 7.99 (978-0-545-03520-0(1), Scholastic Paperbacks) Scholastic, Inc.

—Please Do Not Feed the Weirdo, 4. 2018. (Goosebumps SlappyWorld Ser.). (ENG.). 160p. (J). (gr. 4-7). 22.44 (978-1-5364-3367-8(5)) Scholastic, Inc.

—Please Do Not Feed the Weirdo. 2018. (Goosebumps SlappyWorld Ser.: 4). 135p. (J). lib. bdg. 18.40 (978-0-606-41161-5(5)) Turtleback.

—Please Do Not Feed the Weirdo (Goosebumps SlappyWorld #4) 2018. (Goosebumps SlappyWorld Ser.: 4). (ENG.). 160p. (J). (gr. 3-7). pap. 7.99 (978-1-338-06847-4(4), Scholastic Paperbacks) Scholastic, Inc.

—Revenge of the Lawn Gnomes (Classic Goosebumps #19) 2011. (Classic Goosebumps Ser.: 19). (ENG.). 160p. (J). (gr. 3-7). pap. 7.99 (978-0-545-29835-3(0), Scholastic Paperbacks) Scholastic, Inc.

—Revenge of the Living Dummy. 2008. (Goosebumps HorrorLand Ser.: No. 1). 128p. (J). (gr. 4-7). 13.65 (978-0-7569-8816-6(0)) Perfection Learning Corp.

—Revenge of the Living Dummy. 2008. (Goosebumps HorrorLand Ser.: 1). 128p. (gr. 4-7). lib. bdg. 17.20 (978-1-4178-1891-4(3)) Turtleback.

—A Shocker on Shock Street. 2015. (Goosebumps Ser.: 23). lib. bdg. 17.20 (978-0-606-37064-6(1)) Turtleback.

—Werewolf of Fever Swamp (Classic Goosebumps #11) 2009. (Classic Goosebumps Ser.: 11). (ENG.). 160p. (J). (gr. 3-7). 7.99 (978-0-545-15886-2(9), Scholastic Paperbacks) Scholastic, Inc.

—You Can't Scare Me! (Classic Goosebumps #17) 2010. (Classic Goosebumps Ser.: 17). (ENG.). 160p. (J). (gr. 3-7). pap. 7.99 (978-0-545-17796-2(0), Scholastic Paperbacks) Scholastic, Inc.

Stone, Jon. The Monster at the End of This Book. Smollin, Michael, illus. 2015. (ENG.). 26p. (J). (— 1). bds. 7.99 (978-0-553-50873-4(3), Golden Bks.) Random Hse. Children's Bks.

Stone, Kate & Accord Publishing, Accord. One Spooky Night: A Halloween Adventure. 2011. (ENG.). 36p. (J). pap. 11.99 (978-1-4494-0330-0(1)) Andrews McMeel Publishing.

Storrie, Paul D. #02 Made for Each Other. Cowgur, Eldon, illus. 2011. (My Boyfriend Is a Monster Ser.). 128p. (YA). pap. 56.72 (978-0-7613-7604-0(6), Graphic Universe™) Lerner Publishing Group.

Strachan, Linda. Hamish Mchaggis & the Search for the Loch Ness Monster. Collins, Sally J., illus. 2005. 32p. (J). pap. 9.00 (978-0-9546701-5-3(9)) GW Publishing GBR. Dist: Gatewood Pr.

Streed, Sam. Alfred's Book of Monsters. Streed, Sam, illus. 2019. (Illus.). 32p. (J). (gr. -1-2). lib. bdg. 15.99 (978-1-58089-833-1(5)) Charlesbridge Publishing, Inc.

Strelitz Haber, Tiffany. The Monster Who Lost His Mean. Edmunds, Kirstie, illus. 2012. (ENG.). 40p. (J). (gr. -1-3). 18.99 (978-0-8050-9375-9(3), 900073740, Holt, Henry & Co. Bks. For Young Readers) Holt, Henry & Co.

Stumpe, Jennifer. Aunt Jo Jo's Magical Gifts: Amazing Underwater Adventure. 2011. 32p. (gr. 1-2). pap. 14.95 (978-1-4567-3160-1(2)) AuthorHouse.

Styles, Walker. Mystery Mountain Getaway. Whitehouse, Ben, illus. 2017. (Rider Woofson Ser.: 9). (ENG.). 128p. (J). (gr. k-4). 16.99 (978-1-4814-9896-8(7)); pap. 5.99 (978-1-4814-9895-1(9)) Little Simon. (Little Simon).

Suarez, Sergio Lopez. Huakala! a los Miedos. Suarez, Sergio Lopez, illus. 2003. (SPA., Illus.). 32p. (J). (gr. k-3). 9.95 (978-968-19-0556-9(3)) Aguilar, Altea, Taurus, Alfaguara, S.A. de C.V MEX. Dist: Santillana USA Publishing Co., Inc.

Sutton, Laurie S. The Heart of Hades. Lozano, Omar, illus. 2019. (You Choose Stories: Wonder Woman Ser.). (ENG.). 112p. (J). (gr. 2-6). pap. 6.95 (978-1-4965-8438-0(4), 140963); lib. bdg. 32.65 (978-1-4965-8348-2(5), 140642) Capstone. (Stone Arch Bks.).

—Mud Menace! Brizuela, Dario, illus. 2019. (Amazing Adventures of Batman! Ser.). (ENG.). 32p. (J). (gr. k-2). lib. bdg. 25.32 (978-1-5158-3979-8(6), 139705, Stone Arch Bks.) Capstone.

—The Portal of Doom. Doescher, Erik, illus. 2018. (You Choose Stories: Justice League Ser.). (ENG.). 112p. (J). (gr. 2-6). pap. 6.95 (978-1-4965-6558-7(4), 138571, Stone Arch Bks.) Capstone.

—Wonder Woman vs. Circe, 1 vol. Vecchio, Luciano, illus. 2013. (DC Super Heroes Ser.). (ENG.). 56p. (J). (gr. 3-6). lib. bdg. 26.65 (978-1-4342-6014-7(3), 123074, Stone Arch Bks.) Capstone.

Swore, Wendy S. A Monster Like Me. 2019. (ENG.). 304p. (J). (gr. 3-6). 16.99 (978-1-62972-555-0(2), 5214782, Shadow Mountain) Shadow Mountain Publishing.

Tadjo, Veronique. Mamy Wata & the Monster, 8 vols. 2005. (ARA, ENG, VIE, CHI & BEN., Illus.). 24p. (J). pap. 9.95 (978-1-84059-264-1(8)) Milet Publishing.

Tagg, Christine. Who Will You Meet on Scary Street? Nine Pop-up Nightmares! Fuge, Charles, illus. 2004. 20p. (J). reprint ed. 15.00 (978-0-7567-8003-6(9)) DIANE Publishing Co.

Tamura, Mitsuhisa. BakéGyamon, Vol. 1. 2009. (Bakégyamon Ser.: 1). (ENG., Illus.). 200p. (J). pap. 7.99 (978-1-4215-1793-3(0)) Viz Media.

—BakéGyamon, Vol. 2. 2009. (Bakégyamon Ser.: 2). (ENG., Illus.). 200p. (J). pap. 7.99 (978-1-4215-1794-0(9)) Viz Media.

Taplin, Sam. This Is My Monster. Furukawa, Masumi, illus. 2008. (Noisy Touchy-Feely Board Bks). 10p. (J). bds. 16.99 (978-0-7945-2353-4(6), Usborne) EDC Publishing.

Tatulli, Mark. Desmond Pucket & the Cloverfield Junior High Carnival of Horrors. 2016. (Desmond Pucket Ser.: 3). (ENG., Illus.). 240p. (J). 13.99 (978-1-4494-6628-2(1)) Andrews McMeel Publishing.

—Desmond Pucket & the Mountain Full of Monsters. 2015. (Desmond Pucket Ser.). (ENG.). 240p. (J). pap. 9.99 (978-1-4494-7140-8(4)) Andrews McMeel Publishing.

—Desmond Pucket & the Mountain Full of Monsters. 2015. (Desmond Pucket Ser.: 2). lib. bdg. 20.85 (978-0-606-38232-8(1)) Turtleback.

—Desmond Pucket Makes Monster Magic. (ENG.). 240p. (J). 2015. pap. 9.99 (978-1-4494-7139-2(0)) 2013. (Desmond Pucket Ser.: 1). 13.99 (978-1-4494-3548-6(3)) Andrews McMeel Publishing.

—Desmond Pucket Makes Monster Magic. 2015. (Desmond Pucket Ser.: 1). lib. bdg. 20.85 (978-0-606-38231-1(3)) Turtleback.

—Lio: There's a Monster in My Socks. 2012. (Lio Ser.: 7). (ENG., Illus.). 224p. (J). (gr. 3-5). pap. 9.99 (978-1-4494-2304-9(3)) Andrews McMeel Publishing.

Tavares, Victor, illus. Beauty & the Beast. 2007. (Usborne Young Reading: Series Two Ser.). 63p. (J). 8.99 (978-0-7945-1456-3(1), Usborne) EDC Publishing.

Tayler, Amber. What Do Monsters Look Like? Birth, Ryan, illus. 2009. 36p. pap. 11.25 (978-1-935125-51-8(6)) Robertson Publishing.

Taylor, Greg. Killer Pizza: the Slice. 2012. (ENG.). 368p. (YA). (gr. 5-9). pap. 16.99 (978-1-250-00478-9(0), 900080730) Square Fish.

Taylor, Phillip J. Brian, His Granddad & the Cup of Ages. 2012. 310p. pap. (978-1-78003-422-5(9)) Pen Pr. Pubs., Ltd.

Taylor, Sean. I Want to Be in a Scary Story. Jullien, Jean, illus. 2017. (ENG.). 32p. (J). (-k). 15.99 (978-0-7636-8953-7(X)) Candlewick Pr.

Testa, Susan L. Myra the House Cat & the Garbage Can Monster. 2011. 44p. pap. 24.95 (978-1-4560-4887-7(2)) America Star Bks.

Tetri, Emily. Tiger vs. Nightmare. Tetri, Emily, illus. 2018. (ENG., Illus.). 64p. (J). 18.99 (978-1-62672-535-5(7), 900160471, First Second Bks.) Roaring Brook Pr.

Thaler, Mike. Black Lagoon, 6 vols., Set. Lee, Jared, illus. Incl. Gym Teacher from the Black Lagoon. lib. bdg. 31.36 (978-1-59961-794-7(3), 3620); Librarian from the Black Lagoon. lib. bdg. 31.36 (978-1-59961-795-4(1), 3621); Music Teacher from the Black Lagoon. lib. bdg. 31.36 (978-1-59961-796-1(X), 3622); Principal from the Black Lagoon. lib. bdg. 31.36 (978-1-59961-797-8(8), 3623); School Nurse from the Black Lagoon. lib. bdg. 31.36 (978-1-59961-798-5(6), 3624); Teacher from the Black Lagoon. lib. bdg. 31.36 (978-1-59961-799-2(4), 3625); (J). (gr. k-4). (Black Lagoon Ser.: 6). (ENG., Illus.). 32p. 2011. Set lib. bdg. 188.16 (978-1-59961-793-0(5), 3619, Picture Bk.) Spotlight.

—Meatloaf Monster from the School Cafeteria. Lee, Jared D., illus. 2012. (J). pap. (978-0-545-48570-8(3)) Scholastic, Inc.

—The School Carnival from the Black Lagoon. Lee, Jared, illus. 2005. 64p. (J). pap. (978-0-439-80075-4(7)) Scholastic, Inc.

—The School Carnival from the Black Lagoon, 1 vol. Lee, Jared, illus. 2012. (Black Lagoon Adventures Ser.: No. 2). (ENG.). 64p. (J). (gr. 2-6). 31.36 (978-1-59961-962-0(8), 3606, Chapter Bks.) Spotlight.

—The Secret Santa from the Black Lagoon. Lee, Jared D., illus. 2014. 64p. (J). (978-0-545-78519-8(7)) Scholastic, Inc.

—The Secret Santa from the Black Lagoon. Lee, Jared, illus. 2016. (Black Lagoon Adventures Set 4 Ser.). (ENG.). 64p. (J). (gr. 2-6). lib. bdg. 31.36 (978-1-61479-607-7(6), 24340, Chapter Bks.) Spotlight.

—The Thanksgiving Day from the Black Lagoon. Lee, Jared, illus. 2009. 64p. (J). (978-0-545-16812-0(0)) Scholastic, Inc.

—Valentine's Day from the Black Lagoon, 1 vol. Lee, Jared, illus. 2014. (Black Lagoon Adventures Ser.). (ENG.). 64p. (J). (gr. 2-6). lib. bdg. 31.36 (978-1-61479-209-3(7), 3618, Chapter Bks.) Spotlight.

There's a Monster under the Sheets. 2004. (J). pap. 8.00 (978-0-8059-6461-5(4)) Dorrance Publishing Co., Inc.

Thomas, Colleen. No Monster Here. 2009. (978-1-61584-910-9(6)) Independent Pub.

Thompson, Jill. The Revenge of Jimmy. 2006. (Illus.). 48p. pap. 9.95 (978-1-57989-071-1(7)) Sirius Entertainment, Inc.

—Scary Godmother. 2005. (Illus.). 48p. pap. 9.95 (978-1-57989-070-4(9)) Sirius Entertainment, Inc.

Thompson, Jill, creator. Scary Godmother: The Mystery Date. 2004. (Illus.). 48p. pap. 9.95 (978-1-57989-072-8(5)) Sirius Entertainment, Inc.

Thomson, Malcolm. Saga of the Vegvisir. 2012. (Illus.). 68p. pap. 32.03 (978-1-4772-4741-9(6)) AuthorHouse.

Ticktock Media, Ltd. Staff. The Unexplained: Encounters with Ghosts, Monsters, & Aliens. 2008. (ENG.). 96p. (J). (gr. 2-4). pap. 9.95 (978-1-84696-807-5(0), TickTock Books) Octopus Publishing Group GBR. Dist: Independent Pubs. Group.

Tolonen, Tuutikki. Monster Nanny. Silver, Annira, tr. Pitkanen, Pasi, illus. 2017. (ENG.). 304p. (J). (gr. 3-7). 16.99 (978-0-544-94354-4(6), 1659015, Clarion Bks.) HarperCollins Pubs.

Tombo. The Magic Nickel: A Fable about an Unhappy Salesman, a Sad Retired Person, & an Invisible Monster. 2012. 26p. pap. 16.99 (978-1-4624-0280-9(1), Inspiring Voices) Author Solutions, LLC.

Top That Publishing Staff, ed. Mini Monsters. 2005. (Illus.). 24p. pap. (978-1-84510-159-6(6)) Top That! Publishing PLC.

Toreeva, Natalia G. Greg & the Sea Monster. 2011. 34p. pap. 14.50 (978-1-61204-332-6(1), Eloquent Bks.) Strategic Book Publishing & Rights Agency (SBPRA).

Toufexis, George. MONSTER MASH-Up — Rise of the Predators. 2014. (ENG., Illus.). 48p. (J). (gr. 4). pap. 4.99 (978-0-486-49224-7(9)) Dover Pubns., Inc.

—Monster Matrix Activity Book. 2013. (Dover Children's Activity Bks.). (ENG.). 48p. (J). (gr. 3-8). pap. 4.99 (978-0-486-49963-5(4)) Dover Pubns., Inc.

ToyBox Innovations, creator. Disney's Monsters, Inc. Read-along. 2006. (Disney's Read Along Ser.). (ENG., Illus.). 24p. (J). pap. (978-0-7634-2175-5(8)) Walt Disney Records.

Trapani, Iza. Gabe & Goon. Trapani, Iza, illus. 2016. (Illus.). 32p. (J). (gr. -1-1). lib. bdg. 16.95 (978-1-58089-640-5(5)) Charlesbridge Publishing, Inc.

Trayer, Edward H. Struggles of Felicity Brady: Articulus Quest. 2005. (YA). per. 14.95 (978-1-59571-091-8(4)) Word Association Pubs.

Tremblay, Carole. Floop in the Dark, 1 vol. Beshwaty, Steve, illus. 2009. (Floop Ser.). (ENG.). 24p. (J). (gr. -1-k). 27.27 (978-1-60754-341-1(9), f9f994d3-11e5-46ab-b443-f75e57a42e33, Windmill Bks.) Rosen Publishing Group, Inc., The.

Troupe, Thomas Kingsley. The Misplaced Mummy, 1 vol. Gilpin, Stephen, illus. 2014. (Furry & Flo Ser.). (ENG.). 128p. (J). (gr. 2-3). 25.32 (978-1-4342-6396-4(7), 123874, Stone Arch Bks.) Capstone.

—The Skeletons in City Park, 1 vol. Gilpin, Stephen, illus. 2014. (Furry & Flo Ser.). (ENG.). 128p. (J). (gr. 2-3). 25.32 (978-1-4342-6397-1(5), 123875, Stone Arch Bks.) Capstone.

—The Solemn Golem. Gilpin, Stephen, illus. 2015. (Furry & Flo Ser.). (ENG.). 128p. (J). (gr. 2-3). lib. bdg. 25.32 (978-1-4342-9646-7(6), 126933, Stone Arch Bks.) Capstone.

Ttofa, Juliette. How Monsters Wish to Feel: A Story about Emotional Resilience. 2017. (Nurturing Emotional Resilience Storybooks Ser.). (ENG., Illus.). 28p. pap. 15.95 (978-1-909301-84-9(1), Y328998) Routledge.

—How Monsters Wish to Feel & Other Picture Books: Seven Storybooks Set. 2018. (Nurturing Emotional Resilience Storybooks Ser.). (ENG.). 138p. pap. 70.95 (978-1-138-55647-8(5), Y380599) Routledge.

Tucholke, April Genevieve. The Boneless Mercies. 2020. (ENG.). 368p. (YA). pap. 10.99 (978-1-250-21150-7(6), 900178964) Square Fish.

Tuxford, Jenny & Brazier, Jenny. Fredd Boggitt & the Loch Ness Monster. 2009. 152p. pap. 11.99 (978-1-4389-9593-9(8)) AuthorHouse.

Twin Sister Produtions & Shepherd, Jodie. Sesame Street Big Red Riding Hood. 2010. (J). (gr. k-2). 14.99 (978-1-59922-635-4(9)) Twin Sisters IP, LLC.

Twin Sister Produtions Staff & Shepherd, Jodie. Sesame Street Big Red Riding Hood. 2010. (J). (gr. k-2). 14.99 (978-1-59922-526-5(3)) Twin Sisters IP, LLC.

Tyrrell, Colm. Snow Day. 2015. (Illus.). 32p. (J). (978-1-5182-0102-8(4)) Disney Publishing Worldwide.

Tyrrell, Melissa. Beauty & the Beast. McMullen, Nigel, illus. 2005. (Fairytale Friends Ser.). 12p. (J). bds. 5.95 (978-1-58117-153-2(6), Intervisual/Piggy Toes) Bendon, Inc.

Ugo, Kachi. Mewranters: Attack of the Sea Monster: A Novel. 2019. 238p. (YA). lib. bdg. 22.95 (978-1-64279-076-4(1)) Morgan James Publishing.

Underwood, Deborah. Monster & Mouse Go Camping. Chapman, Jared, illus. 2018. (ENG.). 32p. (J). (gr. -1-3). 17.99 (978-0-544-64832-6(3), 1621605, Clarion Bks.) HarperCollins Pubs.

Uram, Maggie. Good Night Good Knight. 2004. (Illus.). 39p. (J). per. (978-1-932077-38-4(3)) Athena Pr.

V, Vasanthi. The Toy-Gobbling Monster. Lee, Anais, illus. 2013. (ENG.). (J). 14.95 (978-1-62086-330-5(8)) Amplify Publishing Group.

Valentino, Serena. Beast Within, the-Villains, Book 2. 2014. (Villains Ser.). (ENG., Illus.). 224p. (YA). (gr. 7-12). 17.99 (978-1-4231-5912-4(8), Disney Press Books) Disney Publishing Worldwide.

Vallejo-Nagera, Alejandra. Los Cazadores de Monstruos.Tr. of Monsters Hunters. (SPA.). 32p. (J). 10.95 (978-84-204-4955-5(5)) Ediciones Alfaguara ESP. Dist: Santillana USA Publishing Co., Inc.

Van Dusen, Chris. Hattie & Hudson. Van Dusen, Chris, illus. 2017. (ENG., Illus.). 40p. (J). (gr. -1-3). 17.99 (978-0-7636-6545-6(2)) Candlewick Pr.

van Haeringen, Annemarie. How to Knit a Monster. van Haeringen, Annemarie, illus. 2018. (ENG., Illus.). 32p. (J). (gr. -1-3). 17.99 (978-1-328-84210-7(X), 1691968, Clarion Bks.) HarperCollins Pubs.

Van, Muon Thi. The Most Terrible of All. Myers, Matt, illus. 2019. (ENG.). 40p. (J). (gr. -1-3). 17.99 (978-1-5344-1716-8(8), McElderry, Margaret K. Bks.) McElderry, Margaret K. Bks.

Van Slyke, Rebecca. Monster's Trucks. Sutphin, Joe, illus. 2020. (ENG.). 40p. (J). 17.99 (978-1-68119-301-4(9), 900165544, Bloomsbury Children's Bks.) Bloomsbury Publishing USA.

Vana, Dan. Joey & the Magic Dream Pillow. Ware, Quinton, illus. 2013. 20p. pap. 24.95 (978-1-4626-7872-3(6)) America Star Bks.

VanRiper, Gary & VanRiper, Justin. Legend of the Lake Monster. 2009. (Adirondack Kids Ser.: Vol. 9). 96p. (J). (gr. 2-7). pap. 9.95 (978-0-9707044-9-8(6)) Adirondack Kids Pr.

Varley, Dax. Graveyard Dirt. Proctor, Jon, illus. 2016. (Demon Slayer Ser.). (ENG.). 48p. (J). (gr. 3-7). lib. bdg. 34.21 (978-1-62402-158-9(1), 21563, Spellbound) Magic Wagon.

—Hideout. Proctor, Jon, illus. 2016. (Demon Slayer Ser.). (ENG.). 48p. (J). (gr. 3-7). lib. bdg. 34.21 (978-1-62402-157-2(3), 21561, Spellbound) Magic Wagon.

Vega, Denise. If Your Monster Won't Go to Bed. OHora, Zachariah, illus. 2017. 40p. (J). (gr. -1-2). 18.99 (978-0-553-49655-0(7), Knopf Bks. for Young Readers) Random Hse. Children's Bks.

Velthuijs, Max. The Kind-Hearted Monster. 2015. (ENG., Illus.). 64p. (J). (gr. -1-2). 19.95 (978-0-7358-4107-9(1)) North-South Bks., Inc.

Venditti, Robert & Riordan, Rick. The Sea of Monsters. 2013. (Percy Jackson & the Olympians Graphic Novels Ser.: 2). (J). lib. bdg. 24.50 (978-0-606-23611-9(2)) Turtleback.

Vere, Ed. A Dormir, Monstruos! 2012. (SPA.). 32p. (J). (gr. -1-1). pap. 21.99 (978-84-261-3890-3(X)) Juventud, Editorial ESP. Dist: Lectorum Pubns., Inc.

Viguié, Debbie. The Fall of Candy Corn, 1 vol. 2008. (Sweet Seasons Novel Ser.: 2). (ENG., Illus.). 224p. (YA). (gr. 8-11). pap. 9.99 (978-0-310-71559-7(8)) Zondervan.

Villarreal, Jennifer. The Monster under My Bed. 2008. 20p. pap. 13.50 (978-1-4389-0371-2(5)) AuthorHouse.

Villeneuve, Anne. Loula & Mister the Monster. Villeneuve, Anne, illus. 2015. (Loula Ser.). (ENG., Illus.). 32p. (J). (gr. -1-2). 16.95 (978-1-77138-326-4(7)) Kids Can Pr., Ltd. CAN. Dist: Hachette Bk. Group.

Wacholtz, Anthony. The Monster in the Mirror: A Tale of Terror. Epelbaum, Mariano, illus. 2018. (Michael Dahl Presents: Phobia Ser.). (ENG.). 72p. (J). (gr. 4-6). lib. bdg. 25.32 (978-1-4965-7341-4(2), 138928, Stone Arch Bks.) Capstone.

Waisanen, Emily. The Book Monster. Konecny, John, illus. 2012. 24p. pap. 8.99 (978-1-937165-25-3(6)) Orange Hat Publishing.

Wallace, Adam & Wallace, Adam. How to Catch a Monster. Elkerton, Andy, illus. 2017. (How to Catch Ser.: 0). (ENG.). 40p. (J). (gr. k-3). 10.99 (978-1-4926-4894-9(9)) Sourcebooks, Inc.

Wallace, Lizzie. My Sister's Turning into a Monster. 2011. (Illus.). 20p. 10.96 (978-1-4520-9930-9(8)) AuthorHouse.

Walstead, Alice. How to Catch a Witch. Joyce, Megan, illus. 2022. (How to Catch Ser.). 40p. (J). (gr. k-5). 10.99 (978-1-7282-1035-3(6)) Sourcebooks, Inc.

Walton, Rick. 10 Little Monsters Visit Oregon. Smiley, Jess Smart, illus. 2014. (ENG.). 32p. (J). (gr. -1-3). 16.95 (978-1-939629-29-6(2), 552929) Familius LLC.

Wang, Andrea. The Nian Monster. Chau, Alina, illus. 2016. (ENG.). 32p. (J). (gr. -1-3). 17.99 (978-0-8075-5642-9(4), 807556424) Whitman, Albert & Co.

Ward, Nick. Another Rumpus. Ward, Nick, illus. 2015. (ENG., Illus.). 24p. (J). (gr. -1-3). 7.99 (978-1-85733-728-0(X)) Lerner Publishing Group.

Ward-Showers, Latanya. Could It Be a Monster in the Attic? 2013. 24p. pap. 17.99 (978-1-4817-0542-4(3)) AuthorHouse.

Warren, Celia. A Big Surprise, 4 vols. 2005. (Read On (QEB) Ser.). (Illus.). 24p. (J). (gr. 1-4). lib. bdg. 15.95 (978-1-59566-092-3(5)) QEB Publishing Inc.

Washer, S. N. The Wingate Adventures: Our New Friends. 2006. 164p. pap. 11.95 (978-1-59800-510-3(3)) Outskirts Pr., Inc.

Wasserman, Robin. Scooby-Doo & the Missing Scooby-Snacks, 1 vol. Sur, Duendes del, illus. 2016. (Scooby-Doo Early Reading Adventures Ser.). (ENG.). 24p. (J). (gr. -1-2). lib. bdg. 31.36 (978-1-61479-467-7(7), 21380) Spotlight.

Watkins, Sam. Creature Teacher. O'Connell, David, illus. 2017. (Creature Teacher Ser.). (ENG.). 176p. (J). (gr. 2-4). pap. 6.95 (978-1-4965-5681-3(X), 136595); pap., pap., pap. 27.80 (978-1-4965-5682-0(8), 27297); lib. bdg. 24.65

(978-1-4965-5702-5(6), 136591) Capstone. (Stone Arch Bks.).
Watson Dubisch, Carolyn. The Horribles. 2011. (ENG.). 73p. pap. 16.96 (978-0-557-35938-7(4)) Lulu Pr., Inc.
Watson, Michael. Search, Secrets, & Spies. 2011. 32p. pap. 13.00 (978-1-61204-357-9(7), Strategic Bk. Publishing) Strategic Book Publishing & Rights Agency (SBPRA).
Watt, Fiona. That's Not My Monster. Wells, Rachel, illus. 2004. 10p. (J). 7.99 (978-0-7945-0818-0(9), Usborne) EDC Publishing.
Watters, Shannon & Kat Leyh. Stone Cold. 2018. (Lumberjanes (Graphic Novels) Ser.: 8). lib. bdg. 26.95 (978-0-606-41185-1(2)) Turtleback.
Watters, Shannon, et al. Band Together. 2016. (Lumberjanes (Graphic Novels) Ser.: 5). lib. bdg. 26.95 (978-0-606-39484-0(2)) Turtleback.
Wayne, Matt. Panic of the Composite Creatures. Suriano, Andy & Davis, Dan W., illus. 2012. (Batman: the Brave & the Bold Ser.). (ENG.). 32p. (J). (gr. 2-5). lib. bdg. 22.60 (978-1-4342-4545-8(4), 120505, Stone Arch Bks.) Capstone.
Webb, Rita. Tears. 2012. 350p. pap. 12.99 (978-0-615-51355-3(7)) Robot Playground, Inc.
Weekes, Patrick. Feeder. 2018. (ENG., Illus.). 304p. (YA). (gr. 9). 17.99 (978-1-5344-0016-0(8), McElderry, Margaret K. Bks.) McElderry, Margaret K. Bks.
Weigand, Jessica. I Have a Monster under My Bed. 2009. 20p. pap. 10.49 (978-1-4389-7503-0(1)) AuthorHouse.
Weinberg, Jennifer Liberts. Happy Birthday, Mike! 2014. (Step into Reading Level 2 Ser.). lib. bdg. 13.55 (978-0-606-36006-7(9)) Turtleback.
Weiner, Jennifer. The Littlest Bigfoot. (Littlest Bigfoot Ser.: 1). (ENG.). (J). (gr. 3-7). 2017. 352p. pap. 8.99 (978-1-4814-7075-9(2)) 2016. (Illus.). 304p. 16.99 (978-1-4814-7074-2(4)) Simon & Schuster Children's Publishing. (Aladdin).
—The Littlest Bigfoot. 2017. (Littlest Bigfoot Ser.: 1). lib. bdg. 18.40 (978-0-606-40206-4(3)) Turtleback.
Weiss, Ellen. Whatever You Do, I Love You. Williams, Sam, illus. 2010. (ENG.). 16p. (J). (gr. -1 — 1). bds. 7.99 (978-1-4424-0809-8(X), Little Simon) Little Simon.
Wellington, Stanley. Where Monsters Hide. 2003. 223p. (YA). per. 16.95 (978-1-59196-384-4(2)) 2nd ed. 2004. 237p. per. 17.95 (978-1-59196-481-0(4)) Instant Pub.
West, David & West, David. Ten of the Best Monster Stories. West, David, illus. 2014. (Ten of the Best: Myths, Legends & Folk Stories Ser.). (ENG., Illus.). 24p. (J). (gr. 3-4). (978-0-7787-0783-7(0)) Crabtree Publishing Co.
West, Robert. Attack of the Spider Bots, 1 vol. 2008. (Star-Fighters of Murphy Street Ser.: 2). (ENG., Illus.). 160p. (J). (gr. 4-7). pap. 6.99 (978-0-310-71426-2(5)) Zonderkidz.
West, Tracey. Masquerade Brawl. 2009. (Bakugan Battle Brawlers Ser.). (ENG.). 32p. (J). (gr. 2-4). 16.19 (978-0-545-13121-6(9)) Scholastic, Inc.
Wheeler, Kim. Even More Adventures of Jonny Plumb. 2013. 186p. pap. (978-0-7552-1570-6(2), Bright Pen) Authors OnLine, Ltd.
Wheeler, Lisa. Boogie Knights. Siegel, Mark, illus. 2008. (ENG.). 40p. (J). (gr. -1-3). 16.99 (978-0-689-87639-4(4), Atheneum/Richard Jackson Bks.) Simon & Schuster Children's Publishing.
—Even Monsters Go to School. Van Dusen, Chris, illus. 2019. (ENG.). 32p. (J). (gr. -1-3). 17.99 (978-0-06-236642-9(4), Balzer & Bray) HarperCollins Pubs.
—Even Monsters Need to Sleep. 2017. (ENG., Illus.). 32p. (J). (gr. -1-3). 17.99 (978-0-06-236640-5(8), Balzer & Bray) HarperCollins Pubs.
Where The Wild Things Are. 2005. (J). (978-1-59564-831-0(3)) Steps To Literacy, LLC.
White, Kiersten. The Dark Descent of Elizabeth Frankenstein. 2019. 320p. (YA). (gr. 7). pap. 11.99 (978-0-525-57796-6(3), Ember) Random Hse. Children's Bks.
Whitesides, Tyler. Curse of the Broomstaff. 2013. (Janitors Ser.: 3). (ENG., Illus.). 384p. (J). (gr. 5). 18.99 (978-1-60907-605-4(2), 5107237, Shadow Mountain) Shadow Mountain Publishing.
—Heroes of the Dustbin. 2015. (Janitors Ser.: 5). (ENG., Illus.). 416p. (J). (gr. 5). 18.99 (978-1-62972-065-4(8), 5136476, Shadow Mountain) Shadow Mountain Publishing.
—Janitors. 2011. (Janitors Ser.: Bk. 1). pap. 34.99 (978-1-60908-075-4(0)) Deseret Bk. Co.
—Janitors. (Janitors Ser.: 1). (ENG., Illus.). (J). (gr. 5). 2012. 320p. pap. 9.99 (978-1-60907-065-6(8), 5078581) 2011. 312p. 17.99 (978-1-60908-056-3(4), 5057487) Shadow Mountain Publishing. (Shadow Mountain).
—Secrets of New Forest Academy. 2013. (Janitors Ser.: 2). (ENG., Illus.). 368p. (J). (gr. 5). pap. 8.99 (978-1-60907-546-0(3), 5105035, Shadow Mountain) Shadow Mountain Publishing.
—Strike of the Sweepers. 2014. (Janitors Ser.: 4). (ENG., Illus.). 400p. (J). (gr. 5). 18.99 (978-1-60907-907-9(8), 5121465, Shadow Mountain) Shadow Mountain Publishing.
Whitten, A. J. The Well. 2009. (ENG., Illus.). 336p. (YA). (gr. 7-18). pap. 18.95 (978-0-547-23229-4(2), 1082742, Clarion Bks.) HarperCollins Pubs.
Wigger, Sherry. Scary Stories for Brave Kids, 1 vol. 2009. 73p. pap. 16.95 (978-1-61582-308-6(5)) PublishAmerica, Inc.
Wilden, Beverley. Who Said Monsters Don't Exist? 2010. (Illus.). 32p. pap. 12.99 (978-1-4490-7313-8(1)) AuthorHouse.
Wiley, Chris. The Purloined Boy. 2018. (J). pap. (978-1-947644-40-3(8), Canonball Bks.) Canon Pr.
Willems, Mo. A Busy Creature's Day Eating! (ENG.). 32p. (J). (gr. -1-k). 2019. bds. 8.99 (978-1-368-04129-4(9)) 2018. (Illus.). 17.99 (978-1-368-01352-9(X)) Disney Publishing Worldwide. (Hyperion Books for Children).
—Leonardo, the Terrible Monster. 2005. (ENG., Illus.). 48p. (J). (gr. -1-k). 18.99 (978-0-7868-5294-9(1), Hyperion Books for Children) Disney Publishing Worldwide.
—Sam, the Most Scaredycat Kid in the Whole World: A Leonardo, the Terrible Monster Companion. 2017. (ENG., Illus.). 48p. (J). (gr. -1-k). 17.99 (978-1-368-00214-1(5), Hyperion Books for Children) Disney Publishing Worldwide.
Willems, Mo, narrated by. Leonardo, the Terrible Monster. 2011. (Illus.). (J). (gr. -1-3). 29.95 (978-0-439-02766-3(7), WHCD801) Weston Woods Studios, Inc.
Williams, Harland, illus. The Kid with Too Many Nightmares. 2004. (J). (978-0-8431-1582-6(3), Price Stern Sloan) Penguin Publishing Group.
Williams, Kristen. Sheepy Sue & the Bedtime Blues. 2012. 28p. pap. 12.95 (978-1-105-48819-1(5)) Lulu.com GBR. Dist: Lulu Pr., Inc.
Williams, Rozanne. Five Little Monsters Went to School. 2017. (Learn-To-Read Ser.). (ENG., Illus.). (J). pap. 3.49 (978-1-68310-244-1(4)) Pacific Learning, Inc.
—There's a Monster in the Tree. 2017. (Learn-To-Read Ser.). (ENG., Illus.). (J). pap. 3.49 (978-1-68310-207-6(X)) Pacific Learning, Inc.
—Where Do Monsters Live? 2017. (Learn-To-Read Ser.). (ENG., Illus.). (J). pap. 3.49 (978-1-68310-193-2(6)) Pacific Learning, Inc.
Williams, Rozanne Lanczak. Little Monster Becomes an Author. Hefferan, Rob, illus. 2006. (Learn to Write Ser.). 16p. (J). (gr. k-2). pap. 3.49 (978-1-59198-300-2(2), 6192) Creative Teaching Pr., Inc.
—Little Monster Becomes an Author. Maio, Barbara, ed. Hefferan, Rob, illus. 2006. (J). per. 8.99 (978-1-59198-349-1(5)) Creative Teaching Pr., Inc.
Williams, Tim & Williams, Tony. Timmy's Bedtime: A Monster Bear Tale. 2011. 28p. pap. 12.50 (978-1-61204-171-1(X), Eloquent Bks.) Strategic Book Publishing & Rights Agency (SBPRA).
Williams, Walter. A Monster for Tea. Williams, Walter, illus. 2013. (ENG., Illus.). 32p. (J). (gr. -1-2). 17.99 (978-0-9890698-3-0(4)) Fernwood & Hedges Bks.
Williamson, Joshua. Sketch Monsters Vol. 1: Escape of the Scribbles. Navarrete, Vicente, illus. 2011. (Sketch Monsters Ser.: 1). (ENG.). 48p. (J). 12.99 (978-1-934964-69-9(7), 9781934964699, Lion Forge) Oni Pr., Inc.
Willis, Jeanne. La Tormenta Monstruosa. (Cotton Cloud Ser.). (SPA.). (J). (gr. 1-3). pap. (978-84-480-0180-3(X)) Timun Mas, Editorial S.A. ESP. Dist: Lectorum Pubns., Inc.
Wilson, A. c. & Wilson, A. C. Ambersil - the Legacy of Mr Harrison. 2011. 496p. pap. (978-1-908105-45-5(3)) Grosvenor Hse. Publishing Ltd.
Wilson-Timmons, Karen. Agha the Eight-Mile Monster. Dubois, Marie Thérèse, illus. rev. ed. 2012. (ENG.). 32p. (J). (gr. -1). 16.99 (978-1-60887-124-7(X)) Mandala Publishing.
Wilson, W. Shane. The sprite Adventure. 2010. 97p. pap. 12.99 (978-0-557-42603-4(0)) Lulu Pr., Inc.
Windsor, Herbert C. The Colour Monster. 2009. (Illus.). 32p. pap. 12.99 (978-1-4490-1056-0(3)) AuthorHouse.
Windsor, M. L. Jack Death. 2016. (ENG., Illus.). 163p. (J). (gr. 4-6). 12.99 (978-1-939547-28-6(8), 21f8be44-e783-4b5f-86f7-2ee741f8fb21) Creston Bks.
Winick, Judd. Hilo Book 2: Saving the Whole Wide World: (a Graphic Novel) 2016. (Hilo Ser.: 2). (ENG., Illus.). 208p. (J). (gr. 3-7). 16.99 (978-0-385-38624-1(9));Bk. 2. 13.99 (978-0-385-38623-4(0)) Penguin Random Hse. LLC.
Wong, Angi Ma. Who Ate My Socks? 2005. (Illus.). 32p. (J). 11.98 (978-1-928753-00-1(0)) Pacific Heritage Bks.
Wright, Terry. The One-Eyed Monster. 2006. 48p. pap. 16.95 (978-1-4241-3696-4(2)) PublishAmerica, Inc.
Wynne-Jones, Tim. On Tumbledown Hill, 1 vol. Petricic, Dusan, illus. 2008. (ENG.). 32p. (J). (gr. k-3). pap. 5.95 (978-0-88995-409-0(7), b535b8c2-8843-44c4-a062-fb6fcb6cb8f6) Red Deer Pr. CAN. Dist: Firefly Bks., Ltd.
X, Sulayman. King of Storms. 2016. (Five Kingdoms Ser.: Vol. 2). (ENG., Illus.). (YA). 29.99 (978-1-63533-038-0(6), Harmony Ink Pr.) Dreamspinner Pr.
Yancey, Rick. The Curse of the Wendigo. 2011. (Monstrumologist Ser.: 2). (ENG.). 464p. (YA). (gr. 9). pap. 13.99 (978-1-4169-8451-1(8), Simon & Schuster Bks. For Young Readers) Simon & Schuster Bks. For Young Readers.
—The Final Descent. 2013. (Monstrumologist Ser.: 4). (ENG., Illus.). 320p. (YA). (gr. 9). 18.99 (978-1-4424-5153-7(X), Simon & Schuster Bks. For Young Readers) Simon & Schuster Bks. For Young Readers.
—The Isle of Blood. (Monstrumologist Ser.: 3). (ENG.). 560p. (YA). (gr. 9). 2012. pap. 13.99 (978-1-4169-8453-5(4)) 2011. (Illus.). 18.99 (978-1-4169-8452-8(6)) Simon & Schuster Bks. For Young Readers. (Simon & Schuster Bks. For Young Readers).
—The Monstrumologist. 2010. (Monstrumologist Ser.: 1). (ENG.). 464p. (YA). (gr. 9). pap. 13.99 (978-1-4169-8449-8(6), Simon & Schuster Bks. For Young Readers) Simon & Schuster Bks. For Young Readers.
—The Monstrumologist Collection: The Monstrumologist; the Curse of the Wendigo; the Isle of Blood; the Final Descent. 2014. (Monstrumologist Ser.). (ENG., Illus.). 1808p. (YA). (gr. 9). pap. 51.99 (978-1-4814-3012-8(2), Simon & Schuster Bks. For Young Readers) Simon & Schuster Bks. For Young Readers.
Yarlett, Emma, illus. Nibbles: The Book Monster. 2016. (J). (978-1-61067-467-6(7)) Kane Miller.
Yohn-Rhodes, Phyllis. The Monster. 2005. (Special Kids of Sharon Ser.). (ENG., Illus.). 34p. (J). (gr. -1-3). per. 15.99 (978-1-4134-8516-5(2)) Xlibris Corp.
Yolen, Jane. Creepy Monsters, Sleepy Monsters. Murphy, Kelly, illus. 2013. (ENG.). 32p. (J). (gr. -1-2). 8.99 (978-0-7636-6283-7(6)) Candlewick Pr.
Yorinks, Arthur. Maurice Sendak's Seven Little Monsters: Hide & Seek. 6th rev. ed. 2004. 24p. (J). pap. 3.99 (978-0-7868-1780-1(1)) Hyperion Pr.
—Maurice Sendak's Seven Little Monsters: Take a Hike. 5th rev. ed. 2004. 24p. (J). pap. 3.99 (978-0-7868-1779-5(8)) Hyperion Pr.
Young, Billy. Teddy the Bear. 2007. 27p. 19.95 (978-1-84799-068-6(1)) Lulu Pr., Inc.
Young, Laurie. I See a Monster! Mahoney, Daniel J., illus. 2007. (Touch & Feel Ser.). 12p. (gr. -1-k). 15.95 (978-1-58117-574-5(4), Intervisual/Piggy Toes) Bendon, Inc.
Yovanoff, Brenna. The Replacement. 2011. (ENG.). 368p. (YA). (gr. 7-18). 8.99 (978-1-59514-381-5(5), Razorbill) Penguin Young Readers Group.
Zappa, Ahmet. Because I'm Your Dad. Santat, Dan, illus. (ENG.). 32p. (J). (gr. -1-k). 2016. bds. 7.99 (978-1-4847-2661-7(8)) 2013. 18.99 (978-1-4231-4774-9(X)) Little, Brown Bks. for Young Readers.
Zenz, Aaron. Monsters Go Night-Night. 2018. (ENG., Illus.). 32p. (J). (gr. -1-k). pap. 5.99 (978-1-4197-3201-0(3), 1105303, Abrams Bks. for Young Readers) Abrams, Inc.
—Monsters Go Night-Night. 2019. (ENG.). 32p. (J). (gr. k-1). 13.89 (978-1-64310-971-8(5)) Penworthy Co., LLC, The.
Zimet, Sara Goodman. The Monster Solution. Parish, Shannon, illus. 2005. 32p. (J). 16.95 (978-0-9645159-1-8(1), 1245168) Discovery Pr. Pubns., Inc.
Zindel, Paul. Loch. 2005. 209p. (YA). (gr. 7-12). 13.65 (978-0-7569-6001-8(0)) Perfection Learning Corp.
Zombie, Zack. Diario de un Zombie de Minecraft: Un Libro No Oficial Sobre Minecraft. 2017. (SPA.). 60p. (J). (gr. 2-4). pap. 12.95 (978-987-46163-5-7(0)) Lectura Colaborativa ARG. Dist: Independent Pubs. Group.
—Diary of a Minecraft Zombie Book 10: One Bad Apple. 2016. (Diary of a Minecraft Zombie Ser.: Vol. 10). (ENG., Illus.). (J). (gr. 3-6). 13.99 (978-1-943330-74-4(3), Zack Zombie Publishing) Herobrine Publishing.
—Diary of a Minecraft Zombie Book 11: Insides Out. 2016. (Diary of a Minecraft Zombie Ser.: Vol. 11). (ENG., Illus.). (J). (gr. 3-6). 13.99 (978-1-943330-75-1(1), Zack Zombie Publishing) Herobrine Publishing.
—Diary of a Minecraft Zombie Book 4: Zombie Swap. 2015. (Diary of a Minecraft Zombie Ser.: Vol. 4). (ENG., Illus.). (J). (gr. 3-6). 12.99 (978-1-943330-40-9(9), Zack Zombie Publishing) Herobrine Publishing.
—Diary of a Minecraft Zombie Book 5: School Daze. 2015. (Diary of a Minecraft Zombie Ser.: Vol. 5). (ENG., Illus.). (J). (gr. 3-6). 12.99 (978-1-943330-41-6(7), Zack Zombie Publishing) Herobrine Publishing.
—Diary of a Minecraft Zombie Book 6: Zombie Goes to Camp. 2015. (Diary of a Minecraft Zombie Ser.: Vol. 6). (ENG., Illus.). (J). (gr. 3-6). 12.99 (978-1-943330-42-3(5), Zack Zombie Publishing) Herobrine Publishing.
—Diary of a Minecraft Zombie Book 7: Zombie Family Reunion. 2015. (Diary of a Minecraft Zombie Ser.: Vol. 7). (ENG., Illus.). (J). (gr. 3-6). 12.99 (978-1-943330-43-0(3), Zack Zombie Publishing) Herobrine Publishing.
—Diary of a Minecraft Zombie Book 8: Back to Scare School. 2015. (Diary of a Minecraft Zombie Ser.: Vol. 8). (ENG., Illus.). (J). (gr. 3-6). 13.99 (978-1-943330-44-7(1), Zack Zombie Publishing) Herobrine Publishing.
—Diary of a Minecraft Zombie Book 9: Zombie's Birthday Apocalypse. 2015. (Diary of a Minecraft Zombie Ser.: Vol. 9). (ENG., Illus.). (J). (gr. 3-6). 13.99 (978-1-943330-45-4(X), Zack Zombie Publishing) Herobrine Publishing.
—Herobrine Goes on Vacation. 2017. (Herobrine's Wacky Adventures Ser.: Vol. 4). (ENG., Illus.). (J). (gr. 3-6). pap. 9.99 (978-1-943330-84-3(0), Zack Zombie Publishing) Herobrine Publishing.
Zornow, Jeff. Werewolf, 1 vol. Zornow, Jeff, illus. 2007. (Graphic Horror Ser.). (ENG., Illus.). 32p. (J). (gr. 3-6). 32.79 (978-1-60270-062-8(1), 9078, Graphic Planet - Fiction) Magic Wagon.
Zucker, Jonny. Mission 5: Subzero. Woodman, Ned, illus. 2013. (Max Flash Ser.: 5). (ENG.). 144p. (J). (gr. 2-5). pap. 7.95 (978-1-4677-1481-5(X), 22dac0fb-3d86-41f9-9639-7ae52c412c75, Darby Creek) Lerner Publishing Group.
Zuckerman, Heather. A Monster Named Criney Who Makes Kids Whiney. Delice, Shelly Meredith, illus. 2005. 32p. (J). (gr. -1-3). 15.95 (978-0-9744307-0-6(6)) Merry Lane Pr.

MONSTROSITIES

see Monsters

MONTANA

Alt, David D. & Hyndman, Donald W. Roadside Geology of Montana. rev. ed. (Roadside Geology Ser.). (Illus.). 435p. (J). (gr. 4). pap. 20.00 (978-0-87842-202-9(1), 212) Mountain Pr. Publishing Co., Inc.
Bailer, Darice. What's Great about Montana? 2014. (Our Great States Ser.). (ENG., Illus.). 32p. (J). (gr. 2-5). lib. bdg. 26.65 (978-1-4677-3387-8(3), 2722c288-d6c9-4c6f-bdde-3c67bd0fdc73, Lerner Pubns.) Lerner Publishing Group.
Bakker, Robert T. Raptor Pack. Skrepnick, Michael William, illus. 2003. (Step into Reading: Step 5 Ser.). (ENG.). 48p. (J). (gr. 2-4). lib. bdg. 16.19 (978-0-375-92303-6(9)) Random House Publishing Group.
—Raptor Pack. Skrepnick, Mike, illus. 2003. (Step into Reading Ser.). 48p. (J). (gr. 2-4). pap. 5.99 (978-0-375-82303-9(4), Random Hse. Bks. for Young Readers) Random Hse. Children's Bks.
Bennett, Clayton. Montana, 1 vol. 2003. (Celebrate the States (First Edition) Ser.). (ENG., Illus.). 144p. (gr. 6-6). lib. bdg. 39.79 (978-0-7614-1312-7(X), cda4a350-6f8f-4737-805d-d212466f24d8) Cavendish Square Publishing LLC.
Bennett, Clayton & Mead, Wendy. Montana, 1 vol. 2nd rev. ed. 2010. (Celebrate the States (Second Edition) Ser.). (ENG.). 144p. (gr. 6-6). 39.79 (978-0-7614-4731-3(8), c5e11447-3cb0-48f0-a02a-f3fc584fd3d2) Cavendish Square Publishing LLC.
Bjorklund, Ruth. Montana, 1 vol. Santoro, Christopher, illus. 2004. (It's My State! (First Edition)(r) Ser.). (ENG.). 80p. (gr. 4-4). lib. bdg. 34.07 (978-0-7614-1689-0(7), cd801c82-b9b6-44f2-b197-059c0bf39993) Cavendish Square Publishing LLC.
—Montana, 1 vol. 2nd rev. ed. 2013. (It's My State! (Second Edition)(r) Ser.). (ENG.). 80p. (gr. 4-4). pap. 18.64 (978-1-62712-100-2(5), a63326cd-e46d-41d9-8ec6-9f1e3a6ec770) Cavendish Square Publishing LLC.
Brown, Jonatha A. Montana, 1 vol. 2006. (Portraits of the States Ser.). (ENG.). 32p. (gr. 3-5). pap. 11.50 (978-0-8368-4719-2(9), 1ea6e38a-d883-4cfb-89c8-77c3cd03cf75); (Illus.). lib. bdg. 28.67 (978-0-8368-4702-4(4), 3e7fbfa7-c222-441c-ab60-165cc7e5c1da) Stevens, Gareth Publishing LLLP. (Gareth Stevens Learning Library).
Brown, Vanessa. Montana. 2009. (Bilingual Library of the United States of America Ser.). (SPA.). 32p. (gr. 2-2). 47.90 (978-1-60853-371-8(9), Editorial Buenas Letras) Rosen Publishing Group, Inc., The.
—Montana, 1 vol. Brusca, Maria Cristina, tr. 2005. (Bilingual Library of the United States of America Ser.: Set 2). (ENG & SPA., Illus.). 32p. (J). (gr. 2-2). lib. bdg. 28.93 (978-1-4042-3091-0(2), a03e475d-feba-4297-99c6-842d48931684) Rosen Publishing Group, Inc., The.
Bruchac, Joseph. Buffalo Song. Farnsworth, Bill, illus. 2008. (J). Lee & Low Bks., Inc.
Collard, Sneed B., III & Collard, Sneed B. B Is for Big Sky Country: A Montana Alphabet. Yardley, Joanna, illus. 2003. (Discover America State by State Ser.). (ENG.). 40p. (J). (gr. 1-3). 18.99 (978-1-58536-098-7(8), 201978) Sleeping Bear Pr.
Heinrichs, Ann. Montana. Kania, Matt, illus. 2017. (U. S. A. Travel Guides). (ENG.). 40p. (J). (gr. 2-5). lib. bdg. 38.50 (978-1-5038-1966-5(3), 211603) Child's World, Inc, The.
Hirschmann, Kris. Montana, 1 vol. 2003. (World Almanac(r) Library of the States Ser.). (ENG., Illus.). 48p. (gr. 4-6). pap. 15.05 (978-0-8368-5324-7(5), 4f87a9c7-e838-4be1-a15e-9c54de9112a0); lib. bdg. 33.67 (978-0-8368-5153-3(6), e60a7bfa-cfcd-4a51-9467-55d6761b1e1e) Stevens, Gareth Publishing LLLP. (Gareth Stevens Learning Library).
Kuedee, Jaycee. How to Draw Montana's Sights & Symbols. 2009. (Kid's Guide to Drawing America Ser.). 32p. (gr. k-k). 50.50 (978-1-61511-075-9(5), PowerKids Pr.) Rosen Publishing Group, Inc., The.
LaDoux, Rita. Montana. 2012. (J). lib. bdg. 25.26 (978-0-7613-4542-8(6), Lerner Pubns.) Lerner Publishing Group.
Lawson, Cheri. Chip the Buffalo: Based on a True Story. Lawson, J., illus. Beerntsen, Tammy, photos by. 2006. 32p. (J). lib. bdg. 14.95 (978-1-930580-61-9(4), Luminary Media Group) Pine Orchard, Inc.
Marsh, Carole. Montana Current Events Projects: 30 Cool, Activities, Crafts, Experiments & More for Kids to Do to Learn about Your State! 2003. (Montana Experience Ser.). 32p. (gr. k-5). pap. 5.95 (978-0-635-02045-1(9), Marsh, Carole Bks.) Gallopade International.
—Montana Geography Projects: 30 Cool, Activities, Crafts, Experiments & More for Kids to Do to Learn about Your State! 2003. (Montana Experience Ser.). 32p. (gr. k-5). pap. 5.95 (978-0-635-01845-8(4), Marsh, Carole Bks.) Gallopade International.
—Montana Government Projects: 30 Cool, Activities, Crafts, Experiments & More for Kids to Do to Learn about Your State! 2003. (Montana Experience Ser.). 32p. (gr. k-5). pap. 5.95 (978-0-635-01945-5(0), Marsh, Carole Bks.) Gallopade International.
—Montana People Projects: 30 Cool, Activities, Crafts, Experiments & More for Kids to Do to Learn about Your State! 2003. (Montana Experience Ser.). 32p. (gr. k-5). pap. 5.95 (978-0-635-01995-0(7), Marsh, Carole Bks.) Gallopade International.
—Montana Symbols & Facts Projects: 30 Cool, Activities, Crafts, Experiments & More for Kids to Do to Learn about Your State! 2003. (Montana Experience Ser.). 32p. (gr. k-5). pap. 5.95 (978-0-635-01895-3(0), Marsh, Carole Bks.) Gallopade International.
McLuskey, Krista. Montana. 2011. (Guide to American States Ser.). (Illus.). 48p. (YA). (gr. 3-6). 29.99 (978-1-61690-798-3(3)) Weigl Pubs., Inc.
Miles, Stephanie & Farley, Christin. M Is for Montana. Kaliaha, Volha, illus. 2018. (ABC Regional Board Bks.). (ENG.). 20p. (J). (gr. -1 — 1). bds. 12.99 (978-1-945547-88-1(X), 554788) Familius LLC.
Murray, Julie. Montana, 1 vol. 2006. (Buddy Book Ser.). (ENG., Illus.). 32p. (gr. 2-4). 27.07 (978-1-59197-685-1(5), Buddy Bks.) ABDO Publishing Co.

MONTANA—FICTION

Andrews, Neva. Stormy & Stub. 2008. 108p. pap. 10.95 (978-0-595-52854-7(6), iUniverse, Inc.) iUniverse, Inc.
Brammer, Deb. Moose. 2007. 132p. (YA). (gr. 8-12). per. 8.99 (978-1-59166-722-3(4)) BJU Pr.
Charles L. Wilson. The Search Is On: The Wild Adventures of Lester & Dora. 2009. 200p. 24.99 (978-1-4269-1813-1(5)); pap. 14.99 (978-1-4269-1812-4(7)) Trafford Publishing.
Collard, Sneed B., III. The Governor's Dog Is Missing. 2011. (Slate Stephens Mysteries Ser.). 176p. (J). (gr. 4-6). 16.00 (978-0-9844460-1-8(X)) Bucking Horse Bks.
Danforth, Emily M. The Miseducation of Cameron Post. (ENG.). 480p. (YA). (gr. 9). 2013. pap. 12.99 (978-0-06-202057-4(9)) 2012. 17.99 (978-0-06-202056-7(0)) HarperCollins Pubs. (Balzer & Bray).
—The Miseducation of Cameron Post Movie Tie-In Edition. movie tie-in ed. 2018. (ENG.). 480p. (J). (gr. 9). pap. 9.99 (978-0-06-288449-7(2), Balzer & Bray) HarperCollins Pubs.
Davis, Trisha. Wildfire! 2011. 112p. (gr. 4-6). 20.95 (978-1-4620-1615-0(4)); pap. 10.95 (978-1-4620-1616-7(2)) iUniverse, Inc.
Eberhard, Phyllis Lunde Brees. Little Miss Neat-As-A-Pin. Jacoby, Nickolina Dye, illus. 2007. (J). (978-0-9722741-7-3(0)) Publishing Factory, The.
Ellison, Laura. Hard Rock, Hard Times: Coming of Age in Butte Montana, 1911-1917. 2005. 195p. (YA). per. (978-0-9722217-7-1(8)) Horse Creek Pubns.
Farnes, Catherine. Snowblind. 2004. 108p. (J). (978-1-59166-329-4(6)) BJU Pr.
Ficklin, Jonene H. Orinoco Intrigue. 2005. (YA). 14.95 (978-0-9761188-1-7(5)) Victor's Crown Publishing.
Gavila, Robert. Nisha: Montana. 2004. (YA). 2.25 (978-0-9748466-0-6(0)) Gavila Publishing.
A Gift to Share. 2005. (J). 17.00 (978-0-9721457-1-8(0)) Silent Moon Bks.
Giles, Jeff. The Brink of Darkness. 2018. (Edge of Everything Ser.). (ENG.). 352p. (YA). 18.99 (978-1-61963-755-9(3), 900147530, Bloomsbury Young Adult) Bloomsbury Publishing USA.
Gilliland, Hap. Alone in the Wilderness. 2003. (Illus.). 160p. (YA). (gr. 6-10). pap. 14.95 (978-0-87961-257-3(6)) Naturegraph Pubs., Inc.
Harmon, Michael. The Last Exit to Normal. 2008. (ENG.). 288p. (J). (gr. 9-12). lib. bdg. 21.19 (978-0-375-94098-9(7), Knopf Bks. for Young Readers) Random Hse. Children's Bks.
Hiaasen, Carl. Squirm. (ENG.). (J). (gr. 5-7). 2020. 304p. 8.99 (978-0-593-17767-9(3), Yearling) 2020. 304p. pap. 9.99 (978-0-385-75300-5(4), Ember) 2018. 288p. 18.99 (978-0-385-75297-8(0), Knopf Bks. for Young Readers) Random Hse. Children's Bks.

Hill, Janet Muirhead. The Horse & the Crow: A Miranda & Starlight Story. 2015. (ENG.). 268p. (J). pap. 13.00 *(978-1-937849-27-6(9))* Raven Publishing Inc. of Montana.

Hipp, Diane. Stuart the Donkey: A Tale of His Tail. Hill, T. J., illus. 2010. 52p. pap. 21.99 *(978-1-4520-3420-1(6))* AuthorHouse.

Hodder, Beth. The Ghost of Schafer Meadows. 2007. (J). per. 7.99 *(978-0-9793963-0-4(1))* Grizzly Ridge Publishing.

—Stealing the Wild. 2010. 166p. (J). pap. 11.95 *(978-0-9793963-1-1(X))* Grizzly Ridge Publishing.

Ingold, Jeanette. The Big Burn: Teddy Roosevelt & the Fire That Saved America. 2003. (Illus.). 301p. (YA). (gr. 8-12). 14.60 *(978-0-7569-4283-0(7))* Perfection Learning Corp.

—Hitch. 2006. (ENG., Illus.). 288p. (YA). (gr. 7-12). pap. 9.99 *(978-0-15-205619-3(X)*, 1196901, Clarion Bks.) HarperCollins Pubs.

—Mountain Solo. 2005. (ENG.). 320p. (YA). (gr. 7-12). pap. 15.95 *(978-0-15-205358-1(1)*, 1062824, Clarion Bks.) HarperCollins Pubs.

Jacobs, Lily. The Littlest Bunny in Montana: An Easter Adventure. Dunn, Robert, illus. 2015. (Littlest Bunny Ser.). (ENG.). 32p. (J). (gr. -1-3). 9.99 *(978-1-4926-1129-5(8)*, Hometown World) Sourcebooks, Inc.

James, Eric. Santa's Sleigh Is on Its Way to Montana: A Christmas Adventure. Dunn, Robert, illus. 2016. (Santa's Sleigh Is on Its Way Ser.). (ENG.). 32p. (J). (gr. k-2). 12.99 *(978-1-4926-4338-8(6)*, 9781492643388, Hometown World) Sourcebooks, Inc.

—The Spooky Express Montana. Piwowarski, Marcin, illus. 2017. (Spooky Express Ser.). (ENG.). 32p. (J). (gr. k-6). 9.99 *(978-1-4926-5374-5(8)*, Hometown World) Sourcebooks, Inc.

—Tiny the Montana Easter Bunny. 2018. (Tiny the Easter Bunny Ser.). (ENG.). 40p. (J). (gr. k-3). 9.99 *(978-1-4926-5941-9(X)*, Hometown World) Sourcebooks, Inc.

Johnson, Terry Lynn. Falcon Wild. 2017. 176p. (J). (gr. 5). lib. bdg. 16.99 *(978-1-58089-788-4(6))* Charlesbridge Publishing, Inc.

Kevtherev. Riddle Tails: The Golden Fruit. 2012. 28p. pap. 30.70 *(978-1-4634-0617-2(7))* AuthorHouse.

Konigsberg, Bill. The Porcupine of Truth. 2015. (ENG.). 336p. (YA). (gr. 9). 17.99 *(978-0-545-64893-6(9)*, Levine, Arthur A. Bks.) Scholastic, Inc.

Krovatin, Christopher. Gravediggers: Mountain of Bones. 2013. (Gravediggers Ser.: 1). (ENG.). 352p. (J). (gr. 3-7). pap. 6.99 *(978-0-06-207741-7(4)*, Tegen, Katherine Bks) HarperCollins Pubs.

Larson, Kirby. Hattie Big Sky. (Hattie Ser.: 1). (YA). (gr. 7-7). 2008. (ENG.). 304p. 8.99 *(978-0-385-73595-7(2)*, Yearling) 2007. 336p. pap. 9.99 *(978-0-440-23941-3(9)*, Ember) Random Hse. Children's Bks.

—Hattie Big Sky. l.t. ed. 2007. (Literacy Bridge Young Adult Ser.). 381p. (YA). (gr. 7-12). 23.95 *(978-0-7862-9697-2(6))* Thorndike Pr.

Lemna, Don. Out in Left Field. Collins, Matt, illus. 2013. (ENG.). 224p. (J). (gr. 4-6). 22.44 *(978-0-8234-2313-2(1))* Holiday Hse., Inc.

Lenz, Dave. Jack Crow: Indian Healer. 2014. (J). *(978-0-9801744-7-2(3))* Barnhardt & Ashe Publishing, Inc.

Maynard, Joyce. The Cloud Chamber. 2006. (ENG.). 288p. (YA). (gr. 7-7). pap. 13.99 *(978-1-4169-2699-3(2)*, Simon Pulse) Simon Pulse.

McMann, Lisa. Cryer's Cross. 2011. (ENG.). 256p. (YA). (gr. 9). pap. 9.99 *(978-1-4169-9482-4(3)*, Simon Pulse) Simon Pulse.

Meddaugh, Susan. Martha & Skits Out West. 2011. (Martha Speaks Ser.). (ENG., Illus.). 96p. (J). (gr. 1-4). pap. 5.99 *(978-0-547-21074-2(4))* Houghton Mifflin Harcourt Publishing Co.

Melton, Marcia. The Boarding House. Doran, Fran, illus. 2012. 153p. (J). pap. 12.00 *(978-1-937849-03-0(1))* Raven Publishing Inc. of Montana.

—Joe Henry's Journey. 2014. (Illus.). 169p. (J). pap. 12.00 *(978-1-937849-20-7(1))* Raven Publishing Inc. of Montana.

Miller, Paula. One-Eyed Jack. Forrest, Chris, illus. (J). 2007. (ENG.). 133p. (gr. 2-7). pap. 8.95 *(978-0-9769417-0-5(8))* 2006. 144p. 13.95 *(978-0-9718348-8-0(1))* Blooming Tree Pr.

O'Neill, Elizabeth. Alfred Visits Montana. 2009. 24p. pap. 12.00 *(978-0-9822288-6-9(4))* Funny Bone Bks.

Ore, Stephen. Round Trip: A Novel. 2018. (Illus.). 220p. (YA). pap. *(978-1-937849-49-8(X))* Raven Publishing Inc. of Montana.

Out of the Blue. 2014. (J). pap. *(978-0-8163-5016-2(7))* Pacific Pr. Publishing Assn.

Palmer, Robin. Girl vs. Superstar, 1. 2010. (Yours Truly, Lucy B. Parker Ser.: 1). 224p. (J). (gr. 6-8). 21.19 *(978-0-14-241500-9(6))* Penguin Young Readers Group.

Philips, Fleur. Beautiful Girl: A Novel. 2015. (ENG.). 150p. (YA). pap. 17.00 *(978-1-940716-47-3(0))* SparkPr. (a Bks.parks Imprint).

—Crumble. 2013. 168p. (YA). pap. 8.99 *(978-0-9889299-0-6(2))* Philips, Fleur.

Piper, William Bowman. Giraffe of Montana, Volume 1, 1. 2005. (Giraffe of Montana Ser.). (Illus.). 152p. (J). 19.95 *(978-0-9763359-4-8(8)*, 0-9763359) Little Pemberley Pr.

—Giraffe of Montana, Volume 3. 2007. (Giraffe of Montana Ser.). (Illus.). 144p. (J). 19.95 *(978-0-9763359-6-2(4))* Little Pemberley Pr.

Porter, Pamela. Sky. 1 vol. Gerber, Mary Jane, illus. 2004. (ENG.). 104p. (J). (gr. 3-7). pap. 9.95 *(978-0-88899-607-7(1)*, Libros Tigrillo) Groundwood Bks. CAN. Dist: Publishers Group West (PGW).

Sanderson, Nancy. Summer of the Painted Horse. 2009. 188p. pap. 14.49 *(978-1-4490-2312-6(6))* AuthorHouse.

Sargent, Dave & Sargent, Pat. Sweetpea: (Purple Corn Welsh) Be Happy, 30 vols., Vol. 58. Lenoir, Jane, illus. 2003. (Saddle up Ser.: Vol. 58). 42p. (J). pap. 10.95 *(978-1-56763-816-5(3))*; lib. bdg. 23.60 *(978-1-56763-815-8(5))* Ozark Publishing.

Schaaf, Ron. BearClaw: Finding Courage Within. 2007. (J). *(978-0-9787555-1-5(0))* Hickory Tales Publishing.

Seidler, Tor. Firstborn. Sheban, Chris, illus. 2015. (ENG.). 240p. (J). (gr. 4-9). 16.99 *(978-1-4814-1017-5(2)*, Atheneum Bks. for Young Readers) Simon & Schuster Children's Publishing.

Sigafus, Kim. Nowhere to Hide. 2019. (Autumn's Dawn Trilogy Ser.: 1). (ENG.). 112p. (YA). (gr. 8-12). pap. 9.95 *(978-1-939053-21-3(8)*, 7th Generation) BPC.

Smith, Michael. Thomas the T. Rex: The Journey of a Young Dinosaur to Los Angeles. Roski, Gayle Garner, illus. 2011. (J). *(978-0-9832278-4-7(5))* East West Discovery Pr.

Smith, Michael & Roski, Gayle Garner. Thomas the T. Rex: The Journey of a Young Dinosaur to Los Angeles. Roski, Gayle Garner, illus. 2011. (SPA & ENG., Illus.). (J). *(978-0-9832278-2-3(9))* East West Discovery Pr.

Stine, Faye. Wolf: A Story of the Wild. 2012. (ENG.). 64p. pap. 10.95 *(978-1-4787-2054-6(9))* Outskirts Pr., Inc.

Sully, Katherine. Night-Night Montana. Poole, Helen, illus. 2017. (Night-Night Ser.). (ENG.). 20p. (J). (gr. -1-1). bds. 9.99 *(978-1-4926-5486-5(8)*, Hometown World) Sourcebooks, Inc.

Swinger-Ellbogen, Sue. Campfire Kids, 1 vol. 2010. 54p. pap. 16.95 *(978-1-4489-5493-3(2))* America Star Bks.

Tarshis, Lauren. I Survived: The Attack of the Grizzlies, 1967, Vol. 17. 2018. (I Survived Ser.: 17). (ENG., Illus.). 144p. (J). (gr. 3-7). lib. bdg. 16.99 *(978-0-545-91983-8(5)*, Scholastic Paperbacks) Scholastic, Inc.

—I Survived the Attack of the Grizzlies 1967, 17. 2019. (I Survived Ser.). (ENG.). 144p. (J). (gr. 4-6). 15.96 *(978-1-64310-822-3(0))* Penworthy Co., LLC, The.

Thomas, Jane Resh. Blind Mountain. 2006. (ENG.). 128p. (J). (gr. 5-7). 15.00 *(978-0-618-64872-6(0)*, 100463, Clarion Bks.) HarperCollins Pubs.

Thomas, Jeanne Taylor. Kerry Mcdaniels & the Cave. 2012. (ENG.). 276p. pap. 18.95 *(978-1-4327-7296-3(1))* Outskirts Pr., Inc.

Ward, Kaitlin. Girl in a Bad Place. 2017. (ENG.). 272p. (YA). (gr. 7-7). 17.99 *(978-1-338-10105-8(6))* Scholastic, Inc.

Yep, Laurence. When the Circus Came to Town. Wang, Suling, illus. 2004. 112p. (J). (gr. 3-5). 13.65 *(978-0-7569-2969-5(5))* Perfection Learning Corp.

MONTANA—HISTORY

Bjorklund, Ruth. Montana, 1 vol. 2nd rev. ed. 2013. (It's My State! (Second Edition)(r) Ser.). (ENG.). 80p. (gr. 4-4). 35.93 *(978-0-7614-7999-4(6)*, f787c7a9-9208-4fe7-a82f-e2a0491a9ecd) Cavendish Square Publishing LLC.

Bjorklund, Ruth, et al. Montana, 1 vol. 3rd rev. ed. 2015. (It's My State! (Third Edition)(r) Ser.). (ENG., Illus.). 80p. (gr. 4-4). 35.93 *(978-1-62713-204-6(X)*, dc15a574-9cf5-4101-a1c7-16db3430a71a) Cavendish Square Publishing LLC.

Blake, Kevin. Deadly Mine: Libby, Montana. 2017. (Eco-Disasters Ser.). (ENG., Illus.). 32p. (J). (gr. 2-7). 19.95 *(978-1-68402-222-9(3))* Bearport Publishing Co., Inc.

Collard, Sneed B., III. The World Famous Miles City Bucking Horse Sale. 2010. 64p. 18.00 *(978-0-9844460-0-1(1))* Bucking Horse Bks.

Gamble, Adam. Good Night Montana. 2013. (Good Night Our World Ser.). (ENG., Illus.). 20p. (J). (— 1). bds. 9.95 *(978-1-60219-080-1(1))* Good Night Bks.

Gregory, Josh. Montana (a True Book: My United States) (Library Edition) 2018. (True Book (Relaunch) Ser.). (ENG., Illus.). 48p. (J). (gr. 3-5). 31.00 *(978-0-531-23563-8(7)*, Children's Pr.) Scholastic Library Publishing.

Hamilton, John. Montana, 1 vol. 2016. (United States of America Ser.). (ENG., Illus.). 48p. (J). (gr. 5-9). 34.21 *(978-1-68078-328-5(9)*, 21641, Abdo & Daughters) ABDO Publishing Co.

Jerome, Kate B. Lucky to Live in Montana. 2017. (Arcadia Kids Ser.). (ENG., Illus.). 32p. (J). 16.99 *(978-0-7385-2803-8(X))* Arcadia Publishing.

—The Wise Animal Handbook Montana. 2017. (Arcadia Kids Ser.). (ENG., Illus.). 32p. (J). 16.99 *(978-0-7385-2829-8(3))* Arcadia Publishing.

Jones, Donald M., photos by. Buffalo Country: America's National Bison Range. 2005. (ENG., Illus.). 72p. per. 14.95 *(978-1-931832-56-4(0)*, 8667872363) Riverbend Publishing.

Kopp, Megan. Montana: The Treasure State. 2012. (J). *(978-1-61913-371-6(7))*; pap. *(978-1-61913-372-3(5))* Weigl Pubs., Inc.

Lusted, Marcia Amidon. Montana: The Treasure State, 1 vol. 2010. (Our Amazing States Ser.). (ENG.). 24p. (J). (gr. 3-3). pap. 9.25 *(978-1-4488-0758-1(1)*, c8e358d5-cb3c-49cd-ae34-a7b09f30baba); lib. bdg. 26.27 *(978-1-4488-0662-1(3)*, 92d7c45c-6c8e-4a78-88d2-d98781fb5371) Rosen Publishing Group, Inc., The. (PowerKids Pr.).

Marsh, Carole. Exploring Montana Through Project-Based Learning: Geography, History, Government, Economics & More. 2016. (Montana Experience Ser.). (ENG.). (J). pap. 9.99 *(978-0-635-12350-3(9))* Gallopade International.

—I'm Reading about Montana. 2014. (Montana Experience Ser.). (ENG., Illus.). (J). pap., pap. 8.99 *(978-0-635-11301-6(5))* Gallopade International.

—Montana History Projects: 30 Cool, Activities, Crafts, Experiments & More for Kids to Do to Learn about Your State! 2003. (Montana Experience Ser.). 32p. (gr. k-5). pap. 5.95 *(978-0-635-01795-6(4)*, Marsh, Carole Bks.) Gallopade International.

McLuskey, Krista. Montana: The Treasure State. 2016. (J). *(978-1-4896-4893-8(3))* Weigl Pubs., Inc.

Merrill-Maker, Andrea. Montana: People & Their Stories. 2004. (Illus.). 371p. (J). 32.09 *(978-0-913205-28-0(1))* Sage Hill Pubs., LLC.

Mills, Jordan & Parker, Bridget. Montana. 2016. (States Ser.). (ENG., Illus.). 32p. (J). (gr. 3-6). lib. bdg. 27.99 *(978-1-5157-0413-3(0)*, 132024, Capstone Pr.) Capstone.

Montana History Notebook Map. 2004. (J). *(978-0-9759433-6-6(7))* Maps For Kids Inc.

Patent, Dorothy Hinshaw. Call of the Osprey. Muñoz, William, illus. 2015. (Scientists in the Field Ser.). (ENG.). 80p. (J). (gr. 5-7). 18.99 *(978-0-544-23268-6(2)*, 1564093, Clarion Bks.) HarperCollins Pubs.

Peterson, Sheryl. Montana. 2009. (This Land Called America Ser.). 32p. (YA). (gr. 3-6). 19.95 *(978-1-58341-779-9(6))* Creative Co., The.

Porterfield, Jason. Montana: Past & Present, 1 vol. 2010. (United States: Past & Present Ser.). (ENG.). 48p. (YA). (gr. 5-5). pap. 12.75 *(978-1-4358-9513-3(4)*, f6028e77-1fbf-43c2-bfa7-b9b48a5d3faa); lib. bdg. 34.47 *(978-1-4358-9486-0(3)*, 0b3d05c3-5e4e-42ee-a350-e82afc27edd0) Rosen Publishing Group, Inc., The. (Rosen Reference).

Solberg, Jessica L. First Dog: Unleashed in the Montana Capitol. Rath, Robert, illus. 2007. (J). 11.95 *(978-1-56037-419-0(5))* Farcountry Pr.

Stein, R. Conrad. America the Beautiful: Montana (Revised Edition) 2014. (America the Beautiful, Third Ser. (Revised Edition) Ser.). (ENG.). 144p. (J). lib. bdg. 40.00 *(978-0-531-28283-0(X))* Scholastic Library Publishing.

Westcott, Jim. Upper Plains: Montana, North Dakota, South Dakota, Vol. 19. 2015. (Let's Explore the States Ser.). (Illus.). 64p. (J). (gr. 5). 23.95 *(978-1-4222-3336-8(7))* Mason Crest.

Williams, Judith M. Montana. 2009. (From Sea to Shining Sea, Second Ser.). (ENG.). 80p. (J). pap. 7.95 *(978-0-531-21135-9(5)*, Children's Pr.) Scholastic Library Publishing.

MONTEREY (CALIF.)

Abbink, Emily. Monterey Bay Area Missions. 2007. (Exploring California Missions Ser.). (ENG., Illus.). 64p. (gr. 4-7). lib. bdg. 27.93 *(978-0-8225-0887-8(7)*, Lerner Pubns.) Lerner Publishing Group.

Feldman, Thea. A Sea Otter to the Rescue: Ready-To-Read Level 2. Sanson, Rachel, illus. 2019. (Tails from History Ser.). (ENG.). 32p. (J). (gr. k-2). pap. 4.99 *(978-1-5344-4337-2(1)*, Simon Spotlight) Simon Spotlight.

MONTEREY (CALIF.)—FICTION

Collins, Yvonne & Rideout, Sandy. The Black Sheep. 2007. 348p. (J). *(978-1-4287-4665-7(X))* Hyperion Pr.

MONTESSORI, MARIA, 1870-1952

Bach, Nancy. Maria Montessori & Her Quiet Revolution: A Picture Book about Maria Montessori & Her School Method. Lätti, Leo, illus. 2013. 24p. pap. *(978-1-938712-10-4(2))* Roxby Media Ltd.

Sharpe, Paula A. Maria Montessori. Ward, Patricia R. & Pigford, Grady A., illus. 2010. 51p. (J). *(978-1-892142-47-4(3))* Cedar Tree Bks.

MONTEZUMA II, EMPEROR OF MEXICO, 1480-1520

Conklin, Wendy. Moctezuma: Aztec Ruler, 1 vol. rev. ed. 2007. (Social Studies: Informational Text Ser.). (ENG.). 32p. (J). (gr. 4-8). pap. 11.99 *(978-0-7439-0457-5(5))* Teacher Created Materials, Inc.

Green, Carl R. Cortés: Conquering the Powerful Aztec Empire, 1 vol. 2009. (Great Explorers of the World Ser.). (ENG., Illus.). 112p. (gr. 6-7). 35.93 *(978-1-59845-099-6(9)*, 5d911ead-c3fc-4a96-8038-2ff81f92b380) Enslow Publishing, LLC.

Schulz, Elizabeth. Montezuma II, 1 vol. 2017. (Great Military Leaders Ser.). (ENG.). 128p. (YA). (gr. 9-9). 47.36 *(978-1-5026-2789-6(2)*, 922400b8-71f4-4451-b223-951ff9855275) Cavendish Square Publishing LLC.

MONTEZUMA, CARLOS, 1866-1923

Capaldi, Gina. A Boy Named Beckoning: The True Story of Dr. Carlos Montezuma, Native American Hero. Capaldi, Gina, illus. (ENG., Illus.). (J). (gr. 3-6). 2019. 40p. 9.99 *(978-1-5415-7837-1(6)*, 0f80bbd2-6515-4a10-8d4b-4e7529959c34) 2008. 32p. lib. bdg. 18.99 *(978-0-8225-7644-0(9)*, 12a62db4-6a87-4a34-a1de-c81c778ec779) Lerner Publishing Group. (Carolrhoda Bks.).

MONTGOLFIER, JOSEPH MICHEL, 1740-1810

Henry, Jason. Up & Away! How Two Brothers Invented the Hot-Air Balloon. 2018. (Illus.). 48p. (J). (gr. k). 18.99 *(978-1-4549-2360-2(1))* Sterling Publishing Co., Inc.

Lowery, Lawrence F. Up, up in a Balloon. 2013. (I Wonder Why Ser.). (ENG., Illus.). 36p. (J). (gr. k-3). pap. 13.99 *(978-1-938946-14-1(6))* National Science Teachers Assn.

MONTGOMERY, L. M. (LUCY MAUD), 1874-1942

MacLeod, Elizabeth. Lucy Maud Montgomery. Mantha, John, illus. 2008. 32p. (J). (gr. 1-3). 14.95 *(978-1-55453-055-7(5))* Kids Can Pr., Ltd. CAN. Dist: Hachette Bk. Group.

MONTGOMERY (ALA.)—RACE RELATIONS

Aretha, David. The Story of Rosa Parks & the Montgomery Bus Boycott in Photographs, 1 vol. 2014. (Story of the Civil Rights Movement in Photographs Ser.). (ENG.). 48p. (gr. 5-6). 27.93 *(978-0-7660-4234-6(0)*, e21f5d8c-f41e-4022-be0d-e634268e951a) Enslow Publishing, LLC.

Banting, Erinn. Rosa Parks. 2005. (Great African American Women for Kids Ser.). (Illus.). 24p. (J). (gr. 2-3). lib. bdg. 26.00 *(978-1-59036-336-2(1))*; (gr. 3-7). per. 8.95 *(978-1-59036-342-3(6))* Weigl Pubs., Inc.

Bjornlund, Lydia D. Rosa Parks & the Montgomery Bus Boycott, 1 vol. 2007. (Lucent Library of Black History Ser.). (ENG., Illus.). 104p. (gr. 7-7). lib. bdg. 41.03 *(978-1-4205-0010-3(4)*, 6776b446-a900-4bd3-a78f-f2f693a22225, Lucent Pr.) Greenhaven Publishing LLC.

Brandt, Keith & Mattern, Joanne. Rosa Parks: Freedom Rider. Griffith, Gershom, illus. 2006. 54p. (J). pap. *(978-0-439-66045-7(9))* Scholastic, Inc.

Brindell Fradin, Dennis. The Montgomery Bus Boycott, 1 vol. 2010. (Turning Points in U. S. History Ser.). (ENG.). 48p. (gr. 4-4). 34.07 *(978-0-7614-4258-5(8)*, 0d3787c1-13eb-4d62-aab1-b3d95ad87102) Cavendish Square Publishing LLC.

Brown, Jonatha A. Rosa Parks, 1 vol. (People We Should Know Ser.). (Illus.). 24p. (gr. 2-4). 2006. (ENG.). lib. bdg. 24.67 *(978-0-8368-4748-2(2)*, 3fd2247d-ef71-4f76-8f9d-fe2565b41a2e, Weekly Reader Leveled Readers) 2005. (SPA., pap. 9.15 *(978-0-8368-4769-7(5)*, dc6d6549-aadd-4a94-970a-bd4b21cb8052, Weekly Reader Leveled Readers) 2005. (ENG., pap. 9.15 *(978-0-8368-4755-0(5)*, 04e24c04-67e0-444b-8563-13ff52afad09, Weekly Reader Leveled Readers) 2005. (SPA., lib. bdg. 24.67 *(978-0-8368-4762-8(8)*, 8ef1c1f4-f871-42b6-b2cd-befae7e48778) Stevens, Gareth Publishing LLLP.

Connors, Kathleen. The Life of Rosa Parks, 1 vol., Vol. 1. 2013. (Famous Lives Ser.). (ENG.). 24p. (J). (gr. 1-2). 25.27 *(978-1-4824-0419-7(2)*, b2f69321-8d88-4e1e-a43f-20dde8903ca5) Stevens, Gareth Publishing LLLP.

Dubowski, Cathy East. Rosa Parks: Don't Give In! 2005. (Defining Moments Ser.). (Illus.). 32p. (J). (gr. 2-5). lib. bdg. 28.50 *(978-1-59716-078-0(4))* Bearport Publishing Co., Inc.

Edwards, Pamela Duncan. The Bus Ride That Changed History. Shanahan, Danny, illus. 2009. (ENG.). 32p. (J). (gr. -1-3). pap. 7.99 *(978-0-547-07674-4(6)*, 1042031, Clarion Bks.) HarperCollins Pubs.

Freedman, Russell. Freedom Walkers: The Story of the Montgomery Bus Boycott. 2009. (ENG., Illus.). 112p. (J). (gr. 5-7). pap. 14.99 *(978-0-8234-2195-4(3))* Holiday Hse., Inc.

Giovanni, Nikki. Rosa. Collier, Bryan, illus. rev. ed. 2005. (ENG.). 40p. (J). (gr. -1-3). 19.99 *(978-0-8050-7106-1(7)*, 900029805, Holt, Henry & Co. Bks. For Young Readers) Holt, Henry & Co.

—Rosa. Collier, Bryan, illus. 2007. (ENG.). 40p. (J). (gr. -1-3). per. 8.99 *(978-0-312-37602-4(2)*, 900048322) Square Fish.

—Rosa. Collier, Bryan, illus. 2011. (J). (gr. 2-5). 29.95 *(978-0-545-04261-1(5))* Weston Woods Studios, Inc.

Haldy, Emma E. Rosa Parks SP. Bane, Jeff, illus. 2018. (My Early Library: Mi Mini Biografía (My Itty-Bitty Bio) Ser.). (SPA.). 24p. (J). (gr. k-1). lib. bdg. 30.64 *(978-1-5341-2999-3(5)*, 212044) Cherry Lake Publishing.

Hoose, Phillip. Claudette Colvin: Twice Toward Justice. 2010. (ENG., Illus.). 160p. (YA). (gr. 8-12). pap. 12.99 *(978-0-312-66105-2(3)*, 900070657) Square Fish.

Hull, Mary, et al. Rosa Parks. 2nd rev. ed. 2008. (ENG.). 128p. (gr. 6-12). pap. 11.95 *(978-1-60413-325-7(2)*, P158536, Checkmark Bks.) Infobase Holdings, Inc.

Hurt, Avery Elizabeth. Rosa Parks: Civil Rights Activist, 1 vol. 2017. (Spotlight on Civic Courage: Heroes of Conscience Ser.). (ENG., Illus.). 48p. (J). (gr. 6-6). 33.47 *(978-1-5383-8105-2(2)*, 3ea91743-5014-4485-998a-c4da0612e0d4) Rosen Publishing Group, Inc., The.

Kishel, Ann-Marie. Rosa Parks: A Life of Courage. 2006. (Pull Ahead Books-Biographies Ser.). (ENG., Illus.). 32p. (gr. k-3). lib. bdg. 22.60 *(978-0-8225-3478-5(9)*, Lerner Pubns.) Lerner Publishing Group.

—Rosa Parks: Una Vida de Valentia. Translations.com Staff, tr. 2006. (Libros para Avanzar-Biografías (Pull Ahead Books-Biographies) Ser.). (ENG & SPA., Illus.). 32p. (gr. k-3). lib. bdg. 22.60 *(978-0-8225-6239-9(1))* Lerner Publishing Group.

Kittinger, Jo S. Rosa's Bus: The Ride to Civil Rights. Walker, Steven, illus. 2010. (ENG.). 40p. (J). (gr. 2-5). 17.99 *(978-1-59078-722-9(6)*, Calkins Creek) Highlights Pr., c/o Highlights for Children, Inc.

Mara, Wil. Rosa Parks. (Rookie Biographies Ser.). (ENG., Illus.). 32p. (J). (gr. 1-2). 2004. pap. 4.95 *(978-0-516-27916-9(5))* 2007. pap. 4.95 *(978-0-531-12592-2(0))* Scholastic Library Publishing. (Children's Pr.).

Marsico, Katie. The Montgomery Bus Boycott: Milestone of the Civil Rights Movement, 1 vol. 2012. (Perspectives On Ser.). (ENG., Illus.). 112p. (YA). (gr. 8-8). 42.64 *(978-1-60870-447-7(5)*, 7a8b73a1-b062-4460-9723-365cd161b44a) Cavendish Square Publishing LLC.

McDonough, Yona Zeldis & Who HQ. Who Was Rosa Parks? Marchesi, Stephen, illus. 2010. (Who Was? Ser.). 112p. (J). (gr. 3-7). pap. 5.99 *(978-0-448-45442-9(4)*, Penguin Workshop) Penguin Young Readers Group.

Meltzer, Brad. I Am Rosa Parks. Eliopoulos, Christopher, illus. 2014. (Ordinary People Change the World Ser.). 40p. (J). (gr. k-4). 15.99 *(978-0-8037-4085-3(9)*, Dial Bks) Penguin Young Readers Group.

Miller, Connie Colwell. Rosa Parks & the Montgomery Bus Boycott, 1 vol. Kalal, Dan, illus. 2006. (Graphic History Ser.). (ENG.). 32p. (J). (gr. 3-9). per. 8.10 *(978-0-7368-9658-0(9)*, 93445) Capstone.

Miller, Jake. The Montgomery Bus Boycott: Integrating Public Buses. 2009. (Library of the Civil Rights Movement Ser.). 24p. (gr. 3-3). 42.50 *(978-1-60853-895-9(8)*, PowerKids Pr.) Rosen Publishing Group, Inc., The.

Mis, Melody S. Meet Rosa Parks. 2009. (Civil Rights Leaders Ser.). 24p. (gr. 2-3). 42.50 *(978-1-61511-855-7(1)*, PowerKids Pr.) Rosen Publishing Group, Inc., The.

Morris, Roz. Rosa Parks: Mother of the Civil Rights Movement. 2003. (Alabama Roots Biography Ser.). (ENG., Illus.). 109p. (J). *(978-1-878561-57-2(X))* Seacoast Publishing, Inc.

Rinaldo, Denise. Rosa Parks: With a Discussion of Courage. 2003. (Values in Action Ser.). (J). *(978-1-59203-061-3(0))* Learning Challenge, Inc.

Ringgold, Faith. If a Bus Could Talk: The Story of Rosa Parks. Ringgold, Faith, illus. 2003. (ENG., Illus.). 32p. (J). (gr. k-4). pap. 8.99 *(978-0-689-85676-1(8)*, Aladdin) Simon & Schuster Children's Publishing.

Sepahban, Lois. 12 Incredible Facts about the Montgomery Bus Boycott. 2015. (Turning Points in US History Ser.). (ENG., Illus.). 32p. (J). (gr. 3-5). 32.80 *(978-1-63235-132-6(3)*, 12-Story Library) Bookstaves, LLC.

Shone, Rob. Rosa Parks: The Life of a Civil Rights Heroine. 2009. (Graphic Nonfiction Biographies Ser.). (ENG.). 48p. (YA). (gr. 4-5). 58.50 *(978-1-61513-026-9(8)*, Rosen Reference) Rosen Publishing Group, Inc., The.

—Rosa Parks: The Life of a Civil Rights Heroine, 1 vol. Spender, Nick, illus. 2006. (Graphic Nonfiction Biographies Ser.). (ENG.). 48p. (J). (gr. 4-5). lib. bdg. 37.13 *(978-1-4042-0864-3(X)*, 6428da22-86f3-4701-b64a-9c47ea50d2f3) Rosen Publishing Group, Inc., The.

—Rosa Parks: The Life of a Civil Rights Heroine, 1 vol. Spender, Nik, illus. 2006. (Graphic Nonfiction Biographies Ser.). (ENG.). 48p. (gr. 4-5). pap. 14.05 *(978-1-4042-0927-5(1)*, c2923d67-40d0-41b6-a57f-742175328325) Rosen Publishing Group, Inc., The.

Time for Kids Editors. Rosa Parks: Civil Rights Pioneer. 2007. (Time for Kids Biographies Ser.). (Illus.). 44p. (gr. 2-4). 14.00 *(978-0-7569-8110-5(7))* Perfection Learning Corp.

Vaughn, Wally G. & Davis, Mattie Campbell, eds. The Selma Campaign, 1963-1965: The Decisive Battle of the Civil Rights Movement. 2006. (ENG., Illus.). 244p. pap. 19.95 *(978-0-912469-44-7(7))* Majority Pr., The.

Walsh, Francis. The Montgomery Bus Boycott, 1 vol. 2003. (Landmark Events in American History Ser.). (ENG., Illus.). 48p. (gr. 5-8). pap. 15.05 *(978-0-8368-5403-9(9)*,

31d0b62a-3d44-4f13-8aa6-0a231d93be21, Gareth Stevens Secondary Library) Stevens, Gareth Publishing LLLP.

Walsh, Francis & O'Hern, Kerri. The Montgomery Bus Boycott, 1 vol. 2005. (Graphic Histories Ser.). (ENG., Illus.). 32p. (gr. 3-3). pap. 11.50 *(978-0-8368-6257-7(0),* 61142692-e7fa-45f6-914a-055a214c827d) Stevens, Gareth Publishing LLLP.

Weidt, Maryann N. Rosa Parks. (History Maker Bios Ser.). (Illus.). (J). 2004. 48p. pap. 8.95 *(978-0-8225-4805-8(4))* 2003. 47p. 26.60 *(978-0-8225-4673-3(6))* Lerner Publishing Group. (Lerner Pubns.).

Weston Woods Staff, creator. Rosa. 2011. 18.95 *(978-0-545-14962-4(2))*; 38.75 *(978-0-545-14963-1(0))* Weston Woods Studios, Inc.

Wheeler, Jill C. Rosa Parks, Set II. 2003. (Breaking Barriers Ser.). 64p. (gr. 3-8). lib. bdg. 27.07 *(978-1-57765-640-1(7),* Abdo & Daughters) ABDO Publishing Co.

Whiting, Jim. Rosa Parks. 2007. (What's So Great About... ? Ser.). (Illus.). 32p. (YA). (gr. 2-4). lib. bdg. 25.70 *(978-1-58415-573-7(6))* Mitchell Lane Pubs.

MONTHS

Brode, Robyn. April, 1 vol. 2nd rev. ed. 2009. (Months of the Year (Second Edition) Ser.). (ENG.). 24p. (J). (gr. 1-1). pap. 9.15 *(978-1-4339-2097-4(2),* a0799db3-8e0b-4f65-9c4a-c30a4d92b0e3); lib. bdg. 24.67 *(978-1-4339-1920-6(6),* 80c9e860-0476-4789-9641-24fbb0f10c7f) Stevens, Gareth Publishing LLLP. (Weekly Reader Leveled Readers).

—April / Abril, 1 vol. 2009. (Months of the Year / Meses Del Ano Ser.). (ENG & SPA.). 24p. (J). (gr. 1-1). pap. 9.15 *(978-1-4339-2109-4(X),* 00b7e47e-eeb2-47d0-bced-74a8ef9fc932); lib. bdg. 24.67 *(978-1-4339-1932-9(X),* 901f9bc7-a39e-4b04-bd6f-cd31a2143530) Stevens, Gareth Publishing LLLP. (Weekly Reader Leveled Readers).

—August, 1 vol. 2nd rev. ed. 2009. (Months of the Year (Second Edition) Ser.). (ENG.). 24p. (J). (gr. 1-1). pap. 9.15 *(978-1-4339-2101-8(4),* 015f85e0-a7b6-4cb8-843d-828d84578e73); lib. bdg. 24.67 *(978-1-4339-1924-4(9),* 638b22d0-feb3-41e3-acf2-920df1dcaf80) Stevens, Gareth Publishing LLLP. (Weekly Reader Leveled Readers).

—August / Agosto, 1 vol. 2009. (Months of the Year / Meses Del Ano Ser.). (ENG & SPA.). 24p. (J). (gr. 1-1). pap. 9.15 *(978-1-4339-2113-1(8),* d36b8b35-00b4-4af4-b447-613d09d265d7); lib. bdg. 24.67 *(978-1-4339-1936-7(2),* 08c615d4-1b6c-43c9-8fb5-bd85c05faaa7) Stevens, Gareth Publishing LLLP. (Weekly Reader Leveled Readers).

—December / Diciembre, 1 vol. 2009. (Months of the Year / Meses Del Ano Ser.). (ENG & SPA.). 24p. (J). (gr. 1-1). pap. 9.15 *(978-1-4339-2117-9(0),* 3b06ac47-d44d-4347-8e3c-7c1fdf22247b); lib. bdg. 24.67 *(978-1-4339-1940-4(0),* 7da791ed-2b48-408e-818d-ce6b301fbd5b) Stevens, Gareth Publishing LLLP. (Weekly Reader Leveled Readers).

—February, 1 vol. 2nd rev. ed. 2009. (Months of the Year (Second Edition) Ser.). (ENG.). 24p. (J). (gr. 1-1). pap. 9.15 *(978-1-4339-2095-0(6),* fad4d013-a112-437f-b2d8-4d82ebc6c7a7); lib. bdg. 24.67 *(978-1-4339-1918-3(4),* e35fc70b-2438-453f-ac90-08fbbeac70d6) Stevens, Gareth Publishing LLLP. (Weekly Reader Leveled Readers).

—February / Febrero, 1 vol. 2009. (Months of the Year / Meses Del Ano Ser.). (ENG & SPA.). 24p. (J). (gr. 1-1). pap. 9.15 *(978-1-4339-2107-0(3),* bb90e354-93e6-41f4-8331-1a1781090645); lib. bdg. 24.67 *(978-1-4339-1930-5(3),* 80e531d7-2cdb-4419-9e61-5ab6ac4d7abd) Stevens, Gareth Publishing LLLP. (Weekly Reader Leveled Readers).

—January, 1 vol. 2nd rev. ed. 2009. (Months of the Year (Second Edition) Ser.). (ENG.). 24p. (J). (gr. 1-1). pap. 9.15 *(978-1-4339-2094-3(8),* 597faa33-9fd9-4084-ae57-542e675298e6); lib. bdg. 24.67 *(978-1-4339-1917-6(6),* c125702c-12f7-4be4-98fc-9bb9b92af5a3) Stevens, Gareth Publishing LLLP. (Weekly Reader Leveled Readers).

—January / Enero, 1 vol. 2009. (Months of the Year / Meses Del Ano Ser.). (ENG & SPA.). 24p. (J). (gr. 1-1). pap. 9.15 *(978-1-4339-2106-3(5),* ab729847-401e-41a7-a7ac-37a33e21a3ae); lib. bdg. 24.67 *(978-1-4339-1929-9(X),* 622b9688-bbf2-476c-9d4f-96d6af31c399) Stevens, Gareth Publishing LLLP. (Weekly Reader Leveled Readers).

—July, 1 vol. 2nd rev. ed. 2009. (Months of the Year (Second Edition) Ser.). (ENG.). 24p. (J). (gr. 1-1). pap. 9.15 *(978-1-4339-2100-1(6),* 999cfeb5-7ef8-4978-bcf5-819f6475df27); lib. bdg. 24.67 *(978-1-4339-1923-7(0),* 7de8a18b-0bee-4b00-af54-422c26607453) Stevens, Gareth Publishing LLLP. (Weekly Reader Leveled Readers).

—July / Julio, 1 vol. 2009. (Months of the Year / Meses Del Ano Ser.). (ENG & SPA.). 24p. (J). (gr. 1-1). pap. 9.15 *(978-1-4339-2112-4(X),* 1ee4ff40-6e00-42d8-8a61-dcdefff29e49); lib. bdg. 24.67 *(978-1-4339-1935-0(4),* d0545bf3-4d53-4a8e-a1bb-119ee57a2ee6) Stevens, Gareth Publishing LLLP. (Weekly Reader Leveled Readers).

—June, 1 vol. 2nd rev. ed. 2009. (Months of the Year (Second Edition) Ser.). (ENG.). 24p. (J). (gr. 1-1). pap. 9.15 *(978-1-4339-2099-8(9),* 27670c9b-e702-4961-b8e3-1196acfb07ba); lib. bdg. 24.67 *(978-1-4339-1922-0(2),* 3ef7b3c4-0a78-4148-a18f-cf5ff8636a5c) Stevens, Gareth Publishing LLLP. (Weekly Reader Leveled Readers).

—June / Junio, 1 vol. 2009. (Months of the Year / Meses Del Ano Ser.). (ENG & SPA.). 24p. (J). (gr. 1-1). pap. 9.15 *(978-1-4339-2111-7(1),* a8158983-22af-48a8-85b7-9219e41ee6c5); lib. bdg. 24.67 *(978-1-4339-1934-3(6),* 542b9c05-bb20-4ea6-bfd9-6f1cf22a59c7) Stevens, Gareth Publishing LLLP. (Weekly Reader Leveled Readers).

—March, 1 vol. 2nd rev. ed. 2009. (Months of the Year (Second Edition) Ser.). (ENG.). 24p. (J). (gr. 1-1). pap. 9.15 *(978-1-4339-2096-7(4),* 62e73f46-8aaf-4d7d-b091-291322a7e869); lib. bdg. 24.67 *(978-1-4339-1919-0(2),* fac8673a-5f8d-4e68-ba95-ff92f245184c) Stevens, Gareth Publishing LLLP. (Weekly Reader Leveled Readers).

—March / Marzo, 1 vol. 2009. (Months of the Year / Meses Del Ano Ser.). (ENG & SPA.). 24p. (J). (gr. 1-1). pap. 9.15 *(978-1-4339-2108-7(1),* 839d1464-433a-405f-8f81-b9f61b190a66); lib. bdg. 24.67 *(978-1-4339-1931-2(1),* 2f0d421e-b6a6-43f7-9bcd-639b5b03d6b6) Stevens, Gareth Publishing LLLP. (Weekly Reader Leveled Readers).

—May, 1 vol. 2nd rev. ed. 2009. (Months of the Year (Second Edition) Ser.). (ENG.). 24p. (J). (gr. 1-1). pap. 9.15 *(978-1-4339-2098-1(0),* a6c97378-63c3-4e60-9d3c-56328769676e); lib. bdg. 24.67 *(978-1-4339-1921-3(4),* eb7e4c47-8139-4d4b-92fe-3ee509d598af) Stevens, Gareth Publishing LLLP. (Weekly Reader Leveled Readers).

—November, 1 vol. 2nd rev. ed. 2009. (Months of the Year (Second Edition) Ser.). (ENG.). 24p. (J). (gr. 1-1). pap. 9.15 *(978-1-4339-2104-9(9),* 8e00d03e-5afe-4f00-8cec-16f82d421f7e); lib. bdg. 24.67 *(978-1-4339-1927-5(3),* 5654d3e9-91bb-4be0-bbd6-32ec2fa68259) Stevens, Gareth Publishing LLLP. (Weekly Reader Leveled Readers).

—November / Noviembre, 1 vol. 2009. (Months of the Year / Meses Del Ano Ser.). (ENG & SPA.). 24p. (J). (gr. 1-1). pap. 9.15 *(978-1-4339-2116-2(2),* 26f8ce6a-51fc-45f2-bfc8-7182c4443bf7); lib. bdg. 24.67 *(978-1-4339-1939-8(7),* 24dca8ed-a0aa-4518-a8b4-a25013236e2f) Stevens, Gareth Publishing LLLP. (Weekly Reader Leveled Readers).

—October, 1 vol. 2nd rev. ed. 2009. (Months of the Year (Second Edition) Ser.). (ENG.). 24p. (J). (gr. 1-1). pap. 9.15 *(978-1-4339-2103-2(0),* c9daad70-d624-439e-befb-216d8eba9835); lib. bdg. 24.67 *(978-1-4339-1926-8(5),* 6869c58d-80fc-4afb-ac14-f4142165b12d) Stevens, Gareth Publishing LLLP. (Weekly Reader Leveled Readers).

—October / Octubre, 1 vol. 2009. (Months of the Year / Meses Del Ano Ser.). (ENG & SPA.). 24p. (J). (gr. 1-1). pap. 9.15 *(978-1-4339-2115-5(4),* ebd550c8-db50-4860-904d-0cc68e76f449); lib. bdg. 24.67 *(978-1-4339-1938-1(9),* 2ab4377a-6c38-4e37-8f5e-e32c76dcc628) Stevens, Gareth Publishing LLLP. (Weekly Reader Leveled Readers).

—September, 1 vol. 2nd rev. ed. 2009. (Months of the Year (Second Edition) Ser.). (ENG.). 24p. (J). (gr. 1-1). pap. 9.15 *(978-1-4339-2102-5(2),* d2de7b12-af8d-467b-9221-4cebbe7e4231); lib. bdg. 24.67 *(978-1-4339-1925-1(7),* a21f7560-f08c-4bcb-9afb-b6f052b42682) Stevens, Gareth Publishing LLLP. (Weekly Reader Leveled Readers).

—September / Septiembre, 1 vol. 2009. (Months of the Year / Meses Del Ano Ser.). (ENG & SPA.). 24p. (J). (gr. 1-1). pap. 9.15 *(978-1-4339-2114-8(6),* bf5c68c9-e199-447d-814f-8688aa3736eb); lib. bdg. 24.67 *(978-1-4339-1937-4(0),* 148d6df9-3806-4c4a-a8b4-532892d4e712) Stevens, Gareth Publishing LLLP. (Weekly Reader Leveled Readers).

Clark, Claire. How Long Is a Month? 2012. (Calendar Ser.). (ENG.). 24p. (gr. k-1). pap. 41.70 *(978-1-4296-8335-7(X),* Capstone Pr.) Capstone.

Cohn, Scotti. One Wolf Howls, 1 vol. Detwiler, Susan, illus. 2009. (ENG.). 32p. (J). (gr. -1-3). 16.95 *(978-1-934359-92-1(0))* Arbordale Publishing.

Havercroft, Elizabeth. A Year in the World of Dinosaurs. 2008. (Time Goes By Ser.). (ENG.). (gr. k-2). pap. 39.62 *(978-0-7613-4714-9(3))* Lerner Publishing Group.

Hunt, Darleen L. Bob's Busy Year: Months of the Year. Komarck, Michael, illus. 2003. (Sherman's Math Corner Ser.). (J). (gr. -1-3). *(978-1-929591-03-9(9))* Reading Rock, Inc.

Kesselring, Mari. April, 1 vol. Dumm, Brian Caleb, illus. 2009. (Months of the Year Ser.). (ENG.). 24p. (J). (gr. k-2). 31.36 *(978-1-60270-631-6(X),* 11569, Looking Glass Library) Magic Wagon.

—August, 1 vol. Collier-Morales, Roberta, illus. 2009. (Months of the Year Ser.). (ENG.). 24p. (J). (gr. k-2). 31.36 *(978-1-60270-635-4(2),* 11577, Looking Glass Library) Magic Wagon.

—December, 1 vol. Billin-Frye, Paige, illus. 2009. (Months of the Year Ser.). (ENG.). 24p. (J). (gr. k-2). 31.36 *(978-1-60270-639-2(5),* 11585, Looking Glass Library) Magic Wagon.

—February, 1 vol. Billin-Frye, Paige, illus. 2009. (Months of the Year Ser.). (ENG.). 24p. (J). (gr. k-2). 31.36 *(978-1-60270-629-3(8),* 11565, Looking Glass Library) Magic Wagon.

—January, 1 vol. Billin-Frye, Paige, illus. 2009. (Months of the Year Ser.). (ENG.). 24p. (J). (gr. k-2). 31.36 *(978-1-60270-628-6(X),* 11563, Looking Glass Library) Magic Wagon.

—July, 1 vol. Collier-Morales, Roberta, illus. 2009. (Months of the Year Ser.). (ENG.). 24p. (J). (gr. k-2). 31.36 *(978-1-60270-634-7(4),* 11575, Looking Glass Library) Magic Wagon.

—June, 1 vol. Collier-Morales, Roberta, illus. 2009. (Months of the Year Ser.). (ENG.). 24p. (J). (gr. k-2). 31.36 *(978-1-60270-633-0(6),* 11573, Looking Glass Library) Magic Wagon.

—March, 1 vol. Dumm, Brian Caleb, illus. 2009. (Months of the Year Ser.). (ENG.). 24p. (J). (gr. k-2). 31.36 *(978-1-60270-630-9(1),* 11567, Looking Glass Library) Magic Wagon.

—May, 1 vol. Dumm, Brian Caleb, illus. 2009. (Months of the Year Ser.). (ENG.). 24p. (J). (gr. k-2). 31.36 *(978-1-60270-632-3(8),* 11571, Looking Glass Library) Magic Wagon.

—Months of the Year, 12 vols., Set. Incl. April. Dumm, Brian Caleb, illus. 31.36 *(978-1-60270-631-6(X),* 11569); August. Collier-Morales, Roberta, illus. 31.36 *(978-1-60270-635-4(2),* 11577); December. Billin-Frye, Paige, illus. 31.36 *(978-1-60270-639-2(5),* 11585); February. Billin-Frye, Paige, illus. 31.36 *(978-1-60270-629-3(8),* 11565); January. Billin-Frye, Paige, illus. 31.36 *(978-1-60270-628-6(X),* 11563); July. Collier-Morales, Roberta, illus. 31.36 *(978-1-60270-634-7(4),* 11575); June. Collier-Morales, Roberta, illus. 31.36 *(978-1-60270-633-0(6),* 11573); March. Dumm, Brian Caleb, illus. 31.36 *(978-1-60270-630-9(1),* 11567); May. Dumm, Brian Caleb, illus. 31.36 *(978-1-60270-632-3(8),* 11571); November. Rooney, Ronnie, illus. 31.36 *(978-1-60270-638-5(7),* 11583); October. Rooney, Ronnie, illus. 31.36 *(978-1-60270-637-8(9),* 11581); September. Rooney, Ronnie, illus. 31.36 *(978-1-60270-636-1(0),* 11579); (J). (gr. k-2). (Months of the Year Ser.). (ENG.). 24p. 2009. 376.32 *(978-1-60270-627-9(1),* 11561, Looking Glass Library) Magic Wagon.

—November, 1 vol. Rooney, Ronnie, illus. 2009. (Months of the Year Ser.). (ENG.). 24p. (J). (gr. k-2). 31.36 *(978-1-60270-638-5(7),* 11583, Looking Glass Library) Magic Wagon.

—October, 1 vol. Rooney, Ronnie, illus. 2009. (Months of the Year Ser.). (ENG.). 24p. (J). (gr. k-2). 31.36 *(978-1-60270-637-8(9),* 11581, Looking Glass Library) Magic Wagon.

—September, 1 vol. Rooney, Ronnie, illus. 2009. (Months of the Year Ser.). (ENG.). 24p. (J). (gr. k-2). 31.36 *(978-1-60270-636-1(0),* 11579, Looking Glass Library) Magic Wagon.

Mitten, Luana K. Mi Calendario: Los Meses Del Año/My Calendar: Months of the Year. 2008. (SPA & ENG., Illus.). 24p. (J). 22.79 *(978-1-60472-492-9(7))* Rourke Educational Media.

Months of the Year (Second Edition), 24 vols. 2nd rev. ed. 2009. (Months of the Year (Second Edition) Ser.). (ENG.). 24p. (J). (gr. 1-1). lib. bdg. 296.04 *(978-1-4339-1994-7(X),* 16c47412-8451-4c16-9230-325a17422b43, Weekly Reader Leveled Readers) Stevens, Gareth Publishing LLLP.

Months of the Year;Meses del Año, 24 vols. 2nd rev. ed. 2009. (Months of the Year / Meses Del Ano Ser.). (ENG & SPA.). 24p. (J). (gr. 1-1). lib. bdg. 296.04 *(978-1-4339-1995-4(8),* f65e9bfb-74aa-40ad-b1f5-75705b008250, Weekly Reader Leveled Readers) Stevens, Gareth Publishing LLLP.

Morris, Sheila L. Sweet Baby's Fun Months of the Year. 2013. 16p. pap. 9.99 *(978-1-61897-424-2(6),* Strategic Bk. Publishing) Strategic Book Publishing & Rights Agency (SBPRA).

Murray, Julie. April. 2017. (Months Ser.). (ENG., Illus.). 24p. (J). (gr. -1-2). lib. bdg. 31.36 *(978-1-5321-0018-5(3),* 25118, Abdo Kids) ABDO Publishing Co.

—August. 2017. (Months Ser.). (ENG., Illus.). 24p. (J). (gr. -1-2). lib. bdg. 31.36 *(978-1-5321-0022-2(1),* 25126, Abdo Kids) ABDO Publishing Co.

—February. 2017. (Months Ser.). (ENG., Illus.). 24p. (J). (gr. -1-2). lib. bdg. 31.36 *(978-1-5321-0016-1(7),* 25114, Abdo Kids) ABDO Publishing Co.

—January. 2017. (Months Ser.). (ENG., Illus.). 24p. (J). (gr. -1-2). lib. bdg. 31.36 *(978-1-5321-0015-4(9),* 25112, Abdo Kids) ABDO Publishing Co.

—July. 2017. (Months Ser.). (ENG., Illus.). 24p. (J). (gr. -1-2). lib. bdg. 31.36 *(978-1-5321-0021-5(3),* 25124, Abdo Kids) ABDO Publishing Co.

—June. 2017. (Months Ser.). (ENG., Illus.). 24p. (J). (gr. -1-2). lib. bdg. 31.36 *(978-1-5321-0020-8(5),* 25122, Abdo Kids) ABDO Publishing Co.

—March. 2017. (Months Ser.). (ENG., Illus.). 24p. (J). (gr. -1-2). lib. bdg. 31.36 *(978-1-5321-0017-8(5),* 25116, Abdo Kids) ABDO Publishing Co.

—May. 2017. (Months Ser.). (ENG., Illus.). 24p. (J). (gr. -1-2). lib. bdg. 31.36 *(978-1-5321-0019-2(1),* 25120, Abdo Kids) ABDO Publishing Co.

—November. 2017. (Months Ser.). (ENG., Illus.). 24p. (J). (gr. -1-2). lib. bdg. 31.36 *(978-1-5321-0025-3(6),* 25132, Abdo Kids) ABDO Publishing Co.

—October. 2017. (Months Ser.). (ENG., Illus.). 24p. (J). (gr. -1-2). lib. bdg. 31.36 *(978-1-5321-0024-6(8),* 25130, Abdo Kids) ABDO Publishing Co.

—September. 2017. (Months Ser.). (ENG., Illus.). 24p. (J). (gr. -1-2). lib. bdg. 31.36 *(978-1-5321-0023-9(X),* 25128, Abdo Kids) ABDO Publishing Co.

Randolph, Joanne. All about A Months/Los Meses, 1 vol. Brusca, Maria Cristina, tr. 2007. (It's about Time / Los Libros Del Tiempo Ser.). (SPA & ENG., Illus.). 24p. (J). (gr. 1-1). lib. bdg. 26.27 *(978-1-4042-7628-4(9),* 7a299ee6-755c-4d3a-aee7-b3087c44e510) Rosen Publishing Group, Inc., The.

—All about the Months. (It's about Time Ser.). 24p. (gr. 1-1). 2009. 42.50 *(978-1-61513-632-2(0),* PowerKids Pr.) 2007. (ENG., Illus.). (J). lib. bdg. 26.27 *(978-1-4042-3769-8(0),* 88c02ccf-5148-47b3-a3f5-869459c20c06) Rosen Publishing Group, Inc., The.

—All about the Months/Los Meses. 2009. (It's about Time/Los libros del tiempo Ser.). (SPA.). 24p. (gr. 1-1). 42.50 *(978-1-61513-628-5(2),* Editorial Buenas Letras) Rosen Publishing Group, Inc., The.

Wahl, Ellen. Full Moon Lore. Stewart, Ashley, illus. 2017. (ENG.). 32p. (J). (gr. k-3). 16.99 *(978-1-58536-965-2(9),* 204301) Sleeping Bear Pr.

MONTHS—FICTION

Blackstone, Stella. Jump into January. Carluccio, Maria, illus. 2004. (ENG.). 32p. (J). 15.99 *(978-1-84148-629-1(9))* Barefoot Bks., Inc.

—On y Danse les Saisons. Carluccio, Maria, illus. 2016. (FRE.). (J). pap. *(978-1-78285-298-8(0))* Barefoot Bks., Inc.

—Un Recorrido Por Los Estaciones. Carluccio, Maria, illus. 2009. (SPA.). 32p. (J). (gr. -1-2). pap. 9.99 *(978-1-84686-291-5(4))* Barefoot Bks., Inc.

—Skip Through the Seasons. Carluccio, Maria, illus. 32p. (J). 2009. 16.99 *(978-1-84686-293-9(0))* 2006. (ENG.). (gr. -1-k). pap. 9.99 *(978-1-905236-71-8(9))* Barefoot Bks., Inc.

Gravett, Emily. The Rabbit Problem. Gravett, Emily, illus. 2010. (ENG., Illus.). 32p. (J). (gr. -1-3). 24.99 *(978-1-4424-1255-2(0),* Simon & Schuster Bks. For Young Readers) Simon & Schuster Bks. For Young Readers.

Inkpen, Mick. One Year with Kipper. 2015. (ENG., Illus.). 32p. (J). (gr. -1-k). pap. 10.99 *(978-1-4449-1820-5(6))* Hodder & Stoughton GBR. Dist: Hachette Bk. Group.

Martin Jr, Bill. The Turning of the Year. Shed, Greg, illus. 2007. (ENG.). 28p. (J). (gr. -1-3). pap. 7.99 *(978-0-15-204555-5(4),* 1193717, Clarion Bks.) HarperCollins Pubs.

Menge, Dawn & Rhoades, Heath. Queen Vernita Meets Sir HeathyBean the Astronomer. 2010. 33p. (J). pap. 19.95 *(978-1-4327-3120-5(3))* Outskirts Pr., Inc.

Parker, Sandy. What Month Is It? Hofher, Cathy, illus. l.t. ed. 2004. 32p. (J). 15.95 *(978-0-9643462-5-3(7),* Just Think Bks.) Canary Connect Pubns.

Rylant, Cynthia. Long Night Moon. Siegel, Mark, illus. 2004. (ENG.). 32p. (J). (gr. -1-3). 18.99 *(978-0-689-85426-2(9),* Simon & Schuster Bks. For Young Readers) Simon & Schuster Bks. For Young Readers.

Scelsa, Greg. Months of the Year. Faulkner, Stacey, ed. Fulcher, Roz, illus. 2006. (J). pap. 2.99 *(978-1-59198-320-0(7))* Creative Teaching Pr., Inc.

Tudor, Tasha. Around the Year. Tudor, Tasha, illus. 2004. (ENG., Illus.). 64p. (J). (gr. -1-3). 8.99 *(978-0-689-87350-8(6),* Aladdin) Simon & Schuster Children's Publishing.

Walsh, Susanne. My Very Favorite Time of Year: Featuring the Whimsy Kids. 2007. 34p. pap. 24.95 *(978-1-4241-9090-4(8))* America Star Bks.

MONTHS—POETRY

Sendak, Maurice. Chicken Soup with Rice: A Book of Months. Sendak, Maurice, illus. 2018. (ENG., Illus.). 32p. (J). (gr. -1-3). pap. 9.95 *(978-0-06-285440-7(2),* HarperCollins) HarperCollins Pubs.

Weston Woods Staff, creator. Chicken Soup with Rice. 2004. (J). 18.95 *(978-1-55592-801-8(3))* Weston Woods Studios, Inc.

MONTREAL (QUEBEC)

Coster, Patience & Rowe, Percy. Montreal, 1 vol. 2004. (Great Cities of the World Ser.). (ENG., Illus.). 48p. (gr. 5-8). lib. bdg. 33.67 *(978-0-8368-5039-0(4),* 70630cfd-09fc-4cb0-8132-7e425d3abaf6, Gareth Stevens Secondary Library) Stevens, Gareth Publishing LLLP.

MONTREAL (QUEBEC)—FICTION

Bayle, B. J. Perilous Passage. 2007. (ENG.). 184p. (YA). (gr. k-7). pap. 11.99 *(978-1-55002-689-4(5))* Dundurn Pr. CAN. Dist: Publishers Group West (PGW).

Delaney, Rachelle. The Bonaventure Adventures. 2018. (ENG.). 288p. (J). (gr. 3-7). pap. 8.99 *(978-0-14-319851-2(3),* Puffin Canada) PRH Canada Young Readers CAN. Dist: Penguin Random Hse. LLC.

Frechette, Carole. In the Key of Do, 1 vol. Ouriou, Susan, tr. 2003. (ENG.). 96p. (YA). (gr. 6-8). pap. 6.95 *(978-0-88995-254-6(X),* 95682455-5e97-40d2-aefe-80f0fd843f45) Red Deer Pr. CAN. Dist: Firefly Bks., Ltd.

Gamble, Adam. Good Night Montreal. Kelly, Cooper, illus. 2007. (Good Night Our World Ser.). (ENG.). 20p. (J). (gr. k — 1). bds. 9.95 *(978-1-60219-012-2(7))* Good Night Bks.

Goodwin, Catherine. Seeking Shelter. 2006. (ENG., Illus.). 156p. (J). per. *(978-1-55380-033-0(8))* Ronsdale Pr.

Kimmel, Elizabeth Cody. Suddenly Supernatural: Crossing Over. 2011. (Suddenly Supernatural Ser.: 4). (ENG.). 256p. (J). (gr. 3-7). pap. 14.99 *(978-0-316-13345-6(0))* Little, Brown Bks. for Young Readers.

Launier, Veronique. Deliverance. 2014. (Hearts of Stone Ser.: 2). (ENG.). 288p. (YA). pap. 9.99 *(978-0-7387-3075-2(0),* Flux) Llewellyn Pubns.

Polak, Monique. Finding Elmo, 1 vol. 2007. (Orca Currents Ser.). (ENG.). 128p. (J). (gr. 4-7). per. 9.95 *(978-1-55143-686-9(8))* Orca Bk. Pubs. USA.

—Pyro, 1 vol. 2012. (Orca Currents Ser.). (ENG.). 128p. (J). (gr. 4-7). pap. 9.95 *(978-1-4598-0228-5(4))* Orca Bk. Pubs. USA.

Zweig, Eric. Fever Season. 2009. (ENG.). 256p. (YA). (gr. 4-18). pap. 10.99 *(978-1-55488-432-2(2))* Dundurn Pr. CAN. Dist: Publishers Group West (PGW).

MONUMENTS

see also Pyramids

Booker, Dwayne. Looking for Landmarks: Working at the Same Time, 1 vol. 2017. (Computer Kids: Powered by Computational Thinking Ser.). (ENG.). 24p. (J). (gr. 3-4). 25.27 *(978-1-5383-2408-0(3),* 9224c20b-8d4c-4216-a81a-fa3f8aafdf2b, PowerKids Pr.); pap. *(978-1-5081-3771-9(4),* ec341aba-a604-4d92-9c68-9b44ff81a369, Rosen Classroom) Rosen Publishing Group, Inc., The.

Bryant, Tamera. We Remember: State Monuments & Historic Sites. 2004. (ZB Reads Trio Books). (Illus.). iii, 43p. (gr. 3-5). pap., tchr. ed. 4.50 *(978-0-7367-1783-0(8))* Zaner-Bloser, Inc.

Ferry, Joseph. Vietnam Veterans Memorial: Remembering a Generation & a War. Moreno, Barry, ed. 2014. (Patriotic Symbols of America Ser.: 20). 48p. (J). (gr. 4-18). lib. bdg. 20.95 *(978-1-4222-3136-4(4))* Mason Crest.

Galván, Victor. Texas Monuments, 1 vol. 2018. (Explore Texas Ser.). (ENG.). 24p. (gr. 9-12). 26.27 *(978-1-5081-8662-5(6),* bd5da2b8-4942-4542-a8ec-be18004381ff, Rosen Young Adult) Rosen Publishing Group, Inc., The.

Gamble, Adam & Jasper, Mark. Good Night Statue of Liberty. Stevenson, Harvey, illus. 2017. (Good Night Our World Ser.). 20p. (J). (gr. -1 — 1). bds. 9.95 *(978-1-60219-429-8(7))* Good Night Bks.

Gray, Leon. Solving the Mysteries of Stonehenge, 1 vol. 2009. (Digging into History Ser.). (ENG.). 32p. (gr. 3-3). lib. bdg. 32.64 *(978-0-7614-3110-7(1),* b0b5ff60-fdf0-406c-b18c-1b052d14bad4) Cavendish Square Publishing LLC.

Hargrove, Julia. Bostons Trail to Freedom. 2003. (Historic Monuments Ser.). (Illus.). 48p. (J). (gr. 4-8). pap. 6.95 *(978-1-57310-403-6(5))* Teaching & Learning Co.

Hoobler, Dorothy & Hoobler, Thomas. Where Is the Taj Mahal? 2017. (Where Is... ? Ser.). lib. bdg. 16.00 *(978-0-606-39777-3(9))* Turtleback.

Jango-Cohen, Judith. Mount Rushmore. 2010. pap. 45.32 *(978-0-7613-6990-5(2))* Lerner Publishing Group.

Keenan, Sheila. O, Say Can You See? America's Symbols, Landmarks, & Important Words. Boyajian, Ann, illus. 2007. (ENG.). 64p. (J). (gr. -1-3). pap. 7.99 *(978-0-439-59360-1(3),* Scholastic Nonfiction) Scholastic, Inc.

Kelley, True. Where Is Stonehenge? Hinderliter, John & Groff, David, illus. 2016. (Where Is... ? Ser.). (ENG.). 112p. (J). (gr. 3-7). 16.00 *(978-0-606-39317-1(X))* Turtleback.

McNeilly, Linden. Historic Monuments. 2017. (State Guides). (ENG.). 48p. (gr. 4-8). 35.64 *(978-1-68342-402-4(6),* 9781683424024) Rourke Educational Media.

Moore Niver, Heather. 20 Fun Facts about U. S. Monuments, 1 vol. 2013. (Fun Fact File: U. S. History! Ser.). (ENG.). 32p.

(J). (gr. 2-3). 27.93 (978-1-4339-9208-7(6), 71db2ea8-b877-4214-9110-e6c2fba6afe7); pap. 11.50 (978-1-4339-9209-4(4), c4e7a34e-cdb1-47d4-b488-988da7e97ce6) Stevens, Gareth Publishing LLLP.

Moriarty, Siobhan. Visit the Statue of Liberty, 1 vol. 2012. (Landmarks of Liberty Ser.). (ENG., Illus.). 24p. (J). (gr. 2-3). pap. 9.15 (978-1-4339-6402-2(3), 7d937197-1526-4045-8011-fa2ca79ec733, Gareth Stevens Learning Library); lib. bdg. 25.27 (978-1-4339-6400-8(7), 1f1d79cd-bcdd-49f0-afc6-fb3962804988) Stevens, Gareth Publishing LLLP.

National Geographic Learning. World Windows 3 (Social Studies): Famous Landmarks: Content Literacy, Nonfiction Reading, Language & Literacy. 2011. (World Windows Ser.). (ENG.). 16p. stu. ed. 10.95 (978-1-133-56616-8(2)) Cengage Heinle.

Niver, Heather Moore. 20 Fun Facts about US Monuments. 2013. (Fun Fact File: US History! Ser.). 32p. (J). (gr. 3-6). pap. 63.00 (978-1-4339-9210-0(8)) Stevens, Gareth Publishing LLLP.

O'connor, Jim. Where Is the Colosseum? 2017. (Where Is... ? Ser.). lib. bdg. 16.00 (978-0-606-39776-6(0)) Turtleback.

O'Donnell, Kerri. The Great Wall of China. 2009. (Reading Room Collection 2 Ser.). 24p. (gr. 3-4). 42.50 (978-1-60851-994-1(5), PowerKids Pr.) Rosen Publishing Group, Inc., The.

Owings, Lisa. Stonehenge. 2015. (Unexplained Mysteries Ser.). (ENG., Illus.). 24p. (J). (gr. 3-7). lib. bdg. 26.95 (978-1-62617-204-3(8), Epic Bks.) Bellwether Media.

Peterson, Megan Cooley. Stonehenge: Who Built This Stone Formation? 2018. (History's Mysteries Ser.). (ENG.). 32p. (J). (gr. 4-6). pap. 9.99 (978-1-64466-259-5(0), 12289); (Illus.). lib. bdg. (978-1-68072-412-7(6), 12288) Black Rabbit Bks. (Bolt).

Phillips, Cynthia & Priwer, Shana. Ancient Monuments. 2009. (ENG., Illus.). 115p. (C). (gr. 6-18). lib. bdg. 180.00 (978-0-7656-8123-2(4), Y181320) Routledge.

Prior, Jennifer. Engineering Marvels: Landmarks Around the World: Addition & Subtraction (Grade 2) 2018. (Mathematics in the Real World Ser.). (ENG., Illus.). 32p. (J). (gr. 2-3). pap. 10.99 (978-1-4258-5749-3(3)) Teacher Created Materials, Inc.

Prior, Jennifer Overend. America's Man-Made Landmarks. rev. ed. 2014. (Social Studies: Informational Text Ser.). (ENG., Illus.). 32p. (gr. 2-4). pap. 11.99 (978-1-4333-7370-1(X)) Teacher Created Materials, Inc.

—Monumentos Del Mundo: Suma y Resta. rev. ed. 2018. (Mathematics in the Real World Ser.). (SPA., Illus.). 32p. (J). (gr. 2-3). pap. 10.99 (978-1-4258-2866-0(3)) Teacher Created Materials, Inc.

Putnam, Jeff. National Monuments: Events & Times. 2004. (ZB Reads Trio Books). (Illus.). iii, 75p. (gr. 4-6). pap. 5.00 (978-0-7367-1787-8(0)) Zaner-Bloser, Inc.

—National Monuments: Nature. 2004. (ZB Reads Trio Books). (Illus.). iii, 92p. (gr. 4-6). pap. 5.00 (978-0-7367-1788-5(9)) Zaner-Bloser, Inc.

Ridley, Sarah. Remembering the Fallen of the First World War. 2019. (ENG., Illus.). 48p. (J). (gr. 6-12). pap. 10.99 (978-1-4451-4834-2(X), Franklin Watts) Hachette Children's Group GBR. Dist: Hachette Bk. Group.

Riggs, Kate. Stonehenge. 2009. (Places of Old Ser.). 24p. (J). (gr. 1-5). lib. bdg. 24.25 (978-1-58341-711-9(7), Creative Education) Creative Co., The.

—Taj Mahal. 2009. (Places of Old Ser.). 24p. (J). (gr. 1-5). lib. bdg. 24.25 (978-1-58341-712-6(5), Creative Education) Creative Co., The.

Schwartz, Heather E. & Salzano, Tammi. Around the World: An Amazing World. 2009. (Illus.). 48p. (J). pap. (978-0-545-17229-5(2)) Scholastic, Inc.

Scott, Dan. Big Buildings of the Ancient World. 2015. (Inside Eye Ser.). (Illus.). 32p. (gr. 3-6). 31.35 (978-1-906370-75-6(3)) Book Hse. GBR. Dist: Black Rabbit Bks.

Silate, Jennifer. The Statue of Liberty. (Primary Sources of American Symbols Ser.). 24p. (gr. 3-3). 2009. 42.50 (978-1-60851-510-3(9), PowerKids Pr.) 2006. (ENG., Illus.). (J). lib. bdg. 26.27 (978-1-4042-2696-8(6), 021195ea-ca45-478d-8e1d-a934079862f0) Rosen Publishing Group, Inc., The.

World Book, Inc. Staff, contrib. by. The Mysteries of Stonehenge. 2014. (J). (978-0-7166-2667-1(5)) World Bk., Inc.

Yasuda, Anita. The 12 Most Amazing American Monuments & Symbols. 2015. (Amazing America Ser.). (ENG., Illus.). 32p. (J). (gr. 3-6). 32.80 (978-1-63235-009-1(2), 11548, 12-Story Library) Bookstaves, LLC.

MONUMENTS, NATURAL

see Natural Monuments

MONUMENTS—UNITED STATES

Ashley, Susan. Mount Rushmore, 1 vol. 2004. (Places in American History Ser.). (ENG., Illus.). 24p. (gr. 2-4). pap. 9.15 (978-0-8368-4149-7(2), 55d1b36c-93a5-4fd0-b7d7-03c3cb2fe286); lib. bdg. 24.67 (978-0-8368-4142-8(5), 9854fe32-021b-4357-99c8-c9e528fba86e) Stevens, Gareth Publishing LLLP. (Weekly Reader Leveled Readers).

—The Washington Monument, 1 vol. 2004. (Places in American History Ser.). (ENG., Illus.). 24p. (gr. 2-4). pap. 9.15 (978-0-8368-4151-0(4), 547d763f-7d2b-4752-aecd-39c122e10340); lib. bdg. 24.67 (978-0-8368-4144-2(1), 186daaba-3f29-4939-9870-8d97bbb8d4dc) Stevens, Gareth Publishing LLLP. (Weekly Reader Leveled Readers).

Britton, Tamara L. Devil's Tower. 2005. (Symbols, Landmarks, & Monuments Set 3 Ser.). (Illus.). 32p. (gr. k-6). 27.07 (978-1-59197-833-6(5), Checkerboard Library) ABDO Publishing Co.

Byrd, Robert. Liberty Arrives! How America's Grandest Statue Found Her Home. Byrd, Robert, illus. 2019. (Illus.). 40p. (J). (gr. 1-4). 17.99 (978-0-7352-3082-8(X), Dial Bks) Penguin Young Readers Group.

Cain, Marie Mowery. Monumental America. 2013. (Big Books, Red Ser.). (ENG & SPA., Illus.). 16p. pap. 33.00 (978-1-59246-224-7(3)) Big Books, by George!

Dickerson, Joy E. Pack & Go. 2004. (ZB Reads Trio Books). (Illus.). iii, 75p. (gr. 3-5). pap. 5.00 (978-0-7367-1785-4(4)) Zaner-Bloser, Inc.

Eggers, Dave. Her Right Foot (American History Books for Kids, American History for Kids) 2017. (ENG., Illus.). 104p. (J). (gr. k-3). 19.99 (978-1-4521-6281-2(6)) Chronicle Bks. LLC.

Ferry, Joseph. The Jefferson Memorial. 2004. (American Symbols & Their Meanings Ser.). (Illus.). 48p. (J). (gr. 4-18). lib. bdg. 19.95 (978-1-59084-034-4(8)) Mason Crest.

—Jefferson Memorial: A Monument to Greatness. Moreno, Barry, ed. 2014. (Patriotic Symbols of America Ser.: 20). 48p. (J). (gr. 4-18). lib. bdg. 20.95 (978-1-4222-3125-8(9)) Mason Crest.

—The Vietnam Veterans Memorial. 2004. (American Symbols & Their Meanings Ser.). (Illus.). 48p. (J). (gr. 4-18). lib. bdg. 19.95 (978-1-59084-039-9(9)) Mason Crest.

Foran, Jill. Statues & Monuments. 2004. (American Symbols Ser.). (Illus.). 24p. (J). (gr. 4-7). per. 8.95 (978-1-59036-178-8(4)) Weigl Pubs., Inc.

Gunderson, Jessica & Murray, Robb. Monumental History, 1 vol. 2014. (Monumental History Ser.). (ENG.). 32p. (J). (gr. 3-6). 119.96 (978-1-4914-0207-8(5), 21376, Capstone Pr.) Capstone.

Healy, Nick. The Statue of Liberty. 2003. (J). pap. (978-1-58417-117-1(0)); lib. bdg. (978-1-58417-054-9(9)) Lake Street Pubs.

Jango-Cohen, Judith. Mount Rushmore. 2003. (Pull Ahead Books — American Symbols Ser.). (ENG., Illus.). 32p. (J). (gr. k-3). pap. 7.99 (978-0-8225-3755-7(9), 06363896-3e29-4b53-b7be-6b9f9152da33, First Avenue Editions) Lerner Publishing Group.

Kasson, Joseph E. The Making of the Star of Texas. 2003. (Illus.). 32p. (J). lib. bdg. 14.95 (978-0-9729435-8-1(7)) Kasson Publishing.

Kissock, Heather. Lincoln Memorial. 2017. (Illus.). 24p. (J). (978-1-5105-0602-2(0)) SmartBook Media, Inc.

Lavelett, Lucille. Through the Years at Monument, Colorado, 1 Vol. 5th ed. 2004. (Illus.). 168p. (YA). per. (978-0-9755989-0-0(2)) Palmer Lake Historical Society.

Lindeen, Mary. History Rocks!, 1 vol. (Wonder Readers: Social Studies). (ENG.). (gr. -1-2). 2012. 20p. (J). lib. bdg. 25.32 (978-1-4296-9614-2(1), 120530) 2011. 16p. (J). pap. 6.25 (978-1-4296-7927-5(1), 118259) 2011. 16p. pap. 35.94 (978-1-4296-8262-6(0)) Capstone. (Capstone Pr.).

Marcovitz, Hal. Liberty Bell: Let Freedom Ring. 2015. (Illus.). 48p. (J). (978-1-4222-3117-3(8)) Mason Crest.

Mattern, Joanne. Martin Luther King, Jr. National Memorial: A Stone of Hope. 2017. (Core Content Social Studies — Let's Celebrate America Ser.). (ENG., Illus.). 32p. (J). (gr. 2-5). pap. 8.99 (978-1-63440-237-8(5), 0cb298c1-d6e0-443a-a3c8-833b15dd797f); lib. bdg. 26.65 (978-1-63440-227-9(8), e01c5cb3-4ce1-4148-88fa-1ab88866015b) Red Chair Pr.

Mayfield, Marilee Joy. My First Book of United States Monuments & Parks. 2017. (Illus.). 51p. (J). (978-1-4351-6637-0(X)) Barnes & Noble, Inc.

Nelson, Kristin L. The Lincoln Memorial. 2003. (Pull Ahead Books — American Symbols Ser.). (ENG., Illus.). 32p. (J). (gr. k-3). pap. 7.99 (978-0-8225-3761-8(3), 384a595f-45c2-4185-bd52-7127ca59c4d5, First Avenue Editions) Lerner Publishing Group.

—The Washington Monument. (Lightning Bolt Bks.). (Illus.). 32p. (J). (gr. k-2). 2010. lib. bdg. 25.26 (978-0-7613-6019-3(0), Lerner Pubns.) 2003. (ENG., pap. 7.99 (978-0-8225-3759-5(1), 4a0d1f3a-9731-4c87-b938-ac6605d7826f, First Avenue Editions) Lerner Publishing Group.

Reed, Ellis M. The National September 11 Memorial. 2018. (US Symbols Ser.). (ENG., Illus.). 24p. (J). (gr. 1-1). pap. 8.95 (978-1-63517-835-7(5), 1635178355) North Star Editions.

—The National September 11 Memorial. 2018. (US Symbols Ser.). (ENG., Illus.). 24p. (J). (gr. k-3). lib. bdg. 31.36 (978-1-5321-6047-9(X), 28726, Pop! Cody Koala) Pop!

RJF Publishing Staff & Hankins, Chelsey. The Gateway Arch. 2009. (Symbols of American Freedom Ser.). 48p. (gr. 4-6). 30.00 (978-1-60413-513-8(1), Chelsea Clubhse.) Infobase Holdings, Inc.

Rowell, Rebecca. The 12 Most Amazing American Natural Wonders. 2015. (Amazing America Ser.). (ENG.). 32p. (J). (gr. 3-6). 32.80 (978-1-63235-011-4(4), 11550, 12-Story Library) Bookstaves, LLC.

Stein, R. Conrad. The Oklahoma City National Memorial. 2003. (Cornerstones of Freedom Ser.). (ENG., Illus.). 48p. (YA). (gr. 4-7). 26.00 (978-0-516-24205-7(9)) Scholastic Library Publishing.

Trumbauer, Lisa. Set in Stone. 2005. (Yellow Umbrella Fluent Level Ser.). (ENG.). 16p. (gr. k-1). pap. 35.70 (978-0-7368-5308-8(1), Capstone Pr.) Capstone.

Wachtel, Roger. Cornerstones of Freedom: the Tomb of the Unknown Soldier. 2003. (Cornerstones of Freedom Ser.). (ENG., Illus.). 48p. (YA). (gr. 4-7). 26.00 (978-0-516-24215-6(6)) Scholastic Library Publishing.

Yasuda, Anita. The 12 Most Amazing American Monuments & Symbols. 2015. (Amazing America Ser.). (ENG., Illus.). 32p. (J). (gr. 3-6). pap. 9.95 (978-1-63235-069-5(6), 11554, 12-Story Library) Bookstaves, LLC.

MOODY, JUDY (FICTITIOUS CHARACTER)—FICTION

Jones, Lucinda. Moody: What Moody Likes to Do. 2010. 28p. pap. 15.99 (978-1-4535-3794-7(5)) Xlibris Corp.

Mcdonald, Megan. Around the World in 8 1/2 Days. 2007. (Judy Moody Ser.: 7). (SPA.). (J). 1.25 (978-1-4281-3376-1(3)) Recorded Bks., Inc.

—Jessica Finch in Pig Trouble. 2014. (Judy Moody & Friends Ser.: 1). (Illus.). 60p. (J). lib. bdg. 14.75 (978-0-606-35162-1(0)) Turtleback.

McDonald, Megan. Judy Moody. Reynolds, Peter H., illus. (Judy Moody Ser.: 1). (ENG.). (J). (gr. 1-4). 2018. 176p. pap. 5.99 (978-1-5362-0071-3(9)) 2010. 160p. 16.99 (978-0-7636-4850-3(7)) Candlewick Pr.

Mcdonald, Megan. Judy Moody. 2010. (Judy Moody Ser.: 1). lib. bdg. 16.00 (978-0-606-12330-3(X)) Turtleback.

McDonald, Megan. Judy Moody & Friends: Jessica Finch in Pig Trouble. Madrid, Erwin, illus. 2014. (Judy Moody & Friends Ser.: 1). (ENG.). 64p. (J). (gr. -1-1). pap. 5.99 (978-0-7636-7027-6(8)) Candlewick Pr.

—Judy Moody & Friends: Judy Moody, Tooth Fairy. Madrid, Erwin, illus. 2017. (Judy Moody & Friends Ser.: 9). (ENG.). 64p. (J). (gr. -1-1). pap. 5.99 (978-0-7636-9168-4(2)) Candlewick Pr.

—Judy Moody & Friends: One, Two, Three, ROAR! Books 1-3. Madrid, Erwin, illus. 2017. (Judy Moody & Friends Ser.). (ENG.). 200p. (J). (gr. -1-1). pap. 8.99 (978-0-7636-9576-7(9)) Candlewick Pr.

—Judy Moody & Friends: Stink Moody in Master of Disaster. Madrid, Erwin, illus. 2015. (Judy Moody & Friends Ser.: 5). (ENG.). 64p. (J). (gr. -1-1). 12.99 (978-0-7636-7218-8(1)) Candlewick Pr.

—Judy Moody & Stink: the Big Bad Blackout. Reynolds, Peter H., illus. 2015. (Judy Moody & Stink Ser.: 3). (ENG.). 144p. (J). (gr. 1-4). pap. 7.99 (978-0-7636-7665-0(9)) Candlewick Pr.

—Judy Moody & Stink: the Wishbone Wish. Reynolds, Peter H., illus. 2015. (Judy Moody & Stink Ser.: 4). (ENG.). 128p. (J). (gr. 1-4). 14.99 (978-0-7636-7206-5(8)) Candlewick Pr.

—Judy Moody & the Bucket List. Reynolds, Peter H., illus. 2018. (Judy Moody Ser.: 13). (ENG.). 176p. (J). (gr. 1-4). pap. 5.99 (978-1-5362-0082-9(4)) Candlewick Pr.

—Judy Moody & the NOT Bummer Summer. Reynolds, Peter H., illus. 2018. (Judy Moody Ser.: 10). (ENG.). 208p. (J). (gr. 1-4). pap. 5.99 (978-1-5362-0084-3(0)) Candlewick Pr.

Mcdonald, Megan. Judy Moody & the Not Bummer Summer. (Judy Moody Ser.: 10). 2018. lib. bdg. 16.00 (978-0-606-41200-1(X)) 2012. lib. bdg. 16.00 (978-0-606-23800-7(X)) Turtleback.

McDonald, Megan. Judy Moody: Around the World in 8 1/2 Days. Reynolds, Peter H., illus. (Judy Moody Ser.: 7). (ENG.). 176p. (J). (gr. 1-4). 2018. pap. 5.99 (978-1-5362-0077-5(8)) 2010. 15.99 (978-0-7636-4864-0(7)) Candlewick Pr.

—Judy Moody Declares Independence. Reynolds, Peter H., illus. 2018. (Judy Moody Ser.: 6). (ENG.). 160p. (J). (gr. 1-4). pap. 5.99 (978-1-5362-0076-8(X)) Candlewick Pr.

—Judy Moody Gets Famous! Reynolds, Peter H., illus. 2018. (Judy Moody Ser.: 2). (ENG.). 144p. (J). (gr. 1-4). pap. 5.99 (978-1-5362-0073-7(5)) Candlewick Pr.

—Judy Moody, Girl Detective. Reynolds, Peter H., illus. 2018. (Judy Moody Ser.: 9). (ENG.). 192p. (J). (gr. 1-4). pap. 5.99 (978-1-5362-0079-9(4)) Candlewick Pr.

Mcdonald, Megan. Judy Moody, Girl Detective. 2018. (Judy Moody Ser.: 9). lib. bdg. 16.00 (978-0-606-41199-8(2)) Turtleback.

—Judy Moody Goes to College. 2018. (Judy Moody Ser.: 8). lib. bdg. 16.00 (978-0-606-41198-1(4)) Turtleback.

McDonald, Megan. Judy Moody, M. D. The Doctor Is In! Reynolds, Peter H., illus. 2018. (Judy Moody Ser.: 5). (ENG.). 176p. (J). (gr. 1-4). pap. 5.99 (978-1-5362-0074-4(3)) Candlewick Pr.

Mcdonald, Megan. Judy Moody, M. D. The Doctor Is In! 2018. (Judy Moody Ser.: 5). lib. bdg. 16.00 (978-0-606-41195-0(X)) Turtleback.

—Judy Moody, Mood Martian. Reynolds, Peter H., illus. 2014. (Judy Moody Ser.: 12). 208p. (J). (gr. 1-4). 15.99 (978-0-7636-6698-9(X)) Candlewick Pr.

—Judy Moody, Mood Martian. 2018. (Judy Moody Ser.: 12). lib. bdg. 16.00 (978-0-606-41202-5(6)) Turtleback.

McDonald, Megan. The Judy Moody Most Mood-Tastic Collection Ever: Books 1-12, 12 vols. Reynolds, Peter H., illus. 2018. (Judy Moody Ser.). (ENG.). 2080p. (J). (gr. 1-4). pap. 71.88 (978-1-5362-0359-2(9)) Candlewick Pr.

—Judy Moody Predicts the Future. Reynolds, Peter H., illus. 2018. (Judy Moody Ser.: 4). (ENG.). 160p. (J). (gr. 1-4). pap. 5.99 (978-1-5362-0075-1(1)) Candlewick Pr.

—Judy Moody Saves the World! Reynolds, Peter H., illus. (Judy Moody Ser.: 3). (ENG.). 160p. (J). (gr. 1-4). 2018. pap. 5.99 (978-1-5362-0072-0(7)) 2010. 16.99 (978-0-7636-4860-2(4)) Candlewick Pr.

Mcdonald, Megan. Judy Moody Saves the World! 2010. (Judy Moody Ser.: 3). 144p. lib. bdg. 16.00 (978-0-606-12340-2(7)) Turtleback.

—Judy Moody Was in a Mood. 2018. (Judy Moody Ser.: 1). lib. bdg. 16.00 (978-0-606-41191-2(7)) Turtleback.

—Rocky Zang in the Amazing Mr. Magic. 2014. (Judy Moody & Friends Ser.: 2). lib. bdg. 14.75 (978-0-606-35163-8(9)) Turtleback.

—The Wishbone Wish. Reynolds, Peter H., illus. 2016. (Judy Moody & Stink Ser.: 4). (ENG.). 116p. (J). (gr. 1-4). lib. bdg. 18.40 (978-0-606-39093-4(6)) Turtleback.

Mcdonald, Megan & Michalak, Jamie. Judy Moody & the Poop Picnic (Judy Moody Movie Tie-In) Reynolds, Peter H. & Candlewick Press Staff, illus. 2011. (Judy Moody Ser.). (ENG.). 48p. (J). (gr. k-3). pap. 3.99 (978-0-7636-5553-2(8)) Candlewick Pr.

Mcdonald, Megan & Reynolds, Peter H. Judy Moody & Stink: The Wishbone Wish. 2015. (Illus.). 128p. (J). pap. (978-1-4063-6659-4(5)) Candlewick Pr.

Michalak, Jamie. Judy Moody & the Thrill Points Race (Judy Moody Movie Tie-In) Candlewick Press, illus. 2011. (Judy Moody Ser.). (ENG.). 48p. (J). (gr. k-3). pap. 3.99 (978-0-7636-5552-5(X)) Candlewick Pr.

MOON, LOTTIE, 1840-1912

Meloche, Renee. Heroes for Young Readers - Lottie Moon: A Generous Offering. Pollard, Bryan, illus. 2004. (Heroes for Young Readers Ser.). (ENG.). 32p. (J). 8.99 (978-1-57658-243-5(4)) YWAM Publishing.

Vogel, Cara Lynn. The Lottie & Annie Upside-down Book. Adkins, Loretta B., illus. 2003. 16p. (J). 8.99 (978-1-56309-627-3(7)) Woman's Missionary Union.

MOON, MOLLY (FICTITIOUS CHARACTER)—FICTION

Byng, Georgia. Molly Moon Detiene el Mundo. 2004. (SPA.). 358p. (gr. 5-8). 18.99 (978-84-348-9610-9(9)) SM Ediciones ESP. Dist: Lectorum Pubns., Inc.

—Molly Moon, Micky Minus, & the Mind Machine. (Molly Moon Ser.). (ENG.). (J). (gr. 3-7). 2007. 384p. 16.99 (978-0-06-075036-7(7))4. 2008. 416p. pap. 7.99 (978-0-06-075038-1(3), HarperCollins) HarperCollins Pubs.

—Molly Moon Stops the World. (Illus.). (J). 2004. 384p. 16.99 (978-0-06-051410-5(8)) 2005. (Molly Moon Ser.: 2). (ENG., 416p. (gr. 3-7). reprint ed. pap. 7.99 (978-0-06-051415-0(9), HarperCollins) HarperCollins Pubs.

—Molly Moon Viaja a Traes del Tiempo. Crispin, Maria Dolores, tr. 2005. (SPA.). 350p. (978-84-675-0570-2(2)) SM Ediciones.

—Molly Moon y el Increible Libro. 2003. (SPA.). 349p. (J). 18.99 (978-84-348-9076-3(3)) SM Ediciones ESP. Dist: Lectorum Pubns., Inc.

—Molly Moon's Hypnotic Time Travel Adventure. (ENG.). 400p. (J). 2006. (Molly Moon Ser.: 3). (gr. 3-7). pap. 8.99 (978-0-06-075034-3(0), HarperCollins) 2005. (Illus.). 16.99 (978-0-06-075032-9(4)) HarperCollins Pubs.

—Molly Moon's Hypnotic Time-Travel Adventure. 2005. (Illus.). 400p. (J). lib. bdg. 18.89 (978-0-06-075033-6(2)) HarperCollins Pubs.

—Molly Moon's Incredible Book of Hypnotism. 2003. 135.92 (978-0-06-057217-4(5)) 2003. (Molly Moon Ser.: 1). (ENG., Illus.). 384p. (J). (gr. 3-7). 17.99 (978-0-06-051406-8(X), HarperCollins) 2004. (Molly Moon Ser.: 1). (ENG., Illus.). 384p. (J). (gr. 3-7). reprint ed. pap. 7.99 (978-0-06-051409-9(4), HarperCollins) HarperCollins Pubs.

MOON

see also Tides

Adams, Alison. Our Moon. 2011. (Early Connections Ser.). (J). (978-1-61672-531-0(1)) Benchmark Education Co.

Adamson, Thomas K. The Moon [Scholastic]. 2011. (Exploring the Galaxy Ser.). 24p. pap. 0.50 (978-1-4296-6289-5(1), Capstone Pr.) Capstone.

Aguilar, David A. Luna: The Science & Stories of Our Moon. 2019. (Illus.). 64p. (J). (gr. 5-9). 17.99 (978-1-4263-3322-4(6)); (ENG., lib. bdg. 27.90 (978-1-4263-3323-1(4)) Disney Publishing Worldwide. (National Geographic Kids).

Alexander, richard. Exploring the Moon. 2017. (Journey Through Our Solar System Ser.). 24p. (gr. 1-2). 49.50 (978-1-5345-2249-7(2), KidHaven Publishing); (ENG.). pap. 9.25 (978-1-5345-2293-0(X), 38c5d3b3-9e77-4c8e-9c83-36ea608f4448); (ENG.). lib. bdg. 26.23 (978-1-5345-2277-0(8), 062af313-e9bd-4fc4-a8ad-094563340e43) Greenhaven Publishing LLC.

Allyn, Daisy. The Moon, 1 vol. 2010. (Our Solar System Ser.). (ENG.). 24p. (J). (gr. k-2). pap. 9.15 (978-1-4339-3831-3(6), 8779b81c-28a6-46cd-a80f-1cd4132a8acd); (Illus.). lib. bdg. 25.27 (978-1-4339-3830-6(8), f5c31915-1741-44f2-9e26-9959373caa13) Stevens, Gareth Publishing LLLP.

Anderson, Michael. Earth & Its Moon, 1 vol. 2011. (Solar System Ser.). (ENG.). 96p. (gr. 8-8). lib. bdg. 35.29 (978-1-61530-515-5(7), 51508e2f-511d-477c-9ee1-78f1c44da8c5) Rosen Publishing Group, Inc., The.

Applesauce, Press. Discovering Planets & Moons: The Ultimate Guide to the Most Fascinating Features of Our Solar System (Features Glow in Dark Book Cov. 2018. (Discovering Ser.). (ENG., Illus.). 96p. (J). 19.95 (978-1-60433-800-3(8), Applesauce Pr.) Cider Mill Pr. Bk. Pubs., LLC.

Ashby, Ruth. The Earth & Its Moon. 2003. (New Solar System Ser.). (J). lib. bdg. 28.50 (978-1-58340-287-0(X)) Black Rabbit Bks.

Aspen-Baxter, Linda. La Luna, with Code. 2012. (Mirando Al Cielo Ser.). (SPA., Illus.). 24p. (J). (gr. k-2). lib. bdg. 27.13 (978-1-61913-214-6(1), AV2 by Weigl) Weigl Pubs., Inc.

Beaton, Kathryn. The Moon Changes Shape. 2015. (Tell Me Why Library). (ENG., Illus.). 24p. (gr. 2-5). 29.21 (978-1-63362-000-1(X), 205912) Cherry Lake Publishing.

Beaver, Simon. A Light in the Night: the Moon Beginning Book with Online Access, 1 vol. 2014. (ENG., Illus.). 24p. (J). pap., E-Book, E-Book 9.50 (978-1-107-64756-5(8)) Cambridge Univ. Pr.

Bowman, Donna H. What Is the Moon Made Of? And Other Questions Kids Have about Space, 1 vol. Lubach, Peter, illus. 2010. (Kids' Questions Ser.). (ENG.). 24p. (J). (gr. k-2). pap. 7.49 (978-1-4048-6726-0(0), 115554, Picture Window Bks.) Capstone.

Branley, Franklyn M. The Moon Seems to Change. Emberley, Barbara & Ed, illus. 2015. (Let's-Read-And-Find-Out Science 2 Ser.). (ENG.). 32p. (J). (gr. -1-3). pap. 6.99 (978-0-06-238206-1(3), HarperCollins) HarperCollins Pubs.

Brinkman, Patricia. Discover the Moon. 2006. (J). pap. (978-1-4108-6478-9(2)) Benchmark Education Co.

—The Moon. 2006. (J). pap. (978-1-4108-6475-8(8)) Benchmark Education Co.

Buckley, James. The Moon. 2016. (Smithsonian Ser.). (ENG., Illus.). 48p. (J). (gr. 3-4). pap. 5.99 (978-0-448-49020-5(X), Penguin Young Readers) Penguin Young Readers Group.

Cain, Marie Mowery. A Trip to the Moon. 2013. (Big Books, Red Ser.). (ENG & SPA., Illus.). 16p. pap. 33.00 (978-1-59246-211-7(1)) Big Books, by George!

Carlin, Lydia. The Moon. 2007. (Illus.). 16p. (J). 3.95 (978-0-545-00732-0(1)) Scholastic, Inc.

Carroll, Jillian. Zoom Around a Moon. 2003. (J). pap. (978-1-58417-241-3(X)); lib. bdg. (978-1-58417-240-6(1)) Lake Street Pubs.

Carson, Mary Kay. Far-Out Guide to the Moon, 1 vol. 2010. (Far-Out Guide to the Solar System Ser.). (ENG., Illus.). 48p. (J). (gr. 4-6). 27.93 (978-0-7660-3189-0(6), 826e8346-b03a-4610-8f7d-5061c75e655c); pap. 11.53 (978-1-59845-184-9(7), f8c0fc43-18f4-42c5-822b-3c4cfab1bf73, Enslow Elementary) Enslow Publishing, LLC.

Crabtree Editors & Miller, Reagan. The Moon. 2012. (Journey Through Space Ser.). (ENG.). 24p. (J). (gr. 3-6). lib. bdg. (978-0-7787-5306-3(9)) Crabtree Publishing Co.

Crelin, Bob. Faces of the Moon. Evans, Leslie, illus. 2009. 36p. (J). (gr. 1-4). 16.95 (978-1-57091-785-1(X)) Charlesbridge Publishing, Inc.

Dale, Jay. To the Moon. Dybing, Michelle, illus. 2012. (Wonder Words Ser.). (ENG.). 16p. (J). (gr. k-2). pap. 36.94 (978-1-4296-8905-2(6), 18348, Capstone Pr.) Capstone.

Dale, Jay & Scott, Kay. To the Moon, 1 vol. Dybing, Michelle, illus. 2012. (Wonder Words Ser.). (ENG.). 16p. (J). (gr. k-2). pap. 6.99 (978-1-4296-8904-5(8), 119955, Capstone Pr.) Capstone.

DeCristofano, Carolyn Cinami. The Sun & the Moon. Morley, Taia, illus. 2016. (Let's-Read-And-Find-Out Science 1 Ser.). (ENG.). 40p. (J). (gr. -1-3). pap. 7.99 (978-0-06-233803-7(X), HarperCollins) HarperCollins Pubs.

deMarin, Layne. The Moon Book, 1 vol. 2011. (Wonder Readers Fluent Level Ser.). (ENG.). 16p. (gr. -1-2). (J). pap.

6.25 *(978-1-4296-7942-8(5)*, 118274); pap. 35.94 *(978-1-4296-8169-8(1))* Capstone. (Capstone Pr.).
Di Piazza, Domenica. Space Engineer & Scientist Margaret Hamilton. 2017. (STEM Trailblazer Bios Ser.). (ENG., Illus.). 32p. (J). (gr. 2-5). 26.65 *(978-1-5124-3450-7(7)*, 00361086-11f1-4e7d-80a7-8140621d385a, Lerner Pubns.) Lerner Publishing Group.
Dickmann, Nancy. Exploring Planet Earth & the Moon, 1 vol. 2015. (Spectacular Space Science Ser.). (ENG., Illus.). 48p. (J). (gr. 5-6). 33.47 *(978-1-4994-3625-9(4)*, 4fcedff1-c3c5-4408-bb4a-188aba9702fd, Rosen Central) Rosen Publishing Group, Inc., The.
—The Moon, 1 vol. 2018. (Space Facts & Figures Ser.). (ENG.). 32p. (gr. 2-3). 28.93 *(978-1-5081-9663-1(X)*, 61ce2a01-cb7b-4c9e-9277-92cf68c230c9, Windmill Bks.) Rosen Publishing Group, Inc., The.
Dils, Tracey E. Around the Moon 1,2,3: A Space Counting Book. 2015. (1, 2, 3... Count with Me Ser.). (ENG., Illus.). 24p. (J). (gr. k-2). 19.95 *(978-1-60753-714-4(1))* Amicus Learning.
Doudna, Kelly. The Moon. 2016. (Exploring Our Universe Ser.). (ENG., Illus.). 32p. (J). (gr. 3-6). lib. bdg. 32.79 *(978-1-68078-405-3(6)*, 23669, Checkerboard Library) ABDO Publishing Co.
Dyson, Laurence. Journey to the Moon, 1 vol. 2014. (Spotlight on Space Science Ser.). (ENG.). 32p. (J). (gr. 5-5). pap. 12.75 *(978-1-4994-0373-2(9)*, ec84f562-6fac-4eaa-b1c7-12b9df235f0d, PowerKids Pr.) Rosen Publishing Group, Inc., The.
Eckart, Edana. Watching the Moon. 2004. (Wel-Watching Nature Ser.). (Illus.). 24p. (J). 19.00 *(978-0-516-27598-7(4)*, Children's Pr.) Scholastic Library Publishing.
Galat, Joan Marie. Dot to Dot in the Sky: Stories of the Moon, 1 vol. Bennett, Lorna, illus. 2004. (Dot to Dot in the Sky Ser.: 0). (ENG.). 64p. (J). (gr. 6-8). pap. 12.95 *(978-1-55285-610-9(0)*, ce2944fd-71ac-49da-be71-f792cc696a3e) Whitecap Bks., Ltd. CAN. Dist: Firefly Bks., Ltd.
Gardner, Robert. Science Fair Projects about the Sun & the Moon, 1 vol. 2016. (Hands-On Science Ser.). (ENG.). 48p. (gr. 4-4). pap. 12.70 *(978-0-7660-8215-1(6)*, ca703e88-3c77-48ff-9f01-4cc20ad03da7) Enslow Publishing, LLC.
Gendell, Megan & Connolly, Rachel. Your Home in Space: Everything You Wanted to Know about Earth, the Sun, & the Moon. 2008. (Illus.). 32p. (J). *(978-0-545-04457-8(X))* Scholastic, Inc.
Gibbons, Gail. The Moon Book (New & Updated Edition) 2019. (Illus.). 32p. (J). (gr. -1-3). 18.99 *(978-0-8234-4324-6(8))*; pap. 8.99 *(978-0-8234-4323-9(X))* Holiday Hse., Inc.
Goldstein, Margaret J. The Moon. 2005. (Pull Ahead Bks.). (Illus.). 32p. (gr. 2-4). lib. bdg. 22.60 *(978-0-8225-4658-0(2))* Lerner Publishing Group.
Graham, Ian. Our Moon. 2015. (Space Ser.). (ENG., Illus.). 24p. (J). (gr. 1-3). lib. bdg. 28.50 *(978-1-62588-209-7(2)*, 17403) Black Rabbit Bks.
Gregory, Cam. Why Does the Moon Look Different? 2012. (Level E Ser.). (ENG., Illus.). 16p. (J). (gr. k-2). pap. 7.95 *(978-1-927136-46-1(6)*, 19464) RiverStream Publishing.
Hansen, Grace. The Moon. 2017. (Our Galaxy Ser.). (ENG., Illus.). 24p. (J). (gr. -1-2). lib. bdg. 32.79 *(978-1-5321-0053-6(1)*, 25180, Abdo Kids) ABDO Publishing Co.
Hantula, Richard & Asimov, Isaac. La Luna (the Moon), 1 vol. 2003. (Isaac Asimov's Biblioteca Del Universo Del Siglo XXI (Isaac Asimov's 21st Century Library of the Universe) Ser.).Tr. of Moon. (SPA., Illus.). 32p. (gr. 3-5). (J). pap. 9.95 *(978-0-8368-3868-8(8)*, 54c656b2-16c8-49d4-aa51-588af726dc25, Weekly Reader); lib. bdg. 28.67 *(978-0-8368-3855-8(6)*, e186285f-763c-407c-b6e7-c647e44523d1, Gareth Stevens Learning Library) Stevens, Gareth Publishing LLLP.
Harman, Alice. Moon, 1 vol., 1. 2015. (Fact Finders: Space Ser.). (ENG., Illus.). 24p. (J). (gr. 2-2). pap. 9.25 *(978-1-5081-9129-2(8)*, cc9e5148-5a10-4b1b-aace-bbe2966c1816, Windmill Bks.) Rosen Publishing Group, Inc., The.
HB Staff. Let's Visit the Moon. 97th ed. 2003. (Signatures Ser.). (gr. 1-18). pap. 19.20 *(978-0-15-308181-1(3))* Harcourt Schl. Pubs.
Hicks, Terry Allan. Earth & the Moon, 1 vol. 2010. (Space! Ser.). (ENG.). 64p. (gr. 5-5). lib. bdg. 35.50 *(978-0-7614-4254-7(5)*, b684035f-a814-47fc-8233-c422509a6af0) Cavendish Square Publishing LLC.
Hill, Christina. Earth's Moon, 1 vol. 2015. (Science: Informational Text Ser.). (ENG., Illus.). 32p. (gr. 3-4). pap. 11.99 *(978-1-4807-4651-0(7))* Teacher Created Materials, Inc.
Hutmacher, Kimberly. The Night Sky. 2012. (My Science Library). (ENG.). 24p. (gr. 3-4). pap. 8.95 *(978-1-61810-225-6(7)*, 9781618102256) Rourke Educational Media.
Hutson, Matt. The Inside Story of the Moon. 2006. (J). 7.80 *(978-1-933798-05-9(X))* Sally Ride Science.
Ipcizade, Catherine. Phases of the Moon: A 4D Book. 2018. (Cycles of Nature Ser.). (ENG., Illus.). 24p. (J). (gr. -1-2). lib. bdg. 29.32 *(978-1-9771-0040-5(6)*, 138182, Capstone Pr.) Capstone.
Jacobson, Bray. Cycles in Space, 1 vol. 2019. (Look at Nature's Cycles Ser.). (ENG.). 32p. (gr. 2-2). pap. 11.50 *(978-1-5382-4102-8(1)*, 7760a719-9624-474b-a10c-07e61e7af6b8) Stevens, Gareth Publishing LLLP.
Jefferis, David. The Moon: Earth's Neighbor. 2008. (Exploring Our Solar System Ser.). (ENG., Illus.). 32p. (J). (gr. 3-7). pap. *(978-0-7787-3747-6(0))* Crabtree Publishing Co.
Kissock, Heather. Moon. 2011. (J). *(978-1-61690-600-9(6))*; *(978-1-61690-954-3(4))* Weigl Pubs., Inc.
Koontz, Robin. Hide & Seek Moon: The Moon Phases, 1 vol. Davidson, Chris, illus. 2010. (First Graphics: Nature Cycles Ser.). (ENG.). 24p. (J). (gr. 1-2). pap. 6.29 *(978-1-4296-6229-1(8)*, 1321992) Capstone.
—Hide & Seek Moon: The Moon Phases. Davidson, Chris, illus. 2010. (First Graphics: Nature Cycles Ser.). (ENG.). 24p. (J). (gr. 1-2). pap. 38.74 *(978-1-4296-6398-4(7)*, 16146) Capstone.
Koontz, Robin Michal. Hide & Seek Moon: The Moon Phases, 1 vol. Davidson, Chris, illus. 2010. (First Graphics: Nature Cycles Ser.). (ENG.). 24p. (J). (gr. 1-3). 24.65 *(978-1-4296-5365-7(5)*, 1321992) Capstone.
Labrecque, Ellen. The Moon & Other Satellites. 2019. (Our Place in the Universe Ser.). (ENG., Illus.). 24p. (J). (gr. 1-3). pap. 7.95 *(978-1-9771-1019-0(3)*, 140962, Pebble) Capstone.
Lawrence, Ellen. The Moon: Our Neighbor in Space. 2013. (Zoom into Space Ser.). (ENG., Illus.). 24p. (J). (gr. -1-3). lib. bdg. 23.99 *(978-1-909673-08-3(0)*, 907b8a46-2653-48c8-b81b-2f428ac4f0cd) Ruby Tuesday Books Limited GBR. Dist: Lerner Publishing Group.
Lilly, Melinda. Sun & Moon. Thompson, Scott M., photos by. 2005. (Rourke Discovery Library). (Illus.). 24p. (J). (gr. 1-4). lib. bdg. 14.95 *(978-1-59515-405-7(1)*, 1244276) Rourke Educational Media.
Lipschultz, Wes. All about the Moon. 2009. (Reading Room Collection 2 Ser.). 24p. (gr. 3-4). 42.50 *(978-1-60851-955-2(4)*, PowerKids Pr.) Rosen Publishing Group, Inc., The.
Llewellyn, Claire. The Moon. 2003. (Starters Ser.). 24p. (J). lib. bdg. 21.35 *(978-1-58340-260-3(8))* Black Rabbit Bks.
Lockhart, Barbara M. Circle the Moon. Grunden, Kimberly, illus. 2008. 24p. pap. 10.95 *(978-1-934246-96-2(4))* Peppertree Pr., The.
Lockyer, John. The Moon, 1 vol. 2015. (ENG., Illus.). 16p. (-2). pap. *(978-1-77654-140-9(5)*, Red Rocket Readers) Flying Start Bks.
Lucas, Debra. Our Moon. 2005. (Yellow Umbrella Fluent Level Ser.). (ENG., Illus.). 16p. (gr. k-1). pap. 35.70 *(978-0-7368-5296-8(4)*, Capstone Pr.) Capstone.
Malam, John. Man Walks on the Moon. 2003. (Dates with History Ser.). 45p. (J). lib. bdg. 28.50 *(978-1-58340-407-2(4))* Black Rabbit Bks.
Maloof, Torrey. Earth & Moon, 1 vol. rev. ed. (Science: Informational Text Ser.). (ENG., Illus.). 24p. (gr. 1-2). 2015. lib. bdg. 22.96 *(978-1-4938-1158-8(4))* 2014. pap. 9.99 *(978-1-4807-4571-1(5))* Teacher Created Materials, Inc.
Mattern, Joanne. Our Moon. 2010. (Solar System & Beyond Ser.). (ENG.). 32p. (gr. 3-4). pap. 48.60 *(978-1-4296-6408-0(8)*, 16153); (Illus.). pap. 8.10 *(978-1-4296-6239-0(5)*, 115391) Capstone. (Capstone Pr.).
McAnulty, Stacy. Moon! Earth's Best Friend. Lewis, Stevie, illus. 2019. (Our Universe Ser.: 3). (ENG.). 40p. (J). 19.99 *(978-1-250-19934-8(4)*, 900194811, Holt, Henry & Co. Bks. For Young Readers) Holt, Henry & Co.
McNeil, Niki, et al. The Moon. 2007. (In the Hands of a Child: Project Pack Continent Study Ser.). (Illus.). 73p. spiral bd. 16.50 *(978-1-60308-100-9(3))* In the Hands of a Child.
McNulty, Faith. If You Decide to Go to the Moon. Kellogg, Steven, illus. 2005. (ENG.). 48p. (J). (gr. -1-k). 18.99 *(978-0-590-48359-9(5)*, Scholastic Pr.) Scholastic, Inc.
Metebole, Mattie. The Lunar Cycle: Phases of the Moon. 2009. (Amazing Science Ser.). 24p. (gr. 3-3). 42.50 *(978-1-61511-330-9(4)*, PowerKids Pr.) Rosen Publishing Group, Inc., The.
Michele, Tracey. The Moon. 2011. (Learn-Abouts Ser.). (Illus.). 16p. (J). pap. 7.95 *(978-1-59920-625-7(0))* Black Rabbit Bks.
Milbourne, Anna. On the Moon. 2004. (On the Moon Ser.). 24p. (J). 9.95 *(978-0-7945-0617-9(8)*, Usborne) EDC Publishing.
Miller, Derek L. Earth, Sun, & Moon: Cyclic Patterns of Lunar Phases, Eclipses, & the Seasons, 1 vol. 2016. (Space Systems Ser.). (ENG., Illus.). 112p. (J). (gr. 8-8). 44.50 *(978-1-5026-2291-4(2)*, 57747697-6be6-413c-89a6-556ec9ddfb6e) Cavendish Square Publishing LLC.
Miller, Ron. Earth & the Moon. 2003. (Worlds Beyond Ser.). (Illus.). 96p. (gr. 7-18). lib. bdg. 27.93 *(978-0-7613-2358-7(9)*, Twenty-First Century Bks.) Lerner Publishing Group.
Mitchell, Melanie. Moon. 2004. (First Step Nonfiction — Space Ser.). (ENG., Illus.). 24p. (J). (gr. k-2). pap. 6.99 *(978-0-8225-3591-1(2)*, eb11f127-a381-449d-8737-1837b2fa2617) Lerner Publishing Group.
Mitchell, Melanie S. Moon. 2004. (First Step Nonfiction). (ENG., Illus.). 24p. (gr. k-2). lib. bdg. 23.93 *(978-0-8225-0188-6(0))* Lerner Publishing Group.
Mora, Pat. The Night the Moon Fell: A Maya Myth, 1 vol. Domi, illus. 2009. (ENG.). 32p. (J). (gr. k-k). pap. 6.95 *(978-0-88899-938-2(0))* Groundwood Bks. CAN. Dist: Publishers Group West (PGW).
—La Noche Que Se Cayó la Luna. Domi, illus. 2nd ed. 2009. (SPA.). 32p. (J). (gr. -1-k). pap. 6.95 *(978-0-88899-963-4(1))* Groundwood Bks. CAN. Dist: Publishers Group West (PGW).
Morgan, Emily. Next Time You See the Moon. 2014. (Next Time You See Ser.). (ENG.). 32p. (J). (gr. k-5). pap. 13.99 *(978-1-938946-33-2(2)*, P241373) National Science Teachers Assn.
—La Próxima Vez Que Veas la Luna. 2016. (Next Time You See Ser.). (SPA.). 32p. (J). (gr. 2-4). pap. 12.95 *(978-1-68140-286-4(6))* National Science Teachers Assn.
Mortensen, Lori. Our Moon. 2018. (Let's Learn Ser.). (ENG., Illus.). 16p. (gr. -1-2). lib. bdg. 28.50 *(978-1-64156-176-1(9)*, 9781641561761) Rourke Educational Media.
Nagelhout, Ryan. What Is a Moon?, 1 vol. 2014. (Let's Find Out! Space Science Ser.). (ENG.). 32p. (J). (gr. 2-3). 26.06 *(978-1-62275-466-3(2)*, 69130890-627f-4f2a-9f1e-0f1236a5c654) Rosen Publishing Group, Inc., The.
—20 Fun Facts about the Moon, 1 vol. 2014. (Fun Fact File: Space! Ser.). (ENG.). 32p. (J). (gr. 2-3). 20.95 *(978-1-4824-1018-1(4)*, 0ec35251-049e-45ff-a53c-58296471d322) Stevens, Gareth Publishing LLLP.
National Geographic Learning. Reading Expeditions (Science: Earth Science): Earth, Sun, Moon. 2007. (ENG., Illus.). 32p. (J). pap. 18.95 *(978-0-7922-4573-5(3))* CENGAGE Learning.
Nelson, Robin. El Cielo de Noche (the Night Sky) 2012. (Mi Primer Paso Al Mundo Real — Descubriendo Los Ciclos de la Naturaleza (First Step Nonfiction — Discovering Nature's Cycles) Ser.). (SPA., Illus.). 24p. (J). (gr. k-2). pap. 6.99 *(978-0-7613-9360-3(9)*, 276bf67c-db3b-468c-b7d8-e0c721559465, Ediciones Lerner) Lerner Publishing Group.
—The Night Sky. 2010. (First Step Nonfiction — Discovering Nature's Cycles Ser.). (gr. k-2). (ENG., Illus.). 24p. (J). pap. 6.99 *(978-0-7613-5683-7(5)*, f865d96d-610f-4798-8484-0fc16d881d8e); pap. 33.92 *(978-0-7613-6917-2(1))* Lerner Publishing Group.
Nuestro Satelite: La Luna. (SPA.). (J). 10.00 *(978-84-342-1811-6(9))* Parramon Ediciones S.A. ESP. Dist: Distribuidora Norma, Inc.
Olien, Rebecca. Exploring the Moon, 1 vol. 2007. (Objects in the Sky Ser.). (ENG., Illus.). 24p. (J). (gr. 3-3). lib. bdg. 26.27 *(978-1-4042-3466-6(7)*, 003b77c6-da98-40f1-897b-ea98f1c4d440, PowerKids Pr.) Rosen Publishing Group, Inc., The.
Olson, Gillia M. Phases of the Moon, 1 vol. Miller, Jo, illus. 2006. (Patterns in Nature Ser.). (ENG.). 24p. (gr. k-1). 24.65 *(978-0-7368-6340-7(0)*, Capstone Pr.) Capstone.
O'Mara, Genevieve. The Lunar Cycle: Phases of the Moon, 1 vol. (Amazing Science Ser.). (ENG.). 24p. (gr. 3-3). 2009. (J). lib. bdg. 26.27 *(978-1-4358-2973-2(5)*, 1715dc9c-cc81-46a3-ac08-5aec8f137a35, PowerKids Pr.) 2008. pap. 8.25 *(978-1-4358-0002-1(8)*, 9213a466-88e6-4a5b-8310-4025524ffd5a, Rosen Classroom) Rosen Publishing Group, Inc., The.
Orme, Helen & Orme, David. Let's Explore the Moon, 1 vol. 2007. (Space Launch! Ser.). (ENG., Illus.). 24p. (gr. 2-4). lib. bdg. 25.67 *(978-0-8368-7943-8(0)*, 81e27e23-ac75-4ea7-9755-c7c26969ef75, Gareth Stevens Learning Library) Stevens, Gareth Publishing LLLP.
Orr, Tamra. I Spy in the Sky the Moon. 2011. (Randy's Corner Ser.). (Illus.). 32p. (J). (gr. k-3). lib. bdg. 25.70 *(978-1-58415-973-5(1))* Mitchell Lane Pubs.
Oxlade, Chris. Earth & Its Moon, 1 vol. 2007. (Earth & Space Ser.). (ENG., Illus.). 48p. (YA). (gr. 6-6). lib. bdg. 34.47 *(978-1-4042-3734-6(8)*, ed6daa5e-0d9c-490c-a60c-77d0face0312) Rosen Publishing Group, Inc., The.
—The Moon. 2010. (Eye on Space Ser.). 24p. (J). pap. 8.25 *(978-1-61532-546-7(8)*, PowerKids Pr.); (ENG.). (gr. 1-1). lib. bdg. 26.27 *(978-1-61532-541-2(7)*, 46e50f19-85f1-40a9-83de-9e71bf1de938) Rosen Publishing Group, Inc., The.
Paris, Stephanie. 20th Century: Race to the Moon, 1 vol. 2nd rev. ed. 2013. (TIME for KIDS(r): Informational Text Ser.). (ENG., Illus.). 64p. (J). (gr. 4-8). pap. 14.99 *(978-1-4333-4899-0(3))* Teacher Created Materials, Inc.
Peters, Elisa. The Moon, 1 vol. 2012. (PowerKids Readers: the Universe Ser.). (ENG., Illus.). 24p. (J). (gr. k-k). pap. 9.25 *(978-1-4488-7466-8(1)*, fd2af38d-db00-45bb-83ff-e36eab0370e7); lib. bdg. 26.27 *(978-1-4488-7386-9(X)*, 1a549a68-791a-4ec3-847d-37c7aafc031e) Rosen Publishing Group, Inc., The. (PowerKids Pr.).
—The Moon: La Luna, 1 vol. 2012. (PowerKids Readers: el Universo / the Universe Ser.). (SPA & ENG., Illus.). 24p. (J). (gr. k-k). lib. bdg. 26.27 *(978-1-4488-7822-2(5)*, bccd1d87-8622-456f-889f-23b1af6238eb, PowerKids Pr.) Rosen Publishing Group, Inc., The.
Podesto, Martine. The Moon, 1 vol. 2008. (My Science Notebook Ser.). (ENG., Illus.). 104p. (YA). (gr. 4-5). lib. bdg. 33.67 *(978-0-8368-9215-4(1)*, e794d5c4-8de1-4366-8914-50d2eebe66b7) Stevens, Gareth Publishing LLLP.
Portillo, Athena Yvette. Sun & Moon. 2007. (Illus.). 32p. (J). pap. 8.00 *(978-0-8059-7278-8(1))* Dorrance Publishing Co., Inc.
Portman, Michael. Where Did the Moon Come From?, 1 vol. 2013. (Space Mysteries Ser.). (ENG., Illus.). 32p. (J). (gr. 2-3). 29.27 *(978-1-4339-8277-4(3)*, 5fef08f7-7592-4b4d-9e37-8a62bc26ca00); pap. 11.50 *(978-1-4339-8278-1(1)*, 1596ae51-b0c3-496f-8a1c-adef59de9ae4) Stevens, Gareth Publishing LLLP. (Gareth Stevens Learning Library).
Rathburn, Betsy. Moons. 2018. (Space Science Ser.). (ENG., Illus.). 24p. (J). (gr. 3-7). lib. bdg. 26.95 *(978-1-62617-860-1(7)*, Torque Bks.) Bellwether Media.
Read, John A. 50 Things to See on the Moon: A First-Time Stargazer's Guide. 2019. (Beginner's Guide to Space Ser.). (ENG., Illus.). 80p. (J). (gr. 2-5). 26.65 *(978-1-4595-0522-3(0)*, 2f4ed98d-d6f3-45eb-ba9e-0cd7c0efc468) Formac Publishing Co., Ltd. CAN. Dist: Lerner Publishing Group.
Reilly, Carmel. The Moon, 1 vol. 2012. (Sky Watching Ser.). (ENG.). 32p. (gr. 5-5). 31.21 *(978-1-60870-581-8(1)*, b04b8cbc-6448-4f42-9a30-9e3d37122916) Cavendish Square Publishing LLC.
Rice, Clay. Mama, Let's Make a Moon. (ENG.). 32p. (J). 2012. E-Book 9.99 *(978-1-938301-05-6(6)*, 9781938301056) 2013. (gr. -1-k). 16.95 *(978-1-938301-06-3(4)*, 559106) Familius LLC.
Riley, Peter. Earth, Moon & Sun. 2007. (Essential Science/Watts Ser.). (Illus.). 32p. (YA). (gr. 3-6). lib. bdg. 28.50 *(978-1-59920-025-5(2))* Black Rabbit Bks.
Robbins, Dean. Margaret & the Moon. Knisley, Lucy, illus. 2017. 40p. (J). (gr. -1-3). 18.99 *(978-0-399-55185-7(9)*, Knopf Bks. for Young Readers) Random Hse. Children's Bks.
Roesser, Marie. Why Does the Moon Change Shape?, 1 vol. 2020. (Everyday Mysteries Ser.). (ENG.). 24p. (gr. 1-2). pap. 9.15 *(978-1-5382-5667-1(3)*, 948575e2-6c07-43ff-abdb-025d723fbcc6) Stevens, Gareth Publishing LLLP.
Rushworth, Gary. Our Solar System the Moon: Set Of 6. 2011. (Navigators Ser.). (J). pap. 44.00 net. *(978-1-4108-6221-1(6))* Benchmark Education Co.
—Our Solar System: the Moon: Text Pairs. 2008. (Bridges/Navigators Ser.). (J). (gr. 3). 89.00 *(978-1-4108-8370-4(1))* Benchmark Education Co.
Rustad, Martha E. H. La Luna/the Moon. 2012. (En el Espacio/Out in Space Ser.). (MUL.). 24p. (gr. k-1). pap. 35.70 *(978-1-4296-8553-5(0))* Capstone.
—The Moon. 2016. (Space Ser.). (ENG., Illus.). 24p. (J). (gr. -1-2). lib. bdg. 22.65 *(978-1-4914-8323-7(7)*, 130796, Capstone Pr.) Capstone.
—The Moon: Revised Edition. rev. ed. 2008. (Out in Space Ser.). (ENG., Illus.). 24p. (J). (gr. -1-2). pap. 6.29 *(978-1-4296-2811-2(1)*, 95331) Capstone.
—The Moon [Scholastic]: Revised Edition. 2009. (Out in Space Ser.). 24p. (gr. k-1). pap. 2.50 *(978-1-4296-4048-0(0)*, Pebble) Capstone.
Ryback, Carol. The Moon, 1 vol. 2005. (In the Sky Ser.). (ENG., Illus.). 24p. (gr. 2-4). pap. 9.15 *(978-0-8368-6348-2(8)*, 62264a12-3f44-4db1-9572-f666dc348e31); lib. bdg. 24.67 *(978-0-8368-6343-7(7)*, b6c4043a-9a4c-471a-9a0f-62d60ebe62a4) Stevens, Gareth Publishing LLLP. (Weekly Reader Leveled Readers).
Salas, Laura Purdie. If You Were the Moon. Kim, Jaime, illus. 2017. (ENG.). 32p. (J). (gr. k-2). 19.99 *(978-1-4677-8009-4(X)*, 85307bf0-f95b-493d-8e79-002bc9c23e22); E-Book 30.65 *(978-1-5124-2838-4(8))* Lerner Publishing Group. (Millbrook Pr.).
Sasek, Miroslav. This Is the Way to the Moon: A Children's Classic. 2009. (This Is ... Ser.). (ENG., Illus.). 64p. (J). (gr. 2-12). 17.95 *(978-0-7893-1842-8(3))* Universe Publishing.
Sawyer, J. Clark. Nuestra Luna: El Objeto MÁS Brillante Del Cielo Nocturno. 2015. (Fuera de Este Mundo Ser.). (SPA., Illus.). 24p. (J). (gr. -1-3). lib. bdg. 26.99 *(978-1-62724-594-4(4))* Bearport Publishing Co., Inc.
—Our Moon: Brightest Object in the Night Sky. 2015. (Out of This World Ser.). (ENG.). 24p. (J). (gr. -1-3). lib. bdg. 26.99 *(978-1-62724-570-8(7))* Bearport Publishing Co., Inc.
Sexton, Colleen. The Moon. 2010. (Exploring Space Ser.). (ENG., Illus.). 24p. (J). (gr. k-3). lib. bdg. 26.95 *(978-1-60014-401-1(2)*, Blastoff! Readers) Bellwether Media.
Seymour, Arlene. The Moon Book: A Lunar Pop-up Celebration. Seymour, Arlene, illus. 2004. (Illus.). 14p. (YA). (gr. k-4). reprint ed. 22.00 *(978-0-7567-7645-9(7))* DIANE Publishing Co.
Sikkens, Crystal. Day & Night. 2019. (Full STEAM Ahead! - Science Starters Ser.). (Illus.). 24p. (J). (gr. 1-1). *(978-0-7787-6187-7(8))* Crabtree Publishing Co.
Simon, Seymour. The Moon. rev. ed. 2003. (ENG., Illus.). 32p. (J). (gr. 2-6). 19.99 *(978-0-689-83563-6(9)*, Simon & Schuster Bks. For Young Readers) Simon & Schuster Bks. For Young Readers.
Slade, Suzanne. The Phases of the Moon. 2009. (Cycles in Nature Ser.). 24p. (gr. 3-3). 42.50 *(978-1-61512-115-1(3)*, PowerKids Pr.) Rosen Publishing Group, Inc., The.
Sohn, Emily. Sun, Moon, & Stars. 2019. (iScience Ser.). (ENG., Illus.). 32p. (J). (gr. 3-4). pap. 13.26 *(978-1-68404-386-6(7))* Norwood Hse. Pr.
Sommer, Nathan. The Moon. 2019. (Space Science Ser.). (ENG., Illus.). 24p. (J). (gr. 3-7). lib. bdg. 26.95 *(978-1-62617-975-2(1)*, Torque Bks.) Bellwether Media.
Sparrow, Giles. Destination the Moon, 1 vol. 2009. (Destination Solar System Ser.). (ENG.). 32p. (J). (gr. 3-4). lib. bdg. 28.93 *(978-1-4358-3445-3(3)*, 03f096a0-83da-4397-83d9-313b4e5034bf); (Illus.). pap. 11.00 *(978-1-4358-3465-1(8)*, 54763f66-7a02-4317-bc37-71e5c557c43e) Rosen Publishing Group, Inc., The. (PowerKids Pr.).
Stewart, Melissa. Why Does the Moon Change Shape?, 1 vol. 2009. (Tell Me Why, Tell Me How Ser.). (ENG., Illus.). 32p. (gr. 3-3). lib. bdg. 32.64 *(978-0-7614-2921-0(2)*, 987f45f3-fac5-4e9b-b94c-2badafe0992c) Cavendish Square Publishing LLC.
Storad, Conrad J. Day & Night. 2011. (My Science Library). (ENG., Illus.). 24p. (gr. k-1). pap. 9.95 *(978-1-61741-926-3(5)*, 9781617419263) Rourke Educational Media.
Turnbull, Stephanie. Sun, Moon & Stars. Chen, Kuo Kang & Mayer, Uwe, illus. 2006. (Beginners Nature: Level 2 Ser.). 32p. (J). (gr. 1-3). 4.99 *(978-0-7945-1399-3(9)*, Usborne) EDC Publishing.
Wahl, Ellen. Full Moon Lore. Stewart, Ashley, illus. 2017. (ENG.). 32p. (J). (gr. k-3). 16.99 *(978-1-58536-965-2(9)*, 204301) Sleeping Bear Pr.
Waxman, Laura Hamilton. The Moon. 2010. (Early Bird Astronomy Ser.). (ENG.). 48p. (gr. 2-5). lib. bdg. 26.60 *(978-0-7613-3872-7(1))*; (Illus.). pap. 8.95 *(978-0-7613-4983-9(9)*, 1306462, Lerner Pubns.) Lerner Publishing Group.
Wilberforce, Bert. The Moon, 1 vol. 2020. (Look at Space Science Ser.). (ENG.). 32p. (gr. 2-2). pap. 11.50 *(978-1-5382-5926-9(5)*, ae9c2580-e643-410b-882e-ac6043027fdf) Stevens, Gareth Publishing LLLP.
Wilkins, Mary-Jane. The Moon. 2017. (Our Solar System Ser.). (ENG.). 24p. (J). (gr. 2-4). 28.50 *(978-1-78121-365-0(8)*, 16655) Brown Bear Bks.
Wishinsky, Frieda. Could We Live on the Moon? 2004. (ENG., Illus.). 24p. (J). (gr. 2-2). pap. 10.92 *(978-0-7652-5178-7(7)*, Celebration Pr.) Savvas Learning Co.
World Book, Inc. Staff, contrib. by. Earth & Earth's Moon. (J). 2010. *(978-0-7166-9540-0(5))* 2006. 63p. *(978-0-7166-9503-5(0))* 2nd ed. 2007. (Illus.). 64p. *(978-0-7166-9512-7(X))* World Bk., Inc.
Zimmerman, W. Our Colorful Moon: Beautiful Images to Energize & Delight. 2007. 40p. per. 18.27 *(978-1-934840-04-7(1))* Nimble Bks. LLC.

MOON—EXPLORATION

Adamson, Thomas K. Apollo 11 Moon Landing: An Interactive Space Exploration Adventure. 2016. (You Choose: Space Ser.). (ENG., Illus.). 112p. (J). (gr. 3-7). lib. bdg. 32.65 *(978-1-4914-8103-5(X)*, 130587, Capstone Pr.) Capstone.
—Do You Really Want to Visit the Moon? Fabbri, Daniele, illus. 2013. (Do You Really Want to Visit the Solar System? Ser.). (ENG.). 24p. (J). (gr. 1-4). 27.10 *(978-1-60753-197-5(6)*, 16266) Amicus.
—The First Moon Landing, 1 vol. Purcell, Gordon & Beatty, Terry, illus. 2006. (Graphic History Ser.). (ENG.). 32p. (J). (gr. 3-9). per. 8.10 *(978-0-7368-9654-2(6)*, 93409) Capstone.
Alexander, richard. Exploring the Moon. 2017. (Journey Through Our Solar System Ser.). 24p. (gr. 1-2). 49.50 *(978-1-5345-2249-7(2)*, KidHaven Publishing); (ENG.). pap. 9.25 *(978-1-5345-2293-0(X)*, 38c5d3b3-9e77-4c8e-9c83-36ea608f4448); (ENG.). lib. bdg. 26.23 *(978-1-5345-2277-0(8)*,

M N O

062af313-e9bd-4fc4-a8ad-094563340e43) Greenhaven Publishing LLC.

Allien Cave Explorers: Meet NASA Inventor William "Red" Whittaker & His Team's. 2017. (J). *(978-0-7166-6163-4(2))* World Bk., Inc.

Baker, David & Kissock, Heather. Living on the Moon. 2009. (Exploring Space Ser.). (Illus.). 32p. (J). (gr. 2-4). lib. bdg. 26.00 *(978-1-60596-021-0(7))* Weigl Pubs., Inc.

—Moon Base: Exploring Space. 2009. (Exploring Space Ser.). (Illus.). 32p. (J). (gr. 2-4). pap. 9.95 *(978-1-60596-022-7(5))* Weigl Pubs., Inc.

Bredeson, Carmen & Dyson, Marianne. Exploring the Moon, 1 vol. 2015. (Launch into Space! Ser.). (ENG.). 32p. (gr. 3-4). pap. 11.52 *(978-0-7660-6821-6(8),* 4d9c449b-9f32-43fa-b75d-43f50a51759c); (Illus.). 26.93 *(978-0-7660-6823-0(4),* 6cb0a1c2-32fb-4671-a089-fa872ea1c484) Enslow Publishing, LLC.

Brinkley, Douglas. American Moonshot Young Readers' Edition: John F. Kennedy & the Great Space Race. 2019. (ENG., Illus.). 272p. (J). (gr. 3-7). 16.99 *(978-0-06-266028-2(4),* HarperCollins) HarperCollins Pubs.

Close, Edward. Moon Missions, 1 vol., 1. 2014. (Discovery Education: Earth & Space Science Ser.). (ENG.). 32p. (gr. 4-5). 28.93 *(978-1-4777-6178-6(0),* 3a958377-1ebb-4f7a-814b-0b9ad8ffa8bf, PowerKids Pr.) Rosen Publishing Group, Inc., The.

Crane, Cody. The Moon (Rookie Read-About Science: the Universe) 2018. (Rookie Read-About Science Ser.). (ENG., Illus.). 32p. (J). (gr. 1-2). pap. 5.95 *(978-0-531-22862-3(2),* Children's Pr.) Scholastic Library Publishing.

Dyer, Alan. Mission to the Moon: (Book & DVD) 2009. (ENG., Illus.). 80p. (J). (gr. 3-7). 19.99 *(978-1-4169-7935-7(2),* Simon & Schuster Bks. For Young Readers) Simon & Schuster Bks. For Young Readers.

Dyson, Marianne. Home on the Moon: Living on a Space Frontier. 2003. (ENG., Illus.). 64p. (J). (gr. 3-7). 18.95 *(978-0-7922-7193-2(9),* National Geographic Children's Bks.) National Geographic Society.

Glatzer, Jenna. The Exploration of the Moon. 2004. (Exploration & Discovery Ser.). (Illus.). 64p. (YA). (gr. 5-18). lib. bdg. 19.95 *(978-1-59084-048-1(8))* Mason Crest.

Jefferis, David. The Astronauts: Space Survival. 2019. (Moon Flight Atlas Ser.). (Illus.). 32p. (J). (gr. 5-5). *(978-0-7787-5411-4(1))*; pap. *(978-0-7787-5420-6(0))* Crabtree Publishing Co.

—Exploring the Moon: 1969-1972. 2019. (Moon Flight Atlas Ser.). (Illus.). 32p. (J). (gr. 5-5). *(978-0-7787-5409-1(X))*; pap. *(978-0-7787-5418-3(9))* Crabtree Publishing Co.

—Project Apollo: the Race to Land on the Moon. 2019. (Moon Flight Atlas Ser.). (Illus.). 32p. (J). (gr. 5-5). *(978-0-7787-5410-7(3))*; pap. *(978-0-7787-5419-0(7))* Crabtree Publishing Co.

Jefferis, David & Irvine, Mat. Return to the Moon. 2007. (Humans in Space Ser.). (ENG., Illus.). 32p. (J). (gr. 4-7). lib. bdg. *(978-0-7787-3103-0(0))*; pap. *(978-0-7787-3117-7(0))* Crabtree Publishing Co.

Klepeis, Alicia Z. Moon Base & Beyond: The Lunar Gateway to Deep Space. 2019. (Future Space Ser.). (ENG., Illus.). 32p. (J). (gr. 3-9). pap. 7.95 *(978-1-5435-7515-6(3),* 141046); lib. bdg. 28.65 *(978-1-5435-7267-4(7),* 140598) Capstone.

Mahoney, Emily. What Is on the Far Side of the Moon?, 1 vol. 2018. (Space Mysteries Ser.). (ENG.). 32p. (gr. 2-3). 29.27 *(978-1-5382-1963-8(8),* fe28b8d8-1939-4ac8-bf39-cd53bc7bca0c) Stevens, Gareth Publishing LLLP.

Olien, Rebecca. Exploring the Moon. 2009. (Objects in the Sky Ser.). 24p. (gr. 3-3). 42.50 *(978-1-60851-140-2(5),* PowerKids Pr.) Rosen Publishing Group, Inc., The.

Olson, Elsie. Breakthroughs in Moon Exploration. 2019. (Cosmos Chronicles (Alternator Books (r)) Ser.). (ENG., Illus.). 32p. (J). (gr. 3-6). pap. 10.99 *(978-1-5415-7369-7(2),* 5ff50d8f-8878-4f7d-ab5d-e8341f177e7e); lib. bdg. 29.32 *(978-1-5415-5596-9(1),* 49e56b8f-bdaa-4a09-9ea0-63920cff5d63) Lerner Publishing Group. (Lerner Pubns.).

Owen, Ruth. The Moon, 1 vol. 2013. (Explore Outer Space Ser.). (ENG.). 32p. (J). (gr. 2-3). pap. 11.00 *(978-1-61533-759-0(8),* b5059f1f-0ac9-400d-8ced-3f5216df1109); lib. bdg. 29.93 *(978-1-61533-721-7(0),* a2f2cc80-70ef-42c2-9814-3527653aadb8) Rosen Publishing Group, Inc., The. (Windmill Bks.).

—The Moon. 2013. (Explore Outer Space Ser.). 32p. (J). (gr. 3-6). pap. 60.00 *(978-1-61533-760-6(1))* Windmill Bks.

Scott, Elaine. Our Moon: New Discoveries about Earth's Closest Companion. 2016. (ENG., Illus.). 72p. (J). (gr. 5-7). 18.99 *(978-0-547-48394-8(5),* 1439925, Clarion Bks.) HarperCollins Pubs.

Shepherd, Jodie. To the Moon! Byrne, Mike, illus. 2017. (Cloverleaf Books (tm) — Space Adventures Ser.). (ENG.). 24p. (J). (gr. k-2). 25.32 *(978-1-5124-2536-9(2),* f4260f28-62aa-4c30-b7af-1bdb6e6753bb); E-Book 38.65 *(978-1-5124-3893-2(6),* 9781512438932); E-Book 38.65 *(978-1-5124-2833-9(7))*; E-Book 4.99 *(978-1-5124-3894-9(4),* 9781512438949) Lerner Publishing Group. (Millbrook Pr.).

Slade, Suzanne. Daring Dozen: The Twelve Who Walked on the Moon. Marks, Alan, illus. 2019. 48p. (J). (gr. k-4). lib. bdg. 17.99 *(978-1-58089-773-0(8))* Charlesbridge Publishing, Inc.

Wilkinson, Philip. Spacebusters. 2012. (DK Reader Level 3 Ser.). lib. bdg. 13.55 *(978-0-606-26544-7(9))* Turtleback.

MOON—EXPLORATION—FICTION

Anderson, Matthew. Feed. 2004. 320p. (J). (gr. 7-18). pap. 38.00 incl. audio *(978-1-4000-9022-8(9),* Listening Library) Random Hse. Audio Publishing Group.

Hillert, Margaret. Up, up, & Away. Scott Spinks, illus. 2016. (Beginning-To-Read Ser.). (ENG.). 32p. (J). (gr. k-2). pap. 13.26 *(978-1-60357-947-6(8))* Norwood Hse. Pr.

Montgomery, Anson. Moon Quest. Semionov, Vladimir, illus. 2008. (ENG.). 144p. (J). (gr. 4-8). pap. 7.99 *(978-1-933390-26-0(3))* Chooseco LLC.

Newbery, Linda. Andie's Moon. 2009. (Historical House Ser.). 208p. (YA). (gr. 5-18). pap. 5.99 *(978-0-7945-2333-6(1),* Usborne) EDC Publishing.

Palmer, S. Y. May's Moon. 2015. (May's Moon Ser.: Book I). (ENG., Illus.). 184p. (J). (gr. -1-12). pap. 11.95 *(978-1-78279-780-7(7),* Our Street Bks.) Hunt, John Publishing Ltd. GBR. Dist: National Bk. Network.

Rockwood, Roy. Lost on the Moon. 2008. 132p. 24.95 *(978-1-60664-737-0(7))* Rodgers, Alan Bks.

Todd, Ruthven. Space Cat. Galdone, Paul, illus. 2018. (ENG.). 80p. (gr. 1-5). 16.95 *(978-0-486-82272-3(9),* 822729) Dover Pubns., Inc.

Verne, Jules. From the Earth to the Moon. 2008. (Bring the Classics to Life Ser.). (ENG., Illus.). 72p. (gr. 4-12). pap., act. bk. ed. 10.95 *(978-1-55576-181-3(X),* EDCTR-407B) EDCON Publishing Group.

MOON—FICTION

Akers, Darla G. The Man, the Moon, & the Star. 2008. 24p. per. 24.95 *(978-1-60474-030-1(2))* PublishAmerica, Inc.

Allen, Page. Madison's Descent: A Child's Journey. (Illus.). (J). 2006. pap. 25.00 *(978-0-9752516-2-1(7))* 2004. lib. bdg. 60.00 *(978-0-9752516-1-4(9))* Otis & Randolph Pr.

Almond, David. The Boy Who Climbed into the Moon. Dunbar, Polly, illus. 2010. (ENG.). 128p. (J). (gr. 3-7). 15.99 *(978-0-7636-4217-4(7))* Candlewick Pr.

and Film Studio, Shanghai Animation & Tang, Sanmu. An Attempt to Scoop up the Moon. Ying, Wu, tr. 2010. (Favorite Childrens Cartoons from China Ser.). (ENG., Illus.). 32p. (gr. -1-3). pap. 5.95 *(978-1-60220-971-8(5))* Shanghai Pr.

Andersen, D. R. Why the Moon Changes in the Night Sky. 2005. (J). pap. *(978-1-4108-4190-2(1))* Benchmark Education Co.

Anderson, M. T. Feed. 2012. (ENG., Illus.). 320p. (YA). (gr. 9). pap. 11.99 *(978-0-7636-6262-2(3))* Candlewick Pr.

Artus, William. The King on the Moon. 2008. 32p. pap. 20.95 *(978-1-4092-3044-1(9))* Lulu Pr., Inc.

Asch, Frank. Happy Birthday, Moon. Asch, Frank, illus. 2014. (Moonbear Ser.). (ENG., Illus.). 32p. (J). (gr. -1-3). 8.99 *(978-1-4424-9400-8(X),* Aladdin) Simon & Schuster Children's Publishing.

—Mooncake. Asch, Frank, illus. 2014. (Moonbear Ser.). (ENG., Illus.). 32p. (J). (gr. -1-3). 8.99 *(978-1-4424-9403-9(4),* Aladdin) Simon & Schuster Children's Publishing.

—Moondance. Asch, Frank, illus. 2014. (Moonbear Ser.). (ENG., Illus.). 32p. (J). (gr. -1-3). 17.99 *(978-1-4424-6659-3(6),* Aladdin) Simon & Schuster Children's Publishing.

—Moongame. Asch, Frank, illus. 2014. (Moonbear Ser.). (ENG., Illus.). 32p. (J). (gr. -1-3). 8.99 *(978-1-4424-9406-0(9),* Aladdin) Simon & Schuster Children's Publishing.

Asch, Frank & Asch, Frank. Happy Birthday, Moon. Asch, Frank & Asch, Frank, illus. 2005. (Stories to Go! Ser.). (ENG., Illus.). 32p. (J). 4.99 *(978-1-4169-0307-9(0),* Simon & Schuster/Paula Wiseman Bks.) Simon & Schuster/Paula Wiseman Bks.

Astro, Ian. Moon School, 1 vol. 2006. (Neighborhood Readers Ser.). (ENG.). 16p. (gr. 1-2). pap. 6.50 *(978-1-4042-7196-8(1),* 5462beef-9025-4a84-b0cd-78c50d2a7eb8, Rosen Classroom) Rosen Publishing Group, Inc., The.

Baker, Theo. Do Robots Get Space Sick? López, Àlex, illus. 2017. (Galaxy Games Ser.). (ENG.). 48p. (gr. 3-5). pap. 8.95 *(978-1-68342-434-5(4),* 9781683424345) Rourke Educational Media.

Belle, Deborah A. The Day the Sun Called Out Sick!!! Collenberger, Chris, illus. 2013. 30p. pap. 12.99 *(978-0-9853406-0-5(6))* Scribez, Scarebz & Vibez.

Bencivengo, Mary Ann. The Man in the Moon. 2011. 56p. pap. *(978-1-77067-302-1(4))* FriesenPress.

Bennett, Jeffrey. Max Goes to the Moon: A Science Adventure with Max the Dog. Okamoto, Alan, illus. 2nd ed. 2012. (Science Adventures with Max the Dog Ser.). (ENG.). 32p. (J). (gr. 2-4). 15.00 *(978-1-937548-20-9(1))* Big Kid Science.

Berggren, Jeff. My Moon Lagoon. Hansen, Tammy A., ed. Berggren, Jeff, illus. 2007. (Illus.). (J). per. 14.95 *(978-0-9755033-1-7(6))* Deep Dish Design.

Bewley, Elizabeth. The Moon Followed Me Home. Furukawa, Masumi, illus. 2007. (ENG.). 6p. (J). (gr. -1-3). 12.95 *(978-1-58117-598-1(1),* Intervisual/Piggy Toes) Bendon, Inc.

Biviano, David J. True Moon. 2009. 36p. pap. 17.95 *(978-1-4490-1693-7(6))* AuthorHouse.

Black, Robert A. Lunar Pioneers. 2008. 280p. (YA). pap. 14.99 *(978-1-59092-397-9(9))* Blue Forge Pr.

Bolden, Tonya. Beautiful Moon. 2014. (ENG., Illus.). 32p. (J). (gr. -1-3). 16.95 *(978-1-4197-0792-6(2),* 679501, Abrams Bks. for Young Readers) Abrams, Inc.

Bonnell, Kris. The Happy Moon. 2006. (J). pap. 5.95 *(978-1-933727-30-1(6))* Reading Reading Bks., LLC.

Bootsma, Verner. Talking to the Moon. LaGrange, Tiffany, illus. 2007. 32p. per. 12.95 *(978-1-934246-70-2(0))* Peppertree Pr., The.

Boyce, Frank Cottrell. Chitty Chitty Bang Bang over the Moon. Berger, Joe, illus. 2015. (Chitty Chitty Bang Bang Ser.: 4). (ENG.). 304p. (J). (gr. 4-7). pap. 6.99 *(978-0-7636-7666-7(7))* Candlewick Pr.

Branson, Terri. Tyler on the Moon. Taylor, Chet, illus. l.t. ed. 24p. (J). 2005. lib. bdg. 24.95 *(978-0-9765786-2-8(X))* 2004. 18.99 *(978-0-9755888-2-6(6))* Dragonfly Publishing, Inc.

Brickwood, L. M. Children of the Moon. 2007. 216p. pap. 14.95 *(978-1-920153-03-8(9))* Zulu Planet Pubs. ZAF. Dist: APG Sales & Distribution Services.

Bronn, Charles Heil. The Sun, the Moon, & the Gardener's Son. Kami, Y. Z., illus. 2006. 30p. (J). (gr. 4-12). reprint ed. 16.00 *(978-1-4223-5222-9(6))* DIANE Publishing Co.

Brooks. Mary Will Not Watch Moon. Date not set. 32p. (J). (gr. -1-1). 14.99 *(978-0-06-024491-0(7))* HarperCollins Pubs.

—Mary Will Not Watch the Moon. Date not set. 32p. (J). (gr. -1-1). lib. bdg. 15.89 *(978-0-06-024492-7(5))* HarperCollins Pubs.

Brown, Betisa Garagozlu. Sister Sun & Sister Moon. 2012. 28p. pap. 13.95 *(978-1-4525-4635-3(5))* Balboa Pr.

Brown, Margaret Wise. Buenas Noches, Luna: Goodnight Moon (Spanish Edition), 1 vol. Hurd, Clement, illus. 2006. Tr. of Goodnight Moon. (SPA.). 32p. (J). (gr. -1-3). 18.99 *(978-0-06-026214-3(1),* HC0528); pap. 8.99 *(978-0-06-443416-4(8),* HC0527) HarperCollins Español.

—Goodnight Moon 123 Board Book: A Counting Book. Hurd, Clement, illus. 2008. (ENG.). 30p. (J). (gr. -1-k). bds. 8.99 *(978-0-06-112597-3(0),* HarperFestival) HarperCollins Pubs.

—Goodnight Moon 123 Lap Edition. Hurd, Clement, illus. 2008. (ENG.). 30p. (J). (gr. -1 — 1). bds. 12.99 *(978-0-06-166755-8(2),* HarperFestival) HarperCollins Pubs.

—Goodnight Moon Classic Library: Contains Goodnight Moon, the Runaway Bunny, & My World. Hurd, Clement, illus. 2011. (ENG.). 32p. (J). (gr. -1-1). 17.99 *(978-0-06-199823-2(0),* HarperCollins) HarperCollins Pubs.

—Over the Moon: a Collection of First Books: Goodnight Moon, the Runaway Bunny, & My World. Hurd, Clement, illus. 2006. (ENG.). 108p. (J). (gr. -1-1). 19.99 *(978-0-06-076162-2(8),* HarperCollins) HarperCollins Pubs.

Brown-Wood, Janay. Imani's Moon. Mitchell, Hazel, illus. 2014. (ENG.). 32p. (J). (gr. 1-4). pap. 7.95 *(978-1-934133-58-3(2))* Charlesbridge Publishing, Inc.

Byrne, Barbara. Megan's Moon. 2004. 18p. 14.87 *(978-1-4116-1008-8(3))* Lulu Pr., Inc.

Carle, Eric. Coccinelle Mal Lune. pap. 18.95 *(978-2-87142-287-7(7))* Mijade Editions BEL. Dist: Distribooks, Inc.

Carrington, Samala. Sally Sunshine Mandy Moon. 2011. 20p. (gr. -1). pap. 12.99 *(978-1-4567-6708-2(9))* AuthorHouse.

Carroll, James Christopher. The Boy & the Moon. Carroll, James Christopher, illus. 2010. (ENG., Illus.). 32p. (J). (gr. 1-4). 19.99 *(978-1-58536-521-0(1),* 202209) Sleeping Bear Pr.

Casado, Alicia & Casado, Dami. La Luna. 2005. (Yo Te Hablare De... Ser.). (SPA., Illus.). 14p. (J). per., bds. 8.99 *(978-84-272-7386-3(X))* Molino, Editorial ESP. Dist: Santillana USA Publishing Co., Inc.

Castelli, Jeanette. Los Gatos en la Luna/the Cats on the Moon. Santana, Andrea, illus. 2005. (Bilingual Collection). (SPA.). 51p. (J). (gr. k-2). *(978-958-30-1767-4(1))* Panamericana Editorial.

Chafe, Justin. Bunny Rabbit on the Moon. 2007. (Illus.). 28p. (J). 14.95 *(978-0-9787660-0-9(8))* Baboosic Enterprises, LLC.

Christenson, Lisa & Christenson, Emme Jo. Who Ate the Moon? Christenson, Lisa & Christenson, Emme Jo, illus. 2006. (Illus.). (J). per. *(978-0-9725311-2-2(2),* Pickled Eggs Press (TM)) Loucks Studios Inc.

Cole, Rachael. City Moon. Gómez, Blanca, illus. 2017. 40p. (J). (gr. -1-2). 18.99 *(978-0-553-49707-6(3))* Random Hse. Children's Bks.

Conway, David. Shine Moon Shine. Kolanovic, Dubravka, illus. 2008. 32p. (J). (gr. -1-2). 15.95 *(978-1-58925-073-4(7))* Tiger Tales.

Cooper, Floyd. Max & the Tag-Along Moon. Cooper, Floyd, illus. (Illus.). 32p. (J). (gr. -1-2). 2015. 8.99 *(978-0-14-751546-9(7),* Puffin Books) 2013. (ENG., 17.99 *(978-0-399-23342-5(3),* Philomel Bks.) Penguin Young Readers Group.

Craft, Mahlon. Christmas Moon. Craft, K. Y., illus. 2003. 32p. (J). 15.95 *(978-1-58717-056-0(6))*; lib. bdg. *(978-1-58717-057-7(4))* Chronicle Bks. LLC. (SeaStar Bks.).

Cundiff, Joe. Fly to the Moon on a Witch's Broom. 2013. (ENG.). 34p. (J). pap. 15.95 *(978-1-4787-2306-6(8))* Outskirts Pr., Inc.

Curtis, Carolyn. I Took the Moon for a Walk. Jay, Alison, illus. (ENG.). 32p. (J). 2012. (gr. -1-2). pap. 9.99 *(978-1-84148-803-5(8))* 2008. (gr. -1-2). bds. 14.99 *(978-1-84686-200-7(0))* 2004. 16.99 *(978-1-84148-611-6(6))* Barefoot Bks., Inc.

—Lleve la Luna a Pasear. Jay, Alison, illus. 2014. (SPA.). 32p. (J). (gr. -1-2). pap. 9.99 *(978-1-78285-084-7(8))* Barefoot Bks., Inc.

Dabell, John. Moon People. 2011. 266p. pap. *(978-1-908105-66-0(6))* Grosvenor Hse. Publishing Ltd.

Danilo, Roberto. Mylene & the Moon. 2011. 24p. pap. 12.99 *(978-1-4634-1196-1(0))* AuthorHouse.

de Brunhoff, Laurent. Babar Raconte la Course a la Lune. (Babar Ser.). (FRE., Illus.). 48p. (J). (gr. -1-3). 19.95 *(978-0-7859-8820-5(3))* French & European Pubns., Inc.

De Lint, Charles. Wolf Moon. 2004. (ENG., Illus.). 256p. (Orig.). (YA). (gr. 7-18). 6.99 *(978-0-14-240077-7(7),* Firebird) Penguin Young Readers Group.

Delessert, Etienne. Moon Theater. 2010. (ENG.). 32p. (J). (gr. 1-3). 17.95 *(978-1-56846-208-0(5),* 22053, Creative Editions) Creative Co., The.

Duffy, Carol Ann. The Tear Thief. Ceccoli, Nicoletta, illus. 2007. (ENG.). 32p. (J). (gr. -1-3). 16.99 *(978-1-84686-045-4(8))* Barefoot Bks., Inc.

Duffy, Carol Ann & Stevenson, Juliet. The Tear Thief. Ceccoli, Nicoletta, illus. 2011. 32p. (J). (gr. k-4). 9.99 *(978-1-84686-622-7(7))* Barefoot Bks., Inc.

Dyan, Penelope. I Am the Moon. 2011. 34p. pap. 11.95 *(978-1-935630-91-3(1))* Bellissima Publishing, LLC.

Eastridge, Jim. Gregory & the Moon. 2008. 12p. pap. 24.95 *(978-1-4241-9008-9(8))* America Star Bks.

Ehlert, Lois. Moon Rope. 2003. Orig. Title: Un Lazo a la Luna. (SPA & ENG.). (gr. k-3). lib. bdg. 18.40 *(978-0-613-70661-2(7))* Turtleback.

Elliott, Miriam Isabel. Solita & the Purple Moon: Solita y la Luna Morada. 2007. (ENG.). 24p. per. 11.49 *(978-1-4343-4932-3(2))* AuthorHouse.

Eubanks-Adkison, Eufa. When the Moon Was Born, 1 vol. Spinks, Stefphany (Snider), illus. 2010. 16p. 24.95 *(978-1-4512-1367-6(0))* PublishAmerica, Inc.

Farias, Juan. Los Caminos de la Luna. (SPA., Illus.). 96p. (J). *(978-84-207-8293-5(9))* Grupo Anaya, S.A. ESP. Dist: Lectorum Pubns., Inc.

Farnol, Jeffery. Money Moon. 2006. pap. 13.95 *(978-1-4218-3066-7(3))* 1st World Publishing, Inc.

Feder, Sandra V. The Moon Inside, 1 vol. Sicuro, Aimée, illus. 2016. (ENG.). 32p. (J). (gr. -1-k). 17.95 *(978-1-55498-823-5(3))* Groundwood Bks. CAN. Dist: Publishers Group West (PGW).

Fischer, Kelly. The Moon Throws a Birthday Party. Duckworth, Michelle, illus. 2011. 32p. (J). 19.50 *(978-1-58385-237-8(9))* ktf-writers-studio.

Fletcher, Ralph. Hello, Harvest Moon. Kiesler, Kate, illus. 2017. (ENG.). 32p. (J). (gr. -1-3). pap. 8.99 *(978-1-328-74049-6(8),* 1677015, Clarion Bks.) HarperCollins Pubs.

Fluharty, Kristi and T. Lively. Fool Moon Rising. Fluharty, T. Lively, illus. 2009. (ENG.). 40p. (J). 16.99 *(978-1-4335-0682-6(3))* Crossway.

Foster, Marilyn. Moon Tricks. Vega, Alison, illus. 2012. 48p. pap. *(978-1-77097-960-4(3))* FriesenPress.

Franco, Franco & Aureliani, Franco. Dino-Mike & the Lunar Showdown. Franco, Franco et al, illus. 2016. (Dino-Mike! Ser.). (ENG.). 128p. (J). (gr. 2-3). lib. bdg. 25.32 *(978-1-4965-2492-8(6),* 130424, Stone Arch Bks.) Capstone.

Froud, Brian, illus. Chelsea Morning. 2004. 32p. (J). *(978-0-689-03593-7(4),* Milk & Cookies) ibooks, Inc.

Galliez, Roxane Marie. Give Me Moon. Delanssay, Cathy, illus. 2009. 44p. (J). (gr. -1-3). 14.99 *(978-0-8416-7138-6(9))* Hammond World Atlas Corp.

Galloway, Emily Ledford. Nimby the Cloud. 2008. 32p. pap. 24.95 *(978-1-60441-779-1(X))* America Star Bks.

Gardner, Sally. Maggot Moon. Crouch, Julian, illus. (ENG.). 288p. (YA). (gr. 7). 2014. pap. 9.99 *(978-0-7636-7169-3(X))* 2013. 16.99 *(978-0-7636-6553-1(3))* Candlewick Pr.

Gay, Marie-Louise. Mademoiselle Moon, 1 vol. 2006. (ENG., Illus.). 32p. (J). (gr. k-2). pap. 7.95 *(978-1-55005-134-6(2),* ba7c0bef-e090-42f1-bc8b-ebc662fbd603) Fitzhenry & Whiteside, Ltd. CAN. Dist: Firefly Bks., Ltd.

Gibbs, Stuart. Space Case. 2015. (Moon Base Alpha Ser.). (ENG., Illus.). 368p. (J). (gr. 3-7). pap. 8.99 *(978-1-4424-9487-9(5),* Simon & Schuster Bks. For Young Readers) Simon & Schuster Bks. For Young Readers.

—Space Case. 2015. (Moon Base Alpha Ser.: 1). lib. bdg. 18.40 *(978-0-606-37883-3(9))* Turtleback.

—Spaced Out. (Moon Base Alpha Ser.). (ENG.). (J). (gr. 3-7). 2017. 368p. pap. 8.99 *(978-1-4814-2337-3(1))* 2016. (Illus.). 352p. 18.99 *(978-1-4814-2336-6(3))* Simon & Schuster Bks. For Young Readers. (Simon & Schuster Bks. For Young Readers).

—Spaced Out. 2017. (Moon Base Alpha Ser.: 2). lib. bdg. 18.40 *(978-0-606-39762-9(0))* Turtleback.

—Waste of Space. (Moon Base Alpha Ser.). (ENG.). (J). (gr. 3-7). 2019. 368p. pap. 8.99 *(978-1-4814-7780-2(3))* 2018. (Illus.). 336p. 18.99 *(978-1-4814-7779-6(X))* Simon & Schuster Bks. For Young Readers. (Simon & Schuster Bks. For Young Readers).

Gigot, Jami. Mae & the Moon. 2015. (ENG., Illus.). 36p. (J). (gr. k-2). 17.99 *(978-0-9913866-2-8(0))* Ripple Grove Pr.

Gill, Michael. Mitsuki. 2008. 32p. pap. 19.99 *(978-1-4363-0938-7(7))* Xlibris Corp.

Gillmor, Don. Yuck, a Love Story, 1 vol. Gay, Marie-Louise, illus. 2010. (ENG.). 32p. (J). (gr. k-2). pap. 9.95 *(978-1-55455-172-9(2),* 22c06c67-ac15-4283-b0c3-cb6c296fd01e) Trifolium Bks., Inc. CAN. Dist: Firefly Bks., Ltd.

Golde, Justin F. Yes, My Dear, Alligators Do Belong on the Moon. 2012. 24p. pap. 11.50 *(978-1-62212-188-5(0),* Strategic Bk. Publishing) Strategic Book Publishing & Rights Agency (SBPRA).

Graham, Judith A. The Didley-Doo's, 1 vol. 2009. 36p. pap. 24.95 *(978-1-60836-035-2(0))* America Star Bks.

Guess What the Moon Saw? Individual Title Six-Packs. (gr. -1-2). 23.00 *(978-0-7635-8807-6(5))* Rigby Education.

Guettier, Nancy. Jude's Moon. Walsh, Tina, illus. (ENG.). 32p. (gr. -1-4). 2015. 19.95 *(978-1-63047-725-7(7))* 2014. pap. 9.95 *(978-1-61448-964-1(5))* Morgan James Publishing.

Gutierrez, Lorna. Hello, Mr. Moon. Watkins, Laura, illus. 2016. (J). *(978-1-4351-6412-3(1))* Barnes & Noble, Inc.

Haaji. Black Moon. 2004. 176p. per. 15.00 *(978-0-9747017-2-1(6))* Neshee Pubn.

Handa, Nimret. Good Night Stories. 2004. (Illus.). 20p. (J). *(978-81-291-0373-4(7))* Rupa & Co.

Hano, Patricia. Tyler Meets the Moon. 2010. 28p. pap. 11.99 *(978-1-60911-189-2(3),* Eloquent Bks.) Strategic Book Publishing & Rights Agency (SBPRA).

Hanson, Anders. Night Owl. Haberstroh, Anne, illus. 2006. (Fact & Fiction Ser.). 24p. (J). pap. 48.42 *(978-1-59679-954-7(4))* ABDO Publishing Co.

Hanson, Robert. Bluey & the Great Spirit Moon. 2013. 48p. pap. 17.45 *(978-1-4525-0845-0(3))* Balboa Pr.

Hare, John. Field Trip to the Moon. 2019. (Field Trip Adventures Ser.). (ENG., Illus.). 40p. (J). (gr. -1-3). 17.99 *(978-0-8234-4253-9(5),* Margaret Ferguson Books) Holiday Hse., Inc.

Harley, Bill. Bear's All-Night Party. Ferreira, Melissa, illus. 2005. (ENG.). 32p. (J). (gr. -1-2). 15.95 *(978-0-87483-572-4(0))* August Hse. Pubs., Inc.

Harstad, Johan. 172 Hours on the Moon. 2012. (ENG.). 368p. (YA). (gr. 7-17). 36.99 *(978-0-316-18288-1(5))* Little, Brown Bks. for Young Readers.

Hawthorne, Rachel. Dark Guardian #2: Full Moon. 2009. (Dark Guardian Ser.: 2). (ENG.). 272p. (YA). (gr. 9-18). pap. 8.99 *(978-0-06-170956-2(5),* HarperTeen) HarperCollins Pubs.

Hayes, Vicki C. Home Planet, 1 vol. 2015. (Red Rhino Ser.). (ENG.). 72p. (J). (gr. 4-7). mass mkt. 9.95 *(978-1-62250-966-9(8))* Saddleback Educational Publishing, Inc.

Heather Rose Brabant. The Moon Princess. 2009. 20p. pap. 11.95 *(978-1-4389-2980-4(3))* AuthorHouse.

Heimdallson, Freydis, et al. Kindertales: Stories Old & New for the Children of the Folk. 2008. 100p. pap. 19.50 *(978-1-4357-2563-8(8))* Lulu Pr., Inc.

Heller, Janet Ruth. How the Moon Regained Her Shape, 1 vol. Hodson, Ben, illus. 2006. (ENG.). 32p. (J). (gr. 1-5). 15.95 *(978-0-9764943-4-8(5))* Arbordale Publishing.

Hendrick-Lockyer, Veronica. Moon Boy. 2013. 18p. pap. *(978-1-84903-209-4(2))* Schiel & Denver Publishing Ltd.

Henkes, Kevin. Kitten's First Full Moon: A Caldecott Award Winner. Henkes, Kevin, illus. 2004. (ENG., Illus.). 40p. (J). (gr. -1-3). 19.99 *(978-0-06-058828-1(4),* Greenwillow Bks.) HarperCollins Pubs.

—Kitten's First Full Moon Board Book: A Caldecott Award Winner. Henkes, Kevin, illus. 2015. (ENG., Illus.). 34p. (J). (gr. -1 — 1). bds. 9.99 *(978-0-06-241710-7(X),* Greenwillow Bks.) HarperCollins Pubs.

—La Primera Luna Llena de Gatita: A Caldecott Award Winner, 1 vol. Henkes, Kevin, illus. 2006. Orig. Title: Kitten's First Full Moon. (SPA., Illus.). 40p. (J). (gr. -1-3). 17.99 *(978-0-06-087223-6(3))* HarperCollins Español.

Heo, Yumi. Sun & Moon Have a Tea Party. Stoop, Naoko, illus. 2020. 40p. (J). (gr. -1-2). 17.99 *(978-0-385-39033-0(5),* Schwartz & Wade Bks.) Random Hse. Children's Bks.

Hergé. Destination Moon.Tr. of Objectif Lune. (J). (gr. 3-8). ring bd. 19.95 *(978-0-8288-5026-1(7))*; (Illus.). 62p. 19.95 *(978-0-8288-5027-8(5))* French & European Pubns., Inc.

—Objectif Lune.Tr. of Destination Moon. (FRE., Illus.). (J). (gr. 7-9). ring bd. 19.95 *(978-0-8288-5051-3(8))* French & European Pubns., Inc.

—On a Marche sur la Lune. (Tintin Ser.).Tr. of Explorers on the Moon. (FRE., Illus.). 62p. (J). pap. 21.95 *(978-2-203-00116-9(X))* Casterman, Editions FRA. Dist: Distribooks, Inc.

—On a Marche sur la Lune.Tr. of Explorers on the Moon. (FRE., Illus.). (J). (gr. 7-9). ring bd. 19.95 *(978-0-8288-5053-7(4))* French & European Pubns., Inc.

Hija del Sol y de Luna (Daughter of Sun & Moon) (SPA.). 24p. (J). 4.95 *(978-84-246-1610-6(3))* La Galera, S.A. Editorial ESP. Dist: AIMS International Bks., Inc.

Hill, Susanna Leonard. Moon's First Friends: One Giant Leap for Friendship. Paganelli, Elisa, illus. 2019. (ENG.). 40p. (J). (gr. k-3). 17.99 *(978-1-4926-5680-7(1))* Sourcebooks, Inc.

Hillert, Margaret. Up, up & Away. 2016. (BeginningtoRead Ser.). (ENG., Illus.). 32p. (J). (gr. 1-2). 22.60 *(978-1-59953-806-8(7))* Norwood Hse. Pr.

Holland, Trish. Lasso the Moon. Petrone, Valeria, illus. 2005. (Little Golden Book Ser.). 24p. (J). (gr. -1-2). 5.99 *(978-0-375-83289-5(0)*, Golden Bks.) Random Hse. Children's Bks.

Holmes-Merritt, Angela. LINK Fairflies & Fairies. 2008. 36p. 17.50 *(978-0-615-17415-0(9))* AngiesInk.

Hooten, K. J. The Egg Nanny Tales. 2008. 98p. pap. 19.95 *(978-1-60563-722-8(X))* America Star Bks.

Hopkins, Leslie. A World Apart. 2012. 20p. pap. 17.99 *(978-1-4772-6783-7(2))* AuthorHouse.

Hosford, Kate. Big Birthday. Clifton-Brown, Holly, illus. 2012. (Carolrhoda Picture Bks.). (ENG.). 32p. (J). (gr. k-2). lib. bdg. 16.95 *(978-0-7613-5410-9(7))* Lerner Publishing Group.

Hughes, Ann. Kaitlyn & the Moonman. 2008. (Illus.). 56p. pap. *(978-1-84748-470-3(0))* Athena Pr.

Hunter, R. C. Moon Kids. 2010. 64p. pap. 11.99 *(978-1-4490-7846-1(X))* AuthorHouse.

Ikeda, Daisaku. The Princess & the Moon. McCraughrean, Geraldine, tr. from JPN. Wildsmith, Brian, illus. 2013. 6.95 *(978-1-935523-58-1(9))* World Tribune Pr.

Ikin, Susan. Alex & the Night-tide Dragon. 2010. (Illus.). 68p. pap. 18.95 *(978-1-4461-4894-5(7))* Lulu Pr., Inc.

Isadora, Rachel. Mr. Moon. Date not set. (J). 15.99 *(978-0-06-029821-0(9))*; lib. bdg. 16.89 *(978-0-06-029822-7(7))* HarperCollins Pubs.

Ishwaran, Wobine. A Journey into Space: Kary to the Moon. 2008. 24p. pap. 11.49 *(978-1-4343-6717-4(7))* AuthorHouse.

Ives, Frances. Maybe the Moon. 2019. (ENG., Illus.). 32p. (J). (gr. -1-k). pap. 9.99 *(978-1-910552-84-1(4))* O'Mara, Michael Bks., Ltd. GBR. Dist: Independent Pubs. Group.

Jackson, Bridgett. The Monster on the Moon: Book Three of Tales from the Creek. 2009. 40p. pap. 18.49 *(978-1-4389-3540-9(4))* AuthorHouse.

Jeffers, Oliver. The Way Back Home. Jeffers, Oliver, illus. 2008. (ENG., Illus.). 32p. (J). (gr. -1-3). 18.99 *(978-0-399-25074-3(3)*, Philomel Bks.) Penguin Young Readers Group.

Jones, Alexandra. Moon Magic. 2012. 28p. pap. 21.99 *(978-1-4771-3995-0(8))* Xlibris Corp.

Joyce, William. The Man in the Moon. Joyce, William, illus. 2011. (Guardians of Childhood Ser.). (ENG., Illus.). 56p. (J). (gr. -1-3). 19.99 *(978-1-4424-3041-9(9)*, Atheneum Bks. for Young Readers) Simon & Schuster Children's Publishing.

—The Sandman: The Story of Sanderson Mansnoozie. Joyce, William, illus. 2012. (Guardians of Childhood Ser.). (ENG., Illus.). 48p. (J). (gr. -1-3). 19.99 *(978-1-4424-3042-6(7)*, Atheneum Bks. for Young Readers) Simon & Schuster Children's Publishing.

Joyce, William & Geringer, Laura. Nicholas St. North & the Battle of the Nightmare King. Joyce, William, illus. 2018. (Guardians Ser.: 1). (ENG., Illus.). 256p. (J). (gr. 2-6). pap. 8.99 *(978-1-4424-3049-5(4)*, Atheneum Bks. for Young Readers) Simon & Schuster Children's Publishing.

—Nicholas St. North & the Battle of the Nightmare King, Bk. 1. Joyce, William, illus. 2011. (Guardians Ser.: 1). (ENG., Illus.). 240p. (J). (gr. 2-6). 18.99 *(978-1-4424-3048-8(6)*, Atheneum Bks. for Young Readers) Simon & Schuster Children's Publishing.

Kalz, Jill. Tuckerbean on the Moon, 1 vol. Mahan, Benton, illus. 2009. (Read-It! Readers: Adventures of Tuckerbean Ser.). (ENG.). 24p. (J). (gr. -1-3). 22.65 *(978-1-4048-5234-1(4)*, 95522, Picture Window Bks.) Capstone.

Kemble, Mai S. The Moon & the Night Sweeper. Kemble, Mai S., illus. 2008. (Illus.). (J). pap. 6.95 *(978-1-60108-023-3(9))* Red Cygnet Pr.

Kemble, Mai S., illus. The Moon & the Night Sweeper. 2007. 30p. (J). (gr. -1-2). 15.95 *(978-1-60108-013-4(1))* Red Cygnet Pr.

Kherdian, David. Come Back, Moon. Hogrogian, Nonny, illus. 2013. (ENG.). 32p. (J). (gr. -1-3). 17.99 *(978-1-4424-5887-1(9)*, Beach Lane Bks.) Beach Lane Bks.

Kim, Cecil. Little Moon's Christmas: Imagination - Objects. Horacek, Petr, illus. 2015. (Step up — Creative Thinking Ser.). (ENG.). 32p. (J). (gr. -1-2). 27.99 *(978-1-925186-39-0(3)*, 33d2428e-eca5-4009-9861-ee5fc79e6245, Big and SMALL) ChoiceMaker Pty. Ltd., The AUS. Dist: Lerner Publishing Group.

King, Thomas. Coyote Sings to the Moon. Wales, Johnny, illus. 2008. (ENG.). 36p. (J). pap. *(978-1-55263-868-2(5))* Magma.

Kitze, Carrie A. We See the Moon. Jinshan Painting Academy, illus. l.t. ed. 2003. 32p. (J). (gr. -1-3). 16.95 *(978-0-9726244-0-4(6))* EMK Pr.

Koksal, Erin. Bedtime for Abbie. 2010. 23p. (J). pap. 11.95 *(978-1-4327-5693-2(1))* Outskirts Pr., Inc.

Komai, Asuka, illus. October Moon. 2009. (J). *(978-1-60108-017-2(4))* Red Cygnet Pr.

Koren, Robert. The Moon in the Man. 2010. 28p. pap. 15.99 *(978-1-4535-3946-0(8))* Xlibris Corp.

Kraatz, Jeramey. Space Runners #1: the Moon Platoon. (Space Runners Ser.: 1). (ENG.). (J). (gr. 3-7). 2018. 368p. pap. 7.99 *(978-0-06-244598-8(7))* 2017. 352p. 16.99 *(978-0-06-244597-1(9))* HarperCollins Pubs. (HarperCollins).

—Space Runners #2: Dark Side of the Moon. 2018. (Space Runners Ser.: 2). (ENG.). (J). (gr. 3-7). 368p. pap. 6.99 *(978-0-06-244601-5(0))*; 352p. 16.99 *(978-0-06-244600-8(2))* HarperCollins Pubs. (HarperCollins).

—Space Runners #4: the Fate of Earth. 2019. (Space Runners Ser.: 4). (ENG.). 320p. (J). (gr. 3-7). 16.99 *(978-0-06-244606-0(1)*, HarperCollins) HarperCollins Pubs.

Krans, Kim. Whose Moon Is That? 2017. (Illus.). 48p. (J). (gr. -1-2). 17.99 *(978-1-101-93227-8(9)*, Random Hse. Bks. for Young Readers) Random Hse. Children's Bks.

Krouskop, Adrienne. The Bakers Moon. 2013. 24p. pap. 10.50 *(978-1-938743-92-4(X))* Reimann Bks.

Lamar, Gail Renfroe. Moon of the Wishing Night. Mask, Cynthia, illus. 2004. 32p. (J). 17.95 *(978-1-57966-047-5(9)*, River City Kids) River City Publishing.

Lascurain, Anna. Apollo in the Moon House. 2006. Orig. Title: The Moonboy. (J). per. 7.99 *(978-0-9769612-3-9(7))* Darker Intentions Pr.

Lemieux, Jean. Toby Shoots for Infinity. Cummins, Sarah, tr. Casson, Sophie, illus. 2005. (Formac First Novels Ser.: 55). (ENG.). 64p. (J). (gr. 2-5). 14.95 *(978-0-88780-685-8(6)*, 685); 4.95 *(978-0-88780-684-1(8)*, 684) Formac Publishing Co., Ltd. CAN. Dist: Formac Lorimer Bks. Ltd.

Lin, Grace. A Big Mooncake for Little Star (Caldecott Honor Book) 2018. (ENG., Illus.). 40p. (J). (gr. -1-3). 18.99 *(978-0-316-40448-8(9))* Little, Brown Bks. for Young Readers.

—Starry River of the Sky. 2014. (ENG., Illus.). 320p. (J). (gr. 3-7). pap. 11.99 *(978-0-316-12597-0(0))* Little, Brown Bks. for Young Readers.

—Starry River of the Sky. 2014. (J). lib. bdg. 20.85 *(978-0-606-32277-5(9))* Turtleback.

—Thanking the Moon: Celebrating the Mid-Autumn Moon Festival. 2010. (ENG.). 32p. (J). (gr. -1-2). 18.99 *(978-0-375-86101-7(7)*, Knopf Bks. for Young Readers) Random Hse. Children's Bks.

—Where the Mountain Meets the Moon. 2011. (ENG., Illus.). 278p. (gr. 4-7). 19.00 *(978-1-61383-087-1(4))* Perfection Learning Corp.

—Where the Mountain Meets the Moon. 2011. (J). lib. bdg. 22.10 *(978-0-606-16233-3(X))* Turtleback.

—Where the Mountain Meets the Moon (Newbery Honor Book) (ENG., Illus.). (J). (gr. 3-7). 2011. 320p. pap. 12.99 *(978-0-316-03863-8(6))* 2009. 288p. 18.99 *(978-0-316-11427-1(8))* Little, Brown Bks. for Young Readers.

Liniers. Buenas Noches, Planeta: TOON Level 2. 2017. (SPA., Illus.). 36p. (J). (gr. k-1). 12.99 *(978-1-943145-21-8(0)*, 9781943145218, TOON Books) Astra Publishing Hse.

—Buenas Noches, Planeta: TOON Level 2. 2017. (SPA., Illus.). 36p. (J). (gr. k-1). pap. 7.99 *(978-1-943145-19-5(9)*, 9781943145195, Toon Books) Candlewick Pr.

—Good Night, Planet: TOON Level 2. 2017. (ENG., Illus.). 36p. (J). (gr. k-2). 12.99 *(978-1-943145-20-1(2)*, 9781943145201, TOON Books) Astra Publishing Hse.

Longstreet, Olivia. Edgar's Moon. 2011. 24p. pap. 15.99 *(978-1-4568-6524-5(2))* Xlibris Corp.

Lopez, Sixto. Snarloff Duwaki's Adventures. 2011. 24p. pap. 24.95 *(978-1-4626-2557-4(6))* America Star Bks.

The Lotus Caves. 2014. (ENG., Illus.). 288p. (J). (gr. 4-8). pap. 7.99 *(978-1-4814-1837-9(8)*, Aladdin) Simon & Schuster Children's Publishing.

The Lotus Caves. 2014. (ENG., Illus.). 288p. (J). (gr. 4-8). 17.99 *(978-1-4814-1838-6(6)*, Simon & Schuster/Paula Wiseman Bks.) Simon & Schuster/Paula Wiseman Bks.

Loveridge, Pamela. The Man in the Moon. 2012. 28p. pap. 32.70 *(978-1-4797-5423-6(4))* Xlibris Corp.

Lowe, Tom. Louie the Loon & the Moon. Leadlove, Ben, illus. 2011. 28p. pap. 11.00 *(978-1-61170-030-5(2))* Robertson Publishing.

Mackin, Joan Marie. It's Just the Moon. 2004. (J). pap. 9.00 *(978-0-8059-6315-1(4))* Dorrance Publishing Co., Inc.

MacLachlan, Patricia. The Moon's Almost Here. dePaola, Tomie, illus. 2016. (ENG.). 32p. (J). (gr. -1-3). 17.99 *(978-1-4814-2062-4(3)*, McElderry, Margaret K. Bks.) McElderry, Margaret K. Bks.

Madison's Descent: A Child's Journey. collector's ed. 2004. (J). 75.00 *(978-0-9752516-0-7(0))* Otis & Randolph Pr.

Maher, Mickle Brandt. Master Stitchum & the Moon. Dousias, Spiro, illus. 2003. (J). 19.99 *(978-1-932188-01-1(0))* Bollix Bks.

Mai, Lily. Bertie Boom's Trip to the Moon. 2010. (Illus.). 20p. 12.49 *(978-1-4520-1379-4(9))* AuthorHouse.

Martin-Duttmann, Robin. Zoo on the Moon. 2013. 24p. pap. 12.97 *(978-1-62212-735-1(8)*, Strategic Bk. Publishing) Strategic Book Publishing & Rights Agency (SBPRA).

Martin, Gina. Mother Moon: Magic Pool in the Sky. 2008. 28p. pap. 12.49 *(978-1-4389-0138-1(0))* AuthorHouse.

MaryAnn, Aunt. Spooky Journey down Riverside Drive the Night of the Full Moon. 2010. (ENG.). 40p. pap. 15.95 *(978-0-557-31081-4(4))* Lulu Pr., Inc.

Matula, Christina. The Shadow in the Moon. Law, Pearl, illus. 2018. 32p. (J). (gr. k-3). lib. bdg. 17.99 *(978-1-58089-746-4(0))* Charlesbridge Publishing, Inc.

McCluire, Brian D. The Sun & the Moon. 2006. (Illus.). 36p. (J). 14.95 *(978-1-933426-09-9(8))* Universal Flag Publishing.

McKellop, Holly R. To the Moon. 2012. 32p. pap. 24.95 *(978-1-4626-8034-4(8))* America Star Bks.

McKinnon, Yolanda Amos. Why Is the Moon Following Me? 2012. 24p. pap. 15.99 *(978-1-4771-3081-0(0))* Xlibris Corp.

Meschenmoser, Sebastian. Mr. Squirrel & the Moon. 2015. (ENG., Illus.). 48p. (J). (gr. -1-1). 18.95 *(978-0-7358-4156-7(X))* North-South Bks., Inc.

Micchelli, Lauren. The Snootzytime Adventures of Maddie & Murphy - to the Moon & Back. 2015. (ENG., Illus.). 40p. (J). pap. 14.95 *(978-1-62287-843-7(4))* First Edition Design Publishing.

Milbourne, A. & Wells, R. Mouse on the Moon. 2004. (Touchy-Feely Board Bks.). (Illus.). 10p. (J). (gr. -1-18). 4.95 *(978-0-7945-0163-1(X)*, Usborne) EDC Publishing.

Miller, Jules, illus. When Night Became Day. 2015. (ENG.). 32p. (J). (gr. -1-k). 16.95 *(978-1-62914-632-4(3)*, Sky Pony Pr.) Skyhorse Publishing Co., Inc.

Mindler, Jason. Giralon. 2003. 122p. (YA). 20.95 *(978-0-595-74854-9(6))*; pap. 10.95 *(978-0-595-28581-5(3))* iUniverse, Inc. (Writers Club Pr.).

Moon Stories. 2004. (YA). 11.95 *(978-0-9752801-1-9(2))* Beres, Nancy.

Morrissey, Dean & Krensky, Stephen. The Crimson Comet. Morrissey, Dean, illus. 2006. (Illus.). 32p. (J). (gr. k-4). 17.89 *(978-0-06-008070-9(1))* HarperCollins Pubs.

Mortensen, Lori. Cindy Moo. 2012. (ENG., Illus.). 32p. (J). (gr. -1-2). 16.99 *(978-0-06-204393-1(5)*, HarperCollins) HarperCollins Pubs.

Murphy, Bobby. Ted the Turtle's Trip to the Moon. 2013. 24p. pap. 11.50 *(978-1-62212-431-2(6)*, Strategic Bk. Publishing) Strategic Book Publishing & Rights Agency (SBPRA).

Mutuku, E. M. When the Sun Challenged the Moon. 2012. 20p. pap. 15.50 *(978-1-4634-4718-2(3))* AuthorHouse.

My Trip to the Moon. 2004. (J). ring bd. 4.50 *(978-0-9762740-0-1(0)*, Flat Kids) Smart Smiles Co., The.

Neira, Elsy. The Kid That Flew to the Moon: El niño que volo a la Luna. 2011. 40p. pap. *(978-1-4269-6986-7(4))* Trafford Publishing (UK) Ltd.

Nickel, Scott. Blastoff to the Secret Side of the Moon!, 1 vol. Bradley, Jess, illus. 2013. (Comics Land Ser.). (ENG.). 32p. (J). (gr. k-2). 7.95 *(978-1-4342-4273-0(0)*, 120359, Stone Arch Bks.) Capstone.

Oddo, Joanne. The Strawberry Moon. 2004. (Illus.). 24.99 *(978-1-4134-5075-0(X))* Xlibris Corp.

Ofanansky, Allison Maile. New Month, New Moon. Alpern, Eliyahu, photos by. 2014. (ENG., Illus.). 32p. (J). (gr. -1-2). 16.95 *(978-1-4677-1945-2(5)*, e6eba705-31d0-4590-8f0c-2c4a44088e85, Kar-Ben Publishing) Lerner Publishing Group.

Olker, Constance. The Punctuation Pals Go to the Moon. 2005. (Illus.). (J). 64p. per. 24.95 *(978-1-933449-13-5(6))*; per. 19.95 *(978-0-9761289-6-0(9))* Nightengale Pr.

Orobosa-Ogbeide, Kathryn. The Boy & the Moon. 2012. 12p. pap. 12.68 *(978-1-4669-1894-8(2))* Trafford Publishing.

Overton, Lou Ann. Thank You, Moon. 2013. 24p. pap. 12.45 *(978-1-4908-0030-1(1)*, WestBow Pr.) Author Solutions, LLC.

Palazzolo, Gail M. Mommy, How Can We Catch the Moon? 2008. 15p. pap. 24.95 *(978-1-60672-864-2(4))* America Star Bks.

Paraskevas, Michael. Mr. Moon. 2017. (Illus.). 34p. (J). (gr. -1-2). bds. 7.99 *(978-0-399-54995-3(1)*, Crown Books For Young Readers) Random Hse. Children's Bks.

Petrone, Catherine. Moon Worms. 2010. 27p. (J). pap. 12.95 *(978-1-4327-1477-2(5))* Outskirts Pr., Inc.

Plunkett, Windyann. Fiddle Me a Riddle & Bring Me the Moon. Davidson, Mary, illus. 2011. 24p. pap. 24.95 *(978-1-4626-3920-5(8))* America Star Bks.

Porter, Pamela. Yellow Moon, Apple Moon, 1 vol. James, Matt, illus. 2008. (ENG.). 32p. (J). (gr. k — 1). 17.95 *(978-0-88899-809-5(0))* Groundwood Bks. CAN. Dist: Publishers Group West (PGW).

Posnock, Michael A. The Adventures of Wilbur the Wave. 2013. (ENG.). 44p. pap. 17.99 *(978-1-4808-0132-5(1))* Archway Publishing.

Potts, Molly. The Falling Moon. 2012. 26p. 24.95 *(978-1-4626-6596-9(9))* America Star Bks.

Reed, Lynn Rowe. Swim to the Moon. 2009. 32p. pap. 12.99 *(978-1-4389-4980-2(4))* AuthorHouse.

Reynolds, Paul A. Sydney & Simon: to the Moon! Reynolds, Peter H., illus. 2017. (Sydney & Simon Ser.: 3). 48p. (J). (gr. 1-4). pap. 4.99 *(978-1-58089-680-1(4))*; lib. bdg. 12.99 *(978-1-58089-679-5(0))* Charlesbridge Publishing, Inc.

Robinson, Hilary. Over the Moon. Abbott, Jane, illus. 2009. (Tadpoles Ser.). (ENG.). 24p. (J). (gr. k-2). pap. *(978-0-7787-3899-2(X))*; lib. bdg. *(978-0-7787-3868-8(X))* Crabtree Publishing Co.

Rosario, Joann. Where Did Sabrina Go? Rosario, Joann, illus. 2004. (Illus.). 13p. (J). (gr. -1-5). pap. 10.00 *(978-0-9758746-1-5(6))* J.G.R. Enterprises.

ROSE ANNE ST ROMAIN. Moon's Cloud Blanket, 1 vol. 2003. (ENG., Illus.). 32p. (J). (gr. k-3). 16.99 *(978-1-56554-922-7(8)*, Pelican Publishing) Arcadia Publishing.

Ross, Daisy T. Ty & the Moon. 2012. 80p. pap. 25.25 *(978-1-4772-6950-3(9))* AuthorHouse.

Routley, Becky. Moon Golf. 2009. (Illus.). 28p. pap. 12.49 *(978-1-4490-4713-9(0))* AuthorHouse.

Ryan, Karlene Kay. Genevieve & the Moon. Johnson, Meredith, illus. 2013. 34p. pap. 9.99 *(978-0-9888843-3-5(X))* Ryan, Karlene Kay Author.

Rylant, Cynthia. Long Night Moon. Siegel, Mark, illus. 2004. (ENG.). 32p. (J). (gr. -1-3). 18.99 *(978-0-689-85426-2(9)*, Simon & Schuster Bks. For Young Readers) Simon & Schuster Bks. For Young Readers.

Saikia, Mayur, illus. Anansi & His Children. 2010. 24p. (J). *(978-1-60617-139-4(9))* Teaching Strategies, LLC.

Samuels, Gregory Robert. Mommy, Where Does Everything Come From? Brennan, Craig, illus. 2008. 11p. pap. 24.95 *(978-1-60610-437-8(3))* America Star Bks.

Scott, Janine. Mars Mouse, 1 vol. Wood, Hannah, illus. 2009. (Treasure Chest Readers Ser.). (ENG.). 24p. (J). (gr. 1-1). pap. 9.15 *(978-1-60754-677-1(9)*, 91ae73ab-a879-4fb8-9c38-fd87648aaf30); lib. bdg. 27.27 *(978-1-60754-676-4(0)*, c87bb159-35dd-4473-a072-85a046b4d8b0) Rosen Publishing Group, Inc., The. (Windmill Bks.).

Sharpe, Jemima. Mr Moon Wakes Up. Sharpe, Jemima, illus. 2016. (Child's Play Library). (ENG., Illus.). 32p. (J). *(978-1-84643-694-9(X))* Child's Play International Ltd.

Shelton, C. M. Cosmic Chaos. 2015. (ENG., Illus.). 226p. (J). pap. 8.99 *(978-1-941720-25-7(0))* Ashberry Lane.

Sills, Elizabeth & Patrice, Elena. Nana Star. Saker, Linda, illus. 2007. 32p. (J). (gr. -1-3). 15.95 *(978-0-9753843-5-0(X))* ee publishing & productions, inc.

—Nana Star & the Moonman. Saker, Linda, illus. 2008. 32p. (J). (gr. -1-3). 15.95 *(978-0-9753843-6-7(8))* ee publishing & productions, inc.

Sinke, Janet Mary. Priscilla Mcdoodlenut Doodle Mcmae Asks, Why? Pennington, Craig, illus. 2007. 40p. (J). 17.95 *(978-0-9742732-8-0(7))* My Grandma & Me Pubs.

Slayton, Fran Cannon. Snowball Moon. Bishop, Tracy, illus. (ENG.). (J). (gr. -1-k). 2019. 26p. bds. 7.99 *(978-1-4998-0991-6(3))* 2017. 32p. 16.99 *(978-1-4998-0495-9(4))* Little Bee Books Inc.

Smith, Buckley. Moonsailors. Smith, Buckley, illus. 2007. (ENG., Illus.). 40p. (J). (gr. -1-7). 14.95 *(978-0-937822-95-1(7))* WoodenBoat Pubns.

Smith, Richard G. When the Moon Fell Down. Date not set. 32p. (J). (gr. -1-18). pap. 4.99 *(978-0-06-443550-5(4))* HarperCollins Pubs.

Smith, Rosemarie. Meet the Bubblechomps - & the Bubblechomps Go Skiing. 2010. (Illus.). 36p. pap. *(978-1-907652-00-4(0))* Grosvenor Hse. Publishing Ltd.

Soetoro-Ng, Maya. Ladder to the Moon. Morales, Yuyi, illus. 2017. (ENG.). 48p. (J). (gr. -1-3). 8.99 *(978-0-7636-9343-5(X))* Candlewick Pr.

—Ladder to the Moon with CD. Morales, Yuyi, illus. 2012. (ENG.). 48p. (J). (gr. -1-3). 19.99 *(978-0-7636-6006-2(X))* Candlewick Pr.

Solner Heimer, Patricia. Li'l Earth. Solner Heimer, Patricia, illus. 2010. (Illus.). 32p. (J). (gr. k-4). 15.99 *(978-0-9844453-0-1(7))* Maple Road Publishing, Inc.

Sonneborn, Scott. The Man of Steel: Superman vs. the Moon Bandits. Cavallaro, Mike, illus. 2013. (Man of Steel Ser.). (ENG.). 88p. (J). (gr. 3-7). 26.65 *(978-1-4342-4093-4(2)*, 119812); pap. 5.95 *(978-1-4342-4223-5(4)*, 120281) Capstone. (Stone Arch Bks.).

Space Case. 2014. (Moon Base Alpha Ser.). (ENG., Illus.). 352p. (J). (gr. 3-7). 18.99 *(978-1-4424-9486-2(7)*, Simon & Schuster Bks. For Young Readers) Simon & Schuster Bks. For Young Readers.

The Spotted Moon & Deputy KC: Chase the Big Orange Ball. 2008. (J). spiral bd. *(978-0-9793930-3-7(5))* Dandelion Publishing.

Stead, Philip C. Music for Mister Moon. Stead, Erin E., illus. 2019. 40p. (J). (gr. -1-3). 18.99 *(978-0-8234-4160-0(1)*, Neal Porter Bks) Holiday Hse., Inc.

Steadman, Ralph. Flowers for the Moon. 2004. (Illus.). 42p. 100.00 *(978-0-9760742-0-5(6))* Sylph Pubns.

Steinmann, Donna. Hello, Grand Mamoon! Guion, Tamara, illus. 2005. 32p. (J). 16.95 *(978-0-9663286-4-6(7))* EarthTime Pubns.

Stokholm, Susan Mary. Between a Shadow & the Moon. 2010. (ENG.). 264p. pap. 14.49 *(978-1-4520-1752-5(2))* AuthorHouse.

Sutherland, Suzanne. Under the Dusty Moon. 2016. (ENG.). 272p. (YA). pap. 14.99 *(978-1-4597-3202-5(2))* Dundurn Pr. CAN. Dist: Publishers Group West (PGW).

Swarbrick, David E. Peggy's Play House. 2011. 24p. pap. 24.95 *(978-1-4626-1989-4(4))* America Star Bks.

Taylor, Rosemary. Eddie's Rocket Adventure. 2011. 28p. pap. 13.54 *(978-1-4670-2537-9(2))* AuthorHouse.

Teckentrup, Britta. Moon: a Peek-Through Picture Book. 2018. (ENG., Illus.). 32p. (J). (gr. -1-2). 17.99 *(978-1-5247-6966-6(5)*, Doubleday Bks. for Young Readers) Random Hse. Children's Bks.

Torgerson, Scotty Delray. Jacob Goes to the Moon. 2nd l.t. ed. 2005. (Illus.). 32p. (J). 10.00 *(978-0-9767116-0-5(5))* Torgerson Meadows Publishing.

Udry, Janice May. The Moon Jumpers: A Caldecott Honor Award Winner. Sendak, Maurice, illus. 2013. (ENG.). 32p. (J). (gr. -1-3). 17.95 *(978-0-06-028460-2(9)*, HarperCollins) HarperCollins Pubs.

Ungerer, Tomi. El Hombre de la Luna. (SPA., Illus.). 40p. (J). (gr. k-2). 7.95 *(978-84-204-3746-0(8)*, AF0456) Santillana USA Publishing Co., Inc.

—El Hombre de la Luna. Ungerer, Tomi, illus. 2003. (Picture Books Collection). (SPA., Illus.). 40p. (J). (gr. k-3). pap. 10.95 *(978-968-19-0661-0(6))* Santillana USA Publishing Co., Inc.

van Genechten, Guido. Moon Is Sad. 2010. (ENG.). 12p. (J). (gr. k — 1). bds. 8.95 *(978-1-60537-048-4(7))* Clavis Publishing.

Varando, Alberto. Get the Moon. Colvin, Andrea, ed. 2020. (ENG., Illus.). 52p. (J). 14.99 *(978-1-941302-59-0(9)*, e05419b7-2bda-42d6-b1c2-356991d1fb31) Magnetic Pr.

Veil, Karney. Sun & Moon Play Hide & Seek: A Children's Story. 2012. 24p. (-18). pap. 24.95 *(978-1-4626-9401-3(2))* America Star Bks.

Vere, Ed. Max at Night. 2016. (Max Ser.: 2). (ENG., Illus.). 32p. (J). (gr. -1-2). 16.99 *(978-1-4926-3296-2(1)*, 9781492632962, Sourcebooks Jabberwocky) Sourcebooks, Inc.

Waller, C. L. Lady Sun & the Man in the Moon. 2008. 16p. per. 24.95 *(978-1-4241-8670-9(6))* America Star Bks.

Ward, Helen. Moon Dog. 2005. (Illus.). 40p. (J). *(978-1-84011-864-3(4))* Templar Publishing.

Wartko, Karen J. I Know My Daddy Works on the Moon. 2004. (J). lib. bdg. 17.95 *(978-0-9748979-0-5(6))* Spreeda Publishing.

Weston Woods Staff, creator. Happy Birthday Moon. 2004. 29.95 *(978-1-55592-842-1(0))*; (J). 18.95 *(978-1-55592-805-6(6))*; (J). 38.75 *(978-1-55592-822-3(6))* Weston Woods Studios, Inc.

—Kitten's First Full Moon. 2011. 29.95 *(978-0-545-37422-4(7))* Weston Woods Studios, Inc.

Williams, John Joseph. The Frightened Garden. 2013. 98p. (J). pap. *(978-1-78299-167-0(0))* FeedARead.com.

Wilson, Land. The Girl Who Spoke to the Moon: A Story about Friendship & Loving Our Earth. Cornelison, Sue, illus. 2nd rev. ed. 2020. (ENG.). 40p. (J). (gr. k-2). 17.99 *(978-1-4926-9873-9(3)*, Little Pickle Pr.) Sourcebooks, Inc.

—Sofia's Dream. Cornelison, Sue, illus. 2010. (ENG.). 40p. (J). (gr. -1-2). 18.95 *(978-0-9829938-1-1(1)*, Little Pickle Pr.) Sourcebooks, Inc.

Yakola, Carrie. Full Moon Maxi. 2008. 36p. pap. 19.99 *(978-1-4343-3966-9(1))* AuthorHouse.

Yankey, Lindsey. Sun & Moon. 2015. (Illus.). 32p. (J). (gr. -1-3). 16.95 *(978-1-927018-60-6(9))* Simply Read Bks. CAN. Dist: Ingram Publisher Services.

Yolen, Jane & Stemple, Heidi E. A Kite for Moon, 1 vol. Phelan, Matt, illus. 2019. (ENG.). 32p. (J). 17.99 *(978-0-310-75642-2(1))* Zonderkidz.

Young, Katharine Anne. Grandmother Moon & Roy G Biv: A Colorful Bedtime Story for All Ages. EXPLORE the AMAZING SECRETS of COLOR. 2009. 72p. pap. 23.49 *(978-1-4389-7844-4(8))* AuthorHouse.

Zumwalt, Susan. Shine on Me. 2007. 16p. per. 24.95 *(978-1-4241-8836-9(9))* America Star Bks.

MOON, VOYAGES TO

see Space Flight to the Moon

MOON PROBES

see Lunar Probes

MOORE, HENRY, 1898-1986

O'Reilly, Sally. Henry Moore. 2003. (Artists in Their Time Ser.). (ENG., Illus.). 48p. (J). 24.00 *(978-0-531-12241-9(7)*, Watts, Franklin) Scholastic Library Publishing.

M
N
O

MOORISH ART
see Islamic Art

MOORS (PEOPLE)
see Muslims

MOORS (WETLANDS)—FICTION

Overington, Marcus. Lost on Bodmin Moor. 2012. (Illus.). 50p. pap. *(978-1-909039-36-0(5))* Legend Pr.

MOOSE

Albertson, Al. Moose. 2020. (Animals of the Forest Ser.). (ENG.). 24p. (J). (gr. k-3). lib. bdg. 26.95 *(978-1-64487-128-7(9),* Blastoff! Readers) Bellwether Media.
Borgert-Spaniol, Megan. Moose. 2015. (North American Animals Ser.). (ENG., Illus.). 24p. (J). (gr. k-3). lib. bdg. 26.95 *(978-1-62617-260-9(9),* Blastoff! Readers) Bellwether Media.
Carr, Aaron. Moose. 2014. (Illus.). 24p. (J). *(978-1-62127-212-0(5))* Weigl Pubs., Inc.
Early Macken, JoAnn. Moose, 1 vol. (Animals That Live in the Forest (First Edition) Ser.). (ENG., Illus.). 24p. (gr. 1-1). 2004. lib. bdg. 25.27 *(978-0-8368-4482-5(3),* a1cd7189-0572-49c9-b7e0-6d7f8c128366) 2nd rev. ed. 2009. (J). pap. 9.15 *(978-1-4339-2480-4(3),* c0a5087c-ae24-44ed-965c-d316be888290) 2nd rev. ed. 2009. (J). lib. bdg. 25.27 *(978-1-4339-2404-0(8),* 3a0f8a14-d516-4c27-afb2-a71fd523d7d7) Stevens, Gareth Publishing LLLP.
—Moose / Alces, 1 vol. 2nd rev. ed. 2009. (Animals That Live in the Forest / Animales Del Bosque Ser.). (SPA & ENG.). 24p. (J). (gr. 1-1). lib. bdg. 25.27 *(978-1-4339-2436-1(6),* 0bc5735e-455a-4628-8e7e-827c93a90b72, Weekly Reader Leveled Readers) Stevens, Gareth Publishing LLLP.
Estigarribia, Diana. Moose, 1 vol. 2007. (Animals, Animals Ser.). (ENG., Illus.). 48p. (gr. 5-5). lib. bdg. 32.64 *(978-0-7614-1870-2(9),* 21ffb3b6-375a-41c1-bf15-f67985f9040b) Cavendish Square Publishing LLC.
Gannij, Joan. Elusive Moose. Beaton, Clare, illus. 2011. 32p. (J). (gr. -1-k). pap. 7.99 *(978-1-84686-075-1(X))* Barefoot Bks., Inc.
Gannij, Joan & Grannij, Joan. Elusive Moose. 2006. (Hide-and-Seek Books (Barefoot Books) Ser.). (Illus.). 32p. (J). (gr. -1-3). 15.99 *(978-1-905236-75-6(1))* Barefoot Bks., Inc.
Gish, Melissa. Living Wild - Moose. 2010. (Living Wild Ser.). (ENG., Illus.). 48p. (J). (gr. 5-8). 23.95 *(978-1-58341-973-1(X),* 22190, Creative Education) Creative Co., The.
Hemstock, Annie. Moose, 1 vol. 2012. (North American Animals Ser.). (ENG.). 24p. (J). (gr. -1-2). lib. bdg. 27.32 *(978-1-4296-7705-9(8),* 117302); (gr. k-1). pap. 41.70 *(978-1-4296-8360-9(0))* Capstone. (Capstone Pr.).
Krauskopf, Sharma. Moose Family Close Up. Holdsworth, Henry, photos by. 2007. (Illus.). 28p. per. *(978-0-9543367-4-5(7))* Scottish Radiance Pubns.
Loh-Hagan, Virginia. Moose. Bane, Jeff, illus. 2017. (My Early Library: My Favorite Animal Ser.). (ENG.). 24p. (J). (gr. k-1). lib. bdg. 30.64 *(978-1-63472-834-8(3),* 209762) Cherry Lake Publishing.
Love, Pamela. A Moose's Morning. Sochor, Lesia, illus. 2007. (ENG.). 32p. (J). (gr. -1-3). 15.95 *(978-0-89272-733-9(0))* Down East Bks.
Magby, Meryl. Moose, 1 vol. 2012. (American Animals Ser.). (ENG., Illus.). 24p. (J). (gr. 2-3). pap. 9.25 *(978-1-4488-6325-9(2),* b07fafaf-1abe-4f73-9969-ec2315d582fe, PowerKids Pr.); lib. bdg. 26.27 *(978-1-4488-6183-5(7),* 571b8490-cc32-4989-9675-c01da812bc8b) Rosen Publishing Group, Inc., The.
Meister, Cari. Do You Really Want to Meet a Moose? Fabbri, Daniele, illus. 2015. (Do You Really Want to Meet ... ? Ser.). (ENG.). 24p. (J). (gr. 1-4). lib. bdg. 19.95 *(978-1-60753-736-6(2),* 15267) Amicus.
Mihaly, Christy. Moose. 2017. (Animals of North America Ser.). (ENG., Illus.). 32p. (J). (gr. 2-3). pap. 9.95 *(978-1-63517-091-7(5),* 1635170915, Focus Readers) North Star Editions.
The Moose, 6 vols. (gr. 4-18). 39.95 *(978-0-7368-8500-3(5),* Red Brick Learning) Capstone.
Owen, Ruth. Moose, 1 vol., 1. 2013. (Dr. Bob's Amazing World of Animals Ser.). (ENG.). 32p. (J). (gr. 2-3). pap. 12.75 *(978-1-4777-9037-3(3),* 5c695c97-4dc2-45cc-b9f2-5bda3140b8b2); lib. bdg. 31.27 *(978-1-4777-9036-6(5),* d6242cf5-7df6-46d7-ae05-663e1c329d83) Rosen Publishing Group, Inc., The. (Windmill Bks.).
Owings, Lisa. Moose Attack. 2012. (Animal Attacks Ser.). (ENG., Illus.). 24p. (J). (gr. 3-7). lib. bdg. 26.95 *(978-1-60014-788-3(7),* Torque Bks.) Bellwether Media.
Riggs, Kate. Moose. 2012. 24p. (J). 25.65 *(978-1-60818-111-7(1),* Creative Education) Creative Co., The.
Rogers, Amy B. Moose, 1 vol., 1. 2015. (North America's Biggest Beasts Ser.). (ENG., Illus.). 24p. (J). (gr. 3-4). pap. 9.25 *(978-1-5081-4296-6(3),* 497bec6b-ba10-4d5b-b35d-7278ee1ece15, PowerKids Pr.) Rosen Publishing Group, Inc., The.
Schuetz, Kristin. Moose. 2014. (Backyard Wildlife Ser.). (ENG.). 24p. (J). (gr. k-3). lib. bdg. 26.95 *(978-1-60014-969-6(3),* Blastoff! Readers) Bellwether Media.
Shea, Mary Molly. Massive Moose, 1 vol. 2016. (Cutest Animals... That Could Kill You! Ser.). (ENG., Illus.). 24p. (J). (gr. 2-3). 24.27 *(978-1-4824-4913-6(7),* d038e997-a1b5-4217-b379-ce9d8c26f075) Stevens, Gareth Publishing LLLP.
Stewart, Anne. I Saw a Moose Today. 2007. (Illus.). 32p. (J). (gr. 1-2). 12.95 *(978-0-9766264-6-6(2))* Raven Productions, Inc.
Terp, Gail. Moose. 2016. (Wild Animal Kingdom Ser.). (ENG.). 32p. (J). (gr. 4-6). pap. 9.99 *(978-1-64466-171-0(3),* 10401); (Illus.). 31.35 *(978-1-68072-053-2(8),* 10400) Black Rabbit Bks. (Bolt).
Terp, Gail, contrib. by. Moose. 2018. (Wild Animal Kingdom Ser.). (ENG., Illus.). 32p. (gr. 2-7). pap. 9.95 *(978-1-68072-310-6(3))* RiverStream Publishing.
Winnick, Nick. Moose. 2010. (Backyard Animals Ser.). (Illus.). 24p. (gr. 2-4). (J). pap. 11.95 *(978-1-60596-947-3(8))*; (YA). lib. bdg. 25.70 *(978-1-60596-946-6(X))* Weigl Pubs., Inc.

MOOSE—FICTION

Ayton, Shalanna. The Adventures of Missy the Moose. 2009. 68p. pap. 26.99 *(978-1-4389-7827-7(8))* AuthorHouse.
Beckhorn, Susan Williams. Moose Eggs: Or, Why Moose Has Flat Antlers. Stevens, Helen, illus. 2007. (ENG.). 32p. (J). (gr. -1-3). 15.95 *(978-0-89272-689-9(X))* Down East Bks.
Bingham, Kelly. Circle, Square, Moose. Zelinsky, Paul O., illus. 2014. (ENG.). 48p. (J). (gr. -1-3). 17.99 *(978-0-06-229003-8(7),* Greenwillow Bks.) HarperCollins Pubs.
—Z Is for Moose. Zelinsky, Paul O., illus. 2012. (ENG.). 32p. (J). (gr. -1-2). 17.99 *(978-0-06-079984-7(6))*; lib. bdg. 17.89 *(978-0-06-079985-4(4))* HarperCollins Pubs. (Greenwillow Bks.).
Blizzard on Moose Mountain. 2007. (J). pap. *(978-0-9794542-0-2(4))* Battat, Inc.
Bourgeois, Paulette. Franklin's New Friend. Clark, Brenda, illus. (Franklin Ser.). (ENG.). 32p. (J). (gr. -1-3). *(978-1-55074-363-0(5))* Kids Can Pr., Ltd.
—Franklin's New Friend. 2004. (Illus.). (J). (gr. k-3). spiral bd. *(978-0-616-01590-2(9))*; spiral bd. *(978-0-616-01591-9(7))* Canadian National Institute for the Blind/Institut National Canadien pour les Aveugles.
Brightwood, Laura, illus. Red Hat / Blue Hat. Brightwood, Laura, . 2006. (J). *(978-0-9779290-5-4(1))* 3-C Institute for Social Development.
Calmenson, Stephanie. There Are No Moose on This Island, 1 vol. Thermes, Jennifer, illus. 2013. (ENG.). 32p. (J). 17.95 *(978-1-934031-34-6(8),* 61a87c0b-3c77-4592-b779-225f25f016bb) Islandport Pr., Inc.
Carlson, Amanda. Sultenfuss Moose's Lost Slipper. 2006. 26p. 18.03 *(978-1-4116-7729-6(3))* Lulu Pr., Inc.
Carpenter, Chad. Morry Moose's Time-Traveling Outhouse Adventure. 2013. (ENG.). 48p. (J). pap. 12.95 *(978-1-62343-163-1(8))* Willow Creek Pr., Inc.
Casanova, Mary. Moose Tracks. Lt. ed. 2004. (LRS Large Print Cornerstone Ser.). 117p. (J). lib. bdg. 27.95 *(978-1-58118-117-3(5))* LRS.
—Moose Tracks. 2nd ed. 2010. (J). *(978-0-9793444-3-5(3))* Quercus Pr.
—Moose Tracks. 2013. (Fesler-Lampert Minnesota Heritage Ser.). (ENG.). 128p. pap. 9.95 *(978-0-8166-9019-0(7))* Univ. of Minnesota Pr.
Chapman, Karean. The Adventures of Northern the Moose & a Dragon Named Zeus. Ciesinka, Izabela, illus. 2010. 38p. pap. 12.95 *(978-1-935268-44-4(9))* Halo Publishing International.
Charron, Ashley. Hello Green Mountains: It's a Soggy Spring. 2013. (ENG.). 26p. (J). 21.95 *(978-1-4787-0803-2(4))* Outskirts Pr., Inc.
The Chocolate Moose. 2007. (Illus.). 48p. (J). per. 13.00 *(978-0-9767189-5-6(2))* Better Day Publishing.
Chronicle Books & ImageBooks. Little Moose: Finger Puppet Book: (Finger Puppet Book for Toddlers & Babies, Baby Books for First Year, Animal Finger Puppets) 2015. (ENG., Illus.). 12p. (J). (gr. -1 — 1). 7.99 *(978-1-4521-4231-9(9))* Chronicle Bks. LLC.
Claflin, Willy. The Little Moose Who Couldn't Go to Sleep. Stimson, James, illus. 2014. (ENG.). 36p. 18.95 *(978-1-939160-67-6(7))* August Hse. Pubs., Inc.
—Rapunzel & the Seven Dwarfs: A Maynard Moose Tale. Stimson, James, illus. 2011. (ENG.). 33p. (J). (gr. -1-3). 18.95 *(978-0-87483-914-2(9))* August Hse. Pubs., Inc.
—The Uglified Ducky: A Maynard Moose Tale. Stimson, James, illus. 2011. (ENG.). 32p. (J). (gr. -1-3). 9.95 *(978-0-87483-953-1(X))* August Hse. Pubs., Inc.
Clarke, Jacqueline A. Moose's Loose Tooth. McNally, Bruce, illus. 2003. (J). *(978-0-439-41183-7(1))* Scholastic, Inc.
Cook, Sherry & Johnson, Terri. Mary Motion, 26 vols. Kuhn, Jesse, illus. Lt. ed. 2006. (Quirkles — Exploring Phonics through Science Ser.: 13). 32p. (J). 7.99 *(978-1-933815-12-1(4),* Quirkles, The) Creative 3, LLC.
Cook, Terry. A Moose at the Bus Stop. Cook, Terry, illus. 2013. (Illus.). 24p. pap. 10.95 *(978-1-61633-378-2(2))* Guardian Angel Publishing, Inc.
Custard, Stefanie. The Story of Baby Moose Joe. 2008. (Illus.). 32p. pap. 20.99 *(978-1-4343-9138-4(8))* AuthorHouse.
Derrick, Patricia & Sibbett, Joyce. Montgomery the Moose Can Shake His Caboose. Martinez, J-P Loppo, illus. 2007. 32p. (J). (gr. -1). 18.95 incl. audio compact disk *(978-1-933818-18-4(2))* Animalations.
deRubertis, Barbara. Maxwell Moose's Mountain Monster. Alley, R. W., illus. 2011. (Animal Antics A to Z Ser.). 32p. (J). pap. 45.32 *(978-0-7613-7659-0(3))*; (ENG.). lib. bdg. 22.60 *(978-1-57565-334-1(6))* Astra Publishing Hse.
deRubertis, Barbara & DeRubertis, Barbara. Maxwell Moose's Mountain Monster. Alley, R. W., illus. 2012. (Animal Antics A to Z Ser.). 32p. (J). (gr. 2 — 1). cd-rom 7.95 *(978-1-57565-406-5(7))* Astra Publishing Hse.
Dixon, Karen S. Alexander the Moose. Crouch, Frances, illus. 2004. 23p. pap. 24.95 *(978-1-4137-3626-7(2))* PublishAmerica, Inc.
Dyan, Penelope. Ba-Ba-Ba-Bad — -The Story of One Mean Moose. Dyan, Penelope, illus. 2012. (Illus.). 34p. pap. 11.95 *(978-1-61477-053-4(0))* Bellissima Publishing, LLC.
—Molly Moose Is on the Loose. Dyan, Penelope, illus. 2012. (Illus.). 34p. pap. 11.95 *(978-1-61477-025-1(5))* Bellissima Publishing, LLC.
Evans, Sarah. The Moose, the Flea, the Fly. 2007. 16p. pap. 24.95 *(978-1-4241-8533-7(5))* America Star Bks.
Fraggalosch, Audrey. Let's Explore, Moose! Forest, Crista, illus. 2005. (ENG.). 32p. (J). (gr. -1-1). pap. 3.95 *(978-1-59249-151-3(0),* S2017) Soundprints.
Fraggolosch, Audrey. Northern Refuge: A Story of a Canadian Boreal Forest. Fraggalosch, Crista, illus. 2005. (Soundprints' Wild Habitats Ser.). (ENG.). 36p. (J). (gr. 1-4). 8.95 *(978-1-59249-100-1(6),* SC7012) Soundprints.
Gauthier, Pamela. The Adventures of Bernie the Moose: Bernie Meets Maria. 2009. 20p. pap. 10.49 *(978-1-4490-3019-3(X))* AuthorHouse.
Greene, Stephanie. Moose Crossing, 0 vols. Mathieu, Joe, illus. 2012. (Moose & Hildy Ser.: 2). (ENG.). 64p. (J). (gr. 1-3). pap. 9.99 *(978-0-7614-5699-5(6),* 9780761456995, Two Lions) Amazon Publishing.
—Moose's Big Idea, 0 vols. Mathieu, Joe, illus. 2012. (Moose & Hildy Ser.: 1). (ENG.). 64p. (J). (gr. 1-3). pap. 6.99 *(978-0-7614-5698-8(8),* 9780761456988, Two Lions) Amazon Publishing.
—Pig Pickin', 0 vols. Mathieu, Joe, illus. 2013. (Moose & Hildy Ser.: 3). (ENG.). 68p. (J). (gr. 1-3). pap. 9.99 *(978-1-4778-1684-4(4),* 9781477816844, Two Lions) Amazon Publishing.
Guthrie, Arlo. Whose Moose Am I? Bradley, Cindy, illus. 2014. (ENG.). (J). 15.00 *(978-0-9915370-3-7(3))* Rising Son International, Ltd.
Hatch, Thomas. Larry the Moose. 2009. 32p. pap. 15.99 *(978-1-4389-8533-6(9))* AuthorHouse.
Hermann, Peter. If the S in Moose Comes Loose. Cordell, Matthew, illus. 2018. (ENG.). 48p. (J). (gr. -1-3). 18.99 *(978-0-06-229510-1(1),* HarperCollins) HarperCollins Pubs.
Hoff, Syd. Santa's Moose. 2017. (I Can Read Level 1 Ser.). (ENG., Illus.). 32p. (J). (gr. -1-3). pap. 4.99 *(978-0-06-264307-0(X),* HarperCollins) HarperCollins Pubs.
—Santa's Moose: A Christmas Holiday Book for Kids. Hoff, Syd, illus. 2017. (I Can Read Level 1 Ser.). (ENG., Illus.). 32p. (J). (gr. -1-3). 16.99 *(978-0-06-264308-7(8),* HarperCollins) HarperCollins Pubs.
Hulet, Paul. Bruce the Moose Is on the Loose. 2009. (Illus.). 36p. (gr. -1-7). pap. 13.95 *(978-1-60860-473-9(X),* Strategic Bk. Publishing) Strategic Book Publishing & Rights Agency (SBPRA).
Jeffers, Oliver. This Moose Belongs to Me. Jeffers, Oliver, illus. 2012. (ENG., Illus.). 32p. (J). (gr. -1-2). 19.99 *(978-0-399-16103-2(1),* Philomel Bks.) Penguin Young Readers Group.
Kaiser, Lori. Megan the Moody Moose. Kaiser, Lori, illus. 2013. (Illus.). 26p. pap. *(978-0-9883770-5-9(5))* Roxby Media Ltd.
Kaut, Joy. Matilda Moose Learns about Being Unique. 2013. 32p. pap. 13.95 *(978-1-4497-9362-3(2),* WestBow Pr.) Author Solutions, LLC.
Kawecki, Daniel. The Mad Moose. 2009. 32p. pap. 13.00 *(978-1-60693-888-1(6),* Eloquent Bks.) Strategic Book Publishing & Rights Agency (SBPRA).
Kellogg, Catherine Berry. The Moose Who Ate My Fort: Stories from Bella Sage. 2008. 36p. pap. 24.95 *(978-1-60441-696-1(3))* America Star Bks.
Kems, Kim A. Moose on the Loose: Moose Capades Book 1. 2011. 21p. (J). pap. 6.99 *(978-0-615-40229-1(1))* KAK.
Larsen, Jill. There's a Moose on the Loose Coloring Book. 2004. (J). pap. 4.99 *(978-0-9755200-0-0(8))* Kids, Critters & Country Publishing.
Lindwall, Erika. The Moose & the Goose. Lindwall, Erika, illus. 2013. (Illus.). 32p. pap. 11.95 *(978-1-940728-01-8(0),* Simple Faith Bks.) Sunrise Mountain Bks.
Macy-Mills, Phyllis. Murphy Moose & Garrett Goose. Russell, Kay, illus. 2003. (J). spiral bd. *(978-1-932303-48-3(0),* Lumina Pr.) Aeon Publishing Inc.
Majestic's Search. 2004. (J). *(978-0-615-12544-2(1))* Jadenaila Publishing.
Martin, Ruth. The Little Moose. Boey, Stephanie, illus. 2008. (ENG.). 35p. (J). *(978-1-55168-332-4(6))* Fenn, H. B. & Co., Ltd.
McArthur, Cathy E. The Story of Chris Moose, 1 vol. Stutz, Chris, illus. 2009. 24p. pap. 24.95 *(978-1-4489-0928-5(7))* America Star Bks.
Messy Moose: Take-Home Book. 2005. (Emergent Library: Vol. 2). (YA). (gr. -1-1). 12.60 *(978-0-8215-7251-1(2))* Sadlier, William H. Inc.
Miller, Janie Evans. How Randy the Moose Turned His Frown Upside Down. 2013. 50p. pap. 23.95 *(978-1-4908-0936-6(8),* WestBow Pr.) Author Solutions, LLC.
Mooney, Silk Waters. Puka the Moose. 2006. (YA). 24.95 *(978-0-9776608-1-0(8))* Silk Waters Mooney.
Morgan, Roxy. Melvin the Moose & Mr. Bluefish. 2007. (Illus.). 35p. (J). lib. bdg. 18.95 *(978-0-9768052-4-3(3))* New Century Publishing, LLC.
Mott, Chuck. The Hannukah Moose. 2009. 48p. pap. 19.99 *(978-1-4490-4974-4(5))* AuthorHouse.
Munsch, Robert. Moose! Martchenko, Michael, illus. 2015. 28p. (J). pap. *(978-0-545-82631-0(4))* Scholastic, Inc.
Nelson-Schmidt, Michelle. Bob Is a Unicorn. 2014. (ENG., Illus.). 28p. (J). 14.99 *(978-1-61067-155-2(4))* Kane Miller.
Northcutt, Allen. The Legend of Chris Moose: The Most Beautiful Moose in the World. 2015. (ENG.). 48p. (J). 17.95 *(978-1-938462-01-6(7),* ab80d21c-658f-46ea-8913-8c1c1da8f348) Old Stone Pr.
Numeroff, Laura Joffe. If You Give a Moose a Matzoh. Date not set. (J). pap. *(978-0-06-443558-1(X))* HarperCollins Pubs.
—If You Give a Moose a Muffin. Bond, Felicia, illus. Date not set. (J). bds. 6.99 *(978-0-694-01426-2(5))* HarperCollins Pubs.
—If You Give a Moose a Muffin: Book & Doll. Bond, Felicia, illus. Date not set. (J). 19.99 *(978-0-694-01421-7(4))* HarperCollins Pubs.
—Moose Stroller Songs. Bond, Felicia, illus. Date not set. (J). 9.99 *(978-0-694-01424-8(9))* HarperCollins Pubs.
Oldland, Nicholas. Making the Moose Out of Life. Oldland, Nicholas, illus. (Life in the Wild Ser.). (ENG., Illus.). 32p. (J). (gr. -1-2). 2015. pap. 7.99 *(978-1-55453-627-6(8))* 2010. 16.99 *(978-1-55453-580-4(8))* Kids Can Pr., Ltd. CAN. Dist: Hachette Bk. Group.
Pace, Anne Marie. Groundhug Day. Denise, Christopher, illus. 2017. (ENG.). 48p. (J). (gr. -1-k). 18.99 *(978-1-4847-5356-9(9))* Little, Brown Bks. for Young Readers.
Palatini, Margie. Moosestache. 32p. pap. *(978-0-7868-1497-8(7))* Hyperion Bks. for Children.
Plourde, Paulette. Smitty Moose, Petey & Me - Episode One, the Witch. Golen, Jessica, illus. Lt. ed. 2005. 32p. (J). per. 9.95 *(978-1-59879-038-2(2))* Lifevest Publishing, Inc.
Rayner, Catherine. Ernest, the Moose Who Doesn't Fit. Rayner, Catherine, illus. 2010. (ENG., Illus.). 32p. (J). (gr. -1-1). 19.99 *(978-0-374-32217-5(1),* 900065793, Farrar, Straus & Giroux (BYR)) Farrar, Straus & Giroux.
Rea, Monique. Toulouse the Moose. 2003. (J). 3.50 *(978-1-891030-30-7(2))* Paragon Agency, The.
—Toulouse the Moose & the Mystery Guests. 2012. 34p. pap. 13.99 *(978-0-9788926-4-7(X))* Trails of Discovery.
Rea, Monique F. The Original Story of Toulouse the Moose & His Friends: Book & CD. 2007. (J). *(978-0-9788926-2-3(3))* Trails of Discovery.
—Toulouse the Moose Coloring Book. 2007. (J). *(978-0-9788926-3-0(1))* Trails of Discovery.
Restrepo, Bettina. Moose & Magpie, 1 vol. Rogers, Sherry, illus. 2009. (ENG.). 32p. (J). (gr. -1-3). 16.95 *(978-1-934359-97-6(1))*; pap. 9.95 *(978-1-60718-042-5(1))* Arbordale Publishing.
Rivard, Erin. Agattu: The Alaskan Caribou. 2013. (J). pap. 9.95 *(978-1-59433-344-6(0))* Publication Consultants.
Root, Phyllis. Looking for a Moose. Cecil, Randy, illus. 2008. (ENG.). 40p. (J). (gr. -1-2). pap. 8.99 *(978-0-7636-3885-6(4))* Candlewick Pr.
Rouncville, Bibi. Sea Bugs & Moose Eggs. 2009. 52p. pap. 9.50 *(978-1-4357-4004-4(1))* Lulu Pr., Inc.
Savage, Doug. Disco Fever. 2017. (Illus.). 142p. (J). *(978-1-5379-7394-4(0))* Andrews McMeel Publishing.
—Laser Moose & Rabbit Boy. 2016. (Laser Moose & Rabbit Boy Ser.: 1). (ENG., Illus.). 144p. (J). pap. 9.99 *(978-1-4494-7094-4(7))* Andrews McMeel Publishing.
—Laser Moose & Rabbit Boy: Disco Fever. 2017. (Laser Moose & Rabbit Boy Ser.: 2). (ENG., Illus.). 144p. (J). pap. 9.99 *(978-1-4494-8687-7(8))* Andrews McMeel Publishing.
Scaling, Sam T. Marv the Moose Is on the Loose. Stanley, Susan, illus. 2012. 32p. (J). *(978-0-9798806-4-3(5))* STS Publishing.
Schwartz, Corey Rosen & Gomez, Rebecca J. What about Moose? Yamaguchi, Keika, illus. 2015. (ENG.). 40p. (J). (gr. -1-3). 19.99 *(978-1-4814-0496-9(2),* Atheneum Bks. for Young Readers) Simon & Schuster Children's Publishing.
Scott, Joanna I. Stanley the Moose: Book One of the Woodsie Tails Series. 2009. (Illus.). 40p. (J). 19.95 net. *(978-0-9795678-1-0(5))* Cherakota Publishing.
Shankman, Ed. I Met a Moose in Maine One Day. O'Neill, Dave, illus. 2008. (Shankman & O'Neill Ser.). (ENG.). 32p. (J). (gr. -1-3). 17.99 *(978-1-933212-77-7(2),* Commonwealth Editions) Applewood Bks.
Shuttlewood, Craig. Awesome! Shuttlewood, Craig, illus. 2018. (ENG., Illus.). 32p. (J). (gr. k-2). 15.95 *(978-1-68446-013-7(1),* 138906, Capstone Editions) Capstone.
Skrentny, Jan. The Christmas Moose. 2008. 36p. pap. 18.95 *(978-1-4389-2807-4(6))* AuthorHouse.
Spinelle, Nancy Louise. Moose's Loose Tooth. Gedeon, Gloria, illus. Lt. ed. 2005. (ENG.). 16p. (gr. k-2). pap. 7.95 *(978-1-57874-032-1(0),* Kaeden Bks.) Kaeden Corp.
Swinney, Kay. Marty Moose & the Mystical Reunion, 1 vol. 2009. 73p. pap. 19.95 *(978-1-61546-867-6(6))* America Star Bks.
Turner, Tracie & Dyson, Kyree. The Adventures of Kyree the Chocolate Moose. 2013. 20p. pap. 24.95 *(978-1-62709-178-7(5))* America Star Bks.
Van Laan, Nancy. Busy, Busy Moose. Rusch, Amy, illus. 2003. (ENG.). 48p. (J). (gr. k-2). tchr. ed. 21.19 *(978-0-395-96091-2(6))* Houghton Mifflin Harcourt Publishing Co.
VanRiper, Gary & VanRiper, Justin. Mystery of the Missing Moose. 2007. (Adirondack Kids Ser.: Vol. 7). 77p. (J). (gr. 2-7). pap. 9.95 *(978-0-9707044-7-4(X),* ADK7) Adirondack Kids Pr.
Wargin, Kathy-jo. Moose on the Loose. Bendall-Brunello, John, illus. 2009. (ENG.). 32p. (J). (gr. -1-4). 16.99 *(978-1-58536-427-5(4),* 202158) Sleeping Bear Pr.
William H. Sadlier Staff. Messy Moose. 2005. (Emergent Library: Vol. 2). (gr. -1-1). 24.00 net. *(978-0-8215-8921-2(0))* Sadlier, William H. Inc.
Wilson, Karma. Moose Tracks! 2006. (ENG., Illus.). 32p. (J). (gr. -1-2). 19.99 *(978-0-689-83437-0(3),* McElderry, Margaret K. Bks.) McElderry, Margaret K. Bks.
Womack, Rowena. Yellowstone Moose. 2013. 28p. pap. 13.95 *(978-1-61160-597-6(0))* Whiskey Creek Restorations.
Yellowstone Moose. 2004. (Illus.). (J). spiral bd. 9.95 *(978-0-9754913-1-7(8),* Gap Tooth Publishing) Charles River Pr.
Yoon, Salina. Found. 2014. (ENG., Illus.). 40p. (J). (gr. -1-1). 14.99 *(978-0-8027-3559-1(2),* 900121351, Bloomsbury USA Childrens) Bloomsbury Publishing USA.

MORAL EDUCATION

ABDO Publishing Company Staff & Salzmann, Mary Elizabeth. Building Character, Set. 2003. (Building Character Ser.: 3). (ENG.). (J). (gr. k-3). lib. bdg. 72.63 *(978-1-57765-824-5(8),* SandCastle) ABDO Publishing Co.
Aguilera, Dana, et al. Character in Motion! Real Life Stories Series 5th Grade Student Workbook. 2006. 68p. (J). per. 5.95 *(978-0-9765722-8-2(1))* Positively for Kids, Inc.
Bakhtiar, Laleh. Islamic Ethics: An Interfaith Perspective: Grade 2: the Moral Education Series. 2005. 32p. (J). pap., pupil's gde. ed. 4.95 net. *(978-1-56744-722-4(8))* Kazi Pubns., Inc.
—Islamic Ethics: An Interfaith Perspective: Grade 3: the Moral Education Textbook Series. 2005. 32p. (J). 4.95 net. *(978-1-56744-723-1(6))* Kazi Pubns., Inc.
—Islamic Ethics: An Interfaith Perspective: the Moral Education Textbook Series. 2005. (Islamic Books for Children). 32p. (J). pupil's gde. ed. 4.95 net. *(978-1-56744-721-7(X))* Kazi Pubns., Inc.
Bergstrom, Amy, et al. The Seventh Generation: Native Students Speak about Finding the Good Path. 2003. 300p. (YA). (gr. 7-12). pap. 25.00 *(978-1-880785-25-6(0))* ERIC Clearinghouse on Rural Education & Small Schls.
Boritzer, Etan. What Is Right? Sale, Graham, illus. Lt. ed. 2005. (What Is? Ser.). 40p. (J). (gr. k-5). pap. 6.95 *(978-0-9762743-0-8(2))* Lane, Veronica Bks.
Brooks, Diane L. Readings & Activities for Character Education. 220p. (YA). (gr. 4-18). ring bd. 69.95 *(978-0-8126-7550-4(9))* Cricket Bks.
Character Ed Says Courtesy Is Contagious. 2006. (J). 4.95 *(978-1-55548-055-4(1),* 676) Human Relations Media.
Character Ed Says Honesty Counts. 2006. (J). 4.95 *(978-1-55548-057-8(8),* 678) Human Relations Media.
Character Ed Says Keep Your Cool. 2006. (J). 4.95 *(978-1-55548-056-1(X),* 677) Human Relations Media.
Clifford, Kathleen & Uy, Megan Black. Great Lives, Vital Lessons: A Character Education Curriculum Resource for Grades 5-8. Bohlin, Karen E. & Lerner, Bernice, eds. 2005. (gr. 5-8). pap. 19.95 *(978-1-892056-41-2(0))* Character Development Group, Inc.

Deroche, Ed, et al. Character: A Guide for Middle Grade Students. 2004. (ENG.). 176p. pap., wbk. ed. 9.95 (978-1-55864-152-5(1), JIST Life) JIST Publishing.

Dunagan, Cindy. Journaling Toward Moral Excellence Volume Four for Young Adults: A Character Building Workbook of 100 Thought-Provoking Questions to Help the Young Discover the Value of Moral Strength. 2004. (Journaling Toward Moral Excellence Ser.: Vol. 4). 107p. (YA). (gr. 11-18). 11.95 (978-0-9759871-3-1(5)) Straight Paths Pr.

—Journaling Toward Moral Excellence Volume One for Young Writers. 2004. (Journaling Toward Moral Excellence Ser.: Vol. 1). 107p. (J). (gr. 1-4). 11.95 (978-0-9759871-0-0(0)) Straight Paths Pr.

—Journaling Toward Moral Excellence Volume Three for Teenagers: A Character Building Workbook of 100 Thought-Provoking Questions to Help the Young Discover the Value of Moral Strength. 2004. (Journaling Toward Moral Excellence Ser.: Vol. 3). 107p. (YA). (gr. 8-10). 11.95 (978-0-9759871-2-4(7)) Straight Paths Pr.

—Journaling Toward Moral Excellence Volume Two for Pre-Teens Vol. 2: A Character Building Workbook of 100 Thought-Provoking Questions to Help the Young Discover the Value of Moral Strength. 2004. (Journaling Toward Moral Excellence Ser.: Vol. 2). 107p. (J). (gr. 5-7). 11.95 (978-0-9759871-1-7(9)) Straight Paths Pr.

Everyday Character Education, 12 vols., Set. 2005. (Everyday Character Education Ser.). (ENG., Illus.). 24p. (gr. 1-2). 49.30 (978-0-7368-4410-9(4), Capstone Pr.) Capstone.

Handley, Rod, et al. Team Studies on Character: Inspiration for Life & Sports. 2004. (YA). pap. 6.99 (978-1-929478-65-1(8)) Cross Training Publishing.

It's Good 2b Good Staff & Zerner, Sandra. It's Good 2B Good: Why It's Not Bad to Be Good. 2011. (ENG., Illus.). 106p. (J). pap. 12.95 (978-0-615-51275-4(5)) It's Good 2B Good LLC.

James, Emily. Character Matters. 2017. (Character Matters Ser.). (ENG.). 32p. (J). (gr. -1-2). 119.96 (978-1-5157-7238-5(1), 26691, Capstone Pr.) Capstone.

Keuss, Jeff & Sloth, Lia. Character in Motion! Athlete Series. 2006. (Illus.). 136p. (YA). per. 5.95 (978-0-9765722-0-6(6)) Positively for Kids, Inc.

Lang, Carol, et al. Character in Motion! Real Life Stories Series 3rd Grade Student Workbook. 2006. 63p. (J). per. 5.95 (978-0-9765722-9-9(X)) Positively for Kids, Inc.

Lewis, Barbara A. What Do You Stand For? Character Building. 2006. (ENG., Illus.). 60p. (gr. 1-6). 13.99 (978-1-57542-217-6(4), 1125) Free Spirit Publishing Inc.

—What Do You Stand For? For Kids: a Guide to Building Character. 2005. (ENG., Illus.). 176p. (J). (gr. 3-7). pap. 17.99 (978-1-57542-174-2(7), 617) Free Spirit Publishing Inc.

—What Do You Stand For? For Teens: a Guide to Building Character. 2005. (ENG., Illus.). 288p. (YA). (gr. 5-9). pap. 29.99 (978-1-57542-029-5(5), 461) Free Spirit Publishing Inc.

Merino, Noël, ed. Should Character Be Taught in School?, 1 vol. 2010. (At Issue Ser.). (ENG.). 120p. (gr. 10-12). 41.03 (978-0-7377-4890-1(7), 74220b68-539b-42ff-9c7f-362176999dcc, Greenhaven Publishing) Greenhaven Publishing LLC.

—Should Character Be Taught in School?, 1 vol. 2010. (At Issue Ser.). (ENG.). 120p. (gr. 10-12). pap. 28.80 (978-0-7377-4891-8(5), ef4e2722-a7b1-4a15-b6dd-1c2a417e52be, Greenhaven Publishing) Greenhaven Publishing LLC.

Munroe, Terri, et al. Rachel's Challenge: A Columbine Legacy Student Workbook. 2006. (YA). per. 5.95 (978-0-9765722-4-4(9)) Positively for Kids, Inc.

Murphy, John Paul. Watt's Special Purpose. 2012. 20p. pap. 17.99 (978-1-4685-5344-4(5)) AuthorHouse.

Murphy, Madonna M. & Banas, Sharon L. Character Education Set. 2009. (ENG.). (gr. 6-12). 175.00 (978-1-60413-642-5(1), P166839, Facts On File) Infobase Holdings, Inc.

Murray, Amy R. The Character & Career Connection. 2005. (ENG., Illus.). 78p. (gr. k-5). per. 19.95 (978-1-931636-45-2(1)) National Ctr. For Youth Issues.

Murray, Julie. Respect. 2017. (Character Education (Abdo Kids Junior) Ser.). (ENG., Illus.). 24p. (J). (gr. -1-2). lib. bdg. 31.36 (978-1-5321-0011-6(6), 25106, Abdo Kids) ABDO Publishing Co.

Neuberger, Anne. All God's Children: 42 Short & Joyful Stories for Kids (ages 3 Through 8) 2010. (Illus.). 104p. (J). pap. 14.95 (978-1-58595-797-2(6)) Twenty-Third Pubns./Bayard.

Perez, Claire M. & Fox, Mary. Peacemakers: The New Generation Practical Group Activities for Grades 6-8. 2003. (Illus.). 76p. (YA). (gr. 6-8). pap. 20.00 (978-1-893757-32-5(3), E T Nedder) Paulist Pr.

Stein, Lee. Generation Communication: For Teens Who Want to Get Ahead in the World. 2011. 60p. (YA). per. 9.99 (978-0-9786663-1-6(3)) Paradoxical Pr., The.

Stephens, Wayne. Building Character Through Music - Elementary Song Book. 2004. spiral bd. 39.95 (978-1-892056-32-0(1)) Character Development Group, Inc,.

—Building Character Through Music - High School Song Book. 2004. (YA). spiral bd. 39.95 (978-1-892056-36-8(4)) Character Development Group, Inc,.

Tracy, Jean. Character Building on BackTalk Street. 2004. 110p. (J). spiral bd. 25.00 (978-0-9749244-0-3(7)) KidsDiscuss.com.

Wiley, Lori. Character Education Activities. 2004. (Illus.). 176p. (J). per. 9.95 (978-1-55864-154-9(8), K1548, KIDSRIGHTS) JIST Publishing.

MORAL EDUCATION—FICTION

Adeleke, Abraham Ajibade. Beauty Contest in the Animal Kingdom. 2011. 40p. pap. 16.46 (978-1-4269-5773-4(4)) Trafford Publishing.

Brezenoff, Steve. Cheaters, 1 vol. Pinelli, Amerigo, illus. 2013. (Ravens Pass Ser.). (ENG.). 96p. (J). (gr. 3-6). lib. bdg. 25.32 (978-1-4342-4616-5(7), 120605, Stone Arch Bks.) Capstone.

Cr. Adventures of Jenni & Jake. 2011. 28p. pap. 12.99 (978-1-4568-8677-6(0)) Xlibris Corp.

Farnsworth-Simpson, Patricia Ann. Stories to Thrill & Delight. 2008. (ENG.). 142p. pap. 12.95 (978-1-4357-3275-9(8)) Lulu Pr., Inc.

Ferrin, Wendy Wakefield. Germs on Their Fingers! Tono, Lucia, tr. Broyles, Beverly Ashley, illus. 2003.Tr. of Germenes en Tus Manos! (SPA & ENG.). 64p. (J). (gr. 1-7). 17.95 (978-0-9703632-1-3(4)); pap. 12.95 (978-0-9703632-0-6(6)) Wakefield Connection, The.

Hamilton, Elizabeth L. Christopher Cat's Character Club. 2003. (Character Critters Ser.: No. 1). (Illus.). 32p. (J). (gr. -1-3). per. 5.95 (978-0-9713749-2-8(9), Character-in-Action) Quiet Impact, Inc.

—Cubby Bear's Big Responsibility. 2004. (Character Critters Ser.: No. 8). (Illus.). 32p. (J). per. 5.95 (978-0-9754629-4-2(6), Character-in-Action) Quiet Impact, Inc.

—Date with Responsibility. 2004. (Character-in-Action Ser.: No. 2). (Illus.). 384p. (YA). per. 19.95 (978-0-9713749-0-4(2), Character-in-Action) Quiet Impact, Inc.

—Georgey Giraffe's Giant Respect: Character Critter Series #6. 2004. (Character Critters Ser.: No. 6). (Illus.). 32p. (J). per. 5.95 (978-0-9754629-1-1(1), Character-in-Action) Quiet Impact, Inc.

—Jeremy Rabbit's Honesty Pie. 2003. (Character Critters Ser.: No. 2). (Illus.). 32p. (J). (gr. -1-3). per. 5.95 (978-0-9713749-5-9(3), Character-in-Action) Quiet Impact, Inc.

—Little Zoh's Submissive Trunk. 2003. (Character Critters Ser.: No. 3). (Illus.). 32p. (J). (gr. -1-3). per. 5.95 (978-0-9713749-9-7(6), Character-in-Action) Quiet Impact, Inc.

—Lost on Superstition Mountain. 2004. (Character Mystery Ser.: No. 3). (Illus.). 144p. (J). per. 9.95 (978-0-9754629-5-9(4), Character-in-Action) Quiet Impact, Inc.

—Mystery at Lake Cachuma. 2003. (Character Mystery Ser.: No. 1). (Illus.). 114p. (J). (gr. 3-6). per. 9.95 (978-0-9713749-4-2(5), Character-in-Action) Quiet Impact, Inc.

—Pandora Puppy's Caring Circle. 2004. (Character Critters Ser.: No. 5). (Illus.). 32p. (J). per. 5.95 (978-0-9754629-0-4(3), Character-in-Action) Quiet Impact, Inc.

—Pansy Pig's Patience Pit. 2004. (Character Critters Ser.: No. 7). (Illus.). 32p. (J). per. 5.95 (978-0-9754629-3-5(8), Character-in-Action) Quiet Impact, Inc.

—Stinky Skunk's Self-Control. 2004. (Character Critters Ser.: No. 4). (Illus.). 32p. (J). (gr. -1-3). per. 5.95 (978-0-9713749-6-6(1), Character-in-Action) Quiet Impact, Inc.

—Surprise at Pearl Harbor. 2004. (Character Mystery Ser.: No. 2). (Illus.). 144p. (J). per. 9.95 (978-0-9754629-2-8(X), Character-in-Action) Quiet Impact, Inc.

Hank. 2003. (ENG.). 192p. (J). 19.95 (978-1-890862-22-0(3), 827a2b88-c50e-44f2-ad1d-6733447b1879) Bancroft Pr.

Harvey, Sharon M. Virginia's Travel Basket. 2008. 76p. pap. 10.95 (978-1-4327-3424-4(5)) Outskirts Pr., Inc.

Henry, Heather French. What Freedom Means to Me: A Flag Day Story. Henry, Heather French, illus. 2004. (Claire's Holiday Adventures Ser.). (Illus.). 32p. (J). (gr. k-4). (ENG.). 15.95 (978-0-9706341-2-2(9), 1231611); pap. 8.95 (978-0-9706341-9-1(6)) Cubbie Blue Publishing.

Knisley, Lucy. Heart: Seed Snow Circuit. 2007. 20p. pap. 10.00 (978-0-9789427-7-9(9)) Epigraph Bks.

Mbonu, Ngozi Elizabeth. Tatiana. Taylor, Kristen Michelle, illus. 2013. (ENG.). (J). 14.95 (978-1-62086-307-7(3)) Amplify Publishing Group.

Miller, Jay. Opal, Herby, & Squeaky. 2008. 44p. pap. 18.99 (978-1-4389-1808-2(9)) AuthorHouse.

Olsen EdS, Marci. Lessons to Live by: Character Building Books for School-Age Children. 2008. 52p. pap. 24.95 (978-1-60474-501-6(0)) America Star Bks.

Suparna. The Science Playground: Fun with Science Concepts & Nature. 2009. (ENG.). 46p. pap. 24.99 (978-1-4389-3466-2(1)) AuthorHouse.

MORAL PHILOSOPHY

see Ethics

MORALITY

see Ethics

MORALS

see Behavior; Ethics

MORE, THOMAS, SIR, SAINT, 1478-1535

Hobbes, Emma. Thomas More & Utopia. 2016. (J). lib. bdg. (978-1-68048-551-6(2)) Rosen Publishing Group, Inc., The.

Wallace, Susan Helen & Jablonski, Patricia E. Saint Thomas More: Courage, Conscience, & the King. Lachuk, Dani, illus. 2014. (ENG.). 144p. (J). pap. 8.95 (978-0-8198-9021-4(9)) Pauline Bks. & Media.

MORGAN, DANIEL, 1736-1802

Gallagher, Jim. Daniel Morgan: Fighting Frontiersman. 2006. (J). pap. (978-1-59556-020-9(3)); (Illus.). 88p. (gr. 5-11). lib. bdg. 23.95 (978-1-59556-015-5(7)) OTTN Publishing.

MORGAN, HENRY, SIR, 1635-1688

Sullivan, Laura L. Sir Henry Morgan. 2015. (J). lib. bdg. (978-1-62713-308-1(9)) Cavendish Square Publishing LLC.

Weintraub, Aileen. Henry Morgan: 17th-Century Buccaneer. 2009. (Library of Pirates Ser.). 24p. (gr. 3-3). 42.50 (978-1-60853-812-6(5), PowerKids Pr.) Rosen Publishing Group, Inc., The.

MORMONS AND MORMONISM

Andersen, Susan. Nephi Breaks His Bow. 2009. 20p. pap. 5.95 (978-1-60641-115-5(2)) Deseret Bk. Co.

Bagley, Val. Gospel Truths from the Book of Mormon. 2004. (Seek & Ye Shall Find Flap Book Ser.). (Illus.). (J). bds. 13.95 (978-1-59156-279-5(1)) Covenant Communications, Inc.

Bagley, Val Chadwick, illus. I Will Follow God's Plan for Me. 2004. (J). (978-1-59156-579-6(0)) Covenant Communications.

Bagley, Val Chadwick & Mullins, Amy. My Favorite Stories from the Book of Mormon. 2007. (Carry-Along Lift-The-Flap Book Ser.). (Illus.). (J). (978-1-59811-385-3(2)) Covenant Communications.

Barnes, Kathleen. I Love to See the Temple Reprint. 2009. 32p. pap. 8.95 (978-1-60641-112-4(8)) Deseret Bk. Co.

—Sacrament Time. 2009. 32p. pap. 9.95 (978-1-60641-113-1(6)) Deseret Bk. Co.

Bernice, Janet. Tiny Talks: I Will Follow God's Plan for Me, Vol. 5. 2004. (J). pap. 7.95 (978-1-55517-815-4(4)) Cedar Fort, Inc./CFI Distribution.

Bowman, David. The Great Plan of Happiness. 2010. (Illus.). (J). 15.99 (978-1-59955-451-8(8)) Cedar Fort, Inc./CFI Distribution.

—The Great Plan of Happiness. 2010. (J). (978-1-60641-637-2(5)) Deseret Bk. Co.

—Who's Your Hero? Boxed Set of Five Books. 2009. pap. 45.95 (978-1-60641-152-0(7)) Deseret Bk. Co.

—Who's Your Hero? Vol. 1: Book of Mormon Stories Applied to Children, Vol. 1. 2006. (Illus.). 74p. (J). pap. 15.95 (978-1-59038-573-9(X)) Deseret Bk. Co.

—Who's Your Hero? Vol. 2: Book of Mormon Stories Applied to Children. Bowman, David, illus. 2006. (Illus.). 80p. (J). pap. 14.95 (978-1-59038-691-0(4)) Deseret Bk. Co.

—Who's Your Hero? Vol. 4: Book of Mormon Stories Applied to Children. 2008. 80p. pap. 14.95 (978-1-59038-928-7(X)) Deseret Bk. Co.

Bowman, David, illus. Beyond Bethlehem: A Book of Mormon Christmas. 2008. 32p. (J). pap. 11.95 (978-1-59038-991-1(3)) Deseret Bk. Co.

Brown, Toni Sorenson. Heroes of the Book of Mormon. 2004. bds. 10.95 (978-1-59156-056-2(X)) Covenant Communications, Inc.

Buck, Deanna. My First Articles of Faith BK. 2008. 32p. pap. 6.95 (978-1-59038-931-7(X)) Deseret Bk. Co.

—My First Church HIST Stories. 2008. 32p. pap. 8.95 (978-1-60641-078-3(4)) Deseret Bk. Co.

Buck, Deanna Draper;. My First Book of Temples. Nelson, Casey, illus. 2012. 28p. (J). bds. 15.99 (978-1-60907-158-5(1)) Deseret Bk. Co.

—The Whole Armor of God. Hochstrasser, Karin, illus. 2019. (J). 12.99 (978-1-62972-577-2(3)) Deseret Bk. Co.

Bytheway, John. Are Your Standards Fences or Guardrails? 2003. (Illus.). xiv, 97p. (J). pap. (978-1-57008-990-9(6)) Deseret Bk. Co.

Carnesecca, Michele. How Does the Holy Ghost Make Me Feel? Xanthos, Carol, illus. 2010. 44p. (978-1-60641-245-9(0)) Deseret Bk. Co.

Carter, Molly. Guess Who's in the Book of Mormon? 2018. (ENG., Illus.). (J). 14.99 (978-1-4621-2197-7(7)) Cedar Fort, Inc./CFI Distribution.

Christensen, Laurel. LYFSGUD: If God Sent You a Text Message. 2009. xi, 115p. (J). (978-1-60641-108-7(X)) Deseret Bk. Co.

Coltrane, R. Book of Mormon Adventures. 2017. (ENG.). (J). (gr. -1-2). 14.99 (978-1-4621-2089-5(X)) Cedar Fort, Inc./CFI Distribution.

Craner, Ben, tr. & illus. I Can Be a Missionary, Too. Craner, Ben, illus. 2003. (J). (978-1-57008-965-7(5)) Deseret Bk. Co.

Daybell, Chad. The Aaronic Priesthood: Seven Principles That Will Make This Power a Part of Your Daily Life. Murray, Rhett E., illus. 2003. 100p. (J). pap. 8.95 (978-1-55517-717-1(4), 77174) Cedar Fort, Inc./CFI Distribution.

—Book of Mormon Numbers. Bonham, Bob, illus. 2004. (J). bds. 8.95 (978-1-55517-755-3(7), 77557) Cedar Fort, Inc./CFI Distribution.

Dean, Arlan. The Mormon Pioneer Trail: From Nauvoo, Illinois to the Great Salt Lake, Utah. 2009. (Famous American Trails Ser.). 24p. (gr. 3-3). 42.50 (978-1-61512-488-6(8), PowerKids Pr.) Rosen Publishing Group, Inc., The.

Dobson, Cynthia Lund. I'm Trying to Be Like Jesus. Dewey, Simon, illus. 2010. (J). 19.99 (978-1-60641-846-8(7)) Deseret Bk. Co.

Doxey, Heidi. Tiny Talks, Volume 15. 2014. pap. 8.99 (978-1-4621-1511-2(X), Horizon Pubs.) Cedar Fort, Inc./CFI Distribution.

—1, 2, 3 with Nephi & Me! Konopasek, Emily, illus. 2015. 9.99 (978-1-4621-1636-2(1), Horizon Pubs.) Cedar Fort, Inc./CFI Distribution.

Durrant, George D. Seven Years Old & Preparing for Baptism. 2007. (Illus.). 68p. (J). pap. 7.95 (978-1-932898-74-3(3)) Spring Creek Bk. Co.

Eden, Kristena. Book of Mormon 1-2-3s. Silvestri, Linda, illus. 2016. (ENG.). (J). 14.99 (978-1-4621-1651-5(5)) Cedar Fort, Inc./CFI Distribution.

Eden, Kristina. Prophet Joseph's 1-2-3s. Silvestri, Linda, illus. 2016. (ENG.). (gr. -1-1). 14.99 (978-1-4621-1949-3(2)) Cedar Fort, Inc./CFI Distribution.

Encyclopaedia Britannica, Inc. Staff, compiled by. Brigham Young. 2008. 49.95 (978-1-59339-525-4(6)) Encyclopaedia Britannica, Inc.

Gibby, Shauna. Exploring the Pioneer Trail: A Flashlight Discovery Book. Nelson, Casey, illus. 2019. (J). 16.99 (978-1-62972-575-8(7)) Deseret Bk. Co.

—Follow the Prophet: A Flashlight Discovery Book. Beech, Bryan, illus. 2019. (J). 16.99 (978-1-62972-576-5(5)) Deseret Bk. Co.

—Heroic Stories from the Book of Mormon: A Flashlight Discovery Book. Nelson, Casey, illus. 2017. (J). 16.99 (978-1-62972-319-8(3)) Deseret Bk. Co.

Gowans, Floyd W. Covenant Verses: The Book of Mormon. 2004. 276p. (YA). per. 19.95 (978-1-58982-160-6(2), Millennial Mind Publishing) American Bk. Publishing Group.

Gudmundson, C. J. When I Take the Sacrament, I Remember Jesus. Tenney, Shawna J. C., illus. 2012. (J). (978-1-62108-020-6(X)) Covenant Communications, Inc.

Hall, Annalisa. The Holy Ghost Is Like a Blanket. Egbert, Corey, illus. 2014. 12.99 (978-1-4621-1419-1(9), Horizon Pubs.) Cedar Fort, Inc./CFI Distribution.

—I Want to Be Baptized. Egbert, Corey, illus. 2015. (J). 10.99 (978-1-4621-1670-6(1), Horizon Pubs.) Cedar Fort, Inc./CFI Distribution.

Johnson, Alice W. & Warner, Allison H. Believe & You're There When Lehi Left Jerusalem. Harston, Jerry, illus. 2010. (J). (978-1-60641-246-6(9)) Deseret Bk. Co.

Krishna, McArthur & Spalding, Bethany Brady. Girls Who Choose God: Stories of Strong Women from the Book of Mormon. Peterson, Kathleen, illus. 2015. (J). 18.99 (978-1-62972-101-9(8)) Deseret Bk. Co.

Madsen, Susan Arrington. I Walked to Zion: True Stories of Young Pioneers on the Mormon Trail. 2008. 192p. pap. 9.95 (978-1-59038-930-0(1)) Deseret Bk. Co.

Marsh, Dilleen, tr. & illus. What Happens When People Die? Marsh, Dilleen, illus. 2003. (J). 12.95 (978-1-57008-954-1(X)) Deseret Bk. Co.

McKellar, Tyler. Book of Mormon Family Reader. Burr, Dan, illus. 2017. viii, 292p. 24.99 (978-1-62972-334-1(7)) Deseret Bk. Co.

—The Book of Mormon Family Reader: Spanish Edition. Burr, Dan, illus. 2019. (SPA.). viii, 292p. pap. 19.99 (978-1-62972-624-3(9)) Deseret Bk. Co.

Merrill, Alexis. My Book of Mormon Friends. 2018. (Illus.). (J). bds. 14.99 (978-1-62972-470-6(X)) Deseret Bk. Co.

Millett, Melanie. Teeny Tiny Talks: Junior Primary: I Will Follow God's Plan for Me, Vol. 1. Millett, Melanie, illus. 2004. (Illus.). (J). per. 12.95 (978-1-55517-778-2(6), Cedar Fort, Inc.) Cedar Fort, Inc./CFI Distribution.

Morton, William A. From Plowboy to Mormon Prophet Being a Short History of Joseph Smith for Children. Ramsey, L. A., illus. 2004. reprint ed. pap. 30.95 (978-1-4179-6860-2(5)) Kessinger Publishing, LLC.

Mullins, Amy. I'm Reverent When- Bagley, Val Chadwick, illus. 2005. ("Move-About" Book Ser.). (J). (978-1-59156-951-0(6)) Covenant Communications.

Naden, Corinne J. & Blue, Rose. Mormonism. 2004. (Illus.). 112p. (J). 29.95 (978-1-59018-452-3(1), Lucent Bks.) Cengage Gale.

Newell, Karmel H. Come Follow Me: A Child's Guide to Faith, Hope, & Charity. Smith, Mary Ann Free, illus. 2003. (J). 16.95 (978-1-57008-809-4(8), Bookcraft, Inc.) Deseret Bk. Co.

Oaks, Kristen M. My Home Can Be a Holy Place. Burr, Dan, illus. 2015. (J). 18.99 (978-1-62972-099-9(2)) Deseret Bk. Co.

Oaks, Kristen M. & Phillips, JoAnn. The Testimony Glove. Burr, Dan, illus. 2010. 31p. (J). (gr. -1-4). 17.99 (978-1-60641-151-3(9)) Deseret Bk. Co.

Oaks, Robert C. Believe! Helping Youth Learn to Trust in the Lord. 2003. (Illus.). xiii, 126p. (J). pap. 14.95 (978-1-59038-203-5(X)) Deseret Bk. Co.

Olsen, Bevan Lloyd. The Littlest Nephite in Nephi & the Brass Plates. Miller, Rebecca, illus. 2008. 14p. (J). (gr. 3-7). 15.99 (978-1-59955-087-9(3)) Cedar Fort, Inc./CFI Distribution.

Palmer, Alison. Simply Singing Time. 2009. 96p. (J). pap. 8.99 (978-0-88290-970-7(3)) Cedar Fort, Inc./CFI Distribution.

Poelman, Heidi. I Can Love Like Jesus. 2017. (ENG., Illus.). (J). (gr. -1-2). 14.99 (978-1-4621-1940-0(9)) Cedar Fort, Inc./CFI Distribution.

Pruett, Jason. Seek & Find: Book of Mormon Stories (Board Book) 2017. (ENG., Illus.). (gr. -1). bds. 12.99 (978-1-4621-2099-4(7)) Cedar Fort, Inc./CFI Distribution.

—Seek & Find Book of Mormon Stories. 2015. 14.99 (978-1-4621-1528-0(4), Horizon Pubs.) Cedar Fort, Inc./CFI Distribution.

Rich, J. Milton. Heavenly Fathers Plan of Salvation Coloring Book. Knaupp, Andrew & Koford, Adam, illus. 2003. 108p. (J). per. 7.95 (978-0-9726670-2-9(4)) Rich Publishing.

Richards, Claude. The Temple Letters: A Rewarding Path to Happiness on Earth & Everlasting Treasures in Heaven. 2011. 228p. 46.95 (978-1-258-05537-0(6)) Literary Licensing, LLC.

Rostrom, Laura Lee. My First Book of Mormon Activity Book, Vol. 1. 2011. 64p. pap. 3.99 (978-1-59955-957-5(9)) Cedar Fort, Inc./CFI Distribution.

Rowley, Deborah Pace. White Dresses: A Baptism Keepsake for Girls. Hodson, Jewel, illus. 2006. 32p. (J). 16.99 (978-1-59038-632-3(9)) Deseret Bk. Co.

—White Shirts: A Baptism Keepsake for Boys. Call, Brian, illus. 2006. 32p. (J). 16.99 (978-1-59038-633-0(7)) Deseret Bk. Co.

Sanford, William R. & Green, Carl R. Brigham Young: Courageous Mormon Leader, 1 vol. 2013. (Courageous Heroes of the American West Ser.). (ENG., Illus.). 48p. (J). (gr. 5-7). 25.27 (978-0-7660-4004-5(6), 1af10d1c-95b1-437f-899f-75c721185f12); pap. 11.53 (978-1-4644-0089-6(X), 739c4ab8-19fe-43ed-9eb1-b1824bf5d05b) Enslow Publishing, LLC.

Setzer, Lee Ann. I Am a Child of God. Harmon, Glenn, illus. 2007. (Tiny Talks Ser.). 74p. (J). per. 7.99 (978-1-59955-076-3(8)) Cedar Fort, Inc./CFI Distribution.

—I Am Ready for Baptism. 2006. 30p. (J). pap. 4.99 (978-1-55517-944-1(4)) Cedar Fort, Inc./CFI Distribution.

—Tiny Talks: My Savior, Jesus Christ, Vol. 10. 2009. 86p. (J). pap. 8.99 (978-1-59955-375-7(9)) Cedar Fort, Inc./CFI Distribution.

—Tiny Talks #6: I will Trust in Heavenly Father & His Son, Jesus Christ-Their Promises are Sure, Vol. 6. 2005. (J). pap. 7.99 (978-1-55517-889-5(8)) Cedar Fort, Inc./CFI Distribution.

Staker, Sara. My Baptism Keepsake. 2009. (Illus.). (J). (978-1-59811-837-7(4)) Covenant Communications, Inc.

Turley, Richard & Littke, Lael. Stories from the Life of Joseph Smith. 2008. 192p. pap. 16.95 (978-1-60641-080-6(6)) Deseret Bk. Co.

Turley, Richard E. & Littke, Lael. Stories from the Life of Joseph Smith. 2003. (Illus.). viii, 184p. (J). (978-1-57008-915-2(9)) Deseret Bk. Co.

Wells, Anita. Nephi, Nephi, the Scriptures Are True. Anderson, Neal, illus. 2004. 32p. (J). (gr. -1-2). 17.95 (978-1-59038-307-0(9)) Deseret Bk. Co.

MORMONS AND MORMONISM—FICTION

Andersen, C. B. The Book of Mormon Sleuth Vol. 3: The Hidden Path. 2003. ix, 214p. (J). pap. (978-1-57008-988-6(4)) Deseret Bk. Co.

—The Forgotten Treasure. 2004. 215p. (J). pap. (978-1-59038-314-8(1)) Deseret Bk. Co.

—The Secret Mission. 2008. (J). (978-1-59038-906-5(9)) Deseret Bk. Co.

Bateman, Anya. I Just Got a Letter from Allyson Pringle. 2008. 256p. (YA). pap. 15.95 (978-1-60641-028-8(8)) Deseret Bk. Co.

—The Makeover of James Orville Wickenbee. 2007. 262p. (J). pap. (978-1-59038-707-8(4)) Deseret Bk. Co.

Bell, Michele Ashman. Dragon's Jaw: A Heart-Pounding Adventure. 2005. 241p. (J). (978-1-59156-880-3(3)) Covenant Communications.

Bennett, Carolyn Hart. Seven Sisters: The Voyage. 2008. 232p. 25.95 (978-0-595-51213-3(5)); pap. 15.95 (978-0-595-52242-2(4)) iUniverse, Inc.

Bessey, Siân Ann. Uprising in Samoa: A Novel. 2004. 178p. (J). (978-1-59156-890-2(0)) Covenant Communications.

Blackmore, Katherine, illus. Because of You, Mom. 2019. (J). 13.99 (978-1-62972-520-8(X)) Deseret Bk. Co.

Bowman, David. Who's Your Hero? Vol. 3: Book of Mormon Stories Applied to Children. 2007. 80p. pap. 14.95 *(978-1-59038-759-7(7))* Deseret Bk. Co.
Boyack, Merrilee. The Mismatched Nativity. Tenney, Shawna J. C., illus. 2016. (J). 18.99 *(978-1-62972-239-9(1))* Deseret Bk. Co.
Brown, Toni Sorenson. I Can't Go to Church. Jolley, Mack, illus. 2005. (J). *(978-1-59156-270-2(8))* Covenant Communications.
C. Larene Hall. Martha's Freedom Train. 2009. 100p. pap. 10.49 *(978-1-4389-7977-9(0))* AuthorHouse.
Call, Brian D., tr. & illus. Sarah's Cloud. Call, Brian D., illus. 2003. (J). 15.95 *(978-1-57008-955-8(8))* Deseret Bk. Co.
Cannon, A. E. Charlotte's Rose. 2011. (ENG., Illus.). 256p. (gr. 4). pap. 9.95 *(978-1-60781-141-1(3)*, P196472) Univ. of Utah Pr.
Condie, Ally. Being Sixteen. 2010. 249p. (YA). *(978-1-60641-233-6(7))* Deseret Bk. Co.
—First Day. 2007. 304p. (YA). pap. 15.95 *(978-1-59038-775-7(9))* Deseret Bk. Co.
—Reunion. 2008. 288p. (YA). pap. 15.95 *(978-1-59038-989-8(1))* Deseret Bk. Co.
—Yearbook. 2006. 208p. (YA). pap. 14.95 *(978-1-59038-690-3(6))* Deseret Bk. Co.
Crane, Cheri J. Moment of Truth: A Novel. 2005. 238p. (YA). *(978-1-59156-727-1(0))* Covenant Communications.
Deseret Book Company. Because of You, Dad. Keele, Kevin, illus. 2018. (J). 13.99 *(978-1-62972-561-1(7))* Deseret Bk. Co.
Durrant, George D. Shakespeare's Best Work: A Novel of Unexpected Family Ties & Uncommon Faith. 2003. 130p. pap. 10.95 *(978-1-55517-709-6(3)*, 77093) Cedar Fort, Inc./CFI Distribution.
Evans, Loralee. The King's Heir. 2006. 287p. (YA). (gr. 8-12). per. 18.99 *(978-1-55517-865-9(0)*, Bonneville Bks.) Cedar Fort, Inc./CFI Distribution.
Fechner, Maggie. Growing Up Gracie. 2010. 240p. pap. 15.99 *(978-1-59955-453-2(4))* Cedar Fort, Inc./CFI Distribution.
Ficklin, Jonene H. The Garden Gate. 2005. (YA). 14.95 *(978-0-9761188-2-4(3))* Victor's Crown Publishing.
Gavin, Sherrie. Baptism & Boomerangs. 2015. (Illus.). (J). 14.99 *(978-1-4621-1681-2(7))* Cedar Fort, Inc./CFI Distribution.
Greene, Michele Dominguez. Keep Sweet. 2011. (ENG.). 224p. (YA). (gr. 9). pap. 9.99 *(978-1-4424-0977-4(0)*, Simon Pulse) Simon Pulse.
Harman, Debbie G. My Baptism: The Best Day Ever. 2007. (Illus.). 31p. (J). *(978-1-59156-564-2(2))* Covenant Communications.
Heimerdinger, Chris. Escape from Zarahemla. 2011. 263p. (YA). pap. *(978-1-60861-539-1(1))* Covenant Communications.
—Kingdoms & Conquerors: A Novel. 2005. 434p. (YA). *(978-1-59156-740-0(8))* Covenant Communications.
—Tower of Thunder Vol. 9: A Novel. 2004. (Tennis Shoes Adventure Ser.). 406p. pap. 14.95 *(978-1-59156-177-4(9))* Covenant Communications, Inc.
Hughes, Dean. As Wide As the River. 2005. 156p. (J). pap. *(978-1-59038-450-3(4))* Deseret Bk. Co.
—Under the Same Stars. 2005. viii, 152p. (J). pap. *(978-1-59038-448-0(2))* Deseret Bk. Co.
Hulet, Debra. Independence Rock. 2011. 208p. pap. 13.99 *(978-1-59955-441-9(0)*, Bonneville Bks.) Cedar Fort, Inc./CFI Distribution.
Johnson, Alice W. & Warner, Allison H. Believe & You're There When Ammon Was a Missionary. Harston, Jerry, illus. 2010. (J). *(978-1-60641-247-3(7))* Deseret Bk. Co.
Johnson-Choong, Shelly. A Light to Come Home By. 2nd unabr. ed. 2004. 212p. (C). reprint ed. pap. 12.95 *(978-1-932280-52-4(9)*, 80529) Granite Publishing & Distribution.
Kearns, Ann. Dell's Discovery. 2006. 108p. (YA). per. 9.95 *(978-0-9710696-6-4(2))* Jorlan Publishing, Inc.
Littke, Lael. Searching for Selene. 2003. 203p. (J). pap. 13.95 *(978-1-59038-179-3(3))* Deseret Bk. Co.
Luce, Willard. Jerry Lindsey: Explorer to the San Juan. Collett, Farrell R., illus. 2011. 88p. 38.95 *(978-1-258-07330-5(7))* Literary Licensing, LLC.
Mangum, Kay Lynn. When the Bough Breaks. 2007. 352p. (YA). pap. 15.95 *(978-1-59038-748-1(1))* Deseret Bk. Co.
Mercer, Michael, illus. From the Dust #1: The Last King of Judah. 2012. (ENG.). 110p. (J). pap. 14.99 *(978-0-9859884-1-8(X))* Spider Comics.
Millett, Melanie. CTR Boy. 2006. (Illus.). (J). *(978-1-59811-062-3(4))* Covenant Communications.
Monson, Marianne. The Enchanted Tunnel Vol. 3: Journey to Jerusalem. Burr, Dan, illus. 2011. 85p. (YA). (gr. 3-6). pap. 7.99 *(978-1-60908-068-6(8))* Deseret Bk. Co.
—The Enchanted Tunnel Vol. 4: Wandering in the Wilderness. Burr, Dan, illus. 2011. 85p. (YA). (gr. 3-6). pap. 7.99 *(978-1-60908-069-3(6))* Deseret Bk. Co.
—Escape from Egypt. 2010. (Illus.). 85p. (J). *(978-1-60641-670-9(7))* Deseret Bk. Co.
Morrison, Angela. Taken by Storm. 2009. (ENG.). 304p. (YA). (gr. 7-12). 22.44 *(978-1-59514-238-2(X))* Penguin Young Readers Group.
Nelson, Wendy Watson. The Not Even Once Club: My Promise to Heavenly Father. Dorman, Brandon, illus. 2013. 18.99 *(978-1-60907-337-4(1))* Deseret Bk. Co.
Norton, Tamra. Comfortable in My Own Genes: A Novel. 2004. 175p. (J). pap. 15.95 *(978-1-55517-772-0(7))* Cedar Fort, Inc./CFI Distribution.
—Molly Mormon? Myth or Me? 2011. (Illus.). 170p. (YA). pap. 11.99 *(978-1-55517-606-8(2)*, Bonneville Bks.) Cedar Fort, Inc./CFI Distribution.
Parker, Emma Rae. Papa's Book of Mormon Christmas. 2015. (Illus.). (J). 14.99 *(978-1-4621-1741-3(4))* Cedar Fort, Inc./CFI Distribution.
Peterson, David. 10 Days Until Forever. 2011. 32p. 14.99 *(978-1-59955-266-8(3)*, Bonneville Bks.) Cedar Fort, Inc./CFI Distribution.
Pike, Kenneth & Stewart, Isaac. Jacob's Journal of Doom: Confessions of an Almost-Deacon. 2012. (Illus.). 196p. (J). 14.99 *(978-1-60907-016-8(X))* Deseret Bk. Co.
Rowley, Deborah. The Miracle of the Wooden Shoes. 2008. 32p. (J). 18.95 *(978-1-59038-990-4(5))* Deseret Bk. Co.
Rowley, Deborah Pace. Easter Walk: A Treasure Hunt for the Real Meaning of Easter. Burr, Dan, illus. 2010. (J). *(978-1-60641-055-4(5))* Deseret Bk. Co.
Sebra, Diane. Making Mountains Out of Moles. 2003. 120p. pap. 9.95 *(978-1-55517-712-6(3)*, 77123) Cedar Fort, Inc./CFI Distribution.
Setzer, Lee Ann. Sariah McDuff: Primary Program Diva. Officer, Robyn, illus. 2004. 61p. (J). pap. 4.95 *(978-1-55517-786-7(7))* Cedar Fort, Inc./CFI Distribution.
Smith, Robert F. Bitten: A Romantic Comedy. 2008. 510p. (YA). pap. *(978-1-59038-904-1(2))* Deseret Bk. Co.
Sorenson, Toni. I Will Go, I Will Do: A Book of Mormon Story. 2008. (Illus.). (J). *(978-1-59811-627-4(4))* Covenant Communications.
Sume, Lori Anne, illus. Sorry, Sorry, Sorry: Learning to Choose the Right. 2004. (J). bds. 9.95 *(978-1-59156-298-6(8))* Covenant Communications, Inc.
Talley, Rebecca Cornish. Heaven Scent. 2008. 229p. (gr. 8-12). pap. 15.99 *(978-1-59955-100-5(4))* Cedar Fort, Inc./CFI Distribution.
Thompson, Michelle. Taming the Wind. 2010. 176p. pap. 12.99 *(978-1-59955-379-5(1))* Cedar Fort, Inc./CFI Distribution.
Weyland, Jack. As Always, Dave. 2003. 320p. (YA). pap. 15.95 *(978-1-59038-849-5(6))* Deseret Bk. Co.
Wiles, Patricia. Early-Morning Cemetery: A Novel. 2006. 243p. (YA). pap. *(978-1-59811-077-7(2))* Covenant Communications.
—The Final Farewell: A Novel. 2007. 246p. (J). *(978-1-59811-353-2(4))* Covenant Communications.
Wood, Holly J. Invaluable. 2011. (YA). pap. 14.99 *(978-1-60908-835-4(2))* Deseret Bk. Co.
Yates, Alma J. Sammy's Song: A Novel. 2005. 272p. (J). *(978-1-59156-945-9(1))* Covenant Communications.

MOROCCO

Beardsley, Kurt. Under Saharan Skies. 2004. (Illus.). 96p. per. 25.00 *(978-0-9761103-0-9(X)*, 1000) International Vaquero Productions.
Cassanos, Lynda Cohen. Morocco. 2010. (Major Muslim Nations Ser.). 128p. (YA). (gr. 5-18). lib. bdg. 25.95 *(978-1-4222-1391-9(9))* Mason Crest.
Fordyce, Deborah. Welcome to Morocco, 1 vol. 2004. (Welcome to My Country Ser.). (ENG., Illus.). 48p. (gr. 2-4). lib. bdg. 29.67 *(978-0-8368-2561-9(6)*, 48ebdcac-1a26-4f09-8ce1-9109e19ce4ee) Stevens, Gareth Publishing LLLP.
Markovics, Joyce L. Morocco. 2019. (Countries We Come From Ser.). (ENG., Illus.). 32p. (J). (gr. k-3). 19.95 *(978-1-64280-532-1(7))* Bearport Publishing Co., Inc.
Raabe, Emily. A Primary Source Guide to Morocco. (Countries of the World). 24p. 2009. (gr. 2-3). 42.50 *(978-1-61512-040-6(8))* 2004. (ENG., Illus.). (gr. 3-4). lib. bdg. 26.27 *(978-1-4042-2755-2(5)*, 6822dde0-9df6-4858-9353-79a4a44d66b0) Rosen Publishing Group, Inc., The. (PowerKids Pr.).
Seward, Pat & Hargraves, Orin. Morocco, 1 vol. 2nd rev. ed. 2006. (Cultures of the World (Second Edition)(r) Ser.). (ENG., Illus.). 144p. (gr. 5-5). lib. bdg. 49.79 *(978-0-7614-2051-4(7)*, 47413024-07af-4701-afb5-7fee1e2fd2a5) Cavendish Square Publishing LLC.
U. S. A. Global Investment Center Staff. Morocco Customs, Trade Regulations & Procedures Handbook. 2003. (World Investment & Business Library). pap. 99.95 *(978-0-7397-5590-7(0))* Global Pro Info USA.

MOROCCO—FICTION

Baker, Jeannie. Mirror. Baker, Jeannie, illus. 2010. (ENG., Illus.). 48p. (J). (gr. k-4). 21.99 *(978-0-7636-4848-0(5))* Candlewick Pr.
Demetrios, Heather. Blood Passage. 2016. (Dark Caravan Cycle Ser.: 2). (ENG.). 512p. (YA). (gr. 8). 17.99 *(978-0-06-231859-6(4)*, Balzer & Bray) HarperCollins Pubs.
Dixon, Ken. Cobweb Jack & the Sacred Khunjar. 2009. 210p. pap. 28.50 *(978-1-4092-8919-7(2))* Lulu Pr., Inc.
Feuerman, Ruchama King. The Mountain Jews & the Mirror. Calderón, Marcela & Kosec, Polona, illus. 2015. (ENG.). 32p. (J). (gr. k-4). 7.99 *(978-1-4677-3896-5(4)*, 58813890-5c4f-483b-8b19-5aaa197f5b95, Kar-Ben Publishing) Lerner Publishing Group.
Friedman, J. S. Casablanca. Beatrice, Chris, illus. 2013. (Maurice's Valises Ser.: Vol. 3). (ENG.). 53p. (J). (gr. k-4). 16.95 *(978-94-91613-09-8(X))* Mouse Prints Pr. NLD. Dist: Ingram Publisher Services.
Klaus, Sandra. Mustafas Geheimnis: Ein Moslemischer Junge auf der Suche nach Gott. Date not set.Tr. of Mustapha's Secret - A Muslim Boy's Search to Know God. (GER., Illus.). (J). (gr. 2-7). pap. *(978-0-9617490-6-4(7))* Gospel Missionary Union.
—Tainata na Mustapha. Date not set.Tr. of Mustapha's Secret. (BUL.). (J). (gr. 2-7). pap. *(978-1-890940-04-1(6))* Gospel Missionary Union.
Laurie, Victoria. Oracles of Delphi Keep. (Oracles of Delphi Keep Ser.: 1). (J). 2010. 576p. (gr. 3-7). 8.99 *(978-0-440-42258-7(2)*, Yearling)1. 2009. (ENG.). 560p. (gr. 6-8). lib. bdg. 22.44 *(978-0-385-90561-9(0)*, Delacorte Pr.) Random Hse. Children's Bks.
O'Neill, Joe. Legends of the Rif, bk. 3. 2015. (Red Hand Adventures Ser.: 3). (ENG., Illus.). 311p. (gr. 3-7). pap. 9.95 *(978-0-9851969-8-1(X))* Black Ship Publishing.
Peterson, Will. Triskellion 2: the Burning. 2009. (Triskellion Ser.: 2). (ENG., Illus.). 480p. (J). (gr. 9-8). 16.99 *(978-0-7636-4223-5(1))* Candlewick Pr.
Sewell, Helen & Coatsworth, Elizabeth. The White Horse. 2005. (ENG., Illus.). 169p. (J). (gr. 3-4). per. 11.95 *(978-1-883937-86-7(8))* Ignatius Pr.
Tóth-Jones, Dee S. The Street Cats of Marrakech. Stevenson, Seline, illus. 2013. 34p. pap. *(978-1-908794-08-6(9))* Chiaroscuro Bks.
Turk, Evan. The Storyteller. Turk, Evan, illus. 2016. (ENG., Illus.). 48p. (J). (gr. -1-3). 18.99 *(978-1-4814-3518-5(3))* Simon & Schuster Children's Publishing.

MOROCCO—HISTORY

Ayo's Awesome Adventures in Rabat: Capital of Morocco. 2018. (J). *(978-0-7166-3643-4(3))* World Bk., Inc.
Drummond, Allan. Solar Story: How One Community Lives Alongside the World's Biggest Solar Plant. 2020. (Green Power Ser.). (ENG., Illus.). 40p. (J). 18.99 *(978-0-374-30899-5(3)*, 900188024, Farrar, Straus & Giroux (BYR)) Farrar, Straus & Giroux.
Kavanaugh, Dorothy. Morocco. 2012. (J). *(978-1-4222-2227-0(6))* Mason Crest.
—Morocco. Rotberg, Robert I., ed. 2012. (Evolution of Africa's Major Nations Ser.). (Illus.). 88p. (J). (gr. 7). 22.95 *(978-1-4222-2199-0(7))* Mason Crest.
Klepeis, Alicia Z. Morocco. 2020. (Country Profiles Ser.). (ENG., Illus.). 32p. (J). (gr. 3-8). lib. bdg. 27.95 *(978-1-64487-170-6(X)*, Blastoff! Discovery) Bellwether Media.
Leavitt, Amie Jane. We Visit Morocco. 2012. (J). lib. bdg. 33.95 *(978-1-61228-306-7(3))* Mitchell Lane Pubs.
Mattern, Joanne. Morocco, 1 vol. 2020. (Exploring World Cultures (First Edition) Ser.). (ENG.). 32p. (gr. 3-3). pap. 12.16 *(978-1-5026-5677-3(9)*, 1d0c5e50-77ba-4d26-9f44-96512478c57d) Cavendish Square Publishing LLC.
Perritano, John. Morocco. 2018. (Illus.). 32p. (J). *(978-1-4896-7510-1(8)*, AV2 by Weigl) Weigl Pubs., Inc.
Seward, Pat, et al. Morocco, 1 vol. 3rd rev. ed. 2016. (Cultures of the World (Third Edition)(r) Ser.). (ENG., Illus.). 144p. (gr. 5-5). 48.79 *(978-1-5026-1699-9(8)*, a575fa74-2ccd-4e87-b123-dd347557fd07) Cavendish Square Publishing LLC.
Sheen, Barbara. Foods of Morocco, 1 vol. 2011. (Taste of Culture Ser.). (ENG., Illus.). 64p. (gr. 3-6). lib. bdg. 36.83 *(978-0-7377-5865-8(1)*, 95ec6e0b-fa56-4197-a175-d6fec14f5ff2, KidHaven Publishing) Greenhaven Publishing LLC.
Simmons, Walter. Morocco. 2012. (Exploring Countries Ser.). (ENG., Illus.). 32p. (J). (gr. 3-7). lib. bdg. 27.95 *(978-1-60014-731-9(3)*, Blastoff! Readers) Bellwether Media.

MORPHOLOGY

see Anatomy; Anatomy, Comparative; Biology

MORRISON, TONI, 1931-2019

Crayton, Lisa A. Reading & Interpreting the Works of Toni Morrison, 1 vol. 2015. (Lit Crit Guides). (ENG., Illus.). 152p. (gr. 8-8). lib. bdg. 41.60 *(978-0-7660-7352-4(1)*, 5d908acb-db14-40b7-8e12-c57d6bbf6f58) Enslow Publishing, LLC.
Kramer, Barbara. Toni Morrison: A Biography of a Nobel Prize-Winning Writer, 1 vol. 2013. (African-American Icons Ser.). (ENG.). 104p. (gr. 6-7). pap. 13.88 *(978-1-59845-392-8(0)*, 12cd162e-0984-4bfd-a54a-bb1b20113d05) Enslow Publishing, LLC.
Novel Units. The Bluest Eye Novel Units Student Packet. 2019. (ENG.). (YA). pap., stu. ed., wbk. ed. 13.99 *(978-1-58130-709-2(8)*, Novel Units, Inc.) Classroom Library Co.
Watson, Galadriel Findlay. Toni Morrison. 2005. (Great African American Women for Kids Ser.). (Illus.). 24p. (J). (gr. 2-3). lib. bdg. 24.45 *(978-1-59036-334-8(5))* Weigl Pubs., Inc.

MORSE, SAMUEL FINLEY BREESE, 1791-1872

Davis, Lynn. Samuel Morse, 1 vol. 2015. (Amazing Inventors & Innovators Ser.). (ENG., Illus.). 24p. (J). (gr. k-3). 32.79 *(978-1-62403-725-2(9)*, 17956, Super SandCastle) ABDO Publishing Co.
Kerby, Mona. Samuel Morse. 2018. (ENG., Illus.). 48p. (J). (gr. 4-6). pap. 7.99 *(978-0-9993790-6-6(2))* MK Pubs.
Maurer, Tracy Nelson. Samuel Morse, That's Who! The Story of the Telegraph & Morse Code. Ramón, El Primo, illus. 2019. (ENG.). 40p. (J). 19.99 *(978-1-62779-130-4(2)*, 900136046, Holt, Henry & Co. Bks. For Young Readers) Holt, Henry & Co.
Seidman, David. Samuel Morse & the Telegraph, 1 vol. Whigham, Rod, illus. 2007. (Inventions & Discovery Ser.). (ENG.). 32p. (J). (gr. 3-9). pap. 8.10 *(978-0-7368-7898-2(X)*, 93896, Capstone Pr.) Capstone.
Zannos, Susan. Samuel Morse & the Telegraph. 2004. (Uncharted, Unexplored, & Unexplained Ser.). (Illus.). 48p. (J). (gr. 4-8). lib. bdg. 29.95 *(978-1-58415-269-9(9))* Mitchell Lane Pubs.

MORTUARY CUSTOMS

see Funeral Rites and Ceremonies

MOSAICS

Brack, Amanda. Amazing Brick Mosaics: Fantastic Projects to Build with Lego Blocks You Already Have. 2018. (ENG., Illus.). 160p. (J). pap. 19.99 *(978-1-250-16361-5(7)*, 900186485) St. Martin's Pr.
Harris, Nathaniel. Mosaics, 1 vol. 2008. (Stories in Art Ser.). (ENG., Illus.). 32p. (J). (gr. 4-4). lib. bdg. 30.27 *(978-1-4042-4438-2(7)*, be16b7c9-1e09-4993-acd4-ff790d50f5b5, PowerKids Pr.) Rosen Publishing Group, Inc., The.
Henry, Sally & Cook, Trevor. Making Mosaics, 1 vol. 2010. (Make Your Own Art Ser.). (ENG., Illus.). 32p. (J). (gr. 3-4). 30.27 *(978-1-4488-1585-2(1)*, b486d950-5a61-4480-bf95-a93f3b05f98a); pap. 12.75 *(978-1-4488-1617-0(3)*, 25c5cda6-397a-4e44-8024-552d7f3dbf66) Rosen Publishing Group, Inc., The. (PowerKids Pr.).
Mosaics: Creative Tiled Projects. 2013. (Kits for Kids Ser.). (ENG., Illus.). 64p. (J). (gr. 1-7). *(978-1-77132-052-8(4))* SpiceBox Products Ltd.
The American Mosaic: Immigration Today, 12 vols. 2014. (American Mosaic: Immigration Today Ser.). (ENG.). 24p. (J). (gr. 2-3). 151.62 *(978-1-4777-6653-8(7)*, 6aabddc0-37eb-4657-84f3-b3526bcdaa8c, PowerKids Pr.) Rosen Publishing Group, Inc., The.

MOSCOW (RUSSIA)

Goldsworthy, Steve. Kremlin. 2014. (Illus.). 24p. (J). *(978-1-62127-464-3(0))* Weigl Pubs., Inc.
Hopkinson, Deborah & Who HQ. Where Is the Kremlin? Putra, Dede, illus. 2019. (Where Is? Ser.). 112p. (J). (gr. 3-7). 5.99 *(978-1-5247-8974-9(7))*; 15.99 *(978-1-5247-8975-6(5))* Penguin Young Readers Group. (Penguin Workshop).
Mason Crest. Moscow, Vol. 8. 2016. (Major World Cities Ser.: Vol. 8). (ENG., Illus.). 48p. (J). (gr. 5-8). 20.95 *(978-1-4222-3542-3(4))* Mason Crest.
Maule, David. What Makes a Place Special? Moscow, Egypt, Australia, 1 vol. 2014. (ENG., Illus.). 24p. (J). pap., E-Book 9.50 *(978-1-107-63317-9(6))* Cambridge Univ. Pr.
Steele, Philip. Moscow, 1 vol. 2003. (Great Cities of the World Ser.). (ENG., Illus.). 48p. (gr. 5-8). lib. bdg. 33.67 *(978-0-8368-5024-6(6)*, 91168811-5012-4a7c-9033-a5ccb9cb1a4b, Gareth Stevens Secondary Library) Stevens, Gareth Publishing LLLP.

MOSCOW (RUSSIA)—FICTION

Angel, Ido. Vipo in Moscow: The Siberian Tiger Is Hungry! 2015. (AV2 Animated Storytime Ser.). (ENG.). (J). lib. bdg. 29.99 *(978-1-4896-3914-1(4)*, AV2 by Weigl) Weigl Pubs., Inc.
Brodsky, Slava. Funny Children's Stories (in Russian - Smeshnye detskie Rasskazy) 2006. (RUS.). 144p. pap. 8.76 *(978-0-615-16120-4(0))* Manhattan Academia.
Evans, Connie. Sasha & Babushka: A Story of Russia. Schpitalnik, Vladimir, illus. (Make Friends Around the World Ser.). (ENG.). 32p. (J). (gr. k-3). 8.95 *(978-1-59249-446-0(3)*, SC8007) Soundprints.
Evans, Cornelia & Shpitalnik, Vladimir. Sasha & Babushka: A Story of Russia. 2005. (Make Friends Around the World Ser.). (ENG., Illus.). 32p. (J). (gr. k-3). 19.95 *(978-1-59249-445-3(5)*, BC8007) Soundprints.
Friedman, J. S. The Micetro of Moscow. Beatrice, Chris, illus. 2013. (Maurice's Valises Ser.: Vol. 2). (ENG.). 44p. (J). (gr. k-4). 16.95 *(978-94-91613-06-7(5))* Mouse Prints Pr. NLD. Dist: Ingram Publisher Services.
Grant, Myrna. Ivan & the Daring Escape. rev. ed. 2006. (Flamingo Fiction 9-13s Ser.). (ENG., Illus.). 144p. (J). (gr. 4-7). per. 6.99 *(978-1-84550-132-7(2)*, 6a061cd0-b8f2-4a06-bb6c-179f7a430555) Christian Focus Pubns. GBR. Dist: Baker & Taylor Publisher Services (BTPS).
—Ivan & the Moscow Circus. 2006. (Flamingo Fiction 9-13s Ser.). (ENG., Illus.). 160p. (J). (gr. 4-7). per. 11.99 *(978-1-84550-135-8(7)*, 40bfabff-5df7-44fd-a846-b5a56c6d4c58) Christian Focus Pubns. GBR. Dist: Baker & Taylor Publisher Services (BTPS).
Lane, Andrew. Black Ice. 2013. (Sherlock Holmes: the Legend Begins Ser.: 3). (ENG.). 304p. (YA). (gr. 7-12). pap. 13.99 *(978-1-250-03654-4(2)*, 900122027) Square Fish.
Shpitalnik, Vladimir & Evans, Connie. Sasha & Babushka: A Story of Russia. 2005. (Make Friends Around the World Ser.). (ENG., Illus.). 32p. (J). (gr. k-3). pap. 6.95 *(978-1-59249-444-6(7)*, S8007) Soundprints.
Shpitalnik, Vladimir & Evans, Cornelia. Sasha & Babushka: A Story of Russia. 2005. (Make Friends Around the World Ser.). (ENG., Illus.). 32p. (J). (gr. k-3). 15.95 *(978-1-59249-443-9(9)*, B8007) Soundprints.

MOSES (BIBLICAL LEADER)

The Adventures of Moses: A Bible Story to Color. (Illus.). 16p. (J). pap. 1.50 *(978-0-87162-849-7(X)*, E6023) Warner Pr., Inc.
Andrews, Jackie. Moses in the Bulrushes. de Klerk, Roger, illus. 2012. (ENG.). 24p. (J). 8.50 *(978-1-84135-807-9(X))* Award Pubns. Ltd. GBR. Dist: Parkwest Pubns., Inc.
Award, Anna. Moses in the Bulrushes: See the Picture & Say the Word. 2012. (ENG., Illus.). 24p. (J). pap. 6.50 *(978-1-84135-602-0(6))* Award Pubns. Ltd. GBR. Dist: Parkwest Pubns., Inc.
Bader, Joanne. Moses & the Long Walk. von der Sterre, Johanna, illus. 2006. (ENG.). 16p. (J). pap. 1.99 *(978-0-7586-0874-1(8))* Concordia Publishing Hse.
Blyton, Enid. Moses in the Bulrushes: See the Picture & Say the Word. 2012. 24p. (J). 9.95 *(978-1-84135-747-8(2))* Award Pubns. Ltd. GBR. Dist: Parkwest Pubns., Inc.
Booth, Bradley. God Said It #3: The Life of Moses. 2018. (J). pap. *(978-0-8163-6482-4(6))* Pacific Pr. Publishing Assn.
Bower, Gary. The Hurry-Up Exit from Egypt. Chotiner, Barbara, illus. 2017. (Faith That God Built Book Ser.). (ENG.). 32p. (J). 14.99 *(978-1-4964-1745-9(3)*, 20_28620, Tyndale Kids) Tyndale Hse. Pubs.
Dietrich, Julie. Tiny Baby Moses. Clark, Bill, illus. 2003. (Arch Bks.). (ENG.). 16p. (J). (gr. k-4). 1.99 *(978-0-570-07581-3(5))* Concordia Publishing Hse.
Fernandez, Francisco. Moises. Osorio, Sergio, illus. 2005. (Historia de la Biblia Ser.). (SPA.). 64p. (J). pap. 4.70 *(978-970-643-875-1(0))* Selector, S.A. de C.V. MEX. Dist: Spanish Pubs., LLC.
Fogle, Robin. Baby Moses Coloring Book. 2007. (Illus.). 16p. (J). pap. 1.89 *(978-1-59317-189-6(7))* Warner Pr., Inc.
Frank, Penny. Let My People Go! Morris, Tony, illus. 2nd rev. ed. (ENG.). 24p. pap. 2.99 *(978-0-7459-4108-0(7)*, Lion Books) Lion Hudson PLC GBR. Dist: Trafalgar Square Publishing.
—The Princess & the Baby. Morris, Tony, illus. 2nd rev. ed. (ENG.). 24p. pap. 2.99 *(978-0-7459-4107-3(9)*, Lion Books) Lion Hudson PLC GBR. Dist: Trafalgar Square Publishing.
Gallaudet, Thomas H. Scripture Biography for the Young: Vol. 3 - Moses Part 1. 2009. 224p. pap. 18.00 *(978-1-59925-235-3(X))* Solid Ground Christian Bks.
—Scripture Biography for the Young: Vol. 4 - Moses Part 2. 2009. 276p. pap. 20.00 *(978-1-59925-236-0(8))* Solid Ground Christian Bks.
Gamblin, Rose Tooley. Baby Moses. 2007. (J). *(978-0-8127-0466-2(5))* Autumn Hse. Publishing Co.
Hyatt, Greg. Moses & the Bronze Snake. 2008. (Arch Bks.). (Illus.). 16p. (J). (gr. k-4). pap. 1.99 *(978-0-7586-1456-8(X))* Concordia Publishing Hse.
Kerensa, Paul. Moses & the Exodus Express. Liz and Kate Pope, illus. 2018. (ENG.). 32p. (J). pap. 12.99 *(978-0-281-07757-1(6)*, 033c59b4-d7b6-42f2-9d50-3065de2a4784) SPCK Publishing GBR. Dist: Baker & Taylor Publisher Services (BTPS).
Koralek, Jenny. The Moses Basket. Baynes, Pauline, illus. 2004. 32p. (J). 16.00 *(978-0-8028-5251-9(3))* Eerdmans, William B. Publishing Co.
Kovacs, Victoria. Miriam/Daniel Flip-Over Book. Krome, Mike & Ryley, David, illus. 2015. (Little Bible Heroes(tm) Ser.). (ENG.). 32p. (J). (gr. k-2). pap. 5.99 *(978-1-4336-8717-4(8)*, 005742017, B&H Kids) B&H Publishing Group.
Lafond, Pascale. The Story of Moses. Flowerpot Press, ed. 2012. (Illus.). 32p. (J). *(978-1-77093-388-0(3))* Flowerpot Children's Pr. Inc.
Lashbrook, Marilyn. Who Needs a Boat? Britt, Stephanie McFetridge, illus. 2012. 32p. (J). pap. 8.00 *(978-1-935014-39-3(0))* Hutchings, John Pubs.

MacKenzie, Carine. Moses the Child: Kept by God. 2008. (Bible Alive Ser.). (ENG., Illus.). 24p. (J). 4.50 (978-1-84550-330-7(9), f64d7a0c-5400-4a67-b1f6-7b57d6837c3d) Christian Focus Pubns. GBR. Dist: Baker & Taylor Publisher Services (BTPS).

—Moses the Leader: Used by God. 2008. (Bible Alive Ser.). (ENG., Illus.). 24p. (J). 4.50 (978-1-84550-332-1(5), d8740529-989a-4ddc-8325-23bae535913c) Christian Focus Pubns. GBR. Dist: Baker & Taylor Publisher Services (BTPS).

—Moses the Shepherd: Chosen by God. 2008. (Bible Alive Ser.). (ENG., Illus.). 24p. (J). 4.50 (978-1-84550-331-4(7), 4298e5cb-f0bc-4be0-a7e9-d4159bf0b327) Christian Focus Pubns. GBR. Dist: Baker & Taylor Publisher Services (BTPS).

—Moses the Traveller: Guided by God. 2008. (Bible Alive Ser.). (ENG., Illus.). 24p. (J). 4.50 (978-1-84550-333-8(3), e50659d1-646a-491c-9dae-4988694763fe) Christian Focus Pubns. GBR. Dist: Baker & Taylor Publisher Services (BTPS).

Martin, Oscar, Jr., creator. The Story of Moses l.t. ed. 2003. (Illus.). 25p. (J). E-Book 19.95 incl. cd-rom (978-0-9748416-2-5(5)) Build Your Story.

Miller, Mary R. Moses, the Meekest Man. Higgins, Tabitha & Shirk, Linda, illus. 2016. (ENG.). 32p. (J). (gr. -1). 3.25 (978-0-7399-2536-2(9)) Rod & Staff Pubs., Inc.

Moises (Moses) (Divertidas Historias Biblicas para Ninos Ser.). (SPA.). (J). 3.49 (978-0-7899-0597-0(3), 496644) Editorial Unilit.

Moses: God's Man of the Hour — Activity Book. 2005. pap. 1.69 (978-1-59317-109-4(9)) Warner Pr., Inc.

Nolan, Allia Zobel. Moses' Big Adventure. Cox, Steve, illus. 2004. 12p. (J). bds. 10.99 (978-0-8254-5521-6(9)) Kregel Pubns.

Roberts, Catrin, et al. Mawredd Mawr Moses! 16 Sesiwn Beiblaidd Ar Gyfer Clwb Plant Neu'r Ysgol Sul. 2005. (WEL., Illus.). 76p. pap. (978-1-85994-034-1(X)) Cyhoeddiadau'r Gair.

Smith, Brendan Powell. Baby Moses: The Brick Bible for Kids. 2016. (Brick Bible for Kids Ser.). (ENG., Illus.). 32p. (J). (gr. -1-k). 12.99 (978-1-5107-1266-9(6), Sky Pony Pr.) Skyhorse Publishing Co., Inc.

Stowell, Gordon. Y Ddihangfa Anhygoel! Llyfr Drysfa Beiblaidd. Davies, Aled, ed. Wyn, Delyth, tr. Richardson-Jones, Tessa, illus. 2005. (WEL.). 12p. (978-1-85994-469-1(8)) Cyhoeddiadau'r Gair.

Thomas, Sylvia A. Moses & the Exodus from Egypt. 2012. 34p. pap. 19.99 (978-1-61904-669-6(5)) Salem Author Services.

Van Der Veer, Andrew. Bible Lessons for Juniors, Book 1: Creation Through Moses. 2007. 88p. (J). 6.00 (978-1-60178-012-6(5)) Reformation Heritage Bks.

Whiting, Jim. The Life & Times of Moses. 2005. (Biography from Ancient Civilizations Ser.). (Illus.). 48p. (J). (gr. -1-7). lib. bdg. 29.95 (978-1-58415-340-5(7)) Mitchell Lane Pubs.

Zondervan Bibles Staff. Moses & the King, 1 vol. Pulley, Kelly, illus. 2009. (I Can Read! / the Beginner's Bible Ser.). (ENG.). 32p. (J). pap. 4.99 (978-0-310-71800-0(7)) Zonderkidz.

Zondervan Staff. Moses, God's Brave Servant, 1 vol. Jones, Dennis G., illus. 2010. (I Can Read! / Dennis Jones Ser.). (ENG.). 32p. (J). (gr. -1-2). pap. 4.99 (978-0-310-71882-6(1)) Zonderkidz.

—Moses Leads the People, 1 vol. Miles, David, illus. 2014. (I Can Read! / Adventure Bible Ser.). (ENG.). 32p. (J). pap. 4.99 (978-0-310-73236-5(0)) Zondervan.

Zondervan Staff & The Beginner's Bible. Baby Moses & the Princess, 1 vol. Pulley, Kelly, illus. 2009. (I Can Read! / the Beginner's Bible Ser.). (ENG.). 32p. (J). pap. 5.99 (978-0-310-71767-6(1)) Zonderkidz.

MOSES (BIBLICAL LEADER)—FICTION

Adler, David A. Brothers in Egypt. abr. ed. (Prince of Egypt Ser.). (ENG.). 64p. pap. (978-0-582-36482-0(5)) Addison-Wesley Longman, Inc.

Baby Moses. 2005. (J). bds. 5.99 (978-0-9753127-9-7(0)) Family Bks. at Home.

Booth, Bradley. Escape from Egypt. 2009. (J). pap. 11.99 (978-0-8163-2305-0(4)) Pacific Pr. Publishing Assn.

—Plagues in the Palace. 2006. 159p. (J). 10.99 (978-0-8163-2143-8(4)) Pacific Pr. Publishing Assn.

CrossStaff Publishing, creator. The Ten Commandments Movie Coloring Book, Part 2. 2007. (Epic Stories of the Bible Ser.). (Illus.). 32p. (J). (gr. -1-3). 5.99 (978-0-9743876-3-5(0)) CrossStaff Publishing.

Lester, Julius. Pharaoh's Daughter: A Novel of Ancient Egypt. 2009. (ENG., Illus.). 192p. (YA). (gr. 7). pap. 7.99 (978-0-15-206662-8(4), 1099001, Clarion Bks.) HarperCollins Pubs.

Monson, Marianne. Escape from Egypt. 2010. (Illus.). 85p. (J). (978-1-60641-670-9(7)) Deseret Bk. Co.

Rothero, C. Moses in the Bulrushes. 2005. (See & Say Storybook Ser.). (Illus.). 20p. (J). 5.95 (978-965-483-008-9(6), Devora Publishing) Simcha Media Group.

Thomas, M. J. The Secret of the Hidden Scrolls: the Great Escape, Book 3. 2018. (Secret of the Hidden Scrolls Ser.: 3). (ENG., Illus.). 128p. (J). (gr. 1-4). pap. 6.99 (978-0-8249-5689-9(3), Worthy Kids/Ideals) Worthy Publishing.

MOSES, GRANDMA, 1860-1961

Ketchum, William C. Grandma Moses: An American Original, Vol. 8. 2018. (American Artists Ser.). 80p. (J). (gr. 7). 33.27 (978-1-4222-4160-8(2)) Mason Crest.

Kopp, Megan. Grandma Moses. 2016. (Illus.). 32p. (J). (978-1-4896-4621-7(3)) Weigl Pubs., Inc.

Stephens, Pamela. Dropping in on Grandma Moses. McNeill, Jim, illus. 2008. 32p. (J). 15.95 (978-1-56290-598-9(8)) Crystal Productions.

Venezia, Mike. Grandma Moses. Venezia, Mike, illus. 2004. (Getting to Know the World's Greatest Artists Ser.). (ENG., Illus.). 32p. (J). (gr. 3-4). pap. 6.95 (978-0-516-27913-8(0), Children's Pr.) Scholastic Library Publishing.

MOSLEM ART

see Islamic Art

MOSQUITOES

Abraham, Anika. Mosquitoes, 1 vol. 2018. (Creepy Crawlers Ser.). (ENG.). 24p. (gr. 1-1). pap. 9.22 (978-1-5026-4228-8(X), 9a817c36-27fd-4211-a2e3-fa1866e2a29b) Cavendish Square Publishing LLC.

Bearden, Stacy. Boudreaux the Louisiana Mosquiteaux, 1 vol. 2017. (ENG., Illus.). 32p. (J). (gr. k-3). pap. 9.95 (978-1-4556-2247-4(8), Pelican Publishing) Arcadia Publishing.

Braun, Eric. Great White Shark vs. Mosquito. 2018. (Versus! Ser.). (ENG.). 24p. (J). (gr. 4-6). pap. 9.99 (978-1-64466-332-5(5), 12163); (Illus.). lib. bdg. (978-1-68072-349-6(9), 12162) Black Rabbit Bks. (Hi Jinx).

Carr, Aaron. Mosquitoes. 2014. (J). (978-1-4896-3200-5(X)) Weigl Pubs., Inc.

Dessen, Maci. Look Out for the Mosquito!, 1 vol. 2015. (Surprisingly Scary! Ser.). (ENG.). 24p. (J). (gr. 2-3). 25.27 (978-1-4994-0942-0(7), 6f4b801d-c932-45e3-b808-b85e43709681, PowerKids Pr.) Rosen Publishing Group, Inc., The.

DiConsiglio, John. Bitten! Mosquitoes Infect New York. 2011. (Illus.). 48p. (J). (978-0-545-32807-4(1)) Scholastic, Inc.

Diconsiglio, John. Blood Suckers! Deadly Mosquito Bites. 2007. (24/7: Science Behind the Scenes Ser.). (ENG., Illus.). 64p. (J). (gr. 9-12). pap. 7.95 (978-0-531-17529-3(4), Watts, Franklin) Scholastic Library Publishing.

Ford, Jeanne Marie. Malaria: How a Parasite Changed History. 2019. (Infected! Ser.). (ENG., Illus.). 32p. (J). (gr. 3-9). lib. bdg. 28.65 (978-1-5435-5505-9(5), 139377, Capstone Pr.) Capstone.

Goldish, Meish. Bloodthirsty Mosquitoes. (No Backbone! Insects Ser.). 24p. (J). (gr. k-3). 2018. (ENG.). 7.99 (978-1-64280-081-4(3)) 2008. (Illus.). lib. bdg. 26.99 (978-1-59716-585-3(9)) Bearport Publishing Co., Inc.

—Murderous Mosquitoes. 2019. (Bugged Out! the World's Most Dangerous Bugs Ser.). (ENG., Illus.). 24p. (J). (gr. 2-7). lib. bdg. 19.45 (978-1-64280-166-8(6)) Bearport Publishing Co., Inc.

Hansen, Grace. Becoming a Mosquito. 2018. (Changing Animals Ser.). (ENG., Illus.). 24p. (J). (gr. -1-2). lib. bdg. 32.79 (978-1-5321-0817-4(6), 28195, Abdo Kids) ABDO Publishing Co.

—Mosquitoes, 1 vol. 2014. (Insects (Abdo Kids) Ser.). (ENG.). 24p. (J). (gr. -1-2). lib. bdg. 32.79 (978-1-62970-041-0(X), 1454, Abdo Kids) ABDO Publishing Co.

Hunt, Santana. Bloodsucking Mosquitoes, 1 vol. 2015. (Real-Life Vampires Ser.). (ENG., Illus.). 24p. (J). (gr. 2-3). pap. 9.15 (978-1-4824-3955-7(7), 5a29a02b-b0f6-428c-8731-b09f61896f17) Stevens, Gareth Publishing LLLP.

Kalman, Bobbie. El Ciclo de Vida del Mosquito. 2005. (Serie Ciclos de Vida Ser.). (SPA., Illus.). 32p. (J). lib. bdg. (978-0-7787-8667-2(6)); (gr. 1-7). pap. (978-0-7787-8713-6(3)) Crabtree Publishing Co.

—The Life Cycle of a Mosquito. 2003. (Life Cycle Ser.). (ENG., Illus.). 32p. (J). pap. (978-0-7787-0695-3(8)) Crabtree Publishing Co.

—Les Moustiques. Briere, Marie-Josee, tr. from ENG. 2006. (Petit Monde Vivant Ser.). (FRE., Illus.). 32p. (J). (gr. -1-3). pap. 9.95 (978-2-89579-077-8(9)) Bayard Canada Livres CAN. Dist: Crabtree Publishing Co.

Kravetz, Jonathan. Mosquitoes. (Gross Bugs Ser.). 24p. (gr. 3-4). 2009. 42.50 (978-1-61513-229-4(5)) 2005. (ENG., Illus.). (J). lib. bdg. 26.27 (978-1-4042-3044-6(0), 6f52bc54-f3b7-43a6-8866-8280d2b39576) Rosen Publishing Group, Inc., The. (PowerKids Pr.).

Lew, Kristi. Mosquito-Borne Illnesses, 1 vol. 2010. (Health Alert Ser.). (ENG.). 64p. (gr. 4-4). 35.50 (978-0-7614-3980-6(3), 1cea95ec-a87b-4efe-b7d4-61f9984c7c5b) Cavendish Square Publishing LLC.

Markle, Sandra. Mosquitoes. 2008. pap. 52.95 (978-1-58013-284-8(7)) Lerner Publishing Group.

—Mosquitoes: Tiny Insect Troublemakers. 2008. (Insect World Ser.). (ENG., Illus.). 48p. (gr. 4-8). lib. bdg. 27.93 (978-0-8225-7299-2(0), Lerner Pubns.) Lerner Publishing Group.

Mitchell, Kirstin. Madame Anopheles. 2008.Tr. of Seòora Anopheles. (Illus.). 26p. (J). pap. 20.00 (978-0-9816301-0-6(3)) Alexander, Raine.

Orr, Tamra B. Understanding Insects. 2014. (Explorer Library: Science Explorer Ser.). (ENG., Illus.). 32p. (J). (gr. 4-8). 32.07 (978-1-62431-783-5(9), 203328) Cherry Lake Publishing.

Perish, Patrick. Mosquitoes. 2018. (Insects up Close Ser.). (ENG., Illus.). 24p. (J). (gr. k-3). lib. bdg. 26.95 (978-1-62617-717-8(1), Blastoff! Readers) Bellwether Media.

Piehl, Janet. Flying Mosquitoes. 2006. (Pull Ahead Bks.). (Illus.). 32p. (J). (gr. 3-7). lib. bdg. 22.60 (978-0-8225-5932-0(3), Lerner Pubns.) Lerner Publishing Group.

Reher, Matt. The Life of a Mosquito. 2016. (2G Bugs Ser.). (ENG., Illus.). 24p. (J). pap. 9.60 (978-1-63437-503-0(3)) American Reading Co.

—Mosquito Moms. 2016. (2G Bugs Ser.). (ENG., Illus.). 24p. (J). pap. 9.60 (978-1-63437-510-8(6)) American Reading Co.

Richter, Abigail. Deadly Mosquitoes, 1 vol. 2011. (Small but Deadly Ser.). (ENG., Illus.). 24p. (J). (gr. 2-3). pap. 9.15 (978-1-4339-5740-6(X), 38f74c8b-9345-4c8c-9797-7868c7938c5c); lib. bdg. 25.27 (978-1-4339-5738-3(8), c5d7c266-d6b4-418b-9f62-ebfd0847ebff) Stevens, Gareth Publishing LLLP. (Gareth Stevens Learning Library).

Rustad, Martha E. H. Mosquitoes. 2007. (World of Insects Ser.). (ENG., Illus.). 24p. (J). (gr. k-3). lib. bdg. 26.95 (978-1-60014-078-5(5)) Bellwether Media.

Schuh, Mari. Mosquitoes. 2014. (Illus.). 24p. (J). lib. bdg. 25.65 (978-1-62031-085-4(6), Bullfrog Bks.) Jump! Inc.

Scott, Jane Beecher. The Amazing Mosquito Bridge Secret. Scott, Jane Beecher, ed. Scott, Jane Beecher, illus. Scott, Jane Beecher, photos by. 5th ed. 2004. (Illus.). 32p. (J). (gr. k-12). 12.95 (978-0-9763077-0-9(7)) Beecher Scott.

Siemens, Jared. Mosquitoes. 2017. (Illus.). 24p. (J). (978-1-5105-0641-1(1)) SmartBook Media, Inc.

Siy, Alexandra. Mosquito Bite. Kunkel, Dennis, illus. 32p. (J). (gr. 2-5). 2006. pap. 7.95 (978-1-57091-592-5(X)) 2005. 16.95 (978-1-57091-591-8(1)) Charlesbridge Publishing, Inc.

Somervill, Barbara A. Mosquitoes: Hungry for Blood. (Bloodsuckers Ser.). 24p. (gr. 2-3). 2009. 42.50 (978-1-61511-635-5(4), PowerKids Pr.) 2007. (ENG., Illus.). (J). lib. bdg. 26.27 (978-1-4042-3802-2(6), 046849d5-b64f-45c1-a721-da94c8492e12) Rosen Publishing Group, Inc., The.

Walker, Sally M. Mosquitoes. 2008. (Early Bird Nature Books Ser.). (Illus.). 48p. (J). (gr. 2-5). 26.60 (978-0-8225-1375-9(7)) Lerner Publishing Group.

Webster, Christine. Mosquitoes. 2009. (Backyard Animals Ser.). (Illus.). 24p. (J). (gr. 3-5). pap. 8.95 (978-1-60596-087-6(X)); lib. bdg. 24.45 (978-1-60596-086-9(1)) Weigl Pubs., Inc.

MOTELS

see Hotels, Motels, etc.

MOTHER AND CHILD

see also Mothers and Daughters; Mothers and Sons

April, Elyse. Ready to Wean: The Return of the Dangling Red Earrings. Iverson, Diane, illus. 2012. (Family & World Health / We Like To Ser.). (ENG.). 32p. (J). pap. 9.95 (978-1-935387-30-5(8)) Hohm Pr.

Arzón, Robin. Strong Mama. Sonda, Addy Rivera, illus. 2022. (ENG.). 40p. (J). (gr. -1-3). 17.99 (978-0-316-29994-7(4)) Little, Brown Bks. for Young Readers.

Barry, Ron & Fitzgerald, Paula. Me 'n Mom: A Keepsake Scrapbook Journal. Sharp, Chris, illus. 2009. (ENG.). 33p. pap. 14.99 (978-0-8249-1435-6(X), Ideals Pubns.) Worthy Publishing.

Berry, Joy. I Love Mommies & Daddies. Regan, Dana, illus. 2010. (Teach Me About Ser.). (ENG.). 20p. (J). (gr. k — 1). pap. 5.99 (978-1-60577-001-7(9)) Berry, Joy Enterprises.

Catt, Thessaly. My Mom, 1 vol. 2010. (My Family Ser.). (ENG.). 24p. (J). (gr. 1-2). pap. 9.25 (978-1-4488-1490-9(1), f4a76970-8e18-4a92-b1e7-c65748eacfd3); lib. bdg. 26.27 (978-1-4488-1462-6(6), 29fc2fb0-2a8a-4acf-801b-9810b42b3ca1) Rosen Publishing Group, Inc., The. (PowerKids Pr.).

—My Mom(Mi Mamá), 1 vol. 2010. (My Family / Mi Familia Ser.). (SPA & ENG.). 24p. (gr. 1-2). lib. bdg. 26.27 (978-1-4488-0717-8(4), 5c24e066-7844-428e-aa3f-9fe9ce6fadbc) Rosen Publishing Group, Inc., The.

D'Costa, Jasmine. Real Justice: Branded a Baby Killer: The Story of Tammy Marquardt. 2015. (Lorimer Real Justice Ser.). (ENG., Illus.). 120p. (YA). (gr. 9-12). pap. 12.95 (978-1-4594-0993-4(0)) James Lorimer & Co. Ltd., Pubs. CAN. Dist: Casemate Pubs. & Bk. Distributors, LLC.

Elkus, Julie. Cuando Mi Mama Me Lee/When My Mama Reads to Me. Fagin, Cristina, tr. from ENG. Nunez, Jose Luis, illus. 2005. (SPA & ENG.). 24p. (J). (gr. -1-3). 8.95 (978-1-933197-06-7(4)) Orange Frazer Pr.

Fitzgerald, Juniper. How Mamas Love Their Babies. Peterson, Elise, illus. 2018. (ENG.). 48p. (J). (gr. -1-3). 16.95 (978-1-936932-00-9(8)) Feminist Pr. at The City Univ. of New York.

Gamble, Adam & Jasper, Mark. Good Night Mommy. Kelly, Cooper, illus. 2015. (Good Night Our World Ser.). (ENG.). 20p. (J). (— 1). bds. 9.95 (978-1-60219-230-0(8)) Good Night Bks.

Gervais, Josephine. Mommies Are Protecting Their Children. 2013. 20p. pap. 24.95 (978-1-62709-538-9(1)) America Star Bks.

—Mommies Are Special People. 2013. 24p. pap. 24.95 (978-1-62709-537-2(3)) America Star Bks.

Greven, Alec. How to Talk to Moms. Acedera, Kei, illus. 2009. (ENG.). 48p. (J). (gr. 1-5). 9.99 (978-0-06-171001-8(6), HarperCollins) HarperCollins Pubs.

Jackson, Toneal M. Four Girls: A Lot of Choices. 2011. 40p. pap. 24.95 (978-1-4560-8518-6(2)) PublishAmerica, Inc.

Legg, Brook. The Healing Rhythms of Home: 30 Days of Devotion for the Homeschool Mom. 2012. 74p. pap. 9.95 (978-1-4497-5587-4(9), WestBow Pr.) Author Solutions, LLC.

L'Heureux, Christine. Caillou: I Love You. Brignaud, Pierre, illus. 2012. (Hand in Hand Ser.). (ENG.). 24p. (J). (gr. -1-k). 5.99 (978-2-89450-860-2(3)) Caillouet, Gerry.

Liles, Rebecca. My Mommy's a Soldier, 2 bks. 2003. (Illus.). 16p. (J). 4.99 (978-0-9744346-1-2(2)) Rebecca's Bks.

Lindsay, Jeanne Warren & Brunelli, Jean. Nurturing Your Newborn: Young Parents' Guide to Baby's First Month. 2nd ed. 2006. (Illus.). 96p. (J). pap. (978-1-932538-38-0(0)) Morning Glory Pr., Inc.

Meeker, Clare Hodgson. Growing up Gorilla: How a Zoo Baby Brought Her Family Together. 2019. (ENG., Illus.). 48p. (J). (gr. 3-6). 31.99 (978-1-5415-4240-2(1), 10f080ef-eeb6-432b-99a4-0ebfbc30939e, Millbrook Pr.) Lerner Publishing Group.

Moore, M. Meet My Mom: Learning the M Sound. 2009. (PowerPhonics Ser.). 24p. (gr. 1-1). 39.90 (978-1-60851-459-5(5), PowerKids Pr.) Rosen Publishing Group, Inc., The.

Moore-Mallinos, Jennifer & Roca, Nuria. Mi Mama Tiene Cancer! My Mom Has Cancer! (Spanish-Language Edition) Fabrega, Marta, illus. 2008. (Hablemos de Esto! / Let's Talk about It! Ser.). (SPA.). 32p. (J). (gr. k-3). 22.44 (978-0-7641-4075-4(2), B.E.S. Publishing) Peterson's.

Moulton, Alison. When Mommy Is Home with Me. Beckett, Kinsey, illus. 2017. (J). 14.99 (978-1-4622-0093-1(1), Horizon Pubs.) Cedar Fort, Inc./CFI Distribution.

Neumann, Rachel. Baby Present. McConnell, Ericka, photos by. 2016. (Illus.). 22p. (J). (gr. -1 — 1). bds. 9.95 (978-1-941529-24-9(0), Plum Blossom Bks.) Parallax Pr.

Newell, Cheri Cameron. An Angel Just Like You. 2012. (ENG.). (J). pap. (978-1-4675-5356-8(5)) Independent Pub.

Nilsen, Anna. My Mum's Best. Dodd, Emma, illus. 2011. 24p. bds. (978-1-84089-679-4(5)) Zero to Ten, Ltd.

Page, Liza & Innovative Kids Staff. Mommies & Babies. Larrañaga, Ana Martín, illus. 2008. (ENG.). 12p. (J). (gr. -1 — 1). bds. 5.99 (978-1-58476-656-8(5)) Innovative Kids.

Parr, todd. The Mommy Book. 2016. (ENG., Illus.). 20p. (J). (gr. -1 — 1). bds. 7.99 (978-0-316-33774-8(9)) Little, Brown Bks. for Young Readers.

Raucy, Elise. Mom's Busy Days. Meens, Estelle, illus. 2018. 32p. (J). (978-1-4338-2820-1(0), Magination Pr.) American Psychological Assn.

Richmond, Marianne. Thank You Mom. 2004. (Illus.). 40p. (YA). 7.95 (978-0-9741465-6-0(0), Marianne Richmond Studios, Inc.) Sourcebooks, Inc.

Riehle, Mary Ann McCabe. M Is for Mom: A Child's Alphabet. Ellison, Chris, illus. 2009. (ENG.). 32p. (J). (gr. 1-4). 17.95 (978-1-58536-458-9(4), 202181) Sleeping Bear Pr.

Schaefer, Lola M. Mothers: Revised Edition. rev. ed. 2008. (Families Ser.). (ENG., Illus.). 24p. (J). (gr. -1-2). per. 6.29 (978-1-4296-1756-7(X), 94803) Capstone.

Silva Escalera, Manuel. Ale y Su Estrellit. 2009. 80p. pap. 26.49 (978-1-4490-2217-4(0)) AuthorHouse.

Snead, Kathi. My Mom Has a Job. Grove, Christine, illus. 2004. (J). (978-0-9747385-0-5(6)) City of Manassas Department of Social Services.

Staehli, Melissa. I Love You to the Moon. 2011. 28p. pap. 11.95 (978-1-935268-88-8(0)) Halo Publishing International.

Steigemeyer, Julie. Mommy Promises. Ong, Wilson, illus. 2008. 32p. pap. 7.49 (978-0-7586-1479-7(9)) Concordia Publishing Hse.

Tobel, Susan Von. Mei-Ling's Forever Mommy. 2012. 40p. pap. 21.99 (978-1-4691-2578-7(1)) Xlibris Corp.

Vast, Émilie. From Mother to Mother. Vast, Émilie, illus. 2018. (ENG., Illus.). 14p. (J). (— 1). bds. 7.99 (978-1-58089-813-3(0)) Charlesbridge Publishing, Inc.

Wang, Holman. Great Job, Mom! 2019. (Great Job Ser.: 2). (Illus.). 32p. (J). (gr. -1-2). 16.99 (978-0-7352-6408-3(2), Tundra Bks.) Tundra Bks. CAN. Dist: Penguin Random Hse. LLC.

Washburn, Sandi. Good Night, Grandma. Roehler, Yvonne Fetig, illus. 2009. (ENG.). 16p. (J). 17.95 (978-1-934367-09-4(5)) Growing Art Pr.

Why Mom Deserves a Diamond(r) 2012 Anthology - A Gift of Love. 2012. 39.95 (978-1-891665-46-2(4)) Moon Over Mountains Publishing (M.O.M.).

MOTHER AND CHILD—FICTION

Abbott, Donna. Cjam, the Unique Camel. 2008. 24p. pap. 24.95 (978-1-60610-228-2(1)) America Star Bks.

Abegg, Rainbow. Mom, Are You There? 2004. (Illus.). (J). (978-1-59156-437-9(9)) Covenant Communications.

Allan, Delores. Magical Moments with Roy & Toni: Have You Hugged Your Mother Today. 2012. 24p. pap. 17.99 (978-1-4685-7584-2(8)) AuthorHouse.

Alvarez, Miguel, et al. Why, Mommy!!, 1 vol. Pastrovicchio, Lorenzo, illus. 2009. 17p. pap. 24.95 (978-1-60749-429-4(9)) America Star Bks.

Anastas, Margaret. Mommy's Best Kisses Board Book. Winter, Susan, illus. 2008. (ENG.). 34p. (J). (gr. -1-k). bds. 8.99 (978-0-06-124130-7(X), HarperFestival) HarperCollins Pubs.

and Film Studio, Shanghai Animation & Tang, Sanmu. Tadpoles Looking for Their Mother. Xiaozhen, Wu, tr. 2010. (Favorite Childrens Cartoons from China Ser.). (ENG., Illus.). 32p. (gr. -1-3). pap. 5.95 (978-1-60220-972-5(3)) Shanghai Pr.

Andreae, Giles. I Love My Mommy. Dodd, Emma, illus. 2013. (ENG.). 26p. (J). (gr. -1 — 1). bds. 7.99 (978-1-4231-6825-6(9)) Hyperion Pr.

Appelt, Kathi. Oh My Baby, Little One. Dyer, Jane, illus. 2006. (ENG.). 32p. (J). (gr. -1 — 1). pap. 5.99 (978-0-15-206031-2(6), 1198114, Clarion Bks.) HarperCollins Pubs.

Aragon, Quina. Love Made: A Story of God's Overflowing, Creative Heart. 2019. (ENG., Illus.). 32p. (J). (gr. -1-2). 17.99 (978-0-7369-7436-3(9), 6974363) Harvest Hse. Pubs.

Armstrong-Ellis, Carey F. I Love You More Than Moldy Ham. 2015. (ENG., Illus.). 32p. (J). (gr. -1-3). 14.95 (978-1-4197-1646-1(8), 1102101, Abrams Bks. for Young Readers) Abrams, Inc.

Atkinson, Olympia J. Kendahl's Plans. 2010. 24p. 11.99 (978-1-4490-8371-7(4)) AuthorHouse.

Averbeck, Jim. Oh No, Little Dragon! Averbeck, Jim, illus. 2012. (ENG., Illus.). 40p. (J). (gr. -1-1). 19.99 (978-1-4169-9545-6(5), Atheneum Bks. for Young Readers) Simon & Schuster Children's Publishing.

Baguley, Elizabeth. Just Like Brothers. Blanz, Aurélie, illus. 2018. (ENG.). 32p. (J). (gr. -1-2). 16.99 (978-1-78285-345-9(6)) Barefoot Bks., Inc.

Bailey, Melissa. Well, for Goodness Sake Little Jake. 2009. 24p. pap. 11.50 (978-1-60693-675-7(1), Eloquent Bks.) Strategic Book Publishing & Rights Agency (SBPRA).

Baker, Liza. Grandma Loves You Because You're You. McPhail, David, illus. 2018. (ENG.). 20p. (J). (gr. -1 — 1). bds. 8.99 (978-1-338-27143-0(1), Cartwheel Bks.) Scholastic, Inc.

—I Love You Because You're You. McPhail, David, illus. 2008. (ENG.). 24p. (J). (gr. -1-k). bds. 8.99 (978-0-545-02931-5(7), Cartwheel Bks.) Scholastic, Inc.

Baker, Rhiannon. My Mummy's Brain Is Sick. 2019. (ENG.). 26p. 37.94 (978-1-7960-0156-3(2)); (Illus.). pap. 24.14 (978-1-7960-0155-6(4)) Xlibris Corp.

Balas, Vincent. Where Is Your Mama? Slide & See Board Book. Durbiano, Lucie, illus. 2011. (ENG.). 8p. (J). (gr. -1-3). bds. 5.99 (978-0-547-54807-4(9), 1449290, Clarion Bks.) HarperCollins Pubs.

Ballard, George Anne. Flowers along the Way. Ballard, George Anne & Bolton, Georgia Helen, illus. 2012. 26p. pap. 12.00 (978-0-9855312-2-5(3)) Bolton Publishing LLC.

Balsley, Tilda. Soo's Boo-Boos: She's Got 10! McNicholas, Shelagh, illus. 2013. (ENG.). 32p. (J). (gr. -1-2). 12.95 (978-1-58925-118-2(0)) Tiger Tales.

Banks, Kate. Pup & Bear. Stoop, Naoko, illus. 2017. 32p. (J). (gr. -1-2). 17.99 (978-0-399-55409-4(2), Schwartz & Wade Bks.) Random Hse. Children's Bks.

Barcelo, François. My Mommy's Hands, 1 vol. Mongeau, Marc, illus. 2009. (My First Stories Ser.). (ENG.). 24p. (J). (gr. -1-3). 27.27 (978-1-60754-362-6(1), 4d8a7194-ee07-411a-835c-5142445204f1, Windmill Bks.) Rosen Publishing Group, Inc., The.

Bardhan-Quallen, Sudipta. Chicks Run Wild. Jenkins, Ward, illus. 2011. (ENG.). 32p. (J). (gr. -1-1). 19.99 (978-1-4424-0673-5(9), Simon & Schuster Bks. For Young Readers) Simon & Schuster Bks. For Young Readers.

—Rutabaga Boo! Adamson, Bonnie, illus. 2017. (ENG.). 40p. (J). (gr. -1-3). 15.99 (978-1-4814-2461-5(0)) Simon & Schuster Children's Publishing.

Baron, Michael & Aronica, Lou. A Winter Discovery. 2011. 60p. pap. 4.99 *(978-1-61188-027-4(0))* Story Plant, The.

Beaty, Andrea. Hush, Baby Ghostling. Lemaitre, Pascal, illus. 2009. (ENG.). 32p. (J). (gr. -1-3). 14.99 *(978-1-4169-2545-3(7),* McElderry, Margaret K. Bks.) McElderry, Margaret K. Bks.

Beek, Rosheena. Mommy Says! Maye, Warren L., illus. 2nd ed. 2013. (ENG.). 24p. pap. *(978-1-927750-20-9(2))* Bermuda National Trust.

Bendall-Brunello, John, illus. Dinosnore! 2016. (J). *(978-1-4351-6490-1(3))* Barnes & Noble, Inc.

Berenstain, Jan & Berenstain, Mike. We Love Our Mom! 2012. (Berenstain Bears Ser.). (J). lib. bdg. 13.55 *(978-0-606-23578-5(7))* Turtleback.

Bergren, Lisa Tawn. How Big Is God? Bryant, Laura J., illus. 2008. (ENG.). 32p. (J). (gr. -1-2). 10.99 *(978-0-06-113174-5(1),* HarperCollins) HarperCollins Pubs.

Berry, Ron. Where Is Mommy? Smart Kids Publishing Staff, ed. 2009. (ENG.). 20p. (J). bds. 7.99 *(978-0-8249-1404-2(X),* Ideals Pubns.) Worthy Publishing.

Bertram, Debbie & Bloom, Susan. The Best Place to Read. Garland, Michael, illus. 2007. 32p. (J). (gr. -1-2). pap. 8.99 *(978-0-375-83757-9(4),* Dragonfly Bks.) Random Hse. Children's Bks.

—The Best Place to Read. 2007. lib. bdg. 18.40 *(978-1-4177-9097-5(0))* Turtleback.

Billingsley, Franny. Big Bad Bunny. Karas, G. Brian, illus. 2008. (ENG.). 40p. (J). (gr. k-3). 19.99 *(978-1-4169-0601-8(0),* Atheneum/Richard Jackson Bks.) Simon & Schuster Children's Publishing.

Blackmore, Katherine, illus. Because of You, Mom. 2019. (J). 13.99 *(978-1-62972-520-8(X))* Deseret Bk. Co.

Bonnell, Kris. Presents for Mom. 2007. (J). pap. 6.95 *(978-1-933727-61-5(6))* Reading Reading Bks., LLC.

Booth, Tom. This Is Christmas. Booth, Tom, illus. 2018. (Jeter Publishing Ser.). (ENG., Illus.). 40p. (J). (gr. -1-3). 19.99 *(978-1-5344-1090-9(2),* Aladdin) Simon & Schuster Children's Publishing.

Bourguignon, Laurence. Heart in the Pocket. D'heur, Valérie, illus. 2008. 26p. (J). (gr. -1-3). 16.50 *(978-0-8028-5343-1(9))* Eerdmans, William B. Publishing Co.

Bower, Gary. Mommy Love. Bower, Jan, illus. 2012. (Little Lovable Board Bks.). (ENG.). 16p. (J). bds. 8.50 *(978-0-9845236-0-3(X))* Storybook Meadow Publishing.

Bowman, Crystal. Mommy, May I Hug the Fish?, 1 vol. Christensen, Donna, illus. 2007. (I Can Read! Ser.).Tr. of Mamá, Puedo Abrazar Al Pez? (ENG.). 32p. (J). (gr. -1-1). pap. 4.99 *(978-0-310-71468-2(0))* Zonderkidz.

Boynton, Sandra. What's Wrong, Little Pookie? Boynton, Sandra, illus. 2017. (Little Pookie Ser.). (ENG., Illus.). 18p. (J). (gr. -1-k). bds. 6.99 *(978-1-4814-9769-5(3))* Simon & Schuster, Inc.

Bradley, Jeanette. Love, Mama. Bradley, Jeanette, illus. 2019. (ENG., Illus.). 28p. (J). bds. 7.99 *(978-1-250-24035-4(2),* 900211506) Roaring Brook Pr.

Braun, Sebastien. I Love My Mommy Board Book. Braun, Sebastien, illus. 2017. (ENG., Illus.). 26p. (J). (gr. -1 — 1). bds. 8.99 *(978-0-06-256424-5(2),* Tegen, Katherine Bks) HarperCollins Pubs.

Brewer, Sarah. Our New Garden. Brewer, Sarah & Brewer, Dean, illus. 2013. 20p. pap. 24.95 *(978-1-63004-768-9(6))* America Star Bks.

Brill, Calista. Little Wing Learns to Fly. Bell, Jennifer A., illus. 2016. (Little Wing Ser.). (ENG.). 32p. (J). (gr. -1-3). 17.99 *(978-0-06-236033-5(7),* HarperCollins) HarperCollins Pubs.

Brown, Jo. Where's My Mommy? Brown, Jo, illus. 2006. (Storytime Board Bks.). (Illus.). 18p. (J). (gr. -1-3). bds. 6.95 *(978-1-58925-795-5(2))* Tiger Tales.

Brown, Palmer. Something for Christmas. Brown, Palmer, illus. 2011. (ENG., Illus.). 40p. (J). (gr. -1-2). 14.95 *(978-1-59017-462-3(3),* NYR Children's Collection) New York Review of Bks., Inc., The.

Brown, Ruby. Cuddles for Mommy. Macnaughton, Tina, illus. 2016. (ENG.). 32p. (J). (gr. -1-3). 16.99 *(978-1-4998-0203-0(X))* Little Bee Books Inc.

Brown, Toni Sorenson. I Can't Go to Church. Jolley, Mack, illus. 2005. (J). *(978-1-59156-270-2(8))* Covenant Communications.

Browne, Anthony. My Mom. Browne, Anthony, illus. 2009. (ENG., Illus.). 32p. (J). (gr. k-3). pap. 8.99 *(978-0-374-40026-2(1),* 900058756) Square Fish.

Bruno, Debra. Petey's Tale: A Story of Survival Inspired by Actual Events. 2010. 28p. pap. 12.49 *(978-1-4490-6597-3(X))* AuthorHouse.

Buller, Jon & Schade, Susan. I Love You, Good Night: Lap Edition. Pons, Bernadette, illus. 2013. (ENG.). 28p. (J). (gr. -1 — 1). bds. 12.99 *(978-1-4424-8539-6(6),* Little Simon) Little Simon.

Bunting, Eve. Pirate Boy. Fortenberry, Julie, illus. 2012. (ENG.). 32p. (J). (gr. -1-3). pap. 8.99 *(978-0-8234-2546-4(0))* Holiday Hse., Inc.

Burden-Evans, Patricia. A Steep Mountain to Climb. 2008. 151p. pap. 9.95 *(978-0-615-15120-5(5))* Burden-Evans, Patricia.

Burlingham, Abigail. All Grown Up, 1 vol. Everitt-Stewart, Andy, illus. 2009. (Stories to Grow With Ser.). (ENG.). 24p. (J). (gr. 1-2). 27.27 *(978-1-60754-469-2(5),* 9a1658ce-e9e3-4679-8f17-ee20181e6304); pap. 9.15 *(978-1-60754-470-8(9),* 8d0efe7a-0bcb-4991-805f-c28dc359e4b2) Rosen Publishing Group, Inc., The. (Windmill Bks.).

Burnett, Frances. Esmeralda, Mère Giraud's Little Daughter, Little Saint Elizabeth & Other Stories: A Collection of Short Stories by Frances Hodgson Burnett. 2012. 378p. *(978-1-78139-164-8(5))* Benediction Classics.

Burroughs, Denise. The Story of the Day You Were Born. 2012. (ENG.). 28p. (J). pap. 16.00 *(978-1-4772-4547-7(2))* AuthorHouse.

Burton, Linda K. A Mother's Prayer. Meyer, Jennifer, illus. 2018. (J). 17.99 *(978-1-62972-471-3(8))* Deseret Bk. Co.

Busheri, Devora. In the Jerusalem Forest. Kelner, Noa, illus. 2019. (ENG.). 32p. (J). (gr. -1-3). 17.99 *(978-1-5415-3472-8(7),* 44f7f14e-ddaf-4dfe-9235-7200edce6859, Kar-Ben Publishing) Lerner Publishing Group.

Buzzeo, Toni. Stay Close to Mama. Wohnoutka, Mike, illus. 2012. (ENG.). 32p. (J). (gr. -1-3). 15.99 *(978-1-4231-3482-4(6))* Little, Brown Bks. for Young Readers.

Byrne, Jean Livingstone. Legends of Newgrange. 2014. 54p. pap. 12.99 *(978-1-84386-818-7(0))* Vanguard Pr.

Cabrera, Jane. There Was an Old Woman Who Lived in a Shoe. 2017. (Jane Cabrera's Story Time Ser.). (ENG.). 32p. (J). (gr. -1-k). 7.99 *(978-0-8234-3771-9(X))* Holiday Hse., Inc.

Calhoun, Megan. Oscar the Pig: Mommy Goes to Work. 2008. 32p. 18.50 *(978-0-615-25193-6(5))* Silly String Media.

Capucilli, Alyssa Satin. My Mom & Me. Mitchell, Susan, illus. 2009. (ENG.). 16p. (J). (gr. -1-1). 7.99 *(978-1-4169-5829-1(0),* Little Simon) Little Simon.

Carle, Eric, illus. I Love Mom with the Very Hungry Caterpillar. 2017. (World of Eric Carle Ser.). (ENG.). 32p. (J). (-k). 9.99 *(978-0-451-53346-3(1))* Penguin Young Readers Group.

Carlisle, Kelly. My Mommy Is A Rocker. 2007. (Illus.). 21p. (J). lib. bdg. *(978-0-9795046-2-4(7))* Kwist, Karla.

Carpenter, Donna. A Triple Treat. 2007. (Illus.). 20p. (J). 14.95 *(978-0-9793987-0-4(3))* DFC Pubs.

Carrick, Carol. Mothers Are Like That. Carrick, Paul, illus. 2007. (ENG.). 32p. (J). (gr. -1-k). 7.99 *(978-0-618-75241-6(2),* 100523, Clarion Bks.) HarperCollins Pubs.

Cavaliere, Lisa. Lainey Lemonade's Cupcake Parade. 2008. 32p. pap. 24.95 *(978-1-60474-860-4(5))* America Star Bks.

Chaffin, Dawn Marie. My Love. 2010. 20p. 11.99 *(978-1-4520-0031-2(X))* AuthorHouse.

Chalker Browne, Susan. Freddy's Day at the Races, 1 vol. Rose, Hilda, illus. 2008. (ENG.). 32p. (J). (gr. 1-8). *(978-1-897174-36-4(5))* Breakwater Bks., Ltd.

Chamberlin, Ann. Dumpling. 2012. (Illus.). 32p. pap. 21.99 *(978-1-4691-6313-0(6))* Xlibris Corp.

Chen, Julie. When I Grow Up. Goode, Diane, illus. 2018. (ENG.). 32p. (J). (gr. -1-3). 17.99 *(978-1-4814-9719-0(7),* Simon & Schuster/Paula Wiseman Bks.) Simon & Schuster/Paula Wiseman Bks.

Chichester Clark, Emma. My Baby Sister (Humber & Plum, Book 2), Book 2. Chichester Clark, Emma, illus. 2nd ed. 2009. (Humber & Plum Ser.: 2). (ENG., Illus.). 32p. (J). (gr. -1-k). 9.99 *(978-0-00-727324-9(X),* HarperCollins Children's Bks.) HarperCollins Pubs. Ltd. GBR. Dist: HarperCollins Pubs.

Childress, Story. Momma, What's Love?, 1 vol. 2010. 28p. 24.95 *(978-1-61546-067-0(5))* PublishAmerica, Inc.

Choclate-Brown, Honey. Mama never told Me. 2005. (J). 9.95 *(978-0-9765467-0-2(1))* Creative Bk. Pubs.

Chou, Yih-fen. Mimi Tidies Up. Chen, Zhiyuan, illus. 2011. (J). *(978-0-9845523-6-8(7))* Heryin Publishing Corp.

Chronicle Books & ImageBooks. Snow Baby: Finger Puppet Book. 2011. (Little Finger Puppet Board Bks.). (ENG.). 12p. (J). (gr. -1 — 1). 6.99 *(978-1-4521-0220-7(1))* Chronicle Bks. LLC.

Cinderella. 2005. 124p. 26.95 *(978-1-4218-0600-6(2),* 1st World Library - Literary Society) 1st World Publishing, Inc.

Clark, Amy. Mom Just Said No! 2012. 28p. pap. 21.99 *(978-1-4691-5104-5(9))* Xlibris Corp.

Clark, Danell. Daisy. Irwin, April, illus. 2008. 28p. pap. 11.95 *(978-1-59858-642-8(4))* Dog Ear Publishing, LLC.

Clark, Sally. Where's My Hug? 2015. (ENG., Illus.). 24p. (J). bds. 8.99 *(978-0-8249-1952-8(1),* Ideals Pubns.) Worthy Publishing.

Cline, H. R. Just Mommy & Me. 2009. 16p. pap. 9.95 *(978-1-4389-3879-0(9))* AuthorHouse.

Cole, Rachael. Mousie, I Will Read to You. Crowton, Melissa, illus. 2018. 40p. (J). (gr. -1-2). 17.99 *(978-1-5247-1536-6(0),* Schwartz & Wade Bks.) Random Hse. Children's Bks.

Collier, Kelly L. Mommy, Why am I Different? 2011. 16p. (gr. 1-2). pap. 10.99 *(978-1-4634-0357-7(7))* AuthorHouse.

Collum, Karen. Blow Me a Kiss. Geddes, Serena, illus. 2012. (J). *(978-1-4351-4513-9(5))* Barnes & Noble, Inc.

Conroy, Christine. Mama Wants a Llam. 2012. 16p. pap. 15.99 *(978-1-4772-1605-7(7))* AuthorHouse.

Cook, Jessica & Stephens, Michael. What If Mommy Took a Vacation? 2011. 28p. pap. 13.99 *(978-1-4634-3601-8(7))* AuthorHouse.

Cook, Kajsa. Discoveries in the Shriver Family Attic: How a Woman & Her Children Dealt with the Battle of Gettysburg. 2009. (Illus.). 122p. (J). (gr. 4-8). pap. 8.95 *(978-1-57249-398-8(4),* White Mane Kids) White Mane Publishing Co., Inc.

Cooper, Bernice Soroka. The Little Elf-Frog. 2012. 24p. pap. 17.99 *(978-1-4772-9525-0(9))* AuthorHouse.

Costain, Meredith. Mommies Are Amazing. Lovsin, Polona, illus. 2018. (ENG.). 28p. (J). bds. 8.99 *(978-1-250-10721-3(0),* 900164823, Holt, Henry & Co. Bks. For Young Readers) Holt, Henry & Co.

Cousins, Lucy. Hooray for Fish! Cousins, Lucy, illus. 2005. (ENG., Illus.). 40p. (J). (gr. k-k). 17.99 *(978-0-7636-2741-6(0))* Candlewick Pr.

Couteaud, Cheryl. A Monster for Halloween. Couteaud, Cheryl, illus. 2009. (Illus.). 24p. pap. 10.96 *(978-1-4251-8563-3(0))* Trafford Publishing.

Cranford, Elizabeth A. I Love You Out Loud Mommy: I Love You Out Loud Children's Book Collection-Book #1. 2007. (ENG.). 36p. per. 15.99 *(978-1-4257-6723-5(0))* Xlibris Corp.

Craver, Marcella Marino. Joey Daring, Caring, & Curious. Lew-Vriethoff, Joanne, illus. 2014. 32p. (J). pap. *(978-1-4338-1653-6(9),* Magination Pr.) American Psychological Assn.

—Joey Daring Caring & Curious: How a Mischief Maker Uncovers Unconditional Love. Lew-Vriethoff, Joanne, illus. 2014. 32p. (J). *(978-1-4338-1652-9(0),* Magination Pr.) American Psychological Assn.

Crimi, Carolyn. Where's My Mummy? Manders, John, illus. 32p. (J). (gr. -1-3). 2009. (ENG.). 7.99 *(978-0-7636-4337-9(8))* 2008. 15.99 *(978-0-7636-3196-3(5))* Candlewick Pr.

Crosby, June. A Monster in the Attic. Chapman, Michelle, illus. 2011. 16p. pap. 24.95 *(978-1-4560-6959-9(4))* America Star Bks.

Crumbaugh, David. The Primrose Kids. 2006. 81p. pap. 16.95 *(978-1-4241-3250-8(9))* PublishAmerica, Inc.

Cummings, Pat. Where Is Mommy? 2019. (I Like to Read Ser.). (Illus.). 32p. (J). (gr. -1-3). 15.99 *(978-0-8234-3935-5(6))* Holiday Hse., Inc.

Dahl, Michael. Bear Says Thank You. Vidal, Oriol, illus. 2012. (Hello Genius Ser.). (ENG.). 20p. (J). (gr. -1 — 1). bds. 7.99 *(978-1-4048-6786-4(4),* 116224, Picture Window Bks.) Capstone.

—Penguin Misses Mom. Vidal, Oriol, illus. 2016. (Hello Genius Ser.). (ENG.). 20p. (J). (gr. -1 — 1). bds. 7.99 *(978-1-4795-8739-1(7),* 131128, Picture Window Bks.) Capstone.

Dalmatian Press Staff. Mommy, Is That You? 2008. (ENG.). 5p. bds. 4.95 *(978-1-58117-714-5(3),* Intervisual/Piggy Toes) Bendon, Inc.

Darling, Helen. Hide-n-seek Monday. Glickstein, Jennifer, ed. Sona and Jacob, illus. 2007. (J). 10.00 *(978-0-9797674-0-1(7))* My Darling-Tots Pubns.

Dauphin, Lili. I Will Fly Again: The Restavek. 2007. 284p. 29.95 *(978-0-9748329-9-9(5))* MiraQuest.

Davis, Terrance. Mom & Me. 2012. 24p. (-18). pap. 24.95 *(978-1-4626-9502-7(7))* America Star Bks.

De Blumenthal, Verra X. K. Folk Tales from the Russian. 2008. 88p. pap. 8.95 *(978-1-60664-152-1(2))* Aegypan.

de Las Casas, Dianne. Mama's Bayou, 1 vol. Stone-Barker, Holly, illus. 2010. (ENG.). 32p. (J). (gr. k-k). 16.99 *(978-1-58980-787-7(1),* Pelican Publishing) Arcadia Publishing.

Deflitch, Jennifer L. Where Do You Go? 2013. 24p. pap. 24.95 *(978-1-62709-307-1(9))* America Star Bks.

Derrick, David G., Jr. Animals Don't, So I Won't! 2012. (ENG., Illus.). 36p. (J). (gr. -1-3). 15.95 *(978-1-59702-029-9(X))* Immedium.

Deshmukh, Manisha. Chinu's Day Out. 2008. 24p. pap. 11.49 *(978-1-4389-0601-0(3))* AuthorHouse.

Dewdney, Anna. Llama Llama Birthday Party! Dewdney, Anna, illus. 2013. (Llama Llama Ser.). (Illus.). 16p. (J). (gr. -1-k). 7.99 *(978-0-448-45880-9(2),* Grosset & Dunlap) Penguin Young Readers Group.

—Llama Llama Holiday Drama. (Llama Llama Ser.). (Illus.). (J). 2018. 36p. (— 1). bds. 14.99 *(978-1-9848-3558-1(0))* 2017. 36p. (— 1). bds. 9.99 *(978-0-425-29181-8(2))* 2010. 40p. (gr. -1-k). 18.99 *(978-0-670-01161-2(4))* Penguin Young Readers Group. (Viking Books for Young Readers).

—Llama Llama Home with Mama. 2011. (Llama Llama Ser.). (ENG., Illus.). 40p. (J). (gr. -1-k). 18.99 *(978-0-670-01232-9(7),* Viking Books for Young Readers) Penguin Young Readers Group.

—Llama Llama Mad at Mama. Dewdney, Anna, illus. 2007. (Llama Llama Ser.). (ENG., Illus.). 40p. (J). (gr. -1-k). 18.99 *(978-0-670-06240-9(5),* Viking Books for Young Readers) Penguin Young Readers Group.

—Llama Llama Mad at Mama. 2009. (Illus.). (J). *(978-0-545-15933-3(4))* Scholastic, Inc.

—Llama Llama Red Pajama. Dewdney, Anna, illus. (Llama Llama Ser.). (ENG., Illus.). (J). 2018. 34p. (-k). bds. 15.99 *(978-0-451-48063-7(5))* 2005. 40p. (gr. -1-k). 18.99 *(978-0-670-05983-6(8))* Penguin Young Readers Group. (Viking Books for Young Readers).

—Llama Llama Red Pajama. *(978-0-439-90665-4(2));* 2006. lp *(978-0-439-90679-1(2))* Scholastic, Inc.

—Llama Llama Red Pajama: Gift Edition. Dewdney, Anna, illus. 2014. (Llama Llama Ser.). (ENG., Illus.). 40p. (J). (gr. -1-k). 26.99 *(978-0-451-46990-8(9),* Viking Books for Young Readers) Penguin Young Readers Group.

Di Santo, Melina. Mel & her Magic Journey. 2010. (Illus.). 32p. 14.49 *(978-1-4490-6889-9(8))* AuthorHouse.

Diaz, Cynthia. Sunny & Cubby's Real Life: ... Venturing Through Darkness. 2012. 24p. pap. 14.93 *(978-1-4669-4316-2(5))* Trafford Publishing.

Diggs, Taye. Chocolate Me! Book & CD Storytime Set: Book & CD Storytime Set. Evans, Shane W., illus. unabr. ed. 2019. (ENG.). 1p. (J). 12.99 *(978-1-250-22256-5(7),* 900208043) Feiwel & Friends.

DK. I Love You Little One. 2018. (ENG.). 18p. (J). (— 1). bds. 12.99 *(978-1-4654-8016-3(1),* DK Children) Dorling Kindersley Publishing, Inc.

Dodd, Emma. Happy. Dodd, Emma, illus. (Emma Dodd's Love You Bks.). (ENG., Illus.). (J). (— 1). 2017. 22p. bds. 10.99 *(978-0-7636-9642-9(0))* 2015. 24p. 12.99 *(978-0-7636-8008-4(7))* Candlewick Pr.

—When I Grow Up. Dodd, Emma, illus. 2015. (Emma Dodd's Love You Bks.). (ENG., Illus.). 24p. (J). (-k). 14.99 *(978-0-7636-7985-9(2),* Templar) Candlewick Pr.

—Wish. Dodd, Emma, illus. (Emma Dodd's Love You Bks.). (ENG., Illus.). (J). (— 1). 2017. 22p. bds. 9.99 *(978-0-7636-9643-6(9))* 2015. 24p. 14.99 *(978-0-7636-8009-1(5))* Candlewick Pr.

Doerrfeld, Cori. Wild Baby. Doerrfeld, Cori, illus. 2019. (ENG., Illus.). 32p. (J). (gr. -1-3). 17.99 *(978-0-06-269894-0(X),* HarperCollins) HarperCollins Pubs.

—Wild Baby Board Book. Doerrfeld, Cori, illus. 2019. (ENG., Illus.). 36p. (J). (gr. -1 — 1). bds. 7.99 *(978-0-06-269893-3(1),* HarperFestival) HarperCollins Pubs.

Doman, Regina. Angel in the Waters. Hatke, Ben, illus. 2004. 48p. (J). (gr. -1-3). pap. 6.95 *(978-1-928832-81-2(4))* Sophia Institute Pr.

—Mi Angelito en Las Aguas. Hatke, Ben, illus. 2006. (SPA.). 40p. (J). (gr. -1-3). pap. 6.95 *(978-1-933184-22-7(1))* Sophia Institute Pr.

Dwyer, Mindy. It's Only the Wind. 2017. (ENG., Illus.). 32p. (J). (gr. k-3). 16.99 *(978-1-5132-6074-7(X),* West Winds Pr.) West Margin Pr.

Dyan, Penelope. A New Bag! Dyan, Penelope, illus. 2012. (Illus.). 34p. pap. 11.95 *(978-1-61477-054-1(9))* Bellissima Publishing, LLC.

Earhardt, Ainsley. Take Heart, My Child: A Mother's Dream. Kim, Jaime, illus. 2018. (ENG.). 34p. (J). (gr. -1-k). bds. 8.99 *(978-1-5344-2631-3(0),* Little Simon) Little Simon.

—Take Heart, My Child: A Mother's Dream. Kim, Jaime, illus. 2016. (ENG.). 32p. (J). (gr. -1-3). 18.99 *(978-1-4814-6622-6(4),* Aladdin) Simon & Schuster Children's Publishing.

—Through Your Eyes: My Child's Gift to Me. Kim, Ji-Hyuk, illus. 2017. (ENG.). 32p. (J). (gr. -1-3). 19.99 *(978-1-5344-0959-0(9),* Aladdin) Simon & Schuster Children's Publishing.

Edwards, Christine. The Charmed Enchanted Book. 2010. 24p. pap. 16.49 *(978-1-4490-7091-5(4))* AuthorHouse.

Elmquist, Laurie. Forest Baby, 1 vol. Robinson, Shantaia, illus. 2018. (ENG.). 24p. (J). (gr. -1 — 1). bds. 10.95 *(978-1-4598-1333-5(2))* Orca Bk. Pubs. USA.

Enriquez, Lucy Rivas. Dj's Lullaby: A Mother's Love Song. 2013. (ENG.). 26p. (J). pap. 12.95 *(978-1-4787-1148-3(5))* Outskirts Pr., Inc.

Fallon, Jimmy. Everything Is Mama. Ordonez, Miguel, illus. (ENG.). (J). 2019. 32p. bds. 7.99 *(978-1-250-12583-5(9),* 900174972) 2017. 40p. 16.99 *(978-1-250-12584-2(7),* 900174971) Feiwel & Friends.

Felts, C. C. My Best Friend Mommy. 2008. 12p. pap. 24.95 *(978-1-60703-671-5(1))* America Star Bks.

Fernandez, Texanna. My Mighty Mother. 2010. 16p. pap. 9.00 *(978-1-4490-5409-0(9))* AuthorHouse.

Fleuriel, Allison. Are You Done Sleeping? 2006. (J). pap. 16.00 *(978-0-8059-7115-6(7))* Dorrance Publishing Co., Inc.

Frey, Cathy. Muttin's Puttins. 2010. 24p. pap. 13.99 *(978-1-4490-6753-3(0))* AuthorHouse.

Friester, Paul. Owl Howl Board Book. Goossens, Philippe, illus. 2nd rev. ed. 2016. (ENG.). 26p. (J). (gr. -1-1). bds. 8.95 *(978-0-7358-4234-2(5))* North-South Bks., Inc.

Furrow, Rebecca. You Grew in My Heart: An Adoption Story. 2012. 32p. pap. 16.95 *(978-1-4497-6064-9(3),* WestBow Pr.) Author Solutions, LLC.

Gabriel, Andrea. My Favorite Bear. 2014. 32p. pap. 8.00 *(978-1-61003-310-7(8))* Center for the Collaborative Classroom.

Gaichies, Sarah. Mirabelle the Lost Kitten. 2010. (Illus.). 76p. pap. 24.99 *(978-1-4490-5593-6(1))* AuthorHouse.

Galvin, Laura. I Love My Mommy. 2009. (I Love My... Ser.). (ENG., Illus.). 16p. (J). 12.95 *(978-1-59249-801-7(9))* Soundprints.

Galvin, Laura, told to. I Love My Mommy. 2007. (ENG., Illus.). 16p. (J). (gr. -1-k). bds. 6.95 *(978-1-59249-730-0(6))* Soundprints.

Galvin, Laura G. & Galvin, Laura. I Love My Mommy (with Download) 2011. (ENG.). 16p. (J). *(978-1-60727-345-5(4))* Soundprints.

Galvin, Laura Gates. Baby Koala & Mommy. 2007. (Baby Animals Ser.). (ENG., Illus.). 16p. (J). (gr. -1-k). 6.95 *(978-1-59249-744-7(6))* Soundprints.

Gates, Margo. My Baby Elephant. Jennings, Sarah, illus. 2019. (Let's Look at Animal Habitats (Pull Ahead Readers — Fiction) Ser.). (ENG.). 16p. (J). (gr. -1-1). 27.99 *(978-1-5415-5864-9(2),* 919a2771-d332-4bf1-a2ff-0e5b7a325b2d, Lerner Pubns.) Lerner Publishing Group.

Gaylord, Laurel Porter. Quiero a Mi Mama Porque (I Love My Mommy Because Eng/Span Ed) Wolff, Ashley, illus. 2004.Tr. of I Love My Mommy Because. 22p. (J). (gr. -1 — 1). bds. 7.99 *(978-0-525-47248-3(7),* Dutton Books for Young Readers) Penguin Young Readers Group.

Georges, Theodore K. Forever in My Arms. 2011. 28p. pap. 13.99 *(978-1-4634-1494-8(3))* AuthorHouse.

Gessner, Kati. What Do You See When You Look at Me. 2012. 32p. pap. 19.99 *(978-1-4772-2106-8(9))* AuthorHouse.

Gibby, Bayne. You Mean the World to Me. Walker, David, illus. 2013. (ENG.). 24p. (J). (gr. -1-k). bds. 8.99 *(978-0-545-40570-6(X),* Cartwheel Bks.) Scholastic, Inc.

Goode, Molly. Mama Loves. McCue, Lisa, illus. 2015. (Step into Reading Ser.). 32p. (J). (gr. -1-1). 4.99 *(978-0-553-53896-0(9),* Random Hse. Bks. for Young Readers) Random Hse. Children's Bks.

Gore, Leonid. Mommy, Where Are You? Gore, Leonid, illus. 2009. (ENG., Illus.). 32p. (J). (gr. -1-2). 18.99 *(978-1-4169-5505-4(4),* Atheneum Bks. for Young Readers) Simon & Schuster Children's Publishing.

Graham, Georgia. Cub's Journey Home, 1 vol. Graham, Georgia, illus. 2015. (ENG., Illus.). 32p. (J). (gr. -1-2). 18.95 *(978-0-88995-516-5(6),* 4942dc77-a658-4536-ab24-ffddb6e88f0a) Trifolium Bks., Inc. CAN. Dist: Firefly Bks., Ltd.

Gray, Susannah. Gotta See Nathan! Jones, Nathan, illus. 2012. 20p. pap. 15.00 *(978-1-4575-1315-2(3))* Dog Ear Publishing, LLC.

Green, Jose. Castro's Diary. 2004. 174p. pap. 24.95 *(978-1-4137-4556-6(3))* America Star Bks.

Griffune, Donna L. I Love You with My Heart. 2007. 44p. (J). pap. 8.99 *(978-1-59092-391-7(X))* Blue Forge Pr.

Grimes, Nikki. Bedtime for Sweet Creatures. Zunon, Elizabeth, illus. 2020. (ENG.). 32p. (J). (gr. -1-3). 17.99 *(978-1-4926-3832-2(3),* Sourcebooks Jabberwocky) Sourcebooks, Inc.

Gummelt, Donna & Melchiorre, Dondino. Your Name Is Mud. Wall, Randy Hugh, ed. Varela, Carmen, tr. Varela, Juan D., illus. Lt. ed. 2006.Tr. of Tu nombre es Mud. 34p. (J). 14.95 *(978-0-9764798-3-3(4))* Story Store Collection Publishing.

Gutman, Anne & Hallensleben, Georg. Mommy Snuggles: (Motherhood Books for Kids, Toddler Board Books) 2017. (Daddy, Mommy Ser.). (ENG., Illus.). 14p. (J). (gr. -1 — 1). bds. 5.99 *(978-1-4521-5822-8(3))* Chronicle Bks. LLC.

Hahn, Kathryn. My Wish for You: Lessons from My Six-Year-Old Daughter. Barrager, Brigette, illus. 2018. (ENG.). 40p. (J). (gr. -1-3). 17.99 *(978-1-338-15040-7(5),* Orchard Bks.) Scholastic, Inc.

Halfmann, Janet. Good Night, Little Sea Otter: Burmese Karen/English, 1 vol. Williams, Wish, illus. 2012. (ENG.). 24p. (J). 5.95 *(978-1-59572-371-0(4))* Star Bright Bks., Inc.

—Good Night, Little Sea Otter: Burmese/English, 1 vol. Williams, Wish, illus. 2012. (ENG.). 24p. (J). pap. 5.95 *(978-1-59572-370-3(6))* Star Bright Bks., Inc.

—Good Night, Little Sea Otter: English, 1 vol. Williams, Wish, illus. (ENG.). (J). 2012. 24p. 15.95 *(978-1-59572-277-5(7))* 2010. 32p. (gr. -1-3). pap. 5.95 *(978-1-59572-254-6(8))* Star Bright Bks., Inc.

—Good Night, Little Sea Otter: Hmong/English, 1 vol. Williams, Wish, illus. 2012. (ENG.). 24p. (J). pap. 5.95 *(978-1-59572-365-9(X))* Star Bright Bks., Inc.

—Good Night, Little Sea Otter: Portugese/English, 1 vol. Williams, Wish, illus. 2012. (ENG.). 24p. (J). pap. 5.95 *(978-1-59572-359-8(5))* Star Bright Bks., Inc.

Hall, Annalisa. Momma, I hold You. 2009. 32p. pap. 7.99 *(978-0-557-05470-1(2))* Lulu Pr., Inc.

Hall, Hannah C. Mommy Cuddles. Szmidt, Aleksandra, illus. 2019. (ENG.). 20p. (J). (gr. -1-k). bds. 7.99 *(978-0-8249-5695-0(8))* Worthy Publishing.

Hallinan, P. K. My Mother & I: A Picture Book for Moms & Their Loving Children. 2020. (ENG.). 24p. (J). (-1). 9.99 *(978-1-5107-4546-9(7),* Sky Pony Pr.) Skyhorse Publishing Co., Inc.

Hamilton, Clarice. Special Delivery. 2010. (ENG.). 24p. (YA). pap. 13.99 *(978-1-4520-4199-5(7))* AuthorHouse.

Hao, K. T. Where's My Mommy? Toni, Alessandra, illus. 2008. (ENG.). 32p. (J). (gr. -1). 15.95 *(978-1-933327-40-2(5))* Purple Bear Bks., Inc.

—Where's My Mommy? Toni, Alessandra, illus. 2008. (ENG.). 32p. (J). (gr. -1). 16.50 *(978-1-933327-41-9(3))* Purple Bear Bks., Inc.

Hardesty, Michael. Who Made the Sun, Mommy? 2011. 28p. 15.95 *(978-1-4520-7721-5(5))* AuthorHouse.

Hardin, Melinda. Hero Mom. Langdo, Bryan, illus. 2013. 24p. pap. 12.99 *(978-1-4778-6645-0(0))* Amazon Publishing.

Harms, Carol. What If? Heshmat, Claire, illus. 2010. (ENG.). 24p. pap. 10.49 *(978-1-4520-8463-3(7))* AuthorHouse.

Harper, Jo. Teresa's Journey. 2006. (ENG., Illus.). 162p. (J). (gr. 4-6). per. 17.95 *(978-0-89672-591-1(X)*, P171799) Texas Tech Univ. Pr.

Hart, Linda. When Mummy Says. 2009. (Illus.). 32p. pap. 18.99 *(978-1-4490-1291-5(4))* AuthorHouse.

Harvey, Jacqueline. Clementine Rose Collection Three. 2018. (Clementine Rose Ser.: 3). 448p. (J). (gr. 1-3). 18.99 *(978-0-14-379019-8(6))* Random Hse. Australia AUS. Dist: Independent Pubs. Group.

Harvey Mph, Janera P. What Mommy Does. Utley, J. Stacy, illus. 2012. 24p. pap. 24.95 *(978-1-4560-4180-9(0))* America Star Bks.

Haughton, Chris. Little Owl Lost. Haughton, Chris, illus. 2010. (ENG., Illus.). 32p. (J). (gr. -1-k). 17.99 *(978-0-7636-5022-3(6))* Candlewick Pr.

Hayes, Geoffrey. Patrick in a Teddy Bear's Picnic & Other Stories: Toon Books Level 2. 2011. (ENG., Illus.). 32p. (J). (gr. -1-3). 12.95 *(978-1-935179-09-2(8)*, Toon Books) Astra Publishing Hse.

Heath, Paulette Powell. In the Mist. 2012. 24p. pap. 15.99 *(978-1-4797-4354-4(2))* Xlibris Corp.

Henkes, Kevin. Words of Stone. 2005. (ENG.). 160p. (J). (gr. 3-7). reprint ed. pap. 6.99 *(978-0-06-078230-6(7)*, Greenwillow Bks.) HarperCollins Pubs.

Heroux, Matthew & Kirwan, Wednesday. Owl Love You. 2018. (ENG., Illus.). 32p. (J). (gr. -1-3). 16.95 *(978-1-944903-35-0(6)*, 1320501, Cameron Kids) Cameron + Co.

Hicks, Constance. Florabelle Bunny & the Sparrow. 2011. 24p. pap. 12.99 *(978-1-4490-9969-5(6))* AuthorHouse.

Higgins, M. G. Trouble in the City. Taylor, Jo, illus. 2016. (Sibling Split Ser.). (ENG.). 112p. (J). (gr. 3-6). lib. bdg. 25.32 *(978-1-4965-2591-8(4)*, 130720, Stone Arch Bks.) Capstone.

Hodgman, Ann. That's My Mommy! Logan, Laura, illus. 2013. (ENG.). 22p. bds. *(978-1-58925-645-3(X))* Tiger Tales.

Huber, Mike. Mama's Gloves. Cowman, Joseph, illus. 2014. (ENG.). 32p. (gr. -1). 15.95 *(978-1-60554-210-2(5))* Redleaf Pr.

Huether, Michael & Huether, Amy. Ju Ju & the Sunblock. 2012. 32p. pap. 10.95 *(978-1-60494-729-8(2))* Wheatmark, Inc.

Hwang, Sun-mi. The Hen Who Dreamed She Could Fly. 2013. lib. bdg. 28.20 *(978-0-606-35094-5(2))* Turtleback.

Ivey, Pamela. Mom! I'm Special I Am Fearfully & Wonderfully Made! 2011. 28p. pap. 12.99 *(978-1-4634-3830-2(3))* AuthorHouse.

Iwai, Melissa. Soup Day. Iwai, Melissa, illus. 2017. (ENG., Illus.). 32p. (J). bds. 8.99 *(978-1-250-12772-3(6)*, 900175517, Holt, Henry & Co. Bks. For Young Readers) Holt, Henry & Co.

—Soup Day: a Picture Book. Iwai, Melissa, illus. 2010. (ENG., Illus.). 40p. (J). (gr. -1-k). 18.99 *(978-0-8050-9004-8(5)*, 900058965, Holt, Henry & Co. Bks. For Young Readers) Holt, Henry & Co.

James, Helen Foster. Mommy Loves You! Brown, Petra, illus. 2017. (ENG.). 32p. (J). (gr. -1-k). 15.99 *(978-1-58536-941-6(1)*, 204232) Sleeping Bear Pr.

Jenkins, T. L. On the Bed & off the Bed. 2009. (ENG.). 26p. pap. 12.49 *(978-1-4389-2648-3(0))* AuthorHouse.

Jensen, Bonnie Rickner. God Loves Mommy & Me, 1 vol. 2017. (ENG., Illus.). 20p. (J). bds. 9.99 *(978-0-7180-9178-1(7)*, Tommy Nelson) Nelson, Thomas Inc.

Jeram, Anita. Bunny My Honey. Jeram, Anita, illus. 2009. (ENG., Illus.). 22p. (J). (gr. k-k). bds. 7.99 *(978-0-7636-4645-5(8))* Candlewick Pr.

Johnson, Wyletta. Your Precious Eyes. 2013. 16p. pap. 9.99 *(978-0-9897168-3-3(X))* Mindstir Media.

Johnston, Tony. Loving Hands. Bates, Amy June, illus. 2018. (ENG.). 32p. (J). (gr. -1-1). 16.99 *(978-0-7636-7993-4(3))* Candlewick Pr.

Katz, Karen. Mommy Hugs. Katz, Karen, illus. 2007. (Classic Board Bks.). (ENG., Illus.). 32p. (J). (gr. -1 — 1). bds. 7.99 *(978-1-4169-4121-7(5)*, Little Simon) Little Simon.

—Mommy Hugs. 2006. (ENG., Illus.). 32p. (J). (gr. -1-3). 19.99 *(978-0-689-87772-8(2)*, McElderry, Margaret K. Bks.) McElderry, Margaret K. Bks.

—Mommy Hugs: Lap Edition. Katz, Karen, illus. 2010. (ENG., Illus.). 26p. (J). (gr. -1 — 1). bds. 12.99 *(978-1-4424-0791-6(3)*, Little Simon) Little Simon.

Katz, Susan B. My Mama Earth. Launay, Melissa, illus. 2012. (ENG.). 24p. (J). 16.99 *(978-1-84686-418-6(6))* Barefoot Bks., Inc.

—My Mama Hung the World for Me. Newey, Gail, illus. 2009. (J). *(978-1-84686-269-4(8))* Barefoot Bks., Inc.

Kaus, Cathy. The Bean Bandit, 1 vol. 2010. 24p. 24.95 *(978-1-4489-2202-4(X))* PublishAmerica, Inc.

Keller, Holly. Miranda's Beach Day. Keller, Holly, illus. 2009. (Illus.). 32p. (J). (gr. -1). lib. bdg. 18.89 *(978-0-06-158300-1(6)*, Greenwillow Bks.) HarperCollins Pubs.

Kelley, Louise. Stretch the Giraffe. 2012. 32p. pap. 19.99 *(978-1-4772-2161-7(1))* AuthorHouse.

Kelly, Mij. The Bump. Allan, Nicholas, illus. 2012. (ENG.). 32p. (J). *(978-1-58925-107-6(5))* Tiger Tales.

Ketteman, Helen. Goodnight, Little Monster, 0 vols. Leick, Bonnie, illus. 2012. (Little Monster Ser.: 1). (ENG.). 32p. (J). (gr. k-2). 16.99 *(978-0-7614-5683-4(X)*, 9780761456834, Two Lions) Amazon Publishing.

—If Beaver Had a Fever, 0 vols. O'Malley, Kevin, illus. 2012. (ENG.). 32p. (J). (gr. -1-3). 16.99 *(978-0-7614-5951-4(0)*, 9780761459514, Two Lions) Amazon Publishing.

Keys, Dalen. Just a Quilt? Sponaugle, Kim, illus. 2nd ed. 2012. (ENG.). 32p. (J). 16.00 *(978-1-886068-56-8(9))* Fruitbearer Publishing, LLC.

Kimla, Lenka J. I Love My Mommy. Golds, Alexandra Kimla, illus. 2008. 22p. pap. 24.95 *(978-1-60703-126-0(4))* America Star Bks.

King, Frances. The Roundabout Boy. 2012. 28p. pap. 16.50 *(978-1-4772-8059-1(6))* AuthorHouse.

Kirchner, Janette. I Love You So Much. 2011. 20p. pap. 24.95 *(978-1-4137-5952-5(1))* America Star Bks.

Klise, Kate. Little Rabbit & the Meanest Mother on Earth. Klise, M. Sarah, illus. 2015. (ENG.). 32p. (J). (gr. -1-3). 6.99 *(978-0-544-45611-2(4)*, 1599396, Clarion Bks.) HarperCollins Pubs.

Konrad, Marla Stewart. Just Like You: Beautiful Babies Around the World, 1 vol. Wang, Lin., illus. 2010. (ENG.). 32p. (J). (gr. -1-2). 15.99 *(978-0-310-71478-1(8))* Zonderkidz.

Kotb, Hoda. I've Loved You since Forever. Mason, Suzie, illus. 2018. (ENG.). 32p. (J). (gr. -1-3). 18.99 *(978-0-06-284174-2(2)*, HarperCollins) HarperCollins Pubs.

—You Are My Happy. Mason, Suzie, illus. 2019. (ENG.). 32p. (J). (gr. -1-3). 18.99 *(978-0-06-288789-4(0)*, HarperCollins) HarperCollins Pubs.

Kroll, Steve. Nina in That Makes Me Mad!, 1 vol. Knight, Hilary, illus. 2013. (Toon Bks.). (ENG.). 36p. (J). (gr. 1-2). lib. bdg. 32.79 *(978-1-61479-153-9(8)*, 14845) Spotlight.

La Coccinella. Look & See: Mommy, Where Are You? 2014. (Look & See! Ser.). (ENG., Illus.). 24p. (J). (gr. -1 — 1). bds. 8.95 *(978-1-4549-0615-5(4))* Sterling Publishing Co., Inc.

Laible, Steve William, ed. Dandylion. Berry, VacieAnna, illus. 2012. (ENG.). 38p. (J). pap. 9.95 *(978-0-9844784-6-0(9)*, Empire Holdins - Literary Division for Young Readers) Kodel Group, LLC, The.

Lampson, Rosalie. Give Mom a Minute. 2009. 32p. pap. 13.99 *(978-1-4490-1407-0(0))* AuthorHouse.

The Land Beyond Forever. 2006. 25.00 *(978-0-9785570-0-3(X))* Three Sisters Publishing Hse., Ltd.

Landers, Gail J. Late for the Race. 2008. 24p. pap. 24.95 *(978-1-60441-371-7(9))* America Star Bks.

LaPoint, Crystal Godfrey. When My Mommy Cries: A Story to Help Families Cope with Sadness. Eldridge, Crystal, illus. 2012. (ENG.). 32p. (gr. k-6). pap. 19.99 *(978-1-4525-4241-6(4)*, 7529fdad-44ef-45a0-9351-f4e3e18c4d7c, Balboa Pr.) Author Solutions, LLC.

Lawson-Miller, Barb. I Love Mommy Because... 2004. (Illus.). 14p. bds. *(978-0-9688553-1-7(8))* Barbamel Bks., Inc.

Lee, Calee M. I Love You! Tharp, Tricia, illus. 2013. (ENG.). 32p. (J). (gr. -1-k). pap. 9.99 *(978-1-62395-471-0(1))* Xist Publishing.

Lee, Spike & Lee, Tonya Lewis. Please, Baby, Please. Nelson, Kadir, illus. 2007. (Classic Board Bks.). (ENG.). 32p. (J). (gr. -1-k). bds. 8.99 *(978-1-4169-4911-4(9)*, Little Simon) Little Simon.

Lewis, Anne Margaret. The Runaway Mitten: A Michigan Adventure Story. Zenz, Aaron, illus. 2015. (ENG.). 40p. (J). (gr. -1-k). 15.99 *(978-1-63450-213-9(2)*, Sky Pony Pr.) Skyhorse Publishing Co., Inc.

—The Runaway Pumpkin. Zenz, Aaron, illus. 2018. (ENG.). 22p. (J). (gr. -1-2). bds. 5.99 *(978-1-5107-2764-9(7)*, Sky Pony Pr.) Skyhorse Publishing Co., Inc.

—The Runaway Pumpkin: A Halloween Adventure Story. Zenz, Aaron, illus. 2015. (ENG.). 40p. (J). (gr. -1-k). 15.99 *(978-1-63450-214-6(0)*, Sky Pony Pr.) Skyhorse Publishing Co., Inc.

Lewis, Paeony. I'll Always Love You. Ives, Penny, illus. (J). (gr. -1-2). 2013. (ENG.). 32p. pap. 3.99 *(978-1-58925-441-1(4))* 2008. 12p. bds. 7.95 *(978-1-58925-833-4(9))* Tiger Tales.

Lin, Grace. A Big Bed for Little Snow. 2019. (ENG., Illus.). 40p. (J). (gr. -1-3). 18.99 *(978-0-316-47836-6(9))* Little, Brown Bks. for Young Readers.

Link, Amy. My Mommy Wears a Wig. 2009. 16p. pap. 17.95 *(978-1-4490-0218-3(8))* AuthorHouse.

Little Bee Books. Kisses & Cuddles. 2015. (ENG., Illus.). 16p. (J). (gr. -1 — 1). bds. 5.99 *(978-1-4998-0151-4(3))* Little Bee Books Inc.

The Little Saguaro. 2007. (YA). pap. 15.95 *(978-1-886679-37-5(1))* Arizona Sonora Desert Museum Pr.

Lois, Lowry. Son. l.t. ed. 2013. (Giver Quartet Ser.). (ENG.). 422p. 23.99 *(978-1-4104-5448-5(7))* Thorndike Pr.

—Son. 2014. (Giver Quartet Ser.: 4). lib. bdg. 20.85 *(978-0-606-35979-5(6))* Turtleback.

Looper, Grace W. Great-Grandpa's Hidden Treasure. 2006. (YA). pap. *(978-1-933523-18-7(2))* Bella Rosa Bks.

Love, Judy. Praise Be & Rainbows. 2006. 51p. pap. 16.95 *(978-1-4241-0333-1(9))* PublishAmerica, Inc.

Lowry, Lois. Son. (Giver Quartet Ser.: 4). (ENG.). 400p. (YA). (gr. 7). 2014. pap. 9.99 *(978-0-544-33625-4(9)*, 1584171) 2012. 17.99 *(978-0-547-88720-3(5)*, 1507673) HarperCollins Pubs. (Clarion Bks.).

Ltd Mommy Loves/Mommy Kisses. 2005. (J). bds. 11.90 *(978-0-8118-9934-5(9))* Chronicle Bks. LLC.

Luebs, Robin. Please Pick Me up, Mama! Luebs, Robin, illus. 2009. (ENG., Illus.). 40p. (J). (gr. -1-k). 15.99 *(978-1-4169-7977-7(8)*, Beach Lane Bks.) Beach Lane Bks.

Maltese, John. I Love You the Most. 2009. (ENG.). 33p. pap. 16.40 *(978-0-557-09465-3(8))* Lulu Pr., Inc.

Mariam, Sahra Mire - Umm. I Love Making Mummy Happy. 2011. (Illus.). 28p. pap. 15.99 *(978-1-4628-9341-6(4))* Xlibris Corp.

Marr, Melissa. Bunny Roo, I Love You. White, Teagan, illus. 2015. 32p. (J). (gr. -1 — 1). 18.99 *(978-0-399-16742-3(0)*, Nancy Paulsen Books) Penguin Young Readers Group.

Marrero-Martinez, Gloria. Darling Daughter: What Will You Be? Kozak, Maria, illus. 2006. (ENG.). 44p. per. 26.90 *(978-1-4259-4235-9(0))* AuthorHouse.

Martin, Bill, Jr. Baby Bear, Baby Bear, What Do You See? Carle, Eric, illus. (Brown Bear & Friends Ser.). (ENG.). (J). (gr. -1-k). 2014. 28p. bds. 12.99 *(978-0-8050-9949-2(2)*, 900127480) 2011. 40p. 9.99 *(978-0-8050-9291-2(9)*, 900069194) 2007. 32p. 19.99 *(978-0-8050-8336-1(7)*, 900044467) Holt, Henry & Co. (Holt, Henry & Co. Bks. For Young Readers).

—Baby Bear, Baby Bear, What Do You See? Big Book. Carle, Eric, illus. 2011. (Brown Bear & Friends Ser.). (ENG.). 32p. (J). (gr. -1-k). pap. 27.99 *(978-0-8050-9345-2(1)*, 900072447, Holt, Henry & Co. Bks. For Young Readers) Holt, Henry & Co.

—Baby Bear, Baby Bear, What Do You See? Board Book. Carle, Eric, illus. 2009. (Brown Bear & Friends Ser.). (ENG.). 28p. (J). (gr. -1-k). bds. 8.99 *(978-0-8050-8990-5(X)*, 900058689, Holt, Henry & Co. Bks. For Young Readers) Holt, Henry & Co.

Mayer, Ellen. Red Socks: English, bks. 7, bk. 2. Hu, Ying-Hwa, illus. 2015. (ENG.). 18p. (J). pap. 6.99 *(978-1-59572-706-0(X))* Star Bright Bks., Inc.

Mayer, Mercer. Little Critter's Family Treasury. 2018. (Illus.). 176p. (J). (gr. -1-2). 9.99 *(978-1-5247-6619-1(4)*, Random Hse. Bks. for Young Readers) Random Hse. Children's Bks.

McBratney, Sam. I Love It When You Smile. Fuge, Charles, illus. 2012. (ENG.). 32p. (J). (gr. -1-3). 10.99 *(978-0-06-222133-9(7)*, HarperCollins) HarperCollins Pubs.

McCloskey, Robert. Blueberries for Sal. (J). (gr. -1-k). pap. 12.95 incl. audio. 2004. 29.95 *(978-1-55592-841-4(2))*; 2004. (J). 18.95 *(978-1-55592-799-8(8))*; 2004. (J). 38.75 *(978-1-55592-816-2(1))* Weston Woods Studios, Inc.

McCourt, Lisa. Goodnight, Stinky Face. Moore, Cyd, illus. 2016. (ENG.). 32p. (J). (— 1). bds. 7.99 *(978-0-545-90592-3(3)*, Cartwheel Bks.) Scholastic, Inc.

—Happy Halloween, Stinky Face. Moore, Cyd, illus. 2011. (ENG.). 32p. (J). (gr. k — 1). bds. 6.99 *(978-0-545-28542-1(9)*, Cartwheel Bks.) Scholastic, Inc.

—I Miss You, Stinky Face (Board Book) Moore, Cyd, illus. 2014. (ENG.). 32p. (J). (gr. -1 — 1). bds. 7.99 *(978-0-545-74848-3(8)*, Cartwheel Bks.) Scholastic, Inc.

—Merry Christmas, Stinky Face. Moore, Cyd, illus. 2016. (ENG.). 32p. (J). (gr. -1 — 1). 3.99 *(978-1-338-02919-2(3)*, Cartwheel Bks.) Scholastic, Inc.

—Ready for Kindergarten, Stinky Face? Moore, Cyd, illus. 2010. (Scholastic Reader: Level 1 Ser.). (ENG.). 32p. (J). (gr. -1-1). 16.19 *(978-0-545-11518-6(3))* Scholastic, Inc.

—Thank You, Stinky Face. Moore, Cyd, illus. 2018. (ENG.). 20p. (J). (gr. -1 — 1). bds. 7.99 *(978-1-338-27020-4(6)*, Cartwheel Bks.) Scholastic, Inc.

—You Can Do It, Stinky Face!: a Stinky Face Book. Moore, Cyd, illus. 2016. (ENG.). 32p. (J). (— 1). bds. 7.99 *(978-0-545-80648-0(8)*, Cartwheel Bks.) Scholastic, Inc.

Mcdonnell, Patrick. Art. 2011. (J). (gr. -1-3). 29.95 *(978-0-545-10697-9(4))* Weston Woods Studios, Inc.

McDonnell, Patrick. Art. 2006. (ENG., Illus.). 48p. (J). (gr. -1-3). 17.99 *(978-0-316-11491-2(X))* Little, Brown Bks. for Young Readers.

Mcdoogle, Farrah. A Sweet Surprise for Mom. 2015. (Olivia 8x8 Ser.). lib. bdg. 13.55 *(978-0-606-36319-8(X))* Turtleback.

Mcghee, Alison. Someday. 2014. pap. 29.95 *(978-0-545-79756-6(X))* Scholastic, Inc.

—Someday. Reynolds, Peter H., illus. 2008. (J). (gr. -1-2). 29.95 incl. audio compact disk *(978-0-8045-4200-5(7))*; 27.95 incl. audio *(978-0-8045-6975-0(4))* Spoken Arts, Inc.

McGhee, Alison. Someday. Reynolds, Peter H., illus. 2015. (ENG.). 42p. (J). (gr. -1). bds. 9.99 *(978-1-4814-6012-5(9)*, Little Simon) Little Simon.

—Someday. Reynolds, Peter H., illus. 2007. (ENG.). 40p. (J). (gr. -1-3). 17.99 *(978-1-4169-2811-9(1)*, Atheneum Bks. for Young Readers) Simon & Schuster Children's Publishing.

McGinty, Alice B. Eliza's Kindergarten Surprise, 0 vols. Speir, Nancy, illus. 2013. (ENG.). 34p. (J). (gr. -1-1). pap. 9.99 *(978-1-4778-1683-7(6)*, 9781477816837, Two Lions) Amazon Publishing.

McGowen, Julie. Virginia's Voyage. 2007. 48p. per. 16.95 *(978-1-4241-6672-5(1))* America Star Bks.

McKoin, Cathy Taylor. Little Pup Finds a Home! 2009. 28p. pap. 15.99 *(978-1-4415-3407-1(5))* Xlibris Corp.

Meade, L. A Little Mother to the Others. 2006. pap. 36.99 *(978-1-4219-7036-3(8))* IndyPublish.com.

Melmed, Laura Krauss. Before We Met. Tsong, Jing Jing, illus. 2016. (ENG.). 32p. (J). (gr. -1-3). 17.99 *(978-1-4424-4156-9(9)*, Beach Lane Bks.) Beach Lane Bks.

Mendelsohn, Jeffrey. Grumpalina. 2012. (ENG.). 30p. (J). 25.95 *(978-1-4327-7830-9(7))* Outskirts Pr., Inc.

Merrick, Laurie K. Mama, Don't! Eremeyev, Margarita, illus. 2008. 20p. per. 24.95 *(978-1-4241-9868-9(2))* America Star Bks.

Miller, Victoria, illus. Flowers for Mami Unicorn! 2010. (Dora the Explorer Ser.). (ENG.). 24p. (J). (gr. -1-2). pap. 3.99 *(978-1-4169-9064-2(X)*, Simon Spotlight/Nickelodeon) Simon Spotlight/Nickelodeon.

Milligan, Domino. The Sandman. Spiller, Michael, illus. 2008. 16p. pap. 24.95 *(978-1-60703-728-6(9))* America Star Bks.

Mitton, Tony. The Somethingosaur. Ayto, Russell, illus. 2014. (ENG.). 32p. (J). 17.99 *(978-0-00-758395-9(8)*, HarperCollins Children's Bks.) HarperCollins Pubs. Ltd. GBR. Dist: HarperCollins Pubs.

Mommy You're My Hero. 2nd ed. 2005. (J). bds. 12.99 *(978-0-9729264-3-0(7)*, Books for Brats) Little Redhaired Girl Publishing, Inc.

Moneer, Simi. Once upon a Time: Part (1) 2012. (Illus.). 92p. pap. 35.08 *(978-1-4685-0353-1(7))* AuthorHouse.

Monreal, Jeannie. What Will I Be? Asked Little Miss Christina Magee. 2010. 30p. pap. 12.99 *(978-1-60860-791-4(7)*, Eloquent Bks.) Strategic Book Publishing & Rights Agency (SBPRA).

Moore, Diane. Aniville Tales Presents: O. C.'s Big Lesson. 2009. 15p. (J). pap. 12.95 *(978-1-4327-3630-9(2))* Outskirts Pr., Inc.

Moore, Rita M. Big Bell Goes Shopping. 2005. (J). pap. 8.00 *(978-0-8059-6514-8(9))* Dorrance Publishing Co., Inc.

Morgan, Cythia. The Day I Met You & You Met Me! Cable, Annette, illus. 2008. 32p. pap. 5.95 *(978-0-9802497-0-5(8))* King'S Land Pr. Inc.

Morgan, Mary. Pip Sits. 2017. (I Like to Read Ser.). (ENG., Illus.). 24p. (J). (gr. -1-3). 14.95 *(978-0-8234-3676-7(4))* Holiday Hse., Inc.

Morris, C. J. The Stone Children. 2005. (YA). per. 13.95 *(978-1-58597-314-9(9))* Leathers Publishing.

Morris, Deborah K. Here I Am Look at Me! Morris, Douglas, illus. 2010. 36p. pap. 13.95 *(978-1-60911-739-9(5)*, Eloquent Bks.) Strategic Book Publishing & Rights Agency (SBPRA).

MosesAntoinette. The Girl at the Window Starter/Beginner. 2007. (Cambridge English Readers Ser.). (ENG., Illus.). 32p. pap. 14.75 *(978-0-521-70585-1(1))* Cambridge Univ. Pr.

Mukherjee, Aiswarya & S., Bijan, illus. My Family! ABCs with Keesha. 2011. (J). pap. 2.99 *(978-0-9767273-9-2(0))* Dodi Pr.

Muldrow, Diane E. Where Do Giggles Come From? Kennedy, Anne, illus. 2011. (Little Golden Book Ser.). 24p. (J). (gr. -1-2). 5.99 *(978-0-375-86133-8(5)*, Golden Bks.) Random Hse. Children's Bks.

Munsch, Robert. Love You Forever. McGraw, Sheila, illus. 2018. (ENG.). 32p. (J). (gr. -1-1). bds. 8.95 *(978-0-2281-0104-8(2)*, 93279bc2-9280-4ed0-8e4f-216516529c98) Firefly Bks., Ltd.

—Love You Forever Pop-Up Edition. McGraw, Sheila, illus. 2017. (ENG.). 14p. (J). (gr. -1-1). 29.95 *(978-1-77085-965-4(9)*, a9e2dca8-f177-424e-8b80-a3c02dd73a41) Firefly Bks., Ltd.

Murphy, Mary. Are You My Mommy? Murphy, Mary, illus. 2015. (ENG., Illus.). 16p. (J). (gr. -1 — 1). bds. 7.99 *(978-0-7636-7372-7(2))* Candlewick Pr.

Murray, Kirsty. Puddle Hunters. Blair, Karen, illus. 2019. (ENG.). 32p. (J). (gr. -1-1). 16.99 *(978-1-76029-674-2(0))* Allen & Unwin AUS. Dist: Independent Pubs. Group.

Nelson, Thomas. Mommy Loves You So Much, 1 vol. 2015. (ENG., Illus.). 20p. (J). bds. 9.99 *(978-0-529-12338-1(X)*, Tommy Nelson) Nelson, Thomas Inc.

Nethaway, Misty. I Know My Mommy Loves Me. 2008. 17p. pap. 24.95 *(978-1-60672-475-0(4))* America Star Bks.

Nia, Nikki. Mommy's Love. 2007. 19.95 *(978-0-9792151-0-0(2))* Global Pr.

Numeroff, Laura. Nighty-Night, Cooper. Munsinger, Lynn, illus. 2013. (ENG.). 32p. (J). (gr. -1-3). 17.99 *(978-0-547-40205-5(8)*, 1427979, Clarion Bks.) HarperCollins Pubs.

O'Connor, Crystal Ball. Gift/ Book Combo. Hollinger, Valerie Bunch, illus. 2005. (J). 25.00 *(978-0-9774038-0-6(7))* Monarch Pubs.

—Jake & the Migration of the Monarch. Hollinger, Valerie Bunch, illus. 2005. 32p. (J). 17.95 *(978-0-615-12659-3(6))* Monarch Pubs.

—Jake y la Migraci'on de la Monarca. Brenes-Sotela, Guillermo J. & Quave, Gloria Martinez, trs. from ENG. Hollinger, Valerie Bunch, illus. 2005. (SPA.). (J). 17.95 *(978-0-9774038-2-0(3))* Monarch Pubs.

Ohanesian, Diane. Hugga Bugga Love. Flint, Gillian, illus. (ENG.). (J). (gr. -1-k). 2018. 26p. bds. 7.99 *(978-1-4998-0744-8(9))* 2017. 32p. 16.99 *(978-1-4998-0395-2(8))* Little Bee Books Inc.

Ohlin, Nancy. Beauty. 2013. (ENG., Illus.). 208p. (YA). (gr. 7). pap. 9.99 *(978-1-4424-7265-5(0)*, Simon Pulse) Simon Pulse.

Ostermann, Riley. So Big. 2009. 24p. pap. 12.00 *(978-1-60693-970-3(X)*, Eloquent Bks.) Strategic Book Publishing & Rights Agency (SBPRA).

Palazzolo, Gail M. Mommy, How Can We Catch the Moon? 2008. 15p. pap. 24.95 *(978-1-60672-864-2(4))* America Star Bks.

Parragon Staff, ed. Corderito. 2010. pap. 5.95 *(978-1-4054-4914-4(4))* Parragon, Inc.

Patricelli, Leslie. Tubby. Patricelli, Leslie, illus. 2010. (Leslie Patricelli Board Bks.). (ENG., Illus.). 28p. (J). (— 1). bds. 7.99 *(978-0-7636-4567-0(2))* Candlewick Pr.

Pauly, Natalie. Mommy Mayhem. 2009. (Illus.). 28p. pap. 13.99 *(978-1-4389-6254-2(1))* AuthorHouse.

Pelley, Kathleen T. & Harper, Ruth E. Happy Mamas. 2016. (ENG., Illus.). 30p. 14.95 *(978-1-58760-160-6(5)*, P544297, CWLA Pr.) Child Welfare League of America, Inc.

Pendleton, Claudette M. I'm Mommy's Little Helper. Scott, Christopher L., illus. 2012. 46p. 24.95 *(978-1-4626-9303-0(2))* America Star Bks.

Penn, Audrey. Chester Raccoon & the Acorn Full of Memories. Gibson, Barbara, illus. 2009. (Kissing Hand Ser.). (ENG.). 32p. (J). (gr. -1-3). 16.99 *(978-1-933718-29-3(3))* Tanglewood Pr.

—A Pocket Full of Kisses. Gibson, Barbara Leonard, illus. 2004. (New Child & Family Press Titles Ser.). 32p. (J). (gr. -1-1). 16.95 *(978-0-87868-894-4(3)*, 8943, Child & Family Pr.) Child Welfare League of America, Inc.

—A Pocket Full of Kisses. Gibson, Barbara, illus. 2006. (Kissing Hand Ser.). (ENG.). 32p. (J). (gr. -1-3). 18.99 *(978-1-933718-02-6(1))* Tanglewood Pr.

Peterson, Willa. It's a Mommy Day! 2011. 28p. pap. 13.99 *(978-1-4634-3592-9(4))* AuthorHouse.

Phyllarry (Rittmueller), Kathryn. Beauregart the Bear. 2009. (ENG., Illus.). 64p. (J). 12.95 *(978-0-943972-80-0(9))* Homestead Publishing.

Pick Me up, Mama! 2014. (ENG., Illus.). 34p. (J). (gr. -1-k). bds. 6.99 *(978-1-4814-1633-7(2)*, Little Simon) Little Simon.

Pierce, Terry. Mama Loves You So. Shin, Simone, illus. 2017. (New Books for Newborns Ser.). (ENG.). 16p. (J). (gr. -1 — 1). bds. 7.99 *(978-1-4814-8159-5(2)*, Little Simon) Little Simon.

Pitts, Daphne. What Makes God Laugh. 2012. 30p. 25.99 *(978-1-62419-299-9(8))*; pap. 15.99 *(978-1-62419-298-2(X))* Salem Author Services.

Platt, Cynthia. Little Bit of Love. Whitty, Hannah, illus. 2011. (ENG.). 32p. (J). (gr. -1-2). pap. 7.95 *(978-1-58925-426-8(0))* Tiger Tales.

Polacco, Patricia. Mommies Say Shh! Polacco, Patricia, illus. 2007. (Illus.). 34p. (J). (gr. -1 — 1). bds. 8.99 *(978-0-399-24720-0(3)*, Philomel Bks.) Penguin Young Readers Group.

popular, Tradición. Estaba la pájara pinta. 2011. (SPA.). 14p. (J). (gr. -1-k). pap. 8.99 *(978-980-257-026-3(5))* Ekare, Ediciones VEN. Dist: Lectorum Pubns., Inc.

Potvin, Amy K. I Miss Daddy. 2009. 28p. pap. 13.99 *(978-1-4259-1705-0(4))* AuthorHouse.

Propaganda, Amanda. People Flavors. 2006. (Illus.). (J). 6.00 *(978-1-60149-000-1(3))* Punkin Pr.

Publications International Ltd. Staff, creator. Mother Goose. 2007. (Pop-up Treasury Ser.). (Illus.). 16p. (J). (gr. -1-3). 12.98 *(978-1-4127-8833-5(1))* Publications International, Ltd.

Quintart, Natalie. Mama Bear. Blanchart, Stephanie, illus. 2005. (Tiger Tales Ser.). 32p. (J). (gr. -1-2). 6.95 *(978-1-58925-394-0(9))* Tiger Tales.

Raab, Brigitte. Mama, I Can't Sleep. Olten, Manuela, illus. 2012. (ENG.). 32p. (J). (gr. -1-k). 16.95 *(978-1-61608-965-8(2)*, 608965, Sky Pony Pr.) Skyhorse Publishing Co., Inc.

Racek, Jennifer. Cadberry's Letters. 2008. 33p. 13.90 *(978-1-4357-0566-1(1))* Lulu Pr., Inc.

Ramos, Angelica. If My Mommy Was an Octopus. 2008. 12p. pap. 24.95 *(978-1-60563-821-8(8))* PublishAmerica, Inc.

Raquel, Israel & Sissom, Carol. Help Mommy Clean-Up! 2006. (Help Mommy Clen-Up! Ser.: Vol. 1). (Illus.). 16p. (J). mass mkt. 7.99 *(978-1-4243-2034-9(8))* Independent Publisher Services.

Reed, Jennifer Bond. That's a Lot of Love. Houdeshell, Jennifer Thomas, illus. 2011. 16p. pap. 9.95 *(978-1-61633-172-6(0))* Guardian Angel Publishing, Inc.

Rex, Michael. The Runaway Mummy: A Petrifying Parody. 2012. lib. bdg. 17.20 *(978-0-606-26086-2(2))* Turtleback.

—Runaway Mummy: a Petrifying Parody. 2012. 32p. (J). (gr. -1-k). pap. 7.99 *(978-0-14-242121-5(9)*, Puffin Books) Penguin Young Readers Group.

Reyes, S. L. Mommy Does a Lot So I Want to Too, 1 vol. Taylor, Amber, illus. 2010. 30p. 24.95 *(978-1-4489-5420-9(7))* PublishAmerica, Inc.

Reynolds, Alison. Why I Love My Mom. Geddes, Serena, illus. 2015. (ENG.). 22p. (J). (gr. -1-1). 9.99 *(978-1-4998-0020-3(7))* Little Bee Books Inc.

Richards, Dan. Can One Balloon Make an Elephant Fly? Newman, Jeff, illus. 2016. (ENG.). 40p. (J). (gr. -1-3). 17.99 *(978-1-4424-5215-2(3))* Simon & Schuster Bks. For Young Readers.

Richmond, Marianne. I Wished for You: An Adoption Story. 2008. (Marianne Richmond Ser.). (Illus.). 40p. (J). (gr. -1-3). 17.99 *(978-1-934082-06-5(6)*, Sourcebooks Jabberwocky) Sourcebooks, Inc.

Riebel, Jessica Mire. Katrina & the Rinky-Dink Sewing Machine. Herpin, K. K., illus. 2008. 32p. pap. 24.95 *(978-1-60813-545-5(4))* America Star Bks.

Rigo, Laura. Little Duckling. 2011. (Mini Look at Me Bks.). (Illus.). 10p. (J). bds. 8.99 *(978-0-7641-6425-5(2))* Sourcebooks, Inc.

—Little Pony. 2011. (Look at Me Bks.). (Illus.). 10p. (J). (gr. -1). bds. 8.99 *(978-0-7641-6448-4(1))* Sourcebooks, Inc.

—Little Reindeer. 2011. (Mini Look at Me Bks.). (Illus.). 10p. (J). (gr. -1). bds. 7.99 *(978-0-7641-6450-7(3))* Sourcebooks, Inc.

Rigo, Laura, illus. Little Chimp. 2011. (Mini Look at Me Bks.). 10p. (J). (gr. -1). bds. 7.99 *(978-0-7641-6428-6(7))* Sourcebooks, Inc.

—Little Elephant. 2011. (Look at Me Bks.). 10p. (J). (gr. -1). bds. 8.99 *(978-0-7641-6426-2(0))* Sourcebooks, Inc.

Rinker, Sherri Duskey. Silly Wonderful You. McDonnell, Patrick, illus. 2016. (ENG.). 40p. (J). (gr. -1-3). 17.99 *(978-0-06-227105-1(9)*, Balzer & Bray) HarperCollins Pubs.

Ritchie, Kate. I Just Couldn't Wait to Meet You. Somerville, Hannah, illus. 2015. 32p. (J). (-k). 22.99 *(978-0-85798-970-3(7))* Random Hse. Australia AUS. Dist: Independent Pubs. Group.

Romano, Melissa. Mama, Lions Don't Listen. 2008. 24p. pap. 11.99 *(978-1-4343-9907-6(9))* AuthorHouse.

Romeo, Fran & Romeo, Fran. Once upon A Dream. 2007. (ENG., Illus.). 18p. 14.99 *(978-0-8249-5901-2(9)*, Ideals Pubns.) Worthy Publishing.

Ron, Berry. Mommy Do You Love Me. 2009. (ENG.). 20p. bds. 5.99 *(978-0-8249-1422-6(8)*, Ideals Pubns.) Worthy Publishing.

Root, Phyllis. Flip, Flap, Fly! A Book for Babies Everywhere. Walker, David M., illus. 2011. (ENG.). 32p. (J). (gr. -1 — 1). bds. 7.99 *(978-0-7636-5325-5(X))* Candlewick Pr.

Roper, Shannon L. Mommy's Garden. 2012. 26p. 24.95 *(978-1-4626-5327-0(8))* America Star Bks.

Rosland, Linsey. How Much Do I Love You? 2012. 20p. pap. 14.99 *(978-1-4567-4880-7(7))* AuthorHouse.

Roth, Kapra Lynn. The Healing Bugs. 2008. 24p. pap. 24.95 *(978-1-60703-169-7(8))* America Star Bks.

Rowland, Kelly & Mckay, Jessica. Always with You, Always with Me. Liem, Fanny, illus. 2022. 19.99 *(978-1-7339049-5-7(6))* Hightree Publishing.

Rowland, Kelly & McKay, Jessica. Always with You, Always with Me. Liem, Fanny, illus. 2022. (ENG.). 40p. (J). (gr. -1-2). 17.99 *(978-0-593-46551-6(2)*, Viking Books for Young Readers) Penguin Young Readers Group.

Russell, B. M. My Friend Bianca. 2010. 32p. 13.95 *(978-1-4497-0168-0(X)*, WestBow Pr.) Author Solutions, LLC.

Ryder, Joanne. Bear of My Heart. Moore, Margie, illus. 2009. (ENG.). 32p. (J). (gr. -1 — 1). bds. 9.99 *(978-1-4169-5472-9(4)*, Little Simon) Little Simon.

Sagendorph, Jean. Starry Night, Hold Me Tight. Siebold, Kim, illus. 2015. (ENG.). 18p. (J). (gr. -1 — 1). bds. 6.95 *(978-0-7624-5853-0(4)*, Running Pr. Kids) Running Pr.

Sakai, Komako. The Snow Day. 2009. (J). pap. *(978-0-545-01322-2(4)*, Levine, Arthur A. Bks.) Scholastic, Inc.

Sala, Laurenne. You Made Me a Mother. Glasser, Robin Preiss, illus. 2016. (ENG.). 32p. (J). (gr. -1-3). 16.99 *(978-0-06-235886-8(3)*, HarperCollins) HarperCollins Pubs.

Samuels, Gregory Robert. Mommy, Where Does Everything Come From? Brennan, Craig, illus. 2008. 11p. pap. 24.95 *(978-1-60610-437-8(3))* America Star Bks.

Sandau, Carol E. Prairie Patchwork. 2012. 88p. (gr. 4-6). pap. 9.95 *(978-1-4759-4807-3(7))* iUniverse, Inc.

Sands, Monty. King of Nine Mile Canyon. 2008. 124p. 11.99 *(978-0-615-25788-4(7))* Sands, Monty.

Sanna, Francesca. The Journey. 2016. (ENG., Illus.). 48p. (J). (gr. k-2). 17.99 *(978-1-909263-99-4(0))* Flying Eye Bks. GBR. Dist: Penguin Random Hse. LLC.

Schad, Kristine. Do You Love Me Best? Timmons, Gayle, illus. 2007. 40p. (J). lib. bdg. 23.95 *(978-1-58374-156-6(9))* Chicago Spectrum Pr.

Schulz, Kathy. I Need a Little Help. Iosa, Ann, illus. 2011. (Rookie Ready to Learn — All about Me! Ser.). 32p. (J). (gr. -1-k). lib. bdg. 25.00 *(978-0-531-26526-0(9)*, Children's Pr.) Scholastic Library Publishing.

—Rookie Ready to Learn en Español: Necesito una Ayudita. Iosa, Ann, illus. 2011. (Rookie Ready to Learn Español Ser.). Orig. Title: Rookie Ready to Learn: I Need a Little Help. (SPA.). 32p. (J). pap. 5.95 *(978-0-531-26782-0(2)*, Children's Pr.) Scholastic Library Publishing.

Scott, Ann Herbert. On Mother's Lap/en Las Piernas de Mamá: Bilingual English-Spanish. Coalson, Glo, illus. 2007.Tr. of On Mother's Lap. (ENG.). 14p. (J). (gr. k — 1). bds. 5.95 *(978-0-618-75247-8(1)*, 100529, Clarion Bks.) HarperCollins Pubs.

Seif Simpson, Martha. What NOT to Give Your Mom on Mother's Day, 0 vols. Christy, Jana, illus. 2013. (ENG.). 24p. (J). (gr. -1-2). 12.99 *(978-1-4778-1647-9(X)*, 9781477816479, Two Lions) Amazon Publishing.

Senir, Mirik & Shubow, Mary Jane. When I First Held You: A Lullaby from Israel. 2009. (J). lib. bdg. 17.95 *(978-0-7613-5096-5(9)*, Kar-Ben Publishing) Lerner Publishing Group.

Sewell, Jaime. When Mommy Went on Strike. 2010. 28p. pap. 15.49 *(978-1-4490-8726-5(4))* AuthorHouse.

Shaffer, Jennifer. I Want to Play! 2012. 26p. 24.95 *(978-1-4626-5779-7(6))* America Star Bks.

Shaw, Stephanie. Piece by Piece. Daigneault, Sylvie, illus. 2017. (ENG.). 32p. (J). (gr. 1-4). 16.99 *(978-1-58536-999-7(3)*, 204318) Sleeping Bear Pr.

Sheehy-Culhane, Roisin. WHEN MAMA GOES to WORK: DEVIN'S STORY. 2006. (ENG.). 32p. per. 19.99 *(978-1-4257-0596-1(0))* Xlibris Corp.

Shepherd, Melissa L. On Mother's Day. 2012. 24p. pap. 14.93 *(978-1-4669-1165-9(4))* Trafford Publishing.

Sher, Emil. Away, 1 vol. Leng, Qin, illus. 2017. (ENG.). 32p. (J). (gr. k-2). 18.95 *(978-1-55498-483-1(1))* Groundwood Bks. CAN. Dist: Publishers Group West (PGW).

Sherwood, Mary Marth. The History of Lucy Clare. 2004. reprint ed. pap. 15.95 *(978-1-4191-6620-4(4))* Kessinger Publishing, LLC.

Sherwood, Mary Martha. The History of Lucy Clare. 2004. reprint ed. pap. 1.99 *(978-1-4192-6620-1(9))* Kessinger Publishing, LLC.

Sigmon-Heck, Christina. A Smile for Only You! 2012. 24p. 24.95 *(978-1-4626-6197-8(1))* America Star Bks.

Sills, Kathy & Sills, Karen. Feelings, Feelings, Feelings. 2012. 19p. 19.00 *(978-1-4349-8743-3(4)*, RoseDog Bks.) Dorrance Publishing Co., Inc.

Silva, Abbey. She Came to Heal. 2008. 136p. pap. 11.50 *(978-1-4389-1086-4(X))* AuthorHouse.

Simons, Paullina. I Love My Baby Because... Thomas, Cassia, illus. 2015. (ENG.). 24p. (J). 17.99 *(978-0-00-810211-1(2)*, HarperCollins Children's Bks.) HarperCollins Pubs. Ltd. GBR. Dist: HarperCollins Pubs.

—Poppet Gets Two Big Brothers. 2015. (ENG., Illus.). 32p. (J). 17.99 *(978-0-00-811041-3(7)*, HarperCollins Children's Bks.) HarperCollins Pubs. Ltd. GBR. Dist: HarperCollins Pubs.

Skougaard, Shari. Grumpy Goo, I Love You. 2009. 24p. pap. 13.50 *(978-1-60860-454-8(3)*, Eloquent Bks.) Strategic Book Publishing & Rights Agency (SBPRA).

Slade, Cheryl. Mummy Is Sick, but I Love You. 2019. (ENG.). 28p. 37.94 *(978-1-9845-0474-6(6))*; (Illus.). pap. 24.14 *(978-1-9845-0473-9(8))* Xlibris Corp.

Sliwerski, Jessica Reid. Cancer Hates Kisses. Song, Mika, illus. 2017. 40p. (J). (-k). 18.99 *(978-0-7352-2781-1(0)*, Dial Bks) Penguin Young Readers Group.

Smith, Andrea Neile. Who Aiden Was. 2012. 38p. pap. 14.95 *(978-1-60594-879-9(9))* Aeon Publishing Inc.

Smith, Joye. What Does It Mean to Be Poor? 2005. (Illus.). 30p. (J). 8.99 *(978-1-56309-880-2(6))* Woman's Missionary Union.

Smith, Rosie. My Mom's the Best. Whatley, Bruce, illus. 2013. (J). *(978-0-545-60361-4(7))* Scholastic, Inc.

Smith, Sarah, illus. Where's My Mommy? 2009. (J). *(978-0-7607-8404-4(3))* Barnes & Noble, Inc.

Sperring, Mark. The Shape of My Heart. Paterson, Alys, illus. 2015. (ENG.). 32p. (J). (gr. -1-1). bds. 8.99 *(978-1-68119-017-4(6)*, 900155505, Bloomsbury USA Childrens) Bloomsbury Publishing USA.

Spillett-Sumner, Tasha. I Sang You down from the Stars. Goade, Michaela, illus. 2021. (ENG.). 32p. (J). (gr. -1-3). 18.99 *(978-0-316-49316-1(3))* Little, Brown Bks. for Young Readers.

Spinelli, Jerry. Mama Seeton's Whistle. 2015. (ENG., Illus.). 40p. (J). (gr. -1-3). 17.00 *(978-0-316-12217-7(3))* Little, Brown Bks. for Young Readers.

Spooner, Carol. I Love You Best. 2012. 24p. pap. 24.95 *(978-1-4626-5803-9(2))* America Star Bks.

Stanwood, Jane. Squeak's Bus Company. 2008. 28p. per. 11.95 *(978-1-4327-1964-7(5))* Outskirts Pr., Inc.

Stein, David Ezra. Pouch! Stein, David Ezra, illus. 2012. (ENG., Illus.). 32p. (J). (gr. -1 — 1). bds. 8.99 *(978-0-399-25738-4(1)*, Nancy Paulsen Books) Penguin Young Readers Group.

Stevens, Jennifer. Love You More. 2013. 24p. pap. 24.95 *(978-1-63004-655-2(8))* America Star Bks.

Stewart, Patricia. Do You Want To Know Why My Mother Margaret Swallowed a Fly? Leago, Shirley Moore, illus. 2008. (ENG.). 36p. pap. 14.99 *(978-1-4343-5674-1(4))* AuthorHouse.

Stewart, Shawna. Amazing Tails of Zomber Doodles & Buttons, 1 vol. 2010. 30p. pap. 24.95 *(978-1-4489-7913-4(7))* PublishAmerica, Inc.

Stott, Ann. Always. Phelan, Matt, illus. 2008. (ENG.). 32p. (J). (gr. k-k). 15.99 *(978-0-7636-3232-8(5))* Candlewick Pr.

—I'll Be There. Phelan, Matt, illus. 2011. (ENG.). 32p. (J). (gr. -1-2). 14.99 *(978-0-7636-4711-7(X))* Candlewick Pr.

Stram, Dawn. Fat Ladies Shouldn't Have Orange Hair! 2011. 56p. pap. 31.99 *(978-1-4568-5804-9(1))* Xlibris Corp.

Strelitski, Mies & Hartog, Arnold. Woobie Dreams Hc. 2006. (Illus.). 32p. (J). 16.95 *(978-1-59249-554-2(0))* Soundprints.

Summer, Laura LeClair. Mommy will always come Home. White, Kathy, illus. 2006. 35p. (J). per. 24.95 *(978-1-4276-0158-2(5))* Aardvark Global Publishing.

Sundaram, Renuka. Sammy, the Galapagos Sea Lion. 2011. 32p. pap. 15.00 *(978-1-61286-015-2(X))* Avid Readers Publishing Group.

Surrisi, Cynthia. The Best Mother. Goode, Diane, illus. 2018. (ENG.). 32p. (J). (gr. -1-2). 16.99 *(978-1-4197-2534-0(3)*, 1144001, Abrams Bks. for Young Readers) Abrams, Inc.

Sutton, Jane. What's up with This Chicken?, 1 vol. Welling, Peter, illus. 2015. (ENG.). 32p. (J). (gr. k-3). 16.99 *(978-1-4556-2085-2(8)*, Pelican Publishing) Arcadia Publishing.

Swain, Cynthia. The Birthday Flowers. 2006. (Early Explorers Ser.). (J). pap. *(978-1-4108-6025-5(6))* Benchmark Education Co.

Swinburne, Stephen R. Safe in a Storm. Bell, Jennifer, illus. 2016. (J). *(978-0-545-66987-0(1))* Scholastic, Inc.

Tafuri, Nancy. Five Little Chicks. Tafuri, Nancy, illus. 2011. (Classic Board Bks.). (ENG., Illus.). 34p. (J). (gr. -1 — 1). bds. 8.99 *(978-1-4424-0722-0(0)*, Little Simon) Little Simon.

—Five Little Chicks. Tafuri, Nancy, illus. 2006. (ENG., illus.). 32p. (J). (gr. -1-3). 19.99 *(978-0-689-87342-3(5)*, Simon & Schuster Bks. For Young Readers) Simon & Schuster Bks. For Young Readers.

—Whose Chick Are You? 2007. (ENG., Illus.). 40p. (J). (gr. -1-k). 16.99 *(978-0-06-082514-0(6)*, Greenwillow Bks.) HarperCollins Pubs.

—Whose Chick Are You? Board Book: An Easter & Springtime Book for Kids. Tafuri, Nancy, illus. 2019. (ENG., Illus.). 38p. (J). (gr. -1 — 1). bds. 7.99 *(978-0-06-285739-2(8)*, Greenwillow Bks.) HarperCollins Pubs.

Tanco, Miguel. Mom & Me, Me & Mom (Mother Daughter Gifts, Mother Daughter Books, Books for Moms, Motherhood Books) 2019. (You & Me, Me & You Ser.). (ENG., Illus.). 36p. (J). (gr. -1-k). 12.99 *(978-1-4521-7190-6(4))* Chronicle Bks. LLC.

Thiel Annie. The Playdate Kids Dakota's Mom Goes to the Hospital 2ED 2007. 2007. 32p. 12.95 *(978-1-933721-30-9(8))*; pap. 6.95 *(978-1-933721-26-2(X))* Playdate Kids Publishing.

Thiel, Annie & Fanning, Tena. Dakota Gets Lost. Edwards, William M., illus. 2007. (Playdate Kids: Let's Be Friends! Ser.). 27p. (J). (gr. -1-3). per. 6.95 *(978-1-933721-20-0(0))* Playdate Kids Publishing.

Thomas, Christie. Quinn Says Goodbye: Friends May Go Away, but God Is Here to Stay. 2019. (ENG., Illus.). 32p. (J). (gr. -1-2). 16.99 *(978-0-7369-7434-9(2)*, 6974349) Harvest Hse. Pubs.

Thomas, Martin. My Mom Is There. Jatkowska, Ag, illus. 2018. (ENG.). 20p. (gr. -1 — 1). bds. 8.99 *(978-1-5107-3616-0(6)*, Sky Pony Pr.) Skyhorse Publishing Co., Inc.

Thomas, Pam. Mamarswpial. 2005. (WEL., Illus.). 128p. pap. *(978-0-86243-360-4(6))* Y Lolfa.

Thompson, Lauren. Leap Back Home to Me. Cordell, Matthew, illus. 2011. (ENG.). 32p. (J). (gr. -1-3). 19.99 *(978-1-4169-0664-3(9)*, McElderry, Margaret K. Bks.) McElderry, Margaret K. Bks.

—Mouse Loves Spring. 2018. (Simon & Schuster Ready-To-Read Level 1 Ser.). lib. bdg. 13.55 *(978-0-606-40862-2(2))* Turtleback.

—Mouse Loves Spring: Ready-To-Read Pre-Level 1. Erdogan, Buket, illus. 2018. (Mouse Ser.). (ENG.). 32p. (J). (gr. -1-k). 17.99 *(978-1-5344-0185-3(7))*; pap. 4.99 *(978-1-5344-0184-6(9))* Simon Spotlight. (Simon Spotlight).

—Mouse's First Spring. Erdogan, Buket, illus. 2012. (Classic Board Bks.). (ENG.). 34p. (J). (gr. -1-3). bds. 8.99 *(978-1-4424-3431-8(7)*, Little Simon) Little Simon.

Thuma, Chris. Cigarette Sue. 2008. 24p. per. 12.95 *(978-1-59858-561-2(4))* Dog Ear Publishing, LLC.

Todorov, Vladimir. Oliver's Tantrums. 2013. (ENG., Illus.). 34p. (J). (gr. k-4). 16.95 *(978-1-897476-67-3(1))* Simply Read Bks. CAN. Dist: Ingram Publisher Services.

Tomey, Ingrid. The Queen of Dreamland. 2004. 179p. (YA). (gr. 6-10). reprint ed. 15.00 *(978-0-7567-7151-5(X))* DIANE Publishing Co.

Tompert, Ann. Little Fox Goes to the End of the World, 0 vols. Bryant, Laura J., illus. 2012. (ENG.). 32p. (J). (gr. -1-3). 16.99 *(978-0-7614-5703-9(8)*, 9780761457039, Two Lions) Amazon Publishing.

Top That Publishing Staff, ed. Who's My Mommy. 2005. 12p. bds. *(978-1-84510-067-4(0))* Top That! Publishing PLC.

Torres, Jos A. & Torres, Jose A. Joey Kanga Roo: Plays the Trumpet. 2009. 36p. pap. 15.99 *(978-1-4389-7434-7(5))* AuthorHouse.

The Trail of the Wooden Horse. 2007. 32p. pap. 4.50 *(978-0-8341-2284-0(7)*, 083-412-2847) Beacon Hill Pr. of Kansas City.

Trimmer, Christian. Teddy's Favorite Toy. Valentine, Madeline, illus. 2018. (ENG.). 40p. (J). (gr. -1-3). 17.99 *(978-1-4814-8079-6(0)*, Atheneum Bks. for Young Readers) Simon & Schuster Children's Publishing.

Vagnozzi, Barbara, illus. Jack & the Beanstalk. 2007. (Flip-Up Fairy Tales Ser.). 24p. (J). (gr. -1-2). pap. incl. audio compact disk *(978-1-84643-086-2(0))* Child's Play International Ltd.

van Genechten, Guido. Because I Love You So Much. 2006. (Illus.). 12p. (J). (gr. -1-3). 15.95 *(978-1-58925-794-8(4))* Tiger Tales.

Van, Muon. The Little Tree. Adinolfi, JoAnn, illus. 2015. (ENG.). 32p. (J). (gr. k-3). 16.95 *(978-1-939547-19-4(9)*, 1405f785-4f8e-4f2f-adbe-93dcf2ee9cb1) Creston Bks.

Velde, Marie. Laundry Day. 2007. (Illus.). (J). bds. 22.95 *(978-1-933156-17-0(1)*, Visikid Bks.) GSVQ Publishing.

Vella, Sylvia. It's Okay to Tell. 2011. 28p. 13.59 *(978-1-4567-1912-8(2))* AuthorHouse.

Vision, David, et al. My Very Breast Friend. Alcantara, Ignacio, illus. 2009. (ENG.). 40p. 17.00 *(978-0-9659538-5-6(8))* Vitally Important.

Voskoboinikov, Valery & Linnamagi, Anne. The Icicle. 2007. (POL & ENG., Illus.). 32p. (J). pap. 16.95 *(978-1-60195-100-7(0))* International Step by Step Assn.

Waddell, Martin. Owl Babies. Benson, Patrick, illus. (ENG.). (J). 2017. 32p. (gr. -1-2). 17.99 *(978-0-7636-9519-4(X))* 2015. 22p. (— 1). bds. 7.99 *(978-0-7636-7961-3(5))* Candlewick Pr.

—Owl Babies: Padded Board Book. Benson, Patrick, illus. 2019. (ENG.). 24p. (J). (— 1). bds. 9.99 *(978-1-5362-0963-1(5))* Candlewick Pr.

—Owl Babies Book & Toy Gift Set. Benson, Patrick, illus. 2016. (ENG.). 22p. (J). (-k). bds. 15.99 *(978-0-7636-8898-1(3))* Candlewick Pr.

—Owl Babies Lap-Size Board Book. Benson, Patrick, illus. 2018. (ENG.). 22p. (J). (— 1). bds. 12.99 *(978-0-7636-9520-0(3))* Candlewick Pr.

Walker, Anna. I Love My Mom. Walker, Anna, illus. 2010. (ENG., Illus.). 32p. (J). (gr. -1-1). 9.99 *(978-1-4169-8318-7(X)*, Simon & Schuster Bks. For Young Readers) Simon & Schuster Bks. For Young Readers.

Walker, Susan Eileen. I Know the Quigglebush Heroes. 2008. 53p. pap. 16.95 *(978-1-60672-587-0(4))* America Star Bks.

Walsh, Ann. Horse Power, 1 vol. 2007. (Orca Currents Ser.). (ENG.). 112p. (J). (gr. 4-7). lib. bdg. 14.95 *(978-1-55143-883-2(6))* Orca Bk. Pubs. USA.

Walters, Eric. Visions. 2011. (ENG.). 208p. (J). pap. *(978-1-55455-122-4(6))* Fitzhenry & Whiteside, Ltd.

Wan, Joyce. Are You My Mommy? Wan, Joyce, illus. 2014. (ENG.). 18p. (J). (gr. -1 — 1). bds. 6.99 *(978-0-545-54047-6(X)*, Cartwheel Bks.) Scholastic, Inc.

Weiss, Ellen. I Love You, Little Monster. Arnold, Ali, illus. 2012. (ENG.). 16p. (J). (gr. -1 — 1). bds. 7.99 *(978-1-4424-2850-8(3)*, Little Simon) Little Simon.

Wells, Jason. Why Children Should Listen to Their Mothers. 2013. 28p. pap. 24.95 *(978-1-62709-489-4(X))* America Star Bks.

Wells, Rosemary. Yoko Finds Her Way. 2014. (Yoko Book Ser.). (ENG.). 32p. (J). (gr. -1-3). 16.99 *(978-1-4231-6512-5(8))* Little, Brown Bks. for Young Readers.

Weninger, Brigitte. Davy Loves His Mommy. Tharlet, Eve, illus. 2014. (ENG.). 32p. (J). (gr. k-3). 15.95 *(978-0-7358-4164-2(0))* North-South Bks., Inc.

Wheeler, Laura C. I'll Kiss You A Promise. 2010. 24p. pap. 12.99 *(978-1-4520-0790-8(X))* AuthorHouse.

White, Gloria. Something More Important. 2013. 24p. pap. *(978-1-4602-1115-1(4))* FriesenPress.

Willis, Jeanne. Slug Needs a Hug! Ross, Tony, illus. 2015. (ENG.). 32p. (J). (gr. -1-3). 17.99 *(978-1-4677-9309-4(4)*, 7f9d8f68-27c2-42e6-aeaf-961d4351753a); E-Book 27.99 *(978-1-4677-9317-9(5))* Lerner Publishing Group.

—Upside down Babies. Reynolds, Adrian, illus. 2014. (ENG.). 32p. (J). (gr. -1-3). 16.95 *(978-1-4677-3424-0(1)*, 2e46e88c-1ead-4934-b5c4-8599ee20187c) Lerner Publishing Group.

Wilson, Karma. Mama Always Comes Home. Dyer, Brooke, illus. 2007. (ENG.). 32p. (J). (gr. -1-1). pap. 6.99 *(978-0-06-057507-6(7)*, Harper Trophy) HarperCollins Pubs.

—Mama, Why? Mendez, Simon, illus. 2011. (ENG.). 40p. (J). (gr. -1-2). 16.99 *(978-1-4169-4205-4(X)*, McElderry, Margaret K. Bks.) McElderry, Margaret K. Bks.

Wilson, Sarah. Moms Are the Best! 2014. (Spongebob Squarepants Step into Reading Ser.). lib. bdg. 13.55 *(978-0-606-35203-1(1))* Turtleback.

Wilt, Gerri Ann, et al. My Little One: A Mother's Lullaby. Sargent, Shannon Marie, illus. 2008. (J). *(978-0-87839-299-5(8))* North Star Pr. of St. Cloud.

Winters, Kari-Lynn. On My Walk, 1 vol. Leist, Christina, illus. 2010. (On My ... Ser.: 1). (ENG.). 32p. (J). (gr. -1-k). 16.95 *(978-1-896580-61-6(0))* Tradewind Bks. CAN. Dist: Orca Bk. Pubs. USA.

Wolff, Ashley. Where, Oh Where, Is Baby Bear? Wolff, Ashley, illus. 2017. (Baby Bear Ser.). (ENG., Illus.). 32p. (J). (-3). 18.99 *(978-1-4814-9916-3(5)*, Beach Lane Bks.) Beach Lane Bks.

Wolnik, Charlotte. The Chocolate Chip Ghost. 2008. 40p. pap. 24.95 *(978-1-4241-8896-3(2))* America Star Bks.

Woodson, Jacqueline. Pecan Pie Baby. Blackall, Sophie, illus. (ENG.). 32p. (J). (gr. k-3). 2013. 8.99 *(978-0-14-751128-7(3)*, Puffin Books) 2010. 17.99 *(978-0-399-23987-8(1)*, G.P. Putnam's Sons Books for Young Readers) Penguin Young Readers Group.

Wright, Gina. My Mommy Has Breast Cancer. 2009. 32p. pap. 13.49 *(978-1-4490-2150-4(6))* AuthorHouse.

Wright, Velma. Fuzz, an Impatient Chick. 2010. 12p. 12.68 *(978-1-4269-3430-8(0))* Trafford Publishing.

Yellowknife, Jessica. Spring Break Adventure. 2011. 84p. pap. 11.11 *(978-1-4269-6952-2(X))* Trafford Publishing.

Yolen, Jane & Stemple, Heidi E. Y. You Nest Here with Me. Sweet, Melissa, illus. 2019. 28p. (J). (— 1). bds. 7.99 *(978-1-68437-371-0(9)*, Astra Young Readers) Astra Publishing Hse.

Yoshitake, Shinsuke. Still Stuck. 2017. (ENG., Illus.). 32p. (J). (gr. -1-2). 12.95 *(978-1-4197-2699-6(4)*, 1192801, Abrams Bks. for Young Readers) Abrams, Inc.

Young, Michael. Portrait of a Mother. 2011. 16p. pap. 2.99 *(978-1-59955-810-3(6)*, Bonneville Bks.) Cedar Fort, Inc./CFI Distribution.

MOTHER GOOSE

Greenaway, Kate. Mother Goose Coloring Book. Perkins, Nancy, illus. 2013. (Dover Classic Stories Coloring Book Ser.). (ENG.). 48p. (J). (gr. -1-8). pap. 4.99 *(978-0-486-22883-9(5)*, 228835) Dover Pubns., Inc.

Hysom, Dennis Joe & Walker, Christine. Wooleycat's Musical Theater. Walker, Christine, illus. 2003. (ENG., Illus.). 32p. (J). (gr. -1-3). 11.95 *(978-1-889910-26-0(0))*; 18.95 *(978-1-889910-25-3(2))* Tortuga Pr.

Provensen, Alice & Provensen, Martin. The Golden Mother Goose. 2017. (Illus.). 72p. (J). (— 1). 16.99 *(978-1-5247-1578-6(6)*, Golden Bks.) Random Hse. Children's Bks.

MOTHER GOOSE—SONGS AND MUSIC

Beall, Pamela Conn & Nipp, Susan Hagen. Wee Sing Mother Goose, 1 vol. Guida, Liisa & Klein, Nancy, illus. 2006. (Wee Sing Ser.). 64p. (J). (gr. -1-2). 10.99 *(978-0-8431-0485-1(6)*, Price Stern Sloan) Penguin Young Readers Group.

MOTHERS

Arzón, Robin. Strong Mama. Sonda, Addy Rivera, illus. 2022. (ENG.). 40p. (J). (gr. -1-3). 17.99 *(978-0-316-29994-7(4))* Little, Brown Bks. for Young Readers.

Ashford, Kathy. Around & Back Around Again: A Metaphor, 1 vol. 2010. 48p. pap. 16.95 *(978-1-4489-5883-2(0))* America Star Bks.

Auld, Mary. Mi Mamá (My Mom), 1 vol. 2004. (Conoce la Familia (Meet the Family) Ser.). (SPA., Illus.). 24p. (gr. k-2). lib. bdg. 24.67 *(978-0-8368-3932-6(3)*, 09a7108c-fe6c-4f22-aac9-75bde0928475, Gareth Stevens Learning Library) Stevens, Gareth Publishing LLLP.

—My Mom, 1 vol. 2004. (Meet the Family Ser.). (ENG., Illus.). 24p. (gr. k-2). lib. bdg. 24.67 *(978-0-8368-3927-2(7)*, a2e78d11-e383-4d61-a7f9-e07ebf756630, Gareth Stevens Learning Library) Stevens, Gareth Publishing LLLP.

Barbara, Diane & Donnier, Christine. Mom & Me. 2004. (ENG., Illus.). 48p. (J). (gr. -1-3). 16.95 *(978-0-8109-4820-4(6))* Abrams, Inc.

Bedford, David & Worthington, Leonie. Mums. 2007. (Illus.). 16p. *(978-1-921049-78-1(2))* Little Hare Bks. AUS. Dist: HarperCollins Pubs. Australia.

Campbell, Carol P. & Orr, Tamra. Frequently Asked Questions about Teen Pregnancy, 1 vol. 2011. (FAQ: Teen Life Ser.). (ENG.). 64p. (J). (gr. 5-6). lib. bdg. 37.13 *(978-1-4488-4627-6(7)*,

9a2b4b13-04ad-47a8-ba3e-25c407cf0820) Rosen Publishing Group, Inc., The.

Catt, Thessaly. My Mom, 1 vol. 2010. (My Family Ser.). (ENG.). 24p. (J). (gr. 1-2). pap. 9.25 *(978-1-4488-1490-9(1),* f4a76970-8e18-4a92-b1e7-c65748eacfd3); lib. bdg. 26.27 *(978-1-4488-1462-6(6),* 29fc2fb0-2a8a-4acf-801b-9810b42b3ca1) Rosen Publishing Group, Inc., The. (PowerKids Pr.).

—My Mom(Mi Mamá), 1 vol. 2010. (My Family / Mi Familia Ser.). (SPA & ENG.). 24p. (gr. 1-2). lib. bdg. 26.27 *(978-1-4488-0717-8(4),* 5c24e066-7844-428e-aa3f-9fe9ce6fadbc) Rosen Publishing Group, Inc., The.

Edgehill, S. D. To Honor Thy Mother. 2003. 380p. (YA). mass mkt. 21.95 *(978-0-9744027-0-3(2))* Cahill Publishing.

Gamble, Adam & Jasper, Mark. Good Night Mommy. Kelly, Cooper, illus. 2015. (Good Night Our World Ser.). (ENG.). 20p. (J). (— 1). bds. 9.95 *(978-1-60219-230-0(8))* Good Night Bks.

Greven, Alec. How to Talk to Moms. Acedera, Kei, illus. 2009. (ENG.). 48p. (J). (gr. 1-5). 9.99 *(978-0-06-171001-8(6),* HarperCollins) HarperCollins Pubs.

Halteman, Laverne K. Mommy Goes to Heaven. 2003. (Illus.). (J). *(978-0-87813-612-4(6))* Christian Light Pubns., Inc.

Hammerslough, Jane. Everything You Need to Know about Teen Motherhood. 2009. (Need to Know Library). 64p. (gr. 5-5). 58.50 *(978-1-60854-090-7(1))* Rosen Publishing Group, Inc., The.

Jeffries, Joyce. I Learn from My Mom, 1 vol. 2016. (Things I Learn Ser.). (ENG., Illus.). 24p. (J). (gr. 1-1). pap. 9.25 *(978-1-4994-2371-6(3),* 59129858-e04c-4450-8154-377efad71bd5, PowerKids Pr.) Rosen Publishing Group, Inc., The.

Moore, M. Meet My Mom: Learning the M Sound. 2009. (PowerPhonics Ser.). 24p. (gr. 1-1). 39.90 *(978-1-60851-459-5(5),* PowerKids Pr.) Rosen Publishing Group, Inc., The.

Mothers. 7.50 *(978-0-8054-5972-2(3))* B&H Publishing Group.

Newkirk, Stephanie. I'm So Madd!!! 2009. 28p. pap. 12.99 *(978-1-4389-6022-7(0))* AuthorHouse.

Nilsen, Anna. My Mum's Best. Dodd, Emma, illus. 2011. 24p. bds. *(978-1-84089-679-4(5))* Zero to Ten, Ltd.

Parr, todd. The Mommy Book. 2016. (ENG., Illus.). 20p. (J). (gr. -1 — 1). bds. 7.99 *(978-0-316-33774-8(9))* Little, Brown Bks. for Young Readers.

Poole, H. W. Teen Parents, Vol. 12. 2016. (Families Today Ser.). (Illus.). 48p. (J). (gr. 5). 20.95 *(978-1-4222-3624-6(2))* Mason Crest.

Raatma, Lucia. Mothers Are Part of a Family. 2017. (Our Families Ser.). (ENG., Illus.). 24p. (J). (gr. 1-2). lib. bdg. 22.65 *(978-1-5157-7465-5(1),* 135810, Capstone Pr.) Capstone.

Riehle, Mary Ann McCabe. M Is for Mom: A Child's Alphabet. Ellison, Chris, illus. 2009. (ENG.). 32p. (J). (gr. 1-4). 17.95 *(978-1-58536-458-9(4),* 202181) Sleeping Bear Pr.

Schaefer, Lola M. Mothers: Revised Edition. rev. ed. 2008. (Families Ser.). (ENG., Illus.). 24p. (J). (gr. -1-2). per. 6.29 *(978-1-4296-1756-7(X),* 94803) Capstone.

Sourcebooks. To the Best Mom Ever! 2016. (Sealed with a Kiss Ser.: 0). (ENG.). 48p. (J). (gr. 1-4). pap. 7.99 *(978-1-4926-3329-7(1))* Sourcebooks, Inc.

Stewart, Kelsey. The Best for You. 2009. 24p. pap. 12.49 *(978-1-4490-0832-1(1))* AuthorHouse.

Stewart, Sheila. Sometimes My Mom Drinks Too Much. (Kids Have Troubles Too Ser.). (Illus.). 48p. (YA). (gr. 5-18). 2010. lib. bdg. 19.95 *(978-1-4222-1704-7(3))* 2009. pap. 7.95 *(978-1-4222-1917-1(8))* Mason Crest.

Wang, Holman. Great Job, Mom! 2019. (Great Job Ser.: 2). (Illus.). 32p. (J). (gr. -1-2). 16.99 *(978-0-7352-6408-3(2),* Tundra Bks.) Tundra Bks. CAN. Dist: Penguin Random Hse. LLC.

MOTHERS—FICTION

Abbott, Tony. Knights of the Ruby Wand, 36. Fitzgerald, Royce & Jessell, Tim, illus. 2010. (Secrets of Droon Ser.: 36). (ENG.). 128p. (J). (gr. 2-4). 17.44 *(978-0-545-09886-1(6))* Scholastic, Inc.

Andreae, Giles. I Love My Mommy. Dodd, Emma, illus. 2013. (ENG.). 26p. (J). (gr. -1 — 1). bds. 7.99 *(978-1-4231-6825-6(9))* Hyperion Pr.

Armstrong, Rachel. Fair Folk in Knob's End. 2013. 274p. pap. 14.99 *(978-1-60820-851-7(6))* MLR Pr., LLC.

Arno, Ronni. Dear Poppy. 2016. (Mix Ser.). (ENG., Illus.). 256p. (J). (gr. 4-8). 17.99 *(978-1-4814-3760-8(7),* Simon & Schuster/Paula Wiseman Bks.) Simon & Schuster/Paula Wiseman Bks.

Balian, Lorna. Mother's Mother's Day, 1 vol. 2004. (ENG., Illus.). 32p. (J). 8.95 *(978-1-932065-39-8(3))* Star Bright Bks., Inc.

Banting, Celia. I Only Said I Didn't Want You Because I Was Terrified. 2006. (I Only Said Ser.: 4). 240p. (YA). pap. 14.99 *(978-0-9786648-3-1(3))* Wighita Pr.

Barbara E. Barber. Saturday at the New You, 1 vol. 2013. (ENG., Illus.). 32p. (J). (gr. 1-4). reprint ed. pap. 11.95 *(978-1-880000-43-4(1),* leelowbooks) Lee & Low Bks., Inc.

Barkow, Henriette. That's My Mum. Brazell, Derek, illus. 2004. 28p. (J). (ENG & YOR.). pap. *(978-1-84444-381-9(7));* (ALB & ENG.). pap. *(978-1-85269-595-8(1))* Mantra Lingua.

Baskin, Nora Raleigh. All We Know of Love. 2008. (ENG., Illus.). 208p. (YA). (gr. 9-12). 16.99 *(978-0-7636-3623-4(1))* Candlewick Pr.

Bauer, Marion Dane. My Mother Is Mine. Elwell, Peter, illus. 2009. (Classic Board Bks.). (ENG.). 36p. (J). (gr. -1-k). bds. 8.99 *(978-1-4169-6090-4(2),* Little Simon) Little Simon.

—My Mother Is Mine. Elwell, Peter, illus. 2004. (ENG.). 40p. (J). (gr. -1-k). reprint ed. 7.99 *(978-0-689-86695-1(X),* Simon & Schuster Bks. For Young Readers) Simon & Schuster Bks. For Young Readers.

Beasley, Kate. Gertie's Leap to Greatness. 2018. (ENG., Illus.). 272p. (J). pap. 12.99 *(978-1-250-14374-7(8),* 900180551) Square Fish.

Beha, Eileen. The Secrets of Eastcliff-By-the-Sea: The Story of Annaliese Easterling & Throckmorton, Her Simply Remarkable Sock Monkey. Wright, Sarah Jane, illus. 2015. (ENG.). 288p. (J). (gr. 3-7). pap. 8.99 *(978-1-4424-9841-9(2),* Beach Lane Bks.) Beach Lane Bks.

Berenstain, Stan & Berenstain, Jan. The Berenstain Bears & the Mama's Day Surprise. 2004. (First Time Books(R) Ser.). (Illus.). 32p. (J). (gr. -1-2). pap. 4.99 *(978-0-375-81132-6(X),* Random Hse. Bks. for Young Readers) Random Hse. Children's Bks.

A Big Surprise for Mom. 2005. (J). per. *(978-0-9765950-1-4(X))* Carlson, Debra R.

Blackmore, Charlotte Lozano. Jeanette Is Called Retard, 1 vol. Francis, Amber Rose, illus. 2010. 34p. 24.95 *(978-1-4489-4096-7(6))* PublishAmerica, Inc.

Bonnell, Kris. Mother Animals. 2007. (J). pap. 5.95 *(978-1-933727-49-3(7))* Reading Reading Bks., LLC.

Brez, Lisa. Hickerdoodle Gets Lost. l.t. ed. 2003. (Illus.). 32p. (J). per. 6.99 *(978-0-9743758-4-7(5))* Red Engine Pr.

Brown, Rena Cherry. Otter Lee Brave, 1 vol. 2012. (ENG., Illus.). 48p. (J). (gr. -1-3). 16.99 *(978-0-7643-4155-7(3),* 4632) Schiffer Publishing, Ltd.

Browne, Anthony. My Mom. Browne, Anthony, illus. 2009. (ENG., Illus.). 32p. (J). (gr. k-3). pap. 8.99 *(978-0-374-40026-2(1),* 900058756) Square Fish.

Bruno, Cristina. The Mother Store. 2009. 52p. pap. 30.00 *(978-1-4389-2875-3(0))* AuthorHouse.

Buller, Jon. I Love You, Good Night. 2006. (ENG., Illus.). 28p. (J). (gr. -1 — 1). bds. 8.99 *(978-0-689-86212-0(1),* Little Simon) Little Simon.

Burns, Laura J. & Metz, Melinda. Crave, 1. 2010. (ENG.). 288p. (YA). (gr. 9-12). pap. 9.99 *(978-1-4424-0816-6(2))* Simon & Schuster, Inc.

Callen, Sharon. Happy Faces Leave Home, 1 vol. rev. ed. 2013. (Literary Text Ser.). (ENG., Illus.). 28p. (gr. 2-3). pap. 9.99 *(978-1-4333-5560-8(4))* Teacher Created Materials, Inc.

Cameron, Kristy. The Adventures of Herb the Wild Turkey - Herb Goes Camping. Shickle, Ian, illus. 2012. 38p. pap. *(978-0-9859790-0-3(3))* LP Publishing.

Carey Nevin, Judy. What Mommies Like. Six, Stephanie, illus. 2018. (ENG.). 32p. (J). (gr. -1-3). 16.99 *(978-1-4998-0528-4(4))* Little Bee Books Inc.

Carlson, Nancy. Poor Carl. Carlson, Nancy, illus. 2012. (Nancy Carlson Picture Bks.). (Illus.). 32p. (J). (gr. k-2). 56.72 *(978-0-7613-9305-4(6),* Carolrhoda Bks.) Lerner Publishing Group.

Carpenter, Angie. Digewi Deer: The Tale of a Blind Deer. Berner Coble, Lynn, ed. 2013. 82p. (J). pap. 8.99 *(978-0-9846724-3-1(5))* Paws and Claws Publishing, LLC.

Casey, Dawn. The Children of Lir: A Celtic Legend. Mayo, Diana, illus. 2004. 32p. (J). pap. *(978-1-85269-818-8(7));* pap. *(978-1-85269-823-2(3));* pap. *(978-1-85269-838-6(1));* pap. *(978-1-85269-828-7(4));* (PAN.). pap. *(978-1-85269-843-0(8));* pap. *(978-1-85269-848-5(9));* pap. *(978-1-85269-853-9(5));* pap. *(978-1-85269-858-4(6));* pap. *(978-1-85269-897-3(7));* pap. *(978-1-85269-892-8(6));* pap. *(978-1-85269-887-4(X));* pap. *(978-1-85269-878-2(0));* pap. *(978-1-85269-873-7(X));* (ARA.). pap. *(978-1-85269-872-0(1));* pap. *(978-1-85269-868-3(3));* pap. *(978-1-85269-867-6(5));* pap. *(978-1-85269-863-8(2))* Mantra Lingua.

Cebulski, Megan Elizabeth. The Brave Little Butterfly. 2008. 32p. pap. 24.95 *(978-1-60474-739-3(0))* America Star Bks.

Celcer, Iréné. George & Will Have a Baby: The Gift of Family. Gatto, Horacio, illus. 2018. (J). pap. *(978-1-938313-24-0(0))* Graphite Pr.

Celcer, Irene. The Gift of Surrogacy. Gatto, Horacio, illus. 2007. (Hope & Will Have a Baby Ser.). 32p. (J). (gr. k-3). pap. 19.95 *(978-0-9755810-4-9(X),* 9780975581049) Graphite Pr.

Chambers, Pamela G. My Mommy's Getting Married. Stewart, Muriel, illus. 2009. 32p. (gr. -1-3). 17.95 *(978-0-9799487-0-1(3))* Infinity Publishing Co.

Chang, Victoria. Is Mommy? Frazee, Marla, illus. 2015. (ENG.). 40p. (J). (gr. -1-k). 15.99 *(978-1-4814-0292-7(7),* Beach Lane Bks.) Beach Lane Bks.

Cleary, Beverly. Emily's Runaway Imagination. Dockray, Tracy, illus. 2008. (ENG.). 288p. (J). (gr. 3-7). pap. 7.99 *(978-0-380-70923-6(6),* HarperCollins) HarperCollins Pubs.

—Emily's Runaway Imagination. 221p. (J). (gr. 2-4). pap. 4.95 *(978-0-8072-1416-9(7),* Listening Library) Random Hse. Audio Publishing Group.

Clough, Lisa. Country Girl, City Girl. 2009. (ENG.). 192p. (YA). (gr. 7). pap. 12.95 *(978-0-547-22322-3(6),* 1061786, Clarion Bks.) HarperCollins Pubs.

Connor, Leslie. Waiting for Normal. (ENG.). (J). (gr. 5). 2010. 320p. pap. 7.99 *(978-0-06-089090-2(8))* 2008. 304p. 16.99 *(978-0-06-089088-9(6))* HarperCollins Pubs. (Tegen, Katherine Bks).

Cooper, Jennifer. Guardian Angel. 2009. 155p. pap. 12.87 *(978-0-557-09330-4(9))* Lulu Pr., Inc.

Corbett, Sue. 12 Again. 2007. 240p. (J). (gr. 5-18). 6.99 *(978-0-14-240729-5(1),* Puffin Books) Penguin Young Readers Group.

Crayon, Paula. An Angel in My Pocket. 2010. 44p. (J). pap. 17.99 *(978-1-4490-9921-3(1))* AuthorHouse.

Cronin, Doreen. M. O. M. (Mom Operating Manual) Cornell, Laura, illus. 2011. (ENG.). 56p. (J). (gr. -1-3). 16.99 *(978-1-4169-6150-5(X),* Atheneum Bks. for Young Readers) Simon & Schuster Children's Publishing.

Curtis, Christopher Paul. Bucking the Sarge. 2006. (ENG.). 288p. (YA). (gr. 7-7). reprint ed. mass mkt. 8.99 *(978-0-440-41331-8(1),* Laurel Leaf) Random Hse. Children's Bks.

Curtis, Jamie Lee. My Mommy Hung the Moon: A Love Story. Date not set. 32p. (J). (gr. -1-3). pap. 6.99 *(978-0-06-443696-0(9))* HarperCollins Pubs.

—My Mommy Hung the Moon: A Love Story. Cornell, Laura, illus. 2010. (ENG.). 40p. (J). (gr. -1-3). 17.99 *(978-0-06-029016-0(1),* HarperCollins) HarperCollins Pubs.

Cushman, Jean, et al. Little Golden Book Mommy Stories. Wilkin, Eloise & Meisel, Paul, illus. 2015. 80p. (J). (-k). 7.99 *(978-0-385-39273-0(7),* Golden Bks.) Random Hse. Children's Bks.

Dean, James. Rock on, Mom & Dad! Dean, James, illus. 2015. (Pete the Cat (HarperCollins) Ser.). (Illus.). (J). lib. bdg. 17.20 *(978-0-606-36490-4(0))* Turtleback.

Dean, James & Dean, Kimberly. Pete the Cat: Rock on, Mom & Dad! A Father's Day Gift Book from Kids. Dean, James, illus. 2015. (Pete the Cat Ser.). (ENG., Illus.). 24p. (J). (gr. -1-3). pap. 6.99 *(978-0-06-230408-7(9),* HarperFestival) HarperCollins Pubs.

Deem, James M. 3 NBs of Julian Drew. 2004. (ENG.). 208p. (YA). (gr. 7-18). pap. 13.95 *(978-0-618-43907-2(2),* 484394, Clarion Bks.) HarperCollins Pubs.

Dixon, Heather. Entwined. 2012. (ENG.). 480p. (YA). (gr. 8). pap. 10.99 *(978-0-06-200104-7(3),* Greenwillow Bks.) HarperCollins Pubs.

DK. I Love You Little One. 2018. (ENG.). 18p. (J). (— 1). bds. 12.99 *(978-1-4654-8016-3(1),* DK Children) Dorling Kindersley Publishing, Inc.

Dodd, Christina. Back to School Mom, 18 Copies. 2003. mass mkt. 128.88 *(978-0-06-056267-0(6))* HarperCollins Pubs.

Dorsey, Angela & Miller, Marina. Sun Chaser. 2012. 112p. pap. *(978-1-927100-21-9(6))* Enchanted Pony Bks.

Downing, Julie. Where Is My Mommy? Downing, Julie, illus. 2003. (ENG., Illus.). 32p. (J). (gr. -1-18). 15.99 *(978-0-688-17824-6(3))* HarperCollins Pubs.

Doyle, Roddy. Her Mother's Face. Blackwood, Freya, illus. 2008. (J). pap. *(978-0-439-81502-4(9),* Levine, Arthur A. Bks.) Scholastic, Inc.

Dufresne, Michèle. Mom Dresses Up. 2003. (Mom & Dad Ser.). (J). pap. 7.33 *(978-1-58453-254-5(8))* Pioneer Valley Bks.

Dukes, Alicia. Ms. Mabel's Fables. 2010. 94p. pap. 42.20 *(978-0-557-31374-7(0))* Lulu Pr., Inc.

Duncan, Alice Faye. Honey Baby Sugar Child. Keeter, Susan, illus. 2005. (ENG.). 32p. (J). (gr. -1-1). 19.99 *(978-0-689-84678-6(9),* Simon & Schuster Bks. For Young Readers) Simon & Schuster Bks. For Young Readers.

Dunn, Pintip. The Darkest Lie. 2016. viii, 292p. (YA). *(978-1-5182-2703-5(1),* Kensington Bks.) Kensington Publishing Corp.

Dyan, Penelope. Baylee's Giraffes! Sometimes Only a Giraffe Will Do. Dyan, Penelope, illus. 2013. (Illus.). 34p. pap. 11.95 *(978-1-61477-085-5(9))* Bellissima Publishing, LLC.

Eastman, P. D. Are You My Mother? 2015. (Big Bright & Early Board Book Ser.). (ENG., Illus.). 24p. (J). (— 1). bds. 7.99 *(978-0-553-49680-2(8),* Random Hse. Bks. for Young Readers) Random Hse. Children's Bks.

—Are You My Mother?/¿Eres Tú Mi Mamá? (Bilingual Edition) 2016. (SPA., Illus.). 72p. (J). (gr. 1-4). 17.99 *(978-0-553-53990-5(6),* Random Hse. Bks. for Young Readers) Random Hse. Children's Bks.

—¿Eres Tú Mi Mamá? (Are You My Mother? Spanish Edition) 2016. (Beginner Books(R) Ser.). (SPA., Illus.). 72p. (J). (gr. -1-2). 9.99 *(978-0-553-53989-9(2),* Random Hse. Bks. for Young Readers) Random Hse. Children's Bks.

Edge, Christopher. The Many Worlds of Albie Bright. 2019. (ENG.). 192p. (J). (gr. 4-7). 6.99 *(978-1-5247-1360-7(0),* Yearling) Random Hse. Children's Bks.

Erhard, Lorie. Mama's Many Hats. Kalis, Jennifer, illus. 2014. (ENG.). 32p. (J). 18.99 *(978-0-9914701-4-3(1))* Bumble Bee Bks.

Evans, Edie. I Love You, Mommy! Demmer, Melanie, illus. 2019. (Little Golden Book Ser.). 16p. (J). (-k). 4.99 *(978-1-9848-5257-1(4),* Golden Bks.) Random Hse. Children's Bks.

Evans, Stephanie. Steven James: I Just Can't Pay Attention. 2011. 28p. 12.03 *(978-1-4567-2707-9(9))* AuthorHouse.

Finley, Martha. Elsie's Motherhood. 2006. 29.95 *(978-1-4218-2995-1(9));* pap. 14.95 *(978-1-4218-3095-7(7))* 1st World Publishing, Inc.

—Elsie's Motherhood. 2018. (ENG., Illus.). 252p. (YA). (gr. 7-12). pap. *(978-93-5297-358-3(5))* Alpha Editions.

—Elsie's Motherhood. 2017. (ENG., Illus.). (J). 25.95 *(978-1-374-95817-3(4))* Capital Communications, Inc.

—Elsie's Motherhood, Vol. 5. 320p. (gr. 7-12). pap. 5.95 *(978-1-58182-068-3(2),* Cumberland Hse.) Sourcebooks, Inc.

Flaherty, Kathleen Marion. An Octopus Named Mom. Donehey, Jennifer Caulfield, illus. 2012. (ENG.). 32p. (J). 16.95 *(978-0-9767276-8-2(4))* Three Bean Pr.

The Flower Pot Bunnies Return. 2006. (J). *(978-0-9755390-2-6(7))* Fifth Ave Pr.

Fontinalis. The Far Shore. 2011. 76p. pap. 6.99 *(978-1-61667-309-3(5))* Raider Publishing International.

Frantz, Donna. Silly Gilly Gil - Gay L-U-V. Evans, Gabriel, illus. 2013. 30p. pap. *(978-1-921883-38-5(3),* MBS Pr.) Pick-a-Woo Woo Pubs.

Fruisen, Catherine Myler. My Mother's Pearls. 2005. (Illus.). 32p. (J). pap. 5.95 *(978-1-59572-005-4(7))* Star Bright Bks., Inc.

Fusco, Kimberly Newton. Tending to Grace. 2005. 175p. (gr. 7-12). 16.50 *(978-0-7569-5478-9(9))* Perfection Learning Corp.

Gabriel, Andrea. My Favorite Bear. Gabriel, Andrea, illus. 2004. (Illus.). 32p. (J). (-k). pap. 7.95 *(978-1-58089-039-7(3))* Charlesbridge Publishing, Inc.

Gantos, Jack. The Love Curse of the Rumbaughs. 2008. (ENG.). 192p. (YA). (gr. 9-12). pap. 15.99 *(978-0-312-38052-6(6),* 900050683) Square Fish.

Garner, Em. Contaminated. 2014. (Contaminated Ser.). (ENG.). 336p. (YA). (gr. 7-12). pap. 9.99 *(978-1-60684-542-4(X),* 2c54e8bc-3921-4e4c-83a2-24e18c5d6d0c, Carolrhoda Lab™) Lerner Publishing Group.

Gay, Michel. El Cochecito. 2003. (SPA.). 68p. *(978-84-8470-084-5(4))* Corimbo, Editorial S.L.

George, Mindy Lee. These Hands. Hagan, Donell, illus. 2013. 30p. pap. *(978-0-9878208-4-6(2))* Catching Rainbows.

Gilliland, Raquel Vasquez. Sia Martinez & the Moonlit Beginning of Everything. 2020. (ENG., Illus.). 432p. (YA). (gr. 7). 19.99 *(978-1-5344-4863-6(2),* Simon Pulse) Simon Pulse.

Glaser, P. H. Chrystallia & the Source of Light. 2011. (Illus.). 196p. (J). 18.99 *(978-1-60832-232-9(7))* Greenleaf Book Group.

Glines, Abbi. After the Game. 2018. (Field Party Ser.). (ENG., Illus.). 368p. (YA). (gr. 9). pap. 12.99 *(978-1-4814-3892-6(1),* Simon Pulse) Simon Pulse.

—After the Game: A Field Party Novel. 2017. (YA). *(978-1-5344-0168-6(7),* Simon Pulse) Simon Pulse.

Graves, Kimberlee. Mom Can Fix Anything. 2017. (Learn-To-Read Ser.). (ENG., Illus.). (J). (gr. -1-2). pap. 3.49 *(978-1-68310-187-1(1))* Pacific Learning, Inc.

Greban, Quentin. Mommy, I Love You. 2007. (ENG., Illus.). 32p. (J). (gr. -1-3). 9.95 *(978-1-59687-184-7(9))* IBks., Inc.

Gutman, Anne & Hallensleben, Georg. Mommy Hugs. 2003. (DaddyMommy Ser.). (ENG., Illus.). 14p. (J). (gr. -1-7). bds. 5.99 *(978-0-8118-3916-7(8))* Chronicle Bks. LLC.

Haddix, Margaret Peterson. Escape from Memory. 2012. (ENG.). 272p. (YA). (gr. 7). pap. 8.99 *(978-1-4424-4602-1(1),* Simon & Schuster Bks. For Young Readers) Simon & Schuster Bks. For Young Readers.

—Escape from Memory. 2003. (ENG., Illus.). 224p. (YA). (gr. 7). 17.99 *(978-0-689-85421-7(8))* Simon & Schuster, Inc.

—Takeoffs & Landings. 2004. 201p. (gr. 5-9). 17.00 *(978-0-7569-4255-7(1))* Perfection Learning Corp.

Hallinan, P. K. We're Very Good Friends, My Mother & I. 24p. (J). 7.95 *(978-0-8249-5373-7(8));* 5.95 *(978-0-8249-5374-4(6))* Worthy Publishing. (Ideals Pubns.).

Hardin, Melinda. Hero Mom, 0 vols. Langdo, Bryan, illus. 2013. (ENG.). 24p. (J). (gr. -1-3). 12.99 *(978-1-4778-1645-5(3),* 9781477816455, Two Lions) Amazon Publishing.

Harding, Susan. Here I Am! 2008. 20p. pap. 24.95 *(978-1-60474-093-6(0))* America Star Bks.

Harrington, Claudia. My Single Mom. Persico, Zoe, illus. 2017. (My Family Set 2 Ser.). (ENG.). 32p. (J). (gr. -1-4). lib. bdg. 32.79 *(978-1-5321-3020-5(1),* 25542, Looking Glass Library) Magic Wagon.

—My Two Moms, 1 vol. Persico, Zoe, illus. 2015. (My Family Ser.). (ENG.). 32p. (J). (gr. -1-3). 32.79 *(978-1-62402-110-7(7),* 18162, Looking Glass Library) Magic Wagon.

Harris, Kandi. Princess, the Future Queen: A Mother's Guidance. Rippon, Jor-El, illus. l.t. ed. 2006. 32p. (J). bds. 12.99 *(978-0-9770331-1-9(2))* Harris, K Publishing, Inc.

Harvey, Jacqueline. The Sound of the Sea. Crossett, Warren, illus. 2005. 32p. (J). *(978-0-7344-0742-9(4),* Lothian Children's Bks.) Hachette Australia.

Hello!Lucky & Moyle, Sabrina. My Mom Is Magical! (a Hello!Lucky Book) Moyle, Eunice, illus. 2018. (Hello!Lucky Book Ser.). (ENG.). 24p. (J). (gr. -1 — 1). bds. 7.99 *(978-1-4197-2962-1(4),* 1212110) Abrams, Inc.

Hill, Nancy. If Body Parts Could Grow on Trees. 2010. 32p. pap. 12.99 *(978-1-4520-0661-1(X))* AuthorHouse.

Hill, Tara Theresa. What Can You Do with Two Mommies? 2012. (ENG.). 37p. 18.00 *(978-1-105-50649-9(5))* Lulu Pr., Inc.

Hodgman, Ann. That's My Mommy! Logan, Laura, illus. 2013. (ENG.). 22p. bds. *(978-1-58925-645-3(X))* Tiger Tales.

Hodkin, Faith. What Was My Mother Thinking? Militello, Joy, illus. 2013. (J). 22.95 *(978-1-933420-02-8(2))* Ravenwood Studios.

Hopkins, Ellen. Fallout. (Crank Trilogy Ser.). (ENG., (YA). (gr. 9). 2013. Illus.). 720p. pap. 14.99 *(978-1-4424-7180-1(8))* 2010. 672p. 18.99 *(978-1-4169-5009-7(5))* McElderry, Margaret K. Bks. (McElderry, Margaret K. Bks.).

Hutchins, Pat. Where, Oh Where, Is Rosie's Chick? Hutchins, Pat, illus. 2016. (ENG., Illus.). 32p. (J). (gr. -1-3). 17.99 *(978-1-4814-6071-2(4),* Simon & Schuster Bks. For Young Readers) Simon & Schuster Bks. For Young Readers.

Jessica Hoel. Adam B Brave. Samantha Nowak, illus. 2009. 20p. pap. 12.49 *(978-1-4389-3240-8(5))* AuthorHouse.

Jiménez Martínez, Ángeles. Macarena, la anguila. 2004. (SPA., Illus.). 26p. pap. 8.00 *(978-84-931888-0-1(8))* Editorial Brief ESP. Dist: Independent Pubs. Group.

Johansson, Cecilia, illus. Just Like Mommy. 2006. (ENG.). 16p. (J). (gr. -1 — 1). bds. 7.99 *(978-1-4169-1218-7(5),* Little Simon) Little Simon.

Johnson, Gerald J. J. Betty, the Chubby Butterfly. Miltenberger, Jeri and Dave, illus. 2011. 24p. pap. 24.95 *(978-1-4489-3990-9(9))* America Star Bks.

Jones, Kelly. Mama. Kewley, Ken, illus. 2004. 32p. (J). *(978-0-9745930-0-5(1))* Stunt Publishing.

Jordan, Deloris. Did I Tell You I Love You Today? Evans, Shane W., illus. 2004. (ENG.). 32p. (J). (gr. -1-3). 19.99 *(978-0-689-85271-8(1),* Simon & Schuster/Paula Wiseman Bks.) Simon & Schuster/Paula Wiseman Bks.

Kalman, Maira & Kalman, Alex. Sara Berman's Closet. 2018. (ENG., Illus.). 128p. 27.99 *(978-0-06-284640-2(X),* Harper) HarperCollins Pubs.

Kane, Kimberly Brougham. Every Time You Call Me Mommy-an Adoption Blessing. 2007. 32p. 16.50 *(978-0-615-17610-9(0))* Kane, Kimberly Brougham.

Kasza, Keiko. A Mother for Choco. 2003. (ENG.). 30p. (J). (gr. -1 — 1). bds. 7.99 *(978-0-399-24191-8(4),* G.P. Putnam's Sons Books for Young Readers) Penguin Young Readers Group.

Kent, Nicola. The Strongest Mom. Kent, Nicola, illus. 2018. (ENG., Illus.). 32p. (J). (gr. -1-3). 17.99 *(978-0-8075-7616-8(6),* 807576166) Whitman, Albert & Co.

Kephart, Beth. Nothing but Ghosts. 2009. (ENG.). 288p. (J). (gr. 8-18). 17.99 *(978-0-06-166796-1(X),* HarperTeen) HarperCollins Pubs.

Kilgore, Mary & Kilgore, Mitchell. Where Is My Mommy? Coping When a Parent Leaves (and Doesn't Come Back) Pillo, Cary, illus. 2010. (ENG.). 32p. (J). (gr. -1-4). pap. 14.99 *(978-1-884734-46-5(4))* Parenting Pr., Inc.

Kormos, Lawrence A. There Is A Place I Go. 2007. (Illus.). (J). *(978-1-55452-245-3(5))* Essence Publishing.

—What Is Love Mama? 2007. (Illus.). (J). *(978-1-55452-190-6(4))* Essence Publishing.

Krivinskas, Carol Italiano. Barnyard Babies to the Rescue. 2008. 20p. pap. 13.95 *(978-1-4327-2183-1(6))* Outskirts Pr., Inc.

Lake, Mary. Piccolo. Collier, Kevin Scott, illus. 2007. 25p. (J). (gr. -1-3). 14.99 *(978-1-59879-358-1(6))* Lifevest Publishing, Inc.

Lasky, Kathryn. Before I Was Your Mother. Pham, LeUyen, illus. 2007. (ENG.). 40p. (J). (gr. k-2). 18.69 *(978-0-15-201464-3(0))* Houghton Mifflin Harcourt Publishing Co.

—Tangled in Time: the Portal. 2019. (ENG.). (J). (gr. 3-7). 400p. pap. 6.99 *(978-0-06-269326-6(3));* (Illus.). 384p. 16.99 *(978-0-06-269325-9(5))* HarperCollins Pubs. (HarperCollins).

Lee, Marie Myung-Ok. Somebody's Daughter: A Novel. 2006. 280p. per. 21.00 *(978-0-8070-8389-5(5),* Beacon Pr.) Beacon Pr.

Leeson, Christine. Just for You! Ellis, Andy, illus. 2008. (Tiger Tales Ser.). 24p. (J). (gr. -1-2). pap. 6.95 *(978-1-58925-408-4(2))* Tiger Tales.

Leicht, Martin & Neal, Isla. The World Forgot. 2015. 279p. (YA). pap. *(978-1-4424-2967-3(4),* Simon & Schuster Bks. For Young Readers) Simon & Schuster Bks. For Young Readers.

M
N
O

Lewis, Carolyn. Hairy Beary Book Two Bk. 2,Vol. 2: The Great Waterfall, 3 bks. DeVince, James, ed. Porcheron, Tammy, illus. 2003. (Hairy Beary Ser.: 2). 42p. (J). pap. 9.95 (978-0-9712641-1-3(2)) J M D's Business Services.

Lewis-Long, Carla. Why I'm So Special: A Book about Surrogacy. 2010. 44p. pap. 19.95 (978-1-4389-9656-1(X)) AuthorHouse.

Lewis, Stewart. You Have Seven Messages. 2012. (ENG.). 304p. (YA). (gr. 7). pap. 11.99 (978-0-385-74029-6(8), Ember) Random Hse. Children's Bks.

Liddle, Elizabeth. Pip & the Edge of Heaven. Jones, Lara, illus. 2003. (ENG.). 48p. (J). pap. 6.99 (978-0-7459-4694-8(1), f8e64969-3bf5-47f1-a80a-70891845ad22, Lion Children's) Lion Hudson PLC GBR. Dist: Baker & Taylor Publisher Services (BTPS).

Lindsay, Maud. More Mother Stories. Sanborn, F. C. & Railton, Fanny, illus. 2008. 160p. pap. 9.95 (978-1-59915-168-7(5)) Yesterday's Classics.

Love, Mary Angelean. Mama's House. 2005. (ENG.). 42p. per. 17.99 (978-1-4257-0254-0(6)) Xlibris Corp.

Lowell, Pamela. Returnable Girl, 0 vols. 2012. (ENG.). 240p. (YA). (gr. 7-12). pap. 9.99 (978-0-7614-5592-9(2), 9780761455929, Skyscape) Amazon Publishing.

—Returnable Girl. 2006. 229p. (YA). (gr. 8-12). 16.99 (978-0-7614-5317-8(2)) Marshall Cavendish Corp.

Lyons, Belinda. Meet My Air Force Mommy. 2008. 20p. pap. 24.95 (978-1-60563-673-3(8)) America Star Bks.

Mac, Carrie. Charmed, 1 vol. 2004. (Orca Soundings Ser.). (ENG.). 128p. (YA). (gr. 8-12). pap. 9.95 (978-1-55143-321-9(4)) Orca Bk. Pubs. USA.

Maclachlan, Patricia. More Perfect Than the Moon. 2004. (Sarah, Plain & Tall Ser.). 96p. (J). (gr. 3-5). 14.99 (978-0-06-027558-7(8), Cotler, Joanna Books) HarperCollins Pubs.

Magden, Loretta. The Treetop Bird Family. Barringer, J. M., illus. 2007. 28p. (J). 15.95 (978-0-9788771-0-1(1)) Level Green Bks.

Martin, Ann M. Here Today. 2005. 308p. (gr. 5-9). 18.00 (978-0-7569-5104-7(6)) Perfection Learning Corp.

McAllister, Angela. My Mom Has X-Ray Vision. Smith, Alex T., illus. 2011. (ENG.). 32p. (J). (gr. -1-2). 15.95 (978-1-58925-097-0(4)) Tiger Tales.

McCourt, Lisa. I Love You, Stinky Face. Moore, Cyd, illus. (ENG.). 32p. (J). (gr. -1 — 1). 2004. bds. 6.99 (978-0-439-63572-1(1)) 2003. pap. 6.99 (978-0-439-63469-4(5)) Scholastic, Inc.

Mceldowney, Connie. Josiah's Journey. 2009. 34p. pap. 12.99 (978-1-4490-0489-7(X)) AuthorHouse.

McIntosh, Kenneth. The Trickster's Image: Forensic Art. 2009. (J). pap. 24.95 (978-1-4222-1452-7(4)) 2007. (Illus.). 144p. (YA). (gr. 8-12). pap. 9.95 (978-1-4222-0873-1(7)) Mason Crest.

—The Trickster's Image: Forensic Art, 3 vols. Miller, Justin, illus. 2007. (Crime Scene Club Ser.). 144p. (YA). (gr. 9-12). lib. bdg. 24.95 (978-1-4222-0249-4(6)) Mason Crest.

Melmed, Laura Krauss. I Love You As Much... Board Book & Picture Frame. 2003. (Illus.). 22p. (J). (gr. -1-2). 12.99 (978-0-06-008659-6(9), HarperFestival) HarperCollins Pubs.

Messaoudi, Michele. My Mum Is a Wonder. 2016. (ENG., Illus.). 24p. (J). (gr. -1). 8.95 (978-0-86037-298-1(7)) Kube Publishing Ltd. GBR. Dist: Consortium Bk. Sales & Distribution.

Miller, Constances. Mommy Always Comes Back. 2011. 28p. pap. 16.99 (978-1-257-13201-0(6)) Lulu Pr., Inc.

Mogk, Matt. That's Not Your Mommy Anymore: A Zombie Tale. Mulford, Aja, illus. 2011. (ENG.). 32p. pap. 10.00 (978-1-56975-926-4(X)) Ulysses Pr.

Moore, David Barclay. The Stars Beneath Our Feet. Lt. ed. 2018. (ENG.). 340p. 22.99 (978-1-4328-4916-0(6)) Cengage Gale.

—The Stars Beneath Our Feet. 2019. (Penworthy Picks Middle School Ser.). (ENG.). 294p. (J). (gr. 6-8). 20.49 (978-1-64310-932-9(4)) Penworthy Co., LLC, The.

—The Stars Beneath Our Feet. 2019. 304p. (J). (gr. 5). 8.99 (978-1-5247-0127-7(0), Yearling) Random Hse. Children's Bks.

Moore, Karen. Mommy Loves Me. Stanley, Mandy, illus. gif. ed. 2005. 10p. (J). (gr. -1-1). per., bds. 6.99 (978-1-57791-182-1(2)) Brighter Minds Children's Publishing.

Moore, Mel. Mother's Little Helper. 2006. (Illus.). 16p. (J). per. (978-0-9775919-5-4(6)) Carpe Diem Publishing.

Morgan, Sally. Dream Little One, Dream. 2020. 32p. (J). (— 1). 14.99 (978-0-14-350721-5(4), Puffin) Penguin Random Hse. AUS. Dist: Independent Pubs. Group.

Muñoz, Isabel. Just Like Mom. Mazali, Gustavo, illus. 2005. 22p. (J). pap. (978-0-439-78844-1(7)) Scholastic, Inc.

Munsch, Robert. I'm So Embarrassed! 2007. (J). 12.65 (978-0-7569-7624-8(3)) Perfection Learning Corp.

Murphy, Jill. Five Minutes' Peace. Murphy, Jill, illus. 2012. (ENG., Illus.). 24p. (J). (gr. -1 — 1). bds. 8.99 (978-0-399-25707-0(1), G.P. Putnam's Sons Books for Young Readers) Penguin Young Readers Group.

My Big Book of Beginner Books about Me. 2011. (Beginner Books(R) Ser.). (ENG., Illus.). 208p. (J). (gr. -1-2). 16.99 (978-0-307-93183-2(8), Random Hse. Bks. for Young Readers) Random Hse. Children's Bks.

My Stepmother: Individual Title Six-Packs. (gr. -1-2). 27.00 (978-0-7635-9466-4(0)) Rigby Education.

Nellist, Glenys. God Made Mommy Special, 1 vol. Corke, Estelle, illus. 2018. (ENG.). 20p. (J). bds. 9.99 (978-0-310-76233-1(2)) Zonderkidz.

Njenga, Wamoro P. Wow, What a Mama!! Webber, Penny, illus. 2012. 58p. pap. 13.70 (978-0-9787461-2-7(1)) Prop-Abilities Inc.

Old Mother Hubbard: 6 Small Books. (gr. k-2). 23.00 (978-0-7635-8496-2(7)) Rigby Education.

O'Maley, Elizabeth. By Freedom's Light. 2009. 188p. (J). 15.95 (978-0-87195-273-8(4)); pap. 7.95 (978-0-87195-274-5(2)) Indiana Historical Society.

Ortiz, Estrella. A Bailar: Let's Dance. Valdivia, Paloma, illus. 2015. (ENG & SPA.). (J). (978-0-545-85368-2(0)) Scholastic, Inc.

Ostow, Micol & Ostow, David. So Punk Rock: And Other Ways to Disappoint Your Mother. 2009. (ENG., Illus.). 264p. (YA). (gr. 6-8). 26.19 (978-0-7387-1471-4(2), Flux) North Star Editions.

Painter, Grace. The Harry Bear Story. Kacer, Stephen, illus. 2011. 28p. pap. 24.95 (978-1-4626-3327-2(7)) America Star Bks.

Paratore, Coleen Murtagh. Catching the Sun. 2010. (J). (978-0-618-45780-9(1)) Houghton Mifflin Harcourt Publishing Co.

Parker, Amy. A Night Night Prayer, 1 vol. 2014. (Night Night Ser.). (ENG., Illus.). 20p. (J). bds. 9.99 (978-1-4003-2431-6(9), Tommy Nelson) Nelson, Thomas Inc.

Parr, todd. The Mommy Book. 2010. (ENG., Illus.). 32p. (J). (gr. -1-1). pap. 8.99 (978-0-316-07044-7(0)) Little, Brown Bks. for Young Readers.

Paschalis, Juli. Druan O Mam! 2005. (WEL., Illus.). 16p. pap. (978-0-86174-149-6(8)) Drake Educational Assocs. Ltd.

Petty, J. T. & Pope, Paul. The Fall of the House of West. Rubin, David, illus. 2015. 157p. (J). (978-1-5182-0095-3(8), First Second Bks.) Roaring Brook Pr.

Phillips, Dee. Baby's Day. 2009. (Flip Flap Fun Bks.). (ENG.). 5p. (J). (gr. -1-k). bds. 5.95 (978-1-84696-087-1(8), TickTock Books) Octopus Publishing Group GBR. Dist: Independent Pubs. Group.

Podos, Rebecca. The Mystery of Hollow Places. 2016. (ENG.). 304p. (YA). (gr. 9). 17.99 (978-0-06-237334-2(X), Balzer & Bray) HarperCollins Pubs.

Polacco, Patricia. In Our Mothers' House. Polacco, Patricia, illus. 2009. (ENG., Illus.). 48p. (J). (gr. k-3). 18.99 (978-0-399-25076-7(X), Philomel Bks.) Penguin Young Readers Group.

Potter, Ellen. The Kneebone Boy. 2011. (ENG.). 304p. (J). (gr. 4-7). pap. 17.99 (978-0-312-67432-8(5), 900072847) Square Fish.

Pullman, Philip. Sally y el Tigre en el Pozo. 2003. (SPA.). 512p. (YA). 16.95 (978-84-95618-49-8(4), Umbriel) Ediciones Urano S. A. ESP. Dist: Spanish Pubs., LLC.

Ramljak, Marijan. Are You My Mommy? 2009. (Look for Me Bks.). (Illus.). (J). bds. 9.99 (978-1-934650-65-3(X)) Just For Kids Pr., LLC.

Ramos, Angelica. If My Mommy Was an Octopus. 2008. 12p. pap. 24.95 (978-1-60563-821-8(8)) PublishAmerica, Inc.

Reagan, Jean. How to Raise a Mom. 2021. (How to Pic Bks). (ENG., Illus.). 25p. (J). (gr. k-1). 19.96 (978-1-64697-736-9(X)) Penworthy Co., LLC, The.

—How to Raise a Mom. Wildish, Lee, illus. 2017. (How to Ser.). (ENG.). 32p. (J). (gr. -1-3). 17.99 (978-0-553-53829-8(2), Knopf Bks. for Young Readers) Random Hse. Children's Bks.

Reagan, Jean & Wildish, Lee. How to Raise a Mom. (How to Ser.). (ENG.). (J). 2021. 32p. (gr. -1-3). pap. 7.99 (978-0-593-30191-3(9), Dragonfly Bks.) 2019. (Illus.). 26p. (— 1). bds. 8.99 (978-1-9848-4960-1(3), Knopf Bks. for Young Readers) Random Hse. Children's Bks.

Reid-Tulloch, Joseth. Manu's Special Day. 2012. 16p. pap. 14.99 (978-1-4520-9150-1(1)) AuthorHouse.

Reinhardt, Dana. A Brief Chapter in My Impossible Life. 2007. (ENG.). 256p. (YA). (gr. 9-12). pap. 8.99 (978-0-375-84691-5(3), Ember) Random Hse. Children's Bks.

Reynolds Naylor, Phyllis. Alice on Her Way. 2006. (Alice McKinley Ser.: No. 17). 322p. (gr. 9-12). 17.00 (978-0-7569-6909-7(3)) Perfection Learning Corp.

—Polo's Mother. Daniel, Alan, illus. 2006. (Cat Pack Ser.). (ENG.). 176p. (J). (gr. 3-7). pap. 7.99 (978-0-689-87404-8(9), Atheneum Bks. for Young Readers) Simon & Schuster Children's Publishing.

Richter, Bernd & Richter, Susan. The Little Bear Who Didn't Want to Hibernate. Green, Sue, illus. 2003. 42p. pap. 9.95 (978-1-931353-10-6(7)) Saddle Pal Creations, Inc.

Richter, Jutta. The Summer of the Pike. 2006. (ENG., Illus.). 132p. (J). (gr. 8-12). per. 6.95 (978-1-57131-672-1(8)) Milkweed Editions.

—The Summer of the Pike. Brailovsky, Anna, tr. 2006. (ENG., Illus.). 132p. (J). (gr. 2-8). 16.95 (978-1-57131-671-4(X)) Milkweed Editions.

Rigby Education Staff. Old Mother Big Book. (gr. k-2). 21.00 (978-0-7635-2408-1(5)) Rigby Education.

Ringgold, Robyn. My Mom Hugs Trees. Vasudevan, Vidya, illus. 2006. 24p. (J). per. 15.95 (978-0-9785326-1-9(9)) Solar Publishing LLC.

Rinker, Sherri Duskey. Silly Wonderful You. McDonnell, Patrick, illus. 2016. (ENG.). 40p. (J). (gr. -1-3). 17.99 (978-0-06-227105-1(9), Balzer & Bray) HarperCollins Pubs.

Ritchie, Kate. I Just Couldn't Wait to Meet You. Somerville, Hannah, illus. 2015. 32p. (J). (-k). 22.99 (978-0-85798-970-3(7)) Random Hse. Australia AUS. Dist: Independent Pubs. Group.

Roberts, Pauline. Oh! I Wish. Bates, Lindsey E. & Wiggan, Desmond, illus. 2012. 24p. pap. 9.95 (978-0-9848243-3-5(2)) Beckham Pubns. Co.

Ruby, Laura. Play Me. 2009. (ENG.). 336p. (YA). (gr. 9). pap. 9.99 (978-0-06-124329-5(9), HarperTeen) HarperCollins Pubs.

Rushton, Rosie. Just Don't Make a Scene, Mum! 2005. 224p. (J). pap. 5.99 (978-0-7868-5186-7(4)) Hyperion Bks. for Children.

Ryan, Nancy. The Bookworm & His New Book. 2012. 32p. pap. 24.95 (978-1-4626-6492-4(X)) America Star Bks.

Sala, Laurenne. You Made Me a Mother. Glasser, Robin Preiss, illus. 2016. (ENG.). 32p. (J). (gr. -1-3). 16.99 (978-0-06-235886-8(3), HarperCollins) HarperCollins Pubs.

Salan, Felipe Lopez, illus. Jack & the Beanstalk. 2006. (ENG.). 32p. (J). (gr. -1). 15.95 (978-1-933327-11-2(1)) Purple Bear Bks., Inc.

Sanderson, Brandon. The Knights of Crystallia: Alcatraz vs. the Evil Librarians. 2016. (Alcatraz Versus the Evil Librarians Ser.: 3). (ENG., Illus.). 320p. (J). 23.99 (978-0-7653-7898-9(1), 900141065, Starscape) Doherty, Tom Assocs., LLC.

Sautereau, Francois. La Extrana Navidad de Jonas.Tr. of Jonas's Extraordinary Christmas. (SPA.). 92p. (YA). (gr. 5-8). (978-84-279-3163-3(8), NG3472) Noguer y Caralt Editores, S. A. ESP. Dist: Lectorum Pubns., Inc.

Say, Allen. Tree of Cranes: A Christmas Holiday Book for Kids. 2009. (ENG., Illus.). 32p. (J). (gr. -1-3). pap. 7.99 (978-0-547-24830-1(X), 1100745, Clarion Bks.) HarperCollins Pubs.

Schreiber, Hannah & Hartsock, Conner. One in a Buzzillion. Foster, Jack, illus. 2011. 16p. pap. 9.95 (978-1-61633-154-2(2)) Guardian Angel Publishing, Inc.

Scott, Kieran. This Is So Not Happening. 2013. (He's So/She's So Trilogy Ser.). (ENG., Illus.). 320p. (YA). (gr. 7). pap. 9.99 (978-1-4169-9956-0(6), Simon & Schuster Bks. For Young Readers) Simon & Schuster Bks. For Young Readers.

The Secrets of Eastcliff-By-the-Sea: The Story of Annaliese Easterling & Throckmorton, Her Simply Remarkable Sock Monkey. 2014. (ENG., Illus.). 288p. (J). (gr. 3-7). 16.99 (978-1-4424-9640-2(4), Beach Lane Bks.) Beach Lane Bks.

Setterington, Ken. Mom & Mum Are Getting Married!, 1 vol. Priestley, Alice, illus. 2004. (ENG.). 24p. (J). (gr. -1-3). 14.95 (978-1-896764-84-9(3)) Second Story Pr. CAN. Dist: Orca Bk. Pubs. USA.

Shahan, Sherry. Death Mountain, 1 vol. 2007. 208p. (J). (gr. 5-9). pap. 8.95 (978-1-56145-428-0(1)) Peachtree Publishing Co. Inc.

Shanahan, Lisa. My Mom Tarzan. Guthridge, Bettina, illus. 2008. (ENG.). 32p. (J). (gr. -1-3). (978-1-59692-239-6(7)) MacAdam/Cage Publishing, Inc.

Silberberg, Alan. Milo: Sticky Notes & Brain Freeze. Silberberg, Alan, illus. (ENG., Illus.). 288p. (J). (gr. 4-8). 2011. pap. 7.99 (978-1-4169-9431-2(9)) 2010. 15.99 (978-1-4169-9430-5(0)) Simon & Schuster Children's Publishing. (Aladdin).

Simmons, Jane. Come On. 2005. (Daisy Ser.). (Illus.). (Orig.). (J). (ARA, ENG, VIE, CHI & BEN.). 36p. pap. 11.95 (978-1-84059-217-7(6)); (VIE, ENG, CHI, ARA & BEN., 3p. (gr. -1-1). pap. 11.95 (978-1-84059-183-5(8)); (URD, ENG, VIE, CHI & ARA., 36p. (gr. -1-1). pap. 11.95 (978-1-84059-182-8(X)) Milet Publishing.

Sinclair, Gardine. Keira at Stageschool. 2013. 186p. (J). pap. (978-1-78299-387-2(8)) FeedARead.com.

Sitomer, Alan Lawrence. Daddies Do It Different. Carter, Abby, illus. 2012. (ENG.). 40p. (J). (gr. -1 — 1). 16.99 (978-1-4231-3315-5(3)) Little, Brown Bks. for Young Readers.

Skougaard, Shari. Grumpy Goo, I Love You. 2009. 24p. pap. 13.50 (978-1-60860-454-8(3), Eloquent Bks.) Strategic Book Publishing & Rights Agency (SBPRA).

Smith, Roland. Independence Hall. (I, Q Ser.: Bk. 1). (ENG.). 312p. (YA). (gr. 6-8). 2009. illus. 15.95 (978-1-58536-468-8(1), 202188) 2008. pap. 12.99 (978-1-58536-325-4(1), 202289) Sleeping Bear Pr.

Smith, Rosie. My Mom's the Best. Whatley, Bruce, illus. 2013. (J). (978-0-545-60361-4(7)) Scholastic, Inc.

Snead, Kathi. My Mom Has a Job. Christine, Grove, illus. 2004. (J). (978-0-9747385-1-2(4)) City of Manassas Department of Social Services.

Snyder, Laurel. Charlie & Mouse Even Better: Book 3 in the Charlie & Mouse Series (Beginning Chapter Books, Beginning Chapter Book Series, Funny Books for Kids, Kids Book Series), Bk. 3. Hughes, Emily, illus. 2019. (Charlie & Mouse Ser.: 3). (ENG.). 40p. (J). (gr. 1-4). 14.99 (978-1-4521-7065-7(7)) Chronicle Bks. LLC.

Somper, Justin. Vampirates: Black Heart. 2010. (Vampirates Ser.: 4). (ENG.). 512p. (J). (gr. 3-7). pap. 22.99 (978-0-316-02088-6(5)) Little, Brown Bks. for Young Readers.

Sparks, Favre. The Ugly Brown Cup. 2013. 12p. pap. 9.00 (978-1-62516-468-1(8), Strategic Bk. Publishing) Strategic Book Publishing & Rights Agency (SBPRA).

St. Anthony, Jane. Grace above All. 2015. (Fesler-Lampert Minnesota Heritage Ser.). (ENG.). 176p. pap. 9.95 (978-0-8166-9814-1(7)) Univ. of Minnesota Pr.

Stevens, Rob. Would the Real Stanley Carrot Please Stand Up? 2015. (ENG.). 272p. (J). (gr. 4-6). pap. 12.99 (978-1-78344-228-7(X)) Andersen Pr. GBR. Dist: Independent Pubs. Group.

Stewart, Kiera. Fetching. 2012. (ENG.). 304p. (J). (gr. 5-9). pap. 7.99 (978-1-4231-4245-4(4)) Little, Brown Bks. for Young Readers.

Sutton, Michelle. It's Not about Him. 2012. (Second Glances Ser.). (ENG.). 228p. pap. 12.99 (978-0-9838836-0-9(2)) Sword of the Spirit Publishing.

Swanson, A. M. Momma's Biscuits. 2010. 19p. (J). pap. 14.95 (978-1-4327-4699-5(5)) Outskirts Pr., Inc.

Tamaro, Susanna. Castello Dei Sogni Storie Che. pap. 18.95 (978-88-04-50610-2(5)) Mondadori ITA. Dist: Distribooks, Inc.

Tarver, Whitney B. When Mommy Went Back to Work. 2011. 20p. (gr. 1-2). pap. 13.95 (978-1-4269-6833-4(7)) Trafford Publishing.

Tattum, Stephan. Mom. 2005. (J). 4.95 (978-1-59792-006-3(1)) F.A.S.T. Learning LLC.

Tayleur, Karen. Famous (Scholastic) The Awesome Life of David Mortimore Baxter. Garvey, Brann, illus. 2009. (David Mortimore Baxter Ser.). 88p. pap. 0.80 (978-1-4342-2503-0(8), Stone Arch Bks.) Capstone.

Thomson, Sarah L. Mercy: The Last New England Vampire, 1 vol. 2011. (ENG.). 178p. (J). pap. 16.95 (978-1-934031-36-0(4), 53a309a3-c71e-4f20-bdd3-f4fe46e103af) Islandport Pr., Inc.

Toon, Paige. The Accidental Life of Jessie Jefferson. 2016. (Jessie Jefferson Novels Ser.: 1). (ENG.). 336p. (J). pap. 9.99 (978-1-4711-4582-7(4), Simon & Schuster Children's) Simon & Schuster, Ltd. GBR. Dist: Simon & Schuster, Inc.

Trilling, Richard J. Still More Stories of Stephanie & Friends: Volume 3 in the Stephanie Series. 2011. 72p. pap. 21.00 (978-1-61204-546-7(4), Strategic Bk. Publishing) Strategic Book Publishing & Rights Agency (SBPRA).

Tucker, Mark. Super Phil & the Missing Mom. Patete, Christine, illus. 2003. 24p. (J). 4.50 (978-1-882440-01-6(3)) God's World Pubns. Inc.

Valentino, Serena. Mother Knows Best-Villains, Book 5. 2018. (Villains Ser.: 5). (ENG.). 400p. (YA). (gr. 7-12). 17.99 (978-1-368-00902-7(6), Disney Press Books) Disney Publishing Worldwide.

van Gageldonk, Mack. Mommy, Look What I Can Do! 2013. (ENG., Illus.). 14p. (J). (— 1). bds. 10.95 (978-1-60537-169-6(6)) Clavis Publishing.

van Genechten, Guido. Porque Te Quiero Tanto. 2003. (SPA., Illus.). 28p. (J). (gr. k-3). 15.95 (978-970-29-0912-5(0)) Santillana USA Publishing Co., Inc.

Waddell, Martin. Owl Babies. (Illus.). 25p. (J). (ENG, VIE, URD, TUR & CHI.). (978-1-85430-348-6(1), 93442); (CHI, ENG, URD, TUR & VIE., (978-1-85430-343-1(0), 93441) Little Tiger Pr. Group.

Walsh, Joanna. I Love Mom. Abbot, Judi, illus. 2019. (Classic Board Bks.). (ENG.). 28p. (J). (gr. -1 — 1). bds. 7.99 (978-1-5344-3900-9(5), Little Simon) Little Simon.

—I Love Mom. Abbot, Judi, illus. 2014. (ENG.). 32p. (J). (gr. -1-3). 16.99 (978-1-4814-2808-8(X), Simon & Schuster/Paula Wiseman Bks.) Simon & Schuster/Paula Wiseman Bks.

Weatherly, L. A. Watcher. 2012. (Stoke Books Titles Ser.). (ENG.). 64p. (YA). (gr. 8-12). pap. 6.95 (978-1-78112-106-1(0)); lib. bdg. 22.60 (978-1-78112-107-8(9)) Lerner Publishing Group.

Webb, Holly. Rose & the Silver Ghost. 2015. (Rose Ser.: 4). (ENG.). 224p. (J). (gr. 3-6). pap. 10.99 (978-1-4926-0433-4(X)) Sourcebooks, Inc.

Webster, Michelle B. The Christmas of Miracles. 2004. 136p. per. 12.95 (978-0-9753117-0-7(0)) Four Sonkist Angels.

Wells, Rosemary. La Estupenda Mama de Roberta. (SPA.). (J). 16.95 (978-84-372-1612-6(5)) Santillana USA Publishing Co., Inc.

Werlin, Nancy. Impossible. 2011. 11.04 (978-0-7848-3488-6(1), Everbind) Marco Bk. Co.

White, Ruth. Belle Prater's Boy. unabr. ed. 2004. 196p. (J). (gr. 5-9). pap. 38.00 incl. audio (978-0-8072-8682-1(6), YA234SP, Listening Library) Random Hse. Audio Publishing Group.

Willard, Renee. The Mama Who Didn't Work. 2012. 48p. pap. 24.95 (978-1-4626-6930-1(1)) America Star Bks.

Williams-Garcia, Rita. One Crazy Summer. 2009. (KOR.). 272p. (J). pap. (978-89-7199-494-8(0)) Dolbegae Publishing Co.

—One Crazy Summer. 2011. (ENG.). 240p. (J). (gr. 3-7). pap. 9.99 (978-0-06-076090-8(7), Quill Tree Bks.) HarperCollins Pubs.

—One Crazy Summer. (J). 2011. 1.25 (978-1-4498-2201-9(0)) 2010. 69.75 (978-1-4498-2197-5(9)) 2010. 67.75 (978-1-4498-2199-9(5)) Recorded Bks., Inc.

—One Crazy Summer. 2011. (J). lib. bdg. 17.20 (978-0-606-23555-6(8)) Turtleback.

—One Crazy Summer: A Newbery Honor Award Winner. 2010. (ENG.). 224p. (J). (gr. 3-7). 18.99 (978-0-06-076088-5(5)); lib. bdg. 16.89 (978-0-06-076089-2(3)) HarperCollins Pubs. (Quill Tree Bks.).

Williams, Jane. Heeey Ma. Date not set. (Illus.). 40p. (J). (gr. -1-1). pap. 5.99 (978-0-06-443601-4(2)) HarperCollins Pubs.

Williams, Vera B. A Chair for My Mother: A Caldecott Honor Award Winner. Williams, Vera B., illus. 25th anniv. ed. 2007. (ENG., Illus.). 32p. (J). (gr. -1-3). pap. 8.99 (978-0-688-04074-1(8), Greenwillow Bks.) HarperCollins Pubs.

—Un Sillón para Mi Mamá: A Caldecott Honor Award Winner, 1 vol. Williams, Vera B., illus. 25th anniv. ed. 2007. (SPA., Illus.). 32p. (J). (gr. -1-3). reprint ed. pap. 7.99 (978-0-688-13200-2(6), MR5678) HarperCollins Español.

Wilson, Sarah. Moms Are the Best! 2014. (Spongebob Squarepants Step into Reading Ser.). lib. bdg. 13.55 (978-0-606-35203-1(1)) Turtleback.

Wolff, Virginia Euwer. Make Lemonade: A Novel. 2006. (ENG.). 208p. (YA). (gr. 5-9). pap. 9.99 (978-0-8050-8070-4(8), 900038834) Square Fish.

Woodson, J. L. Superwoman's Child: Son of a Single Mother. Malone, Susan Mary, ed. 2005. 204p. pap. 14.95 (978-0-9754130-8-1(2)) Macro Publishing Group.

Yeh, Kat. The Truth about Twinkie Pie. 2015. (ENG.). 352p. (J). E-Book (978-0-316-23671-3(3)) Little Brown & Co.

Young, Andrew. The Giving Mother. 2006. (J). (978-1-933554-36-5(3)) Primordia.

Zhang, Kat. The Memory of Forgotten Things. (ENG.). (J). (gr. 3-7). 2019. 304p. pap. 8.99 (978-1-4814-7866-3(4)) 2018. (Illus.). 288p. 17.99 (978-1-4814-7865-6(6)) Simon & Schuster Children's Publishing. (Aladdin).

MOTHERS—POETRY

Grover, Lorie Ann. Loose Threads. 2007. (ENG.). 304p. (J). (gr. 4-7). pap. 14.95 (978-1-4169-5562-7(3), McElderry, Margaret K. Bks.) McElderry, Margaret K. Bks.

Toison, Hannah, illus. My Mommy Is a Hero. 2018. 32p. 12.99 (978-1-61067-721-9(8)) Kane Miller.

MOTHERS AND DAUGHTERS

Biestman, Margot. Grammie Stories: True Stories about People Living in the Real World. 2009. (YA). audio compact disk (978-0-936865-06-5(7)) Pergot Pr.

Cammarata, Jan. Karli's Kritters. 2009. (ENG.). 24p. pap. 12.00 (978-1-4389-6726-4(8)) AuthorHouse.

Farrin, Patty. The Teacup Café. Davis, Hilary, illus. 2018. (J). 19.95 (978-1-63381-142-3(5)); pap. 15.95 (978-1-63381-143-0(3)) Maine Authors Publishing.

Fowler, Leona. I Don't Want to Be Grumpy Anymore! Martins, Ann-Kathrin & Fowler, Romana, illus. 2011. 19p. (J). 12.95 (978-1-58909-804-6(8)) Bookstand Publishing.

Guipre, Jewel Moreland. Dance with Me. 2012. 32p. 24.95 (978-1-4560-6044-2(9)) America Star Bks.

Harper, Lisa. You Belong to Me Little One. 2011. 16p. (gr. -1). pap. 8.99 (978-1-4634-1371-2(8)) AuthorHouse.

Khalifé, Fatima & Mouazen, Deema. If Your Mom Was.... What Will You Do? 2012. 28p. pap. 19.99 (978-1-4772-6951-0(7)) AuthorHouse.

McDonald, Stacy. Raising Maidens of Virtue: A Study of Feminine Loveliness for Mothers & Daughters. 2004. (Illus.). 226p. (YA). 18.00 (978-0-9743390-1-6(6)) Bks. on the Path.

Noonan, Helen. Mom Let Me Be Me. 2009. 28p. pap. 15.95 (978-1-4389-7414-9(0)) AuthorHouse.

Polacco, Patricia. Betty Doll. 2004. 18.00 (978-0-7569-3208-4(4)) Perfection Learning Corp.

Summer Rogers Martin. Kaylea Grows Up: Mommy & Me Days. Debi Rogers, illus. 2009. 20p. pap. 10.99 (978-1-4389-5908-5(7)) AuthorHouse.

Zweber, Rhonda. Mommy's Hats. 2009. 36p. pap. 18.50 (978-1-60860-204-9(4), Eloquent Bks.) Strategic Book Publishing & Rights Agency (SBPRA).

MOTHERS AND DAUGHTERS—FICTION

Acampora, Paul. Confusion Is Nothing New. 2018. (ENG.). 192p. (J). (gr. 3-7). 16.99 (978-1-338-20999-0(X), Scholastic Pr.) Scholastic, Inc.

Acorn, Alesa. Diary of the Beloved Book One: The Hidden. 2011. 512p. 31.95 *(978-1-4634-0276-1(7))* AuthorHouse.
Adams, Thomas J. My Mommy Went to Sea Today. 2012. 16p. pap. 15.99 *(978-1-4772-8476-6(1))* AuthorHouse.
Adewoyin, Beverly. Inside the Mommie Pond. 2013. (ENG.). 28p. (J). pap. 11.95 *(978-1-4327-9703-4(4))* Outskirts Pr., Inc.
Adhikary, Anita B. My Daughters Are Smart! D Is for Daughters & S Is for Smart. Russo, Blythe, illus. 2014. (ENG.). 24p. (J). (gr. -1-3). 14.95 *(978-1-62086-429-6(0))* Amplify Publishing Group.
The Adventures of Molly. 2004. pap. 13.95 *(978-1-59526-180-9(X))* Aeon Publishing Inc.
Afandalor, Indu. Moooooooom, Do You Love Me? 2012. 28p. pap. 15.50 *(978-1-4670-7132-1(3))* AuthorHouse.
Albert, Melissa. The Hazel Wood. l.t. ed. 2018. (ENG.). 458p. 21.99 *(978-1-4328-4617-6(5))* Cengage Gale.
—The Hazel Wood: A Novel. (Hazel Wood Ser.: 1). (ENG., Illus.). (YA). 2019. 400p. pap. 10.99 *(978-1-250-14793-6(X)*, 900181824) 2018. 368p. 16.99 *(978-1-250-14790-5(5)*, 900181823) Flatiron Bks.
Alegre, Mari. Destiny. 2011. 174p. 29.99 *(978-1-4568-2040-4(0))*; pap. 19.99 *(978-1-4568-2039-8(7))* Xlibris Corp.
Alegria, Malin. Estrella's Quinceañera. (ENG.). (gr. 7-18). 2007. 288p. (YA). pap. 11.99 *(978-0-689-87810-7(9))* 2006. (Illus.). 272p. (J). 15.99 *(978-0-689-87809-1(5))* Simon & Schuster Bks. For Young Readers. (Simon & Schuster Bks. For Young Readers).
Alexander, Jill S. The Sweetheart of Prosper County. 2010. (ENG.). 240p. (YA). (gr. 7-12). pap. 18.99 *(978-0-312-54857-5(5)*, 900055795) Square Fish.
Alexander, R. C. Unfamiliar Magic. 2011. 368p. (J). (gr. 3-7). pap. 8.99 *(978-0-375-85855-0(5)*, Yearling) Random Hse. Children's Bks.
Alexander, William. A Properly Unhaunted Place. Murphy, Kelly, illus. 2017. (ENG.). 192p. (J). (gr. 3-7). 16.99 *(978-1-4814-6915-9(0)*, McElderry, Margaret K. Bks.) McElderry, Margaret K. Bks.
—A Properly Unhaunted Place. 2019. (Penworthy Picks Middle School Ser.). (ENG.). 182p. (J). (gr. 4-5). 18.96 *(978-1-64310-942-8(1))* Penworthy Co., LLC, The.
Alexandria, Shalayne. Nyville High No. 2: Mother May I. 2007. 130p. (YA). pap. 10.00 *(978-0-9786180-4-9(1))* 5 Muses Publishing.
Alfonsi, Alice, adapted by. 'Rents: Lizzie Mcguire. 2005. 134p. (J). lib. bdg. 16.92 *(978-1-4242-0689-6(8))* Fitzgerald Bks.
Allen, Crystal. The Wall of Fame Game. 2018. (Magnificent Mya Tibbs Ser.: 2). (J). lib. bdg. 17.20 *(978-0-606-41018-2(X))* Turtleback.
Almond, David. My Name Is Mina. 2012. (ENG.). 304p. (J). (gr. 6-8). 21.19 *(978-0-375-98964-3(1))*; (gr. 5). 7.99 *(978-0-375-87327-0(9))* Random Hse. Children's Bks. (Yearling).
Alpine, Rachele. You Throw Like a Girl. 2017. (Mix Ser.). (ENG., Illus.). 272p. (J). (gr. 4-8). pap. 8.99 *(978-1-4814-5984-6(8)*, Simon & Schuster/Paula Wiseman Bks.) Simon & Schuster/Paula Wiseman Bks.
Altieri, Maria. Mom, Tell Me a Story. 2012. 20p. pap. 24.95 *(978-1-62709-702-4(3))* America Star Bks.
Ambatchew, Daniel. Mimi Mystery. 2012. (Illus.). 39p. pap. 10.95 *(978-9988-647-83-4(2))* Sub-Saharan Pubs. & Traders GHA. Dist: African Bks. Collective, Ltd.
Amelia Asks Why... Book of Fun. 2007. (J). 1.09 *(978-0-9726075-7-5(9))* EPI Bks.
An, Na. Wait for Me. 2017. (ENG., Illus.). (YA). (gr. 7). 192p. 19.99 *(978-1-4814-4242-8(2))*; 208p. pap. 10.99 *(978-1-4814-4243-5(0))* Simon & Schuster Children's Publishing. (Atheneum/Caitlyn Dlouhy Books).
Anderson, Jessica Lee. Calli. 2011. (ENG.). 198p. (J). (gr. 6). 16.95 *(978-1-57131-702-5(3))*; pap. 8.00 *(978-1-57131-699-8(X))* Milkweed Editions.
Anselmo, Robert Louis. We're All Different & yet Still the Same. l.t. ed. 2006. (Illus.). 22p. (J). 14.99 *(978-1-59879-107-5(9))*; per. 9.99 *(978-1-59879-088-7(9))* Lifevest Publishing, Inc.
Appelt, Kathi. Keeper. Hall, August, illus. (ENG.). (J). (gr. 3-7). 2012. 432p. pap. 9.99 *(978-1-4169-5061-5(3))* 2010. 416p. 17.99 *(978-1-4169-5060-8(5))* Simon & Schuster Children's Publishing. (Atheneum Bks. for Young Readers).
Applegate, Katherine & Grant, Michael. Eve & Adam. 2013. (ENG.). 304p. (YA). (gr. 8-12). pap. 15.99 *(978-1-250-03419-9(1)*, 900120591) Square Fish.
Arcos, Carrie. We Are All That's Left. 2018. 400p. (YA). (gr. 7). 17.99 *(978-0-399-17554-1(7)*, Philomel Bks.) Penguin Young Readers Group.
Arno, Ronni. Dear Poppy. 2016. (Mix Ser.). (ENG., Illus.). 256p. (J). (gr. 4-8). pap. 7.99 *(978-1-4814-3759-2(3)*, Aladdin) Simon & Schuster Children's Publishing.
Arnold, Elana K. Infandous. 2015. (ENG.). 200p. (YA). (gr. 8-12). 18.99 *(978-1-4677-3849-1(2)*, 5f116506-df41-46d9-aaec-833557c7c676, Carolrhoda Lab™) Lerner Publishing Group.
Aschermann, Kurt. Bj & the Amazing Doctor Directions. 2008. 172p. pap. 11.99 *(978-1-4343-7708-1(3))* AuthorHouse.
AZ Books, creator. Lamb Searches for Her Mom. 2012. (Plush Baby Ser.). (ENG., Illus.). 10p. (J). (gr. -1 — 1). 11.95 *(978-1-61889-218-8(5))* AZ Bks. LLC.
Babbitt, Kelli. You Grew in My Heart Instead. 2008. 36p. pap. 24.95 *(978-1-60474-981-6(4))* America Star Bks.
Bachorz, Pam. Drought. 2011. (ENG.). 400p. (YA). (gr. 7-12). 17.99 *(978-0-61684-016-0(9)*, 287c1b93-a51d-4c11-892e-c61df04d0ed9, Carolrhoda Lab™) Lerner Publishing Group.
Baier, Hiltrud. Greta in Schweden. 2009. 114p. pap. *(978-3-8391-2523-6(5))* Books on Demand GmbH.
Baker, Andrea. Worlds Apart: Leah. 2013. 284p. pap. 14.99 *(978-0-9892854-3-8(X))* Taylor Street Publishing LLC.
Banks, Taylor. Rock Princess. 2009. 102p. pap. 15.99 *(978-1-4415-4288-5(4))* Xlibris Corp.
Baratz-Logsted, Lauren. Secrets of My Suburban Life. 2008. (ENG.). 240p. (YA). (gr. 9-18). pap. 7.99 *(978-1-4169-2525-5(2)*, Simon Pulse) Simon Pulse.
Bardsley-Sirois, Lois. Katherine's Winter Garden. 2012. 24p. pap. 12.99 *(978-1-4525-6269-8(5))* Balboa Pr.
Barkow, Henriette. Buri & the Marrow. Finlay, Lizzie, illus. 2004. (ENG & FRE.). 24p. (J). pap. *(978-1-85269-583-5(8))* Mantra Lingua.
Barnhart, Judy. Sand Angels in the Snow. 2007. 68p. per. 8.95 *(978-0-595-45154-8(3))* iUniverse, Inc.
Barr, Barbara Jean. My Mom Inside My Pocket, 1 vol. Stutz, Chris, illus. 2010. 16p. 24.95 *(978-1-4489-5704-0(4))* America Star Bks.
Barry, Debra R. Debbie's Eyes. Tessier, Beth Marie, photos by. 2011. (Illus.). 32p. pap. 24.95 *(978-1-4560-5272-0(1))* America Star Bks.
Barter, Catherine. Troublemakers. 2018. (ENG.). 360p. (YA). (gr. 7-12). 17.99 *(978-1-5124-7549-4(1)*, 6501f552-14c0-47e0-aa58-d3647a7e0d10, Carolrhoda Lab™) Lerner Publishing Group.
Baskin, Nora Raleigh. Ruby on the Outside. 2015. (ENG., Illus.). 176p. (J). (gr. 3-7). 18.99 *(978-1-4424-8503-7(5)*, Simon & Schuster Bks. For Young Readers) Simon & Schuster Bks. For Young Readers.
Bauer, Joan. Almost Home. 2013. (ENG.). 288p. (J). (gr. 5). pap. 8.99 *(978-0-14-242748-4(9)*, Puffin Books) Penguin Young Readers Group.
Beale, Fleur. The Boy in the Olive Grove. 2013. 368p. pap. *(978-1-4596-5723-6(3))* ReadHowYouWant.com, Ltd.
—I Am Not Esther. 2013. 246p. pap. *(978-1-4596-5748-9(9))* ReadHowYouWant.com, Ltd.
Bedford, David A. Angela. 2009. 190p. 25.50 *(978-1-60860-755-6(0)*, Eloquent Bks.) Strategic Book Publishing & Rights Agency (SBPRA).
Bell, Clare. Ratha's Challenge. 2011. (Named Ser.: Bk. 4). (ENG.). 252p. (YA). pap. 14.95 *(978-0-9745603-9-7(1))* Imaginator Pr.
Bell, Hilari. Sword of Waters. Willis, Drew, illus. 2009. (Shield, Sword, & Crown Ser.: 2). (ENG.). 384p. (J). (gr. 3-7). pap. 6.99 *(978-1-4169-0597-4(9)*, Aladdin) Simon & Schuster Children's Publishing.
—Sword of Waters, No. 2. Willis, Drew, illus. 2008. (Shield, Sword, & Crown Ser.: 2). (ENG.). 368p. (J). (gr. 3-7). 16.99 *(978-1-4169-0596-7(0)*, Simon & Schuster/Paula Wiseman Bks.) Simon & Schuster/Paula Wiseman Bks.
Benton, Jim. Bad Hair Day. Benton, Jim, illus. 2019. (Franny K. Stein, Mad Scientist Ser.: 8). (ENG., Illus.). 112p. (J). (gr. 1-5). 15.99 *(978-1-5344-1337-5(5)*, Simon & Schuster Bks. For Young Readers) Simon & Schuster Bks. For Young Readers.
Berke, Lindsey Jensen. Am I Pretty? 2013. 28p. 22.99 *(978-1-4808-0106-6(2))*; pap. 16.99 *(978-1-4808-0108-0(9))* Archway Publishing.
Bernal, Estela. Can You See Me Now? 2014. (ENG.). v, 161p. (J). pap. 10.95 *(978-1-55885-783-4(4)*, Piñata Books) Arte Publico Pr.
Bernard, Margaret Mitchell. Kate & the Family Tree. Duncan, Shirley, ed. Ciesinska, Izabela, illus. 2009. 24p. pap. 14.99 *(978-1-4251-7408-8(6))* Trafford Publishing.
Black, Amber. A Day with Miss Sassy. 2008. 16p. pap. 24.95 *(978-1-60610-338-8(5))* PublishAmerica, Inc.
Black, Teri Bailey. Girl at the Grave. 2019. (ENG.). 336p. (YA). pap. 9.99 *(978-0-7653-9949-6(0)*, 900185196, Tor Teen) Doherty, Tom Assocs., LLC.
Blake, Ashley Herring. How to Make a Wish. (ENG.). (YA). (gr. 9). 2018. 352p. pap. 11.99 *(978-1-328-86932-6(6)*, 1696697) 2017. 336p. 17.99 *(978-0-544-81519-3(X)*, 1642371) HarperCollins Pubs. (Clarion Bks.).
—How to Make a Wish. 2018. lib. bdg. 20.85 *(978-0-606-40996-4(3))* Turtleback.
Blanchard, Amy Ella. A Sweet Little Maid. 2017. (ENG., Illus.). (J). 22.95 *(978-1-374-97343-5(2))*; pap. 12.95 *(978-1-374-97342-8(4))* Capital Communications, Inc.
Bliss, Barbara. Abigail Elliot & the Dollhouse Family. 2008. (ENG.). 258p. pap. 9.99 *(978-1-4196-7615-4(6))* CreateSpace Independent Publishing Platform.
Blocker, Ariel S. Beauty in Me. 2012. 24p. pap. 12.45 *(978-1-4497-6363-3(4)*, WestBow Pr.) Author Solutions, LLC.
Blos, Joan W. Letters from the Corrugated Castle: A Novel of Gold Rush California, 1850-1852. 2008. (ENG.). 320p. (J). (gr. 5-9). pap. 5.99 *(978-0-689-87078-1(7)*, Atheneum Bks. for Young Readers) Simon & Schuster Children's Publishing.
Blue Moon. 2014. (Dead City Ser.: 2). (ENG., Illus.). 336p. (J). (gr. 4-8). pap. 8.99 *(978-1-4424-4132-3(1)*, Aladdin) Simon & Schuster Children's Publishing.
Blume, Lesley M. M. Tennyson. 2008. (ENG.). 240p. (J). (gr. 6-8). lib. bdg. 21.19 *(978-0-375-94703-2(5))* Random House Publishing Group.
Bone, Angela M. Spotted Jeans & Speckled Faces. 2005. (ENG.). 24p. per. 12.99 *(978-1-4134-6895-3(0))* Xlibris Corp.
Bonnell, Kris. We Like the Beach. 2007. (J). pap. 5.95 *(978-1-933727-55-4(1))* Reading Reading Bks., LLC.
Bonnett-Rampersaud, Louise. Bubble & Squeak, 1 vol. Banta, Susan, illus. 2006. (ENG.). 24p. (J). (gr. -1-2). 14.99 *(978-0-7614-5310-9(5))* Marshall Cavendish Corp.
Booth, Coe. Kendra. 2010. (Push Fiction Ser.). (ENG.). 304p. (J). (gr. 9-12). 22.44 *(978-0-439-92537-2(1))* Scholastic, Inc.
Bosworth, Jennifer. The Killing Jar. 2016. (ENG.). 352p. (YA). 34.99 *(978-0-374-34137-4(0)*, 900126267, Farrar, Straus & Giroux (BYR)) Farrar, Straus & Giroux.
Boudreau, Helene. Real Mermaids Don't Hold Their Breath. 2012. (ENG.). 240p. (J). (gr. 4-8). pap. 9.99 *(978-1-4022-6446-7(1))* Sourcebooks, Inc.
Bowe, Julie. Birthday Glamour! 2015. (Victoria Torres, Unfortunately Average Ser.). (ENG., Illus.). 160p. (J). (gr. 4-8). lib. bdg. 27.99 *(978-1-4965-0533-0(6)*, 128605, Stone Arch Bks.) Capstone.
Bowman, Akemi Dawn. Starfish. (ENG.). (YA). (gr. 7). 2018. 368p. pap. 12.99 *(978-1-4814-8773-3(6))* 2017. (Illus.). 352p. 19.99 *(978-1-4814-8772-6(8))* Simon Pulse. (Simon Pulse).
Braswell, Liz. As Old As Time: A Twisted Tale. (Twisted Tale Ser.). (ENG.). (YA). (gr. 7-12). 2018. 512p. pap. 10.99 *(978-1-4847-0731-9(1))* 2016. 496p. 17.99 *(978-1-4847-0728-9(1))* Disney Publishing Worldwide. (Disney-Hyperion).
—As Old As Time: A Twisted Tale. 2018. (YA). lib. bdg. 20.85 *(978-0-606-39964-7(X))* Turtleback.
Braxton-Smith, Ananda. Merrow. 2016. (ENG.). 240p. (YA). (gr. 9). 16.99 *(978-0-7636-7924-8(0))* Candlewick Pr.
Brewer, Melanie. Sweep Away the Bad Day. 2009. 20p. pap. 12.99 *(978-1-4490-1605-0(7))* AuthorHouse.
Bright, Amy. Swimmers, 1 vol. 2014. (ENG.). 216p. (YA). (gr. 9-11). pap. 12.95 *(978-0-88995-513-4(1)*, 60e31062-21d7-46b5-b9ab-20d07d3700db) Trifolium Bks., Inc. CAN. Dist: Firefly Bks., Ltd.
Broberg, Janel. Catie the Cute, Curious & Sometimes Crooked Caterpillar. 2012. 24p. pap. 12.00 *(978-1-61170-073-2(6))* Robertson Publishing.
Brothers, Marilee. Moonstone. 2008. 236p. (YA). pap. 14.95 *(978-0-9802453-4-9(6)*, Bell Bridge Bks.) BelleBks., Inc.
Brown, Teri. Born of Illusion. 2013. (ENG.). 384p. (YA). pap. 9.99 *(978-0-06-227720-6(0))* HarperCollins Pubs.
Brucke, Candice Yarbray. Night-Night Town. 2009. 28p. pap. 15.00 *(978-1-4389-7467-5(1))* AuthorHouse.
Bruha, Ginger. Lilly's Breakfast Time. 2004. 20p. pap. 24.95 *(978-1-4137-3133-0(3))* PublishAmerica, Inc.
Bryant, Cathy. The Doctor Said I Have Leukemi. Bunker, Thomas, illus. 2012. 24p. pap. 24.95 *(978-1-4560-6929-2(2))* America Star Bks.
Budhos, Marina. Tell Us We're Home. 2011. (ENG.). 320p. (YA). (gr. 7). pap. 12.99 *(978-1-4424-2128-8(2)*, Atheneum Bks. for Young Readers) Simon & Schuster Children's Publishing.
Burian, Natalka. Welcome to the Slipstream. 2017. (ENG., Illus.). 272p. (YA). (gr. 9-12). 18.99 *(978-1-5072-0075-9(7)*, Simon Pulse) Simon Pulse.
Burkart, Tammy Jayne. Lillie, 1 vol. 2009. 48p. pap. 16.95 *(978-1-60813-680-3(9))* America Star Bks.
Burt, Marissa. The 12 Dares of Christa. 2017. (ENG.). 304p. (J). (gr. 3-7). 16.99 *(978-0-06-241618-6(9)*, Tegen, Katherine Bks) HarperCollins Pubs.
Bush, Rosetta Bowman. My Name Is Violet. 2013. 20p. pap. 24.95 *(978-1-63000-515-3(0))* America Star Bks.
By Kaleena Ma. Glasses for Me? Oh No! Dawn Phillips, illus. 2009. 40p. pap. 18.49 *(978-1-4389-5418-9(2))* AuthorHouse.
Cabrera, Cozbi A. Me & Mama. Cabrera, Cozbi A., illus. 2020. (ENG., Illus.). 40p. (J). (gr. -1-3). 18.99 *(978-1-5344-5421-7(7))* Simon & Schuster, Inc.
Cala, C. J. Mother Dandy's Nonmalmani. 2011. 58p. pap. 6.95 *(978-1-257-37974-3(7))* Lulu Pr., Inc.
Caletti, Deb. Girl, Unframed. 2020. (ENG.). 368p. (YA). (gr. 9). 18.99 *(978-1-5344-2697-9(3)*, Simon Pulse) Simon Pulse.
—The Queen of Everything. 2008. (ENG.). 352p. (YA). (gr. 7-12). pap. 11.99 *(978-1-4169-5781-2(2)*, Simon Pulse) Simon Pulse.
—The Six Rules of Maybe. 2011. (ENG.). 352p. (YA). (gr. 7). pap. 12.99 *(978-1-4169-7971-5(9)*, Simon Pulse) Simon Pulse.
Callender, Kacen. Hurricane Child (Scholastic Gold) (ENG.). (J). (gr. 3-7). 2019. 240p. pap. 8.99 *(978-1-338-12931-1(7))* 2018. 224p. 17.99 *(978-1-338-12930-4(9))* Scholastic, Inc. (Scholastic Pr.).
Callender, Simone. Rosa's Paw-Paw Tree: An inspiring tale about a daughter's deep love for her Mother. Downer, Romeo, illus. 2011. 24p. pap. 8.99 *(978-1-4575-0596-6(7))* Dog Ear Publishing, LLC.
Cameron, Ann. The Secret Life of Amanda K. Woods. 2014. (ENG.). 208p. (J). (gr. 5-9). pap. 14.99 *(978-1-250-04419-8(7)*, 900128307) Square Fish.
Cameron, Josephine. Maybe a Mermaid. 2019. (ENG.). 288p. (J). 16.99 *(978-0-374-30642-7(7)*, 900176074, Farrar, Straus & Giroux (BYR)) Farrar, Straus & Giroux.
Campbell-Fells. Blue Ribbon Girls. 2005. 145p. pap. 13.95 *(978-0-7414-2593-5(9))* Infinity Publishing.
Carey, Janet Lee. Dragon's Keep. 2007. 302p. (J). *(978-1-4287-3929-1(7))* Harcourt Trade Pubs.
Carkhuff, Denise. Mama's Heart Fits Two. 2015. (ENG., Illus.). 32p. (J). (gr. -1-2). 16.95 *(978-1-62634-222-4(9))* Greenleaf Book Group.
Carlson, Melody. A Not-So-Simple Life: Maya: Book 1. 2008. (Diary of a Teenage Girl Ser.: 13). (ENG.). 256p. (YA). (gr. 7). pap. 14.99 *(978-1-60142-117-3(6)*, Multnomah) Crown Publishing Group, The.
Carlson, Nancy. It's Going to Be Perfect! Carlson, Nancy, illus. 2012. (Nancy Carlson Picture Bks). (Illus.). 32p. (J). (gr. k-2). 56.72 *(978-0-7613-9299-6(8)*, Carolrhoda Bks.) Lerner Publishing Group.
Carlstrom, Nancy White. It's Your First Day of School, Annie Claire. Moore, Margie, illus. 2009. (ENG.). 32p. (J). (gr. k-2). 16.95 *(978-0-8109-4057-4(4)*, 639801, Abrams Bks. for Young Readers) Abrams, Inc.
Carter, Caela. One Speck of Truth. 2019. (ENG.). 288p. (J). (gr. 3-7). 16.99 *(978-0-06-267266-7(5)*, Quill Tree Bks.) HarperCollins Pubs.
Carter, Olivia. Through My Eyes, Book One: Jake. 2013. (ENG.). 235p. (YA). (gr. 7). pap. 10.95 *(978-1-935089-63-6(3))* Acacia Publishing, Inc.
Carttar, Debra. Picturing Lucy. 2010. pap. 14.95 *(978-0-7414-6195-7(1))* Infinity Publishing.
The Case of the Secret Box. 2007. 56p. pap. 7.75 *(978-0-8341-2288-8(X)*, 083-412-288X) Beacon Hill Pr. of Kansas City.
Cassidy, Cathy. Love from Lexie (the Lost & Found) 2019. (Lost & Found Ser.: 1). (Illus.). 336p. (J). (gr. 4-6). pap. 9.99 *(978-0-14-138512-9(X))* Penguin Random Hse. AUS. Dist: Independent Pubs. Group.
Castro, Edmund Lee. Crystal & Her Flying Adventure. 2010. 44p. 16.99 *(978-1-4490-6867-7(7))* AuthorHouse.
—Crystal & the Not-So-Scary Night. 2008. 36p. pap. 24.95 *(978-1-60672-236-7(0))* America Star Bks.
Chang, Hae-Kyung. Oh No, School! Bisaillon, Josée, illus. 2014. 32p. (J). 18.99 *(978-1-4338-1333-7(5)*, Magination Pr.) American Psychological Assn.
Chappas, Bess. Kiki & the Red Shoes. Branam, Sandy, illus. 2007. (J). 17.99 *(978-1-60131-012-5(9))* Big Tent Bks.
Charles, Bob. A Trip to the Market & una visita al Mercado: 6 English, 6 Spanish Adaptations. 2011. (ENG & SPA.). (J). 75.00 net. *(978-1-4108-5642-5(9))* Benchmark Education Co.
Cheever, Karen J. The Tuck-In: (a Child's Event) 2012. 24p. (-18). pap. 17.99 *(978-1-4772-7546-7(0))* AuthorHouse.
Chen, Justina. Nothing but the Truth (and a Few White Lies) 2007. (Justina Chen Novel Ser.). (ENG.). 256p. (J). (gr. 7-17). per. 15.99 *(978-0-316-01131-0(2))* Little, Brown Bks. for Young Readers.
Chew, Ruth. A Matter-Of-Fact Magic Book: Witch's Broom. 2015. (Matter-Of-Fact Magic Book Ser.). (Illus.). 144p. (J). (gr. 2-5). pap. 5.99 *(978-0-449-81578-6(1)*, Random Hse. Bks. for Young Readers) Random Hse. Children's Bks.
Clare, Cassandra. The Mortal Instruments, the Complete Collection: City of Bones; City of Ashes; City of Glass; City of Fallen Angels; City of Lost Souls; City of Heavenly Fire. 2014. (Mortal Instruments Ser.). (ENG., Illus.). 3248p. (YA). (gr. 9). 149.99 *(978-1-4814-4296-1(1)*, McElderry, Margaret K. Bks.) McElderry, Margaret K. Bks.
Clark, Kristin Elizabeth. Jess, Chunk, & the Road Trip to Infinity. 2016. (ENG.). 272p. (YA). 21.00 *(978-0-374-38006-9(6)*, 900096882, Farrar, Straus & Giroux (BYR)) Farrar, Straus & Giroux.
Clark, Kristina. The Great Adventures of Ella: The Magic Desk. 2010. 28p. 12.95 *(978-1-4520-2412-7(X))* AuthorHouse.
Clark, M. H. T. L. C. 2015. 36p. 16.95 *(978-1-938298-42-4(X))* Compendium, Inc., Publishing & Communications.
Clark Sherryl Staff. Bone Song. 2008. (Cutting Edge Ser.). (ENG.). 200p. pap. *(978-1-84167-751-4(5))* Ransom Publishing Ltd.
Clarke, E. J. Oakwing: A Fairy's Tale. 2017. (Oakwing Ser.: 1). (ENG., Illus.). 192p. (J). (gr. 2-6). 16.99 *(978-1-4814-8191-5(6)*, Aladdin) Simon & Schuster Children's Publishing.
—Oakwing: A Fairy's Tale. 2018. (Oakwing Ser.: 1). (ENG.). 208p. (J). (gr. 2-6). pap. 6.99 *(978-1-4814-8190-8(8)*, Simon & Schuster/Paula Wiseman Bks.) Simon & Schuster/Paula Wiseman Bks.
Clavette, Taylor. Shapeshifter's Mark. 2012. 168p. (gr. 10-12). pap. 12.95 *(978-1-4697-9264-4(8))* iUniverse, Inc.
Clough, Lisa. Me, Penelope. 2009. (ENG.). 208p. (YA). (gr. 9). pap. 12.99 *(978-0-547-07632-4(0)*, 1042010, Clarion Bks.) HarperCollins Pubs.
Clow, Alexine. Jenny's Dreams. Clow, Alexine, illus. 2010. (Illus.). 20p. pap. 10.95 *(978-1-936051-89-2(3))* Peppertree Pr., The.
Coates, Angel J. Mommy Loves No ! 2008. (Illus.). 48p. pap. 19.95 *(978-1-4343-8642-7(2))* AuthorHouse.
Cochran, Cheryl. The Mini Message Man & the Great Candy Caper. Cochran, Christina, illus. 2011. 40p. pap. 24.95 *(978-1-4560-7565-1(9))* America Star Bks.
Cochrane, Mick. The Girl Who Threw Butterflies. 2010. (ENG.). 192p. (J). (gr. 3-7). 7.99 *(978-0-375-84610-6(7)*, Yearling) Random Hse. Children's Bks.
Cohn, Rachel. Shrimp, 7 vols. 2005. (YA). 171.75 *(978-1-4193-5253-9(9))* Recorded Bks., Inc.
Coker, Rachel. Interrupted: A Life Beyond Words, 1 vol. 2013. (ENG.). 256p. (YA). pap. 9.99 *(978-0-310-72810-8(X))* Zondervan.
Connors, Faith Raymond. Love, Midgie. Connors, Tracy D., ed. 2008. (ENG., Illus.). 308p. pap. 12.95 *(978-0-9640138-1-0(9)*, 9780964013810) BelleAire Pr.
Cooney, Caroline B. The Lost Songs. 2013. (ENG.). 256p. (YA). (gr. 7). pap. 8.99 *(978-0-385-73967-2(2)*, Ember) Random Hse. Children's Bks.
Cornwell, Betsy. Mechanica. 2016. lib. bdg. 19.65 *(978-0-606-37999-1(1))* Turtleback.
Cotter, Charis. The Painting. 2017. (Illus.). 288p. (J). (gr. 4-7). 16.99 *(978-1-101-91887-6(X)*, Tundra Bks.) Tundra Bks. CAN. Dist: Penguin Random Hse. LLC.
Cowling, Chani. Cookie Baker, Sweet & Sour. 2008. 24p. pap. 24.95 *(978-1-60703-021-8(7))* America Star Bks.
Cox, Tracey M. Angels Do That. Movshina, Marina, illus. 2012. 16p. pap. 9.95 *(978-1-61633-299-0(9))* Guardian Angel Publishing, Inc.
Coyle, Carmela Lavigna. Do Princesses Wear Hiking Boots? Gordon, Mike & Gordon, Carl, illus. 2003. (Do Princesses Ser.). (ENG.). 32p. (J). (gr. -1-2). 15.95 *(978-0-87358-828-7(2))* Cooper Square Publishing Llc.
Crosby, Sherry. A Bad Case of the Grownies. Sy, Jan Michael Vincent & Graves, Freedom, illus. 2012. (ENG.). 28p. pap. 16.09 *(978-1-4669-3554-9(5))* Trafford Publishing.
Crossan, Sarah. The Weight of Water. 2018. (ENG., Illus.). 240p. (J). pap. 10.99 *(978-1-68119-954-2(8)*, 900194338, Bloomsbury Young Adult) Bloomsbury Publishing USA.
—The Weight of Water. 2018. (J). lib. bdg. 22.10 *(978-0-606-41077-9(5))* Turtleback.
CRUTCHFIELD, Shannon. Arion's Way. 2010. 10p. 11.50 *(978-0-557-54457-8(2))* Lulu Pr., Inc.
Dale, Jay. Our Baby. Everitt-Stewart, Andrew, illus. 2012. (Engage Literacy Green Ser.). (ENG.). 16p. (J). (gr. k-2). pap. 36.94 *(978-1-4296-9025-6(9)*, 18404, Capstone Pr.) Capstone.
Dale, Jay & Scott, Kay. Our Baby, 1 vol. Everitt-Stewart, Andrew, illus. 2012. (Engage Literacy Green Ser.). (ENG.). 16p. (J). (gr. k-2). pap. 6.99 *(978-1-4296-9023-2(2)*, 120022, Capstone Pr.) Capstone.
Danticat, Edwidge. Mama's Nightingale: A Story of Immigration & Separation. Staub, Leslie, illus. 2015. 32p. (J). (gr. k-3). 17.99 *(978-0-525-42809-1(7)*, Dial Bks) Penguin Young Readers Group.
Danziger, Paula. Amber Brown Is Green with Envy. 2014. (Amber Brown Ser.: 9). (ENG., Illus.). 176p. (J). (gr. 2-5). pap. 7.99 *(978-0-14-242699-9(7)*, Puffin Books) Penguin Young Readers Group.
—Amber Brown Is Green with Envy. Ross, Tony, illus. 2004. (Amber Brown Ser.: No. 9). 151p. (J). (gr. 2-5). 12.65 *(978-0-7569-2978-7(4))* Perfection Learning Corp.
—Amber Brown Wants Extra Credit. Ross, Tony, illus. 2008. (Amber Brown Ser.: 4). (ENG.). 144p. (J). (gr. 2-5). 6.99 *(978-0-14-241049-3(7)*, Puffin Books) Penguin Young Readers Group.
Dao, Cindy. Mama? 2005. (Illus.). 36p. (J). per. 8.99 *(978-1-932338-79-9(9))* Lifevest Publishing, Inc.
Dauphin, Lili. I Will Fly Again: The Restavek. 2007. 284p. per. 18.95 *(978-0-9748329-8-2(7))* MiraQuest.
Davenport, Jennifer. Anna Begins. 2008. (ENG.). 150p. 21.95 *(978-0-930773-83-0(7))* Black Heron Pr.
David, Kate. Murphy & the Magical Hat. 2012. (ENG.). 26p. (J). 18.95 *(978-1-4327-8582-6(6))* Outskirts Pr., Inc.
Davis, Chasta. Maggie's Little Strawberry, 1 vol. 2010. 20p. pap. 24.95 *(978-1-4489-5486-5(X))* PublishAmerica, Inc.
Davis, Jacky. Ladybug Girl & Her Mama. Soman, David, illus. 2013. (Ladybug Girl Ser.). 12p. (J). (gr. -1 — 1). bds. 8.99 *(978-0-8037-3891-1(9)*, Dial Bks) Penguin Young Readers Group.
—Ladybug Girl Loves... Soman, David, illus. 2010. (Ladybug Girl Ser.). 12p. (J). (gr. -1 — 1). bds. 6.99 *(978-0-448-45374-3(6)*, Grosset & Dunlap) Penguin Young Readers Group.

MNO

Dawn, Sasha. Splinter. 2018. (ENG.). 304p. (YA). (gr. 8-12). pap. 9.99 (978-1-5415-3845-0(5), e570372a-60e4-45dc-8e51-088b983b546f, Carolrhoda Lab™) Lerner Publishing Group.

Deal-Trainor, Carol. Marilee: A Manatee's First Journey to the Springs. 2008. 48p. pap. 16.95 (978-1-60563-660-3(6)) America Star Bks.

Deaver, Julie Reece. The Night I Disappeared. 2012. (ENG.). 256p. (YA). (gr. 7). pap. 12.99 (978-1-4424-7298-3(7), Simon Pulse) Simon Pulse.

Dee, Barbara. Trauma Queen. 2011. (Mix Ser.). (ENG.). 272p. (J). (gr. 4-8). pap. 8.99 (978-1-4424-0923-1(1), Aladdin) Simon & Schuster Children's Publishing.

Dellaira, Ava. In Search of Us. 2020. (ENG.). 416p. (YA). pap. 10.99 (978-1-250-29461-6(4), 900163346) Square Fish.

Delmonte, Ellis. Miracle Girl. 2007. (ENG.). 208p. (YA). per. (978-0-9555096-4-3(5)) Hawkwood Bks.

DeNomme, Donna & Proctor, Tina. Ophelia's Oracle: Discovering the Healthy, Happy, Self-aware, & Competant Girl in the Mirror. 2009. (YA). pap. 16.95 (978-1-61539-958-1(5)) Independent Pub.

Deriso, Christine Hurley. Talia Talk. 2009. 184p. (J). pap. (978-0-375-84496-6(1), Delacorte Pr) Random House Publishing Group.

Devlin, Calla. Right Where You Left Me. 2017. (ENG., Illus.). 256p. (YA). (gr. 9). 17.99 (978-1-4814-8699-6(3), Atheneum Bks. for Young Readers) Simon & Schuster Children's Publishing.

—Tell Me Something Real. 2016. (ENG., Illus.). 304p. (YA). (gr. 9). 17.99 (978-1-4814-6115-3(X), Atheneum Bks. for Young Readers) Simon & Schuster Children's Publishing.

Diesen, Deborah. Catch a Kiss. McLeod, Kris Aro, illus. 2016. (ENG.). 32p. (J). (gr. k-2). 15.99 (978-1-58536-961-4(6), 204037) Sleeping Bear Pr.

Dixon, Linda A. Cupcakes for Cristina! 2010. 16p. 9.99 (978-1-4520-6650-9(7)) AuthorHouse.

Dodd, Kelly. Gregarious Gabby & Her Gabbyful Life: Moving Day. 2011. 28p. 13.59 (978-1-4567-2890-8(3)) AuthorHouse.

Dorros, Arthur. Mama & Me. Gutierrez, Rudy, illus. 2011. (ENG.). 32p. (J). (gr. -1-3). 16.99 (978-0-06-058160-2(3), HarperCollins) HarperCollins Pubs.

Doty, Kathryn Adams. Wild Orphan. 2006. (ENG.). 144p. (gr. 3-7). per. 14.95 (978-1-889020-20-4(6)) Edinborough Pr.

Dougherty, Meghan. Dorothy's Derby Chronicles: Woe of Jade Doe. Birnbach, Alece, illus. 2015. (Dorothy's Derby Chronicles Ser.: 2). 288p. (J). (gr. 4-7). pap. 6.99 (978-1-4926-0147-0(0)) Sourcebooks, Inc.

Dower, Laura. Gabi & the Great Big Bakeover. Lazuli, Lilly, illus. 2016. (Dessert Diaries). (ENG.). 160p. (J). (gr. 4-8). lib. bdg. 26.65 (978-1-4965-3119-3(1), 132190, Stone Arch Bks.) Capstone.

—Gabi & the Great Big Bakeover. Lazuli, Lilly, illus. 2017. (ENG.). 160p. (J). pap. (978-1-4747-2213-1(X), Stone Arch Bks.) Capstone.

Downham, Jenny. Unbecoming, 1 vol. (ENG.). 384p. (YA). (gr. 9-9). 2017. pap. 12.99 (978-1-338-16072-7(9)) 2016. 17.99 (978-0-545-90717-0(9)) Scholastic, Inc.

D'Souza, Barbara. If We Were Snowflakes. 2018. (YA). pap. (978-1-59719-091-6(8)) Pearlsong Pr.

Dube, Pierrette. How to Become a Perfect Princess in Five Days, 1 vol. Melanson, Luc, illus. 2009. (Rainy Day Readers Ser.). (ENG.). 32p. (J). (gr. 1-2). 27.27 (978-1-60754-376-3(1), d475ad4c-eaa9-491c-b8ae-c2c376868dd9, Windmill Bks.) Rosen Publishing Group, Inc., The.

Duble, Kathleen Benner. The Sacrifice. 2007. (ENG.). 224p. (J). (gr. 5-9). pap. 8.99 (978-0-689-87651-6(3), McElderry, Margaret K. Bks.) McElderry, Margaret K. Bks.

Dubrule, Jackie. Miranda, God & the Park. Swope, Brenda, illus. 2011. 32p. pap. 24.95 (978-1-4560-0966-3(4)) America Star Bks.

Duncan, Alice Faye. Just Like a Mama. Barlow, Charnelle Pinkney, illus. 2020. (ENG.). 40p. (J). (gr. -1-3). 17.99 (978-1-5344-6183-3(3)) Simon & Schuster, Inc.

Dunn, Pintip. Seize Today. 2017. (Forget Tomorrow Ser.: 3). (ENG.). 300p. (YA). 17.99 (978-1-63375-818-6(4), 9781633758186) Entangled Publishing, LLC.

Durgan, Lori Origer. The Little Scrub Lady. 2012. 28p. pap. 15.99 (978-1-4797-4259-2(7)) Xlibris Corp.

Durst, Sarah Beth. Into the Wild. 2007. (ENG.). 278p. (J). (gr. 6-8). 22.44 (978-1-59514-156-9(1), Razorbill) Penguin Young Readers Group.

Dyan, Penelope. Introducing Fabulous Marie, a Girl with a Good Head on Her Shoulders. Dyan, Penelope, illus. 2009. (Illus.). 44p. pap. 11.95 (978-1-935118-55-8(2)) Bellissima Publishing, LLC.

—Lovely Libby. Dyan, Penelope, illus. 2010. (Illus.). 34p. pap. 11.95 (978-1-935630-28-9(8)) Bellissima Publishing, LLC.

Dyer, Hadley. Johnny Kellock Died Today. 2007. (ENG.). 192p. (J). (gr. 5-9). mass mkt. 8.99 (978-0-00-639534-8(1), Harper Trophy) HarperCollins Pubs.

Eagar, Lindsay. The Bigfoot Files. 2018. (ENG.). 384p. (J). (gr. 5-9). 16.99 (978-0-7636-9234-6(4)) Candlewick Pr.

Earhardt, Ainsley. Through Your Eyes: My Child's Gift to Me. Kim, Ji-Hyuk, illus. 2017. (ENG.). 32p. (J). (gr. -1-3). 19.99 (978-1-5344-0959-0(9), Aladdin) Simon & Schuster Children's Publishing.

Easton, Kelly. To Be Mona. (ENG.). 224p. (YA). (gr. 7). 2009. pap. 7.99 (978-1-4169-0055-9(1)) 2008. 16.99 (978-1-4169-0054-2(3)) McElderry, Margaret K. Bks. (McElderry, Margaret K. Bks.).

Ehrlich, Amy. Joyride. 2008. (ENG., Illus.). 256p. (YA). (gr. 7). pap. 8.99 (978-0-7636-2321-0(0)) Candlewick Pr.

Eilrich, Dinah Kay. Teeny Tessie's Big Baking Adventure. 2009. 28p. pap. 13.99 (978-1-4490-2277-8(4)) AuthorHouse.

Eisenberg, Kristy. When I Grow Up. Joslin, Irene, illus. 2009. 28p. pap. 12.49 (978-1-4389-0183-1(6)) AuthorHouse.

Ekster, Carol Gordon. Before I Sleep I Say Thank You. Rojas, Mary, illus. 2015. (J). 14.95 (978-0-8198-1225-4(0)) Pauline Bks. & Media.

Elliott, Miriam Isabel. Solita & the Purple Moon: Solita y la Luna Morada. 2007. (ENG.). 24p. per. 11.49 (978-1-4343-4932-3(2)) AuthorHouse.

Ellis, Amanda & Block, Maggie. Jwenlapaix in the Bateyes. 2009. 52p. pap. 24.00 (978-1-4389-4391-6(1)) AuthorHouse.

Elovitz Marshall, Linda. Rainbow Weavery, 1 vol. Chavarri, Elisa, illus. 2016. (ENG.). 40p. (J). (gr. k-4). 20.95 (978-0-89239-374-9(2), leelowcbp) Lee & Low Bks., Inc.

Erlich, Bev. Pink Roses Everywhere. gif. ed. 2004. (Illus.). 64p. (J). 14.95 (978-0-9743913-0-4(1)) Snojoy Publishing.

Evetts-Secker, Josephine. Mother & Daughter Tales. Cann, Helen, illus. 2011. 40p. (J). 21.99 (978-1-84686-572-5(7)) Barefoot Bks., Inc.

Faris, Stephanie. Piper Morgan Plans a Party. Fleming, Lucy, illus. 2017. (Piper Morgan Ser.: 5). (ENG.). 96p. (J). (gr. 1-4). 16.99 (978-1-5344-0386-4(8)); pap. 5.99 (978-1-5344-0385-7(X));5. 18.69 (978-1-5364-2740-0(3)) Simon & Schuster Children's Publishing. (Aladdin).

Farish, Terry. The Good Braider, 0 vols. 2013. (ENG.). 224p. (YA). (gr. 7-12). pap. 9.99 (978-1-4778-1628-8(3), 9781477816288, Skyscape) Amazon Publishing.

—The Good Braider. 2014. (ENG.). 221p. (YA). (gr. 9-12). lib. bdg. 21.80 (978-1-5311-8306-6(9)) Perfection Learning Corp.

Feiffer, Kate. My Mom Is Trying to Ruin My Life. Goode, Diane, illus. 2009. (ENG.). 32p. (J). (gr. -1-3). 19.99 (978-1-4169-4100-2(2), Simon & Schuster/Paula Wiseman Bks.) Simon & Schuster/Paula Wiseman Bks.

Fenderson, Shani. Mommy, Why Is the Sky So Blue? Fenderson, David, illus. 2009. 24p. pap. 24.95 (978-1-60749-550-5(3)) America Star Bks.

Fessler, Jennifer. Precious Is Worried. 2008. 16p. 11.30 (978-0-615-24258-3(8)) Twin Sisters Publishing Co.

Filigenzi, Courtney & Bersani, Shennen. Let My Colors Out. Bersani, Shennen, illus. 2009. (ENG., Illus.). 16p. (J). (gr. -1-k). 11.95 (978-1-60443-011-0(7), 1604430117) American Cancer Society, Inc.

Fisher, Rusty. Littlest Vampire's Story, 1 vol. 2014. (Story Time for Little Monsters Ser.). (ENG., Illus.). 24p. (J). (gr. -1-4). lib. bdg. 31.36 (978-1-62402-020-9(8), 626, Looking Glass Library) Magic Wagon.

—Littlest Werewolf's Story, 1 vol. 2014. (Story Time for Little Monsters Ser.). (ENG.). 24p. (J). (gr. -1-4). lib. bdg. 31.36 (978-1-62402-021-6(6), 628, Looking Glass Library) Magic Wagon.

—Littlest Witch's Story, 1 vol. 2014. (Story Time for Little Monsters Ser.). (ENG., Illus.). 24p. (J). (gr. -1-4). lib. bdg. 31.36 (978-1-62402-022-3(4), 630, Looking Glass Library) Magic Wagon.

—Littlest Zombie's Story, 1 vol. 2014. (Story Time for Little Monsters Ser.). (ENG., Illus.). 24p. (J). (gr. -1-4). lib. bdg. 31.36 (978-1-62402-023-0(2), 632, Looking Glass Library) Magic Wagon.

Fitzmaurice, Kathryn. Destiny, Rewritten. 2015. (ENG.). 368p. (J). (gr. 3-7). pap. 6.99 (978-0-06-162503-9(5), Tegen, Katherine Bks) HarperCollins Pubs.

Fixmer, Elizabeth. Down from the Mountain. 2015. (ENG.). 288p. (YA). (gr. 8-12). 16.99 (978-0-8075-8370-8(7), 807583707) Whitman, Albert & Co.

Flinn, Alex. Diva. 2013. (ENG.). 304p. (YA). (gr. 9). pap. 9.99 (978-0-06-212434-0(X)) 2007. (ENG.). 304p. (J). (gr. 9-12). pap. 8.99 (978-0-06-056846-7(1)) 2006. 263p. (YA). (gr. 7-12). 16.99 (978-0-06-056843-6(7)) 2006. 263p. (YA). (gr. 7-12). lib. bdg. 18.89 (978-0-06-056845-0(3)) HarperCollins Pubs. (HarperTeen).

Floyd, Brandi. Alex's Choice. 2012. 38p. 24.95 (978-1-4626-6028-5(2)) America Star Bks.

Fonner, Deborah K. An Extra Ordinary Day. VonBokel, Jan, illus. 2012. 24p. 19.95 (978-1-4327-8342-6(4)) Outskirts Pr., Inc.

Fox, Mem. This & That. Horacek, Judy, illus. 2017. (ENG.). 32p. (J). (gr. -1-k). 17.99 (978-1-338-03780-7(3), Scholastic Pr.) Scholastic, Inc.

France, Emily. Zen & Gone. 2019. (ENG.). 1p. (YA). (gr. 9). pap. 10.99 (978-1-64129-031-9(5), Soho Teen) Soho Pr., Inc.

Frederick, Heather Vogel. Dear Pen Pal. (Mother-Daughter Book Club Ser.). (ENG.). (J). (gr. 4-7). 2010. 432p. pap. 8.99 (978-1-4424-0848-7(0)) 2009. 416p. 19.99 (978-1-4169-7430-7(X)) Simon & Schuster Bks. For Young Readers. (Simon & Schuster Bks. For Young Readers).

—Home for the Holidays. (Mother-Daughter Book Club Ser.). (ENG.). (J). (gr. 4-9). 2012. 384p. pap. 8.99 (978-1-4424-0686-5(0)) 2011. 352p. 18.99 (978-1-4424-0685-8(2)) Simon & Schuster Bks. For Young Readers. (Simon & Schuster Bks. For Young Readers).

—The Mother-Daughter Book Club. (Mother-Daughter Book Club Ser.). (ENG.). (J). 2008. 288p. (gr. 4-7). pap. 8.99 (978-1-4169-7079-8(7)) 2007. (Illus.). 256p. (gr. 5-7). 19.99 (978-0-689-86412-4(4)) Simon & Schuster Bks. For Young Readers. (Simon & Schuster Bks. For Young Readers).

—Much Ado about Anne. (Mother-Daughter Book Club Ser.). (ENG., Illus.). (J). (gr. 4-7). 2009. 352p. pap. 8.99 (978-1-4169-8269-2(8)) 2008. 336p. 18.99 (978-0-689-85566-5(4)) Simon & Schuster Bks. For Young Readers. (Simon & Schuster Bks. For Young Readers).

—Pies & Prejudice. (Mother-Daughter Book Club Ser.). (ENG.). (J). (gr. 4-7). 2011. 400p. pap. 8.99 (978-1-4424-2019-9(7)) 2010. 384p. 15.99 (978-1-4169-7431-4(8)) Simon & Schuster Bks. For Young Readers. (Simon & Schuster Bks. For Young Readers).

—Wish You Were Eyre. 2013. (Mother-Daughter Book Club Ser.). (ENG.). 480p. (J). (gr. 4-9). pap. 8.99 (978-1-4424-3065-5(6), Simon & Schuster Bks. For Young Readers) Simon & Schuster Bks. For Young Readers.

Friedman, Aimee. Two Summers. 2016. (ENG.). 368p. (YA). (gr. 7). 17.99 (978-0-545-51807-9(5)) Scholastic, Inc.

Friedman, Robin. The Importance of Wings. 2017. 176p. (J). (gr. 5). pap. 7.99 (978-1-58089-331-2(7)) Charlesbridge Publishing, Inc.

Friend, Natasha. For Keeps. 2011. (YA). (ENG.). 256p. (gr. 8-12). 22.44 (978-0-670-01190-2(8)); 272p. (gr. 7-18). 7.99 (978-0-14-241846-8(3), Speak) Penguin Young Readers Group.

Froemming, Kaylee. My Mama's Hair Is Everywhere: It just won't go Away!! 2008. 12p. pap. 8.49 (978-1-4389-0385-9(5)) AuthorHouse.

Galang, M. Evelina. Angel de la Luna & the 5th Glorious Mystery. 2013. (ENG.). 304p. (J). (gr. 6). pap. 16.95 (978-1-56689-333-6(X)) Coffee Hse. Pr.

Galante, Cecilia. The Strays Like Us. 2018. (ENG.). 320p. (J). (gr. 3-7). 16.99 (978-1-338-04300-6(5), Scholastic Pr.) Scholastic, Inc.

—The Summer of May. 2011. (ENG., Illus.). 256p. (J). (gr. 4-8). 16.99 (978-1-4169-8023-0(7), Aladdin) Simon & Schuster Children's Publishing.

—The Summer of May. 2012. (ENG., Illus.). 256p. (J). (gr. 4-8). pap. 7.99 (978-1-4169-8304-0(X), Simon & Schuster/Paula Wiseman Bks.) Simon & Schuster/Paula Wiseman Bks.

Gardner, Sally. I, Coriander. 2007. (ENG., Illus.). 288p. (J). (gr. 5-18). 7.99 (978-0-14-240763-9(1), Puffin Books) Penguin Young Readers Group.

Garner, Paula. Relative Strangers. 2018. (ENG.). 368p. (YA). (gr. 9). 17.99 (978-0-7636-9469-2(X)) Candlewick Pr.

Garnett, Tarreka. The Sleepover. Damon Danielson, illus. 2013. 32p. pap. 14.97 (978-1-62212-249-3(6), Strategic Bk. Publishing) Strategic Book Publishing & Rights Agency (SBPRA).

Garton, Carol. Isabella Barella. 2013. (ENG.). 300p. (YA). 32.95 (978-1-4787-1339-5(9)); pap. 17.95 (978-1-4787-1490-3(5)) Outskirts Pr., Inc.

Gayton, Sam. The Adventures of Lettie Peppercorn. Bernatene, Poly, illus. 2016. (ENG.). 304p. (J). (gr. 3-7). 16.99 (978-1-4814-4769-0(6), McElderry, Margaret K. Bks.) McElderry, Margaret K. Bks.

Gelenius, Deb. My Mom, My Teacher. 2013. 28p. pap. 11.95 (978-1-61244-135-1(1)) Halo Publishing International.

George, Jessica Day. The Queen's Secret. 2019. (Rose Legacy Ser.). (ENG.). 256p. (J). 16.99 (978-1-5476-0089-2(6), 900198455, Bloomsbury Children's Bks.) Bloomsbury Publishing USA.

Giff, Patricia Reilly. Jubilee. 2017. (ENG.). 160p. (J). (gr. 3-7). 6.99 (978-0-385-74489-8(7), Yearling) Random Hse. Children's Bks.

Gillis, Jennifer B. What Do You Say? 2006. (Reader's Clubhouse Level 2 Reader Ser.). (Illus.). 24p. (J). (gr. k-1). pap. 3.99 (978-0-7641-3298-8(9)) Sourcebooks, Inc.

Glasgow, Kathleen. How to Make Friends with the Dark. (ENG.). (YA). (gr. 9). 2020. 448p. pap. 12.99 (978-1-101-93478-4(6), Ember) 2019. 432p. 18.99 (978-1-101-93475-3(1), Delacorte Pr.) 2019. 432p. lib. bdg. 21.99 (978-1-101-93477-7(8), Delacorte Pr.) Random Hse. Children's Bks.

Glocke, Robin. Tiny Fish. 2006. 56p. pap. 16.95 (978-1-4241-3777-0(2)) PublishAmerica, Inc.

Goerzen, Christy. Farmed Out, 1 vol. 2011. (Orca Currents Ser.). (ENG.). 128p. (J). (gr. 4-7). pap. 9.95 (978-1-55469-910-0(X)) Orca Bk. Pubs. USA.

Gomes, Filomena. My Mom Loves Me More Than Sushi. Spires, Ashley, illus. 2006. 24p. (J). pap. (978-1-897187-13-5(0)) Second Story Pr.

—My Mom Loves Me More Than Sushi, 1 vol. Spires, Ashley, illus. 2006. (ENG.). 24p. (J). (gr. -1-3). 15.95 (978-1-897187-09-8(2)) Second Story Pr. CAN. Dist: Orca Bk. Pubs. USA.

Gonzalez, Noni. Dream of Wings. Gonzalez, Tom, illus. 2013. (ENG.). 40p. (J). pap. 9.99 (978-1-939337-20-7(8)); 14.99 (978-1-939337-71-9(2)) Telemachus Pr., LLC.

Graves, Sue. A Cake for Dinner. 2011. (Tadpoles Ser.: No. 26). (ENG., Illus.). 24p. (J). (gr. k-3). pap. (978-0-7787-0583-3(8)) Crabtree Publishing Co.

Gray, Dianne. Holding up the Earth. 2006. (ENG.). 210p. (J). (gr. 5-7). pap. 12.95 (978-0-618-73747-5(2), 486718, Clarion Bks.) HarperCollins Pubs.

Gray, Kes. Daisy & the Trouble with Life. Parsons, Garry & Sharratt, Nick, illus. 2007. (Daisy Ser.: 12). (ENG.). 240p. (J). (gr. 2-4). pap. 11.95 (978-1-86230-167-2(0), Red Fox) Random House Children's Books GBR. Dist: Independent Pubs. Group.

Gray, Kristin L. Vilonia Beebe Takes Charge. (ENG.). 208p. (J). (gr. 3-7). 2018. pap. 7.99 (978-1-4814-5843-6(4)) 2017. (Illus.). 16.99 (978-1-4814-5842-9(6)) Simon & Schuster/Paula Wiseman Bks. (Simon & Schuster/Paula Wiseman Bks.).

Greathouse, Cindy. Sophie the Missing Bunny. 2011. 20p. pap. 24.95 (978-1-4489-5607-4(2)) America Star Bks.

Greenacres, Levi. Mommy's New Tattoo: A Bedtime Story for People, 1 vol. 2013. (ENG., Illus.). 32p. 16.99 (978-0-7643-4389-6(0), 4803) Schiffer Publishing, Ltd.

Greene, Bette. The Drowning of Stephan Jones. 2012. 220p. pap. 9.99 (978-0-9834681-3-4(3)) Greene & Sandell.

Greenwald, Lisa. My Life in Pink & Green. 2010. (Pink & Green Ser.). (ENG.). 300p. (J). (gr. 3-7). pap. 9.99 (978-0-8109-8984-9(0), 656603, Amulet Bks.) Abrams, Inc.

Grimes, Nikki. Poems in the Attic, 1 vol. Zunon, Elizabeth, illus. 2015. (ENG.). 48p. (J). (gr. 1-6). 21.95 (978-1-62014-027-7(6), leelowbooks) Lee & Low Bks., Inc.

Guest, Jacqueline. Dream Racer, 1 vol. 2006. (Lorimer SideStreets Ser.). (ENG.). 136p. (YA). (gr. 9-12). 16.95 (978-1-55028-945-9(4), 945); 8.99 (978-1-55028-942-8(X), 3e6017e8-ebd0-4258-b41b-aa688f1f6c49) James Lorimer & Co. Ltd., Pubs. CAN. Dist: Formac Lorimer Bks. Ltd., Lerner Publishing Group.

Gummer, Chlele. A Family of Geese. 2013. 34p. pap. 16.95 (978-1-4808-0026-7(0)) Archway Publishing.

Gunning, Monica. A Shelter in Our Car, 1 vol. 2014. (ENG., Illus.). 32p. (J). (gr. k-2). pap. 11.95 (978-0-89239-308-4(4), leelowcbp, Children's Book Press) Lee & Low Bks., Inc.

Hackney, Stacy. Forever Glimmer Creek. 2020. (ENG.). 320p. (J). (gr. 3-7). 17.99 (978-1-5344-4484-3(X), Simon & Schuster Bks. For Young Readers) Simon & Schuster Bks. For Young Readers.

Haddix, Margaret Peterson. Full Ride. 2014. (ENG.). 368p. (YA). (gr. 7). pap. 12.99 (978-1-4424-4279-5(4), Simon & Schuster Bks. For Young Readers) Simon & Schuster Bks. For Young Readers.

Hahn, Mary Downing. Deep & Dark & Dangerous: A Ghost Story. (ENG.). (J). (gr. 5-7). 2008. 200p. pap. 7.99 (978-0-547-07645-4(2), 1042023) 2007. 192p. 16.99 (978-0-618-66545-7(5), 100471) HarperCollins Pubs. (Clarion Bks.).

Hahn, Mary Downing & Giblin, James Cross. Tallahassee Higgins. 2007. (ENG.). 192p. (J). (gr. 5-7). pap. 6.95 (978-0-618-75246-1(3), 100528, Clarion Bks.) HarperCollins Pubs.

Halahmy, Miriam. Behind Closed Doors. 2017. (978-0-8234-3792-4(2)) Holiday Hse., Inc.

Hall, Deirdre Riordan. Pearl, 0 vols. 2016. (ENG.). 352p. (YA). (gr. 9-12). pap. 9.99 (978-1-5039-4858-7(7), 9781503948587, Skyscape) Amazon Publishing.

Hamilton, Deborah E. Why are You my Mother? A Mother's Response to Her Adopted Daughter. Andrules, Jamie L., illus. 2006. (J). 9.99 net. (978-0-9789202-0-3(1)) Dreams Due Media Group, Inc.

Hargrave, Kiran Millwood. The Island at the End of Everything. 2018. (ENG.). 256p. (J). (gr. 5). lib. bdg. 19.99 (978-0-553-53533-4(1), Knopf Bks. for Young Readers) Random Hse. Children's Bks.

Harlow, Joan Hiatt. The Watcher. 2015. (ENG.). 304p. (J). (gr. 3-7). pap. 8.99 (978-1-4424-2912-3(7), McElderry, Margaret K. Bks.) McElderry, Margaret K. Bks.

Harmon, Michael. Brutal. 2011. 240p. (YA). (gr. 9). pap. 8.99 (978-0-440-23995-6(8), Knopf Bks. for Young Readers) Random Hse. Children's Bks.

Harrell, Mary. The Mythmaker. 2018. (YA). pap. (978-1-63051-500-3(0)); (ENG., Illus.). 148p. (J). pap. 14.95 (978-1-63051-503-4(5)) Chiron Pubns.

Harrington, Claudia. My Two Moms, 1 vol. Persico, Zoe, illus. 2015. (My Family Ser.). (ENG.). 32p. (J). (gr. -1-3). 32.79 (978-1-62402-110-7(7), 18162, Looking Glass Library) Magic Wagon.

Harrington, Janine. Soul Sister. 2012. 244p. pap. (978-1-78176-139-7(6)) FeedARead.com.

Harris, Angela. Night Light. 2008. 28p. pap. 12.95 (978-1-4389-1971-3(9)) AuthorHouse.

Harris, Annaka. I Wonder. Rowe, John, illus. 2013. 32p. (J). 16.95 (978-1-940051-04-8(5)) Four Elephants Pr.

Harris, Dee. I Am Not a Hippopotamus, I Am a Little Girl , Book. Bohart, Lisa, illus. 2011. 24p. pap. 12.95 (978-1-61493-005-1(8)) Peppertree Pr., The.

Harris, Teresa E. The Perfect Place. 2014. (ENG.). 272p. (J). (gr. 5-7). 17.99 (978-0-547-25519-4(5), 1388242, Clarion Bks.) HarperCollins Pubs.

Harrison, Emma. Toe the Line: A Rival High Novel. 2008. (YA). (978-1-4114-0526-4(9), Spark Publishing Group) Sterling Publishing Co., Inc.

Harrold, A. F. The Imaginary. Gravett, Emily, illus. 2015. (ENG.). 240p. (J). (gr. 3-6). 16.99 (978-0-8027-3811-0(7), 900141005, Bloomsbury USA Childrens) Bloomsbury Publishing USA.

Hartley, Julie. The Finding Place, 1 vol. 2015. (ENG., Illus.). 244p. (J). (gr. 6-10). pap. 10.95 (978-0-88995-533-2(6), 643bfd24-b97a-4add-bd50-76f88f65b38b) Red Deer Pr. CAN. Dist: Firefly Bks., Ltd.

Hartman, Carrie. Child of Mine. 2007. (ENG., Illus.). 32p. (J). lib. bdg. 11.99 (978-1-934277-12-6(6)) Mam Green Publishing, Inc.

Haydel, Catherine. Uno the Cat & Hurricane Katrina. 2006. 18.00 (978-0-8059-7341-9(9)) Dorrance Publishing Co., Inc.

Hayes-Knoll, Carolyn. Ista Cante. 2004. (Illus.). 32p. (J). (978-0-9755646-6-0(8)) Westview Publishing Co., Inc.

Heasley, Gwendolyn. Don't Call Me Baby. 2014. (ENG.). 304p. (YA). (gr. 8). pap. 9.99 (978-0-06-220852-1(7), HarperTeen) HarperCollins Pubs.

Heidicker, Christian McKay. Attack of the 50 Foot Wallflower. Bosma, Sam, illus. (ENG.). 320p. (YA). (gr. 9). 2019. pap. 11.99 (978-1-4814-9914-9(9)) 2018. 18.99 (978-1-4814-9913-2(0)) Simon & Schuster Bks. For Young Readers. (Simon & Schuster Bks. For Young Readers).

Heller, Maryellen. My Big Sister's First Day of School. Soman, David, illus. 2009. (J). (978-0-8037-3246-9(5), Dial) Penguin Publishing Group.

Henderson, Susan Sinclair. Penelope's Journey Home. 2013. 48p. pap. 9.99 (978-1-4908-0420-0(X), WestBow Pr.) Author Solutions, LLC.

Henig, Sherry. Sara Makes Her Mother Proud & Learns Good Behavior: A Children's Book. 2nd ed. 2006. per. 6.95 (978-0-9777203-2-3(2)) Brenner Publishing, LLC.

Hernandez, Jo Ann Yolanda. The Throwaway Piece. 2006. 246p. (J). (gr. 6). per. 9.95 (978-1-55885-353-9(7), Piñata Books) Arte Publico Pr.

Herring, Bruce D. The Wizard of Wonderland, 1 vol. 2010. 192p. pap. 24.95 (978-1-4489-5844-3(X)) America Star Bks.

Hibbs, Lisa. Allie Doogledorf & the Mighty Mess. 2009. 36p. pap. 21.99 (978-1-4500-0777-1(5)) Xlibris Corp.

Hichens, Joanne. Stained. 2008. (Cutting Edge Ser.). (ENG.). 200p. pap. (978-1-84167-715-6(9)) Ransom Publishing Ltd.

Hill, Tara Theresa. What Can You Do with Two Mommies? 2012. (ENG.). 37p. 18.00 (978-1-105-50649-9(5)) Lulu Pr., Inc.

Hillyer, Brenda L. Mystery in the Marsh. 2008. 48p. pap. 16.95 (978-1-60703-784-2(X)) America Star Bks.

Hines, Thomas, illus. The Bubble Machine. l.t. ed. 2003. 26p. (J). per. (978-1-887636-02-5(1)) Creative Writing & Publishing Co.

Hirota, Denise. The Circus Poster. 2011. 58p. pap. 9.99 (978-1-60911-292-9(X), Eloquent Bks.) Strategic Book Publishing & Rights Agency (SBPRA).

Hitchcock, Shannon. One True Way. (ENG.). 224p. (J). (gr. 4-7). 2019. pap. 8.99 (978-1-338-18174-6(2)) 2018. (Illus.). 17.99 (978-1-338-18172-2(6)) Scholastic, Inc. (Scholastic Pr.).

Ho, Joanna. Eyes That Kiss in the Corners. Ho, Dung, illus. 2021. (ENG.). 40p. (J). (gr. -1-3). 17.99 (978-0-06-291562-7(2), HarperCollins) HarperCollins Pubs.

Hobbs, Valerie. Carolina Crow Girl. 2013. 146p. pap. 12.95 (978-1-62352-008-3(8)) IntoPrint Publishing LLC.

Hoffman, Diana / Lynne. Lighting the Earth. Brough, Karen, illus. 2014. 34p. (J). 23.95 (978-0-9891296-4-0(0), Aurora Books) Eco-Justice Pr., LLC.

Holcomb, T. Toot-Toot & Her Troubles: Name Calling. 2008. 12p. pap. 24.95 (978-1-60563-472-2(7)) America Star Bks.

Holmes, Kathryn. How It Feels to Fly. 2016. (ENG.). 368p. (YA). (gr. 8). 17.99 (978-0-06-238734-9(0), HarperTeen) HarperCollins Pubs.

Hoover, P. J. Solstice. 2013. (ENG.). 384p. (YA). (gr. 8). 34.99 (978-0-7653-3469-5(0), 900096814, Tor Teen) Doherty, Tom Assocs., LLC.

Howard, A. G. Splintered. 2013. (Splintered Ser.). (ENG.). 384p. (YA). (gr. 8-17). pap. 8.95 (978-1-4197-0627-1(6)) Abrams, Inc.

—Splintered. 2014. (Splintered Ser.: 1). (J). lib. bdg. 19.60 (978-0-606-35235-2(X)) Turtleback.

—Unhinged. 2014. (Splintered Ser.). (ENG.). 384p. (YA). (gr. 8-17). pap. 8.95 *(978-1-4197-1047-6(8))* Abrams, Inc.

—Unhinged. 2015. (Splintered Ser.: 2). (J). lib. bdg. 19.60 *(978-0-606-36565-9(6))* Turtleback.

—Unhinged (Splintered Series #2) 2015. (Splintered Ser.). (ENG.). 416p. (YA). (gr. 8-17). pap. 10.99 *(978-1-4197-1373-6(6)*, 1036403) Abrams, Inc.

Howard, J. J. That Time I Joined the Circus. 2013. (ENG.). 272p. (YA). (gr. 7). 17.99 *(978-0-545-43381-5(9))* Scholastic, Inc.

Hurwitz, Laura. Disappear Home. 2015. (ENG.). 256p. (YA). (gr. 8-12). 16.99 *(978-0-8075-2468-8(9)*, 807524689) Whitman, Albert & Co.

Hyde, Catherine Ryan. Jumpstart the World. 2011. 192p. (YA). (gr. 9). pap. 7.99 *(978-0-375-86626-5(4)*, Ember) Random Hse. Children's Bks.

Hysen, Sylvia. A Very Dairy Christmas. 2005. 290p. 24.95 *(978-0-9763365-6-3(1))* 1st Impression Publishing.

Ibbotson, Eva. The Star of Kazan. 2006. (ENG., Illus.). 416p. (J). (gr. 3-7). reprint ed. 10.99 *(978-0-14-240582-6(5)*, Puffin Books) Penguin Young Readers Group.

Ifueko, Jordan. Raybearer. (Raybearer Ser.). (ENG., Illus.). (YA). (gr. 7-17). 2021. 400p. pap. 10.99 *(978-1-4197-3983-5(2)*, 1297003) 2020. 368p. 18.99 *(978-1-4197-3982-8(4)*, 1297001) Abrams, Inc.

Jackson, Everett E. Kimme Meets Squirrelly D. Jimboy, Sarah, illus. 2008. (ENG.). 28p. pap. 16.95 *(978-1-4389-0971-4(3))* AuthorHouse.

Jacobs, John. I Wanna Be. 2006. (Illus.). 144p. 9.95 *(978-0-9774659-6-5(9))* Cameo Pubns., LLC.

Jalonen, Riitta. Tundra Mouse Mountain. Ledgard, J. M., tr. from FIN. Louhi, Kristiina, illus. 2006. (Picture books from around the World Seri Ser.). (ENG.). 56p. (J). (gr. k-2). 20.95 *(978-1-905341-05-4(9))* WingedChariot Pr. GBR. Dist: Independent Pubs. Group.

James, Debra & James, Jessica. The Social Pyramid. 2010. 57p. pap. 7.50 *(978-0-557-40789-7(3))* Lulu Pr., Inc.

Janice Turner & Colleen Connelly. Colleen Goes to the Farmer's Market. Ron Frazier, photos by. 2009. (Illus.). 20p. pap. 12.49 *(978-1-4389-6085-2(9))* AuthorHouse.

Jansen, Karen. The Coming of an Astronaut. 2009. 68p. pap. 9.99 *(978-1-60911-076-5(5)*, Eloquent Bks.) Strategic Book Publishing & Rights Agency (SBPRA).

Jefferson, Coretta Carte. Beautiful Lizzie. 2012. 24p. pap. 24.95 *(978-1-4626-8988-0(4))* America Star Bks.

Johnson, Andrea N. Mommy & Me. 2013. 20p. pap. 24.95 *(978-1-4626-9892-9(1))* America Star Bks.

Johnson, Christine. Nocturne. 2011. (ENG.). 368p. (YA). (gr. 7). 16.99 *(978-1-4424-0776-3(X)*, Simon Pulse) Simon Pulse.

—Nocturne: A Claire de Lune Novel. 2012. (ENG.). 384p. (YA). (gr. 7). pap. 9.99 *(978-1-4424-0777-0(8)*, Simon Pulse) Simon Pulse.

Johnson, D. C. & Turner, Sandra. Let's Be Friends. Johnson, D. C. & Johnson, Darnell, illus. 2007. (J). per. 9.95 *(978-1-933556-66-6(8))* Publishers' Graphics, L.L.C.

Johnson, Varian. The Parker Inheritance (Scholastic Gold) (ENG.). (J). (gr. 3-7). 2019. 368p. pap. 8.99 *(978-0-545-95278-1(6))* 2018. 352p. 18.99 *(978-0-545-94617-9(4))* Scholastic, Inc. (Levine, Arthur A. Bks.).

Johnston, Wayne M. North Fork. 2016. (ENG.). 210p. (YA). (gr. 7-12). pap. 14.95 *(978-1-936364-20-6(4))* Black Heron Pr.

Jones, Callie Carol Rodgers. A Good Cry. 2013. 20p. pap. 17.99 *(978-1-4772-9414-7(7))* AuthorHouse.

Jones, Erin. Tinfoil Crowns. 2019. (ENG.). 352p. (YA). (gr. 9-12). pap. 14.99 *(978-1-63583-032-3(X)*, 163583032X, Flux) North Star Editions.

Jones, Jen. Maren's New Family. Franco, Paula, illus. 2015. (Sleepover Girls Ser.). (ENG.). 128p. (J). (gr. 3-5). lib. bdg. 22.65 *(978-1-4965-0540-8(9)*, 128612, Stone Arch Bks.) Capstone.

Jones M.A., Yvette. I Know I Love You. 2008. 36p. pap. 24.95 *(978-1-60474-474-3(X))* America Star Bks.

Jones, Patrick. Outburst. 2014. (Alternative Ser.). (ENG.). 104p. (YA). (gr. 6-12). pap. 7.95 *(978-1-4677-4484-3(0)*, 19373d2e-a571-4166-b228-9cdb9f563141, Darby Creek) Lerner Publishing Group.

—Raising Heaven. 2015. (Locked Out Ser.). (ENG.). 96p. (YA). (gr. 6-12). E-Book 6.99 *(978-1-4677-7697-4(1)*, 9781467776974, Darby Creek) Lerner Publishing Group.

Joosse, Barbara M. Mama, Do You Love Me? 2014. (J). lib. bdg. 18.40 *(978-0-606-35289-5(9))* Turtleback.

—Mama, Do You Love Me? & Papa, Do You Love Me? Boxed Set: (Children's Emotions Books, Parent & Child Stories, Family Relationship Books for Kids), Set. Lavallee, Barbara, illus. 2017. (Mama & Papa, Do You Love Me? Ser.). (ENG.). 62p. (J). (gr. -1 — 1). bds. 14.99 *(978-1-4521-6612-4(9))* Chronicle Bks. LLC.

June, Christina. Everywhere You Want to Be, 1 vol. 2018. (ENG.). 288p. (YA). pap. 12.99 *(978-0-310-76333-8(9))* Blink.

June, Kimberly. It's No Fun Sucking Your Thumb. 2012. 28p. pap. 15.99 *(978-1-4691-8228-5(9))* Xlibris Corp.

Kade, Stacey. Finding Felicity. 2018. (ENG., Illus.). 304p. (YA). (gr. 9). 17.99 *(978-1-4814-6425-3(6)*, Simon & Schuster Bks. For Young Readers) Simon & Schuster Bks. For Young Readers.

Kadohata, Cynthia. Outside Beauty. (ENG.). (YA). (gr. 7). 2009. 288p. pap. 8.99 *(978-1-4169-9818-1(7))* 2008. (Illus.). 272p. 16.99 *(978-0-689-86575-6(9))* Simon & Schuster Children's Publishing. (Atheneum Bks. for Young Readers).

Kalmbach, Nicole. Lilly J, What Did I Say? 2011. 20p. 10.03 *(978-1-4520-9318-5(0))* AuthorHouse.

Kanady, Mary Ellen Murdock. Mommy & Me. 2008. (Illus.). 32p. (J). pap. 8.00 *(978-0-8059-7728-8(7))* Dorrance Publishing Co., Inc.

Kann, Victoria. Pinkalicious & the Perfect Present. Kann, Victoria, illus. 2014. (I Can Read Level 1 Ser.). (ENG., Illus.). 32p. (J). (gr. -1-3). 16.99 *(978-0-06-218789-5(9))*; pap. 4.99 *(978-0-06-218788-8(0))* HarperCollins Pubs. (HarperCollins).

Karandeev, Oleg. Dmitri II: The Kind Storyteller Book Two of Five. Ciesinska, Izabela, illus. 2007. 76p. (YA). per. 15.95 *(978-0-9793944-3-0(0))* Digi-Tall Media.

Katies Choice. 2005. (YA). per. *(978-1-59872-217-8(4))* Instant Pub.

Kats, Jewel. Snow White's Seven Patches: A Vitiligo Fairy Tale. Goodfellow, Dan, illus. 2013. 40p. (J). pap. 14.95 *(978-1-61599-206-5(5))* Loving Healing Pr., Inc.

Katschke, Judy. I Love My Mami! Aikins, Dave, illus. 2006. (Dora the Explorer Ser.: 9). (ENG.). 24p. (J). (gr. -1-k). pap. 3.99 *(978-1-4169-0650-6(9)*, Simon Spotlight/Nickelodeon) Simon Spotlight/Nickelodeon.

Kay, Sjoukje & Kay, Sjoukje. The Donut Yogi. Vita, Ariela, illus. 2007. (ENG.). 32p. (J). 2.50 *(978-0-9789698-1-3(2))* Kay, Sjoukje.

Kelsey, Annie. Love & Chicken Nuggets. Larsen, Kate, illus. 2017. (Pippa Morgan's Diary Ser.: 2). (ENG.). 176p. (J). (gr. 3-7). pap. 9.99 *(978-1-4926-4794-2(2))* Sourcebooks, Inc.

Kelso, Mary Jean. Birds in the Flower Basket. Hammond, Julie, illus. 2012. 26p. 19.95 *(978-1-61633-343-0(X))* Guardian Angel Publishing, Inc.

Kelso, Mary Jean & Hammond, Julie. Birds in the Flower Basket. 2012. 26p. pap. 11.95 *(978-1-61633-344-7(8))* Guardian Angel Publishing, Inc.

Kenneally, Miranda. Stealing Parker. 2012. (Hundred Oaks Ser.: 2). 256p. (YA). (gr. 7-12). pap. 10.99 *(978-1-4022-7187-8(5))* Sourcebooks, Inc.

Kennedy, Marlane. Me & the Pumpkin Queen. 2009. (ENG.). 192p. (J). (gr. 3-7). pap. 5.99 *(978-0-06-114024-2(4)*, Greenwillow Bks.) HarperCollins Pubs.

Kent, Trilby. Stones for My Father. 2011. 176p. (YA). (gr. 7-18). 19.95 *(978-1-77049-252-3(6)*, Tundra Bks.) Tundra Bks. CAN. Dist: Penguin Random Hse. LLC.

Keonna-E'nea. Momzilla, 1 vol. Joane', E'nea, illus. 2009. 18p. pap. 24.95 *(978-1-60749-607-6(0))* America Star Bks.

Kephart, Beth. House of Dance. 2010. (ENG.). 272p. (J). (gr. 8). pap. 10.99 *(978-0-06-142930-9(9))* 2008. 263p. (YA). (gr. 7-18). lib. bdg. 17.89 *(978-0-06-142929-3(5))* HarperCollins Pubs. (HarperTeen).

Kew, Trevor. Trading Goals, 1 vol. 2009. (Lorimer Sports Stories Ser.). (ENG.). 144p. (J). (gr. 3-7). 26.19 *(978-1-55277-425-0(2)*, 425) James Lorimer & Co. Ltd., Pubs. CAN. Dist: Children's Plus, Inc.

Khan, Sabina. The Love & Lies of Rukhsana Ali. (ENG.). 336p. (gr. 9). 2020. (J). pap. 10.99 *(978-1-338-58215-4(1))* 2019. (YA). 17.99 *(978-1-338-22701-7(7))* Scholastic, Inc. (Scholastic Pr.).

Kimmel, Elizabeth Cody. Suddenly Supernatural: Crossing Over. 2011. (Suddenly Supernatural Ser.: 4). (ENG.). 256p. (J). (gr. 3-7). pap. 14.99 *(978-0-316-13345-6(0))* Little, Brown Bks. for Young Readers.

—Suddenly Supernatural: Scaredy Kat. 2010. (Suddenly Supernatural Ser.: 2). (ENG.). 272p. (J). (gr. 3-7). pap. 15.99 *(978-0-316-08745-2(9))* Little, Brown Bks. for Young Readers.

—Suddenly Supernatural: School Spirit. 2010. (Suddenly Supernatural Ser.: 1). (ENG.). 336p. (J). (gr. 3-7). pap. 17.99 *(978-0-316-07821-4(2))* Little, Brown Bks. for Young Readers.

Kinsella, Sophie, pseud. Fairy Mom & Me #1. Kissi, Marta, illus. 2019. (Fairy Mom & Me Ser.: 1). (ENG.). 160p. (J). (gr. 2-5). pap. 5.99 *(978-1-5247-6993-2(2)*, Yearling) Random Hse. Children's Bks.

Kirby, Jessi. Golden. (ENG.). 288p. (YA). (gr. 7). 2014. pap. 9.99 *(978-1-4424-5218-3(8))* 2013. 16.99 *(978-1-4424-5216-9(1))* Simon & Schuster Bks. For Young Readers. (Simon & Schuster Bks. For Young Readers).

Kirby, Matthew J. The Arctic Code. 2015. (Dark Gravity Sequence Ser.: 1). (ENG.). 336p. (J). (gr. 3-7). 16.99 *(978-0-06-222487-3(5)*, Balzer & Bray) HarperCollins Pubs.

Kittredge, Caitlin. Dreaming Darkly. 2019. (ENG.). 368p. (YA). (gr. 9). 17.99 *(978-0-06-266562-1(6)*, Tegen, Katherine Bks) HarperCollins Pubs.

Klein, Alina. Rape Girl. 2012. 132p. (YA). 18.95 *(978-1-60898-123-6(1))*; pap. 9.95 *(978-1-60898-124-3(X))* namelos llc.

Klein, J. M. New School, New Me!, 1 vol. 2018. (Totally Secret Diary of Dani D. Ser.). (ENG.). 64p. (YA). (gr. 2-3). 23.25 *(978-1-5383-8196-0(6)*, 765fbfc3-1486-4ed4-94b5-27d0895051d1); pap. 13.35 *(978-1-5383-8195-3(8)*, ca0db874-610c-4d21-a737-ad4327ae802c) Enslow Publishing, LLC.

Knight, Andrew. Dead Beckoning. (Thumbprint Mysteries Ser.). 32.86 *(978-0-8092-0421-2(5))* McGraw-Hill/Contemporary.

Korelitz, Jean Hanff. Interference Powder, 0 vols. 2006. (ENG.). 146p. (J). (gr. 4-6). pap. 7.99 *(978-0-7614-5275-1(3)*, 9780761452751, Two Lions) Amazon Publishing.

Kulper, Kendall. Salt & Storm. 2014. (ENG.). 416p. (YA). E-Book *(978-0-316-40456-3(X))* Little Brown & Co.

Lacamara, Laura. Floating on Mama's Song. Morales, Yuyi, illus. 2010. (ENG.). 32p. (J). (gr. -1-2). 17.99 *(978-0-06-084368-7(3)*, Tegen, Katherine Bks) HarperCollins Pubs.

LaFaye, A. Nissa's Place. 2010. (ENG.). 256p. (J). (gr. 2-8). pap. 8.00 *(978-1-57131-697-4(3))* Milkweed Editions.

—The Year of the Sawdust Man. 2008. (ENG.). 224p. (J). (gr. 2-8). pap. 6.95 *(978-1-57131-679-0(5))* Milkweed Editions.

Laird, Chynna. Dark Water. 2012. 166p. pap. *(978-1-926997-76-6(X))* Imajin Bks.

Lakshmi, Padma. Tomatoes for Neela. Martinez-Neal, Juana, illus. 2021. 40p. (J). (gr. -1-2). 17.99 *(978-0-593-20270-8(8)*, Viking Books for Young Readers) Penguin Young Readers Group.

Lambert, Susan Dodd. Clarence the Clam. 2017. (ENG., Illus.). (J). (gr. k-3). 12.95 *(978-0-9984606-4-2(8))* Borgo Publishing.

—Clarence the Clam. Modugno, Tina, illus. 2013. 28p. pap. 6.95 *(978-0-9883893-5-9(5))* Borgo Publishing.

Lanagan, Margo. Tender Morsels. 2010. (ENG.). 464p. (YA). (gr. 9-18). pap. 11.99 *(978-0-375-84305-1(1)*, Ember) Random Hse. Children's Bks.

Lane, Dakota. The Orpheus Obsession. 2008. (ENG., Illus.). 288p. (YA). (gr. 9). pap. 8.99 *(978-0-06-074175-4(9)*, HarperTeen) HarperCollins Pubs.

Lasky, Kathryn. The Escape. 2014. (Horses of the Dawn Trilogy Ser.: 1). lib. bdg. 17.20 *(978-0-606-36034-0(4))* Turtleback.

—Horses of the Dawn #1: the Escape. 2014. (Horses of the Dawn Ser.: 1). (ENG.). 240p. (J). (gr. 3-7). pap. 6.99 *(978-0-545-39730-8(8)*, Scholastic Pr.) Scholastic, Inc.

Lasota, Mary. Kitty Piper, Angel Cat, Book 3, A Surprise for Ashley. 2011. 48p. (gr. 1-2). pap. 11.66 *(978-1-4634-1031-5(X))* AuthorHouse.

Laurie, Cook, illus. Amelia Asks Why. 2007. (J). 3.99 *(978-0-9726075-4-4(4))* EPI Bks.

Lawless, Freda. Shauna's Chance. 2013. 24p. pap. 24.95 *(978-1-62709-601-0(9))* America Star Bks.

Lawson, Jessica. Under the Bottle Bridge. 2017. (ENG., Illus.). 352p. (J). (gr. 3-7). 16.99 *(978-1-4814-4842-0(0)*, Simon & Schuster Bks. For Young Readers) Simon & Schuster Bks. For Young Readers.

Lawson, Kate. Mum's the Word. 2011. (ENG.). 400p. 14.99 *(978-1-84756-052-0(0)*, Avon Bks.) HarperCollins Pubs.

Leavitt, Caroline. Girls in Trouble: A Novel. 2005. (ENG.). 368p. pap. 22.99 *(978-0-312-33973-9(9)*, 900028982, St. Martin's Griffin) St. Martin's Pr.

Lee, Kyanna Shanae. Stepdad? No Thanks...! 2008. 60p. pap. 19.95 *(978-1-60563-422-7(0))* America Star Bks.

Lee, P. Janet. Ella Elephant: And Her Fear of Mice. 2007. (ENG., Illus.). 36p. (J). per. 15.95 *(978-1-59800-713-8(0))* Outskirts Pr., Inc.

Lemon, Emily. Little Hands. 2012. 24p. pap. 15.99 *(978-1-4771-4875-4(2))* Xlibris Corp.

Leonard, Marcia. Mi Dia de Campamento. Translations.com Staff, tr. from ENG. Handelman, Dorothy, photos by. 2007. (Lecturas para niños de Verdad - Nivel 1 (Real Kids Readers - Level 1) Ser.).Tr. of My Camp-Out. (SPA., Illus.). 32p. (gr. k-2). per. 5.95 *(978-0-8225-7798-0(4)*, Ediciones Lerner) Lerner Publishing Group.

—Mi Dia de Campamento; My Camp Out. 2008. pap. 34.95 *(978-0-8225-9496-3(X))* Lerner Publishing Group.

Leszczynski, Diana. Fern Verdant & the Silver Rose. 2009. (Playaway Children Ser.). (J). 59.99 *(978-1-4332-7708-5(5))* Findaway World, LLC.

Lietaert, Kelly Jean. I Wish I Was Big. 2017. (ENG.). (J). 14.95 *(978-1-68401-396-8(8))* Amplify Publishing Group.

Liner, Robin. Your Own Little Silly Mcgilly. Rogers, Madalyn V., illus. 2013. 38p. pap. 9.99 *(978-0-9910342-0-8(1))* East Stream Group, LLC.

Lisa Catanzarite. What the World Is Like to Bea Moore: Dear Santa. 2009. 60p. pap. 16.43 *(978-1-4269-2115-5(2))* Trafford Publishing.

Little, Cynthia. Mom's Imaginary Child. 2008. pap. *(978-0-9747707-2-7(8))* Sleepless Warrior Publishing.

Little, Kimberley Griffiths. Circle of Secrets. 2011. 326p. (J). *(978-0-545-38523-7(7)*, Scholastic Pr.) Scholastic, Inc.

Liu, Liana. The Memory Key. 2015. (ENG.). 368p. (YA). (gr. 8). 17.99 *(978-0-06-230664-7(2)*, HarperTeen) HarperCollins Pubs.

Lloyd, Natalie. A Snicker of Magic. 2015. lib. bdg. 17.20 *(978-0-606-37089-9(7))* Turtleback.

—A Snicker of Magic (Scholastic Gold) 2015. (ENG.). 336p. (J). (gr. 3-7). pap. 7.99 *(978-0-545-55273-8(7)*, Scholastic Pr.) Scholastic, Inc.

—A Snicker of Magic (Scholastic Gold) (Unabridged Edition), 2 vols. unabr. ed. 2014. (ENG.). 2p. (J). (gr. 3-7). audio compact disk 34.99 *(978-0-545-70679-7(3))* Scholastic, Inc.

Lloyd, Natalie, et al. A Snicker of Magic. 2014. (ENG.). mass mkt. *(978-0-545-68447-7(1))* Scholastic, Inc.

Lopresti, Kirsten. Bright Coin Moon: A Novel. 2014. (ENG.). 272p. (J). (gr. 6-6). 16.95 *(978-1-62914-751-2(6)*, Sky Pony Pr.) Skyhorse Publishing Co., Inc.

Lord, Emery. The Names They Gave Us. 2017. (ENG.). 400p. (YA). 17.99 *(978-1-61963-958-4(0)*, 900153588, Bloomsbury USA Childrens) Bloomsbury Publishing USA.

Lorimer, Janet. The Mystery Quilt, 1 vol. unabr. ed. 2010. (Q Reads Ser.). (ENG.). 32p. (YA). (gr. 9-12). pap. 8.50 *(978-1-61651-183-8(4))* Saddleback Educational Publishing, Inc.

Love, D. Anne. Semiprecious. (ENG.). 304p. (J). (gr. 5-9). 2009. pap. 6.99 *(978-0-689-87389-8(1))* 2006. (Illus.). 17.99 *(978-0-689-85638-9(5))* McElderry, Margaret K. Bks. (McElderry, Margaret K. Bks.).

Lovett, Louise Sheppa, illus. A Happy Day. Lovett, Louise Sheppa, . 2008. 32p. (J). 18.50 *(978-0-9793419-0-8(6))* Tish & Co. LLC.

Lowe, Natasha. The Courage of Cat Campbell. 2015. (Poppy Pendle Ser.). (ENG., Illus.). 288p. (J). (gr. 3-7). 16.99 *(978-1-4814-1870-6(X)*, Simon & Schuster/Paula Wiseman Bks.) Simon & Schuster/Paula Wiseman Bks.

Lowry, Lois. Find a Stranger, Say Goodbye. 2018. (ENG.). 240p. (YA). (gr. 7). pap. 9.99 *(978-1-328-90105-7(X)*, 1700162, Clarion Bks.) HarperCollins Pubs.

Lyons, Kelly Starling. Tiara's Hat Parade. Tadgell, Nicole, illus. 2020. (ENG.). 32p. (J). (gr. -1-3). 16.99 *(978-0-8075-7945-9(9)*, 807579459) Whitman, Albert & Co.

Mack, Winnie. After All, You're Callie Boone. 2013. (ENG.). 192p. (J). (gr. 4-7). pap. 14.99 *(978-1-250-02735-1(7)*, 900098307) Square Fish.

Mackler, Carolyn. Guyaholic. 2009. (ENG., Illus.). 192p. (YA). (gr. 9). pap. 7.99 *(978-0-7636-2801-7(8))* Candlewick Pr.

Maclachlan, Patricia. More Perfect Than the Moon. 2005. 16.00 *(978-0-7569-5437-6(1))* Perfection Learning Corp.

Maclean, Heather. Toward a Secret Sky, 1 vol. 2018. (ENG.). 384p. (YA). pap. 10.99 *(978-0-310-75487-9(9))* Blink.

Maddox, Jake. Power Play. 2016. (Jake Maddox JV Girls Ser.). (ENG., Illus.). 96p. (J). (gr. 4-8). lib. bdg. 26.65 *(978-1-4965-3673-0(8)*, 132924, Stone Arch Bks.) Capstone.

—Spinning Away. 2017. (Jake Maddox JV Girls Ser.). (ENG., Illus.). 96p. (J). (gr. 4-8). lib. bdg. 26.65 *(978-1-4965-4927-3(9)*, 135824, Stone Arch Bks.) Capstone.

—Tae Kwon Do Clash. 2016. (Jake Maddox JV Ser.). (ENG., Illus.). 96p. (J). (gr. 4-6). lib. bdg. 26.65 *(978-1-4965-3981-6(8)*, 133204, Stone Arch Bks.) Capstone.

Madonia, Kristen-Paige. Fingerprints of You. (ENG., Illus.). 272p. (YA). (gr. 9). 2013. pap. 9.99 *(978-1-4424-2921-5(6))* 2012. 16.99 *(978-1-4424-2920-8(8))* Simon & Schuster Bks. For Young Readers. (Simon & Schuster Bks. For Young Readers).

Madrigal, Antonio Hernandez. Erandi's Braids. dePaola, Tomie, illus. 2015. 32p. pap. 7.00 *(978-1-61003-530-9(5))* Center for the Collaborative Classroom.

Maguire, Gregory. Matchless: An Illumination of Hans Christian Andersen's Classic the Little Match Girl. 2010. (ENG., Illus.). 112p. pap. 14.99 *(978-0-06-200482-6(4)*, William Morrow Paperbacks) HarperCollins Pubs.

Makechnie, Amy. The Unforgettable Guinevere St. Clair. (ENG.). 336p. (J). (gr. 3-7). 2019. pap. 8.99 *(978-1-5344-1447-1(9))* 2018. (Illus.). 18.99 *(978-1-5344-1446-4(0))* Simon & Schuster Children's Publishing. (Atheneum Bks. for Young Readers).

Mancini, Kristen Belmont. A Bunny Named Boo. 2011. 24p. pap. *(978-1-4269-7640-7(2))* Trafford Publishing (UK) Ltd.

Manushkin, Fran. Katie's Happy Mother's Day. Lyon, Tammie, illus. 2015. (Katie Woo Ser.). (ENG.). 32p. (J). (gr. k-2). 21.32 *(978-1-4795-6179-7(7)*, 127896, Picture Window Bks.) Capstone.

Marchese, Allison Marie. Patty's Best Friend. 2008. (Illus.). 16p. (J). 7.00 *(978-0-8059-7533-8(0))* Dorrance Publishing Co., Inc.

Marciniak, Christine. Lights, Camera, Ali! 2013. 232p. (J). pap. 13.99 *(978-1-61271-214-7(2))* Zumaya Pubns. LLC.

Marie, Jessica. Keeping Broken Promises, 1 vol. 2010. 182p. pap. 24.95 *(978-1-4489-5273-1(5))* America Star Bks.

Marler, Jerilyn. Lily Hates Goodbyes. Stoltenberg, Nathan, illus. 2012. 32p. pap. 6.95 *(978-1-936214-78-5(4))* Wyatt-MacKenzie Publishing.

Marlow, Herb. A Long Way Home. l.t. ed. 2003. (Illus.). 14p. (J). 19.95 *(978-1-893595-35-4(8))* Four Seasons Bks., Inc.

Marr, Kendra Lynn. I Was Rufus. 2013. 20p. pap. 24.95 *(978-1-4626-9917-9(0))* America Star Bks.

Marrone, Amanda. The Shape-Shifter's Curse, 2. 2010. (Magic Repair Shop Ser.: 2). (ENG.). 240p. (J). (gr. 3-7). pap. 5.99 *(978-1-4169-9034-5(8)*, Aladdin) Simon & Schuster Children's Publishing.

Martin-Fluet, Marie T. The Fairies' Century Celebration. 2011. 40p. pap. 18.62 *(978-1-4567-2477-1(0))* AuthorHouse.

Martinez, Jessica. Virtuosity. (ENG.). (YA). (gr. 9). 2012. 320p. pap. 9.99 *(978-1-4424-2053-3(7))* 2011. 304p. 16.99 *(978-1-4424-2052-6(9))* Simon Pulse. (Simon Pulse).

Mason-Black, Jennifer. Devil & the Bluebird. 2016. (ENG.). 336p. (J). (gr. 8-17). 17.95 *(978-1-4197-2000-0(7)*, 1135901, Amulet Bks.) Abrams, Inc.

Mason, Christopher. Little Bunny Comfy Pants. 2011. 20p. pap. 24.95 *(978-1-4626-0900-0(7))* America Star Bks.

Mathieu, Jennifer. Moxie: A Novel. 2018. (ENG.). 352p. (YA). pap. 10.99 *(978-1-250-10426-7(2)*, 900163699) Square Fish.

Mathis, Tabitha. The Princess & the Tyger. 2012. 28p. pap. 24.95 *(978-1-4626-8265-2(0))* America Star Bks.

Mathisen, Michael. Abby & the Helping Mommy. Estill, Amy, illus. 2009. 28p. pap. 13.99 *(978-1-4389-5327-4(5))* AuthorHouse.

Mayhew, Julie. Red Ink. 2016. (ENG.). 320p. (YA). (gr. 9). 16.99 *(978-0-7636-7731-2(0))* Candlewick Pr.

Mazer, Norma Fox. Missing Pieces. 2007. (ENG., Illus.). 160p. (YA). (gr. 7-12). pap. 11.95 *(978-0-15-206271-2(8)*, 1198796, Clarion Bks.) HarperCollins Pubs.

Mazurick, Shannon K. Gemm: The Search for the Gem. 2011. 24p. pap. 15.00 *(978-1-4634-4265-1(3))* AuthorHouse.

McCahan, Erin. I Now Pronounce You Someone Else. 2010. (ENG.). 272p. (J). (gr. 7-18). 16.99 *(978-0-545-08818-3(6)*, Levine, Arthur A. Bks.) Scholastic, Inc.

McCartney, Jenny. The Stone Bird. Benson, Patrick, illus. 2018. (ENG.). 32p. (J). (gr. -1-3). 17.99 *(978-1-5415-1455-3(6)*, 992b2066-f683-4ace-96cd-689c95cba14b) Lerner Publishing Group.

McCormick, Michelle. Priscilla Willa, Party Planner: Night at the Haunted Hotel. 2013. (ENG.). 108p. (YA). pap. 9.95 *(978-1-4787-0890-2(5))* Outskirts Pr., Inc.

McDaniel, Lurlene. Garden of Angels. 2005. 272p. (gr. 7). 16.50 *(978-0-7569-5756-8(7))* Perfection Learning Corp.

McDowell, Kara. Just for Clicks. 2019. (ENG.). 250p. (YA). pap. 12.99 *(978-1-948705-19-6(2))* Amberjack Publishing Co.

McElreath, Kim. Pouring in Love. l.t. ed. 2005. (Illus.). 30p. (J). 13.95 *(978-0-9769271-0-5(1))* McElreath, K.M.

McElroy, Lisa Tucker. Love, Lizzie: Letters to a Military Mom. Paterson, Diane, illus. 2009. (ENG.). 32p. (J). (gr. -1-3). pap. 7.99 *(978-0-8075-4778-6(6)*, 807547786) Whitman, Albert & Co.

McFarlane, Sheryl. The Smell of Paint, 1 vol. 2006. (ENG.). 280p. (YA). (gr. 6-9). pap. 7.95 *(978-1-55041-457-8(7)*, 85c13ada-495b-4550-b661-085b7998e4ff) Fitzhenry & Whiteside, Ltd. CAN. Dist: Firefly Bks., Ltd.

McGee, Pamela M. Keri. Miller, Dawn Ellen, illus. 2012. 20p. pap. 24.95 *(978-1-4626-8593-6(5))* America Star Bks.

—Keri: Dandelions. Miller, Dawn Ellen, illus. 2012. 24p. pap. 24.95 *(978-1-4626-9977-3(4))* America Star Bks.

—Keri: The Wedding. Miller, Dawn Ellen, illus. 2013. 20p. pap. 24.95 *(978-1-63004-171-7(8))* America Star Bks.

McGinnis, Mindy. Not a Drop to Drink. (ENG.). (YA). (gr. 9). 2014. 352p. pap. 9.99 *(978-0-06-219851-8(3))* 2013. 320p. 17.99 *(978-0-06-219850-1(5))* HarperCollins Pubs. (Tegen, Katherine Bks).

McKenny, Stephanie L. Pearls of My Own. 2012. 102p. pap. 10.00 *(978-0-9705008-5-4(8))* J & J Publishing Co.

McKenzie, Paige. The Haunting of Sunshine Girl. 2016. (Haunting of Sunshine Girl Ser.: Vol. 1). (ENG.). 320p. (YA). (gr. 7-17). lib. bdg. 21.80 *(978-1-5311-8307-3(7))* Perfection Learning Corp.

—The Haunting of Sunshine Girl: Book One. 2016. (Haunting of Sunshine Girl Ser.: 1). (ENG.). 320p. (YA). (gr. 7-17). pap. 10.99 *(978-1-60286-302-6(4))* Hachette Bk. Group.

—The Haunting of Sunshine Girl: Book One. 2015. (Haunting of Sunshine Girl Ser.: 1). (ENG.). 304p. (YA). (gr. 7-17). 16.00 *(978-1-60286-272-2(9))* Hachette Bks.

Meldrum, Christina. Madapple. 2010. 416p. (YA). (gr. 9-18). pap. 10.99 *(978-0-375-85177-3(1)*, Knopf Bks. for Young Readers) Random Hse. Children's Bks.

Mentyka, Sharon. Chasing at the Surface: A Novel. 2016. (ENG., Illus.). 228p. (J). (gr. 3-7). pap. 12.99 *(978-1-943328-60-4(9)*, West Winds Pr.) West Margin Pr.

Meyers, Susan York. Stone Girl. 2018. (ENG.). 96p. (J). (gr. 4-8). 14.99 *(978-0-9972351-5-9(2))* Doodle and Peck Publishing.

Micinilio, Leanne Plein. Tia's Troubles: The First in a series of Tia's Adventures. 2011. 40p. pap. 16.99 *(978-1-4490-4695-8(9))* AuthorHouse.

MNO

Mickelson, Marcia. The Huaca. 2013. (J). pap. 16.99 *(978-1-4621-1190-9(4)*, Horizon Pubs.) Cedar Fort, Inc./CFI Distribution.

Miller-Johnston, Renee. Double Trouble for Courtney Logan Kennedy, 1 vol. 2009. 88p. pap. 19.95 *(978-1-60836-384-1(8))* America Star Bks.

Miller, Kymberly. My Mommy's Having a Baby. 2012. 36p. (-18). pap. 18.99 *(978-1-4772-8660-9(8))* AuthorHouse.

Miller, Mary Beth. Aimee. 2005. 276p. (gr. 9-12). 17.00 *(978-0-7569-6303-3(6))* Perfection Learning Corp.

Mills, Wendy. Positively Beautiful. 2016. (ENG.). 368p. (YA). pap. 9.99 *(978-1-68119-025-9(7)*, 9781681190259, Bloomsbury USA Childrens) Bloomsbury Publishing USA.

Mincin, Sabrina. Catching a Shooting Star. 2012. 28p. pap. 12.95 *(978-1-4575-0862-2(1))* Dog Ear Publishing, LLC.

Minix, Holly. What Does Mommy Do at Night? 2009. 68p. pap. 25.00 *(978-1-60693-705-1(7)*, Strategic Bk. Publishing) Strategic Book Publishing & Rights Agency (SBPRA).

Miranda, Megan. The Safest Lies. 2017. (ENG.). 384p. (YA). (gr. 9). pap. 11.99 *(978-0-553-53754-3(7)*, Ember) Random Hse. Children's Bks.

Mitchell, Rae. Anna's Wish. 2009. 24p. pap. 13.50 *(978-1-60860-441-8(1)*, Eloquent Bks.) Strategic Book Publishing & Rights Agency (SBPRA).

Molesworth, Mary Louisa S. Rosy. 2008. 120p. pap. 9.95 *(978-1-60664-226-9(X))* Rodgers, Alan Bks.

Monnar, Alberto. The Girl & the Mirror. Weiner, Linda, ed. Morton, Lisa, illus. 2008. per. 14.99 *(978-0-9768035-8-4(5))* Readers Are Leaders U.S.A.

Montijo, Rhode. Gum Luck. 2018. (Gum Girl Ser.: 2). (J). lib. bdg. 17.20 *(978-0-606-40644-4(1))* Turtleback.

Montijo, Rhode & Reynolds, Luke. The Gumazing Gum Girl! Gum Luck. Montijo, Rhode, illus. 2017. (Gumazing Gum Girl! Ser.: 2). (ENG., Illus.). 160p. (J). (gr. 1-5). 14.99 *(978-1-4231-6117-2(3))* Hyperion Bks. for Children.

Moon, Sarah. Sparrow. 2019. (ENG.). 272p. (YA). (gr. 7-7). pap. 10.99 *(978-1-338-31286-7(3)*, Levine, Arthur A. Bks.) Scholastic, Inc.

Mora, Oge. Saturday. 2019. (ENG., Illus.). 40p. (J). (gr. -1-3). 18.99 *(978-0-316-43127-9(3))* Little, Brown Bks. for Young Readers.

Moranville, Sharelle Byars. Surprise Lily. 2019. (ENG., Illus.). 240p. (J). (gr. 3-7). 15.99 *(978-0-8234-4264-5(0))* Holiday Hse., Inc.

Morgan, Phillip. Abused, Alone & Forsaken: Mommy, Don't Leave Me. 2009. 212p. pap. 24.95 *(978-1-4489-2733-3(1))* America Star Bks.

Morrissey, Donna. What Beautiful Mistake Did You Make Today? 2012. 24p. pap. 13.95 *(978-1-4772-5669-5(5))* AuthorHouse.

Moser, Fiadhnait. The Flourishing of Floralie Laurel. 2018. (ENG., Illus.). 336p. (J). (gr. 4-9). 16.99 *(978-1-4998-0668-7(X)*, Yellow Jacket) Bonnier Publishing USA.

—The Serendipity of Flightless Things. 2019. (ENG.). 320p. (J). (gr. 4-9). 16.99 *(978-1-4998-0843-8(7)*, Yellow Jacket) Bonnier Publishing USA.

Mullaly Hunt, Lynda. One for the Murphys. (J). (gr. 5). 2013. 256p. pap. 8.99 *(978-0-14-242652-4(0)*, Puffin Books) 2012. 240p. 17.99 *(978-0-399-25615-8(6)*, Nancy Paulsen Books) Penguin Young Readers Group.

Muñoz, Isabel. Just Like Mom. Mazali, Gustavo, illus. 2005. 22p. (J). pap. *(978-0-439-78844-1(7))* Scholastic, Inc.

Mureddu, R. The Laundromat. 2011. 96p. pap. 19.95 *(978-1-4560-8389-2(9))* America Star Bks.

Murray, Victoria Christopher. Aaliyah. 2009. (Divas Ser.). (ENG.). 224p. pap. 14.99 *(978-1-4165-6351-8(2)*, Gallery Bks.) Gallery Bks.

Myers, Lily. This Impossible Light. 2017. 352p. (YA). (gr. 7). 17.99 *(978-0-399-17372-1(2)*, Philomel Bks.) Penguin Young Readers Group.

Myracle, Lauren. The Forgetting Spell. 2018. (Wishing Day Ser.: 2). (ENG.). 368p. (J). (gr. 3-7). pap. 6.99 *(978-0-06-234210-2(X)*, Tegen, Katherine Bks) HarperCollins Pubs.

Napoli, Donna Jo. Zel. 2005. 240p. (J). (gr. 5-9). 21.00 *(978-0-8446-7278-6(5)*, 3593) Smith, Peter Pub., Inc.

Nation, Kay. Jamie Learns to Love. 2006. pap. 10.00 *(978-1-4257-0534-3(0))* Xlibris Corp.

Neel, Julien. Secret Diary. Neel, Julien, illus. 2012. (Lou! Ser.). (Illus.). 48p. (J). (gr. 4-8). pap. 51.02 *(978-0-7613-9285-9(8))*; (ENG., (gr. 6-9). pap. 8.95 *(978-0-7613-8868-5(0))* Lerner Publishing Group. (Graphic Universe™).

—Summertime Blues. Neel, Julien, illus. 2012. (Lou! Ser.). (Illus.). 48p. (J). (gr. 4-8). pap. 51.02 *(978-0-7613-9286-6(6)*, Graphic Universe™) Lerner Publishing Group.

Newman, Leslea. Heather Has Two Mommies. Cornell, Laura, illus. 2015. (ENG.). 32p. (J). (gr. -1-2). 18.99 *(978-0-7636-6631-6(9))* Candlewick Pr.

Nickles, Clay & Ayres, Ella. Ali's Treasure. l.t. ed. 2005. (Illus.). 38p. (J). per. 16.95 *(978-1-59879-006-1(4))* Lifevest Publishing, Inc.

Nielsen-Fernlund, Susin. The Magic Beads. Côté, Geneviève, illus. 2007. (ENG.). 32p. (J). (gr. -1-3). 16.95 *(978-1-894965-47-7(7))* Simply Read Bks. CAN. Dist: Ingram Publisher Services.

Nilsson, Ulf. Detective Gordon: a Case for Buffy. Spee, Gitte, illus. 2018. (Detective Gordon Ser.). (ENG.). 108p. (J). (gr. k-5). 16.99 *(978-1-77657-178-9(9)*, c920efa5-2f2a-4261-a17f-c17d9ea10668) Gecko Pr. NZL. Dist: Lerner Publishing Group.

Nix, Josef. My Mama's War. 2009. 104p. pap. 9.99 *(978-1-60860-666-5(X)*, Strategic Bk. Publishing) Strategic Book Publishing & Rights Agency (SBPRA).

Nona Theresa Perez - Bayanin. The Birth of Nadia Mei. 2012. 24p. pap. 15.99 *(978-1-4771-0387-6(2))* Xlibris Corp.

Novak, Ali. Paper Hearts. 2017. (Heartbreak Chronicles Ser.: 2). 400p. (YA). (gr. 8-12). pap. 10.99 *(978-1-4926-5336-3(5))* Sourcebooks, Inc.

Noyes, Deborah. Angel & Apostle. 2007. 304p. per. 14.95 *(978-1-932961-29-4(1))* Unbridled Bks.

Oakes, Cory Putman. Witchtown. 2017. (ENG.). 320p. (YA). (gr. 7). 17.99 *(978-0-544-76557-3(5)*, 1635515, Clarion Bks.) HarperCollins Pubs.

Oates, Joyce Carol. Freaky Green Eyes. 2005. 341p. (YA). 15.65 *(978-0-7569-6308-8(7))* Perfection Learning Corp.

O'Brien, Claudia Moore. My Mom's Apron. Friar, Joanne, illus. 2005. (ENG.). 12p. (J). 5.75 *(978-1-57274-753-1(6)*, 2772, Bks. for Young Learners) Owen, Richard C. Pubs., Inc.

Ofelia, Dumas Lachtman. Big Enough Bastante Grande. Enrique, Sanchez, illus. 2008. 32p. (J). pap. 7.95 *(978-1-55885-239-6(5))* Arte Publico Pr.

Oliver, Jan. Heart of Fire. 2009. 176p. pap. 18.95 *(978-1-4092-6660-0(5))* Lulu Pr., Inc.

Olson, Gretchen. Call Me Hope. 2008. (ENG.). 288p. (J). (gr. 3-7). pap. 15.99 *(978-0-316-01239-3(4))* Little, Brown Bks. for Young Readers.

One Last Garden. 2006. (J). per. 10.95 *(978-1-933505-20-6(6))* Quantum Manifestations Publishing.

O'Reilly, Jane. The Secret of Goldenrod. (ENG.). (J). (gr. 3-6). 2018. 392p. pap. 9.99 *(978-1-5415-1493-5(9)*, 75e9b3c2-a2d3-4066-85fe-25aea387aa08) 2016. 376p. 17.99 *(978-1-5124-0135-6(8)*, c4a3f32f-d495-461e-8c14-f8580406f616) 2016. 376p. E-Book 27.99 *(978-1-5124-0894-2(8))* Lerner Publishing Group. (Carolrhoda Bks.).

Ormerod, Jan. Lizzie Nonsense. 2006. (Illus.). 32p. pap. *(978-1-877003-93-6(X))* Little Hare Bks. AUS. Dist: HarperCollins Pubs. Australia.

Palmer, Ingrid. All Out of Pretty. 2018. (ENG.). 344p. (YA). (gr. 7-12). 16.99 *(978-1-939547-48-4(2)*, 8fe2a0c1-3f0e-4034-be6e-b825aed9d232) Creston Bks.

Paoline, Dyann. Cecilia's Fitness Adventure. 2011. 24p. pap. 15.75 *(978-1-4634-0797-1(1))* AuthorHouse.

Paratore, Coleen Murtagh. Sunny Holiday. 2008. (Sunny Holiday Ser.: 1). (ENG.). 176p. (J). (gr. 2-4). 18.69 *(978-0-545-07588-6(2))* Scholastic, Inc.

—The Wedding Planner's Daughter. McGregor, Barbara, illus. 2006. (Wedding Planner's Daughter Ser.). (ENG.). 208p. (J). (gr. 3-8). reprint ed. pap. 7.99 *(978-1-4169-1854-7(X)*, Simon & Schuster Bks. For Young Readers) Simon & Schuster Bks. For Young Readers.

Parish, Herman. Amelia Bedelia by the Yard. Avril, Lynne, illus. 2016. (I Can Read Level 1 Ser.). (ENG.). 32p. (J). (gr. -1-3). pap. 4.99 *(978-0-06-233427-5(1)*, Greenwillow Bks.) HarperCollins Pubs.

—Amelia Bedelia Chalks One Up. 2014. (I Can Read Level 1 Ser.). (ENG., Illus.). 32p. (J). (gr. -1-3). 16.99 *(978-0-06-233422-0(0)*, Greenwillow Bks.) HarperCollins Pubs.

—Amelia Bedelia Chalks One Up! 2014. (I Can Read Level 1 Ser.). (ENG., Illus.). 32p. (J). (gr. -1-3). pap. 4.99 *(978-0-06-233421-3(2)*, Greenwillow Bks.) HarperCollins Pubs.

—Amelia Bedelia Chalks One Up. 2014. (Amelia Bedelia: I Can Read! Ser.). (J). lib. bdg. 13.55 *(978-0-606-35947-4(8))* Turtleback.

Pascal, Francine. Falsas Apariencias. Orig. Title: Jumping to Conclusions. (SPA., Illus.). 128p. (J). 6.95 *(978-84-272-3794-0(4))* Molino, Editorial ESP. Dist: AIMS International Bks., Inc.

Patron, Susan. Maybe Yes, Maybe No, Maybe Maybe. Halpin, Abigail, illus. 2009. (ENG.). 128p. (J). (gr. 3-5). pap. 5.99 *(978-1-4169-6176-5(3)*, Atheneum Bks. for Young Readers) Simon & Schuster Children's Publishing.

Patterson, Valerie O. The Other Side of Blue. 2011. (ENG.). 240p. (YA). (gr. 7). pap. 13.99 *(978-0-547-55215-6(7)*, 1450660, Clarion Bks.) HarperCollins Pubs.

Peakler, Nicole Danette. Tayno Ti & the Legend of the Coqui. 2012. 28p. 24.95 *(978-1-4626-5940-1(3))* America Star Bks.

Pearce, Valarie. When Mommy Needs a Timeout. Johnson, Meredith, illus. 2012. 26p. pap. 10.99 *(978-0-9843111-5-6(7))* ImaRa Publishing.

Perelman-Bernstein, Helen. Feel the Noise! Tips & Tricks to Rockin' Camp. 2009. (ENG.). 40p. (J). 4.99 *(978-1-4231-2219-7(4))* Disney Pr.

Peterka, Edward S. Zoe Isabella Goes to the Zoo. 2011. 32p. pap. 12.77 *(978-1-4520-0305-4(X))* AuthorHouse.

Peterson, Lois. Three Good Things, 1 vol. 2015. (Orca Currents Ser.). (ENG.). 144p. (J). (gr. 4-7). pap. 9.95 *(978-1-4598-0985-7(8))* Orca Bk. Pubs. USA.

Pfoutz, Sally. Missing Person. 2009. 192p. (gr. 7-18). pap. 12.95 *(978-1-4401-5108-8(3))* iUniverse, Inc.

Philbin, Joanna. The Daughters Take the Stage. 2011. (Daughters Ser.: 3). (ENG.). 304p. (YA). (gr. 7-17). pap. 16.99 *(978-0-316-04908-5(5)*, Poppy) Little, Brown Bks. for Young Readers.

Philips, Fleur. Beautiful Girl: A Novel. 2015. (ENG.). 150p. (YA). pap. 17.00 *(978-1-940716-47-3(0))* SparkPr. (a Bks.parks Imprint).

Phillips, Linda Vigen. Crazy. 2014. (ENG.). 320p. (YA). pap. 9.00 *(978-0-8028-5437-7(0)*, Eerdmans Bks For Young Readers) Eerdmans, William B. Publishing Co.

Pickett, Anola. Whisper Island. 2013. (ENG.). 235p. (J). (gr. 3-7). pap. 14.99 *(978-1-4621-1167-1(X)*, Sweetwater Bks.) Cedar Fort, Inc./CFI Distribution.

Picoult, Jodi & van Leer, Samantha. Between the Lines. (ENG., Illus.). 368p. (YA). (gr. 7). 2013. pap. 15.99 *(978-1-4516-3581-2(8))* 2012. 19.99 *(978-1-4516-3575-1(3))* Atria/Emily Bestler Bks. (Atria/Emily Bestler Bks.).

Pierres, Marianne De. Serious Sas & Messy Magda. Bridgen, Rachel Annie, illus. 2013. 32p. pap. *(978-1-909423-04-6(1))* Bks. to Treasure.

Pierro, Rita. A Horse in the House, 1 vol. French, David, illus. 2009. 29p. pap. 24.95 *(978-1-60836-410-7(0))* America Star Bks.

Piontek, Victoria. The Spirit of Cattail County. 2018. (ENG.). 288p. (J). (gr. 3-7). 16.99 *(978-1-338-16705-4(7)*, Scholastic Pr.) Scholastic, Inc.

Polsky, Sara. This Is How I Find Her. 2015. (ENG.). 272p. (YA). (gr. 8-12). pap. 9.99 *(978-0-8075-7880-3(0)*, 807578800) Whitman, Albert & Co.

Ponnay, Brenda & Ponnay, Brenda. Secret Agent Josephine in Paris. 2013. 32p. pap. 9.99 *(978-1-62395-552-6(1))* Xist Publishing.

Ponti, James. Dead City. (Dead City Ser.: 1). (ENG., Illus.). (J). (gr. 4-8). 2013. 304p. pap. 8.99 *(978-1-4424-4130-9(5))* 2012. 288p. 19.99 *(978-1-4424-4129-3(1))* Simon & Schuster Children's Publishing. (Aladdin).

Poston, Karen. A Baby for Mabel & Frederick. 2005. 20p. (J). 11.28 *(978-1-4116-6024-3(2))* Lulu Pr., Inc.

Potter, Dawn. Isobel's Tree. 2010. 16p. pap. 9.99 *(978-1-60860-966-6(9)*, Eloquent Bks.) Strategic Book Publishing & Rights Agency (SBPRA).

Powers, J. L. This Thing Called the Future, 1 vol. 2011. (ENG.). 208p. (YA). (gr. 9-12). 16.95 *(978-1-933693-95-8(9)*, 23353382, Cinco Puntos Press) Lee & Low Bks., Inc.

Pressler, Mirjam. Malka. Murdoch, Brian, tr. 2005. 280p. (YA). (gr. 7-12). 13.65 *(978-0-7569-5217-4(4))* Perfection Learning Corp.

Price, M. J. The Skin I'm In. 2013. 32p. pap. 24.95 *(978-1-63000-967-0(9))* America Star Bks.

Puentes, Christina. On the Way to Granny's House. 2005. 28p. per. 17.32 *(978-1-4134-3612-9(9))* Xlibris Corp.

Pullman, Philip. Le Miroir d'Ambre. (FRE.). pap. 18.95 *(978-2-07-054376-2(5))* Gallimard, Editions FRA. Dist: Distribooks, Inc.

Pyles, Mary Kay. Rise & Shine Rosie. 2013. 134p. pap. 11.95 *(978-0-9887836-9-0(X))* Taylor and Seale Publishing.

Quirk, Katie. A Girl Called Problem. 2013. (ENG., Illus.). 256p. (J). pap. 8.50 *(978-0-8028-5404-9(4)*, Eerdmans Bks For Young Readers) Eerdmans, William B. Publishing Co.

Rahlens, Holly-Jane. Prince William, Maximilian Minsky, & Me. 2007. (ENG.). 320p. (YA). (gr. 7-11). per. 7.99 *(978-0-7636-3299-1(6))* Candlewick Pr.

Rando, Licia. The Warmest Place of All. Jewett, Anne, illus. 2009. (ENG.). 32p. (J). (gr. -1-k). 16.95 *(978-0-9792035-8-9(9))* Pleasant St. Pr.

Rao, Sandhya. My Mother's Sari. Sabnani, Nina, illus. 2009. (ENG.). 28p. (J). (gr. -1-3). 8.95 *(978-0-7358-2233-7(6))* North-South Bks., Inc.

Ratcliffe-Kitchingman, Linda. Lindylou in I Hate Porridge. 2012. 32p. pap. 8.99 *(978-1-62419-173-2(8))* Salem Author Services.

Ratliff, Lana. A Blanket Full of Blessings. 2012. 32p. 29.99 *(978-1-62230-245-1(1))*; pap. 19.99 *(978-1-62230-244-4(3))* Salem Author Services.

Raymundo, Peter. Third Grade Mermaid. 2017. (ENG., Illus.). 208p. (J). (gr. 1-3). 14.99 *(978-0-545-91816-9(2)*, Scholastic Pr.) Scholastic, Inc.

Reed, Amy. Over You. (ENG., Illus.). (YA). (gr. 9). 2014. 336p. pap. 9.99 *(978-1-4424-5697-6(3))* 2013. 320p. 16.99 *(978-1-4424-5696-9(5))* Simon Pulse. (Simon Pulse).

Reeves, Dia. Bleeding Violet. 2010. (ENG.). 480p. (YA). (gr. 9). pap. 20.99 *(978-1-4169-8619-5(7)*, Simon Pulse) Simon Pulse.

Reichert, Amy. Take Your Mama to Work Today. Boiger, Alexandra, illus. 2012. (ENG.). 40p. (J). (gr. -1-8). 16.99 *(978-1-4169-7095-8(9)*, Atheneum Bks. for Young Readers) Simon & Schuster Children's Publishing.

Reiser, Lynn. Tortillas & Lullabies/Tortillas y Cancioncitas: Bilingual English-Spanish. Corazones Valientes, Corazones, illus. 2008.Tr. of Tortillas & Lullabies. (ENG.). 48p. (J). (gr. -1-3). pap. 8.99 *(978-0-06-089185-5(8)*, Greenwillow Bks.) HarperCollins Pubs.

Remington, Laurel. Secrets & Scones. 2018. (Secret Recipe Book Ser.: 1). (ENG.). 288p. (J). (gr. 3-7). pap. 7.99 *(978-1-4926-6964-7(4))* Sourcebooks, Inc.

Renfrew, Regan. Orphans of the Heart: A Young Girl & a Paint Filly Heal Each Other's Broken Hearts. 2013. (ENG.). 163p. (YA). pap. 12.95 *(978-1-4787-1686-0(X))* Outskirts Pr., Inc.

Resau, Laura. The Indigo Notebook. 2010. (Notebook Ser.: 1). 336p. (YA). (gr. 7). pap. 9.99 *(978-0-375-84524-6(0)*, Ember) Random Hse. Children's Bks.

—The Ruby Notebook. 2012. (Notebook Ser.). 384p. (YA). (gr. 7). pap. 9.99 *(978-0-375-84525-3(9)*, Ember) Random Hse. Children's Bks.

Reschke, Kathleen. Grandma, Mommy & Me. 2010. 20p. pap. 12.95 *(978-1-4490-5550-9(8))* AuthorHouse.

Rice, Luanne. The Beautiful Lost. (ENG.). 304p. (YA). (gr. 7-7). 2019. pap. 9.99 *(978-1-338-31631-5(1))* 2017. 18.99 *(978-1-338-11107-1(8))* Scholastic, Inc.

Richards, Katherine. My Favorite Run. Fieldhouse, Vicky, illus. 2013. (ENG.). 32p. (J). 16.99 *(978-0-9895095-2-7(4))* Fit Kids Publishing.

Rim, Sujean. Birdie's Big-Girl Hair. 2014. (Birdie Ser.). (ENG., Illus.). 40p. (J). (gr. -1-3). 17.00 *(978-0-316-22791-9(9))* Little, Brown Bks. for Young Readers.

Rinaldi, Ann. The Family Greene. 2011. (ENG.). 256p. (YA). (gr. 7). pap. 14.95 *(978-0-547-57723-4(0)*, 1458519, Clarion Bks.) HarperCollins Pubs.

Rivers, Karen. Finding Ruby Starling. 2014. (ENG.). 304p. (J). (gr. 5-9). 17.99 *(978-0-545-53479-6(8)*, Levine, Arthur A. Bks.) Scholastic, Inc.

—A Possibility of Whales. 2019. (ENG.). 288p. (gr. 3-7). pap. 8.95 *(978-1-61620-926-1(7)*, 73926) Algonquin Young Readers.

Rivers, Phoebe. Yesterday & Today. 2013. (Saranormal Ser.: 11). (ENG., Illus.). 160p. (J). (gr. 3-7). 15.99 *(978-1-4424-8962-2(6))*; pap. 5.99 *(978-1-4424-8961-5(8))* Simon Spotlight. (Simon Spotlight).

Roash, Riki. Mom, I Can Sleep in My Bed Tonight! 2013. 24p. pap. 24.95 *(978-1-4626-8255-3(3))* America Star Bks.

Robberecht, Thierry. Back into Mommy's Tummy. Goossens, Philippe, illus. 2005. (ENG.). 32p. (J). (gr. -1 — 1). 15.00 *(978-0-618-58106-1(5)*, 100424, Clarion Bks.) HarperCollins Pubs.

Robinson, Kathleen Marie. Snowflake Sandwiches. 2007. 15p. pap. 24.95 *(978-1-4241-8620-4(X))* America Star Bks.

Rodgers, Mary. Freaky Friday. 2005. 176p. (YA). (gr. 5-9). 21.25 *(978-0-8446-7273-1(4)*, 3588) Smith, Peter Pub., Inc.

Rosenthal, Amy Krouse. Bedtime for Mommy. Pham, LeUyen, illus. 2010. (ENG.). 32p. (J). (gr. -1-k). 18.99 *(978-1-59990-341-5(5)*, 900055542, Bloomsbury USA Childrens) Bloomsbury Publishing USA.

Roske, Melissa. Kat Greene Comes Clean. 2017. 192p. (J). (gr. 4-7). lib. bdg. 16.99 *(978-1-58089-776-1(2))* Charlesbridge Publishing, Inc.

Rubi, Nicholas. My Mom's Not Cool. Maia, Chavez Larkin, illus. 2008. 24p. (J). per. 12.95 *(978-0-9776906-4-0(4))* Blueline Publishing.

Ruby, Laura. Lily's Ghosts. 2005. (Illus.). 258p. (J). (gr. 5-9). 13.65 *(978-0-7569-5115-3(1))* Perfection Learning Corp.

Rundell, Katherine. The Wolf Wilder. 2015. (ENG., Illus.). 240p. (J). (gr. 3-7). 19.99 *(978-1-4814-1942-0(0)*, Simon & Schuster Bks. For Young Readers) Simon & Schuster Bks. For Young Readers.

Russo, Angela B. Beautiful. 2013. 28p. pap. 24.95 *(978-1-62709-040-7(1))* America Star Bks.

Sackier, Shelley. Dear OPL. 2015. (ENG.). 240p. (J). (gr. 5-8). pap. 12.99 *(978-1-4926-0859-2(9)*, 9781492608592) Sourcebooks, Inc.

Salazar, Aida. The Moon Within (Scholastic Gold), 1 vol. 2019. (ENG., Illus.). 240p. (J). (gr. 3-7). 17.99 *(978-1-338-28337-2(5)*, Levine, Arthur A. Bks.) Scholastic, Inc.

Salma, Hammad. I am Beautiful. 2007. (Illus.). 20p. (J). mass mkt. *(978-0-9787849-9-7(5))* Lucent Interpretations, LLC.

Salter, Sydney. My Big Nose & Other Natural Disasters. 2009. (ENG., Illus.). 352p. (YA). (gr. 7-18). pap. 19.95 *(978-0-15-206643-7(8)*, 1099023, Clarion Bks.) HarperCollins Pubs.

Sánchez, Erika L. I Am Not Your Perfect Mexican Daughter. 2019. (ENG.). lib. bdg. 22.80 *(978-1-6636-2193-1(4))* Perfection Learning Corp.

—I Am Not Your Perfect Mexican Daughter. (ENG.). (YA). (gr. 9). 2019. 368p. pap. 12.99 *(978-1-5247-0051-5(7)*, Ember) 2017. 352p. 19.99 *(978-1-5247-0048-5(7)*, Knopf Bks. for Young Readers) Random Hse. Children's Bks.

Sand-Eveland, Cyndi. A Tinfoil Sky. (Illus.). (YA). (gr. 7). 2014. (ENG.). 216p. pap. 9.99 *(978-1-77049-510-4(X))* 2012. 224p. 17.95 *(978-1-77049-277-6(1))* Tundra Bks. CAN. (Tundra Bks.). Dist: Penguin Random Hse. LLC.

Satterfield, Barbara. Answer Why for Mee Mee. 2004. (Illus.). 32p. (J). pap. 11.50 *(978-0-9748715-1-6(6)*, 314-004) Vision Harmony Publishing.

Sauer, Tammi. Dear Jack. 2004. 164p. (YA). mass mkt. 6.99 *(978-0-9753367-0-0(3))* Onstage Publishing, LLC.

Scanlon, Liz Garton. The Great Good Summer. 2015. (ENG., Illus.). 224p. (J). (gr. 3-7). 16.99 *(978-1-4814-1147-9(0)*, Beach Lane Bks.) Beach Lane Bks.

Schaeffer, Rebecca. Not Even Bones. (Market of Monsters Ser.: 1). (ENG.). (YA). (gr. 9). 2019. 384p. pap. 9.99 *(978-0-358-10825-2(X)*, 1748891) 2018. 368p. 17.99 *(978-1-328-86354-6(9)*, 1694449) HarperCollins Pubs. (Clarion Bks.).

Schantz, Sarah Elizabeth. Fig. 2016. (ENG.). 352p. (YA). (gr. 9). pap. 11.99 *(978-1-4814-2359-5(2)*, McElderry, Margaret K. Bks.) McElderry, Margaret K. Bks.

Schena, Maghan. When I Grow Up. 2011. (ENG.). 18p. (J). pap. 11.95 *(978-1-4327-8203-0(7))* Outskirts Pr., Inc.

Schnell, Selynn. The Backpack Jungle. 2011. 48p. pap. 16.95 *(978-1-4560-3332-3(8))* America Star Bks.

Schoenbohm, Ann. Rising above Shepherdsville. 2019. (ENG., Illus.). 320p. (J). (gr. 3-7). 17.99 *(978-1-4814-5283-0(5)*, Beach Lane Bks.) Beach Lane Bks.

Schoettler, Joan. Good Fortune in a Wrapping Cloth. Lanan, Jessica, illus. 2011. (ENG.). 32p. (J). (gr. k-3). 17.95 *(978-1-885008-40-4(6)*, leelowshens, Shen's Bks.) Lee & Low Bks., Inc.

Schrader, Margaret. Green Knee-High Farm. Schrader, Kimberly, illus. 2009. 28p. pap. 12.95 *(978-1-60844-000-9(1))* Dog Ear Publishing, LLC.

Schraff, Anne. The Fairest, 1 vol. unabr. ed. 2010. (Urban Underground Ser.). (ENG.). 179p. (YA). (gr. 9-12). pap. 11.95 *(978-1-61651-007-7(2))* Saddleback Educational Publishing, Inc.

Schraff, Anne E. Misjudged. 2014. (Urban Underground — Cesar Chavez High School Ser.). (YA). lib. bdg. 20.80 *(978-0-606-35589-6(8))* Turtleback.

Schröder, Monika & Schröder, Monika. Be Light Like a Bird. 2016. (ENG.). 240p. (J). (gr. 3-7). lib. bdg. 14.95 *(978-1-62370-749-1(8)*, 132439, Capstone Young Readers) Capstone.

Schroeder, Lisa. It's Raining Cupcakes. 2011. (ENG., Illus.). 208p. (J). (gr. 3-7). pap. 7.99 *(978-1-4169-9085-7(2)*, Aladdin) Simon & Schuster Children's Publishing.

—My Secret Guide to Paris: a Wish Novel. (Wish Ser.). (ENG.). 224p. (J). (gr. 3-7). 2016. pap. 6.99 *(978-0-545-70810-4(9))* 2015. 16.99 *(978-0-545-70808-1(7)*, Scholastic Pr.) Scholastic, Inc.

Schumacher, Julie. The Unbearable Book Club for Unsinkable Girls. (ENG.). 240p. (YA). (gr. 7). 2013. pap. 8.99 *(978-0-375-85127-8(5)*, Ember) 2012. 24.94 *(978-0-385-90685-2(4)*, Delacorte Pr.) Random Hse. Children's Bks.

Schwartz, Dana. And We're Off. 2018. 272p. (YA). (gr. 7). pap. 9.99 *(978-0-448-49382-4(9)*, Razorbill) Penguin Young Readers Group.

Selby, Vicki L. Sleepy Sierra & the Great Blanket Adventure. 2011. 20p. (gr. 1-2). pap. 11.32 *(978-1-4567-3099-4(1))* AuthorHouse.

Sharenow, Robert. My Mother the Cheerleader. 2009. (ENG.). 320p. (YA). (gr. 8). pap. 10.99 *(978-0-06-114898-9(9)*, Balzer & Bray) 2007. 304p. (J). (gr. 7-18). 16.99 *(978-0-06-114896-5(2)*, Geringer, Laura Book) 2007. 304p. (J). (gr. 7-18). lib. bdg. 17.89 *(978-0-06-114897-2(0)*, Geringer, Laura Book) HarperCollins Pubs.

Shaw, Laura. Priscilla & the Big Red Ball, 1 vol. Shaw, Yvonne, illus. 2009. 19p. pap. 24.95 *(978-1-60749-523-9(6))* America Star Bks.

Shaw, Susan. Black-Eyed Suzie. 2007. (ENG.). 176p. (J). (gr. 1-4). pap. 9.95 *(978-1-59078-533-1(9)*, Astra Young Readers) Astra Publishing Hse.

Shemin, Craig. Families Are Forever. McCoy, John, illus. 2006. 34p. (J). (gr. -1-2). 16.95 *(978-0-9728666-6-8(3))* As Simple As That Publishing.

Sher, Emil. Away, 1 vol. Leng, Qin, illus. 2017. (ENG.). 32p. (J). (gr. k-2). 18.95 *(978-1-55498-483-1(1))* Groundwood Bks. CAN. Dist: Publishers Group West (PGW).

Sherrard, Valerie. Searching for Yesterday: A Shelby Belgarden Mystery. 2008. (ENG.). 224p. (YA). (gr. 6-10). pap. 12.99 *(978-1-55002-788-4(3))* Dundurn Pr. CAN. Dist: Publishers Group West (PGW).

Shimizu, Michio. Ding Dong. McLaughlin, Sako, tr. Yamamoto, Matsuko, illus. 2009. 32p. 14.95 *(978-1-74126-440-1(5))* R.I.C. Pubns. AUS. Dist: SCB Distributors.

Shofner, Corabel. Almost Paradise. 2018. (ENG.). 304p. (J). pap. 19.99 *(978-1-250-15858-1(3)*, 900157543) Square Fish.

—Almost Paradise. 2018. (J). lib. bdg. 18.40 *(978-0-606-41107-3(0))* Turtleback.

Simner, Janni Lee. Faerie Winter, 2. 2012. (Bones of Faerie Trilogy Ser.). (ENG.). 288p. (J). (gr. 8-12). 24.94 *(978-0-375-96671-2(4))* Random House Publishing Group.

—Secret of the Three Treasures. 2006. (ENG.). 160p. (YA). (gr. 8-12). 16.95 *(978-0-8234-1914-2(2))* Holiday Hse., Inc.

Simon, Sandy. Sylvie. 2012. 16p. pap. 15.99 *(978-1-4772-4899-7(4))* AuthorHouse.

Sinclair, Mehded Maryam. When Wings Expand. 2013. (ENG., Illus.). 150p. (J). (gr. 5-9). pap. 9.95 *(978-0-86037-499-2(8))* Kube Publishing Ltd. GBR. Dist: Consortium Bk. Sales & Distribution.

Singleton, Paul. Sometimes Mama's Just Like That. 2013. 30p. pap. 17.99 *(978-0-578-13425-3(X))* Drinking Gourd Pr.

Sinois, Latrice J. You Are My Sunshine. 2012. 20p. pap. 17.99 *(978-1-4772-5731-9(4))* AuthorHouse.

Slegers, Liesbet. Laura Ayuda a Su Mama/ Laura Helps Her Mom. 2008. (SPA.). 28p. 10.95 *(978-84-263-6492-0(6))* Vives, Luis Editorial (Edelvives) ESP. Dist: Baker & Taylor Bks.

Smith, Craig. The Dinky Donkey (a Wonky Donkey Book) Cowley, Katz, illus. 2019. (ENG.). 24p. (J). (gr. -1-k). pap. 7.99 *(978-1-338-60083-4(4))* Scholastic, Inc.

Smith, Rosemary. Three Wishes for Maddy. 2012. 48p. pap. 10.00 *(978-1-61204-798-0(X)*, Strategic Bk. Publishing) Strategic Book Publishing & Rights Agency (SBPRA).

Snyder, Laurel. Seven Stories Up. 2015. 240p. (J). (gr. 3-7). 7.99 *(978-0-375-87326-3(0)*, Yearling) Random Hse. Children's Bks.

Soda, Cynthia. Lolly's Basement Crawlies. 2011. 28p. (gr. 1-2). pap. 13.59 *(978-1-4567-4562-2(X))* AuthorHouse.

Sonnenblick, Jordan. Falling over Sideways. (ENG.). 272p. (YA). (gr. 7). 2017. pap. 10.99 *(978-0-545-86325-4(2))* 2016. 17.99 *(978-0-545-86324-7(4)*, Scholastic Pr.) Scholastic, Inc.

Soo, Kean. Jellaby: The Lost Monster. 2014. (Jellaby Ser.). (ENG., Illus.). 160p. (J). (gr. 4-8). pap. 12.95 *(978-1-4342-6420-6(3)*, 123935, Stone Arch Bks.) Capstone.

Sorrells, Walter. Club Dread. 2007. (Hunted Ser.: 2). (ENG.). 272p. (YA). (gr. 7-18). 8.99 *(978-0-14-240904-6(9)*, Puffin Books) Penguin Young Readers Group.

—Fake ID. 2007. (Hunted Ser.: 1). (ENG.). 336p. (YA). (gr. 7-18). 9.99 *(978-0-14-240762-2(3)*, Puffin Books) Penguin Young Readers Group.

Speaker, Cathy. The Road Home. Rosteck, Rachel, illus. 2012. (ENG.). 45p. (J). pap. 15.95 *(978-1-4327-9146-9(X))* Outskirts Pr., Inc.

Springer, Nancy. Possessing Jessie. 2010. (ENG.). 128p. (YA). (gr. 7-18). pap. 16.95 *(978-0-8234-2259-3(3))* Holiday Hse., Inc.

Spyri, Johanna. Gritli's Children. 2006. 144p. (gr. 4-7). per. 11.95 *(978-1-59818-921-6(2))*; 24.95 *(978-1-59818-413-6(X))* Aegypan.

St. Anthony, Jane. The Summer Sherman Loved Me. 2015. (Fesler-Lampert Minnesota Heritage Ser.). (ENG.). 144p. pap. 9.95 *(978-0-8166-9815-8(5))* Univ. of Minnesota Pr.

Stamm, Linda J. Phoebe's Family: A Story about Egg Donation. Clipp, Joan, illus. 2015. (J). pap. *(978-0-9755810-7-0(4))* Graphite Pr.

—Scarlett's Story: A Tale about Embryo Donation. Clipp, Joan, illus. 2017. (J). pap. *(978-1-938313-17-2(8))* Graphite Pr.

Stan, Jaskiel, illus. Families are Forever Learning & Activity Guide. 2007. 20p. (J). 9.95 *(978-0-9728666-2-0(0))* As Simple As That Publishing.

Standish, Ali. August Isle. 2019. (ENG.). 368p. (J). (gr. 3-7). 16.99 *(978-0-06-243341-1(5)*, HarperCollins) HarperCollins Pubs.

Staniszewski, Anna. Once upon a Cruise: a Wish Novel. 2016. (Wish Ser.). (ENG.). 256p. (J). (gr. 3-7). pap. 6.99 *(978-0-545-87986-6(8)*, Scholastic Paperbacks) Scholastic, Inc.

Steffen, Tim. Mom's Cup of Coffee: The (Incr)Edible Adventures of Allie Quirk. 2012. (Illus.). 65p. (J). pap. *(978-0-9779518-5-7(5))* Cardinal Pr.

Stern, A. J. Fashion Frenzy. Marts, Doreen Mulryan, illus. 2011. (Frankly, Frannie Ser.: 6). 128p. (J). (gr. 1-3). pap. 6.99 *(978-0-448-45544-0(7)*, Grosset & Dunlap) Penguin Young Readers Group.

Sternberg, Julie. Bedtime at Bessie & Lil's. Gudeon, Adam, illus. 2015. (ENG.). 32p. (J). (gr. -1-2). 16.95 *(978-1-59078-934-6(2)*, Astra Young Readers) Astra Publishing Hse.

Stiverson, Charlotte L. Nellie's Walk. Aitken, Kati, illus. 2016. (J). *(978-1-935864-62-2(9))* Oncology Nursing Society.

Stone, Heather Duffy. Over the Tracks. 2015. (Suspended Ser.). (ENG.). 96p. (YA). (gr. 6-12). 27.99 *(978-1-4677-5711-9(X)*, a27c9ee2-e68b-48fe-b301-4ac7ea30dcaa, Darby Creek) Lerner Publishing Group.

Stone, Jade. Whispering Willow Woods. 2005. 73p. pap. 19.95 *(978-1-4137-4264-0(5))* America Star Bks.

Stone, Laura. Little Lulu Learns a Lesson. 2010. 34p. pap. 16.95 *(978-0-557-33222-9(2))* Lulu Pr., Inc.

Stone, Phoebe. Paris for Two. 2016. (J). (ENG.). 272p. (gr. 3-7). 16.99 *(978-0-545-44362-3(8))*; 257p. *(978-1-338-04510-9(5))* Scholastic, Inc. (Levine, Arthur A. Bks.).

Stratton-Porter, Gene. A Girl of the Limberlost. Benda, Wladyslaw T., illus. 2005. reprint ed. pap. 38.95 *(978-0-7661-9424-3(8))* Kessinger Publishing, LLC.

—A Girl of the Limberlost. 2006. 336p. (YA). 21.95 *(978-1-934169-30-8(7))*; pap. 10.95 *(978-1-934169-31-5(5))* Norilana Bks.

—A Girl of the Limberlost. 2011. 266p. pap. 17.99 *(978-1-61279-071-8(2))* Publishing in Motion.

—Wonder, Hope, Love, & Loss: The Selected Novels of Gene Stratton-Porter. 2015. (ENG.). 784p. (gr. 6-6). pap. 17.99 *(978-1-63220-320-5(0)*, Sky Pony Pr.) Skyhorse Publishing Co., Inc.

Stringam, Jean. How Not to Cry in Public. 2013. 390p. pap. 16.99 *(978-0-9855540-1-9(0))* Dollison Road Bks.

Struyk-Bonn, Chris. Nice Girls Endure. 2016. (ENG.). 256p. (YA). (gr. 9-12). 16.95 *(978-1-63079-047-9(8)*, 131502, Switch Pr.) Capstone.

Stuart, Carrie. Lenore's Chores, 1 vol. 2006. (Neighborhood Readers Ser.). (ENG.). 8p. (gr. 1-2). pap. 5.15 *(978-1-4042-6823-4(5)*, eec6a475-0c34-4f4b-9475-9762929c2498, Rosen Classroom) Rosen Publishing Group, Inc., The.

Suchy, Julianne. Leaf Me Alone. 2009. 36p. pap. 13.95 *(978-1-60693-300-8(0)*, Eloquent Bks.) Strategic Book Publishing & Rights Agency (SBPRA).

Sudo, Kumiko. Coco-Chan's Kimono. Sudo, Kumiko, illus. 2010. (ENG., Illus.). 32p. (J). (gr. k-2). 16.95 *(978-1-933308-26-5(5))* Breckling Pr.

Sugiura, Misa. This Time Will Be Different. 2019. (ENG.). 400p. (YA). (gr. 8). 17.99 *(978-0-06-247344-8(1)*, HarperTeen) HarperCollins Pubs.

Suma, Nova Ren. Fade Out. 2012. (ENG.). 288p. (YA). (gr. 7). pap. 9.99 *(978-1-4169-7565-6(9)*, Simon Pulse) Simon Pulse.

Summy, Barrie. I So Don't Do Famous. 2012. (I So Don't Do... Ser.). (ENG.). 304p. (J). (gr. 5). 7.99 *(978-0-385-73791-3(2)*, Yearling) Random Hse. Children's Bks.

—I So Don't Do Makeup. 2011. (I So Don't Do... Ser.). (ENG.). 288p. (J). (gr. 3-7). 7.99 *(978-0-385-73789-0(0)*, Yearling) Random Hse. Children's Bks.

—I So Don't Do Mysteries. 2009. (I So Don't Do... Ser.). (ENG.). 288p. (J). (gr. 3-7). 7.99 *(978-0-385-73603-9(7)*, Yearling) Random Hse. Children's Bks.

—I So Don't Do Spooky. (I So Don't Do... Ser.). (ENG.). (J). 2011. 288p. (gr. 6-8). lib. bdg. 21.19 *(978-0-385-90584-8(X))* 2010. 304p. (gr. 3-7). 7.99 *(978-0-385-73605-3(3))* Random Hse. Children's Bks. (Yearling).

Supplee, Suzanne. Artichoke's Heart. 2009. 288p. (YA). (gr. 7-18). 8.99 *(978-0-14-241427-9(1)*, Speak) Penguin Young Readers Group.

Sutton, Katisha Barner. Caring & Sharing. 2011. 26p. pap. 12.50 *(978-1-60976-177-6(4)*, Strategic Bk. Publishing) Strategic Book Publishing & Rights Agency (SBPRA).

Sweeney, Joyce. Waiting for June, 0 vols. 2012. (ENG.). 158p. (YA). (gr. 7-12). pap. 7.99 *(978-0-7614-5329-1(6)*, 9780761453291, Skyscape) Amazon Publishing.

Swore, Wendy S. A Monster Like Me. 2019. (ENG.). 304p. (J). (gr. 3-6). 16.99 *(978-1-62972-555-0(2)*, 5214782, Shadow Mountain) Shadow Mountain Publishing.

Sydor, Colleen. My Mother Is a French Fry & Further Proof of My Fuzzed-Up Life. 2008. 256p. (J). (gr. 7-9). pap. 8.95 *(978-1-55453-184-4(5))* Kids Can Pr., Ltd. CAN. Dist: Hachette Bk. Group.

Symons, Brandy. Lemonade Kisses. 2009. 24p. pap. 12.95 *(978-1-4389-7251-0(2))* AuthorHouse.

Tait, Elena. Mommy Why Wasn't I at Your Wedding? 2009. 24p. pap. 11.49 *(978-1-4389-5426-4(3))* AuthorHouse.

Tate, Nikki. Home Base: A Mother-Daughter Story. Kath, Katie, illus. 2020. 32p. (J). (gr. -1-3). 18.99 *(978-0-8234-3663-7(2))* Holiday Hse., Inc.

Taylor, Cora. Finding Melissa, 1 vol. 2013. (ENG.). 184p. (J). (gr. 6-10). pap. 12.95 *(978-1-55455-274-0(5)*, 270cb0c0-5f1b-47d2-a33e-2aea755f76ae) éditeur, Annika Parance CAN. Dist: Firefly Bks., Ltd.

Taylor, Kim. Cissy Funk. Date not set. 224p. (YA). (gr. 5-18). mass mkt. 4.99 *(978-0-06-440880-6(9))* HarperCollins Pubs.

Telma, Tante. Telma's Day at Magens Bay. 2012. 16p. pap. 15.99 *(978-1-4772-7776-8(5))* AuthorHouse.

Templeton, Donna L. Mother's Surprise. Berlinger, Nancy A., illus. 2009. (ENG.). 32p. (J). pap. 9.99 *(978-0-9764336-6-8(4))* MJS Publishing Group LLC.

The Calaiacovo Family. The Amazing Adventures of Ruby & Rubette: San Francisco. 2010. 32p. pap. 14.49 *(978-1-4490-6948-3(7))* AuthorHouse.

The Story Pirates & West, Jacqueline. The Story Pirates Present. Aly, Hatem, illus. 2019. (Story Pirates Ser.: 2). 288p. (J). (gr. 3-7). 13.99 *(978-1-63565-091-4(7)*, 9781635650914, Random Hse. Bks. for Young Readers) Random Hse. Children's Bks.

Thomas, Chericia. Buffy the Football Player. 2010. 20p. 12.49 *(978-1-4490-9708-0(1))* AuthorHouse.

Thompkins-Bigelow, Jamilah. Mommy's Khimar. Glenn, Ebony, illus. 2018. (ENG.). 40p. (J). (gr. -1-3). 18.99 *(978-1-5344-0059-7(1)*, Salaam Reads) Simon & Schuster Bks. For Young Readers.

Tilly, Meg. First Time, 1 vol. 2008. (Orca Soundings Ser.). (ENG.). (YA). (gr. 8-12). 128p. pap. 9.95 *(978-1-55143-944-0(1))*; 112p. 16.95 *(978-1-55143-946-4(8))* Orca Bk. Pubs. USA.

Tinsley, Helen. Me & My Grandma: A Story for Children about AIDS. 2012. Tr. of 32. (Illus.). 34p. (J). pap. 14.95 *(978-1-937622-21-3(5)*, Nefu Bks.) Africana Homestead Legacy Pubs., Inc.

Tracey, Rhian. True Colours. 2007. 272p. (J). (gr. 4-7). per. 11.95 *(978-0-7475-8941-9(0))* Bloomsbury Publishing Plc GBR. Dist: Independent Pubs. Group.

Train, Mary. Time for the Fair. Hayes, Karel, illus. 2005. (ENG.). 28p. (J). (gr. k-1). 15.95 *(978-0-89272-694-3(6))* Down East Bks.

Tuminelly, Nancy. Horse Shoes. Nobens, C. A., illus. 2006. (Fact & Fiction Ser.). 24p. (J). pap. 48.42 *(978-1-59679-944-8(7))* ABDO Publishing Co.

Turner, Juliette. That's Not Hay in My Hair, 1 vol. 2016. (ENG.). 240p. (J). pap. 8.99 *(978-0-310-73244-0(1))* Zonderkidz.

Turner, Nicci. Milky's Story, 1 vol. 2010. 18p. pap. 24.95 *(978-1-4489-6808-4(9))* PublishAmerica, Inc.

Tyler, Bridget. The Pioneer. 2020. (ENG.). 384p. (YA). (gr. 8). pap. 10.99 *(978-0-06-265807-4(7)*, HarperTeen) HarperCollins Pubs.

V., Patti. My Na Na Stories. 2005. 18.00 *(978-0-8059-9806-1(3))* Dorrance Publishing Co., Inc.

Vail, Rachel. Brilliant. 2011. (Avery Sisters Trilogy Ser.: 3). (ENG., Illus.). 256p. (YA). (gr. 8-12). pap. 9.99 *(978-0-06-089051-3(7)*, HarperTeen) HarperCollins Pubs.

van Dam, Katrin. Come November. (ENG.). 384p. (YA). (gr. 7-7). 2020. pap. 10.99 *(978-1-338-26843-0(0))* 2018. 18.99 *(978-1-338-26842-3(2)*, Scholastic Pr.) Scholastic, Inc.

Van Draanen, Wendelin. Sammy Keyes & the Hollywood Mummy. 2008. (Sammy Keyes Ser.: Bk. 6). (J). 64.99 *(978-1-60640-641-0(8))* Findaway World, LLC.

—Sammy Keyes & the Showdown in Sin City. 2013. (Sammy Keyes Ser.: 16). (ENG.). 304p. (J). (gr. 5). pap. 7.99 *(978-0-307-93061-3(0)*, Yearling) Random Hse. Children's Bks.

van Genechten, Guido. Kangaroo Christine. van Genechten, Guido, illus. 2005. (Illus.). 24p. (J). (gr. 3-7). pap. 6.95 *(978-1-58925-396-4(5))* Tiger Tales.

Van Winkle, Amy. The Flower Fairy, 1 vol. 2010. 13p. pap. 24.95 *(978-1-61582-729-9(3))* PublishAmerica, Inc.

Vande Velde, Vivian. The Book of Mordred. 2007. (ENG.). 352p. (YA). (gr. 7-12). pap. 8.99 *(978-0-618-80916-5(3)*, 497456, Clarion Bks.) HarperCollins Pubs.

Vander Zee, Ruth. Always with You. Himler, Ron, illus. 2008. (ENG.). 32p. (J). (gr. -1-3). 17.00 *(978-0-8028-5295-3(5)*, Eerdmans Bks For Young Readers) Eerdmans, William B. Publishing Co.

Vaughn, Trudy D. Bugs Beware My Mom Doesn't Care! 2012. (ENG.). 24p. pap. 10.95 *(978-1-4497-3635-4(1)*, WestBow Pr.) Author Solutions, LLC.

Velásquez, Gloria. Rudy's Memory Walk. 2009. (Roosevelt High School Ser.). 140p. (YA). (gr. 6-18). pap. 9.95 *(978-1-55885-593-9(9))* Arte Publico Pr.

Verdi, Jessica. And She Was. 2018. (ENG.). 368p. (YA). (gr. 9). 18.99 *(978-1-338-15053-7(7)*, Scholastic Pr.) Scholastic, Inc.

—The Summer I Wasn't Me. 2014. (ENG.). 352p. (YA). (gr. 7-12). pap. 13.99 *(978-1-4022-7788-7(1)*, 9781402277887) Sourcebooks, Inc.

Vernick, Shirley Reva. The Black Butterfly, 1 vol. 2014. (ENG.). 226p. (J). (gr. 8-12). 19.95 *(978-1-935955-79-5(9)*, 23353382, Cinco Puntos Press) Lee & Low Bks., Inc.

Vescovi, Laura A. Good Morning Sleepyhead. 2004. 15.95 *(978-0-9763219-0-3(4))* Vescovi, Laura.

Vita. Head in the Clouds. 2004. (Illus.). 108p. pap. 44.50 *(978-0-9760062-0-6(0))* Magic Woman Pubns.

Wait for Me. 2007. 169p. (gr. 4-7). 18.00 *(978-0-7569-7959-1(5))* Perfection Learning Corp.

Waldman, Debby & Feutl, Rita. Room Enough for Daisy, 1 vol. Revell, Cindy, illus. 2011. (ENG.). 32p. (J). (gr. -1-k). 19.95 *(978-1-55469-255-2(5))* Orca Bk. Pubs. USA.

Walker, D. S. Delightfully Different. 2010. 160p. (gr. -1). 22.95 *(978-1-4502-6051-0(9))*; pap. 12.95 *(978-1-4502-6050-3(0))* iUniverse, Inc.

Wallace, Carey. The Ghost in the Glass House. 2014. (ENG.). 240p. (YA). (gr. 7). pap. 13.99 *(978-0-544-33618-6(6)*, 1584164, Clarion Bks.) HarperCollins Pubs.

Wallis, Quvenzhané. A Night Out with Mama. Brantley-Newton, Vanessa, illus. 2017. (ENG.). 40p. (J). (gr. -1-3). 17.99 *(978-1-4814-5880-1(9)*, Simon & Schuster Bks. For Young Readers) Simon & Schuster Bks. For Young Readers.

Walsh, Ann. Flower Power. 2006. (Orca Currents Ser.). 107p. (gr. 5-9). 19.95 *(978-0-7569-6874-8(7))* Perfection Learning Corp.

Waters, Tawni. The Long Ride Home. 2017. (ENG.). 240p. (YA). (gr. 8-12). pap. 10.99 *(978-1-4926-4543-6(5))* Sourcebooks, Inc.

Watson, J. A. Nocturnal Symphony: A Bat Detector's Journal. Olbey, Arpad, illus. 2019. (Science Squad Set 2 Ser.). (ENG.). 192p. (J). (gr. 3-4). 28.50 *(978-1-63163-299-0(X)*, 163163299X, Jolly Fish Pr.) North Star Editions.

Watts, Julia. Revived Spirits. 2011. (ENG.). 170p. (J). (gr. 7). pap. 8.95 *(978-0-9831032-2-6(4)*, BeanPole Bks.) OH Industries.

Weber, Lori. Tattoo Heaven, 1 vol. 2005. (Lorimer SideStreets Ser.). (ENG.). 168p. (YA). (gr. 9-12). 16.95 *(978-1-55028-903-9(9)*, 903); 8.99 *(978-1-55028-902-2(0)*, 13526657-8e5a-41db-be9d-fb60af7971e9) James Lorimer & Co. Ltd., Pubs. CAN. Dist: Formac Lorimer Bks. Ltd., Lerner Publishing Group.

Weeks, Sarah. Pie (Scholastic Gold) 2013. (ENG.). 192p. (J). (gr. 3-7). pap. 7.99 *(978-0-545-27012-0(X)*, Scholastic Paperbacks) Scholastic, Inc.

—So B. It (ENG.). (J). (gr. 5). 2005. 288p. pap. 9.99 *(978-0-06-441047-2(1))* 2004. 256p. 16.99 *(978-0-06-623622-3(3))* HarperCollins Pubs. (HarperCollins).

—So B. It. 2009. 9.00 *(978-0-7848-3326-1(5)*, Everbind) Marco Bk. Co.

—So B. It. 2005. 17.00 *(978-0-7569-5112-2(7))* Perfection Learning Corp.

—So B. It. 2007. (J). 1.25 *(978-1-4193-7988-8(7))* Recorded Bks., Inc.

Welch, Jenna Evans. Love & Gelato. (ENG., Illus.). 400p. (YA). (gr. 7). 2017. pap. 11.99 *(978-1-4814-3255-9(9))* 2016. 19.99 *(978-1-4814-3254-2(0))* Simon Pulse. (Simon Pulse).

Welsh, Kenneth Wilbur. Magic Chalk. 2011. 16p. pap. 12.00 *(978-1-4520-6078-1(9))* AuthorHouse.

Wessel-Estes, Pam. A Quilt & a Home. 2012. 36p. pap. 14.95 *(978-1-4575-1489-0(3))*; 24.95 *(978-1-4575-1490-6(7))* Dog Ear Publishing, LLC.

West, Kasie. The Distance Between Us. 2013. (ENG.). 320p. (YA). (gr. 8). pap. 9.99 *(978-0-06-223565-7(6)*, HarperTeen) HarperCollins Pubs.

Whincup, Sara. The St John's Cross Spider. Yapsangco, Kenn, illus. 2015. (ENG.). 28p. (J). pap. 28.22 *(978-1-5035-0985-6(0))* Xlibris Corp.

White, Kathryn. Ruby's School Walk. Latimer, Miriam, illus. 2010. 32p. (J). (gr. -1-2). 16.99 *(978-1-84686-275-5(2))* Barefoot Bks., Inc.

Wiggin, Kate Douglas. Polly Oliver's Problem. 2007. 108p. per. 9.95 *(978-1-60312-369-3(5))*; 22.95 *(978-1-60312-707-3(0))* Aegypan.

—Polly Oliver's Problem. 2016. (ENG., Illus.). (J). 24.95 *(978-1-357-78791-2(X))* Creative Media Partners, LLC.

Wiggin, Kate Douglas Smith. Polly Oliver's Problem. 2017. (ENG., Illus.). (J). 22.95 *(978-1-374-96499-0(9))* Capital Communications, Inc.

Williams, Carol Lynch. Glimpse. (ENG., (YA). (gr. 9). 2012. Illus.). 512p. pap. 13.99 *(978-1-4169-9731-3(8))* 2010. 496p. 16.99 *(978-1-4169-9730-6(X))* Simon & Schuster/Paula Wiseman Bks. (Simon & Schuster/Paula Wiseman Bks.).

—Miles from Ordinary: A Novel. 2012. (ENG.). 208p. (YA). (gr. 8-12). 26.19 *(978-0-312-55512-2(1))* St. Martin's Pr.

—Signed, Skye Harper. 2014. (ENG., Illus.). 304p. (YA). (gr. 7). 17.99 *(978-1-4814-0032-9(0)*, Simon & Schuster/Paula Wiseman Bks.) Simon & Schuster/Paula Wiseman Bks.

Williams, Jamie L. Mommy's Little Helper, 1 vol. 2010. 26p. 24.95 *(978-1-4512-9232-9(5))* PublishAmerica, Inc.

Williams, Lori Aurelia. Broken China. 2006. (ENG., Illus.). 272p. (YA). (gr. 7-12). reprint ed. mass mkt. 8.99 *(978-1-4169-1618-5(0)*, Simon Pulse) Simon Pulse.

Williams, Marilyn & Caspersen, Barbara. Peggy & Barbie on the Farm. 2013. 24p. pap. 24.95 *(978-1-63004-043-7(6))* America Star Bks.

Williams, Nicole. Almost Impossible. 2018. 272p. (YA). (gr. 9). pap. 9.99 *(978-0-553-49881-3(9)*, Crown Books For Young Readers) Random Hse. Children's Bks.

Williams, Rozanne Lanczak. How Can I Get a Pet? Reid, Mick, illus. 2006. (Learn to Write Ser.). 8p. (J). (gr. k-2). pap. *(978-1-59198-290-6(1)*, 6184) Creative Teaching Pr., Inc.

—How Can I Get a Pet? Maio, Barbara & Faulkner, Stacey, eds. Reid, Mick, illus. 2006. (J). per. 6.99 *(978-1-59198-363-7(0))* Creative Teaching Pr., Inc.

Williams, Shanica. Amy Goes Shopping for School. 2012. 16p. pap. 15.99 *(978-1-4772-1360-5(0))* AuthorHouse.

Willis, Meredith Sue. Meli's Way. 2015. 178p. (YA). *(978-1-932727-15-9(9))* Montemayor Pr.

Wilner-Pardo, Gina. Prettiest Doll. 2012. (ENG.). 240p. (J). (gr. 5-7). 16.99 *(978-0-547-68170-2(4)*, 1476079, Clarion Bks.) HarperCollins Pubs.

Wilson, Annette. K'Nyah's Big Celebration. 2012. 28p. pap. 24.95 *(978-1-4626-9925-4(1))* America Star Bks.

Wilson, Jacqueline. The Story of Tracy Beaker. Sharratt, Nick, illus. 2004. (ENG.). 133p. 16.00 *(978-0-7569-3205-3(X))* Perfection Learning Corp.

Winston, Sherri. Jada Sly, Artist & Spy. 2019. (ENG., Illus.). 272p. (J). (gr. 3-7). 32.99 *(978-0-316-50536-9(6))* Little, Brown Bks. for Young Readers.

Wittlinger, Ellen. Blind Faith. 2007. (ENG.). 304p. (YA). (gr. 7-12). pap. 9.99 *(978-1-4169-4906-0(2)*, Simon & Schuster Bks. For Young Readers) Simon & Schuster Bks. For Young Readers.

Wolf, Elaine. Camp. 2012. (ENG.). 256p. (YA). (gr. 6-6). 16.95 *(978-1-61608-657-2(2)*, 608657, Sky Pony Pr.) Skyhorse Publishing Co., Inc.

Wood, Gail. Lizzie & the Big Lake Mystery. 2015. (Illus.). ix, 93p. (J). pap. *(978-1-57249-416-9(6)*, White Mane Kids) White Mane Publishing Co., Inc.

Woodson, Jacqueline. Show Way. Talbott, Hudson, illus. 2005. (ENG.). 48p. (J). (gr. -1-3). 18.99 *(978-0-399-23749-2(6)*, G.P. Putnam's Sons Books for Young Readers) Penguin Young Readers Group.

Wrede, Patricia. Snow White & Rose Red. 2009. (ENG.). 288p. (YA). (gr. 7-18). 8.99 *(978-0-14-241121-6(3)*, Firebird) Penguin Young Readers Group.

Wyeth, Sharon Dennis. The Granddaughter Necklace. Ibatoulline, Bagram, illus. (J). 2013. (ENG.). 32p. (gr. -1-3). 18.99 *(978-0-545-08125-2(4))* 2012. pap. *(978-0-545-23983-7(4))* Scholastic, Inc. (Levine, Arthur A. Bks.).

Yee, Lisa. Absolutely Maybe. 2009. (ENG.). 288p. (J). (gr. 7-7). 16.99 *(978-0-439-83844-3(4)*, Levine, Arthur A. Bks.) Scholastic, Inc.

Young, Karen Romano. A Girl, a Raccoon, & the Midnight Moon: (Juvenile Fiction, Mystery, Young Reader Detective Story, Light Fantasy for Kids) Bagley, Jessixa, illus. 2020. (ENG.). 392p. (J). (gr. 5-9). 16.99 *(978-1-4521-6952-1(7))* Chronicle Bks. LLC.

Young, Ruth. Aunty Marmalade. 2009. 218p. pap. 13.78 *(978-1-60693-893-5(2)*, Eloquent Bks.) Strategic Book Publishing & Rights Agency (SBPRA).

Younge-Ullman, Danielle. Everything Beautiful Is Not Ruined. 2017. (ENG.). 368p. (YA). (gr. 9). 17.99 *(978-0-425-28759-0(9)*, Viking Books for Young Readers) Penguin Young Readers Group.

Zabel, Vivian. I Like Pink. Nielson, Ginger, illus. 2013. 28p. pap. 12.99 *(978-0-9889617-1-5(7))* 4RV Pub.

Zarr, Sara. How to Save a Life. 2012. (ENG.). 368p. (YA). (gr. 7-17). pap. 18.99 *(978-0-316-03605-4(6))* Little, Brown Bks. for Young Readers.

Zerza, Safoora Z. Sophia V. Is Flower Girl. 2012. 24p. pap. 17.99 *(978-1-4685-5136-5(1))* AuthorHouse.

Zimmerman, Diana S. Kandide & the Secret of the Mists. Gadd, Maxine, illus. 2008. (Calabiyau Chronicles Ser.: Bk. 1). 296p. (YA). (gr. 5-18). 17.99 *(978-0-9794328-3-5(9))*; Bk. 1. 290p. (J). (gr. 4-7). pap. 9.99 *(978-0-9794328-2-8(0))* Noesis Publishing.

Zimmerman, Mary Joyce. Just Four. 2005. (Illus.). 32p. (J). (gr. -1-5). 2.70 *(978-0-7399-2340-5(4)*, 2779) Rod & Staff Pubs., Inc.

Zirin, David. My Name Is Erica Montoya de la Cruz. White, Deborah, illus. 2005. (ENG.). 16p. (J). 5.75 *(978-1-57274-732-6(3)*, 2779, Bks. for Young Learners) Owen, Richard C. Pubs., Inc.

1, 2, 3 Happy Family. 2005. (J). bds. *(978-0-9769910-2-1(0))* Terrific Twins LLC.

MOTHERS AND SONS

Anderson, Nancy. My Mother Helps Me with Homework, 1 vol. 2016. (Rosen REAL Readers: Social Studies Nonfiction / Fiction: Myself, My Community, My World Ser.). (ENG.). 8p. (gr. k-1). pap. 5.46 *(978-1-5081-2284-5(9)*, 6e193f52-b570-465f-b717-bb53f61227be, Rosen Classroom) Rosen Publishing Group, Inc., The.

Cargile, Phillip & Miss Cheryl. The Wagon Man: The Untold Story of the Go-Burn Kids. 2009. 54p. pap. 16.95 *(978-1-60703-939-6(7))* America Star Bks.

Hoge, Robert. Ugly. 2016. (ENG., Illus.). 208p. (J). (gr. 3-7). 16.99 *(978-0-425-28775-0(0)*, Viking Books for Young Readers) Penguin Young Readers Group.

L'heureux, Christine. Caillou Loves His Mommy. Brignaud, Pierre, illus. 2018. (Caillou's Essentials Ser.). (ENG.). 24p. (J). (gr. -1-k). bds. 7.99 *(978-2-89718-441-4(8))* Caillouet, Gerry.

Lynch, Chris. Angry Young Man. 2012. (ENG.). 192p. (YA). (gr. 7). pap. 10.99 *(978-1-4424-5419-4(9)*, Simon & Schuster Bks. For Young Readers) Simon & Schuster Bks. For Young Readers.

Morales, Yuyi. Dreamers. 2018. (Illus.). 40p. (J). (gr. -1-3). 18.99 *(978-0-8234-4055-9(9)*, Neal Porter Bks) Holiday Hse., Inc.

Selzer, Anita. I Am Sasha. 2019. 336p. (YA). (gr. 7). 14.99 *(978-0-14-378574-3(5))* Penguin Random Hse. AUS. Dist: Independent Pubs. Group.

MOTHERS AND SONS—FICTION

Acevedo, Ari. Juan Bobo Sends the Pig to Mass. Wrenn, Tom, illus. 2008. (Story Cove Ser.). (SPA & ENG.). 24p. (J). (gr. -1-3). pap. 4.95 *(978-0-87483-883-1(5))* August Hse. Pubs., Inc.

Addison, George R. Iii. When Mom Came Home. 2012. 32p. pap. 21.99 *(978-1-4691-6406-9(X))* Xlibris Corp.

M N O

Akiona, Micalynn. My Mom Can Do Anything. 2011. 28p. pap. 15.99 *(978-1-4568-2006-0(0))* Xlibris Corp.

Alan E. And Lisa J. Laird. Cows Can Be Scary. 2009. 40p. pap. 18.49 *(978-1-4389-8150-5(3))* AuthorHouse.

Alger, Horatio. Herbert Carter's Legacy. 2006. pap. *(978-1-4065-0710-2(5))* Dodo Pr.

Alger Jr. Horatio Staff. Andy Grants Pluck. rev. ed. 2006. 312p. 29.95 *(978-1-4218-1762-0(4))*; pap. 14.95 *(978-1-4218-1862-7(0))* 1st World Publishing, Inc. (1st World Library - Literary Society).

—Do & Dare. rev. ed. 2006. 272p. 28.95 *(978-1-4218-1757-6(8))*; pap. 13.95 *(978-1-4218-1857-3(4))* 1st World Publishing, Inc. (1st World Library - Literary Society).

—Herbert Carter's Legacy. rev. ed. 2006. 264p. 28.95 *(978-1-4218-1756-9(X))*; pap. 13.95 *(978-1-4218-1856-6(6))* 1st World Publishing, Inc. (1st World Library - Literary Society).

Allen, George L. Thelma's Boy. 2010. (ENG.). 60p. 24.99 *(978-1-4415-8326-0(2))*; pap. 15.99 *(978-1-4415-8325-3(4))* Xlibris Corp.

Anderson, Alice. Danny Be Good! 2012. 24p. pap. 17.99 *(978-1-4685-6433-4(1))* AuthorHouse.

Anderson, Jane. Inspector Insector. 2005. (J). pap. *(978-1-4108-4196-4(0))* Benchmark Education Co.

Ankhnu Feaster, Teraab & Campbell, Rochelle. The Magic Seeds. 2009. 42p. pap. 19.25 *(978-1-4490-0784-3(8))* AuthorHouse.

Appelt, Kathi. When Otis Courted Mama. McElmurry, Jill, illus. 2015. (ENG.). 40p. (J). (gr. -1-3). 17.99 *(978-0-15-216688-5(2)*, 1201655, Clarion Bks.) HarperCollins Pubs.

Armand, Glenda. Love Twelve Miles Long, 1 vol. Bootman, Colin, illus. (ENG.). 32p. (J). 2015. (gr. 1-6). pap. 11.95 *(978-1-62014-254-7(6)*, leelowbooks) 2013. 17.95 *(978-1-60060-245-0(2))* Lee & Low Bks., Inc.

Arrington, R. Region. Billy Buckins & the Pirates Map, 1 vol. 2010. 64p. pap. 19.95 *(978-1-4512-2087-2(1))* America Star Bks.

Ashley, Sharon. I Wish I Could See. 2013. 24p. pap. 24.95 *(978-1-4626-9700-7(3))* America Star Bks.

Asim, Jabari. Boy of Mine. Pham, LeUyen, illus. 2010. (ENG.). 20p. (J). (gr. -1 — 1). bds. 8.99 *(978-0-316-73577-3(9))* Little, Brown Bks. for Young Readers.

Auch, M. J. Wing Nut. 2008. (ENG.). 256p. (J). (gr. 6-8). pap. 15.99 *(978-0-312-38420-3(3)*, 900053321) Square Fish.

Baggett, Shirley Reed. Adventures of Bandit: A Little Racoon Goes into the Forbidden Forest. 2011. 16p. (gr. 1-2). pap. 9.99 *(978-1-4567-6575-0(2))* AuthorHouse.

Bailey, Loren. Becoming Prince Charming. 2018. (Suddenly Royal Ser.). (ENG., Illus.). 112p. (YA). (gr. 6-12). 26.65 *(978-1-5415-2570-2(1)*, db07567d-4f85-40c4-82b7-cbee65cfe97a, Darby Creek) Lerner Publishing Group.

Ball, Jacqueline A. Timmy's My Hero, Who's Yours? 2007. 36p. per. 24.95 *(978-1-4137-0063-3(2))* America Star Bks.

Banerjee, Anjali. The Silver Spell. Fiegenshuh, Emily, illus. 2005. (Knights of the Silver Dragon Ser.: Bk. 8). 174p. (J). *(978-1-4156-1645-1(0)*, Mirrorstone) Wizards of the Coast.

Banks, Lynne Reid. The Indian in the Cupboard. 2010. (Indian in the Cupboard Ser.). (ENG.). 240p. (J). (gr. 3-7). 8.99 *(978-0-375-84753-0(7)*, Yearling) Random Hse. Children's Bks.

Banting, Celia. I Only Said I Had No Choice. 2006. (I Only Said Ser.). (Illus.). 202p. (YA). pap. 14.99 *(978-0-9786648-0-0(9))* Wighita Pr.

Barchers, Suzanne I. Read with Gus, 1 vol. rev. ed. 2011. (Phonics Ser.). (ENG.). 16p. (gr. k-1). 6.99 *(978-1-4333-2420-8(2))* Teacher Created Materials, Inc.

Barnes, John. Tales of the Madman Underground. 2011. (ENG.). 544p. (YA). (gr. 9-18). pap. 9.99 *(978-0-14-241702-7(5)*, Speak) Penguin Young Readers Group.

Barry, Debra R. Brady Pickles. 2011. 32p. pap. 24.95 *(978-1-4626-3716-4(7))* America Star Bks.

—Let's Go to the Market. 2012. 28p. pap. 24.95 *(978-1-4626-8533-2(1))* America Star Bks.

Bates, Melinda. Nick Pricer: An American Heir. 2012. 88p. 19.95 *(978-1-4697-8478-6(5))*; pap. 9.95 *(978-1-4697-8476-2(9))* iUniverse, Inc.

Bean, Jonathan. Big Snow. Bean, Jonathan, illus. 2013. (ENG., Illus.). 32p. (J). (gr. -1-1). 17.99 *(978-0-374-30696-0(6)*, 900087739, Farrar, Straus & Giroux (BYR)) Farrar, Straus & Giroux.

Bell, Liz. Mohawk, Fro or Crew, It Is up to You. 2011. 24p. pap. 24.95 *(978-1-4626-3196-4(7))* America Star Bks.

Benavides, Desiree. Little Henry's Adventures: Henry's Trip to the Supermarket. 2008. 24p. pap. 24.95 *(978-1-60563-011-3(X))* America Star Bks.

Benjamin, Rick A. The Hunt for Lost Treasure, 1 vol. 2010. 56p. pap. 16.95 *(978-1-4489-6417-8(2))* America Star Bks.

Benwell, Sarah. The Last Leaves Falling. 2015. (ENG., Illus.). 368p. (YA). (gr. 9). 17.99 *(978-1-4814-3065-4(3))* Simon & Schuster Children's Publishing.

Bernstein, David D. The Enchanted Rope. 2010. 25p. (J). pap. 13.95 *(978-1-4327-5175-3(1))* Outskirts Pr., Inc.

Bevan, Lizzie. Never Far When in My Heart. 2013. (ENG., Illus.). 31p. (J). pap. 15.95 *(978-1-4787-1027-1(6))* Outskirts Pr., Inc.

Bilan Hochenberg, Nerissa. Mommy Works. Bilan, Edgar, illus. 2013. 24p. pap. *(978-1-4602-2602-5(X))* FriesenPress.

Binns, Barbara. Courage. 2018. (ENG.). 368p. (J). (gr. 3-7). 16.99 *(978-0-06-256165-7(0)*, HarperCollins) HarperCollins Pubs.

Bird, James. The Brave. 2022. (ENG., Illus.). 320p. (J). pap. 7.99 *(978-1-250-79174-0(X)*, 900214708) Square Fish.

Bird, Jodi Stiriz. Going on a Tree Hunt: A Tree Identification Book for Young Children. 2011. 28p. (gr. 1-2). pap. 14.99 *(978-1-4490-8308-3(0))* AuthorHouse.

Bishop, Brandy. The Christmas Mice, 1 vol. 2010. 30p. 24.95 *(978-1-4489-4438-5(4))* PublishAmerica, Inc.

Blackmon, Rodney Allan. A Kitten Named Buddy: Buddy Goes Outside. 2013. 20p. pap. 24.95 *(978-1-62709-677-5(9))* America Star Bks.

Blake, Colleen H. Robley. Don't You Wish Your Momma Could Cook Like Mine? Jennings, Randy, illus. 2012. 40p. pap. 16.97 *(978-1-61204-876-5(5)*, Strategic Bk. Publishing) Strategic Book Publishing & Rights Agency (SBPRA).

Blake, Jocelyn. Mama Is on an Airplane. Blake, Jocelyn, illus. 2006. (Illus.). (J). per. 9.99 *(978-0-9790572-0-5(5))* Kreativ Kaos.

Blevins, Wiley. Jack & the Bloody Beanstalk. Cox, Steve, illus. 2016. (Scary Tales Retold Ser.). (ENG.). 24p. (J). (gr. k-3). lib. bdg. 27.99 *(978-1-63440-099-2(2)*, 0a9b4164-d9db-40ec-9e2c-fdb082ac7993) Red Chair Pr.

Boles, Rhonda G. Why Does the Sun Set, Mommy? 2009. 24p. pap. 10.99 *(978-1-4389-8112-3(0))* AuthorHouse.

Bombaci, James J. The Million Dollar Dog. 2010. 32p. pap. 14.99 *(978-1-4490-4936-2(2))* AuthorHouse.

Bonilla, Rocío & Lethem, Mara. Max & the Superheroes. Bonilla, Rocío & Malet, Oriol, illus. 2018. (ENG.). 48p. (J). (gr. -1-3). lib. bdg. 14.99 *(978-1-58089-844-7(0))* Charlesbridge Publishing, Inc.

Bradley, A. M. Finnegan's Magic Sunglasses. 2013. 24p. pap. 24.95 *(978-1-62709-814-4(3))* America Star Bks.

Bratcher, Shirley Kay. Tudy Goes to the Zoo. 2013. 24p. pap. 24.95 *(978-1-4626-9560-7(4))* America Star Bks.

—Tudy Won't Count - Three. 2012. 16p. pap. 24.95 *(978-1-4626-8886-9(1))* America Star Bks.

Broach, Elise. When Dinosaurs Came with Everything. Small, David, illus. (ENG.). 40p. (J). (gr. -1-3). 2019. 8.99 *(978-1-5344-5227-5(3))* 2007. 18.99 *(978-0-689-86922-8(3))* Simon & Schuster Children's Publishing. (Atheneum Bks. for Young Readers).

Buckle, J. A. Half My Facebook Friends Are Ferrets, 1 vol. 2014. (ENG.). 224p. (YA). (gr. 9-12). 16.95 *(978-1-63079-000-4(1)*, 126761, Switch Pr.) Capstone.

Cakal, Kimberly. Today I Hugged a Porcupine. 2007. 20p. per. 24.95 *(978-1-4241-8561-0(0))* America Star Bks.

Cali, Davide. Piano, Piano. Rivers, Randi, tr. from FRE. Heliot, Eric, illus. 2007. 28p. (J). (gr. 4-7). 15.95 *(978-1-58089-191-2(8))* Charlesbridge Publishing, Inc.

Callender, Kacen. This Is Kind of an Epic Love Story. 2019. (ENG.). 304p. (YA). (gr. 9). pap. 10.99 *(978-0-06-282023-5(0)*, Balzer & Bray) HarperCollins Pubs.

Callender, Kheryn. This Is Kind of an Epic Love Story. 2018. (ENG.). 304p. (YA). (gr. 9). 17.99 *(978-0-06-282022-8(2)*, Balzer & Bray) HarperCollins Pubs.

Campbell, Suzy. Pennies for Christmas, 1 vol. 2010. 24p. 24.95 *(978-1-4512-0553-4(8))* PublishAmerica, Inc.

Carr, Kathy. Granny, Where Did My Mommy Go? 2008. 24p. pap. 24.95 *(978-1-60610-324-1(5))* America Star Bks.

Castillo, Elizabeth. Jaden Christian. 2012. 24p. pap. 24.95 *(978-1-4626-7624-8(3))* America Star Bks.

Celcer, Iréné. Hope & Rosie Have a Baby: The Gift of Family. Gatto, Horacio, illus. 2018. (J). pap. *(978-1-938313-22-6(4))* Graphite Pr.

—Hope Has a Baby: The Gift of Family. Gatto, Horacio, illus. 2018. (J). pap. *(978-1-938313-20-2(8))* Graphite Pr.

Childers, Amy. You're My Boy! 2011. 36p. (gr. -1). pap. 17.95 *(978-1-4567-5514-0(5))* AuthorHouse.

Christie, Douglas, Jr. Dougie Goes to School. 2009. 32p. (J). pap. 16.50 *(978-0-9794827-7-9(1))* Infinite Love Publishing.

Ciccone, Tiziana & Linardi, Franca. No More Peanut Butter, Daniel! Bucci, Gino, illus. 2012. 36p. pap. 13.95 *(978-1-61897-718-2(0)*, Strategic Bk. Publishing) Strategic Book Publishing & Rights Agency (SBPRA).

Clifton, Lutricia. Freaky Fast Frankie Joe. 2013. (ENG.). 272p. (J). (gr. 3-7). pap. 7.99 *(978-0-8234-2867-0(2))* Holiday Hse., Inc.

Coleman, Candace. Zubie the Lightning Bug - I Want to Remember Your Thoughts. 2006. (J). 15.99 *(978-0-9774998-0-9(4))* Parent Brigade Company, The.

Colfer, Eoin. Artemis Fowl, 3 vols., Set. 2010. (Artemis Fowl Ser.). (ENG.). 944p. (J). (gr. 5-17). pap. 19.99 *(978-1-4231-3681-1(0))* Disney Pr.

—Artemis Fowl. (Artemis Fowl Ser.: Bk. 1). (FRE.). pap. 34.95 *(978-2-07-054681-7(0))* Gallimard, Editions FRA. Dist: Distribooks, Inc.

—Artemis Fowl. (Artemis Fowl Ser.: Bk. 1). pap. 34.95 *(978-88-04-49788-2(2))* Mondadori ITA. Dist: Distribooks, Inc.

—Artemis Fowl. (Artemis Fowl Ser.: 1). (YA). 2007. 1.25 *(978-1-4193-6020-6(5))* 2006. 52.75 *(978-1-4193-6023-7(X))* 2006. 54.75 *(978-1-4193-6021-3(3))* 2006. 54.75 *(978-1-4193-6026-8(4))* 2006. 132.75 *(978-1-4193-6022-0(1))* 2005. 56.75 *(978-1-4193-6024-4(8))* Recorded Bks., Inc.

—Artemis Fowl. 2009. (Artemis Fowl Ser.: 1). (J). (gr. 5-8). lib. bdg. 19.65 *(978-0-613-60637-0(X))* Turtleback.

—Eoin Colfer: Artemis Fowl: the Graphic Novel. 2019. (Artemis Fowl Ser.). (ENG., Illus.). 128p. (J). (gr. 3-7). 21.99 *(978-1-368-04314-4(3)*, Disney-Hyperion) Disney Publishing Worldwide.

—EL MUNDO SUBTERRÁNEO (ARTEMIS FOWL 1) (Artemis Fowl Ser.: Bk. 1). (SPA.). 288p. pap. *(978-84-8441-115-4(X)*, MO31567) Grijalbo Mondadori, S.A.-Montena.

Connell, Julie. The Adventures of Cutie Pie & Mr. Squishy. 2008. 12p. pap. 24.95 *(978-1-60703-826-9(9))* America Star Bks.

Cook, Sonya Correll. Quest for a Family Pet: The Adventures of Nique, Nick, & Nelle. Transou, Devora & Watkins, Karen, illus. 2008. (ENG.). 24p. pap. 11.49 *(978-1-4343-5043-5(6))* AuthorHouse.

Cooley, Judy. Mom Says I Can. 2008. (Illus.). 32p. (J). (gr. -1-3). lib. bdg. 17.95 *(978-1-59038-872-3(0)*, Shadow Mountain) Shadow Mountain Publishing.

Cooper & the Enchanted Metal Detector. 2013. (ENG.). 250p. (J). pap. 9.95 *(978-1-60898-150-2(9))* namelos llc.

Cornish, Linda Sowa Young. Pong's Birthday Journey. 2006. (J). pap. 15.00 *(978-0-8059-6993-1(4))* Dorrance Publishing Co., Inc.

Craig, Joni. A Shoulder for Oscar. Haddad-Hamwi, Louise, illus. 2013. 40p. pap. 11.95 *(978-0-9887836-6-9(5))* Taylor and Seale Publishing.

Cumyn, Alan. North to Benjamin. 2018. (ENG., Illus.). 304p. (J). (gr. 5-9). 17.99 *(978-1-4814-9752-7(9))* Simon & Schuster Children's Publishing.

D'Agata, Tabatha Jean. Storm Tunes: Yes, I Can Read! Nature Series, Book 2. Lineberger, Judy, illus. 2006. (Yes, I Can Read! Ser.: Bk. 2). 30p. (J). pap. 6.95 *(978-1-934138-02-1(9))* Bouncing Ball Bks., Inc.

Davis, Ashley. The Big Storm, 1 vol. 2006. (Neighborhood Readers Ser.). (ENG.). 16p. (gr. 1-2). pap. 6.50 *(978-1-4042-7192-0(9)*, acd57e4e-3518-4d62-8b03-069c49727692, Rosen Classroom) Rosen Publishing Group, Inc., The.

Dean, James, illus. Pete the Cat & the Surprise Teacher. 2017. 32p. (J). *(978-1-5182-3399-9(6))* Harper & Row Ltd.

deGroat, Diane. Happy Birthday to You, You Belong in a Zoo. deGroat, Diane, illus. 2007. (Gilbert & Friends Ser.). (Illus.). (gr. -1-3). 17.00 *(978-0-7569-8108-2(5))* Perfection Learning Corp.

Denman, K. L. La Cache, 1 vol. 2012. (Orca Currents en Français Ser.). (FRE.). 128p. (J). (gr. 4-7). pap. 9.95 *(978-1-4598-0314-5(0))* Orca Bk. Pubs. USA.

Dieterle, Amber. Will You Miss Me? 2008. 14p. pap. 24.95 *(978-1-60672-485-9(1))* PublishAmerica, Inc.

Dodd, Emma. Together. Dodd, Emma, illus. (Emma Dodd's Love You Bks.). (ENG., Illus.). (J). (— 1). 2018. 22p. bds. 9.99 *(978-0-7636-9940-6(3))* 2016. 24p. 14.99 *(978-0-7636-8940-7(8))* Candlewick Pr.

Duff, Justin. Alex Goes Apple Picking. 2012. 32p. pap. 21.99 *(978-1-4771-2845-9(X))* Xlibris Corp.

Duksta, Laura. I Love You More. Keesler, Karen, illus. (J). 2009. 24p. bds. 6.99 *(978-1-4022-2460-7(5))* 2007. 34p. 17.99 *(978-1-4022-1126-3(0))* Sourcebooks, Inc. (Sourcebooks Jabberwocky).

—Te Quiero Más. Keesler, Karen, illus. 2013. 24p. (J). bds. 7.99 *(978-1-4022-8177-8(3)*, Sourcebooks Jabberwocky) Sourcebooks, Inc.

Duley, Wayla C. Strawberry Soup & Other Crazy Things. 2013. 28p. pap. 24.95 *(978-1-63000-952-6(0))* America Star Bks.

Edwards, Carol. Jacy Meets Betsy: Jacy's Search for Jesus Book 2. Frey, Daniel, illus. 2006. 32p. (J). 15.95 *(978-0-9755314-1-9(7))* Majestic Publishing, LLC.

Elizabeth Arkward Newton. The Little Boy Who Wished God Had Not Given Him a Brain: Big Momma Books. 2009. 36p. pap. 18.99 *(978-1-4389-0133-6(X))* AuthorHouse.

Espinoza, Olivia G. Jay-Dylan's Cat & Fish. 2011. 24p. (gr. -1). pap. 14.39 *(978-1-4567-5119-7(0))* AuthorHouse.

Feiffer, Jules. I'm Not Bobby! Feiffer, Jules, illus. 2006. (Illus.). 28p. (J). (gr. k-4). reprint ed. 16.00 *(978-0-7567-9853-6(1))* DIANE Publishing Co.

Feldmann, Claudia, tr. ARTEMIS FOWL. (Artemis Fowl Ser.: Bk. 1). (GER.). pap. 24.95 *(978-3-548-60320-9(3))* Ullstein-Taschenbuch-Verlag DEU. Dist: Distribooks, Inc.

Fleming, Chula. Spooky Old Tree, 1 vol. 2010. 26p. pap. 24.95 *(978-1-4489-9166-2(8))* PublishAmerica, Inc.

Fogg, K. L. Serpent Tide. 2006. 16.95 *(978-1-59156-861-2(7))* Covenant Communications, Inc.

Ford, J. One in Four. 2007. pap. *(978-1-84747-173-4(0))* Chipmunkapublishing.

French, Simon. Where in the World, 1 vol. 2008. (ENG.). 208p. (J). (gr. 5-7). pap. 7.95 *(978-1-56145-443-3(5))* Peachtree Publishing Co. Inc.

Friend, Gaythel Boggs & Miller, Dalton. Foundation of a Clown, 1 vol. 2010. 58p. pap. 19.95 *(978-1-4489-8253-0(7))* America Star Bks.

Furniss, Alice. The Happiest Mommy Ever. 2009. (Illus.). 32p. (J). 17.95 *(978-1-60641-056-1(3))* Deseret Bk. Co.

Garcia, Cindy Booth. Rat-a-Tat-Tat Not That!, 1 vol. 2010. 22p. 24.95 *(978-1-4489-7425-2(9))* PublishAmerica, Inc.

González, Rigoberto. Antonio's Card: La Tarjeta de Antonio, 1 vol. Álvarez, Cecilia, illus. 2016. (ENG.). 32p. (J). (gr. 2-5). pap. 11.95 *(978-0-89239-387-9(4)*, leelowcbp, Children's Book Press) Lee & Low Bks., Inc.

Goobie, Beth. Jason's Why, 1 vol. 2012. (ENG.). 80p. (J). (gr. 4-6). pap. 8.95 *(978-0-88995-484-7(4)*, 9c7bbc8b-0448-4e1b-911b-a87fc6d00ec2) Red Deer Pr. CAN. Dist: Firefly Bks., Ltd.

Goode, Diane. The Most Perfect Spot. Goode, Diane, illus. 2006. (ENG., Illus.). 32p. (J). (gr. -1-3). 16.99 *(978-0-06-072697-3(0))* HarperCollins Pubs.

Gooding-Alber, Karry. Red Shoelace, 1 vol. 2010. 16p. pap. 24.95 *(978-1-4489-6255-6(2))* America Star Bks.

Gorbachev, Valeri. Pizza-Pie Snowman. 2018. (Illus.). 40p. (J). (gr. -1-3). pap. 8.99 *(978-0-8234-4040-5(0))* Holiday Hse., Inc.

Graham, Frederick. Why Me? 2008. 98p. pap. 13.95 *(978-1-4303-1628-2(4))* Lulu Pr., Inc.

Green, Tim. Lost Boy. (ENG.). (J). (gr. 3-7). 2016. 320p. pap. 9.99 *(978-0-06-231709-4(1))* 2015. 304p. 16.99 *(978-0-06-231708-7(3))* HarperCollins Pubs. (HarperCollins).

Grimshaw, Luke. Sniffle, Sneeze, Cough... Back Off!, 1 vol. Brzozowski, Christina, illus. 2010. 22p. 24.95 *(978-1-4512-1034-7(5))* America Star Bks.

Gutman, Dan. Abner & Me. 2007. (Baseball Card Adventures Ser.). (ENG., Illus.). 176p. (J). (gr. 5-9). pap. 7.99 *(978-0-06-053445-5(1)*, HarperCollins) HarperCollins Pubs.

—Abner & Me. 2007. (Baseball Card Adventures Ser.). (Illus.). 166p. (gr. 5-9). 16.00 *(978-0-7569-7920-1(X))* Perfection Learning Corp.

Hall, Christina. Can Checkers Come Too? Hall, Lowell, illus. 2011. 36p. pap. 24.95 *(978-1-4560-7753-2(8))* America Star Bks.

Hamilton, S. J. The Cat's Eye View. 2012. 186p. pap. 24.95 *(978-1-4626-6056-8(8))* America Star Bks.

Hanington, John G. The Adventures of Quick Fox. 2006. (ENG.). 92p. per. 9.95 *(978-0-7414-3223-0(4))* Infinity Publishing.

Hanning, Jacob. Mommy's Little Helper: That's Me. 2012. 28p. pap. 24.95 *(978-1-4626-5649-3(8))* America Star Bks.

Hansen, MaryAnn Shelley. Sam the Second. 2010. 32p. 14.49 *(978-1-4520-2408-0(1))* AuthorHouse.

Harel, Moshe. Elf Prince. 2012. (ENG.). 258p. pap. *(978-965-550-089-9(6))* Contento De Semrik.

Harris, Angela L. Mommy What Is a Ceo? Chapman, Debbie, illus. 2013. 32p. pap. 10.00 *(978-0-615-62527-0(4))* ALHsiccesslines.

Hazelton, Tanya & Bonanni, Constance. Ian's Golden Passage. 2009. 168p. pap. 9.99 *(978-1-935105-33-6(7))* Avid Readers Publishing Group.

HB Staff. My Wild Woolly. 97th ed. 2003. (First-Place Reading Ser.). (gr. 1-18). pap. 16.50 *(978-0-15-308163-7(5))* Harcourt Schl. Pubs.

Heaney Dunn, John, illus. The Little Red House with No Doors & No Windows & A Star Inside. 2011. 25p. (J). pap. 15.95 *(978-1-58909-915-9(X))* Bookstand Publishing.

Hest, Amy. Don't You Feel Well, Sam? Jeram, Anita, illus. 2007. (Sam Bks.). (ENG.). 32p. (J). (gr. -1-k). 5.99 *(978-0-7636-2408-8(X))* Candlewick Pr.

Hill, Eric. Spot Loves His Mommy. Hill, Eric, illus. 2006. (Spot Ser.). (ENG., Illus.). 14p. (J). (gr. -1 — 1). bds. 6.99 *(978-0-399-24511-4(1)*, Warne) Penguin Young Readers Group.

Hillert, Margaret. The Magic Beans. Farida Zaman, illus. 2016. (Beginning-To-Read Ser.). (ENG.). 32p. (J). (gr. k-2). pap. 13.26 *(978-1-60357-910-0(9))* Norwood Hse. Pr.

Himes, Rachel. Princess & the Peas. Himes, Rachel, illus. 2017. (Illus.). 32p. (J). (gr. k-3). 16.99 *(978-1-58089-718-1(5))* Charlesbridge Publishing, Inc.

Hiris, Monica. Just Like Mom. Sierra, Holly, illus. 2005. (ENG.). 8p. (gr. k-1). pap. 7.95 *(978-1-57874-088-8(6)*, Kaeden Bks.) Kaeden Corp.

Hoban, Russell. Emmet Otter's Jug-Band Christmas. Hoban, Lillian, illus. 2017. (ENG.). 48p. (J). (gr. -1-2). 16.99 *(978-1-5247-1457-4(7)*, Doubleday Bks. for Young Readers) Random Hse. Children's Bks.

Hoover, Paulette. What's That Lump in Your Bed? 2011. 28p. pap. 21.95 *(978-1-4567-1859-6(2))* AuthorHouse.

Howard, Max. Fifteen & Change, 1 vol. 2018. (YA Verse Ser.). (ENG.). 200p. (YA). (gr. 3-4). 25.80 *(978-1-5383-8260-8(1)*, e9a0fb0b-a424-40b8-906b-73974d4d5ccb); pap. 16.35 *(978-1-5383-8259-2(8)*, 4665e9f6-dce1-4935-bbfa-07b260172900) Enslow Publishing, LLC.

Howe, James. Also Known As Elvis. (Misfits Ser.). (ENG., Illus.). (J). (gr. 5-9). 2015. 304p. pap. 8.99 *(978-1-4424-4511-6(4))* 2014. 288p. 16.99 *(978-1-4424-4510-9(6)*, Atheneum Bks. for Young Readers) Simon & Schuster Children's Publishing.

Hughes, Shirley. Alfie Gets in First. 2009. (Alfie Ser.). (Illus.). 32p. (J). (gr. -1-k). pap. 14.99 *(978-1-86230-783-4(0)*, Red Fox) Random House Children's Books GBR. Dist: Independent Pubs. Group.

Iacovone, Lauren Marie. Here Lies Thomas Crawford, 1 vol. 2010. 252p. pap. 27.95 *(978-1-61582-690-2(4))* America Star Bks.

Ireland, Justina. Zach Lopez vs. the Unicorns of Doom. Champion, Tyler, illus. 2017. (Devils' Pass Ser.). (ENG.). 128p. (J). (gr. 4-8). lib. bdg. 25.99 *(978-1-4965-4989-1(9)*, 135881, Stone Arch Bks.) Capstone.

Jasper, J. J. When I Grow Up. Bullock, Brad, illus. 2003. 16p. (J). *(978-0-9727279-8-3(1))* Pine Hill Graphics.

Jenkins, Amanda & Benchmark Education Co., LLC. The Secret Life of Wally Smithers. Fagan, Martin, illus. 2014. (Text Connections Ser.). (J). (gr. 3). *(978-1-4509-9656-3(6))* Benchmark Education Co.

Johnson, Gail. Chasing the Sun. 2009. 40p. pap. 17.99 *(978-1-4389-2192-1(6))* AuthorHouse.

Johnson, Gerald J. J. A Boy Called Tiny Tim. 2013. 20p. pap. 24.95 *(978-1-62709-865-6(8))* America Star Bks.

Jonell, Lynne. The Sign of the Cat. 2016. (J). lib. bdg. 18.40 *(978-0-606-39559-5(8))* Turtleback.

Joosse, Barbara. I Love You the Purplest (Love Board Book, Sibling Book for Kids, Family Board Book) Whyte, Mary, illus. 2019. (ENG.). 24p. (J). (gr. -1 — 1). bds. 9.99 *(978-1-4521-7771-7(6))* Chronicle Bks. LLC.

Judd, Christopher M. Bearable Moments. 2005. (Illus.). (J). 16.95 *(978-0-9766666-1-5(8))* Arcadian Hse.

Judd-Leisten, Betty. Tell It for a Toll, Toll It for a Tale. 2005. 102p. per. 7.95 *(978-1-59824-057-3(9))* E-BookTime LLC.

Jue, Thea. Remember the Love. Lenz, Mary, illus. 2013. 36p. pap. 13.95 *(978-0-9827753-3-2(4))* Interdimensional Pr.

Jules, Jacqueline. Freddie Ramos Tracks down a Drone. Benítez, Miguel, illus. 2020. (Zapato Power Ser.: 9). (ENG.). 96p. (J). (gr. 1-5). 14.99 *(978-0-8075-9544-2(6)*, 807595446) Whitman, Albert & Co.

Kaufman, Sashi. The Other Way Around. 2014. (ENG.). 288p. (YA). (gr. 8-12). 17.95 *(978-1-4677-0262-1(5))* Lerner Publishing Group.

Keeley, Holly M. The Journey of a Grape. 2009. 20p. pap. 12.49 *(978-1-4490-3060-5(2))* AuthorHouse.

Kelley, Maria Felicia. Buz Words: Discovering Words in Pairs. Kelley, Maria Felicia, illus. 2007. (Illus.). 32p. (J). (gr. -1-3). 14.95 *(978-0-9650918-1-7(3))* April Arts Press & Productions.

Kenyon, Sherrilyn. The Dark-Hunters: Infinity, Vol. 1, Vol. 1. 2013. (Dark-Hunters Ser.: 1). (ENG., Illus.). 240p. (gr. 11-17). 13.00 *(978-0-316-19053-4(5)*, Yen Pr.) Yen Pr. LLC.

—Infinity: Chronicles of Nick. 2011. (Chronicles of Nick Ser.: 1). (ENG.). 480p. (YA). (gr. 7-18). pap. 14.00 *(978-0-312-60304-5(5)*, 900064303, St. Martin's Griffin) St. Martin's Pr.

Kim, HoJeong. Kanga & Anger. Kim, SookKyeong, illus. rev. ed. 2014. (MySELF Bookshelf Ser.). (ENG.). 32p. (J). (gr. k-2). pap. 11.94 *(978-1-60357-652-9(5))*; lib. bdg. 25.27 *(978-1-59953-643-9(9))* Norwood Hse. Pr.

Kim, Patti. I'm Ok. 2018. (ENG., Illus.). 288p. (J). (gr. 5). 16.99 *(978-1-5344-1929-2(2)*, Atheneum Bks. for Young Readers) Simon & Schuster Children's Publishing.

Kingsbury, Karen. Whatever You Grow up to Be, 1 vol. Docampo, Valeria, illus. rev. ed. 2014. (ENG.). 32p. (J). 17.99 *(978-0-310-71646-4(2))* Zonderkidz.

Knudson, Mike & Wilkinson, Steve. Raymond & Graham: Bases Loaded. Curtis, Stacy, illus. 2011. (Raymond & Graham Ser.: 3). 160p. (J). (gr. 3-7). 6.99 *(978-0-14-241751-5(3)*, Puffin Books) Penguin Young Readers Group.

Koertge, Ron. Where the Kissing Never Stops. 2005. (ENG.). 256p. (YA). (gr. 9-18). per. 6.99 *(978-0-7636-2696-9(1))* Candlewick Pr.

Konigsberg, Bill. The Music of What Happens, 1 vol. 2019. (ENG.). 352p. (YA). (gr. 9-9). 17.99 *(978-1-338-21550-2(7)*, Levine, Arthur A. Bks.) Scholastic, Inc.

Kraatz, Jeramey. The Cloak Society. (Cloak Society Ser.: 1). (ENG.). (J). (gr. 3-7). 2013. 304p. pap. 7.99 *(978-0-06-209548-0(X))* 2012. 288p. 16.99 *(978-0-06-209547-3(1))* HarperCollins Pubs. (HarperCollins).

Kraegel, Kenneth. Wild Honey from the Moon. Kraegel, Kenneth, illus. 2019. (ENG., Illus.). 64p. (J). (gr. -1-3). 18.99 *(978-0-7636-8169-2(5))* Candlewick Pr.

Kreie, Chris. Take Shelter. 2018. (Attack on Earth Ser.). (ENG.). 112p. (YA). (gr. 6-12). pap. 7.99 *(978-1-5415-2631-0(7)*, f97b38d8-1c87-40b0-8b19-ebd5c2f36aaf); lib. bdg. 26.65 (978-1-5415-2578-8(7), d2b53f7d-5a7e-42ff-a7fb-3a6c8be8e7ef) Lerner Publishing Group. (Darby Creek).

Kropp, Paul. Winner! (978-1-897039-31-1(X)) High Interest Publishing (HIP).

Kumara, Mark. The Tr-Youth Truth: Knowledge, Apprehens. 2005. (Illus.). 206p. pap. 24.75 (978-1-4120-6960-1(2)) Trafford Publishing.

Kuracka, Vicki. When the Sun Sleeps. 2010. 16p. pap. 9.99 (978-1-60911-509-8(0), Eloquent Bks.) Strategic Book Publishing & Rights Agency (SBPRA).

Kurstedt, Rosanne. And I Thought about You. Carletta-Vietes, Lisa, illus. 2012. (J). 14.95 (978-1-937406-65-3(2)) Amplify Publishing Group.

LaFaye, A. Walking Home to Rosie Lee, 1 vol. Shepherd, Keith D., illus. 2019. (ENG.). 32p. (J). (gr. 1-6). pap. 11.95 (978-1-941026-57-1(5), 23353382, Cinco Puntos Press) Lee & Low Bks., Inc.

Lang, Gregory E. & Hill, Susanna Leonard. Why a Son Needs a Mom. Yerrill, Gail, illus. 2021. (Always in My Heart Ser.). (ENG.). 40p. (J). (gr. k-3). 10.99 (978-1-7282-3584-4(7)) Sourcebooks, Inc.

LaRochelle, David. The Best Pet of All. 2009. (Illus.). 32p. (J). (gr. -1-k). pap. 8.99 (978-0-14-241272-5(4), Puffin Books) Penguin Young Readers Group.

Lawrence, David Herbert. The Rocking-Horse Winner. 2010. (Creative Short Stories Ser.). (ENG., Illus.). 48p. (J). (gr. 5-8). 19.95 (978-1-58341-924-3(1), 22130, Creative Education) Creative Co., The.

Leonard, Marcia. Pantalones Nuevos, No! Handelman, Dorothy, photos by. 2005.Tr. of No New Pants! (Illus.). 32p. (J). (ENG & SPA.). (gr. -1-1). pap. 4.99 (978-0-8225-3297-2(2)); (SPA., (gr. 1-1). per. 5.95 (978-0-8225-3296-5(4), Ediciones Lerner) Lerner Publishing Group.

Lerangis, Peter. The Code. 2004. (Spy X Ser.: No. 1). 139p. (Orig.). (J). (978-0-439-70242-3(9)) Scholastic, Inc.

Lewis, Gill. I Love You More Each Day. Ho, Louise, illus. 2017. (Padded Board Books for Babies Ser.). (ENG.). 20p. (J). (gr. -1 — 1). bds. 6.99 (978-1-68412-042-0(X), Silver Dolphin Bks.) Printers Row Publishing Group.

Licciardi, Paula. Wasting Calvin's Time. 2006. 9.00 (978-0-8059-8138-4(1)) Dorrance Publishing Co., Inc.

Little Bee Books. Kisses & Cuddles. 2015. (ENG., Illus.). 16p. (J). (gr. -1 — 1). bds. 5.99 (978-1-4998-0151-4(3)) Little Bee Books Inc.

Lloyd, A. Wallis. Das Monster-Musical. 2013. 32p. pap. (978-3-944704-02-9(9)) Nothnagle, Alan. Edition Graugans.

López, Lorraine. Call Me Henri. 2012. (ENG.). 242p. (gr. 9-17). pap. 19.95 (978-0-8101-2893-4(4)) Curbstone Pr.

Lord, Pia. The Day the Sun Went Out. 2012. 30p. 24.95 (978-1-4626-6797-0(X)) America Star Bks.

Lupica, Mike. The Batboy. 2011. (ENG.). 272p. (J). (gr. 5-18). 8.99 (978-0-14-241782-9(3), Puffin Books) Penguin Young Readers Group.

—The Batboy. 2011. lib. bdg. 18.40 (978-0-606-15352-2(7)) Turtleback.

Mai, Resa. Toy for Chantelle. 2007. 32p. per. 12.95 (978-1-59858-338-0(7)) Dog Ear Publishing, LLC.

Mankell, Henning. Journey to the End of the World. 2011. (Joel Gustafsson Ser.: No. 4). (ENG.). 208p. (YA). (gr. 7). pap. 8.99 (978-0-385-73498-1(0), Delacorte Bks. for Young Readers) Random Hse. Children's Bks.

Mannion, Mary. Roaring Rory. Fitzgerald, Brian, illus. 2010. 68p. pap. (978-1-907276-63-7(7)) Lapwing Pubns.

Marcotte, David A. Be Wary of Strangers. 2005. (ENG., Illus.). 36p. per. 14.95 (978-1-932672-47-3(8)) Outskirts Pr., Inc.

Mardani, Parisa. Nathan Sees a Monster But... . 2012. 16p. pap. 15.99 (978-1-4685-9405-8(2)) AuthorHouse.

Marr, Nikki. Marty Misbehaves. 2008. 40p. pap. 17.99 (978-1-4389-3171-5(9)) AuthorHouse.

Marshall, Peter, et al. Nate Donovan: Revolutionary Spy. 2007. 208p. (J). pap. 9.99 (978-0-8054-4394-3(0), B&H Bks.) B&H Publishing Group.

Martin, Brian. The Gold of Angel Island. McDonald, Kim, illus. 2007. 46p. (J). (978-0-9798059-0-5(2)) Lunchbox Stories Inc.

Marvin, Dan. But I Don't Eat Ants. Fry, Kelly, illus. 2017. (ENG.). 32p. (J). (gr. -1-2). 16.99 (978-1-57687-837-8(6), powerHouse Bks.) powerHse. Bks.

Mayer, Mercer. Just Me & My Mom. 2014. (Little Critter Ser.). lib. bdg. 14.75 (978-0-606-35555-1(3)) Turtleback.

Mayo, Jason. Do Witches Make Fishes? 2010. 36p. pap. 16.99 (978-1-4520-6944-9(1)) AuthorHouse.

McAllister, Angela. My Mom Has X-Ray Vision. Smith, Alex T., illus. 2011. (ENG.). 32p. (J). (gr. -1-2). 15.95 (978-1-58925-097-0(4)); pap. 7.95 (978-1-58925-428-2(7)) Tiger Tales.

McAnulty, Stacy. Max Explains Everything: Grocery Store Expert. Hocking, Deborah, illus. 2018. 32p. (J). (gr. -1-2). 16.99 (978-1-101-99644-7(7), G.P. Putnam's Sons Books for Young Readers) Penguin Young Readers Group.

McC, Meg. Goodnap, Brewer, 1 vol. 2010. 32p. 24.95 (978-1-4512-1447-5(2)) PublishAmerica, Inc.

McClure, Brian D. The Bubble. 2006. (Illus.). 64p. (J). 14.95 (978-1-933426-05-1(5)) Universal Flag Publishing.

McCourt, Lisa. I Miss You, Stinky Face, 1 vol. Moore, Cyd, illus. 2009. (Stinky Face Ser.). (ENG.). (J). (gr. -1-3). pap. 9.99 incl. audio compact disk (978-0-545-13849-9(3)) Scholastic, Inc.

McCullough, Myrina D. Feet. Schafrath, Ty, illus. 2013. 28p. pap. 15.00 (978-0-9847740-1-2(7)) Systems Group, Inc., The.

McFadden, Jennifer. Rusty My Playful Cat. 2010. 24p. pap. 11.49 (978-1-4490-5101-3(4)) AuthorHouse.

McKinty, Adrian. The Lighthouse Land. 2006. (ENG., Illus.). 200p. (YA). (gr. 6-10). 16.95 (978-0-8109-5480-9(X)) Abrams, Inc.

Mencio, Anna. The Day the Wind Changed. 2012. 24p. pap. 28.03 (978-1-4691-8232-2(7)) Xlibris Corp.

Messner, Kate. The Exact Location of Home. (ENG.). (J). 2018. 272p. pap. 8.99 (978-1-68119-898-9(3), 900191676, Bloomsbury Children's Bks.) 2017. 256p. 16.99 (978-1-68119-548-3(8), 900177288, Bloomsbury USA Childrens) Bloomsbury Publishing USA.

Minarik, Else Holmelund. Little Bear. Sendak, Maurice, illus. 2003. (I Can Read Level 1 Ser.). (ENG.). 64p. (J). (gr. k-3). pap. 4.95 (978-0-06-444004-2(4), HarperCollins) HarperCollins Pubs.

—Little Bear. 2003. (Little Bear: I Can Read! Ser.). (J). (gr. k-3). lib. bdg. 13.55 (978-0-8085-2618-6(9)) Turtleback.

—Osito. Aguilar, Joaquina, tr. Sendak, Maurice, illus. 2003. (Infantil Alfaguara Ser.: 25).Tr. of Little Bear. (SPA.). 60p. (J). (gr. k-3). pap. 8.95 (978-84-204-3044-7(7), AF1346) Santillana USA Publishing Co., Inc.

Mitchell, Hazel. 1, 2, 3 ... by the Sea. 2013. (ENG., Illus.). 36p. (J). (gr. k-3). pap. 18.69 (978-1-935279-94-5(7)) Kane Miller.

Mitchell, Mary Esther. The Adventures of Timmy Gills. 2005. (J). pap. 20.00 (978-0-8059-9660-9(5), RoseDog Bks.) Dorrance Publishing Co., Inc.

Mohamoud, Ashlee. Brown Is Beautiful, 1 vol. 2010. 18p. 24.95 (978-1-4512-0064-5(1)) PublishAmerica, Inc.

Mommy Has a Tattoo. 2006. (GER, ITA & SPA., Illus.). 32p. (J). (gr. 3-7). 16.95 (978-0-9770232-7-1(3)) Mommy Has Tattoos.

Moon, Adam. The Fuzzle. 2007. (J). per. 7.95 (978-1-934345-28-3(8)) GoodLife Publishing.

Morgenroth, Kate. Jude. 2006. (ENG., Illus.). 288p. (YA). (gr. 7-12). reprint ed. mass mkt. 8.99 (978-1-4169-1267-5(3), Simon Pulse) Simon Pulse.

Mosby, Pamela. I'm So Angry. Brever, Amy, illus. 2013. 28p. pap. 7.99 (978-0-9886272-4-6(8)) Brothers N Publishing Corp.

Mosel, Arlene. Tikki Tikki Tembo Book & CD Storytime Set. Lent, Blair, illus. unabr. ed. 2012. (Macmillan Young Listeners Story Time Sets Ser.). (ENG.). (J). 12.99 (978-1-4272-3211-3(3), 900121709) Macmillan Audio.

Mowry, Jess. Skeleton Key. 2007. 280p. (YA). pap. 14.99 (978-1-59092-353-5(7)) Blue Forge Pr.

Mrazovic, Ivan. Phobias - Crash Course. 2010. (ENG.). 48p. pap. 20.99 (978-0-557-38257-6(2)) Lulu Pr., Inc.

Mullin, Mike. Surface Tension. 2018. (ENG.). 424p. (YA). (gr. 8-12). 17.99 (978-1-939100-16-0(X)) Tanglewood Pr.

Munson, Kayla, illus. Night Night. 2013. (ENG.). 34p. (J). pap. 12.95 (978-0-9821956-3-5(X)) Fleur De Lis Publishing, LLC.

Muse, Ludi. My Day at the Park. 2007. 32p. per. 13.95 (978-1-4259-6563-1(6)) AuthorHouse.

Myers, Jason. Blazed. 2014. (ENG., Illus.). 528p. (YA). (gr. 11-11). pap. 13.99 (978-1-4424-8721-5(6), Simon Pulse) Simon Pulse.

Ness, Patrick. A Monster Calls: Inspired by an Idea from Siobhan Dowd. Kay, Jim, illus. (ENG.). 224p. (YA). (gr. 7). 2013. pap. 12.00 (978-0-7636-6065-9(5)) 2011. 22.99 (978-0-7636-5559-4(7)) Candlewick Pr.

—A Monster Calls: Inspired by an Idea from Siobhan Dowd. 2011. (Playaway Children Ser.). (YA). (gr. 7-12). 54.99 (978-1-4558-4499-9(3)) Findaway World, LLC.

—A Monster Calls: Inspired by an Idea from Siobhan Dowd. 2013. lib. bdg. 23.30 (978-0-606-31603-3(5)) Turtleback.

—A Monster Calls: a Novel (Movie Tie-In) Inspired by an Idea from Siobhan Dowd. 2016. (ENG.). 240p. (YA). (gr. 7). pap. 9.99 (978-0-7636-9215-5(8)) Candlewick Pr.

Newman, Leslea. Donovan's Big Day. Dutton, Mike, illus. 2011. (ENG.). 32p. (J). (gr. -1-2). 17.99 (978-1-58246-332-2(8), Tricycle Pr.) Random Hse. Children's Bks.

Nicolas, Stephanie. A Forged Report Card. 2004. (J). pap. 8.00 (978-0-8059-6420-2(7)) Dorrance Publishing Co., Inc.

Nielsen, Kelli & Benham, Kelly. You Will Always Be My Son. 2009. 36p. pap. 13.95 (978-1-60844-018-4(4)) Dog Ear Publishing, LLC.

Nielsen, Susin. No Fixed Address. 2020. (ENG., Illus.). 288p. (J). (gr. 5). pap. 8.99 (978-1-5247-6837-9(5), Yearling) Random Hse. Children's Bks.

—Word Nerd. (ENG.). (J). (gr. 4-7). 2010. 264p. pap. 12.95 (978-0-88776-990-0(X)) 2008. 256p. 18.95 (978-0-88776-875-0(X)) Tundra Bks. CAN. (Tundra Bks.). Dist: Penguin Random Hse. LLC.

Norris, Gayle A. Bed Bug, 1 vol. 2009. 23p. pap. 24.95 (978-1-60836-088-8(1)) America Star Bks.

Northrop, Michael. The Final Kingdom (TombQuest, Book 5) 2016. (TombQuest Ser.: 5). (ENG.). 192p. (J). (gr. 3-7). 16.99 (978-0-545-87111-2(5), Scholastic Pr.) Scholastic, Inc.

—The Stone Warriors (TombQuest, Book 4) 2015. (TombQuest Ser.: 4). (ENG.). 192p. (J). (gr. 3-7). 12.99 (978-0-545-72341-1(8), Scholastic Pr.) Scholastic, Inc.

Ochsner, Gina. The Hidden Letters of Velta B. 2017. (ENG.). 320p. pap. 14.99 (978-0-544-70304-9(9), 1628112, Harper Perennial) HarperCollins Pubs.

Odezi, Jesse. Little Sunny & the Giants: The World's Greatest. 2012. 76p. pap. 30.00 (978-1-4669-0270-1(1)) Trafford Publishing.

Olvera, Jillann. Christian's Lullaby. 2006. 29p. pap. 24.95 (978-1-4241-1909-7(X)) PublishAmerica, Inc.

Osterweil, Adam. Cooper & the Enchanted Metal Detector. 2013. (ENG.). 250p. (J). 18.95 (978-1-60898-149-6(5)) namelos llc.

Panagopoulos, Janie Lynn. Mark of the Bear Claw. 2007. 224p. (J). pap. 8.95 (978-0-938682-83-7(0)) River Road Pubns., Inc.

Pastis, Stephan. Timmy Failure: the Book You're Not Supposed to Have. Pastis, Stephan, illus. (Timmy Failure Ser.: 5). (ENG., Illus.). 304p. (J). (gr. 3-7). 2019. pap. 7.99 (978-1-5362-0908-2(2)) 2016. 15.99 (978-0-7636-9004-5(X)) Candlewick Pr.

Patron, Susan. Lucky for Good. McGuire, Erin, illus. 2012. (ENG.). 224p. (J). (gr. 3-7). pap. 8.99 (978-1-4169-9059-8(3), Atheneum Bks. for Young Readers) Simon & Schuster Children's Publishing.

—Lucky for Good, 3. McGuire, Erin, illus. 2011. (ENG.). 224p. (J). (gr. 3-7). 16.99 (978-1-4169-9058-1(5)) Simon & Schuster, Inc.

Paul, J. D. The Little Lost Dog, 1 vol. 2010. 12p. pap. 24.95 (978-1-4489-9251-5(6)) PublishAmerica, Inc.

Paulsen, Gary. The Glass Cafe or, the Stripper & the State: How My Mother Started a War with the System That Made Us Kind of Rich & a Little Bit Famous. 2004. 99p. (J). 13.65 (978-0-7569-3105-6(3)) Perfection Learning Corp.

Pavon, Mar. Could It Happen to Anyone? Brokenbrow, Jon, tr. Wimmer, Sonja, illus. 2011. 32p. (J). (gr. k-3). 14.95 (978-84-15241-03-4(8)) Cuento de Luz SL ESP. Dist: Publishers Group West (PGW).

Pen, Chenda. Dara Learns How to Ride a Bike! An Autism Story. 2010. 24p. pap. 14.99 (978-1-4490-6943-8(6)) AuthorHouse.

Penn, Audrey. Un Beso en Mi Mano (the Kissing Hand) Harper, Ruth, illus. 2006. (ENG.). 32p. (J). (gr. -1-3). 18.99 (978-1-933718-01-9(3)) Tanglewood Pr.

—The Kissing Hand. Harper, Ruth, illus. 2007. (ENG.). 32p. (J). (gr. -1-3). 28.95 (978-1-933718-07-1(2)) Tanglewood Pr.

—A Kissing Hand for Chester Raccoon. Gibson, Barbara, illus. 2014. (Kissing Hand Ser.). (ENG.). 14p. (J). (gr. -1-2). bds. 8.99 (978-1-933718-77-4(3)) Tanglewood Pr.

Penn, Audrey, et al, illus. The Kissing Hand. 2010. 23.05 (978-0-7569-9299-6(0)) Natl Bk. Network.

Pennington, Norma C. & Schuller, Sheldon V. The Unopened Gift, 1 vol. 2010. 18p. 24.95 (978-1-4489-7670-6(7)) PublishAmerica, Inc.

Pentz, Jane A. Horatio's Magical Journeys - the Secret. 2007. 108p. pap. 10.00 (978-1-892426-11-6(0)) LMA Publishing.

Perry, Fred. Grossery Games. 2012. (ENG., Illus.). 128p. (J). (gr. 4-7). pap. 10.99 (978-0-9850925-5-9(6), baf71806-dc15-4c9c-a7f7-67e5a6bd9621) Antarctic Pr., Inc.

—Playing Dead. 2012. (ENG., Illus.). 128p. (J). pap. 10.99 (978-0-9850925-4-2(8), fd0c2d86-94c4-479a-ada8-c3f0d61fbb76) Antarctic Pr., Inc.

Pham, LeUyen. All the Things I Love about You. Pham, LeUyen, illus. 2010. (ENG., Illus.). 40p. (J). (gr. -1-3). 14.99 (978-0-06-199029-8(9), Balzer & Bray) HarperCollins Pubs.

Pick, Alice. Jamey's Promise, 1 vol. 2009. 61p. pap. 19.95 (978-1-61582-547-9(9)) America Star Bks.

Pignataro, Anna. Mama, Will You Hold My Hand? Pignataro, Anna, illus. 2010. (ENG., Illus.). 32p. (J). (gr. -1-k). pap. 4.99 (978-0-545-16986-8(0), Cartwheel Bks.) Scholastic, Inc.

Poh, Jennie. Herbie's Big Adventure. Poh, Jennie, illus. 2019. (ENG., Illus.). 30p. (gr. -1-2). bds. 7.99 (978-1-68446-092-2(1), 141307, Capstone Editions) Capstone.

Powell, Randy. Tribute to Another Dead Rock Star. 2003. (ENG.). 224p. (YA). (gr. 7-12). pap. 15.99 (978-0-374-47968-8(2), 900021239, Farrar, Straus & Giroux (BYR)) Farrar, Straus & Giroux.

Prevost, Jeanne. It's Raining Cats — And Cats! Hansen, Amelia, illus. 2008. (ENG.). 24p. (J). (gr. k-2). 16.95 (978-0-940719-06-4(1)) Gryphon Pr., The.

Prince Apple Head Humpledink. 2006. 38p. (J). 13.68 (978-1-4116-7232-1(1)) Lulu Pr., Inc.

Quiller-Couch, Arthur Thomas. Naughts & Crosses. 2009. 188p. 26.95 (978-1-60664-671-7(0)) Rodgers, Alan Bks.

Quiller-Couch, Arthur Thomas & Q. Naughts & Crosses. 2009. 188p. pap. 13.95 (978-1-60664-299-3(5)) Rodgers, Alan Bks.

Rabley, Stephen. Danny's Blog/El Blog de Daniel. Martin, Rosa Maria, tr. Ursell, Martin, illus. 2008. (Let's Read! Spanish-English Ser.).Tr. of El Blog de Daniel. (ENG.). 30p. (J). (gr. k-3). 17.44 (978-0-7641-4047-1(7), B.E.S. Publishing) Peterson's.

Rahnama, Seyed Javad. Minty Ear. 2011. (Illus.). 20p. pap. 14.11 (978-1-4567-8188-0(X)) AuthorHouse.

Ramdayal, Mia. Learning How to Fly. 2012. 28p. pap. 15.99 (978-1-4691-5897-6(3)) Xlibris Corp.

Ramsey, Jo. Nail Polish & Feathers. 2016. (ENG., Illus.). (YA). (gr. 9-12). 24.99 (978-1-63533-050-2(5), Harmony Ink Pr.) Dreamspinner Pr.

Ramthun, Bonnie. The White Gates. 2008. (ENG.). 256p. (J). (gr. 6-8). lib. bdg. 22.44 (978-0-375-94554-0(7)) Random House Publishing Group.

Reibstein, Mark. Yugen. Young, Ed, illus. 2019. 32p. (J). (gr. -1-2). 17.95 (978-1-60980-865-5(7), Triangle Square) Seven Stories Pr.

Renero, Joaquin. The Enchanted Scrapbook: Welcome to the Wilburton Society. 2011. 320p. 29.95 (978-1-4502-6140-1(X)); pap. 19.95 (978-1-4502-6138-8(8)) iUniverse, Inc.

Reynolds, Aaron. Back of the Bus. Cooper, Floyd, illus. 2013. 32p. (J). (gr. 1-3). 8.99 (978-0-14-751058-7(9), Puffin Books) Penguin Young Readers Group.

Rhodes, Terry. Marley's Big Day. 2008. 16p. pap. 24.95 (978-1-60474-947-2(4)) America Star Bks.

Richardson, Tom. Dominic Is Strong. 2005. (Illus.). 26p. (J). lib. bdg. 16.95 (978-1-932338-99-7(3)) Lifevest Publishing, Inc.

Richmond, Lori. Bunny Business (Mama's Day at Work) 2020. (ENG., Illus.). 32p. (J). (gr. -1-k). 18.99 (978-0-545-92590-7(8), Scholastic Pr.) Scholastic, Inc.

Ringo, Mary Lou. That's Not Fair. 2012. 28p. pap. 24.95 (978-1-4626-5153-5(4)) America Star Bks.

Rivera, Veronica. Mommy's Little Helper. 2012. 32p. pap. 17.49 (978-1-4691-9026-6(5)) Xlibris Corp.

Rockliff, Mara. Me & Momma & Big John. Low, William, illus. 2012. (ENG.). 32p. (J). (gr. -1-2). 16.99 (978-0-7636-4359-1(9)) Candlewick Pr.

Romagnoli, L. M. Memories of Me, 1 vol. 2009. 22p. pap. 24.95 (978-1-60836-084-0(9)) America Star Bks.

Rossell, Judith. Oliver. Rossell, Judith, illus. 2012. (ENG., Illus.). 32p. (J). (gr. -1-2). 16.99 (978-0-06-202210-3(5), HarperCollins) HarperCollins Pubs.

Rudolph, Shaina & Royer, Danielle. All My Stripes: A Story for Children with Autism. Zivoin, Jennifer, illus. 2014. (J). pap. (978-1-4338-1917-9(1), Magination Pr.) American Psychological Assn.

Ryan, Pam Muñoz. Yo, Naomi León. 2005. (SPA.). 272p. (J). (gr. 4-7). pap. 8.99 (978-0-439-75572-6(7), Scholastic en Espanol) Scholastic, Inc.

Ryan, Patrick. In Mike We Trust. 2009. 321p. (J). lib. bdg. 17.89 (978-0-06-085814-8(1), HarperTeen) HarperCollins Pubs.

Rylant, Cynthia. A Kindness. Date not set. (Sky Bks.). 104p. pap. 54.75 (978-0-582-08106-2(8)) Addison-Wesley Longman, Ltd. GBR. Dist: Trans-Atlantic Pubns., Inc.

Sabo, J. Mamma's Boy. 2012. 30p. 24.95 (978-1-4626-6928-8(X)) America Star Bks.

Samuel, Lynette M. Mommy's Hat. Capps, Leigh, illus. 2005. (J). per. (978-0-9727703-3-0(X)) P.R.A. Publishing.

Saunders, Brianna. The Magic Marble. 2013. 32p. pap. 24.95 (978-1-63004-598-2(5)) America Star Bks.

Sawyer, Louise. Mother's Storybook Signs, Vol. 1. 2004. (YA). spiral bd. 19.95 (978-0-9719842-0-2(4)) Martin & Brothers.

Schmid, Lisa. Ollie Oxley & the Ghost: The Search for Lost Gold. 2019. (ENG.). 220p. (J). (gr. 3-7). pap. 11.99 (978-1-63163-289-1(2), 1631632892, Jolly Fish Pr.) North Star Editions.

Schmidt, Shawntay. Invincible Me. Du Pont, Brittany, illus. 2013. 24p. pap. 8.99 (978-1-937165-61-1(2)) Orange Hat Publishing.

Scholastic. My Mommy (Peppa Pig) 2014. (ENG.). 16p. (J). (gr. -1-k). bds. 7.99 (978-0-545-46804-6(3)) Scholastic, Inc.

Schraff, Anne. To Be a Man. 2011. (Urban Underground — Harriet Tubman High School Ser.). (YA). lib. bdg. 20.80 (978-0-606-14815-3(9)) Turtleback.

Scraper, Katherine. The Yard Sale. 2006. (Early Explorers Ser.). (J). pap. (978-1-4108-6043-9(4)) Benchmark Education Co.

Seghetti, Nancy & Esseveld, Nelson. The Day Mom Quit. 2009. 36p. pap. 16.99 (978-1-4389-2168-6(3)) AuthorHouse.

Sexauer, Donald E. The Standoff & Kramer Too! 2012. 24p. pap. 12.56 (978-1-4669-4577-7(X)) Trafford Publishing.

Shea, John & Harmon, Michael B. A Kid from Southie. 2011. 240p. (YA). (gr. 9-18). 16.95 (978-1-934813-53-9(2)) Westside Bks.

Shutz, Ashley. Little Ricky Roo. 2012. 28p. 24.95 (978-1-4512-6491-3(7)) America Star Bks.

Smith, Andrew Christopher John. Soi. 2009. (Illus.). 40p. pap. 16.99 (978-1-4490-3591-4(4)) AuthorHouse.

Smith, Dan. Boy X. 2017. 274p. (J). (978-1-338-17150-1(X)) Scholastic, Inc.

Smith, Latoya K. My Favorite Trey. 2009. 24p. pap. 11.49 (978-1-4490-4220-2(1)) AuthorHouse.

Snyder, Laurel. Hungry Jim: (Children's Emotion Books, Animal Books for Kids, Funny Children Books) 2019. (ENG., Illus.). 56p. (J). (gr. -1-k). 17.99 (978-1-4521-4987-5(9)) Chronicle Bks. LLC.

Solomon, Enid. Toby Visits Mommy: A Book for Children Who See Their Parents Only During Scheduled Visitations. 2010. 32p. pap. 13.25 (978-1-4490-0683-9(3)) AuthorHouse.

Sonnenblick, Jordan. The Secret Sheriff of Sixth Grade. 2017. (ENG.). 208p. (J). (gr. 5-9). 16.99 (978-0-545-86320-9(1), Scholastic Pr.) Scholastic, Inc.

Sosna-Spear, Quinn. The Remarkable Inventions of Walter Mortinson. 2019. (ENG., Illus.). 336p. (J). (gr. 3-7). 17.99 (978-1-5344-2080-9(0), Simon & Schuster Bks. For Young Readers) Simon & Schuster Bks. For Young Readers.

Sprenger, Luke. Sommer in Canvas Bay. 2008. (GER.). 92p. pap. 13.95 (978-1-4092-3213-1(1)) Lulu Pr., Inc.

Stanley, Dan. Danny the Fisherman, 1 vol. LaRue, Athena Mariah, illus. 2010. 46p. 24.95 (978-1-4512-9695-2(9)) PublishAmerica, Inc.

Star, Eloney. Heavy Duty Trucker. 2007. 28p. (J). per. 7.99 (978-1-59879-287-4(3)) Lifevest Publishing, Inc.

Stinson, Kathy. The Man with the Violin. Petricic, Dusan, illus. 2016. 32p. (J). (gr. k-3). pap. 9.95 (978-1-55451-564-6(5)) Annick Pr., Ltd. CAN. Dist: Publishers Group West (PGW).

Stultz, Janice. Harry Turnaround. 2012. 24p. pap. 15.99 (978-1-4691-7141-8(4)) Xlibris Corp.

Sullivan, Paula. Todd's Box. Westcott, Nadine Bernard, illus. 2004. (J). (gr. -1-1). 11.60 (978-0-7569-5629-5(3)) Perfection Learning Corp.

Surplice, Holly. I Love You, Little One. Surplice, Holly, illus. 2019. (ENG., Illus.). 24p. (J). (-k). bds. 9.99 (978-1-5362-0578-7(8)) Candlewick Pr.

Suter, Lorenzo. TrYouth Truth Knowledge Apprehension Cog. 2005. (Illus.). 206p. 27.55 (978-1-4122-0095-0(4)) Trafford Publishing.

Swain, Cynthia. No, Tim! 2006. (Early Explorers Ser.). (J). pap. (978-1-4108-6029-3(9)) Benchmark Education Co.

Taylor, Brigid. How I Turn My Mom into a Momster! 2009. 16p. pap. 9.95 (978-1-4389-9755-1(8)) AuthorHouse.

Thomas, Alease Allen. Bobby Jones of Beardsley Terrace. 2006. 18.00 (978-0-8059-9829-0(2)) Dorrance Publishing Co., Inc.

Thompson, Lisa. The Light Jar. 2019. (ENG.). 240p. (J). (gr. 3-7). 17.99 (978-1-338-21630-1(9), Scholastic Pr.) Scholastic, Inc.

Thompson, Mary G. Wuftoom. 2013. (ENG.). 256p. (YA). (gr. 7). pap. 14.99 (978-0-544-02247-8(5), 1528482, Clarion Bks.) HarperCollins Pubs.

Tommasi, Michael Richard. Stinky Mcgee. 2008. 16p. pap. 9.95 (978-1-4343-6004-5(0)) AuthorHouse.

Torres, Jose A. Joey Kanga Roo: First Day of School. 2009. 36p. pap. 15.99 (978-1-4389-3964-3(7)) AuthorHouse.

Travis, Allison J. Bundy. One More Wake Up: With Faith All Things Are Possible-Even Surviving the Loss of a Loved One. 2012. 34p. 24.95 (978-1-4626-5862-6(8)) America Star Bks.

Truly Blessed Ink. I Know You Won't Forget. Jordan, Carol, illus. 2007. (ENG.). 40p. (J). 16.95 (978-0-9789066-1-0(6)) Square Circle Pr. LLC.

Tulloch, Scott. Willy's Mum. 2008. (Illus.). 32p. pap. (978-1-86950-682-7(0)) HarperCollins Pubs. Australia.

Turnbull-Kennedy, Tiffany. No School for Evil Eraser! 2011. (Illus.). 48p. pap. 16.59 (978-1-4634-3965-1(2)) AuthorHouse.

Turpin, Nick. Samuel, lo Siento. Nascimbeni, Barbara, illus. 2006. (Lectores Relampago / Lightning Readers: Level P Ser.). (SPA.). 32p. (J). (gr. -1-k). 16.19 (978-0-7696-4216-1(0)) School Specialty, Incorporated.

Tyburski, Kimberly. Pesty Boy. 2011. 24p. pap. 15.99 (978-1-4628-9302-7(3)) Xlibris Corp.

Underwood, Deborah. Pirate Mom. Gilpin, Stephen, illus. 2006. (Step into Reading Ser.: Vol. 3). 48p. (J). (gr. k-3). per. 5.99 (978-0-375-83323-6(4), Random Hse. Bks. for Young Readers) Random Hse. Children's Bks.

Urban, Linda. Road Trip with Max & His Mom. Kath, Katie, illus. 2018. (ENG.). 160p. (J). (gr. 3-7). 16.99 (978-0-544-80912-3(2), 1641407, Clarion Bks.) HarperCollins Pubs.

Varley, Dax. The Crow. Proctor, Jon, illus. 2016. (Demon Slayer Ser.). (ENG.). 48p. (J). (gr. 3-7). lib. bdg. 34.21 (978-1-62402-160-2(3), 21567, Spellbound) Magic Wagon.

—Graveyard Dirt. Proctor, Jon, illus. 2016. (Demon Slayer Ser.). (ENG.). 48p. (J). (gr. 3-7). lib. bdg. 34.21 (978-1-62402-158-9(1), 21563, Spellbound) Magic Wagon.

—The Locket. Proctor, Jon, illus. 2016. (Demon Slayer Ser.). (ENG.). 48p. (J). (gr. 3-7). lib. bdg. 34.21 (978-1-62402-159-6(X), 21565, Spellbound) Magic Wagon.

Villareal, Ray. Don't Call Me Hero. 2011. (J). pap. 10.95 *(978-1-55885-711-7(7)*, Piñata Books) Arte Publico Pr.

Wallace, Nancy Elizabeth. Shells! Shells! Shells!, 0 vols. Wallace, Nancy Elizabeth, illus. 2013. (ENG.). 40p. (J). (gr. 1-3). pap. 9.99 *(978-1-4778-1679-0(8)*, 9781477816790, Two Lions) Amazon Publishing.

Walter, Chris. Tell Your Dreams to Me. 2008. 32p. pap. 14.95 *(978-1-4389-0162-6(3))* AuthorHouse.

Walters, Celeste. Deception. 2005. 288p. (YA). pap. *(978-0-7022-3527-6(X))* Univ. of Queensland Pr.

Walters, Eric. The Falls. 2008. (ENG.). 336p. (J). (gr. 3-7). 12.00 *(978-0-14-331246-8(4)*, Puffin Canada) PRH Canada Young Readers CAN. Dist: Penguin Random Hse. LLC.

Ward Appleton's Pancakes a Special Way. 2005. 10.95 *(978-0-9754779-6-0(X))* Chosen Word Publishing.

Weatherall, Barry. Jay & the Worm Save the Day. 2005. 40p. 14.28 *(978-1-4116-4717-6(3))* Lulu Pr., Inc.

Weatherford, Carole Boston. In Your Hands. Pinkney, Brian, illus. 2017. (ENG.). 32p. (J). (gr. -1-3). 17.99 *(978-1-4814-6293-8(8))* Simon & Schuster Children's Publishing.

Weiner, Brian. Toad Catchers' Creek. Weintraub, Claudia & Frederick, Robin, eds. Cannon, Martin, illus. 2005. 40p. (J). lib. bdg. 17.99 *(978-1-932949-58-2(5))* Illusion Factory, The.

Welsh, Karen Leis. Eh, Spaghetti You Say? 2012. 36p. pap. 20.99 *(978-1-4772-0473-3(3))* AuthorHouse.

Wheelwright, Ryan. Olivar & the Forbidden Plum Patch. 2011. 21p. (J). pap. 11.95 *(978-1-4327-6689-4(9))* Outskirts Pr., Inc.

Whitten, A. J. The Well. 2009. (ENG., Illus.). 336p. (YA). (gr. 7-18). pap. 18.95 *(978-0-547-23229-4(2)*, 1082742, Clarion Bks.) HarperCollins Pubs.

Wilderness, Dale. Drift in Your Pillow's Eyes. 2013. pap. 9.95 *(978-1-59433-155-8(3))* Publication Consultants.

Williams-Garcia, Rita. Clayton Byrd Goes Underground. 2019. (Penworthy Picks Middle School Ser.). (ENG.). 166p. (J). (gr. 4-5). 18.49 *(978-1-64310-913-8(8))* Penworthy Co., LLC, The.

Williams, Tova. The Boy Who Did Not Want to Read, 1 vol. Suggs, Aisha, illus. 2010. 36p. pap. 24.95 *(978-1-4489-5705-7(2))* PublishAmerica, Inc.

Williamson, Jennifer. Timmy the Tow Truck, 6 vols. Williamson, Alan, 8th, illus. 2005. 28p. (J). pap. *(978-0-9771678-1-4(X))* Theee Hole Punch Publishing.

Willis, Jeanne. Cottonball Colin. Ross, Tony, illus. 2008. 26p. (J). (gr. -1-4). 16.00 *(978-0-8028-5331-8(5)*, Eerdmans Bks For Young Readers) Eerdmans, William B. Publishing Co.

Wilson, N. D. Leepike Ridge. 2007. (ENG., Illus.). 224p. (J). (gr. 4-6). lib. bdg. 22.44 *(978-0-375-93873-3(7))* Random House Publishing Group.

—Leepike Ridge. 2008. (ENG., Illus.). 256p. (J). (gr. 3-7). 8.99 *(978-0-375-83874-3(0)*, Yearling) Random Hse. Children's Bks.

Winkler, Henry & Oliver, Lin. Always Watch Out for the Flying Potato Salad! #9. Garrett, Scott, illus. 2017. (Here's Hank Ser.: 9). 128p. (J). (gr. 1-3). 6.99 *(978-1-101-99583-9(1)*, Penguin Workshop) Penguin Young Readers Group.

Wood, Courtney. Just the Way It Was. 2013. 28p. pap. 19.99 *(978-1-4817-0734-3(5))* AuthorHouse.

Wood, Frank. Little Ray's Trip to the Doctor. 2012. 58p. pap. 40.00 *(978-1-60746-263-7(X))* FastPrncil, Inc.

Woodson, Jacqueline. From the Notebooks of Melanin Sun. 2011. 9.68 *(978-0-7848-3512-8(8))* 2009. 7.84 *(978-0-7848-2356-9(1))* Marco Bk. Co. (Everbind).

—From the Notebooks of Melanin Sun. 2010. (ENG.). 176p. (J). (gr. 5-18). 7.99 *(978-0-14-241641-9(X)*, Puffin Books) Penguin Young Readers Group.

—From the Notebooks of Melanin Sun. 2003. (Point Ser.). (ENG.). 141p. (YA). (gr. 7). 13.65 *(978-0-7807-7292-2(X))* Perfection Learning Corp.

Young, Candice June. My Name Is Wes & My Mema Has Ms. 2013. 24p. pap. 24.95 *(978-1-4137-7777-2(5))* America Star Bks.

Yum, Hyewon. Mom, It's My First Day of Kindergarten!, 1 vol. Yum, Hyewon, illus. 2012. (ENG., Illus.). 40p. (J). (gr. -1-2). 19.99 *(978-0-374-35004-8(3)*, 900077454, Farrar, Straus & Giroux (BYR)) Farrar, Straus & Giroux.

—Puddle. 2016. (ENG., Illus.). 40p. (J). 18.99 *(978-0-374-31695-2(3)*, 900147132, Farrar, Straus & Giroux (BYR)) Farrar, Straus & Giroux.

Zolotow, Charlotte. The Seashore Book. Minor, Wendell, illus. 2017. 32p. (J). (-k). lib. bdg. 18.99 *(978-1-58089-787-7(8))* Charlesbridge Publishing, Inc.

—The Seashore Book. Minor, Wendell, illus. 2004. (Reading Rainbow Bks.). (gr. -1-3). 17.00 *(978-0-7569-4234-2(9))* Perfection Learning Corp.

MOTHER'S DAY

Day, Erin. Happy Mother's Day!, 1 vol. 2016. (Celebrations Ser.). (ENG.). 24p. (J). (gr. 1-1). pap. 9.25 *(978-1-4994-2765-3(4)*, f6aebcbe-1946-4134-abf9-be0989d52511, PowerKids Pr.) Rosen Publishing Group, Inc., The.

Erlbach, Arlene & Erlbach, Herbert. Fun Mother's Day Crafts, 1 vol. 2014. (Kid Fun Holiday Crafts! Ser.). (ENG.). 32p. (gr. 3-4). 25.60 *(978-0-7660-6245-0(7)*, 0e3226d2-fe55-49c2-af92-faf5edb0471e); pap. 10.35 *(978-0-7660-6246-7(5)*, b273f000-174a-4717-9301-b0f0b19345df, Enslow Elementary) Enslow Publishing, LLC.

Fowler, Eleri. My Mother, My Heart: A Joyful Book to Color. Fowler, Eleri, illus. 2016. (ENG., Illus.). 96p. (J). (gr. -1). pap. 15.99 *(978-0-06-247938-9(5)*, HarperFestival) HarperCollins Pubs.

Gilpin, Rebecca. Things to Make for Mother's Day. 2004. (ENG., Illus.). 32p. (J). pap. 8.95 *(978-0-7945-0693-3(3)*, Usborne) EDC Publishing.

Honoring Mothers. 7.50 *(978-0-8054-5928-9(6))* B&H Publishing Group.

Lim, Annalees. Mother's & Father's Day Crafts, 1 vol., 1. 2015. (10-Minute Crafts Ser.). (ENG., Illus.). 24p. (J). (gr. 2-3). 28.93 *(978-1-5081-9095-0(X)*, 619b12ed-7ec8-481a-a140-aa4173f75cd6); pap. 11.60 *(978-1-5081-9093-6(3)*, 8da527ad-6c19-4d40-bcde-2a0f5d555bad) Rosen Publishing Group, Inc., The. (Windmill Bks.).

Miller, Reagan. Mother's Day & Other Family Days. 2010. (Celebrations in My World Ser.). (ENG.). 32p. (J). (gr. k-3). pap. *(978-0-7787-4937-0(1))*; lib. bdg. *(978-0-7787-4930-1(4))* Crabtree Publishing Co.

Nelid, Piper. Mother's Day with My Moms, 1 vol., 1. 2015. (Rosen REAL Readers: Social Studies Nonfiction / Fiction: Myself, My Community, My World Ser.). (ENG.). 8p. (J). (gr. k-1). pap. 5.46 *(978-1-5081-1647-9(4)*, 48f82c02-34e3-4161-9853-513ec81040fb, Rosen Classroom) Rosen Publishing Group, Inc., The.

Rey, H. A. Mother's Day Surprise. 2018. (Curious George TV Tie-In Early Reader Ser.). lib. bdg. 13.55 *(978-0-606-41009-0(0))* Turtleback.

Ross, Kathy. All New Crafts for Mother's Day & Father's Day. Holm, Sharon Lane, illus. 2007. (All New Holiday Crafts for Kids Ser.). (ENG.). 48p. (gr. k-3). per. 7.95 *(978-0-8225-6368-6(1)*, First Avenue Editions) Lerner Publishing Group.

—All New Holiday Crafts for Mother's & Father's Day. Holm, Sharon Lane, illus. 2007. (All New Holiday Crafts for Kids Ser.). (ENG.). 48p. (gr. k-3). lib. bdg. 25.26 *(978-0-8225-6367-9(3)*, Millbrook Pr.) Lerner Publishing Group.

Watson, Michael C., frwd. Why Mom Deserves a Diamond(r) -Twelve Years of Love: Twelve Years of Love. 2005. 144p. (YA). lib. bdg. 29.95 *(978-1-891665-35-6(9))* Moon Over Mountains Publishing (M.O.M.).

Williams, Colleen Madonna Flood. My Adventure on Mother's Day. 2007. 44p. (J). 8.99 *(978-1-59092-552-2(1))* Blue Forge Pr.

MOTHER'S DAY—FICTION

Berenstain, Jan & Berenstain, Mike. We Love Our Mom! 2012. (Berenstain Bears Ser.). (J). lib. bdg. 13.55 *(978-0-606-23578-5(7))* Turtleback.

Berenstain, Jan & Mike. The Berenstain Bears Spring Storybook Favorites: Includes 7 Stories Plus Stickers!: a Springtime Book for Kids. Berenstain, Mike, illus. 2019. (Berenstain Bears Ser.). (ENG.). 192p. (J). (gr. -1-3). 13.99 *(978-0-06-288310-0(0)*, HarperCollins) HarperCollins Pubs.

Berenstain, Mike. The Berenstain Bears Mother's Day Blessings, 1 vol. 2016. (Berenstain Bears/Living Lights: a Faith Story Ser.). (ENG., Illus.). 32p. (J). pap. 3.99 *(978-0-310-74869-4(0))* Zonderkidz.

Britt, Paige. The Lost Track of Time. White, Lee, illus. 2015. (ENG.). 320p. (J). (gr. 3-7). 17.99 *(978-0-545-53812-1(2)*, Scholastic Pr.) Scholastic, Inc.

Carle, Eric, illus. I Love Mom with the Very Hungry Caterpillar. 2017. (World of Eric Carle Ser.). (ENG.). 32p. (J). (-k). 9.99 *(978-0-451-53346-3(1))* Penguin Young Readers Group.

González, Rigoberto. Antonio's Card: La Tarjeta de Antonio, 1 vol. Álvarez, Cecilia, illus. 2016. (ENG.). 32p. (J). (gr. 2-5). pap. 11.95 *(978-0-89239-387-9(4)*, leelowcbp, Children's Book Press) Lee & Low Bks., Inc.

González, Rigoberto & Alvarez, Cecilia Concepcion. Antonio's Card/la Tarjeta de Antonio. 2013. (ENG & SPA., Illus.). 32p. (J). 17.95 *(978-0-89239-204-9(5))* Lee & Low Bks., Inc.

Grambling, Lois G. T. Rex & the Mother's Day Hug. Davis, Jack E., illus. 2011. (ENG.). 32p. (J). (gr. -1-1). pap. 7.99 *(978-0-06-053128-7(2)*, Tegen, Katherine Bks) HarperCollins Pubs.

Hapka, Catherine, pseud. Sofia the First: Our Mother's Day Surprise. 2015. (Sofia the First Ser.). (Illus.). 24p. (J). lib. bdg. 14.75 *(978-0-606-35913-9(3))* Turtleback.

Hillert, Margaret. Happy Mother's Day, Dear Dragon. Starfall Education, illus. 2005. (ENG.). 32p. (J). pap. *(978-1-59577-023-3(2))* Starfall Education.

Kann, Victoria. Pinkalicious: Mother's Day Surprise. Kann, Victoria, illus. 2015. (Pinkalicious Ser.). (ENG., Illus.). 24p. (J). (gr. -1-3). pap. 6.99 *(978-0-06-224587-8(2)*, HarperFestival) HarperCollins Pubs.

Knudsen, Michelle. Mother's Day Ribbons. Wallace, John, illus. 2005. (ENG.). 12p. (J). bds. 6.99 *(978-0-689-86381-3(0)*, Little Simon) Little Simon.

Lampson, Rosalie. Give Mom a Minute. 2009. 32p. pap. 13.99 *(978-1-4490-1407-0(0))* AuthorHouse.

Manushkin, Fran. Katie Woo Tries Something New. Lyon, Tammie, illus. 2015. (Katie Woo Ser.). (ENG.). 96p. (J). (gr. k-2). pap., pap., pap. 4.95 *(978-1-4795-6182-7(7)*, 127899, Picture Window Bks.) Capstone.

—Katie's Happy Mother's Day. Lyon, Tammie, illus. 2015. (Katie Woo Ser.). (ENG.). 32p. (J). (gr. k-2). 21.32 *(978-1-4795-6179-7(7)*, 127896, Picture Window Bks.) Capstone.

May, Eleanor. The Best Mother's Day Ever. Pilz, M. H., illus. 2010. (Social Studies Connects Ser.). 32p. (J). (gr. 1-4). pap. 6.99 *(978-1-57565-299-3(4)*, 10a30778-f71f-4dc6-9aae-05d93685d79f, Kane Press) Astra Publishing Hse.

McCarthy, Rebecca. A Very Special Mama's Day. Artful Doodlers Ltd. Staff, illus. 2013. (Zoobles! Ser.). (ENG.). 24p. (J). (gr. -1-1). 17.44 *(978-0-448-46316-2(4))* Penguin Young Readers Group.

McClatchy, Lisa. Eloise's Mother's Day Surprise: Ready-To-Read Level 1. Lyon, Tammie, illus. (Eloise Ser.). (ENG.). 32p. (J). (gr. -1-1). 2018. 17.99 *(978-1-4814-7678-2(5))* 2009. pap. 4.99 *(978-1-4169-7889-3(5))* Simon Spotlight. (Simon Spotlight).

McDonald, Kirsten. El Error Rico (the Yummy Mistake) Meza, Erika, illus. 2018. (Carlos & Carmen (Spanish Version) (Calico Kid) Ser.). (SPA.). 32p. (J). (gr. -1-3). lib. bdg. 32.79 *(978-1-5321-3324-4(3)*, 28511, Calico Chapter Bks) Magic Wagon.

—The Yummy Mistake. Meza, Erika, illus. 2016. (Carlos & Carmen Ser.). (ENG.). 32p. (J). (gr. -1-3). 32.79 *(978-1-62402-145-9(X)*, 21557, Calico Chapter Bks) Magic Wagon.

O'Connor, Jane. Fancy Nancy: The Marvelous Mother's Day Brunch. 2011. (Fancy Nancy Ser.). (ENG., Illus.). 16p. (J). (gr. -1-3). pap. 6.99 *(978-0-06-170380-5(X)*, HarperFestival) HarperCollins Pubs.

Pratt, Laura. La Fête des Mères: Les Célébrations Canadiennes. Karvonen, Tanjah, tr. from ENG. 2011. (FRE.). 24p. (gr. k-3). *(978-1-77071-398-7(0))* Weigl Educational Pubs. Ltd.

Remkiewicz, Frank. Gus Makes a Gift. Remkiewicz, Frank, illus. 2012. (Scholastic Reader, Pre-Level 1 Ser.). (ENG., Illus.). 24p. (J). (gr. -1-1). pap. 3.99 *(978-0-545-24469-5(2)*, Cartwheel Bks.) Scholastic, Inc.

Ricci, Christine. I Love My Abuela! Miller, Victoria, illus. 2009. (Dora the Explorer Ser.: 28). (ENG.). 24p. (J). pap. 3.99 *(978-1-4169-6866-5(0)*, Simon Spotlight/Nickelodeon) Simon Spotlight/Nickelodeon.

Rylant, Cynthia. Henry & Mudge & the Funny Lunch. Bracken, Carolyn, illus. 2005. (Henry & Mudge Ready-To-Read Ser.: 24). 40p. (gr. k-2). lib. bdg. 13.55 *(978-1-4176-7107-6(6))* Turtleback.

Schiffer, Miriam B. Stella Brings the Family. 2015. (ENG., Illus.). 36p. (J). (gr. k-3). 16.99 *(978-1-4521-1190-2(1))* Chronicle Bks. LLC.

Self Simpson, Martha. What NOT to Give Your Mom on Mother's Day, 0 vols. Christy, Jana, illus. 2013. (ENG.). 24p. (J). (gr. -1-2). 12.99 *(978-1-4778-1647-9(X)*, 9781477816479, Two Lions) Amazon Publishing.

Weninger, Brigitte. Davy Loves His Mommy. Tharlet, Eve, illus. 2014. (ENG.). 32p. (J). (gr. k-3). 15.95 *(978-0-7358-4164-2(0))* North-South Bks., Inc.

Wiseman, Blaine. La Fête des Pères: Les Célébrations Canadiennes. Karvonen, Tanjah, tr. from ENG. 2011. (FRE.). 24p. (gr. k-3). *(978-1-77071-396-3(4))* Weigl Educational Pubs. Ltd.

MOTHS

see also Butterflies; Caterpillars; Silkworms

Adams, Alison. Butterflies & Moths. #N/A. ed. 2011. (Early Connections Ser.). (ENG.). (J). (gr. 2). 8.00 net. *(978-1-61672-629-4(6))* Benchmark Education Co.

Bedoyere, Camilla De La, et al. Butterflies & Moths. 2017. (Illus.). 96p. (J). pap. 9.95 *(978-1-78209-169-1(6))* Miles Kelly Publishing, Ltd. GBR. Dist: Parkwest Pubns., Inc.

Bishop, Nic. Butterflies & Moths. Bishop, Nic, photos by. 2009. (ENG., Illus.). 48p. (J). (gr. -1-3). 19.99 *(978-0-439-87757-2(1)*, Scholastic Nonfiction) Scholastic, Inc.

Black, Nessa. Moths. 2019. (Spot Creepy Crawlies Ser.). (ENG.). 16p. (J). (gr. -1-2). lib. bdg. *(978-1-68151-538-0(5)*, 14499) Amicus.

Bodden, Valerie. Creepy Creatures: Moths. 2014. (Creepy Creatures Ser.). (ENG.). 24p. (J). (gr. 1-3). pap. 9.99 *(978-0-89812-937-3(0)*, 21500, Creative Paperbacks) Creative Co., The.

—Moths. 2014. (Creepy Creatures Ser.). (ENG.). 24p. (J). (gr. 1-4). *(978-1-60818-358-6(0)*, 21499, Creative Education) Creative Co., The.

Burns, Loree. You're Invited to a Moth Ball: A Nighttime Insect Celebration. Harasimowicz, Ellen, illus. 2020. 40p. (J). (gr. k-3). lib. bdg. 16.99 *(978-1-58089-686-3(3))* Charlesbridge Publishing, Inc.

Carr, Aaron. Moths. 2014. (J). *(978-1-4896-1042-3(1))*; *(978-1-4896-1044-7(8))* Weigl Pubs., Inc.

Coleman, Miriam. Moths Drink Tears!, 1 vol., 1. 2013. (Disgusting Animal Dinners Ser.). (ENG.). 24p. (J). (gr. 2-3). 26.27 *(978-1-4777-2883-3(X)*, 2e9153b3-d750-421b-a638-f9bc3d7d5ae5, PowerKids Pr.) Rosen Publishing Group, Inc., The.

DK. Butterflies & Moths: Explore Nature with Fun Facts & Activities. 2018. (Nature Explorers Ser.). (ENG., Illus.). 64p. (J). (gr. 1-3). 9.99 *(978-1-4654-7340-0(8)*, DK Children) Dorling Kindersley Publishing, Inc.

Early Macken, JoAnn. The Life Cycle of a Moth, 1 vol. 2005. (Things with Wings Ser.). (ENG., Illus.). 24p. (J). (gr. k-2). pap. 9.15 *(978-0-8368-6391-8(7)*, 8a7f198d-27b0-4994-a11a-07a179785dcc); lib. bdg. 24.67 *(978-0-8368-6384-0(4)*, f2e05255-4c8a-4d54-b709-d60caa673b8c) Stevens, Gareth Publishing LLLP. (Weekly Reader Leveled Readers).

Farndon, John. Butterflies & Moths: A Comprehensive Guide to the Brief but Brilliant Lives of These Fascinating Creatures, with over 200 Pictures. 2015. (Illus.). 64p. (J). (gr. -1-k). 12.99 *(978-1-86147-407-0(5)*, Armadillo) Anness Publishing GBR. Dist: National Bk. Network.

Gallagher, Belinda. Spot 50 Butterflies & Moths. Kelly, Richard, ed. 2017. (ENG., Illus.). 56p. (J). pap. 9.95 *(978-1-84810-597-3(5))* Miles Kelly Publishing, Ltd. GBR. Dist: Parkwest Pubns., Inc.

Gish, Ashley. Moths. 2018. (X-Books: Insects Ser.). (ENG.). 32p. (J). (gr. 3-5). pap. 9.99 *(978-1-62832-619-2(0)*, 20008, Creative Paperbacks); *(978-1-60818-992-2(9)*, 20000, Creative Education) Creative Co., The.

Gray, Karlin. An Extraordinary Ordinary Moth. Doneva, Steliyana, illus. 2018. (ENG.). 32p. (J). (gr. k-3). 16.99 *(978-1-58536-372-8(3)*, 204401) Sleeping Bear Pr.

Helget, Nicole. Moths. 2007. (Bugbooks Ser.). (Illus.). 24p. (J). (gr. -1-3). lib. bdg. 24.25 *(978-1-58341-543-6(2)*, Creative Education) Creative Co., The.

Leaf, Christina. Butterfly or Moth? 2019. (Spotting Differences Ser.). (ENG., Illus.). 24p. (J). (gr. k-3). lib. bdg. 26.95 *(978-1-64487-032-7(0)*, Blastoff! Readers) Bellwether Media.

Light, Kate. Why Do Some Moths Mimic Wasps? And Other Odd Insect Adaptations, 1 vol. 2018. (Odd Adaptations Ser.). (ENG.). 32p. (gr. 3-4). 28.27 *(978-1-5382-2027-6(X)*, ec9f1245-a81c-4197-baa2-2c3f750a69e9) Stevens, Gareth Publishing LLLP.

Lundgren, Julie K. Butterflies & Moths. 2010. (Life Cycles Ser.). (ENG., Illus.). 24p. (gr. 1-4). pap. 8.95 *(978-1-61590-547-8(2)*, 9781615905478) Rourke Educational Media.

Markle, Sandra. Luna Moths. 2008. pap. 52.95 *(978-1-58013-283-1(9))* Lerner Publishing Group.

—Luna Moths: Masters of Change. 2008. (Insect World Ser.). (ENG., Illus.). 48p. (gr. 4-8). lib. bdg. 27.93 *(978-0-8225-7302-9(4)*, Lerner Pubns.) Lerner Publishing Group.

Martinez, Claudia Guadalupe. Not a Bean. Gonzalez, Laura, illus. 2019. 32p. (J). (gr. -1-2). lib. bdg. 16.99 *(978-1-58089-815-7(7))* Charlesbridge Publishing, Inc.

Mitchell, Susan K. Biggest vs. Smallest Things with Wings, 1 vol. 2010. (Biggest vs. Smallest Animals Ser.). (ENG., Illus.). 24p. (gr. k-2). 25.27 *(978-0-7660-3578-2(6)*, 7f7567d6-b8e9-4028-9317-1f79b3ca91bb, Enslow Elementary) Enslow Publishing, LLC.

Moth. 2003. (J). 36.95 *(978-0-8136-9268-5(7))*; 38.95 *(978-0-8136-4161-4(6))* Modern Curriculum Pr.

Orenstein, Ronald. Weird Butterflies & Moths. Marent, Thomas, photos by. 2016. (ENG., Illus.). 64p. (J). (gr. 5-8). pap. 9.95 *(978-1-77085-814-5(8)*, a5ba8696-e685-45ab-8e09-f6e174f21fb3) Firefly Bks., Ltd.

Orr, Tamra. Butterfly or Moth. 2019. (21st Century Junior Library: Which is Which? Ser.). (ENG., Illus.). 24p. (J). (gr. 2-5). pap. 12.79 *(978-1-5341-5024-9(2)*, 213403); lib. bdg. 30.64 *(978-1-5341-4738-6(1)*, 213402) Cherry Lake Publishing.

Pallotta, Jerry. Not a Butterfly Alphabet Book: It's about Time Moths Had Their Own Book! Bersani, Shennen, illus. 2019. 32p. (J). (gr. -1-2). lib. bdg. 17.99 *(978-1-58089-689-4(8))* Charlesbridge Publishing, Inc.

Perish, Patrick. Moths. 2018. (Insects up Close Ser.). (ENG., Illus.). 24p. (J). (gr. k-3). lib. bdg. 26.95 *(978-1-62617-718-5(X)*, Blastoff! Readers) Bellwether Media.

Reagan, Naomi. Butterflies & Moths: Represent & Interpret Data, 1 vol. 2014. (Rosen Math Readers Ser.). (ENG., Illus.). 24p. (J). (gr. 3-3). pap. 8.25 *(978-1-4777-4901-2(2)*, 54c99c90-81a3-471c-b797-cc45572303ae, Rosen Classroom) Rosen Publishing Group, Inc., The.

Rustad, Martha E. H. Magnificent Moths. 2017. (Bugs Are Beautiful! Ser.). (ENG., Illus.). 32p. (J). (gr. -1-2). lib. bdg. 27.99 *(978-1-5157-4499-3(X)*, 134198, Capstone Pr.) Capstone.

—Moths. 2007. (World of Insects Ser.). (ENG., Illus.). 24p. (J). (gr. k-3). lib. bdg. 26.95 *(978-1-60014-107-2(2))* Bellwether Media.

Sajjad, Mohammad. Insecticide Resistance Management in Tomato Fruit Borer. 2011. 232p. pap. *(978-3-8443-8248-8(8))* Lap Lambert Academic Publishing GmbH & Co. KG.

Schuh, Mari. Moths. 2014. (Illus.). 24p. (J). lib. bdg. 25.65 *(978-1-62031-086-1(4)*, Bullfrog Bks.) Jump! Inc.

Silverman, Buffy. Can You Tell A Butterfly from A Moth? 2011. (Animal Look-Alikes Ser.). pap. 45.32 *(978-0-7613-8383-3(2))* Lerner Publishing Group.

Stewart, Melissa. Butterfly or Moth? How Do You Know?, 1 vol. 2011. (Which Animal Is Which? Ser.). (ENG., Illus.). 24p. (gr. k-2). pap. 10.35 *(978-1-59845-235-8(5)*, 6f85c8df-84e1-4057-b035-8e75c028e9f0, Enslow Elementary); lib. bdg. 25.27 *(978-0-7660-3678-9(2)*, 96b3db59-e37d-4467-adba-80ce26633d14) Enslow Publishing, LLC.

Upgrade kit dsm-3 Butterflies&moths. (J). 2004. *(978-1-59242-526-6(7))* 2003. *(978-1-59242-409-2(0))* Delta Education, LLC.

MOTION

see also Force and Energy; Mechanics; Speed

Ballard, Carol. Exploring Forces & Movement, 1 vol. 2007. (How Does Science Work? Ser.). (ENG., Illus.). 32p. (J). (gr. 2-3). lib. bdg. 30.27 *(978-1-4042-4277-7(5)*, dc4364d5-8fa3-4349-b9a2-243494ca9804) Rosen Publishing Group, Inc., The.

Bell, Samantha. Pushing & Pulling. Bane, Jeff, illus. 2018. (Mi Mini Biografía (My Itty-Bitty Bio): My Early Library). (ENG.). 24p. (J). (gr. k-1). pap. 12.79 *(978-1-5341-0820-2(3)*, 210644); lib. bdg. 30.64 *(978-1-5341-0721-2(5)*, 210643) Cherry Lake Publishing.

Benchmark Education Company. Newton & His Laws (Teacher Guide) 2005. *(978-1-4108-4670-9(9))* Benchmark Education Co.

—Objects in Motion (Teacher Guide) 2005. *(978-1-4108-4663-1(6))* Benchmark Education Co.

—The Three Laws of Motion (Teacher Guide) 2005. *(978-1-4108-4677-8(6))* Benchmark Education Co.

Benchmark Education Company, LLC Staff, compiled by. Bodies in Motion & Body Systems. 2005. spiral bd. 225.00 *(978-1-4108-5824-5(3))* Benchmark Education Co.

—Forces & Motion. 2006. spiral bd. 330.00 *(978-1-4108-7014-8(6))* 2006. (J). 178.00 *(978-1-4108-7030-8(8))* 2005. (J). spiral bd. 265.00 *(978-1-4108-5760-6(3))* Benchmark Education Co.

—Forces & Motion: Theme Set. 2006. (J). 183.00 *(978-1-4108-7146-6(0))* Benchmark Education Co.

—Science Theme: Forces & Motion. 2005. spiral bd. 115.00 *(978-1-4108-5312-7(8))* Benchmark Education Co.

Biskup, Agnieszka. The Gripping Truth about Forces & Motion, 1 vol. Lum, Bernice, illus. 2012. (LOL Physical Science Ser.). (ENG.). 32p. (J). (gr. 3-6). pap. 8.10 *(978-1-4296-9298-4(7)*, 120361, Capstone Pr.) Capstone.

—The Gripping Truth about Forces & Motion. Lum, Bernice, illus. 2012. (LOL Physical Science Ser.). (ENG.). 32p. (J). (gr. 3-4). pap. 49.60 *(978-1-4296-9299-1(5)*, 18531, Capstone Pr.) Capstone.

—The Powerful World of Energy with Max Axiom, Super Scientist, 1 vol. Martin, Cynthia & Timmons, Anne, illus. 2009. (Graphic Science Ser.). (ENG.). 32p. (J). (gr. 3-9). pap. 8.10 *(978-1-4296-3450-2(2)*, 95993) Capstone.

Blanche, Lynn. What Makes It Go? 2004. (ENG., Illus.). 8p. (J). (gr. k-k). pap. 7.56 *(978-0-7652-5138-1(8)*, Celebration Pr.) Savvas Learning Co.

Bonnet, Robert L. & Keen, Dan. Home Run! Science Projects with Baseball & Softball, 1 vol. 2009. (Score! Sports Science Projects Ser.). (ENG., Illus.). 104p. (gr. 5-6). lib. bdg. 35.93 *(978-0-7660-3365-8(1)*, dba14f41-8d17-48fa-a413-92e4bc29a7a0) Enslow Publishing, LLC.

Boothroyd, Jennifer. Give it A Push! Give it A Pull! 2010. pap. 45.32 *(978-0-7613-6931-8(7))* Lerner Publishing Group.

—Give It a Push! Give It a Pull! A Look at Forces. 2010. (Lightning Bolt Books (r) — Exploring Physical Science Ser.). (ENG., Illus.). 32p. (J). (gr. 1-3). lib. bdg. 29.32 *(978-0-7613-5431-4(X)*, 7297cbe0-b208-4a02-88a8-5627cb41f46c, Lerner Pubns.) Lerner Publishing Group.

—Many Ways to Move. 2010. pap. 45.32 *(978-0-7613-6932-5(5))* Lerner Publishing Group.

—Many Ways to Move: A Look at Motion. 2010. (Lightning Bolt Books (r) — Exploring Physical Science Ser.). (ENG., Illus.). 32p. (J). (gr. 1-3). pap. 9.99 *(978-0-7613-6060-5(3)*, e0ac9898-fe98-4596-8a29-5d14b33dfead) Lerner Publishing Group.

Bortz, Fred. Laws of Motion & Isaac Newton, 1 vol. 2013. (Revolutionary Discoveries of Scientific Pioneers Ser.). (ENG., Illus.). 80p. (J). (gr. 6-6). 38.41 *(978-1-4777-1808-7(7)*, 874ae16c-2d37-4d79-a8df-bb2a415e1f52) Rosen Publishing Group, Inc., The.

Brannon, Barbara. Discover Motion. 2005. (J). pap. (978-1-4108-5126-0(5)) Benchmark Education Co.

—Discover the Laws of Motion. 2005. (J). pap. (978-1-4108-5128-4(1)) Benchmark Education Co.

Braun, Eric. Curious Pearl Kicks off Forces & Motion: 4D an Augmented Reading Science Experience. Lewis, Anthony, illus. 2018. (Curious Pearl, Science Girl 4D Ser.). (ENG.). 24p. (J). (gr. k-2). lib. bdg. 25.99 (978-1-5158-2970-6(7), 138573, Picture Window Bks.) Capstone.

Capstone Classroom & Stead, Tony. Could a Mouse Push a Car? 2017. (What's the Point? Reading & Writing Expository Text Ser.). (ENG., Illus.). 16p. (J). (gr. 2-2). pap. 6.95 (978-1-4966-0747-8(3), 132382, Capstone Classroom) Capstone.

Carlson Berne, Emma. Speeding! Mechanical Energy, 1 vol. 2013. (Energy Everywhere Ser.). (ENG., Illus.). 24p. (J). (gr. 2-3). 26.27 (978-1-4488-9651-6(7), 35f8944f-e054-4e0b-b6ef-5d20aead914e); pap. 9.25 (978-1-4488-9760-5(2), 6a727174-7ef7-46c7-938e-23e73d45abc3) Rosen Publishing Group, Inc., The. (PowerKids Pr.).

Challoner, Jack & Hewson, Maggie. Hands-On Science: Forces & Motion. 2013. (Hands-On Science Ser.). (ENG., Illus.). 32p. (J). (gr. 2-5). pap. 7.99 (978-0-7534-6972-9(3), 900088157, Kingfisher) Roaring Brook Pr.

Chiang, Mona. Isaac Newton & His Laws of Motion: Text Pairs. 2008. (Bridges/Navigators Ser.). (J). (gr. 6). 94.00 (978-1-4108-8442-8(2)) Benchmark Education Co.

Claybourne, Anna. Pushes & Pulls. 2012. (ENG., Illus.). 24p. (gr. k-4). pap. 7.95 (978-1-926853-59-8(8)) Saunders Bk. Co. CAN. Dist: RiverStream Publishing.

Close, Edward. Force & Motion, 1 vol., 1. 2014. (Discovery Education: How It Works). (ENG.). 32p. (gr. 4-5). 28.93 (978-1-4777-6317-9(1), eebde530-eb2d-4ed6-9a19-ebf34d7aec72, PowerKids Pr.) Rosen Publishing Group, Inc., The.

Cobb, Vicki. Whirlers & Twirlers: Science Fun with Spinning. Haefele, Steve, illus. 2007. (Science Fun with Vicki Cobb Ser.). (J). (gr. 4-7). per. 7.95 (978-0-8225-7025-7(4), First Avenue Editions) Lerner Publishing Group.

Connors, Kathleen. Forces & Motion, 1 vol. 2018. (Look at Physical Science Ser.). (ENG.). 32p. (gr. 2-2). 28.27 (978-1-5382-2143-3(8), 41962def-a88f-4b80-813a-dfe5cd0df539) Stevens, Gareth Publishing LLLP.

Delta Education. Sci Res Bk Foss Grade 3 Next Gen Ea. 2014. (Illus.). 274p. (J). lib. bdg. (978-1-62571-375-9(4)) Delta Education, LLC.

Dicker, Katie. Forces & Motion, 1 vol. 2010. (Sherlock Bones Looks at Physical Science Ser.). (ENG.). 32p. (YA). (gr. 5-5). lib. bdg. 29.93 (978-1-61533-211-3(1), 32381219-84c8-404b-b8d7-a094d38c5139, Windmill Bks.) Rosen Publishing Group, Inc., The.

Dolz, Jordi Bayarri. Isaac Newton & the Laws of Motion. Dolz, Jordi Bayarri, illus. 2020. (Graphic Science Biographies Ser.). (ENG., Illus.). 40p. (J). (gr. 5-8). 30.65 (978-1-5415-7824-1(4), f4e739d4-966f-428f-b673-126f76a0245c, Graphic Universe™) Lerner Publishing Group.

Drozd, Anne & Drozd, Jerzy. Science Comics: Rockets: Defying Gravity. 2018. (Science Comics Ser.). (ENG., Illus.). 128p. (J). 21.99 (978-1-62672-826-4(7), 900174978, First Second Bks.) Roaring Brook Pr.

Duke, Shirley. Forces & Motion at Work. 2011. (Let's Explore Science Ser.). (ENG., Illus.). 48p. (gr. 4-6). pap. 10.95 (978-1-61741-990-4(7), 9781617419904) Rourke Educational Media.

Enz, Tammy Laura Lynn. Motion at the Amusement Park. 2019. (Amusement Park Science Ser.). (ENG., Illus.). 32p. (J). (gr. 3-6). 27.99 (978-1-5435-7285-8(5), 140607) Capstone.

Evans Ogden, Lesley J. Forces & Motion. 2011. (J). (gr. 4-6). pap. 12.95 (978-1-61690-733-4(9), AV2 by Weigl); (Illus.). 24p. (gr. 3-6). 27.13 (978-1-61690-729-7(0)) Weigl Pubs., Inc.

—Studying Forces & Motion. 2016. (Illus.). 24p. (J). (978-1-5105-1124-8(5)) SmartBook Media, Inc.

Farndon, John. Motion, 1 vol. 2003. (Science Experiments Ser.). (ENG., Illus.). 32p. (gr. 4-4). 32.64 (978-0-7614-1471-1(1), c93dcbee-b6aa-4161-b38a-04ffbca56a18) Cavendish Square Publishing LLC.

Ferrie, Chris. Newtonian Physics for Babies. 2017. (Baby University Ser.: 0). (Illus.). 24p. (J). (gr. -1-k). bds. 9.99 (978-1-4926-5620-3(8)) Sourcebooks, Inc.

Fiedler, Julie. Learning about Force & Motion with Graphic Organizers, 1 vol. 2006. (Graphic Organizers in Science Ser.: Vol. 3). (ENG., Illus.). 24p. (J). (gr. 3-4). lib. bdg. 26.27 (978-1-4042-3410-9(1), a7daaff3-ce78-409f-b36e-8d4f29be3adf) Rosen Publishing Group, Inc., The.

Forest, Christopher. Focus on Momentum. 2017. (Hands-On STEM Ser.). (ENG., Illus.). 32p. (J). (gr. 2-3). pap. 9.95 (978-1-63517-351-2(5), 1635173515); lib. bdg. 31.35 (978-1-63517-286-7(1), 1635172861) North Star Editions. (Focus Readers).

Frisch-Schmoll, Joy. Motion & Movement. 2008. (Simple Science Ser.). (Illus.). 24p. (J). (gr. -1). lib. bdg. 24.25 (978-1-58341-578-8(5), Creative Education) Creative Co., The.

Frost, Adriana. Making Things Move: Force & Motion. 2013. (InfoMax Readers Ser.). (ENG.). 24p. (J). (gr. 2-3). pap. 49.50 (978-1-4777-2336-4(6)); (Illus.). pap. 8.25 (978-1-4777-2335-7(8), 0e1973e9-6ebc-461d-8248-03bac4b9f4a9) Rosen Publishing Group, Inc., The. (Rosen Classroom).

Funk, Tara. Newton & His Laws. 2005. (J). pap. (978-1-4108-4622-8(9)) Benchmark Education Co.

—Objects in Motion. 2005. (J). pap. (978-1-4108-4615-0(6)) Benchmark Education Co.

—The Three Laws of Motion. 2005. (J). pap. (978-1-4108-4629-7(6)) Benchmark Education Co.

Gardner, Robert. The Physics of Sports Science Projects, 1 vol. 2013. (Exploring Hands-On Science Projects Ser.). (ENG.). 128p. (gr. 5-6). pap. 13.88 (978-1-4644-0222-7(1), 0257ffe0-eddf-4a37-8257-690a9f6c4745); lib. bdg. 30.60 (978-0-7660-4146-2(8), 1cfcb805-a91a-4b9a-91f7-951871acdc1a) Enslow Publishing, LLC.

Gianopoulos, Andrea & Barnett, Charles, III. Isaac Newton & the Laws of Motion, 1 vol. Miller, Phil, illus. 2007. (Inventions & Discovery Ser.). (ENG.). 32p. (J). (gr. 3-9). pap. 8.10 (978-0-7368-7899-9(8), 93895, Capstone Pr.) Capstone.

Glass, Maya. The Jumping Book, 1 vol. 2003. (Let's Get Moving Ser.). (ENG., Illus.). 24p. (J). (gr. k-k). lib. bdg. 26.27 (978-1-4042-2513-8(7), 70dec572-ab98-435e-8817-b4ff0b11e950, Editorial Buenas Letras) Rosen Publishing Group, Inc., The.

—The Jumping Book/Saltar, 1 vol. Brusca, Maria Cristina, tr. 2003. (Let's Get Moving / Diviértete en Movimiento Ser.). (ENG & SPA., Illus.). 24p. (J). (gr. k-1). lib. bdg. 26.27 (978-1-4042-7513-3(4), 5d5623b7-150c-46e5-a9a0-ef310ede8fe8) Rosen Publishing Group, Inc., The.

Goodstein, Madeline. Goal! Science Projects with Soccer, 1 vol. 2009. (Score! Sports Science Projects Ser.). (ENG., Illus.). 104p. (gr. 5-6). lib. bdg. 35.93 (978-0-7660-3106-7(3), 4e2da253-e69d-416f-a848-a59dec36c85f) Enslow Publishing, LLC.

Graham, Stella. Forces & Motion at the Playground, 1 vol. 2008. (Real Life Readers Ser.). (ENG.). 16p. (gr. 2-3). pap. 7.05 (978-1-4358-0057-1(5), 7485c6ad-80e1-46c7-b923-cad6a6b01230, Rosen Classroom) Rosen Publishing Group, Inc., The.

Gray, Leon. Forces & Motion, 1 vol. 2013. (Physical Science Ser.). 48p. (J). (gr. 4-5). (ENG.). pap. 15.05 (978-1-4339-9505-7(0), 98f1f480-0f9d-4bc0-adbf-9fc211bf9ca4); pap. 84.30 (978-1-4339-9506-4(9)); (ENG., Illus.). lib. bdg. 34.61 (978-1-4339-9504-0(2), 324aa4c8-028e-4a02-a237-3d140d5ed806) Stevens, Gareth Publishing LLLP.

Gray, Susan H. Experiments with Motion. (True Book: Experiments Ser.). (ENG., Illus.). 48p. (J). 2012. (gr. 3-5). lib. bdg. 21.19 (978-0-531-26346-4(0)) 2011. pap. 6.95 (978-0-531-26646-5(X)) Scholastic Library Publishing. (Children's Pr.).

Grudzina, Rebecca. Motion. 2017. (Text Connections Guided Close Reading Ser.). (J). (gr. k). (978-1-4900-1763-1(1)) Benchmark Education Co.

Haber-Schaim, Uri, et al. Force, Motion, & Energy Assessment Package. 2003. pap. (978-1-882057-15-3(5), SCI-777-3393) Science Curriculum, Inc.

Hansen, Grace. Motion. 2018. (Beginning Science Ser.). (ENG., Illus.). 24p. (J). (gr. -1-2). lib. bdg. 32.79 (978-1-5321-0811-2(7), 28183, Abdo Kids) ABDO Publishing Co.

Hewitt, Sally. Amazing Forces & Movement. 2007. (Amazing Science Ser.). (ENG.). 32p. (J). pap. (978-0-7787-3625-7(3)) Crabtree Publishing Co.

—Forces & Motion. (Illus.). 32p. (YA). (gr. 2-18). lib. bdg. 27.10 (978-1-932333-32-9(0)) Chrysalis Education.

Higgins, Nadia. Marvelous Motion Site CD+Book. Martinez Ricci, Andres, illus. 2010. (Science Rocks! Set 2 Site CD+Book Ser.). 32p. lib. bdg. 84.14 incl. cd-rom (978-1-61641-010-0(8)) ABDO Publishing Co.

Hirsch, Rebecca. Science Lab: Motion & Forces. 2011. (Explorer Library: Language Arts Explorer Ser.). (ENG.). 32p. (gr. 4-8). pap. 14.21 (978-1-61080-294-9(2), 201216) Cherry Lake Publishing.

—Science Lab: Motion & Forces. 2011. (Explorer Library: Language Arts Explorer Ser.). (ENG., Illus.). 32p. (gr. 4-8). 32.07 (978-1-61080-205-5(5), 201186) Cherry Lake Publishing.

Hoffmann, Sara E. Going from Here to There. 2012. (First Step Nonfiction — Balance & Motion Ser.). (ENG., Illus.). 8p. (J). (gr. k-2). pap. 5.99 (978-1-4677-0516-5(0), 53770875-9819-464e-931c-d48a571719d9) Lerner Publishing Group.

—Spinning. 2012. (First Step Nonfiction — Balance & Motion Ser.). (ENG., Illus.). 8p. (J). (gr. k-2). pap. 5.99 (978-1-4677-0513-4(6), a93706f1-c11a-4fa8-88e3-59d209902b48) Lerner Publishing Group.

Holt, Rinehart and Winston Staff. Holt Science & Technology Chapter 5: Physical Science: Matter in Motion. 5th ed. 2004. (Illus.). pap. 12.86 (978-0-03-030376-0(1)) Holt McDougal.

Holzweiss, Kristina A. Amazing MakerSpace DIY Movers (a True Book: Makerspace Projects) (Library Edition) 2017. (True Book (Relaunch) Ser.). (ENG., Illus.). 48p. (J). (gr. 3-5). lib. bdg. 31.00 (978-0-531-23847-9(4), Children's Pr.) Scholastic Library Publishing.

Housel, Debra J. Motion, 1 vol. rev. ed. 2014. (Science: Informational Text Ser.). (ENG.). 32p. (gr. 2-3). pap. 10.99 (978-1-4807-4607-7(X)) Teacher Created Materials, Inc.

Hyde, Natalie. Changing Direction. 2014. (Motion Close-Up Ser.). (ENG., Illus.). 24p. (J). (-1). (978-0-7787-0528-4(5)) Crabtree Publishing Co.

—Pushing & Pulling. 2014. (Motion Close-Up Ser.). (ENG., Illus.). 24p. (J). (-1). (978-0-7787-0529-1(3)) Crabtree Publishing Co.

—What Is Motion? 2014. (Motion Close-Up Ser.). (ENG., Illus.). 24p. (J). (-1). (978-0-7787-0527-7(7)) Crabtree Publishing Co.

Ives, Rob. Fun Experiments with Forces & Motion: Hovercrafts, Rockets, & More. Sassin, Eva, illus. 2017. (Amazing Science Experiments Ser.). (ENG.). 32p. (J). (gr. 3-6). lib. bdg. 27.99 (978-1-5124-3217-6(2), c09d5541-0bb3-4fc3-ae1d-2b1d07224398, Hungry Tomato (r)) Lerner Publishing Group.

James, Emily. The Simple Science of Motion. 2018. (Simply Science Ser.). (ENG., Illus.). 32p. (J). (gr. -1-2). lib. bdg. 27.99 (978-1-5435-1227-4(5), 137735, Capstone Pr.) Capstone.

Jonath, Leslie & Nash, Josh. On the Go: A Mini AniMotion Book. 2010. (ENG., Illus.). 12p. (J). (gr. -1). 9.99 (978-0-7407-9800-9(6)) Andrews McMeel Publishing.

Jones, Tammy. I Go! 2009. (Sight Word Readers Set A Ser.). (J). 3.49 net. (978-1-60719-143-8(1)) Newmark Learning LLC.

Juettner, Bonnie. Motion. 2004. (KidHaven Science Library). (ENG., Illus.). 48p. (J). (gr. 4-7). 27.50 (978-0-7377-1536-1(7), Greenhaven Pr., Inc.) Cengage Gale.

Kelley, Jennifer. Ways Things Move. 2006. (Science Leveled Readers Ser.). (ENG., Illus.). 8p. (gr. k-k). pap. 5.40 (978-0-15-365319-3(1)) Harcourt Schl. Pubs.

Kelly, Lynne. Simple Concepts in Physics: Motion. (Illus.). (J). (gr. 3-6). pap. (978-1-875739-35-6(1)) Wizard Bks.

Kenney, Karen Latchana. The Science of Race Cars: Studying Forces & Motion. 2015. (Science in Action Ser.). (ENG., Illus.). 32p. (J). (gr. 3-6). 32.79 (978-1-62403-963-8(4), 19423, Checkerboard Library) ABDO Publishing Co.

Kook, Ima. Newton's Laws: They Tell How Things Move. 2008. (Illus.). 24p. (J). pap. 12.00 (978-1-892298-24-9(4)) Abique Pub.

Lawrence, Debbie & Lawrence, Richard. Machines & Motion: God's Design for the Physical World. 2005. (Illus.). 160p. per. (978-0-9725365-9-2(0)) Boarding House Publishing.

Lawrence, Ellen. Motion. 2013. (Science Slam: FUN-Damental Experiments Ser.). 24p. (J). (gr. -1-3). lib. bdg. 26.99 (978-1-61772-739-9(3)) Bearport Publishing Co., Inc.

Llewellyn, Claire. Forces & Movement. 2010. (Start-Up Connections Ser.). (ENG., Illus.). 24p. (J). (gr. 2-4). pap. 14.99 (978-0-237-54172-9(6)) Evans Brothers, Ltd. GBR. Dist: Independent Pubs. Group.

Macken, JoAnn Early. Toys. 2010. (Everyday Science Ser.). (ENG.). 24p. (J). (gr. k-2). lib. bdg. 25.65 (978-1-60753-017-6(1), 17138) Amicus.

Manolis, Kay. Motion. 2008. (First Science Ser.). (ENG., Illus.). 24p. (J). (gr. 2-5). lib. bdg. 26.95 (978-1-60014-225-3(7)) Bellwether Media.

—Motion. 2011. (Blastoff! Readers Ser.). 24p. (J). pap. 5.95 (978-0-531-28458-2(1), Children's Pr.) Scholastic Library Publishing.

Mason, Adrienne. Move It! Motion, Forces & You. Dávila, Claudia, illus. 2005. (Primary Physical Science Ser.). (ENG.). 32p. (J). (gr. -1-2). pap. 8.99 (978-1-55337-759-7(1)) Kids Can Pr., Ltd. CAN. Dist: Hachette Bk. Group.

Monroe, Tilda. What Do You Know about Forces & Motion?, 1 vol. 2010. (20 Questions: Physical Science Ser.). (ENG.). 24p. (J). (gr. 2-3). pap. 9.25 (978-1-4488-1254-7(2), bac3292d-94df-40df-a347-af6f2b867938, PowerKids Pr.); lib. bdg. 26.27 (978-1-4488-0673-7(9), 034751f9-b968-4dd9-98c4-1a75df8da1be) Rosen Publishing Group, Inc., The.

Motion & Force: Integrated Physics & Chemistry / Algebra I Instructional Unit. 2003. (Region IV ESC Resources for Mathematics & Science Ser.). stu. ed., per. (978-1-932524-69-7(X)) Region 4 Education Service Ctr.

Murphy, Brian. Movement. 2004. (Experiment with Ser.). (ENG., Illus.). 32p. (J). (gr. 2-5). 9.95 (978-1-58728-248-5(8), Two-Can Publishing) T&N Children's Publishing.

Murray, Julie. Fast & Slow. 2018. (Opposites Ser.). (ENG., Illus.). 24p. (J). (gr. -1-2). lib. bdg. 31.36 (978-1-5321-8178-8(7), 29829, Abdo Kids) ABDO Publishing Co.

National Geographic Learning. Reading Expeditions (Science: Physical Science): Introduction to Energy. 2007. (Nonfiction Reading & Writing Workshops Ser.). (ENG., Illus.). 32p. (J). pap. 18.95 (978-0-7922-4580-3(6)) CENGAGE Learning.

—Reading Expeditions (Science: Physical Science): Newton's Laws. 2007. (ENG., Illus.). 32p. (J). pap. 18.95 (978-0-7922-4584-1(9)) CENGAGE Learning.

Nelson, Robin. Cómo Se Mueven Las Cosas. Translations.com Staff, tr. from ENG. 2007. (Mi Primer Paso Al Mundo Real - Fuerzas y Movimiento (First Step Nonfiction - Forces & Motion) Ser.). (SPA., Illus.). 24p. (gr. k-2). lib. bdg. 23.93 (978-0-8225-7811-6(5), Ediciones Lerner) Lerner Publishing Group.

—Ways Things Move. (Forces & Motion Ser.). (Illus.). (J). 2005. 22p. pap. 5.95 (978-0-8225-5300-7(7)) 2004. 24p. lib. bdg. 18.60 (978-0-8225-5136-2(5)) Lerner Publishing Group.

Newton, Joan. Gravity in Action: Roller Coasters!, 1 vol. (Amazing Science Ser.). (ENG.). 24p. (gr. 3-3). 2009. (J). lib. bdg. 26.27 (978-1-4358-2976-3(X), eda3b8c6-ae6e-4679-8363-19dca5d4bb8c, PowerKids Pr.) 2008. pap. 8.25 (978-1-4358-0008-3(7), 79e1719f-5a98-4533-bbd1-df5f32edd1f4, Rosen Classroom) Rosen Publishing Group, Inc., The.

Nsrc. Science & Technology for Children Books: Motion & Design. 2004. (Illus.). 64p. (J). (978-1-933008-03-5(2)) Smithsonian Science Education Ctr. (SSEC).

O'Donnell, Kerri. Sir Isaac Newton: Using the Laws of Motion to Solve Problems, 1 vol. (Math for the REAL World Ser.). 32p. (gr. 5-5). 2009. (ENG., Illus.). pap. 10.00 (978-1-4042-6079-5(X), ce33957a-c41c-4955-bcc4-d67057e0f665) 2009. 47.90 (978-1-60851-366-6(1), PowerKids Pr.) 2006. (ENG., Illus.). (YA). lib. bdg. 28.93 (978-1-4042-3363-8(6), f0654ff1-b3f5-49ff-b288-9b7bdf626c27) Rosen Publishing Group, Inc., The.

O'Leary, Denyse. What Are Newton's Laws of Motion? 2010. (Shaping Modern Science Ser.). (ENG.). 64p. (J). (gr. 5-8). pap. (978-0-7787-7207-1(1)); (Illus.). (gr. 6-6). lib. bdg. (978-0-7787-7200-2(4)) Crabtree Publishing Co.

Orr, Tamra. Motion & Forces, 1 vol. 2011. (Science Made Simple Ser.). (ENG., Illus.). 64p. (YA). (gr. 7-7). lib. bdg. 37.13 (978-1-4488-1232-5(1), 3a451b7e-074f-47f0-9ea0-ec37351d9324) Rosen Publishing Group, Inc., The.

Orr, Tamra B. Motion & Forces, 1 vol. 2011. (Science Made Simple Ser.). (ENG.). 64p. (YA). (gr. 7-7). pap. 13.95 (978-1-4488-2240-9(8), 8cb34cf3-fcef-4857-bfd5-218dc88df7af) Rosen Publishing Group, Inc., The.

Oxlade, Chris. Forces & Motion: An Investigation, 1 vol. 2007. (Science Investigations Ser.). (ENG., Illus.). 32p. (YA). (gr. 4-5). lib. bdg. 30.27 (978-1-4042-4283-8(X), 22f2ed8f-6833-4a24-bc06-984ad90bf957) Rosen Publishing Group, Inc., The.

—Simple Experiments with Inclined Planes, 1 vol. 2013. (Science Experiments with Simple Machines Ser.). (ENG.). 32p. (J). (gr. 2-3). 31.17 (978-1-61533-752-1(0), 2c1b48f5-4d72-4d74-885c-1fe571cab294); pap. 12.75 (978-1-61533-821-4(7), 81808ed5-9e4b-4eac-b4d7-a06c9973b73f) Rosen Publishing Group, Inc., The. (Windmill Bks.).

—Simple Experiments with Inclined Planes. 2013. (Science Experiments with Simple Machines Ser.). 32p. (J). (gr. k-3). pap. 70.50 (978-1-61533-822-1(5)) Windmill Bks.

Pamplona, Alberto Hernández. A Visual Guide to Energy & Movement, 1 vol. 2017. (Visual Exploration of Science Ser.). (ENG.). 104p. (J). (gr. 8-8). 38.80 (978-1-5081-7582-7(9), 0062be71-2b5a-472e-86ca-f9de42611940, Rosen Young Adult) Rosen Publishing Group, Inc., The.

Peters, Katie. Pull & Push. 2019. (Science All Around Me (Pull Ahead Readers — Nonfiction) Ser.). (ENG., Illus.). 16p. (J). (gr. -1-1). pap. 8.99 (978-1-5415-7329-1(3), 591de7e0-f16c-4f9a-8782-ea3f328bce1f); lib. bdg. 27.99 (978-1-5415-5846-5(4), f62b4474-20a9-41f8-9459-0d11d616dec8) Lerner Publishing Group. (Lerner Pubns.).

Petersen, Kristen. Understanding the Laws of Motion. 2015. (J). lib. bdg. (978-1-62713-427-9(1)) Cavendish Square Publishing LLC.

Peterson, Megan Cooley. Motion. 2019. (Little Physicist Ser.). (ENG., Illus.). 32p. (J). (gr. 1-3). pap. 6.95 (978-1-9771-1066-4(5), 141140); lib. bdg. 28.65 (978-1-9771-0963-7(2), 140554) Capstone. (Pebble).

—Scooby-Doo! a Science of Forces & Motion Mystery: The Rogue Robot. Brizuela, Dario, illus. 2016. (Scooby-Doo Solves It with S. T. E. M. Ser.). (ENG.). 32p. (J). (gr. 3-6). 28.65 (978-1-5157-2590-9(1), 132934, Capstone Pr.) Capstone.

Phelan, Glen. Forces & Motion in Sports: Set Of 6. 2011. (Navigators Ser.). (J). pap. 50.00 net. (978-1-4108-5088-1(9)) Benchmark Education Co.

—Forces & Motion on Earth: Set Of 6. 2011. (Navigators Ser.). (J). pap. 50.00 net. (978-1-4108-5087-4(0)) Benchmark Education Co.

Rand, Casey. Forces & Motion. rev. ed. 2016. (Sci-Hi: Physical Science Ser.). (ENG.). 48p. (J). (gr. 6-10). pap. 8.99 (978-1-4109-8633-7(0), 134719, Raintree) Capstone.

Rivera, Andrea. Motion. 2017. (Science Concepts Ser.). (ENG., Illus.). 24p. (J). (gr. -1-2). lib. bdg. 31.36 (978-1-5321-2054-1(0), 25358, Abdo Zoom-Launch) ABDO Publishing Co.

Rossiter, Brienna. Fast & Slow. 2019. (Opposites Ser.). (ENG., Illus.). 16p. (J). (gr. k-1). 25.64 (978-1-64185-345-3(X), 164185345X, Focus Readers) North Star Editions.

Rowell, Rebecca. Forces & Motion Through Infographics. Dean, Venitia, illus. 2013. (Super Science Infographics Ser.). (ENG.). 32p. (J). (gr. 3-5). pap. 8.99 (978-1-4677-1591-1(3), 67522118-a31b-4cf9-aa33-5a08c2408268); lib. bdg. 26.65 (978-1-4677-1291-0(4), beb481a6-f946-4a8e-9659-b68f7f65d7b9, Lerner Pubns.) Lerner Publishing Group.

Royston, Angela. Forces: Pushes & Pulls, 1 vol. 2011. (Science Corner Ser.). (ENG., Illus.). 24p. (J). (gr. 2-2). lib. bdg. 26.27 (978-1-4488-5292-5(7), 6c6f3e53-1387-47cb-82ee-827ee503777d) Rosen Publishing Group, Inc., The.

—Race That Bike! Forces in Vehicles. 2015. (Feel the Force Ser.). (ENG., Illus.). 48p. (J). (gr. 3-6). 35.99 (978-1-4846-2599-6(4), 130081, Heinemann) Capstone.

—Win That Sprint! Forces in Sport. 2015. (Feel the Force Ser.). (ENG., Illus.). 48p. (J). (gr. 3-6). 35.99 (978-1-4846-2597-2(8), 130075, Heinemann) Capstone.

Schneider, Christa. Move It! Projects You Can Drive, Fly, & Roll. 2017. (Cool Makerspace Gadgets & Gizmos Ser.). (ENG., Illus.). 32p. (J). (gr. 3-6). lib. bdg. 34.21 (978-1-5321-1254-6(8), 27585, Checkerboard Library) ABDO Publishing Co.

Science & Technology for Children Books, Motion & Design Set, 8 vols. 2004. (Illus.). 64p. (J). (978-1-933008-15-8(6)) Smithsonian Science Education Ctr. (SSEC).

Science Stories Foss Spanish Balance & Motion EA CR05. 2005. (J). (978-1-59242-582-2(8)) Delta Education, LLC.

Sheehan, Thomas F. Playground Science. 2005. (City Science Ser.). (ENG.). 24p. (gr. k-3). pap. 8.95 (978-1-62717-235-6(1), 9781627172356) Rourke Educational Media.

Silverman, Buffy. Pull It, Push It. 2012. (My Science Library). (ENG.). 24p. (gr. 3-4). pap. 8.95 (978-1-61810-229-4(X), 9781618102294) Rourke Educational Media.

Silverstein, Alvin, et al. Forces & Motion. 2008. (Science Concepts, Second Ser.). (ENG., Illus.). 112p. (gr. 6-8). lib. bdg. 31.93 (978-0-8225-7514-6(0)) Lerner Publishing Group.

Sohn, Emily. Experiments in Forces & Motion with Toys & Everyday Stuff. 2015. (Fun Science Ser.). (ENG., Illus.). 24p. (J). (gr. 1-3). lib. bdg. 27.99 (978-1-4914-5032-1(0), 128756, Capstone Pr.) Capstone.

Sohn, Emily & Brennan, Joseph K. Balance & Motion. 2019. (IScience Ser.). (ENG., Illus.). 24p. (J). (gr. k-2). 23.94 (978-1-68450-972-0(6)) Norwood Hse. Pr.

Solway, Andrew. Exploring Forces & Motion, 1 vol. 2007. (Exploring Physical Science Ser.). (ENG., Illus.). 48p. (YA). (gr. 6-6). lib. bdg. 34.47 (978-1-4042-3747-6(X), df96f96c-2d23-4012-ba28-07bc6130c285) Rosen Publishing Group, Inc., The.

Spilsbury, Richard. Investigating Forces & Motion. 2018. (Investigating Science Challenges Ser.). (ENG., Illus.). 32p. (J). (gr. 4-4). (978-0-7787-4205-0(9)); pap. (978-0-7787-4253-1(9)) Crabtree Publishing Co.

Stille, Darlene R. El Movimiento: Tira y Empuja, Rápido y Despacio. Robledo, Sol, tr. Boyd, Sheree, illus. 2007. (Ciencia Asombrosa Ser.). (SPA.). 24p. (J). (gr. k-4). lib. bdg. 27.32 (978-1-4048-3222-0(X), 93763, Picture Window Bks.) Capstone.

Sullivan, Laura. What Is Motion?, 1 vol. 2015. (Unseen Science Ser.). (ENG., Illus.). 32p. (gr. 3-3). pap. 11.58 (978-1-5026-0914-4(2), bcf4056f-6f36-46e2-abc7-da51db6c0012) Cavendish Square Publishing LLC.

Sullivan, Laura L. How Do Objects Move?, 1 vol. 2018. (How Does It Move? Forces & Motion Ser.). (ENG.). 32p. (gr. 3-3). 30.21 (978-1-5026-3764-2(2), f19a2166-d3df-4698-9b8e-f55ca1b2e5eb) Cavendish Square Publishing LLC.

Thiel, Kristin. Investigating Forces & Motion Through Modeling, 1 vol. 2019. (Science Investigators Ser.). (ENG.). 48p. (J). (gr. 5-5). pap. 13.93 (978-1-5026-5243-0(9), 8765dffd-7790-459e-a224-3f5aac28a4be) Cavendish Square Publishing LLC.

Troupe, Thomas Kingsley. Move on up That Beanstalk, Jack! The Fairy-Tale Physics of Forces & Motion. Tejido, Jomike, illus. 2018. (STEM-Twisted Fairy Tales Ser.). (ENG.). 32p.

(J). (gr. k-3). pap. 7.95 *(978-1-5158-2898-3(0),* 138420); lib. bdg. 27.99 *(978-1-5158-2894-5(8),* 138416) Capstone. (Picture Window Bks.).

Uttley, Colin. Experiments with Force & Motion, 1 vol. 2010. (Cool Science Ser.). (ENG., Illus.). 32p. (J). (gr. 4-5). pap. 11.50 *(978-1-4339-3460-5(4),* fa3c19f0-e4bb-4c31-afed-83a1c3867c7a); lib. bdg. 30.67 *(978-1-4339-3459-9(0),* a0829e7c-b83d-4d0e-991b-f236b497ce34) Stevens, Gareth Publishing LLLP. (Gareth Stevens Learning Library).

Ventura, Marne. Motion Projects to Build On: 4D an Augmented Reading Experience. 2019. (Take Making to the Next Level 4D Ser.). (ENG., Illus.). 48p. (J). (gr. 3-5). lib. bdg. 33.99 *(978-1-5435-2847-3(3),* 138337, Capstone Classroom) Capstone.

Wadsworth, Pamela. Golwg Gyntaf Ar Bethau'n Symud. 2005. (WEL., Illus.). 24p. pap. *(978-1-85596-252-1(7))* Dref Wen.

Way, Jennifer. The Hopping Book, 1 vol. 2003. (Let's Get Moving Ser.). (ENG., Illus.). 24p. (J). (gr. k-k). lib. bdg. 26.27 *(978-1-4042-2514-5(5),* eab22b73-f21b-49cc-86e7-e49eee35462c, PowerKids Pr.) Rosen Publishing Group, Inc., The.

—The Hopping Book/Brincar en un Pie, 1 vol. Brusca, Maria Cristina, tr. 2003. (Let's Get Moving / Diviértete en Movimiento Ser.). (ENG & SPA., Illus.). 24p. (J). (gr. k-1). lib. bdg. 26.27 *(978-1-4042-7514-0(2),* 053c44c2-524a-4447-a63a-29a179f2ba9b) Rosen Publishing Group, Inc., The.

Weakland, Mark Andrew. Zombis, Fuerzas y Movimiento. Flocco, Gervasio Benítez, illus. 2019. (Ciencias Monstruosas Ser.). (SPA.). 32p. (J). (gr. 3-9). lib. bdg. 31.32 *(978-1-5435-8262-8(1),* 141272) Capstone.

Weir, Jane. Investigating Forces & Motion, 1 vol. rev. ed. 2007. (Science: Informational Text Ser.). (ENG.). 32p. (J). (gr. 3-6). pap. 12.99 *(978-0-7439-0573-2(3))* Teacher Created Materials, Inc.

What Makes It Move? KinderFacts Individual Title Six-Packs. (Kinderstarters Ser.). 8p. (gr. -1-1). 21.00 *(978-0-7635-8755-0(9))* Rigby Education.

Whitehouse, Patty. Moving Machines. 2006. (Construction Forces Discovery Library). (Illus.). 24p. (J). (gr. k-2). lib. bdg. 22.79 *(978-1-60044-192-9(0))* Rourke Educational Media.

Whiting, Jim. The Science of Hitting a Home Run: Forces & Motion in Action. 2010. (Action Science Ser.). (ENG.). 32p. (gr. 3-4). pap. 47.70 *(978-1-4296-5076-2(1),* Capstone Pr.) Capstone.

Wood, Matthew Brenden. Projectile Science: The Physics Behind Kicking a Field Goal & Launching a Rocket with Science Activities for Kids. 2018. (Build It Yourself Ser.). (ENG., Illus.). 128p. (J). (gr. 4-10). 22.95 *(978-1-61930-676-9(X),* 19bcbe53-156f-49fa-aaec-7ea095e84ba4) Nomad Pr.

World Book, Inc. Staff, contrib. by. Learning about Energy, Forces, & Motion. 2011. (J). *(978-0-7166-0233-0(4))* World Bk., Inc.

Zubek, Adeline. Fast or Slow?, 1 vol. 2019. (All about Opposites Ser.). (ENG.). 24p. (gr. k-k). 24.27 *(978-1-5382-3716-8(4),* 60fb01b2-8fb8-4e67-96a0-20fcc3052a0f) Stevens, Gareth Publishing LLLP.

Zuravicky, Orli. The Galloping Book, 1 vol. 2003. (Let's Get Moving Ser.). (ENG., Illus.). 24p. (J). (gr. k-k). lib. bdg. 26.27 *(978-1-4042-2517-6(X),* 93f4ee31-3bb8-4c5f-b212-a108220370dd, PowerKids Pr.) Rosen Publishing Group, Inc., The.

—The Galloping Book/Trotar, 1 vol. De Leon, Mauricio Velzaquez, tr. 2003. (Let's Get Moving / Diviértete en Movimiento Ser.). (ENG & SPA., Illus.). 24p. (J). (gr. k-1). lib. bdg. 26.27 *(978-1-4042-7517-1(7),* 95c80a27-7d66-4290-9c81-fe601e972c4a) Rosen Publishing Group, Inc., The.

—The Skipping Book: Avanzar a Saltitos, 1 vol. Brusca, Maria C., tr. 2003. (Let's Get Moving / Diviértete en Movimiento Ser.). (ENG & SPA., Illus.). 24p. (J). (gr. k-1). lib. bdg. 26.27 *(978-1-4042-7515-7(0),* db545fdb-02b7-4163-b307-0101fd6cbf0b) Rosen Publishing Group, Inc., The.

MOTION PICTURE CARTOONS

see Animated Films

MOTION PICTURE INDUSTRY

Anastasio, Dina & Who HQ. Where Is Hollywood? Foley, Tim, illus. 2019. (Where Is? Ser.). 112p. (J). (gr. 3-7). 7.99 *(978-1-5247-8644-1(6),* Penguin Workshop) Penguin Young Readers Group.

Animation. 2010. (ENG., Illus.). 208p. (gr. 6-12). 32.95 *(978-0-8160-8015-1(1),* P178868, Ferguson Publishing Company) Infobase Holdings, Inc.

Brown, Don. Mack Made Movies. Brown, Don, illus. 2008. (Illus.). (J). (gr. 2-5). 25.95 incl. audio compact disk *(978-1-4301-0432-2(5));* pap. 16.95 incl. audio *(978-1-4301-0431-5(7))* Live Oak Media.

Burgan, Michael. Ronald Reagan. 2011. 128p. pap. 14.99 *(978-0-7566-7739-8(4))* Dorling Kindersley Publishing, Inc.

Cartlidge, Cherese. Leonardo Dicaprio, 1 vol. 2011. (People in the News Ser.). (ENG.). 96p. (gr. 7-7). lib. bdg. 41.03 *(978-1-4205-0427-9(4),* 02b1037a-6e1d-4064-8de1-4a111d151218, Lucent Pr.) Greenhaven Publishing LLC.

Davies, Monika. On the Job: Filmmakers: Adding & Subtracting Mixed Numbers (Grade 5) 2018. (Mathematics in the Real World Ser.). (ENG., Illus.). 32p. (J). (gr. 4-8). pap. 11.99 *(978-1-4258-5814-8(7))* Teacher Created Materials, Inc.

Downing, Todd. Filmmaking, 1 vol. 2010. (Master This! Ser.). (ENG.). 32p. (J). (gr. 4-4). lib. bdg. 28.93 *(978-1-61532-597-9(2),* 17b2050a-0dc9-40de-a170-e9a86f416690, PowerKids Pr.) Rosen Publishing Group, Inc., The.

Espejo, Roman, ed. The Film Industry, 1 vol. 2009. (Opposing Viewpoints Ser.). (ENG., Illus.). 224p. (gr. 10-12). 50.43 *(978-0-7377-4364-7(6),* b22b3b30-6022-49ba-80fa-2ce33ce6d76c); pap. 34.80 *(978-0-7377-4363-0(8),* 4a905bf6-5f41-48cc-b9df-37b17e861a35) Greenhaven Publishing LLC. (Greenhaven Publishing).

Garza, Sarah. Action! Making Movies, 1 vol. 2nd rev. ed. 2013. (TIME for KIDS(r): Informational Text Ser.). (ENG., Illus.). 64p. (J). (gr. 4-8). lib. bdg. 31.96 *(978-1-4333-7448-7(X))* Teacher Created Materials, Inc.

Gosling, Maureen, et al. You Can Be a Woman Movie Maker. l.t. ed. 2003. (Illus.). 80p. (J). 19.95 incl. DVD *(978-1-880599-64-8(3));* pap. 14.95 incl. DVD *(978-1-880599-63-1(5))* Cascade Pass, Inc.

Great Filmmakers, 12 vols. 2014. (Great Filmmakers Ser.). (ENG.). 80p. (YA). (gr. 7-7). 224.16 *(978-1-62713-134-6(5),* 1f715ff4-b9f2-4ec6-83bc-dab086c9d8ea, Cavendish Square) Cavendish Square Publishing LLC.

Hindman, Susan. Working at a Movie Theater. 2011. (21st Century Junior Library: Careers Ser.). (ENG., Illus.). 24p. (gr. 2-5). lib. bdg. 29.21 *(978-1-60279-979-0(2),* 200948) Cherry Lake Publishing.

Kennon, Michou. Queen Latifah, 1 vol. 2011. (Hip-Hop Headliners Ser.). (ENG., Illus.). 32p. (J). (gr. 1-1). lib. bdg. 27.93 *(978-1-4339-4808-4(7),* 4d494ccf-d9fb-49c7-88a9-dc55103f5049) Stevens, Gareth Publishing LLLP.

Korté, Steve & Who HQ. What Is the Story of Looney Tunes? Hinderliter, John, illus. 2020. (What Is the Story Of? Ser.). (ENG.). 112p. (J). (gr. 3-7). 6.99 *(978-1-5247-8836-0(8));* 15.99 *(978-1-5247-8837-7(6))* Penguin Young Readers Group. (Penguin Workshop).

Mapua, Jeff. Lana Wachowski, 1 vol. 2016. (Transgender Pioneers Ser.). (ENG., Illus.). 112p. (J). (gr. 7-7). 38.80 *(978-1-5081-7160-7(2),* 1c8beab0-561b-4ac8-aacf-658a66e31483) Rosen Publishing Group, Inc., The.

Mara, Wil. The Movie Industry. 2018. (21st Century Skills Library: Global Citizens: Modern Media Ser.). (ENG., Illus.). 32p. (J). (gr. 4-7). lib. bdg. 32.07 *(978-1-5341-2927-6(8),* 211752) Cherry Lake Publishing.

Menkes Kushner, Jill. Johnny Depp: Movie Megastar, 1 vol. 2009. (Hot Celebrity Biographies Ser.). (ENG., Illus.). 48p. (gr. 5-7). lib. bdg. 27.93 *(978-0-7660-3567-6(0),* d749e9e0-c204-4e91-b014-9b4e1c3386a2) Enslow Publishing, LLC.

Millar, Colin & Breakwell, Spike. Movie World 4 Voyagers. 2017. (Cambridge Reading Adventures Ser.). (ENG., Illus.). 48p. pap. 11.00 *(978-1-108-40106-7(6))* Cambridge Univ. Pr.

Mullins, Matt. Special Effects Technician. 2011. (21st Century Skills Library: Cool Arts Careers Ser.). (ENG., Illus.). 32p. (gr. 4-8). lib. bdg. 32.07 *(978-1-61080-134-8(2),* 201146) Cherry Lake Publishing.

Rauf, Don. Choose a Career Adventure in Hollywood. 2016. (Bright Futures Press: Choose a Career Adventure Ser.). (ENG., Illus.). 32p. (J). (gr. 4-6). 32.07 *(978-1-63471-911-7(5),* 208965) Cherry Lake Publishing.

Scholastic, Inc. Staff. The Hunger Games Official Illustrated Movie Companion. 2012. (Illus.). 158p. (YA). lib. bdg. 31.80 *(978-0-606-23704-8(6))* Turtleback.

Schuman, Michael A. Halle Berry: A Biography of an Oscar-Winning Actress, 1 vol. 2013. (African-American Icons Ser.). (ENG.). 104p. (gr. 6-7). pap. 13.88 *(978-1-59845-396-6(3),* eef7a7d5-54c1-4d16-b5c8-b669ebfe953f) Enslow Publishing, LLC.

Skogen, Jenny. Film. 2014. (Urban Entrepreneurs Ser.). (gr. 3-8). pap. 8.99 *(978-1-61570-872-7(3))* Scobre Pr. Corp.

Spinner, Stephanie & Who HQ. Who Is Steven Spielberg? Mather, Daniel, illus. 2013. (Who Was? Ser.). 112p. (J). (gr. 3-7). 6.99 *(978-0-448-47935-4(4),* Penguin Workshop) Penguin Young Readers Group.

Vander Hook, Sue. Steven Spielberg: Groundbreaking Director, 1 vol. 2009. (Essential Lives Set 4 Ser.). (ENG., Illus.). 112p. (YA). (gr. 6-12). lib. bdg. 41.36 *(978-1-60453-704-8(3),* 6699, Essential Library) ABDO Publishing Co.

Weitzman, Elizabeth. Hollywood Trivia: What You Never Knew about Celebrity Life, Fame, & Fortune. 2018. (Not Your Ordinary Trivia Ser.). (ENG., Illus.). 32p. (J). (gr. 3-9). lib. bdg. 28.65 *(978-1-5435-2528-1(8),* 138025, Capstone Pr.) Capstone.

Wood, Alix. Be a Film Director: Direct with Confidence, 1 vol. 2017. (Moviemakers' Film Club Ser.). (ENG.). 32p. (J). (gr. 4-5). 27.93 *(978-1-5383-2276-5(5),* 91651b21-56ef-4adc-9008-088d9d57a53b); pap. 11.00 *(978-1-5383-2372-4(9),* 953fd88c-4eb5-43df-9cf2-e9dd39ab045d) Rosen Publishing Group, Inc., The. (PowerKids Pr.).

Zannos, Susan. Ron Howard. l.t. ed. 2003. (Billboard Biography Ser.). (Illus.). 32p. (J). (gr. 3-8). lib. bdg. 25.70 *(978-1-58415-185-2(4))* Mitchell Lane Pubs.

MOTION PICTURE INDUSTRY—FICTION

Baron, Jeff. Sean Rosen Is Not for Sale. 2015. (ENG.). 384p. (J). (gr. 3-7). pap. 6.99 *(978-0-06-218751-2(1),* Greenwillow Bks.) HarperCollins Pubs.

Bentley, Sue. Star of the Show #4, 4 vols. Swan, Angela, illus. 2009. (Magic Puppy Ser.: 4). (ENG.). 128p. (J). (gr. 1-3). pap. 6.99 *(978-0-448-45047-6(X),* Grosset & Dunlap) Penguin Young Readers Group.

Blake, Ashley Herring. The Mighty Heart of Sunny St. James. 2019. (ENG.). 384p. (J). (gr. 3-7). 16.99 *(978-0-316-51553-5(1))* Little, Brown Bks. for Young Readers.

Boné, Thomas H., illus. The Teacher Who Would Not Retire Becomes a Movie Star. 2012. (J). *(978-0-9792918-6-9(0))* Blue Marlin Pubns.

Castellucci, Cecil. Boy Proof, 4 vols. 2005. (YA). 62.75 *(978-1-4193-5131-0(1))* Recorded Bks., Inc.

Coleman, Rowan. Ruby Parker: Film Star. 2011. (ENG., Illus.). 320p. (gr. 6-9). pap. 11.99 *(978-0-00-719039-3(5),* HarperCollins Children's Bks.) HarperCollins Pubs. Ltd. GBR. Dist: HarperCollins Pubs.

—Ruby Parker: Shooting Star. 2011. (ENG.). 256p. (gr. 6-9). pap. 9.99 *(978-0-00-725812-3(7),* HarperCollins Children's Bks.) HarperCollins Pubs. Ltd. GBR. Dist: HarperCollins Pubs.

Dixon, Franklin W. Movie Mayhem: Book Three in the Deathstalker Trilogy. 2012. (Hardy Boys (All New) Undercover Brothers Ser.: 39). (ENG.). 176p. (J). (gr. 3-7). pap. 7.99 *(978-1-4424-0260-7(1),* Aladdin) Simon & Schuster Children's Publishing.

—Movie Menace: Book One in the Deathstalker Trilogy. 2011. (Hardy Boys (All New) Undercover Brothers Ser.: 37). (ENG.). 176p. (J). (gr. 3-7). pap. 5.99 *(978-1-4424-0258-4(X),* Aladdin) Simon & Schuster Children's Publishing.

Gentry, Brad. The Hollywood Princess. 2009. 40p. pap. 20.99 *(978-1-4490-3545-7(0))* AuthorHouse.

Handford, Martin. Where's Waldo? in Hollywood: Deluxe Edition. Handford, Martin, illus. deluxe ed. 2013. (Where's Waldo? Ser.). (ENG., Illus.). 32p. (J). (gr. k-4). 17.99 *(978-0-7636-4527-4(3))* Candlewick Pr.

Hapka, Catherine, pseud. Rio 2: Vacation in the Wild. 2014. (I Can Read Level 2 Ser.). (ENG.). 32p. (J). (gr. -1-3). pap. 3.99 *(978-0-06-228499-0(1))* HarperCollins Pubs.

Harris, Rachel. My Not So Super Sweet Life. 2017. (ENG., Illus.). (YA). pap. 14.99 *(978-1-68281-443-7(2))* Entangled Publishing, LLC.

Harrison, Emma. That's a Wrap: A Rival High Novel. 2008. (YA). *(978-1-4114-0527-1(7),* Spark Publishing Group) Sterling Publishing Co., Inc.

Keene, Carolyn. Movie Madness. Francis, Peter, illus. 2016. (Nancy Drew Clue Book Ser.: 5). (ENG.). 96p. (J). (gr. 1-4). 16.99 *(978-1-4814-5821-4(3),* Simon & Schuster/Paula Wiseman Bks.) Simon & Schuster/Paula Wiseman Bks.

—A Script for Danger. 2015. (Nancy Drew Diaries: 10). (ENG., Illus.). 192p. (J). (gr. 3-7). 7.99 *(978-1-4814-3810-0(7),* Aladdin) Simon & Schuster Children's Publishing.

Klise, Kate. Hollywood, Dead Ahead. Klise, M. Sarah, illus. 2014. (43 Old Cemetery Road Ser.: 5). (ENG.). 144p. (J). (gr. 3-7). pap. 7.99 *(978-0-544-33661-2(5),* 1584183, Clarion Bks.) HarperCollins Pubs.

Lombardo, Constance. Mr. Puffball: Stunt Cat to the Stars. Lombardo, Constance, illus. 2015. (Mr. Puffball Ser.: 1). (ENG., Illus.). 240p. (J). (gr. 3-7). 12.99 *(978-0-06-232065-0(3),* HarperCollins) HarperCollins Pubs.

Naylor, Clare & Hare, Mimi. The First Assistant: A Continuing Tale from Behind the Hollywood Curtain. 2007. (Lizzie Miller Ser.). (ENG.). 288p. (gr. 12-18). 15.00 *(978-0-452-28836-2(3),* Plume) Penguin Publishing Group.

Nielsen, Susin. Dear George Clooney: Please Marry My Mom. 2012. (ENG., Illus.). 240p. (J). (gr. 5-9). pap. 10.95 *(978-1-77049-295-0(X),* Tundra Bks.) Tundra Bks. CAN. Dist: Penguin Random Hse. LLC.

Salisbury, Graham. Calvin Coconut #9: Extra Famous. Rogers, Jacqueline, illus. 2014. (Calvin Coconut Ser.: 9). 176p. (J). (gr. 2-5). pap. 6.99 *(978-0-307-93075-0(0),* Yearling) Random Hse. Children's Bks.

Schraff, Anne. The Lost, 1 vol. unabr. ed. 2011. (Urban Underground Ser.). (ENG.). 198p. (YA). (gr. 9-12). pap. 11.95 *(978-1-61651-585-0(6))* Saddleback Educational Publishing, Inc.

MOTION PICTURE MUSIC

Hom, Geoffrey M. Movie Soundtracks & Sound Effects, 1 vol. 2006. (Making Movies Ser.). (ENG., Illus.). 32p. (J). (gr. 3-3). lib. bdg. 28.67 *(978-0-8368-6839-5(0),* ac22cb96-807c-4749-8b5b-dc88d421f4a9) Stevens, Gareth Publishing LLLP.

Toybox Innovations, creator. Disney's Enchanted. 2007. (Disney's Read along Collection). (Illus.). 24p. (J). (gr. -1-3). pap. *(978-0-7634-2197-7(9))* Walt Disney Records.

MOTION PICTURE PLAYS

Rowling, J. K. Fantastic Beasts & Where to Find Them. 2016. lib. bdg. 39.15 *(978-0-606-39668-4(3))* Turtleback.

—Fantastic Beasts & Where to Find Them: the Original Screenplay. 2016. (ENG.). 304p. (J). (gr. 3-3). 24.99 *(978-1-338-10906-1(5),* Levine, Arthur A. Bks.) Scholastic, Inc.

—Fantastic Beasts & Where to Find Them: the Original Screenplay (Library Edition) 2016. (ENG.). 304p. (J). (gr. 3). 27.99 *(978-1-338-13208-3(3),* Levine, Arthur A. Bks.) Scholastic, Inc.

—Fantastic Beasts: the Crimes of Grindelwald — the Original Screenplay. 2018. (ENG., Illus.). 304p. (J). (gr. 5-5). 24.99 *(978-1-338-26389-3(7),* Levine, Arthur A. Bks.) Scholastic, Inc.

MOTION PICTURES

Abdo, Kenny. Jason Voorhees. 2019. (Hollywood Monsters Ser.). (ENG., Illus.). 24p. (J). (gr. 2-8). lib. bdg. 31.36 *(978-1-5321-2746-5(4),* 31699, Abdo Zoom-Fly) ABDO Publishing Co.

—Leatherface. 2019. (Hollywood Monsters Ser.). (ENG., Illus.). 24p. (J). (gr. 2-8). lib. bdg. 31.36 *(978-1-5321-2747-2(2),* 31701, Abdo Zoom-Fly) ABDO Publishing Co.

Abrams Books, Abrams. Moviemaking Magic of Star Wars: Creatures & Aliens. 2018. (ENG., Illus.). 144p. (J). (gr. 5-17). 29.99 *(978-1-4197-2819-8(9),* 1199101, Abrams Bks. for Young Readers) Abrams, Inc.

Adams, Colleen. Jake Gyllenhaal. 2009. (Stars in the Spotlight Ser.). 32p. (gr. 4-4). 47.90 *(978-1-60853-202-5(X),* PowerKids Pr.) Rosen Publishing Group, Inc., The.

—Orlando Bloom. (Stars in the Spotlight Ser.). 32p. (gr. 4-4). 2009. 47.90 *(978-1-60853-205-6(4),* PowerKids Pr.) 2006. (ENG., Illus.). (YA). lib. bdg. 28.93 *(978-1-4042-3517-5(5),* 03d2093e-2498-4d4c-9201-3005bd36a08b) Rosen Publishing Group, Inc., The.

Anniss, Matthew. Create Your Own Movie or TV Show. 2016. (Media Genius Ser.). (ENG., Illus.). 48p. (J). (gr. 5-8). lib. bdg. 35.99 *(978-1-4109-8110-3(X),* 131004, Raintree) Capstone.

Apel, Melanie. Cool Careers Without College for Film & Television Buffs, 1 vol. 2nd ed. 2007. (Cool Careers Without College (2002-2006) Ser.). (ENG., Illus.). 144p. (YA). (gr. 7-7). lib. bdg. 41.13 *(978-1-4042-1429-3(1),* 4e780e00-46b4-4ac3-a97b-870aa31075ec) Rosen Publishing Group, Inc., The.

Bacher, Lindsay. Biblical Allusions, 1 vol. 2015. (Essential Literary Themes Ser.). (ENG., Illus.). 112p. (YA). (gr. 6-12). 41.36 *(978-1-62403-802-0(6),* 17802, Essential Library) ABDO Publishing Co.

Beecroft, Simon. Pirates ... & Worse! Dorling Kindersley Publishing Staff, ed. 2009. (Star Wars: the Clone Wars DK Readers Ser.). lib. bdg. 13.55 *(978-0-606-07064-5(8))* Turtleback.

Bell, Elisa. Sleepover Movie Scrapbook. 2004. (Illus.). 48p. (J). *(978-0-439-66058-7(0))* Scholastic, Inc.

Bell, Samantha S. You Can Work in Movies. 2018. (You Can Work in the Arts Ser.). (ENG., Illus.). 32p. (J). (gr. 4-6). lib. bdg. 28.65 *(978-1-5435-4143-4(7),* 139097, Capstone Pr.) Capstone.

Benjamin, Daniel. American Life & Movies from the Ten Commandments to Twilight, 1 vol. 2013. (Pop Culture Ser.). (ENG.). 112p. (YA). (gr. 7-7). 42.64 *(978-1-60870-921-2(3),* 76de748f-b110-44b5-a6fd-b2ace39cd79a); pap. 20.99 *(978-1-62712-121-7(8),* a4728844-5774-460f-8fe2-273e39366bc8) Cavendish Square Publishing LLC.

Bjorklund, Ruth. Set Design in TV & Film, 1 vol. 2018. (Exploring Careers in TV & Film Ser.). (ENG.). 96p. (gr. 7-7). pap. 20.99 *(978-1-5026-4152-6(6),* c1daa181-8265-4f92-94ab-9f75dfff778c) Cavendish Square Publishing LLC.

BookSource Staff, compiled by. Who Saved the Galaxy? 2012. (Star Wars DK Readers Level 1 Ser.). lib. bdg. 13.55 *(978-0-606-26677-2(1))* Turtleback.

Boothroyd, Jennifer. Coco Top 10s: The Power of Music. 2019. (My Top 10 Disney Ser.). (ENG., Illus.). 32p. (J). (gr. 1-4). 27.99 *(978-1-5415-3910-5(9));* pap. 8.99 *(978-1-5415-4660-8(1))* Lerner Publishing Group. (Lerner Pubns.).

—Frozen Quizzes: All Good Things. 2019. (Disney Quiz Magic Ser.). (ENG., Illus.). 32p. (J). (gr. 1-4). 29.32 *(978-1-5415-5472-6(8),* Lerner Pubns.) Lerner Publishing Group.

—How to Be a Hero: Responsibility with the Incredibles. 2019. (Disney Great Character Guides). (ENG., Illus.). 32p. (J). (gr. 1-4). pap. 8.99 *(978-1-5415-4602-8(4));* lib. bdg. 27.99 *(978-1-5415-3900-6(1))* Lerner Publishing Group. (Lerner Pubns.).

—How to Be a Zootopia Police Officer: Grit with Judy Hopps. 2019. (Disney Great Character Guides). (ENG., Illus.). 32p. (J). (gr. 1-4). 27.99 *(978-1-5415-3898-6(6),* Lerner Pubns.) Lerner Publishing Group.

—The Incredibles Top 10s: No Guts, No Glory. 2019. (My Top 10 Disney Ser.). (ENG., Illus.). 32p. (J). (gr. 1-4). 27.99 *(978-1-5415-3908-2(7));* pap. 8.99 *(978-1-5415-4663-9(6))* Lerner Publishing Group. (Lerner Pubns.).

—Toy Story Quizzes: Giddyup, Partner! 2019. (Disney Quiz Magic Ser.). (ENG., Illus.). 32p. (J). (gr. 1-4). pap. 8.99 *(978-1-5415-7398-7(6),* 9781541573987, Lerner Pubns.) Lerner Publishing Group.

—Toy Story Quizzes: Reach for the Sky. 2019. (Disney Quiz Magic Ser.). (ENG., Illus.). 32p. (J). (gr. 1-4). 29.32 *(978-1-5415-5476-4(0),* 9781541554764, Lerner Pubns.) Lerner Publishing Group.

Bradley, Timothy. History of Monster Movies (Grade 6) 2nd rev. ed. 2016. (TIME(r): Informational Text Ser.). (ENG., Illus.). 48p. (J). (gr. 5-8). pap. 13.99 *(978-1-4938-3596-6(3))* Teacher Created Materials, Inc.

Bradley, Timothy J. History of Monster Movies. 2016. (Time for Kids Nonfiction Readers Ser.). (ENG.). (J). (gr. 5-8). lib. bdg. 20.85 *(978-0-606-39532-8(6))* Turtleback.

A Brief Guide for the High School Moviemaker. 2003. 56p. (YA). per. *(978-0-9753076-0-1(6))* Kerr, Alex.

Bringle, Jennifer. Vampires in Film & Television, 1 vol. 2011. (Vampires Ser.). (ENG.). 64p. (gr. 5-5). pap. 13.95 *(978-1-4488-2229-4(7),* 74e88c1c-e073-4985-b5f0-c9824f5f43d3, Rosen Reference); (ENG.). 64p. (YA). (gr. 5-5). lib. bdg. 37.13 *(978-1-4488-1226-4(7),* dca51e21-a3a6-4b5b-9c60-e6f87e25e9a8); 77.70 *(978-1-4488-2236-2(X),* Rosen Reference) Rosen Publishing Group, Inc., The.

Brodie, Ian. Cameras in Narnia: How the Lion, the Witch & the Wardrobe Came to Life. 2005. (Illus.). 72p. (J). pap. *(978-1-86950-580-6(8))* HarperCollins Pubs. New Zealand.

Brooks, Riley & Scholastic, Inc. Staff. Edward or Jacob? Quick Quizzes for Fans of the Twilight Saga. 2010. (ENG., Illus.). 96p. (J). (gr. 3-7). pap. 5.99 *(978-0-545-24842-6(6))* Scholastic, Inc.

Buckley, Annie. Movies. 2008. (21st Century Skills Innovation Library: Innovation in Entertainment Ser.). (ENG., Illus.). 32p. (gr. 4-8). lib. bdg. 32.07 *(978-1-60279-222-7(4),* 200153) Cherry Lake Publishing.

Buller, Laura. DK Readers L1: Star Wars: What Is a Wookiee? 2015. (DK Readers Level 1 Ser.). (ENG., Illus.). 48p. (J). (gr. k-2). pap. 3.99 *(978-1-4654-3386-2(4),* DK Children) Dorling Kindersley Publishing, Inc.

Candlewick Press Staff & Barba, Rick. Fantastic Beasts & Where to Find Them. 2016. (ENG.). 48p. (J). (gr. 5). 19.99 *(978-0-7636-9590-3(4))* Candlewick Pr.

Capek, Michael. Zorro. 2017. 25.70 *(978-1-61228-972-4(X))* Mitchell Lane Pubs.

Casey, Joe & Saunders, Catherine. Darth Maul: Sith Apprentice. 2012. (Star Wars DK Readers Level 4 Ser.). lib. bdg. 13.55 *(978-0-606-26563-8(5))* Turtleback.

Centore, Michael. Pixar, Disney, Dreamworks, & Digital Animation, Vol. 6. 2018. (Tech 2. 0: World-Changing Entertainment Companies Ser.). (Illus.). 64p. (J). (gr. 7). 31.93 *(978-1-4222-4057-1(6))* Mason Crest.

Chambers, Jo. Making Movies. 2007. (Trackers-Math Ser.). (gr. 2-5). pap. 5.00 *(978-1-59055-932-1(0))* Pacific Learning, Inc.

Chapman, Patricia. The Bible in the Hunger Games: A "Bibleizing" Study Guide. 2012. (ENG., Illus.). 52p. (J). (gr. 17-17). pap. 9.95 *(978-1-77064-565-3(9))* Wood Lake Publishing, Inc. CAN. Dist: Westminster John Knox Pr.

El Cine. (Coleccion Biblioteca Visual).Tr. of Cinema. (SPA.). (YA). (gr. 5-8). 14.95 *(978-84-372-3767-1(X))* Altea, Ediciones, S.A. - Grupo Santillana ESP. Dist: Lectorum Pubns., Inc.

Clare, John. Braveheart. 2009. (Hodder History: Concepts & Processes Ser.). (ENG., Illus.). 48p. pap. 23.50 *(978-0-340-95771-4(9))* Hodder Education Group GBR. Dist: Trans-Atlantic Pubns., Inc.

Clark, Katie. Animal Actors. 2013. (We Work! Animals with Jobs Ser.). (Illus.). 24p. (J). (gr. -1-3). lib. bdg. 25.65 *(978-1-61772-897-6(7))* Bearport Publishing Co., Inc.

Combs, Maggie. Love, 1 vol. 2015. (Essential Literary Themes Ser.). (ENG., Illus.). 112p. (YA). (gr. 6-12). 41.36 *(978-1-62403-806-8(9),* 17810, Essential Library) ABDO Publishing Co.

Connolly, Sean. Movies & Video. 2010. (Illus.). 46p. 34.25 *(978-1-59920-346-1(4))* Black Rabbit Bks.

Corporate Contributor Staff & Johnson, Robin. The Economics of Making a Movie. 2013. (ENG.). 48p. (J). *(978-0-7787-7971-1(8));* pap. *(978-0-7787-7976-6(9))* Crabtree Publishing Co.

Croce, Nicholas. The History of Film, 1 vol. 2015. (Britannica Guide to the Visual & Performing Arts Ser.). (ENG., Illus.). 240p. (YA). (gr. 9-10). 47.59 *(978-1-68048-076-4(6),* 7bde680b-9baa-43ba-89ce-fdf35bd1ef4b, Britannica Educational Publishing) Rosen Publishing Group, Inc., The.

Dichter, Paul. The Pacific Islands: A Moana Discovery Book. Disney Storybook Artists, illus. 2018. (Disney Learning Discovery Bks.). (ENG.). 48p. (J). (gr. 2-5). pap. 8.99 *(978-1-5415-3276-2(7),* Lerner Pubns.) Lerner Publishing Group.

—The Pacific Islands: A Moana Discovery Book. Disney Storybook Artists, Disney Storybook, illus. 2018. (Disney Learning Discovery Bks.). (ENG.). 48p. (J). (gr. 2-5). lib. bdg. 31.99 *(978-1-5415-3258-8(9),* Lerner Pubns.) Lerner Publishing Group.

Disney Publishing Creative Development (Firm) Staff, et al, contrib. by. Learn to Draw Disney/Pixar Toy Story: Featuring Favorite Characters from Toy Story 2 & Toy Story 3! 2010. (Learn to Draw Favorite Characters Ser.). 32p. (J). (gr. k-3). 28.50 *(978-1-936309-00-9(9))* Quarto Publishing Group USA.

Disney Storybook Artists Staff, contrib. by. Learn to Draw Plus Disney Pixar Toy Story: Featuring Favorite Characters from Toy Story 2 & Toy Story 3! 2012. (J). *(978-1-936309-69-6(6))* Quarto Publishing Group USA.

DK. DK Readers L2: Star Wars: Lightsaber Battles. 2018. (DK Readers Level 2 Ser.). (ENG., Illus.). 48p. (J). (gr. k-2). pap. 4.99 *(978-1-4654-6758-4(0),* DK Children) Dorling Kindersley Publishing, Inc.

—LEGO Star Wars Visual Dictionary, New Edition: With Exclusive Finn Minifigure. 2019. (ENG., Illus.). 160p. (J). (gr. 2-4). 21.99 *(978-1-4654-7888-7(4),* DK Children) Dorling Kindersley Publishing, Inc.

—Ultimate Sticker Book: Star Wars: More Than 60 Reusable Full-Color Stickers. 2004. (Ultimate Sticker Book Ser.). (ENG.). 16p. (J). (gr. k-2). pap. 6.99 *(978-0-7566-0764-7(7),* DK Children) Dorling Kindersley Publishing, Inc.

Dorling Kindersley Publishing Staff. Ahsoka in Action! 2012. (Star Wars: the Clone Wars DK Readers Ser.). lib. bdg. 13.55 *(978-0-606-31472-5(5))* Turtleback.

—Character Encyclopedia. 2011. 208p. pap. *(978-0-7566-8885-1(X))* Dorling Kindersley Publishing, Inc.

—Star Wars: Jedi Battles. 2013. (DK Adventures Ser.). lib. bdg. 16.00 *(978-0-606-35319-9(4))* Turtleback.

—Star Wars: Sith Wars. 2013. (DK Adventures Ser.). lib. bdg. 16.00 *(978-0-606-35320-5(8))* Turtleback.

Dorling Kindersley Publishing Staff & East Dubowski, Cathy. Masters of the Force. 2013. (DK Readers Pre-Level 1: Star Wars Ser.). (ENG.). 32p. (J). (gr. -1-1). 16.19 *(978-1-4654-0586-9(0))* Dorling Kindersley Publishing, Inc.

Downey, Glen R. & Malara, Maria. The 10 Hottest Hollywood Cars. 2007. 14.99 *(978-1-55448-526-0(6))* Scholastic Library Publishing.

Drake, Carol. The 10 Best Movies from Books. 2007. (J). 14.99 *(978-1-55448-463-8(4))* Scholastic Library Publishing.

Dunn, Mary R. I Want to Make Movies. (Dream Jobs Ser.). 24p. (gr. 2-3). 2009. 42.50 *(978-1-61512-216-5(8),* PowerKids Pr.) 2008. (ENG., Illus.). (YA). lib. bdg. 26.27 *(978-1-4042-4473-3(5),* 83cc834f-3f81-4abb-895f-2dcb536fd764) Rosen Publishing Group, Inc., The.

—Quiero Hacer Películas, 1 vol. 2009. (Trabajos de Ensueño (Dream Jobs) Ser.). (SPA.). 24p. (gr. 2-3). pap. 8.25 *(978-1-4358-3429-3(1),* 875bb39b-084e-4212-9a1d-22eda9101f3d, PowerKids Pr.); (Illus.). (J). lib. bdg. 26.27 *(978-1-4042-8155-4(X),* 19b1df87-48d8-4bc3-9ea2-c995f2ed8df5) Rosen Publishing Group, Inc., The.

Editors of Topix Media Lab, Editors of. Star Wars: the Force Awakens: The Official Collector's Edition. 2016. (ENG., Illus.). 96p. (YA). (gr. 6-12). 33.22 *(978-1-5124-1791-3(2),* 23180e97-bfce-44f6-b71f-0c00b7d13f58, Twenty-First Century Bks.) Lerner Publishing Group.

Elish, Dan. Screenplays, 1 vol. 2012. (Craft of Writing Ser.). (ENG.). 96p. (YA). (gr. 7-7). 36.93 *(978-1-60870-501-6(3),* f797ecf8-e65c-4c5e-8a08-2d16f301495e) Cavendish Square Publishing LLC.

Fields, Jan. Asking Questions about How Hollywood Movies Get Made. 2015. (21st Century Skills Library: Asking Questions about Media Ser.). (ENG., Illus.). 32p. (J). (gr. 4-8). pap. 14.21 *(978-1-63362-504-4(4),* 206861) Cherry Lake Publishing.

Firth, Melissa. Behind the Scenes at a Movie Set, 1 vol. 2014. (VIP Tours Ser.). (ENG.). 48p. (gr. 4-4). 33.07 *(978-1-62713-025-7(X),* 9d584ad0-8a53-4cec-b85a-6d1f5b8852f5) Cavendish Square Publishing LLC.

Fiscus, James W. Meet King Kong, 1 vol. 2005. (Famous Movie Monsters Ser.). (ENG., Illus.). 48p. (gr. 6-6). lib. bdg. 34.47 *(978-1-4042-0270-2(6),* 833b03fc-170d-497a-b195-ab32cf25eb89) Rosen Publishing Group, Inc., The.

Fletcher's Seasons. 2018. 59.95 *(978-1-338-23224-0(X))* Weston Woods Studios, Inc.

Ford, Jeanne Marie. Screenwriting, 1 vol. 2018. (Exploring Careers in TV & Film Ser.). (ENG.). 96p. (gr. 7-7). pap. 20.99 *(978-1-5026-4146-5(1),* 6497182e-0d23-49e5-b176-30d35c6ebbe6) Cavendish Square Publishing LLC.

Franks, Katie. I Want to Be a Movie Star. (Dream Jobs Ser.). 24p. (gr. 2-3). 2009. 42.50 *(978-1-61512-207-3(9),* PowerKids Pr.) 2006. (ENG., Illus.). (YA). lib. bdg. 26.27 *(978-1-4042-3619-6(8),* 173dd864-0ee6-4483-b772-e364699a0208) Rosen Publishing Group, Inc., The.

Freedman, Jeri. Acting in TV & Film, 1 vol. 2018. (Exploring Careers in TV & Film Ser.). (ENG.). 96p. (J). (gr. 7-7). pap. 20.99 *(978-1-5026-4011-6(2),* c72655be-19d3-4df7-8ddc-46954c219fe7) Cavendish Square Publishing LLC.

Garza, Sarah. Action! Making Movies, 1 vol. 2nd rev. ed. 2013. (TIME for KIDS(r): Informational Text Ser.). (ENG.). 64p. (gr. 4-8). pap. 14.99 *(978-1-4333-4949-2(3))* Teacher Created Materials, Inc.

Gitlin, Marty. Tyler Perry: A Biography of a Movie Mogul, 1 vol. 2014. (African-American Icons Ser.). (ENG.). 104p. (gr. 6-7). lib. bdg. 30.61 *(978-0-7660-4241-4(3),* cc8a68e4-21b8-4dec-b5ed-a0770e1398ef) Enslow Publishing, LLC.

Graham, P. J. Directing in TV & Film, 1 vol. 2018. (Exploring Careers in TV & Film Ser.). (ENG.). 96p. (gr. 7-7). pap. 20.99 *(978-1-5026-4053-6(8),* 366134e2-23e8-4c53-92aa-86ef5f63c1c9) Cavendish Square Publishing LLC.

Grayson, Robert. Performers, 1 vol. 2011. (Working Animals Ser.). (ENG.). 64p. (gr. 5-5). 31.21 *(978-1-60870-165-0(4),* 060ee4d6-1293-4c2d-ad41-fc5792bd7360) Cavendish Square Publishing LLC.

Greatest Movie Monsters. 2015. (Greatest Movie Monsters Ser.). (ENG.). 48p. (J). (gr. 5-6). pap., pap., pap. 493.50 *(978-1-4777-8622-2(8),* Rosen Central) Rosen Publishing Group, Inc., The.

Green, Julie. Shooting Video to Make Learning Fun. 2010. (Explorer Library: Information Explorer Ser.). (ENG., Illus.). 32p. (gr. 4-8). lib. bdg. 32.07 *(978-1-60279-955-4(5),* 200635) Cherry Lake Publishing.

Green, Naima. Meet Frankenstein. (Famous Movie Monsters Ser.). 48p. (gr. 6-6). 2009. 53.00 *(978-1-61512-529-6(9))* 2005. (ENG., Illus.). lib. bdg. 34.47 *(978-1-4042-0268-9(4),* 36a18341-8b66-4d0f-861a-019b54f73510) Rosen Publishing Group, Inc., The.

Green, Sara. Animal Performers. 2018. (Movie Magic Ser.). (ENG., Illus.). 32p. (J). (gr. 3-8). lib. bdg. 27.95 *(978-1-62617-845-8(3),* Blastoff! Discovery) Bellwether Media.

—Costumes & Props. 2018. (Movie Magic Ser.). (ENG., Illus.). 32p. (J). (gr. 3-8). lib. bdg. 27.95 *(978-1-62617-847-2(X),* Blastoff! Discovery) Bellwether Media.

—Star Wars. 2017. (Brands We Know Ser.). (ENG., Illus.). 24p. (J). (gr. 3-8). lib. bdg. 27.95 *(978-1-62617-656-0(6),* Pilot Bks.) Bellwether Media.

Greenberger, Robert. Meet Godzilla, 1 vol. 2005. (Famous Movie Monsters Ser.). (ENG., Illus.). 48p. (gr. 6-6). lib. bdg. 34.47 *(978-1-4042-0269-6(2),* ac3c18b1-8a70-4a89-9192-d8427ebc7d1c) Rosen Publishing Group, Inc., The.

Gulko, Candace S. Film. 2010. (Career Launcher Ser.). 176p. (C). (gr. 9). pap. 14.95 *(978-0-8160-7981-0(1),* Checkmark Bks.) Infobase Holdings, Inc.

Harland, Joan & Timmons, Nick. As Film Studies. 2006. (ENG., Illus.). 240p. (YA). pap. 49.50 *(978-0-7487-9030-2(6))* Nelson Thornes Ltd. GBR. Dist: Trans-Atlantic Pubns., Inc.

Harmon, Daniel E. Werewolves, 1 vol. 2015. (Greatest Movie Monsters Ser.). (ENG., Illus.). 48p. (J). (gr. 5-6). 33.47 *(978-1-4994-3521-4(5),* 01e8d145-644e-43d8-bfe5-88a8e26b68eb, Rosen Central) Rosen Publishing Group, Inc., The.

Harper, Benjamin. DK Readers L3: Star Wars: Feel the Force! 2011. (DK Readers Level 3 Ser.). (ENG.). 48p. (J). (gr. 2-4). 4.99 *(978-0-7566-7126-6(4),* DK Children) Dorling Kindersley Publishing, Inc.

Hermansson, Casie. Parental Guidance Ratings. 2013. (Hot Topics in Media Ser.). (ENG.). 48p. (J). (gr. 4-8). pap. 18.50 *(978-1-61783-784-5(9),* 10758) ABDO Publishing Co.

Hibbert, Clare & Hachette Children's Books Staff. Movie Star: Find Out How Your Favorite Movie Stars Made It! 2012. (Celeb Ser.). (ENG., Illus.). 32p. (J). (gr. 4-6). lib. bdg. 28.50 *(978-1-59771-332-0(5))* Sea-To-Sea Pubns.

Hill, Mary. Let's Go to a Movie. 2004. (Welcome Bks.). (ENG.). 24p. (J). (gr. -1-2). pap. 4.95 *(978-0-516-25917-8(2),* Children's Pr.) Scholastic Library Publishing.

Hirschmann, Kris. The Science of Super Powers: An Incredibles Discovery Book. 2019. (Disney Learning Discovery Bks.). (ENG., Illus.). 48p. (J). (gr. 2-5). pap. 8.99 *(978-1-5415-7390-1(0),* 9781541573901); lib. bdg. 31.99 *(978-1-5415-5489-4(2),* 9781541554894) Lerner Publishing Group. (Lerner Pubns.).

Hofer, Charles. Meet Dracula. (Famous Movie Monsters Ser.). 48p. (gr. 6-6). 2009. 53.00 *(978-1-61512-528-9(0))* 2005. (ENG., Illus.). 34.47 *(978-1-4042-0267-2(6),* e2b21aef-ba34-4c9b-b2f7-5648b152b084) Rosen Publishing Group, Inc., The.

Holzer, Harold. Lincoln: How Abraham Lincoln Ended Slavery in America: A Companion Book for Young Readers to the Steven Spielberg Film. 2012. (ENG., Illus.). 240p. 16.99 *(978-0-06-226509-8(1),* Newmarket for It Bks.) HarperCollins Pubs.

Horn, Geoffrey M. Writing, Producing, & Directing Movies, 1 vol. 2006. (Making Movies Ser.). (ENG., Illus.). 32p. (gr. 3-3). lib. bdg. 28.67 *(978-0-8368-6841-8(2),* 2a69c765-5cc2-468f-97b6-ec05aa3d7f23) Stevens, Gareth Publishing LLLP.

Horning, Nicole. Robert Downey Jr: Superhero Superstar, 1 vol. 2019. (People in the News Ser.). (ENG.). 104p. (gr. 7-7). pap. 20.99 *(978-1-5345-6769-6(0),* 5c0b9854-aef7-4d42-bada-cc4b57a9aeb9, Lucent Pr.) Greenhaven Publishing LLC.

Howard, Kate. The Lego Movie: Junior Novel. 2013. (Illus.). 133p. (J). lib. bdg. 16.00 *(978-0-606-35406-6(9))* Turtleback.

Indovino, Shaina Carmel. Dracula & Beyond: Famous Vampires & Werewolves in Literature & Film. 2010. (Making of a Monster Ser.). (Illus.). 64p. (YA). (gr. 7-18). pap. 9.95 *(978-1-4222-1956-0(9));* lib. bdg. 22.95 *(978-1-4222-1803-7(1))* Mason Crest.

Jantner, Janos, illus. Drawing Horror-Movie Monsters, 1 vol. 2013. (How to Draw Monsters Ser.). (ENG.). 32p. (J). (gr. 4-5). 30.27 *(978-1-4777-0308-3(X),* 26524055-cc98-462e-aa4a-d9238a2a2844); pap. 12.75 *(978-1-4777-0338-0(1),* c664f382-188f-4699-ba23-5045b0c609ea) Rosen Publishing Group, Inc., The. (PowerKids Pr.).

Johnson, Marlys. Careers in the Movies. 2009. (Career Resource Library). 192p. (gr. 7-12). 63.90 *(978-1-60853-406-7(5))* Rosen Publishing Group, Inc., The.

Jones, Bruce Patrick. Action Stars Paper Dolls. Jones, Bruce Patrick, illus. 2010. (Dover Celebrity Paper Dolls Ser.). (ENG., Illus.). 32p. (J). (gr. 3-5). 9.99 *(978-0-486-47606-3(5))* Dover Pubns., Inc.

Jones, Sarah. Film. 2003. (Media Wise Ser.). (Illus.). 64p. (J). lib. bdg. 28.50 *(978-1-58340-256-6(X))* Black Rabbit Bks.

Kassnoff, David. Transformers, Robots, & Cyborgs, 1 vol. 2015. (Greatest Movie Monsters Ser.). (ENG., Illus.). 48p. (J). (gr. 5-6). 33.47 *(978-1-4994-3529-0(0),* 0db40ea9-6425-47bb-951d-5f01aff02976, Rosen Central) Rosen Publishing Group, Inc., The.

Kent, Lindsay. DK Readers L4: Star Wars: Ultimate Duels: Find Out about the Deadliest Battles! 2011. (DK Readers Level 4 Ser.). (ENG.). 48p. (J). (gr. 3-7). 4.99 *(978-0-7566-8263-7(0),* DK Children) Dorling Kindersley Publishing, Inc.

Kinney, Jeff. The Wimpy Kid Movie Diary: The Next Chapter. 2017. (Diary of a Wimpy Kid Ser.). (ENG., Illus.). 208p. (J). (gr. 3-7). 16.95 *(978-1-4197-2752-8(4),* 1207501) Abrams, Inc.

—The Wimpy Kid Movie Diary (Dog Days Revised & Expanded Edition) 2012. (ENG., Illus.). 256p. (YA). (gr. 3-7). 15.95 *(978-1-4197-0642-4(X))* Abrams, Inc.

Krasner, Barbara. The 12 Most Influential Movies of All Time. 2018. (Most Influential Ser.). (ENG., Illus.). 32p. (J). (gr. 3-6). 32.80 *(978-1-63235-410-5(1),* 13747, 12-Story Library) Bookstaves, LLC.

Kuromiya, Jun. The Future of Entertainment. 2020. (Searchlight Books (tm) — Future Tech Ser.). (ENG., Illus.). 32p. (J). (gr. 3-5). 30.65 *(978-1-5415-9734-1(6),* e50c9475-d602-403d-8653-5753277b8860, Lerner Pubns.) Lerner Publishing Group.

La Bella, Laura. Drones & Entertainment, 1 vol. 2016. (Inside the World of Drones Ser.). (ENG.). 64p. (J). (gr. 7-7). 36.13 *(978-1-5081-7339-7(7),* 8300ba43-9f9e-465a-a6ac-dd705e2f28d1) Rosen Publishing Group, Inc., The.

Lace, William W. Blacks in Film, 1 vol. 2008. (Lucent Library of Black History Ser.). (ENG., Illus.). 104p. (gr. 7-7). 41.03 *(978-1-4205-0084-4(8),* 1ab142e5-ace0-44a9-8eb6-0a7f7cad1d1b, Lucent Pr.) Greenhaven Publishing LLC.

Larson, Jeff. FX! Lighting & Sound. 2017. (Time for Kids Nonfiction Readers Ser.). lib. bdg. 22.10 *(978-0-606-40269-9(1))* Turtleback.

Last, Shari. Star Wars: Rebel Heroes. 2017. (Illus.). 63p. (J). *(978-1-5182-3539-9(5))* Dorling Kindersley Publishing, Inc.

Lewis, Daniel. Computers, Communications & the Arts, Vol. 10. 2018. (Careers in Demand for High School Graduates Ser.). 112p. (J). (gr. 7). 34.60 *(978-1-4222-4134-9(3))* Mason Crest.

Lindeen, Mary. Cars Top 10s: It's Drive Time! 2019. (My Top 10 Disney Ser.). (ENG., Illus.). 32p. (J). (gr. 1-4). pap. 8.99 *(978-1-5415-4659-2(8),* Lerner Pubns.) Lerner Publishing Group.

—Frozen Top 10s: Some People Are Worth Melting For. 2019. (My Top 10 Disney Ser.). (ENG., Illus.). 32p. (J). (gr. 1-4). pap. 8.99 *(978-1-5415-4662-2(8),* Lerner Pubns.) Lerner Publishing Group.

—Toy Story Top 10s: To Infinity & Beyond. 2019. (My Top 10 Disney Ser.). (ENG., Illus.). 32p. (J). (gr. 1-4). pap. 8.99 *(978-1-5415-4664-6(4),* Lerner Pubns.) Lerner Publishing Group.

Little Sparrow. 2004. pap. 9.99 *(978-0-307-14298-6(1))* Random Hse., Inc.

Lockyer, John & Holden, Pam. Making a Movie, 1 vol. 2009. (Red Rocket Readers Ser.). (ENG., Illus.). 19p. (gr. 2-2). pap. *(978-1-877435-50-8(3),* Red Rocket Readers) Flying Start Bks.

Loh-Hagan, Virginia. Documentary Film. 2017. (D. I. Y. Make It Happen Ser.). (ENG., Illus.). 32p. (J). (gr. 4-8). lib. bdg. 32.07 *(978-1-63472-879-9(3),* 209942, 45th Parallel Press) Cherry Lake Publishing.

—Sound Effects Artist. 2015. (Illus.). 32p. (J). pap. 9.95 *(978-1-63470-056-6(2))* Cherry Lake Publishing.

Margles, Samantha. Star Wars: Science Fair Book. 2013. lib. bdg. 20.85 *(978-0-606-32399-4(6))* Turtleback.

Markegard, Blake. John Cena. 2014. (Wrestling Superstars Ser.). (ENG., Illus.). 24p. (J). (gr. 3-7). pap. 8.99 *(978-1-61891-244-2(5),* 11989, Epic Bks.) Bellwether Media.

Matthews, John. DVDs. 2008. (21st Century Skills Library: Global Products Ser.). (ENG., Illus.). 32p. (gr. 4-8). lib. bdg. 32.07 *(978-1-60279-253-1(4),* 200120) Cherry Lake Publishing.

McAlpine, Margaret. Working in Film & Television, 1 vol. 2005. (My Future Career Ser.). (ENG., Illus.). 64p. (gr. 4-6). lib. bdg. 29.67 *(978-0-8368-4237-1(5),* a8151ada-0e90-4192-a2bd-1a6bc6a0f619, Gareth Stevens Learning Library) Stevens, Gareth Publishing LLLP.

McCarthy, Cecilia Pinto. The Science of Movies, 1 vol. 2016. (Super-Awesome Science Ser.). (ENG., Illus.). 48p. (J). (gr. 4-8). lib. bdg. 35.64 *(978-1-68078-247-9(9),* 22095) ABDO Publishing Co.

McClintock Miller, Shannon & Hoena, Blake. A Stop-Motion Animation Mission. Brown, Alan, illus. 2019. (Adventures in Makerspace Ser.). (ENG.). 32p. (J). (gr. 3-5). lib. bdg. 30.65 *(978-1-4965-7951-5(8),* 139760, Stone Arch Bks.) Capstone.

Miller, Connie Colwell. Movie Animals. 2013. (Animals with Jobs Ser.). (ENG.). 32p. (J). (gr. 2-5). 28.50 *(978-1-60753-379-5(0),* 16291) Amicus.

Morgan, Kathryn. Zombies, 1 vol. 2015. (Greatest Movie Monsters Ser.). (ENG., Illus.). 48p. (J). (gr. 5-6). 33.47 *(978-1-4994-3545-0(2),* 0bd2be59-09f9-42e3-956d-c6466dd38169, Rosen Central) Rosen Publishing Group, Inc., The.

Morina, Barbara, concept. Movie Journal (Kraft) Journals Unlimited. 2003. (Write It down Ser.). (Illus.). 200p. spiral bd. 21.95 *(978-1-892033-34-5(8))* Journals Unlimited, Inc.

Mosqueda, Olga T. & Tucker, Marianne, illus. Learn to Draw Plus Disney Winnie the Pooh. 2012. (J). *(978-1-936309-68-9(8))* Quarto Publishing Group USA.

Moviemakers' Film Club: Direct with Confidence (Set), 12 vols. 2017. (Moviemakers' Film Club Ser.). (ENG.). (J). (gr. 4-5). lib. bdg. 167.58 *(978-1-5081-6271-1(9),* bd1f3cbe-0841-4528-abe4-88366af01896, PowerKids Pr.) Rosen Publishing Group, Inc., The.

Mullins, Matt. Scriptwriter. 2011. (21st Century Skills Library: Cool Arts Careers Ser.). (ENG., Illus.). 32p. (gr. 4-8). lib. bdg. 32.07 *(978-1-61080-135-5(0),* 201148) Cherry Lake Publishing.

Murdico, Suzanne J. Meet the Blob, 1 vol. 2005. (Famous Movie Monsters Ser.). (ENG., Illus.). 48p. (gr. 6-6). lib. bdg. 34.47 *(978-1-4042-0271-9(4),* 4f46f2c0-e2af-4676-af06-466e88799905) Rosen Publishing Group, Inc., The.

Murphy, Maggie. Johnny Depp, 1 vol. 2011. (Movie Superstars Ser.). (ENG., Illus.). 32p. (J). (gr. 4-4). pap. 11.00 *(978-1-4488-2721-3(3),* 465f689e-8cdf-48ab-8354-ae3b2cc54cf2, PowerKids Pr.) Rosen Publishing Group, Inc., The.

—Movie Superstars, 12 vols., Set. Incl. Johnny Depp. 28.93 *(978-1-4488-2566-0(0),* b5dd275b-d832-4a8f-a471-ff05df4c8053); Megan Fox. lib. bdg. 28.93 *(978-1-4488-2567-7(9),* 0c28d94b-16ba-4b64-b7ee-6868cead796b); Reese Witherspoon. lib. bdg. 28.93 *(978-1-4488-2568-4(7),* 763ce019-29b0-4036-a20a-6efe2bc56468); Shia Labeouf. 28.93 *(978-1-4488-2563-9(6),* 8cde57c8-3759-4311-952a-c2f52264abfc); Taylor Lautner. lib. bdg. 28.93 *(978-1-4488-2564-6(4),* d104c531-1eb7-4646-a004-e4cb34014baa); Zoe Saldana. lib. bdg. 28.93 *(978-1-4488-2565-3(2),* 578064c9-f92b-4b0e-85a3-52b8b251d772); (J). (gr. 4-4). (Movie Superstars Ser.). (ENG., Illus.). 32p. 2011. Set lib. bdg. 173.58 *(978-1-4488-2907-1(0),* b9cd6b7e-1a16-458f-a4f4-178fb613e1ef, PowerKids Pr.) Rosen Publishing Group, Inc., The.

Murray, Helen & Dorling Kindersley Publishing Staff. The LEGO Movie 2: The Awesomest, Amazing, Most Epic Movie Guide in the Universe! 2019. (ENG., Illus.). 96p. (J). *(978-0-241-36045-3(5))* Dorling Kindersley Publishing, Inc.

Nagelhout, Ryan. Dwayne Johnson: The Rock's Rise to Fame, 1 vol. 2018. (People in the News Ser.). (ENG.). 104p. (gr. 7-7). 41.03 *(978-1-5345-6329-2(6),* 0637fc73-bd43-4a86-a4c6-2207323effc8, Lucent Pr.) Greenhaven Publishing LLC.

Naha, Ed. The Ten Commandments Movie Storybook. 2007. (Epic Stories of the Bible Ser.). (Illus.). 77p. (J). (gr. -1-3). 14.99 *(978-0-9743876-4-2(9))* CrossStaff Publishing.

Nardo, Don. Careers in Film, TV, & Theater. 2019. (Careers for Creative People Ser.). (ENG.). 80p. (J). (gr. 6-12). 41.27 *(978-1-68282-681-2(3))* ReferencePoint Pr., Inc.

Nesworthy, Lauren. Ultimate Sticker Book: Disney Pixar Cars 3. 2017. (Ultimate Sticker Book Ser.). (ENG.). 16p. (J). (gr. k-4). pap. 6.99 *(978-1-4654-5560-4(4),* DK Children) Dorling Kindersley Publishing, Inc.

Niver, Heather Moore. Dracula & Other Vampires, 1 vol. 2015. (Greatest Movie Monsters Ser.). (ENG., Illus.). 48p. (J). (gr. 5-6). 33.47 *(978-1-4994-3525-2(8),* a8e71e42-240c-46d7-bbe9-22739181bf88, Rosen Central) Rosen Publishing Group, Inc., The.

O'Neill, Joseph. Movie Director. 2009. (21st Century Skills Library: Cool Careers Ser.). (ENG., Illus.). 32p. (gr. 4-8). lib. bdg. 32.07 *(978-1-60279-499-3(5),* 200310) Cherry Lake Publishing.

Patz, Deborah. Write! Shoot! Edit! The Complete Guide for Teen Filmmakers. 2017. (ENG., Illus.). 210p. (YA). pap. 23.95 *(978-1-61593-264-1(X))* Wiese, Michael Productions.

Pelusey, Michael & Pelusey, Jane. Film & Television. 2005. (Media Ser.). (ENG., Illus.). 32p. (gr. 5-8). lib. bdg. 21.95 *(978-0-7910-8802-9(2),* P114423, Facts On File) Infobase Holdings, Inc.

Perritano, John. The Science of Movies, 1 vol. 2016. (Red Rhino Nonfiction Ser.). (ENG., Illus.). 60p. (J). (gr. 4-7). pap. 11.95 *(978-1-68021-050-7(5))* Saddleback Educational Publishing, Inc.

Perritano, Johnrau Dana M. The Science of Movies. 2017. (Red Rhino Nonfiction Ser.). (J). lib. bdg. 19.60 *(978-0-606-39892-3(9))* Turtleback.

Pinede, Nadine. Women in Film. 2018. (Women in the Arts Ser.). (ENG., Illus.). 48p. (J). (gr. 4-8). lib. bdg. 35.64 *(978-1-5321-1475-5(3),* 29142) ABDO Publishing Co.

Pipe, Jim. Make a Movie! 2013. (Find Your Talent Ser.). 32p. (gr. 5-8). 28.50 *(978-1-84858-573-7(X))* Arcturus Publishing GBR. Dist: Black Rabbit Bks.

Pollack, Pam & Meg Belviso. Who Is George Lucas? 2014. (Who Is... ? Ser.). (Illus.). 105p. (J). lib. bdg. 16.00 *(978-0-606-35690-9(8))* Turtleback.

Pollack, Pamela D. & Belviso, Meg. Who Was Alfred Hitchcock? 2014. (Who Was... ? Ser.). lib. bdg. 14.75 *(978-0-606-36176-7(6))* Turtleback.

Price, Roger & Stern, Leonard. Star Wars Mad Libs: World's Greatest Word Game. 2008. (Star Wars Ser.). (ENG.). 48p. (J). (gr. 3-7). 5.99 *(978-0-8431-3271-7(X),* Mad Libs) Penguin Young Readers Group.

Publishing, Ferguson. Film. 2012. (Career Launcher Ser.). (ENG.). 176p. (gr. 9). 34.95 *(978-0-8160-7959-9(5),* P179128, Ferguson Publishing Company) Infobase Holdings, Inc.

Revenson, Jody. Harry Potter: Diagon Alley: a Movie Scrapbook. 2018. (Harry Potter Ser.). (ENG., Illus.). 48p. (J). (gr. 5). 19.99 *(978-0-7636-9592-7(0))* Candlewick Pr.

—J. K. Rowling's Wizarding World: Movie Magic Volume One: Extraordinary People & Fascinating Places. 2016. (J. K. Rowling's Wizarding World Ser.). (ENG., Illus.). 96p. (J). (gr. 5). 29.99 *(978-0-7636-9582-8(3))* Candlewick Pr.

—J. K. Rowling's Wizarding World: the Dark Arts: a Movie Scrapbook. 2017. (J. K. Rowling's Wizarding World Ser.). (ENG., Illus.). 48p. (J). (gr. 5). 19.99 *(978-0-7636-9591-0(2))* Candlewick Pr.

Richards, Andrea. Girl Director: A How-to-Guide for the First-Time, Flat-Broke Filmaker (and Videomaker) (ENG., Illus.). 106p. (YA). pap. 17.95 *(978-1-931497-00-8(1))* Girl Pr., Inc.

Riordan, Rick. Percy Jackson & the Olympians: Ultimate Guide, the-Percy Jackson & the Olympians. 2010. (Percy Jackson & the Olympians Ser.). (ENG., Illus.). 156p. (J). (gr. 5-9). 12.99 *(978-1-4231-2171-8(6),* Disney-Hyperion) Disney Publishing Worldwide.

Rodgers, Kelly. Communicate! Documentaries (Level 5) 2017. (TIME for KIDS(r): Informational Text Ser.). (ENG., Illus.). 48p. (gr. 4-8). pap. 13.99 *(978-1-4258-4986-3(5))* Teacher Created Materials, Inc.

Roussos, Eleni. The Moviemaking Magic of Marvel Studios: Heroes & Villains. 2019. (ENG., Illus.). 176p. (gr. 5-17). 29.99 *(978-1-4197-3587-5(X),* 1269701, Abrams Bks. for Young Readers) Abrams, Inc.

Running Press. Fantastic Beasts & Where to Find Them: Newt Scamander's Case: With Sound. 2017. (RP Minis Ser.). (ENG., Illus.). 48p. pap. 12.95 *(978-0-7624-6072-4(5),* Running Pr. Minature Editions) Running Pr.

Saunders, Catherine. Are Ewoks Scared of Stormtroopers? 2013. (Star Wars DK Readers Level 1 Ser.). lib. bdg. 13.55 (978-0-606-35205-5(8)) Turtleback.

—DK Readers L3: Star Wars: the Legendary Yoda: Discover the Secret of Yoda's Life! 2013. (DK Readers Level 3 Ser.). (ENG., Illus.). 48p. (J). (gr. 2-4). pap. 4.99 (978-1-4654-0184-7(9), DK Children) Dorling Kindersley Publishing, Inc.

Scholastic, Inc. Staff, contrib. by. The World of Harry Potter: Harry Potter Poster Book. 2011. (Illus.). 125p. (J). pap. (978-0-545-31482-4(8)) Scholastic, Inc.

Schwartz, Heather E. The Lion King Quizzes: Hakuna Matat. 2019. (Disney Quiz Magic Ser.). (ENG., Illus.). 32p. (J). (gr. 1-4). 29.32 (978-1-5415-5473-3(6), 9781541554733, Lerner Pubns.) Lerner Publishing Group.

—Wreck-It Ralph Quizzes: When the Game Is over, the Fun Begins. 2019. (Disney Quiz Magic Ser.). (ENG., Illus.). 32p. (J). (gr. 1-4). 29.32 (978-1-5415-5474-0(4), 9781541554740); pap. 8.99 (978-1-5415-7399-4(4), 9781541573994) Lerner Publishing Group. (Lerner Pubns.).

Segall, Miriam. Career Building Through Digital Moviemaking. 2009. (Digital Career Building Ser.). 64p. (gr. 6-6). 58.50 (978-1-61512-164-9(1)) Rosen Publishing Group, Inc., The.

Shea, Therese. Godzilla, 1 vol. 2015. (Greatest Movie Monsters Ser.). (ENG., Illus.). 48p. (J). (gr. 5-6). 33.47 (978-1-4994-3533-7(9), 279ab90f-c3fc-4e13-b5da-342f18fe05fb, Rosen Central) Rosen Publishing Group, Inc., The.

Sichol, Lowey Bundy. From an Idea to Disney: How Imagination Built a World of Magic. Jennings, C. S., illus. 2019. (From an Idea To Ser.). (ENG.). 112p. (J). (gr. 1-5). 16.99 (978-1-328-45360-0(X), 1711801); pap. 6.99 (978-1-328-45361-7(8), 1711803) HarperCollins Pubs. (Clarion Bks.).

Sinyard, Neil. George Stevens: The Films of a Hollywood Giant, 1 vol. 2019. (ENG., Illus.). 222p. pap. 45.00 (978-0-7864-7775-3(X), dd9b7441-718d-4826-8b2f-afe9611655b1) McFarland & Co., Inc. Pubs.

Slaby, Nette. Movies I've Seen. 2006. 65p. (J). per. (978-0-9774118-5-6(0)) SLABYPRESS.

Small, Cathleen. Frankenstein's Monster, 1 vol. 2015. (Creatures of Fantasy Ser.). (ENG., Illus.). 64p. (gr. 6-6). lib. bdg. 35.93 (978-1-5026-0936-6(3), f88a5e0f-745c-4078-940f-f116a0755d0b) Cavendish Square Publishing LLC.

Somervill, Barbara A. Actor. 2011. (21st Century Skills Library: Cool Arts Careers Ser.). (ENG., Illus.). 32p. (gr. 4-8). lib. bdg. 32.07 (978-1-61080-129-4(6), 201136) Cherry Lake Publishing.

Spencer, Liv. Love Bites: The Unofficial Saga of Twilight. 2010. (ENG., Illus.). 203p. (YA). (gr. 7). pap. 14.95 (978-1-55022-930-1(3), 5794965c-1c31-4a08-9c84-7624b5b00c5d) ECW Pr. CAN. Dist: Baker & Taylor Publisher Services (BTPS).

Star Wars Block (an Abrams Block Book) Over 100 Words Every Fan Should Know. 2018. (Abrams Block Book Ser.). (ENG., Illus.). 104p. (gr. -1-17). 17.99 (978-1-4197-2831-0(8), 1213610) Abrams, Inc.

Stewart, Mark. Movie Blockbusters, 1 vol. 2009. (Ultimate 10: Entertainment Ser.). (ENG.). 48p. (gr. 3-3). (J). pap. 11.50 (978-1-4339-2211-4(8), 73f43888-ba9c-49c7-9fbf-5bf243b46799); (YA). lib. bdg. 33.67 (978-0-8368-9163-8(5), 91f4fc7f-d73e-4102-8570-7778bc8f1717) Stevens, Gareth Publishing LLLP.

—Movie Characters, 1 vol. 2009. (Ultimate 10: Entertainment Ser.). (ENG.). 48p. (gr. 3-3). (J). pap. 11.50 (978-1-4339-2212-1(6), 38b755eb-290b-4946-ac9f-16eb7ee92caa); (YA). lib. bdg. 33.67 (978-0-8368-9164-5(3), c662166d-675a-4b4d-a6cf-1ca93a9f3a7d) Stevens, Gareth Publishing LLLP.

Stierle, Cynthia. Let It Grow: A Frozen Guide to Gardening. 2019. (ENG., Illus.). 32p. (J). (gr. 2-5). 27.99 (978-1-5415-3913-6(3), Lerner Pubns.) Lerner Publishing Group.

Stock, Lisa. DK Readers L1: Star Wars: What Is a Droid? 2018. (DK Readers Level 1 Ser.). (ENG., Illus.). 24p. (J). (gr. k-2). pap. 4.99 (978-1-4654-6753-9(X), DK Children) Dorling Kindersley Publishing, Inc.

Stoller, Bryan Michael. Harry Potter: Imagining Hogwarts: A Beginner's Guide to Moviemaking. 2018. (ENG., Illus.). 64p. (J). 19.99 (978-1-68383-399-4(6)) Insight Editions.

Sublette, Guen. Here's Lookin' at Lizzie. (978-0-312-32669-2(6)) St. Martin's Pr.

The Beatles. Yellow Submarine. Edelmann, Heinz, illus. 2018. (ENG.). 40p. (J). (gr. 2-5). 15.99 (978-1-5362-0145-1(6)) Candlewick Pr.

Die Theatre der Welt.Tr. of Theater of the World. (GER., Illus.). (YA). 31.95 (978-3-411-09061-7(8)) Bibliographisches Institut & F. A. Brockhaus AG DEU. Dist: Continental Bk. Co., Inc.

Thomas, William David. Movie Stunt Worker, 1 vol. 2011. (Dirty & Dangerous Jobs Ser.). (ENG.). 32p. (gr. 3-3). 31.21 (978-1-60870-172-8(7), 7cc30088-65c1-4022-a31f-837489fdd344) Cavendish Square Publishing LLC.

Tolkien, J. R. R. Como Se Hizo el Senor de los Anillos. 2003. (Lord of the Rings Ser.). (SPA., Illus.). 192p. (J). 14.95 (978-84-450-7414-5(8)) Minotauro Ediciones ESP. Dist: Planeta Publishing Corp.

—Guia de Fotos. 2003. (Lord of the Rings Ser.). (SPA., Illus.). 48p. (J). 7.95 (978-84-450-7415-2(6)) Minotauro Ediciones ESP. Dist: Planeta Publishing Corp.

Triumph Books Staff. Hilary Duff: Total Hilary, Metamorphosis, Lizzie McGuire. . . & More. 2003. (Illus.). 80p. pap. 9.95 (978-1-57243-625-1(5)) Triumph Bks.

Troupe, Thomas Kingsley. Shoot Epic Short Documentaries: 4D an Augmented Reading Experience. 2019. (Make a Movie! 4D Ser.). (ENG., Illus.). 48p. (J). (gr. 3-5). lib. bdg. 33.99 (978-1-5435-4008-6(2), 139042) Capstone.

Tucker, Marianne & Phillipson, Andy, illus. Learn to Draw Plus Disney Pixar Cars. 2012. (978-1-936309-70-2(X)) Quarto Publishing Group USA.

Uhl, Xina M. Using Computer Science in Film & Television Careers, 1 vol. 2018. (Coding Your Passion Ser.). (ENG.). 80p. (gr. 7-7). pap. 16.30 (978-1-5081-8393-8(7), 0c9a4817-caed-44cd-b1f2-8b94f6d5ae48, Rosen Young Adult) Rosen Publishing Group, Inc., The.

Universal. Despicable Me 3: Gru's Gadget Guide. 2017. (ENG., Illus.). 24p. (J). pap. (978-0-316-47618-8(8)) Little, Brown Bks. for Young Readers.

Valentine, Emily. Steven Spielberg: With a Discussion of Imagination. 2004. (Values in Action Biographies Ser.). (J). (978-1-59203-072-9(6)) Learning Challenge, Inc.

Valle, Suzette. 101 Movies to See Before You Grow Up. 2017. (101 Ser.). (ENG., Illus.). 144p. (J). (gr. 3-5). lib. bdg. 33.32 (978-1-942875-15-4(0), 10344934-fd16-4443-96d0-a8ccf7fa2049, Walter Foster Jr) Quarto Publishing Group USA.

Walter Foster Jr. Creative Team, Walter. Learn to Draw Disney Brave: Featuring Favorite Characters from the Disney∙Pixar Film, Including Merida & Angus. Disney Storybook Artists, Disney Storybook, illus. 2015. (Learn to Draw Favorite Characters: Expanded Edition Ser.). (ENG.). 64p. (J). (gr. 3-5). 33.32 (978-1-939581-45-7(1), c035ea1c-1b52-43a6-8081-afec265ed790, Walter Foster Jr) Quarto Publishing Group USA.

Wessling, Katherine. High Interest Books: Backstage Pass: Backstage at a Movie Set. 2003. (High Interest Bks.). (ENG., Illus.). 48p. (J). (gr. 7-12). pap. 6.95 (978-0-516-24387-0(X), Children's Pr.) Scholastic Library Publishing.

Whos Who at the Zoo. 2004. pap. 9.99 (978-0-307-14272-6(8)) Random Hse., Inc.

Willian, Michael. The Essential It's a Wonderful Life Film Guidebook: A scene by scene look at a holiday Classic. 2004. (Illus.). 140p. per. 15.95 (978-0-9762429-0-1(7)) Kerpluggo Bks. LLC.

Willoughby, Nick. Digital Filmmaking for Kids for Dummies. 2015. (For Kids for Dummies Ser.). (ENG., Illus.). 336p. pap. 34.99 (978-1-119-02740-9(3), For Dummies) Wiley, John & Sons, Inc.

Windham Ryder & Dorling Kindersley Publishing Staff. Journey Through Space. 2015. (ENG., Illus.). 48p. (J). (978-0-241-18633-6(1)) Dorling Kindersley Publishing, Inc.

Wood, Alix. Be a Film Editor: Polish the Performance, 1 vol. 2017. (Moviemakers' Film Club Ser.). (ENG.). 32p. (J). (gr. 4-5). pap. 11.00 (978-1-5383-2374-8(5), 71a23be7-2120-47e2-852b-dbc768452316); lib. bdg. 27.93 (978-1-5081-6266-7(2), 80eb03a7-021a-4360-8885-dce0d31b7016) Rosen Publishing Group, Inc., The. (PowerKids Pr.).

—Be a Screenwriter: Turn Your Idea into a Script, 1 vol. 2017. (Moviemakers' Film Club Ser.). (ENG.). 32p. (J). (gr. 4-5). 27.93 (978-1-5383-2280-2(3), 56d06c19-0ce4-4014-b0b5-a975821f5591); pap. 11.00 (978-1-5383-2378-6(8), e5f821ca-9537-4694-9465-ae368b600b4d) Rosen Publishing Group, Inc., The. (PowerKids Pr.).

Woog, Adam. Vampires in the Movies. 2010. (Vampire Library). (Illus.). 80p. (J). (gr. 7-12). lib. bdg. 41.27 (978-1-60152-135-4(9)) ReferencePoint Pr., Inc.

Wooley, John & Price, Michael H. The Big Book of Biker Flicks: 40 of the Best Motorcycle Movies of All Times, 1. 2005. (Illus.). 168p. pap. 24.95 (978-1-930709-45-4(5)) HAWK Publishing Group.

Wright, Greg. Peter Jackson in Perspective: The Power Behind Cinema's the Lord of the Rings: A Look at Hollywood's Take on Tolkien's Epic Tale. 2004. 212p. per. 13.95 (978-0-9759577-0-7(8)) Methow Pr.

Wyss, Johann. The Swiss Family Robinson Graphic Novel. 2010. (Illustrated Classics Ser.). (ENG., Illus.). 64p. (YA). (gr. 4-12). per. 11.95 (978-1-56254-938-1(3)) Saddleback Educational Publishing, Inc.

Zahed, Ramin. J. K. Rowling's Wizarding World: Movie Magic Volume Two: Curious Creatures. 2017. (J. K. Rowling's Wizarding World Ser.). (ENG., Illus.). 104p. (J). (gr. 5). 29.99 (978-0-7636-9583-5(1)) Candlewick Pr.

MOTION PICTURES—BIOGRAPHY

see also Actors and Actresses

Abrams, Dennis. Gregory Hines: Entertainer. 2008. (ENG., Illus.). 98p. (gr. 6-12). lib. bdg. 35.00 (978-0-7910-9718-2(8), P145796, Facts On File) Infobase Holdings, Inc.

Adams, Colleen. Keira Knightley. 2009. (Stars in the Spotlight Ser.). 32p. (gr. 4-4). 47.90 (978-1-60853-203-2(8), PowerKids Pr.) Rosen Publishing Group, Inc., The.

—Kelly Clarkson. 2009. (Stars in the Spotlight Ser.). 32p. (gr. 4-4). 47.90 (978-1-60853-204-9(6), PowerKids Pr.) Rosen Publishing Group, Inc., The.

Bjornlund, Lydia D. Angelina Jolie. 2010. (Modern Role Models Ser.). (Illus.). 64p. (YA). (gr. 7-12). 22.95 (978-1-4222-0504-4(5)) Mason Crest.

Borgert-Spaniol, Megan. Hedy Lamarr: Reimagining Radio. 2017. (STEM Superstar Women Ser.). (ENG., Illus.). 32p. (J). (gr. 3-6). lib. bdg. 32.79 (978-1-5321-1282-9(3), 27606, Checkerboard Library) ABDO Publishing Co.

Boshier, Rosa. Ronald Reagan: 40th US President, 1 vol. 2013. (Essential Lives Set 8 Ser.). (ENG.). 112p. (YA). (gr. 6-12). lib. bdg. 41.36 (978-1-61783-895-8(0), 6767, Essential Library) ABDO Publishing Co.

Brown, Don. Mack Made Movies. Brown, Don, illus. 2008. (Illus.). (J). (gr. 2-5). 25.95 incl. audio compact disk (978-1-4301-0432-2(5)); pap. 16.95 incl. audio (978-1-4301-0431-5(7)); pap. 39.95 incl. audio compact disk (978-1-4301-0436-0(8));Set. pap. 37.95 incl. audio (978-1-4301-0433-9(3)) Live Oak Media.

Brown, Jonatha A. Steven Spielberg, 1 vol. 2004. (Gente Que Hay Que Conocer (People We Should Know) Ser.). 24p. (gr. 2-4). (SPA.). pap. 9.15 (978-0-8368-4592-1(7), 7832285f-eedc-4679-aae5-f9b7a496ef82); (SPA.). lib. bdg. 24.67 (978-0-8368-4585-3(4), 3d84b2cc-727e-4137-8f4b-a9cf9bc2fd8e); (ENG., Illus.). pap. 9.15 (978-0-8368-4476-4(9), 51833d36-af77-4bc2-99c8-a04f28687352); (ENG., Illus.). lib. bdg. 24.67 (978-0-8368-4469-6(6), 8bb8aef9-8957-4145-93f5-3ed4d37aedfe) Stevens, Gareth Publishing LLLP. (Weekly Reader Leveled Readers).

Cartlidge, Cherese. Jennifer Hudson, 1 vol. 2011. (People in the News Ser.). (ENG., Illus.). 96p. (gr. 7-7). lib. bdg. 41.03 (978-1-4205-0607-5(2), acf0d5fd-fe32-4165-a7c0-6407ff4c7800, Lucent Pr.) Greenhaven Publishing LLC.

Custance, Petrice. Emma Watson. 2018. (Superstars! Ser.). (ENG., Illus.). 32p. (J). (gr. 4-4). (978-0-7787-4834-2(0)); pap. (978-0-7787-4860-1(X)) Crabtree Publishing Co.

Dakers, Diane. Oprah Winfrey: Media Legend & Inspiration to Millions. 2015. (Crabtree Groundbreaker Biographies Ser.). (ENG., Illus.). 112p. (J). (gr. 6-6). (978-0-7787-2559-6(6)) Crabtree Publishing Co.

Davidson, Avelyn. Elle Fanning, 1 vol. 2012. (Rising Stars Ser.). (ENG., Illus.). 32p. (J). (gr. 1-1). 27.93 (978-1-4339-7280-5(8), ec5971a8-0b58-4991-a0fe-56e884c3d313); pap. 11.50 (978-1-4339-7281-2(6), b503aa61-1717-4f05-9e35-cece1ce99aea) Stevens, Gareth Publishing LLLP.

—KeKe Palmer, 1 vol. 2012. (Rising Stars Ser.). (ENG., Illus.). 32p. (J). (gr. 1-1). 27.93 (978-1-4339-7287-4(5), 19dd6a07-21c0-4cb6-8d9f-3d5c2c223f50); pap. 11.50 (978-1-4339-7284-3(0), 9c292b37-b419-48aa-8b25-ea140055e387) Stevens, Gareth Publishing LLLP.

Doeden, Matt. Will Smith. 2007. (Illus.). 112p. (J). pap. 9.95 (978-0-8225-7064-6(5)) Lerner Publishing Group.

Dougherty, Terri. Jennifer Lopez: Entertainer, 1 vol. 2007. (Twentieth Century's Most Influential Hispanics Ser.). (ENG., Illus.). 104p. (gr. 7-10). 41.03 (978-1-4205-0021-9(X), fa12b1bc-34f1-4cda-ac35-ec6191d53bfc, Lucent Pr.) Greenhaven Publishing LLC.

Dudley Gold, Susan. Kathryn Bigelow, 1 vol. 2014. (Great Filmmakers Ser.). (ENG.). 80p. (YA). (gr. 7-7). lib. bdg. 37.36 (978-1-62712-939-8(1), ac5e09e6-6bad-484f-abb6-b010400a2f36) Cavendish Square Publishing LLC.

—Sofia Coppola, 1 vol. 2014. (Great Filmmakers Ser.). (ENG.). 80p. (YA). (gr. 7-7). lib. bdg. 37.36 (978-1-62712-945-9(6), aef0b32c-6f48-413c-ab71-f389d1a6ac6e) Cavendish Square Publishing LLC.

Edge, Laura B. Steven Spielberg: Director of Blockbuster Films, 1 vol. 2009. (People to Know Today Ser.). (ENG., Illus.). 128p. (gr. 6-7). lib. bdg. 35.93 (978-0-7660-2888-3(7), ba11e0a8-9d3d-4698-a8d8-eb8845991838) Enslow Publishing, LLC.

Fleischman, Sid. Sir Charlie: Chaplin, the Funniest Man in the World. 2010. (ENG.). 288p. (J). (gr. 4-18). 19.99 (978-0-06-189640-8(3), Greenwillow Bks.) HarperCollins Pubs.

Flor Ada, Alma & Campoy, F. Isabel, contrib. by. Pasos. (Literature Collection of Puertas Al Sol Ser.).Tr. of Steps. (SPA.). 32p. (J). (gr. k-6). pap. 13.95 (978-1-59437-704-4(9)) Santillana USA Publishing Co., Inc.

—Voces. (Literature Collection of Puertas Al Sol Ser.).Tr. of Voices. (SPA.). 32p. (J). (gr. k-6). pap. 13.95 (978-1-59437-707-5(3)) Santillana USA Publishing Co., Inc.

Furstinger, Nancy. Today's 12 Hottest Movie Superstars. 2015. (Today's Superstars Ser.). (ENG., Illus.). 32p. (J). (gr. 3-6). 32.80 (978-1-63235-019-0(X), 11576, 12-Story Library) Bookstaves, LLC.

Gagne, Tammy. What It's Like to Be Cameron Diaz. 2012. (SPA & ENG., Illus.). 32p. (J). lib. bdg. 25.70 (978-1-61228-323-4(3)) Mitchell Lane Pubs.

Galaxy of Superstars. 2005. (Galaxy of Superstars Ser.). (gr. 6-12). 375.00 (978-0-7910-9145-6(7), Facts On File) Infobase Holdings, Inc.

Gogerly, Liz. Film Stars, 1 vol. 2012. (Celebrity Secrets Ser.). (ENG., Illus.). 24p. (J). (gr. 5-6). pap. 9.25 (978-1-4488-7084-4(4), eb04e1d6-868f-4340-b0cc-50b1388423a6); lib. bdg. 26.27 (978-1-4488-7037-0(2), 07338316-b48b-4242-865e-3f0db0440d85) Rosen Publishing Group, Inc., The. (PowerKids Pr.).

González, Juan Carlos. Francois Truffaut -una vida hecha Cine. 2005. (SPA.). 150p. (YA). (978-958-30-1686-8(1)) Panamericana Editorial.

Gosling, Maureen, et al. You Can Be a Woman Movie Maker. l.t. ed. 2003. (Illus.). 80p. (J). 19.95 incl. DVD (978-1-880599-64-8(3)); pap. 14.95 incl. DVD (978-1-880599-63-1(5)) Cascade Pass, Inc.

Grabowski, John F. Johnny Depp, 1 vol. 2011. (People in the News Ser.). (ENG., Illus.). 104p. (gr. 7-7). 41.03 (978-1-4205-0292-3(1), ef632e0c-c4cf-467b-97c6-ad276542bcda, Lucent Pr.) Greenhaven Publishing LLC.

Graziano, Jim. Johnny Depp. 2008. (Pop Culture Ser.). (Illus.). 64p. (YA). (gr. 3-7). lib. bdg. 22.95 (978-1-4222-0200-5(3)) Mason Crest.

Hansen, Grace. George Lucas: Filmmaker & Creator of Star Wars. 2017. (History Maker Biographies (Abdo Kids Jumbo) Ser.). (ENG., Illus.). 24p. (J). (gr. -1-2). lib. bdg. 32.79 (978-1-5321-0425-1(1), 26551, Abdo Kids) ABDO Publishing Co.

Hart, Haley. I (Heart) Zac Efron. 2010. 144p. (YA). (gr. 7-18). pap. 4.95 (978-1-60747-707-5(6), Dove Books and Audio) Phoenix Bks., Inc.

Hasday, Judy L. Extraordinary People: Extraordinary People in the Movies. 2003. (Extraordinary People Ser.). (ENG., Illus.). 288p. (J). (gr. 6-18). 40.00 (978-0-516-22348-3(8), Children's Pr.) Scholastic Library Publishing.

Henricks, Dana. George Clooney. (Sharing the American Dream Ser.). 64p. (YA). (gr. 7-12). 2009. 22.95 (978-1-4222-0600-3(9)) 2007. pap. 9.95 (978-1-4222-0741-3(2)) Mason Crest.

Herringshaw, DeAnn. Dorothy Dandridge: Singer & Actress, 1 vol. 2011. (Essential Lives Set 6 Ser.). (ENG., Illus.). 112p. (J). (gr. 6-12). lib. bdg. 41.36 (978-1-61714-779-1(6), 6723, Essential Library) ABDO Publishing Co.

Hopman, Philip. For Audrey with Love: Audrey Hepburn & Givenchy. De Clercq-Foley, Ann, tr. 2018. (ENG., Illus.). 32p. (J). (gr. -1-3). 17.95 (978-0-7358-4314-1(7)) North-South Bks., Inc.

Jensen Shaffer, Jody & Who HQ. Who Is Jackie Chan? Copeland, Gregory, illus. 2020. (Who Was? Ser.). 112p. (J). (gr. 3-7). 6.99 (978-1-5247-9162-9(8)); 15.99 (978-1-5247-9163-6(6)) Penguin Young Readers Group. (Penguin Workshop).

Johns, Michael-Anne. School Cool. 2009. (Illus.). 48p. (J). (978-0-545-15901-2(6)) Scholastic, Inc.

Johnson, Robin. Kristen Stewart. 2010. (Superstars! Ser.). (ENG.). 32p. (J). (gr. 3-6). lib. bdg. (978-0-7787-7248-4(9)) Crabtree Publishing Co.

—Robert Pattinson. 2010. (Superstars! Ser.). (ENG., Illus.). 32p. (J). (gr. 3-6). lib. bdg. (978-0-7787-7251-4(9)) Crabtree Publishing Co.

Kawa, Katie. Brie Larson Is Captain Marvel(r), 1 vol. 2019. (Human Behind the Hero Ser.). (ENG.). 32p. (gr. 1-2). pap. 11.50 (978-1-5382-4819-5(0), 075d6473-0a02-45c0-8a54-1dbadc28f4ef) Stevens, Gareth Publishing LLLP.

—Scarlett Johansson Is Black Widow(r), 1 vol. 2019. (Human Behind the Hero Ser.). (ENG.). 32p. (gr. 1-2). pap. 11.50 (978-1-5382-4835-5(2), f665887e-abbe-4229-9e49-833b6940be24) Stevens, Gareth Publishing LLLP.

Latinos in the Limelight. 2005. (Latinos in the Limelight Ser.). (gr. 5-8). 165.00 (978-0-7910-8728-2(X), Facts On File) Infobase Holdings, Inc.

Lawrence, Katherine. Jean-Claude Van Damme. 2009. (Martial Arts Masters Ser.). 112p. (gr. 5-5). 63.90 (978-1-61514-373-3(4)) Rosen Publishing Group, Inc., The.

Lee, T. S. The Stephen Spielberg Story: The First Stephen Spielberg Comic Biogrhaphy. 2010. 177p. (J). pap. 14.95 (978-0-9819542-7-1(8)) DASANBOOKS.

Lewis, J. Patrick. Michelangelo's World. 2008. (ENG., Illus.). 40p. (J). (gr. 2-5). 17.95 (978-1-56846-167-0(4), 22052, Creative Editions) Creative Co., The.

Lunzer, Lee. Betty Grable Paper Dolls. Lunzer, Lee, illus. 2007. (ENG., Illus.). 16p. pap. 12.00 (978-0-9790668-7-0(5)) Paper Studio Pr.

Lynette, Rachel. Tim Burton: Filmmaker, 1 vol. 2006. (Innovators Ser.). (ENG., Illus.). 64p. (gr. 4-8). lib. bdg. 30.38 (978-0-7377-3556-7(2), 1ad2cf62-72e3-4f4c-93bd-374413e6de43, KidHaven Publishing) Greenhaven Publishing LLC.

MacKay, Jennifer. James Cameron, 1 vol. 2013. (People in the News Ser.). (ENG., Illus.). 96p. (gr. 7-7). lib. bdg. 41.03 (978-1-4205-0885-7(7), 3788c2df-1c84-481a-8699-8fcb4f5befbc, Lucent Pr.) Greenhaven Publishing LLC.

Madan, Fredric C. Greer Garson Paper Dolls. Madan, Fredric C. & Ernst, Clara, illus. 2007. (ENG.). 16p. pap. 12.00 (978-0-9790668-6-3(7)) Paper Studio Pr.

Magid, Jennifer. Angelina Jolie, 1 vol. 2008. (Today's Superstars Ser.). (ENG.). 32p. (YA). (gr. 3-3). lib. bdg. 34.60 (978-0-8368-9234-5(8), ba7517f1-566f-4076-8a1b-bba28c1aeeb3) Stevens, Gareth Publishing LLLP.

Mara, Wil. Clint Eastwood, 1 vol. 2014. (Great Filmmakers Ser.). (ENG.). 80p. (YA). (gr. 7-7). lib. bdg. 37.36 (978-1-62712-948-0(0), 78f94036-5f74-4da1-90b2-4302cb4210be) Cavendish Square Publishing LLC.

—James Cameron, 1 vol. 2014. (Great Filmmakers Ser.). (ENG.). 80p. (YA). (gr. 7-7). lib. bdg. 37.36 (978-1-62712-951-0(0), 785f8712-26c4-4ebf-9073-450fe00b9f5f) Cavendish Square Publishing LLC.

—Peter Jackson, 1 vol. 2014. (Great Filmmakers Ser.). (ENG., Illus.). 80p. (YA). (gr. 7-7). lib. bdg. 37.36 (978-1-62712-942-8(1), 22307fb1-f1e8-4fa0-9d66-ca9558e19a87) Cavendish Square Publishing LLC.

—Rookie Biographies: Steven Spielberg. 2005. (Rookie Biographies Ser.). (ENG., Illus.). 32p. (gr. 1-2). 20.50 (978-0-516-21842-7(5), Children's Pr.) Scholastic Library Publishing.

—Steven Spielberg, 1 vol. 2014. (Great Filmmakers Ser.). (ENG.). 80p. (YA). (gr. 7-7). lib. bdg. 37.36 (978-1-62712-936-7(7), c80c73ce-f5bb-43fd-8681-5f7be59c143e) Cavendish Square Publishing LLC.

Marcovitz, Hal. Owen & Luke Wilson. 2007. (Popular Culture: A View from the Paparazzi Ser.). (Illus.). 64p. (YA). (gr. 3-7). pap. 7.95 (978-1-4222-0365-1(4)) Mason Crest.

Markegard, Blake. John Cena. 2014. (Wrestling Superstars Ser.). (ENG.). 24p. (J). (gr. 3-7). 26.95 (978-1-62617-141-1(6), Epic Bks.) Bellwether Media.

Marx, Christy. Jet Li. 2009. (Martial Arts Masters Ser.). 112p. (gr. 5-5). 63.90 (978-1-61514-374-0(2)) Rosen Publishing Group, Inc., The.

—The Wachowski Brothers: Creators of the Matrix. 2009. (Famous Families Ser.). 48p. (gr. 5-5). 53.00 (978-1-61512-511-1(6)) Rosen Publishing Group, Inc., The.

Mattern, Joanne. Keke Palmer. 2010. (Robbie Reader Ser.). (Illus.). 32p. (J). (gr. 2-5). lib. bdg. 25.70 (978-1-58415-896-7(4)) Mitchell Lane Pubs.

—Tyler Perry. 2012. (J). lib. bdg. 25.70 (978-1-61228-334-0(9)) Mitchell Lane Pubs.

Menkes Kushner, Jill. Johnny Depp: Movie Megastar, 1 vol. 2009. (Hot Celebrity Biographies Ser.). (ENG., Illus.). 48p. (gr. 5-7). pap. 11.53 (978-0-7660-3631-4(6), c68d07e5-3a09-42ff-bff4-4c3fbe481c97, Enslow Elementary) Enslow Publishing, LLC.

Miller, Kat. I Love Robert Pattinson, 1 vol. 2010. (Fan Club Ser.). (ENG.). 24p. (gr. 2-3). lib. bdg. 27.27 (978-1-61533-057-7(7), ceef3ced-9367-4bd4-9077-f9c1231d1d91); (Illus.). (J). pap. 9.15 (978-1-61533-058-4(5), 271d51df-7a48-4257-bfbf-a987d9ec01e3) Rosen Publishing Group, Inc., The. (Windmill Bks.).

Mingo, Norman. Alice Faye Paper Dolls: Glamorous Movie Star Paper Dolls & Costumes. Mingo, Norman & Ernst, Clara, illus. 2007. 8p. pap. 12.00 (978-0-9795053-0-0(5)) Paper Studio Pr.

—Bette Davis Paper Dolls. Taliadoros, Jenny, ed. Mingo, Norman & Ernst, Clara, illus. 2007. (ENG.). 16p. pap. 12.00 (978-0-9790668-2-5(4)) Paper Studio Pr.

—Deanna Durbin Paper Dolls. Mingo, Norman & Emt, Clara, illus. 2007. 16p. pap. 12.00 (978-0-9790668-5-6(9)) Paper Studio Pr.

—Rita Hayworth Paper Dolls. Taliadoros, Jenny, ed. Mingo, Norman & Ernst, Clara, illus. 2006. 16p. pap. 12.00 (978-0-9790668-0-1(8)) Paper Studio Pr.

Mochizuki, Ken. Be Water, My Friend: The Early Years of Bruce Lee, 1 vol. Lee, Dom, illus. 2006. (ENG.). 32p. (J). (gr.

1-6). pap. 11.95 *(978-1-62014-164-9(7),* leelowbooks) Lee & Low Bks., Inc.

Moening, Kate. Kathleen Kennedy: Movie Producer. 2019. (Women Leading the Way Ser.). (ENG., Illus.). 24p. (J). (gr. k-3). pap. 7.99 *(978-1-61891-723-2(4),* 12304); lib. bdg. 26.95 *(978-1-64487-100-3(9))* Bellwether Media. (Blastoff! Readers).

Murphy, Maggie. Johnny Depp, 1 vol. 2011. (Movie Superstars Ser.). (ENG., Illus.). 32p. (J). (gr. 4-4). 28.93 *(978-1-4488-2566-0(0),* b5dd275b-d832-4a8f-a471-ff05df4c8053, PowerKids Pr.) Rosen Publishing Group, Inc., The.

—Miley Cyrus: Rock Star, 1 vol. 2010. (Young & Famous Ser.). (ENG., Illus.). 24p. (J). (gr. 1-2). 26.27 *(978-1-4488-0643-0(7),* 956473f8-e7ee-43d7-9aeb-b0c0e055fe7c); pap. 9.85 *(978-1-4488-1799-3(4),* f0e8ec27-d6b2-42ac-a676-611f61c40f46, PowerKids Pr.) Rosen Publishing Group, Inc., The.

—Reese Witherspoon, 1 vol. 2011. (Movie Superstars Ser.). (ENG., Illus.). 32p. (J). (gr. 4-4). pap. 11.00 *(978-1-4488-2725-1(6),* 64ffedc2-328b-496d-94d9-1ed914f849ae); lib. bdg. 28.93 *(978-1-4488-2568-4(7),* 763ce019-29b0-4036-a20a-6efe2bc56468) Rosen Publishing Group, Inc., The. (PowerKids Pr.).

Nagle, Jeanne. Jennifer Hudson, 1 vol. 2008. (Who's Your Idol? Ser.). (ENG., Illus.). 48p. (J). (gr. 5-5). lib. bdg. 34.47 *(978-1-4042-1372-2(4),* 3ef5c3a9-5cb6-43cd-88e3-ab4dc364f611) Rosen Publishing Group, Inc., The.

Nelson, Maria. Robert Pattinson, 1 vol. 2011. (Rising Stars Ser.). (ENG.). 32p. (J). (gr. 1-1). pap. 11.50 *(978-1-4339-5900-4(3),* 3d2bb9f6-8890-44ed-a1ce-72db276866a7); lib. bdg. 27.93 *(978-1-4339-5898-4(8),* 637ae504-22f8-4d7f-8afa-a7d6d8bbf68e) Stevens, Gareth Publishing LLLP.

Norwich, Grace. Daniel Radcliffe: No Ordinary Wizard. 2008. (ENG.). 128p. (J). (gr. 4-9). pap. 5.99 *(978-1-4169-6771-2(0),* Simon Spotlight) Simon Spotlight.

Novesky, Amy. Mary Blair's Unique Flair: The Girl Who Became One of the Disney Legends. 2019. (ENG., Illus.). 40p. (J). (gr. 1-3). 17.99 *(978-1-4847-5720-8(3),* Disney Press Books) Disney Publishing Worldwide.

Omoth, Tyler. Jennifer Lawrence: Movie Star. 2017. (Superstar Stories Ser.). (ENG.). 24p. (J). (gr. 3-6). lib. bdg. 32.79 *(978-1-5038-1994-8(9),* 211870) Child's World, Inc, The.

Orr, Tamra. Robert Pattison. 2010. (Blue Banner Biography Ser.). (Illus.). 32p. (YA). (gr. 4-7). lib. bdg. 25.70 *(978-1-58415-905-6(7))* Mitchell Lane Pubs.

O'Shea, Mick. Beyond District 12: The Stars of the Hunger Games. 2012. (ENG., Illus.). 160p. pap. 16.95 *(978-0-85965-487-6(7))* Plexus Publishing, Ltd. GBR. Dist: Publishers Group West (PGW).

Owings, Lisa. Marilyn Monroe: Hollywood Icon, 1 vol. 2012. (Lives Cut Short Set 2 Ser.). (ENG.). 112p. (YA). (gr. 6-12). lib. bdg. 41.36 *(978-1-61783-481-3(5),* 11197, Essential Library) ABDO Publishing Co.

Parvis, Sarah. Taylor Lautner. 2010. (ENG.). 80p. 5.99 *(978-0-7407-9962-4(2))* Andrews McMeel Publishing.

Paul Yoo. Shining Star: the Anna May Wong Story, 1 vol. 2009. (ENG., Illus.). 32p. (J). (gr. 1-6). pap. 11.95 *(978-1-62014-257-8(0),* leelowbooks) Lee & Low Bks., Inc.

Peppas, Lynn. Zac Efron. 2010. (Superstars! Ser.). (ENG., Illus.). 32p. (J). (gr. 3-6). lib. bdg. *(978-0-7787-7254-5(3))* Crabtree Publishing Co.

Pollack, Pam, et al. Who Is George Lucas? Hammond, Ted, illus. 2014. (Who Was? Ser.). 112p. (J). (gr. 3-7). 5.99 *(978-0-448-47947-7(8),* Penguin Workshop) Penguin Young Readers Group.

—Who Was Alfred Hitchcock? Moore, Jonathan, illus. 2014. (Who Was? Ser.). 112p. (J). (gr. 3-7). pap. 5.99 *(978-0-448-48237-8(1),* Penguin Workshop) Penguin Young Readers Group.

Powers, Tom. Steven Spielberg. (Just the Facts Biographies Ser.). (Illus.). 112p. 2004. (ENG.). (gr. 5-12). 27.93 *(978-0-8225-2473-1(2))* 2003. (J). (gr. 6-18). pap. 7.95 *(978-0-8225-9694-3(6))* Lerner Publishing Group.

Rechner, Amy. Movie Director. 2019. (Cool Careers Ser.). (ENG., Illus.). 24p. (J). (gr. 3-7). lib. bdg. 26.95 *(978-1-64487-063-1(0),* Torque Bks.) Bellwether Media.

Richardson, Adele D. The Story of Disney. 2003. (Built for Success Ser.). (Illus.). 48p. (J). 19.95 *(978-1-58340-291-7(8))* Black Rabbit Bks.

Sanchez Vegara, Maria Isabel. Audrey Hepburn, Volume 7. Arrazola, Amaia, illus. 2017. (Little People, BIG DREAMS Ser.: 7). (ENG.). 32p. (J). (gr. -1-2). 15.99 *(978-1-78603-053-5(5),* Frances Lincoln Children's Bks.) Quarto Publishing Group UK GBR. Dist: Hachette Bk. Group.

Sapet, Kerrily. Halle Berry. (Transcending Race in America Ser.). (Illus.). 64p. (J). 2010. (gr. 4-8). 22.95 *(978-1-4222-1612-5(8))* 2009. (gr. 5-18). pap. 9.95 *(978-1-4222-1626-2(8))* Mason Crest.

—Halle Berry: Academy Award Winning Actress. 2012. (Transcending Race Ser.). 64p. (J). (gr. 5). 22.95 *(978-1-4222-2729-9(4))* Mason Crest.

Schuman, Michael A. Halle Berry: A Biography of an Oscar-Winning Actress, 1 vol. 2013. (African-American Icons Ser.). (ENG.). 104p. (gr. 6-7). lib. bdg. 30.61 *(978-0-7660-3993-3(5),* 2f964dc2-7e18-48c3-94eb-9e4e68409bd6) Enslow Publishing, LLC.

—Robert Pattinson: Shining Star, 1 vol. 2012. (Hot Celebrity Biographies Ser.). (ENG., Illus.). 48p. (gr. 5-7). pap. 11.53 *(978-1-59845-284-6(3),* bb7ddf14-ee71-4a3e-a7b6-770baebedf85); lib. bdg. 27.93 *(978-0-7660-3872-1(6),* bb5546f7-6954-4777-82b7-99aeb83fcca9) Enslow Publishing, LLC.

Shea, Therese M. Before Ronald Reagan Was President, 1 vol. 2018. (Before They Were President Ser.). (ENG.). 24p. (gr. 2-3). lib. bdg. 24.27 *(978-1-5382-2911-8(0),* dc9577f9-9282-4610-8848-188518851e6d) Stevens, Gareth Publishing LLLP.

Sheen, Barbara. J. J. Abrams, 1 vol. 2015. (People in the News Ser.). (ENG., Illus.). 104p. (gr. 7-7). 41.03 *(978-1-4205-1249-6(8),* 0ec43891-8e0f-4c2f-af93-f5400570308a, Lucent Pr.) Greenhaven Publishing LLC.

Simoni, Suzanne. Fantastic Female Filmmakers, 1 vol. 2008. (Women's Hall of Fame Ser.: 12). (ENG., Illus.). 122p. (J). (gr. 5-8). pap. 10.95 *(978-1-897187-36-4(X))* Second Story Pr. CAN. Dist: Orca Bk. Pubs. USA.

Snyder, Gail. Jake Gyllenhaal. 2008. (Pop Culture Ser.). (Illus.). 64p. (YA). (gr. 3-7). lib. bdg. 22.95 *(978-1-4222-0203-6(8))* Mason Crest.

Spence, Kelly. Emma Stone. 2015. (Superstars! Ser.). (ENG., Illus.). 32p. (J). (gr. 4-4). *(978-0-7787-8078-6(3))* Crabtree Publishing Co.

Spencer, Liv. The Miranda Cosgrove & iCarly Spectacular! Unofficial & Unstoppable. 2010. (ENG., Illus.). 142p. (J). (gr. 4-7). pap. 14.95 *(978-1-55022-929-5(X),* a320d589-d63c-4e2d-af5b-ec96858d718a) ECW Pr. CAN. Dist: Baker & Taylor Publisher Services (BTPS).

Spinner, Stephanie. Who Is Steven Spielberg? 2013. (Who Is...? Ser.). lib. bdg. 16.00 *(978-0-606-34157-8(9))* Turtleback.

Stair, Nancy L. Michelle Yeoh. 2009. (Martial Arts Masters Ser.). 112p. (gr. 5-5). 63.90 *(978-1-61514-375-7(0))* Rosen Publishing Group, Inc., The.

Stone, Adam. John Cena. 2011. (Pro Wrestling Champions Ser.). (ENG., Illus.). 24p. (J). (gr. 3-7). lib. bdg. 26.95 *(978-1-60014-636-7(8),* Torque Bks.) Bellwether Media.

Stone, Amy M. Jim Carrey, 1 vol. 2007. (Today's Superstars Ser.). (ENG., Illus.). 32p. (gr. 3-3). lib. bdg. 34.60 *(978-0-8368-8197-4(4),* b2bdc58a-0929-4e4d-803e-b856d13c1149) Stevens, Gareth Publishing LLLP.

Sutcliffe, Jane & Walt Disney Company Staff. Walt Disney. 2009. (History Maker Biographies Ser.). (gr. 3-6). 26.60 *(978-1-58013-704-1(0),* Lerner Pubns.) Lerner Publishing Group.

Taliadoros, Jenny, ed. Doris Day Paper Dolls. 2007. (ENG., Illus.). 16p. pap. 12.00 *(978-0-9790668-4-9(0))* Paper Studio Pr.

Thomas, William David. Johnny Depp, 1 vol. 2007. (Today's Superstars Ser.). (ENG., Illus.). 32p. (gr. 3-3). lib. bdg. 34.60 *(978-0-8368-7650-5(4),* a3a191af-b45e-4d6f-ac86-763b46605f47) Stevens, Gareth Publishing LLLP.

Toler, Pamela D. Matt Damon. 2012. (Role Model Entertainers Ser.). 64p. (J). (gr. 7). 22.95 *(978-1-4222-2718-3(9))* Mason Crest.

Torres, Jennifer. Kate Hudson. 2005. (Blue Banner Biography Ser.). (Illus.). 32p. (J). (gr. 3-8). lib. bdg. 25.70 *(978-1-58415-381-8(4))* Mitchell Lane Pubs.

Tracy, Kathleen. Johnny Depp. 2007. (Blue Banner Biography Ser.). (Illus.). 32p. (J). (gr. 4-7). lib. bdg. 25.70 *(978-1-58415-614-7(7))* Mitchell Lane Pubs.

Uschan, Michael V. Halle Berry, 1 vol. 2012. (People in the News Ser.). (ENG., Illus.). 104p. (J). (gr. 7-7). lib. bdg. 41.03 *(978-1-4205-0817-8(2),* b3d6dfc9-1d9a-4841-8635-7b33e5b26926, Lucent Pr.) Greenhaven Publishing LLC.

—Tyler Perry, 1 vol. 2010. (People in the News Ser.). (ENG.). 96p. (gr. 7-7). 41.03 *(978-1-4205-0309-8(X),* 8f0a4aa0-35ed-4241-9d42-57b3b698e2d5, Lucent Pr.) Greenhaven Publishing LLC.

Valliant, Regina. Judy Garland Cut-Out Dolls. Valliant, Regina & Lunzer, Lee, illus. 2007. (ENG.). 16p. pap. 12.00 *(978-0-9790668-9-4(1))* Paper Studio Pr.

Watson, Stephanie. Heath Ledger: Talented Actor, 1 vol. 2010. (Lives Cut Short Set 1 Ser.). (ENG., Illus.). 112p. (YA). (gr. 6-12). lib. bdg. 41.36 *(978-1-60453-789-5(2),* 11187, Essential Library) ABDO Publishing Co.

Weber, Terri Smith. Halle Berry: Fighting for First. 2003. (J). pap. *(978-0-9740180-8-9(2));* lib. bdg. *(978-0-9740180-7-2(4))* Panda Publishing, L.L.C. (Bios for Kids).

White, Katherine. The Wayans Brothers. 2009. (Famous Families Ser.). 48p. (gr. 5-5). 53.00 *(978-1-61512-512-8(4))* Rosen Publishing Group, Inc., The.

Williams, Mel. Stars in the Arena: Meet the Hotties of the Hunger Games. 2012. (ENG., Illus.). 48p. (YA). (gr. 7). pap. 9.99 *(978-1-4424-5363-0(X),* Simon Pulse) Simon Pulse.

Yasuda, Anita. James Cameron. 2010. (Remarkable People Ser.). (Illus.). 24p. (J). (gr. 4-6). pap. 11.95 *(978-1-61690-176-9(4));* lib. bdg. 25.70 *(978-1-61690-175-2(6))* Weigl Pubs., Inc.

—Johnny Depp. 2012. (J). 27.13 *(978-1-61913-536-9(1))* Weigl Pubs., Inc.

—Mike Meyers. 2012. (J). *(978-1-61913-587-1(6));* pap. *(978-1-61913-593-2(0))* Weigl Pubs., Inc.

Yoo, Paula. The Story of Movie Star Anna May Wong, 1 vol. Wang, Lin, illus. 2019. (Story Of Ser.). (ENG.). 64p. (J). (gr. 4-8). 10.95 *(978-1-62014-853-2(6),* leelowbooks) Lee & Low Bks., Inc.

MOTION PICTURES—FICTION

Abela, Deborah. Mission: Hollywood. O'Connor, George, illus. 2007. (Spy Force Ser.: 4). (ENG.). 240p. (J). (gr. 3-7). pap. 10.99 *(978-1-4169-3969-6(5),* Aladdin) Simon & Schuster Children's Publishing.

Acton, Vanessa. Director's Cut. 2016. (Atlas of Cursed Places Ser.). (ENG.). 104p. (YA). (gr. 6-12). lib. bdg. 26.65 *(978-1-5124-1324-3(0),* db233274-947c-4149-bc01-a3c095c9c457, Darby Creek) Lerner Publishing Group.

Appelt, Kathi. Bat Jamboree. Sweet, Melissa, illus. 2004. 17.00 *(978-0-7569-4074-4(5))* Perfection Learning Corp.

Appleton, Victor. The Moving Picture Boys on the Coast or Showing up the Perils of the Deep. 2004. reprint ed. pap. 24.95 *(978-1-4179-1612-2(5))* Kessinger Publishing, LLC.

—Tom Swift & his Wizard Camera. 2005. 26.95 *(978-1-4218-1507-7(9));* 196p. pap. 11.95 *(978-1-4218-1607-4(5))* 1st World Publishing, Inc. (1st World Library - Literary Society).

—Tom Swift & His Wizard Camera or Thril. 2006. pap. *(978-1-4065-0912-0(4))* Dodo Pr.

Arnold, Ted. Fly Guy & the Alienzz. 2019. (Scholastic Readers Ser.). (SPA.). 29p. (J). (gr. k-1). 13.89 *(978-0-87617-739-6(9))* Penworthy Co., LLC, The.

Arnold, Tedd. Fly Guy & the Alienzz (Fly Guy #18) 2018. (Fly Guy Ser.: 18). (ENG., Illus.). 32p. (J). (gr. k-2). 6.99 *(978-0-545-66318-2(0),* Cartwheel Bks.) Scholastic, Inc.

Ashworth, Sherry. Close-Up. 2006. (ENG.). 256p. (J). (gr. 7). pap. 11.95 *(978-1-4169-0474-8(3),* Simon & Schuster Children's) Simon & Schuster, Ltd. GBR. Dist: Simon & Schuster, Inc.

Beecroft, Simon. R2-D2 & Friends. 2008. (Star Wars DK Readers Level 2 Ser.). (Illus.). 32p. lib. bdg. 13.55 *(978-1-4364-5044-7(6))* Turtleback.

Blume, Lesley M. M. The Wondrous Journals of Dr. Wendell Wellington Wiggins. Foote, David, illus. 2013. (ENG.). 256p. (J). (gr. 3-7). pap. 8.99 *(978-0-375-87218-1(3),* Knopf Bks. for Young Readers) Random Hse. Children's Bks.

Boyle Crompton, Laurie. Freaky in Fresno, 1 vol. 2020. (ENG.). 352p. (YA). 18.99 *(978-0-310-76747-3(4))* Blink.

Bracegirdle, P. J. Sinister Scenes. (Joy of Spooking Ser.). (ENG.). 320p. (J). (gr. 3-7). 2012. pap. 6.99 *(978-1-4169-3421-9(9))* 2011. 15.99 *(978-1-4169-3420-2(0))* McElderry, Margaret K. Bks. (McElderry, Margaret K. Bks.).

Brashear, Amy. The Incredible True Story of the Making of the Eve of Destruction. 2019. (ENG., Illus.). 312p. (YA). (gr. 9). pap. 10.99 *(978-1-64129-048-7(X),* Soho Teen) Soho Pr., Inc.

Carlson, Bryce. Wall- E: Out There. Luthi, Morgan, illus. 2010. (ENG.). 112p. (J). (gr. 3-6). pap. 9.99 *(978-1-60886-568-0(1))* BOOM! Studios.

Clement, Emily. Thea Stilton & the Hollywood Hoax. Pellizzari, Barbara & Balleello, Chiara, illus. 2015. 159p. (J). *(978-1-5182-1175-1(5))* Scholastic, Inc.

Coleman, K. R. Off Course. 2020. (Road Trip Ser.). (ENG.). 112p. (YA). (gr. 6-12). 26.65 *(978-1-5415-5688-1(7),* 9357fa30-bd0d-473d-a077-2f69a92d5727, Darby Creek) Lerner Publishing Group.

Coloma, Cindy Martinusen. Ruby Unscripted, 1 vol. 2009. (ENG.). 272p. (YA). (gr. 7-18). pap. 12.99 *(978-1-59554-356-1(2))* Nelson, Thomas Inc.

Conford, Ellen. Annabel the Actress Starring in Camping It Up. Andriani, Renee W., illus. 2005. (Annabel the Actress Ser.). 60p. (J). (gr. 2-5). 11.65 *(978-0-7569-5555-7(6))* Perfection Learning Corp.

—Annabel the Actress Starring in Camping It Up. Andriani, Renee W., illus. 2013. (ENG.). 64p. (J). (gr. 2-5). pap. 13.99 *(978-1-4814-0147-0(5),* Simon & Schuster Bks. For Young Readers) Simon & Schuster Bks. For Young Readers.

—Annabel the Actress Starring in Just a Little Extra. Andriani, Renee W., illus. 2013. (ENG.). 64p. (J). (gr. 4-6). pap. 13.99 *(978-1-4814-0148-7(3),* Simon & Schuster Bks. For Young Readers) Simon & Schuster Bks. For Young Readers.

Cousins, Lucy. Maisy Goes to the Movies. 2014. (Maisy First Experiences Ser.). lib. bdg. 17.20 *(978-0-606-35156-0(6))* Turtleback.

Cowley, Joy. Meanies Night Out. 2009. pap. 8.25 *(978-1-60559-229-9(3))* Hameray Publishing Group, Inc.

Darke, J. A. Do Not Watch. Evans, Neil, illus. 2016. (Spine Shivers Ser.). (ENG.). 128p. (J). (gr. 4-6). lib. bdg. 27.32 *(978-1-4965-3071-4(3),* 131947, Stone Arch Bks.) Capstone.

Davies, Beth. Rise of the Rogues. 2017. (Illus.). 48p. (J). *(978-1-5182-3600-6(6))* Dorling Kindersley Publishing, Inc.

—Team Batman. 2017. (Illus.). 24p. (J). *(978-1-5182-3634-1(0))* Dorling Kindersley Publishing, Inc.

De la Cruz, Melissa. Girl Stays in the Picture. 2009. (Girl Ser.: Bk. 1). (ENG.). 208p. (YA). (gr. 9-12). 26.19 *(978-1-4169-6096-6(1))* Simon & Schuster, Inc.

Dixon, Franklin W. Deception on the Set. 2015. (Hardy Boys Adventures Ser.: 8). (ENG., Illus.). 128p. (J). (gr. 3-7). pap. 6.99 *(978-1-4814-1406-7(2),* Aladdin) Simon & Schuster Children's Publishing.

—Movie Menace: Book One in the Deathstalker Trilogy. 2011. (Hardy Boys (All New) Undercover Brothers Ser.: 37). (ENG.). 176p. (J). (gr. 3-7). pap. 5.99 *(978-1-4424-0258-4(X),* Aladdin) Simon & Schuster Children's Publishing.

—Movie Mission: Book Two in the Deathstalker Trilogy, 38. 2011. (Hardy Boys (All New) Undercover Brothers Ser.: 38). (ENG.). 176p. (J). (gr. 3-7). pap. 6.99 *(978-1-4424-0266-9(0),* Aladdin) Simon & Schuster Children's Publishing.

Doctorow, Cory. Pirate Cinema. 2013. (ENG.). 384p. (YA). (gr. 7). pap. 18.99 *(978-0-7653-2909-7(3),* 90007453, Tor Teen) Doherty, Tom Assocs., LLC.

Dorling Kindersley Publishing Staff. The Adventures of C-3PO. 2014. (Star Wars DK Readers Level 2 Ser.). lib. bdg. 13.55 *(978-0-606-35324-3(0))* Turtleback.

Dower, Laura. The Slime That Would Not Die, 1. Schlafman, Dave, illus. 2009. (Monster Squad Ser.: 1). (ENG.). 144p. (J). (gr. 4-6). 17.44 *(978-0-448-44912-8(9))* Penguin Young Readers Group.

Duncan, Lois. Movie for Dogs. 2011. (ENG.). 208p. (J). (gr. 4-6). 18.69 *(978-0-545-10931-4(0))* Scholastic, Inc.

Encyclopaedia Britannica, Inc. Staff, compiled by. How the Elephant Got His Trunk. 2008. 49.95 *(978-1-59339-556-8(6))* Encyclopaedia Britannica, Inc.

Enderle, Dotti & McWilliam, Howard. Ghost Detectors Book 12: Monsters!, 1 vol. 2011. (Ghost Detectors Ser.). (ENG., Illus.). 80p. (J). (gr. 2-5). 35.64 *(978-1-61641-628-7(9),* 8824, Calico Chapter Bks.) ABDO Publishing Co.

Evans, Jonathan, adapted by. Meet the Cast! 2018. (Illus.). 32p. (J). *(978-0-316-48709-2(0))* Little Brown & Co.

Fleming, Candace. Strongheart: Wonder Dog of the Silver Screen. Rohmann, Eric, illus. 2018. 256p. (J). (gr. 3-7). 17.99 *(978-1-101-93410-4(7),* Schwartz & Wade Bks.) Random Hse. Children's Bks.

Fox, Hugh. Wobbley Zombies. 2004. 64p. (J). per. 5.95 *(978-1-930648-80-7(4))* Goose River Pr.

Gaiman, Neil. MirrorMask (children's Edition) McKean, Dave, illus. 2005. (ENG.). 80p. (J). (gr. 5). 16.99 *(978-0-06-082109-8(4),* HarperCollins) HarperCollins Pubs.

Gorgas, Paula Blais. Little Lost Leprechaun. 2006. (Illus.). 24p. (J). lib. bdg. 24.95 *(978-0-9778651-4-7(2))* Dragonfly Publishing, Inc.

Grace, N. B. Lights, Camera, Action! 14th ed. 2009. (ENG.). 128p. (J). pap. 4.99 *(978-1-4231-1609-7(7))* Disney Pr.

Hamilton, Sable. Free Spirit. 2015. (Stardust Stables Ser.). (ENG.). 160p. (J). (gr. 3-6). lib. bdg. 22.65 *(978-1-4342-9792-1(6),* 127174, Stone Arch Bks.) Capstone.

Handford, Martin. Where's Waldo? in Hollywood. 2007. (Where's Waldo? Ser.). (Illus.). 24p. (gr. 4-7). lib. bdg. 18.40 *(978-1-4178-2425-0(5))* Turtleback.

Harrison, Lisi. Dial L for Loser. 2008. (Clique Novels Ser.). 268p. 20.00 *(978-1-60686-291-9(X))* Perfection Learning Corp.

Hart, Kevin. Marcus Makes a Movie, 1. 2022. (Marcus Ser.). (ENG.). 202p. (J). (gr. 3-7). 19.96 ***(978-1-68505-541-7(9))*** Penworthy Co., LLC, The.

—Marcus Makes a Movie. Cooper, David, illus. (Marcus Ser.). (J). (gr. 3-7). 2022. 224p. pap. 8.99 *(978-0-593-17917-8(X),* Yearling) 2021. 208p. 16.99 *(978-0-593-17914-7(5),* Crown Books For Young Readers) 2021. (ENG.). 208p. lib. bdg. 19.99 *(978-0-593-17915-4(3),* Crown Books For Young Readers) Random Hse. Children's Bks.

Hartinger, Brent. Split Screen: Attack of the Soul-Sucking Brain Zombies; Bride of the Soul-Sucking Brain Zombies. 2007. 304p. (YA). (gr. 9-12). lib. bdg. 17.89 *(978-0-06-082409-9(3),* HarperTeen) HarperCollins Pubs.

Harvey, Jacqueline. Clementine Rose & the Movie Magic. 2015. (Clementine Rose Ser.: 9). (ENG., Illus.). 128p. (J). (gr. 1-3). pap. 8.99 *(978-0-85798-518-7(3))* Random Hse. Australia AUS. Dist: Independent Pubs. Group.

Harvey, Jacqueline & Yi Anne, Anne. Alice-Miranda in Hollywood. 2018. (Alice-Miranda Ser.: 16). (ENG.). 362p. (J). (gr. 3-7). 10.99 *(978-0-14-378061-8(1))* Random Hse. Australia AUS. Dist: Independent Pubs. Group.

Heidicker, Christian McKay. Attack of the 50 Foot Wallflower. Bosma, Sam, illus. (ENG.). 320p. (YA). (gr. 9). 2019. pap. 11.99 *(978-1-4814-9914-9(9))* 2018. 18.99 *(978-1-4814-9913-2(0))* Simon & Schuster Bks. For Young Readers. (Simon & Schuster Bks. For Young Readers).

Holm, Jennifer L. Lights, Camera, Middle School! Holm, Matthew, illus. 2017. (Babymouse Tales from the Locker Ser.: 1). (ENG.). 208p. (J). (gr. 3-7). 13.99 *(978-0-399-55438-4(6),* Random Hse. Bks. for Young Readers) Random Hse. Children's Bks.

Holm, Jennifer L. & Holm, Matthew. Squish #6: Fear the Amoeba, No. 6. Holm, Jennifer L. & Holm, Matthew, illus. 2014. (Squish Ser.: 6). (Illus.). 96p. (J). (gr. 2-5). pap. 6.99 *(978-0-307-98302-2(1),* Random Hse. Bks. for Young Readers) Random Hse. Children's Bks.

Jones, Buck. Buck Jones Rangers-Cowboys Collection. 2011. 68p. 36.95 *(978-1-258-07141-7(X))* Literary Licensing, LLC.

Kalman, Maira. Max in Hollywood, Baby. 2018. (Illus.). 48p. (J). (gr. k-3). 18.95 *(978-1-68137-234-1(7),* NYR Children's Collection) New York Review of Bks., Inc., The.

Kaplan-Taylor, Maeve. At the Movies with Maeve. 2004. (Illus.). 36p. (J). 3.99 *(978-0-9746587-4-2(X),* Beacon Street Girls) B*tween Productions, Inc.

Katschke, Judy. Hooray for Shoppywood! 2017. (Illus.). 62p. (J). *(978-1-5182-4211-3(1))* Scholastic, Inc.

Keene, Carolyn. Movie Madness. Francis, Peter, illus. 2016. (Nancy Drew Clue Book Ser.: 5). (ENG.). 96p. (J). (gr. 1-4). pap. 5.99 *(978-1-4814-5820-7(5),* Aladdin) Simon & Schuster Children's Publishing.

Kidd, Ronald. The Year of the Bomb. 2009. (ENG.). 208p. (YA). (gr. 7). pap. 5.99 *(978-1-4169-9625-5(7));* 16.99 *(978-1-4169-5892-5(4))* Simon & Schuster Bks. For Young Readers. (Simon & Schuster Bks. For Young Readers).

—Year of the Bomb. 2009. 208p. 5.99 *(978-1-4169-9504-3(8))* Studio Fun International.

Kinney, Jeff. Double Down. 2016. (Diary of a Wimpy Kid Ser.: Bk. 11). (ENG., Illus.). 224p. (J). (gr. 3-7). E-Book 13.49 *(978-1-61312-992-0(0),* Amulet Bks.) Abrams, Inc.

—Double Down. 2016. (Diary of a Wimpy Kid Ser.: 11). (J). lib. bdg. 25.70 *(978-0-606-38998-3(9))* Turtleback.

Kyi, Tanya Lloyd. Anywhere but Here. 2013. (ENG., Illus.). 320p. (YA). (gr. 9). 17.99 *(978-1-4424-8070-4(X));* pap. 9.99 *(978-1-4424-8069-8(6))* Simon Pulse. (Simon Pulse).

Lasky, Kathryn. The Extra. 2013. (ENG.). 320p. (YA). (gr. 7). 16.99 *(978-0-7636-3972-3(9))* Candlewick Pr.

Mass, Wendy. Finally: a Wish Novel. 2016. (ENG.). 304p. (J). (gr. 3-7). pap. 8.99 *(978-0-545-05243-6(2),* Scholastic Paperbacks) Scholastic, Inc.

McFarlane, Susannah. Drama Queen: EJ12 Girl Hero. 2017. (Illus.). 128p. (J). pap. 5.99 *(978-1-61067-509-3(6))* Kane Miller.

McKean, Dave. Mirrormask. McKean, Dave, illus. 2005. (Illus.). 80p. (J). lib. bdg. 17.89 *(978-0-06-082110-4(8))* HarperCollins Pubs.

Meister, Cari. Movie Madness: A 4D Book. Burns, Heather, illus. 2018. (Three Horses Ser.). (ENG.). 56p. (J). (gr. k-2). pap. 4.95 *(978-1-5158-2954-6(5),* 138501); lib. bdg. 23.99 *(978-1-5158-2950-8(2),* 138497) Capstone. (Picture Window Bks.).

Morgan, Melissa J. Extra Credit #22, 22. 2009. (Camp Confidential Ser.: 22). 160p. (J). (gr. 4-7). 4.99 *(978-0-448-45216-6(2),* Grosset & Dunlap) Penguin Young Readers Group.

Myers, Bill. My Life As Alien Monster Bait, 1 vol. 2019. (Incredible Worlds of Wally Mcdoogle Ser.: 2). (ENG.). 144p. (J). pap. 8.99 *(978-0-7852-3114-1(5),* Tommy Nelson) Nelson, Thomas Inc.

Paige, D. M. Box-Office Smash. (Opportunity Ser.). (ENG.). 112p. (YA). (gr. 6-12). 2013. pap. 7.95 *(978-1-4677-1494-5(1),* 30d81f99-0711-4ecc-8b1c-fb590bdba390, Darby Creek) 2013. lib. bdg. 27.99 *(978-1-4677-1371-9(6),* 7a3889e2-2cf2-4587-8dfd-699ca5c56544, Darby Creek) 2015. E-Book 53.32 *(978-1-4677-6012-6(9),* 9781467760126, Lerner Digital) Lerner Publishing Group.

Pauley, Kimberly. Cat Girl's Day Off, 1 vol. (ENG.). (YA). 2018. 352p. (gr. 6-12). pap. 13.95 *(978-1-64379-050-3(1),* leelowtu) 2012. 336p. 17.95 *(978-1-60060-883-4(3))* Lee & Low Bks., Inc. (Tu Bks.).

Pfeffer, Susan Beth. Revenge of the Aztecs. 2004. 118p. (J). lib. bdg. 16.92 *(978-1-4242-0763-3(0))* Fitzgerald Bks.

Pflugfelder, Bob & Hockensmith, Steve. Nick & Tesla's Special Effects Spectacular: A Mystery with Animatronics, Alien Makeup, Camera Gear, & Other Movie Magic You Can Make Yourself! 2015. (Nick & Tesla Ser.: 5). (Illus.). 256p. (J). (gr. 4-7). 12.95 *(978-1-59474-760-1(1))* Quirk Bks.

MNO

Poulsen, David A. The Hunk Machine. 2nd rev. ed. 2007. (Salt & Pepper Chronicles). (ENG.). 160p. (J). (gr. 4-7). 6.95 *(978-1-55263-723-4(9))* Leaf Storm Pr.
Qualey, Marsha. Gracie Laroo on the Big Screen. Litten, Kristyna, illus. 2017. (Gracie Laroo Ser.). (ENG.). 40p. (J). (gr. k-2). lib. bdg. 21.32 *(978-1-5158-1441-2(6)*, 135711, Picture Window Bks.) Capstone.
Rey. Vive le Cinema. 16.95 *(978-2-09-250166-5(6))* Nathan, Fernand FRA. Dist: Distribooks, Inc.
Rippin, Sally. The Night Fright. Fukuoka, Aki, illus. 2015. (Billie B. Brown Ser.). (ENG.). 43p. (J). *(978-1-61067-451-5(0))* Kane Miller.
—The Night Fright: Billie B Brown. Fukuoka, Aki, illus. 2016. (ENG.). 48p. (J). pap. 4.99 *(978-1-61067-391-4(3))* Kane Miller.
Ruditis, P. J. Love, Hollywood Style. 2013. (Romantic Comedies Ser.). (ENG., Illus.). 272p. (YA). (gr. 7). pap. 13.99 *(978-1-4814-1539-2(5)*, Simon Pulse) Simon Pulse.
Saxon, Victoria. Big Trouble in Little Rodentia. 2016. (Illus.). (J). *(978-1-5182-0883-6(5))* Random House Children's Books.
Shaler, Robert. The Boy Scouts with the Motion Picture P. 2005. pap. 21.95 *(978-1-885529-59-6(7))* Stevens Publishing.
Shan, Darren, pseud. Slawter. 2007. (Demonata Ser.: 3). (ENG.). 240p. (J). (gr. 10-17). pap. 13.99 *(978-0-316-01388-8(9))* Little, Brown Bks. for Young Readers.
Shaw, Tucker. Oh Yeah, Audrey! 2014. (ENG., Illus.). 256p. (YA). (gr. 8-17). 16.95 *(978-1-4197-1223-4(3)*, 1077501, Amulet Bks.) Abrams, Inc.
Smith, Alex T. Claude on the Big Screen, 1 vol. 2017. (Claude Ser.: 7). (ENG., Illus.). 96p. (J). (gr. 2-4). 12.95 *(978-1-68263-009-9(9))* Peachtree Publishing Co. Inc.
Snider, Brandon T., adapted by. Meet Quicksnadow. 2017. (Illus.). 31p. (J). *(978-1-5182-4447-6(5))* Little Brown & Co.
Sortland, Bjorn. The Dream Factory Starring Anna & Henry. Christianson, Emily V. & Hedin, Robert, trs. from NOR. Elling, Lars, illus. 2003. (Picture Bks.). 40p. (J). (gr. -1-3). 15.95 *(978-0-87614-009-3(6)*, Carolrhoda Bks.) Lerner Publishing Group.
Star Wars Villains. 2011. (Illus.). (J). *(978-0-545-28664-0(6))* Scholastic, Inc.
Steel, Danielle. Pretty Minnie in Hollywood. Valiant, Kristi, illus. 2016. 32p. (J). (gr. -1-2). 17.99 *(978-0-553-53755-0(5)*, Doubleday Bks. for Young Readers) Random Hse. Children's Bks.
Steele, Michael Anthony. Movie Magic Madness. Lozano, Omar, illus. 2019. (You Choose Stories: Wonder Woman Ser.). (ENG.). 112p. (J). (gr. 2-6). pap. 6.95 *(978-1-4965-8440-3(6)*, 140965); lib. bdg. 32.65 *(978-1-4965-8350-5(7)*, 140644) Capstone. (Stone Arch Bks.).
Stevens, Mark. Tailspin Tommy: The Mystery of the Midnight Patrol. Beebe, Robb, illus. 2011. 226p. 44.95 *(978-1-258-10164-0(5))* Literary Licensing, LLC.
Stilton, Thea. Thea Stilton & the Hollywood Hoax. 2016. (Thea Stilton Ser.: 23). lib. bdg. 18.40 *(978-0-606-38799-6(4))* Turtleback.
Strand, Jeff. The Greatest Zombie Movie Ever. 2016. 272p. (YA). (gr. 6-12). pap. 12.99 *(978-1-4926-2814-9(X)*, 9781492628149) Sourcebooks, Inc.
Strange, Jason. To Wake the Dead, 1 vol. Parks, Phil, illus. 2011. (Jason Strange Ser.). (ENG.). 72p. (gr. 3-6). (J). 25.32 *(978-1-4342-2963-2(7)*, 114196); pap. 6.25 *(978-1-4342-3094-2(5)*, 114734) Capstone. (Stone Arch Bks.).
Struyk-Bonn, Chris. Nice Girls Endure. 2016. (ENG.). 256p. (YA). (gr. 9-12). 16.95 *(978-1-63079-047-9(8)*, 131502, Switch Pr.) Capstone.
Suma, Nova Ren. Fade Out. 2012. (ENG.). 288p. (YA). (gr. 7). pap. 9.99 *(978-1-4169-7565-6(9)*, Simon Pulse) Simon Pulse.
Tashjian, Janet. My Life As a Stuntboy. Tashjian, Jake, illus. 2015. (My Life Ser.: 2). (ENG.). 288p. (J). (gr. 4-7). pap. 8.99 *(978-1-250-01038-4(1)*, 900084784) Square Fish.
Thompson, Kay. Eloise in Hollywood. 2006. (Eloise Ser.). (ENG., Illus.). 70p. (J). (gr. -1-3). 19.99 *(978-0-689-84289-4(9)*, Simon & Schuster Bks. For Young Readers) Simon & Schuster Bks. For Young Readers.
Toffler-Corrie, Laura. Noah Green Saves the World. Pamintuan, Macky, illus. 2020. (ENG.). 280p. (J). (gr. 4-7). 17.99 *(978-1-5415-6036-9(1)*, 4e539792-d4b9-48b5-a143-9e038eaf9c09, Kar-Ben Publishing) Lerner Publishing Group.
Wheeler, Shannon & Torres, J. Wall E Vol. 1: Recharge. Luthi, Morgan, illus. 2010. (ENG.). (J). 24.99 *(978-1-60886-554-3(1))* BOOM! Studios.
Wheeler, Shannon, et al. Wall-E Vol. 1: Recharge. Luthi, Morgan & Barks, Carl, illus. 2010. (ENG.). 112p. (J). pap. 9.99 *(978-1-60886-512-3(6))* BOOM! Studios.
Wild, Ailsa. Squishy Taylor & the Mess Makers. 2018. (Squishy Taylor Ser.). (ENG., Illus.). 128p. (J). (gr. 2-4). pap. 6.95 *(978-1-5158-1973-8(6)*, 136645, Picture Window Bks.) Capstone.
Wild, Ailsa. Squishy Taylor & the Mess-Makers. Wood, Ben, illus. 2017. (Squishy Taylor Ser.). (ENG.). 128p. (J). (gr. 2-4). lib. bdg. 25.32 *(978-1-5158-1957-8(4)*, 136640, Picture Window Bks.) Capstone.
Wilsdon, Christina. Lights! Action! California! Hockerman, Dennis, illus. 2006. 26p. (J). 7.99 *(978-1-59939-009-3(4))* Cornerstone Pr.
Wittlinger, Ellen. Saturdays with Hitchcock. 272p. (J). (gr. 5). 2019. pap. 8.99 *(978-1-58089-986-4(2))* 2017. lib. bdg. 16.99 *(978-1-58089-775-4(4))* Charlesbridge Publishing, Inc.

MOTION PICTURES—PLAY WRITING
see Motion Picture Plays

MOTION PICTURES IN EDUCATION
Fernandez, Elizabeth. Screenwriting & Directing for Secondary Schools. 2010. 181p. pap. 68.95 *(978-1-4452-9245-8(9))* Lulu Pr., Inc.

MOTOR BOATS
see Motorboats

MOTOR BUSES
see Buses

MOTOR CARS
see Automobiles

MOTOR COURTS
see Hotels, Motels, etc.

MOTOR CYCLES
see Motorcycles

MOTOR SPORTS
see also Automobile Racing
2004. (Machines at Work Ser.). 24p. (J). (gr. -1-3). lib. bdg. 21.36 Child's World, Inc, The.
Adamson, Thomas K. Freestyle Motocross. 2010. (Dirt Bike World Ser.). (ENG.). 32p. pap. 47.70 *(978-1-4296-5707-5(3)*, Capstone Pr.) Capstone.
—Motocross Racing. 2010. (Dirt Bike World Ser.). (ENG.). 32p. (gr. 1-2). pap. 47.70 *(978-1-4296-5706-8(5)*, Capstone Pr.) Capstone.
Carney, Larry. Jeff Gordon. PC Treasures Staff, ed. Houghton, Chris & Morrison, Jeff, illus. 2009. (Nascar Drivers Coloring/Sticker Book Ser.). (ENG.). 96p. (J). pap. 6.95 *(978-1-60072-162-5(1))* PC Treasures, Inc.
Carr, Aaron. Motocross. 2013. (Deportes de Moda Ser.). (SPA., Illus.). 24p. (J). (gr. k-2). lib. bdg. 27.13 *(978-1-62127-629-6(5)*, AV2 by Weigl) Weigl Pubs., Inc.
Crawford, Cindy. Drag Racing Basics: Christmas Tree to Finish Line Has Something for All Drag Racing Enthusiasts. 2003. (ENG., Illus.). 168p. pap. 24.95 *(978-0-929758-22-0(6)*, 0929758226) Beeman Jorgensen, Inc.
Gifford, Clive. The Inside Story of Motorsports, 1 vol. 2011. (Sports World Ser.). (ENG.). 48p. (YA). (gr. 5-5). lib. bdg. 34.47 *(978-1-4488-4848-5(2)*, a8a7bcb7-4d55-483e-993a-f518a42f0ad4) Rosen Publishing Group, Inc., The.
Inside the Speedway, 6 vols. 2014. (Inside the Speedway Ser.: 6). (ENG.). 48p. (J). (gr. 3-6). lib. bdg. 205.32 *(978-1-62403-401-5(2)*, 1455, SportsZone) ABDO Publishing Co.
Mapua, Jeff. Extreme Motorsports, 1 vol. 2015. (Sports to the Extreme Ser.). (ENG., Illus.). 48p. (J). (gr. 5-6). 33.47 *(978-1-4994-3549-8(5)*, d6a61ed0-27e4-4924-8c97-758d1e50445b, Rosen Central) Rosen Publishing Group, Inc., The.
Mason, Paul. Motorcycles. 2010. (Motorsports Ser.). 32p. (J). (gr. 3-6). 28.50 *(978-1-60753-121-0(6))* Amicus Learning.
Mezzanotte, Jim. Supermoto, 1 vol. 2005. (Carreras de Motos: a Toda Velocidad (Motorcycle Racing: the Fast Track) Ser.). (SPA., Illus.). 24p. (gr. 3-3). lib. bdg. 25.67 *(978-0-8368-6444-1(1)*, ab757cba-9c93-4418-bc05-8015caf0b480, Gareth Stevens Learning Library) Stevens, Gareth Publishing LLLP.
Mikoley, Kate. Truck & Tractor Pulls, 1 vol. 2019. (Motorsports Maniacs Ser.). (ENG.). 32p. (gr. 1-2). pap. 11.50 *(978-1-5382-4098-4(X)*, 235042a6-91dc-4947-9a09-74c7650bc9cd); lib. bdg. 28.27 *(978-1-5382-4100-4(5)*, 73c6d770-b54d-4159-92bb-ae7535ffc677) Stevens, Gareth Publishing LLLP.
NASCAR Staff, ed. Speedway Superstars. 2004. (NASCAR Chapter Bks.). (ENG., Illus.). 94p. (J). (gr. 3-6). 17.44 *(978-0-7944-0406-2(5)*, Reader's Digest Children's Bks.) Studio Fun International.
Parker, Steve. On the Race Track. 2010. (J). 28.50 *(978-1-59920-287-7(5))* Black Rabbit Bks.
PC Treasures Staff, ed. Jimmie Johnson, Vol. 48. 2009. (Nascar Drivers Coloring/Sticker Book Ser.). (ENG., Illus.). 96p. (J). 6.95 *(978-1-60072-161-8(3))* PC Treasures, Inc.
Tyson, Carolee. Factory Ride. 2004. 198p. (YA). per. 6.99 *(978-0-9754459-0-7(1))* Pumpkin Ridge Publishing.
Weber, M. Wild Moments of Motorsports. 2017. (Wild Moments of Motorsports Ser.). (ENG., Illus.). 32p. (J). (gr. 3-9). 122.60 *(978-1-5157-7424-2(4)*, 26753, Capstone Pr.) Capstone.
—Wild Moments of Stock Car Racing. 2017. (Wild Moments of Motorsports Ser.). (ENG., Illus.). 32p. (J). (gr. 3-9). lib. bdg. 28.65 *(978-1-5157-7408-2(2)*, 135729, Capstone Pr.) Capstone.
—Wild Moments of Truck Racing. 2017. (Wild Moments of Motorsports Ser.). (ENG., Illus.). 32p. (J). (gr. 3-9). lib. bdg. 28.65 *(978-1-5157-7407-5(4)*, 135728, Capstone Pr.) Capstone.
—Wild Moments on Dirt Bikes. 2017. (Wild Moments of Motorsports Ser.). (ENG., Illus.). 32p. (J). (gr. 3-9). lib. bdg. 28.65 *(978-1-5157-7406-8(6)*, 135727, Capstone Pr.) Capstone.
Woods, Bob. Snowmobile Racers, 1 vol. 2010. (Kid Racers Ser.). (ENG., Illus.). 48p. (gr. 5-7). 27.93 *(978-0-7660-3487-7(9)*, 7e2b1dd4-8261-47c8-9aa8-c9bfa4c00c66); pap. 11.53 *(978-0-7660-3756-4(8)*, e37fe124-de78-4017-b123-8b89ec0fc78c) Enslow Publishing, LLC.

MOTOR TRUCKS
see Trucks

MOTORBOAT RACING
Bach, Rachel. The Boat Race. 2016. (Let's Race Ser.). (ENG., Illus.). 16p. (J). (gr. -1-1). pap. 7.99 *(978-1-68152-130-5(X)*, 15496); lib. bdg. 17.95 *(978-1-60753-911-7(X)*, 15488) Amicus.
Bullard, Lisa. Powerboats. 2004. (Pull Ahead Books-Mighty Movers Ser.). (ENG., Illus.). 32p. (gr. k-3). lib. bdg. 22.60 *(978-0-8225-0744-4(7))* Lerner Publishing Group.
Hauenstein, Michael. Speedboat Racers, 1 vol. 2010. (Kid Racers Ser.). (ENG., Illus.). 48p. (gr. 5-7). 27.93 *(978-0-7660-3485-3(2)*, 5925c404-ecca-46cf-b50f-51c7fbc56366); pap. 11.53 *(978-0-7660-3755-7(X)*, d18260f6-9694-45b2-bbc8-22ef58912fe8) Enslow Publishing, LLC.
Hetrick, Hans. Hydroplanes, 1 vol. 2010. (Full Throttle Ser.). (ENG.). 32p. (J). (gr. 3-9). lib. bdg. 28.65 *(978-1-4296-4753-3(1)*, 103290, Capstone Pr.) Capstone.
—Sport Bikes, 1 vol. 2010. (Full Throttle Ser.). (ENG.). 32p. (J). (gr. 3-9). lib. bdg. 28.65 *(978-1-4296-4751-9(5)*, 103288, Capstone Pr.) Capstone.
Hofer, Charles. Speedboats. (World's Fastest Machines Ser.). 24p. (gr. 2-3). 2009. 42.50 *(978-1-60854-856-9(2))* 2007. (ENG., Illus.). (J). lib. bdg. 26.27 *(978-1-4042-4176-3(0)*, d96be8c8-cfbb-4bcc-bdc7-81ea2467356a) Rosen Publishing Group, Inc., The. (PowerKids Pr.).
MacArthur, Collin. Inside a Speedboat, 1 vol. 2014. (Life in the Fast Lane Ser.). (ENG.). 48p. (gr. 4-4). 33.07 *(978-1-62713-037-0(3)*, 3b2a79ed-9d89-4fc6-902a-5520fa8cc582) Cavendish Square Publishing LLC.
Rickard, Steve. Powerboat Race. 2008. (321 Go! Ser.). (ENG., Illus.). 36p. pap. *(978-1-84167-786-6(8))* Ransom Publishing Ltd.
Sherman, Jill. Racing Personal Watercraft (Sea-Doos), 1 vol. 2017. (Speed Racers Ser.). (ENG.). 48p. (gr. 6-6). 29.60 *(978-0-7660-9271-6(2)*, 106932ea-8daf-42b5-b0fe-b2aa8d8ad3c6) Enslow Publishing, LLC.

MOTORBOAT RACING—FICTION
Farber, E. S. Fish Finelli (Book 2) Operation Fireball. Beene, Jason, illus. 2014. (Fish Finelli Ser.). (ENG.). 172p. (J). (gr. 3-7). 15.99 *(978-1-4521-1083-7(2))* Chronicle Bks. LLC.
Kay, Ross. The Go Ahead Boys & the Racing Motor-Boat. 2007. 176p. per. *(978-1-4065-1858-0(1))* Dodo Pr.
—Go Ahead Boys & the Racing Motorboat. 2017. (ENG., Illus.). (J). 23.95 *(978-1-374-88610-0(6))*; pap. 13.95 *(978-1-374-88609-4(2))* Capital Communications, Inc.

MOTORBOATS
Bullard, Lisa. Powerboats. 2004. (Pull Ahead Books-Mighty Movers Ser.). (ENG., Illus.). 32p. (gr. k-3). lib. bdg. 22.60 *(978-0-8225-0744-4(7))* Lerner Publishing Group.
Eason, Sarah. How Does a Powerboat Work?, 1 vol. 2010. (How Does It Work? Ser.). (ENG.). 32p. (J). (gr. 3-4). lib. bdg. 28.67 *(978-1-4339-3474-2(4)*, 4e2d6a26-4b5c-46f9-b469-940558747c24); (Illus.). pap. 11.50 *(978-1-4339-3475-9(2)*, 161987b4-a654-4fa5-95b9-d70f6878f81e) Stevens, Gareth Publishing LLLP. (Gareth Stevens Learning Library).
Gabrielson, Curt. Kinetic Contraptions: Build a Hovercraft, Airboat, & More with a Hobby Motor. 2010. (ENG., Illus.). 192p. (J). (gr. 7-18). pap. 18.99 *(978-1-55652-957-3(0))* Chicago Review Pr., Inc.
Hofer, Charles. Speedboats. 2009. (World's Fastest Machines Ser.). 24p. (gr. 2-3). 42.50 *(978-1-60854-856-9(2)*, PowerKids Pr.) Rosen Publishing Group, Inc., The.
Jacobson, Bob. Ole Evinrude & His Outboard Motor. 2009. (Badger Biographies Ser.). (ENG., Illus.). 78p. (J). (gr. 3-7). pap. 12.95 *(978-0-87020-420-3(3))* Wisconsin Historical Society.
MacArthur, Collin. Inside a Speedboat, 1 vol. 2014. (Life in the Fast Lane Ser.). (ENG.). 48p. (gr. 4-4). 33.07 *(978-1-62713-037-0(3)*, 3b2a79ed-9d89-4fc6-902a-5520fa8cc582) Cavendish Square Publishing LLC.
McClellan, Ray & Finn, Denny Von. Hydroplanes. 2008. (Cool Rides Ser.). (ENG., Illus.). 24p. (J). (gr. 3-7). lib. bdg. 26.95 *(978-1-60014-211-6(7))* Bellwether Media.
Riggs, Kate. Seedlings: Speedboats. 2015. (Seedlings Ser.). (ENG.). 24p. (J). (gr. -1-1). pap. 8.99 *(978-1-62832-123-4(7)*, 21254, Creative Paperbacks) Creative Co., The.
—Speedboats. (Seedlings Ser.). 24p. (J). (gr. -1-k). 2015. (ENG.). *(978-1-60818-523-8(0)*, 21253) 2010. 16.95 *(978-1-58341-915-1(2))* Creative Co., The. (Creative Education).
Von Finn, Denny. Powerboats. 2009. (World's Fastest Ser.). (ENG., Illus.). 24p. (J). (gr. 3-7). lib. bdg. 26.95 *(978-1-60014-282-6(6)*, Torque Bks.) Bellwether Media.
Werther, Scott P. Powerboats / Lanchas Motorizadas. 2009. (Extreme Machines / Máquinas extremas Ser.). (ENG & SPA.). 24p. (gr. 1-2). 42.50 *(978-1-61512-448-0(9)*, Editorial Buenas Letras) Rosen Publishing Group, Inc., The.

MOTORCYCLES
Abdo, Kenny. Dirt Bikes. 2017. (Off Road Vehicles Ser.). (ENG., Illus.). 24p. (J). (gr. 2-8). lib. bdg. 31.36 *(978-1-5321-2100-5(8)*, 26783, Abdo Zoom-Fly) ABDO Publishing Co.
Adamson, Thomas K. Motocross Freestyle. 2015. (Extreme Sports Ser.). (ENG., Illus.). 24p. (J). (gr. 3-7). lib. bdg. 26.95 *(978-1-62617-275-3(7)*, Epic Bks.) Bellwether Media.
Aloian, Molly. Motorcycles. 2011. (ENG., Illus.). 32p. (J). lib. bdg. *(978-0-7787-2730-9(0))*; (Vehicles on the Move Ser.: No. 16). pap. *(978-0-7787-2737-8(8))* Crabtree Publishing Co.
Aloian, Molly, contrib. by. Les Motocyclettes. 2011. (FRE.). 32p. (J). pap. *(978-2-89579-490-5(1))* Crabtree Publishing Co.
Armentrout, David & Armentrout, Patricia. Dirt Bikes. 2005. (Motorcycle Mania Ser.). (Illus.). 24p. (J). (gr. 3-6). lib. bdg. 27.07 *(978-1-59515-453-8(1)*, 1244371) Rourke Educational Media.
—Sportbikes. 2005. (Motorcycle Mania Ser.). (Illus.). 24p. (J). (gr. 3-6). lib. bdg. 27.07 *(978-1-59515-456-9(6)*, 1244375) Rourke Educational Media.
—Stunts, Tricks, & Jumps. 2007. (Motorcycle Mania (High Interest) Ser.). (Illus.). 24p. (J). (gr. 3-7). lib. bdg. 27.07 *(978-1-60044-591-0(8))* Rourke Educational Media.
Arnold, Quinn M. Scooters. 2019. (Seedlings: on the Go Ser.). (ENG.). 24p. (J). (gr. -1-1). pap. 8.99 *(978-1-62832-734-2(0)*, 19130, Creative Paperbacks) Creative Co., The.
Bailey, Diane. Yamaha: Sport Racing Legend, 1 vol. 2013. (Motorcycles: a Guide to the World's Best Bikes Ser.). (Illus.). 48p. (J). (gr. 5-5). (ENG.). 34.41 *(978-1-4777-1859-9(1)*, c76bab15-c371-466b-bb36-5a27e6fb700d); (ENG., pap. 12.75 *(978-1-4777-1878-0(8)*, 54b1cc5a-d9fd-40a5-9003-5f1d7fd57bc7); pap. 70.50 *(978-1-4777-1879-7(6))* Rosen Publishing Group, Inc., The. (Rosen Reference).
Bailey, Katharine. Sport Bikes. rev. ed. 2007. (Automania! Ser.). (ENG., Illus.). 32p. (J). (gr. 4-7). pap. *(978-0-7787-3035-4(2)*, 1266046) Crabtree Publishing Co.
Barnes, Pete. Harley & the Davidsons: Motorcycle Legends. 2007. (Badger Biographies Ser.). (ENG., Illus.). 112p. (J). (gr. 4-8). per. 12.95 *(978-0-87020-380-0(0))* Wisconsin Historical Society.
Barrington, Richard. Ducati: High Performance Italian Racer, 1 vol. 2013. (Motorcycles: a Guide to the World's Best Bikes Ser.). (Illus.). 48p. (J). (gr. 5-5). (ENG.). 34.41 *(978-1-4777-1856-8(7)*, 0d6de9fc-93de-4cb2-8570-fb80f15ff33f); (ENG., pap. 12.75 *(978-1-4777-1870-4(2)*, 129a8690-097e-43c2-adab-2773b2be5ced); pap. 70.50 *(978-1-4777-1871-1(0))* Rosen Publishing Group, Inc., The. (Rosen Reference).
Belcher, Andy. Motorcycles. Cambridge Reading Adventures. Turquoise Band. 2016. (Cambridge Reading Adventures Ser.). (ENG., Illus.). 24p. pap. 8.80 *(978-1-107-57624-7(5))* Cambridge Univ. Pr.
Bender, Lionel. Cars & Motorcycles. 2006. (J). *(978-1-59389-262-3(4))* Chrysalis Education.
Besel, Tucker. Build Your Own Motorcycle Bot. Gould, Grant, illus. 2018. (Bot Maker Ser.). (ENG.). 24p. (J). (gr. 4-6). lib. bdg. *(978-1-68072-325-0(1)*, 12084, Hi Jinx) Black Rabbit Bks.
—Build Your Own Motorcycle Bot. 2018. (Bot Maker Ser.). (ENG.). (J). (gr. 3-7). pap. 8.95 *(978-1-68072-649-7(8))* Hi Jinx Pr.
Beyer, Mark. Motocicletas Del Pasado, 1 vol. 2003. (Transporte Ayer y Hoy (Transportation Through the Ages) Ser.). (SPA., Illus.). 24p. (J). (gr. 1-2). lib. bdg. 26.27 *(978-0-8239-6854-1(5)*, be3b7eeb-f2a8-44bb-85d7-162f1cc8b1b5) Rosen Publishing Group, Inc., The.
—Motocicletas del pasado (Motorcycles of the Past) 2009. (transporte ayer y hoy (Transportation Through the Ages) Ser.). 24p. (gr. 1-2). 42.50 *(978-1-61512-255-4(9)*, Editorial Buenas Letras) Rosen Publishing Group, Inc., The.
—Motorcycles of the Past. 2009. (Transportation Through the Ages Ser.). 24p. (gr. 1-1). 42.50 *(978-1-60854-589-6(X)*, PowerKids Pr.) Rosen Publishing Group, Inc., The.
Blaine, Victor. Mi Patineta / My Scooter, 1 vol. 2014. (¡Mírame, Ahí Voy! / Watch Me Go! Ser.). (ENG & SPA., Illus.). 24p. (J). (gr. 1-2). 25.27 *(978-1-4994-0288-9(0)*, 40aaabde-fd0f-4d0e-80d8-c056c5fe9e2c, PowerKids Pr.) Rosen Publishing Group, Inc., The.
Bodensteiner, Peter. Les Choppers. 2016. (Passion Mécanique Ser.). (FRE., Illus.). 32p. (J). (gr. 4-6). *(978-1-77092-365-2(9)*, 10438, Bolt) Black Rabbit Bks.
—Choppers. 2016. (Gearhead Garage Ser.). (ENG.). 32p. (J). (gr. 4-6). pap. 9.99 *(978-1-64466-124-6(1)*, 10201); (Illus.). 31.35 *(978-1-68072-028-0(7)*, 10200) Black Rabbit Bks. (Bolt).
—Les Motos de Sport. 2016. (Passion Mécanique Ser.). (FRE., Illus.). 32p. (J). (gr. 4-6). *(978-1-77092-368-3(3)*, 10441, Bolt) Black Rabbit Bks.
—Sport Bikes. 2016. (Gearhead Garage Ser.). (ENG.). 32p. (J). (gr. 4-6). pap. 9.99 *(978-1-64466-127-7(6)*, 10213); (Illus.). 31.35 *(978-1-68072-034-1(1)*, 10212) Black Rabbit Bks. (Bolt).
Bowman, Chris. Motorcycles. 2018. (Mighty Machines in Action Ser.). (ENG., Illus.). 24p. (J). (gr. k-3). lib. bdg. 26.95 *(978-1-62617-758-1(9)*, Blastoff! Readers) Bellwether Media.
Brooklyn, Billie. Motorcycle Racing, 1 vol. 2014. (Checkered Flag Ser.). (ENG., Illus.). 32p. (J). (gr. 4-5). lib. bdg. 27.93 *(978-1-4994-0158-5(2)*, 4564440f-e04e-4e5c-97d0-fc60a6da46c0, PowerKids Pr.) Rosen Publishing Group, Inc., The.
Brown, Roland & Scarborough, Kate. Hot Bikes. 2012. (Fast Facts Ser.). (ENG.). 32p. (gr. 4-6). pap. 28.50 *(978-1-59771-326-9(0))* Sea-To-Sea Pubns.
Burns, Ricky. How to Restore Suzuki 2-Stroke Triples GT350, GT550 & GT750 1971 To 1978: YOUR Step-By-step Colour Illustrated Guide to Complete Restoration. 2016. (Enthusiast's Restoration Manual Ser.). (ENG., Illus.). 176p. pap. 59.95 *(978-1-84584-820-0(9))* Veloce Publishing Ltd. GBR. Dist: National Bk. Network.
Capstone Press. Dirt Bike World, 1 vol. 2010. (Dirt Bike World Ser.). (ENG.). 32p. lib. bdg. 101.28 *(978-1-4296-5931-4(9)*, Capstone Pr.) Capstone.
Castellano, Peter. Motocross, 1 vol. 2015. (Daredevil Sports Ser.). (ENG., Illus.). 32p. (J). (gr. 1-1). lib. bdg. 28.27 *(978-1-4824-2985-5(3)*, 824f37e6-6020-4bdd-a60d-c459b50b79c8) Stevens, Gareth Publishing LLLP.
Caswell, Deanna. Dirt Bikes. 2017. (Gearhead Garage Ser.). (ENG., Illus.). 32p. (J). (gr. 4-6). lib. bdg. *(978-1-68072-134-8(8)*, 10444, Bolt) Black Rabbit Bks.
—Motos Todoterreno. 2018. (SPA., Illus.). 31p. (J). lib. bdg. *(978-1-68072-573-5(4))* Black Rabbit Bks.
—Les Motos Tout Terrain. 2017. (Passion Mécanique Ser.). (FRE.). 32p. (J). (gr. 4-6). *(978-1-77092-413-0(2)*, 10607, Bolt) Black Rabbit Bks.
Ciovacco, Justine. All about Motorcycles, 1 vol. 2016. (Let's Find Out! Transportation Ser.). (ENG., Illus.). 32p. (J). (gr. 2-3). lib. bdg. 26.06 *(978-1-68048-441-0(9)*, 105bfa71-3734-4ac9-bf46-cbb2f598f860) Rosen Publishing Group, Inc., The.
Clark, Willow. Motorcycles on the Move, 1 vol. 2010. (Transportation Station Ser.). (ENG., Illus.). 24p. (J). (gr. 2-3). pap. 9.25 *(978-1-4358-9758-8(7)*, e3200cdb-b183-42ff-b214-c00ba2a9a670); lib. bdg. 26.27 *(978-1-4358-9335-1(2)*, 0c0944d0-7e08-443e-bc21-89bb20db596a) Rosen Publishing Group, Inc., The. (PowerKids Pr.).
Colson, Rob. Motorbikes, 1 vol. 2013. (Ultimate Machines Ser.). (ENG., Illus.). 24p. (J). (gr. 5-5). 26.27 *(978-1-4777-0066-2(8)*, 2916254a-a6dd-4624-83c3-b06b1e055445); pap. 9.25 *(978-1-4777-0117-1(6)*, 63601fdf-9a55-4948-bf55-8edf34482441) Rosen Publishing Group, Inc., The. (PowerKids Pr.).
Crabtree Editors & Stuckey, Rachel. Ride It Bmx. 2012. (Sports Starters Ser.). (ENG., Illus.). 32p. (J). (gr. 1-4). lib. bdg. *(978-0-7787-3150-4(2))* Crabtree Publishing Co.
David, Jack. Choppers. 2007. (Motorcycles Ser.). (ENG., Illus.). 24p. (J). (gr. 3-7). lib. bdg. 26.95 *(978-1-60014-131-7(5))* Bellwether Media.
—Cruisers. 2007. (Motorcycles Ser.). (ENG., Illus.). 24p. (J). (gr. 3-7). lib. bdg. 26.95 *(978-1-60014-132-4(3))* Bellwether Media.
—Enduro Motorcycles. 2007. (Motorcycles Ser.). (ENG., Illus.). 24p. (J). (gr. 3-7). lib. bdg. 26.95 *(978-1-60014-133-1(1))* Bellwether Media.
—Harley-Davidson Motorcycles. 2007. (Motorcycles Ser.). (ENG., Illus.). 24p. (J). (gr. 3-7). lib. bdg. 26.95 *(978-1-60014-134-8(X))* Bellwether Media.
—Moto-X Freestyle. 2007. (Action Sports Ser.). (ENG., Illus.). 24p. (J). (gr. 3-7). lib. bdg. 26.95 *(978-1-60014-125-6(0))* Bellwether Media.

—Motocross Cycles. 2008. (Cool Rides Ser.). (ENG., Illus.). 24p. (J). (gr. 3-7). lib. bdg. 26.95 *(978-1-60014-152-2(8))* Bellwether Media.
—Motocross Racing. 2007. (Action Sports Ser.). (ENG., Illus.). 24p. (J). (gr. 3-7). lib. bdg. 26.95 *(978-1-60014-124-9(2))* Bellwether Media.
—Sport Bikes. 2007. (Motorcycles Ser.). (ENG., Illus.). 24p. (J). (gr. 3-7). lib. bdg. 26.95 *(978-1-60014-135-5(8))* Bellwether Media.
—Supercross Racing. 2008. (Action Sports Ser.). (ENG., Illus.). 24p. (J). (gr. 3-7). lib. bdg. 26.95 *(978-1-60014-200-0(1))* Bellwether Media.
—Touring Motorcycles. 2007. (Motorcycles Ser.). (ENG., Illus.). 24p. (J). (gr. 3-7). lib. bdg. 26.95 *(978-1-60014-136-2(6))* Bellwether Media.
David West. Motorcycle. 2006. (Illus.). 32p. (J). pap. *(978-1-4109-2561-9(7))* Steck-Vaughn.
Davidson, Jean. My Daddy Makes the Best Motorcycles in the Whole Wide World, the Harley-Davidson. Hammerquist, Theresa, illus. 2004. (J). 16.95 *(978-1-930596-26-9(X))* Amherst Pr.
Dayton, Connor. Choppers, 1 vol. 2007. (Motorcycles: Made for Speed Ser.). (Illus.). 24p. (J). (gr. 1-1). (ENG.). lib. bdg. 26.27 *(978-1-4042-3654-7(6),* b30a0a21-84a5-4ab6-88a5-c62bd11b0575); (SPA & ENG.). lib. bdg. 26.27 *(978-1-4042-7612-3(2),* 49fdf4e1-81ff-4f5a-bde6-3383b56858a1) Rosen Publishing Group, Inc., The.
—Cool Bikes/Motos Cool, 1 vol. Alaman, Eduardo, tr. 2007. (Motorcycles: Made for Speed / Motocicletas: a Toda Velocidad Ser.). (SPA & ENG., Illus.). 24p. (J). (gr. 1-1). lib. bdg. 26.27 *(978-1-4042-7613-0(0),* f30c5551-25af-4218-a0a5-a2b5a940cbee) Rosen Publishing Group, Inc., The.
—Dirt Bikes, 1 vol. 2007. (Motorcycles: Made for Speed Ser.). (ENG., Illus.). 24p. (J). (gr. 1-1). lib. bdg. 26.27 *(978-1-4042-3652-3(X),* 9b61f873-a01a-4c35-98d5-b28de3f22beb) Rosen Publishing Group, Inc., The.
—Dirt Bikes, 1 vol. Alaman, Eduardo, tr. 2007. (Motorcycles: Made for Speed / Motocicletas: a Toda Velocidad Ser.). (SPA & ENG., Illus.). 24p. (J). (gr. 1-1). lib. bdg. 26.27 *(978-1-4042-7610-9(6),* b67a3669-7e62-464f-9f8d-7ad154269fd3) Rosen Publishing Group, Inc., The.
—Motorcycles: Made for Speed: Set, 8 vols. Incl. Choppers. lib. bdg. 26.27 *(978-1-4042-3654-7(6),* b30a0a21-84a5-4ab6-88a5-c62bd11b0575); Dirt Bikes. lib. bdg. 26.27 *(978-1-4042-3652-3(X),* 9b61f873-a01a-4c35-98d5-b28de3f22beb); Street Bikes. lib. bdg. 26.27 *(978-1-4042-3656-1(2),* 4f82e69a-f4ff-4ab8-b76b-1691ff516978); Superbikes. lib. bdg. 26.27 *(978-1-4042-3653-0(8),* 8cec671a-7441-49c6-9ae7-d2536f7f4480); Tricks with Bikes. lib. bdg. 26.27 *(978-1-4042-3657-8(0),* 17cd17ea-d925-4c6d-b917-55103864052c); (Illus.). 24p. (J). (gr. 1-1). (Motorcycles: Made for Speed Ser.). (ENG.). 2007. Set lib. bdg. 105.08 *(978-1-4042-3604-2(X),* 39cba7c8-4ebb-4a0f-bcf3-083f7f8defeb) Rosen Publishing Group, Inc., The.
—Street Bikes, 1 vol. 2007. (Motorcycles: Made for Speed Ser.). (ENG., Illus.). 24p. (J). (gr. 1-1). lib. bdg. 26.27 *(978-1-4042-3656-1(2),* 4f82e69a-f4ff-4ab8-b76b-1691ff516978) Rosen Publishing Group, Inc., The.
—Street Bikes/Motos de Calle, 1 vol. Alaman, Eduardo, tr. 2007. (Motorcycles: Made for Speed / Motocicletas: a Toda Velocidad Ser.). (SPA & ENG., Illus.). 24p. (J). (gr. 1-1). lib. bdg. 26.27 *(978-1-4042-7614-7(9),* 73b5ea07-143b-4d79-9c77-10be96de9075) Rosen Publishing Group, Inc., The.
—Superbikes, 1 vol. 2007. (Motorcycles: Made for Speed Ser.). (ENG., Illus.). 24p. (J). (gr. 1-1). lib. bdg. 26.27 *(978-1-4042-3653-0(8),* 8cec671a-7441-49c6-9ae7-d2536f7f4480) Rosen Publishing Group, Inc., The.
—Superbikes, 1 vol. Alaman, Eduardo, tr. 2007. (Motorcycles: Made for Speed / Motocicletas: a Toda Velocidad Ser.). (SPA & ENG., Illus.). 24p. (J). (gr. 1-1). lib. bdg. 26.27 *(978-1-4042-7611-6(4),* 7297b43f-8789-4714-8603-6954af6f290f) Rosen Publishing Group, Inc., The.
—Tricks with Bikes/Trucos con la Moto, 1 vol. Alaman, Eduardo, tr. 2007. (Motorcycles: Made for Speed / Motocicletas: a Toda Velocidad Ser.). (SPA & ENG., Illus.). 24p. (J). (gr. 1-1). lib. bdg. 26.27 *(978-1-4042-7615-4(7),* 114c80ad-5625-4254-916c-744d9b09eb48) Rosen Publishing Group, Inc., The.
Dieker, Wendy Strobel. Las Motocicletas. 2019. (Máquinas Poderosas Ser.). (SPA.). 16p. (J). (gr. -1-2). *(978-1-68151-865-5(6),* 10830) Amicus.
—Motorcycles. 2019. (Spot Mighty Machines Ser.). (ENG.). 16p. (J). (gr. -1-2). lib. bdg. *(978-1-68151-646-2(2),* 10778) Amicus.
Dinmont, Kerry. Motorcycles on the Go. 2016. (Bumba Books (r) — Machines That Go Ser.). (ENG., Illus.). 24p. (J). (gr. -1-1). 26.65 *(978-1-5124-1446-2(8),* ac13f9b0-6a43-4ca9-8b75-358d5284bafa, Lerner Pubns.) Lerner Publishing Group.
Dirt Bike World. 2010. (Dirt Bike World Ser.). (ENG.). 32p. (gr. 1-2). pap. 190.80 *(978-1-4296-5712-9(X),* Capstone Pr.) Capstone.
Doeden, Matt. Choppers. 2008. pap. 52.95 *(978-1-58013-661-7(3));* (ENG., Illus.). 48p. (gr. 4-7). lib. bdg. 26.60 *(978-0-8225-7288-6(5))* Lerner Publishing Group.
—Dirt Bikes. 2018. (Horsepower Ser.). (ENG., Illus.). 32p. (J). (gr. 3-9). lib. bdg. 27.32 *(978-1-5435-2463-5(X),* 137971, Capstone Pr.) Capstone.
—Motocross. 2019. (Todo Motor Ser.). (SPA., Illus.). 32p. (J). (gr. 3-9). lib. bdg. 27.32 *(978-1-5435-8256-7(7),* 141266) Capstone.
—Supercross. 2010. (Dirt Bike World Ser.). (ENG.). 32p. (gr. 1-2). pap. 47.70 *(978-1-4296-5708-2(1),* Capstone Pr.) Capstone.
Dowds, Alan. High-Speed Superbikes, 1 vol. 2006. (Cool Wheels Ser.). (ENG., Illus.). 32p. (gr. 3-5). lib. bdg. 28.67 *(978-0-8368-6826-5(9),* 2764572b-abe7-4b6b-a4bd-b9ea8084fe70, Gareth Stevens Learning Library) Stevens, Gareth Publishing LLLP.
Dubowski, Mark. Superfast Motorcycles. 2005. (Ultimate Speed Ser.). (Illus.). 32p. (J). (gr. 3-6). lib. bdg. 28.50 *(978-1-59716-081-0(4))* Bearport Publishing Co., Inc.
Eagen, Rachel. Street Bikes, 1 vol. rev. ed. 2007. (Automania! Ser.). (ENG., Illus.). 32p. (J). (gr. 4-7). pap. *(978-0-7787-3036-1(0))* Crabtree Publishing Co.
Early Macken, JoAnn. Bike Riding, 1 vol. 2004. (After-School Fun Ser.). (ENG., Illus.). 24p. (gr. k-2). lib. bdg. 23.67 *(978-0-8368-4512-9(9),* a930a909-57d3-461b-b753-58a2053c3a59, Weekly Reader Leveled Readers) Stevens, Gareth Publishing LLLP.
Enz, Tammy. Batmobiles & Batcycles: The Engineering Behind Batman's Vehicles, 1 vol. 2014. (Batman Science Ser.). (ENG., Illus.). 32p. (J). (gr. 5-9). 27.99 *(978-1-4765-3940-9(5),* 123940, Stone Arch Bks.) Capstone.
—Building Vehicles That Roll. 2017. (Young Engineers Ser.). (ENG., Illus.). 32p. (J). (gr. 1-3). lib. bdg. 29.99 *(978-1-4846-3748-7(8),* 134191, Heinemann) Capstone.
Finn, Denny Von. Drag Racing Motorcycles. 2011. (World's Fastest Ser.). (ENG., Illus.). 24p. (J). (gr. 3-7). lib. bdg. 26.95 *(978-1-60014-586-5(8),* Torque Bks.) Bellwether Media.
—Racing Motorcycles. 2009. (World's Fastest Ser.). (ENG., Illus.). 24p. (J). (gr. 3-7). lib. bdg. 26.95 *(978-1-60014-291-8(5),* Torque Bks.) Bellwether Media.
Franchino, Vicky. Motorcycles. 2008. (21st Century Skills Innovation Library: Innovation in Transportation Ser.). (ENG., Illus.). 32p. (gr. 4-8). lib. bdg. 32.07 *(978-1-60279-238-8(0),* 200168) Cherry Lake Publishing.
Franks, Katie. Choppers. 2009. (Motorcycles: Made for Speed Ser.). 24p. (gr. 1-1). 42.50 *(978-1-61514-676-5(8),* PowerKids Pr.); (ENG & SPA.). 42.50 *(978-1-61514-670-3(9),* Editorial Buenas Letras) Rosen Publishing Group, Inc., The.
—Cool Bikes. 2009. (Motorcycles: Made for Speed Ser.). 24p. (gr. 1-1). 42.50 *(978-1-61514-677-2(6),* PowerKids Pr.) Rosen Publishing Group, Inc., The.
—Cool Bikes/Motos Cool. 2009. (Motorcycles Made for Speed/Motocicletas a toda velocidad Ser.). (ENG & SPA.). 24p. (gr. 1-1). 42.50 *(978-1-61514-671-0(7),* Editorial Buenas Letras) Rosen Publishing Group, Inc., The.
—Dirt Bikes. 2009. (Motorcycles: Made for Speed Ser.). 24p. (gr. 1-1). 42.50 *(978-1-61514-678-9(4),* PowerKids Pr.); (ENG & SPA.). 42.50 *(978-1-61514-672-7(5),* Editorial Buenas Letras) Rosen Publishing Group, Inc., The.
—Street Bikes. 2009. (Motorcycles: Made for Speed Ser.). 24p. (gr. 1-1). 42.50 *(978-1-61514-679-6(2),* PowerKids Pr.) Rosen Publishing Group, Inc., The.
—Street Bikes/Motos de Calle. 2009. (Motorcycles Made for Speed/Motocicletas a toda velocidad Ser.). (ENG & SPA.). 24p. (gr. 1-1). 42.50 *(978-1-61514-673-4(3),* Editorial Buenas Letras) Rosen Publishing Group, Inc., The.
—Superbikes. 2009. (Motorcycles Made for Speed/Motocicletas a toda velocidad Ser.). 24p. (gr. 1-1). (ENG & SPA.). 42.50 *(978-1-61514-674-1(1),* Editorial Buenas Letras); 42.50 *(978-1-61514-680-2(6),* PowerKids Pr.) Rosen Publishing Group, Inc., The.
—Tricks with Bikes. 2009. (Motorcycles: Made for Speed Ser.). 24p. (gr. 1-1). 42.50 *(978-1-61514-681-9(4),* PowerKids Pr.) Rosen Publishing Group, Inc., The.
—Tricks with Bikes/Trucos con la Moto. 2009. (Motorcycles Made for Speed/Motocicletas a toda velocidad Ser.). (ENG & SPA.). 24p. (gr. 1-1). 42.50 *(978-1-61514-675-8(X),* Editorial Buenas Letras) Rosen Publishing Group, Inc., The.
Freeman, Gary. Motocross, 1 vol. 2012. (To the Limit Ser.). (ENG., Illus.). 32p. (J). (gr. 3-6). pap. 11.00 *(978-1-4488-7062-2(3),* 856ef75f-863e-4b7c-8765-82e956f93da4); lib. bdg. 28.93 *(978-1-4488-7027-1(5),* 044f2376-852e-40b7-8ec4-bc9a0809ed8e) Rosen Publishing Group, Inc., The. (PowerKids Pr.).
Gibbs, Lynne. Mega Book of Motorcycles. 2003. (Illus.). 32p. (YA). pap. *(978-1-903954-57-7(6),* Pavilion Children's Books) Pavilion Bks.
Gifford, Clive. Ducati. 2009. (Red-Hot Bikes Ser.). (YA). (gr. 2-5). 28.50 *(978-1-59771-135-7(7))* Sea-To-Sea Pubns.
—Motorbikes. 2012. (ENG.). 24p. (J). lib. bdg. *(978-0-7787-7475-4(9));* (Illus.). pap. *(978-0-7787-7480-8(5))* Crabtree Publishing Co.
Gillespie, Leslie. Motorcycles. 2011. (Discovery Adventures Ser.). 80p. (J). pap. 8.99 *(978-0-7945-2565-1(2),* Usborne) EDC Publishing.
Glover, David & Glover, Penny. Motorcycles in Action, 1 vol. 2007. (On the Go Ser.). (ENG., Illus.). 24p. (J). (gr. 1-2). lib. bdg. 26.27 *(978-1-4042-4311-8(9),* a40b5b01-c2ee-4447-8cb8-249c589f658f, PowerKids Pr.) Rosen Publishing Group, Inc., The.
Goodman, Susan E. Motorcycles! Doolittle, Michael, illus. 2007. (Step into Reading: Step 3 Ser.). (ENG.). 48p. (J). (gr. k-2). lib. bdg. 16.19 *(978-0-375-94116-0(9))* Random Hse. Bks. for Young Readers.
—Motorcycles! Doolittle, Michael J., illus. 2007. (Step into Reading Ser.). 48p. (J). (gr. k-3). per. 4.99 *(978-0-375-84116-3(4),* Random Hse. Bks. for Young Readers) Random Hse. Children's Bks.
Graham, Ian. Bikes. 2017. (Mighty Machines Ser.). (ENG., Illus.). 24p. (J). (gr. -1-2). pap. 5.95 *(978-1-77085-849-7(0),* 9c2672b7-7144-4620-87a0-b2350673e8d3) Firefly Bks., Ltd.
—Motorcycles. 2015. (Wonderwise Ser.). (Illus.). 32p. (gr. 2-6). 31.35 *(978-1-62588-360-5(9))* Black Rabbit Bks.
Graham, Ian & Salariya, David. Super Bikes. Hewetson, N. J., illus. 2014. (Time Shift Speed Ser.). 32p. (gr. 3-6). 31.35 *(978-1-908973-96-2(X))* Book Hse. GBR. Dist: Black Rabbit Bks.
Gunston, Bill Tudor & Parker, Steve. Fasten Your Seatbelt! Mind-Boggling Machines. 2010. (ENG.). 96p. (J). (gr. 2-4). pap. 9.95 *(978-1-84696-205-9(6),* TickTock Books) Octopus Publishing Group GBR. Dist: Independent Pubs. Group.
Harrison, Paul. Superbikes. 2013. (Illus.). 32p. (J). *(978-1-84858-563-8(2))* Arcturus Pubs., Inc.
Hatter, Hilda E. Bananas & Balloons: Inspirational Stories of Motorcycling Adventures. 2004. 307p. (YA). per. 15.99 *(978-0-9761167-0-7(7))* TIGO & Co.
Hawkins, Clyde. Harley Davidson, Vol. 8. 2015. (Classic Cars & Bikes Collection). (Illus.). 64p. (J). (gr. 7). lib. bdg. 23.95 *(978-1-4222-3280-4(8))* Mason Crest.
Hill, David. Speed King: Burt Munro, the World's Fastest Indian. Morris, Phoebe, illus. 2016. 32p. (J). 17.99 *(978-0-14-350722-2(2))* Penguin Group New Zealand, Ltd. NZL. Dist: Independent Pubs. Group.
Hill, Lee Sullivan. Motorcycles. 2004. (Pull Ahead Books — Mighty Movers Ser.). (ENG., Illus.). 32p. (J). (gr. k-3). pap. 7.99 *(978-0-8225-9924-1(4),* a7abed57-d6b9-4cf1-a24b-8d2a601d6174, First Avenue Editions) Lerner Publishing Group.
—Motorcycles on the Move. 2011. (Lightning Bolt Books Vroom-Vroom Ser.). 32p. pap. 45.32 *(978-0-7613-7619-4(4))* Lerner Publishing Group.
Hinote Lanier, Wendy. Choppers. 2017. (Let's Roll Ser.). (ENG., Illus.). 32p. (J). (gr. 2-3). pap. 9.95 *(978-1-63517-110-5(5),* 1635171105); lib. bdg. 31.35 *(978-1-63517-054-2(0),* 1635170540) North Star Editions. (Focus Readers).
—Dirt Bikes. 2017. (Let's Roll Ser.). (ENG., Illus.). 32p. (J). (gr. 2-3). pap. 9.95 *(978-1-63517-109-9(1),* 1635171091); lib. bdg. 31.35 *(978-1-63517-053-5(2),* 1635170532) North Star Editions. (Focus Readers).
Hobbs, Mike. Superbikes, Vol. 8. 2015. (Classic Cars & Bikes Collection). (Illus.). 64p. (J). (gr. 7). lib. bdg. 23.95 *(978-1-4222-3282-8(4))* Mason Crest.
Hofer, Charles. Motorcycles, 1 vol. 2007. (World's Fastest Machines Ser.). (ENG., Illus.). 24p. (J). (gr. 2-3). lib. bdg. 26.27 *(978-1-4042-4177-0(9),* ce9d5c96-1723-438b-81c4-cf50583583cd, PowerKids Pr.) Rosen Publishing Group, Inc., The.
Holter, James. Dirt Bike Racers, 1 vol. 2010. (Kid Racers Ser.). (ENG., Illus.). 48p. (gr. 5-7). 27.93 *(978-0-7660-3483-9(6),* 1ef2da01-4cb4-4423-ad61-a89d573b16d1) Enslow Publishing, LLC.
—Racing Dirt Bikes, 1 vol. 2017. (Speed Racers Ser.). (ENG.). 48p. (gr. 6-6). 29.60 *(978-0-7660-9275-4(5),* 66881dc9-1ba6-4978-9303-6e2da193f733) Enslow Publishing, LLC.
Johnson, Ben. Motocross. 2008. (Crabtree Contact Ser.). (ENG., Illus.). 32p. (J). (gr. 3-7). pap. *(978-0-7787-3786-5(1));* lib. bdg. *(978-0-7787-3764-3(0))* Crabtree Publishing Co.
Kamberg, Mary-Lane. Kawasaki: World's Fastest Bike, 1 vol. 2013. (Motorcycles: a Guide to the World's Best Bikes Ser.). (ENG.). 48p. (J). (gr. 5-5). pap. 12.75 *(978-1-4777-1874-2(5),* b8e42a5b-97d2-4706-9f2c-d1fa8774bb5b, Rosen Reference) Rosen Publishing Group, Inc., The.
Kawasaki: World's Fastest Bike. 2013. (Motorcycles: a Guide to the World's Best Bikes Ser.). 48p. (J). (gr. 5-8). pap. 70.50 *(978-1-4777-1875-9(3),* Rosen Reference) Rosen Publishing Group, Inc., The.
Levy, Janey. Freestyle Motocross. (Motocross Ser.). 32p. (gr. 4-5). 2009. 47.90 *(978-1-61514-662-8(8))* 2007. (ENG., Illus.). (J). lib. bdg. 28.93 *(978-1-4042-3694-3(5),* fd7400cc-0227-46a1-bc43-b5ec0f700c82) Rosen Publishing Group, Inc., The. (PowerKids Pr.).
—Motocross. 2007. 36p. (gr. 3-7). pap. 23.95 *(978-1-4358-3836-9(X));* (ENG., Illus.). 32p. (J). (gr. 4-5). lib. bdg. 28.93 *(978-1-4042-3692-9(9),* 484b1da7-34d8-440e-b011-9aaee7391185) Rosen Publishing Group, Inc., The. (PowerKids Pr.).
—Motocross, 12 vols., Set. Incl. Freestyle Motocross. lib. bdg. 28.93 *(978-1-4042-3694-3(5),* fd7400cc-0227-46a1-bc43-b5ec0f700c82); lib. bdg. 28.93 *(978-1-4042-3692-9(9),* 484b1da7-34d8-440e-b011-9aaee7391185); Motocross Races. lib. bdg. 28.93 *(978-1-4042-3696-7(1),* 6b71ced9-efee-48ec-8180-c8fc14a3e803); Motocross Superstars. lib. bdg. 28.93 *(978-1-4042-3695-0(3),* 43b92e34-7cbf-4509-b5da-cfc400a95363); Motocross Tricks. lib. bdg. 28.93 *(978-1-4042-3697-4(X),* 70c4a1fb-e86b-4575-820b-7ce0eae03363); Supercross. lib. bdg. 28.93 *(978-1-4042-3693-6(7),* cba2bef7-313e-4537-87e5-6a8f78b8ac00); (Illus.). 32p. (J). (gr. 4-5). 2007., PowerKids Pr. (Motocross Ser.). (ENG.). 2006. Set lib. bdg. 173.58 *(978-1-4042-3611-0(2),* 71321050-3222-4f9b-ab04-ab26c9fb1eb7) Rosen Publishing Group, Inc., The.
—Motocross Races, 1 vol. 2007. (Motocross Ser.). (ENG., Illus.). 32p. (J). (gr. 4-5). lib. bdg. 28.93 *(978-1-4042-3696-7(1),* 6b71ced9-efee-48ec-8180-c8fc14a3e803, PowerKids Pr.) Rosen Publishing Group, Inc., The.
—Motocross Superstars, 1 vol. 2007. (Motocross Ser.). (ENG., Illus.). 32p. (J). (gr. 4-5). lib. bdg. 28.93 *(978-1-4042-3695-0(3),* 43b92e34-7cbf-4509-b5da-cfc400a95363, PowerKids Pr.) Rosen Publishing Group, Inc., The.
—Motocross Tricks, 1 vol. 2007. (Motocross Ser.). (ENG., Illus.). 32p. (J). (gr. 4-5). lib. bdg. 28.93 *(978-1-4042-3697-4(X),* 70c4a1fb-e86b-4575-820b-7ce0eae03363, PowerKids Pr.) Rosen Publishing Group, Inc., The.
—Supercross. (Motocross Ser.). 32p. (gr. 4-5). 2009. 47.90 *(978-1-61514-669-7(5))* 2007. (ENG., Illus.). (J). lib. bdg. 28.93 *(978-1-4042-3693-6(7),* cba2bef7-313e-4537-87e5-6a8f78b8ac00) Rosen Publishing Group, Inc., The. (PowerKids Pr.).
Louck, Cheryl. The ABC's of Motocross. Zielinski, Dave, photos by. 2003. (Illus.). 24p. (J). per. 14.95 *(978-0-9744230-0-5(9))* Louck, Cheryl.
Mahaney, Ian F. Travis Pastrana: Motorcross Champion, 1 vol. 2004. (Extreme Sports Biographies Ser.). (ENG., Illus.). 24p. (J). (gr. 3-4). 26.27 *(978-1-4042-2748-4(2),* e24f14c9-91ea-4851-87bb-6f26989de6a0, PowerKids Pr.) Rosen Publishing Group, Inc., The.
Mara, Wil. Extreme Motocross, 1 vol. 2013. (Sports on the Edge Ser.). (ENG.). 48p. (gr. 4-4). pap. 13.93 *(978-1-62712-132-3(3),* b21aa671-7f4e-4054-8537-4ad942622195) Cavendish Square Publishing LLC.
Marshall, Jane. Superbikes. 2013. (Wild Rides Ser.). 32p. (gr. 2-4). *(978-1-84898-621-3(1),* TickTock Books) Octopus Publishing Group.
Marx, Mandy R. Choppers. 2018. (Horsepower Ser.). (ENG., Illus.). 32p. (J). (gr. 3-9). pap. 7.95 *(978-1-5435-2470-3(2),* 137978); lib. bdg. 27.32 *(978-1-5435-2462-8(1),* 137970) Capstone. (Capstone Pr.).
—Choppers. Aparicio Publishing LLC, Aparicio Publishing, tr. from ENG. 2019. (Todo Motor Ser.). (SPA., Illus.). 32p. (J). (gr. 3-9). lib. bdg. 27.32 *(978-1-5435-8255-0(9),* 141265) Capstone.
Mason, Paul. Motorcycles. 2010. (Motorsports Ser.). 32p. (J). (gr. 3-6). 28.50 *(978-1-60753-121-0(6))* Amicus Learning.
Mattern, Joanne. Staying Safe on My Bike, 1 vol. 2007. (Safety First Ser.). (ENG., Illus.). 24p. (gr. k-2). pap. 9.15 *(978-0-8368-7801-1(9),* 6172f468-320b-490f-93ef-119f79ee8878); lib. bdg. 24.67 *(978-0-8368-7794-6(2),* 8f1e2c53-4f85-4e83-a93b-809bc1d9289a) Stevens, Gareth Publishing LLLP. (Weekly Reader Leveled Readers).
—Staying Safe on My Bike / la Seguridad en Mi Bicicleta, 1 vol. 2007. (Safety First / la Seguridad Es lo Primero Ser.). (SPA & ENG., Illus.). 24p. (gr. k-2). lib. bdg. 24.67 *(978-0-8368-8059-5(5),* 00aaf97c-8673-4d88-aaa5-e359bbc56f21, Weekly Reader Leveled Readers) Stevens, Gareth Publishing LLLP.
McClellan, Ray. SuperMoto. 2008. (Action Sports Ser.). (ENG., Illus.). 24p. (J). (gr. 3-7). lib. bdg. 26.95 *(978-1-60014-144-7(7))* Bellwether Media.
Mezzanotte, Jim. Motocross, 1 vol. 2005. (Motorcycle Racing: the Fast Track Ser.). (ENG., Illus.). 24p. (gr. 3-3). pap. 9.15 *(978-0-8368-6572-1(3),* e583013d-fd37-487d-9b97-43a849c3c73c); lib. bdg. 25.67 *(978-0-8368-6423-6(9),* 7894778b-fee2-43ad-8832-28851324fafa) Stevens, Gareth Publishing LLLP.
—Superbike, 1 vol. 2005. (Motorcycle Racing: the Fast Track Ser.). (ENG., Illus.). 24p. (gr. 3-3). pap. 9.15 *(978-0-8368-6573-8(1),* 8fa027a0-3e45-4ce9-828d-1839c80c3028); lib. bdg. 25.67 *(978-0-8368-6424-3(7),* 18f31513-463b-42d7-a46e-288dc9db3c9f) Stevens, Gareth Publishing LLLP.
—Supercross, 1 vol. 2005. (Motorcycle Racing: the Fast Track Ser.). (ENG., Illus.). 24p. (gr. 3-3). lib. bdg. 25.67 *(978-0-8368-6425-0(5),* a3096841-f8f9-4f78-92ae-6fc1f17701db) Stevens, Gareth Publishing LLLP.
—Supermoto, 1 vol. 2005. (Motorcycle Racing: the Fast Track Ser.). (ENG., Illus.). 24p. (gr. 3-3). pap. 9.15 *(978-0-8368-6575-2(8),* 53d747c4-8a36-451c-a66e-48c787a51641) Stevens, Gareth Publishing LLLP.
Mitton, Tony. Marvelous Motorcycles. Parker, Ant, illus. 2018. (Amazing Machines Ser.). (ENG.). 20p. (J). bds. 6.99 *(978-0-7534-7419-8(0),* 900187154, Kingfisher) Roaring Brook Pr.
Morey, Allan. Motorcycles. 2014. (Illus.). 24p. (J). lib. bdg. 25.65 *(978-1-62031-103-5(8),* Bullfrog Bks.) Jump! Inc.
Motor Bike. 2004. (Press-Out & Build Ser.). (Illus.). 24p. (J). per. *(978-1-84229-724-7(4))* Top That! Publishing PLC.
Motorcycles: a Guide to the World's Best Bikes: A Guide to the World's Best Bikes, 12 vols. 2013. (Motorcycles: a Guide to the World's Best Bikes Ser.). 48p. (J). (gr. 5-5). (ENG.). 206.46 *(978-1-4777-1867-4(2),* 58919035-c882-4326-808b-14a54a8063a7); pap. 423.00 *(978-1-4777-7800-5(4));* pap. 70.50 *(978-1-4777-7801-2(2))* Rosen Publishing Group, Inc., The. (Rosen Reference).
Mr Mcdoodle & His Scooter: 3-in-1 Package. (Sails Literacy Ser.). 24p. (gr. 2-18). 57.00 *(978-0-7578-6831-3(2))* Rigby Education.
Mr Mcdoodle & His Scooter: Big Book Only. (Sails Literacy Ser.). 24p. (gr. 2-18). 27.00 *(978-0-7578-6819-1(3))* Rigby Education.
Murray, Julie. Bmw. 2018. (Motorcycles Ser.). (ENG., Illus.). 24p. (J). (gr. k-4). lib. bdg. 31.36 *(978-1-5321-2302-3(7),* 28371, Abdo Zoom-Dash) ABDO Publishing Co.
—Harley-Davidson. 2018. (Motorcycles Ser.). (ENG., Illus.). 24p. (J). (gr. k-4). lib. bdg. 31.36 *(978-1-5321-2303-0(5),* 28373, Abdo Zoom-Dash) ABDO Publishing Co.
—Honda. 2018. (Motorcycles Ser.). (ENG., Illus.). 24p. (J). (gr. k-4). lib. bdg. 31.36 *(978-1-5321-2304-7(3),* 28375, Abdo Zoom-Dash) ABDO Publishing Co.
—Kawasaki. 2018. (Motorcycles Ser.). (ENG., Illus.). 24p. (J). (gr. k-4). lib. bdg. 31.36 *(978-1-5321-2305-4(1),* 28377, Abdo Zoom-Dash) ABDO Publishing Co.
—Triumph. 2018. (Motorcycles Ser.). (ENG., Illus.). 24p. (J). (gr. k-4). lib. bdg. 31.36 *(978-1-5321-2306-1(X),* 28379, Abdo Zoom-Dash) ABDO Publishing Co.
—Yamaha. 2018. (Motorcycles Ser.). (ENG., Illus.). 24p. (J). (gr. k-4). lib. bdg. 31.36 *(978-1-5321-2307-8(8),* 28381, Abdo Zoom-Dash) ABDO Publishing Co.
Nix, Harvey. How to Ride a Bike: My Very First Learn-To Book. 2006. 92p. 14.95 *(978-0-944353-22-6(3))* Rivendell Bk. Factory.
Nixon, James. Motorcycles. 2010. (Machines on the Move Ser.). (ENG.). 32p. (J). (gr. 1-3). lib. bdg. 28.50 *(978-1-60753-060-2(0),* 17213) Amicus.
—Motorcycles. 2012. (ENG., Illus.). 32p. (gr. 1-3). pap. 8.95 *(978-1-926722-70-2(1))* Saunders Bk. Co. CAN. Dist: RiverStream Publishing.
Norman, Tony. Motorbike Racing, 1 vol. 2005. (Action Sports Ser.). (ENG., Illus.). 32p. (gr. 3-5). lib. bdg. 28.67 *(978-0-8368-6368-0(2),* 95eb382b-d5f3-41d8-986b-c4e817f2b426, Gareth Stevens Learning Library) Stevens, Gareth Publishing LLLP.
Norris, Ashley P. Watson. The World's Fastest Motorcycles. 2016. (World Record Breakers Ser.). (ENG., Illus.). 32p. (J). (gr. 3-9). lib. bdg. 28.65 *(978-1-4914-8178-3(1),* 130654, Capstone Pr.) Capstone.
Oxlade, Chris. Motorcycles. (Mighty Machines Ser.). (Illus.). (gr. 4-7). 2009. 31p. (J). pap. 7.95 *(978-1-59920-255-6(7))* 2007. 32p. (YA). lib. bdg. 28.50 *(978-1-59920-041-5(4))* Black Rabbit Bks.
—Motorcycles. 2009. (How Machines Work Ser.). (ENG., Illus.). 32p. (J). (gr. -1-3). pap. *(978-1-897563-44-1(2))* Saunders Bk. Co.
—Motorcycles Inside & Out, 1 vol. 2009. (Machines Inside Out Ser.). (ENG., Illus.). 32p. (J). (gr. 4-4). pap. 11.00 *(978-1-4358-2942-8(5),*

M N O

bf9a00ae-cb7e-414d-931e-0e5abbdf030f, PowerKids Pr.) Rosen Publishing Group, Inc., The.

Parker, Steve. Cars Trucks & Bikes. 2010. (How It Works Ser.). (Illus.). 40p. (J). (gr. 3-18). lib. bdg. 19.95 *(978-1-4222-1792-4(2),* 1317905) Mason Crest.

Perritano, John. American MX: From Backwater to World Leaders. 2008. (MXplosion! Ser.). (ENG., Illus.). 32p. (J). (gr. 3-7). pap. *(978-0-7787-3999-9(6));* (gr. 4-7). lib. bdg. *(978-0-7787-3986-9(4))* Crabtree Publishing Co.

—Mx Bikes: Evolution from Primitive Street Machines to State of the Art Off-Road Machines. 2008. (MXplosion! Ser.). (ENG., Illus.). 32p. (J). (gr. 3-7). pap. *(978-0-7787-4001-8(3));* lib. bdg. *(978-0-7787-3988-3(0))* Crabtree Publishing Co.

Peterson, Blaire & Peterson, Brent. The Bike Race, 1 vol. 2013. (Rosen Math Readers Ser.). (ENG.). 24p. (J). (gr. 1-1). pap. 8.25 *(978-1-4777-2022-6(7),* 3e4c4f60-3d4f-439f-aac6-8310f5469f07, Rosen Classroom) Rosen Publishing Group, Inc., The.

Peterson, Brent. The Bike Race: Add Within 20. 2013. (Rosen Math Readers Ser.). (ENG.). 24p. (J). (gr. 1-2). pap. 49.50 *(978-1-4777-2023-3(5),* Rosen Classroom) Rosen Publishing Group, Inc., The.

Polydoros, Lori. Dirt Bikes, 1 vol. 2010. (Full Throttle Ser.). (ENG.). 32p. (J). (gr. 3-9). lib. bdg. 28.65 *(978-1-4296-3940-8(7),* 102550, Capstone Pr.) Capstone.

Raby, Philip & Nix, Simon. Motorbikes. 2005. (Need for Speed Ser.). (Illus.). 32p. (J). (gr. 3-5). pap. 7.95 *(978-0-8225-9854-1(X))* Lerner Publishing Group.

Riggs, Kate. Motorcycles. (Seedlings Ser.). 24p. (J). (gr. -1-k). 2015. (ENG.). *(978-1-60818-522-1(2),* 21237) 2010. 16.95 *(978-1-58341-914-4(4))* 2007. (Illus.). lib. bdg. 24.25 *(978-1-58341-528-3(9))* Creative Co., The. (Creative Education).

—Seedlings: Motorcycles. 2015. (Seedlings Ser.). (ENG.). 24p. (J). (gr. -1-1). pap. 10.99 *(978-1-62832-122-7(9),* 21238, Creative Paperbacks) Creative Co., The.

Rosenberg, Aaron. Kick Scooters: Techniques & Tricks. 2009. (Rad Sports: Techniques & Tricks Ser.). 48p. (gr. 5-8). 53.00 *(978-1-60851-934-7(1),* Rosen Reference) Rosen Publishing Group, Inc., The.

Roza, Greg. Harley-Davidson: An All-American Legend, 1 vol. 2013. (Motorcycles: a Guide to the World's Best Bikes Ser.). (Illus.). 48p. (J). (gr. 5-5). (ENG.). 34.41 *(978-1-4777-1855-1(9),* 75339a8c-d999-4fd5-9e29-3510f7608b4a); (ENG., pap. 12.75 *(978-1-4777-1872-8(9),* 7241b197-6ba2-4be2-a3c7-7f810ddf3d96); pap. 70.50 *(978-1-4777-1873-5(7))* Rosen Publishing Group, Inc., The. (Rosen Reference).

Ruck, Colleen. Motorcycles. 2011. (My Favorite Machines Ser.). 24p. (gr. 2-5). 28.50 *(978-1-59920-676-9(5))* Black Rabbit Bks.

Savage, Jeff. Choppers, 1 vol. 2010. (Full Throttle Ser.). (ENG.). 32p. (J). (gr. 3-9). lib. bdg. 28.65 *(978-1-4296-3939-2(3),* 102549, Capstone Pr.) Capstone.

—James Stewart. 2008. pap. 40.95 *(978-0-8225-9286-0(X))* Lerner Publishing Group.

—Motorcycles. collector's ed. 2005. (Race Car Legends: Collector's Edition Ser.). (ENG., Illus.). 80p. (gr. 5-9). lib. bdg. 25.00 *(978-0-7910-8695-7(X),* P114393, Facts On File) Infobase Holdings, Inc.

—Travis Pastrana. 2006. (Amazing Athletes Ser.). (Illus.). 32p. (J). (gr. 2-5). per. 5.95 *(978-0-8225-3433-4(9),* First Avenue Editions) Lerner Publishing Group.

Schuette, Sarah L. Bike Safety. 2019. (Staying Safe! Ser.). (ENG., Illus.). 24p. (J). (gr. -1-2). 24.65 *(978-1-9771-0873-9(3),* 140484, Pebble) Capstone.

Schuh, Mari. Motorcycles. 2020. (Wild about Wheels Ser.). (ENG., Illus.). 24p. (J). (gr. k-2). lib. bdg. 29.99 *(978-1-9771-2478-4(X),* 200490, Pebble) Capstone.

Shaffer, Lindsay. Motocross Cycles. 2018. (Full Throttle Ser.). (ENG., Illus.). 24p. (J). (gr. 3-7). lib. bdg. 26.95 *(978-1-62617-875-5(5),* Epic Bks.) Bellwether Media.

Sharkey, Alex. Classic Bikes, Vol. 8. 2015. (Classic Cars & Bikes Collection). (Illus.). 64p. (J). (gr. 7). lib. bdg. 23.95 *(978-1-4222-3277-4(8))* Mason Crest.

Shofner, Shawndra. How It Happens at the Motorcycle Plant. Wolfe, Bob & Wolfe, Diane, photos by. 2006. (How It Happens Ser.). (Illus.). 32p. (J). (gr. 2-5). lib. bdg. 19.95 *(978-1-881508-99-1(4))* Oliver Pr., Inc.

Slingerland, Janet. Superfast Motorcycle Racing. 2020. (Extreme Speed (Lerner (tm) Sports) Ser.). (ENG., Illus.). 32p. (J). (gr. 2-5). pap. 8.99 *(978-1-5415-8738-0(3),* 258e51a6-b6d4-48d5-9b22-0ea8b34919e6); lib. bdg. 29.32 *(978-1-5415-7721-3(3),* 17d9db3a-173b-433d-b562-a6ea263e0e8e) Lerner Publishing Group. (Lerner Pubns.).

Smith, Elliott. Enduro & Other Extreme Mountain Biking. 2019. (Natural Thrills Ser.). (ENG., Illus.). 32p. (J). (gr. 3-9). lib. bdg. 28.65 *(978-1-5435-7324-4(X),* 140624) Capstone.

Stealey, Bryan. Motocross, 1 vol. 2010. (Racing Mania Ser.). (ENG.). 48p. (gr. 4-4). lib. bdg. 34.07 *(978-0-7614-4386-5(X),* 6f7b6a63-c7b6-400a-8871-54c4840a402d) Cavendish Square Publishing LLC.

Storm, Marysa. Motorcycles. 2020. (Wild Rides Ser.). (ENG.). 24p. (J). (gr. k-3). pap. 8.99 *(978-1-64466-121-5(7),* 23007, Bolt Jr.) Black Rabbit Bks.

Streissguth, Thomas. Mini Bikes. 2008. (Motorcycles Ser.). (ENG., Illus.). 24p. (J). (gr. 3-7). lib. bdg. 26.95 *(978-1-60014-155-3(2))* Bellwether Media.

—Off-Road Motorcycles. 2008. (Motorcycles Ser.). (ENG., Illus.). 24p. (J). (gr. 3-7). lib. bdg. 26.95 *(978-1-60014-156-0(0))* Bellwether Media.

—Pocket Bikes. 2008. (Motorcycles Ser.). (ENG., Illus.). 24p. (J). (gr. 3-7). lib. bdg. 26.95 *(978-1-60014-157-7(9))* Bellwether Media.

—Scooters. 2008. (Motorcycles Ser.). (ENG., Illus.). 24p. (J). (gr. 3-7). lib. bdg. 26.95 *(978-1-60014-158-4(7))* Bellwether Media.

—Standard Motorcycles. 2008. (Motorcycles Ser.). (ENG., Illus.). 24p. (J). (gr. 3-7). lib. bdg. 26.95 *(978-1-60014-159-1(5))* Bellwether Media.

—Trials Bikes. 2008. (Motorcycles Ser.). (ENG., Illus.). 24p. (J). (gr. 3-7). lib. bdg. 26.95 *(978-1-60014-160-7(9))* Bellwether Media.

Stuckey, Rachel. Ride It Bmx. 2012. (ENG., Illus.). 32p. (J). pap. *(978-0-7787-3161-0(8))* Crabtree Publishing Co.

Taylor, Trace. Bikes. Taylor, Trace, illus. 2015. (1-3Y Getting Around Ser.). (ENG., Illus.). 24p. (J). (gr. k-2). pap. 8.00 *(978-1-59301-465-0(1))* American Reading Co.

Tiner, John Hudson. Motorcycles. (Illus.). 32p. 2004. pap. 8.95 *(978-0-89812-389-0(5),* Creative Paperbacks) 2003. (J). lib. bdg. 18.95 *(978-1-58341-285-5(9),* Creative Education) Creative Co., The.

Tudhope, Simon. Build Your Own Motorcycles Sticker Book. 2015. (Build Your Own Sticker Bks.). (ENG.). 24+10p. (J). (gr. k-5). pap. 8.99 *(978-0-7945-3546-9(1),* Usborne) EDC Publishing.

West, David. Motorcycles. 2015. (Mechanic Mike's Machines (continuation) Ser.). (Illus.). 24p. (gr. k-3). 27.10 *(978-1-62588-064-2(2))* Black Rabbit Bks.

Wiseman, Blaine. MotoX. 2010. (Record Breakers Ser.). (Illus.). 24p. (YA). (gr. 3-6). lib. bdg. 27.13 *(978-1-61690-115-8(2));* (J). (gr. 4-6). pap. 12.95 *(978-1-61690-116-5(0))* Weigl Pubs., Inc.

Woods, Bob. Motocross History: From Local Scrambling to World Championship MX to Freestyle. 2008. (MXplosion! Ser.). (ENG., Illus.). 32p. (J). (gr. 3-7). pap. *(978-0-7787-4000-1(5));* lib. bdg. *(978-0-7787-3987-6(2))* Crabtree Publishing Co.

—Smokin' Motorcycles, 1 vol. 2013. (Fast Wheels! Ser.). (ENG.). 48p. (gr. 4-6). pap. 11.53 *(978-1-62285-086-0(6),* cfe7fbd8-0baf-4c88-8fab-bc6a78276160) Enslow Publishing, LLC.

Worms, Penny. Motorcycles. 2016. (Motormania Ser.). 32p. (gr. 2-7). 31.35 *(978-1-59920-996-8(9),* Smart Apple Media) Black Rabbit Bks.

Young, Jeff C. Motorcycles: The Ins & Outs of Superbikes, Choppers, & Other Motorcycles. 2010. (Rpm Ser.). (ENG.). 48p. (gr. 3-4). pap. 59.70 *(978-1-4296-5127-1(X))* Capstone.

Zobel, Derek. Motorcycles. 2009. (Mighty Machines Ser.). (ENG., Illus.). 24p. (J). (gr. k-3). lib. bdg. 26.95 *(978-1-60014-269-7(9))* Bellwether Media.

Zuehlke, Jeffrey. Motorcycle Road Racing. 2009. pap. 52.95 *(978-0-7613-4792-7(5))* Lerner Publishing Group.

—Supercross. 2008. pap. 52.95 *(978-1-58013-709-6(1))* Lerner Publishing Group.

MOTORCYCLES—FICTION

Appleton, Victor. Tom Swift & his Motor-Cycle. 2005. 26.95 *(978-1-4218-1502-2(8));* 192p. pap. 11.95 *(978-1-4218-1602-9(4))* 1st World Publishing, Inc. (1st World Library - Literary Society).

—Tom Swift & His Motor Cycle. 2004. reprint ed. pap. 1.99 *(978-1-4192-8459-5(2))* Kessinger Publishing, LLC.

—Tom Swift & His Motor-Cycle, Tom Swift & His Motor-Boat, Tom Swift & His Airship. 2007. 292p. per. 12.99 *(978-1-60459-097-5(1))* Wilder Pubns., Corp.

—Tom Swift & His MotorCycle. 2006. pap. *(978-1-4068-0727-1(3))* Echo Library.

—Tom Swift & His MotorCycle or Fun and. 2006. pap. *(978-1-4065-0905-2(1))* Dodo Pr.

Aronson, Jeff & Aronson, Miriam. Little Mike & Maddie's Black Hill's Adventure. Aronson, Jeff & Zephyr, Jay, illus. 2007. 33p. (J). 16.00 *(978-0-9795302-1-0(0),* CrumbGobbler Pr.) Downtown Wetmore Pr.

—Little Mike & Maddie's First Motorcycle Ride. Aronson, Jeff & Zephyr, Jay, illus. 2007. 32p. (J). 16.00 *(978-0-9795302-0-3(2),* CrumbGobbler Pr.) Downtown Wetmore Pr.

Blake, Quentin. Mrs. Armitage, Queen of the Road. 2003. (ENG., Illus.). 32p. (J). (gr. -1-3). 15.95 *(978-1-56145-287-3(4))* Peachtree Publishing Co. Inc.

The Box. 2012. (ENG.). 30p. (J). (gr. -1-k). 16.95 *(978-1-60537-134-4(3))* Clavis Publishing.

Burger, Kyle. The Adventures of Buddy the Motocross Bike: Buddy Learns about Confidence. 2012. 32p. pap. 19.99 *(978-1-4685-0609-9(9))* AuthorHouse.

Caldwell, Bruce. Sidecar Scooter. Hawyard, Charlie O., illus. 2008. 32p. (J). pap. 9.95 *(978-0-9792612-9-9(5))* Blue Gate Bks.

Charles, Norma. Chasing a Star. 2009. (ENG., Illus.). 182p. (YA). (gr. 5-8). pap. *(978-1-55380-077-4(X))* Ronsdale Pr.

Christopher, Matt. Dirt Bike Runaway. 2008. (New Matt Christopher Sports Library). 176p. (J). (gr. 4-6). lib. bdg. 26.60 *(978-1-59953-215-8(8))* Norwood Hse. Pr.

Cross, Carrie. Skylar Robbins: The Mystery of the Hidden Jewels. 2014. (ENG., Illus.). 249p. (J). (gr. 4-9). pap. 11.99 *(978-0-9894143-2-6(9))* Ward Design, LLC DBA Teen Mystery Pr.

Davidson, Jean. My Grandma Rides a Harley: She's Cool! Bauknecht, Julie, illus. 2007. (J). *(978-1-930596-79-5(0))* Amherst Pr.

Duff, Ms. Michelle Ann. Five Cats, One Dog, a Motorcycle & a Lady in a Hot Pink Jacket. 2012. 146p. pap. *(978-0-9685706-7-8(4))* Mad8 Publishing.

Jamiol, Paul. Bikers Are Animals: A Children's Book on Motorcycling. Habib, Linda, ed. 2009. 38p. pap. 14.95 *(978-1-60844-232-4(2))* Dog Ear Publishing, LLC.

—Bikers Are Animals 4: Working & Riding. 2013. (Illus.). 38p. pap. 14.95 *(978-1-4575-2323-6(X))* Dog Ear Publishing, LLC.

Kirkpatrick, Brenna. My Motorcycle & Me: A Trip in the Mountains. 2011. 28p. pap. 14.56 *(978-1-4634-0469-7(7))* AuthorHouse.

Link, C. Edward. The Little Motorcycle. Serfass, Jim, illus. 2004. (J). 9.95 *(978-0-9749615-0-7(7))* Roadracing World Publishing, Inc.

Maddox, Jake. Motocross Double-Cross. Tiffany, Sean, illus. 2007. (Jake Maddox Sports Stories Ser.). (ENG.). 72p. (J). (gr. 3-6). pap. 5.95 *(978-1-59889-897-2(3),* 94321, Stone Arch Bks.) Capstone.

Matson, Carole. Jesus Loves Dirt Bikes Too!! 2011. (ENG.). 33p. pap. 15.40 *(978-0-557-15092-2(2))* Lulu Pr., Inc.

Meadows, Michelle. Traffic Pups. Andreasen, Dan, illus. 2011. (ENG.). 32p. (J). (gr. -1-3). 15.99 *(978-1-4169-2485-2(X),* Simon & Schuster Bks. For Young Readers) Simon & Schuster Bks. For Young Readers.

Mount, Jill. The Mystery of the Dirty Bike. 2005. 9.00 *(978-0-8059-9778-1(4))* Dorrance Publishing Co., Inc.

Nelson, Scott. Patch the Porcupine & the Bike Shop Job. Nelson, Scott, illus. 2004. (Illus.). 28p. (J). 14.95 *(978-0-9745715-3-9(9))* KRBY Creations, LLC.

O'Mailey, Kevin. Once upon a Cool Motorcycle Dude. O'Mailey, Kevin & Heyer, Carol, illus. 2005. (ENG.). 32p. (J). (gr. 1-5). 17.99 *(978-0-8027-8947-1(1),* 900034867, Bloomsbury USA Childrens) Bloomsbury Publishing USA.

Pakalne, Violeta. A Motorcyclist Croaker Lee. 2010. 80p. pap. 29.49 *(978-1-4520-9578-3(7))* AuthorHouse.

Parker, John. Sucked In. 2008. (Lightning Strikes Ser.). (ENG.). 96p. (J). pap. *(978-1-921150-62-3(9))* Walker Bks. Australia Pty. Ltd.

Quigley, Daniel. A Face Full of Wind. 2003. 106p. (YA). pap. 10.95 *(978-0-7414-1798-5(7))* Infinity Publishing.

Quintero, Isabel. My Papi Has a Motorcycle. Peña, Zeke, illus. 2019. (ENG.). 40p. (J). (gr. -1-3). 18.99 *(978-0-525-55341-0(X),* Kokila) Penguin Young Readers Group.

Ralphson, G. Harvey. Boy Scouts on Motorcycles. 2007. 100p. per. *(978-1-4068-3731-5(8))* Echo Library.

Randolph, Robert. Their Very Own Bike, 1 vol. 2010. 28p. 24.95 *(978-1-4489-8322-3(3))* PublishAmerica, Inc.

Roy, James. Queasy Rider. 2008. (Lightning Strikes Ser.). (ENG.). 96p. (J). pap. *(978-1-921150-57-9(2))* Walker Bks. Australia Pty. Ltd.

Rush, Jennifer. Devils & Thieves. 2017. (Devils & Thieves Ser.: 1). (ENG.). 336p. (YA). (gr. 9-17). 17.99 *(978-0-316-39089-7(5))* Little, Brown Bks. for Young Readers.

Siebert, Diane. Motorcycle Song. Jenkins, Leonard, illus. Date not set. 32p. (J). (gr. -1-3). 5.99 *(978-0-06-443632-8(2))* HarperCollins Pubs.

Strange, David. Why Grandpa Rides a Harley. 2005. 16.95 *(978-0-9772771-0-0(0))* Cherry Tree Pr. LLC.

Togden, Ra Chel. The Legendary Rabbit of Death - Volume One [Paperback]. 2013. 108p. pap. *(978-1-898185-27-7(1))* Aro Bks. worldwide.

Walters, Celeste. The Glass Mountain. 2003. 280p. (YA). pap. *(978-0-7022-3297-8(1))* Univ. of Queensland Pr.

MOTORING

see Automobile Travel

MOTORS

see Electric Motors; Engines

MOTT, LUCRETIA, 1793-1880

Marsico, Katie. Lucretia Mott: Abolitionist & Women's Rights Leader, 1 vol. 2008. (Essential Lives Set 2 Ser.). (ENG., Illus.). 112p. (YA). (gr. 6-12). lib. bdg. 41.36 *(978-1-60453-039-1(1),* 6659, Essential Library) ABDO Publishing Co.

MOUNDS AND MOUND BUILDERS

see also Excavations (Archaeology)

Anthony, David. Who Were the Mound Builders?, 1 vol. 2013. (Rosen Readers Ser.). (ENG.). 24p. (J). (gr. 3-3). pap. 8.25 *(978-1-4777-2623-5(3),* fa39f180-a193-48d8-bff3-97e0d471c9bc); pap. 49.50 *(978-1-4777-2624-2(1))* Rosen Publishing Group, Inc., The. (Rosen Classroom).

Malone, Bobbie & Rosebrough, Amy. Water Panthers, Bears, & Thunderbirds: Exploring Wisconsin's Effigy Mounds. 2003. (ENG., Illus.). 48p. (J). (gr. 4-7). pap. 12.95 *(978-0-87020-357-2(6))* Wisconsin Historical Society.

Steele, Kris. Journey to Cahokia. Steele, Kris, illus. (Illus.). 32p. (Orig.). (J). (gr. 4-6). pap. 4.95 *(978-1-881563-02-0(2))* Cahokia Mounds Museum Society.

MOUNT RUSHMORE NATIONAL MEMORIAL (S.D.)

Ashley, Susan. Mount Rushmore, 1 vol. 2004. (Places in American History Ser.). (ENG., Illus.). 24p. (gr. 2-4). pap. 9.15 *(978-0-8368-4149-7(2),* 55d1b36c-93a5-4fd0-b7d7-03c3cb2fe286); lib. bdg. 24.67 *(978-0-8368-4142-8(5),* 9854fe32-021b-4357-99c8-c9e528fba86e) Stevens, Gareth Publishing LLLP. (Weekly Reader Leveled Readers).

Bauer, Marion Dane. Mount Rushmore. Wallace, John, illus. 2007. (Ready-To-Read Level 1 Ser.). (ENG.). 32p. (J). (gr. -1-1). lib. bdg. 16.19 *(978-1-4169-3478-3(2),* Aladdin) Simon & Schuster Children's Publishing.

—Mount Rushmore: Ready-To-Read Level 1. Wallace, John, illus. (Wonders of America Ser.). (ENG.). 32p. (J). (gr. -1-1). 2018. 17.99 *(978-1-5344-3030-3(X))* 2007. pap. 4.99 *(978-1-4169-3477-6(4))* Simon Spotlight. (Simon Spotlight).

Calkhoven, Laurie. Mount Rushmore's Hidden Room & Other Monumental Secrets: Monuments & Landmarks (Ready-To-Read Level 3) Fabbretti, Valerio, illus. 2018. (Secrets of American History Ser.). (ENG.). 48p. (J). (gr. 1-3). 17.99 *(978-1-5344-2925-3(5));* pap. 4.99 *(978-1-5344-2924-6(7))* Simon Spotlight. (Simon Spotlight).

Chang, Kirsten. Mount Rushmore. 2019. (Symbols of American Freedom Ser.). (ENG., Illus.). 24p. (J). (gr. k-3). pap. 7.99 *(978-1-61891-494-1(4),* 12144, Blastoff! Readers) Bellwether Media.

Conley, Kate. Engineering Mount Rushmore. 2017. (Building by Design Ser.). (ENG., Illus.). 48p. (J). (gr. 4-8). lib. bdg. 35.64 *(978-1-5321-1162-4(2),* 25900) ABDO Publishing Co.

Dittmer, Lori. Mount Rushmore. 2019. (Landmarks of America Ser.). (ENG.). 24p. (J). (gr. 1-4). *(978-1-64026-127-3(3),* 18977, Creative Education); pap. 8.99 *(978-1-62832-690-1(5),* 18978, Creative Paperbacks) Creative Co., The.

Eldridge, Alison & Eldridge, Stephen. Mount Rushmore: An American Symbol, 1 vol. 2012. (All about American Symbols Ser.). (ENG.). 24p. (gr. -1-1). 25.27 *(978-0-7660-4060-1(7),* eabf30d7-6f84-441c-b4fb-7653c131b250); (Illus.). pap. 10.35 *(978-1-4644-0049-0(0),* b158bc12-7293-4fb5-87ac-def0994a572a) Enslow Publishing, LLC. (Enslow Publishing).

Goldsworthy, Kaite. Mount Rushmore with Code. 2012. (AV2 American Icons Ser.). (ENG., Illus.). 24p. (J). pap. 12.95 *(978-1-61913-302-0(4));* lib. bdg. 27.13 *(978-1-61913-079-1(3))* Weigl Pubs., Inc. (AV2 by Weigl).

Gunderson, Jessica. Mount Rushmore: Myths, Legends, & Facts, 1 vol. 2014. (Monumental History Ser.). (ENG., Illus.). 32p. (J). (gr. 3-6). lib. bdg. 27.99 *(978-1-4914-0203-0(2),* 125786, Capstone Pr.) Capstone.

Hahn, Laura. Mount Rushmore: Memorial to Our Greatest Presidents. Moreno, Barry, ed. 2014. (Patriotic Symbols of America Ser.: 20). 48p. (J). (gr. 4-18). lib. bdg. 20.95 *(978-1-4222-3128-9(3))* Mason Crest.

Jango-Cohen, Judith. Mount Rushmore. (Lightning Bolt Bks.). (gr. k-2). 2010. (Illus.). 32p. (J). lib. bdg. 25.26 *(978-0-7613-6021-6(2),* Lerner Pubns.) 2010. pap. 45.32 *(978-0-7613-6990-5(2))* 2003. (ENG., Illus.). 32p. (J). pap. 7.99 *(978-0-8225-3755-7(9),* 06363896-3e29-4b53-b7be-6b9f9152da33, First Avenue Editions) Lerner Publishing Group.

Kelley, True. Where Is Mount Rushmore? 2015. (Where Is... ? Ser.). lib. bdg. 16.00 *(978-0-606-36589-5(3))* Turtleback.

Kelley, True & Who HQ. Where Is Mount Rushmore? Hinderliter, John, illus. 2015. (Where Is? Ser.). 112p. (J). (gr. 3-7). 5.99 *(978-0-448-48356-6(4),* Penguin Workshop) Penguin Young Readers Group.

Klepeis, Alicia Z. Building Mount Rushmore, 1 vol. 2017. (Engineering North America's Landmarks Ser.). (ENG.). 32p. (gr. 3-3). pap. 11.58 *(978-1-5026-2952-4(6),* 15d7b337-41d6-445d-afcd-92eec56ff691) Cavendish Square Publishing LLC.

Linde, Barbara M. Mount Rushmore, 1 vol. 2018. (Symbols of America Ser.). (ENG.). 24p. (gr. 1-2). 24.27 *(978-1-5382-2898-2(X),* 12e83fe3-3dea-4a49-b778-c7998c922109) Stevens, Gareth Publishing LLLP.

Mattern, Joanne. Mount Rushmore: Faces of Our History. 2017. (Core Content Social Studies — Let's Celebrate America Ser.). (ENG., Illus.). 32p. (J). (gr. 2-5). pap. 8.99 *(978-1-63440-236-1(7),* 6bea6138-6169-493d-8ec7-8200775503e7); lib. bdg. 26.65 *(978-1-63440-226-2(X),* 84d9c69c-2df6-4420-9c01-65c14712eb9f) Red Chair Pr.

Mojica, Barbara Ann. Little Miss History Travels to Mount Rushmore. Mojica, Victor Ramon, illus. 2012. 36p. pap. 13.95 *(978-0-9885030-0-7(X))* eugenus STUDIOS.

Murray, Julie. Mount Rushmore. 2016. (US Landmarks Ser.). (ENG., Illus.). 24p. (J). (gr. -1-2). lib. bdg. 31.36 *(978-1-68080-913-8(X),* 23301, Abdo Kids) ABDO Publishing Co.

O'Mara, Mary. Visit Mount Rushmore, 1 vol. 2012. (Landmarks of Liberty Ser.). (ENG.). 24p. (J). (gr. 2-3). pap. 9.15 *(978-1-4339-6390-2(6),* 9f9f0021-2b4a-4a45-bb96-9ee943f545ea, Gareth Stevens Learning Library); lib. bdg. 25.27 *(978-1-4339-6388-9(4),* 39e32d3d-8529-4dd0-8fc0-af06197f6b93) Stevens, Gareth Publishing LLLP.

Patrick, Jean L. S. Face to Face with Mount Rushmore. Patrick, Jean L. S. & Faricy, Patrick, illus. 2008. (J). *(978-0-9798823-1-9(1))* Mount Rushmore Bookstores.

—Who Carved the Mountain? The Story of Mount Rushmore. Graef, Renee, illus. 2005. 37p. (J). 16.99 *(978-0-9752617-4-3(6))* Mount Rushmore Bookstores.

Riggs, Kate. Mount Rushmore. 2009. (Now That's Big Ser.). 24p. (J). (gr. 1-5). lib. bdg. 24.25 *(978-1-58341-705-8(2),* Creative Education) Creative Co., The.

RJF Publishing Staff & Thomas, William David. Mount Rushmore. 2009. (Symbols of American Freedom Ser.). (Illus.). 48p. (J). (gr. 4-6). 30.00 *(978-1-60413-515-2(8),* Chelsea Clubhse.) Infobase Holdings, Inc.

The Seasons of Mount Rushmore Coloring Book. 2006. (J). *(978-0-9752617-7-4(0))* Mount Rushmore Bookstores.

Simms, Susan Rose. Mount Rushmore. 2018. (US Symbols Ser.). (ENG., Illus.). 24p. (J). (gr. k-3). lib. bdg. 31.36 *(978-1-5321-6046-2(1),* 28724, Pop! Cody Koala) Pop!

Troupe, Thomas Kingsley. Mount Rushmore, 1 vol. Skeens, Matthew, illus. 2009. (American Symbols Ser.). (ENG.). 24p. (J). (gr. 1-3). lib. bdg. 27.32 *(978-1-4048-5168-9(2),* 95495, Picture Window Bks.) Capstone.

MOUNT VERNON (VA.: ESTATE)

Dyan, Penelope. This Is the House George Built! a Kid's Guide to Mount Vernon. Weigand, John D., photos by. 2009. (Illus.). 44p. pap. 11.95 *(978-1-935118-63-1(8))* Bellissima Publishing, LLC.

Rinaldi, Ann. Sarah's Ground. 2012. (ENG.). 192p. (YA). (gr. 7). pap. 9.99 *(978-1-4424-8107-7(2),* Simon & Schuster Bks. For Young Readers) Simon & Schuster Bks. For Young Readers.

Thomas, Peggy. Farmer George Plants a Nation. Johnson, Layne, illus. 2013. (ENG.). 40p. (J). (gr. 2-5). pap. 9.99 *(978-1-62091-029-0(2),* Calkins Creek) Highlights Pr., c/o Highlights for Children, Inc.

MOUNTAIN CLIMBING

see Mountaineering

MOUNTAIN LIFE—SOUTHERN STATES

Santella, Andrew. Mountain Men. 2003. (Cornerstones of Freedom Ser.). (ENG., Illus.). 48p. (YA). (gr. 4-7). 26.00 *(978-0-516-24216-3(4))* Scholastic Library Publishing.

MOUNTAIN LIFE—SOUTHERN STATES—FICTION

Bare, Bart. Girl. 2010. 188p. (YA). pap. 11.95 *(978-0-9825396-4-4(9))* Canterbury Hse. Publishing, Ltd.

Spyri, Johanna. Heidi. Marks, Alan, illus. 2006. 63p. (J). (gr. 2). 8.99 *(978-0-7945-1237-8(2),* Usborne) EDC Publishing.

MOUNTAINEERING

Athans, Sandra K. Secrets of the Sky Caves: Danger & Discovery on Nepal's Mustang Cliffs. 2014. (ENG., Illus.). 64p. (J). (gr. 4-8). lib. bdg. 33.32 *(978-1-4677-0016-0(9),* 72d8d6df-062d-4285-a9a5-05b384d9a7cb, Millbrook Pr.) Lerner Publishing Group.

Benjamin, Daniel. Extreme Rock Climbing, 1 vol. 2013. (Sports on the Edge Ser.). (ENG.). 48p. (gr. 4-4). pap. 13.93 *(978-1-62712-133-0(1),* 65137fcc-4074-4ecd-a69b-249a1d794ef0); (Illus.). 32.64 *(978-1-60870-223-7(5),* 035e7556-588f-4881-9b21-aa4e9be6c16b) Cavendish Square Publishing LLC.

Black, Nessa. Rock Climbing. 2020. (Spot Outdoor Fun Ser.). (ENG.). 16p. (J). (gr. -1-2). lib. bdg. *(978-1-68151-814-5(7),* 10688) Amicus.

Bodden, Valerie. To the Top of Mount Everest. 2011. (Great Expeditions Ser.). (ENG., Illus.). 48p. (J). (gr. 5-8). lib. bdg. 34.25 *(978-1-60818-070-7(0),* 22156, Creative Education) Creative Co., The.

Bramucci, Steve. National Geographic Kids Chapters: Rock Stars! 2018. (NGK Chapters Ser.). (Illus.). 112p. (J). (gr. 3-7). pap. 5.99 *(978-1-4263-3049-0(9));* (ENG.). lib. bdg. 14.90 *(978-1-4263-3050-6(2))* Disney Publishing Worldwide. (National Geographic Kids).

Brown, Alex. Mountain Adventures. 2009. (Difficult & Dangerous Ser.). (J). 28.50 *(978-1-59920-157-3(7))* Black Rabbit Bks.

—Mountain Adventures. 2009. (Difficult & Dangerous Ser.). (ENG., Illus.). 32p. (J). pap. *(978-1-897563-25-0(6))* Saunders Bk. Co.

Champion, Neil. Rock Climbing, 1 vol. 2009. (Get Outdoors Ser.). (ENG., Illus.). 32p. (gr. 4-4). (J). pap. 11.00 *(978-1-4358-3051-6(2),* 15a92134-be50-4831-ab84-b51d56b462b2, PowerKids Pr.); (YA). lib. bdg. 28.93 *(978-1-4358-3043-1(1),* e8705b55-1322-4389-8dc6-a91906d7217a) Rosen Publishing Group, Inc., The.

—Wild Rock Climbing & Mountaineering. 2012. (Adventure Outdoors Ser.). (ENG., Illus.). 32p. (J). (gr. 3-6). lib. bdg. 28.50 *(978-1-59920-807-7(5),* 17251, Smart Apple Media) Black Rabbit Bks.

Chapman, Simon. In the Himalayas. Chapman, Simon, illus. 2005. (Illus.). 103p. (J). lib. bdg. 20.00 *(978-1-4242-0626-1(X))* Fitzgerald Bks.

Cleare, John. Epic Climbs. 2011. (Illus.). 64p. (J). (gr. 3-6). 19.99 *(978-0-7534-6473-1(X))* Larousse Kingfisher Chambers, Inc.

Cohn, Jessica. Mountain Climbing, 1 vol. 2013. (Incredibly Insane Sports Ser.). (ENG., Illus.). 48p. (J). (gr. 4-5). 34.60 *(978-1-4339-8830-1(5),* 5773225e-5f07-41ce-803f-2e7e83c36be2, Gareth Stevens Learning Library) Stevens, Gareth Publishing LLLP.

Dean, Cynthia A. Rock Climbing: Making It to the Top. 2005. (High Five Reading - Blue Ser.). (ENG., Illus.). 48p. (gr. 3-4). per. 9.00 *(978-0-7368-5745-1(1))* Capstone.

Dugan, Christine. Defying Gravity! Rock Climbing, 1 vol. 2nd rev. ed. 2012. (TIME for KIDS(r): Informational Text Ser.). (ENG.). 48p. (gr. 4-5). pap. 13.99 *(978-1-4333-4830-3(6))* Teacher Created Materials, Inc.

Endres, Hollie. Rock Climbing. 2007. (Action Sports Ser.). (ENG., Illus.). 24p. (J). (gr. 3-7). lib. bdg. 26.95 *(978-1-60014-127-0(7))* Bellwether Media.

Fandel, Jennifer. Rock Climbing. 2007. (Active Sports Ser.). (ENG., Illus.). 24p. (J). (gr. 1-4). lib. bdg. 24.25 *(978-1-58341-468-2(1),* 22077, Creative Education) Creative Co., The.

Follett, Katherine. One Giant Leap. Urbanovic, Jackie; Follett, illus. 2004. (Reader's Theater Content-Area Concepts Ser.). (ENG.). (J). (gr. 3-5). 5.00 net. *(978-1-4108-1147-9(6))* Benchmark Education Co.

Fowler Hicks, Ginny. Mountain Star: A Story about a Mountaineer That Will Teach You How to Draw a Star! Fowler, Charlie, photos by. 2008. (Illus.). 24p. (J). 18.95 *(978-0-9763309-3-6(8))* Mountain World Media LLC.

Frisch-Schmoll, Joy. Rock Climbing. 2017. (Odysseys in Outdoor Adventures Ser.). (ENG., Illus.). 80p. (J). (gr. 7-10). *(978-1-60818-689-1(X),* 20328, Creative Education) Creative Co., The.

Genereux, Andy. Yamnuska Rock: The Crown Jewel of Canadian Rockies Traditional Climbing, 1 vol. 2010. (ENG., Illus.). 320p. pap. *(978-1-894765-74-9(5))* RMB Rocky Mountain Bks.

Goldish, Meish. Lost on a Mountain. 2015. (Illus.). 32p. (J). lib. bdg. 28.50 *(978-1-62724-292-9(9))* Bearport Publishing Co., Inc.

Graf, Mike. Rock Climbing. 2004. (Illus.). 56p. pap. 9.00 *(978-0-7891-6043-0(9));* (J). (gr. 4-7). lib. bdg. 17.95 *(978-0-7569-1385-4(3))* Perfection Learning Corp.

Green, Sara. Mountain Climbing. 2013. (Outdoor Adventures Ser.). (ENG., Illus.). 24p. (J). (gr. 3-8). lib. bdg. 27.95 *(978-1-60014-892-7(1),* Pilot Bks.) Bellwether Media.

Herman, Gail & Amatrula, Michele. Climbing Everest (Totally True Adventures) How Two Friends Reached Earth's Highest Peak. 2015. (Totally True Adventures Ser.). (Illus.). 112p. (J). (gr. 2-5). 5.99 *(978-0-553-50986-1(1),* Random Hse. Bks. for Young Readers) Random Hse. Children's Bks.

Hoena, Blake. Surviving Mount Everest: An Interactive Extreme Sports Adventure. 2017. (You Choose: Surviving Extreme Sports Ser.). (ENG., Illus.). 112p. (J). (gr. 3-7). lib. bdg. 32.65 *(978-1-5157-7169-2(5),* 135542, Capstone Pr.) Capstone.

Hyde, Natalie. Conquering Everest, 1 vol. 2013. (ENG., Illus.). 48p. (J). pap. *(978-0-7787-1175-9(7))* Crabtree Publishing Co.

Iversen, Sandra. A Day on the Mountain. 2010. (Quick60 Factual Bks.). (ENG., Illus.). 12p. (J). pap. *(978-1-77540-220-6(7))* Iversen Publishing Ltd.

Jankowski, Emily. Reaching Everest's Summit, 1 vol. 2014. (Incredible True Adventures Ser.). (ENG., Illus.). 32p. (J). (gr. 3-4). pap. 11.50 *(978-1-4824-2046-3(5),* d7e1260e-ad83-44a2-85ec-fbfde2e4bef0) Stevens, Gareth Publishing LLLP.

Johnson, Robin. Conquering Everest. 2013. (ENG., Illus.). 48p. (J). *(978-0-7787-1167-4(6))* Crabtree Publishing Co.

Kalman, Bobbie & Crossingham, John. Extreme Climbing. 2003. (Extreme Sports No Limits! Ser.). (ENG., Illus.). 32p. (J). pap. *(978-0-7787-1717-1(8));* lib. bdg. *(978-0-7787-1671-6(6))* Crabtree Publishing Co.

Loh-Hagan, Virginia. Aron Ralston: Trapped in the Desert. 2018. (True Survival Ser.). (ENG.). 32p. (J). (gr. 4-8). pap. 14.21 *(978-1-5341-0872-1(6),* 210852); (Illus.). lib. bdg. 32.07 *(978-1-5341-0773-1(8),* 210851) Cherry Lake Publishing. (45th Parallel Press).

—Extreme Mountain Climbing. 2016. (Nailed It! Ser.). (ENG., Illus.). 32p. (J). (gr. 4-8). 32.07 *(978-1-63470-491-5(6),* 207695) Cherry Lake Publishing.

—Extreme Rock Climbing. 2015. (Nailed It! Ser.). (ENG., Illus.). 32p. (J). (gr. 4-8). 32.07 *(978-1-63470-020-7(1),* 206728) Cherry Lake Publishing.

Luke, Andrew. Mountain Sports. 2017. (Illus.). 48p. (J). *(978-1-4222-3707-6(9))* Mason Crest.

Marsico, Katie. Surviving a Canyon: Aron Ralston. 2019. (They Survived (Alternator Books (r)) Ser.). (ENG., Illus.). 32p. (J). (gr. 3-6). 29.32 *(978-1-5415-2351-7(2),* 25cbef04-4875-4507-a597-0f782f7e1392, Lerner Pubns.) Lerner Publishing Group.

McFee, Shane. Rock Climbing. (Living on the Edge Ser.). 24p. (gr. 2-3). 2009. 42.50 *(978-1-61514-297-2(5),* PowerKids Pr.) 2008. (ENG., Illus.). (J). lib. bdg. 26.27 *(978-1-4042-4220-3(1),* 6e3107f1-0944-4b08-86f8-58c6de423347) Rosen Publishing Group, Inc., The.

Mountaineering Adventures, 6 vols. (gr. 4-18). 39.95 *(978-0-7368-9029-8(7),* Red Brick Learning) Capstone.

Oxlade, Chris. Rock Climbing. 2003. (Extreme Sports Ser.). (ENG., Illus.). 32p. (gr. 3-6). lib. bdg. 22.60 *(978-0-8225-1240-0(8))* Lerner Publishing Group.

Payment, Simone. Extreme Rock Climbing, 1 vol. 2019. (Extreme Sports & Stunts Ser.). (ENG.). 48p. (gr. 5-5). pap. 12.75 *(978-1-7253-4745-8(8),* 2758d0de-09c4-45c8-a420-1e88bfda9b72) Rosen Publishing Group, Inc., The.

Rajczak Nelson, Kristen. Climbing Mount Everest, 1 vol. 2013. (Thrill Seekers Ser.). (ENG., Illus.). 32p. (J). (gr. 3-4). lib. bdg. 29.27 *(978-1-4824-0142-4(8),* a0f0af1a-f88d-4c9f-a6a8-1131ba51303e) Stevens, Gareth Publishing LLLP.

Randall, Jory. My Day in the Mountains, 1 vol. 2009. (Kid's Life! Ser.). (ENG.). 24p. (J). (gr. 1-1). pap. 9.25 *(978-1-4358-2471-3(7),* 6223e9b1-7244-441a-95d7-e7a80eb2d16f); (Illus.). lib. bdg. 26.27 *(978-1-4042-8076-2(6),* ccc44f2-01f1-4594-8856-a01ecd531ea4) Rosen Publishing Group, Inc., The. (PowerKids Pr.).

Rapparlie, Leslie & Wurdinger, Scott. Rock Climbing. 2006. (Adventure Sports Ser.). (Illus.). 48p. (YA). (gr. 5-9). lib. bdg. 21.95 *(978-1-58341-394-4(4))* Creative Co., The.

Romero, Jordan. No Summit Out of Sight: The True Story of the Youngest Person to Climb the Seven Summits. 2014. (ENG., Illus.). 368p. (YA). (gr. 7). 21.99 *(978-1-4767-0962-8(9),* Simon & Schuster Bks. For Young Readers) Simon & Schuster Bks. For Young Readers.

Salkeld, Audrey. Climbing Everest: Tales of Triumph & Tragedy on the World's Highest Mountain. 2003. (ENG., Illus.). 128p. (J). (gr. 5-9). 21.00 *(978-0-7922-5105-7(9))* National Geographic Society.

Scherer, Glenn. True Mountain Rescue Stories, 1 vol. 2011. (True Rescue Stories Ser.). (ENG.). 48p. (gr. 5-7). lib. bdg. 25.27 *(978-0-7660-3572-0(7),* 7ad3f39a-dcbd-4ddb-ae21-efa5b1cd92c8) Enslow Publishing, LLC.

Schindler, John. Rock Climbing, 1 vol. 2004. (Extreme Sports Ser.). (ENG., Illus.). 24p. (gr. 2-4). pap. 9.15 *(978-0-8368-4548-8(X),* 51b0aa2d-ddb0-4e04-bf2e-67238ab0f840); lib. bdg. 25.67 *(978-0-8368-4541-9(2),* ebf2a090-b2eb-4401-9378-42f26c8bd4b9) Stevens, Gareth Publishing LLLP. (Gareth Stevens Learning Library).

Shackleton, Caroline. Trapped! The Aron Ralston Story High Intermediate Book with Online Access, 1 vol. 2014. (ENG., Illus.). 28p. (J). pap., E-Book 9.50 *(978-1-107-66998-7(7))* Cambridge Univ. Pr.

Shea, Therese. Rock & Ice Climbing, 1 vol. 2015. (Sports to the Extreme Ser.). (ENG., Illus.). 48p. (J). (gr. 5-6). 33.47 *(978-1-4994-3557-3(6),* ad0c6083-dc99-4186-b6ab-913efa45954a, Rosen Central) Rosen Publishing Group, Inc., The.

Sheehan, Robert. Conquering Mount Everest, 1 vol. 2013. (Discovery Education: Sensational True Stories Ser.). (ENG., Illus.). 32p. (J). (gr. 4-5). pap. 11.00 *(978-1-4777-0109-6(5),* faa7bb8c-5067-4b0c-856e-0dc556c29d96); lib. bdg. 28.93 *(978-1-4777-0062-4(5),* 0e455370-ccbf-4bf2-834b-d3872f238a00) Rosen Publishing Group, Inc., The. (PowerKids Pr.).

Shone, Rob. Defying Death in the Mountains. Spender, Nick, illus. 2010. (Graphic Survival Stories Ser.). 48p. (YA). 58.50 *(978-1-61532-901-4(3),* Rosen Reference) Rosen Publishing Group, Inc., The.

—Defying Death in the Mountains, 1 vol. Spender, Nik, illus. 2010. (Graphic Survival Stories Ser.). (ENG.). 48p. (YA). (gr. 5-5). 37.13 *(978-1-4358-3532-0(8),* 07fd218d-4cd0-4b93-9f8e-bc58bdcb39b9); pap. 15.05 *(978-1-61532-866-6(1),* 0ff7e3c8-0165-4567-b4ab-294b843bb172) Rosen Publishing Group, Inc., The. (Rosen Reference).

Skreslet, Laurie & MacLeod, Elizabeth. To the Top of Everest. 2003. (ENG., Illus.). 56p. (J). (gr. 5-17). 11.99 *(978-1-55074-814-7(9))* Kids Can Pr., Ltd. CAN. Dist: Hachette Bk. Group.

Smith, Elliott. Free Soloing & Other Extreme Rock Climbing. 2019. (Natural Thrills Ser.). (ENG., Illus.). 32p. (J). (gr. 3-9). lib. bdg. 28.65 *(978-1-5435-7325-1(8),* 140625) Capstone.

Spilsbury, Louise. How to Survive on a Mountain, 1 vol. 2012. (Tough Guides). (ENG., Illus.). 32p. (J). (gr. 4-5). pap. 11.00 *(978-1-4488-7936-6(1),* 47227724-b281-4cca-8dc2-29baac1bb2f4); lib. bdg. 28.93 *(978-1-4488-7871-0(3),* a92196a4-9d79-44e2-83fd-cb506f4f1fba) Rosen Publishing Group, Inc., The. (PowerKids Pr.).

Stewart, Alexandra. Everest: the Remarkable Story of Edmund Hillary & Tenzing Norgay. Todd-Stanton, Joe, illus. 2020. (ENG.). 64p. (J). 21.99 *(978-1-5476-0159-2(0),* 900200537, Bloomsbury Children's Bks.) Bloomsbury Publishing USA.

Taylor-Butler, Christine. Sacred Mountain: Everest. 2009. (ENG., Illus.). 48p. (J). (gr. 2-7). 19.95 *(978-1-60060-255-9(X))* Lee & Low Bks., Inc.

Teitelbaum, Michael. Rock Climbing. 2007. (21st Century Skills Library: Healthy for Life Ser.). (ENG., Illus.). 32p. (gr. 4-8). lib. bdg. 32.07 *(978-1-60279-014-8(0),* 200031) Cherry Lake Publishing.

Thomas, William David. Mountain Rescuer, 1 vol. 2008. (Cool Careers: Helping Careers Ser.). (ENG.). 32p. (gr. 3-3). pap. 11.50 *(978-0-8368-9328-1(X),* 0564e2d3-24a3-4549-ab7d-a94967e1b592); lib. bdg. 28.67 *(978-0-8368-9195-9(3),* bd25c45f-06de-4de4-bd70-2c6a4c8dc77a) Stevens, Gareth Publishing LLLP.

Tomljanovic, Tatiana. Rock Climbing. (J). 2013. *(978-1-62127-359-2(8))* 2013. pap. *(978-1-62127-365-3(2))* 2007. (Illus.). 24p. (gr. 4-7). lib. bdg. 24.45 *(978-1-59036-667-7(0))* 2007. (Illus.). 24p. (gr. 4-7). per. 8.95 *(978-1-59036-668-4(9))* Weigl Pubs., Inc.

Turnbull, Stephanie. Rock Climbing. 2016. (Adventure Sports Ser.). 24p. (gr. 2-6). 28.50 *(978-1-62588-386-5(2),* Smart Apple Media) Black Rabbit Bks.

Weingarten, A. J. Rock Climbing, 1 vol. 2012. (Great Outdoors Ser.). (ENG., Illus.). 24p. (J). (gr. 2-3). pap. 9.15 *(978-1-4339-7108-2(9),* e87b0c71-aca2-4c1e-9f12-7a22b7c9799c); lib. bdg. 25.27 *(978-1-4339-7107-5(0),* 077db253-7207-4acf-90da-92c8a38aa538) Stevens, Gareth Publishing LLLP.

Weintraub, Aileen. Mount Everest: The Highest Mountain. 2009. (Great Record Breakers in Nature Ser.). 24p. (gr. 3-4). 42.50 *(978-1-61513-181-5(7),* PowerKids Pr.) Rosen Publishing Group, Inc., The.

—Rock Climbing. 2003. (High Interest Bks.). (ENG., Illus.). 48p. (J). 24.50 *(978-0-516-24319-1(5),* Children's Pr.); (YA). (gr. 7-12). pap. 6.95 *(978-0-516-24381-8(0),* Watts, Franklin) Scholastic Library Publishing.

Whiting, Jim. Ultra Running with Scott Jurek. 2006. (Extreme Sports Ser.). (Illus.). 32p. (J). (gr. 1-4). lib. bdg. 25.70 *(978-1-58415-484-6(5))* Mitchell Lane Pubs.

Willet, Edward. Rock Sport Climbing: Techniques & Tricks. 2009. (Rad Sports: Techniques & Tricks Ser.). 48p. (gr. 5-8). 53.00 *(978-1-60851-936-1(8),* Rosen Reference) Rosen Publishing Group, Inc., The.

MOUNTAINEERING—BIOGRAPHY

see Mountaineers

MOUNTAINEERING—FICTION

Baillie, Helen. The Azura Stones. 2007. 212p. (YA). per. 18.00 *(978-1-58982-374-7(5),* Bedside Bks.) American Bk. Publishing Group.

Barwin, Steven. Rock Dogs, 1 vol. 2009. (Lorimer Sports Stories Ser.). (ENG.). 104p. (J). (gr. 4-8). 16.95 *(978-1-55277-028-3(1),* 028); 8.95 *(978-1-55277-027-6(3),* 027) James Lorimer & Co. Ltd., Pubs. CAN. Dist: Formac Lorimer Bks. Ltd.

Coleman, K. R. Deadman Anchor. 2016. (Atlas of Cursed Places Ser.). (ENG.). 112p. (YA). (gr. 6-12). lib. bdg. 26.65 *(978-1-5124-1326-7(7),* d57daced-b1d4-4b36-ac89-658a52c6a375, Darby Creek) Lerner Publishing Group.

Curlin, Tera. Pat's Mountain, 1 vol. 2010. 16p. 24.95 *(978-1-4489-4356-2(6))* PublishAmerica, Inc.

Dale, Jay. I Go Up. Gulliver, Amanda, illus. 2012. (Engage Literacy Magenta Ser.). (ENG.). 16p. (J). (gr. k-2). pap. 36.94 *(978-1-4296-8840-6(8),* 18306); pap. 6.99 *(978-1-4296-8832-1(7),* 119888) Capstone. (Capstone Pr.).

Doyle, Bill & Borgenicht, David. Everest: You Decide How to Survive! 2015. (Worst-Case Scenario Ultimate Adventure Ser.). (ENG., Illus.). 204p. (J). (gr. 3-8). 47.10 *(978-1-59920-978-4(0),* 19401, Smart Apple Media) Black Rabbit Bks.

Drake, Raelyn. On Edge. 2019. (To the Limit Ser.). (ENG.). 104p. (YA). (gr. 6-12). 26.65 *(978-1-5415-4038-5(7),* f4eab6d3-de77-4267-8203-8d9d4bd9d376, Darby Creek) Lerner Publishing Group.

Fawcett, Heather. Even the Darkest Stars. (Even the Darkest Stars Ser.: 1). (ENG.). (YA). (gr. 8). 2018. 448p. pap. 9.99 *(978-0-06-246339-5(X))* 2017. 432p. 17.99 *(978-0-06-246338-8(1))* HarperCollins Pubs. (Balzer & Bray).

Fuerst, Jeffrey B. Bear Went over the Mountain. Oliver, Mark, illus. 2010. (Rising Readers Ser.). (J). 3.49 *(978-1-60719-686-0(7))* Newmark Learning LLC.

Holtfreter, Nastja. Colorful World: Mountain. Holtfreter, Nastja, illus. 2017. (ENG., Illus.). 14p. (J). bds. 5.99 *(978-1-61067-579-6(7))* Kane Miller.

Johnson, D. B. Henry Climbs a Mountain. 2019. (Henry Book Ser.). (ENG., Illus.). 32p. (J). (gr. -1-3). pap. 7.99 *(978-0-358-11205-1(2),* 1749851, Clarion Bks.) HarperCollins Pubs.

Jones, V. M. Out of Reach, 0 vols. unabr. ed. 2013. (ENG.). 272p. (YA). (gr. 7-12). pap. 9.99 *(978-1-4778-1705-6(0),* 9781477817056, Skyscape) Amazon Publishing.

Korman, Gordon. The Climb (Everest, Book 2) 2012. (Everest Ser.). (ENG.). 160p. (J). (gr. 3-7). pap. 7.99 *(978-0-545-39233-4(0))* Scholastic, Inc.

—The Contest (Everest, Book 1) 2012. (Everest Ser.: 1). (ENG.). 144p. (J). (gr. 3-7). pap. 7.99 *(978-0-545-39232-7(2))* Scholastic, Inc.

—The Summit (Everest, Book 3), Vol. 3. 2012. (Everest Ser.). (ENG.). 160p. (J). (gr. 3-7). pap. 7.99 *(978-0-545-39234-1(9))* Scholastic, Inc.

Lasher, Kathy. Heinrich Streudleman Climbs Mt. Baker. 2010. 32p. pap. 14.49 *(978-1-4520-2090-7(6))* AuthorHouse.

Maddox, Jake. Climbing Strong. 2019. (Jake Maddox JV Ser.). (ENG.). 96p. (J). (gr. 4-6). lib. bdg. 25.99 *(978-1-4965-7524-1(5),* 139146, Stone Arch Bks.) Capstone.

Mantell, Paul. Mountain Bike Mania. 2005. (Sports Classics IV Ser.). 151p. (J). lib. bdg. 15.00 *(978-1-59054-764-9(0))* Fitzgerald Bks.

Marshall, Catherine. The Bridge to Cutter Gap, 1 vol. 2018. (Christy of Cutter Gap Ser.: 1). 112p. (J). pap. 7.99 *(978-1-68370-157-6(7))* Evergreen Farm.

—Silent Superstitions, 1 vol. 2018. (Christy of Cutter Gap Ser.: 2). 112p. (J). pap. 7.99 *(978-1-68370-159-0(3))* Evergreen Farm.

Monroy, Eva. Little Mountain. 2004. (J). pap. 8.00 *(978-0-8059-6535-3(1))* Dorrance Publishing Co., Inc.

Montgomery, R. A. The Abominable Snowman: (Choose Your Own Adventure #1) Peguy, Laurence, illus. 2006. (ENG.). 144p. (J). (gr. 4-8). per. 7.99 *(978-1-933390-01-7(8),* CHCL01) Chooseco LLC.

Myers, Edward. Climb or Die. 2nd ed. 2016. 154p. (J). pap. *(978-1-932727-12-8(4))* Montemayor Pr.

—Solos en la Montaña. 2016. (SPA.). 157p. (J). pap. *(978-1-932727-18-0(3))* Montemayor Pr.

Newman, Gwill York. Bingo Bear Was Here: A Toy Bear's Climb to the Top of Africa's Highest Mountain. Babcock, Jeff, illus. 2003. 48p. (J). pap. 8.95 *(978-0-86534-395-5(0))* Sunstone Pr.

Orme, Helen. Wet! 2008. (Siti's Sisters Ser.). (ENG., Illus.). 36p. pap. *(978-1-84167-688-3(8))* Ransom Publishing Ltd.

Paulsen, Gary & Roberts, Esyllt Nest. Craig y Diafol. 2005.Tr. of Devil's Wall. (WEL.). 64p. pap. *(978-0-86381-684-0(3))* Gwasg Carreg Gwalch.

Rockwell, Anne. Hiking Day. Rockwell, Lizzy, illus. 2018. (My First Experience Book Ser.). (ENG.). 32p. (J). (gr. -1-3). 17.99 *(978-1-4814-2737-1(7),* Aladdin) Simon & Schuster Children's Publishing.

Simpson, Joe & Bembibre, Cecilia. Tocando el Vacío, 1 vol. 2014. (SPA., Illus.). 64p. pap., stu. ed. 15.00 incl. audio compact disk *(978-84-9848-133-4(3))* Edinumen, Editorial ESP. Dist: Cambridge Univ. Pr.

Smelcer, John. Savage Mountain. 2015. (ENG., Illus.). 160p. (J). (gr. 6). pap. 12.00 *(978-1-935248-65-1(0))* Leapfrog Pr.

Smith, Roland. Ascent. 2018. (Peak Marcello Adventure Ser.: 3). (ENG.). 240p. (YA). (gr. 7). 17.99 *(978-0-544-86759-8(9),* 1648549, Clarion Bks.) HarperCollins Pubs.

—The Edge. 2016. (Peak Marcello Adventure Ser.: 2). (ENG.). 240p. (YA). (gr. 7). pap. 7.99 *(978-0-544-81354-0(5),* 1641953, Clarion Bks.) HarperCollins Pubs.

—Peak. 2008. (Peak Marcello Adventure Ser.: 1). (ENG., Illus.). 256p. (YA). (gr. 7). pap. 9.99 *(978-0-15-206268-2(8),* 1198787, Clarion Bks.) HarperCollins Pubs.

Sterling, James Milton. Willy the Mountain Climber. 2012. 32p. pap. 24.95 *(978-1-4626-8242-3(1))* America Star Bks.

Stilton, Gerónimo. I'm Too Fond of My Fur! Wolf, Matt, illus. 2004. (Geronimo Stilton Ser.: No. 4). 116p. (J). lib. bdg. 10.00 *(978-1-4242-0698-8(7))* Fitzgerald Bks.

Thomas, Jane Resh. Blind Mountain. 2006. (ENG.). 128p. (J). (gr. 5-7). 15.00 *(978-0-618-64872-6(0),* 100463, Clarion Bks.) HarperCollins Pubs.

VanRiper, Gary & VanRiper, Justin. Islands in the Sky. 2005. (Adirondack Kids Ser.: Vol. 5). 78p. (J). (gr. 2-7). pap. 9.95 *(978-0-9707044-5-0(3))* Adirondack Kids Pr.

Wild, Ailsa. Squishy Taylor & the Mess Makers. 2018. (Squishy Taylor Ser.). (ENG., Illus.). 128p. (J). (gr. 2-4). pap. 6.95 *(978-1-5158-1973-8(6),* 136645, Picture Window Bks.) Capstone.

MOUNTAINEERS

Bodden, Valerie. To the Top of Mount Everest. 2011. (Great Expeditions Ser.). (ENG., Illus.). 48p. (J). (gr. 5-8). pap. 12.00 *(978-0-89812-668-6(1),* 22162, Creative Paperbacks); lib. bdg. 34.25 *(978-1-60818-070-7(0),* 22156, Creative Education) Creative Co., The.

Bramucci, Steve. National Geographic Kids Chapters: Rock Stars! 2018. (NGK Chapters Ser.). (Illus.). 112p. (J). (gr. 3-7). pap. 5.99 *(978-1-4263-3049-0(9));* (ENG., lib. bdg. 14.90 *(978-1-4263-3050-6(2))* Disney Publishing Worldwide. (National Geographic Kids).

Crompton, Samuel Willard. Sir Edmund Hillary. 2009. (Great Explorers Ser.). (ENG., Illus.). 112p. (gr. 6-12). 30.00 *(978-1-60413-420-9(8),* P173416, Facts On File) Infobase Holdings, Inc.

Elish, Dan. Edmund Hillary: First to the Top, 1 vol. 2007. (Great Explorations Ser.). (ENG., Illus.). 80p. (gr. 6-6). lib. bdg. 36.93 *(978-0-7614-2224-2(2),* 0ffc39f0-72d2-424d-bd4f-1d1714700be7) Cavendish Square Publishing LLC.

Hyde, Natalie. Conquering Everest, 1 vol. 2013. (ENG., Illus.). 48p. (J). pap. *(978-0-7787-1175-9(7))* Crabtree Publishing Co.

Iversen, Sandra. A Day on the Mountain. 2010. (Quick60 Factual Bks.). (ENG., Illus.). 12p. (J). pap. *(978-1-77540-220-6(7))* Iversen Publishing Ltd.

Johnson, Robin. Conquering Everest. 2013. (ENG., Illus.). 48p. (J). *(978-0-7787-1167-4(6))* Crabtree Publishing Co.

Jones, Brenn. Learning about Teamwork from the Lives of Sir Edmund Hillary & Tenzing Norgay. 2009. (Character Building Book Ser.). 24p. (gr. 2-3). 42.50 *(978-1-60854-968-9(2),* PowerKids Pr.) Rosen Publishing Group, Inc., The.

Marsico, Katie. Surviving a Canyon: Aron Ralston. 2019. (They Survived (Alternator Books (r)) Ser.). (ENG., Illus.). 32p. (J). (gr. 3-6). 29.32 *(978-1-5415-2351-7(2),* 25cbef04-4875-4507-a597-0f782f7e1392, Lerner Pubns.) Lerner Publishing Group.

Niver, Heather Moore. Sir Edmund Hillary Explores Mount Everest, 1 vol. 2018. (Real-Life Scientific Adventures Ser.). (ENG., Illus.). 32p. (gr. 4-5). 29.27 *(978-1-5081-6862-1(8),* 9151c8b2-49b1-4af1-8a3a-d214baeaded1, PowerKids Pr.) Rosen Publishing Group, Inc., The.

Rolfe, Helen. Women Explorers (JR) 100 Years of Mountain Adventure. 2007. (Amazing Stories Ser.). (ENG., Illus.). 96p. (J). (gr. 4-5). pap. 9.95 *(978-1-55439-709-9(X),* 709) James Lorimer & Co. Ltd., Pubs. CAN. Dist: Formac Lorimer Bks. Ltd.

Romero, Jordan. No Summit Out of Sight: The True Story of the Youngest Person to Climb the Seven Summits. 2014. (ENG., Illus.). 368p. (YA). (gr. 7). 21.99 *(978-1-4767-0962-8(9),* Simon & Schuster Bks. For Young Readers) Simon & Schuster Bks. For Young Readers.

—No Summit Out of Sight: The True Story of the Youngest Person to Climb the Seven Summits. 2015. lib. bdg. 24.50 *(978-0-606-37139-1(7))* Turtleback.

Stewart, Alexandra. Everest: the Remarkable Story of Edmund Hillary & Tenzing Norgay. Todd-Stanton, Joe, illus. 2020. (ENG.). 64p. (J). 21.99 *(978-1-5476-0159-2(0),* 900200537, Bloomsbury Children's Bks.) Bloomsbury Publishing USA.

Trussell-Cullen, Alan. Edmund Hillary. 2009. pap. 13.25 *(978-1-60559-058-5(4))* Hameray Publishing Group, Inc.

Whipple, Heather. Hillary & Norgay: To the Top of Mount Everest. 2007. (In the Footsteps of Explorers Ser.). (ENG., Illus.). 32p. (J). (gr. 3-7). lib. bdg. *(978-0-7787-2418-6(2));* pap. *(978-0-7787-2454-4(9))* Crabtree Publishing Co.

Yomtov, Nel. Amelia Earhart Flies Across the Atlantic. 2015. (Extraordinary Explorers Ser.). (ENG., Illus.). 24p. (J). (gr. 3-8). lib. bdg. 29.95 *(978-1-62617-290-6(0),* Black Sheep) Bellwether Media.

—Edmund Hillary Reaches the Top of Everest. 2015. (Extraordinary Explorers Ser.). (ENG., Illus.). 24p. (J). (gr. 3-8). lib. bdg. 29.95 *(978-1-62617-291-3(9),* Black Sheep) Bellwether Media.

MOUNTAINS

see also Mountaineering; Volcanoes

also names of mountain ranges, e.g. Rocky Mountains; etc.

Adams, Alison. Mountains. 2011. (Early Connections Ser.). (J). *(978-1-61672-644-7(X))* Benchmark Education Co.

Anderson, Sheila. Mountains. 2008. pap. 34.95 *(978-0-8225-9937-1(6))* 2008. (ENG., Illus.). 24p. (J). pap. 6.99 *(978-0-8225-8605-0(3),* 0e913505-99ae-4164-bc04-952cecfdf062) 2008. (ENG., Illus.). 24p. lib. bdg. 23.93 *(978-0-8225-8590-9(1),* Lerner Pubns.) 2015. (ENG., Illus.). 24p. (J). E-Book 35.99 *(978-1-5124-1043-3(8),* Lerner Pubns.) Lerner Publishing Group.

Arnold, Quinn M. Mountains. 2016. (Seedlings Ser.). (ENG., Illus.). 24p. (J). (gr. -1-k). *(978-1-60818-742-3(X),* 20735, Creative Education); pap. 8.99 *(978-1-62832-338-2(8),* 20733, Creative Paperbacks) Creative Co., The.

MNO

Atwal, Shalini. Mighty U. S. Mountains, 1 vol. 2013. (InfoMax Readers Ser.). (ENG.). 24p. (J). (gr. 3-3). pap. 8.25 (978-1-4777-2485-9(0), 9abbffec-4fa1-42fe-829d-b1e9724b0dc1); pap. 49.50 (978-1-4777-2486-6(9)) Rosen Publishing Group, Inc., The. (Rosen Classroom).

Bailey, Gerry. Trapped on the Rock. Noyes, Leighton, illus. 2014. (Science to the Rescue Ser.). (ENG.). 32p. (J). (gr. 4-4). (978-0-7787-0433-1(5)) Crabtree Publishing Co.

Banting, Erinn. Mountains. 2016. (Illus.). 32p. (J). (978-1-5105-0873-6(2)) SmartBook Media, Inc.

—Mountains. (J). 2013. (Illus.). 32p. 13.95 (978-1-61913-236-8(2)) 2013. (Illus.). 32p. 28.55 (978-1-61913-073-9(4)) 2006. (Illus.). 32p. (gr. 3-7). lib. bdg. 26.00 (978-1-59036-444-4(9)) 2006. 9.95 (978-1-59036-445-1(7)) Weigl Pubs., Inc.

Barber, Nicola. Mountain Homes. 2007. (Homes Around the World Ser.). (ENG., Illus.). 32p. (J). (gr. 3-7). pap. (978-0-7787-3557-1(5)) Crabtree Publishing Co.

Barnes, J. Lou. 101 Facts about Mountains, 1 vol. 2003. (101 Facts about Our World Ser.). (ENG., Illus.). 32p. (gr. 2-4). lib. bdg. 28.67 (978-0-8368-3708-7(8), 4de6e9dc-eb25-4511-9bfa-0975935a48ff, Gareth Stevens Learning Library) Stevens, Gareth Publishing LLLP.

Benduhn, Tea. Living in Mountains, 1 vol. 2007. (Life on the Edge Ser.). (ENG.). 24p. (gr. 2-4). pap. 9.15 (978-0-8368-8347-3(0), c289e4ea-d128-481e-92b9-95e56b52eaa0); (Illus.). lib. bdg. 24.67 (978-0-8368-8342-8(X), 692c984e-65f8-4989-a97e-75d9e4490122) Stevens, Gareth Publishing LLLP. (Weekly Reader Leveled Readers).

Best, B. J. How Are Mountains Formed?, 1 vol. 2017. (Nature's Formations Ser.). (ENG., Illus.). 24p. (gr. 1-1). pap. 9.22 (978-1-5026-2545-8(8), a6b07534-def5-4557-a599-5833cfeec36a) Cavendish Square Publishing LLC.

Bodden, Valerie. Mountains. 2006. (Our World Ser.). (Illus.). 24p. (J). (gr. -1-3). lib. bdg. 16.95 (978-1-58341-463-7(0), Creative Education) Creative Co., The.

Callery, Sean. Life Cycles: Mountain. 2018. (Lifecycles Ser.). (ENG.). 32p. (J). 12.99 (978-0-7534-7432-7(8), 900187457, Kingfisher) Roaring Brook Pr.

—Mountains. 2018. (Lifecycles Ser.). (ENG.). 32p. (J). pap. 7.99 (978-0-7534-7424-2(7), 900187156, Kingfisher) Roaring Brook Pr.

Carlson Berne, Emma. Hills. 2009. (Geography Zone: Landforms Ser.). 24p. (gr. 2-3). 42.50 (978-1-61512-710-8(0), PowerKids Pr.) Rosen Publishing Group, Inc., The.

Casado, Dami & Casado, Alicia. Las Montanas. 2005. (Yo Te Hablare De... Ser.). (SPA., Illus.). 14p. (J). per., bds. 8.99 (978-84-272-7388-7(6)) Molino, Editorial ESP. Dist: Santillana USA Publishing Co., Inc.

Clarke, Penny. Scary Creatures of the Mountains. 2008. (Scary Creatures Ser.). (ENG.). 32p. (J). 27.00 (978-0-531-21748-1(5), Watts, Franklin) Scholastic Library Publishing.

Claybourne, Anna. Mountains. 2004. (Geography Fact Files Ser.). (Illus.). (J). lib. bdg. 28.50 (978-1-58340-426-3(0)) Black Rabbit Bks.

Cole, Melissa S. Mountain. 2003. (Wild America Habitats Ser.). (Illus.). 24p. (J). 21.20 (978-1-56711-806-3(2), Blackbirch Pr., Inc.) Cengage Gale.

Duhig, Holly. Life in the Mountains. 2019. (Human Habitats Ser.). (ENG.). 24p. (J). (gr. 2-2). pap. (978-0-7787-6483-0(4), 0807309d-52e0-45fe-ac42-bc6ccfcf00f7); lib. bdg. (978-0-7787-6477-9(X), 576baefc-8cf3-4767-b29e-82236628c730) Crabtree Publishing Co.

Early Macken, JoAnn. Montañas (Mountains), 1 vol. 2005. (¿Conoces la Tierra? Geografía Del Mundo (Where on Earth? World Geography) Ser.). (SPA., Illus.). 24p. (gr. 2-4). pap. 9.15 (978-0-8368-6553-0(7), 96a8ee19-25e8-403c-a1ab-3832a75b3ae3); lib. bdg. 24.67 (978-0-8368-6546-2(4), a916ceff-43c8-420c-8ab7-09781747d6db) Stevens, Gareth Publishing LLLP. (Weekly Reader Leveled Readers).

—Mountains, 1 vol. 2005. (Where on Earth? World Geography Ser.). (ENG., Illus.). 24p. (gr. 2-4). pap. 9.15 (978-0-8368-6402-1(6), ffa1609e-8889-46d2-b463-9585d134ed34); lib. bdg. 24.67 (978-0-8368-6395-6(X), 0a90ec45-269e-42cc-adec-bbb1f7f4ab81) Stevens, Gareth Publishing LLLP. (Weekly Reader Leveled Readers).

Frankston, Evan. Mountains & Valleys: What's the Difference? 2013. (InfoMax Readers Ser.). (ENG.). 24p. (J). (gr. 3-4). pap. 49.50 (978-1-4777-2464-4(8)); (Illus.). pap. 8.25 (978-1-4777-2463-7(X), 9bbb2a78-2025-4a94-a20f-298a43e9ef05) Rosen Publishing Group, Inc., The. (Rosen Classroom).

Freedman, Jeri. Land Formation: The Shifting, Moving, Changing Earth: The Creation of Mountains. 2009. (J). 77.70 (978-1-4358-5599-1(X)); (ENG.). 64p. (YA). (gr. 5-6). pap. 13.95 (978-1-4358-5598-4(1), 9edcc6d0-f3af-4507-aa2d-be16169fb0d4); (ENG., Illus.). 64p. (YA). (gr. 5-6). lib. bdg. 37.13 (978-1-4358-5300-3(8), d5e68f51-9cbc-4dc0-a0f3-7f40a5cf3d94) Rosen Publishing Group, Inc., The.

Furgang, Kathy. Mountains, 1 vol. 2019. (Investigate Earth Science Ser.). (ENG.). 24p. (gr. 2-2). pap. 10.95 (978-1-9785-0871-2(9), 39ff04d8-5b5f-4d11-aa09-b8f7933eabac) Enslow Publishing, LLC.

Gamble, Adam & Jasper, Mark. Good Night Mountains. 2013. (Good Night Our World Ser.). (ENG., Illus.). 24p. (J). (— 1). bds. 9.95 (978-1-60219-090-0(9)) Good Night Bks.

Gill, Shelley. Up on Denali: Alaska's Wild Mountain. Cartwright, Shannon, illus. 2006. (Paws IV Ser.). (ENG.). 32p. (J). (gr. -1-2). pap. 11.99 (978-1-57061-365-4(6), Little Bigfoot) Sasquatch Bks.

Gordon, Sharon. At Home on the Mountain, 1 vol. (At Home Ser.). (ENG.). 32p. (gr. k-2). 2008. pap. 9.23 (978-0-7614-3310-1(4), ae7f817d-2bcc-4b96-8894-9644ef2505e5) 2007. (Illus.). lib. bdg. 25.50 (978-0-7614-1961-7(6), bd851989-7051-4d9b-926e-8e41df196b16) Cavendish Square Publishing LLC.

—Mi Casa en la Montana / at Home on the Mountain, 1 vol. 2008. (Mi Casa / at Home Ser.). (ENG & SPA., Illus.). 32p. (gr. k-2). lib. bdg. 25.50 (978-0-7614-2455-0(5), dcbe2edd-904f-4295-9f45-4e86dfe0ed75) Cavendish Square Publishing LLC.

—Mi Casa en la Montana (at Home on the Mountain), 1 vol. 2008. (Mi Casa (at Home) Ser.). (SPA., Illus.). 32p. (gr. k-2). lib. bdg. 25.50 (978-0-7614-2376-8(1), c16ed840-15ee-4199-a210-23594653be58) Cavendish Square Publishing LLC.

Great Mountain Ranges of the World, 10 vols. 2003. (Great Mountain Ranges of the World Ser.). (ENG., Illus.). (J). (gr. 3-3). 131.35 (978-0-8239-6995-1(9), 8be8e5b1-5b4c-436a-b718-591e3ada3433) Rosen Publishing Group, Inc., The.

Green, Emily K. Mountains. 2006. (Learning about the Earth Ser.). (ENG., Illus.). 24p. (J). (gr. k-3). lib. bdg. 26.95 (978-1-60014-038-9(6)) Bellwether Media.

—Mountains. 2011. (Blastoff! Readers Ser.). 24p. (J). pap. 5.95 (978-0-531-26031-9(3), Children's Pr.) Scholastic Library Publishing.

Green, Jen. Mountains, 1 vol. 2011. (Geography Wise Ser.). (ENG., Illus.). 32p. (YA). (gr. 2-3). lib. bdg. 30.27 (978-1-4488-3281-1(0), 31b4abe7-f7a0-4931-a8fc-b8b74f057b38) Rosen Publishing Group, Inc., The.

—Mountains Around the World, 1 vol. 2009. (Geography Now! Ser.). (ENG.). 32p. (gr. 5-5). (YA). lib. bdg. 30.27 (978-1-4358-2869-8(0), 1bc6732f-59db-4dda-bfc7-4629102bf21f); (Illus.). (J). pap. 11.00 (978-1-4358-2955-8(7), 48283ac1-877a-4a77-8106-cc485df7ebc6, PowerKids Pr.) Rosen Publishing Group, Inc., The.

Hewitt, Sally. Mountains. 2010. (Starting Geography Ser.). 32p. (J). (gr. 2-5). 28.50 (978-1-60753-127-2(5)) Amicus Learning.

Hicks, Terry Allan. How Do Mountains Form?, 1 vol. 2010. (Tell Me Why, Tell Me How Ser.). (ENG.). 32p. (gr. 3-3). 32.64 (978-0-7614-3992-9(7), a8f8a923-b56f-4c40-8251-d52754e27fdd) Cavendish Square Publishing LLC.

Holland, Gini. I Live in the Mountains, 1 vol. 2004. (Where I Live Ser.). (ENG., Illus.). 24p. (gr. k-2). pap. 9.15 (978-0-8368-4088-9(7), 1d664e5f-fbe2-4d96-a08c-120321f70030); lib. bdg. 24.67 (978-0-8368-4081-0(X), 39f9bd58-b3b7-4bef-adbd-82a4057403c2) Stevens, Gareth Publishing LLLP. (Weekly Reader Leveled Readers).

—I Live in the Mountains / Vivo en Las Montañas, 1 vol. 2004. (Where I Live / Donde Vivo Ser.). (ENG & SPA., Illus.). 24p. (gr. k-2). lib. bdg. 24.67 (978-0-8368-4129-9(8), dcec776f-e33c-4977-9181-662bd79ef361) Stevens, Gareth Publishing LLLP.

Howell, Izzi. Mountain Geo Facts. 2018. (Geo Facts Ser.). (Illus.). 32p. (J). (gr. 5-5). (978-0-7787-4384-2(5)) Crabtree Publishing Co.

Hudak, Heather C. Map & Track Mountains. 2019. (Map & Track Biomes & Animals Ser.). (Illus.). 32p. (J). (gr. 4-5). (978-0-7787-5368-1(9)); pap. (978-0-7787-5380-3(8)) Crabtree Publishing Co.

Huntington, Amy. How to Make a Mountain: In Just 9 Simple Steps & Only 100 Million Years! Lemon, Nancy, illus. 2022. (ENG.). 68p. (J). (gr. k-3). 18.99 (978-1-4521-7588-1(8)) Chronicle Bks. LLC.

Hynes, Margaret. Discover Science: Mountains. 2017. (Discover Science Ser.). (ENG.). 56p. (J). pap. 7.99 (978-0-7534-7335-1(6), 9780753473351, Kingfisher) Roaring Brook Pr.

Jeffries, Joyce. Mountains of the United States, 1 vol. 2013. (Rosen Readers Ser.). (ENG.). 24p. (J). (gr. 3-3). pap. 8.25 (978-1-4777-2471-2(0), 181f12b8-f9d7-4095-a8de-6088d132f442); pap. 49.50 (978-1-4777-2472-9(9)) Rosen Publishing Group, Inc., The. (Rosen Classroom).

Jennings, Terry J. Massive Mountains. 2009. (Amazing Planet Earth Ser.). 32p. (gr. 4-7). 31.35 (978-1-59920-370-6(7)) Black Rabbit Bks.

Kalman, Bobbie. Earth's Mountains. 2008. (Looking at Earth Ser.). (ENG., Illus.). 32p. (J). (gr. 1-4). pap. (978-0-7787-3217-4(7)); lib. bdg. (978-0-7787-3207-5(X)) Crabtree Publishing Co.

—Las Montañas de la Tierra. 2009. (SPA.). 32p. (J). (978-0-7787-8238-4(7)); pap. (978-0-7787-8255-1(7)) Crabtree Publishing Co.

—Where on Earth Are Mountains? 2014. (Explore the Continents Ser.). (ENG., Illus.). 32p. (J). (gr. 2-3). (978-0-7787-0501-7(3)) Crabtree Publishing Co.

Ladybird. BBC Earth: Mountains - Ladybird Readers Level 2. 2018. (Ladybird Readers Ser.). (Illus.). 48p. (J). (gr. k-2). pap. 8.99 (978-0-241-31948-2(X)) Penguin Bks., Ltd. GBR. Dist: Independent Pubs. Group.

Le Tord, Bijou. A Mountain Is to Climb. Le Tord, Bijou, illus. Date not set. (Illus.). 40p. (J). 5.99 (978-0-06-443591-8(1)) HarperCollins Pubs.

Levin, Judy. Life at a High Altitude. (Life in Extreme Environments Ser.). 64p. (gr. 5-8). 2009. 53.00 (978-1-61514-268-2(1)) 2003. (ENG., Illus.). (J). lib. bdg. 37.13 (978-0-8239-3987-9(1), 3a2a6e6b-5626-4085-a669-94587389891f) Rosen Publishing Group, Inc., The. (Rosen Reference).

Levy, Janey. Discovering Mountains. (World Habitats Ser.). 32p. (gr. 4-5). 2009. 47.90 (978-1-60854-835-4(X), PowerKids Pr.) 2007. (ENG., Illus.). (YA). lib. bdg. 28.93 (978-1-4042-3785-8(2), 2ac6df07-ee79-413e-b264-c8f55598578d) Rosen Publishing Group, Inc., The.

London, Martha. Mountains. 2018. (Landforms Ser.). (ENG., Illus.). 32p. (J). (gr. 2-3). pap. 9.95 (978-1-63517-995-8(5), 1635179955); lib. bdg. 31.35 (978-1-63517-894-4(0), 1635178940) North Star Editions. (Focus Readers).

Marsico, Katie. Mountains. 2009. (21st Century Skills Library: Real World Math Ser.). (ENG.). 32p. (gr. 4-8). lib. bdg. 32.07 (978-1-60279-492-4(8), 200316) Cherry Lake Publishing.

Masterson, Josephine. The Big Hill, 1 vol. 2015. (Rosen REAL Readers: STEM & STEAM Collection). (ENG.). 8p. (gr. k-1). pap. 5.46 (978-1-4994-9683-3(4), 5a7b2e75-f879-4097-a3f0-9594bc1531d8, Rosen Classroom) Rosen Publishing Group, Inc., The.

Maynard, Charles W. The Appalachians, 1 vol. 2003. (Great Mountain Ranges of the World Ser.). (ENG., Illus.). 24p. (YA). (gr. 3-3). lib. bdg. 26.27 (978-0-8239-6695-0(X), ec5629f2-c7ce-4a7f-814b-f94506191422) Rosen Publishing Group, Inc., The.

—The Ural Mountains. (Great Mountain Ranges of the World Ser.). 24p. (gr. 3-3). 2009. 42.50 (978-1-61513-172-3(8)) 2003. (ENG., Illus.). (J). lib. bdg. 26.27 (978-0-8239-6699-8(2), ff6e7413-7033-41e5-a17f-9e21a8c762d1) Rosen Publishing Group, Inc., The. (PowerKids Pr.).

McCurry, Kristin. Mountain Babies. 2006. (Animal Babies Ser.). (ENG., Illus.). 22p. (J). (gr. -1 — 1). bds. 5.95 (978-1-55971-940-7(0)) Cooper Square Publishing Llc.

Minden, Cecilia. The World Around Us: Mountains. 2010. (21st Century Basic Skills Library: the World Around Us Ser.). (ENG., Illus.). 24p. (gr. k-3). lib. bdg. 26.35 (978-1-60279-860-1(5), 200586) Cherry Lake Publishing.

Mis, Melody S. Exploring Mountains. 2009. (Geography Zone: Landforms Ser.). 24p. (gr. 2-3). 42.50 (978-1-61512-704-7(6)); (ENG.). (J). pap. 9.25 (978-1-4358-3113-1(6), 30d23f7a-f25f-4ca1-ad82-4488f762d32e); (ENG., Illus.). (J). lib. bdg. 26.27 (978-1-4358-2715-8(5), bec2cced-170e-4a8f-932e-41de349828b6) Rosen Publishing Group, Inc., The. (PowerKids Pr.).

Morley, Catherine Weyerhaeuser. Where Do Mountains Come from, Momma? 2012. (Illus.). (J). (978-0-87842-582-2(9)) Mountain Pr. Publishing Co., Inc.

Nadeau, Isaac. Mountains. (Library of Landforms Ser.). 24p. (gr. 3-4). 2009. 42.50 (978-1-60853-727-3(7), PowerKids Pr.) 2005. (ENG., Illus.). (J). lib. bdg. 26.27 (978-1-4042-3127-6(7), 827f8806-29eb-4a15-bfc2-a7bdefc17626) Rosen Publishing Group, Inc., The.

National Geographic Learning. Reading Expeditions (Social Studies: the Land Around Us): Mountains. 2007. (ENG., Illus.). 32p. (J). pap. 18.95 (978-0-7922-4562-9(8)) CENGAGE Learning.

Northcott, Richard. In the Mountains. 2013. (ENG., Illus.). 40p. pap. 11.00 (978-0-19-464687-1(4)) Oxford Univ. Pr., Inc.

O'DellKathryn. SURVIVAL GUIDE: LOST IN THE MOUNTAINS LOW INTERMEDIATE BOOK WITH ONLINE ACCESS, 1 vol. 2014. (ENG., Illus.). 28p. (J). pap., E-Book, E-Book 9.50 (978-1-107-64328-4(7)) Cambridge Univ. Pr.

Oxlade, Chris. Mountains, 1 vol. 2003. (Science Files: Earth Ser.). (ENG., Illus.). 32p. (gr. 3-5). lib. bdg. 28.67 (978-0-8368-3569-4(7), d0ffc7e7-1f63-4ec5-bb22-0b8999009dfe) Stevens, Gareth Publishing LLLP.

Pyers, Greg. Biodiversity of Alpine Zones, 1 vol. 2012. (Biodiversity Ser.). (ENG.). 32p. (gr. 4-4). 31.21 (978-1-60870-528-3(5), 4e59c39a-cf9d-4650-a1ff-f35a527b41b2) Cavendish Square Publishing LLC.

Randall, Jory. My Day in the Mountains, 1 vol. 2009. (Kid's Life! Ser.). (ENG.). 24p. (J). (gr. 1-1). pap. 9.25 (978-1-4358-2471-3(7), 6223e9b1-7244-441a-95d7-e7a80eb2d16f); (Illus.). lib. bdg. 26.27 (978-1-4042-8076-2(6), cccc44f2-01f1-4594-8856-a01ecd531ea4) Rosen Publishing Group, Inc., The. (PowerKids Pr.).

Rice, Dona Herweck. Mountain Travel (Grade 1) 2018. (See Me Read! Everyday Words Ser.). (ENG., Illus.). 12p. (J). (gr. k-1). 6.99 (978-1-4938-9856-5(6)) Teacher Created Materials, Inc.

Richardson, Gillian. Mountain Extremes. 2008. (Extreme Nature Ser.). (ENG., Illus.). 32p. (J). (gr. 2-3). pap. (978-0-7787-4520-4(1)); lib. bdg. (978-0-7787-4503-7(1)) Crabtree Publishing Co.

Rissman, Rebecca. Living & Nonliving in the Mountains, 1 vol. 2013. (Is It Living or Nonliving? Ser.). (ENG.). 24p. (J). (gr. k-2). pap. 6.95 (978-1-4109-5392-6(0), 123332, Raintree) Capstone.

Roumanis, Alexis. Mountains. 2014. (Illus.). 24p. (J). (978-1-4896-3010-0(4)) Weigl Pubs., Inc.

Samuel, Nigel. The 10 Mightiest Mountains. 2007. (Illus.). (J). 14.99 (978-1-55448-509-3(6)) Scholastic Library Publishing.

Sill, Cathryn. About Habitats: Mountains, 1 vol. Sill, John, illus. 2009. (About Habitats Ser.: 3). 48p. (J). (gr. -1-2). 16.95 (978-1-56145-469-3(9)) Peachtree Publishing Co. Inc.

Snedden, Robert. Protecting Mountain Habitats, 1 vol. 2005. (Protecting Habitats Ser.). (ENG., Illus.). 32p. (gr. 4-6). lib. bdg. 28.67 (978-0-8368-4991-2(4), d6669367-6317-4961-a89c-e17a60a660c8, Gareth Stevens Learning Library) Stevens, Gareth Publishing LLLP.

Staub, Frank. America's Mountains. 2003. (Illus.). 48p. (J). (gr. 2-6). 16.95 (978-1-59034-870-3(2)); (978-1-59034-872-7(9)) Mondo Publishing.

Tanumihardja, Pat. Amazing Mountains Around the World. 2019. (Passport to Nature Ser.). (ENG., Illus.). 32p. (J). (gr. 4-6). lib. bdg. 28.65 (978-1-5435-5775-6(9), 139731) Capstone.

Taylor, Chad. Our Community Is in the Mountains, 1 vol. 2016. (Rosen REAL Readers: Social Studies Nonfiction / Fiction: Myself, My Community, My World Ser.). (ENG.). 8p. (gr. k-1). pap. 5.46 (978-1-5081-2299-9(7), 53b80c12-210e-4fae-8824-671f0bd892da, Rosen Classroom) Rosen Publishing Group, Inc., The.

Thomson, Ruth. Mountains. 2012. (Geography Corner Ser.). (ENG., Illus.). 24p. (J). (gr. k-3). 21.25 (978-1-4488-6617-5(0), PowerKids Pr.) Rosen Publishing Group, Inc., The.

Watson, Galadriel Findlay. Mount Kilimanjaro. 2008. (Natural Wonders Ser.). (Illus.). 32p. (J). (gr. 5-6). pap. 9.95 (978-1-59036-935-7(1)) Weigl Pubs., Inc.

Waxman, Laura Hamilton. Life on a Mountain. 2016. (Biomes Alive! Ser.). (ENG., Illus.). 24p. (J). (gr. k-3). lib. bdg. 26.95 (978-1-62617-319-4(2), Blastoff! Readers) Bellwether Media.

Webster, Christine. K2. 2008. (Natural Wonders Ser.). 32p. (J). (gr. 5-6). lib. bdg. 26.00 (978-1-59036-938-8(6)); (Illus.). pap. 9.95 (978-1-59036-939-5(4)) Weigl Pubs., Inc.

Wilkes, Angela. Wild Places: Combined Volume. 2009. (Explainers Ser.). 96p. (J). pap. 12.99 (978-0-7945-2499-9(0), Usborne) EDC Publishing.

Woods, Michael & Woods, Mary B. Seven Natural Wonders of Africa. 2009. (Seven Wonders Ser.). (ENG., Illus.). 80p. (gr. 5-8). lib. bdg. 33.26 (978-0-8225-9071-2(9)) Lerner Publishing Group.

World Book, Inc. Staff, contrib. by. Mountains, Deserts, & Grasslands. 2008. 64p. (J). (978-0-7166-1403-6(0)) World Bk., Inc.

—Nature's Skyscrapers. 2017. (Illus.). 40p. (J). (978-0-7166-3368-6(X)) World Bk., Inc.

Youssef, Jagger. Mountains, 1 vol. 2017. (Our Exciting Earth! Ser.). (ENG.). 24p. (J). (gr. k-k). pap. 9.15 (978-1-5382-0965-3(9), 965e654a-4610-453f-a53e-7901b67d4af1) Stevens, Gareth Publishing LLLP.

Zoehfeld, Kathleen Weidner. How Mountains Are Made. Hale, James Graham, illus. 2015. (Let's-Read-And-Find-Out Science 2 Ser.). (ENG.). 32p. (J). (gr. -1-3). pap. 7.99 (978-0-06-238203-0(9), HarperCollins) HarperCollins Pubs.

—How Mountains Are Made. 2015. (Let's-Read-And-Find-Out Science: Stage 2 Ser.). (J). lib. bdg. 17.20 (978-0-606-37637-2(2)) Turtleback.

Zolty, Howard. Mountain View A through Z. A Colorful Reader for Children of All Ages. 2006. 28p. 14.99 (978-1-4116-5708-3(X)) Lulu Pr., Inc.

MOUNTIES

see Royal Canadian Mounted Police

MOURNING CUSTOMS

see Funeral Rites and Ceremonies

MOUSE

see Mice

MOUTH ORGAN

see Harmonica

MOVIES

see Motion Pictures

MOVING, HOUSEHOLD

Amos, Janine. Moving, 1 vol. 2009. (Changes Ser.). (ENG., Illus.). 32p. (J). (gr. 2-2). 27.27 (978-1-60754-487-6(3), a0030150-8b3a-4895-964b-b04d127f2cb8); pap. 11.55 (978-1-60754-488-3(1), 55021282-6838-46af-adc4-07c502ee52f1) Rosen Publishing Group, Inc., The. (Windmill Bks.).

Barber, Nicola. Moving to a New House, 1 vol. (Big Day! Ser.). (ENG., 24p. (J). (gr. 1-1). 2009. Illus.). pap. 9.25 (978-1-4358-2897-1(6), a7aa3d8a-a919-4807-84ee-f8459976a31f) 2008. 26.27 (978-1-4358-2841-4(0), 8b8f9641-0d0d-4328-8d52-b2492c3cb00e) Rosen Publishing Group, Inc., The. (PowerKids Pr.).

Berry, Joy. Good Answers to Tough Questions about Moving. 2009. (ENG.). 52p. (J). (gr. k-7). pap. 7.95 (978-1-60577-503-6(7)) Berry, Joy Enterprises.

—Good Answers to Tough Questions Moving. Bartholomew, illus. 2010. (Good Answers to Tough Questions Ser.). (ENG.). 48p. (J). (gr. k-7). pap. 7.99 (978-1-60577-508-1(8)) Berry, Joy Enterprises.

Civardi, Anne. Moving House Sticker Book. 2009. (First Experiences Sticker Bks). 18p. (J). pap. 6.99 (978-0-7945-2430-2(3), Usborne) EDC Publishing.

Davis, Gabriel. The Moving Book: A Kids' Survival Guide. Dennen, Sue, illus. 2nd ed. 2008. 160p. (J). spiral bd. 22.95 (978-0-912301-92-1(9)) First Bks.

Glasser, Debbie & Schenck, Emily. New Kid, New Scene: A Guide to Moving & Switching Schools. 2011. (Illus.). 112p. (J). pap. 9.95 (978-1-4338-1038-1(7), Magination Pr.) American Psychological Assn.

Glasser, Debbie, et al. New Kid, New Scene: A Guide to Moving & Switching Schools. 2011. (Illus.). 112p. (J). 14.95 (978-1-4338-1039-8(5), Magination Pr.) American Psychological Assn.

Lott, Ruth. BK's Big Move Across the Country: From Philadelphia to Los Angeles. 2012. (Illus.). 104p. (J). (978-1-58982-846-9(1), Millennial Mind Publishing) American Bk. Publishing Group.

McAneney, Caitlin. Moving, 1 vol. 2014. (Let's Talk about It Ser.). (ENG.). 24p. (J). (gr. 2-2). pap. 9.25 (978-1-4777-5801-4(1), 28090683-50d5-46f4-bbb4-b6e72895f833, PowerKids Pr.) Rosen Publishing Group, Inc., The.

A New House. 2004. (J). pap. 6.95 (978-0-9760646-0-2(X)) Grape Elephant MarketPr.

Rober, Harold. Moving Day. 2017. (Bumba Books (r) — Fun Firsts Ser.). (ENG., Illus.). 24p. (J). (gr. -1-1). E-Book 39.99 (978-1-5124-3686-0(0), 9781512436860); E-Book 4.99 (978-1-5124-3687-7(9), 9781512436877); E-Book 39.99 (978-1-5124-2747-9(0)) Lerner Publishing Group. (Lerner Pubns.).

Sportelli-Rehak, Angela. Moving Again Mom! Hinlicky, Gregg, illus. (J). 2004. (Uncle Sam's Kids Ser.: Bk. 2). 40p. (gr. -1-7). pap. 7.95 (978-0-9714515-0-6(8)) 2003. (gr. k-7). pap. (978-0-9714515-3-7(2)) Abidenme Bks.

—Uncle Sam's Kids: Moving Again Mom. Hinlicky, Gregg, illus. 2004. (Uncle Sam's Kids Ser.: Bk. 2). 40p. (gr. k-6). 16.95 (978-0-9714515-2-0(4)) Abidenme Bks.

MOVING, HOUSEHOLD—FICTION

Absolutely Truly. 2014. (Pumpkin Falls Mystery Ser.). (ENG., Illus.). 368p. (J). (gr. 3-7). 19.99 (978-1-4424-2972-7(0), Simon & Schuster Bks. For Young Readers) Simon & Schuster Bks. For Young Readers.

Acampora, Paul. Rachel Spinelli Punched Me in the Face. 2013. (ENG.). 192p. (J). (gr. 8-12). pap. 14.99 (978-1-250-01669-0(X), 900087083) Square Fish.

Allbright, Lauren. Exit Strategy. (Max Ser.). (ENG.). 176p. (J). (gr. 4-8). 2018. pap. 7.99 (978-1-4814-7913-4(X)) 2017. (Illus.). 16.99 (978-1-4814-7912-7(1)) Simon & Schuster Children's Publishing. (Aladdin).

Allen, Nancy. Amazing Grace: A Kentucky Girl with Gumption During World War II. Shapiro, Meryl R. B., illus. 2014. Orig. Title: Amazing Grace: a Kentucky Girl with Gumption During World War II. (ENG.). 160p. (gr. 4-7). 29.99 (978-1-62619-405-2(X), History Pr., The) Arcadia Publishing.

Almond, David. Skellig. 2009. 9.14 (978-0-7848-2973-8(X), Everbind) Marco Bk. Co.

Amato, Mary. Invisible Lines. Caparó, Antonio Javier, illus. 2011. (ENG.). 336p. (gr. 4-6). lib. bdg. 22.44 (978-1-60684-043-6(6)) Farshore GBR. Dist: Children's Plus, Inc.

Anderson, Laurie Halse. Helping Hands. 2013. (Vet Volunteers Ser.: 15). (ENG.). 144p. (J). (gr. 3-7). pap. 7.99 *(978-0-14-241677-8(0)*, Puffin Books) Penguin Young Readers Group.
—New Beginnings, 13 vols., 13. 2012. (Vet Volunteers Ser.: 13). (ENG.). 192p. (J). (gr. 3-7). 7.99 *(978-0-14-241675-4(4)*, Puffin) Penguin Young Readers Group.
Arno, Ronni. Dear Poppy. 2016. (Mix Ser.). (ENG., Illus.). 256p. (J). (gr. 4-8). pap. 7.99 *(978-1-4814-3759-2(3)*, Aladdin) Simon & Schuster Children's Publishing.
—Dear Poppy. 2016. (Mix Ser.). (ENG., Illus.). 256p. (J). (gr. 4-8). 17.99 *(978-1-4814-3760-8(7)*, Simon & Schuster/Paula Wiseman Bks.) Simon & Schuster/Paula Wiseman Bks.
Arnold, Elana K. Far from Fair. 2016. (ENG.). 240p. (J). (gr. 5-7). 16.99 *(978-0-544-60227-4(7)*, 1616935, Clarion Bks.) HarperCollins Pubs.
—The Question of Miracles. 2016. (ENG.). 256p. (J). (gr. 5-7). pap. 7.99 *(978-0-544-66852-2(9)*, 1625476, Clarion Bks.) HarperCollins Pubs.
Atkinson, Elizabeth. From Alice to Zen & Everyone in Between. 2008. (Exceptional Reading & Language Arts Titles for Intermediate Grades Ser.). 247p. (YA). (gr. 4-7). 16.95 *(978-0-8225-7271-8(0))* Lerner Publishing Group.
Auch, M. J. Wing Nut. 2008. (ENG.). 256p. (J). (gr. 6-8). pap. 15.99 *(978-0-312-38420-3(3)*, 900053321) Square Fish.
Bagley, Jessixa. Before I Leave: A Picture Book. 2016. (ENG., Illus.). 40p. (J). (gr. 1-3). 18.99 *(978-1-62672-040-4(1)*, 900132813) Roaring Brook Pr.
Banks, Lynne Reid. The Mystery of the Cupboard. Newsom, Tom, illus. 2004. (ENG.). 256p. (J). (gr. 4-18). pap. 7.99 *(978-0-380-72013-2(2)*, HarperCollins) HarperCollins Pubs.
Barnes, Jennifer Lynn. The Fixer. 2016. (ENG.). 400p. (YA). pap. 11.99 *(978-1-61963-598-2(4)*, 900141877, Bloomsbury USA Childrens) Bloomsbury Publishing USA.
Barnett, Mac. Terrible Two Get Worse (UK Edition) 2016. (Terrible Two Ser.). (ENG., Illus.). 224p. (J). (gr. 3-7). pap. 7.95 *(978-1-4197-1925-7(4))* Abrams, Inc.
—Terrible Two Go Wild (UK Edition) 2018. (Terrible Two Ser.). (ENG., Illus.). 224p. (J). (gr. 3-7). pap. 7.99 *(978-1-4197-2341-4(3))* Abrams, Inc.
Barnett, Mac & John, Jory. The Terrible Two. Cornell, Kevin, illus. 2017. (Terrible Two Ser.). (ENG.). 240p. (J). (gr. 3-7). pap. 8.99 *(978-1-4197-2737-5(0)*, 1196503, Amulet Bks.) Abrams, Inc.
—The Terrible Two. 2017. (Terrible Two Ser.: 1). (J). lib. bdg. 18.40 *(978-0-606-40723-6(5))*; lib. bdg. 18.40 *(978-0-606-40724-3(3))* Turtleback.
—The Terrible Two Get Worse. Cornell, Kevin, illus. 2016. (Terrible Two Ser.). (ENG.). 224p. (J). (gr. 3-7). 15.99 *(978-1-4197-1680-5(8)*, 1093701, Amulet Bks.) Abrams, Inc.
—The Terrible Two Go Wild. Cornell, Kevin, illus. 2018. (Terrible Two Ser.). (ENG.). 240p. (J). (gr. 3-7). pap. 8.99 *(978-1-4197-3205-8(6)*, 1093803) Abrams, Inc.
—Terrible Two Go Wild. Cornell, Kevin, illus. 2018. (Terrible Two Ser.). (ENG.). 224p. (J). (gr. 3-7). 13.99 *(978-1-4197-2185-4(2)*, 1093801, Amulet Bks.) Abrams, Inc.
Barshaw, Ruth McNally. The Ellie Mcdoodle Diaries: New Kid in School. 2013. (Ellie Mcdoodle Diaries). (ENG., Illus.). 192p. (YA). (gr. 3-6). 13.99 *(978-1-61963-174-8(1)*, 900123470, Bloomsbury USA Childrens) Bloomsbury Publishing USA.
Beake, Lesley. Home Now. Littlewood, Karin, illus. 2007. 32p. (J). (ENG.). (gr. -1-3). pap. 6.95 *(978-1-58089-163-9(2))*; (gr. k-3). 16.95 *(978-1-58089-162-2(4))* Charlesbridge Publishing, Inc.
Bean, Raymond. First Family in Space. Vimislik, Matthew, illus. 2016. (Out of This World Ser.). (ENG.). 112p. (J). (gr. 2-5). lib. bdg. 32.65 *(978-1-4965-3617-4(7)*, 132833, Stone Arch Bks.) Capstone.
Beiko, S. M. The Lake & the Library. l.t. ed. 2013. 542p. pap. *(978-1-4596-6871-3(5))* ReadHowYouWant.com, Ltd.
Bennett, Jenn. Alex, Approximately. 2017. (ENG., Illus.). 400p. (YA). (gr. 9). 18.99 *(978-1-4814-7877-9(X)*, Simon Pulse) Simon Pulse.
Benson, Linda. Finding Chance. Lane, Nancy, illus. 2006. 112p. (J). *(978-1-59336-696-4(5))* Mondo Publishing.
Bentley, Sue. Chocolate Wishes #1. Swan, Angela, illus. 2013. (Magic Bunny Ser.: 1). (ENG.). 128p. (J). (gr. 1-3). pap. 6.99 *(978-0-448-46727-6(5)*, Grosset & Dunlap) Penguin Young Readers Group.
—A Puzzle of Paws. 2014. (Magic Kitten Ser.: 12). lib. bdg. 14.75 *(978-0-606-35682-4(7))* Turtleback.
—A Puzzle of Paws #12. Swan, Angela, illus. 2014. (Magic Kitten Ser.: 12). (ENG.). 128p. (J). (gr. 1-3). 5.99 *(978-0-448-46795-5(X)*, Grosset & Dunlap) Penguin Young Readers Group.
—Seaside Mystery. 2013. (Magic Kitten Ser.: 9). lib. bdg. 16.00 *(978-0-606-32121-1(7))* Turtleback.
Berman, Ali. Misdirected: A Novel. 2014. (Illus.). 288p. (YA). (gr. 7). 18.95 *(978-1-60980-573-9(9)*, Triangle Square) Seven Stories Pr.
Berry, Eileen M. Looking for Home. Manning, Maurie J., illus. 2006. 75p. (J). (gr. -1-3). per. *(978-1-59166-493-2(4))* BJU Pr.
Berube, Amelinda. Here There Are Monsters. 2019. (ENG., Illus.). 352p. (YA). (gr. 8-12). pap. 10.99 *(978-1-4926-7101-5(0))* Sourcebooks, Inc.
Bietz, Barbara. The Sundown Kid: A Southwestern Shabbat. 2017. (ENG., Illus.). 32p. (J). (gr. k-2). pap. 8.95 *(978-1-939160-94-2(4))* August Hse. Pubs., Inc.
Binns, B. A. & McKenzie, C. Lee. The Princess of Las Pulgas. 2010. 334p. (YA). (gr. 8-18). 16.95 *(978-1-934813-44-7(3))* Westside Bks.
Birle, Pete. Locals Only. 2013. (Av2 Audio Chapter Bks.). (ENG.). 121p. (J). 27.13 *(978-1-62127-985-3(5)*, AV2 by Weigl) Weigl Pubs., Inc.
Blakemore, Megan Frazer. The Water Castle. 2014. (ENG.). 368p. (YA). (gr. 3-8). pap. 9.99 *(978-0-8027-3593-5(2)*, 900123283, Bloomsbury USA Childrens) Bloomsbury Publishing USA.
Blecher, Jennifer. Out of Place. Liddiard, Merrilee, illus. 2019. (ENG.). 304p. (J). (gr. 3-7). 16.99 *(978-0-06-274859-1(9)*, Greenwillow Bks.) HarperCollins Pubs.
Blume, Judy. Starring Sally J. Freedman As Herself. 2014. (ENG., Illus.). (J). (gr. 3-7). 384p. 18.99 *(978-1-4814-1437-1(2))*; 400p. pap. 8.99 *(978-1-4814-1355-8(4))* Simon & Schuster Children's Publishing. (Atheneum Bks. for Young Readers).
Blythe, Daniel. Shadow Breakers. 2013. (J). *(978-0-545-47980-6(0)*, Chicken Hse., The) Scholastic, Inc.
Border, Terry. Peanut Butter & Cupcake. Border, Terry, illus. 2014. (Illus.). 32p. (J). (gr. -1-2). 18.99 *(978-0-399-16773-7(0)*, Philomel Bks.) Penguin Young Readers Group.
Bostrom, Kathleen Long. The Worst Christmas Ever. Porfirio, Guy, illus. 2019. (ENG.). 48p. (J). (gr. -1-1). 17.00 *(978-1-947888-09-8(9)*, Flyaway Bks.) Westminster John Knox Pr.
Bottner, Barbara. Rosa's Room, 1 vol. Spiegel, Beth, illus. 2014. 32p. (J). (gr. -1-3). pap. 7.99 *(978-1-56145-776-2(0))* Peachtree Publishing Co. Inc.
Bouwman, H. M. Owen & Eleanor Move In. Alder, Charlie, illus. 2018. (Owen & Eleanor Ser.: 1). 133p. (J). (gr. 2-5). pap. 7.99 *(978-1-5064-3972-3(1)*, Sparkhouse Family) 1517 Media.
Bowers, Tim. A New Home. Bowers, Tim, illus. 2003. (Green Light Readers Level 1 Ser.). (ENG., Illus.). 24p. (J). (gr. -1-3). pap. 4.99 *(978-0-15-204848-8(0)*, 1194639, Clarion Bks.) HarperCollins Pubs.
Boyack, Merrilee. The Mismatched Nativity. Tenney, Shawna J. C., illus. 2016. (J). 18.99 *(978-1-62972-239-9(1))* Deseret Bk. Co.
Brandon, Anthony G. Moving Day. Yee, Wong Herbert, illus. 2005. (ENG.). 32p. (J). (gr. -1-3). pap. 4.99 *(978-0-15-205652-0(1)*, 1196995, Clarion Bks.) HarperCollins Pubs.
Branford, Anna. Violet Mackerel's Personal Space. Allen, Elanna, illus. 2013. (Violet Mackerel Ser.). (ENG.). 128p. (J). (gr. 1-5). 15.99 *(978-1-4424-3591-9(7))*; pap. 6.99 *(978-1-4424-3592-6(5))* Simon & Schuster Children's Publishing. (Atheneum Bks. for Young Readers).
—Violet Mackerel's Possible Friend. Allen, Elanna, illus. 2014. (Violet Mackerel Ser.). (ENG.). 128p. (J). (gr. 1-5). 17.99 *(978-1-4424-9455-8(7)*, Atheneum Bks. for Young Readers) Simon & Schuster Children's Publishing.
Braver, Vanita. Madison & the New Neighbors, 1 vol. Brown, Jonathan, illus. 2014. (ENG.). 32p. (J). 15.99 *(978-1-59572-686-5(1))* Star Bright Bks., Inc.
Brennan-Nelson, Denise. Willow & the Snow Day Dance. Moore, Cyd, illus. 2010. (ENG.). 32p. (J). (gr. 1-4). lib. bdg. 16.95 *(978-1-58536-522-7(X)*, 202210) Sleeping Bear Pr.
Brewer, Heather. The Cemetery Boys. 2016. (ENG.). 304p. (YA). (gr. 8). pap. 9.99 *(978-0-06-230789-7(4)*, HarperTeen) HarperCollins Pubs.
—The Cemetery Boys. 2016. (YA). lib. bdg. 20.85 *(978-0-606-38741-5(2))* Turtleback.
Brezenoff, Steve. No Place Like Home. 2013. (Ravens Pass Ser.). (ENG.). 96p. (J). (gr. 2-3). pap. 36.90 *(978-1-4342-6292-9(8)*, 20263, Stone Arch Bks.) Capstone.
—No Place Like Home, 1 vol. Pinelli, Amerigo, illus. 2013. (Ravens Pass Ser.). (ENG.). 96p. (J). (gr. 3-6). pap. 6.15 *(978-1-4342-6215-8(4)*, 123513); lib. bdg. 25.32 *(978-1-4342-4615-8(9)*, 120604) Capstone. (Stone Arch Bks.).
Brown, Gavin. Josh Baxter Levels Up. 2016. (ENG., Illus.). 192p. (J). (gr. 3-7). 12.99 *(978-0-545-77294-5(X)*, Scholastic Pr.) Scholastic, Inc.
Bullard, Lisa. Trick-or-Treat on Milton Street. Oeltjenbruns, Joni, illus. (Carolrhoda Picture Books Ser.). 32p. (J). 2004. (gr. k-4). pap. 6.95 *(978-1-57505-793-4(X))* 2003. (gr. -1-3). 15.95 *(978-1-57505-158-1(3)*, Carolrhoda Bks.) Lerner Publishing Group.
Bundy, Tamara. Walking with Miss Millie. 2018. 240p. (J). (gr. 5). 8.99 *(978-0-399-54457-6(7)*, Puffin Books) Penguin Young Readers Group.
Burkhart, Jessica. Wild Hearts. 2015. (If Only... Ser.). (ENG.). 368p. (YA). (gr. 7). 17.99 *(978-1-61963-258-5(6)*, 9781619632585, Bloomsbury USA Childrens) Bloomsbury Publishing USA.
Bustard, Anne. Anywhere but Paradise. 2018. (ENG., Illus.). 288p. (J). (gr. 5-12). pap. 9.99 *(978-1-5415-1481-2(5)*, 8e45d442-59ae-45b4-b23c-96b160e2e472, Carolrhoda Bks.) Lerner Publishing Group.
Buxbaum, Julie. Tell Me Three Things. 2017. (ENG.). 352p. (YA). (gr. 7). pap. 11.99 *(978-0-553-53567-9(6)*, Ember) Random Hse. Children's Bks.
Buyea, Rob. Mr. Terupt Falls Again. 2013. (Mr. Terupt Ser.: 2). 400p. (J). (gr. 3-7). 8.99 *(978-0-307-93046-0(7)*, Yearling) Random Hse. Children's Bks.
—Mr. Terupt Falls Again. 2013. lib. bdg. 18.40 *(978-0-606-32236-2(1))* Turtleback.
Buzbee, Lewis. Steinbeck's Ghost. 2010. (ENG.). 368p. (J). (gr. 4-6). pap. 19.99 *(978-0-312-60211-6(1)*, 900064224) Square Fish.
Cabot, Meg. Moving Day. 2009. (Allie Finkle's Rules for Girls Ser.: 1). lib. bdg. 17.20 *(978-0-606-06818-5(X))* Turtleback.
Calhoun, Dia. After the River the Sun. Slater, Kate, illus. 2013. (ENG.). 368p. (J). (gr. 4-7). 16.99 *(978-1-4424-3985-6(8))* Simon & Schuster Children's Publishing.
Callaghan, Cindy. Sydney Mackenzie Knocks 'Em Dead. (ENG., Illus.). 256p. (J). (gr. 4-8). 2018. pap. 7.99 *(978-1-4814-6568-7(6))* 2017. 17.99 *(978-1-4814-6569-4(4))* Simon & Schuster/Paula Wiseman Bks. (Simon & Schuster/Paula Wiseman Bks.).
Calonita, Jen. Belles. 2012. (Belles Ser.: 1). (ENG.). 384p. (YA). (gr. 7-17). pap. 19.99 *(978-0-316-09112-1(X)*, Poppy) Little, Brown Bks. for Young Readers.
Campbell, Isaiah. AbrakaPOW. Perillo, Dave, illus. 2016. (ENG.). 400p. (J). (gr. 3-7). 16.99 *(978-1-4814-2634-3(6)*, Simon & Schuster Bks. For Young Readers) Simon & Schuster Bks. For Young Readers.
Carey, Janet Lee. The Double Life of Zoe Flynn. 2007. (ENG.). 240p. (J). (gr. 3-7). pap. 12.95 *(978-1-4169-6754-5(0)*, Simon & Schuster/Paula Wiseman Bks.) Simon & Schuster/Paula Wiseman Bks.
Carlson, Nancy. My Best Friend Moved Away. Carlson, Nancy, illus. 2012. (Nancy Carlson Picture Bks). (Illus.). 32p. (J). (gr. k-2). 56.72 *(978-0-7613-9309-2(9)*, Carolrhoda Bks.) Lerner Publishing Group.
Carmean, John. Moving Day: Adventures in Hogtown. l.t. ed. 2011. (ENG., Illus.). 33p. (J). pap. 16.99 *(978-0-9839799-1-3(X))* Carmean Productions LLC.
Cassidy, Cathy. Indigo Blue. 2006. (ENG.). 240p. (J). (gr. 5-18). 7.99 *(978-0-14-240703-5(8)*, Puffin Books) Penguin Young Readers Group.
Castle, Jennifer. Butterfly Wishes 1: the Wishing Wings. 2017. (Butterfly Wishes Ser.). (ENG., Illus.). 128p. (J). 15.99 *(978-1-68119-491-2(0)*, 9781681194912, Bloomsbury USA Childrens) Bloomsbury Publishing USA.
Castrillon, Melissa. The Balcony. Castrillon, Melissa, illus. 2019. (ENG., Illus.). 48p. (J). (gr. -1-3). 18.99 *(978-1-5344-0588-2(7)*, Simon & Schuster/Paula Wiseman Bks.) Simon & Schuster/Paula Wiseman Bks.
Chamberlin, Ann. Dumpling. 2012. (Illus.). 32p. pap. 21.99 *(978-1-4691-6313-0(6))* Xlibris Corp.
Chambliss Bertman, Jennifer. Book Scavenger. 2016. (Book Scavenger Ser.: 1). (ENG.). 368p. (J). pap. 8.99 *(978-1-250-07980-0(2)*, 900154628) Square Fish.
Charles, Tami. Daphne Definitely Doesn't Do Sports. Calo, Marcos, illus. 2018. (Daphne, Secret Vlogger Ser.). (ENG.). 96p. (J). (gr. 4-7). lib. bdg. 24.65 *(978-1-4965-6294-4(1)*, 138020, Stone Arch Bks.) Capstone.
Chen, Justina. Return to Me. (ENG.). (YA). (gr. 7-17). 2014. 368p. pap. 19.99 *(978-0-316-10258-2(X))* 2013. 352p. 17.99 *(978-0-316-10255-1(5))* Little, Brown Bks. for Young Readers.
Cheng, Andrea. The Year of the Garden. Barton, Patrice, illus. 2018. (Anna Wang Novel Ser.: 5). (ENG.). 128p. (J). (gr. 1-4). pap. 6.99 *(978-1-328-90017-3(7)*, 1700051, Clarion Bks.) HarperCollins Pubs.
Christopher, Matt. The Extreme Team: One Smooth Move. 2004. (Extreme Team Ser.: 1). (ENG., Illus.). 64p. (J). (gr. 1-4). pap. 8.99 *(978-0-316-73749-4(6))* Little, Brown Bks. for Young Readers.
—Hot Shot. 2010. (ENG.). 128p. (J). (gr. 3-7). pap. 9.99 *(978-0-316-04482-0(2))* Little, Brown Bks. for Young Readers.
—Hot Shot. 2018. (Matt Christopher: the #1 Sports Series for Kids Ser.). (ENG.). 128p. (J). (gr. 3-7). lib. bdg. 31.36 *(978-1-5321-4267-3(6)*, 31077, Chapter Bks.) Spotlight.
Citra, Becky. Duke's Den, 1 vol. 2016. (ENG.). 208p. (J). (gr. 4-7). pap. 10.95 *(978-1-4598-0901-7(7))* Orca Bk. Pubs. USA.
Civardi, Anne. Moving House. Bates, Michelle, ed. Cartwright, Stephen, illus. rev. ed. 2005. 16p. (J). (gr. -1-17). pap. 4.95 *(978-0-7945-1009-1(4)*, Usborne) EDC Publishing.
Clark, Eleanor. Katie Sue: Heading West. 2007. (Eleanor Ser.: Bk. 3). 220p. 14.99 *(978-0-9788726-0-1(6))* HonorNet.
Clements, Andrew. Lost & Found. Elliott, Mark, illus. 2010. (ENG.). 192p. (J). (gr. 3-7). pap. 7.99 *(978-1-4169-0986-6(9)*, Atheneum Bks. for Young Readers) Simon & Schuster Children's Publishing.
Cline-Ransome, Lesa. Finding Langston. (Finding Langston Trilogy Ser.). 112p. (J). (gr. 3-7). 2020. pap. 7.99 *(978-0-8234-4582-0(8))* 2018. 16.99 *(978-0-8234-3960-7(7))* Holiday Hse., Inc.
—Leaving Lymon. 2020. (Finding Langston Trilogy Ser.: 2). 208p. (J). (gr. 3-7). 17.99 *(978-0-8234-4442-7(2))* Holiday Hse., Inc.
Clough, Lisa. Nothing but Blue. 2013. (ENG.). 224p. (YA). (gr. 9-7). 16.99 *(978-0-618-95961-7(0)*, 1021899, Clarion Bks.) HarperCollins Pubs.
Coates, Charmian. Secret Staircase. 2011. (Illus.). 88p. pap. 27.76 *(978-1-4567-8715-8(2))* AuthorHouse.
Coben, Harlan. Shelter. l.t. ed. 2011. (Mickey Bolitar Ser.: Bk. 1). (ENG.). 354p. (J). (gr. 9-12). 23.99 *(978-1-4104-4365-6(5))* Thorndike Pr.
—Shelter. 2012. (Mickey Bolitar Ser.: 1). lib. bdg. 20.85 *(978-0-606-26669-7(0))* Turtleback.
—Shelter (Book One) A Mickey Bolitar Novel, Bk. 1. 2012. (Mickey Bolitar Novel Ser.: 1). (ENG.). 336p. (YA). (gr. 7). pap. 11.99 *(978-0-14-242203-8(7)*, Speak) Penguin Young Readers Group.
Cochrane, Ian. Shian & the Corryvreckan. 2013. (Illus.). 96p. pap. *(978-1-909465-09-1(7))* Cloister Hse. Pr., The.
Cody, Matthew. Powerless. 2011. 288p. (J). (Supers of Noble's Green Ser.: 1). (gr. 3-7). 8.99 *(978-0-375-84489-8(9)*, Yearling); 1. (Supers of Noble Green Ser.). (ENG.). (gr. 4-6). lib. bdg. 18.69 *(978-0-375-95595-2(X)*, Knopf Bks. for Young Readers) Random Hse. Children's Bks.
Collins, A. L. Redworld: Year One. Tikulin, Tomislav, illus. 2018. (Redworld Ser.). (ENG.). 320p. (J). (gr. 3-8). pap., pap., pap. 8.95 *(978-1-62370-986-0(5)*, 137317, Capstone Young Readers) Capstone.
Coloma, Cindy Martinusen. Ruby Unscripted, 1 vol. 2009. (ENG.). 272p. (YA). (gr. 7-18). pap. 12.99 *(978-1-59554-356-1(2))* Nelson, Thomas Inc.
Cook, Eileen. Unraveling Isobel. 2012. (ENG.). 320p. (YA). (gr. 9). pap. 9.99 *(978-1-4424-1328-3(X)*, Simon Pulse) Simon Pulse.
Corriveau, Art. How I, Nicky Flynn, Finally Get a Life (and a Dog) 2010. (ENG.). 288p. (YA). (gr. 3-7). 16.95 *(978-0-8109-8298-7(6)*, 661601, Amulet Bks.) Abrams, Inc.
Cosgrove, Stephen. Bee Double Bopp: Respecting Others. Arroyo, Fian, illus. 2004. (J). *(978-1-58804-350-4(9))* P C I Education.
Couloumbis, Audrey. Not Exactly a Love Story. 2014. (ENG.). 288p. (YA). (gr. 7). pap. 9.99 *(978-0-375-86606-7(X)*, Ember) Random Hse. Children's Bks.
Cox, Phil Roxbee. Mouse Moves House. Tyler, Jenny, ed. Cartwright, Stephen, illus. rev. ed. 2006. (Phonic Readers Ser.). 16p. (J). (gr. -1-3). pap. 6.99 *(978-0-7945-1507-2(X)*, Usborne) EDC Publishing.
Creech, Sharon. Moo. 2018. (Penworthy Picks Middle School Ser.). (ENG.). 278p. (J). (gr. 5-7). 17.96 *(978-1-64310-363-1(6))* Penworthy Co., LLC, The.
—Moo. 2017. (J). lib. bdg. 17.20 *(978-0-606-40402-0(3))* Turtleback.
—Moo: A Novel. (ENG.). 288p. (J). (gr. 3-7). 2017. pap. 9.99 *(978-0-06-241526-4(3))* 2016. 16.99 *(978-0-06-241524-0(7))* 2016. lib. bdg. 17.89 *(978-0-06-241525-7(5))* HarperCollins Pubs. (HarperCollins).
Crimi, Carolyn. The Louds Move In!, 1 vol. Dunnick, Regan, illus. 2006. (ENG.). 32p. (J). (gr. -1-3). 14.95 *(978-0-7614-5221-8(4))* Marshall Cavendish Corp.
Croza, Laurel. From There to Here, 1 vol. James, Matt, illus. 2014. (ENG.). 32p. (J). (gr. -1-2). 18.95 *(978-1-55498-365-0(7))* Groundwood Bks. CAN. Dist: Publishers Group West (PGW).
Cumbie, Patricia. Where People Like Us Live. 2008. 224p. (YA). (gr. 7-18). lib. bdg. 17.89 *(978-0-06-137598-9(5)*, Geringer, Laura Book) HarperCollins Pubs.
Cumming, Hannah. The Red Boat. Cumming, Hannah, illus. 2012. (Child's Play Library). (Illus.). 32p. (J). *(978-1-84643-481-5(5))* Child's Play International Ltd.
Cumyn, Alan. North to Benjamin. 2018. (ENG., Illus.). 304p. (J). (gr. 5-9). 17.99 *(978-1-4814-9752-7(9))* Simon & Schuster Children's Publishing.
Cutler, Jane. Susie Q Fights Back. 2018. (ENG.). 112p. (J). (gr. 3-7). pap. 6.99 *(978-0-8234-3993-5(3))* Holiday Hse., Inc.
Danielson, Diane K. There Is a Mouse That Is Haunting Our House. 2012. (ENG.). 28p. (J). pap. 14.99 *(978-0-9885157-0-3(9))* SDP Publishing.
Danziger, Paula. Amber Brown Is Green with Envy. 2014. (Amber Brown Ser.: 9). (ENG., Illus.). 176p. (J). (gr. 2-5). pap. 7.99 *(978-0-14-242699-9(7)*, Puffin Books) Penguin Young Readers Group.
—Amber Brown Is Green with Envy. Ross, Tony, illus. 2004. (Amber Brown Ser.: No. 9). 151p. (J). (gr. 2-5). 12.65 *(978-0-7569-2978-7(4))* Perfection Learning Corp.
—Amber Brown Is Not a Crayon. Ross, Tony, illus. 2006. (Amber Brown Ser.: 1). (ENG.). 96p. (J). (gr. 2-5). 6.99 *(978-0-14-240619-9(8)*, Puffin Books) Penguin Young Readers Group.
—Amber Brown Is Not a Crayon. (Amber Brown Ser.: No. 1). 80p. (J). (gr. 3-6). pap. 3.50 *(978-0-8072-1289-9(X)*, Listening Library) Random Hse. Audio Publishing Group.
Danziger, Paula & Martin, Ann M. P. S. Longer Letter Later. (Tara Starr & Elizabeth Ser.). 240p. (J). (gr. 3-5). pap. 4.99 *(978-0-8072-1537-1(6)*, Listening Library) Random Hse. Audio Publishing Group.
Danziger, Paula, et al. Amber Brown Is on the Move. Lewis, Anthony, illus. 2014. (Amber Brown Ser.: 11). (ENG.). 192p. (J). (gr. 2-5). pap. 7.99 *(978-0-14-751223-9(9)*, Puffin Books) Penguin Young Readers Group.
Daswani, Kavita. Lovetorn. 2012. (ENG.). 256p. (YA). (gr. 8). 17.99 *(978-0-06-167311-5(0)*, HarperTeen) HarperCollins Pubs.
Davies, Nicola. King of the Sky. Carlin, Laura, illus. 2017. (ENG.). 48p. (J). (gr. -1-3). 18.99 *(978-0-7636-9568-2(8))* Candlewick Pr.
Davis, Dana L. Tiffany Sly Lives Here Now. 2018. (ENG.). 336p. (YA). 18.99 *(978-1-335-99413-4(0)*, Harlequin Teen) Harlequin Enterprises ULC CAN. Dist: HarperCollins Pubs.
De Bode, Ann & Broere, Rien. Leave Me Alone! 2011. (Side by Side Ser.). (Illus.). 32p. (J). (gr. k-3). lib. bdg. 28.50 *(978-1-60753-182-1(8))* Amicus Learning.
Dee, Barbara. Trauma Queen. 2011. (Mix Ser.). (ENG.). 272p. (J). (gr. 4-8). pap. 8.99 *(978-1-4424-0923-1(1)*, Aladdin) Simon & Schuster Children's Publishing.
DeFelice, Cynthia. Signal. 2011. (ENG.). 176p. (J). (gr. 5-8). pap. 16.99 *(978-0-312-61776-9(3)*, 900076913) Square Fish.
Dellasega, Cheryl. Nugrl90 (Sadie), 0 vols. LaPierre, Karina, illus. 2012. (Bloggrls Ser.: 1). (ENG.). 192p. (YA). (gr. 7-12). pap. 9.99 *(978-0-7614-5396-3(2)*, 9780761453963, Skyscape) Amazon Publishing.
Delton, Judy. Angel Bites the Bullet. Weber, Jill, illus. 2003. (ENG.). 144p. (J). (gr. 3-7). pap. 10.95 *(978-0-618-36920-1(1)*, 484409, Clarion Bks.) HarperCollins Pubs.
deRubertis, Barbara. Nina Nandu's Nervous Noggin. Alley, R. W., illus. 2011. (Animal Antics A to Z Ser.). 32p. (J). pap. 45.32 *(978-0-7613-7660-6(7))*; (ENG.). lib. bdg. 22.60 *(978-1-57565-335-8(4))* Astra Publishing Hse.
deRubertis, Barbara & DeRubertis, Barbara. Nina Nandu's Nervous Noggin. Alley, R. W., illus. 2012. (Animal Antics A to Z Ser.). 32p. (J). (gr. 2 — 1). cd-rom 7.95 *(978-1-57565-407-2(5))* Astra Publishing Hse.
Dicamillo, Kate. Louisiana's Way Home. 2018. 232p. (J). *(978-1-4063-8754-4(1))* Candlewick Pr.
DiCamillo, Kate. Louisiana's Way Home. (ENG.). 240p. (J). (gr. 5). 2020. pap. 7.99 *(978-1-5362-0799-6(3))* 2018. 16.99 *(978-0-7636-9463-0(0))* Candlewick Pr.
DiCerto, Joseph J. The Wall People: In Search of a Home. 2014. (Illus.). 128p. (J). pap. 14.00 *(978-0-87842-633-1(7))* Mountain Pr. Publishing Co., Inc.
Dickson, Darnell G. Small Town, Big Dreams: A Dane Jordan Sports Novel. 2008. pap. 14.99 *(978-1-59955-229-3(9))* Cedar Fort, Inc./CFI Distribution.
Doerrfeld, Cori. Goodbye, Friend! Hello, Friend! 2019. (ENG., Illus.). 40p. (J). (gr. -1-3). 18.99 *(978-0-525-55423-3(8)*, Dial Bks) Penguin Young Readers Group.
—The Welcome Wagon: A Cubby Hill Tale. 2020. (Cubby Hill Tale Ser.). (ENG., Illus.). 40p. (J). (gr. -1-2). 17.99 *(978-1-4197-4417-4(8)*, 1688701, Abrams Bks. for Young Readers) Abrams, Inc.
Dougherty, Meghan. Rise of the Undead Redhead. Birnbach, Alece, illus. 2014. (Dorothy's Derby Chronicles Ser.: 1). 256p. (J). (gr. 3-6). pap. 10.99 *(978-1-4022-9535-5(9))* Sourcebooks, Inc.
Drummond, Ree. Little Ree #2 (signed Edition) Rogers, Jacqueline, illus. 2018. (Little Ree Ser.). 32p. (J). (gr. -1-3). 17.99 *(978-0-06-282077-8(X))* HarperCollins Pubs.
Duckett, Brenda. Summit Lane. 2005. 79p. pap. 10.99 *(978-1-4116-3897-6(2))* Lulu Pr., Inc.
Dunham, Wendy. My Name Is River. 2015. (ENG.). 144p. (J). (gr. 2-6). pap. 8.99 *(978-0-7369-6461-6(4)*, 6964616) Harvest Hse. Pubs.
Earhart, Kristin. Welcome Home! Geddes, Serena, illus. 2015. (Marguerite Henry's Misty Inn Ser.: 1). (ENG.). 128p. (J). (gr. 2-5). 16.99 *(978-1-4814-1414-2(3)*, Aladdin) Simon & Schuster Children's Publishing.
—Welcome Home! 2015. (Marguerite Henry's Misty Inn Ser.: 1). lib. bdg. 16.00 *(978-0-606-37126-1(5))* Turtleback.
Eggers, Dave. The Lifters. (ENG.). 352p. (J). (gr. 3-7). 2019. pap. 9.99 *(978-1-5247-6419-7(1)*, Yearling) 2018. lib. bdg. 20.99 *(978-1-5247-6417-3(5)*, Knopf Bks. for Young Readers) Random Hse. Children's Bks.
Ellis, Sarah. Ben Says Goodbye. La Fave, Kim, illus. 2016. (ENG.). 32p. (J). (gr. -1-1). 16.95 *(978-1-927485-79-8(7))* Pajama Pr. CAN. Dist: Publishers Group West (PGW).
Emmer, E. R. Me, Minerva & the Flying Flora. Huerta, Catherine, illus. 2nd rev. ed. 2005. (Going to Ser.). Orig. Title: Me, Minera & the Flying Car. (ENG.). 133p. (J). (gr. 4-8).

MNO

pap. 6.95 *(978-1-893577-10-7(4))* Four Corners Publishing Co., Inc.

English, Karen. Dog Days: The Carver Chronicles, Book One, 1 vol. Humaran, Aurora & Monge, Leticia, trs. Freeman, Laura, illus. 2014. (Carver Chronicles Ser.). (ENG.). 128p. (J). (gr. 1-4). pap. 6.99 *(978-0-544-33912-5(6)*, eeece7c5-4442-418b-a3f1-08e1410d9daf, Clarion Bks.) HarperCollins Pubs.

Escklsen, Erik E. Offsides. 2004. (ENG.). 176p. (J). (gr. 5-7). tchr. ed. 15.00 *(978-0-618-46284-1(8)*, 543211, Clarion Bks.) HarperCollins Pubs.

Evans, Richard Paul. If Only. 2015. (ENG., Illus.). 288p. (YA). (gr. 9). pap. 12.99 *(978-1-4814-4853-6(6)*, Simon Pulse) Simon Pulse.

Faris, Stephanie. Piper Morgan Joins the Circus. Fleming, Lucy, illus. 2016. (Piper Morgan Ser.: 1). (ENG.). 112p. (J). (gr. 1-4). 16.99 *(978-1-4814-5709-5(8)*, Simon & Schuster/Paula Wiseman Bks.) Simon & Schuster/Paula Wiseman Bks.

Faruqi, Reem. Lailah's Lunchbox: A Ramadan Story, 1 vol. Lyon, Lea, illus. 2015. (ENG.). 32p. (J). (gr. 1-7). 16.95 *(978-0-88448-431-8(9)*, 884431) Tilbury Hse. Pubs.

Feagan, Robert. Arctic Thunder. 2010. (ENG.). 288p. (YA). (gr. 7). pap. 12.99 *(978-1-55488-700-2(3))* Dundurn Pr. CAN. Dist: Publishers Group West (PGW).

Fehlbaum, Beth. Big Fat Disaster. (ENG.). (YA). 2015. 286p. pap. 9.99 *(978-1-4405-9267-6(5))* 2014. 288p. 17.99 *(978-1-4405-7048-3(5))* Simon Pulse. (Simon Pulse).

Feinstein, John. The Walk On. 2015. (Triple Threat Ser.: 1). lib. bdg. 18.40 *(978-0-606-37704-1(2))* Turtleback.

—The Walk on (the Triple Threat, 1) 2015. (Triple Threat Ser.: 1). 384p. (J). (gr. 5). pap. 8.99 *(978-0-385-75349-4(7)*, Yearling) Random Hse. Children's Bks.

Ferrell, Miralee. A Horse for Kate. 2015. (Horses & Friends Ser.: 1). (ENG.). 208p. (J). pap. 8.99 *(978-0-7814-1114-1(9)*, 129562) Cook, David C.

Ferruolo, Jeanne Zulick. Ruby in the Sky. 2020. (ENG.). 320p. (J). pap. 9.99 *(978-1-250-23329-5(1)*, 900188386) Square Fish.

Figley, Marthy Rhodes & Figley, Marty Rhodes. The Night the Chimneys Fell. Marschall, Felicia, illus. 2011. 48p. (J). pap. 6.95 *(978-0-7613-3939-7(6)*, First Avenue Editions) Lerner Publishing Group.

Figley, Marty Rhodes. The Night the Chimneys Fell. Marschall, Felicia, illus. 2011. (On My Own History Ser.). 48p. (J). pap. 39.62 *(978-0-7613-7622-4(4)*, First Avenue Editions) Lerner Publishing Group.

—The Night the Chimneys Fell. Marshall, Felicia, illus. 2009. (On My Own History Ser.). (ENG.). 48p. (gr. 2-4). 25.26 *(978-0-8225-7894-9(8))* Lerner Publishing Group.

Filliozat, Isabelle. Anger: An Inside Out Story. 2020. (J). *(978-1-5415-9857-7(1))* Lerner Publishing Group.

Fleming, Anne. The Goat. 1 vol. 2019. (ENG.). 120p. (J). (gr. 4-6). 9.95 *(978-1-77306-299-0(9))* Groundwood Bks. CAN. Dist: Publishers Group West (PGW).

Fleming, Candace. Lowji Discovers America. 2008. (ENG.). 160p. (J). (gr. 2-6). pap. 7.99 *(978-1-4169-5832-1(0)*, Aladdin) Simon & Schuster Children's Publishing.

Fletcher, Ralph. Spider Boy. 2009. (ENG.). 192p. (J). (gr. 5-7). pap. 7.99 *(978-0-547-24820-2(2)*, 1100710, Clarion Bks.) HarperCollins Pubs.

Flor, Ada Alma. My Name Is Maria Isabel. 2014. (ENG.). 64p. (J). (gr. 12-12). 9.24 *(978-1-63245-189-7(1))* Lectorum Pubns., Inc.

Foutz, Ian. Year of the Dragon. Miller, Madeline, illus. 2014. (J). *(978-1-62086-634-4(X))* Amplify Publishing Group.

Fox, Kir & Coats, M. Shelley. A Friendly Town That's Almost Always by the Ocean! 2018. (Secrets of Topsea Ser.: 1). (ENG.). 208p. (J). (gr. 3-7). E-Book 45.00 *(978-1-368-00051-2(7))* Little, Brown Bks. for Young Readers.

Franklin, Miriam Spitzer. Call Me Sunflower. (ENG.). (J). (gr. 2-7). 2019. 256p. pap. 8.99 *(978-1-5107-3914-7(9))* 2017. 272p. 15.99 *(978-1-5107-1179-2(1))* Skyhorse Publishing Co., Inc. (Sky Pony Pr.).

Frederick, Heather Vogel. Absolutely Truly. 2015. (Pumpkin Falls Mystery Ser.). (ENG., Illus.). 368p. (J). (gr. 3-7). pap. 8.99 *(978-1-4424-2973-4(9)*, Simon & Schuster Bks. For Young Readers) Simon & Schuster Bks. For Young Readers.

French, Gillian. The Missing Season. 2019. (ENG.). 304p. (YA). (gr. 8). 17.99 *(978-0-06-280333-7(6)*, HarperTeen) HarperCollins Pubs.

French, Simon. Where in the World. 2nd ed. 2008. 198p. *(978-1-921272-57-8(0))* Little Hare Bks. AUS. Dist: HarperCollins Pubs. Australia.

Friedland, Joyce, ed. Lizzie Bright & the Buckminster Boy: Novel-Ties Study Guide. 2007. 36p. pap. 16.95 *(978-0-7675-3558-8(8))* Learning Links Inc.

Friedman, Laurie. Back to School, Mallory. Schmitz, Tamara, illus. 2005. (Mallory Ser.: 2). (ENG.). 176p. (J). (gr. 2-5). per. 7.99 *(978-1-57505-865-8(0)*, bb96daab-2d2d-475e-94ad-0d7331a6e756, Darby Creek) Lerner Publishing Group.

—Mallory Se Muda. Schmitz, Tamara. illus. 2007. (Mallory en español (Mallory in Spanish) Ser.). (SPA.). 160p. (J). (gr. 4-7). per. 5.95 *(978-0-8225-7493-4(4)*, Ediciones Lerner) Lerner Publishing Group.

Friend, Natasha. Where You'll Find Me. 2017. (YA). lib. bdg. 20.85 *(978-0-606-39591-5(1))* Turtleback.

Galante, Cecilia. Willowood. 2011. (ENG.). 288p. (J). (gr. 4-8). pap. 6.99 *(978-1-4169-8303-3(1)*, Aladdin) Simon & Schuster Children's Publishing.

—Willowood. 2010. (ENG.). 272p. (J). (gr. 4-8). 16.99 *(978-1-4169-8022-3(9)*, Simon & Schuster/Paula Wiseman Bks.) Simon & Schuster/Paula Wiseman Bks.

Garland, Michael. Daddy Played the Blues, 1 vol. 2017. (ENG., Illus.). 48p. (J). (gr. 1-5). 17.95 *(978-0-88448-588-9(9)*, 884588) Tilbury Hse. Pubs.

Garrott, Dawn E. How Riley Tamed the Invisible Monster. Mazibuko, Luthando, illus. 2009. (How Riley Ser.). (ENG.). 65p. (J). (gr. 2-7). pap. 9.95 *(978-0-87743-709-3(2))* Baha'i Publishing.

Georgieva, Zoia. Herman the Earth Worm: Illustrated by Emma C. Van Dyke. 2008. pap. 18.00 *(978-0-8059-8630-3(8))* Dorrance Publishing Co., Inc.

Gibson, Marley. Ghost Huntress Book 1: the Awakening. 2009. (Ghost Huntress Ser.: 1). (ENG.). 352p. (YA). (gr. 7-18). pap. 19.99 *(978-0-547-15093-2(8)*, 1051747, Clarion Bks.) HarperCollins Pubs.

—Ghost Huntress Book 2: the Guidance. 2009. (Ghost Huntress Ser.: 2). (ENG.). 320p. (YA). (gr. 7-18). pap. 16.95 *(978-0-547-15094-9(6)*, 1051748, Clarion Bks.) HarperCollins Pubs.

Giff, Patricia Reilly. Meet the Crew at the Zoo. Carter, Abby, illus. 2020. (Mysteries on Zoo Lane Ser.: 1). 112p. (J). (gr. 2-5). 16.99 *(978-0-8234-4666-7(2))* Holiday Hse., Inc.

—R My Name Is Rachel. 2012. (ENG.). 176p. (J). (gr. 4-7). pap. 6.99 *(978-0-440-42176-4(4)*, Yearling) Random Hse. Children's Bks.

Glaser, Linda. Hannah's Way. Gustavson, Adam, illus. 2012. 32p. (J). (gr. k-3). (ENG.). pap. 7.95 *(978-0-7613-5138-2(8)*, 59392402-0f00-41e2-b7cf-f8230b7c8ebc); lib. bdg. 17.95 *(978-0-7613-5137-5(X))* Lerner Publishing Group. (Kar-Ben Publishing).

Gleeson, Libby. Half a World Away. Blackwood, Freya, illus. 2007. (J). pap. *(978-0-439-88978-0(2)*, Levine, Arthur A. Bks.) Scholastic, Inc.

Gonzalez, Gabriela & Triana, Gaby. Backstage Pass. 2004. (Illus.). 224p. (J). (gr. 7-18). 15.99 *(978-0-06-056017-1(7))*; lib. bdg. 16.89 *(978-0-06-056018-8(5))* HarperCollins Pubs.

Gownley, Jimmy. Amelia in into Graceland, 1 vol. Gownley, Jimmy, illus. 2013. (Amelia Rules! Ser.). (ENG., Illus.). 36p. (J). (gr. 2-6). 31.36 *(978-1-61479-071-6(X)*, 2390, Graphic Novels) Spotlight.

Grabenstein, Chris. The Crossroads. 2009. (Haunted Mystery Ser.: 1). (ENG.). 352p. (J). (gr. 3-7). 8.99 *(978-0-375-84698-4(0)*, Yearling) Random Hse. Children's Bks.

Graff, Lisa. Double Dog Dare. 2013. (ENG.). (J). 320p. (gr. 3-7). pap. 8.99 *(978-0-14-242412-4(9)*, Puffin Books); 304p. (gr. 4-6). 22.44 *(978-0-399-25516-8(8))* Penguin Young Readers Group.

Green, D. L. Making Friends & Horsing Around: A 4D Book. Rosa, Leandra La, illus. 2018. (Funny Girl Ser.). (ENG.). 112p. (J). (gr. 3-5). pap. 7.95 *(978-1-4965-6471-9(5)*, 138380); lib. bdg. 26.65 *(978-1-4965-6467-2(7)*, 138376) Capstone. (Stone Arch Bks.).

Green, Tim. First Team. 2015. (ENG.). 352p. (J). (gr. 3-7). pap. 7.99 *(978-0-06-220876-7(4)*, HarperCollins) HarperCollins Pubs.

—First Team. 2014. (ENG.). 336p. (J). (gr. 3-7). 16.99 *(978-0-06-220875-0(6)*, HarperCollins) HarperCollins Pubs.

—First Team. 2015. (J). lib. bdg. 17.20 *(978-0-606-37616-7(X))* Turtleback.

—New Kid. (ENG.). (J). (gr. 3-7). 2015. 336p. pap. 9.99 *(978-0-06-220873-6(X))* 2014. 320p. 16.99 *(978-0-06-220872-9(1))* HarperCollins Pubs. (HarperCollins).

Greene, Stephanie. Falling into Place. 2006. (ENG.). 128p. (J). (gr. 5-7). pap. 8.95 *(978-0-618-68928-6(1)*, 100487, Clarion Bks.) HarperCollins Pubs.

Griffin, Adele. The Becket List: A Blackberry Farm Story. Pham, LeUyen, illus. 2019. (ENG.). 208p. (gr. 2-6). 16.95 *(978-1-61620-790-8(6)*, 73790) Algonquin Young Readers.

Griffith, Gretchen. When Christmas Feels Like Home. Farias, Carolina, illus. 2014. (AV2 Fiction Readalong Ser.: Vol. 119). (ENG.). 32p. (J). (gr. k-3). lib. bdg. 34.28 *(978-1-4896-2392-8(2)*, AV2 by Weigl) Weigl Pubs., Inc.

Grimes, Nikki. Make Way for Dyamonde Daniel. Christie, R. Gregory, illus. (Dyamonde Daniel Book Ser.: 1). (ENG.). (J). (gr. 2-4). 2010. 112p. pap. 6.99 *(978-0-14-241555-9(3)*, Puffin Books) 2009. 96p. 12.99 *(978-0-399-25175-7(8)*, G.P. Putnam's Sons Books for Young Readers) Penguin Young Readers Group.

—Poems in the Attic, 1 vol. Zunon, Elizabeth, illus. 2015. (ENG.). 48p. (J). (gr. 1-6). 21.95 *(978-1-62014-027-7(6)*, leelowbooks) Lee & Low Bks., Inc.

—Southwest Sunrise. Minor, Wendell, illus. 2020. (ENG.). 40p. (J). 18.99 *(978-1-5476-0082-3(9)*, 900197954, Bloomsbury Children's Bks.) Bloomsbury Publishing USA.

Grimes, Shaunta. The Astonishing Maybe. 2020. (ENG.). 256p. (J). pap. 20.99 *(978-1-250-23363-9(1)*, 900192879) Square Fish.

Gunnery, Sylvia. Out of Bounds. 2004. (Sports Stories Ser.). (ENG.). 104p. (J). (gr. 3-8). *(978-1-55028-827-8(X))* James Lorimer & Co. Ltd., Pubs. CAN. Dist: Casemate Pubs. & Bk. Distributors, LLC.

Hale, Marian. The Truth about Sparrows. 2007. (ENG.). 288p. (YA). (gr. 6-8). pap. 11.99 *(978-0-312-37133-3(0)*, 900044661) Square Fish.

Hale, Shannon & Hale, Dean. The Unbeatable Squirrel Girl: Squirrel Meets World. 2018. (YA). lib. bdg. 19.65 *(978-0-606-40715-1(4))* Turtleback.

Hall, Kirsten. My New Town. Suzan, Gerardo, illus. 2005. (My First Reader Ser.). (ENG.). 32p. (J). (gr. k-1). lib. bdg. 18.50 *(978-0-516-24877-6(4)*, Children's Pr.) Scholastic Library Publishing.

Hand, Cynthia. Unearthly. 2011. (Unearthly Ser.: 1). (ENG.). 464p. (YA). (gr. 8). pap. 9.99 *(978-0-06-199617-7(3)*, HarperTeen) HarperCollins Pubs.

Harmon, Michael. Brutal. 2011. 240p. (YA). (gr. 9). pap. 8.99 *(978-0-440-23995-6(8)*, Knopf Bks. for Young Readers) Random Hse. Children's Bks.

Harris, Danielle. The Big Move to the Little House. 2013. 24p. pap. 24.95 *(978-1-4626-8725-1(3))* America Star Bks.

Harris, Teresa E. The Perfect Place. 2018. (ENG.). 272p. (J). (gr. 5-7). pap. 7.99 *(978-1-328-78418-6(5)*, 1683760, Clarion Bks.) HarperCollins Pubs.

—The Perfect Place. 2018. lib. bdg. 18.40 *(978-0-606-40433-4(3))* Turtleback.

Hart, Melissa. Avenging the Owl. (ENG.). 224p. (J). (gr. 5-8). 2018. pap. 9.99 *(978-1-5107-2628-4(4))* 2016. 15.99 *(978-1-63450-147-7(0))* Skyhorse Publishing Co., Inc. (Sky Pony Pr.).

Haskins, Lori. Butterfly Fever. Smath, Jerry, illus. 2004. 31p. (J). lib. bdg. 20.00 *(978-1-4242-1087-9(9))* Fitzgerald Bks.

—Locura Por Las Mariposas (Butterfly Fever) Smath, Jerry, illus. 2009. (Science Solves It! (r) en Espanol Ser.). (SPA.). (gr. 1-3). pap. 33.92 *(978-0-7613-4799-6(2))* Lerner Publishing Group.

Hautman, Pete. The Big Crunch. 2011. (ENG.). 288p. (J). (gr. 9-8). 17.99 *(978-0-545-24075-8(1)*, Scholastic Pr.) Scholastic, Inc.

Havill, Juanita. Jamaica's Blue Marker. O'Brien, Anne Sibley, illus. 2003. (ENG.). 32p. (J). (gr. -1-3). pap. 8.99 *(978-0-618-36917-1(1)*, 487457, Clarion Bks.) HarperCollins Pubs.

Hawes, Adrienne Hill. Moving Danielle. 2008. 22p. pap. 24.95 *(978-1-4241-4977-3(0))* America Star Bks.

Haxhia, Miranda. Andy's Cherry Tree. Deisadze, Zaur, illus. 2007. (POL & ENG.). 32p. (J). pap. 12.95 *(978-1-60195-094-9(2))* International Step by Step Assn.

Haydu, Corey Ann. Eventown. 2019. (ENG.). 336p. (J). (gr. 3-7). 16.99 *(978-0-06-268980-1(0)*, Tegen, Katherine Bks) HarperCollins Pubs.

Heasley, Gwendolyn. Where I Belong. 2011. (Where I Belong Ser.: 1). (ENG.). 304p. (YA). (gr. 8-18). pap. 9.99 *(978-0-06-197884-5(1)*, HarperTeen) HarperCollins Pubs.

Hees, Miriam. The Adventures of Jilly & Brad: Noises in the Attic. Kinneman, D. Michael, illus. 2003. 128p. (J). pap. 5.95 *(978-0-9718348-4-2(9))* Blooming Tree Pr.

Helmore, Jim. The Snow Lion. Jones, Richard, illus. rev. ed. 2018. (ENG.). 32p. (J). (gr. -1-3). 17.95 *(978-1-68263-048-8(X))* Peachtree Publishing Co. Inc.

Hepler, Heather. The Cupcake Queen. 2010. (ENG.). 256p. (YA). (gr. 7-18). 7.99 *(978-0-14-241668-6(1)*, Speak) Penguin Young Readers Group.

Hermes, Patricia. Emma Dilemma, the Nanny, & the Best Horse Ever, 0 vols. Carter, Abby, illus. 2013. (Emma Dilemma Ser.: 6). (ENG.). 144p. (J). (gr. 3-6). pap. 9.99 *(978-1-4778-1633-2(X)*, 9781477816332, Two Lions) Amazon Publishing.

Heyne, Kara. The Locket's Secret. 2013. (ENG.). 162p. (J). pap. 8.95 *(978-0-8198-7484-9(1))* Pauline Bks. & Media.

Hill, Ryan. J P Trouble. 2012. 32p. pap. 12.95 *(978-1-886057-15-9(X))* Warren Publishing, Inc.

Hobbs, William. Leaving Protection. 2004. 192p. (J). (gr. 5-18). lib. bdg. 16.89 *(978-0-06-051632-1(1))* HarperCollins Pubs.

Hoberman, Mary Ann. Strawberry Hill. Halperin, Wendy Anderson, illus. 2009. (ENG.). 240p. (J). (gr. 4-6). 21.19 *(978-0-316-04136-2(X))* Little Brown & Co.

—Strawberry Hill. 2010. (ENG., Illus.). 240p. (J). (gr. 3-7). pap. 13.99 *(978-0-316-04135-5(1))* Little, Brown Bks. for Young Readers.

Hoffman, Mary. Bravo, Grace! 2011. (ENG.). 112p. (J). (gr. 3-7). 5.99 *(978-0-14-241850-5(1)*, Puffin Books) Penguin Young Readers Group.

Hofmann-Maniyar, Ariane. Ice in the Jungle. Hofmann-Maniyar, Ariane, illus. 2016. (Child's Play Library). (Illus.). 32p. (J). pap. *(978-1-84643-730-4(X))* Child's Play International Ltd.

Hogan, Mary. The Serious Kiss. 2005. (ENG.). 256p. (YA). (gr. 7-18). 16.99 *(978-0-06-072206-7(1))* HarperCollins Pubs.

Holder, Nancy & Viguie, Debbie. Unleashed. 2012. (Wolf Spring Chronicles Ser.: 1). (ENG.). 400p. (YA). (gr. 7). pap. 9.99 *(978-0-385-74099-9(9)*, Ember) Random Hse. Children's Bks.

Holt, Kimberly Willis. Piper Reed, Forever Friend, 6. Davenier, Christine, illus. 2012. (Piper Reed Ser.: 6). (ENG.). 160p. (J). (gr. 3-6). 18.69 *(978-0-8050-9008-6(8)*, 900058970, Holt, Henry & Co.) Holt, Henry & Co.

—Piper Reed, Forever Friend. Davenier, Christine, illus. 2013. (Piper Reed Ser.: 6). (ENG.). 176p. (J). (gr. 3-6). pap. 8.99 *(978-1-250-02725-2(X)*, 900098296) Square Fish.

—Piper Reed, Navy Brat. Davenier, Christine, illus. 2011. (Piper Reed Ser.: 1). (ENG.). 176p. (J). (gr. 3-6). pap. 9.99 *(978-0-312-62548-1(0)*, 900077153) Square Fish.

Horn, Lorri. Dewey Fairchild, Parent Problem Solver. 2018. (Dewey Fairchild Ser.: 1). (ENG., Illus.). 252p. (J). (gr. 4-7). pap. 7.99 *(978-1-948705-12-7(5))* Amberjack Publishing Co.

—Dewey Fairchild, Parent Problem Solver: Parent Problem Solver. 2017. (Dewey Fairchild Ser.: 1). (ENG., Illus.). 252p. (J). (gr. 4-7). 13.99 *(978-1-944995-16-4(1))* Amberjack Publishing Co.

House of Wooden Santas, 1 vol. 2003. (ENG., Illus.). 96p. (J). (gr. 4-6). 22.95 *(978-0-88995-166-2(7)*, f1ebd2a2-a16f-4d44-ab93-4ad9394f2bfa) Red Deer Pr. CAN. Dist: Firefly Bks., Ltd.

Howland, Leila. Hello, Sunshine. 2018. (ENG.). 368p. (YA). (gr. 9-17). pap. 9.99 *(978-1-4847-2850-5(5))* Hyperion Bks. for Children.

Hundal, Nancy. Kaleidoscopes & Butterfly Dreams. 2009. (ENG.). 112p. (YA). (gr. 5-9). pap. 12.95 *(978-0-88982-256-6(5))* Oolichan Bks. CAN. Dist: Univ. of Toronto Pr.

Hurst, Carol Otis. The Wrong One. 2003. (ENG.). 160p. (J). (gr. 5-7). tchr. ed. 15.00 *(978-0-618-27599-1(1)*, 588811, Clarion Bks.) HarperCollins Pubs.

Hyde, Catherine Ryan. Jumpstart the World. 2011. 192p. (YA). (gr. 9). pap. 7.99 *(978-0-375-86626-5(4)*, Ember) Random Hse. Children's Bks.

Inacio, Maria St. Katie's Big Move! 2013. 20p. pap. 17.99 *(978-1-4772-8703-3(5))* AuthorHouse.

Ives, Frances. Maybe the Moon. 2019. (ENG., Illus.). 32p. (J). (gr. -1-k). pap. 9.99 *(978-1-910552-84-1(4))* O'Mara, Michael Bks., Ltd. GBR. Dist: Independent Pubs. Group.

Jakubowski, Michele. Brushes & Basketballs. Fekete, Hédi, illus. 2016. (Ashley Small & Ashlee Tall Ser.). (ENG.). 64p. (J). (gr. 1-3). lib. bdg. 20.65 *(978-1-5158-0010-1(5)*, 131847, Picture Window Bks.) Capstone.

Janowitz, Jessie. The Doughnut Fix. (Doughnut Fix Ser.: 1). (ENG., Illus.). (J). (gr. 3-7). 2019. 336p. pap. 7.99 *(978-1-4926-7148-0(7))* 2018. 304p. 16.99 *(978-1-4926-5541-1(4))* Sourcebooks, Inc.

Johnson-Choong, Shelly. The Jewelry Box. 2nd ed. 2004. (YA). reprint ed. pap. 10.95 *(978-1-932280-40-1(5)*, 80405) Granite Publishing & Distribution.

Johnson, Janet. The Last Great Adventure of the PB & J Society. 2016. (ENG., Illus.). 256p. (J). (gr. 4-8). 12.95 *(978-1-62370-636-4(X)*, 131285, Capstone Young Readers) Capstone.

Johnson, Jimmie. Somewhere Else. 2017. (ENG., Illus.). 30p. (J). pap. 12.95 *(978-0-9976010-8-0(0))* Black Sugar Pr.

Jonell, Lynne. Hamster Magic. Dorman, Brandon, illus. 2012. (Magical Mix-Ups Ser.: 1). (ENG.). 112p. (J). (gr. 1-4). pap. 6.99 *(978-0-375-86616-6(7)*, Random Hse. Bks. for Young Readers) Random Hse. Children's Bks.

Jordan, Sophie. Firelight. (Firelight Ser.: 1). (ENG.). (YA). (gr. 8). 2011. 352p. pap. 9.99 *(978-0-06-193509-1(3))* 2010. 336p. 16.99 *(978-0-06-193508-4(5))* HarperCollins Pubs. (HarperCollins).

Joseph, Bruchac. Eagle Song. 2014. (ENG.). 80p. (J). (gr. 12-12). 9.24 *(978-1-63245-103-3(4))* Lectorum Pubns., Inc.

Joyce, Melanie. A New House, 1 vol. 2008. (Fred Bear & Friends Ser.). (ENG., Illus.). 24p. (gr. k-1). pap. 9.15 *(978-0-8368-8974-1(6)*, 729ef204-73a0-4460-ae95-d8361712127e, Gareth Stevens Learning Library) Stevens, Gareth Publishing LLLP.

Jukes, Mavis. The New Kid. (ENG.). 288p. (J). (gr. 4-6). 2013. lib. bdg. 21.19 *(978-0-375-95879-3(7)*, Knopf Bks. for Young Readers) 2012. 7.99 *(978-0-375-85367-8(7)*, Yearling) Random Hse. Children's Bks.

Jules, Jacqueline. What a Way to Start a New Year! A Rosh Hashanah Story. Stead, Judy, illus. 2013. (ENG.). 24p. (J). (gr. -1-2). 7.95 *(978-0-7613-8117-4(1)*, f7438181-666c-4652-8821-3d6f7f9a904b, Kar-Ben Publishing) Lerner Publishing Group.

Juster, Norton. Neville. Karas, G. Brian, illus. 2011. 32p. (J). (gr. -1-3). 17.99 *(978-0-375-86765-1(1)*, Schwartz & Wade Bks.) Random Hse. Children's Bks.

Kehret, Peg & the Cat, Pete. The Stranger Next Door. 2008. (Pete the Cat Ser.: 1). (ENG.). 176p. (J). (gr. 3-7). 5.99 *(978-0-14-241248-0(1)*, Puffin Books) Penguin Young Readers Group.

Kelley, Jane. The Girl Behind the Glass. 2012. (ENG.). 192p. (J). (gr. 4-7). pap. 6.99 *(978-0-375-86219-9(6)*, Yearling) Random Hse. Children's Bks.

Kelly, Katy. Lucy Rose: Here's the Thing about Me. Rex, Adam, illus. 2006. (Lucy Rose Ser.: 1). 160p. (J). (gr. 3-7). reprint ed. per. 7.99 *(978-0-440-42026-2(1)*, Yearling) Random Hse. Children's Bks.

Kennedy, Pamela. Moving Day for Sam: A Story about Change. Petrov, Anton, illus. 2007. 32p. (J). (gr. -1-3). 8.99 *(978-0-8249-5558-8(7)*, Ideals Pubns.) Worthy Publishing.

Kent, Rose. Rocky Road. 2012. (ENG.). 304p. (J). (gr. 4-6). 21.19 *(978-0-375-86344-8(3)*, Knopf Bks. for Young Readers); (gr. 3-7). 7.99 *(978-0-375-86345-5(1)*, Yearling) Random Hse. Children's Bks.

Kidd, Ronald. Room of Shadows. (ENG.). 256p. (J). (gr. 3-7). 2018. pap. 9.99 *(978-0-8075-6807-1(4)*, 807568074) 2017. 16.99 *(978-0-8075-6805-7(8)*, 807568058) Whitman, Albert & Co.

Kimmel, Jordan L. The Magic Gown. 2007. (Illus.). 144p. (J). (gr. 3-6). pap. *(978-0-9785007-0-2(9))* Spring Tree Pr.

Kingsbury, Karen & Russell, Tyler. Best Family Ever. 2019. (Baxter Family Children Story Ser.). (ENG., Illus.). 288p. (J). (gr. 3-7). 17.99 *(978-1-5344-1215-6(8)*, Simon & Schuster Bks. For Young Readers) Simon & Schuster Bks. For Young Readers.

—Finding Home. 2020. (Baxter Family Children Story Ser.). (ENG., Illus.). 320p. (J). (gr. 3-7). 18.99 *(978-1-5344-1218-7(2)*, Simon & Schuster Bks. For Young Readers) Simon & Schuster Bks. For Young Readers.

—Finding Home. 2021. (Baxter Family Children Story Ser.). (ENG.). 336p. (J). (gr. 3-7). pap. 8.99 *(978-1-5344-1219-4(0)*, Simon & Schuster/Paula Wiseman Bks.) Simon & Schuster/Paula Wiseman Bks.

Kirby, Jessi. Moonglass. (ENG.). (YA). (gr. 7). 2012. 256p. pap. 11.99 *(978-1-4424-1695-6(5))* 2011. 240p. 16.99 *(978-1-4424-1694-9(7))* Simon & Schuster Bks. For Young Readers. (Simon & Schuster Bks. For Young Readers).

Kirby, Stan. Captain Awesome to the Rescue! O'Connor, George, illus. 2012. (Captain Awesome Ser.: 1). (ENG.). 128p. (J). (gr. k-2). 17.99 *(978-1-4424-4090-6(2))*; pap. 5.99 *(978-1-4424-3561-2(5))* Little Simon. (Little Simon).

—Captain Awesome to the Rescue! 2012. (Captain Awesome Ser.: 1). lib. bdg. 16.00 *(978-0-606-26322-1(5))* Turtleback.

Kirsch, Vincent. How I Learned to Fall Out of Trees. 2019. (ENG., Illus.). 40p. (J). (gr. -1-3). 16.99 *(978-1-4197-3413-7(X)*, 1255501, Abrams Bks. for Young Readers) Abrams, Inc.

Klein, Adria F. Tia Tape Measure & the Move, 1 vol. Rowland, Andrew, illus. 2012. (Tool School Ser.). (ENG.). 32p. (J). (gr. 1-3). lib. bdg. 22.65 *(978-1-4342-4023-1(1)*, 118404, Stone Arch Bks.) Capstone.

—Tia Tape Measure & the Move, 1 vol. Rowland, Andrew, illus. 2012. (Tool School Ser.). (ENG.). 32p. (J). (gr. 1-3). pap. 6.25 *(978-1-4342-4236-5(6)*, 120293, Stone Arch Bks.) Capstone.

Koponen, Libby. Blow Out the Moon. 2006. (ENG., Illus.). 224p. (gr. 8-17). per. 13.99 *(978-0-316-01480-9(X))* Little, Brown Bks. for Young Readers.

Korman, Gordon. Pop. (ENG.). 272p. (YA). (gr. 8). 2019. pap. 9.99 *(978-0-06-174261-3(9))* 2009. 16.99 *(978-0-06-174228-6(7))* HarperCollins Pubs. (Balzer & Bray).

Kraus, Daniel. Rotters. 2012. (ENG.). 464p. (YA). (gr. 9). pap. 10.99 *(978-0-385-73858-3(7)*, Ember) Random Hse. Children's Bks.

Krech, Bob. Love Puppies & Corner Kicks. 2010. (ENG.). 192p. (J). (gr. 6-8). 22.44 *(978-0-525-42197-9(1))* Penguin Young Readers Group.

Krishnaswami, Uma. The Grand Plan to Fix Everything. Halpin, Abigail, illus. 2013. (ENG.). 288p. (J). (gr. 3-7). pap. 8.99 *(978-1-4169-9590-6(0)*, Atheneum Bks. for Young Readers) Simon & Schuster Children's Publishing.

Krishnaswami, Uma & Bhabha, Shiraaz. The Closet Ghosts. Bhabha, Shiraaz, illus. 2013. (ENG., Illus.). 32p. (J). (gr. 2). 16.95 *(978-0-89239-208-7(8))* Lee & Low Bks., Inc.

Krulik, Nancy. Super Burp! #1, No. 1. Blecha, Aaron, illus. 2010. (George Brown, Class Clown Ser.: 1). 128p. (J). (gr. 2-4). pap. 6.99 *(978-0-448-45367-5(3)*, Grosset & Dunlap) Penguin Young Readers Group.

Kurtz, Jane. Anna Was Here. 2013. (ENG.). 288p. (J). (gr. 3-7). 16.99 *(978-0-06-056493-3(8)*, Greenwillow Bks.) HarperCollins Pubs.

—Lemon Sand. 2011. (J). lib. bdg. 17.89 *(978-0-06-056494-0(6)*, Greenwillow Bks.) HarperCollins Pubs.

Lachtman, Ofelia Dumas. Pepita on Pepper Street/Pepita en la Calle Pepper. Monsivais, Maria Estela, tr. from ENG. Delange, Alex Pardo, illus. 2008. (SPA & ENG.). 32p. (J). (gr. -1-3). 16.95 *(978-1-55885-443-7(6)*, Piñata Books) Arte Publico Pr.

—Pepita Packs Up: Pepita Empaca. Ventura, Gabriela Baeza, tr. from ENG. Delange, Alex Pardo, illus. 2005. 48p. (J). (gr.

-1-k). lib. bdg. 16.95 (978-1-55885-431-4(2), Piñata Books) Arte Publico Pr.

LaFleur, Suzanne. Listening for Lucca. 2015. (ENG.). 240p. (J). (gr. 4-7). pap. 8.99 (978-0-307-98030-4(8), Yearling) Random Hse. Children's Bks.

Lahan, Tim. Nosyhood. 2016. (ENG., Illus.). 60p. (J). (gr. -1). 16.95 (978-1-938073-93-9(2), dd483dac-25f1-4cac-881a-2cc37d3ee21d) McSweeney's Publishing.

Lam, Thao. Wallpaper. 2018. (ENG., Illus.). 32p. (J). (gr. -1-3). 18.95 (978-1-77147-283-8(9)) Owlkids Bks. Inc. CAN. Dist: Publishers Group West (PGW).

Landgraf, James, Jr. Monsters Monsters Go Away. Warrick, Jessica, illus. 2008. 40p. (J). 8.99 (978-0-9819283-0-2(7)) Makdan Publishing.

Latimer, Alex. Lula & the Sea Monster, 1 vol. 2019. (ENG., Illus.). 32p. (J). (gr. -1-3). 16.95 (978-1-68263-122-5(2)) Peachtree Publishing Co. Inc.

Ledyard, Stephanie. Home Is a Window. Sasaki, Chris, illus. 2019. 40p. (J). (gr. -1-3). 18.99 (978-0-8234-4156-3(3), Neal Porter Bks) Holiday Hse., Inc.

Lemon, Sarah Nicole. Valley Girls. 2018. (ENG., Illus.). 400p. (gr. 7-17). 18.99 (978-1-4197-2964-5(0), 1218701, Amulet Bks.) Abrams, Inc.

Liliom, Laura. You Are a Really Good Friend of Mine. Vagharshyan, Lilit, illus. 2007. 32p. (J). (ARA & ENG.). pap. 16.95 (978-1-60195-310-0(0)); (POL & ENG.). pap. 16.95 (978-1-60195-107-6(8)) International Step by Step Assn.

Littman, Sarah Darer. Life, After. 2010. (ENG.). 288p. (J). (gr. 7-18). 17.99 (978-0-545-15144-3(9), Scholastic Pr.) Scholastic, Inc.

Lockington, Mariama J. For Black Girls Like Me. 2019. (ENG.). 336p. (J). 16.99 (978-0-374-30804-9(7), 900184172, Farrar, Straus & Giroux (BYR)) Farrar, Straus & Giroux.

Loe, Steve. The Hot Hurry of Mercurial Fleeting. 2016. (YA). pap. 9.99 (978-0-88092-303-3(2)) Royal Fireworks Publishing Co.

Lord, Bette Bao. In the Year of the Boar & Jackie Robinson. Simont, Marc, illus. 2019. (ENG.). 176p. (J). (gr. 3-7). pap. 7.99 (978-0-06-440175-3(8), HarperCollins) HarperCollins Pubs.

—In the Year of the Boar & Jackie Robinson. 2009. 8.32 (978-0-7848-0826-9(0), Everbind) Marco Bk. Co.

—In the Year of the Boar & Jackie Robinson. (J). 2008. 67.75 (978-1-4281-8016-1(8)) 2004. 46.75 (978-1-4025-9147-1(0)) Recorded Bks., Inc.

—In the Year of the Boar & Jackie Robinson. 2003. (J). (gr. 3-6). 16.00 (978-0-8085-7599-3(6)) Turtleback.

Lore, Pittacus. I Am Number Four. (Lorien Legacies Ser.: 1). (ENG.). (YA). (gr. 9). 2011. 496p. pap. 15.99 (978-0-06-196957-7(5)) 2010. 448p. 18.99 (978-0-06-196955-3(9)) HarperCollins Pubs. (HarperCollins).

—I Am Number Four. 2009. (Lorien Legacies Ser.: Bk. 1). 11.04 (978-0-7848-3715-3(5), Everbind) Marco Bk. Co.

—I Am Number Four. 2011. (I Am Number Four Ser.: Vol. 1). (ENG.). 440p. (gr. 9-12). 20.00 (978-1-61383-207-3(9)) Perfection Learning Corp.

—I Am Number Four. 2011. (Lorien Legacies Ser.: 1). (YA). lib. bdg. 20.85 (978-0-606-23545-7(0)) Turtleback.

—I Am Number Four Movie Tie-In Edition. movie tie-in ed. 2011. (Lorien Legacies Ser.: 1). (ENG.). (YA). (gr. 9). 496p. pap. 9.99 (978-0-06-211655-0(X)); 480p. 17.99 (978-0-06-202624-8(0)) HarperCollins Pubs. (HarperCollins).

—I Am Number Four: the Lost Files: Rebel Allies. 2015. (Lorien Legacies: the Lost Files Ser.). (ENG.). 416p. (YA). (gr. 9). pap. 10.99 (978-0-06-236404-3(9), HarperCollins) HarperCollins Pubs.

—I Am Number Four: the Lost Files: Secret Histories. 2013. (Lorien Legacies: the Lost Files Ser.). (ENG.). 416p. (YA). (gr. 9). pap. 10.99 (978-0-06-222367-8(4), HarperCollins) HarperCollins Pubs.

—I Am Number Four: the Lost Files: Zero Hour. 2016. (Lorien Legacies: the Lost Files Ser.). (ENG.). 416p. (YA). (gr. 9). pap. 11.99 (978-0-06-238771-4(5), HarperCollins) HarperCollins Pubs.

—Secret Histories. 2013. (Lorien Legacies: the Lost Files Ser.). (YA). lib. bdg. 20.85 (978-0-606-31823-5(2)) Turtleback.

Lorenz, Albert. The Exceptionally, Extraordinarily Ordinary First Day of School. 2010. (ENG., Illus.). 32p. (J). (gr. 1-4). 16.95 (978-0-8109-8960-3(3), 649501, Abrams Bks. for Young Readers) Abrams, Inc.

Lorenzi, Natalie Dias. Flying the Dragon. 240p. (J). (gr. 4-7). 2014. (ENG.). pap. 8.95 (978-1-58089-435-7(6)) 2012. 16.95 (978-1-58089-434-0(8)) Charlesbridge Publishing, Inc.

Lovelace, Maud Hart & Lovelace, M. Betsy-Tacy. 2007. (Betsy-Tacy Ser.). (J). (gr. 3-6). lib. bdg. 16.00 (978-0-8335-1338-0(9)) Turtleback.

Lucido, Aimee. Emmy in the Key of Code. 2019. (ENG.). 416p. (J). (gr. 3-7). 16.99 (978-0-358-04082-8(5), 1740459, Versify) HarperCollins Pubs.

Lupica, Mike. Shoot-Out. 2018. (ENG.). 208p. (J). (gr. 3-7). pap. 8.99 (978-0-451-47934-1(3), Puffin Books) Penguin Young Readers Group.

Lynch, Chris. The Gravedigger's Cottage. 2004. (ENG.). 208p. (J). (gr. 7-18). 15.99 (978-0-06-623940-8(0)) HarperCollins Pubs.

Maclachlan, Patricia. What You Know First. 2007. 17.00 (978-0-7569-7908-9(0)) Perfection Learning Corp.

Macomber, Debbie. The Yippy, Yappy Yorkie in the Green Doggy Sweater. Lambert, Sally Anne, illus. 2011. (ENG.). 32p. (J). (gr. -1-2). 17.99 (978-0-06-165096-3(X), HarperCollins) HarperCollins Pubs.

Maddox, Jake. Beach Bully. Aburto, Jesus, illus. 2013. (Jake Maddox Sports Stories Ser.). (ENG.). 72p. (J). (gr. 2-3). pap. 35.70 (978-1-4342-6234-9(0), 20039); (gr. 3-6). pap. 5.95 (978-1-4342-6206-6(5), 123504); (gr. 3-6). lib. bdg. 25.99 (978-1-4342-5973-8(0), 122930) Capstone. (Stone Arch Bks.).

—Board Rebel. Tiffany, Sean, illus. 2007. (Jake Maddox Sports Stories Ser.). (ENG.). 72p. (J). (gr. 3-6). pap. 5.95 (978-1-59889-414-1(5), 93561); lib. bdg. 25.99 (978-1-59889-319-9(X), 93515) Capstone. (Stone Arch Bks.).

—Dance Team Drama. 2016. (Jake Maddox JV Girls Ser.). (ENG., Illus.). 96p. (J). (gr. 4-8). pap. 5.95 (978-1-4965-3678-5(9), 132929); lib. bdg. 26.65 (978-1-4965-3674-7(6), 132925) Capstone. (Stone Arch Bks.).

—El Rebelde de la Patineta, 1 vol. Heck, Claudia, tr. Tiffany, Sean, illus. 2012. (Jake Maddox en Español Ser.). (SPA.). 72p. (J). (gr. 3-6). 25.32 (978-1-4342-3816-0(4), 117505, Stone Arch Bks.) Capstone.

—Touchdown Triumph. Aburto, Jesus, illus. 2015. (Jake Maddox Sports Stories Ser.). (ENG.). 72p. (J). (gr. 3-6). lib. bdg. 25.99 (978-1-4965-0492-0(5), 128564, Stone Arch Bks.) Capstone.

Madonia, Kristen-Paige. Fingerprints of You. (ENG., Illus.). 272p. (YA). (gr. 9). 2013. pap. 9.99 (978-1-4424-2921-5(6)) 2012. 16.99 (978-1-4424-2920-8(8)) Simon & Schuster Bks. For Young Readers. (Simon & Schuster Bks. For Young Readers).

Madonna. The English Roses: Goodbye, Grace. 2018. (ENG., Illus.). 144p. (J). (gr. -1-k). 14.95 (978-0-935112-70-2(7)) Callaway Editions, Inc.

Major, Kevin. The House of Wooden Santas, 1 vol. Pratt, Ned, photos by. gif. ed. 2004. (ENG., Illus.). 96p. (J). 34.95 (978-0-88995-249-2(3)) Red Deer Pr. CAN. Dist: Fitzhenry & Whiteside, Ltd.

Makechnie, Amy. The Unforgettable Guinevere St. Clair. (ENG.). 336p. (J). (gr. 3-7). 2019. pap. 8.99 (978-1-5344-1447-1(9)) 2018. (Illus.). 18.99 (978-1-5344-1446-4(0)) Simon & Schuster Children's Publishing. (Atheneum Bks. for Young Readers).

Mancusi, Mari. Gamer Girl. 2010. 256p. (YA). (gr. 7-18). 7.99 (978-0-14-241509-2(X), Speak) Penguin Young Readers Group.

Manushkin, Fran. Moving Day, 1 vol. Lyon, Tammie, illus. 2010. (Katie Woo Ser.). (ENG.). 32p. (J). (gr. k-2). pap. 5.95 (978-1-4048-6059-9(2), 103149, Picture Window Bks.) Capstone.

Marciano, Johnny & Chenoweth, Emily. Klawde: Evil Alien Warlord Cat #1. Mommaerts, Robb, illus. 2019. (Klawde: Evil Alien Warlord Cat Ser.: 1). 224p. (J). (gr. 3-7). 14.99 (978-1-5247-8720-2(5), Penguin Workshop) Penguin Young Readers Group.

Marsden, Carolyn. The Gold-Threaded Dress. 2006. (ENG.). 80p. (J). (gr. 2-4). reprint ed. per. 7.99 (978-0-7636-2993-9(6)) Candlewick Pr.

—The Gold-Threaded Dress. 2006. 73p. (gr. 2-4). 17.00 (978-0-7569-6574-7(8)) Perfection Learning Corp.

Martin, Rebecca. Joanna's Journey. Yoder, Laura & Weaver, Lisa, illus. 2006. 168p. (YA). pap. 9.99 (978-1-933753-01-0(3)) Carlisle Pr.- Walnut Creek.

Mast, Dorcas R. The Cranberry House. 2015. (ENG.). 249p. (YA). 11.50 (978-0-7399-2507-2(5)) Rod & Staff Pubs., Inc.

Mayhall, Robin. He Loves Me, He Loves Me Not: Book 7, No. 7. Irwin, Jane Elizabeth et al, illus. 2013. (My Boyfriend Is a Monster Ser.: 7). (ENG.). 128p. (YA). (gr. 7-12). lib. bdg. 29.32 (978-0-7613-6005-6(0), ae79c15f-787b-43fa-9d0a-94255bbea1be, Graphic Universe™) Lerner Publishing Group.

Mazer, Norma Fox. What I Believe. 2007. (ENG., Illus.). 176p. (J). (gr. 5-9). pap. 12.95 (978-0-15-206283-5(1)) Houghton Mifflin Harcourt Publishing Co.

McCranie, Stephen. Stephen Mccranie's Space Boy Volume 1, Vol. 1. 2018. (ENG., Illus.). 220p. (J). (gr. 7). pap. 12.99 (978-1-5067-0648-1(7), Dark Horse Books) Dark Horse Comics.

—Stephen Mccranie's Space Boy Volume 2. McCranie, Stephen, illus. 2018. (Illus.). 240p. (J). (gr. 5-9). pap. 12.99 (978-1-5067-0680-1(0), Dark Horse Books) Dark Horse Comics.

—Stephen Mccranie's Space Boy Volume 3. McCranie, Stephen, illus. 2019. (ENG., Illus.). 240p. (J). (gr. 5-9). pap. 12.99 (978-1-5067-0842-3(0), Dark Horse Books) Dark Horse Comics.

McDonald, Kirsten. The Nighttime Noise, 1 vol. Meza, Erika, illus. 2015. (Carlos & Carmen Ser.). (ENG.). 32p. (J). (gr. k-3). 32.79 (978-1-62402-139-8(5), 19075, Calico Chapter Bks) Magic Wagon.

—The One-Tire House, 1 vol. Meza, Erika, illus. 2015. (Carlos & Carmen Ser.). (ENG.). 32p. (J). (gr. k-3). 32.79 (978-1-62402-140-4(9), 19077, Calico Chapter Bks) Magic Wagon.

McDonald, Marion. The Missing Mom. McDonald, Marion & Brown, Marion, illus. 2012. 30p. pap. 9.00 (978-1-4349-8628-3(4), RoseDog Bks.) Dorrance Publishing Co., Inc.

McGuirk, Leslie. The Moogees Move House. McGuirk, Leslie, illus. 2012. (ENG., Illus.). 32p. (J). (gr. -1-2). 14.99 (978-0-7636-5558-7(9)) Candlewick Pr.

McKay, Hilary. Binny for Short. Player, Micah, illus. (ENG.). (J). (gr. 3-7). 2014. 288p. pap. 8.99 (978-1-4424-8276-0(1)) 2013. 304p. 16.99 (978-1-4424-8275-3(3)) McElderry, Margaret K. Bks. (McElderry, Margaret K. Bks.).

McKenzie, C. Lee. The Princess of Las Pulgas. 2010. (ENG.). 348p. (YA). (978-1-934813-46-1(X)) Westside Bks.

Mcmann, Lisa. Predator vs. Prey. 2018. (Going Wild Ser.: 2). (J). lib. bdg. 17.20 (978-0-606-41375-6(8)) Turtleback.

McManus, Karen M. Two Can Keep a Secret. 2019. (ENG.). 352p. lib. bdg. 21.80 (978-1-6636-2970-8(6)) Perfection Learning Corp.

—Two Can Keep a Secret. (ENG.). 352p. (YA). (gr. 9). 2021. pap. 12.99 (978-1-5247-1471-0(2), Ember) 2019. 19.99 (978-1-5247-1472-7(0), Delacorte Pr.) Random Hse. Children's Bks.

McQuestion, Karen. Life on Hold, 0 vols. unabr. ed. 2011. (ENG.). 196p. (YA). (gr. 3-6). pap. 9.95 (978-1-935597-27-8(2), 9781935597278, Skyscape) Amazon Publishing.

McVoy, Terra Elan. After the Kiss. 2011. (ENG.). 416p. (YA). (gr. 9). pap. 10.99 (978-1-4424-0216-4(4), Simon Pulse) Simon Pulse.

Mead, Emi. Ryan Is Moving Away. 2009. 32p. pap. 12.99 (978-1-4389-7226-8(1)) AuthorHouse.

Meltzer, Amy. A Mezuzah on the Door. Fried, Janice, illus. 2007. (Jewish Identity Ser.). 32p. (J). (gr. -1-3). 17.95 (978-1-58013-249-7(9), Kar-Ben Publishing) Lerner Publishing Group.

Meyerhoff, Jenny. Green Thumbs-Up! Chatelain, Éva & Chatelain, Éva, illus. 2015. (Friendship Garden Ser.: 1). (ENG.). 176p. (J). (gr. 2-5). pap. 6.99 (978-1-4814-3904-6(9), Aladdin) Simon & Schuster Children's Publishing.

Michelin, Linda. Zuzu's Wishing Cake. Johnson, D. B., illus. 2006. (ENG.). 32p. (J). (gr. -1-3). 16.00 (978-0-618-64640-1(X), 518747, Clarion Bks.) HarperCollins Pubs.

Miedoso, Andres. The Haunted House Next Door. Rivas, Victor, illus. 2017. (Desmond Cole Ghost Patrol Ser.: 1). (ENG.). 128p. (J). (gr. k-4). 17.99 (978-1-5344-1039-8(2)); pap. 6.99 (978-1-5344-1038-1(4)) Little Simon. (Little Simon).

Millner, Denene. Fresh Princess. Jose, Gladys, illus. 2019. (ENG.). 32p. (J). (gr. -1-3). 18.99 (978-0-06-288457-2(3), HarperCollins) HarperCollins Pubs.

Moore, Stephanie Perry. True Friends, 1. 2005. (Carmen Browne Ser.: 1). (ENG.). 128p. (YA). (gr. 4-6). pap. 6.99 (978-0-8024-8172-6(8)) Moody Pubs.

Moradian, Afsaneh. Jamie Is Jamie: A Book about Being Yourself & Playing Your Way. Bogade, Maria, illus. 2018. (Jamie Is Jamie Ser.). (ENG.). 32p. (J). (gr. -1-3). 15.99 (978-1-63198-139-5(0), 81395) Free Spirit Publishing Inc.

Morgan, Alex. Saving the Team. (Kicks Ser.). (ENG., Illus.). (J). (gr. 3-7). 2014. 192p. pap. 7.99 (978-1-4424-8571-6(X)) 2013. 176p. 17.99 (978-1-4424-8570-9(1)) Simon & Schuster Bks. For Young Readers. (Simon & Schuster Bks. For Young Readers).

—Saving the Team. 2021. (Kicks Ser.). (ENG.). 176p. (J). (gr. 3-7). lib. bdg. 31.36 (978-1-5321-4994-8(8), 36990, Chapter Bks.) Spotlight.

Moss, Alexandra, pseud. Ellie's Chance to Dance #1. 2005. (Royal Ballet School Diaries: 1). 144p. (J). (gr. 3-7). mass mkt. 5.99 (978-0-448-43535-0(7), Grosset & Dunlap) Penguin Young Readers Group.

Moss, Marissa. Amelia's Notebook. Moss, Marissa, illus. 2006. (Amelia Ser.). (ENG., Illus.). (J). 5.99 (978-1-4169-1286-6(X)); 40p. (gr. 2-5). 14.99 (978-1-4169-0905-7(2)) Simon & Schuster/Paula Wiseman Bks. (Simon & Schuster/Paula Wiseman Bks.).

Moss, Peggy. One of Us, 1 vol. 2010. (ENG., Illus.). 32p. (J). (gr. 1-7). 16.95 (978-0-88448-322-9(3), 884322) Tilbury Hse. Pubs.

Mowry, Tia & Mowry, Tamera. Twintuition: Double Vision. 2015. (Twintuition Ser.: 1). (ENG.). 208p. (J). (gr. 3-7). 16.99 (978-0-06-237286-4(6), HarperCollins) HarperCollins Pubs.

Munro, Sandie. Karlee's Other Family. 2006. 84p. pap. 8.95 (978-1-60126-000-0(8)) Masthof Pr.

Murphy, Stuart J. Emma Hace Amigos. 2011. (I See I Learn Ser.: 17). (Illus.). 32p. (J). (-k). 14.95 (978-1-58089-482-1(8)); pap. 6.95 (978-1-58089-483-8(6)) Charlesbridge Publishing, Inc.

—Emma's Friendwich. 2010. (I See I Learn Ser.: 1). (Illus.). 32p. (J). (gr. -1-k). 14.95 (978-1-58089-450-0(X)) Charlesbridge Publishing, Inc.

Nelson, Marilyn. Pemba's Song. 2008. (ENG.). 112p. (J). (gr. 7-7). 16.99 (978-0-545-02076-3(X), Scholastic Pr.) Scholastic, Inc.

Newton, A. I. The Alien Next Door 7: up, up, & Away! Sarkar, Anjan, illus. 2019. (Alien Next Door Ser.: 7). (ENG.). 112p. (J). (gr. k-3). 16.99 (978-1-4998-0806-3(2)); pap. 5.99 (978-1-4998-0805-6(4)) Little Bee Books Inc.

Nicholls, Claire. In it to win It. 2011. 160p. (gr. 4-6). pap. 14.09 (978-1-4567-7994-8(X)) AuthorHouse.

Noonan, Diana. The Old Things (Paperback) Copyright 2016. 2015. (ENG.). (gr. k-6). pap. 6.97 (978-0-328-83269-9(3), Scott Foresman) Savvas Learning Co.

Norfleet, Mary Crockett. Hand Me down House. Mallory, Edgar, illus. 2011. 98p. 38.95 (978-1-258-07946-8(1)) Literary Licensing, LLC.

O'Byrne, Nicola. Where Is Home, Daddy Bear? 2019. (ENG., Illus.). 32p. (J). (gr. -1-1). 17.00 (978-1-947888-14-2(5), Flyaway Bks.) Westminster John Knox Pr.

O'Connor, Barbara. Wonderland. 2019. (ENG.). 288p. (J). pap. 7.99 (978-1-250-21138-5(7), 900193345) Square Fish.

Old Cat & the Kitten. 2014. (ENG., Illus.). 128p. (J). (gr. 3-7). pap. 6.99 (978-1-4814-1938-3(2), Aladdin) Simon & Schuster Children's Publishing.

O'Maley, Elizabeth. By Freedom's Light. 2009. 188p. (J). 15.95 (978-0-87195-273-8(4)); pap. 7.95 (978-0-87195-274-5(2)) Indiana Historical Society.

O'Neill, Joy. Why Do We Have to Move? 2013. (Illus.). 32p. pap. (978-0-7552-1525-6(7), Bright Pen) Authors OnLine, Ltd.

O'Reilly, Jane. The Secret of Goldenrod. (ENG.). (J). (gr. 3-6). 2018. 392p. pap. 9.99 (978-1-5415-1493-5(9), 75e9b3c2-a2d3-4066-85fe-25aea387aa08) 2016. 376p. 17.99 (978-1-5124-0135-6(8), c4a3f32f-d495-461e-8c14-f8580406f616) 2016. 376p. E-Book 27.99 (978-1-5124-0894-2(8)) Lerner Publishing Group. (Carolrhoda Bks.).

O'Ryan, Ray. Hello, Nebulon! Jack, Colin, illus. 2013. (Galaxy Zack Ser.: 1). (ENG.). 128p. (J). (gr. k-4). 17.99 (978-1-4424-5387-6(7)); pap. 6.99 (978-1-4424-5386-9(9)) Little Simon. (Little Simon).

—Hello, Nebulon! 2013. (Galaxy Zack Ser.: 1). lib. bdg. 16.00 (978-0-606-32442-7(9)) Turtleback.

Palmer, Iva-Marie. Gabby Garcia's Ultimate Playbook #3: Sidelined. Kissi, Marta, illus. 2019. (Gabby Garcia's Ultimate Playbook Ser.: 3). (ENG.). 288p. (J). (gr. 3-7). 12.99 (978-0-06-239186-5(0), Tegen, Katherine Bks) HarperCollins Pubs.

Paris, Harper. The Mystery of the Gold Coin. Calo, Marcos, illus. 2014. (Greetings from Somewhere Ser.: 1). (ENG.). 128p. (J). (gr. k-4). pap. 5.99 (978-1-4424-9718-4(1), Little Simon) Little Simon.

Parish, Herman. Amelia Bedelia on the Move. Avril, Lynne, illus. 2017. (I Can Read Level 1 Ser.). (ENG.). 32p. (J). (gr. -1-3). 16.99 (978-0-06-265886-9(7)); pap. 4.99 (978-0-06-265885-2(9)) HarperCollins Pubs. (Greenwillow Bks.).

Parker, David. My Best Friend Is Moving. Lucas, Margeaux, illus. 2007. (J). (978-0-545-00389-6(X)) Scholastic, Inc.

Patrick, Cat. Revived. 2013. (ENG.). 368p. (YA). (gr. 7-17). pap. 18.99 (978-0-316-09463-4(3)) Little, Brown Bks. for Young Readers.

Patron, Susan. Maybe Yes, Maybe No, Maybe Maybe. Halpin, Abigail, illus. 2009. (ENG.). 128p. (J). (gr. 3-5). pap. 5.99 (978-1-4169-6176-5(3), Atheneum Bks. for Young Readers) Simon & Schuster Children's Publishing.

Payton, Belle. A Whole New Ball Game. 2014. (It Takes Two Ser.: 1). (ENG., Illus.). 160p. (J). (gr. 3-7). 16.99 (978-1-4814-0642-0(6)); pap. 7.99 (978-1-4814-0641-3(8)) Simon Spotlight. (Simon Spotlight).

Peck, Richard. A Season of Gifts. 2010. (ENG.). 208p. (J). (gr. 5-18). 8.99 (978-0-14-241729-4(7), Puffin Books) Penguin Young Readers Group.

Pennypacker, Sara. Meet the Dullards. Salmieri, Daniel, illus. 2015. (ENG.). 32p. (J). (gr. -1-3). 17.99 (978-0-06-219856-3(4), Balzer & Bray) HarperCollins Pubs.

Perry, Hailey. On the Move. 2010. 188p. pap. 12.00 (978-1-60844-428-1(7)) Dog Ear Publishing, LLC.

Philippe, Ben. The Field Guide to the North American Teenager. (ENG.). 384p. (YA). (gr. 8). 2020. pap. 11.99 (978-0-06-282412-7(0)) 2019. 18.99 (978-0-06-282411-0(2)) HarperCollins Pubs. (Balzer & Bray).

Phillips, Dee. Grind, 1 vol. unabr. ed. 2010. (Right Now! Ser.). (ENG., Illus.). 45p. (YA). (gr. 9-12). pap. 10.75 (978-1-61651-250-7(4)) Saddleback Educational Publishing, Inc.

Pirc, Jerri J. Kate & Caboodle. Smith, Jane, illus. 2015. pap. (978-0-473-32583-1(7)) Pirc, Jerri J.

Plastow, Joan. Adventures of Joe. 2003. (Illus.). 68p. pap. (978-1-84401-144-5(5)) Athena Pr.

Polacco, Patricia. The Graves Family. Polacco, Patricia, illus. 2006. (Illus.). (gr. k-3). 17.00 (978-0-7569-6715-4(5)) Perfection Learning Corp.

—Holes in the Sky. Polacco, Patricia, illus. 2018. (Illus.). 48p. (J). (gr. 1-4). 19.99 (978-1-5247-3948-5(0), G.P. Putnam's Sons Books for Young Readers) Penguin Young Readers Group.

Preller, James. Bystander. 2011. (ENG.). 256p. (YA). (gr. 5-9). pap. 8.99 (978-0-312-54796-7(X), 900074323) Square Fish.

—Home Sweet Horror. Bruno, Iacopo, illus. 2013. (Scary Tales Ser.: 1). (ENG.). 112p. (J). (gr. 2-5). pap. 9.99 (978-1-250-01887-8(0), 900087724) Feiwel & Friends.

Prendergast, Gabrielle. Audacious, 1 vol. 2015. (ENG.). 336p. (YA). (gr. 8-12). pap. 12.95 (978-1-4598-0264-3(0)) Orca Bk. Pubs. USA.

Quirk, Katie. A Girl Called Problem. 2013. (ENG., Illus.). 256p. (J). pap. 8.50 (978-0-8028-5404-9(4), Eerdmans Bks For Young Readers) Eerdmans, William B. Publishing Co.

Ramthun, Bonnie. The White Gates. 2008. (ENG.). 256p. (J). (gr. 6-8). lib. bdg. 22.44 (978-0-375-94554-0(7)) Random House Publishing Group.

Randle, Kristen. The Only Alien on the Planet. 2009. 240p. (YA). (gr. 7-12). pap. 11.99 (978-1-4022-2669-4(1), 9781402226694) Sourcebooks, Inc.

Ransom, Candice. Seeing Sky-Blue Pink. 2007. (Exceptional Reading & Language Arts Titles for Intermediate Grades Ser.). 122p. (J). (gr. 4-7). 16.95 (978-0-8225-7142-1(0), Carolrhoda Bks.) Lerner Publishing Group.

Reed, Ken. Sara's Big Challenge: Who's the Real Me? A Sara Thompson Sports Book. 2008. 188p. (J). pap. 9.95 (978-1-4327-0624-1(1)) Outskirts Pr., Inc.

Reynolds, Alison. A Year with Marmalade. McKenzie, Heath, illus. 2013. (ENG.). 40p. (J). (gr. -1-1). 15.99 (978-1-4424-8105-3(6), Little Simon) Little Simon.

RH Disney. Inside Out (Disney/Pixar Inside Out) Batson, Alan, illus. 2016. (Little Golden Book Ser.). (ENG.). 24p. (J). (-k). 5.99 (978-0-7364-3629-8(4), Golden/Disney) Random Hse. Children's Bks.

—Journey into the Mind (Disney/Pixar Inside Out) RH Disney, illus. 2015. (Step into Reading Ser.). (ENG., Illus.). 32p. (J). (gr. -1-1). 5.99 (978-0-7364-3316-7(3), RH/Disney) Random Hse. Children's Bks.

Rim, Sujean. Chee-Kee: a Panda in Bearland. 2017. (ENG., Illus.). 40p. (J). (gr. -1-3). 17.99 (978-0-316-40744-1(5)) Little, Brown Bks. for Young Readers.

Ripken Jr., Cal. Cal Ripken Jr. 's All-Stars Super-Sized Slugger. Cowherd, Kevin, illus. 2013. (Cal Ripken Jr. 's All Stars Ser.: 2). (ENG.). 208p. (J). (gr. 3-7). pap. 6.99 (978-1-4231-4004-7(4)) Hyperion Pr.

Rivers, Phoebe. Ghost Town, 1. 2012. (Saranormal Ser.: 1). (ENG.). 160p. (J). (gr. 4-6). 18.69 (978-1-4424-5378-4(8), Simon Spotlight) Simon & Schuster Children's Publishing.

—Ghost Town. 2012. (Saranormal Ser.: 1). (ENG.). 160p. (J). (gr. 3-7). pap. 5.99 (978-1-4424-4038-8(4), Simon Spotlight) Simon Spotlight.

Rodman, Sean. Firewall, 1 vol. 2017. (Orca Soundings Ser.). (ENG.). 144p. (YA). (gr. 8-12). pap. 9.95 (978-1-4598-1453-0(3)) Orca Bk. Pubs. USA.

Romito, Dee. No Place Like Home. 2017. 234p. (J). (978-965-278-469-8(9), Simon & Schuster/Paula Wiseman Bks.) Simon & Schuster/Paula Wiseman Bks.

Rosensweig, Jay B. & Repka, Janice. The Stupendous Dodgeball Fiasco. Dibley, Glin, illus. 2012. 181p. (J). (gr. 4-6). 21.19 (978-0-525-47346-6(7)) Penguin Young Readers Group.

Ross, Tony. I Want to Go Home! Ross, Tony, illus. 2014. (ENG., Illus.). 32p. (J). (gr. -1-3). 16.95 (978-1-4677-5095-0(6)) Lerner Publishing Group.

Rouss, Sylvia A. Sammy Spider's New Friend. Kahn, Katherine, illus. 2012. (Kar-Ben Favorites Ser.). (ENG.). 32p. (J). (gr. -1-2). lib. bdg. 17.95 (978-0-7613-6663-8(6), Kar-Ben Publishing) Lerner Publishing Group.

Rowland, Patty. Marvelous Max, the Mansion Mouse. Rasmussen, Wendy, tr. Rasmussen, Wendy, illus. 2003. 32p. (J). 17.95 (978-0-9649934-4-0(9)) Norfleet Pr., Inc.

Sadu, Itah. Greetings, Leroy, 1 vol. Delinois, Alix, illus. 2017. (ENG.). 32p. (J). (gr. k-2). 18.95 (978-1-55498-760-3(1)) Groundwood Bks. CAN. Dist: Publishers Group West (PGW).

Salisbury, Linda G. The Wild Women of Lake Anna: A Bailey Fish Adventure. 2005. (Illus.). 159p. (J). (978-1-881539-37-7(7)) Tabby Hse. Bks.

Sanchez, Mary Louise, illus. The Wind Called My Name, 1 vol. 2018. (ENG.). 288p. (J). (gr. 3-7). 20.95 (978-1-62014-780-1(7), leelowtu, Tu Bks.) Lee & Low Bks., Inc.

Schröder, Monika & Schröder, Monika. Be Light Like a Bird. 2016. (ENG.). 240p. (J). (gr. 3-7). lib. bdg. 14.95 (978-1-62370-749-1(8), 132439, Capstone Young Readers) Capstone.

Schultz, Jan Neubert. Firestorm. 2003. (Adventures in Time Ser.). 204p. (YA). (gr. 4-7). 15.95 (978-0-87614-276-9(5), Carolrhoda Bks.) Lerner Publishing Group.

Scieszka, Jon. The All-Purpose SPHDZ Boxed Set: SPHDZ Book #1!; SPHDZ Book #2!; SPHDZ Book #3!; SPHDZ 4 Life!, Set. Prigmore, Shane, illus. 2013. (Spaceheadz Ser.). (ENG.). 864p. (J). (gr. 2-5). pap. 23.99 (978-1-4424-9858-7(7), Simon & Schuster Bks. For Young Readers) Simon & Schuster Bks. For Young Readers.

—SPHDZ Book #1! Prigmore, Shane, illus. (Spaceheadz Ser.: 1). (ENG.). (J). (gr. 2-5). 2011. 192p. pap. 7.99 (978-1-4424-1986-5(5)) 2010. 176p. 14.99 (978-1-4169-7951-7(4)) Simon & Schuster Bks. For Young Readers. (Simon & Schuster Bks. For Young Readers).

Sedita, Francesco. Miss Popularity. 2007. 120p. (J). pap. (978-0-545-00828-0(X)) Scholastic, Inc.

Seely, Debra. Grasslands. 2017. (ENG., Illus.). (J). (gr. 4-6). pap. 9.99 (978-0-922820-18-4(X)) Watermark Pr., Inc.

Seybold, Celisa. The Keys to Adventure. 2010. 62p. pap. 9.95 (978-0-557-55086-9(6)) Lulu Pr., Inc.

Seyfert, Ella Maie. Amish Moving Day. Jones, Henrietta, illus. 2011. 132p. 40.95 (978-1-258-01315-8(0)) Literary Licensing, LLC.

Sheinmel, Courtney. The Kindness Club: Chloe on the Bright Side. 2016. (Kindness Club Ser.). (ENG.). 224p. (J). 15.99 (978-1-68119-091-4(5), 900158417, Bloomsbury USA Childrens) Bloomsbury Publishing USA.

Sheriff, Jeanne. Walkabout Kid. 2013. 172p. pap. 12.95 (978-1-4787-2130-7(8)) Outskirts Pr., Inc.

Shmuel, Naomi. Too Far from Home. Katz, Avi, illus. 2020. (ENG.). 96p. (J). (gr. 3-7). 15.99 (978-1-5415-4671-4(7), 15d83bab-1d1f-4e49-9c2f-6edeed30b6ae, Kar-Ben Publishing) Lerner Publishing Group.

Siebold, Jan. Rope Burn. 2012. (ENG.). 82p. (J). (gr. 2-4). 17.44 (978-0-8075-7109-5(1)) Whitman, Albert & Co.

Simpson, Lesley. The Purim Surprise. Church, Peter, illus. 2004. (Purim Ser.). (ENG.). 32p. (J). (gr. -1-3). pap. 6.95 (978-1-58013-090-5(9), Kar-Ben Publishing) Lerner Publishing Group.

Slater, Teddy. Patty & the Pink Princesses. Springer, Sally, illus. 2007. (J). pap. (978-0-439-89707-5(6)) Scholastic, Inc.

Smallman, Jeff. Stump's in the Cellar. 2008. 100p. pap. 13.95 (978-0-557-03091-0(9)) Lulu Pr., Inc.

Smith, Heather. Baygirl, 1 vol. 2013. (ENG.). 288p. (YA). (gr. 8-12). pap. 12.95 (978-1-4598-0274-2(8)) Orca Bk. Pubs. USA.

Sones, Sonya. One of Those Hideous Books Where the Mother Dies. (ENG., (YA). (gr. 7). 2013. Illus.). 288p. pap. 12.99 (978-1-4424-9383-4(6)) 2005. 272p. reprint ed. pap. 7.99 (978-1-4169-0788-6(2)) Simon & Schuster Bks. For Young Readers. (Simon & Schuster Bks. For Young Readers).

Sorenson, Margo. Aloha for Carol Ann. Burris, Priscilla, illus. 2011. 32p. (J). (gr. -1-3). pap. 8.95 (978-1-60349-027-6(2), Marimba Bks.) Just Us Bks., Inc.

Soup, Cuthbert. A Whole Nother Story. Timmins, Jeffrey Stewart, illus. 2010. (Whole Nother Story Ser.). (ENG.). 288p. (YA). (gr. 3-6). pap. 8.99 (978-1-59990-518-1(3), 900068450, Bloomsbury USA Childrens) Bloomsbury Publishing USA.

Spencer, Octavia. The Case of the Time-Capsule Bandit. To, Vivienne, illus. 2013. (Randi Rhodes, Ninja Detective Ser.: 1). (ENG.). 224p. (J). (gr. 3-7). 16.99 (978-1-4424-7681-3(8), Simon & Schuster Bks. For Young Readers) Simon & Schuster Bks. For Young Readers.

Spiegelman, Nadja. Lost in NYC: A Subway Adventure. Sánchez, Sergio García, illus. 2016. (Toon Graphics Ser.). (ENG.). 52p. (J). (gr. 3-6). lib. bdg. 34.21 (978-1-61479-499-8(5), 21435, Graphic Novels) Spotlight.

—Lost in NYC: a Subway Adventure: A TOON Graphic. Garcia Sanchez, Sergio, illus. 2015. 52p. (J). (gr. 3-7). 16.99 (978-1-935179-81-8(0), TOON Books) Astra Publishing Hse.

Springstubb, Tricia. Mo Wren, Lost & Found. Ross, Heather, illus. 2011. (Fox Street Ser.: 2). (ENG.). 256p. (J). (gr. 3-7). 15.99 (978-0-06-199039-7(6), Balzer & Bray) HarperCollins Pubs.

Stahler, David, Jr. Gathering of Shades. 2006. (ENG.). 256p. pap. (978-0-06-052296-4(8)) HarperCollins Canada, Ltd.

—A Gathering of Shades. 2005. (ENG.). 304p. (J). 15.99 (978-0-06-052294-0(1), HarperTeen) HarperCollins Pubs.

Stanley, Brenda. I Am Nuchu. 2010. 334p. (YA). (gr. 9-18). 16.95 (978-1-934813-47-8(8)) Westside Bks.

Stanley, George E. Night Fires. 2009. (ENG.). 192p. (J). (gr. 3-7). 15.99 (978-1-4169-7559-5(4), Aladdin) Simon & Schuster Children's Publishing.

—Night Fires. 2011. (ENG.). 192p. (J). (gr. 3-7). pap. 6.99 (978-1-4169-1250-7(9), Simon & Schuster/Paula Wiseman Bks.) Simon & Schuster/Paula Wiseman Bks.

Stead, Philip C. Lenny & Lucy. Stead, Erin E., illus. 2015. (ENG.). 40p. (J). (gr. -1-2). 21.99 (978-1-59643-932-0(7), 900122425) Roaring Brook Pr.

Stever, Karen Malloy. Jabin, the Talking Donkey: In Jerusalem. 2012. 24p. pap. 24.95 (978-1-4626-8285-0(5)) America Star Bks.

Stine, R. L. First Evil. 2011. (Fear Street Cheerleaders Ser.: 1). (ENG.). 176p. (YA). (gr. 9). pap. 9.99 (978-1-4424-3086-0(9), Simon Pulse) Simon Pulse.

—Here Comes the Shaggedy. 2016. (Goosebumps Most Wanted Ser.: 9). (Illus.). 140p. (J). lib. bdg. 17.20 (978-0-606-38587-9(8)) Turtleback.

—Here Comes the Shaggedy (Goosebumps Most Wanted #9), Vol. 9. 2016. (Goosebumps Most Wanted Ser.: 9). (ENG., Illus.). 160p. (J). (gr. 3-7). pap. 6.99 (978-0-545-82547-4(4), Scholastic Paperbacks) Scholastic, Inc.

Stockham, Jess, illus. Moving Day! 2011. (Helping Hands Ser.). 24p. (J). (978-1-84643-414-3(9)) Child's Play International Ltd.

Stoddard, Lindsey. Right As Rain. 2019. (ENG.). 304p. (J). (gr. 3-7). 16.99 (978-0-06-265294-2(X), HarperCollins) HarperCollins Pubs.

Stromberg, Ronica. A Shadow in the Dark. 2009. (J). pap. (978-0-88092-751-2(8)); lib. bdg. (978-0-88092-750-5(X)) Royal Fireworks Publishing Co.

Strow, Lorie. The Shimmers. 2011. 32p. pap. 21.99 (978-1-4568-8133-7(7)) Xlibris Corp.

Suen, Anastasia. In the Big City. Myer, Ed, illus. 2012. (Little Birdie Bks.). (ENG.). 24p. (gr. k-1). pap. 9.95 (978-1-61810-302-4(4), 9781618103024) Rourke Educational Media.

Sumner, Jamie. Roll with It. 2019. (Roll with It Ser.). (ENG., Illus.). 256p. (J). (gr. 5). 19.99 (978-1-5344-4255-9(3), Atheneum Bks. for Young Readers) Simon & Schuster Children's Publishing.

Sumner Johnson, Janet. The Last Great Adventure of the PB & J Society. 2016. (Middle-Grade Novels Ser.). (ENG., Illus.). 256p. (J). (gr. 4-8). lib. bdg. 26.65 (978-1-4965-2695-3(3), 131275, Stone Arch Bks.) Capstone.

Tabby, Abigail. The KnitWits Make a Move! Wildish, Lee, illus. Frost, Michael, photos by. 2013. (ENG.). 32p. (J). (gr. -1-1). 14.99 (978-1-4424-5342-5(7), Little Simon) Little Simon.

Tanaka, Shelley. Nobody Knows, 1 vol. 2012. (ENG., Illus.). 144p. (J). (gr. 4-5). 16.95 (978-1-55498-140-3(9)) Groundwood Bks. CAN. Dist: Publishers Group West (PGW).

Telgemeier, Raina. Ghosts: a Graphic Novel. Telgemeier, Raina, illus. 2016. (ENG., Illus.). 256p. (J). (gr. 3-7). 24.99 (978-0-545-54061-2(5), Graphix) Scholastic, Inc.

Thomas, Kara. Little Monsters. 2018. (ENG.). 368p. (YA). (gr. 9). pap. 10.99 (978-0-553-52152-8(7), Ember) Random Hse. Children's Bks.

Tooke, Wes. Lucky: Maris, Mantle, & My Best Summer Ever. (ENG.). 192p. (J). (gr. 3-7). 2011. pap. 6.99 (978-1-4169-8664-5(2)) 2010. 15.99 (978-1-4169-8663-8(4)) Simon & Schuster Bks. For Young Readers. (Simon & Schuster Bks. For Young Readers).

Townsend, Michael. Kit Feeny: On the Move, 1. 2009. (Kit Feeny Ser.). (ENG., Illus.). 96p. (J). (gr. 3-6). lib. bdg. 18.69 (978-0-375-95614-0(X), Knopf Bks. for Young Readers) Random Hse. Children's Bks.

Tregay, Sarah. Love & Leftovers. 2011. (ENG.). 448p. (YA). (gr. 8). 17.99 (978-0-06-202358-2(6), Tegen, Katherine Bks) HarperCollins Pubs.

Urban, Linda. Mabel & Sam at Home: (Imagination Books for Kids, Children's Books about Creative Play) Hooper, Hadley, illus. 2018. (ENG.). 60p. (J). (gr. k-3). 17.99 (978-1-4521-3996-8(2)) Chronicle Bks. LLC.

Vega, Danielle. The Haunted. 2019. (Haunted Ser.). (ENG.). 256p. (YA). (gr. 9). 17.99 (978-0-451-48146-7(1), Razorbill) Penguin Young Readers Group.

Venditti, Robert. Attack of the Alien Horde. Higgins, Dusty, illus. 2015. (Miles Taylor & the Golden Cape Ser.: 1). (ENG.). 304p. (J). (gr. 4-7). 16.99 (978-1-4814-0542-3(X)) Simon & Schuster, Inc.

Villeneuve, Marie-Paule & Audet, Patrice. Qui a Enleve Polka? 2004. (FRE., Illus.). 122p. (J). 8.95 (978-2-922565-81-2(5)) Editions de la Paix CAN. Dist: World of Reading, Ltd.

Viorst, Judith. Alexander, Who's Not (Do You Hear Me? I Mean It!) Going to Move. Glasser, Robin Preiss, illus. 2015. 32p. pap. 9.00 (978-1-61003-597-2(6)) Center for the Collaborative Classroom.

Vrabel, Beth. A Blind Guide to Stinkville. (ENG.). (J). (gr. 2-7). 2016. 280p. pap. 7.99 (978-1-5107-0382-7(9)) 2015. 264p. 16.99 (978-1-63450-157-6(8)) Skyhorse Publishing Co., Inc. (Sky Pony Pr.).

Vrettos, Adrienne Maria. Best Friends for Never. 2016. (ENG.). 240p. (J). (gr. 3-7). 16.99 (978-0-545-56149-5(3), Scholastic Pr.) Scholastic, Inc.

Vries, Lizzette de & Vries, Cecile de. How the Tooth Mouse Met the Tooth Fairy. Suwannakit, Tul, illus. 2010. (J). 19.95 (978-0-86715-507-5(8)) Quintessence Publishing Co., Inc.

Wade, Rebecca. The Whispering House. 2012. (ENG.). 272p. (J). (gr. 3-7). 16.99 (978-0-06-077497-4(5), Tegen, Katherine Bks) HarperCollins Pubs.

Walker, Anna. Florette. Walker, Anna, illus. 2018. (ENG., Illus.). 40p. (J). (gr. -1-3). 17.99 (978-0-544-87683-5(0), 1649580, Clarion Bks.) HarperCollins Pubs.

Wallace, Ian. Mr. Kneebone's New Digs. Wallace, Ian, illus. (Illus.). (J). 16.95 (978-0-88899-143-0(6)) Groundwood Bks. CAN. Dist: Publishers Group West (PGW).

Wallace, Rich. Southpaw. 2006. 105p. (J). lib. bdg. 15.38 (978-1-4242-2166-0(8)) Fitzgerald Bks.

—Southpaw. 2006. (Winning Season Ser.). (ENG.). 112p. (J). (gr. 3-6). 17.44 (978-0-670-06053-5(4)) Penguin Young Readers Group.

—Southpaw: Winning Season. 6th ed. 2007. (Winning Season Ser.: 6). 128p. (J). (gr. 3-7). 5.99 (978-0-14-240785-1(2), Puffin Books) Penguin Young Readers Group.

Watson, Philip & Ofiesh, Nicole. The Treasure Chest. 2011. 52p. 20.50 (978-1-4269-5350-7(X)); pap. 10.50 (978-1-4269-5269-2(4)) Trafford Publishing.

Watt, Fiona. Complete Book of First Experiences. rev. ed. 2011. (First Experiences Ser.). 144p. (J). ring bd. 19.99 (978-0-7945-2948-2(8), Usborne) EDC Publishing.

Watt, Mélanie & Watt, Mélanie. Augustine. Watt, Mélanie & Watt, Mélanie, illus. 2008. (ENG., Illus.). 32p. (J). (gr. -1-2). pap. 9.99 (978-1-55453-268-1(X)) Kids Can Pr., Ltd. CAN. Dist: Hachette Bk. Group.

Watts, Jeri. A Piece of Home. Yum, Hyewon, illus. 2016. (ENG.). 32p. (J). (gr. k-3). 17.99 (978-0-7636-6971-3(7)) Candlewick Pr.

Weitzman, Jacqueline Preiss. Superhero Joe & the Creature Next Door. Barrett, Ron, illus. 2013. (ENG.). 32p. (J). (gr. -1-3). 16.99 (978-1-4424-1268-2(2), Simon & Schuster Bks. For Young Readers) Simon & Schuster Bks. For Young Readers.

Welch, Ginger. The Dream Reader. 2012. 76p. 19.95 (978-1-4626-7276-9(0)); pap. 19.95 (978-1-4626-8291-1(X)) America Star Bks.

Wenberg, Michael. Stringz. 2010. 216p. (YA). (gr. 6-10). 16.95 (978-1-934813-33-1(8)) Westside Bks.

Wertheim, L. Jon & Moskowitz, Tobias J. The Rookie Bookie. 2015. (ENG., Illus.). 272p. (J). (gr. 3-7). pap. 15.99 (978-0-316-24979-9(3)) Little, Brown Bks. for Young Readers.

Whelan, Gloria. A Haunted House in Starvation Lake. 2003. (Starvation Lake Ser.). (ENG., Illus.). 80p. (J). (gr. 3-6). lib. bdg. 16.19 (978-0-307-46516-0(0)) Random House Publishing Group.

Wigington, Patti. Summer's Ashes. 2007. (ENG.). 208p. (gr. 8-12). per. 15.00 (978-0-9766805-9-8(9)) Keene Publishing.

Williams, Alicia D. Genesis Begins Again. 2019. (ENG., Illus.). 384p. (J). (gr. 4-8). 17.99 (978-1-4814-6580-9(5), Atheneum/Caitlyn Dlouhy Books) Simon & Schuster Children's Publishing.

Williams, Sarah DeFord. Palace Beautiful. 2011. (ENG.). (J). 224p. (gr. 6-8). 21.19 (978-0-399-25298-3(3)); 240p. (gr. 5-18). 6.99 (978-0-14-241745-4(9), Puffin Books) Penguin Young Readers Group.

Wilson, Nathaniel. Jessie's Big Move. Shoopik, Marina, illus. 2010. (ENG.). 54p. (J). 16.95 (978-0-9744935-7-2(0)) Allwrite Publishing.

Wolf, Maria. Black Dog. 2013. 12p. pap. 15.99 (978-1-4817-0405-2(2)) AuthorHouse.

Wong, Janet S. Homegrown House. Lewis, E. B., illus. 2009. (ENG.). 40p. (J). (gr. -1-3). 19.99 (978-0-689-84718-9(1), McElderry, Margaret K. Bks.) McElderry, Margaret K. Bks.

Wood, Fiona. Six Impossible Things. 2016. (ENG.). 304p. (YA). (gr. 7-17). pap. 16.99 (978-0-316-29941-1(3), Poppy) Little, Brown Bks. for Young Readers.

Wynne-Jones, Tim. Rex Zero, the Great Pretender. 2013. (Rex Zero Ser.). (ENG.). 240p. (J). (gr. 4-6). 21.19 (978-1-250-01673-7(8)) Square Fish.

Yee, Wong Herbert. Did You See Chip? Ovresat, Laura, illus. 2004. (ENG.). 24p. (J). (gr. -1-3). pap. 4.99 (978-0-15-205096-2(5), 1195388, Clarion Bks.) HarperCollins Pubs.

Yeh, Kat. The Truth about Twinkie Pie. 2015. (ENG.). 352p. (J). E-Book (978-0-316-23671-3(3)) Little Brown & Co.

Yoo, Paula. Lily's New Home (Confetti Kids), 1 vol. 2016. (Confetti Kids Ser.: 1). (ENG., Illus.). 32p. (J). (gr. k-2). 14.95 (978-1-62014-249-3(X), leelowbooks) Lee & Low Bks., Inc.

Young, Karen Romano. Doodlebug: A Novel in Doodles. 2012. (ENG., Illus.). 128p. (J). (gr. 3-7). pap. 15.99 (978-1-250-01020-9(9), 900084757) Square Fish.

Ziegler, Jennifer. How Not to Be Popular. 2010. 352p. (YA). (gr. 7). mass mkt. 8.99 (978-0-440-24024-2(7), Delacorte Bks. for Young Readers) Random Hse. Children's Bks.

Ziegler, Maddie. The Audition. 2017. (Maddie Ziegler Ser.: 1). (ENG., Illus.). 256p. (J). (gr. 4-8). 16.99 (978-1-4814-8636-1(5), Aladdin) Simon & Schuster Children's Publishing.

—The Audition. 2018. (Maddie Ziegler Ser.: 1). (ENG.). 272p. (J). (gr. 4-8). pap. 7.99 (978-1-4814-8637-8(3), Simon & Schuster/Paula Wiseman Bks.) Simon & Schuster/Paula Wiseman Bks.

Zink, Michelle. Lies I Told. 2015. (Lies I Told Ser.: 1). (ENG.). 352p. (YA). (gr. 8). pap. 9.99 (978-0-06-232713-0(5), HarperTeen) HarperCollins Pubs.

50 Cent, 50. Playground. Akana, Lizzi, illus. 2012. (ENG.). 320p. (YA). (gr. 7). pap. 10.99 (978-1-59514-478-2(1), Razorbill) Penguin Young Readers Group.

MOWGLI (FICTITIOUS CHARACTER)—FICTION

Kipling, Rudyard. All the Mowgli Stories. Tresilian, Stuart, illus. 2017. (ENG.). 328p. 12.99 (978-1-5098-3076-3(6), 900176730, Collector's Library, The) Pan Macmillan GBR. Dist: Macmillan.

—The Jungle Book. 2019. (Arcturus Children's Classics Ser.). (ENG.). 192p. (J). pap. 6.99 (978-1-78950-474-3(0), 3cf8edfc-ed95-4f41-865a-75ea532f7420) Arcturus Publishing GBR. Dist: Baker & Taylor Publisher Services (BTPS).

—The Jungle Book. (ENG.). (J). 2019. 104p. (gr. -1). pap. 17.82 (978-0-368-70953-1(1)) 2019. 104p. (gr. -1). pap. 20.02 (978-0-368-70955-5(8)) 2019. 104p. (gr. -1). pap. 20.92 (978-0-368-70958-6(2)) 2019. 172p. (gr. -1). 19.99 (978-0-368-49137-5(4)) 2019. 172p. (gr. -1). pap. 6.99 (978-0-368-49138-2(2)) 2019. 188p. (gr. -1). pap. 10.66 (978-0-368-35469-4(5)) 2019. 92p. (gr. -1). pap. 12.55 (978-0-368-28346-8(1)) 2017. (Illus.). (gr. 2-4). 28.99 (978-1-366-55592-2(9)) Blurb, Inc.

—The Jungle Book. 2019. (ENG.). 136p. (J). (gr. -1). pap. (978-5-519-65715-0(7)) Books on Demand.

—The Jungle Book. 2017. (ENG., Illus.). (J). pap. 13.95 (978-1-374-94816-7(0)); (gr. 2-4). 23.95 (978-1-374-94817-4(9)) Capital Communications, Inc.

—The Jungle Book. 2018. (ENG., Illus.). 76p. (J). (gr. -1). pap. 5.99 (978-1-9781-2043-3(5)) CreateSpace Independent Publishing Platform.

—The Jungle Book. (ENG.). (J). (gr. -1). 2019. 294p. pap. (978-3-337-72574-7(0)) 2017. 328p. pap. (978-3-337-31131-5(8)) Creation Pubs.

—The Jungle Book. 2019. (ENG.). 314p. (J). (gr. -1). 26.95 (978-0-526-09355-7(2), Wentworth Pr.) 2019. (ENG.). 314p. (J). (gr. -1). pap. 16.95 (978-0-526-09354-0(4), Wentworth Pr.) 2018. (ENG., Illus.). 330p. (J). pap. 16.95 (978-1-376-44541-1(7)) 2016. (ENG., Illus.). (J). 26.95 (978-1-357-82751-9(2)) 2016. (ENG., Illus.). (J). 26.95 (978-1-357-82674-1(5)) 2016. (ENG., Illus.). (J). (gr. 4-7). 24.95 (978-1-355-20838-9(6)) 2016. (ENG., Illus.). (J). (gr. 4-7). 26.95 (978-1-357-34691-1(3)) 2016. (ENG., Illus.). (J). (gr. 4-7). 26.95 (978-1-354-97623-4(1)) 2015. (ENG., Illus.). (J). (gr. 4-7). 25.95 (978-1-347-30815-8(6)) 2015. (ENG., Illus.). (J). (gr. 4-7). 25.95 (978-1-347-82513-6(4)) 2010. 318p. (gr. 3-7). pap. 30.75 (978-1-142-79715-7(5)) Creative Media Partners, LLC.

—The Jungle Book. Detmold, Edward J. & Detmold, Maurice, illus. 2010. (Calla Editions Ser.). (ENG.). 192p. 30.00 (978-1-60660-009-2(5), 600095) Dover Pubns., Inc.

—The Jungle Book. 2008. (Bring the Classics to Life Ser.). (ENG., Illus.). 72p. (gr. 1-12). pap., act. bk. ed. 10.95 (978-1-55576-355-8(3), EDCTR-109B) EDCON Publishing Group.

—The Jungle Book. 2019. (Faber Children's Classics Ser.). (ENG.). 272p. pap. 8.95 (978-0-571-33490-2(3), Faber & Faber Children's Bks.) Faber & Faber, Inc.

—The Jungle Book. 2009. 122p. (gr. 3-7). pap. 19.99 (978-1-4589-2084-3(4)) General Bks. LLC.

—The Jungle Book. 2017. (ENG., Illus.). (J). (gr. 2-4). pap. (978-3-95940-265-1(1)) Henkea.

—The Jungle Book. (ENG.). (J). 2019. 340p. (gr. 3-9). pap. 36.99 (978-1-7069-2902-4(1)) 2019. 340p. (gr. -1). pap. 14.99 (978-1-7018-2163-7(X)) 2019. 340p. (gr. -1). pap. 14.99 (978-1-6996-3068-6(2)) 2019. 242p. (gr. -1). pap. 12.95 (978-1-6978-9129-4(2)) 2019. 340p. (gr. -1). pap. 19.99 (978-1-6967-9051-2(4)) 2019. 340p. (gr. -1). pap. 19.99 (978-1-6907-1574-0(X)) 2019. 340p. (gr. -1). pap. 19.99 (978-1-6949-5906-5(6)) 2019. 124p. (gr. -1). pap. 7.00 (978-1-6891-0648-1(4)) 2019. 586p. (gr. -1). pap. 38.99 (978-1-0894-9198-9(0)) 2019. 140p. (gr. -1). pap. 9.99 (978-1-0873-5813-0(2)) 2019. 518p. (gr. -1). pap. 34.99 (978-1-0823-8177-5(2)) 2019. 526p. (gr. -1). pap. 31.99 (978-1-0816-6781-8(8)) 2019. 526p. (gr. -1). pap. 29.99 (978-1-0774-0389-5(5)) 2019. 276p. (gr. -1). pap. 29.99 (978-1-0783-8621-0(8)) 2019. 314p. (gr. -1). pap. 21.99 (978-1-0798-9920-7(0)) 2019. 172p. (gr. -1). pap. 12.99 (978-1-0707-4596-1(0)) 2019. 274p. (gr. -1). pap. 19.99 (978-1-0745-7855-8(4)) 2019. 526p. (gr. -1). pap. 29.99 (978-1-0756-3575-5(6)) 2019. 340p. (gr. -1). pap. 23.99 (978-1-0756-8845-4(0)) 2019. 302p. (gr. -1). pap. 17.99 (978-1-0996-1758-4(8)) 2019. 526p. (gr. -1). pap. 29.99 (978-1-0985-3827-9(7)) 2019. 340p. (gr. -1). pap. 19.99 (978-1-0973-3543-5(7)) 2019. 340p. (gr. -1). pap. 19.99 (978-1-0705-9737-9(6)) 2019. 174p. (gr. -1). pap. 12.99 (978-1-0956-3174-4(8)) 2019. 318p. (gr. -1). pap. 17.99 (978-1-0917-4744-9(X)) 2018. (Illus.). 96p. (gr. -1). pap. 7.00 (978-1-7921-9104-6(9)) 2018. (Illus.). 134p. (gr. -1). pap. 12.99 (978-1-7919-1172-0(2)) 2018. (Illus.). 96p. (gr. -1). pap. 7.00 (978-1-7921-6282-4(0)) 2018. (Illus.). 96p. (gr. -1). pap. 7.00 (978-1-7919-5702-5(1)) 2018. 128p. (gr. -1). pap. 6.99 (978-1-7286-4787-6(8)) Independently Published.

—The Jungle Book. 2017. (ENG., Illus.). 110p. (J). (gr. k-2). pap. (978-1-387-29886-0(0)) Lulu Pr., Inc.

—The Jungle Book. 2016. (ENG., Illus.). (J). (gr. 4-7). pap. 7.77 (978-1-62910-056-2(0)) Peach Tree Pr.

—The Jungle Book. 2020. (Green Puffin Classics Ser.). (Illus.). 240p. (J). pap. 15.99 (978-0-241-44075-9(0), Puffin) Penguin Bks., Ltd. GBR. Dist: Independent Pubs. Group.

—The Jungle Book. 2013. (Vintage Children's Classics Ser.). (Illus.). 256p. (J). (gr. 4-7). pap. 10.99 (978-0-09-957302-9(4)) Penguin Random Hse. GBR. Dist: Independent Pubs. Group.

—The Jungle Book. (ENG., Illus.). (J). 2018. 164p. (gr. -1). 24.30 (978-1-7317-0682-9(0)) 2018. 164p. (gr. -1). pap. 12.24 (978-1-7317-0683-6(9)) 2018. 164p. (gr. -1). 12.42 (978-1-7317-0235-7(3)) 2018. 164p. (gr. -1). pap. 5.64 (978-1-7317-0236-4(1)) 2011. 13.99 (978-1-61382-850-2(0)) Simon & Brown.

—The Jungle Book. (ENG., 202p. (J). 2018. Illus.). (978-93-87669-33-8(5)) 2017. (gr. -1). pap. (978-81-935458-6-7(9)) Sumaiyah Distributors Pvt Ltd.

—The Jungle Book. 2018. (ENG., Illus.). 124p. (J). 12.99 (978-1-5154-2892-3(3)) Wilder Pubns., Corp.

—The Jungle Book. 2016. (ENG., Illus.). (J). (gr. 4-7). 16.99 (978-1-4794-2259-3(2)); pap. 5.99 (978-1-4794-2223-4(1)) Wildside Pr., LLC.

—Jungle Book. (ENG.). (J). (gr. 3-9). 2020. 170p. pap. (978-1-77426-042-5(5)) 2019. 142p. pap. (978-1-77426-002-9(6)) East India Publishing Co.

—Jungle Book: The Classic Edition. 2014. (ENG., Illus.). 64p. (J). (gr. -1). 19.99 (978-1-60433-475-3(4)) Cider Mill Pr. Bk. Pubs., LLC.

—The Jungle Books. 2013. (ENG.). 384p. (gr. 12). mass mkt. 5.95 (978-0-451-41918-7(9), Signet) Penguin Publishing Group.

—The Jungle Books. Nagai, Kaori, ed. 2013. 448p. (gr. 12). 11.00 (978-0-14-119665-7(3), Penguin Classics) Penguin Publishing Group.

—The Jungle Books: The Mowgli Stories. Blau, Aljosha, illus. 2015. (ENG.). 240p. (J). (gr. -1-2). 26.95 (978-0-7358-4226-7(4)) North-South Bks., Inc.

Kipling, Rudyard, creator. The Jungle Book. 2016. (ENG., Illus.). (J). (gr. 4-7). pap. (978-1-318-74332-2(X)) HardPr.

Kipling, Rudyard & Ladybird Books Staff. The Jungle Book. Bernstein, Galia, illus. 2015. (Ladybird Classics Ser.). 72p. (J). (gr. 3-7). 10.99 (978-1-4093-1358-8(1)) Penguin Bks., Ltd. GBR. Dist: Independent Pubs. Group.

Kipling, Rudyard & Riazi, Karuna. The Jungle Book. 2019. (Ghostwriter Ser.). 144p. (J). (gr. 3-9). 12.99 (978-1-7282-2153-3(6)) Sourcebooks, Inc.

Kipling, Rudyard, et al. The Jungle Book. (ENG.). (J). 2019. 368p. (gr. -1). 27.95 (978-0-526-38229-3(5), Wentworth Pr.) 2019. 368p. (gr. -1). pap. 17.95 (978-0-526-38228-6(7), Wentworth Pr.) 2016. (Illus.). (gr. 4-7). 26.95 (978-1-356-03624-0(4)) Creative Media Partners, LLC.

Rowe, John, ed. The Jungle Book. (J). reprint ed. lib. bdg. 24.95 (978-0-88411-819-0(3)) Amereon Ltd.

Thorne, Jenny, illus. The Jungle Book. 2016. 24p. (J). (gr. -1-12). pap. 7.99 (978-1-86147-814-6(3), Armadillo) Anness Publishing GBR. Dist: National Bk. Network.

MOZART, WOLFGANG AMADEUS, 1756-1791

Allman, Barbara. Musical Genius: A Story about Wolfgang Amadeus Mozart. Hamlin, Janet, illus. 2004. (Creative Minds Biographies Ser.). (ENG.). 64p. (gr. 4-8). (J). per. 9.99 (978-1-57505-637-1(2), c8fa1f85-1761-4416-8dc7-c1f46f8efdc2); 22.60 (978-1-57505-604-3(6)) Lerner Publishing Group.

Bailey, Gerry & Foster, Karen. Mozart's Wig, 1 vol. 2008. (Stories of Great People Ser.). (ENG., Illus.). 40p. (J). (gr. 3-6). pap. (978-0-7787-3718-6(7)) Crabtree Publishing Co.

—Mozart's Wig. Noyes, Leighton & Radford, Karen, illus. 2008. (Stories of Great People Ser.). (ENG.). 40p. (J). (gr. 3-6). lib. bdg. (978-0-7787-3696-7(2)) Crabtree Publishing Co.

Beth, Georgia. 18th Century Superstar: Mozart. 2nd rev. ed. 2017. (TIME(r): Informational Text Ser.). (ENG., Illus.). 32p. (J). (gr. 6-8). pap. 13.99 (978-1-4938-3631-4(5)) Teacher Created Materials, Inc.

—18th Century Superstar: Mozart. 2017. (Time for Kids Nonfiction Readers Ser.). lib. bdg. 19.65 (978-0-606-40268-2(3)) Turtleback.

Bodden, Valerie. Wolfgang Amadeus Mozart. 2017. (Odysseys in Artistry Ser.). (ENG., Illus.). 80p. (J). (gr. 7-11). pap. 14.99 (978-1-62832-318-4(3), 20666, Creative Paperbacks) Creative Co., The.

Brighton, Catherine. Mozart. 2004. (Illus.). 30p. (J). pap. (978-1-84507-212-4(X)) ReiseArt Buchhandlung GmbH.

Cook, Diane. Wolfgang Amadeus Mozart: World-Famous Composer. (Illus.). 32p. (J). 2013. (People of Importance Ser.: 21). (gr. 4-18). 19.95 (978-1-4222-2860-9(6)) 2004. (Great Names Ser.). (gr. 3-18). lib. bdg. 19.95 (978-1-59084-159-4(X)) Mason Crest.

Cooke, Tim. Mozart, 1 vol. 2016. (Meet the Greats Ser.). (ENG.). 48p. (J). (gr. 5-5). pap. 15.65 (978-1-4824-5956-2(6), 9e3bb5eb-2c2f-4548-b951-1e5f2c130541) Stevens, Gareth Publishing LLLP.

Dunn, Mary. My Adventure with Mozart. 2006. 44p. (J). 8.99 *(978-1-59092-459-4(2))* Blue Forge Pr.

Kaufmann, Helen L. The Story of Mozart. Meadowcroft, Enid Lamonte, ed. Simon, Eric M., illus. 2011. 190p. 42.95 *(978-1-258-06631-4(9))* Literary Licensing, LLC.

Loh-Hagan, Virginia. The Real Wolfgang Amadeus Mozart. 2019. (History Uncut Ser.). (ENG., Illus.). 32p. (J). (gr. 4-8). pap. 14.21 *(978-1-5341-3991-6(5),* 212793); lib. bdg. 32.07 *(978-1-5341-4335-7(1),* 212792) Cherry Lake Publishing. (45th Parallel Press).

Loria, Laura. Wolfgang Amadeus Mozart, 1 vol. 2014. (Britannica Beginner Bios Ser.). (ENG.). 32p. (J). (gr. 2-3). 26.06 *(978-1-62275-681-0(9),* 1feb4e0b-c798-4803-914c-168cd3814afa, Britannica Educational Publishing) Rosen Publishing Group, Inc., The.

McDonough, Yona Zeldis. Who Was Wolfgang Amadeus Mozart? 2003. (Who Was... ? Ser.). (gr. 3-6). 16.00 *(978-0-613-61669-0(3))* Turtleback.

McDonough, Yona Zeldis & Who HQ. Who Was Wolfgang Amadeus Mozart? Robbins, Carrie, illus. 2003. (Who Was? Ser.). 112p. (J). (gr. 3-7). pap. 5.99 *(978-0-448-43104-8(1),* Penguin Workshop) Penguin Young Readers Group.

Murtagh, Ciaran. The Making of Mozart: Band 12/Copper. 2017. (Collins Big Cat Ser.). (ENG., Illus.). 32p. (J). pap. 7.99 *(978-0-00-820876-9(X))* HarperCollins Pubs. Ltd. GBR. Dist: Independent Pubs. Group.

Riggs, Kate. Wolfgang Amadeus Mozart. (Odysseys in Artistry Ser.). (ENG., Illus.). (J). 2016. 80p. (gr. 7-10). *(978-1-60818-722-5(5),* 20667) 2008. 48p. (gr. 5-8). lib. bdg. 22.95 *(978-1-58341-664-8(1),* 22319) Creative Co., The. (Creative Education).

Ross, Stewart. The Story of Wolfgang Amadeus Mozart. (Lifetimes Ser.). (Illus.). 48p. (J). lib. bdg. 28.50 *(978-1-931983-14-3(3))* Chrysalis Education.

Sís, Peter. Play, Mozart, Play! Sís, Peter, illus. 2006. (Illus.). 32p. (J). (gr. -1-3). 16.99 *(978-0-06-112181-4(9),* Greenwillow Bks.) HarperCollins Pubs.

Summerer, Eric. Wolfgang Amadeus Mozart. 2006. 36p. pap. 21.25 *(978-1-4358-3796-6(7),* PowerKids Pr.) Rosen Publishing Group, Inc., The.

Summerer, Eric Michael. Wolfgang Amadeus Mozart. 2009. (Primary Source Library of Famous Composers Ser.). 32p. (gr. 4-4). 42.50 *(978-1-60854-115-7(0),* PowerKids Pr.) Rosen Publishing Group, Inc., The.

Turner, Barrie Carson. Mozart. 2003. (Famous Childhoods Ser.). (Illus.). (J). lib. bdg. 24.25 *(978-1-59389-115-2(6))* Chrysalis Education.

Weeks, Marcus. World History Biographies: Mozart: The Boy Who Changed the World with His Music. 2013. (National Geographic World History Biographies Ser.). (Illus.). 64p. (J). (gr. 3-7). pap. 7.99 *(978-1-4263-1451-3(5),* National Geographic Kids) Disney Publishing Worldwide.

MOZART, WOLFGANG AMADEUS, 1756-1791—FICTION

Lu, Marie. The Kingdom of Back. 336p. (YA). (gr. 7). 2021. pap. 12.99 *(978-1-5247-3903-4(0),* Penguin Books) 2020. (Illus.). 18.99 *(978-1-5247-3901-0(4),* G.P. Putnam's Sons Books for Young Readers) Penguin Young Readers Group.

—The Kingdom of Back. 2019. (ENG.). 336p. lib. bdg. 22.80 *(978-1-6636-2728-5(2))* Perfection Learning Corp.

Muir, Sabine. Meeting Wolfie: A Story about Mozart. 2006. 129p. pap. 19.95 *(978-1-4241-3968-2(6))* PublishAmerica, Inc.

Stilton, Geronimo. Geronimo Stilton Graphic Novels #8: Play It Again, Mozart!, Vol. 8. 2011. (Geronimo Stilton Graphic Novels Ser.: 8). (ENG., Illus.). 56p. (J). (gr. 2-6). 9.99 *(978-1-59707-276-2(1),* 900078848, Papercutz) Mad Cave Studios.

Turnbull, Ann. Mary Ann & Miss Mozart. 2009. (Historical House Ser.). 166p. (YA). (gr. 5-18). pap. 5.99 *(978-0-7945-2332-9(3))* Usborne) EDC Publishing.

MUDGE (FICTITIOUS CHARACTER)—FICTION

Henry & Mudge Book Set 800925, 6 vols. 2005. (J). pap. *(978-1-59794-090-0(9))* Environments, Inc.

Rylant, Cynthia. Annie & Snowball & the Teacup Club: Ready-To-Read Level 2. Stevenson, Suçie & Stevenson, Suçie, illus. 2009. (Annie & Snowball Ser.: 3). (ENG.). 40p. (J). (gr. k-2). pap. 4.99 *(978-1-4169-1461-7(7),* Simon Spotlight) Simon Spotlight.

—Henry & Mudge & a Very Merry Christmas: Ready-To-Read Level 2. Stevenson, Suçie & Stevenson, Suçie, illus. 2004. (Henry & Mudge Ser.: 25). (ENG.). 40p. (J). (gr. k-2). 17.99 *(978-0-689-81168-5(3),* Simon Spotlight) Simon Spotlight.

—Henry & Mudge & Mrs. Hopper's House: Ready-To-Read Level 2. Bracken, Carolyn, illus. (Henry & Mudge Ser.: 22). (ENG.). 40p. (J). (gr. k-2). 2004. pap. 4.99 *(978-0-689-83446-2(2))* 2003. 17.99 *(978-0-689-81153-1(5))* Simon Spotlight. (Simon Spotlight).

—Henry & Mudge & the Big Sleepover: Ready-To-Read Level 2. Stevenson, Suçie et al, illus. 2006. (Henry & Mudge Ser.: 28). (ENG.). 40p. (J). (gr. k-2). 17.99 *(978-0-689-81171-5(3),* Simon Spotlight) Simon Spotlight.

—Henry & Mudge & the Big Sleepover: Ready-To-Read Level 2, Bk. 28. Stevenson, Suçie & Stevenson, Suçie, illus. 2007. (Henry & Mudge Ser.: 28). (ENG.). 40p. (J). (gr. k-2). pap. 4.99 *(978-0-689-83451-6(9),* Simon Spotlight) Simon Spotlight.

—Henry & Mudge & the Funny Lunch: Ready-To-Read Level 2. Bracken, Carolyn, illus. 2004. (Henry & Mudge Ser.: 24). (ENG.). 40p. (J). (gr. k-2). 17.99 *(978-0-689-81178-4(0),* Simon Spotlight) Simon Spotlight.

—Henry & Mudge & the Great Grandpas: Ready-To-Read Level 2. Stevenson, Suçie et al, illus. 2005. (Henry & Mudge Ser.: 26). (ENG.). 40p. (J). (gr. k-2). 17.99 *(978-0-689-81170-8(5),* Simon Spotlight) Simon Spotlight.

—Henry & Mudge & the Tumbling Trip: Ready-To-Read Level 2. Bracken, Carolyn, illus. 2005. (Henry & Mudge Ser.: 27). (ENG.). 40p. (J). (gr. k-2). 17.99 *(978-0-689-81180-7(2),* Simon Spotlight) Simon Spotlight.

—Henry & Mudge & the Wild Goose Chase: Ready-To-Read Level 2. 2004. (Henry & Mudge Ser.: 23). (ENG., Illus.). 40p. (J). (gr. k-2). pap. 4.99 *(978-0-689-83450-9(0),* Simon Spotlight) Simon Spotlight.

—Henry & Mudge & the Wild Goose Chase: Ready-To-Read Level 2. Bracken, Carolyn, illus. 2003. (Henry & Mudge Ser.: 23). (ENG.). 40p. (J). (gr. k-2). 17.99 *(978-0-689-81172-2(1),* Simon Spotlight) Simon Spotlight.

—Puppy Mudge Has a Snack: Ready-To-Read Pre-Level 1. Mones, Isidre, illus. 2004. (Puppy Mudge Ser.). (ENG.). 32p. (J). (gr. -1-k). pap. 4.99 *(978-0-689-86995-2(9),* Simon Spotlight) Simon Spotlight.

Stevenson, Suçie, illus. Henry & Mudge Collector's Set (Boxed Set) Henry & Mudge; Henry & Mudge in Puddle Trouble; Henry & Mudge in the Green Time; Henry & Mudge under the Yellow Moon; Henry & Mudge in the Sparkle Days; Henry & Mudge & the Forever Sea. 2014. (Henry & Mudge Ser.). (ENG.). 280p. (J). (gr. k-2). pap. 17.99 *(978-1-4814-2147-8(6),* Simon Spotlight) Simon Spotlight.

MUHAMMAD, PROPHET, -632

Abou El Azm, Mohsen, illus. Muhammad: The Life of the Prophet. adapted ed. 2014. (ENG.). 64p. pap. 7.95 *(978-1-906230-62-3(5))* Real Reads Ltd. GBR. Dist: Casemate Pubs. & Bk. Distributors, LLC.

Büyüksahin, Mehmet, et al. Khadija Bint Khuwaylid. 2016. (Age of Bliss Ser.). (ENG.). 80p. (J). (gr. 4-8). pap. 5.95 *(978-1-59784-375-1(X),* Tughra Bks.) Blue Dome, Inc.

Caglaroglu, Nurefsan. Awaiting the Prophet. (J). (gr. 2-5). 2019. (Illus.). 96p. pap. 16.95 *(978-1-59784-935-7(9))* 2008. (ENG.). 16p. pap. 12.95 *(978-1-59784-126-9(9))* Blue Dome, Inc. (Tughra Bks.).

Cohn, Jessica. Muhammad: Prophet of Islam, 1 vol. rev. ed. 2012. (Social Studies: Informational Text Ser.). (ENG.). 32p. (gr. 4-8). pap. 11.99 *(978-1-4333-5004-7(1))* Teacher Created Materials, Inc.

Haylamaz, Resit. Abu Bakr: The Pinnacle of Truthfulness. 2011. (ENG.). 175p. (J). (gr. 8-11). pap. 9.95 *(978-1-59784-250-1(8),* Tughra Bks.) Blue Dome, Inc.

—Ali: Hero of Chivalry. 2011. 142p. (J). (gr. 5-8). pap. 9.95 *(978-1-59784-253-2(2),* Tughra Bks.) Blue Dome, Inc.

—The Luminous Life of Our Prophet. 2014. (ENG.). 365p. pap. 14.95 *(978-1-59784-310-2(5),* Tughra Bks.) Blue Dome, Inc.

—Zayd: The Rose That Bloomed in Captivity. 2011. 88p. (J). (gr. -1-12). pap. 7.50 *(978-1-59784-247-1(8),* Tughra Bks.) Blue Dome, Inc.

Murad, Khurram. Stories of the Broken Idol & the Jewish Rabbi. 2007. (ENG., Illus.). 28p. pap. 3.95 *(978-0-86037-151-9(4))* Kube Publishing Ltd. GBR. Dist: Consortium Bk. Sales & Distribution.

—The Wise Poet: Story of Al-Tufayl Bin'Amir. 2007. (ENG., Illus.). 24p. pap. 3.95 *(978-0-86037-150-2(6))* Kube Publishing Ltd. GBR. Dist: Consortium Bk. Sales & Distribution.

Oral, Osman. I Believe in the Prophets. 2013. (J). *(978-1-59784-305-8(9),* Tughra Bks.) Blue Dome, Inc.

Oze, Ozkan. I Wonder about the Prophet. Ayduz, Selma, tr. 2016. (ENG., Illus.). 120p. (J). pap. 10.95 *(978-0-86037-508-1(0))* Kube Publishing Ltd. GBR. Dist: Consortium Bk. Sales & Distribution.

Pike, E. Royston. Mohammed: Founder of the Religion of Islam. 2011. 134p. 40.95 *(978-1-258-00657-0(X))* Literary Licensing, LLC.

Taib, Saadah. Prophet Muhammad & the Crying Camel Activity Book. Rosli, Shazana, illus. 2019. (Prophets of Islam Activity Bks.). (ENG.). 16p. (J). pap. 3.95 *(978-0-86037-634-7(6))* Kube Publishing Ltd. GBR. Dist: Consortium Bk. Sales & Distribution.

Tarantino, Mardijah Aldrich. Marvelous Stories from the Life of Muhammad. 2012. (ENG., Illus.). 120p. (J). (gr. 2-7). pap. 8.95 *(978-0-86037-103-8(4))* Kube Publishing Ltd. GBR. Dist: Consortium Bk. Sales & Distribution.

MUHAMMAD ALI, 1942-

see Ali, Muhammad, 1942-2016

MUIR, JOHN, 1838-1914

Archer, Jules. To Save the Earth: The American Environmental Movement. 2016. (Jules Archer History for Young Readers Ser.). (ENG., Illus.). 200p. (J). (gr. 6-6). 16.99 *(978-1-63450-196-5(9),* Sky Pony Pr.) Skyhorse Publishing Co., Inc.

Danneberg, Julie. John Muir Wrestles a Waterfall. Hogan, Jamie, illus. 2015. (ENG.). 32p. (J). (gr. -1-3). lib. bdg. 17.99 *(978-1-58089-586-6(7))* Charlesbridge Publishing, Inc.

Devera, Czeena. John Muir. Bane, Jeff, illus. 2017. (My Early Library: My Itty-Bitty Bio Ser.). (ENG.). 24p. (J). (gr. k-1). lib. bdg. 30.64 *(978-1-63472-814-0(9),* 209682) Cherry Lake Publishing.

Elliot, Henry. John Muir: Protecting & Preserving the Environment. 2009. (Voices for Green Choices Ser.). (ENG., Illus.). 48p. (J). (gr. 5-9). pap. *(978-0-7787-4681-2(X));* lib. bdg. *(978-0-7787-4668-3(2))* Crabtree Publishing Co.

Goldstein, Natalie. John Muir. 2011. (ENG., Illus.). 144p. (gr. 6-12). 35.00 *(978-1-60413-945-7(5),* P189956, Facts On File) Infobase Holdings, Inc.

Kiely Miller, Barbara. John Muir, 1 vol. 2007. (Grandes Personajes (Great Americans) Ser.). 24p. (gr. 2-4). (SPA.). pap. 9.15 *(978-0-8368-8339-8(X),* 027deba2-1d65-4f22-afdd-b25c74e7ca0c); (ENG.). lib. bdg. 24.67 *(978-0-8368-8318-3(7),* 86d24b9e-cde3-4ee8-a2b1-a311970c63af); (SPA.). lib. bdg. 24.67 *(978-0-8368-8332-9(2),* fc2fd432-5fd4-462b-87ac-0011ba6ede2f) Stevens, Gareth Publishing LLLP. (Weekly Reader Leveled Readers).

Koehler-Pentacoff, Elizabeth. John Muir & Stickeen: An Alaskan Adventure. Swanson, Karl W., illus. 2003. (Single Titles Ser.). 32p. (J). 14.95 *(978-0-7613-1997-9(2))* Lerner Publishing Group.

—John Muir & Stickeen: An Alaskan Adventure. Swanson, Karl, illus. 2003. (Single Titles Ser.). (ENG.). 32p. (J). (gr. 4-8). lib. bdg. 15.95 *(978-0-7613-2769-1(X),* Millbrook Pr.) Lerner Publishing Group.

Locker, Thomas. John Muir: America's Naturalist. 2010. (ENG.). 32p. (J). (gr. -1-3). pap. 12.95 *(978-1-55591-705-0(4))* Fulcrum Publishing.

Maynard, Charles W. John Muir: Naturalist & Explorer. 2009. (Famous Explorers of the American West Ser.). 24p. (gr. 3-4). 42.50 *(978-1-61512-504-3(3),* PowerKids Pr.) Rosen Publishing Group, Inc., The.

Muir, John. Stickeen. Buell, Carl Dennis, illus. Date not set. 94p. (J). 16.95 *(978-0-8488-2803-5(8))* Amereon Ltd.

—Stickeen. 2017. (ENG., Illus.). (J). pap. 6.90 *(978-1-366-50427-2(5))* Blurb, Inc.

—Stickeen. (ENG.). (J). 2022. 90p. 24.95 *(978-1-01-546358-5(4))* 2022. 90p. pap. 12.95 *(978-1-01-546823-8(3))* 2018. 92p. pap. 10.95 *(978-0-341-70482-9(2))* 2018. 90p. pap. 10.95 *(978-0-343-00064-6(4))* 2017. (Illus.). pap. 10.95 *(978-1-375-43113-2(7))* 2017. (Illus.). pap. 10.95 *(978-1-376-05017-2(X))* 2016. (Illus.). 21.95 *(978-1-359-77363-0(0))* Creative Media Partners, LLC.

—Stickeen. 2020. (ENG.). 24p. (J). pap. 5.99 *(978-1-4209-7046-3(1))* Digireads.com Publishing.

—Stickeen. 2019. (ENG., (J), Illus.). 40p. pap. 6.97 *(978-1-6913-8242-2(6));* 34p. pap. 5.87 *(978-1-0869-5120-2(4));* 34p. pap. 5.98 *(978-1-0867-1738-9(4));* (Illus.). 34p. pap. 6.55 *(978-1-6876-4452-7(7))* Independently Published.

—Stickeen. 2017. (ENG., Illus.). (J). pap. *(978-0-649-39800-3(9))* Trieste Publishing Pty Ltd.

—Stickeen. Buell, Carl Dennis, illus. 2008. (ENG.). 96p. (J). (gr. 3-5). reprint ed. pap. 10.00 *(978-0-930588-48-9(7))* Heyday.

Rosenstock, Barb. The Camping Trip That Changed America: Theodore Roosevelt, John Muir, & Our National Parks. Gerstein, Mordecai, illus. 2012. 32p. (J). (gr. 1-3). 18.99 *(978-0-8037-3710-5(6),* Dial Bks) Penguin Young Readers Group.

Wadsworth, Ginger. Camping with the President. Dugan, Karen, illus. 2009. (ENG.). 32p. (J). (gr. 2-5). 16.99 *(978-1-59078-497-6(9),* Calkins Creek) Highlights Pr., c/o Highlights for Children, Inc.

MULDER, FOX (FICTITIOUS CHARACTER)—FICTION

Smith, Kim, illus. The X-Files: Earth Children Are Weird: A Picture Book. 2017. (Pop Classics Ser.: 2). 40p. (J). (gr. -1-3). 18.99 *(978-1-59474-979-7(5))* Quirk Bks.

MULES

Goldish, Meish & Parkhurst, Anthony. Horses, Donkeys, & Mules in the Marines. 2012. (America's Animal Soldiers Ser.). 24p. (J). (gr. 1-6). lib. bdg. 26.99 *(978-1-61772-453-4(X))* Bearport Publishing Co., Inc.

Graubart, Norman D. Mules in American History, 1 vol. 2014. (How Animals Shaped History Ser.). (ENG., Illus.). 24p. (J). (gr. 2-3). 25.27 *(978-1-4777-6769-6(X),* 2acdea89-51bd-4468-909e-d1f96826461c, PowerKids Pr.) Rosen Publishing Group, Inc., The.

Schmid, Diana J. Samule the Worthless White Mule. 2009. 24p. pap. 12.49 *(978-1-4490-0032-5(0))* AuthorHouse.

MULES—FICTION

Buzel, Alita. The Adventures of Jedediah the Mule: Book One. 2010. (ENG.). 116p. 24.95 *(978-1-4520-4336-4(1));* pap. 12.95 *(978-1-4520-4337-1(X))* AuthorHouse.

Coxe, Molly. Blues for Unicorn. 2019. (Bright Owl Bks.). (Illus.). 40p. (J). (gr. -1-2). 17.99 *(978-1-63592-109-0(0),* 4d7b72dd-81cd-4c1e-814c-6500c4591452); pap. 6.99 *(978-1-63592-110-6(4),* 52e6d08c-51b4-4aad-91f4-67b0c8896404) Astra Publishing Hse. (Kane Press).

Grovet, Heather. Sarah Lee & a Mule Named Maybe. 2003. (Pathfinder Junior Book Club Ser.). 136p. (J). pap. 7.99 *(978-0-8280-1725-1(5),* 191-530) Review & Herald Publishing Assn.

Hammond, Jenna. Downward Mule. Page, Steve, illus. 2017. (ENG.). (J). (gr. k-4). 17.99 *(978-1-365-44567-5(4));* pap. 13.99 *(978-1-365-44564-4(X))* Lulu Pr., Inc.

—Downward Mule Dyslexic Font. Page, Steve, illus. 2017. (ENG.). (J). (gr. k-6). pap. 13.99 *(978-1-365-44566-8(6))* Lulu Pr., Inc.

Hodges, Meredith. Jasper: A Christmas Caper. Shields, Bonnie, illus. 2004. 85p. (J). 24.95 *(978-1-928624-20-2(0))* Lucky 3 Ranch, Inc.

—Jasper: A Fabulous Fourth. Shields, Bonnie, illus. 2006. 83p. (J). *(978-1-928624-24-0(3))* Lucky 3 Ranch, Inc.

—Jasper: The Story of a Mule. Shields, Bonnie, illus. 2003. 245p. (J). (gr. k-7). 39.95 *(978-0-9702309-8-0(2))* Lucky 3 Ranch, Inc.

Hopkinson, Deborah. From Slave to Soldier: Based on a True Civil War Story (Ready-To-Read Level 3) Floca, Brian, illus. (Ready-To-Read Ser.). (ENG.). 48p. (J). (gr. 1-3). 2007. pap. 4.99 *(978-0-689-83966-5(9))* 2005. 16.99 *(978-0-689-83965-8(0))* Simon Spotlight. (Simon Spotlight).

Huston, Donna. Mr. O'Toole, the Diabetic Mule. 2006. (J). spiral bd. 19.95 *(978-0-9771192-2-6(X))* Shayne Publishing.

Nash, Andy. Melinda & Her Mule: For Kids Blessed with a Strong Will. 2008. (J). *(978-0-8127-0453-2(3))* Autumn Hse. Publishing Co.

Rae Strawn, Evelyn. Moncho the Mule. 2010. 24p. 12.99 *(978-1-4389-8751-4(X))* AuthorHouse.

Ramsey, Calvin Alexander & Stroud, Bettye. Belle, the Last Mule at Gee's Bend: A Civil Rights Story. Holyfield, John, illus. 2016. (ENG.). 32p. (J). (gr. k-3). 8.99 *(978-0-7636-8769-4(3))* Candlewick Pr.

Root, Alice. A Job for Deirdre. 2010. (ENG.). 69p. pap. 24.70 *(978-0-557-23363-2(1))* Lulu Pr., Inc.

—What Is a Mule? 2010. 17p. 9.10 *(978-0-557-19648-7(5))* Lulu Pr., Inc.

Schmauss, Judy Kentor. Luke's Mule. 2006. (Reader's Clubhouse Level 2 Reader Ser.). (Illus.). 24p. (J). (gr. k-1). pap. 3.99 *(978-0-7641-3297-1(0))* Sourcebooks, Inc.

Sommer, Carl. Tied up in Knots(Enredados) Budwine, Greg, illus. 2009. (Another Sommer-Time Story Bilingual Ser.). (SPA & ENG.). 48p. (J). lib. bdg. 16.95 *(978-1-57537-169-6(3))* Advance Publishing, Inc.

Wilson, Douglas. Maude, the Flop-Eared Mule. Fore, Elizabeth, illus. 2012. 38p. 24.95 *(978-1-4626-7455-8(0))* America Star Bks.

MULTICULTURAL EDUCATION

Alexander, Linda B. & Kwon, Nahyun. Multicultural Programs for Tweens & Teens. 2010. (ENG.). 216p. pap. 52.00 *(978-0-8389-3582-8(6))* American Library Assn.

Pugliano-Martin, Carol. Making Crafts from Around the World & Artesanías del Mundo: 6 English, 6 Spanish Adaptations. 2011. (ENG & SPA.). (J). 89.00 net. *(978-1-4108-5674-6(7))* Benchmark Education Co.

Tabor, Nancy Maria Grande. Somos un Arco Iris (We Are a Rainbow) Tabor, Nancy Maria Grande, illus. 2006. (ENG & SPA., Illus.). 28p. (gr. -1-3). 17.95 *(978-0-7569-7027-7(X))* Perfection Learning Corp.

MULTICULTURAL EDUCATION—FICTION

Mycek-Wodecki, Anna. The Bilingual Dog, 1 vol. Abt, Diana, tr. Mycek-Wodecki, Anna, illus. 2008. (Minutka Ser.). (ENG., Illus.). 48p. (J). (gr. -1-k). 9.95 *(978-1-84059-509-3(4))* Milet Publishing.

—The Bilingual Dog/Iki Dili Kopek, 1 vol. Erdogan, Fatih, tr. Mycek-Wodecki, Anna, illus. 2008. (Minutka Ser.). (ENG., Illus.). 48p. (J). (gr. -1-k). 9.95 *(978-1-84059-510-9(8))* Milet Publishing.

MULTICULTURALISM

Here are entered works on policies or programs that foster the preservation of different cultural identities, including customs, languages, and beliefs, within a unified society such as a state or nation.

Ajmera, Maya, et al. Healthy Kids. 2013. (Global Fund for Children Bks.). (Illus.). 32p. (J). (gr. -1-3). (ENG.). pap. 7.95 *(978-1-58089-437-1(2));* lib. bdg. 17.95 *(978-1-58089-436-4(4))* Charlesbridge Publishing, Inc.

Anderson, Joanna. The Many People of America, 1 vol. 2012. (I'm an American Citizen Ser.). (ENG., Illus.). 24p. (J). (gr. 1-2). 26.27 *(978-1-4488-8591-6(4),* d0f7d528-ba0f-4f24-85e6-957351610874, PowerKids Pr.) Rosen Publishing Group, Inc., The.

Anthony, David. What's Diversity?, 1 vol. 2018. (What's the Issue? Ser.). (ENG.). 24p. (gr. 3-3). pap. 9.25 *(978-1-5345-2800-0(8),* 06d4ff8f-09d1-4f72-8a92-8ba702fbbee4, KidHaven Publishing) Greenhaven Publishing LLC.

Behrens, Janice. We Are Alike, We Are Different. 2009. (Scholastic News Nonfiction Readers Ser.). (ENG.). 24p. (J). (gr. 1-2). lib. bdg. 22.00 *(978-0-531-21347-6(1))* Scholastic Library Publishing.

—We Are Alike, We Are Different (Scholastic News Nonfiction Readers: We the Kids) 2009. (Scholastic News Nonfiction Readers Ser.). (ENG.). 24p. (J). (gr. 1-2). pap. 6.95 *(978-0-531-21447-3(8),* Children's Pr.) Scholastic Library Publishing.

Crayton, Lisa A. Everything You Need to Know about Cultural Appropriation, 1 vol. 2018. (Need to Know Library). (ENG.). 64p. (gr. 6-6). 36.13 *(978-1-5081-7918-4(2),* 70cd9e07-163a-45d5-821d-570c5cbb28fc) Rosen Publishing Group, Inc., The.

Fox, Mem. Whoever You Are Board Book. Staub, Leslie, illus. 2017.Tr. of Sé de¿it Mak Ó. (ENG.). 28p. (J). (— 1). bds. 7.99 *(978-1-328-89581-3(5),* 1699665, Clarion Bks.) HarperCollins Pubs.

Geisen, Cynthia. You Are You, I Am Me: Understanding Diversity. Alley, R. W., illus. 2016. 32p. (J). pap. 7.95 *(978-0-87029-699-4(X))* Abbey Pr.

Gitlin, Martin, ed. National Identity, 1 vol. 2019. (Global Viewpoints Ser.). (ENG.). 176p. (gr. 10-12). pap. 32.70 *(978-1-5345-0655-8(1),* e1c9680f-d5bd-4eb3-8533-196aa93e1e71, Greenhaven Publishing) Greenhaven Publishing LLC.

Higgins, Melissa. We All Come from Different Cultures, 1 vol. 2012. (Celebrating Differences Ser.). (ENG.). 24p. (J). (gr. -1-2). pap. 7.29 *(978-1-4296-7887-2(9),* 118219); (gr. k-1). pap. 41.70 *(978-1-4296-8320-3(1),* Capstone Pr.) Capstone.

Hindley, Anna Forgerson & Nat'l Mus Afr Am Hist Culture, Nat'l Mus. A Is for All the Things You Are: A Joyful ABC Book. Bobo, Keturah A., illus. 2019. 26p. (J). (— 1). bds. 9.95 *(978-1-58834-650-6(1),* Smithsonian Bks.) Smithsonian Institution Scholarly Pr.

Kerley, Barbara. A Cool Drink of Water. 2006. (Barbara Kerley Photo Inspirations Ser.). (Illus.). 32p. (J). (gr. -1-k). pap. 7.95 *(978-0-7922-5489-8(9),* National Geographic Kids) Disney Publishing Worldwide.

Loewen, Nancy & Skelley, Paula. People of the World. 2015. (Go Go Global Ser.). (ENG., Illus.). 32p. (J). (gr. -1-2). lib. bdg. 27.99 *(978-1-4914-3920-3(3),* 128629, Capstone Pr.) Capstone.

Mader, Jan. Learning about Other People & Cultures, 1 vol. 2017. (Active Citizenship Today Ser.). (ENG.). 32p. (gr. 3-3). pap. 11.58 *(978-1-5026-2924-1(0),* c6316537-0aef-4338-a0e9-6258d0756ed9) Cavendish Square Publishing LLC.

Marwah, Gauri. Tikki Tikki Tembo. 2013. 12p. pap. 7.95 *(978-1-4828-1424-8(2))* Partridge Pub.

McAneney, Caitie. Different but Equal: Appreciating Diversity. 2019. (Spotlight on Social & Emotional Learning Ser.). (ENG.). 24p. (gr. 4-6). 60.00 *(978-1-7253-0670-7(0),* PowerKids Pr.) Rosen Publishing Group, Inc., The.

McIntosh, Kenneth & Walker, Ida. Interpreting an Alien World: Youth with Cultural/Language Differences. 2007. (Helping Youth with Mental, Physical, & Social Challenges Ser.). (Illus.). 128p. (YA). (gr. 8-12). pap. 14.95 *(978-1-4222-0441-2(3))* Mason Crest.

Meet Our New Student, 12 vols., Set. 2008. (J). (gr. 1-5). lib. bdg. 359.40 *(978-1-58415-658-1(9))* Mitchell Lane Pubs.

Ogden, Charlie. Equality & Diversity. 2017. (Our Values - Level 3 Ser.). 32p. (J). (gr. 5-6). *(978-0-7787-3265-5(7))* Crabtree Publishing Co.

Peters, Jennifer, ed. Critical Perspectives on Political Correctness, 1 vol. 2017. (Analyzing the Issues Ser.). (ENG.). 216p. (gr. 8-8). 50.93 *(978-0-7660-9167-2(8),* 361a61f9-0f14-4274-b971-c07f3fc3eb36) Enslow Publishing, LLC.

Robins, Maureen Picard. One Land, Many Cultures. 2012. (Little World Social Studies). (ENG.). 24p. (gr. k-2). pap. 9.95 *(978-1-61810-276-8(1),* 9781618102768) Rourke Educational Media.

Routes of Cross-Cultural Exchange, 16 vols. 2017. (Routes of Cross-Cultural Exchange Ser.). (ENG.). 96p. (gr. 8-8). lib. bdg. 356.00 *(978-1-5026-2681-3(0),* b0344cca-04bd-40ac-abee-f808ce07562a, Cavendish Square) Cavendish Square Publishing LLC.

Samuels, Barbara. Canada's Multicultural Society Today: Multiculturalism in Canada. 2011. 32p. (gr. 5-8). *(978-1-77071-706-0(4));* pap. *(978-1-77071-709-1(9))* Weigl Educational Pubs. Ltd.

—Multiculturalism in Early Canada: Multiculturalism in Canada. 2011. 32p. (gr. 5-8). *(978-1-77071-704-6(8))* Weigl Educational Pubs. Ltd.

Santos, Rita. Appreciating Diversity. 2019. (Working for Social Justice Ser.). (ENG.). 24p. (gr. 3-4). 63.18 *(978-1-9785-0796-8(8))* Enslow Publishing, LLC.

Schramm, Linda Anette. Don't Let the Ziglers into the Zoo! 2004. 31p. pap. 24.95 *(978-1-4137-1541-5(9))* PublishAmerica, Inc.

M N O

Taylor, Charlotte. The United States: a Melting Pot, 1 vol. 2020. (Being a U. S. Citizen Ser.). (ENG.). 24p. (gr. 1-2). pap. 10.35 (978-1-9785-1755-4(6), d09067b2-7a80-40f3-bb12-79a58f1f30c9) Enslow Publishing, LLC.

Teichmann, Iris. A Multicultural World. 2006. (Understanding Immigration Ser.). (Illus.). 44p. (YA). (gr. 5-9). lib. bdg. 31.35 (978-1-58340-969-5(6)) Black Rabbit Bks.

Wachtel, Alan. Southeast Asian Americans, 1 vol. 2010. (New Americans Ser.). (ENG.). 80p. (gr. 5-5). 38.36 (978-0-7614-4312-4(6), b09ef946-1007-40e2-a566-e5a5a14e9a8a) Cavendish Square Publishing LLC.

MULTICULTURALISM—FICTION

Aunt Judy. Chickens on the Go! Chickens from different locations around the World. Aunt Judy, illus. 2nd ed. 2006. (Illus.). 40p. (J). pap. 7.00 (978-0-9780693-0-8(7)) McEwen, Judith A.

Constantine, Cara J. I Can Choose to Be Happy. Barge III, John S., illus. 2012. 32p. 24.95 (978-1-4626-4731-6(6)) America Star Bks.

Gomes, Linda Nunes. Special Words: A Story about Multicultural Families & Their Pets. Levine, Lenora D., illus. 2007. (YA). per. 12.99 (978-1-934400-02-9(5)) Rock Village Publishing.

Gonzales, Mark. Yo Soy Muslim: A Father's Letter to His Daughter. Amini, Mehrdokht, illus. 2017. (ENG.). 32p. (J). (gr. -1-3). 18.99 (978-1-4814-8936-2(4), Simon & Schuster Bks. For Young Readers) Simon & Schuster Bks. For Young Readers.

Hartley, A. J. Guardian: Book 3 in the Steeplejack Series. 2019. (Steeplejack Ser.: 3). (ENG.). 320p. (YA). pap. 17.99 (978-0-7653-8816-2(2), 900162382, Tor Teen) Doherty, Tom Assocs., LLC.

Iyengar, Malathi Michelle. Romina's Rangoli. 2007. (Romina's Rangoli Ser.). (ENG., Illus.). 32p. (J). (gr. -1-3). 16.95 (978-1-885008-32-9(5), Shen's Bks.) Lee & Low Bks., Inc.

Kendi, Ibram X. Antiracist Baby Board Book. Lukashevsky, Ashley, illus. 2020. 24p. (J). (— 1). bds. 8.99 (978-0-593-11041-6(2), Kokila) Penguin Young Readers Group.

—Antiracist Baby Picture Book. Lukashevsky, Ashley, illus. 2020. (ENG.). 32p. (J). (— 1). 8.99 (978-0-593-11050-8(1), Kokila) Penguin Young Readers Group.

Khan, Rukhsana, et al. Many Windows: Six Kids, Five Faiths, One Community. 2008. (ENG., Illus.). 88p. (J). (gr. 4-18). pap. 14.99 (978-1-894917-56-8(1), Napoleon & Co.) Dundurn Pr. CAN. Dist: Publishers Group West (PGW).

Minaki, Christina. Zoe's Extraordinary Holiday Adventures, 1 vol. 2007. (ENG.). 146p. (J). (gr. 2-5). pap. 8.95 (978-1-897187-26-5(2)) Second Story Pr. CAN. Dist: Orca Bk. Pubs. USA.

Murray, Victoria Christopher. Veronique. 2009. (Divas Ser.). (ENG., Illus.). 257p. pap. 11.00 (978-1-4165-6350-1(4), Gallery Bks.) Gallery Bks.

Murrell, Belinda. Lulu Bell & the Arabian Nights. Geddes, Serena, illus. 2015. (Lulu Bell Ser.). 96p. (J). (gr. 1-3). pap. 7.99 (978-0-85798-558-3(2)) Random Hse. Australia AUS. Dist: Independent Pubs. Group.

Penfold, Alexandra. All Are Welcome. Kaufman, Suzanne, illus. 2018. (ENG.). 44p. (J). (gr. -1-3). 17.99 (978-0-525-57964-9(8), Knopf Bks. for Young Readers) Random Hse. Children's Bks.

Reynolds, Peter H. ¡Di Algo! (Say Something!), 1 vol. Reynolds, Peter H., illus. 2019. (SPA., Illus.). 40p. (J). (gr. -1-k). pap. 7.99 (978-1-338-56596-6(6), Scholastic en Espanol) Scholastic, Inc.

—Say Something! Reynolds, Peter H., illus. 2019. (ENG., Illus.). 40p. (J). (gr. -1-3). 17.99 (978-0-545-86503-6(4), Orchard Bks.) Scholastic, Inc.

Robertson, Tammy. Konnichiwa & Hello: Celebrating Diversity. Mash, Brittany, illus. 2014. (J). 19.99 (978-1-945384-07-3(7)) Hawaii Way Publishing.

Rodari, Gianni. One & Seven. Anglin, David, tr. from ITA. Alemagna, Beatrice, illus. 2005. (SPA.). 26p. (J). (gr. k-3). 17.95 (978-0-9628720-6-8(7)) Iaconi, Mariuccia Bk. Imports.

Rusu, Meredith. C Train: A New Beginning. Atuesta, Ángela, illus. 2023. (ENG & SPA.). 32p. (J). 18.99 Circle Tales, The.

Saunders, Sara. Swirly. Pierce, Matthew, illus. 2012. 32p. (J). 7.99 (978-0-8280-2681-9(5)) Review & Herald Publishing Assn.

Selected Children's Stories - Multi Cultural, 3 bks. (Illus.). (J). lib. bdg. 38.85 (978-1-56674-906-0(9)) Forest Hse. Publishing Co., Inc.

Smith Jr., Charles R. I Am the World. 2013. (ENG., Illus.). 48p. (J). (gr. -1-2). 17.99 (978-1-4424-2302-2(1)) Simon & Schuster Children's Publishing.

Suter, Lorenzo. TrYouth Truth Knowledge Apprehension Cog. 2005. (Illus.). 206p. 27.55 (978-1-4122-0095-0(4)) Trafford Publishing.

Theo & the Sisters of Sage: From the Creator of We Are All the Same Inside. 2003. (We Are All the Same Inside Ser.: Vol. 3). (Illus.). 32p. (J). pap. 9.95 (978-0-9718232-1-1(9)) T.I.M.M.-E. Co., Inc.

Tutu, Desmond & Abrams, Douglas Carlton. God's Dream. Pham, LeUyen, illus. 2010. (ENG.). 32p. (J). (— 1). bds. 8.99 (978-0-7636-4742-1(X)) Candlewick Pr.

Winkler, Henry & Oliver, Lin. Holy Enchilada! #6. 2004. (Hank Zipzer Ser.: 6). (ENG., Illus.). 160p. (J). (gr. 3-7). pap. 6.99 (978-0-448-43353-0(2), Grosset & Dunlap) Penguin Young Readers Group.

—The Zippity Zinger #4: The Zippity Zinger the Mostly True Confessions of the World's Best Underachiever, 4 vols. 2004. (Hank Zipzer Ser.: 4). (ENG., Illus.). 160p. (J). (gr. 3-7). mass mkt. 6.99 (978-0-448-43193-2(9), Grosset & Dunlap) Penguin Young Readers Group.

MUMMIES

Ashman, Iain. Egyptian Mummy. 2004. (Cut-Out Models Ser.). (Illus.). 32p. (J). pap. 9.95 (978-0-7945-0255-3(5), Usborne) EDC Publishing.

Biskup, Agnieszka & Ward, Krista. Uncovering Mummies: An Isabel Soto Archaeology Adventure. rev. ed. 2016. (Graphic Expeditions Ser.). (ENG., Illus.). 32p. (J). (gr. 3-9). pap. 8.10 (978-1-5157-6190-7(8), 135046) Capstone.

Bow, James. Forensic Investigations of the Ancient Egyptians. 2018. (Forensic Footprints of Ancient Worlds Ser.). (Illus.). 32p. (J). (gr. 5-5). (978-0-7787-4941-7(X)) Crabtree Publishing Co.

Bower, Tamara. The Mummy Makers of Egypt. 2016. (Illus.). 40p. (J). (gr. 2-5). 18.95 (978-1-60980-600-2(X), Triangle Square) Seven Stories Pr.

Burgan, Michael. Mummy Lairs. 2012. (Scary Places Ser.). 32p. (J). (gr. 4-8). lib. bdg. 25.27 (978-1-61772-568-5(4)) Bearport Publishing Co., Inc.

Carney, Elizabeth. National Geographic Readers: Mummies. 2009. (Readers Ser.). (Illus.). 32p. (J). (gr. 1-3). (ENG.). 14.90 (978-1-4263-0529-0(X)); pap. 4.99 (978-1-4263-0528-3(1)) Disney Publishing Worldwide. (National Geographic Kids).

Cheatham, Mark. Mummies, 1 vol. 2012. (Jr. Graphic Monster Stories Ser.). (ENG.). 24p. (J). (gr. 2-3). pap. 11.60 (978-1-4488-6409-6(7), e986e40e-fe33-4097-bb1e-9ccca4bae23c); lib. bdg. 28.93 (978-1-4488-6225-2(6), 2fcf1765-29ab-4c99-bab8-4c1cdefb9163) Rosen Publishing Group, Inc., The. (PowerKids Pr.).

Clarke, Penny. The Story of Mummies. 2013. (Illus.). 63p. (J). (978-1-4351-5032-4(5)) Barnes & Noble, Inc.

Claybourne, Anna. Mummies Around the World. 2010. (Big Picture: People & Culture Ser.). (ENG.). 24p. (gr. 1-2). pap. 41.70 (978-1-4296-5821-8(5), Capstone Pr.) Capstone.

Davis, Kenneth C. Don't Know Much about Mummies. Date not set. 48p. (J). pap. 5.99 (978-0-06-443645-8(4)) HarperCollins Pubs.

Deem, James M. Bodies from the Ice: Melting Glaciers & the Recovery of the Past. 2008. (ENG., Illus.). 64p. (J). (gr. 3-7). 18.99 (978-0-618-80045-2(X), 552123, Clarion Bks.) HarperCollins Pubs.

Donald, Rhonda Lucas. If a Mummy Could Talk. . 2019. (ENG.). 32p. (J). (gr. k-2). 19.96 (978-1-64310-837-7(9)) Penworthy Co., LLC, The.

Donald, Rhonda Lucas & Morrison, Cathy. Si una Momia Pudiera Hablar... de la Torre, Alejandra, tr. from ENG. Morrison, Cathy, illus. 2019. (SPA., Illus.). (J). pap. 11.95 (978-1-60718-748-6(5)) Arbordale Publishing.

Farndon, John. How to Live Like an Egyptian Mummy Maker. Campidelli, Maurizio, illus. 2016. (How to Live Like ... Ser.). (ENG.). 32p. (J). (gr. 3-6). 27.99 (978-1-5124-0629-0(5), 867fcaa2-0f83-423c-987c-06a8048eb1c1, Hungry Tomato (r)) Lerner Publishing Group.

Fleury, Kevin. Mummies. (Up Close Ser.). 24p. (gr. 3-3). 2009. 47.90 (978-1-60854-698-5(5)) 2006. (ENG., Illus.). (J). lib. bdg. 28.93 (978-1-4042-3761-2(5), d6b05db2-2f1a-43a0-addc-2a00fa28798e) Rosen Publishing Group, Inc., The. (PowerKids Pr.).

Frisch, Aaron. Mummies. 2013. 24p. (J). 25.65 (978-1-60818-247-3(9), Creative Education) Creative Co., The.

Ganeri, Anita. Mummies & Ancient Egypt. 2009. (History Explorers Ser.). (ENG.). 24p. (J). (gr. k-2). pap. 5.95 (978-1-84696-210-3(2), TickTock Books) Octopus Publishing Group GBR. Dist: Independent Pubs. Group.

Griffey, Harriet. Secrets of the Mummies. 2013. (DK Reader Level 4 Ser.). lib. bdg. 13.55 (978-0-606-32438-0(0)) Turtleback.

Hall, Brianna. Mummies of Ancient Egypt. 2012. (Ancient Egyptian Civilization Ser.). (ENG.). 32p. (gr. 3-4). pap. 47.70 (978-1-4296-8403-3(8), Capstone Pr.) Capstone.

Harrison, Paul. Uncovering Mummies & Other Mysteries of the Ancient World. 2010. (Extreme! Ser.). (ENG.). 32p. (gr. 3-4). pap. 47.70 (978-1-4296-5117-2(2), Capstone Pr.) Capstone.

Keyes, Anna. Pharaohs, Pyramids Mummies & Faraones, pirámides y Momias: 6 English, 6 Spanish Adaptations. 2011. (ENG & SPA.). (J). 101.00 net. (978-1-4108-5732-3(8)) Benchmark Education Co.

Knapp, Ron. Mummy Secrets Uncovered, 1 vol. 2011. (Bizarre Science Ser.). (ENG., Illus.). 48p. (gr. 5-7). pap. 11.53 (978-1-59845-222-8(3), ad8860fb-0096-47ca-abfd-86b515141d41); lib. bdg. 27.93 (978-0-7660-3670-3(7), 95e993ce-540d-4db8-b262-4c5ee8377db0) Enslow Publishing, LLC.

—Mysterious Mummies, 1 vol. 2018. (Creepy, Kooky Science Ser.). (ENG.). 48p. (gr. 5-5). 29.60 (978-1-9785-0452-3(7), 8903dbd3-8e9c-4ac7-91b5-bc7052aefeae) Enslow Publishing, LLC.

Krensky, Stephen. The Mummy. 2006. (Monster Chronicles Ser.). (Illus.). 48p. (J). (gr. 5-8). lib. bdg. 26.60 (978-0-8225-5924-5(2), Lerner Pubns.) Lerner Publishing Group.

Lace, William W. Mummification & Death Rituals of Ancient Egypt. 2012. (ENG., Illus.). 80p. (J). lib. bdg. (978-1-60152-254-2(1)) ReferencePoint Pr., Inc.

Logan Hollihan, Kerrie. Mummies Exposed! Creepy & True #1. 2019. (Creepy & True Ser.). (ENG., Illus.). 208p. (J). (gr. 5-9). 16.99 (978-1-4197-3167-9(X), 1171201) Abrams, Inc.

Lucas Donald, Rhonda. If a Mummy Could Talk ... Morrison, Cathy, illus. 2018. (ENG.). 32p. (J). (gr. 1-3). 17.95 (978-1-60718-737-0(X), 9781607187370) Arbordale Publishing.

MacDonald, Fiona. The Amazing History of Mummies & Tombs: Uncover the Secrets of the Egyptian Pyramids & Other Ancient Burial Sites, Shown in over 350 Exciting Pictures. 2016. (Illus.). 64p. (J). (gr. -1-12). 12.99 (978-1-86147-735-4(X), Armadillo) Anness Publishing GBR. Dist: National Bk. Network.

—The Egyptian Mummy. 2011. (History Detectives Ser.). (ENG.). 32p. (J). (gr. 4-7). spiral bd. 9.95 (978-1-84898-186-7(4), TickTock Books) Octopus Publishing Group GBR. Dist: Independent Pubs. Group.

Malam, John. Mummies. (Amazing History Ser.). (Illus.). (J). (gr. 2-6). 2009. 32p. pap. 7.95 (978-1-59920-207-5(7)) 2008. pap. 28.50 (978-1-59920-106-1(2)) Black Rabbit Bks.

—Mummies. 2010. (Remarkable Man & Beast Ser.). 48p. (J). (gr. 3-18). lib. bdg. 19.95 (978-1-4222-1971-3(2)) Mason Crest.

—Mummies, 1 vol. 2014. (100 Facts You Should Know Ser.). (ENG., Illus.). 48p. (J). (gr. 4-5). lib. bdg. 33.60 (978-1-4824-2177-4(1), 60641d9c-6562-49c5-8ece-373b8af2129a) Stevens, Gareth Publishing LLLP.

Malam, John & Kelly, Miles. Mummies. Kelly, Richard, ed. 2017. (Illus.). 48p. (J). pap. 9.95 (978-1-84810-106-7(6)) Miles Kelly Publishing, Ltd. GBR. Dist: Parkwest Pubns., Inc.

Markovics, Joyce. Mummy Tombs. 2017. (Tiptoe into Scary Places Ser.). (ENG., Illus.). 24p. (J). (gr. k-3). lib. bdg. 26.99 (978-1-68402-271-7(1)) Bearport Publishing Co., Inc.

Mason, Roger. Mummies - Mysteries of the Past. 2004. pap. 48.30 (978-1-4109-0283-2(8)) Harcourt Schl. Pubs.

McCall, Henrietta. Egyptian Mummies. 2015. (ENG., Illus.). 32p. (J). pap. 9.95 (978-1-910184-26-4(8)) RiverStream Publishing.

—Mummies. 2015. (Time Shift History Ser.). (Illus.). 32p. (gr. 3-6). 31.35 (978-1-905638-41-3(8)) Book Hse. GBR. Dist: Black Rabbit Bks.

McNeil, Niki, et al. Egyptian Mummies. 2007. (In the Hands of a Child: Project Pack Continent Study Ser.). (Illus.). 52p. spiral bd. 12.50 (978-1-60308-064-4(3)) In the Hands of a Child.

Meachen Rau, Dana. Mummies, 1 vol. 2011. (Surprising Science Ser.). (ENG.). 24p. (gr. 2-2). 25.50 (978-0-7614-4869-3(1), d779c46b-eace-49dc-b188-7cb55ddf827e) Cavendish Square Publishing LLC.

Merwin, E. Tumbas de Momias. 2018. (De Puntillas en Lugares Escalofriantes/Tiptoe into Scary Places Ser.). (SPA.). 24p. (J). (gr. k-3). 18.95 (978-1-68402-615-9(6)) Bearport Publishing Co., Inc.

Momias. 2003. (Megabites Ser.). (SPA., Illus.). (J). pap. 8.95 (978-0-9715256-6-5(8)) Planeta Publishing Corp.

O'Hearn, Michael. Zombies vs. Mummies: Clash of the Living Dead. Moffet, Patricia, illus. 2011. (Monster Wars Ser.). (ENG.). 32p. (gr. 3-4). pap. 47.70 (978-1-4296-7268-9(4), Capstone Pr.) Capstone.

Orme, David. Mummies. 2009. (Fact to Fiction Ser.). (Illus.). 36p. (J). 16.95 (978-0-7569-9281-1(8)); pap. 6.95 (978-0-7891-7904-3(0)) Perfection Learning Corp.

Orme David, David. Mummies. 2007. (Trailblazers Ser.). (ENG., Illus.). 36p. pap. (978-1-84167-427-8(3)) Ransom Publishing Ltd.

Owings, Lisa. The Mummy's Curse. 2015. (Unexplained Mysteries Ser.). (ENG., Illus.). 24p. (J). (gr. 3-7). lib. bdg. 26.95 (978-1-62617-203-6(X), Epic Bks.) Bellwether Media.

Pearson, Marie. Mummies. 2019. (Monster Histories Ser.). (ENG., Illus.). 32p. (J). (gr. 4-6). pap. 7.95 (978-1-5435-7501-9(3), 141031); lib. bdg. 28.65 (978-1-5435-7124-0(7), 140406) Capstone.

Peterson, Megan Cooley. Bog Mummies: Where Did They Come From? 2018. (History's Mysteries Ser.). (ENG.). 32p. (J). (gr. 4-6). pap. 9.99 (978-1-64466-254-0(X), 12269); (Illus.). lib. bdg. (978-1-68072-407-3(X), 12268) Black Rabbit Bks. (Bolt).

Putnam, James. DK Eyewitness Books: Mummy: Discover the Secrets of Mummies — From the Early Embalming, to Bodies Preserved In. 2009. (DK Eyewitness Ser.). (ENG., Illus.). 72p. (J). (gr. 3-7). 16.99 (978-0-7566-4541-0(7), DK Children) Dorling Kindersley Publishing, Inc.

Rice, Dona Herweck. Making a Mummy. rev. ed. 2018. (Smithsonian: Informational Text Ser.). (ENG., Illus.). 32p. (J). (gr. 3-4). pap. 11.99 (978-1-4938-6679-3(6)) Teacher Created Materials, Inc.

Shea, Therese. Mummies of Ancient Egypt, 1 vol. 2008. (Real Life Readers Ser.). (ENG.). 24p. (gr. 3-4). pap. 8.25 (978-1-4358-0052-6(4), 42fd3d07-7209-4b03-a6f9-d6d73181c01d, Rosen Classroom) Rosen Publishing Group, Inc., The.

Shea, Therese M. Mummies Multiply!, 1 vol. 2018. (Monsters Do Math! Ser.). (ENG.). 24p. (gr. 2-3). 24.27 (978-1-5382-2934-7(X), 1b210d55-b27e-4597-9420-d073a046fd31) Stevens, Gareth Publishing LLLP.

Skillet, Helen. Mummies! Unwrapping the Secrets of Ancient Egypt. 2005. (YA). cd-rom (978-1-4105-0411-1(5)) Building Wings LLC.

Sloan, Christopher. Mummies: Dried, Tanned, Sealed, Drained, Frozen, Embalmed, Stuffed, Wrapped, & Smoked... & We're Dead Serious. 2010. (Illus.). 48p. (J). (gr. 3-7). 17.95 (978-1-4263-0695-2(4), National Geographic Kids) Disney Publishing Worldwide.

Small, Cathleen. Mummies, 1 vol. 2016. (Creatures of Fantasy Ser.). (ENG., Illus.). 64p. (gr. 6-6). 35.93 (978-1-5026-1854-2(0), 7dd45538-019f-4ebb-9340-bbddcb8d74f4) Cavendish Square Publishing LLC.

Stewart, David. Creepy Egyptian Mummies, 1 vol. Antram, David, illus. 2010. (Top 10 Worst Ser.). (ENG.). 32p. (J). (gr. 3-5). pap. 11.50 (978-1-4339-4080-4(9), 61cd7c1d-4faf-4b8a-8ce2-e66fd1ae82a9); lib. bdg. 29.27 (978-1-4339-4079-8(5), 67231d0d-c088-4d78-a4c9-820db8a8d9d0) Stevens, Gareth Publishing LLLP. (Gareth Stevens Learning Library).

—You Wouldn't Want to... Be an Egyptian Mummy! Antram, David, illus. rev. ed. 2013. (You Wouldn't Want To... Ser.). (ENG.). 32p. (J). (gr. 4-6). lib. bdg. 26.19 (978-0-531-27501-6(9), Watts, Franklin) Scholastic Library Publishing.

Strom, Laura Layton. The Egyptian Science Gazette. 2008. (Illus.). 36p. (J). pap. (978-0-531-18813-2(2)) Children's Pr., Ltd.

Taplin, Sam. Mummies & Pyramids. 2004. (Discovery Program Ser.). (Illus.). 48p. (J). pap. 8.95 (978-0-7945-0317-8(9), Usborne); lib. bdg. 16.95 (978-1-58086-479-4(1)) EDC Publishing.

Tieck, Sarah. Mummies, 1 vol. 2015. (Creepy Creatures Ser.). (ENG.). 32p. (J). (gr. 2-5). 34.21 (978-1-62403-766-5(6), 17834, Big Buddy Bks.) ABDO Publishing Co.

Tyler, Madeline. Surviving the Rise of the Mummies, 1 vol. 2018. (Surviving the Impossible Ser.). (ENG.). 32p. (gr. 4-5). pap. 11.50 (978-1-5382-3526-3(9), 3e3de852-3379-4781-86b3-ba463c26bf83) Stevens, Gareth Publishing LLLP.

Weakland, Mark Andrew & Collins, Terry Lee. The Truth Behind Mummies. 2016. (ENG., Illus.). 24p. (J). pap. (978-1-4062-8897-1(7)) Capstone.

Wood, Alix. Mummification, 1 vol. Wood, Alix, illus. 2013. (Why'd They Do That? Strange Customs of the Past Ser.). (Illus.). 32p. (J). (gr. 4-5). (ENG.). 29.27 (978-1-4339-9588-0(3), 2c19be32-fcd7-4202-9467-45668cd1e3a2); (ENG., pap. 11.50 (978-1-4339-9589-7(1), f8f72729-84ba-42ce-9d2a-4830bed36ff6); pap. 63.00 (978-1-4339-9590-3(5)) Stevens, Gareth Publishing LLLP.

Woog, Adam. Mummies. 2008. (Mysterious & Unknown Ser.). 104p. (YA). (gr. 7-12). lib. bdg. 41.27 (978-1-60152-054-8(9)) ReferencePoint Pr., Inc.

MUMMIES—FICTION

Bosch, Pseudonymous. You Have to Stop This. (Secret Ser.: 5). (ENG.). (J). (gr. 3-7). 2012. 368p. pap. 9.99 (978-0-316-07627-2(9)) 2011. 352p. 17.99 (978-0-316-07626-5(0)) Little, Brown Bks. for Young Readers.

—You Have to Stop This. 2012. (Secret Ser.: 5). (J). lib. bdg. 18.45 (978-0-606-26695-6(X)) Turtleback.

Bradman, Tony. The Mummy Family Find Fame. 2006. (Red Bananas Ser.). (ENG., Illus.). 48p. (J). (gr. -1-3). lib. bdg. (978-0-7787-1076-9(9)) Crabtree Publishing Co.

Bradman, Tony & Chatterton, Martin. The Surprise Party. 2005. (Red Bananas Ser.). (ENG., Illus.). 48p. (J). (gr. 1-3). (978-0-7787-1084-4(X)) Crabtree Publishing Co.

Branzei, Sylvia. Ickstory: Unraveling the Icky History of Mummies. Keely, Jack, illus. 2009. (Penguin Young Readers, Level 4 Ser.). 48p. (J). (gr. 3-4). mass mkt. 4.99 (978-0-448-45033-9(X), Penguin Young Readers) Penguin Young Readers Group.

Brezenoff, Steve. The Mummy at Midnight. Prothero, Tiffany, illus. 2008. (Shade Bks.). (ENG.). 80p. (J). (gr. 5-9). 25.32 (978-1-4342-0797-5(8), 95202, Stone Arch Bks.) Capstone.

Bright, J. E. Savage Sands, 1 vol. Schoening, Dan, illus. 2011. (Green Lantern Ser.). (ENG.). 56p. (J). (gr. 3-6). pap. 4.95 (978-1-4342-3405-6(3), 116418); lib. bdg. 26.65 (978-1-4342-2619-8(0), 113664) Capstone. (Stone Arch Bks.).

Chatterton, Martin & Bradman, Tony. The Surprise Party. Chatterton, Martin, illus. 2005. (Red Bananas Ser.). (ENG., Illus.). 48p. (J). lib. bdg. (978-0-7787-1068-4(8)) Crabtree Publishing Co.

Crimi, Carolyn. Where's My Mummy? Manders, John, illus. 2008. 32p. (J). (gr. -1-3). 15.99 (978-0-7636-3196-3(5)) Candlewick Pr.

de Gieter, Lucien. The Evil Mummies. Spear, Luke, tr. 2010. (Papyrus Ser.: 4). (Illus.). 46p. (J). (gr. 4-7). pap. 11.95 (978-1-84918-027-6(X)) CineBook GBR. Dist: National Bk. Network.

Donbavand, Tommy. Scream Street: Heart of the Mummy, Bk. 3. Cartoon Saloon, Ltd., illus. 2010. (Scream Street Ser.: 3). (ENG.). 128p. (J). (gr. 3-7). pap. 5.99 (978-0-7636-4636-3(9)) Candlewick Pr.

—Scream Street: Skull of the Skeleton, 5. Cartoon Saloon, Ltd., illus. 2010. (Scream Street Ser.: 5). (ENG.). 128p. (J). (gr. 3-7). pap. 5.99 (978-0-7636-4635-6(0)) Candlewick Pr.

Dougherty, Brandi. The Littlest Mummy (the Littlest Series) Todd, Michelle, illus. 2018. (Littlest Ser.). (ENG.). 24p. (J). (gr. -1-k). pap. 3.99 (978-0-545-81091-3(4), Cartwheel Bks.) Scholastic, Inc.

Duey, Kathleen. Time Soldiers - Mummy. Epstein, Eugene, illus. Gould, Robert, photos by. 2005. (Time Soldiers Ser.: 5). (ENG.). (J). (gr. k-2). 48p. 15.95 (978-1-929945-50-4(7)); 96p. per. 5.95 (978-1-929945-57-3(4)) Big Guy Bks., Inc.

Enderle, Dotti & McWilliam, Howard. Ghost Detectors Book 10: Curses!, 1 vol. 2011. (Ghost Detectors Ser.). (ENG., Illus.). 80p. (J). (gr. 2-5). 35.64 (978-1-61641-626-3(2), 8820, Calico Chapter Bks.) ABDO Publishing Co.

Ewert, Marcus. Mummy Cat. Brown, Lisa, illus. 2015. (ENG.). 48p. (J). (gr. 1-4). 16.99 (978-0-544-34082-4(5), 1584824, Clarion Bks.) HarperCollins Pubs.

Feder, Jane. Spooky Friends. Downing, Julie, illus. 2013. (ENG.). 40p. (J). (gr. 1-2). 16.99 (978-0-545-47815-1(4), Scholastic Pr.) Scholastic, Inc.

Hawksley, Gerald. Mommies & Babies on the Farm. Calitri, Susan, illus. 2004. (J). bds. 11.99 (978-1-890647-11-7(X)) TOMY International, Inc.

Howe, James. Howie Monroe & the Screaming Mummies of the Pharoah's Tomb II. 2004. (Tales from the House of Bunnicula Ser.). 112p. (J). (gr. 3-6). pap. 17.00 incl. audio (978-1-4000-8635-1(3), Listening Library) Random Hse. Audio Publishing Group.

Kinney, Jeff. Rowley Jefferson's Awesome Friendly Spooky Stories. 2021. (ENG., Illus.). 224p. (J). (gr. 3-7). 14.99 (978-1-4197-5697-9(4), 1748601) Abrams, Inc.

McBrier, Page. Abracadabra Tut. 2014. (ENG.). (J). pap. 9.99 (978-0-9960794-0-2(8)) Palm Canyon Pr.

McCann, Jesse Leon. Scooby-Doo & Museum Madness, 1 vol. Sur, Duendes Del, illus. 2011. (Scooby-Doo! Ser.: No. 2). (ENG.). 24p. (J). (gr. k-4). lib. bdg. 31.36 (978-1-59961-867-8(2), 13245, Picture Bk.) Spotlight.

Nesbit, Troy. The Indian Mummy Mystery. 2013. (Wilderness Mystery Ser.). (ENG., Illus.). 276p. (J). (gr. 3-7). pap. 12.95 (978-1-58979-813-7(9)) Taylor Trade Publishing.

Night, P. J. Off the Wall. 2013. (You're Invited to a Creepover Ser.: 14). (ENG., Illus.). 160p. (J). (gr. 3-7). pap. 5.99 (978-1-4424-7238-9(3), Simon Spotlight) Simon Spotlight.

O'Reilly, Sean. The Missing Mummy, 1 vol. 2011. (Mighty Mighty Monsters Ser.). (ENG., Illus.). 48p. (J). (gr. 2-4). lib. bdg. 23.99 (978-1-4342-3218-2(2), 116190, Stone Arch Bks.) Capstone.

Osborne, Mary Pope. Una Momia Al Amanecer. 2004. (Casa del Arbol Ser.: 3). (SPA.). (J). pap. 6.99 (978-1-930332-51-5(3)) Lectorum Pubns., Inc.

—Una Momia en la Manana. 2003. (Magic Tree House Ser.: 3). (SPA.). (gr. 3-6). lib. bdg. 16.00 (978-0-613-64609-3(6)) Turtleback.

—Mummies in the Morning. unabr. ed. 2004. (Magic Tree House Ser.: No. 3). 65p. (J). (gr. k-5). pap. 17.00 incl. audio (978-0-8072-0332-3(7), Listening Library) Random Hse. Audio Publishing Group.

Preller, James. Jigsaw Jones: the Case of the Mummy Mystery. 2017. (Jigsaw Jones Mysteries Ser.). (ENG., Illus.). 96p. (J). pap. 6.99 (978-1-250-11082-4(3), 900169770) Feiwel & Friends.

Rex, Michael. The Runaway Mummy: A Petrifying Parody. 2012. lib. bdg. 17.20 (978-0-606-26086-2(2)) Turtleback.

—Runaway Mummy: a Petrifying Parody. 2012. 32p. (J). (gr. -1-k). pap. 7.99 (978-0-14-242121-5(9), Puffin Books) Penguin Young Readers Group.

Rogers, Kirsteen. Mummies & Pyramids: Internet-Linked. 2009. (Discovery Nature Ser.). 48p. (J). 6.99 *(978-0-7945-2239-1(4),* Usborne) EDC Publishing.
Roy, Ron. The Missing Mummy. (A to Z Mystery Ser.: Vol. 13). (J). 11.32 *(978-0-7383-3465-3(0))* Booksource, The.
Schachner, Judy. Skippyjon Jones in Mummy Trouble. 2008. (Skippyjon Jones Ser.). 32p. (J). (gr. -1-k). pap. 8.99 *(978-0-14-241211-4(2),* Puffin Books) Penguin Young Readers Group.
—Skippyjon Jones in Mummy Trouble. 2009. (Skippyjon Jones Ser.). 17.00 *(978-1-60686-418-0(1))* Perfection Learning Corp.
Scheidt, Dave. Wrapped up Vol. 2. McMahon, Scoot, illus. 2018. (ENG.). 144p. (J). pap. 12.99 *(978-1-941302-70-5(X),* 41dfa637-7f8b-4c36-9590-b8766c99c3ec, Lion Forge) Oni Pr., Inc.
Shreve, Steve. The Mummy: Or Another Great Use for Toilet Paper. 2010. (Adventures of Charlie Ser.). (Illus.). 32p. pap. *(978-0-237-54285-6(4))* Evans Brothers, Ltd.
Shultz, D. B. The World Adventures of Sahara the Mummy: The Magical Exploration of Ancient Egypt. 2012. 28p. pap. 17.99 *(978-1-4772-3310-8(5))* AuthorHouse.
Stine, R. L. The Curse of the Mummy's Tomb. 2009. (Goosebumps Ser.: 6). lib. bdg. 17.20 *(978-0-606-00243-1(X))* Turtleback.
—Curse of the Mummy's Tomb (Classic Goosebumps #6) 2009. (Classic Goosebumps Ser.: 6). (ENG.). 160p. (J). (gr. 3-7). 7.99 *(978-0-545-03523-1(6),* Scholastic Paperbacks) Scholastic, Inc.
—Return of the Mummy (Classic Goosebumps #18) 2010. (Classic Goosebumps Ser.: 18). (ENG.). 160p. (J). (gr. 3-7). pap. 7.99 *(978-0-545-17794-8(4),* Scholastic Paperbacks) Scholastic, Inc.
—Who's Your Mummy? 2009. (Goosebumps HorrorLand Ser.: No. 7). 160p. (J). pap. *(978-1-4071-0755-4(0))* Scholastic, Inc.
—Who's Your Mummy? 2009. (Goosebumps HorrorLand Ser.: 6). lib. bdg. 17.20 *(978-0-606-05328-0(X))* Turtleback.
Stoker, Bram. Mummy, 1 vol. Miroglio, Brian, illus. 2007. (Graphic Horror Ser.). (ENG.). 32p. (J). (gr. 3-6). 32.79 *(978-1-60270-061-1(3),* 9076, Graphic Planet - Fiction) Magic Wagon.
Troupe, Thomas Kingsley. The Misplaced Mummy, 1 vol. Gilpin, Stephen, illus. 2014. (Furry & Flo Ser.). (ENG.). 128p. (J). (gr. 2-3). 25.32 *(978-1-4342-6396-4(7),* 123874, Stone Arch Bks.) Capstone.

MUMPS

Colligan, L. H. Measles & Mumps, 1 vol. 2011. (Health Alert Ser.). (ENG., Illus.). 64p. (gr. 4-4). 35.50 *(978-0-7614-4819-8(5),* 681b0fec-1dd6-4100-bce9-dc5d0d01f398) Cavendish Square Publishing LLC.
Hecht, Alan. Mumps. 2011. (Deadly Diseases & Epidemics Ser.). (J). 34.95 *(978-1-61753-019-7(0),* Facts On File) Infobase Holdings, Inc.

MUNICH (GERMANY)

Dyan, Penelope. The Big Clock! a Kid's Guide to Munich, Germany. Weigand, John D., photos by. 2013. (Illus.). 34p. pap. 11.95 *(978-1-61477-080-0(8))* Bellissima Publishing, LLC.
Sasek, M. This Is Munich: A Children's Classic. 2012. (This Is ... Ser.). (ENG., Illus.). 64p. (J). (gr. 2-12). 17.95 *(978-0-7893-2426-9(1))* Universe Publishing.
Sonneborn, Liz. Murder at the 1972 Olympics in Munich. 2009. (Terrorist Attacks Ser.). 64p. (gr. 5-5). 58.50 *(978-1-60853-308-4(5))* Rosen Publishing Group, Inc., The.

MUNICIPAL ADMINISTRATION

see Municipal Government

MUNICIPAL EMPLOYEES

see Civil Service; Municipal Government

MUNICIPAL ENGINEERING

see also Refuse and Refuse Disposal; Water-Supply

Hellebuyck, Adam & Medvinsky, Mike. Using Tools & Building a City in Minecraft. 2019. (21st Century Skills Innovation Library: Minecraft & STEAM Ser.). (ENG., Illus.). 32p. (J). (gr. 4-8). pap. 14.21 *(978-1-5341-3969-5(9),* 212705) Cherry Lake Publishing.
—Using Tools & Building a City in Minecraft: Technology. 2019. (21st Century Skills Innovation Library: Minecraft & STEAM Ser.). (ENG., Illus.). 32p. (J). (gr. 4-8). lib. bdg. 32.07 *(978-1-5341-4313-5(0),* 212704) Cherry Lake Publishing.
Porter, Esther. Peeking under the City. Lozano, Andrés, illus. 2016. (What's Beneath Ser.). (ENG.). 32p. (J). (gr. -1-3). lib. bdg. 27.99 *(978-1-4795-8665-3(X),* 130863, Picture Window Bks.) Capstone.
Rodger, Ellen. Underground City Systems Cities. 2018. (Underground Worlds Ser.). (Illus.). 32p. (J). (gr. 4-4). *(978-0-7787-6081-8(2))* Crabtree Publishing Co.

MUNICIPAL GOVERNMENT

see also Cities and Towns; Public Administration

Bozzo, Linda. Community Helpers of the Past, Present, & Future, 1 vol. 2010. (Imagining the Future Ser.). (ENG., Illus.). 24p. (gr. k-2). lib. bdg. 25.27 *(978-0-7660-3435-8(6),* 108b0403-8f84-4ea1-979c-c4cb392f95bd, Enslow Elementary) Enslow Publishing, LLC.
Cuthbert, Megan & Siemens, Jared. City Hall. 2016. (Illus.). 24p. (J). *(978-1-5105-1881-0(9))* SmartBook Media, Inc.
Goldsworthy, Steve. Municipal Government. 2010. (Illus.). 32p. *(978-1-55388-679-2(8))*; pap. *(978-1-55388-683-9(6))* Weigl Educational Pubs. Ltd.
Manning, Jack. The City Mayor, 1 vol. 2014. (Our Government Ser.). (ENG.). 24p. (J). (gr. 1-3). 27.99 *(978-1-4914-0336-5(5),* 125849, Capstone Pr.) Capstone.
Muschal, Frank. Local Action. 2007. (21st Century Skills Library: Citizens & Their Governments Ser.). (ENG., Illus.). 32p. (gr. 4-8). lib. bdg. 32.07 *(978-1-60279-061-2(2),* 200007) Cherry Lake Publishing.
Raatma, Lucia. Working at City Hall. 2011. (21st Century Junior Library: Careers Ser.). (ENG., Illus.). 24p. (gr. 2-5). lib. bdg. 29.21 *(978-1-60279-981-3(4),* 200952) Cherry Lake Publishing.
Silate, Jennifer. Your Mayor: Local Government in Action. (Primary Source Library of American Citizenship Ser.). 32p. (gr. 5-5). 2009. 47.90 *(978-1-61511-237-1(5))* 2003. (ENG., Illus.). lib. bdg. 29.13 *(978-0-8239-4481-1(6),* 85072cd8-c6b7-4740-b7b5-1bdeadb5b181) Rosen Publishing Group, Inc., The. (Rosen Reference).

MUNICIPAL IMPROVEMENTS

see Civic Improvement

MUNICIPALITIES

see Cities and Towns; Municipal Government

MUNITIONS

see Military Weapons

MUNOZ MARIN, LUIS, 1898-1980

Ebon Research Systems Staff. Dare to Be Vol. 4: Luis Munoz Marion. I.t. ed. 2003.Tr. of Atrevete Ser... Un Heroe Luis Munoz Marin. (ENG & SPA., Illus.). 14p. (J). 3.99 *(978-0-9648313-7-7(6))* Ebon Research Systems Publishing, LLC.

MURAL PAINTING AND DECORATION

see Cave Paintings; Mosaics

MURDER

see also Assassination

Allman, Toney. The Homicide Detective, 1 vol. 2009. (Crime Scene Investigations Ser.). (ENG., Illus.). 104p. (gr. 7-7). 42.03 *(978-1-4205-0109-4(7),* 3c567097-d68b-4655-be76-32163c1f5de4, Lucent Pr.) Greenhaven Publishing LLC.
—Poisoning, 1 vol. 2008. (Crime Scene Investigations Ser.). (ENG., Illus.). 104p. (gr. 7-7). lib. bdg. 42.03 *(978-1-4205-0064-6(3),* ed3b8003-5d96-405e-86a5-442bcde78291, Lucent Pr.) Greenhaven Publishing LLC.
Alphin, Elaine Marie. An Unspeakable Crime: The Prosecution & Persecution of Leo Frank. 152p. (YA). (gr. 9-12). 2014. (ENG., Illus.). pap. 9.99 *(978-1-4677-4630-4(4),* 1f53664b-7683-4869-a740-b6f520307983, Carolrhoda Bks.) 2009. lib. bdg. 22.95 *(978-0-8225-8944-0(3))* Lerner Publishing Group.
Anniss, Matt. Cold Cases, 1 vol. 2013. (Crime Science Ser.). (Illus.). 48p. (J). (gr. 4-5). (ENG.). pap. 15.05 *(978-1-4339-9477-7(1),* e6567d7b-377d-4f82-bc29-9dce5904a3ff); (ENG., lib. bdg. 34.61 *(978-1-4339-9476-0(3),* 952b447a-a4a5-4d55-ba62-4739374ade59); pap. 84.30 *(978-1-4339-9478-4(X))* Stevens, Gareth Publishing LLLP.
Dicker, Katie. Unsolved Crimes. 2015. (Mystery! Ser.). (ENG.). 24p. (J). (gr. 2-5). 28.50 *(978-1-62588-205-9(X),* 17362) Black Rabbit Bks.
Faryon, Cynthia J. Real Justice: Guilty of Being Weird: The Story of Guy Paul Morin, 1 vol. 2012. (Lorimer Real Justice Ser.). (ENG., Illus.). 144p. (YA). (gr. 9-12). pap. 12.95 *(978-1-4594-0092-4(5),* 3b40e44c-6d03-446e-936a-8c36c517fb89) James Lorimer & Co. Ltd., Pubs. CAN. Dist: Lerner Publishing Group.
Heing, Bridey. Investigating Mass Shootings in the United States, 1 vol. 2017. (Terrorism in the 21st Century: Causes & Effects Ser.). (ENG., Illus.). 64p. (J). (gr. 6-6). lib. bdg. 36.13 *(978-1-5081-7462-2(8),* f207921a-c863-4560-9ce2-26eb19249bfa, Rosen Young Adult) Rosen Publishing Group, Inc., The.
Heits, Rudolph T. Mass Murderers. 2013. (J). 34.98 *(978-1-61900-034-6(2))* Eldorado Ink.
Hinton, Kerry. The Trial of Sacco & Vanzetti: A Primary Source Account. 2009. (Great Trials of the Twentieth Century Ser.). 64p. (gr. 5-8). 58.50 *(978-1-61513-220-1(1))* Rosen Publishing Group, Inc., The.
Honders, Christine. Tracking Serial Killers: How to Catch a Murderer, 1 vol. 2017. (Crime Scene Investigations Ser.). (ENG.). 104p. (gr. 7-7). lib. bdg. 42.03 *(978-1-5345-6069-8(6),* 143a24ad-bd7d-4136-936c-8742866be51e, Lucent Pr.) Greenhaven Publishing LLC.
Innes, Brian. Serial Murders, Vol. 20. Gomez, Manny, ed. 2016. (Crime & Detection Ser.). (Illus.). 96p. (J). (gr. 7). 24.95 *(978-1-4222-3486-0(X))* Mason Crest.
Joyce, Jaime. Going Ballistic: Who Pulled the Trigger in a Gangland Massacre? 2011. (J). pap. *(978-0-545-32801-2(2))* Scholastic, Inc.
Kovatch, Johnny. 59 Hours. 2018. (Simon True Ser.). (ENG.). 224p. (YA). (gr. 9). 19.99 *(978-1-4814-7660-7(2))*; (Illus.). pap. 12.99 *(978-1-4814-7659-1(9))* Simon Pulse. (Simon Pulse).
Latta, Sara L. Medical Serial Killers, 1 vol. 2015. (Psychology of Serial Killers Ser.). (ENG.). 128p. (gr. 9-9). lib. bdg. 38.93 *(978-0-7660-7296-1(7),* 8804b3a1-ae79-4c62-8ff2-2ab8f940f2e3) Enslow Publishing, LLC.
Loker, Aleck. The Murder of Joseph Henry Ching: A Legend Examined. 2003. (Illus.). 28p. 6.00 *(978-1-928874-04-1(5))* Solitude Pr.
Miller, Sarah. The Borden Murders: Lizzie Borden & the Trial of the Century. 2019. 336p. (J). (gr. 5). pap. 9.99 *(978-1-9848-9244-7(4),* Schwartz & Wade Bks.) Random Hse. Children's Bks.
Orr, Tamra. Murder. 2008. (Man's Inhumanities Ser.). (YA). (gr. 7-12). 23.95 *(978-1-60217-977-6(8))* Erickson Pr.
Orr, Tamra B. Tucson Shooting & Gun Control. 2017. (Perspectives Library: Modern Perspectives Ser.). (ENG., Illus.). 32p. (J). (gr. 4-7). lib. bdg. 32.07 *(978-1-63472-865-2(3),* 209886) Cherry Lake Publishing.
Rogers, Kate. The Zodiac Killer: Terror in California, 1 vol. 2017. (Crime Scene Investigations Ser.). (ENG.). 112p. (gr. 7-7). 42.03 *(978-1-5345-6085-7(8),* f4ec6f43-dc6d-436e-82bc-0d39f2ffd70f, Lucent Pr.) Greenhaven Publishing LLC.
Royston, Angela. Homicide, 1 vol. 2013. (Crime Science Ser.). (Illus.). 48p. (J). (gr. 4-5). (ENG.). pap. 15.05 *(978-1-4339-9493-7(3),* a3e2b269-b99e-4e1a-99bb-77c5ae0bf7fd); (ENG., lib. bdg. 34.61 *(978-1-4339-9492-0(5),* 4c9e24c0-54d1-4238-bd07-9e2afb2004c7); pap. 84.30 *(978-1-4339-9494-4(1),* 1358485) Stevens, Gareth Publishing LLLP.
Schauer, Pete. The People Behind Cult Murders, 1 vol. 2016. (Psychology of Mass Murderers Ser.). (ENG., Illus.). 144p. (gr. 8-8). 38.93 *(978-0-7660-7610-5(5),* f26f5969-ad8d-4808-bae8-6092ae96b6af) Enslow Publishing, LLC.
Stewart, Gail B. Cold Cases, 1 vol. 2010. (Crime Scene Investigations Ser.). (ENG.). 104p. (gr. 7-7). 42.03 *(978-1-4205-0323-4(5),* 3f377c23-05fa-4019-9e97-8f1f3baa4058, Lucent Pr.) Greenhaven Publishing LLC.
Swan, Bill. Real Justice: Fourteen & Sentenced to Death: The Story of Steven Truscott. 2012. (Lorimer Real Justice Ser.). (ENG., Illus.). 152p. (YA). (gr. 9-12). 18.95 *(978-1-4594-0075-7(5),* f3bdbdde-f4e6-46d9-8aff-3f6f3d2a87ca); pap. 12.95 *(978-1-4594-0074-0(7),* c345611f-10f4-4e3e-8fbf-e9a28442e0bb) James Lorimer & Co. Ltd., Pubs. CAN. Dist: Lerner Publishing Group.
Townsend, John. Searching for Murder Clues. 2013. (Amazing Crime Scene Science Ser.). (ENG., Illus.). 32p. (J). (gr. 4-8). pap. *(978-1-77092-020-0(X),* 17103) Amicus.
—Unsolved Crimes. 2009. (Amazing Mysteries Ser.). (ENG.). 32p. (J). (gr. 3-6). 28.50 *(978-1-59920-367-6(7),* 19255, Smart Apple Media) Black Rabbit Bks.
Wolf, Allan. Who Killed Christopher Goodman?: Based on a True Crime. 2017. (ENG.). 288p. (YA). (gr. 9). 17.99 *(978-0-7636-5613-3(5))* Candlewick Pr.
Wright, Simeon & Boyd, Herb. Simeon's Story: An Eyewitness Account of the Kidnapping of Emmett Till. 2011. (ENG., Illus.). 160p. (J). (gr. 7). pap. 14.99 *(978-1-56976-819-8(6),* Hill, Lawrence Bks.) Chicago Review Pr., Inc.
Yancey, Diane. The Case of the Zodiac Killer, 1 vol. 2008. (Crime Scene Investigations Ser.). (ENG., Illus.). 112p. (gr. 7-7). lib. bdg. 42.03 *(978-1-4205-0063-9(5),* 76c61d01-48fb-48ef-a461-c81f3db84640, Lucent Pr.) Greenhaven Publishing LLC.
—Murder: Inside the Crime Lab, 1 vol. 2006. (Crime Scene Investigations Ser.). (ENG., Illus.). 112p. (gr. 7-7). lib. bdg. 42.03 *(978-1-59018-619-0(2),* 8d9f8d4f-1c3f-4438-bbbc-0082e7d98f04, Lucent Pr.) Greenhaven Publishing LLC.

MURDER—FICTION

Abrahams, Peter. Down the Rabbit Hole. 2006. (Echo Falls Mystery Ser.: 1). (ENG.). 448p. (J). (gr. 5-9). reprint ed. pap. 8.99 *(978-0-06-073703-0(4),* HarperCollins) HarperCollins Pubs.
—Into the Dark. 2009. (Echo Falls Mystery Ser.: 3). (ENG.). 352p. (J). (gr. 5-18). pap. 7.99 *(978-0-06-073710-8(7),* HarperCollins) HarperCollins Pubs.
Acosta, Daniel. Iron River, 1 vol. 2018. (ENG.). 224p. (YA). (gr. 9-12). 19.95 *(978-1-941026-93-9(1),* 23353382); pap. 13.95 *(978-1-941026-94-6(X),* 23353382) Lee & Low Bks., Inc. (Cinco Puntos Press).
Adler, Irene. The Mystery of the Scarlet Rose. McGuinness, Nanette, tr. Bruno, Iacopo, illus. 2015. (Sherlock, Lupin, & Me Ser.). (ENG.). 256p. (J). (gr. 4-8). lib. bdg. 26.65 *(978-1-4342-6524-1(2),* 124281, Stone Arch Bks.) Capstone.
Ahdieh, Renée. The Beautiful. (Beautiful Quartet Ser.: 1). (ENG.). (YA). (gr. 7). 2021. 480p. pap. 5.99 *(978-1-5247-3819-8(0),* Penguin Books) 2021. 480p. pap. 12.99 *(978-0-593-46266-9(1),* G.P. Putnam's Sons Books for Young Readers) 2019. 448p. 18.99 *(978-1-5247-3817-4(4),* G.P. Putnam's Sons Books for Young Readers) Penguin Young Readers Group.
—The Wrath & the Dawn. (Wrath & the Dawn Ser.: 1). (ENG.). (YA). (gr. 7). 2016. 432p. pap. 11.99 *(978-0-14-751385-4(5),* Penguin Books) 2015. (Illus.). 416p. 18.99 *(978-0-399-17161-1(4),* G.P. Putnam's Sons Books for Young Readers) Penguin Young Readers Group.
—The Wrath & the Dawn. 2016. lib. bdg. 22.10 *(978-0-606-38849-8(4))* Turtleback.
Alderson, Sarah. The Sound. 2014. (ENG., Illus.). 320p. (YA). (gr. 9). 17.99 *(978-1-4424-9933-1(8),* Simon Pulse) Simon Pulse.
Alphin, Elaine Marie. The Perfect Shot. 2011. (ENG.). 360p. (YA). (gr. 6-12). pap. 9.99 *(978-0-7613-8138-9(4),* bbde24bb-9d6a-4b93-9b20-9a4a886372a1, Carolrhoda Lab™) Lerner Publishing Group.
Anderson, Jennifer. Spider. 2013. 174p. pap. 10.99 *(978-1-62237-146-4(1))* Turquoise Morning Pr.
Anderson, Natalie C. City of Saints & Thieves. 2018. (ENG.). 432p. (YA). (gr. 7). pap. 11.99 *(978-0-399-54759-1(2),* Speak) Penguin Young Readers Group.
Anderson, R. J. A Little Taste of Poison. 2016. (ENG., Illus.). 368p. (J). (gr. 4-7). 18.99 *(978-1-4814-3774-5(7),* Atheneum Bks. for Young Readers) Simon & Schuster Children's Publishing.
—A Pocket Full of Murder. 2015. (ENG., Illus.). 352p. (J). (gr. 4-7). 18.99 *(978-1-4814-3771-4(2))* Simon & Schuster Children's Publishing.
Armstrong, Robert. Buyer Beware. 2016. (ENG.). 94p. (YA). (gr. 10-12). 10.95 *(978-1-78554-474-3(8),* 8d6f3a35-f0de-4e80-b69c-ac8e49656faa) Austin Macauley Pubs. Ltd. GBR. Dist: Baker & Taylor Publisher Services (BTPS).
Ballantyne, R. M. Blown to Bits; or, the Lonely Man of Rak. 2006. pap. *(978-1-4065-0515-3(3))* Dodo Pr.
Ballesteros, Jason. Sideways. 2010. 145p. pap. 14.72 *(978-0-557-28699-7(9))* Lulu Pr., Inc.
Barnes, Jennifer Lynn. All In. 2015. (Naturals Ser.: 3). (ENG.). 384p. (YA). (gr. 7-12). 36.99 *(978-1-4847-1643-4(4))* Little, Brown Bks. for Young Readers.
Barrett, Jennifer. Lethal Delivery, Postage Prepaid. (Thumbprint Mysteries Ser.). 32.86 *(978-0-8092-0425-0(8))* McGraw-Hill/Contemporary.
Bellucci, Arianna, illus. Sherlock Holmes: a Study in Scarlet. adapted abr. ed. 2019. (Sweet Cherry Easy Classics Ser.: 1). (ENG.). 216p. (J). (gr. 4-8). 6.95 *(978-1-78226-575-7(9),* fc905307-5e05-4111-883c-9cda0989b378) Sweet Cherry Publishing GBR. Dist: Baker & Taylor Publisher Services (BTPS).
Berk, Josh. The Dark Days of Hamburger Halpin. 2011. 256p. (YA). (gr. 7). pap. 8.99 *(978-0-375-84625-0(5),* Ember) Random Hse. Children's Bks.
—Strike Three, You're Dead. 2014. (Lenny & the Mikes Ser.: 1). (ENG.). 272p. (J). (gr. 3-7). 7.99 *(978-0-307-93006-4(8),* Yearling) Random Hse. Children's Bks.
Bernard, Romily. Never Apart. 2017. (ENG.). 400p. (J). 17.99 *(978-1-63375-822-3(2),* 9781633758223) Entangled Publishing, LLC.
Bick, Ilsa J. The Sin-Eater's Confession. 2014. (ENG., Illus.). 296p. (YA). (gr. 9-12). pap. 9.95 *(978-1-4677-3705-0(4),* d1d2a2d6-a315-4ec1-843c-4b7c1da54080, Carolrhoda Lab™) Lerner Publishing Group.
Blundell, Judy. Strings Attached (Unabridged Edition), 2 vols. unabr. ed. 2011. (ENG.). 2p. (YA). (gr. 8-8). audio compact disk 29.99 *(978-0-545-28280-2(2))* Scholastic, Inc.
Boaz, Ashley. The Mystery of the Midnight Blaze. 2005. (J). *(978-0-9761033-6-3(2))* Waldenhouse Pubs., Inc.
Bowler, Tim. Blade: Playing Dead. 2010. (Blade Ser.: 1). (ENG.). 256p. (YA). (gr. 9-18). 7.99 *(978-0-14-241600-6(2),* Speak) Penguin Young Readers Group.
Brambles, Lindsay. Becoming Darkness. 2015. (ENG.). 496p. (YA). (gr. 9). 17.95 *(978-1-63079-017-2(6),* 128563, Switch Pr.) Capstone.
Bray, Libba. Before the Devil Breaks You. 2017. (Diviners Ser.: 3). (ENG.). 560p. (YA). (gr. 10-17). 21.99 *(978-0-316-12606-9(3))* Little, Brown Bks. for Young Readers.
—The Diviners. 2012. 578p. (YA). 9.99 *(978-0-316-23242-5(4))* Little Brown & Co.
—The Diviners. (Diviners Ser.: 1). (ENG.). (YA). (gr. 10-17). 2013. 496p. pap. 16.99 *(978-0-316-12610-6(1))* 2012. 800p. 52.99 *(978-0-316-22426-0(X))* Little, Brown Bks. for Young Readers.
—The Diviners. 2013. (Diviners Ser.: 1). 468p. (YA). lib. bdg. 24.50 *(978-0-606-32284-3(1))* Turtleback.
Brewer, Amy J. The Mystery of Murder. 2012. 28p. pap. 16.95 *(978-1-62709-595-2(0))* America Star Bks.
Brian, Kate, pseud. Ambition. 2008. (Private Ser.: No. 7). (ENG.). 288p. (YA). (gr. 9-18). pap. 12.99 *(978-1-4169-5882-6(7),* Simon & Schuster Bks. For Young Readers) Simon & Schuster Bks. For Young Readers.
—Confessions. 2009. (Private Ser.: No. 4). (ENG.). 240p. (YA). pap. 9.99 *(978-1-4169-9949-2(3),* Simon & Schuster Bks. For Young Readers) Simon & Schuster Bks. For Young Readers.
—Last Christmas: The Private Prequel. 2010. (Private Ser.). (ENG.). 288p. (YA). (gr. 9). pap. 9.99 *(978-1-4169-1370-2(X),* Simon & Schuster Bks. For Young Readers) Simon & Schuster Bks. For Young Readers.
—Ominous. 2011. (Private Ser.). (ENG.). 224p. (YA). (gr. 9-18). pap. 9.99 *(978-1-4169-8472-6(0),* Simon & Schuster Bks. For Young Readers) Simon & Schuster Bks. For Young Readers.
—Privilege. 2008. (Privilege Ser.: No. 1). (ENG.). 304p. (YA). (gr. 9-18). pap. 9.99 *(978-1-4169-6759-0(1),* Simon & Schuster Bks. For Young Readers) Simon & Schuster Bks. For Young Readers.
Bunce, Elizabeth C. Liar's Moon. 2011. (YA). pap. *(978-0-545-13607-5(5),* Levine, Arthur A. Bks.) Scholastic, Inc.
Burke, Morgan. Get It Started. 2010. (Party Room Ser.: 1). (ENG.). 272p. (J). (gr. 11). pap. 12.99 *(978-1-4424-1420-4(0),* Simon Pulse) Simon Pulse.
Butcher, Kristin. Return to Bone Tree Hill. 2009. (ENG.). 176p. (J). pap. 12.95 *(978-1-897235-58-4(5))* Thistledown Pr., Ltd. CAN. Dist: Univ. of Toronto Pr.
Byars, Betsy. Death's Door. 2006. (Herculeah Jones Mystery Ser.: 4). (ENG.). 144p. (J). (gr. 3-7). 6.99 *(978-0-14-240565-9(5),* Puffin Books) Penguin Young Readers Group.
—Tarot Says Beware. 2006. (Herculeah Jones Mystery Ser.). 151p. (gr. 3-7). 16.00 *(978-0-7569-6737-6(6))* Perfection Learning Corp.
Cabot, Meg. The Mediator #4: Darkest Hour. 2004. (Mediator Ser.: 4). (ENG.). 336p. (YA). (gr. 8-18). pap. 10.99 *(978-0-06-072514-3(1),* HarperTeen) HarperCollins Pubs.
—Safe House. 2011. (1-800-Where-R-You Ser.: 3). (ENG.). 272p. (YA). (gr. 9). pap. 12.99 *(978-1-4424-3084-6(2),* Simon Pulse) Simon Pulse.
—Vanished Books Three & Four: Safe House; Sanctuary. 2011. (Vanished Ser.: Bks. 3 & 4). (ENG.). 512p. (YA). (gr. 7-12). pap. 15.99 *(978-1-4424-0631-5(3),* Simon Pulse) Simon Pulse.
Caletti, Deb. The Queen of Everything. 2008. (ENG.). 352p. (YA). (gr. 7-12). pap. 11.99 *(978-1-4169-5781-2(2),* Simon Pulse) Simon Pulse.
Capetta, A. R. Echo after Echo. 2017. (ENG.). 432p. (YA). (gr. 9). 17.99 *(978-0-7636-9164-6(X))* Candlewick Pr.
Capin, Hannah. Foul Is Fair: A Novel. 2020. (ENG.). 336p. (YA). 18.99 *(978-1-250-23954-9(0),* 900211181, Wednesday Bks.) St. Martin's Pr.
Carey, Anna. Blackbird. 2014. (Blackbird Ser.: 1). (ENG.). 256p. (YA). (gr. 9). 17.99 *(978-0-06-229973-4(5),* HarperTeen) HarperCollins Pubs.
—Blackbird. 2015. (SPA.). 240p. (YA). (gr. 9-12). pap. 17.99 *(978-987-612-909-1(0))* Lectorum Pubns., Inc.
—Deadfall. 2015. 256p. (Blackbird Ser.: 2). (ENG.). (YA). (gr. 9). 17.99 *(978-0-06-229976-5(X),* HarperTeen); (J). pap. *(978-0-06-242788-5(1))* HarperCollins Pubs.
Carter, Ally. Take the Key & Lock Her Up. 2018. (Embassy Row Ser.: 3). lib. bdg. 20.85 *(978-0-606-41138-7(0))* Turtleback.
—Take the Key & Lock Her up (Embassy Row, Book 3) (Embassy Row Ser.: 3). (ENG.). (YA). (gr. 7). 2017. 336p. pap. 12.99 *(978-0-545-65501-9(3))* 2016. 2p. audio compact disk 39.99 *(978-0-545-81400-3(6))* Scholastic, Inc.
Carter, T. E. I Stop Somewhere. 2019. (ENG.). 336p. (YA). pap. 17.99 *(978-1-250-29459-3(2),* 900174482) Square Fish.
Cassidy, Anne. Looking for Jj. 2009. (ENG., Illus.). 336p. (YA). (gr. 7). pap. 20.95 *(978-0-15-206638-3(1),* 1099009, Clarion Bks.) HarperCollins Pubs.
Cavallaro, Brittany. A Study in Charlotte. 2016. (Charlotte Holmes Novel Ser.: 1). (ENG.). 336p. (YA). (gr. 8). 17.99 *(978-0-06-239890-1(3),* Tegen, Katherine Bks) HarperCollins Pubs.
Chadwick, Robert. Vengeful Impulse. 2003. 70p. pap. 8.95 *(978-0-595-27876-3(0))* iUniverse, Inc.
Chandler, Elizabeth. The Back Door of Midnight. 2010. (Dark Secrets Ser.: Vol. 5). (ENG.). 320p. (YA). (gr. 7-18). pap. 9.99 *(978-1-4424-0626-1(7),* Simon Pulse) Simon Pulse.
—Everlasting. (Kissed by an Angel Ser.). (ENG.). (YA). (gr. 7). 2013. 336p. pap. 11.99 *(978-1-4424-0917-0(7))* 2012. 320p. 16.99 *(978-1-4424-0921-7(5))* Simon Pulse. (Simon Pulse).
Chee, Traci. The Reader. (Reader Ser.: 1). 464p. (YA). (gr. 7). 2017. pap. 11.99 *(978-0-14-751805-7(9),* Speak)Bk. 1.

MNO

2016. 19.99 *(978-0-399-17677-7(2),* G.P. Putnam's Sons Books for Young Readers) Penguin Young Readers Group.
—The Reader. 2017. (Sea of Ink & Gold Ser.: 1). lib. bdg. 22.10 *(978-0-606-40001-5(X))* Turtleback.
Chima, Cinda Williams. The Sorcerer Heir. 2016. (Heir Chronicles Ser.: 5). (ENG.). 560p. (YA). (gr. 7-12). pap. 11.99 *(978-1-4231-9475-0(6))* Little, Brown Bks. for Young Readers.
Cho, Kat. Wicked Fox. 2019. 448p. (YA). (gr. 7). 18.99 *(978-1-9848-1234-6(3),* G.P. Putnam's Sons Books for Young Readers) Penguin Young Readers Group.
Choyce, Lesley. Rat, 1 vol. 2012. (Orca Soundings Ser.). (ENG.). 128p. (YA). (gr. 8-12). pap. 9.95 *(978-1-4598-0300-8(0))* Orca Bk. Pubs. USA.
Clark, Melissa. Bear Witness: A Novel. 2015. (ENG.). 118p. pap. 13.00 *(978-1-940716-75-6(6))* SparkPr. (a Bks.parks Imprint).
Coben, Harlan. Seconds Away. l.t. ed. 2012. (Mickey Bolitar Ser.: 2). (ENG.). 396p. 23.99 *(978-1-4104-5348-8(0))* Thorndike Pr.
—Seconds Away. 2013. (Mickey Bolitar Ser.: 2). lib. bdg. 20.85 *(978-0-606-32141-9(1))* Turtleback.
—Seconds Away (Book Two) A Mickey Bolitar Novel, Bk. 2. 2013. (Mickey Bolitar Novel Ser.: 2). (ENG.). 368p. (YA). (gr. 7). pap. 11.99 *(978-0-14-242635-7(0),* Speak) Penguin Young Readers Group.
Collins, Amberly & Collins, Brandilyn. Final Touch, 1 vol. 2010. (Rayne Tour Ser.). (ENG.). 224p. (YA). (gr. 8-11). pap. 9.99 *(978-0-310-71933-5(X))* Zondervan.
Connor, Leslie. The Truth As Told by Mason Buttle. (ENG.). (J). (gr. 3-7). 2020. 352p. pap. 9.99 *(978-0-06-249145-9(8))* 2018. 336p. 16.99 *(978-0-06-249143-5(1))* HarperCollins Pubs. (Tegen, Katherine Bks).
Conradt, Christine. Murdered At 17. 2018. (At 17 Ser.: 3). (ENG.). 400p. (YA). (gr. 9). pap. 11.99 *(978-0-06-265168-6(4),* HarperTeen) HarperCollins Pubs.
Cook, Eileen. You Owe Me a Murder. 2019. (ENG.). 368p. (YA). (gr. 9). 17.99 *(978-1-328-51902-3(3),* 1720627, Clarion Bks.) HarperCollins Pubs.
Cooney, Caroline B. Enter Three Witches: A Story of Macbeth. l.t. ed. 2007. (Thorndike Literacy Bridge Young Adult Ser.). 343p. (YA). (gr. 8-12). 22.95 *(978-0-7862-9889-1(8))* Thorndike Pr.
—No Such Person. 2016. (ENG.). 256p. (YA). (gr. 7). pap. 9.99 *(978-0-385-74292-4(4),* Ember) Random Hse. Children's Bks.
Cooney, Caroline B. & Shakespeare, William. Enter Three Witches: A Story of Macbeth. 2007. 281p. (YA). pap. *(978-0-545-01972-9(9))* Scholastic, Inc.
Cormier, Robert. Tenderness. 2004. 229p. 19.00 *(978-0-7569-3636-5(5))* Perfection Learning Corp.
Crawford, Ann Fears. Keechee: The Witch of the Woods. 2005. (J). *(978-1-931823-21-0(9))* Halcyon Pr.
Cray, Jordan. Shiver. 2009. (Danger. com Ser.: 9). (ENG.). 224p. (YA). (gr. 7). pap. 10.99 *(978-1-4169-9853-2(5),* Simon Pulse) Simon Pulse.
Cusick, Richie Tankersley. Starstruck. 2013. (ENG., Illus.). 240p. (YA). (gr. 7). pap. 15.99 *(978-1-4814-0161-6(0),* Simon Pulse) Simon Pulse.
Dahl, Michael. The Man Behind the Mask. Schoening, Dan, illus. 2019. (Batman Ser.). (ENG.). 56p. (J). (gr. 3-6). pap. 6.95 *(978-1-4965-8654-4(9),* 141342); lib. bdg. 27.32 *(978-1-4965-8650-6(6),* 141341) Capstone. (Stone Arch Bks.).
Dekker, James C. Scum, 1 vol. 2008. (Orca Soundings Ser.). (ENG.). 112p. (YA). (gr. 8-12). pap. 9.95 *(978-1-55143-924-2(7))* Orca Bk. Pubs. USA.
Derting, Kimberly. The Body Finder. 2011. (Body Finder Ser.: 1). (ENG.). 352p. (YA). (gr. 9). pap. 10.99 *(978-0-06-177983-1(0),* HarperCollins) HarperCollins Pubs.
—Desires of the Dead. 2012. (Body Finder Ser.: 2). (ENG.). 384p. (YA). (gr. 9). pap. 8.99 *(978-0-06-177986-2(5),* HarperCollins) HarperCollins Pubs.
Devine, Eric. Look Past. 2016. (ENG.). 288p. (YA). (gr. 8-17). 17.99 *(978-0-7624-5921-6(2),* Running Pr. Kids) Running Pr.
Dix, Catherine R. Rosetta Stones. 2009. (ENG.). 213p. (J). pap. 14.95 *(978-0-9798452-2-2(X),* 9780979845222) Central Ave. Pr.
Dixon, Franklin. Top Ten Ways to Die. 2006. 169p. (J). lib. bdg. 16.92 *(978-1-4242-0390-1(2))* Fitzgerald Bks.
Doherty, Patrick. Cold Waves, Cold Blood. Struntz, D. J., photos by. 2015. (ENG., Illus.). 256p. (YA). (gr. 9-12). pap. 11.95 *(978-0-9963756-3-4(5))* All About Kids Publishing.
Donnelly, Jennifer. A Northern Light. 2004. 396p. (gr. 9-12). 20.00 *(978-0-7569-3614-3(4))* Perfection Learning Corp.
—A Northern Light: A Printz Honor Winner. 2019. (ENG.). 416p. (YA). (gr. 9). pap. 9.99 *(978-0-358-06368-1(X),* 1743697, Clarion Bks.) HarperCollins Pubs.
Doyle, Arthur Conan. A Study in Scarlet. 2020. (ENG.). (J). (gr. 4-6). 130p. 16.95 *(978-1-61895-797-9(X));* 128p. pap. 9.95 *(978-1-61895-796-2(1))* Bibliotech Pr.
—A Study in Scarlet. 2019. (ENG.). 144p. (J). (gr. 2-3). pap. 9.92 *(978-0-368-71706-2(2))* Blurb, Inc.
—A Study in Scarlet. (ENG.). 128p. (J). 2020. (gr. 4-6). pap. *(978-1-77426-027-2(1))* 2018. (gr. 2-3). pap. *(978-1-989201-31-2(8))* East India Publishing Co.
—A Study in Scarlet. 2019. (ENG.). (J). 118p. (gr. 4-6). pap. 15.99 *(978-1-7066-3080-7(8));* 90p. (gr. 4-6). pap. 9.99 *(978-1-7080-7089-2(3));* 430p. (gr. 4-6). pap. 17.99 *(978-1-6971-6365-0(3));* 270p. (gr. 4-6). pap. 12.99 *(978-1-6992-5432-5(X));* 270p. (gr. 4-6). pap. 12.99 *(978-1-7017-6352-4(4));* 250p. (gr. 4-6). pap. 18.99 *(978-1-6938-2841-6(3));* 268p. (gr. 4-6). pap. 16.99 *(978-1-6907-9956-6(0));* 108p. (gr. 4-6). pap. 7.99 *(978-1-6949-0361-7(3));* 268p. (gr. 4-8). pap. 16.99 *(978-1-0898-5479-1(X));* 428p. (gr. 4-8). pap. 26.99 *(978-1-0896-6977-7(1));* 268p. (gr. 2-3). pap. 19.99 *(978-1-0825-6321-8(8));* 252p. (gr. 2-3). pap. 14.99 *(978-1-0794-5609-7(0));* 268p. (gr. 2-3). pap. 19.99 *(978-1-0800-8053-3(8));* 244p. (gr. 2-3). pap. 14.99 *(978-1-0795-3080-3(0));* 162p. (gr. 2-3). pap. 9.99 *(978-1-0710-7921-8(2));* 244p. (gr. 2-3). pap. 18.99 *(978-1-0724-9435-5(3));* 108p. (gr. 2-3). pap. 7.99 *(978-1-0749-8357-4(2));* 428p. (gr. 2-3). pap. 24.99 *(978-1-0772-0458-4(2));* 268p. (gr. 2-3). pap. 21.99 *(978-1-0755-4026-4(7));* 108p. (gr. 2-3). pap. 7.99 *(978-1-0968-7413-3(X));* 268p. (gr. 2-3). pap. 16.99 *(978-1-0985-1181-4(6));* 254p. (gr. 2-3). pap. 15.99 *(978-1-0988-6658-7(4));* 244p. (gr. 2-3). pap. 18.98 *(978-1-0706-2207-1(9));* 264p. (gr. 2-3). pap. 17.99 *(978-1-0921-4528-2(1))* Independently Published.
—A Study in Scarlet. Blake, Sheba, ed. 2020. (ENG.). 128p. (J). (gr. 4-6). pap. 11.99 *(978-1-222-29323-4(4))* Indy Pub.
—A Study in Scarlet. 2020. (ENG.). 98p. (J). (gr. 4-6). pap. 4.95 *(978-1-68422-459-3(4))* Martino Fine Bks.
—A Study in Scarlet. 2018. (VIE.). (J). (gr. 2-3). pap. *(978-604-960-780-6(X))* Publishing Hse. of Writers's Assn.
Dunn, Pintip. Before Tomorrow. 2016. (ENG., Illus.). (YA). pap. 12.99 *(978-1-68281-336-2(3))* Entangled Publishing, LLC.
Durango, Julia. Sea of the Dead. 2009. (ENG.). 144p. (J). (gr. 3-7). 16.99 *(978-1-4169-5778-2(2),* Simon & Schuster Bks. For Young Readers) Simon & Schuster Bks. For Young Readers.
Electric Chair or Taser Fried: Malicious Murder; Good Cop, Bad Cop. 2004. (YA). per. 25.00 *(978-0-9760909-0-8(2))* Yost-Haynes, Melissa.
Elston, Ashley. The Rules for Breaking. 2014. (Rules Ser.). (ENG.). 320p. (J). (gr. 7-12). 16.99 *(978-1-4231-6898-0(4))* Hyperion Bks. for Children.
Fahy, Thomas. Sleepless. 2010. (ENG.). 224p. (YA). (gr. 7). pap. 8.99 *(978-1-4169-5902-1(5),* Simon & Schuster Bks. For Young Readers) Simon & Schuster Bks. For Young Readers.
—Sleepless. 2009. (ENG.). 224p. (YA). (gr. 7-12). 15.99 *(978-1-4169-5901-4(7))* Simon & Schuster, Inc.
—The Unspoken. 2008. (ENG.). 176p. (YA). (gr. 7-18). 15.99 *(978-1-4169-4007-4(3),* Simon & Schuster Bks. For Young Readers) Simon & Schuster Bks. For Young Readers.
—The Unspoken. 2009. (ENG.). 256p. (YA). (gr. 7). mass mkt. 6.99 *(978-1-4169-4008-1(1),* Simon Pulse) Simon Pulse.
Fama, Elizabeth. Monstrous Beauty. 2013. (ENG.). 352p. (YA). (gr. 7-12). pap. 17.99 *(978-1-250-03425-0(6),* 900120598) Square Fish.
Ferguson, Alane. The Angel of Death. 2008. (Forensic Mystery Ser.). 258p. 17.00 *(978-0-7569-8929-3(9))* Perfection Learning Corp.
Fiore, Kelly. Thicker Than Water. 2016. (ENG.). 320p. (YA). (gr. 9). 17.99 *(978-0-06-232473-3(X),* HarperTeen) HarperCollins Pubs.
Fisher, Linda C. A Will of Her Own. 2006. (YA). pap. *(978-0-88092-641-6(4));* lib. bdg. *(978-0-88092-640-9(6))* Royal Fireworks Publishing Co.
Flinn, Alex. Nothing to Lose. 2005. (ENG.). 304p. (YA). (gr. 9-12). pap. 8.99 *(978-0-06-051752-6(2),* HarperTeen) HarperCollins Pubs.
Forrest. Sign of Blood. (Thumbprint Mysteries Ser.). 32.86 *(978-0-8092-0408-3(8))* McGraw-Hill/Contemporary.
Fredericks, Mariah. The Girl in the Park. 2013. (ENG.). 224p. (YA). (gr. 9). pap. 8.99 *(978-0-449-81591-5(9),* Ember) Random Hse. Children's Bks.
French, Gillian. The Door to January, 1 vol. 2nd ed. 2019. (ENG.). 212p. (YA). pap. 14.95 *(978-1-944762-61-2(2),* bfd61ab4-190b-41be-a973-f62e0568c1f7) Islandport Pr., Inc.
Frost, Heather. Guardians. 2013. (Seers - Trilogy Ser.: Vol. 3). (ENG.). 424p. (J). (gr. 8-12). pap. 17.99 *(978-1-4621-1035-3(5),* Sweetwater Bks.) Cedar Fort, Inc./CFI Distribution.
Gailey, Sarah. When We Were Magic. 2020. (ENG.). 352p. (YA). (gr. 9). 18.99 *(978-1-5344-3287-1(6),* Simon Pulse) Simon Pulse.
Giles, Gail. Right Behind You. 2008. (ENG.). 320p. (J). (gr. 10-17). pap. 17.99 *(978-0-316-16637-9(5))* Little, Brown Bks. for Young Readers.
Giles, Lamar. Spin. (ENG.). 400p. (gr. 7-7). 2020. (J). pap. 12.99 *(978-1-338-58218-5(6))* 2019. (Illus.). (YA). 18.99 *(978-1-338-21921-0(9),* Scholastic Pr.) Scholastic, Inc.
Girard, Geoffrey. Project Cain. 2013. (ENG., Illus.). 368p. (YA). (gr. 9). 17.99 *(978-1-4424-7696-7(6),* Simon & Schuster Bks. For Young Readers) Simon & Schuster Bks. For Young Readers.
Godfrey. Murder in the Shadows. (Thumbprint Mysteries Ser.). 32.86 *(978-0-8092-0418-2(5))* McGraw-Hill/Contemporary.
Gonzalez, Christina Diaz. Moving Target. (ENG.). 256p. (J). (gr. 3-7). 2016. pap. 8.99 *(978-0-545-77319-5(9))* 2015. 17.99 *(978-0-545-77318-8(0))* Scholastic, Inc. (Scholastic Pr.).
Goodwin, Vincent. Moonlit Road, 1 vol. 2014. (Graphic Horror Ser.). (ENG.). 32p. (J). (gr. 5-8). lib. bdg. 32.79 *(978-1-62402-016-2(X),* 9102, Graphic Planet - Fiction) Magic Wagon.
Grabenstein, Chris. The Black Heart Crypt. 2012. (Haunted Mystery Ser.: 4). 336p. (J). (gr. 3-7). 8.99 *(978-0-375-87301-0(5),* Yearling) Random Hse. Children's Bks.
Gratz, Alan. Something Rotten, 1. 2007. (Horatio Wilkes Mystery Ser.). (ENG.). 208p. (J). (gr. 7-12). 21.19 *(978-0-8037-3216-2(3))* Penguin Young Readers Group.
—Something Wicked, 2. 2008. (Horatio Wilkes Mystery Ser.). (ENG.). 272p. (YA). (gr. 7-12). 22.44 *(978-0-8037-3666-5(5),* Dial) Penguin Publishing Group.
Gratz, Alan M. Something Rotten. 2009. 224p. (YA). (gr. 7-18). 8.99 *(978-0-14-241297-8(X),* Speak) Penguin Young Readers Group.
—Something Wicked. 2009. 238p. (YA). (gr. 7-18). 10.99 *(978-0-14-241496-5(4),* Speak) Penguin Young Readers Group.
Gray, Clio. Peder & the Skincatcher. 2013. 188p. (J). pap. *(978-1-78299-157-1(3))* FeedARead.com.
Gray, Keith. Ghosting. 2012. (Stoke Books Titles Ser.). (ENG.). 72p. (YA). (gr. 8-12). pap. 6.95 *(978-1-78112-103-0(6));* lib. bdg. 22.60 *(978-1-78112-104-7(4))* Lerner Publishing Group.
Green, Jacqueline. Secrets & Lies. 2014. (Truth or Dare Ser.: 2). (ENG.). 336p. (YA). (gr. 10-17). pap. 17.99 *(978-0-316-22030-9(2),* Poppy) Little, Brown Bks. for Young Readers.
Green, Ken. Not a Chance. (Thumbprint Mysteries Ser.). 32.86 *(978-0-8092-0422-9(3))* McGraw-Hill/Contemporary.
Grisham, John. Kid Lawyer. l.t. ed. 2010. (Theodore Boone Ser.: Bk. 1). (ENG.). 278p. (J). 24.99 *(978-1-4104-3050-2(2))* Thorndike Pr.
—Kid Lawyer. 2011. (Theodore Boone Ser.: 1). lib. bdg. 19.65 *(978-0-606-23071-1(8))* Turtleback.
—Theodore Boone: Kid Lawyer. 2014. lthr. 79.00 *(978-1-62715-259-4(8))* Leatherbound Bestsellers.
—Theodore Boone: Kid Lawyer. 2011. 18.00 *(978-1-60686-999-4(X))* Perfection Learning Corp.
—Theodore Boone: Kid Lawyer. 2011. (Theodore Boone Ser.: 1). (ENG.). 288p. (J). (gr. 3-7). 8.99 *(978-0-14-241722-5(X),* Puffin Books) Penguin Young Readers Group.
Groot, De. Black Moon. Spear, Luke, tr. Rodrigue, illus. 2007. (Clifton Ser.: 4). 48p. (J). (gr. 4-7). pap. 9.99 *(978-1-905460-30-4(9))* CineBook GBR. Dist: National Bk. Network.
Hahn, Mary Downing. Closed for the Season. 2010. (ENG.). 192p. (J). (gr. 5-7). pap. 7.99 *(978-0-547-39853-2(0),* 1427651, Clarion Bks.) HarperCollins Pubs.
—Mister Death's Blue-Eyed Girls. 2013. (ENG.). 336p. (YA). (gr. 7). pap. 10.99 *(978-0-544-02224-9(6),* 1528481, Clarion Bks.) HarperCollins Pubs.
Hale, Kathleen. No One Else Can Have You. 2014. (Kippy Bushman Ser.). (ENG.). 384p. (YA). (gr. 9). 17.99 *(978-0-06-221119-4(6),* HarperTeen) HarperCollins Pubs.
Hammel, Sara. The Underdogs. 2017. (J). lib. bdg. 18.40 *(978-0-606-39936-4(4))* Turtleback.
Handwerk, Marina. Hey Cool, I've Never Seen a Teacher with His Head Cut off Before! 2007. 284p. per. 11.95 *(978-1-4327-0332-5(3))* Outskirts Pr., Inc.
Hansen, Lynne & Bosco, Sally. AltDeath.com. 2004. 152p. (YA). pap. 9.00 *(978-0-7599-4572-2(1))* Hard Shell Word Factory.
Hathaway, Jill. Slide, 1. 2013. (Slide Ser.: 1). (ENG.). 272p. (YA). (gr. 9-12). pap. 9.99 *(978-0-06-207796-7(1),* Balzer & Bray) HarperCollins Pubs.
Henderson, Lauren. Kiss in the Dark, 3. 2011. (Scarlett Wakefield Novels Ser.). (ENG.). 256p. (J). (gr. 8-12). lib. bdg. 24.94 *(978-0-385-90690-6(0),* Delacorte Pr.) Random Hse. Children's Bks.
—Kiss Me Kill Me. 2009. (Scarlett Wakefield Ser.). 272p. (YA). (gr. 9). pap. 10.99 *(978-0-385-73488-2(3),* Delacorte Pr.) Random Hse. Children's Bks.
—Kisses & Lies, 2. 2009. (Scarlett Wakefield Novels Ser.). (ENG.). 320p. (J). (gr. 9-12). lib. bdg. 26.19 *(978-0-385-90486-5(X),* Delacorte Pr.) Random Hse. Children's Bks.
Henn, Pamela. Nick & Slim: The Legend of the Falcon Mine. 2006. (Illus.). 472p. (YA). 19.95 *(978-0-9760654-0-1(1))* White Wolf Studio, Inc.
Henry, April. The Lonely Dead. 2020. (ENG.). 240p. (YA). pap. 14.99 *(978-1-250-23376-9(3),* 900185223) Square Fish.
Herren, Greg. Sleeping Angel. 2011. (ENG.). 288p. (J). (gr. 7). pap. 13.95 *(978-1-60282-214-6(X))* Bold Strokes Bks.
Hill, Will. Department 19: First Edition, 1. 2012. (Department Nineteen Ser.: 1). (ENG.). 544p. (YA). (gr. 9-12). pap. 9.99 *(978-1-59514-485-0(4),* Razorbill) Penguin Young Readers Group.
Hodkin, Michelle. The Retribution of Mara Dyer. 2014. (Mara Dyer Trilogy Ser.: 3). (ENG., Illus.). 480p. (YA). (gr. 9). 18.99 *(978-1-4424-8423-8(3),* Simon & Schuster Bks. For Young Readers) Simon & Schuster Bks. For Young Readers.
—The Unbecoming of Mara Dyer. (Mara Dyer Trilogy Ser.: 1). (ENG., Illus.). (YA). (gr. 9). 2012. 480p. pap. 14.99 *(978-1-4424-2177-6(0))* 2011. 464p. 24.99 *(978-1-4424-2176-9(2))* Simon & Schuster Bks. For Young Readers. (Simon & Schuster Bks. For Young Readers).
Hofmeyr, Dianne. Eye of the Moon. 2011. (ENG.). 336p. (J). (gr. 3-7). pap. 9.99 *(978-1-4424-1188-3(0),* Aladdin) Simon & Schuster Children's Publishing.
Holland, Sara. Havenfall. 2020. (Havenfall Ser.: 1). (ENG.). 320p. (YA). 18.99 *(978-1-5476-0379-4(8),* 900215313, Bloomsbury Young Adult) Bloomsbury Publishing USA.
Hounam, Donald. A Dangerous Magic. 2017. (ENG., Illus.). 352p. (YA). (gr. 5-12). 17.99 *(978-1-5124-3232-9(6),* ce27e1d0-1960-495f-a52b-2d7bd78c0eca, Carolrhoda Lab™) Lerner Publishing Group.
Ireland, Justina. Vengeance Bound. 2013. (ENG.). 320p. (YA). (gr. 9). 17.99 *(978-1-4424-4462-1(2),* Simon & Schuster Bks. For Young Readers) Simon & Schuster Bks. For Young Readers.
Ius, Dawn. Lizzie. 2018. (ENG., Illus.). 336p. (YA). (gr. 7). 18.99 *(978-1-4814-9076-4(1),* Simon Pulse) Simon Pulse.
Jablonski, Carla. Book One of the Travelers, Bk. 1. 2009. (Pendragon: Before the War Ser.: 1). (ENG., Illus.). 256p. (J). (gr. 5-9). pap. 8.99 *(978-1-4169-6522-0(X),* Aladdin) Simon & Schuster Children's Publishing.
Jayne, Hannah. Copycat. 2018. (ENG.). 272p. (YA). (gr. 8-12). pap. 10.99 *(978-1-4926-4739-3(X))* Sourcebooks, Inc.
—Twisted. 2016. (ENG.). 320p. (YA). (gr. 8-12). pap. 10.99 *(978-1-4926-3179-8(5),* 9781492631798) Sourcebooks, Inc.
Joelson, Penny. I Have No Secrets. 2019. (ENG.). 304p. (YA). (gr. 8-12). 16.99 *(978-1-4926-9336-9(7))* Sourcebooks, Inc.
Johnson, Alaya Dawn. Detective Frankenstein. Ota, Yuko, illus. 2011. (Twisted Journeys Ser.: 17). (ENG.). 112p. (J). (gr. 4-7). pap. 45.32 *(978-0-7613-7613-2(5),* Graphic Universe™) Lerner Publishing Group.
Johnson, Maureen. The Madness Underneath: Book 2. 2013. (Shades of London Ser.: 2). (ENG.). 304p. (YA). (gr. 7). pap. 10.99 *(978-0-14-242754-5(3),* Speak) Penguin Young Readers Group.
—The Name of the Star. 2012. (Shades of London Ser.: 1). (ENG.). 400p. (YA). (gr. 7). pap. 12.99 *(978-0-14-242205-2(3),* Speak) Penguin Young Readers Group.
—The Vanishing Stair. 2019. (Truly Devious Ser.: 2). (ENG.). (YA). (gr. 9). 400p. pap. 12.99 *(978-0-06-233809-9(9));* 384p. 17.99 *(978-0-06-233808-2(0));* 400p. E-Book *(978-0-06-233810-5(2),* 9780062338105) HarperCollins Pubs. (Tegen, Katherine Bks).
Johnston, Jeffry W. Following. 2019. 288p. (YA). (gr. 8-12). pap. 10.99 *(978-1-4926-6461-1(8))* Sourcebooks, Inc.
Jones, Rob Lloyd. Wild Boy. 2013. (ENG.). 304p. (J). (gr. 5). 16.99 *(978-0-7636-6252-3(6))* Candlewick Pr.
Jordan, Sophie. Uninvited. 2015. (Uninvited Ser.: 1). (ENG.). 400p. (YA). (gr. 8). pap. 9.99 *(978-0-06-223364-6(5),* HarperTeen) HarperCollins Pubs.
Kam, Jennifer Wolf. Devin Rhodes Is Dead. 2014. (YA). 200p. (gr. 7). 16.95 *(978-1-934133-59-0(0),* Mackinac Island Press, Inc.); 228p. *(978-1-60734-706-4(7))* Charlesbridge Publishing, Inc.
Kittscher, Kristen. The Tiara on the Terrace. 2016. (ENG.). 400p. (J). (gr. 3-7). 16.99 *(978-0-06-222798-0(X),* HarperCollins) HarperCollins Pubs.
Klingele, Lindsey. The Truth Lies Here. 2018. (ENG.). 416p. (YA). (gr. 8). 17.99 *(978-0-06-238039-5(7),* HarperTeen) HarperCollins Pubs.
Kollar, J. P. Three Tomato Brand. 2005. 127p. per. 12.95 *(978-1-59879-076-4(5))* Lifevest Publishing, Inc.
Kraus, Daniel. The Death & Life of Zebulon Finch, Volume Two: Empire Decayed. 2017. (Zebulon Finch Ser.: 2). (ENG.). 800p. (YA). (gr. 9). pap. 14.99 *(978-1-4814-1143-1(8))* Simon & Schuster Children's Publishing.
—The Death & Life of Zebulon Finch, Volume Two Vol. 2: Empire Decayed. 2016. (Zebulon Finch Ser.: 2). (ENG., Illus.). 784p. (YA). (gr. 9). 19.99 *(978-1-4814-1142-4(X),* Simon & Schuster Bks. For Young Readers) Simon & Schuster Bks. For Young Readers.
Kunze, Nansi. Kill the Music. l.t. ed. 2013. 330p. pap. *(978-1-4596-6983-3(5))* ReadHowYouWant.com, Ltd.
Kyi, Tanya Lloyd. Truth. 2003. (YA). (gr. 7-18). pap. 7.95 *(978-1-55143-235-9(8))* Orca Bk. Pubs. USA.
—Truth. 2004. (Orca Soundings Ser.). 108p. 19.95 *(978-0-7569-4346-2(9))* Perfection Learning Corp.
Lane, Andrew. Black Ice. 2013. (Sherlock Holmes: the Legend Begins Ser.: 3). (ENG.). 304p. (YA). (gr. 7-12). pap. 13.99 *(978-1-250-03654-4(2),* 900122027) Square Fish.
—Death Cloud. 2012. (ENG.). (YA). (gr. 7-12). 64.99 *(978-1-4272-2800-0(0))* Findaway World, LLC.
—Death Cloud. 2011. (Sherlock Holmes: the Legend Begins Ser.: 1). (ENG.). 336p. (YA). (gr. 7-12). pap. 10.99 *(978-0-312-56371-4(X),* 900074762) Square Fish.
—Death Cloud. l.t. ed. 2011. (Young Sherlock Holmes Ser.). (ENG.). 367p. 23.99 *(978-1-4104-3971-0(2))* Thorndike Pr.
—Death Cloud. 2011. (Sherlock Holmes: the Legend Begins Ser.: 1). (YA). lib. bdg. 22.10 *(978-0-606-23781-9(X))* Turtleback.
Latham, Jennifer. Dreamland Burning. 2018.Tr. of s. (ENG.). 400p. (YA). (gr. 9-17). pap. 11.99 *(978-0-316-38490-2(9))* Little, Brown Bks. for Young Readers.
Latimer, E. Witches of Ash & Ruin. 2020. (ENG.). 384p. (YA). (gr. 9-17). 18.99 *(978-1-368-05225-2(8))* Disney Publishing Worldwide.
Lawrence, Caroline. The Assassins of Rome. 2005. (Roman Mysteries Ser.). (Illus.). 161p. (J). (gr. 3-7). 14.65 *(978-0-7569-5879-4(2))* Perfection Learning Corp.
—The Fugitive from Corinth, Bk. 10. 2006. (ENG., Illus.). 240p. (gr. 4-6). pap. 10.99 *(978-1-84255-515-6(4),* Orion Children's Bks.) Hachette Children's Group GBR. Dist: Hachette Bk. Group.
Lee, Y. S. The Agency 2: the Body at the Tower. 2010. (Agency Ser.: 2). (ENG., Illus.). 352p. (YA). (gr. 7-18). 16.99 *(978-0-7636-4968-5(6))* Candlewick Pr.
—The Agency 3: the Traitor in the Tunnel. 2012. (Agency Ser.: 3). (ENG., Illus.). 384p. (YA). (gr. 7). 16.99 *(978-0-7636-5316-3(0))* Candlewick Pr.
Leonard, Julia Platt. Cold Case. 2011. (ENG., Illus.). 288p. (J). (gr. 3-7). 15.99 *(978-1-4424-2009-0(X),* Simon & Schuster/Paula Wiseman Bks.) Simon & Schuster/Paula Wiseman Bks.
Lester, Julius. When Dad Killed Mom. 2003. (YA). (gr. 7-12). mass mkt. 6.95 *(978-0-15-524698-0(4),* Silver Whistle) Harcourt Trade Pubs.
—When Dad Killed Mom. 2003. (ENG.). 216p. (YA). (gr. 7-12). pap. 13.95 *(978-0-15-204698-9(4),* 1194150, Clarion Bks.) HarperCollins Pubs.
Lindsey, Julie Anne. Deceived. 2013. (ENG.). 320p. (YA). 17.99 *(978-1-4405-6389-8(6),* Simon Pulse) Simon Pulse.
—Reinventing Chloe. 2013. 278p. pap. 13.99 *(978-1-62237-152-5(6))* Turquoise Morning Pr.
Lo, Malinda. A Line in the Dark. 2017. 288p. (YA). (gr. 9). 17.99 *(978-0-7352-2742-2(X),* Dutton Books for Young Readers) Penguin Young Readers Group.
Lyga, Barry. I Hunt Killers. 2013. (I Hunt Killers Ser.: 1). (ENG.). 384p. (YA). (gr. 10-17). pap. 11.99 *(978-0-316-12583-3(0))* Little, Brown Bks. for Young Readers.
MacColl, Michaela. The Revelation of Louisa May: A Novel of Intrigue & Romance. 2015. (ENG.). 272p. (J). (gr. 7-12). 16.99 *(978-1-4521-3357-7(3))* Chronicle Bks. LLC.
MacGregor, Roy. Murder at the Winter Games (#18), No. 18. 2004. (Screech Owls Ser.: 18). (ENG., Illus.). 128p. (J). (gr. 3-7). mass mkt. 4.95 *(978-0-7710-5647-5(8),* Screech Owls) McClelland & Stewart CAN. Dist: Penguin Random Hse. LLC.
MacGregor, Roy & MacGregor, Roy. The Complete Screech Owls, Volume 4, Vol. 4. 2006. (Complete Screech Owls Ser.: 4). (ENG.). 488p. (J). (gr. 3-7). per. 15.95 *(978-0-7710-5491-4(2),* Screech Owls) McClelland & Stewart CAN. Dist: Penguin Random Hse. LLC.
Mackall, Dandi Daley. The Silence of Murder. 2012. 336p. (YA). (gr. 9). pap. 10.99 *(978-0-375-87293-8(0),* Ember) Random Hse. Children's Bks.
Maniscalco, Kerri. Escaping from Houdini. (Stalking Jack the Ripper Ser.: 3). (ENG., Illus.). (YA). (gr. 10-17). 2019. 480p. pap. 12.99 *(978-0-316-55172-4(4))* 2018. 448p. 19.99 *(978-0-316-55170-0(8))* Little Brown & Co. (Jimmy Patterson).
—Hunting Prince Dracula. (Stalking Jack the Ripper Ser.: 2). (ENG., Illus.). (YA). (gr. 10-17). 2018. 480p. pap. 12.99 *(978-0-316-55167-0(8))* 2017. 448p. 19.99 *(978-0-316-55166-3(X))* Little Brown & Co. (Jimmy Patterson).
—Stalking Jack the Ripper. 2018. (Stalking Jack the Ripper Ser.: 1). (ENG.). 416p. (YA). (gr. 10-17). mass mkt. 8.99 *(978-1-5387-6118-2(1))* Grand Central Publishing.
—Stalking Jack the Ripper. (Stalking Jack the Ripper Ser.: 1). (ENG., (YA). (gr. 10-17). 2017. Illus.). 352p. pap. 12.99 *(978-0-316-27351-0(1))* 2016. (Illus.). 336p. 19.99 *(978-0-316-27349-7(X))* 2016. 464p. 39.99 *(978-0-316-46428-4(7))* Little Brown & Co. (Jimmy Patterson).
Markus, Deborah. The Letting Go. 2018. (ENG.). 360p. (YA). (gr. 9-9). 16.99 *(978-1-5107-3405-0(8),* Sky Pony Pr.) Skyhorse Publishing Co., Inc.
Martin, Ann M. Abby & the Secret Society (the Baby-Sitters Club Mystery #23) 2016. (Geronimo Stilton & the Kingdom of Fantasy Ser.: 23). (ENG.). 160p. (J). (gr. 2-5). E-Book 14.99 *(978-0-545-79228-8(2),* Scholastic Paperbacks) Scholastic, Inc.

Mason, Simon. Kid Alone: a Garvie Smith Mystery: A Garvie Smith Mystery. 2017. (ENG.). 384p. (YA). (gr. 9). 18.99 *(978-1-338-03649-7(1))* Scholastic, Inc.

Matthews. Death in the Desert. (Thumbprint Mysteries Ser.). 32.86 *(978-0-8092-0416-8(9))* McGraw-Hill/Contemporary.

McAndrew, Matthew. Headshot: A Thriller. 2017. (ENG., Illus.). 178p. (YA). pap. 10.99 *(978-0-692-97450-6(4))* Dark Mantle Publishing.

McBride, Kristina. The Bakersville Dozen. 2017. (ENG.). 320p. (J). (gr. 8-8). 17.99 *(978-1-5107-0805-1(7),* Sky Pony Pr.) Skyhorse Publishing Co., Inc.

McCaughrean, Geraldine. Stories from Shakespeare. 2017. (ENG.). 176p. (J). (gr. 4-6). pap. 7.99 *(978-1-5101-0145-6(4),* Orion Children's Bks.) Hachette Children's Group GBR. Dist: Hachette Bk. Group.

McClintock, Norah. Bang, 1 vol. 2007. (Orca Soundings Ser.). (ENG.). 112p. (YA). (gr. 8-12). per. 9.95 *(978-1-55143-654-8(X))* Orca Bk. Pubs. USA.

—Change of Heart, No. 7. 2013. (Robyn Hunter Mysteries Ser.: 7). (ENG.). 224p. (YA). (gr. 6-12). lib. bdg. 27.99 *(978-0-7613-8317-8(4),* 3a767ef8-7c9d-4c63-bddd-279ad2c330c3, Darby Creek) Lerner Publishing Group.

—Dead & Gone. 2014. (Mike & Riel Mysteries Ser.: No. 3). (ENG.). 224p. (YA). (gr. 6-12). lib. bdg. 27.99 *(978-1-4677-2607-8(9),* 56cd1991-1fd6-4b8b-a437-e30a99fe3231);No. 3. pap. 8.95 *(978-1-4677-2615-3(X),* 65e36658-00a1-4803-9dae-db038268b3f4) Lerner Publishing Group. (Darby Creek).

—Dooley Takes the Fall, 1 vol. 2007. (Dooley Ser.). (ENG.). 256p. (YA). (gr. 7-12). per. 12.95 *(978-0-88995-403-8(8),* 4f86ceaa-f9c8-4d68-a820-8fb4039fda28) Trifolium Bks., Inc. CAN. Dist: Firefly Bks., Ltd.

—From Above, 1 vol. 2016. (Riley Donovan Ser.: 2). (ENG.). 240p. (YA). (gr. 8-12). pap. 10.95 *(978-1-4598-0933-8(5))* Orca Bk. Pubs. USA.

—Guilty, 1 vol. 2012. (ENG.). 224p. (YA). (gr. 8-12). pap. 12.95 *(978-1-55469-989-6(4))* Orca Bk. Pubs. USA.

—I, Witness, 1 vol. Deas, Mike, illus. 2012. (ENG.). 144p. (YA). (gr. 8-12). pap. 16.95 *(978-1-55469-789-2(1))* Orca Bk. Pubs. USA.

—Out of Tune, 1 vol. 2017. (Riley Donovan Ser.: 3). (ENG.). 240p. (YA). (gr. 8-12). pap. 10.95 *(978-1-4598-1465-3(7))* Orca Bk. Pubs. USA.

—Tell. 2007. (Orca Soundings Ser.). 100p. (gr. 4-7). 19.95 *(978-0-7569-8069-6(0))* Perfection Learning Corp.

—Truth & Lies, No. 2. 2014. (Mike & Riel Mysteries Ser.: 2). (ENG.). 216p. (YA). (gr. 6-12). pap. 8.95 *(978-1-4677-2613-9(3),* c47f99a6-46ce-4283-b828-f5ce465ae132, Darby Creek) Lerner Publishing Group.

McDaniel, Lurlene. Angels in Pink: Raina's Story. 2006. (Angels in Pink Ser.). (ENG.). 208p. (YA). (gr. 7-12). mass mkt. 6.99 *(978-0-440-23866-9(8),* Laurel Leaf) Random Hse. Children's Bks.

Mcentire, Myra. Hourglass, 1. 2012. (Hourglass Ser.). (ENG.). 400p. (YA). (gr. 9-12). 26.19 *(978-1-60684-144-0(0))* Farshore GBR. Dist: Children's Plus, Inc.

McGill, Nichole. Girl #3. 2009. (ENG.). 224p. (YA). (gr. 7-18). pap. *(978-1-55470-143-8(0))* Me to We.

McGowan, Anthony. The Knife That Killed Me. 2011. (ENG.). 224p. (YA). (gr. 9). pap. 8.99 *(978-0-375-85516-0(5),* Ember) Random Hse. Children's Bks.

McIntosh, Kenneth. Close-Up: Forensic Photography. 2009. (J). pap. 24.95 *(978-1-4222-1455-8(9))* Mason Crest.

—Close-Up: Forensic Photography, 5 vols. Sanborn, Casey, illus. 2007. (Crime Scene Club Ser.: Bk. 5). 144p. (YA). (gr. 9-12). lib. bdg. 24.95 *(978-1-4222-0251-7(8))* Mason Crest.

McManus, Karen M. Two Can Keep a Secret. 2019. (ENG.). 352p. lib. bdg. 21.80 *(978-1-6636-2970-8(6))* Perfection Learning Corp.

—Two Can Keep a Secret. (ENG.). 352p. (YA). (gr. 9). 2021. pap. 12.99 *(978-1-5247-1471-0(2),* Ember) 2019. 19.99 *(978-1-5247-1472-7(0),* Delacorte Pr.) Random Hse. Children's Bks.

McNeil, Gretchen. Get Dirty. 2015. (Don't Get Mad Ser.). (ENG.). 384p. (YA). (gr. 8). pap. 10.99 *(978-0-06-226087-1(1),* Balzer & Bray) HarperCollins Pubs.

—Ten. 2013. (ENG.). 320p. (YA). (gr. 8). pap. 10.99 *(978-0-06-211879-0(X),* Balzer & Bray) HarperCollins Pubs.

McVoy, Terra Elan. Criminal. (ENG., (YA). (gr. 9). 2014. Illus.). 304p. pap. 9.99 *(978-1-4424-2163-9(0))* 2013. 288p. 16.99 *(978-1-4424-2162-2(2))* Simon Pulse. (Simon Pulse).

Medina, Meg. Burn Baby Burn. (ENG.). 320p. (YA). (gr. 9). 2018. pap. 8.99 *(978-1-5362-0027-0(1))* 2016. 17.99 *(978-0-7636-7467-0(2))* Candlewick Pr.

Meldrum, Christina. Madapple. 2010. 416p. (YA). (gr. 9-18). pap. 10.99 *(978-0-375-85177-3(1),* Knopf Bks. for Young Readers) Random Hse. Children's Bks.

Mele, Dana. People Like Us. 2018. 384p. (YA). (gr. 7). 18.99 *(978-1-5247-4170-9(1),* G.P. Putnam's Sons Books for Young Readers) Penguin Young Readers Group.

Michaels, Rune. Genesis Alpha. 2007. (ENG.). 208p. (YA). (gr. 7-12). 23.80 *(978-1-4287-4620-6(X),* Follettbound) Follett School Solutions.

—Genesis Alpha. 2011. (ENG.). 224p. (YA). (gr. 7). pap. 10.99 *(978-1-4169-6500-8(9),* Atheneum Bks. for Young Readers) Simon & Schuster Children's Publishing.

Milman, Derek. Swipe Right for Murder. 2019. (ENG.). 368p. (YA). (gr. 10-17). 17.99 *(978-0-316-45106-2(1),* Jimmy Patterson) Little Brown & Co.

Moldavsky, Goldy. Kill the Boy Band. 2017. lib. bdg. 20.85 *(978-0-606-39701-8(9))* Turtleback.

Moriarty, Chris. The Watcher in the Shadows. Geyer, Mark Edward, illus. 2014. (ENG.). 336p. (J). (gr. 5-7). pap. 18.99 *(978-0-544-22776-7(X),* 1563388, Clarion Bks.) HarperCollins Pubs.

Mussi, Sarah. The Door of No Return. (ENG.). 400p. (YA). (gr. 7). 2009. pap. 10.99 *(978-1-4169-6825-2(3))* 2008. 17.99 *(978-1-4169-1550-8(8))* McElderry, Margaret K. Bks. (McElderry, Margaret K. Bks.).

Myers, Walter Dean. Monster. 2019. (ENG., Illus.). 336p. (YA). (gr. 8). reprint ed. pap. 12.99 *(978-0-06-440731-1(4),* Amistad) HarperCollins Pubs.

—Monster: A Graphic Novel. Anyabwile, Dawud, illus. 2015. (Monster Ser.). (ENG.). 160p. (J). (gr. 8). pap. 15.99 *(978-0-06-227499-1(6),* Quill Tree Bks.) HarperCollins Pubs.

Neal, Terry L. The Find It Club. 2007. 80p. per. 19.95 *(978-1-4241-7490-4(2))* America Star Bks.

Nelson, Blake. Paranoid Park. 2008. (ENG.). 192p. (YA). (gr. 7-18). 6.99 *(978-0-14-241156-8(6),* Puffin Books) Penguin Young Readers Group.

Newsome, Richard. The Mask of Destiny, 3. Duddle, Jonny, illus. 2013. (ENG.). 384p. (J). (gr. 3-7). pap. 6.99 *(978-0-06-194495-6(5),* Waldon Pond Pr.) HarperCollins Pubs.

Nixon & Brush. Champagne with a Corpse. (Thumbprint Mysteries Ser.). 32.86 *(978-0-8092-0420-5(7))* McGraw-Hill/Contemporary.

Nixon, Joan Lowery. Nightmare. 2005. 166p. (gr. 5-7). 17.00 *(978-0-7569-5239-6(5))* Perfection Learning Corp.

Nordin, Ruth Ann. Witness to a Murder. 2007. 140p. per. 11.95 *(978-0-595-45089-3(X))* iUniverse, Inc.

Oakes, Stephanie. The Sacred Lies of Minnow Bly. 2015. (ENG.). 400p. (YA). (gr. 9). 17.99 *(978-0-8037-4070-9(0),* Dial Bks) Penguin Young Readers Group.

Oates, Joyce Carol. Freaky Green Eyes. 2003. 352p. (J). 16.99 *(978-0-06-623759-6(9))* 2005. (ENG.). 368p. (YA). (gr. 8). reprint ed. pap. 10.99 *(978-0-06-447348-4(1))* HarperCollins Pubs. (HarperTeen).

—Freaky Green Eyes. 2005. 341p. (YA). 15.65 *(978-0-7569-6308-8(7))* Perfection Learning Corp.

Okorafor, Nnedi. Akata Witch. (Nsibidi Scripts Ser.: 1). (ENG.). (YA). (gr. 7). 2017. 384p. pap. 11.99 *(978-0-14-242091-1(3),* Speak) 2011. 368p. 18.99 *(978-0-670-01196-4(7),* Viking Books for Young Readers) Penguin Young Readers Group.

—Akata Witch. 2017. (Akata Witch Ser.: 1). lib. bdg. 22.10 *(978-0-606-40101-2(6))* Turtleback.

O'Leary, Edward J. Murder in the I. R. S. 2003. (YA). per. 18.95 *(978-0-9708590-9-9(0))* First Word Publishing, The.

Olsen, Nora. Maxine Wore Black. 2014. (ENG.). 264p. (J). (gr. 7). pap. 11.95 *(978-1-62639-208-3(0))* Bold Strokes Bks.

Ormsbee, K. E. The House in Poplar Wood: (Fantasy Middle Grade Novel, Mystery Book for Middle School Kids) 2018. (ENG., Illus.). 344p. (J). (gr. 3-7). 16.99 *(978-1-4521-4986-8(0))* Chronicle Bks. LLC.

Patterson, James & Paetro, Maxine. The Private School Murders. 2014. (Confessions Ser.: 2). (YA). lib. bdg. 20.85 *(978-0-606-35945-0(1))* Turtleback.

Peacock, Kathleen. Hemlock. 2013. (Shifters Novel Ser.: 1). (ENG.). 432p. (YA). (gr. 9). pap. 9.99 *(978-0-06-204866-0(X),* Tegen, Katherine Bks) HarperCollins Pubs.

Peacock, Shane. The Dark Missions of Edgar Brim: Monster. 2019. (Dark Missions of Edgar Brim Ser.: 2). 288p. (YA). (gr. 7). pap. 9.99 *(978-0-7352-6273-7(X),* Penguin Teen) PRH Canada Young Readers CAN. Dist: Penguin Random Hse. LLC.

Pearsall, Shelley. Crooked River. 2007. 249p. (gr. 5-9). 17.00 *(978-0-7569-7771-9(1))* Perfection Learning Corp.

Perez, Marlene. Dead Is Just a Dream. 2014. (Dead Is Ser.: 8). lib. bdg. 18.40 *(978-0-606-35990-0(7))* Turtleback.

Perkins, Stephanie. There's Someone Inside Your House. (ENG.). (YA). (gr. 9). 2018. 320p. pap. 10.99 *(978-0-14-242498-8(6),* Speak) 2017. 304p. 18.99 *(978-0-525-42601-1(9),* Dutton Books for Young Readers) Penguin Young Readers Group.

Perkins, T. J. In the Grand Scheme of Things: A Kim & Kelly Mystery. 2007. (Illus.). 151p. (YA). 10.99 *(978-0-9777538-4-0(0))* GumShoe Press.

Perkins, TJ. Fantasies Are Murder: A Kim & Kelly Mystery. novel ed. 2005. (Illus.). 148p. (YA). 10.99 *(978-0-9777538-0-2(8))* GumShoe Press.

Pierce, Tamora. Magic Steps. 2006. (Circle Opens Ser.: No. 1). 264p. 18.00 *(978-0-7569-6588-4(8))* Perfection Learning Corp.

Pitcher, Chelsea. This Lie Will Kill You. 2018. (ENG., Illus.). 320p. (YA). (gr. 9). 17.99 *(978-1-5344-4324-2(X),* McElderry, Margaret K. Bks.) McElderry, Margaret K. Bks.

Preston, Natasha. You Will Be Mine. 2018. (ENG., Illus.). 304p. (YA). (gr. 8-12). pap. 10.99 *(978-1-4926-5432-2(9))* Sourcebooks, Inc.

Price, Charlie. Dead Connection. 2008. (ENG.). 240p. (YA). (gr. 6-8). pap. 18.99 *(978-0-312-37966-7(8),* 900050316) Square Fish.

Priest, Cherie. The Agony House. O'Connor, Tara, illus. (ENG.). 272p. (gr. 7-7). 2020. (J). pap. 10.99 *(978-1-338-58217-8(8))* 2018. (YA). 18.99 *(978-0-545-93429-9(X))* Scholastic, Inc. (Levine, Arthur A. Bks.).

Priestley, Chris. Death & the Arrow: A Gripping Tale of Murder & Revenge. 2007. (Tom Marlowe Ser.). (ENG., Illus.). 240p. (YA). (gr. 7). per. 12.95 *(978-0-552-55475-6(8))* Transworld Publishers Ltd. GBR. Dist: Independent Pubs. Group.

Project Cain. 2014. (ENG., Illus.). 384p. (YA). (gr. 9). pap. 11.99 *(978-1-4424-7698-1(2),* Simon & Schuster Bks. For Young Readers) Simon & Schuster Bks. For Young Readers.

Prophet, John M. Body in the Salt Marsh Boatyard: A Casey Miller Mystery. 2004. 162p. (YA). pap. 13.95 *(978-0-595-30991-7(7),* Mystery & Suspense Pr.) iUniverse, Inc.

Purdie, Kathryn. Burning Glass. (Burning Glass Ser.: 1). (ENG.). (YA). (gr. 9). 2017. 528p. pap. 9.99 *(978-0-06-241237-9(X))* 2016. (Illus.). 512p. 17.99 *(978-0-06-241236-2(1))* HarperCollins Pubs. (Tegen, Katherine Bks).

Ray, Michelle. Falling for Hamlet. 2012. (ENG.). 368p. (YA). (gr. 10-17). pap. 19.99 *(978-0-316-10161-5(3),* Poppy) Little, Brown Bks. for Young Readers.

Reeves, Dia. Slice of Cherry. 2011. (ENG.). (YA). (gr. 9). 528p. pap. 14.99 *(978-1-4169-8621-8(9));* 512p. 16.99 *(978-1-4169-8620-1(0))* Simon Pulse. (Simon Pulse).

Revis, Beth. Across the Universe. 2012. (Across the Universe Trilogy: Bk. 1). (ENG.). (YA). (gr. 7-12). 54.99 *(978-1-61587-857-4(2),* Penguin AudioBooks) Penguin Publishing Group.

—Across the Universe, 1. 2011. (Across the Universe Ser.: 1). (ENG.). 448p. (YA). (gr. 9-12). pap. 11.99 *(978-1-59514-467-6(6),* Razorbill) Penguin Young Readers Group.

—Across the Universe. 2011. (Across the Universe Trilogy Ser.: 1). lib. bdg. 20.85 *(978-0-606-23139-8(0))* Turtleback.

Reynolds, Jason. Long Way Down. 2022. (ENG.). 205p. (J). (gr. 6-8). 24.46 ***(978-1-68505-416-8(1))*** Penworthy Co., LLC, The.

—Long Way Down. (ENG., Illus.). (YA). (gr. 7). 2019. 336p. pap. 12.99 *(978-1-4814-3826-1(3),* Atheneum Bks. for Young Readers) 2017. 320p. 19.99 *(978-1-4814-3825-4(5),* Atheneum/Caitlyn Dlouhy Books) 2017. 320p. E-Book *(978-1-4814-3827-8(1),* Atheneum/Caitlyn Dlouhy Books) Simon & Schuster Children's Publishing.

Reynolds Naylor, Phyllis. Saving Shiloh. unabr. ed. 2004. 137p. (J). (gr. 3-7). pap. 29.00 incl. audio *(978-0-8072-0456-6(0),* Listening Library) Random Hse. Audio Publishing Group.

Ribay, Randy. Patron Saints of Nothing. 2019. (ENG., Illus.). 352p. (YA). (gr. 9). 19.99 *(978-0-525-55491-2(2),* Kokila) Penguin Young Readers Group.

Roberts, Willo Davis. Nightmare. 2012. (ENG.). 224p. (J). (gr. 5-9). pap. 10.99 *(978-1-4424-7229-7(4),* Atheneum Bks. for Young Readers) Simon & Schuster Children's Publishing.

Roehrig, Caleb. White Rabbit. 2019. (ENG.). 352p. (YA). pap. 13.99 *(978-1-250-29475-3(4),* 900195091) Square Fish.

Rogers, Anne. The magic rainbow large Print. 2008. 332p. pap. 30.95 *(978-1-4092-3059-5(7))* Lulu Pr., Inc.

—The magic rainbow very large Print. 2008. 502p. pap. 39.50 *(978-1-4092-3065-6(1))* Lulu Pr., Inc.

Russell, Kristin. A Sky for Us Alone. 2019. (ENG.). 336p. (YA). (gr. 8). 17.99 *(978-0-06-269702-8(1),* Tegen, Katherine Bks) HarperCollins Pubs.

Ryan, Tom. Keep This to Yourself. 2019. (ENG.). 320p. (YA). (gr. 8-12). 17.99 *(978-0-8075-4151-7(6),* 807541516) Whitman, Albert & Co.

Salerni, Dianne K. The Caged Graves. 2014. (ENG.). 336p. (YA). (gr. 7). pap. 10.99 *(978-0-544-33622-3(4),* 1584168, Clarion Bks.) HarperCollins Pubs.

Samms, Olivia. Sketchy. 2013. pap. *(978-1-4778-6650-4(7))* Amazon Publishing.

Sampson, Jeff. Vesper. 2011. (Deviants Ser.: 1). (ENG.). 304p. (YA). (gr. 8-18). 16.99 *(978-0-06-199276-6(3),* Balzer & Bray) HarperCollins Pubs.

Sanders, Scott Loring. Gray Baby. 2009. (ENG.). 336p. (YA). (gr. 7-18). 17.00 *(978-0-547-07661-4(4),* 1042029, Clarion Bks.) HarperCollins Pubs.

Sanderson, Brandon. The Rithmatist. McSweeney, Ben, illus. (ENG.). (YA). 2019. 448p. 14.99 *(978-1-250-24271-6(1),* 900211978) 2014. 384p. (gr. 7). pap. 11.99 *(978-0-7653-3844-0(0),* 900126287) Doherty, Tom Assocs., LLC. (Tor Teen).

—The Rithmatist. McSweeney, Ben & McSweeney, Ben, illus. 2013. (ENG.). 384p. (YA). (gr. 7). 19.99 *(978-0-7653-2032-2(0),* 900050488, Tor Teen) Doherty, Tom Assocs., LLC.

—The Rithmatist. 2014. (YA). lib. bdg. 22.10 *(978-0-606-38512-1(6))* Turtleback.

Schraff, Anne. One of Us. 2010. (Urban Underground — Harriet Tubman High School Ser.). (YA). lib. bdg. 20.80 *(978-0-606-14267-0(3))* Turtleback.

Schrefer, Eliot. The Deadly Sister. 2010. (ENG.). 320p. (J). (gr. 7-18). 17.99 *(978-0-545-16574-7(1),* Scholastic Pr.) Scholastic, Inc.

Shalvey, Declan & Cardy, Jason, illus. Sweeney Todd: The Demon Barber of Fleet Street. 2012. (ENG.). 176p. pap. 16.95 *(978-1-907127-10-6(0),* Classical Comics, Ltd.); pap. 16.95 *(978-1-907127-09-0(7),* Classical Comics, Ltd.); (gr. 9). lib. bdg. 24.95 *(978-1-907127-82-3(8))* Classical Comics GBR. Dist: Publishers Group West (PGW).

Shankman, Adam & Sullivan, Laura L. Murder among the Stars: A Lulu Kelly Mystery. 2017. (ENG., Illus.). 320p. (YA). (gr. 9). 17.99 *(978-1-4814-4790-4(4),* Atheneum Bks. for Young Readers) Simon & Schuster Children's Publishing.

Shaw, Susan. Tunnel Vision. (ENG.). 272p. (YA). (gr. 7). 2012. pap. 8.99 *(978-1-4424-0840-1(5))* 2011. 16.99 *(978-1-4424-0839-5(1))* McElderry, Margaret K. Bks. (McElderry, Margaret K. Bks.).

Shepard, Sara. The Amateurs. 2016. (Amateurs Ser.: 1). (ENG.). 320p. (YA). (gr. 9-17). 17.99 *(978-1-4847-4227-3(3))* Little, Brown Bks. for Young Readers.

—Deadly. 2014. (Pretty Little Liars Ser.: 14). (YA). lib. bdg. 20.85 *(978-0-606-35972-6(9))* Turtleback.

—The Good Girls. 2015. (Perfectionists Ser.: 2). (ENG.). 368p. (YA). (gr. 9). 17.99 *(978-0-06-207452-2(0),* HarperTeen); 341p. (J). *(978-0-06-239115-5(1))* HarperCollins Pubs.

—Hide & Seek. 2012. (Lying Game Ser.: Bk. 4). 289p. (YA). 9.99 *(978-0-06-219369-8(4),* HarperTeen) HarperCollins Pubs.

—The Lying Game. (Lying Game Ser.: 1). (ENG.). (YA). (gr. 9-18). 2010. 320p. 17.99 *(978-0-06-186970-9(8))*1. 2011. 336p. pap. 11.99 *(978-0-06-186971-6(6))* HarperCollins Pubs. (HarperTeen).

—The Lying Game. 2011. (Lying Game (Quality) Ser.: Vol. 1). (ENG.). (YA). (gr. 9). lib. bdg. 20.60 *(978-1-61383-667-5(8))* Perfection Learning Corp.

—The Lying Game #2: Never Have I Ever. (Lying Game Ser.: 2). (ENG.). (YA). (gr. 9). 2012. 336p. pap. 10.99 *(978-0-06-186973-0(2))* 2011. 320p. 16.99 *(978-0-06-186972-3(4))* HarperCollins Pubs. (HarperTeen).

—The Lying Game #3: Two Truths & a Lie. (Lying Game Ser.: 3). (ENG.). (YA). (gr. 9). 2013. 320p. pap. 10.99 *(978-0-06-186975-4(9))* 2012. 304p. 17.99 *(978-0-06-186974-7(0))* HarperCollins Pubs. (HarperTeen).

—The Lying Game #4: Hide & Seek. 2013. (Lying Game Ser.: 4). (ENG.). 320p. (YA). (gr. 9). pap. 10.99 *(978-0-06-186977-8(5),* HarperTeen) HarperCollins Pubs.

—The Lying Game #6: Seven Minutes in Heaven. 2014. (Lying Game Ser.: 6). (ENG.). 400p. (YA). (gr. 9). pap. 11.99 *(978-0-06-212823-2(X),* HarperTeen) HarperCollins Pubs.

—The Perfectionists. 2014. (Perfectionists Ser.: 1). (ENG.). 336p. (YA). (gr. 9). 17.99 *(978-0-06-207469-0(5),* HarperTeen) HarperCollins Pubs.

—Pretty Little Liars #16: Vicious. 2014. (Pretty Little Liars Ser.: 16). (ENG.). 352p. (YA). (gr. 9). 17.99 *(978-0-06-228704-5(4),* HarperTeen) HarperCollins Pubs.

Shusterman, Neal. Scythe. (Arc of a Scythe Ser.: 1). (ENG., Illus.). (YA). (gr. 7). 2017. 464p. pap. 13.99 *(978-1-4424-7243-3(X))* 2016. 448p. 19.99 *(978-1-4424-7242-6(1))* Simon & Schuster Bks. For Young Readers. (Simon & Schuster Bks. For Young Readers).

—Thunderhead. (Arc of a Scythe Ser.: 2). (ENG., Illus.). 512p. (YA). (gr. 7). 2019. pap. 13.99 *(978-1-4424-7246-4(4))* 2018. 19.99 *(978-1-4424-7245-7(6))* Simon & Schuster Bks. For Young Readers. (Simon & Schuster Bks. For Young Readers).

—Thunderhead. 2018. (Arc of a Scythe Ser.: 2). (ENG., Illus.). 512p. (YA). (gr. 7). pap. 12.99 *(978-1-5344-1786-1(9))* Simon & Schuster Children's Publishing.

—Thunderhead. l.t. ed. 2020. (Arc of a Scythe Ser.: 2). (ENG.). lib. bdg. 22.99 *(978-1-4328-7667-8(8))* Thorndike Pr.

—The Toll. (Arc of a Scythe Ser.: 3). (ENG.). 640p. (YA). (gr. 7). 2020. pap. 13.99 *(978-1-4814-9707-3(3))* 2019. (Illus.). 19.99 *(978-1-4814-9706-0(5))* Simon & Schuster Bks. For Young Readers. (Simon & Schuster Bks. For Young Readers).

Sirowy, Alexandra. The Creeping. 2015. (ENG., Illus.). 400p. (YA). (gr. 7). 17.99 *(978-1-4814-1886-7(6))* Simon & Schuster Children's Publishing.

—The Telling. 2016. (ENG., Illus.). 400p. (YA). (gr. 7). 17.99 *(978-1-4814-1889-8(0),* Simon & Schuster Bks. For Young Readers) Simon & Schuster Bks. For Young Readers.

Smith, Amber. The Last to Let Go. 2018. (ENG.). 384p. (YA). (gr. 9). pap. 12.99 *(978-1-5344-2601-6(9));* (Illus.). 17.99 *(978-1-4814-8073-4(1),* McElderry, Margaret K. Bks.) McElderry, Margaret K. Bks.

Smith, Sasha Peyton. The Witch Haven. 2022. (ENG., Illus.). 464p. (YA). (gr. 9). pap. 13.99 *(978-1-5344-5439-2(X),* Simon & Schuster Bks. For Young Readers) Simon & Schuster Bks. For Young Readers.

Snicket, Lemony, pseud. The Composer Is Dead. Ellis, Carson, illus. 2009. (ENG.). 40p. (J). (gr. k-5). 17.99 *(978-0-06-123627-3(6),* HarperCollins) HarperCollins Pubs.

Snyder, Zilpha Keatley. The Egypt Game. 2014. (ENG.). 240p. (J). (gr. 3-7). 11.24 *(978-1-63245-327-3(4))* Lectorum Pubns., Inc.

—The Egypt Game. Raible, Alton, illus. 2009. (ENG.). 240p. (J). (gr. 3-7). pap. 8.99 *(978-1-4169-9051-2(8),* Atheneum Bks. for Young Readers) Simon & Schuster Children's Publishing.

Sorrells, Walter. Book Two of the Travelers, Bk. 2. 2009. (Pendragon: Before the War Ser.: 2). (ENG.). 240p. (J). (gr. 5-9). pap. 8.99 *(978-1-4169-6523-7(8),* Aladdin) Simon & Schuster Children's Publishing.

—Club Dread. 2007. (Hunted Ser.: 2). (ENG.). 272p. (YA). (gr. 7-18). 8.99 *(978-0-14-240904-6(9),* Puffin Books) Penguin Young Readers Group.

—Fake ID. 2007. (Hunted Ser.: 1). (ENG.). 336p. (YA). (gr. 7-18). 9.99 *(978-0-14-240762-2(3),* Puffin Books) Penguin Young Readers Group.

—First Shot. 2009. (ENG.). 288p. (YA). (gr. 7-18). 8.99 *(978-0-14-241421-7(2),* Speak) Penguin Young Readers Group.

St. Claire, Roxanne. They All Fall Down. 2016. (ENG.). 352p. (YA). (gr. 7). pap. 10.99 *(978-0-385-74272-6(X),* Ember) Random Hse. Children's Bks.

Stampler, Ann Redisch. How to Disappear. 2016. (ENG., Illus.). 416p. (YA). (gr. 9). 18.99 *(978-1-4814-4393-7(3),* Simon Pulse) Simon Pulse.

Starinobets, Anna. A Predator's Rights: A Beastly Crimes Book (#2) Bugaeva, Jane, tr. 2019. (ENG., Illus.). 112p. (gr. 2-6). 16.99 *(978-0-486-82951-7(0),* 829510) Dover Pubns., Inc.

Steiner. Murder Takes a Fast Track. (Thumbprint Mysteries Ser.). 32.86 *(978-0-8092-0417-5(7))* McGraw-Hill/Contemporary.

Stelmach, Orest. The Boy Who Stole from the Dead, 0 vols. 2014. (Nadia Tesla Ser.: 2). (ENG.). 366p. pap. 14.95 *(978-1-4778-0948-8(1),* 9781477809488, Thomas & Mercer) Amazon Publishing.

Stevens, B. K. Fighting Chance. 2015. (ENG.). 336p. (YA). pap. 18.99 *(978-1-929345-14-4(3),* Poisoned Pen Press) Sourcebooks, Inc.

Stevens, Robin. Jolly Foul Play. (Murder Most Unladylike Mystery Ser.). (ENG.). (J). (gr. 5). 2019. 384p. pap. 8.99 *(978-1-4814-8910-2(0))* 2018. (Illus.). 368p. 19.99 *(978-1-4814-8909-6(7))* Simon & Schuster Bks. For Young Readers. (Simon & Schuster Bks. For Young Readers).

—Mistletoe & Murder. (Murder Most Unladylike Mystery Ser.). (ENG., Illus.). (J). (gr. 5). 2019. 368p. pap. 8.99 *(978-1-4814-8913-3(5))* 2018. 352p. 19.99 *(978-1-4814-8912-6(7))* Simon & Schuster Bks. For Young Readers. (Simon & Schuster Bks. For Young Readers).

—Murder Is Bad Manners. 2015. (Murder Most Unladylike Mystery Ser.). (ENG., Illus.). 320p. (J). (gr. 5). 19.99 *(978-1-4814-2212-3(X),* Simon & Schuster Bks. For Young Readers) Simon & Schuster Bks. For Young Readers.

—Poison Is Not Polite. 2016. (Murder Most Unladylike Mystery Ser.). (ENG., Illus.). 336p. (J). (gr. 5). 19.99 *(978-1-4814-2215-4(4),* Simon & Schuster Bks. For Young Readers) Simon & Schuster Bks. For Young Readers.

Stine, R. L. The Confession. 2005. (Fear Street Ser.: Bk. 39). 150p. (J). lib. bdg. 13.00 *(978-1-4242-1000-8(3))* Fitzgerald Bks.

—Fear Street Super Thriller. 2015. (Fear Street Ser.). (ENG.). 592p. (YA). (gr. 7-12). pap. 12.99 *(978-1-250-07693-9(5),* 900152585, St. Martin's Griffin) St. Martin's Pr.

—Midnight Games. 2005. (Fear Street Nights Ser.: No. 2). 183p. (YA). lib. bdg. 20.00 *(978-1-4242-1119-7(0))* Fitzgerald Bks.

—A Midsummer Night's Scream. 2014. (ENG.). 256p. (YA). (gr. 7-12). pap. 17.99 *(978-1-250-04434-1(0),* 900128329) Square Fish.

Strange, Jason. 23 Crow's Perch, 1 vol. Evergreen, Nelson & Kendall, Bradford, illus. 2012. (Jason Strange Ser.). (ENG.). 72p. (J). (gr. 3-6). pap. 6.25 *(978-1-4342-3885-6(7),* 118066, Stone Arch Bks.) Capstone.

Strasser, Todd. Blood on My Hands. 2011. (ENG.). 304p. (YA). (gr. 9-12). pap. 8.99 *(978-1-60684-228-7(5),* fc739d70-6a40-42fa-b8e1-d93dc4d8aac1, Carolrhoda Lab™) Lerner Publishing Group.

Taylor, Kara. Prep School Confidential. 2013. (Prep School Confidential Novel Ser.: 1). (ENG.). 336p. (YA). (gr. 7). pap. 22.99 *(978-1-250-01759-8(9),* 900087397, St. Martin's Griffin) St. Martin's Pr.

MNO

This Is How It Ends. 2014. (ENG., Illus.). 320p. (YA). (gr. 9). pap. 11.99 (978-1-4814-0210-1(2), Simon Pulse) Simon Pulse.

Thomas, Kara. The Darkest Corners. 2017. 352p. (YA). (gr. 9). pap. 9.99 (978-0-553-52148-1(9), Ember) Random Hse. Children's Bks.

Thomas, Leah. Wild & Crooked. 2019. (ENG.). 448p. (YA). 18.99 (978-1-5476-0002-1(0), 900194772, Bloomsbury Young Adult) Bloomsbury Publishing USA.

A Thousand Pieces of You. 2014. (Firebird Ser.: 1). (ENG.). 368p. (YA). (gr. 9). 18.99 (978-0-06-227896-8(7), HarperTeen) HarperCollins Pubs.

Thrace, Mischa. My Whole Truth. 2018. (ENG.) 320p. (YA). (gr. 9-12). pap. 11.99 (978-1-63583-024-8(9), 1635830249, Flux) North Star Editions.

Tims, Laura. Please Don't Tell. 2016. (ENG.). 336p. (YA). (gr. 8). 17.99 (978-0-06-231732-2(6), HarperTeen) HarperCollins Pubs.

Turman, Joe Garner. Sling Creek. 2007. (ENG., Illus.). 124p. (J). pap. 10.99 (978-0-692-14181-6(2)) Turman, Joe Garner.

Turnage, Sheila. Three Times Lucky. 2013. (Mo & Dale Mysteries Ser.). (Illus.). 336p. (J). (gr. 5). pap. 9.99 (978-0-14-242605-0(9), Puffin Books) Penguin Young Readers Group.

—Three Times Lucky. 2013. (Mo & Dale Mystery Ser.: 1). lib. bdg. 18.40 (978-0-606-34168-4(4)) Turtleback.

Turner, Henry. Ask the Dark. 2016. (ENG.). 256p. (YA). (gr. 9). pap. 9.99 (978-0-544-81353-3(7), 1641941, Clarion Bks.) HarperCollins Pubs.

Vande Velde, Vivian. Magic Can Be Murder. 2009. (ENG.). 208p. (YA). (gr. 7). pap. 12.99 (978-0-547-25872-0(0), 1402326, Clarion Bks.) HarperCollins Pubs.

—Never Trust a Dead Man. 2008. (ENG., Illus.). 208p. (YA). (gr. 7). pap. 13.95 (978-0-15-206448-8(6), 1199267, Clarion Bks.) HarperCollins Pubs.

Vehlmann, Fabien. Green Manor Pt. 1: Assassins & Gentleman. Bodart, Denis, illus. 2008. (Expresso Collection). 56p. pap. 13.95 (978-1-905460-53-3(8)) CineBook GBR. Dist: National Bk. Network.

Villani, Donna. The Capture of Art. 2008. 244p. pap. 14.95 (978-1-60693-104-2(0), Eloquent Bks.) Strategic Book Publishing & Rights Agency (SBPRA).

Volponi, Paul. Rucker Park Setup. 2007. (ENG.). 149p. (YA). (gr. 7-12). 21.19 (978-0-670-06130-3(1), Viking) Penguin Publishing Group.

—Rucker Park Setup. 2008. 160p. (YA). (gr. 7-18). 8.99 (978-0-14-241207-7(4), Speak) Penguin Young Readers Group.

Walden, Mark. Rogue. (H. I. V. E. Ser.: 5). (ENG.). (J). (gr. 3-7). 2012. 320p. pap. 8.99 (978-1-4424-1369-6(7)) 2011. 304p. 18.99 (978-1-4424-2187-5(8)) Simon & Schuster Bks. For Young Readers. (Simon & Schuster Bks. For Young Readers).

Walkup, Jennifer. Second Verse. 2013. 270p. pap. 15.95 (978-1-935462-87-3(3)); (ENG.). 200p. (YA). (gr. 7-12). pap. 11.95 (978-1-935462-85-9(7)) Luminis Bks., Inc.

Wallace, Becky. The Storyspinner. 2015. (Keepers' Chronicles Ser.). (ENG., Illus.). 432p. (YA). (gr. 9). 17.99 (978-1-4814-0565-2(9), McElderry, Margaret K. Bks.) McElderry, Margaret K. Bks.

Wallace, Kali. Shallow Graves. 2017. (ENG.). 384p. (YA). (gr. 9). pap. 9.99 (978-0-06-236621-4(1), Tegen, Katherine Bks) HarperCollins Pubs.

Wallace, Rich. A Deadly Fall. Volpari, Daniela, illus. 2016. (Haunted Ser.). (ENG.). 48p. (J). (gr. 3-7). 34.21 (978-1-62402-147-3(6), 21571, Spellbound) Magic Wagon.

Warstler, Mary Lu. Michael's Angel, 1 vol. 2009. 227p. pap. 24.95 (978-1-61546-723-5(8)) PublishAmerica, Inc.

Waters, Daniel. Break My Heart 1,000 Times. 2013. (ENG., Illus.). 352p. (J). (gr. 7-17). pap. 9.99 (978-1-4231-2228-9(3)) Hyperion Pr.

Weber, Richard D. Elvis & Me. 2004. 511p. (YA). per. 17.41 (978-1-4116-0549-7(7)) Lulu Pr., Inc.

Welch, Jim. Steven Stevens' Killer App. 2012. (ENG.). 196p. pap. 16.50 (978-1-105-06310-7(0)) Lulu Pr., Inc.

Welshman, Kate. Anais Butt & the Hairy-Handed Gent. 2013. 164p. pap. 16.50 (978-1-61213-187-0(5)) Writer's Coffee Shop, The.

White, Kiersten. The Dark Descent of Elizabeth Frankenstein. 2019. 320p. (YA). (gr. 7). pap. 11.99 (978-0-525-57796-6(3), Ember) Random Hse. Children's Bks.

Wilcox. The Hidden Men. (Thumbprint Mysteries Ser.). 32.86 (978-0-8092-0415-1(0)) McGraw-Hill/Contemporary.

Wolf, Jennifer Shaw. Dead Girls Don't Lie. (ENG.). 2014. 368p. (YA). (gr. 9). pap. 12.99 (978-0-8027-3753-3(6), 900135679) 2013. 304p. E-Book 7.99 (978-0-8027-3450-1(2)) Bloomsbury Publishing USA. (Bloomsbury USA Childrens).

Wright, Betty Ren. The Dollhouse Murders (35th Anniversary Edition) 35th ed. 2018. 160p. (J). (gr. 3-7). 17.99 (978-0-8234-4030-6(3)) Holiday Hse., Inc.

Wynne-Jones, Tim. The Boy in the Burning House. braille ed. 2003. (J). (gr. 2). spiral bd. (978-0-616-15275-1(2)) Canadian National Institute for the Blind/Institut National Canadien pour les Aveugles.

—The Boy in the Burning House. 2003. (ENG.). 224p. (J). (gr. 5-9). pap. 13.99 (978-0-374-40887-9(4), 900021225, Farrar, Straus & Giroux (BYR)) Farrar, Straus & Giroux.

—The Boy in the Burning House, 1 vol. (ENG.). 232p. pap. 8.95 (978-0-88899-500-1(8)) Groundwood Bks. CAN. Dist: Publishers Group West (PGW).

—The Ruinous Sweep. 400p. (YA). (gr. 9). 2019. pap. 9.99 (978-1-5362-0879-5(5)) 2018. (ENG.). 18.99 (978-0-7636-9745-7(1)) Candlewick Pr.

MURPHY, JIMMY, 1894-1924

Briggs, Raymond. Jimmy Murphy & the White Duesenberg. 2006. (Illus.). (J). (978-0-9766683-0-5(0)) Racemaker Pr. LLC.

MURRY FAMILY (FICTITIOUS CHARACTER)—FICTION

L'Engle, Madeleine. Many Waters. 2007. (Wrinkle in Time Quintet Ser.: 3). (ENG.). 368p. (J). (gr. 5-9). per. 7.99 (978-0-312-36857-9(7), 900042674) Square Fish.

—A Swiftly Tilting Planet. 228p. (YA). (gr. 5-18). pap. 5.50 (978-0-8072-1495-4(7), Listening Library) Random Hse. Audio Publishing Group.

—A Swiftly Tilting Planet. 2007. (Wrinkle in Time Quintet Ser.: 4). (ENG.). 320p. (J). (gr. 5-9). per. 7.99 (978-0-312-36856-2(9), 900042673) Square Fish.

—A Wind in the Door. 211p. (YA). (gr. 5-18). pap. 5.50 (978-0-8072-1466-4(3), Listening Library) Random Hse. Audio Publishing Group.

—A Wind in the Door. 2007. (Wrinkle in Time Quintet Ser.: 2). (ENG.). 256p. (J). (gr. 5-9). per. 8.99 (978-0-312-36854-8(2), 900042671) Square Fish.

—A Wrinkle in Time, 2 vols., Set. 20.00 (978-0-89064-014-2(9)) National Assn. for Visually Handicapped.

—A Wrinkle in Time. 211p. (YA). (gr. 5-18). pap. 5.99 (978-0-8072-1460-2(4), Listening Library) Random Hse. Audio Publishing Group.

—A Wrinkle in Time. l.t. ed. 2005. 273p. pap. 10.95 (978-0-7862-7335-5(6), Large Print Pr.) Thorndike Pr.

—The Wrinkle in Time Quintet - Digest Size Boxed Set, Set. 2007. (Wrinkle in Time Quintet Ser.). (ENG.). 244p. (J). (gr. 5-9). 44.95 (978-0-312-37351-1(1), 900048381) Square Fish.

MUSA, SULTAN OF MALI, ACTIVE 1324

Krasner, Barbara. Mansa Musa, 1 vol. 2016. (Silk Road's Greatest Travelers Ser.). (ENG.). 112p. (J). (gr. 6-6). 38.80 (978-1-5081-7151-5(3), b17cbd0a-277d-43eb-90c0-166677ab31c7) Rosen Publishing Group, Inc., The.

National Geographic Learning. Reading Expeditions (Social Studies: Civilizations Past to Present): Mali. 2007. (ENG., Illus.). 24p. (J). pap. 15.95 (978-0-7922-4539-1(3)) CENGAGE Learning.

Zamosky, Lisa. Mansa Musa: Leader of Mali, 1 vol. rev. ed. 2007. (Social Studies: Informational Text Ser.). (ENG.). 32p. (gr. 4-8). pap. 11.99 (978-0-7439-0439-1(7)) Teacher Created Materials, Inc.

MUSCLES

Abramovitz, Melissa. Muscular Dystrophy, 1 vol. 2008. (Diseases & Disorders Ser.). (ENG., Illus.). 104p. (gr. 7-7). lib. bdg. 41.53 (978-1-4205-0073-8(2), 7f06e0bf-2266-4435-8246-ab6893c29f95, Lucent Pr.) Greenhaven Publishing LLC.

Bailey, Jacqui. What Happens When You Move?, 1 vol. 2008. (How Your Body Works (2008) Ser.). (ENG.). 32p. (gr. 3-3). pap. 10.60 (978-1-4358-2617-5(5), 54f75ecd-28b9-4f22-805c-ae07d6fece3e, Rosen Classroom) Rosen Publishing Group, Inc., The.

Ballard, Carol. The Skeleton & Muscles. 2005. (Exploring the Human Body Ser.). (ENG., Illus.). 32p. (J). (gr. 3-6). lib. bdg. 27.80 (978-0-7377-3022-7(6), Greenhaven Pr., Inc.) Cengage Gale.

Beevor, Lucy. Understanding Our Muscles. 2017. (Brains, Body, Bones! Ser.). (ENG., Illus.). 32p. (J). (gr. 3-6). lib. bdg. 33.32 (978-1-4109-8581-1(4), 134422, Raintree) Capstone.

Berger, Melvin & Berger, Gilda. Your Muscles. 2005. (Illus.). pap. (978-0-439-77371-3(7)) Scholastic, Inc.

Biskup, Agnieszka. The Science Behind Superman's Strength. 2017. (Science Behind Superman Ser.). (ENG., Illus.). 24p. (J). (gr. 1-3). lib. bdg. 27.99 (978-1-5157-5099-4(X), 134629, Stone Arch Bks.) Capstone.

—Stopping Runaway Trains: Superman & the Science of Strength. 2016. (Superman Science Ser.). (ENG., Illus.). 32p. (J). (gr. 3-9). lib. bdg. 27.99 (978-1-5157-0914-5(0), 132212, Stone Arch Bks.) Capstone.

Biskup, Agnieszka & Enz, Tammy. Superman Science: The Real-World Science Behind Superman's Powers. 2017. (ENG., Illus.). 144p. (J). (gr. 3-9). pap. 9.95 (978-1-62370-702-6(1), 132245, Stone Arch Bks.) Capstone.

Brett, Flora. Your Muscular System Works! 2015. (Your Body Systems Ser.). (ENG., Illus.). 24p. (J). (gr. 1-3). lib. bdg. 27.99 (978-1-4914-2065-2(0), 127543, Capstone Pr.) Capstone.

Brynie, Faith Hickman. 101 Questions about Muscles: To Stretch Your Mind & Flex Your Brain. 2007. (101 Questions... Ser.). (ENG., Illus.). 176p. (gr. 7-12). lib. bdg. 30.60 (978-0-8225-6380-8(0)) Lerner Publishing Group.

Burstein, John. The Mighty Muscular & Skeletal Systems: How Do My Bones & Muscles Work? 2009. (Slim Goodbody's Body Buddies Ser.). (ENG., Illus.). 32p. (J). (gr. 3-5). lib. bdg. (978-0-7787-4419-1(1)) Crabtree Publishing Co.

—The Mighty Muscular-Skeletal System: How Do My Bones & Muscles Work?, 1 vol. 2009. (Slim Goodbody's Body Buddies Ser.). (ENG., Illus.). 32p. (J). (gr. 3-5). pap. (978-0-7787-4433-7(7)) Crabtree Publishing Co.

Canavan, Thomas. How Many Muscles Make Your Smile? Questions about Muscles & Movement, 1 vol. 2016. (Human Body FAQ Ser.). (ENG.). 32p. (J). (gr. 3-3). pap. 11.00 (978-1-4994-3166-7(X), 89a8508a-a01a-454d-9e8d-5d93d3b3b2d0, PowerKids Pr.) Rosen Publishing Group, Inc., The.

Cole, Tayler. 20 Fun Facts about the Muscular System, 1 vol. 2018. (Fun Fact File: Body Systems Ser.). (ENG.). 32p. (gr. 2-3). 27.93 (978-1-5382-2923-1(4), 831b0d48-93c0-473c-9640-dbe5c0267e39) Stevens, Gareth Publishing LLLP.

Colligan, L. H. Muscles, 1 vol. 2010. (Amazing Human Body Ser.). (ENG.). 80p. (gr. 6-6). 36.93 (978-0-7614-4038-3(0), bf6b24e8-621f-49c8-a90b-2f4e73226f49) Cavendish Square Publishing LLC.

Farndon, John. Stickmen's Guide to Your Mighty Muscles & Bones. Dean, Venitia, illus. 2017. (Stickmen's Guides to Your Awesome Body Ser.). (ENG.). 32p. (J). (gr. 3-6). 27.99 (978-1-5124-3214-5(8), 990019ba-4a9d-4469-928c-8dd242e45d82, Hungry Tomato (r)) Lerner Publishing Group.

Fitzpatrick, Anne. The Muscles. 2003. (Illus.). 24p. (J). lib. bdg. 21.35 (978-1-58340-309-9(4)) Black Rabbit Bks.

Furgang, Kathy. Using Your Muscles, 1 vol. 2019. (Investigate the Human Body Ser.). (ENG.). 24p. (gr. 2-2). pap. 10.95 (978-1-9785-1301-3(1), d151365c-2ca9-48ca-9c15-db741b4d9499) Enslow Publishing, LLC.

Green, Emily & Manolis, Kay. The Muscular System. 2009. (Body Systems Ser.). (ENG., Illus.). 24p. (J). (gr. 2-5). lib. bdg. 26.95 (978-1-60014-244-4(3)) Bellwether Media.

Houghton, Gillian. Muscles: The Muscular System. 2009. (Body Works Ser.). 24p. (gr. 2-3). 42.50 (978-1-61511-645-4(1), PowerKids Pr.) Rosen Publishing Group, Inc., The.

—Muscles: the Muscular System, 1 vol. 2006. (Body Works). (ENG., Illus.). 24p. (YA). (gr. 2-3). lib. bdg. 26.27 (978-1-4042-3475-8(6), 9e85e2fd-0a51-4218-9de7-519470c54a38) Rosen Publishing Group, Inc., The.

—The Muscular System, 1 vol. 2006. (Human Body: a Closer Look Ser.). (ENG., Illus.). 24p. (gr. 2-3). pap. 9.25 (978-1-4042-2184-0(0), 66847c31-c1e2-4b8b-9329-a4f006848f41, PowerKids Pr.) Rosen Publishing Group, Inc., The.

Ipcizade, Catherine. The Strongest Animals. 2011. (Extreme Animals Ser.). (ENG.). 24p. (gr. k-1). pap. 41.70 (978-1-4296-6381-6(2), Capstone Pr.) Capstone.

Johnson, Rebecca L. The Muscular System. 2005. (Early Bird Body Systems Ser.). (Illus.). 48p. (J). (gr. 2-4). lib. bdg. 25.26 (978-0-8225-1248-6(3)) Lerner Publishing Group.

—Muscular System. 2005. (Early Bird Body Systems Ser.). (ENG., Illus.). 48p. (gr. 2-5). pap. 7.95 (978-0-8225-2520-2(8), Lerner Pubns.) Lerner Publishing Group.

—El Sistema Muscular (The Muscular System) 2007. (Libros Sobre el Cuerpo Humano para Madrugadores Ser.). (Illus.). 48p. (J). (gr. -1-3). per. 8.95 (978-0-8225-6650-2(8)) Lerner Publishing Group.

Kenney, Karen Latchana. Strength Training for Teen Athletes: Exercises to Take Your Game to the Next Level, 1 vol. 2012. (Sports Training Zone Ser.). (ENG.). 48p. (J). (gr. 5-9). pap. 8.19 (978-1-4296-8002-8(4), 118334) Capstone.

Kirk, Bill. Muscles Make Us Move. Ruble, Eugene, illus. 2011. 32p. pap. 10.95 (978-1-61633-134-4(8)) Guardian Angel Publishing, Inc.

Leading Women 2, 12 vols. 2013. (Leading Women Ser.). (ENG.). (gr. 7-7). 255.84 (978-1-62712-000-5(9), 3ce9d6f3-7fbe-4bf6-871a-1cbd3820ec67, Cavendish Square) Cavendish Square Publishing LLC.

Lowell, Barbara. The Muscular System. 2018. (Amazing Human Body Ser.). (ENG.). 32p. (gr. 2-7). 9.95 (978-1-68072-683-1(8)); (Illus.). (J). (gr. 4-6). lib. bdg. (978-1-68072-389-2(8), 23160); (J). (gr. 4-6). pap. 9.99 (978-1-64466-236-6(1), 12201) Black Rabbit Bks. (Bolt).

—El Sistema Muscular. 2018. (Asombroso Cuerpo Humano Ser.). (SPA., Illus.). 32p. (J). (gr. 4-6). lib. bdg. (978-1-68072-959-7(4), 12426, Bolt) Black Rabbit Bks.

—Le Système Musculaire. 2018. (Incroyable Corps Humain Ser.). (FRE.). 32p. (J). (gr. 4-6). (978-1-77092-444-4(2), 12440, Bolt) Black Rabbit Bks.

Manolis, Kay. The Muscular System. 2009. (Blastoff! Readers Ser.). (ENG., Illus.). 24p. (J). (gr. k-3). 20.00 (978-0-531-21703-0(5), Children's Pr.) Scholastic Library Publishing.

Martin, Bobi. The Muscles in Your Body, 1 vol. 2014. (Let's Find Out! the Human Body Ser.). (ENG.). 32p. (J). (gr. 2-3). 26.06 (978-1-62275-651-3(7), 1d84e3ed-fa1b-4692-9cc6-d201d7c6eb10, Britannica Educational Publishing) Rosen Publishing Group, Inc., The.

Meachen Rau, Dana. Huesos y Músculos / My Bones & Muscles, 1 vol. 2008. (Qué Hay Dentro de Mí? / What's Inside Me? Ser.). (ENG & SPA., Illus.). 32p. (gr. 1-2). lib. bdg. 25.50 (978-0-7614-2479-6(2), a578cb17-5eab-47ad-be77-ee7b5a1af0a0) Cavendish Square Publishing LLC.

—Huesos y Músculos (My Bones & Muscles), 1 vol. 2008. (Qué Hay Dentro de Mí? (What's Inside Me?) Ser.). (SPA., Illus.). 32p. (gr. 1-2). lib. bdg. 25.50 (978-0-7614-2401-7(6), e3b3b8dd-0a44-4863-b5b3-acf75c3f17e0) Cavendish Square Publishing LLC.

—My Bones & Muscles, 1 vol. (Bookworms: My Body Ser.). (ENG.). 2013. 24p. (gr. 2-2). pap. 9.23 (978-1-62712-032-6(7), 7be28f8f-5349-438f-905c-e59889cb009a) 2006. (Illus.). 32p. (gr. 1-2). 25.50 (978-0-7614-1777-4(X), d00042a8-5ea5-4f19-a814-858c311d0029) 2nd ed. 2013. 24p. (gr. 2-2). 24.07 (978-1-60870-433-0(5), 1bfc8363-389e-4472-a4f4-f80dea3693c4) Cavendish Square Publishing LLC.

El Musculo, Organo de la Fuerza. (Coleccion Mundo Invisible).Tr. of How Are Muscles Work. (SPA.). (YA). (gr. 5-8). pap. 8.00 (978-958-04-3225-8(2)) Norma S.A. COL. Dist: Distribuidora Norma, Inc.

Musculo, Organo de la Fuerza. (SPA.). 88p. (J). 10.00 (978-84-342-1740-9(6)) Parramon Ediciones S.A. ESP. Dist: Distribuidora Norma, Inc.

National Geographic Learning. Reading Expeditions (Science: the Human Body): Bones & Muscles. 2007. (ENG., Illus.). 32p. (J). pap. 18.95 (978-0-7922-4585-8(7)) CENGAGE Learning.

Ollhoff, Jim. Muscles & Bones. 2012. (J). (978-1-61783-256-7(1)) ABDO Publishing Co.

Olson, Gillia M. Muscles & Bones (a Repulsive Augmented Reality Experience) 2020. (Gross Human Body in Action: Augmented Reality Ser.). (ENG., Illus.). 32p. (J). (gr. 3-5). 31.99 (978-1-5415-9811-9(3), 5a000a7a-c788-4b2c-af11-7fbe47fa2e40, Lerner Pubns.) Lerner Publishing Group.

Pettiford, Rebecca. The Muscular System. 2019. (Your Body Systems Ser.). (ENG., Illus.). 24p. (J). (gr. k-3). lib. bdg. 26.95 (978-1-64487-020-4(7), Blastoff! Readers) Bellwether Media.

Rau, Dana Meachen. My Bones & Muscles. 2014. (Illus.). 23p. (J). pap. (978-1-6721-2032-6(2)) Musa Publishing.

Rose, Simon. Muscles: All about the Muscular System. 2017. (Illus.). 32p. (J). (978-1-5105-0890-3(2)) SmartBook Media, Inc.

Ross, Veronica. Muscles. 2004. (Body Ser.). (Illus.). 32p. (J). (gr. -1-3). lib. bdg. 27.10 (978-1-59389-166-4(0)) Chrysalis Education.

Rushworth, Gary. Body Systems: Set of 6: Skeletal & Muscular. 2011. (Navigators Ser.). (J). pap. (978-1-4108-5085-0(4)) Benchmark Education Co.

Shaffer, Jody Jensen. My Muscles. Alberini, Teresa, illus. 2015. (Inside My Body Ser.). (ENG.). 24p. (J). (gr. 1-4). lib. bdg. 19.95 (978-1-60753-757-1(5), 15287) Amicus.

Spilsbury, Louise & Spilsbury, Richard. The Science of the Skeleton & Muscles. 2017. (Flowchart Smart Ser.). 48p. (gr. 4-5). pap. 84.30 (978-1-5382-0686-7(2)) Stevens, Gareth Publishing LLLP.

Treays, Rebecca. Understanding Your Muscles & Bones: Internet-Linked. Fox, Christyan, illus. rev. ed. 2006. (Usborne Science for Beginners Ser.). 32p. (J). (gr. 3-7). per. 7.99 (978-0-7945-0813-5(8), Usborne) EDC Publishing.

Williams, Ben. Look Inside: Your Skeleton & Muscles, 1 vol. 2nd rev. ed. 2013. (TIME for KIDS(r): Informational Text Ser.). (ENG., Illus.). 28p. (J). (gr. 2-3). lib. bdg. 23.96 (978-1-4807-1056-6(3)) Teacher Created Materials, Inc.

—Your Skeleton & Muscles, 1 vol. 2nd rev. ed. 2011. (TIME for KIDS(r): Informational Text Ser.). (ENG.). 28p. (gr. 2-3). pap. 10.99 (978-1-4333-3635-5(9)) Teacher Created Materials, Inc.

MUSEUMS

see also Art Museums

also names of countries, cities, etc. with the subdivision Galleries and Museums (e.g. United States—Galleries and Museums; etc.); and names of galleries and museums, e.g. New York Metropolitan Museum of Art

Andersen, Jill. My Favorite Museum, 1 vol. 2016. (Rosen REAL Readers: Social Studies Nonfiction / Fiction: Myself, My Community, My World Ser.). (ENG.). 8p. (gr. k-1). pap. 5.46 (978-1-5081-2266-1(0), a056ff97-46b5-44bc-bf4d-e7a3bbced8c1, Rosen Classroom) Rosen Publishing Group, Inc., The.

Bishop, Celeste. A Day at the Children's Museum, 1 vol. 2016. (Places in My Community Ser.). (ENG., Illus.). 24p. (J). (gr. 1-1). pap. 9.25 (978-1-4994-2773-8(5), f4429cb3-1c49-447d-abd2-8a14d9603f16, PowerKids Pr.) Rosen Publishing Group, Inc., The.

Bolden, Tonya. How to Build a Museum: Smithsonian's National Museum of African American History & Culture. 2016. (Smithsonian Ser.). (Illus.). 64p. (J). (gr. 5-7). 17.99 (978-0-451-47637-1(9), Viking Books for Young Readers) Penguin Young Readers Group.

Broom, Jenny. Animalium: Welcome to the Museum. Scott, Katie, illus. 2014. (Welcome to the Museum Ser.). (ENG.). 112p. (J). (gr. 3-7). 37.99 (978-0-7636-7508-0(3), Big Picture Press) Candlewick Pr.

Candlewick Press. The Louvre: a 3D Expanding Pocket Guide. McMenemy, Sarah, illus. 2014. (Panorama Pops Ser.). (ENG.). 64p. (J). (gr. k-4). 8.99 (978-0-7636-7506-6(7)) Candlewick Pr.

Clark, Rosalyn. A Visit to the Museum. 2017. (Bumba Books (r) — Places We Go Ser.). (ENG., Illus.). 24p. (J). (gr. -1-1). 26.65 (978-1-5124-3371-5(3), 5b868384-61e6-4647-9901-d196c3bed7e4, Lerner Pubns.) Lerner Publishing Group.

Cooley Peterson, Megan. The National Air & Space Museum. 2017. (Smithsonian Field Trips Ser.). (ENG., Illus.). 32p. (J). (gr. 2-5). lib. bdg. 28.65 (978-1-5157-7974-2(2), 136046, Capstone Pr.) Capstone.

—The National Museum of American History. 2017. (Smithsonian Field Trips Ser.). (ENG., Illus.). 32p. (J). (gr. 2-5). lib. bdg. 28.65 (978-1-5157-7976-6(9), 136047, Capstone Pr.) Capstone.

Cuthbert, Megan & Siemens, Jared. Museum. 2016. (J). (978-1-5105-1885-8(1)) SmartBook Media, Inc.

Ducatteau, Florence. A Day at the Museum. Peten, Chantal, illus. 2013. (Want to Know Ser.: 3). (ENG.). 32p. (J). (gr. k-2). 16.95 (978-1-60537-142-9(4)) Clavis Publishing.

First Sticker Book Museums. 2017. (First Sticker Bks.). (ENG.). (J). pap. 6.99 (978-0-7945-3999-3(8), Usborne) EDC Publishing.

Gamble, Adam & Jasper, Mark. Good Night Aerospace Museum. Leonard, David, illus. 2018. (Good Night Our World Ser.). 20p. (J). (— 1). bds. 9.95 (978-1-60219-679-7(6)) Good Night Bks.

—Good Night Children's Museum. Veno, Joe, illus. 2018. (Good Night Our World Ser.). 20p. (J). (— 1). bds. 9.95 (978-1-60219-578-3(1)) Good Night Bks.

—Good Night Museums. Kelly, Cooper, illus. 2018. (Good Night Our World Ser.). 20p. (J). (— 1). bds. 9.95 (978-1-60219-576-9(5)) Good Night Bks.

Gloor, Elizabeth. The Cultural Institutions of New York City, 1 vol. 2011. (My Community Ser.). (ENG., Illus.). 12p. (gr. 2-2). pap. 6.95 (978-1-4488-5716-6(3), 3beefc8a-3df4-4e55-b576-8f98f7f37532, Rosen Classroom) Rosen Publishing Group, Inc., The.

Gregory, Joy. The Field Museum of Natural History. 2014. (Illus.). 24p. (J). (978-1-4896-3252-4(2)) Weigl Pubs., Inc.

Guggenheim, Jaenet & Lucas, Spencer G. Triassic Hall: Building the Triassic Exhibit from the Ground Up. Lucas, Spencer G., ed. Guggenheim, Jaenet, photos by. 2011. (ENG., Illus.). 130p. 25.00 (978-1-929115-21-1(0)) Azro Pr., Inc.

Guidone, Lisa M. What Happens at a Museum?, 1 vol. 2008. (Where People Work Ser.). (ENG.). 24p. (gr. k-2). (J). lib. bdg. 24.67 (978-0-8368-9276-5(3), 5dbb82f8-26d1-4cc3-9242-89c1264a6df4); pap. 9.15 (978-0-8368-9375-5(1), 3fc9a32a-1912-41b5-8f89-dd4269e77a15) Stevens, Gareth Publishing LLLP. (Weekly Reader Leveled Readers).

Hayes, Amy. Discovering STEM at the Museum, 1 vol. 2015. (STEM in the Real World Ser.). (ENG., Illus.). 24p. (J). (gr. 2-3). pap. 9.25 (978-1-4994-0919-2(2), 2a356b88-ed5d-49b0-b2d2-ace25e58189e, PowerKids Pr.) Rosen Publishing Group, Inc., The.

Hill, Mary. Let's Go to a Science Center. 2004. (Welcome Bks.). (ENG.). 24p. (J). (gr. -1-2). pap. 4.95 (978-0-516-25920-8(2), Children's Pr.) Scholastic Library Publishing.

Honey, Alison. My Ashmolean Discovery Book. 2010. (ENG., Illus.). 24p. (J). (gr. -1-3). pap. 9.95 (978-1-85444-242-0(2)) Ashmolean Museum GBR. Dist: National Bk. Network.

Hopper, Whitney. Time to Go to the Science Museum! Work with Time, 1 vol. 2014. (Math Masters: Measurement & Data Ser.). (ENG.). 24p. (J). (gr. 2-2). 25.27 (978-1-4777-6406-0(2), 0b60b671-2de3-4651-839b-bef3c3dceaf8); pap. 8.25 (978-1-4777-4819-0(9), 3d4f306a-11c5-4baf-9205-f39ebd8c3f6b) Rosen Publishing Group, Inc., The. (Rosen Classroom).

Howse, Jennifer. The British Museum. 2014. (J). (978-1-4896-1186-4(X)) Weigl Pubs., Inc.

—Museum Volunteer. 2016. 32p. (J). (978-1-4896-5851-7(3)) Weigl Pubs., Inc.

Kelley, K. C. Museum. 2018. (Field Trips, Let's Go! Ser.). (ENG.). 16p. (J). (gr. k-2). lib. bdg. 25.65 *(978-1-68151-303-4(X)*, 14862) Amicus.

Korrell, Emily B. Awesome Adventures at the Smithsonian: The Official Kids Guide to the Smithsonian Institution. 2013. (Illus.). 128p. (gr. 2-5). pap. 14.95 *(978-1-58834-349-9(9)*, Smithsonian Bks.) Smithsonian Institution Scholarly Pr.

Kreisman, Rachelle. Things We Do: A Kids' Guide to Community Activity. Haggerty, Tim, illus. 2015. (Start Smart (tm) — Community Ser.). (ENG.). 32p. (J). (gr. 1-3). E-Book 39.99 *(978-1-937529-51-2(7))* Red Chair Pr.

Laks Gorman, Jacqueline. The Museum, 1 vol. 2005. (I Like to Visit Ser.). (ENG., Illus.). 24p. (gr. k-2). pap. 9.15 *(978-0-8368-4460-3(2)*, 4aaec0f6-4e75-404b-b6bb-44f621c3c2ce, Weekly Reader Leveled Readers) Stevens, Gareth Publishing LLLP.

—The Museum / el Museo, 1 vol. 2004. (I Like to Visit / Me Gusta Visitar Ser.). (Illus.). 24p. (gr. k-2). (ENG & SPA.). pap. 9.15 *(978-0-8368-4604-1(4)*, 31d2c1b8-4892-48f0-b362-08153df41d29); (SPA & ENG., lib. bdg. 24.67 *(978-0-8368-4597-6(8)*, 487344fd-ff44-4bbd-9ee1-78fbc6f7f3de) Stevens, Gareth Publishing LLLP. (Weekly Reader Leveled Readers).

Lee, Michelle. Guggenheim Museum. 2015. (How Did They Build That? Ser.). (ENG., Illus.). 32p. (gr. 3-8). 27.99 *(978-1-62920-563-2(X))* Scobre Pr. Corp.

Lindeen, Carol K. What Is a Museum?, 6 vols., Set. 2004. (Phonics Readers Books 37-72 Ser.). (ENG.). 8p. (gr. k-1). pap. 35.70 *(978-0-7368-4076-7(1))* Capstone.

Macken, JoAnn Early. The Dinosaur Museum. 2010. (My Community Ser.). (ENG.). 24p. (J). (gr. k-2). lib. bdg. 25.65 *(978-1-60753-023-7(6)*, 17148) Amicus.

Mark, Jan. The Museum Book: A Guide to Strange & Wonderful Collections. Holland, Richard, illus. (ENG.). 56p. (J). 2014. (gr. 2-5). 8.99 *(978-0-7636-7500-4(8))* 2007. (gr. 3-7). 18.99 *(978-0-7636-3370-7(4))* Candlewick Pr.

Markovics, Joyce L. Spooky Museums. 2018. (Scary Places Ser.). (ENG.). 32p. (J). (gr. 4-8). 19.95 *(978-1-68402-437-7(4))* Bearport Publishing Co., Inc.

Mattern, Joanne. Museums. 2018. (Kids' Day Out Ser.). (ENG., Illus.). 32p. (J). (gr. 2-4). lib. bdg. 25.32 *(978-1-63440-390-0(8)*, 0cef5936-0a93-4930-98b5-28227f75c17d) Red Chair Pr.

Metropolitan Museum of Art, compiled by. Nyc ABC. 2016. (ENG., Illus.). 60p. (J). (gr. -1-3). 4.98 *(978-0-7893-2597-6(7)*, Rizzoli Universe Promotional Bks.) Rizzoli International Pubns., Inc.

Museum Activity Book. 2017. (ENG.). 80p. pap. 12.99 *(978-0-7945-4019-7(8)*, Usborne) EDC Publishing.

Nelson, Jo. Historium: Welcome to the Museum. Wilkinson, Richard, illus. 2015. (Welcome to the Museum Ser.). (ENG.). 112p. (J). (gr. 3-7). 37.99 *(978-0-7636-7984-2(4)*, Big Picture Press) Candlewick Pr.

Pioch, Marc. Art & Culture: Exploring the Louvre: Shapes (Grade 3) 2017. (Mathematics in the Real World Ser.). (ENG., Illus.). 32p. (J). (gr. 3-4). pap. 11.99 *(978-1-4807-5813-1(2))* Teacher Created Materials, Inc.

Quinlivan, Kelly. Science Museum Time! Work with Time, 1 vol. 2014. (InfoMax Math Readers Ser.). (ENG.). 24p. (J). (gr. 2-2). pap. 8.25 *(978-1-4777-4755-1(9)*, 68b398e6-85ee-4415-b7ff-f070e3d99e72, Rosen Classroom) Rosen Publishing Group, Inc., The.

Rissman, Rebecca. Going to a Museum, 1 vol. 2012. (World of Field Trips Ser.). (ENG.). 24p. (gr. -1-1). pap. 6.29 *(978-1-4329-6076-6(8)*, 117906, Heinemann) Capstone.

Watson, Joan & Creed, Murray. The Accidental Farmer: The Story of Ross Farm, 1 vol. 2017. (Stories of Our Past Ser.). (ENG., Illus.). 128p. pap. 15.95 *(978-1-77108-527-4(4)*, 39e531ec-2366-4499-a968-326aa3a282c6) Nimbus Publishing, Ltd. CAN. Dist: Baker & Taylor Publisher Services (BTPS).

Wells, Naomi. Stars at the Science Museum: What Will Happen?, 1 vol. 2017. (Computer Science for the Real World Ser.). (ENG.). 12p. (gr. 1-2). pap. *(978-1-5383-5152-9(8)*, 1ae7216c-8301-425a-b2f8-8526e44c5d9f, Rosen Classroom) Rosen Publishing Group, Inc., The.

Wight, Karol. Paperweight Pals. 2012. (Illus.). 22p. (J). *(978-0-87290-191-9(2))* Corning Museum of Glass.

Wilson, Becky. Lonely Planet Kids Sticker World - Museum 1. Basil, Aviel, illus. 2018. (Lonely Planet Kids Ser.). (ENG.). 40p. (J). (gr. 1-3). 6.99 *(978-1-78701-135-9(6)*, 5697) Lonely Planet Global Ltd. IRL. Dist: Hachette Bk. Group.

Yenawine, Philip. Places. 2006. (Illus.). 22p. (J). (gr. 4-8). reprint ed. 15.00 *(978-1-4223-5407-0(5))* DIANE Publishing Co.

MUSEUMS—FICTION

Adler, David A. Bones & the Dinosaur Mystery. Newman, Barbara Johansen, illus. 2005. (Jeffrey Bones Mystery Ser.: No. 4). 32p. (J). *(978-0-670-05970-6(6)*, Viking Adult) Penguin Publishing Group.

—Bones & the Dinosaur Mystery, No. 4. Johansen Newman, Barbara, illus. 2009. (Bones Ser.: 4). (ENG.). 32p. (J). (gr. 1-3). mass mkt. 4.99 *(978-0-14-241341-8(0)*, Penguin Young Readers) Penguin Young Readers Group.

Ali, Raydin. The Mystic Museum. 2010. 64p. pap. 12.00 *(978-1-4269-1138-5(6))* Trafford Publishing.

Arrhenius, Ingela P., illus. Bookscape Board Books: a Marvelous Museum: (Artist Board Book, Colorful Art Museum Toddler Book) 2019. (Bookscape Board Bks.). (ENG.). 10p. (J). (gr. -1 — 1). bds. 8.99 *(978-1-4521-7492-1(X))* Chronicle Bks. LLC.

Asselin, Kristine & Malone, Jen. The Art of the Swap. (ENG., Illus.). 352p. (J). (gr. 3-7). 2019. pap. 8.99 *(978-1-4814-7872-4(9))* 2018. 17.99 *(978-1-4814-7871-7(0))* Simon & Schuster Children's Publishing. (Aladdin).

Aureliani, Franco, illus. Dino-Mike & the Museum Mayhem. 2015. (J). lib. bdg. *(978-1-4062-9391-3(1)*, Stone Arch Bks.) Capstone.

Bailer, Darice. The Last Rail. 2011. (ENG.). 32p. (J). 9.95 *(978-1-60727-173-4(7))* Soundprints.

—The Pony Express. Antonishak, Tom, illus. 3rd ed. 2003. (Soundprints' Read-and-Discover Ser.). (ENG.). 48p. (J). (gr. -1-3). pap. 3.95 *(978-1-59249-019-6(0)*, S2008) Soundprints.

Bakewell, Lori. Savannah Adventure: Pirate's Treasure. 2007. 173p. (J). pap. 12.95 *(978-0-9799473-9-1(1))* Tailwind Press.

Barkley, Callie. Liz's Night at the Museum. Bishop, Tracy, illus. 2016. (Critter Club Ser.: 15). (ENG.). 128p. (J). (gr. k-4). pap. 6.99 *(978-1-4814-7164-0(3)*, Little Simon) Little Simon.

Battista, Mary Jane. Danny's Day at the Children's Museum. 2009. 24p. pap. 11.49 *(978-1-4389-4396-1(2))* AuthorHouse.

The Battle of Bayport. 2014. (Hardy Boys Adventures Ser.: 6). (ENG., Illus.). 160p. (J). (gr. 3-7). 17.99 *(978-1-4814-0007-7(X)*, Aladdin) Simon & Schuster Children's Publishing.

Brett, Jan. Mossy. Brett, Jan, illus. 2012. (Illus.). 32p. (J). (gr. -1-k). 19.99 *(978-0-399-25782-7(9)*, G.P. Putnam's Sons Books for Young Readers) Penguin Young Readers Group.

Brezenoff, Steve. The Case of the Counterfeit Painting. Weber, Lisa K., illus. 2016. (Museum Mysteries Ser.). (ENG.). 128p. (J). (gr. 3-6). pap. 6.95 *(978-1-4965-2522-2(1)*, 130495, Stone Arch Bks.) Capstone.

—The Case of the New Professor. Weber, Lisa K., illus. 2019. (Museum Mysteries Ser.). (ENG.). 128p. (J). (gr. 3-6). lib. bdg. 26.65 *(978-1-4965-7818-1(X)*, 139246, Stone Arch Bks.) Capstone.

—The Case of the Soldier's Ghost. Weber, Lisa K., illus. 2016. (Museum Mysteries Ser.). (ENG.). 128p. (J). pap. 42.70 *(978-1-4965-2531-4(0)*, 23937); (gr. 3-6). lib. bdg. 26.65 *(978-1-4965-2519-2(1)*, 130492) Capstone. (Stone Arch Bks.).

—Field Trip Mysteries: the Crook That Made Kids Cry. Calo, Marcos, illus. 2013. (Field Trip Mysteries Ser.). (ENG.). 88p. (J). (gr. 2-3). pap. 35.70 *(978-1-4342-6232-5(4)*, 20038); (gr. 3-6). pap. 5.95 *(978-1-4342-6210-3(3)*, 123508) Capstone. (Stone Arch Bks.).

—Field Trip Mysteries: the Dinosaur That Disappeared. Calo, Marcos, illus. 2013. (Field Trip Mysteries Ser.). (ENG.). 88p. (J). (gr. 2-3). pap. 35.70 *(978-1-4342-6233-2(2)*, 20037, Stone Arch Bks.) Capstone.

—The Messed-Up Museum: An Interactive Mystery Adventure. Calo, Marcos, illus. 2019. (You Choose Stories: Field Trip Mysteries Ser.). (ENG.). 112p. (J). (gr. 3-7). lib. bdg. 32.65 *(978-1-4965-4859-7(0)*, 135458, Stone Arch Bks.) Capstone.

—The Outlaw from Outer Space: An Interactive Mystery Adventure. Calo, Marcos, illus. 2017. (You Choose Stories: Field Trip Mysteries Ser.). (ENG.). 112p. (J). (gr. 3-7). lib. bdg. 32.65 *(978-1-4965-2644-1(9)*, 131208, Stone Arch Bks.) Capstone.

Brezenoff, Steven. The Case of the Haunted History Museum. Weber, Lisa K., illus. 2015. (Museum Mysteries Ser.). (ENG.). 128p. (J). (gr. 3-6). lib. bdg. 26.65 *(978-1-4342-9687-0(3)*, 126996, Stone Arch Bks.) Capstone.

—The Case of the Missing Museum Archives. Weber, Lisa K., illus. 2015. (Museum Mysteries Ser.). (ENG.). 128p. (J). (gr. 3-6). lib. bdg. 26.65 *(978-1-4342-9688-7(1)*, 126997, Stone Arch Bks.) Capstone.

—The Case of the Portrait Vandal. Weber, Lisa K., illus. 2015. (Museum Mysteries Ser.). (ENG.). 128p. (J). (gr. 3-6). lib. bdg. 26.65 *(978-1-4342-9685-6(7)*, 126994, Stone Arch Bks.) Capstone.

—The Case of the Stolen Space Suit. Weber, Lisa K., illus. 2016. (Museum Mysteries Ser.). (ENG.). 128p. (J). (gr. 3-6). 26.65 *(978-1-4965-2516-1(7)*, 130489, Stone Arch Bks.) Capstone.

Brown, Marc. Arthur Lost in the Museum. 2005. (Step into Reading Ser.). (Illus.). 24p. (J). (gr. k-3). pap. 5.99 *(978-0-375-82973-4(3)*, Random Hse. Bks. for Young Readers) Random Hse. Children's Bks.

Burke, Arlene Avery & Hamilton, Phyllis McAllister. Grandma's Fairy Tale Museum. 2009. 40p. pap. 21.99 *(978-1-4415-0607-8(1))* Xlibris Corp.

Caim, Barbara. Gatsby's Grand Adventure: Book 2 Renoir's the Apple Seller. Ruble, Eugene, illus. 2013. 16p. pap. 9.95 *(978-1-61633-387-4(1))* Guardian Angel Publishing, Inc.

Cali, Davide & Chaud, Benjamin. A Funny Thing Happened at the Museum ... (Funny Children's Books, Educational Picture Books, Adventure Books for Kids) 2017. (Funny Thing Happened Ser.). (ENG., Illus.). 44p. (J). (gr. 1-4). 12.99 *(978-1-4521-5593-7(3))* Chronicle Bks. LLC.

Candlewick Press. Peppa Pig & the Day at the Museum. 2015. (Peppa Pig Ser.). (ENG., Illus.). 32p. (J). (-k). 12.99 *(978-0-7636-8060-2(5)*, Candlewick Entertainment) Candlewick Pr.

Chokshi, Roshani. Aru Shah & the End of Time, 1. 2019. (Pandava Ser.). (ENG.). 376p. (gr. 4-6). 24.94 *(978-1-5364-5430-7(3)*, Riordan, Rick) Disney Pr.

—Aru Shah & the End of Time. 2022. (Pandava Ser.). (ENG.). 126p. (J). (gr. 4-5). 24.46 ***(978-1-68505-435-9(8))*** Penworthy Co., LLC, The.

—Aru Shah & the End of Time. 2019. (Pandava Ser.: Vol. 1). (ENG.). 384p. lib. bdg. 19.80 *(978-1-6636-2563-2(8))* Perfection Learning Corp.

—Rick Riordan Presents Aru Shah & the End of Time (a Pandava Novel, Book 1) 2018. (Pandava Ser.: 1). (ENG.). 368p. (J). (gr. 3-7). 16.99 *(978-1-368-01235-5(3)*, Riordan, Rick) Disney Publishing Worldwide.

—Rick Riordan Presents Aru Shah & the End of Time (a Pandava Novel Book 1) 2019. (Pandava Ser.: 1). (ENG.). 384p. (J). (gr. 3-7). pap. 8.99 *(978-1-368-02356-6(8)*, Riordan, Rick) Disney Publishing Worldwide.

Cousins, Lucy. Maisy Goes to the Museum: A Maisy First Experience Book. Cousins, Lucy, illus. 2009. (Maisy Ser.). (ENG., Illus.). 32p. (J). (gr. k-k). pap. 6.99 *(978-0-7636-4370-6(X))* Candlewick Pr.

Crain, Kira. SEK Statton. 2009. (GER.). 136p. 29.95 *(978-1-4092-6127-8(1))* Lulu Pr., Inc.

Cummings, Troy. The Notebook of Doom #6: Pop of the Bumpy Mummy (a Branches Book) - Library Edition. 2014. (Notebook of Doom Ser.: 6). (ENG.). 96p. (J). (gr. 1-3). 15.99 *(978-0-545-69899-3(5))* Scholastic, Inc.

—Pop of the Bumpy Mummy: a Branches Book (the Notebook of Doom #6) Cummings, Troy, illus. 2014. (Notebook of Doom Ser.: 6). (ENG., Illus.). 96p. (J). (gr. 1-3). pap. 5.99 *(978-0-545-69898-6(7))* Scholastic, Inc.

Czernecki, Stefan. Mystery at Midnight Museum. Date not set. 32p. (J). 14.99 *(978-0-06-026199-3(4))* HarperCollins Pubs.

David Wiggles: Individual Title Six-Packs. (gr. -1-2). 27.00 *(978-0-7635-9445-9(8))* Rigby Education.

Davis, Jacky. Ladybug Girl's Day Out with Grandpa. Soman, David, illus. 2017. (Ladybug Girl Ser.). 40p. (J). (-k). 17.99 *(978-0-8037-4032-7(8)*, Dial Bks) Penguin Young Readers Group.

de Brunhoff, Laurent. Babar's Museum of Art, 65 vols. 2003. (ENG., Illus.). 48p. (J). (gr. -1-17). 24.99 *(978-0-8109-4597-5(5))* Abrams, Inc.

Deutsch, Stacia. A Picture's Worth a Thousand Clues. Boyden, Robin, illus. 2017. (Mysterious Makers of Shaker Street Ser.). (ENG.). 112p. (J). (gr. 2-4). pap. 6.95 *(978-1-4965-4681-4(4)*, 135210); lib. bdg. 22.65 *(978-1-4965-4677-7(6)*, 135202) Capstone. (Stone Arch Bks.).

Dixon, Franklin W. The Battle of Bayport. 2014. (Hardy Boys Adventures Ser.: 6). (ENG., Illus.). 160p. (J). (gr. 3-7). pap. 6.99 *(978-1-4814-0006-0(1)*, Aladdin) Simon & Schuster Children's Publishing.

—Fossil Frenzy. Burroughs, Scott, illus. 2014. (Hardy Boys: the Secret Files Ser.: 14). (ENG.). 96p. (J). (gr. 1-4). pap. 5.99 *(978-1-4424-9043-7(8)*, Aladdin) Simon & Schuster Children's Publishing.

Evans, Michelle D. I Don't Belong in the Jungle. 2011. 20p. pap. 24.95 *(978-1-4626-1382-3(9))* America Star Bks.

Finchler, Judy & O'Malley, Kevin. Miss Malarkey's Field Trip. O'Malley, Kevin, illus. 2004. (Miss Malarkey Ser.). (ENG., Illus.). 32p. (J). (gr. k-2). 21.19 *(978-0-8027-8913-6(7)*, 9780802789136) Walker & Co.

Floca, Brian. The Frightful Story of Harry Walfish. Floca, Brian, illus. 2004. (Illus.). 26p. (J). (gr. k-4). reprint ed. pap. *(978-0-7567-7852-1(2))* DIANE Publishing Co.

Fogle, Christina Melato, illus. Museum Mouse. 2017. (J). pap. *(978-1-5393-7488-6(2))* CreateSpace Independent Publishing Platform.

Frade, B. A. & Deutsch, Stacia. Haunted Sleepover. 2017. (Tales from the Scaremaster Ser.: 6). (ENG.). 160p. (J). (gr. 3-7). pap. 5.99 *(978-0-316-43802-5(2))* Little, Brown Bks. for Young Readers.

—Haunted Sleepover. 2017. (Tales of the Scaremaster Ser.). (J). lib. bdg. 16.00 *(978-0-606-40631-4(X))* Turtleback.

Gannon, Nicholas. The Doldrums. (ENG.). 368p. (J). (gr. 3-7). 2017. pap. 7.99 *(978-0-06-232095-7(5))* 2015. (Illus.). 17.99 *(978-0-06-232094-0(7))* HarperCollins Pubs. (Greenwillow Bks.).

García Gurevich, Marina. Mateo de paseo por el prado. 2004. (SPA.). 42p. (J). 18.99 *(978-84-8488-070-7(2))* Serres, Ediciones, S. L. ESP. Dist: Lectorum Pubns., Inc.

Garton, Sam. Otter in Space. Garton, Sam, illus. 2015. (ENG., Illus.). 32p. (J). (gr. -1-3). 16.99 *(978-0-06-224776-6(X)*, Balzer & Bray) HarperCollins Pubs.

Gayle, Sharon Shavers. Emma's Escape: A Story of America's Underground Railroad. Velasquez, Eric, illus. 3rd ed. 2003. (Soundprints' Read-and-Discover Ser.). (ENG.). 48p. (J). (gr. -1-3). pap. 3.95 *(978-1-59249-021-9(2)*, S2009) Soundprints.

Gilman, Grace. Dixie & the School Trip. 2012. (Dixie: I Can Read Ser.). (J). lib. bdg. 13.55 *(978-0-606-26284-2(9))* Turtleback.

Goldman, Leslie. Night at the Museum: A Junior Novelization. 2006. (Illus.). 144p. (J). (gr. 4-6). per. 4.99 *(978-0-7641-3576-7(7))* Sourcebooks, Inc.

Griffin, Molly Beth. Field Trip Trouble. Deas, Mike, illus. 2019. (School Sidekicks Ser.). (ENG.). 32p. (J). (gr. -1-2). lib. bdg. 21.32 *(978-1-5158-4416-7(1)*, 140510, Picture Window Bks.) Capstone.

Gutiérrez, Elisa. Picturescape. rev. ed. 2007. (ENG., Illus.). 40p. (J). (gr. -1-3). pap. 9.95 *(978-1-894965-65-1(5))* Simply Read Bks. CAN. Dist: Ingram Publisher Services.

Gutman, Dan. My Weird School Goes to the Museum. Paillot, Jim, illus. 2016. 30p. (J). *(978-1-5182-2157-6(2))* Harper & Row Ltd.

—My Weird School Goes to the Museum. Paillot, Jim, illus. 2016. (I Can Read Level 2 Ser.). (ENG.). 32p. (J). (gr. -1-3). pap. 5.99 *(978-0-06-236742-6(0)*, HarperCollins) HarperCollins Pubs.

Harrison, Zac. Frozen Enemies, 1 vol. 2013. (Hyperspace High Ser.). (ENG.). 288p. (J). (gr. 4-8). 27.32 *(978-1-4342-6307-0(X)*, 123753, Stone Arch Bks.) Capstone.

Henry, James. The Cabinet of Curiosities. 2010. 240p. pap. 21.50 *(978-0-9559851-0-2(2))* Blue Cat GBR. Dist: Lulu Pr., Inc.

Huffman, Mindy. Sofia Goes to the Science Museum: What Will Happen?, 1 vol. 2017. (Computer Science for the Real World Ser.). (ENG.). 12p. (gr. 1-2). pap. *(978-1-5383-5150-5(1)*, 15f4a9ce-65b7-49c9-b170-6aced00391d8, Rosen Classroom) Rosen Publishing Group, Inc., The.

Hunt, Elizabeth Singer. Secret Agent Jack Stalwart: Book 1: the Escape of the Deadly Dinosaur: USA. 2007. (Secret Agent Jack Stalwart Ser.: 1). (ENG., Illus.). 128p. (J). (gr. 1-4). per. 5.99 *(978-1-60286-004-9(1)*, Running Pr. Kids) Running Pr.

—Secret Agent Jack Stalwart: Book 3: the Mystery of the Mona Lisa: France, Bk. 3. 2007. (Secret Agent Jack Stalwart Ser.: 3). (ENG., Illus.). 128p. (J). (gr. 1-4). per. 5.99 *(978-1-60286-001-8(7)*, Running Pr. Kids) Running Pr.

Hutchins, Hazel & Herbert, Gail. Anna at the Art Museum. Crump, Lil, illus. (ENG.). (J). (gr. k-2). 2020. 36p. pap. 9.95 *(978-1-77321-042-1(4))* 2018. 32p. 18.95 *(978-1-77321-043-8(2))* Annick Pr., Ltd. CAN. Dist: Publishers Group West (PGW).

Isaacson, Rick. The Magic Museum. 2013. 34p. pap. 19.95 *(978-0-9844938-4-5(0))* Lexingford Publishing.

Jaggi, Harleen. Mystery at the Book Store. 2007. (J). per. *(978-0-9790896-0-2(3))* Booksmart Pubns.

Jakubowski, Michele. The Professor's Discovery. Pinelli, Amerigo, illus. 2016. (Sleuths of Somerville Ser.). (ENG.). 144p. (J). (gr. 4-6). lib. bdg. 25.99 *(978-1-4965-3177-3(9)*, 132216, Stone Arch Bks.) Capstone.

—The Professor's Discovery. Pinelli, Amerigo, illus. 2017. (Sleuths of Somerville Ser.). (ENG.). 144p. (J). (gr. 4-6). pap. 6.95 *(978-1-4965-3181-0(7)*, Stone Arch Bks.) Capstone.

Jane, Pamela. Winky Blue Goes Wild! Tilley, Debbie, illus. 2003. 64p. (J). 13.95 *(978-1-59034-588-7(6))*; pap. *(978-1-59034-589-4(4))* Mondo Publishing.

Johnson-Simon, Anaya. Anaya Visits the James E Lewis Museum of Art at Morgan State University. 2009. 40p. pap. 16.99 *(978-1-4490-1884-9(X))* AuthorHouse.

Jules, Jacqueline. Freddie Ramos Hears It All. Benítez, Miguel, illus. (Zapato Power Ser.: 7). (ENG.). 96p. (J). (gr. 1-5). 2019. pap. 5.99 *(978-0-8075-9542-8(X)*, 080759542X) 2018. 14.99 *(978-0-8075-9500-8(4)*, 807595004) Whitman, Albert & Co.

Keene, Carolyn. Butterfly Blues. Francis, Peter, illus. 2015. (Nancy Drew & the Clue Crew Ser.: 40). (ENG.). 96p. (J). (gr. 1-4). pap. 5.99 *(978-1-4814-1470-8(4)*, Aladdin) Simon & Schuster Children's Publishing.

—Hidden Pictures. 2020. (Nancy Drew Diaries: 19). (ENG.). 192p. (J). (gr. 3-7). pap. 6.99 *(978-1-5344-2102-8(5)*, Simon & Schuster/Paula Wiseman Bks.) Simon & Schuster/Paula Wiseman Bks.

Kelley, Marty. Three . . . Two . . .one . . . Blastoff! Kelley, Marty, illus. 2018. (Molly Mac Ser.). (ENG., Illus.). 56p. (J). (gr. k-2). pap. 4.95 *(978-1-5158-2391-9(1)*, 137206, Picture Window Bks.) Capstone.

—Three ... Two ... One ... Blastoff! Kelley, Marty, illus. 2018. (Molly Mac Ser.). (ENG., Illus.). 56p. (J). (gr. k-2). lib. bdg. 22.65 *(978-1-5158-2387-2(3)*, 137202, Picture Window Bks.) Capstone.

Kelly, Katherine, text. Albert Bear & the Big Celebration. 2005. (J). 12.95 *(978-0-9773481-0-7(5))* Kelly, Katherine.

Kelly, Kathy & Feder, Debbie. Jelly Bean's Art Museum Adventure. 2012. 40p. pap. 20.99 *(978-1-4772-4828-7(5))* AuthorHouse.

Kenah, Katharine. The Best Seat in Second Grade. Carter, Abby, illus. 2006. (I Can Read Bks.). 48p. (J). (gr. -1-3). 11.65 *(978-0-7569-6979-0(4))* Perfection Learning Corp.

—The Best Seat in Second Grade: A Back to School Book for Kids. Carter, Abby, illus. 2006. (I Can Read Level 2 Ser.). (ENG.). 48p. (J). (gr. k-3). pap. 5.99 *(978-0-06-000736-2(2)*, HarperCollins) HarperCollins Pubs.

Kientz, Chris & Hockensmith, Steve. It's Treason, by George! Nielsen, Lee, illus. 2017. (Secret Smithsonian Adventures Ser.: 3). 64p. (gr. 3-7). pap. 10.95 *(978-1-58834-586-8(6)*, Smithsonian Bks.) Smithsonian Institution Scholarly Pr.

—The Wrong Wrights. Nielsen, Lee, illus. 2016. (Secret Smithsonian Adventures Ser.: 1). 64p. (gr. 4-7). 10.95 *(978-1-58834-541-7(6)*, Smithsonian Bks.) Smithsonian Institution Scholarly Pr.

Kirby, Stan. Captain Awesome & the Mummy's Treasure. O'Connor, George, illus. 2015. (Captain Awesome Ser.: 15). (ENG.). 128p. (J). (gr. k-4). pap. 6.99 *(978-1-4814-4438-5(7)*, Little Simon) Little Simon.

Kirk, Daniel. Library Mouse: A Museum Adventure. 2012. (ENG., Illus.). 32p. (J). (gr. -1-3). 18.99 *(978-1-4197-0173-3(8)*, 1007501, Abrams Bks. for Young Readers) Abrams, Inc.

—Museum Adventure. 2012. (ENG., Illus.). 32p. (J). (gr. k-2). pap. 7.95 *(978-1-4197-0318-8(8))* UK Abrams Bks. for Young Readers.

Konigsburg, E. L. From the Mixed-up Files of Mrs. Basil E. Frankweiler. 2007. (Illus.). 74p. (J). pap. *(978-0-545-04173-7(2))* Scholastic, Inc.

—From the Mixed-up Files of Mrs. Basil E. Frankweiler. l.t. ed. 2005. 186p. pap. 10.95 *(978-0-7862-7358-4(5)*, Large Print Pr.) Thorndike Pr.

Krulik, Nancy. Don't Be Such a Turkey! John and Wendy, illus. 2010. (Katie Kazoo, Switcheroo Ser.). 160p. (J). (gr. 2-4). pap. 6.99 *(978-0-448-45448-1(3)*, Grosset & Dunlap) Penguin Young Readers Group.

—No Bones about It #12. John and Wendy, illus. 12th ed. 2004. (Katie Kazoo, Switcheroo Ser.: 12). 80p. (J). (gr. 2-4). pap. 5.99 *(978-0-448-43358-5(3)*, Grosset & Dunlap) Penguin Young Readers Group.

Kruse, Donald W. Jasper Has Left the Building! Crank, Donny, illus. 2013. 50p. pap. 12.95 *(978-1-59663-863-1(X)*, Castle Keep Pr.) Rock, James A. & Co. Pubs.

LaFevers, R. L. Theodosia & the Eyes of Horus. Tanaka, Yoko, illus. 2011. (Theodosia Ser.: 3). (ENG.). 384p. (J). (gr. 3-7). pap. 7.99 *(978-0-547-55011-4(1)*, 1450219, Clarion Bks.) HarperCollins Pubs.

—Theodosia & the Last Pharaoh, 4. Tanaka, Yoko, illus. 2012. (Theodosia Ser.: 4). (ENG.). 400p. (J). (gr. 4-6). 21.19 *(978-0-547-39018-5(1))* Houghton Mifflin Harcourt Publishing Co.

—Theodosia & the Serpents of Chaos. Tanaka, Yoko, illus. 2008. (Theodosia Ser.: 1). (ENG.). 352p. (J). (gr. 3-7). pap. 8.99 *(978-0-618-99976-7(0)*, 1027887, Clarion Bks.) HarperCollins Pubs.

—Theodosia & the Serpents of Chaos, 1. Tanaka, Yoko, illus. 2007. (Theodosia Ser.). (ENG.). 352p. (J). (gr. 4-6). 22.44 *(978-0-618-75638-4(8))* Houghton Mifflin Harcourt Publishing Co.

LaPorte, Tom. Hembree Heiroglyphs. 2008. 98p. pap. 9.42 *(978-1-4357-5970-1(2))* Lulu Pr., Inc.

Lattimore, Deborah Nourse. Mystery at Midnight Museum. Date not set. 32p. (J). 15.89 *(978-0-06-026202-0(8))* HarperCollins Pubs.

Lehman, Barbara. Museum Trip. (ENG., Illus.). 40p. (J). (gr. -1-3). 2017. pap. 9.99 *(978-1-328-74051-9(X)*, 1677019) 2006. 17.99 *(978-0-618-58125-2(1)*, 592181) HarperCollins Pubs. (Clarion Bks.).

Lithgow, John. Carnival of the Animals. Kulikov, Boris, illus. 2004. (ENG.). 40p. (J). (gr. -1-3). 19.99 *(978-0-689-86721-7(2)*, Simon & Schuster Bks. For Young Readers) Simon & Schuster Bks. For Young Readers.

—Micawber. Payne, C. F., illus. 2005. (ENG.). 40p. (J). (gr. -1-3). reprint ed. 9.99 *(978-0-689-83542-1(6)*, Simon & Schuster Bks. For Young Readers) Simon & Schuster Bks. For Young Readers.

Loux, Matthew. The Time Museum. 2017. (Time Museum Ser.: 1). (ENG., Illus.). 256p. (J). pap. 15.99 *(978-1-59643-849-1(5)*, 900097185, First Second Bks.) Roaring Brook Pr.

—The Time Museum. 2017. (J). lib. bdg. 26.95 *(978-0-606-40348-1(5))* Turtleback.

Lucas, David. Christmas at the Toy Museum. Lucas, David, illus. 2012. (ENG., Illus.). 32p. (J). (gr. -1-2). 15.99 *(978-0-7636-5868-7(5))* Candlewick Pr.

Lytton, Deborah. The Great Museum Mix-Up & Other Surprise Endings. 2019. (Ruby Starr Ser.: 3). (ENG.). 240p. (J). (gr. 3-7). pap. 7.99 *(978-1-4926-4583-2(4))* Sourcebooks, Inc.

Macnamara, Peggy & Macnamara, Katie. Rosie the Tarantula: A True Adventure in Chicago's Field Museum. 2017. (ENG., Illus.). 48p. (J). (gr. 1-6). 17.95 *(978-0-8101-3657-1(0))* Northwestern Univ. Pr.

MNO

Marsh, Carole. The Mystery at Hollywood. 2011. (Carole Marsh Mysteries Ser.). (J). pap. 7.99 *(978-0-635-07959-6(3)*, Marsh, Carole Mysteries) Gallopade International.

—The Mystery of the Missing Dinosaurs. 2009. (Real Kids, Real Places Ser.). 146p. (J). 18.99 *(978-0-635-06995-5(4)*, Marsh, Carole Mysteries) Gallopade International.

Matyas, Diane. The Terrible Captain Jack Visits the Museum: Or A Guide of Museum Manners for Incorrigible Pirates & the Like. 2008. (Illus.). 24p. (J). *(978-0-9623017-2-8(8))* Noble Maritime Collection, The.

May, Eleanor. Lost in the Mouseum. 2018. (Mouse Math Ser.). (ENG.). 32p. (J). (gr. -1-1). lib. bdg. 34.28 *(978-1-4896-8291-8(0)*, AV2 by Weigl) Weigl Pubs., Inc.

Mayer, Mercer. Little Critter: My Trip to the Science Museum. Mayer, Mercer, illus. 2017. (Little Critter Ser.). (ENG., Illus.). 24p. (J). (gr. -1-3). pap. 4.99 *(978-0-06-147809-3(1)*, HarperFestival) HarperCollins Pubs.

—My Trip to the Science Museum. 2017. (Little Critter Ser.). (J). lib. bdg. 13.55 *(978-0-606-39625-7(X))* Turtleback.

Mayhew, James. Katie & the Dinosaurs. 2014. (Katie Ser.). (ENG., Illus.). 32p. (J). (gr. -1-k). 9.99 *(978-1-4083-3191-0(8))* Hodder & Stoughton GBR. Dist: Hachette Bk. Group.

Mayhew, James & McQuillan, Mary. Katie & the Waterlily Pond. 2015. (Katie Ser.). (ENG., Illus.). 32p. (J). (gr. -1-k). pap. 10.99 *(978-1-4083-3245-0(0))* Hodder & Stoughton GBR. Dist: Hachette Bk. Group.

McCann, Jesse Leon. Scooby-Doo & Museum Madness. 1 vol. Sur, Duendes Del, illus. 2011. (Scooby-Doo! Ser.: No. 2). (ENG.). 24p. (J). (gr. k-4). lib. bdg. 31.36 *(978-1-59961-867-8(2)*, 13245, Picture Bk.) Spotlight.

McClatchy, Lisa. Eloise & the Dinosaurs: Ready-To-Read Level 1. Lyon, Tammie, illus. (Eloise Ser.). (ENG.). 32p. (J). (gr. -1-1). 2017. 16.99 *(978-1-4814-9980-4(7))* 2007. pap. 4.99 *(978-0-689-87453-6(7))* Simon Spotlight. (Simon Spotlight).

McKay, Sindy. We Both Read Bilingual Edition-Museum Day/Dia Del Museo. Johnson, Meredith, illus. 2015.Tr. of Dia Del Museo. (ENG & SPA.). 44p. (J). (gr. k-1). pap. 5.99 *(978-1-60115-064-6(4))* Treasure Bay, Inc.

Menchin, Scott. Grandma in Blue with Red Hat. Bliss, Harry, illus. 2015. (ENG.). 32p. (J). (gr. -1-3). 16.95 *(978-1-4197-1484-9(8)*, 1067501, Abrams Bks. for Young Readers) Abrams, Inc.

Meredith-Markowitz, Susan. Charlie's Museum Adventure: Set Of 6. 2010. (Early Connections Ser.). (J). pap. 37.00 net. *(978-1-4108-1367-1(3))* Benchmark Education Co.

Messner, Kate. Fergus & Zeke. Ross, Heather, illus. 2018. (Candlewick Sparks Ser.). (ENG.). 56p. (J). (gr. k-4). pap. 5.99 *(978-0-7636-9953-6(5))* Candlewick Pr.

Metcalf, Dan. The Catacombs of Chaos: A Lottie Lipton Adventure. Panagarry, Rachelle, illus. 2017. (Adventures of Lottie Lipton Ser.). (ENG.). 80p. (J). (gr. 2-5). pap. 6.99 *(978-1-5124-8185-3(8)*, bf98dbb4-ffb2-40d9-baa2-c10e0ea72223, Darby Creek) Lerner Publishing Group.

—The Curse of the Cairo Cat: A Lottie Lipton Adventure. Panagarry, Rachelle, illus. 2017. (Adventures of Lottie Lipton Ser.). (ENG.). 80p. (J). (gr. 2-5). pap. 6.99 *(978-1-5124-8186-0(6)*, 3975037b-5b5e-4526-9f37-bde5fcb634f9); lib. bdg. 25.32 *(978-1-5124-8179-2(3)*, dd400f92-d4b7-4c17-9548-8f21bf3bb34a) Lerner Publishing Group. (Darby Creek).

—The Eagle of Rome: A Lottie Lipton Adventure. Panagarry, Rachelle, illus. 2017. (Adventures of Lottie Lipton Ser.). (ENG.). 80p. (J). (gr. 2-5). pap. 6.99 *(978-1-5124-8187-7(4)*, c93d2499-cc33-4c5f-a008-6dd45c987a49, Darby Creek) Lerner Publishing Group.

—The Egyptian Enchantment: A Lottie Lipton Adventure. Panagarry, Rachelle, illus. 2017. (Adventures of Lottie Lipton Ser.). (ENG.). 96p. (J). (gr. 2-5). pap. 6.99 *(978-1-5124-8188-4(2)*, 4fed1583-9683-4856-8a90-024c82752f05); lib. bdg. 25.32 *(978-1-5124-8182-2(3)*, b8fef38d-820d-4af0-a6d3-a069159248c1) Lerner Publishing Group. (Darby Creek).

—The Scroll of Alexandria: A Lottie Lipton Adventure. Panagarry, Rachelle, illus. 2017. (Adventures of Lottie Lipton Ser.). (ENG.). 80p. (J). (gr. 2-5). pap. 6.99 *(978-1-5124-8189-1(0)*, dfbd8d06-f168-40b7-bf38-f172f4cf1a82); 25.32 *(978-1-5124-8181-5(5)*, 7e3fdca9-4b61-427f-8b63-58a43b320696) Lerner Publishing Group. (Darby Creek).

—The Secrets of the Stone: A Lottie Lipton Adventure. Panagarry, Rachelle, illus. 2017. (Adventures of Lottie Lipton Ser.). (ENG.). 80p. (J). (gr. 2-5). pap. 6.99 *(978-1-5124-8190-7(4)*, 9c7ccc0f-a907-4c6a-8fa3-2ac8144c8825, Darby Creek) Lerner Publishing Group.

Muñoz, Isabel. Eric & Julieta: en el Museo / at the Museum (Bilingual) (Bilingual Edition) Mazali, Gustavo, illus. 2011. (Eric & Julieta Ser.).Tr. of At the Museum. (SPA.). 24p. (J). (gr. -1-3). pap. 3.99 *(978-0-545-34512-5(X)*, Scholastic en Espanol) Scholastic, Inc.

Museum Mayhem. 2014. (Nancy Drew & the Clue Crew Ser.: 39). (ENG., Illus.). 96p. (J). (gr. 1-4). pap. 5.99 *(978-1-4424-9967-6(2)*, Aladdin) Simon & Schuster Children's Publishing.

Nesbit, Sara E. Mary Wants to Be an Artist. 2009. 28p. pap. 12.49 *(978-1-4490-2609-7(5))* AuthorHouse.

Neubecker, Robert. Linus the Vegetarian T. Rex. Neubecker, Robert, illus. 2013. (ENG., Illus.). 40p. (J). (gr. -1-3). 18.99 *(978-1-4169-8512-9(3)*, Beach Lane Bks.) Beach Lane Bks.

Nicholson, Mike. Museum Mystery Squad & the Case of the Curious Coins, 32 vols. Phillips, Mike, illus. 2017. (Museum Mystery Squad Ser.: 3). 128p. (J). pap. 6.95 *(978-1-78250-363-7(3)*, Kelpies) Floris Bks. GBR. Dist: Consortium Bk. Sales & Distribution.

—Museum Mystery Squad & the Case of the Hidden Hieroglyphics, 30 vols. Phillips, Mike, illus. 2017. (Museum Mystery Squad Ser.: 2). 128p. (J). pap. 6.95 *(978-1-78250-362-0(5)*, Kelpies) Floris Bks. GBR. Dist: Consortium Bk. Sales & Distribution.

—Museum Mystery Squad & the Case of the Moving Mammoth, 30 vols. Phillips, Mike, illus. 2017. (Museum Mystery Squad Ser.: 1). 128p. (J). pap. 6.95 *(978-1-78250-361-3(7)*, Kelpies) Floris Bks. GBR. Dist: Consortium Bk. Sales & Distribution.

Night, P. J. Off the Wall. 2013. (You're Invited to a Creepover Ser.: 14). (ENG., Illus.). 160p. (J). (gr. 3-7). pap. 5.99 *(978-1-4424-7238-9(3)*, Simon Spotlight) Simon Spotlight.

Nolan, Han. When We Were Saints. 2005. (ENG.). 312p. (YA). (gr. 7-12). pap. 15.95 *(978-0-15-205322-2(0)*, 1196035, Clarion Bks.) HarperCollins Pubs.

Nord, Kristin Magnuson. Moosh & Grizzle. 2011. 28p. (gr. 1-2). 13.95 *(978-1-4269-6167-0(7))* Trafford Publishing.

O'Connor, Jane. Fancy Nancy at the Museum. 2008. (I Can Read Level 1 Ser.). (ENG., Illus.). 32p. (J). (gr. -1-3). pap. 4.99 *(978-0-06-123607-5(1)*, HarperCollins) HarperCollins Pubs.

—Fancy Nancy at the Museum. Glasser, Robin Preiss, illus. 2008. (I Can Read Level 1 Ser.). (ENG.). 32p. (J). (gr. -1-3). 17.99 *(978-0-06-123608-2(X)*, HarperCollins) HarperCollins Pubs.

O'Connor, Jane & Harper Collins / LeapFrog. Fancy Nancy at the Museum. Glasser, Robin Preiss, illus. 2008. (Fancy Nancy Ser.). (J). 13.99 *(978-1-59319-940-1(6))* LeapFrog Enterprises, Inc.

Oliver, Lauren & Chester, H. C. Curiosity House: the Shrunken Head. Lacombe, Benjamin, illus. 2015. (Curiosity House Ser.: 1). (ENG.). 368p. (J). (gr. 3-7). 16.99 *(978-0-06-227081-8(8)*, HarperCollins) HarperCollins Pubs.

ón, Raúl. Imagine! ón, Raúl, illus. 2018. (ENG., Illus.). 48p. (J). (gr. -1-3). 17.99 *(978-1-4814-6273-0(3)*, Simon & Schuster/Paula Wiseman Bks.) Simon & Schuster/Paula Wiseman Bks.

O'neal, Katherine Pebley. The Fume in the Tomb. Collins, Daryl, illus. 2004. 68p. (J). lib. bdg. 15.00 *(978-1-4242-0901-9(3))* Fitzgerald Bks.

Orloff, Karen Kaufman. Nightlight Detective: Mystery at the Museum. Smith, Jamie, illus. 2013. 42p. spiral bd. 12.99 *(978-1-4413-1228-0(5))* Peter Pauper Pr. Inc.

Papademetriou, Lisa. Apartment 1986. 2017. (ENG.). 272p. (J). (gr. 3-7). 16.99 *(978-0-06-237108-9(8)*, HarperCollins) HarperCollins Pubs.

Parish, Herman. Amelia Bedelia's Backpack Bundle. Sweat, Lynn, illus. 2012. 192p. (J). *(978-1-4351-4392-0(2)*, Greenwillow Bks.) HarperCollins Pubs.

—Amelia Bedelia's Masterpiece. 2008. (I Can Read Level 2 Ser.). (ENG., Illus.). 64p. (J). (gr. k-3). pap. 4.99 *(978-0-06-084357-1(8)*, Greenwillow Bks.) HarperCollins Pubs.

—Amelia Bedelia's Masterpiece. Sweat, Lynn, illus. 2007. (Amelia Bedelia Ser.). (ENG.). 64p. (J). (gr. k-4). 16.99 *(978-0-06-084355-7(1)*, Greenwillow Bks.) HarperCollins Pubs.

Parsons, Tom. Pinky the Rat at the Brussels Sprout Museum. 2007. 194p. 27.76 *(978-1-4303-1538-4(5))* Lulu Pr., Inc.

Perelstein, Jennifer. Who Moved the Masterpieces? A Visit to the Mcnay Art Museum. 2010. 30p. pap. 15.99 *(978-1-60844-585-1(2))* Dog Ear Publishing, LLC.

Perkins, Lynne Rae. The Museum of Everything. 2021. (ENG., Illus.). 40p. (J). (gr. -1-3). 17.99 *(978-0-06-298630-6(9)*, Greenwillow Bks.) HarperCollins Pubs.

The Phantom of Nantucket. 2014. (Nancy Drew Diaries: 7). (ENG., Illus.). 192p. (J). (gr. 3-7). pap. 7.99 *(978-1-4814-0015-2(0)*, Aladdin) Simon & Schuster Children's Publishing.

Pifferson Sisters, the. Zach & Lucy & the Museum of Natural Wonders: Ready-To-Read Level 3. Chambers, Mark, illus. 2016. (Zach & Lucy Ser.). (ENG.). 40p. (J). (gr. 1-3). pap. 4.99 *(978-1-4814-3935-0(9)*, Simon Spotlight) Simon Spotlight.

Prime, D. Van al Museo. (Serie Sara y Pablo - Sarah & Paul Ser.: No. 5).Tr. of Go to the Museum. (SPA.). (J). 2.99 *(978-0-7899-0499-7(3)*, 498899) Editorial Unilit.

Prime, Derek. Sarah & Paul Go to the Museum. 2006. (Sarah & Paul Ser.). (ENG., Illus.). 128p. (J). (gr. 2-5). per. 6.99 *(978-1-84550-161-7(6)*, 2998b457-4155-49a3-83f2-dd09f61c5ae7) Christian Focus Pubns. GBR. Dist: Baker & Taylor Publisher Services (BTPS).

Rau, Dana. Moon Walk. Buchs, Thomas, illus. 3rd ed. 2003. (Soundprints' Read-and-Discover Ser.). (ENG.). 48p. (J). (gr. -1-3). pap. 4.35 *(978-1-59249-015-8(8)*, S2006) Soundprints.

Rau, Dana Meachen. Moon Walk. Buchs, Thomas, illus. 2004. (Soundprints' Read-and-Discover Ser.). 48p. (gr. -1-3). 13.95 *(978-0-7569-3370-8(6))* Perfection Learning Corp.

Richardson, Deborra. Treasures at the Museum. 2011. (Illus.). 64p. (J). pap. 5.99 *(978-0-9824945-1-6(3))* Elevator Group, The.

Rim, Sujean. Birdie's Happiest Halloween. 2016. (ENG., Illus.). 40p. (J). (gr. -1-3). 16.99 *(978-0-316-40746-5(1))* Little, Brown Bks. for Young Readers.

Ripley's Believe It or Not Editors. Haunted Hotel. 2011. (Ripley RBI Ser.). 128p. (J). pap. 4.99 *(978-1-893951-65-5(0))* Ripley Entertainment, Inc.

Robertson, K. A. Fright at the Museum. Wood, Katie, illus. 2017. (G. H. O. S. T. Squad Ser.). (ENG.). 48p. (gr. 3-5). pap. 8.95 *(978-1-68342-437-6(9)*, 9781683424376) Rourke Educational Media.

Rock, Zack. Homer Henry Hudson's Curio Museum. 2014. (ENG., Illus.). 32p. (J). (gr. 5-8). 18.99 *(978-1-56846-260-8(3)*, 21312, Creative Editions) Creative Co., The.

Rosen, Michael. You're Thinking about Doughnuts. Tisdall, Sarah, illus. 2006. 90p. (J). (gr. 2-4). per. 6.95 *(978-1-903015-03-2(0))* Barn Owl Bks, London GBR. Dist: Independent Pubs. Group.

Roy, Ron. A to Z Mysteries Super Edition #10: Colossal Fossil. Gurney, John Steven, illus. 2018. (to Z Mysteries Ser.: 10). 144p. (J). (gr. 1-4). 6.99 *(978-0-399-55198-7(0)*, Random Hse. Bks. for Young Readers) Random Hse. Children's Bks.

Rush, Barbara & Stratton, Jane. The Boat in the Attic. 2012. (ENG.). 30p. pap. 15.00 *(978-1-938002-02-1(4)*, Hummingbird World Media) Double Edge Pr.

Ruurs, Margriet. Bus to the Badlands. Dávila, Claudia, illus. 2018. 80p. (J). *(978-1-5490-7424-0(5))* Orca Bk. Pubs.

Sagner, Sibel, et al. A Day at the Museum Blue Band. Pérez, Moni, illus. 2016. (Cambridge Reading Adventures Ser.). (ENG.). 16p. pap. 7.95 *(978-1-316-50320-1(8))* Cambridge Univ. Pr.

Sale, Carolyn. How to Read a Dinosaur & Other Museum Tales. Dubinsky, Lon, ed. 2004. (Illus.). 96p. *(978-1-895766-27-1(3)*, Pacific Educational Pr.) Univ. of British Columbia Pr.

Sally's Picture: Individual Title Six-Packs. (Literatura 2000 Ser.). (gr. 1-2). 28.00 *(978-0-7635-0108-2(5))* Rigby Education.

Sanders, Addie Meyer. I Don't Want to Go. l.t. ed. 2012. 43p. (J). pap. *(978-1-4596-3449-7(7))* ReadHowYouWant.com, Ltd.

Santopolo, Jill. Nina, the Pinta, & the Vanishing Treasure (an Alec Flint Mystery #1). 1. 2009. (ENG.). 192p. (J). (gr. 2-5). mass mkt. 6.99 *(978-0-439-90353-0(X)*, Scholastic Paperbacks) Scholastic, Inc.

Scieszka, Jon. 2095. Smith, Lane, illus. 2005. (Time Warp Trio Ser.: No. 5). 72p. (gr. 4-7). 15.00 *(978-0-7569-5989-0(6))* Perfection Learning Corp.

—2095 #5. Smith, Lane, illus. 2004. (Time Warp Trio Ser.: 5). 80p. (J). (gr. 2-4). pap. 6.99 *(978-0-14-240044-9(0)*, Puffin Books) Penguin Young Readers Group.

Selznick, Brian. Wonderstruck. 1 vol. Selznick, Brian, illus. 2011. (ENG., Illus.). 640p. (J). (gr. 4-7). 29.99 *(978-0-545-02789-2(6)*, Scholastic Pr.) Scholastic, Inc.

Shaskan, Trisha Speed. Meteorite or Meteor-Wrong? Case 2, Bk. 2. Shaskan, Stephen, illus. 2018. (Q & Ray Ser.). (ENG.). 48p. (J). (gr. 2-5). 26.65 *(978-1-5124-1148-5(5)*, ac6051f7-42ca-4332-8dd7-363184dbe085, Graphic Universe™) Lerner Publishing Group.

Shields, Kathleen J. Hamilton Troll Meets Dinosaurs. Klug, Leigh A. & Bryant, Carol W., illus. 6th ed. 2013. 36p. 14.00 *(978-0-9882745-5-6(8))* Erin Go Bragh Publishing.

Smith, Alex T. Mr. Penguin & the Lost Treasure. 2019. (Mr. Penguin Ser.: 1). (ENG., Illus.). 208p. (J). (gr. 3-7). 16.95 *(978-1-68263-120-1(6))* Peachtree Publishing Co. Inc.

Snyder, Karen. Mona Lisa's Makeover. LaGrange, Tiffany, illus. 2010. 24p. pap. 12.95 *(978-1-936343-15-7(0))* Peppertree Pr., The.

Steele, Michael Anthony. Secret of the Tomb: Night at the Museum: Nick's Tales. 3rd ed. 2014. (Night at the Museum: Nick's Tales Ser.). 176p. (J). (gr. 3-7). pap. 5.99 *(978-1-4380-0524-9(5))* Sourcebooks, Inc.

Stine, R. L. Fright Knight & the Ooze: Twice Terrifying Tales. 2010. (R. L. Stine's Ghosts of Fear Street Ser.). (ENG.). 240p. (J). (gr. 3-7). pap. 7.99 *(978-1-4169-9135-9(2)*, Aladdin) Simon & Schuster Children's Publishing.

Strohm, Stephanie Kate. Pilgrims Don't Wear Pink. 2012. (ENG.). 208p. (YA). (gr. 7-12). pap. 12.99 *(978-0-547-56459-3(7)*, 1454809, Clarion Bks.) HarperCollins Pubs.

Suen, Anastasia. Dino Hunt: A Robot & Rico Story. Laughead, Michael, illus. 2010. (Robot & Rico Ser.). (ENG.). 32p. (J). (gr. 1-2). pap. 6.25 *(978-1-4342-2300-5(0)*, 103169, Stone Arch Bks.) Capstone.

Teitelbaum, Michael. The Phantom Pharaoh. 2015. (Cold Whispers Ser.). (ENG., Illus.). 32p. (J). (gr. 2-6). lib. bdg. 28.50 *(978-1-62724-810-5(2))* Bearport Publishing Co., Inc.

Thomas, Debbie. Dead Hairy. MacDonald, Stella, illus. unabr. ed. 2011. (ENG.). 256p. (J). pap. 14.95 *(978-1-85635-678-7(7))* Mercier Pr., Ltd., The IRL. Dist: Dufour Editions, Inc.

Town, Vicky. Mayhem in the Museum. 2013. 74p. pap. 9.99 *(978-1-61720-974-1(0))* Wilder Pubns., Corp.

Trenc, Milan. The Night at the Museum. 2006. (Illus.). 32p. (J). (gr. k-2). pap. 6.99 *(978-0-7641-3631-3(3)*, Sourcebooks Jabberwocky) Sourcebooks, Inc.

Vajda, Tibor Timothy. The End of the World. 2008. 96p. pap. 9.95 *(978-0-595-52914-8(3))* iUniverse, Inc.

Verde, Susan. The Museum. Reynolds, Peter H., illus. 2013. (ENG.). 32p. (J). (gr. -1-2). 17.99 *(978-1-4197-0594-6(6)*, 1048601, Abrams Bks. for Young Readers) Abrams, Inc.

Waite, Judy. Digging for Dinosaurs. Parsons, Garry, illus. 2003. (Flying Foxes Ser.). (ENG.). 48p. (J). lib. bdg. *(978-0-7787-1483-5(7))* Crabtree Publishing Co.

Wallace, Nancy Elizabeth. Stars! Stars! Stars!, 0 vols. Wallace, Nancy Elizabeth, illus. 2012. (ENG., Illus.). 40p. (J). (gr. 1-3). 17.99 *(978-0-7614-5612-4(0)*, 9780761456124, Two Lions) Amazon Publishing.

We Both Read-Museum Day. 2014. (Illus.). 44p. (J). 9.95 *(978-1-60115-265-7(5))*; pap. 5.99 *(978-1-60115-266-4(3))* Treasure Bay, Inc.

Wells, Helen. Cherry Ames, Companion Nurse. 2007. (Cherry Ames Nurse Stories Ser.). 224p. (J). (gr. 3-7). 14.95 *(978-0-8261-0431-2(2))* Springer Publishing Co., Inc.

Weston Woods Staff, creator. Norman the Doorman. 2011. 29.95 *(978-0-439-78648-5(7))* Weston Woods Studios, Inc.

Weyn, Suzanne. The Titanic Locket. 2014. (Hauntings: the Haunted Museum Ser.: 1). lib. bdg. 17.20 *(978-0-606-35809-5(9))* Turtleback.

Wilburn, Mary Lynne. Sam's Toy Museum. 2012. 24p. pap. 15.99 *(978-1-4653-4029-0(7))* Xlibris Corp.

Wilkins, James Francis. The Queen & Mr Brown: a Night in the Natural History Museum. 2016. (Queen & Mr Brown Ser.). (ENG., Illus.). 48p. (J). (gr. -1-2). 17.99 *(978-0-565-09376-1(2))* Natural History Museum Pubns. GBR. Dist: Independent Pubs. Group.

—The Queen & Mr Brown: Meet the Rats. (Queen & Mr Brown Ser.). (ENG., Illus.). 48p. (J). (gr. k-2). 2019. pap. 12.99 *(978-0-565-09446-1(7))* 2017. 17.99 *(978-0-565-09438-6(6))* Natural History Museum Pubns. GBR. Dist: Independent Pubs. Group.

Yee, Wong Herbert. Hammy & Gerbee: Mummies at the Museum. Yee, Wong Herbert, illus. 2018. (ENG., Illus.). 112p. (J). pap. 13.99 *(978-1-62779-462-6(X)*, 900151451, Holt, Henry & Co. Bks. For Young Readers) Holt, Henry & Co.

MUSHROOMS

see also Fungi

Bowers, A., et al. Mushrooms of the World with Pictures to Color. 2013. (Dover Nature Coloring Book Ser.). (ENG., Illus.). 48p. (J). (gr. 3-12). pap. 4.99 *(978-0-486-24643-7(4)*, 246434) Dover Pubns., Inc.

Mushroom. 2003. stu. ed. 36.95 *(978-0-8136-9261-6(X))*; 38.95 *(978-0-8136-4122-5(5))* Modern Curriculum Pr.

Owings, Lisa. From Spore to Mushroom. 2017. (Start to Finish, Second Ser.). (ENG., Illus.). 24p. (J). (gr. k-3). 23.99 *(978-1-5124-3441-5(8)*, 267d55a1-ec64-4a08-bf88-1b8517a37132, Lerner Pubns.); pap. 7.99 *(978-1-5124-5626-4(8)*, 4db889d2-32ec-45a3-85cf-11bc6b52b2ab) Lerner Publishing Group.

MUSIAL, STAN, 1920-2013

Giglio, James N. Stan Musial: Baseball Hero. 2015. (ENG., Illus.). 48p. (J). pap. 24.00 *(978-1-61248-151-7(5))* Truman State Univ. Pr.

MUSIC

see also Church Music; Concerts; Jazz; Musicians; Singing; Sound

also Orchestral Music; Organ Music; Piano music; etc. and headings beginning with the words Music and Musical

Abdo, Kenny. Music Concerts. 2018. (Arena Events Ser.). (ENG.). 24p. (J). (gr. 2-8). lib. bdg. 31.36 *(978-1-5321-2536-2(4)*, 30081, Abdo Zoom-Fly) ABDO Publishing Co.

Aksomitis, Linda, ed. Downloading Music, 1 vol. 2007. (Issues That Concern You Ser.). (ENG., Illus.). 112p. (gr. 7-10). lib. bdg. 43.63 *(978-0-7377-3646-5(1)*, ec1221b0-225a-46ae-81db-eeb62d9808a7, Greenhaven Publishing) Greenhaven Publishing LLC.

Albrecht, Sally K., et al. I Sing, You Sing, Too! 30 Echo Songs for Young Singers. 2008. (I Sing, You Sing Ser.). (ENG.). 68p. pap. 19.95 *(978-0-7390-5259-4(4))* Alfred Publishing Co., Inc.

—I Sing, You Sing, Too! 30 Echo Songs for Young Singers, Book & CD. 2008. (I Sing, You Sing Ser.). (ENG.). 68p. pap. 44.95 *(978-0-7390-5257-0(8))* Alfred Publishing Co., Inc.

Aliki. ¡Musica! 2004. (SPA.). 28p. (J). (gr. k-3). 22.99 *(978-84-261-3343-4(6))* Juventud, Editorial ESP. Dist: Lectorum Pubns., Inc.

Allan, Delores. Magical Moments with Roy & Toni: The Magic of Music. 2011. 20p. pap. 11.99 *(978-1-4634-2686-6(0))* AuthorHouse.

Allman, Toney. Downloading Music. 2007. (Ripped from the Headlines Ser.). 64p. (J). (gr. 7-12). 23.95 *(978-1-60217-006-3(1))* Erickson Pr.

Ancona, George. Ole Flamenco. Ancona, George, photos by. 2010. (ENG., Illus.). 47p. (J). (gr. 2-6). 19.95 *(978-1-60060-361-7(0))* Lee & Low Bks., Inc.

Anniss, Matt. The Story of Techno & Dance Music. 2013. (Pop Histories Ser.). (Illus.). 32p. (gr. 4-7). 31.35 *(978-1-59920-967-8(5))* Black Rabbit Bks.

Apostoli, Andrea, ed. What Great Music! Classical Selections to Hear & to See. Dufey, Alexandra, illus. 2011. (ENG.). 48p. (J). (-1). pap. 19.95 *(978-1-57999-841-7(0))* G I A Pubns., Inc.

Archuleta, Michael, concept. Mariachi Method Book for Vihuela. 2nd ed. 2005. (YA). 24.95 *(978-0-9675951-3-9(4))* Mixta Publishing Co.

Ardley, Neil. La Musica.Tr. of Music. (SPA.). 64p. (YA). (gr. 5-8). *(978-84-372-3711-4(4))* Altea, Ediciones, S.A. - Grupo Santillana.

Barden, Christine H., et al. Music for Little Mozarts Little Mozarts Perform the Nutcracker: 8 Favorites Form Tchaikovsky's Nutcracker Suite. 2007. (Music for Little Mozarts Ser.). (ENG.). 24p. (J). pap. 7.99 *(978-0-7390-4822-1(8))* Alfred Publishing Co., Inc.

Bass Schule. 2004. (GER.). (YA). cd-rom *(978-1-891155-18-5(0))* EMedia Corp.

Ben-Hur, Roni Amos. Talk Jazz Guitar: A Comprehensive Collection of Be Bop Studies for the Aspiringand Professional Jazz Guitarist. 2004. 268p. (YA). pap. 34.00 net. *(978-0-9744943-1-9(3))* Bohobza Music.

Bennett, Paul. The Seven Harmonies of Music: A Field Guide, 1. 2004. (Illus.). 80p. ring bd. 19.95 *(978-0-9753599-0-7(8))* Music Awareness.

Bernard, Yves & Fredette, Nathalie. Le Guide de la Musique du Monde. 2004. (FRE., Illus.). 230p. (J). pap. *(978-2-89021-662-4(4))* Diffusion du livre Mirabel (DLM).

Between the Lions - Early Literacy Kit - Zoop! Zoop!, 1 cass., 1 bk. 2005. (Between the Lions Ser.). 36p. (J). VHS 29.95 *(978-1-59375-287-3(3)*, WG38653) WGBH Boston Video.

Billet, Marion. I Love Music: My First Sound Book. Billet, Marion, illus. 2016. (ENG., Illus.). 16p. (J). (gr. -1 — 1). 9.99 *(978-1-338-03261-1(5)*, Cartwheel Bks.) Scholastic, Inc.

Birthday Party Songs. (Early Learning Ser.). (J). incl. audio. 7.98 incl. audio NewSound, LLC.

Bissinger, Wendy & Wendy Bissinger. Sequenced Scale Studies for Cello. 2004. (Illus.). 108p. (J). spiral bd. *(978-0-9755624-0-6(1))* Boshu Pr.

Black, Dave & Houghton, Steve. Alfred's Kid's Drum Course, Bk 1: The Easiest Drum Method Ever!, Starter Kit (Sound Shape(tm) Included) 2005. (Kid's Drum Course Ser.: Bk 1). (ENG.). 999p. pap. 25.99 *(978-0-7390-3742-3(0))* Alfred Publishing Co., Inc.

Blair, Cathy. Music Baseball: Name That Style. 2005. act. bk. ed., instr.'s gde. ed. 29.95 *(978-0-89328-174-8(3)*, 30/2006H) Heritage Music Pr.

—Rhythm Rally! Level 1, Grades 3-5: Six Fun & Fast-Paced Rhythm Games in One! 2004. act. bk. ed. 29.95 *(978-0-89328-176-2(X)*, 30/1908H) Heritage Music Pr.

—Rhythm Rally! Level 2, Grades 5-7: Six Fun & Fast-Paced Rhythm Games in One! 2004. act. bk. ed. 29.95 *(978-0-89328-177-9(8)*, 30/1909H) Heritage Music Pr.

—Rhythms of the World: Discovering the Indigenous Rhythms of Africa, India, Cuba, & Brazil; Grades 5-8. 2005. 34.95 *(978-0-89328-173-1(5)*, 30/1989H) Heritage Music Pr.

Blending Music Styles Videotape: Videotape Packages. 2003. (Share the Music Ser.). (gr. 4-8). *(978-0-02-295486-4(4))* Macmillan/McGraw-Hill Schl. Div.

Boom, Tap-n-Play Bells & Boomwhackers. 2006. cd-rom 19.95 *(978-1-933260-16-7(5))* Vision Pubns.

Boytim, Joan Frey. Daffodils, Violets & Snowflakes - Low Voice: 24 Classical Songs for Young Women Ages Ten to Mid-Teens. 2003. (ENG.). 88p. pap. 16.99 *(978-0-634-06212-4(3)*, 00740245) Leonard, Hal Corp.

Boytim, Joan Frey, ed. Daffodils, Violets & Snowflakes - High Voice: Classical Songs for Young Women High Voice Edition. 2003. (ENG.). 88p. (gr. 5-18). pap. 17.99 *(978-0-634-06181-3(X)*, 00740244) Leonard, Hal Corp.

Burch, Lynda S. Meet Me at the Park! Burch, Lynda S., photos by. 2005. (Illus.). 64p. (J). E-Book 6.00 incl. cd-rom *(978-1-933090-15-3(4))* Guardian Angel Publishing, Inc.

—Wicky Wacky Things that Go! Airplanes 1. Roberts, MarySue, photos by. 2004. (Illus.). 28p. (J). E-Book 9.95 incl.

cd-rom *(978-1-933090-07-8(3))* Guardian Angel Publishing, Inc.
—Wicky Wacky Things that Go! Tractors. Burch, Lynda S., photos by. 2004. (Illus.). 28p. (J). E-Book 9.95 incl. cd-rom *(978-1-933090-09-2(X))* Guardian Angel Publishing, Inc.
—Wicky Wacky Things that Go! Trains 1. Burch, Lynda S., photos by. 2004. (Illus.). 16p. (J). E-Book 9.95 incl. cd-rom *(978-1-933090-02-3(2))* Guardian Angel Publishing, Inc.
—Wicky Wacky Things That Go! Trucks. Burch, Lynda S., photos by. 2004. (Illus.). 28p. (J). E-Book 9.95 incl. cd-rom *(978-1-933090-11-5(1))* Guardian Angel Publishing, Inc.
—Zoom Zoom Zoom Come Count with Me! Burch, Lynda S., photos by. 2005. (Illus.). 20p. (J). E-Book 6.00 incl. cd-rom *(978-1-933090-14-6(6))* Guardian Angel Publishing, Inc.
Can't Help Falling in Love. Date not set. 32p. 15.99 *(978-0-06-027796-3(3))* HarperCollins Pubs.
Carolus, Mario. Music for New Zealand, Years 9 & 10. 2013. (ENG.). pap., stu. ed. *(978-1-107-61206-8(3))* Cambridge Univ. Pr.
Casterline, L. C. The Sounds of Music, 1 vol. 2004. (Sounds of Music Ser.). (ENG., Illus.). 16p. (gr. k-2). lib. bdg. 22.67 *(978-0-8368-4100-8(X),* 0d0ff6f2-b524-4be2-a0f5-0430febd1d63, Gareth Stevens Learning Library) Stevens, Gareth Publishing LLLP.
Cefrey, Holly. Career Building Through Music, Video, & Software Mashups. 2009. (Digital Career Building Ser.). 64p. (gr. 6-6). 58.50 *(978-1-61512-169-4(2))* Rosen Publishing Group, Inc., The.
Celia, Shannon Casey. Nature's Music: Musical Colors Series 2003. (ENG., Illus.). 12p. (J). spiral bd. 10.95 *(978-1-931844-07-9(0),* PP1019) Piano Pr.
Claudio, Abbado. Yo Sere Director de Orquesta. 2007. (SPA.). 48p. (J). (gr. 4-5). 23.99 *(978-84-8470-052-4(6))* Corimbo, Editorial S.L. ESP. Dist: Lectorum Pubns., Inc.
Compact Discs. 2003. (Share the Music Ser.). (gr. 2-18). *(978-0-02-295437-6(6));* (gr. 3-18). *(978-0-02-295438-3(4));* (gr. 4-18). *(978-0-02-295439-0(2));* (gr. 5-18). *(978-0-02-295440-6(6));* (gr. 7-18). *(978-0-02-295442-0(2))* Macmillan/McGraw-Hill Schl. Div.
Congratulations - Grade 1 Alto Sax & Piano. (YA). 9.95 *(978-1-85909-666-6(2),* Warner Bros. Pubns.) Alfred Publishing Co., Inc.
Conley, Eddie And Uchenna. Team Conley: Elaykim's Life Lessons for the Love of Music. 2011. 28p. pap. 13.99 *(978-1-4634-0144-3(2))* AuthorHouse.
Creating Musical Moods Videotape: Videotape Packages. 2003. (Share the Music Ser.). (gr. 3-6). *(978-0-02-295484-0(8))* Macmillan/McGraw-Hill Schl. Div.
Dahl, Roald, et al. Collins Musicals - Roald Dahl's Cinderella (Book + Downloads), 1 vol. Blake, Quentin & Eccles, Jane, illus. 2008. (and C Black Musicals Ser.). (ENG.). 64p. (J). (gr. 2-6). pap. 42.95 *(978-0-7136-8195-6(0))* HarperCollins Pubs. Ltd. GBR. Dist: Independent Pubs. Group.
—Collins Musicals - Roald Dahl's the Three Little Pigs (Book + CD/CD-ROM): a Tail-Twistingly Treacherous Musical, 1 vol. Blake, Quentin, illus. 2007. (and C Black Musicals Ser.). (ENG.). 64p. (J). (gr. 2-6). pap. 42.95 incl. cd-rom *(978-0-7136-8202-1(7))* HarperCollins Pubs. Ltd. GBR. Dist: Independent Pubs. Group.
Dale, Monica. Eurhythmics for Young Children: Six Lessons for Winter. 2003. (Illus.). 108p. pap. 24.95 *(978-0-9701416-1-3(0))* MusiKinesis.
Davidson, Susanna. Swan Lake with Music. 2012. (Picture Books with Music Ser.). 24p. (J). bds. 18.99 *(978-0-7945-3301-4(9),* Usborne) EDC Publishing.
Diamond, Eileen. Let's Make Music Fun! Songs to Sing, Action Songs, Rounds & Songs with Percussion Instruments. (Let's Make Music Fun Ser.). 14.95 *(978-1-85909-417-4(1),* Warner Bros. Pubns.) Alfred Publishing Co., Inc.
District License Package: Technology: Music with MIDI. 2003. (Share the Music Ser.). (gr. 1-18). *(978-0-02-295470-3(8));* (gr. 2-18). *(978-0-02-295471-0(6));* (gr. 3-18). *(978-0-02-295472-7(4));* (gr. 4-18). *(978-0-02-295473-4(2));* (gr. 5-18). *(978-0-02-295474-1(0));* (gr. 6-18). *(978-0-02-295475-8(9));* (gr. 7-18). *(978-0-02-295298-3(5));* (gr. 8-18). *(978-0-02-295299-0(3))* Macmillan/McGraw-Hill Schl. Div.
Doug Smith's Classical Guitar Method, Reading Book 1: Introduction to the Natural Notes in the First Position. 2004. (J). 24.95 *(978-0-9729879-1-2(6))* Musictech College Pr.
Dream Theater. Dream Theater - Awake. 2007. (ENG.). 160p. pap. 29.99 *(978-0-89724-608-8(X),* 00700142) Alfred Publishing Co., Inc.
EMedia Fortgeschrittene Gitarren Schule. 2004. (GER.). (YA). cd-rom *(978-1-891155-16-1(4))* EMedia Corp.
eMedia Klavier & Keyboard Einstieg. CD-ROM für Windows XP/ME/2000/NT/98//95 und Macintosh: Die ersten Schritte auf dem Klavier und Keyboard. 2004. (GER.). (YA). cd-rom *(978-1-891155-22-2(9))* EMedia Corp.
Emmer, Rae. Band: Banda, 1 vol. 2003. (School Activities / Actividades Escolares Ser.). (SPA & ENG., Illus.). 24p. (J). (gr. 1-2). lib. bdg. 26.27 *(978-0-8239-6902-9(9),* 7d4bc4df-b5f5-440f-a287-abdaca07cc74) Rosen Publishing Group, Inc., The.
—Chorus. 2009. (School Activities Ser.). 24p. (gr. 1-1). 42.50 *(978-1-60852-996-4(7),* PowerKids Pr.) Rosen Publishing Group, Inc., The.
—Chorus: Coro, 1 vol. 2003. (School Activities / Actividades Escolares Ser.). (SPA & ENG., Illus.). 24p. (J). (gr. 1-2). lib. bdg. 26.27 *(978-0-8239-6903-6(7),* bdf4bf28-fa41-453b-85f2-430a5418c933) Rosen Publishing Group, Inc., The.
—Chorus / Coro. 2009. (School Activities / Actividades escolares Ser.). (ENG & SPA.). 24p. (gr. 1-2). 42.50 *(978-1-60853-002-1(7),* Editorial Buenas Letras) Rosen Publishing Group, Inc., The.
Feierabend, John M. The Book of Beginning Circle Games: Let's Make a Circle. 2004. (First Steps in Music Ser.). (ENG., Illus.). 84p. (J). (gr. -1-2). pap. 15.95 *(978-1-57999-266-8(8),* G-5878) G I A Pubns., Inc.
Feierabend, John M. & Kahan, Jane. The Book of Movement Exploration: Can You Move Like This? 2004. (First Steps in Music Ser.). (ENG., Illus.). 86p. (J). (gr. -1-2). pap. 14.95 *(978-1-57999-264-4(1),* G-5876) G I A Pubns., Inc.
Feldstein, Sandy. Rhythm Party Guide. 2004. audio compact disk 24.95 *(978-1-932895-16-2(7))* PlayinTime Productions, Inc.
Feldstein, Sandy & Clark, Larry. Antiphony. 2004. (YA). pap. 40.00 *(978-1-932895-03-2(5))* PlayinTime Productions, Inc.
—Fanfare Minuet - Trombone/Baritone/Basson Solo with Piano Acc. 2005. (YA). pap. 9.95 incl. audio compact disk *(978-1-932895-53-7(1))* PlayinTime Productions, Inc.
—Fanfare Minuet -Trumpet/Baritone Solo with Piano Acc. 2005. (YA). pap. 9.95 incl. audio compact disk *(978-1-932895-51-3(5))* PlayinTime Productions, Inc.
—The Fifers. 2005. (YA). pap. 10.95 *(978-1-932895-81-0(7))* PlayinTime Productions, Inc.
—Honor March. 2005. (YA). pap. 40.00 *(978-1-932895-99-5(X))* PlayinTime Productions, Inc.
—Jupiter. 2004. (YA). pap. 40.00 *(978-1-932895-00-1(0))* PlayinTime Productions, Inc.
—Jupiter - Conductor's Score. 2004. (YA). pap. 6.00 *(978-1-932895-01-8(9))* PlayinTime Productions, Inc.
—Outback Rhapsody. 2004. (YA). pap. 40.00 *(978-1-932895-06-3(X))* PlayinTime Productions, Inc.
—Outback Rhapsody - Conductor's Score. 2004. (YA). pap. 8.00 *(978-1-932895-07-0(8))* PlayinTime Productions, Inc.
—Scherzando - Alto Sax/Bari. Sax Solo with Piano Acc. W/CD. 2005. (YA). pap. 9.95 *(978-1-932895-28-5(0))* PlayinTime Productions, Inc.
—Scherzando - Keyboard Percussion Solo with piano acc. W/CD. 2005. (YA). pap. 9.95 *(978-1-932895-34-6(5))* PlayinTime Productions, Inc.
—Scherzando - Snare Drum Solo with Piano Acc. W/CD. 2005. (YA). pap. 9.95 *(978-1-932895-35-3(3))* PlayinTime Productions, Inc.
—Scherzando - Trombone/Baritone/Bassoon Solo with Piano Acc. W/CD. 2005. (YA). pap. 9.95 *(978-1-932895-32-2(9))* PlayinTime Productions, Inc.
—Scherzando - Tuba Solo with Piano Acc. W/CD. 2005. (YA). pap. 9.95 *(978-1-932895-33-9(7))* PlayinTime Productions, Inc.
—Scherzando -Trumpet/Baritone Solo with Piano Acc. w/ CD. 2005. (YA). pap. 9.95 *(978-1-932895-30-8(2))* PlayinTime Productions, Inc.
—Scherzando Tenor Sax Solo with Piano Acc. W/CD. 2005. (YA). pap. 9.95 *(978-1-932895-29-2(9))* PlayinTime Productions, Inc.
—Sentinel. 2004. (YA). pap. 40.00 *(978-1-932895-10-0(8))* PlayinTime Productions, Inc.
—Sentinel - conductor's Score. 2004. (YA). pap. 6.00 *(978-1-932895-11-7(6))* PlayinTime Productions, Inc.
Feldstein, Sandy & Firth, Vic. Vic Firth/SandyFeldstein Percussion Series - complete Score. 2004. (YA). 24.95 *(978-1-932895-12-4(4))* PlayinTime Productions, Inc.
Fox, Donna Brink, et al. Classroom Music for Little Mozarts — the Big Music Book, Bk.3: 10 Sequential Lessons for Ages 4-6. Big Book. 2010. (Music for Little Mozarts Ser.: Bk 3). (ENG.). 999p. (J). pap. 59.99 *(978-0-7390-4564-0(4))* Alfred Publishing Co., Inc.
Gameplan - Grade One: An Active Music Curriculum for Children. 2005. spiral bd. 80.00 net. *(978-0-9767650-0-4(4))* KiD Sounds.
Gardner, Jane P. Music Science, Vol. 11. Lewin, Russ, ed. 2015. (Science 24/7 Ser.). (Illus.). 48p. (J). (gr. 5). 20.95 *(978-1-4222-3412-9(6))* Mason Crest.
George, Francis. Mr G Clef & Friends. Wasvary, Marcia, illus. 2012. 32p. 24.95 *(978-1-4560-9642-7(7))* America Star Bks.
Gitarren Einstieg. 2004. (GER.). (YA). cd-rom *(978-1-891155-21-5(0))* EMedia Corp.
Godula, Ellen Kjelgaard & Godula, Brian. Queen Mab, Musical Verses Volume 3. 2007. (J). audio compact disk 16.99 *(978-0-9764109-3-5(1))* Pillar Rock Publishing.
Gordon, Edwin E. Am I Musical? Discover Your Musical Potential (Adults & Children Ages 7 & Up) 2004. (ENG., Illus.). 40p. pap. 18.95 *(978-1-57999-222-4(6),* G-6092) G I A Pubns., Inc.
Grade: Gr 7 Te Share the Music 2000. 2003. (Share the Music Ser.). (gr. 7-18). *(978-0-02-295393-5(0))* Macmillan/McGraw-Hill Schl. Div.
Grade: Gr 8 CDs Share the Music 2000. 2003. (Share the Music Ser.). (gr. 8-18). *(978-0-02-295443-7(0))* Macmillan/McGraw-Hill Schl. Div.
Grade: Gr 8 Te Share the Music 2000. 2003. (Share the Music Ser.). (gr. 8-18). *(978-0-02-295394-2(9))* Macmillan/McGraw-Hill Schl. Div.
Gray, Susan H. Zebra Mussel. 2008. (21st Century Skills Library: Animal Invaders Ser.). (ENG., Illus.). 32p. (gr. 4-8). lib. bdg. 32.07 *(978-1-60279-111-4(2),* 200113) Cherry Lake Publishing.
The Grey House Performing Arts Directory. 4th ed. 2004. 1,500p. 185.00 *(978-1-59237-023-8(3),* Universal Reference Pubns.) Grey Hse. Publishing.
Hal Leonard Corp. Staff. Children's Songs for Ukulele Strummers. 2012. (ENG.). 56p. pap. 16.99 *(978-1-4768-1275-5(6),* 00101925) Leonard, Hal Corp.
Hal Leonard Corp. Staff, contrib. by. Experiencing Choral Music, Advanced Mixed: Grades 9-12. 2004. (Illus.). 281p. stu. ed., per. 30.61 *(978-0-07-861129-2(6),* 9780078611292) Glencoe/McGraw-Hill.
Hal Leonard Corp. Staff, creator. Disney Movie Hits: Alto Sax. 2003. (ENG.). 20p. pap. 12.95 incl. audio compact disk *(978-0-634-00095-9(0),* 0634000950) Leonard, Hal Corp.
—Disney Movie Hits - Clarinet Book/Online Audio. 2003. (ENG.). 20p. pap. 14.99 *(978-0-634-00094-2(2),* 00841421) Leonard, Hal Corp.
—Disney Movie Hits for Cello: Play along with a Full Symphony Orchestra! 2003. (ENG.). 20p. pap. 14.99 *(978-0-634-00101-7(9),* 00841428) Leonard, Hal Corp.
—Disney Movie Hits for French Horn: Play along with a Full Symphony Orchestra! 2003. (ENG.). 20p. pap. 14.99 *(978-0-634-00097-3(7),* 00841424) Leonard, Hal Corp.
—Disney Movie Hits for Trombone/Baritone B. C. Play along with a Full Symphony Orchestra! 2003. (ENG.). 20p. pap. 14.99 *(978-0-634-00098-0(5),* 00841425) Leonard, Hal Corp.
—Disney Movie Hits for Trumpet: Play along with a Full Symphony Orchestra! 2003. (ENG.). 20p. pap. 14.99 *(978-0-634-00096-6(9),* 00841423) Leonard, Hal Corp.
Hamilton, Jill, ed. The Music Industry, 1 vol. 2009. (Introducing Issues with Opposing Viewpoints Ser.). (ENG.). 144p. (gr. 7-10). 43.63 *(978-0-7377-4339-5(5),* a1a5177b-70b9-41bd-853b-b74082bb6b7d, Greenhaven Publishing) Greenhaven Publishing LLC.
Hapka, Catherine, pseud. Together We Can Do It. 2004. (Star Power Ser.: 4). (ENG.). 160p. (J). (gr. 4-8). pap. 4.99 *(978-0-689-86790-3(5),* Aladdin) Simon & Schuster Children's Publishing.
Harding, James. From Wibbleton to Wobbleton: Adventures with the Elements of Music & Movement. Noyes, Eli, illus. 2014. (Pentatonic Press Integrated Learning Ser.: 3). (ENG.). 201p. pap. 32.00 *(978-0-9773712-5-9(5))* Pentatonic Pr.
Hellebuyck, Adam & Medvinsky, Mike. Sight & Sound in Minecraft. 2019. (21st Century Skills Innovation Library: Minecraft & STEAM Ser.). (ENG., Illus.). 32p. (J). (gr. 4-8). pap. 14.21 *(978-1-5341-3971-8(0),* 212713) Cherry Lake Publishing.
—Sight & Sound in Minecraft: Art. 2019. (21st Century Skills Innovation Library: Minecraft & STEAM Ser.). (ENG., Illus.). 32p. (J). (gr. 4-8). lib. bdg. 32.07 *(978-1-5341-4315-9(7),* 212712) Cherry Lake Publishing.
Hemperly, Ilona K. & Nanni, Lyn. Koa'e Kea. (Illus.). (J). pap. 11.95 *(978-0-9639279-0-3(6))* Sunset Beach Music.
Hilderbrand, Karen Mitzo & Thompson, Kim Mitzo. Essential Preschool Skills. 2008. (J). 44.99 *(978-1-59922-321-6(X))* Findaway World, LLC.
Holl, Kristi. Shazam & Chris Barton, Philip Inghelbrecht, Dhiraj Mukherjee, & Avery Wang, 1 vol. 2014. (Internet Biographies Ser.). (ENG., Illus.). 128p. (J). (gr. 7-7). 39.80 *(978-1-4777-7925-5(6),* bf3db782-e6af-49ab-ab26-99313de94cfb, Rosen Young Adult) Rosen Publishing Group, Inc., The.
Houlihan, Brian. Nickelodeon Bubble Guppies: Let's Rock! Moore, Harry, illus. 2014. (ENG.). 12p. (J). bds. 15.99 *(978-1-4508-7489-2(4),* 1590, PI Kids) Phoenix International Publications, Inc.
Hull, Bunny. Dream a World: A Child's Journey to Self-Discovery Dreamer's Activity Kit. Saint-James, Synthia, illus. 2004. 24p. (J). 16.95 incl. cd-rom *(978-0-9721478-3-5(7))* BrassHeart Music.
Hyde, Heidi Smith. Mendel's Accordion. van der Sterre, Johanna, illus. 2007. 30p. (J). (gr. 3-7). lib. bdg. 16.95 *(978-1-58013-212-1(X),* Kar-Ben Publishing) Lerner Publishing Group.
Im Kindergarten. 2005. (GER.). (J). pap. 14.25 *(978-3-411-09841-5(4))* Langenscheidt Publishing Group.
Introduction to the Computer in Music Videotape: Videotape Packages. 2003. (Share the Music Ser.). (gr. 3-8). *(978-0-02-295492-5(9))* Macmillan/McGraw-Hill Schl. Div.
Jackson, Tom. Music Technology. 2015. (Technology Timelines Ser.). (ENG., Illus.). 32p. (J). (gr. 2-4). 31.35 *(978-1-78121-240-0(6),* 16811) Brown Bear Bks.
Kallen, Stuart A. The History of R & B & Soul Music, 1 vol. 2013. (Music Library). (ENG., Illus.). 128p. (gr. 7-10). lib. bdg. 41.03 *(978-1-4205-0899-4(7),* b071b40b-8484-4a9c-b9ac-26edad34b142, Lucent Pr.) Greenhaven Publishing LLC.
Kelly, Tracey. Computer Technology: From Punch Cards to Supercomputers. 2019. (History of Inventions Ser.). (ENG.). 24p. (J). (gr. 2-4). lib. bdg. *(978-1-78121-454-1(9),* 16731) Brown Bear Bks.
Kennedy, Steven. Crescent City Collection: Marimba Tunes from the Big Easy for Grades 4 - 8. Holl, Brent, ed. 2012. 40p. (J). spiral bd. 29.95 *(978-0-9832648-9-7(9))* Beatin' Path Pubns., LLC.
Kocienda, Genevieve. The Magic of Music Low Intermediate Book with Online Access, 1 vol. 2014. (ENG., Illus.). 24p. (J). pap., E-Book, E-Book 9.50 *(978-1-107-66558-3(2))* Cambridge Univ. Pr.
Koopmans, Andy. The History of the Blues. 2005. (Music Library). (ENG., Illus.). 112p. (J). (gr. 4-7). lib. bdg. 33.45 *(978-1-59018-767-8(9),* Lucent Bks.) Cengage Gale.
Learn to Play the Recorder. 2004. (Fun Kits Ser.). (Illus.). 48p. (J). *(978-1-84229-730-8(9))* Top That! Publishing PLC.
Listening Map Transparencies. 2003. (Share the Music Ser.). (gr. k-18). *(978-0-02-295494-9(5));* (gr. 1-18). *(978-0-02-295495-6(3));* (gr. 2-18). *(978-0-02-295496-3(1));* (gr. 3-18). *(978-0-02-295497-0(X));* (gr. 4-18). *(978-0-02-295498-7(8));* (gr. 5-18). *(978-0-02-295499-4(6));* (gr. 6-18). *(978-0-02-295500-7(3))* Macmillan/McGraw-Hill Schl. Div.
Lorenz, Geoff, et al, creators. The Ultimate Music Game Book: Grades K-6+ 2005. (Illus.). 96p. spiral bd. 29.95 *(978-0-89328-031-4(3),* 30/2013H) Heritage Music Pr.
Lorenz, Geoff & Vogt, Janet, creators. Music Out of a Hat, Grades 4-6: 7 Card Games for Classroom Fun! 2005. act. bk. ed. 39.95 *(978-0-89328-025-3(9),* 30/2008H) Heritage Music Pr.
—Music Out of a Hat, Grades K-3: 7 Card Games for Classroom Fun! 2005. act. bk. ed. 39.95 *(978-0-89328-024-6(0),* 30/2007H) Heritage Music Pr.
Lowe, Marilyn, et al. Music Moves for Two. 2004. (J). Bk. 1. 15.95 *(978-1-57999-347-4(8),* G-6443)Bk. 2. 22p. 7.95 *(978-1-57999-348-1(6),* G-6444) G I A Pubns., Inc.
MacGregor, Helen & Umansky, Kaye. The Threes - Three Rocking Crocs. 2006. (Threes Ser.). (ENG., Illus.). 80p. (J). (gr. -1-k). pap. 22.95 *(978-0-7136-7756-0(2))* HarperCollins Pubs. Ltd. GBR. Dist: Independent Pubs. Group.
Maestro in the Making. 2006. cd-rom 24.95 *(978-1-933260-15-0(7))* Vision Pubns.
Making Music Videotape: Videotape Packages. 2003. (Share the Music Ser.). (gr. 4-8). *(978-0-02-295487-1(2))* Macmillan/McGraw-Hill Schl. Div.
Martin, Oscar, Jr., creator. History of Music I.t. ed. 2003. (Illus.). 25p. (J). E-Book 19.95 incl. cd-rom *(978-0-9748416-7-0(6))* Build Your Story.
Mason, Antony. Music. 2004. (Culture Encyclopedia Ser.). (Illus.). 40p. (YA). (gr. 5-18). lib. bdg. 19.95 *(978-1-59084-479-3(3))* Mason Crest.
McCarthy, Cecilia Pinto. The Science of Music. 2016. (Super-Awesome Science Ser.). (ENG., Illus.). 48p. (J). (gr. 4-8). lib. bdg. 35.64 *(978-1-68078-248-6(7),* 22097) ABDO Publishing Co.
McGraw Hill. Experiencing Choral Music, Beginning Unison 2-Part/3-Part, Student Edition Pt. 2 & 3. 2004. (Experiencing Choral Music Beginning Se Ser.). (ENG., Illus.). 261p. (gr. 6-12). stu. ed., per. 50.08 *(978-0-07-861104-9(0),* 0078611040) McGraw-Hill Education.
—Experiencing Choral Music, Intermediate Mixed Voices, Student Edition. 2004. (Experiencing Choral Music Intermediate Se Ser.). (ENG.). (gr. 6-12). pap., stu. ed. 47.68 *(978-0-07-861108-7(3),* 0078611083) McGraw-Hill Education.
—Experiencing Choral Music, Proficient Mixed Voices, Student Edition. 2004. (Experiencing Choral Music Proficient Se Ser.). (ENG., Illus.). 288p. (gr. 9-12). stu. ed., per. 50.08 *(978-0-07-861119-3(9),* 0078611199) McGraw-Hill Education.
—Experiencing Choral Music, Proficient Tenor Bass Voices, Student Edition. 2004. (Experiencing Choral Music Proficient Se Ser.). (ENG., Illus.). 263p. (gr. 9-12). stu. ed., per. 47.68 *(978-0-07-861125-4(3),* 0078611253) McGraw-Hill Education.
—Experiencing Choral Music, Proficient Treble Voices, Student Edition. 2004. (Experiencing Choral Music Proficient Se Ser.). (ENG., Illus.). 287p. (gr. 9-12). stu. ed., per. 50.08 *(978-0-07-861122-3(9),* 0078611229) McGraw-Hill Education.
McGraw-Hill-Glencoe Staff. Experiencing Choral Music. 2004. (Experiencing Choral Music Intermediate Se Ser.). (ENG., Illus.). 256p. (gr. 7-9). stu. ed., per. 39.88 *(978-0-07-861114-8(8),* 0078611148) McGraw-Hill Higher Education.
McGraw-Hill Staff. Grade: Gr 4-8 Sound Perc. Video Share Music 2000. 2003. (Share the Music Ser.). (gr. 4-8). *(978-0-02-295485-7(6))* Macmillan/McGraw-Hill Schl. Div.
—Grade: Gr 6 Playing Guitar Share Music 2000. 2003. (Share the Music Ser.). (gr. 6-18). *(978-0-02-295406-2(6))* Macmillan/McGraw-Hill Schl. Div.
—Grade: Gr K CDs Share the Music 2000. 2003. (Share the Music Ser.). (gr. k-18). *(978-0-02-295435-2(X))* Macmillan/McGraw-Hill Schl. Div.
—Grade: Gr1 Cd(8) Share the Music. 2003. (Share the Music Ser.). (gr. 1-18). *(978-0-02-295436-9(8))* Macmillan/McGraw-Hill Schl. Div.
—Videocassette: Video Gr 3-6 Signing Share Music 2000. 2003. (Share the Music Ser.). (gr. 3-6). *(978-0-02-295480-2(5))* Macmillan/McGraw-Hill Schl. Div.
Michael, Judah Israel. The New Music. 2004. 60p. (YA). per. 12.95 *(978-1-59196-665-4(5))* Instant Pub.
MiDisaurus. 2003. (Share the Music Ser.). (gr. 1-3). *(978-0-02-295528-1(3)); (978-0-02-295557-1(7))* Macmillan/McGraw-Hill Schl. Div.
The Mischievous Bugs. 2003. (J). pap., tchr. ed., act. bk. ed. 17.95 *(978-0-9722673-2-8(8))* Audrey Productions.
Mitchell, Loretta. Ready-to-Use Music Reading Activities Kit: A Complete Sequential Program for Use with Mallet & Keyboard Instruments. 2003. (Illus.). 228p. pap. 29.95 *(978-0-89328-156-4(5),* 30/1801H) Heritage Music Pr.
Modern Music Masters, vols. 3, vol. 3. Incl. Reggae Poet: The Story of Bob Marley. Miller, Calvin Craig. 128p. (YA). (gr. 9-18). 2007. lib. bdg. 27.95 *(978-1-59935-071-4(8));* Revolution: The Story of John Lennon. Duggleby, John. 176p. 2007. lib. bdg. 28.95 *(978-1-59935-034-9(3));* Say It with Music: The Story of Irving Berlin. Furstinger, Nancy. 128p. (gr. 6-12). 2003. 28.95 *(978-1-931798-12-9(5));* Spin: The Story of Michael Jackson. O'Keefe, Sherry. 144p. (YA). (gr. 6-9). 2011. 28.95 *(978-1-59935-134-6(X));* Uh Huh! The Story of Ray Charles. Duggleby, John. 160p. (gr. 9-12). 2005. lib. bdg. 28.95 *(978-1-931798-65-5(6));* (Illus.). 2010. Set lib. bdg. 92.85 *(978-1-59935-007-3(6))* Reynolds, Morgan Inc.
Mueller, Todd & Boland, Hank. Soup du Jour (mus) 2003. (YA). (gr. 10). pap. 7.50 *(978-1-58342-179-6(3),* SH7) Dramatic Publishing Co.
Music. Gr 1 Share the Music Pe. 2003. (Share the Music Ser.). (gr. 1-18). *(978-0-02-295563-2(1))* Macmillan/McGraw-Hill Schl. Div.
—Gr 6 Share the Music Pe. 2003. (Share the Music Ser.). (gr. 6-18). *(978-0-02-295568-7(2))* Macmillan/McGraw-Hill Schl. Div.
—Gr K-3 Stm Music & Moveme. 2003. (Share the Music Ser.). (gr. k-3). *(978-0-02-295482-6(1))* Macmillan/McGraw-Hill Schl. Div.
—Instrmnts of the Orch(Cd- 2003. (Share the Music Ser.). (gr. 1-8). *(978-0-02-295594-6(1))* Macmillan/McGraw-Hill Schl. Div.
—Instrmnts of the World(Cd. 2003. (Share the Music Ser.). (gr. 3-8). *(978-0-02-295595-3(X))* Macmillan/McGraw-Hill Schl. Div.
—Instrumental Sounds. 2003. (Share the Music Ser.). (gr. 1-8). incl. audio compact disk *(978-0-02-295596-0(8))* Macmillan/McGraw-Hill Schl. Div.
—Share the Music Big Book Grade 1. 2003. (Share the Music Ser.). (gr. 1-18). *(978-0-02-295384-3(1))* Macmillan/McGraw-Hill Schl. Div.
—Share the Music Big Book Grade 2. 2003. (Share the Music Ser.). (gr. 2-18). *(978-0-02-295385-0(X))* Macmillan/McGraw-Hill Schl. Div.
Music Ace. 2003. (Technology: Music Ser.). *(978-0-02-295318-8(3)); (978-0-02-295319-5(1)); (978-0-02-295320-1(5)); (978-0-02-295321-8(3)); (978-0-02-295327-0(2)); (978-0-02-295328-7(0))* Macmillan/McGraw-Hill Schl. Div.
Music Ace 2. 2003. (Technology: Music Ser.). *(978-0-02-295333-1(7)); (978-0-02-295334-8(5)); (978-0-02-295335-5(3)); (978-0-02-295344-7(2)); (978-0-02-295336-2(1))* Macmillan/McGraw-Hill Schl. Div.
Music Alive Magazine Classroom Set. 2003. (Share the Music Ser.). (gr. 6-8). *(978-0-02-295618-9(2))* Macmillan/McGraw-Hill Schl. Div.
Music Express Magazine Classroom Set. 2003. (Share the Music Ser.). (gr. k-6). *(978-0-02-295671-4(9))* Macmillan/McGraw-Hill Schl. Div.
Music Time. 1.85 *(978-0-7673-6158-3(X));* 2005. 1.95 *(978-0-633-17857-4(8));* 2005. 1.95 *(978-0-633-17659-4(1));* 2004. 1.95 *(978-0-633-17464-4(5));* 2004. 1.95 *(978-0-633-08665-7(7));* 2004. 1.95 *(978-0-633-08415-8(8));* 2004. 1.95 *(978-0-633-08163-8(9));* 2003. 1.95 *(978-0-633-07791-4(7))* Lifeway Christian Resources.
Music Time. 2003. (Technology: Music Ser.). *(978-0-02-295243-3(8)); (978-0-02-295245-7(4))* Macmillan/McGraw-Hill Schl. Div.
Musica para todos Handbook: Additional Components. 2003. (Share the Music Ser.). (gr. k-2). *(978-0-02-295444-4(9));* (gr. 3-6). *(978-0-02-295445-1(7))* Macmillan/McGraw-Hill Schl. Div.

M N O

Musical Expression Videotape: Videotape Packages. 2003. (Share the Music Ser.). (gr. 3-6). *(978-0-02-295483-3(X))* Macmillan/McGraw-Hill Schl. Div.

Musik. 3rd ed. (Duden-Schuelerduden Ser.). (GER.). 504p. (YA). *(978-3-411-05393-3(3))* Bibliographisches Institut & F. A. Brockhaus AG DEU. Dist: International Bk. Import Service, Inc.

Naji, Jamilla. Musical Storyland: A Sing-A-Long Book with Musical Disc. Lt. ed. 2004. (Illus.). 32p. (J). per. 19.99 *(978-0-9745568-0-2(7))* Worlds In Ink Publishing, Inc.

Ochs, Bill. The Clarke Learn-to-Play Tin Whistle Set: Includes Clarke Original D Tin Whistle on Blister Card: Book, Whistle & Compact Disc. 2003. (Illus.). 80p. audio compact disk 29.95 *(978-0-9727516-0-5(2))* Pennywhistler's Pr.

Orchestrations for Orff Instruments. 2003. (Share the Music Ser.). (gr. 1-18). *(978-0-02-295407-9(4))*; (gr. 2-18). *(978-0-02-295408-6(2))*; (gr. 3-18). *(978-0-02-295409-3(0))*; (gr. 4-18). *(978-0-02-295410-9(4))*; (gr. 5-18) *(978-0-02-295411-6(2))*; (gr. 6-18). *(978-0-02-295412-3(0))* Macmillan/McGraw-Hill Schl. Div.

Parker, Josephine. I Wonder Why Mice Are Musical: And Other Questions about Music. 2007. (I Wonder Why Ser.). (ENG., Illus.). 32p. (J). (gr. k-3). pap. 21.19 *(978-0-7534-6084-9(X))*, 9780753460849) Kingfisher Publications, plc GBR. Dist: Children's Plus, Inc.

Patrick, Chris. Beyoncé & Destiny's Child. 2005. (Illus.). 122p. (J). *(978-0-439-80832-3(4))* Scholastic, Inc.

Penton. Masterpieces Set. 2003. (Baby's First Ser.). (ENG.). (J). 23.95 *(978-1-59125-335-8(7))* Penton Overseas, Inc.

—Sleep Little Baby Set. 2003. (Relaxation Ser.). (ENG.). (J). 23.95 *(978-1-59125-336-5(5))* Penton Overseas, Inc.

Performance Supplement Kit: Additional Components. 2003. (Share the Music Ser.). (gr. k-18). *(978-0-02-295664-6(6))*; (gr. 1-18). *(978-0-02-295665-3(4))*; (gr. 2-18). *(978-0-02-295666-0(2))*; (gr. 3-18). *(978-0-02-295667-7(0))*; (gr. 4-18). *(978-0-02-295668-4(9))*; (gr. 5-18). *(978-0-02-295669-1(7))*; (gr. 6-18). *(978-0-02-295670-7(0))* Macmillan/McGraw-Hill Schl. Div.

Perucca, Nancy Call & Evans, Renee Call. Sea Notes on the Keyboard: The Fast & Fun Way to Learn the Notes on the Keyboard! Perucca, Nancy Call, illus. 2004. (Illus.). 32p. (J). pap. 9.95 *(978-0-9748074-1-6(9))* Nancy's Artworks.

Playing the Recorder. 2003. (Share the Music Ser.). (gr. 3-18). *(978-0-02-295402-4(3))*; (gr. 4-18). *(978-0-02-295403-1(1))*; (gr. 5-18). *(978-0-02-295404-8(X))*; (gr. 6-18). *(978-0-02-295405-5(8))* Macmillan/McGraw-Hill Schl. Div.

Potter, Giselle, illus. C'mon an' Swing in My Tree! 2005. 14p. (J). bds. 16.95 incl. audio compact disk *(978-0-9763012-0-2(2))* Cow Heard Records.

Price, Roger & Stern, Leonard. Rock 'n' Roll Mad Libs: World's Greatest Word Game. 2010. (Mad Libs Ser.). 48p. (J). (gr. 3-7). 5.99 *(978-0-8431-2695-2(7)*, Mad Libs) Penguin Young Readers Group.

Publications International Ltd. Staff, creator. Get Ready for Fun! 2007. (Sesame Street Music Works). (Illus.). 6p. (J). bds. 9.98 *(978-1-4127-8746-8(7))* Publications International, Ltd.

Publications International Ltd. Staff, ed. Xylophone Dora. 2010. 24p. (J). bds. 19.98 *(978-1-4127-4554-3(3))* Phoenix International Publications, Inc.

Pugliano-Martin, Carol. Around the World with Music: Set Of 6. 2010. (Early Connections Ser.). (J). pap. 37.00 net. *(978-1-4108-1081-6(X))* Benchmark Education Co.

Pupil Edition. 2003. (Share the Music Ser.). (gr. 2-18). *(978-0-02-295564-9(X))*; (gr. 3-18). *(978-0-02-295565-6(8))*; (gr. 4-18). *(978-0-02-295566-3(6))*; (gr. 5-18). *(978-0-02-295567-0(4))* Macmillan/McGraw-Hill Schl. Div.

Quill, Charlie. History of the Blues. 2009. (Reading Room Collection 2 Ser.). 24p. (gr. 3-4). 42.50 *(978-1-60851-968-2(6)*, PowerKids Pr.) Rosen Publishing Group, Inc., The.

Rands, Bernard. Concerto, No. 1. 2006. (ENG.). 92p. pap. 100.00 *(978-1-4234-0305-0(3)*, 49013168) Schott Musik International GmbH & Co. KG DEU. Dist: Leonard, Hal Corp.

Ridgley, Sara & Mole, Gavin. Sing It & Say - France. (Illus.). 124p. 10.95 *(978-1-85909-301-6(9)*, Warner Bros. Pubns.) Alfred Publishing Co., Inc.

Ridgley, Sara, et al. Sing It & Say - Festivals. (Illus.). 128p. 10.95 *(978-1-85909-304-7(3)*, Warner Bros. Pubns.) Alfred Publishing Co., Inc.

Rigby Education Staff. Bingo. (Illus.). (J). suppl. ed. 20.00 *(978-0-7635-6473-5(7)*, 764737C99) Rigby Education.

Rutland, Jonathan. Abracadabra Woodwind - Abracadabra Saxophone (Pupil's Book + 2 CDs): the Way to Learn Through Songs & Tunes, 1 vol. 3rd ed. 2008. (Abracadabra Ser.). (ENG., Illus.). 72p. (J). pap., stu. ed. 15.95 incl. audio compact disk *(978-1-4081-0529-0(2))* HarperCollins Pubs. Ltd. GBR. Dist: Independent Pubs. Group.

Scholastic, Inc. Staff. Clifford Musical Memory Games. 2004. (J). cd-rom 9.99 *(978-0-439-44355-5(5))* Scholastic, Inc.

Schwaeber, Barbie Heit. Alphabet of Music. Santillan, Jorge & Clark, Debbie, illus. 2011. (Alphabet Bks.). (ENG.). 40p. (J). (gr. -1-3). 9.95 *(978-1-60727-445-2(0))* Soundprints.

—Alphabet of Music. Clark, Debbie, illus. 2009. (ENG.). 40p. 9.95 *(978-1-59249-995-3(3))* Soundprints.

—Alphabet of Music. Santillan, Jorge, illus. 2008. (ENG.). 40p. (J). (gr. k-2). 15.95 *(978-1-59249-770-6(5))* Soundprints.

Schwartz, Betty Ann. What Makes Music? A Magic Ribbon Book. Turner, Dona, illus. 2005. (Stories to Share Ser.). 16p. (J). (gr. -1-3). act. bk. ed. 11.95 *(978-1-58117-139-6(0)*, Intervisual/Piggy Toes) Bendon, Inc.

Share Caribbean Music: Additional Components. 2003. (Share the Music Ser.). (gr. 3-5). incl. audio compact disk *(978-0-02-295598-4(4))* Macmillan/McGraw-Hill Schl. Div.

Share the Music Big Book. 2003. (Share the Music Ser.). (gr. k-18). *(978-0-02-295366-9(3))* Macmillan/McGraw-Hill Schl. Div.

Signing for Primary Grades Videotape: Videotape Packages. 2003. (Share the Music Ser.). (gr. k-2). *(978-0-02-295479-6(1))* Macmillan/McGraw-Hill Schl. Div.

Sing a Song Set 800867, 3 vols. 2005. (J). pap. *(978-1-59794-052-8(6))* Environments, Inc.

Site License Package: Technology: Music with MIDI. 2003. (Share the Music Ser.). (gr. 4-18). *(978-0-02-295467-3(8))*; (gr. 7-18). *(978-0-02-295237-2(3))*; (gr. 8-18). *(978-0-02-295238-9(1))* Macmillan/McGraw-Hill Schl. Div.

Smith, Douglas W. Doug Smith's Classical Guitar Method, Reading Book 2: Beginning Pieces for the First Position. 2004. (J). 24.95 *(978-0-9729879-2-9(4))* Musictech College Pr.

Smith, Sydney. Music Is for Everyone, 1 vol. Barber, Jill, illus. 2017. 32p. (J). (gr. 1-3). pap. 12.95 *(978-1-77108-535-9(5)*, 543fec31-c625-4cf5-ba12-d3e5fe12a9eb) Nimbus Publishing, Ltd. CAN. Dist: Baker & Taylor Publisher Services (BTPS).

SRA Publications Staff. Grade: Gr 6 CDs Share the Music. 2003. (Share the Music Ser.). (gr. 6-18). *(978-0-02-295441-3(4))* Macmillan/McGraw-Hill Schl. Div.

Standard Package: Technology: Music with MIDI. 2003. (Share the Music Ser.). (gr. 4-18). *(978-0-02-295461-1(9))*; (gr. 7-18). *(978-0-02-295231-0(4))*; (gr. 8-18). *(978-0-02-295232-7(2))* Macmillan/McGraw-Hill Schl. Div.

Stephens, Wayne. Building Character Through Music - Elementary Song Book. 2004. spiral bd. 39.95 *(978-1-892056-32-0(1))* Character Development Group, Inc.

—Building Character Through Music - High School Song Book. 2004. (YA). spiral bd. 39.95 *(978-1-892056-36-8(4))* Character Development Group, Inc.

Sturm, Jeanne. MP3 Players. 2008. (Let's Explore Science Ser.). (Illus.). 48p. (J). (gr. 4-8). lib. bdg. 31.36 *(978-1-60472-332-8(7))* Rourke Educational Media.

Swain, Cynthia & Benchmark Education Co. Staff. Folksongs: The Music of My Life. 2014. (Text Connections Ser.). (J). (gr. 6). *(978-1-4900-1520-0(5))* Benchmark Education Co.

Television Themes Alto Sax. 13.95 incl. audio compact disk *(978-1-85909-718-2(9)*, Warner Bros. Pubns.) Alfred Publishing Co., Inc.

Television Themes Clarinet. 13.95 incl. audio compact disk *(978-1-85909-717-5(0)*, Warner Bros. Pubns.) Alfred Publishing Co., Inc.

Television Themes Flute. 13.95 incl. audio compact disk *(978-1-85909-716-8(2)*, Warner Bros. Pubns.) Alfred Publishing Co., Inc.

Theory for Young Musicians. (J). Bk. 1. *(978-0-7390-0232-2(5)*, 18513)Bk. 2. *(978-0-7390-0235-3(X)*, 18516) Alfred Publishing Co., Inc.

Thomson, Ryan J. Left Handed Fiddling for Beginners: A Teach Yourself Method, 1 bk, 1 CD. 2004. (Illus.). 22p. 22.95 *(978-0-931877-44-5(X))* Captain Fiddle Pubns.

Thyberg, Kathleen. Pianomouse's Musical Circus: Lesson Book 1, vols. , vol. 2. 2013. (ENG., Illus.). 72p. pap. 9.95 *(978-0-9889068-0-8(5))* Pianomouse Productions.

Tomaselli, Anthony. Play Guitar 1. 2003. cd-rom *(978-0-9714299-5-6(2))* I Save A Tree.

Troupe, Thomas Kingsley. Make Mind-Blowing Music Videos: 4D an Augmented Reading Experience. 2019. (Make a Movie! 4D Ser.). (ENG., Illus.). 48p. (J). (gr. 3-5). lib. bdg. 33.99 *(978-1-5435-4009-3(0)*, 139043) Capstone.

Turck, Mary C. Freedom Song: Young Voices & the Struggle for Civil Rights. 2008. (ENG., Illus.). 160p. (J). (gr. 4). pap. 18.95 *(978-1-55652-773-9(X))* Chicago Review Pr., Inc.

Turnbull, Elizabeth, ed. Music from the Romantic Era: Violin & Piano. 2004. (gr. 4-7). 19.95 *(978-0-8256-1843-7(6)*, BOE005012) Music Sales Corp.

Turner, Gary. Keyboard Method for Young Beginners, Book 1. Stewart, James, illus. 2006. (Young Beginner Giant Coloring Bks.). 48p. pap. incl. audio compact disk *(978-1-86469-097-2(6))* LearnToPlayMusic.com Pty Ltd.

—Recorder Method for Young Beginners, Book 1. Stewart, James, illus. 2006. (Young Beginner Giant Coloring Bks.). 36p. pap. *(978-1-86469-099-6(2))* LearnToPlayMusic.com Pty Ltd.

Wadsworth, Pamela. Golwg Gyntaf Ar Sain a Cherddoriaeth. 2005. (WEL., Illus.). 24p. pap. *(978-1-85596-247-7(0))* Dref Wen.

Walker, Carolina. You Can Work in Music. 2018. (You Can Work in the Arts Ser.). (ENG., Illus.). 32p. (J). (gr. 4-6). lib. bdg. 28.65 *(978-1-5435-4141-0(0)*, 139095, Capstone Pr.) Capstone.

Wargin, Kathy-jo. M Is for Melody: A Music Alphabet. Larson, Katherine, illus. 2006. (Art & Culture Ser.). (ENG.). 40p. (J). (gr. 1-4). 16.95 *(978-1-58536-215-8(8)*, 202129); pap. 9.99 *(978-1-58536-332-2(4)*, 202295) Sleeping Bear Pr.

Warner, Dennis. Beads on One String. 2004. (Illus.). 31p. (J). lib. bdg. 24.95 *(978-0-9747147-7-6(1))* MK Publishing.

Washburn, Sandi. Good Night, Grandma. Roehler, Yvonne Fetig, illus. 2009. (ENG.). 16p. (J). 17.95 *(978-1-934367-09-4(5))* Growing Art Pr.

Weeks, Sarah. Z Is for Zoe. Date not set. 32p. (J). (gr. -1-3). 15.99 *(978-0-06-028138-0(3))* HarperCollins Pubs.

Wu, Miriam, et al. Scaling the Tenor Clef Dragon: A Tenor Clef Workbook for Cellists. 2004. 28p. (J). 8.95 *(978-0-9755624-1-3(X))* Boshu Pr.

Yes I Can Staff. A Mariachi I'll Be. (J). stu. ed. 12.95 *(978-0-8136-4418-9(6))* Modern Curriculum Pr.

Zimmerman Rutledge, Jill S. Prom: The Big Night Out. 2017. (ENG., Illus.). 80p. (YA). (gr. 8-12). E-Book 54.65 *(978-1-5124-2850-6(7))*; E-Book 54.65 *(978-1-5124-3918-2(5)*, 9781512439182); E-Book 9.99 *(978-1-5124-3917-5(7)*, 9781512439175) Lerner Publishing Group. (Twenty-First Century Bks.).

Zoo-phonics Music that Teaches. 2004. (J). cd-rom 19.95 *(978-1-886441-43-9(X))* Zoo-phonics, Inc.

MUSIC—ACOUSTICS AND PHYSICS

see also Sound

Albertson, Margaret & Emick, Paula. Music: the Sound of Science. 2018. (Project: STEAM Ser.). (ENG., Illus.). 48p. (gr. 4-8). pap. 10.95 *(978-1-64156-589-9(6)*, 9781641565899) Rourke Educational Media.

Allen, Kathy. The Science of a Rock Concert: Sound in Action. 2010. (Action Science Ser.). (ENG.). 32p. (gr. 3-4). pap. 47.70 *(978-1-4296-5075-5(3)*, Capstone Pr.) Capstone.

Anduri, Stefanie. Music. 2021. (High-Interest STEAM Ser.: 10). (ENG.). 80p. (J). (gr. 7-12). 34.60 *(978-1-4222-4523-1(3))* Mason Crest.

Claybourne, Anna. The Science of a Guitar, 1 vol. 2009. (Science Of... Ser.). (ENG., Illus.). 32p. (YA). (gr. 4-5). lib. bdg. 28.67 *(978-1-4339-0042-6(4)*, 9837157f-1dfb-45cd-86ed-976f05989798) Stevens, Gareth Publishing LLLP.

Flesch Connors, Abigail. Exploring the Science of Sounds: 100 Musical Activities for Young Children. 2017. (ENG., Illus.). 216p. (gr. 13). pap. 16.95 *(978-0-87659-731-6(2)*, Gryphon House Inc) Gryphon Hse., Inc.

Jennings, Terry J. Sound. 2009. (J). 28.50 *(978-1-59920-275-4(1))* Black Rabbit Bks.

Kenney, Karen Latchana. The Science of Music: Discovering Sound. 2015. (Science in Action Ser.). (ENG., Illus.). 32p. (J). (gr. 3-6). 32.79 *(978-1-62403-962-1(6)*, 19421, Checkerboard Library) ABDO Publishing Co.

Rowe, Brooke. Playing Musical Bottles. Bane, Jeff, illus. 2016. (My Early Library: My Science Fun Ser.). (ENG.). 24p. (J). (gr. k-1). 30.64 *(978-1-63471-028-2(2)*, 208192) Cherry Lake Publishing.

MUSIC, AMERICAN

Kuzma, Gregory. On the Field from Denver, Colorado... the Blue Knights! One Member's Experience of the 1994 Summer National Tour. 2004. 206p. (YA). pap. 17.95 *(978-0-595-32278-7(6))* iUniverse, Inc.

Lindeen, Mary. Cool Latin Music: Create & Appreciate What Makes Music Great! 2008. (Cool Music Ser.). (ENG., Illus.). 32p. (J). (gr. 3-6). 34.21 *(978-1-59928-972-4(5)*, 368, Checkerboard Library) ABDO Publishing Co.

MUSIC—ANALYSIS, APPRECIATION

see Music Appreciation

MUSIC—APPRECIATION

see Music Appreciation

MUSIC—BIOGRAPHY

see Musicians

MUSIC—DICTIONARIES

Krull, Kathleen. M Is for Music. Innerst, Stacy, illus. 2009. (ENG.). 48p. (J). (gr. -1-3). pap. 7.99 *(978-0-15-206479-2(6)*, 1099014, Clarion Bks.) HarperCollins Pubs.

Munoz, Miguel. Diccionario Juvenil de Musica.Tr. of Children's Music Dictionary. (SPA.). (J). (gr. 3-5). pap. 11.20 *(978-958-33-1357-8(2))* Botero de Borrero, Beatriz & Martha Olga Botero de Gomez COL. Dist: Lectorum Pubns., Inc.

—Sonodiccionario: Asi Suenan los Instrumentos. (SPA.). (J). (gr. k-2). pap. 8.76 *(978-958-33-1556-5(7))* Botero de Borrero, Beatriz & Martha Olga Botero de Gomez COL. Dist: Lectorum Pubns., Inc.

MUSIC, DRAMATIC

see Opera

MUSIC—FICTION

Adoff, Arnold. Roots & Blues: A Celebration. Christie, R. Gregory, illus. 2011. (ENG.). 96p. (J). (gr. 5-7). 17.99 *(978-0-547-23554-7(2)*, 1083184, Clarion Bks.) HarperCollins Pubs.

The Adventures of Max & Millie: At the Pond. 2003. (Illus.). 32p. (J). 8.95 *(978-0-9744427-0-9(4))* Music Bks. & Games.

Alexander, Carol. Percy Mcgoo. 2012. 24p. pap. 15.99 *(978-1-4771-2359-1(8))* Xlibris Corp.

Alexander, William. Ghoulish Song. (ENG., Illus.). (J). (gr. 3-7). 2014. 192p. pap. 6.99 *(978-1-4424-2730-3(2))* 2013. 176p. 16.99 *(978-1-4424-2729-7(9))* McElderry, Margaret K. Bks. (McElderry, Margaret K. Bks.).

Almond, David. The Dam. Pinfold, Levi, illus. 2018. (ENG.). 32p. (J). (gr. k-4). 17.99 *(978-0-7636-9597-2(1))* Candlewick Pr.

Anaya, Hector. Cuenta Cuenta. Moreno, Sergio, illus. 2nd rev. ed. 2005. (Castillo de la Lectura Verde Ser.). (SPA & ENG.). 184p. (J). (gr. -1-7). pap. 7.95 *(978-970-20-0135-5(8))* Castillo, Ediciones, S. A. de C. V. MEX. Dist: Macmillan.

Angus, John. Beautiful Music A Children's Concert. 2009. 21p. pap. 10.99 *(978-0-9716411-0-5(2))* APG Sales & Distribution Services.

Arkin, Alan. Cassie Loves Beethoven. Lt. ed. 2003. (Children's Large Print Ser.). 28.95 *(978-1-58118-108-1(6))* LRS.

AZ Books Staff. Merry Orchestra. Tulup, Natalia, ed. 2012. (Tra-La-la Ser.). (ENG.). 14p. (J). (-k). bds. 10.95 *(978-1-61889-056-6(5))* AZ Bks. LLC.

—Musical Animals. Tulup, Natalia, ed. 2012. (Tra-La-la Ser.). (ENG.). 14p. (J). (-k). bds. 10.95 *(978-1-61889-057-3(3))* AZ Bks. LLC.

—Musical Machines. Tulup, Natalia, ed. 2012. (Tra-La-la Ser.). (ENG.). 14p. (J). (-k). bds. 10.95 *(978-1-61889-055-9(7))* AZ Bks. LLC.

Ball, Marcia. Christmas Fais Do-Do. 2006. (Illus.). 36p. (J). per. 14.95 *(978-1-58939-972-3(2))* Virtualbookworm.com Publishing, Inc.

Banks, Steven. The Song That Never Ends. DePorter, Vince, illus. 2004. (Spongebob Squarepants Ser.). 32p. (J). (gr. k-2). 11.65 *(978-0-7569-5374-4(X))* Perfection Learning Corp.

Basore, Polly M. Santa's Stray in A Piano for Christmas. Williams, Carlene H., illus. 2005. 32p. (J). per. *(978-0-9771749-1-1(3))* AngelBooks.

Becker, Mary R. Woodland Party. 2013. 10.95 *(978-0-7414-8170-2(7))* Infinity Publishing.

—Woodland Party - Color. 2013. pap. 19.95 *(978-0-7414-8171-9(5))* Infinity Publishing.

Bergen, Lara. Drama Queen. 2007. 164p. (J). pap. *(978-0-545-03702-0(6))* Scholastic, Inc.

Bigelow, Lisa Jenn. Drum Roll, Please. (ENG.). (J). (gr. 3-7). 2019. 336p. pap. 9.99 *(978-0-06-279115-3(X))* 2018. 320p. 17.99 *(978-0-06-279114-6(1))* HarperCollins Pubs. (HarperCollins).

Black, Allyson. Fashion Face-off. Johnson, Shane L., illus. 2011. (Scarlett & Crimson Ser.). (ENG.). 112p. (J). (gr. 3-7). pap. 6.99 *(978-1-4169-5937-3(8)*, Simon Spotlight) Simon Spotlight.

Bloom, Stephanie. The Drummer Who Lost His Beat. Keylon, Joe, illus. 2005. 40p. (J). lib. bdg. 16.95 *(978-1-931969-47-5(7))* Bloom & Grow Bks.

Bonnett-Rampersaud, Louise. The Spring Un-Fair, 0 vols. McHeffey, Adam, illus. 2015. (Secret Knock Club Ser.: 2). (ENG.). 112p. (J). (gr. 1-4). pap. 9.99 *(978-0-7614-6326-9(7)*, 9780761463269, Two Lions) Amazon Publishing.

Brandt, Courney. A Fine Line. 2008. 164p. pap. 12.95 *(978-0-595-52500-3(8))* iUniverse, Inc.

Brennan-Nelson, Denise. Maestro Stu Saves the Zoo. Bowers, Tim, illus. 2012. (ENG.). 32p. (J). (gr. -1-3). 15.95 *(978-1-58536-802-0(4)*, 202340) Sleeping Bear Pr.

Brenner, Vida. The Magic Music Shop. Sharp, Mary, ed. Sharpnack, Joe, illus. 2013. 102p. pap. 12.95 *(978-1-57216-094-1(2))* Penfield Bks.

Bronson, Matthew Shane & Bronson, Tammy Carter. Kaleidonotes & the Mixed-up Orchestra. Bronson, Tammy Carter, illus. 2nd rev. ed. 2003. (Illus.). 24p. (J). lib. bdg. 12.99 *(978-0-9678167-6-0(9))* Bookaroos Publishing, Inc.

Brouwer, Sigmund & Morgan, Cindy. True Blue, 1 vol. 2018. (Orca Limelights Ser.). (ENG.). 128p. (J). (gr. 4-7). pap. 9.95 *(978-1-4598-1580-3(7)*, 1459815807) Orca Bk. Pubs. USA.

Burch, Sharon. Freddie the Frog & the Mysterious Wahooooo: 3rd Adventure: Tempo Island. 2010. (ENG.). 34p. 24.99 incl. audio compact disk *(978-0-9747454-7-3(2)*, 09971503) Mystic Publishing.

Burnell, Cerrie. Harper & the Fire Star. Anderson, Laura Ellen, illus. 2018. (Harper Ser.: 4). (ENG.). 168p. (J). (gr. 1-3). 14.99 *(978-1-5107-3613-9(1)*, Sky Pony Pr.) Skyhorse Publishing Co., Inc.

Byng, Georgia. Molly Moon & the Monster Music. 2013. (Molly Moon Ser.: 6). (ENG.). 320p. (J). (gr. 3-7). 16.99 *(978-0-06-166163-1(5)*, HarperCollins) HarperCollins Pubs.

Cabrera, Jane. The 12 Days of Christmas. 2017. (Jane Cabrera's Story Time Ser.). (ENG.). 28p. (J). (gr. -1 — 1). bds. 7.99 *(978-0-8234-3783-2(3))* Holiday Hse., Inc.

Caines-Floyd, Eydi. The Story of Wanton Desire. 2009. 64p. (J). pap. 26.49 *(978-1-4389-3156-2(5))* AuthorHouse.

La Cancion de Roldan. (SPA., Illus.). 160p. (YA). 11.95 *(978-84-7281-076-1(3)*, AF1076) Auriga, Ediciones S.A. ESP. Dist: Continental Bk. Co., Inc.

Carolan, Joanna F. Old Makana Had a Taro Farm. Carolan, Joanna F., illus. 2008. (Illus.). 48p. 17.95 *(978-0-9715333-9-4(3))* Banana Patch Pr.

Carr, Heather. The Jiggleworm. Carr, Greg, illus. 2005. 18p. (J). 21.95 incl. audio compact disk *(978-0-9768450-0-3(8)*, Giggletins) Le Bk. Moderne, LLC.

Castonguay, Leo. Piper Peter. 2012. 44p. 24.95 *(978-1-4626-8604-9(4))*; pap. 24.95 *(978-1-4626-8078-8(X))* America Star Bks.

Celenza, Anna Harwell. Bach's Goldberg Variations. Kitchel, JoAnn E., illus. 2016. (Once upon a Masterpiece Ser.: 3). 32p. (J). (gr. 1-4). lib. bdg. 16.95 *(978-1-58089-529-3(8))* Charlesbridge Publishing, Inc.

Chaviano, Daina. Pais de Dragones. 2003. (Fables & Legends Ser.). (SPA., Illus.). 136p. (J). 9.95 *(978-84-239-6346-1(2)*, EC30627) Espasa Calpe, S.A. ESP. Dist: Lectorum Pubns., Inc., Planeta Publishing Corp.

Cheerios Counting Songs. 2004. (Illus.). (J). *(978-0-7853-9953-7(4))* Publications International, Ltd.

Chewins, Hayley. The Turnaway Girls. 2018. (ENG.). 272p. (J). (gr. 5-9). 16.99 *(978-0-7636-9792-1(3))* Candlewick Pr.

Clark, Platte F. Good Ogre. 2015. (Bad Unicorn Trilogy Ser.: 3). (ENG., Illus.). 384p. (J). (gr. 3-7). 17.99 *(978-1-4424-5018-9(5)*, Aladdin) Simon & Schuster Children's Publishing.

Clarkson, Kelly. River Rose & the Magical Lullaby. Hughes, Laura, illus. 2016. (ENG.). 32p. (J). (gr. -1-3). 18.99 *(978-0-06-242756-4(3)*, HarperCollins) HarperCollins Pubs.

Clements, Andrew. The Last Holiday Concert. 2006. (ENG., Illus.). 176p. (J). (gr. 3-7). pap. 7.99 *(978-0-689-84525-3(1)*, Atheneum Bks. for Young Readers) Simon & Schuster Children's Publishing.

—The Last Holiday Concert. rev. Lt. ed. 2007. (Literacy Bridge Middle Reader Ser.). 165p. (J). (gr. 3-7). 22.95 *(978-0-7862-9374-2(8))* Thorndike Pr.

—Things Hoped For. 2008. (ENG.). 176p. (J). (gr. 5-18). 7.99 *(978-0-14-241073-8(X)*, Puffin Books) Penguin Young Readers Group.

—Things Hoped For. 2008. 167p. (gr. 5-9). 17.00 *(978-0-7569-8933-0(7))* Perfection Learning Corp.

—Things Hoped For. Lt. ed. 2008. (Thorndike Literacy Bridge Ser.). 207p. 23.95 *(978-1-4104-0500-5(1))* Thorndike Pr.

Clendenan, Megan. Offbeat, 1 vol. 2018. (Orca Limelights Ser.). (ENG.). 144p. (J). (gr. 4-7). pap. 9.95 *(978-1-4598-1792-0(3))* Orca Bk. Pubs. USA.

Clifford the Best Helper. (Illus.). 10p. (J). bds. 9.98 *(978-0-7853-9948-3(8)*, 7208900) Publications International, Ltd.

Cline, Thornton. The Amazing Incredible Shrinking Drums. 2017. (ENG.). 44p. pap. 9.99 *(978-1-57424-344-4(6)*, 00231633) Centerstream Publishing.

Cole, Barbara H. Wash Day, 1 vol. Himler, Ronald, illus. 2004. (ENG.). 32p. (J). 15.95 *(978-1-932065-36-7(9)*, 7187849112) Star Bright Bks., Inc.

Collins, Pat Lowery. Hidden Voices: The Orphan Musicians of Venice. 2009. (ENG., Illus.). 352p. (YA). (gr. 7). 17.99 *(978-0-7636-3917-4(6))* Candlewick Pr.

Cook, Jacqueline. The Little Bear Who Worried Too Much: Suzie Bear & the Music Festival. 2010. 32p. pap. 13.00 *(978-1-60860-529-3(9)*, Strategic Bk. Publishing) Strategic Book Publishing & Rights Agency (SBPRA).

Coveleskie, Sally & Goodrich, Peter. Henry the Steinway Tours the World. Friedman, Laura, illus. 2005. (Henry the Steinway Ser.: 3). 32p. (J). (gr. -1-3). 15.95 *(978-0-9729427-8-2(5))* Yorkville Pr.

Coveleskie, Sally & Peter, Goodrich. Henry the Steinway a Star Is Born. Friedman, Laura, illus. 2003. (Henry the Steinway Ser.: Vol. 2). 32p. (J). (gr. k-3). *(978-0-9729427-1-3(8))* Yorkville Pr.

Coveleskie, Sally, et al. Henry the Steinway & the Piano Recital. Friedman, Laura, illus. 2003. (Henry the Steinway Ser.: Vol. 1). 32p. (J). (gr. k-3). *(978-1-931721-05-9(X))* Night Heron Media.

Cowley, Joy. Miss Doll & Friends: Toy Music. Bordicchia, Gaia, illus. 2014. (ENG.). 8p. pap. *(978-0-927244-59-6(4)*, Joy Cowley Club) Flying Start Bks.

Cowling, Douglas. Vivaldi's Ring of Mystery. Fernandez, Laura & Jacobson, Rick, illus. 2004. (ENG.). 44p. (J). *(978-0-439-96904-8(2)*, North Winds Pr) Scholastic Canada, Ltd.

Cox, Steven. Justin's Very Own Drum. Saavedra, Anthony, illus. 2009. 24p. pap. 24.95 *(978-1-60749-553-6(8))* America Star Bks.

Crew, Gary. Pig on the Titanic: A True Story. Whatley, Bruce, illus. 2005. 32p. (J). 15.99 *(978-0-06-052305-3(0))* HarperCollins Pubs.

Culbertson, Kim. Songs for a Teenage Nomad. 2010. (ENG.). 256p. (YA). (gr. 7-12). pap. 12.99 *(978-1-4022-4301-1(4))* Sourcebooks, Inc.

Daddy Saved the Day: Six-Pack. (Greetings Ser.: Vol. 3). 24p. (gr. 2-3). 31.00 *(978-0-7635-9417-6(2))* Rigby Education.

d'Allancé, Mireille. No, No Y No! 2005. (SPA., Illus.). (J). 15.99 *(978-84-8470-114-9(X))* Corimbo, Editorial S.L. ESP. Dist: Iaconi, Mariuccia Bk. Imports.

Dapre, Alan & Rooney, Ronnie. Brum Big Town Songs. 2004. (Illus.). 10p. (J). bds. *(978-0-7853-9898-1(8))* Publications International, Ltd.

Decker, Tim. The Punk Ethic. Decker, Tim, illus. 2012. (ENG., Illus.). 188p. (YA). 18.95 *(978-1-60898-120-5(7))*; pap. 9.95 *(978-1-60898-121-2(5))* namelos llc.

Decter, Nora. How Far We Go & How Fast. 1 vol. 2018. (ENG.). 264p. (YA). (gr. 8-12). pap. 14.95 *(978-1-4598-1688-6(9))* Orca Bk. Pubs. USA.

Delacre, Lulu. Rafi & Rosi: Music!. 1 vol. Delacre, Lulu, illus. 2019. (Rafi & Rosi Ser.). (ENG., Illus.). 64p. (J). (gr. 2-2). pap. 11.95 *(978-0-89239-431-9(5),* leelowcbp, Children's Book Press) Lee & Low Bks., Inc.

—Rafi y Rosi ¡Música!. 1 vol. Delacre, Lulu, illus. 2019. (Rafi & Rosi Ser.). (SPA., Illus.). 64p. (J). (gr. k-3). pap. 10.95 *(978-0-89239-432-6(3),* leelowcbp, Children's Book Press) Lee & Low Bks., Inc.

DeLand, M. Maitland. Busy Bees on Broadway. Martin, Lyn, illus. 2011. 32p. 15.95 *(978-1-60832-063-9(4))* Greenleaf Book Group.

Delporte, Yvan & Peyo. The Smurfs #2: The Smurfs & the Magic Flute. 2010. (Smurfs Graphic Novels Ser.: 2). (ENG., Illus.). 64p. (J). (gr. 2-5). pap. 5.99 *(978-1-59707-208-3(7),* 900070210, Papercutz) Mad Cave Studios.

Denman, K. L. Stuff We All Get. 1 vol. 2011. (Orca Currents Ser.). (ENG.). 128p. (J). (gr. 4-7). pap. 9.95 *(978-1-55469-820-2(0))*; lib. bdg. 16.95 *(978-1-55469-821-9(9))* Orca Bk. Pubs. USA.

Desrosiers, Sylvie. Aimez-Vous la Musique? Sylvestre, Daniel, illus. 2004. (Roman Jeunesse Ser.). (FRE.). 96p. (J). (gr. 4-7). pap. *(978-2-89021-709-6(4))* Diffusion du livre Mirabel (DLM).

Destiny, A. & Lenhard, Elizabeth. Our Song. 2015. 225p. (YA). *(978-1-4424-8407-8(1),* Simon Pulse) Simon Pulse.

Dimopoulos, Elaine. Material Girls. 2016. (ENG.). 336p. (YA). (gr. 9). pap. 8.99 *(978-0-544-67173-7(2),* 1625822, Clarion Bks.) HarperCollins Pubs.

Disney Junior. Disney Junior Music Player Storybook. Stierle, Cynthia, ed. 2018. (Music Player Storybook Ser.). (ENG., Illus.). 32p. (J). (gr. -1-k). 19.99 *(978-1-68412-261-5(9),* Reader's Digest Children's Bks.) Studio Fun International.

Donald, David R. Gogo's Song. 2012. 64p. (-18). pap. 15.99 *(978-1-4797-1024-9(5))* Xlibris Corp.

Donegan, Noel & Donegan, Luz. The Hot-Headed Bassoon. 2013. (Magical Mozart & His Musical Ser.). (ENG.). 32p. (J). pap. 8.95 *(978-1-84730-392-9(7))* Veritas Pubns. IRL. Dist: Casemate Pubs. & Bk. Distributors, LLC.

—The Noisy Blue Drum. 2013. (Magical Mozart & His Musical Ser.). (ENG.). 32p. (J). pap. 8.95 *(978-1-84730-391-2(9))* Veritas Pubns. IRL. Dist: Casemate Pubs. & Bk. Distributors, LLC.

—The Sad Little Violin. 2013. (Magical Mozart & His Musical Ser.). (ENG.). 32p. (J). pap. 8.95 *(978-1-84730-393-6(5))* Veritas Pubns. IRL. Dist: Casemate Pubs. & Bk. Distributors, LLC.

Dowell, Frances O'Roark. Ten Miles Past Normal. 2011. (ENG.). 224p. (YA). (gr. 7-18). 16.99 *(978-1-4169-9585-2(4),* Atheneum Bks. for Young Readers) Simon & Schuster Children's Publishing.

Downing, Johnette. Spooky Second Line. 1 vol. 2019. (ENG., Illus.). 32p. (J). pap. 9.95 *(978-1-4556-2505-5(1),* Pelican Publishing) Arcadia Publishing.

Drachman, Eric. Ellison the Elephant. Muscarello, James, illus. 2005. (ENG.). 32p. (J). (gr. -1-2). 18.95 incl. audio compact disk *(978-0-9703809-1-3(7))* Kidwick Bks.

Druvert, Hélène & Druvert, Hélène. New York Melody. 2018. (ENG., Illus.). 36p. (J). (gr. k-3). 24.95 *(978-0-500-65173-5(6),* 565173) Thames & Hudson.

Duchesne, Christiane. W Is for Wapiti! An Alphabet Songbook. Kunigis, Paul, illus. 2012. (ENG.). 48p. (J). (gr. -1-k). 16.95 *(978-2-923163-83-3(4))* La Montagne Secrete CAN. Dist: Independent Pubs. Group.

Dyan, Penelope. The Musical Family — Sometimes a Song Says It All. Dyan, Penelope, illus. 2009. (Illus.). 42p. pap. 11.95 *(978-1-935118-81-7(1))* Bellissima Publishing, LLC.

EarTwiggle's Adventure 1: Twiggle Book. 2004. (J). 1.99 *(978-0-9762573-1-8(9))* Ear Twiggles Productions, Inc.

Elerya. One Step Higher: Piano Paradise Book II. 1 vol. 2009. 79p. pap. 16.95 *(978-1-60749-477-5(9))* PublishAmerica, Inc.

Engle, Margarita. Drum Dream Girl: How One Girl's Courage Changed Music. López, Rafael & López, Rafael, illus. 2015. (ENG.). 48p. (J). (gr. -1-3). 19.99 *(978-0-544-10229-3(0),* 1540161, Clarion Bks.) HarperCollins Pubs.

Evensen, Rachelle. Finn's Marching Band: A Story of Counting, Colors, & Playing Together. 2009. 32p. (J). 14.95 *(978-0-8091-6749-4(2),* Ambassador Bks.) Paulist Pr.

Ewing, Lynne. Motown Anthology. 2003. (ENG.). 96p. (J). 22.99 *(978-0-7868-0854-0(3))* Hyperion Pr.

Fagan, Cary. Banjo of Destiny. 1 vol. Demirel, Selcuk, illus. 2011. (ENG.). 128p. (J). (gr. 3-4). pap. 8.95 *(978-1-55498-086-4(0))* Groundwood Bks. CAN. Dist: Publishers Group West (PGW).

Federle, Tim. Better Nate Than Ever. 2013. (Nate Ser.). (ENG., Illus.). 288p. (J). (gr. 4-8). 18.99 *(978-1-4424-4689-2(7),* Simon & Schuster Bks. For Young Readers) Simon & Schuster Bks. For Young Readers.

—Five, Six, Seven, Nate! 2014. (Nate Ser.). (ENG., Illus.). 298p. (J). (gr. 5-9). 19.99 *(978-1-4424-4693-9(5),* Simon & Schuster Bks. For Young Readers) Simon & Schuster Bks. For Young Readers.

Fertig, Michael P. Musical Mystery Scooby Doo! McKee, Darren, illus. 2007. (Scooby Doo Ser.). (J). (gr. -1-3). 12.98 *(978-1-4127-7429-1(2))* Publications International, Ltd.

Fischel, Ana. The Twelve Quests - Book 3, the Pied Piper's Flute. 2009. 158p. pap. *(978-1-84923-875-5(8))* YouWriteOn.

Fishman, Linda Charles. The Little Girl Who Loves Music: Book Three of Grandma's Girls. 2012. 24p. pap. 17.99 *(978-1-4772-6156-9(7))* AuthorHouse.

Fitzer, Robin. Summer Stories. 2008. 45p. pap. 24.95 *(978-1-60563-742-6(4))* America Star Bks.

Fogelin, Adrian. The Big Nothing. 2006. (Neighborhood Novels Ser.: 4). 224p. (J). (gr. 3-7). pap. 7.99 *(978-1-56145-388-7(9))* Peachtree Publishing Co. Inc.

Foley, Greg. Kat Writes a Song. Foley, Greg, illus. 2018. (ENG., Illus.). 40p. (J). (gr. -1-2). 14.99 *(978-1-5344-0680-3(8),* Little Simon) Little Simon.

French, Simon. Where in the World. 2nd ed. 2008. 198p. *(978-1-921272-57-8(0))* Little Hare Bks. AUS. Dist: HarperCollins Pubs. Australia.

Friesel, Uwe. Tim, the Peacemaker. Wilkon, Jozef, illus. 32p. (J). (gr. -1-3). 13.95 *(978-0-87592-052-8(7))* Scroll Pr., Inc.

Galvin, Laura Gates. If Cookie Had a Cookie. Wood, Damian, illus. 2009. (Sesame Street Read, Play & Go Ser.). 20p. (J). (gr. -1). 9.99 incl. audio compact disk *(978-1-59069-867-9(3))* Studio Mouse LLC.

—I've Been Working on the Railroad. Brown, Dan, illus. 2008. (ENG.). 32p. (J). (gr. k-2). 14.95 *(978-1-59249-771-3(3))*; 8.95 *(978-1-59249-772-0(1))* Soundprints.

—Musical Safari - Little Einsteins. 2009. (Little Einstein Audio Tales). (ENG.). 20p. (J). (gr. -1). 8.99 *(978-1-59069-774-0(X))* Studio Mouse LLC.

Garland, Michael. Daddy Played the Blues. 1 vol. 2017. (ENG., Illus.). 48p. (J). (gr. 1-5). 17.95 *(978-0-88448-588-9(9),* 884588) Tilbury Hse. Pubs.

Gillmor, Don. Fabuleuse Melodie De. Gay, Marie-Louise, illus. 2013. (ENG.). 44p. (J). (gr. -1-k). 16.95 *(978-2-923163-30-7(3))* La Montagne Secrete CAN. Dist: Independent Pubs. Group.

Godinez, Flory. The Adventures of Max & Millie: The Notable Orchard. 2004. (Illus.). 32p. (J). 9.95 *(978-0-9744427-1-6(2))* Music Bks. & Games.

Goembel, Ponder. Animal Fair. 0 vols. Goembel, Ponder, illus. 2012. (ENG., Illus.). 24p. (J). (gr. -1-1). 12.99 *(978-0-7614-5642-1(2),* 9780761456421, Two Lions) Amazon Publishing.

Gohmann, Johanna. Shock & Roll, Bk. 2. Zoloti?, Aleksandar, illus. 2018. (Electric Zombie Ser.). (ENG.). 112p. (J). (gr. 2-5). lib. bdg. 38.50 *(978-1-5321-3362-6(6),* 31147, Calico Chapter Bks.) ABDO Publishing Co.

Gold, Gina, et al. Harvest Hoedown. 2017. (Illus.). (J). *(978-1-5182-5126-9(9))* Harcourt.

Gorman, Amanda. Change Sings: A Children's Anthem. Long, Loren, illus. 2021. (ENG.). 32p. (J). (gr. -1-3). 18.99 *(978-0-593-20322-4(4),* Viking Books for Young Readers) Penguin Young Readers Group.

Gray, Michael Loyd. King Biscuit. 2013. (J). pap. *(978-1-938237-04-1(8))* Tempest Bk. Shop.

Gregorich, Barbara & Witty, Bruce. A Different Tune, Level 3. Hoffman, Joan, ed. 3rd ed. 2011. (ENG., Illus.). 16p. (J). (gr. -1-2). pap. 3.49 *(978-0-88743-028-2(7),* ca042b29-74b3-4e66-a208-22927a529587) School Zone Publishing Co.

Gripe, Maria. Elvis Karlsson. Gripe, Harold, illus. 2003. (SPA.). 148p. (J). (gr. 3-5). pap. 9.95 *(978-958-24-0181-8(8))* Santillana USA Publishing Co., Inc.

Gutknecht, Allison. Sing Like Nobody's Listening. 2018. (Mix Ser.). (ENG.). 256p. (J). (gr. 4-8). 18.99 *(978-1-4814-7157-2(0))*; (Illus.). pap. 7.99 *(978-1-4814-7156-5(2))* Simon & Schuster Children's Publishing. (Aladdin).

Haak, Harold H. The Mubox Bugs. lt. ed. 2003. (Illus.). 20p. (J). 5.95 *(978-1-931474-82-5(6))* Creative Teaching Assocs.

Harrison, John. Fergal Onions. 2005. (Illus.). 32p. pap. *(978-0-7022-3481-1(8))* Univ. of Queensland Pr.

Hart, Barbara. The Adventures of Octopus Rex. Baron, Andrew, illus. 2003. (SPA.). (J). 18.95 *(978-0-9760348-1-0(6))* Bh Pubns.

Hartman, Rachel. Seraphina. 2014. (Seraphina Ser.: 1). (ENG.). 528p. (YA). (gr. 7). pap. 13.99 *(978-0-375-86622-7(1),* Ember) Random Hse. Children's Bks.

Harvey, Jacqueline. Alice-Miranda Keeps the Beat. 2020. (Alice-Miranda Ser.: 18). (Illus.). 384p. (J). (gr. 3-7). 9.99 *(978-0-14-378603-0(2),* Puffin) Penguin Random Hse. AUS. Dist: Independent Pubs. Group.

Harvey, Jeanne Walker. My Hands Sing the Blues: Romare Bearden's Childhood Journey. 0 vols. Zunon, Elizabeth, illus. 2012. (ENG.). 40p. (J). (gr. 1-3). 17.99 *(978-0-7614-5810-4(7),* 9780761458104, Two Lions) Amazon Publishing.

Hayes, Mj. Emma's House of Sound. Robinson-Chavez, Kathryn A. & Madzel, D. E., illus. 2012. 80p. pap. 12.95 *(978-0-9819634-4-0(7))* Mary Jane Hayes.

Helguera, Luis Ignacio. Gracias a Johannes. Morales, Judith, illus. 2003. (SPA.). *(978-968-494-086-4(6),* CI5287) Centro de Informacion y Desarrollo de la Comunicacion y la Literatura MEX. Dist: Lectorum Pubns., Inc.

Heller, Sarah. Tinker Bell My Music MP3 Player: Storybook & Personal Music Player. 2008. (RD Innovative Book & Player Format Ser.). (ENG.). 36p. (YA). bds. 24.99 *(978-0-7944-1673-7(X))* Reader's Digest Assn., Inc., The.

Henkes, Kevin. Penny & Her Song. Henkes, Kevin, illus. 2012. (I Can Read Level 1 Ser.). (ENG., Illus.). 32p. (J). (gr. -1-3). pap. 4.99 *(978-0-06-208197-1(7))*; 12.99 *(978-0-06-208195-7(0))*; lib. bdg. 14.89 *(978-0-06-208196-4(9))* HarperCollins Pubs. (Greenwillow Bks.).

—Penny & Her Song. 2012. (J). lib. bdg. 13.55 *(978-0-606-26847-9(2))* Turtleback.

Herrera, Alberto. Músic: A Delightfully Harmonic Tale of the Origin of Music. 2012. 26p. 25.95 *(978-1-4327-8807-0(8))* Outskirts Pr., Inc.

Hertz, Kellen. Tenney. 1. 2018. (American Girl Contemporary Ser.). (ENG.). 172p. (J). (gr. 3-5). 17.96 *(978-1-64310-321-1(0))* Penworthy Co., LLC, The.

—Tenney Shares the Stage. 2017. 189p. (J). *(978-1-338-16722-1(7))* Scholastic, Inc.

—Tenney Shares the Stage. 2017. (American Girl Contempory Middle Grade Ser.: 3). lib. bdg. 20.85 *(978-0-606-40161-6(X))* Turtleback.

Hoffman, Amalia. Klezmer Bunch. 2009. (ENG.). 36p. 15.95 *(978-965-229-447-0(0))* Gefen Publishing Hse., Ltd ISR. Dist: Strauss Consultants.

Hoffman, Don & Palmer, Priscilla. Find Your Music. Dakins, Todd, illus. 2016. (ENG.). 32p. (J). (gr. -1-k). pap. 3.99 *(978-1-943154-06-7(6))* Peek-A-Boo Publishing.

Hoffmann, Burton R. Millicent the Magnificent. du Houx, Emily C., illus. 2004. 64p. pap. 12.00 *(978-1-882190-68-3(8))* Solon Ctr. for Research & Publishing.

Holm, Jennifer L. & Holm, Matthew. Babymouse #10: the Musical. Holm, Jennifer L. & Holm, Matthew, illus. 2009. (Babymouse Ser.: 10). (ENG., Illus.). 96p. (J). (gr. 2-5). pap. 6.99 *(978-0-375-84388-4(4))*; lib. bdg. 12.99 *(978-0-375-93791-0(9))* Penguin Random Hse. LLC.

Houran, Lori Haskins. Too Many Cats. Mathieu, Joe, illus. 2009. (Step into Reading: Step 1 Ser.). (ENG.). 32p. (J). (gr. -1-1). lib. bdg. 16.19 *(978-0-375-95197-8(0))* Random House Publishing Group.

—Too Many Cats. Mathieu, Joe, illus. 2009. (Step into Reading Ser.). 32p. (J). (gr. -1-1). pap. 5.99 *(978-0-375-85197-1(6),* Random Hse. Bks. for Young Readers) Random Hse. Children's Bks.

Howie, Vicki. Silent Night. Kallai, Kriszta Nagy, illus. 2009. 32p. (J). (gr. -1). pap. 13.49 *(978-0-7586-1779-8(8))* Concordia Publishing Hse.

Humble, Mark. Elmo Raps. 2009. (Sesame Street Step by Step Ser.). 10p. (J). (gr. -1). bds. 15.99 *(978-1-59069-870-9(3))* Studio Mouse LLC.

Ibbitson, John. The Landing. 2008. 160p. (J). (gr. 7-9). 17.95 *(978-1-55453-234-6(5))*; pap. 7.95 *(978-1-55453-238-4(8))* Kids Can Pr., Ltd. CAN. Dist: Hachette Bk. Group.

Jacobson, John & Huff, Mac. North Pole Musical: One Singular Sensational Holiday Revue. 2010. (Illus.). 72p. (J). pap. *(978-1-4234-7661-0(1))* Leonard, Hal Corp.

Jae-Jones, S. Shadowsong: A Novel. 2019. (ENG.). 400p. (YA). pap. 16.00 *(978-1-250-30818-4(6),* 900198098, Wednesday Bks.) St. Martin's Pr.

James, Karim. The Kids Time to Rhyme: Read & Rhyme at the same Time. 2009. 16p. pap. 14.99 *(978-1-4490-0424-8(5))* AuthorHouse.

Kalman, Esther. Tchaikovski Descubre America. 2003. (SPA., Illus.). 38p. (J). (gr. 3-5). 10.95 *(978-1-58105-123-0(9),* SAN1239) Santillana USA Publishing Co., Inc.

Katz, Alan. Where Did They Hide My Presents? Silly Dilly Christmas Songs. Catrow, David, illus. 2008. (ENG.). 32p. (J). (gr. -1-3). 6.99 *(978-1-4169-6830-6(X),* McElderry, Margaret K. Bks.) McElderry, Margaret K. Bks.

Kelly, Erin Entrada. Blackbird Fly. Peterschmidt, Betsy, illus. 2015. (ENG.). 304p. (J). (gr. 3-7). 16.99 *(978-0-06-223861-0(2),* Greenwillow Bks.) HarperCollins Pubs.

Khoury, Jessica. The Mystwick School of Musicraft. 2020. (ENG., Illus.). 368p. (J). (gr. 5-7). 16.99 *(978-1-328-62563-2(X),* 1734231, Clarion Bks.) HarperCollins Pubs.

Kidd, Ronald. Lord of the Mountain. 2018. (ENG.). 296p. (J). (gr. 3-7). 16.99 *(978-0-8075-4751-9(4),* 807547514) Whitman, Albert & Co.

Kimmel, Eric A. The Three Cabritos. 0 vols. Gilpin, Stephen, illus. 2012. (ENG.). 32p. (J). (gr. -1-3). pap. 7.99 *(978-0-7614-6309-2(7),* 9780761463092, Two Lions) Amazon Publishing.

Kimpton, Paul & Kimpton, Ann Kaczkowski. Dog Tags: A Young Musician's Sacrifice During WWII. 2012. (Adventures with Music Ser.: 2). (ENG.). 120p. (J). (gr. 4-7). pap. 8.95 *(978-1-57999-882-0(8))* G I A Pubns., Inc.

—Summer of Firsts: WWII Is Ending, but the Music Adventures Are Just Beginning. 2013. (Adventures with Music Ser.: 3). (ENG., Illus.). 288p. (J). (gr. 4-7). pap. 8.95 *(978-1-57999-972-8(7))* G I A Pubns., Inc.

Kirsch - Gambrell, Deneen. No Music for Mouseville. 2012. 32p. pap. 19.99 *(978-1-4772-7151-3(1))* AuthorHouse.

Kirwan, Wednesday. Baby Loves to Rock! Kirwan, Wednesday, illus. 2013. (ENG., Illus.). 28p. (J). (gr. -1 — 1). bds. 7.99 *(978-1-4424-5989-2(1),* Little Simon) Little Simon.

Knight, Hilary. A Firefly in a Fir Tree: A Carol for Mice. Knight, Hilary, illus. 2004. (Illus.). 32p. (J). (gr. -1-3). lib. bdg. 15.89 *(978-0-06-000992-2(6),* Tegen, Katherine Bks) HarperCollins Pubs.

Kormos, Lawrence. It Happened One Night in the Barn. Purdy, Joanne, illus. 2007. 24p. *(978-1-55452-192-0(0))* Essence Publishing.

Kristen, Judith. Once upon a Time in Liverpool. Cash, Eric, illus. 2012. 40p. pap. 15.95 *(978-0-9849505-2-2(4))* Aquinas & Krone Publishing, LLC.

Lacaille, Link. Roots, Rock, Rap & Reggae. 1 vol. 2009. 25p. pap. 24.95 *(978-1-60836-930-0(7))* America Star Bks.

Langham, Tony. Creepy Crawly Calypso. Harter, Debbie, illus. 2004. (ENG.). 32p. (J). 16.99 *(978-1-84148-699-4(X))* Barefoot Bks., Inc.

Langham, Tony & Harter, Debbie. Creepy Crawly Calypso. 2005. (ENG.). 32p. (J). pap. 9.99 *(978-1-902283-46-3(5))* Barefoot Bks., Inc.

Lauture, Mireille B. Gade Yon Kado Remi Jwenn / Remi's Magical Gift: Mancy's Haitian Folktale Collection. 2012. 28p. pap. 16.99 *(978-1-4685-5546-2(4))* AuthorHouse.

LeFlore, Lyah B. The World Is Mine. Warfield, D. L., illus. 2009. (Come Up Ser.). (ENG.). 304p. (YA). (gr. 9-18). pap. 8.99 *(978-1-4169-7963-0(8),* Simon Pulse) Simon Pulse.

Lewman, David. Drop the Beat! Laguna, Fabio & Matta, Gabriella, illus. 2017. 24p. (J). *(978-1-5379-5751-7(1))* Random Hse., Inc.

—Drop the Beat! 2017. (Step into Reading - Level 1 Ser.). lib. bdg. 14.75 *(978-0-606-40252-1(7))* Turtleback.

Lies, Brian. Bats in the Band. Lies, Brian, illus. 2014. (Bat Book Ser.). (ENG., Illus.). 32p. (J). (gr. -1-3). 17.99 *(978-0-544-10569-0(9),* 1540826, Clarion Bks.) HarperCollins Pubs.

Lionni, Leo. Geraldine, the Music Mouse. (Illus.). 32p. (J). (gr. -1-2). 2016. (ENG.). 20.99 *(978-0-394-94238-4(8),* Knopf Bks. for Young Readers) 2009. 8.99 *(978-0-375-85514-6(9),* Dragonfly Bks.) Random Hse. Children's Bks.

Lipsyte, Robert. Yellow Flag. 2009. (ENG.). 256p. (YA). (gr. 8). pap. 10.99 *(978-0-06-055709-6(5),* HarperCollins) HarperCollins Pubs.

Litchfield, David. The Bear & the Piano. Litchfield, David, illus. 2016. (ENG., Illus.). 40p. (J). (gr. -1-3). 17.99 *(978-0-544-67454-7(5),* 1626244, Clarion Bks.) HarperCollins Pubs.

—The Bear, the Piano, the Dog, & the Fiddle. Litchfield, David, illus. 2019. (ENG., Illus.). 40p. (J). (gr. -1-3). 17.99 *(978-1-328-59589-8(7),* 1731276, Clarion Bks.) HarperCollins Pubs.

Lupton, Hugh. Tales of Wisdom & Wonder. Sharkey, Niamh, illus. 2008. 64p. (J). 19.99 *(978-1-84686-243-4(4))* Barefoot Bks., Inc.

MacHado, Ana Maria. Un Buen Coro. (Torre de Papel Ser.). (SPA., Illus.). (J). 7.95 *(978-958-04-4525-8(7),* NR30643) Norma S.A. COL. Dist: Lectorum Pubns., Inc., Distribuidora Norma, Inc.

Madden, Kerry. Gentle's Holler. 2007. (Maggie Valley Ser.). 237p. (gr. 4-7). 17.00 *(978-0-7569-8090-0(9))* Perfection Learning Corp.

Maddox, Jake. Block & Rock. 2017. (Jake Maddox JV Ser.). (ENG., Illus.). 96p. (J). (gr. 4-6). lib. bdg. 26.65 *(978-1-4965-4942-6(2),* 135847, Stone Arch Bks.) Capstone.

Maloney, Andrew. The Master Song. 2014. (Blue Time Ser.: 1). (ENG., Illus.). 352p. (gr. 7). pap. 15.99 *(978-1-62911-176-6(7),* 770172) Whitaker Hse.

—Verse of Valor. 2015. (Blue Time Ser.: 2). (ENG.). 288p. (gr. 7). pap. 15.99 *(978-1-62911-357-9(3),* 770306) Whitaker Hse.

Manning, Sarra. Guitar Girl. 2005. 217p. (gr. 9-12). 17.00 *(978-0-7569-5702-5(8))* Perfection Learning Corp.

Mantchev, Lisa & Dallas, Glenn. Sugar Skulls. 0 vols. 2015. (ENG.). 333p. (YA). (gr. 10-12). pap. 9.99 *(978-1-5039-4971-3(0),* 9781503949713, Skyscape) Amazon Publishing.

Manushkin, Fran. Katie's Noisy Music. Lyon, Tammie, illus. 2015. (Katie Woo Ser.). (ENG.). 32p. (J). (gr. k-2). 21.32 *(978-1-4795-5893-3(1),* 127034, Picture Window Bks.) Capstone.

Martin, Amy. Symphony City. 2011. (ENG., Illus.). 48p. (J). (gr. -1-4). 17.95 *(978-1-936365-39-5(1),* 4506c646-7825-42ba-9674-8978332756b5) McSweeney's Publishing.

Mason-Black, Jennifer. Devil & the Bluebird. 2016. (ENG.). 336p. (J). (gr. 8-17). 17.95 *(978-1-4197-2000-0(7),* 1135901, Amulet Bks.) Abrams, Inc.

Mayer, Mercer. Little Critter: Just a Little Music. Mayer, Mercer, illus. 2009. (Little Critter Ser.). (ENG., Illus.). 24p. (J). (gr. -1-3). pap. 4.99 *(978-0-06-053962-7(3),* HarperFestival) HarperCollins Pubs.

Mayerhofer, Felix. Horace the Great Harmonica King. MacFarlane, John, illus. 2006. 31p. (J). (gr. -1-7). per. 16.95 *(978-1-60002-255-5(3),* 4313) Mountain Valley Publishing, LLC.

Mazer, Anne. It's Music to My Ears. 2005. (Amazing Days of Abby Hayes Ser.). (Illus.). 110p. (J). (gr. 3-7). 12.65 *(978-0-7569-5910-4(1))* Perfection Learning Corp.

—Mabel Strikes a Chord. 4. Brown, Bill, illus. 2008. (Sister Magic Ser.). (ENG.). 86p. (J). (gr. 3-6). 17.44 *(978-0-439-87249-2(9))* Scholastic, Inc.

McCanna, Tim. Barnyard Boogie! Black, Allison, illus. 2017. (ENG.). 24p. (J). (gr. -1-k). 12.95 *(978-1-4197-2346-9(4),* 1163801, Abrams Appleseed) Abrams, Inc.

McGowan, Jayme. One Bear Extraordinaire. 2015. (ENG., Illus.). 32p. (J). (gr. -1-3). 16.95 *(978-1-4197-1654-6(9),* 1095601, Abrams Bks. for Young Readers) Abrams, Inc.

Meadows, Daisy. Alyssa the Star-Spotter Fairy. 2013. (Rainbow Magic — the Superstar Fairies Ser.: 6). lib. bdg. 14.75 *(978-0-606-31518-0(7))* Turtleback.

—Frankie the Makeup Fairy. 2013. (Rainbow Magic — the Superstar Fairies Ser.: 5). lib. bdg. 14.75 *(978-0-606-31517-3(9))* Turtleback.

—Jessie the Lyrics Fairy. 2013. (Rainbow Magic — the Superstar Fairies Ser.: 1). lib. bdg. 14.75 *(978-0-606-31513-5(6))* Turtleback.

Melki-Wegner, Skye. The Hush. 2017. (ENG.). 386p. (J). (gr. 6-6). 16.99 *(978-1-5107-1248-5(8),* Sky Pony Pr.) Skyhorse Publishing Co., Inc.

Merveille, David. Juke Box. Merveille, David, illus. 2008. (ENG., Illus.). 48p. (J). (gr. 4-7). 9.99 *(978-1-933605-72-2(3))* Kane Miller.

Middlemiss, David. The Great Hamstini. Middlemiss, Laura B., illus. 2010. 108p. *(978-1-907211-18-8(7))* Grosvenor Hse. Publishing Ltd.

Middleton, William. The Chipmunk Jamboree. 2013. 24p. pap. 12.45 *(978-1-4624-0669-2(6),* Inspiring Voices) Author Solutions, LLC.

Miles, David W. Allegro: A Musical Journey Through 11 Musical Masterpieces. Barghigiani, Anita, illus. 2018. (ENG.). 32p. (J). (gr. k-3). 24.99 *(978-1-64170-038-2(6),* 550038) Familius LLC.

Miller, Karl. Bongo Boy's Magical Drums. 2011. 72p. pap. 31.27 *(978-1-4567-7102-7(7))* AuthorHouse.

Miller, Sara. My Pod: Libro de Cuentos y Reproductor Personal de Musica. Peterson, Stacy & Maberry, Maranda, illus. 2007. (SPA.). 38p. (J). (gr. -1-3). *(978-970-718-495-4(7),* Silver Dolphin en Español) Advanced Marketing, S. de R. L. de C. V.

Mit musik geht alles Besser. pap. 12.95 *(978-3-89748-676-8(8))* Dino Entertainment AG DEU. Dist: Distribooks, Inc.

Moss, Lloyd. Zin! Zin! Zin! A Violin. Priceman, Marjorie, illus. 2004. (gr. -1-3). 18.00 *(978-0-7569-1919-1(3))* Perfection Learning Corp.

—Zin! Zin! Zin! A Violin. Priceman, Marjorie, illus. 2005. (Stories to Go! Ser.). (ENG.). 32p. (J). (gr. -1-3). 4.99 *(978-1-4169-0838-8(2),* Simon & Schuster/Paula Wiseman Bks.) Simon & Schuster/Paula Wiseman Bks.

Moulton, Mark Kimball. A Cricket's Carol. Blowers, Lisa, illus. 2004. 32p. (J). 14.95 *(978-0-8249-5488-8(2),* Ideals Pubns.) Worthy Publishing.

Nall, Gail. Out of Tune. 2017. (Mix Ser.). (ENG.). 352p. (J). (gr. 4-8). pap. 7.99 *(978-1-4814-5816-0(7),* Aladdin) Simon & Schuster Children's Publishing.

—Out of Tune. 2016. (Mix Ser.). (ENG., Illus.). 336p. (J). (gr. 4-9). 17.99 *(978-1-4814-5817-7(5),* Simon & Schuster/Paula Wiseman Bks.) Simon & Schuster/Paula Wiseman Bks.

Newton, Jill, illus. Crash Bang Donkey! 2015. 32p. (J). *(978-1-4896-3858-8(X))* Weigl Pubs., Inc.

Norman, Tyler & Perez, Jose S. The Banjoman/El Hombre del Banjo. Perez, Jose S., illus. 2004. (ENG & SPA., Illus.). 32p. (J). 12.95 *(978-1-57072-292-9(7))* Overmountain Pr.

Nowlin, Laura. This Song Is (Not) for You. 2016. 240p. (YA). (gr. 8-12). pap. 12.99 *(978-1-4926-0290-3(6),* 9781492602903) Sourcebooks, Inc.

M N O

Ode, Eric. Dan, the Taxi Man. 2012. (Picture Book Ser.). (ENG., Illus.). 32p. (J). 14.99 *(978-1-61067-072-2(8))* Kane Miller.
O'Neill, Richard & Quarmby, Katharine. Ossiri & the Bala Mengro. Tolson, Hannah, illus. 2017. (Travellers Tales Ser.). (ENG.). 32p. (J). *(978-1-84643-925-4(6))* Child's Play International Ltd.
Paige, D. M. Chart Topper. 2015. (Opportunity Ser.). (ENG.). 112p. (YA). (gr. 6-12). E-Book 53.32 *(978-1-4677-6014-0(5)*, 9781467760140, Lerner Digital) Lerner Publishing Group.
Parenteau, Shirley. Bears in a Band. Walker, David M., illus. 2016. (Bears on Chairs Ser.). (ENG.). 32p. (J). (-k). 15.99 *(978-0-7636-8147-0(4))* Candlewick Pr.
Parton, Dolly & Perl, Erica S. Dolly Parton's Billy the Kid Makes It Big. Haley, MacKenzie, illus. 2023. (ENG.). 40p. (J). (gr. -1-2). 19.99 ***(978-0-593-66157-4(5)***, Penguin Workshop) Penguin Young Readers Group.
Patrick, Wendy. When Passion Wins. 2012. 186p. (gr. 4-6). pap. 14.50 *(978-1-4669-7131-8(2))* Trafford Publishing.
Pattou, Edith. Hero's Song: The First Song of Eirren. 2005. (ENG., Illus.). 348p. (J). (gr. 7-12). pap. 15.95 *(978-0-15-205542-4(8)*, Clarion Bks.) HarperCollins Pubs.
Payne, C. C. Something to Sing About. 2008. (ENG.). 167p. (J). (gr. 4-7). pap. 8.50 *(978-0-8028-5344-8(7))* Eerdmans, William B. Publishing Co.
Payne, Sandy. Find Your Magic. Goodpaster, Nancy, illus. 2013. 50p. pap. 12.95 *(978-1-937508-16-6(1))* Bearhead Publishing, LLC.
Perelman, Helen. Heart to Heart. 2007. (High School Musical Stories from East High Ser.). 125p. (J). (gr. 3-7). 12.65 *(978-0-7569-8340-6(1))* Perfection Learning Corp.
Perez, Marlene. Dead Is a Killer Tune. 2012. (Dead Is Ser.: 7). lib. bdg. 18.40 *(978-0-606-26623-9(2))* Turtleback.
Plant, Marilyn. Trinka's Music Lessons. 2013. 48p. pap. *(978-1-4602-1273-8(8))* FriesenPress.
Polacco, Patricia. The Bravest Man in the World. Polacco, Patricia, illus. 2019. (ENG., Illus.). 56p. (J). (gr. -1-3). 17.99 *(978-1-4814-9461-8(9)*, Simon & Schuster Bks. For Young Readers) Simon & Schuster Bks. For Young Readers.
Politi, Leo. Pedro: The Angel of Olvera Street. 2009. (ENG., Illus.). 32p. (gr. 1). 15.95 *(978-0-89236-990-4(6))* Oxford Univ. Pr., Inc.
Poulsen, David A. Jeremy's Song. 2004. 110p. (YA). pap. 3.99 *(978-1-55035-027-8(4))* Cygnet Publishing Group, Inc./Coolreading.com CAN. Dist: Orca Bk. Pubs. USA.
—Jeremy's Song. 2008. (Lawrence High Yearbook Ser.). (ENG.). 96p. (YA). (gr. 7-18). pap. *(978-1-55470-098-1(1))* Me to We.
Poupart, Jean-Marie. Des Pianos Qui S'Envolent. 2003. (Roman Jeunesse Ser.). (FRE.). 96p. (YA). (gr. 4-7). pap. *(978-2-89021-173-5(8))* Diffusion du livre Mirabel (DLM).
Powell, Amy. Hope Music. Farley, Katherine, illus. 2006. 32p. (J). (gr. -1-3). per. 12.00 *(978-0-9773608-4-0(9))* Shiny Red Ball Publishing.
Priddy, Roger. The 12 Days of Christmas: A Lift-The-tab Book. 2018. (Lift-The-Flap Tab Bks.: 1). (ENG., Illus.). 24p. (J). bds. 7.99 *(978-0-312-52743-3(8)*, 900190067) St. Martin's Pr.
Prinz, Yvonne. The Vinyl Princess. 2011. 336p. (J). pap. 8.99 *(978-0-06-171585-3(9)*, HarperTeen) 2009. (ENG.). 320p. (YA). (gr. 8-18). 16.99 *(978-0-06-171583-9(2))* HarperCollins Pubs.
Pritchett, Dylan. The First Music. Banks, Erin, illus. 2006. (ENG.). 32p. (J). (gr. -1-3). 16.95 *(978-0-87483-776-6(6))* August Hse. Pubs., Inc.
Publications International Ltd. Staff, creator. High School Musical: Let's Text. 2008. (High School Musical Ser.). (Illus.). 24p. (J). (gr. 4-7). 19.98 *(978-1-4127-7569-4(8))* Publications International, Ltd.
—Pooh Surprise Sing-along. 2007. (Surprise Mirror Book Ser.). (Illus.). (gr. -1-k). 15.98 *(978-1-4127-7418-5(7))* Publications International, Ltd.
Publications International Ltd. Staff, ed. Baby Einstein: Look, Listen, & Discover. 2010. 14p. (J). bds. 22.98 *(978-1-4127-4517-8(9)*, 1412745179) Phoenix International Publications, Inc.
—Barney Favorite Things. 2010. 12p. (J). bds. 10.98 *(978-1-4127-4465-2(2)*, PIL Kids) Publications International, Ltd.
—Hello Kitty I Love to Play Piano. 2013. 12p. (J). (gr. k-3). bds. 16.99 *(978-1-4508-6168-7(7)*, 3621dc87-b55b-4629-b450-4e32aa29210f) Phoenix International Publications, Inc.
—Look & Find Elmo. 2010. 24p. (J). 7.98 *(978-1-60553-766-5(7))* Phoenix International Publications, Inc.
—Musical Pop up Disney Princess. 2008. (SPA.). (J). 15.98 *(978-1-4127-8980-6(X))* Publications International, Ltd.
—Sesame Street (Musical Treasury) 2011. 40p. (J). bds. 15.98 *(978-1-4508-1081-4(0))* Publications International, Ltd.
Pugliano-Martin, Carol. The Very Mean King & el rey Malo: 6 English, 6 Spanish Adaptations. 2011. (ENG & SPA.). (J). 75.00 net. *(978-1-4108-5648-7(8))* Benchmark Education Co.
Quinn, Jordan. The Bard & the Beast. McPhillips, Robert, illus. 2015. (Kingdom of Wrenly Ser.: 9). (ENG.). 128p. (J). (gr. k-4). pap. 6.99 *(978-1-4814-4396-8(8)*, Little Simon) Little Simon.
Rankin, Joan & Hartmann, Wendy. The African Orchestra. 2017. (ENG., Illus.). 32p. (J). (gr. 1-2). 17.95 *(978-1-56656-048-1(9)*, Crocodile Bks.) Interlink Publishing Group, Inc.
Rey, H. A. Curious George Harvest Hoedown (CGTV 8 X 8) 2017. (Curious George Ser.). (ENG., Illus.). 24p. (J). (gr. -1-3). pap. 4.99 *(978-1-328-69597-0(2)*, 1671310, Clarion Bks.) HarperCollins Pubs.
Reynolds, Paul A. Sydney & Simon: Go Green! Reynolds, Peter H., illus. 2015. (Sydney & Simon Ser.: 2). 48p. (J). (gr. 1-4). lib. bdg. 12.95 *(978-1-58089-677-1(4))* Charlesbridge Publishing, Inc.
Reynolds, Peter H. Playing from the Heart. Reynolds, Peter H., illus. 2016. (ENG., Illus.). 32p. (J). (gr. k-4). 15.99 *(978-0-7636-7892-0(9))* Candlewick Pr.
RH Disney. Coco Little Golden Book (Disney/Pixar Coco) The Disney Storybook Art Team, illus. 2017. (Little Golden Book Ser.). (ENG.). 24p. (J). (-k). 5.99 *(978-0-7364-3800-1(9)*, Golden/Disney) Random Hse. Children's Bks.
Richards, Chip & De Alessi, O. B. Flutes in the Garden. 2015. (ENG.). 68p. pap. 13.95 *(978-0-7387-4658-6(4))* Llewellyn Pubns.
Richardson, Bill. I Would Have Gone to Woodstock. 2007. 28p. (YA). per. 12.95 *(978-1-4327-1256-3(X))* Outskirts Pr., Inc.
Rivera, Liz. Miguel's Music (Disney/Pixar Coco) The Disney Storybook Art Team, illus. 2017. (Step into Reading Ser.). (ENG.). 32p. (J). (gr. -1-1). pap. 5.99 *(978-0-7364-3811-7(4)*, RH/Disney) Random Hse. Children's Bks.
Roach. Monstrous Stories #3: Frogosaurus vs. the Bog Monster, 3. 2013. (Dr. Roach's Monstrous Stories Ser.: 3). (ENG.). 64p. (J). (gr. 2-4). 17.44 *(978-0-545-42556-8(5))* Scholastic, Inc.
Robinson, Fiona. What Animals Really Like. 2011. (ENG., Illus.). 24p. (J). (gr. k-2). pap. 7.95 *(978-1-4197-0121-4(5))* UK Abrams Bks. for Young Readers.
Rodman, Mercedes. My Blue Butterfly. 2012.Tr. of Mi Mariposa Azul. (SPA & ENG., Illus.). 64p. (J). pap. 19.95 *(978-0-9827146-7-6(X))* Vineyard Stories.
Rodriguez Ferrer, Janel. The Arts-Angels Track 1: Drawn to You. 2012. 252p. pap. 8.99 *(978-1-936214-91-4(1))* Wyatt-MacKenzie Publishing.
Rollins, Barbara B. Syncopated Summer. unabr. ed. 2006. (J). per. 9.95 *(978-1-932196-97-9(8))* WordWright.biz, Inc.
Romanelli, Serena. El Pequeno Coco. Lamas, Blanca Rosa, tr. from GER. De Beer, Hans, illus. 2004.Tr. of Kleiner Dodo was Spielst du?. (SPA.). 24p. (J). (gr. k-4). reprint ed. 16.00 *(978-0-7567-7707-4(0))* DIANE Publishing Co.
Rosenberg, Michael. The Little Lost Tune: More Adventures from Bendalot. 2010. 30p. pap. 13.00 *(978-1-60911-881-5(2)*, Eloquent Bks.) Strategic Book Publishing & Rights Agency (SBPRA).
Rosenstock, Barb. Blue Grass Boy: The Story of Bill Monroe, Father of Bluegrass Music. Fotheringham, Edwin, illus. 2018. (ENG.). 40p. (J). (gr. 2-5). 17.95 *(978-1-62979-439-6(2)*, Calkins Creek) Highlights Pr., c/o Highlights for Children, Inc.
Roth, Susan. Do Re Mi: If You Can Read Music, Thank Guido D'Arezzo. 2007. (ENG., Illus.). 40p. (J). (gr. -1-3). 18.99 *(978-0-618-46572-9(3)*, 595305, Clarion Bks.) HarperCollins Pubs.
Russell, D. Z. The Amazing Adventures of Andy Owl: A Children's Guide to Understanding Music. Stone, John, illus. 2003. 34p. (J). per. 7.95 *(978-0-9725398-0-7(8))* World Famous Children's Bks.
Ryan, Pam Muñoz. Echo, 1 vol. 2015. (ENG., Illus.). 592p. (J). (gr. 5-9). 19.99 *(978-0-439-87402-1(5)*, Scholastic Pr.) Scholastic, Inc.
—Echo (Unabridged Edition), 1 vol. unabr. ed. 2015. (ENG.). (J). (gr. 5-9). 4p. audio compact disk 39.99 *(978-0-545-78836-6(8))*; Vol. 8. audio compact disk 79.99 *(978-0-545-78837-3(4))* Scholastic, Inc.
Santillo, LuAnn. The Tune. Santillo, LuAnn, ed. 2003. (Half-Pint Kids Readers Ser.). (Illus.). 7p. (J). (gr. -1-1). pap. 1.00 *(978-1-59256-102-5(0))* Half-Pint Kids, Inc.
Schreiber, Sam. Raise Your Voice. 2004. (Illus.). 187p. (J). pap. *(978-0-439-73083-9(X))* Scholastic, Inc.
Sesame Street. Sesame Street Elmo's Musical Hugs. 2014. (Hugs Book Ser.: 5). (ENG.). 32p. (J). 19.99 *(978-0-7944-2862-4(2))* Reader's Digest Assn., Inc., The.
Shammas, Anna. Recorder Karate. Guzza, Victor, illus. 2012. 32p. pap. 8.95 *(978-0-9843869-2-5(0)*, Castlebridge Bks.) Big Tent Bks.
Shankman, Ed. The Bourbon Street Band Is Back. O'Neill, Dave, illus. 2011. (Shankman & O'Neill Ser.). (ENG.). 32p. (J). (gr. -1-3). 14.95 *(978-1-933212-79-1(9)*, Commonwealth Editions) Applewood Bks.
Shefelman, Janice. Anna Maria's Gift. Papp, Robert, illus. 2011. (Stepping Stone Book(TM) Ser.). 112p. (J). (gr. 2-5). pap. 4.99 *(978-0-375-85882-6(2)*, Random Hse. Bks. for Young Readers) Random Hse. Children's Bks.
Shefelman, Janice Jordan. Anna Maria's Gift. Papp, Robert, illus. 2010. (Stepping Stones Chapter Book: History Ser.). (ENG.). 112p. (J). (gr. 1-4). lib. bdg. 17.44 *(978-0-375-95881-6(9))* Random House Publishing Group.
Sing with Your Baby. 2006. (ENG., Illus.). 36p. (gr. -1). 12.99 *(978-1-59069-494-7(5)*, 1P800) Studio Mouse LLC.
St. Jean, Alan. The Legend of OinkADoodleMoo. St. Jean, Alan, ed. Krock, Libby Carruth, illus. 2013. 32p. 19.95 *(978-0-9777272-9-2(7))* Oren Village, LLC.
Staunton, Ted. Accord de Puissance, 1 vol. 2012. (Orca Currents en Français Ser.). (FRE.). 128p. (J). (gr. 4-7). pap. 9.95 *(978-1-4598-0311-4(6))* Orca Bk. Pubs. USA.
Steve Cormey. The Brothers Foot: A Hare Raising Story. Ronda Eden, illus. 2009. 56p. pap. 21.99 *(978-1-4389-4269-8(9))* AuthorHouse.
Stilton, Gerónimo. Singing Sensation. 2009. (Geronimo Stilton Ser.: 39). lib. bdg. 18.40 *(978-0-606-00230-1(8))* Turtleback.
Stilwell, Norma Mintum. Making Beautiful Music. LaGrange, Tiffany, illus. 2011. 28p. pap. 14.95 *(978-1-936343-92-8(4))* Peppertree Pr., The.
Stinson, Kathy. The Man with the Violin. Petricic, Dusan, illus. (J). (gr. k-3). 2016. 32p. pap. 9.95 *(978-1-55451-564-6(5))* 5th ed. 2013. (ENG.). 36p. 19.95 *(978-1-55451-565-3(3)*, 9781554515653) Annick Pr. Ltd. CAN. Dist: Publishers Group West (PGW).
Stone, Laura. Miss Clarissa & Her Musical Shoes. 2010. 32p. pap. 16.95 *(978-0-557-33226-7(5))* Lulu Pr., Inc.
Stosuy, Brandon. Music Is ... Martin, Amy, illus. 2016. (ENG.). 32p. (J). (gr. -1 — 1). bds. 8.99 *(978-1-4814-7702-4(1)*, Little Simon) Little Simon.
Stuchner, Joan Betty. The Kugel Valley Klezmer Band. Row, Richard, illus. 2010. (ENG.). 32p. (J). (gr. -1-3). pap. 7.95 *(978-1-56656-782-4(3)*, Crocodile Bks.) Interlink Publishing Group, Inc.
Studio Mouse Staff. Musical Fun: Colors & Patterns. rev. ed. 2008. (ENG., Illus.). 24p. (J). 4.99 *(978-1-59069-605-7(0))* Studio Mouse LLC.
Supplee, Suzanne. Somebody Everybody Listens To. 2011. 288p. (YA). (gr. 7-12). 8.99 *(978-0-14-241886-4(2)*, Speak) Penguin Young Readers Group.
Taddonio, Lea. Book 4: Solo ACT. Aly, Hatem, illus. 2017. (Along for the Ride Ser.). (ENG.). 48p. (J). (gr. 3-7). lib. bdg. 34.21 *(978-1-5321-3004-5(X)*, 25554, Spellbound) Magic Wagon.
Taylor, Je'. The Animal Dance. 2009. 32p. pap. 14.49 *(978-1-4490-2626-4(5))* AuthorHouse.
Taylor, Vincent. Cornbread Has a Bad Habit. 2007. (Illus.). 96p. (J). pap. 4.99 *(978-0-9704512-5-5(3))* TriEclipse, Inc.
Tey, Rachel. Tea in Pajamas. 2019. 170p. (J). (gr. 2-4). pap. 16.95 *(978-981-4828-85-7(8))* Marshall Cavendish International (Asia) Private Ltd. SGP. Dist: Independent Pubs. Group.
Thaler, Mike. The Music Teacher from the Black Lagoon, 1 vol. Lee, Jared, illus. 2011. (Black Lagoon Ser.: No. 1). (ENG.). 32p. (J). (gr. k-4). lib. bdg. 31.36 *(978-1-59961-796-1(X)*, 3622, Picture Bk.) Spotlight.
The Library Fairy. The Magical Tree & Musical Wind. Faust, Laurie A., illus. 2008. 32p. pap. 16.95 *(978-1-59858-604-6(1))* Dog Ear Publishing, LLC.
Thomas, Maria Jose & Thomas, María José. !Bravo, Rosina! Muñoz, Claudio, illus. 2005. (SPA.). 48p. (J). (gr. -1-5). 10.40 *(978-980-257-242-7(X)*, EK33833) Ekare, Ediciones VEN. Dist: Lectorum Pubns., Inc.
Thomas, Terri. J Mac Is the Freestyle King! Sefcik, Wendy, illus. 2010. 38p. pap. 20.00 *(978-1-60844-453-3(8))* Dog Ear Publishing, LLC.
Thompson, Carol. Music. Thompson, Carol, illus. 2018. (Amazing Me! Ser.: 4). (Illus.). 12p. (J). (gr. k-k). spiral bd. *(978-1-84643-961-2(2))* Child's Play International Ltd.
Thompson, Kate. The New Policeman. (Illus.). 2008. (New Policeman Trilogy Ser.: 1). (ENG.). 464p. (YA). (gr. 8-12). pap. 9.99 *(978-0-06-117429-2(7))* 2007. 448p. (J). (gr. 7-12). 16.99 *(978-0-06-117427-8(0))* HarperCollins Pubs. (Greenwillow Bks.).
—The New Policeman. pap. 1.00 *(978-1-4074-4550-2(2))* Recorded Bks., Inc.
Thompson, Vivian L. Kimo Makes Music. Nomura, Beverly, photos by. 2005. (ENG., Illus.). 24p. pap. 14.99 *(978-1-4120-1137-2(X))* Trafford Publishing.
Tibo, Gilles. Simon et la Musique. 2004.Tr. of Simon Makes Music. (FRE.). (J). (gr. -1-2). spiral bd. *(978-0-616-01845-3(2))* Canadian National Institute for the Blind/Institut National Canadien pour les Aveugles.
—Simon Makes Music. 2004. (J). (gr. -1-2). spiral bd. *(978-0-616-01793-7(6))*; spiral bd. *(978-0-616-01792-0(8))* Canadian National Institute for the Blind/Institut National Canadien pour les Aveugles.
Tomlinson, Heather. Aurelie: A Faerie Tale. 2010. (ENG.). 208p. (YA). (gr. 7-12). pap. 18.99 *(978-0-312-60275-8(8)*, 900064245) Square Fish.
Toon, Paige. All about the Hype. 2017. (Jessie Jefferson Novels Ser.: 3). (ENG.). 320p. (J). 9.99 *(978-1-4711-4610-7(3)*, Simon & Schuster Children's) Simon & Schuster, Ltd. GBR. Dist: Simon & Schuster, Inc.
Torgan, Keith & Siesel, Barbara. Green Golly & Her Golden Flute. Langelier-Lebeda, Suzanne, illus. 2013. 58p. pap. 19.99 *(978-1-936172-61-0(5))* Elfrig Publishing.
Urban, Linda. A Crooked Kind of Perfect. 2009. (ENG., Illus.). 224p. (J). (gr. 5-7). pap. 7.99 *(978-0-15-206608-6(X)*, 1099010, Clarion Bks.) HarperCollins Pubs.
Van Dyne, Edith. Aunt Jane's Nieces Abroad. 2017. (ENG., Illus.). (J). pap. 13.95 *(978-1-374-81521-6(7))* Capital Communications, Inc.
Velasquez, Eric. Grandma's Records. Velasquez, Eric, illus. 2004. (ENG., Illus.). 32p. (J). (gr. k-3). pap. 9.99 *(978-0-8027-7660-0(4)*, 900032898, Bloomsbury USA Childrens) Bloomsbury Publishing USA.
—Grandma's Records. 2014. 32p. pap. 9.00 *(978-1-61003-346-6(9))* Center for the Collaborative Classroom.
—Grandma's Records. 2004. (Illus.). 32p. (J). (gr. k-3). 17.85 *(978-0-8027-8761-3(4))*; 16.95 *(978-0-8027-8760-6(6))* Walker & Co.
Vigneault, Gilles. Un Cadeau Pour Sophie: Conte et Chansons. Jorisch, Stéphane, illus. 2013. (ENG.). 40p. (J). (gr. k-2). 16.95 *(978-2-923163-38-3(9))* La Montagne Secrete CAN. Dist: Independent Pubs. Group.
Vipont, Elfrida. The Lark in the Morn. Freeman, T. R., illus. 2007. (Young Adult Historical Bookshelf Ser.). (ENG.). 196p. (J). (gr. 7-9). pap. 12.95 *(978-1-932350-22-7(5))* Ignatius Pr.
Wallace, Suzanne. The Man Who Loved Violins. 2011. 28p. pap. 15.99 *(978-1-4568-7753-8(4))* Xlibris Corp.
Walton, K. M., et al. Behind the Song. 2017. (ENG.). 376p. (YA). (gr. 8-12). pap. 14.99 *(978-1-4926-3881-0(1))* Sourcebooks, Inc.
Walton, O. F. Christie's Old Organ. rev. ed. 2008. (Classic Fiction Ser.). (ENG.). 176p. (J). (gr. 4-7). mass mkt. 7.99 *(978-1-85792-523-4(8)*, 6c4a8b80-df9a-4516-a3af-3e9f769f9d8c) Christian Focus Pubns. GBR. Dist: Baker & Taylor Publisher Services (BTPS).
Watt, Fiona. Little Children's Christmas Music Book. 2012. (Little Children's Music Book Ser.). 24p. (J). bds. 18.99 *(978-0-7945-3328-1(0)*, Usborne) EDC Publishing.
—Sing-Along Christmas Carols. Bonnet, Rosalinde, illus. 2010. (Baby Board Books with CD Ser.). 10p. (J). bds. 14.99 incl. audio compact disk *(978-0-7945-2660-3(8)*, Usborne) EDC Publishing.
Watts, Leander. Beautiful City of the Dead. 2007. (ENG.). 256p. (YA). (gr. 7-12). pap. 14.99 *(978-0-618-59499-3(X)*, 474084, Clarion Bks.) HarperCollins Pubs.
Weidt, Maryann N. Daddy Played Music for the Cows. Sorensen, Henri, illus. 2nd ed. 2004. (ENG.). 32p. (J). pap. 7.95 *(978-0-89317-060-8(7)*, WW-0607, Windward Publishing) Finney Co., Inc.
Weinstone, David. Music Class Today! Vogel, Vin, illus. 2015. (ENG.). 40p. (J). (gr. -1 — 1). 19.99 *(978-0-374-35131-1(7)*, 900138002, Farrar, Straus & Giroux (BYR)) Farrar, Straus & Giroux.
Wekelo, Kerry. Audrey's Journey: Round & Round Yoga. 2012. 16p. pap. 15.99 *(978-1-4685-9645-8(4))* AuthorHouse.
Wells, Tina. Mackenzie Blue #4 Mixed Messages. 2013. (Mackenzie Blue Ser.: 4). (ENG.). 224p. (J). (gr. 3-7). pap. 6.99 *(978-0-06-158319-3(7)*, HarperCollins) HarperCollins Pubs.
Wheeler, Lisa. Jazz Baby. Christie, R. Gregory, illus. 2007. (ENG.). 40p. (J). (gr. -1-3). 18.99 *(978-0-15-202522-9(7)*, 1193042, Clarion Bks.) HarperCollins Pubs.
Where's Henry?, 6 Pack. (gr. k-1). 23.00 *(978-0-7635-8828-1(8))* Rigby Education.
Whitaker, Alecia. The Way Back Home. 2016. (Wildflower Ser.: 3). (ENG.). 336p. (YA). (gr. 7-17). 17.99 *(978-0-316-25144-0(5)*, Poppy) Little, Brown Bks. for Young Readers.
Williams-Garcia, Rita. Clayton Byrd Goes Underground. Morrison, Frank, illus. (ENG.). 176p. (J). (gr. 3-7). 2018. pap. 9.99 *(978-0-06-221593-2(0))* 2017. 16.99 *(978-0-06-221591-8(4))* 2017. E-Book *(978-0-06-221594-9(9)*, 9780062215949) HarperCollins Pubs. (Quill Tree Bks.).
Witte, Anna. El Fandango de Lola. Archer, Micha, illus. 2011. 32p. (J). (gr. k-5). 9.99 *(978-1-84686-359-2(7))* Barefoot Bks., Inc.
Woodfolk, Ashley. The Beauty That Remains. 336p. (YA). (gr. 9). 2019. pap. 9.99 *(978-1-5247-1590-8(5)*, Ember) 2018. (Illus.). 17.99 *(978-1-5247-1587-8(5)*, Delacorte Pr.) Random Hse. Children's Bks.
Yager, Fred. Sound from a Star: A Novel. 2011. 150p. (YA). 31.95 *(978-1-889262-90-1(0))* Hannacroix Creek Bks., Inc.
Zappa, Shana Muldoon, et al. Astra's Mixed-Up Mission, 8. 2016. (Star Darlings Ser.). (ENG.). 176p. (J). (gr. 3-6). 21.19 *(978-1-4844-8084-7(8))* Disney Pr.
Zimelman, Nathan. Evening Song. Morrison, Cathy, illus. 2003. (Books for Young Learners). (ENG.). 12p. (J). 5.75 net. *(978-1-57274-536-0(3)*, 2741, Bks. for Young Learners) Owen, Richard C. Pubs., Inc.
Ziskind, Hélio & Duchesne, Christiane. Le Géant de la Forêt: Un Voyage Musical. Pratt, Pierre, illus. 2014. (ENG.). 48p. (J). (gr. k-2). 16.95 *(978-2-923163-36-9(2))* La Montagne Secrete CAN. Dist: Independent Pubs. Group.

MUSIC—HISTORY AND CRITICISM

Aliki. Ah Music. 2005. (ENG., Illus.). 48p. (J). (gr. k-5). pap. 7.99 *(978-0-06-446236-5(6)*, HarperCollins) HarperCollins Pubs.
Ancona, George. Mi Musica. 2006. (Somos Latinos (We Are Latinos) Ser.).Tr. of My Music. (SPA., Illus.). 32p. (J). (gr. 1-3). per. 8.95 *(978-0-516-25494-4(4)*, Children's Pr.) Scholastic Library Publishing.
Barlex, David & Wadsworth, Pamela. Rhagor Am Sain a Cherddoriaeth. 2005. (WEL., Illus.). 24p. pap. *(978-1-85596-240-8(3))* Dref Wen.
—Sain a Cherddoriaeth. 2005. (WEL., Illus.). 24p. pap. *(978-1-85596-239-2(X))* Dref Wen.
Birkenshaw, Lois. Music for Fun, Music for Learning. 4th ed. 2006. (Illus.). 394p. per. 46.00 *(978-1-891278-43-3(6))* Barcelona Pubs.
Boone, Mary. Dizzy Gillespie. 2012. 48p. (J). (gr. 4-8). lib. bdg. 29.95 *(978-1-61228-272-5(5))* Mitchell Lane Pubs.
Buckley, Annie. Music. 2008. (21st Century Skills Innovation Library: Innovation in Entertainment Ser.). (ENG., Illus.). 32p. (gr. 4-8). lib. bdg. 32.07 *(978-1-60279-220-3(8)*, 200151) Cherry Lake Publishing.
Cameron, Andrea. The 10 Most Revolutionary Songs. 2008. 14.99 *(978-1-55448-493-5(6))* Scholastic Library Publishing.
Carr, Aaron. Blues. 2015. (J). *(978-1-4896-3573-0(4))* Weigl Pubs., Inc.
—Country. 2015. (J). *(978-1-4896-3577-8(7))* Weigl Pubs., Inc.
Carroll, Jamuna. Edm. 2019. (Music Scene Ser.). (ENG.). 80p. (J). (gr. 6-12). 41.27 *(978-1-68282-639-3(2))* ReferencePoint Pr., Inc.
Ellis, Carol. Landmark Hip-Hop Hits. 2012. (Illus.). 64p. (J). pap. *(978-1-4222-2134-1(2))*; (gr. 4). 22.95 *(978-1-4222-2121-1(0))* Mason Crest.
Fullman, Joe. The Ultimate Guide to Music: A Fascinating Introduction to Music & the Instruments of the Orchestra. 2016. (Y Ser.). (ENG., Illus.). 96p. (J). (gr. 3-7). 19.95 *(978-1-78312-091-8(6))* Carlton Kids GBR. Dist: Two Rivers Distribution.
Gershenson, Harold P. America the Musical 1900-2000: A Nation's History Through Music. Chesworth, Michael, illus. 2006. (J). *(978-1-58987-201-1(0))* Kindermusik International.
Handyside, Chris. A History of Blues. 2006. (J). *(978-1-4109-1811-6(4))* Steck-Vaughn.
—A History of Country. 2006. (J). *(978-1-4109-1814-7(9))* Steck-Vaughn.
—A History of Soul & R&B. 2006. (J). *(978-1-4109-1816-1(5))* Steck-Vaughn.
Hill, Z. B. Music & Musicians. 2014. (Art Today! Ser.: 10). 64p. (J). (gr. 7-18). 23.95 *(978-1-4222-3172-2(0))* Mason Crest.
Kallen, Stuart A. Country Music. 2019. (Music Scene Ser.). (ENG.). 80p. (J). (gr. 6-12). 41.27 *(978-1-68282-637-9(6))* ReferencePoint Pr., Inc.
—Electronic Dance Music DJs. 2016. (ENG., Illus.). 80p. (J). (gr. 5-12). *(978-1-60152-966-4(X))* ReferencePoint Pr., Inc.
—The History of American Pop, 1 vol. 2012. (Music Library). (ENG., Illus.). 136p. (gr. 7-10). lib. bdg. 41.03 *(978-1-4205-0672-3(2)*, 52f04563-53a7-42aa-a896-c22a84914530, Lucent Pr.) Greenhaven Publishing LLC.
—The History of Classical Music, 1 vol. 2013. (Music Library). (ENG., Illus.). 128p. (gr. 7-10). lib. bdg. 41.03 *(978-1-4205-0944-1(6)*, 6e17e7cd-5e9e-4db2-a5a6-632791280b4b, Lucent Pr.) Greenhaven Publishing LLC.
—The History of Country Music, 1 vol. 2012. (Music Library). (ENG., Illus.). 136p. (gr. 7-10). lib. bdg. 41.03 *(978-1-4205-0737-9(0)*, 3eebee30-502a-453b-8e7b-3038ada89597, Lucent Pr.) Greenhaven Publishing LLC.
—The History of Latin Music, 1 vol. 2013. (Music Library). (ENG., Illus.). 128p. (gr. 7-10). lib. bdg. 41.03 *(978-1-4205-0947-2(0)*, d4693430-b0e5-4412-9286-bcbeb05dde14, Lucent Pr.) Greenhaven Publishing LLC.
—The History of Reggae. 2005. (Music Library). (ENG., Illus.). 112p. (J). (gr. 4-7). lib. bdg. 33.45 *(978-1-59018-740-1(7)*, Lucent Bks.) Cengage Gale.
—The History of Rock & Roll, 1 vol. 2012. (Music Library). (ENG., Illus.). 128p. (gr. 7-10). lib. bdg. 41.03 *(978-1-4205-0694-5(3)*, e2b60ede-194e-4c08-9bf2-938d88b92cad, Lucent Pr.) Greenhaven Publishing LLC.
—The History of World Music, 1 vol. 2006. (Music Library). (ENG., Illus.). 112p. (J). (gr. 7-10). lib. bdg. 35.08 *(978-1-59018-741-8(5)*, 4e308be3-a252-4900-95b3-6fb129e4e72d, Lucent Pr.) Greenhaven Publishing LLC.

Kaufmann, Helen L. The Story of Beethoven. Meadowcroft, Enid Lamonte, ed. Kredel, Fritz, illus. 2011. 192p. 42.95 *(978-1-258-10000-1(2))* Literary Licensing, LLC.

—The Story of Mozart. Meadowcroft, Enid Lamonte, ed. Simon, Eric M., illus. 2011. 190p. 42.95 *(978-1-258-06631-4(9))* Literary Licensing, LLC.

Kenney, Karen Latchana. Cool Reggae Music: Create & Appreciate What Makes Music Great! 2008. (Cool Music Ser.). (ENG., Illus.). 32p. (J). (gr. 3-6). 34.21 *(978-1-59928-973-1(3)*, 370, Checkerboard Library) ABDO Publishing Co.

Killcoyne, Hope Lourie. The History of Music, 1 vol. 2015. (Britannica Guide to the Visual & Performing Arts Ser.). (ENG., Illus.). 240p. (J). (gr. 9-10). 47.59 *(978-1-68048-091-7(X)*, 57911283-690f-4459-b2f6-ff61f4295f53, Britannica Educational Publishing) Rosen Publishing Group, Inc., The.

Killcoyne, Hope Lourie, ed. The History of Music, 4 vols. 2015. (Britannica Guide to the Visual & Performing Arts Ser.). (ENG.). 240p. (YA). (gr. 9-10). 95.18 *(978-1-68048-092-4(8)*, 0a9c745c-266e-4b13-a96a-2cea3795a523, Britannica Educational Publishing) Rosen Publishing Group, Inc., The.

Kuhtz, Russell. Music: Techniques, Styles, Instruments, & Practice, 1 vol. 2016. (Britannica's Practical Guide to the Arts Ser.). (ENG.). 128p. (J). (gr. 10-10). lib. bdg. 37.82 *(978-1-68048-372-7(2)*, 65edc87e-a8ec-4fdd-8071-12584e408888, Britannica Educational Publishing) Rosen Publishing Group, Inc., The.

Mendelson, Aaron. American R & B: Gospel Grooves, Funky Drummers, & Soul Power. 2012. (American Music Milestones Ser.). (ENG., Illus.). 64p. (J). (gr. 5-12). lib. bdg. 30.65 *(978-0-7613-4501-5(9)*, 9684d58f-bebf-445f-9664-39d4953cd91e, Twenty-First Century Bks.) Lerner Publishing Group.

Mills, Nathan & Wesolowski, Harriet. The Songs We Sing: Honoring Our Country, 1 vol. 2012. (Rosen Readers Ser.). (ENG., Illus.). 24p. (J). (gr. 1-2). pap. 8.25 *(978-1-4488-8821-4(2)*, 45c822f8-b9c7-4ecb-af47-3e5ded263e4b, Rosen Classroom) Rosen Publishing Group, Inc., The.

O'Brien, Eileen. The Usborne Story of Music. Danes, Emma & Hooper, Caroline, eds. Cuzik, David, illus. 2006. (Story of Music Ser.). 32p. (J). (gr. 4). lib. bdg. 15.99 *(978-1-58086-935-5(1)*, Usborne) EDC Publishing.

—The Usborne Story of Music. Danes, Emma, ed. Cuzik, David, illus. 2006. 32p. (J). (gr. 4-7). per. 7.99 *(978-0-7945-1403-7(0)*, Usborne) EDC Publishing.

Our Musical Past 16p. (YA). pap. 16.95 incl. audio *(978-0-88432-403-4(6)*, S11020) Pavilion Pubs.

Rice, Dona & Austin, Elizabeth. Making Music. rev. ed. 2019. (Smithsonian: Informational Text Ser.). (ENG., Illus.). 24p. (J). (gr. 1-2). pap. 8.99 *(978-1-4938-6649-6(4))* Teacher Created Materials, Inc.

Rice, Dona Herweck. The History of Listening to Music: Displaying Data. 2019. (Mathematics in the Real World Ser.). (ENG., Illus.). 32p. (gr. 5-8). pap. 11.99 *(978-1-4258-5894-0(5))* Teacher Created Materials, Inc.

Riggs, Kate. Classical Music. 2008. (World of Music Ser.). (Illus.). 24p. (J). (gr. -1). lib. bdg. 24.25 *(978-1-58341-564-1(5)*, Creative Education) Creative Co., The.

—Country Music. 2008. (World of Music Ser.). (Illus.). 24p. (J). (gr. -1). lib. bdg. 24.25 *(978-1-58341-565-8(3)*, Creative Education) Creative Co., The.

—Folk Music. 2008. (World of Music Ser.). (Illus.). 24p. (J). (gr. -1). lib. bdg. 24.25 *(978-1-58341-566-5(1)*, Creative Education) Creative Co., The.

Shoup, Kate. My Country 'Tis of Thee. 2019. (America's Songs Ser.). (ENG.). 32p. (gr. 3-3). 63.48 *(978-1-5026-4870-9(9))* Cavendish Square Publishing LLC.

Sombart, Elisabeth & Lafaye, Jean-Jacques. Doce Vidas para la Musica.Tr. of Twelve Composers. (SPA.). 118p. (J). 17.95 *(978-84-261-3115-7(8)*, JV11155) Juventud, Editorial ESP. Dist: Lectorum Pubns., Inc.

Stratton, Connor. We Make Music. 2019. (Activities We Do Ser.). (ENG., Illus.). 16p. (J). (gr. k-1). pap. 7.95 *(978-1-64185-870-0(2)*, 1641858702); lib. bdg. 25.64 *(978-1-64185-801-4(X)*, 164185801X) North Star Editions. (Focus Readers).

Turner, Cherie. Everything You Need to Know about the Riot Grrrl Movement: The Feminism of a New Generation. 2009. (Need to Know Library). 64p. (gr. 5-5). 58.50 *(978-1-60854-095-2(2))* Rosen Publishing Group, Inc., The.

Uschan, Michael V. The Blues, 1 vol. 2011. (Lucent Library of Black History Ser.). (ENG., Illus.). 112p. (gr. 7-7). lib. bdg. 41.03 *(978-1-4205-0658-7(7)*, a073e2bd-ad28-4327-bc80-21225e7a62f7, Lucent Pr.) Greenhaven Publishing LLC.

Walker, Ida. Around the World. 2009. (Hip-Hop Ser.). (Illus.). 64p. (YA). (gr. 4-7). pap. 7.95 *(978-1-4222-0350-7(6))* Mason Crest.

Wargin, Kathy-jo. M Is for Melody: A Music Alphabet. Larson, Katherine, illus. 2006. (Art & Culture Ser.). (ENG.). 40p. (J). (gr. 1-4). 16.95 *(978-1-58536-215-8(8)*, 202129) Sleeping Bear Pr.

Weatherford, Carole. The Sound That Jazz Makes. 2003. (ENG., Illus.). 32p. (J). (gr. 2-4). pap. 7.95 *(978-0-8027-7674-7(4)*, c621b412-1796-420c-90f6-7495f41e7acb) Fitzhenry & Whiteside, Ltd. CAN. Dist: Firefly Bks., Ltd.

Wesolowski, Harriet. The Songs We Sing: Honoring Our Country, 1 vol. 2012. (I'm an American Citizen Ser.). (ENG., Illus.). 24p. (J). (gr. 1-2). 26.27 *(978-1-4488-8581-7(7)*, d0e84b88-61f5-4cdc-a0e5-8c808b2c9380, PowerKids Pr.) Rosen Publishing Group, Inc., The.

What Jazz & Blues Can I Play - Alto Sax. 20p. 6.95 *(978-1-85909-426-6(0)*, Warner Bros. Pubns.) Alfred Publishing Co., Inc.

Wheeler, Opal. Handel: at the Court of Kings. Greenwalt, Mary, illus. 2006. 166p. per. 13.95 *(978-1-933573-03-8(1)*, 4481) Zeezok Publishing, LLC.

Wheeler, Opal & Deucher, Sybil. Joseph Haydn: the Merry Little Peasant. Greenwalt, Mary, illus. 2005. 118p. per. 13.95 *(978-1-933573-00-7(7))* Zeezok Publishing, LLC.

Woog, Adam. The History of Gospel Music, 1 vol. 2014. (Music Library). (ENG., Illus.). 136p. (gr. 7-10). lib. bdg. 41.03 *(978-1-4205-0945-8(4)*, 8751f184-f116-455c-bf56-5a8bb4494010, Lucent Pr.) Greenhaven Publishing LLC.

MUSIC, INDIAN

see Indians of North America—Music

MUSIC—INSTRUCTION AND STUDY

see Music—Study and Teaching

MUSIC—NOTATION

see Musical Notation

MUSIC, POPULAR

see Popular Music

MUSIC, SACRED

see Church Music

MUSIC—STUDY AND TEACHING

Aruffo, Christopher, tr. We Hear & Play. 2005. (J). Vol. 1. 112p. ring bd. 44.95 *(978-0-9761435-2-9(6))* Vol. 2. 112p. ring bd. 44.95 *(978-0-9761435-3-6(4))* Vol. 3. ring bd. 49.95 *(978-0-9761435-4-3(2))* Acoustic Learning Inc.

Atlantic, Leonard. We Play Music!, 1 vol. 2017. (Ways to Play Ser.). (ENG.). 24p. (J). (gr. k-k). pap. 9.15 *(978-1-4824-6349-1(0)*, 4d79aca9-0052-4955-9a2a-8d3286cf6d6c) Stevens, Gareth Publishing LLLP.

Barden, Christine H., et al. Music for Little Mozarts — Little Mozarts Go to Church, Bk 1-2: 10 Favorite Hymns, Spirituals & Sunday School Songs. 2008. (Music for Little Mozarts Ser.: Bk 1-2). (ENG.). 24p. (J). pap. 7.99 *(978-0-7390-5689-9(1))* Alfred Publishing Co., Inc.

—Music for Little Mozarts — Little Mozarts Go to Church, Bk 3-4: 10 Favorite Hymns, Spirituals & Sunday School Songs. 2008. (Music for Little Mozarts Ser.: Bk 3-4). (ENG.). 24p. (J). pap. 6.95 *(978-0-7390-5690-5(5))* Alfred Publishing Co., Inc.

Battaglia, Stephen. Mr. Mcsymphony's It's All about Classical Music. 2008. (ENG.). 32p. pap. 9.99 *(978-1-4196-8085-4(4))* CreateSpace Independent Publishing Platform.

—Mr. Mcsymphony's It's All about Jazz. 2008. (ENG.). 28p. pap. 9.99 *(978-1-4196-8086-1(2))* CreateSpace Independent Publishing Platform.

Blair, Peter, compiled by. Concert Ensembles for Everyone: Works for Instrumental Ensembles with Limited or Non-Traditional Instrumentation, Grades 3-4 (Alto Saxophone - WW 3 And 4) 2006. 8.95 *(978-0-89328-262-2(6))* Heritage Music Pr.

—Concert Ensembles for Everyone: Works for Instrumental Ensembles with Limited or Non-Traditional Instrumentation, Grades 3-4 (Bass - Tuba/Bass, Baritone Saxophone & Bass Clarinet) 2006. 8.95 *(978-0-89328-268-4(5))* Heritage Music Pr.

—Concert Ensembles for Everyone: Works for Instrumental Ensembles with Limited or Non-Traditional Instrumentation, Grades 3-4 (Clarinet A - WW 1 And 2) 2006. 8.95 *(978-0-89328-260-8(X))* Heritage Music Pr.

—Concert Ensembles for Everyone: Works for Instrumental Ensembles with Limited or Non-Traditional Instrumentation, Grades 3-4 (Clarinet B - WW 2 And 3) 2006. 8.95 *(978-0-89328-261-5(8))* Heritage Music Pr.

—Concert Ensembles for Everyone: Works for Instrumental Ensembles with Limited or Non-Traditional Instrumentation, Grades 3-4 (F Horn - Brass 3 And 4) 2006. 8.95 *(978-0-89328-266-0(9))* Heritage Music Pr.

—Concert Ensembles for Everyone: Works for Instrumental Ensembles with Limited or Non-Traditional Instrumentation, Grades 3-4 (Tenor Saxophone - WW 4 & Brass 4) 2006. 8.95 *(978-0-89328-263-9(4))* Heritage Music Pr.

—Concert Ensembles for Everyone: Works for Instrumental Ensembles with Limited or Non-Traditional Instrumentation, Grades 3-4 (Trombone/Baritone B. C./Bassoon - Brass 4 & Bass) 2006. 8.95 *(978-0-89328-267-7(7))* Heritage Music Pr.

—Concert Ensembles for Everyone: Works for Instrumental Ensembles with Limited or Non-Traditional Instrumentation, Grades 3-4 (Trumpet A - Brass 1 And 2) 2006. 8.95 *(978-0-89328-264-6(2))* Heritage Music Pr.

—Concert Ensembles for Everyone: Works for Instrumental Ensembles with Limited or Non-Traditional Instrumentation, Grades 3-4 (Trumpet B - Brass 2 And 3) 2006. 8.95 *(978-0-89328-265-3(0))* Heritage Music Pr.

Brewer, Mike & Harris, Paul. Improve Your Sight-Singing! Elementary Low / Medium Treble. 2003. (Faber Edition Ser.). (ENG.). 40p. (gr. 1-5). pap. 9.99 *(978-0-571-51766-4(8))* Faber & Faber, Ltd. GBR. Dist: Alfred Publishing Co., Inc.

Bridges, Doreen. Music, Young Children & You: A Parent-Teacher Guide to Music for 0-5 Year-Olds. (Illus.). 160p. (J). (gr. -1-k). pap. *(978-0-86806-530-4(7)*, Hale & Iremonger) GHR Pr., The.

Bridges, Madeline. Sing Together, Children. 2008. (J). mass mkt. 39.95 *(978-1-929187-21-8(1))* Choristers Guild.

Burch, Sharon. Sticks! 2013. (ENG.). 56p. pap. 32.99 *(978-1-4803-4266-8(1)*, 35029029) Shawnee Pr., Inc.

Burton, Leon H. & Kudo, Takeo. SoundPlay: Understanding Music Through Creative Movement. 2006. (ENG., Illus.). 120p. 66.00 *(978-1-56545-130-8(9)*, 3003) Rowman & Littlefield Education.

Celik, Vladislav. You Too Can Play Piano & Organ Without Teacher, Vol. 1. (Music Instructional Ser.). (Illus.). 96p. (J). pap. 12.95 incl. audio *(978-0-9624062-1-8(X))* Music Institute of California.

Chadwick, Stephen. Music Express - Music Express: Age 10-11 (Book + 3CDs + DVD-ROM): Complete Music Scheme for Primary Class Teachers, 1 vol. 2nd ed. 2014. (Music Express Ser.). (ENG., Illus.). 64p. (J). (gr. 5-6). pap. 47.95 incl. audio compact disk *(978-1-4729-0022-7(7))* HarperCollins Pubs. Ltd. GBR. Dist: Independent Pubs. Group.

Coates, Dan. The Kids' Music Collection, Vol. 2. 2005. (ENG.). 124p. pap. 14.95 *(978-0-7579-3763-7(2)*, AFM0416) Alfred Publishing Co., Inc.

Concert Ensembles for Everyone: Works for Instrumental Ensembles with Limited or Non-Traditional Instrumentation, Grades 3-4 (Conductor's Score with CD) 2006. 29.95 *(978-0-89328-258-5(8))* Heritage Music Pr.

Dale, Monica. Eurhythmics for Young Children: Six Lessons for Spring. 2003. (Illus.). 90p. pap. 24.95 *(978-0-9701416-2-0(9))* MusiKinesis.

Dyke, Sylvie. Piano Music Made Easy. 2012. (Illus.). 28p. pap. *(978-1-78148-794-5(4))* Grosvenor Hse. Publishing Ltd.

Early Macken, JoAnn. Music Lessons, 1 vol. 2004. (After-School Fun Ser.). (ENG., Illus.). 24p. (gr. k-2). lib. bdg. 23.67 *(978-0-8368-4515-0(3)*, a0428294-4eb6-459b-aec2-4352cd8bb61b, Weekly Reader Leveled Readers) Stevens, Gareth Publishing LLLP.

Edwards, Linda Carol, et al. Music: A Way of Life for the Young Child. 5th ed. 2004. (ENG., Illus.). 288p. pap. 49.33 *(978-0-13-111676-4(2))* Prentice Hall PTR.

Flohr, John W. & Trollinger, Valerie L. Music in Elementary Education. 2010. (Illus.). xiii, 244p. *(978-0-205-76035-0(X))* Prentice Hall PTR.

Francis, Dale. The Quelbe Method: Music Fundamentals in Quelbe Ensembles. 2012. 256p. (gr. -1). pap. 27.95 *(978-1-4759-2684-2(7))* iUniverse, Inc.

Frostick, Richard. Sound Beginnings. 2003. (Faber Edition Ser.). (ENG., Illus.). 999p. pap. 11.99 *(978-0-571-51991-0(1))* Faber Music, Ltd. GBR. Dist: Alfred Publishing Co., Inc.

The Fundamental Guitar Method Book 2: The Science of Harmony. 2004. (YA). spiral bd. *(978-0-9771357-1-4(3))* Sound Craft Designs.

Greer, Eileen. Loud & Quiet in Music Class, 1 vol. 2017. (Opposites at School Ser.). (ENG.). 24p. (J). (gr. 1-1). 25.27 *(978-1-5081-6353-4(7)*, a1afe78c-764c-4449-a8aa-8bc2758df403, PowerKids Pr.) Rosen Publishing Group, Inc., The.

Hamilton, Robert M. Do Music & Art Classes Matter?, 1 vol. 2018. (Points of View Ser.). (ENG.). 24p. (J). (gr. 3-3). 26.23 *(978-1-5345-2567-2(X)*, 82d8321b-8825-4668-9321-1e3e892bdc40, KidHaven Publishing) Greenhaven Publishing LLC.

Hammond, Susan. Susan Hammond's Classical Kids: A New Music-Based Curriculum: Grades K-8. 2008. (Classical Kids Ser.). (J). (gr. -1-8). *(978-1-897166-42-0(7))* Children's Group, The.

Hamsberger, L. C. & Manus, Ron. Alfred's Kid's Guitar Course Movie & TV Songbook 1 And 2: 13 Fun Arrangements That Make Learning Even Easier!, Book & Online Audio. 2009. (Kid's Guitar Course Ser.). (ENG.). 24p. pap. 15.99 *(978-0-7390-6419-1(3))* Alfred Publishing Co., Inc.

Heritage & Almeida, Artie. Music Proficiency: Doggone Dynamics. 2005. ring bd. 14.95 *(978-0-89328-029-1(1))* Lorenz Corp., The.

Hooper, Caroline. Learn Songwriting. 2004. (Learn to Play Ser.). (Illus.). 48p. (YA). (gr. 1-18). lib. bdg. 17.95 *(978-1-58086-222-6(5))* EDC Publishing.

Huang, Annie. Notes & the Keyboard. 2006. (ENG.). 32p. pap. 14.99 *(978-1-4257-0279-3(1))* Xlibris Corp.

Kenney, Karen Latchana. Cool Reggae Music: Create & Appreciate What Makes Music Great! 2008. (Cool Music Ser.). (ENG., Illus.). 32p. (J). (gr. 3-6). 34.21 *(978-1-59928-973-1(3)*, 370, Checkerboard Library) ABDO Publishing Co.

Key Porter Books, creator. Music Play: Inspired Ways to Explore Music. rev. ed. 2007. (Gymboree Play & Music Ser.). (ENG., Illus.). 36p. (J). (gr. -1-2). bds. *(978-1-55263-964-1(9))* Magma.

Kurz, Ron. The Inner Music Experience. l.t. ed. 2003. 124p. (YA). 75.00 *(978-0-939829-07-1(X)*, Item#3) Kurz, Ron.

Lindeen, Mary. Cool Latin Music: Create & Appreciate What Makes Music Great! 2008. (Cool Music Ser.). (ENG., Illus.). 32p. (J). (gr. 3-6). 34.21 *(978-1-59928-972-4(5)*, 368, Checkerboard Library) ABDO Publishing Co.

Lindeman, Carolynn. Musical Children: Engaging Children in Musical Experiences. 2010. (ENG.). 264p. (C). pap. 65.95 *(978-0-13-604384-3(4)*, Y204706) Routledge.

MacGregor, Helen. Music Express - Music Express: Age 7-8 (Book + 3CDs + DVD-ROM): Complete Music Scheme for Primary Class Teachers, 1 vol. 2nd ed. 2014. (Music Express Ser.). (ENG., Illus.). 64p. (J). (gr. 2-3). pap. 47.95 incl. audio compact disk *(978-1-4729-0019-7(7))* HarperCollins Pubs. Ltd. GBR. Dist: Independent Pubs. Group.

—Music Express - Music Express: Age 8-9 (Book + 3CDs + DVD-ROM): Complete Music Scheme for Primary Class Teachers, 1 vol. 2nd ed. 2014. (Music Express Ser.). (ENG., Illus.). 64p. (J). (gr. 3-4). pap. 47.95 incl. audio compact disk *(978-1-4729-0020-3(0))* HarperCollins Pubs. Ltd. GBR. Dist: Independent Pubs. Group.

—Music Express - Music Express: Age 9-10 (Book + 3CDs + DVD-ROM): Complete Music Scheme for Primary Class Teachers, 1 vol. 2nd ed. 2014. (Music Express Ser.). (ENG., Illus.). 64p. (J). (gr. 4-5). pap. 47.95 incl. audio compact disk *(978-1-4729-0021-0(9))* HarperCollins Pubs. Ltd. GBR. Dist: Independent Pubs. Group.

Mister C's Beginning Drums, Vol. 1. 2004. (Illus.). (J). spiral bd. 14.99 *(978-0-9755333-0-7(4))* Mister C Music.

Morgan, Jeanette, ed. Activate!: Music, Movement & More: The Music Magazine for Grades K-6. 2011. (Illus.). 84p. pap. 19.95 incl. audio compact disk *(978-0-89328-376-6(2))* Heritage Music Pr.

Neelly, Linda Page. Musical ConverSings with Children. 2007. (ENG., Illus.). 161p. 79.00 *(978-1-60021-708-1(7))* Nova Science Pubs., Inc.

O'Brien, Eileen. Introduction to Music. Alaverdy, Melissa, illus. 2004. (ENG.). 96p. (J). 7.95 *(978-0-7945-0276-8(8)*, Usborne) EDC Publishing.

Parker, Ben. My First Keyboard - Learn to Play: Kids. 2013. (Illus.). 42p. pap. *(978-1-908707-15-4(1))* Kyle Craig Publishing.

—My First Recorder - Learn to Play: Kids. 2013. 38p. pap. *(978-1-908707-18-5(6))* Kyle Craig Publishing.

Parker, Kate & Parker, Zac. Nos Gusta Tocar Musica: We Like to Play Music. 2009. (SPA., Illus.). 32p. pap. 10.95 *(978-1-890772-90-1(9))* Kalindi Pr.

—We Like to Play Music. 2015. (ENG.). 48p. pap. 9.95 *(978-1-890772-85-7(2))* Kalindi Pr.

Price, Melissa. Luke & Lori's Musical Journey: Learning the Basic Elements of Music. Keren Weaver Graphics, illus. 2003. 48p. (J). spiral bd. *(978-0-9747792-0-1(2))* Luke & Lori Bks.

Publications International Ltd. Staff, ed. Electronic Time for Learning: Music. 2011. 120p. (J). *(978-1-4508-0260-4(5))* Publications International, Ltd.

—Princess Songs Play & Learn. 2010. 24p. (J). 12.98 *(978-1-4508-0113-3(7))* Phoenix International Publications, Inc.

Purton, Michael. Show Me How: I Can Make Music. 2015. (ENG., Illus.). 48p. (J). (gr. -1-12). 7.99 *(978-1-86147-297-7(8)*, Armadillo) Anness Publishing GBR. Dist: National Bk. Network.

Rowsell, Cyrilla & Vinden, David. Jolly Music Player: Beginners: (Physical CD) Lamb, Karen, illus. 2018. (ENG.). (J). cd-rom 43.95 *(978-1-84414-491-4(7)*, Jolly Music) Jolly Learning, Ltd. GBR. Dist: American International Distribution Corp.

—Jolly Music Player: Level 1: (Physical CD) Lamb, Karen, illus. 2018. (ENG.). (J). cd-rom 43.95 *(978-1-84414-492-1(5)*, Jolly Music) Jolly Learning, Ltd. GBR. Dist: American International Distribution Corp.

—Jolly Music Player: Level 2. Lamb, Karen, illus. 2018. (ENG.). (J). cd-rom 43.95 *(978-1-84414-493-8(3)*, Jolly Music) Jolly Learning, Ltd. GBR. Dist: American International Distribution Corp.

—Jolly Music Player: Level 3. Lamb, Karen, illus. 2018. (ENG.). (J). cd-rom 43.95 *(978-1-84414-494-5(1)*, Jolly Music) Jolly Learning, Ltd. GBR. Dist: American International Distribution Corp.

—The Music Handbook, Level 2: Teaching Music Skills to Children Through Singing, 1 vol. Lamb, Karen, illus. 2012. (ENG.). 212p. (J). spiral bd. 59.95 incl. audio compact disk *(978-1-84414-265-1(5)*, Jolly Learning) Jolly Learning, Ltd. GBR. Dist: American International Distribution Corp.

Scott, Patricia, et al. Music Express - Music Express Early Years Foundation Stage: Complete Music Scheme for Early Years Foundation Stage - Second Edition, 1 vol. 2nd ed. 2012. (Music Express Ser.). (ENG., Illus.). 88p. pap. 55.00 incl. audio compact disk *(978-1-4081-8707-4(8))* HarperCollins Pubs. Ltd. GBR. Dist: Independent Pubs. Group.

Sebba, Jane & Moses, David. Recorder Magic - Recorder Magic (Book 1 + Practice CD), 1 vol. Sanderson, Ana & Haward, Emily, eds. 2003. (Recorder Magic Ser.). (ENG., Illus.). 32p. (J). pap. 11.95 incl. audio compact disk *(978-0-7136-6581-9(5))* HarperCollins Pubs. Ltd. GBR. Dist: Independent Pubs. Group.

Snitkin, Harvey R. Practicing for Young Musicians: You Are Your Own Teacher. 2nd rev. ed. 2011. (Illus.). 153p. (Orig.). (gr. 4-18). pap. 14.95 *(978-1-888732-00-9(8))* H M S Pubns., Inc.

Stultz, Marie. Innocent Sounds, Book II: Building Choral Tone & Artistry in Your Children's Choir. 2008. 240p. per. *(978-0-944529-45-4(3))* Morning Star Music Pubs.

Sullivan, Erin Ash. Music Counts & Cálculos Musicales: 6 English, 6 Spanish Adaptations. 2011. (ENG & SPA.). (J). 89.00 net. *(978-1-4108-5675-3(5))* Benchmark Education Co.

Vogt, Janet. Music Brain Teasers. 2006. pap. 19.95 *(978-0-89328-248-6(0))* Lorenz Corp., The.

Wedgwood, Pam. Up-Grade! Flute: Grade 1-2. 2003. (Faber Edition: up-Grade! Ser.). (ENG.). 999p. (gr. 2). pap. 11.99 *(978-0-571-51818-0(4))* Faber & Faber, Ltd. GBR. Dist: Alfred Publishing Co., Inc.

Whykes, Susan. Let's Practise: Be a Better Musician. 2009. 216p. pap. 14.49 *(978-1-4389-2933-0(1))* AuthorHouse.

Young, Susan. Music 3-5. 2008. (Essential Guides for Early Years Practitioners Ser.). (ENG.). 128p. (C). 83.95 *(978-0-415-43056-2(9)*, RU44504); 40.95 *(978-0-415-43057-9(7)*, RU44505) Routledge.

MUSIC—THEORY

see Music Theory

MUSIC—VOCATIONAL GUIDANCE

Anniss, Matt. Start a Band! 2013. (Find Your Talent Ser.). (Illus.). 32p. (J). (gr. 5-8). 28.50 *(978-1-84858-571-3(3))* Arcturus Publishing GBR. Dist: Black Rabbit Bks.

Barden, Christine H., et al. Music for Little Mozarts — Little Mozarts Go to Hollywood, Bk 1-2: 10 Favorites from TV, Movies & Radio. 2008. (Music for Little Mozarts Ser.: Bk 1-2). (ENG., Illus.). 24p. (J). pap. 8.99 *(978-0-7390-5013-2(3))* Alfred Publishing Co., Inc.

Burling, Alexis. Working in Music. 2018. (Career Files Ser.). (ENG.). 32p. (J). (gr. 3-6). 32.80 *(978-1-63235-447-1(0)*, 13840, 12-Story Library) Bookstaves, LLC.

Culp, Jennifer. Using Computer Science in Digital Music Careers, 1 vol. 2017. (Coding Your Passion Ser.). (ENG., Illus.). 80p. (J). (gr. 7-7). 37.47 *(978-1-5081-7517-9(9)*, 2be9d75c-d4d1-4fdd-9711-827a91b2c331, Rosen Young Adult) Rosen Publishing Group, Inc., The.

Erickson, Marty. Work in the Music Industry. 2019. (Career Finder Ser.). (ENG.). 80p. (YA). (gr. 6-12). 41.27 *(978-1-68282-731-4(3))* ReferencePoint Pr., Inc.

Feierabend, John. First Steps in Music Vocal Development Kit. 2004. 21p. (J). 79.95 *(978-1-57999-326-9(5)*, G-6400) G I A Pubns., Inc.

Harvey, M. A. Wannabes Pop Diva: For Girls Who Know What They Want to Be. 2004. (Illus.). 128p. (J). pap. *(978-1-84458-049-1(0)*, Pavilion Children's Books) Pavilion Bks.

Hasan, Heather. How to Produce, Release, & Market Your Music, 1 vol. 2011. (Garage Bands Ser.). (ENG.). 64p. (YA). (gr. 5-5). pap. 13.95 *(978-1-4488-5662-6(0)*, bd54478a-2800-47d4-97fb-0a67518e0393); lib. bdg. 37.13 *(978-1-4488-5658-9(2)*, 3a61a987-323c-497e-9421-cf0f7886414c) Rosen Publishing Group, Inc., The.

Hill, Z. B. Music & Musicians. 2014. (Art Today! Ser.: 10). 64p. (J). (gr. 7-18). 23.95 *(978-1-4222-3172-2(0))* Mason Crest.

Hinton, Kerry. Cool Careers Without College for Music Lovers. 2007. (Cool Careers Without College Ser.). (Illus.). 140p. (YA). (gr. 8-12). lib. bdg. 33.25 *(978-1-4042-0872-8(0))* Rosen Publishing Group, Inc., The.

Kallen, Stuart A. Careers in Music. 2019. (Careers for Creative People Ser.). (ENG.). 80p. (J). (gr. 6-12). 41.27 *(978-1-68282-683-6(X))* ReferencePoint Pr., Inc.

Liebman, Dan & Liebman, Dan. I Want to Be a Musician. 2003. (I Want to Be Ser.). (ENG., Illus.). 24p. (J). (gr. -1-2). 14.95 *(978-1-55297-760-6(9)*, 29086ba5-8806-4472-a4f5-ce1ad4e48070); pap. 3.99 *(978-1-55297-759-0(5)*, c7fc3675-1995-4c11-ae9c-2328d7845042) Firefly Bks., Ltd.

—Quiero Ser Musico. 2003. (Quiero Ser.).Tr. of I Want to Be a Musician. (SPA., Illus.). 24p. (J). (gr. -1-2). pap. 5.99 *(978-1-55297-761-3(7)*, 91bff97b-49f4-4b70-a081-abfc3676368d) Firefly Bks., Ltd.

MNO

Miller, Connie Colwell. I'll Be a Musician. Baroncelli, Silvia, illus. 2016. (When I Grow Up Ser.). (ENG.). 24p. (J). (gr. 1-4). lib. bdg. 20.95 *(978-1-60753-762-5(1),* 15574) Amicus.
—Musicienne. Baroncelli, Silvia, illus. 2016. (Plus Tard, Je Serai... Ser.). (FRE.). 24p. (J). (gr. 1-4). *(978-1-77092-356-0(X),* 17619) Amicus.
Mooney, Carla. Cool Careers Without College for People Who Love Music, 1 vol. 2nd ed. 2013. (Cool Careers Without College Ser.). (ENG.). 144p. (YA). (gr. 7-7). 41.12 *(978-1-4777-1819-3(2),* 670afe84-75c0-47b7-8d2d-74185b6f873c) Rosen Publishing Group, Inc., The.
Parks, Peggy J. Musician. 2003. (Illus.). 48p. (J). 26.20 *(978-0-7377-2067-9(0),* Greenhaven Pr., Inc.) Cengage Gale.
Payment, Simone. Taking Your Band Online, 1 vol. 2011. (Garage Bands Ser.). (ENG.). 64p. (YA). (gr. 5-5). pap. 13.95 *(978-1-4488-5664-0(7),* a8fa51f4-155f-42c5-9992-1e72444ab666); lib. bdg. 37.13 *(978-1-4488-5660-2(4),* 81d62c04-0de4-482a-bb3f-52c4ccba2e29) Rosen Publishing Group, Inc., The.
Roberts, Laura. Careers If You Like Music. 2017. (ENG.). 80p. (YA). (gr. 5-12). *(978-1-68282-138-1(2))* ReferencePoint Pr., Inc.
Somervill, Barbara A. Musician. 2011. (21st Century Skills Library: Cool Arts Careers Ser.). (ENG., Illus.). 32p. (gr. 4-8). lib. bdg. 32.07 *(978-1-61080-132-4(6),* 201142) Cherry Lake Publishing.
Spaulding, Jeffrey & Gisnash, Sahara. Career Building Through Digital Sampling & Remixing, 1 vol. 2008. (Digital Career Building Ser.). (ENG., Illus.). 64p. (J). (gr. 6-6). lib. bdg. 37.13 *(978-1-4042-1355-5(4),* fea69e93-414a-4cb3-bb75-c9b631d49d41) Rosen Publishing Group, Inc., The.

MUSIC APPRECIATION

Adams, Dena C. & Clark, Claire D. This Is Music! Preschool, Vol 1: Itsy Bitsy Music, Book & CD. 2008. (This Is Music! Ser.: Vol 1). (ENG.). 224p. pap. 64.95 *(978-0-7390-4723-1(X))* Alfred Publishing Co., Inc.
Ajmera, Maya, et al. Music Everywhere! 2014. (Global Fund for Children Bks.). (ENG., Illus.). 32p. (J). (gr. -1-3). pap. 7.95 *(978-1-57091-937-4(2))* Charlesbridge Publishing, Inc.
Baldwin, Lillian. Music for Young Listeners: The Blue Book. 2012. 128p. 40.95 *(978-1-258-23857-5(8));* pap. 25.95 *(978-1-258-24708-9(9))* Literary Licensing, LLC.
—Music for Young Listeners: The Crimson Book. 2012. 128p. 40.95 *(978-1-258-23856-8(X));* pap. 25.95 *(978-1-258-24709-6(7))* Literary Licensing, LLC.
Bernard, Yves & Fredette, Nathalie. Le Guide de la Musique du Monde. 2004. (FRE., Illus.). 230p. (J). pap. *(978-2-89021-662-4(4))* Diffusion du livre Mirabel (DLM).
Buchanan, Fannie R. Magic Music Story Interpretations. 2006. (Illus.). pap. 21.95 *(978-1-4286-5945-2(5))* Kessinger Publishing, LLC.
Labrecque, Ellen. How Did That Get to My House? Music. 2009. (Community Connections: How Did That Get to My House? Ser.). (ENG.). 24p. (gr. 2-5). lib. bdg. 29.21 *(978-1-60279-481-8(2),* 200246) Cherry Lake Publishing.
Lindeen, Mary. Cool Classical Music: Create & Appreciate What Makes Music Great! 2008. (Cool Music Ser.). (ENG.). 32p. (J). (gr. 3-6). 34.21 *(978-1-59928-969-4(5),* 362, Checkerboard Library) ABDO Publishing Co.
Moore Niver, Heather. Songs, 1 vol. 2018. (Let's Learn about Literature Ser.). (ENG.). 24p. (gr. 1-2). 24.27 *(978-0-7660-9759-9(5),* 7b81f67e-bcd6-4614-b91b-5e6a89833ff3) Enslow Publishing, LLC.
Parker, Kate & Parker, Zac. Nos Gusta Tocar Musica: We Like to Play Music. 2009. (SPA., Illus.). 32p. pap. 10.95 *(978-1-890772-90-1(9))* Kalindi Pr.
—We Like to Play Music. 2015. (ENG.). 48p. pap. 9.95 *(978-1-890772-85-7(2))* Kalindi Pr.
Persons, Marjorie Kiel. Themes to Remember, 3, Vol. 1. Nellis, Philip, illus. 2007. 124p. (J). lib. bdg. 31.95 incl. audio compact disk *(978-0-9794947-0-3(2))* Classical Magic, Inc.
—Themes to Remember, Volume 2, Vol. 2. Nellis, Philip & Johnson, George Ann, illus. rev. ed. 2004. 128p. (J). lib. bdg. 31.95 *(978-0-9675997-5-5(X))* Classical Magic, Inc.

MUSIC THEORY

Alexander, Dennis, et al. Alfred's Premier Piano Course: Performance 3. Manus, Morton, ed. 2007. (Alfred's Premier Piano Course Ser.). (Illus.). 32p. pap. 6.95 *(978-0-7390-4743-9(4))* Alfred Publishing Co., Inc.
—Premier Piano Course Assignment Book: Level 1A-6. 2007. (Premier Piano Course Ser.). (ENG.). 80p. pap. 6.95 *(978-0-7390-4877-1(5))* Alfred Publishing Co., Inc.
—Premier Piano Course Lesson Book, Bk 3. 2007. (Premier Piano Course Ser.: Bk 3). (ENG., Illus.). 48p. pap. 8.99 *(978-0-7390-4639-5(X))* Alfred Music.
—Premier Piano Course Theory, Bk 3. 2007. (Premier Piano Course Ser.: Bk 3). (ENG., Illus.). 32p. pap. 9.99 *(978-0-7390-4750-7(7))* Alfred Publishing Co., Inc.
Biklou, Eliyana. Lady Treble & the Seven Notes. 2010. (ENG., Illus.). 32p. (J). (gr. -1-3). 16.95 *(978-1-897476-21-5(3))* Simply Read Bks. CAN. Dist: Ingram Publisher Services.
Danes, E. Music Theory for Beginners. rev. ed. 2004. (ENG.). 48p. (J). pap. 8.95 *(978-0-7945-0389-5(6))* EDC Publishing.
Danes, Emma. Music Theory for Beginners. Wood, Gerald, illus. 2006. (Music Theory Ser.). 48p. (J). (gr. 4). lib. bdg. 16.95 *(978-1-58086-562-3(3))* EDC Publishing.
Day, Jonathan. The Politics of Navigation: Globalisation, Music & Composition. 2008. 180p. pap. *(978-3-639-07208-2(1))* AV Akademikerverlag GmbH & Co. KG.
Sharp, M. Theory of Music for Young Musicians. 2013. 57p. reprint ed. lthr. 79.00 *(978-0-7812-9322-8(7))* Reprint Services Corp.

MUSICAL APPRECIATION

see Music Appreciation

MUSICAL COMEDIES

see Musicals

MUSICAL CRITICISM

see Music—History and Criticism

MUSICAL EDUCATION

see Music—Study and Teaching

MUSICAL INSTRUCTION

see Music—Study and Teaching

MUSICAL INSTRUMENTS

see also Orchestra

also groups of instruments, e.g. Percussion Instruments; Stringed Instruments; Wind Instruments; etc.; also names of musical instruments, e.g. Drum; etc.

Alfred Music. Suzuki Cello School, Vol 5: Cello Part, Vol. 5. rev. ed. 2003. (Suzuki Cello School Ser.: Vol 5). (ENG., Illus.). 16p. (gr. k-12). pap. 14.99 *(978-0-87487-267-5(7),* Suzuki) Alfred Publishing Co., Inc.
—Suzuki Cello School, Vol 6: Piano Acc, Vol. 6. rev. ed. 2003. (Suzuki Cello School Ser.: Vol 6). (ENG., Illus.). 32p. (gr. 6-12). pap. 13.99 *(978-0-87487-271-2(5),* Warner Bros. Pubns.) Alfred Publishing Co., Inc.
Almeida, Artie. Recorder Express (Soprano Recorder Method for Classroom or Individual Use) Soprano Recorder Method for Classroom or Individual Use, Book & CD. 2007. (ENG.). 48p. pap. 14.95 *(978-0-7390-4726-2(4))* Alfred Publishing Co., Inc.
Anduri, Stefanie. Music. 2021. (High-Interest STEAM Ser.: 10). (ENG.). 80p. (J). (gr. 7-12). 34.60 *(978-1-4222-4523-1(3))* Mason Crest.
Battaglia, Stephen. Mr. Mcsymphony's Musicians & their Instruments. 2008. (ENG.). 28p. pap. 9.99 *(978-1-4196-8077-9(3))* CreateSpace Independent Publishing Platform.
Blackwell, Kathy & Blackwell, David. String Time Joggers: 14 Pieces for Flexible Ensemble. 2007. (String Time Ensembles Ser.). (ENG.). 24p. 11.25 *(978-0-19-335915-4(4));* 11.25 *(978-0-19-335914-7(6));* 11.25 *(978-0-19-335913-0(8))* Oxford Univ. Pr., Inc.
Blair, Peter, compiled by. Concert Ensembles for Everyone: Works for Instrumental Ensembles with Limited or Non-Traditional Instrumentation, Grades 3-4 (Flute/Oboe - WW 1 And 2) 2006. 8.95 *(978-0-89328-259-2(6))* Heritage Music Pr.
Blane, Francisco. I Can Play Music: Lap Book. 2009. (My First Reader's Theater Set B Ser.). (J). 28.00 *(978-1-935441-03-8(5))* Benchmark Education Co.
Burchett, Jan & Vogler, Sara. Collins Big Cat Phonics for Letters & Sounds - Tap Tap: Band 01A/Pink A, Bd. 1A. 2018. (Collins Big Cat Ser.). (ENG., Illus.). 16p. (J). pap. 7.99 *(978-0-00-823017-3(X))* HarperCollins Pubs. Ltd. GBR. Dist: Independent Pubs. Group.
Canetti, Yanitzia. ABeCedario Musical. 2010. (SPA.). 40p. (J). pap. 8.99 *(978-1-59835-222-1(9),* BrickHouse Education) Cambridge BrickHouse, Inc.
—Musical ABCs. 2010. 40p. (J). pap. 8.99 *(978-1-59835-221-4(0),* BrickHouse Education) Cambridge BrickHouse, Inc.
—Musical Colors/Colores Musicales: A World of Color. 2010. 24p. (J). pap. 6.99 *(978-1-59835-267-2(9),* BrickHouse Education) Cambridge BrickHouse, Inc.
Casterline, L. C. The Sounds of Music, 1 vol. 2004. (Sounds of Music Ser.). (ENG., Illus.). 16p. (gr. k-2). lib. bdg. 22.67 *(978-0-8368-4100-8(X),* 0d0ff6f2-b524-4be2-a0f5-0430febd1d63, Gareth Stevens Learning Library) Stevens, Gareth Publishing LLLP.
Claudio, Abbado. Yo Sere Director de Orquesta. 2007. (SPA.). 48p. (J). (gr. 4-5). 23.99 *(978-84-8470-052-4(6))* Corimbo, Editorial S.L. ESP. Dist: Lectorum Pubns., Inc.
Clyne, Margaret & Griffiths, Rachel. Let's Make Music. 2004. (ENG., Illus.). 16p. (J). (gr. 1-1). pap. 10.92 *(978-0-7652-5155-8(8),* Celebration Pr.) Savvas Learning Co.
Congratulations - Grade 1 Clarinet/Piano. (J). 9.95 *(978-1-85909-667-3(0),* Warner Bros. Pubns.) Alfred Publishing Co., Inc.
Congratulations- Grade 2 Alto Sax/Piano. 9.95 *(978-1-85909-816-5(9),* Warner Bros. Pubns.) Alfred Publishing Co., Inc.
Congratulations: Grade 2 Clarinet. (J). 9.95 *(978-1-85909-814-1(2),* Warner Bros. Pubns.) Alfred Publishing Co., Inc.
Congratulations: Grade 2 Flute. 9.95 *(978-1-85909-815-8(0),* Warner Bros. Pubns.) Alfred Publishing Co., Inc.
Coulthard, Emma. Recorder Wizard. 2005. (ENG.). 40p. pap. 8.95 incl. audio compact disk *(978-0-8256-3338-6(9),* 14033356, Chester Music) Music Sales Corp.
Daly, Ruth. Bagpipes. 2020. (J). *(978-1-7911-1632-3(9),* AV2 by Weigl) Weigl Pubs., Inc.
—Banjos. 2019. (J). *(978-1-7911-1628-6(0),* AV2 by Weigl) Weigl Pubs., Inc.
—Clarinets. 2020. (J). *(978-1-7911-1624-8(8),* AV2 by Weigl) Weigl Pubs., Inc.
—Tubas. 2020. (J). *(978-1-7911-1616-3(7),* AV2 by Weigl) Weigl Pubs., Inc.
D'Cruz, Anna-Marie. Make Your Own Musical Instruments, 1 vol. 2009. (Do It Yourself Projects! Ser.). (ENG., Illus.). 24p. (J). (gr. 4-4). pap. 10.40 *(978-1-4358-2925-1(5),* 6729205c-7f84-4af0-9f31-0ff37573536e, PowerKids Pr.) Rosen Publishing Group, Inc., The.
Deane-Pratt, Ade. Musical Instruments, 1 vol. 2011. (How Things Work Ser.). (ENG., Illus.). 32p. (J). (gr. 4-4). lib. bdg. 30.27 *(978-1-4488-5280-2(3),* 3998b40a-1801-4dca-8a3c-7fdbe88558eb) Rosen Publishing Group, Inc., The.
Dearling, Robert. Encyclopedia of Musical Instruments, 5 vols., Set. 2005. (Encyclopedia of Musical Instruments Ser.). (Illus.). 48p. (gr. 6-12). 91.80 *(978-0-7910-6090-2(X),* Facts On File) Infobase Holdings, Inc.
Dobson, Jolie. Bang Bang Plink Plink. 2014. (Snappy Sounds Ser.). (ENG., Illus.). 22p. (J). (gr. -1 — 1). bds. 5.95 *(978-1-77085-438-3(X),* 1cf7eee8-4063-4d9a-bf4f-6d2144912006) Firefly Bks., Ltd.
Dyke, Sylvie. "Descant" Recorder Music Made Easy - Just for Little Fingers! 2013. 36p. pap. *(978-1-78148-611-5(5))* Grosvenor Hse. Publishing Ltd.
Equipo Staff & Josephine, Paker. Las lautas Tienen Agujeros. 2003. (Enciclopedia Me Pregunto Por Que). (SPA., Illus.). 32p. (J). (gr. 3-5). 12.99 *(978-84-241-1968-3(1),* EV2041) Everest Editora ESP. Dist: Lectorum Pubns., Inc.
Faine, Edward Allan. Bebop Babies. 2003. (Illus.). 22p. (J). bds. 5.95 *(978-0-9716911-3-1(4))* IM Pr.
Frogs Play Cellos: And Other Fun Facts. 2014. (Did You Know? Ser.). (ENG., Illus.). 32p. (J). (gr. -1-3). pap. 6.99 *(978-1-4814-1425-8(9),* Little Simon) Little Simon.
Froseth, James O. Alto Saxophone Home Helper First Lessons at School & at Home. 2005. 16p. 7.95 *(978-1-57999-499-0(7),* M574) G I A Pubns., Inc.
—Baritone BC Home Helper First Lessons at School & at Home. 2005. 16p. 7.95 *(978-1-57999-505-8(5),* M580) G I A Pubns., Inc.
—Bassoon Home Helper First Lessons at School & at Home. 2005. 16p. 7.95 *(978-1-57999-498-3(9),* M573) G I A Pubns., Inc.
—Clarinet Home Helper First Lessons at School & at Home. 2005. 16p. 7.95 *(978-1-57999-496-9(2),* M571) G I A Pubns., Inc.
George, Francis. Mr G Clef & Friends. Wasvary, Marcia, illus. 2012. 32p. 24.95 *(978-1-4560-9642-7(7))* America Star Bks.
George, Gale. We're in the Band: Develop Understanding of Fractions & Numbers, 1 vol. 2014. (Rosen Math Readers Ser.). (ENG., Illus.). 24p. (J). (gr. 3-3). pap. 8.25 *(978-1-4777-4927-2(6),* a1c6afd6-6aae-4419-88f9-ab63c6856bf9, Rosen Classroom) Rosen Publishing Group, Inc., The.
Greenwood, Mark. Drummer Boy of John John. Lessac, Frané, illus. 2006. (ENG.). 40p. (J). 18.95 *(978-1-60060-652-6(0))* Lee & Low Bks., Inc.
Haynes, Norma Jean, et al. Make Music! A Kid's Guide to Creating Rhythm, Playing with Sound, & Conducting & Composing Music. 2019. (ENG.). 144p. (J). (gr. k-17). pap. 16.95 *(978-1-63586-035-1(0),* 626035) Storey Publishing, LLC.
Helenek, Sophie. My First Book MUSICAL INSTRUMENTS: GOLD Mom's Choice Awards Recipient. 2014. (My First Book Ser.). (ENG., Illus.). 16p. (J). (gr. -1 — 1). bds. 5.99 *(978-0-9894505-2-2(X))* Nursery Bks.
Holden, Pam. Musical Instruments, 1 vol. 2015. (ENG., Illus.). 16p. (-1). pap. *(978-1-77654-116-4(2),* Red Rocket Readers) Flying Start Bks.
Hutmacher, Kimberly. Djembes. 2020. (J). *(978-1-7911-1620-0(5),* AV2 by Weigl) Weigl Pubs., Inc.
Jackson, Jake. Chords for Kids (Pick up & Play) Quick Start, Easy Diagrams. 2018. (Pick up & Play Ser.). (ENG., Illus.). 176p. spiral bd. 15.99 *(978-1-78664-801-3(6),* ae4faeda-16e2-419a-9b6a-6fc8848f7480) Flame Tree Publishing GBR. Dist: Atlas Bks.
Kallen, Stuart A. The Instruments of Music, 1 vol. 2013. (Music Library). (ENG., Illus.). 136p. (gr. 7-10). lib. bdg. 41.03 *(978-1-4205-0946-5(2),* c71a8845-09ea-4349-b2d9-f9543b226c39, Lucent Pr.) Greenhaven Publishing LLC.
Kenney, Karen Latchana. The Science of Music: Discovering Sound. 2015. (Science in Action Ser.). (ENG., Illus.). 32p. (J). (gr. 3-6). 32.79 *(978-1-62403-962-1(6),* 19421, Checkerboard Library) ABDO Publishing Co.
—Tuneful Tubes. Heinsz, Joshua, illus. 2019. (Physics of Music Ser.). (ENG.). 24p. (J). (gr. k-2). lib. bdg. 33.99 *(978-1-68410-345-4(2),* 140265) Cantata Learning.
The Lac Hong Music Group: Six-Pack. (Greetings Ser.: Vol. 1). (gr. 3-5). 31.00 *(978-0-7635-1750-2(X))* Rigby Education.
Landau, Elaine. Is the Flute for You? 2010. (Ready to Make Music Ser.). (ENG., Illus.). 40p. (gr. 4-6). lib. bdg. 27.93 *(978-0-7613-5420-8(4),* Lerner Pubns.) Lerner Publishing Group.
—Is the Saxophone for You? 2010. (Ready to Make Music Ser.). (ENG.). 40p. (gr. 4-6). lib. bdg. 27.93 *(978-0-7613-5425-3(5),* Lerner Pubns.) Lerner Publishing Group.
—Is the Trumpet for You? 2010. (Ready to Make Music Ser.). (ENG., Illus.). 40p. (gr. 4-6). lib. bdg. 27.93 *(978-0-7613-5422-2(0),* Lerner Pubns.) Lerner Publishing Group.
Langham, Tony. Creepy Crawly Calypso. Harter, Debbie, illus. 2012. (Barefoot Singalongs Ser.). (ENG.). 32p. (J). (gr. -1-2). pap. 10.99 *(978-1-84686-828-3(9))* Barefoot Bks., Inc.
Lemmerz, Claudia Baumgaertner. My Book about Musical Instruments. 2011. (ENG.). 64p. (J). 19.95 *(978-0-9837585-3-2(0))* Touch the Music.
Marks, Anthony. Recorder for Beginners IR. 2018. (Activity Kits Ser.). (ENG.). 32p. 19.99 *(978-0-7945-4216-0(6),* Usborne) EDC Publishing.
Martin, Iain C., illus. Complete Theory Fun Factory. 2004. (ENG.). 96p. pap. 27.99 *(978-0-85162-181-4(3),* 48011786) Boosey & Hawkes, Inc.
McGraw-Hill Interactive Recorder. 2003. (Share the Music Ser.). (gr. 3-6). cd-rom *(978-0-02-295529-8(1))* Macmillan/McGraw-Hill Schl. Div.
McKean, Helen. Abracadabra Woodwind - Abracadabra Oboe (Pupil's Book + 2 CDs): the Way to Learn Through Songs & Tunes, 1 vol. 3rd ed. 2008. (Abracadabra Ser.). (ENG., Illus.). 64p. (J). pap., stu. ed. 15.95 incl. audio compact disk *(978-1-4081-0528-3(4))* HarperCollins Pubs. Ltd. GBR. Dist: Independent Pubs. Group.
Michele, Tracey. Musical Instruments. 2011. (Learn-Abouts Ser.). (Illus.). 16p. (J). pap. 7.95 *(978-1-59920-642-4(0))* Black Rabbit Bks.
Milet Publishing Staff. Music, 1 vol. 2012. (My First Bilingual Book Ser.). (ENG., Illus.). 24p. (J). (gr. k — 1). bds. 8.99 *(978-1-84059-718-9(6));* bds. 7.99 *(978-1-84059-716-5(X));* bds. 8.99 *(978-1-84059-724-0(0))* Milet Publishing.
—Music - English-Spanish, 1 vol. 2012. (My First Bilingual Book Ser.). (ENG & SPA., Illus.). 24p. (J). (gr. k — 1). bds. 8.99 *(978-1-84059-728-8(3))* Milet Publishing.
—Music - My First Bilingual Book, 1 vol. 2012. (My First Bilingual Book Ser.). (ENG & ITA., Illus.). 24p. (J). (gr. k — 1). bds. 7.99 *(978-1-84059-722-6(4));* bds. 7.99 *(978-1-84059-725-7(9))* Milet Publishing.
—La Musique, 1 vol. 2012. (My First Bilingual Book Ser.).Tr. of Music. (ENG & FRE., Illus.). 24p. (J). (gr. k — 1). bds. 7.99 *(978-1-84059-720-2(8))* Milet Publishing.
—My First Bilingual Book-Music, 1 vol. 2012. (My First Bilingual Book Ser.). (ENG., Illus.). 24p. (J). (gr. k — 1). bds. 7.99 *(978-1-84059-717-2(8))* Milet Publishing.
—My First Bilingual Book-Music (English-Farsi), 1 vol. 2012. (My First Bilingual Book Ser.). (ENG., Illus.). 24p. (J). (gr. k — 1). bds. 7.99 *(978-1-84059-719-6(4))* Milet Publishing.
—My First Bilingual Book-Music (English-German), 1 vol. 2012. (My First Bilingual Book Ser.). (ENG & GER., Illus.). 24p. (J). (gr. k — 1). bds. 7.99 *(978-1-84059-721-9(6))* Milet Publishing.
—My First Bilingual Book-Music (English-Korean), 1 vol. 2012. (My First Bilingual Book Ser.). (ENG., Illus.). 24p. (J). (gr. k — 1). bds. 7.99 *(978-1-84059-723-3(2))* Milet Publishing.
—My First Bilingual Book-Music (English-Russian), 1 vol. 2012. (My First Bilingual Book Ser.). (ENG., Illus.). 24p. (J). (gr. k — 1). bds. 7.99 *(978-1-84059-726-4(7))* Milet Publishing.
—My First Bilingual Book-Music (English-Somali), 1 vol. 2012. (My First Bilingual Book Ser.). (ENG., Illus.). 24p. (J). (gr. k — 1). bds. 8.99 *(978-1-84059-727-1(5))* Milet Publishing.
—My First Bilingual Book-Music (English-Turkish), 1 vol. 2012. (My First Bilingual Book Ser.). (ENG., Illus.). 24p. (J). (gr. k — 1). bds. 7.99 *(978-1-84059-729-5(1))* Milet Publishing.
—My First Bilingual Book-Music (English-Urdu), 1 vol. 2012. (My First Bilingual Book Ser.). (ENG., Illus.). 24p. (J). (gr. k — 1). bds. 7.99 *(978-1-84059-730-1(5))* Milet Publishing.
—My First Bilingual Book-Music (English-Vietnamese), 1 vol. 2012. (My First Bilingual Book Ser.). (ENG., Illus.). 24p. (J). (gr. k — 1). bds. 7.99 *(978-1-84059-731-8(3))* Milet Publishing.
Miller, Randy. The Fiddler's Throne: A Selection of 375 Tunes for Contra Dances, Sessions, & House Parties 2004. (Illus.). 246p. spiral bd. 25.00 *(978-0-9770530-1-8(6))* Miller, Randy.
Murphy, Maggie. High-Tech DIY Projects with Musical Instruments. 2014. (Maker Kids Ser.). (ENG., Illus.). 32p. (J). (gr. 3-6). pap. 70.50 *(978-1-4777-6661-3(8))* Rosen Publishing Group, Inc., The.
Music. Gr K-3 Stm Instrument Sou. 2003. (Share the Music Ser.). (gr. k-3). *(978-0-02-295481-9(3))* Macmillan/McGraw-Hill Schl. Div.
National Geographic Kids. Look & Learn: Let's Make Music. 2018. (Look & Learn Ser.). (Illus.). 24p. (J). (gr. -1-k). bds. 6.99 *(978-1-4263-2991-3(1),* National Geographic Kids) Disney Publishing Worldwide.
Norgaard, Martin. Jazz Cello/Bass Wizard Junior, Book 2, 1 vol., Bk. 2. 2005. (ENG., Illus.). 64p. pap. 17.95 *(978-0-7866-6655-3(2),* 20869BCD) Mel Bay Pubns., Inc.
—Jazz Fiddle Wizard Junior, Book 2, 1 vol., Book. 2. 2005. (ENG., Illus.). 64p. 19.99 *(978-0-7866-6644-7(7),* 20726BCD) Mel Bay Pubns., Inc.
—Jazz Viola Wizard Junior, Book 2, 1 vol., Bk. 2. 2005. (ENG., Illus.). 64p. 17.95 *(978-0-7866-6653-9(6),* 20868BCD) Mel Bay Pubns., Inc.
O'Hara, Shelley. ICan IPod. 2005. (ENG., Illus.). 160p. (J). per. 12.99 *(978-0-7897-3527-0(X))* Que.
Parker, Ben. My First Keyboard - Learn to Play: Kids. 2013. (Illus.). 42p. pap. *(978-1-908707-15-4(1))* Kyle Craig Publishing.
—My First Recorder - Learn to Play: Kids. 2013. 38p. pap. *(978-1-908707-18-5(6))* Kyle Craig Publishing.
Passchier, Maja. Abracadabra Strings - Abracadabra Cello (Pupil's Book + 2 CDs): the Way to Learn Through Songs & Tunes, 1 vol. 3rd rev. ed. 2009. (Abracadabra Ser.). (ENG., Illus.). 64p. (J). pap. 17.95 incl. audio compact disk *(978-1-4081-1462-9(3))* HarperCollins Pubs. Ltd. GBR. Dist: Independent Pubs. Group.
PI Kids. Sesame Street: 12 Board Books. Mathieu, Joe et al, illus. 2010. (ENG.). 120p. (J). 16.99 *(978-1-4127-0515-8(0),* 4867, PI Kids) Phoenix International Publications, Inc.
Pollock, Malcolm. Abracadabra Woodwind - Abracadabra Flute (Pupils' Book + 2 CDs): the Way to Learn Through Songs & Tunes, 1 vol. 3rd ed. 2008. (Abracadabra Ser.). (ENG., Illus.). 72p. (J). (gr. k-4). pap., stu. ed. 15.95 incl. audio compact disk *(978-1-4081-0527-6(6))* HarperCollins Pubs. Ltd. GBR. Dist: Independent Pubs. Group.
Ponto, Joanna & Lowenstein Niven, Felicia. Kids Love Music Crafts, 1 vol. 2018. (Kids Love Crafts Ser.). (ENG.). 32p. (J). (gr. 3-3). 26.93 *(978-1-9785-0199-7(4),* 07b8f5ab-1e5d-4fa9-97db-f9c10b234489) Enslow Publishing, LLC.
Purton, Michael. Show Me How: I Can Make Music. 2015. (ENG., Illus.). 48p. (J). (gr. -1-12). 7.99 *(978-1-86147-297-7(8),* Armadillo) Anness Publishing GBR. Dist: National Bk. Network.
Rice, Dona Herweck. I Have Music. 2018. (See Me Read! Everyday Words Ser.). (ENG., Illus.). 12p. (J). (gr. -1-k). 6.99 *(978-1-4938-9822-0(1))* Teacher Created Materials, Inc.
Riggs, Kate. Flute. 2014. (Making Music Ser.). (ENG.). 24p. (J). (gr. 1-4). pap. 9.99 *(978-0-89812-946-5(X),* 21528, Creative Paperbacks) Creative Co., The.
—Trumpet. 2014. (Making Music Ser.). (ENG.). 24p. (J). (gr. 1-4). pap. 9.99 *(978-0-89812-949-6(4),* 21537, Creative Paperbacks) Creative Co., The.
Roberts, Gregory. Chin Music. 2007. 208p. (J). pap. 12.99 *(978-0-14-305573-0(9))* Penguin Publishing Group.
Robson, Kirsteen. Listen & Learn Musical Instruments. 2018. (Listen & Learn Ser.). (ENG.). 4p. (J). 19.99 *(978-0-7945-4115-6(1),* Usborne) EDC Publishing.
Rowe, Brooke. Playing Musical Bottles. Bane, Jeff, illus. 2016. (My Early Library: My Science Fun Ser.). (ENG.). 24p. (J). (gr. k-1). 30.64 *(978-1-63471-028-2(2),* 208192) Cherry Lake Publishing.
Roza, Greg. Getting the Most Out of Makerspaces to Make Musical Instruments. 2014. (Makerspaces Ser.). 64p. (J). (gr. 6-12). pap. 77.70 *(978-1-4777-7826-5(8));* (ENG.). 36.13 *(978-1-4777-7823-4(3),* 9d238719-57f4-42d3-9124-f2dc64563153); (ENG.). pap. 13.95 *(978-1-4777-7825-8(X),* ffc5b182-4f08-462d-892a-c84f0185b43b) Rosen Publishing Group, Inc., The.
Rutland, Jonathan. Abracadabra Clarinet (Pupil's Book + 2 CDs) The Way to Learn Through Songs & Tunes, 1 vol. 3rd ed. 2008. (ENG., Illus.). 72p. (J). pap., stu. ed. 15.95 incl. audio compact disk *(978-1-4081-0530-6(6))* HarperCollins Pubs. Ltd. GBR. Dist: Independent Pubs. Group.
—Abracadabra Woodwind - Abracadabra Saxophone (Pupil's Book + 2 CDs): the Way to Learn Through Songs & Tunes, 1 vol. 3rd ed. 2008. (Abracadabra Ser.). (ENG., Illus.). 72p. (J). pap., stu. ed. 15.95 incl. audio compact disk *(978-1-4081-0529-0(2))* HarperCollins Pubs. Ltd. GBR. Dist: Independent Pubs. Group.
Schwartz, Betty Ann. What Makes Music? A Magic Ribbon Book. Turner, Dona, illus. 2005. (Stories to Share Ser.). 16p. (J). (gr. -1-3). act. bk. ed. 11.95 *(978-1-58117-139-6(0),* Intervisual/Piggy Toes) Bendon, Inc.

Sjonger, Rebecca. Maker Projects for Kids Who Love Music. 2016. (Be a Maker! Ser.). (ENG., Illus.). 32p. (J). (978-0-7787-2252-6(X)) Crabtree Publishing Co.

Smith, A. G. Little Mandalas Stained Glass Coloring Book. 2006. (Dover Stained Glass Coloring Book Ser.). (ENG., Illus.). 8p. (J). (gr. k-3). 1.99 (978-0-486-44937-1(8), 449378) Dover Pubns., Inc.

Smith, Erica. Making Music with Stringed Instruments. 2009. (Reading Room Collection 2 Ser.). 24p. (gr. 3-4). 42.50 (978-1-60851-979-8(1), PowerKids Pr.) Rosen Publishing Group, Inc., The.

Smith, Melanie. Beginner Cello Theory for Children, Book One, 1 vol. 2005. (ENG., Illus.). 84p. pap. 19.99 (978-0-7866-7088-8(6), 20451) Mel Bay Pubns., Inc.

Taplin, Sam. My First Xylophone Book IR. 2018. (My First Musical Books* Ser.). (ENG.). 22p. (J). 24.99 (978-0-7945-4114-9(3), Usborne) EDC Publishing.

Tarantino, Scott & Ruggiero, David. High Sticking: Xylophone & Marimba Pieces for Grades 4 - 8. 2011. 32p. (J). pap. 19.95 (978-0-9832648-2-8(1)) Beatin' Path Pubns., LLC.

Urquhart, Kristina Mercedes. Making Music with Magnets. rev. ed. 2018. (Smithsonian: Informational Text Ser.). (ENG., Illus.). 32p. (J). (gr. 4-8). pap. 12.99 (978-1-4938-6713-4(X)) Teacher Created Materials, Inc.

Verderosa, Laura. In the Band. 2010. (Sight Word Readers Ser.). (J). 3.49 (978-1-60719-612-9(3)) Newmark Learning LLC.

Watt, Fiona. Little Children's Music Book. 2012. (Little Children's Music Book Ser.). 24p. (J). bds. 18.99 (978-0-7945-3168-3(7), Usborne) EDC Publishing.

Wearing, Katie & Henry, Frankie. Abracadabra Strings Beginners - Abracadabra Cello Beginner (Pupil's Book + CD), 1 vol. rev. ed. 2007. (Abracadabra Ser.). (ENG., Illus.). 32p. (J). pap. 11.95 incl. audio compact disk (978-0-7136-9366-9(5)) HarperCollins Pubs. Ltd. GBR. Dist: Independent Pubs. Group.

Wearing, Katie & Maybank, Chris. Abracadabra Strings Beginners - Abracadabra Double Bass Beginner (Pupil's Book + CD), 1 vol. 2007. (Abracadabra Ser.). (ENG., Illus.). 32p. (J). pap. 11.95 incl. audio compact disk (978-0-7136-8163-5(2)) HarperCollins Pubs. Ltd. GBR. Dist: Independent Pubs. Group.

Whykes, Susan. Let's Practise: Be a Better Musician. 2009. 216p. pap. 14.49 (978-1-4389-2933-0(1)) AuthorHouse.

MUSICAL INSTRUMENTS—FICTION

Adair, Amy. Jay Jay's Special Delivery. 2003. (Illus.). (J). 15.98 (978-0-7853-8625-4(4)) Publications International, Ltd.

Albee, Sarah. Max Can Fix That. Schick, Joel, illus. 2006. (Step-By-Step Readers Ser.). (J). pap. (978-1-59939-055-0(8), Reader's Digest Young Families, Inc.) Studio Fun International.

Barton, Chris. 88 Instruments. Thomas, Louis, illus. 2016. 32p. (J). (gr. -1-2). 17.99 (978-0-553-53814-4(4), Knopf Bks. for Young Readers) Random Hse. Children's Bks.

Benator, Eileen. A Marching Band for Bears. Benator, Seth, illus. 2004. 32p. (J). lib. bdg. 15.95 (978-0-9748478-5-6(2)) Lion's Tale Pr., LLC.

Binding, Tim. Sylvie & the Songman. 2011. (ENG.). 352p. (J). (gr. 4-6). lib. bdg. 22.44 (978-0-385-75159-9(1), Yearling) Random Hse. Children's Bks.

Blackaby, Susan & Cicciarelli, Joellyn. Leo's Gift. Schuler, Carrie, illus. 2017. (ENG.). 32p. (J). (gr. 1-7). 19.95 (978-0-8294-4600-5(1)) Loyola Pr.

Blumberg, Margie. Avram's Gift. McGaw, Laurie, illus. 2005. (ENG.). 48p. (YA). pap. 12.95 (978-0-9624166-3-7(0)) MB Publishing, LLC.

Blume, Lesley M. M. The Rising Star of Rusty Nail. 2009. (ENG.). 288p. (J). (gr. 3-7). 7.99 (978-0-440-42111-5(X), Yearling) Random Hse. Children's Bks.

Bowe, Julie. Face the Music. 2015. (Victoria Torres, Unfortunately Average Ser.). (ENG., Illus.). 160p. (J). (gr. 4-8). pap. 5.95 (978-1-4965-0538-5(7), 128610, Stone Arch Bks.) Capstone.

Call, Davide. Piano, Piano. Rivers, Randi, tr. from FRE. Heliot, Eric, illus. 2007. 28p. (J). (gr. 4-7). 15.95 (978-1-58089-191-2(8)) Charlesbridge Publishing, Inc.

Castonguay, Leo. Piper Peter. 2012. 44p. 24.95 (978-1-4626-8604-9(4)) America Star Bks.

Christie, Tory. Curious Mccarthy's Not-So-Perfect Pitch. Price, Mina, illus. 2017. (Curious Mccarthy Ser.). (ENG.). 112p. (J). (gr. 2-4). pap. 6.95 (978-1-5158-1647-8(8), 136302, Picture Window Bks.) Capstone.

Curtis, Gavin. The Bat Boy & His Violin. 2004. (Illus.). (J). (gr. k-3). spiral bd. (978-0-616-07254-7(6)) Canadian National Institute for the Blind/Institut National Canadien pour les Aveugles.

Dagostino, Argus. Stop the Lute. 2009. (ENG.). 34p. pap. 20.00 (978-0-557-24546-8(X)) Lulu Pr., Inc.

Donegan, Noel & Donegan, Luz. The Hot-Headed Bassoon. 2013. (Magical Mozart & His Musical Ser.). (ENG.). 32p. (J). pap. 8.95 (978-1-84730-392-9(7)) Veritas Pubns. IRL. Dist: Casemate Pubs. & Bk. Distributors, LLC.

—The Noisy Blue Drum. 2013. (Magical Mozart & His Musical Ser.). (ENG.). 32p. (J). pap. 8.95 (978-1-84730-391-2(9)) Veritas Pubns. IRL. Dist: Casemate Pubs. & Bk. Distributors, LLC.

—The Sad Little Violin. 2013. (Magical Mozart & His Musical Ser.). (ENG.). 32p. (J). pap. 8.95 (978-1-84730-393-6(5)) Veritas Pubns. IRL. Dist: Casemate Pubs. & Bk. Distributors, LLC.

Errico, Jessica / C. Grandpa's Magical Accordion. Star, Brenda, illus. 2007. 28p. (J). pap. 17.95 incl. cd-rom (978-0-9800577-0-6(1)) Three Part Harmony LLC.

Falconer, Ian. Olivia Forms a Band. Falconer, Ian, illus. 2006. (ENG., Illus.). 50p. (J). (gr. -1-3). 19.99 (978-1-4169-2454-8(X), Atheneum Bks. for Young Readers) Simon & Schuster Children's Publishing.

Farmer, Zoe. Practice Makes Perfect. Farmer, Zoe, illus. 2007. (Illus.). 74p. (gr. -1-k). pap. (978-1-58690-029-8(3)) Mould, Paul Publishing.

Forman, Gayle. Where She Went. l.t. ed. 2015. (If I Stay Ser.: BK.2). (ENG.). 288p. (YA). 23.99 (978-1-4104-7562-6(X)) Cengage Gale.

—Where She Went. (ENG.). (YA). (gr. 9-18). 2012. 304p. 10.99 (978-0-14-242089-8(1), Speak) 2011. 272p. 17.99 (978-0-525-42294-5(3), Dutton Books for Young Readers) Penguin Young Readers Group.

—Where She Went. 2012. (If I Stay Ser.: BK.2). (YA). 21.00 (978-1-61383-394-0(6)) Perfection Learning Corp.

—Where She Went. l.t. ed. 2015. (If I Stay Ser.: BK.2). (ENG.). 286p. (YA). pap. 12.99 (978-1-59413-855-3(9), Large Print Pr.) Thorndike Pr.

—Where She Went. 2012. (If I Stay Ser.: BK.2). (YA). lib. bdg. 22.10 (978-0-606-23644-7(9)) Turtleback.

Free Kazoos. 2003. (978-0-375-88484-9(X)) Random Hse. Children's Bks.

Garriel, Barbara S. I Know a Shy Fellow Who Swallowed a Cello. O'Brien, John, illus. (ENG.). 32p. (J). (gr. k-2). 2012. pap. 8.99 (978-1-59078-946-9(6)) 2004. 17.99 (978-1-59078-043-5(4)) Astra Publishing Hse. (Astra Young Readers).

George Trad. The Symph - in Search of Harmony. Beniamino Brady, illus. 2012. 38p. 30.50 (978-1-61897-519-5(6), Strategic Bk. Publishing) Strategic Book Publishing & Rights Agency (SBPRA).

Gifford, Peggy Elizabeth. Moxy Maxwell Does Not Love Practicing the Piano: (But She Does Love Being in Recitals) Fisher, Valorie, illus. Fisher, Valorie, photos by. 2009. (Moxy Maxwell Ser.). (ENG.). 192p. (J). (gr. 4-6). lib. bdg. 21.19 (978-0-375-96688-0(9), Yearling) Random Hse. Children's Bks.

Gillmor, Don. Fabuleuse Melodie De. Gay, Marie-Louise, illus. 2013. (ENG.). 44p. (J). (gr. -1-k). 16.95 (978-2-923163-30-7(3)) La Montagne Secrete CAN. Dist: Independent Pubs. Group.

Ginsberg, Mort. Ukey & His Magical Ukulele. 2008. 75p. pap. 19.95 (978-1-60610-395-1(4)) America Star Bks.

Harris, Lee. Carla & the Great Talent Show. 2009. 80p. pap. 10.00 (978-1-60860-515-6(9), Strategic Bk. Publishing) Strategic Book Publishing & Rights Agency (SBPRA).

Keller, Jessica. Mia's Marvelous Musical Group. 2009. (Illus.). 64p. (gr. -1-3). pap. 26.99 (978-1-4389-8160-4(0)) AuthorHouse.

Laird, Judie. I Don't Want to Play the Piano! 2009. 20p. pap. 10.95 (978-1-4490-1496-4(8)) AuthorHouse.

—Lori Takes Piano Lessons. 2009. 20p. pap. 10.95 (978-1-4490-1205-2(1)) AuthorHouse.

Landon, Kristen. Life in the Pit. 2008. (ENG., Illus.). 248p. (YA). (gr. 5-13). pap. 8.95 (978-1-933831-08-4(1)) Blooming Tree Pr.

Langham, Tony. Creepy Crawly Calypso. Harter, Debbie, illus. 2004. (ENG.). 32p. (J). 16.99 (978-1-84148-699-4(X)) Barefoot Bks., Inc.

Langham, Tony & Harter, Debbie. Creepy Crawly Calypso. 2005. (ENG.). 32p. (J). pap. 9.99 (978-1-902283-46-3(5)) Barefoot Bks., Inc.

Lithgow, John. The Remarkable Farkle Mcbride. Payne, C. F., illus. 2003. (ENG.). 40p. (J). (gr. -1-3). pap. 9.99 (978-0-689-83541-4(8), Simon & Schuster Bks. For Young Readers) Simon & Schuster Bks. For Young Readers.

Manning, Sarra. Guitar Girl. 2003. (ENG.). 256p. (YA). pap. (978-0-340-86071-7(5)) Hodder & Stoughton.

Manushkin, Fran. Katie's Noisy Music. Lyon, Tammie, illus. 2015. (Katie Woo Ser.). (ENG.). 32p. (J). (gr. k-2). 21.32 (978-1-4795-5893-3(1), 127034, Picture Window Bks.) Capstone.

Meadows, Daisy. Danni the Drum Fairy #4. 2010. (ENG.). 80p. (J). lib. bdg. 15.39 (978-1-4242-4729-5(2)) Fitzgerald Bks.

—Fiona the Flute Fairy #3. 2010. (ENG.). 80p. (J). lib. bdg. 15.39 (978-1-4242-4731-8(4)) Fitzgerald Bks.

—Maya the Harp Fairy #5. 2010. (ENG.). 80p. (J). lib. bdg. 15.39 (978-1-4242-4732-5(2)) Fitzgerald Bks.

—Poppy the Piano Fairy #1. 2010. (ENG.). 80p. (J). lib. bdg. 15.39 (978-1-4242-4733-2(0)) Fitzgerald Bks.

—Sadie the Saxophone Fairy #7. 2010. (ENG.). 80p. (J). lib. bdg. 15.39 (978-1-4242-4734-9(9)) Fitzgerald Bks.

Meehl, Brian. Blowback '07: When the Only Way Forward Is Back. 2016. (Illus.). 346p. (J). pap. 12.95 (978-1-63505-185-8(1)) Salem Author Services.

Megerdichian, Janet. Pine Needle Pedro. Adams, Allysa, illus. 2010. 36p. pap. 16.99 (978-1-4520-4422-4(8)) AuthorHouse.

Montparker, Carol. Polly & the Piano: With Online Resource. 2004. (Amadeus Ser.). (ENG., Illus.). 40p. pap. 25.00 (978-1-57467-093-6(X), 157467093X, Amadeus Press) Leonard, Hal Corp.

Moss, Lloyd. Zin! Zin! Zin! A Violin. Priceman, Marjorie, illus. 2004. (gr. -1-3). 18.00 (978-0-7569-1919-1(3)) Perfection Learning Corp.

—Zin! Zin! Zin! A Violin. 2004. 29.95 (978-1-55592-131-6(0)); 18.95 (978-1-55592-118-7(3)); 38.75 (978-1-55592-650-2(9)) Weston Woods Studios, Inc.

Mulder, Michelle. Out of the Box. 2011. (ENG.). 160p. (J). E-Book (978-1-55469-329-0(2)) Orca Bk. Pubs.

Omololu, C. J. Transcendence. 2012. (ENG.). 336p. (YA). (gr. 8-12). 26.19 (978-0-8027-2370-3(5), 9780802723703) Walker & Co.

Pellegata, Donna, illus. The Harp Mouse Chooses Her Home: The Adventure Begins. 2008. 24p. (J). pap. 6.95 (978-0-9742174-1-3(7)) Heart & Harp LLC.

Perkins, Lynne Rae. The Cardboard Piano. Perkins, Lynne Rae, illus. 2008. (ENG., Illus.). 32p. (J). (gr. -1-2). 17.99 (978-0-06-154265-7(2), Greenwillow Bks.) HarperCollins Pubs.

pierSath, Chath. Sinat & the Instrument of the Heart: A Story of Cambodia. Nath, Vann & Pouriseth, Phal, illus. 2010. (Make Friends Around the World Ser.). (ENG.). 32p. (J). (gr. k-3). 9.95 (978-1-60727-116-1(8)); 9.95 (978-1-60727-098-0(6)); 19.95 (978-1-60727-097-3(8)); 9.95 (978-1-60727-117-8(6)); 16.95 (978-1-60727-087-4(0)); pap. 6.95 (978-1-60727-088-1(9)) Soundprints.

Potter, Debra, illus. I Am the Music Man. (Classic Books with Holes 8x8 Ser.). 16p. (J). 2018. (ENG.). pap. (978-1-78628-129-6(5)) 2006. (gr. -1-3). spiral bd. (978-1-84643-010-7(0)) Child's Play International Ltd.

Publications International Ltd. Staff. Dora PNO BK Follow Music. 2008. 10p. (J). 16.98 (978-1-4127-8996-7(6), PIL Kids) Publications International, Ltd.

Ray, Mary Lyn. A Violin for Elva. Tusa, Tricia, illus. 2015. (ENG.). 32p. (J). (gr. -1-3). 16.99 (978-0-15-225483-4(8), 1202633, Clarion Bks.) HarperCollins Pubs.

Rovetch, L. Bob. I Need a Kazoot! Castillon, Carly, illus. 2006. (J). (978-1-58987-055-0(7)) Kindermusik International.

Rumbley, Rose-Mary. Dear Santa: Thanks for the Piano. 2004. (Illus.). 46p. (J). pap. 8.95 (978-1-57168-466-0(2)) Eakin Pr.

Rylant, Cynthia. The Case of the Puzzling Possum. Karas, G. Brian, illus. 2003. (High-Rise Private Eyes Ser.: No. 3). (J). (gr. -1-3). 25.95 incl. audio (978-1-59112-198-5(1)); (gr. k-3). pap. 29.95 incl. audio (978-1-59112-199-2(X)) Live Oak Media.

Seybold, Celisa. The Keys to Adventure. 2010. 62p. pap. 9.95 (978-0-557-55086-9(6)) Lulu Pr., Inc.

Shahan, Sherry. The Jazzy Alphabet. Thelen, Mary, illus. 2006. 30p. (J). (gr. k-4). reprint ed. 16.00 (978-1-4223-5730-9(9)) DIANE Publishing Co.

Snicket, Lemony, pseud. The Composer Is Dead. Ellis, Carson, illus. 2009. (ENG.). 40p. (J). (gr. k-5). 17.99 (978-0-06-123627-3(6), HarperCollins) HarperCollins Pubs.

Spinner, Cala. Super Cat Speed! 2018. (Ready-To-Read Ser.). (ENG.). 32p. (J). (gr. -1-1). 12.89 (978-1-64310-648-9(1)) Penworthy Co., LLC, The.

Spinner, Cala, adapted by. Super Cat Speed! Ready-To-Read Level 1. 2017. (PJ Masks Ser.). (ENG., Illus.). 32p. (J). (gr. -1-1). 16.99 (978-1-5344-0926-2(2)); pap. 4.99 (978-1-5344-0925-5(4)) Simon Spotlight. (Simon Spotlight).

Stewart, Kymberly M. Play It Again, Rachel. 2003. 74p. (J). pap. 10.95 (978-0-9740653-0-4(7)) Neema's Children Literature Assn., Inc.

Stilwell, Norma Mintum. Making Beautiful Music. LaGrange, Tiffany, illus. 2011. 28p. pap. 14.95 (978-1-936343-92-8(4)) Peppertree Pr., The.

Studio Mouse Staff. Sesame Street My First Instrument. 2008. (ENG.). 24p. (J). (gr. -1). 4.99 (978-1-59069-737-5(5)) Studio Mouse LLC.

Sullivan, Kate. What Do You Hear?, 1 vol. 2018. (ENG., Illus.). 24p. (J). bds. 12.99 (978-0-7643-5601-8(1), 16179) Schiffer Publishing, Ltd.

Taylor, Lillian Webb. Santa's Musical Elves. 2009. 28p. pap. 12.25 (978-1-60860-146-2(3), Strategic Bk. Publishing) Strategic Book Publishing & Rights Agency (SBPRA).

Tripp, Paul. Tubby the Tuba. Cole, Henry, illus. 2006. 32p. (J). (gr. -1-3). 17.99 (978-0-525-47717-4(9), Dutton Books for Young Readers) Penguin Young Readers Group.

Weston Woods Staff, creator. Dem Bones. 2004. 29.95 (978-1-55592-702-8(5)) Weston Woods Studios, Inc.

Yoo, Paula. Good Enough. 2012. (ENG.). 336p. (YA). (gr. 8). pap. 7.99 (978-0-06-079090-5(3), HarperTeen) HarperCollins Pubs.

Young, Jessica. Play This Book. Wiseman, Daniel, illus. 2018. (ENG.). 32p. (J). 15.99 (978-1-68119-506-3(2), 900175599, Bloomsbury Children's Bks.) Bloomsbury Publishing USA.

Zobel-Nolan, Allia. Animal Parade. Maddocks, Maria, illus. 2008. 10p. (J). (gr. -1). 12.95 (978-1-932915-63-1(X)) Sandvik Innovations, LLC.

MUSICAL NOTATION

Biklou, Eliyana. Lady Treble & the Seven Notes. 2010. (ENG., Illus.). 32p. (J). (gr. -1-3). 16.95 (978-1-897476-21-5(3)) Simply Read Bks. CAN. Dist: Ingram Publisher Services.

Collins, Kathleen. Music Math: Exploring Different Interpretations of Fractions, 1 vol. (Math for the REAL World Ser.). 32p. (gr. 4-5). 2010. (ENG., Illus.). (J). pap. 10.00 (978-0-8239-8877-8(5), cddf00e8-4b12-4f3c-8a76-6e4705e95cd1) 2009. 47.90 (978-1-60851-398-7(X)) 2003. (ENG., Illus.). (J). lib. bdg. 28.93 (978-0-8239-8984-3(4), b8125844-a06d-4fcb-9ad6-8809328dfed8) Rosen Publishing Group, Inc., The. (PowerKids Pr.).

Yazbeck, Peter & Castano, Clara. Learning Cards(tm) Musical Symbols in Q&A Form, Secondary Level, 3 bks., Bk. 3. 2007. (Illus.). 150p. ring bd. 9.95 (978-0-9785118-5-2(9)) CCRiddles.

MUSICALS

Buck, Sammy. Like You Like It. 2016. (Illus.). 106p. pap. 9.99 (978-1-68069-064-4(7)) Playscripts, Inc.

Capaccio, Nancy. How the Lion King Made It to the Stage, 1 vol. 2018. (Getting to Broadway Ser.). (ENG.). 96p. (YA). (gr. 8-8). 45.93 (978-1-5026-3508-2(9), 63f04ba5-bcd8-43d0-aa08-a429554efa50) Cavendish Square Publishing LLC.

Freedman, Jeri. How Wicked Made It to the Stage, 1 vol. 2018. (Getting to Broadway Ser.). (ENG.). 96p. (YA). (gr. 8-8). lib. bdg. 45.93 (978-1-5026-3514-3(3), 9e6d7045-7aa0-46f3-ab39-febb5b79c3c3) Cavendish Square Publishing LLC.

Glore, John. The Stinky Cheese Man & Other Fairly Stupid Tales. 2015. 42p. (J). pap. 9.99 (978-1-62384-970-2(5)) Playscripts, Inc.

Hal Leonard Corp. Staff, creator. Teaching Little Fingers to Play More Broadway Songs: Mid to Later Elementary Level. 2012. (ENG.). 32p. pap. 12.99 incl. audio compact disk (978-1-4584-1768-8(9), 00416929) Willis Music Co.

Isenberg, Barbara. Making It Big: The Diary of a Broadway Musical. 2004. (Limelight Ser.). (ENG., Illus.). 238p. 29.95 (978-0-87910-088-9(5), 0879100885, Limelight Editions) Leonard, Hal Corp.

McMahon, James P. & Ryan, Nancy. Buttonbush. 2003. (Musicals Ser.). 55p. (Orig.). (J). (gr. k-7). pap. 10.00 (978-0-88734-526-5(3)) Players Pr., Inc.

Nelson, Penelope S. Lin-Manuel Miranda. 2018. (Influential People Ser.). (ENG., Illus.). 32p. (J). (gr. 4-6). lib. bdg. 28.65 (978-1-5435-4129-8(1), 139083, Capstone Pr.) Capstone.

Picoult, Jodi & van Leer, Jake. Over the Moon: A Musical Play. 2011. (ENG., Illus.). 240p. (YA). (gr. 7-18). pap. 15.99 (978-1-4424-2132-5(0), Simon Pulse) Simon Pulse.

Robinson, Peg. How Cats Made It to the Stage, 1 vol. 2018. (Getting to Broadway Ser.). (ENG.). 96p. (YA). (gr. 8-8). 45.93 (978-1-5026-3502-0(X), 773c6cce-78da-47aa-8064-ad6e2b62cbb0) Cavendish Square Publishing LLC.

MUSICIANS

see also African American Musicians; Composers; Pianists; Rap Musicians; Singers; Violinists

Aberback, Brian. Black Sabbath: Pioneers of Heavy Metal, 1 vol. 2011. (Rebels of Rock Ser.). (ENG., Illus.). 112p. (gr. 5-6). pap. 13.88 (978-1-59845-212-9(6), 72a29380-bdba-4282-8f0b-2abba039cac2) Enslow Publishing, LLC.

Adams, Michelle Medlock. Tim Mcgraw. 2006. (Blue Banner Biography Ser.). (Illus.). 32p. (YA). (gr. 4-7). lib. bdg. 25.70 (978-1-58415-501-0(9)) Mitchell Lane Pubs.

Alagna, Magdalena. Elvis Presley. 2009. (Rock & Roll Hall of Famers Ser.). 112p. (gr. 5-8). 63.90 (978-1-60852-474-7(4), Rosen Reference) Rosen Publishing Group, Inc., The.

Allen, Richard, contrib. by. Charlie Parker Played Be Bop. 2003. (Illus.). (J). (gr. -1-2). pap. 35.95 incl. audio compact disk (978-1-59112-602-7(9)) Live Oak Media.

—Mysterious Thelonious. abr. ed. 2003. (Illus.). (J). (gr. -1-2). audio compact disk 28.95 (978-1-59112-422-1(0)) Live Oak Media.

Anderson, Jennifer Joline. John Lennon: Legendary Musician & Beatle, 1 vol. 2010. (Lives Cut Short Set 1 Ser.). (ENG.). 112p. (YA). (gr. 6-12). lib. bdg. 41.36 (978-1-60453-790-1(6), 11189, Essential Library) ABDO Publishing Co.

Anderson, Kirsten. Who Is Elton John? 2016. (Who Is... ? Ser.). lib. bdg. 16.00 (978-0-606-38396-7(4)) Turtleback.

Anderson, Kirsten & Who HQ. Who Is Elton John? Qiu, Joseph J. M., illus. 2016. (Who Was? Ser.). 112p. (J). (gr. 3-7). pap. 6.99 (978-0-448-48846-2(9), Penguin Workshop) Penguin Young Readers Group.

Anderson, Michelle. A Dj. 2018. (So You Wanna Be Ser.). (ENG., Illus.). 32p. (gr. 4-8). lib. bdg. 32.79 (978-1-64156-472-4(5), 9781641564724) Rourke Educational Media.

Angel, Ann. Janis Joplin: Rise up Singing. 2010. (ENG., Illus.). 120p. (YA). (gr. 8-17). 24.95 (978-0-8109-8349-6(4), 641601, Amulet Bks.) Abrams, Inc.

Anniss, Matt. Music, Fashion, & Style. 2015. (Music Scene Ser.). (J). lib. bdg. 37.10 (978-1-59920-912-8(8)) Black Rabbit Bks.

Ashley, Susan. Yo-Yo Ma, 1 vol. 2004. (Trailblazers of the Modern World Ser.). (ENG., Illus.). 48p. (gr. 5-8). pap. 15.05 (978-0-8368-5266-0(4), 4c179bea-aac3-4693-960a-c19578a643d5); lib. bdg. 33.67 (978-0-8368-5497-8(7), 62462dad-376d-4b88-a97e-d857841a2294) Stevens, Gareth Publishing LLLP. (Gareth Stevens Secondary Library).

Bailey, Ellen. One Dream, One Direction. 2012. (ENG.). 64p. (J). (gr. 3-7). pap. 9.99 (978-1-4424-7308-9(8), Aladdin) Simon & Schuster Children's Publishing.

Bailey, Tom. Hank Williams Sr: Country Music Legend. 2008. (Illus.). 104p. (J). (978-1-59421-043-3(8)) Seacoast Publishing, Inc.

Ball, Heather. Magnificent Women in Music, 1 vol. 2005. (Women's Hall of Fame Ser.: 7). (ENG., Illus.). 110p. (J). (gr. 4-8). pap. 10.95 (978-1-897187-02-9(5)) Second Story Pr. CAN. Dist: Orca Bk. Pubs. USA.

Bankston, John. Jay-Z. l.t. ed. 2004. (Blue Banner Biography Ser.). (Illus.). 32p. (J). (gr. 3-8). lib. bdg. 25.70 (978-1-58415-223-1(0)) Mitchell Lane Pubs.

—The Life & Times of Duke Ellington. 2004. (Masters of Music Ser.). (Illus.). 48p. (gr. 4-8). lib. bdg. 20.95 (978-1-58415-248-4(6)) Mitchell Lane Pubs.

Battaglia, Stephen. Mr. Mcsymphony's Musicians & their Instruments. 2008. (ENG.). 28p. pap. 9.99 (978-1-4196-8077-9(3)) CreateSpace Independent Publishing Platform.

Behnke, Alison. Death of a Dreamer: The Assassination of John Lennon. 2012. (Single Titles Ser.). (ENG.). 96p. (gr. 6-12). lib. bdg. 33.26 (978-0-8225-9036-1(0), Twenty-First Century Bks.) Lerner Publishing Group.

Beyer, Mark. Stevie Wonder. 2009. (Rock & Roll Hall of Famers Ser.). 112p. (gr. 5-8). 63.90 (978-1-60852-475-4(2), Rosen Reference) Rosen Publishing Group, Inc., The.

Bisantz, Kate & Bisantz, Max. Who Was Selena? Qiu, Joseph J. M., illus. 2018. 108p. (J). (978-1-5444-0832-3(3), Penguin Workshop) Penguin Young Readers Group.

Bisantz, Max & Bisantz, Kate. Who Was Selena? 2018. (Who Was... ? Ser.). lib. bdg. 16.00 (978-0-606-41325-1(1)) Turtleback.

Bisantz, Max, et al. Who Was Selena? Qiu, Joseph J. M., illus. 2018. (Who Was? Ser.). 112p. (J). (gr. 3-7). 5.99 (978-1-101-99549-5(1)); lib. bdg. 15.99 (978-1-5247-8675-5(6)) Penguin Young Readers Group. (Penguin Workshop).

Blue Banner Biographies, 26 Bks, Set. (gr. 3-8). (Illus.). lib. bdg. (978-1-58415-323-8(7)); 2005. (J). lib. bdg. 745.80 (978-1-58415-412-9(8)) Mitchell Lane Pubs.

Bodden, Valerie. One Direction. 2015. (Big Time Ser.). (ENG.). 24p. (J). (gr. 1-4). (978-1-60818-497-2(8), 21167, Creative Education) Creative Co., The.

Bolte, Mari. Rock Star Style: Fun Fashions You Can Sketch, 1 vol. Dahl, Sarah, illus. 2013. (Drawing Fun Fashions Ser.). (ENG.). 32p. (J). (gr. 3-9). lib. bdg. 28.65 (978-1-62065-036-3(3), 120716) Capstone.

Boone, Mary. Behind-The-Scenes Music Careers. 2017. (Behind the Glamour Ser.). (ENG., Illus.). 64p. (J). (gr. 4-8). lib. bdg. 31.99 (978-1-5157-4898-4(7), 134483, Capstone Pr.) Capstone.

Borus, Audrey & Miller, Heather. The Rolling Stones, 1 vol. 2018. (Bands That Rock! Ser.). (ENG.). 112p. (YA). (gr. 7-7). 38.93 (978-1-9785-0353-3(9), 16e9ce7a-92e6-4c6f-85d0-883b06ce4617) Enslow Publishing, LLC.

Bowe, Brian J. The Clash, 1 vol. 2018. (Bands That Rock! Ser.). (ENG.). 112p. (YA). (gr. 7-7). pap. 20.95 (978-1-9785-0522-3(1), 2d3dbc2c-d513-4c3e-937e-47ebc4882ea7) Enslow Publishing, LLC.

—The Clash: Punk Rock Band, 1 vol. 2011. (Rebels of Rock Ser.). (ENG., Illus.). 112p. (gr. 5-6). pap. 13.88 (978-1-59845-211-2(8), 2dfa1fac-36e7-4edb-8a07-1af0d1405d51) Enslow Publishing, LLC.

—Judas Priest: Metal Gods, 1 vol. 2009. (Rebels of Rock Ser.). (ENG., Illus.). 112p. (gr. 5-6). pap. 13.88 (978-0-7660-3621-5(9), 072641fc-78a7-4a7a-943b-33042288ea08); lib. bdg. 35.93 (978-0-7660-3029-9(6), 7fa2ddaf-900e-403d-8613-b00a3a04bf1f) Enslow Publishing, LLC.

—The Ramones: American Punk Rock Band, 1 vol. 2011. (Rebels of Rock Ser.). (ENG., Illus.). 128p. (gr. 5-6). pap. 13.88 (978-1-59845-213-6(4),

9bde1a09-784c-43d9-acaf-023915c18d66) Enslow Publishing, LLC.

Braidich, Shelby. Faith Hill, 1 vol. 2010. (Country Music Stars Ser.). (ENG., Illus.). 32p. (J). (gr. 1-1). pap. 11.50 *(978-1-4339-3614-2(3),* 397af1e8-466e-4be7-8431-aee746775093); lib. bdg. 27.93 *(978-1-4339-3613-5(5),* 5a0be484-c168-4a55-85b2-3b1f8d2c74c5) Stevens, Gareth Publishing LLLP.

Braun, Eric. Prince: The Man, the Symbol, the Music. 2017. (Gateway Biographies Ser.). (ENG.). 48p. (J). (gr. 4-8). 12.99 *(978-1-5124-3861-1(8));* 39.99 *(978-1-5124-3860-4(X));* (Illus.). 31.99 *(978-1-5124-3456-9(6),* 0dbaac1c-fa77-45e4-a8c8-e7eaf94a8897); (Illus.). E-Book 47.99 *(978-1-5124-3457-6(4))* Lerner Publishing Group. (Lerner Pubns.).

Breguet, Amy. Yellowcard. 2009. (Contemporary Musicians & Their Music Ser.). 48p. (gr. 6-6). 53.00 *(978-1-61511-948-6(5))* Rosen Publishing Group, Inc., The.

Broadbent, Paul. Rock Stars. 2007. (Trackers-Math Ser.). (gr. 2-5). pap. 5.00 *(978-1-59055-939-0(8))* Pacific Learning, Inc.

Brooks, Riley. Up Close! [25 of Your Fave Stars Inside!]. 2013. (Illus.). 48p. (J). pap. *(978-0-545-54126-8(3))* Scholastic, Inc.

Brown, Risa. Blake Shelton. 2014. (Illus.). 32p. (J). 25.70 *(978-1-61228-641-9(0))* Mitchell Lane Pubs.

Buckley, Annie. Yo-Yo Ma. 2007. (21st Century Skills Library: Life Skills Biographies Ser.). (ENG., Illus.). 48p. (gr. 4-8). lib. bdg. 34.93 *(978-1-60279-077-3(9),* 200049) Cherry Lake Publishing.

Burlingame, Jeff. Aerosmith: Hard Rock Superstars, 1 vol. 2011. (Rebels of Rock Ser.). (ENG., Illus.). 112p. (gr. 5-6). pap. 13.88 *(978-1-59845-210-5(X),* 34b3bf7c-ad65-4176-8725-8c2abe0d2c5e) Enslow Publishing, LLC.

—John Lennon: Fighting for World Peace, 1 vol. 2017. (Rebels with a Cause Ser.). (ENG.). 128p. (gr. 8-8). 38.93 *(978-0-7660-9260-0(7),* 2fac6fb8-4cad-44f6-b30a-6f7f4e799187); pap. 20.95 *(978-0-7660-9564-9(9),* 357c1e29-2022-4086-8779-5216383c67ed) Enslow Publishing, LLC.

—Taylor Swift: Music Superstar, 1 vol. 2012. (Hot Celebrity Biographies Ser.). (ENG., Illus.). 48p. (gr. 5-7). pap. 11.53 *(978-1-59845-286-0(X),* 30da60cc-4fd0-4672-97bc-a610677e8fb1) Enslow Publishing, LLC.

Capaldi, Gina & Pearce, Q. L. Red Bird Sings: The Story of Zitkala-Sa, Native American Author, Musician, & Activist. Capaldi, Gina, illus. 2019. (ENG., Illus.). 32p. (J). (gr. 3-6). 9.99 *(978-1-5415-7836-4(8),* 83dbf92b-8b47-42bc-a6c1-bc8ee2b3c024, Carolrhoda Bks.) Lerner Publishing Group.

Christenson, Maren. Just Like Joan. 2011. 36p. pap. 15.14 *(978-1-4634-3848-7(6))* AuthorHouse.

Cline-Ransome, Lesa. Just a Lucky So & So: The Story of Louis Armstrong. Ransome, James E., illus. 2016. (ENG.). 40p. (J). (gr. 1-4). 18.99 *(978-0-8234-3428-2(1))* Holiday Hse., Inc.

Croft, Malcolm. One Direction in 3D. 2015. (Y Ser.). (ENG., Illus.). 48p. (gr. 4). 12.95 *(978-1-78097-564-1(3))* Carlton Bks., Ltd. GBR. Dist: Two Rivers Distribution.

Da Coll, Ivar. Azucar! Da Coll, Ivar, illus. 2005. (SPA., Illus.). (J). 14.99 *(978-1-930332-65-2(3))* Lectorum Pubns., Inc.

Dakers, Diane. The Beatles: Leading the British Invasion, 1 vol. 2013. (ENG., Illus.). 112p. (J). pap. *(978-0-7787-1045-5(9))* Crabtree Publishing Co.

Dann, Sarah. Beyonce, 1 vol. 2013. (ENG., Illus.). 32p. (J). pap. *(978-0-7787-0039-5(9))* Crabtree Publishing Co.

Doeden, Matt. Green Day: Keeping Their Edge. 2006. (Gateway Biographies Ser.). (ENG., Illus.). 48p. (gr. 4-8). lib. bdg. 26.60 *(978-0-8225-6390-7(8),* Lerner Pubns.) Lerner Publishing Group.

Dominguez, Angela. Sing, Don't Cry. Dominguez, Angela, illus. 2017. (ENG., Illus.). 32p. (J). 17.99 *(978-1-62779-839-6(0),* 900160652, Holt, Henry & Co. Bks. For Young Readers) Holt, Henry & Co.

Earl, C. F. Timbaland. 2012. (J). *(978-1-4222-2554-7(2));* (Illus.). 48p. (gr. 3-4). 19.95 *(978-1-4222-2528-8(3))* Mason Crest.

Edward, Herman. Pink Floyd. 2008. (Pop Rock Ser.). (Illus.). 64p. (YA). (gr. 3-7). lib. bdg. 22.95 *(978-1-4222-0214-2(3))* Mason Crest.

Eggleton, Jill. Up to the Challenge. 2007. (Connectors Ser.). (gr. 2-5). pap. *(978-1-877453-21-2(8))* Global Education Systems Ltd.

Elish, Dan. Louis Armstrong & the Jazz Age. 2005. (Cornerstones of Freedom Ser.). (ENG., Illus.). 48p. (J). (gr. 4-7). 26.00 *(978-0-516-23629-2(6))* Scholastic Library Publishing.

Ellison, Katie. Who Was Bob Marley? 2017. (Who Was... ? Ser.). lib. bdg. 16.00 *(978-0-606-40115-9(6))* Turtleback.

Etinde-Crompton, Charlotte & Crompton, Samuel Willard. Miles Davis: Jazz Musician & Composer, 1 vol. 2019. (Celebrating Black Artists Ser.). (ENG.). 104p. (gr. 7-7). 38.93 *(978-1-9785-1474-4(3),* 10d8d4d4-adb6-44ae-b2de-41b5044d37c8) Enslow Publishing, LLC.

Flynn, Noa. The Who. 2008. (Pop Rock Ser.). (Illus.). 64p. (YA). (gr. 3-7). lib. bdg. 22.95 *(978-1-4222-0196-1(1))* Mason Crest.

Ford, Jeanne Marie. Adele: Music Sensation. 2017. (Superstar Stories Ser.). (ENG.). 24p. (J). (gr. 3-6). lib. bdg. 32.79 *(978-1-5038-1993-1(0),* 211869) Child's World, Inc, The.

—The 12 Most Influential Musicians of All Time. 2018. (Most Influential Ser.). (ENG., Illus.). 32p. (J). (gr. 3-6). 32.80 *(978-1-63235-411-2(X),* 13748, 12-Story Library) Bookstaves, LLC.

Forget, Thomas. The Rolling Stones. 2009. (Rock & Roll Hall of Famers Ser.). 112p. (gr. 5-8). 63.90 *(978-1-60852-478-5(7),* Rosen Reference) Rosen Publishing Group, Inc., The.

Fyffe, Daniel. Indoor Percussion Ensembles & Drum Corps. 2009. (Team Spirit! Ser.). 64p. (gr. 6-6). 53.00 *(978-1-60853-270-4(4))* Rosen Publishing Group, Inc., The.

Gagne, Tammy. Brett Eldridge. 2018. lib. bdg. 25.70 *(978-1-68020-152-9(2))* Mitchell Lane Pubs.

—Chris Stapleton. 2018. 25.70 *(978-1-68020-154-3(9))* Mitchell Lane Pubs.

—Darius Rucker. 2014. (Illus.). 32p. (J). (gr. 1-4). 25.70 *(978-1-61228-639-6(9))* Mitchell Lane Pubs.

—Dierks Bentley. 2018. lib. bdg. 25.70 *(978-1-68020-156-7(5))* Mitchell Lane Pubs.

—Eric Church. 2018. lib. bdg. 25.70 *(978-1-68020-158-1(1))* Mitchell Lane Pubs.

Gallagher, James. The Beatles. 2008. (Pop Rock Ser.). (Illus.). 64p. (YA). (gr. 4-7). lib. bdg. 22.95 *(978-1-4222-0186-2(4))* Mason Crest.

Galletti, Barbara. A Baltimore Symphony Chorus Retrospective. 2004. (Illus.). 56p. pap. 24.00 *(978-0-9748737-0-1(5))* Galletti, Barbara.

Greenwood, Mark. Drummer Boy of John John. Lessac, Frané, illus. 2006. (ENG.). 40p. (J). 18.95 *(978-1-60060-652-6(0))* Lee & Low Bks., Inc.

Gregory, Peter. The Allman Brothers. 2008. (Pop Rock Ser.). (Illus.). 64p. (YA). (gr. 3-7). lib. bdg. 22.95 *(978-1-4222-0188-6(0))* Mason Crest.

—Queen. 2008. (Pop Rock Ser.). (Illus.). 64p. (YA). (gr. 4-7). lib. bdg. 22.95 *(978-1-4222-0193-0(7))* Mason Crest.

Hakit, Ruben. Keith Urban, 1 vol. 2010. (Country Music Stars Ser.). (ENG., Illus.). 32p. (J). (gr. 1-1). pap. 11.50 *(978-1-4339-3605-0(4),* 33d8c8f8-3fe1-4f14-bf92-28b4296ab85f); lib. bdg. 27.93 *(978-1-4339-3604-3(6),* 3c060ad1-db5d-452b-943e-6aebd7503f77) Stevens, Gareth Publishing LLLP.

Hetrick, Hans. The Rolling Stones: Pushing Rock's Boundaries. 2015. (Legends of Rock Ser.). (ENG., Illus.). 32p. (J). (gr. 3-9). lib. bdg. 28.65 *(978-1-4914-1817-8(6),* 127261, Capstone Pr.) Capstone.

Hetrick, Hans, et al. Legends of Rock. 2015. (Legends of Rock Ser.). (ENG.). 32p. (J). (gr. 3-9). 122.60 *(978-1-4914-1819-2(2),* 22172, Capstone Pr.) Capstone.

Hibbert, Clare & Hachette Children's Group. Pop Star - Celeb: Find Out How Your Favorite Pop Stars Made It! 2012. (Celeb Ser.). (ENG., Illus.). 32p. (gr. 4-6). lib. bdg. 28.50 *(978-1-59771-333-7(3))* Sea-To-Sea Pubns.

Hill, Susan. The Rolling Stones. (Unseen Archives Ser.). (Illus.). 384p. (YA). 29.95 *(978-0-7525-8971-8(7))* Parragon, Inc.

Hill, Z. B. Usher. 2012. (J). pap. *(978-1-4222-2557-8(7));* (Illus.). 48p. (gr. 3-4). 19.95 *(978-1-4222-2531-8(3))* Mason Crest.

—50 Cent. 2012. (J). pap. *(978-1-4222-2535-6(6));* (Illus.). 48p. (gr. 3-4). 19.95 *(978-1-4222-2509-7(7))* Mason Crest.

Hinman, Bonnie. John Legend. 2009. (Blue Banner Biography Ser.). (Illus.). 32p. (YA). (gr. 4-7). lib. bdg. 25.70 *(978-1-58415-774-8(7))* Mitchell Lane Pubs.

Holcomb, Mark. The Beach Boys. 2009. (Rock & Roll Hall of Famers Ser.). 112p. (gr. 5-8). 63.90 *(978-1-60852-476-1(0),* Rosen Reference) Rosen Publishing Group, Inc., The.

Hollow, Michele C. Grateful Dead: What a Long, Strange Trip It's Been, 1 vol. 2009. (Rebels of Rock Ser.). (ENG., Illus.). 104p. (gr. 5-6). pap. 13.88 *(978-0-7660-3620-8(0),* 051c6d59-07e4-4c68-b3bb-52ba1002e61b); lib. bdg. 35.93 *(978-0-7660-3028-2(8),* 0ab61506-0b7e-4e82-84eb-73d1b93bf997) Enslow Publishing, LLC.

Hood, Susan. Ada's Violin: The Story of the Recycled Orchestra of Paraguay. Comport, Sally Wern, illus. 2016. (ENG.). 40p. (J). (gr. -1-3). 18.99 *(978-1-4814-3095-1(5),* Simon & Schuster Bks. For Young Readers) Simon & Schuster Bks. For Young Readers.

—El Violín de Ada (Ada's Violin) La Historia de la Orquesta de Instrumentos Reciclados Del Paraguay. McConnell, Shelley, tr. Comport, Sally Wern, illus. 2016. (SPA.). 40p. (J). (gr. -1-3). 19.99 *(978-1-4814-6657-8(7),* Simon & Schuster Bks. For Young Readers) Simon & Schuster Bks. For Young Readers.

Horn, Geoffrey M. Usher, 1 vol. 2005. (Today's Superstars Ser.). (ENG., Illus.). 32p. (gr. 3-3). lib. bdg. 34.60 *(978-0-8368-4235-7(9),* 70baebbd-89cc-4e21-b509-8a24150118af) Stevens, Gareth Publishing LLLP.

Hudak, Heather C. Creative Podcast Producers. 2018. (It's a Digital World! Ser.). (ENG., Illus.). 32p. (J). (gr. 3-6). lib. bdg. 32.79 *(978-1-5321-1531-8(8),* 28916, Checkerboard Library) ABDO Publishing Co.

Huston, Jennifer L. U2: Changing the World Through Rock 'n' Roll. 2015. (Legends of Rock Ser.). (ENG., Illus.). 32p. (J). (gr. 3-9). lib. bdg. 28.65 *(978-1-4914-1818-5(4),* 127262, Capstone Pr.) Capstone.

Hyde, Natalie. Stay Strong: A Musician's Journey from Congo to Canada, 1 vol. 2015. (Arrivals Ser.: 1). (ENG.). 141p. (YA). (gr. 8-12). pap. 12.95 *(978-0-9939351-2-1(5),* 66c60121-95f3-4061-95c0-a26546d26865) Clockwise Pr. CAN. Dist: Firefly Bks., Ltd.

Jeffrey, Laura S. Def Leppard: Arena Rock Band, 1 vol. 2011. (Rebels of Rock Ser.). (ENG., Illus.). 104p. (gr. 5-6). 35.93 *(978-0-7660-3234-7(5),* 6741372a-ce49-457b-b885-09116514c20a); pap. 13.88 *(978-1-59845-208-2(8),* 3af2a85c-0a9a-4f5f-b645-c6cd85887ac2) Enslow Publishing, LLC.

—Pink Floyd: The Rock Band, 1 vol. 2010. (Rebels of Rock Ser.). (ENG., Illus.). 112p. (gr. 5-6). pap. 13.88 *(978-0-7660-3622-2(7),* 70bc7696-3a56-4628-927c-79ae53766b0d); lib. bdg. 35.93 *(978-0-7660-3030-5(X),* af616bdb-0fe2-4368-98b4-23e92a5701e2) Enslow Publishing, LLC.

Johnson, Robin. The Jonas Brothers. 2010. (Superstars! Ser.). (ENG.). 32p. (J). (gr. 3-6). lib. bdg. *(978-0-7787-7247-7(0))* Crabtree Publishing Co.

—Robert Pattinson. 2010. (Superstars! Ser.). (ENG., Illus.). 32p. (J). pap. *(978-0-7787-7260-6(8))* Crabtree Publishing Co.

Jones, Grace. People Who Changed the World: Science & Arts. 2018. (Ideas, Inventions, & Innovators Ser.). (Illus.). 32p. (J). (gr. 4-4). *(978-0-7787-5828-0(1))* Crabtree Publishing Co.

Josephson, Judith P. Louis Armstrong. 2008. (History Maker Biographies Ser.). (Illus.). 47p. (J). (gr. 3-7). lib. bdg. 26.60 *(978-0-8225-7169-8(2),* Lerner Pubns.) Lerner Publishing Group.

Juzwiak, Rich. Lifehouse. 2009. (Contemporary Musicians & Their Music Ser.). 48p. (gr. 6-6). 53.00 *(978-1-61511-941-7(8))* Rosen Publishing Group, Inc., The.

Kallen, Stuart A. The Beatles: British Pop Sensation, 1 vol. 2011. (Innovators Ser.). (ENG., Illus.). 48p. (gr. 4-8). lib. bdg. 36.23 *(978-0-7377-5868-9(6),* 6459cc2f-f708-4473-bbd1-021e6e3069ce, KidHaven Publishing) Greenhaven Publishing LLC.

—Bono. (Role Model Entertainers Ser.). (Illus.). 64p. (YA). 2010. (gr. 7-12). 22.95 *(978-1-4222-0499-3(5))* 2007. pap. 9.95 *(978-1-4222-0786-4(2))* Mason Crest.

Kamberg, Mary-Lane. Bono: Fighting World Hunger & Poverty. (Celebrity Activists Ser.). 112p. (gr. 8-8). 2009. 66.50 *(978-1-61511-828-1(4))* 2008. (ENG., Illus.). (YA). lib. bdg. 39.80 *(978-1-4042-1760-7(6),* 28bf93ac-7a11-4a16-b03f-af526f48b122) Rosen Publishing Group, Inc., The.

—Bono Fighting World Hunger & Poverty. Lt. ed. 2012. 188p. pap. *(978-1-4596-3374-2(1))* ReadHowYouWant.com, Ltd.

Keedle, Jayne. Jonas Brothers, 1 vol. 2009. (Today's Superstars Ser.). (ENG.). 48p. (J). (gr. 3-3). pap. 15.05 *(978-1-4339-2163-6(4),* f7ea20a1-27a4-499c-bc3c-bbc790feacf1); lib. bdg. 34.60 *(978-1-4339-1970-1(2),* 2bf2ddd2-0209-4fc1-890a-56281f589188) Stevens, Gareth Publishing LLLP.

Klepeis, Alicia Z. Music Trivia: What You Never Knew about Rock Stars, Recording Studios, & Smash-Hit Songs. 2018. (Not Your Ordinary Trivia Ser.). (ENG., Illus.). 32p. (J). (gr. 3-9). lib. bdg. 28.65 *(978-1-5435-2529-8(6),* 138026, Capstone Pr.) Capstone.

Konieczny, Vladimir. Struggling for Perfection: The Story of Glenn Gould. 2009. (Stories of Canada Ser.: 5). (ENG., Illus.). 104p. (J). (gr. 4-7). per. 14.95 *(978-1-894917-48-3(0),* Napoleon & Co.) Dundurn Pr. CAN. Dist: Publishers Group West (PGW).

Krohn, Katherine. Michael Jackson: Ultimate Music Legend. 2015. (Gateway Biographies Ser.). (ENG., Illus.). 48p. (J). (gr. 4-8). E-Book 46.65 *(978-1-4677-5976-2(7),* 9781467759762, Lerner Digital) Lerner Publishing Group.

Krull, Kathleen. Lives of the Musicians: Good Times, Bad Times (and What the Neighbors Thought) Hewitt, Kathryn, illus. 2013. (Lives Of ... Ser.). (ENG.). 96p. (J). (gr. 5-7). pap. 8.99 *(978-0-544-23806-0(0),* 1564791, Clarion Bks.) HarperCollins Pubs.

La Bella, Laura. My Chemical Romance. 2009. (Contemporary Musicians & Their Music Ser.). 48p. (gr. 6-6). 53.00 *(978-1-61511-943-1(4))* Rosen Publishing Group, Inc., The.

Lajiness, Katie. One Direction, 1 vol. 2015. (Big Buddy Pop Biographies Ser.). (ENG., Illus.). 32p. (J). (gr. 2-5). lib. bdg. 34.21 *(978-1-68078-056-7(5),* 19039, Big Buddy Bks.) ABDO Publishing Co.

—5 Seconds of Summer, 1 vol. 2015. (Big Buddy Pop Biographies Ser.). (ENG., Illus.). 32p. (J). (gr. 2-5). lib. bdg. 34.21 *(978-1-68078-052-9(2),* 19031, Big Buddy Bks.) ABDO Publishing Co.

Lawson, Carlie. John Legend. 2019. (Hip-Hop & R&B: Culture, Music & Storytelling Ser.). (Illus.). 80p. (J). (gr. 12). lib. bdg. 34.60 *(978-1-4222-4364-0(8))* Mason Crest.

Leavitt, Amie Jane. Keith Urban. 2007. (Blue Banner Biography Ser.). (Illus.). 32p. (YA). (gr. 4-7). lib. bdg. 25.70 *(978-1-58415-619-2(8))* Mitchell Lane Pubs.

—What It's Like to Be the Jonas Brothers: Que Se Siente Al Ser Los Hermanos Jonas. Vega, Eida de la, tr. 2009. (What It's Like to Be/Que se Siente al Ser Ser.). (SPA & ENG., Illus.). 32p. (J). (gr. -1-2). 25.70 *(978-1-58415-842-4(5))* Mitchell Lane Pubs.

Liebman, Dan & Liebman, Dan. I Want to Be a Musician. 2003. (I Want to Be Ser.). (ENG., Illus.). 24p. (J). (gr. -1-2). 14.95 *(978-1-55297-760-6(9),* 29086ba5-8806-4472-a4f5-ce1ad4e48070); pap. 3.99 *(978-1-55297-759-0(5),* c7fc3675-1995-4c11-ae9c-2328d7845042) Firefly Bks., Ltd.

—Quiero Ser Musico. 2003. (Quiero Ser.) Tr. of I Want to Be a Musician. (SPA., Illus.). 24p. (J). (gr. -1-2). pap. 5.99 *(978-1-55297-761-3(7),* 91bff97b-49f4-4b70-a081-abfc3676368d) Firefly Bks., Ltd.

Loh-Hagan, Virginia. Band. 2016. (D. I. Y. Make It Happen Ser.). (ENG., Illus.). 32p. (J). 32.07 *(978-1-63470-498-4(3),* 207723) Cherry Lake Publishing.

Lord, Michelle. A Song for Cambodia, 1 vol. Arihara, Shino, illus. 2008. (ENG.). 32p. (J). (gr. 1-6). 16.95 *(978-1-60060-139-2(1))* Lee & Low Bks., Inc.

Lord, Raymond. Usher. 2008. (Hip-Hop Ser.). (Illus.). 64p. (YA). (gr. 7-12). lib. bdg. 22.95 *(978-1-4222-0131-2(7))* Mason Crest.

Louie, Ai-Ling. Yo-Yo & Yeou-Cheng Ma, Finding Their Way: Amazing Asian Americans. Peng, Cathy, illus. 2012. (Biographies of Amazing Asian Americans Ser.: 2). (ENG.). 48p. (J). pap. 16.99 *(978-0-9787465-0-6(3))* Dragoneagle Pr.

Markel, Rita J. & Poole, Rebecca. Jimi Hendrix. 2006. (Just the Facts Biographies Ser.). (ENG., Illus.). 112p. (gr. 5-12). 27.93 *(978-0-8225-3532-4(7),* Lerner Pubns.) Lerner Publishing Group.

Marlowe, Christie. Dj. 2013. (Earning $50,000 - $100,000 with a High School Diploma or Less Ser.: 14). 64p. (J). (gr. 7-18). 22.95 *(978-1-4222-2892-0(4))* Mason Crest.

Mattern, Joanne. Jonas Brothers. 2008. (Robbie Reader Ser.). (Illus.). 32p. (YA). (gr. 2-5). lib. bdg. 25.70 *(978-1-58415-721-2(6))* Mitchell Lane Pubs.

—Selena. 2011. (Blue Banner Biography Ser.). (Illus.). 32p. (YA). (gr. 4-7). lib. bdg. 25.70 *(978-1-61228-054-7(4))* Mitchell Lane Pubs.

Matthews, Sheelagh. Bono. 2007. (Remarkable People Ser.). (Illus.). 24p. (J). (gr. 3-7). pap. 8.95 *(978-1-59036-638-7(7));* lib. bdg. 24.45 *(978-1-59036-637-0(9))* Weigl Pubs., Inc.

McDonough, Yona Zeldis & Who HQ. Who Was Louis Armstrong? O'Brien, John, illus. 2004. (Who Was? Ser.). 112p. (J). (gr. 3-7). pap. 5.99 *(978-0-448-43368-4(0),* Penguin Workshop) Penguin Young Readers Group.

McIntosh Wooten, Sara. Tim McGraw: Celebrity with Heart, 1 vol. 2010. (Celebrities with Heart Ser.). (ENG., Illus.). 128p. (gr. 6-7). 35.93 *(978-0-7660-3405-1(4),* 36998e15-0543-4afa-b120-f45fd4383d86) Enslow Publishing, LLC.

Medina, Tony. I & I: Bob Marley. Watson, Jesse Joshua, illus. 2009. (ENG.). 48p. (J). (gr. 3-6). 19.95 *(978-1-60060-257-3(6))* Lee & Low Bks., Inc.

Megastars, 12 vols., Set. Incl. Jonas Brothers. Orr, Tamra. (YA). 34.47 *(978-1-4358-3572-6(7),* 0ad7c82e-e565-463e-a30b-931e449c18a6, Rosen Reference); Lady Gaga. Heos, Bridget. (YA). lib. bdg. 34.47 *(978-1-4358-3574-0(3),* ac5215f1-d02d-4c52-9c46-dd59e686674f); Miley Cyrus. Bailey, Diane. (J). lib. bdg. 34.47 *(978-1-4358-3573-3(5),* 89cb6f5f-7cc9-47c7-89df-91d4b8cfb96c, Rosen Reference); Pink. Sirota, Lyn. (YA). 34.47 *(978-1-4358-3577-1(8),* d65a001e-d585-441a-ab57-3087a5179d18, Rosen Reference); Rihanna. Heos, Bridget. (YA). lib. bdg. 34.47 *(978-1-4358-3576-4(X),* 36d91b06-06ef-4e73-8b43-42626cedf983); Taylor Swift. Cefrey, Holly. (YA). 34.47 *(978-1-4358-3575-7(1),* 921b07f9-abfa-4faa-a863-86a1f80465d8, Rosen Reference); (gr. 5-5). 2011. (Megastars Ser.). (ENG., Illus.). 48p. 2010. Set lib. bdg. 206.82 *(978-1-4358-9418-1(9),* 12b67d6a-f1e8-4a07-bc98-028820e0cabf, Rosen Reference) Rosen Publishing Group, Inc., The.

Micklos, John & Micklos, John, Jr. Elvis Presley: I Want to Entertain People, 1 vol. 2010. (American Rebels Ser.). (ENG., Illus.). 160p. (YA). (gr. 9-10). 38.60 *(978-0-7660-3382-5(1),* 9ac42541-9ac9-4a42-be15-4e574dc78d7e) Enslow Publishing, LLC.

Milet Publishing Staff. Music, 1 vol. 2012. (My First Bilingual Book Ser.). (ENG & ARA., Illus.). 24p. (J). (gr. k — 1). bds. 7.99 *(978-1-84059-716-5(X));* bds. 8.99 *(978-1-84059-718-9(6))* Milet Publishing.

—Music - English-Spanish, 1 vol. 2012. (My First Bilingual Book Ser.). (ENG & SPA., Illus.). 24p. (J). (gr. k — 1). bds. 8.99 *(978-1-84059-728-8(3))* Milet Publishing.

—Music - My First Bilingual Book, 1 vol. 2012. (My First Bilingual Book Ser.). (ENG., Illus.). 24p. (J). (gr. k — 1). bds. 7.99 *(978-1-84059-725-7(9));* bds. 7.99 *(978-1-84059-722-6(4))* Milet Publishing.

—La Musique, 1 vol. 2012. (My First Bilingual Book Ser.).Tr. of Music. (ENG & FRE., Illus.). 24p. (J). (gr. k — 1). bds. 7.99 *(978-1-84059-720-2(8))* Milet Publishing.

—My First Bilingual Book-Music, 1 vol. 2012. (My First Bilingual Book Ser.). (ENG., Illus.). 24p. (J). (gr. k — 1). bds. 7.99 *(978-1-84059-717-2(8))* Milet Publishing.

—My First Bilingual Book-Music (English-Farsi), 1 vol. 2012. (My First Bilingual Book Ser.). (ENG., Illus.). 24p. (J). (gr. k — 1). bds. 7.99 *(978-1-84059-719-6(4))* Milet Publishing.

—My First Bilingual Book-Music (English-German), 1 vol. 2012. (My First Bilingual Book Ser.). (ENG & GER., Illus.). 24p. (J). (gr. k — 1). bds. 7.99 *(978-1-84059-721-9(6))* Milet Publishing.

—My First Bilingual Book-Music (English-Korean), 1 vol. 2012. (My First Bilingual Book Ser.). (ENG., Illus.). 24p. (J). (gr. k — 1). bds. 7.99 *(978-1-84059-723-3(2))* Milet Publishing.

—My First Bilingual Book-Music (English-Russian), 1 vol. 2012. (My First Bilingual Book Ser.). (ENG., Illus.). 24p. (J). (gr. k — 1). bds. 7.99 *(978-1-84059-726-4(7))* Milet Publishing.

—My First Bilingual Book-Music (English-Somali), 1 vol. 2012. (My First Bilingual Book Ser.). (ENG., Illus.). 24p. (J). (gr. k — 1). bds. 8.99 *(978-1-84059-727-1(5))* Milet Publishing.

—My First Bilingual Book-Music (English-Turkish), 1 vol. 2012. (My First Bilingual Book Ser.). (ENG., Illus.). 24p. (J). (gr. k — 1). bds. 7.99 *(978-1-84059-729-5(1))* Milet Publishing.

—My First Bilingual Book-Music (English-Urdu), 1 vol. 2012. (My First Bilingual Book Ser.). (ENG., Illus.). 24p. (J). (gr. k — 1). bds. 7.99 *(978-1-84059-730-1(5))* Milet Publishing.

—My First Bilingual Book-Music (English-Vietnamese), 1 vol. 2012. (My First Bilingual Book Ser.). (ENG., Illus.). 24p. (J). (gr. k — 1). bds. 7.99 *(978-1-84059-731-8(3))* Milet Publishing.

Miller, Calvin Craig. Reggae Poet: The Story of Bob Marley. 2007. (Modern Music Masters Ser.). (Illus.). 128p. (YA). (gr. 9-18). lib. bdg. 27.95 *(978-1-59935-071-4(8))* Reynolds, Morgan Inc.

Miller, Heather. AC / DC: Hard Rock Band, 1 vol. 2010. (Rebels of Rock Ser.). (ENG., Illus.). 104p. (gr. 5-6). pap. 13.88 *(978-0-7660-3623-9(5),* 17d2886a-0294-450b-9206-8c2f2fb4e4ad); lib. bdg. 35.93 *(978-0-7660-3031-2(8),* 96bf0553-baa8-407c-bdbc-e4dc3d9a50a4) Enslow Publishing, LLC.

—The Rolling Stones: The Greatest Rock Band, 1 vol. 2011. (Rebels of Rock Ser.). (ENG., Illus.). 112p. (gr. 5-6). 35.93 *(978-0-7660-3231-6(0),* 97b99dd5-182c-4d85-88e1-ead26d5e0ca4); pap. 13.88 *(978-1-59845-209-9(6),* 713c78dc-ad48-42cd-8c63-69d3ef3bf71a) Enslow Publishing, LLC.

Miller, Kat. I Love the Jonas Brothers, 1 vol. 2010. (Fan Club Ser.). (ENG.). 24p. (J). (gr. 2-3). lib. bdg. 27.27 *(978-1-61533-048-5(8),* 53b5250a-83d0-440e-adc6-967ffac16fb0); (Illus.). pap. 9.15 *(978-1-61533-049-2(6),* d03d3ae6-628e-4d5a-82dc-2c493062d86a) Rosen Publishing Group, Inc., The. (Windmill Bks.).

Mitchell Lane Publishers Inc. Staff. Blue Banner Biographies-Child Stars. 2004. (Blue Banner Biography Ser.). (Illus.). (J). (gr. 3-8). lib. bdg. 179.90 *(978-1-58415-354-2(7))* Mitchell Lane Pubs.

—Masters of Music: The World's Greatest Composers, 24 vols., Set. 2003. (Illus.). (gr. 4-8). lib. bdg. 502.80 *(978-1-58415-318-4(0))* Mitchell Lane Pubs.

Mitchells, Brett. Dixie Chicks. 2009. (Contemporary Musicians & Their Music Ser.). 48p. (gr. 6-6). 53.00 *(978-1-61511-932-5(9))* Rosen Publishing Group, Inc., The.

Moore Niver, Heather. Taylor Swift: Singer & Songwriter, 1 vol. 2017. (Junior Biographies Ser.). (ENG.). 24p. (gr. 3-4). pap. 10.35 *(978-0-7660-9057-6(4),* 713fbcfc-92bd-49f4-abca-d6f6263e7ba0) Enslow Publishing, LLC.

Morgan, Joe L. DJ Khaled, Vol. 11. 2018. (Hip-Hop & R & B: Culture, Music & Storytelling Ser.). (Illus.). 80p. (J). (gr. 7). lib. bdg. 33.27 *(978-1-4222-4187-5(4))* Mason Crest.

Morreale, Marie. Real Bios: One Direction. 2014. (ENG.). 48p. (J). pap. 7.95 (978-0-531-21271-4(8)) Scholastic Library Publishing.
Mour, Stanley I. Innovators of American Jazz, 1 vol. 2013. (Inspiring Collective Biographies Ser.). (ENG.). 112p. (gr. 5-6). pap. 13.88 (978-1-4644-0271-5(X), be0b49d6-18d3-40a0-a1ac-31f5d32dc3ae) Enslow Publishing, LLC.
Murphy, Maggie. The Jonas Brothers: Rock Stars, 1 vol. 2010. (Young & Famous Ser.). (ENG.). 24p. (J). (gr. 1-2). lib. bdg. 26.27 (978-1-4488-0646-1(1), 93b62d02-4549-46ad-9a6e-462e2c331f77) Rosen Publishing Group, Inc., The.
—Taylor Swift: Country Music Star, 1 vol. 2010. (Young & Famous Ser.). (ENG.). 24p. (J). (gr. 1-2). lib. bdg. 26.27 (978-1-4488-0645-4(3), f185df64-b096-47f3-b628-aabee44fa0f3) Rosen Publishing Group, Inc., The.
Nagle, Jeanne & Chippendale, Lisa A. Yo-Yo Ma: Grammy Award-Winning Cellist, 1 vol. 2016. (Influential Asians Ser.). (ENG.). 128p. (gr. 6-7). 38.93 (978-0-7660-7899-4(X), 1954119d-e466-414b-866f-f99615f6ecd3) Enslow Publishing, LLC.
Napoli, Tony. Justin Timberlake: Breakout Music Superstar, 1 vol. 2009. (Hot Celebrity Biographies Ser.). (ENG., Illus.). 48p. (gr. 5-7). lib. bdg. 27.93 (978-0-7660-3566-9(2), 54e4c888-84be-4319-8098-1590e0df089d) Enslow Publishing, LLC.
Neimark, Anne E. Johnny Cash: A Twentieth-Century Life. 2007. (Up Close Ser.). (Illus.). 207p. (J). (978-1-4287-3958-1(0), Viking Adult) Penguin Publishing Group.
Newkey-Burden, Chas. One Way Street: One Direction: The Story of Britain's Biggest Boy Band. 2012. (ENG.). 96p. (YA). (gr. 8-12). pap. (978-1-907823-28-2(X)) Grange Communications Ltd.
O'Keefe, Sherry. Spin: The Story of Michael Jackson. 2011. (Modern Music Masters Ser.). (Illus.). 144p. (YA). (gr. 6-9). 28.95 (978-1-59935-134-6(X)) Reynolds, Morgan Inc.
O'Mahony, John. Elton John. 2003. (World Musicmakers Ser.). (Illus.). 64p. (J). 26.20 (978-1-56711-972-5(7), Blackbirch Pr., Inc.) Cengage Gale.
O'Shea, Mick. One Direction: No Limits. 2012. (ENG., Illus.). 198p. (gr. 3). pap. 12.95 (978-0-85965-493-7(1)) Plexus Publishing, Ltd. GBR. Dist: Publishers Group West (PGW).
Parks, Peggy J. Musician. 2003. (Illus.). 48p. (J). 26.20 (978-0-7377-2067-9(0), Greenhaven Pr., Inc.) Cengage Gale.
Patrick, Joseph. Robert Johnson, 1 vol. 2010. (Inspiring Lives Ser.). (ENG.). 32p. (J). (gr. 1-1). lib. bdg. 27.93 (978-1-4339-3619-7(4), d02ef22f-d331-49b3-9bab-402b4c6c5120); (Illus.). pap. 11.50 (978-1-4339-3620-3(8), 463257ef-4ac7-4a7d-b227-2ea187424359) Stevens, Gareth Publishing LLLP.
Patton, Julie. Maximizing Your Studio's Potential: the Student Log Book: Skill Assessment & Progress Management Tools for the College-Level Musician. 2004. 200p. (C). stu. ed., spiral bd. 24.95 (978-0-9762902-0-9(0)) Purple Lizard Pr. LLC.
Peppas, Lynn. M. I. A. 2010. (Superstars! Ser.). (ENG., Illus.). 32p. (J). (gr. 3-6). lib. bdg. (978-0-7787-7249-1(7)) Crabtree Publishing Co.
—One Direction. 2013. (ENG., Illus.). 32p. (J). (978-0-7787-1049-3(1)); pap. (978-0-7787-1053-0(X)) Crabtree Publishing Co.
Polark, Kelly. Rockabet: Classic Edition. Little, Kelli Ann, illus. 2013. 32p. pap. 10.49 (978-0-9888462-0-3(9)) Big Smile Pr., LLC.
Pollack, Pam, et al. Who Is Bono? Thomson, Andrew, illus. 2018. (Who Was? Ser.). 112p. (J). (gr. 3-7). 6.99 (978-0-448-48868-4(X)); lib. bdg. 15.99 (978-1-5247-8851-3(1)) Penguin Young Readers Group. (Penguin Workshop).
Pop Rock: Popular Rock Superstars of Yesterday & Today, 17 vols., Set. Incl. AC/DC. Schlesinger, Ethan. (gr. 3-7). lib. bdg. 22.95 (978-1-4222-0183-1(X)); Aerosmith. Schlesinger, Ethan. (gr. 3-7). lib. bdg. 22.95 (978-1-4222-0184-8(8)); Allman Brothers. Gregory, Peter. (gr. 3-7). lib. bdg. 22.95 (978-1-4222-0188-6(0)); Beatles. Gallagher, James. (gr. 4-7). lib. bdg. 22.95 (978-1-4222-0186-2(4)); Billy Joel. Schlesinger, Ethan. (gr. 3-7). lib. bdg. 22.95 (978-1-4222-0185-5(6)); Bob Marley & the Wailers. Waters, Rosa. (gr. 7-18). lib. bdg. 22.95 (978-1-4222-0192-3(9)); Bruce Springsteen. Simons, Rae. (gr. 4-7). lib. bdg. 22.95 (978-1-4222-0187-9(2)); Doors. Simons, Rae. (gr. 3-7). lib. bdg. 22.95 (978-1-4222-0190-9(2)); Elton John. Schlesinger, Ethan. (gr. 3-7). lib. bdg. 22.95 (978-1-4222-0189-3(9)); Grateful Dead. McIntosh, Kenneth. (gr. 4-7). lib. bdg. 22.95 (978-1-4222-0191-6(0)); Led Zeppelin. Schlesinger, Ethan. (gr. 3-7). lib. bdg. 22.95 (978-1-4222-0212-8(7)); Lynyrd Skynrd. Walker, Ida. (gr. 4-7). lib. bdg. 22.95 (978-1-4222-0213-5(5)); Pink Floyd. Edward, Herman. (gr. 3-7). lib. bdg. 22.95 (978-1-4222-0214-2(3)); Queen. Gregory, Peter. (gr. 4-7). lib. bdg. 22.95 (978-1-4222-0193-0(7)); Rolling Stones. Schlesinger, Ethan. (gr. 3-7). lib. bdg. 22.95 (978-1-4222-0194-7(5)); Who. Flynn, Noa. (gr. 3-7). lib. bdg. 22.95 (978-1-4222-0196-1(1)); (Illus.). 64p. (YA). 2008. 2007. Set lib. bdg. 390.15 (978-1-4222-0182-4(1)) Mason Crest.
Pratt, Mary K. Michael Jackson: King of Pop. (Lives Cut Short Ser.). (YA). 2011. (gr. 7-12). 71.36 (978-1-61641-447-4(2)) 2010. (ENG.). 112p. (gr. 6-12). lib. bdg. 41.36 (978-1-60453-788-8(4), 11185) ABDO Publishing Co. (Essential Library).
Rappaport, Doreen. John's Secret Dreams: The Life of John Lennon. Collier, Bryan, illus. 2016. (Big Words Book Ser.: 2). (ENG.). 48p. (J). (gr. 1-3). pap. 8.99 (978-1-4847-4962-3(6)) Little, Brown Bks. for Young Readers.
Raschka, Chris. Mysterious Thelonious. Raschka, Chris, illus. (Illus.). pap. 18.95 incl. audio compact disk (978-1-59112-421-4(2)) Live Oak Media.
Rawson, Katherine. The Jonas Brothers, 1 vol. 2009. (Kid Stars! Ser.). (ENG.). 24p. (J). (gr. 2-3). pap. 10.40 (978-1-4358-3402-6(X), c9e9a18c-fbd2-4b5b-a945-38ab7f2f73b2); (Illus.). lib. bdg. 26.27 (978-1-4042-8134-9(7), a7294132-466b-4350-819f-0e4c457b934b) Rosen Publishing Group, Inc., The.
—Taylor Swift, 1 vol. 2009. (Kid Stars! Ser.). (ENG.). 24p. (J). (gr. 2-3). pap. 10.40 (978-1-4358-3410-1(0), 9f7a4f22-9409-42e8-aedf-302381f7a233); (Illus.). lib. bdg. 26.27 (978-1-4042-8138-7(X), 2921c389-8394-49cb-ba64-07cf5324fe10) Rosen Publishing Group, Inc., The. (PowerKids Pr.).
Reisfeld, Randi. This Is the Sound: The Best of Alternative Rock. 2011. (ENG.). 144p. (YA). (gr. 9). pap. 8.99 (978-1-4424-3098-3(2), Simon Pulse) Simon Pulse.
Richards, Keith. Gus & Me: The Story of My Granddad & My First Guitar. Richards, Theodora, illus. 2014. (ENG.). 32p. (J). (gr. -1-3). 18.00 (978-0-316-32065-8(X)) Little, Brown Bks. for Young Readers.
Robertson, Robbie, et al. Legends, Icons & Rebels: Music That Changed the World. 2016. (Illus.). 128p. (J). (gr. 4-7). pap. 18.99 (978-1-101-91868-5(3), Tundra Bks.) Tundra Bks. CAN. Dist: Penguin Random Hse. LLC.
Robertson, Sebastian. Rock & Roll Highway: The Robbie Robertson Story. Gustavson, Adam, illus. 2014. (ENG.). 40p. (J). (gr. 1-4). 21.99 (978-0-8050-9473-2(3), 900079390, Holt, Henry & Co. Bks. For Young Readers) Holt, Henry & Co.
Robinson, Lisa. Madame Saqui: Revolutionary Rope Dancer. Green, Rebecca, illus. 2020. 44p. (J). (gr. -1-3). 17.99 (978-0-525-57997-7(4), Schwartz & Wade Bks.) Random Hse. Children's Bks.
Robson, David. Prince: Singer-Songwriter, Musician, & Record Producer. (Transcending Race in America Ser.). 64p. (YA). 2010. (Illus.). (gr. 4-8). lib. bdg. 22.95 (978-1-4222-1614-9(4)) 2009. (gr. 5-18). pap. 9.95 (978-1-4222-1628-6(4)) Mason Crest.
Rosen, Steven & Steventon, John. History of Rock. 2009. (Crabtree Contact Ser.). (ENG., Illus.). 32p. (J). (gr. 6-8). pap. (978-0-7787-3844-2(2)); lib. bdg. (978-0-7787-3823-7(X)) Crabtree Publishing Co.
Rubin, Susan Goldman. Music Was IT: Young Leonard Bernstein. 2015. (ENG., Illus.). 192p. (J). (gr. 4-7). pap. 12.95 (978-1-58089-345-9(7)) Charlesbridge Publishing, Inc.
Russell-Brown, Katheryn. A Voice Named Aretha. Freeman, Laura, illus. 2020. (ENG.). 40p. (J). 17.99 (978-1-68119-850-7(9), 900189371, Bloomsbury Children's Bks.) Bloomsbury Publishing USA.
Ryals, Lexi. More Jammin' with the Jonas Brothers: An Unauthorized Biography. 2009. (Unauthorized Biographies Ser.). (ENG.). 192p. (J). (gr. 5-8). 17.44 (978-0-8431-8929-2(0)) Penguin Young Readers Group.
Saddleback Educational Publishing Staff. Jay-Z. 2013. (Hip-Hop Biographies (Saddleback Publishing) Ser.). (YA). lib. bdg. 23.25 (978-0-606-31484-8(9)) Turtleback.
—Nicki Minaj. 2013. (Hip-Hop Biographies (Saddleback Publishing) Ser.). (YA). lib. bdg. 23.25 (978-0-606-31487-9(3)) Turtleback.
—Pitbull. 2013. (Hip-Hop Biographies (Saddleback Publishing) Ser.). (YA). lib. bdg. 23.25 (978-0-606-31488-6(1)) Turtleback.
Saddleback Educational Publishing Staff, ed. The Beatles, 1 vol. unabr. ed. 2007. (Graphic Biographies Ser.). (ENG., Illus.). 25p. (YA). (gr. 4-12). pap. 9.75 (978-1-59905-216-8(4)) Saddleback Educational Publishing, Inc.
Saucerman, Linda. Ozzy & Kelly Osbourne, 1 vol. 2004. (Famous Families Ser.). (ENG., Illus.). 48p. (J). (gr. 5-5). lib. bdg. 34.47 (978-1-4042-0262-7(5), ebe31881-b3b8-4f53-aa2f-1f214014ea28) Rosen Publishing Group, Inc., The.
—Ozzy Osbourne & Kelly Osbourne. 2009. (Famous Families Ser.). 48p. (gr. 5-5). 53.00 (978-1-61512-509-8(4)) Rosen Publishing Group, Inc., The.
Saulmon, Greg. Linkin Park. 2009. (Contemporary Musicians & Their Music Ser.). 48p. (gr. 6-6). 53.00 (978-1-61511-942-4(6)) Rosen Publishing Group, Inc., The.
Sauver, Dennis St. Finn Wolfhard. 2018. (Big Buddy Pop Biographies Ser.). (ENG.). 32p. (J). (gr. 2-5). lib. bdg. 34.21 (978-1-5321-1804-3(X), 30654, Big Buddy Bks.) ABDO Publishing Co.
Schilling, Vincent. Native Musicians in the Groove, 1 vol. 2009. (Native Trailblazers Ser.: 2). (ENG.). 132p. (YA). (gr. 8-12). pap. 9.95 (978-0-9779183-4-8(3), 7th Generation) BPC.
Schlesinger, Ethan. Billy Joel. (Pop Rock Ser.). (Illus.). 64p. (YA). (gr. 3-7). 2008. lib. bdg. 22.95 (978-1-4222-0185-5(6)) 2007. pap. 7.95 (978-1-4222-0315-6(8)) Mason Crest.
—Led Zeppelin. 2007. (Popular Rock Superstars of Yesterday & Today Ser.). (Illus.). 64p. (YA). (gr. 3-7). pap. 7.95 (978-1-4222-0324-8(7)) Mason Crest.
—The Rolling Stones. 2008. (Pop Rock Ser.). (Illus.). 64p. (YA). (gr. 3-7). lib. bdg. 22.95 (978-1-4222-0194-7(5)) Mason Crest.
Schlessinger Media Staff, prod. My Family from Japan. 2003. (Families Around the World Ser.). (J). (gr. k-4). pap., tchr. ed. 19.95 incl. VHS (978-1-57225-644-6(3)) Schlessinger Media.
Schuman, Michael A. Led Zeppelin, 1 vol. 2018. (Bands That Rock! Ser.). (ENG.). 112p. (YA). (gr. 7-7). 38.93 (978-1-9785-0349-6(0), 5c643f02-7544-4912-90cc-b41a1490a211) Enslow Publishing, LLC.
—Led Zeppelin: Legendary Rock Band, 1 vol. 2010. (Rebels of Rock Ser.). (ENG., Illus.). 112p. (gr. 5-6). lib. bdg. 35.93 (978-0-7660-3026-8(1), fe9b58c7-919c-495f-bb29-b790cda4a7c1) Enslow Publishing, LLC.
Shea, Mary Molly. Taylor Swift, 1 vol. 2010. (Country Music Stars Ser.). (ENG., Illus.). 32p. (J). (gr. 1-1). pap. 11.50 (978-1-4339-3611-1(9), aa8d0ab2-3397-4baa-bf59-d898a1fdb738); lib. bdg. 27.93 (978-1-4339-3610-4(0), a102993e-ed47-4b72-ad14-5f0f33e34f60) Stevens, Gareth Publishing LLLP.
Shea, Therese M. John Lee Hooker, 1 vol. 2010. (Inspiring Lives Ser.). (ENG.). 32p. (J). (gr. 1-1). lib. bdg. 27.93 (978-1-4339-3625-8(9), 931a8baf-a146-4de5-96b6-4fb5c5340c41); (Illus.). pap. 11.50 (978-1-4339-3626-5(7), 31dd1041-73ae-444a-addd-441cfa8d13b2) Stevens, Gareth Publishing LLLP.
Sierra i Fabra, Jordi. John Lennon - Imagina que esto fue Real. 2005. (SPA.). 168p. (YA). (978-958-30-1702-5(7)) Panamericana Editorial.
Simons, Rae. Bruce Springsteen. (Pop Rock Ser.). (Illus.). 64p. (YA). (gr. 4-7). 2008. lib. bdg. 22.95 (978-1-4222-0187-9(2)) 2007. pap. 7.95 (978-1-4222-0321-7(2)) Mason Crest.
—The Doors. 2008. (Pop Rock Ser.). (Illus.). 64p. (YA). (gr. 3-7). lib. bdg. 22.95 (978-1-4222-0190-9(2)) Mason Crest.
Slavicek, Louise Chipley. Carlos Santana. 2006. (Great Hispanic Heritage Ser.). (ENG., Illus.). 112p. (gr. 6-12). lib. bdg. 35.00 (978-0-7910-8844-9(8), P114456, Facts On File) Infobase Holdings, Inc.
Sloate, Susan. Ray Charles: Find Another Way! 2006. (Defining Moments Ser.). (Illus.). 32p. (J). (gr. 2-5). lib. bdg. 28.50 (978-1-59716-267-8(1)) Bearport Publishing Co., Inc.
Smith Weber, Terri. Dixie Chicks. 2004. (J). pap. (978-0-9740180-9-6(0), Bios for Kids) Panda Publishing, L.L.C.
Snellgrove, Chris. Bruno Mars, Vol. 11. 2018. (Hip-Hop & R & B: Culture, Music & Storytelling Ser.). (Illus.). 80p. (J). (gr. 7). lib. bdg. 33.27 (978-1-4222-4178-3(5)) Mason Crest.
Sooner, Jeffrey. Rascal Flatts, 1 vol. 2010. (Country Music Stars Ser.). (ENG., Illus.). 32p. (J). (gr. 1-1). pap. 11.50 (978-1-4339-3617-3(8), 428c8905-e347-4574-85ab-a1269ba154b3); lib. bdg. 27.93 (978-1-4339-3616-6(X), 1f2d9b52-fcbd-4fcb-8bb9-e4827e63c664) Stevens, Gareth Publishing LLLP.
Spencer, Liv. Taylor Swift: Every Day Is a Fairytale - The Unofficial Story. 2010. (ENG., Illus.). 155p. (YA). (gr. 7-18). pap. 14.95 (978-1-55022-931-8(1), a74e0eb1-f39d-41b8-99fe-5a351074977a) ECW Pr. CAN. Dist: Baker & Taylor Publisher Services (BTPS).
Stassi, Laura. Pink Floyd, 1 vol. 2018. (Bands That Rock! Ser.). (ENG.). 112p. (YA). (gr. 7-7). 38.93 (978-1-9785-0350-2(4), b35fb468-8b0a-465d-ac4b-fca511c94d55) Enslow Publishing, LLC.
Stevens, Cara J. Bts: Rise of Bangtan. 2018. (ENG., Illus.). 96p. (J). (gr. 3-7). pap. 8.99 (978-0-06-288648-4(7), HarperCollins) HarperCollins Pubs.
Steventon, John. DJing. 2009. (Crabtree Contact Ser.). (ENG., Illus.). 32p. (J). (gr. 6-8). pap. (978-0-7787-3840-4(X)); lib. bdg. (978-0-7787-3819-0(1)) Crabtree Publishing Co.
Stewart, Mark. Music Legends, 1 vol. 2009. (Ultimate 10: Entertainment Ser.). (ENG.). 48p. (gr. 3-3). (J). pap. 11.50 (978-1-4339-2213-8(4), 5545e1c1-8bf0-4979-828b-2c94ed101110); (YA). lib. bdg. 33.67 (978-0-8368-9165-2(1), 5f494f81-e911-4c16-8b2a-fb4ea4d5c341) Stevens, Gareth Publishing LLLP.
Strand, Jennifer. Beyoncé. 2016. (Stars of Music Ser.). (ENG.). 24p. (J). (gr. -1-2). lib. bdg. 31.36 (978-1-68079-917-0(7), 24138, Abdo Zoom-Launch) ABDO Publishing Co.
Subset 2: Masters of Music. (Illus.). 9p. (gr. 4-8). lib. bdg. (978-1-58415-352-8(0)) Mitchell Lane Pubs.
Thomson, Cindy. Kenny Chesney. 2009. (Sharing the American Dream Ser.). 64p. (YA). (gr. 7-12). 22.95 (978-1-4222-0594-5(0)) Mason Crest.
Thorpe, Jack. Little Mix: Test Your Super-Fan Status. 2019. (ENG.). 96p. (J). (gr. 4-6). pap. 9.99 (978-1-78055-604-8(7)) O'Mara, Michael Bks., Ltd. GBR. Dist: Independent Pubs. Group.
Tierney, Tom. Rock & Roll Legends of the 1950s Paper Dolls. 2007. (Dover Celebrity Paper Dolls Ser.). (ENG., Illus.). 32p. (J). (gr. 4-8). pap. 6.95 (978-0-486-45660-7(9)) Dover Pubns., Inc.
Timmons, Angie. U2, 1 vol. 2018. (Bands That Rock! Ser.). (ENG.). 112p. (YA). (gr. 7-7). 38.93 (978-1-9785-0354-0(7), 10e7a089-5d76-4ba0-9c53-5b089db65dc1) Enslow Publishing, LLC.
Trachtenberg, Martha P. Bono: Rock Star Activist, 1 vol. 2008. (People to Know Today Ser.). (ENG., Illus.). 128p. (gr. 6-7). lib. bdg. 35.93 (978-0-7660-2695-7(7), 0212d014-ce56-4d7e-9e0e-33424331bb2c) Enslow Publishing, LLC.
Tracy, Kathleen. Gwen Stefani. 2006. (Blue Banner Biography Ser.). (Illus.). 32p. (YA). (gr. 4-7). lib. bdg. 25.70 (978-1-58415-514-0(0)) Mitchell Lane Pubs.
—Mario. 2006. (Blue Banner Biography Ser.). (Illus.). 32p. (J). (gr. 3-8). lib. bdg. 25.70 (978-1-58415-391-7(1)) Mitchell Lane Pubs.
—Orianthi. 2010. (Blue Banner Biography Ser.). (Illus.). 32p. (YA). (gr. 4-7). lib. bdg. 25.70 (978-1-58415-913-1(8)) Mitchell Lane Pubs.
Triumph Books Staff. One Direction: Where We Are. 2014. (ENG.). 112p. (YA). (gr. 7). pap. 12.95 (978-1-62937-019-4(3)) Triumph Bks.
Ungs, Tim. Paul McCartney & Stella McCartney, 1 vol. 2004. (Famous Families Ser.). (ENG., Illus.). 48p. (J). (gr. 5-5). lib. bdg. 34.47 (978-1-4042-0263-4(3), e941e498-bc77-4ada-9e55-05fee787dc87) Rosen Publishing Group, Inc., The.
—Paul Mccartney & Stella Mccartney. 2009. (Famous Families Ser.). 48p. (gr. 5-5). 53.00 (978-1-61512-510-4(8)) Rosen Publishing Group, Inc., The.
Venezia, Mike. Duke Ellington (Revised Edition) (Getting to Know the World's Greatest Composers) (Library Edition) Venezia, Mike, illus. 2017. (Getting to Know the World's Greatest Composers Ser.). (ENG., Illus.). 40p. (J). (gr. 3-4). lib. bdg. 29.00 (978-0-531-22658-2(1), Children's Pr.) Scholastic Library Publishing.
—Leonard Bernstein (Revised Edition) (Getting to Know the World's Greatest Composers) Venezia, Mike, illus. rev. ed. 2017. (Getting to Know the World's Greatest Composers Ser.). (ENG., Illus.). 40p. (J). (gr. 3-4). pap. 7.95 (978-0-531-23034-3(1), Children's Pr.) Scholastic Library Publishing.
—Leonard Bernstein (Revised Edition) (Getting to Know the World's Greatest Composers) (Library Edition) Venezia, Mike, illus. 2017. (Getting to Know the World's Greatest Composers Ser.). (ENG., Illus.). 40p. (J). (gr. 3-4). lib. bdg. 29.00 (978-0-531-22656-8(5), Children's Pr.) Scholastic Library Publishing.
Waters, Rosa. Bob Marley & the Wailers. (Pop Rock Ser.). (Illus.). 64p. (YA). 2008. (gr. 7-18). lib. bdg. 22.95 (978-1-4222-0192-3(9)) 2007. pap. 7.95 (978-1-4222-0317-0(4)) Mason Crest.
Watson, Cindy. Out of Darkness: The Jeff Healey Story. 2010. (ENG., Illus.). 134p. (YA). (gr. k-6). pap. 21.99 (978-1-55488-706-4(2), 9781554887064) Dundurn Pr. CAN. Dist: Ingram Publisher Services.
Waxman, Laura Hamilton. Cool Kid Musicians. 2020. (Lightning Bolt Books (r) — Kids in Charge! Ser.). (ENG., Illus.). 24p. (J). (gr. 1-3). 29.32 (978-1-5415-7704-6(3), 2e289793-ef75-400a-bbbf-5f263e82b28c, Lerner Pubns.) Lerner Publishing Group.
Weintraub, Aileen. Kiss: I Wanna Rock & Roll All Night, 1 vol. 2009. (Rebels of Rock Ser.). (ENG., Illus.). 112p. (gr. 5-6). lib. bdg. 35.93 (978-0-7660-3027-5(X), e5140a54-8143-4870-abd7-f936c142f440) Enslow Publishing, LLC.
Wentzel, Jim. The Beatles. 2009. (Rock & Roll Hall of Famers Ser.). 112p. (gr. 5-8). 63.90 (978-1-60852-477-8(9), Rosen Reference) Rosen Publishing Group, Inc., The.
Wheeler, Jill C. Faith Hill. 2003. (Star Tracks Ser.). (Illus.). 64p. (gr. 3-8). lib. bdg. 27.07 (978-1-57765-771-2(3), Abdo & Daughters) ABDO Publishing Co.
Wheeler, Opal & Deucher, Sybil. Sebastian Bach: the Boy from Thuringia. Greenwalt, Mary, illus. l.t. ed. 2005. 126p. per. 13.95 (978-0-9746505-1-7(X), 4354) Zeezok Publishing, LLC.
White, Danny. One Direction: La Historia. 2nd ed. 2013. (Corazon Joven Ser.). (SPA., Illus.). 256p. (YA). pap. 15.95 (978-84-15579-15-1(2)) Ediciones B ESP. Dist: Spanish Pubs., LLC.
White, Katherine. Elton John. 2009. (Rock & Roll Hall of Famers Ser.). 112p. (gr. 5-8). 63.90 (978-1-60852-473-0(6), Rosen Reference) Rosen Publishing Group, Inc., The.
Whiting, Jim. The Life & Times of Gilbert & Sullivan. 2004. (Masters of Music Ser.). (Illus.). 48p. (gr. 4-8). lib. bdg. 20.95 (978-1-58415-276-7(1)) Mitchell Lane Pubs.
Wilcox, Christine. Justin Bieber, 1 vol. 2013. (People in the News Ser.). (ENG., Illus.). 96p. (gr. 7-7). lib. bdg. 41.03 (978-1-4205-0756-0(7), 5564123d-8ab4-4a6e-b2c9-c6f22d23d414, Lucent Pr.) Greenhaven Publishing LLC.
Willett, Edward. Jimi Hendrix: Kiss the Sky, 1 vol. 2010. (American Rebels Ser.). (ENG., Illus.). 160p. (gr. 9-10). lib. bdg. 38.60 (978-0-7660-2449-6(0), 707a1bd2-198f-443c-a2a8-daa8c888d782) Enslow Publishing, LLC.
Williams, Imogen. 5 Seconds of Summer: 100% Unofficial. 2014. (ENG., Illus.). 24p. (J). (gr. 3-7). pap. 7.99 (978-1-4814-4365-4(8), Aladdin) Simon & Schuster Children's Publishing.
Wilson, Rosie. Kenny Chesney, 1 vol. 2010. (Country Music Stars Ser.). (ENG., Illus.). 32p. (J). (gr. 1-1). pap. 11.50 (978-1-4339-3608-1(9), f554fced-6d02-451b-9b5e-28a2ce0a7c4f); lib. bdg. 27.93 (978-1-4339-3607-4(0), 0c18087d-6a08-4a61-b389-2e6201cf95d3) Stevens, Gareth Publishing LLLP.
Winter, Jonah. Dizzy. Qualls, Sean, illus. 2006. (J). 16.99 (978-0-439-50736-3(7), Levine, Arthur A. Bks.) Scholastic, Inc.
—Elvis Is King! Red Nose Studio, illus. 2019. 40p. (J). (gr. -1-3). 18.99 (978-0-399-55470-4(X), Schwartz & Wade Bks.) Random Hse. Children's Bks.
Wittenstein, Barry. Sonny's Bridge: Jazz Legend Sonny Rollins Finds His Groove. Mallett, Keith, illus. 2019. 40p. (J). (gr. 1-4). lib. bdg. 17.99 (978-1-58089-881-2(5)) Charlesbridge Publishing, Inc.
Wood, Ramona. The Goat Woman of Smackover: An Arkansas Legend. Wood, Ramona, . 2006. (Illus.). 32p. (J). pap. 11.00 (978-0-9758622-1-6(9)) ABC Pr.
Woog, Adam. Blake Shelton, 1 vol. 2015. (People in the News Ser.). (ENG., Illus.). 104p. (gr. 7-7). 41.03 (978-1-4205-1225-0(0), 40ee8d43-1f4b-4de5-a025-dfc3757e0506, Lucent Pr.) Greenhaven Publishing LLC.
Wyckoff, Edwin Brit. Electric Guitar Man: The Genius of les Paul, 1 vol. 2008. (Genius at Work! Great Inventor Biographies Ser.). (ENG., Illus.). 32p. (gr. 3-3). lib. bdg. 26.60 (978-0-7660-2847-0(X), 276b0fc5-16a0-4a8e-b418-483fafe20c1f, Enslow Elementary) Enslow Publishing, LLC.
Wyner, Zach. Music. 2014. (Urban Entrepreneurs Ser.). (gr. 3-8). pap. 8.99 (978-1-61570-873-4(1)) Scobre Pr. Corp.
Yasuda, Anita. Taylor Swift. 2010. (Remarkable People Ser.). (Illus.). 24p. (J). (gr. 4-6). pap. 11.95 (978-1-61690-158-5(6)); lib. bdg. 25.70 (978-1-61690-157-8(8)) Weigl Pubs., Inc.
Zimmerman, Robert K. Switchfoot, 1 vol. 2006. (Contemporary Musicians & Their Music Ser.). (ENG., Illus.). 48p. (YA). (gr. 6-6). lib. bdg. 34.47 (978-1-4042-0709-7(0), dad774c2-9a4c-4e0f-b792-3c54d034aeb5) Rosen Publishing Group, Inc., The.

MUSICIANS, AFRICAN AMERICAN

see African American Musicians

MUSICIANS, BLACK

see African American Musicians

MUSICIANS—FICTION

Acampora, Paul. Rachel Spinelli Punched Me in the Face. 2013. (ENG.). 192p. (J). (gr. 8-12). pap. 14.99 (978-1-250-01669-0(X), 900087083) Square Fish.
Albertalli, Becky. Leah on the off Beat. 2019. (ENG.). (YA). (gr. 9). lib. bdg. 21.80 (978-1-6636-2843-5(2)) Perfection Learning Corp.
—Leah on the Offbeat. (ENG.). 368p. (YA). (gr. 9). 2019. pap. 10.99 (978-0-06-264381-0(9)) 2018. 17.99 (978-0-06-264380-3(0)) HarperCollins Pubs. (Balzer & Bray).
Alexander, Kwame. Acoustic Rooster & His Barnyard Band. Bowers, Tim, illus. 2011. (ENG.). 32p. (J). (gr. 1-4). lib. bdg. 17.99 (978-1-58536-688-0(9), 202227) Sleeping Bear Pr.
Alexander, Kwame & Rand Hess, Mary. Solo, 1 vol. 2019. (ENG., Illus.). 464p. (YA). (gr. 8). pap. 15.99 (978-0-310-76188-4(3), Clarion Bks.) HarperCollins Pubs.
Alger, Horatio. Phil the Fiddler. rev. ed. 2006. (ENG.). 224p. 27.95 (978-1-4218-2091-0(9), 1st World Library - Literary Society) 1st World Publishing, Inc.
—Phil the Fiddler. 2006. pap. (978-1-4068-0667-0(6)) Echo Library.

—The Young Musician. reprint ed. pap. 79.00 *(978-1-4047-3629-0(8))* Classic Textbooks.

—The Young Musician. 2006. pap. *(978-1-4068-0673-1(0))* Echo Library.

Amato, Mary. Get Happy. 2014. (ENG.). 244p. (YA). (gr. 7-12). 16.99 *(978-1-60684-522-6(5),* 037db3b0-4e02-4a16-b6fd-3f2e64eeac4d, Carolrhoda Lab™) Lerner Publishing Group.

—Guitar Notes. 2014. (ENG., Illus.). 320p. (YA). (gr. 7-12). pap. 10.99 *(978-1-60684-503-5(9),* 012af6c8-2b15-4576-82cf-476ac42f8d26, Carolrhoda Lab™) Lerner Publishing Group.

Andrews, Jesse. The Haters. 2017. (ENG.). 336p. (YA). (gr. 8-17). pap. 9.95 *(978-1-4197-2370-4(7),* 1140003, Amulet Bks.) Abrams, Inc.

—The Haters. 2017. (YA). lib. bdg. 20.80 *(978-0-606-39688-2(8))* Turtleback.

Andrews, Julie. Simeon's Gift. 2003. (J). 169.90 *(978-0-06-056905-1(0))*; 169.90 *(978-0-06-056906-8(9))* HarperCollins Pubs. (Julie Andrews Collection).

Andrews, Julie & Hamilton, Emma Walton. Simeon's Gift. Spirin, Gennady, illus. 2006. 30p. (J). (gr. 4-8). reprint ed. 17.00 *(978-1-4223-5855-9(0))* DIANE Publishing Co.

—Simeon's Gift. Spirin, Gennady, illus. 2003. (Julie Andrews Collection). 40p. (J). 17.89 *(978-0-06-008915-3(6),* Julie Andrews Collection) HarperCollins Pubs.

Andrews, Julie, et al. Simeon's Gift. Spirin, Gennady, illus. 2003. (Julie Andrews Collection). (ENG.). 40p. (J). (gr. k-4). 19.99 *(978-0-06-008914-6(8))* HarperCollins Pubs.

Armstrong, Samuel, illus. Gene Autry & the Lost Dogie. 2011. 30p. 35.95 *(978-1-258-02476-5(4))* Literary Licensing, LLC.

Asphyxia. The Grimstones Collection. Asphyxia, illus. 2015. (Grimstones Ser.). (ENG., Illus.). 488p. (J). (gr. 3-7). pap. 17.99 *(978-1-76011-391-9(3))* Allen & Unwin AUS. Dist: Independent Pubs. Group.

Auch, M. J. Guitar Boy. 2012. (ENG.). 288p. (J). (gr. 5-9). pap. 15.99 *(978-0-312-64124-5(9),* 900077675) Square Fish.

Autry, Gene. Gene Autry & the Land Grab Mystery. 2011. 286p. 48.95 *(978-1-258-02327-0(X))* Literary Licensing, LLC.

Beaudoin, Sean. Wise Young Fool. 2013. (ENG.). 448p. (YA). (gr. 9-17). 18.00 *(978-0-316-20379-1(3))* Little, Brown Bks. for Young Readers.

Berlin, Eric. The Puzzler's Mansion: The Puzzling World of Winston Breen. 2013. (Puzzling World of Winston Breen Ser.: 3). 272p. (J). (gr. 3-7). 8.99 *(978-0-14-242643-2(1),* Puffin Books) Penguin Young Readers Group.

Blake, Ashley Herring. How to Make a Wish. 2017. (ENG.). 336p. (YA). (gr. 9). 17.99 *(978-0-544-81519-3(X),* 1642371, Clarion Bks.) HarperCollins Pubs.

Blevins, Wiley. The Bremen Town Ghosts. Cox, Steve, illus. 2017. (Scary Tales Retold Ser.). (ENG.). 24p. (J). (gr. k-3). pap. 6.99 *(978-1-63440-169-2(7),* 7d3fe735-8925-41c9-b3bf-b28bcf5166db) Red Chair Pr.

Blume, Lesley M. M. The Rising Star of Rusty Nail. 2009. (ENG.). 288p. (J). (gr. 3-7). 7.99 *(978-0-440-42111-5(X),* Yearling) Random Hse. Children's Bks.

Bradford, Chris. Bodyguard: Target (Book 7) 2018. (Bodyguard Ser.: 7). (ENG.). 288p. (J). (gr. 5). pap. 8.99 *(978-1-5247-3935-5(9),* Philomel Bks.) Penguin Young Readers Group.

—Bodyguard: Traitor (Book 8) 2018. (Bodyguard Ser.: 8). (ENG., Illus.). 224p. (J). (gr. 5). pap. 8.99 *(978-1-5247-3937-9(5),* Philomel Bks.) Penguin Young Readers Group.

Brezenoff, Steve. Guitarist Wanted. 2017. (Boy Seeking Band Ser.). (ENG., Illus.). 96p. (J). (gr. 5-8). lib. bdg. 25.99 *(978-1-4965-4448-3(X),* 134762, Stone Arch Bks.) Capstone.

Brouwer, Sigmund. Rock the Boat. 1 vol. 2015. (Orca Limelights Ser.). (ENG.). 128p. (J). (gr. 4-7). pap. 9.95 *(978-1-4598-0455-5(4))* Orca Bk. Pubs. USA.

Brouwer, Sigmund & Morgan, Cindy. True Blue. 1 vol. 2018. (Orca Limelights Ser.). (ENG.). 128p. (J). (gr. 4-7). pap. 9.95 *(978-1-4598-1580-3(7),* 1459815807) Orca Bk. Pubs. USA.

Brown, Bea. Wally the Cockeyed Cricket. 2017. (ENG., Illus.). (J). pap. 9.95 *(978-1-947825-63-5(1))* Yorkshire Publishing Group.

Brown, Dan. Wild Symphony. Batori, Susan, illus. 2020. (ENG.). 44p. (J). (gr. -1-2). 19.99 *(978-0-593-12384-3(0),* Rodale Kids) Random Hse. Children's Bks.

Brown, Dan. Wild Symphony. Batori, Susan, illus. 2023. (ENG.). 44p. (J). (gr. -1-2). pap. 8.99 ***(978-0-593-70423-3(1),*** Dragonfly Bks.) Random Hse. Children's Bks.

Burstein, Lisa. MIA & the Bad Boy. 2015. (ENG., Illus.). 220p. (J). pap. 14.99 *(978-1-943336-18-0(0))* Entangled Publishing, LLC.

Burton, Shovon. Banton Hits A Homerun. 2010. (ENG.). 46p. pap. 21.99 *(978-1-4500-7165-9(1))* Xlibris Corp.

Caine, Rachel, pseud. Kiss of Death: The Morganville Vampires, 8 vols. 2010. (Morganville Vampires Ser.: 8). (ENG.). 256p. (YA). (gr. 9-18). 6.99 *(978-0-451-22973-1(8),* Berkley) Penguin Publishing Group.

—The Morganville Vampires, Volume 4, Vol. 4. 2011. (Morganville Vampires Ser.: Bks. 7-8). (ENG.). 464p. (YA). (gr. 9-18). 12.99 *(978-0-451-23426-1(X),* Berkley) Penguin Publishing Group.

Caletti, Deb. Love Is All You Need: Wild Roses; the Nature of Jade. 2013. (ENG.). 608p. (YA). (gr. 7-7). pap. 11.99 *(978-1-4424-6636-4(7),* Simon Pulse) Simon Pulse.

—Wild Roses. 2008. (ENG.). 320p. (YA). (gr. 7-12). pap. 8.99 *(978-1-4169-5782-9(0),* Simon Pulse) Simon Pulse.

Calmenson, Stephanie. Jazzmatazz! Degen, Bruce, illus. 2008. 32p. (J). (gr. -1). lib. bdg. 17.89 *(978-0-06-077290-1(5))* HarperCollins Pubs.

Calvani, Mayra. The Luthier's Apprentice. 2014. (ENG.). 184p. (J). pap. 15.95 *(978-1-60619-029-6(6))* Twilight Times Bks.

Camp Rock: Second Session: Super Special: under the Mistletoe (Camp Rock: Second Session) 2009. 256p. pap. 6.99 *(978-1-4231-2222-7(4))* Disney Pr.

Capetta, Amy Rose. Entangled. 2013. (ENG.). 336p. (YA). (gr. 9). 17.99 *(978-0-544-08744-6(5),* 1538242, Clarion Bks.) HarperCollins Pubs.

Carlon, Mick. Riding on Duke's Train. 2011. (LeapKids Ser.). (ENG.). 160p. (J). (gr. k-7). pap. 9.95 *(978-1-935248-06-4(5))* Leapfrog Pr.

—Travels with Louis. 2012. (LeapKids Ser.). (ENG.). 240p. (J). (gr. 2-10). pap. 9.95 *(978-1-935248-35-4(9))* Leapfrog Pr.

Carter, Nikki. Doing My Own Thing. 2011. (Fab Life Ser.: 3). (ENG., Illus.). 282p. (YA). (gr. 9). 9.95 *(978-0-7582-5558-7(6),* K-Teen/Dafina) Kensington Publishing Corp.

Castellucci, Cecil. Beige. (ENG., 320p. (YA). 2009. Illus.). (gr. 9). pap. 8.99 *(978-0-7636-4232-7(0))* 2007. (Illus.). (gr. 9-18). 16.99 *(978-0-7636-3066-9(7))* 2007. 25.66 *(978-1-4287-4767-8(2))* Candlewick Pr.

Celenza, Anna Harwell. Duke Ellington's Nutcracker Suite. Tate, Don, illus. 2018. (Once upon a Masterpiece Ser.: 5). 32p. (J). (gr. 1-4). 16.99 *(978-1-57091-701-1(9))* Charlesbridge Publishing, Inc.

Colbert, Brandy. Finding Yvonne. 2018. (ENG.). 288p. (YA). (gr. 9-17). 17.99 *(978-0-316-34905-5(4))* Little, Brown Bks. for Young Readers.

Cosgrove, Stephen. Cricket Clickett: Finding Your Talents. Arroyo, Fian, illus. 2004. (J). *(978-1-58804-382-5(7))* P C I Education.

Coxe, Molly. Blues for Unicorn. 2019. (Bright Owl Bks.). (Illus.). 40p. (J). (gr. -1-2). 17.99 *(978-1-63592-109-0(0),* 4d7b72dd-81cd-4c1e-814c-6500c4591452, Kane Press) Astra Publishing Hse.

Cross, Kady. Sisters of Salt & Iron. 2016. (Sisters of Blood & Spirit Ser.: 2). (ENG.). 352p. (YA). 18.99 *(978-0-373-21176-0(7),* Harlequin Teen) Harlequin Enterprises ULC CAN. Dist: HarperCollins Pubs.

Cross, Mimi. Before Goodbye. 0 vols. 2016. (ENG.). 399p. (YA). (gr. 8-12). pap. 9.99 *(978-1-5039-4972-0(9),* 9781503949720, Skyscape) Amazon Publishing.

Crow, Kristyn. Skeleton Cat. 2012. lib. bdg. 17.20 *(978-0-606-26209-5(1))* Turtleback.

Dachman, Adam. The Player Piano Mouse. Julich, Jenniffer, illus. 2008. 32p. (J). 14.99 *(978-0-9797794-0-4(5))* Player Piano Mouse Productions (PPMP).

Dakers, Diane. Strings Attached. 1 vol. 2017. (Orca Limelights Ser.). (ENG.). 144p. (J). (gr. 4-7). pap. 9.95 *(978-1-4598-0970-3(X))* Orca Bk. Pubs. USA.

Darden, Floyd. Drumdee makes a Drum. 2007. 15.95 *(978-1-59526-711-5(5))* Aeon Publishing Inc.

Davidson, Susanna. The Musicians of Bremen. Gordon, Mike & Gordon, Carl, illus. 2007. (Usborne First Reading: Level 3 Ser.). 48p. (J). 8.99 *(978-0-7945-1911-7(3),* Usborne) EDC Publishing.

Dawn, Sasha. Panic. 2019. (ENG.). 312p. (YA). (gr. 8-12). 18.99 *(978-1-5415-3574-9(X),* 26749504-7b38-4af7-a92f-4ed6911ffbbd, Carolrhoda Lab™) Lerner Publishing Group.

Decter, Nora. How Far We Go & How Fast. 1 vol. 2018. (ENG.). 264p. (YA). (gr. 8-12). pap. 14.95 *(978-1-4598-1686-9(6))* Orca Bk. Pubs. USA.

Deen, Natasha. In the Key of Nira Ghani. 2019. (ENG.). 304p. (YA). (gr. 7-17). 17.99 *(978-0-7624-6547-7(6),* Running Pr. Kids) Running Pr.

Derubertis, Barbara. Xavier Ox's Xylophone Experiment. Alley, R. W., illus. 2011. (Animal Antics A to Z Set III Ser.). pap. 45.32 *(978-0-7613-8433-5(2))* Astra Publishing Hse.

deRubertis, Barbara. Xavier Ox's Xylophone Experiment. Alley, R. W., illus. 2011. (Animal Antics A to Z Ser.). 32p. (J). (gr. -1-3). pap. 7.95 *(978-1-57565-349-5(4),* 65fbdd96-a532-4d2d-bc28-c31fd51103d9, Kane Press) Astra Publishing Hse.

deRubertis, Barbara & DeRubertis, Barbara. Xavier Ox's Xylophone Experiment. Alley, R. W., illus. 2012. (Animal Antics A to Z Ser.). 32p. (J). (gr. 2 — 1). cd-rom 7.95 *(978-1-57565-417-1(2))* Astra Publishing Hse.

DiCamillo, Kate. Great Joy (midi Edition) Ibatoulline, Bagram, illus. 2010. (ENG.). 32p. (J). (gr. -1-3). 12.00 *(978-0-7636-4996-8(1))* Candlewick Pr.

Doktorski, Jennifer. August & Everything After. 2018. 320p. (YA). (gr. 8-12). pap. 10.99 *(978-1-4926-5715-6(8))* Sourcebooks, Inc.

Donbavand, Tommy. Scream Street: Flesh of the Zombie, Bk. 4. Cartoon Saloon, Ltd., illus. 2010. (Scream Street Ser.: 4). (ENG.). 128p. (J). (gr. 3-7). pap. 5.99 *(978-0-7636-4637-0(7))* Candlewick Pr.

Donnelly, Jennifer. Revolution. 2011. (ENG.). 512p. (YA). (gr. 9). pap. 10.99 *(978-0-385-73764-7(5),* Ember) Random Hse. Children's Bks.

Draper, Polly. Cry Wolff. 2007. 89p. (J). pap. *(978-0-545-02570-6(2))* Scholastic, Inc.

Dunlap Cather, Katherine. Boyhood Stories of Famous Men. 2013. 292p. pap. *(978-3-95507-921-5(X))* DOGMA. in Europäischer Hochschulverlag GmbH & Co. KG.

Edwards, Pamela Duncan. The Leprechaun's Gold. Cole, Henry, illus. 2006. (ENG.). 40p. (J). (gr. -1-2). reprint ed. 7.99 *(978-0-06-443878-0(3),* Tegen, Katherine Bks) HarperCollins Pubs.

Ehrhardt, Karen. This Jazz Man. Roth, R. G., illus. 2010. (J). (gr. 1-5). 28.95 incl. audio compact disk *(978-1-4301-0740-8(5))* Live Oak Media.

Enderle, Dotti. Book 15: Rock & Roll!, 1 vol. 2014. (Ghost Detectors Ser.). (ENG., Illus.). 80p. (J). (gr. 2-5). lib. bdg. 35.64 *(978-1-62402-003-2(8),* 8832, Calico Chapter Bks.) ABDO Publishing Co.

Engle, Margarita. Drum Dream Girl: How One Girl's Courage Changed Music. López, Rafael & López, Rafael, illus. 2015. (ENG.). 48p. (J). (gr. -1-3). 19.99 *(978-0-544-10229-3(0),* 1540161, Clarion Bks.) HarperCollins Pubs.

FableVision. Spf 40. Reynolds, Peter H., illus. 2013. (Zebrafish Ser.). (ENG.). 128p. (J). (gr. 5-9). pap. 9.99 *(978-1-4169-9709-2(1),* Atheneum Bks. for Young Readers) Simon & Schuster Children's Publishing.

Falconer, Ian. Olivia Forms a Band. Falconer, Ian, illus. 2006. (ENG., Illus.). 50p. (J). (gr. -1-3). 19.99 *(978-1-4169-2454-8(X),* Atheneum Bks. for Young Readers) Simon & Schuster Children's Publishing.

Fannin, Cole. Gene Autry & the Golden Stallion. Hampton, John, illus. 2011. 284p. 48.95 *(978-1-258-02563-2(9))* Literary Licensing, LLC.

Ferron, Joanne. Luis Saves the Llama. 2012. (ENG.). 35p. (J). pap. 17.95 *(978-1-4327-7623-7(1))* Outskirts Pr., Inc.

Fisher, Catherine. The Oracle Betrayed. 2005. (Oracle Prophecies Ser.). (Illus.). 332p. (YA). (gr. 7-12). 14.65 *(978-0-7569-5269-3(7))* Perfection Learning Corp.

Fletcher, Steffi. Gene Autry. Crawford, Mel, illus. 2011. 32p. pap. 35.95 *(978-1-258-02076-7(9))* Literary Licensing, LLC.

Forman, Gayle. If I Stay. 2011. (If I Stay Ser.: BK.1). (YA). 10.36 *(978-0-7848-3573-9(X),* Everbind) Marco Bk. Co.

—If I Stay. (ENG.). (YA). (gr. 7). 2021. 272p. pap. 5.99 *(978-0-593-40384-6(3),* Penguin Books) 2018. 288p. mass mkt. 7.99 *(978-0-451-48064-4(3),* Speak) 2010. 320p. 11.99 *(978-0-14-241543-6(X),* Speak) Penguin Young Readers Group.

—If I Stay. 2010. (If I Stay Ser.: BK.1). (ENG.). 262p. (YA). (gr. 9-12). 18.45 *(978-1-60686-742-6(3))* Perfection Learning Corp.

—If I Stay. l.t. ed. 2014. (If I Stay Ser.: BK.1). (ENG.). (YA). 482p. 23.99 *(978-1-4104-7543-5(3))*; 480p. pap. 12.99 *(978-1-59413-814-0(1),* Large Print Pr.) Thorndike Pr.

—If I Stay. 2018. lib. bdg. 18.40 *(978-0-606-41304-6(9))* 2010. (If I Stay Ser.: BK.1). (YA). lib. bdg. 22.10 *(978-0-606-14395-0(5))* Turtleback.

Forsythe, Matthew. Pokko & the Drum. Forsythe, Matthew, illus. 2019. (ENG., Illus.). 64p. (J). (gr. -1-3). 18.99 *(978-1-4814-8039-0(1),* Simon & Schuster/Paula Wiseman Bks.) Simon & Schuster/Paula Wiseman Bks.

Fox, Paula. The Slave Dancer. unabr. ed. 2004. 152p. (J). (gr. 5-9). pap. 38.00 incl. audio *(978-0-8072-0458-0(7),* Listening Library) Random Hse. Audio Publishing Group.

Frank, Lucy. Lucky Stars. 2014. (ENG.). 304p. (J). (gr. 5-9). pap. 14.99 *(978-1-4814-2901-6(9),* Atheneum Bks. for Young Readers) Simon & Schuster Children's Publishing.

French, Simon. Where in the World. 1 vol. 2008. (ENG.). 208p. (J). (gr. 5-7). pap. 7.95 *(978-1-56145-443-3(5))* Peachtree Publishing Co. Inc.

Friedman, J. S. The Micetro of Moscow. Beatrice, Chris, illus. 2013. (Maurice's Valises Ser.: Vol. 2). (ENG.). 44p. (J). (gr. k-4). 16.95 *(978-94-91613-06-7(5))* Mouse Prints Pr. NLD. Dist: Ingram Publisher Services.

Fullerton, Alma. In the Garage. 1 vol. 2006. (ENG.). 112p. (YA). (gr. 8-10). per. 4.95 *(978-0-88995-371-0(6),* 2289f886-9775-4b48-b28c-83ab098fbab4) Red Deer Pr. CAN. Dist: Firefly Bks., Ltd.

Gallagher, Denise, illus. A Tip Tap Tale. 2017. (J). *(978-1-946160-09-6(1))* Univ. of Louisiana at Lafayette Pr.

Gansworth, Eric. Give Me Some Truth. (ENG.). 432p. (gr. 9-9). 2022. (J). pap. 12.99 *(978-1-338-58216-1(X))* 2018. (Illus.). (YA). 18.99 *(978-1-338-14354-6(9))* Scholastic, Inc. (Levine, Arthur A. Bks.).

Garcia, Kami & Stohl, Margaret. Dangerous Deception. 2015. (ENG.). 352p. (YA). (gr. 7-17). 19.00 *(978-0-316-37034-9(7))* Little, Brown Bks. for Young Readers.

Garza, Fabiola, illus. Coco. 2017. (J). *(978-1-5379-5892-7(5),* Golden Bks.) Random Hse. Children's Bks.

Garza, Xavier. Just One Itsy Bitsy Little Bite / Sólo un Mordadita Chiquitita. de Vita, Flor, illus. 2018. (ENG & SPA.). 32p. (J). (gr. -1-3). 17.95 *(978-1-55885-872-5(5),* Piñata Books) Arte Publico Pr.

Gershenson, Harold P. Freddy Flamingo & the Kindertown Five. Mills, Christopher, illus. 2005. 27p. (J). *(978-1-58987-070-3(0))* Kindermusik International.

Gillmor, Don. The Fabulous Song. Gay, Marie-Louise, illus. 2003. 32p. (J). pap. 7.95 *(978-1-929132-48-5(4))* Kane Miller.

—The Fabulous Song. Gay, Marie-Louise, illus. 2006. (ENG.). 44p. (J). (gr. -1-2). 16.95 *(978-2-923163-17-8(6))* La Montagne Secrete CAN. Dist: Independent Pubs. Group.

Ginsberg, Mort. Ukey & His Magical Ukulele. 2008. 75p. pap. 19.95 *(978-1-60610-395-1(4))* America Star Bks.

Glines, Abbi. Bad for You. 2015. (Sea Breeze Ser.). (ENG., Illus.). 320p. (YA). (gr. 11). pap. 12.99 *(978-1-4814-2074-7(7),* Simon Pulse) Simon Pulse.

—Breathe. 2013. (Sea Breeze Ser.). (ENG., Illus.). 352p. (YA). (gr. 11). pap. 11.99 *(978-1-4424-8869-4(7),* Simon Pulse) Simon Pulse.

—Breathe. 2011. 166p. (gr. 8-12). pap. 9.99 *(978-1-61798-004-6(8))* Wild Child Publishing.

—Misbehaving. 2014. (Sea Breeze Ser.). (ENG., Illus.). 352p. (YA). (gr. 11). 17.99 *(978-1-4814-0674-1(4))*; pap. 12.99 *(978-1-4814-0673-4(6))* Simon Pulse. (Simon Pulse).

Gohmann, Johanna. Knock 'Em Dead, Bk. 4. Zoloti?, Aleksandar, illus. 2018. (Electric Zombie Ser.). (ENG.). 112p. (J). (gr. 2-5). lib. bdg. 38.50 *(978-1-5321-3364-0(2),* 31151, Calico Chapter Bks.) ABDO Publishing Co.

—Lurching to the Beat, Bk. 1. Zoloti?, Aleksandar, illus. 2018. (Electric Zombie Ser.). (ENG.). 112p. (J). (gr. 2-5). lib. bdg. 38.50 *(978-1-5321-3361-9(8),* 31145, Calico Chapter Bks.) ABDO Publishing Co.

—Pleased to Eat You: Book 3. Zoloti?, Aleksandar, illus. 2018. (Electric Zombie Ser.). (ENG.). 112p. (J). (gr. 2-5). lib. bdg. 38.50 *(978-1-5321-3363-3(4),* 31149, Calico Chapter Bks.) ABDO Publishing Co.

Going, K. L. Fat Kid Rules the World. 2004. (ENG.). 224p. (YA). (gr. 7-18). reprint ed. pap. 10.99 *(978-0-14-240208-5(7),* Penguin Books) Penguin Young Readers Group.

Gollub, Matthew. Jazz Fly 2: The Jungle Pachanga. 2010. (Jazz Fly Ser.). (ENG., Illus.). 32p. (J). (gr. k-2). 18.95 *(978-1-889910-44-4(9))* Tortuga Pr.

—Jazz Fly 2: The Jungle Pachanga. Hanke, Karen, illus. 2010. (J). *(978-1-889910-45-1(7))* Tortuga Pr.

Gonzalez, Gabriela & Triana, Gaby. Backstage Pass. 2004. (Illus.). 224p. (J). (gr. 7-18). 15.99 *(978-0-06-056017-1(7))*; lib. bdg. 16.89 *(978-0-06-056018-8(5))* HarperCollins Pubs.

Goodan, Till. Gene Autry & Raiders of the Range. 2011. 350p. 51.95 *(978-1-258-02137-5(4))* Literary Licensing, LLC.

Graham, Hilary Weisman. Reunited. 2013. (ENG., Illus.). 336p. (YA). (gr. 7). pap. 9.99 *(978-1-4424-0687-2(9),* Simon & Schuster Bks. For Young Readers) Simon & Schuster Bks. For Young Readers.

Greene, Janice. The Dark Lady. 1 vol. unabr. ed. 2010. (Q Reads Ser.). (ENG.). 32p. (YA). (gr. 9-12). pap. 8.50 *(978-1-61651-215-6(6))* Saddleback Educational Publishing, Inc.

Greene, Kimberly. My Sister's a Pop Star. 2011. (My Sister's a Pop Star Ser.). (ENG.). 277p. (J). (gr. 4-6). 18.69 *(978-0-7945-2899-7(6))* EDC Publishing.

GRIMM. The Bremen Town Musicians. 1 vol. Bell, Anthea, ed. Bell, Anthea, tr. Lai, Hsin-Shih, illus. 2007. (ENG.). 32p. (J). (gr. -1-3). 17.95 *(978-0-88010-583-5(6),* Bell Pond Bks.) SteinerBooks, Inc.

Grimm, Jacob & Grimm, Wilhelm K. The Bremen Town Musicians: A Tale about Working Together. Catalano, Dominic, illus. 2006. (Famous Fables Ser.). (J). *(978-1-59939-039-0(6),* Reader's Digest Young Families, Inc.) Studio Fun International.

Grosso, Mike. I Am Drums. (ENG.). 256p. (J). (gr. 5-7). 2019. pap. 7.99 *(978-1-328-90013-5(4),* 1700043) 2016. 17.99 *(978-0-544-70710-8(9),* 1628642) HarperCollins Pubs. (Clarion Bks.).

Gunderson, Jessica. Honestly, Our Music Stole the Show! The Story of the Bremen Town Musicians As Told by the Donkey. Bernardini, Cristian, illus. 2018. (Other Side of the Story Ser.). (ENG.). 24p. (J). (gr. -1-3). lib. bdg. 27.99 *(978-1-5158-2296-7(6),* 137005, Picture Window Bks.) Capstone.

Hannigan, Paula. Music Star. Slade, Christian, illus. 2011. (ENG.). 16p. (J). (gr. -1-3). 14.99 *(978-1-4494-0173-3(2))* Andrews McMeel Publishing.

Harris, Fiona. Super Moopers: Musical Markus. Edgar, Scott, illus. 2017. (Super Moopers Ser.). (ENG.). 48p. (J). pap. 11.99 *(978-1-76040-650-9(3))* Bonnier Publishing GBR. Dist: Independent Pubs. Group.

Haus, Jean. With the Band. 0 vols. 2014. (Luminescent Juliet Ser.: 3). (ENG.). 286p. (gr. 7-12). pap. 7.99 *(978-1-4778-4709-1(X),* 9781477847091, Skyscape) Amazon Publishing.

Hedderwick, Mairi. Katie Morag & the Grand Concert. 2010. (Katie Morag Ser.: 6). (Illus.). 32p. (J). (gr. k-2). pap. 12.99 *(978-1-84941-087-8(9),* Red Fox) Random House Children's Books GBR. Dist: Independent Pubs. Group.

Heim, Robert. The Squeaking Earl. 2009. 32p. pap. 16.50 *(978-1-60693-711-2(1),* Strategic Bk. Publishing) Strategic Book Publishing & Rights Agency (SBPRA).

Heuiser Hill, Melanie. Giant Pumpkin Suite. 2017. (ENG.). 448p. (J). (gr. 4-7). 18.99 *(978-0-7636-9155-4(0))* Candlewick Pr.

Hillerman, Tony. Buster Mesquite's Cowboy Band. 2006. (J). reprint ed. lib. bdg. 14.95 *(978-0-914001-12-6(4))* Sidewinder Publishing LLC.

Hoffman, Amalia. Klezmer Bunch. 2009. (ENG.). 36p. 15.95 *(978-965-229-447-0(0))* Gefen Publishing Hse., Ltd ISR. Dist: Strauss Consultants.

Houran, Lori Haskins. Too Many Cats. Mathieu, Joe, illus. 2009. (Step into Reading: Step 1 Ser.). (ENG.). 32p. (J). (gr. -1-1). lib. bdg. 16.19 *(978-0-375-95197-8(0))* Random House Publishing Group.

Huelin, Jodi. Alvin's Easter Break. 2014. (ENG., Illus.). 24p. (J). (gr. -1-3). pap. 3.99 *(978-0-06-225222-7(4),* HarperFestival) HarperCollins Pubs.

Hughes, Mark Peter. Lemonade Mouth: Adapted Movie Tie-In Edition. movie tie-in ed. 2011. (ENG.). 352p. (YA). (gr. 7-7). pap. 8.99 *(978-0-385-74208-5(8),* Ember) Random Hse. Children's Bks.

Hurd, Thacher. Mama Don't Allow. 2003. (Illus.). (J). (gr. -1-2). pap. 35.95 incl. audio compact disk *(978-1-59112-605-8(3))* Live Oak Media.

—Mama Don't Allow 25th Anniversary Edition. Hurd, Thacher, illus. 25th anniv. ed. 2008. (ENG., Illus.). 40p. (J). (gr. -1-3). pap. 8.99 *(978-0-06-443078-4(2),* HarperCollins) HarperCollins Pubs.

Hurd, Thacher & Hurd, T. Mama Don't Allow. 2008. (Illus.). (J). (gr. -1-2). 17.20 *(978-0-8085-3698-7(2))* Turtleback.

Jackson, Ellen B. Cinnamon Brown & the Seven Dwarfs. Brown, Elbrite, illus. 2006. (J). *(978-0-670-06106-8(9),* Viking Adult) Penguin Publishing Group.

Jackson, Tiffany D. Let Me Hear a Rhyme. (ENG.). (YA). (gr. 8). 2020. 400p. pap. 11.99 *(978-0-06-284033-2(9))* 2019. 384p. 19.99 *(978-0-06-284032-5(0))* HarperCollins Pubs. (Tegen, Katherine Bks).

Janover, Caroline D. Zipper: The Kid with ADHD. 2007. 172p. per. 12.95 *(978-0-595-47615-2(5),* Backinprint.com) iUniverse, Inc.

Johnson, Angela. Violet's Music. Huliska-Beith, Laura, illus. 2004. 32p. (J). (gr. -1-3). 18.99 *(978-0-8037-2740-3(2),* Dial Bks) Penguin Young Readers Group.

Johnson, Christine. The Gathering Dark. (ENG., (YA). (gr. 9). 2014. Illus.). 528p. pap. 9.99 *(978-1-4424-3904-7(1))* 2013. 512p. 16.99 *(978-1-4424-3903-0(3))* Simon Pulse. (Simon Pulse).

Kadence, Sam. Unicorns & Rainbow Poop. (J). 2016. (ENG., Illus.). 27.99 *(978-1-63477-988-3(6),* Harmony Ink Pr.) 2014. 246p. pap. *(978-1-63216-417-9(5))* Dreamspinner Pr.

Kamata, Suzanne. Screaming Divas. 2014. (ENG.). 208p. (YA). 17.99 *(978-1-4405-7279-1(8),* Simon Pulse) Simon Pulse.

Keil, Michelle Ruiz. All of Us with Wings. 2019. (ENG., Illus.). 360p. (YA). (gr. 11). 18.99 *(978-1-64129-034-0(X),* Soho Teen) Soho Pr., Inc.

Keller, Jessica. Mia's Marvelous Musical Group. 2009. (Illus.). 64p. (gr. -1-3). pap. 26.99 *(978-1-4389-8160-4(0))* AuthorHouse.

Kerick, Mia. Intervention. 2016. (ENG., Illus.). (J). 24.99 *(978-1-63533-036-6(X),* Harmony Ink Pr.) Dreamspinner Pr.

—Intervention [Library Edition]. 2014. 230p. pap. 14.99 *(978-1-62798-336-5(8),* Harmony Ink Pr.) Dreamspinner Pr.

Kerner, Charlotte. Blueprint. Crawford, Elizabeth D., tr. from GER. 2003. (Young Adult Fiction Ser.). 192p. (YA). (gr. 9-12). 16.95 *(978-0-8225-0080-3(9),* Carolrhoda Bks.) Lerner Publishing Group.

Kimmel, Elizabeth Cody. Suddenly Supernatural: Scaredy Kat. 2010. (Suddenly Supernatural Ser.: 2). (ENG.). 272p. (J). (gr. 3-7). pap. 15.99 *(978-0-316-08745-2(9))* Little, Brown Bks. for Young Readers.

Kogler, Jennifer Anne. Ruby Tuesday. 2005. (ENG.). 320p. (J). (gr. 7-18). 15.99 *(978-0-06-073956-0(8))* HarperCollins Pubs.

Koosis, Lisa A. Resurrecting Sunshine. 2016. (ENG.). 320p. (YA). (gr. 8-12). 16.99 *(978-0-8075-6943-6(7),* 807569437) Whitman, Albert & Co.

Krosoczka, Jarrett J. Punk Farm. 2010. (Punk Farm Bks.). 40p. (J). (gr. -1-2). pap. 8.99 *(978-0-440-41793-4(7),* Dragonfly Bks.) Random Hse. Children's Bks.

Krulik, Nancy. She's Got the Beat. 2010. (Romantic Comedies Ser.). (ENG.). 320p. (YA). (gr. 9). pap. 14.99 *(978-1-4424-1419-8(7),* Simon Pulse) Simon Pulse.

Larson, Hope. All Together Now. Larson, Hope, illus. 2020. (Eagle Rock Ser.: 2). (ENG., Illus.). 192p. (J). 21.99 *(978-0-374-31162-9(5),* 900195864); pap. 12.99

(978-0-374-31365-4(2), 900215357) Farrar, Straus & Giroux. (Farrar, Straus & Giroux (BYR)).
Lewis, Stewart. Stealing Candy. 2017. (ENG.). 288p. (YA). (gr. 8-12). pap. 10.99 *(978-1-4926-3888-9(9),* 9781492638889) Sourcebooks, Inc.
Litchfield, David. The Bear, the Piano, the Dog, & the Fiddle. Litchfield, David, illus. 2019. (ENG., Illus.). 40p. (J). (gr. -1-3). 17.99 *(978-1-328-59589-8(7),* 1731276, Clarion Bks.) HarperCollins Pubs.
Loewen, Nancy. The Ants & the Grasshopper, Narrated by the Fanciful but Truthful Grasshopper. Arbat, Carles, illus. 2018. (Other Side of the Fable Ser.). (ENG.). 24p. (J). (gr. -1-3). lib. bdg. 27.99 *(978-1-5158-2868-6(9),* 138406, Picture Window Bks.) Capstone.
Loney, Andrea J. Double Bass Blues. Gutierrez, Rudy, illus. 2019. 32p. (J). (gr. -1-3). 18.99 *(978-1-5247-1852-7(1),* Knopf Bks. for Young Readers) Random Hse. Children's Bks.
Lu, Marie. The Kingdom of Back. 336p. (YA). (gr. 7). 2021. pap. 12.99 *(978-1-5247-3903-4(0),* Penguin Books) 2020. (Illus.). 18.99 *(978-1-5247-3901-0(4),* G.P. Putnam's Sons Books for Young Readers) Penguin Young Readers Group.
—The Kingdom of Back. 2019. (ENG.). 336p. lib. bdg. 22.80 *(978-1-6636-2728-5(2))* Perfection Learning Corp.
Mahin, Michael. Stalebread Charlie & the Razzy Dazzy Spasm Band. Tate, Don, illus. 2018. (ENG.). 40p. (J). (gr. -1-3). 17.99 *(978-0-547-94201-8(X),* 1517145, Clarion Bks.) HarperCollins Pubs.
Man-Kong, Mary. Star Power. 2012. (Barbie Step into Reading Level 2 Ser.). lib. bdg. 13.55 *(978-0-606-26550-8(3))* Turtleback.
Marchetta, Melina. The Piper's Son. 2011. (ENG., Illus.). 336p. (YA). (gr. 9-18). 17.99 *(978-0-7636-4758-2(6))* Candlewick Pr.
Martinez, Jessica. Virtuosity. (ENG.). (YA). (gr. 9). 2012. 320p. pap. 9.99 *(978-1-4424-2053-3(7))* 2011. 304p. 16.99 *(978-1-4424-2052-6(9))* Simon Pulse. (Simon Pulse).
Massenot, Véronique & Hie, Vanessa. The Three Musicians: A Children's Book Inspired by Pablo Picasso. 2013. (Children's Books Inspired by Famous Artworks Ser.). (ENG., Illus.). 32p. (J). (gr. -1-3). 14.95 *(978-3-7913-7151-1(7))* Prestel Verlag GmbH & Co KG. DEU. Dist: Penguin Random Hse. LLC.
McCarry, Sarah. All Our Pretty Songs: A Novel. 2013. (Metamorphoses Trilogy Ser.: 1). (ENG.). 240p. (YA). (gr. 8-12). pap. 19.99 *(978-1-250-02708-5(X),* 900098096, St. Martin's Griffin) St. Martin's Pr.
McClintock, Norah. Out of Tune, 1 vol. 2017. (Riley Donovan Ser.: 3). (ENG.). 240p. (YA). (gr. 8-12). pap. 10.95 *(978-1-4598-1465-3(7))* Orca Bk. Pubs. USA.
McRobb, Will & Viscardi, Chris. Battle of the Bands. 2007. 87p. (J). pap. *(978-0-545-02571-3(0))* Scholastic, Inc.
Milanes, Janelle. The Victoria in My Head. (ENG.). (YA). (gr. 7). 2018. 416p. pap. 12.99 *(978-1-4814-8090-1(1))* 2017. (Illus.). 400p. 17.99 *(978-1-4814-8089-5(8))* Simon Pulse. (Simon Pulse).
Montano, Josie. Pop Starlets. 2005. (Illus.). 142p. pap. *(978-0-7344-0446-6(8),* Lothian Children's Bks.) Hachette Australia.
Mutchnick, Brenda & Casden, Ron. A Noteworthy Tale. Penney, Ian, illus. 2004. 30p. (J). (gr. k-4). reprint ed. 19.00 *(978-0-7567-7654-1(6))* DIANE Publishing Co.
Myers, Walter Dean. Jazz. Myers, Christopher, illus. 2006. (ENG.). 48p. (J). (gr. 3-7). 18.95 *(978-0-8234-1545-8(7))* Holiday Hse., Inc.
Nelson, Jandy. The Sky Is Everywhere. 2011. (ENG.). 320p. (YA). (gr. 9-18). 9.99 *(978-0-14-241780-5(7),* Speak) Penguin Young Readers Group.
—The Sky Is Everywhere. 2011. (ENG., Illus.). 275p. (gr. 9-12). 19.00 *(978-1-61383-223-3(0))* Perfection Learning Corp.
Nichols, Travis. Matthew Meets the Man. 2012. (ENG., Illus.). 176p. (YA). (gr. 6-9). 24.99 *(978-1-59643-545-2(3),* 900061886) Roaring Brook Pr.
Noel, Alyson. Infamous. 2018. (ENG.). 432p. (YA). (Beautiful Idols Ser.: 3). (gr. 9). 17.99 *(978-0-06-232458-0(6));* *(978-0-06-279645-5(3))* HarperCollins Pubs. (Tegen, Katherine Bks).
Ohlin, Nancy. Consent. 2015. (ENG., Illus.). 288p. (YA). (gr. 9). 17.99 *(978-1-4424-6490-2(9),* Simon Pulse) Simon Pulse.
Omololu, C. J. Transcendence. 2012. (ENG.). 336p. (YA). (gr. 8-12). 26.19 *(978-0-8027-2370-3(5),* 9780802723703) Walker & Co.
Ostrander, P. Martin. P Martin Ostrander's Dangerous Four Series: Book #1. 2007. 112p. 20.95 *(978-0-595-68250-8(2))* iUniverse, Inc.
Parent, David D. Drummers Forward! Marching with Angels: The Exciting Tale of a Drummer Boy Serving with the First Vermont Brigade & His Adventures During the Americ. 2013. 188p. pap. 13.50 *(978-1-62516-582-4(X),* Strategic Bk. Publishing) Strategic Book Publishing & Rights Agency (SBPRA).
Parker, Vic, compiled by. The Musicians of Bremen & Other Silly Stories, 1 vol. 2015. (Silly Stories Ser.). (ENG.). 40p. (J). (gr. 2-3). pap. 15.05 *(978-1-4824-4207-6(8),* 72908de5-c396-4c31-b7c3-2411d14bc812) Stevens, Gareth Publishing LLLP.
Patten, Lewis B. Gene Autry & Arapaho War Drums. Hampton, John W., illus. 2011. 280p. 47.95 *(978-1-258-04495-4(1))* Literary Licensing, LLC.
—Gene Autry & the Ghost Riders. Bartram, Bob & Eggers, James, illus. 2011. 280p. 47.95 *(978-1-258-02621-9(X))* Literary Licensing, LLC.
Pearson, Maggie. The Pop Star Pirates. 2015. (Race Further with Reading Ser.). (ENG., Illus.). 48p. (J). (gr. 3-3). *(978-0-7787-2089-8(6))* Crabtree Publishing Co.
Philips, L. Sometime after Midnight. 2018. 400p. (YA). (gr. 9). 18.99 *(978-0-425-29163-4(4),* Viking Books for Young Readers) Penguin Young Readers Group.
Phillips, Dee. Scout, 1 vol. unabr. ed. 2010. (Right Now! Ser.). (ENG., Illus.). 45p. (YA). (gr. 9-12). pap. 10.75 *(978-1-61651-252-1(0))* Saddleback Educational Publishing, Inc.
Pittman, Samuel, II. Alligator Jazz, 1 vol. Bailey, Sheila, illus. 2018. (ENG.). 32p. (J). (gr. -1-3). 16.99 *(978-1-4556-2422-5(5),* Pelican Publishing) Arcadia Publishing.
Potter, Debra, illus. I Am the Music Man. (Classic Books with Holes 8x8 Ser.). 16p. (J). 2018. (ENG.). pap. *(978-1-78628-129-6(5))* 2006. (gr. -1-3). spiral bd. *(978-1-84643-010-7(0))* Child's Play International Ltd.
Pratchett, Terry. The Amazing Maurice & His Educated Rodents. 2008. (ENG.). 368p. (YA). (gr. 8-18). pap. 11.99 *(978-0-06-001235-9(8),* Clarion Bks.) HarperCollins Pubs.
—The Amazing Maurice & His Educated Rodents. 2003. (ENG.). 340p. (gr. 7). 19.00 *(978-0-7569-1458-5(2))* Perfection Learning Corp.
—The Amazing Maurice & His Educated Rodents. 2008. (Discworld Ser.: 33). (YA). (gr. 5-8). 19.65 *(978-0-613-65757-0(8))* Turtleback.
Prendergast, Gabrielle. The Frail Days, 1 vol. 2015. (Orca Limelights Ser.). (ENG.). 128p. (J). (gr. 4-7). pap. 9.95 *(978-1-4598-0464-7(3))* Orca Bk. Pubs. USA.
—Pinch Me, 1 vol. 2017. (Orca Soundings Ser.). (ENG.). 144p. (YA). (gr. 8-12). pap. 9.95 *(978-1-4598-1364-9(2))* Orca Bk. Pubs. USA.
RH Disney. Coco Little Golden Book (Disney/Pixar Coco) The Disney Storybook Art Team, illus. 2017. (Little Golden Book Ser.). (ENG.). 24p. (J). (-k). 5.99 *(978-0-7364-3800-1(9),* Golden/Disney) Random Hse. Children's Bks.
Ritter, John H. Under the Baseball Moon. 2008. (Illus.). 283p. (gr. 8-12). 17.00 *(978-0-7569-8934-7(5))* Perfection Learning Corp.
Rivera, Liz. Miguel's Music (Disney/Pixar Coco) The Disney Storybook Art Team, illus. 2017. (Step into Reading Ser.). (ENG.). 32p. (J). (gr. -1-1). pap. 5.99 *(978-0-7364-3811-7(4),* RH/Disney) Random Hse. Children's Bks.
Rivers, Olivia. Tone Deaf. (ENG.). (J). (gr. 8). 2017. 296p. pap. 9.99 *(978-1-5107-2627-7(6))* 2016. 288p. 17.99 *(978-1-63450-707-3(0))* Skyhorse Publishing Co., Inc. (Sky Pony Pr.).
Robinson, Craig & Mansbach, Adam. Jake the Fake Keeps It Real. Knight, Keith, illus. 2018. (Jake the Fake Ser.: 1). 160p. (J). (gr. 3-7). 7.99 *(978-0-553-52354-6(6),* Yearling) Random Hse. Children's Bks.
Ross, Jeff. At Ease, 1 vol. 2015. (Orca Limelights Ser.). (ENG.). 144p. (J). (gr. 4-7). pap. 9.95 *(978-1-4598-0800-3(2))* Orca Bk. Pubs. USA.
Ross, Susan. Searching for Lottie. 2019. (ENG., Illus.). 176p. (J). (gr. 3-7). 17.99 *(978-0-8234-4166-2(0))* Holiday Hse., Inc.
Roy, Jennifer. Mindblind, 0 vols. unabr. ed. 2013. (ENG.). 254p. (YA). (gr. 7-12). pap. 9.99 *(978-1-4778-1712-4(3),* 9781477817124, Skyscape) Amazon Publishing.
Roy, Ron. A to Z Mysteries: the X'ed-Out X-Ray. Gurney, John Steven, illus. 2005. (to Z Mysteries Ser.: 24). 96p. (J). (gr. 1-4). 6.99 *(978-0-375-82481-4(2),* Random Hse. Bks. for Young Readers) Random Hse. Children's Bks.
Rubens, Michael. The Bad Decisions Playlist. 2017. (ENG.). 304p. (YA). (gr. 9). pap. 9.99 *(978-1-328-74208-7(3),* 1677324, Clarion Bks.) HarperCollins Pubs.
Ryan, Tom. Totally Unrelated, 1 vol. 2013. (Orca Limelights Ser.). (J). (ENG.). 128p. (gr. 4-7). pap. 9.95 *(978-1-4598-0458-6(9));* 120p. *(978-1-4598-0648-1(4))* Orca Bk. Pubs. USA.
Sachar, Louis. Small Steps. 2008. (Holes Ser.: 2). (ENG.). 288p. (YA). (gr. 7-9). pap. 10.99 *(978-0-385-73315-1(1),* Ember) Random Hse. Children's Bks.
Schwabach, Karen. The Storm Before Atlanta. 2011. 320p. (J). (gr. 3-7). pap. 7.99 *(978-0-375-85867-3(9),* Yearling) Random Hse. Children's Bks.
Sedgwick, Chantele. Interlude. 2018. (Love, Lucas Novel Ser.: 3). (ENG.). 284p. (YA). (gr. 7-13). 16.99 *(978-1-5107-1515-8(0),* Sky Pony Pr.) Skyhorse Publishing Co., Inc.
Seidler, Tor. Toes. Beddows, Eric, illus. 2004. 176p. (J). (gr. 3-18). (ENG.). 15.99 *(978-0-06-054099-9(0));* lib. bdg. 16.89 *(978-0-06-054100-2(8))* HarperCollins Pubs. (Geringer, Laura Book).
Shahegh, Mahvash. The Green Musician. Ewart, Claire, illus. 2015. 36p. (J). (gr. k-3). 16.95 *(978-1-937786-42-7(0),* Wisdom Tales) World Wisdom, Inc.
Shaskan, Trisha Speed. Punk Skunks. Shaskan, Stephen, illus. 2016. (ENG.). 40p. (J). (gr. -1-3). 17.99 *(978-0-06-236396-1(4),* HarperCollins) HarperCollins Pubs.
Shlasko, Robert. Molly & the Sword Diamond, Donna, illus. 2004. 32p. (J). 15.95 *(978-0-9745077-4-3(1))* Jane & Street Pubs. Ltd.
Shoulders, Michael. Crossing the Deadline: Stephen's Journey Through the Civil War. 2016. (ENG.). 384p. (YA). (gr. 4-7). 16.99 *(978-1-58536-951-5(9),* 204098) Sleeping Bear Pr.
Skuse, C. J. Rockoholic. 2012. (YA). *(978-0-545-44251-0(6))* Scholastic, Inc.
Smith-Ready, Jeri. Shade. (ENG.). (YA). (gr. 9). 2011. 336p. pap. 9.99 *(978-1-4169-9407-7(6))* 2010. 320p. 17.99 *(978-1-4169-9406-0(8))* Simon Pulse. (Simon Pulse).
—Shift. (ENG.). (YA). (gr. 9). 2012. 400p. pap. 9.99 *(978-1-4169-9409-1(2))* 2011. 384p. 17.99 *(978-1-4169-9408-4(4))* Simon Pulse. (Simon Pulse).
Smith, Roland. Independence Hall. (I, Q Ser.: Bk. 1). (ENG., 312p. (YA). (gr. 6-8). 2009. Illus.). 15.95 *(978-1-58536-468-8(1),* 202188) 2008. pap. 12.99 *(978-1-58536-325-4(1),* 202289) Sleeping Bear Pr.
Smith, Roland & Spradlin, Michael P. The Alamo. 2013. (I, Q Ser.). (ENG.). 288p. (YA). (gr. 5-8). 16.99 *(978-1-58536-822-8(9),* 202356); pap. 9.99 *(978-1-58536-821-1(0),* 202369) Sleeping Bear Pr.
—Alcatraz. 2014. (I, Q Ser.). (ENG.). 272p. (J). (gr. 5-7). 16.99 *(978-1-58536-826-6(1),* 203667);Bk. 6. pap. 9.99 *(978-1-58536-825-9(3),* 203727) Sleeping Bear Pr.
—I, Q the Windy City. Bk.5. 2014. (I, Q Ser.). (ENG.). 240p. (YA). (gr. 5-7). 9.99 *(978-1-58536-823-5(7),* 202902) Sleeping Bear Pr.
Solomon, Rachel Lynn. Our Year of Maybe. 2019. (ENG., Illus.). 384p. (YA). (gr. 9). 18.99 *(978-1-4814-9776-3(6),* Simon Pulse) Simon Pulse.
Sonnenblick, Jordan. Are You Experienced? 2015. (YA). lib. bdg. 20.85 *(978-0-606-37592-4(9))* Turtleback.
—Notes from the Midnight Driver. 2009. 265p. 18.00 *(978-1-60686-516-3(1))* Perfection Learning Corp.
—Notes from the Midnight Driver. 2007. (ENG.). 288p. (J). (gr. 7-12). pap. 11.99 *(978-0-439-75781-2(9),* Scholastic Paperbacks) Scholastic, Inc.
Sorrells, Walter. Fake ID. 2007. (Hunted Ser.: 1). (ENG.). 336p. (YA). (gr. 7-18). 9.99 *(978-0-14-240762-2(3),* Puffin Books) Penguin Young Readers Group.
Staunton, Ted. Power Chord, 1 vol. 2011. (Orca Currents Ser.). (ENG.). 128p. (J). (gr. 4-7). pap. 9.95 *(978-1-55469-903-2(7))* Orca Bk. Pubs. USA.
Stead, Philip C. Music for Mister Moon. Stead, Erin E., illus. 2019. 40p. (J). (gr. -1-3). 18.99 *(978-0-8234-4160-0(1),* Neal Porter Bks) Holiday Hse., Inc.
Stern, A. J. Rocking Out! Marts, Doreen Mulryan, illus. 2012. (Frankly, Frannie Ser.: 8). 128p. (J). (gr. 1-3). pap. 6.99 *(978-0-448-45750-5(4),* Grosset & Dunlap) Penguin Young Readers Group.
Stiefvater, Maggie. Lament: The Faerie Queen's Deception. 2008. (Lament Novel Ser.: 1). (ENG., Illus.). 336p. (YA). (gr. 9-12). pap. 9.95 *(978-0-7387-1370-0(8),* 0738713708, Flux) North Star Editions.
Sugg, Zoe. Girl Online: On Tour. 2016. (ENG.). (J). pap. 13.00 *(978-1-5011-5958-9(5))* Simon & Schuster.
—Girl Online: on Tour: The Second Novel by Zoella. 2016. (Girl Online Book Ser.: 2). (ENG.). 368p. (gr. 7). pap. 11.99 *(978-1-5011-0034-5(3),* Atria Bks.) Simon & Schuster.
Sullivan, Kate. What Do You Hear?, 1 vol. 2018. (ENG., Illus.). 24p. (J). bds. 12.99 *(978-0-7643-5601-8(1),* 16179) Schiffer Publishing, Ltd.
Tangerine, Tracey. Buddy Zooka: In the French Quarter & Beyond. 2010. (ENG.). 201p. (J). (gr. 7-12). pap. 16.00 *(978-0-9741995-8-0(3))* Chin Music Pr.
Taylor, Debbie A. Sweet Music in Harlem. Morrison, Frank, illus. 2014. 32p. pap. 9.00 *(978-1-61003-220-9(9))* Center for the Collaborative Classroom.
—Sweet Music in Harlem, 1 vol. Morrison, Frank, illus. 2004. (ENG.). 32p. (J). 17.95 *(978-1-58430-165-3(1));* (gr. 1-4). pap. 11.95 *(978-1-62014-080-2(2),* leelowbooks) Lee & Low Bks., Inc.
Thompson, Kate. The Last of the High Kings. 2008. 323p. (YA). (gr. 7-18). lib. bdg. 17.89 *(978-0-06-117596-1(X),* HarperTeen) HarperCollins Pubs.
Thorne, Jenn Marie. Night Music. 2019. 400p. (YA). (gr. 9). 17.99 *(978-0-7352-2877-1(9),* Dial Bks) Penguin Young Readers Group.
Torres, Jennifer. Finding the Music: En Pos de la Música, 1 vol. Alarcão, Renato, illus. 2015.Tr. of En Pos de la Música. (ENG.). 40p. (J). 18.95 *(978-0-89239-291-9(6))* Lee & Low Bks., Inc.
Townley, Roderick. Sky. 2010. (ENG.). 272p. (YA). (gr. 7). pap. 12.99 *(978-1-4423-3973-6(X),* Atheneum Bks. for Young Readers) Simon & Schuster Children's Publishing.
Trine, Greg. The Grateful Fred. Montijo, Rhode, illus. 3rd rev. ed. 2006. (Melvin Beederman, Superhero Ser.: 3). (ENG.). 144p. (J). (gr. 2-5). pap. 9.99 *(978-0-8050-7922-7(X),* 900031581) Square Fish.
Trout, Robert J. Drumbeat: The Story of a Civil War Drummer Boy. 2007. 190p. (J). (gr. 4-9). pap. 12.95 *(978-1-57249-390-2(9),* White Mane Kids) White Mane Publishing Co., Inc.
Vagnozzi, Barbara, illus. The Musicians of Bremen. 2007. (Flip-Up Fairy Tales Ser.). 24p. (J). (gr. 1-2). *(978-1-84643-115-9(8))* Child's Play International Ltd.
Verde, Susan. Rock 'n' Roll Soul. Cordell, Matthew, illus. 2018. (ENG.). 32p. (J). (gr. k-2). 16.99 *(978-1-4197-2849-5(0),* 697701, Abrams Bks. for Young Readers) Abrams, Inc.
Vernick, Audrey. Teach Your Buffalo to Play Drums. Jennewein, Daniel, illus. 2011. (ENG.). 32p. (J). (gr. -1-3). 16.99 *(978-0-06-176253-6(9),* Balzer & Bray) HarperCollins Pubs.
Walsh, Alice. A Gift of Music: Emile Benoit & His Fiddle, 1 vol. Butler, Geoff, illus. 2010. (ENG.). 32p. (J). (gr. k-5). *(978-1-897174-52-4(7))* Breakwater Bks., Ltd.
Warga, Jasmine. Here We Are Now. 2017. 292p. (YA). *(978-0-06-269404-1(9))* Addison Wesley.
—Here We Are Now. 2017. (ENG.). 304p. (YA). (gr. 9). 17.99 *(978-0-06-232470-2(5),* Balzer & Bray) HarperCollins Pubs.
Weatherford, Carole Boston. Becoming Billie Holiday. Cooper, Floyd, illus. 2008. (ENG.). 120p. (YA). (gr. 4-7). 19.95 *(978-1-59078-507-2(X),* Wordsong) Highlights Pr., c/o Highlights for Children, Inc.
Wells, Helen. Cherry Ames, Private Duty Nurse. 2006. (Cherry Ames Nurse Stories Ser.). 224p. (J). (gr. 3-7). 14.95 *(978-0-8261-0398-7(7))* Springer Publishing Co., Inc.
Wenberg, Michael. Stringz. 2010. 216p. (YA). (gr. 6-10). 16.95 *(978-1-934813-33-1(8))* Westside Bks.
Whitaker, Alecia. The Way Back Home. 2016. (Wildflower Ser.: 3). (ENG.). 336p. (YA). (gr. 7-17). 17.99 *(978-0-316-25144-0(5),* Poppy) Little, Brown Bks. for Young Readers.
Wilde, Jen. The Brightsiders. 2019. (ENG.). 320p. (YA). pap. 10.99 *(978-1-250-30914-3(X),* 900192313) Square Fish.
Willems, Mo. Because. Ren, Amber, illus. 2019. (ENG.). 40p. (J). (gr. -1-k). 17.99 *(978-1-368-01901-9(3),* Hyperion Books for Children) Disney Publishing Worldwide.
Williams, Sean. Impossible Music. 2019. (ENG.). 320p. (YA). (gr. 9). 17.99 *(978-0-544-81620-6(X),* 1642320, Clarion Bks.) HarperCollins Pubs.
Winters, Ben H. The Secret Life of Ms. Finkleman. 2011. (ENG.). 272p. (J). (gr. 3-7). pap. 5.99 *(978-0-06-196543-2(X),* HarperCollins) HarperCollins Pubs.
Wolff, Virginia Euwer. The Mozart Season. 2007. (ENG.). 272p. (J). (gr. 6-8). per. 12.99 *(978-0-312-36745-9(7),* 900042350) Square Fish.
Yoo, Paula. Good Enough. 2012. (ENG.). 336p. (YA). (gr. 8). pap. 7.99 *(978-0-06-079090-5(3),* HarperTeen) HarperCollins Pubs.

MUSICIANS, NEGRO

see African American Musicians

MUSICIANS—UNITED STATES

Adams, Michelle Medlock. Kenny Chesney. 2006. (Blue Banner Biography Ser.). (Illus.). 32p. (YA). (gr. 4-7). lib. bdg. 25.70 *(978-1-58415-502-7(7),* 1259607) Mitchell Lane Pubs.
Andrews, Troy. Trombone Shorty. Collier, Bryan, illus. 2015. (ENG.). 40p. (J). (gr. -1-3). 19.99 *(978-1-4197-1465-8(1),* 1071101, Abrams Bks. for Young Readers) Abrams, Inc.
Andrews, Troy & Taylor, Bill. The 5 o'Clock Band. Collier, Bryan, illus. 2018. (ENG.). 40p. (J). (gr. -1-3). 19.99 *(978-1-4197-2836-5(9),* 1196201, Abrams Bks. for Young Readers) Abrams, Inc.
Azzarelli, Ally. Drake! Hip-Hop Celebrity, 1 vol. 2013. (Sizzling Celebrities Ser.). (ENG.). 48p. (gr. 4-6). pap. 11.53 *(978-1-4644-0275-3(2),* 3996c7d4-201b-42d2-9766-92dafb905bfb) Enslow Publishing, LLC.
Bankston, John. The Life & Times of Scott Joplin. 2004. (Masters of Music Ser.). (Illus.). 48p. (gr. 4-8). lib. bdg. 20.95 *(978-1-58415-270-5(2))* Mitchell Lane Pubs.
Bodden, Valerie. Carrie Underwood: Big Time. 2013. (Big Time Ser.). (ENG.). 24p. (J). (gr. 1-4). 23.09 *(978-1-60818-476-7(5),* 21704) Creative Co., The.
Books, Triumph, ed. Taylor Swift: Seeing Red. 2013. (ENG., Illus.). 96p. (J). pap. 9.99 *(978-1-60078-902-1(1))* Triumph Bks.
Boone, Mary. Dizzy Gillespie. 2012. 48p. (J). (gr. 4-8). lib. bdg. 29.95 *(978-1-61228-272-5(5))* Mitchell Lane Pubs.
—Ornette Coleman. 2012. (J). lib. bdg. 29.95 *(978-1-61228-268-8(7))* Mitchell Lane Pubs.
Bowe, Brian J. The Ramones, 1 vol. 2018. (Bands That Rock! Ser.). (ENG.). 112p. (YA). (gr. 7-7). 38.93 *(978-1-9785-0352-6(0),* d6c565b1-020d-4a94-8983-10f7a1530302) Enslow Publishing, LLC.
Breguet, Amy. Yellowcard, 1 vol. 2006. (Contemporary Musicians & Their Music Ser.). (ENG., Illus.). 48p. (YA). (gr. 6-6). lib. bdg. 34.47 *(978-1-4042-0714-1(7),* a5e362dc-3ec6-4c31-aec5-96612780c49a) Rosen Publishing Group, Inc., The.
Brooks, Riley. Taylor Swift: Fearless Star. 2010. (Illus.). 48p. (J). *(978-0-545-30382-8(6))* Scholastic, Inc.
Brown, Monica. Tito Puente, Mambo King/Tito Puente, Rey Del Mambo: Bilingual English-Spanish. Lopez, Rafael, illus. 2013. (ENG.). 32p. (J). (gr. -1-3). 19.99 *(978-0-06-122783-7(8))* HarperCollins Español.
Burlingame, Jeff. Taylor Swift: Music Superstar, 1 vol. 2012. (Hot Celebrity Biographies Ser.). (ENG., Illus.). 48p. (gr. 5-7). lib. bdg. 27.93 *(978-0-7660-3870-7(X),* c037aea0-2249-4265-80c6-d52d3ec5f273) Enslow Publishing, LLC.
Burns, Kylie. Carrie Underwood. 2013. (ENG., Illus.). 32p. (J). *(978-0-7787-0024-1(0));* pap. *(978-0-7787-0043-2(7))* Crabtree Publishing Co.
Cefrey, Holly. Taylor Swift, 1 vol. 2011. (Megastars Ser.). (ENG., Illus.). 48p. (YA). (gr. 5-5). 34.47 *(978-1-4358-3575-7(1),* 921b07f9-abfa-4faa-a863-86a1f80465d8); pap. 12.75 *(978-1-4488-2261-4(0),* e4a0ec47-97a8-4fd9-9147-9b1092b26f46) Rosen Publishing Group, Inc., The. (Rosen Reference).
Cham, Stephanie. Yo-Yo Ma. 2018. (Illus.). 24p. (J). *(978-81-515-7997-2(8))* Capstone.
Christensen, Bonnie. Elvis: The Story of the Rock & Roll King. Christensen, Bonnie, illus. 2015. (ENG., Illus.). 32p. (J). (gr. 1-4). 18.99 *(978-0-8050-9447-3(4),* 900077612, Holt, Henry & Co. Bks. For Young Readers) Holt, Henry & Co.
Cline-Ransome, Lesa. Benny Goodman & Teddy Wilson: Taking the Stage As the First Black-And-White Jazz Band in History. Ransome, James E., illus. 2014. (ENG.). 32p. (J). (gr. 3-7). 18.99 *(978-0-8234-2362-0(X))* Holiday Hse., Inc.
Collins, Terry. King of Pop: The Story of Michael Jackson, 1 vol. Byers, Michael, illus. 2012. (American Graphic Ser.). (ENG.). 32p. (J). (gr. 3-9). 31.32 *(978-1-4296-6015-0(5),* 114952, Capstone Pr.) Capstone.
—Louis Armstrong: Jazz Legend, 1 vol. Pope, Richmond & Pope, Richmond, illus. 2012. (American Graphic Ser.). (ENG.). 32p. (J). (gr. 3-9). pap. 8.10 *(978-1-4296-9336-3(3),* 120376, Capstone Pr.) Capstone.
Cupp, Tonya. Taylor Swift. 2015. (Illus.). 48p. (J). lib. bdg. *(978-1-62713-310-4(0))* Cavendish Square Publishing LLC.
Currie-McGhee, Leanne K. Alicia Keys, 1 vol. 2012. (People in the News Ser.). (ENG.). 96p. (gr. 7-7). lib. bdg. 41.03 *(978-1-4205-0782-9(6),* 88270efe-9636-4195-96f5-94df5329153c, Lucent Pr.) Greenhaven Publishing LLC.
Dann, Sarah. Beyoncé. 2013. (ENG., Illus.). 32p. (J). *(978-0-7787-0019-7(4))* Crabtree Publishing Co.
Dylan, Bob. Forever Young. Rogers, Paul, illus. 2008. (ENG.). 40p. (J). (gr. -1-4). 18.99 *(978-1-4169-5808-6(8),* Atheneum Bks. for Young Readers) Simon & Schuster Children's Publishing.
Earl, C. F. Kanye West. 2012. (Superstars of Hip-Hop Ser.). (Illus.). 48p. (J). (gr. 3-4). 19.95 *(978-1-4222-2533-2(X))* Mason Crest.
Edgers, Geoff. Who Was Elvis Presley? O'brien, John, illus. 2007. (Who Was...? Ser.). 105p. (gr. 2-5). 15.00 *(978-0-7569-8164-8(6))* Perfection Learning Corp.
Engle, Susan. John Birks "Dizzy" Gillespie. Mazibuko, Luthando, illus. 2020. (Change Maker Ser.). (ENG.). 90p. (J). (gr. 4-7). pap. 9.95 *(978-1-61851-153-9(X))* Baha'i Publishing.
Franke, Amim. Julianne Hough, 1 vol. 2010. (Country Music Stars Ser.). (ENG.). 32p. (J). (gr. 1-1). pap. 11.50 *(978-1-4339-3933-4(9),* 975f373e-a92a-4511-91ca-c5bc577e1a9c); lib. bdg. 27.93 *(978-1-4339-3932-7(0),* df7fa4eb-2534-473e-9cbd-c51f5bea2eb1) Stevens, Gareth Publishing LLLP.
—Miranda Lambert, 1 vol. 2010. (Country Music Stars Ser.). (ENG.). 32p. (J). (gr. 1-1). pap. 11.50 *(978-1-4339-3936-5(3),* 1ac6038a-53ca-4aca-aa55-8f7b554a8f05); lib. bdg. 27.93 *(978-1-4339-3935-8(5),* 22afc16e-ef22-4cc4-9739-21c0b2c61a8f) Stevens, Gareth Publishing LLLP.
French, Holly. One Direction. 2015. (Pop Icons Ser.). (Illus.). 64p. (J). (gr. 7). lib. bdg. 23.95 *(978-1-4222-3249-1(2))* Mason Crest.
Frisch, Aaron. Taylor Swift. 2013. (Big Time Ser.). (ENG., Illus.). 24p. (J). (gr. 1-4). 25.65 *(978-1-60818-333-3(5),* 21818, Creative Education) Creative Co., The.
Gagne, Tammy. Jake Owen. 2018. lib. bdg. 25.70 *(978-1-68020-162-8(X))* Mitchell Lane Pubs.
—Kacey Musgraves. 2018. lib. bdg. 25.70 *(978-1-68020-160-4(3))* Mitchell Lane Pubs.
Giddens, Sandra. Chris Daughtry. (Who's Your Idol? Ser.). 48p. (gr. 5-5). 2009. 53.00 *(978-1-60854-786-9(8),* Rosen Reference) 2008. (ENG., Illus.). (J). lib. bdg. 34.47 *(978-1-4042-1371-5(6),*

MNO

3b547ecf-03e5-4ed7-81d8-d2529fcde407) Rosen Publishing Group, Inc., The.

Gigliotti, Jim. Bruno Mars. 2018. (Amazing Americans: Pop Music Stars Ser.). (ENG.). 24p. (J). (gr. -1-3). 26.99 *(978-1-68402-459-9(5))* Bearport Publishing Co., Inc.

Gigliotti, Jim & Roshell, Starshine. Blake Shelton. 2018. (Amazing Americans: Country Music Stars Ser.). (ENG.). 24p. (J). (gr. -1-3). 26.99 *(978-1-68402-682-1(2))* Bearport Publishing Co., Inc.

—Miranda Lambert. 2018. (Amazing Americans: Country Music Stars Ser.). (ENG.). 24p. (J). (gr. -1-3). lib. bdg. 18.45 *(978-1-68402-684-5(9))* Bearport Publishing Co., Inc.

Gitlin, Martin. Chaz Bono, 1 vol. 2016. (Transgender Pioneers Ser.). (ENG., Illus.). 112p. (J). (gr. 7-7). 38.80 *(978-1-5081-7157-7(2),* 80aa16a0-c36f-49c7-bb3a-774de0ab3d61) Rosen Publishing Group, Inc., The.

Gnojewski, Carol. Madonna: Fighting for Self-Expression, 1 vol. 2017. (Rebels with a Cause Ser.). (ENG.). 128p. (gr. 8-8). 38.93 *(978-0-7660-9255-6(0),* 8361f07d-bca5-4de3-b8d4-edc5249c8e78) Enslow Publishing, LLC.

Golio, Gary. Bird & Diz. Young, Ed, illus. 2015. (ENG.). 26p. (J). (gr. -1-3). 19.99 *(978-0-7636-6660-6(2))* Candlewick Pr.

—Jimi: Sounds Like a Rainbow: A Story of the Young Jimi Hendrix. Steptoe, Javaka, illus. 2010. (ENG.). 32p. (J). (gr. 1-4). 17.99 *(978-0-618-85279-6(4),* 100567, Clarion Bks.) HarperCollins Pubs.

Gourley, Robbin. Talkin' Guitar: A Story of Young Doc Watson. 2015. (ENG., Illus.). 40p. (J). (gr. -1-3). 16.99 *(978-0-544-12988-7(1),* 1544783, Clarion Bks.) HarperCollins Pubs.

Griffiths, Katie. Beyoncé: Entertainment Industry Icon, 1 vol. 2017. (Leading Women Ser.). (ENG., Illus.). 112p. (YA). (gr. 7-7). 41.64 *(978-1-5026-2705-6(1),* ea49be16-bf57-49ea-879d-1ec72e415a89) Cavendish Square Publishing LLC.

Hamilton, Toby G. Busta Rhymes. 2009. (Hip Hop (Mason Crest Paperback) Ser.). (Illus.). 64p. (YA). (gr. 4-7). pap. 7.95 *(978-1-4222-0333-0(6))* Mason Crest.

Hampton, Wilborn. Elvis Presley: A Twentieth Century Life. 2007. (ENG., Illus.). 192p. (YA). (gr. 7). 26.16 *(978-1-4287-4879-8(2))* Follett School Solutions.

Horning, Nicole. Justin Timberlake: Musical Megastar, 1 vol. 2019. (People in the News Ser.). (ENG.). 104p. (gr. 7-7). pap. 20.99 *(978-1-5345-6837-2(9),* 34102f88-b22f-409a-8ac8-d64b0c63fdbf, Lucent Pr.) Greenhaven Publishing LLC.

Jacobson, Bob. Les Paul: Guitar Wizard. 2012. (Badger Biographies Ser.). (ENG., Illus.). 112p. (J). (gr. 4-6). pap. 12.95 *(978-0-87020-488-3(2))* Wisconsin Historical Society.

Janic, Susan & Thomas, Scott. Jonas Brothers Forever: The Unofficial Story of Kevin, Joe & Nick. 2009. (ENG., Illus.). 158p. (J). (gr. 4-7). pap. 14.95 *(978-1-55022-851-9(X),* 58085575-3f03-4566-a4d1-2abb5f8b42b6) ECW Pr. CAN. Dist: Baker & Taylor Publisher Services (BTPS).

Jemaine, Bret. Sugarland, 1 vol. 2010. (Country Music Stars Ser.). (ENG.). 32p. (J). (gr. 1-1). pap. 11.50 *(978-1-4339-3939-6(8),* 2181b101-4e77-4b55-9ad0-bec324030773); lib. bdg. 27.93 *(978-1-4339-3938-9(X),* 3590bc32-f3b2-4627-a7c8-00fc0921ff27) Stevens, Gareth Publishing LLLP.

—Tim Mcgraw, 1 vol. 2010. (Country Music Stars Ser.). (ENG.). 32p. (J). (gr. 1-1). pap. 11.50 *(978-1-4339-3942-6(8),* a17be525-e5e2-41a4-85af-46bd4ac3d5c1); lib. bdg. 27.93 *(978-1-4339-3941-9(X),* e97506e4-2d54-41b6-9a25-dd6b332e879d) Stevens, Gareth Publishing LLLP.

Kallen, Stuart A. Gwen Stefani. (Role Model Entertainers Ser.). (Illus.). 64p. (YA). 2010. (gr. 7-12). 22.95 *(978-1-4222-0510-5(X))* 2007. pap. 9.95 *(978-1-4222-0797-0(8))* Mason Crest.

Kawa, Katie & Cartlidge, Cherese. Taylor Swift: Superstar Singer, 1 vol. 2016. (People in the News Ser.). (ENG.). 104p. (J). (gr. 7-7). lib. bdg. 41.03 *(978-1-5345-6025-3(4),* ac227de1-650d-4244-a457-698940f8a45a, Lucent Pr.) Greenhaven Publishing LLC.

Kelley, K. C. Michael Jackson. 2018. (Amazing Americans: Pop Music Stars Ser.). (ENG.). 24p. (J). (gr. -1-3). lib. bdg. 26.99 *(978-1-68402-679-1(2))* Bearport Publishing Co., Inc.

—Taylor Swift. 2018. (Amazing Americans: Pop Music Stars Ser.). (ENG.). 24p. (J). (gr. -1-3). lib. bdg. 26.99 *(978-1-68402-456-8(0))* Bearport Publishing Co., Inc.

Kelley, True & Who HQ. Who Is Dolly Parton? Marchesi, Stephen, illus. 2014. (Who Was? Ser.). 112p. (J). (gr. 3-7). 5.99 *(978-0-448-47892-0(7),* Penguin Workshop) Penguin Young Readers Group.

La Bella, Laura. My Chemical Romance, 1 vol. 2008. (Contemporary Musicians & Their Music Ser.). (ENG., Illus.). 48p. (gr. 6-6). (J). lib. bdg. 34.47 *(978-1-4042-1818-5(1),* 4cb39b1a-962b-4483-bb30-876a0e557f8c); pap. 12.75 *(978-1-4358-5126-9(9),* f3a16fb9-a843-4c87-8140-3b0226003f5c) Rosen Publishing Group, Inc., The.

Lajiness, Katie. Blake Shelton. 2017. (Big Buddy Pop Biographies Set 2 Ser.). (ENG., Illus.). 32p. (J). (gr. 2-5). lib. bdg. 34.21 *(978-1-5321-1063-4(4),* 25702, Big Buddy Bks.) ABDO Publishing Co.

—R5, 1 vol. 2015. (Big Buddy Pop Biographies Ser.). (ENG., Illus.). 32p. (J). (gr. 2-5). 34.21 *(978-1-68078-058-1(1),* 19043, Big Buddy Bks.) ABDO Publishing Co.

—Riker Lynch, 1 vol. 2015. (Big Buddy Pop Biographies Ser.). (ENG., Illus.). 32p. (J). (gr. 2-5). 34.21 *(978-1-68078-054-3(9),* 19035, Big Buddy Bks.) ABDO Publishing Co.

—Taylor Swift, 1 vol. 2015. (Big Buddy Pop Biographies Ser.). (ENG., Illus.). 32p. (J). (gr. 2-5). 34.21 *(978-1-68078-060-4(3),* 19047, Big Buddy Bks.) ABDO Publishing Co.

Leavitt, Amie Jane. Bruno Mars. 2012. (Illus.). 32p. (J). lib. bdg. 25.70 *(978-1-61228-316-6(0))* Mitchell Lane Pubs.

—Toby Keith. 2008. (Blue Banner Biography Ser.). (Illus.). 32p. (YA). (gr. 4-7). lib. bdg. 25.70 *(978-1-58415-678-9(3))* Mitchell Lane Pubs.

Linde, Barbara M. Taylor Swift, 1 vol. 2010. (Today's Superstars Ser.). (ENG.). 48p. (J). (gr. 3-3). pap. 15.05 *(978-1-4339-4002-6(7),* 853b9cb5-e1e9-463b-8a39-ca65dff46301); lib. bdg. 34.60 *(978-1-4339-4001-9(9),* a1aef9a3-eda1-47da-8a35-4b06a9204418) Stevens, Gareth Publishing LLLP.

Lynette, Rachel. Miles Davis: Legendary Jazz Musician, 1 vol. 2010. (Innovators Ser.). (ENG., Illus.). 48p. (gr. 4-8). 36.23 *(978-0-7377-5034-8(0),* 3294fa0d-68af-4bb1-bd8b-19d4f9a076e8, KidHaven Publishing) Greenhaven Publishing LLC.

Maccarry, Noel. Who Was Pete Seeger? 2017. (Who Was... ? Ser.). lib. bdg. 16.00 *(978-0-606-40116-6(4))* Turtleback.

Magram, Clara. John Legend. (Pop Culture Ser.). (Illus.). 64p. (YA). (gr. 4-7). 2008. lib. bdg. 22.95 *(978-1-4222-0076-6(0))* 2007. pap. 7.95 *(978-1-4222-0360-6(3))* Mason Crest.

Mahin, Michael. Muddy: The Story of Blues Legend Muddy Waters. Turk, Evan, illus. 2017. (ENG.). 48p. (J). (gr. -1-3). 17.99 *(978-1-4814-4349-4(6))* Simon & Schuster Children's Publishing.

—When Angels Sing: The Story of Rock Legend Carlos Santana. Ramirez, Jose, illus. 2018. (ENG.). 48p. (J). (gr. -1-3). 17.99 *(978-1-5344-0413-7(9))* Simon & Schuster Children's Publishing.

Marcovitz, Hal. Chris Daughtry. 2009. (Dream Big: American Idol Superstars Ser.). 64p. (YA). (gr. 5-18). 22.95 *(978-1-4222-1508-1(3));* pap. 9.95 *(978-1-4222-1595-1(4))* Mason Crest.

Markel, Rita J. Jimi Hendrix. 2003. (Biography Ser.). (Illus.). 112p. (YA). (gr. 6-18). pap. 7.95 *(978-0-8225-9697-4(0),* Carolrhoda Bks.) Lerner Publishing Group.

Marron, Maggie. Jonas Brothers: Tasty Celebrity Bios. 2009. (Junk Food: Tasty Celebrity Bios Ser.). (ENG.). 112p. (J). (gr. 3-6). pap. 22.44 *(978-0-531-21721-4(3))* Scholastic Library Publishing.

Marvis, Barbara. Day by Day with Beyonce. 2010. (Randy's Corner Ser.). (Illus.). 32p. (J). (gr. -1-2). lib. bdg. 25.70 *(978-1-58415-859-2(X))* Mitchell Lane Pubs.

Mattern, Joanne. Benny Goodman. 2012. (J). lib. bdg. 29.95 *(978-1-61228-269-5(5))* Mitchell Lane Pubs.

—Count Basie. 2012. (J). lib. bdg. 29.95 *(978-1-61228-270-1(9))* Mitchell Lane Pubs.

McDougall, Chros. Kurt Cobain: Alternative Rock Innovator, 1 vol. 2012. (Lives Cut Short Set 2 Ser.). (ENG., Illus.). 112p. (YA). (gr. 6-12). 41.36 *(978-1-61783-480-6(7),* 11195, Essential Library) ABDO Publishing Co.

McIntosh, Kenneth. The Grateful Dead. 2008. (Pop Rock Ser.). (Illus.). 64p. (YA). (gr. 4-7). lib. bdg. 22.95 *(978-1-4222-0191-6(0))* Mason Crest.

Mckissack, Patricia & Mckissack, Fredrick. Louis Armstrong: King of Jazz, 1 vol. 2013. (Famous African Americans Ser.). (ENG., Illus.). 24p. (gr. k-2). 25.27 *(978-0-7660-4106-6(9),* d3383f77-34de-4fe1-84ea-a9a0b5cf7a92); pap. 10.35 *(978-1-4644-0200-5(0),* 38ea6494-964a-4dc1-b96a-2d5a5193aabb) Enslow Publishing, LLC. (Enslow Elementary).

McNeese, Tim. Tito Puente. 2008. (ENG., Illus.). 118p. (gr. 6-12). lib. bdg. 35.00 *(978-0-7910-9666-6(1),* P145665, Facts On File) Infobase Holdings, Inc.

Mellark, Kat. Louis Armstrong: American Musician. 2013. (InfoMax Readers Ser.). (ENG.). 24p. (J). (gr. 2-3). pap. 49.50 *(978-1-4777-2429-3(X));* (Illus.). pap. 8.25 *(978-1-4777-2428-6(1),* 0b07c8ef-5ec9-4ab8-a957-2217333dca90) Rosen Publishing Group, Inc., The. (Rosen Classroom).

Merwin, E. & Roshell, Starshine. Carrie Underwood. 2018. (Amazing Americans: Country Music Stars Ser.). (ENG.). 24p. (J). (gr. -1-3). lib. bdg. 18.45 *(978-1-68402-683-8(0))* Bearport Publishing Co., Inc.

Micklos, John & Micklos, John, Jr. Elvis Presley: Fighting for the Right to Rock, 1 vol. 2017. (Rebels with a Cause Ser.). (ENG.). 128p. (J). (gr. 8-8). 38.93 *(978-0-7660-9258-7(5),* 5908d67d-754a-4219-b3d7-6ea667662142); pap. 20.95 *(978-0-7660-9549-6(5),* b5ea81c8-5ee6-4f61-97e4-afe4efbaaad3) Enslow Publishing, LLC.

Mitchells, Brett. The Dixie Chicks, 1 vol. 2008. (Contemporary Musicians & Their Music Ser.). (ENG., Illus.). 48p. (J). (gr. 6-6). lib. bdg. 34.47 *(978-1-4042-1817-8(3),* 9f3ce705-6314-489a-885b-db3eeac89120) Rosen Publishing Group, Inc., The.

—Dixie Chicks, 1 vol. 2008. (Contemporary Musicians & Their Music Ser.). (ENG., Illus.). 48p. (gr. 6-6). pap. 12.75 *(978-1-4358-5125-2(0),* 311a4104-afec-4cd1-96d3-ed1986a7ebb2, Rosen Classroom) Rosen Publishing Group, Inc., The.

Mooney, Carla. Jonas Brothers, 1 vol. 2009. (People in the News Ser.). (ENG., Illus.). 96p. (gr. 7-7). 41.03 *(978-1-4205-0236-7(0),* 9e06352f-b3c8-44ef-8691-b262cd85bdf1, Lucent Pr.) Greenhaven Publishing LLC.

Morganelli, Adrianna. Bruno Mars. 2013. (ENG., Illus.). 32p. (J). pap. *(978-0-7787-0041-8(0))* Crabtree Publishing Co.

Morreale, Marie. Taylor Swift. 2015. (ENG.). 48p. (J). pap. 7.95 *(978-0-531-21429-9(X),* Children's Pr.) Scholastic Library Publishing.

Mour, Stanley I. Innovators of American Jazz, 1 vol. 2013. (Inspiring Collective Biographies Ser.). (ENG.). 112p. (gr. 5-6). 35.93 *(978-0-7660-4166-0(2),* 9f6b5c9e-1d71-4d4b-94b9-d79be9f7275d) Enslow Publishing, LLC.

Murphy, Maggie. The Jonas Brothers: Rock Stars, 1 vol. 2010. (Young & Famous Ser.). (ENG., Illus.). 24p. (J). (gr. 1-2). pap. 9.85 *(978-1-4488-1805-1(2),* d9e376a5-7be9-4907-8e4d-60e5cfe372b7, PowerKids Pr.) Rosen Publishing Group, Inc., The.

—Taylor Swift: Country Music Star, 1 vol. 2010. (Young & Famous Ser.). (ENG., Illus.). 24p. (J). (gr. 1-2). pap. 9.85 *(978-1-4488-1803-7(6),* 899798c1-96d8-4871-a465-12883b3eb207, PowerKids Pr.) Rosen Publishing Group, Inc., The.

Napoli, Tony. Justin Timberlake: Breakout Music Superstar, 1 vol. 2009. (Hot Celebrity Biographies Ser.). (ENG., Illus.). 48p. (gr. 5-7). pap. 11.53 *(978-0-7660-3632-1(4),* 553ba8ca-bfd1-4144-8161-944cf4df140b, Enslow Elementary) Enslow Publishing, LLC.

Newsome, Joel. Louis Armstrong: Jazz Musician, 1 vol. 2017. (History Makers Ser.). (ENG.). 144p. (YA). (gr. 9-9). 47.36 *(978-1-5026-3292-0(6),* f407f0ce-1c17-4c24-8582-2725df99846b) Cavendish Square Publishing LLC.

Nolan, Nina. Mahalia Jackson: Walking with Kings & Queens. Holyfield, John, illus. 2015. (ENG.). 32p. (J). (gr. -1-3). 17.99 *(978-0-06-087944-0(0),* HarperCollins) HarperCollins Pubs.

O'Connor, Jim. Who Is Bob Dylan? 2013. (Who Is... ? Ser.). lib. bdg. 16.00 *(978-0-606-31685-9(X))* Turtleback.

O'Connor, Jim & Who HQ. Who Is Bob Dylan? O'Brien, John, illus. 2013. (Who Was? Ser.). 112p. (J). (gr. 3-7). pap. 5.99 *(978-0-448-46461-9(6),* Penguin Workshop) Penguin Young Readers Group.

Old, Wendie C. The Life of Duke Ellington: Giant of Jazz, 1 vol. 2014. (Legendary African Americans Ser.). (ENG., Illus.). 96p. (gr. 6-7). 31.61 *(978-0-7660-6127-9(2),* 19358b88-58fa-4c94-a96a-d9248b4afa1e) Enslow Publishing, LLC.

—The Life of Louis Armstrong: King of Jazz, 1 vol. 2014. (Legendary African Americans Ser.). (ENG., Illus.). 96p. (gr. 6-7). 31.61 *(978-0-7660-6142-2(6),* c3122453-2823-4435-951a-9b12a7999ca0) Enslow Publishing, LLC.

Omoth, Tyler. Taylor Swift: Music Icon. 2017. (Superstar Stories Ser.). (ENG.). 24p. (J). (gr. 3-6). lib. bdg. 32.79 *(978-1-5038-1999-3(X),* 211875) Child's World, Inc, The.

Orr, Tamra. The Jonas Brothers, 1 vol. 2011. (Megastars Ser.). (ENG., Illus.). 48p. (YA). (gr. 5-5). 34.47 *(978-1-4358-3572-6(7),* 0ad7c82e-e565-463e-a30b-931e449c18a6, Rosen Reference) Rosen Publishing Group, Inc., The.

—Louis Armstrong. 2012. (J). lib. bdg. 29.95 *(978-1-61228-264-0(4))* Mitchell Lane Pubs.

—Miles Davis. 2012. (Illus.). 47p. (J). lib. bdg. 29.95 *(978-1-61228-265-7(2))* Mitchell Lane Pubs.

Orr, Tamra B. The Jonas Brothers, 1 vol. 2011. (Megastars Ser.). (ENG., Illus.). 48p. (YA). (gr. 5-5). pap. 12.75 *(978-1-4488-2258-4(0),* 5fb1ba55-202a-42a7-afbc-1e04e567e472, Rosen Reference) Rosen Publishing Group, Inc., The.

Peppas, Lynn. Taylor Swift. 2010. (Superstars! Ser.). (ENG.). 32p. (J). (gr. 3-6). lib. bdg. *(978-0-7787-7252-1(7))* Crabtree Publishing Co.

Rajczak Nelson, Kristen. Bruno Mars: Singer & Songwriter. 2017. (Illus.). 24p. (J). pap. *(978-80-7660-784-2(1))* Enslow Publishing, LLC.

—China Anne Mcclain: Actress, Singer, & Songwriter, 1 vol. 2016. (Junior Biographies Ser.). (ENG.). 24p. (gr. 3-4). pap. 10.35 *(978-0-7660-8184-0(2),* 4ae7f475-4d94-4da0-b37c-2ca3d5b2459c) Enslow Publishing, LLC.

Rau, Dana Meachen. Who Are the Rolling Stones? 2017. (Who Is... ? Ser.). (Illus.). 107p. (J). lib. bdg. 16.00 *(978-0-606-39778-0(7))* Turtleback.

Reef, Catherine. Leonard Bernstein & American Music. 2012. (Modern Music Masters Ser.). (gr. 7-12). 27.95 *(978-1-59935-125-4(0))* Reynolds, Morgan Inc.

Reusser, Kayleen. Day by Day with Taylor Swift. 2010. (Randy's Corner Ser.). (Illus.). 32p. (J). (gr. -1-2). lib. bdg. 25.70 *(978-1-58415-857-8(3))* Mitchell Lane Pubs.

—Taylor Swift. 2008. (Blue Banner Biography Ser.). (Illus.). 32p. (YA). (gr. 4-7). lib. bdg. 25.70 *(978-1-58415-675-8(9))* Mitchell Lane Pubs.

Rice, Earle. Charlie Parker. 2012. (Illus.). 47p. (J). lib. bdg. 29.95 *(978-1-61228-266-4(0))* Mitchell Lane Pubs.

Riddle, Sharon Kay & Sanders, Nancy/Ida. Tony Loved to Learn. Mendoza, Megan Elizabeth, illus. 2007. 32p. (J). pap. 15.00 *(978-0-9761583-6-3(1))* Olive Leaf Pubns.

Rivera, Ursula. Aretha Franklin. 2009. (Rock & Roll Hall of Famers Ser.). 112p. (gr. 5-8). 63.90 *(978-1-60852-467-9(1),* Rosen Reference) Rosen Publishing Group, Inc., The.

Roberts, Russell. Alicia Keys: Singer-Songwriter, Musician, Actress, & Producer. 2012. (Transcending Race Ser.). 64p. (J). (gr. 5). 22.95 *(978-1-4222-2727-5(8))* Mason Crest.

Roza, Greg. Bo Diddley, 1 vol. 2010. (Inspiring Lives Ser.). (ENG.). 32p. (J). (gr. 1-1). lib. bdg. 27.93 *(978-1-4339-3622-7(4),* b9d7faa7-ca31-4cce-87de-664ce246da79); (Illus.). pap. 11.50 *(978-1-4339-3623-4(2),* 6a37788e-1c1b-4de9-91ab-59b8f0dd2f2d) Stevens, Gareth Publishing LLLP.

Rubin, Laurie. Do You Dream in Color? Insights from a Girl Without Sight. 2012. (Illus.). 400p. (J). (gr. 7). pap. 18.95 *(978-1-60980-424-4(4),* Triangle Square) Seven Stories Pr.

Russell-Brown, Katheryn. Little Melba & Her Big Trombone, 1 vol. Morrison, Frank, illus. 2014. (ENG.). 40p. (J). (gr. 1-5). 20.95 *(978-1-60060-898-8(1),* leelowbooks) Lee & Low Bks., Inc.

Sabol, Stephanie & Who HQ. Who Is Bruce Springsteen? Copeland, Gregory, illus. 2016. (Who Was? Ser.). 112p. (J). (gr. 3-7). 5.99 *(978-0-448-48703-8(9),* Penguin Workshop) Penguin Young Readers Group.

Saddleback Educational Publishing Staff. Usher. 2013. (Hip-Hop Biographies (Saddleback Publishing) Ser.). (YA). lib. bdg. 23.25 *(978-0-606-31490-9(3))* Turtleback.

Saddleback Educational Publishing Staff, ed. Elvis Presley, 1 vol. unabr. ed. 2007. (Graphic Biographies Ser.). (ENG., Illus.). 25p. (YA). (gr. 4-12). pap. 9.75 *(978-1-59905-221-2(0))* Saddleback Educational Publishing, Inc.

Sarantou, Katlin. Stevie Wonder. Bane, Jeff, illus. 2019. (My Early Library: My Itty-Bitty Bio Ser.). (ENG.). 24p. (J). (gr. k-1). pap. 12.79 *(978-1-5341-4988-5(0),* 213259); lib. bdg. 30.64 *(978-1-5341-4702-7(0),* 213258) Cherry Lake Publishing.

Sauver, Dennis St. Shawn Mendes. 2018. (Big Buddy Pop Biographies Ser.). (ENG.). 32p. (J). (gr. 2-5). lib. bdg. 34.21 *(978-1-5321-1801-2(5),* 30648, Big Buddy Bks.) ABDO Publishing Co.

Sawyer, Sarah. Fall Out Boy. (Contemporary Musicians & Their Music Ser.). 48p. (gr. 6-6). 2009. 53.00 *(978-1-61511-935-6(3))* 2008. (ENG., Illus.). (J). lib. bdg. 34.47 *(978-1-4042-1819-2(X),* fd4c205b-a073-4907-bd6f-3958fde5e4df) 2008. (ENG., Illus.). pap. 12.75 *(978-1-4358-5127-6(7),* 1d41538c-e188-4221-8853-3253c3e0fa8a) Rosen Publishing Group, Inc., The.

Schuman, Michael A. Beyoncé: A Biography of a Legendary Singer, 1 vol. 2014. (African-American Icons Ser.). (ENG.). 112p. (gr. 6-7). lib. bdg. 30.61 *(978-0-7660-4230-8(8),* 4e11f61e-4a47-4641-b4c0-ee2508c62796) Enslow Publishing, LLC.

—Led Zeppelin: Legendary Rock Band, 1 vol. 2010. (Rebels of Rock Ser.). (ENG., Illus.). 112p. (gr. 5-6). pap. 13.88 *(978-0-7660-3618-5(9),* 84a344ae-7d19-4a41-9e0b-7335f5b4cda4) Enslow Publishing, LLC.

Schwartz, Heather E. Taylor Swift: Superstar Singer & Songwriter. 2019. (Gateway Biographies Ser.). (ENG., Illus.). 48p. (J). (gr. 4-8). 31.99 *(978-1-5415-2885-7(9),* bef4f13b-67d4-4169-bed1-7a4b2850fc21, Lerner Pubns.) Lerner Publishing Group.

Shea, Therese M. Brad Paisley, 1 vol. 2010. (Country Music Stars Ser.). (ENG.). 32p. (J). (gr. 1-1). pap. 11.50 *(978-1-4339-3930-3(4),* 9e198d1b-4275-4392-9566-7e9ce5f618bc); lib. bdg. 27.93 *(978-1-4339-3929-7(0),* 7c3f65c0-025e-465b-b097-19f057d93e83) Stevens, Gareth Publishing LLLP.

—Toby Keith, 1 vol. 2010. (Country Music Stars Ser.). (ENG.). 32p. (J). (gr. 1-1). pap. 11.50 *(978-1-4339-3945-7(2),* 6b7835cc-e392-4590-8955-f93d53149255); lib. bdg. 27.93 *(978-1-4339-3944-0(4),* 55a7cfec-3a7b-41a5-a7a7-d99ad6a2933d) Stevens, Gareth Publishing LLLP.

—Usher, 1 vol. 2011. (Hip-Hop Headliners Ser.). (ENG., Illus.). 32p. (gr. 1-1). pap. 11.50 *(978-1-4339-4813-8(3),* f9697ac7-bbc3-4e95-81ce-4087158155b2); (J). 27.93 *(978-1-4339-4812-1(5),* 0147663d-f70b-4386-b541-04fd20c28edf) Stevens, Gareth Publishing LLLP.

Sheafer, Silvia Anne. The Life of Aretha Franklin: Queen of Soul, 1 vol. 2014. (Legendary African Americans Ser.). (ENG.). 96p. (gr. 6-6). 31.61 *(978-0-7660-6225-2(2),* 8d530108-f814-45f8-865b-bc40724b292f) Enslow Publishing, LLC.

Spence, Kelly. Taylor Swift: Pop Music Superstar, 1 vol. 2016. (Leading Women Ser.). (ENG., Illus.). 112p. (J). (gr. 7-7). 41.64 *(978-1-5026-1991-4(1),* 7262e2c1-3b9b-4a88-9043-694d1e10493d) Cavendish Square Publishing LLC.

Stark, William N. Aerosmith: Living the Rock 'n' Roll Dream. 2015. (Legends of Rock Ser.). (ENG., Illus.). 32p. (J). (gr. 3-9). lib. bdg. 28.65 *(978-1-4914-1815-4(X),* 127259, Capstone Pr.) Capstone.

Stine, Megan. Who Was Michael Jackson? 2015. (Who Was... ? Ser.). lib. bdg. 16.00 *(978-0-606-37559-7(7))* Turtleback.

Strand, Jennifer. Bruno Mars. 2016. (Stars of Music Ser.). (ENG.). 24p. (J). (gr. -1-2). lib. bdg. 31.36 *(978-1-68079-918-7(5),* 24140, Abdo Zoom-Launch) ABDO Publishing Co.

—Justin Timberlake. 2016. (Stars of Music Ser.). (ENG.). 24p. (J). (gr. -1-2). lib. bdg. 31.36 *(978-1-68079-921-7(5),* 24146, Abdo Zoom-Launch) ABDO Publishing Co.

—Pharrell Williams. 2016. (Stars of Music Ser.). (ENG.). 24p. (J). (gr. -1-2). lib. bdg. 31.36 *(978-1-68079-922-4(3),* 24148, Abdo Zoom-Launch) ABDO Publishing Co.

Sullivan, Laura L. Yo-Yo Ma: Cellist, 1 vol. 2019. (Barrier-Breaker Bios Ser.). (ENG.). 32p. (gr. 2-2). pap. 11.58 *(978-1-5026-4968-3(3),* 12baee61-7360-43ef-a002-2a67cd89d851) Cavendish Square Publishing LLC.

Tomsic, Kim. Guitar Genius: How les Paul Engineered the Solid-Body Electric Guitar & Rocked the World (Children's Music Books, Picture Books, Guitar Books, Music Books for Kids) Helquist, Brett, illus. 2019. (ENG.). 56p. (J). (gr. k-3). 17.99 *(978-1-4521-5919-5(X))* Chronicle Bks. LLC.

Torres, John A. Timbaland. 2008. (Blue Banner Biography Ser.). (Illus.). 32p. (YA). (gr. 4-7). lib. bdg. 25.70 *(978-1-58415-671-0(6))* Mitchell Lane Pubs.

Tracy, Kathleen. Chris Daughtry. 2007. (Blue Banner Biography Ser.). (Illus.). 32p. (YA). (gr. 4-7). lib. bdg. 25.70 *(978-1-58415-629-1(5))* Mitchell Lane Pubs.

Walker, Ida. Lynyrd Skynrd. 2008. (Pop Rock Ser.). (Illus.). 64p. (YA). (gr. 4-7). lib. bdg. 22.95 *(978-1-4222-0213-5(5))* Mason Crest.

—Lynyrd Skynyrd. 2007. (Popular Rock Superstars of Yesterday & Today Ser.). (Illus.). 64p. (YA). (gr. 4-7). pap. 7.95 *(978-1-4222-0320-0(4))* Mason Crest.

Wallenfeldt, Jeff, ed. The Birth of Rock & Roll: Music in the 1950s Through the 1960s, 1 vol. 2012. (Popular Music Through the Decades Ser.). (ENG., Illus.). 240p. (J). (gr. 9-9). lib. bdg. 48.59 *(978-1-61530-906-1(3),* cc269c07-99ff-4435-bc80-79ea03a6b91b) Rosen Publishing Group, Inc., The.

—The Birth of Rock & Roll: Music in the 1950S Through The 1960S, 4 vols. 2012. (Popular Music Through the Decades Ser.). (ENG., Illus.). 240p. (YA). (gr. 9-9). 97.18 *(978-1-61530-915-3(2),* 9a381669-fb5b-457e-96c5-932383442833) Rosen Publishing Group, Inc., The.

Watson, Stephanie. Elvis Presley: Rock & Roll's King, 1 vol. 2012. (Lives Cut Short Set 2 Ser.). (ENG.). 112p. (YA). (gr. 6-12). 41.36 *(978-1-61783-482-0(3),* 11199, Essential Library) ABDO Publishing Co.

We, Why Don't. Why Don't We: In the Limelight. 2018. (ENG., Illus.). 240p. (J). (gr. 3-7). 21.99 *(978-0-06-287131-2(5),* HarperCollins) HarperCollins Pubs.

Weatherford, Carole Boston. Before John Was a Jazz Giant: A Song of John Coltrane. Qualls, Sean, illus. 2008. (ENG.). 32p. (J). (gr. k-4). 18.99 *(978-0-8050-7994-4(7),* 900034598, Holt, Henry & Co. Bks. For Young Readers) Holt, Henry & Co.

Webster, Christine. The Jonas Brothers. 2009. (Remarkable People Ser.). (Illus.). 24p. (J). (gr. 4-6). pap. 8.95 *(978-1-60596-627-4(4));* lib. bdg. 24.45 *(978-1-60596-626-7(6))* Weigl Pubs., Inc.

Wells, Peggy Sue. Soulja Boy Tell 'Em. 2008. (Blue Banner Biography Ser.). (Illus.). 32p. (YA). (gr. 4-7). lib. bdg. 25.70 *(978-1-58415-676-5(7))* Mitchell Lane Pubs.

Willett, Edward. Johnny Cash: Fighting for the Underdog, 1 vol. 2017. (Rebels with a Cause Ser.). (ENG.). 128p. (gr. 8-8). 38.93 *(978-0-7660-9257-0(7),* aae449b8-b42c-43b5-9b3d-305e8dd97f72); pap. 20.95

(978-0-7660-9565-6(7), 7bad3686-2af4-44f5-8edf-ec48047aa239) Enslow Publishing, LLC.

Wyckoff, Edwin Brit. The Man Who Invented the Electric Guitar: The Genius of les Paul, 1 vol. 2013. (Genius Inventors & Their Great Ideas Ser.). (ENG., Illus.). 48p. (gr. 3-3). 27.93 (978-0-7660-4137-0(9), a1488d31-b620-40ad-abd7-502cbab2829d); pap. 11.53 (978-1-4644-0207-4(8), d3a286dc-2db3-4ccb-9208-124635f626aa, Enslow Elementary) Enslow Publishing, LLC.

Zimmerman, Robert. Switchfoot. 2009. (Contemporary Musicians & Their Music Ser.). 48p. (gr. 6-6). 53.00 (978-1-61511-946-2(9)) Rosen Publishing Group, Inc., The.

MUSKOX

Alkire, Jessie. Musk Oxen. 2018. (Arctic Animals at Risk Ser.). (ENG., Illus.). 32p. (J). (gr. 3-6). lib. bdg. 32.79 (978-1-5321-1697-1(7), 30682, Checkerboard Library) ABDO Publishing Co.

Markle, Sandra. Musk Oxen. (Animal Prey Ser.). 2008. (Illus.). 39p. (J). (gr. 3-7). per. 7.95 (978-0-8225-6067-8(4), First Avenue Editions) 2008. pap. 46.95 (978-0-8225-9320-1(3)) 2007. (ENG., Illus.). 40p. (J). (gr. 3-6). lib. bdg. 25.32 (978-0-8225-6064-7(X), f1f1d7b1-831f-441e-b2d4-ac2ce62a54e3, Lerner Pubns.) Lerner Publishing Group.

Niptanatiak, Allen. Animals Illustrated: Muskox, 1 vol. McLeod, Kagan, illus. 2016. (Animals Illustrated Ser.: 3). (ENG.). 24p. (J). (gr. 1-3). 12.95 (978-1-77227-122-5(5)) Inhabit Media Inc. CAN. Dist: Consortium Bk. Sales & Distribution.

Owen, Ruth. Musk Oxen, 1 vol. 2013. (Polar Animals: Life in the Freezer Ser.). (ENG., Illus.). 32p. (J). (gr. 2-3). pap. 11.00 (978-1-4777-0225-3(3), f2b59435-67de-438c-9b1d-11d518ef636f); lib. bdg. 29.93 (978-1-4777-0219-2(9), 44e6ace6-c9af-426b-adea-c2126e269eb6) Rosen Publishing Group, Inc., The. (Windmill Bks.).

Patrick, Roman. Musk Oxen, 1 vol. 2010. (Animals That Live in the Tundra Ser.). (ENG.). 24p. (J). (gr. 1-1). pap. 9.15 (978-1-4339-3903-7(7), 2f268f52-73bc-4e7f-b36e-bf3d3afc8492); lib. bdg. 25.27 (978-1-4339-3902-0(9), 544d024c-eb49-4054-9fb6-95d50dfdfadb) Stevens, Gareth Publishing LLLP.

Pratt, Laura. Les Boelig;ufs Musqueacute;s: Les Animaux du Canada. Karvonen, Tanjah, tr. from ENG. 2011. (FRE.). 24p. (gr. 3-6). (978-1-77071-414-4(6)) Weigl Educational Pubs. Ltd.

—Muskox. 2010. (Illus.). 24p. (978-1-55388-668-6(2)); pap. (978-1-55388-669-3(0)) Weigl Educational Pubs. Ltd.

MUSKOX—FICTION

Brett, Jan. Cozy. Brett, Jan, illus. 2020. (Illus.). 32p. (J). (gr. -1-3). 18.99 (978-0-593-10979-3(1), G.P. Putnam's Sons Books for Young Readers) Penguin Young Readers Group.

Brown, Tricia. The Itchy Little Musk Ox. Dubac, Debra, illus. 2006. (ENG.). 32p. (J). (gr. -1-3). pap. 12.99 (978-0-88240-614-5(0), Alaska Northwest Bks.) West Margin Pr.

Cabatingan, Erin. A Is for Musk Ox. Myers, Matthew, illus. 2012. (Musk Ox Ser.: 1). (ENG.). 40p. (J). (gr. k-2). 19.99 (978-1-59643-676-3(X), 900071112) Roaring Brook Pr.

MUSKRATS

Albertson, Al. Muskrats. 2019. (North American Animals Ser.). (ENG., Illus.). 24p. (J). (gr. k-3). lib. bdg. 26.95 (978-1-62617-984-4(0), Blastoff! Readers) Bellwether Media.

Gaertner, Meg. Muskrats. 2019. (Pond Animals Ser.). (ENG., Illus.). 24p. (J). (gr. 1-1). pap. 8.95 (978-1-64185-580-8(0), 1641855800) North Star Editions.

—Muskrats. 2018. (Pond Animals Ser.). (ENG., Illus.). 24p. (J). (gr. k-3). lib. bdg. 31.36 (978-1-5321-6209-1(X), 30201, Pop! Cody Koala) Pop!

Lawrence, Ellen. Muskrat. 2016. (Swamp Things: Animal Life in a Wetland Ser.). (ENG.). 24p. (J). (gr. -1-3). 26.99 (978-1-944102-55-5(8)) Bearport Publishing Co., Inc.

MUSKRATS—FICTION

Burgess, Thornton W. The Adventures of Jerry Muskrat. 2007. 108p. (gr. 2-5). per. 9.95 (978-1-60312-336-5(9)); 22.95 (978-1-60312-674-8(0)) Aegypan.

—The Adventures of Jerry Muskrat. 2006. pap. 9.95 (978-1-59605-676-3(2), Cosimo Classics) Cosimo, Inc.

—The Adventures of Jerry Muskrat. 2011. 108p. 23.95 (978-1-4638-9564-8(X)) Rodgers, Alan Bks.

—Jerry Muskrat at Home. (J). 18.95 (978-0-8488-0399-5(X)) Amereon Ltd.

Chaconas, Dori. The Babysitters. McCue, Lisa, illus. 2014. (Cork & Fuzz Ser.: 6). 32p. (J). (gr. 1-3). pap. 4.99 (978-0-448-48050-3(6), Penguin Young Readers) Penguin Young Readers Group.

—Best Friends No. 1. McCue, Lisa, illus. 2010. (Cork & Fuzz Ser.: 1). 32p. (J). (gr. 1-3). mass mkt. 4.99 (978-0-14-241593-1(6), Penguin Young Readers) Penguin Young Readers Group.

—The Collectors, 4 vols. McCue, Lisa, illus. 2010. (Cork & Fuzz Ser.: 4). 32p. (J). (gr. 1-3). mass mkt. 4.99 (978-0-14-241714-0(9), Penguin Young Readers) Penguin Young Readers Group.

—Finders Keepers, 5 vols. McCue, Lisa, illus. 2011. (Cork & Fuzz Ser.: 5). 32p. (J). (gr. 1-3). mass mkt. 4.99 (978-0-14-241869-7(2), Penguin Young Readers) Penguin Young Readers Group.

—Good Sports. McCue, Lisa, illus. 2010. (Cork & Fuzz Ser.: 3). 32p. (J). (gr. 1-3). mass mkt. 4.99 (978-0-14-241713-3(0), Penguin Young Readers) Penguin Young Readers Group.

—Short & Tall. McCue, Lisa, illus. 2006. (Penguin Young Readers: Level 3 Ser.: 2). (ENG.). 32p. (J). (gr. 1-3). 16.19 (978-0-670-05985-0(4), Viking) Penguin Publishing Group.

—Short & Tall No. 2, 2 vols. McCue, Lisa, illus. 2010. (Cork & Fuzz Ser.: 2). 32p. (J). (gr. 1-3). mass mkt. 4.99 (978-0-14-241594-8(4), Penguin Young Readers) Penguin Young Readers Group.

—The Swimming Lesson. McCue, Lisa, illus. 2014. (Cork & Fuzz Ser.: 7). 32p. (J). (gr. 1-3). pap. 5.99 (978-0-448-48051-0(4), Penguin Young Readers) Penguin Young Readers Group.

—Wait a Minute. McCue, Lisa, illus. 2015. (Cork & Fuzz Ser.: 9). 32p. (J). (gr. 1-3). 4.99 (978-0-14-750856-0(8), Penguin Young Readers) Penguin Young Readers Group.

Garis, Howard Roger. Sammie & Susie Littletail. 2005. 182p. pap. 11.95 (978-1-4218-1565-7(6), 1st World Library - Literary Society) 1st World Publishing, Inc.

Hoban, Russell. Harvey's Hideout. Hoban, Lillian, illus. 2018. (ENG.). 42p. (J). (gr. -1-3). 16.00 (978-0-87486-138-9(1)) Plough Publishing Hse.

McSorley, Paul J. & Bearss, Patricia. The Adventures of Forealdo: Finding Millie. 2012. 34p. 24.95 (978-1-4626-6721-5(X)) America Star Bks.

Savageau, Cheryl. Muskrat Will Be Swimming, 1 vol. Hynes, Robert, illus. 2006. (ENG.). 32p. (J). (gr. 3-7). 9.95 (978-0-88448-280-2(4), 884280) Tilbury Hse. Pubs.

MUSLIMS

Here are entered works on the community of believers in Islam. Works on the religion of which Muhammad is the prophet are entered under Islam.

Abdullah, Noorah Kathryn. What Do We Say? A Guide to Islamic Manners. 2nd ed. 2010. (ENG., Illus.). 24p. (J). (gr. -1-k). 8.95 (978-0-86037-350-6(9)) Kube Publishing Ltd. GBR. Dist: Consortium Bk. Sales & Distribution.

ARAB-AMERICAN & MUSLIM WRITERS. 2010. (Multicultural Voices Ser.). (ENG., Illus.). 130p. (gr. 6-12). 35.00 (978-1-60413-377-6(5), P179271, Facts On File) Infobase Holdings, Inc.

Demi. Muhammad. Demi, illus. 2003. (ENG., Illus.). 48p. (J). (gr. 2-5). 24.99 (978-0-689-85264-0(9), McElderry, Margaret K. Bks.) McElderry, Margaret K. Bks.

Diaz, Wendy Umm Uthman. Nuestros Oficios. 2012. (ENG.). (J). pap. 12.99 (978-1-4675-3282-2(7)) Independent Pub.

Ejaz, Khadija. My Friend Is Muslim. 2015. (ENG., Illus.). 47p. (J). 29.95 (978-1-62469-096-9(3)) Purple Toad Publishing, Inc.

Ergün, Erol. 100 Hadiths for Children. 2014. (Illus.). 112p. (J). (gr. 3-7). pap. 11.95 (978-1-59784-320-1(2), Tughra Bks.) Blue Dome, Inc.

Faust, Daniel R. Ibtihaj Muhammad: Muslim American Champion Fencer & Olympian, 1 vol. 2017. (Breakout Biographies Ser.). (ENG., Illus.). 32p. (J). (gr. 4-5). 27.93 (978-1-5081-6060-1(0), edb48c2a-7335-4060-9e9d-88433e3aab1f, PowerKids Pr.) Rosen Publishing Group, Inc., The.

Flatt, Lizann. Early Islamic Empires, 1 vol. 2013. (Life in the Early Islamic World Ser.). (ENG., Illus.). 48p. (J). pap. (978-0-7787-2178-9(7)) Crabtree Publishing Co.

Gunderson, Jessica. X: a Biography of Malcolm X. Hayden, William, illus. 2010. (American Graphic Ser.). (ENG.). 32p. (J). (gr. 3-9). pap. 8.10 (978-1-4296-6267-3(0), 115414, Capstone Pr.) Capstone.

Hafiz, Dilara, et al. The American Muslim Teenager's Handbook. 2009. (ENG., Illus.). 192p. (YA). (gr. 7-18). pap. 14.99 (978-1-4169-8578-5(6), Atheneum Bks. for Young Readers) Simon & Schuster Children's Publishing.

Hodges, Rick. What Muslims Think, & How They Live. 2005. (Introducing Islam Ser.). (Illus.). 112p. (YA). lib. bdg. 24.95 (978-1-59084-702-2(4)) Mason Crest.

Ismail, Vehbi. Muhammad: The Last Prophet. 2011. 190p. 42.95 (978-1-258-03217-3(1)) Literary Licensing, LLC.

Kavanaugh, Dorothy. The Muslim World: An Overview. 2010. (World of Islam Ser.). (Illus.). 64p. (J). (gr. 4-7). lib. bdg. 22.95 (978-1-4222-0532-7(0)) Mason Crest.

Kayani, M.S. Love All Creatures. 2007. (ENG., Illus.). 36p. pap. 3.95 (978-0-86037-077-2(1)) Kube Publishing Ltd. GBR. Dist: Consortium Bk. Sales & Distribution.

Kemmetmueller, Donna Jean. My Muslim Friend: A Young Catholic Learns about Islam. Jacobsen, Laura, illus. 2006. 47p. (J). 15.95 (978-0-8198-4844-4(1)) Pauline Bks. & Media.

Khan, Hena. Night of the Moon: A Muslim Holiday Story. Paschkis, Julie, illus. 2018. (ENG.). 36p. (J). (gr. -1-k). pap. 7.99 (978-1-4521-6896-8(2)) Chronicle Bks. LLC.

Melman, Anna. Muslims in America. 2010. (World of Islam Ser.). (Illus.). 64p. (YA). (gr. 4-7). lib. bdg. 22.95 (978-1-4222-0535-8(5)) Mason Crest.

Mir, Saira. Muslim Girls Rise: Inspirational Champions of Our Time. Jaleel, Aaliya, illus. 2019. (ENG.). 48p. (J). (gr. 1). 19.99 (978-1-5344-1888-2(1)) Simon & Schuster, Inc.

Peppas, Lynn. Cultural Traditions in Iran. 2015. (Cultural Traditions in My World Ser.). (ENG., Illus.). 32p. (J). (gr. 2-3). (978-0-7787-8061-8(9)) Crabtree Publishing Co.

Sanna, Ellyn. Gallup Guides for Youth Facing Persistent Prejudice Muslims. 2012. (Gallup Guides for Youth Facing Persistent Prejudice Ser.). 64p. (J). (gr. 7-8). 22.95 (978-1-4222-2468-7(6)) Mason Crest.

—People with Mental & Physical Challenges. 2012. (Gallup Guides for Youth Facing Persistent Prejudice Ser.). (Illus.). 64p. (J). (gr. 7-8). 22.95 (978-1-4222-2470-0(8)) Mason Crest.

Sears, Evelyn. Muslims & the West. 2005. (Introducing Islam Ser.). (Illus.). 112p. (YA). lib. bdg. 24.95 (978-1-59084-700-8(8)) Mason Crest.

Shabazz, Ilyasah & Magoon, Kekla. X: A Novel. 2016. (ENG.). 384p. (YA). (gr. 9). 19.65 (978-0-606-39098-9(7)) Turtleback.

Syed, Tayyaba. Islam, 1 vol. 2018. (Let's Find Out! Religion Ser.). (ENG.). 32p. (gr. 2-3). lib. bdg. 26.06 (978-1-5081-0686-9(X), b89e6474-7e47-42d3-9a2d-e2c21b62c527, Britannica Educational Publishing) Rosen Publishing Group, Inc., The.

Vietze, Andrew. The Life & Death of Malcolm X, 1 vol. 2017. (Spotlight on the Civil Rights Movement Ser.). (ENG.). 48p. (J). (gr. 6-6). pap. 12.75 (978-1-5383-8031-4(5), 482e1ecb-a26d-4a6b-8991-514724ac5e84, Rosen Young Adult) Rosen Publishing Group, Inc., The.

Wolny, Philip. Muslims Around the World Today. 2009. (Understanding Islam Ser.). 64p. (gr. 6-6). 58.50 (978-1-60854-626-8(8)) Rosen Publishing Group, Inc., The.

Zaidi, Anbara. Muslims in America, Vol. 8. Pecastaing, Camille, ed. 2016. (Understanding Islam Ser.: Vol. 8). (ENG., Illus.). 112p. (J). (gr. 7-12). 25.95 (978-1-4222-3676-5(5)) Mason Crest.

MUSLIMS, BLACK

see Black Muslims

MUSLIMS—FICTION

Abdel-Fattah, Randa. Does My Head Look Big in This? 2007. 360p. (YA). 25.66 (978-1-4287-4610-7(2), Follettbound) Follett School Solutions.

—Does My Head Look Big in This? 2008. (ENG.). 368p. (J). (gr. 7). pap. 11.99 (978-0-439-92233-3(X), Scholastic Paperbacks) Scholastic, Inc.

—The Lines We Cross. 2017. (ENG.). 400p. (YA). (gr. 7-7). 18.99 (978-1-338-11866-7(8), Scholastic Pr.) Scholastic, Inc.

Abdelsalam, Lisa. A Song for Me: A Muslim Holiday Story. Nielsen, Janet Marie, illus. 2006. 34p. (J). (978-0-9755975-1-4(5)) Abdelsalam Corp.

Addasi, Maha. Time to Pray. Gannon, Ned, illus. 2010. (ENG.). 32p. (J). (gr. 2-4). 17.95 (978-1-59078-611-6(4), Astra Young Readers) Astra Publishing Hse.

Ahmed, Samira. Internment. (ENG.). 400p. (YA). (gr. 7-17). 2020. pap. 11.99 (978-0-316-52270-0(8)) 2019. 17.99 (978-0-316-52269-4(4)) Little, Brown Bks. for Young Readers.

—Love, Hate & Other Filters. (ENG.). (YA). (gr. 9). 2019. 312p. pap. 10.99 (978-1-61695-999-9(1)) 2018. 288p. 18.99 (978-1-61695-847-3(2)) Soho Pr., Inc. (Soho Teen).

Ali, Anila & Gottlieb, Karen. Mommy, Am I A ? Seiders, Marian, illus. 2010. 28p. pap. 11.95 (978-1-935105-45-9(0)) Avid Readers Publishing Group.

Ali, S. K. Love from a to Z. 2019. (ENG., Illus.). 352p. (YA). (gr. 9). 19.99 (978-1-5344-4272-6(3), Salaam Reads) Simon & Schuster Bks. For Young Readers.

—Saints & Misfits. 2017. (Saints & Misfits Ser.). (ENG., Illus.). 336p. (YA). (gr. 9). 18.99 (978-1-4814-9924-8(6), Salaam Reads) Simon & Schuster Bks. For Young Readers.

Barto, Linda "iLham", illus. Where the Ghost Camel Grins: Muslim Fables for Families of All Faiths. 2009. (ENG.). 119p. (gr. 5). 19.95 (978-1-879402-24-9(6)) Tahrike Tarsile Quran, Inc.

Baten, Kim Nisha. Nadia Hears the Shahadah. Lu, Marisa, illus. 2018. 30p. (J). (gr. -1-2). 14.95 (978-1-59784-934-0(0), Tughra Bks.) Blue Dome, Inc.

Bradbury, Jennifer. A Moment Comes. (ENG.). 288p. (YA). (gr. 7). 2019. pap. 11.99 (978-1-5344-3949-8(8), Atheneum/Caitlyn Dlouhy Books) 2013. (Illus.). 18.99 (978-1-4169-7876-3(3)) Simon & Schuster Children's Publishing.

Cerra, Kerry O'Malley. Just a Drop of Water. 2016. (ENG.). 320p. (J). (gr. 2-7). pap. 8.99 (978-1-5107-1234-8(8), Sky Pony Pr.) Skyhorse Publishing Co., Inc.

Cunnane, Kelly. Deep in the Sahara. Hadadi, Hoda, illus. 2018. 40p. (J). (gr. -1-3). 8.99 (978-0-525-64566-5(7), Schwartz & Wade Bks.) Random Hse. Children's Bks.

Doller, Trish. In a Perfect World. (ENG.). (YA). (gr. 7). 2019. 320p. pap. 11.99 (978-1-4814-7989-9(X)) 2017. (Illus.). 304p. 18.99 (978-1-4814-7988-2(1)) Simon Pulse. (Simon Pulse).

Ellis, Deborah & Walters, Eric. Bifocal, 1 vol. 2007. (ENG.). 280p. (YA). (gr. 7-12). per. 12.95 (978-1-55455-062-3(9), 40c1a241-5a17-43bc-857e-e8bb6cabba4f) Fitzhenry & Whiteside, Ltd. CAN. Dist: Firefly Bks., Ltd.

—Bifocal, 1 vol. 2007. (ENG.). 240p. (YA). (gr. 7-12). 17.95 (978-1-55455-036-4(X), 81472636-fc44-4218-a9bb-bdaa0b47264c) Trifolium Bks., Inc. CAN. Dist: Firefly Bks., Ltd.

Faruqi, Reem. Lailah's Lunchbox: A Ramadan Story, 1 vol. Lyon, Lea, illus. 2015. (ENG.). 32p. (J). (gr. 1-7). 16.95 (978-0-88448-431-8(9), 884431) Tilbury Hse. Pubs.

Faruqi, Saadia. Yasmin, la Guardiana Del Zoo. Aparicio Publishing LLC, Aparicio Publishing, tr. from ENG. Aly, Hatem, illus. 2020. (Yasmin en Español Ser.).Tr. of Yasmin the Zookeeper. (SPA.). 32p. (J). (gr. k-2). pap. 5.95 (978-1-5158-5735-8(2), 142100); lib. bdg. 20.65 (978-1-5158-5731-0(X), 142096) Capstone. (Picture Window Bks.).

—Yasmin la Maestra. Aparicio Publishing LLC, Aparicio Publishing, tr. from ENG. Aly, Hatem, illus. 2020. (Yasmin en Español Ser.).Tr. of Yasmin the Teacher. (SPA.). 32p. (J). (gr. k-2). pap. 5.95 (978-1-5158-5732-7(8), 142097); lib. bdg. 20.65 (978-1-5158-5728-0(X), 142092) Capstone. (Picture Window Bks.).

—Yasmin la Superheroína. Aparicio Publishing LLC, Aparicio Publishing, tr. from ENG. Aly, Hatem, illus. 2020. (Yasmin en Español Ser.).Tr. of Yasmin the Superhero. (SPA.). 32p. (J). (gr. k-2). pap. 5.95 (978-1-5158-5733-4(6), 142099); lib. bdg. 20.65 (978-1-5158-5729-7(8), 142094) Capstone. (Picture Window Bks.).

—Yasmin the Explorer. Aly, Hatem, illus. 2018. (Yasmin Ser.). (ENG.). 32p. (J). (gr. k-2). 22.65 (978-1-5158-2729-0(1), 137933, Picture Window Bks.) Capstone.

—Yasmin the Fashionista. Aly, Hatem, illus. 2018. (Yasmin Ser.). (ENG.). 32p. (J). (gr. k-2). 22.65 (978-1-5158-3103-7(5), 138807, Picture Window Bks.) Capstone.

—Yasmin the Painter. Aly, Hatem, illus. 2018. (Yasmin Ser.). (ENG.). 32p. (J). (gr. k-2). 22.65 (978-1-5158-2728-3(3), 137932, Picture Window Bks.) Capstone.

—Yasmin the Superhero. Aly, Hatem, illus. 2019. (Yasmin Ser.). (ENG.). 32p. (J). (gr. k-2). pap. 5.95 (978-1-5158-4579-9(6), 141179); lib. bdg. 22.65 (978-1-5158-3783-1(1), 139365) Capstone. (Picture Window Bks.).

—Yasmin the Teacher. Aly, Hatem, illus. 2019. (Yasmin Ser.). (ENG.). 32p. (J). (gr. k-2). pap. 5.95 (978-1-5158-4580-5(X), 141180); lib. bdg. 22.65 (978-1-5158-3782-4(3), 139364) Capstone. (Picture Window Bks.).

—Yasmin the Zookeeper. Aly, Hatem, illus. 2019. (Yasmin Ser.). (ENG.). 32p. (J). (gr. k-2). pap. 5.95 (978-1-5158-4581-2(8), 141181); lib. bdg. 22.65 (978-1-5158-3785-5(8), 139367) Capstone. (Picture Window Bks.).

Gilani-Williams, Fawzia. Yaffa & Fatima: Shalom, Salaam. Fedele, Chiara, illus. 2017. (ENG.). 24p. (J). (gr. -1-3). 17.99 (978-1-4677-8938-7(0), 8b6f0d02-4214-4d99-9d3c-9fb65bc60527, Kar-Ben Publishing) Lerner Publishing Group.

Gonzales, Mark. Yo Soy Muslim: A Father's Letter to His Daughter. Amini, Mehrdokht, illus. 2017. (ENG.). 32p. (J). (gr. -1-3). 18.99 (978-1-4814-8936-2(4), Simon & Schuster Bks. For Young Readers) Simon & Schuster Bks. For Young Readers.

Grant, K. M. Blaze of Silver, 3. 2008. (De Granville Trilogy Ser.). (ENG.). 261p. (YA). (gr. 6-8). 22.44 (978-0-8027-9625-7(7), 9780802796257) Walker & Co.

Hamed, Maissa. The Last Night of Ramadan, 1 vol. El Wakil, Mohamed, illus. 2007. (ENG.). (J). (gr. -1-3). (978-0-88010-586-6(0), Bell Pond Bks.) SteinerBooks, Inc.

Helwani, Najiyah Diana. Sophia's Journal: Time Warp 1857. 2008. (YA). per. (978-0-9793577-2-5(1)) Muslim Writers Publishing.

Hingoro, Samira, creator. A Marriage Proposal. 2003. (YA). per. 12.95 (978-0-9743167-0-3(9)) Faith Pubns.

Hiranandani, Veera. The Night Diary. (J). (gr. 3-7). 2019. (Illus.). 288p. 8.99 (978-0-7352-2852-8(3), Puffin Books) 2018. 272p. 17.99 (978-0-7352-2851-1(5), Kokila) Penguin Young Readers Group.

Holm, M. S. How Mohammed Saved Miss Liberty: The Story of a Good Muslim Boy. 2008. (ENG., Illus.). 270p. (YA). (gr. 7-12). pap. 12.00 (978-0-9796199-0-8(4), Sentry Bks.) Great West Publishing.

Husain, Aliya. Neither This nor That. 2010. 260p. pap. 19.99 (978-0-557-22302-2(4)) Lulu Pr., Inc.

Jalali, Reza. Moon Watchers: Shirin's Ramadan Miracle, 1 vol. Sibley O'Brien, Anne, illus. 2017. (ENG.). 32p. (J). (gr. 1-7). pap. 9.95 (978-0-88448-587-2(0), 884587) Tilbury Hse. Pubs.

Jolin, Paula. In the Name of God. 2008. (ENG.). 224p. (YA). (gr. 9-12). pap. 18.99 (978-0-312-38455-5(6), 900053460) Square Fish.

Karim, Sheba. That Thing We Call a Heart. 2017. (ENG.). 288p. (YA). (gr. 8). 17.99 (978-0-06-244570-4(7), Quill Tree Bks.) HarperCollins Pubs.

Kayani, M. S. Assalamu Alaykum. 2nd ed. 2009. (ENG., Illus.). 22p. (J). (gr. -1-1). 8.95 (978-0-86037-347-6(9)) Kube Publishing Ltd. GBR. Dist: Consortium Bk. Sales & Distribution.

Khan, Farheen. Ibrahim Khan & the Mystery of the Roaring Lion. 2010. (Ibrahim Khan Ser.). (ENG., Illus.). 56p. (J). (gr. 2-6). pap. 7.50 (978-0-86037-467-1(X)) Kube Publishing Ltd. GBR. Dist: Consortium Bk. Sales & Distribution.

Khan, Hena. Amina's Voice. 2019. (Penworthy Picks Middle School Ser.). (ENG.). 208p. (J). (gr. 4-5). 19.36 (978-1-64310-938-1(3)) Penworthy Co., LLC, The.

—Amina's Voice. 2017. (Amina's Voice Ser.). (ENG., Illus.). 208p. (J). (gr. 3-7). 17.99 (978-1-4814-9206-5(3), Salaam Reads) Simon & Schuster Bks. For Young Readers.

—Amina's Voice. 2018. (Amina's Voice Ser.). (ENG.). 208p. (J). (gr. 3-7). pap. 7.99 (978-1-4814-9207-2(1)) Simon & Schuster, Inc.

—Amina's Voice. 2018. lib. bdg. 18.40 (978-0-606-40842-4(8)) Turtleback.

—Crescent Moons & Pointed Minarets: A Muslim Book of Shapes (Islamic Book of Shapes for Kids, Toddler Book about Religion, Concept Book for Toddlers) Amini, Mehrdokht, illus. 2018. (Muslim Book of Concepts Ser.). (ENG.). 32p. (J). (gr. -1-k). 17.99 (978-1-4521-5541-8(0)) Chronicle Bks. LLC.

—Golden Domes & Silver Lanterns: A Muslim Book of Colors. Amini, Mehrdokht, illus. 2012. (Muslim Book of Concepts Ser.). (ENG.). 32p. (J). (gr. -1-2). 17.99 (978-0-8118-7905-7(4)) Chronicle Bks. LLC.

—More to the Story. 2019. (ENG., Illus.). 272p. (J). (gr. 3-7). 17.99 (978-1-4814-9209-6(8), Salaam Reads) Simon & Schuster Bks. For Young Readers.

—Under My Hijab, 1 vol. Jaleel, Aaliya, illus. 2019. (ENG.). 32p. (J). (gr. -1-3). 19.95 (978-1-62014-792-4(0), leelowbooks) Lee & Low Bks., Inc.

Kheiriyeh, Rashin. Saffron Ice Cream. Kheiriyeh, Rashin, illus. 2018. (ENG., Illus.). 40p. (J). (gr. -1-3). 18.99 (978-1-338-15052-0(9), Levine, Arthur A. Bks.) Scholastic, Inc.

Klaus, Sandra. Mustafas Geheimnis: Ein Moslemischer Junge auf der Suche nach Gott. Date not set.Tr. of Mustapha's Secret - A Muslim Boy's Search to Know God. (GER., Illus.). (J). (gr. 2-7). pap. (978-0-9617490-6-4(7)) Gospel Missionary Union.

—Tainata na Mustapha. Date not set.Tr. of Mustapha's Secret. (BUL.). (J). (gr. 2-7). pap. (978-1-890940-04-1(6)) Gospel Missionary Union.

Krantz, Hazel. In the Garden of the Caliph. 2012. 132p. (gr. 4-6). 23.14 (978-1-4669-2888-6(3)); (J). pap. 13.14 (978-1-4669-2886-2(7)) Trafford Publishing.

Lat. Kampung Boy. Lat, illus. rev. ed. 2006. Orig. Title: The Kampung Boy. (ENG., Illus.). 144p. (YA). (gr. 7-8). pap. 21.99 (978-1-59643-121-8(0), 900031942, First Second Bks.) Roaring Brook Pr.

Lipp, Frederick. Fatima. Lindmark, Margaret, illus. 2006. 32p. (J). pap. (978-1-59336-302-4(8)) Mondo Publishing.

Mafi, Tahereh. A Very Large Expanse of Sea. (ENG.). (YA). (gr. 8). 2019. 336p. pap. 12.99 (978-0-06-286657-8(5)) 2018. 320p. 18.99 (978-0-06-286656-1(7)) HarperCollins Pubs. (HarperCollins).

Mahmoodian, Maryam. Muslim Teens In: Pitfalls & Pranks. 2008. (YA). per. 10.95 (978-0-9793577-3-2(X)) Muslim Writers Publishing.

Marsden, Carolyn. The White Zone. 2012. (Exceptional Reading & Language Arts Titles for Intermediate Grades Ser.). (ENG.). 192p. (J). (gr. 4-8). 17.95 (978-0-7613-7383-4(7), Carolrhoda Bks.) Lerner Publishing Group.

Mian, Zanib. Planet Omar: Accidental Trouble Magnet. Mafaridik, Nasaya, illus. 2020. (Planet Omar Ser.: 1). (ENG.). 224p. (J). (gr. 2-5). 13.99 (978-0-593-10921-2(X), G.P. Putnam's Sons Books for Young Readers) Penguin Young Readers Group.

—Planet Omar: Unexpected Super Spy. Mafaridik, Nasaya, illus. 2020. (Planet Omar Ser.: 2). (ENG.). 224p. (J). (gr. 2-5). 13.99 (978-0-593-10924-3(4), G.P. Putnam's Sons Books for Young Readers) Penguin Young Readers Group.

Mills, Wendy. All We Have Left. 2017. (ENG.). 368p. (YA). pap. 10.99 (978-1-68119-432-5(5), 900172651, Bloomsbury USA Childrens) Bloomsbury Publishing USA.

Mitchell, Jane. Without Refuge. 2018. (ENG.). 288p. (J). (gr. 4-7). 16.99 (978-1-5415-0050-1(4), bbf255d3-caab-431e-aef2-238a34400f75, Carolrhoda Bks.) Lerner Publishing Group.

Mobin-Uddin, Asma. My Name Is Bilal. Kiwak, Barbara, illus. 2005. (ENG.). 32p. (J). (gr. 1-4). 17.99

(978-1-59078-175-3(9), Astra Young Readers) Astra Publishing Hse.

Muhammad, Ibtihaj. The Proudest Blue: A Story of Hijab & Family. Aly, Hatem, illus. 2019. (ENG.). 40p. (J). (gr. -1-3). 17.99 *(978-0-316-51900-7(6))* Little, Brown Bks. for Young Readers.

Muhammad, Khaleel. Helping the Polonskys. 2013. (ENG., Illus.). 80p. (J). (gr. 2-6). pap. 8.95 *(978-0-86037-454-1(8))* Kube Publishing Ltd. GBR. Dist: Consortium Bk. Sales & Distribution.

Munshey, Sana. We're off to Make 'Umrah. 2011. (ENG., Illus.). 32p. (J). (gr. -1-k). 10.95 *(978-0-86037-458-9(0))* Kube Publishing Ltd. GBR. Dist: Consortium Bk. Sales & Distribution.

Muschla, Gary Robert. The Sword & the Cross. 2009. (YA). lib. bdg. *(978-0-88092-471-9(3))* Royal Fireworks Publishing Co.

Nelson, Colleen. Sadia. 2018. (ENG.). 240p. (YA). pap. 12.99 *(978-1-4597-4029-7(7))* Dundurn Pr. CAN. Dist: Publishers Group West (PGW).

Nolan, Han. A Summer of Kings. 2006. 334p. (J). *(978-1-4156-7340-9(3))* Harcourt Trade Pubs.

—A Summer of Kings. 2006. (ENG., Illus.). 352p. (YA). (gr. 7-8). 17.00 *(978-0-15-205108-2(2))*, 1195424, Clarion Bks.) HarperCollins Pubs.

Nuurali, Siman. Sadiq & the Desert Star. Sarkar, Anjan, illus. 2019. (Sadiq Ser.). (ENG.). 64p. (J). (gr. 1-3). 23.32 *(978-1-5158-3878-4(1)*, 139596, Picture Window Bks.) Capstone.

—Sadiq & the Fun Run. Sarkar, Anjan, illus. 2019. (Sadiq Ser.). (ENG.). 64p. (J). (gr. 1-3). pap. 6.95 *(978-1-5158-4566-9(4)*, 141154, Picture Window Bks.) Capstone.

—Sadiq & the Green Thumbs. Sarkar, Anjan, illus. 2019. (Sadiq Ser.). (ENG.). 64p. (J). (gr. 1-3). pap. 6.95 *(978-1-5158-4567-6(2)*, 141155, Picture Window Bks.) Capstone.

—Sadiq & the Pet Problem. Sarkar, Anjan, illus. 2019. (Sadiq Ser.). (ENG.). 64p. (J). (gr. 1-3). pap. 6.95 *(978-1-5158-4568-3(0)*, 141156, Picture Window Bks.) Capstone.

Paterson, Katherine. The Day of the Pelican. 2010. (ENG.). 160p. (J). (gr. 5-7). pap. 7.99 *(978-0-547-40627-5(4)*, 1428505, Clarion Bks.) HarperCollins Pubs.

Radwan, Hassan. Rashid & the Haupmann Diamond. 2010. (ENG., Illus.). 112p. (J). (gr. 2-6). pap. 6.50 *(978-0-86037-357-5(6))* Kube Publishing Ltd. GBR. Dist: Consortium Bk. Sales & Distribution.

—Rashid & the Missing Body. 2010. (ENG., Illus.). 80p. (J). (gr. 2-6). pap. 5.95 *(978-0-86037-395-7(9))* Kube Publishing Ltd. GBR. Dist: Consortium Bk. Sales & Distribution.

Riazi, Karuna. The Battle. 2019. (ENG., Illus.). 304p. (J). (gr. 3-7). 17.99 *(978-1-5344-2872-0(0)*, Salaam Reads) Simon & Schuster Bks. For Young Readers.

—The Gauntlet. 2018. (ENG., Illus.). 304p. (J). (gr. 3-7). pap. 8.99 *(978-1-4814-8697-2(7)*, Salaam Reads) Simon & Schuster Bks. For Young Readers.

Robert, Na'ima Bint. The Swirling Hijaab. Mistry, Nilesh, illus. 2004. 24p. (J). *(978-1-85269-910-9(8))*; (CZE & ENG.). pap. *(978-1-85269-629-0(X))*; (TAM & ENG.). pap. *(978-1-85269-188-2(3))*; (SOM & ENG.). pap. *(978-1-85269-181-3(6))*; (SER & ENG.). pap. *(978-1-85269-180-6(8))*; (TUR & ENG.). pap. *(978-1-85269-189-9(1))*; (SPA & ENG.). pap. *(978-1-85269-182-0(4))*; (ARA & ENG.). pap. *(978-1-85269-119-6(0))*; (URD & ENG.). pap. *(978-1-85269-143-1(3))*; (BEN & ENG.). pap. *(978-1-85269-160-8(3))*; (PER & ENG.). pap. *(978-1-85269-163-9(8))*; (GER & ENG.). pap. *(978-1-85269-165-3(4))*; (ITA & ENG.). pap. *(978-1-85269-167-7(0))*; (PAN & ENG.). pap. *(978-1-85269-178-3(6))*; (POR & ENG.). pap. *(978-1-85269-179-0(4))* Mantra Lingua.

Robert, Naima Bint, tr. The Swirling Hijaab: Le Foulard Qui Tourbillonne. Mistry, Nilesh, illus. 2004. (FRE & ENG.). 24p. (J). pap. *(978-1-85269-164-6(6))* Mantra Lingua.

Rosenblatt, Darcey. Lost Boys. 2018. (ENG.). 288p. (J). pap. 12.99 *(978-1-250-15882-6(6)*, 900159430) Square Fish.

Schaenen, Inda. All the Cats of Cairo. 2007. 225p. (J). (gr. -1-10). per. 8.95 *(978-0-9768126-5-4(7))* Brown Barn Bks.

Sharif, Medeia. Bestest. Ramadan. Ever. 2011. (ENG.). 312p. (YA). (gr. 9-12). pap. 9.95 *(978-0-7387-2323-5(1)*, 0738723231, Flux) North Star Editions.

Silverman, Laura. You Asked for Perfect. 2019. (ENG.). 288p. (YA). (gr. 8-12). pap. 11.99 *(978-1-4926-5827-6(8))* Sourcebooks, Inc.

Stolz, Joelle. The Shadows of Ghadames. 2006. (ENG.). 128p. (J). (gr. 3-7). 5.99 *(978-0-440-41949-5(2)*, Yearling) Random Hse. Children's Bks.

Stratton, Allan. Borderline. 2012. (ENG.). 320p. (YA). (gr. 8). pap. 10.99 *(978-0-06-145113-3(4)*, HarperTeen) HarperCollins Pubs.

Thompkins-Bigelow, Jamilah. Mommy's Khimar. Glenn, Ebony, illus. 2018. (ENG.). 40p. (J). (gr. -1-3). 18.99 *(978-1-5344-0059-7(1)*, Salaam Reads) Simon & Schuster Bks. For Young Readers.

Westlund, Emmaline. Fatim. 2012. 42p. pap. 16.95 *(978-1-4626-9660-4(0))* America Star Bks.

Youree, Barbara. Senegal Sleuths. 2006. 56p. 7.75 *(978-0-8341-2226-0(X))* Beacon Hill Pr. of Kansas City.

Zalben, Jane Breskin. A Moon for Moe & Mo. Amini, Mehrdokht, illus. 2018. 48p. (J). (gr. -1-2). lib. bdg. 17.99 *(978-1-58089-727-3(4))* Charlesbridge Publishing, Inc.

Zia, Farhana. The Garden of My Imaan. 1 vol. 2016. 192p. (J). (gr. 3-7). pap. 8.99 *(978-1-56145-921-6(6))* Peachtree Publishing Co. Inc.

MUSSOLINI, BENITO, 1883-1945

Benchmark Education Company. Three Twentieth Century Dictators (Teacher Guide) 2004. *(978-1-4108-2593-3(0))* Benchmark Education Co.

Ruby, India. Three Twentieth Century Dictators: Set Of 6. 2011. (Navigators Ser.). (J). pap. 50.00 net. *(978-1-4108-2578-0(7))* Benchmark Education Co.

MUSTELIDAE

Klobuchar, Lisa. Badgers & Other Mustelids. 2005. (World Book's Animals of the World Ser.). (Illus.). 64p. (J). *(978-0-7166-1265-0(8))* World Bk., Inc.

Morgan, Sally. The Weasel Family. 2004. (J). lib. bdg. *(978-1-59389-173-2(3))* Cherrytree Bks.

Paulsen, Rosalie. My Ferrets. 2009. 84p. pap. 19.95 *(978-1-4489-9257-7(5))* America Star Bks.

MUTATION (BIOLOGY)

see Evolution

MYCENAE (EXTINCT CITY)

Schlitz, Laura Amy. The Hero Schliemann: The Dreamer Who Dug for Troy. Byrd, Robert, illus. 2013. (ENG.). 80p. (J). (gr. 4-7). pap. 8.99 *(978-0-7636-6504-3(5))* Candlewick Pr.

MYCOLOGY

see Fungi

MYSTERY AND DETECTIVE STORIES

A. Gunderson, Jessica. Pick your Poison Apple. 2009. 187p. pap. 14.32 *(978-0-557-19188-8(2))* Lulu Pr., Inc.

Abbott, Tony. The Mysterious Talent Show Mystery. 4. Madden, Colleen, illus. 2013. (Goofballs Ser.: No. 4). (ENG.). 112p. (J). (gr. 2-4). 17.44 *(978-1-60684-167-9(X))* Farshore GBR. Dist: Children's Plus, Inc.

Abdo Publishing & Gelsey, James. Scooby-Doo Mysteries, 4 vols., Set. Sur, Duendes Del, illus. 2013. (Scooby-Doo Mysteries Ser.: 6). (ENG.). 64p. (J). (gr. 3-6). lib. bdg. 125.44 *(978-1-61479-041-9(8)*, 13221, Chapter Bks.) Spotlight.

The Abominable Snowman, 6 Vols., Pack. (Bookweb Ser.). 32p. (gr. 3-18). 34.00 *(978-0-7635-3935-1(X))* Rigby Education.

The Abominable Snowman Doesn't Roast Marshmallows, 6 bks., Pack. 2005. 96p. (J). pap. 3.99 *(978-0-439-86573-9(5))* Scholastic, Inc.

Abrahams, Peter. Behind the Curtain. 2007. (Echo Falls Mystery Ser.: 2). (ENG.). 400p. (J). (gr. 5-18). pap. 6.99 *(978-0-06-073706-1(9)*, HarperCollins) HarperCollins Pubs.

—Down the Rabbit Hole. 2006. (Echo Falls Mystery Ser.: 1). (ENG.). 448p. (J). (gr. 5-9). reprint ed. pap. 8.99 *(978-0-06-073703-0(4)*, HarperCollins) HarperCollins Pubs.

—Into the Dark. 2009. (Echo Falls Mystery Ser.: 3). (ENG.). 352p. (J). (gr. 5-18). pap. 7.99 *(978-0-06-073710-8(7)*, HarperCollins) HarperCollins Pubs.

Absolutely Truly. 2014. (Pumpkin Falls Mystery Ser.). (ENG., Illus.). 368p. (J). (gr. 3-7). 19.99 *(978-1-4424-2972-7(0)*, Simon & Schuster Bks. For Young Readers) Simon & Schuster Bks. For Young Readers.

Abuhamda, Nasser. 6 Tales of Adventure. 2009. 84p. pap. 14.95 *(978-1-59858-833-0(8))* Dog Ear Publishing, LLC.

Ackerman, Helen. Casper's Paper Caper. 2013. 36p. pap. 18.41 *(978-1-4669-7448-7(6))* Trafford Publishing.

Acton, Vanessa. Tracks. 2018. (Mason Falls Mysteries Ser.). (ENG.). 104p. (YA). (gr. 6-12). pap. 7.99 *(978-1-5415-0121-8(7)*, 013e8880-d624-43f4-9f49-8dbf6563ea4a); lib. bdg. 25.32 *(978-1-5415-0112-6(8)*, e7831c22-3231-4acf-adf6-c7fd5c57a480) Lerner Publishing Group. (Darby Creek).

Adam, Paul. Escape from Shadow Island. (ENG.). 304p. (J). (gr. 5). 2011. (Max Cassidy Ser.: Bk. 1). pap. 5.99 *(978-0-06-186325-7(4))* 2010. 16.99 *(978-0-06-186323-3(8))* HarperCollins Pubs. (Waldon Pond Pr.).

Adams, Andy. The African Ivory Mystery: A Biff Brewster Mystery Adventure. 2011. 184p. 42.95 *(978-1-258-09296-2(4))* Literary Licensing, LLC.

—Mystery of the Ambush in Indi: A Biff Brewster Mystery. 2011. 180p. 42.95 *(978-1-258-09701-1(X))* Literary Licensing, LLC.

—Mystery of the Mexican Treasure: A Biff Brewster Mystery Adventure. 2011. 192p. 42.95 *(978-1-258-10141-1(6))* Literary Licensing, LLC.

Adamson, Heather & Adamson, Thomas K. Solve It with Scooby-Doo!: Math. Neely, Scott, illus. 2017. (Solve It with Scooby-Doo!: Math Ser.). (ENG.). 24p. (J). (gr. k-2). 183.90 *(978-1-5157-7924-7(6)*, 26952, Capstone Pr.) Capstone.

Adappur, Georgekutty. Jack Batson & the Secret in the Manuscript. 2009. 142p. pap. 24.95 *(978-1-4489-8439-8(4))* America Star Bks.

Adler, David A. Andy Russell, Not Wanted by the Police. Franson, Leanne, illus. 2005. (Andy Russell Ser.: Bk. 5). (ENG.). 128p. (J). (gr. 1-4). pap. 7.99 *(978-0-15-216719-6(6)*, 1201719, Clarion Bks.) HarperCollins Pubs.

—Bones & the Apple Pie Mystery. Johansen Newman, Barbara, illus. 2014. (Bones Ser.: 10). (ENG.). 32p. (J). (gr. 1-3). pap. 4.99 *(978-0-448-48231-6(2)*, Penguin Young Readers) Penguin Young Readers Group.

—Bones & the Big Yellow Mystery, No. 1. Johansen Newman, Barbara, illus. 2008. (Bones Ser.: 1). (ENG.). 32p. (J). (gr. 1-3). mass mkt. 4.99 *(978-0-14-241042-4(X)*, Penguin Young Readers) Penguin Young Readers Group.

—Bones & the Big Yellow Mystery. Newman, Barbara Johansen, illus. 2008. (Puffin Easy-to-Read Ser.). 32p. (gr. k-3). 14.00 *(978-0-7569-8914-9(0))* Perfection Learning Corp.

—Bones & the Birthday Mystery, No. 5. Newman, Barbara, illus. 2009. (Bones Ser.: 5). (ENG.). 32p. (J). (gr. 1-3). mass mkt. 4.99 *(978-0-14-241432-3(8)*, Penguin Young Readers) Penguin Young Readers Group.

—Bones & the Clown Mix-Up Mystery, No. 8. Johansen Newman, Barbara, illus. 2011. (Bones Ser.: 8). (ENG.). 32p. (J). (gr. 1-3). 4.99 *(978-0-14-241825-3(0)*, Penguin Young Readers) Penguin Young Readers Group.

—Bones & the Cupcake Mystery, No. 3. Johansen Newman, Barbara, illus. 2008. (Bones Ser.: 3). (ENG.). 32p. (J). (gr. 1-3). mass mkt. 4.99 *(978-0-14-241147-6(7)*, Penguin Young Readers) Penguin Young Readers Group.

—Bones & the Dinosaur Mystery. Newman, Barbara Johansen, illus. 2005. (Jeffrey Bones Mystery Ser.: No. 4). 32p. (J). *(978-0-670-05970-5(6)*, Viking Adult) Penguin Publishing Group.

—Bones & the Dinosaur Mystery, No. 4. Johansen Newman, Barbara, illus. 2009. (Bones Ser.: 4). (ENG.). 32p. (J). (gr. 1-3). mass mkt. 4.99 *(978-0-14-241341-8(0)*, Penguin Young Readers) Penguin Young Readers Group.

—Bones & the Dog Gone Mystery, No. 2. Johansen Newman, Barbara, illus. 2008. (Bones Ser.: 2). (ENG.). 32p. (J). (gr. 1-3). mass mkt. 4.99 *(978-0-14-241043-1(8)*, Penguin Young Readers) Penguin Young Readers Group.

—Bones & the Dog Gone Mystery. Newman, Barbara Johansen, illus. 2008. (Puffin Easy-to-Read Ser.: Bk. 2). 32p. (gr. k-3). 14.00 *(978-0-7569-8916-3(7))* Perfection Learning Corp.

—Bones & the Football Mystery. 2013. (Bones Ser.: 9). (ENG.). 32p. (J). (gr. 1-3). pap. 4.99 *(978-0-448-47942-2(7)*, Penguin Young Readers) Penguin Young Readers Group.

—Bones & the Football Mystery. 2013. (Bones Penguin Young Readers Ser.: 9). lib. bdg. 13.55 *(978-0-606-32450-2(X))* Turtleback.

—Bones & the Math Test. 2010. (Bones Penguin Young Readers Ser.: 6). lib. bdg. 13.55 *(978-0-606-10585-9(9))* Turtleback.

—Bones & the Math Test Mystery. Johansen Newman, Barbara, illus. 2010. (Bones Ser.: 6). (ENG.). 32p. (J). (gr. 1-3). mass mkt. 5.99 *(978-0-14-241519-1(7)*, Penguin Young Readers) Penguin Young Readers Group.

—Cam Jansen: The Mystery of the Babe Ruth Baseball. (Cam Jansen Ser.: No. 6). 57p. (J). (gr. 2-4). pap. 3.99 *(978-0-8072-1347-6(0)*, Listening Library) Random Hse. Audio Publishing Group.

—Cam Jansen & the Catnapping Mystery. Natti, Susanna, illus. 2005. (Cam Jansen Ser.). 58p. (gr. 2-5). 14.00 *(978-0-7569-5045-3(7))* Perfection Learning Corp.

—Cam Jansen & the Graduation Day Mystery. 2012. (Cam Jansen Ser.: 31). lib. bdg. 14.75 *(978-0-606-26663-5(1))* Turtleback.

—Cam Jansen & the Graduation Day Mystery #31. 2012. (Cam Jansen Ser.: 31). (ENG.). 64p. (J). (gr. 2-5). pap. 4.99 *(978-0-14-242208-3(8)*, Puffin Books) Penguin Young Readers Group.

—Cam Jansen & the Millionaire Mystery. Allen, Joy, illus. 2013. (Cam Jansen Ser.: 32). (ENG.). 64p. (J). (gr. 2-5). pap. 4.99 *(978-0-14-242747-7(0)*, Puffin Books) Penguin Young Readers Group.

—Cam Jansen & the Secret Service Mystery #26. Natti, Susanna, illus. 2008. (Cam Jansen Ser.: 26). (ENG.). 64p. (J). (gr. 2-5). 4.99 *(978-0-14-241074-5(8)*, Puffin Books) Penguin Young Readers Group.

—Cam Jansen & the Spaghetti Max Mystery. Allen, Joy, illus. 2014. (Cam Jansen Ser.: 33). (ENG.). 64p. (J). (gr. 2-5). pap. 4.99 *(978-0-14-751232-1(8)*, Puffin Books) Penguin Young Readers Group.

—Cam Jansen & the Sports Day Mysteries. Allen, Joy, illus. 2009. (Cam Jansen: A Super Special Ser.). 118p. 16.00 *(978-1-60686-431-9(9))* Perfection Learning Corp.

—Cam Jansen & the Sports Day Mysteries: A Super Special. 2009. (Cam Jansen Ser.). lib. bdg. 16.00 *(978-0-606-00110-6(7))* Turtleback.

—Cam Jansen: Cam Jansen & the Mystery Writer Mystery #27. Allen, Joy, illus. 27th ed. 2008. (Cam Jansen Ser.: 27). (ENG.). 64p. (J). (gr. 2-5). 5.99 *(978-0-14-241194-0(9)*, Puffin Books) Penguin Young Readers Group.

—Cam Jansen: Cam Jansen & the Sports Day Mysteries: A Super Special. Allen, Joy, illus. 2009. (Cam Jansen Ser.). 128p. (J). (gr. 2-5). 5.99 *(978-0-14-241225-1(2)*, Puffin Books) Penguin Young Readers Group.

—Cam Jansen: Cam Jansen & the Summer Camp Mysteries: A Super Special. Allen, Joy, illus. 2007. (Cam Jansen Ser.). 128p. (J). (gr. 2-5). 6.99 *(978-0-14-240742-4(9)*, Puffin Books) Penguin Young Readers Group.

—Cam Jansen: Cam Jansen & the Valentine Baby Mystery #25. Natti, Susanna, illus. 25th ed. 2006. (Cam Jansen Ser.: 25). (ENG.). 80p. (J). (gr. 2-5). 4.99 *(978-0-14-240694-6(5)*, Puffin Books) Penguin Young Readers Group.

—Cam Jansen: Cam Jansen & the Wedding Cake Mystery #30, 30 vols. Allen, Joy, illus. 2011. (Cam Jansen Ser.: 30). (ENG.). 64p. (J). (gr. 2-5). 5.99 *(978-0-14-241958-8(3)*, Puffin Books) Penguin Young Readers Group.

—Cam Jansen: the Barking Treasure Mystery #19. Natti, Susanna, illus. 2005. (Cam Jansen Ser.: 19). (ENG.). 64p. (J). (gr. 2-5). 4.99 *(978-0-14-240319-8(9)*, Puffin Books) Penguin Young Readers Group.

—Cam Jansen: the Basketball Mystery #29, 29 vols., No. 29. Allen, Joy, illus. 2010. (Cam Jansen Ser.: 29). (ENG.). 64p. (J). (gr. 2-5). 5.99 *(978-0-14-241671-6(1)*, Puffin Books) Penguin Young Readers Group.

—Cam Jansen: the Birthday Mystery #20. Natti, Susanna, illus. 2005. (Cam Jansen Ser.: 20). (ENG.). 64p. (J). (gr. 2-5). 5.99 *(978-0-14-240354-9(7)*, Puffin Books) Penguin Young Readers Group.

—Cam Jansen: the Catnapping Mystery #18, 18 vols. Natti, Susanna, illus. 2005. (Cam Jansen Ser.: 18). (ENG.). 64p. (J). (gr. 2-5). 5.99 *(978-0-14-240289-4(3)*, Puffin Books) Penguin Young Readers Group.

—Cam Jansen: the Chocolate Fudge Mystery #14, 14 vols. Natti, Susanna, illus. 2004. (Cam Jansen Ser.: 14). (ENG.). 64p. (J). (gr. 2-5). 5.99 *(978-0-14-240211-5(7)*, Puffin Books) Penguin Young Readers Group.

—Cam Jansen: the First Day of School Mystery #22, 22 vols. Natti, Susanna, illus. 2005. (Cam Jansen Ser.: 22). (ENG.). 64p. (J). (gr. 2-5). 4.99 *(978-0-14-240326-6(1)*, Puffin Books) Penguin Young Readers Group.

—Cam Jansen: the Ghostly Mystery #16, Vol. 16. Natti, Susanna, illus. 2005. (Cam Jansen Ser.: 16). (ENG.). 64p. (J). (gr. 2-5). 5.99 *(978-0-14-240287-0(7)*, Puffin Books) Penguin Young Readers Group.

—Cam Jansen: the Green School Mystery #28, No. 28. Allen, Joy, illus. 2009. (Cam Jansen Ser.: 28). (ENG.). 64p. (J). (gr. 2-5). 5.99 *(978-0-14-241456-9(5)*, Puffin Books) Penguin Young Readers Group.

—Cam Jansen: the Mystery of Flight 54 #12, 12 vols. Natti, Susanna, illus. 2004. (Cam Jansen Ser.: 12). (ENG.). 64p. (J). (gr. 2-5). 5.99 *(978-0-14-240179-8(X)*, Puffin Books) Penguin Young Readers Group.

—Cam Jansen: the Mystery of the Carnival Prize #9, 9 vols. Natti, Susanna, illus. 2004. (Cam Jansen Ser.: 9). (ENG.). 64p. (J). (gr. 2-5). 5.99 *(978-0-14-240018-0(1)*, Puffin Books) Penguin Young Readers Group.

—Cam Jansen: the Mystery of the Circus Clown #7, 7 vols. Natti, Susanna, illus. 2004. (Cam Jansen Ser.: 7). 64p. (J). (gr. 2-5). 5.99 *(978-0-14-240016-6(5)*, Puffin Books) Penguin Young Readers Group.

—Cam Jansen: the Mystery of the Gold Coins #5, 5 vols. Natti, Susanna, illus. 2004. (Cam Jansen Ser.: 5). 64p. (J). (gr. 2-5). 5.99 *(978-0-14-240014-2(9)*, Puffin Books) Penguin Young Readers Group.

—Cam Jansen: the Mystery of the Monkey House #10. Natti, Susanna, illus. 2004. (Cam Jansen Ser.: 10). (ENG.). 64p. (J). (gr. 2-5). 5.99 *(978-0-14-240019-7(X)*, Puffin Books) Penguin Young Readers Group.

—Cam Jansen: the Mystery of the Monster Movie #8, 8 vols. Natti, Susanna, illus. 2004. (Cam Jansen Ser.: 8). (ENG.). 64p. (J). (gr. 2-5). 5.99 *(978-0-14-240017-3(3)*, Puffin Books) Penguin Young Readers Group.

—Cam Jansen: the Mystery of the Stolen Corn Popper #11, 11 vols. Natti, Susanna, illus. 2004. (Cam Jansen Ser.: 11). (ENG.). 64p. (J). (gr. 2-5). 5.99 *(978-0-14-240178-1(1)*, Puffin Books) Penguin Young Readers Group.

—Cam Jansen: the Mystery of the Stolen Diamonds #1. Natti, Susanna, illus. 2004. (Cam Jansen Ser.: 1). (ENG.). 64p. (J). (gr. 2-5). pap. 5.99 *(978-0-14-240010-4(6)*, Puffin Books) Penguin Young Readers Group.

—Cam Jansen: the Mystery of the Television Dog #4, 4 vols. Natti, Susanna, illus. 2004. (Cam Jansen Ser.: 4). 64p. (J). (gr. 2-5). 5.99 *(978-0-14-240013-5(0)*, Puffin Books) Penguin Young Readers Group.

—Cam Jansen: the Mystery of the U. F. O. #2, 2 vols. Natti, Susanna, illus. 2004. (Cam Jansen Ser.: 2). (ENG.). 64p. (J). (gr. 2-5). 5.99 *(978-0-14-240011-1(4)*, Puffin Books) Penguin Young Readers Group.

—Cam Jansen: the Scary Snake Mystery #17. Natti, Susanna, illus. 2005. (Cam Jansen Ser.: 17). (ENG.). 64p. (J). (gr. 2-5). 5.99 *(978-0-14-240288-7(5)*, Puffin Books) Penguin Young Readers Group.

—Cam Jansen: the School Play Mystery #21. Natti, Susanna, illus. 2005. (Cam Jansen Ser.: 21). (ENG.). 64p. (J). (gr. 2-5). 5.99 *(978-0-14-240355-6(5)*, Puffin Books) Penguin Young Readers Group.

—Cam Jansen: the Snowy Day Mystery #24, 24 vols. Natti, Susanna, illus. 2005. (Cam Jansen Ser.: 24). 64p. (J). (gr. 2-5). 5.99 *(978-0-14-240417-1(9)*, Puffin Books) Penguin Young Readers Group.

—Cam Jansen: the Triceratops Pops Mystery #15, 15 vols. Natti, Susanna, illus. 2004. (Cam Jansen Ser.: 15). (ENG.). 64p. (J). (gr. 2-5). 5.99 *(978-0-14-240206-1(0)*, Puffin Books) Penguin Young Readers Group.

—The Mystery of Flight 427: Inside a Crash Investigation. Natti, Susanna, illus. 2004. (Cam Jansen Ser.: No. 12). 56p. (J). pap. *(978-0-439-13384-5(X)*, Puffin) Penguin Publishing Group.

—The Secret Service Mystery. Natti, Susanna, illus. 2008. (Cam Jansen Ser.: Bk. 26). 57p. (J). (gr. 2-5). 11.65 *(978-0-7569-8917-0(5))* Perfection Learning Corp.

—Young Cam Jansen & the 100th Day of School Mystery, 15 vols. Natti, Susanna, illus. 2010. (Young Cam Jansen Ser.: 15). (ENG.). 32p. (J). (gr. 1-3). mass mkt. 4.99 *(978-0-14-241685-3(1)*, Penguin Young Readers) Penguin Young Readers Group.

—Young Cam Jansen & the Circus Mystery. Natti, Susanna, illus. 2013. (Young Cam Jansen Ser.: 17). (ENG.). 32p. (J). (gr. 1-3). pap. 4.99 *(978-0-448-46614-9(7)*, Penguin Young Readers) Penguin Young Readers Group.

—Young Cam Jansen & the Double Beach Mystery. Natti, Susanna, illus. 2003. (Young Cam Jansen Ser.: 8). (ENG.). 32p. (J). (gr. 1-3). mass mkt. 4.99 *(978-0-14-250079-8(8)*, Penguin Young Readers) Penguin Young Readers Group.

—Young Cam Jansen & the Double Beach Mystery. Natti, Susanna, illus. 2003. (Young Cam Jansen — Penguin Young Readers Level 3 Ser.: 8). 30p. (gr. -1-3). lib. bdg. 13.55 *(978-0-613-67477-5(4))* Turtleback.

—Young Cam Jansen & the Goldfish Mystery. Natti, Susanna, illus. 2014. (Young Cam Jansen Ser.: 19). (ENG.). 32p. (J). (gr. 1-3). pap. 4.99 *(978-0-14-242224-3(X)*, Penguin Young Readers) Penguin Young Readers Group.

—Young Cam Jansen & the Knock, Knock Mystery. Natti, Susanna, illus. 2015. (Young Cam Jansen Ser.: 20). (ENG.). 32p. (J). (gr. 1-3). pap. 4.99 *(978-0-14-242225-0(8)*, Penguin Young Readers) Penguin Young Readers Group.

—Young Cam Jansen & the Lions' Lunch Mystery, No. 13. Natti, Susanna, illus. 2008. (Young Cam Jansen Ser.: 13). (ENG.). 32p. (J). (gr. 1-3). mass mkt. 4.99 *(978-0-14-241176-6(0)*, Penguin Young Readers) Penguin Young Readers Group.

—Young Cam Jansen & the Magic Bird Mystery. Natti, Susanna, illus. 2013. (Young Cam Jansen Ser.: 18). (ENG.). 32p. (J). (gr. 1-3). pap. 4.99 *(978-0-448-46613-2(9)*, Penguin Young Readers) Penguin Young Readers Group.

—Young Cam Jansen & the Molly Shoe Mystery, No. 14. Natti, Susanna, illus. 2009. (Young Cam Jansen Ser.: 14). (ENG.). 32p. (J). (gr. 1-3). mass mkt. 4.99 *(978-0-14-241402-6(6)*, Penguin Young Readers) Penguin Young Readers Group.

—Young Cam Jansen & the New Girl Mystery. Natti, Susanna, illus. 2005. (Young Cam Jansen Ser.: 10). (ENG.). 32p. (J). (gr. 1-3). mass mkt. 5.99 *(978-0-14-240353-2(9)*, Penguin Young Readers) Penguin Young Readers Group.

—Young Cam Jansen & the New Girl Mystery. Natti, Susanna, illus. 2005. (Young Cam Jansen Ser.: Bk. 10). 32p. (gr. k-2). 14.00 *(978-0-7569-5522-9(X))* Perfection Learning Corp.

—Young Cam Jansen & the Speedy Car Mystery, 16 vols. Natti, Susanna, illus. 2011. (Young Cam Jansen Ser.: 16). (ENG.). 32p. (J). (gr. 1-3). mass mkt. 4.99 *(978-0-14-241868-0(4)*, Penguin Young Readers) Penguin Young Readers Group.

—Young Cam Jansen & the Spotted Cat Mystery, No. 12. Natti, Susanna, illus. 2007. (Young Cam Jansen Ser.: 12). (ENG.). 32p. (J). (gr. 1-3). pap. 4.99 *(978-0-14-241012-7(8)*, Penguin Young Readers) Penguin Young Readers Group.

—Young Cam Jansen & the Spotted Cat Mystery. Natti, Susanna, illus. 2007. (Young Cam Jansen (prebound) Ser.). 31p. (gr. -1-3). 14.00 *(978-0-7569-8155-6(7))* Perfection Learning Corp.

—Young Cam Jansen & the Zoo Note Mystery. Natti, Susanna, illus. 2013. (Puffin Young Readers, L3 Ser.). (ENG.). 31p. (J). (gr. -1-3). pap. 3.99 *(978-0-448-46633-0(3)*, Puffin) Penguin Publishing Group.

—Young Cam Jansen & the Zoo Note Mystery. Natti, Susanna, illus. 2004. (Young Cam Jansen Ser.: 9). (ENG.). 32p. (J). (gr. 1-3). mass mkt. 4.99 *(978-0-14-240204-7(4)*, Penguin Young Readers) Penguin Young Readers Group.

Adler, Irene. The Cathedral of Fear. McGuinness, Nanette, tr. Bruno, Iacopo, illus. 2015. (Sherlock, Lupin, & Me Ser.). (ENG.). 256p. (J). (gr. 4-8). lib. bdg. 26.65 *(978-1-4965-0490-6(9)*, 128559, Stone Arch Bks.) Capstone.

—The Mystery of the Scarlet Rose. McGuinness, Nanette, tr. Bruno, Iacopo, illus. 2015. (Sherlock, Lupin, & Me Ser.). (ENG.). 256p. (J). (gr. 4-8). lib. bdg. 26.65 *(978-1-4342-6524-1(2),* 124281, Stone Arch Bks.) Capstone.

Ahdieh, Renée. The Beautiful. (Beautiful Quartet Ser.: 1). (ENG.). (YA). (gr. 7). 2021. 480p. pap. 5.99 *(978-1-5247-3819-8(0),* Penguin Books) 2021. 480p. pap. 12.99 *(978-0-593-46266-9(1),* G.P. Putnam's Sons Books for Young Readers) 2019. 448p. 18.99 *(978-1-5247-3817-4(4),* G.P. Putnam's Sons Books for Young Readers) Penguin Young Readers Group.

Aili, Olivia. The Portrait Pathway. 2012. 62p. 19.95 *(978-1-4626-7206-6(X));* pap. 12.99 *(978-1-4626-7937-9(4))* America Star Bks.

Albin, Colin. Tom's Tales. 2013. 136p. pap. *(978-1-78407-043-4(2))* FeedARead.com.

Alderson, Sarah. Out of Control. 2015. (ENG., Illus.). 320p. (YA). (gr. 9). 17.99 *(978-1-4814-2716-6(4),* Simon Pulse) Simon Pulse.

Alessio, Amy. Taking the High Ground. 2013. 128p. pap. 19.99 *(978-1-940310-00-8(8))* 4RV Pub.

Alexander, Heather. The Case of the Tattooed Cat. 2003. (New Adventures of Mary-Kate & Ashley Ser.). (Illus.). 83p. (J). (gr. 1-5). 12.65 *(978-0-7569-5351-5(0))* Perfection Learning Corp.

—Wallace & Grace & the Cupcake Caper. Zarrin, Laura, illus. 2017. (Wallace & Grace Ser.). (ENG.). 80p. (J). 9.99 *(978-1-68119-010-5(9),* 900154813, Bloomsbury USA Childrens) Bloomsbury Publishing USA.

Alexander, Yvonne. Adventure in Autou. 2012. 230p. pap. 15.99 *(978-1-62230-262-8(1))* Salem Author Services.

Alexandria, Vincent. Marvelous Martin: Case of the Freckle-Faced Bully. 2009. 64p. (J). (gr. 2-7). 7.95 *(978-1-60349-015-3(9),* Marimba Bks.) Just Us Bks., Inc.

—Marvelous Marvin. 2009. 64p. 4.99 *(978-1-60349-013-9(2),* Marimba Bks.) Just Us Bks., Inc.

Alfonsi, Alice. The Almost Invisible Cases. Harrington, Rich, illus. 2007. 96p. (J). *(978-0-545-01585-1(5))* Scholastic, Inc.

—The Code Red Cases. Harrington, Rich, illus. 2006. 96p. (J). *(978-0-439-91447-5(7))* Scholastic, Inc.

—The Playing Card Cases. Harrington, Rich, illus. 2007. 96p. (J). *(978-0-545-01087-0(X))* Scholastic, Inc.

Alger, Horatio. The Store Boy. 2005. 256p. 28.95 *(978-1-4218-0954-0(0),* 1st World Library - Literary Society) 1st World Publishing, Inc.

—The Store Boy. 2007. (ENG.). 170p. pap. 19.99 *(978-1-4264-4359-6(5))* Creative Media Partners, LLC.

—The Store Boy. 2006. pap. *(978-1-4065-0722-5(9))* Dodo Pr.

—The Store Boy. 2007. 116p. per. *(978-1-4068-1617-4(5))* Echo Library.

—Timothy Crump's Ward. 2005. 27.95 *(978-1-4218-1451-3(X));* 220p. pap. 12.95 *(978-1-4218-1551-0(6))* 1st World Publishing, Inc. (1st World Library - Literary Society).

Alison, Hart. Spy on the Home Front. Jean-P, Tibbles, illus. 2005. (American Girls Collection). (ENG.). 176p. (J). 10.95 *(978-1-58485-996-3(2),* American Girl) American Girl Publishing, Inc.

Allen, Betsy. The Mystery of the Ruby Queens: Connie Blair Mystery Series. 2011. 192p. 42.95 *(978-1-258-09539-0(4))* Literary Licensing, LLC.

—The Silver Secret: A Connie Blair Mystery. 2011. 184p. 42.95 *(978-1-258-09883-4(0))* Literary Licensing, LLC.

Allen, Michelle. Grandma Nell's Basement. 2009. 24p. pap. 15.00 *(978-1-4490-1551-0(4))* AuthorHouse.

Allen, Quincy. The Outdoor Chums at Cabin Point: Or the Golden Cup Mystery. Lt. ed. 2007. (ENG.). 166p. pap. 21.99 *(978-1-4346-3239-5(3))* Creative Media Partners, LLC.

Allison, Jennifer. Gilda Joyce: the Ladies of the Lake. 2007. (Gilda Joyce Ser.: 2). (ENG.). 352p. (J). (gr. 5-18). 10.99 *(978-0-14-240907-7(3),* Puffin Books) Penguin Young Readers Group.

—The Ladies of the Lake. 2006. (Gilda Joyce Ser.). (ENG.). 339p. (J). (gr. 6-8). 22.44 *(978-0-525-47693-1(8))* Penguin Young Readers Group.

Allison, John. Bad Machinery Vol. 1: The Case of the Team Spirit, Pocket Edition. 2017. (Bad Machinery Ser.: 1). (ENG., Illus.). 136p. pap. 9.99 *(978-1-62010-387-6(7),* 9781620103876, Lion Forge) Oni Pr., Inc.

—Bad Machinery Vol. 3 Vol. 3: The Case of the Simple Soul, Pocket Edition. 2017. (Bad Machinery Ser.: 3). (ENG., Illus.). 136p. pap. 12.99 *(978-1-62010-443-9(1),* 9781620104439, Lion Forge) Oni Pr., Inc.

—Bad Machinery Vol. 7: The Case of the Forked Road. 2017. (Bad Machinery Ser.: 7). (ENG., Illus.). 128p. (YA). pap. 14.99 *(978-1-62010-390-6(7),* 9781620103906, Lion Forge) Oni Pr., Inc.

Alpine, Rachele. A Void the Size of the World. 2017. (ENG., Illus.). 368p. (YA). (gr. 9). 17.99 *(978-1-4814-8571-5(7),* Simon Pulse) Simon Pulse.

Altebrando, Tara. The Leaving. 2016. (ENG.). 432p. (YA). 18.99 *(978-1-61963-803-7(7),* 900149146, Bloomsbury USA Childrens) Bloomsbury Publishing USA.

—The Opposite of Here. 2018. (ENG.). 256p. (YA). 17.99 *(978-1-68119-706-7(5),* 900182256, Bloomsbury Young Adult) Bloomsbury Publishing USA.

Amato, Carol J. The Lost Treasure of the Golden Sun. 2005. 172p. (J). *(978-0-9713756-3-5(1))* Stargazer Publishing Co.

—The Secret of Blackhurst Manor. 2017. (ENG.). 232p. (J). pap. 9.95 *(978-1-933277-02-8(5))* Stargazer Publishing Co.

Amato, Mary. Edgar Allan's Official Crime Investigation Notebook. 2010. (ENG.). 176p. (J). (gr. 4-6). 21.19 *(978-0-8234-2271-5(2))* Holiday Hse., Inc.

Anastasiu, Heather & Brown, Anne Greenwood. Girl Last Seen. 2016. (ENG.). 272p. (YA). (gr. 8-12). 16.99 *(978-0-8075-8140-7(2),* 807581402); pap. 9.99 *(978-0-8075-8141-4(0),* 807581410) Whitman, Albert & Co.

Andersen, C. B. The Secret Mission. 2008. (J). *(978-1-59038-906-5(9))* Deseret Bk. Co.

Anderson, Connie Kingrey. Toadies. 2013. (Creepers Mysteries Ser.: Bk. 2). (ENG.). 142p. (J). pap. 7.99 *(978-1-935793-03-8(9))* Movies for the Ear, LLC.

Anderson, Jennifer. Spider. 2013. 174p. pap. 10.99 *(978-1-62237-146-4(1))* Turquoise Morning Pr.

Anderson, Jessica. Shaky, Breaky School Sleuth. 2015. (Rourke's Mystery Chapter Bks.). (ENG.). 64p. (gr. 3-6). 28.50 *(978-1-63430-387-3(3),* 9781634303873) Rourke Educational Media.

Anderson, M. T. Agent Q, or the Smell of Danger! Cyrus, Kurt, illus. 2011. (Pals in Peril Tale Ser.). (ENG.). 320p. (J). (gr. 5-9). pap. 8.99 *(978-1-4424-2640-5(3),* Beach Lane Bks.) Beach Lane Bks.

—The Clue of the Linoleum Lederhosen. Cyrus, Kurt, illus. 2010. (Pals in Peril Tale Ser.). (ENG.). (J). (gr. 5-9). 272p. pap. 8.99 *(978-1-4424-0702-2(6));* 2. 256p. 17.99 *(978-1-4424-0697-1(6))* Beach Lane Bks. (Beach Lane Bks.).

—Jasper Dash & the Flame-Pits of Delaware. Cyrus, Kurt, illus. (Pals in Peril Tale Ser.). (ENG.). (J). (gr. 5-9). 2010. 448p. pap. 8.99 *(978-1-4424-0838-8(3))*3. 2009. 432p. 16.99 *(978-1-4169-8639-3(1))* Beach Lane Bks. (Beach Lane Bks.).

Anderson, Matthew. Agent Q, or the Smell of Danger! Cyrus, Kurt, illus. 2010. (Pals in Peril Tale Ser.). (ENG.). 304p. (J). (gr. 5-9). 16.99 *(978-1-4169-8640-9(5),* Beach Lane Bks.) Beach Lane Bks.

Anderson, Max Elliott. Mountain Cabin Mystery. 2004. (Tweener Press Adventure Ser.). (Illus.). 123p. (J). (gr. 3). per. 10.95 *(978-0-9729256-3-1(5),* Tweener Pr.) Baker Trittin Pr.

Anderson, R. J. A Little Taste of Poison. 2016. (ENG., Illus.). 368p. (J). (gr. 4-7). 18.99 *(978-1-4814-3774-5(7),* Atheneum Bks. for Young Readers) Simon & Schuster Children's Publishing.

—A Pocket Full of Murder. 2015. (ENG., Illus.). 352p. (J). (gr. 4-7). 18.99 *(978-1-4814-3771-4(2))* Simon & Schuster Children's Publishing.

Ando, Yuma. Sherlock Bones 1, Vol. 1. Sato, Yuki, illus. 2013. (Sherlock Bones Ser.: 1). 200p. (gr. 8-12). pap. 10.99 *(978-1-61262-444-0(8))* Kodansha America, Inc.

—Sherlock Bones 3, Vol. 3. Sato, Yuki, illus. 2014. (Sherlock Bones Ser.: 3). 208p. (gr. 8-12). pap. 10.99 *(978-1-61262-446-4(4))* Kodansha America, Inc.

—Sherlock Bones 4, Vol. 4. Sato, Yuki, illus. 2014. (Sherlock Bones Ser.: 4). 208p. (gr. 8-12). pap. 10.99 *(978-1-61262-447-1(2))* Kodansha America, Inc.

—Sherlock Bones 5. Sato, Yuki, illus. 2014. (Sherlock Bones Ser.: 5). 192p. (gr. 8-12). pap. 10.99 *(978-1-61262-545-4(2))* Kodansha America, Inc.

Andrews, John. Beck's Missing Shoes. 2013. 28p. pap. 9.95 *(978-1-4787-2524-4(9))* Outskirts Pr., Inc.

Angleberger, Tom. The Da Vinci Cold. 2016. (Inspector Flytrap Ser.: 1). (J). lib. bdg. 15.95 *(978-0-606-38200-7(3))* Turtleback.

—Inspector Flytrap in the Goat Who Chewed Too Much (Inspector Flytrap #3) Bell, Cece, illus. 2017. (Flytrap Files Ser.). (ENG.). 112p. (J). (gr. 1-4). 14.95 *(978-1-4197-0956-2(9),* 1065101, Amulet Bks.) Abrams, Inc.

—Inspector Flytrap in the President's Mane Is Missing (Inspector Flytrap #2). 2. Bell, Cece, illus. 2016. (Flytrap Files Ser.). (ENG.). 112p. (J). (gr. 1-4). 14.95 *(978-1-4197-0955-5(0),* 1065001, Amulet Bks.) Abrams, Inc.

—Inspector Flytrap (Inspector Flytrap #1) Bell, Cece, illus. 2016. (Flytrap Files Ser.). (ENG.). 112p. (J). (gr. 1-4). pap. 6.99 *(978-1-4197-0965-4(8),* 1064903, Amulet Bks.) Abrams, Inc.

—The President's Mane Is Missing. 2016. (Inspector Flytrap Ser.: 2). (J). lib. bdg. 15.95 *(978-0-606-38201-4(1))* Turtleback.

Anyone's Guess Teen Kits: A Murderous Melodrama. 2004. 39.95 *(978-1-932146-26-4(1),* Upstart Bks.) Highsmith Inc.

Anza, Ana Luisa. El Misterio de la Casa Chueca (y el Bulto Color Mugre) The Mystery of the Crooked House. Escobar, Antonio Rocha, illus. rev. ed. 2006. (Castillo de la Lectura Naranja Ser.). (SPA & ENG.). 120p. (J). (gr. 4-7). pap. 7.95 *(978-970-20-0200-0(1))* Castillo, Ediciones, S. A. de C. V. MEX. Dist: Macmillan.

Appleton, Victor. Moving Picture Boys at Panama. 2006. pap. *(978-1-4065-0890-1(X))* Dodo Pr.

—The Moving Picture Boys on the Coast or Showing up the Perils of the Deep. 2004. reprint ed. pap. 24.95 *(978-1-4179-1612-2(5))* Kessinger Publishing, LLC.

—Moving Picture Boys on the War Front or. 2006. pap. *(978-1-4065-0891-8(8))* Dodo Pr.

Appleton, Victor & Appleton, Victor, II. On Top of the World. 2007. (Tom Swift, Young Inventor Ser.: 5). (ENG.). 160p. (J). (gr. 3-7). pap. 6.99 *(978-1-4169-3643-5(2),* Aladdin) Simon & Schuster Children's Publishing.

Applewood Books. Black Cat's Clue #23, No. 23. Doane, Pelagie, illus. 2008. (Judy Bolton Ser.). (ENG.). 224p. (J). (gr. 4-7). pap. 14.95 *(978-1-4290-9043-8(X))* Applewood Bks.

Archer, Dosh. The Case of Piggy's Bank (Detective Paw of the Law: Time to Read, Level 3) Archer, Dosh, illus. 2018. (Time to Read Ser.: 1). (ENG., Illus.). 48p. (J). (gr. k-2). 12.99 *(978-0-8075-1557-0(4),* 807515574) Whitman, Albert & Co.

—The Case of the Icky Ice Cream (Detective Paw of the Law: Time to Read, Level 3) Archer, Dosh, illus. 2020. (Time to Read Ser.). (ENG., Illus.). 48p. (J). (gr. k-2). 12.99 *(978-0-8075-1571-6(X),* 080751571X) Whitman, Albert & Co.

—The Case of the Stolen Drumsticks (Detective Paw of the Law: Time to Read, Level 3) Archer, Dosh, illus. 2018. (Time to Read Ser.: 2). (ENG., Illus.). 48p. (J). (gr. k-2). 12.99 *(978-0-8075-1556-3(6),* 807515566) Whitman, Albert & Co.

Arensen, Shel. The Poison Arrow Tree. 2003. (Rugendo Rhino Ser.). (Illus.). 128p. (J). pap. 5.99 *(978-0-8254-2041-2(5))* Kregel Pubns.

Armstrong, Robert. Buyer Beware. 2016. (ENG.). 94p. (YA). (gr. 10-12). 10.95 *(978-1-78554-474-3(8),* 8d6f3a35-f0de-4e80-b69c-ac8e49656faa) Austin Macauley Pubs. Ltd. GBR. Dist: Baker & Taylor Publisher Services (BTPS).

—Escape from Camp Bedlam. 2018. (ENG.). 128p. (J). 17.95 *(978-1-78629-886-7(4),* cb5c0f1d-32c9-4657-86b0-13b731e03b12) Austin Macauley Pubs. Ltd. GBR. Dist: Baker & Taylor Publisher Services (BTPS).

Arnett, Mindee. The Nightmare Dilemma. 2015. (Arkwell Academy Ser.: 2). (ENG.). 400p. (YA). (gr. 8-12). pap. 10.99 *(978-0-7653-3337-7(6),* 900084950, Tor Teen) Doherty, Tom Assocs., LLC.

Arnold, Chirley. Double Trouble: A Novel. 160p. (YA). pap. 7.95 *(978-1-56236-454-0(5))* Aspen Bks.

Asad, Megan Emily. The Juggler's Journey. 2005. 144p. pap. 9.95 *(978-0-7599-4470-1(9))* Hard Shell Word Factory.

Ashby, Freya Katrina. Summer at the Dunes: A Deirdre Carlisle Mystery. 2007. 108p. per. 9.95 *(978-0-595-43663-7(3))* iUniverse, Inc.

Ashley, Bernard. Solitaire. 2012. (Fiction Ser.). 338p. (J). pap. 6.99 *(978-0-7945-3031-0(1),* Usborne) EDC Publishing.

Ashley, Elana. Splunkunio Splunkey Detective & Peacemaker Detective y Pacificador: Case One: The Missing Friendship Bracelet Caso Primero: El Brazalete de la Amistad Desaparecido. Nikolov, Stefan V., tr. Ashley, Elana, photos by. 2005. (SPA & ENG., Illus.). 32p. (J). (gr. k-3). 17.95 *(978-0-9744812-1-0(1))* Dream Image Pr., LLC.

Ashton, Brodi. Diplomatic Immunity. 2016. (ENG.). 368p. (YA). (gr. 8). 17.99 *(978-0-06-236856-0(7),* Balzer & Bray) HarperCollins Pubs.

Ashton, Kenneth. Gale's Gold Ring: The Legend of Lincoln's Lost Gold. Ashton-Briggs, Shelley, illus. 2012. (ENG.). 198p. pap. 14.95 *(978-1-4327-8224-5(X))* Outskirts Pr., Inc.

Asselin, Kristine & Malone, Jen. The Art of the Swap. (ENG., Illus.). 352p. (J). (gr. 3-7). 2019. pap. 8.99 *(978-1-4814-7872-4(9))* 2018. 17.99 *(978-1-4814-7871-7(0))* Simon & Schuster Children's Publishing. (Aladdin).

Atanacio, Frank. Aggravating Factors: From the Nick Barnum Sealed Case File a Nick Barnum Novel II. 2003. 128p. (YA). pap. 10.95 *(978-0-595-26985-3(0),* Writers Club Pr.) iUniverse, Inc.

Atkins, Ron. Abby & the Bicycle Caper. 2004. 48p. pap. 8.95 *(978-0-595-30565-0(2))* iUniverse, Inc.

Atwater-Rhodes, Amelia. Midnight Predator. 2003. (Den of Shadows Ser.: 4). 256p. (YA). (gr. 7). mass mkt. 7.99 *(978-0-440-23797-6(1),* Laurel Leaf) Random Hse. Children's Bks.

Auerbach, Annie. Scooby-Doo in the Coolsville Contraption Contest, 1 vol. 2015. (Scooby-Doo! Ser.). (ENG., Illus.). 32p. (J). (gr. k-4). lib. bdg. 31.36 *(978-1-61479-409-7(X),* 19448, Picture Bk.) Spotlight.

—Scooby-Doo in the Mystery Mansion, 1 vol. 2015. (Scooby-Doo! Ser.). (ENG., Illus.). 32p. (J). (gr. k-4). lib. bdg. 31.36 *(978-1-61479-411-0(1),* 19450, Picture Bk.) Spotlight.

Austin, Rikey. Captain's Treasure: Alice's Bear Shop. 2012. 28p. pap. *(978-1-78092-149-5(7))* MX Publishing, Ltd.

Austin, Su. The Salterns House Mystery. 2013. 186p. pap. *(978-1-78299-194-6(8))* FeedARead.com.

Averbeck, Jim. A Hitch at the Fairmont. Bertozzi, Nick, illus. (ENG.). 416p. (J). (gr. 3-7). 2015. pap. 9.99 *(978-1-4424-9448-0(4))* 2014. 16.99 *(978-1-4424-9447-3(6),* Atheneum Bks. for Young Readers) Simon & Schuster Children's Publishing.

Avi. City of Orphans. Ruth, Greg, illus. 2012. (ENG.). 368p. (J). (gr. 5-9). pap. 8.99 *(978-1-4169-7108-5(4),* Atheneum Bks. for Young Readers) Simon & Schuster Children's Publishing.

—The Man Who Was Poe. 2013. (ENG.). 224p. (J). (gr. 6-8). 21.19 *(978-0-545-50523-9(2))* Scholastic, Inc.

—Murder at Midnight. 2011. (ENG.). 256p. (J). (gr. 3-7). pap. 7.99 *(978-0-545-08091-0(6),* Scholastic Paperbacks) Scholastic, Inc.

—The Traitors' Gate. Raude, Karina, illus. 2010. (ENG.). 368p. (J). (gr. 5-8). pap. 8.99 *(978-0-689-85336-4(X),* Atheneum Bks. for Young Readers) Simon & Schuster Children's Publishing.

—Wolf Rider. 2008. (ENG.). 208p. (YA). (gr. 7-12). mass mkt. 8.99 *(978-1-4169-5444-6(9),* Simon Pulse) Simon Pulse.

Awad, Shelley. The Greenhouse Kids: Dan Dellon's Secret. Zonta, Rose, illus. 2009. 127p. (J). pap. *(978-0-88887-379-8(4))* Borealis Pr.

Awdry, W. Blue Mountain Mystery (Thomas & Friends) Golden Books, illus. 2012. (Little Golden Book Ser.). (ENG.). 24p. (J). (gr. k-k). 5.99 *(978-0-307-97590-4(8),* Golden Bks.) Random Hse. Children's Bks.

Axelsson, Carina. Model Undercover: London. 2016. (Model Undercover Ser.: 3). (ENG.). 368p. (J). (gr. 5-8). pap. 6.99 *(978-1-4926-2088-4(2))* Sourcebooks, Inc.

—Model Undercover: New York. 2015. (Model Undercover Ser.: 2). (ENG.). 320p. (J). (gr. 4-8). pap. 10.99 *(978-1-4926-0785-4(1))* Sourcebooks, Inc.

—Paris. 2014. (Model Undercover Ser.: 1). (ENG.). 368p. (J). (gr. 4-7). pap. 10.99 *(978-1-4022-8587-5(6))* Sourcebooks, Inc.

Babbitt, Natalie. El Cerro del Abismo. 2003.Tr. of Knee-Knock Rise. (SPA., Illus.). 128p. (J). (gr. 3-5). *(978-84-236-3420-0(5),* ED0964) Edebé ESP. Dist: Lectorum Pubns., Inc.

—Goody Hall. Babbitt, Natalie, illus. 2007. (ENG., Illus.). 192p. (J). (gr. 3-7). per. 18.99 *(978-0-312-36983-5(2),* 900044327) Square Fish.

—Kneeknock Rise. Babbitt, Natalie, illus. 2007. (ENG., Illus.). 144p. (J). (gr. 3-7). per. 7.99 *(978-0-312-37009-1(1),* 900044346) Square Fish.

Baccalario, P. d. Century #2: Star of Stone. Janeczko, Leah D., tr. 2011. (Century Ser.: 2). 336p. (J). (gr. 3-7). 8.99 *(978-0-375-85796-6(6),* Yearling) Random Hse. Children's Bks.

Baccalario, P. D. Century #3: City of Wind. Janeczko, Leah D., tr. 2012. (Century Ser.: 3). (Illus.). 336p. (J). (gr. 5-8). 8.99 *(978-0-375-85797-3(4),* Yearling) Random Hse. Children's Bks.

Baccalario, Pierdomenico. Star of Stone, 2. Janeczko, Leah D., tr. Bruno, Iacopo, illus. 2012. (Century Quartet Ser.). (ENG.). 304p. (J). (gr. 6-8). lib. bdg. 22.44 *(978-0-375-95896-0(7))* Random House Publishing Group.

Bacigalupi, Paolo. The Doubt Factory: A Page-Turning Thriller of Dangerous Attraction & Unscrupulous Lies. 2016. (ENG.). 512p. (YA). (gr. 10-17). pap. 12.99 *(978-0-316-22076-7(0))* Little, Brown Bks. for Young Readers.

Backman, Aidel, illus. & adapted by. The Money in the Honey. Backman, Aidel, adapted by. 2003. 32p. (J). 13.95 *(978-0-8266-0030-1(1))* Merkos L'Inyonei Chinuch.

Backues, E. Sharol. Stories of a Dragonfly Spy, a Dog Named Droop & a Little Calf That Wondered Why? 2011. 28p. pap. 21.99 *(978-1-4653-6343-5(2))* Xlibris Corp.

Badeaux, Dewey. Sam & Skully. Ball, Lauren, illus. 2013. 126p. pap. 12.99 *(978-0-9884057-4-5(1))* Alligator Pr.

Baglio, Ben M. Help Find Honey! 2006. (Pet Finders Club Ser.: Vol. 10). (Illus.). 157p. (J). *(978-0-439-87143-3(3))* Scholastic, Inc.

—Max Is Missing. 2005. (Pet Finders Club Ser.: Vol. 2). (Illus.). 126p. (J). pap. *(978-0-439-68884-0(1))* Scholastic, Inc.

—Runaway Rascal. 2006. (Illus.). 157p. (J). *(978-0-439-79250-9(9))* Scholastic, Inc.

—Vanishing Point. Ettinger, Doris, illus. 2007. 158p. (J). pap. *(978-0-439-87145-7(X))* Scholastic, Inc.

Bailey, Linda. How Can a Brilliant Detective Shine in the Dark?, No. 6. 2003. (Stevie Diamond Mystery Ser.). (ENG.). 200p. (J). (gr. 13-18). 14.95 *(978-1-55074-896-3(3))* Kids Can Pr., Ltd. CAN. Dist: Hachette Bk. Group.

—What's a Serious Detective Like Me Doing in Such a Silly Movie? 2003. (Stevie Diamond Mystery Ser.). 192p. (YA). *(978-1-55337-639-2(0))* Kids Can Pr., Ltd.

Bailey, Mary. Vhan Zeely & the Time Prevaricators. 2009. 192p. 25.50 *(978-1-60693-477-7(5),* Eloquent Bks.) Strategic Book Publishing & Rights Agency (SBPRA).

Bailie, Helen. The Azura Stones. 2007. 212p. (YA). per. 18.00 *(978-1-58982-374-7(5),* Bedside Bks.) American Bk. Publishing Group.

The Baker Street Bunch & the Missing Honeybees Mystery. 2005. (J). per. *(978-0-9754241-5-5(7))* MiMar Publishing.

Balaban, Mariah. Scooby-Doo! & the Haunted Diner. 2010. (Illus.). 31p. (J). *(978-0-545-20882-6(3))* Scholastic, Inc.

—Scooby-Doo & the Rotten Robot, 1 vol. Sur, Duendes Del, illus. 2011. (Scooby-Doo! Ser.: No. 2). (ENG.). 24p. (J). (gr. k-4). lib. bdg. 31.36 *(978-1-59961-868-5(0),* 13246, Picture Bk.) Spotlight.

—Scooby-Doo & the Scary Snowman, 1 vol. Sur, Duendes Del, illus. 2011. (Scooby-Doo! Ser.: No. 2). (ENG.). 24p. (J). (gr. k-4). lib. bdg. 31.36 *(978-1-59961-869-2(9),* 13247, Picture Bk.) Spotlight.

—Scooby-Doo & the Thanksgiving Terror, 1 vol. Duendes Del Sur Staff, illus. 2011. (Scooby-Doo! Ser.: No. 2). (ENG.). 24p. (J). (gr. k-4). lib. bdg. 31.36 *(978-1-59961-870-8(2),* 13248, Picture Bk.) Spotlight.

Balasubramanian, Lalitha. The Twins at the Ancient Villa, 1 vol. 2009. 48p. pap. 16.95 *(978-1-61582-601-8(7))* America Star Bks.

Baldwin, Faith. Judy: A Story of Divine Corners. Beebe, Robb, illus. 2011. 264p. 47.95 *(978-1-258-08877-4(0))* Literary Licensing, LLC.

Baldwin, Rich & Jones, Sandie. The Detective Company. Dawn, Baumer, illus. 2004. 183p. (YA). pap. 9.95 *(978-0-9742920-0-7(1),* 2001) Buttonwood Pr.

Balian, Lorna. Humbug Witch: Spanish, 1 vol. 2003.Tr. of Humbug Witch. (SPA., Illus.). 32p. (J). (gr. -1). pap. 4.95 *(978-1-59572-011-5(1))* Star Bright Bks., Inc.

Ball, Duncan. An Eyeful of Emily. 2007. 336p. *(978-0-7322-8568-5(2))* HarperCollins Pubs. Australia.

—Selby Supersnoop. 2003. (ENG., Illus.). 176p. *(978-0-207-20005-2(X))* HarperCollins Pubs. Australia.

Balliett, Blue. The Calder Game. Helquist, Brett, illus. 2010. (ENG.). 416p. (J). (gr. 4-7). 7.99 *(978-0-439-85208-1(0),* Scholastic Paperbacks) Scholastic, Inc.

—Chasing Vermeer (Scholastic Gold), 1 vol. Helquist, Brett, illus. 2005. (ENG.). 304p. (gr. 4-7). reprint ed. pap. 8.99 *(978-0-439-37297-8(6))* Scholastic, Inc.

—The Danger Box. 2010. (ENG.). 320p. (J). (gr. 4-18). 16.99 *(978-0-439-85209-8(9),* Scholastic Pr.) Scholastic, Inc.

—Hold Fast. 2015. (ENG.). 288p. (J). (gr. 3-7). pap. 8.99 *(978-0-545-29989-3(6),* Scholastic Paperbacks) Scholastic, Inc.

—The Wright 3. Helquist, Brett, illus. 2008. 318p. (gr. 4-7). 18.00 *(978-0-7569-8942-2(6))* Perfection Learning Corp.

—The Wright 3. Helquist, Brett, illus. 2007. (ENG.). 352p. (J). (gr. 4-7). pap. 8.99 *(978-0-439-69368-4(3),* Scholastic Paperbacks) Scholastic, Inc.

Balmer, Fred. Festus & the Hole in the Fence Gang. Newcomb, Kristene, illus. 2005. 33p. (J). per. 7.00 *(978-0-9760790-3-3(8))* Folsom Fallies Pr.

—Festus & the Missing Bag of Feed. Newcomb, Kristene, illus. 2004. 26p. (J). per. 7.00 *(978-0-9760790-0-2(3))* Folsom Fallies Pr.

Balog, Cyn. Alone. 2018. (ENG.). 304p. (YA). (gr. 8-12). pap. 10.99 *(978-1-4926-6086-6(8))* Sourcebooks, Inc.

Banim, Lisa. In the Doghouse. 2005. 124p. (J). lib. bdg. 16.92 *(978-1-4242-0685-8(5))* Fitzgerald Bks.

Banim, Lisa & Minsky, Terri. The Case of the Kate Haters. 2005. (Illus.). 124p. (J). *(978-1-4156-3927-6(2))* Disney Pr.

Banks, Lynne Reid. The Mystery of the Cupboard. Newsom, Tom, illus. 2004. (ENG.). 256p. (J). (gr. 4-18). pap. 7.99 *(978-0-380-72013-2(2),* HarperCollins) HarperCollins Pubs.

—The Mystery of the Cupboard. (ENG., Illus.). 208p. pap. *(978-0-00-714901-8(8))* HarperCollins Pubs. Ltd.

—The Mystery of the Cupboard. (Indian in the Cupboard Ser.: No. 4). 246p. (J). (gr. 4-7). pap. 4.99 *(978-0-8072-1459-6(0),* Listening Library) Random Hse. Audio Publishing Group.

Banyard, Jen. Riddle Gully Secrets. 2016. (Riddle Gully Ser.). 188p. (J). 9.95 *(978-1-925163-95-7(4))* Fremantle Pr. AUS. Dist: Independent Pubs. Group.

Baratz-Logsted, Lauren & Logsted, Jackie. Marcia's Madness. Weber, Lisa K., illus. 2010. (Sisters Eight Ser.: 5). (ENG.). 128p. (J). (gr. 1-4). pap. 6.99 *(978-0-547-32864-5(8),* 1416978, Clarion Bks.) HarperCollins Pubs.

Baratz-Logsted, Lauren, et al. Marcia's Madness, 5. Weber, Lisa K., illus. 2010. (Sisters 8 Ser.: 5). (ENG.). 128p. (J). (gr. 2-4). 18.69 *(978-0-547-33401-1(X))* Houghton Mifflin Harcourt Publishing Co.

Barba, Rick. The Quantum Quandary. 2006. (Spy Gear Adventures Ser.: 3). (ENG.). 208p. (J). (gr. 3-7). pap. 10.99 *(978-1-4169-0889-0(1),* Aladdin) Simon & Schuster Children's Publishing.

Barbo, Maria S. Scooby-Doo & the Kitty Cat Caper, 1 vol. Sur, Duendes del, illus. 2016. (Scooby-Doo Early Reading Adventures Ser.). (ENG.). 24p. (J). (gr. -1-2). lib. bdg. 31.36 *(978-1-61479-465-3(0),* 21378) Spotlight.

Barbo, Maria S. & Preller, James. The Case of the Four-Leaf Clover. Smith, Jamie, illus. 2008. 104p. (J). pap. *(978-0-545-03837-9(5))* Scholastic, Inc.

Barclay, Linwood. Chase. 2019. (Chase Ser.). (ENG.). 256p. (J). (gr. 4-7). 10.99 *(978-1-5101-0219-4(1),* Orion Children's Bks.) Hachette Children's Group GBR. Dist: Hachette Bk. Group.

Barklem, Jill. La Escalera Secreta.Tr. of Secret Staircase. (SPA.). 30p. (J). 8.95 *(978-84-233-2765-2(5))* Ediciones Destino ESP. Dist: Planeta Publishing Corp.

MNO

—The Secret Staircase (Brambly Hedge) Barklem, Jill, illus. 2018. (Brambly Hedge Ser.). (ENG., Illus.). 32p. (J). 9.99 *(978-0-00-826914-2(9),* HarperCollins Children's Bks.) HarperCollins Pubs. Ltd. GBR. Dist: HarperCollins Pubs.

Barkley, Callie. Amy & the Missing Puppy. Riti, Marsha, illus. 2013. (Critter Club Ser.: 1). (ENG.). 128p. (J). (gr. k-4). 17.99 *(978-1-4424-5770-6(8));* pap. 5.99 *(978-1-4424-5769-0(4))* Little Simon. (Little Simon).

—Amy & the Missing Puppy. 2013. (Critter Club Ser.: 1). lib. bdg. 16.00 *(978-0-606-27023-6(X))* Turtleback.

Barnes, Jennifer Lynn. All In. 2015. (Naturals Ser.: 3). (ENG.). 384p. (YA). (gr. 7-12). 36.99 *(978-1-4847-1643-4(4))* Little, Brown Bks. for Young Readers.

—Bad Blood. 2016. (Naturals Ser.: 4). (ENG.). 384p. (YA). (gr. 7-12). 36.99 *(978-1-4847-5732-1(7))* Hyperion Bks. for Children.

—The Long Game: A Fixer Novel. 2017. (ENG.). 368p. (YA). pap. 12.99 *(978-1-61963-599-9(2),* 900141878, Bloomsbury USA Childrens) Bloomsbury Publishing USA.

Barnes, Phil. My Teacher's a Spy! 2017. (ENG.). 66p. (J). pap. 10.95 *(978-1-78629-497-5(4),* 718f7420-02c0-4e75-ab7b-c2d3d49bf9ff) Austin Macauley Pubs. Ltd. GBR. Dist: Baker & Taylor Publisher Services (BTPS).

Barnett, Angela. Mystic Grove. 2006. pap. 10.00 *(978-1-4257-1912-8(0))* Xlibris Corp.

Barnett, Mac. Brixton Brothers Mysterious Case of Cases: The Case of the Case of Mistaken Identity; the Ghostwriter Secret; It Happened on a Train; Danger Goes Berserk. Rex, Adam & Myers, Matt, illus. 2013. (Brixton Brothers Ser.). (ENG.). 1024p. (J). (gr. 3-7). pap. 33.99 *(978-1-4424-9818-1(8),* Simon & Schuster Bks. For Young Readers) Simon & Schuster Bks. For Young Readers.

—The Case of the Case of Mistaken Identity. Rex, Adam, illus. (Brixton Brothers Ser.: 1). (ENG.). (J). (gr. 3-7). 2010. 208p. pap. 7.99 *(978-1-4169-7816-9(X))* 2009. 192p. 15.99 *(978-1-4169-7815-2(1))* Simon & Schuster Bks. For Young Readers. (Simon & Schuster Bks. For Young Readers).

—Danger Goes Berserk. Myers, Matt, illus. (Brixton Brothers Ser.: 4). (ENG.). 256p. (J). (gr. 3-7). 2013. pap. 8.99 *(978-1-4424-3978-8(5))* 2012. 17.99 *(978-1-4424-3977-1(7))* Simon & Schuster Bks. For Young Readers. (Simon & Schuster Bks. For Young Readers).

—The Ghostwriter Secret. Rex, Adam, illus. (Brixton Brothers Ser.: 2). (ENG.). (J). (gr. 3-7). 2011. 256p. pap. 7.99 *(978-1-4169-7818-3(6))* 2010. 240p. 17.99 *(978-1-4169-7817-6(8))* Simon & Schuster Bks. For Young Readers. (Simon & Schuster Bks. For Young Readers).

—The Impossible Crime (Mac B., Kid Spy #2) Lowery, Mike, illus. 2018. (Mac B., Kid Spy Ser.: 2). (ENG.). 160p. (J). (gr. 2-5). 12.99 *(978-1-338-14368-3(9),* Orchard Bks.) Scholastic, Inc.

—It Happened on a Train. Rex, Adam, illus. 2012. (Brixton Brothers Ser.: 3). (ENG.). 304p. (J). (gr. 3-7). pap. 8.99 *(978-1-4169-7820-6(8),* Simon & Schuster Bks. For Young Readers) Simon & Schuster Bks. For Young Readers.

Barnholdt, Lauren. Girl Meets Ghost. 2013. (Girl Meets Ghost Ser.: 1). (ENG.). 224p. (J). (gr. 4-9). 15.99 *(978-1-4424-4246-7(8),* Aladdin) Simon & Schuster Children's Publishing.

—The Harder the Fall. 2014. (Girl Meets Ghost Ser.: 2). (ENG., Illus.). 256p. (J). (gr. 4-9). pap. 7.99 *(978-1-4424-2147-9(9),* Aladdin) Simon & Schuster Children's Publishing.

Barnickle, Angela. Miles Gardner & the Secret of Blissville: A Blissville Mystery Series. 2011. 128p. (gr. 4-6). 23.89 *(978-1-4634-1675-1(X));* pap. 12.01 *(978-1-4634-1676-8(8))* AuthorHouse.

Barr, Robert. The Clue of the Silver Spoons. 2004. reprint ed. pap. 15.95 *(978-1-4191-5701-1(9));* pap. 1.99 *(978-1-4192-5701-8(3))* Kessinger Publishing, LLC.

Barrett, Cheryl. Andy Goes Crab Fishin' 2010. 32p. pap. 12.99 *(978-1-4490-7459-3(6))* AuthorHouse.

Barrett, Jennifer. Lethal Delivery, Postage Prepaid. (Thumbprint Mysteries Ser.). 32.86 *(978-0-8092-0425-0(8))* McGraw-Hill/Contemporary.

Barrett, Tracy. The Beast of Blackslope. 2011. (Sherlock Files Ser.: 2). (ENG., Illus.). 192p. (J). (gr. 3-7). pap. 9.99 *(978-0-312-65918-9(0),* 900070505) Square Fish.

—The Case That Time Forgot. 3. 2011. (Sherlock Files Ser.: 3). (ENG., Illus.). 176p. (J). (gr. 4-6). pap. 10.99 *(978-0-312-56358-5(2),* 900074759) Square Fish.

—The Missing Heir. 2012. (Sherlock Files Ser.: 4). (J). lib. bdg. 19.65 *(978-0-606-26131-9(1))* Turtleback.

Barriman, Lydia. The Runaway Puppy No. 8: A Mystery with Probability. Grutzik, Rebecca Ann, illus. 2011. (Manga Math Mysteries Ser.: 8). (ENG.). 48p. (J). (gr. 3-5). pap. 6.99 *(978-0-7613-8137-2(6),* 2a91e8d7-a279-4bef-9712-d2028c1e96fb, Graphic Universe™) Lerner Publishing Group.

—#8 the Runaway Puppy: A Mystery with Probability. Grutzik, Becky, illus. 2011. (Manga Math Mysteries Set II Ser.). pap. 39.62 *(978-0-7613-8365-9(4),* Graphic Universe™) Lerner Publishing Group.

Barrows, Annie. Ivy & Bean Take the Case. 2014. (Ivy & Bean Ser.: 10). (J). lib. bdg. 16.00 *(978-0-606-36537-6(0))* Turtleback.

—Ivy & Bean Take the Case (Book 10) (Books for Curious Children, Books for Young Girls), Volume 10. Blackall, Sophie, illus. 2014. (Ivy & Bean Ser.). (ENG.). 136p. (J). (gr. 1-4). pap. 5.99 *(978-1-4521-2871-9(5))* Chronicle Bks. LLC.

Barry, Nick. Escape of the Terra-Cotta Soldiers: An Ethan Sparks Adventure. 2008. 180p. 23.95 *(978-0-595-49365-4(3));* pap. 13.95 *(978-0-595-45413-6(5))* iUniverse, Inc.

Bartlett, Philip A. Mystery of the Circle of Fire: A Roy Stover Story. 2011. 258p. 47.95 *(978-1-258-09666-3(8))* Literary Licensing, LLC.

The Baseball Heroes, 6 vols. (Woodland Mysteriestm Ser.). 133p. (gr. 3-7). 42.50 *(978-0-7802-7931-5(X))* Wright Group/McGraw-Hill.

Basil of Baker Street, 1 vol. 2016. (Your Reading Path Ser.: 1). (Illus.). 112p. (J). (gr. 4-4). pap. *(978-1-4814-6401-7(9),* c557f760-fd35-4d9b-81b4-60e49570d332, Rosen Classroom) Rosen Publishing Group, Inc., The.

Bates, Sonya Spreen. Topspin, 1 vol. 2013. (Orca Sports Ser.). (ENG.). 160p. (J). (gr. 4-7). pap. 9.95 *(978-1-4598-0385-5(X))* Orca Bk. Pubs. USA.

Bath, K. P. Flip Side. 2009. (YA). 16.99 *(978-0-316-03836-2(9))* Little Brown & Co.

The Battle of Bayport. 2014. (Hardy Boys Adventures Ser.: 6). (ENG., Illus.). 160p. (J). (gr. 3-7). 17.99 *(978-1-4814-0007-7(X),* Aladdin) Simon & Schuster Children's Publishing.

Baucom, Ian. Through the Skylight. Gerard, Justin, illus. (ENG.). 400p. (J). (gr. 4-8). 2014. pap. 6.99 *(978-1-4424-8167-1(6))* 2013. 17.99 *(978-1-4169-1777-9(2))* Simon & Schuster Children's Publishing. (Atheneum Bks. for Young Readers).

Bauer, Joan. Tell Me. 2015. 288p. (J). (gr. 5). 8.99 *(978-0-14-751314-4(6),* Puffin Books) Penguin Young Readers Group.

Baughman, Sarah R. The Light in the Lake. 2019. (ENG., Illus.). 320p. (J). (gr. 3-7). 16.99 *(978-0-316-42242-0(8))* Little, Brown Bks. for Young Readers.

Baum, L. Frank. Mary Louise in the Country. 2011. 188p. pap. 14.95 *(978-1-4638-0069-7(X))* Rodgers, Alan Bks.

Baum, L. Frank & van Dyne, Edith. Mary Louise in the Country. 2011. 188p. 26.95 *(978-1-4638-9605-8(0))* Rodgers, Alan Bks.

—Mary Louise Solves a Mystery. 2011. 140p. 24.95 *(978-1-4638-9498-6(8))* Rodgers, Alan Bks.

Baumgartner, Edward Louis. Wabash Boy. 2011. 236p. (gr. 4-6). pap. 16.26 *(978-1-4269-7615-5(1))* Trafford Publishing.

Baumgartner, John Robert. Like Losing Your Left Hand. 2011. 244p. pap. 24.95 *(978-1-4560-4043-7(X))* America Star Bks.

Beard, Elizabeth. Liza & the Mysteries. 2004. 70p. (J). per. *(978-1-59196-640-1(X))* Instant Pub.

Beardsley, Martyn. The Ghosts of Blackbottle Rock. 2017. (ENG., Illus.). 128p. (J). (gr. 4-12). pap. 12.95 *(978-1-78535-615-5(1),* Our Street Bks.) Hunt, John Publishing Ltd. GBR. Dist: National Bk. Network.

Beatty, Robert. Willa of the Wood: Willa of the Wood, Book 1. 2019. (Willa of the Wood Ser.: 1). (ENG.). 400p. (J). (gr. 3-7). pap. 7.99 *(978-1-368-00947-8(6),* Disney-Hyperion) Disney Publishing Worldwide.

Beatty, Scott. Murder in Mind, Vol. 4. Guice, Butch et al, illus. 2004. (Ruse Ser.: Vol. 4). 160p. (YA). pap. 15.95 *(978-1-59314-047-2(9))* CrossGeneration Comics, Inc.

Beaufrand, M. J. Useless Bay. 2016. (ENG., Illus.). 240p. (YA). (gr. 8-17). 17.95 *(978-1-4197-2138-0(0),* 1135401, Amulet Bks.) Abrams, Inc.

Beauregard, Lynda. Summer Camp Science Mysteries. Helmer, Der-shing, illus. 2012. (Summer Camp Science Mysteries Ser.). (ENG.). 48p. (gr. 3-6). pap. 52.82 *(978-0-7613-9272-9(6));*Pack, Set. pap. 316.92 *(978-0-7613-9273-6(4))* Lerner Publishing Group. (Graphic Universe™).

—Summer Camp Science Mysteries: Spring 2012 New Releases. Helmer, Der-shing, illus. 2012. (Summer Camp Science Mysteries Ser.). 48p. (J). (gr. 3-6). lib. bdg. 117.08 *(978-0-7613-5688-2(6),* Graphic Universe™) Lerner Publishing Group.

Beck, W. H. Malcolm at Midnight. Lies, Brian, illus. 2015. (ENG.). 272p. (J). (gr. 3-7). pap. 7.99 *(978-0-544-33666-7(6),* 1584188, Clarion Bks.) HarperCollins Pubs.

Beer, Henry. Girl Defective. 2015. (ENG., Illus.). 320p. (YA). (gr. 9). pap. 10.99 *(978-1-4424-9761-0(0))* Simon & Schuster Children's Publishing.

Behems, Kathryn J. Breakdown. 2016. (Atlas of Cursed Places Ser.). (ENG.). 96p. (YA). (gr. 6-12). lib. bdg. 26.65 *(978-1-5124-1323-6(2),* db301279-6588-4513-88e6-fa63ae4be1cc, Darby Creek) Lerner Publishing Group.

Beil, Michael D. Lantern Sam & the Blue Streak Bandits. 2015. (ENG., Illus.). 288p. (J). (gr. 3-7). pap. 7.99 *(978-0-385-75320-3(9),* Yearling) Random Hse. Children's Bks.

—The Red Blazer Girls: the Mistaken Masterpiece. 2012. (Red Blazer Girls Ser.: 3). (ENG.). 336p. (J). (gr. 5). 8.99 *(978-0-375-86494-0(6),* Yearling) Random Hse. Children's Bks.

—The Red Blazer Girls: the Ring of Rocamadour. 2010. (Red Blazer Girls Ser.: 1). (ENG.). 320p. (J). (gr. 3-7). 7.99 *(978-0-375-84303-7(5),* Yearling) Random Hse. Children's Bks.

—The Red Blazer Girls: the Secret Cellar. 2013. (Red Blazer Girls Ser.: 4). (ENG., Illus.). 288p. (J). (gr. 5). pap. 8.99 *(978-0-375-86495-7(4),* Yearling) Random Hse. Children's Bks.

—The Red Blazer Girls: the Vanishing Violin. 2011. (Red Blazer Girls Ser.: 2). (ENG.). 336p. (J). (gr. 3-7). 8.99 *(978-0-375-85454-5(1),* Yearling) Random Hse. Children's Bks.

—The Ring of Rocamadour, 1. 2009. (Red Blazer Girls Ser.). (ENG.). 304p. (J). (gr. 6-8). lib. bdg. 21.19 *(978-0-375-94814-5(7),* Knopf Bks. for Young Readers) Random Hse. Children's Bks.

—Summer at Forsaken Lake. Kneen, Maggie, illus. 2013. (ENG.). 336p. (J). (gr. 5). pap. 10.99 *(978-0-375-86496-4(2),* Yearling) Random Hse. Children's Bks.

Bell, Juliet. Kepler's Dream. 2013. 256p. (J). (gr. 5-8). 6.99 *(978-0-14-242648-7(2),* Puffin Books) Penguin Young Readers Group.

Bellairs, John. The Chessmen of Doom (A Johnny Dixon Mystery: Book Seven) 2011. 114p. pap. 14.95 *(978-1-61756-348-5(X))* Open Road Integrated Media, Inc.

—The Curse of the Blue Figurine (A Johnny Dixon Mystery: Book One) 2011. 150p. pap. 15.95 *(978-1-61756-324-9(2))* Open Road Integrated Media, Inc.

—The Eyes of the Killer Robot (A Johnny Dixon Mystery: Book Five) 2011. 126p. pap. 14.95 *(978-1-61756-340-9(4))* Open Road Integrated Media, Inc.

—The House with a Clock in Its Walls. Gorey, Edward, illus. 2004. (Lewis Barnavelt Ser.: Bk. 1). (ENG.). 192p. (J). (gr. 3-7). pap. 7.99 *(978-0-14-240257-3(5),* Puffin Books) Penguin Young Readers Group.

—The House with a Clock in Its Walls. Gorey, Edward, illus. 2004. (John Bellairs Mysteries Ser.). 179p. (J). (gr. 3-7). 13.65 *(978-0-7569-5257-0(3))* Perfection Learning Corp.

—The House with a Clock in Its Walls. (Lewis Barnavelt Ser.: Bk. 1). 179p. (J). (gr. 4-6). pap. 4.50 *(978-0-8072-1423-7(X),* Listening Library) Random Hse. Audio Publishing Group.

—The House with a Clock in Its Walls. 2004. 17.20 *(978-1-4176-3513-9(4))* Turtleback.

—The Mummy, the Will, & the Crypt (A Johnny Dixon Mystery: Book Two) 2011. 126p. pap. 14.95 *(978-1-61756-328-7(5))* Open Road Integrated Media, Inc.

—The Secret of the Underground Room (A Johnny Dixon Mystery: Book Eight) 2011. 96p. pap. 14.95 *(978-1-61756-352-2(8))* Open Road Integrated Media, Inc.

—The Spell of the Sorcerer's Skull. Gorey, Edward, illus. 2004. 170p. (J). (gr. 4-7). 13.65 *(978-0-7569-4965-5(3))* Perfection Learning Corp.

—The Spell of the Sorcerer's Skull (A Johnny Dixon Mystery: Book Three) 2011. 124p. pap. 14.95 *(978-1-61756-332-4(3))* Open Road Integrated Media, Inc.

Bellingham, Brenda. La Maldicion del Cofre de Plata. (SPA.). (YA). 8.95 *(978-958-04-7079-3(0))* Norma S.A. COL. Dist: Distribuidora Norma, Inc.

Bellino, Sarah. The Little Miss Detectives: Case Number 1. 2012. 32p. pap. 14.51 *(978-1-4669-6867-7(2))* Trafford Publishing.

Bellucci, Arianna, illus. Sherlock Holmes: a Study in Scarlet. adapted abr. ed. 2019. (Sweet Cherry Easy Classics Ser.: 1). (ENG.). 216p. (J). (gr. 4-8). 6.95 *(978-1-78226-575-7(9),* fc905307-5e05-4111-883c-9cda0989b378) Sweet Cherry Publishing GBR. Dist: Baker & Taylor Publisher Services (BTPS).

Benjamin, Ruth. The Lost Treasure of Chelton. 2004. viii, 170p. (J). 13.95 *(978-1-932443-02-8(9))* Judaica Pr., Inc., The.

—The Mysterious Lighthouse of Chelton. 2006. (ENG.). 160p. (J). 14.95 *(978-1-932443-57-8(6))* Judaica Pr., Inc., The.

Bennett, Jenn. Serious Moonlight. 2019. (ENG., Illus.). 432p. (YA). (gr. 9). 19.99 *(978-1-5344-2514-9(4),* Simon Pulse) Simon Pulse.

Bennett, Marcia Allen. Mystery at Saddlecreek. 2003. (Illus.). 162p. (J). pap. 12.95 *(978-1-57168-494-3(8),* Eakin Pr.) Eakin Pr.

Bennett, Marcia Allen & Eckhardt, Jason C. Mystery at Saddlecreek. 2004. (Illus.). 162p. (J). 17.95 *(978-1-57168-336-6(4),* Eakin Pr.) Eakin Pr.

Bennicke, Rune Brandt. The Mystery Hat. Jensen, Jakob Hjort, illus. 2014. (ENG.). 32p. (J). (gr. -1-k). 16.95 *(978-1-62914-621-8(8),* Sky Pony Pr.) Skyhorse Publishing Co., Inc.

Benoit, Charles. Cold Calls. 2016. (ENG.). 304p. (YA). (gr. 7). pap. 8.99 *(978-0-544-54121-4(9),* 1608880, Clarion Bks.) HarperCollins Pubs.

Benson, Amber. Among the Ghosts. Grace, Sina, illus. 2011. (ENG.). 256p. (J). (gr. 3-7). pap. 6.99 *(978-1-4169-9426-8(2),* Aladdin) Simon & Schuster Children's Publishing.

—Among the Ghosts. Grace, Sina, illus. 2010. (ENG.). 256p. (J). (gr. 3-7). 15.99 *(978-1-4169-9405-3(X),* Simon & Schuster/Paula Wiseman Bks.) Simon & Schuster/Paula Wiseman Bks.

Bentley, Maria. Summer Sounds Level 1 Beginner/Elementary. 2010. (Cambridge Experience Readers Ser.). (ENG., Illus.). 46p. pap. 14.75 *(978-0-521-18158-7(5))* Cambridge Univ. Pr.

Beresford, Elisabeth. The Great Cake Mystery. (ENG., Illus.). 16p. (J). (gr. k-6). pap. *(978-0-340-74672-1(6))* Hodder & Stoughton.

Berk, Josh. The Dark Days of Hamburger Halpin. 2011. 256p. (YA). (gr. 7). pap. 8.99 *(978-0-375-84625-0(5),* Ember) Random Hse. Children's Bks.

—Guy Langman, Crime Scene Procrastinator. 2013. 240p. (YA). (gr. 7). pap. 8.99 *(978-0-375-84627-4(1),* Ember) Random Hse. Children's Bks.

—Say It Ain't So. 2015. (Lenny & the Mikes Ser.: 2). (ENG.). 288p. (J). (gr. 3-7). pap. 9.99 *(978-0-307-93007-1(6),* Yearling) Random Hse. Children's Bks.

—Strike Three, You're Dead. 2014. (Lenny & the Mikes Ser.: 1). (ENG.). 272p. (J). (gr. 3-7). 7.99 *(978-0-307-93006-4(8),* Yearling) Random Hse. Children's Bks.

Berlin, Eric. The Puzzler's Mansion: The Puzzling World of Winston Breen. 2013. (Puzzling World of Winston Breen Ser.: 3). 272p. (J). (gr. 3-7). 8.99 *(978-0-14-242643-2(1),* Puffin Books) Penguin Young Readers Group.

—The Puzzling World of Winston Breen. (J). 2009. (Puzzling World of Winston Breen Ser.: 1). 256p. (gr. 3-7). pap. 7.99 *(978-0-14-241388-3(7),* Puffin Books) 2007. (Puzzling World of Winston Breen Ser.). (ENG., Illus.). 215p. (gr. 4-6). 18.69 *(978-0-399-24693-7(2))* Penguin Young Readers Group.

Bern, Dave. Best Friends. 2006. 28p. pap. 9.95 *(978-1-4327-0036-2(7))* Outskirts Pr., Inc.

Bernard, Romily. Find Me. 2014. (Find Me Ser.: 1). (ENG.). 336p. (YA). (gr. 8). pap. 9.99 *(978-0-06-222904-5(4),* HarperTeen) HarperCollins Pubs.

—Remember Me. 2014. (Find Me Ser.: 2). (ENG.). 368p. (YA). (gr. 8). 17.99 *(978-0-06-222906-9(0),* HarperTeen) HarperCollins Pubs.

Berne, Emma Carlson. The Lady's Slipper: A Melody Mystery. 2017. 183p. (J). *(978-1-5182-4313-4(4),* American Girl) American Girl Publishing, Inc.

Berry, Julie. All the Truth That's in Me. 2014. (ENG.). 304p. (YA). (gr. 7). pap. 9.99 *(978-0-14-242730-9(6),* Speak) Penguin Young Readers Group.

Betancourt, Jeanne. Pony Mysteries #1: Penny & Pepper (Scholastic Reader, Level 3) Riley, Kellee, illus. 2011. (Scholastic Reader, Level 3 Ser.). (ENG.). 48p. (J). (gr. 1-3). pap. 3.99 *(978-0-545-11508-7(6),* Cartwheel Bks.) Scholastic, Inc.

Bevins, Pegi & Conan Doyle, Arthur. Sherlock Holmes. 2003. (Retold Classics Anthologies Ser.). (Illus.). 282p. (J). pap. 9.99 *(978-0-7891-5931-1(7))* Perfection Learning Corp.

Bhagwat, B. R. Faster Fenay at Fort Pratapgad. Modak, Tejas, tr. 2013. 120p. 10.00 *(978-0-14-333201-5(5))* Penguin Group India IND. Dist: Penguin Publishing Group.

Bial, Raymond. Shadow Island: A Tale of Lake Superior. 2006. 172p. (J). (gr. 3-7). 18.95 *(978-1-883953-37-9(5));* per. 12.95 *(978-1-883953-36-2(7))* Great Lakes Literary, LLC. (Blue Horse Books).

Bichoman Vuelve de la Tumba. (Fantasmas de Fear Street Coleccion). (SPA.). (YA). (gr. 5-8). pap. 7.95 *(978-950-04-1718-1(9),* EM9292) Emecé Editores S.A. ARG. Dist: Lectorum Pubns., Inc., Planeta Publishing Corp.

Biedrzycki, David. Ace Lacewing, Bug Detective: the Big Swat. Biedrzycki, David, illus. (Ace Lacewing, Bug Detective Ser.). (Illus.). 44p. (J). (gr. k-4). 2012. pap. 8.95 *(978-1-57091-748-6(5))* 2010. 16.95 *(978-1-57091-747-9(7))* Charlesbridge Publishing, Inc.

—Bad Bugs Are My Business. Biedrzycki, David, illus. 2011. (Ace Lacewing, Bug Detective Ser.). (Illus.). 44p. (J). (gr. k-4). pap. 8.95 *(978-1-57091-693-9(4))* Charlesbridge Publishing, Inc.

Bills, Randall N. Detective Mysteries. 2008. 92p. pap. 6.95 *(978-0-9796392-1-0(2))* Adventure Boys Inc.

Birney, Betty G. Mysteries According to Humphrey. 2013. (Humphrey Ser.: 8). (ENG.). 176p. (J). (gr. 3-7). pap. 7.99 *(978-0-14-242669-2(5),* Puffin Books) Penguin Young Readers Group.

—Mysteries According to Humphrey. 2013. (According to Humphrey Ser.: 8). lib. bdg. 16.00 *(978-0-606-31699-6(X))* Turtleback.

Blackburn, Gary. Pickerel Lake, 1 vol. 2010. 220p. pap. 24.95 *(978-1-4489-4971-7(8))* America Star Bks.

Blackwell-Burke, Melissa & Kunkel, Kristen. The Messy Mystery. 2003. (J). spiral bd. 14.95 *(978-1-58605-958-3(0),* LeapFrog Schl. Hse.) LeapFrog Enterprises, Inc.

Blaine, John. The Blue Ghost Mystery: A Rick Brant Science Adventure Story. 2011. 188p. 42.95 *(978-1-258-09526-0(2))* Literary Licensing, LLC.

—The Caves of Fear: A Rick Brant Science Adventure Story. 2011. 220p. 44.95 *(978-1-258-09271-9(9))* Literary Licensing, LLC.

—The Egyptian Cat Mystery: A Rick Brant Science Adventure Story. 2011. 192p. 42.95 *(978-1-258-09449-2(5))* Literary Licensing, LLC.

—The Pirates of Shan: A Rick Brant Science Adventure Story. 2011. 190p. 42.95 *(978-1-258-10086-5(X))* Literary Licensing, LLC.

—The Scarlet Lake Mystery: A Rick Brant Science Adventure Story. 2011. 192p. 42.95 *(978-1-258-09823-0(7))* Literary Licensing, LLC.

—Smuggler's Reef: A Rick Brant Science Adventure Story. 2011. 220p. 44.95 *(978-1-258-04085-7(9))* Literary Licensing, LLC.

Blaine, John & Goodwin, Harold Leland. The Caves of Fear. 2011. 150p. 24.95 *(978-1-4638-9614-0(X));* pap. 13.95 *(978-1-4638-0073-4(8))* Rodgers, Alan Bks.

Blaisdell, Patty. The Haunted Shed, 1 vol. 2009. 32p. pap. 24.95 *(978-1-60836-674-3(X))* America Star Bks.

Blake-Garrett, Andrea. The Adventures of Izzy & Juju: Twin Detective Investigators (T. D. I.) 2012. 28p. pap. 19.99 *(978-1-4685-0683-9(8))* AuthorHouse.

Blakemore, Megan Frazer. The Spy Catchers of Maple Hill. 2014. (ENG.). 320p. (J). (gr. 3-6). 16.99 *(978-1-61963-348-3(5),* 900134200, Bloomsbury USA Childrens) Bloomsbury Publishing USA.

Blankman, Anne. Prisoner of Night & Fog. 2014. (ENG.). 416p. (YA). (gr. 8). 17.99 *(978-0-06-227881-4(9),* Balzer & Bray) HarperCollins Pubs.

Blum, Paul. Dawn of the Zombies, 1 vol. 2007. (Extraordinary Files Ser.). (ENG., Illus.). 48p. (J). (gr. 4-7). pap. 10.99 *(978-1-84680-250-8(4))* Evans Brothers, Ltd. GBR. Dist: Independent Pubs. Group.

—Day of Judgement, 1 vol. 2007. (Extraordinary Files Ser.). (ENG., Illus.). 48p. (J). (gr. 4-7). pap. 11.99 *(978-1-84680-251-5(2))* Evans Brothers, Ltd. GBR. Dist: Independent Pubs. Group.

—Gene Machine, 1 vol. 2007. (Extraordinary Files Ser.). (ENG., Illus.). 48p. (J). (gr. 4-7). pap. 10.99 *(978-1-84680-252-2(0))* Evans Brothers, Ltd. GBR. Dist: Independent Pubs. Group.

—Killer Robot, 1 vol. 2007. (Extraordinary Files Ser.). (ENG., Illus.). 48p. (J). (gr. 4-7). pap. 10.99 *(978-1-84680-178-5(8))* Evans Brothers, Ltd. GBR. Dist: Independent Pubs. Group.

—Puppet Master, 1 vol. 2007. (Extraordinary Files Ser.). (ENG., Illus.). 48p. (J). (gr. 4-7). pap. 10.99 *(978-1-84680-182-2(6))* Evans Brothers, Ltd. GBR. Dist: Independent Pubs. Group.

—Secrets & Lies, 1 vol. 2007. (Extraordinary Files Ser.). (ENG., Illus.). 48p. (J). (gr. 4-7). pap. 10.99 *(978-1-84680-249-2(0))* Evans Brothers, Ltd. GBR. Dist: Independent Pubs. Group.

—Sleep Walker, 1 vol. 2007. (Extraordinary Files Ser.). (ENG., Illus.). 48p. (J). (gr. 4-7). pap. 10.99 *(978-1-84680-174-7(5))* Evans Brothers, Ltd. GBR. Dist: Independent Pubs. Group.

—Spider Invasion, 1 vol. 2007. (Extraordinary Files Ser.). (ENG., Illus.). 48p. (J). (gr. 4-7). pap. 10.99 *(978-1-84680-183-9(4))* Evans Brothers, Ltd. GBR. Dist: Independent Pubs. Group.

—Werewolf Eclipse, 1 vol. 2007. (Extraordinary Files Ser.). (ENG., Illus.). 48p. (J). (gr. 4-7). pap. 10.99 *(978-1-84680-180-8(X))* Evans Brothers, Ltd. GBR. Dist: Independent Pubs. Group.

Blythe, Daniel. Shadow Breakers. 2013. (J). *(978-0-545-47980-6(0),* Chicken Hse., The) Scholastic, Inc.

Blyton, Enid. The Adventure of the Strange Ruby. (ENG., Illus.). 128p. (J). pap. 5.95 *(978-0-09-958230-4(9))* Penguin Random Hse. GBR. Dist: Trafalgar Square Publishing.

—The Ragamuffin Mystery: A Barney Mystery. 2013. (ENG., Illus.). 199p. (J). pap. 9.99 *(978-1-84135-733-1(2))* Award Pubns. Ltd. GBR. Dist: Parkwest Pubns., Inc.

—The Rat-a-Tat Mystery. 2013. 220p. (J). pap. 9.99 *(978-1-84135-732-4(4))* Award Pubns. Ltd. GBR. Dist: Parkwest Pubns., Inc.

—The Rilloby Fair Mystery. 2013. 284p. (J). pap. 9.99 *(978-1-84135-729-4(4))* Award Pubns. Ltd. GBR. Dist: Parkwest Pubns., Inc.

—The Ring O' Bells Mystery. 2013. 276p. (J). pap. 9.99 *(978-1-84135-730-0(8))* Award Pubns. Ltd. GBR. Dist: Parkwest Pubns., Inc.

—The Rockingdown Mystery. 2013. (ENG.). 295p. (J). pap. 9.99 *(978-1-84135-728-7(6))* Award Pubns. Ltd. GBR. Dist: Parkwest Pubns., Inc.

—The Rubadub Mystery. 2013. 280p. (J). pap. 9.99 *(978-1-84135-731-7(6))* Award Pubns. Ltd. GBR. Dist: Parkwest Pubns., Inc.

—The Secret of Cliff Castle: 3 Great Adventure Stories. Downer, Maggie, illus. 2013. (ENG.). 288p. (J). 16.50 *(978-1-84135-588-7(7))* Award Pubns. Ltd. GBR. Dist: Parkwest Pubns., Inc.

—The Secret of the Lost Necklace: 3 Great Adventure Stories. Biro, Val, illus. 2013. (ENG.). 272p. (J). 16.50

(978-1-84135-587-0(9)) Award Pubns. Ltd. GBR. Dist: Parkwest Pubns., Inc.

Boaz, Ashley. The Mystery of the Midnight Blaze. 2005. (J). *(978-0-9761033-6-3(2))* Waldenhouse Pubs., Inc.

Bodeen, S. A. The Fallout. 2014. (Compound Ser.: 2). (ENG.). 352p. (YA). (gr. 7-12). pap. 11.99 *(978-1-250-05078-6(2),* 900134149) Square Fish.

Bohannon, C. S. Spatula Boy: And the Secret of the Mysterious Old House. 2007. 52p. per. 16.95 *(978-1-4241-6956-6(9))* America Star Bks.

Boldt, Claudia. The Mystery of the Missing Cake. 2018. (ENG., Illus.). 32p. (J). (gr. -1-3). 16.95 *(978-1-84976-485-8(9))* Tate Publishing, Ltd. GBR. Dist: Hachette Bk. Group.

Bolger, Z. C. Danny Calloway & the Puzzle House. Robinson, Garrett, ed. Tallent, Alyssa, illus. 2013. 346p. 24.99 *(978-1-939898-01-2(3))* Story Road Publishing, Inc.

Bollback, Anthony G. Capture of the Twin Dragon. 2012. 152p. pap. 8.99 *(978-0-9849359-1-8(6))* Finding the Cause, LLC.

—Hijacked. 2012. 176p. pap. 8.99 *(978-0-9849359-5-6(9))* Finding the Cause, LLC.

—Mystery of the Counterfeit Money. 2012. 170p. (gr. 4-7). pap. 8.99 *(978-0-9849359-2-5(4))* Finding the Cause, LLC.

—Rescue at Cripple Creek. 2012. 178p. pap. 8.99 *(978-0-9849359-3-2(2))* Finding the Cause, LLC.

—Smugglers in Hong Kong. 2012. 156p. pap. 8.99 *(978-0-9849359-0-1(8))* Finding the Cause, LLC.

—The Tiger Shark Strikes Again. 2012. 172p. pap. 8.99 *(978-0-9849359-4-9(0))* Finding the Cause, LLC.

Bomback, Mark & Craze, Galaxy. Mapmaker. 2017. (ENG.). 272p. (YA). (gr. 9). pap. 10.99 *(978-1-61695-633-2(X),* Soho Teen) Soho Pr., Inc.

Bonar, Troy A. Safety = Caring. 2013. 28p. pap. 9.95 *(978-1-4787-0745-5(3))* Outside the Box Publishing, LLC.

Bond, Gwenda. Strange Alchemy. 2017. (ENG., Illus.). 336p. (YA). (gr. 9-12). 17.95 *(978-1-63079-076-9(1),* 134212, Switch Pr.) Capstone.

Bonham, T. J. SPI: the Case of the Dark Shadow: The Case of the Dark Shadow, 1 vol. 2012. (ENG.). 112p. pap. 12.99 *(978-0-7643-4132-8(4),* 4550) Schiffer Publishing, Ltd.

Bonk, John J. Madhattan Mystery. 2012. (ENG., Illus.). 304p. (J). (gr. 4-6). 22.44 *(978-0-8027-2349-9(7),* 9780802723499) Walker & Co.

Bonner, Anne. Intrigue at Pine Haven: Civil War in Florida. Akridge, Bill, illus. 2006. 220p. (YA). 12.95 net. *(978-1-878398-76-5(8),* Blue Note Bks.) Blue Note Pubns.

BookSource Staff, compiled by. Balloon Blow-Up. 2013. (Hardy Boys: Secret Files Ser.: 13). lib. bdg. 16.00 *(978-0-606-32328-4(7))* Turtleback.

—The Great Coaster Caper. 2012. (Hardy Boys: Secret Files Ser.: 9). lib. bdg. 14.75 *(978-0-606-26321-4(7))* Turtleback.

—Lights, Camera... Zombies! 2013. (Hardy Boys: Secret Files Ser.: 12). lib. bdg. 14.75 *(978-0-606-32033-7(4))* Turtleback.

—Robot Rumble. 2013. (Hardy Boys: Secret Files Ser.: 11). lib. bdg. 16.00 *(978-0-606-27027-4(2))* Turtleback.

Bosch, Pseudonymous. The Name of This Book Is Secret. 2008. (Secret Ser.: 1). (ENG.). 400p. (J). (gr. 3-7). pap. 9.99 *(978-0-316-11369-4(7))* Little, Brown Bks. for Young Readers.

—The Name of This Book Is Secret. 2009. 18.00 *(978-1-60686-518-7(8))* Perfection Learning Corp.

—The Name of This Book Is Secret. 2008. (Secret Ser.: 1). (J). lib. bdg. 19.65 *(978-1-4178-2975-0(3))* Turtleback.

—The Secret Series Complete Collection. 2012. (ENG.). 2016p. (J). (gr. 3-7). pap. 38.99 *(978-0-316-21981-5(9))* Little, Brown Bks. for Young Readers.

—Write This Book: A Do-It-Yourself Mystery. (Secret Ser.). (ENG., Illus.). (J). (gr. 3-7). 2014. 304p. pap. 8.99 *(978-0-316-20780-5(2))* 2013. 288p. 16.99 *(978-0-316-20781-2(0))* Little, Brown Bks. for Young Readers.

Bossley, Michele Martin. Bio-Pirate, 1 vol. 2008. (Orca Currents Ser.). (ENG.). (J). (gr. 4-7). 112p. 16.95 *(978-1-55143-895-5(X))*; 128p. pap. 9.95 *(978-1-55143-893-1(3))* Orca Bk. Pubs. USA.

—Cracked, 1 vol. 2007. (Orca Currents Ser.). (ENG.). 128p. (J). (gr. 4-7). per. 9.95 *(978-1-55143-700-2(7))* Orca Bk. Pubs. USA.

—Swiped, 1 vol. 2011. (Orca Currents Ser.). (ENG.). 109p. (J). (gr. 6-8). 26.19 *(978-1-55143-652-4(3))* Orca Bk. Pubs. USA.

—Tampered, 1 vol. 2013. (Orca Currents Ser.). (ENG.). 136p. (J). (gr. 4-7). pap. 9.95 *(978-1-4598-0356-5(6))* Orca Bk. Pubs. USA.

Bow, James. The Unwritten Girl: The Unwritten Books. 2006. (Unwritten Bks.: 1). (ENG.). 180p. (YA). (gr. 7). pap. 12.99 *(978-1-55002-604-7(6))* Dundurn Pr. CAN. Dist: Publishers Group West (PGW).

Bow, Patricia. The Spiral Maze, 1 vol. 2006. (ENG., Illus.). 192p. pap. 11.00 *(978-1-895449-68-6(5))* Thistledown Pr., Ltd. CAN. Dist: Univ. of Toronto Pr.

Bowditch, Eden Unger. The Atomic Weight of Secrets or the Arrival of the Mysterious Men in Black. 2011. (Young Inventors Guild Ser.: 1). (ENG.). 320p. (YA). 19.95 *(978-1-61088-002-2(1),* 3affde56-4139-4a62-9c5d-612313bb8c2d) Bancroft Pr.

Bowen, Carl. The Murders in the Rue Morgue, 1 vol. Dimaya, Emerson, illus. 2013. (Edgar Allan Poe Graphic Novels Ser.). (ENG.). 72p. (J). (gr. 5-9). 28.65 *(978-1-4342-3033-1(3),* 114578); pap. 6.10 *(978-1-4342-4259-4(5),* 120321) Capstone. (Stone Arch Bks.).

Bowler, Tim. Frozen Fire. 2010. (ENG.). 352p. (YA). (gr. 7-18). 8.99 *(978-0-14-241465-1(4),* Speak) Penguin Young Readers Group.

Boyd, David. Beware the Vikings. Rooth, Mike, illus. 2007. 48p. (J). lib. bdg. 23.08 *(978-1-4242-1624-6(9))* Fitzgerald Bks.

Bracegirdle, P. J. Fiendish Deeds. 2009. (Joy of Spooking Ser.: 1). (ENG.). 224p. (J). (gr. 3-7). pap. 5.99 *(978-1-4169-3417-2(0),* McElderry, Margaret K. Bks.) McElderry, Margaret K. Bks.

Bradford, Quebe Merritt. In the Absence of My Father: Grief. Grit. Gangs. Guts. Grace. 2011. 188p. 24.79 *(978-1-4567-4026-9(1))*; pap. 14.99 *(978-1-4567-3968-3(9))* AuthorHouse.

Brafman, Bonnie. Treasure in Marci's House. 2007. (J). pap. 8.00 *(978-0-8059-7418-8(0))* Dorrance Publishing Co., Inc.

Bramlett, Timothy A. Sharkey Explores the Unknown. 2007. pap. 14.95 *(978-0-9796444-0-5(2))* Azuria Bks.

Brannigan's Folly. 64p. (YA). (gr. 6-12). pap. *(978-0-8224-2360-7(X))* Globe Fearon Educational Publishing.

Branning, Debe. The Adventures of Chickolet Pigolet: The Bribe of Frankenbeans. Knold, Nijlon, illus. 2008. 48p. pap. 7.95 *(978-1-935137-40-5(9))* Guardian Angel Publishing, Inc.

Brasch, Nicolas & Webb, Melissa. The Mystery of the Missing Bike. 2008. (Rigby Focus Forward: Level F Ser.). (Illus.). 24p. (J). (gr. 4-7). pap. *(978-1-4190-3688-0(2),* Rigby) Pearson Education Australia.

Bray, Libba. Before the Devil Breaks You. 2017. (Diviners Ser.: 3). (ENG.). 560p. (YA). (gr. 10-17). 21.99 *(978-0-316-12606-9(3))* Little, Brown Bks. for Young Readers.

—The Diviners. 2012. 578p. (YA). 9.99 *(978-0-316-23242-5(4))* Little Brown & Co.

—The Diviners. (Diviners Ser.: 1). (ENG.). (YA). (gr. 10-17). 2013. 496p. pap. 16.99 *(978-0-316-12610-6(1))* 2012. 800p. 52.99 *(978-0-316-22426-0(X))* Little, Brown Bks. for Young Readers.

—The Diviners. 2013. (Diviners Ser.: 1). 468p. (YA). lib. bdg. 24.50 *(978-0-606-32284-3(1))* Turtleback.

—Lair of Dreams: A Diviners Novel. 2015. (Diviners Ser.: 2). (ENG.). 624p. (YA). (gr. 7-17). E-Book 45.00 *(978-0-316-36488-1(6))* Little, Brown Bks. for Young Readers.

Brewer, Zac. The Blood Between Us. 2017. (ENG.). 304p. (YA). (gr. 8). pap. 9.99 *(978-0-06-230792-7(4),* HarperTeen) HarperCollins Pubs.

Brezenoff, Steve. The Carnival Caper: An Interactive Mystery Adventure. Calo, Marcos, illus. 2017. (You Choose Stories: Field Trip Mysteries Ser.). (ENG.). 112p. (J). (gr. 3-7). lib. bdg. 32.65 *(978-1-4965-2645-8(7),* 131209, Stone Arch Bks.) Capstone.

—The Case of the Counterfeit Painting. Weber, Lisa K., illus. 2016. (Museum Mysteries Ser.). (ENG.). 128p. (J). pap. 42.70 *(978-1-4965-2530-7(2),* 23936); (gr. 3-6). lib. bdg. 26.65 *(978-1-4965-2518-5(3),* 130491) Capstone. (Stone Arch Bks.).

—The Case of the New Professor. Weber, Lisa K., illus. 2019. (Museum Mysteries Ser.). (ENG.). 128p. (J). (gr. 3-6). lib. bdg. 26.65 *(978-1-4965-7818-1(X),* 139246, Stone Arch Bks.) Capstone.

—The Case of the Soldier's Ghost. Weber, Lisa K., illus. 2016. (Museum Mysteries Ser.). (ENG.). 128p. (J). pap. 42.70 *(978-1-4965-2531-4(0),* 23937); (gr. 3-6). pap. 6.95 *(978-1-4965-2523-9(X),* 130496); (gr. 3-6). lib. bdg. 26.65 *(978-1-4965-2519-2(1),* 130492) Capstone. (Stone Arch Bks.).

—The Cave That Shouldn't Collapse. Calo, Marcos, illus. 2011. (Field Trip Mysteries Ser.). (ENG.). 88p. (J). (gr. 3-6). pap. 5.95 *(978-1-4342-3430-8(4),* 116451, Stone Arch Bks.) Capstone.

—The Disappearing Fruit: An Interactive Mystery Adventure. Calo, Marcos, illus. 2017. (You Choose Stories: Field Trip Mysteries Ser.). (ENG.). 112p. (J). (gr. 3-7). lib. bdg. 32.65 *(978-1-4965-2643-4(0),* 131206, Stone Arch Bks.) Capstone.

—Field Trip Mysteries: the Ballgame with No One at Bat. Calo, Marcos, illus. 2013. (Field Trip Mysteries Ser.). (ENG.). 88p. (J). (gr. 2-3). pap. 35.70 *(978-1-4342-6230-1(8),* 20035); (gr. 3-6). pap. 5.95 *(978-1-4342-6211-0(1),* 123509); (gr. 3-6). lib. bdg. 25.32 *(978-1-4342-5978-3(1),* 122935) Capstone. (Stone Arch Bks.).

—Field Trip Mysteries: the Bowling Lane Without Any Strikes. Calo, Marcos, illus. 2013. (Field Trip Mysteries Ser.). (ENG.). 88p. (J). (gr. 2-3). pap. 35.70 *(978-1-4342-6231-8(6),* 20036, Stone Arch Bks.) Capstone.

—Field Trip Mysteries: the Burglar Who Bit the Big Apple. Canga, Chris, illus. 2010. (Field Trip Mysteries Ser.). (ENG.). 88p. (J). (gr. 3-6). 25.32 *(978-1-4342-2139-1(3),* 102869); pap. 5.95 *(978-1-4342-2771-3(5),* 114038) Capstone. (Stone Arch Bks.).

—Field Trip Mysteries: the Crook That Made Kids Cry. Calo, Marcos, illus. 2013. (Field Trip Mysteries Ser.). (ENG.). 88p. (J). (gr. 2-3). pap. 35.70 *(978-1-4342-6232-5(4),* 20038); (gr. 3-6). pap. 5.95 *(978-1-4342-6210-3(3),* 123508) Capstone. (Stone Arch Bks.).

—Field Trip Mysteries: the Crook Who Crossed the Golden Gate Bridge. Canga, Chris, illus. 2010. (Field Trip Mysteries Ser.). (ENG.). 88p. (J). (gr. 3-6). 25.32 *(978-1-4342-2138-4(5),* 102868); pap. 5.95 *(978-1-4342-2770-6(7),* 114037) Capstone. (Stone Arch Bks.).

—Field Trip Mysteries: the Dinosaur That Disappeared. Calo, Marcos, illus. 2013. (Field Trip Mysteries Ser.). (ENG.). 88p. (J). (gr. 2-3). pap. 35.70 *(978-1-4342-6233-2(2),* 20037); (gr. 3-6). pap. 5.95 *(978-1-4342-6213-4(8),* 123512); (gr. 3-6). lib. bdg. 25.32 *(978-1-4342-5980-6(3),* 122937) Capstone. (Stone Arch Bks.).

—Field Trip Mysteries: the Everglades Poacher Who Pretended. Canga, Chris & Calo, Marcos, illus. 2012. (Field Trip Mysteries Ser.). (ENG.). 88p. (J). (gr. 3-6). pap. 5.95 *(978-1-4342-4197-9(1),* 120255); lib. bdg. 25.32 *(978-1-4342-3790-3(7),* 117089) Capstone. (Stone Arch Bks.).

—Field Trip Mysteries: the Ghost Who Haunted the Capitol. Canga, Chris, illus. 2010. (Field Trip Mysteries Ser.). (ENG.). 88p. (J). (gr. 3-6). 25.32 *(978-1-4342-2140-7(7),* 102870); pap. 5.95 *(978-1-4342-2772-0(3),* 114039) Capstone. (Stone Arch Bks.).

—Field Trip Mysteries: the Grand Canyon Burros That Broke. Canga, Chris & Calo, Marcos, illus. 2012. (Field Trip Mysteries Ser.). (ENG.). 88p. (J). (gr. 3-6). pap. 5.95 *(978-1-4342-4198-6(X),* 120256); lib. bdg. 25.32 *(978-1-4342-3788-0(5),* 117087) Capstone. (Stone Arch Bks.).

—Field Trip Mysteries: the Mount Rushmore Face That Couldn't See. Canga, Chris & Calo, Marcos, illus. 2012. (Field Trip Mysteries Ser.). (ENG.). 88p. (J). (gr. 3-6). pap. 5.95 *(978-1-4342-4199-3(8),* 120257, Stone Arch Bks.) Capstone.

—Field Trip Mysteries: the Ride That Was Really Haunted. Calo, Marcos, illus. 2011. (Field Trip Mysteries Ser.). (ENG.). 88p. (J). (gr. 3-6). pap. 5.95 *(978-1-4342-3427-8(4),* 116448, Stone Arch Bks.) Capstone.

—Field Trip Mysteries: the Seals That Wouldn't Swim. Calo, Marcos, illus. 2011. (Field Trip Mysteries Ser.). (ENG.). 88p. (J). (gr. 3-6). pap. 5.95 *(978-1-4342-3428-5(2),* 116449, Stone Arch Bks.) Capstone.

—Field Trip Mysteries: the Symphony That Was Silent. Calo, Marcos, illus. 2011. (Field Trip Mysteries Ser.). (ENG.). 88p. (J). (gr. 3-6). pap. 5.95 *(978-1-4342-3429-2(0),* 116450, Stone Arch Bks.) Capstone.

—Field Trip Mysteries: the Teacher Who Forgot Too Much. Canga, Chris, illus. 2009. (Field Trip Mysteries Ser.). (ENG.). 88p. (J). (gr. 3-6). lib. bdg. 25.32 *(978-1-4342-1609-0(8),* 95782, Stone Arch Bks.) Capstone.

—Field Trip Mysteries: the Village That Almost Vanished. Canga, Chris, illus. 2009. (Field Trip Mysteries Ser.). (ENG.). 88p. (J). (gr. 3-6). lib. bdg. 25.32 *(978-1-4342-1611-3(X),* 95785, Stone Arch Bks.) Capstone.

—Field Trip Mysteries: the Yellowstone Kidnapping That Wasn't. Canga, Chris & Calo, Marcos, illus. 2012. (Field Trip Mysteries Ser.). (ENG.). 88p. (J). (gr. 3-6). pap. 5.95 *(978-1-4342-4200-6(5),* 120258); lib. bdg. 25.32 *(978-1-4342-3789-7(3),* 117088) Capstone. (Stone Arch Bks.).

—Field Trip Mysteries: the Zoo with the Empty Cage. Canga, Chris, illus. 2009. (Field Trip Mysteries Ser.). (ENG.). 88p. (J). (gr. 3-6). lib. bdg. 25.32 *(978-1-4342-1610-6(1),* 95784, Stone Arch Bks.) Capstone.

—I Dare You! Hilliker, Phillip, illus. 2008. (Vortex Bks.). (ENG.). 112p. (J). (gr. 5-9). 26.65 *(978-1-4342-0798-2(6),* 95203, Stone Arch Bks.) Capstone.

—The Outlaw from Outer Space: An Interactive Mystery Adventure. Calo, Marcos, illus. 2017. (You Choose Stories: Field Trip Mysteries Ser.). (ENG.). 112p. (J). (gr. 3-7). lib. bdg. 32.65 *(978-1-4965-2644-1(9),* 131208, Stone Arch Bks.) Capstone.

—The Zombie Who Visited New Orleans, 1 vol. Canga, Chris, illus. 2010. (Field Trip Mysteries Ser.). (ENG.). 88p. (J). (gr. 3-6). 25.32 *(978-1-4342-2141-4(5),* 102871); pap. 5.95 *(978-1-4342-2773-7(1),* 114040) Capstone. (Stone Arch Bks.).

Brezenoff, Steve & Calo, Marcos. Field Trip Mysteries, 16 vols. 2013. (Field Trip Mysteries Ser.). (ENG.). 88p. (J). (gr. 3-6). pap., pap., pap. 95.20 *(978-1-4342-6223-3(5),* 20028, Stone Arch Bks.) Capstone.

—Field Trip Mysteries Classroom Collection. 2013. (Field Trip Mysteries Ser.). (ENG.). 88p. (J). (gr. 2-3). 571.20 *(978-1-4342-6318-6(5),* 20303, Stone Arch Bks.) Capstone.

Brezenoff, Steven. The Case of the Haunted History Museum. Weber, Lisa K., illus. 2015. (Museum Mysteries Ser.). (ENG.). 128p. (J). (gr. 3-6). lib. bdg. 26.65 *(978-1-4342-9687-0(3),* 126996, Stone Arch Bks.) Capstone.

—The Case of the Missing Museum Archives. Weber, Lisa K., illus. 2015. (Museum Mysteries Ser.). (ENG.). 128p. (J). (gr. 3-6). lib. bdg. 26.65 *(978-1-4342-9688-7(1),* 126997, Stone Arch Bks.) Capstone.

—The Case of the Portrait Vandal. Weber, Lisa K., illus. 2015. (Museum Mysteries Ser.). (ENG.). 128p. (J). (gr. 3-6). lib. bdg. 26.65 *(978-1-4342-9685-6(7),* 126994, Stone Arch Bks.) Capstone.

—The Case of the Stolen Space Suit. Weber, Lisa K., illus. 2016. (Museum Mysteries Ser.). (ENG.). 128p. (J). (gr. 3-6). 26.65 *(978-1-4965-2516-1(7),* 130489, Stone Arch Bks.) Capstone.

—The Missing Bully: An Interactive Mystery Adventure. Calo, Marcos, illus. 2017. (You Choose Stories: Field Trip Mysteries Ser.). (ENG.). 112p. (J). (gr. 3-7). lib. bdg. 32.65 *(978-1-4965-2642-7(2),* 131205, Stone Arch Bks.) Capstone.

Brian, Kate, pseud. Inner Circle. 2007. (Private Ser.: No. 5). (ENG.). 224p. (YA). (gr. 9-12). pap. 9.99 *(978-1-4169-5041-7(9),* Simon & Schuster Bks. For Young Readers) Simon & Schuster Bks. For Young Readers.

—Revelation. 2008. (Private Ser.: No. 8). (ENG.). 288p. (YA). (gr. 9-18). pap. 11.99 *(978-1-4169-5883-3(5),* Simon & Schuster Bks. For Young Readers) Simon & Schuster Bks. For Young Readers.

Brignole, Giancarla, tr. El Misterio del Condor. Polastri, Rosa Elena, illus. (Fabulas De Familia Ser.). (SPA.). 32p. *(978-970-20-0270-3(2))* Castillo, Ediciones, S. A. de C. V.

Brisland, Toni. DemiChat & the Lost Mummy. de los reyes Cruz, Cheryl, illus. 2013. 142p. (J). pap. 14.95 *(978-1-60131-173-3(7))* Big Tent Bks.

Broach, Elise. Masterpiece. 2010. 18.00 *(978-1-60686-888-1(8))* Perfection Learning Corp.

—Masterpiece. Murphy, Kelly, illus. 2010. (Masterpiece Adventures Ser.). (ENG.). 320p. (J). (gr. 4-6). pap. 8.99 *(978-0-312-60870-5(5),* 900065170) Square Fish.

—Masterpiece. 2010. (J). lib. bdg. 18.40 *(978-0-606-14604-3(0))* Turtleback.

—Revenge of Superstition Mountain. Ivanov, Aleksey & Olga, illus. 2015. (Superstition Mountain Mysteries Ser.: 3). (ENG.). 320p. (J). (gr. 3-7). pap. 16.99 *(978-1-250-05686-3(1),* 900139059) Square Fish.

—Shakespeare's Secret. 2007. (Illus.). 258p. (gr. 4-9). 17.00 *(978-0-7569-8204-1(9))* Perfection Learning Corp.

—Shakespeare's Secret. 2007. (ENG.). 272p. (YA). (gr. 6-8). pap. 8.99 *(978-0-312-37132-6(2),* 900044660) Square Fish.

—Shakespeare's Secret. l.t. ed. 2006. (Thorndike Literacy Bridge Ser.). (Illus.). 263p. (J). (gr. 5-10). 22.95 *(978-0-7862-8735-2(7))* Thorndike Pr.

—Treasure on Superstition Mountain. Caparo, Antonio Javier, illus. 2014. (Superstition Mountain Mysteries Ser.: 2). (ENG.). 304p. (J). (gr. 3-7). pap. 11.99 *(978-1-250-03990-3(8),* 900123693) Square Fish.

Broaddus, Maurice. The Usual Suspects. 2019. (ENG., Illus.). 288p. (J). (gr. 3-7). 17.99 *(978-0-06-279631-8(3),* Tegen, Katherine Bks) HarperCollins Pubs.

Broberg, Penelope Northrop. Sleuthy Gumshoe: The Remarkable Detective. 2011. 32p. (gr. -1). pap. 14.39 *(978-1-4567-6404-3(7))* AuthorHouse.

Bronstein, S. N. Private Eye Cats: Book One: the Case of the Neighborhood Burglars. 2012. 108p. (gr. 4-6). 23.99 *(978-1-4685-4557-9(4))*; pap. 14.95 *(978-1-4685-4558-6(2))* AuthorHouse.

—Private Eye Cats Book Two: The Case of the Kidnapped Dog. 2013. 116p. (gr. 4-6). 23.99 *(978-1-4817-2421-0(5))*; pap. 14.95 *(978-1-4817-2422-7(3))* AuthorHouse.

Brooks, Dawn Marie. Cat-Ice. 2004. 175p. pap. 13.95 *(978-0-7414-2240-8(9))* Infinity Publishing.

Brooks, Kevin. Born Scared. 2018. (ENG.). 256p. (J). (gr. 7). 16.99 *(978-0-7636-9565-1(3))* Candlewick Pr.

Brooks, Martha. Traveling on into the Light: And Other Stories. 160p. (J). reprint ed. 7.95 *(978-0-88899-237-6(8))* Groundwood Bks. CAN. Dist: Publishers Group West (PGW).

Brooks, Walter R. Freddy the Detective. Wiese, Kurt, illus. 2010. (ENG.). 272p. (YA). (gr. 4-13). 11.99 *(978-1-59020-418-4(2),* 1453803, Amulet Bks.) Abrams, Inc.

Brouwer, Sigmund. Absolute Pressure, 1 vol. 2009. (Orca Sports Ser.). (ENG.). 176p. (J). (gr. 4-7). pap. 10.95 *(978-1-55469-130-2(3))* Orca Bk. Pubs. USA.

—All-Star Pride, 1 vol. 2006. (Orca Sports Ser.). (ENG.). 176p. (J). (gr. 4-7). per. 9.95 *(978-1-55143-635-7(3))* Orca Bk. Pubs. USA.

—Hurricane Power, 1 vol. 2007. (Orca Sports Ser.). (ENG.). 176p. (J). (gr. 4-7). per. 9.95 *(978-1-55143-865-8(8))* Orca Bk. Pubs. USA.

Brown, Gary. Sam's Mission Call. Tanner, Stephanie, illus. 24p. (J). 12.95 *(978-0-910523-13-4(4))* Grandin Bk. Co.

Brown, Jeff. Flat Stanley & the Missing Pumpkins. Pamintuan, Macky, illus. 2017. (I Can Read Level 2 Ser.). (ENG.). 32p. (J). (gr. -1-3). 16.99 *(978-0-06-236598-9(3))*; pap. 5.99 *(978-0-06-236594-1(0))* HarperCollins Pubs. (HarperCollins).

—Flat Stanley's Worldwide Adventures #11: Framed in France. Pamintuan, Macky, illus. 2014. (Flat Stanley's Worldwide Adventures Ser.: 11). (ENG.). 128p. (J). (gr. 1-5). 15.99 *(978-0-06-218985-1(9))*; pap. 4.99 *(978-0-06-218984-4(0))* HarperCollins Pubs. (HarperCollins).

—Framed in France. 2014. (Flat Stanley's Worldwide Adventures Ser.: 11). (J). lib. bdg. 14.75 *(978-0-606-35480-6(8))* Turtleback.

Brown, Jennifer. Break Us. 2018. (Shade Me Ser.: 3). (ENG.). 384p. (YA). (gr. 9). 17.99 *(978-0-06-232449-8(7),* Tegen, Katherine Bks) HarperCollins Pubs.

—Dare You. 2018. (Shade Me Ser.: 2). (ENG.). 496p. (YA). (gr. 9). pap. 9.99 *(978-0-06-232447-4(0),* Tegen, Katherine Bks) HarperCollins Pubs.

—Pennybaker School Is Headed for Disaster. 2018. (J). lib. bdg. 18.40 *(978-0-606-41073-1(2))* Turtleback.

—Shade Me. 2017. (Shade Me Ser.: 1). (ENG.). 464p. (YA). (gr. 9). pap. 9.99 *(978-0-06-232444-3(6),* Tegen, Katherine Bks) HarperCollins Pubs.

Brown, Jim. The Foster Twins in the Mystery at Moore's Lake. 2005. 164p. 22.95 *(978-0-595-67087-1(3))* iUniverse, Inc.

Brown, Liz. Misty's Revenge. (Illus.). 65p. *(978-1-897039-21-2(2))* High Interest Publishing (HIP).

Brown, Marc. Arthur's Mystery Babysitter. Brown, Marc, illus. 2004. (ENG., Illus.). 24p. (J). (gr. -1-1). pap. 3.99 *(978-0-316-73394-6(6),* Tingley, Megan Bks.) Little, Brown Bks. for Young Readers.

Brown, Ruth. A Dark, Dark Tale. 2004. (Illus.). 27p. (J). *(978-1-85269-457-9(2))* Mantra Lingua.

Brown, Shannon L. The Feather Chase. 2016. (ENG.). 24.95 *(978-0-9898438-9-8(0))* 2014. pap. 12.95 *(978-0-9898438-0-5(7))* Sienna Bay Pr.

—The Treasure Key: (the Crime-Solving Cousins Mysteries Book 2), vol. 2. 2016. (the Crime-Solving Cousins Mysteries Ser.: Vol. 2). (ENG., Illus.). 216p. (J). (gr. 3-6). 24.95 *(978-0-9898438-7-4(4))* Sienna Bay Pr.

Bruchac, Joseph. Skeleton Man. 2003. (Skeleton Man Ser.: 1). (ENG., Illus.). 128p. (J). (gr. 3-8). pap. 9.99 *(978-0-06-440888-2(4),* HarperCollins) HarperCollins Pubs.

—Skeleton Man. Comport, Sally Wern, illus. 2003. 114p. (J). (gr. 5). 12.65 *(978-0-7569-3399-9(4))* Perfection Learning Corp.

Bruzon, Louise A. The Grimstone Galleries. 2010. 192p. pap. *(978-1-907652-17-2(5))* Grosvenor Hse. Publishing Ltd.

Bryant, Annie. Ghost Town. 2007. (Beacon Street Girls Ser.: No. 11). (Illus.). 217p. (J). (gr. 4-7). per. 7.10 *(978-1-933566-09-2(4))* B*tween Productions, Inc.

Bryant, Jen. Kaleidoscope Eyes. 2010. 272p. (J). (gr. 3-7). 7.99 *(978-0-440-42190-0(X),* Yearling) Random Hse. Children's Bks.

Buckey, Sarah M. The Hidden Gold. Bernstein, Galia & Giovine, Sergio, illus. 2012. (American Girl Mysteries Ser.). (ENG.). 150p. (J). (gr. 4-6). pap. 21.19 *(978-1-59369-902-4(6))* American Girl Publishing, Inc.

Buckey, Sarah Masters. Clue in the Castle Tower: A Samantha Mystery. Ross, Peg, ed. Giovine, Sergio, illus. 2011. (American Girl Mysteries Ser.). (ENG.). 184p. (YA). (gr. 4-6). pap. 21.19 *(978-1-59369-752-5(X))* American Girl Publishing, Inc.

—The Light in the Cellar: A Molly Mystery. 2003. (American Girl Mysteries Ser.). (ENG., Illus.). 176p. (gr. 4-7). 10.95 *(978-1-59369-159-2(9))* American Girl Publishing, Inc.

—The Stolen Sapphire. 2007. (American Girl Mysteries Ser.). (Illus.). 181p. (gr. 4-7). 17.45 *(978-0-7569-8278-2(2))* Perfection Learning Corp.

Buckley, Michael. The Council of Mirrors. (Sisters Grimm Ser.: 9). 2018. lib. bdg. 19.65 *(978-0-606-41062-5(7))* 2013. (J). lib. bdg. 18.40 *(978-0-606-31650-7(7))* Turtleback.

—The Council of Mirrors (the Sisters Grimm #9) 10th Anniversary Edition. 10th ed. 2018. (Sisters Grimm Ser.). (ENG., Illus.). 304p. (J). (gr. 3-7). pap. 9.99 *(978-1-4197-2009-3(0),* 696406, Amulet Bks.) Abrams, Inc.

—The Everafter War (the Sisters Grimm #7) 10th Anniversary Edition. 10th ed. 2018. (Sisters Grimm Ser.). (ENG., Illus.). 272p. (J). (gr. 3-7). pap. 8.99 *(978-1-4197-2011-6(2),* 660206, Amulet Bks.) Abrams, Inc.

—The Fairy-Tale Detectives. (Sisters Grimm Ser.: 1). (J). 2008. 81.45 *(978-1-4361-0398-5(3))* 2007. 214.75 *(978-1-4193-6197-5(X))* 2007. 1.25 *(978-1-4193-6193-7(7))* 2006. 71.75 *(978-1-4193-6198-2(8))* 2006. 74.75 *(978-1-4193-6196-8(1))* 2006. 86.75 *(978-1-4193-8749-4(9))* 2006. 89.75 *(978-1-4193-8747-0(2))* Recorded Bks., Inc.

—The Fairy-Tale Detectives. 2017. (Sisters Grimm Ser.: 1). (J). lib. bdg. 19.60 *(978-0-606-39685-1(3))* Turtleback.

—The Inside Story, 6 vols. 2010. (Sisters Grimm Ser.: 8). (J). 89.75 *(978-1-4498-1969-9(9))*; 1.25 *(978-1-4498-1973-6(7))*; 87.75 *(978-1-4498-1971-2(0))*; 72.75 *(978-1-4498-1967-5(2))*; 219.75 *(978-1-4498-1966-8(4))* Recorded Bks., Inc.

—The Inside Story (the Sisters Grimm #8) 10th Anniversary Edition. 10th ed. 2018. (Sisters Grimm Ser.). (ENG., Illus.).

MNO

240p. (J). (gr. 3-7). pap. 9.99 (978-1-4197-2006-2(6), 660306, Amulet Bks.) Abrams, Inc.

—Magic & Other Misdemeanors (the Sisters Grimm #5) 10th Anniversary Edition. Ferguson, Peter, illus. 10th ed. 2017. (Sisters Grimm Ser.). (ENG.). 280p. (J). (gr. 3-7). pap. 9.99 (978-1-4197-2010-9(4), 608806, Amulet Bks.) Abrams, Inc.

—Once upon a Crime (the Sisters Grimm #4) 10th Anniversary Edition. Ferguson, Peter, illus. 10th anniv. ed. 2017. (Sisters Grimm Ser.). (ENG.). 272p. (J). (gr. 3-7). pap. 9.99 (978-1-4197-2007-9(4), 608706, Amulet Bks.) Abrams, Inc.

—The Problem Child: The Sisters Grimm. 2007. (Sisters Grimm Ser.: 3). (YA). lib. bdg. 18.40 (978-1-4178-0733-8(4)) Turtleback.

—Tales from the Hood (the Sisters Grimm #6) 10th Anniversary Edition. 10th ed. 2017. (Sisters Grimm Ser.). (ENG., Illus.). 256p. (J). (gr. 3-7). pap. 8.99 (978-1-4197-2012-3(0), 608906, Amulet Bks.) Abrams, Inc.

—The Unusual Suspects. 2006. (Sisters Grimm Ser.: Bk. 2). 1.00 (978-1-4237-8623-8(8)) Recorded Bks., Inc.

—The Unusual Suspects. (Sisters Grimm Ser.: 2). (J). 2017. lib. bdg. 19.60 (978-0-606-39686-8(1)) 2007. lib. bdg. 18.40 (978-1-4178-0732-1(6)) Turtleback.

—The Unusual Suspects (the Sisters Grimm #2) 10th Anniversary Edition. Ferguson, Peter, illus. 10th anniv. ed. 2017. (Sisters Grimm Ser.). (ENG.). 288p. (J). (gr. 3-7). pap. 8.95 (978-1-4197-2008-6(2), 580506, Amulet Bks.) Abrams, Inc.

—A Very Grimm Guide. Ferguson, Peter, illus. 2012. (Sisters Grimm Ser.). (ENG.). 128p. (J). (gr. 3-7). 17.99 (978-1-4197-0201-3(7), 1019601, Amulet Bks.) Abrams, Inc.

Buckmaster, Heath L. The Venus Diary, 3 bks., Bk. 2. ltd. ed. 2008. 132p. (YA). lib. bdg. 19.95 (978-0-9771802-6-4(3)) Transaltar Publishing.

Bunce, Elizabeth C. Liar's Moon. 2011. (YA). pap. (978-0-545-13607-5(5), Levine, Arthur A. Bks.) Scholastic, Inc.

Bundy, E. A. Phillip Marrow, Jr. 2013. (ENG.). 206p. (YA). pap. 10.99 (978-1-61955-008-7(3)) Singing Winds Pr.

Bunting, Eve. The Man with the Red Bag. 2007. 230p. (J). (gr. 5-9). 15.99 (978-0-06-081828-9(X), Cotler, Joanna Books) HarperCollins Pubs.

Bunting, Eve & Giblin, James Cross. The Ghost Children. 2005. (ENG.). 176p. (J). (gr. 5-7). pap. 12.95 (978-0-618-60477-7(4), 100434, Clarion Bks.) HarperCollins Pubs.

Bunzl, Peter. Moonlocket. 2019. (Cogheart Adventures Ser.). (ENG.). 384p. (J). (gr. 3-7). pap. 12.99 (978-1-63163-375-1(9), 1631633759, Jolly Fish Pr.) North Star Editions.

The Buried Eye, 6 vols. (Woodland Mysteriestm Ser.). 133p. (gr. 3-7). 42.50 (978-0-7802-7932-2(8)) Wright Group/McGraw-Hill.

Burke, Anjalena Anita. Ghost: The Dead End Series Book 1, 1. vol. 2009. 73p. pap. 16.95 (978-1-61582-686-5(6)) PublishAmerica, Inc.

Burke, Bob. The Third Pig Detective Agency: The Complete Casebook. 2015. (ENG.). 432p. 8.99 (978-0-00-747940-5(9), Friday Project) HarperCollins Pubs. Ltd. GBR. Dist: HarperCollins Pubs.

Burke, Morgan. Get It Started. 2010. (Party Room Ser.: 1). (ENG.). 272p. (J). (gr. 11). pap. 12.99 (978-1-4424-1420-4(0), Simon Pulse) Simon Pulse.

Burket, Shelia. Detective Morris Norris & the Case of the Missing Socks. 2011. 20p. pap. 24.95 (978-1-4626-2822-3(2)) America Star Bks.

Burnell, Cerrie. Harper & the Fire Star. Anderson, Laura Ellen, illus. 2018. (Harper Ser.: 4). (ENG.). 168p. (J). (gr. 1-3). 14.99 (978-1-5107-3613-9(1), Sky Pony Pr.) Skyhorse Publishing Co., Inc.

Burns, Emily. Manitou Art Caper. 2003. (Rocky Mountain Mysteries Ser.: 2). (Illus.). 128p. (J). per. 4.95 (978-0-9723259-1-2(3), RMM2) Covered Wagon Publishing LLC.

—Marked Evidence. 2003. (Rocky Mountain Mysteries Ser.: 3). (J). per. 4.95 (978-0-9723259-2-9(1), RMM3) Covered Wagon Publishing LLC.

Burt, Steve. Oddest Yet: Even More Stories to Chill the Heart. Hagerman, Jessica, illus. 2004. 144p. (gr. 5-18). pap. 14.95 (978-0-9741407-1-1(6)) Burt, Steven E.

Bustani, Juma. Adventure in Nairobi. 2005. (Illus.). 72p. pap. (978-9966-46-842-0(0)) Heinemann Kenya, Limited (East African Educational Publishers Ltd E.A.E.P.) KEN. Dist: Michigan State Univ. Pr.

Butcher, A. J. Spy High Mission Three: the Serpent Scenario. 2004. (ENG.). 224p. (YA). (gr. 5-8). pap. 13.99 (978-0-316-73766-1(6)) Little, Brown Bks. for Young Readers.

Butcher, Kristin. Return to Bone Tree Hill. 2009. (ENG.). 176p. (J). pap. 12.95 (978-1-897235-58-4(5)) Thistledown Pr., Ltd. CAN. Dist: Univ. of Toronto Pr.

—Zach & Zoe & the Bank Robber, 1 vol. 2008. (Lorimer Streetlights Ser.). (ENG.). 112p. (J). (gr. 2-4). 8.95 (978-1-55277-015-3(X), 015) James Lorimer & Co. Ltd., Pubs. CAN. Dist: Formac Lorimer Bks. Ltd.

Butler, Darren J. The Masterpiece: An Abbie Girl Spy Mystery. Casteel, Kay, illus. 2004. (Abbie, Girl Spy Ser.: 4). (ENG.). 278p. (J). mass mkt. 8.50 (978-0-9753367-3-1(8)) Onstage Publishing, LLC.

—The Secret of Crybaby Hollow. 2004. (YA). mass mkt. 6.99 (978-0-9753367-5-5(4)) Onstage Publishing, LLC.

Butler, Dori. Detective Cluck & the Missing Hens. 2005. (J). pap. (978-1-4108-4192-6(8)) Benchmark Education Co.

Butler, Dori H. Campus Attack, Sabotage! 2011. (Readers' & Writers' Genre Workshop Ser.). (YA). pap. (978-1-4509-3018-5(2)) Benchmark Education Co.

—The Hide-And-Seek Ghost. 2016. (Haunted Library: 8). lib. bdg. 14.75 (978-0-606-38838-2(9)) Turtleback.

Butler, Dori Hillestad. The Case of the Fire Alarm, 4. Tugeau, Jeremy, illus. 2011. (Buddy Files Ser.: 4). (ENG.). 128p. (J). (gr. 1-3). 17.44 (978-0-8075-0913-5(2)) Whitman, Albert & Co.

—The Case of the Fire Alarm Bk. 4. Tugeau, Jeremy, illus. 2011. (Buddy Files Ser.: 4). (ENG.). 144p. (J). (gr. 1-5). pap. 5.99 (978-0-8075-0935-7(3), 807509353) Whitman, Albert & Co.

—The Case of the Library Monster. Tugeau, Jeremy, illus. 2012. (Buddy Files Ser.: 5). (J). lib. bdg. 16.00 (978-0-606-23839-7(5)) Turtleback.

—The Case of the Missing Family, 1 vol., Bk. 3. Tugeau, Jeremy, illus. 2010. (Buddy Files Ser.: 3). (ENG.). 144p. (J). (gr. 1-5). pap. 5.99 (978-0-8075-0934-0(5), 807509345) Whitman, Albert & Co.

—The Case of the School Ghost. 2013. (Buddy Files Ser.: 6). lib. bdg. 16.00 (978-0-606-31843-3(7)) Turtleback.

—The Five O'Clock Ghost #4, No. 4. Damant, Aurore, illus. 2015. (Haunted Library: 4). 144p. (J). (gr. 1-3). bds. 6.99 (978-0-448-46248-6(6), Grosset & Dunlap) Penguin Young Readers Group.

—The Ghost at the Fire Station #6, No. 6. Damant, Aurore, illus. 2015. (Haunted Library: 6). 128p. (J). (gr. 1-3). bds. 6.99 (978-0-448-48334-4(3), Grosset & Dunlap) Penguin Young Readers Group.

—The Ghost Backstage #3. Damant, Aurore, illus. 2014. (Haunted Library: 3). 128p. (J). (gr. 1-3). 6.99 (978-0-448-46246-2(X), Grosset & Dunlap) Penguin Young Readers Group.

—The Ghost in the Attic #2, No. 2. Damant, Aurore, illus. 2014. (Haunted Library: 2). 128p. (J). (gr. 1-3). 6.99 (978-0-448-46244-8(3), Grosset & Dunlap) Penguin Young Readers Group.

—The Ghost in the Tree House #7. Damant, Aurore, illus. 2016. (Haunted Library: 7). 128p. (J). (gr. 1-3). bds. 6.99 (978-0-448-48940-7(6), Grosset & Dunlap) Penguin Young Readers Group.

—The Ghosts at the Movie Theater. 2017. (Haunted Library: 9). (Illus.). 127p. (J). lib. bdg. 16.00 (978-0-606-39772-8(8)) Turtleback.

—The Ghosts at the Movie Theater #9. Damant, Aurore, illus. 2017. (Haunted Library: 9). 128p. (J). (gr. 1-3). 6.99 (978-0-451-53435-4(2), Grosset & Dunlap) Penguin Young Readers Group.

—The Haunted Library #1. Damant, Aurore, illus. 2014. (Haunted Library: 1). 128p. (J). (gr. 1-3). 6.99 (978-0-448-46242-4(7), Grosset & Dunlap) Penguin Young Readers Group.

—King & Kayla & the Case of Found Fred. Meyers, Nancy, illus. 2019. (King & Kayla Ser.: 5). 48p. (J). (gr. 2-4). 14.95 (978-1-68263-052-5(8)) Peachtree Publishing Co. Inc.

—King & Kayla & the Case of the Lost Tooth, 1 vol. Meyers, Nancy, illus. 2018. (King & Kayla Ser.: 4). 48p. (J). (gr. 2-4). pap. 6.99 (978-1-68263-018-1(8)); 14.99 (978-1-56145-880-6(5)) Peachtree Publishing Co. Inc.

—King & Kayla & the Case of the Mysterious Mouse. Meyers, Nancy, illus. (King & Kayla Ser.: 3). 48p. (J). (gr. 2-4). 2018. pap. 6.99 (978-1-68263-017-4(X)) 2017. 14.99 (978-1-56145-879-0(1)) Peachtree Publishing Co. Inc.

—King & Kayla & the Case of the Secret Code, 1 vol. Meyers, Nancy, illus. (King & Kayla Ser.: 2). 48p. (J). (gr. 2-4). 2018. pap. 6.99 (978-1-68263-016-7(1)) 2017. 14.95 (978-1-56145-878-3(3)) Peachtree Publishing Co. Inc.

—King & Kayla & the Case of the Unhappy Neighbor. Meyers, Nancy, illus. 2020. (King & Kayla Ser.: 6). 48p. (J). (gr. 2-4). 14.99 (978-1-68263-055-6(2)) Peachtree Publishing Co. Inc.

Butler, Heather. The Milkshake Detectives. 2017. (ENG.). 208p. (J). (gr. 4-6). pap. 7.99 (978-0-349-12410-0(8)) Little, Brown Bks. for Young Readers.

Butler, William S. Scraper Jones: Treasure Hunter. 2007. 320p. pap. 19.95 (978-1-59663-770-2(6), Castle Keep Pr.) Rock, James A. & Co. Pubs.

Byars, Betsy. The Black Tower. 2007. (Herculeah Jones Mystery Ser.: 7). 144p. (J). (gr. 3-7). 6.99 (978-0-14-240937-4(5), Puffin Books) Penguin Young Readers Group.

—The Blossoms & the Green Phantom. (Blossom Family Ser.: Bk. 3). 146p. (J). (gr. 4-6). pap. 3.99 (978-0-8072-1443-5(4), Listening Library) Random Hse. Audio Publishing Group.

—The Dark Stairs. 2006. (Herculeah Jones Mystery Ser.: 1). (ENG.). 160p. (J). (gr. 3-7). pap. 6.99 (978-0-14-240592-5(2), Puffin Books) Penguin Young Readers Group.

—The Dark Stairs. 2006. (Herculeah Jones Mystery Ser.). 130p. (gr. 3-7). 16.00 (978-0-7569-6736-9(8)) Perfection Learning Corp.

—The Dark Stairs. (Herculeah Jones Mystery Ser.). 160p. (J). (gr. 3-5). pap. 4.99 (978-0-8072-1478-7(7), Listening Library) Random Hse. Audio Publishing Group.

—Dead Letter. 2006. (Herculeah Jones Mystery Ser.: 3). 160p. (J). (gr. 3-7). 5.99 (978-0-14-240564-2(7), Puffin Books) Penguin Young Readers Group.

—Death's Door. 2006. (Herculeah Jones Mystery Ser.: 4). (ENG.). 144p. (J). (gr. 3-7). 6.99 (978-0-14-240565-9(5), Puffin Books) Penguin Young Readers Group.

—Disappearing Acts. 2006. (Herculeah Jones Mystery Ser.: 5). (ENG.). 144p. (J). (gr. 3-7). 6.99 (978-0-14-240566-6(3), Puffin Books) Penguin Young Readers Group.

—King of Murder. 2007. (Herculeah Jones Mystery Ser.: 6). 144p. (J). (gr. 3-7). 5.99 (978-0-14-240759-2(3), Puffin Books) Penguin Young Readers Group.

—Tarot Says Beware, No. 2. 2006. (Herculeah Jones Mystery Ser.: 2). (ENG.). 160p. (J). (gr. 3-7). 5.99 (978-0-14-240593-2(0), Puffin Books) Penguin Young Readers Group.

—Tarot Says Beware. 2006. (Herculeah Jones Mystery Ser.). 151p. (gr. 3-7). 16.00 (978-0-7569-6737-6(6)) Perfection Learning Corp.

Byrne, Marlene F. Treasure Hunt. Graber, Jesse, illus. 2009. 36p. (J). 14.99 (978-0-9777135-0-9(4)) Good Stories Publishing.

Cabot, Meg. The Mediator #3: Reunion. 2004. (Mediator Ser.: 3). (ENG.). 304p. (YA). (gr. 8-18). pap. 10.99 (978-0-06-072513-6(3), HarperTeen) HarperCollins Pubs.

—The Mediator #4: Darkest Hour. 2004. (Mediator Ser.: 4). (ENG.). 336p. (YA). (gr. 8-18). pap. 10.99 (978-0-06-072514-3(1), HarperTeen) HarperCollins Pubs.

—The Mediator: Shadowland & Ninth Key. 2010. (Mediator Ser.). (ENG.). 544p. (YA). (gr. 8). pap. 9.99 (978-0-06-204020-6(0), HarperTeen) HarperCollins Pubs.

—Safe House. 2011. (1-800-Where-R-You Ser.: 3). (ENG.). 272p. (YA). (gr. 9). pap. 12.99 (978-1-4424-3084-6(2), Simon Pulse) Simon Pulse.

—Sanctuary. 2007. (1-800-Where-R-You Ser.: No. 4). (ENG., Illus.). 240p. (YA). (gr. 9-12). mass mkt. 6.99 (978-1-4169-2707-5(7), Simon Pulse) Simon Pulse.

—Vanished Books One & Two: When Lightning Strikes; Code Name Cassandra. 2010. (Vanished Ser.: Bks. 1 & 2). (ENG., Illus.). 560p. (YA). (gr. 7). pap. 15.99 (978-1-4424-0629-2(1), Simon Pulse) Simon Pulse.

—Vanished Books Three & Four: Safe House; Sanctuary. 2011. (Vanished Ser.: Bks. 3 & 4). (ENG.). 512p. (YA). (gr. 7-12). pap. 15.99 (978-1-4424-0631-5(3), Simon Pulse) Simon Pulse.

Cadose, Linda A. The Hidden Chamber in the Great Sphinx. 2012. 110p. (gr. 4-6). 23.99 (978-1-4685-0806-2(7)); pap. 14.95 (978-1-4685-0807-9(5)) AuthorHouse.

Caine, Paul. Jake's Journey. 2010. 68p. pap. 10.49 (978-1-4520-0508-9(7)) AuthorHouse.

Calandrelli, Emily. Ada Lace & the Impossible Mission. Kurilla, Renée, illus. 2018. (Ada Lace Adventure Ser.: 4). (ENG.). 112p. (J). (gr. 1-5). pap. 6.99 (978-1-5344-1684-0(6), Simon & Schuster Bks. For Young Readers) Simon & Schuster Bks. For Young Readers.

—Ada Lace & the Suspicious Artist. Kurilla, Renée, illus. 2019. (Ada Lace Adventure Ser.: 5). (ENG.). 112p. (J). (gr. 1-5). pap. 6.99 (978-1-5344-1687-1(0), Simon & Schuster Bks. For Young Readers) Simon & Schuster Bks. For Young Readers.

—Ada Lace, on the Case. Kurilla, Renée, illus. 2017. (Ada Lace Adventure Ser.: 1). (ENG.). 128p. (J). (gr. 1-5). pap. 6.99 (978-1-4814-8598-2(9), Simon & Schuster Bks. For Young Readers) Simon & Schuster Bks. For Young Readers.

—Ada Lace Sees Red. Kurilla, Renée, illus. 2017. (Ada Lace Adventure Ser.: 2). (ENG.). 144p. (J). (gr. 1-5). 17.99 (978-1-4814-8602-6(0)); pap. 6.99 (978-1-4814-8601-9(2)) Simon & Schuster Bks. For Young Readers. (Simon & Schuster Bks. For Young Readers).

—Ada Lace, Take Me to Your Leader. Kurilla, Renée, illus. 2018. (Ada Lace Adventure Ser.: 3). (ENG.). 96p. (J). (gr. 1-5). 17.99 (978-1-4814-8605-7(5)); pap. 6.99 (978-1-4814-8604-0(7)) Simon & Schuster Bks. For Young Readers. (Simon & Schuster Bks. For Young Readers).

Calderon, Eduardo Caballero. Bolívar: Una Historia que Parece un Cuento. 2011. (SPA.). 64p. (gr. 5-8). pap. 15.99 (978-958-04-7161-5(4)) Norma S.A. COL. Dist: Lectorum Pubns., Inc.

Caletti, Deb. Girl, Unframed. 2020. (ENG.). 368p. (YA). (gr. 9). 18.99 (978-1-5344-2697-9(3), Simon Pulse) Simon Pulse.

Call of the Selkie: Individual Title Six-Packs. (Action Packs Ser.). 104p. (gr. 3-5). 44.00 (978-0-7635-2991-8(5)) Rigby Education.

Callaghan, Cindy. Sydney Mackenzie Knocks 'Em Dead. (ENG., Illus.). 256p. (J). (gr. 4-8). 2018. pap. 7.99 (978-1-4814-6568-7(6)) 2017. 17.99 (978-1-4814-6569-4(4)) Simon & Schuster/Paula Wiseman Bks. (Simon & Schuster/Paula Wiseman Bks.).

Cameron, Bill. Property of the State: The Legend of Joey. 2016. (ENG.). 288p. (gr. 9-13). pap. 18.99 (978-1-929345-22-9(4), Poisoned Pen Press) Sourcebooks, Inc.

Campbell, Julie. The Secret of the Mansion: Trixie Belden. 2004. 236p. (J). (gr. 3-7). pap. 29.00 incl. audio (978-1-4000-9000-6(8), Listening Library) Random Hse. Audio Publishing Group.

Campbell, Morgan. Shots, Lies, & That Party. 2013. 178p. pap. 19.95 (978-1-4489-4324-1(8)) America Star Bks.

Campbell, R. W. Merrick Tumbledorf: The Last Talcomite Dragon. 2013. (ENG.). 250p. (YA). pap. 15.95 (978-1-4787-1312-8(7)) Outskirts Pr., Inc.

Carey, Anna. Blackbird. 2014. (Blackbird Ser.: 1). (ENG.). 256p. (YA). (gr. 9). 17.99 (978-0-06-229973-4(5), HarperTeen) HarperCollins Pubs.

—Blackbird. 2015. (SPA.). 240p. (YA). (gr. 9-12). pap. 17.99 (978-987-612-909-1(0)) Lectorum Pubns., Inc.

—Deadfall. 2015. 256p. (J). pap. (978-0-06-242788-5(1)) HarperCollins Pubs.

Carlson, Caroline. The World's Greatest Detective. 2017. (ENG.). 368p. (J). (gr. 3-7). 16.99 (978-0-06-236827-0(3), HarperCollins) HarperCollins Pubs.

Carman, Patrick. The Black Circle. 2009. (Playaway Children Ser.: Bk. 5). (J). 49.99 (978-1-61545-995-7(2)) Findaway World, LLC.

—The Black Circle. 2009. (Illus.). 160p. (J). (978-0-545-15291-4(7)) Scholastic, Inc.

—The Black Circle (the 39 Clues, Book 5), Volume 5. 2009. (39 Clues Ser.: 5). (ENG., Illus.). 176p. (J). (gr. 3-7). 13.99 (978-0-545-06045-5(1)) Scholastic, Inc.

Caron, Eleonore. Gizmo & Ellen Mysteries: The Case of the Missing Boy. 2012. 24p. pap. 24.95 (978-1-4626-6747-5(3)) America Star Bks.

Carr, Annie Roe. Nan Sherwood at Pine Camp or the Old Lum. 2007. pap. (978-1-4065-1294-6(X)) Dodo Pr.

—Nan Sherwood at Rose Ranch. 2007. 124p. per. (978-1-4068-4396-5(2)) Echo Library.

—Nan Sherwood at Rose Ranch or the Old Me. 2007. pap. (978-1-4065-1295-3(8)) Dodo Pr.

—Nan Sherwoods Winter Holidays or Rescuin. 2007. pap. (978-1-4065-1296-0(6)) Dodo Pr.

Carr, Debra. The Curry Comb Caper. Carr, Stephen, illus. 2006. 48p. per. 8.95 (978-1-933912-59-2(6)) Westview Publishing Co., Inc.

—The Feed Trough Thriller. Carr, Stephen, illus. 2007. 56p. per. 8.95 (978-1-933912-66-0(9)) Westview Publishing Co., Inc.

—Misty Is Missing. Carr, Stephen, illus. 2008. 52p. pap. 8.95 (978-0-9816172-7-5(1)) Westview Publishing Co., Inc.

Carr, Patrick W. The Legend's Granddaughter: Not Quite Super, Book 1. Dabbs, Douglas, illus. 2007. 281p. (J). pap. (978-0-9793168-0-7(4)) NQSBks.

Carson, Donna Wren. The Mystery of Grimly Manor. 2012. 114p. 29.99 (978-1-4771-5508-0(2)); pap. 19.99 (978-1-4771-5507-3(4)) Xlibris Corp.

Carter, Ally. Don't Judge a Girl by Her Cover. 2016. (Gallagher Girls Ser.: 3). (ENG.). 288p. (YA). (gr. 7-17). pap. 10.99 (978-1-4847-8504-1(5)) Hyperion Bks. for Children.

—Perfect Scoundrels. 2014. (Heist Society Novel Ser.: 3). (ENG.). 336p. (J). (gr. 7-12). pap. 9.99 (978-1-4231-6681-8(7)) Hyperion Bks. for Children.

Carter, Keisha. Maloni's Shoes. 2013. 28p. pap. 9.95 (978-1-4327-9958-8(4)) Outskirts Pr., Inc.

Carthew, Natasha. The Light That Gets Lost. 2016. (ENG.). 320p. (YA). pap. (978-1-4088-3587-6(8), 226733, Bloomsbury Children's Bks.) Bloomsbury Publishing Plc.

Cartwright, Stephen, illus. Find the Duck. 2007. (Find-its Board Bks). 12p. (J). (gr. -1-k). bds. 6.99 (978-0-7945-1804-2(4), Usborne) EDC Publishing.

—Find the Kitten. 2007. (Find-its Board Bks). 12p. (J). (gr. -1-k). bds. 6.99 (978-0-7945-1803-5(6), Usborne) EDC Publishing.

—Find the Puppy. 2007. (Find-its Board Bks). 12p. (J). (gr. -1-k). bds. 6.99 (978-0-7945-1802-8(8), Usborne) EDC Publishing.

Casanova, Mary. The Showstopper: A Rebecca Mystery. 2018. 209p. (J). (978-1-5444-0746-3(7), American Girl) American Girl Publishing, Inc.

—The Turtle-Hatching Mystery, 5. Rayyan, Omar, illus. 2008. (Dog Watch Ser.: 6). (ENG.). 144p. (J). (gr. 3-7). pap. 8.99 (978-1-4169-4783-7(3)) Simon & Schuster, Inc.

Case, Linda. Brigits Day of Fun. 2006. 28p. pap. 9.95 (978-1-4327-0001-0(4)) Outskirts Pr., Inc.

The Case of the Myface Kidnapper (W. T.) 2012. (Hardy Boys (All New) Undercover Brothers Ser.: 40). (ENG.). 160p. (J). pap. 5.99 (978-1-4424-2235-3(1), Simon & Schuster/Paula Wiseman Bks.) Simon & Schuster/Paula Wiseman Bks.

The Case of the Secret Box. 2007. 56p. pap. 7.75 (978-0-8341-2288-8(X), 083-412-288X) Beacon Hill Pr. of Kansas City.

Casey, Barbara. The Cadence of Gypsies. 2011. (ENG.). 272p. (J). (gr. 7-12). 16.95 (978-0-9820812-8-0(6), Hungry Goat Pr.) Gauthier Pubns. Inc.

Casey, Jane. Hide & Seek. 2015. (Jess Tennant Mysteries Ser.: 3). (ENG.). 288p. (YA). (gr. 8). 36.99 (978-1-250-04067-1(1), 900123900, St. Martin's Griffin) St. Martin's Pr.

Cashore, Kristin. Jane, Unlimited. 2018. (Illus.). 480p. (YA). (gr. 9). pap. 10.99 (978-0-14-751310-6(3), Speak) Penguin Young Readers Group.

A Castle Mystery. 2013. (Illus.). (J). (978-1-4351-4945-8(9)) Disney Pr.

Castle, Regina F. Henry Hopper. 2011. 20p. pap. 24.95 (978-1-4560-6563-8(7)) America Star Bks.

Castleberry, Stephen B., Sr. & Castleberry, Susie. The History Mystery. 2005. (Farm Mystery Ser.). per. 8.50 (978-1-891907-16-6(6)) Castleberry Farms Pr.

—Where There's Smoke. 2004. (Farm Mystery Ser.). (J). per. 8.50 (978-1-891907-14-2(X)) Castleberry Farms Pr.

Castor, Daniel & Castor, Harriet. Jam Sponge & Sneakers. (ENG., Illus.). 60p. (J). pap. 7.99 (978-0-340-63441-7(3)) Hodder & Stoughton GBR. Dist: Trafalgar Square Publishing.

Caswell, Brian. Double Exposure. 2005. 240p. (YA). pap. (978-0-7022-3533-7(4)) Univ. of Queensland Pr.

Caszatt-Allen, Wendy, et al. Raptor's Revenge. 2007. (PaleoJoe's Dinosaur Detective Club Ser.). 187p. (J). (gr. 2-5). pap. 8.95 (978-1-934133-37-8(X), Mackinac Island Press, Inc.) Charlesbridge Publishing, Inc.

Caton, Peter. Josh: Hero. 2012. 114p. pap. (978-1-908128-40-9(2)) Spiderwize.

Caulfield, Annie. Solves Crimes: And So On... 2006. (Katie Milk Ser.). (ENG.). 208p. (J). (gr. 4-7). pap. 9.95 (978-0-440-86686-2(3)) Transworld Publishers Ltd. GBR. Dist: Independent Pubs. Group.

Cavallaro, Brittany. The Case for Jamie. 2018. (Charlotte Holmes Novel Ser.: 3). (ENG., Illus.). 368p. (YA). (gr. 8). 17.99 (978-0-06-239897-0(0), Tegen, Katherine Bks) HarperCollins Pubs.

—The Last of August. (Charlotte Holmes Novel Ser.: 2). (ENG.). (YA). (gr. 8). 2018. 352p. pap. 10.99 (978-0-06-239895-6(4)) 2017. (Illus.). 336p. 17.99 (978-0-06-239894-9(6)) HarperCollins Pubs. (Tegen, Katherine Bks).

—A Study in Charlotte. (Charlotte Holmes Novel Ser.: 1). (ENG.). (YA). (gr. 8). 2017. 352p. pap. 11.99 (978-0-06-239891-8(1)) 2016. 336p. 17.99 (978-0-06-239890-1(3)) HarperCollins Pubs. (Tegen, Katherine Bks).

Cavendish, Grace. The Grace Mysteries: Assassin & Betrayal. 2011. (Grace Mysteries Ser.). (ENG.). 384p. (J). (gr. 3-7). pap. 6.99 (978-0-385-74005-0(0), Delacorte Bks. for Young Readers); 1. (gr. 6-8). lib. bdg. 21.19 (978-0-385-90821-4(0), Delacorte Pr.) Random Hse. Children's Bks.

Chadda, Sarwat. Mission Atomic (the 39 Clues: Doublecross, Book 4) 2018. (Follow Me Around... Ser.: 4). (ENG.). 256p. (J). (gr. 3-4). E-Book 27.00 (978-0-545-76936-5(1)) Scholastic, Inc.

Chaisson, Samuel Jam. Larry & Joe's Detective Agency. 2005. pap. 26.50 (978-1-4184-6878-1(9)) AuthorHouse.

Chambliss Bertman, Jennifer. Book Scavenger. 2016. (Book Scavenger Ser.: 1). (ENG.). 368p. (J). pap. 8.99 (978-1-250-07980-0(2), 900154628) Square Fish.

—The Unbreakable Code. 2018. (Book Scavenger Ser.: 2). (ENG.). 384p. (J). pap. 8.99 (978-1-250-15839-0(7), 900179194) Square Fish.

Chan, Marty. The Mystery of the Frozen Brains, 1 vol. 2004. (ENG.). 112p. (J). pap. 10.95 (978-1-894345-71-2(1)) Thistledown Pr., Ltd. CAN. Dist: Univ. of Toronto Pr.

—The Mystery of the Mad Science Teacher. 2008. (ENG.). 127p. (J). (gr. 2-7). pap. 10.95 (978-1-897235-38-6(0)) Thistledown Pr., Ltd. CAN. Dist: Univ. of Toronto Pr.

Chancey, Loren. Blue Sneaker Breakdown. 2010. 146p. (J). pap. 6.99 (978-0-9844649-1-3(3)) DIASOT Pubns.

Chand, Emlyn. Davey the Detective: A Bird Brain Book. Shaw, Sarah, illus. l.t. ed. 2012. (ENG.). 42p. (gr. k-1). 21.95 (978-1-62253-107-3(8)); pap. 10.95 (978-1-62253-119-6(1)) Evolved Publishing.

Chandler, Elizabeth. The Back Door of Midnight. 2004. (Dark Secrets Ser.: 5). (ENG.). 224p. (YA). mass mkt. 5.99 (978-0-689-86642-5(9), Simon Pulse) Simon Pulse.

—Dark Secrets 1: Legacy of Lies & Don't Tell. 2009. (Dark Secrets Ser.: 1). (ENG., Illus.). 496p. (YA). (gr. 7-18). pap. 13.99 (978-1-4169-9461-9(0), Simon Pulse) Simon Pulse.

—Dark Secrets 2 No. 2: No Time to Die; the Deep End of Fear. 2010. (Dark Secrets Ser.: 2). (ENG.). 624p. (YA). (gr. 7). pap. 9.99 (978-1-4169-9462-6(9), Simon Pulse) Simon Pulse.

Chapman, Brenda. Hiding in Hawk's Creek: A Jennifer Bannon Mystery. 2006. (Jennifer Bannon Mystery Ser.: 2). (ENG.). 144p. (YA). per. 9.95 *(978-1-894917-24-7(3),* Napoleon & Co.) Dundurn Pr. CAN. Dist: Publishers Group West (PGW).
—Trail of Secrets: A Jennifer Bannon Mystery. 2009. (Jennifer Bannon Mystery Ser.: 4). (ENG.). 144p. (YA). (gr. 7-18). pap. 9.95 *(978-1-894917-76-6(6),* Napoleon & Co.) Dundurn Pr. CAN. Dist: Publishers Group West (PGW).
Chari, Sheela. Finding Mighty. 2019. (ENG.). 336p. (J). (gr. 5-9). pap. 9.99 *(978-1-4197-3479-3(2),* 1144603, Amulet Bks.) Abrams, Inc.
Chase, L. P. Elliot Stone & the Mystery of the Summer Vacation Sea Monster. DiRocco, Carl, illus. 2011. (ENG.). 165p. (J). pap. 8.99 *(978-0-9792918-7-6(9))* Blue Marlin Pubns.
—Elliott Stone & the Mystery of the Backyard Treasure. 2008. 122p. (J). pap. 11.95 *(978-0-7414-4804-0(1))* Infinity Publishing.
Chatterton, Martin. The Brain Finds a Leg. 2007. 207p. *(978-1-921049-79-8(0))* Little Hare Bks. AUS. Dist: HarperCollins Pubs. Australia.
Cherub: The Recruit; the Dealer; Maximum Security. 2013. (Cherub Ser.). (ENG.). 1008p. (YA). (gr. 7). pap. 29.99 *(978-1-4424-8376-7(8),* Simon Pulse) Simon Pulse.
Cheshire, Simon. The Treasure of Dead Man's Lane & Other Case Files: Saxby Smart, Private Detective: Book 2. Alley, R. W., illus. 2011. (Saxby Smart, Private Detective Ser.: 2). (ENG.). 224p. (J). (gr. 3-7). pap. 14.99 *(978-0-312-67434-2(1),* 900072849) Square Fish.
Chesterman, Simon. Being Arcadia. 2018. (Raising Arcadia Trilogy Ser.). 456p. (YA). (gr. 7). pap. 19.95 *(978-981-4751-52-0(9))* Marshall Cavendish International (Asia) Private Ltd. SGP. Dist: Independent Pubs. Group.
Chick, Bryan. The Secret Zoo: Secrets & Shadows. 2011. (Secret Zoo Ser.: 2). (ENG.). 272p. (J). (gr. 3-7). pap. 7.99 *(978-0-06-198926-1(6));* 16.99 *(978-0-06-198925-4(8))* HarperCollins Pubs. (Greenwillow Bks.).
Chicken Squad: The First Misadventure, 1 vol. 2015. (Your Reading Path Ser.: 1). (Illus.). 112p. (J). (gr. 3-3). pap. *(978-1-4424-9677-4(0),* 04928386-0b45-4e55-b035-177f94c93034, Rosen Classroom) Rosen Publishing Group, Inc., The.
Child, Lauren. Clarice Bean, Don't Look Now. Child, Lauren, illus. 2008. (Clarice Bean Ser.: 3). (ENG., Illus.). 256p. (J). (gr. 3-7). pap. 7.99 *(978-0-7636-3935-8(4))* Candlewick Pr.
—Ruby Redfort Blink & You Die. Child, Lauren, illus. (Ruby Redfort Ser.: 6). (ENG., Illus.). 544p. (J). (gr. 5-9). 2019. pap. 8.99 *(978-1-5362-0863-4(9))* 2018. 18.99 *(978-0-7636-5472-6(8))* Candlewick Pr.
—Ruby Redfort Catch Your Death. Child, Lauren, illus. (Ruby Redfort Ser.: 3). (ENG., Illus.). (J). (gr. 5-9). 2018. 528p. pap. 7.99 *(978-0-7636-8846-2(0))* 2015. 432p. 17.99 *(978-0-7636-5469-6(8))* Candlewick Pr.
—Ruby Redfort Feel the Fear. Child, Lauren, illus. (Ruby Redfort Ser.: 4). (ENG., Illus.). 528p. (J). (gr. 5-9). 2018. pap. 7.99 *(978-0-7636-9452-4(5))* 2016. 16.99 *(978-0-7636-5470-2(1))* Candlewick Pr.
—Ruby Redfort Look into My Eyes. Child, Lauren, illus. 2018. (Ruby Redfort Ser.: 1). (ENG., Illus.). 400p. (J). (gr. 5-9). pap. 8.99 *(978-1-5362-0047-8(6))* Candlewick Pr.
—Ruby Redfort Pick Your Poison. Child, Lauren, illus. (Ruby Redfort Ser.: 5). (ENG., Illus.). 528p. (J). (gr. 5-9). 2018. pap. 7.99 *(978-1-5362-0049-2(2))* 2017. 16.99 *(978-0-7636-5471-9(X))* Candlewick Pr.
—Ruby Redfort Take Your Last Breath. Child, Lauren, illus. (Ruby Redfort Ser.: 2). (ENG., Illus.). 432p. (J). (gr. 5-9). 2018. pap. 7.99 *(978-1-5362-0048-5(4))* 2013. 16.99 *(978-0-7636-5468-9(X))* Candlewick Pr.
—Utterly Me, Clarice Bean. Child, Lauren, illus. 2005. (Clarice Bean Ser.). (ENG., Illus.). (J). 190p. (gr. 4-6). 18.69 *(978-0-7636-2186-5(2));* 208p. (gr. 3-7). reprint ed. pap. 7.99 *(978-0-7636-2788-1(7))* Candlewick Pr.
—Utterly Me, Clarice Bean. Child, Lauren, illus. 2006. (Clarice Bean Ser.). (Illus.). 16.00 *(978-0-7569-6567-9(5))* Perfection Learning Corp.
Christian, Anna. The Newcomer. 2013. 56p. pap. 6.99 *(978-0-9799273-5-5(8))* Dadielte Production.
Christie, Agatha. Asesinato en el Orient Expreso.Tr. of Murder on the Orient Express. (SPA.). 240p. (J). 7.95 *(978-84-272-0005-0(6))* Molino, Editorial ESP. Dist: AIMS International Bks., Inc.
Christopher, Lucy. The Killing Woods. 2014. (ENG.). 384p. (J). (gr. 9). pap. 11.99 *(978-0-545-46101-6(4),* Chicken Hse., The) Scholastic, Inc.
Christopher, Matt. The Hockey Machine. 2008. (New Matt Christopher Sports Library). 128p. (J). (gr. 4-6). lib. bdg. 26.60 *(978-1-59953-214-1(X))* Norwood Hse. Pr.
—The Mystery under Fugitive House. 2016. (ENG., Illus.). 114p. (J). pap. 9.95 *(978-1-62268-067-2(7))* Bella Rosa Bks.
—Skateboard Tough. 2007. (New Matt Christopher Sports Library). 167p. (J). (gr. 4-6). lib. bdg. 26.60 *(978-1-59953-115-1(1))* Norwood Hse. Pr.
Churchman, Jennifer & Churchman, John. The Easter Surprise. (Sweet Pea & Friends Ser.: 5). (ENG., Illus.). (J). (gr. -1 — 1). 2020. 22p. bds. 8.99 *(978-0-316-53822-0(1))* 2019. 40p. 17.99 *(978-0-316-41166-0(3))* Little, Brown Bks. for Young Readers.
Ciminera, Siobhan & Faulkner, Keith. A Yummy Mystery: A Scratch-and-Sniff Story. 2007. (Puppy Scooby-Doo Ser.). 16p. (J). pap. 5.99 *(978-0-448-44406-2(2),* Grosset & Dunlap) Penguin Publishing Group.
The Circus Mystery, 6 vols., Vol. 2. (Woodland Mysteriestm Ser.). 133p. (gr. 3-7). 42.50 *(978-0-7802-7942-1(5))* Wright Group/McGraw-Hill.
Cirrone, Dorian. The Big Scoop, 1 vol. Woodruff, Liza, illus. 2006. (Marshall Cavendish Chapter Book Ser.). (ENG.). 74p. (J). (gr. 2-5). 14.99 *(978-0-7614-5323-9(7))* Marshall Cavendish Corp.
—The Missing Silver Dollar, 1 vol. Woodruff, Liza, illus. 2006. (Lindy Blues Ser.). (ENG.). 32p. (J). (gr. -1-3). 14.95 *(978-0-7614-5284-3(2))* Marshall Cavendish Corp.
Citra, Becky. Missing, 1 vol. 2011. (ENG.). 184p. (J). (gr. 4-7). pap. 9.95 *(978-1-55469-345-0(4))* Orca Bk. Pubs. USA.
Clark, Hannah L. Uncovering Cobbogoth. 2014. pap. 17.99 *(978-1-4621-1426-9(1))* Cedar Fort, Inc./CFI Distribution.
Clark, Joan. Penny Nichols & the Black Imp. 2012. 136p. pap. *(978-1-78139-156-3(4))* Benediction Classics.
—Penny Nichols & the Knob Hill Mystery. 2012. 124p. pap. *(978-1-78139-157-0(2))* Benediction Classics.
—Penny Nichols & the Mystery of the Lost Key. 2012. 124p. pap. *(978-1-78139-155-6(6))* Benediction Classics.
—Penny Nichols Finds a Clue. 2012. 128p. pap. *(978-1-78139-154-9(8))* Benediction Classics.
—Penny Nichols Omnibus - Finds a Clue, Mystery of the Lost Key, Black Imp, & Knob Hill Mystery. 2012. 484p. *(978-1-78139-158-7(0))* Benediction Classics.
Clark, Lisa M. The Messengers: Concealed. 2017. (ENG.). 317p. (J). (gr. 7-12). pap. 12.99 *(978-0-7586-5657-5(2))* Concordia Publishing Hse.
Clasicos de Misterio. (Clasicos Juveniles Coleccion).Tr. of Classic Mystery Stories II. (SPA.). (YA). (gr. 5-8). pap. *(978-950-11-1279-5(9),* SG4720) Sigmar ARG. Dist: Lectorum Pubns., Inc.
Class 1-208. Pizza Place Ghost, 1 vol. Sur, Duendes Del, illus. 2013. (Scooby-Doo! Picture Clue Bks.). (ENG.). 24p. (J). (gr. k-2). lib. bdg. 31.36 *(978-1-61479-038-9(8),* 13232) Spotlight.
Clement, Emily. Thea Stilton & the Hollywood Hoax. Pellizzari, Barbara & Balleello, Chiara, illus. 2015. 159p. (J). *(978-1-5182-1175-1(5))* Scholastic, Inc.
Clements, Andrew. Fear Itself. Stower, Adam, illus. 2011. (Benjamin Pratt & the Keepers of the School Ser.: 2). (ENG.). 240p. (J). (gr. 2-5). pap. 8.99 *(978-1-4169-3908-5(3),* Atheneum Bks. for Young Readers) Simon & Schuster Children's Publishing.
—In Harm's Way. Stower, Adam, illus. (Benjamin Pratt & the Keepers of the School Ser.: 4). (ENG.). (J). (gr. 2-5). 2014. 240p. pap. 8.99 *(978-1-4169-3910-8(5))* 2013. 224p. 14.99 *(978-1-4169-3889-7(3))* Simon & Schuster Children's Publishing. (Atheneum Bks. for Young Readers).
—The Map Trap. Andreasen, Dan, illus. 2016. (ENG.). 160p. (J). (gr. 3-7). pap. 7.99 *(978-1-4169-9728-3(8))* Simon & Schuster Children's Publishing.
—The Map Trap. 2016. lib. bdg. 18.40 *(978-0-606-38977-8(6))* Turtleback.
—Room One: A Mystery or Two. Elliott, Mark, illus. (ENG.). (J). (gr. 3-7). 2008. 192p. pap. 7.99 *(978-0-689-86687-6(9))* 2006. 176p. 19.99 *(978-0-689-86686-9(0))* Simon & Schuster Children's Publishing. (Atheneum Bks. for Young Readers).
—We Hold These Truths. Stower, Adam, illus. 2013. (Benjamin Pratt & the Keepers of the School Ser.: 5). (ENG.). 272p. (J). (gr. 2-5). 14.99 *(978-1-4169-3890-3(7),* Atheneum Bks. for Young Readers) Simon & Schuster Children's Publishing.
—We the Children. 2011. (Benjamin Pratt & the Keepers of the School Ser.: 1). (ENG.). 176p. (J). (gr. 2-5). pap. 8.99 *(978-1-4169-3907-8(5),* Atheneum Bks. for Young Readers) Simon & Schuster Children's Publishing.
—The Whites of Their Eyes. Stower, Adam, illus. 2013. (Benjamin Pratt & the Keepers of the School Ser.: 3). (ENG.). 240p. (J). (gr. 2-5). pap. 7.99 *(978-1-4169-3909-2(1),* Atheneum Bks. for Young Readers) Simon & Schuster Children's Publishing.
Cleverly, Sophie. The Curse in the Candlelight: a Scarlet & Ivy Mystery. 2019. (ENG.). 384p. (J). 7.99 *(978-0-00-830822-3(5),* HarperCollins Children's Bks.) HarperCollins Pubs. Ltd. GBR. Dist: HarperCollins Pubs.
—The Dance in the Dark. 2018. (Scarlet & Ivy Ser.: 3). (ENG.). 320p. (J). (gr. 5-8). pap. 7.99 *(978-1-4926-3409-6(3))* Sourcebooks, Inc.
—The Last Secret: a Scarlet & Ivy Mystery. 2019. (ENG.). 320p. (J). 7.99 *(978-0-00-830823-0(3),* HarperCollins Children's Bks.) HarperCollins Pubs. Ltd. GBR. Dist: HarperCollins Pubs.
—The Lights under the Lake: a Scarlet & Ivy Mystery. 2018. (ENG.). 304p. (J). 7.99 *(978-0-00-830821-6(7),* HarperCollins Children's Bks.) HarperCollins Pubs. Ltd. GBR. Dist: HarperCollins Pubs.
—The Lost Twin. 2017. (Scarlet & Ivy Ser.: 1). (ENG.). 320p. (J). (gr. 5-8). 7.99 *(978-1-4926-4792-8(6),* 9781492647928) Sourcebooks, Inc.
—The Whispers in the Walls. 2017. (Scarlet & Ivy Ser.: 2). (ENG.). 288p. (J). (gr. 5-8). pap. 12.99 *(978-1-4926-3406-5(9),* 9781492634065) Sourcebooks, Inc.
Clewarth, John. Firestorm Rising. 2012. (Illus.). 200p. pap. *(978-1-4710-3681-1(2))* Lulu.com.
—Firestorm Rising. 2018. (ENG., Illus.). 216p. (J). (gr. 4-6). pap. *(978-1-912513-70-3(6))* Silver Quill Publishing.
Clover, Andrew. Rory Branagan: Detective #1. Lazar, Ralph, illus. 2020. (Rory Branagan: Detective Ser.: 1). (ENG.). 352p. (J). (gr. 2-7). pap. 9.99 *(978-1-5247-9364-7(7),* Penguin Workshop) Penguin Young Readers Group.
The Clue in the Castle, 6 vols., Vol. 2. (Woodland Mysteriestm Ser.). 133p. (gr. 3-7). 42.50 *(978-0-7802-7935-3(2))* Wright Group/McGraw-Hill.
Coben, Harlan. Seconds Away. l.t. ed. 2012. (Mickey Bolitar Ser.: 2). (ENG.). 396p. 23.99 *(978-1-4104-5348-8(0))* Thorndike Pr.
—Seconds Away. 2013. (Mickey Bolitar Ser.: 2). lib. bdg. 20.85 *(978-0-606-32141-9(1))* Turtleback.
—Seconds Away (Book Two) A Mickey Bolitar Novel, Bk. 2. 2013. (Mickey Bolitar Novel Ser.: 2). (ENG.). 368p. (YA). (gr. 7). pap. 11.99 *(978-0-14-242635-7(0),* Speak) Penguin Young Readers Group.
—Shelter. l.t. ed. 2011. (Mickey Bolitar Ser.: Bk. 1). (ENG.). 354p. (J). (gr. 9-12). 23.99 *(978-1-4104-4365-6(5))* Thorndike Pr.
—Shelter. 2012. (Mickey Bolitar Ser.: 1). lib. bdg. 20.85 *(978-0-606-26669-7(0))* Turtleback.
—Shelter (Book One) A Mickey Bolitar Novel, Bk. 1. 2012. (Mickey Bolitar Novel Ser.: 1). (ENG.). 336p. (YA). (gr. 7). pap. 11.99 *(978-0-14-242203-8(7),* Speak) Penguin Young Readers Group.
Cody, Matthew. Powerless. 2011. 288p. (J). (Supers of Noble's Green Ser.: 1). (gr. 3-7). 8.99 *(978-0-375-84489-8(9),* Yearling);1. (Supers of Noble Green Ser.). (ENG.). (gr. 4-6). lib. bdg. 18.69 *(978-0-375-95595-2(X),* Knopf Bks. for Young Readers) Random Hse. Children's Bks.
—Villainous. 2015. (Supers of Noble's Green Ser.: 3). (ENG.). 320p. (J). (gr. 3-7). 8.99 *(978-0-385-75492-7(2),* Yearling) Random Hse. Children's Bks.
Cofer, Amadeus. Mystery of the Golden Pearls: A Halloween Adventure in Clarkesville, 1. l.t. ed. 2004. (Illus.). 36p. (J). 14.00 *(978-1-932957-02-0(2))* Legacy Pubs.
Coffey, M. Carol. Zoe Lucky & the Green Gables' Mystery. 2008. 156p. pap. 12.95 *(978-1-4327-3190-8(4))* Outskirts Pr., Inc.
—Zoe Lucky & the Mystery of the Pink Pearl Necklace. 2013. 176p. pap. 12.95 *(978-1-4327-9789-8(1))* Outskirts Pr., Inc.
Coleman, Evelyn. The Cameo Necklace: A Cecile Mystery. Giovine, Sergio, illus. 2012. (American Girl Mysteries Ser.). (ENG.). 192p. (J). (gr. 4-6). pap. 18.69 *(978-1-59369-900-0(X))* American Girl Publishing, Inc.
—Shadows on Society Hill. 2007. (American Girl Mysteries Ser.). (ENG., Illus.). 192p. (J). (gr. 4-7). 10.95 *(978-1-59369-163-9(7),* American Girl) American Girl Publishing, Inc.
Coleman, Tamala J. Donovan's Shoes. 2010. 28p. pap. 9.95 *(978-1-4327-5801-1(2))* Outskirts Pr., Inc.
Coles, William E., Jr. Compass in the Blood: A Reissue of the Simon & Schuster Original Novel. 2004. (YA). per. 9.95 *(978-1-59571-034-5(5))* Word Association Pubs.
Colfer, Eoin. Half-Moon Investigations. 2006. 290p. (J). *(978-1-4156-7354-6(3))* Hyperion Bks. for Children.
Collard, Sneed B., III. Dog 4491. 2013. (Illus.). 256p. (J). 13.99 *(978-0-9844460-4-9(4))* Bucking Horse Bks.
Collard, Sneed B., 3rd. Dog 4491. 2013. (ENG., Illus.). 256p. (J). pap. 8.00 *(978-0-9844460-5-6(2))* Mountain Pr. Publishing Co., Inc.
Collard, Sneed B., III. The Governor's Dog Is Missing. 2011. (Slate Stephens Mysteries Ser.). 176p. (J). (gr. 4-6). 16.00 *(978-0-9844460-1-8(X))* Bucking Horse Bks.
Collicutt, Paul. Murder on the Robot City Express. Collicutt, Paul, illus. 2010. (Robot City Ser.: 4). (ENG., Illus.). 48p. (J). (gr. 3-7). pap. 8.99 *(978-0-7636-5015-5(3),* Templar) Candlewick Pr.
Collier, Christine. Twelve Months of Mystery. 2003. 72p. pap. 8.95 *(978-0-595-29943-0(1),* Mystery & Suspense Pr.) iUniverse, Inc.
Collier, Kathy Lynn. Walter S. (Spy) Pigeon, 1 vol. Pace, Brittany Lee Ann, illus. 2009. 20p. pap. 24.95 *(978-1-60813-543-1(8))* America Star Bks.
Collins, Amberly & Collins, Brandilyn. Final Touch, 1 vol. 2010. (Rayne Tour Ser.). (ENG.). 224p. (YA). (gr. 8-11). pap. 9.99 *(978-0-310-71933-5(X))* Zondervan.
Colvin, S. R. R. The Krybosian Stairpath: Magnetic Reversal. 2009. 200p. pap. 14.95 *(978-1-4401-5927-5(0))* iUniverse, Inc.
Comeau, Ceara. Adventures of the Young & Curious. 2008. (ENG.). 136p. pap. 10.94 *(978-0-557-00914-5(6))* Lulu Pr., Inc.
Conan Doyle, Arthur. The Adventures of Sherlock Holmes. Caparo, Antonio Javier, illus. 2011. (Calico Illustrated Classics Ser.: No. 4). (ENG.). 112p. (J). (gr. 2-5). 38.50 *(978-1-61641-610-2(6),* 4035, Calico Chapter Bks.) ABDO Publishing Co.
—The Adventures of Sherlock Holmes: With a Discussion of Curiosity. Butterfield, Ned, tr. Butterfield, Ned, illus. 2003. (Values in Action Illustrated Classics Ser.). (J). *(978-1-59203-045-3(9))* Learning Challenge, Inc.
—The Boys' Sherlock Holmes. Haycraft, Howard, ed. 2011. 366p. 51.95 *(978-1-258-00844-4(0))* Literary Licensing, LLC.
—The Hound of the Baskervilles. 2004. (Fast Track Classics Ser.). (Illus.). 48p. (J). pap. *(978-0-237-52402-9(3))* Evans Brothers, Ltd.
—The Man with the Twisted Lip - Lego - the Adventures of Sherlock Holmes. Macaluso, James, illus. 2014. (ENG.). pap. *(978-1-78092-698-8(7))* MX Publishing, Ltd.
—Sherlock Holmes. 2003. (Retold Ser.). (Illus.). 282p. (J). (gr. 7-18). 15.99 *(978-0-7569-1196-6(6))* Perfection Learning Corp.
—Sherlock Holmes & a Scandal in Bohemia: Case 1, No. 1. Rohrbach, Sophie, illus. 2010. (On the Case with Holmes & Watson Ser.: 1). (ENG.). 48p. (J). (gr. 4-6). pap. 9.99 *(978-0-7613-6197-8(9),* 32653730-1bc9-4a3e-a5c2-62bec3acce70, Graphic Universe™) Lerner Publishing Group.
—Sherlock Holmes & the Adventure of Black Peter. Rohrbach, Sophie & Morrow, J. T., illus. 2012. (On the Case with Holmes & Watson Ser.). 48p. (J). (gr. 4-6). pap. 39.62 *(978-0-7613-9274-3(2),* Graphic Universe™) Lerner Publishing Group.
—Sherlock Holmes & the Adventure of the Cardboard Box. Rohrbach, Sophie & Morrow, J. T., illus. 2012. (On the Case with Holmes & Watson Ser.). 48p. (J). (gr. 4-6). pap. 39.62 *(978-0-7613-9275-0(0),* Graphic Universe™) Lerner Publishing Group.
—Sherlock Holmes & the Adventure of the Speckled Band: Case 5, No. 5. Rohrbach, Sophie, illus. 2010. (On the Case with Holmes & Watson Ser.: 5). (ENG.). 48p. (J). (gr. 4-6). pap. 9.99 *(978-0-7613-6198-5(7),* da1d6bdc-4673-4aa3-94e6-93dad2ea71a5, Graphic Universe™) Lerner Publishing Group.
—Sherlock Holmes & the Adventure of the Three Garridebs. Rohrbach, Sophie & Morrow, J. T., illus. 2012. (On the Case with Holmes & Watson Ser.). 48p. (J). (gr. 4-6). pap. 39.62 *(978-0-7613-9276-7(9),* Graphic Universe™) Lerner Publishing Group.
—Sherlock Holmes & the Case of the Hound of the Baskervilles. Vogel, Malvina G., ed. Marcos, Pablo, illus. 2006. 237p. (YA). (gr. 4-8). 10.00 *(978-0-7567-9834-5(5))* DIANE Publishing Co.
—Sherlock Holmes & the Gloria Scott. Rohrbach, Sophie & Morrow, J. T., illus. 2012. (On the Case with Holmes & Watson Ser.). 48p. (J). (gr. 4-6). pap. 39.62 *(978-0-7613-9277-4(7),* Graphic Universe™) Lerner Publishing Group.
—Sherlock Holmes & the Hound of the Baskervilles, 1 vol. Caparó, Antonio Javier, illus. 2011. (Calico Illustrated Classics Ser.: No. 3). (ENG.). 112p. (J). (gr. 2-5). 38.50 *(978-1-61641-109-1(0),* 4025, Calico Chapter Bks.) ABDO Publishing Co.
—#07 Sherlock Holmes & the Redheaded League. Rohrbach, Sophie & Morrow, Jt, illus. 2011. (On the Case with Holmes & Watson Set II Ser.). pap. 39.62 *(978-0-7613-7609-5(7),* Graphic Universe™) Lerner Publishing Group.
—#08 Sherlock Holmes & the Adventure at the Copper Beeches. Rohrbach, Sophie & Morrow, Jt, illus. 2011. (On the Case with Holmes & Watson Set II Ser.). (J). pap. 39.62 *(978-0-7613-7610-1(0),* Graphic Universe™) Lerner Publishing Group.
—#09 Sherlock Holmes & the Adventure of the Six Napoleons. Rohrbach, Sophie & Morrow, Jt, illus. 2011. (On the Case with Holmes & Watson Set II Ser.). pap. 39.62 *(978-0-7613-7611-8(9),* Graphic Universe™) Lerner Publishing Group.
—#10 Sherlock Holmes & the Boscombe Valley Mystery. Rohrbach, Sophie & Morrow, Jt, illus. 2011. (On the Case with Holmes & Watson Set II Ser.). pap. 39.62 *(978-0-7613-7612-5(7),* Graphic Universe™) Lerner Publishing Group.
Conford, Ellen. A Case for Jenny Archer. Palmisciano, Diane, illus. 2nd ed. 2006. (ENG.). 64p. (J). (gr. 1-4). per. 8.99 *(978-0-316-01486-1(9))* Little, Brown Bks. for Young Readers.
Conn, Bruce. The Curse of Durgan's Reef. 2004. 142p. (YA). 21.95 *(978-0-595-66223-4(4));* pap. 11.95 *(978-0-595-30935-1(6))* iUniverse, Inc.
Conrad, Hy. Kids' Whodunits Vol. 2: Crack the Cases!, 2. Blanchard, Sue, illus. 2009. (Jonah Bixby Mystery: Kid Detective! Ser.). (ENG.). 96p. (J). (gr. 2-4). 21.19 *(978-1-4027-5398-5(5))* Sterling Publishing Co., Inc.
Conrad, Joseph & Snyder, John K., III. The Secret Agent. (Classics Illustrated Ser.). (Illus.). 52p. (YA). pap. 4.95 *(978-1-57209-017-0(0))* Classics International Entertainment, Inc.
Conrique, Samantha. The Pod-Poppers. 2007. (J). pap. 8.00 *(978-0-8059-7200-9(5))* Dorrance Publishing Co., Inc.
The Contagious Colors of Mumpley Middle School. 2014. (ENG., Illus.). 288p. (J). (gr. 2-5). pap. 8.99 *(978-1-4424-7830-5(6),* Atheneum Bks. for Young Readers) Simon & Schuster Children's Publishing.
Cook, Eileen. The Hanging Girl. 2017. (ENG.). 320p. (YA). (gr. 9). 17.99 *(978-0-544-82982-4(4),* 1644036, Clarion Bks.) HarperCollins Pubs.
—One Lie Too Many. 2019. (ENG.). 336p. (YA). (gr. 9). pap. 9.99 *(978-1-328-61841-2(2),* 1733754, Clarion Bks.) HarperCollins Pubs.
—You Owe Me a Murder. 2019. (ENG.). 368p. (YA). (gr. 9). 17.99 *(978-1-328-51902-3(3),* 1720627, Clarion Bks.) HarperCollins Pubs.
Cook, Gerri. Where the Buffalo Jump. Yu, Chao & Wang, Jue, illus. 2003. (Dinosaur Soup Ser.). 120p. (YA). (gr. 3-5). pap. 9.95 *(978-1-895836-95-0(6))* River Bks. CAN. Dist: Fitzhenry & Whiteside, Ltd.
Cooke, Tobias. The Secret of the Lost Soul: A Ben Street Mystery. 2011. 272p. pap. *(978-1-907499-80-7(6))* Pen Pr. Pubs., Ltd.
Cool by the Pool: Coloring/Activity Book. 2005. (Illus.). (J). 2.99 *(978-0-9770455-2-5(8))* Mighty Kids Media.
Cool by the Pool: Picture Book (English) 2005. (Illus.). 47p. (J). 5.99 *(978-0-9770455-3-2(6))* Mighty Kids Media.
Coombs, Charles. Detective Stories: Young Readers. Geer, Charles H., illus. 2011. 194p. 42.95 *(978-1-258-10586-0(1))* Literary Licensing, LLC.
—Ranch Mystery: Young Readers. Priscilla, Louis, illus. 2011. 188p. 42.95 *(978-1-258-09854-4(7))* Literary Licensing, LLC.
Cooney, Caroline B. No Such Person. 2016. (ENG.). 256p. (YA). (gr. 7). pap. 9.99 *(978-0-385-74292-4(4),* Ember) Random Hse. Children's Bks.
—The Terrorist. 2012. (ENG.). 144p. (YA). (gr. 7-12). pap. 6.99 *(978-1-4532-7467-5(7))* Open Road Integrated Media, Inc.
Coons, Mary. The Piglys & the Hundred-Year Mystery. 2013. 216p. (gr. 4-6). 33.99 *(978-1-4808-0141-7(0));* pap. 15.99 *(978-1-4808-0139-4(9))* Archway Publishing.
Cooper, Brigitte Henry. Spooky Spots. Napoli, Elena, illus. 2018. (Odd Jobs Ser.). (ENG.). 48p. (J). (gr. 3-7). lib. bdg. 34.21 *(978-1-5321-3190-5(9),* 28485, Spellbound) Magic Wagon.
—Terrifying Tales. Napoli, Elena, illus. 2018. (Odd Jobs Ser.). (ENG.). 48p. (J). (gr. 3-7). lib. bdg. 34.21 *(978-1-5321-3191-2(7),* 28487, Spellbound) Magic Wagon.
Cooper, Dolores Thorne. The Story of the Knus. 2005. (Illus.). 64p. (J). pap. 9.95 *(978-1-881539-38-4(5),* Strathmoor) Tabby Hse. Bks.
Cooper, E. E. Avenged. 2016. (Vanished Ser.: 2). (ENG.). 352p. (YA). (gr. 9). 17.99 *(978-0-06-229392-3(3),* Tegen, Katherine Bks) HarperCollins Pubs.
—Vanished. 2015. (Vanished Ser.: 1). (ENG.). 320p. (YA). (gr. 9). 17.99 *(978-0-06-229390-9(7),* Tegen, Katherine Bks) HarperCollins Pubs.
Coren, Alan. Railroad Arthur. 2004. (Illus.). 64p. *(978-0-903895-92-7(7),* Robson Bks. Ltd.) Pavilion Bks.
Corrossi, Steven A. Angus & the Hidden Fort. 2003. 162p. pap. 9.95 *(978-0-595-27540-3(0),* Writer's Showcase Pr.) iUniverse, Inc.
Corley, Sandra Y. The Crochet Detective Case #101: The Case of the Missing African Treasure. 2011. 36p. (gr. 4-6). pap. 16.86 *(978-1-4567-4678-0(2))* AuthorHouse.
Cormier, Robert. I Am the Cheese. l.t. ed. 2005. 255p. pap. 10.95 *(978-0-7862-7336-2(4),* Large Print Pr.) Thorndike Pr.
—The Rag & Bone Shop. 2003. (ENG.). 176p. (YA). (gr. 7). mass mkt. 7.99 *(978-0-440-22971-1(5),* Laurel Leaf) Random Hse. Children's Bks.
Corona, Sarah. El Misterio del Tiempo Robado. (Barril Sin Fondo Ser.). (SPA.). (J). (gr. 3-5). pap. *(978-968-6465-16-7(2))* Casa de Estudios de Literatura y Talleres Artisticos Amaquemecan A.C. MEX. Dist: Lectorum Pubns., Inc.
Corriveau, Art. How I, Nicky Flynn, Finally Get a Life (and a Dog) 2010. (ENG.). 288p. (YA). (gr. 3-7). 16.95 *(978-0-8109-8298-7(6),* 661601, Amulet Bks.) Abrams, Inc.
Cortez, Sarah, ed. You Don't Have a Clue: Latino Mystery Stories for Teens. 2011. 320p. (YA). (gr. 6-18). pap. *(978-1-55885-692-9(7))* Arte Publico Pr.
Cosson, M. J. The Mystery of the Old Car. 2005. (Cover-to-Cover Kooties Club Mysteries Ser.). (Illus.). 56p. (J). (gr. k-3). lib. bdg. 14.95 *(978-0-7569-4606-7(9))* Perfection Learning Corp.
—Sherlock Holmes & A Scandal in Bohemia. rev. ed. 2010. pap. 39.62 *(978-0-7613-6954-7(6))* Lerner Publishing Group.
—Sherlock Holmes & the Adventure at the Abbey Grange. 2nd rev. ed. 2010. pap. 39.62 *(978-0-7613-6957-8(0))* Lerner Publishing Group.

—Sherlock Holmes & the Adventure of the Blue Gem. 3rd rev. ed. 2010. pap. 39.62 *(978-0-7613-6959-2(7))* Lerner Publishing Group.

—Sherlock Holmes & the Adventure of the Dancing Men. 4th rev. ed. 2010. pap. 39.62 *(978-0-7613-6961-5(9))* Lerner Publishing Group.

—Sherlock Holmes & the Adventure of the Speckled Band. 5th rev. ed. 2010. pap. 39.62 *(978-0-7613-6962-2(7))* Lerner Publishing Group.

—Sherlock Holmes & the Adventure of the Sussex Vampire. 6th rev. ed. 2010. pap. 39.62 *(978-0-7613-6963-9(5))* Lerner Publishing Group.

Côté, Denis. La Machination du Scorpion Noir. 2004. (Mon Roman Ser.). (FRE.). 160p. (J). (gr. 2). pap. *(978-2-89021-667-9(5))* Diffusion du livre Mirabel (DLM).

Cote, Denis. Un Parfum de Mystere. 2003. (Premier Roman Ser.). (Illus.). 64p. (J). (gr. 2-5). pap. *(978-2-89021-352-4(8))* Diffusion du livre Mirabel (DLM).

Cousineau-Peiffer, Trisha. Have You Ever Heard of a Rainbow Farm. Everett-Hawkes, Bonnie, illus. 2006. 32p. (J). 12.95 *(978-0-9792084-1-6(6))* Dream Ridge Pr.

—Have You Ever Heard of a Rainbow Farm: The Missing Color Kittens. Everett-Hawkes, Bonnie, illus. 2007. 48p. (J). per. 15.95 *(978-0-9792084-2-3(4))* Dream Ridge Pr.

Covington, Nichole. Melinda the Miserable: Eeriness in the Attic. 2011. 116p. pap. 19.95 *(978-1-4560-7250-6(1))* America Star Bks.

Cowan, C. C. The Case of the Missing Pooch: Amanda's Amazing Adventures - Book One, 6 vols., Vol. 1. Bauer, Cindy, ed. Rashid, Abdul, illus. 2009. (ENG.). 100p. (J). pap. 14.95 *(978-0-9677385-1-2(2))* CCP Publishing & Entertainment.

—The Misadventures of Buck the Puppy Duck: The Case of the Missing Pooch, 6 vols., Vol. 1. Khatri, Mudassir, illus. 2018. (ENG.). 40p. (J). pap. 12.00 *(978-0-9677385-0-5(4))* CCP Publishing & Entertainment.

Cox, James. Earth Dogs Don't Speak. 2009. (Illus.). 112p. pap. 31.99 *(978-1-4389-3990-2(6))* AuthorHouse.

Cox, Judy. The Case of the Purloined Professor, 0 vols. Rayyan, Omar, illus. 2009. (Tails of Frederick & Ishbu Ser.: 0). (ENG.). 256p. (J). (gr. 5-7). 16.99 *(978-0-7614-5544-8(2)*, 9780761455448, Two Lions) Amazon Publishing.

—The Mystery of the Burmese Bandicoot, 1 vol. Rayyan, Omar, illus. 2007. (Tails of frederick & Ishbu Ser.). (ENG.). 224p. (J). (gr. 5-9). lib. bdg. 16.99 *(978-0-7614-5376-5(8))* Marshall Cavendish Corp.

—The Mystery of the Burmese Bandicoot. 2012. 254p. (gr. 4-6). pap. 15.95 *(978-1-4759-3838-8(1))* iUniverse, Inc.

Cox, Katherine. The Missing Fox. 2015. (Scholastic Reader Level 2 Ser.). lib. bdg. 13.55 *(978-0-606-37748-5(4))* Turtleback.

Cox, M. M. Accidental Mobster. 2012. 252p. pap. *(978-1-927134-89-4(7))* Bluewood Publishing, Ltd.

Cox, Suzy. The Dead Girls Detective Agency. 2012. (ENG.). 368p. (YA). (gr. 9). pap. 9.99 *(978-0-06-202064-2(1)*, HarperTeen) HarperCollins Pubs.

Crain, Kira. SEK Statton. 2009. (GER.). 136p. 29.95 *(978-1-4092-6127-8(1))* Lulu Pr., Inc.

Crawford, Clint. The Rag Tag Gang, 1 vol. 2009. 83p. pap. 19.95 *(978-1-4489-9697-1(X))* America Star Bks.

Crawford, K. Michael. The Mystery of Journeys Crowne-an Adventure Drawing Game. Crawford, K. Michael, illus. 2008. (Illus.). 52p. pap. 14.95 *(978-0-9817940-0-6(9))* Virtualbookworm.com Publishing, Inc.

Crawford, Ruth. Squirrel Boy & Brad: Solve a Mystery. 2010. 24p. pap. 12.99 *(978-1-4490-1612-8(X))* AuthorHouse.

Cray, Jordan. Dead Man's Hand. 2009. (Danger. com Ser.: 8). (ENG.). 224p. (YA). (gr. 7). pap. 10.99 *(978-1-4169-9852-5(7)*, Simon Pulse) Simon Pulse.

—Most Wanted. 2009. (Danger. com Ser.: 7). (ENG.). 240p. (YA). (gr. 7). pap. 11.99 *(978-1-4169-9851-8(9)*, Simon Pulse) Simon Pulse.

—Shadow Man. 2009. (Danger. com Ser.: 3). (ENG.). 192p. (YA). (gr. 7). pap. 9.99 *(978-1-4169-9848-8(9)*, Simon Pulse) Simon Pulse.

—Shiver. 2009. (Danger. com Ser.: 9). (ENG.). 224p. (YA). (gr. 7). pap. 10.99 *(978-1-4169-9853-2(5)*, Simon Pulse) Simon Pulse.

—Stalker. 2009. (Danger. com Ser.: 5). (ENG.). 224p. (YA). (gr. 7). pap. 10.99 *(978-1-4169-9850-1(0)*, Simon Pulse) Simon Pulse.

Crilley, Paul. The Osiris Curse: A Tweed & Nightingale Adventure. 2013. (Tweed & Nightingale Adventures Ser.). (ENG.). 287p. (YA). (gr. 7). 17.99 *(978-1-61614-857-7(8)*, Pyr) Start Publishing LLC.

Cronin, Doreen. Bear Country: Bearly a Misadventure. Gilpin, Stephen, illus. (Chicken Squad Ser.: 6). (ENG.). 112p. (J). (gr. 2-5). 2019. pap. 7.99 *(978-1-5344-0575-2(5))* 2018. 12.99 *(978-1-5344-0574-5(7)*, Atheneum/Caitlyn Dlouhy Books) Simon & Schuster Children's Publishing.

—The Case of the Weird Blue Chicken: The Next Misadventure. 2015. (Chicken Squad Ser.: 2). 35.75 *(978-1-4906-4049-5(5))* Recorded Bks., Inc.

—The Chicken Squad. Cornell, Kevin, illus. 2014. 92p. (J). *(978-0-605-90609-9(2))* Simon & Schuster Children's Publishing.

—The Chicken Squad: The First Misadventure. 2014. (Chicken Squad Ser.: 1). 35.75 *(978-1-4906-2065-7(6))*; 1.25 *(978-1-4906-2066-4(4))*; 33.75 *(978-1-4906-2064-0(8))* Recorded Bks., Inc.

—The Chicken Squad: The First Misadventure. Cornell, Kevin, illus. 2014. (Chicken Squad Ser.: 1). (ENG.). 112p. (J). (gr. 2-5). 12.99 *(978-1-4424-9676-7(2)*, Atheneum Bks. for Young Readers) Simon & Schuster Children's Publishing.

—Dark Shadows. 2018. (Chicken Squad Ser.: 4). lib. bdg. 17.20 *(978-0-606-40643-1(6))* Turtleback.

—Into the Wild: Yet Another Misadventure. Gilpin, Stephen, illus. (Chicken Squad Ser.: 3). (ENG.). 112p. (J). (gr. 2-5). 2017. pap. 7.99 *(978-1-4814-5047-8(6))* 2016. 12.99 *(978-1-4814-5046-1(8)*, Atheneum/Caitlyn Dlouhy Books) Simon & Schuster Children's Publishing.

—The Legend of Diamond Lil: A J. J. Tully Mystery. Cornell, Kevin, illus. (ENG.). 144p. (J). (gr. 1-5). 2013. pap. 5.99 *(978-0-06-177997-8(0))* 2012. lib. bdg. 15.89 *(978-0-06-198578-2(3))* HarperCollins Pubs. (Balzer & Bray).

—The Trouble with Chickens: A J. J. Tully Mystery. Cornell, Kevin, illus. (ENG.). (J). (gr. 1-5). 2012. 144p. pap. 9.99 *(978-0-06-121534-6(1))* 2011. 128p. 14.99 *(978-0-06-121532-2(5))* HarperCollins Pubs. (Balzer & Bray).

Cross, P. C. Summer Job: A Virgil & Cy Mystery. 2008. 260p. pap. 16.95 *(978-0-595-50921-8(5))* iUniverse, Inc.

Crossman, D. A. The Legend of Burial Island: A Bean & Ab Mystery. 2009. (J). pap. *(978-0-89272-812-1(4))* Down East Bks.

Crossman, David. The Legend of Burial Island: A Bean & Ab Mystery. 2009. (ENG.). 201p. (J). (gr. 3-7). pap. 11.95 *(978-0-89272-797-1(7))* Down East Bks.

Crowley, Ashley. Officer Panda: Fingerprint Detective. Crowley, Ashley, illus. 2015. (Officer Panda Ser.: 1). (ENG., Illus.). 32p. (J). (gr. -1-3). 17.99 *(978-0-06-236626-9(2)*, HarperCollins) HarperCollins Pubs.

Crowley, Kieran Mark. Colm & the Ghost's Revenge. 2012. (ENG.). 320p. (J). pap. 13.95 *(978-1-85635-997-9(2))* Mercier Pr., Ltd., The IRL. Dist: Dufour Editions, Inc.

—Colm & the Lazarus Key. 2009. (ENG., Illus.). 224p. (J). pap. 14.95 *(978-1-85635-646-6(9))* Mercier Pr., Ltd., The IRL. Dist: Dufour Editions, Inc.

Crutcher, Chris. Period 8. 2013. (ENG.). 288p. (YA). (gr. 9). 17.99 *(978-0-06-191480-5(0)*, Greenwillow Bks.) HarperCollins Pubs.

Cullen-Skowronski, Fiona. The Smugglers' Caves. 2009. 284p. pap. *(978-1-84923-435-1(3))* YouWriteOn.

Cummings, Pat. Where Is Mommy? 2019. (I Like to Read Ser.). (Illus.). 32p. (J). (gr. -1-3). 15.99 *(978-0-8234-3935-5(6))* Holiday Hse., Inc.

Cunliffe, John. Postman Pat & the Mystery Tour. (Postman Pat Ser.: Bk. 13). (ENG., Illus.). 32p. (J). pap. 8.99 *(978-0-340-71333-4(X))* Hodder & Stoughton GBR. Dist: Trafalgar Square Publishing.

Cunning, Concord. Scripture Sleuth 3. 2004. pap. 8.95 *(978-1-885904-39-3(8))* Focus Publishing.

Currie, Lindsay. The Peculiar Incident on Shady Street. 2017. (ENG., Illus.). 304p. (J). (gr. 3-7). 17.99 *(978-1-4814-7704-8(8)*, Aladdin) Simon & Schuster Children's Publishing.

Curtis, Christopher Paul. Mr. Chickee's Funny Money. 2007. (Mr. Chickee's Ser.: 1). (ENG.). 160p. (J). (gr. 3-7). 6.99 *(978-0-440-22919-3(7)*, Yearling) Random Hse. Children's Bks.

—Mr. Chickee's Messy Mission. 2008. (Mr. Chickee's Ser.: 2). (ENG., Illus.). 240p. (J). (gr. 3-7). 6.99 *(978-0-440-22922-3(7)*, Yearling) Random Hse. Children's Bks.

Curtiss, A. B. & Curtiss, A. B. Hanner & the Bullies. Brown, Jason, illus. 2012. 140p. pap. 9.99 *(978-0-932529-63-3(1))* Oldcastle Publishing.

Cushman, Doug. Dirk Bones & the Mystery of the Haunted House. Cushman, Doug, illus. 2009. (I Can Read Level 1 Ser.). (ENG., Illus.). 32p. (J). (gr. k-3). pap. 4.99 *(978-0-06-073767-2(0)*, HarperCollins) HarperCollins Pubs.

—Dirk Bones & the Mystery of the Haunted House. 2009. (I Can Read! Level 1 Ser.). (J). lib. bdg. 13.55 *(978-0-606-04778-4(6))* Turtleback.

—Dirk Bones & the Mystery of the Missing Books. Cushman, Doug, illus. 2009. (I Can Read Level 1 Ser.). (ENG., Illus.). 32p. (J). (gr. -1-3). 16.99 *(978-0-06-073768-9(9)*, HarperCollins) HarperCollins Pubs.

Cusick, Richie Tankersley. Starstruck. 2013. (ENG., Illus.). 240p. (YA). (gr. 7). pap. 15.99 *(978-1-4814-0161-6(0)*, Simon Pulse) Simon Pulse.

—Summer of Secrets. 2013. (ENG., Illus.). 224p. (YA). (gr. 7). pap. 15.99 *(978-1-4814-0160-9(2)*, Simon Pulse) Simon Pulse.

Czernecki, Stefan. Mystery at Midnight Museum. Date not set. 32p. (J). 14.99 *(978-0-06-026199-3(4))* HarperCollins Pubs.

Dadey, Debbie. The Narwhal Problem. Avakyan, Tatevik, illus. 2019. (Mermaid Tales Ser.: 19). (ENG.). 112p. (J). (gr. 1-4). 18.99 *(978-1-4814-8715-3(9))*; pap. 6.99 *(978-1-4814-8714-6(0))* Simon & Schuster Children's Publishing. (Aladdin).

Dahl, Michael. The Assistant Vanishes!, 1 vol. Weber, Lisa K., illus. 2013. (Hocus Pocus Hotel Ser.). (ENG.). 112p. (J). (gr. 3-6). lib. bdg. 25.32 *(978-1-4342-4101-6(7)*, 119822, Stone Arch Bks.) Capstone.

—Curtains! A High School Musical Mystery. Prothero, Tiffany, illus. 2008. (Vortex Bks.). (ENG.). 112p. (J). (gr. 5-9). 26.65 *(978-1-4342-0801-9(X)*, 95206, Stone Arch Bks.) Capstone.

—The Horizontal Man. 2008. (Finnegan Zwake Ser.: 1). (ENG., Illus.). 192p. (YA). (gr. 7). pap. 9.99 *(978-1-4169-8668-3(5)*, Simon Pulse) Simon Pulse.

—Out the Rear Window, 1 vol. Weber, Lisa K., illus. 2012. (Hocus Pocus Hotel Ser.). (ENG.). 112p. (J). (gr. 3-6). lib. bdg. 25.32 *(978-1-4342-4038-5(X)*, 118479, Stone Arch Bks.) Capstone.

—The Return of Abracadabra. Weber, Lisa K., illus. 2015. (Hocus Pocus Hotel Ser.). (ENG.). 208p. (J). (gr. 3-6). pap., pap. 7.95 *(978-1-4965-2486-7(1)*, 130343, Stone Arch Bks.) Capstone.

—The Ruby Raven. 2008. (Finnegan Zwake Ser.: 3). (ENG.). 192p. (YA). (gr. 7). pap. 9.99 *(978-1-4169-8666-9(9)*, Simon Pulse) Simon Pulse.

—The Thirteenth Mystery. Weber, Lisa K., illus. 2016. (Hocus Pocus Hotel Ser.). (ENG.). 224p. (J). (gr. 3-6). pap., pap. 7.95 *(978-1-4965-0755-6(X)*, 128800, Stone Arch Bks.) Capstone.

—The Viking Claw. 2011. (Finnegan Zwake Ser.: 4). (ENG.). 192p. (YA). (gr. 7). pap. 9.99 *(978-1-4424-3101-0(6)*, Simon Pulse) Simon Pulse.

—The Worm Tunnel. 2008. (Finnegan Zwake Ser.: 2). (ENG., Illus.). 176p. (YA). (gr. 7). pap. 9.99 *(978-1-4169-8667-6(7)*, Simon Pulse) Simon Pulse.

Dale, Elizabeth. The Detective Club. O'Neill, Kelly, illus. 2021. (Early Bird Readers — Gold (Early Bird Stories (tm)) Ser.). (ENG.). 32p. (J). (gr. k-3). 30.65 *(978-1-5415-9008-3(2)*, 3a2c3181-610a-499d-9829-1965afcab114, Lerner Pubns.) Lerner Publishing Group.

Dalton, Andrew & Boatfield, Jonny. The Lost People of Malplaquet. 2007. (Malplaquet Trilogy Ser.). (ENG., Illus.). (C). (gr. 4-7). 180p. 34.00 *(978-0-7188-3049-6(0))*; 176p. per. 17.00 *(978-0-7188-3050-2(4))* Lutherworth Pr., The GBR. Dist: ISD.

Daly, Joseph M. Strange Town Volume One: The Woods Behind Trevor Malone's House. 2007. 265p. (YA). pap. 9.99 net. *(978-0-9779921-0-2(1))* Wolfs Corner Publishing.

Damico, Gina. Wax. 2016. (ENG.). 368p. (YA). (gr. 7). 17.99 *(978-0-544-63315-5(6)*, 1619758, Clarion Bks.) HarperCollins Pubs.

Dandridge, Gwen. The Stone Lions. 2013. 230p. pap. 10.99 *(978-0-9893157-8-4(9))* Hickory Tree Publishing.

Daneshvari, Gitty. School of Fear: Class Is Not Dismissed! 2011. (School of Fear Ser.: 2). (ENG.). 336p. (J). (gr. 3-7). pap. 17.99 *(978-0-316-03329-9(4))* Little, Brown Bks. for Young Readers.

Daniels, W. J. The Empress Academy: The Secret of Glittershine. 2009. 144p. pap. 16.95 *(978-1-4327-2335-4(9))* Outskirts Pr., Inc.

Davidson, Michele R. Stowaways to Smith Island: Hayden & Chloe's Enchanted Journey with the Nurses to Maryland's Mysterious Smith Island. Watjen, Laureen, illus. 2004. 128p. (J). pap. 8.95 *(978-0-9754170-1-0(0))* Smith Island Foundation.

Davies, Jacqueline. The Bell Bandit. (Lemonade War Ser.: 3). (ENG., Illus.). 192p. (J). (gr. 3-7). 2022. pap. 9.99 *(978-0-544-02274-4(2)*, 1528495) 2012. 18.99 *(978-0-547-56737-2(5)*, 1455332) HarperCollins Pubs. (Clarion Bks.).

—The Bell Bandit. 2013. (Lemonade War Ser.: 3). lib. bdg. 18.40 *(978-0-606-31669-9(8))* Turtleback.

Davies, Nicola. Escape from Silver Street Farm. McEwen, Katharine, illus. 2013. (Silver Street Farm Ser.). (ENG.). 80p. (J). (gr. 2-5). 12.99 *(978-0-7636-6133-5(3))* Candlewick Pr.

Davis, Christy. Newshounds. 2010. 156p. pap. 12.50 *(978-1-4389-7869-7(3))* AuthorHouse.

Davis, Tim, illus. The Case of the Purple Diamonds. 2011. 88p. pap. 9.95 *(978-1-934606-07-0(3))* TAG Publishing, LLC.

Dawn, Sasha. Blink. 2018. (ENG.). 344p. (YA). (gr. 8-12). 17.99 *(978-1-5124-3977-9(0)*, df9a5d50-6f73-45f3-8467-9620d5e1b05f, Carolrhoda Lab™) Lerner Publishing Group.

De Campi, Alex. Kat & Mouse Vol. 1: Teacher Torture, 1 vol. Manfredi, Federica, illus. 2008. (Tokyopop Ser.). (ENG.). 96p. (J). (gr. 2-6). 32.79 *(978-1-59961-564-6(9)*, 14807, Graphic Novels) Spotlight.

—Kat & Mouse Vol. 2: Tripped, 1 vol. Manfredi, Federica, illus. 2008. (Tokyopop Ser.). (ENG.). 96p. (J). (gr. 2-6). 32.79 *(978-1-59961-565-3(7)*, 14808, Graphic Novels) Spotlight.

De felice, Cynthia. Devil's Bridge. 2008. (ENG.). 96p. (YA). (gr. 7). pap. 9.99 *(978-1-4169-8307-1(4)*, Atheneum Bks. for Young Readers) Simon & Schuster Children's Publishing.

de Groot, Bob. Clifton Vol. 6: Kidnapping. 2009. (Clifton Ser.: 6). (Illus.). 48p. (J). (gr. 3-17). pap. 11.95 *(978-1-905460-87-8(2))* CineBook GBR. Dist: National Bk. Network.

de los Santos, Marisa. Saving Lucas Biggs. 2015. (ENG.). 320p. (J). (gr. 3-7). pap. 7.99 *(978-0-06-227463-2(5)*, HarperCollins) HarperCollins Pubs.

DeAnda, Diane. The Monster in the Mattress & Other Stories: El Monstruo en el Colchón y Otros Cuentos. 2011. (SPA & ENG., Illus.). 90p. (J). (gr. 3-7). pap. 9.95 *(978-1-55885-693-6(5)*, Piñata Books) Arte Publico Pr.

DeArville, J. It's Kambri Time! 2007. 28p. per. 9.95 *(978-1-4327-0812-2(0))* Outskirts Pr., Inc.

Death at the Border. 64p. (YA). (gr. 6-12). pap. *(978-0-8224-2361-4(8))* Globe Fearon Educational Publishing.

Deathman Don't Follow Me. 2003. (J). pap. 2.95 *(978-0-590-44006-6(3))* Scholastic, Inc.

Deborah Strandberg, Rebecca Reynolds and. Trammler Triplet Tales #2 - HIDDEN in TIME. 2007. 116p. pap. 8.94 *(978-1-4303-2097-5(4))* Lulu Pr., Inc.

—Trammler Triplet Tales Advente #4 MYSTERIOUS ABBY. 2007. (ENG.). 113p. pap. 8.90 *(978-1-4357-0651-4(X))* Lulu Pr., Inc.

DeDonato, Rick. Pipsie, Nature Detective: the Lunchnapper, 0 vols. Bishop, Tracy, illus. 2016. (Pipsie, Nature Detective Ser.). (ENG.). 40p. (J). (gr. -1-2). 17.99 *(978-1-5039-5061-0(1)*, 9781503950610, Two Lions) Amazon Publishing.

DeFelice, Cynthia. The Ghost & Mrs. Hobbs. 2010. (Ghost Mysteries Ser.: 2). (ENG.). 208p. (J). (gr. 3-7). pap. 14.99 *(978-0-312-62909-0(5)*, 900066873) Square Fish.

—The Ghost of Cutler Creek. 2011. (Ghost Mysteries Ser.: 3). (ENG.). 208p. (J). (gr. 3-7). pap. 14.99 *(978-0-312-62967-0(2)*, 900066886) Square Fish.

Defelice, Cynthia. The Light on Hogback Hill. 2008. (ENG.). 128p. (J). (gr. 3-7). pap. 7.99 *(978-1-4169-8691-1(X)*, Simon & Schuster/Paula Wiseman Bks.) Simon & Schuster/Paula Wiseman Bks.

DeFelice, Cynthia. The Missing Manatee: A Mystery about Fishing & Family. 2008. (ENG.). 192p. (J). (gr. 3-7). pap. 11.99 *(978-0-374-40020-0(2)*, 900050873) Square Fish.

DeFelice, Cynthia C. The Ghost of Cutler Creek. 2006. (Ghost Mysteries Ser.). 181p. (J). (gr. 3-7). 13.60 *(978-0-7569-8185-3(9))* Perfection Learning Corp.

—The Missing Manatee. 2005. (ENG.). 192p. (J). (gr. 4-6). 22.44 *(978-0-374-31257-2(5)*, Farrar, Straus & Giroux) Farrar, Straus & Giroux.

Defreitas, Henrietta. Henratty Mortimer: The Meerville Myth. 2011. (Illus.). 88p. pap. 28.14 *(978-1-4520-8237-0(5))* AuthorHouse.

Degrado, Louis Paul. The Questors' Adventures: The Round House & the Moaning Walls. 2012. 326p. 29.95 *(978-1-4759-4469-3(1))*; pap. 19.95 *(978-1-4759-4470-9(5))* iUniverse, Inc.

Deiss, A. The Sullivan Girls & the Mystery of Moonhouse. 2003. 104p. (Orig.). pap. 9.95 *(978-0-595-29580-7(0))* iUniverse, Inc.

Dekker, James C. Scum, 1 vol. 2008. (Orca Soundings Ser.). (ENG.). 112p. (YA). (gr. 8-12). pap. 9.95 *(978-1-55143-924-2(7))* Orca Bk. Pubs. USA.

Delashmit, Margaret V. Thief! 2012. 148p. (gr. 4-6). pap. 12.99 *(978-1-4624-0348-6(4)*, Inspiring Voices) Author Solutions, LLC.

De'Leon, Lunden. Oops Loops. 2006. 28p. pap. 9.95 *(978-1-4327-0114-7(2))* Outskirts Pr., Inc.

DeMeulemeester, Linda. The Forgotten Secret. 2016. (Grim Hill Ser.). (ENG.). 192p. (J). (gr. 4-7). pap. 12.95 *(978-1-77203-100-3(3)*, Wandering Fox) Heritage Hse. CAN. Dist: Orca Bk. Pubs. USA.

Deming, Lynette. Day in Matthews Shoes. 2006. 28p. pap. 9.95 *(978-1-4327-0100-0(2))* Outskirts Pr., Inc.

DeMitchell, Terri A. You Will Come Back - the First in the Olde Locke Beach Mysteries. 2004. (ENG., Illus.). 176p. 14.95 *(978-1-932278-02-6(8))* Mayhaven Publishing, Inc.

Denton, Shannon Eric & Warner, Gertrude Chandler. The Boxcar Children, 1 vol. Dubisch, Michael, illus. 2009. (Boxcar Children Graphic Novels Ser.). (ENG.). 32p. (J). (gr. 3-8). lib. bdg. 32.79 *(978-1-60270-586-9(0)*, 3669, Graphic Planet - Fiction) Magic Wagon.

Dernavich, Drew. Elvin Link, Please Report to the Principal's Office! Dernavich, Drew, illus. 2021. (ENG., Illus.). 224p. (J). pap. 7.99 *(978-1-250-79170-2(7)*, 900238557) Square Fish.

Derting, Kimberly. The Last Echo: A Body Finder Novel, 3. 2013. (Body Finder Ser.: 3). (ENG.). 384p. (YA). (gr. 9-12). pap. 10.99 *(978-0-06-208220-6(5)*, HarperCollins) HarperCollins Pubs.

DeSio, Delores . Up a Tree with Mary Mcphee: A Mystery for Children. 2006. 86p. pap. 16.95 *(978-1-4241-4309-2(8))* PublishAmerica, Inc.

Deutsch, Stacia. The Hole Nine Yards. Boyden, Robin, illus. 2017. (Mysterious Makers of Shaker Street Ser.). (ENG.). 112p. (J). (gr. 2-4). pap. 6.95 *(978-1-4965-4683-8(0)*, 135213); lib. bdg. 22.65 *(978-1-4965-4679-1(2)*, 135204) Capstone. (Stone Arch Bks.).

—A Picture's Worth a Thousand Clues. Boyden, Robin, illus. 2017. (Mysterious Makers of Shaker Street Ser.). (ENG.). 112p. (J). (gr. 2-4). pap. 6.95 *(978-1-4965-4681-4(4)*, 135210); lib. bdg. 22.65 *(978-1-4965-4677-7(6)*, 135202) Capstone. (Stone Arch Bks.).

—Sounds Like Trouble. Boyden, Robin, illus. 2017. (Mysterious Makers of Shaker Street Ser.). (ENG.). 112p. (J). (gr. 2-4). pap. 6.95 *(978-1-4965-4680-7(6)*, 135211); lib. bdg. 22.65 *(978-1-4965-4676-0(8)*, 135201) Capstone. (Stone Arch Bks.).

—That's the Spirit! Boyden, Robin, illus. 2017. (Mysterious Makers of Shaker Street Ser.). (ENG.). 112p. (J). (gr. 2-4). pap. 6.95 *(978-1-4965-4682-1(2)*, 135212); lib. bdg. 22.65 *(978-1-4965-4678-4(4)*, 135203) Capstone. (Stone Arch Bks.).

Devine, Eric. Look Past. 2016. (ENG.). 288p. (YA). (gr. 8-17). 17.99 *(978-0-7624-5921-6(2)*, Running Pr. Kids) Running Pr.

Devine, Ginger. The Missing Goose Egg: A Sam the Lamb Mystery. 2009. 32p. pap. 14.95 *(978-1-4389-8839-9(7))* AuthorHouse.

Devlin Affair. 64p. (YA). (gr. 6-12). pap. *(978-0-8224-2362-1(6))* Globe Fearon Educational Publishing.

Devlin, Wende. Cranberry Halloween. Devlin, Harry, illus. 2013. (Cranberryport Ser.). (ENG.). (J). (gr. -1-3). 18.95 *(978-1-930900-69-1(4))* Purple Hse. Pr.

Diamond, Jill. Lou Lou & Pea & the Mural Mystery. Vamos, Lesley, illus. 2018. (Lou Lou & Pea Ser.). (ENG.). 288p. (J). pap. 10.99 *(978-1-250-14373-0(X)*, 900180548) Square Fish.

The Diamond of Doom, 6 vols. (Woodland Mysteriestm Ser.). 133p. (gr. 3-7). 42.50 *(978-0-7802-7927-8(1))* Wright Group/McGraw-Hill.

Diaz, Enrique Perez. Los Pelusos, Cuentos Policiacos. Martinez, Enrique, illus. 2003. (SPA.). 95p. (J). (gr. 3-5). pap. 8.95 *(978-968-19-1018-1(4))* Santillana USA Publishing Co., Inc.

Dickens, Charles. Great Expectations: And Related Readings. 2006. (McDougal Littell Literature Connections Ser.). (ENG., Illus.). 704p. (gr. 10-10). lib. bdg. 18.50 *(978-0-395-87484-4(X)*, 2-70843) Great Source Education Group, Inc.

Dickey, Janet. Anyone's Guess Jr: Who's a Fraidy Kat? 2003. 39.95 *(978-1-57950-093-1(5)*, Upstart Bks.) Highsmith Inc.

Dickson, Diane. 3 Things That Might Have Happened. 2010. 100p. pap. 15.50 *(978-1-4452-3414-4(9))* Lulu Pr., Inc.

Dickson, Robert. Sam Ferret Mysteries. 2010. 88p. pap. 14.95 *(978-1-4259-2741-7(6))* AuthorHouse.

Dillon, Eilis. The Island of Horses. 2018. (ENG.). 224p. (J). (gr. 4-7). pap. 11.99 *(978-1-68137-306-5(8)*, NYRB Kids) New York Review of Bks., Inc., The.

Dillon, Kimberly M. The Ghosts of Wolf Creek. 2008. 73p. pap. 19.95 *(978-1-60563-996-3(6))* America Star Bks.

Dionne, Erin. Moxie & the Art of Rule Breaking: A 14 Day Mystery. 2014. (14 Day Mystery Ser.). (ENG.). 288p. (J). (gr. 5). pap. 7.99 *(978-0-14-242614-2(8)*, Puffin Books) Penguin Young Readers Group.

DiOrio, Ariel, illus. The Mystery of the Missing Menorahs: A Hanukkah Humdinger! 2007. 52p. (J). pap. 9.95 *(978-0-9659546-4-8(1))* Oak Leaf Systems.

DiTocco, Robyn & DiTocco, Tony. Atlas' Revenge: Another Mad Myth Mystery. 2005. 234p. 19.95 *(978-0-9723429-2-6(3))*; pap. 11.95 *(978-0-9723429-3-3(1))* Brainstorm Pubns., Inc.

Dittman, Jeffery. Jungle Heroes. 2013. 36p. pap. 15.95 *(978-1-4327-9935-9(5))* Outskirts Pr., Inc.

Diver, Lucienne. Faultlines. 2016. (ENG., Illus.). 254p. (YA). (gr. 7-12). pap. 14.95 *(978-1-62268-100-6(2))* Bella Rosa Bks.

Dixon, Franklin. Burned. 2005. 154p. (J). lib. bdg. 16.92 *(978-1-4242-0391-8(0))* Fitzgerald Bks.

—Camping Chaos. 2014. (Hardy Boys: Secret Files Ser.: 16). lib. bdg. 16.00 *(978-0-606-36100-2(6))* Turtleback.

—A con Artist in Paris. 2017. (Hardy Boys Adventures Ser.: 15). (ENG.). 128p. (J). (gr. 3-7). 17.99 *(978-1-4814-9007-8(9)*, Aladdin) Simon & Schuster Children's Publishing.

—A con Artist in Paris. 2017. 122p. (J). *(978-1-5379-7447-7(5)*, Simon & Schuster/Paula Wiseman Bks.) Simon & Schuster/Paula Wiseman Bks.

—The Dangerous Transmission. 2005. (Hardy Boys II Ser.: No. 184). 147p. (J). lib. bdg. 15.00 *(978-1-59054-850-9(7))* Fitzgerald Bks.

—Farming Fear. 2005. (Hardy Boys II Ser.: No. 188). 154p. (J). lib. bdg. 15.00 *(978-1-59054-839-4(6))* Fitzgerald Bks.

—Fossil Frenzy. 2014. (Hardy Boys: Secret Files Ser.: 14). lib. bdg. 16.00 *(978-0-606-35434-9(4))* Turtleback.

—The Great Pumpkin Smash. Gutierrez, Santy, illus. 2019. (Hardy Boys Clue Book Ser.: 10). (ENG.). 96p. (J). (gr. 1-4). pap. 5.99 *(978-1-5344-3123-2(3)*, Simon & Schuster/Paula Wiseman Bks.) Simon & Schuster/Paula Wiseman Bks.

—In Plane Sight. 2005. (Hardy Boys I Ser.: No. 176). 148p. (J). lib. bdg. 15.00 *(978-1-59054-842-4(6))* Fitzgerald Bks.

—Kickoff to Danger. 2005. (Hardy Boys I Ser.: No. 170). 149p. (J). lib. bdg. 15.00 *(978-1-59054-843-1(4))* Fitzgerald Bks.

—Line of Fire. (Illus.). (J). mass mkt. 2.95 *(978-0-671-70492-6(3)*, Simon Pulse) Simon Pulse.

—Motocross Madness. 2005. (Hardy Boys II Ser.: No. 190). 154p. (J). lib. bdg. 15.00 *(978-1-59054-844-8(2))* Fitzgerald Bks.

—The Mystery of the Black Rhino. 2005. (Hardy Boys I Ser.: No. 178). 151p. (J). lib. bdg. 15.00 *(978-1-59054-851-6(5))* Fitzgerald Bks.

—No Way Out. 2005. (Hardy Boys II Ser.: No. 187). 149p. (J). lib. bdg. 15.00 *(978-1-59054-845-5(0))* Fitzgerald Bks.

—One False Step. 2005. (Hardy Boys II Ser.: No. 189). 150p. (J). lib. bdg. 15.00 *(978-1-59054-846-2(9))* Fitzgerald Bks.

—Passport to Danger. 2005. (Hardy Boys I Ser.: No. 179). 147p. (J). lib. bdg. 15.00 *(978-1-59054-847-9(7))* Fitzgerald Bks.

—The Race Is On. 2015. (Hardy Boys: Secret Files Ser.: 19). lib. bdg. 16.00 *(978-0-606-37840-6(5))* Turtleback.

—Running on Fumes. 2005. 150p. (J). lib. bdg. 16.92 *(978-1-4242-0384-0(8))* Fitzgerald Bks.

—The Secret of the Soldier's Gold. 2005. (Hardy Boys II Ser.: No. 182). 147p. (J). lib. bdg. 15.00 *(978-1-59054-852-3(3))* Fitzgerald Bks.

—Ship of Secrets. 2014. (Hardy Boys: Secret Files Ser.: 15). lib. bdg. 14.75 *(978-0-606-35781-4(5))* Turtleback.

—Skin & Bones. 2005. (Hardy Boys I Ser.: No. 164). 148p. (J). lib. bdg. 15.00 *(978-1-59054-848-6(5))* Fitzgerald Bks.

—Speed Times Five. 2005. (Hardy Boys I Ser.: No. 173). 150p. (J). lib. bdg. 15.00 *(978-1-59054-849-3(3))* Fitzgerald Bks.

—Stolen Identity. 2018. (Hardy Boys Adventures Ser.: 16). (ENG.). 144p. (J). (gr. 3-7). 17.99 *(978-1-4814-9967-5(X)*, Aladdin) Simon & Schuster Children's Publishing.

—Talent Show Tricks. David, Matt, illus. 2016. (Hardy Boys Clue Book Ser.: 4). (ENG.). 96p. (J). (gr. 1-4). 16.99 *(978-1-4814-5181-9(2)*, Simon & Schuster/Paula Wiseman Bks.) Simon & Schuster/Paula Wiseman Bks.

—Top Ten Ways to Die. 2006. 169p. (J). lib. bdg. 16.92 *(978-1-4242-0390-1(2))* Fitzgerald Bks.

—Training for Trouble. 2005. (Hardy Boys I Ser.: No. 161). 147p. (J). lib. bdg. 15.00 *(978-1-59054-853-0(1))* Fitzgerald Bks.

—Trick-or-Trouble. 2005. (Hardy Boys I Ser.: No. 175). 154p. (J). lib. bdg. 15.00 *(978-1-59054-854-7(X))* Fitzgerald Bks.

—Trouble in Warp Space. 2005. (Hardy Boys I Ser.: No. 172). 154p. (J). lib. bdg. 15.00 *(978-1-59054-855-4(8))* Fitzgerald Bks.

—The Video Game Bandit. David, Matt, illus. 2016. (Hardy Boys Clue Book Ser.: 1). (ENG.). 96p. (J). (gr. 1-4). 17.99 *(978-1-4814-5053-9(0)*, Aladdin) Simon & Schuster Children's Publishing.

—Warehouse Rumble. 2005. (Hardy Boys II Ser.: No. 183). 152p. (J). lib. bdg. 15.00 *(978-1-59054-858-5(2))* Fitzgerald Bks.

—Water-Ski Wipeout. David, Matt, illus. 2016. (Hardy Boys Clue Book Ser.: 3). (ENG.). 96p. (J). (gr. 1-4). 16.99 *(978-1-4814-5056-0(5)*, Simon & Schuster/Paula Wiseman Bks.) Simon & Schuster/Paula Wiseman Bks.

—Wreck & Roll. 2005. (Hardy Boys II Ser.: No. 185). 153p. (J). lib. bdg. 15.00 *(978-1-59054-859-2(0))* Fitzgerald Bks.

Dixon, Franklin W. Attack of the Bayport Beast. 2017. (Hardy Boys Adventures Ser.: 14). (ENG., Illus.). 112p. (J). (gr. 3-7). pap. 7.99 *(978-1-4814-6834-3(0)*, Simon & Schuster/Paula Wiseman Bks.) Simon & Schuster/Paula Wiseman Bks.

—Balloon Blow-Up. Burroughs, Scott, illus. 2013. (Hardy Boys: the Secret Files Ser.: 13). (ENG.). 112p. (J). (gr. 1-4). pap. 5.99 *(978-1-4424-5371-5(0)*, Aladdin) Simon & Schuster Children's Publishing.

—The Battle of Bayport. 2014. (Hardy Boys Adventures Ser.: 6). (ENG., Illus.). 160p. (J). (gr. 3-7). pap. 6.99 *(978-1-4814-0006-0(1)*, Aladdin) Simon & Schuster Children's Publishing.

—Bayport Buccaneers. 16th ed. 2007. (Hardy Boys (All New) Undercover Brothers Ser.: 16). (ENG., Illus.). 176p. (J). (gr. 3-7). pap. 5.99 *(978-1-4169-3403-5(0)*, Aladdin) Simon & Schuster Children's Publishing.

—The Bicycle Thief. Burroughs, Scott, illus. 2011. (Hardy Boys: the Secret Files Ser.: 6). (ENG.). 96p. (J). (gr. 1-4). pap. 5.99 *(978-1-4169-9396-4(7)*, Aladdin) Simon & Schuster Children's Publishing.

—Blown Away. 10th ed. 2006. (Hardy Boys (All New) Undercover Brothers Ser.: 10). (ENG., Illus.). 160p. (J). (gr. 3-7). pap. 7.99 *(978-1-4169-1173-9(1)*, Aladdin) Simon & Schuster Children's Publishing.

—Boardwalk Bust, Vol. 3. 3rd ed. 2005. (Hardy Boys (All New) Undercover Brothers Ser.: 3). (ENG.). 176p. (J). (gr. 3-7). pap. 7.99 *(978-1-4169-0004-7(7)*, Aladdin) Simon & Schuster Children's Publishing.

—Bound for Danger. 2016. (Hardy Boys Adventures Ser.: 13). (ENG., Illus.). 144p. (J). (gr. 3-7). pap. 6.99 *(978-1-4814-6831-2(6)*, Aladdin) Simon & Schuster Children's Publishing.

—Bound for Danger. 2016. (Hardy Boys Adventures Ser.: 13). (ENG., Illus.). 144p. (J). (gr. 3-7). 17.99 *(978-1-4814-6832-9(4)*, Simon & Schuster/Paula Wiseman Bks.) Simon & Schuster/Paula Wiseman Bks.

—Burned, 6. 6th ed. 2005. (Hardy Boys (All New) Undercover Brothers Ser.: 6). (ENG., Illus.). 160p. (J). (gr. 3-7). pap. 5.99 *(978-1-4169-0008-5(X))* Simon & Schuster, Inc.

—The Children of the Lost: Book One in the Lost Mystery Trilogy, Bk. 1. 2010. (Hardy Boys (All New) Undercover Brothers Ser.: 34). (ENG.). 192p. (J). (gr. 3-7). pap. 5.99 *(978-1-4424-0262-1(8)*, Aladdin) Simon & Schuster Children's Publishing.

—Comic con Artist. 21st ed. 2008. (Hardy Boys (All New) Undercover Brothers Ser.: 21). (ENG., Illus.). 192p. (J). (gr. 3-7). pap. 6.99 *(978-1-4169-5498-9(8)*, Aladdin) Simon & Schuster Children's Publishing.

—A con Artist in Paris. 2017. (Hardy Boys Adventures Ser.: 15). (ENG.). 128p. (J). (gr. 3-7). pap. 7.99 *(978-1-4814-9006-1(0)*, Aladdin) Simon & Schuster Children's Publishing.

—The Curse of the Ancient Emerald. 2015. (Hardy Boys Adventures Ser.: 9). (ENG., Illus.). 128p. (J). (gr. 3-7). pap. 6.99 *(978-1-4814-2475-2(0)*, Aladdin) Simon & Schuster Children's Publishing.

—Death & Diamonds. 15th ed. 2007. (Hardy Boys (All New) Undercover Brothers Ser.: 15). (ENG., Illus.). 176p. (J). (gr. 3-7). pap. 5.99 *(978-1-4169-3402-8(2)*, Aladdin) Simon & Schuster Children's Publishing.

—Deception on the Set. 2015. (Hardy Boys Adventures Ser.: 8). (ENG., Illus.). 128p. (J). (gr. 3-7). pap. 6.99 *(978-1-4814-1406-7(2)*, Aladdin) Simon & Schuster Children's Publishing.

—The Disappearance. 2019. (Hardy Boys Adventures Ser.: 18). (ENG.). 160p. (J). (gr. 3-7). 17.99 *(978-1-5344-1489-1(4))*; (Illus.). pap. 7.99 *(978-1-5344-1488-4(6))* Simon & Schuster Children's Publishing. (Aladdin).

—Double Deception: Book Three in the Double Danger Trilogy, 27. 2009. (Hardy Boys (All New) Undercover Brothers Ser.: 27). (ENG.). 176p. (J). (gr. 3-7). pap. 6.99 *(978-1-4169-6766-8(4))* Simon & Schuster, Inc.

—Double Down: Book Two in the Double Danger Trilogy, 26. 26th ed. 2008. (Hardy Boys (All New) Undercover Brothers Ser.: 26). (ENG.). 172p. (J). (gr. 3-7). pap. 7.99 *(978-1-4169-7446-8(6))* Simon & Schuster, Inc.

—Double Trouble: Book One in the Double Danger Trilogy. 25th ed. 2008. (Hardy Boys (All New) Undercover Brothers Ser.: 25). (ENG.). 176p. (J). (gr. 3-7). pap. 7.99 *(978-1-4169-6765-1(6)*, Aladdin) Simon & Schuster Children's Publishing.

—Dungeons & Detectives. 2019. (Hardy Boys Adventures Ser.: 19). (ENG., Illus.). 208p. (J). (gr. 3-7). pap. 6.99 *(978-1-5344-2105-9(X)*, Simon & Schuster/Paula Wiseman Bks.) Simon & Schuster/Paula Wiseman Bks.

—Extreme Danger. 2005. (Hardy Boys (All New) Undercover Brothers Ser.: 1). (ENG.). 176p. (J). (gr. 3-7). pap. 7.99 *(978-1-4169-0002-3(0)*, Aladdin) Simon & Schuster Children's Publishing.

—Feeding Frenzy. 20th ed. 2008. (Hardy Boys (All New) Undercover Brothers Ser.: 20). (ENG., Illus.). 160p. (J). (gr. 3-7). pap. 6.99 *(978-1-4169-5499-6(6)*, Aladdin) Simon & Schuster Children's Publishing.

—Forever Lost: Book Three in the Lost Mystery Trilogy. 2011. (Hardy Boys (All New) Undercover Brothers Ser.: 36). (ENG.). 160p. (J). (gr. 3-7). pap. 6.99 *(978-1-4424-0264-5(4)*, Aladdin) Simon & Schuster Children's Publishing.

—Foul Play. 19th ed. 2007. (Hardy Boys (All New) Undercover Brothers Ser.: 19). (ENG., Illus.). 192p. (J). (gr. 3-7). pap. 6.99 *(978-1-4169-4977-0(1)*, Aladdin) Simon & Schuster Children's Publishing.

—The Gray Hunter's Revenge. 2018. (Hardy Boys Adventures Ser.: 17). (ENG.). 144p. (J). (gr. 3-7). (Illus.). 17.99 *(978-1-5344-1151-7(8))*; pap. 6.99 *(978-1-5344-1150-0(X))* Simon & Schuster Children's Publishing. (Aladdin).

—The Great Coaster Caper. Burroughs, Scott, illus. 2012. (Hardy Boys: the Secret Files Ser.: 9). (ENG.). 112p. (J). (gr. 1-4). pap. 5.99 *(978-1-4424-1669-7(6)*, Aladdin) Simon & Schuster Children's Publishing.

—The Great Escape. Burroughs, Scott, illus. 2015. (Hardy Boys: the Secret Files Ser.: 17). (ENG.). 112p. (J). (gr. 1-4). pap. 5.99 *(978-1-4814-2267-3(7)*, Aladdin) Simon & Schuster Children's Publishing.

—The Hardy Boys Secret Files Collection Books 1-5 (Boxed Set) Trouble at the Arcade; the Missing Mitt; Mystery Map; Hopping Mad; a Monster of a Mystery. Burroughs, Scott, illus. 2014. (Hardy Boys: the Secret Files Ser.). (ENG.). 496p. (J). (gr. 1-4). pap. 29.99 *(978-1-4814-1473-9(9)*, Aladdin) Simon & Schuster Children's Publishing.

—Haunted. 2008. (Hardy Boys Undercover Brothers: Super Mystery Ser.). (ENG., Illus.). 192p. (J). (gr. 3-7). pap. 6.99 *(978-1-4169-6169-7(0)*, Aladdin) Simon & Schuster Children's Publishing.

—Hazed. 14th ed. 2007. (Hardy Boys (All New) Undercover Brothers Ser.: 14). (ENG., Illus.). 160p. (J). (gr. 3-7). pap. 6.99 *(978-1-4169-1803-5(5)*, Aladdin) Simon & Schuster Children's Publishing.

—House Arrest: Book Two in the Murder House Trilogy, 23. 23rd ed. 2008. (Hardy Boys (All New) Undercover Brothers Ser.: 23). (ENG., Illus.). 176p. (J). (gr. 3-7). pap. 5.99 *(978-1-4169-6171-0(2))* Simon & Schuster, Inc.

—The House on the Cliff #2, Bk. 2. 2016. (Hardy Boys Ser.: 2). (Illus.). 192p. (J). (gr. 3-7). 10.99 *(978-0-448-48953-7(8)*, Grosset & Dunlap) Penguin Young Readers Group.

—Hurricane Joe. 11th ed. 2006. (Hardy Boys (All New) Undercover Brothers Ser.: 11). (ENG., Illus.). 160p. (J). (gr. 3-7). pap. 6.99 *(978-1-4169-1174-6(X)*, Aladdin) Simon & Schuster Children's Publishing.

—Into Thin Air. 2013. (Hardy Boys Adventures Ser.: 4). (ENG., Illus.). 128p. (J). (gr. 3-7). 17.99 *(978-1-4424-7345-4(2))*; pap. 7.99 *(978-1-4424-5983-0(2))* Simon & Schuster Children's Publishing. (Aladdin).

—Kidnapped at the Casino. 2007. (Hardy Boys Undercover Brothers: Super Mystery Ser.: 2). (ENG., Illus.). 240p. (J). (gr. 3-7). pap. 5.99 *(978-1-4169-3923-8(7)*, Aladdin) Simon & Schuster Children's Publishing.

—Killer Mission: Book One in the Killer Mystery Trilogy. 2009. (Hardy Boys (All New) Undercover Brothers Ser.: 31). (ENG.). 192p. (J). (gr. 3-7). pap. 6.99 *(978-1-4169-8695-9(2)*, Aladdin) Simon & Schuster Children's Publishing.

—Lights, Camera ... Zombies! Burroughs, Scott, illus. 2013. (Hardy Boys: the Secret Files Ser.: 12). (ENG.). 96p. (J). (gr. 1-4). pap. 5.99 *(978-1-4424-5369-2(9)*, Aladdin) Simon & Schuster Children's Publishing.

—Lost Brother: Book Two in the Lost Mystery Trilogy. 2010. (Hardy Boys (All New) Undercover Brothers Ser.: 35). (ENG.). 160p. (J). (gr. 3-7). pap. 6.99 *(978-1-4424-0256-0(3)*, Aladdin) Simon & Schuster Children's Publishing.

—The Madman of Black Bear Mountain. 2016. (Hardy Boys Adventures Ser.: 12). (ENG., Illus.). 144p. (J). (gr. 3-7). pap. 6.99 *(978-1-4814-3880-3(8)*, Aladdin) Simon & Schuster Children's Publishing.

—The Missing Chums #4. 2016. (Hardy Boys Ser.: 4). (Illus.). 192p. (J). (gr. 3-7). 8.99 *(978-0-448-48955-1(4)*, Grosset & Dunlap) Penguin Young Readers Group.

—The Missing Mitt. Burroughs, Scott, illus. 2010. (Hardy Boys: the Secret Files Ser.: 2). (ENG.). 112p. (J). (gr. 1-4). pap. 5.99 *(978-1-4169-9394-0(0)*, Aladdin) Simon & Schuster Children's Publishing.

—The Missing Playbook. David, Matt, illus. 2016. (Hardy Boys Clue Book Ser.: 2). (ENG.). 96p. (J). (gr. 1-4). pap. 5.99 *(978-1-4814-5177-2(4)*, Aladdin) Simon & Schuster Children's Publishing.

—A Monster of a Mystery. Burroughs, Scott, illus. 2011. (Hardy Boys: the Secret Files Ser.: 5). (ENG.). 96p. (J). (gr. 1-4). pap. 5.99 *(978-1-4169-9166-3(2)*, Aladdin) Simon & Schuster Children's Publishing.

—Movie Mayhem: Book Three in the Deathstalker Trilogy. 2012. (Hardy Boys (All New) Undercover Brothers Ser.: 39). (ENG.). 176p. (J). (gr. 3-7). pap. 7.99 *(978-1-4424-0260-7(1)*, Aladdin) Simon & Schuster Children's Publishing.

—Movie Menace: Book One in the Deathstalker Trilogy. 2011. (Hardy Boys (All New) Undercover Brothers Ser.: 37). (ENG.). 176p. (J). (gr. 3-7). pap. 5.99 *(978-1-4424-0258-4(X)*, Aladdin) Simon & Schuster Children's Publishing.

—The Mummy's Curse. 13th ed. 2006. (Hardy Boys (All New) Undercover Brothers Ser.: 13). (ENG., Illus.). 176p. (J). (gr. 3-7). pap. 7.99 *(978-1-4169-1507-2(9)*, Aladdin) Simon & Schuster Children's Publishing.

—Murder at the Mall. 17th ed. 2007. (Hardy Boys (All New) Undercover Brothers Ser.: 17). (ENG., Illus.). 176p. (J). (gr. 3-7). pap. 6.99 *(978-1-4169-3930-6(X)*, Aladdin) Simon & Schuster Children's Publishing.

—Murder House: Book Three in the Murder House Trilogy, Bk. 3. 24th ed. 2008. (Hardy Boys (All New) Undercover Brothers Ser.: 24). (ENG.). 160p. (J). (gr. 3-7). pap. 6.99 *(978-1-4169-6409-4(6)*, Aladdin) Simon & Schuster Children's Publishing.

—Mystery Map, 3. Burroughs, Scott, illus. 2010. (Hardy Boys: the Secret Files Ser.: 3). (ENG.). 96p. (J). (gr. 1-4). pap. 5.99 *(978-1-4169-9165-6(4)*, Aladdin) Simon & Schuster Children's Publishing.

—The Mystery of the Black Rhino. 178th ed. 2003. (Hardy Boys Ser.: 178). (ENG., Illus.). 160p. (J). (gr. 3-7). pap. 6.99 *(978-0-689-85598-6(2)*, Aladdin) Simon & Schuster Children's Publishing.

—Mystery of the Phantom Heist. 2013. (Hardy Boys Adventures Ser.: 2). (ENG.). 160p. (J). (gr. 3-7). 17.99 *(978-1-4424-6586-2(7))*; pap. 7.99 *(978-1-4424-2237-7(8))* Simon & Schuster Children's Publishing. (Aladdin).

—Passport to Danger, Vol. 179. 179th ed. 2003. (Hardy Boys Ser.: 179). (ENG., Illus.). 160p. (J). (gr. 3-7). pap. 5.99 *(978-0-689-85779-9(9)*, Aladdin) Simon & Schuster Children's Publishing.

—Peril at Granite Peak. 2014. (Hardy Boys Adventures Ser.: 5). (ENG., Illus.). 160p. (J). (gr. 3-7). pap. 7.99 *(978-1-4424-9395-7(X)*, Aladdin) Simon & Schuster Children's Publishing.

—Private Killer: Book Two in the Killer Mystery Trilogy, Bk. 2. Frost, Michael, photos by. 2010. (Hardy Boys (All New) Undercover Brothers Ser.: 32). (ENG., Illus.). 160p. (J). (gr. 3-7). pap. 5.99 *(978-1-4169-8697-3(9)*, Aladdin) Simon & Schuster Children's Publishing.

—Pushed. 18th ed. 2007. (Hardy Boys (All New) Undercover Brothers Ser.: 18). (ENG., Illus.). 160p. (J). (gr. 3-7). pap. 7.99 *(978-1-4169-4802-5(3)*, Aladdin) Simon & Schuster Children's Publishing.

—The Race Is On. Burroughs, Scott, illus. 2015. (Hardy Boys: the Secret Files Ser.: 19). (ENG.). 96p. (J). (gr. 1-4). pap. 5.99 *(978-1-4814-2271-0(5)*, Aladdin) Simon & Schuster Children's Publishing.

—Robot Rumble, 11. Burroughs, Scott, illus. 2013. (Hardy Boys: the Secret Files Ser.: 11). (ENG.). 96p. (J). (gr. 1-4). pap. 5.99 *(978-1-4424-5367-8(2)*, Aladdin) Simon & Schuster Children's Publishing.

—A Rockin' Mystery. Burroughs, Scott, illus. 2012. (Hardy Boys: the Secret Files Ser.: 10). (ENG.). 96p. (J). (gr. 1-4). pap. 5.99 *(978-1-4424-1671-0(8)*, Aladdin) Simon & Schuster Children's Publishing.

—Running on Fumes, Vol. 2. 2nd ed. 2005. (Hardy Boys (All New) Undercover Brothers Ser.: 2). (ENG.). 160p. (J). (gr. 3-7). pap. 6.99 *(978-1-4169-0003-0(9)*, Aladdin) Simon & Schuster Children's Publishing.

—Scavenger Hunt Heist. David, Matt, illus. 2017. (Hardy Boys Clue Book Ser.: 5). (ENG.). 96p. (J). (gr. 1-4). pap. 5.99 *(978-1-4814-8516-6(4)*, Simon & Schuster/Paula Wiseman Bks.) Simon & Schuster/Paula Wiseman Bks.

—The Secret of the Caves #7, Bk. 7. 2017. (Hardy Boys Ser.: 7). 192p. (J). (gr. 3-7). 8.99 *(978-0-515-15909-7(3)*, Grosset & Dunlap) Penguin Young Readers Group.

—Secret of the Red Arrow. 2013. (Hardy Boys Adventures Ser.: 1). (ENG.). 176p. (J). (gr. 3-7). 17.99 *(978-1-4424-6585-5(9))*; pap. 7.99 *(978-1-4424-4615-1(3))* Simon & Schuster Children's Publishing. (Aladdin).

—Shadows at Predator Reef. 2014. (Hardy Boys Adventures Ser.: 7). (ENG., Illus.). 128p. (J). (gr. 3-7). pap. 7.99 *(978-1-4814-0009-1(6)*, Aladdin) Simon & Schuster Children's Publishing.

—The Shore Road Mystery #6, Bk. 6. 2017. (Hardy Boys Ser.: 6). (Illus.). 192p. (J). (gr. 3-7). 8.99 *(978-0-515-15908-0(5)*, Grosset & Dunlap) Penguin Young Readers Group.

—Showdown at Widow Creek. 2016. (Hardy Boys Adventures Ser.: 11). (ENG., Illus.). 128p. (J). (gr. 3-7). 17.99 *(978-1-4814-3878-0(6)*, Aladdin) Simon & Schuster Children's Publishing.

—Stolen Identity. 2018. (Hardy Boys Adventures Ser.: 16). (ENG., Illus.). 144p. (J). (gr. 3-7). pap. 6.99 *(978-1-4814-9966-8(1)*, Aladdin) Simon & Schuster Children's Publishing.

—Talent Show Tricks. David, Matt, illus. 2016. (Hardy Boys Clue Book Ser.: 4). (ENG.). 96p. (J). (gr. 1-4). pap. 5.99 *(978-1-4814-5180-2(4)*, Aladdin) Simon & Schuster Children's Publishing.

—The Tower Treasure #1. 2016. (Hardy Boys Ser.: 1). (Illus.). 192p. (J). (gr. 3-7). 9.99 *(978-0-448-48952-0(X)*, Grosset & Dunlap) Penguin Young Readers Group.

—Trouble at the Arcade, 1. Burroughs, Scott, illus. 2010. (Hardy Boys: the Secret Files Ser.: 1). (ENG.). 96p. (J). (gr. 1-4). pap. 5.99 *(978-1-4169-9164-9(6)*, Aladdin) Simon & Schuster Children's Publishing.

—Trouble in Paradise. 12th ed. 2006. (Hardy Boys (All New) Undercover Brothers Ser.: 12). (ENG., Illus.). 176p. (J). (gr. 3-7). pap. 6.99 *(978-1-4169-1178-4(2)*, Aladdin) Simon & Schuster Children's Publishing.

—Tunnel of Secrets. 2015. (Hardy Boys Adventures Ser.: 10). (ENG., Illus.). 144p. (J). (gr. 3-7). pap. 6.99 *(978-1-4814-3874-2(3)*, Aladdin) Simon & Schuster Children's Publishing.

—Typhoon Island, Vol. 180. 2003. (Hardy Boys Ser.: 180). (ENG., Illus.). 160p. (J). (gr. 3-7). pap. 5.99 *(978-0-689-85884-0(1)*, Aladdin) Simon & Schuster Children's Publishing.

—The Vanishing Game. 2013. (Hardy Boys Adventures Ser.: 3). (ENG.). 144p. (J). (gr. 3-7). 17.99 *(978-1-4424-7344-7(4))*; (Illus.). pap. 7.99 *(978-1-4424-5981-6(6))* Simon & Schuster Children's Publishing. (Aladdin).

—The Video Game Bandit. David, Matt, illus. 2016. (Hardy Boys Clue Book Ser.: 1). (ENG.). 96p. (J). (gr. 1-4). pap. 5.99 *(978-1-4814-5052-2(2)*, Aladdin) Simon & Schuster Children's Publishing.

—Wanted. 2006. (Hardy Boys Undercover Brothers: Super Mystery Ser.: 1). (ENG., Illus.). 192p. (J). (gr. 3-7). pap. 7.99 *(978-1-4169-1258-3(4)*, Aladdin) Simon & Schuster Children's Publishing.

—Water-Ski Wipeout. David, Matt, illus. 2016. (Hardy Boys Clue Book Ser.: 3). (ENG.). 96p. (J). (gr. 1-4). pap. 5.99 *(978-1-4814-5055-3(7)*, Aladdin) Simon & Schuster Children's Publishing.

—Who Let the Frogs Out? Gutierrez, Santy, illus. 2019. (Hardy Boys Clue Book Ser.: 9). (ENG.). 96p. (J). (gr. 1-4). pap. 5.99 *(978-1-5344-1485-3(1)*, Simon & Schuster/Paula Wiseman Bks.) Simon & Schuster/Paula Wiseman Bks.

—The X-Factor: Book Three in the Galaxy X Trilogy, 30. 2009. (Hardy Boys (All New) Undercover Brothers Ser.: 30). (ENG.). 176p. (J). (gr. 3-7). pap. 7.99 *(978-1-4169-7802-2(X)*, Aladdin) Simon & Schuster Children's Publishing.

—X-Plosion: Book Two in the Galaxy X Trilogy, 29. 2009. (Hardy Boys (All New) Undercover Brothers Ser.: 29). (ENG.). 160p. (J). (gr. 3-7). pap. 6.99 *(978-1-4169-7870-1(4))* Simon & Schuster, Inc.

Dixon, Franklin W. & Keene, Carolyn. Bonfire Masquerade. 2011. (Nancy Drew/Hardy Boys Ser.: 5). (ENG.). 176p. (J). (gr. 3-7). pap. 6.99 *(978-1-4424-0328-4(4)*, Aladdin) Simon & Schuster Children's Publishing.

d'Lacey, Chris. The Fire Eternal (the Last Dragon Chronicles #4) 2010. (Last Dragon Chronicles Ser.: 4). (ENG.). 512p. (J). (gr. 4-7). 9.99 *(978-0-545-05164-4(9)*, Orchard Bks.) Scholastic, Inc.

Doane, Pelagie. Clue in the Patchwork Quilt #14, No. 14. Doane, Pelagie, illus. 2008. (Judy Bolton Ser.). (ENG., Illus.). 228p. (J). (gr. 4-7). pap. 14.95 *(978-1-4290-9034-6(0))* Applewood Bks.

—Clue in the Ruined Castle, No. 26. Doane, Pelagie, illus. 2008. (Judy Bolton Ser.). (ENG., Illus.). 192p. (gr. 4-7). pap. 14.95 *(978-1-4290-9046-9(4))* Applewood Bks.

—Clue of the Stone Lantern #21, No. 21. Doane, Pelagie, illus. 2008. (Judy Bolton Ser.). (ENG., Illus.). 224p. (J). (gr. 4-7). pap. 14.95 *(978-1-4290-9041-4(3))* Applewood Bks.

—Haunted Attic #2, No. 2. Doane, Pelagie, illus. 2008. (Judy Bolton Ser.). (ENG., Illus.). 240p. (J). (gr. 4-7). pap. 14.95 *(978-1-4290-9022-3(7))* Applewood Bks.

—Haunted Fountain, No. 28. Doane, Pelagie, illus. 2008. (Judy Bolton Ser.). (ENG., Illus.). 196p. (gr. 4-7). pap. 14.95 *(978-1-4290-9048-3(0))* Applewood Bks.

—Invisible Chimes #3, No. 3. Doane, Pelagie, illus. 2008. (Judy Bolton Ser.). (ENG., Illus.). 236p. (J). (gr. 4-7). pap. 14.95 *(978-1-4290-9023-0(5))* Applewood Bks.

—Midnight Visitor #12, No. 12. Doane, Pelagie, illus. 2008. (Judy Bolton Ser.). (ENG.). 264p. (J). (gr. 4-7). pap. 14.95 *(978-1-4290-9032-2(4))* Applewood Bks.

—Mystic Ball #7, No. 7. Doane, Pelagie, illus. 2008. (Judy Bolton Ser.). (ENG., Illus.). 236p. (J). (gr. 4-7). pap. 14.95 *(978-1-4290-9027-8(8))* Applewood Bks.

—Seven Strange Clues #4, No. 4. Doane, Pelagie, illus. 2008. (Judy Bolton Ser.). (ENG., Illus.). 236p. (J). (gr. 4-7). pap. 14.95 *(978-1-4290-9024-7(3))* Applewood Bks.

—Trail of the Green Doll #27, No. 27. Doane, Pelagie, illus. 2008. (Judy Bolton Ser.). (ENG., Illus.). 196p. (gr. 4-7). pap. 14.95 *(978-1-4290-9047-6(2))* Applewood Bks.

—Unfinished House #11, No. 11. Doane, Pelagie, illus. 2008. (Judy Bolton Ser.). (ENG., Illus.). 264p. (J). (gr. 4-7). pap. 14.95 *(978-1-4290-9031-5(6))* Applewood Bks.

—Vanishing Shadow #1, No. 1. Doane, Pelagie, illus. 2008. (Judy Bolton Ser.). (ENG.). 240p. (J). (gr. 4-7). pap. 14.95 *(978-1-4290-9021-6(9))* Applewood Bks.

Dobinson, Tony. The Crossing. 2006. 158p. (YA). (gr. 8-12). per. 10.00 *(978-1-84427-003-3(3))* Send The Light Distribution LLC.

Doerr, Bonnie J. Kenzie's Key. Aberle, Xylena Apotheloz, illus. 2003. 211p. (J). 16.95 *(978-0-9619155-6-8(0))* Laurel & Herbert, Inc.

Dogar, Sharon. Waves. 2007. (ENG.). 327p. (J). (gr. 7-12). 22.44 *(978-0-545-10178-3(6))* Scholastic, Inc.

Dolzer, Krista Van. The Multiplying Mysteries of Mount Ten. 2019. (ENG.). 272p. (J). 16.99 *(978-1-68119-770-8(7)*, 900185876, Bloomsbury Children's Bks.) Bloomsbury Publishing USA.

Dominguez, Elaudy. The Mountain Mystery, 1 vol. 2006. (Neighborhood Readers Ser.). (ENG.). 16p. (gr. 1-2). pap. 6.50 *(978-1-4042-7124-1(4)*, 396bbca4-e713-4eb4-a6d0-c0c146995eab, Rosen Classroom) Rosen Publishing Group, Inc., The.

Donbavand, Tommy. Read on - Cyber Shock. 2014. (Read On Ser.). (ENG., Illus.). 640p. (YA). (gr. 7). 9.99 *(978-0-00-746473-9(8))* HarperCollins Pubs. Ltd. GBR. Dist: Independent Pubs. Group.

Donnell, Annie Hamilton. Four Girls & a Compact. 2005. 76p. pap. 10.95 *(978-1-59540-606-4(9)*, 1st World Library - Literary Society) 1st World Publishing, Inc.

—Four Girls & A Compact. 2005. 26.95 *(978-1-4218-0906-9(0)*, 1st World Library - Literary Society) 1st World Publishing, Inc.

—Four Girls & A Compact. 2004. reprint ed. pap. 15.95 *(978-1-4191-2048-0(4))*; pap. 1.99 *(978-1-4192-2048-7(9))* Kessinger Publishing, LLC.

Dorato, A. P. Arthur, Donna, & the Magic Crown of Tiabora. 2006. pap. 24.95 *(978-1-4137-8898-3(X))* PublishAmerica, Inc.

Doro, Ann. The Missing Canary. l.t. ed. 2005. 93p. 12.95 *(978-0-9745052-2-0(6)*, Peeper & Friends) Tree Of Life Publishing.

MNO

Dorpinghaus, Penny. Fear Balls & Button Wads. 2006. 52p. pap. 16.95 *(978-1-4241-2281-3(3))* PublishAmerica, Inc.
Dowd, Siobhan. The London Eye Mystery. 2009. (ENG.). 336p. (J). (gr. 3-7). 8.99 *(978-0-385-75184-1(2),* Yearling) Random Hse. Children's Bks.
—The London Eye Mystery. 2009. (London Eye Mystery Ser.: 1). lib. bdg. 18.40 *(978-0-606-14413-1(7))* Turtleback.
Dowell, Frances O'Roark. Sam the Man & the Secret Detective Club Plan. Bates, Amy June, illus. 2018. (Sam the Man Ser.: 4). (ENG.). 192p. (J). (gr. 1-4). 16.99 *(978-1-5344-1258-3(1),* Atheneum/Caitlyn Dlouhy Books) Simon & Schuster Children's Publishing.
Dower, Laura. On the Case. 2004. 170p. (J). lib. bdg. 16.92 *(978-1-4242-0648-3(0))* Fitzgerald Bks.
Doyle, Arthur Conan. The Extraordinary Cases of Sherlock Holmes. 2010. (Puffin Classics Ser.). 304p. (J). (gr. 5-7). pap. 8.99 *(978-0-14-133004-4(X),* Puffin Books) Penguin Young Readers Group.
—The Hound of the Baskervilles. 2012. (Puffin Classics Ser.). 262p. (J). (gr. 5). pap. 7.99 *(978-0-14-132939-0(4),* Puffin Books) Penguin Young Readers Group.
—Sherlock Holmes. Love, Mike, illus. 2014. 46p. (J). *(978-1-4351-5822-1(9))* Barnes & Noble, Inc.
—A Study in Scarlet. 2020. (ENG.). (J). (gr. 4-6). 130p. 16.95 *(978-1-61895-797-9(X));* 128p. pap. 9.95 *(978-1-61895-796-2(1))* Bibliotech Pr.
—A Study in Scarlet. 2019. (ENG.). 144p. (J). (gr. 2-3). pap. 9.92 *(978-0-368-71706-2(2))* Blurb, Inc.
—A Study in Scarlet. (ENG.). 128p. (J). 2020. (gr. 4-6). pap. *(978-1-77426-027-2(1))* 2018. (gr. 2-3). pap. *(978-1-989201-31-2(8))* East India Publishing Co.
—A Study in Scarlet. 2019. (ENG.). (J). 90p. (gr. 4-6). pap. 9.99 *(978-1-7080-7089-2(3));* 118p. (gr. 4-6). pap. 15.99 *(978-1-7066-3080-7(8));* 270p. (gr. 4-6). pap. 12.99 *(978-1-6992-5432-5(X));* 430p. (gr. 4-6). pap. 17.99 *(978-1-6971-6365-0(3));* 270p. (gr. 4-6). pap. 12.99 *(978-1-7017-6352-4(4));* 108p. (gr. 4-6). pap. 7.99 *(978-1-6949-0361-7(3));* 250p. (gr. 4-6). pap. 18.99 *(978-1-6938-2841-6(3));* 268p. (gr. 4-6). pap. 16.99 *(978-1-6907-9956-6(0));* 428p. (gr. 4-8). pap. 26.99 *(978-1-0896-6977-7(1));* 268p. (gr. 4-8). pap. 16.99 *(978-1-0898-5479-1(X));* 268p. (gr. 2-3). pap. 19.99 *(978-1-0825-6321-8(8));* 268p. (gr. 2-3). pap. 19.99 *(978-1-0800-8053-3(8));* 244p. (gr. 2-3). pap. 14.99 *(978-1-0795-3080-3(0));* 252p. (gr. 2-3). pap. 14.99 *(978-1-0794-5609-7(0));* 268p. (gr. 2-3). pap. 21.99 *(978-1-0755-4026-4(7));* 108p. (gr. 2-3). pap. 7.99 *(978-1-0749-8357-4(2));* 244p. (gr. 2-3). pap. 18.99 *(978-1-0724-9435-5(3));* 162p. (gr. 2-3). pap. 9.99 *(978-1-0710-7921-8(2));* 428p. (gr. 2-3). pap. 24.99 *(978-1-0772-0458-4(2));* 108p. (gr. 2-3). pap. 7.99 *(978-1-0968-7413-3(X));* 244p. (gr. 2-3). pap. 18.98 *(978-1-0706-2207-1(9));* 254p. (gr. 2-3). pap. 15.99 *(978-1-0988-6658-7(4));* 268p. (gr. 2-3). pap. 16.99 *(978-1-0985-1181-4(6));* 264p. (gr. 2-3). pap. 17.99 *(978-1-0921-4528-2(1))* Independently Published.
—A Study in Scarlet. Blake, Sheba, ed. 2020. (ENG.). 128p. (J). (gr. 4-6). pap. 11.99 *(978-1-222-29323-4(4))* Indy Pub.
—A Study in Scarlet. 2020. (ENG.). 98p. (J). (gr. 4-6). pap. 4.95 *(978-1-68422-459-3(4))* Martino Fine Bks.
—A Study in Scarlet. 2018. (VIE.). (J). (gr. 2-3). pap. *(978-604-960-780-6(X))* Publishing Hse. of Writers's Assn.
Doyle, Arthur Conan, ed. The Hound of the Baskervilles. 2008. (Bring the Classics to Life Ser.). (Illus.). 72p. (gr. 5-12). pap., act. bk. ed. 10.95 *(978-0-931334-67-2(5),* EDCTR-502B) EDCON Publishing Group.
Doyle, Bill. Betrayed! The 1977 Journal of Zeke Moorie. 4th ed. 2006. (Crime Through Time Ser.: 4). (ENG., Illus.). 144p. (J). (gr. 3-7). per. 10.99 *(978-0-316-05741-7(X))* Little, Brown Bks. for Young Readers.
—Trapped! The 2031 Journal of Otis Fitzmorgan. 6th ed. 2006. (Crime Through Time Ser.: 6). (ENG., Illus.). 144p. (J). (gr. 3-7). per. 10.99 *(978-0-316-05754-7(1))* Little, Brown Bks. for Young Readers.
Doyle, Bill H. Swindled! The 1906 Journal of Fitz Morgan. 2006. (Crime Through Time Ser.). (ENG., Illus.). 138p. (J). (gr. 3-6). 18.69 *(978-0-316-05736-3(3))* Little Brown & Co.
Doyle, Patrick H. T. Edgar Font's Hunt for a House to Haunt: Adventure Three: the Flint Island Treehouse. 2008. (Illus.). 300p. (J). per. 7.99 *(978-0-9786132-2-8(8))* Armadillo Bks.
—Edgar Font's Hunt for a House to Haunt: Adventure Two: the Fakersville Power Station. Doyle, Patrick H. T., illus. 2007. (Edgar Font's Hunt for a House to Haunt Ser.). (Illus.). 303p. (J). (gr. 4-7). per. 7.99 *(978-0-9786132-1-1(X))* Armadillo Bks.
Drake, Raelyn. The House. 2018. (Mason Falls Mysteries Ser.). (ENG.). 104p. (YA). (gr. 6-12). pap. 7.99 *(978-1-5415-0117-1(9),* ecf14180-5c91-4f54-af67-cf9919eff52e); lib. bdg. 25.32 *(978-1-5415-0113-3(6),* c1b63664-3e5c-420a-8032-5981f16c5cce) Lerner Publishing Group. (Darby Creek).
Draper, Sharon M. The Buried Bones Mystery. Watson, Jesse Joshua, illus. 2011. (Clubhouse Mysteries Ser.: 1). (ENG.). 112p. (J). (gr. 3-7). pap. 6.99 *(978-1-4424-2709-9(4),* Aladdin) Simon & Schuster Children's Publishing.
—The Buried Bones Mystery. Watson, Jesse Joshua, illus. 2011. (Clubhouse Mysteries Ser.: 1). (ENG.). 112p. (J). (gr. 3-7). lib. bdg. 16.99 *(978-1-4424-2710-5(8),* Simon & Schuster/Paula Wiseman Bks.) Simon & Schuster/Paula Wiseman Bks.
—Shadows of Caesar's Creek. Watson, Jesse Joshua, illus. 2011. (Clubhouse Mysteries Ser.: 3). (ENG.). 128p. (J). (gr. 3-7). 15.99 *(978-1-4424-2712-9(4));* pap. 6.99 *(978-1-4424-2711-2(6))* Simon & Schuster Children's Publishing. (Aladdin).
Dubisch, Mike, illus. Mike's Mystery, No. 5. 2009. (Boxcar Children Graphic Novels Ser.). (ENG.). 32p. (J). (gr. 2-5). 6.99 *(978-0-8075-2871-6(4))* Whitman, Albert & Co.
Ducharme, Huguette. Enquete Tres Speciale. Caron, Romi, illus. 2004. (Collection des 6 Ans: Vol. 32). (FRE.). 68p. (YA). 7.95 *(978-2-922565-94-2(7))* Editions de la Paix CAN. Dist: World of Reading, Ltd.
Duckett, Brenda. Casey's Shadow. 2008. pap. 10.96 *(978-0-615-17289-7(X))* Duckett, Brenda.
Dudley, Sean. Who's Afraid of the Pumpkin Man??? 2009. 47p. pap. 10.01 *(978-0-557-12616-3(9))* Lulu Pr., Inc.
Duey, Kathleen. Arthur. Epstein, Eugene, illus. Gould, Robert, photos by. 2005. (Time Soldiers Ser.: Vol. 4). (ENG.). 96p. (J). (gr. k-2). per. 5.95 *(978-1-929945-56-6(6))* Big Guy Bks., Inc.
—Leonardo. Epstein, Eugene, illus. 2009. (Time Soldiers Ser.). (ENG.). (J). (gr. k-2). 95p. 9.95 *(978-1-929945-89-4(2));*Bk. 8. 48p. 15.95 *(978-1-929945-88-7(4))* Big Guy Bks., Inc.
—Time Soldiers - Patch. Epstein, Eugene, illus. Gould, Robert, photos by. 2005. (Time Soldiers Ser.: Bk. 3). (ENG.). 96p. (J). (gr. k-2). per. 5.95 *(978-1-929945-55-9(8))* Big Guy Bks., Inc.
Duff, Hilary. Devoted: An Elixir Novel. 2012. (Elixir Ser.). (ENG.). 368p. (YA). (gr. 9). pap. 9.99 *(978-1-4424-0856-2(1),* Simon & Schuster Bks. For Young Readers) Simon & Schuster Bks. For Young Readers.
—Elixir. 2011. (Playaway Young Adult Ser.). (YA). 59.99 *(978-1-4417-7416-3(5))* Findaway World, LLC.
—Elixir. 2011. (Elixir Ser.). (ENG.). 336p. (YA). (gr. 9). pap. 12.99 *(978-1-4424-0854-8(5),* Simon & Schuster Bks. For Young Readers) Simon & Schuster Bks. For Young Readers.
—True: An Elixir Novel. (Elixir Ser.). (ENG., 304p. (YA). (gr. 7). 2014. Illus.). pap. 12.99 *(978-1-4424-0858-6(8))* 2013. 17.99 *(978-1-4424-0857-9(X))* Simon & Schuster Bks. For Young Readers. (Simon & Schuster Bks. For Young Readers).
Duffy, James. Desaparecida. (SPA.). 142p. (YA). (gr. 5-8). *(978-84-279-3200-5(6),* NG4451) Noguer y Caralt Editores, S. A. ESP. Dist: Lectorum Pubns., Inc.
Dufris, William, reader. The Case of the Climbing Cat. 2004. (High-Rise Private Eyes Ser.: No. 2). (Illus.). (J). (gr. -1-2). pap. 31.95 incl. audio compact disk *(978-1-59112-612-6(6))* Live Oak Media.
Dumas Lachtman, Ofelia. Looking for la Unica. 2004. (ENG & SPA., Illus.). 190p. (J). pap. 9.95 *(978-1-55885-412-3(6),* Piñata Books) Arte Publico Pr.
Duncan, Lois. Don't Look Behind You. 2010. (ENG.). 240p. (J). (gr. 7-17). pap. 13.99 *(978-0-316-12658-8(6))* Little, Brown Bks. for Young Readers.
—Don't Look Behind You, 6 vols. 2004. (J). 82.75 *(978-1-4025-5005-8(7));* 1.25 *(978-1-4025-6754-4(5))* Recorded Bks., Inc.
—Don't Look Behind You. 2010. (YA). lib. bdg. 19.65 *(978-0-606-15155-9(9))* Turtleback.
—I Know What You Did Last Summer. 2011. (ENG.). 200p. (gr. 6-10). 19.00 *(978-1-60686-921-5(3))* Perfection Learning Corp.
—Killing Mr. Griffin. 2009. 7.61 *(978-0-7848-3597-5(7),* Everbind) Marco Bk. Co.
—Killing Mr. Griffin. 223p. (YA). (gr. 7-18). pap. 4.50 *(978-0-8072-1373-5(X),* Listening Library) Random Hse. Audio Publishing Group.
—Locked in Time. 2011. (ENG.). 272p. (YA). (gr. 7-17). pap. 15.99 *(978-0-316-09902-8(3))* Little, Brown Bks. for Young Readers.
—Stranger with My Face. 235p. (YA). (gr. 7-18). pap. 4.99 *(978-0-8072-1371-1(3),* Listening Library) Random Hse. Audio Publishing Group.
—The Third Eye. 2012. (ENG.). 288p. (J). (gr. 7-17). pap. 15.99 *(978-0-316-09908-0(2))* Little, Brown Bks. for Young Readers.
Dunkleberger, Amy. Write a Mystery in 5 Simple Steps, 1 vol. 2013. (Creative Writing in 5 Simple Steps Ser.). (ENG., Illus.). 48p. (gr. 5-6). 27.93 *(978-0-7660-3835-6(1),* b58dfb52-a02c-4eb3-bbe6-481182587ea3) Enslow Publishing, LLC.
Dunlop, Ed. Sherlock Jones: The Assassination Plot. 2004. 116p. (J). 8.99 *(978-1-59166-315-7(6))* BJU Pr.
—Sherlock Jones: The Missing Diamond. 2005. (Sherlock Jones Ser.). 109p. (J). (gr. 3-7). per. 8.99 *(978-1-59166-316-4(4))* BJU Pr.
—Sherlock Jones: The Willoughby Bank Robbery. 2004. 96p. (J). 8.99 *(978-1-59166-314-0(8))* BJU Pr.
Dunn, Joeming & Warner, Gertrude Chandler. The Lighthouse Mystery, 1 vol., Bk. 14. Dunn, Ben, illus. 2011. (Boxcar Children Graphic Novels Ser.). (ENG.). 32p. (J). (gr. 2-8). 32.79 *(978-1-61641-122-0(8),* 3684, Graphic Planet - Fiction) Magic Wagon.
—The Woodshed Mystery, 1 vol., Bk. 13. Dunn, Ben, illus. 2011. (Boxcar Children Graphic Novels Ser.). (ENG.). 32p. (J). (gr. 3-8). 32.79 *(978-1-61641-121-3(X),* 3683, Graphic Planet - Fiction) Magic Wagon.
Durant, Alan. Humpty Dumpty's Great Fall. Heming, Leah-Ellen, illus. 2012. (ENG.). 32p. (J). *(978-0-7787-8028-1(7));* pap. *(978-0-7787-8039-7(2))* Crabtree Publishing Co.
—Little Bo-Peep's Missing Sheep. Heming, Leah-Ellen, illus. 2012. (ENG.). 32p. (J). *(978-0-7787-8029-8(5));* pap. *(978-0-7787-8040-3(6))* Crabtree Publishing Co.
—Little Miss Muffet's Big Scare. Heming, Leah-Ellen, illus. 2012. (ENG.). 32p. (J). *(978-0-7787-8030-4(9));* pap. *(978-0-7787-8041-0(4))* Crabtree Publishing Co.
—Old Mother Hubbard's Stolen Bone. Heming, Leah-Ellen, illus. 2012. (ENG.). 32p. (J). *(978-0-7787-8031-1(7));* pap. *(978-0-7787-8042-7(2))* Crabtree Publishing Co.
Dyan, Penelope. Tammy's Left Shoe — -As Opposed to Her Right. Dyan, Penelope, illus. 2008. (Illus.). 44p. pap. 11.95 *(978-1-935118-41-1(2))* Bellissima Publishing, LLC.
Earhart, Kristin. Buttercup Mystery. Geddes, Serena, illus. 2015. (Marguerite Henry's Misty Inn Ser.: 2). (ENG.). 128p. (J). (gr. 2-5). pap. 6.99 *(978-1-4814-1416-6(X),* Aladdin) Simon & Schuster Children's Publishing.
—Buttercup Mystery. 2015. (Marguerite Henry's Misty Inn Ser.: 2). lib. bdg. 16.00 *(978-0-606-37127-8(3))* Turtleback.
East, Bob. Tommy Cat & the Haunted Well, 1 vol. 2009. 42p. pap. 24.95 *(978-1-60703-754-5(8))* America Star Bks.
Ecton, Emily. Night of the Living Lawn Ornaments. 2009. (ENG.). 240p. (J). (gr. 3-7). pap. 5.99 *(978-1-4169-6451-3(7),* Aladdin) Simon & Schuster Children's Publishing.
Eden, Alexandra. The Duchess to the Rescue: A Bones & the Duchess Mystery. 2006. (Bones & the Duchess Mysteries Ser.). 120p. (J). (gr. 3-7). 16.00 *(978-1-888310-55-9(3))* Knoll, Allen A. Pubs.
—Holy Smoke: A Bones & the Duchess Mystery. 2004. (ENG., Illus.). 117p. (J). 16.00 *(978-1-888310-46-7(4));* 128p. (YA). pap. 8.00 *(978-1-888310-47-4(2))* Knoll, Allen A. Pubs.
Edge, Christopher. Twelve Minutes to Midnight. 2014. (Penelope Tredwell Mysteries Ser.: 1). (ENG.). 256p. (J). (gr. 3-7). 16.99 *(978-0-8075-8133-9(X),* 080758133X) Whitman, Albert & Co.
Edwards, Julie Andrews & Hamilton, Emma Walton. Dragon: Hound of Honor. 2005. (ENG.). 208p. (J). (gr. 4-18). pap. 7.99 *(978-0-06-057121-4(7),* HarperCollins) HarperCollins Pubs.
Edwards, Leo. Jerry Todd & the Rose-Colored Cat. 2007. 264p. 29.95 *(978-1-4344-9192-3(7));* per. 19.95 *(978-1-4344-9098-8(X))* Wildside Pr., LLC.
—Poppy Ott Hits the Trail. Salg, Bert, illus. 2011. 218p. 44.95 *(978-1-258-10146-6(7))* Literary Licensing, LLC.
Eggleton, Jill. The Mystery of Missing Big Wig. (Sails Literacy Ser.). 24p. (gr. 3-18). 27.00 *(978-0-7578-6982-2(3))* Rigby Education.
Eisenstein, Ann. Fallen Prey, a Sean Gray Junior Special Agent Mystery. Waugh, Leslie, ed. 2013. 190p. pap. 9.99 *(978-1-935711-31-5(8))* Peak City Publishing, LLC.
Eisenstein, Ann E. Hiding Carly, a Sean Gray Junior Special Agent Mystery. 2013. 162p. pap. 9.99 *(978-1-935711-27-8(X))* Peak City Publishing, LLC.
Ellen, Raskin. The Westing Game. 2014. (Puffin Modern Classics Ser.). (ENG.). 192p. (J). (gr. 5-12). 12.24 *(978-1-63245-142-2(5))* Lectorum Pubns., Inc.
Elliott, Julia. Where Did God Come From? Elliott, Julia, illus. 2005. (Illus.). (J). 15.95 *(978-0-9764129-0-8(X))* Rain Tree Bks.
Elliott, Rebecca. Trip to the Pumpkin Farm. 11. 2020. (Branches Early Ch Bks). (ENG.). 72p. (J). (gr. 2-3). 15.36 *(978-1-64697-304-0(6))* Penworthy Co., LLC, The.
—Trip to the Pumpkin Farm: a Branches Book (Owl Diaries #11) Elliott, Rebecca, illus. 2019. (Owl Diaries: 11). (ENG., Illus.). 80p. (J). (gr. k-2). pap. 6.99 *(978-1-338-29864-2(X))* Scholastic, Inc.
—Trip to the Pumpkin Farm: a Branches Book (Owl Diaries #11) (Library Edition) Elliott, Rebecca, illus. 2019. (Owl Diaries: 11). (ENG., Illus.). 80p. (J). (gr. k-2). lib. bdg. 24.99 *(978-1-338-29865-9(8))* Scholastic, Inc.
Ellis, Sarah. Odd Man Out, 1 vol. 2006. (ENG.). 160p. (J). (gr. 4-7). pap. 8.95 *(978-0-88899-703-6(5))* Groundwood Bks. CAN. Dist: Publishers Group West (PGW).
Ellwand, Ruth & Ellwand, David. The Mystery of the Fool & the Vanisher. Ellwand, David, photos by. 2008. (ENG., Illus.). 104p. (J). (gr. 5). 18.99 *(978-0-7636-2096-7(3))* Candlewick Pr.
Elston, Ashley. The Lying Woods. (ENG.). 336p. (YA). (gr. 9-12). 2019. pap. 9.99 *(978-1-368-01591-2(3))* 2018. 17.99 *(978-1-368-01478-6(X))* Hyperion Bks. for Children.
—The Rules for Disappearing. 2014. (Rules Ser.). (ENG.). 336p. (J). (gr. 7-12). pap. 8.99 *(978-1-4231-6926-0(3))* Hyperion Bks. for Children.
—This Is Our Story. (ENG.). 320p. (YA). (gr. 7-12). 2017. pap. 11.99 *(978-1-4847-3412-4(2))* 2016. 17.99 *(978-1-4847-3089-8(5))* Hyperion Bks. for Children.
Elys Dayton, Arwen. Seeker. 2015. (Seeker Ser.: 1). (ENG.). 480p. (YA). (gr. 9). pap. 9.99 *(978-0-385-74408-9(0),* Ember) Random Hse. Children's Bks.
Emerson, Kevin. The Demon Hunter, 4. 2009. (Oliver Nocturne Ser.: 4). (ENG.). 224p. (J). (gr. 6-8). pap. 18.69 *(978-0-545-05804-9(X))* Scholastic, Inc.
Emerson, Scott. The Case of the Cat with the Missing Ear: From the Notebooks of Edward R. Smithfield D. V. M. Mullett, Viv, illus. 2011. (Adventures of Samuel Blackthorne Ser.: 1). (ENG.). 240p. (J). (gr. 3-7). pap. 11.99 *(978-0-689-87615-8(7),* Simon & Schuster Bks. For Young Readers) Simon & Schuster Bks. For Young Readers.
Encyclopedia Brown & the Case of the Exploding Plumbing & Other Stories. 2003. (J). pap. 2.95 *(978-0-590-44093-6(4))* Scholastic, Inc.
Enright, Elizabeth. The Four-Story Mistake. Enright, Elizabeth, illus. 3rd ed. 2008. (Melendy Quartet Ser.: 2). (ENG., Illus.). 208p. (J). (gr. 3-7). per. 9.99 *(978-0-312-37599-7(9),* 900048318) Square Fish.
—Spiderweb for Two: A Melendy Maze. Enright, Elizabeth, illus. 3rd ed. 2008. (Melendy Quartet Ser.: 4). (ENG., Illus.). 224p. (J). (gr. 3-7). per. 11.99 *(978-0-312-37601-7(4),* 900048320) Square Fish.
Ensor, Rod. Getting It. 2007. 216p. per. 14.95 *(978-0-595-44800-5(3))* iUniverse, Inc.
Eppler, Jamie. Suzy & the Sewing Room Mystery. 2017. (ENG., Illus.). 30p. (J). (gr. -1-3). pap. 9.95 *(978-1-947491-29-8(6))* Yorkshire Publishing Group.
Erickson, John. The Big Question. Holmes, Gerald L., illus. 2012. 128p. (J). pap. *(978-1-59188-160-5(9))* Maverick Bks.
—The Big Question. Holmes, Gerald L., illus. 2012. (Hank the Cowdog Ser.: Vol. 60). (ENG.). 128p. (J). (gr. 3-6). 15.99 *(978-1-59188-260-2(5))* Maverick Bks., Inc.
—The Case of the Black-Hooded Hangmans. Holmes, Gerald L., illus. 2011. (Hank the Cowdog Ser.). (ENG.). 113p. (J). (gr. 3-6). pap. 5.99 *(978-1-59188-124-7(2))* Maverick Bks., Inc.
—The Case of the Burrowing Robot. Holmes, Gerald L., illus. 2011. (Hank the Cowdog Ser.). (ENG.). 125p. (J). (gr. 3-6). pap. 5.99 *(978-1-59188-142-1(0))* Maverick Bks., Inc.
—The Case of the Deadly Ha-Ha Game. Holmes, Gerald L., illus. 2011. (Hank the Cowdog Ser.). (ENG.). 128p. (J). (gr. 3-6). pap. 5.99 *(978-1-59188-137-7(4))* Maverick Bks., Inc.
—The Case of the Falling Sky. Holmes, Gerald L., illus. 2011. (Hank the Cowdog Ser.: No. 45). (ENG.). 129p. (J). (gr. 3-6). pap. 5.99 *(978-1-59188-145-2(5))* Maverick Bks., Inc.
—The Case of the Fiddle-Playing Fox. Holmes, Gerald L., illus. 2011. (Hank the Cowdog Ser.: No. 12). (ENG.). 118p. (J). (gr. 3-6). pap. 5.99 *(978-1-59188-112-4(9))* Maverick Bks., Inc.
—The Case of the Halloween Ghost. Holmes, Gerald L., illus. 2011. (Hank the Cowdog Ser.). (ENG.). 123p. (J). (gr. 3-6). pap. 5.99 *(978-1-59188-109-4(9))* Maverick Bks., Inc.
—The Case of the Kidnapped Collie. Holmes, Gerald L., illus. 2011. (Hank the Cowdog Ser.). (ENG.). 113p. (J). (gr. 3-6). pap. 5.99 *(978-1-59188-126-1(9))* Maverick Bks., Inc.
—The Case of the Midnight Rustler. Holmes, Gerald L., illus. 2011. (Hank the Cowdog Ser.: No. 19). (ENG.). 113p. (J). (gr. 3-6). pap. 5.99 *(978-1-59188-119-3(6))* Maverick Bks., Inc.
—The Case of the Most Ancient Bone. Holmes, Gerald L., illus. 2011. (Hank the Cowdog Ser.). (ENG.). 239p. (J). (gr. 3-6). pap. 5.99 *(978-1-59188-150-6(1))* Maverick Bks., Inc.
—The Case of the One-Eyed Killer Stud Horse. Holmes, Gerald L., illus. 2011. (Hank the Cowdog Ser.: No. 8). (ENG.). 120p. (J). (gr. 3-6). pap. 5.99 *(978-1-59188-108-7(0))* Maverick Bks., Inc.
—The Case of the Perfect Dog. Holmes, Gerald L., illus. 2012. 127p. (J). *(978-1-59188-259-6(1))* Maverick Bks.
—The Case of the Perfect Dog. Holmes, Gerald L., illus. 2012. (Hank the Cowdog (Quality) Ser.). (ENG.). 127p. (J). (gr. 3-6). pap. 5.99 *(978-1-59188-159-9(5))* Maverick Bks., Inc.
—The Case of the Secret Weapon. Holmes, Gerald L., illus. 2011. (Hank the Cowdog Ser.). (ENG.). 125p. (J). (gr. 3-6). pap. 5.99 *(978-1-59188-155-1(2))* Maverick Bks., Inc.
—The Case of the Tender Cheeping Chickies. Holmes, Gerald L., illus. 2011. (Hank the Cowdog Ser.). (ENG.). 129p. (J). (gr. 3-6). pap. 5.99 *(978-1-59188-147-6(1))* Maverick Bks., Inc.
—The Case of the Tricky Trap. Holmes, Gerald L., illus. 2011. (Hank the Cowdog Ser.). (ENG.). 126p. (J). (gr. 3-6). pap. 5.99 *(978-1-59188-146-9(3))* Maverick Bks., Inc.
—The Case of the Vampire Cat. Holmes, Gerald L., illus. 2011. (Hank the Cowdog Ser.). (ENG.). 115p. (J). (gr. 3-6). pap. 5.99 *(978-1-59188-121-6(8))* Maverick Bks., Inc.
—The Curse of the Incredible Priceless Corncob. Holmes, Gerald L., illus. 2011. (Hank the Cowdog Ser.: No. 7). (ENG.). 127p. (J). (gr. 3-6). pap. 5.99 *(978-1-59188-107-0(2))* Maverick Bks., Inc.
—The Disappearance of Drover. Holmes, Gerald L., illus. 2011. (Hank the Cowdog Ser.). (ENG.). 122p. (J). (gr. 3-6). pap. 5.99 *(978-1-59188-157-5(9))* Maverick Bks., Inc.
—The Garbage Monster from Outer Space. Holmes, Gerald L., illus. 2011. (Hank the Cowdog Ser.). (ENG.). 126p. (J). (gr. 3-6). pap. 5.99 *(978-1-59188-132-2(3))* Maverick Bks., Inc.
—It's a Dog's Life. Holmes, Gerald L., illus. (Hank the Cowdog Ser.: No. 3). 100p. (J). (gr. 2-5). 9.95 *(978-0-916941-04-8(3))* Maverick Bks., Inc.
—Murder in the Middle Pasture. Holmes, Gerald L., illus. 2011. (Hank the Cowdog Ser.). (ENG.). 120p. (J). (gr. 3-6). pap. 5.99 *(978-1-59188-104-9(8))* Maverick Bks., Inc.
—The Original Adventures of Hank the Cowdog. Holmes, Gerald L., illus. (ENG.). 127p. (J). (gr. 3-6). 2012. (Hank the Cowdog Ser.: Vol. 1). 15.99 *(978-1-59188-201-5(X))* 2011. (Hank the Cowdog Ser.: No. 1). pap. 5.99 *(978-1-59188-101-8(3))* Maverick Bks., Inc.
—The Phantom in the Mirror. Holmes, Gerald L., illus. 2011. (Hank the Cowdog Ser.: No. 20). (ENG.). 114p. (J). (gr. 3-6). pap. 5.99 *(978-1-59188-120-9(X))* Maverick Bks., Inc.
—The Quest for the Great White Quail. Holmes, Gerald L., illus. 2011. (Hank the Cowdog Ser.). (ENG.). 123p. (J). (gr. 3-6). pap. 5.99 *(978-1-59188-152-0(8))* Maverick Bks., Inc.
—The Return of the Charlie Monsters. Holmes, Gerald L., illus. 2014. 128p. (J). pap. *(978-1-59188-163-6(3))* Maverick Bks., Inc.
Erickson, John & Holmes, Gerald L., illus. The Case of the Prowling Bear. 2013. 126p. (J). *(978-1-59188-261-9(3));* pap. *(978-1-59188-161-2(7))* Maverick Bks.
Erickson, Mary Ellen. What Happened to the Deer? Peanut Butter Club Mysteries. 2007. 182p. (J). 23.95 *(978-0-595-68396-3(7));* per. 13.95 *(978-0-595-42799-4(5))* iUniverse, Inc.
—Who Jinxed the CG Ranch? 2009. 196p. 24.95 *(978-1-4401-4218-5(1));* pap. 14.95 *(978-1-4401-4216-1(5))* iUniverse, Inc.
Ernst, Kathleen. Midnight in Lonesome Hollow: A Kit Mystery. 2007. (American Girl Mysteries Ser.). (ENG., Illus.). 192p. (gr. 4-7). 10.95 *(978-1-59369-161-5(0),* American Girl) American Girl Publishing, Inc.
Ervin, Randy. Maycroft From 232nd. 2010. 150p. (J). pap. 10.00 *(978-0-578-05732-3(8))* Ervin, Randy.
Erway, Chad Lee. An Appointment with Fear. 2019. (ENG., Illus.). 184p. (J). (gr. 2-7). pap. 9.99 *(978-1-7335610-1-3(3))* Parallel Vortex.
Erwin, Vicki Berger. Elizabeth Bryan Mysteries Set, 6 vols. (Elizabeth Bryan Mysteries Ser.). (J). 29.99 *(978-0-7586-0008-0(9))* Concordia Publishing Hse.
Eschler, Linda. The Strawberry Fairies & the Secret of Mystery Island. 2008. 57p. pap. 16.95 *(978-1-60610-960-1(X))* America Star Bks.
—The Strawberry Fairies Save Sandcastle Island. 2007. 52p. per. 16.95 *(978-1-4241-9175-8(0))* America Star Bks.
Escott, John. Level 2: the Ghost of Genny Castle. 2nd ed. 2008. (Pearson English Graded Readers Ser.). (ENG., Illus.). 48p. pap. 13.32 *(978-1-4058-6953-9(4),* Pearson ELT) Pearson Education.
Eskeland, N. L. Menace in the Walls: A Summer Project Turns Treacherous. 2004. (Joshua Keegan Mysteries Ser.). 142p. (J). per. 10.95 *(978-0-9673811-6-9(9))* Science2Discover, Inc.
Estes, Eleanor. The Alley. Ardizzone, Edward, illus. 2003. (ENG.). 288p. (J). (gr. 3-7). pap. 18.95 *(978-0-15-204918-8(5),* 1194852, Clarion Bks.) HarperCollins Pubs.
—The Alley. Ardizzone, Edward, illus. 2004. (Odyssey/Harcourt Young Classic Ser.). 283p. 15.95 *(978-0-7569-3475-0(3))* Perfection Learning Corp.
Etherly, L. D. Winter Arrives This Summer. 2012. 34p. pap. 12.95 *(978-0-9833877-1-8(0))* Inkspil Publishing.
Etienne, Doris. The Jewels of Sofia Tate. 2009. (ENG.). 272p. (J). (gr. 6). pap. 12.99 *(978-1-55488-230-4(3))* Dundurn Pr. CAN. Dist: Publishers Group West (PGW).
Eulberg, Elizabeth. The Great Shelby Holmes. 2017. (ENG., Illus.). 272p. (J). pap. 8.99 *(978-1-68119-053-2(2),* 900157428, Bloomsbury USA Childrens) Bloomsbury Publishing USA.
—The Great Shelby Holmes. 2017. (Great Shelby Holmes Ser.: 1). (J). lib. bdg. 18.40 *(978-0-606-40594-2(1))* Turtleback.
—The Great Shelby Holmes: Girl Detective. 2016. (ENG., Illus.). 256p. (J). 16.99 *(978-1-68119-051-8(6),* 900157427, Bloomsbury USA Childrens) Bloomsbury Publishing USA.
—The Great Shelby Holmes & the Coldest Case. 2018. (ENG., Illus.). 224p. (J). 16.99 *(978-1-68119-057-0(5),* 900157430, Bloomsbury Children's Bks.) Bloomsbury Publishing USA.

—The Great Shelby Holmes & the Haunted Hound. 2019. (ENG., Illus.). 256p. (J). 16.99 *(978-1-5476-0147-9(7)*, 900199958, Bloomsbury Children's Bks.) Bloomsbury Publishing USA.
—The Great Shelby Holmes Meets Her Match. 2017. (ENG., Illus.). 240p. (J). 16.99 *(978-1-68119-054-9(0)*, 900157431, Bloomsbury USA Childrens) Bloomsbury Publishing USA.
Eustace, Robert & Meade, L. T. A Master of Mysteries. Walton, J. Ambrose, illus. 2013. 106p. pap. 8.00 *(978-1-927558-41-6(7))* Birch Tree Publishing.
Evatt, Harriet. The Mystery of the Alpine Castle. 2011. 242p. 46.95 *(978-1-258-08839-2(8))* Literary Licensing, LLC.
Everett, George W. G. W. Frog & the Haunted House in Misty Meadows. 2010. 44p. 16.95 *(978-1-4497-0752-1(1)*, WestBow Pr.) Author Solutions, LLC.
Everheart, Chris. Concrete Gallery. 2015. (Tartan House Ser.). (ENG.). 96p. (J). (gr. 3-6). *(978-1-63235-053-4(X)*, 11680, 12-Story Library) Bookstaves, LLC.
Extreme Danger. 2007. 15.00 *(978-0-7569-7603-3(0))* Perfection Learning Corp.
Fairchild, Simone. The Plight of the Queen Bee. Key, Pamela, illus. 2006. 34p. (J). per. 17.95 *(978-0-9767732-3-8(6))* W & B Pubs.
—Queen Bee's Midnight Caper, 3 vols. Key, Pamela Marie, illus. 2006. 33p. (J). (gr. -1-3). per. 17.95 *(978-0-9771971-4-9(X))* W & B Pubs.
Fairlie, Emily. The Magician's Bird. Caparo, Antonio Javier, illus. 2014. (Tuckernuck Mysteries Ser.: 2). (ENG.). 288p. (J). (gr. 3-7). pap. 6.99 *(978-0-06-211894-3(3)*, Tegen, Katherine Bks) HarperCollins Pubs.
Falcone, L. M. The Ghost & Max Monroe, Case #1: The Magic Box. Smith, Kim, illus. 2014. (Ghost & Max Monroe Ser.). (ENG.). 88p. (J). (gr. 1-4). pap. 6.95 *(978-1-77138-017-1(9))* Kids Can Pr., Ltd. CAN. Dist: Hachette Bk. Group.
Falconer, Ian. Olivia y el Juguete Desaparecido. Miawer, Teresa, tr. from ENG. Falconer, Ian, illus. 2004. (Olivia Ser.).Tr. of Olivia & the Missing Toy. (SPA., Illus.). 30p. (J). 16.95 *(978-1-930332-71-3(8))* Lectorum Pubns., Inc.
Fanning, Kieran. Code Crackers: Trapdoor to Treachery. 2010. (Dover Children's Classics Ser.). (ENG., Illus.). 128p. (J). (gr. 3-5). pap. 5.99 *(978-0-486-47880-7(7))* Dover Pubns., Inc.
—Code Crackers: Voyage to Victory. 2010. (Dover Kids Activity Books: Fantasy Ser.). (ENG., Illus.). 128p. (J). (gr. 3-5). pap. 5.99 *(978-0-486-47881-4(5)*, 478815) Dover Pubns., Inc.
Fantaskey, Beth. Isabel Feeney, Star Reporter. 2017. (ENG.). (J). (gr. 5-7). lib. bdg. 18.40 *(978-0-606-39809-1(0))* Turtleback.
Farrell-Whelan, Max. Something Fishy Aboard the Red Herring: Can You Catch the Killer? 2013. 130p. pap. 11.95 *(978-1-61204-239-8(2)*, Strategic Bk. Publishing) Strategic Book Publishing & Rights Agency (SBPRA).
Faulkner, Michael H. The Pearl Necklace: Miss Kitty Mysteries. 2006. (Illus.). 43p. (J). per. 21.95 *(978-1-59858-150-8(3))* Dog Ear Publishing, LLC.
Feagins, Sistah L. E. T. M. E. TELL'YA Bernadine, Hakim & Terrance Shadow Mystery ! 2009. (ENG.). 68p. pap. 15.72 *(978-0-557-09041-9(5))* Lulu Pr., Inc.
Feehan-Vileria, Elaine. The Legend of Old Mr. Clarke. 2004. 58p. per. 17.95 *(978-1-4116-1523-6(9))* Lulu Pr., Inc.
Feiffer, Kate. Signed by Zelda. (ENG.). 240p. (J). (gr. 3-7). 2013. pap. 6.99 *(978-1-4424-3332-8(9))* 2012. (Illus.). 16.99 *(978-1-4424-3331-1(0))* Simon & Schuster/Paula Wiseman Bks. (Simon & Schuster/Paula Wiseman Bks.).
Fein, Eric. Mystery at Manzanar: A WWII Internment Camp Story, 1 vol. Hartman, Kurt, illus. 2008. (Historical Fiction Ser.). (ENG.). 56p. (J). (gr. 3-6). pap. 6.25 *(978-1-4342-0847-7(8)*, 95208, Stone Arch Bks.) Capstone.
Feinstein, John. Change-Up: Mystery at the World Series (the Sports Beat, 4) 2010. (Sports Beat Ser.: 4). 336p. (J). (gr. 5). 8.99 *(978-0-375-84759-2(6)*, Yearling) Random Hse. Children's Bks.
—Cover-Up: Mystery at the Super Bowl (the Sports Beat, 3)   2008. (Sports Beat Ser.: 3). (ENG.). 320p. (J). (gr. 5). 8.99 *(978-0-440-42205-1(1)*, Yearling) Random Hse. Children's Bks.
—Last Shot: Mystery at the Final Four (the Sports Beat, 1) 2006. (Sports Beat Ser.: 1). (ENG.). 272p. (J). (gr. 7-9). reprint ed. per. 8.99 *(978-0-553-49460-0(0)*, Yearling) Random Hse. Children's Bks.
—Rush for the Gold: Mystery at the Olympics (the Sports Beat, 6) 2013. (Sports Beat Ser.: 6). 320p. (J). (gr. 5). pap. 10.99 *(978-0-375-87168-9(3)*, Yearling) Random Hse. Children's Bks.
—Vanishing Act: Mystery at the U. S. Open (the Sports Beat, 2) 2008. (Sports Beat Ser.: 2). (ENG.). 304p. (J). (gr. 3-7). 9.99 *(978-0-440-42125-2(X)*, Yearling) Random Hse. Children's Bks.
Feld, Ellen F. Annie: The Mysterious Morgan Horse. Mellin, Jeanne, illus. 2007. 206p. (J). per. 9.95 *(978-0-9709002-9-6(5))* Willow Bend Publishing.
Ferguson, Alane. The Angel of Death. 2008. (Forensic Mystery Ser.). 258p. 17.00 *(978-0-7569-8929-3(9))* Perfection Learning Corp.
—The Christopher Killer. 2006. (Forensic Mystery Ser.). (ENG.). 288p. (YA). (gr. 7-18). 21.19 *(978-0-670-06008-5(9))* Penguin Young Readers Group.
—The Christopher Killer. 2008. (Forensic Mystery Ser.). 274p. (gr. 7-12). 17.00 *(978-0-7569-8930-9(2))* Perfection Learning Corp.
—Mysteries in Our National Parks: Deadly Waters: A Mystery in Everglades National Park. 2007. (Mysteries in Our National Park Ser.). (Illus.). 160p. (J). (gr. 3-7). 4.99 *(978-1-4263-0093-6(X)*, National Geographic Kids) Disney Publishing Worldwide.
—Mysteries in Our National Parks: Ghost Horses: A Mystery in Zion National Park. 2007. (Mysteries in Our National Park Ser.). (Illus.). 160p. (J). (gr. 3-7). per. 4.99 *(978-1-4263-0108-7(1)*, National Geographic Kids) Disney Publishing Worldwide.
—Mysteries in Our National Parks: over the Edge: A Mystery in Grand Canyon National Park. 2008. (Mysteries in Our National Park Ser.). (Illus.). 160p. (J). (gr. 3-7). per. 4.99 *(978-1-4263-0177-3(4)*, National Geographic Kids) Disney Publishing Worldwide.
—Mysteries in Our National Parks: Valley of Death: A Mystery in Death Valley National Park. 2008. (Mysteries in Our National Park Ser.). (Illus.). 160p. (J). (gr. 3-7). per. 4.99 *(978-1-4263-0178-0(2)*, National Geographic Kids) Disney Publishing Worldwide.
—Night of the Black Bear: A Mystery in Great Smoky Mountains National Park. 2007. (Mysteries in Our National Park Ser.). (Illus.). 160p. (J). (gr. 3-7). 4.99 *(978-1-4263-0094-3(8)*, National Geographic Kids) Disney Publishing Worldwide.
Ferguson, Donald. Chums of Scranton High on the Cinder Pat. 2006. 25.95 *(978-1-4218-2937-1(1))*; pap. 10.95 *(978-1-4218-3037-7(X))* 1st World Publishing, Inc.
—The Chums of Scranton High on the Cinder Path. 2007. 124p. per. *(978-1-4065-2363-8(1))* Dodo Pr.
Ferguson, Dwayne. Ghost Ranch: The Legend of Mad Jake, 2004. (Kid Caramel: Bk. 4). (J). pap. 4.50 *(978-0-940975-17-0(3)*, Sankofa Bks.) Just Us Bks., Inc.
Ferraro, Maureen. Sugar & Els: The Mystery. 2011. 28p. pap. 15.99 *(978-1-4628-5347-2(1))* Xlibris Corp.
Ferrell, Deen. Cryptic Spaces: Book One: Foresight. 2013. 396p. pap. 16.95 *(978-1-60047-864-2(6)*, Curio Creative) Wasteland Pr.
Fertig, Michael P. Musical Mystery Scooby Doo! McKee, Darren, illus. 2007. (Scooby Doo Ser.). (J). (gr. -1-3). 12.98 *(978-1-4127-7429-1(2))* Publications International, Ltd.
Fickey, Brenda. Whispering Darkness. 2007. (ENG.). 136p. per. 24.95 *(978-1-4241-6932-0(7))* America Star Bks.
Fiedler, Lisa. The Green-Eyed Monster. 2012. 168p. (J). *(978-0-545-48424-4(3))* Scholastic, Inc.
Fields, Jan. Ghost Light Burning: An Up2U Mystery Adventure, 1 vol. Fabbretti, Valerio, illus. 2015. (Up2U Adventures Ser.). (ENG.). 80p. (J). (gr. 2-5). 35.64 *(978-1-62402-092-6(5)*, 17353, Calico Chapter Bks.) ABDO Publishing Co.
—Lost in Space: An Up2U Action Adventure. Vidal, Oriol, illus. 2017. (Up2U Adventures Set 3 Ser.). (ENG.). 80p. (J). (gr. 2-5). lib. bdg. 35.64 *(978-1-5321-3030-4(9)*, 25508, Calico Chapter Bks.) ABDO Publishing Co.
The Fiji Flood, 6 vols. (Woodland Mysteriestm Ser.). 133p. (gr. 3-7). 42.50 *(978-0-7802-7925-4(5))* Wright Group/McGraw-Hill.
Finding Conway: Seek the Truth. 2006. (YA). *(978-0-9771114-1-1(5))* LIP Publishing LLC.
Finding the Forger. 2004. (ENG.). 192p. (J). 19.95 *(978-1-890862-32-9(0)*, 36c09b8d-21aa-4f44-a8ac-089832ec9c92) Bancroft Pr.
Fine, Sarah. Beneath the Shine. 2017. (ENG.). 304p. (YA). (gr. 10-13). pap. 9.99 *(978-1-4778-2327-9(1)*, 9781477823279, Skyscape) Amazon Publishing.
—Uncanny. 2017. (ENG.). 316p. (YA). (gr. 10-12). pap. 9.99 *(978-1-5420-4646-6(7)*, 9781542046466, Skyscape) Amazon Publishing.
Finley, Leah. Ms T. 2007. 108p. (J). per. 8.95 *(978-0-9794815-1-2(1))* Bellissima Publishing, LLC.
—The One & Only Mr C. 2009. 82p. pap. 8.95 *(978-1-935118-75-6(7))* Bellissima Publishing, LLC.
Fisch, Sholly. Scooby-Doo in Fangs, but No Fangs!, 1 vol. Deporter, Vincent, illus. 2013. (Scooby-Doo Graphic Novels Ser.). (ENG.). 24p. (J). (gr. 2-6). lib. bdg. 31.36 *(978-1-61479-051-8(5)*, 584, Graphic Novels) Spotlight.
Fisher, Aleah & Riddle, Debbie. Hunter & the Aliens. 2010. (ENG.). 24p. pap. 15.99 *(978-1-4500-0684-2(1))* Xlibris Corp.
The Fishy, Flashy Fourth, 6 vols., Vol. 3. (Woodland Mysteriestm Ser.). 133p. (gr. 3-7). 42.50 *(978-0-322-02373-4(4))* Wright Group/McGraw-Hill.
Fitzgerald, John D. More Adventures of the Great Brain. Mayer, Mercer, illus. 2004. (Great Brain Ser.: 2). (ENG.). 176p. (J). (gr. 3-7). pap. 8.99 *(978-0-14-240065-4(3)*, Puffin Books) Penguin Young Readers Group.
—More Adventures of the Great Brain. 2004. (Great Brain Ser.). 142p. (J). (gr. 3-7). pap., tchr.'s training gde. ed. 36.00 incl. audio *(978-0-8072-0860-1(4)*, Listening Library) Random Hse. Audio Publishing Group.
Fitzgerald, Laura Marx. The Gallery. 2017. lib. bdg. 18.40 *(978-0-606-40088-6(5))* Turtleback.
—Under the Egg. 2015. 272p. (J). (gr. 3-7). 8.99 *(978-0-14-242765-1(9)*, Puffin Books) Penguin Young Readers Group.
Fitzhugh, Louise. The Long Secret. unabr. ed. 2004. 224p. (J). (gr. 3-7). pap. 38.00 incl. audio *(978-0-8072-0666-9(0)*, LYA 303 SP, Listening Library) Random Hse. Audio Publishing Group.
Fiz. George & the Treasure Box Mysteries. 2012. (ENG., Illus.). 105p. pap. 8.49 *(978-1-78035-223-7(9)*, Fastprint Publishing) Upfront Publishing Ltd. GBR. Dist: Printondemand-worldwide.com.
Fleischman, Paul. The Dunderheads. 2012. lib. bdg. 17.20 *(978-0-606-23804-5(2))* Turtleback.
—The Dunderheads Behind Bars. Roberts, David, illus. 2012. (ENG.). 48p. (J). (gr. 1-4). 16.99 *(978-0-7636-4543-4(5))* Candlewick Pr.
Fleischman, Sid. Jim Ugly. Smith, Jos. A., illus. 2003. (ENG.). 144p. (J). (gr. 3-7). pap. 6.99 *(978-0-06-052121-9(X)*, Greenwillow Bks.) HarperCollins Pubs.
Fletcher, J. S. Scarhaven Keep. 2011. (YA). *(978-1-60682-173-2(3))* BJU Pr.
Flint, Garrison. The Butler Did It! A Raymond Masrters Mystery. 2003. (Raymond Masters Mystery: 10). 206p. per. 13.99 *(978-1-885631-72-5(3))* Hutchison, G.F. Pr.
—Sanity in Search of Peter Alexander. 2003. 198p. (YA). per. 13.95 *(978-1-885631-73-2(1))* Hutchison, G.F. Pr.
Floreen, Tim. Tattoo Atlas. 2016. (ENG., Illus.). 384p. (YA). (gr. 9). 17.99 *(978-1-4814-3280-1(X)*, Simon Pulse) Simon Pulse.
Flower, Amanda. Andi under Pressure: An Andi Boggs Novel. 2014. 176p. (J). pap. *(978-0-310-74022-3(3))* Zondervan.
Floyd, Brandi. Alex's Choice. 2012. 38p. 24.95 *(978-1-4626-6028-5(2))* America Star Bks.
Födi, Lee Edward. Kendra Kandlestar & the Crack in Kazah. Födi, Lee Edward, illus. 2011. (ENG., Illus.). 282p. (J). (gr. 4-7). 16.95 *(978-1-61254-018-4(X))* Brown Books Publishing Group.
Fogelin, Adrian. Some Kind of Magic, 1 vol. 2015. (Neighborhood Novels Ser.: 6). 232p. (J). (gr. 3-7). 15.95 *(978-1-56145-820-2(1))* Peachtree Publishing Co. Inc.
Fontes, Justine & Fontes, Ron. Casebook: Atlantis, 1 vol. 2009. (Top Secret Graphica Mysteries Ser.). (ENG., Illus.). 48p. (YA). (gr. 4-4). 33.93 *(978-1-60754-588-0(8)*, fdbcb500-f892-4f54-8fcb-d11606c4b86d); pap. 12.75 *(978-1-60754-590-3(X)*, aabdb817-7905-4ffb-8f55-866bee2d0f25) Rosen Publishing Group, Inc., The. (Windmill Bks.).
The Forgotten Hiding Place, 6 vols., Vol. 3. (Woodland Mysteriestm Ser.). 133p. (gr. 3-7). 42.50 *(978-0-322-02376-5(9))* Wright Group/McGraw-Hill.
Forman, Gayle. I Was Here. l.t. ed. 2015. 420p. 24.99 *(978-1-4104-8255-6(3))* Cengage Gale.
—I Was Here. 2016. (ENG.). 304p. (YA). (gr. 9). pap. 10.99 *(978-0-14-751403-5(7)*, Speak) Penguin Young Readers Group.
—I Was Here. 2016. lib. bdg. 22.10 *(978-0-606-38404-9(9))* Turtleback.
Forrest. Sign of Blood. (Thumbprint Mysteries Ser.). 32.86 *(978-0-8092-0408-3(8))* McGraw-Hill/Contemporary.
Foster, Martha S. Ginger Box. Geer, Charles, illus. 2011. 126p. 40.95 *(978-1-258-06588-1(6))* Literary Licensing, LLC.
Fox, Janet. The Charmed Children of Rookskill Castle. 2017. 400p. (J). (gr. 5). 9.99 *(978-0-14-751713-5(3)*, Puffin Books) Penguin Young Readers Group.
Fox, R. J. Stuart & His Incredibly Obnoxious Magical Book: Soccer, 1 vol. 2009. 86p. pap. 19.95 *(978-1-4489-9833-3(6))* America Star Bks.
Fox, Valerie P. Deefa: Seek the Vixen. 2008. 92p. pap. 10.49 *(978-1-4389-0723-9(0))* AuthorHouse.
Frade, B. A. & Deutsch, Stacia. Haunted Sleepover. 2017. (Tales from the Scaremaster Ser.: 6). (ENG.). 160p. (J). (gr. 3-7). pap. 5.99 *(978-0-316-43802-5(2))* Little, Brown Bks. for Young Readers.
—Haunted Sleepover. 2017. (Tales of the Scaremaster Ser.). (J). lib. bdg. 16.00 *(978-0-606-40631-4(X))* Turtleback.
Francis, Suzanne, adapted by. Zootopia: The Junior Novelization. 2016. (Illus.). 121p. (J). *(978-1-5182-0840-9(1))* Random Hse., Inc.
Fraustino, Lisa Rowe. The Hole in the Wall. 2010. (ENG.). 280p. (J). (gr. 2-7). 16.95 *(978-1-57131-696-7(5))* Milkweed Editions.
Frazier, Janet. The Case of the Theme Park Cry. l.t. ed. 2004. 90p. (J). per. *(978-1-59196-737-8(6))* Instant Pub.
Frazier, Janet L. The Mysterious Mall Disappearance: P. K. Mystery Series # 2. 2004. 100p. (J). per. *(978-1-59196-811-5(9))* Instant Pub.
Frederick, Heather Vogel. Absolutely Truly. 2015. (Pumpkin Falls Mystery Ser.). (ENG., Illus.). 368p. (J). (gr. 3-7). pap. 8.99 *(978-1-4424-2973-4(9)*, Simon & Schuster Bks. For Young Readers) Simon & Schuster Bks. For Young Readers.
Fredericks, Mariah. The Girl in the Park. 2013. (ENG.). 224p. (YA). (gr. 9). pap. 8.99 *(978-0-449-81591-5(9)*, Ember) Random Hse. Children's Bks.
Fredo, Sophia E. The Girls of Oak Court: Death at Whitford Pond. 2012. 172p. (gr. 10-12). pap. 13.95 *(978-1-4759-4057-2(2))* iUniverse, Inc.
Freedom's Whisper. 2007. (J). *(978-1-933343-52-5(4)*, PONY) Stabenfeldt Inc.
Freeman, J. Miller. Creak in the Night - Mystery of the Crypts. Lavender, Todd, illus. 2012. 74p. pap. 9.99 *(978-0-9850410-1-4(3))* Akmaeon Publishing, LLC.
Freeman, Martha. The Case of the Diamond Dog Collar, 2. 2nd ed. 2012. (First Kids Mysteries Ser.: 2). (ENG.). 144p. (J). (gr. 2-4). 21.19 *(978-0-8234-2337-8(9))* Holiday Hse., Inc.
—The Case of the Rock 'N' Roll Dog, 1. 2012. (First Kids Mysteries Ser.: 1). (ENG., Illus.). 128p. (J). (gr. 2-4). 21.19 *(978-0-8234-2267-8(4))* Holiday Hse., Inc.
—Effie Starr Zook Has One More Question. (ENG.). (J). (gr. 3-7). 2018. 240p. pap. 7.99 *(978-1-4814-7265-4(8))* 2017. (Illus.). 224p. 16.99 *(978-1-4814-7264-7(X))* Simon & Schuster/Paula Wiseman Bks. (Simon & Schuster/Paula Wiseman Bks.).
—Zap! 2018. (ENG., Illus.). 304p. (J). (gr. 3-7). 18.99 *(978-1-5344-0557-8(7)*, Simon & Schuster/Paula Wiseman Bks.) Simon & Schuster/Paula Wiseman Bks.
Freese, Thomas, reader. Fog Swirler & 11 Other Ghost Stories. 2006. (J). Pt. 1. cd-rom 13.95 *(978-0-9789511-0-8(7))*Pt. 2. cd-rom 13.95 *(978-0-9789511-1-5(5))*Pt. 3. cd-rom 13.95 *(978-0-9789511-2-2(3))* Illumination Pubns.
Frey, Hildegard G. The Camp Fire Girls Go Motoring. 2004. reprint ed. pap. 20.95 *(978-1-4191-5583-3(0))*; pap. 1.99 *(978-1-4192-5583-0(5))* Kessinger Publishing, LLC.
Freyburger, Nancy. The Case of the Hiccuping Clown. 2008. 108p. pap. 10.99 *(978-1-4389-2699-5(5))* AuthorHouse.
Friedman, Kinky. Curse of the Missing Puppet Head. 2003. lib. bdg. 29.95 *(978-0-9702383-6-8(3)*, CMPH01) Vandam Pr., Inc.
Friedman, Mel. The Mystery of the Backlot Banshee: A ClueFinders Mystery Adventure. 2004. (Illus.). 96p. (J). pap. *(978-0-7630-7620-7(1))* Magma.
Friedmann, Patty. Taken Away. 2010. (ENG.). 427p. (J). (gr. 6). pap. 18.95 *(978-0-9845318-2-0(3))* Tiny Stachel Pr.
Fry, Rosalie K. Secret of the Ron Mor Skerry. Fry, Rosalie K., illus. 2017. (Illus.). 104p. (J). (gr. 3-7). 16.95 *(978-1-68137-166-5(9)*, NYR Children's Collection) New York Review of Bks., Inc., The.
Fultz, Steven D. The Adventures of the Barnyard Detectives: Where's Mr. Peacock, 1 vol. 2009. 79p. pap. 19.95 *(978-1-60749-965-7(7))* America Star Bks.
Funaro, Gregory. Watch Hollow. Griffin, Matthew, illus. (Watch Hollow Ser.: 1). (ENG.). (J). (gr. 3-7). 2020. 272p. pap. 7.99 *(978-0-06-264346-9(0))* 2019. 256p. 16.99 *(978-0-06-264345-2(2))* HarperCollins Pubs. (HarperCollins).
Funk, Josh. Mission Defrostable. Kearney, Brendan, illus. 2018. (Lady Pancake & Sir French Toast Ser.: 3). (ENG.). 40p. (J). (gr. -1-3). 17.99 *(978-1-4549-2811-9(5))* Sterling Publishing Co., Inc.
Funke, Cornelia. The Thief Lord. Birmingham, Christian, illus. 2010.Tr. of Herr der Diebe. (ENG.). 368p. (J). (gr. 4-7). pap. 9.99 *(978-0-545-22770-4(4))* Scholastic, Inc.
Fuss, Kevin. The Brothers Geek. 2010. 180p. 24.99 *(978-1-4490-7366-4(2))*; pap. 14.49 *(978-1-4490-7365-7(4))* AuthorHouse.
Gaetz, Dayle Campbell. Crossbow, 1 vol. 2007. (Orca Currents Ser.). (ENG.). 112p. (J). (gr. 4-7). pap. 9.95 *(978-1-55143-841-2(0))* Orca Bk. Pubs. USA.
Gallagher, Mary. The Legend of Lisnashee. 2006. (ENG., Illus.). 100p. (J). pap. 10.95 *(978-1-903464-71-7(4)*, Collins Pr., The) M.H. Gill & Co. U. C. IRL. Dist: Dufour Editions, Inc.
Galvin, Larry J. The Pythagoras Solution. 2008. 102p. pap. 19.95 *(978-1-60441-990-0(3))* America Star Bks.
Ganeri, Anita. Mystery Stories: Writing Stories, 1 vol. 2013. (Writing Stories Ser.). (ENG.). 32p. (J). (gr. 1-3). pap. 8.95 *(978-1-4329-7539-5(0)*, 122436, Heinemann) Capstone.
Gant, Gene. Always Leaving. 2016. (ENG., Illus.). (YA). (gr. 8-12). 24.99 *(978-1-63477-934-0(7)*, Harmony Ink Pr.) Dreamspinner Pr.
Gantos, Jack. From Norvelt to Nowhere. 2015. (J). lib. bdg. 18.40 *(978-0-606-37280-0(6))* Turtleback.
Gardner, Sally. Operation Bunny: Book One. Roberts, David, illus. 2014. (Wings & Co Ser.: 1). (ENG.). 208p. (J). (gr. 2-5). pap. 8.99 *(978-1-250-05053-3(7)*, 900134108) Square Fish.
Garis, Howard R. The Curlytops & Their Playmates. 2009. 120p. 22.95 *(978-1-60664-610-6(9))*; pap. 10.95 *(978-1-60664-342-6(8))* Rodgers, Alan Bks.
Garmon, Larry Mike. The Calamari Code: an Agatha Pixie Mystery. 2007. 244p. pap. 15.49 *(978-0-615-15267-7(8))* Zu Bks.
Garrett, Kelly. The Last to Die. 2017. (ENG.). 208p. (YA). (gr. 8-12). pap. 18.99 *(978-1-929345-30-4(5)*, Poisoned Pen Press) Sourcebooks, Inc.
Garthwaite, Lynn D. Dirkle Smat Inside Mount Flatbottom. Howarth, Craig, illus. 2006. 48p. (J). pap. 9.95 *(978-1-59663-512-8(6)*, Castle Keep Pr.) Rock, James A. & Co. Pubs.
Garton, Kevan. The Cockleton Mystery. 2006. 68p. pap. *(978-1-84401-788-1(5))* Athena Pr.
Gary R Kirby. Stories of Sunshine & Funtime of Wonder & Thunder of Mystery & Magic for the Young to Grow On. 2009. 404p. pap. 22.95 *(978-1-4401-8640-0(5))* iUniverse, Inc.
Garza, Xavier. Vincent Ventura & the Mystery of the Chupacabra / Vincent Ventura y el Misterio Del Chupacabras. 2018. (ENG & SPA., Illus.). 80p. (J). (gr. 4-8). pap. 9.95 *(978-1-55885-869-5(5)*, Piñata Books) Arte Publico Pr.
Garza, Xavier & Gabriela, Baeza Ventura. Vincent Ventura & the Mystery of the Witch Owl / Vincent Ventura y el Misterio de la Bruja Lechuza: A Monster Fighter Mystery / Serie Exterminador de Monstruos. 2019. (SPA & ENG., Illus.). 122p. (J). (gr. 4-7). pap. 9.95 *(978-1-55885-890-9(3)*, Piñata Books) Arte Publico Pr.
Gauthier, Gail. Happy Kid! 2006. 230p. (J). *(978-1-4156-6311-0(4)*, Putnam Juvenile) Penguin Publishing Group.
Gavin, Rohan. 3 of a Kind. 2016. (Knightley & Son Ser.: 3). (ENG.). 288p. (J). pap. *(978-1-4088-6008-3(2)*, 260862, Bloomsbury Children's Bks.) Bloomsbury Publishing Plc.
Gayle, Juliet V. Emily & Beautiful & the Great Strawberry Whipped Cream Pie Mystery. 2011. 24p. pap. 13.95 *(978-1-4520-9744-2(5))* AuthorHouse.
Gee, Maurice. The Fire Raiser. 2007. (ENG.). 176p. (J). (gr. 5-7). pap. 11.95 *(978-0-618-75041-2(X)*, 486378, Clarion Bks.) HarperCollins Pubs.
Geesey, Kathleen. Black Fog. 2011. 200p. pap. 24.95 *(978-1-4560-7000-7(2))* America Star Bks.
Gegner, Rose G. Detective Rooster Rue. 2014. 32p. pap. 22.54 *(978-1-4828-9517-9(X))* Partridge Pub.
Geiger, A. V. Follow Me Back. 2017. (Follow Me Back Ser.: 1). 368p. (YA). (gr. 8-12). pap. 10.99 *(978-1-4926-4523-8(0))* Sourcebooks, Inc.
Gelsey, James. The Baseball Boogeyman. 2004. (Illus.). 44p. (J). *(978-0-439-55713-9(5))* Scholastic, Inc.
—Scooby-Doo! & the Carnival Creeper, 1 vol. Sur, Duendes Del, illus. 2013. (Scooby-Doo Mysteries Ser.). (ENG.). 64p. (J). (gr. 3-6). lib. bdg. 31.36 *(978-1-61479-042-6(6)*, 13222, Chapter Bks.) Spotlight.
—Scooby-Doo! & the Gruesome Goblin, 1 vol. Sur, Duendes Del, illus. 2013. (Scooby-Doo Mysteries Ser.). (ENG.). 64p. (J). (gr. 3-6). lib. bdg. 31.36 *(978-1-61479-045-7(0)*, 13225, Chapter Bks.) Spotlight.
—Scooby-Doo! & the Spooky Strikeout, 1 vol. Sur, Duendes Del, illus. 2013. (Scooby-Doo Mysteries Ser.). (ENG.). 64p. (J). (gr. 3-6). lib. bdg. 31.36 *(978-1-61479-047-1(7)*, 13227, Chapter Bks.) Spotlight.
Gentile, Joe. Mysterious Traveler. 2003. (ENG., Illus.). 48p. (gr. 12-18). pap. 5.50 *(978-0-9721668-5-0(8)*, 69962463-033c-4c38-aadd-6cd41685080a) Moonstone.
George, J. A. Camp Aconyte. 2008. 65p. pap. 19.95 *(978-1-60610-631-0(7))* America Star Bks.
Gerwitz, Felice & Gerwitz, Christina. Dinosaur Quest at Diamond Peak, 3, Vol. 2. 2nd rev. ed. 2007. (Truth Seeker's Mystery Ser.). 208p. (YA). per. 8.99 *(978-1-931941-11-2(4))* Media Angels, Inc.
—The Missing Link: Found, 3, Vol. 1. 2nd rev. ed. 2004. (Truth Seeker's Mystery Ser.). 208p. (YA). per. 8.99 *(978-1-931941-08-2(4))* Media Angels, Inc.
Ghost Detectors Set 2, 6 vols. 2011. (Ghost Detectors Ser.: 6). (ENG., Illus.). 80p. (J). (gr. 2-5). 213.84 *(978-1-61641-622-5(X)*, 8812, Calico Chapter Bks.) ABDO Publishing Co.
Gibbons, Alan. End Game. 2016. (ENG.). 304p. (YA). (gr. 7-12). pap. 7.99 *(978-1-78062-181-4(7)*, Orion Children's Bks.) Hachette Children's Group GBR. Dist: Hachette Bk. Group.
—They Saw Too Much. 2019. (ENG.). 240p. (YA). (gr. 7-17). 10.99 *(978-1-78062-248-4(1)*, Orion Children's Bks.) Hachette Children's Group GBR. Dist: Hachette Bk. Group.
Gibbs, Anna. The Mystery of the Healing Waters. 2005. 55p. pap. 10.00 *(978-1-4134-4533-6(0))* Xlibris Corp.
Gibbs, Gretchen. The Book of Maggie Bradstreet. 2012. (Bradstreet Chronicles). (ENG.). 183p. (YA). pap. 9.99 *(978-0-9852948-0-9(9))* Glenmere Pr.
Gibbs, Stuart. Bear Bottom. (FunJungle Ser.). (ENG., Illus.). (J). (gr. 3-7). 2022. 336p. pap. 8.99 *(978-1-5344-7947-0(3))* 2021. 320p. 17.99 *(978-1-5344-7946-3(5))* Simon & Schuster Bks. For Young Readers. (Simon & Schuster Bks. For Young Readers).
—Belly Up. 2011. (ENG.). (J). (gr. 4-7). lib. bdg. 18.60 *(978-1-61383-640-8(6))* Perfection Learning Corp.
—Belly Up. (FunJungle Ser.). (ENG.). (J). (gr. 3-7). 2011. 320p. pap. 8.99 *(978-1-4169-8732-1(0))* 2010. (Illus.). 304p. 18.99

M N O

(978-1-4169-8731-4(2)) Simon & Schuster Bks. For Young Readers. (Simon & Schuster Bks. For Young Readers).

—Big Game. 2015. (FunJungle Ser.). (ENG., Illus.). 352p. (J). (gr. 3-7). 18.99 *(978-1-4814-2333-5(9)*, Simon & Schuster Bks. For Young Readers) Simon & Schuster Bks. For Young Readers.

—Even More FunJungle: Panda-Monium; Lion down; Tyrannosaurus Wrecks. 2020. (FunJungle Ser.). (ENG., Illus.). 1040p. (J). (gr. 3-7). 53.99 *(978-1-5344-6783-5(1)*, Simon & Schuster Bks. For Young Readers) Simon & Schuster Bks. For Young Readers.

—The FunJungle Mystery Madness Collection: Panda-Monium; Lion down; Tyrannosaurus Wrecks. 2021. (FunJungle Ser.). (ENG., Illus.). 1120p. (J). (gr. 3-7). pap. 26.99 *(978-1-6659-0048-5(2)*, Simon & Schuster Bks. For Young Readers) Simon & Schuster Bks. For Young Readers.

—The FunJungle Paperback Collection (Boxed Set) Belly up; Poached; Big Game. 2021. (FunJungle Ser.). (ENG., Illus.). 1040p. (J). (gr. 3-7). pap. 26.99 *(978-1-6659-0042-3(3)*, Simon & Schuster Bks. For Young Readers) Simon & Schuster Bks. For Young Readers.

—Lion Down. 2019. (FunJungle Ser.). (ENG., Illus.). 352p. (J). (gr. 3-7). 18.99 *(978-1-5344-2473-9(3)*, Simon & Schuster Bks. For Young Readers) Simon & Schuster Bks. For Young Readers.

—Panda-Monium. (FunJungle Ser.). (ENG.). (J). (gr. 3-7). 2018. 384p. pap. 8.99 *(978-1-4814-4568-9(5))* 2017. (Illus.). 352p. 18.99 *(978-1-4814-4567-2(7))* Simon & Schuster Bks. For Young Readers. (Simon & Schuster Bks. For Young Readers).

—Panda-Monium. 2018. (Funjungle (Teddy Fitzroy) Ser.: 4). lib. bdg. 18.40 *(978-0-606-40849-3(5))* Turtleback.

—Poached. (FunJungle Ser.). (ENG., Illus.). 352p. (J). (gr. 3-7). 2015. pap. 8.99 *(978-1-4424-6778-1(9))* 2014. 18.99 *(978-1-4424-6777-4(0))* Simon & Schuster Bks. For Young Readers. (Simon & Schuster Bks. For Young Readers).

—Space Case. 2015. (Moon Base Alpha Ser.). (ENG., Illus.). 368p. (J). (gr. 3-7). pap. 8.99 *(978-1-4424-9487-9(5)*, Simon & Schuster Bks. For Young Readers) Simon & Schuster Bks. For Young Readers.

—Space Case. 2015. (Moon Base Alpha Ser.: 1). lib. bdg. 18.40 *(978-0-606-37883-3(9))* Turtleback.

—Spaced Out. (Moon Base Alpha Ser.). (ENG.). (J). (gr. 3-7). 2017. 368p. pap. 8.99 *(978-1-4814-2337-3(1))* 2016. (Illus.). 352p. 18.99 *(978-1-4814-2336-6(3))* Simon & Schuster Bks. For Young Readers. (Simon & Schuster Bks. For Young Readers).

—Spaced Out. 2017. (Moon Base Alpha Ser.: 2). lib. bdg. 18.40 *(978-0-606-39762-9(0))* Turtleback.

—Tyrannosaurus Wrecks. (FunJungle Ser.). (ENG., Illus.). (J). (gr. 3-7). 2021. 368p. pap. 8.99 *(978-1-5344-4376-1(2))* 2020. 336p. 17.99 *(978-1-5344-4375-4(4))* Simon & Schuster Bks. For Young Readers. (Simon & Schuster Bks. For Young Readers).

—Waste of Space. (Moon Base Alpha Ser.). (ENG.). (J). (gr. 3-7). 2019. 368p. pap. 8.99 *(978-1-4814-7780-2(3))* 2018. (Illus.). 336p. 18.99 *(978-1-4814-7779-6(X))* Simon & Schuster Bks. For Young Readers. (Simon & Schuster Bks. For Young Readers).

—Whale Done. 2023. (FunJungle Ser.). (ENG., Illus.). 320p. (J). (gr. 3-7). 17.99 *(978-1-5344-9931-7(8)*, Simon & Schuster Bks. For Young Readers) Simon & Schuster Bks. For Young Readers.

Giff, Patricia Reilly. Animal at Large. Carter, Abby, illus. 2020. (Mysteries on Zoo Lane Ser.: 2). 128p. (J). (gr. 2-5). 16.99 *(978-0-8234-4667-4(0))* Holiday Hse., Inc

—Meet the Crew at the Zoo. Carter, Abby, illus. 2020. (Mysteries on Zoo Lane Ser.: 1). 112p. (J). (gr. 2-5). 16.99 *(978-0-8234-4666-7(2))* Holiday Hse., Inc.

—The Mystery of the Blue Ring. 73p. (J). (gr. 1-2). pap. 3.99 *(978-0-8072-1272-1(5)*, Listening Library) Random Hse. Audio Publishing Group.

—The Powder Puff Puzzle. 75p. (J). pap. 3.99 *(978-0-8072-1275-2(X)*, Listening Library) Random Hse. Audio Publishing Group.

—The Riddle of the Red Purse. 68p. (J). pap. 3.99 *(978-0-8072-1273-8(3)*, Listening Library) Random Hse. Audio Publishing Group.

Giffen, Keith. Scooby Apocalypse Vol. 1. 2017. lib. bdg. 29.40 *(978-0-606-39806-0(6))* Turtleback.

Gilbert, D. Hide & Seek: A Mystery Novel for Children. 2005. 187p. pap. 24.95 *(978-1-4137-9748-0(2))* PublishAmerica, Inc.

Gilbert, Kelly Loy. Conviction. 2018. (YA). lib. bdg. 20.85 *(978-0-606-39170-2(3))* Turtleback.

Giles, Lamar. Endangered. 2016. (ENG.). 304p. (YA). (gr. 9). pap. 10.99 *(978-0-06-229757-0(0)*, HarperTeen) HarperCollins Pubs.

—Fake ID. 2014. (ENG.). 320p. (YA). (gr. 8). 17.99 *(978-0-06-212184-4(7)*, Amistad) HarperCollins Pubs.

—Spin. (ENG.). 400p. (gr. 7-7). 2020. (J). pap. 12.99 *(978-1-338-58218-5(6))* 2019. (Illus.). (YA). 18.99 *(978-1-338-21921-0(9)*, Scholastic Pr.) Scholastic, Inc.

Gilligan, Shannon. The Case of the Silk King. Pornkerd, Vorrarit et al, illus. 2006. (ENG.). 144p. (J). (gr. 4-8). per. 7.99 *(978-1-933390-14-7(X)*, CHCL14) Chooseco LLC.

—The Case of the Silk King. 2005. 116p. (J). pap. *(978-0-7608-9702-7(6))* Sundance/Newbridge Educational Publishing.

—Choose Your Own Adventure: The Case of the Silk King. 2007. 144p. (J). pap. *(978-1-74169-069-9(2))* Chooseco LLC.

—The Mystery of Ura Senke. 2005. (Illus.). 120p. (Orig.). (J). *(978-0-7608-9701-0(8))* Sundance/Newbridge Educational Publishing.

Gilman, David. Blood Sun. 2012. (Danger Zone Ser.: 3). (ENG.). 432p. (YA). (gr. 7). pap. 10.99 *(978-0-440-42241-9(8)*, Ember) Random Hse. Children's Bks.

Ginns, Russell. Samantha Spinner & the Spectacular Specs. 2019. (Samantha Spinner Ser.: 2). (Illus.). 416p. (J). (gr. 3-7). 16.99 *(978-1-5247-2004-9(6)*, Delacorte Bks. for Young Readers) Random Hse. Children's Bks.

—Samantha Spinner & the Super-Secret Plans. Fisinger, Barbara, illus. 2018. (Samantha Spinner Ser.: 1). 208p. (J). (gr. 3-7). 16.99 *(978-1-5247-2000-1(3)*, Delacorte Bks. for Young Readers) Random Hse. Children's Bks.

Giovannoli, Renato. Misterio en Villa Jamaica. 2005. (SPA.). 122p. (J). (gr. 4-5). 7.95 *(978-84-348-6713-0(3))* SM Ediciones ESP. Dist: Iaconi, Mariuccia Bk. Imports.

Gipson, Morrell, ed. Stories of Mystery, Adventure & Fun from Calling All Girls. Dawson, Isabel, illus. 2011. 252p. 46.95 *(978-1-258-10497-9(0))* Literary Licensing, LLC.

Girard, Geoffrey. Truthers. 2017. (ENG.). 360p. (YA). (gr. 7-12). 17.99 *(978-1-5124-2779-0(9)*, 0d09002c-e9fc-4b30-baed-e1251cfe8f3e, Carolrhoda Lab™) Lerner Publishing Group.

Girdner, Randall P. Mr. Ping's Almanac of the Twisted & Weird presents Boyd Mccloyd & the Perpetual Motion Machine. 2009. 473p. pap. 25.00 *(978-0-615-25755-6(0))* Acclimated Spooks, Light, & Power.

Gleason, Colleen. The Chess Queen Enigma: A Stoker & Holmes Novel. (ENG.). 360p. (YA). (gr. 7-12). 2016. pap. 9.99 *(978-1-4521-5649-1(2))* 2015. (Stoker & Holmes Ser.: 3). 17.99 *(978-1-4521-4317-0(X))* Chronicle Bks. LLC.

Godfrey. Murder in the Shadows. (Thumbprint Mysteries Ser.). 32.86 *(978-0-8092-0418-2(5))* McGraw-Hill/Contemporary.

Goerz, Gillian. Shirley & Jamila Save Their Summer. 2020. (Illus.). 224p. (J). (gr. 3-7). 20.99 *(978-0-525-55285-7(5))*; pap. 13.99 *(978-0-525-55286-4(3))* Penguin Young Readers Group. (Dial Bks).

Goguen, Martha M. Andromed: Dream Believe Achieve Series. Walker, Patricia M., illus. 2011. 36p. pap. *(978-1-897435-35-9(5))* Agio Publishing Hse.

Goldish, Meish. Sherlock: A Police Dog Story. Andrae, Tom, illus. 2016. (Hound Town Chronicles Ser.). (ENG.). 32p. (J). (gr. 2-6). 28.50 *(978-1-62724-870-9(6))* Bearport Publishing Co., Inc.

Gonzalez, Christina Diaz. Moving Target. 2015. (ENG.). 256p. (J). (gr. 3-7). 17.99 *(978-0-545-77318-8(0)*, Scholastic Pr.) Scholastic, Inc.

Gordon, Lynn & Idle, Molly. Circus Fantastico: A Magnifying Mystery. 2010. (ENG., Illus.). 38p. (J). (gr. k-3). 16.99 *(978-0-7407-9199-4(0))* Andrews McMeel Publishing.

Gore, E. J. Taya Bayliss - Treasure Hunter. 2012. 86p. (J). pap. *(978-0-9873708-0-8(4))* Coppertop Pr.

Gorman, Karyn. Betty Q Investigates. 2015. (Race Further with Reading Ser.). (ENG., Illus.). 48p. (J). (gr. 3-3). *(978-0-7787-2029-4(2))* Crabtree Publishing Co.

Gosling, Sharon. The Diamond Thief. 2014. (Diamond Thief Ser.). (ENG.). 336p. (J). (gr. 9-12). 16.95 *(978-1-63079-002-8(8)*, 126763, Switch Pr.) Capstone.

—The Ruby Airship. 2015. (Diamond Thief Ser.). (ENG.). 496p. (YA). (gr. 9-12). 16.95 *(978-1-63079-004-2(4)*, 126924, Switch Pr.) Capstone.

—The Sapphire Cutlass. 2016. (Diamond Thief Ser.). (ENG.). 336p. (J). (gr. 9-12). 16.95 *(978-1-63079-041-7(9)*, 131432, Switch Pr.) Capstone.

Gould, Sasha. Cross My Heart. 2013. (ENG.). 272p. (YA). (gr. 8-12). lib. bdg. 24.94 *(978-0-375-99007-6(0)*, Delacorte Pr.) Random Hse. Children's Bks.

Grabenstein, Chris. The Demons' Door. 2017. (Haunted Mystery Ser.: 2). 352p. (J). (gr. 3-7). 8.99 *(978-1-5247-6520-0(1)*, Yearling) Random Hse. Children's Bks.

—Escape from Mr. Lemoncello's Library. (Mr. Lemoncello's Library: 1). (ENG.). (J). (gr. 3-7). 2014. 336p. 8.99 *(978-0-307-93147-4(1)*, Yearling) 2013. 304p. 18.99 *(978-0-375-87089-7(X)*, Random Hse. Bks. for Young Readers) Random Hse. Children's Bks.

—Escape from Mr. Lemoncello's Library. 2014. lib. bdg. 18.40 *(978-0-606-37114-8(1))* Turtleback.

—Home Sweet Motel. 2018. (Welcome to Wonderland Ser.: 1). lib. bdg. 18.40 *(978-0-606-40937-7(8))* Turtleback.

—Riley Mack & the Other Known Troublemakers. 2012. (Riley Mack Ser.: 1). (ENG.). 272p. (J). (gr. 3-7). 16.99 *(978-0-06-202620-0(8))* HarperCollins Pubs.

—Riley Mack Stirs up More Trouble. 2013. (Riley Mack Ser.: 2). (ENG.). 336p. (J). (gr. 3-7). 16.99 *(978-0-06-202622-4(4))* HarperCollins Pubs.

—Welcome to Wonderland #3: Sandapalooza Shake-Up. 2018. (Welcome to Wonderland Ser.: 3). (Illus.). 304p. (J). (gr. 3-7). 13.99 *(978-1-5247-1758-2(4)*, Random Hse. Bks. for Young Readers) Random Hse. Children's Bks.

Grabenstein, Chris, et al. Super Puzzletastic Mysteries: Short Stories for Young Sleuths from Mystery Writers of America. 2020. (ENG.). 384p. (J). (gr. 3-7). 17.99 *(978-0-06-288420-6(4)*, HarperCollins) HarperCollins Pubs.

Graham, Cheryl. Stephanie's Shoes. 2010. 28p. pap. 9.95 *(978-1-4327-5944-5(2))* Outskirts Pr., Inc.

Graham, Deborah. The Magic Comes Back: A Max & Sam Adventure. 2012. 66p. (gr. 2-4). pap. 8.95 *(978-1-4759-4758-8(5))* iUniverse, Inc.

Granny's Favorite Tales. 2006. (Illus.). 156p. (J). per. 39.95 *(978-1-60002-098-8(4)*, 3915) Mountain Valley Publishing, LLC.

Grant, Natalie. Miracle in Music City, 1 vol. 2016. (Faithgirlz / Glimmer Girls Ser.: 3). (ENG.). 208p. (J). pap. 8.99 *(978-0-310-75250-9(7))* Zonderkidz.

Grant, Vicki. Cochonnet, 1 vol. 2011. (Orca Currents en Français Ser.). (FRE.). 112p. (J). (gr. 4-7). pap. 9.95 *(978-1-4598-0006-9(0))* Orca Bk. Pubs. USA.

—Hold the Pickles, 1 vol. 2012. (Orca Currents Ser.). (ENG.). 112p. (J). (gr. 4-7). 16.95 *(978-1-55469-921-6(5))* Orca Bk. Pubs. USA.

—Triggered, 1 vol. 2013. (Orca Soundings Ser.). (ENG.). 128p. (YA). (gr. 8-12). pap. 9.95 *(978-1-4598-0526-2(7))* Orca Bk. Pubs. USA.

Gratz, Alan. Something Rotten, 1. 2007. (Horatio Wilkes Mystery Ser.). (ENG.). 208p. (J). (gr. 7-12). 21.19 *(978-0-8037-3216-2(3))* Penguin Young Readers Group.

—Something Wicked, 2. 2008. (Horatio Wilkes Mystery Ser.). (ENG.). 272p. (YA). (gr. 7-12). 22.44 *(978-0-8037-3666-5(5)*, Dial) Penguin Publishing Group.

Grau, Sheila & Sutphin, Joe. Dr. Critchlore's School for Minions: Book Two: Gorilla Tactics. 2016. (Dr. Critchlore's School for Minions Ser.). (ENG., Illus.). 304p. (J). (gr. 3-7). 14.95 *(978-1-4197-1371-2(X)*, 1091701, Amulet Bks.) Abrams, Inc.

Gray, Jennifer. Atticus Claw Breaks the Law. Ecob, Mark, illus. 2016. (Atticus Claw Ser.). (ENG.). 224p. (gr. 1-4). pap. 7.95 *(978-0-571-28449-8(3))* Faber & Faber, Inc.

The Great Paua Mystery: Kyss Series. 2003. (J). mass mkt. *(978-1-932233-69-8(5))* Aurora Libris Corp.

Green, Jacqueline. Kiss & Tell. 2015. (Truth or Dare Ser.: 3). (ENG.). 288p. (YA). (gr. 10-17). 18.00 *(978-0-316-22033-0(7)*, Poppy) Little, Brown Bks. for Young Readers.

—Secrets & Lies. 2014. (Truth or Dare Ser.: 2). (ENG.). 336p. (YA). (gr. 10-17). pap. 17.99 *(978-0-316-22030-9(2)*, Poppy) Little, Brown Bks. for Young Readers.

Green, Jim. Shadows of the Moon... Dancing. 2007. (YA). pap. 14.95 *(978-1-59705-872-8(6))* Wings ePress, Inc.

Green, John. Paper Towns. 2018. (RUS., Illus.). 338p. *(978-5-519-56613-1(5))*; 322p. *(978-5-519-56615-5(1))*; 338p. pap. *(978-5-519-52003-4(8))*; 322p. pap. *(978-5-519-52005-8(4))* Books on Demand.

—Paper Towns. 2011. 11.04 *(978-0-7848-3497-8(0)*, Everbind) Marco Bk. Co.

—Paper Towns. (ENG.). (YA). (gr. 9-18). 2009. 336p. 12.99 *(978-0-14-241493-4(X)*, Penguin Books) 2008. 320p. 18.99 *(978-0-525-47818-8(3)*, Dutton Books for Young Readers) Penguin Young Readers Group.

—Paper Towns. 2010. (ENG., Illus.). 305p. (gr. 9-12). 20.00 *(978-1-60686-913-0(2))* Perfection Learning Corp.

—Paper Towns. 2009. lib. bdg. 20.85 *(978-0-606-10658-0(8))* Turtleback.

—Penguin Minis: Paper Towns. 2018. (ENG.). 648p. (YA). (gr. 9). pap. 12.00 *(978-0-525-55573-5(0)*, Dutton Books for Young Readers) Penguin Young Readers Group.

Green, Ken. Not a Chance. (Thumbprint Mysteries Ser.). 32.86 *(978-0-8092-0422-9(3))* McGraw-Hill/Contemporary.

Green, Terry. Moonstone. 2010. 188p. pap. 14.49 *(978-1-4520-4634-1(4))* AuthorHouse.

Greene, Janice. The Girl Who Had Everything (Suspense), 1 vol. 2017. (Pageturners Ser.). (ENG.). 80p. (YA). (gr. 9-12). 10.75 *(978-1-68021-407-9(1))* Saddleback Educational Publishing, Inc.

—The White Room, 1 vol. unabr. ed. 2010. (Q Reads Ser.). (ENG.). 32p. (YA). (gr. 9-12). pap. 8.50 *(978-1-61651-197-5(4))* Saddleback Educational Publishing, Inc.

Greenfield, A. B. Ra the Mighty: Cat Detective. Horne, Sarah, illus. (Ra the Mighty Ser.: 1). (ENG.). (J). (gr. 2-5). 2019. 240p. pap. 7.99 *(978-0-8234-4438-0(4))* 2018. 224p. 16.99 *(978-0-8234-4027-6(3))* Holiday Hse., Inc.

—Ra the Mighty: the Great Tomb Robbery. Horne, Sarah, illus. 2019. (Ra the Mighty Ser.: 2). (ENG.). 256p. (J). (gr. 2-5). 16.99 *(978-0-8234-4240-9(3))* Holiday Hse., Inc.

Greenwood, Anna. The Children at St Bartholomew's Hospital. 2008. 172p. pap. 13.95 *(978-1-4401-0558-6(8))* iUniverse, Inc.

Gregory, Nan. How Smudge Came, 1 vol. Lightburn, Ron, illus. 2003. (ENG.). 32p. (J). pap. 6.95 *(978-0-88995-161-7(6)*, 73190597-709c-488c-8ed0-b4192a99dc95) Red Deer Pr. CAN. Dist: Firefly Bks., Ltd.

Griffin, Adele. The Unfinished Life of Addison Stone: a Novel. 2016. (Illus.). 256p. (YA). (gr. 9). pap. 11.99 *(978-1-61695-596-0(1)*, Soho Teen) Soho Pr., Inc.

Griffin, N. Smashie Mcperter & the Mystery of Room 11. Hindley, Kate, illus. 2015. (Smashie Mcperter Investigates Ser.: 1). (ENG.). 256p. (J). (gr. 2-5). 15.99 *(978-0-7636-6145-8(7))* Candlewick Pr.

—Smashie Mcperter & the Mystery of the Missing Goop. Hindley, Kate, illus. (Smashie Mcperter Investigates Ser.: 2). (ENG.). 304p. (J). (gr. 2-5). 2017. pap. 7.99 *(978-0-7636-9795-2(8))* 2016. 15.99 *(978-0-7636-8535-5(6))* Candlewick Pr.

Griffiths, Andy. The 52-Story Treehouse. 2017. (Treehouse Adventures Ser.: 4). (J). lib. bdg. 17.20 *(978-0-606-40350-4(7))* Turtleback.

—The 52-Story Treehouse: Vegetable Villains! Denton, Terry, illus. 2016. (Treehouse Bks.: 4). (ENG.). 336p. (J). (gr. 2-5). 17.99 *(978-1-250-02693-4(8)*, 900098158) Feiwel & Friends.

—The 52-Story Treehouse: Vegetable Villains! Denton, Terry, illus. 2017. (Treehouse Bks.: 4). (ENG.). 352p. (J). pap. 8.99 *(978-1-250-10379-6(7)*, 900163638) Square Fish.

Griggs, Joyce. Imanis Good Deed. 2006. pap. 9.95 *(978-1-4327-0071-3(5))* Outskirts Pr., Inc.

Grigsby, Cynthia. Hollow Creek: A Haunted Beginning, 01. 2006. 163p. (J). 14.95 *(978-0-9786840-0-6(1))* Grigsby, Cynthia.

Grisham, John. The Abduction. 2009. (Theodore Boone Ser.: Bk. 2). 9.68 *(978-0-7848-3783-2(X)*, Everbind) Marco Bk. Co.

—The Abduction. 2012. (Theodore Boone Ser.: 2). lib. bdg. 19.65 *(978-0-606-26079-4(X))* Turtleback.

—The Accused. 2013. (Theodore Boone Ser.: 3). lib. bdg. 18.40 *(978-0-606-31696-5(5))* Turtleback.

—The Fugitive. 2016. (Theodore Boone Ser.: 5). 272p. lib. bdg. 18.40 *(978-0-606-38847-4(8))* Turtleback.

—Kid Lawyer. l.t. ed. 2010. (Theodore Boone Ser.: Bk. 1). (ENG.). 278p. (J). 24.99 *(978-1-4104-3050-2(2))* Thorndike Pr.

—Kid Lawyer. 2011. (Theodore Boone Ser.: 1). lib. bdg. 19.65 *(978-0-606-23071-1(8))* Turtleback.

—Theodore Boone: Kid Lawyer. 2014. lthr. 79.00 *(978-1-62715-259-4(8))* Leatherbound Bestsellers.

—Theodore Boone: Kid Lawyer. 2011. 18.00 *(978-1-60686-999-4(X))* Perfection Learning Corp.

—Theodore Boone: Kid Lawyer. 2011. (Theodore Boone Ser.: 1). (ENG.). 288p. (J). (gr. 3-7). 8.99 *(978-0-14-241722-5(X)*, Puffin Books) Penguin Young Readers Group.

—Theodore Boone: the Abduction, 2 vols. (Theodore Boone Ser.: 2). (ENG.). 256p. (J). (gr. 3-7). 2012. pap. 8.99 *(978-0-14-242137-6(5)*, Puffin Books) 2011. 16.99 *(978-0-525-42557-1(8)*, Dutton Books for Young Readers) Penguin Young Readers Group.

—Theodore Boone: the Accused. 2013. (Theodore Boone Ser.: 3). (ENG.). 304p. (J). (gr. 3-7). pap. 8.99 *(978-0-14-242613-5(X)*, Puffin Books) Penguin Young Readers Group.

—Theodore Boone: the Activist. 2013. (Theodore Boone Ser.: 4). (ENG.). 304p. (J). (gr. 3-7). 17.99 *(978-0-525-42577-9(2)*, Dutton Books for Young Readers) Penguin Young Readers Group.

—Theodore Boone: the Fugitive. 2015. (Theodore Boone Ser.: 5). (ENG.). 256p. (J). (gr. 3-7). 17.99 *(978-0-525-42638-7(8)*, Dutton Books for Young Readers) Penguin Young Readers Group.

—Theodore Boone: the Scandal. 2016. (Theodore Boone Ser.: 6). (ENG.). 224p. (J). (gr. 3-7). 17.99 *(978-0-525-42639-4(6)*, Dutton Books for Young Readers) Penguin Young Readers Group.

Groot, Bob de. Jade Vol. 5. Rodrigue, illus. 2008. (Clifton Ser.: 5). 48p. pap. 11.95 *(978-1-905460-52-6(X))* CineBook GBR. Dist: National Bk. Network.

Groot, De. Black Moon. Spear, Luke, tr. Rodrigue, illus. 2007. (Clifton Ser.: 4). 48p. (J). (gr. 4-7). pap. 9.99 *(978-1-905460-30-4(9))* CineBook GBR. Dist: National Bk. Network.

Guest, Jacqueline. At Risk, 1 vol. 2004. (Lorimer SideStreets Ser.). (ENG.). 192p. (YA). (gr. 9-12). 8.99 *(978-1-55028-846-9(6)*, a7832d31-abee-469d-a271-d933129b851b); 16.95 *(978-1-55028-847-6(4)*, 847) James Lorimer & Co. Ltd., Pubs. CAN. Dist: Lerner Publishing Group, Formac Lorimer Bks. Ltd.

Guidone, Ellen. Scooby-Doo in Lights Out at the Ball Game, 1 vol. Sur, Duendes del, illus. 2016. (Scooby-Doo Early Reading Adventures Ser.). (ENG.). 24p. (J). (gr. -1-2). lib. bdg. 31.36 *(978-1-61479-475-2(8)*, 21388) Spotlight.

Gunderson, Jessica A. How to Keep a Secret for Detectives. 2008. 206p. pap. 15.50 *(978-0-557-01369-2(0))* Lulu Pr., Inc.

Gustafson, Scott. Eddie: The Lost Youth of Edgar Allan Poe. Gustafson, Scott, illus. 2012. (ENG., Illus.). 208p. (J). (gr. 3-7). pap. 6.99 *(978-1-4169-9765-8(2)*, Simon & Schuster Bks. For Young Readers) Simon & Schuster Bks. For Young Readers.

—Eddie: The Lost Youth of Edgar Allan Poe. Gustafson, Scott, illus. 2011. (ENG., Illus.). 208p. (J). (gr. 3-7). 15.99 *(978-1-4169-9764-1(4))* Simon & Schuster, Inc.

Gutman, Dan. The Million Dollar Strike. 2004. 176p. (J). lib. bdg. 18.46 *(978-1-4242-2107-3(2))* Fitzgerald Bks.

—The Million Dollar Strike. 2006. 176p. (J). (gr. 3-7). 13.65 *(978-0-7569-7023-9(7))* Perfection Learning Corp.

Guzaldo, Jessica. Murder & Betrayal DeFalco, Julie & Cowhey, Dennis R., eds. Cowhey, Dennis E., illus. 2003. 72p. (YA). (gr. 7-8). pap. 9.95 *(978-0-9642823-2-2(1))* Key Answer Products, Inc.

Hadcroft, Will. Anne Droyd & the Ghosts of Winter Hill. 2013. 210p. pap. *(978-0-9560537-2-5(6))* Nordic.

Haddix, Margaret Peterson. The House on the Gulf. 2006. (ENG., Illus.). 208p. (J). (gr. 3-7). pap. 7.99 *(978-1-4169-1406-8(4)*, Simon & Schuster Bks. For Young Readers) Simon & Schuster Bks. For Young Readers.

—Into the Gauntlet (the 39 Clues, Book 10), Vol. 10. 2010. (39 Clues Ser.: 10). (ENG.). 336p. (J). (gr. 3-7). 12.99 *(978-0-545-06050-9(8))* Scholastic, Inc.

Hadnot, Victor. The Wheels of God. 2003. 140p. (YA). pap. 11.95 *(978-0-595-27507-6(9)*, Writers Club Pr.) iUniverse, Inc.

Haesche, Richard, Sr. The Mystery of Monster Manor. 2007. (ENG.). 306p. (YA). 11.99 *(978-0-9798536-6-1(4))* Kreative X-Pressions Pubns.

Haesche, Richard Paul, Sr. The Mystery of Dismal Swamp. 2007. 402p. (YA). 10.99 *(978-0-9798536-8-5(0))* Kreative X-Pressions Pubns.

—The Treasure of Pirates Cave. 2007. (ENG.). 378p. (YA). 11.99 *(978-0-9798536-7-8(2))* Kreative X-Pressions Pubns.

Hahn, Mary Downing. Closed for the Season. 2010. (ENG.). 192p. (J). (gr. 5-7). pap. 7.99 *(978-0-547-39853-2(0)*, 1427651, Clarion Bks.) HarperCollins Pubs.

—The Dead Man in Indian Creek. 2009. (gr. 3-6). 17.20 *(978-0-8335-6693-5(8))* Turtleback.

Haight, Jessica & Robinson, Stephanie. Fairday Morrow & the Talking Library. 2017. (ENG., Illus.). 228p. (J). (gr. 3-6). pap. 9.99 *(978-0-9993449-1-0(9))*; (Fairday Morrow Ser.: Vol. 2). 24.99 *(978-0-9993449-0-3(0))* Pronoun, Inc.

Hale, Bruce. The Big Nap. unabr. ed. 2004. (Chet Gecko Mystery Ser.: No. 4). 128p. (J). (gr. 3-6). pap. 17.00 incl. audio *(978-0-8072-1707-8(7)*, S FTR 272 SP, Listening Library) Random Hse. Audio Publishing Group.

—Dial M for Mongoose: A Chet Gecko Mystery. 2010. (Chet Gecko Ser.: 15). (ENG., Illus.). 128p. (J). (gr. 3-7). pap. 6.99 *(978-0-547-48079-4(2)*, 1439406, Clarion Bks.) HarperCollins Pubs.

—Farewell, My Lunchbag. unabr. ed. 2004. (Chet Gecko Mystery Ser.: No. 3). 128p. (J). (gr. 3-6). pap. 17.00 incl. audio *(978-0-8072-1708-5(5)*, S FTR 273 SP, Listening Library) Random Hse. Audio Publishing Group.

—Farewell, My Lunchbag: A Chet Gecko Mystery. Hale, Bruce, illus. 2009. (Chet Gecko Ser.: 3). (ENG., Illus.). 128p. (J). (gr. 3-7). pap. 6.99 *(978-0-15-202629-5(0)*, 1193357, Clarion Bks.) HarperCollins Pubs.

—From Russia with Lunch: A Chet Gecko Mystery. Hale, Bruce, illus. 2010. (Chet Gecko Ser.: 14). (ENG., Illus.). 128p. (J). (gr. 3-7). pap. 6.99 *(978-0-547-32882-9(6)*, 1416990, Clarion Bks.) HarperCollins Pubs.

—Give My Regrets to Broadway. 2005. (Chet Gecko Mystery Ser.). (Illus.). 115p. (gr. 3-7). 16.00 *(978-0-7569-5247-1(6))* Perfection Learning Corp.

—Give My Regrets to Broadway: A Chet Gecko Mystery. Hale, Bruce, illus. 2005. (Chet Gecko Ser.: 9). (ENG., Illus.). 144p. (J). (gr. 3-7). pap. 6.99 *(978-0-15-216730-1(7)*, 1201742, Clarion Bks.) HarperCollins Pubs.

—The Hamster of the Baskervilles: A Chet Gecko Mystery. Hale, Bruce, illus. 2003. (Chet Gecko Ser.: 5). (ENG., Illus.). 144p. (J). (gr. 3-7). pap. 6.99 *(978-0-15-202509-0(X)*, 1063329, Clarion Bks.) HarperCollins Pubs.

—Hiss Me Deadly: A Chet Gecko Mystery. Hale, Bruce, illus. 2009. (Chet Gecko Ser.: 13). (ENG., Illus.). 128p. (J). (gr. 3-7). pap. 6.99 *(978-0-15-206424-2(9)*, 1063327, Clarion Bks.) HarperCollins Pubs.

—Key Lardo: A Chet Gecko Mystery. Hale, Bruce, illus. 2007. (Chet Gecko Ser.: 12). (ENG., Illus.). 128p. (J). (gr. 3-7). pap. 7.99 *(978-0-15-205235-5(6)*, 1195772, Clarion Bks.) HarperCollins Pubs.

—The Malted Falcon. 2004. (Chet Gecko Mystery Ser.: 7). (ENG., Illus.). 128p. (J). (gr. 4-6). 17.44 *(978-0-15-216706-6(4))* Harcourt Children's Bks.

—The Malted Falcon. 2007. (Chet Gecko Mystery Ser.). (Illus.). 107p. (J). (gr. 4-7). pap. 6.60 *(978-1-4189-5239-6(7))* Harcourt Trade Pubs.

—The Malted Falcon: A Chet Gecko Mystery. Hale, Bruce, illus. 2008. (Chet Gecko Ser.: 7). (ENG., Illus.). 128p. (J). (gr. 3-7). pap. 9.99 *(978-0-15-216712-7(9))*, 1201705, Clarion Bks.) HarperCollins Pubs.

—Murder, My Tweet. 2004. (Chet Gecko Mystery Ser.: 10). (ENG., Illus.). 136p. (J). (gr. 4-6). 17.44 *(978-0-15-205012-2(4))* Houghton Mifflin Harcourt Publishing Co.

—Murder, My Tweet. 2005. (Chet Gecko Mystery Ser.). (Illus.). 117p. (gr. 3-7). 16.00 *(978-0-7569-5248-8(4))* Perfection Learning Corp.

—The Mystery of Mr. Nice. unabr. ed. 2004. (Chet Gecko Mystery Ser.: No. 2). 112p. (J). (gr. 3-6). pap. 17.00 incl. audio *(978-0-8072-0343-9(2)*, Listening Library) Random Hse. Audio Publishing Group.

—The Mystery of Mr. Nice: A Chet Gecko Mystery. Hale, Bruce, illus. 2008. (Chet Gecko Ser.: 2). (ENG., Illus.). 128p. (J). (gr. 3-7). pap. 6.99 *(978-0-15-202515-1(4)*, 1193021, Clarion Bks.) HarperCollins Pubs.

—The Possum Always Rings Twice. Hale, Bruce, illus. 2007. (Chet Gecko Ser.: 11). (ENG., Illus.). 128p. (J). (gr. 3-7). pap. 7.99 *(978-0-15-205233-1(X)*, 1195769, Clarion Bks.) HarperCollins Pubs.

—This Gum for Hire. 2007. (Chet Gecko Mystery Ser.). (Illus.). 115p. (J). (gr. 4-7). pap. 6.60 *(978-1-4189-5216-7(8))* Houghton Mifflin Harcourt Supplemental Pubs.

—This Gum for Hire: A Chet Gecko Mystery. Hale, Bruce, illus. 2003. (Chet Gecko Ser.: 6). (ENG., Illus.). 144p. (J). (gr. 3-7). pap. 6.99 *(978-0-15-202497-0(2)*, 1192976, Clarion Bks.) HarperCollins Pubs.

—Trouble Is My Beeswax. Weinman, Brad, illus. 2003. (Chet Gecko Mystery Ser.: 8). (ENG.). 128p. (J). (gr. 4-6). 17.44 *(978-0-15-216718-9(8))* Houghton Mifflin Harcourt Publishing Co.

—Trouble Is My Beeswax. 2004. (Chet Gecko Mystery Ser.). (Illus.). 111p. (gr. 3-7). 16.00 *(978-0-7569-3488-0(5))* Perfection Learning Corp.

—Trouble Is My Beeswax: A Chet Gecko Mystery. Hale, Bruce, illus. 2004. (Chet Gecko Ser.: 8). (ENG., Illus.). 144p. (J). (gr. 3-7). pap. 6.99 *(978-0-15-216724-0(2)*, 1099020, Clarion Bks.) HarperCollins Pubs.

Hale, Kathleen. No One Else Can Have You. 2014. (Kippy Bushman Ser.). (ENG.). 384p. (YA). (gr. 9). 17.99 *(978-0-06-221119-4(6)*, HarperTeen) HarperCollins Pubs.

—Nothing Bad Is Going to Happen. 2017. (Kippy Bushman Ser.). (ENG.). 272p. (YA). (gr. 9). pap. 9.99 *(978-0-06-221123-1(4)*, HarperTeen) HarperCollins Pubs.

Hale, Shannon. The Forgotten Sisters. 2016. (Princess Academy Ser.: 3). (J). lib. bdg. 18.40 *(978-0-606-38441-4(3))* Turtleback.

—Princess Academy: the Forgotten Sisters. 2015. (Princess Academy Ser.: 3). (ENG.). 336p. (YA). (gr. 5-8). 18.99 *(978-1-61963-485-5(6)*, 900138574, Bloomsbury USA Childrens) Bloomsbury Publishing USA.

Hall, Duncan. Brambleholme Summer. 2010. 125p. pap. 12.95 *(978-1-4461-4462-6(3))* Lulu Pr., Inc.

Hall, Jacque. Tommy Turns Dtective. 2009. pap. 10.95 *(978-1-61584-268-1(3))* Independent Pub.

Halley, Jane E. The Unidentified Flight-Less Object. 2008. 52p. pap. 22.49 *(978-1-4343-6491-3(7))* AuthorHouse.

Halliday, Gemma. Social Suicide. 2012. (Deadly Cool Ser.: 2). (ENG.). 288p. (YA). (gr. 8). pap. 8.99 *(978-0-06-200332-4(1)*, HarperTeen) HarperCollins Pubs.

Halverson, Mathew. Concord Cunningham Pursues the Clues: The Scripture Sleuth 5. 2008. (Mystery Ser.). (Illus.). 98p. (J). (gr. 4-7). pap. 8.95 *(978-1-885904-55-3(X))* Focus Publishing.

Hamilton, Elizabeth L. Mystery at Lake Cachuma. 2003. (Character Mystery Ser.: No. 1). (Illus.). 114p. (J). (gr. 3-6). per. 9.95 *(978-0-9713749-4-2(5)*, Character-in-Action) Quiet Impact, Inc.

—Surprise at Pearl Harbor. 2004. (Character Mystery Ser.: No. 2). (Illus.). 144p. (J). per. 9.95 *(978-0-9754629-2-8(X)*, Character-in-Action) Quiet Impact, Inc.

Hamilton, Virginia. The House of Dies Drear. 8.97 *(978-0-13-437491-8(6))* Prentice Hall PTR.

—The House of Dies Drear. 2006. (ENG., Illus.). 256p. (J). (gr. 6-9). pap. 8.99 *(978-1-4169-1405-1(6)*, Aladdin) Simon & Schuster Children's Publishing.

Hamley, Dennis. Very Far from Here. 2007. 208p. per. *(978-1-904529-33-0(X)*, Back to Front) Solidus.

Hancock, H. Irving. Young Engineers on the Gulf: Or, the Dread Mystery of the Million Dollar Breakwater. 2017. (ENG., Illus.). (J). 23.95 *(978-1-374-93150-3(0))*; pap. 13.95 *(978-1-374-93149-7(7))* Capital Communications, Inc.

Handwerk, Marina. Hey Cool, I've Never Seen a Teacher with His Head Cut off Before! 2007. 284p. per. 11.95 *(978-1-4327-0332-5(3))* Outskirts Pr., Inc.

Hannah, Vickie. There's A Schnoozle in My Closet. 2004. (J). lib. bdg. 19.95 *(978-0-9754728-4-2(4))* Big Ransom Studio.

Hannibal, James R. The Lost Property Office. 2016. (Section 13 Ser.: 1). (ENG., Illus.). 400p. (J). (gr. 3-7). 18.99 *(978-1-4814-6709-4(3)*, Simon & Schuster Bks. For Young Readers) Simon & Schuster Bks. For Young Readers.

Hannigan, Kate. The Detective's Assistant. 2016. (ENG.). 368p. (J). (gr. 3-7). pap. 7.99 *(978-0-316-40349-8(0))* Little, Brown Bks. for Young Readers.

Hansen, Ace. Julius Caesar Brown & the Green Gas Mystery. 2013. 114p. pap. *(978-1-77127-424-1(7))* MuseItUp Publishing.

Hansen, Lynne & Bosco, Sally. AltDeath.com. 2004. 152p. (YA). pap. 9.00 *(978-0-7599-4572-2(1))* Hard Shell Word Factory.

Harbourt, Kathi. The Adventures of Kat VanDrat. 2013. (ENG.). 111p. (YA). pap. 11.95 *(978-1-4787-1010-3(1))* Outskirts Pr., Inc.

Hardie, Richard. Leap of Faith. 2013. (Illus.). 272p. pap. *(978-1-909841-26-0(9))* Crooked Cat Publishing.

Harel, Moshe. Elf Prince. 2012. (ENG.). 258p. pap. *(978-965-550-089-9(6))* Contento De Semrik.

Harkrader, Lisa. A Fishy Mystery. Pillo, Cary, illus. 2017. (Math Matters Ser.). 32p. (J). (gr. k-4). 5.99 *(978-1-57565-866-7(6)*, 6d95be58-8319-4d28-9b99-9a327899b7ae, Kane Press) Astra Publishing Hse.

—A Fishy Mystery: Venn Diagrams. Pillo, Cary, illus. 2017. (Math Matters (r) Ser.). (ENG.). 32p. (J). (gr. k-3). E-Book 23.99 *(978-1-57565-869-8(0))* Astra Publishing Hse.

—The Mystery of the Whispering Fountain. 2016. (Spring Forward Ser.). (J). (gr. 1). *(978-1-4900-9400-7(8))* Benchmark Education Co.

Harris, Donna. Ruff Life. 2011. 240p. pap. 17.99 *(978-1-4567-5081-7(X))* AuthorHouse.

Harris, Loretta. A Gangsta's Life. 2007. 26p. (YA). 1.99 *(978-0-9786681-4-3(6))* Triumphant Living Enterprises, Inc.

—The Rise of Death Valley. 2007. 41p. (YA). 1.99 *(978-0-9786681-0-5(3))* Triumphant Living Enterprises, Inc.

Harris, Patricia. Rosalina & Jethro Solve a Mystery, 1 vol. 2017. (Rosalina's Flower Garden Ser.). (ENG.). 24p. (gr. 1-1). pap. 9.25 *(978-1-5383-2105-8(X)*, 6648d9a4-bf83-4ec5-a585-106234bd52a2, PowerKids Pr.) Rosen Publishing Group, Inc., The.

Harris, Robert J. Artie Conan Doyle & the Gravediggers' Club, 50 vols. 2017. (Artie Conan Doyle Mysteries Ser.: 1). 192p. (J). 9.95 *(978-1-78250-353-8(6)*, Kelpies) Floris Bks. GBR. Dist: Consortium Bk. Sales & Distribution.

—Artie Conan Doyle & the Vanishing Dragon, 30 vols. 2018. (Artie Conan Doyle Mysteries Ser.: 2). (Illus.). 192p. (J). 9.95 *(978-1-78250-483-2(4)*, Kelpies) Floris Bks. GBR. Dist: Consortium Bk. Sales & Distribution.

Harris, Tony. Sailing with the Stars. 2006. (ENG.). 218p. (YA). pap. 13.86 *(978-1-4116-9198-8(9))* Lulu Pr., Inc.

Harrison, Michelle. The Thirteen Curses. 2014. (ENG., Illus.). 464p. (YA). pap. 8.99 *(978-1-4711-2168-5(2)*, Simon & Schuster Children's) Simon & Schuster, Ltd. GBR. Dist: Simon & Schuster, Inc.

—The Thirteen Secrets. 2014. (ENG.). 400p. (YA). pap. 8.99 *(978-1-4711-2169-2(0)*, Simon & Schuster Children's) Simon & Schuster, Ltd. GBR. Dist: Simon & Schuster, Inc.

—The Thirteen Treasures. 2014. (ENG., Illus.). 352p. pap. 8.99 *(978-1-4711-2167-8(4)*, Simon & Schuster Children's) Simon & Schuster, Ltd. GBR. Dist: Simon & Schuster, Inc.

—13 Treasures. 2011. (13 Treasures Trilogy Ser.: 1). (ENG.). 384p. (J). (gr. 3-7). pap. 18.99 *(978-0-316-04147-8(5))* Little, Brown Bks. for Young Readers.

Hart, Alison. Fires of Jubilee. 2003. (ENG., Illus.). 192p. (J). (gr. 3-7). pap. 9.99 *(978-0-689-85528-3(1)*, Simon & Schuster/Paula Wiseman Bks.) Simon & Schuster/Paula Wiseman Bks.

—Return of the Gypsy Witch. 2003. (ENG., Illus.). 176p. (J). (gr. 3-7). pap. 9.99 *(978-0-689-85527-6(3)*, Simon & Schuster/Paula Wiseman Bks.) Simon & Schuster/Paula Wiseman Bks.

—Whirlwind. 2010. (Shadow Horse Ser.). 272p. (YA). (gr. 7-8). pap. 8.99 *(978-0-375-86005-8(3)*, Laurel Leaf) Random Hse. Children's Bks.

Hart, Anne. Roman Justice: Too Roman to Handle. 2003. 186p. (YA). pap. 13.95 *(978-0-595-27282-2(7)*, Writers Advantage Pr.) iUniverse, Inc.

Hartinger, Brent. Three Truths & a Lie. 2016. (ENG., Illus.). 272p. (YA). (gr. 9). 17.99 *(978-1-4814-4960-1(5)*, Simon Pulse) Simon Pulse.

Hartley, A. J. Guardian: Book 3 in the Steeplejack Series. 2019. (Steeplejack Ser.: 3). (ENG.). 320p. (YA). pap. 17.99 *(978-0-7653-8816-2(2)*, 900162382, Tor Teen) Doherty, Tom Assocs., LLC.

Hartley, Susan. Stephanie Investigates. 2004. (Shared Connections Ser.). (J). instr.'s gde. ed. 27.00 *(978-1-4108-1618-4(4))* Benchmark Education Co.

—Stephanie Investigates: Small Book. 2004. (Shared Connections Ser.). (J). pap. *(978-1-4108-1642-9(7))* Benchmark Education Co.

Hartnett, Sonya. What the Birds See. 2007. (ENG., Illus.). 208p. (YA). (gr. 9). pap. 7.99 *(978-0-7636-3680-7(0))* Candlewick Pr.

Hartt-Snowbell, Sarah. Vivian Untangled. 2006. (ENG., Illus.). 136p. (J). per. 8.95 *(978-1-894917-25-4(1)*, Napoleon & Co.) Dundurn Pr. CAN. Dist: Publishers Group West (PGW).

Harvey, Jacqueline. Alice-Miranda at School. 2012. (Alice-Miranda Ser.). (ENG.). 272p. (J). (gr. 2-5). 7.99 *(978-0-385-73994-8(X)*, Yearling) Random Hse. Children's Bks.

—Alice-Miranda to the Rescue. 2016. (Alice-Miranda Ser.: 13). (ENG.). 336p. (J). (gr. 3-7). pap. 9.99 *(978-0-85798-522-4(1))* Random Hse. Australia AUS. Dist: Independent Pubs. Group.

Harvey, M. A. Attack of the Jaguar: Dare to Take the Test. 2004. (Illus.). 128p. (J). pap. *(978-1-84458-051-4(2)*, Pavilion Children's Books) Pavilion Bks.

—The Scorpion Secret: Dare to Take the Test. 2004. (Illus.). 128p. (J). pap. *(978-1-84458-050-7(4)*, Pavilion Children's Books) Pavilion Bks.

Hauf, Kyle. Annabelle Discovers the Missing Lunch Money. PA Illustrator, illus. 2011. 36p. pap. 24.95 *(978-1-4560-3656-0(4))* America Star Bks.

Hautman, Pete. The Forgetting Machine. 2016. (Flinkwater Chronicles Ser.: 2). (ENG., Illus.). 224p. (J). (gr. 4-8). 16.99 *(978-1-4814-6438-3(8)*, Simon & Schuster Bks. For Young Readers) Simon & Schuster Bks. For Young Readers.

—Snatched. 2007. (Bloodwater Mysteries Ser.: 1). 224p. (J). (gr. 5-7). 7.99 *(978-0-14-240795-0(X)*, Puffin Books) Penguin Young Readers Group.

Hawke, Rosanne. Spinner. (Illus.). 160p. pap. *(978-0-7344-0318-6(6)*, Lothian Children's Bks.) Hachette Australia.

Hawking, Stephen & Hawking, Lucy. George's Secret Key to the Universe. Parsons, Garry, illus. 2009. (George's Secret Key Ser.). (ENG.). 336p. (J). (gr. 3-7). pap. 12.99 *(978-1-4169-8584-6(0)*, Simon & Schuster Bks. For Young Readers) Simon & Schuster Bks. For Young Readers.

Hay, Sam. Goldfish from Beyond the Grave #4. Cooper, Simon, illus. 2015. (Undead Pets Ser.: 4). (ENG.). 120p. (J). (gr. 1-3). 5.99 *(978-0-448-47798-5(X)*, Grosset & Dunlap) Penguin Young Readers Group.

Hayes, Celeste. The Puzzle Box of Nefertiti: A Sphinx & Trevi Adventure. Bishop, Christina, illus. 2011. 42p. (J). pap. 19.95 *(978-0-9785695-3-2(9))* Adam's Creations Publishing, LLC.

Hayes, Geoffrey. Benny & Penny in the Big No-No! Toon Books Level 2. Hayes, Geoffrey, illus. 2014. (Toon Ser.). (ENG., Illus.). 32p. (J). (gr. -1-1). pap. 7.99 *(978-1-935179-35-1(7)*, TOON Books) Astra Publishing Hse.

Hays, Anna Jane. The Secret of the Circle-K Cave. Smath, Jerry, illus. 2006. (Science Solves It! Ser.). (ENG.). 32p. (J). (gr. k-2). pap. 5.99 *(978-1-57565-189-7(0)*, 3c159770-6a2b-4f79-b62b-9bd5318deb31, Kane Press) Astra Publishing Hse.

Hays, Phillip. Porka-Bella-Snu & the Mystery of the Letters. Spencer, Chip, illus. 2013. 54p. pap. 6.95 *(978-1-938679-05-6(9))* Written World Communications.

Headrick, Tammy Hill. That Famous Bird, Sir Thornton the Third. 2009. 24p. pap. 12.00 *(978-1-4269-0550-6(5))* Trafford Publishing.

Healey, Karen. The Shattering. 2013. (ENG.). 336p. (YA). (gr. 7-17). pap. 8.99 *(978-0-316-12573-4(3))* Little, Brown Bks. for Young Readers.

Hecht, Tracey. The Ominous Eye: The Nocturnals Book 2. Liebman, Kate, illus. 2016. (Nocturnals Ser.: 2). (ENG.). 208p. (J). (gr. 3-5). 15.99 *(978-1-944020-03-3(9)*, Fabled Films Pr. LLC) Fabled Films LLC.

Hechtman, Betty Jacobson. Blue Schwartz & Nefertiti's Necklace: A Mystery with Recipes. 2006. 152p. (J). (gr. 5-9). per. 8.95 *(978-0-9768126-3-0(0))* Brown Barn Bks.

Hees, Miriam. The Adventures of Jilly & Brad: Noises in the Attic. Kinneman, D. Michael, illus. 2003. 128p. (J). pap. 5.95 *(978-0-9718348-4-2(9))* Blooming Tree Pr.

Helou, Sandra & Chown, Xanna Eve. Grover on the Case: Follow the Reader Level 1. 2008. (Sesame Street Ser.). (ENG.). 24p. (J). 24.99 *(978-1-4169-5852-9(5)*, Simon Scribbles) Simon Scribbles.

Heltzel, Anne. Charlie, Presumed Dead. 2016. (ENG.). 272p. (YA). (gr. 9). pap. 8.99 *(978-0-544-66869-0(3)*, 1625496, Clarion Bks.) HarperCollins Pubs.

Henderson, Dianne. The Frightening Old Mansion. 2006. 116p. pap. 19.95 *(978-1-4241-2486-2(7))* PublishAmerica, Inc.

Henderson, Lauren. Kiss in the Dark, 3. 2011. (Scarlett Wakefield Novels Ser.). (ENG.). 256p. (J). (gr. 8-12). lib. bdg. 24.94 *(978-0-385-90690-6(0)*, Delacorte Pr.) Random Hse. Children's Bks.

—Kiss Me Kill Me. 2009. (Scarlett Wakefield Ser.). 272p. (YA). (gr. 9). pap. 10.99 *(978-0-385-73488-2(3)*, Delacorte Pr.) Random Hse. Children's Bks.

—Kisses & Lies, 2. 2009. (Scarlett Wakefield Novels Ser.). (ENG.). 320p. (J). (gr. 9-12). lib. bdg. 26.19 *(978-0-385-90486-5(X)*, Delacorte Pr.) Random Hse. Children's Bks.

Heneghan, James. The Grave, 1 vol. (ENG.). 240p. pap. 8.95 *(978-0-88899-499-8(0))* Groundwood Bks. CAN. Dist: Publishers Group West (PGW).

Henry, April. The Girl I Used to Be. 2017. (YA). lib. bdg. 20.85 *(978-0-606-39999-9(2))* Turtleback.

—The Girl Who Was Supposed to Die. 2014. (ENG.). 240p. (YA). (gr. 9-12). pap. 11.99 *(978-1-250-04437-2(5)*, 900128332) Square Fish.

—The Lonely Dead. 2020. (ENG.). 240p. (YA). pap. 14.99 *(978-1-250-23376-9(3)*, 900185223) Square Fish.

—The Night She Disappeared. 2013. (ENG.). 256p. (YA). (gr. 7-12). pap. 10.99 *(978-1-250-01674-4(6)*, 900087088) Square Fish.

Henry, Regene. The Barefoot Boys of Fayette. Stich, Carolyn R., illus. 2005. 180p. (J). (gr. 4-7). pap. 9.95 *(978-0-9749412-3-3(9))* EDCO Publishing, Inc.

Herman, Gail. Fall Fright. Duendes Del Sur Staff, illus. 2005. (Hello Reader! Ser.). 32p. (J). pap. *(978-0-439-78358-3(5))* Scholastic, Inc.

—Scooby-Doo: A Scooby-Rific Reader. 2012. (Illus.). (J). *(978-1-4351-3986-2(0))* Scholastic, Inc.

—Scooby-Doo in the Lighthouse Mystery, 1 vol. 2015. (Scooby-Doo! Ser.). (ENG., Illus.). 32p. (J). (gr. k-4). lib. bdg. 31.36 *(978-1-61479-410-3(3)*, 19449, Picture Bk.) Spotlight.

Herndon, Lee G. The Land of Always & Forever: The Trilogy, 1 vol. 2009. 77p. pap. 19.95 *(978-1-60836-898-3(X))* America Star Bks.

Herren, Greg. Lake Thirteen. 2013. (ENG.). 264p. (gr. 7). pap. 11.95 *(978-1-60282-894-0(6))* Bold Strokes Bks.

—Sleeping Angel. 2011. (ENG.). 288p. (J). (gr. 7). pap. 13.95 *(978-1-60282-214-6(X))* Bold Strokes Bks.

Herz, Henry. Sherlock Chick & Bunny Watson: The Mislaid Egg. Girouard, Patrick, illus. 2019. (ENG.). 32p. (J). *(978-1-4556-2433-1(0)*, Pelican Publishing) Arcadia Publishing.

Hesse, Monica. Girl in the Blue Coat. (ENG.). 320p. (YA). (gr. 7-17). 2017. pap. 11.99 *(978-0-316-26063-3(0))* 2016. E-Book 45.00 *(978-0-316-26064-0(9))* Little, Brown Bks. for Young Readers.

—Girl in the Blue Coat. 2017. (YA). lib. bdg. 20.85 *(978-0-606-39918-0(6))* Turtleback.

Hiaasen, Carl. Hoot. 2005. 292p. (J). (gr. 5-7). 8.99 *(978-0-440-41939-6(5)*, Yearling) Random Hse. Children's Bks.

—Skink — No Surrender. (ENG.). (YA). (gr. 7). 2015. 304p. pap. 10.99 *(978-0-307-93059-0(9)*, Ember) 2014. 288p. 18.99 *(978-0-375-87051-4(2)*, Knopf Bks. for Young Readers) Random Hse. Children's Bks.

—Squirm. (ENG.). (J). (gr. 5-7). 2020. 304p. 8.99 *(978-0-593-17767-9(3)*, Yearling) 2020. 304p. pap. 9.99 *(978-0-385-75300-5(4)*, Ember) 2018. 288p. 18.99 *(978-0-385-75297-8(0)*, Knopf Bks. for Young Readers) Random Hse. Children's Bks.

Hickey, Tony. Where's Jacko? Myler, Terry, illus. 2006. (ENG.). 64p. (J). pap. *(978-1-901737-47-9(0)*, Anvil Bks.) Mercier Pr., Ltd., The.

Hicks, Clifford B. Alvin Fernald, Mayor for a Day. Sokol, Bill, illus. 2015. 138p. (J). pap. 9.99 *(978-1-930900-86-8(4))* Purple Hse. Pr.

—Alvin Fernald's Incredible Buried Treasure. Bradfield, Roger, illus. 2009. (J). 17.95 *(978-1-930900-43-1(0))* Purple Hse. Pr.

—Alvin's Secret Code. Sokol, Bill, illus. 2015. (J). pap. 9.99 *(978-1-930900-85-1(6))* Purple Hse. Pr.

—The Marvelous Inventions of Alvin Fernald. Geer, Charles, illus. 119p. (J). (gr. 3-7). 2013. (ENG.). pap. 7.99 *(978-1-930900-72-1(4))* 2006. 16.95 *(978-1-930900-21-9(X))* Purple Hse. Pr.

Hicks, Deron R. Secrets of Shakespeare's Grave: The Shakespeare Mysteries, Book 1, Bk. 1. Geyer, Mark Edward, illus. 2013. (Shakespeare Mysteries Ser.: 1). (ENG.). 320p. (J). (gr. 3-7). pap. 7.99 *(978-0-544-10504-1(4)*, 1540806, Clarion Bks.) HarperCollins Pubs.

—Tower of the Five Orders: The Shakespeare Mysteries, Book 2. Geyer, Mark Edward, illus. 2014. (Shakespeare Mysteries Ser.). (ENG.). 320p. (J). (gr. 5-7). pap. 7.99 *(978-0-544-33630-8(5)*, 1584176, Clarion Bks.) HarperCollins Pubs.

—The Van Gogh Deception. 2018. (Lost Art Mysteries Ser.). (ENG.). 320p. (J). (gr. 5-7). pap. 9.99 *(978-1-328-63517-4(1)*, 1735316, Clarion Bks.) HarperCollins Pubs.

The Hidden Hand, 6 vols., Vol. 2. (Woodland Mysteriestm Ser.). 133p. (gr. 3-7). 42.50 *(978-0-7802-7939-1(5))* Wright Group/McGraw-Hill.

Higgins, F. E. The Bone Magician, 2. 2011. (ENG.). 304p. (J). (gr. 6-8). pap. 18.99 *(978-0-312-65944-8(X)*, 900070542) Square Fish.

Higman, Anita. The Living Darkness: Texas Caves. 2nd ed. 2003. (Illus.). xiii, 93p. (J). *(978-1-57168-783-8(1)*, Eakin Pr.) Eakin Pr.

Hill, Janet Muirhead. The Horse & the Crow: A Miranda & Starlight Story. 2015. (ENG.). 268p. (J). pap. 13.00 *(978-1-937849-27-6(9))* Raven Publishing Inc. of Montana.

Hillan, Pam & Dyan, Penelope. Dem Bones, Dem Bones! 2013. 110p. pap. 8.95 *(978-1-61477-122-7(7))* Bellissima Publishing, LLC.

Hillan, Pamela & Dyan, Penelope. The Hidden Treasure at Dragon Lake. 2013. 112p. pap. 8.95 *(978-1-61477-101-2(4))* Bellissima Publishing, LLC.

—The Mystery on Burgundy Street. 2013. 134p. pap. 8.95 *(978-1-61477-086-2(7))* Bellissima Publishing, LLC.

—The Secret at Fort Huachuca. 2013. 130p. pap. 8.95 *(978-1-61477-093-0(X))* Bellissima Publishing, LLC.

Hilton, Nette. A Grave Catastrophe. 2005. (Illus.). 160p. (J). (gr. -1-7). pap. *(978-0-7344-0494-7(8)*, Lothian Children's Bks.) Hachette Australia.

Hirsch, Jennifer. Minute Mysteries: Brainteasers, Puzzlers, & Stories to Solve. 2008. (American Girls Collection Sidelines Ser.). (ENG., Illus.). 64p. (gr. 4-7). pap. 5.95 *(978-1-59369-030-4(4)*, American Girl) American Girl Publishing, Inc.

Hirschmann, Kris. A Serious Case of the Sillies. Jennings, C. S., illus. 2013. 32p. (J). pap. *(978-0-545-56765-7(3))* Scholastic, Inc.

Hitchcock, Alfred. Misterio de la Arana de Plata. (Alfred Hitchcock y los Tres Investigadores Ser.). (SPA.). (YA). 8.95 *(978-84-272-4908-0(X)*, MO60) Molino, Editorial ESP. Dist: Continental Bk. Co., Inc.

—Misterio de la Calavera Parlante. (Alfred Hitchcock y los Tres Investigadores Ser.). (SPA.). (YA). 8.95 *(978-84-272-4911-0(X)*, MO63) Molino, Editorial ESP. Dist: Continental Bk. Co., Inc.

—Misterio de la Cueva de los Lamentos. (Alfred Hitchcock y los Tres Investigadores Ser.). (SPA.). 160p. (YA). 8.95 *(978-84-272-4910-3(1)*, MO62) Molino, Editorial ESP. Dist: Continental Bk. Co., Inc.

—Misterio de la Montana del Monstruo. (Alfred Hitchcock y los Tres Investigadores Ser.). (SPA.). (YA). 8.95 *(978-84-272-4920-2(9)*, MO72) Molino, Editorial ESP. Dist: Continental Bk. Co., Inc.

—Misterio de la Serpiente Susurrante. (Alfred Hitchcock y los Tres Investigadores Ser.). (SPA.). (YA). 8.95 *(978-84-272-4917-2(9)*, MO69) Molino, Editorial ESP. Dist: Continental Bk. Co., Inc.

—Misterio de Leon Mervioso. (Alfred Hitchcock y los Tres Investigadores Ser.). (SPA.). 192p. (YA). 8.95 *(978-84-272-4916-5(0)*, MO68) Molino, Editorial ESP. Dist: Continental Bk. Co., Inc.

—Misterio del Dragon. (Alfred Hitchcock y los Tres Investigadores Ser.). (SPA.). 176p. (YA). 8.95 *(978-84-272-4914-1(4)*, MO66) Molino, Editorial ESP. Dist: Continental Bk. Co., Inc.

—Misterio del Gato de Trapo. (Alfred Hitchcock y los Tres Investigadores Ser.). (SPA.). 152p. (YA). 8.95 *(978-84-272-4913-4(6)*, MO65) Molino, Editorial ESP. Dist: Continental Bk. Co., Inc.

—Misterio del Lago Fantasma. (Alfred Hitchcock y los Tres Investigadores Ser.). (SPA.). 173p. (YA). 8.95 *(978-84-272-4919-6(5)*, MO71) Molino, Editorial ESP. Dist: Continental Bk. Co., Inc.

—Misterio del Testamento Sorprendiente. (Alfred Hitchcock y los Tres Investigadores Ser.). (SPA.). (YA). 8.95 *(978-84-272-4922-6(5)*, MO74) Molino, Editorial ESP. Dist: Continental Bk. Co., Inc.

Hobbs, Constance. Dreamers. 2008. 436p. pap. 50.50 *(978-0-9556783-6-3(6))* Hobbs, Constance GBR. Dist: Lulu Pr., Inc.

Hobbs, Valerie. Sweetie McGinnis Solves Them All. Date not set. (J). *(978-0-374-37352-8(3)*, Farrar, Straus & Giroux (BYR)) Farrar, Straus & Giroux.

Hock, Dan. The Birthday Bash 2 vols. An Iggy & Igor Mystery (#2) Hock, Dan, illus. l.t. ed. 2004. (Illus.). 51p. (J). per. 4.99 *(978-0-9754046-1-4(X))* Anticipation Pr.

Hodder, Beth. Stealing the Wild. 2010. 166p. (J). pap. 11.95 *(978-0-9793963-1-1(X))* Grizzly Ridge Publishing.

Hodges, Meredith. Jasper: A Christmas Caper. Shields, Bonnie, illus. 2004. 85p. (J). 24.95 *(978-1-928624-20-2(0))* Lucky 3 Ranch, Inc.

Hodgson, William Hope. The House on the Borderland. 2019. (ENG.). (J). 126p. pap. 16.54 *(978-0-368-72615-6(0))*; 126p. pap. 15.48 *(978-0-368-72614-9(2))*; 126p. pap. 21.65 *(978-0-368-72613-2(4))*; (Illus.). 218p. pap. 10.60 *(978-1-388-10428-3(8))* Blurb, Inc.

—The House on the Borderland. 2019. (ENG.). 142p. (J). pap. 9.89 *(978-1-9790-2174-6(0))* CreateSpace Independent Publishing Platform.

—The House on the Borderland. (ENG.). (J). 2019. 400p. pap. 16.99 *(978-1-7020-9583-9(5))* 2019. 292p. pap. 16.99 *(978-1-6927-0810-8(4))* 2019. 644p. pap. 36.99 *(978-1-6961-4042-3(0))* 2019. 150p. pap. 9.99 *(978-1-0873-3726-5(7))* 2019. 644p. pap. 41.99 *(978-1-6861-7114-7(5))* 2019. 402p. pap. 24.99 *(978-1-6867-1560-0(9))* 2019. 644p. pap. 42.99 *(978-1-0828-5109-4(4))* 2019. 402p. pap. 24.99 *(978-1-0863-0900-3(6))* 2019. 400p. pap. 26.99 *(978-1-0804-9952-6(0))* 2019. 280p. pap. 16.99 *(978-1-0704-7057-3(0))* 2019. 474p. pap. 26.99 *(978-1-0733-8153-1(6))* 2019. 404p. pap. 24.99 *(978-1-0969-4318-1(2))* 2019. 404p. pap. 24.99 *(978-1-0985-5127-8(3))* 2019. 292p. pap. 16.99 *(978-1-0985-6152-9(X))* 2019. 404p. pap. 24.99

M
N
O

(978-1-0922-3080-3(7)) 2019. 298p. pap. 17.99 *(978-1-0934-9461-7(1))* 2019. 404p. pap. 25.99 *(978-1-0955-4396-2(2))* 2019. 292p. pap. 18.99 *(978-1-0901-2790-7(1))* 2019. 408p. pap. 24.99 *(978-1-7965-6600-0(4))* 2018. (Illus.). 406p. pap. 28.99 *(978-1-7920-3816-7(X))* 2018. (Illus.). 406p. pap. 28.99 *(978-1-7919-9755-7(4))* 2018. (Illus.). 292p. pap. 19.99 *(978-1-7918-7722-4(2))* 2018. (Illus.). 130p. pap. 12.99 *(978-1-7918-1863-0(3))* Independently Published.

Hoeye, Michael. Una Cuestion de Tiempo. (SPA.). 304p. (J). (gr. 6-8). 17.56 *(978-84-8441-167-3(2)*, MO1007) Grijalbo Mondadori, S.A.-Montena ESP. Dist: Lectorum Pubns., Inc.

—The Sands of Time. 2007. (ENG.). 288p. (J). (gr. 3-7). pap. 8.99 *(978-0-14-240983-1(9)*, Puffin Books) Penguin Young Readers Group.

—The Sands of Time: A Hermux Tantamoq AdventureTM. 2004. 288p. (J). (gr. 5-9). pap. 40.00 incl. audio *(978-1-4000-9016-7(4)*, Listening Library) Random Hse. Audio Publishing Group.

—Time Stops for No Mouse. 2003. (Hermux Tantamoq Adventure Ser.). (Illus.). 250p. (J). (gr. 4-7). 18.40 *(978-0-613-62122-9(0))* Turtleback.

—Time Stops for No Mouse: A Hermux Tantarnoq AdventureTM. 2004. 272p. (J). (gr. 5-9). pap. 40.00 incl. audio *(978-0-8072-2280-5(1)*, Listening Library) Random Hse. Audio Publishing Group.

Hoffman, Mary Ann. The Maple Tree Mystery. (Neighborhood Readers Ser.). (ENG.). 16p. 2007. 37.95 *(978-1-4042-7342-9(5))* 2006. (gr. 1-2). pap. 6.50 *(978-1-4042-7220-0(8)*, d2f72e77-c054-4adc-ba36-4f0206c429a1) Rosen Publishing Group, Inc., The. (Rosen Classroom).

—El misterio en el árbol (the Maple Tree Mystery) 2007. (Lecturas del barrio (Neighborhood Readers) Ser.). (SPA.). 16p. 37.95 *(978-1-4042-7343-6(3)*, Rosen Classroom) Rosen Publishing Group, Inc., The.

The Hole in the Hill: Individual Title Six-Packs. (Action Packs Ser.). 104p. (gr. 3-5). 44.00 *(978-0-7635-2993-2(1))* Rigby Education.

Holland, Robert. The Black Queen. 2003. (Books Boys Want to Read). 220p. (J). pap. 12.00 *(978-0-9720922-1-0(8))* Frost Hollow Pubs., LLC.

—Spooks: A Charles Oliver Jones, P.I. 2005. 219p. (J). *(978-0-9720922-5-8(0))* Frost Hollow Pubs., LLC.

Holm, Jennifer L. & Hamel, Jonathan. The Postman Always Brings Mice. Weinman, Brad, illus. 2005. (Stink Files Ser.: No. 1). 129p. (J). 12.65 *(978-0-7569-6529-7(2))* Perfection Learning Corp.

—To Scratch a Thief. Weinman, Brad, illus. (Stink Files Ser.: No. 2). 144p. 2005. pap. 4.99 *(978-0-06-052984-0(9)*, Harper Trophy) 2004. (J). 14.99 *(978-0-06-052982-6(2))* 2004. (J). lib. bdg. 15.89 *(978-0-06-052983-3(0))* HarperCollins Pubs.

Holsather, Kent. Henry of York: The Secret of Juan de Vega. Holsather, Bill, illus. 2003. 176p. (YA). (gr. 5-18). 22.95 *(978-0-9729101-0-1(7))*; 2nd ed. per. 12.95 *(978-0-9729101-1-8(5))* Lonejack Mountain Pr.

Holt, Catherine. Midnight Reynolds & the Agency of Spectral Protection. 2018. (Midnight Reynolds Ser.: 2). (ENG.). 264p. (J). (gr. 3-7). 14.99 *(978-0-8075-5128-8(7)*, 807551287) Whitman, Albert & Co.

Holt, Martha. The Adventures of Jillian & Sam: Tiger in Our Town. 2009. 28p. pap. 12.49 *(978-1-4389-6773-8(X))* AuthorHouse.

Hoobler, Dorothy & Hoobler, Thomas. The Demon in the Teahouse. 2005. 181p. (J). (gr. 4-7). 13.65 *(978-0-7569-6725-3(2))* Perfection Learning Corp.

—The Ghost in the Tokaido Inn. 2005. 240p. (J). (gr. 3-7). 7.99 *(978-0-14-240541-3(8)*, Puffin Books) Penguin Young Readers Group.

—The Ghost in the Tokaido Inn. 2005. 214p. (J). (gr. 4-7). 14.65 *(978-0-7569-6403-0(2))* Perfection Learning Corp.

—In Darkness, Death. 2005. (Puffin Sleuth Novels Ser.). 195p. (J). (gr. 5-9). 14.65 *(978-0-7569-5457-4(6))* Perfection Learning Corp.

—The Sword That Cut the Burning Grass. 2006. 211p. (gr. 5-9). 17.00 *(978-0-7569-6907-3(7))* Perfection Learning Corp.

Hood, Karen Jean Matsko. Lost Medal, Bk.1. Whispering Pine Press International, Inc. Staff, ed. Artistic Design Service, illus. 2014. (Hood Horse Story Ser.). 160p. (J). (gr. 4-8). 25.95 *(978-1-930948-94-5(8))* Whispering Pine Pr. International, Inc.

—Lost Medal, Vol. 1. Whispering Pine Press International, ed. Artistic Design Service, illus. 2014. (Hood Horse Story Ser.). (ENG.). 160p. (J). (gr. 4-8). per. 9.95 *(978-1-930948-95-2(6))* Whispering Pine Pr. International, Inc.

—Lost Medal, Christian Edition: With Bible Verses & Christian Themes. Whispering Pine Press International, ed. Artistic Design Services Staff, illus. 2014. (Hood Christian Horse Story Ser.). 160p. (J). Bk.1. pap. 19.95 *(978-1-59808-618-8(9))* Vol. 1. 29.95 *(978-1-59808-617-1(0))* Whispering Pine Pr. International, Inc.

—Spokane Falls. Whispering Pine Press International, ed. Artistic Design Service, illus. l.t. ed. 2015. (Banacek & Flannigan Mystery Ser.). 224p. pap. 22.95 *(978-1-59434-223-3(7))*; Vol. 1. 29.95 *(978-1-59434-228-8(8))*; Vol. 1. per. 19.95 *(978-1-59434-226-4(1))* Whispering Pine Pr. International, Inc.

Hooks, Gwendolyn. The Cat Food Mystery: A Pet Club Story, 1 vol. Byrne, Mike, illus. 2011. (Pet Club Ser.). (ENG.). 32p. (J). (gr. 1-2). pap. 6.25 *(978-1-4342-3051-5(1)*, 114651, Stone Arch Bks.) Capstone.

Hoopmann, Kathy. Blue Bottle Mystery - the Graphic Novel: An Asperger Adventure. 2015. (Asperger Adventures Ser.). (ENG., Illus.). 68p. (J). 21.95 *(978-1-84905-650-2(1)*, 693887) Kingsley, Jessica Pubs. GBR. Dist: Hachette UK Distribution.

Hope, Kathleen. Isiah Thomas & the Mysterious Castle Mcscary. 2012. (Illus.). 44p. pap. 24.40 *(978-1-4685-0496-5(7))* AuthorHouse.

—Jack Eagle the Pirate & Other Mysterious Tales. 2012. (Illus.). 48p. pap. 24.40 *(978-1-4678-9611-5(X))* AuthorHouse.

Hope, Laura. The Bobbsey Twins on Blueberry Island. 2007. 112p. (gr. 3-9). per. 11.95 *(978-1-4344-0033-8(6))* Wildside Pr., LLC.

—Bobbsey Twins or Merry Days Indoors and. 2006. 18.99 *(978-1-4219-7001-1(5))* IndyPublish.com.

Hope, Laura Lee. The Bobbsey Twins: The First Fifteen Stories, Including Merry Days Indoors & Out, in the Country, at the Seashore, at School, at Snow Lodge, on A. 2013. 1080p. *(978-1-78139-372-7(9))* Benediction Classics.

—The Bobbsey Twins at Meadow Brook. 2004. 200p. pap. 12.95 *(978-1-59540-103-8(2)*, 1st World Library - Literary Society) 1st World Publishing, Inc.

—The Bobbsey Twins at School. 2004. per. 11.95 *(978-1-59540-104-5(0))* 1st World Publishing, Inc.

—The Bobbsey Twins in the Country. 2004. 208p. pap. 12.95 *(978-1-59540-105-2(9)*, 1st World Library - Literary Society) 1st World Publishing, Inc.

—The Bobbsey Twins on a House Boat. 2005. 204p. pap. 12.95 *(978-1-4218-1167-3(7)*, 1st World Library - Literary Society) 1st World Publishing, Inc.

—The Bobbsey Twins on A House Boat. 2005. 27.95 *(978-1-4218-1067-6(0)*, 1st World Library - Literary Society) 1st World Publishing, Inc.

Hope, Lee Laura. Six Little Bunkers at Aunt Jo's. 2007. (ENG.). 144p. pap. 18.99 *(978-1-4346-3234-0(2))* Creative Media Partners, LLC.

Horn, Lorri. Dewey Fairchild, Parent Problem Solver: Parent Problem Solver. 2017. (Dewey Fairchild Ser.: 1). (ENG., Illus.). 252p. (J). (gr. 4-7). 13.99 *(978-1-944995-16-4(1))* Amberjack Publishing Co.

Horowitz, Anthony. South by Southeast. 2005. (Diamond Brothers Ser.). (ENG.). 160p. (J). (gr. 3-7). 6.99 *(978-0-14-240374-7(1)*, Puffin Books) Penguin Young Readers Group.

Horseshoe Canyon. 2005. (J). 30.00 *(978-1-884270-38-3(7))* Hall, Nancy Inc.

Houghton, Jackolyn. Detective Billy Pears & the Missing Hat. 2008. 36p. pap. 24.95 *(978-1-60474-543-6(6))* America Star Bks.

Hounam, Donald. A Dangerous Magic. 2017. (ENG., Illus.). 352p. (YA). (gr. 5-12). 17.99 *(978-1-5124-3232-9(6)*, ce27e1d0-1960-495f-a52b-2d7bd78c0eca, Carolrhoda Lab™) Lerner Publishing Group.

Howard, Jeremy. The Countdown: The Adventures of Starforce. 2005. 114p. 23.45 *(978-1-4208-2398-1(1))*; pap. 11.95 *(978-1-4208-2397-4(3))* AuthorHouse.

Howard, Lee. Giddy-Up, Scooby-Doo, 1 vol. Alcadia, S. N. C., illus. 2015. (Scooby-Doo Leveled Readers Ser.). (ENG.). 32p. (J). (gr. k-4). lib. bdg. 31.36 *(978-1-61479-414-1(6)*, 19437) Spotlight.

—Scooby-Doo & the Snow Monster Mystery, 1 vol. Alcadia, S. N. C., illus. 2015. (Scooby-Doo Leveled Readers Ser.). (ENG.). 32p. (J). (gr. k-4). lib. bdg. 31.36 *(978-1-61479-417-2(0)*, 19440) Spotlight.

Howe, Deborah & Howe, James. Bunnicula: A Rabbit-Tale of Mystery. Daniel, Alan, illus. 2006. (Bunnicula & Friends Ser.). (ENG.). 128p. (J). (gr. 3-7). pap. 8.99 *(978-1-4169-2817-1(0)*, Atheneum Bks. for Young Readers) Simon & Schuster Children's Publishing.

Howe, James. Bud Barkin, Private Eye. Helquist, Brett, illus. 2004. (Tales from the House of Bunnicula Ser.: 5). (ENG.). 112p. (J). (gr. 2-5). pap. 6.99 *(978-0-689-86989-1(4)*, Atheneum Bks. for Young Readers) Simon & Schuster Children's Publishing.

—Howliday Inn. Munsinger, Lynn, illus. 2006. 195p. (gr. 3-7). 16.00 *(978-0-7569-6807-6(0))* Perfection Learning Corp.

—Howliday Inn. unabr. ed. 2004. (Bunnicula Ser.). 195p. (J). (gr. 3-7). pap. 29.00 incl. audio *(978-0-8072-8382-0(7)*, YA179SP, Listening Library) Random Hse. Audio Publishing Group.

—Howliday Inn. Munsinger, Lynn, illus. 2nd ed. 2006. (Bunnicula & Friends Ser.). (ENG.). 224p. (J). (gr. 3-7). pap. 7.99 *(978-1-4169-2815-7(4)*, Atheneum Bks. for Young Readers) Simon & Schuster Children's Publishing.

—Nighty-Nightmare. Morrill, Leslie, illus. 2007. (Bunnicula & Friends Ser.). (ENG.). 144p. (J). (gr. 3-7). pap. 7.99 *(978-1-4169-3966-5(0)*, Atheneum Bks. for Young Readers) Simon & Schuster Children's Publishing.

—Return to Howliday Inn. Daniel, Alan, illus. 2007. (Bunnicula & Friends Ser.). (ENG.). 192p. (J). (gr. 3-7). pap. 7.99 *(978-1-4169-3967-2(9)*, Atheneum Bks. for Young Readers) Simon & Schuster Children's Publishing.

—Return to Howliday Inn. Daniel, Alan, illus. 2007. (Bunnicula Ser.: 5). (gr. 4-7). lib. bdg. 17.20 *(978-1-4177-9044-9(X))* Turtleback.

—The Vampire Bunny. Mack, Jeff, illus. 2005. (Bunnicula & Friends Ser.). 41p. (J). (gr. 1-3). 11.65 *(978-0-7569-6832-8(1))* Perfection Learning Corp.

—The Vampire Bunny: Ready-To-Read Level 3. Mack, Jeff, illus. 2004. (Bunnicula & Friends Ser.: 1). (ENG.). 48p. (J). (gr. 1-3). 17.99 *(978-0-689-85724-9(1)*, Simon Spotlight) Simon Spotlight.

Howell, Kathy. Skoob. Linton, Vera, illus. 2004. (J). per. 6.95 *(978-1-59571-026-0(4))* Word Association Pubs.

—Skoob: The Kingdom Awaits. 2005. (J). per. 7.95 *(978-1-59571-072-7(8))* Word Association Pubs.

Howland, Ashley. Ghostnapped. 2009. 64p. pap. 9.99 *(978-1-60860-145-5(5)*, Strategic Bk. Publishing) Strategic Book Publishing & Rights Agency (SBPRA).

Hubbard, L. Ron, contrib. by. The Carnival of Death: Literature Guide for Teachers & Librarians Based on Common Core ELA Standards for Classrooms 6-9. 2013. (Stories from the Golden Age Ser.). (ENG.). 35p. (gr. 6-9). pap., tchr. ed. 14.95 *(978-1-59212-809-9(2))* Galaxy Pr., LLC.

—Common Core Literature Guide: Dead Men Kill: Literature Guide for Teachers & Librarians Based on Common Core ELA Standards for Classrooms 6-9. 2013. (Stories from the Golden Age Ser.). (ENG.). 35p. (gr. 6-9). pap., tchr. ed. 14.95 *(978-1-61986-218-0(2))* Galaxy Pr., LLC.

Hubner, Carol Korb. The Devora Doresh Mysteries. 2006. (Illus.). 288p. (J). 16.95 *(978-1-932443-59-2(2))* Judaica Pr., Inc., The.

—The Devora Doresh Mysteries 2. 2007. (Illus.). 280p. (J). 16.95 *(978-1-932443-68-4(1))* Judaica Pr., Inc., The.

Hughes, Jenny. Dark Horse. 2014. (ENG.). 224p. (J). (gr. 3-7). pap. 9.95 *(978-1-62124-010-5(X))* Breakaway Bks.

—A Horse by Any Other Name. 2014. (ENG.). 224p. (J). (gr. 3-7). pap. 9.95 *(978-1-62124-009-9(6))* Breakaway Bks.

—Horse in the Diary. 2014. (ENG.). 128p. (J). (gr. 3-7). pap. 9.95 *(978-1-62124-014-3(2))* Breakaway Bks.

—Mystery at Black Horse Farm. 2013. (ENG.). 144p. (J). (gr. 3-7). pap. 9.95 *(978-1-62124-003-7(7))* Breakaway Bks.

Hughes, Shirley. Digby o'Day & the Great Diamond Robbery. Vulliamy, Clara, illus. 2015. (ENG.). 136p. (J). (gr. k-3). 12.99 *(978-0-7636-7445-8(1))* Candlewick Pr.

Hughes, Vi. The Graveyard Hounds, 1 vol. 2009. (ENG., Illus.). 167p. (J). (gr. 4-7). pap. 12.95 *(978-1-896580-49-4(1))* Tradewind Bks. CAN. Dist: Orca Bk. Pubs. USA.

Hummel, Jim. A Bubble C. 2009. 32p. pap. 14.95 *(978-1-4269-0034-1(1))* Trafford Publishing.

Hunt, Elizabeth Singer. The Search for the Sunken Treasure Bk. 2: Australia. 2007. (Illus.). 110p. (J). *(978-1-4242-4190-3(1))* Hachette Bk. Group.

—Secret Agent Jack Stalwart: Book 1: the Escape of the Deadly Dinosaur: USA. 2007. (Secret Agent Jack Stalwart Ser.: 1). (ENG., Illus.). 128p. (J). (gr. 1-4). per. 5.99 *(978-1-60286-004-9(1)*, Running Pr. Kids) Running Pr.

—Secret Agent Jack Stalwart: Book 12: the Fight for the Frozen Land: the Arctic, Bk.12. 2009. (Secret Agent Jack Stalwart Ser.: 12). (ENG., Illus.). 128p. (J). (gr. 1-4). pap. 5.99 *(978-1-60286-099-5(8)*, Running Pr. Kids) Running Pr.

—Secret Agent Jack Stalwart: Book 2: the Search for the Sunken Treasure: Australia. 2007. (Secret Agent Jack Stalwart Ser.: 2). (ENG., Illus.). 128p. (J). (gr. 1-4). per. 5.99 *(978-1-60286-002-5(5)*, Running Pr. Kids) Running Pr.

—Secret Agent Jack Stalwart: Book 3: the Mystery of the Mona Lisa: France, Bk. 3. 2007. (Secret Agent Jack Stalwart Ser.: 3). (ENG., Illus.). 128p. (J). (gr. 1-4). per. 5.99 *(978-1-60286-001-8(7)*, Running Pr. Kids) Running Pr.

—Secret Agent Jack Stalwart: Book 4: the Caper of the Crown Jewels: England, Bk. 4. 2008. (Secret Agent Jack Stalwart Ser.: 4). (ENG., Illus.). 144p. (J). (gr. 1-4). per. 5.99 *(978-1-60286-013-1(0))* Hachette Bk. Group.

—Secret Agents Jack & Max Stalwart: Book 1: the Battle for the Emerald Buddha: Thailand. Williamson, Brian, illus. 2017. (Secret Agents Jack & Max Stalwart Ser.: 1). (ENG.): 144p. (J). (gr. 1-4). pap. 5.99 *(978-1-60286-359-0(8)*, Running Pr. Kids) Running Pr.

Hurd, Thacher. Art Dog. Hurd, Thacher, illus. 2004. (ENG., Illus.). 32p. (J). (gr. -1-3). 18.99 *(978-0-06-024424-8(0)*, HarperCollins) HarperCollins Pubs.

—Mystery on the Docks 25th Anniversary Edition. Hurd, Thacher, illus. 25th anniv. ed. 2008. (ENG., Illus.). 32p. (J). (gr. -1-3). pap. 8.99 *(978-0-06-443058-6(8)*, HarperCollins) HarperCollins Pubs.

Hurst, Melissa E. The Edge of Forever. 2015. (ENG.). 272p. (J). (gr. 6-6). pap. 14.99 *(978-1-63220-424-0(X)*, Sky Pony Pr.) Skyhorse Publishing Co., Inc.

—On Through the Never. 2017. (ENG.). 272p. (J). (gr. 6-6). pap. 14.99 *(978-1-5107-0761-0(1)*, Sky Pony Pr.) Skyhorse Publishing Co., Inc.

Huston, Harriette "Ree". The Rescue of Buster Bus: A True Adventure Mystery with Sparkling Intrigue for All Ages. 2012. 36p. pap. 21.99 *(978-1-4771-1658-6(3))* Xlibris Corp.

Hutton, Sam. Countdown (Special Agents, Book 3), Book 3. 2011. (Special Agents Ser.: 3). (ENG.). 224p. pap. 9.99 *(978-0-00-714843-1(7)*, HarperCollins Children's Bks.) HarperCollins Pubs. Ltd. GBR. Dist: HarperCollins Pubs.

—Deep End (Special Agents) 2010. (Special Agents Ser.). (ENG.). 240p. (gr. 5-7). pap. 9.99 *(978-0-00-714842-4(9)*, HarperCollins Children's Bks.) HarperCollins Pubs. Ltd. GBR. Dist: HarperCollins Pubs.

—Final Shot (Special Agents, Book 2), Book 2. 2010. (Special Agents Ser.: 2). (ENG.). 224p. (J). (gr. 5-7). pap. 9.99 *(978-0-00-714844-8(5)*, HarperCollins Children's Bks.) HarperCollins Pubs. Ltd. GBR. Dist: HarperCollins Pubs.

—Kiss & Kill (Special Agents, Book 4), Book 4. 2004. (Special Agents Ser.: 4). (ENG.). 240p. (gr. 4-7). pap. 9.99 *(978-0-00-714845-5(3)*, HarperCollins Children's Bks.) HarperCollins Pubs. Ltd. GBR. Dist: HarperCollins Pubs.

—Meltdown (Special Agents, Book 6), Book 6. 2005. (Special Agents Ser.: 6). (ENG., Illus.). 224p. pap. 9.99 *(978-0-00-714847-9(X)*, HarperCollins Children's Bks.) HarperCollins Pubs. Ltd. GBR. Dist: HarperCollins Pubs.

Hyde, Natalie. I Owe You One, 1 vol. 2011. (Orca Young Readers Ser.). (ENG.). 136p. (J). (gr. 4-7). pap. 7.95 *(978-1-55469-414-3(0))* Orca Bk. Pubs. USA.

Hymas, Allison K. Arts & Thefts. 2018. (Max Ser.). (ENG., Illus.). 352p. (J). (gr. 4-8). pap. 7.99 *(978-1-4814-6345-4(4)*, Aladdin) Simon & Schuster Children's Publishing.

—Under Locker & Key. 2017. (Max Ser.). (ENG., Illus.). 256p. (J). (gr. 4-8). pap. 7.99 *(978-1-4814-6342-3(X)*, Simon & Schuster/Paula Wiseman Bks.) Simon & Schuster/Paula Wiseman Bks.

Ibbotson, Eva. The Star of Kazan. 2006. (ENG., Illus.). 416p. (J). (gr. 3-7). reprint ed. 10.99 *(978-0-14-240582-6(5)*, Puffin Books) Penguin Young Readers Group.

Ice Water Press Staff. Secrets of the Deep. 2010. (J). pap. *(978-1-921639-95-1(4))* Ripley Entertainment, Inc.

Ikaris, Despoina. The Little Red Jacket: A True Almost Christmas Almost Mystery Almost Ghost Story for Children And Certain Grown-Ups. 2008. 48p. pap. 10.99 *(978-1-60647-898-1(2))* Salem Author Services.

Imfeld, Robert. Baylor's Guide to Dreadful Dreams. 2017. (ENG., Illus.). 320p. (J). (gr. 5-9). 16.99 *(978-1-4814-6639-4(9)*, Aladdin) Simon & Schuster Children's Publishing.

—A Guide to the Other Side. 2016. (Beyond Baylor Ser.: 1). (ENG., Illus.). 320p. (J). (gr. 5-9). 17.99 *(978-1-4814-6636-3(4)*, Aladdin) Simon & Schuster Children's Publishing.

Ingold, Jeanette. Paper Daughter. 2013. (ENG.). 224p. (YA). (gr. 7). pap. 15.99 *(978-0-544-10484-6(6)*, 1540793, Clarion Bks.) HarperCollins Pubs.

Inspector Grub & the Fizzer-X Spy: Individual Title Six-Packs. (Bookweb Ser.). 32p. (gr. 5-18). 34.00 *(978-0-7635-3786-9(1))* Rigby Education.

Inspector Grub & the Gourmet Mystery: Individual Title Six-Packs. (Bookweb Ser.). 32p. (gr. 4-18). 34.00 *(978-0-7635-3726-5(8))* Rigby Education.

Ip, Ivy S. Clues at the Carnival, 1 vol. Sur, Duendes Del, illus. 2013. (Scooby-Doo! Picture Clue Bks.). (ENG.). 24p. (J). (gr. k-2). lib. bdg. 31.36 *(978-1-61479-036-5(1)*, 13230) Spotlight.

Ironside, Meredith. Spoon Creek Mystery. 2009. 244p. pap. 16.95 *(978-0-595-53490-6(2))* iUniverse, Inc.

Jackson, Melanie. High Wire, 1 vol. 2012. (Orca Currents Ser.). (ENG.). 128p. (J). (gr. 4-7). pap. 9.95 *(978-1-4598-0236-0(5))* Orca Bk. Pubs. USA.

Jacobs, Brian C. The Case of the Old Man in the Mailbox. 2010. (Enigma Squad Ser.). (ENG.). 192p. (J). pap. 10.95 *(978-0-9841658-8-9(6)*, Excite Kids Pr.) Publishing Services @ Thomson-Shore.

Jacobs, Edgar P. Atlantis Mystery. 2012. (Blake & Mortimer Ser.: 12). (Illus.). 72p. (J). (gr. 5-12). pap. 15.95 *(978-1-84918-107-5(1))* CineBook GBR. Dist: National Bk. Network.

—Blake & Mortimer Vol. 15: The Secret of the Swordfish Part 1. 2013. (Blake & Mortimer Ser.: 15). (Illus.). 64p. pap. 16.95 *(978-1-84918-148-8(9))* CineBook GBR. Dist: National Bk. Network.

—Blake & Mortimer Vol. 17: the Secret of the Swordfish Part 3. 2014. (Blake & Mortimer Ser.: 17). (Illus.). 64p. pap. 15.95 *(978-1-84918-174-7(8))* CineBook GBR. Dist: National Bk. Network.

—The Mystery of the Great Pyramid. (Blake & Mortimer Ser.: 2). (Illus.). Pt. 1. 2007. 72p. pap. 15.95 *(978-1-905460-37-3(6))*Pt. 2. 2008. 56p. pap. 15.95 *(978-1-905460-38-0(4))* CineBook GBR. Dist: National Bk. Network.

—S. O. S. Meteors. 2009. (Blake & Mortimer Ser.: 6). (Illus.). 64p. pap. 15.95 *(978-1-905460-97-7(X))* CineBook GBR. Dist: National Bk. Network.

—The Secret of the Swordfish. 2013. (Blake & Mortimer Ser.: 16). (Illus.). 64p. pap. 15.95 *(978-1-84918-161-7(6))* CineBook GBR. Dist: National Bk. Network.

—The Yellow "M" 2007. (Blake & Mortimer Ser.: 1). (Illus.). 72p. per. 16.95 *(978-1-905460-21-2(X))* CineBook GBR. Dist: National Bk. Network.

Jacobson, Jennifer Richard. Andy Shane & the Barn Sale Mystery. Carter, Abby, illus. 2010. (Andy Shane Ser.: 5). (ENG.). 64p. (J). (gr. k-3). 5.99 *(978-0-7636-4827-5(2))* Candlewick Pr.

Jaffe, Michele. Bad Kitty. 2006. (Bad Kitty Ser.: Bk. 1). (ENG., Illus.). 288p. (YA). (gr. 7-12). 16.99 *(978-0-06-078108-8(4))* HarperCollins Pubs.

—Kitty Kitty. 2008. (Bad Kitty Ser.: Bk. 2). 320p. (YA). (gr. 7-18). lib. bdg. 17.89 *(978-0-06-078114-9(9)*, HarperTeen) HarperCollins Pubs.

Jager, Hartmut. The Secret of the Green Paint: Annette Vetter Adventure #2. 2007. (Illus.). 196p. (YA). pap. 9.95 *(978-0-944851-28-9(2))* Earth Star Pubns.

Jakubowski, Michele. The Professor's Discovery. Pinelli, Amerigo, illus. 2016. (Sleuths of Somerville Ser.). (ENG.). 144p. (J). (gr. 4-6). lib. bdg. 25.99 *(978-1-4965-3177-3(9)*, 132216, Stone Arch Bks.) Capstone.

—The Professor's Discovery. Pinelli, Amerigo, illus. 2017. (Sleuths of Somerville Ser.). (ENG.). 144p. (J). (gr. 4-6). pap. 6.95 *(978-1-4965-3181-0(7)*, Stone Arch Bks.) Capstone.

—Tour of Trouble. Pinelli, Amerigo, illus. 2016. (Sleuths of Somerville Ser.). (ENG.). 144p. (J). (gr. 4-6). lib. bdg. 25.99 *(978-1-4965-3176-6(0)*, 132215, Stone Arch Bks.) Capstone.

—Tour of Trouble. Pinelli, Amerigo, illus. 2017. (Sleuths of Somerville Ser.). (ENG.). 144p. (J). (gr. 4-6). pap. 6.95 *(978-1-4965-3180-3(9)*, Stone Arch Bks.) Capstone.

James, David. Sherlock Holmes & the Midnight Bell. Wilkes, Ian, ed. unabr. ed. 2003. 164p. (YA). (gr. 4-12). 30.00 *(978-0-86025-292-4(2))* Henry, Ian Pubns. GBR. Dist: Empire Publishing Service.

James, Kristopher. Lyrian. 2009. (Illus.). 171p. pap. 16.95 *(978-1-4092-8986-9(9))* Lulu Pr., Inc.

James, Laura. Fabio the World's Greatest Flamingo Detective: Mystery on the Ostrich Express. Fox, Emily, illus. 2020. (ENG.). 128p. (J). 16.99 *(978-1-5476-0459-3(X)*, 900223954); pap. 6.99 *(978-1-5476-0458-6(1)*, 900223951) Bloomsbury Publishing USA. (Bloomsbury Children's Bks.).

—Fabio the World's Greatest Flamingo Detective: the Case of the Missing Hippo. Fox, Emily, illus. 2019. (Fabio the World's Greatest Flamingo Detective Ser.). (ENG.). 144p. (J). 16.99 *(978-1-5476-0217-9(1)*, 900203642); pap. 7.99 *(978-1-5476-0216-2(3)*, 900203643) Bloomsbury Publishing USA. (Bloomsbury Children's Bks.).

James, Richard E., III. Adventures of the Elements Vol. 3: Dangerous Games. Lyle, Maryann, ed. Welch, Chad, illus. 2004. 169p. (YA). (gr. 3-12). pap. 5.95 *(978-0-9675901-2-7(4))* Alchemy Creative, Inc.

Jan Baer: And the Mystery of the Silent Circus. 2005. (J). per. 10.00 *(978-1-930052-29-1(4))* Cherokee Bks.

Jane, Rebecca. Hamster Heroes to the Rescue: The Mystery of the Shadow in the Yard & Retirement. 2012. 84p. 19.95 *(978-1-4626-6862-5(3))* America Star Bks.

Janeway, Paul. Dragon Eye Connection. 2011. 202p. pap. 14.95 *(978-1-60976-854-6(X)*, Strategic Bk. Publishing) Strategic Book Publishing & Rights Agency (SBPRA).

Jannazo, Michelle A. Isabella's Shoes. 2012. 28p. pap. 11.95 *(978-1-4327-9019-6(6))* Outskirts Pr., Inc.

Jasnoch, Dorothy. Frankie the Bunny: Mystery in the Forest. Korzeniowski, Samson O., ed. Jasnoch, Dorothy, illus. 2013. (Illus.). 32p. 17.99 *(978-1-937752-16-3(X))* Owl About Bks. Pubs.

Jason June, Jason. Whobert Whover, Owl Detective. Pauwels, Jess, illus. 2017. (ENG.). 40p. (J). (gr. -1-1). 17.99 *(978-1-4814-6271-6(7)*, McElderry, Margaret K. Bks.) McElderry, Margaret K. Bks.

Jayne, Hannah. Copycat. 2018. (ENG.). 272p. (YA). (gr. 8-12). pap. 10.99 *(978-1-4926-4739-3(X))* Sourcebooks, Inc.

—The Escape. 2015. (ENG., Illus.). 256p. (YA). (gr. 8-12). pap. 10.99 *(978-1-4926-1654-2(0)*, 9781492616542) Sourcebooks, Inc.

—The Revenge. 2017. (ENG.). 288p. (YA). (gr. 8-12). pap. 10.99 *(978-1-4926-4736-2(5))* Sourcebooks, Inc.

Jeffrey, Leonard J. Journeys of the Mind-Book. 2011. 116p. (J). pap. *(978-1-4269-9333-6(1))* Trafford Publishing (UK) Ltd.

Jenkins, Amanda. The Strong & the Weak Hammurabi's Code, Tomb Robbers! A Story of Ancient Egypt. 2011. (Readers' & Writers' Genre Workshop Ser.). (YA). pap. *(978-1-4509-3020-8(4))* Benchmark Education Co.

Jenkins, Carla LaVern. The Disappearance of Mrs. Brown: A Jenkins Girl Mystery. 2010. 72p. 23.55 *(978-1-4269-4537-3(X))*; pap. 13.55 *(978-1-4251-6659-5(8))* Trafford Publishing.

Jennifer, Chambliss Bertman. The Unbreakable Code. 2017. (Book Scavenger Ser.: 2). (ENG., Illus.). 368p. (J). 16.99 *(978-1-62779-116-8(7))*, 900135626, Holt, Henry & Co. Bks. For Young Readers) Holt, Henry & Co.

Jennings, Sharon. Bats in the Graveyard. 69p. *(978-1-897039-18-2(2))* High Interest Publishing (HIP).

—Bats on Horseback. *(978-1-897039-13-7(1))* High Interest Publishing (HIP).

—Jingle Bats. Malloy, Kalle, illus. 72p. pap. *(978-1-897039-22-9(0))* High Interest Publishing (HIP).

Jennings, Sharon, et al, adapted by. Franklin the Detective. 2004. (Kids Can Read Ser.). (ENG., Illus.). 32p. (J). (gr. 1-2). 14.95 *(978-1-55337-497-8(5))* Kids Can Pr., Ltd. CAN. Dist: Hachette Bk. Group.

Jennings, Sharon, et al. Franklin the Detective. Gagnon, Céleste, illus. 2004. 32p. (J). pap. *(978-0-439-41822-5(4))* Scholastic, Inc.

Jessell, Tim, illus. The Boardwalk Mystery. 2013. (Boxcar Children Mysteries Ser.: 131). (ENG.). 144p. (J). (gr. 2-5). pap. 6.99 *(978-0-8075-0803-9(9))*, 807508039);131. 15.99 *(978-0-8075-0802-2(0))*, 807508020) Random Hse. Children's Bks. (Random Hse. Bks. for Young Readers).

—The Boxcar Children Deluxe Hardcover Boxed Gift Set (#1-3), Set. 2013. (Boxcar Children Mysteries Ser.). (ENG.). 538p. (J). (gr. 2-5). lib. bdg., lib. bdg., lib. bdg. 45.00 *(978-0-8075-0864-0(0))*, 807508640, Random Hse. Bks. for Young Readers) Random Hse. Children's Bks.

—The Garden Thief. 2012. (Boxcar Children Mysteries Ser.: 130). (ENG.). 128p. (J). (gr. 2-5). 15.99 *(978-0-8075-2751-1(3))*, 807527513); 5.99 *(978-0-8075-2752-8(1))*, 807527521) Random Hse. Children's Bks. (Random Hse. Bks. for Young Readers).

—Mystery of the Fallen Treasure. 2013. (Boxcar Children Mysteries Ser.: 132). (ENG.). 128p. (J). (gr. 2-5). 5.99 *(978-0-8075-5506-4(1))*, 807555061); 15.99 *(978-0-8075-5508-8(8))*, 807555088) Random Hse. Children's Bks. (Random Hse. Bks. for Young Readers).

—The Mystery of the Stolen Snowboard. 2014. (Boxcar Children Mysteries Ser.: 134). (ENG.). 128p. (J). (gr. 2-5). 15.99 *(978-0-8075-8728-7(1))*, 807587281, Random Hse. Bks. for Young Readers) Random Hse. Children's Bks.

—The Mystery of the Wild West Bandit. 2014. (Boxcar Children Mysteries Ser.: 135). (ENG.). 128p. (J). (gr. 2-5). 15.99 *(978-0-8075-8725-6(7))*, 807587257, Random Hse. Bks. for Young Readers) Random Hse. Children's Bks.

—The Return of the Graveyard Ghost. 2013. (Boxcar Children Mysteries Ser.: 133). (ENG.). 128p. (J). (gr. 2-5). 5.99 *(978-0-8075-6936-8(4))*, 807569364); 15.99 *(978-0-8075-6935-1(6))*, 807569356) Random Hse. Children's Bks. (Random Hse. Bks. for Young Readers).

Jinks, Catherine. The Reformed Vampire Support Group. 2010. (ENG., Illus.). 368p. (YA). (gr. 7-12). 24.94 *(978-0-15-206609-3(8))* Harcourt Children's Bks.

—The Reformed Vampire Support Group. 2010. (ENG.). 384p. (YA). (gr. 7). pap. 8.99 *(978-0-547-41166-8(9))*, 1429152, Clarion Bks.) HarperCollins Pubs.

Johansen, K. V. The Black Box. 2010. (Illus.). 212p. (J). pap. 13.00 *(978-0-9864974-0-7(1))* Syberfooth, Inc. CAN. Dist: Ingram Content Group.

Johansen, Zdenka. When You Give of Yourself. 2006. 28p. pap. 9.95 *(978-1-4327-0059-1(6))* Outskirts Pr., Inc.

Johnson, Alaya Dawn. Detective Frankenstein. Ota, Yuko, illus. 2011. (Twisted Journeys Ser.: 17). (ENG.). 112p. (J). (gr. 4-7). pap. 45.32 *(978-0-7613-7613-2(5))*, Graphic Universe™) Lerner Publishing Group.

Johnson, Allen, Jr. The Dead House. McMorris, Kelley, illus. 2014. (Blackwater Novels Ser.: Vol. 2). (ENG.). 212p. (J). (gr. 4-7). 14.99 *(978-1-933725-34-5(6))* Premium Pr. America.

Johnson, Carol V. Somerset Dreams. 2011. (Illus.). 112p. pap. 32.12 *(978-1-4567-9012-7(9))* AuthorHouse.

Johnson, Denise Donna. The Veridical Circle. 2011. 78p. pap. 19.95 *(978-1-4626-0472-2(2))* America Star Bks.

Johnson, Lois Walfrid. The Creeping Shadows. 2009. (Orig.). (J). 8.99 *(978-0-88062-277-6(6))* Mott Media.

—The Disappearing Stranger. 2009. (Orig.). (J). 8.99 *(978-0-88062-275-2(X))* Mott Media.

—Disaster on Windy Hill. 2009. (J). 8.99 *(978-0-88062-284-4(9))* Mott Media.

—Grandpa's Stolen Treasure. 2009. (Orig.). (J). 8.99 *(978-0-88062-281-3(4))* Mott Media.

—The Hidden Message. 2009. (Orig.). (J). 8.99 *(978-0-88062-276-9(8))* Mott Media.

—Mystery of the Missing Map. 2009. (J). 8.99 *(978-0-88062-283-7(0))* Mott Media.

—The Runaway Clown. 2009. (Orig.). (J). 8.99 *(978-0-88062-282-0(2))* Mott Media.

—Trouble at Wild River. 2009. (J). 8.99 *(978-0-88062-279-0(2))* Mott Media.

—The Vanishing Footprints. 2009. (J). 8.99 *(978-0-88062-278-3(4))* Mott Media.

Johnson, Maureen. The Madness Underneath: Book 2. 2013. (Shades of London Ser.: 2). (ENG.). 304p. (YA). (gr. 7). pap. 10.99 *(978-0-14-242754-5(3))*, Speak) Penguin Young Readers Group.

—Truly Devious: A Mystery. 2018. (Truly Devious Ser.: 1). (ENG., Illus.). 432p. (YA). (gr. 9). 17.99 *(978-0-06-233805-1(6))*, Tegen, Katherine Bks) HarperCollins Pubs.

—The Vanishing Stair. 2019. (Truly Devious Ser.: 2). (ENG.). (YA). (gr. 9). 400p. pap. 12.99 *(978-0-06-233809-9(9))*; 384p. 17.99 *(978-0-06-233808-2(0))*; 400p. E-Book *(978-0-06-233810-5(2))*, 9780062338105) HarperCollins Pubs. (Tegen, Katherine Bks).

Johnson, Pete. Detective Brother. Philips, Mike, illus. 2019. 106p. (J). pap. 4.99 *(978-1-61067-744-8(7))* Kane Miller.

Johnson, Varian. The Parker Inheritance (Scholastic Gold) (ENG.). (J). (gr. 3-7). 2019. 368p. pap. 8.99 *(978-0-545-95278-1(6))* 2018. 352p. 18.99 *(978-0-545-94617-9(4))* Scholastic, Inc. (Levine, Arthur A. Bks.).

Johnston, Jeffry W. Following. 2019. 288p. (YA). (gr. 8-12). pap. 10.99 *(978-1-4926-6461-1(8))* Sourcebooks, Inc.

—The Truth. 2016. (Illus.). 256p. (YA). (gr. 8-12). pap. 18.99 *(978-1-4926-2320-5(2))*, 9781492623205) Sourcebooks, Inc.

Johnston, K. E. M. The Witness Tree & the Shadow of the Noose: Mystery, Lies, & Spies in Manassas. 2009. 111p. (J). (gr. 5-7). pap. 8.95 *(978-1-57249-397-1(6))*, White Mane Kids) White Mane Publishing Co., Inc.

Johnston, Mark & Spizman, Robyn Freedman. The Secret Agents Strike Back. 2008. (ENG., Illus.). 160p. (J). (gr. 4-7). 16.99 *(978-1-4169-0086-3(1))*, Atheneum Bks. for Young Readers) Simon & Schuster Children's Publishing.

Jones, C. B. The Cats' Meow. Green, Chris, illus. 2017. (Bog Hollow Boys Ser.). (ENG.). 72p. (J). (gr. 4-8). lib. bdg. 25.32 *(978-1-4965-4057-7(3))*, 133365, Stone Arch Bks.) Capstone.

—Gone to the Buzzards. Green, Chris, illus. 2017. (Bog Hollow Boys Ser.). (ENG.). 72p. (J). (gr. 4-8). lib. bdg. 25.32 *(978-1-4965-4058-4(1))*, 133366, Stone Arch Bks.) Capstone.

—Kiss of the Snake. Green, Chris, illus. 2017. (Bog Hollow Boys Ser.). (ENG.). 72p. (J). (gr. 4-8). lib. bdg. 25.32 *(978-1-4965-4056-0(5))*, 133364, Stone Arch Bks.) Capstone.

Jones, Darynda. Death & the Girl He Loves. 2013. (Darklight Ser.: 3). (ENG.). 272p. (YA). (gr. 8-12). pap. 18.99 *(978-0-312-62522-1(7))*, 900076867, St. Martin's Griffin) St. Martin's Pr.

Jones, Kim P. Maggie & the Halloween Bandit. 2007. 124p. per. 19.95 *(978-1-60441-158-4(9))* America Star Bks.

Jones, Lee. Whimper. 2011. (ENG.). 142p. pap. 12.00 *(978-0-557-57961-7(9))* Lulu Pr., Inc.

Jones, Lena. The Secret Key (Agatha Oddly, Book 1) 2019. (Agatha Oddly Ser.: 1). (ENG.). 336p. (J). 7.99 *(978-0-00-834891-5(X))*, HarperCollins Children's Bks.) HarperCollins Pubs. Ltd. GBR. Dist: HarperCollins Pubs.

Jones, Rob Lloyd. Wild Boy. (ENG.). 304p. (J). (gr. 5). 2015. pap. 8.99 *(978-0-7636-7157-0(6))* 2013. 16.99 *(978-0-7636-6252-3(6))* Candlewick Pr.

—Wild Boy & the Black Terror. 2015. (ENG.). 336p. (J). (gr. 5). 16.99 *(978-0-7636-6253-0(4))* Candlewick Pr.

Jones, Ruth Fosdick. Boy of the Pyramids: A Mystery of Ancient Egypt. Morse, Dorothy Bayley, illus. 2011. 150p. 40.95 *(978-1-258-06798-4(6))* Literary Licensing, LLC.

Jonsberg, Barry. Pandora Jones: Reckoning. 2016. (Pandora Jones Ser.). (ENG.). 336p. (YA). (gr. 8). pap. 12.99 *(978-1-74331-813-3(8))* Allen & Unwin AUS. Dist: Independent Pubs. Group.

Joy, Linda. Little Wave & the Mystery of the Lost Whale. 2011. 28p. pap. 15.99 *(978-1-4628-9711-7(8))* Xlibris Corp.

Jozefkowicz, Ewa. The Mystery of the Colour Thief. 2019. (ENG., Illus.). 208p. (J). 13.95 *(978-1-78669-895-7(1))*, 667407, Zephyr) Head of Zeus GBR. Dist: Bloomsbury Publishing Plc.

Juby, Susan. Getting the Girl: A Guide to Private Investigation, Surveillance, & Co Okery. 2010. (ENG.). 352p. (YA). (gr. 8). pap. 8.99 *(978-0-06-076528-6(3))*, HarperTeen) HarperCollins Pubs.

Kantor, Melissa. The Amanda Project. 2011. 287p. (J). 8.99 *(978-0-06-202706-1(9))*, HarperTeen) HarperCollins Pubs.

Kanzaka, Hajime & Yoshinaka, Shoko. Super-Explosive Demon Story: City of Lost Souls, 7 vols., Vol. 5. 2004. (Slayers Ser.). (Illus.). 192p. 9.99 *(978-1-58664-915-9(9))*, CMX 64605G, CPM Manga) Central Park Media Corp.

Karas, G. Brian, illus. The Case of the Missing Monkey. 2004. (High-Rise Private Eyes Ser.: No. 1). (J). (gr. -1-2). pap. 31.95 incl. audio compact disk *(978-1-59112-616-4(9))* Live Oak Media.

—The Case of the Puzzling Possum. 2004. (High-Rise Private Eyes Ser.: No. 3). (J). (gr. -1-2). pap. 31.95 incl. audio compact disk *(978-1-59112-620-1(7))* Live Oak Media.

Karkevandian, Parisa. No Way Out. 2004. 108p. (YA). 20.95 *(978-0-595-66242-5(0))*; pap. 10.95 *(978-0-595-31011-1(7))* iUniverse, Inc.

Karr, Kathleen. The 7th Knot. 1 vol. (ENG., Illus.). (J). 2007. 192p. (gr. 5-9). pap. 5.99 *(978-0-7614-5368-0(7))* 2003. 300p. 15.95 *(978-0-7614-5135-8(8))* Marshall Cavendish Corp.

Kassel, Roger de. Mr P & the Silver Red Bag. 2013. (ENG., Illus.). 12p. pap. 7.00 *(978-1-78035-536-8(X))*, Fastprint Publishing) Upfront Publishing Ltd. GBR. Dist: Printondemand-worldwide.com.

Kastner, Erich. Emil & the Detectives. Trier, Walter, illus. 2014. (ENG.). 224p. (YA). (gr. 4-9). pap. 13.99 *(978-1-4683-0829-7(7))*, 1433003) Abrams, Inc.

Katherine's Story 1848. 2014. (Secrets of the Manor Ser.: 4). (ENG., Illus.). 160p. (J). (gr. 3-7). pap. 6.99 *(978-1-4814-1843-0(2))*, Simon Spotlight) Simon Spotlight.

Keats, Israel. Behind the Screen. 2018. (Mason Falls Mysteries Ser.). (ENG.). 104p. (YA). (gr. 6-12). pap. 7.99 *(978-1-5415-0115-7(2))*, eedc1df0-a0a3-4b02-be8a-d39f3b9a36f5); lib. bdg. 25.32 *(978-1-5415-0114-0(4))*, 62d3269f-d719-4e8f-8994-08e18fd459df) Lerner Publishing Group. (Darby Creek).

Keene, Carolyn. Action!. 2005. (Nancy Drew Ser.: 6). 138p. (J). lib. bdg. 15.00 *(978-1-59054-809-7(4))* Fitzgerald Bks.

—Action!, No. 6. 6th ed. 2004. (Nancy Drew (All New) Girl Detective Ser.: 6). (ENG.). 144p. (J). (gr. 3-7). pap. 6.99 *(978-0-689-86571-8(6))*, Aladdin) Simon & Schuster Children's Publishing.

—The Apple Bandit. Jones, Jan Naimo, illus. 2005. (Nancy Drew Notebooks). 74p. (J). (gr. 1-4). 11.65 *(978-0-7569-6505-1(5))* Perfection Learning Corp.

—The Apple Bandit. Jones, Jan Naimo, illus. 68th ed. 2005. (Nancy Drew Notebooks Ser.: 68). (ENG.). 80p. (J). (gr. 1-4). pap. 5.99 *(978-1-4169-0829-6(3))* Simon & Schuster, Inc.

—April Fool's Day. Pamintuan, Macky, illus. 2009. (Nancy Drew & the Clue Crew Ser.: 19). (ENG.). 96p. (J). (gr. 1-4). pap. 5.99 *(978-1-4169-7518-2(7))*, Aladdin) Simon & Schuster Children's Publishing.

—Babysitting Bandit. Pamintuan, Macky, illus. 2009. (Nancy Drew & the Clue Crew Ser.: 23). (ENG.). 96p. (J). (gr. 1-4). pap. 5.99 *(978-1-4169-7813-8(5))*, Aladdin) Simon & Schuster Children's Publishing.

—Bad Times, Big Crimes. 14th ed. 2005. (Nancy Drew (All New) Girl Detective Ser.: 14). (ENG.). 160p. (J). (gr. 3-7). pap. 7.99 *(978-0-689-87883-1(4))*, Aladdin) Simon & Schuster Children's Publishing.

—The Best of Nancy Drew Classic Collection Vol. 1. 2004. (Nancy Drew Ser.: 1). 544p. (J). (gr. 3-7). 16.99 *(978-0-448-44079-8(2))*, Grosset & Dunlap) Penguin Young Readers Group.

—Big Top Flop. Francis, Peter, illus. 2016. (Nancy Drew Clue Book Ser.: 4). (ENG.). 96p. (J). (gr. 1-4). pap. 5.99 *(978-1-4814-3752-3(6))*, Aladdin) Simon & Schuster Children's Publishing.

—Boo Crew. Francis, Peter, illus. 2018. (Nancy Drew Clue Book Ser.: 10). (ENG.). 112p. (J). (gr. 1-4). 17.99 *(978-1-5344-1389-4(8))*; pap. 5.99 *(978-1-5344-1388-7(X))* Simon & Schuster Children's Publishing. (Aladdin).

—The Bungalow Mystery #3, No. 3. 2014. (Nancy Drew Ser.: 3). 192p. (J). (gr. 3-7). 7.99 *(978-0-448-47971-2(0))*, Grosset & Dunlap) Penguin Young Readers Group.

—The Bunny-Hop Hoax. Jones, Jan Naimo, illus. 64th ed. 2005. (Nancy Drew Notebooks Ser.: 64). (ENG.). 80p. (J). (gr. 1-4). pap. 3.99 *(978-0-689-87754-4(4))*, Simon & Schuster/Paula Wiseman Bks.) Simon & Schuster/Paula Wiseman Bks.

—Butterfly Blues. Francis, Peter, illus. 2015. (Nancy Drew & the Clue Crew Ser.: 40). (ENG.). 96p. (J). (gr. 1-4). pap. 5.99 *(978-1-4814-1470-8(4))*, Aladdin) Simon & Schuster Children's Publishing.

—California Schemin' Book One in the Malibu Mayhem Trilogy. 2011. (Nancy Drew (All New) Girl Detective Ser.: 45). (ENG.). 160p. (J). (gr. 3-7). pap. 7.99 *(978-1-4424-2295-7(5))*, Aladdin) Simon & Schuster Children's Publishing.

—Camp Creepy. Pamintuan, Macky, illus. 2010. (Nancy Drew & the Clue Crew Ser.: 26). (ENG.). 96p. (J). (gr. 1-4). pap. 5.99 *(978-1-4169-9438-1(6))*, Aladdin) Simon & Schuster Children's Publishing.

—Candy Is Dandy. Jones, Jan Naimo, illus. 2004. (Nancy Drew Notebooks). 74p. (gr. 2-4). 17.00 *(978-0-7569-3437-8(0))* Perfection Learning Corp.

—Candy Kingdom Chaos. Francis, Peter, illus. 2017. (Nancy Drew Clue Book Ser.: 7). (ENG.). 96p. (J). (gr. 1-4). pap. 5.99 *(978-1-4814-5826-9(4))*, Simon & Schuster/Paula Wiseman Bks.) Simon & Schuster/Paula Wiseman Bks.

—Cape Mermaid Mystery. Pamintuan, Macky, illus. 2012. (Nancy Drew & the Clue Crew Ser.: 32). (ENG.). 96p. (J). (gr. 1-4). pap. 5.99 *(978-1-4424-4625-0(0))*, Aladdin) Simon & Schuster Children's Publishing.

—Case of the Sneaky Snowman. Pamintuan, Macky, illus. 5th ed. 2006. (Nancy Drew & the Clue Crew Ser.: 5). (ENG.). 96p. (J). (gr. 1-4). pap. 5.99 *(978-1-4169-1254-5(1))*, Aladdin) Simon & Schuster Children's Publishing.

—Chick-Napped! Pamintuan, Macky, illus. 13th ed. 2008. (Nancy Drew & the Clue Crew Ser.: 13). (ENG.). 96p. (J). (gr. 1-4). pap. 5.99 *(978-1-4169-5522-1(4))*, Aladdin) Simon & Schuster Children's Publishing.

—The Cinderella Ballet Mystery. Pamintuan, Macky, illus. 4th ed. 2006. (Nancy Drew & the Clue Crew Ser.: 4). (ENG.). 96p. (J). (gr. 1-4). pap. 5.99 *(978-1-4169-1256-9(8))*, Aladdin) Simon & Schuster Children's Publishing.

—Close Encounters. 21st ed. 2006. (Nancy Drew (All New) Girl Detective Ser.: 21). (ENG.). 176p. (J). (gr. 3-7). pap. 7.99 *(978-1-4169-1245-3(2))*, Aladdin) Simon & Schuster Children's Publishing.

—The Clue in the Diary #7. 2015. (Nancy Drew Ser.: 7). (Illus.). 192p. (J). (gr. 3-7). 9.99 *(978-0-448-48907-0(4))*, Grosset & Dunlap) Penguin Young Readers Group.

—Cooking Camp Disaster. Pamintuan, Macky, illus. 2013. (Nancy Drew & the Clue Crew Ser.: 35). (ENG.). 96p. (J). (gr. 1-4). pap. 5.99 *(978-1-4169-9466-4(1))*, Aladdin) Simon & Schuster Children's Publishing.

—Cupcake Chaos, 34. Pamintuan, Macky, illus. 2013. (Nancy Drew & the Clue Crew Ser.: 34). (ENG.). 96p. (J). (gr. 1-4). pap. 5.99 *(978-1-4424-5351-7(6))*, Aladdin) Simon & Schuster Children's Publishing.

—Curse of the Arctic Star. 2013. (Nancy Drew Diaries: 1). (ENG.). 208p. (J). (gr. 3-7). 16.99 *(978-1-4424-6610-4(3))*; pap. 7.99 *(978-1-4169-9072-7(0))* Simon & Schuster Children's Publishing. (Aladdin).

—Danger on the Great Lakes. 173rd ed. 2003. (Nancy Drew Ser.: 173). (ENG., Illus.). 160p. (J). (gr. 3-7). pap. 6.99 *(978-0-689-86146-8(X))*, 53545777, Simon & Schuster/Paula Wiseman Bks.) Simon & Schuster/Paula Wiseman Bks.

—Dangerous Plays. 16th ed. 2006. (Nancy Drew (All New) Girl Detective Ser.: 16). (ENG.). 160p. (J). (gr. 3-7). pap. 7.99 *(978-1-4169-0605-6(3))*, Aladdin) Simon & Schuster Children's Publishing.

—Designed for Disaster. Pamintuan, Macky, illus. 2011. (Nancy Drew & the Clue Crew Ser.: 29). (ENG.). 96p. (J). (gr. 1-4). pap. 5.99 *(978-1-4169-9439-8(4))*, Aladdin) Simon & Schuster Children's Publishing.

—The Dollhouse Mystery. Jones, Jan Naimo, illus. 2004. (Nancy Drew Notebooks). 68p. (J). (gr. 1-4). 12.65 *(978-0-7569-5524-3(6))* Perfection Learning Corp.

—The Dollhouse Mystery. Jones, Jan Naimo, illus. 58th ed. 2004. (Nancy Drew Notebooks Ser.: 58). (ENG.). 80p. (J). (gr. 1-4). pap. 5.99 *(978-0-689-86534-3(1))*, Aladdin) Simon & Schuster Children's Publishing.

—Double Take. Pamintuan, Macky, illus. 2009. (Nancy Drew & the Clue Crew Ser.: 21). (ENG.). 112p. (J). (gr. 1-4). pap. 5.99 *(978-1-4169-7812-1(7))*, Aladdin) Simon & Schuster Children's Publishing.

—Dressed to Steal. 22nd ed. 2007. (Nancy Drew (All New) Girl Detective Ser.: 22). (ENG.). 160p. (J). (gr. 3-7). pap. 7.99 *(978-1-4169-3385-4(9))*, Aladdin) Simon & Schuster Children's Publishing.

—Earth Day Escapade. Pamintuan, Macky, illus. 2009. (Nancy Drew & the Clue Crew Ser.: 18). (ENG.). 96p. (J). (gr. 1-4). pap. 5.99 *(978-1-4169-7218-1(8))*, Aladdin) Simon & Schuster Children's Publishing.

—En Garde. 17th ed. 2006. (Nancy Drew (All New) Girl Detective Ser.: 17). (ENG.). 160p. (J). (gr. 3-7). pap. 6.99 *(978-1-4169-0603-2(7))*, Aladdin) Simon & Schuster Children's Publishing.

—False Notes. 3rd ed. 2004. (Nancy Drew (All New) Girl Detective Ser.: 3). (ENG.). 160p. (J). (gr. 3-7). pap. 6.99 *(978-0-689-86568-8(6))*, Aladdin) Simon & Schuster Children's Publishing.

—Famous Mistakes. 2019. (Nancy Drew Diaries: 17). (ENG., Illus.). 176p. (J). (gr. 3-7). pap. 6.99 *(978-1-4814-8549-4(0))*, Simon & Schuster/Paula Wiseman Bks.) Simon & Schuster/Paula Wiseman Bks.

—The Fashion Disaster. Pamintuan, Macky, illus. 6th ed. 2007. (Nancy Drew & the Clue Crew Ser.: 6). (ENG.). 96p. (J). (gr. 1-4). pap. 5.99 *(978-1-4169-3485-1(5))*, Aladdin) Simon & Schuster Children's Publishing.

—Fishing for Clues. 26th ed. 2007. (Nancy Drew (All New) Girl Detective Ser.: 26). (ENG., Illus.). 144p. (J). (gr. 3-7). pap. 6.99 *(978-1-4169-3525-4(8))*, Aladdin) Simon & Schuster Children's Publishing.

—The Flower Show Fiasco. Pamintuan, Macky, illus. 2014. (Nancy Drew & the Clue Crew Ser.: 37). (ENG.). 96p. (J). (gr. 1-4). pap. 5.99 *(978-1-4424-8668-3(6))*, Aladdin) Simon & Schuster Children's Publishing.

—Framed. 15th ed. 2006. (Nancy Drew (All New) Girl Detective Ser.: 15). (ENG.). 160p. (J). (gr. 3-7). pap. 6.99 *(978-0-689-87863-3(X))*, Aladdin) Simon & Schuster Children's Publishing.

—Getting Burned. 20th ed. 2006. (Nancy Drew (All New) Girl Detective Ser.: 20). (ENG.). 160p. (J). (gr. 3-7). pap. 5.99 *(978-0-689-87703-2(X))*, Aladdin) Simon & Schuster Children's Publishing.

—The Ghost of Grey Fox Inn. 2016. (Nancy Drew Diaries: 13). (ENG., Illus.). 192p. (J). (gr. 3-7). 17.99 *(978-1-4814-6596-0(1))*, Simon & Schuster/Paula Wiseman Bks.) Simon & Schuster/Paula Wiseman Bks.

—Ghost Stories. 2008. (Nancy Drew (All New) Girl Detective Ser.). (ENG.). 240p. (J). (gr. 3-7). pap. 7.99 *(978-1-4169-5909-0(2))*, Aladdin) Simon & Schuster Children's Publishing.

—Green-Eyed Monster: Book One in the Eco Mystery Trilogy. 2009. (Nancy Drew (All New) Girl Detective Ser.: 39). (ENG.). 176p. (J). (gr. 3-7). pap. 6.99 *(978-1-4169-7844-2(5))*, Aladdin) Simon & Schuster Children's Publishing.

—Green with Envy: Book Two in the Eco Mystery Trilogy, 40. 2010. (Nancy Drew (All New) Girl Detective Ser.: 40). (ENG.). 160p. (J). (gr. 3-7). pap. 7.99 *(978-1-4169-7842-8(9))*, Aladdin) Simon & Schuster Children's Publishing.

—Hidden Pictures. 2020. (Nancy Drew Diaries: 19). (ENG.). 192p. (J). (gr. 3-7). pap. 6.99 *(978-1-5344-2102-8(5))*, Simon & Schuster/Paula Wiseman Bks.) Simon & Schuster/Paula Wiseman Bks.

—The Hidden Staircase #2, No. 2. 2014. (Nancy Drew Ser.: 2). 192p. (J). (gr. 3-7). 9.99 *(978-0-448-47970-5(2))*, Grosset & Dunlap) Penguin Young Readers Group.

—High Risk, 4. 4th ed. 2004. (Nancy Drew (All New) Girl Detective Ser.: 4). (ENG.). 160p. (J). (gr. 3-7). pap. 7.99 *(978-0-689-86569-5(4))* Simon & Schuster, Inc.

—Identity Revealed: Book Three in the Identity Mystery Trilogy. 2009. (Nancy Drew (All New) Girl Detective Ser.: 35). (ENG.). 208p. (J). (gr. 3-7). pap. 7.99 *(978-1-4169-6828-3(8))*, Aladdin) Simon & Schuster Children's Publishing.

—Identity Theft: Book Two in the Identity Mystery Trilogy. 34th ed. 2009. (Nancy Drew (All New) Girl Detective Ser.: 34). (ENG.). 176p. (J). (gr. 3-7). pap. 6.99 *(978-1-4169-6831-3(8))*, Aladdin) Simon & Schuster Children's Publishing.

—Intruder,-27. 27th ed. 2007. (Nancy Drew (All New) Girl Detective Ser.: 27). (ENG.). 160p. (J). (gr. 3-7). pap. 5.99 *(978-1-4169-3526-1(6))* Simon & Schuster, Inc.

—The Kitten Caper. Jones, Jan Naimo, illus. 69th ed. 2005. (Nancy Drew Notebooks Ser.: 69). (ENG.). 80p. (J). (gr. 1-4). pap. 5.99 *(978-1-4169-0830-2(7))*, Simon & Schuster/Paula Wiseman Bks.) Simon & Schuster/Paula Wiseman Bks.

—Last Lemonade Standing. Francis, Peter, illus. 2015. (Nancy Drew Clue Book Ser.: 2). (ENG.). 96p. (J). (gr. 1-4). pap. 5.99 *(978-1-4814-3748-6(8))*, Aladdin) Simon & Schuster Children's Publishing.

—Lights, Camera ..., 5. 5th ed. 2004. (Nancy Drew (All New) Girl Detective Ser.: 5). (ENG., Illus.). 160p. (J). (gr. 3-7). pap. 6.99 *(978-0-689-86570-1(8))* Simon & Schuster, Inc.

—The Magician's Secret. 2015. (Nancy Drew Diaries: 8). (ENG., Illus.). 176p. (J). (gr. 3-7). pap. 7.99 *(978-1-4814-1700-6(2))*, Aladdin) Simon & Schuster Children's Publishing.

—The Make-A-Pet Mystery. Pamintuan, Macky, illus. 2012. (Nancy Drew & the Clue Crew Ser.: 31). (ENG.). 96p. (J). (gr. 1-4). pap. 6.99 *(978-1-4169-9464-0(5))*, Aladdin) Simon & Schuster Children's Publishing.

—Mall Madness. Pamintuan, Macky, illus. 15th ed. 2008. (Nancy Drew & the Clue Crew Ser.: 15). (ENG.). 96p. (J). (gr. 1-4). pap. 5.99 *(978-1-4169-5900-7(9))*, Aladdin) Simon & Schuster Children's Publishing.

—Mardi Gras Masquerade. 28th ed. 2008. (Nancy Drew (All New) Girl Detective Ser.: 28). (ENG.). 144p. (J). (gr. 3-7). pap. 6.99 *(978-1-4169-5103-2(2))*, Aladdin) Simon & Schuster Children's Publishing.

—Model Menace: Book Two in the Model Mystery Trilogy. 2009. (Nancy Drew (All New) Girl Detective Ser.: 37). (ENG.). 176p. (J). (gr. 3-7). pap. 7.99 *(978-1-4169-7843-5(7))*, Aladdin) Simon & Schuster Children's Publishing.

—Model Suspect: Book Three in the Model Mystery Trilogy. 2009. (Nancy Drew (All New) Girl Detective Ser.: 38). (ENG.). 160p. (J). (gr. 3-7). pap. 6.99 *(978-1-4169-7841-1(0))*, Aladdin) Simon & Schuster Children's Publishing.

—Movie Madness. Francis, Peter, illus. 2016. (Nancy Drew Clue Book Ser.: 5). (ENG.). 96p. (J). (gr. 1-4). pap. 5.99 *(978-1-4814-5820-7(5))*, Aladdin) Simon & Schuster Children's Publishing.

—Movie Madness. Francis, Peter, illus. 2016. (Nancy Drew Clue Book Ser.: 5). (ENG.). 96p. (J). (gr. 1-4). 16.99 *(978-1-4814-5821-4(3))*, Simon & Schuster/Paula Wiseman Bks.) Simon & Schuster/Paula Wiseman Bks.

—Murder on the Set. 24th ed. 2007. (Nancy Drew (All New) Girl Detective Ser.: 24). (ENG.). 176p. (J). (gr. 3-7). pap. 7.99 *(978-1-4169-3397-7(2))*, Aladdin) Simon & Schuster Children's Publishing.

—The Mystery at Lilac Inn #4. 2014. (Nancy Drew Ser.: 4). 192p. (J). (gr. 3-7). 10.99 *(978-0-448-47972-9(9))*, Grosset & Dunlap) Penguin Young Readers Group.

—Mystery at Malachite Mansion: Book Two in the Malibu Mayhem Trilogy. 2011. (Nancy Drew (All New) Girl Detective

MNO

Ser.: 46). (ENG.). 144p. (J). (gr. 3-7). pap. 6.99 (978-1-4424-2297-1(1), Aladdin) Simon & Schuster Children's Publishing.

—Mystery at the Moss Covered Mansion #18, No. 18. 2003. (Applewood Bks.). (ENG., Illus.). 228p. (gr. 4-7). 14.95 (978-1-55709-264-9(8)) Applewood Bks.

—Mystery of the Midnight Rider. 2013. (Nancy Drew Diaries: 3). (ENG.). 208p. (J). (gr. 1-7). 17.99 (978-1-4424-7861-9(6)); pap. 7.99 (978-1-4424-7860-2(8)) Simon & Schuster Children's Publishing. (Aladdin).

—A Nancy Drew Christmas. 2018. (Nancy Drew Diaries). (ENG., Illus.). 352p. (J). (gr. 3-7). 18.99 (978-1-5344-3164-5(0), Aladdin) Simon & Schuster Children's Publishing.

—Nancy Drew Diaries (Boxed Set) Curse of the Arctic Star; Strangers on a Train; Mystery of the Midnight Rider; Once upon a Thriller. 2013. (Nancy Drew Diaries). (ENG., Illus.). 768p. (J). (gr. 3-7). pap. 31.99 (978-1-4424-8896-0(4), Aladdin) Simon & Schuster Children's Publishing.

—Nancy's Mysterious Letter #8, Bk. 8. 2015. (Nancy Drew Ser.: 8). (Illus.). 192p. (J). (gr. 3-7). 9.99 (978-0-448-48908-7(2), Grosset & Dunlap) Penguin Young Readers Group.

—Once upon a Crime. 2nd ed. 2006. (Nancy Drew: Girl Detective Super Mystery Ser.: 2). (ENG.). 192p. (J). (gr. 3-7). pap. 6.99 (978-1-4169-1248-4(7), Aladdin) Simon & Schuster Children's Publishing.

—Once upon a Thriller. 2013. (Nancy Drew Diaries: 4). (ENG., Illus.). 144p. (J). (gr. 3-7). 17.99 (978-1-4424-6612-8(X)); pap. 7.99 (978-1-4169-9074-1(7)) Simon & Schuster Children's Publishing. (Aladdin).

—The Orchid Thief. 19th ed. 2006. (Nancy Drew (All New) Girl Detective Ser.: 19). (ENG.). 144p. (J). (gr. 3-7). pap. 6.99 (978-1-4169-0980-4(X), Aladdin) Simon & Schuster Children's Publishing.

—Pageant Perfect Crime: Book One in the Perfect Mystery Trilogy. 30th ed. 2008. (Nancy Drew (All New) Girl Detective Ser.: 30). (ENG.). 160p. (J). (gr. 3-7). pap. 6.99 (978-1-4169-5528-3(3), Aladdin) Simon & Schuster Children's Publishing.

—Perfect Cover: Book Two in the Perfect Mystery Trilogy, 31. 31st ed. 2008. (Nancy Drew (All New) Girl Detective Ser.: 31). (ENG.). 160p. (J). (gr. 3-7). pap. 5.99 (978-1-4169-5530-6(5)) Simon & Schuster, Inc.

—Pets on Parade. Francis, Peter, illus. 2016. (Nancy Drew Clue Book Ser.: 6). (ENG.). 96p. (J). (gr. 1-4). pap. 5.99 (978-1-4814-5823-8(X), Aladdin) Simon & Schuster Children's Publishing.

—Pit of Vipers. 18th ed. 2006. (Nancy Drew (All New) Girl Detective Ser.: 18). (ENG.). 160p. (J). (gr. 3-7). pap. 5.99 (978-1-4169-1180-7(4), Aladdin) Simon & Schuster Children's Publishing.

—Pony Problems. Pamintuan, Macky, illus. 3rd ed. 2006. (Nancy Drew & the Clue Crew Ser.: 3). (ENG.). 96p. (J). (gr. 1-4). pap. 5.99 (978-1-4169-1815-8(9), Aladdin) Simon & Schuster Children's Publishing.

—Pool Party Puzzler. Francis, Peter, illus. 2015. (Nancy Drew Clue Book Ser.: 1). (ENG.). 96p. (J). (gr. 1-4). 17.99 (978-1-4814-3896-4(4), Aladdin) Simon & Schuster Children's Publishing.

—Princess Mix-Up Mystery, No. 24. Pamintuan, Macky, illus. 2009. (Nancy Drew & the Clue Crew Ser.: 24). (ENG.). 96p. (J). (gr. 1-4). pap. 5.99 (978-1-4169-7811-4(9), Aladdin) Simon & Schuster Children's Publishing.

—The Professor & the Puzzle. 2017. (Nancy Drew Diaries: 15). (ENG., Illus.). 192p. (J). (gr. 3-7). pap. 7.99 (978-1-4814-8543-2(1), Aladdin) Simon & Schuster Children's Publishing.

—The Pumpkin Patch Puzzle. Pamintuan, Macky, illus. 2012. (Nancy Drew & the Clue Crew Ser.: 33). (ENG.). 112p. (J). (gr. 1-4). pap. 5.99 (978-1-4169-9465-7(3), Aladdin) Simon & Schuster Children's Publishing.

—Puppy Love Prank. Francis, Peter, illus. 2020. (Nancy Drew Clue Book Ser.: 13). (ENG.). 112p. (J). (gr. 1-4). 16.99 (978-1-5344-3134-8(9), Simon & Schuster/Paula Wiseman Bks.) Simon & Schuster/Paula Wiseman Bks.

—Real Fake. 3rd ed. 2007. (Nancy Drew: Girl Detective Super Mystery Ser.: 3). (ENG.). 224p. (J). (gr. 3-7). pap. 7.99 (978-1-4169-3881-1(8), Aladdin) Simon & Schuster Children's Publishing.

—The Red Slippers. 2015. (Nancy Drew Diaries: 11). (ENG., Illus.). 192p. (J). (gr. 3-7). pap. 7.99 (978-1-4814-3813-1(1), Aladdin) Simon & Schuster Children's Publishing.

—Riverboat Roulette. 2017. (Nancy Drew Diaries: 14). (ENG., Illus.). 176p. (J). (gr. 3-7). pap. 7.99 (978-1-4814-6598-4(8), Simon & Schuster/Paula Wiseman Bks.) Simon & Schuster/Paula Wiseman Bks.

—Sabotage at Willow Woods. 2014. (Nancy Drew Diaries: 5). (ENG., Illus.). 176p. (J). (gr. 3-7). pap. 7.99 (978-1-4424-9392-6(5), Aladdin) Simon & Schuster Children's Publishing.

—Sabotage Surrender: Book Three in the Sabotage Mystery Trilogy. 2011. (Nancy Drew (All New) Girl Detective Ser.: 44). (ENG.). 128p. (J). (gr. 3-7). pap. 6.99 (978-1-4169-9071-0(2), Aladdin) Simon & Schuster Children's Publishing.

—The Scarlet Macaw Scandal. 8th ed. 2004. (Nancy Drew (All New) Girl Detective Ser.: 8). (ENG., Illus.). 160p. (J). (gr. 3-7). pap. 7.99 (978-0-689-86844-3(8), Aladdin) Simon & Schuster Children's Publishing.

—Scream for Ice Cream. Pamintuan, Macky, illus. 2nd ed. 2006. (Nancy Drew & the Clue Crew Ser.: 2). (ENG.). 96p. (J). (gr. 1-4). pap. 5.99 (978-1-4169-1253-8(3), Aladdin) Simon & Schuster Children's Publishing.

—Secret at Mystic Lake. 2014. (Nancy Drew Diaries: 6). (ENG., Illus.). 160p. (J). (gr. 3-7). pap. 7.99 (978-1-4814-0012-1(6), Aladdin) Simon & Schuster Children's Publishing.

—Secret Identity: Book One in the Identity Mystery Trilogy, Bk. 1. 33rd ed. 2008. (Nancy Drew (All New) Girl Detective Ser.: 33). (ENG.). 176p. (J). (gr. 3-7). pap. 6.99 (978-1-4169-6827-6(X), Aladdin) Simon & Schuster Children's Publishing.

—The Secret of Red Gate Farm #6. 2015. (Nancy Drew Ser.: 6). (Illus.). 192p. (J). (gr. 3-7). 10.99 (978-0-448-48906-3(6), Grosset & Dunlap) Penguin Young Readers Group.

—The Secret of Shadow Ranch #5. 2015. (Nancy Drew Ser.: 5). (Illus.). 192p. (J). (gr. 3-7). 9.99 (978-0-448-48905-6(8), Grosset & Dunlap) Penguin Young Readers Group.

—The Secret of the Old Clock #1, Bk. 1. 2014. (Nancy Drew Ser.: 1). 192p. (J). (gr. 3-7). 9.99 (978-0-448-47969-9(9), Grosset & Dunlap) Penguin Young Readers Group.

—Secret of the Spa, Vol. 9. 9th ed. 2005. (Nancy Drew (All New) Girl Detective Ser.: 9). (ENG.). 160p. (J). (gr. 3-7). pap. 6.99 (978-0-689-86858-0(8), Aladdin) Simon & Schuster Children's Publishing.

—Secret Sabotage: Book One in the Sabotage Mystery Trilogy, Bk. 1. 2010. (Nancy Drew (All New) Girl Detective Ser.: 42). (ENG.). 144p. (J). (gr. 3-7). pap. 6.99 (978-1-4169-9069-7(0), Aladdin) Simon & Schuster Children's Publishing.

—Seeing Green: Book Three in the Eco Mystery Trilogy, 41. 2010. (Nancy Drew (All New) Girl Detective Ser.: 41). (ENG.). 160p. (J). (gr. 3-7). pap. 6.99 (978-1-4169-7845-9(3), Aladdin) Simon & Schuster Children's Publishing.

—Serial Sabotage: Book Two in the Sabotage Mystery Trilogy. 2010. (Nancy Drew (All New) Girl Detective Ser.: 43). (ENG.). 144p. (J). (gr. 3-7). pap. 5.99 (978-1-4169-9070-3(4), Aladdin) Simon & Schuster Children's Publishing.

—The Singing Suspects. Jones, Jan Naimo, illus. 2005. (Nancy Drew Notebooks). 69p. (J). (gr. 1-4). 11.65 (978-0-7569-5952-4(7)) Perfection Learning Corp.

—Ski School Sneak. Pamintuan, Macky, illus. 11th ed. 2007. (Nancy Drew & the Clue Crew Ser.: 11). (ENG.). 96p. (J). (gr. 1-4). pap. 5.99 (978-1-4169-4936-7(4), Aladdin) Simon & Schuster Children's Publishing.

—Sleepover Sleuths, 1. Pamintuan, Macky, illus. 2006. (Nancy Drew & the Clue Crew Ser.: 1). (ENG.). 96p. (J). (gr. 1-4). pap. 5.99 (978-1-4169-1255-2(X)) Simon & Schuster, Inc.

—The Snowman Surprise. Casale, Paul, illus. 63rd ed. 2004. (Nancy Drew Notebooks Ser.: 63). (ENG.). 80p. (J). (gr. 1-4). pap. 4.99 (978-0-689-87411-6(1)) Simon & Schuster, Inc.

—Springtime Crime. Francis, Peter, illus. 2018. (Nancy Drew Clue Book Ser.: 9). (ENG.). 112p. (J). (gr. 1-4). 16.99 (978-1-4814-9954-5(8)); pap. 5.99 (978-1-4814-9953-8(X)) Simon & Schuster Children's Publishing. (Aladdin).

—Stalk, Don't Run: Book Three in the Malibu Mayhem Trilogy, 47. 2012. (Nancy Drew (All New) Girl Detective Ser.: 47). (ENG.). 160p. (J). (gr. 3-7). pap. 5.99 (978-1-4424-2299-5(8), Aladdin) Simon & Schuster Children's Publishing.

—A Star Witness. Francis, Peter, illus. 2015. (Nancy Drew Clue Book Ser.: 3). (ENG.). 96p. (J). (gr. 1-4). 16.99 (978-1-4814-3998-5(7), Aladdin) Simon & Schuster Children's Publishing.

—The Stolen Bones. 29th ed. 2008. (Nancy Drew (All New) Girl Detective Ser.: 29). (ENG.). 160p. (J). (gr. 3-7). pap. 5.99 (978-1-4169-3614-5(9), Aladdin) Simon & Schuster Children's Publishing.

—The Stolen Relic. 7th ed. 2004. (Nancy Drew (All New) Girl Detective Ser.: 7). (ENG.). 160p. (J). (gr. 3-7). mass mkt. 6.99 (978-0-689-86843-6(X), Aladdin) Simon & Schuster Children's Publishing.

—The Stolen Show. 2019. (Nancy Drew Diaries: 18). (ENG.). 192p. (J). (gr. 3-7). pap. 6.99 (978-1-5344-0577-6(1), Simon & Schuster/Paula Wiseman Bks.) Simon & Schuster/Paula Wiseman Bks.

—Strangers on a Train. 2013. (Nancy Drew Diaries: 2). (ENG.). 208p. (J). (gr. 3-7). 17.99 (978-1-4424-6611-1(1), Simon & Schuster/Paula Wiseman Bks.) Simon & Schuster/Paula Wiseman Bks.

—Thanksgiving Thief. Pamintuan, Macky, illus. 2008. (Nancy Drew & the Clue Crew Ser.: 16). (ENG.). 96p. (J). (gr. 1-4). pap. 5.99 (978-1-4169-6777-4(X), Aladdin) Simon & Schuster Children's Publishing.

—Ticket Trouble, 10. Pamintuan, Macky, illus. 10th ed. 2007. (Nancy Drew & the Clue Crew Ser.: 10). (ENG.). 96p. (J). (gr. 1-4). pap. 5.99 (978-1-4169-4733-2(7)) Simon & Schuster, Inc.

—Time Thief. Pamintuan, Macky, illus. 2011. (Nancy Drew & the Clue Crew Ser.: 28). (ENG.). 96p. (J). (gr. 1-4). pap. 5.99 (978-1-4169-9458-9(0), Aladdin) Simon & Schuster Children's Publishing.

—The Tortoise & the Scare. Francis, Peter, illus. 2019. (Nancy Drew Clue Book Ser.: 11). (ENG.). 96p. (J). (gr. 1-4). 16.99 (978-1-5344-1483-9(5)); pap. 5.99 (978-1-5344-1482-2(7)) Simon & Schuster Children's Publishing. (Aladdin).

—Trails of Treachery, 25. 25th ed. 2007. (Nancy Drew (All New) Girl Detective Ser.: 25). (ENG.). 144p. (J). (gr. 3-7). pap. 7.99 (978-1-4169-3524-7(X)) Simon & Schuster, Inc.

—Treasure Trouble. Pamintuan, Macky, illus. 2009. (Nancy Drew & the Clue Crew Ser.: 20). (ENG.). 112p. (J). (gr. 1-4). pap. 5.99 (978-1-4169-7809-1(7), Aladdin) Simon & Schuster Children's Publishing.

—Troubled Waters. 23rd ed. 2007. (Nancy Drew (All New) Girl Detective Ser.: 23). (ENG., Illus.). 160p. (J). (gr. 3-7). pap. 7.99 (978-1-4169-2513-2(9), Aladdin) Simon & Schuster Children's Publishing.

—Turkey Trot Plot. Francis, Peter, illus. 2019. (Nancy Drew Clue Book Ser.: 12). (ENG.). 112p. (J). (gr. 1-4). pap. 5.99 (978-1-5344-3129-4(2), Simon & Schuster/Paula Wiseman Bks.) Simon & Schuster/Paula Wiseman Bks.

—Uncivil Acts. 10th ed. 2005. (Nancy Drew (All New) Girl Detective Ser.: 10). (ENG.). 160p. (J). (gr. 3-7). pap. 7.99 (978-0-689-86937-2(1), Aladdin) Simon & Schuster Children's Publishing.

—Unicorn Uproar. Pamintuan, Macky, illus. 2009. (Nancy Drew & the Clue Crew Ser.: 22). (ENG.). 96p. (J). (gr. 1-4). pap. 5.99 (978-1-4169-7810-7(0), Aladdin) Simon & Schuster Children's Publishing.

—Valentine's Day Secret. Pamintuan, Macky, illus. 12th ed. 2007. (Nancy Drew & the Clue Crew Ser.: 12). (ENG.). 96p. (J). (gr. 1-4). pap. 5.99 (978-1-4169-4944-2(5), Aladdin) Simon & Schuster Children's Publishing.

—Where's Nancy? 2005. (Nancy Drew: Girl Detective Super Mystery Ser.: 1). (ENG.). 176p. (J). (gr. 3-7). pap. 5.99 (978-1-4169-0034-4(9), Aladdin) Simon & Schuster Children's Publishing.

—Without a Trace. 2005. (Nancy Drew Ser.: 1). (Illus.). 154p. (J). lib. bdg. 15.00 (978-1-59054-819-6(1)) Fitzgerald Bks.

—Without a Trace, 1. 2004. (Nancy Drew (All New) Girl Detective Ser.: 1). (ENG.). 160p. (J). (gr. 3-7). pap. 7.99 (978-0-689-86566-4(X)) Simon & Schuster, Inc.

—World Record Mystery. Francis, Peter, illus. 2017. (Nancy Drew Clue Book Ser.: 8). (ENG.). 96p. (J). (gr. 1-4). 17.99 (978-1-4814-5836-8(1)); pap. 5.99 (978-1-4814-5835-1(3)) Simon & Schuster Children's Publishing. (Aladdin).

—The Zoo Crew. Pamintuan, Macky, illus. 14th ed. 2008. (Nancy Drew & the Clue Crew Ser.: 14). (ENG.). 96p. (J). (gr. 1-4). pap. 5.99 (978-1-4169-5899-4(1), Aladdin) Simon & Schuster Children's Publishing.

Keene, Carolyn & Dixon, Franklin W. Club Dread. 2009. (Nancy Drew/Hardy Boys Ser.: 3). (ENG.). 192p. (J). (gr. 3-7). pap. 6.99 (978-1-4169-7871-8(2), Aladdin) Simon & Schuster Children's Publishing.

—Danger Overseas. 2008. (Nancy Drew/Hardy Boys Ser.: 2). (ENG., Illus.). 224p. (J). (gr. 3-7). pap. 7.99 (978-1-4169-5777-5(4), Aladdin) Simon & Schuster Children's Publishing.

—Stage Fright, 6. 2012. (Nancy Drew/Hardy Boys Ser.: 6). (ENG.). 176p. (J). (gr. 3-7). pap. 6.99 (978-1-4424-5681-5(7)) Simon & Schuster, Inc.

—Terror on Tour. 2007. (Nancy Drew/Hardy Boys Ser.: 1). (ENG., Illus.). 224p. (J). (gr. 3-7). pap. 7.99 (978-1-4169-2726-6(3), Aladdin) Simon & Schuster Children's Publishing.

Kehret, Peg. Backstage Fright. 2008. (ENG.). 128p. (J). (gr. 3-7). pap. 7.99 (978-1-4169-9107-6(7), Simon & Schuster/Paula Wiseman Bks.) Simon & Schuster/Paula Wiseman Bks.

—Race to Disaster. 2008. (ENG.). 128p. (J). (gr. 3-7). pap. 7.99 (978-1-4169-9108-3(5), Simon & Schuster/Paula Wiseman Bks.) Simon & Schuster/Paula Wiseman Bks.

—Screaming Eagles. 2008. (ENG.). 128p. (J). (gr. 3-7). pap. 7.99 (978-1-4169-9106-9(9), Simon & Schuster/Paula Wiseman Bks.) Simon & Schuster/Paula Wiseman Bks.

Keller, Julia. Dark Mind Rising: A Dark Intercept Novel. 2019. (Dark Intercept Ser.: 2). (ENG.). 288p. (YA). pap. 16.99 (978-0-7653-8767-7(0), 900161508, Tor Teen) Doherty, Tom Assocs., LLC.

Keller, William B. Olivia & the Mystery. 2011. 88p. pap. 14.95 (978-1-4327-7636-7(3)) Outskirts Pr., Inc.

Kelly, David A. The All-Star Joker. Meyers, Mark, illus. 2012. (Ballpark Mysteries Ser.: Bk. 5). lib. bdg. 14.75 (978-0-606-26401-3(9)) Turtleback.

—The Astro Outlaw. 2012. (Ballpark Mysteries Ser.: Bk. 4). lib. bdg. 14.75 (978-0-606-23861-8(1)) Turtleback.

—Ballpark Mysteries #1: the Fenway Foul-Up. Meyers, Mark, illus. 2011. (Ballpark Mysteries Ser.: 1). (ENG.). 112p. (J). (gr. 1-4). pap. 6.99 (978-0-375-86703-3(1), Random Hse. Bks. for Young Readers) Random Hse. Children's Bks.

—Ballpark Mysteries #10: the Rookie Blue Jay. Meyers, Mark, illus. 2015. (Ballpark Mysteries Ser.: 10). (ENG.). 112p. (J). (gr. 1-4). 6.99 (978-0-385-37875-8(0), Random Hse. Bks. for Young Readers) Random Hse. Children's Bks.

—Ballpark Mysteries #11: the Tiger Troubles. Meyers, Mark, illus. 2015. (Ballpark Mysteries Ser.: 11). (ENG.). 112p. (J). (gr. 1-4). pap. 6.99 (978-0-385-37878-9(5), Random Hse. Bks. for Young Readers) Random Hse. Children's Bks.

—Ballpark Mysteries #12: the Rangers Rustlers. Meyers, Mark, illus. 2016. (Ballpark Mysteries Ser.: 12). (ENG.). 112p. (J). (gr. 1-4). pap. 5.99 (978-0-385-37881-9(5), Random Hse. Bks. for Young Readers) Random Hse. Children's Bks.

—Ballpark Mysteries #13: the Capital Catch. Meyers, Mark, illus. 2017. (Ballpark Mysteries Ser.: 13). (ENG.). 112p. (J). (gr. 1-4). 5.99 (978-0-399-55189-5(1), Random Hse. Bks. for Young Readers) Random Hse. Children's Bks.

—Ballpark Mysteries #14: the Cardinals Caper. Meyers, Mark, illus. 2018. (Ballpark Mysteries Ser.: 14). (ENG.). 112p. (J). (gr. 1-4). 5.99 (978-1-5247-6751-8(4), Random Hse. Bks. for Young Readers) Random Hse. Children's Bks.

—Ballpark Mysteries #15: the Baltimore Bandit. Meyers, Mark, illus. 2019. (Ballpark Mysteries Ser.: 15). (ENG.). 112p. (J). (gr. 1-4). 12.99 (978-1-5247-6755-6(7)); pap. 6.99 (978-1-5247-6754-9(9)) Random Hse. Children's Bks. (Random Hse. Bks. for Young Readers).

—Ballpark Mysteries #16: the Colorado Curveball. Meyers, Mark, illus. 2020. (Ballpark Mysteries Ser.: 16). (ENG.). 112p. (J). (gr. 1-4). lib. bdg. 12.99 (978-0-525-57899-4(4), Random Hse. Bks. for Young Readers) Random Hse. Children's Bks.

—Ballpark Mysteries #2: the Pinstripe Ghost. Meyers, Mark, illus. 2011. (Ballpark Mysteries Ser.: 2). (ENG.). 112p. (J). (gr. 1-4). 6.99 (978-0-375-86704-0(X), Random Hse. Bks. for Young Readers) Random Hse. Children's Bks.

—Ballpark Mysteries #3: the L. A. Dodger. Meyers, Mark, illus. 2011. (Ballpark Mysteries Ser.: 3). (ENG.). 112p. (J). (gr. 1-4). 6.99 (978-0-375-86885-6(2), Random Hse. Bks. for Young Readers) Random Hse. Children's Bks.

—Ballpark Mysteries #4: the Astro Outlaw. Meyers, Mark, illus. 2012. (Ballpark Mysteries Ser.: 4). (ENG.). 112p. (J). (gr. 1-4). pap. 6.99 (978-0-375-86883-2(6), Random Hse. Bks. for Young Readers) Random Hse. Children's Bks.

—Ballpark Mysteries #5: the All-Star Joker. Meyers, Mark, illus. 2012. (Ballpark Mysteries Ser.: 5). (ENG.). 112p. (J). (gr. 1-4). 6.99 (978-0-375-86884-9(4), Random Hse. Bks. for Young Readers) Random Hse. Children's Bks.

—Ballpark Mysteries #6: the Wrigley Riddle. Meyers, Mark, illus. 2013. (Ballpark Mysteries Ser.: 6). (ENG.). 112p. (J). (gr. 1-4). pap. 6.99 (978-0-307-97776-2(5), Random Hse. Bks. for Young Readers) Random Hse. Children's Bks.

—Ballpark Mysteries #7: the San Francisco Splash. Meyers, Mark, illus. 2013. (Ballpark Mysteries Ser.: 7). (ENG.). 112p. (J). (gr. 1-4). pap. 6.99 (978-0-307-97779-3(X), Random Hse. Bks. for Young Readers) Random Hse. Children's Bks.

—Ballpark Mysteries #8: the Missing Marlin. Meyers, Mark, illus. 2014. (Ballpark Mysteries Ser.: 8). (ENG.). 112p. (J). (gr. 1-4). 6.99 (978-0-307-97782-3(X), Random Hse. Bks. for Young Readers) Random Hse. Children's Bks.

—Ballpark Mysteries #9: the Philly Fake. Meyers, Mark, illus. 2014. (Ballpark Mysteries Ser.: 9). (ENG.). 112p. (J). (gr. 1-4). 6.99 (978-0-307-97785-4(4), Random Hse. Bks. for Young Readers) Random Hse. Children's Bks.

—Ballpark Mysteries Super Special #1: the World Series Curse. Meyers, Mark, illus. 2016. (Ballpark Mysteries Ser.: 1). (ENG.). 144p. (J). (gr. 1-4). 6.99 (978-0-385-37884-0(X), Random Hse. Bks. for Young Readers) Random Hse. Children's Bks.

—Ballpark Mysteries Super Special #2: Christmas in Cooperstown. Meyers, Mark, illus. 2017. (Ballpark Mysteries Ser.: 2). (ENG.). 144p. (J). (gr. 1-4). 5.99 (978-0-399-55192-5(1), Random Hse. Bks. for Young Readers) Random Hse. Children's Bks.

—Ballpark Mysteries Super Special #3: Subway Series Surprise. Meyers, Mark, illus. 2018. (Ballpark Mysteries Ser.: 3). (ENG.). 128p. (J). (gr. 1-4). 5.99 (978-0-525-57892-5(7), Random Hse. Bks. for Young Readers) Random Hse. Children's Bks.

—Ballpark Mysteries Super Special #4: the World Series Kids. Meyers, Mark, illus. 2019. (Ballpark Mysteries Ser.: 4). (ENG.). 128p. (J). (gr. 1-4). pap. 5.99 (978-0-525-57895-6(1), Random Hse. Bks. for Young Readers) Random Hse. Children's Bks.

—The Capital Catch. 2017. (Ballpark Mysteries Ser.: Bk. 13). lib. bdg. 14.75 (978-0-606-39869-5(4)) Turtleback.

—The Cardinals Caper. 2018. (Ballpark Mysteries Ser.: 14). lib. bdg. 14.75 (978-0-606-40921-6(1)) Turtleback.

—The Missing Marlin. 2014. (Ballpark Mysteries Ser.: Bk. 8). lib. bdg. 14.75 (978-0-606-35565-0(0)) Turtleback.

—MVP #1: the Gold Medal Mess. Brundage, Scott, illus. 2016. (Most Valuable Players Ser.: 1). 128p. (J). (gr. 1-4). 5.99 (978-0-553-51319-6(2), Random Hse. Bks. for Young Readers) Random Hse. Children's Bks.

—The San Francisco Splash. 2013. (Ballpark Mysteries Ser.: Bk. 7). lib. bdg. 14.75 (978-0-606-31940-9(9)) Turtleback.

—The Wrigley Riddle. 2013. (Ballpark Mysteries Ser.: Bk. 6). lib. bdg. 14.75 (978-0-606-26998-8(3)) Turtleback.

Kelly, Erin. The Mystery at the Eiffel Tower: Paris, France. 2005. (Carole Marsh Mysteries Ser.). (Illus.). 144p. (J). (gr. 3-5). pap. 7.99 (978-0-635-03468-7(9)) Gallopade International.

Kelly, Margo. Who R U Really? 2015. (ENG.). 240p. (YA). pap. 9.99 (978-1-4405-9226-3(8), Simon Pulse) Simon Pulse.

Kemmerer, Brigid. Secret. 2014. (Elemental Ser.: 4). (ENG.). 336p. (YA). (gr. 13). pap. 16.95 (978-0-7582-9437-1(9)) Kensington Publishing Corp.

Kenison, Misti. The Lost Race Car: A Fox & Goat Mystery, 1 vol. 2018. (Fox & Goat Mysteries Ser.: 2). (ENG., Illus.). 28p. (J). bds. 12.99 (978-0-7643-5599-8(6), 16098) Schiffer Publishing, Ltd.

Kennedy, Emma. The Case of the Fatal Phantom, 3 vols. Marc, Sylvain, illus. 2012. (Wilma Tenderfoot Ser.: 3). (ENG.). 351p. (J). (gr. 3-6). 17.95 (978-0-8037-3542-2(1)) Penguin Young Readers Group.

—Wilma Tenderfoot: the Case of the Frozen Hearts. 2012. (Wilma Tenderfoot Ser.: 1). (ENG.). 368p. (J). (gr. 3-7). 7.99 (978-0-14-242140-6(5), Puffin Books) Penguin Young Readers Group.

Keoghan, Angela. Inspector Brunswick: the Case of the Missing Eyebrow. Sam Lam, Chris, illus. 2017. (ENG.). 32p. (J). (gr. k-17). 16.95 (978-1-84976-444-5(1), 1307001) Tate Publishing, Ltd. GBR. Dist: Hachette Bk. Group, Abrams, Inc.

Kerbel, Deborah. Lure. 2010. (ENG.). 200p. (YA). (gr. 9). pap. 12.99 (978-1-55488-754-5(2)) Dundurn Pr. CAN. Dist: Publishers Group West (PGW).

Kerrin, Jessica Scott. The Missing Dog Is Spotted, 1 vol. 2015. (ENG.). 208p. (J). (gr. -1-2). 14.95 (978-1-55498-726-9(1)) Groundwood Bks. CAN. Dist: Publishers Group West (PGW).

—The Spotted Dog Last Seen, 1 vol. 2013. (ENG.). 208p. (J). (gr. 4-6). 14.95 (978-1-55498-387-2(8)) Groundwood Bks. CAN. Dist: Publishers Group West (PGW).

Kessler, Liz. Emily Windsnap & the Land of the Midnight Sun. 2014. (Emily Windsnap Ser.: Bk. 5). lib. bdg. 16.00 (978-0-606-35165-2(5)) Turtleback.

—North of Nowhere. 2013. (ENG., Illus.). 272p. (J). (gr. 4-7). 15.99 (978-0-7636-6727-6(7)) Candlewick Pr.

Key, Watt. Hideout. 2018. (ENG.). 336p. (J). pap. 9.99 (978-1-250-14397-6(7), 900160565) Square Fish.

Khan, Farheen. Ibrahim Khan & the Mystery of the Haunted Lake. 2011. (Ibrahim Khan Ser.). (ENG., Illus.). 64p. (J). (gr. k-5). pap. 7.50 (978-0-86037-423-7(8)) Kube Publishing Ltd. GBR. Dist: Consortium Bk. Sales & Distribution.

—Ibrahim Khan & the Mystery of the Roaring Lion. 2010. (Ibrahim Khan Ser.). (ENG., Illus.). 56p. (J). (gr. 2-6). pap. 7.50 (978-0-86037-467-1(X)) Kube Publishing Ltd. GBR. Dist: Consortium Bk. Sales & Distribution.

Kiarie, Vivian W. The Waltz, the Weasel & the Lair. 2008. 50p. pap. 16.95 (978-1-60474-265-7(8)) America Star Bks.

Kidd, Ronald. Undercover Kid: The Comic Book King. Sklar, Andy, illus. 2007. (All Aboard Mystery Reader Ser.). (ENG.). 48p. (J). pap. 3.99 (978-0-448-44438-3(0), Grosset & Dunlap) Penguin Publishing Group.

Kilman, Nancy. The Lockgate Mystery: Level O, 6 vols. (Raging Rivers Ser.). 128p. (gr. 3-6). 36.95 (978-0-322-05895-8(3)) Wright Group/McGraw-Hill.

Kilpatrick, Irene. Nancy Drew. 2007. (Nancy Drew Movie Ser.). (ENG., Illus.). 24p. (J). (gr. k-2). 16.19 (978-1-4169-3901-6(6), Simon Spotlight) Simon & Schuster Children's Publishing.

Kimmel, Elizabeth Cody. Legend of the Ghost Dog. 2012. 200p. (J). pap. (978-0-545-50705-9(7), Scholastic Pr.) Scholastic, Inc.

Kimmelman, Leslie. The Rabbi Slurps Spaghetti. Davey, Sharon, illus. 2019. (ENG.). 24p. (J). 17.95 (978-1-68115-543-2(5), cfe9e5c8-3bf9-48b5-83cb-c43c795375ae, Apples & Honey Pr.) Behrman Hse., Inc.

Kimpton, Diana. Princess Ellie Solves a Mystery. Finlay, Lizzie, illus. 8th rev. ed. 2007. (ENG.). 96p. (gr. 1-4). pap. 3.99 (978-1-4231-0901-3(5)) Hyperion Pr.

—Princess Ellie's Moonlight Mystery. 2015. (Pony-Crazed Princess Ser.). (ENG.). 96p. (J). (gr. k-5). pap. 4.99 (978-0-7945-3431-8(7), Usborne) EDC Publishing.

Kincaid, Jamaica. Party: A Mystery. CortAs, Ricardo, illus. 2019. (ENG.). 32p. (J). 17.95 (978-1-61775-716-7(0)) Akashic Bks.

Kindl, Patrice. Lost in the Labyrinth. 2005. (ENG.). 208p. (J). (gr. 5-7). pap. 13.95 (978-0-618-39402-9(8), 489039, Clarion Bks.) HarperCollins Pubs.

King, Glynda T. Skippy the Flea Is off to see the President. 2010. 52p. pap. 22.49 (978-1-4520-0860-8(4)) AuthorHouse.

King, J. Eric & Graham, Greg. Byron Carmichael Book One: The Human Corpse Trade. Mizer, Lindsay, ed. Warner, Michael, illus. 2008. (ENG.). 408p. (gr. 8-12). 18.95 *(978-0-615-15770-2(X))* G & K Publishing.

King, Jane. Welcome to Chillsville Elementary. 2013. (Ghoul School Ser.: 1). (ENG.). 80p. (J). (gr. 1-4). pap. 13.99 *(978-1-4814-2162-1(X)*, Simon & Schuster/Paula Wiseman Bks.) Simon & Schuster/Paula Wiseman Bks.

King, Jeremy Jordan. Dark Rites. 2015. (ENG.). 264p. (J). (gr. 7). pap. 11.95 *(978-1-62639-245-8(5))* Bold Strokes Bks.

King, Peter. Changels: The Crucible. 2nd ed. 2013. 298p. pap. *(978-1-927264-16-4(2))* King, Peter Publishing.

King, Tiffany. Losing Leah. 2018. (ENG.). 320p. (YA). 29.99 *(978-1-250-12466-1(2)*, 900174487) Feiwel & Friends.

—Losing Leah. 2019. (ENG.). 320p. (YA). pap. 21.99 *(978-1-250-29464-7(9)*, 900174488) Square Fish.

King, Trey. Mystery on the LEGO Express. Wang, Sean, illus. 2014. 24p. (J). *(978-1-4242-6168-0(6))* Scholastic, Inc.

—Mystery on the Lego Express. 2014. (LEGO City 8X8 Ser.). (Illus.). 24p. (J). lib. bdg. 13.55 *(978-0-606-36068-5(9))* Turtleback.

—Mystery on the LEGO Express (LEGO City) 2014. (LEGO City Ser.). (ENG., Illus.). 24p. (J). (gr. -1-3). 3.99 *(978-0-545-60366-9(8))* Scholastic, Inc.

—Wrecking Valentine's Day! Wang, Sean, illus. 2015. 24p. (J). *(978-1-4806-9662-4(5))* Scholastic, Inc.

King, Zelda. The Class Surprise, 1 vol. 2006. (Neighborhood Readers Ser.). (ENG.). 16p. (gr. 1-2). pap. 6.50 *(978-1-4042-6994-1(0)*, ce91d7dc-161e-4b30-94f8-41fcf95a8609, Rosen Classroom) Rosen Publishing Group, Inc., The.

Kirby, Matthew J. The Rogue World. 2017. (Dark Gravity Sequence Ser.: 3). (ENG.). 400p. (J). (gr. 3-7). 16.99 *(978-0-06-222493-4(X)*, Balzer & Bray) HarperCollins Pubs.

Kittscher, Kristen. The Tiara on the Terrace. 2016. (ENG.). 400p. (J). (gr. 3-7). 16.99 *(978-0-06-222798-0(X)*, HarperCollins) HarperCollins Pubs.

Klassen, Jon. The Skull: A Tyrolean Folktale. Klassen, Jon, illus. 2023. (ENG.). 112p. (J). (gr. 1-4). 19.99 ***(978-1-5362-2336-1(0))*** Candlewick Pr.

Klein, Jen. Paranormal Investigator. 2016. 288p. (YA). (gr. 9). pap. 10.99 *(978-1-61695-690-5(9)*, Soho Teen) Soho Pr., Inc.

Kleyla, Mary Pat. Identity Unknown. 2003. 154p. (YA). 22.95 *(978-0-595-65812-1(1))*; pap. 12.95 *(978-0-595-28473-3(6))* iUniverse, Inc.

Klim, Christopher. Firecracker Jones Is on the Case. 2005. (Illus.). 111p. (J). per. 9.95 *(978-0-9726906-7-6(0))* Hopewell Pubns., LLC.

Kline, Suzy. Horrible Harry & the Locked Closet. Remkiewicz, Frank, illus. 2005. (Horrible Harry Ser.: 17). 80p. (J). (gr. 2-4). 4.99 *(978-0-14-240451-5(9)*, Puffin Books) Penguin Young Readers Group.

—Horrible Harry & the Locked Closet. Remkiewicz, Frank, illus. 2005. (Horrible Harry Ser.). 68p. (gr. 2-5). 14.00 *(978-0-7569-5825-1(3))* Perfection Learning Corp.

—Horrible Harry & the Secret Treasure. Wummer, Amy, illus. 2012. (Horrible Harry Ser.: 26). 80p. (J). (gr. 2-4). 5.99 *(978-0-14-242021-8(2)*, Puffin Books) Penguin Young Readers Group.

—Horrible Harry Cracks the Code. Remkiewicz, Frank, illus. 2008. (Horrible Harry Ser.: 21). 80p. (J). (gr. 2-4). 5.99 *(978-0-14-241247-3(3)*, Puffin Books) Penguin Young Readers Group.

Klingele, Lindsey. The Truth Lies Here. 2018. (ENG.). 416p. (YA). (gr. 8). 17.99 *(978-0-06-238039-5(7)*, HarperTeen) HarperCollins Pubs.

Klise, Kate. Regarding the Bathrooms: A Privy to the Past. Klise, M. Sarah, illus. 2008. (Regarding The... Ser.: Bk. 4). (ENG.). 160p. (J). (gr. 3-7). pap. 7.99 *(978-0-15-206261-3(0)*, 1198771, Clarion Bks.) HarperCollins Pubs.

—Regarding the Bathrooms: A Privy to the Past. Klise, Kate & Klise, M. Sarah, illus. 2008. (Regarding the Fountain Ser.: Bk. 4). (ENG.). 160p. (J). (gr. 4-6). 21.19 *(978-0-15-205164-8(3))* Houghton Mifflin Harcourt Publishing Co.

Knight, Andrew. Dead Beckoning. (Thumbprint Mysteries Ser.). 32.86 *(978-0-8092-0421-2(5))* McGraw-Hill/Contemporary.

—The Monster in the Loch. (Thumbprint Mysteries Ser.). 32.86 *(978-0-8092-0411-3(8))* McGraw-Hill/Contemporary.

Knighton, Kate, retold by. Phantom of the Opera. 2008. (Young Reading Series 2 Gift Bks). 64p. (J). 8.99 *(978-0-7945-2082-3(0)*, Usborne) EDC Publishing.

Knox, Regina. The Clintonville Abduction. 2007. 108p. per. 19.95 *(978-1-4241-2996-6(6))* PublishAmerica, Inc.

Konigsburg, E. L. My Father's Daughter. 2nd ed. 2008. (ENG.). 144p. (J). (gr. 3-7). pap. 8.99 *(978-1-4169-5500-9(3)*, Atheneum Bks. for Young Readers) Simon & Schuster Children's Publishing.

Korman, Gordon. Criminal Destiny. 2017. (Masterminds Ser.: 2). (J). lib. bdg. 18.40 *(978-0-606-39612-7(8))* Turtleback.

—Jingle (Swindle #8) 2017. (Swindle Ser.: 8). (ENG.). 208p. (J). (gr. 3-7). pap. 7.99 *(978-0-545-86144-1(6))* Scholastic, Inc.

—Masterminds. (Masterminds Ser.: 1). (ENG.). (J). (gr. 3-7). 2016. 352p. pap. 9.99 *(978-0-06-229999-4(9))* 2015. 336p. 16.99 *(978-0-06-229996-3(4))* HarperCollins Pubs. (Balzer & Bray).

—Masterminds. 2016. (Masterminds Ser.: 1). (J). lib. bdg. 18.40 *(978-0-606-38138-3(4))* Turtleback.

—Masterminds: Criminal Destiny. 2016. (Masterminds Ser.: 2). (ENG.). 320p. (J). (gr. 3-7). 17.99 *(978-0-06-230002-7(4)*, Balzer & Bray) HarperCollins Pubs.

—Masterminds: Criminal Destiny. 2017. (Masterminds Ser.: 2). (ENG.). 336p. (J). (gr. 3-7). 9.99 *(978-0-06-230003-4(2)*, Balzer & Bray) HarperCollins Pubs.

—One False Note (the 39 Clues, Book 2), Volume 2. 2008. (39 Clues Ser.: 2). (ENG.). 176p. (J). (gr. 4-7). 13.99 *(978-0-545-06042-4(7))* Scholastic, Inc.

—Whatshisface. 2019. (ENG.). 240p. (J). (gr. 3-7). pap. 8.99 *(978-1-338-20018-8(6))* Scholastic, Inc.

Kostro, Ed. Mystery of Madera Canyon. 2004. 108p. (gr. -1-7). per. 11.95 *(978-1-59113-622-4(9))* Booklocker.com, Inc.

Kotzwinkle, William. Double Trouble in Bugland. Servello, Joe, illus. 2016. (ENG.). 190p. (J). pap. 14.95 *(978-1-56792-564-7(2))* Godine, David R. Pub.

—Trouble in Bugland: A Collection of Inspector Mantis Mysteries. Servello, Joe, illus. 2015. (ENG.). 190p. (J). (gr. 4-7). reprint ed. pap. 14.95 *(978-1-56792-070-3(5))* Godine, David R. Pub.

Krailing, Tessa. La Mano Verde. (SPA.). 96p. (J). (gr. 3-5). 7.95 *(978-84-88061-84-3(6))* Serres, Ediciones, S. L. ESP. Dist: Lectorum Pubns., Inc.

Kreilein, Debra. The Tombstone Treasure Mystery. 2013. 142p. pap. 12.99 *(978-1-62509-458-2(2))* Salem Author Services.

Krensky, Stephen. Case of the Missing Mice: A Simon Mystery. 2003. (Illus.). 14.95 *(978-1-59319-022-4(0))* LeapFrog Enterprises, Inc.

—Case of the Missing Pail. 2003. (Illus.). (J). 14.95 *(978-1-59319-018-7(2))* LeapFrog Enterprises, Inc.

Kristie Smith-Armand M.Ed Ctvi. Adventures of Abby Diamond: Out of Sight. 2009. 300p. pap. 18.95 *(978-1-4401-7013-3(4))* iUniverse, Inc.

Kristie Smith-Armand M.Ed Tvi. Adventures of Abby Diamond: Abby Diamond in Teenage Wizard & Secrets in the Attic. 2009. 276p. pap. 17.95 *(978-1-4401-6626-6(9))* iUniverse, Inc.

Kristina Takes the Stage. 2008. (Illus.). 56p. (J). mass mkt. 10.95 *(978-0-9792361-3-6(4))* Inspire U., LLC.

Kropp, Paul. The Countess & Me. 2003. 144p. (J). pap. *(978-1-55041-689-3(8))* Fitzhenry & Whiteside, Ltd.

—The Countess & Me, 1 vol. 2003. (ENG., Illus.). 32p. (YA). (gr. 6-8). pap. 8.95 *(978-1-55041-692-3(8)*, 2c0c8a47-53b0-4129-ae17-c5326e906316) Fitzhenry & Whiteside, Ltd. CAN. Dist: Firefly Bks., Ltd.

Krosoczka, Jarrett J. Lunch Lady & the Field Trip Fiasco: Lunch Lady #6. 2011. (Lunch Lady Ser.: 6). (ENG.). 96p. (J). (gr. 2-5). pap. 7.99 *(978-0-375-86730-9(9)*, Knopf Bks. for Young Readers) Random Hse. Children's Bks.

—Lunch Lady & the Mutant Mathletes. 2012. (Lunch Lady Ser.: 7). lib. bdg. 17.20 *(978-0-606-23871-7(9))* Turtleback.

—Lunch Lady & the Mutant Mathletes: Lunch Lady #7. 2012. (Lunch Lady Ser.: 7). (ENG., Illus.). 96p. (J). (gr. 2-5). pap. 6.99 *(978-0-375-87028-6(8)*, Knopf Bks. for Young Readers) Random Hse. Children's Bks.

—Lunch Lady & the Picture Day Peril. 2012. (Lunch Lady Ser.: 8). lib. bdg. 17.20 *(978-0-606-26811-0(1))* Turtleback.

—Lunch Lady & the Picture Day Peril: Lunch Lady #8. 2012. (Lunch Lady Ser.: 8). (ENG., Illus.). 96p. (J). (gr. 2-5). pap. 6.99 *(978-0-375-87035-4(0)*, Knopf Bks. for Young Readers) Random Hse. Children's Bks.

—Lunch Lady & the Schoolwide Scuffle. 2014. (Lunch Lady Ser.: 10). lib. bdg. 17.20 *(978-0-606-32235-5(3))* Turtleback.

—Lunch Lady & the Schoolwide Scuffle: Lunch Lady & the Schoolwide Scuffle. 2014. (Lunch Lady Ser.: 10). (ENG., Illus.). 96p. (J). (gr. 2-5). pap. 6.99 *(978-0-385-75279-4(2)*, Knopf Bks. for Young Readers) Random Hse. Children's Bks.

—Lunch Lady & the Summer Camp Shakedown: Lunch Lady #4. 2010. (Lunch Lady Ser.: 4). (ENG.). 96p. (J). (gr. 2-5). pap. 6.99 *(978-0-375-86095-9(9)*, Knopf Bks. for Young Readers) Random Hse. Children's Bks.

—Lunch Lady & the Video Game Villain. 2013. (Lunch Lady Ser.: 9). lib. bdg. 17.20 *(978-0-606-27003-8(5))* Turtleback.

—Platypus Police Squad: Last Panda Standing. Krosoczka, Jarrett J., illus. 2015. (Platypus Police Squad Ser.: 3). (ENG., Illus.). 256p. (J). (gr. 3-7). 13.99 *(978-0-06-207168-2(8)*, Walden Pond Pr.) HarperCollins Pubs.

—Platypus Police Squad: the Frog Who Croaked. Krosoczka, Jarrett J., illus. 2013. (Platypus Police Squad Ser.: 1). (ENG., Illus.). 240p. (J). (gr. 3-7). 13.99 *(978-0-06-207164-4(5)*, Walden Pond Pr.) HarperCollins Pubs.

—Platypus Police Squad: the Ostrich Conspiracy. Krosoczka, Jarrett J., illus. 2014. (Platypus Police Squad Ser.: 2). (ENG., Illus.). 240p. (J). (gr. 3-7). 13.99 *(978-0-06-207166-8(1)*, Walden Pond Pr.) HarperCollins Pubs.

Kruse, Donald W. Jasper Has Left the Building! Crank, Donny, illus. 2013. 50p. pap. 12.95 *(978-1-59663-863-1(X)*, Castle Keep Pr.) Rock, James A. & Co. Pubs.

Kubica, Jeremy. The CS Detective: An Algorithmic Tale of Crime, Conspiracy, & Computation. 2016. (Illus.). 256p. (YA). (gr. 7-7). pap. 19.99 *(978-1-59327-749-9(0))* No Starch Pr., Inc.

Kubuitsile, Lauri. The Mystery of Sol 2 Wayfarers. Bonet, Xavier, illus. 2017. (Cambridge Reading Adventures Ser.). (ENG.). 32p. pap. 8.60 *(978-1-108-43672-4(2))* Cambridge Univ. Pr.

Kudina Steinberg, Ganna V. The Princess Conspiracy: an Inspector Poopchyk Mystery. 2009. 143p. 30.00 *(978-0-557-08936-9(0))* Lulu Pr., Inc.

Kunze, Nansi. Kill the Music. l.t. ed. 2013. 330p. pap. *(978-1-4596-6983-5(3))* ReadHowYouWant.com, Ltd.

Kupperberg, Paul. Scooby-Doo in over the Boardwalk, 1 vol. Laguna, Fabio, illus. 2013. (Scooby-Doo Graphic Novels Ser.). (ENG.). 24p. (J). (gr. 2-6). lib. bdg. 31.36 *(978-1-61479-052-5(3)*, 585, Graphic Novels) Spotlight.

—Scooby-Doo in Read All about It!, 1 vol. Laguna, Fabio, illus. 2013. (Scooby-Doo Graphic Novels Ser.). (ENG.). 24p. (J). (gr. 2-6). lib. bdg. 31.36 *(978-1-61479-053-2(1)*, 586, Graphic Novels) Spotlight.

Kvasnosky, Laura McGee. Zelda & Ivy: the Big Picture: Candlewick Sparks. Kvasnosky, Laura McGee, illus. 2013. (Candlewick Sparks Ser.). (ENG., Illus.). 48p. (J). (gr. k-4). pap. 5.99 *(978-0-7636-6637-8(8))* Candlewick Pr.

Kwitney, Alisa. Cadaver & Queen. 2018. (ENG.). 320p. (YA). 18.99 *(978-1-335-47046-1(8)*, Harlequin Teen) Harlequin Enterprises ULC CAN. Dist: HarperCollins Pubs.

Labeda, Patricia R. Miko & the Mystery Friend. Labeda, Patricia R., illus. 2007. (Illus.). 73p. (J). (gr. 4-7). per. 10.99 *(978-1-59879-415-1(9)*, Lifevest) Lifevest Publishing, Inc.

LaBree Stute, Lela. Wonder Pugs. 2010. 36p. pap. 19.99 *(978-0-557-42611-9(1))* Lulu Pr., Inc.

LaBrot, Matthew & Daniel, Hale. Green Streak. 2004. (Zeke Armstrong Mysteries Ser.: 2). 236p. (J). per. 8.95 *(978-1-929976-28-7(3))* Top Pubns., Ltd.

Lacey, Josh. Island of Thieves. 2013. (ENG.). 240p. (J). (gr. 5-7). pap. 7.99 *(978-0-544-10485-3(4)*, 1540794, Clarion Bks.) HarperCollins Pubs.

Lachtman, Ofelia Dumas. The Truth about las Mariposas. 2007. 144p. (J). (gr. 6-18). pap. 9.95 *(978-1-55885-494-9(0)*, Piñata Books) Arte Publico Pr.

Lackey, Mercedes & Edghill, Rosemary. Shadow Grail #1: Legacies, No. 1. 2010. (Shadow Grail Ser.: 1). (ENG.). 320p. (YA). (gr. 8-12). pap. 17.99 *(978-0-7653-1761-2(3)*, 900041772, Tor Teen) Doherty, Tom Assocs., LLC.

Ladd, Debbie. Ethan the Ending Eater. Nakasone, Shaun, illus. 2008. 64p. (J). 17.95 *(978-0-9727615-2-9(7))* Deb on Air Bks.

Lagonegro, Melissa. Cars - The Spooky Sound. 2010. (Cars Step into Reading Ser.). lib. bdg. 13.55 *(978-0-606-14562-6(1))* Turtleback.

Laidlaw, S. J. The Voice Inside My Head. 2014. (ENG., Illus.). 252p. (YA). (gr. 9). 17.99 *(978-1-77049-565-4(7)*, Tundra Bks.) Tundra Bks. CAN. Dist: Penguin Random Hse. LLC.

Laing, David. Forest Shadows. 2013. 215p. (YA). 15.97 *(978-0-9873585-7-8(X))* JoJo Publishing AUS. Dist: Baker & Taylor Publisher Services (BTPS).

Laird, Chynna. Dark Water. 2012. 166p. pap. *(978-1-926997-76-6(X))* Imajin Bks.

Lalicki, Tom. Danger in the Dark: A Houdini & Nate Mystery, 1. 2010. (Houdini & Nate Mysteries Ser.: 1). (ENG.). 208p. (J). (gr. 6-8). pap. 15.99 *(978-0-312-60214-7(6)*, 900064229) Square Fish.

—Shots at Sea: A Houdini & Nate Mystery. 2011. (Houdini & Nate Mysteries Ser.). 224p. (J). pap. 6.99 *(978-0-312-65920-2(2))* Square Fish.

Lamotte, Kathleen. The Horsetrailer Mystery. 2008. 49p. pap. 16.95 *(978-1-60474-449-1(9))* America Star Bks.

Lamplighter Staff. What Is Her Name. 2004. 16.00 *(978-1-58474-036-0(1))* Cornerstone Family Ministries/Lamplighter Publishing.

Lancett, Peter. Playing the Dark Game, 1 vol. unabr. ed. 2011. (Dark Man Ser.). (ENG.). 48p. (YA). (gr. 5-12). 8.75 *(978-1-61651-296-5(2))* Saddleback Educational Publishing, Inc.

Land, Linda C. The Mysterious Traveling Trunk. 2011. 156p. 23.50 *(978-1-4269-6160-1(X))*; pap. 13.50 *(978-1-4269-6161-8(8))* Trafford Publishing.

Landon, Lucinda. Meg Mackintosh & the April Fools' Day Mystery: A Solve-It-Yourself Mystery. 2018. (Meg Mackintosh Mystery Ser.). (ENG., Illus.). 48p. (J). (gr. 2-4). pap. 6.95 *(978-1-888695-15-1(3))* Secret Passage Pr.

—Meg Mackintosh & the Mystery at Red Herring Beach: A Solve-It-Yourself Mystery. 2013. (Meg Mackintosh Mystery Ser.). 48p. (J). (gr. 2-4). pap. 6.95 *(978-1-888695-14-4(5))* Secret Passage Pr.

—Meg Mackintosh & the Stage Fright Secret: A Solve-It-Yourself Mystery. 2004. (Meg Mackintosh Mystery Ser.: 8). (ENG., Illus.). 48p. (J). (gr. 2-4). pap. 6.95 *(978-1-888695-07-6(2))* Secret Passage Pr.

—Meg Mackintosh Solves Seven American History Mysteries - Title #9: A Solve-It-Yourself Mystery. 2008. (Meg Mackintosh Mystery Ser.: 9). (ENG.). 96p. (J). (gr. 2-4). pap. 8.95 *(978-1-888695-12-0(9))* Secret Passage Pr.

Lane, Andrew. Black Ice. 2013. (Sherlock Holmes: the Legend Begins Ser.: 3). (ENG.). 304p. (YA). (gr. 7-12). pap. 13.99 *(978-1-250-03654-4(2)*, 900122027) Square Fish.

—Death Cloud. 2012. (ENG.). (YA). (gr. 7-12). 64.99 *(978-1-4272-2800-0(0))* Findaway World, LLC.

—Death Cloud. 2011. (Sherlock Holmes: the Legend Begins Ser.: 1). (ENG.). 336p. (YA). (gr. 7-12). pap. 10.99 *(978-0-312-56371-4(X)*, 900074762) Square Fish.

—Death Cloud. l.t. ed. 2011. (Young Sherlock Holmes Ser.). (ENG.). 367p. 23.99 *(978-1-4104-3971-0(2))* Thorndike Pr.

—Death Cloud. 2011. (Sherlock Holmes: the Legend Begins Ser.: 1). (YA). lib. bdg. 22.10 *(978-0-606-23781-9(X))* Turtleback.

—Fire Storm. 2014. (Sherlock Holmes: the Legend Begins Ser.: 4). (ENG.). 368p. (YA). (gr. 7-12). pap. 16.99 *(978-1-250-05072-4(3)*, 900134143) Square Fish.

—Knife Edge. 2015. (Sherlock Holmes: the Legend Begins Ser.: 6). (ENG.). 320p. (YA). (gr. 7). 34.99 *(978-0-374-38011-3(2)*, 900122988, Farrar, Straus & Giroux (BYR)) Farrar, Straus & Giroux.

LaReau, Kara. The Uncanny Express (the Unintentional Adventures of the Bland Sisters Book 2) Hill, Jen, illus. 2018. (Unintentional Adventures of the Bland Sisters Ser.). (ENG.). (J). (gr. 3-7). 184p. pap. 7.99 *(978-1-4197-3204-1(8)*, 1139403); 176p. 14.99 *(978-1-4197-2568-5(8)*, 1139401) Abrams, Inc. (Amulet Bks.).

Lariviere, Sarah. The Bad Kid. 2016. (ENG., Illus.). 304p. (J). (gr. 3-7). 17.99 *(978-1-4814-3581-9(7)*, Simon & Schuster Bks. For Young Readers) Simon & Schuster Bks. For Young Readers.

Larry, H. I. Zac Power #1: Poison Island: 24 Hours to Save the World ... & Walk the Dog. Oswald, Ash, illus. 2008. (Zac Power Ser.: 1). (ENG.). 96p. (J). (gr. 3-6). pap. 6.99 *(978-0-312-34659-1(X)*, 900042759) Square Fish.

—Zac Power #2: Deep Waters: 24 Hours to Save the World ... & Finish His Homework, 2. Oswald, Ash, illus. 2008. (Zac Power Ser.: 2). (ENG.). 96p. (J). (gr. 2-4). pap. 6.99 *(978-0-312-34655-3(7)*, 900042756) Square Fish.

Larry Sweitzer. The Ghost, the Eggheads, & Babe Ruth's Piano: A Novel. 2009. 180p. 23.95 *(978-1-4401-7103-1(3))*; pap. 13.95 *(978-1-4401-7104-8(1))* iUniverse, Inc.

Larson, Kirby. Audacity Jones Steals the Show (Audacity Jones #2) 2018. lib. bdg. 17.20 *(978-0-606-41131-8(3))* Turtleback.

Larson, Mark. The Adventures of Pinky, the Pink Flamingo. 2008. 24p. pap. 24.95 *(978-1-60610-046-2(7))* America Star Bks.

Larson, Rachel. Jesse Strong & Courageous Runaway: There Comes A Time When the Roads of Destiny Will No Longer Wait... 2011. 192p. (J). (gr. -1). pap. 14.03 *(978-1-4520-0421-1(8))* AuthorHouse.

Larwood, Kieran. Freaks. 2013. (J). *(978-0-545-47425-2(6)*, Chicken Hse., The) Scholastic, Inc.

Lashawn Graves, M. Ed. Listen & Embrace When Children Care. 2012. 28p. pap. 9.95 *(978-1-4327-8895-7(7))* Outskirts Pr., Inc.

Lasky, Kathryn. Double Trouble Squared: A Starbuck Twins Mystery, Book One. 2008. (ENG., Illus.). 240p. (J). (gr. 3-7). pap. 14.99 *(978-0-15-205878-4(8)*, 1197650, Clarion Bks.) HarperCollins Pubs.

—The Rescue. 2004. (Guardians of Ga'Hoole Ser.: 3). (gr. 3-6). lib. bdg. 17.20 *(978-0-613-72136-3(5))* Turtleback.

—Shadows in the Water: A Starbuck Twins Mystery, Book Two. 2008. (ENG., Illus.). 224p. (J). (gr. 3-7). pap. 14.95 *(978-0-15-205874-6(5)*, 1197638, Clarion Bks.) HarperCollins Pubs.

—A Voice in the Wind: A Starbuck Twins Mystery, Book Three. 2008. (ENG., Illus.). 272p. (J). (gr. 3-7). pap. 15.95 *(978-0-15-205875-3(3)*, 1197642, Clarion Bks.) HarperCollins Pubs.

Latham, Jennifer. Dreamland Burning. 2018.Tr. of s. (ENG.). 400p. (YA). (gr. 9-17). pap. 11.99 *(978-0-316-38490-2(9))* Little, Brown Bks. for Young Readers.

—Dreamland Burning. 2018.Tr. of s. (YA). lib. bdg. 22.10 *(978-0-606-40637-6(9))* Turtleback.

—Scarlett Undercover. 2016. (ENG.). 336p. (J). (gr. 7-17). pap. 17.99 *(978-0-316-28394-6(0))* Little, Brown Bks. for Young Readers.

Latimer, Alex. Never Follow a Dinosaur, 1 vol. 2016. (ENG., Illus.). 32p. (J). (gr. -1-3). 16.95 *(978-1-56145-704-5(3))* Peachtree Publishing Co. Inc.

Latta, Ruth. The Revenant & Other Stories for Hallowe'en. 2004. 54p. *(978-0-9683382-8-5(3))* Latta, Roger K.

Lattimore, Deborah Nourse. Mystery at Midnight Museum. Date not set. 32p. (J). 15.89 *(978-0-06-026202-0(8))* HarperCollins Pubs.

Lauren, Whitney. Vanessa & Johnny: The Cabinets. 2011. 84p. pap. 9.99 *(978-1-4269-5827-4(7))* Trafford Publishing.

Laurentine, Florianne Daphne. The Mystery Chronicles: The Amazing Chocolate Mystery & the Case of the Phantom Cat. 2008. 100p. pap. 8.99 *(978-1-934360-61-3(9))* Raider Publishing International.

—The Mystery Chronicles: The Unknown Masterpiece & the Case of the Practical Joker. 2012. 98p. pap. 7.99 *(978-1-61667-427-4(X))* Raider Publishing International.

Laurie, Victoria. Forever, Again. (ENG.). 368p. (J). (gr. 7-12). 2017. pap. 9.99 *(978-1-4847-0151-5(8))* 2016. 17.99 *(978-1-4847-0009-9(0))* Hyperion Bks. for Children.

—When. 2016. (ENG.). 336p. (YA). (gr. 9-17). pap. 10.99 *(978-1-4847-0149-2(6))* Hyperion Bks. for Children.

Law, Felicia & Way, Steve. Castaway Code: Sequencing in Action, 1 vol. Spoor, Mike, illus. 2009. (Mandrill Mountain Math Mysteries Ser.). (ENG.). 32p. (J). (gr. 2-3). 27.27 *(978-1-60754-817-1(8)*, 320e8775-ea88-4765-9f6f-3f39bcf63269); pap. 11.55 *(978-1-60754-822-5(4)*, 45ca3189-6d1a-4aba-bc1e-313695ab5542) Rosen Publishing Group, Inc., The. (Windmill Bks.).

—Crocodile Teeth: Geometric Shapes in Action, 1 vol. Spoor, Mike, illus. 2009. (Mandrill Mountain Math Mysteries Ser.). (ENG.). 32p. (J). (gr. 2-3). 27.27 *(978-1-60754-816-4(X)*, f316fc20-91e6-4a71-a59a-55448d4523ab); pap. 11.55 *(978-1-60754-821-8(6)*, d64648f7-9081-4d51-9365-af6071b54489) Rosen Publishing Group, Inc., The. (Windmill Bks.).

—Mirage in the Mist: Measurements in Action, 1 vol. Spoor, Mike, illus. 2009. (Mandrill Mountain Math Mysteries Ser.). (ENG.). 32p. (J). (gr. 2-3). 27.27 *(978-1-60754-818-8(6)*, 3b46573c-6745-47ea-b321-23dc467821a4, Windmill Bks.) Rosen Publishing Group, Inc., The.

—The Mystery of Nine: Number Place & Value in Action, 1 vol. Spoor, Mike, illus. 2009. (Mandrill Mountain Math Mysteries Ser.). (ENG.). 32p. (J). (gr. 2-3). 27.27 *(978-1-60754-819-5(4)*, eb540fd4-8485-47c7-9a25-12d4c647ff10); pap. 11.55 *(978-1-60754-824-9(0)*, 3d506973-6103-4b56-aa0a-977d78cbb7d1) Rosen Publishing Group, Inc., The. (Windmill Bks.).

—A Storm at Sea: Sorting, Mapping, & Grids in Action, 1 vol. Spoor, Mike, illus. 2009. (Mandrill Mountain Math Mysteries Ser.). (ENG.). 32p. (J). (gr. 2-3). 27.27 *(978-1-60754-815-7(1)*, 8ef36f64-756f-4e9e-ba11-50de241ce395); pap. 11.55 *(978-1-60754-820-1(8)*, 97b78dc7-e6a6-4efd-9acc-1d62e87eeaf2) Rosen Publishing Group, Inc., The. (Windmill Bks.).

Lawrence, Caroline. The Assassins of Rome. 2003. (ENG., Illus.). 224p. (gr. 2-7). pap. 10.99 *(978-1-84255-023-6(3)*, Orion Children's Bks.) Hachette Children's Group GBR. Dist: Hachette Bk. Group.

—The Assassins of Rome. 2005. (Roman Mysteries Ser.). (Illus.). 161p. (J). (gr. 3-7). 14.65 *(978-0-7569-5879-4(2))* Perfection Learning Corp.

—The Case of the Deadly Desperados. 1. 2013. (P. K. Pinkerton Novels Ser.: 1). (ENG.). 272p. (J). (gr. 4-6). 21.19 *(978-0-399-25633-2(4))* Penguin Young Readers Group.

—The Charioteer of Delphi. 2007. (ENG., Illus.). 256p. (gr. 4-6). pap. 10.99 *(978-1-84255-544-6(8)*, Orion Children's Bks.) Hachette Children's Group GBR. Dist: Hachette Bk. Group.

—The Dolphins of Laurentum. 2003. (ENG., Illus.). 224p. (gr. 4-6). pap. 10.99 *(978-1-84255-024-3(1)*, Orion Children's Bks.) Hachette Children's Group GBR. Dist: Hachette Bk. Group.

—The Dolphins of Laurentum. 2005. (Roman Mysteries Ser.). (ENG., Illus.). 176p. (J). (gr. 6-8). 18.69 *(978-0-14-240379-2(2))* Penguin Young Readers Group.

—The Dolphins of Laurentum. 2005. (Roman Mysteries Ser.). (Illus.). 161p. (J). (gr. 6-9). 13.65 *(978-0-7569-6538-9(1))* Perfection Learning Corp.

—The Enemies of Jupiter. 2004. (ENG., Illus.). 224p. (gr. 4-6). pap. 10.99 *(978-1-84255-164-6(7)*, Orion Children's Bks.) Hachette Children's Group GBR. Dist: Hachette Bk. Group.

—The Fugitive from Corinth, Bk. 10. 2006. (ENG., Illus.). 240p. (gr. 4-6). pap. 10.99 *(978-1-84255-515-6(4)*, Orion Children's Bks.) Hachette Children's Group GBR. Dist: Hachette Bk. Group.

—The Gladiators from Capua. 2005. (ENG., Illus.). 224p. (gr. 4-6). pap. 10.99 *(978-1-84255-123-3(X)*, Orion Children's Bks.) Hachette Children's Group GBR. Dist: Hachette Bk. Group.

—The Legionary from Londinium & Other Mini Mysteries. 2013. (ENG., Illus.). 192p. (J). (gr. 7-17). 10.99 *(978-1-84255-192-9(2)*, Orion Children's Bks.) Hachette Children's Group GBR. Dist: Hachette Bk. Group.

—The Man from Pomegranate Street, Bk. 17. 2010. (ENG., Illus.). 272p. (YA). (gr. 7-17). 10.99 *(978-1-84255-608-5(8)*, Orion Children's Bks.) Hachette Children's Group GBR. Dist: Hachette Bk. Group.

—P. K. Pinkerton & the Case of the Deadly Desperados. 2013. (P. K. Pinkerton Ser.: 1). (ENG.). 304p. (J). (gr. 3-7). pap. 8.99 *(978-0-14-242381-3(5)*, Puffin Books) Penguin Young Readers Group.

M N O

—P. K. Pinkerton & the Pistol-Packing Widows. 2015. (P. K. Pinkerton Ser.: 3). (ENG.). 320p. (J). (gr. 3-7). 7.99 (978-0-14-751130-0(5), Puffin Books) Penguin Young Readers Group.

—Los Piratas de Pompeya. 2003. (SPA.). 192p. (978-84-7888-798-9(9), 1952) Emece Editores.

—The Pirates of Pompeii. 2004. (Roman Mysteries Ser.). (Illus.). 159p. (J). (gr. 3-7). 13.65 (978-0-7569-5938-8(1)) Perfection Learning Corp.

—The Prophet from Ephesus: The Roman Mysteries 16. 2009. (ENG., Illus.). 224p. (YA). (gr. 7-17). pap. 10.99 (978-1-84255-606-1(1), Orion Children's Bks.) Hachette Children's Group GBR. Dist: Hachette Bk. Group.

—The Secrets of Vesuvius. 2004. (Roman Mysteries Ser.). (Illus.). 173p. (J). (gr. 3-7). 13.65 (978-0-7569-5947-0(0)) Perfection Learning Corp.

—The Sirens of Surrentum. 2006. (ENG., Illus.). 272p. (gr. 4-6). pap. 10.99 (978-1-84255-506-4(5), Orion Children's Bks.) Hachette Children's Group GBR. Dist: Hachette Bk. Group.

—The Sirens of Surrentum. 2007. (Roman Mysteries Ser.: Bk. 11). (ENG., Illus.). 224p. (J). (gr. 6-9). 16.95 (978-1-59643-084-6(2)) Roaring Brook Pr.

—The Slave-Girl from Jerusalem. 2007. (ENG., Illus.). 240p. (gr. 4-6). pap. 10.99 (978-1-84255-572-9(3), Orion Children's Bks.) Hachette Children's Group GBR. Dist: Hachette Bk. Group.

—The Twelve Tasks of Flavia Gemina. 2003. (ENG., Illus.). 224p. (gr. 2-4). pap. 10.99 (978-1-84255-025-0(X), Orion Children's Bks.) Hachette Children's Group GBR. Dist: Hachette Bk. Group.

Lawrence, Casey. Order in the Court. (Survivor's Club Ser.). (ENG., Illus.). (YA). 2017. 25.99 (978-1-64080-356-5(4)) 2016. 24.99 (978-1-63533-059-5(9)) Dreamspinner Pr. (Harmony Ink Pr.).

Laws, Jamie Lynn. Cameron & the Mysterious Shack. 2008. pap. 16.95 (978-1-60563-434-0(4)) America Star Bks.

Lawson, Jessica. Nooks & Crannies. Andrewson, Natalie, illus. 2015. (ENG.). 336p. (J). (gr. 3-7). 19.99 (978-1-4814-1921-5(8), Simon & Schuster Bks. For Young Readers) Simon & Schuster Bks. For Young Readers.

Lay, Eddie. Mystery of the Hats. 2006. 61p. pap. 16.95 (978-1-4241-2649-1(5)) PublishAmerica, Inc.

Layman, John. Eleanor & the Egret Volume 1. Marts, Mike, ed. 2018. (ENG., Illus.). 120p. (J). pap. 14.99 (978-1-935002-76-5(7), 0e6aa812-51a9-4acb-8441-2416fb2b9919) AfterShock Comics.

Layos, Alexandra. Timeless: Blue Ribbon Days #2, 2, 2. 2005. (Illus.). 128p. (YA). pap. 10.95 (978-0-9655501-4-7(1)) Saddle & Bridle, Inc.

Le Gall, Frank. Rooftop Cat #2. 2012. (Miss Annie Ser.: 2). (ENG., Illus.). 48p. (J). (gr. 2-4). pap. 6.95 (978-0-7613-8547-9(9), Graphic Universe™) Lerner Publishing Group.

Leavitt, Lindsey. Commander in Cheese Super Special #1: Mouse Rushmore. Ford, A. G., illus. 2017. (Commander in Cheese Ser.: 1). 128p. (J). (gr. 2-5). 5.99 (978-1-5247-2047-6(X), Random Hse. Bks. for Young Readers) Random Hse. Children's Bks.

Leblanc, Margaret Ann. Ms Maddy & the Lake Adventure. 2008. 89p. pap. 19.95 (978-1-60474-003-5(5)) America Star Bks.

Lee Hope, Laura. The Bobbsey Twins in the Great West. 2005. 200p. pap. 12.95 (978-1-4218-0465-1(4), 1st World Library - Literary Society) 1st World Publishing, Inc.

—The Bobbsey Twins in the Great West. 2004. reprint ed. pap. 1.99 (978-1-4192-5444-4(8)); pap. 20.95 (978-1-4191-5444-7(3)) Kessinger Publishing, LLC.

Lee, Kathy. The Runaway Train. 2011. 144p. pap. (978-1-84427-505-2(1)) Scripture Union.

Lee, Y. S. The Agency 2: the Body at the Tower. 2010. (Agency Ser.: 2). (ENG., Illus.). 352p. (YA). (gr. 7-18). 16.99 (978-0-7636-4968-5(6)) Candlewick Pr.

—The Agency 3: the Traitor in the Tunnel. 2012. (Agency Ser.: 3). (ENG., Illus.). 384p. (YA). (gr. 7). 16.99 (978-0-7636-5316-3(0)) Candlewick Pr.

—The Agency: a Spy in the House. 2016. (Agency Ser.: 1). (ENG.). 352p. (YA). (gr. 7). pap. 9.99 (978-0-7636-8748-9(0)) Candlewick Pr.

—The Agency: the Body at the Tower. 2016. (Agency Ser.: 2). (ENG.). 352p. (YA). (gr. 7). pap. 9.99 (978-0-7636-8750-2(2)) Candlewick Pr.

—A Spy in the House, 1. 2010. (Agency Ser.: Bk. 1). (ENG., Illus.). 352p. (YA). (gr. 7-12). 22.44 (978-0-7636-4067-5(0)) Candlewick Pr.

Leighton, Noreen. Mr Tilly & the Halloween Mystery. Wilson, Lorna, illus. 2013. 42p. pap. (978-0-9573315-6-3(8)) Tatterdemalion Blue.

Lenard, Steve. The Mysterious Maze #1: The Search for the Skeleton Key. 2009. 60p. pap. 21.99 (978-1-4389-5029-7(2)) AuthorHouse.

L'Engle, Madeleine. Dragons in the Waters. 2011. (Polly O'Keefe Ser.: 2). (ENG.). 320p. (YA). (gr. 6-10). pap. 12.99 (978-0-312-67442-7(2), 900072857) Square Fish.

—Troubling a Star: The Austin Family Chronicles, Book 5. 2008. (Austin Family Ser.: 5). (ENG., Illus.). 336p. (J). (gr. 6-12). pap. 13.99 (978-0-312-37934-6(X), 900050197) Square Fish.

Lenihan, Eddie. Eddie Lenihan's Irish Tales of Mystery. Clarke, Alan, illus. 2006. (ENG.). 224p. (J). 33.95 (978-1-85635-519-3(5)) Mercier Pr., Ltd., The IRL. Dist: Dufour Editions, Inc.

Leonard, Julia Platt. Cold Case. (ENG.). 288p. (J). (gr. 3-7). 2012. pap. 5.99 (978-1-4424-2010-6(3)) 2011. (Illus.). 15.99 (978-1-4424-2009-0(X)) Simon & Schuster/Paula Wiseman Bks. (Simon & Schuster/Paula Wiseman Bks.).

Leonard, M. G. Beetle Boy (Beetle Trilogy, Book 1), Bk. 1. 2017. (Beetle Boy Ser.). (ENG., Illus.). 304p. (J). (gr. 3-7). pap. 6.99 (978-0-545-85347-7(8), Chicken Hse., The) Scholastic, Inc.

Leppard, Lois Gladys. The Mandie Collection. (ENG.). (J). 2011. 366p. (gr. 3-8). pap. 16.00 (978-0-7642-0932-1(9)) 2011. 382p. (gr. 3-8). pap. 16.00 (978-0-7642-0878-2(0)) 2011. 368p. (gr. 3-8). pap. 16.00 (978-0-7642-0877-5(2)) 2011. 368p. (gr. 3-8). pap. 16.00 (978-0-7642-0689-4(3))Bks. 16-20, Vol. 4. 2009. 608p. pap. 19.99 (978-0-7642-0663-4(X)) Vol. 1. 2007. 544p. (gr. 3-8). pap. 16.99 (978-0-7642-0446-3(7)) Vol. 2. 2008. (Illus.). 576p. (gr. 3-8). pap. 17.99 (978-0-7642-0538-5(2)) Bethany Hse. Pubs.

—Mandie Collection, Vol. 3. 2008. (ENG.). 608p. (J). pap. 18.99 (978-0-7642-0593-4(5)) Bethany Hse. Pubs.

Lerangis, Peter. The Code. 2004. (Spy X Ser.: No. 1). 139p. (Orig.). (J). (978-0-439-70242-3(9)) Scholastic, Inc.

—Wow! Blast from the Past! Talbot, Jim, illus. 2003. (Abracadabra Ser.: No. 8). (ENG.). 112p. (J). pap. 3.99 (978-0-439-38939-6(9), Scholastic Paperbacks) Scholastic, Inc.

—Wtf. 2013. (ENG., Illus.). 288p. (YA). (gr. 9). 17.99 (978-1-4424-9369-8(0)); pap. 9.99 (978-1-4424-9368-1(2)) Simon Pulse. (Simon Pulse).

Leung, Julie. Mice of the Round Table #2: Voyage to Avalon. Carr, Lindsey, illus. 2018. (Mice of the Round Table Ser.: 2). (ENG.). 352p. (J). (gr. 3-7). pap. 6.99 (978-0-06-240403-9(2), HarperCollins) HarperCollins Pubs.

Leveen, Tom. Shackled. 2015. (ENG., Illus.). 224p. (YA). (gr. 9). 17.99 (978-1-4814-2249-9(9), Simon Pulse) Simon Pulse.

Levine, Gail Carson. A Tale of Two Castles. Call, Greg, illus. (ENG.). (J). (gr. 3-7). 2012. 352p. pap. 7.99 (978-0-06-122967-1(9)) 2011. 336p. 16.99 (978-0-06-122965-7(2)) HarperCollins Pubs. (HarperCollins).

Levy, Elizabeth. A Hare-Raising Tale. Gerstein, Mordicai, illus. unabr. ed. 2006. (First Chapter Bks.). (J). (gr. 2-4). pap. 20.95 incl. audio compact disk (978-1-59519-705-4(2)); pap. 17.95 incl. audio (978-1-59519-704-7(4)) Live Oak Media.

—The Mixed-Up Mask Mystery: A Fletcher Mystery. Gorstein, Mordicai, illus. unabr. ed. 2006. (First Chapter Bks.). (J). (gr. 2-4). pap. 17.95 incl. audio (978-1-59519-710-8(9)); pap. 20.95 incl. audio compact disk (978-1-59519-711-5(7)) Live Oak Media.

Levy, Elizabeth & Brunkus, Denise. The Mystery of the Missing Dog. (Hello Reader! Ser.). (FRE., Illus.). (J). pap. 5.99 (978-0-590-16010-0(9)) Scholastic, Inc.

Levy, Elizabeth & Coville, Bruce. The Dragon of Doom. Gerstein, Mordicai & Coville, Katherine, illus. 2005. 71p. (J). lib. bdg. 15.00 (978-1-59054-903-2(1)) Fitzgerald Bks.

Levy, Viv. The Mysterious Disappearance at Bird Bridge: A Dog Detective Story. 2013. (ENG., Illus.). 156p. 24.00 (978-0-906362-75-4(X)) Gothic Image Pubns. GBR. Dist: SCB Distributors.

Lewis, Beverly. Cul-De-Sac Kids Collection One: Books 1-6. 2017. (ENG., Illus.). 352p. (J). pap. 14.99 (978-0-7642-3048-6(4)) Bethany Hse. Pubs.

Lewis, J. Patrick & Innocenti, Roberto. El último Refugio. 2003. (Los Especiales de A la Orilla del Viento Ser.). (SPA., Illus.). 48p. (J). (gr. -1-7). 16.99 (978-968-16-6860-0(X)) Fondo de Cultura Economica USA.

Lewman, David. Double Trouble: The Case of the Missing Spatula - The Case of the Vanished Squirrel. Moore, Harry, Jr., illus. 2010. (SpongeBob SquarePants Ser.). (ENG.). 36p. (J). bds. 10.99 (978-1-4424-1337-5(9), Simon Spotlight/Nickelodeon) Simon Spotlight/Nickelodeon.

Liess, Claudia Schmidt. Henry the Magical, Mythical Dragon. 2008. 74p. pap. 19.95 (978-1-60672-956-4(X)) America Star Bks.

Lilly, Suzanne. Untellable. 2013. 158p. pap. 9.99 (978-1-62237-218-8(2)) Turquoise Morning Pr.

Lin, Alex. The Little Detective. 2012. 24p. (-18). pap. 15.99 (978-1-4797-0286-2(2)) Xlibris Corp.

Lincoln, Beth. The Swifts: a Dictionary of Scoundrels. Powell, Claire, illus. 2023. (ENG.). 352p. (J). (gr. 3-7). 17.99 (978-0-593-53323-9(2), Dutton Books for Young Readers) Penguin Young Readers Group.

Lindsey, Julie Anne. Reinventing Chloe. 2013. 278p. pap. 13.99 (978-1-62237-152-5(6)) Turquoise Morning Pr.

Liphardt, Linda. Secret in the Old Barn. 2008. 116p. pap. 19.95 (978-1-60703-615-9(0)) America Star Bks.

Lisbon, Zara. Fake Plastic Girl. 2020. (ENG.). 304p. (YA). pap. 10.99 (978-1-250-23371-4(2), 900184880) Square Fish.

Lively, Penelope. A Stitch in Time (Collins Modern Classics) 2017. (Collins Modern Classics Ser.). (ENG.). 224p. (J). 6.99 (978-0-00-820844-8(1), HarperCollins Children's Bks.) HarperCollins Pubs. Ltd. GBR. Dist: HarperCollins Pubs.

Llama, Gram. The Bunny Fuzz Mystery. 2007. 32p. per. 24.95 (978-1-4241-8371-5(5)) America Star Bks.

Llewellyn, Tom. The Shadow of Seth: A Seth Anomundy Murder Mystery. 2015. (Seth Anomundy Murder Mysteries Ser.: 1). (ENG.). 192p. (YA). pap. 18.99 (978-1-929345-18-2(6), Poisoned Pen Press) Sourcebooks, Inc.

Lloyd, Hugh. Held for Ransom: A Skippy Dare Mystery Story. Fogel, Seymour, illus. 2011. 228p. 46.95 (978-1-258-07879-9(1)) Literary Licensing, LLC.

—The Lonesome Swamp Mystery: A Hal Keen Mystery Story. Salg, Bert, illus. 2011. 278p. 47.95 (978-1-258-10174-9(2)) Literary Licensing, LLC.

—The Lost Mine of the Amazon. Salg, Bert, illus. 2011. 232p. 46.95 (978-1-258-10175-6(0)) Literary Licensing, LLC.

Lloyd, Jennifer. Murilla Gorilla & the Hammock Problem. Lee, Jacqui, illus. 2014. (Murilla Gorilla Ser.: 3). (ENG.). 42p. (J). (gr. -1-3). 9.95 (978-1-927018-47-7(1)) Simply Read Bks. CAN. Dist: Ingram Publisher Services.

—Murilla Gorilla & the Lost Parasol. Lee, Jacqui, illus. 2013. (Murilla Gorilla Ser.: 2). (ENG.). 42p. (J). (gr. -1-3). 9.95 (978-1-927018-23-1(4)) Simply Read Bks. CAN. Dist: Ingram Publisher Services.

Lobdell, Scott. Hardy Boys #19: Chaos at 30,000 Feet!, 19. Henrique, Paulo, illus. 2009. (Hardy Boys Undercover Brothers Graphic Novels Ser.: 19). (ENG.). 96p. (J). (gr. 4-7). 22.44 (978-1-59707-170-3(6)) Papercutz.

Lockhart, E. Genuine Fraud. 2017. (YA). (978-1-5247-7067-9(1), Delacorte Pr) Random House Publishing Group.

—Genuine Fraud. 2019. (ENG.). 288p. (YA). (gr. 7). pap. 11.99 (978-0-385-74478-2(1), Ember) Random Hse. Children's Bks.

Lockwood, Cara. Moby Clique. 2008. (Bard Academy Ser.: No. 3). (ENG.). 304p. (YA). (gr. 9-12). pap. 19.99 (978-1-4165-5050-1(X), MTV Bks.) MTV Books.

Long, Angela Pullam. Salvador the Spy in the Case of the Missing Cats. 2008. 32p. pap. 24.95 (978-1-60672-724-9(9)) America Star Bks.

Long, Loren & Bildner, Phil. Horsin' Around. Long, Loren, illus. 2009. (Sluggers Ser.: 2). (ENG., Illus.). 224p. (J). (gr. 3-7). pap. 8.99 (978-1-4169-1888-2(4), Simon & Schuster Bks. For Young Readers) Simon & Schuster Bks. For Young Readers.

The Long-Lost Friends, 6 vols., Vol. 3. (Woodland Mysteriestm Ser.). 133p. (gr. 3-7). 42.50 (978-0-322-02377-2(7)) Wright Group/McGraw-Hill.

Longley, Joshua. Barnaby's Buccaneers. 2011. 240p. (gr. 4-6). 25.95 (978-1-4620-6112-9(5)); pap. 15.95 (978-1-4620-6110-5(9)) iUniverse, Inc.

Lopez, Joe. Solemates. 2013. 28p. pap. 9.95 (978-1-4787-2494-0(3)) Outskirts Pr., Inc.

Lord, Gabrielle. Malice. 2013. (Illus.). 175p. (J). (978-1-61067-167-5(8)) Kane Miller.

Lord, Kenniston. The Pirates of Peary Village. 2004. (ENG.). 180p. (J). pap. 9.18 (978-1-4116-7893-4(1)) Lulu Pr., Inc.

Lorimer, Janet. The Tiger Lily Code, 1 vol. unabr. ed. 2010. (Q Reads Ser.). (ENG.). 32p. (YA). (gr. 9-12). pap. 8.50 (978-1-61651-195-1(8)) Saddleback Educational Publishing, Inc.

—Tug-of-War, 1 vol. unabr. ed. 2010. (Q Reads Ser.). (ENG.). 32p. (YA). (gr. 9-12). pap. 8.50 (978-1-61651-196-8(6)) Saddleback Educational Publishing, Inc.

Loughead, Deb. Time & Again, 1 vol. 2005. (ENG.). 192p. (YA). (gr. 7-12). pap. (978-1-894549-39-4(2), Sumach Pr.) Canadian Scholars.

Loutzenhiser, Katy. If You're Out There. (ENG.). 320p. (YA). (gr. 8). 2020. pap. 10.99 (978-0-06-286568-7(4)) 2019. 17.99 (978-0-06-286567-0(6)) HarperCollins Pubs. (Balzer & Bray).

Lovegrove, James. Kill Swap. 2012. (Stoke Books Titles Ser.). (ENG.). 64p. (YA). (gr. 8-12). pap. 6.95 (978-1-78112-112-2(5)); lib. bdg. 22.60 (978-1-78112-113-9(3)) Lerner Publishing Group.

Low, A. J. Sherlock Sam & the Ghostly Moans in Fort Canning: Book Two. Tan, Andrew, illus. 2016. (Sherlock Sam Ser.: 2). (ENG.). 120p. (J). pap. 7.99 (978-1-4494-7788-2(7)) Andrews McMeel Publishing.

—Sherlock Sam & the Sinister Letters in Bras Basah. Tan, Andrew, illus. 2017. (Sherlock Sam Ser.: 3). (ENG.). 144p. (J). pap. 7.99 (978-1-4494-7975-6(8)) Andrews McMeel Publishing.

—Sherlock Sam & the Sinister Letters in Bras Basah. 2016. (Sherlock Sam Ser.: Vol. 3). (ENG., Illus.). 127p. (J). (gr. 2-6). 26.99 (978-1-4494-8614-3(2)) Andrews McMeel Publishing.

Loye, Scott. Moon Ring. 2011. 160p. (gr. 10-12). 22.95 (978-1-4502-9682-3(3)); pap. 12.95 (978-1-4502-9680-9(7)) iUniverse, Inc.

Lu, Tina. The Mystery of the Starry Night. Liu, Jenny, ed. 2004. (ENG & CHI., Illus.). 64p. (J). pap. 12.00 net. (978-0-9759126-0-7(7)) Global Alliances.

Lubar, David. Dog Days. 80p. (J). (gr. 4-8). 2011. (ENG.). per. 7.99 (978-1-58196-025-9(5), 6d9bb1e0-1830-48ed-a543-0f23f1ac5e48) 2004. 15.95 (978-1-58196-013-6(1)) Lerner Publishing Group. (Darby Creek).

Lucky, A. E. Kyle the Detective, 1 vol. 2010. 70p. pap. 19.95 (978-1-4512-2042-1(1)) America Star Bks.

Luen Yang, Gene. Secret Coders. 2015. (Secret Coders Ser.: 1). (ENG., Illus.). 96p. (J). (gr. 3-7). pap. 10.99 (978-1-62672-075-6(4), 900134876, First Second Bks.) Roaring Brook Pr.

—Secret Coders: Robots & Repeats. 2017. (Secret Coders Ser.: 4). (ENG., Illus.). 96p. (J). pap. 10.99 (978-1-62672-606-2(X), 900162979, First Second Bks.) Roaring Brook Pr.

Luna, Rachel Nickerson. The Haunting of Captain Snow. 2005. (Eel Grass Girls Mystery Ser.: No. 2). (Illus.). 332p. pap. 11.95 (978-1-886551-08-4(1)) Howard, Emma Bks.

—The Strange Disappearance of Agatha Buck. 2005. (Eel Grass Girls Mystery Ser.: Book 3). (Illus.). 284p. (J). pap. 11.95 (978-1-886551-09-1(X)) Howard, Emma Bks.

Lunsford, Judy. Sally & the Buccaneers. 2009. 77p. pap. 12.98 (978-0-557-10064-4(X)) Lulu Pr., Inc.

Luper, Eric. The Mysterious Moonstone (Key Hunters #1) 2016. (Key Hunters Ser.: 1). (ENG., Illus.). 128p. (J). (gr. 2-5). pap. 5.99 (978-0-545-82204-6(1)) Scholastic, Inc.

—The Wizard's War (Key Hunters #4) 2017. (Key Hunters Ser.: 4). (ENG., Illus.). 128p. (J). (gr. 2-5). pap. 5.99 (978-0-545-82213-8(0), Scholastic Paperbacks) Scholastic, Inc.

Lupica, Mike. The Football Fiasco. 2018. (Zach & Zoe Mysteries Ser.: 3). (ENG., Illus.). 80p. (J). (gr. 1-4). 6.99 (978-0-425-28943-3(5), Puffin Books); 14.99 (978-0-425-28942-6(7), Philomel Bks.) Penguin Young Readers Group.

—The Half-Court Hero. 2018. (Zach & Zoe Mysteries Ser.: 2). (ENG., Illus.). 96p. (J). (gr. 1-4). 6.99 (978-0-425-28940-2(0), Puffin Books) Penguin Young Readers Group.

—The Hockey Rink Hunt. 2019. (Zach & Zoe Mysteries Ser.: 5). (ENG., Illus.). 80p. (J). (gr. 1-4). 14.99 (978-0-425-28948-8(6), Philomel Bks.) Penguin Young Readers Group.

—The Missing Baseball. 2018. (Zach & Zoe Mysteries Ser.: 1). (ENG., Illus.). 80p. (J). (gr. 1-4). 6.99 (978-0-425-28937-2(0), Puffin Books) Penguin Young Readers Group.

Luxa, Sue. One Golden Summer. 2004. (Illus.). 80p. (J). pap. 8.95 (978-1-890437-99-2(9), 1234248) Western Reflections Publishing Co.

Lyall, Casey. Howard Wallace, P. I. 2017. (Howard Wallace, P. I. Ser.). (ENG.). 288p. (J). (gr. 3-7). pap. 6.95 (978-1-4549-2604-7(X)) Sterling Publishing Co., Inc.

Lyga, Barry. Blood of My Blood. 2014. (I Hunt Killers Ser.: 3). (ENG.). 480p. (YA). (gr. 10-17). 18.00 (978-0-316-19870-7(6)) Little, Brown Bks. for Young Readers.

—I Hunt Killers. 2013. (I Hunt Killers Ser.: 1). (ENG.). 384p. (YA). (gr. 10-17). pap. 11.99 (978-0-316-12583-3(0)) Little, Brown Bks. for Young Readers.

Lynch, Chris. Freewill. 2006. 148p. (YA). (gr. 7-10). reprint ed. 16.00 (978-0-7567-9869-7(8)) DIANE Publishing Co.

Lyons, CJ. The Color of Lies, 1 vol. 2019. (ENG.). 336p. (YA). pap. 10.99 (978-0-310-76533-2(1)) Blink.

—The Colour of Lies, 1 vol. 2018. (ENG.). 352p. (YA). 17.99 (978-0-310-76535-6(8)) Blink.

Lysaght, Richard. The Black Bag Mystery. Wolfhound Publishing Editors, ed. (ENG., Illus.). 240p. pap. 6.95 (978-0-86327-886-0(8)) Wolfhound Pr. IRL. Dist: Interlink Publishing Group, Inc.

Lysiak, Hilde & Lysiak, Matthew. Bear on the Loose!: a Branches Book (Hilde Cracks the Case #2) Lew-Vriethoff, Joanne, illus. 2nd ed. 2017. (Hilde Cracks the Case Ser.: 2). (ENG.). 96p. (J). (gr. 1-3). pap. 6.99 (978-1-338-14158-0(9)) Scholastic, Inc.

—Bear on the Loose!: a Branches Book (Hilde Cracks the Case #2) (Library Edition) Lew-Vriethoff, Joanne, illus. 2nd ed. 2017. (Hilde Cracks the Case Ser.: 2). (ENG.). 80p. (J). (gr. 1-3). lib. bdg. 15.99 (978-1-338-14159-7(7)) Scholastic, Inc.

—Fire! Fire! 2018. (Hilde Cracks the Case Ser.: No. 3). lib. bdg. 14.75 (978-0-606-41143-1(7)) Turtleback.

—Fire! Fire!: a Branches Book (Hilde Cracks the Case #3) Lew-Vriethoff, Joanne, illus. 2017. (Hilde Cracks the Case Ser.: 3). (ENG.). 96p. (J). (gr. 1-3). pap. 6.99 (978-1-338-14161-0(9)) Scholastic, Inc.

—Hero Dog!: a Branches Book (Hilde Cracks the Case #1) Lew-Vriethoff, Joanne, illus. 2017. (Hilde Cracks the Case Ser.: 1). (ENG.). 112p. (J). (gr. 1-3). pap. 5.99 (978-1-338-14155-9(4)) Scholastic, Inc.

—Thief Strikes!: a Branches Book (Hilde Cracks the Case #6) Lew-Vriethoff, Joanne, illus. 2019. (Hilde Cracks the Case Ser.: 6). (ENG.). 96p. (J). (gr. 1-3). pap. 5.99 (978-1-338-28391-4(X)) Scholastic, Inc.

—Tornado Hits!: a Branches Book (Hilde Cracks the Case #5) Lew-Vriethoff, Joanne, illus. 2018. (Hilde Cracks the Case Ser.: 5). (ENG.). 96p. (J). (gr. 1-3). pap. 5.99 (978-1-338-26677-1(2)) Scholastic, Inc.

—UFO Spotted!: a Branches Book (Hilde Cracks the Case #4) Lew-Vriethoff, Joanne, illus. 2018. (Hilde Cracks the Case Ser.: 4). (ENG.). 96p. (J). (gr. 1-3). pap. 5.99 (978-1-338-14164-1(3)) Scholastic, Inc.

—UFO Spotted!: a Branches Book (Hilde Cracks the Case #4) (Library Edition) Lew-Vriethoff, Joanne, illus. 2018. (Hilde Cracks the Case Ser.: 4). (ENG.). 96p. (J). (gr. 1-3). lib. bdg. 24.99 (978-1-338-14165-8(1)) Scholastic, Inc.

Mac. Anna Smudge: Professional Shrink: Professional Shrink. 2008. (Professionals Ser.: 1). (ENG., Illus.). 256p. (J). (gr. 4-18). pap. 9.99 (978-1-934906-00-2(X)) Toasted Coconut Media LLC.

MacAndrewRichard. A Little Trouble in the Yorkshire Dales Level 3 Lower Intermediate. 2009. (Cambridge Experience Readers Ser.). (ENG.). 80p. pap. 14.75 (978-84-8323-584-3(6)) Cambridge Univ. Pr.

Macauley, Jo. Treason, 1 vol. 2014. (Secrets & Spies Ser.). (ENG.). 224p. (J). (gr. 4-7). 26.65 (978-1-4342-7946-0(4), 124693, Stone Arch Bks.) Capstone.

MacColl, Michaela. Always Emily. 2014. (ENG.). 282p. (YA). (gr. 7-17). 16.99 (978-1-4521-1174-2(X)) Chronicle Bks. LLC.

—Nobody's Secret. 2014. (ENG.). 256p. (YA). (gr. 7-17). pap. 9.99 (978-1-4521-2854-2(5)) Chronicle Bks. LLC.

—Secrets in the Snow: A Novel of Intrigue & Romance. 2016. (ENG., Illus.). 288p. (YA). (gr. 7-12). 16.99 (978-1-4521-3358-4(1)) Chronicle Bks. LLC.

MacDonald, Bailey. The Secret of the Sealed Room: A Mystery of Young Benjamin Franklin. 2010. (ENG.). 224p. (J). (gr. 3-7). 17.99 (978-1-4169-9760-3(1), Simon & Schuster/Paula Wiseman Bks.) Simon & Schuster/Paula Wiseman Bks.

—Wicked Will: A Mystery of Young William Shakespeare. 2010. (ENG.). 224p. (J). (gr. 4-7). pap. 5.99 (978-1-4169-8661-4(8), Aladdin) Simon & Schuster Children's Publishing.

MacGregor, Roy. The Ghost of the Stanley Cup, 11. 2013. (Screech Owls Ser.: 11). (ENG.). 176p. (J). (gr. 4-7). pap. 8.99 (978-1-77049-416-9(2), Tundra Bks.) Tundra Bks. CAN. Dist: Penguin Random Hse. LLC.

—Mystery at Lake Placid, 1. 2013. (Screech Owls Ser.: 1). (ENG.). 272p. (J). (gr. 4-7). pap. 8.99 (978-1-77049-413-8(8), Tundra Bks.) Tundra Bks. CAN. Dist: Penguin Random Hse. LLC.

—The Night They Stole the Stanley Cup, 2. 2013. (Screech Owls Ser.: 2). (ENG.). 176p. (J). (gr. 4-7). pap. 8.99 (978-1-77049-414-5(6), Tundra Bks.) Tundra Bks. CAN. Dist: Penguin Random Hse. LLC.

—Peril at the World's Biggest Hockey Tournament. 2013. (Screech Owls Ser.: 21). (ENG.). 208p. (J). (gr. 4-7). pap. 8.99 (978-1-77049-417-6(0), Tundra Bks.) Tundra Bks. CAN. Dist: Penguin Random Hse. LLC.

MacHale, D. J. Black Moon Rising (the Library Book 2) (Library: 2). 304p. (J). (gr. 3-7). 2018. pap. 7.99 (978-1-101-93260-5(0), Yearling) 2017. 16.99 (978-1-101-93257-5(0), Random Hse. Bks. for Young Readers) Random Hse. Children's Bks.

—Curse of the Boggin (the Library Book 1) 2016. (Library: 1). 256p. (J). (gr. 3-7). 16.99 (978-1-101-93253-7(8), Random Hse. Bks. for Young Readers) Random Hse. Children's Bks.

—Oracle of Doom (the Library Book 3) 2018. (Library: 3). 304p. (J). (gr. 3-7). 16.99 (978-1-101-93261-2(9), Random Hse. Bks. for Young Readers) Random Hse. Children's Bks.

Mack, Karen. The Magical Adventures of Sun Beams. 2009. 42p. 31.99 (978-1-4415-3636-5(1)) Xlibris Corp.

Mack, Tracy & Citrin, Michael. The Fall of the Amazing Zalindas. 2006. (Illus.). 259p. (J). (978-1-4287-0951-5(7), Orchard Bks.) Scholastic, Inc.

—The Fall of the Amazing Zalindas (Sherlock Holmes & the Baker Street Irregulars #1) Ruth, Greg, illus. 2009. (Sherlock Holmes & the Baker Street Irregulars Ser.: 1). (ENG.). 272p. (J). (gr. 4-7). 6.99 (978-0-545-06939-7(4), Scholastic Paperbacks) Scholastic, Inc.

Mackall, Dandi Daley. Cinnamon Lake Mysteries Set, 6 vols. (Cinnamon Lake Mysteries Ser.). (J). 33.74 (978-0-7586-0006-6(2)) Concordia Publishing Hse.

—The Silence of Murder. 2012. 336p. (YA). (gr. 9). pap. 10.99 (978-0-375-87293-8(0), Ember) Random Hse. Children's Bks.

Mackey, R. Scott. The Bugfish Experiment. 2003. 208p. (978-1-930093-12-6(8)) Brookfield Reader, Inc., The.

MacKnight, Wendy McLeod. The Frame-Up. Schoenherr, Ian, illus. (ENG.). (J). (gr. 3-7). 2019. 400p. pap. 7.99 (978-0-06-266831-8(5)) 2018. 384p. 16.99 (978-0-06-266830-1(7)) HarperCollins Pubs. (Greenwillow Bks.).

The check digit for ISBN-10 appears in parentheses after the full ISBN-13

—It's a Mystery, Pig Face! 2017. (ENG.). 352p. (J). (gr. 2-7). 15.99 (978-1-5107-0621-7(6)); pap. 8.99 (978-1-5107-2280-4(7)) Skyhorse Publishing Co., Inc. (Sky Pony Pr.).

MacLean, Sarah. The Season. (ENG.). 352p. (J). (gr. 7). 2010. 8.99 (978-0-545-04887-3(7)) 2009. 17.99 (978-0-545-04886-6(9)) Scholastic, Inc. (Orchard Bks.).

MacPhail, Cathy. Devil You Know, 22 vols. 2015. 240p. (YA). pap. 9.95 (978-1-78250-179-4(7), Kelpies) Floris Bks. GBR. Dist: Consortium Bk. Sales & Distribution.

Maddock, Lisa. The Bridezilla Who Stole Christmas: A Teddy & Pip Story. 2009. 108p. pap. 9.95 (978-1-60844-258-4(6)) Dog Ear Publishing, LLC.

Madsen, Cindi. All the Broken Pieces. 2016. (ENG., Illus.). (YA). (gr. 9). pap. 15.99 (978-1-68281-305-8(3)) Entangled Publishing, LLC.

Madsen, W. J. Arkeepers: Episode One. 2012. 142p. pap. 7.95 (978-0-9830487-0-1(3)) little m Bks.

—Arkeepers: Episode Two. 2012. 206p. pap. 9.30 (978-0-9830487-1-8(1)) little m Bks.

Maetani, Valynne. Ink & Ashes, 1 vol. 2015. (ENG.). 368p. (YA). (gr. 7-12). 19.95 (978-1-62014-211-0(2), leelowtu, Tu Bks.) Lee & Low Bks., Inc.

Magaziner, Lauren. Case Closed #1: Mystery in the Mansion. 2018. (Case Closed Ser.: 1). (ENG., Illus.). 400p. (J). (gr. 3-7). 16.99 (978-0-06-267627-6(X), Tegen, Katherine Bks) HarperCollins Pubs.

Magill, Sharon L. Chloe Madison & the Beach Heists. 2009. 60p. pap. 10.49 (978-1-4389-4191-2(9)) AuthorHouse.

Mahle, Melissa & Dennis, Kathryn. Lost in Petra. 2012. (Anatolia Steppe Mysteries: 1). (ENG., Illus.). 246p. (J). pap. 10.99 (978-0-9852273-0-2(3)) SpyGirls Pr.

Makechnie, Amy. The Unforgettable Guinevere St. Clair. (ENG.). 336p. (J). (gr. 3-7). 2019. pap. 8.99 (978-1-5344-1447-1(9)) 2018. (Illus.). 18.99 (978-1-5344-1446-4(0)) Simon & Schuster Children's Publishing. (Atheneum Bks. for Young Readers).

The Mall Mystery, 6 vols., Vol. 3. (Woodland Mysteriestm Ser.). 133p. (gr. 3-7). 42.50 (978-0-322-02370-3(X)) Wright Group/McGraw-Hill.

Maloney, Peter. The Big Apple Mystery. 2004. 32p. (978-0-439-67638-0(X)) Scholastic, Inc.

Malton, H. Mel. The Drowned Violin: An Alan Nearing Mystery. 2006. (Alan Nearing Mystery Ser.: 1). (ENG.). 168p. (J). (gr. 3-7). pap. 8.95 (978-1-894917-23-0(5), Napoleon & Co.) Dundurn Pr. CAN. Dist: Publishers Group West (PGW).

—Pioneer Poltergeist: An Alan Nearing Mystery. 2007. (Alan Nearing Mystery Ser.: 2). (ENG.). 208p. (J). pap. 8.95 (978-1-894917-60-5(X), Napoleon & Co.) Dundurn Pr. CAN. Dist: Publishers Group West (PGW).

Maniscalco, Kerri. Escaping from Houdini. (Stalking Jack the Ripper Ser.: 3). (ENG., Illus.). (YA). (gr. 10-17). 2019. 480p. pap. 12.99 (978-0-316-55172-4(4)) 2018. 448p. 19.99 (978-0-316-55170-0(8)) Little Brown & Co. (Jimmy Patterson).

—Hunting Prince Dracula. (Stalking Jack the Ripper Ser.: 2). (ENG., Illus.). (YA). (gr. 10-17). 2018. 480p. pap. 12.99 (978-0-316-55167-0(8)) 2017. 448p. 19.99 (978-0-316-55166-3(X)) Little Brown & Co. (Jimmy Patterson).

—Stalking Jack the Ripper. 2018. (Stalking Jack the Ripper Ser.: 1). (ENG.). 416p. (YA). (gr. 10-17). mass mkt. 8.99 (978-1-5387-6118-2(1)) Grand Central Publishing.

—Stalking Jack the Ripper. (Stalking Jack the Ripper Ser.: 1). (ENG., (YA). (gr. 10-17). 2017. Illus.). 352p. pap. 12.99 (978-0-316-27351-0(1)) 2016. (Illus.). 336p. 19.99 (978-0-316-27349-7(X)) 2016. 464p. 39.99 (978-0-316-46428-4(7)) Little Brown & Co. (Jimmy Patterson).

Manning, Dennis & Crisalli, Joseph. The Emeritus Peabody Mysteries. 2008. 212p. pap. 13.98 (978-1-4303-2186-6(5)) Lulu Pr., Inc.

Manning, Matthew K. The Mystery of the Mayhem Mansion. Neely, Scott, illus. 2016. (You Choose Stories: Scooby-Doo Ser.). (ENG.). 112p. (J). (gr. 2-6). lib. bdg. 32.65 (978-1-4965-2661-8(9), 131220, Stone Arch Bks.) Capstone.

Manushkin, Fran. Pedro's Mystery Club. Lyon, Tammie, illus. 2016. (Pedro Ser.). (ENG.). 32p. (J). (gr. k-2). lib. bdg. 21.32 (978-1-5158-0084-2(9), 132123, Picture Window Bks.) Capstone.

Marathon, creator. Trouble in the Tropics. 2005. (Totally Spies! Ser.: Vol. 3). (Illus.). pap. 14.99 (978-1-59532-817-5(3), Tokyopop Kids) TOKYOPOP, Inc.

Marchi, Sergio. The Emerald Table. 2008. 192p. pap. 19.95 (978-1-84799-226-0(9)) Lulu Pr., Inc.

Marcus, Mary J. The Digger. 2013. 180p. pap. 12.99 (978-1-60820-872-2(9)) MLR Pr., LLC.

Margolin, Phillip & Rome, Ami Margolin. Vanishing Acts. 2011. (ENG.). 176p. (J). (gr. 3-7). 16.99 (978-0-06-188556-3(8)) HarperCollins Pubs.

Margolis, Leslie. Girl's Best Friend. 2011. (Maggie Brooklyn Mystery Ser.). (ENG.). 288p. (J). (gr. 3-12). pap. 7.99 (978-1-59990-690-4(2), 900076050, Bloomsbury USA Childrens) Bloomsbury Publishing USA.

—Secrets at the Chocolate Mansion. 2014. (Maggie Brooklyn Mystery Ser.). (ENG.). 272p. (J). (gr. 3-6). pap. 7.99 (978-1-61963-493-0(7), 900138595, Bloomsbury USA Childrens) Bloomsbury Publishing USA.

—Vanishing Acts. 2013. (Maggie Brooklyn Mystery Ser.). (ENG.). 256p. (J). (gr. 3-6). pap. 7.99 (978-1-59990-981-3(2), 900096404, Bloomsbury USA Childrens) Bloomsbury Publishing USA.

Mariotti, Celine Rose. Olivia Macallister, Who Are You? A Ghost Mystery Set in Maine. Tango-Schurmann, Ann, illus. 2004. 85p. (YA). (gr. 3-6). pap. 12.95 (978-0-9721389-6-3(X)) Rock Village Publishing.

Marks, Burton. Tanya Tinker & the Gizmo Gang. Smath, Jerry, illus. 2003. 20p. (J). (gr. -1-3). reprint ed. 22.00 (978-0-7567-6760-0(1)) DIANE Publishing Co.

Markus, Deborah. The Letting Go. 2018. (ENG.). 360p. (YA). (gr. 9-9). 16.99 (978-1-5107-3405-0(8), Sky Pony Pr.) Skyhorse Publishing Co., Inc.

Marlow, Herb. The Classroom Vandal. 2003. (J). 19.95 (978-1-893595-36-1(6)) Four Seasons Bks., Inc.

Marmon, Jim. Alexander Barnaby Meadowlark. 2007. 132p. per. 19.95 (978-1-4241-7662-5(X)) America Star Bks.

Marois, André & Norman, Taylor. The Poisoned Cake. Doyon, Patrick, illus. 2017. (J). (978-1-4521-4660-7(8)) Chronicle Bks. LLC.

Marquis, Michelle. Mikey & the Mysterious Door. 2008. 32p. pap. 14.99 (978-1-4343-4823-4(7)) AuthorHouse.

Marsh, Carole. Adventure to the Eight Wonders of the World. 2007. (Field Trips (Gallopade International) Ser.). (Illus.). 118p. (J). (gr. 2-9). 14.95 (978-0-635-06391-5(3)) Gallopade International.

—The Awesome Aquarium Mystery. 2006. (Awesome Mystery Ser.). (Illus.). 104p. (J). (gr. 7-14). 14.95 (978-0-635-06227-7(5)) Gallopade International.

—The Awesome Aquarium Mystery! 2006. (Carole Marsh Mysteries: Awesome Mysteries Ser.). (ENG., Illus.). 108p. (J). (gr. 2-4). 18.69 (978-0-635-06225-3(9)) Gallopade International.

—The Baseball Bully. 2006. 64p. (gr. 2-4). 14.95 (978-0-635-06221-5(6)); pap. 3.99 (978-0-635-06215-4(1)) Gallopade International.

—The Baskerville Basketball. 2006. 64p. (gr. 2-4). 14.95 (978-0-635-06222-2(4)); pap. 3.99 (978-0-635-06216-1(X)) Gallopade International.

—The Behemoth Blizzard Mystery. (Masters of Disasters Ser.). (Illus.). 118p. (J). (gr. 3-5). 2008. per. 5.99 (978-0-635-06464-6(2)) 2007. 14.95 (978-0-635-06467-7(7)) Gallopade International.

—The Breathtaking Mystery on Mt. Everest. 2009. (Around the World in 80 Mysteries Ser.). 144p. (J). 18.99 (978-0-635-06836-1(2), Marsh, Carole Bks.) Gallopade International.

—The Case of the Crybaby Cowboy. 2006. (Carole Marsh's Three Amigos Ser.). (Illus.). 54p. (J). (ENG.). (gr. 1-3). 16.19 (978-0-635-06166-9(X)); (gr. 4-7). 14.95 (978-0-635-06199-7(6)) Gallopade International.

—The Case of the Hunchback Hairdresser. 2006. (Criss Cross Applesauce Ser.). (Illus.). 54p. (J). (gr. 4-7). 14.95 (978-0-635-06202-4(X)); per. 4.99 (978-0-635-06169-0(4), Marsh, Carole Bks.) Gallopade International.

—The Castaway Cheerleaders. 2006. 64p. (gr. 2-4). 14.95 (978-0-635-06224-6(0)); pap. 3.99 (978-0-635-06218-5(6)) Gallopade International.

—The Colonial Caper Mystery at Williamsburg. 2009. (Real Kids, Real Places Ser.). (J). (gr. 2-9). lib. bdg. 18.99 (978-0-635-06832-3(X)); (Illus.). 143p. (gr. 4-7). pap. 7.99 (978-0-635-06826-2(5), Marsh, Carole Bks.) Gallopade International.

—The Cookie Thief Girl Scout Mystery. 2016. (Girl Scouts Ser.). (ENG.). (J). (gr. 3-7). pap. 7.99 (978-0-635-12170-7(0)) Gallopade International.

—The Counterfeit Constitution Mystery. (Real Kids, Real Places Ser.). (Illus.). 144p. (J). 2009. lib. bdg. 18.99 (978-0-635-07043-2(X), Marsh, Carole Mysteries) 2008. (gr. 3-5). 14.95 (978-0-635-06517-9(7)) 2008. (gr. 3-5). per. 5.95 (978-0-635-06512-4(6)) Gallopade International.

—The Curse of the Ancient Acropolis: Athens, Greece. 2008. (Carole Marsh Mysteries Ser.). 133p. (J). (gr. 3-5). per. 7.99 (978-0-635-06470-7(7), Marsh, Carole Bks.) Gallopade International.

—Dear Alien: The Little Green Man Mystery. 2007. (Postcard Mysteries Ser.). (Illus.). (J). 115p. (gr. 2-9). 14.95 (978-0-635-06397-7(2), Marsh, Carole Family CD-Rom); (ENG., 116p. (gr. 3-6). 18.69 (978-0-635-06341-0(7)) Gallopade International.

—Dear Bats: The Creepy Cave Caper Mystery. 2007. (Postcard Mysteries Ser.). (Illus.). 115p. (J). (gr. 2-9). per. 5.99 (978-0-635-06342-7(5)) Gallopade International.

—Dear Granny: The Spooky State Fair Fiasco. 2007. (Postcard Mysteries Ser.). 128p. (J). (gr. 2-9). 14.95 (978-0-635-06399-1(9), Marsh, Carole Family CD-Rom) Gallopade International.

—Dear Pirate, the Buried Treasure Mystery. 2007. (Postcard Mysteries Ser.). (Illus.). 114p. (J). (gr. 2-9). per. 5.99 (978-0-635-06343-4(3), Marsh, Carole Family CD-Rom) Gallopade International.

—The Earthshaking Earthquake Mystery!, 1. 2009. (Carole Marsh's Masters of Disasters Ser.). (ENG., Illus.). 118p. (J). (gr. 3-6). 18.69 (978-0-635-06339-7(5)) Gallopade International.

—The Football Phantom. 2006. 64p. (gr. 2-4). 14.95 (978-0-635-06223-9(2)); pap. 3.99 (978-0-635-06217-8(8)) Gallopade International.

—The Gargoyle Golf Course. 2006. 64p. (gr. 2-4). 14.95 (978-0-635-06220-8(8)); pap. 3.99 (978-0-635-06214-7(3)) Gallopade International.

—The Ghost of Pickpocket Plantation. 2006. (Pretty Darn Scary Mysteries Ser.). (Illus.). 109p. (YA). (gr. 7-14). 14.95 (978-0-635-06237-6(2)); (J). (gr. 3-5). per. 7.99 (978-0-635-06233-8(X)) Gallopade International.

—The Ghost of the Golden Gate Bridge. 2009. (Real Kids, Real Places Ser.). (Illus.). 146p. (J). lib. bdg. 18.99 (978-0-635-07047-0(2), Marsh, Carole Mysteries) Gallopade International.

—The Giggling Ghost Girl Scout Mystery. 2012. (Carole Marsh Mysteries: Girl Scout Mysteries Ser.). (ENG., Illus.). 158p. (J). (gr. 4-6). 22.44 (978-0-635-10230-0(7)) Gallopade International.

—The Gosh Awful! Gold Rush Mystery. (Real Kids, Real Places Ser.). (Illus.). 146p. (J). 2009. lib. bdg. 18.99 (978-0-635-07026-5(X), Marsh, Carole Mysteries)19. 2007. (ENG., (gr. 4-6). 22.44 (978-0-635-06334-2(4)) Gallopade International.

—The Horrendous Hurricane Mystery. 2007. (Carole Marsh Mysteries Ser.). (Illus.). 118p. (J). (gr. 2-9). per. 7.99 (978-0-635-06340-3(9)) Gallopade International.

—The Madcap Mystery of the Missing Liberty Bell. 2009. 160p. (J). (gr. 4-7). 18.99 (978-0-635-06834-7(6), Marsh, Carole Bks.) Gallopade International.

—The Mission Possible Mystery at Space Center Houston. 2009. 160p. (J). 18.99 (978-0-635-06833-0(8), Marsh, Carole Bks.) Gallopade International.

—The Mystery at Big Ben, 1. 2006. (Carole Marsh Mysteries: Around the World in 80 Mysteries Ser.). (ENG., Illus.). 129p. (J). (gr. 4-6). 18.69 (978-0-635-03469-4(7)) Gallopade International.

—The Mystery at Cape Cod. 2010. (Real Kids, Real Places Ser.). (Illus.). 158p. (J). pap. 18.99 (978-0-635-07594-9(6), Marsh, Carole Mysteries) Gallopade International.

—The Mystery at Cape Cod. Friedlander, Randolyn, illus. 2010. (Real Kids, Real Places Teacher Guides). 32p. (J). pap. 7.99 (978-0-635-07600-7(4)) Gallopade International.

—The Mystery at Death Valley. 2010. (Real Kids, Real Places Ser.). (Illus.). 158p. (J). 24.99 (978-0-635-07608-3(X)); pap. 7.99 (978-0-635-07596-3(2)) Gallopade International. (Marsh, Carole Mysteries).

—The Mystery at Disney World. (Real Kids, Real Places Ser.). (Illus.). 146p. (J). 2009. lib. bdg. 18.99 (978-0-635-06990-0(3), Marsh, Carole Mysteries) 2003. (gr. 2-8). lib. bdg. 14.95 (978-0-635-02105-2(6)) Gallopade International.

—The Mystery at Dracula's Castle: Transylvania, Romania. 2009. (Around the World in 80 Mysteries Ser.). 133p. (J). 18.99 (978-0-635-07039-5(1), Marsh, Carole Mysteries) Gallopade International.

—The Mystery at Fort Sumter. Friedlander, Randolyn, illus. 2010. (Real Kids, Real Places Ser.). 32p. (J). pap. 7.99 (978-0-635-07432-4(X), Marsh, Carole Mysteries) Gallopade International.

—The Mystery at Fort Thunderbolt. 2007. (Pretty Darn Scary Mysteries Ser.). (Illus.). 113p. (YA). lib. bdg. 18.99 (978-0-635-07021-0(9), Marsh, Carole Mysteries); (YA). (gr. 7-14). 14.95 (978-0-635-06239-0(9));3. (ENG., (J). (gr. 2-4). 18.69 (978-0-635-06235-2(6)) Gallopade International.

—The Mystery at Hollywood. 2011. (Carole Marsh Mysteries Ser.). (J). pap. 7.99 (978-0-635-07959-6(3), Marsh, Carole Mysteries) Gallopade International.

—The Mystery at Jamestown: First Permanent English Colony in America! 2009. (Real Kids, Real Places Ser.). (Illus.). 137p. (J). lib. bdg. 18.99 (978-0-635-07023-4(5), Marsh, Carole Mysteries) Gallopade International.

—The Mystery at Kill Devil Hills. 2009. (Real Kids, Real Places Ser.). (Illus.). 145p. (J). lib. bdg. 18.99 (978-0-635-06999-3(7), Marsh, Carole Mysteries) Gallopade International.

—The Mystery at Motown. Friedlander, Randolyn, illus. 2011. (Carole Marsh Mysteries Ser.). 32p. pap. 7.99 (978-0-635-07962-6(3), Marsh, Carole Mysteries) Gallopade International.

—The Mystery at Mount Fuji: Tokyo, Japan, 7. 2007. (Carole Marsh Mysteries: Around the World in 80 Mysteries Ser.). (ENG., Illus.). 131p. (J). (gr. 4-6). 22.44 (978-0-635-06207-9(0)) Gallopade International.

—The Mystery at Mount Vernon. Friedlander, Randolyn, illus. 2010. (Real Kids, Real Places Ser.). 32p. pap. 7.99 (978-0-635-07444-7(3), Marsh, Carole Mysteries) Gallopade International.

—The Mystery at Mount Vernon: Home of America's First President George Washington. 2010. (Real Kids, Real Places Ser.). (Illus.). 158p. (J). 18.99 (978-0-635-07443-0(5), Marsh, Carole Mysteries) Gallopade International.

—The Mystery at Mt. Fuji: Tokyo, Japan. (Around the World in 80 Mysteries Ser.). 131p. (J). 2009. 18.99 (978-0-635-07016-6(2), Marsh, Carole Mysteries) 2007. (Illus.). (gr. 3-5). 14.95 (978-0-635-06211-6(9)) Gallopade International.

—The Mystery at the Boston Marathon. 2003. 160p. (gr. 2-8). 14.95 (978-0-635-01642-3(7), Marsh, Carole Bks.) Gallopade International.

—The Mystery at the Eiffel Tower. 2009. (Around the World in 80 Mysteries Ser.). (Illus.). 132p. (J). 18.99 (978-0-635-07004-3(9), Marsh, Carole Mysteries) Gallopade International.

—The Mystery at the Kentucky Derby. 2009. (Real Kids, Real Places Ser.). (Illus.). 146p. (J). lib. bdg. 18.99 (978-0-635-07002-9(2), Marsh, Carole Mysteries) Gallopade International.

—The Mystery at the Mayan Ruins: Mexico. 2014. (Around the World in 80 Mysteries Ser.: Vol. 16). (ENG., Illus.). 133p. (J). (gr. 3-5). pap. 7.99 (978-0-635-11163-0(2), Marsh, Carole Bks.) Gallopade International.

—The Mystery at the Roman Coloseum. 2006. (Around the World in 80 Mysteries Ser.). (Illus.). 132p. (J). (gr. 4-7). per. 7.99 (978-0-635-06156-0(2), Marsh, Carole Bks.) Gallopade International.

—The Mystery at the Roman Colosseum. 2006. (Around the World in 80 Mysteries Ser.). (Illus.). 132p. (J). (gr. 4-7). 14.95 (978-0-635-06157-7(0)) Gallopade International.

—Mystery at the Space Needle. 2016. (Real Kids, Real Places Ser.). (ENG.). (J). (gr. 3-7). pap. 7.99 (978-0-635-12432-6(7), Marsh, Carole Mysteries) Gallopade International.

—The Mystery at Yellowstone National Park. 2010. (Real Kids, Real Places Ser.). (Illus.). 158p. (J). 18.99 (978-0-635-07437-9(0), Marsh, Carole Mysteries) Gallopade International.

—The Mystery in Chocolate Town: Hershey, Pennsylvania. (Real Kids, Real Places Ser.). (Illus.). (J). 2009. 143p. lib. bdg. 18.99 (978-0-635-07025-8(1), Marsh, Carole Mysteries) 2007. 145p. (gr. 2-8). 14.95 (978-0-635-06389-2(1)) Gallopade International.

—The Mystery in Chocolate Town Hershey, Pennsylvania. 2007. (Real Kids, Real Places Ser.). (Illus.). 145p. (J). (gr. 2-8). per. 7.99 (978-0-635-06333-5(6)) Gallopade International.

—The Mystery in Hawaii. Friedlander, Randolyn, illus. 2010. (Real Kids, Real Places Ser.). 32p. pap. 7.99 (978-0-635-07447-8(8), Marsh, Carole Mysteries) Gallopade International.

—The Mystery in Hawaii: The 50th State. 2010. (Real Kids, Real Places Ser.). (Illus.). 157p. (J). 18.99 (978-0-635-07446-1(X), Marsh, Carole Mysteries) Gallopade International.

—The Mystery in Las Vegas. 2009. (Real Kids, Real Places Ser.). (Illus.). 145p. (J). lib. bdg. 18.99 (978-0-635-07045-6(6), Marsh, Carole Mysteries) Gallopade International.

—The Mystery in New York City. (Real Kids, Real Places Ser.). 146p. (J). 2009. (Illus.). lib. bdg. 18.99 (978-0-635-06998-6(9), Marsh, Carole Mysteries)10. 2003. (ENG.). (gr. 4-6). 22.44 (978-0-635-02099-4(8)) Gallopade International.

—The Mystery in the Amazon Rainforest: South America. (Around the World in 80 Mysteries Ser.). (Illus.). 131p. (J). 2009. lib. bdg. 18.99 (978-0-635-07017-3(0), Marsh, Carole Mysteries) 2007. (gr. 3-5). 14.95 (978-0-635-06212-3(7))8. 2007. (ENG., (gr. 4-6). 22.44 (978-0-635-06208-6(9)) Gallopade International.

—The Mystery in the Rocky Mountains. 2009. (Real Kids, Real Places Ser.). (Illus.). 145p. (J). lib. bdg. 18.99 (978-0-635-07000-5(6), Marsh, Carole Mysteries) Gallopade International.

—The Mystery in the Twin Cities. Baker, Janice, ed. 2011. (Carole Marsh Mysteries Ser.). (Illus.). (J). pap. 7.99 (978-0-635-07960-2(7), Marsh, Carole Mysteries) Gallopade International.

—The Mystery of Blackbeard the Pirate. Marsh, Carole, photos by. 2009. (Real Kids, Real Places Ser.). (Illus.). 150p. (J). 18.99 (978-0-635-06992-4(X), Marsh, Carole Mysteries) Gallopade International.

—The Mystery of Blackbeard the Pirate. 2003. (Carole Marsh Mysteries Ser.). 160p. (J). (gr. 2-8). 14.95 (978-0-635-01650-8(8)); pap. 7.99 (978-0-635-01648-5(6)) Gallopade International.

—The Mystery of Kill Devil Hills. 2003. (Carole Marsh Mysteries Ser.). 160p. (J). (gr. 2-8). 14.95 (978-0-635-02095-6(5)); pap. 5.95 (978-0-635-02094-9(7)) Gallopade International.

—The Mystery of the Alamo Ghost. (Real Kids, Real Places Ser.). (J). 2009. (Illus.). 146p. lib. bdg. 18.99 (978-0-635-06993-1(8), Marsh, Carole Mysteries) 2003. 160p. (gr. 2-8). 14.95 (978-0-635-01654-6(0)) 2003. 160p. (gr. 2-8). pap. 7.99 (978-0-635-01652-2(4)) Gallopade International.

—The Mystery of the Ancient Pyramid: Cairo, Egypt. 2006. (Around the World in 80 Mysteries Ser.). (Illus.). 128p. (J). lib. bdg. 18.99 (978-0-635-07006-7(5), Marsh, Carole Mysteries); (gr. 4-7). 14.95 (978-0-635-03473-1(5)); (gr. 4-7). per. 5.95 (978-0-635-03470-0(0), Marsh, Carole Bks.) Gallopade International.

—The Mystery of the Biltmore House. 25th ed. 2009. (Real Kids, Real Places Ser.). 148p. (J). 18.99 (978-0-635-06989-4(X), Marsh, Carole Mysteries) Gallopade International.

—The Mystery of the Crystal Castle: Bavaria, Germany. 2009. (Around the World in 80 Mysteries Ser.). 133p. (J). 18.99 (978-0-635-07041-8(3), Marsh, Carole Mysteries) Gallopade International.

—The Mystery of the Ghost of the Grand Canyon, 16. 2004. (Carole Marsh Mysteries: Real Kids, Real Places Ser.). (ENG.). 139p. (J). (gr. 4-6). 18.69 (978-0-635-02395-7(4)) Gallopade International.

—The Mystery of the Graveyard of the Atlantic. 2009. (Real Kids, Real Places Ser.). (Illus.). 144p. (J). lib. bdg. 18.99 (978-0-635-07046-3(4), Marsh, Carole Mysteries) Gallopade International.

—The Mystery of the Haunted Ghost Town. 2009. (Real Kids, Real Places Ser.). 144p. (J). 18.99 (978-0-635-07044-9(8), Marsh, Carole Mysteries) Gallopade International.

—The Mystery of the Lost Colony. 2010. (Real Kids, Real Places Ser.). (Illus.). 158p. (J). 24.99 (978-0-635-07607-6(1), Marsh, Carole Mysteries); pap. 7.99 (978-0-635-07601-4(2), Marsh, Carole Mysteries);36. (ENG., 158p. (J). (gr. 4-6). 22.44 (978-0-635-07595-6(4)) Gallopade International.

—The Mystery of the Missing Dinosaurs. 2009. (Real Kids, Real Places Ser.). 146p. (J). 18.99 (978-0-635-06995-5(4), Marsh, Carole Mysteries) Gallopade International.

—The Mystery on Alaska's Iditarod Trail. 2009. (Real Kids, Real Places Ser.). 145p. (J). 18.99 (978-0-635-06997-9(0), Marsh, Carole Mysteries) Gallopade International.

—Mystery on California Mission Trail, 5. 2003. (Carole Marsh Mysteries: Real Kids, Real Places Ser.). (ENG.). 147p. (J). (gr. 4-6). 22.44 (978-0-635-01656-0(7)) Gallopade International.

—The Mystery on the California Mission Trail. 2009. (Real Kids, Real Places Ser.). (Illus.). 147p. (J). lib. bdg. 18.99 (978-0-635-06994-8(6), Marsh, Carole Mysteries) Gallopade International.

—The Mystery on the California Mission Trail (Hardcover) 2003. 160p. (gr. 2-8). 14.95 (978-0-635-01658-4(3)) Gallopade International.

—The Mystery on the Freedom Trail. (Real Kids, Real Places Ser.). (J). 2009. 148p. 18.99 (978-0-635-06988-7(1), Marsh, Carole Mysteries) 2003. 160p. (gr. 2-8). pap. 5.95 (978-0-635-01640-9(0)) Gallopade International.

—The Mystery on the Great Barrier Reef. 2006. (Around the World in 80 Mysteries Ser.). (Illus.). 132p. (J). (gr. 3-5). per. 5.95 (978-0-635-06206-2(2)) Gallopade International.

—The Mystery on the Great Barrier Reef: Sydney, Austrailia. 2009. (Around the World in 80 Mysteries Ser.). 132p. (J). 18.99 (978-0-635-07015-9(4), Marsh, Carole Mysteries) Gallopade International.

—The Mystery on the Great Barrier Reef: Sydney, Australia. 2006. (Around the World in 80 Mysteries Ser.). (Illus.). 132p. (J). (gr. 3-5). 14.95 (978-0-635-06210-9(0)) Gallopade International.

—The Mystery on the Great Lakes. 2010. (Real Kids, Real Places Ser.). (Illus.). 158p. (J). 18.99 (978-0-635-07449-2(4), Marsh, Carole Mysteries) Gallopade International.

—The Mystery on the Great Wall of China. 2006. (Around the World in 80 Mysteries Ser.). (Illus.). 132p. (J). (gr. 3-5). per. 7.99 (978-0-635-06205-5(4)) Gallopade International.

—The Mystery on the Great Wall of China: Beijing, China. (Around the World in 80 Mysteries Ser.). (Illus.). 132p. (J). 2009. lib. bdg. 18.99 (978-0-635-07014-2(6), Marsh, Carole Mysteries) 2006. (gr. 3-5). 14.95 (978-0-635-06209-3(7)) Gallopade International.

—The Mystery on the Mighty Mississippi. 2009. (Real Kids, Real Places Ser.). (Illus.). 146p. (J). lib. bdg. 18.99 (978-0-635-07001-2(4), Marsh, Carole Mysteries) Gallopade International.

—The Mystery on the Oregon Trail. 2010. (Real Kids, Real Places Ser.). (Illus.). 158p. (J). 18.99 (978-0-635-07440-9(0), Marsh, Carole Mysteries) Gallopade International.

—The Mystery on the Oregon Trail. Friedlander, Randolyn, illus. 2010. (Real Kids, Real Places Ser.). 32p. pap. 7.99 (978-0-635-07441-6(9), Marsh, Carole Mysteries) Gallopade International.

—The Mystery on the Underground Railroad. 2009. (Real Kids, Real Places Ser.). (Illus.). 146p. (J). lib. bdg. 18.99 (978-0-635-06991-7(1), Marsh, Carole Mysteries) Gallopade International.

—The Puzzle of the Indian Arrowhead. 2006. (Three Amigos Ser.). (Illus.). 54p. (J). (gr. 1-3). 14.95 *(978-0-635-06201-7(1))*; (ENG.). 16.19 *(978-0-635-06168-3(6))* Gallopade International.

—The Puzzle of the Shark Surfer Girl. 2006. (Criss Cross Applesauce Ser.). (Illus.). 54p. (J). (gr. 1-3). 14.95 *(978-0-635-06204-8(6))*; (gr. 4-7). per. 3.99 *(978-0-635-06171-3(6))*, Marsh, Carole Bks.) Gallopade International.

—The Riddle of the Missing Puppies. 2006. (Criss Cross Applesauce Ser.). (Illus.). 54p. (J). (gr. 1-3). 14.95 *(978-0-635-06203-1(8))*; per. 4.99 *(978-0-635-06170-6(8))*, Marsh, Carole Bks.) Gallopade International.

—The Riddle of the Oogli Boogli. 2006. (Illus.). 54p. (J). (gr. 4-7). 14.95 *(978-0-635-06200-0(3))* Gallopade International.

—The Riddle of the Ooglie Booglie. 2006. (Three Amigos Ser.). (Illus.). 54p. (J). (gr. 4-7). per. 3.99 *(978-0-635-06167-6(8))*, Marsh, Carole Bks.) Gallopade International.

—The Secret of Eyesocket Island. (Pretty Darn Scary Mysteries Ser.). (Illus.). 113p. 2009. (J). lib. bdg. 18.99 *(978-0-635-07022-7(7))*, Marsh, Carole Mysteries) 2007. (J). (gr. 3-5). per. 5.99 *(978-0-635-06236-9(4))* 2007. (YA). (gr. 7-14). 14.95 *(978-0-635-06240-6(2))* Gallopade International.

—The Secret of Skullcracker Swamp. (Pretty Darn Scary Mysteries Ser.). (Illus.). 113p. 2009. (YA). lib. bdg. 18.99 *(978-0-635-07020-3(0))*, Marsh, Carole Mysteries) 2006. (YA). (gr. 7-14). 14.95 *(978-0-635-06238-3(0))* 2006. (J). (gr. 3-5). per. 7.99 *(978-0-635-06234-5(8))* Gallopade International.

—The Secret Soccer Ball. 2006. 64p. (gr. 2-4). 14.95 *(978-0-635-06219-2(4))*; pap. 3.99 *(978-0-635-06213-0(5))* Gallopade International.

—The Treacherous Tornado Mystery. 2007. (Carole Marsh Mysteries Ser.). (Illus.). 118p. (J). (gr. 2-9). per. 5.99 *(978-0-635-06338-0(7))* Gallopade International.

—The White House Christmas Mystery. (Real Kids, Real Places Ser.). (J). 2009. 146p. 18.99 *(978-0-635-06996-2(2))*, Marsh, Carole Mysteries) 2003. 160p. (gr. 2-8). 14.95 *(978-0-635-01666-9(4))*7. 2006. (ENG.). 146p. (gr. 4-6). 22.44 *(978-0-635-01664-5(8))* Gallopade International.

—The Zany Zoo Mystery. 2008. (Carole Marsh Mysteries: Awesome Mysteries Ser.). (ENG.). 128p. (J). (gr. 2-4). 18.69 *(978-0-635-06332-8(8))* Gallopade International.

Martin, Andreu & Ribero, J. No Pidas Sardinas Fuera de Temporada. 35th ed. 2003. (SPA., Illus.). 178p. (J). (gr. 8-12). pap. 11.95 *(978-84-204-4796-4(X))* Santillana USA Publishing Co., Inc.

Martin, Ann M. Abby & the Mystery Baby (the Baby-Sitters Club Mystery #28) 2012. (Geronimo Stilton Ser.: 28). (ENG.). 144p. (J). (gr. 2-5). E-Book 7.99 *(978-0-545-79313-1(0))*, Scholastic Paperbacks) Scholastic, Inc.

—Abby & the Secret Society (the Baby-Sitters Club Mystery #23) 2016. (Geronimo Stilton & the Kingdom of Fantasy Ser.: 23). (ENG.). 160p. (J). (gr. 2-5). E-Book 14.99 *(978-0-545-79228-8(2))*, Scholastic Paperbacks) Scholastic, Inc.

—Mallory y el Gato Fantasma. Peraire del Molino, Conchita, tr. (Club de las Canguro Misterios Ser.: Vol. 3).Tr. of Mallory & the Ghost Cat. (SPA.). 159p. (J). 9.95 *(978-84-272-2603-6(9))* Molino, Editorial ESP. Dist: AIMS International Bks., Inc.

—The Secret Book Club, 5. 2008. (Main Street Ser.: 5). (ENG., Illus.). 212p. (J). (gr. 4-6). 21.19 *(978-0-439-86883-9(1))* Scholastic, Inc.

—Stacey y el Anillo Perdido. (Club de las Canguro Misterios Ser.: Vol. 1).Tr. of Stacy & the Missing Ring. (SPA.). 134p. (J). 9.95 *(978-84-272-2601-2(2))* Molino, Editorial ESP. Dist: AIMS International Bks., Inc.

Martin, R. T. The Turnaround. 2018. (Mason Falls Mysteries Ser.). (ENG.). 104p. (YA). (gr. 6-12). pap. 7.99 *(978-1-5415-0119-5(5))*, 9d659811-f39e-4341-9e00-79462b3015ea); 25.32 *(978-1-5415-0111-9(X))*, 2b1e3214-da27-43ce-875f-e57fa7bb3dbd) Lerner Publishing Group. (Darby Creek).

Martin, T. H. The Johnson House Mystery. 2017. (ENG., Illus.). (J). pap. 9.95 *(978-1-61984-631-9(4))* Gatekeeper Pr.

Martin, W. D. Dragonfly Valley: When Best Plans Go Awry. 2012. (ENG.). 176p. (J). pap. 11.95 *(978-1-4787-1832-1(3))* Outskirts Pr., Inc.

Marzollo, Jean. I Spy: 4 Picture Riddle Books, 1 vol. Wick, Walter, photos by. 2005. (Scholastic Reader, Level 1 Ser.). (ENG., Illus.). 128p. (J). (gr. -1-3). pap., pap., pap. 6.99 *(978-0-439-76309-7(6))*, Cartwheel Bks.) Scholastic, Inc.

Maselli, Christopher P. N. The Runaway Mission. 2004. 104p. 5.99 *(978-1-57562-805-9(8))* Copeland, Kenneth Pubns.

Maselli, Christopher P. N. & Hoose, Bob. Jones & Parker Case Files. 2022. (Jones & Parker Case Files Ser.: 1). (ENG., Illus.). 128p. (J). pap. 10.99 *(978-1-58997-806-5(4))*, 4622352) Focus on the Family Publishing.

Mason, Adrienne. Secret Spies. Cupples, Patricia & Cupples, Pat, illus. 2008. (Kids Can Read Ser.). 32p. (J). (gr. 1-2). 14.95 *(978-1-55453-276-6(0))* Kids Can Pr., Ltd. CAN. Dist: Hachette Bk. Group.

Mason, Jane B. & Hines-Stephens, Sarah. Let Sleeping Dogs Spy. Phillips, Craig, illus. 2012. 91p. (J). pap. *(978-0-545-37470-5(7))* Scholastic, Inc.

Mason, Jane B. & Stephens, Sarah Hines. Bella Baxter & the Lighthouse Mystery. Shelley, John, illus. 2006. (Bella Baxter Ser.: 3). (ENG.). 80p. (J). (gr. 1-4). pap. 6.99 *(978-0-689-86282-3(2))*, Simon & Schuster/Paula Wiseman Bks.) Simon & Schuster/Paula Wiseman Bks.

—Play Dead, 1. 2013. (Dog & His Girl Mysteries Ser.). (ENG.). 208p. (J). (gr. 4-6). 18.69 *(978-0-545-43624-3(9))* Scholastic, Inc.

Mason, Simon. Kid Alone: a Garvie Smith Mystery: A Garvie Smith Mystery. 2017. (ENG.). 384p. (YA). (gr. 9). 18.99 *(978-1-338-03649-7(1))* Scholastic, Inc.

Matas, Carol. Visions. 2nd rev. ed. 2008. (Freak Ser.). (ENG.). 128p. (J). (gr. 7-18). pap. *(978-1-55263-932-0(0))* Me to We.

Matas, Carol & Nodelman, Perry. The Proof That Ghosts Exist. 2008. (Ghosthunters Ser.: Bk. 1). (ENG.). 216p. (J). (gr. 4-7). *(978-1-55470-014-1(0))* Me to We.

Matheson, Dan. Before: The Smith & Miya Collection. 2016. (ENG., Illus.). (J). (gr. 3-6). pap. *(978-1-925590-11-1(9))* Vivid Publishing.

Matthews. Death in the Desert. (Thumbprint Mysteries Ser.). 32.86 *(978-0-8092-0416-8(9))* McGraw-Hill/Contemporary.

Mayer, Jeni. The Mystery of the Missing Will. 2007. (ENG.). 160p. (J). mass mkt. 6.95 *(978-0-920633-90-8(0))* Thistledown Pr., Ltd. CAN. Dist: Univ. of Toronto Pr.

Mazer, Anne. Now You See It, Now You Don't. 2005. (Amazing Days of Abby Hayes Ser.: Bk. 15). (Illus.). 126p. (J). (gr. 4-7). 12.65 *(978-0-7569-5932-6(2))* Perfection Learning Corp.

Mazzio, Joann. The One Who Came Back. 2015. (ENG.). 192p. (YA). (gr. 7). pap. 8.99 *(978-0-544-33612-4(7))*, 1584158, Clarion Bks.) HarperCollins Pubs.

McArthur, Nancy. The Mystery of the Plant That Ate Dirty Socks. 2004. 162p. pap. 11.95 *(978-0-595-33693-7(0))*, Backinprint.com) iUniverse, Inc.

McArthur, Shallee. The Unhappening of Genesis Lee. 2014. (ENG.). 352p. (J). (gr. 6-6). 16.95 *(978-1-62914-647-8(1))*, Sky Pony Pr.) Skyhorse Publishing Co., Inc.

McBride, Kristina. The Bakersville Dozen. 2017. (ENG.). 320p. (J). (gr. 8-8). 17.99 *(978-1-5107-0805-1(7))*, Sky Pony Pr.) Skyhorse Publishing Co., Inc.

McCall Smith, Alexander. The Great Cake Mystery: Precious Ramotswe's Very First Case. 2012. (Precious Ramotswe Mysteries for Young Readers Ser.: 1). (ENG., Illus.). 96p. (J). (gr. 2-5). pap. 6.99 *(978-0-307-74389-3(6))*, Anchor) Knopf Doubleday Publishing Group.

—Harriet Bean & the League of Cheats. Rankin, Laura, illus. 2007. (Harriet Bean Ser.). (ENG.). 66p. (J). (gr. 3-6). 17.44 *(978-1-59990-054-4(8))*, 9781599900544) Bloomsbury Publishing USA.

—Harriet Bean & the League of Cheats. 2006. (Harriet Bean Ser.: 2). (J). 106.75 *(978-1-4281-0376-4(7))* Recorded Bks., Inc.

—Max & Maddy & the Bursting Balloons Mystery. Pamintuan, Macky, illus. 2008. (Max & Maddy Ser.). (ENG.). 70p. (J). (gr. 3-6). 17.44 *(978-1-59990-035-3(1))*, 9781599900353) Bloomsbury Publishing USA.

—Max & Maddy & the Chocolate Money Mystery. Pamintuan, Macky, illus. 2008. (Max & Maddy Ser.). (ENG.). 72p. (J). (gr. 3-6). 17.44 *(978-1-59990-036-0(X))*, 9781599900360) Bloomsbury Publishing USA.

—Mystery of Meerkat Hill. McIntosh, Iain, illus. 2013. (Precious Ramotswe Mysteries for Young Readers Ser.: 2). (ENG.). 112p. (J). (gr. 2-5). pap. 7.99 *(978-0-345-80446-4(5))*, Anchor) Knopf Doubleday Publishing Group.

—The Mystery of the Missing Lion. 2014. (Precious Ramotswe Mysteries for Young Readers Ser.: 3). (ENG., Illus.). 112p. (J). (gr. 2-5). pap. 7.99 *(978-0-8041-7327-8(3))*, Anchor) Knopf Doubleday Publishing Group.

—Precious & the Puggies: Precious Ramotswe's Very First Case. Robertson, James, tr. from ENG. 2011. (ENG., Illus.). 96p. pap. 10.95 *(978-1-84502-332-4(3))* Black and White Publishing Ltd. GBR. Dist: Interlink Publishing Group, Inc.

—School Ship Tobermory. 2016. (School Ship Tobermory Ser.: 1). (ENG., Illus.). 224p. (J). (gr. 3-7). 15.99 *(978-0-399-55261-8(8))*, Delacorte Bks. for Young Readers) Random Hse. Children's Bks.

McCann, Jesse Leon. Scooby-Doo & Museum Madness, 1 vol. Sur, Duendes Del, illus. 2011. (Scooby-Doo! Ser.: No. 2). (ENG.). 24p. (J). (gr. k-4). lib. bdg. 31.36 *(978-1-59961-867-8(2))*, 13245, Picture Bk.) Spotlight.

—Scooby-Doo & the Fishy Phantom, 1 vol. Sur, Duendes Del, illus. 2011. (Scooby-Doo! Ser.: No. 2). (ENG.). 24p. (J). (gr. k-4). lib. bdg. 31.36 *(978-1-59961-866-1(4))*, 13244, Picture Bk.) Spotlight.

McCann, M. L. The Search for Black January: Third Mystery in the Longjohners' Series. 2004. 100p. per. 15.95 *(978-0-9754823-2-2(7))* Pumpkin Patch Publishing.

McCaughan, Timothy. Crimson Soul. 2005. 200p. per. 12.95 *(978-1-58961-438-3(0))* PageFree Publishing, Inc.

McCaughren, Tom. Children of the Forge. (Illus.). 128p. 3.95 *(978-0-900068-98-0(1))* Penguin Publishing Group.

—Legend of the Corrib King. 2nd rev. ed. 2012. (McCaughren's Legends Trilogy Ser.). (ENG., Illus.). 128p. (J). pap. 14.95 *(978-1-85635-801-9(1))* Mercier Pr., Ltd., The IRL. Dist: Dufour Editions, Inc.

—Legend of the Corrib King. (Illus.). 96p. 2.25 *(978-0-900068-86-7(8))* Penguin Publishing Group.

—Legend of the Golden Key. 2nd rev. ed. 2012. (McCaughren's Legends Trilogy Ser.). (ENG., Illus.). 190p. (J). pap. 14.95 *(978-1-85635-803-3(8))* Mercier Pr., Ltd., The IRL. Dist: Dufour Editions, Inc.

—Legend of the Golden Key. (Illus.). 96p. 3.95 *(978-0-900068-73-7(6))* Penguin Publishing Group.

—Legend of the Phantom Highwayman. 2nd rev. ed. 2012. (McCaughren's Legends Trilogy Ser.). (ENG., Illus.). 128p. (J). pap. 14.95 *(978-1-85635-802-6(X))* Mercier Pr., Ltd., The IRL. Dist: Dufour Editions, Inc.

Mccauley, Plum. It All Started with A Bicycle. 2011. (ENG.). 220p. pap. 11.95 *(978-1-4327-7412-7(3))* Outskirts Pr., Inc.

McCaw, Neil. My Dad the Crab. 2008. (ENG.). 158p. pap. 10.95 *(978-1-4092-0156-4(2))* Lulu Pr., Inc.

McClafferty, Lisa. Is the Sky Really Falling? A Matilda Private Eye Book. 2012. 26p. 24.95 *(978-1-4626-8093-1(3))* America Star Bks.

—Matilda Private Eye: The Case of the Missing Socks. Aines, Diane, illus. 2012. 34p. 29.95 *(978-1-4489-5049-2(X))* America Star Bks.

McClintock, Norah. About That Night, 1 vol. 2014. (ENG.). 248p. (YA). (gr. 8-12). pap. 12.95 *(978-1-4598-0594-1(1))* Orca Bk. Pubs. USA.

—At the Edge, No. 9. 2013. (Robyn Hunter Mysteries Ser.: 9). (ENG.). 200p. (YA). (gr. 6-12). pap. 8.95 *(978-1-4677-0703-9(1))*, b52be5ff-21f5-4a76-997e-9953e77157b9); lib. bdg. 27.99 *(978-0-7613-8319-2(0))*, ecdd6d90-f144-4806-aa64-749d2d1d8854) Lerner Publishing Group. (Darby Creek).

—Change of Heart, No. 7. 2013. (Robyn Hunter Mysteries Ser.: 7). (ENG.). 224p. (YA). (gr. 6-12). lib. bdg. 27.99 *(978-0-7613-8317-8(4))*, 3a767ef8-7c9d-4c63-bddd-279ad2c330c3, Darby Creek) Lerner Publishing Group.

—Dead & Gone. 2014. (Mike & Riel Mysteries Ser.: No. 3). (ENG.). 224p. (YA). (gr. 6-12). lib. bdg. 27.99 *(978-1-4677-2607-8(9))*, 56cd1991-1fd6-4b8b-a437-e30a99fe3231); No. 3. pap. 8.95 *(978-1-4677-2615-3(X))*, 65e36658-00a1-4803-9dae-db038268b3f4) Lerner Publishing Group. (Darby Creek).

—Guilty, 1 vol. 2012. (ENG.). 224p. (YA). (gr. 8-12). pap. 12.95 *(978-1-55469-989-6(4))* Orca Bk. Pubs. USA.

—I, Witness, 1 vol. Deas, Mike, illus. 2012. (ENG.). 144p. (YA). (gr. 8-12). pap. 16.95 *(978-1-55469-789-2(1))* Orca Bk. Pubs. USA.

—In Too Deep, No. 8. 2013. (Robyn Hunter Mysteries Ser.: 8). (ENG.). 224p. (YA). (gr. 6-12). pap. 8.95 *(978-1-4677-0702-2(3))*, 19db96f6-0e11-4371-9352-7fa4a1010d67); lib. bdg. 27.99 *(978-0-7613-8318-5(2))*, acbb334b-c787-4cc4-baca-5a288444976f) Lerner Publishing Group. (Darby Creek).

—Marked, 1 vol. 2008. (Orca Currents Ser.). (ENG.). 128p. (J). (gr. 4-7). pap. 9.95 *(978-1-55143-992-1(1))* Orca Bk. Pubs. USA.

—Marqué, 1 vol. 2011. (Orca Currents en Français Ser.).Tr. of Marked. (FRE.). 128p. (J). (gr. 4-7). pap. 9.95 *(978-1-55469-855-4(3))* Orca Bk. Pubs. USA.

—Shadow of Doubt, No. 5. 2012. (Robyn Hunter Mysteries Ser.: 5). (ENG.). 232p. (YA). (gr. 6-12). lib. bdg. 27.99 *(978-0-7613-8315-4(8))*, b6e28dab-7e3e-402e-87c0-8fa43f0097ef, Darby Creek) Lerner Publishing Group.

—Trial by Fire, 1 vol. 2016. (Riley Donovan Ser.: 1). (ENG.). 240p. (YA). (gr. 8-12). pap. 10.95 *(978-1-4598-0936-9(X))* Orca Bk. Pubs. USA.

—Truth & Lies, No. 2. 2014. (Mike & Riel Mysteries Ser.: 2). (ENG.). 216p. (YA). (gr. 6-12). pap. 8.95 *(978-1-4677-2613-9(3))*, c47f99a6-46ce-4283-b828-f5ce465ae132, Darby Creek) Lerner Publishing Group.

McCollum, Lynn Tragesser. The Green School Caper: The Adventures of the Five Amigos. 2008. 164p. pap. 9.95 *(978-1-4327-2564-8(5))* Outskirts Pr., Inc.

McCormack, Devon. When Ryan Came Back. 2016. (ENG., Illus.). (J). 24.99 *(978-1-63477-994-4(0))*, Harmony Ink Pr.) Dreamspinner Pr.

McCullough, Victoria. Charlotte's Hummock: a Young Adult Woman's Mystery Detective Novel. 2007. 124p. per. 19.95 *(978-1-4241-6703-6(5))* America Star Bks.

McDonald, Ellie. Danger after Dark. 4th ed. 2005. (Creative Girls Club Mystery Book Ser.). (Illus.). 118p. (J). pap. *(978-1-59635-127-1(6))*, Annie's) Annie's Publishing, LLC.

Mcentire, Myra. Hourglass, 1. 2012. (Hourglass Ser.). (ENG.). 400p. (YA). (gr. 9-12). 26.19 *(978-1-60684-144-0(0))* Farshore GBR. Dist: Children's Plus, Inc.

McEwen, Scott & Williams, Hof. The Trigger Mechanism. 2020. (Camp Valor Ser.: 2). (ENG.). 352p. (YA). 18.99 *(978-1-250-08825-3(9))*, 900158034, St. Martin's Griffin) St. Martin's Pr.

McFall, Claire. Bombmaker. 2014. (ENG.). 368p. (YA). (gr. 8). pap. 11.99 *(978-1-84877-767-5(1))* Bonnier Publishing GBR. Dist: Independent Pubs. Group.

McFall, Jessica & McFall, Ernest. Unselfish Love. l.t. ed. 2006. (ENG., Illus.). 28p. per. 9.95 *(978-1-4327-0076-8(6))* Outskirts Pr., Inc.

McFarlane, Susannah. Drama Queen: EJ12 Girl Hero. 2017. (Illus.). 128p. (J). pap. 5.99 *(978-1-61067-509-3(6))* Kane Miller.

—On the Ball: EJ12 Girl Hero. 2017. (Illus.). 128p. (J). pap. 5.99 *(978-1-61067-507-9(X))* Kane Miller.

—Rocky Road. 2015. 121p. (J). *(978-1-61067-384-6(0))* Kane Miller.

McGann, Erika. The Clubhouse Mystery. Reid, Vince, illus. 2017. (Cass & the Bubble Street Gang Ser.: 1). (ENG.). 160p. pap. 13.00 *(978-1-84717-920-3(7))* O'Brien Pr., Ltd., The IRL. Dist: Casemate Pubs. & Bk. Distributors, LLC.

McGee, Pamela M. Keri. Miller, Dawn Ellen, illus. 2012. 20p. pap. 24.95 *(978-1-4626-8593-6(5))* America Star Bks.

—Keri: Dandelions. Miller, Dawn Ellen, illus. 2012. 24p. pap. 24.95 *(978-1-4626-9977-3(4))* America Star Bks.

McGinnis, Mindy. The Female of the Species. (ENG.). (YA). (gr. 9). 2017. 368p. pap. 10.99 *(978-0-06-232090-2(4))* 2016. 352p. 17.99 *(978-0-06-232089-6(0))* HarperCollins Pubs. (Tegen, Katherine Bks).

McGregor, Kristen. Danny & Jacob Case #081548 Savanco Inc, 1 vol. 2010. 76p. pap. 19.95 *(978-1-4489-5931-0(4))* America Star Bks.

McIntosh, Kenneth. Close-Up: Forensic Photography. 2009. (J). pap. 24.95 *(978-1-4222-1455-8(9))* Mason Crest.

—Close-Up: Forensic Photography, 5 vols. Sanborn, Casey, illus. 2007. (Crime Scene Club Ser.: Bk. 5). 144p. (YA). (gr. 9-12). lib. bdg. 24.95 *(978-1-4222-0251-7(8))* Mason Crest.

—Devil's Canyon: Forensic Geography. 2009. (J). 24.95 *(978-1-4222-1450-3(8))* Mason Crest.

—Devil's Canyon: Forensic Geography. Miller, Justin, illus. 2007. (Crime Scene Club Ser.: Bk. 1). 144p. (YA). (gr. 9-12). 24.95 *(978-1-4222-0247-0(X))* Mason Crest.

—The Earth Cries Out: Forensic Chemistry & Environmental Science. 2009. (J). pap. 24.95 *(978-1-4222-1457-2(5))* Mason Crest.

—The Earth Cries Out: Forensic Chemistry & Environmental Science, 8 vols. Miller, Justin, illus. 2007. (Crime Scene Club Ser.: Bk. 9). 144p. (YA). (gr. 9-12). lib. bdg. 24.95 *(978-1-4222-0254-8(2))* Mason Crest.

—Face from the Past: Skull Reconstruction. 2009. (J). pap. 24.95 *(978-1-4222-1454-1(0))* Mason Crest.

—If the Shoe Fits: Footwear Analysis. 2009. (J). pap. 24.95 *(978-1-4222-1456-5(7))* 2007. (Illus.). 144p. (YA). (gr. 8-12). pap. 9.95 *(978-1-4222-0877-9(X))* Mason Crest.

—If the Shoe Fits: Footwear Analysis, 7 vols. Miller, Justin, illus. 2007. (Crime Scene Club Ser.). 144p. (YA). (gr. 9-12). lib. bdg. 24.95 *(978-1-4222-0253-1(4))* Mason Crest.

—Monsoon Murder: Forensic Meteorology. 2009. (J). pap. 24.95 *(978-1-4222-1461-9(3))* Mason Crest.

—Monsoon Murder: Forensic Meteorology, 12 vols. Holland, Joe, illus. 2007. (Crime Scene Club Ser.). 144p. (YA). (gr. 9-12). lib. bdg. 24.95 *(978-1-4222-0258-6(5))* Mason Crest.

—Numbering the Crime: Forensic Mathematics, 11 vols. Golden, John Ashton, illus. 2007. (Crime Scene Club Ser.). 144p. (YA). (gr. 9-12). lib. bdg. 24.95 *(978-1-4222-0257-9(7))* Mason Crest.

—Over the Edge: Forensic Accident Reconstruction. 2009. (J). pap. 24.95 *(978-1-4222-1451-0(6))* Mason Crest.

—Over the Edge: Forensic Accident Reconstruction, 2 vols. Sanborn, Casey, illus. 2007. (Crime Scene Club Ser.: Bk. 2). 144p. (YA). (gr. 9-12). lib. bdg. 24.95 *(978-1-4222-0248-7(8))* Mason Crest.

—Poison & Peril: Forensic Toxicology. 2009. (J). pap. 24.95 *(978-1-4222-1453-4(2))* Mason Crest.

—Poison & Peril: Forensic Toxicology, 4 vols. Miller, Justin, illus. 2007. (Crime Scene Club Ser.). 144p. (YA). (gr. 9-12). lib. bdg. 24.95 *(978-1-4222-0250-0(X))* Mason Crest.

—A Stranger's Voice: Forensic Speech. 2007. (Crime Scene Club: Fact & Fiction Ser.). (Illus.). 144p. (YA). (gr. 8-12). pap. 9.95 *(978-1-4222-0879-3(6))* Mason Crest.

—A Stranger's Voice: Forensic Speech Identification, 9 vols. Golden, John Ashton, illus. 2007. (Crime Scene Club Ser.). 144p. (YA). (gr. 9-12). lib. bdg. 24.95 *(978-1-4222-0255-5(0))* Mason Crest.

—Things Fall Apart: Forensic Engineering. 2009. (J). pap. 24.95 *(978-1-4222-1459-6(1))* 2007. (Illus.). 144p. (YA). (gr. 8-12). pap. 9.95 *(978-1-4222-0880-9(X))* Mason Crest.

—Things Fall Apart: Forensic Engineering, 10 vols. Golden, John Ashton, illus. 2007. (Crime Scene Club Ser.). 144p. (YA). (gr. 9-12). lib. bdg. 24.95 *(978-1-4222-0256-2(9))* Mason Crest.

—The Trickster's Image: Forensic Art. 2009. (J). pap. 24.95 *(978-1-4222-1452-7(4))* 2007. (Illus.). 144p. (YA). (gr. 8-12). pap. 9.95 *(978-1-4222-0873-1(7))* Mason Crest.

—The Trickster's Image: Forensic Art, 3 vols. Miller, Justin, illus. 2007. (Crime Scene Club Ser.). 144p. (YA). (gr. 9-12). lib. bdg. 24.95 *(978-1-4222-0249-4(6))* Mason Crest.

Mcintyre, Mel. Flutter Bunnies. Grady, Kit, illus. 2008. 24p. pap. 10.95 *(978-1-933090-68-9(5))* Guardian Angel Publishing, Inc.

McKain, W. J. Morris Hollett - & St Vernon's Ward for Strange & Unusual Diseases. 2013. 140p. pap. *(978-1-78148-193-6(8))* Grosvenor Hse. Publishing Ltd.

McKay, Lise Y. The Mysterious Well. 2012. 130p. pap. 14.95 *(978-1-59663-865-5(6))*, Mount Helicon Pr.) Rock, James A. & Co. Pubs.

McKenzie, Sophie. All My Secrets. 2018. (ENG.). 304p. (J). pap. 11.99 *(978-1-4711-2221-7(2))*, Simon & Schuster Children's) Simon & Schuster, Ltd. GBR. Dist: Simon & Schuster, Inc.

McLean, Allan Campbell. The Hill of the Red Fox, 40 vols. 2nd ed. 2006. (Kelpies Ser.). (ENG.). 272p. (J). 11.95 *(978-0-86315-556-7(1))* Floris Bks. GBR. Dist: SteinerBooks, Inc.

McLean, Hope. Battle of the Brightest. 2013. 140p. (J). *(978-0-545-48292-9(5))* Scholastic, Inc.

—Jewel Society #4: Battle of the Brightest. 2013. (Jewel Society Ser.: 4). (ENG.). 144p. (J). (gr. 3-7). pap. 5.99 *(978-0-545-60765-0(5))*, Scholastic Paperbacks) Scholastic, Inc.

—Keep Friends Close, Emeralds Closer (Jewel Society #3) 2013. (ENG.). 144p. (J). (gr. 3-7). pap. 5.99 *(978-0-545-60764-3(7))* Scholastic, Inc.

McMahon, P. J. Case of the Psychic Hamster. Manders, John, illus. 2005. 153p. (J). lib. bdg. 15.38 *(978-1-4242-0404-5(6))* Fitzgerald Bks.

—The Case of the Psychic Hamster: Secret File #4. Manders, John, illus. 4th ed. 2005. (Freaky Joe Club Ser.: 4). (ENG.). 160p. (J). (gr. 2-5). pap. 8.99 *(978-0-689-86263-2(6))*, Simon & Schuster/Paula Wiseman Bks.) Simon & Schuster/Paula Wiseman Bks.

—Case of the Singing Sea Dragons. Manders, John, illus. 2005. 153p. (J). lib. bdg. 15.38 *(978-1-4242-0406-9(2))* Fitzgerald Bks.

—Case of the Smiling Shark. Manders, John, illus. 2004. 116p. (J). lib. bdg. 15.38 *(978-1-4242-0402-1(X))* Fitzgerald Bks.

—The Case of the Smiling Shark: Secret File #2. Manders, John, illus. 2004. (Freaky Joe Club Ser.: 2). (ENG.). 128p. (J). (gr. 2-5). pap. 7.99 *(978-0-689-86261-8(X))*, Aladdin) Simon & Schuster Children's Publishing.

—The Mystery of the Morphing Hockey Stick: Secret File #3. Manders, John, illus. 3rd ed. 2004. (Freaky Joe Club Ser.: 3). (ENG.). 144p. (J). (gr. 2-5). pap. 8.99 *(978-0-689-86262-5(8))*, Aladdin) Simon & Schuster Children's Publishing.

—Mystery of the Swimming Gorilla. Manders, John, illus. 2004. 106p. (J). lib. bdg. 15.38 *(978-1-4242-0401-4(1))* Fitzgerald Bks.

—The Mystery of the Swimming Gorilla: Secret File #1, 1. Manders, John, illus. 2004. (Freaky Joe Club Ser.: 1). (ENG.). 112p. (J). (gr. 2-5). pap. 6.99 *(978-0-689-86260-1(1))* Simon & Schuster, Inc.

McMann, Lisa. Cryer's Cross. 2011. (ENG.). (YA). (gr. 9). 256p. pap. 9.99 *(978-1-4169-9482-4(3))*; (Illus.). 240p. 16.99 *(978-1-4169-9481-7(5))* Simon Pulse. (Simon Pulse).

—Don't Close Your Eyes: Wake; Fade; Gone. 2013. (ENG., Illus.). 720p. (YA). (gr. 9). pap. 14.99 *(978-1-4424-9913-3(3))*, Simon Pulse) Simon Pulse.

McManus, Karen M. Two Can Keep a Secret. 2019. (ENG.). 352p. lib. bdg. 21.80 *(978-1-6636-2970-8(6))* Perfection Learning Corp.

—Two Can Keep a Secret. (ENG.). 352p. (YA). (gr. 9). 2021. pap. 12.99 *(978-1-5247-1471-0(2))*, Ember) 2019. 19.99 *(978-1-5247-1472-7(0))*, Delacorte Pr.) Random Hse. Children's Bks.

McMurtrie, Kevin. The Prince That Always Wore His Top Hat. 2013. 40p. pap. 16.26 *(978-1-4669-9602-1(1))* Trafford Publishing.

McNally, Amber. Henry & the World of the Missing Socks. 2008. 60p. pap. 16.95 *(978-1-60563-288-9(0))* America Star Bks.

McNamee, Graham. Acceleration. 2012. (ENG.). 240p. (YA). (gr. 7). pap. 9.99 *(978-0-307-97595-9(9))*, Ember) Random Hse. Children's Bks.

McNeil, Gretchen. Get Dirty. 2015. (Don't Get Mad Ser.). (ENG.). 384p. (YA). (gr. 8). pap. 10.99 *(978-0-06-226087-1(1))*, Balzer & Bray) HarperCollins Pubs.

McNicoll, Sylvia. The Artsy Mistake Mystery: The Great Mistake Mysteries. 2017. (Great Mistake Mysteries Ser.: 2). (ENG.). 208p. (J). pap. 8.99 *(978-1-4597-3880-5(2))* Dundurn Pr. CAN. Dist: Publishers Group West (PGW).

—The Diamond Mistake Mystery: The Great Mistake Mysteries. 2019. (Great Mistake Mysteries Ser.: 4). (ENG.).

224p. (J). pap. 8.99 *(978-1-4597-4493-6(4))* Dundum Pr. CAN. Dist: Publishers Group West (PGW).

—The Snake Mistake Mystery: The Great Mistake Mysteries. 2018. (Great Mistake Mysteries Ser.: 3). (ENG.). 224p. (J). pap. 8.99 *(978-1-4597-3973-4(6))* Dundum Pr. CAN. Dist: Publishers Group West (PGW).

McOmber, Rachel B., ed. McOmber Phonics Storybooks: The Cove of Gloom. rev. ed. (Illus.). (J). *(978-0-944991-83-1(1))* Swift Learning Resources.

McQuestion, Karen. Favorite, 0 vols. unabr. ed. 2011. (ENG.). 172p. (gr. 7-9). pap. 9.95 *(978-1-935597-25-4(6)*, 9781935597254, Skyscape) Amazon Publishing.

McShane, Pol. The Button That Should Never, Ever, Ever Be Pushed! 2008. 140p. pap. 11.95 *(978-0-595-53194-3(6)*, iUniverse, Inc.) iUniverse, Inc.

McSkimming, Geoffrey. Phyllis Wong & the Waking of the Wizard. 2016. (Phyllis Wong Ser.). (ENG.). 400p. (J). (gr. 3-7). pap. 12.99 *(978-1-76011-338-4(7))* Allen & Unwin AUS. Dist: Independent Pubs. Group.

Meacham, Margaret. The Secret of Heron Creek, 1 vol. 2009. (ENG., Illus.). 136p. (Orig.). (gr. 3-6). pap. 7.95 *(978-0-87033-414-6(X)*, 3655, Cornell Maritime Pr./Tidewater Pubs.) Schiffer Publishing, Ltd.

Meddaugh, Susan. Detective Dog. 2013. (Martha Speaks Ser.). (ENG., Illus.). 96p. (J). (gr. 1-4). pap. 5.99 *(978-0-547-77512-8(1))* Houghton Mifflin Harcourt Publishing Co.

—Haunted House. 2010. (Martha Speaks Ser.). (ENG., Illus.). 24p. (J). (gr. -1-3). pap. 3.99 *(978-0-547-21073-5(6))* Houghton Mifflin Harcourt Publishing Co.

—Martha on the Case. 2010. (Martha Speaks Ser.). (ENG., Illus.). 112p. (J). (gr. 1-4). pap. 5.99 *(978-0-547-21055-1(8))* Houghton Mifflin Harcourt Publishing Co.

—Martha Speaks: Detective Dog (Chapter Book) 2013. (Martha Speaks Ser.). (ENG., Illus.). 96p. (J). (gr. 1-4). 14.99 *(978-0-547-86021-3(8))* Houghton Mifflin Harcourt Publishing Co.

—Martha Speaks: Haunted House (Reader) 2010. (Green Light Reader Level 2 Ser.). (ENG., Illus.). 24p. (J). (gr. k-2). 16.19 *(978-0-547-39353-7(9))* Houghton Mifflin Harcourt Publishing Co.

—Martha Speaks: Secret Agent Dog (Chapter Book) 2012. (Martha Speaks Ser.). (ENG., Illus.). 96p. (J). (gr. 1-4). pap. 5.99 *(978-0-547-57660-2(9))* Houghton Mifflin Harcourt Publishing Co.

Meddour, Wendy. The Black Cat Detectives. 2012. (Cinnamon Grove Ser.). (Illus.). 176p. (J). *(978-1-84780-226-2(5)*, White Lion Publishing) Quarto Publishing Group UK.

Meigs, Cornelia. The Windy Hill. 2017. (ENG., Illus.). (J). (gr. 2-6). pap. 14.95 *(978-1-375-93200-4(4))* Creative Media Partners, LLC.

—The Windy Hill. 2017. (ENG.). 144p. pap. 5.99 *(978-0-486-81741-5(5)*, 817415) Dover Pubns., Inc.

—The Windy Hill. 2017. (ENG., Illus.). (J). (gr. 2-6). pap. *(978-0-649-73440-5(8))* Trieste Publishing Pty Ltd.

Meisels, Dovid. Bar Mitzvah & Tefillin Secrets: The Mysteries Revealed. 2004. 245p. 24.95 *(978-1-931681-56-8(2))* Israel Bookshop Pubns.

Mele, Dana. People Like Us. 2018. 384p. (YA). (gr. 7). 18.99 *(978-1-5247-4170-9(1)*, G.P. Putnam's Sons Books for Young Readers) Penguin Young Readers Group.

Mele, Leo. Closet Creeps: A Bedtime Mystery. Demmers, Justina, illus. 2011. 20p. pap. 24.95 *(978-1-4560-9002-9(X))* America Star Bks.

Melissa Strangway. Abigail's Mirror. 2010. 316p. pap. 18.95 *(978-1-4401-6176-6(3))* iUniverse, Inc.

Mellor, Jodie. Missing! Dann, Penny, illus. 2010. (Mystery Pups Ser.). (ENG.). 112p. (J). (gr. k-2). pap. 6.99 *(978-1-84738-226-9(6))* Simon & Schuster, Ltd. GBR. Dist: Independent Pubs. Group.

Meloy, Colin. The Stars Did Wander Darkling. (ENG.). 336p. (J). (gr. 3-7). 2023. pap. 9.99 ***(978-0-06-301552-4(8))*** 2022. 17.99 *(978-0-06-301551-7(X))* HarperCollins Pubs. (Balzer & Bray).

Meloy, Colin. The Whiz Mob & the Grenadine Kid. Ellis, Carson, illus. 2019. (ENG.). 432p. (J). (gr. 3-7). pap. 8.99 *(978-0-06-234246-1(0)*, Balzer & Bray) HarperCollins Pubs.

Merritt, Kory. No Place for Monsters. Merritt, Kory, illus. 2020. (No Place for Monsters Ser.). (ENG., Illus.). 384p. (J). (gr. 3-7). 14.99 *(978-0-358-12853-3(6)*, 1752984, Clarion Bks.) HarperCollins Pubs.

Messner, Kate. Chirp. 2020. (ENG.). 240p. (J). 17.99 *(978-1-5476-0281-0(3)*, 900210016, Bloomsbury Children's Bks.) Bloomsbury Publishing USA.

Metcalf, Dan. The Catacombs of Chaos: A Lottie Lipton Adventure. Panagarry, Rachelle, illus. 2017. (Adventures of Lottie Lipton Ser.). (ENG.). 80p. (J). (gr. 2-5). pap. 6.99 *(978-1-5124-8185-3(8)*, bf98dbb4-ffb2-40d9-baa2-c10e0ea72223, Darby Creek) Lerner Publishing Group.

—The Curse of the Cairo Cat: A Lottie Lipton Adventure. Panagarry, Rachelle, illus. 2017. (Adventures of Lottie Lipton Ser.). (ENG.). 80p. (J). (gr. 2-5). pap. 6.99 *(978-1-5124-8186-0(6)*, 3975037b-5b5e-4526-9f37-bde5fcb634f9); lib. bdg. 25.32 *(978-1-5124-8179-2(3)*, dd400f92-d4b7-4c17-9548-8f21bf3bb34a) Lerner Publishing Group. (Darby Creek).

—The Eagle of Rome: A Lottie Lipton Adventure. Panagarry, Rachelle, illus. 2017. (Adventures of Lottie Lipton Ser.). (ENG.). 80p. (J). (gr. 2-5). pap. 6.99 *(978-1-5124-8187-7(4)*, c93d2499-cc33-4c5f-a008-6dd45c987a49, Darby Creek) Lerner Publishing Group.

—The Egyptian Enchantment: A Lottie Lipton Adventure. Panagarry, Rachelle, illus. 2017. (Adventures of Lottie Lipton Ser.). (ENG.). 96p. (J). (gr. 2-5). pap. 6.99 *(978-1-5124-8188-4(2)*, 4fed1583-9683-4856-8a90-024c82752f05); lib. bdg. 25.32 *(978-1-5124-8182-2(3)*, b8fef38d-820d-4af0-a6d3-a069159248c1) Lerner Publishing Group. (Darby Creek).

—The Scroll of Alexandria: A Lottie Lipton Adventure. Panagarry, Rachelle, illus. 2017. (Adventures of Lottie Lipton Ser.). (ENG.). 80p. (J). (gr. 2-5). pap. 6.99 *(978-1-5124-8189-1(0)*, dfbd8d06-f168-40b7-bf38-f172f4cf1a82); 25.32 *(978-1-5124-8181-5(5)*, 7e3fdca9-4b61-427f-8b63-58a43b320696) Lerner Publishing Group. (Darby Creek).

—The Secrets of the Stone: A Lottie Lipton Adventure. Panagarry, Rachelle, illus. 2017. (Adventures of Lottie Lipton Ser.). (ENG.). 80p. (J). (gr. 2-5). pap. 6.99 *(978-1-5124-8190-7(4)*, 9c7ccc0f-a907-4c6a-8fa3-2ac8144c8825, Darby Creek) Lerner Publishing Group.

Metz, Melinda. S. M. A. R. T. S. & the Droid of Doom. McKenzie, Heath, illus. 2016. (S. M. A. R. T. S. Ser.). (ENG.). 128p. (J). (gr. 3-6). pap. 9.95 *(978-1-4965-3017-2(9)*, 131904); lib. bdg. 22.65 *(978-1-4965-3015-8(2)*, 131902) Capstone. (Stone Arch Bks.).

—S. M. A. R. T. S. & the Mars Mission Mayhem. McKenzie, Heath, illus. 2016. (S. M. A. R. T. S. Ser.). (ENG.). 128p. (J). (gr. 3-6). pap. 9.95 *(978-1-4965-3018-9(7)*, 131905); lib. bdg. 22.65 *(978-1-4965-3016-5(0)*, 131903) Capstone. (Stone Arch Bks.).

—S. M. A. R. T. S. & the Poison Plates. McKenzie, Heath, illus. 2015. (S. M. A. R. T. S. Ser.). (ENG.). 128p. (J). (gr. 3-6). 22.65 *(978-1-4965-0464-7(X)*, 128489, Stone Arch Bks.) Capstone.

Mezrich, Ben & Mezrich, Tonya. Charlie Numbers & the Man in the Moon. 2017. (Charlie Numbers Adventures Ser.). (ENG., Illus.). 208p. (J). (gr. 3-7). 16.99 *(978-1-4814-4847-5(1)*, Simon & Schuster Bks. For Young Readers) Simon & Schuster Bks. For Young Readers.

—Charlie Numbers & the Woolly Mammoth. 2020. (Charlie Numbers Adventures Ser.). (ENG.). 192p. (J). (gr. 3-7). pap. 8.99 *(978-1-5344-4101-9(8)*, Simon & Schuster Bks. For Young Readers) Simon & Schuster Bks. For Young Readers.

Michiko Florence, Debbi. Jasmine Toguchi, Super Sleuth. Vukovic, Elizabet, illus. 2017. (Jasmine Toguchi Ser.: 2). (ENG.). 128p. (J). pap. 5.99 *(978-0-374-30835-3(7)*, 900185578, Farrar, Straus & Giroux (BYR)) Farrar, Straus & Giroux.

Midnight at the August Tree House. 2004. (Illus.). 100p. (J). per. 15.95 *(978-0-9754823-1-5(9))* Pumpkin Patch Publishing.

Miley, Berry. Christmas Village Chronicles & Other Short Stories. 2005. 63p. pap. 8.95 *(978-1-4116-2617-1(6))* Lulu Pr., Inc.

Milford, Kate. Ghosts of Greenglass House: A Greenglass House Story. (Greenglass House Ser.). (ENG., Illus.). (J). (gr. 5-7). 2018. 480p. pap. 9.99 *(978-1-328-59442-6(4)*, 1730255) 2017. 464p. 17.99 *(978-0-544-99146-0(X)*, 1666502) HarperCollins Pubs. (Clarion Bks.).

—Greenglass House. 2015. (CHI.). 352p. (J). (gr. 5-7). pap. *(978-986-320-886-0(8))* Commonwealth Publishing Co., Ltd.

—Greenglass House. 2016. (Greenglass House Ser.: 1). lib. bdg. 18.40 *(978-0-606-38908-2(3))* Turtleback.

—Greenglass House: A National Book Award Nominee. Zollars, Jaime, illus. (Greenglass House Ser.). (ENG.). (J). (gr. 5-7). 2016. 400p. pap. 8.99 *(978-0-544-54028-6(X)*, 1608839) 2014. 384p. 18.99 *(978-0-544-05270-3(6)*, 1533148) HarperCollins Pubs. (Clarion Bks.).

Miller, D. C. Hurricane Hunters: A Craig Hancock Adventure. 2005. (YA). pap. 12.95 *(978-1-59088-646-5(1))* Wings ePress, Inc.

Miller, Daniel, et al. A Miller Cousin Mystery. 2010. 120p. pap. 49.00 *(978-0-557-57235-9(5))*; pap. 17.80 *(978-0-557-57118-5(9))* Lulu Pr., Inc.

Miller, Marvin. You Be the Jury: Courtroom Collection. Roper, Bob, illus. 2005. 361p. pap. *(978-0-439-77480-2(2))* Scholastic, Inc.

Miller, Nathan. The Official Librarian: Bessy's Back! 2009. 124p. pap. 12.49 *(978-1-4490-2391-1(6))* AuthorHouse.

Miller, Robin Caroll. Samantha Sanderson at the Movies, 1 vol. 2014. (FaithGirlz / Samantha Sanderson Ser.: 1). (ENG.). 272p. (J). pap. 8.99 *(978-0-310-74245-6(5))* Zonderkidz.

—Samantha Sanderson on the Scene, 1 vol. 2014. (FaithGirlz / Samantha Sanderson Ser.: 2). (ENG.). 256p. (J). pap. 8.99 *(978-0-310-74247-0(1))* Zonderkidz.

Millman, Calanitte. The Adventures of the Gimmel Gang III: The Cave. 2005. (J). pap. 8.95 *(978-1-931681-84-1(8))* Israel Bookshop Pubns.

Mills, Charles. The Bandit of Benson Park. 2003. (Honors Club Story Ser.: Vol. 1). 127p. (J). *(978-0-8163-1977-0(4))* Pacific Pr. Pubns.

—The Secret of Scarlett Cove. 2004. (Honors Club Story Ser.: Bk. 3). 127p. (J). 7.99 *(978-0-8163-1999-2(5))* Pacific Pr. Publishing Assn.

Mills, Patricia Anne. Oswald Daydreams. 2010. (Illus.). 32p. pap. 12.99 *(978-1-4520-2209-3(7))* AuthorHouse.

Mills, Timothy. The Mystery Kids: the Mystery of Ghost Lake. 2008. (ENG.). 87p. pap. 14.96 *(978-0-557-01282-4(1))* Lulu Pr., Inc.

Milman, Derek. Swipe Right for Murder. 2019. (ENG.). 368p. (YA). (gr. 10-17). 17.99 *(978-0-316-45106-2(1)*, Jimmy Patterson) Little Brown & Co.

Minden, Cecilia. The Case of the Big Fish. 2019. (Little Blossom Stories Ser.). (ENG., Illus.). 16p. (J). (gr. -1-2). pap. 11.36 *(978-1-5341-4972-4(4)*, 213205, Cherry Blossom Press) Cherry Lake Publishing.

—The Case of the Flat Hat. 2019. (Little Blossom Stories Ser.). (ENG., Illus.). 16p. (J). (gr. -1-2). pap. 11.36 *(978-1-5341-4970-0(8)*, 213199, Cherry Blossom Press) Cherry Lake Publishing.

—The Case of the Lost Cat. Down, Becky, illus. 2019. (Little Blossom Stories Ser.). (ENG.). 16p. (J). (gr. -1-2). pap. 11.36 *(978-1-5341-3909-1(5)*, 212477, Cherry Blossom Press) Cherry Lake Publishing.

—The Case of the Lost Frog. Down, Becky, illus. 2019. (Little Blossom Stories Ser.). (ENG.). 16p. (J). (gr. -1-2). pap. 11.36 *(978-1-5341-3910-7(9)*, 212480, Cherry Blossom Press) Cherry Lake Publishing.

—The Case of the Lost Hen. Down, Becky, illus. 2019. (Little Blossom Stories Ser.). (ENG.). 16p. (J). (gr. -1-2). pap. 11.36 *(978-1-5341-3911-4(7)*, 212483, Cherry Blossom Press) Cherry Lake Publishing.

—The Case of the Lost Pig. Down, Becky, illus. 2019. (Little Blossom Stories Ser.). (ENG.). 16p. (J). (gr. -1-2). pap. 11.36 *(978-1-5341-3912-1(5)*, 212486, Cherry Blossom Press) Cherry Lake Publishing.

—The Case of the Lost Pup. Down, Becky, illus. 2019. (Little Blossom Stories Ser.). (ENG.). 16p. (J). (gr. -1-2). pap. 11.36 *(978-1-5341-3913-8(3)*, 212489, Cherry Blossom Press) Cherry Lake Publishing.

—The Case of the Mixed Socks. 2019. (Little Blossom Stories Ser.). (ENG., Illus.). 16p. (J). (gr. -1-2). pap. 11.36 *(978-1-5341-4973-1(2)*, 213208, Cherry Blossom Press) Cherry Lake Publishing.

—The Case of the Stuck Truck. 2019. (Little Blossom Stories Ser.). (ENG., Illus.). 16p. (J). (gr. -1-2). pap. 11.36 *(978-1-5341-4974-8(0)*, 213211, Cherry Blossom Press) Cherry Lake Publishing.

—The Case of the Wet Pet. 2019. (Little Blossom Stories Ser.). (ENG., Illus.). 16p. (J). (gr. -1-2). pap. 11.36 *(978-1-5341-4971-7(6)*, 213202, Cherry Blossom Press) Cherry Lake Publishing.

Minden, Cecilia & Roth, Kate. How to Write a Mystery. 2012. (Explorer Junior Library: Language Arts Explorer Junior Ser.). (ENG.). 24p. (gr. 1-4). pap. 12.79 *(978-1-61080-662-6(X)*, 202272); (Illus.). 29.21 *(978-1-61080-488-2(0)*, 202098) Cherry Lake Publishing.

Miner, Sharon. Octavia's Quest. 2005. 113p. pap. 11.95 *(978-0-7414-2647-5(1))* Infinity Publishing.

The Missing Will, 6 vols., Vol. 3. (Woodland Mysteriestm Ser.). 133p. (gr. 3-7). 42.50 *(978-0-322-02369-7(6))* Wright Group/McGraw-Hill.

Mitchelhill, Barbara. Football Forgery: No. 1 Boy Detective. Ross, Tony, illus. 2018. (No. 1 Boy Detective Ser.). (ENG.). 64p. (J). (gr. 2-4). pap. 9.99 *(978-1-78344-670-4(6))* Andersen Pr. GBR. Dist: Independent Pubs. Group.

—How to Be a Detective (No. 1 Boy Detective) Ross, Tony, illus. 2018. (No. 1 Boy Detective Ser.). (ENG.). 64p. (J). (gr. 2-4). pap. 9.99 *(978-1-78344-664-3(1))* Andersen Pr. GBR. Dist: Independent Pubs. Group.

—The Mega Quiz. Ross, Tony, illus. 2018. (No. 1 Boy Detective Ser.). (ENG.). 64p. (J). (gr. 2-4). pap. 9.99 *(978-1-78344-671-1(4))* Andersen Pr. GBR. Dist: Independent Pubs. Group.

—Serious Graffiti: No. 1 Boy Detective. Ross, Tony, illus. 2018. (No. 1 Boy Detective Ser.). (ENG.). 64p. (J). (gr. 2-4). pap. 9.99 *(978-1-78344-666-7(8))* Andersen Pr. GBR. Dist: Independent Pubs. Group.

Mitchell, Briar Lee & Keely, Jack. The Whistlebrass Clock People. 2018. (Whistlebrass Mysteries Ser.: 3). (ENG.). 240p. pap. 16.00 *(978-1-68261-459-4(X))* Simon & Schuster.

—The Whistlebrass Storm Watcher. 2016. (Whistlebrass Mysteries Ser.: 2). (ENG.). 272p. (YA). pap. 12.95 *(978-1-68261-268-2(6))* Simon & Schuster.

Mitchell, Jack. The Ancient Ocean Blues. 2008. 200p. (J). (gr. 5-8). pap. 9.95 *(978-0-88776-832-3(6)*, Tundra Bks.) Tundra Bks. CAN. Dist: Penguin Random Hse. LLC.

Mitchell, Laurence. The Mean Root of Crowteal Pond: Inside a Hollow Oak Tree, Book #4. 2009. 28p. pap. 12.49 *(978-1-4389-5406-6(9))* AuthorHouse.

Mitchell, Marie & Smith, Mason. Squatch Watch & Other Stories. 2013. 130p. pap. 9.95 *(978-0-692-02010-4(1))* Smith, Mason.

Mobley, Jeannie. Bobby Lee Claremont & the Criminal Element. 2017. (ENG., Illus.). 246p. (J). (gr. 3-7). 16.95 *(978-0-8234-3781-8(7))* Holiday Hse., Inc.

Mockford, Caroline. What's This? (ENG., Illus.). 32p. (J). pap. 6.99 *(978-1-84148-166-1(1))* Barefoot Bks., Inc.

Moiser, Liam. Moore Field School & the Mystery. 2013. 118p. pap. 10.95 *(978-1-62516-787-3(3)*, Strategic Bk. Publishing) Strategic Book Publishing & Rights Agency (SBPRA).

Molnar, Gwen. Hate Cell: A Casey Templeton Mystery. 2009. (Casey Templeton Mystery Ser.: 1). (ENG.). 184p. (YA). (gr. 5). pap. 11.99 *(978-1-55002-850-8(2))* Dundurn Pr. CAN. Dist: Publishers Group West (PGW).

—Old Bones: A Casey Templeton Mystery. 2014. (Casey Templeton Mystery Ser.: 2). (ENG.). 136p. (YA). pap. 12.99 *(978-1-4597-1404-5(0)*, 9781459714045) Dundurn Pr. CAN. Dist: Publishers Group West (PGW).

Moloney, James. Black Taxi. 2005. 272p. (YA). (gr. 7-18). 15.99 *(978-0-06-055937-3(3))* HarperCollins Pubs.

—Black Taxi. 2003. (ENG.). 288p. *(978-0-207-19989-9(2))* HarperCollins Pubs. Australia.

Monir, Alexandra. The Girl in the Picture. 2016. 272p. (YA). (gr. 7). 17.99 *(978-0-385-74390-7(4)*, Delacorte Pr.) Random Hse. Children's Bks.

Monroe, Chris. Monkey with a Tool Belt Blasts Off! Monroe, Chris, illus. 2020. (Monkey with a Tool Belt Ser.). (ENG., Illus.). 32p. (J). (gr. -1-2). 17.99 *(978-1-5415-7757-2(4)*, eed07eba-23fa-4179-a41f-6af4139dabb2, Carolrhoda Bks.) Lerner Publishing Group.

Monroe, Mary A. Tagger: Graffiti Was His Life - & Soul. 2011. 176p. 29.99 *(978-1-4567-5028-2(3))*; pap. 19.99 *(978-1-4567-5029-9(1))* AuthorHouse.

Monsell, Mary Elise. A Fish Named Yum Vol. IV: MR. PIN. 2007. 72p. (gr. 1-4). per. 8.95 *(978-0-595-47246-8(X)*, Backinprint.com) iUniverse, Inc.

—The Mysterious Cases of Mr. Pin, Vol. I. 2007. 68p. (gr. -1-3). per. 8.95 *(978-0-595-47247-5(8)*, Backinprint.com) iUniverse, Inc.

—The Spy Who Came North from the Pole. 2007. 68p. (gr. -1-3). per. 8.95 *(978-0-595-47248-2(6)*, Backinprint.com) iUniverse, Inc.

Montgomery, E. j. Hailey Walker & the Mystery of the Absent Professor. 2013. 180p. pap. 13.95 *(978-1-4575-2068-6(0))* Dog Ear Publishing, LLC.

Montgomery, Lewis B. The Case of the Amazing Zelda, Vol. 4. Wummer, Amy, illus. 2009. (Milo & Jazz Mysteries Ser.). 96p. (J). (gr. k-3). 22.60 *(978-1-57565-298-6(6))* Astra Publishing Hse.

—The Case of the Amazing Zelda. Wummer, Amy, illus. 2012. (Milo & Jazz Mysteries Ser.: Vol. 4). (ENG.). (J). (gr. 2-4). pap. 20.95 incl. audio compact disk *(978-1-4301-1209-9(3))* Live Oak Media.

—The Case of the Amazing Zelda (Book 4) Wummer, Amy, illus. 2009. (Milo & Jazz Mysteries Ser.). 96p. (J). (gr. 2-6). pap. 6.99 *(978-1-57565-296-2(X)*, 5d25f054-5ef2-4513-9e71-ec29da4fff54, Kane Press) Astra Publishing Hse.

—The Case of the Buried Bones. Wummer, Amy, illus. 2014. (Milo & Jazz Mysteries (r) Ser.: 12). 112p. (J). (gr. 2-5). lib. bdg. 22.60 *(978-1-57565-640-3(X))* Astra Publishing Hse.

—The Case of the Crooked Campaign. Wummer, Amy, illus. 2012. (Milo & Jazz Mysteries (r) Ser.: 9). (ENG.). 112p. (J). (gr. 2-5). lib. bdg. 22.60 *(978-1-57565-435-5(0))* Astra Publishing Hse.

—The Case of the Crooked Campaign (Book 9), No. 9. Wummer, Amy, illus. 2012. (Milo & Jazz Mysteries Ser.: 9). 112p. (J). (gr. 2-6). pap. 6.99 *(978-1-57565-436-2(9)*, ba48c164-9388-4a16-9fbf-8e780216d18e, Kane Press) Astra Publishing Hse.

—The Case of the Diamonds in the Desk. Wummer, Amy, illus. 2012. (Milo & Jazz Mysteries Ser.). 96p. (J). (gr. 2-5). pap. 39.62 *(978-0-7613-9207-1(6))*; lib. bdg. 22.60 *(978-1-57565-392-1(3))* Astra Publishing Hse.

—The Case of the Diamonds in the Desk (Book 8), No. 8. Wummer, Amy, illus. 2012. (Milo & Jazz Mysteries Ser.). 96p. (J). (gr. 2-6). pap. 6.99 *(978-1-57565-391-4(5)*, f97daf45-42da-4bca-ba88-456280d60669, Kane Press) Astra Publishing Hse.

—The Case of the Haunted Haunted House, Vol. 3. Wummer, Amy, illus. 2009. (Milo & Jazz Mysteries Ser.). 96p. (J). (gr. k-3). 22.60 *(978-1-57565-297-9(8))* Astra Publishing Hse.

—The Case of the Haunted Haunted House. Wummer, Amy, illus. 2012. (Milo & Jazz Mysteries Ser.: Vol. 3). (ENG.). (J). (gr. 2-4). pap. 20.95 incl. audio compact disk *(978-1-4301-1206-8(9))* Live Oak Media.

—The Case of the Haunted Haunted House (Book 3), Vol. 3. Wummer, Amy, illus. 2009. (Milo & Jazz Mysteries Ser.). 96p. (J). (gr. 2-6). pap. 6.99 *(978-1-57565-295-5(1)*, 9cc65eec-16ba-4a80-b83c-15a3d4b1b5d2, Kane Press) Astra Publishing Hse.

—The Case of the July 4th Jinx (Book 5), No. 5. Wummer, Amy, illus. 2010. (Milo & Jazz Mysteries Ser.). 96p. (J). (gr. 2-6). pap. 6.99 *(978-1-57565-308-2(7)*, f1e2be1d-4ae3-4336-af84-77d46a12d375, Kane Press) Astra Publishing Hse.

—The Case of the Locked Box. Wummer, Amy, illus. 2013. (Milo & Jazz Mysteries Ser.: Vol. 11). (ENG.). 106p. (J). (gr. 2-4). lib. bdg. 22.60 *(978-1-57565-625-0(6))* Astra Publishing Hse.

—The Case of the Locked Box (Book 11), No. 11. Wummer, Amy, illus. 2013. (Milo & Jazz Mysteries Ser.: 11). 112p. (J). (gr. 2-6). pap. 6.99 *(978-1-57565-626-7(4)*, 4eb267cb-73d0-4237-8cdc-45a0c519fde1, Kane Press) Astra Publishing Hse.

—The Case of the Missing Moose. Wummer, Amy, illus. 2011. (Milo & Jazz Mysteries Ser.). 96p. (J). 22.60 *(978-1-57565-331-0(1))*; pap. 39.62 *(978-0-7613-7607-1(0))* Astra Publishing Hse.

—The Case of the Missing Moose (Book 6), No. 6. Wummer, Amy, illus. 2011. (Milo & Jazz Mysteries Ser.: No. 6). 96p. (J). (gr. 2-6). pap. 6.99 *(978-1-57565-322-8(2)*, 53b2d42e-f31f-40b5-a785-522d4e132fc3, Kane Press) Astra Publishing Hse.

—The Case of the Poisoned Pig (Book 2), No. 2. Wummer, Amy, illus. 2009. (Milo & Jazz Mysteries Ser.). 96p. (J). (gr. 2-6). pap. 6.99 *(978-1-57565-286-3(2)*, dccfda40-f72a-4587-96f6-a30894d647f4, Kane Press) Astra Publishing Hse.

—The Case of the Purple Pool. Wummer, Amy, illus. 2011. (Milo & Jazz Mysteries Ser.). pap. 39.62 *(978-0-7613-8358-1(1))*;No. 7. 96p. (J). lib. bdg. 22.60 *(978-1-57565-343-3(5))* Astra Publishing Hse.

—The Case of the Purple Pool (Book 7), No. 7. Wummer, Amy, illus. 2011. (Milo & Jazz Mysteries Ser.). 96p. (J). (gr. 2-6). pap. 6.99 *(978-1-57565-342-6(7)*, 3b6d083b-f85b-48d6-aeec-cf0f69f8882b, Kane Press) Astra Publishing Hse.

—The Case of the Stinky Socks (Book 1), No. 1. Wummer, Amy, illus. 2009. (Milo & Jazz Mysteries Ser.). 96p. (J). (gr. 2-6). pap. 6.99 *(978-1-57565-285-6(4)*, 24dd1235-79fe-474e-8cff-31537c7e08d4, Kane Press) Astra Publishing Hse.

—The Case of the Superstar Scam. Wummer, Amy, illus. 2013. (Milo & Jazz Mysteries (r) Ser.). 112p. (J). (gr. 2-5). 22.60 *(978-1-57565-518-5(7))* Astra Publishing Hse.

—The Case of the Superstar Scam (Book 10), No. 10. Wummer, Amy, illus. 2013. (Milo & Jazz Mysteries Ser.). 112p. (J). (gr. 2-6). pap. 6.99 *(978-1-57565-519-2(5)*, 24e4002f-0980-4892-b561-8343b6b099e5, Kane Press) Astra Publishing Hse.

Montgomery, R. A. Dragonlark Bind Up-#02. 2009. 0192p. pap. 6.99 *(978-1-933390-89-5(1))* Chooseco LLC.

—Fire! Newton, Keith, illus. 2015. (ENG.). 80p. (Orig.). (J). (gr. 3-3). pap. 7.99 *(978-1-937133-49-8(4))* Chooseco LLC.

—Lost on the Amazon. Millet, Jason, illus. 2006. (ENG.). 144p. (J). (gr. 4-8). per. 6.99 *(978-1-933390-09-3(3)*, CHCL09) Chooseco LLC.

Moore, Jordan. The Mystery of the Grand Bazaar, 1 vol. rev. ed. 2013. (Literary Text Ser.). (ENG., Illus.). 32p. (gr. 3-4). pap. 11.99 *(978-1-4333-5645-2(7))* Teacher Created Materials, Inc.

Moore, Nathan. The Little Princess & the Backyard Mystery: A Children's Story. 2008. 27p. pap. 24.95 *(978-1-60610-805-5(0))* America Star Bks.

Morgan, Gloria. The Ducking Stool. 2013. (Illus.). 298p. pap. 24.99 *(978-1-78035-684-6(6)*, Fastprint Publishing) Upfront Publishing Ltd. GBR. Dist: Printondemand-worldwide.com.

Morgan, Winter. Beneath the Blocks. 2018. (Unofficial Minecrafter Mysteries Ser.: 2). lib. bdg. 18.40 *(978-0-606-41297-1(2))* Turtleback.

—Beneath the Blocks: An Unofficial Minecrafters Mysteries Series, Book Two. 2018. (Unofficial Minecraft Mysteries Ser.: 2). (ENG.). 112p. (J). (gr. 4-6). pap. 7.99 *(978-1-5107-3188-2(1)*, Sky Pony Pr.) Skyhorse Publishing Co., Inc.

—The Case of the Missing Overworld Villain (for Fans of Creepers) An Unofficial Minecrafters Mysteries Series, Book Four, Book Four. 2018. (Unofficial Minecraft Mysteries Ser.: 4). (ENG.). 112p. (J). (gr. 4-6). pap. 7.99 *(978-1-5107-3190-5(3)*, Sky Pony Pr.) Skyhorse Publishing Co., Inc.

—Mystery on Mushroom Island: An Unofficial Minecrafters Mysteries Series, Book Six. 2018. (Unofficial Minecraft Mysteries Ser.: 6). (ENG.). 112p. (J). (gr. 4-6). pap. 7.99 *(978-1-5107-3192-9(X)*, Sky Pony Pr.) Skyhorse Publishing Co., Inc.

—The Skeleton Secret: An Unofficial Minecrafters Mysteries Series, Book Three. 2018. (Unofficial Minecraft Mysteries Ser.: 3). (ENG.). 112p. (J). (gr. 4-6). pap. 7.99

(978-1-5107-3189-9(X), Sky Pony Pr.) Skyhorse Publishing Co., Inc.
—Stolen Treasure. 2018. (Unofficial Minecrafter Mysteries Ser.: 1). lib. bdg. 18.40 *(978-0-606-41296-4(4))* Turtleback.
—Stolen Treasure: An Unofficial Minecrafters Mysteries Series, Book One. 2018. (Unofficial Minecraft Mysteries Ser.: 1). (ENG.). 112p. (J). (gr. 4-6). pap. 7.99 *(978-1-5107-3187-5(3),* Sky Pony Pr.) Skyhorse Publishing Co., Inc.
—Trapped in the Temple: An Unofficial Minecrafters Mysteries Series, Book Five. 2018. (Unofficial Minecraft Mysteries Ser.: 5). (ENG.). 112p. (J). (gr. 4-6). pap. 7.99 *(978-1-5107-3191-2(1),* Sky Pony Pr.) Skyhorse Publishing Co., Inc.
Moriarty, Chris. The Inquisitor's Apprentice. Geyer, Mark Edward, illus. 2013. (ENG.). 352p. (J). (gr. 5-7). pap. 7.99 *(978-0-547-85084-9(0),* 1501042, Clarion Bks.) HarperCollins Pubs.
—The Watcher in the Shadows. Geyer, Mark Edward, illus. 2014. (ENG.). 336p. (J). (gr. 5-7). pap. 18.99 *(978-0-544-22776-7(X),* 1563388, Clarion Bks.) HarperCollins Pubs.
Morin, Al. Brandon Abroad: The Mystery of the Ruins. 2017. (ENG., Illus.). (J). pap. 7.99 *(978-1-911079-61-3(1),* Heinemann) Capstone.
Morrill, Stephanie. The Lost Girl of Astor Street, 1 vol. 2018. (ENG.). 352p. (YA). pap. 10.99 *(978-0-310-75840-2(8))* Blink.
Morris, Paula. The Eternal City. 2015. (ENG.). 304p. (YA). (gr. 7). 17.99 *(978-0-545-25133-4(8))* Scholastic, Inc.
—The Eternal City. 2015. 291p. (YA). *(978-0-545-91986-9(X))* Scholastic, Inc.
Morris, Rebecca. Mystery. 2016. (Essential Literary Genres Ser.). (ENG., Illus.). 112p. (J). (gr. 6-12). lib. bdg. 41.36 *(978-1-68078-380-3(7),* 23525, Essential Library) ABDO Publishing Co.
Morrison, Kevin. Ghost Arson. 2006. (ENG.). 165p. pap. 12.99 *(978-1-84728-604-8(6))* Lulu Pr., Inc.
Morton-Shaw, Christine. The Hunt for the Seventh. 2009. (ENG.). 288p. (J). (gr. 5). pap. 7.99 *(978-0-06-072824-3(8),* Tegen, Katherine Bks) HarperCollins Pubs.
Mosso, Tyfanny. The Mud Puddle Gang. 2006. pap. 17.00 *(978-0-8059-9067-6(4))* Dorrance Publishing Co., Inc.
Muldoon, Kathleen M. The Runaway Skeleton. Hilliker, Phillip, illus. 2008. (Vortex Bks.). (ENG.). 112p. (J). (gr. 5-9). 26.65 *(978-1-4342-0800-2(1),* 95205, Stone Arch Bks.) Capstone.
Mulligan, Andy. Return to Ribblestrop. 2016. (Ribblestrop Ser.). (ENG., Illus.). 352p. (J). (gr. 3-7). 17.99 *(978-1-4424-9907-2(9),* Beach Lane Bks.) Beach Lane Bks.
—Ribblestrop. (Ribblestrop Ser.). (ENG., Illus.). (J). (gr. 3-7). 2016. 400p. pap. 7.99 *(978-1-4424-9905-8(2))* 2014. 384p. 16.99 *(978-1-4424-9904-1(4))* Beach Lane Bks. (Beach Lane Bks.).
—Ribblestrop Forever! 2016. (Ribblestrop Ser.). (ENG., Illus.). 320p. (J). (gr. 3-7). 16.99 *(978-1-4424-9910-2(9),* Beach Lane Bks.) Beach Lane Bks.
—Trash. 2011. (ENG., Illus.). 240p. (YA). (gr. 7-12). pap. 11.99 *(978-0-385-75216-9(4),* Ember) Random Hse. Children's Bks.
Mulligan, Richard. Marvin's Mysteries. 2009. (ENG.). 120p. pap. 11.30 *(978-0-557-06550-9(X))* Lulu Pr., Inc.
Mullin, Mike. Surface Tension. 2018. (ENG.). 424p. (YA). (gr. 8-12). 17.99 *(978-1-939100-16-0(X))* Tanglewood Pr.
Munday, Evan. The Dead Kid Detective Agency. 2011. (ENG., Illus.). 320p. (J). (gr. 4-7). pap. 9.95 *(978-1-55022-971-4(0),* befbbee6-e7ed-400b-8efd-911e31048a4d) ECW Pr. CAN. Dist: Baker & Taylor Publisher Services (BTPS).
—Dial M for Morna. 2013. (Dead Kid Detective Agency Ser.: 2). (ENG., Illus.). 320p. (J). (gr. 3-8). pap. 11.95 *(978-1-77041-073-2(2),* 02d4b932-fbca-485e-9ab7-3675a2fa6b88) ECW Pr. CAN. Dist: Baker & Taylor Publisher Services (BTPS).
—Loyalist to a Fault: The Dead Kid Detective Agency #3. 2015. (ENG., Illus.). 304p. (J). (gr. 2-7). pap. 11.95 *(978-1-77041-074-9(0),* 66f4ad47-f8c6-47ec-af19-682ae5eedb9c) ECW Pr. CAN. Dist: Baker & Taylor Publisher Services (BTPS).
Mundy, Charlene & Chapline, Jo. David's Donkey Tales. 2007. (ENG.). 73p. pap. 12.50 *(978-0-615-16825-8(6))* Knee-High Adventures.
Munro, Ken. The Cross Keys Caper. 2006. (Sammy & Brian Mystery Ser.: 18). 154p. pap. 5.95 *(978-1-932864-94-6(6))* Masthof Pr.
—Fireball. 2003. (Sammy & Brian Mystery Ser.: No. 15). (J). pap. 6.95 *(978-1-930353-84-8(7))* Masthof Pr.
—Grandfather's Secret: Sammy & Brian Mystery Series #16. 2004. (Sammy & Brian Mystery Ser.: 16). (J). pap. 6.95 *(978-1-932864-04-5(0))* Masthof Pr.
—The Mysterious Baseball Scorecard: Sammy & Brian Mystery Series #17. 2005. (Sammy & Brian Mystery Ser.: 17). pap. 6.95 *(978-1-932864-31-1(8))* Masthof Pr.
Murphy, Antoinette S. Does It Hurt When You Die? 2004. 30p. (J). pap. 24.95 *(978-1-4137-3520-8(7))* PublishAmerica, Inc.
Murphy, Emily Bain. The Disappearances. 2017. (ENG.). 400p. (YA). (gr. 7). 17.99 *(978-0-544-87936-2(8),* 1650974, Clarion Bks.) HarperCollins Pubs.
Murray Prisant, Guillermo. Mas Que Oscuro. rev. ed. 2005. (Castillo del Terror Ser.). (SPA & ENG.). 136p. (J). (gr. -1-7). pap. 6.95 *(978-970-20-0217-8(6))* Castillo, Ediciones, S. A. de C. V. MEX. Dist: Macmillan.
Museum Mayhem. 2014. (Nancy Drew & the Clue Crew Ser.: 39). (ENG., Illus.). 96p. (J). (gr. 1-4). pap. 5.99 *(978-1-4424-9967-6(2),* Aladdin) Simon & Schuster Children's Publishing.
The Mysteries of Shapeville. l.t. ed. 2005. (Illus.). 48p. (J). 18.95 *(978-0-9747509-1-0(3))* Del Gatto, Maria.
Mysterious Chills & Thrills: 10 creepy, strange, adventurous short stories for kids to tickle the imagination. 2004. (J). per. 6.95 *(978-0-9749013-0-5(X))* LH Pubns. & Productions.
The Mysterious IOU, 6 vols., Vol. 3. (Woodland Mysteriestm Ser.). 133p. (gr. 3-7). 42.50 *(978-0-322-02375-8(0))* Wright Group/McGraw-Hill.
The Mysterious Mansion. (Get a Clue Mystery Puzzles Ser.). 16p. (J). (gr. 5). 12.99 *(978-0-7847-0734-0(0))* Standard Publishing.
Mystery Bay: Individual Title Six-Packs. (Action Packs Ser.). 128p. (gr. 3-5). 44.00 *(978-0-7635-3310-6(6))* Rigby Education.
Mystery Mountain: Individual Title Six-Packs. (Bookweb Ser.). 32p. (gr. 6-18). 34.00 *(978-0-7578-0897-5(2))* Rigby Education.
The Mystery of Moody Manor, 6 vols. (Ragged Island Mysteriestm Ser.). 161p. (gr. 5-7). 42.50 *(978-0-322-01655-2(X))* Wright Group/McGraw-Hill.
The Mystery of October Island. 2003. (Illus.). 50p. (J). per. 12.95 *(978-0-9754823-0-8(0))* Pumpkin Patch Publishing.
The Mystery of the Dark Old House, 6 vols., Vol. 2. (Woodland Mysteriestm Ser.). 133p. (gr. 3-7). 42.50 *(978-0-7802-7940-7(9))* Wright Group/McGraw-Hill.
Mystery of the Desert Giant: Hardy Boys Mystery Stories. 2011. 190p. (gr. 5-9). 42.95 *(978-1-258-10226-5(9))* Literary Licensing, LLC.
The Mystery of the Lion's Tail. 2014. (Greetings from Somewhere Ser.: 5). (ENG., Illus.). 128p. (J). (gr. -1-4). pap. 6.99 *(978-1-4814-1464-7(X),* Little Simon) Little Simon.
The Mystery of the Three Keys, 6 vols., Vol. 3. (Woodland Mysteriestm Ser.). 133p. (gr. 3-7). 42.50 *(978-0-322-02371-0(8))* Wright Group/McGraw-Hill.
The Mystery of the Tiny Key. 2008. 32p. pap. 4.99 *(978-0-8341-2351-9(7),* 083-412-3517) Beacon Hill Pr. of Kansas City.
Mystery on Church Hill. 2013. 196p. (J). pap. 8.99 *(978-0-9893414-3-1(7))* MyBoys3 Pr.
Mystery Valley: Individual Title Six-Packs. (Bookweb Ser.). 32p. (gr. 4-18). 34.00 *(978-0-7635-3730-2(6))* Rigby Education.
Nagle, Jeanne, ed. Great Authors of Mystery, Horror & Thrillers, 1 vol. 2013. (Essential Authors for Children & Teens Ser.). (ENG., Illus.). 184p. (YA). (gr. 8-8). 48.59 *(978-1-62275-094-8(2),* 539bf3bd-a541-45b9-a1b0-425e762e2481) Rosen Publishing Group, Inc., The.
Nalbantsky, Danail. Bludnia Sin (the Prodigal Son) Guetov, Dimitar, ed. 2nd unabr. ed. 2004. (BUL.). 228p. per. 9.99 *(978-0-9753970-3-9(6))* Capricorn Publishing.
Nash, Scott. Tuff Fluff: The Case of Duckie's Missing Brain. Nash, Scott, illus. 2004. (Illus.). (J). 101.94 *(978-0-7636-2503-0(5));* (ENG., 40p. (gr. 1-4). 17.99 *(978-0-7636-1882-7(9))* Candlewick Pr.
Nass, Marcia & Campisi, Stephanie. Mini Mysteries & Kooky Spookies. Innes, Calvin, illus. 2007. 176p. per. 6.99 *(978-0-9795364-2-7(1))* Chowder Bay Bks.
Nayeri, Daniel. Sasha & Puck & the Brew for Brainwash. Lourenço, Estrela, illus. 2020. (Elixir Fixers Ser.: 4). (ENG.). 128p. (J). (gr. 1-5). 14.99 *(978-0-8075-7246-7(2),* 807572462) Whitman, Albert & Co.
—Sasha & Puck & the Cordial Cordial. Mak, Anneliese, illus. 2019. (Elixir Fixers Ser.: 2). (ENG.). 128p. (J). (gr. 1-5). 14.99 *(978-0-8075-7243-6(8),* 807572438) Whitman, Albert & Co.
—Straw House, Wood House, Brick House, Blow: Four Novellas by Daniel Nayeri. 2011. (ENG., Illus.). 432p. (YA). (gr. 9). 19.99 *(978-0-7636-5526-6(0))* Candlewick Pr.
Neenan, Colin. Thick. 2006. 126p. (YA). (gr. 7-16). per. 6.95 *(978-0-9746481-9-4(1))* Brown Barn Bks.
Nelson, Suzanne. The Ghoul Next Door. 2012. 186p. (J). *(978-0-545-48421-3(9))* Scholastic, Inc.
Neri, G. Tru & Nelle. 2016. (ENG., Illus.). 336p. (J). (gr. 3-7). 16.99 *(978-0-544-69960-1(2),* 1627790, Clarion Bks.) HarperCollins Pubs.
—Tru & Nelle: a Christmas Tale: A Christmas Holiday Book for Kids. 2017. (ENG.). 304p. (J). (gr. 5-7). 16.99 *(978-1-328-68598-8(5),* 1670543, Clarion Bks.) HarperCollins Pubs.
Nesbit, E. The Seven Dragons & Other Stories. 2006. 140p. 24.95 *(978-1-59818-171-5(8))* Aegypan.
Nesbit, Troy. Diamond Cave Mystery. 2013. (Wilderness Mystery Ser.). (ENG., Illus.). 280p. (J). (gr. 3-7). pap. 12.95 *(978-1-58979-809-0(0))* Taylor Trade Publishing.
—Forest Fire Mystery. 2014. (Wilderness Mystery Ser.). (ENG., Illus.). 284p. (J). (gr. 3-7). pap. 12.95 *(978-1-58979-869-4(4))* Taylor Trade Publishing.
—Jinx of Payrock Canyon. 2014. (Wilderness Mystery Ser.). (ENG., Illus.). 282p. (J). (gr. 3-7). pap. 12.95 *(978-1-58979-865-6(1))* Taylor Trade Publishing.
—Mystery at Rustlers Fort. 2014. (Wilderness Mystery Ser.). (ENG., Illus.). 282p. (J). (gr. 3-7). pap. 12.95 *(978-1-58979-867-0(8))* Taylor Trade Publishing.
Nettrour, Nelani. The Dragon Lands Bk. 1: The Ripple. Nettrour, Heather, illus. 2003. 100p. pap. 11.95 *(978-1-929381-46-3(8),* Third Millennium Publishing) Sci Fi-Arizona, Inc.
Newcomb, Ambrose. Eagles of the Sky or with Jack Ralston along the Air Lanes. 2005. reprint ed. pap. 26.95 *(978-1-4179-8865-5(7))* Kessinger Publishing, LLC.
Newman, Robin. The Case of the Missing Carrot Cake: A Wilcox & Griswold Mystery. Zemke, Deborah, illus. 2015. (Wilcox & Griswold Mysteries Ser.). (ENG.). 40p. (J). (gr. k-5). 18.99 *(978-1-939547-17-0(2),* 285f447c-52b7-4074-8468-10f43b1fbe81) Creston Bks.
—The Case of the Poached Egg: A Wilcox & Griswold Mystery. Zemke, Deborah, illus. 2017. (Wilcox & Griswold Mysteries Ser.). (ENG.). 48p. (J). (gr. k-5). 15.95 *(978-1-939547-30-9(X),* cbab25a3-2b05-4789-9d4c-891ebca2b9b7) Creston Bks.
Newman, Terry. Detective Strongpak & the Case of the Dead Elf. 2015. (ENG.). 312p. (YA). 11.99 *(978-0-00-812066-5(8),* Harper Voyager) HarperCollins Pubs.
Newsome, Richard. The Billionaire's Curse. Duddle, Jonny, illus. 2011. (ENG.). 384p. (J). (gr. 3-7). pap. 8.99 *(978-0-06-194491-8(2),* Waldon Pond Pr.) HarperCollins Pubs.
—The Emerald Casket. Duddle, Jonny, illus. 2012. (ENG.). 384p. (J). (gr. 3-7). pap. 6.99 *(978-0-06-194493-2(9),* Waldon Pond Pr.) HarperCollins Pubs.
—The Mask of Destiny, 3. Duddle, Jonny, illus. 2013. (ENG.). 384p. (J). (gr. 3-7). pap. 6.99 *(978-0-06-194495-6(5),* Waldon Pond Pr.) HarperCollins Pubs.
Nichols, Travis. Fowl Play. 2017. (J). lib. bdg. 18.40 *(978-0-606-40615-4(8))* Turtleback.
Nicholson, Mike. Museum Mystery Squad & the Case of the Curious Coins, 32 vols. Phillips, Mike, illus. 2017. (Museum Mystery Squad Ser.: 3). 128p. (J). pap. 6.95 *(978-1-78250-363-7(3),* Kelpies) Floris Bks. GBR. Dist: Consortium Bk. Sales & Distribution.
—Museum Mystery Squad & the Case of the Hidden Hieroglyphics, 30 vols. Phillips, Mike, illus. 2017. (Museum Mystery Squad Ser.: 2). 128p. (J). pap. 6.95 *(978-1-78250-362-0(5),* Kelpies) Floris Bks. GBR. Dist: Consortium Bk. Sales & Distribution.
—Museum Mystery Squad & the Case of the Moving Mammoth, 30 vols. Phillips, Mike, illus. 2017. (Museum Mystery Squad Ser.: 1). 128p. (J). pap. 6.95 *(978-1-78250-361-3(7),* Kelpies) Floris Bks. GBR. Dist: Consortium Bk. Sales & Distribution.
—Museum Mystery Squad & the Case of the Roman Riddle, 30 vols. Phillips, Mike, illus. 2018. (Museum Mystery Squad Ser.: 4). 128p. (J). pap. 6.95 *(978-1-78250-364-4(1),* Kelpies) Floris Bks. GBR. Dist: Consortium Bk. Sales & Distribution.
Nickel, Scott. Monster Trouble. Fentz, Mike, illus. 2004. (Scholastic Reader Ser.). 22p. (J). pap. *(978-0-439-66977-1(4))* Scholastic, Inc.
Nickerson, Sara. How to Disappear Completely & Never Be Found. Comport, Sally Wern, illus. 2003. (ENG.). 288p. (J). (gr. 5-18). pap. 5.99 *(978-0-06-441027-4(7))* HarperCollins Pubs.
Nienstedt, L. a. Phineas T Pudgepot & the Mysterious Flying Fish. 2009. 32p. pap. 14.49 *(978-1-4343-5123-4(8))* AuthorHouse.
Night, P. J. The House Next Door. 2013. (You're Invited to a Creepover Ser.: 16). (ENG., Illus.). 160p. (J). (gr. 3-7). pap. 6.99 *(978-1-4424-8233-3(8),* Simon Spotlight) Simon Spotlight.
—You're Invited to a Creepover Collection (Boxed Set) Truth or Dare...; You Can't Come in Here!; Ready for a Scare?; the Show Must Go On! 2012. (You're Invited to a Creepover Ser.). (ENG.). 640p. (J). (gr. 3-7). pap. 31.99 *(978-1-4424-8444-3(6),* Simon Spotlight) Simon Spotlight.
Nilsson, Ulf. Detective Gordon: A Case in Any Case. Spee, Gitte, illus. 2017. (Detective Gordon Ser.). (ENG.). 108p. (gr. k-5). 9.99 *(978-1-77657-110-9(X))* Gecko Pr. NZL. Dist: Lerner Publishing Group.
—Detective Gordon: a Case for Buffy. Spee, Gitte, illus. 2018. (Detective Gordon Ser.). (ENG.). 108p. (J). (gr. k-5). 16.99 *(978-1-77657-178-9(9),* c920efa5-2f2a-4261-a17f-c17d9ea10668) Gecko Pr. NZL. Dist: Lerner Publishing Group.
—Detective Gordon: a Case in Any Case. Spee, Gitte, illus. 2017. (Detective Gordon Ser.). (ENG.). 108p. (J). (gr. k-5). 16.99 *(978-1-77657-108-6(8),* 52e08343-0e42-496c-a046-6f07a0aa8561) Gecko Pr. NZL. Dist: Lerner Publishing Group.
—Detective Gordon: the First Case. Spee, Gitte, illus. 2015. (Detective Gordon Ser.). (ENG.). 96p. (J). (gr. k-5). 16.99 *(978-1-927271-49-0(5),* 0f50d454-d471-44fa-b6e5-5430dcc6baf4) Gecko Pr. NZL. Dist: Lerner Publishing Group.
Nixon & Brush. Champagne with a Corpse. (Thumbprint Mysteries Ser.). 32.86 *(978-0-8092-0420-5(7))* McGraw-Hill/Contemporary.
Nixon, Joan Lowery. A Deadly Game of Magic. 2004. 228p. (YA). (gr. 7). 13.60 *(978-0-7569-7230-1(2))* Perfection Learning Corp.
—The Kidnapping of Christina Lattimore. 2004. (ENG.). 320p. (YA). (gr. 7-12). pap. 8.99 *(978-0-15-205031-3(0),* 1195194, Clarion Bks.) HarperCollins Pubs.
—Nightmare. 2005. 166p. (gr. 5-7). 17.00 *(978-0-7569-5239-6(5))* Perfection Learning Corp.
Nobel, Julia. The Mystery of Black Hollow Lane. 2020. (Black Hollow Lane Ser.: 1). 320p. (J). (gr. 3-7). pap. 8.99 *(978-1-4926-9154-9(2))* Sourcebooks, Inc.
Nobel, Zack. The Twisted Teenage Mysteries. 2009. 48p. pap. 17.49 *(978-1-4389-1127-4(0))* AuthorHouse.
Noble, Sarah. Hannah & Horatio Pea. 2006. (Illus.). 336p. pap. *(978-1-84401-673-0(0))* Athena Pr.
Noël, Alyson. Blacklist. 2017. 448p. (J). *(978-0-06-266688-8(6),* Tegen, Katherine Bks) HarperCollins Pubs.
Noel, Alyson. Blacklist. 2018. (Beautiful Idols Ser.: 2). (ENG.). 464p. (YA). (gr. 9). pap. 9.99 *(978-0-06-232456-6(X),* Tegen, Katherine Bks) HarperCollins Pubs.
—Infamous. 2018. (ENG.). 432p. (YA). (Beautiful Idols Ser.: 3). (gr. 9). 17.99 *(978-0-06-232458-0(6));* *(978-0-06-279645-5(3))* HarperCollins Pubs. (Tegen, Katherine Bks).
—Unrivaled. 2017. (Beautiful Idols Ser.: 1). (ENG.). 448p. (YA). (gr. 9). pap. 9.99 *(978-0-06-232453-5(5),* Tegen, Katherine Bks) HarperCollins Pubs.
Noël, Alyson. Unrivaled. 2017. (Beautiful Idols Ser.: 1). (YA). lib. bdg. 20.85 *(978-0-606-39609-7(8))* Turtleback.
—Unrivaled: A Beautiful Idols Novel. 2016. 420p. (YA). *(978-0-06-245840-7(X))* HarperCollins Pubs.
Nolan, Alan. Destination: Homicide! 2012. (ENG., Illus.). 80p. (J). pap. 12.95 *(978-1-84717-256-3(3))* O'Brien Pr., Ltd., The IRL. Dist: Dufour Editions, Inc.
Nomura, Mizuki. Book Girl & the Captive Fool (light Novel), Volume 3. 2011. (Book Girl Ser.: 3). (ENG., Illus.). 248p. (YA). (gr. 8-17). pap. 13.00 *(978-0-316-07693-7(7),* Yen Pr.) Yen Pr. LLC.
—Book Girl & the Corrupted Angel (light Novel), Volume 4. 2012. (Book Girl Ser.: 4). (ENG., Illus.). 248p. (YA). (gr. 8-17). pap. 13.00 *(978-0-316-07694-4(5),* Yen Pr.) Yen Pr. LLC.
—Book Girl & the Suicidal Mime (light Novel), Volume 1. 2010. (Book Girl Ser.: 1). (ENG., Illus.). 200p. (YA). (gr. 8-17). pap. 13.00 *(978-0-316-07690-6(2),* Yen Pr.) Yen Pr. LLC.
Noni, Lynette. Whisper. 2018. (ENG.). 320p. (J). (gr. 9-12). 17.99 *(978-1-77138-938-9(9))* Kids Can Pr., Ltd. CAN. Dist: Hachette Bk. Group.
Nordin, Ruth Ann. Witness to a Murder. 2007. 140p. per. 11.95 *(978-0-595-45089-3(X))* iUniverse, Inc.
Norman, C. S. The Lockview Logans: Fire One. 2012. 316p. (gr. 4-6). pap. 18.95 *(978-1-4697-9840-0(9))* iUniverse, Inc.
Norris, Elizabeth. Unraveling. 2013. (Unraveling Ser.: 1). (ENG.). 480p. (YA). (gr. 8). pap. 9.99 *(978-0-06-210374-1(1),* Balzer & Bray) HarperCollins Pubs.
Norton, Andre. Ralestone Luck. 2017. (ENG., Illus.). (J). 24.95 *(978-1-374-97169-1(3));* pap. 14.95 *(978-1-374-97168-4(5))* Capital Communications, Inc.
—Ralestone Luck. 2006. pap. *(978-1-4068-3557-1(9))* Echo Library.
Norville, Rod. Moonshine Express: Revised Edition with a History of Moonshine Today & Yesterday. 2003. 178p. (YA). per. 13.95 *(978-1-891929-99-1(2))* Four Seasons Pubs.
Novel Units. Encyclopedia Brown: Boy Detective Novel Units Teacher Guide. 2019. (ENG.). (J). pap. 12.99 *(978-1-56137-282-9(X),* Novel Units, Inc.) Classroom Library Co.
—The House of Dies Drear Novel Units Teacher Guide. 2019. (ENG.). (J). pap. 12.99 *(978-1-56137-516-5(0),* NU5168, Novel Units, Inc.) Classroom Library Co.
—Nate the Great & the Sticky Case Novel Units Teacher Guide. 2019. (Nate the Great Ser.). (ENG.). (J). (gr. 1-4). pap. 12.99 *(978-1-56137-263-8(3),* Novel Units, Inc.) Classroom Library Co.
—The Riddle of Penncroft Farm Novel Units Teacher Guide. 2019. (ENG.). (YA). pap. 12.99 *(978-1-56137-597-4(7),* Novel Units, Inc.) Classroom Library Co.
Nye, Bill & Mone, Gregory. Lost in the Jungle: Jack & the Geniuses Book #3. Iluzada, Nicholas, illus. 2019. (Jack & the Geniuses Ser.). (ENG.). 288p. (J). (gr. 3-7). pap. 7.99 *(978-1-4197-3485-4(7),* 1158103, Amulet Bks.) Abrams, Inc.
Nye, Julie & Nye, Julie. Scout: The Secret at les Cheneaux. 2007. (Illus.). 160p. (YA). per. *(978-0-9767762-1-5(9))* Fieldstone Hill Pr.
O'Brien, Carola. Bobby Dazzler & the Three Rubies of Ishmalan. 2010. 236p. 28.99 *(978-1-60911-285-1(7),* Eloquent Bks.) Strategic Book Publishing & Rights Agency (SBPRA).
O'Brien, Robert C. Z for Zachariah. 2007. 249p. (gr. 7-12). 20.00 *(978-0-7569-8098-6(4))* Perfection Learning Corp.
Obrist, Jurg. Case Closed?! 40 Mini-Mysteries for You to Solve. 2003. (Single Titles Ser.). 96p. (J). pap. 6.95 *(978-0-7613-1999-3(9))* Lerner Publishing Group.
Obrist, Jürg. Case Closed?! 40 Mini-Mysteries for You to Solve. 2003. (Mini-Mysteries for You to Solve Ser.). (ENG.). 96p. (gr. 4-6). 23.93 *(978-0-7613-2739-4(8),* Millbrook Pr.) Lerner Publishing Group.
—Complex Cases: Three Major Mysteries for You to Solve. Obrist, Jürg, illus. 2006. (Mini-Mysteries for You to Solve Ser.). (ENG., Illus.). 96p. (gr. 4-6). 23.93 *(978-0-7613-3419-4(X),* Millbrook Pr.) Lerner Publishing Group.
Obrist, Jurg. Complex Cases: Three Major Mysteries for You to Solve. 2006. (Illus.). (J). pap. 6.95 *(978-0-8225-5975-7(7),* First Avenue Editions) Lerner Publishing Group.
Obrist, Jürg. Open & Shut Cases: 40 More Mini - Mysteries for You to Solve. 2005. (Mini-Mysteries for You to Solve Ser.). (ENG.). 96p. (gr. 4-6). lib. bdg. 23.93 *(978-0-7613-2740-0(1),* Millbrook Pr.) Lerner Publishing Group.
Obrist, Jurg. Open & Shut Cases: 40 More Mini-Mysteries for You to Solve. 2005. (Illus.). 96p. (J). (gr. 4-7). pap. 6.95 *(978-0-7613-2344-0(9),* First Avenue Editions) Lerner Publishing Group.
Ocker, Christa Holder. A Crow Named Robin. 2006. (J). per. *(978-1-59872-712-8(5))* Instant Pub.
O'Connor, Finbar. Wolfgran Returns. Fagan, Martin, illus. 2004. (ENG.). 96p. (J). pap. 10.95 *(978-0-86278-884-1(6))* O'Brien Pr., Ltd., The IRL. Dist: Dufour Editions, Inc.
O'Connor, Jane. Fancy Nancy: Nancy Clancy, Super Sleuth. 2013. (Nancy Clancy Ser.: 1). (J). lib. bdg. 14.75 *(978-0-606-31795-5(3))* Turtleback.
—Fancy Nancy: Nancy Clancy, Super Sleuth. Glasser, Robin Preiss, illus. (Nancy Clancy Ser.: 1). (ENG.). (J). (gr. 1-5). 2013. 144p. pap. 5.99 *(978-0-06-208419-4(4))* 2012. 128p. 9.99 *(978-0-06-208293-0(0))* HarperCollins Pubs. (HarperCollins).
—Fancy Nancy: Nancy Clancy's Tres Charming Chapter Book Box Set: Books 1-3, 3 vols., Set. Glasser, Robin Preiss, illus. 2013. (Nancy Clancy Ser.). (ENG.). 384p. (J). (gr. 1-5). 24.99 *(978-0-06-227793-0(6),* HarperCollins) HarperCollins Pubs.
—Nancy Clancy, Secret of the Silver Key. 2015. (Nancy Clancy Ser.: 4). (J). lib. bdg. 14.75 *(978-0-606-36956-5(2))* Turtleback.
O'Connor, Jane & Glasser, Robin Preiss. Fancy Nancy: Nancy Clancy, Secret of the Silver Key. 2014. (Nancy Clancy Ser.: 4). (ENG., Illus.). 128p. (J). (gr. 1-5). 9.99 *(978-0-06-208299-2(X),* HarperCollins) HarperCollins Pubs.
Odgers, Darrel & Odgers, Sally. The Awful Pawful. Dawson, Janine, illus. 2007. (Jack Russell: Dog Detective Ser.: 5). 96p. (J). (gr. 1-6). pap. 4.99 *(978-1-933605-53-1(7))* Kane Miller.
—The Awful Pawful. 2006. (Illus.). 78p. (J). *(978-0-439-88021-3(1))* Scholastic, Inc.
—The Kitnapped Creature. Dawson, Janine, illus. 2008. (Jack Russell: Dog Detective Ser.: 8). 96p. (J). (gr. 2-6). pap. 4.99 *(978-1-933605-82-1(0))* Kane Miller.
—The Kitnapped Creature. 2008. (Illus.). 76p. (J). pap. *(978-0-545-03338-1(1))* Scholastic, Inc.
—The Lying Postman. 2005. (Illus.). 78p. (J). pap. *(978-0-439-88020-6(3))* Scholastic, Inc.
—The Sausage Situation. Dawson, Janine, illus. 2007. (Jack Russell: Dog Detective Ser.: 6). 96p. (J). (gr. 1-6). pap. 4.99 *(978-1-933605-54-8(5))* Kane Miller.
—The Sausage Situation. 2006. (Jack Russell, Dog Detective Ser.: Bk. 6). (Illus.). 78p. (J). pap. *(978-0-439-92197-8(X))* Scholastic, Inc.
Odgers, Sally & Odgers, Darrel. The Buried Biscuits. Dawson, Janine, illus. 2008. (Jack Russell: Dog Detective Ser.: 7). 96p. (J). (gr. 1-6). pap. 4.99 *(978-1-933605-77-7(4))* Kane Miller.
—Dog Den Mystery. Dawson, Janine, illus. 2006. (Jack Russell: Dog Detective Ser.: 1). 96p. (J). (gr. 1-5). pap. 4.99 *(978-1-933605-18-0(9))* Kane Miller.
O'Doherty, Carolyn. Rewind. (Rewind Ser.: 1). (ENG.). (YA). (gr. 7). 2019. 272p. pap. 8.99 *(978-1-68437-372-7(7))* 2018. 256p. 17.95 *(978-1-62979-814-1(2))* Astra Publishing Hse. (Astra Young Readers).
O'Donnell, Liam. Ganked: Geeked Out Mysteries #1. 2013. 214p. pap. *(978-0-9919281-3-2(X))* Feeding Change Media.
—Tank & Fizz: the Case of Firebane's Folly, 1 vol. Deas, Mike, illus. 2018. (Tank & Fizz Ser.: 4). (ENG.). 256p. (J). (gr. 4-7). pap. 9.95 *(978-1-4598-1261-1(1))* Orca Bk. Pubs. USA.
—Tank & Fizz: the Case of the Battling Bots, 1 vol. Deas, Mike, illus. 2016. (Tank & Fizz Ser.: 2). (ENG.). 176p. (J). (gr. 4-7). pap. 10.95 *(978-1-4598-0813-3(4))* Orca Bk. Pubs. USA.
—Tank & Fizz: the Case of the Missing Mage, 1 vol. Deas, Mike, illus. 2017. (Tank & Fizz Ser.: 3). (ENG.). 208p. (J). (gr. 4-8). pap. 10.95 *(978-1-4598-1258-1(1))* Orca Bk. Pubs. USA.

—West Meadows Detectives: the Case of the Snack Snatcher. Grand, Aurélie, illus. 2018. (West Meadows Detectives Ser.: 1). (ENG.). 128p. (J). (gr. 2-5). pap. 9.95 *(978-1-77147-345-3(2))* Owlkids Bks. Inc. CAN. Dist: Publishers Group West (PGW).

Ogden, Charles. Hot Air. Carton, Rick, illus. 2008. (Edgar & Ellen Nodyssey Ser.: 1). (ENG.). 192p. (J). (gr. 3-7). 9.99 *(978-1-4169-5465-1(1))*, Aladdin) Simon & Schuster Children's Publishing.

Ogilvie, Elizabeth. Masquerade at Sea House. 2007. (J). reprint ed. lib. bdg. 28.95 *(978-0-88411-333-1(7))* Amereon Ltd.

O'Hara, Diarmuid H. The Pool. 2004. 184p. pap. 24.95 *(978-1-4137-2116-4(8))* America Star Bks.

Oldman, James. Superhighway. Ingram, Chris, illus. 2012. 184p. pap. *(978-1-78176-206-6(6))* FeedARead.com.

Olds, Barbara Anne. Haven House. Amatrula, Michele, illus. 2007. (ENG.). 148p. (J). (gr. 4-6). pap. 10.95 *(978-0-9744446-0-4(X))* All About Kids Publishing.

O'Leary, Edward J. Murder in the I. R. S. 2003. (YA). per. 18.95 *(978-0-9708590-9-9(0))* First Word Publishing, The.

Olien, Jessica. Shark Detective! 2015. (ENG., Illus.). 32p. (J). (gr. -1-3). 17.99 *(978-0-06-235714-4(X)*, Balzer & Bray) HarperCollins Pubs.

Oliver, Andrew. Haunted Hill. 2006. (Sam & Stephanie Mystery Ser.). 268p. (J). (gr. 5-9). per. 12.95 *(978-0-9661009-7-6(2))* Adams-Pomeroy Pr.

—If Photos Could Talk. 2005. (Sam & Stephanie Mystery Ser.). 264p. (J). per. 12.95 *(978-0-9661009-6-9(4))* Adams-Pomeroy Pr.

—Scrambled. 2007. 288p. (J). per. 12.95 *(978-0-9661009-8-3(0))* Adams-Pomeroy Pr.

Oliver, Lauren. Panic. 2015. (ENG.). 432p. (gr. 9-12). 28.69 *(978-1-4844-5031-4(0))* 2015. (ENG.). 432p. (YA). (gr. 9). pap. 10.99 *(978-0-06-201456-6(0)*, HarperCollins) 2014. (J). 137.91 *(978-0-06-230092-8(X))* 2014. (ENG.). 416p. (YA). (gr. 9). 18.99 *(978-0-06-201455-9(2)*, HarperCollins) HarperCollins Pubs.

—Panic. 2015. (YA). lib. bdg. 20.85 *(978-0-606-36509-3(5))* Turtleback.

Oliver, Lauren & Chester, H. C. Curiosity House: the Fearsome Firebird. 2018. (Curiosity House Ser.: 3). (ENG.). 336p. (J). (gr. 3-7). pap. 6.99 *(978-0-06-227088-7(5)*, HarperCollins) HarperCollins Pubs.

—Curiosity House: the Screaming Statue. 2017. (Curiosity House Ser.: 2). (ENG.). 384p. (J). (gr. 3-7). pap. 6.99 *(978-0-06-227085-6(0)*, HarperCollins) HarperCollins Pubs.

—Curiosity House: the Shrunken Head. Lacombe, Benjamin, illus. 2015. (Curiosity House Ser.: 1). (ENG.). 368p. (J). (gr. 3-7). 16.99 *(978-0-06-227081-8(8)*, HarperCollins) HarperCollins Pubs.

—The Screaming Statue. 2016. (Illus.). 361p. (J). *(978-0-06-245885-8(X))* Harper & Row Ltd.

Olney, Ross R. Time Dial, 1 vol. 2010. 134p. pap. 24.95 *(978-1-4489-4371-5(X))* America Star Bks.

O'Malley, Kevin. Captain Raptor & the Moon Mystery. O'Brien, Patrick, illus. 2005. (Captain Raptor Ser.). (ENG.). 32p. (J). (gr. k-5). 19.99 *(978-0-8027-8935-8(8)*, 900034813, Bloomsbury USA Childrens) Bloomsbury Publishing USA.

O'Neil-Andrews, Milly. Bandolines & Bubbles. 2011. 88p. pap. 11.25 *(978-1-4269-3089-8(5))* Trafford Publishing.

Orczy, Emmuska. The Old Man in the Corner. 2008. (J). 8.99 *(978-1-59166-952-4(9))* BJU Pr.

—The Old Man in the Corner. 2008. 188p. pap. 13.95 *(978-1-60664-231-3(6))* Rodgers, Alan Bks.

—The Scarlet Pimpernel. 2008. 208p. 27.95 *(978-1-60664-862-9(4))*; pap. 14.95 *(978-1-60664-109-5(3))* Aegypan.

Orlando, Martha Jane. A Trip, a Tryst & a Terror. 2012. 134p. pap. 10.95 *(978-1-939289-03-2(3)*, Little Creek Bks.) Jan-Carol Publishing, INC.

Orloff, Karen Kaufman. Nightlight Detective: Big Top Circus Mystery. Smith, Jamie, illus. 2013. 42p. spiral bd. 12.99 *(978-1-4413-1227-3(7))* Peter Pauper Pr. Inc.

—Nightlight Detective: Mystery at the Museum. Smith, Jamie, illus. 2013. 42p. spiral bd. 12.99 *(978-1-4413-1228-0(5))* Peter Pauper Pr. Inc.

Ormsbee, K. E. The House in Poplar Wood: (Fantasy Middle Grade Novel, Mystery Book for Middle School Kids) 2018. (ENG., Illus.). 344p. (J). (gr. 3-7). 16.99 *(978-1-4521-4986-8(0))* Chronicle Bks. LLC.

Oroge, Sabinah. Oluwatofarati & Friends. 2013. 28p. pap. 9.95 *(978-1-4787-0520-8(5))* Outskirts Pr., Inc.

Orris, Cornelius F. The Curious Adventures of Nigel & Viol. 2010. 94p. 19.99 *(978-1-4500-4463-9(8))* Xlibris Corp.

Orshoski, Paul. We Read Phonics-Who Took the Cookbook? Light, Kelly, illus. 2012. 32p. (J). 9.95 *(978-1-60115-347-0(3))*; pap. 4.99 *(978-1-60115-348-7(1))* Treasure Bay, Inc.

Osborne, Mary Pope, et al. The Fun Starts Here! Four Favorite Chapter Books in One: Junie B. Jones, Magic Tree House, Purrmaids, & a to Z Mysteries. Murdocca, Sal, illus. 2018. (ENG.). 336p. (J). (gr. 1-4). 9.99 *(978-1-9848-3059-3(7)*, Random Hse. Bks. for Young Readers) Random Hse. Children's Bks.

Osorio, Rick. The Great Adventure of Sally Rock & el Lobo. 2007. (ENG.). 96p. per. 19.95 *(978-1-4241-5869-0(9))* America Star Bks.

Ostow, Micol. GoldenGirl. 2009. (Bradford Ser.). (ENG.). 224p. (YA). (gr. 9-18). pap. 9.99 *(978-1-4169-6118-5(6)*, Simon Pulse) Simon Pulse.

Packard, Edward. The Forbidden Castle. Willis, Drew, illus. 2013. (U-Ventures Ser.). (ENG.). 192p. (J). (gr. 3-7). pap. 7.99 *(978-1-4424-3428-8(7)*, Simon & Schuster Bks. For Young Readers) Simon & Schuster Bks. For Young Readers.

Page, Nathan. The Montague Twins: the Witch's Hand: (a Graphic Novel) Shannon, Drew, illus. 2020. (Montague Twins Ser.: 1). 352p. (YA). (gr. 7). pap. 17.99 *(978-0-525-64677-8(9)*, Knopf Bks. for Young Readers) Random Hse. Children's Bks.

PaleoJoe. The Disappearance of Dinosaur SUE(r). Caszatt-Allen, Wendy, illus. 2006. (PaleoJoe's Dinosaur Detective Club Ser.: 1). 144p. (J). (gr. 2-5). pap. 8.95 *(978-1-934133-03-3(5)*, Mackinac Island Press, Inc.) Charlesbridge Publishing, Inc.

PaleoJoe & Caszatt-Allen, Wendy. Mysterious Mammoths. 2008. (PaleoJoe's Dinosaur Detective Club Ser.). (Illus.). 200p. (J). (gr. 2-5). pap. 8.95 *(978-1-934133-43-9(4)*, Mackinac Island Press, Inc.) Charlesbridge Publishing, Inc.

—Secret Sabertooth. 2007. (PaleoJoe's Dinosaur Detective Club Ser.: 3). (Illus.). 168p. (J). (gr. 2-5). pap. 8.95 *(978-1-934133-10-1(8)*, Mackinac Island Press, Inc.) Charlesbridge Publishing, Inc.

Palund, Linda. The Little Black Dress. 2016. (ENG., Illus.). (J). 24.99 *(978-1-63477-970-8(3)*, Harmony Ink Pr.) Dreamspinner Pr.

Panckridge, Michael & Harvey, Pam. Ghost of a Chance. 2007. (ENG.). 208p. *(978-0-207-20063-2(7))* HarperCollins Pubs. Australia.

—Into the Fire. 2008. (ENG.). 194p. (J). *(978-0-207-20061-8(0))* HarperCollins Pubs. Australia.

Panda, Jake G. The Case of the Cursed Dodo. 2014. (Illus.). 173p. (J). pap. 8.99 *(978-0-9909391-1-5(1))* Woolley Family Studios.

Pandanas, Ms L. A. The Slinky Luminescence: Two Plus Who? 2013. 84p. pap. *(978-0-9870702-9-6(0))* Reed, Laura.

Pankhurst, Kate. Mariella Mystery Investigates a Cupcake Conundrum. 2014. (Mariella Mysteries Ser.). (ENG., Illus.). 176p. (J). (gr. 2-6). pap. 5.99 *(978-1-4380-0459-4(1))* Sourcebooks, Inc.

—Mariella Mystery Investigates a Kitty Calamity. 2015. (Mariella Mysteries Ser.). (ENG., Illus.). 176p. (J). (gr. 2-6). pap. 5.99 *(978-1-4380-0704-5(3))* Sourcebooks, Inc.

—Mariella Mystery Investigates the Ghostly Guinea Pig. 2014. (Mariella Mysteries Ser.). (ENG., Illus.). 176p. (J). (gr. 2-6). pap. 5.99 *(978-1-4380-0460-0(5))* Sourcebooks, Inc.

—Mariella Mystery Investigates the Huge Hair Scare. 2014. (Mariella Mysteries Ser.). (ENG., Illus.). 176p. (J). (gr. 2-6). pap. 5.99 *(978-1-4380-0461-7(3))* Sourcebooks, Inc.

Papp, Robert, illus. The Amazing Mystery Show. 2010. (Boxcar Children Mysteries Ser.: 123). (ENG.). 128p. (J). (gr. 2-5). pap. 7.99 *(978-0-8075-0315-7(0)*, 807503150);No. 123. 14.99 *(978-0-8075-0314-0(2)*, 807503142) Random Hse. Children's Bks. (Random Hse. Bks. for Young Readers).

—The Clue in the Recycling Bin. 2011. (Boxcar Children Mysteries Ser.: 126). (ENG.). 128p. (J). (gr. 2-5). pap. 6.99 *(978-0-8075-1209-8(5)*, 807512095); lib. bdg. 14.99 *(978-0-8075-1208-1(7)*, 807512087) Random Hse. Children's Bks. (Random Hse. Bks. for Young Readers).

—The Cupcake Caper. 2010. (Boxcar Children Mysteries Ser.: 125). (ENG.). (J). (gr. 2-5). 104p. 14.99 *(978-0-8075-1373-6(3)*, 807513733);No. 125. 112p. pap. 7.99 *(978-0-8075-1374-3(1)*, 807513741) Random Hse. Children's Bks. (Random Hse. Bks. for Young Readers).

—The Dog-Gone Mystery. 2009. (Boxcar Children Mysteries Ser.: 119). (ENG.). 128p. (J). (gr. 2-5). pap. 6.99 *(978-0-8075-1657-7(0)*, 807516570, Random Hse. Bks. for Young Readers) Random Hse. Children's Bks.

—The Ghost of the Chattering Bones. 2007. (Boxcar Children Ser.). 120p. 15.00 *(978-0-7569-7611-8(1))* Perfection Learning Corp.

—The Great Turkey Heist. 2011. (Boxcar Children Mysteries Ser.: 129). (ENG.) (J). (gr. 2-5). 144p. 6.99 *(978-0-8075-3051-1(4)*, 807530514); 128p. lib. bdg. 14.99 *(978-0-8075-3050-4(6)*, 807530506) Random Hse. Children's Bks. (Random Hse. Bks. for Young Readers).

—Monkey Trouble. 2011. (Boxcar Children Mysteries Ser.: 127). (ENG.). 128p. (J). (gr. 2-5). pap. 7.99 *(978-0-8075-5240-7(2)*, 807552402); lib. bdg. 14.99 *(978-0-8075-5239-1(9)*, 807552399) Random Hse. Children's Bks. (Random Hse. Bks. for Young Readers).

—The Pumpkin Head Mystery. 2010. (Boxcar Children Mysteries Ser.: 124). (ENG.). 128p. (J). (gr. 2-5). 14.99 *(978-0-8075-6668-8(3)*, 807566683);No. 124. pap. 5.99 *(978-0-8075-6669-5(1)*, 807566691) Random Hse. Children's Bks. (Random Hse. Bks. for Young Readers).

—Spooktacular Special. 2013. (Boxcar Children Mysteries Ser.). (ENG.). 400p. (J). (gr. 2-5). 9.99 *(978-0-8075-7605-2(0)*, 807576050, Random Hse. Bks. for Young Readers) Random Hse. Children's Bks.

—The Spy Game. 2009. (Boxcar Children Mysteries Ser.: 118). (ENG.). 128p. (J). (gr. 2-5). 14.99 *(978-0-8075-7603-8(4)*, 807576034); pap. 5.99 *(978-0-8075-7604-5(2)*, 807576042) Random Hse. Children's Bks. (Random Hse. Bks. for Young Readers).

—The Spy in the Bleachers. 2010. (Boxcar Children Mysteries Ser.: 122). (ENG.). 128p. (J). (gr. 2-5). 14.99 *(978-0-8075-7606-9(9)*, 807576069, Random Hse. Bks. for Young Readers) Random Hse. Children's Bks.

—Superstar Watch. 2009. (Boxcar Children Mysteries Ser.: 121). (ENG.). 128p. (J). (gr. 2-5). pap. 6.99 *(978-0-8075-7668-7(9)*, 807576689); lib. bdg. 14.99 *(978-0-8075-7667-0(0)*, 807576670) Random Hse. Children's Bks. (Random Hse. Bks. for Young Readers).

—The Vampire Mystery. 2009. (Boxcar Children Mysteries Ser.: 120). (ENG.). 128p. (J). (gr. 2-5). pap. 6.99 *(978-0-8075-8461-3(4)*, 807584614, Random Hse. Bks. for Young Readers) Random Hse. Children's Bks.

—The Zombie Project. 2011. (Boxcar Children Mysteries Ser.: 128). (ENG.). 128p. (J). (gr. 2-5). 6.99 *(978-0-8075-9493-3(8)*, 807594938); lib. bdg. 14.99 *(978-0-8075-9492-6(X)*, 080759492X) Random Hse. Children's Bks. (Random Hse. Bks. for Young Readers).

Paris, Harper. The Mystery Across the Secret Bridge. Calo, Marcos, illus. 2015. (Greetings from Somewhere Ser.: 7). (ENG.). 128p. (J). (gr. k-4). pap. 6.99 *(978-1-4814-2367-0(3)*, Little Simon) Little Simon.

—The Mystery at the Coral Reef. Calo, Marcos, illus. 2015. (Greetings from Somewhere Ser.: 8). (ENG.). 128p. (J). (gr. k-4). pap. 6.99 *(978-1-4814-2370-0(3)*, Little Simon) Little Simon.

—The Mystery in the Forbidden City. Calo, Marcos, illus. 2014. (Greetings from Somewhere Ser.: 4). (ENG.). 128p. (J). (gr. k-4). pap. 6.99 *(978-1-4814-0299-6(4)*, Little Simon) Little Simon.

—The Mystery of the Gold Coin. Calo, Marcos, illus. 2014. (Greetings from Somewhere Ser.: 1). (ENG.). 128p. (J). (gr. k-4). pap. 5.99 *(978-1-4424-9718-4(1)*, Little Simon) Little Simon.

—The Mystery of the Icy Paw Prints. Calo, Marcos, illus. 2015. (Greetings from Somewhere Ser.: 9). (ENG.). 128p. (J). (gr. k-4). pap. 5.99 *(978-1-4814-2373-1(8)*, Little Simon) Little Simon.

—The Mystery of the Mosaic. Calo, Marcos, illus. 2014. (Greetings from Somewhere Ser.: 2). (ENG.). 128p. (J). (gr. k-2). pap. 6.99 *(978-1-4424-9721-4(1)*, Little Simon) Little Simon.

—The Mystery of the Mosaic. Calo, Marcos, illus. 2014. (Greetings from Somewhere Ser.: Vol. 2). (ENG.). 115p. (J). (gr. k-2). lib. bdg. 16.80 *(978-1-62765-837-9(8))* Perfection Learning Corp.

—The Mystery of the Secret Society. Calo, Marcos, illus. 2016. (Greetings from Somewhere Ser.: 10). (ENG.). 128p. (J). (gr. k-4). pap. 5.99 *(978-1-4814-5171-0(5)*, Little Simon) Little Simon.

—The Mystery of the Stolen Painting. Calo, Marcos, illus. 2014. (Greetings from Somewhere Ser.: 3). (ENG.). 128p. (J). (gr. k-4). pap. 6.99 *(978-1-4814-0296-5(X)*, Little Simon) Little Simon.

—The Mystery of the Suspicious Spices. Calo, Marcos, illus. 2014. (Greetings from Somewhere Ser.: 6). (ENG.). 128p. (J). (gr. k-4). pap. 6.99 *(978-1-4814-1467-8(4)*, Little Simon) Little Simon.

Park, Alexander. The Thunderbolts & the Circle of Power. 2012. 316p. pap. 25.86 *(978-1-60746-939-1(1))* FastPrncl, Inc.

Parker, Robert B. The Boxer & the Spy. 2009. (ENG.). 240p. (YA). (gr. 9-18). pap. 8.99 *(978-0-14-241439-2(5)*, Speak) Penguin Young Readers Group.

Parkhurst, Johanna. Every Inferno. 2016. (ENG., Illus.). (J). 24.99 *(978-1-63533-009-0(2)*, Harmony Ink Pr.) Dreamspinner Pr.

Parkinson, Curtis. Death in Kingsport. 2007. 224p. (YA). (gr. 7-9). per. 11.95 *(978-0-88776-827-9(X)*, Tundra Bks.) Tundra Bks. CAN. Dist: Penguin Random Hse. LLC.

Parks, Tiffany. Midnight in the Piazza. 2018. (ENG.). 304p. (J). (gr. 3-7). 16.99 *(978-0-06-264452-7(1)*, HarperCollins) HarperCollins Pubs.

Parsons, Carol. Mystery at Eagle Harbor Lighthouse. 2006. (J). pap. 11.95 *(978-1-59705-985-5(4))* Wings ePress, Inc.

Parsons, Caroline Renee. The Coffins in the Basement. 2008. 134p. pap. 24.95 *(978-1-60563-140-0(X))* America Star Bks.

Parsons, Tom. Pinky the Rat at the Brussels Sprout Museum. 2007. 194p. 27.76 *(978-1-4303-1538-4(5))* Lulu Pr., Inc.

Parus, M. V. The Adventures of Mamma Simone, Jodie & Zed: The Mystery of the Pirate's Lost Treasure. 2006. 115p. (YA). per. 12.95 *(978-1-58374-148-1(8))* Chicago Spectrum Pr.

Pasha, Georgia. Jelly Bean & Key Mystery. 2005. 17.00 *(978-0-8059-9909-9(4)*, RoseDog Bks.) Dorrance Publishing Co., Inc.

Pastis, Stephan. The Cat Stole My Pants. 2017. (Illus.). 304p. (J). *(978-1-4063-7716-3(3))* Candlewick Pr.

—Mistakes Were Made. 2015. (Timmy Failure Ser.: 1). lib. bdg. 18.40 *(978-0-606-36864-3(7))* Turtleback.

—Now Look What You've Done. 2016. (Timmy Failure Ser.: 2). lib. bdg. 18.40 *(978-0-606-37947-2(9))* Turtleback.

—Timmy Failure: Mistakes Were Made. Pastis, Stephan, illus. (Timmy Failure Ser.: 1). (ENG., Illus.). (J). (gr. 3-7). 2015. 320p. pap. 8.99 *(978-0-7636-6927-0(X))* 2013. 304p. 14.99 *(978-0-7636-6050-5(7))* Candlewick Pr.

—Timmy Failure: Mistakes Were Made. 2013. (Timmy Failure Ser.: 1). (J). 189.75 *(978-1-4703-8572-9(4))*; 189.75 *(978-1-4703-8569-9(4))*; 50.75 *(978-1-4703-8573-6(2))*; 50.75 *(978-1-4703-8570-5(8))*; 1.25 *(978-1-4703-9703-6(X))* Recorded Bks., Inc.

—Timmy Failure: Now Look What You've Done! 2014. (Timmy Failure Ser.: 2). (J). 184.75 *(978-1-4906-0682-8(3))* Recorded Bks., Inc.

—Timmy Failure: Mistakes Were Made: Limited Edition. Pastis, Stephan, illus. ltd. ed. 2013. (Timmy Failure Ser.). (ENG., Illus.). 304p. (J). (gr. 3-7). 100.00 *(978-0-7636-6689-7(0))* Candlewick Pr.

—Timmy Failure: Now Look What Mistakes Were Made. Pastis, Stephan, illus. 2017. (Timmy Failure Ser.). (ENG., Illus.). 592p. (J). (gr. 3-7). pap. 12.99 *(978-0-7636-9760-0(5))* Candlewick Pr.

—Timmy Failure: Now Look What You've Done. Pastis, Stephan, illus. 2016. (Timmy Failure Ser.: 2). (ENG., Illus.). 304p. (J). (gr. 3-7). pap. 7.99 *(978-0-7636-8014-5(1))* Candlewick Pr.

—Timmy Failure: the Book You're Not Supposed to Have. Pastis, Stephan, illus. (Timmy Failure Ser.: 5). (ENG., Illus.). 304p. (J). (gr. 3-7). 2019. pap. 7.99 *(978-1-5362-0908-2(2))* 2018. 15.99 *(978-0-7636-9004-5(X))* Candlewick Pr.

—Timmy Failure: the Cat Stole My Pants. Pastis, Stephan, illus. (Timmy Failure Ser.: 6). (ENG., Illus.). 288p. (J). (gr. 3-7). 2019. pap. 7.99 *(978-1-5362-0909-9(0))* 2017. 14.99 *(978-0-7636-9733-4(8))* Candlewick Pr.

Pastor, Norma. The Young Alchemists & the Vatican's Legion of Evil. 2013. 472p. pap. 30.95 *(978-1-4633-6179-2(3))* Palibrio.

Patchin, Frank Gee. The Pony Rider Boys in the Grand Canyon: The Mystery of Bright Angel Gulch. 2017. (ENG., Illus.). (J). 23.95 *(978-1-374-95129-7(3))*; pap. 13.95 *(978-1-374-95128-0(5))* Capital Communications, Inc.

Paterson, Katherine. La Busqueda de Park. 2003. (Katherine Patterson Ser.). Tr. of Park's Quest. (SPA., Illus.). 208p. (J). (gr. 4-7). 9.95 *(978-84-239-2816-3(0)*, EC3399) Espasa Calpe, S.A. ESP. Dist: Planeta Publishing Corp.

Patterson, Eric. Something Lurking in the Bell Tower. Christopher, Wright, illus. 2007. 99p. (J). pap. 6.95 *(978-0-9797106-1-2(8))* Avid Readers Publishing Group.

Patterson, James. Ali Cross. (Ali Cross Ser.: 1). (ENG.). (J). (gr. 5-9). 2020. 336p. pap. 8.99 *(978-0-316-70568-4(3))* 2019. 320p. 16.99 *(978-0-316-53041-5(7))* Little Brown & Co. (Jimmy Patterson).

—Ali Cross: Like Father, Like Son. (Ali Cross Ser.: 2). (ENG.). (J). (gr. 5-9). 2022. 320p. pap. 8.99 *(978-0-316-42377-9(7))* 2021. (Illus.). 304p. 16.99 *(978-0-316-50013-5(5))* Little Brown & Co. (Jimmy Patterson).

—Ali Cross: the Secret Detective. 2022. (Ali Cross Ser.: 3). (ENG.). 272p. (J). (gr. 5-9). 16.99 *(978-0-316-40991-9(X)*, Jimmy Patterson) Little Brown & Co.

—Expelled. 2017. (ENG.). 304p. (YA). (gr. 10-17). 17.99 *(978-0-316-44039-4(6)*, Jimmy Patterson) Little Brown & Co.

—The Injustice. 2018. (ENG.). 336p. (YA). (gr. 10-17). pap. 9.99 *(978-0-316-47883-0(0)*, Jimmy Patterson) Little Brown & Co.

Patterson, James & Paetro, Maxine. Confessions of a Murder Suspect. (YA). 2013. (Confessions Ser.: 1). (ENG.). 400p. (gr. 7-17). pap. 10.99 *(978-0-316-20700-3(4)*, Jimmy Patterson) 2012. (Confessions Ser.: 1). (ENG.). 384p. (gr. 7-17). 19.99 *(978-0-316-20698-3(9)*, Jimmy Patterson) 2012. 372p. 11.99 *(978-0-316-22641-7(6))* 2012. (Confessions Ser.: 1). (ENG.). 400p. (gr. 7-17). 36.99 *(978-0-316-22418-5(9)*, Jimmy Patterson) Little Brown & Co.

—Confessions of a Murder Suspect. 2013. (Confessions Ser.: 1). lib. bdg. 20.85 *(978-0-606-32278-2(7))* Turtleback.

—Confessions: the Paris Mysteries. 2014. (Confessions Ser.: 3). (ENG.). (YA). (gr. 7-17). 320p. 33.99 *(978-0-316-37084-4(3))*; 352p. 35.99 *(978-0-316-40963-6(4))* Little Brown & Co. (Jimmy Patterson).

—The Paris Mysteries. 2015. (Confessions Ser.: 3). (YA). lib. bdg. 20.85 *(978-0-606-37526-9(0))* Turtleback.

—The Private School Murders. 2014. (Confessions Ser.: 2). (YA). lib. bdg. 20.85 *(978-0-606-35945-0(1))* Turtleback.

Patton, Donna Alice. The Gift of Summer Snow: A Tale from the Garden of Mysteries. 2010. (Illus.). ix, 133p. (J). *(978-0-9826867-3-7(0))* Philothea Pr.

Paul, Naomi. Code Name Komiko, 1 vol. 2014. (Scarlet Voyage Ser.). (ENG.). 288p. (gr. 6-7). 41.27 *(978-1-62324-023-3(9)*, 2a196b31-55b7-46ff-8c6a-6b9f51c5363b) Enslow Publishing, LLC.

Pauley, Kimberly. Cat Girl's Day Off, 1 vol. (ENG.). (YA). 2018. 352p. (gr. 6-12). pap. 13.95 *(978-1-64379-050-3(1)*, leelowtu) 2012. 336p. 17.95 *(978-1-60060-883-4(3))* Lee & Low Bks., Inc. (Tu Bks.).

Paulits, John. Philip & the Case of the Mistaken Identity & Philip & the Baby. 2007. (ENG.). 150p. (YA). pap. 10.95 *(978-1-59705-897-1(1))* Wings ePress, Inc.

Paulson, Michael W. The Baker Street Bunch & the Missing Pig Mystery. l.t. ed. 2004. (Illus.). 90p. (J). per. 3.95 *(978-0-9754241-1-7(4))* MiMar Publishing.

Paulson, Michael William. The Baker Street Bunch & the Hidden Map Mystery. 2005. (Illus.). (J). per. *(978-0-9754241-4-8(9))* MiMar Publishing.

—The Baker Street Bunch & the Missing Bracelet Mystery. 2005. (Illus.). (J). per. *(978-0-9754241-2-4(2))* MiMar Publishing.

—The Baker Street Bunch & the Missing Pie Mystery. 2005. (J). per. *(978-0-9754241-9-3(X))* MiMar Publishing.

Payjack, Amy J. The Valorean. 2012. 426p. 34.99 *(978-1-4771-5239-3(3))*; pap. 23.99 *(978-1-4771-5238-6(5))* Xlibris Corp.

Payson, Howard. Boy Scouts' Mountain Camp. 2005. (Illus.). pap. 28.95 *(978-1-885529-54-1(6))* Stevens Publishing.

Peacock, Kathleen. Hemlock. 2013. (Shifters Novel Ser.: 1). (ENG.). 432p. (YA). (gr. 9). pap. 9.99 *(978-0-06-204866-0(X)*, Tegen, Katherine Bks) HarperCollins Pubs.

—Thornhill. 2015. (Shifters Novel Ser.: 2). (ENG.). 368p. (YA). (gr. 9). pap. 9.99 *(978-0-06-204869-1(4)*, Tegen, Katherine Bks) HarperCollins Pubs.

Peacock, Shane. Eye of the Crow: The Boy Sherlock Holmes, His First Case. 2007. (Boy Sherlock Holmes Ser.: 1). 264p. (YA). (gr. 7-9). 19.95 *(978-0-88776-850-7(4)*, Tundra Bks.) Tundra Bks. CAN. Dist: Penguin Random Hse. LLC.

—The Secret Fiend: The Boy Sherlock Holmes, His Fourth Case. 2012. (Boy Sherlock Holmes Ser.: 4). (Illus.). 256p. (YA). (gr. 7-9). pap. 11.99 *(978-1-77049-385-8(9)*, Tundra Bks.) Tundra Bks. CAN. Dist: Penguin Random Hse. LLC.

—Vanishing Girl: The Boy Sherlock Holmes, His Third Case. 2010. (Boy Sherlock Holmes Ser.: 3). (Illus.). 336p. (YA). (gr. 7-9). pap. 11.99 *(978-1-77049-234-9(8)*, Tundra Bks.) Tundra Bks. CAN. Dist: Penguin Random Hse. LLC.

Pearl, Beverly. Poison Ivy. 2008. (ENG.). 71p. pap. 9.99 *(978-1-4357-1386-4(9))* Lulu Pr., Inc.

Pearson, Ridley. Lock & Key: the Downward Spiral. 2017. (Lock & Key Ser.: 2). (ENG.). 432p. (J). (gr. 3-7). 17.99 *(978-0-06-239904-5(7)*, HarperCollins) HarperCollins Pubs.

—Lock & Key: the Initiation. 2017. (Lock & Key Ser.: 1). (ENG.). 384p. (J). (gr. 3-7). pap. 9.99 *(978-0-06-239902-1(0)*, HarperCollins) HarperCollins Pubs.

Peckham, Lori, ed. Guide's Greatest Mystery Stories. 2007. 155p. (J). per. 11.99 *(978-0-8280-2038-1(8))* Review & Herald Publishing Assn.

Peers, Bobbie. William Wenton & the Lost City. Chace, Tara F., tr. 2019. (William Wenton Ser.: 3). (ENG., Illus.). 256p. (J). (gr. 3-7). 17.99 *(978-1-4814-7831-1(1)*, Aladdin) Simon & Schuster Children's Publishing.

—William Wenton & the Secret Portal. Chace, Tara F., tr. 2019. (William Wenton Ser.: 2). (ENG.). 288p. (J). (gr. 3-7). pap. 7.99 *(978-1-4814-7829-8(X)*, Aladdin) Simon & Schuster Children's Publishing.

Pelosi, Catherine. Quark's Academy. 2019. (ENG.). 240p. (J). (gr. 3-7). 11.99 *(978-0-7344-1780-0(2)*, Lothian Children's Bks.) Hachette Australia AUS. Dist: Hachette Bk. Group.

Penn, Audrey. Blackbeard & the Gift of Silence. 2009. (ENG.). 350p. (J). (gr. 2-7). pap. 8.95 *(978-1-933718-32-3(3))* Tanglewood Pr.

—Blackbeard & the Sandstone Pillar: When Lightning Strikes. 2009. (ENG.). 350p. (J). (gr. 2-7). pap. 8.95 *(978-1-933718-31-6(5))* Tanglewood Pr.

—Mystery at Blackbeard's Cove. 2004. (ENG., Illus.). 263p. (J). (gr. 3-12). per. 7.95 *(978-1-933718-09-5(9))* Tanglewood Pr.

—Mystery at Blackbeard's Cove. Howard, Philip & Miller, Josh, illus. 2004. (ENG.). 200p. (J). (gr. 3-7). 14.95 *(978-0-9749303-1-2(8))* Tanglewood Pr.

Pennell, Kathleen. The Phantom Stallion. Pennell, Lauren, illus. 2003. (Pony Investigators Ser.: Vol. 4). 118p. (J). (gr. 3-7). pap. 5.95 *(978-1-930353-73-2(1))* Masthof Pr.

—The Secret Passage: Pony Investigators Series #5. 2005. (Pony Investigators Ser.: 5). (Illus.). 108p. (J). pap. 5.95 *(978-1-932864-42-7(3))* Masthof Pr.

Penner, Stephen. Professor Barrister's Dinosaur Mysteries #1: The Case of the Truncated Troodon. Penner, Stephen, illus. 2010. (Illus.). 44p. pap. 19.25 *(978-1-60888-005-8(2))* Nimble Bks. LLC.

—Professor Barrister's Dinosaur Mysteries #2: The Case of the Armored Allosaurus. 2010. 54p. pap. 19.60 *(978-1-60888-018-8(4))* Nimble Bks. LLC.

MNO

Penney, Shannon. Decodes a Mystery. 2005. 22p. *(978-0-439-67841-4(2))* Scholastic, Inc.

Peralta, Joaquin. An Almost Private Eye: Mystery of the Starfighter. 2008. 260p. (YA). (gr. 8-18). per. 17.00 *(978-1-934376-17-1(5))* Balona Bks.

Perelman, Helen. Marshmallow Mystery. Waters, Erica-Jane, illus. 2014. (Candy Fairies Ser.: 12). (ENG.). 128p. (J). (gr. 2-5). 15.99 *(978-1-4424-6500-8(X))*; pap. 6.99 *(978-1-4424-5301-2(X))* Simon & Schuster Children's Publishing. (Aladdin).

Peretti, Frank E. Hangman's Curse. 2008. 352p. (YA). mass mkt. 7.99 *(978-1-4003-1016-6(4))* Nelson, Thomas Inc.

—Nightmare Academy. 2008. 352p. (YA). mass mkt. 7.99 *(978-1-4003-1017-3(2))* Nelson, Thomas Inc.

Perkins, T. J. Image in the Tapestry: A Kim & Kelly Mystery. 2005. (Illus.). 155p. (YA). 10.99 *(978-0-9777538-3-3(2))* GumShoe Press.

—In the Grand Scheme of Things: A Kim & Kelly Mystery. 2007. (Illus.). 151p. (YA). 10.99 *(978-0-9777538-4-0(0))* GumShoe Press.

—Mystery of the Attic. 2006. (Illus.). 113p. (YA). 10.99 *(978-0-9777538-6-4(7))* GumShoe Press.

—The Secret in Phantom Forest: A Kim & Kelly Mystery. 2004. (Illus.). 130p. (YA). 10.99 *(978-0-9777538-1-9(6))* GumShoe Press.

—Wound Too Tight. 2006. (Illus.). 141p. (YA). 10.99 *(978-0-9777538-5-7(9))* GumShoe Press.

Perkins, TJ. Fantasies Are Murder: A Kim & Kelly Mystery. novel ed. 2005. (Illus.). 148p. (YA). 10.99 *(978-0-9777538-0-2(8))* GumShoe Press.

—Trade Secret: A Kim & Kelly Mystery. 2004. (Illus.). 175p. (YA). 10.99 *(978-0-9777538-2-6(4))* GumShoe Press.

Perry, Phyllis J. The Secret of the Silver Key. Lipking, Ron, illus. 2003. (Fribble Mouse Library Mystery Ser.). 90p. (J). pap. 16.95 *(978-1-932146-03-5(2))* Highsmith Inc.

—The Secrets of the Rock. Lipking, Ron, illus. 2004. (Fribble Mouse Library Mystery Ser.). 96p. (J). 16.95 *(978-1-932146-22-6(9)*, 1237661) Highsmith Inc.

Perry, R. W. Kelly Mccabe in Slow Boat to Terror. 2003. 160p. (J). (gr. 3-6). pap. 11.95 *(978-0-9745522-0-0(8)*, Greenleaf Book Group Pr.) Greenleaf Book Group.

Peters, Tony. Kids on a Case: The Case of the Ten Grand Kidnapping. 2008. 84p. pap. 9.95 *(978-1-60693-173-8(3)*, Eloquent Bks.) Strategic Book Publishing & Rights Agency (SBPRA).

Peterson Haddix, Margaret. El desafío final: The 39 Clues 10. 2013. (SPA.). 304p. (J). pap. 14.99 *(978-84-08-10876-4(X))* Noguer y Caralt Editores, S. A. ESP. Dist: Lectorum Pubns., Inc.

Peterson, Paige. Logic Lotty: The Fortune Teller's Spoon. Sabater, Gaspar, illus. 2015. (ENG.). 82p. (J). pap. 6.99 *(978-0-9907895-0-5(0))* Hollingale Bks. LLC.

Peterson, Shelley. Christmas at Saddle Creek: The Saddle Creek Series. 2017. (Saddle Creek Ser.: 5). (ENG., Illus.). 176p. (YA). pap. 12.99 *(978-1-4597-4026-6(2))* Dundurn Pr. CAN. Dist: Publishers Group West (PGW).

—Dark Days at Saddle Creek: The Saddle Creek Series. 2017. (Saddle Creek Ser.: 4). (ENG.). 344p. (YA). pap. 12.99 *(978-1-4597-3954-3(X))* Dundurn Pr. CAN. Dist: Publishers Group West (PGW).

—Mystery at Saddle Creek: The Saddle Creek Series. 2017. (Saddle Creek Ser.: 3). (ENG.). 392p. (YA). pap. 12.99 *(978-1-4597-3951-2(5))* Dundurn Pr. CAN. Dist: Publishers Group West (PGW).

—Stagestruck: The Saddle Creek Series. 2017. (Saddle Creek Ser.: 1). (ENG.). 344p. (YA). pap. 12.99 *(978-1-4597-3945-1(0))* Dundurn Pr. CAN. Dist: Publishers Group West (PGW).

Petit, Karen. The Mystery of the Screecher Creature: A Shandon's Ivy League Mystery. 2006. (J). per. 14.95 *(978-1-59872-666-4(8))* Instant Pub.

Petrucha, Stefan. Ripper. (ENG.). 432p. (YA). (gr. 7). 2013. pap. 9.99 *(978-0-14-242418-6(8)*, Speak) 2012. 26.19 *(978-0-399-25524-3(9))* Penguin Young Readers Group.

Petrucha, Stefan & Kinney, Sarah. High School Musical Mystery II: The Lost Verse, 21. Murase, Sho, illus. 2010. (Nancy Drew Girl Detective Graphic Novels Ser.: 21). (ENG.). 96p. (J). (gr. 4-6). 22.44 *(978-1-59707-196-3(X))* Papercutz.

Petrucha, Stefan & Pendleton, Thomas. Wicked Dead: Skin. (Wicked Dead Ser.). 224p. (J). pap. 7.99 *(978-0-06-113854-6(1)*, HarperTeen) HarperCollins Pubs.

Petrucha, Stefan, et al. The Fake Heir. Ross, Daniel Vaughn, illus. 2006. (J). *(978-1-59707-060-7(2))* Papercutz.

Petty, Heather W. Final Fall. (Lock & Mori Ser.). (ENG.). 208p. (YA). (gr. 9). 2018. pap. 11.99 *(978-1-4814-2310-6(X))* 2017. (Illus.). 18.99 *(978-1-4814-2309-0(6))* Simon & Schuster Bks. For Young Readers. (Simon & Schuster Bks. For Young Readers).

—Lock & Mori. 2016. (Lock & Mori Ser.). (ENG.). 272p. (YA). (gr. 9). pap. 10.99 *(978-1-4814-2304-5(5))* Simon & Schuster, Inc.

—Mind Games. (Lock & Mori Ser.). (ENG.). (YA). (gr. 9). 2017. 320p. pap. 11.99 *(978-1-4814-2307-6(X))* 2016. (Illus.). 304p. 17.99 *(978-1-4814-2306-9(1))* Simon & Schuster Bks. For Young Readers. (Simon & Schuster Bks. For Young Readers).

Pfeffer, Susan Beth. Revenge of the Aztecs. 2004. 118p. (J). lib. bdg. 16.92 *(978-1-4242-0763-3(0))* Fitzgerald Bks.

Pfitsch, Patricia Curtis. Riding the Flume. 2004. (ENG., Illus.). 240p. (J). (gr. 5-9). pap. 11.99 *(978-0-689-86692-0(5)*, Simon & Schuster/Paula Wiseman Bks.) Simon & Schuster/Paula Wiseman Bks.

Pflugfelder, Bob & Hockensmith, Steve. Nick & Tesla's Solar-Powered Showdown: A Mystery with Sun-Powered Gadgets You Can Build Yourself. 2016. (Nick & Tesla Ser.: 6). (Illus.). 264p. (J). (gr. 4-7). 12.95 *(978-1-59474-866-0(7))* Quirk Bks.

—Nick & Tesla's Special Effects Spectacular: A Mystery with Animatronics, Alien Makeup, Camera Gear, & Other Movie Magic You Can Make Yourself! 2015. (Nick & Tesla Ser.: 5). (Illus.). 256p. (J). (gr. 4-7). 12.95 *(978-1-59474-760-1(1))* Quirk Bks.

Pfoutz, Sally. Missing Person. 2009. 192p. (gr. 7-18). pap. 12.95 *(978-1-4401-5108-8(3))* iUniverse, Inc.

The Phantom of Nantucket. 2014. (Nancy Drew Diaries: 7). (ENG., Illus.). 192p. (J). (gr. 3-7). pap. 7.99 *(978-1-4814-0015-2(0)*, Aladdin) Simon & Schuster Children's Publishing.

Philbrick, Rodman. Who Killed Darius Drake? A Mystery. 2017. (ENG.). 192p. (J). (gr. 3-7). 17.99 *(978-0-545-78978-3(8)*, Blue Sky Pr., The) Scholastic, Inc.

Phillips, Grant R. Jay Walker & the Case of the Missing Action Figure. 2004. (J). pap. 10.95 *(978-0-9749608-4-5(5))* Quiet Storm Publishing Group.

Pierson, Jan. The Haunted Horse of Gold Hill. 2005. (Ghostowners Ser.: Vol. 4). (Illus.). 109p. (J). per. 9.95 *(978-0-9721800-3-0(6))* WildWest Publishing.

Pike, Christopher, pseud. Chain Letter: Chain Letter; the Ancient Evil. 2013. (ENG., Illus.). 496p. (YA). (gr. 9). pap. 14.99 *(978-1-4424-7215-0(4)*, Simon Pulse) Simon Pulse.

Pitcher, Chelsea. The S-Word. 2013. (ENG.). 320p. pap. 19.99 *(978-1-4516-9516-8(0)*, Gallery Bks.) Gallery Bks.

—This Lie Will Kill You. 2018. (ENG., Illus.). 320p. (YA). (gr. 9). 17.99 *(978-1-5344-4324-2(X)*, McElderry, Margaret K. Bks.) McElderry, Margaret K. Bks.

Platt, Kin. Big Max & the Mystery of the Missing Giraffe. Cravath, Lynne, illus. 2006. (I Can Read Level 2 Ser.). (ENG.). 64p. (J). (gr. k-3). pap. 4.99 *(978-0-06-009920-6(8)*, HarperCollins) HarperCollins Pubs.

—Big Max & the Mystery of the Missing Giraffe. Cravath, Lynne Avril, illus. 2005. (I Can Read Bks.). 64p. (J). (gr. -1). 15.99 *(978-0-06-009918-3(6))*; lib. bdg. 17.89 *(978-0-06-009919-0(4))* HarperCollins Pubs.

Podos, Rebecca. The Mystery of Hollow Places. (ENG.). (YA). (gr. 9). 2017. 320p. pap. 9.99 *(978-0-06-237335-9(8))* 2016. 304p. 17.99 *(978-0-06-237334-2(X))* HarperCollins Pubs. (Balzer & Bray).

Poe, Edgar Allan. Edgar Allan Poe's Tales of Death & Dementia. Grimly, Gris, illus. 2009. (ENG.). 144p. (J). (gr. 6-9). 22.99 *(978-1-4169-5025-7(7)*, Atheneum Bks. for Young Readers) Simon & Schuster Children's Publishing.

Pohl-Weary, Emily. Not Your Ordinary Wolf Girl, 0 vols. 2013. (ENG.). 224p. (YA). (gr. 9-12). pap. 9.99 *(978-1-4778-1688-2(7)*, 9781477816882, Skyscape) Amazon Publishing.

Polak, Monique. All In, 1 vol. 2006. (Lorimer SideStreets Ser.). (ENG.). 168p. (YA). (gr. 9-12). 8.99 *(978-1-55028-912-1(8)*, 161111d9-e21e-413b-9bf2-e9d8917416fe) James Lorimer & Co. Ltd., Pubs. CAN. Dist: Lerner Publishing Group.

Polan, Alex. Catching the Jigglypuff Thief. 2016. (Unofficial Adventures for Pokemon GO Players Ser.: 1). lib. bdg. 18.40 *(978-0-606-39657-8(8))* Turtleback.

Pollock, J. A. Titus & Otis & the Arctic Adventure. 2009. 151p. pap. 12.00 *(978-0-557-03427-7(2))* Lulu Pr., Inc.

Ponti, James. Framed! 2016. (Framed! Ser.: 1). (ENG., Illus.). 304p. (J). (gr. 3-7). 19.99 *(978-1-4814-3630-4(9)*, Aladdin) Simon & Schuster Children's Publishing.

—Trapped! 2018. (Framed! Ser.: 3). (ENG., Illus.). 384p. (J). (gr. 3-7). 19.99 *(978-1-5344-0891-3(6)*, Aladdin) Simon & Schuster Children's Publishing.

—Vanished! (Framed! Ser.: 2). (ENG.). (J). (gr. 3-7). 2018. 400p. pap. 8.99 *(978-1-4814-3634-2(1))* 2017. (Illus.). 384p. 19.99 *(978-1-4814-3633-5(3))* Simon & Schuster Children's Publishing. (Aladdin).

Poole, Gabriella. Darke Academy 01: Secret Lives. 2010. (Darke Academy Ser.). (ENG.). 288p. (YA). (gr. 7-17). pap. 9.99 *(978-0-340-98924-1(6))* Hachette Children's Group GBR. Dist: Hachette Bk. Group.

Poon, Janice. Claire & the Bakery Thief. Poon, Janice, illus. 2008. (Illus.). 104p. (J). (gr. 2-5). 15.95 *(978-1-55453-286-5(8))*; pap. 7.95 *(978-1-55453-245-2(0))* Kids Can Pr., Ltd. CAN. Dist: Hachette Bk. Group.

Pope, Paul, et al. The Fall of the House of West. 2015. (J). lib. bdg. 20.85 *(978-0-606-37806-2(5))* Turtleback.

Portman, Frank. King Dork. 2007. 344p. 19.00 *(978-0-7569-7950-8(1))* Perfection Learning Corp.

Poth, Karen. Listen up, Larry, 1 vol. 2013. (I Can Read! / Big Idea Books / VeggieTales Ser.). (ENG.). 32p. (J). pap. 4.99 *(978-0-310-73215-0(8))* Zonderkidz.

—The Mess Detectives & the Case of the Lost Temper, 1 vol. 2014. (I Can Read! / Big Idea Books / VeggieTales Ser.). (ENG.). 32p. (J). pap. 4.99 *(978-0-310-74170-1(X))* Zonderkidz.

Potter, Ellen. Pish Posh. 2011. (ENG.). 176p. (J). (gr. 3-7). 7.99 *(978-0-14-241906-9(0)*, Puffin Books) Penguin Young Readers Group.

Potter-Kotecki, Kerry. I'm a Doggie Detective. 2008. (J). pap. 10.00 *(978-0-9792371-7-1(3)*, Moo Pr.) Keene Publishing.

Poulsen, David A. The Book of Vampire. 4th rev. ed. 2007. (Salt & Pepper Chronicles). (ENG., Illus.). 160p. (J). (gr. 4-7). 6.95 *(978-1-55263-805-7(7))* Leaf Storm Pr.

—No Time Like the Past. 3rd rev. ed. 2007. (Salt & Pepper Chronicles). (ENG., Illus.). 160p. (J). (gr. 4-7). 6.95 *(978-1-55263-807-1(3))* Leaf Storm Pr.

Povey, Jeff. Delete. 2017. (ENG.). 352p. (J). pap. 9.99 *(978-1-4711-1870-8(3)*, Simon & Schuster Children's) Simon & Schuster, Ltd. GBR. Dist: Simon & Schuster, Inc.

Powell, Martin. Private Eye Princess & the Emerald Pea: A Graphic Novel. Cano, Fernando, illus. 2019. (Far Out Fairy Tales Ser.). (ENG.). 40p. (J). (gr. 3-6). pap. 5.95 *(978-1-4965-8443-4(0)*, 140968); lib. bdg. 25.32 *(978-1-4965-8394-9(9)*, 140685) Capstone. (Stone Arch Bks.).

Preble, Joy. Finding Paris. 2015. (ENG.). 272p. (YA). (gr. 9). 17.99 *(978-0-06-232130-5(7)*, Balzer & Bray) HarperCollins Pubs.

—The Sweet Dead Life. 2014. (Sweet Dead Life Novel Ser.). (Illus.). 244p. (YA). (gr. 9). pap. 10.99 *(978-1-61695-368-3(3)*, Soho Teen) Soho Pr., Inc.

Preller, James. Better off Undead. 2018. (ENG.). 304p. (J). pap. 18.99 *(978-1-250-17905-0(X)*, 900189919) Square Fish.

—Better off Undead. 2018. (J). lib. bdg. 18.40 *(978-0-606-41113-4(5))* Turtleback.

—The Case of the Groaning Ghost. Smith, Jamie & Alley, R. W., illus. 2008. (Jigsaw Jones Mysteries Ser.: Bk. 32). 89p. (gr. 1-5). 15.00 *(978-0-7569-8302-4(9))* Perfection Learning Corp.

—Jigsaw Jones: the Case from Outer Space. 2017. (Jigsaw Jones Mysteries Ser.). (ENG., Illus.). 96p. (J). pap. 6.99 *(978-1-250-11017-6(3)*, 900165779) Feiwel & Friends.

—Jigsaw Jones: the Case of the Best Pet Ever. 2017. (Jigsaw Jones Mysteries Ser.). (ENG., Illus.). 96p. (J). pap. 6.99 *(978-1-250-11093-0(9)*, 900169788) Feiwel & Friends.

—Jigsaw Jones: the Case of the Bicycle Bandit. 2017. (Jigsaw Jones Mysteries Ser.). (ENG., Illus.). 96p. (J). pap. 6.99 *(978-1-250-11084-8(X)*, 900169772) Feiwel & Friends.

—Jigsaw Jones: the Case of the Buried Treasure. 2017. (Jigsaw Jones Mysteries Ser.). (ENG., Illus.). 112p. (J). pap. 6.99 *(978-1-250-11086-2(6)*, 900169774) Feiwel & Friends.

—Jigsaw Jones: the Case of the Disappearing Dinosaur. 2017. (Jigsaw Jones Mysteries Ser.). (ENG., Illus.). 96p. (J). pap. 6.99 *(978-1-250-11088-6(2)*, 900169776) Feiwel & Friends.

—Jigsaw Jones: the Case of the Glow-In-the-Dark Ghost. 2017. (Jigsaw Jones Mysteries Ser.). (ENG., Illus.). 96p. (J). pap. 6.99 *(978-1-250-11020-6(3)*, 900165781) Feiwel & Friends.

—Jigsaw Jones: the Case of the Hat Burglar. Alley, R. W., illus. 2019. (Jigsaw Jones Mysteries Ser.). (ENG.). 96p. (J). pap. 6.99 *(978-1-250-20768-5(1)*, 900201639) Feiwel & Friends.

—Jigsaw Jones: the Case of the Million-Dollar Mystery. 2017. (Jigsaw Jones Mysteries Ser.). (ENG., Illus.). 112p. (J). pap. 6.99 *(978-1-250-11095-4(5)*, 900169793) Feiwel & Friends.

—Jigsaw Jones: the Case of the Mummy Mystery. 2017. (Jigsaw Jones Mysteries Ser.). (ENG., Illus.). 96p. (J). pap. 6.99 *(978-1-250-11082-4(3)*, 900169770) Feiwel & Friends.

—Jigsaw Jones: the Case of the Smelly Sneaker. 2017. (Jigsaw Jones Mysteries Ser.). (ENG., Illus.). 96p. (J). pap. 6.99 *(978-1-250-11080-0(7)*, 900169768) Feiwel & Friends.

Press, Judy. The Case of the Missing Kiddush Cup. 2018. (J). *(978-1-5415-0015-0(6)*, Kar-Ben Publishing) Lerner Publishing Group.

Press, Julian. Operation Yellow Dragon: Get a Clue #3, No. 3. 2008. (Get a Clue Ser.: 3). (ENG., Illus.). 128p. (J). (gr. 2-5). 7.99 *(978-0-448-44875-6(0)*, Grosset & Dunlap) Penguin Young Readers Group.

Preston, Natasha. The Cabin. 2016. 336p. (YA). (gr. 8-12). pap. 10.99 *(978-1-4926-1855-3(1)*, 9781492618553) Sourcebooks, Inc.

—The Cellar. 2014. 368p. (YA). (gr. 10-12). pap. 10.99 *(978-1-4926-0097-8(0)*, 9781492600978) Sourcebooks, Inc.

—You Will Be Mine. 2018. (ENG., Illus.). 304p. (YA). (gr. 8-12). pap. 10.99 *(978-1-4926-5432-2(9))* Sourcebooks, Inc.

Price, Kevin, ed. The Mystery of Love: A Born Storyteller Collection of Mystery Adventure & Science Fiction Stories. 2013. (Illus.). 308p. pap. *(978-0-9872559-6-9(7)*, Crotchet Quaver) Logorythm.

Priest, Cherie. The Agony House. O'Connor, Tara, illus. (ENG.). 272p. (gr. 7-7). 2020. (J). pap. 10.99 *(978-1-338-58217-8(8))* 2018. (YA). 18.99 *(978-0-545-93429-9(X))* Scholastic, Inc. (Levine, Arthur A. Bks.).

Priestley, Chris. Death & the Arrow: A Gripping Tale of Murder & Revenge. 2007. (Tom Marlowe Ser.). (ENG., Illus.). 240p. (YA). (gr. 7). per. 12.95 *(978-0-552-55475-6(8))* Transworld Publishers Ltd. GBR. Dist: Independent Pubs. Group.

—Treasure of the Golden Skull. 2018. (Maudlin Towers Ser.). (ENG., Illus.). 272p. (J). pap. *(978-1-4088-7310-6(9)*, 298240, Bloomsbury Children's Bks.) Bloomsbury Publishing Plc.

Princess Protection Program Staff. The Palace of Mystery, No. 4. 2010. (Princess Protection Program Ser.). 144p. pap. 4.99 *(978-1-4231-2727-7(7))* Disney Pr.

Prins, Piet. The Flying Phantom. 2006. (Illus.). 142p. (J). pap. *(978-1-894666-45-9(3))* Inheritance Pubns.

—The Haunted Castle. 2006. (Illus.). 139p. (J). pap. *(978-1-894666-44-2(5))* Inheritance Pubns.

—The Mystery of the Abandoned Mill. Kramer, Jaap, illus. 2006. 127p. (J). pap. *(978-1-894666-48-0(8))* Inheritance Pubns.

—The Sailing Sleuths. Kramer, Jaap, illus. 2006. 137p. (J). pap. *(978-1-894666-46-6(1))* Inheritance Pubns.

—Scout's Distant Journey. 2006. (Illus.). 141p. (J). pap. *(978-1-894666-49-7(6))* Inheritance Pubns.

—The Treasure of Rodensteyn Castle. Kramer, Jaap, illus. 2006. 132p. (J). pap. *(978-1-894666-47-3(X))* Inheritance Pubns.

Prisant, Guillermo Murray & Murray, Guillermo. Escalofrío. rev. ed. 2007. (Ediciones Castillo Castillo Del Terror Ser.). (SPA & ENG.). 140p. (J). (gr. 6-9). pap. 6.95 *(978-970-20-0293-2(1))* Castillo, Ediciones, S. A. de C. V. MEX. Dist: Macmillan.

—La Gente de Las Sombras. rev. ed. 2007. (Ediciones Castillo Castillo Del Terror Ser.). (ENG.). 104p. (J). (gr. 6-9). pap. 6.95 *(978-970-20-0336-6(9))* Castillo, Ediciones, S. A. de C. V. MEX. Dist: Macmillan.

The Prophesied. 2013. 152p. *(978-1-4602-3111-1(2))* FriesenPress.

Prophet, John. Mystery at the Salt Marsh Winery: A Casey Miller Mystery. 2003. 240p. (YA). pap. 16.95 *(978-0-595-26598-5(7)*, Mystery & Suspense Pr.) iUniverse, Inc.

Prophet, John M. Body in the Salt Marsh Boatyard: A Casey Miller Mystery. 2004. 162p. (YA). pap. 13.95 *(978-0-595-30991-7(7)*, Mystery & Suspense Pr.) iUniverse, Inc.

Pullman, Philip. El Reloj Mecanico. Netzel, Carmen, tr. 2005. (Escritura desatada Ser.). (SPA.). 112p. (J). 15.95 *(978-84-406-8065-5(1))* Ediciones B ESP. Dist: Independent Pubs. Group.

—The Ruby in the Smoke. 2009. 9.84 *(978-0-7848-2919-6(5)*, Everbind) Marco Bk. Co.

—The Ruby in the Smoke. 2008. (Sally Lockhart Mystery Ser.: Bk. 1). (ENG.). 230p. (YA). (gr. 7-18). 22.44 *(978-0-394-98826-9(4))* Random House Publishing Group.

—The Ruby in the Smoke. 2003. (Sally Lockhart Ser.: Bk. 1). (Illus.). (YA). pap. 9.95 *(978-0-375-82545-3(2)*, Knopf Bks. for Young Readers) Random Hse. Children's Bks.

—The Ruby in the Smoke: a Sally Lockhart Mystery. 2008. (Sally Lockhart Ser.: Bk. 1). (ENG.). 256p. (YA). (gr. 7). pap. 10.99 *(978-0-375-84516-1(X)*, Ember) Random Hse. Children's Bks.

—The Shadow in the North. 2003. (Sally Lockhart Ser.: Bk. 2). (Illus.). (J). pap. 9.95 *(978-0-375-82546-0(0)*, Knopf Bks. for Young Readers) Random Hse. Children's Bks.

—The Shadow in the North. 2006. (Sally Lockhart Ser.: Bk. 2). 23.75 *(978-0-8446-7289-2(0))* Smith, Peter Pub., Inc.

—The Shadow in the North: a Sally Lockhart Mystery. 2008. (Sally Lockhart Ser.: Bk. 2). (ENG.). 384p. (J). (gr. 7). pap. 14.99 *(978-0-375-84515-4(1)*, Ember) Random Hse. Children's Bks.

—The Tiger in the Well. 2003. (Sally Lockhart Ser.: Bk. 3). (Illus.). (J). pap. 9.95 *(978-0-375-82547-7(9))* Random Hse. Children's Bks.

—The Tiger in the Well: a Sally Lockhart Mystery. 2008. (Sally Lockhart Ser.: Bk. 3). (ENG.). 432p. (YA). (gr. 7). pap. 9.99 *(978-0-375-84517-8(8)*, Ember) Random Hse. Children's Bks.

—The Tin Princess: a Sally Lockhart Mystery. 2008. (Sally Lockhart Ser.). (ENG.). 304p. (YA). (gr. 7). pap. 11.99 *(978-0-375-84514-7(3)*, Knopf Bks. for Young Readers) Random Hse. Children's Bks.

—Two Crafty Criminals! And How They Were Captured by the Daring Detectives of the New Cut Gang. 2013. (ENG.). 288p. (J). (gr. 3-7). 7.99 *(978-0-307-93035-4(1)*, Yearling) Random Hse. Children's Bks.

Quackenbush, Robert. Detective Mole. 2010. 68p. (J). (gr. k-4). pap. 8.95 *(978-1-4502-1529-9(7))* iUniverse, Inc.

—Dig to Disaster: A QUIX Book. Quackenbush, Robert, illus. 2018. (Miss Mallard Mystery Ser.). (ENG., Illus.). 80p. (J). (gr. k-3). 16.99 *(978-1-5344-1313-9(8))*; pap. 5.99 *(978-1-5344-1312-2(X))* Simon & Schuster Children's Publishing. (Aladdin).

—Dogsled to Dread: A QUIX Book. Quackenbush, Robert, illus. 2019. (Miss Mallard Mystery Ser.). (ENG., Illus.). 80p. (J). (gr. k-3). 16.99 *(978-1-5344-1421-1(5))*; pap. 5.99 *(978-1-5344-1420-4(7))* Simon & Schuster Children's Publishing. (Aladdin).

—Express Train to Trouble: A QUIX Book. Quackenbush, Robert, illus. 2018. (Miss Mallard Mystery Ser.). (ENG., Illus.). 80p. (J). (gr. k-3). 16.99 *(978-1-5344-1403-7(7))*; pap. 5.99 *(978-1-5344-1402-0(9))* Simon & Schuster Children's Publishing. (Aladdin).

—Gondola to Danger: A QUIX Book. Quackenbush, Robert, illus. 2019. (Miss Mallard Mystery Ser.). (ENG., Illus.). 80p. (J). (gr. k-3). 16.99 *(978-1-5344-1406-8(1))*; pap. 5.99 *(978-1-5344-1405-1(3))* Simon & Schuster Children's Publishing. (Aladdin).

—Piet Potter Returns: A Piet Potter Mystery. 2010. 52p. (J). (gr. k-4). pap. 8.95 *(978-1-4502-1352-3(9))* iUniverse, Inc.

—Piet Potter Strikes Again: A Piet Potter Mystery. 2010. 52p. (J). (gr. k-4). pap. 8.95 *(978-1-4502-1530-5(0))* iUniverse, Inc.

—Sherlock Chick's First Case. Quackenbush, Robert, illus. 2019. (Sherlock Chick Ser.). (ENG., Illus.). 48p. (J). (gr. -1-3). 16.99 *(978-1-5344-1521-8(1)*, Aladdin) Simon & Schuster Children's Publishing.

—Surfboard to Peril: A QUIX Book. Quackenbush, Robert, illus. 2019. (Miss Mallard Mystery Ser.). (ENG., Illus.). 80p. (J). (gr. k-3). 16.99 *(978-1-5344-1418-1(5))*; pap. 5.99 *(978-1-5344-1417-4(7))* Simon & Schuster Children's Publishing. (Aladdin).

—Texas Trail to Calamity: A QUIX Book. Quackenbush, Robert, illus. 2018. (Miss Mallard Mystery Ser.). (ENG., Illus.). 80p. (J). (gr. k-3). 16.99 *(978-1-5344-1310-8(3))*; pap. 5.99 *(978-1-5344-1309-2(X))* Simon & Schuster Children's Publishing. (Aladdin).

Quinn, Spencer, pseud. Paw & Order: A Chet & Bernie Mystery. 2015. (Chet & Bernie Mystery Ser.: 7). (ENG.). 336p. pap. 17.99 *(978-1-4767-0340-4(X))* Simon & Schuster, Inc.

—Woof: a Bowser & Birdie Novel. 2016. (ENG.). 304p. (J). (gr. 3-7). pap. 7.99 *(978-0-545-64332-0(5))* Scholastic, Inc.

Raab, Ralph. The Dewey Deception: The First Adventure from the Biblio Files. 2009. (ENG.). 248p. 26.95 *(978-1-4401-4687-9(X))*; pap. 16.95 *(978-1-4401-4685-5(3))* iUniverse, Inc.

Rabley, Stephen. Easystart: Marcel & the Mona Lisa. 2nd ed. 2008. (Pearson English Graded Readers Ser.). (ENG., Illus.). 20p. pap. 11.99 *(978-1-4058-6955-3(0)*, Pearson ELT) Pearson Education.

Rader, Josh. Detective Stephy Wephy Holmes in the Missing Cake. Meyer, Sarah, illus. 2007. 36p. (J). (gr. -1-3). per. 14.99 *(978-1-59879-399-4(3))* Lifevest Publishing, Inc.

Radwan, Hassan. Rashid & the Missing Body. 2010. (ENG., Illus.). 80p. (J). (gr. 2-6). pap. 5.95 *(978-0-86037-395-7(9))* Kube Publishing Ltd. GBR. Dist: Consortium Bk. Sales & Distribution.

Ragged Island Mysteries: Classroom Library Set. (Ragged Island Mysteriestm Ser.). (gr. 5-7). 150.95 *(978-0-322-02634-6(2))* Wright Group/McGraw-Hill.

Raglin, Tim. The Curse of Catunkhamun. 2007. (Illus.). (J). *(978-0-9788969-0-4(4)*, Exhibit A) TR Bks.

Rahim, Rahimah. The Trunk. 2012. 64p. pap. *(978-1-78176-715-3(7))* FeedARead.com.

Rainfield, Cheryl. Stained. 2015. (ENG.). 304p. (YA). (gr. 9). pap. 8.99 *(978-0-544-43947-4(3)*, 1596846, Clarion Bks.) HarperCollins Pubs.

Ralph, Grampa. How Santa Knows. 2007. 56p. pap. 16.95 *(978-1-4241-2284-4(8))* America Star Bks.

Rameaka, T. Mystery of Wolf Den Cave. 2005. 74p. pap. 19.95 *(978-1-4137-5551-0(8))* America Star Bks.

Ramirez, D. a. & Ramirez, D. A. Kingdom of Glass. 2012. 336p. pap. 12.99 *(978-0-9834198-8-4(4))* Vinspire Publishing LLC.

Ramthun, Bonnie. The White Gates. 2008. (ENG.). 256p. (J). (gr. 6-8). lib. bdg. 22.44 *(978-0-375-94554-0(7))* Random House Publishing Group.

Rand, Johnathan. American Chillers #29 Oregon Oceanauts. 2010. 208p. (J). pap. 5.99 *(978-1-893699-24-3(2))* AudioCraft Publishing, Inc.

Ranjalkar, Shreyans. My Sunny British Days - Stories for Children by a Child. 2013. (Illus.). 70p. pap. *(978-1-78148-596-5(8))* Grosvenor Hse. Publishing Ltd.

Ransom, Jeanie Franz. The Crown Affair. Axelsen, Stephen, illus. 2015. (Nursery-Rhyme Mysteries Ser.: 2). (ENG.). 40p. (J). (gr. 1-4). lib. bdg. 16.95 *(978-1-58089-552-1(2))* Charlesbridge Publishing, Inc.

Raskin, Ellen. The Mysterious Disappearance of Leon (I Mean Noel) 2011. (Illus.). 176p. (J). (gr. 3-7). 6.99 *(978-0-14-241700-3(9)*, Puffin Books) Penguin Young Readers Group.

—The Tattooed Potato & Other Clues. 2011. (Illus.). 176p. (J). (gr. 5-8). 7.99 *(978-0-14-241699-0(1)*, Puffin Books) Penguin Young Readers Group.

—The Westing Game. 2003. 182p. (J). lib. bdg. 15.00 (978-1-4242-2271-1(0)) Fitzgerald Bks.

—The Westing Game. 2020. (Be Classic Ser.). 240p. (J). (gr. 3-7). pap. 9.99 (978-0-593-11810-8(3), Puffin Books) Penguin Young Readers Group.

—The Westing Game: Anniversary Edition. 25th anniv. ed. 2003. 192p. (J). (gr. 3-7). 17.99 (978-0-525-47137-0(5), Dutton Books for Young Readers) Penguin Young Readers Group.

—The Westing Game: The Deluxe Anniversary Edition. anniv. ed. 2018. (Illus.). 208p. (J). (gr. 3-7). 10.99 (978-0-451-48098-9(8), Puffin Books) Penguin Young Readers Group.

—The Westing Game (Puffin Modern Classics) 2004. (Puffin Modern Classics Ser.). (Illus.). 192p. (J). (gr. 3-7). 8.99 (978-0-14-240120-0(X), Puffin Books) Penguin Young Readers Group.

Rattle, Alison. V for Violet. 2016. (ENG.). 304p. (YA). (gr. 7). 13.99 (978-1-4714-0381-1(5)) Bonnier Publishing GBR. Dist: Independent Pubs. Group.

Rautenberg, Karen Rita. Ballerina Detective & the Missing Jeweled Tiara. 2009. (ENG.). 198p. (J). (gr. 5-8). pap. (978-1-933255-47-7(1)) DNA Pr.

Ray, Gracie. Falling Slowly. 2012. 270p. (978-1-105-59084-9(4)) Lulu.com.

Rayes, Michael. Bank Robbery! 2007. (J). per. 13.95 (978-0-9779628-0-8(6)) Rafka Pr. LLC.

Raymond, Roger & Savoy, Darryl. Ralph Filmore: Paranormal Investigator. O'Reilly, Sean Patrick, ed. 2012. (Illus.). 78p. (J). pap. 14.95 (978-1-926914-31-2(7)) Arcana Studio, Inc.

Razzi, Jim. The Sherluck Bones Mystery Detective. 2003. 62p. Bk. 1. pap. 9.95 (978-0-595-29088-8(4))Bk. 2. pap. 9.95 (978-0-595-29089-5(2)) iUniverse, Inc. (Mystery Writers of America Presents).

Read, Miss. The Howards of Caxley. (J). 17.95 (978-0-8488-1454-0(1)) Amereon Ltd.

Reece, P. J. Roxy, 1 vol. 2010. (ENG., Illus.). 190p. (YA). (gr. 8-12). pap. 12.95 (978-1-896580-01-2(7)) Tradewind Bks. CAN. Dist: Orca Bk. Pubs. USA.

Reese Martin, Faith. Ghost Train to Freedom: An Adventure on the Underground Railroad. Sachs, Barry, illus. 2012. (JMP Mystery Ser.: Bk. 3). (ENG.). 416p. (YA). pap. 14.99 (978-1-60800-014-2(1), American Literary Publishing) LifeReloaded Specialty Publishing LLC.

Reichs, Kathy. Virals. 2014. lthr. 79.00 (978-1-62715-582-3(1)) Leatherbound Bestsellers.

—Virals. 2011. (Virals Ser.: 1). (ENG.). 480p. (J). (gr. 5-18). 11.99 (978-1-59514-426-3(9), Puffin Books) Penguin Young Readers Group.

—Virals. 2011. 20.00 (978-1-61383-226-4(5)) Perfection Learning Corp.

Reichs, Kathy & Reichs, Brendan. Code. 2013. (Virals Ser.: 3). lib. bdg. 19.65 (978-0-606-32140-2(3)) Turtleback.

—Seizure. 2013. (Virals Ser.: 2). lib. bdg. 20.85 (978-0-606-30050-6(3)) Turtleback.

—Trace Evidence. 2016. (Virals Ser.). lib. bdg. 20.85 (978-0-606-38400-1(6)) Turtleback.

—Virals. 2011. (Virals Ser.: 1). lib. bdg. 20.85 (978-0-606-23069-8(6)) Turtleback.

Reid, F. J. The Midwinter Child. 2009. 224p. pap. (978-1-84923-496-2(5)) YouWriteOn.

Reid, Isabelle. Serafina Moon. 2009. 48p. pap. (978-1-84923-771-0(9)) YouWriteOn.

Reid, Kimberly. Sweet 16 to Life. 2013. 233p. (J). lib. bdg. 20.80 (978-0-606-27166-0(X)) Turtleback.

Reid, Roger. Space. 2008. (ENG.). 160p. (J). 19.95 (978-1-58838-230-6(3), 9002, NewSouth Bks.) NewSouth, Inc.

Reide, Mackenzie. The Adventurers the Mask of the Troll. 2013. 326p. pap. (978-0-9869647-2-5(7)) MR Bks.

Reiner, Carl. Tell Me Another Scary Story... But Not Too Scary! Bennett, James & Bennett, Carl A., illus. 2009. (ENG.). 32p. (J). (gr. k-3). 16.95 (978-1-59777-630-1(0)) Phoenix Bks., Inc.

Reiss, Kathryn. A Bundle of Trouble: A Rebecca Mystery. Giovine, Sergio, illus. 2011. (American Girl Mysteries Ser.). (ENG.). 192p. (YA). (gr. 4-6). pap. 21.19 (978-1-59369-754-9(6)) American Girl Publishing, Inc.

—Message in a Bottle: A Julie Mystery. 2017. 209p. (J). (978-1-5182-4315-8(0), American Girl) American Girl Publishing, Inc.

—The Tangled Web: A Julie Mystery. Tibbles, Jean-Paul, illus. 2009. (ENG.). 168p. (J). (gr. 4-18). 10.95 (978-1-59369-475-3(X)); pap. 21.19 (978-1-59369-476-0(8)) American Girl Publishing, Inc.

Renn, Diana. Tokyo Heist. 2013. (ENG.). 384p. (YA). (gr. 7). pap. 8.99 (978-0-14-242654-8(7), Speak) Penguin Young Readers Group.

Rennie-Pattison, Caroline. The Law of Three: A Sarah Martin Mystery. 2007. (Sarah Martin Mystery Ser.: 2). (ENG.). 232p. (YA). (gr. 6). pap. 10.99 (978-1-55002-733-4(6)) Dundurn Pr. CAN. Dist: Publishers Group West (PGW).

—The Whole, Entire, Complete Truth: A Sarah Martin Mystery. 2006. (Sarah Martin Mystery Ser.: 1). (ENG.). 180p. (YA). pap. 12.99 (978-1-55002-583-5(X)) Dundurn Pr. CAN. Dist: Publishers Group West (PGW).

Reynolds Naylor, Phyllis. Zack & the Turkey Attack! To, Vivienne, illus. (ENG.). (J). (gr. 2-6). 2018. 192p. pap. 7.99 (978-1-4814-3780-6(1)) 2017. 176p. 16.99 (978-1-4814-3779-0(8), Atheneum/Caitlyn Dlouhy Books) Simon & Schuster Children's Publishing.

Rhodes, O. K. The Rock Holler Gang: Jr. Detectives Mystery of the Cornerstone. 2003. 11.99 (978-0-9740799-0-5(1)) Maple Bend Farms Pr.

Ricchi, Brenda. The Grandchildren's Bible Journeys - the Creation Story. 2009. (ENG.). 36p. pap. 17.00 (978-0-557-14903-2(7)) Lulu Pr., Inc.

Ricchiuti, Paul B. Treasure on Spyglass Hill. 2015. 143p. (J). pap. (978-0-8163-5771-0(4)) Pacific Pr. Publishing Assn.

Richards, Justin. The Chaos Code. 2007. (ENG.). 400p. (YA). (gr. 7-12). 17.95 (978-1-59990-124-4(2), 9781599901244, Bloomsbury USA Childrens) Bloomsbury Publishing USA.

Richards, Kitty. Belle: The Mysterious Message. Studio IBOIX Staff, illus. 2011. (Disney Princess Ser.). (ENG.). 96p. (J). (gr. 2-6). 31.36 (978-1-59961-878-4(8), 5178, Chapter Bks.) Spotlight.

Richards, Linda L. Death Was in the Blood. 2013. (ENG.). 332p. 25.95 (978-1-4328-2716-8(2), Five Star Trade) Cengage Gale.

Richards, Natalie D. One Was Lost. (ENG., (YA). (gr. 7-12). 2017. Illus.). 23.99 (978-1-4926-6232-7(1)) 2016. 320p. pap. 12.99 (978-1-4926-1574-3(9), 9781492615743) Sourcebooks, Inc.

Richardson, D. L. Feedback. 2013. 254p. pap. 11.99 (978-1-939194-83-1(0)) Etopia Pr.

Richardson, Travis. Lost in Clover. 2012. 198p. pap. 9.99 (978-1-61187-466-2(1)) Untreed Reads Publishing, LLC.

Richter, Virginia Rose. Taken: A Willow Lane Mystery, #4. 2015. (ENG., Illus.). 114p. (YA). pap. 10.00 (978-1-61187-795-3(4)) Untreed Reads Publishing, LLC.

Riddell, Chris. Ottoline y la Gata Amarilla. 2008. (SPA.). 172p. (J). 13.95 (978-84-263-6832-4(8)) Vives, Luis Editorial (Edelvives) ESP. Dist: Baker & Taylor Bks.

Riehecky, Janet. The Red Door Detective Club Mysteries, 4 bks., Set. Halverson, Lydia, illus. (J). (gr. 3-6). lib. bdg. 51.80 (978-1-56674-900-8(X)) Forest Hse. Publishing Co., Inc.

Rifkin, L. (Lauren). The Nine Lives of Romeo Crumb: Life Three. 2010. (ENG.). 276p. (J). pap. 8.95 (978-0-9743221-5-5(6)) Stratford Road Pr., Ltd.

Rigby Education Staff. The Robbers. (Sails Literacy Ser.). (Illus.). 16p. (gr. 1-2). 27.00 (978-0-7635-9913-3(1), 699131C99) Rigby Education.

Riker, Richard K. Scary Days Daze. l.t. ed. 2005. (Illus.). 224p. (J). 15.95 (978-0-9760416-1-0(8), 3,000) Family Christian Ctr.

Riley, D. H. The Mysterians, 1 vol. 2009. 54p. pap. 16.95 (978-1-60836-374-2(0)) America Star Bks.

Rinehart, Mary Roberts. Bab: A Sub-Deb. 2005. (ENG., Illus.). 300p. pap. 15.95 (978-0-9740636-8-3(1)) ARose Books Publishing, LLC.

Ring, Susan. Pete's Surprise. 2009. (ENG.). 24p. (J). pap. 3.99 (978-1-4231-1827-5(8)) Disney Pr.

Riordan, Rick. The Maze of Bones, Bk. 1. unabr. ed. 2008. (39 Clues Ser.: 1). (ENG.). 96p. (J). (gr. 3-7). 49.95 (978-0-545-14290-8(3)) Scholastic, Inc.

—The Maze of Bones (the 39 Clues, Book 1) (Geronimo Stilton Ser.: 1). (ENG.). 224p. (J). 2021. (gr. 2-5). E-Book 7.99 (978-0-545-29265-8(4))Volume 1. 2008. (gr. 4-7). 13.99 (978-0-545-06039-4(7)) Scholastic, Inc.

Ripken Jr., Cal. Cal Ripken Jr. 's All-Stars Super-Sized Slugger. Cowherd, Kevin, illus. 2013. (Cal Ripken Jr. 's All Stars Ser.: 2). (ENG.). 208p. (J). (gr. 3-7). pap. 6.99 (978-1-4231-4004-7(4)) Hyperion Pr.

Ripley's Believe It or Not Editors. Danger Underground. 2011. (Ripley RBI Ser.). 128p. (J). pap. 4.99 (978-1-893951-64-8(2)) Ripley Entertainment, Inc.

—Haunted Hotel. 2011. (Ripley RBI Ser.). 128p. (J). pap. 4.99 (978-1-893951-65-5(0)) Ripley Entertainment, Inc.

Ripley's Believe It Or Not! Ripley's Bureau of Investigation 7: Shock Horror, 7. 2010. (Rbi Ser.: 7). (ENG.). 128p. (J). (gr. 2-5). pap. 4.99 (978-1-893951-58-7(8)) Ripley Entertainment, Inc.

Rippin, Sally. Code Breakers. 2015. (ENG., Illus.). 96p. (J). pap. 4.99 (978-1-61067-312-9(3)) Kane Miller.

—Code Breakers. Fukuoka, Aki, illus. 2014. (Billie B. Mystery Ser.). (ENG.). 92p. (J). (978-1-61067-333-4(6)) Kane Miller.

—Spooky House. 2015. (ENG., Illus.). 96p. (J). pap. 4.99 (978-1-61067-311-2(5)) Kane Miller.

—Treasure Hunt: A Billie B. Mystery. Fukuoka, Aki, illus. 2016. (ENG.). 96p. (J). pap. 4.99 (978-1-61067-464-5(2)) Kane Miller.

Rippl, Terry. Tippy, Dog Gone Detective: From the Files of the World's Shortest Private Eye. 2012. 36p. pap. 12.99 (978-1-4575-1599-6(7)) Dog Ear Publishing, LLC.

Ritchie, Brendan. Carousel. 2015. 352p. (YA). (gr. 7). 13.95 (978-1-925162-14-1(1)) Fremantle Pr. AUS. Dist: Independent Pubs. Group.

Ritter, William. Beastly Bones. 2016. (Jackaby Ser.: 2). lib. bdg. 20.80 (978-0-606-39017-0(0)) Turtleback.

Rivas, Spelile. The Cucuy Stole My Cascarones / el Coco Me Robó Los Cascarones. Baeza Ventura, Gabriela, tr. Cervantes, Valeria, illus. 2013. (SPA & ENG.). 32p. (J). 17.95 (978-1-55885-771-1(0), Piñata Books) Arte Publico Pr.

Robbins, Trina. The Bark in Space: Book 5, No. 5. Page, Tyler, illus. 2013. (Chicagoland Detective Agency Ser.: 5). (ENG.). 64p. (J). (gr. 4-8). pap. 6.95 (978-1-4677-0725-1(2), 659d0711-80dc-41a4-866d-7c460cfaabf5, Graphic Universe™) Lerner Publishing Group.

Roberts, D. W. Pep Squad Mysteries Book 1: Cavern in the Hills. 2009. (ENG.). 103p. pap. 8.99 (978-0-557-05513-5(X)) Lulu Pr., Inc.

—Pep Squad Mysteries Book 2:the Haunting of Townsand Hall. 2008. (ENG.). 101p. pap. 8.95 (978-0-557-05289-9(0)) Lulu Pr., Inc.

—Pep Squad Mysteries Book 4: Prediction of Danger. 2008. (ENG.). 105p. pap. 8.99 (978-0-557-46495-1(1)) Lulu Pr., Inc.

Roberts, Daniel. Young Pep Squad Mysteries. 2011. 36p. pap. 16.99 (978-1-4567-9640-2(2)) AuthorHouse.

Roberts, Dw. Pep Squad Mysteries Book: Cavern in the Hills. 2008. (ENG., Illus.). 67p. pap. 9.96 (978-0-557-02446-9(3)) Lulu Pr., Inc.

—Pep Squad Mysteries Book: Mystery in the Lions' Maze. 2008. (ENG.). 101p. pap. 9.95 (978-1-257-92360-1(9)) Lulu Pr., Inc.

—Pep Squad Mysteries Book: Trouble on Avalance Mountain. 2008. (ENG., Illus.). 101p. pap. 8.99 (978-0-557-16575-9(X)) Lulu Pr., Inc.

—Pep Squad Mysteries Book 7: The Deadly Doll. 2008. (ENG.). 119p. pap. 9.95 (978-1-105-49215-0(X)) Lulu Pr., Inc.

—Pep Squad Mysteries Book 8: Shock of the Scarecrow. 2012. (ENG., Illus.). 122p. pap. 9.95 (978-1-105-83468-4(9)) Lulu Pr., Inc.

Roberts, Ken. Thumb & the Bad Guys. 2013. 104p. pap. (978-1-4596-6491-3(4)) ReadHowYouWant.com, Ltd.

Roberts, Willo Davis. Baby-Sitting Is a Dangerous Job. 2016. (ENG., Illus.). 224p. (J). (gr. 3-7). pap. 7.99 (978-1-4814-3704-2(6), Aladdin) Simon & Schuster Children's Publishing.

—Megan's Island. 2016. (ENG., Illus.). 288p. (J). (gr. 3-7). pap. 7.99 (978-1-4814-4907-6(9), Aladdin) Simon & Schuster Children's Publishing.

—Nightmare. 2012. (ENG.). 224p. (J). (gr. 5-9). pap. 10.99 (978-1-4424-7229-7(4), Atheneum Bks. for Young Readers) Simon & Schuster Children's Publishing.

—The Old House. 2016. (ENG., Illus.). 272p. (J). (gr. 3-7). pap. 6.99 (978-1-4814-5785-9(3), Aladdin) Simon & Schuster Children's Publishing.

—Pawns. Pohl, David, illus. 2012. (ENG.). 160p. (J). (gr. 5-9). pap. 8.99 (978-0-689-83320-5(2), Simon & Schuster/Paula Wiseman Bks.) Simon & Schuster/Paula Wiseman Bks.

—The Pet-Sitting Peril. 2016. (ENG., Illus.). 256p. (J). (gr. 3-7). pap. 7.99 (978-1-4814-7492-4(8), Aladdin) Simon & Schuster Children's Publishing.

—The Pet-Sitting Peril. 2nd ed. 2012. (ENG., Illus.). 192p. (J). (gr. 3-7). reprint ed. pap. 9.99 (978-0-689-71427-6(0), Simon & Schuster/Paula Wiseman Bks.) Simon & Schuster/Paula Wiseman Bks.

—Rebel. 2005. 153p. (J). (gr. 3-7). 13.65 (978-0-7569-5076-7(7)) Perfection Learning Corp.

—Rebel. 2012. (ENG., Illus.). 160p. (J). (gr. 3-7). pap. 8.99 (978-0-689-85081-3(6), Aladdin) Simon & Schuster Children's Publishing.

—Scared Stiff. 2016. (ENG., Illus.). 256p. (J). (gr. 3-7). pap. 8.99 (978-1-4814-4910-6(9), Aladdin) Simon & Schuster Children's Publishing.

—Secrets at Hidden Valley. 2012. (ENG., Illus.). 160p. (J). (gr. 5-9). pap. 8.99 (978-0-689-81167-8(5), Simon & Schuster/Paula Wiseman Bks.) Simon & Schuster/Paula Wiseman Bks.

—Surviving Summer Vacation: How I Visited Yellowstone Park with the Terrible Rupes. 2015. (ENG., Illus.). 208p. (J). (gr. 3-7). pap. 6.99 (978-1-4814-3718-9(6), Aladdin) Simon & Schuster Children's Publishing.

—The View from the Cherry Tree. 2015. (ENG., Illus.). 256p. (J). (gr. 3-7). pap. 8.99 (978-1-4814-3994-7(4), Aladdin) Simon & Schuster Children's Publishing.

—What Could Go Wrong? 2016. (ENG., Illus.). 240p. (J). (gr. 3-7). pap. 8.99 (978-1-4814-7489-4(8), Aladdin) Simon & Schuster Children's Publishing.

—What Could Go Wrong? 2012. (ENG., Illus.). 176p. (J). (gr. 3-7). reprint ed. pap. 9.99 (978-0-689-71690-4(7), Simon & Schuster/Paula Wiseman Bks.) Simon & Schuster/Paula Wiseman Bks.

Robins, Eleanor. Art Show Mystery, 1 vol. unabr. ed. 2011. (Carter High Mysteries Ser.). (ENG.). 48p. (YA). (gr. 9-12). 9.75 (978-1-61651-560-7(0)) Saddleback Educational Publishing, Inc.

—Aztec Ring Mystery, 1 vol. unabr. ed. 2011. (Carter High Mysteries Ser.). (ENG.). 48p. (YA). (gr. 9-12). 9.75 (978-1-61651-561-4(9)) Saddleback Educational Publishing, Inc.

—Drama Club Mystery, 1 vol. unabr. ed. 2011. (Carter High Mysteries Ser.). (ENG.). 48p. (YA). (gr. 9-12). 9.75 (978-1-61651-562-1(7)) Saddleback Educational Publishing, Inc.

—The Field Trip Mystery, 1 vol. unabr. ed. 2011. (Carter High Mysteries Ser.). (ENG.). 48p. (YA). (gr. 9-12). 9.75 (978-1-61651-563-8(5)) Saddleback Educational Publishing, Inc.

—Library Book Mystery, 1 vol. unabr. ed. 2011. (Carter High Mysteries Ser.). (ENG.). 48p. (YA). (gr. 9-12). 9.75 (978-1-61651-564-5(3)) Saddleback Educational Publishing, Inc.

—Lucky Falcon Mystery, 1 vol. unabr. ed. 2011. (Carter High Mysteries Ser.). (ENG.). 48p. (YA). (gr. 9-12). 9.75 (978-1-61651-565-2(1)) Saddleback Educational Publishing, Inc.

—The Missing Test Mystery, 1 vol. unabr. ed. 2011. (Carter High Mysteries Ser.). (ENG.). 48p. (YA). (gr. 9-12). 9.75 (978-1-61651-566-9(X)) Saddleback Educational Publishing, Inc.

—The Secret Admirer Mystery, 1 vol. unabr. ed. 2011. (Carter High Mysteries Ser.). (ENG.). 48p. (YA). (gr. 9-12). 9.75 (978-1-61651-567-6(8)) Saddleback Educational Publishing, Inc.

—Where Is Mr. Zane?, 1 vol. unabr. ed. 2011. (Carter High Mysteries Ser.). (ENG.). 48p. (YA). (gr. 9-12). 9.75 (978-1-61651-569-0(4)) Saddleback Educational Publishing, Inc.

Robles, Eduardo. La Computadora Maldita. rev. ed. 2007. (Ediciones Castillo Castillo Del Terror Ser.). (SPA & ENG.). 108p. (J). (gr. 4-7). pap. 6.95 (978-970-20-0315-1(6)) Castillo, Ediciones, S. A. de C. V. MEX. Dist: Macmillan.

Rocheleau, Nicole. Ryan, Me, & the Mysterious Book. 2006. (ENG.). 204p. per. 24.95 (978-1-4241-3422-9(6)) PublishAmerica, Inc.

Rochester, B. The Joey Jenkins Mysteries: Something Is Missing at Redding Lake. 2005. 67p. pap. 16.95 (978-1-4241-0065-1(8)) PublishAmerica, Inc.

Rock, Brian. The Deductive Detective, 1 vol. Rogers, Sherry, illus. 2013. (SPA.). 32p. (J). (gr. -1-3). pap. 11.95 (978-1-62855-347-5(2), 51ae7a17-bd39-4045-8844-3feabb101eac) Arbordale Publishing.

Rock, Brian & Rogers, Sherry. El Detective Deductivo, 1 vol. Rogers, Sherry, illus. 2013. (SPA., Illus.). 32p. (J). (gr. -1-2). 17.95 (978-1-60718-708-0(6)) Arbordale Publishing.

Rockley, Frank. Tinderbox Cottage. 2010. 136p. pap. 10.99 (978-1-4490-3120-6(X)) AuthorHouse.

Rodda, Emily. The Ghost of Raven Hill. 2005. (Illus.). 112p. (J). (978-0-439-79770-2(5)) Scholastic, Inc.

Roddy, Lee. Case of the Dangerous Cruise. 2007. (Ladd Family Adventure Ser.: Vol. 11). (Illus.). 145p. (J). (gr. 3-7). per. 7.99 (978-0-88062-260-8(1)) Mott Media.

—The Mystery of the Wild Surfer. 2006. (Ladd Family Adventure Ser.: Vol. 6). (Illus.). 135p. (J). (gr. 4-7). per. 7.99 (978-0-88062-255-4(5)) Mott Media.

—Panic in the Wild Waters. 2007. (Ladd Family Adventure Ser.: Vol. 12). (Illus.). 136p. (J). (gr. 3-7). per. 7.99 (978-0-88062-261-5(X)) Mott Media.

—Terror at Forbidden Falls. 2006. (Ladd Family Adventure Ser.: Vol. 8). (Illus.). 157p. (J). (gr. 3-7). per. 7.99 (978-0-88062-257-8(1)) Mott Media.

Rodrigue, Nancy Temple. Hidden Mickey Adventures 3: The Mermaid's Tale, vol. 3. 2014. (Hidden Mickey Adventures Ser.: 3). (ENG.). 272p. (YA). (gr. 4-17). pap. 14.99 (978-1-938319-05-1(2), DOUBLE-R BKS.) Rodrigue & Sons Co./Double R Books Publishing.

Rodrigues, Naomi. Molly Mouse & the Christmas Mystery. 2013. 24p. pap. 15.99 (978-1-4797-6511-9(2)) Xlibris Corp.

Roe, D. J. The Impossible Dream. 2008. 59p. pap. 16.95 (978-1-60610-173-5(0)) America Star Bks.

Roehrig, Caleb. Death Prefers Blondes. 2020. (ENG.). 464p. (YA). pap. 10.99 (978-1-250-23362-2(3), 900184782) Square Fish.

—Last Seen Leaving. 2018. (ENG.). 352p. (YA). pap. 14.99 (978-1-250-12967-3(2), 900176105) Square Fish.

—White Rabbit. 2019. (ENG.). 352p. (YA). pap. 13.99 (978-1-250-29475-3(4), 900195091) Square Fish.

Roemermann, Jennifer. The Long Grass Tunnel. 2012. 50p. pap. 18.68 (978-1-4797-0300-5(1)) Xlibris Corp.

Rogers, Derek G. Monstrous Myths & Fabulous Fables. 2012. 184p. pap. (978-1-78176-741-2(6)) FeedARead.com.

Rogers, Kelly & ABDO Publishing Company Staff. Rm. 201, 4 vols. Peterschmidt, Betsy, illus. 2016. (Rm. 201 Ser.). (ENG.). 48p. (J). (gr. 3-7). lib. bdg. 136.88 (978-1-62402-166-4(2), 21579, Spellbound) Magic Wagon.

Rohmer, Sax, pseud. The Quest of the Sacred Slipper. 2007. 136p. per. 11.95 (978-1-60312-363-1(6)); 24.95 (978-1-60312-701-1(1)) Aegypan.

—The Sins of Severac Bablon. 2008. 200p. per. 14.95 (978-1-60312-545-1(0)) Aegypan.

RollasonJane. Killer Bees Level 2 Elementary/Lower-Intermediate. 2009. (Cambridge Experience Readers Ser.). (ENG.). 64p. pap. 14.75 (978-84-8323-503-4(X)) Cambridge Univ. Pr.

Rollins, James. Jake Ransom & the Skull King's Shadow. 2010. (Jake Ransom Ser.: 1). (ENG.). 432p. (J). (gr. 5). pap. 7.99 (978-0-06-147381-4(2), HarperCollins) HarperCollins Pubs.

Romeu, Emma. Gregorio Vuelve a Mexico. 2003. (SPA., Illus.). 148p. (J). (gr. 5-8). pap. 9.95 (978-968-19-0367-1(6)) Santillana USA Publishing Co., Inc.

Ronco, Dan. PeaceMaker. Pidlubny, Donna, illus. 2004. (YA). per. 15.49 (978-0-9752711-4-8(8)) Winterwolf Publishing.

Rooney, Anne. Wallace & Gromit's World of Mysteries. 2004. (Illus.). 30p. (gr. 5-9). reprint ed. 30.00 (978-0-7567-7410-3(1)) DIANE Publishing Co.

Rosas, Beverly. The Hand That Scared Jenny. Davis, Jeff, illus. 2008. 47p. pap. 24.95 (978-1-4241-9138-3(6)) PublishAmerica, Inc.

Rose, Simon. The Sphere of Septimus, 1 vol. 2015. (ENG., Illus.), 96p. (J). (gr. 4-7). pap. 9.95 (978-1-896580-75-3(0)) Tradewind Bks. CAN. Dist: Orca Bk. Pubs. USA.

Rosellini, Eleanor. Mystery of the Ancient Coins. 2003. (Illus.). 116p. 18.95 (978-1-57860-122-6(3), Clerisy Pr.) AdventureKEEN.

Rosen, Devora. Mystery in Spain. 2009. 250p. 19.99 (978-1-59826-327-5(7)) Feldheim Pubs.

Rosenberg, Meira. Indiana Bamboo: A Novel. 2017. 166p. (J). pap. (978-1-60454-245-5(4), Iris Pr.) Iris Publishing Group, Inc., The.

Ross, Jeff. Coming Clean, 1 vol. 2012. (Orca Soundings Ser.). (ENG.). 128p. (YA). (gr. 8-12). pap. 9.95 (978-1-4598-0331-2(0), 1459803310) Orca Bk. Pubs. USA.

Ross, Jill. The Real Nitty-Gritty. Pruitt, Gwendolyn, illus. 2010. (ENG.). 60p. (J). (gr. 3-7). pap. 9.95 (978-1-59825-949-0(0)) Shenanigans Series.

Rossell, Judith. Inspector Stilton & the Missing Jewels. Rossell, Judith, illus. 2005. (ENG., Illus.). 32p. pap. (978-1-921049-09-5(X)) Little Hare Bks. AUS. Dist: HarperCollins Pubs. Australia.

—Withering-By-Sea. Rossell, Judith, illus. 2017. (ENG., Illus.). 288p. (J). (gr. 3-7). pap. 8.99 (978-1-4814-4368-5(2)) Simon & Schuster Children's Publishing.

—Wormwood Mire. Rossell, Judith, illus. 2017. (ENG., Illus.). 288p. (J). (gr. 3-7). 16.99 (978-1-4814-4370-8(4), Atheneum Bks. for Young Readers) Simon & Schuster Children's Publishing.

Rouncville, Bibi. Sea Bugs & Moose Eggs. 2009. 52p. pap. 9.50 (978-1-4357-4004-4(1)) Lulu Pr., Inc.

Roux, Madeleine. Asylum. (Asylum Ser.: 1). (ENG.). (YA). (gr. 9). 2014. 336p. pap. 15.99 (978-0-06-222097-4(7)) 2013. (Illus.). 320p. 17.99 (978-0-06-222096-7(9)) HarperCollins Pubs. (HarperCollins).

—Asylum. 2015. (SPA.). 320p. (YA). (gr. 9-12). pap. 20.99 (978-987-612-778-3(0)) V&R Editoras.

—The Asylum Novellas: The Scarlets, the Bone Artists, & the Warden. 2016. (Asylum Novella Ser.). (ENG., Illus.). 352p. (YA). (gr. 9). pap. 10.99 (978-0-06-242446-4(7), HarperCollins) HarperCollins Pubs.

—Sanctum. 2014. (Illus.). 343p. (YA). (978-0-06-235182-1(6)) Harper & Row Ltd.

—Sanctum. 2014. (Asylum Ser.: 2). (ENG., Illus.). 352p. (YA). (gr. 9). 17.99 (978-0-06-222099-8(3), HarperCollins) HarperCollins Pubs.

Rouzer, Walter. Rebel Stone & the Ghost Whisperers. 2009. 304p. 28.95 (978-0-595-51192-1(9)); pap. 18.95 (978-0-595-52313-9(7)) iUniverse, Inc.

Rowe, John. Little Stories for Little People. 2013. 92p. pap. 25.95 (978-1-62516-542-8(0), Strategic Bk. Publishing) Strategic Book Publishing & Rights Agency (SBPRA).

Rowe, W. W. Jerry's Mystery. 2016. (ENG., Illus.). 96p. (J). (gr. 6-9). pap. 8.95 (978-1-936012-70-1(7)) Larson Pubns.

Roy, James. Ichabod Hart & the Lighthouse Mystery. 2003. (Steampunk Ser.). (Illus.). 392p. pap. (978-0-7022-3364-7(1)) Univ. of Queensland Pr.

Roy, Ron. A to Z Mysteries Super Edition #5: The New Year Dragon Dilemma. Gurney, John Steven, illus. 5th ed. 2011. (to Z Mysteries Ser.: 5). 144p. (J). (gr. 1-4). 6.99 (978-0-375-86880-1(1), Random Hse. Bks. for Young Readers) Random Hse. Children's Bks.

—The Absent Author. Gurney, John, illus. unabr. ed. 2004. (A to Z Mysteries Ser.: No. 1). 86p. (J). (gr. k-3). pap. 17.00 incl. audio (978-0-8072-1703-0(4), S FTR 269 SP, Listening Library) Random Hse. Audio Publishing Group.

—April Adventure. 2010. (Calendar Mysteries Ser.: 4). lib. bdg. 14.75 (978-0-606-12465-2(9)) Turtleback.

—August Acrobat. 2012. (Calendar Mysteries Ser.: 8). lib. bdg. 14.75 (978-0-606-26403-7(5)) Turtleback.

—The Bald Bandit. Gurney, John, illus. unabr. ed. 2004. (A to Z Mysteries Ser.: No. 2). 80p. (J). (gr. k-3). pap. 17.00 incl. audio (978-0-8072-1704-7(2), S FTR 270 SP, Listening Library) Random Hse. Audio Publishing Group.

—Calendar Mysteries #1: January Joker. Gurney, John Steven, illus. 2009. (Calendar Mysteries Ser.: 1). 96p. (J). (gr. 1-4). 6.99 (978-0-375-85661-7(7), Random Hse. Bks. for Young Readers) Random Hse. Children's Bks.

—Calendar Mysteries #11: November Night. Gurney, John Steven, illus. 2014. (Calendar Mysteries Ser.: 11). 80p. (J). (gr. 1-4). 7.99 (978-0-385-37165-0(9), Random Hse. Bks. for Young Readers) Random Hse. Children's Bks.

—Calendar Mysteries #12: December Dog. Gurney, John Steven, illus. 2014. (Calendar Mysteries Ser.: 12). 80p. (J). (gr. 1-4). 6.99 (978-0-385-37168-1(3), Random Hse. Bks. for Young Readers) Random Hse. Children's Bks.

—Calendar Mysteries #13: New Year's Eve Thieves. Gurney, John Steven, illus. 2014. (Calendar Mysteries Ser.: 13). 80p. (J). (gr. 1-4). 5.99 (978-0-385-37171-1(3), Random Hse. Bks. for Young Readers) Random Hse. Children's Bks.

—Calendar Mysteries #2: February Friend. Gurney, John Steven, illus. 2009. (Calendar Mysteries Ser.: 2). 80p. (J). (gr. 1-4). 6.99 (978-0-375-85662-4(5), Random Hse. Bks. for Young Readers) Random Hse. Children's Bks.

—Calendar Mysteries #3: March Mischief. Gurney, John Steven, illus. 2010. (Calendar Mysteries Ser.: 3). 80p. (J). (gr. 1-4). 6.99 (978-0-375-85663-1(3), Random Hse. Bks. for Young Readers) Random Hse. Children's Bks.

—Calendar Mysteries #4: April Adventure. Gurney, John Steven, illus. 2010. (Calendar Mysteries Ser.: 4). 80p. (J). (gr. 1-4). 6.99 (978-0-375-86116-1(5), Random Hse. Bks. for Young Readers) Random Hse. Children's Bks.

—Calendar Mysteries #5: May Magic. Gurney, John Steven, illus. 2011. (Calendar Mysteries Ser.: 5). 80p. (J). (gr. 1-4). 6.99 (978-0-375-86111-6(4), Random Hse. Bks. for Young Readers) Random Hse. Children's Bks.

—Calendar Mysteries #6: June Jam. Gurney, John Steven, illus. 2011. (Calendar Mysteries Ser.: 6). 80p. (J). (gr. 1-4). 6.99 (978-0-375-86112-3(2), Random Hse. Bks. for Young Readers) Random Hse. Children's Bks.

—Calendar Mysteries #7: July Jitters. Gurney, John Steven, illus. 2012. (Calendar Mysteries Ser.: 7). 80p. (J). (gr. 1-4). 7.99 (978-0-375-86882-5(8), Random Hse. Bks. for Young Readers) Random Hse. Children's Bks.

—Calendar Mysteries #8: August Acrobat. Gurney, John Steven, illus. 2012. (Calendar Mysteries Ser.: 8). 80p. (J). (gr. 1-4). 6.99 (978-0-375-86886-3(0), Random Hse. Bks. for Young Readers) Random Hse. Children's Bks.

—Calendar Mysteries #9: September Sneakers. Gurney, John Steven, illus. 2013. (Calendar Mysteries Ser.: 9). (ENG.). 80p. (J). (gr. 1-4). 7.99 (978-0-375-86887-0(9), Random Hse. Bks. for Young Readers) Random Hse. Children's Bks.

—The Canary Caper. Gurney, John, illus. unabr. ed. 2004. (A to Z Mysteries Ser.: No. 3). 80p. (J). (gr. k-3). pap. 17.00 incl. audio (978-0-8072-1705-4(0), S FTR 271 SP, Listening Library) Random Hse. Audio Publishing Group.

—Capital Mysteries #10: the Election-Day Disaster. Bush, Timothy, illus. 2008. (Capital Mysteries Ser.: 10). (ENG.). 96p. (J). (gr. 1-4). 5.99 (978-0-375-84805-6(3), Random Hse. Bks. for Young Readers) Random Hse. Children's Bks.

—Capital Mysteries #11: the Secret at Jefferson's Mansion. Bush, Timothy, illus. 2009. (Capital Mysteries Ser.: 11). (ENG.). 96p. (J). (gr. 1-4). 6.99 (978-0-375-84533-8(X), Random Hse. Bks. for Young Readers) Random Hse. Children's Bks.

—Capital Mysteries #12: the Ghost at Camp David. Bush, Timothy, illus. 2010. (Capital Mysteries Ser.: 12). 96p. (J). (gr. 1-4). pap. 5.99 (978-0-375-85925-0(X), Random Hse. Bks. for Young Readers) Random Hse. Children's Bks.

—Capital Mysteries #13: Trapped on the D. C. Train! Bush, Timothy, illus. 2011. (Capital Mysteries Ser.: 13). 96p. (J). (gr. 1-4). 5.99 (978-0-375-85926-7(8), Random Hse. Bks. for Young Readers) Random Hse. Children's Bks.

—Capital Mysteries #14: Turkey Trouble on the National Mall. Bush, Timothy, illus. 2012. (Capital Mysteries Ser.: 14). 96p. (J). (gr. 1-4). 6.99 (978-0-307-93220-4(6), Random Hse. Bks. for Young Readers) Random Hse. Children's Bks.

—Capital Mysteries #4: a Spy in the White House. Bush, Timothy, illus. 2004. (Capital Mysteries Ser.: 4). 96p. (J). (gr. 1-4). 6.99 (978-0-375-82557-6(6), Random Hse. Bks. for Young Readers) Random Hse. Children's Bks.

—Capital Mysteries #5: Who Broke Lincoln's Thumb? Bush, Timothy, illus. 2005. (Capital Mysteries Ser.: 5). 96p. (J). (gr. 1-4). per. 5.99 (978-0-375-82558-3(4), Random Hse. Bks. for Young Readers) Random Hse. Children's Bks.

—Capital Mysteries #7: Trouble at the Treasury. Bush, Timothy, illus. 2006. (Capital Mysteries Ser.: 7). 96p. (J). (gr. 1-4). per. 6.99 (978-0-375-83969-6(0), Random Hse. Bks. for Young Readers) Random Hse. Children's Bks.

—Capital Mysteries #8: Mystery at the Washington Monument. Bush, Timothy, illus. 2007. (Capital Mysteries Ser.: 8). (ENG.). 96p. (J). (gr. 1-4). per. 5.99 (978-0-375-83970-2(4), Random Hse. Bks. for Young Readers) Random Hse. Children's Bks.

—Capital Mysteries #9: a Thief at the National Zoo. Bush, Timothy, illus. 2007. (Capital Mysteries Ser.: 9). 96p. (J). (gr. 1-4). per. 5.99 (978-0-375-84804-9(5), Random Hse. Bks. for Young Readers) Random Hse. Children's Bks.

—The Castle Crime. 2014. (to Z Mysteries Ser.: 32). lib. bdg. 16.00 (978-0-606-35190-4(6)) Turtleback.

—The Election-Day Disaster. Bush, Timothy, illus. 2008. (Capital Mysteries Ser.: No. 10). 87p. (gr. 1-4). 15.00 (978-0-7569-8802-9(0)) Perfection Learning Corp.

—The Ghost at Camp David. 2010. (Capital Mysteries Ser.: 12). lib. bdg. 14.75 (978-0-606-14010-2(7)) Turtleback.

—July Jitters. 2012. (Calendar Mysteries Ser.: 7). lib. bdg. 14.75 (978-0-606-26402-0(7)) Turtleback.

—June Jam, 6. Gurney, John, illus. 2011. (Calendar Mysteries Ser.). (ENG.). 80p. (J). (gr. 1-4). lib. bdg. 18.69 (978-0-375-96112-0(7)) Random House Publishing Group.

—June Jam. 2011. (Calendar Mysteries Ser.: 6). lib. bdg. 14.75 (978-0-606-16114-5(7)) Turtleback.

—March Mischief. 2010. (Calendar Mysteries Ser.: 3). lib. bdg. 14.75 (978-0-606-12460-7(8)) Turtleback.

—Mayflower Treasure Hunt. Gurney, John, illus. 2007. (to Z Mysteries Ser.: 28). 114p. (gr. 4-7). lib. bdg. 16.00 (978-1-4177-9141-5(1)) Turtleback.

—The Missing Mummy. (A to Z Mystery Ser.: Vol. 13). (J). 11.32 (978-0-7383-3465-3(0)) Booksource, The.

—Mystery at the Washington Monument. Bush, Timothy, illus. 2007. (Capital Mysteries Ser.: No. 8). 87p. (gr. 1-4). 15.00 (978-0-7569-7845-7(9)) Perfection Learning Corp.

—Mystery at the Washington Monument, 8. Bush, Timothy, illus. 2007. (Capital Mysteries Ser.: No. 8). (ENG.). 87p. (J). (gr. 3-6). lib. bdg. 17.44 (978-0-375-93970-9(9)) Random House Publishing Group.

—October Ogre. 2013. (Calendar Mysteries Ser.: 10). lib. bdg. 14.75 (978-0-606-32232-4(9)) Turtleback.

—The School Skeleton. Gurney, John, illus. 2003. (to Z Mysteries Ser.: 19). (gr. k-3). lib. bdg. 14.75 (978-0-613-62405-3(X)) Turtleback.

—September Sneakers. 2013. (Calendar Mysteries Ser.: 9). lib. bdg. 14.75 (978-0-606-32231-7(0)) Turtleback.

—Sleepy Hollow Sleepover. 4th ed. 2010. (to Z Mysteries Ser.: 30). lib. bdg. 16.00 (978-0-606-14007-2(7)) Turtleback.

—A Spy in the White House, 4. Bush, Timothy, tr. Bush, Timothy, illus. 2004. (Capital Mysteries Ser.: No. 4). (ENG.). 86p. (J). (gr. 2-4). lib. bdg. 17.44 (978-0-375-92557-3(0)) Random House Publishing Group.

—A Thief at the National Zoo. Bush, Timothy, illus. 2008. (Capital Mysteries Ser.: No. 9). 87p. (gr. k-3). 15.00 (978-0-7569-8329-1(0)) Perfection Learning Corp.

—A Thief at the National Zoo, 9. Bush, Timothy, illus. 2007. (Capital Mysteries Ser.: No. 9). (ENG.). 87p. (J). (gr. 2-4). lib. bdg. 17.44 (978-0-375-94804-6(X)) Random House Publishing Group.

—A to Z Mysteries: Collection #1, No. 1. Gurney, John Steven, illus. 2010. (to Z Mysteries Ser.: Nos. 1-4). (ENG.). 384p. (J). (gr. 1-4). 9.99 (978-0-375-85946-5(2), Random Hse. Bks. for Young Readers) Random Hse. Children's Bks.

—A to Z Mysteries Super Edition 1: Detective Camp. Gurney, John Steven, illus. 2006. (to Z Mysteries Ser.: 1). 144p. (J). (gr. 1-4). per. 6.99 (978-0-375-83534-6(2), Random Hse. Bks. for Young Readers) Random Hse. Children's Bks.

—A to Z Mysteries Super Edition #10: Colossal Fossil. Gurney, John Steven, illus. 2018. (to Z Mysteries Ser.: 10). 144p. (J). (gr. 1-4). 6.99 (978-0-399-55198-7(0), Random Hse. Bks. for Young Readers) Random Hse. Children's Bks.

—A to Z Mysteries Super Edition #11: Grand Canyon Grab. Gurney, John Steven, illus. 2019. (to Z Mysteries Ser.: 11). 144p. (J). (gr. 1-4). 6.99 (978-0-525-57886-4(2), Random Hse. Bks. for Young Readers) Random Hse. Children's Bks.

—A to Z Mysteries Super Edition 2: Mayflower Treasure Hunt. Gurney, John Steven, illus. 2nd ed. 2007. (to Z Mysteries Ser.: 2). 128p. (J). (gr. 1-4). per. 6.99 (978-0-375-83937-5(2), Random Hse. Bks. for Young Readers) Random Hse. Children's Bks.

—A to Z Mysteries Super Edition 3: White House White-Out. Gurney, John Steven, illus. 2008. (to Z Mysteries Ser.: 3). 144p. (J). (gr. 1-4). 6.99 (978-0-375-84721-9(9), Random Hse. Bks. for Young Readers) Random Hse. Children's Bks.

—A to Z Mysteries Super Edition #4: Sleepy Hollow Sleepover. Gurney, John Steven, illus. 4th ed. 2010. (to Z Mysteries Ser.: 4). 144p. (J). (gr. 1-4). pap. 6.99 (978-0-375-86669-2(8), Random Hse. Bks. for Young Readers) Random Hse. Children's Bks.

—A to Z Mysteries Super Edition #6: the Castle Crime. Gurney, John Steven, illus. 2014. (to Z Mysteries Ser.: 6). 144p. (J). (gr. 1-4). 6.99 (978-0-385-37159-9(4), Random Hse. Bks. for Young Readers) Random Hse. Children's Bks.

—A to Z Mysteries Super Edition #8: Secret Admirer. Gurney, John Steven, illus. 2015. (to Z Mysteries Ser.: 8). 144p. (J). (gr. 1-4). 5.99 (978-0-553-52399-7(6), Random Hse. Bks. for Young Readers) Random Hse. Children's Bks.

—A to Z Mysteries Super Edition #9: April Fools' Fiasco. Gurney, John Steven, illus. 2017. (to Z Mysteries Ser.: 9). 144p. (J). (gr. 1-4). 6.99 (978-0-399-55195-6(6), Random Hse. Bks. for Young Readers) Random Hse. Children's Bks.

—A to Z Mysteries: the School Skeleton. Gurney, John Steven, illus. 2003. (to Z Mysteries Ser.: 19). 96p. (J). (gr. 1-4). pap. 6.99 (978-0-375-81368-9(3), Random Hse. Bks. for Young Readers) Random Hse. Children's Bks.

—A to Z Mysteries: the Talking T. Rex. Gurney, John Steven, illus. 2003. (to Z Mysteries Ser.: 20). 96p. (J). (gr. 1-4). pap. 6.99 (978-0-375-81369-6(1), Random Hse. Bks. for Young Readers) Random Hse. Children's Bks.

—A to Z Mysteries: the Unwilling Umpire. Gurney, John Steven, illus. 2004. (to Z Mysteries Ser.: 21). 96p. (J). (gr. 1-4). 6.99 (978-0-375-81370-2(5), Random Hse. Bks. for Young Readers) Random Hse. Children's Bks.

—A to Z Mysteries: the Vampire's Vacation. Gurney, John Steven, illus. 2004. (to Z Mysteries Ser.: 22). 96p. (J). (gr. 1-4). pap. 6.99 (978-0-375-82479-1(0), Random Hse. Bks. for Young Readers) Random Hse. Children's Bks.

—A to Z Mysteries: the White Wolf. Gurney, John Steven, illus. 2004. (to Z Mysteries Ser.: 23). 96p. (J). (gr. 1-4). pap. 6.99 (978-0-375-82480-7(4), Random Hse. Bks. for Young Readers) Random Hse. Children's Bks.

—A to Z Mysteries: the X'ed-Out X-Ray. Gurney, John Steven, illus. 2005. (to Z Mysteries Ser.: 24). 96p. (J). (gr. 1-4). 6.99 (978-0-375-82481-4(2), Random Hse. Bks. for Young Readers) Random Hse. Children's Bks.

—A to Z Mysteries: the Yellow Yacht. Gurney, John Steven, illus. 2005. (to Z Mysteries Ser.: 25). 96p. (J). (gr. 1-4). pap. 6.99 (978-0-375-82482-1(0), Random Hse. Bks. for Young Readers) Random Hse. Children's Bks.

—A to Z Mysteries: the Zombie Zone. Gurney, John Steven, illus. 2005. (to Z Mysteries Ser.: 26). 96p. (J). (gr. 1-4). pap. 6.99 (978-0-375-82483-8(9), Random Hse. Bks. for Young Readers) Random Hse. Children's Bks.

—Trouble at the Treasury, 7. Bush, Timothy, illus. 2003. (Capital Mysteries Ser.: No. 7). (ENG.). 86p. (J). (gr. 2-4). lib. bdg. 17.44 (978-0-375-93969-3(5)) Random House Publishing Group.

—The Unwilling Umpire. Gurney, John, illus. 2004. (to Z Mysteries Ser.: 21). (gr. k-3). lib. bdg. 14.75 (978-0-613-82496-5(2)) Turtleback.

—White House White-Out. Gurney, John, illus. 2008. (A to Z Mysteries Ser.: No. 3). 124p. (gr. 1-4). 15.00 (978-0-7569-8799-2(7)) Perfection Learning Corp.

—Who Broke Lincoln's Thumb?, 5. Bush, Timothy, illus. 2005. (Capital Mysteries Ser.: No. 5). (ENG.). 86p. (J). (gr. 2-4). lib. bdg. 17.44 (978-0-375-92558-0(9)) Random House Publishing Group.

Roy, Ronald. Capital Mysteries #14: Turkey Trouble on the National Mall, 14. Bush, Timothy, illus. 2012. (Capital Mysteries Ser.). (ENG.). 96p. (J). (gr. 1-4). lib. bdg. 17.44 (978-0-375-87004-0(0)) Random House Publishing Group.

—December Dog. 2014. (Calendar Mysteries Ser.: 12). lib. bdg. 14.75 (978-0-606-36019-7(0)) Turtleback.

—New Year's Eve Thieves. 2014. (Calendar Mysteries Ser.: 13). lib. bdg. 14.75 (978-0-606-36020-3(4)) Turtleback.

—November Night. 2014. (Calendar Mysteries Ser.: 11). lib. bdg. 14.75 (978-0-606-36018-0(2)) Turtleback.

Rozum, John. Scooby-Doo in Yankee Doodle Danger, 1 vol. Laguna, Fabio, illus. 2013. (Scooby-Doo Graphic Novels Ser.). (ENG.). 24p. (J). (gr. 2-6). lib. bdg. 31.36 (978-1-61479-054-9(X), 587, Graphic Novels) Spotlight.

Rubin, Sarah. The Impossible Clue. 2017. 293p. (J). pap. (978-0-545-94272-0(1), Chicken Hse., The) Scholastic, Inc.

Ruby, Laura. The Shadow Cipher. 2018. (York Ser.: 1). (J). lib. bdg. 18.40 (978-0-606-41390-9(1)) Turtleback.

—York: The Shadow Cipher. Stevenson, Dave, illus. 2018. (York Ser.: 1). (ENG.). 496p. (J). (gr. 3-7). pap. 9.99 (978-0-06-230694-4(4), Waldon Pond Pr.) HarperCollins Pubs.

—York: the Shadow Cipher. Stevenson, Dave, illus. 2017. (York Ser.: 1). (ENG.). 496p. (J). (gr. 3-7). E-Book (978-0-06-230695-1(2), 9780062306951); 17.99 (978-0-06-230693-7(6)) HarperCollins Pubs. (Waldon Pond Pr.).

Ruby, Lois. Rebel Spirits. 2013. 292p. (YA). (978-0-545-55282-0(6)) Scholastic, Inc.

Rucker, Noah. Mystery of the Shadows. 2005. 27p. (J). 5.00 (978-1-882695-21-8(6)) Patagonia Pr.

Ruiz Zafón, Carlos. Marina. 2009. (Best Seller (Edebe) Ser.). (SPA.). 286p. pap. (978-84-236-8726-8(0)) Edebé.

Runholt, Susan. The Mystery of the Third Lucretia. 2009. (Kari & Lucas Mystery Ser.: 1). (ENG.). 304p. (J). (gr. 5-18). pap. 6.99 (978-0-14-241338-8(0), Puffin Books) Penguin Young Readers Group.

Ruplin, Ferdinand A. The Mystery of Sarah & the Gypsies: Illustrated by Lois L. Ruplin. Ruplin, Lois L., illus. 2004. (ENG.). 38p. pap. 15.99 (978-1-4134-1560-5(1)) Xlibris Corp.

Rusch, Elizabeth. Muddy Max: The Mystery of Marsh Creek. Lawrence, Mike, illus. 2014. (ENG.). 224p. (J). pap. 9.99 (978-1-4494-3561-5(0)) Andrews McMeel Publishing.

Rusch, Elizabeth & Lawrence, Mike. Muddy Max: The Mystery of Marsh Creek. 2016. (ENG., Illus.). (J). (gr. 2-6). 37.99 (978-1-4494-7388-4(1)) Andrews McMeel Publishing.

Rush, Barbara & Stratton, Jane. The Boat in the Attic. 2012. (ENG.). 30p. pap. 15.00 (978-1-938002-02-1(4), Hummingbird World Media) Double Edge Pr.

Rush, Jennifer. Erased. 2014. (Altered Ser.: 2). (ENG.). 352p. (YA). (gr. 7-17). pap. 18.99 (978-0-316-19714-4(9)) Little, Brown Bks. for Young Readers.

—Reborn. 2016. (Altered Ser.: 3). (ENG.). 384p. (YA). (gr. 7-17). pap. 10.99 (978-0-316-19707-6(6)) Little, Brown Bks. for Young Readers.

Rushford, Patricia H. Secrets of Ghost Island. 2007. (J). (978-88-02-46255-4(0)) Moody Pubs.

Russel, Mary. Flickertail & Paint, Barnyard Sleuths, 1 vol. 2010. 96p. pap. 19.95 (978-1-4489-7248-7(5)) America Star Bks.

Russell, Elaine. Martin Mcmillan & the Lost Inca City. Cornell du Houx, Emily M. D., illus. 2005. 128p. (gr. 5-18). pap. 10.00 (978-1-882190-86-7(6)) Solon Ctr. for Research & Publishing.

Russell, Sharman Apt. Teresa of the New World. 2015. (ENG.). 192p. (gr. 6-6). 14.99 (978-1-63158-042-0(6), Yucca Publishing) Skyhorse Publishing Co., Inc.

Ryan, Jessica. The Mystery of Arroyo Seco. Stone, David, illus. 2011. 186p. 42.95 (978-1-258-08470-7(8)) Literary Licensing, LLC.

Ryan, Tom. Keep This to Yourself. 2019. (ENG.). 320p. (YA). (gr. 8-12). 17.99 (978-0-8075-4151-7(6), 807541516) Whitman, Albert & Co.

Rylander, Chris. The Codename Conspiracy #2: Countdown Zero. 2016. (Codename Conspiracy Ser.: 2). (ENG.). 384p. (J). (gr. 3-7). pap. 6.99 (978-0-06-212012-0(3), Waldon Pond Pr.) HarperCollins Pubs.

Rylant, Cynthia. The Case of the Climbing Cat. Karas, G. Brian, illus. 2003. (High-Rise Private Eyes Ser.: No. 2). (J). (gr. k-3). 28.95 incl. audio compact disk (978-1-59112-611-9(8)) Live Oak Media.

—The Case of the Desperate Duck. Karas, G. Brian, illus. 2005. (High-Rise Private Eyes Ser.: No. 8). 48p. (J). (gr. k-3). 14.99 (978-0-06-053451-6(6)); lib. bdg. 15.89 (978-0-06-053452-3(4)) HarperCollins Pubs.

—The Case of the Desperate Duck, 4 bks., Set. 2007. (High-Rise Private Eyes Ser.: Bk. 8). (J). (gr. k-2). pap. 31.95 incl. audio compact disk (978-1-4301-0067-6(2)); pap. 29.95 incl. audio (978-1-4301-0065-2(6)) Live Oak Media.

—The Case of the Desperate Duck. Karas, G. Brian, illus. 2006. (High-Rise Private Eyes Ser.). 48p. (gr. -1-3). 14.00 (978-0-7569-6958-5(1)) Perfection Learning Corp.

—The Case of the Fidgety Fox. Karas, G. Brian, illus. unabr. ed. 2005. (High-Rise Private Eyes Ser.: No. 6). (J). (gr. k-4). 25.95 incl. audio (978-1-59519-405-3(3));Set. pap. 29.95 incl. audio (978-1-59519-406-0(1));Set. pap. 31.95 incl. audio compact disk (978-1-59519-410-7(X)) Live Oak Media.

—The Case of the Fidgety Fox. Karas, G. Brian, illus. 2004. (High-Rise Private Eyes Ser.). 58p. (J). (gr. 1-3). 11.65 (978-0-7569-3210-7(6)) Perfection Learning Corp.

—The Case of the Missing Monkey. Karas, G. Brian, illus. 2003. (High-Rise Private Eyes Ser.: No. 1). 28.95 incl. audio compact disk (978-1-59112-615-7(0)) Live Oak Media.

—The Case of the Puzzling Possum. Karas, G. Brian, illus. 2003. (High-Rise Private Eyes Ser.: No. 3). (J). (gr. k-3). 28.95 incl. audio compact disk (978-1-59112-619-5(3)) Live Oak Media.

—The Case of the Sleepy Sloth. Karas, G. Brian, illus. unabr. ed. 2005. (High-Rise Private Eyes Ser.: No. 5). (J). (gr. k-4). 29.95 incl. audio (978-1-59519-413-8(4)); 28.95 incl. audio compact disk (978-1-59519-417-6(7));Set. pap. 29.95 incl. audio (978-1-59519-414-5(2));Set. pap. 31.95 incl. audio compact disk (978-1-59519-418-3(5)) Live Oak Media.

—The High-Rise Private Eye: The Case of the Troublesome Turtle. Karas, G. Brian, illus. 2003. (High-Rise Private Eyes Ser.: No. 4). (J). (gr. k-3). 28.95 incl. audio compact disk (978-1-59112-623-2(1)); 25.95 incl. audio (978-1-59112-202-9(3)); pap. 31.95 incl. audio compact disk (978-1-59112-624-9(X)); pap. 29.95 incl. audio (978-1-59112-203-6(1)) Live Oak Media.

—The High-Rise Private Eyes #1: the Case of the Missing Monkey. Karas, G. Brian, illus. 2003. (I Can Read Level 2 Ser.: No. 1). (ENG.). 48p. (J). (gr. k-3). pap. 4.99 (978-0-06-444306-7(X), Greenwillow Bks.) HarperCollins Pubs.

—The High-Rise Private Eyes #8: the Case of the Desperate Duck. Karas, G. Brian, illus. 2006. (I Can Read Level 2 Ser.: No. 8). (ENG.). 48p. (J). (gr. k-3). pap. 4.99 (978-0-06-053453-0(2), Greenwillow Bks.) HarperCollins Pubs.

—The High-Rise Private Eyes Series. Karas, G. Brian, illus. 2003. pap. 61.95 incl. audio (978-1-59112-430-6(1)); pap. 68.95 incl. audio compact disk (978-1-59112-858-8(7)) Live Oak Media.

Sadar, Albin. Hamster Holmes: A Mystery Comes Knocking. 2015. (Simon & Schuster Ready-To-Read Level 2 Ser.). lib. bdg. 13.55 (978-0-606-37142-1(7)) Turtleback.

—Hamster Holmes, a Mystery Comes Knocking: Ready-To-Read Level 2. Fabbretti, Valerio, illus. 2015. (Hamster Holmes Ser.: 1). (ENG.). 32p. (J). (gr. k-2). 16.99 (978-1-4814-2037-2(2)); pap. 4.99 (978-1-4814-2036-5(4)) Simon Spotlight. (Simon Spotlight).

—Hamster Holmes, Combing for Clues: Ready-To-Read Level 2. Fabbretti, Valerio, illus. 2015. (Hamster Holmes Ser.: 2). (ENG.). 32p. (J). (gr. k-2). pap. 4.99 (978-1-4814-2039-6(9), Simon Spotlight) Simon Spotlight.

—Hamster Holmes, on the Right Track. 2016. (Simon & Schuster Ready-To-Read Level 2 Ser.). lib. bdg. 13.55 (978-0-606-38245-8(3)) Turtleback.

—Hamster Holmes, on the Right Track: Ready-To-Read Level 2. Fabbretti, Valerio, illus. 2016. (Hamster Holmes Ser.). (ENG.). 32p. (J). (gr. k-2). pap. 4.99 (978-1-4814-2042-6(9), Simon Spotlight) Simon Spotlight.

Sadler, Marilyn & Comstock, Eric. Charlie Piechart & the Case of the Missing Hat. Comstock, Eric, illus. 2016. (Charlie Piechart Ser.). (ENG., Illus.). 40p. (J). (gr. -1-3). 17.99 (978-0-06-237056-3(1), HarperCollins) HarperCollins Pubs.

Sage, Angie. Araminta Spookie 3: Frognapped. Pickering, Jimmy, illus. 2008. (Araminta Spookie Ser.: 3). (ENG.). 224p. (J). (gr. 2-5). pap. 6.99 (978-0-06-077489-9(4), Tegen, Katherine Bks) HarperCollins Pubs.

—Skeleton Island. 2016. (Araminta Spookie Adventure Ser.: 2). (ENG., Illus.). 176p. (J). 16.99 (978-1-61963-945-4(9), 9781619639454, Bloomsbury USA Childrens) Bloomsbury Publishing USA.

Said, S. F. Varjak Paw. McKean, Dave, illus. 2005. (ENG.). 256p. (J). (gr. 3-7). reprint ed. pap. 8.99 (978-0-440-42076-7(8), Yearling) Random Hse. Children's Bks.

Salane, Jeffrey. The Haunting of Hounds Hollow. 2018. 339p. (J). pap. (978-1-338-10550-6(7), Scholastic Pr.) Scholastic, Inc.

Saldana, Rene. Case of Pen Gone Missing/El Caso de la Pluma Perdida. Villarroel, Carolina, tr. from ENG. Mora, Giovanni, illus. 2009. (SPA & ENG.). 80p. (J). (gr. 3-7). pap. 9.95 (978-1-55885-555-7(6), Piñata Books) Arte Publico Pr.

Saldaña, René. The Lemon Tree Caper: A Mickey Rangel Mystery / la Intriga del limonero: Colección Mickey Rangel, detective Privado. Rosales-Yeomans, Natalia, tr. from ENG. 2011. (SPA & ENG.). (J). pap. 9.95 (978-1-55885-709-4(5), Piñata Books) Arte Publico Pr.

Saldana, Rene, Jr. A Mystery Bigger Than Big / un Misterio Mas Grande Que Grandisimo: A Mickey Rangel Mystery / Colección Mickey Rangel, Detective Privado. 2016. (Mickey Rangel Mystery / Coleccion Mickey Rangel, Detective P Ser.). (MUL, ENG & SPA., Illus.). 64p. (J). (gr. 3-6). pap. 9.95 (978-1-55885-824-4(5), Piñata Books) Arte Publico Pr.

Saldaña, René. The Mystery of the Mischievous Marker / el Misterio Del Malvado Marcador: A Mickey Rangel Mystery / Colección Mickey Rangel, Detective Privado. Villarroel, Carolina, tr. from ENG. 2013. (Mickey Rangel Mystery / Colección Mickey Rangel, Detective Privado Ser.). (SPA.). 64p. (J). pap. 9.95 (978-1-55885-776-6(1), Piñata Books) Arte Publico Pr.

Salisbury, Linda G. The Mysterious Jamestown Suitcase: A Bailey Fish Adventure. Grotke, Christopher A., illus. 2006. (Bailey Fish Adventures Ser.). 191p. (J). (gr. 3-7). per. 8.95 (978-1-881539-43-8(1)) Tabby Hse. Bks.

—The Thief at Keswick Inn: A Bailey Fish Adventure. Grotke, Christopher A., illus. 2006. (Bailey Fish Adventures Ser.). 191p. (J). (gr. 3-7). per. 8.95 (978-1-881539-41-4(5)) Tabby Hse. Bks.

Salmon, Charles Ray, afterword by. The Adventures of Pittypat & Tippytoe, 1vol., 1vol. 2004. (ENG.). 232p. (YA). per. 12.99 (978-0-9760045-0-9(X), Reluctant Reader Bks.) Cronus College.

Salote, Ana. Oy Yew. 2013. 276p. pap. (978-1-78299-659-0(1)) FeedARead.com.

Salvatierra, Dante. Latchkey Kids & the Fight for A Free F. 2006. (ENG.). 236p. pap. 13.95 (978-1-4303-0969-7(5)) Lulu Pr., Inc.

Sam, Kagan, illus. Mr. Duz Solves a Mystery. 2007. 24p. (J). 5.95 (978-0-9796226-0-1(3)) MrDuz.com.

Sampson, Brent. Aidan's Shoes. Switzer, Bobbi, illus. 2006. (ENG.). 28p. per. 12.95 (978-1-59800-684-1(3)) Outskirts Pr., Inc.

Sam's Last Summer. 2006. (J). per. 5.95 (978-0-9790796-3-4(2)) PJR Assocs., Ltd.

Sander, Sonia. Scooby-Doo & the Battle of the Snowboarders, 1 vol. Alcadia, S. N. C., illus. 2015. (Scooby-Doo Leveled Readers Ser.). (ENG.). 32p. (J). (gr. k-4). lib. bdg. 31.36 (978-1-61479-415-8(4), 19438) Spotlight.

—Scooby-Doo & the Chocolate Phantom, 1 vol. 2015. (Scooby-Doo Comic Readers Ser.). (ENG., Illus.). 32p. (J). (gr. -1-3). lib. bdg. 31.36 (978-1-61479-451-6(0), 19430, Graphic Novels) Spotlight.

—Scooby-Doo & the International Express. 2009. (Illus.). 32p. (J). pap. (978-0-545-16283-8(1)) Scholastic, Inc.

—Scooby-Doo in Food Fight!, 1 vol. 2015. (Scooby-Doo Comic Readers Ser.). (ENG., Illus.). 32p. (J). (gr. -1-3). lib. bdg. 31.36 (978-1-61479-454-7(5), 19433, Graphic Novels) Spotlight.

—Scooby-Doo in Shiver Me Timbers, 1 vol. 2015. (Scooby-Doo! Ser.). (ENG., Illus.). 32p. (J). (gr. k-4). lib. bdg. 31.36 (978-1-61479-408-0(1), 19447, Picture Bk.) Spotlight.

—Witching Hour. 2009. (Scooby Reader 25 Ser.). (ENG., Illus.). 32p. (J). (gr. -1-3). pap. 3.99 *(978-0-545-16106-0(1))* Scholastic, Inc.

Sanders, Gaye Lynn. Chameleon Girl. 2008. 60p. pap. 16.95 *(978-1-60703-643-2(6))* America Star Bks.

Sanders, Russell J. Special Effect. 2016. (ENG., Illus.). (J). 24.99 *(978-1-63533-074-8(2)*, Harmony Ink Pr.) Dreamspinner Pr.

Sanderson, Nancy. Summer of the Painted Horse. 2009. 188p. pap. 14.49 *(978-1-4490-2312-6(6))* AuthorHouse.

Sands, Kevin. The Assassin's Curse. 2017. (Blackthorn Key Ser.: 3). (ENG., Illus.). 544p. (J). (gr. 5-9). 19.99 *(978-1-5344-0523-3(2)*, Aladdin) Simon & Schuster Children's Publishing.

—The Assassin's Curse. 2018. (Blackthorn Key Ser.: 3). (ENG., Illus.). 560p. (J). (gr. 5-9). pap. 9.99 *(978-1-5344-0524-0(0)*, Simon & Schuster/Paula Wiseman Bks.) Simon & Schuster/Paula Wiseman Bks.

—The Blackthorn Key. 2016. lib. bdg. 18.40 *(978-0-606-38966-2(0))* Turtleback.

—Call of the Wraith. (Blackthorn Key Ser.: 4). (ENG.). 512p. (J). (gr. 5-9). 2019. pap. 9.99 *(978-1-5344-2848-5(8))* 2018. (Illus.). 19.99 *(978-1-5344-2847-8(X))* Simon & Schuster Children's Publishing. (Aladdin).

Santomenna, Joan E. & Santomenna, Marco D. Caribbean Capers. 2003. (Illus.). 144p. (YA). (gr. 3-9). pap. 9.95 *(978-0-9643407-2-5(0))* WindSpirit Publishing.

Sarfati, Sonia. La Comédienne Disparue. 2003. (Roman Jeunesse Ser.). (FRE.). 96p. (YA). (gr. 4-7). pap. *(978-2-89021-211-4(4))* Diffusion du livre Mirabel (DLM).

Sargeant, Glen. Finders Keepers, 1 vol. 2009. 142p. pap. 24.95 *(978-1-61582-202-7(X))* America Star Bks.

—Ghost Ship: A y-Files Mystery. 2012. 128p. pap. 19.95 *(978-1-4626-8020-7(8))* America Star Bks.

Satyajit, Ray. Adventures of Feluda: Mystery of the Elephant God. 2019. (Adventures of Feluda Ser.). (ENG.). 112p. pap. 14.95 *(978-0-14-333574-0(X)*, Puffin) Penguin Bks. India PVT, Ltd IND. Dist: Independent Pubs. Group.

—Adventures of Feluda: the Curse of the Goddess. 2016. (Adventures of Feluda Ser.). (ENG.). 104p. (J). pap. 19.99 *(978-0-14-333451-4(4)*, Puffin) Penguin Bks. India PVT, Ltd IND. Dist: Independent Pubs. Group.

—Adventures of Feluda: the Royal Bengal Mystery. 2016. (Adventures of Feluda Ser.). (ENG.). 112p. (J). pap. 19.99 *(978-0-14-333450-7(6)*, Puffin) Penguin Bks. India PVT, Ltd IND. Dist: Independent Pubs. Group.

Savage, J. Scott. Case File 13 #2: Making the Team. Holgate, Doug, illus. 2015. (Case File 13 Ser.: 2). (ENG.). 288p. (J). (gr. 3-7). pap. 6.99 *(978-0-06-213335-9(7)*, HarperCollins) HarperCollins Pubs.

Savage, Kim. Beautiful Broken Girls. 2018. (ENG.). 352p. (YA). pap. 14.99 *(978-1-250-14416-4(7)*, 900180623) Square Fish.

Savageau, Tony. The Mud House Mystery: A Wild Bunch Adventure. Raditz, JoAnne, illus. 2004. (J). pap. 9.95 *(978-0-9759737-0-7(3))* Blue Mustang Pr.

Saxon, Victoria. Big Trouble in Little Rodentia. 2016. (Illus.). (J). *(978-1-5182-0883-6(5))* Random House Children's Books.

Sazaklis, John. The Mystery of the Maze Monster, 1 vol. Neely, Scott, illus. 2014. (You Choose Stories: Scooby-Doo Ser.). (ENG.). 112p. (J). (gr. 2-6). pap. 6.95 *(978-1-4342-7928-6(6)*, 124639, Stone Arch Bks.) Capstone.

Scanes, Amy. The Chosen: Book Two of the Abon Trilogy. 2007. 304p. per. 18.95 *(978-0-595-45990-2(0))* iUniverse, Inc.

Scarborough, Sheryl. To Catch a Killer: A Novel. 2018. (Erin Blake Ser.: 1). (ENG.). 336p. (YA). pap. 10.99 *(978-0-7653-8192-7(3)*, 900151018, Tor Teen) Doherty, Tom Assocs., LLC.

—To Right the Wrongs. 2019. (Erin Blake Ser.: 2). (ENG.). 320p. (YA). pap. 13.99 *(978-0-7653-8194-1(X)*, 900151025, Tor Teen) Doherty, Tom Assocs., LLC.

Schaedler, Peggy. Dagger & Dash: The Scrimshaw Medallion. 2012. 156p. (gr. 4-6). 30.95 *(978-1-4582-0279-6(8))*; (J). pap. 12.99 *(978-1-4582-0277-2(1))* Author Solutions, LLC. (Abbott Pr.).

Scheunemann, Pam. Cat Tails. Chawla, Neena, illus. 2006. (Fact & Fiction Ser.). 24p. (J). pap. 48.42 *(978-1-59679-928-8(5))* ABDO Publishing Co.

Schindler, Holly. Feral. 2014. (ENG.). 432p. (YA). (gr. 8). 17.99 *(978-0-06-222020-2(9)*, HarperTeen) HarperCollins Pubs.

Schlegl, Stacey Lynn & Schlegl, Abigail. MerMountain. 2012. 84p. (J). pap. 11.95 *(978-0-9850272-2-3(3))* Jan-Carol Publishing, INC.

Schluenderfritz, Theodore & Hicks, Clifford B. Alvin Fernald, Mayor for a Day. 2007. (Alvin Fernald Mystery Ser.). (ENG., Illus.). 142p. (J). (gr. 4-11). pap. 11.95 *(978-1-883937-98-0(1))* Ignatius Pr.

Schmitt, Gary. R. O. Dents in the School. 2009. 73p. pap. 19.95 *(978-1-60813-737-4(6))* America Star Bks.

Scholastic. Peppa's Storybook Collection (Peppa Pig) 2017. (ENG., Illus.). 192p. (J). (gr. -1-k). 12.99 *(978-1-338-21199-3(4))* Scholastic, Inc.

Scholastic, Inc. Staff & Duendes Del Sur Staff, contrib. by. Scooby-Doo! & the Mummy's Curse. 2005. (Illus.). 24p. (J). *(978-1-4156-3913-9(2))* Scholastic, Inc.

Schorr, Titus. The Matzo Mystery, 1 vol., 1. 2015. (Rosen REAL Readers: Social Studies Nonfiction / Fiction: Myself, My Community, My World Ser.). (ENG.). 12p. (J). (gr. k-1). pap. 6.33 *(978-1-5081-1985-2(6)*, ae2ac623-baf1-4c9b-809f-9d83144e5721, Rosen Classroom) Rosen Publishing Group, Inc., The.

Schraff, Anne. The Case of the Bad Seed (Detective), 1 vol. 2017. (Pageturners Ser.). (ENG.). 76p. (YA). (gr. 9-12). 10.75 *(978-1-68021-383-6(0))* Saddleback Educational Publishing, Inc.

—The Case of the Cursed Chalet (Detective), 1 vol. 2017. (Pageturners Ser.). (ENG.). 76p. (YA). (gr. 9-12). 10.75 *(978-1-68021-384-3(9))* Saddleback Educational Publishing, Inc.

—The Case of the Dead Duck (Detective), 1 vol. 2017. (Pageturners Ser.). (ENG.). 76p. (YA). (gr. 9-12). 10.75 *(978-1-68021-385-0(7))* Saddleback Educational Publishing, Inc.

—The Case of the Wanted Man (Detective), 1 vol. 2017. (Pageturners Ser.). (ENG.). 76p. (YA). (gr. 9-12). 10.75 *(978-1-68021-386-7(5))* Saddleback Educational Publishing, Inc.

—The Case of the Watery Grave (Detective), 1 vol. 2017. (Pageturners Ser.). (ENG.). 76p. (YA). (gr. 9-12). 10.75 *(978-1-68021-387-4(3))* Saddleback Educational Publishing, Inc.

—The Cold, Cold Shoulder (Suspense), 1 vol. 2017. (Pageturners Ser.). (ENG.). 76p. (YA). (gr. 9-12). 10.75 *(978-1-68021-406-2(3))* Saddleback Educational Publishing, Inc.

—The Darkest Secret. 2008. (Passages Ser.). 114p. (YA). (gr. 7-9). lib. bdg. 13.95 *(978-0-7569-8376-5(2))* Perfection Learning Corp.

—The Howling House. Miller, Fujiko, illus. rev. ed. 2004. (Standing Tall Mysteries Ser.). 51p. (J). (gr. 4-12). pap. 4.95 *(978-1-58659-083-3(9))* Artesian Pr.

—The Hunter (Mystery), 1 vol. 2017. (Pageturners Ser.). (ENG.). 76p. (YA). (gr. 9-12). 10.75 *(978-1-68021-389-8(X))* Saddleback Educational Publishing, Inc.

—Once upon a Crime (Mystery), 1 vol. 2017. (Pageturners Ser.). (ENG.). 76p. (YA). (gr. 9-12). 10.75 *(978-1-68021-388-1(1))* Saddleback Educational Publishing, Inc.

—The Power of the Rose. 2008. (Passages Ser.). 94p. (YA). (gr. 7-12). pap. 8.50 *(978-0-7891-7541-0(X))*; (J). lib. bdg. 13.95 *(978-0-7569-8381-9(9))* Perfection Learning Corp.

—The Shadow Man. 2008. (Passages Ser.). 134p. (YA). (gr. 7-9). lib. bdg. 13.95 *(978-0-7569-8382-6(7))* Perfection Learning Corp.

—The Shining Mark. 2008. (Passages Ser.). 109p. (J). lib. bdg. 13.95 *(978-0-7569-8383-3(5))* Perfection Learning Corp.

—Sounds of Terror, 1 vol. unabr. ed. 2010. (Q Reads Ser.). (ENG.). 32p. (YA). (gr. 9-12). pap. 8.50 *(978-1-61651-206-4(7))* Saddleback Educational Publishing, Inc.

—Whatever Happened to Megan Marie? (Mystery), 1 vol. 2017. (Pageturners Ser.). (ENG.). 80p. (YA). (gr. 9-12). 10.75 *(978-1-68021-390-4(3))* Saddleback Educational Publishing, Inc.

—When Sleeping Dogs Awaken (Mystery), 1 vol. 2017. (Pageturners Ser.). (ENG.). 76p. (YA). (gr. 9-12). 10.75 *(978-1-68021-391-1(1))* Saddleback Educational Publishing, Inc.

—Where's Dudley? (Mystery), 1 vol. 2017. (Pageturners Ser.). (ENG.). 76p. (YA). (gr. 9-12). 10.75 *(978-1-68021-392-8(X))* Saddleback Educational Publishing, Inc.

Schraff, Anne E. Unbroken. 2012. (Urban Underground — Cesar Chavez High School Ser.: 28). (YA). lib. bdg. 20.80 *(978-0-606-26598-0(8))* Turtleback.

Schroeder, Doris. Annie Oakley in the Ghost Town Secret. Sgroi, Tony, illus. 2011. 280p. 47.95 *(978-1-258-06482-2(0))* Literary Licensing, LLC.

Schuikers, Robert. The Gray Ghost: A Seckatary Hawkins Mystery. 2016. (ENG., Illus.). 352p. 19.95 *(978-0-8131-6794-7(9)*, 978-0-8131-6794-7) Univ. Pr. of Kentucky.

—Stoner's Boy: A Seckatary Hawkins Mystery. 2016. (ENG., Illus.). 382p. 24.95 *(978-0-8131-6791-6(4)*, 978-0-8131-6791-6) Univ. Pr. of Kentucky.

Schurch, Maylan Henry. The Meatless Mayhem Mystery. 2003. (Justin Case Adventures Ser.: 5). 121p. (J). pap. 7.99 *(978-0-8280-1615-5(1)*, 133-650) Review & Herald Publishing Assn.

Schwartz, Ellen. The Case of the Missing Deed. 2011. (Teaspoon Detectives Ser.: 1). (Illus.). 200p. (J). (gr. 4-7). 15.95 *(978-0-88776-959-7(4)*, Tundra Bks.) Tundra Bks. CAN. Dist: Penguin Random Hse. LLC.

Schwarzkopf, Tom. Danger at Mason's Island, 1 vol. 2006. (ENG.). 127p. (J). (gr. 4-7). pap. 10.95 *(978-1-55109-562-2(9)*, 6c93e895-88d1-4aaa-ba25-534b2c668e92) Nimbus Publishing, Ltd. CAN. Dist: Baker & Taylor Publisher Services (BTPS).

Schweizer, Chris. Curse of the Attack-O-Lanterns. 2016. (Creeps Ser.: 3). (J). lib. bdg. 20.80 *(978-0-606-39018-7(9))* Turtleback.

Scieszka, Jon. Guys Read: Thriller. 2011. (Guys Read Ser.: 2). (ENG., Illus.). 288p. (J). (gr. 3-7). pap. 7.99 *(978-0-06-196375-9(5)*, Walden Pond Pr.) HarperCollins Pubs.

—Guys Read: Thriller. Helquist, Brett, illus. 2011. (Guys Read Ser.: 2). (ENG.). 288p. (J). (gr. 3-7). 16.99 *(978-0-06-196376-6(3)*, Walden Pond Pr.) HarperCollins Pubs.

Scott, Christina. All in A Night's Work. 2006. (J). lib. bdg. 19.95 *(978-1-933732-19-0(9))* Big Ransom Studio.

—The Chimney. 2006. (J). lib. bdg. 19.95 *(978-1-933732-18-3(0))* Big Ransom Studio.

Scott, Dan. The Secret of Fort Pioneer: A Bret King Mystery. Beeler, Joe, illus. 2011. 190p. 42.95 *(978-1-258-09951-0(9))* Literary Licensing, LLC.

Scott, Jeff. The Discovery of Monkey Island. 2008. 64p. pap. 19.95 *(978-1-60610-921-2(9))* America Star Bks.

Scott, Kevin John. Frederik Sandwich & the Earthquake That Couldn't Possibly Be. (Frederik Sandwich Ser.: 1). (ENG.). (J). (gr. 3-7). 2019. 336p. pap. 12.99 *(978-1-4926-6799-5(4))* 2018. (Illus.). 320p. 16.99 *(978-1-4926-4853-6(1))* Sourcebooks, Inc.

Scott, Michele. Perfect Harmony: A Vivienne Taylor Horse Lover's Mystery, 0 vols. 2014. (Fairmont Riding Academy Ser.: 3). (ENG.). 274p. (YA). (gr. 7-9). pap. 9.99 *(978-1-4778-4779-4(0)*, 9781477847794, Skyscape) Amazon Publishing.

Scott, Terrence. Bryce Coris Blessing. 2006. 28p. pap. 9.95 *(978-1-4327-0000-3(6))* Outskirts Pr., Inc.

Scotton, Rob. Secret Agent Splat! Scotton, Rob, illus. 2012. (Splat the Cat Ser.). (ENG., Illus.). 40p. (J). (gr. -1-2). 19.99 *(978-0-06-197871-5(X)*, HarperCollins) HarperCollins Pubs.

Seaman, Augusta Huiell. The Boarded-Up House. 2014. (ENG.). 250p. (J). (gr. 6-8). pap. 9.99 *(978-0-486-78188-4(7))* Dover Pubns., Inc.

The Search for the Lost Cave, 6 vols. (Woodland Mysteriestm Ser.). 133p. (gr. 3-7). 42.50 *(978-0-7802-7943-8(3))* Wright Group/McGraw-Hill.

Searcy, Amanda. I'll Find You. 2017. 328p. (YA). *(978-1-5247-0090-4(8)*, Delacorte Pr) Random House Publishing Group.

—The Truth Beneath the Lies. 2018. 352p. (YA). (gr. 9). pap. 9.99 *(978-1-5247-0092-8(4)*, Ember) Random Hse. Children's Bks.

Secret Agent Cat Purse: The Case of the Dog with Golden Wings. 2006. (J). *(978-0-9743359-3-3(2))* Murdock Publishing Co.

The Secret of the Monster Book, 6 vols., Vol. 2. (Woodland Mysteriestm Ser.). 133p. (gr. 3-7). 42.50 *(978-0-7802-7933-9(6))* Wright Group/McGraw-Hill.

The Secret of the Old Oak Trunk, 6 vols. (Woodland Mysteriestm Ser.). 133p. (gr. 3-7). 42.50 *(978-0-7802-7926-1(3))* Wright Group/McGraw-Hill.

The Secret of the Song, 6 vols., Vol. 2. (Woodland Mysteriestm Ser.). 133p. (gr. 3-7). 42.50 *(978-0-7802-7937-7(9))* Wright Group/McGraw-Hill.

A Secret Silver Lining, 6 vols. (Ragged Island Mysteriestm Ser.). 161p. (gr. 5-7). 42.50 *(978-0-322-01647-7(9))* Wright Group/McGraw-Hill.

Secrets of the Greaser Hotel. 2014. (ENG., Illus.). 268p. (J). pap. 25.00 *(978-1-61088-130-2(3)*, d70f995e-b5b9-4c8e-8abc-94c961e92977) Bancroft Pr.

Sedgwick, Julian. The Black Dragon. Moffett, Patricia, illus. 2018. (Mysterium Ser.). (ENG.). 352p. (J). (gr. 4-8). pap. 9.99 *(978-1-5415-1489-8(0)*, 6c0683dc-fa47-4097-b4fd-1f7a2d9c8e98, Carolrhoda Bks.) Lerner Publishing Group.

—Ghosts of Shanghai: Return to the City of Ghosts: Book 3, Bk. 3. 2019. (Ghosts of Shanghai Ser.). (ENG., Illus.). 360p. (J). (gr. 3-7). pap. 9.99 *(978-1-4449-2451-0(6))* Hachette Children's Group GBR. Dist: Hachette Bk. Group.

—The Palace of Memory. Moffett, Patricia, illus. (Mysterium Ser.). (ENG.). 352p. (J). (gr. 4-8). 2019. pap. 9.99 *(978-1-5415-5456-6(6)*, 2cd67a2b-7a5e-48cf-93c8-06585cfed974) 2017. E-Book 29.32 *(978-1-5124-2690-8(3))*No. 2. 2017. 18.99 *(978-1-4677-7568-7(1)*, a33df367-d91f-4e23-aeec-f2976f2a8368) Lerner Publishing Group. (Carolrhoda Bks.).

—The Wheel of Life & Death, No. 3. Moffett, Patricia, illus. 2018. (Mysterium Ser.). (ENG.). 344p. (J). (gr. 4-8). 18.99 *(978-1-4677-7569-4(X)*, e1dc9978-31c7-4613-afa7-14b9bae2030a, Carolrhoda Bks.) Lerner Publishing Group.

Sedgwick, Marcus. She Is Not Invisible. 2015. (ENG.). 240p. (YA). (gr. 7). pap. 11.99 *(978-1-250-05698-6(5)*, 900139107) Square Fish.

Sedoti, Chelsea. The Hundred Lies of Lizzie Lovett. 2017. 416p. (YA). (gr. 9-12). 10.99 *(978-1-4926-5275-5(X))* Sourcebooks, Inc.

—Hundred Lies of Lizzie Lovett. 2017. (ENG.). 400p. (YA). (gr. 8-12). 17.99 *(978-1-4926-3608-3(8)*, 9781492636083) Sourcebooks, Inc.

Selfors, Suzanne. Smells Like Treasure. 2012. (Smells Like Dog Ser.: 2). (ENG.). 432p. (J). (gr. 3-7). pap. 8.99 *(978-0-316-04402-8(4))* Little, Brown Bks. for Young Readers.

Sente, Yves. The Sarcophagi of the Sixth Coninent, Pt. 1, Vol. 9. Juillard, André, illus. 2011. (Blake & Mortimer Ser.: 9). 64p. (J). (gr. -1-12). pap. 15.95 *(978-1-84918-067-2(9))* CineBook GBR. Dist: National Bk. Network.

Sente, Yves & Juillard, Andre. The Gondwana Shrine. 2012. (Blake & Mortimer Ser.: 11). (Illus.). 64p. pap. 15.95 *(978-1-84918-094-8(6))* CineBook GBR. Dist: National Bk. Network.

—The Oath of the Five Swords, Vol. 18. 2014. (Blake & Mortimer Ser.: 18). (Illus.). 72p. pap. 15.95 *(978-1-84918-191-4(8))* CineBook GBR. Dist: National Bk. Network.

—The Sarcophagi of the Sixth Continent, Pt. 2. 2011. (Blake & Mortimer Ser.: 10). (Illus.). 64p. pap. 15.95 *(978-1-84918-077-1(6))* CineBook GBR. Dist: National Bk. Network.

Senzai, N. H. Saving Kabul Corner. 2014. (Kabul Chronicles Ser.). (ENG., Illus.). 288p. (J). (gr. 3-7). 16.99 *(978-1-4424-8494-8(2)*, Simon & Schuster/Paula Wiseman Bks.) Simon & Schuster/Paula Wiseman Bks.

Serrano, Tina. Urban Scavenger Hunt, 1 vol. 2010. 50p. pap. 16.95 *(978-1-4489-4451-4(1))* America Star Bks.

Seykora, Teresa. The Case of the Missing Peanut Butter: The Adventures of Peanut Butter Bob. Drewes, Dan, illus. 2010. 32p. 12.99 *(978-1-4520-2678-7(5))* AuthorHouse.

Shadows at Predator Reef. 2014. (Hardy Boys Adventures Ser.: 7). (ENG., Illus.). 128p. (J). (gr. 3-7). 17.99 *(978-1-4814-0010-7(X)*, Aladdin) Simon & Schuster Children's Publishing.

Shalvey, Declan & Cardy, Jason, illus. Sweeney Todd: The Demon Barber of Fleet Street. 2012. (ENG.). 176p. pap. 16.95 *(978-1-907127-10-6(0)*, Classical Comics, Ltd.); pap. 16.95 *(978-1-907127-09-0(7)*, Classical Comics, Ltd.); (gr. 9). lib. bdg. 24.95 *(978-1-907127-82-3(8))* Classical Comics GBR. Dist: Publishers Group West (PGW).

Shankman, Adam & Sullivan, Laura L. Murder among the Stars: A Lulu Kelly Mystery. 2017. (ENG., Illus.). 320p. (YA). (gr. 9). 17.99 *(978-1-4814-4790-4(4)*, Atheneum Bks. for Young Readers) Simon & Schuster Children's Publishing.

Sharmat, Andrew & Sharmat, Marjorie Weinman. Nate the Great & the Missing Birthday Snake. Wheeler, Jody, illus. 2018. (Nate the Great Ser.). 80p. (J). (gr. 1-4). 5.99 *(978-1-101-93470-8(0)*, Yearling) Random Hse. Children's Bks.

Sharmat, Marjorie Weinman. Nate the Great. Simont, Marc, illus. (Nate the Great Ser.: No. 1). 48p. (J). (gr. 1-4). pap. 4.50 *(978-0-8072-1351-3(9)*, Listening Library) Random Hse. Audio Publishing Group.

—Nate the Great & the Halloween Hunt. Simont, Marc, illus. (Nate the Great Ser.: No. 12). 48p. (J). (gr. 1-4). pap. 4.50 *(978-0-8072-1283-7(0)*, Listening Library) Random Hse. Audio Publishing Group.

—Nate the Great & the Missing Key. Simont, Marc, illus. (Nate the Great Ser.: No. 6). 48p. (J). (gr. 1-4). pap. 4.50 *(978-0-8072-1335-3(7)*, Listening Library) Random Hse. Audio Publishing Group.

—Nate the Great Goes Undercover. Simont, Marc, illus. (Nate the Great Ser.: No. 2). 48p. (J). (gr. 1-4). pap. 4.50 *(978-0-8072-1284-4(9)*, Listening Library) Random Hse. Audio Publishing Group.

—Nate the Great on the Owl Express. Sharmat, Mitchell & Weston, Martha, illus. 2004. (Nate the Great Ser.). (ENG.). 80p. (J). (gr. 1-4). 5.99 *(978-0-440-41927-3(1)*, Yearling) Random Hse. Children's Bks.

—Yo, el Gran Fercho y el Ladron. (Torre de Papel Ser.).Tr. of Nate the Great Goes Undercover. (SPA., Illus.). (J). 7.95 *(978-958-04-2540-3(X))* Norma S.A. COL. Dist: Distribuidora Norma, Inc.

Sharmat, Marjorie Weinman & Sharmat, Andrew. Nate the Great & the Wandering Word. Wheeler, Jody, illus. 2019. (Nate the Great Ser.: Bk. 27). 80p. (J). (gr. 1-4). 6.99 *(978-1-5247-6547-7(3)*, Yearling) Random Hse. Children's Bks.

Sharmat, Marjorie Weinman & Sharmat, Mitchell. The Green Toenails Gang. Brunkus, Denise, illus. 2nd ed. 2005. (Olivia Sharp: Agent for Secrets Ser.). 80p. (J). (gr. 3-7). per. 5.99 *(978-0-440-42063-7(6)*, Yearling) Random Hse. Children's Bks.

—Nate the Great & the Big Sniff. Weston, Martha, illus. 2003. (Nate the Great Ser.: No. 23). (ENG.). 80p. (J). (gr. 1-4). pap. 5.99 *(978-0-440-41502-2(0)*, Yearling) Random Hse. Children's Bks.

—Nate the Great & the Big Sniff. Weston, Martha, illus. 2003. (Nate the Great Ser.: Bk. 23). 47p. (gr. -1-3). lib. bdg. 16.00 *(978-0-613-63966-8(9))* Turtleback.

—Nate the Great & the Hungry Book Club. Wheeler, Jody, illus. 2011. (Nate the Great Ser.: No. 26). 80p. (J). (gr. 1-4). 5.99 *(978-0-375-84548-2(8)*, Yearling) Random Hse. Children's Bks.

—Nate the Great Talks Turkey. Wheeler, Jody, illus. 2007. (Nate the Great Ser.: No. 25). 96p. (J). (gr. 1-4). per. 5.99 *(978-0-440-42126-9(8)*, Yearling) Random Hse. Children's Bks.

—Nate the Great Talks Turkey: With Help from Olivia Sharp. Wheeler, Jody, illus. 2007. (Nate the Great Ser.: Bk. 25). (gr. -1-3). lib. bdg. 16.00 *(978-1-4177-9248-1(5))* Turtleback.

—Nate the Great, Where Are You? Wheeler, Jody, illus. 2015. (Nate the Great Ser.). 80p. (J). (gr. 1-4). 5.99 *(978-0-449-81078-1(X)*, Yearling) Random Hse. Children's Bks.

—The Pizza Monster. Brunkus, Denise, illus. 2nd ed. 2005. (Olivia Sharp: Agent for Secrets Ser.: 1). 80p. (J). (gr. 3-7). reprint ed. 5.99 *(978-0-440-42059-0(8)*, Yearling) Random Hse. Children's Bks.

Sharpe, Luke. Billy Sure, Kid Entrepreneur Is a Spy! Ross, Graham, illus. 2016. 141p. (J). *(978-1-4242-6367-7(0)*, Simon Spotlight) Simon Spotlight.

Shaskan, Trisha Speed. Foul Play at Elm Tree Park: Case 3. Shaskan, Stephen, illus. 2018. (Q & Ray Ser.). (ENG.). 48p. (J). (gr. 2-5). 26.65 *(978-1-5124-1149-2(3)*, 4ca0215d-12ac-4838-90b8-6d7c4d9f7cbc, Graphic Universe™) Lerner Publishing Group.

—Meteorite or Meteor-Wrong? Case 2, Bk. 2. Shaskan, Stephen, illus. 2018. (Q & Ray Ser.). (ENG.). 48p. (J). (gr. 2-5). 26.65 *(978-1-5124-1148-5(5)*, ac6051f7-42ca-4332-8dd7-363184dbe085, Graphic Universe™) Lerner Publishing Group.

Shaw, J. D. Leave No Footprints. 2011. (ENG.). 276p. (J). (gr. 7). pap. 14.95 *(978-0-9845318-6-8(6))* Tiny Stachel Pr.

—The Secrets of Loon Lake. 2010. (ENG.). 338p. (J). (gr. 5). pap. 16.95 *(978-0-9845318-0-6(7))* Tiny Stachel Pr.

Shaw, Sandy. Do You Know Where the Bus Driver Will Go? 2012. (ENG.). 24p. pap. 15.99 *(978-1-4771-2107-8(2))* Xlibris Corp.

Shea, Therese. The School Bus Mystery, 1 vol. 2006. (Neighborhood Readers Ser.). (ENG.). 16p. (gr. 1-2). pap. 6.50 *(978-1-4042-6982-8(7)*, 3cd2526f-0d62-4b12-bd01-561320c79797, Rosen Classroom) Rosen Publishing Group, Inc., The.

Shearer, Alex. Canned. 2008. (J). *(978-0-439-90310-3(6)*, Scholastic Pr.) Scholastic, Inc.

Sheinmel, Alyssa. R. I. P. Eliza Hart. 2017. (ENG.). 336p. (YA). (gr. 7). 18.99 *(978-1-338-08762-8(2)*, Scholastic Pr.) Scholastic, Inc.

Shepard, Sara. The Amateurs. 2016. (Amateurs Ser.: 1). (ENG.). 320p. (YA). (gr. 9-17). 17.99 *(978-1-4847-4227-3(3))* Little, Brown Bks. for Young Readers.

—Deadly. 2014. (Pretty Little Liars Ser.: 14). (YA). lib. bdg. 20.85 *(978-0-606-35972-6(9))* Turtleback.

—Flawless. 2007. (Pretty Little Liars Ser.: No. 2). (ENG.). 352p. (YA). (gr. 9-12). 16.99 *(978-0-06-088733-9(8)*, HarperTeen) HarperCollins Pubs.

—Flawless. 2008. (Pretty Little Liars Ser.: 2). (YA). lib. bdg. 20.85 *(978-0-606-12267-2(2))* Turtleback.

—Follow Me. 2017. (Amateurs Ser.: 2). (ENG.). 272p. (YA). (gr. 9-17). 17.99 *(978-1-4847-4228-0(1))* Little, Brown Bks. for Young Readers.

—Follow Me. 2018. (Amateurs Ser.: 2). (ENG.). 288p. (YA). (gr. 7-17). pap. 9.99 *(978-1-4847-4636-3(8))* Little, Brown Bks. for Young Readers.

—The Good Girls. 2015. (Perfectionists Ser.: 2). (ENG.). 368p. (YA). (gr. 9). 17.99 *(978-0-06-207452-0(0)*, HarperTeen); 341p. (J). *(978-0-06-239115-5(1))* HarperCollins Pubs.

—Hide & Seek. 2012. (Lying Game Ser.: Bk. 4). 289p. (YA). 9.99 *(978-0-06-219369-8(4)*, HarperTeen) HarperCollins Pubs.

—Killer. 2010. (Pretty Little Liars Ser.: 6). (YA). lib. bdg. 20.85 *(978-0-606-12278-8(8))* Turtleback.

—Last Seen. 2012. (Amateurs Ser.: 3). (ENG.). 304p. (YA). (gr. 7-17). 17.99 *(978-1-4847-4229-7(X))* Little, Brown Bks. for Young Readers.

—The Lying Game. (Lying Game Ser.: 1). (ENG.). (YA). (gr. 9-18). 2010. 320p. 17.99 *(978-0-06-186970-9(8))*1. 2011. 336p. pap. 11.99 *(978-0-06-186971-6(6))* HarperCollins Pubs. (HarperTeen).

—The Lying Game. 2011. (Lying Game (Quality) Ser.: Vol. 1). (ENG.). (YA). (gr. 9). lib. bdg. 20.60 *(978-1-61383-667-5(8))* Perfection Learning Corp.

—The Lying Game #2: Never Have I Ever. (Lying Game Ser.: 2). (ENG.). (YA). (gr. 9). 2012. 336p. pap. 10.99 *(978-0-06-186973-0(2))* 2011. 320p. 16.99 *(978-0-06-186972-3(4))* HarperCollins Pubs. (HarperTeen).

—The Lying Game #3: Two Truths & a Lie. (Lying Game Ser.: 3). (ENG.). (YA). (gr. 9). 2013. 320p. pap. 10.99 *(978-0-06-186975-4(9))* 2012. 304p. 17.99 *(978-0-06-186974-7(0))* HarperCollins Pubs. (HarperTeen).

MNO

—The Lying Game #6: Seven Minutes in Heaven. 2014. (Lying Game Ser.: 6). (ENG.). 400p. (YA). (gr. 9). pap. 11.99 *(978-0-06-212823-2(X)*, HarperTeen) HarperCollins Pubs.

—Perfect. 2007. (Pretty Little Liars Ser.: No. 3). (ENG.). 320p. (YA). (gr. 9-12). 16.99 *(978-0-06-088736-0(2)*, HarperTeen) HarperCollins Pubs.

—The Perfectionists. 2014. (Perfectionists Ser.: 1). (ENG.). 336p. (YA). (gr. 9). 17.99 *(978-0-06-207469-0(5)*, HarperTeen) HarperCollins Pubs.

—Pretty Little Liars. 2007. (Pretty Little Liars Ser.: 1). (ENG.). 304p. (YA). (gr. 9-12). pap. 10.99 *(978-0-06-088732-2(X)*, HarperTeen) HarperCollins Pubs.

—Pretty Little Liars #10: Ruthless. 2011. (Pretty Little Liars Ser.: 10). (ENG.). 352p. (YA). (gr. 9). 17.99 *(978-0-06-208186-5(1)*, HarperTeen) HarperCollins Pubs.

—Pretty Little Liars #11: Stunning. 2013. (Pretty Little Liars Ser.: 11). (ENG.). 336p. (YA). (gr. 9). pap. 10.99 *(978-0-06-208190-2(X)*, HarperTeen) HarperCollins Pubs.

—Pretty Little Liars #13: Crushed. 2013. (Pretty Little Liars Ser.: 13). (ENG.). 352p. (YA). (gr. 9). 17.99 *(978-0-06-219971-3(4)*, HarperTeen) HarperCollins Pubs.

—Pretty Little Liars #14: Deadly. 2014. (Pretty Little Liars Ser.: 14). (ENG.). 336p. (YA). (gr. 9). pap. 11.99 *(978-0-06-219975-1(7)*, HarperTeen) HarperCollins Pubs.

—Pretty Little Liars #15: Toxic. 2014. (Pretty Little Liars Ser.: 15). (ENG.). 336p. (YA). (gr. 9). 17.99 *(978-0-06-228701-4(X)*, HarperTeen) HarperCollins Pubs.

—Pretty Little Liars #16: Vicious. (Pretty Little Liars Ser.: 16). (ENG.). (YA). (gr. 9). 2016. 368p. pap. 11.99 *(978-0-06-228705-2(2))* 2014. 352p. 17.99 *(978-0-06-228704-5(4))* HarperCollins Pubs. (HarperTeen).

—Pretty Little Liars #2: Flawless. 2008. (Pretty Little Liars Ser.: 2). (ENG.). 352p. (YA). (gr. 9-12). pap. 10.99 *(978-0-06-088735-3(4)*, HarperTeen) HarperCollins Pubs.

—Pretty Little Liars #3: Perfect, No. 3. 2008. (Pretty Little Liars Ser.: 3). (ENG.). 336p. (YA). (gr. 9-12). pap. 11.99 *(978-0-06-088738-4(9)*, HarperTeen) HarperCollins Pubs.

—Pretty Little Liars #4: Unbelievable. 2008. (Pretty Little Liars Ser.: 4). (ENG.). 368p. (YA). (gr. 9). pap. 11.99 *(978-0-06-088741-4(9)*, HarperTeen) HarperCollins Pubs.

—Pretty Little Liars #6: Killer. (Pretty Little Liars Ser.: 6). (ENG.). (YA). (gr. 9). 2010. 352p. pap. 10.99 *(978-0-06-156613-4(6))*No. 6. 2009. 336p. 16.99 *(978-0-06-156611-0(X))* HarperCollins Pubs. (HarperTeen).

—Pretty Little Liars #7: Heartless. 2010. (Pretty Little Liars Ser.: 7). (ENG.). 304p. (YA). (gr. 9-18). pap. 10.99 *(978-0-06-156616-5(0)*, HarperTeen) HarperCollins Pubs.

—Pretty Little Liars #8: Wanted. (Pretty Little Liars Ser.: 8). (ENG.). (YA). (gr. 9). 2011. 288p. pap. 10.99 *(978-0-06-156619-6(5))* 2010. 272p. 16.99 *(978-0-06-156617-2(9))* HarperCollins Pubs. (HarperTeen).

—Pretty Little Liars #9: Twisted. (Pretty Little Liars Ser.: 9). (ENG.). (YA). (gr. 9). 2012. 336p. pap. 11.99 *(978-0-06-208102-5(0))* 2011. 320p. 16.99 *(978-0-06-208101-8(2))* HarperCollins Pubs. (HarperTeen).

—Pretty Little Liars Bind-Up #2: Perfect & Unbelievable. 2014. (Pretty Little Liars Ser.). (ENG.). 672p. (YA). (gr. 9). pap. 10.99 *(978-0-06-232293-7(1)*, HarperTeen) HarperCollins Pubs.

—Pretty Little Liars Box Set: Books 1 To 4, 4 vols., Set, Bks. 1-4. 2009. (Pretty Little Liars Ser.: Bks. 1-4). (ENG.). (YA). (gr. 9). pap. 39.99 *(978-0-06-180131-0(3)*, HarperTeen) HarperCollins Pubs.

—Stunning. 2013. (Pretty Little Liars Ser.: 11). (YA). lib. bdg. 20.85 *(978-0-606-31813-6(5))* Turtleback.

—Twisted. 2012. (Pretty Little Liars Ser.: 9). (YA). lib. bdg. 20.85 *(978-0-606-26288-0(1))* Turtleback.

—Unbelievable. 2008. (Pretty Little Liars Ser.: No. 4). (ENG.). 352p. (J). (gr. 9-18). 16.99 *(978-0-06-088739-1(7)*, HarperTeen) HarperCollins Pubs.

Shepherd, Kat. The Gemini Mysteries: the Cat's Paw (the Gemini Mysteries Book 2) 2021. (Gemini Mysteries Ser.: 2). (ENG., Illus.). 304p. (J). (gr. 3-7). 16.99 *(978-1-4998-0810-0(0)*, Yellow Jacket) Bonnier Publishing USA.

Sherman, Harold M. Ding Palmer, Air Detective. 2011. 264p. 47.95 *(978-1-258-07222-3(X))* Literary Licensing, LLC.

Sherrard, Valerie. Chasing Shadows: A Shelby Belgarden Mystery. 2004. (ENG.). 216p. (YA). pap. 9.99 *(978-1-55002-502-6(3))* Dundurn Pr. CAN. Dist: Publishers Group West (PGW).

—Eyes of a Stalker: A Shelby Belgarden Mystery. 2006. (ENG.). 180p. (YA). (gr. 6). pap. 12.99 *(978-1-55002-643-6(7))* Dundurn Pr. CAN. Dist: Publishers Group West (PGW).

—Hiding in Plain Sight: A Shelby Belgarden Mystery. 2005. (ENG.). 236p. (YA). (gr. 6). pap. 12.99 *(978-1-55002-546-0(5))* Dundurn Pr. CAN. Dist: Publishers Group West (PGW).

—In Too Deep: A Shelby Belgarden Mystery. 2003. (ENG.). 200p. (YA). pap. 8.99 *(978-1-55002-443-2(4))* Dundurn Pr. CAN. Dist: Publishers Group West (PGW).

—Searching for Yesterday: A Shelby Belgarden Mystery. 2008. (ENG.). 224p. (YA). (gr. 6-10). pap. 12.99 *(978-1-55002-788-4(3))* Dundurn Pr. CAN. Dist: Publishers Group West (PGW).

Sherry, Kevin. Attack of the Kraken (the Yeti Files #3) Sherry, Kevin, illus. 2016. (Yeti Files Ser.: 3). (ENG., Illus.). 128p. (J). (gr. 2-5). 11.99 *(978-0-545-85781-9(3)*, Scholastic Pr.) Scholastic, Inc.

Sherry, Maureen. Walls Within Walls. 2012. (ENG., Illus.). 368p. (J). (gr. 3-7). pap. 9.99 *(978-0-06-176703-6(4)*, Tegen, Katherine Bks) HarperCollins Pubs.

—Walls Within Walls. Stower, Adam, illus. 2010. (ENG.). 368p. (J). (gr. 3-7). 16.99 *(978-0-06-176700-5(X)*, Tegen, Katherine Bks) HarperCollins Pubs.

The Ship in a Bottle, 6 vols. (Ragged Island Mysteriestm Ser.). 161p. (gr. 5-7). 42.50 *(978-0-322-01648-4(7))* Wright Group/McGraw-Hill.

Shoemaker, Tim. Below the Surface, 1 vol. 2015. (Code of Silence Novel Ser.: 3). (ENG.). 416p. (J). pap. 9.99 *(978-0-310-73765-0(6))* Zonderkidz.

Shotz, Jennifer Li. Hero: Rescue Mission. 2017. (Hero Ser.: 3). (ENG.). 192p. (J). (gr. 3-7). pap. 7.99 *(978-0-06-256045-2(X)*, HarperCollins) HarperCollins Pubs.

Siamon, Sharon. Heartbreak Hills, 1 vol. 2011. (Wild Horse Creek Ser.: 0). (ENG., Illus.). 144p. (J). (gr. 2-7). pap. 6.95 *(978-1-55285-998-8(3)*, f09adab9-19c4-44bb-aa66-3294791dc574) Whitecap Bks., Ltd. CAN. Dist: Firefly Bks., Ltd.

Silver, Ruth. Aberrant. 2013. 250p. pap. 14.99 *(978-0-9917897-8-8(4))* Patchwork Pr.

Silvey, Craig. Jasper Jones. 2012. 20.00 *(978-1-61383-806-8(9))* Perfection Learning Corp.

—Jasper Jones. 2012. (ENG.). 320p. (YA). (gr. 7). pap. 9.99 *(978-0-375-86627-2(2)*, Ember) Random Hse. Children's Bks.

Simmons, H. Two Tales from Our Corner Lot. 2004. 68p. pap. 19.95 *(978-1-4137-5251-9(9))* America Star Bks.

Simmons, Lynn Sheffield. Bo & the Roaring Pines, 1 vol. Lyne, Alison Davis, illus. 2008. (Bo Ser.). (ENG.). 120p. (J). (gr. 3-6). pap. 8.95 *(978-1-58980-522-4(4)*, Pelican Publishing) Arcadia Publishing.

Simner, Janni Lee. Secret of the Three Treasures. 2006. (ENG.). 160p. (YA). (gr. 8-12). 16.95 *(978-0-8234-1914-2(2))* Holiday Hse., Inc.

Simon, Scott. Sunnyside Plaza. 2020. (ENG.). 208p. (J). (gr. 3-17). 16.99 *(978-0-316-53120-7(0))* Little, Brown Bks. for Young Readers.

Simon, T. R. Zora & Me: the Cursed Ground. 2018. (Zora & Me Ser.). (ENG.). 272p. (J). (gr. 5-9). 16.99 *(978-0-7636-4301-0(7))* Candlewick Pr.

Simons Làda. 2013. 26p. pap. *(978-91-981097-3-3(1))* Woldekidan Songs.

Simpson, Pat. A Compilation of Tales to Thrill & Chill. 2008. 103p. pap. 15.95 *(978-1-4357-2976-6(5))* Lulu Pr., Inc.

Simukka, Salla & Witesman, Owen. As White As Snow. 2017. (YA). pap. *(978-1-5247-1348-5(1))* Bantam Doubleday Dell Large Print Group, Inc.

Singhee, Meghna. P. I. Pojo: The Killing of Mr Heathcote. 2015. (ENG.). 218p. (J). pap. 19.99 *(978-0-14-333345-6(3)*, Puffin) Penguin Bks. India PVT, Ltd IND. Dist: Independent Pubs. Group.

Singleton, Linda Joy. Dog-Gone Danger. 2018. (Curious Cat Spy Club Ser.: 5). (ENG.). 288p. (J). (gr. 3-7). pap. 9.99 *(978-0-8075-1390-3(3)*, 807513903) Whitman, Albert & Co.

—Kelsey the Spy. 2016. (Curious Cat Spy Club Ser.: 3). (ENG.). (J). (gr. 3-7). 304p. pap. 9.99 *(978-0-8075-1384-2(9)*, 807513849); 288p. 14.99 *(978-0-8075-1380-4(6)*, 807513806) Whitman, Albert & Co.

—Melissa's Mission Impossible. 2003. pap. 4.99 *(978-1-58608-609-1(X))* New Concepts Publishing.

—The Mystery of the Zorse's Mask. (Curious Cat Spy Club Ser.: 2). (ENG.). (J). (gr. 3-7). 2016. 272p. pap. 9.99 *(978-0-8075-1383-5(0)*, 807513830) 2015. 256p. 14.99 *(978-0-8075-1378-1(4)*, 807513784) Whitman, Albert & Co.

—The Secret of the Shadow Bandit. (Curious Cat Spy Club Ser.: 4). (ENG.). (J). (gr. 3-7). 2017. 296p. pap. 9.99 *(978-0-8075-1387-3(3)*, 807513873) 2016. (Illus.). 288p. 14.99 *(978-0-8075-1385-9(7)*, 807513857) Whitman, Albert & Co.

—The Trail of the Ghost Bunny. 2018. (Curious Cat Spy Club Ser.: 6). (ENG.). 272p. (J). (gr. 3-7). pap. 9.99 *(978-0-8075-1392-7(X)*, 080751392X) Whitman, Albert & Co.

Siobhan, Dowd. The London Eye Mystery. 2014. (ENG.). 336p. (J). (gr. 3-7). 12.24 *(978-1-63245-320-4(7))* Lectorum Pubns., Inc.

Sirowy, Alexandra. The Creeping. 2015. (ENG., Illus.). 400p. (YA). (gr. 7). 17.99 *(978-1-4814-1886-7(6))* Simon & Schuster Children's Publishing.

—First We Were IV. (ENG.). (YA). (gr. 7). 2018. 464p. pap. 12.99 *(978-1-4814-7843-4(5))* 2017. (Illus.). 448p. 21.99 *(978-1-4814-7842-7(7))* Simon & Schuster Bks. For Young Readers. (Simon & Schuster Bks. For Young Readers).

Skae, Hilda T. The Adventure League. 2013. 138p. pap. 9.00 *(978-1-927558-40-9(9))* Birch Tree Publishing.

Skelton, Matthew. Endymion Spring. 2008. (ENG.). 416p. (YA). (gr. 7). pap. 9.99 *(978-0-385-73456-1(5)*, Delacorte Bks. for Young Readers) Random Hse. Children's Bks.

Skelton, Vonda Skinner. Bitsy & the Mystery at Amelia Island. 2005. (Bitsy Burroughs Mysteries Ser.). (ENG.). 183p. (J). 15.95 *(978-1-57072-306-3(0)*, Silver Dagger Mysteries) Overmountain Pr.

—Bitsy & the Mystery at Hilton Head Island. 2008. 192p. (J). (gr. 4-7). pap. 8.95 *(978-1-57072-325-4(7))* Overmountain Pr.

—Bitsy & the Mystery at Tybee Island. 2003. (Bitsy Burroughs Mysteries Ser.). 120p. (J). (ENG.). 23.95 *(978-1-57072-253-0(6))*; pap. 13.95 *(978-1-57072-254-7(4))* Overmountain Pr. (Silver Dagger Mysteries).

Skillchecks for Mystery. 2005. (Double Fastback Ser.). (J). (gr. 6-12). 64p. pap. 5.95 *(978-0-13-024473-4(2))*; 32p. pap. 5.95 *(978-0-13-024455-0(4))* Globe Fearon Educational Publishing.

Skilton, Sarah. High & Dry. 2014. (ENG.). 272p. (YA). (gr. 8-17). 16.95 *(978-1-4197-0929-6(1)*, 1064601, Amulet Bks.) Abrams, Inc.

Skofield, James. Detective Dinosaur Undercover. 2010. (I Can Read Level 2 Ser.). (ENG., Illus.). 48p. (J). (gr. -1-3). pap. 4.99 *(978-0-06-444319-7(1)*, HarperCollins) HarperCollins Pubs.

Skofield, James & Alley, R. W. Detective Dinosaur Undercover. 2010. (I Can Read Level 2 Ser.). (ENG., Illus.). 48p. (J). (gr. -1-3). 16.99 *(978-0-06-623878-4(1)*, HarperCollins) HarperCollins Pubs.

Skurzynski, Gloria. Mysteries in Our National Parks: Buried Alive! A Mystery in Denali National Park. 2008. (Mysteries in Our National Park Ser.). (Illus.). 160p. (J). (gr. 3-7). pap. 4.99 *(978-1-4263-0252-7(5)*, National Geographic Kids) Disney Publishing Worldwide.

—Mysteries in Our National Parks: CliffHanger: A Mystery in Mesa Verde National Park. 2007. (Mysteries in Our National Park Ser.). (Illus.). 160p. (J). (gr. 3-7). per. 4.99 *(978-1-4263-0092-9(1)*, National Geographic Kids) Disney Publishing Worldwide.

—Mysteries in Our National Parks: Escape from Fear: A Mystery in Virgin Islands National Park. 2008. (Mysteries in Our National Park Ser.). (Illus.). 160p. (J). (gr. 3-7). mass mkt. 4.99 *(978-1-4263-0181-0(2)*, National Geographic Kids) Disney Publishing Worldwide.

—Mysteries in Our National Parks: Out of the Deep: A Mystery in Acadia National Park. 2008. (Mysteries in Our National Park Ser.). (Illus.). 160p. (J). (gr. 3-7). pap. 4.99 *(978-1-4263-0251-0(7)*, National Geographic Kids) Disney Publishing Worldwide.

—Mysteries in Our National Parks: Wolf Stalker: A Mystery in Yellowstone National Park. 2007. (Mysteries in Our National Park Ser.). (Illus.). 160p. (J). (gr. 3-7). per. 4.99 *(978-1-4263-0096-7(4)*, National Geographic Kids) Disney Publishing Worldwide.

—Running Scared: A Mystery in Carlsbad Caverns National Park. 2008. (Mysteries in Our National Park Ser.). (Illus.). 160p. (J). (gr. 3-7). mass mkt. 4.99 *(978-1-4263-0182-7(0)*, National Geographic Kids) Disney Publishing Worldwide.

Skurzynski, Gloria & Ferguson, Alane. Buried Alive. 2003. (Mysteries in Our National Park Ser.: No. 12). (ENG.). 160p. (J). (gr. 3-7). 15.95 *(978-0-7922-6966-3(7)*, National Geographic Children's Bks.) National Geographic Society.

Skye, Obert. Leven Thumps the Complete Series (Boxed Set) The Gateway; the Whispered Secret; the Eyes of the Want; the Wrath of Ezra; the Ruins of Alder. Sowards, Ben, illus. 2018. (Leven Thumps Ser.). (ENG.). 2208p. (J). (gr. 3-7). pap. 49.99 *(978-1-5344-1876-9(8)*, Aladdin) Simon & Schuster Children's Publishing.

—Mutant Bunny Island #3: Buns of Steel. Vieira, Eduardo, illus. 2019. (ENG.). 208p. (J). (gr. 3-7). 12.99 *(978-0-06-239917-5(9)*, HarperCollins) HarperCollins Pubs.

Sleep, Betty. Purrlock Holmes, & the Case of the Vanishing Valuables. 2004. (J). mass mkt. 8.95 *(978-1-58961-330-0(9))* PageFree Publishing, Inc.

Sleepers. 64p. (YA). (gr. 6-12). pap. *(978-0-8224-2366-9(9))* Globe Fearon Educational Publishing.

Sloane, Roxy. Missing: The Heather Harding Mysteries. 2011. 100p. pap. 15.99 *(978-1-4628-9061-3(X))* Xlibris Corp.

Smi. Screams in the Night. 2004. 92p. pap. *(978-0-14-333575-7(8)*, Puffin) Penguin Publishing Group.

Smith, Alex T. Mr. Penguin & the Fortress of Secrets, 1 vol. 2019. (Mr. Penguin Ser.: 2). (ENG., Illus.). 288p. (J). (gr. 3-7). 16.95 *(978-1-68263-130-0(3))* Peachtree Publishing Co. Inc.

—Mr. Penguin & the Lost Treasure. 2019. (Mr. Penguin Ser.: 1). (ENG., Illus.). 208p. (J). (gr. 3-7). 16.95 *(978-1-68263-120-1(6))* Peachtree Publishing Co. Inc.

Smith-Armand, Kristie. Diamond in the Rough: More Fun Adventures with Abby Diamond. 2010. 256p. pap. 16.95 *(978-1-4502-4618-7(4))* iUniverse, Inc.

Smith, Elise & Smith, Kimanne, illus. The Missing Trumpet Blues. 2003. (ENG.). 56p. (J). (gr. 6-8). pap. 7.97 net. *(978-0-7652-3276-2(6)*, Celebration Pr.) Savvas Learning Co.

Smith, Jeff. Old Man's Cave: a Graphic Novel (BONE #6) Smith, Jeff, illus. 2007. (Bone Ser.: 6).Tr. of BONE #6. (ENG., Illus.). 128p. (J). (gr. 3-7). 26.99 *(978-0-439-70628-5(9))*; pap. 12.99 *(978-0-439-70635-3(1))* Scholastic, Inc. (Graphix).

Smith, Jim. Barry Loser & the Case of the Crumpled Carton (Barry Loser) 2015. (Barry Loser Ser.: 6). (ENG., Illus.). 240p. (J). (gr. 2-4). pap. 5.99 *(978-1-4052-6803-5(4))* Farshore GBR. Dist: HarperCollins Pubs.

Smith, Lauren E. Ashley Enright & the Darnell Diamonds, 1 vol. 2009. 90p. pap. 19.95 *(978-1-60836-332-2(5))* America Star Bks.

Smith, Roger B. The Adventures of Xavier Winfield & His Pal Oggie, EPISODE ONE: The Great Camping Adventure. 2018. (ENG.). 184p. (YA). pap. 9.99 *(978-0-9854439-0-0(1))* Backpack Pubs.

Smith, Roland. Cryptid Hunters. 2006. (ENG.). 352p. (J). (gr. 5-9). pap. 7.99 *(978-0-7868-5162-1(7))* Little, Brown Bks. for Young Readers.

—Independence Hall. (I, Q Ser.: Bk. 1). (ENG.). 312p. (YA). (gr. 6-8). 2009. Illus.). 15.95 *(978-1-58536-468-8(1)*, 202188) 2008. pap. 12.99 *(978-1-58536-325-4(1)*, 202289) Sleeping Bear Pr.

—Kitty Hawk. 2012. (I, Q Ser.: Bk. 3). (ENG., Illus.). 240p. (YA). (gr. 6-8). pap. 9.99 *(978-1-58536-604-0(8)*, 202326);Bk. 3. lib. bdg. 16.99 *(978-1-58536-605-7(6)*, 202327) Sleeping Bear Pr.

—Tentacles (Cryptid Hunters, Book 2), Vol. 2. 2011. (Cryptid Hunters Ser.: 2). (ENG.). 336p. (J). (gr. 4-7). pap. 9.99 *(978-0-545-17816-7(9)*, Scholastic Paperbacks) Scholastic, Inc.

Smith, Roland & Spradlin, Michael P. The Alamo. 2013. (I, Q Ser.). (ENG.). 288p. (YA). (gr. 5-8). 16.99 *(978-1-58536-822-8(9)*, 202356); pap. 9.99 *(978-1-58536-821-1(0)*, 202369) Sleeping Bear Pr.

—Alcatraz. 2014. (I, Q Ser.). (ENG.). 272p. (J). (gr. 5-7). 16.99 *(978-1-58536-826-6(1)*, 203667);Bk. 6. pap. 9.99 *(978-1-58536-825-9(3)*, 203727) Sleeping Bear Pr.

—I, Q the Windy City, Bk.5. 2014. (I, Q Ser.). (ENG.). 240p. (YA). (gr. 5-7). 9.99 *(978-1-58536-823-5(7)*, 202902) Sleeping Bear Pr.

Smith, Sherry Weaver. Search for the Hidden Garden: A Discovery with Saint Thérèse. Thornburgh, Rebecca McKillip, illus. 2016. 128p. (J). pap. 9.95 *(978-0-8198-9050-4(2))* Pauline Bks. & Media.

Smith, Steven K. Summer of the Woods. 2013. 158p. pap. 7.99 *(978-0-9893414-1-7(0))* MyBoys3 Pr.

Smith, Timothy R. The Owls Don't Give a Hoot. 2007. (Buck Wilder's Adventure Ser.: 4). (Illus.). 80p. (J). (gr. -1-3). per. 5.95 *(978-1-934133-11-8(6)*, Mackinac Island Press, Inc.) Charlesbridge Publishing, Inc.

—The Salmon Stop Running. 2008. (ENG., Illus.). 80p. (J). pap. 5.95 *(978-1-934133-34-7(5)*, Mackinac Island Press, Inc.) Charlesbridge Publishing, Inc.

Snell, Roy J. Curlie Carson Listens In. 2009. 108p. 22.95 *(978-1-60664-674-8(5))*; 100p. pap. 8.95 *(978-1-60664-303-7(7))* Rodgers, Alan Bks.

Snicket, Lemony, pseud. File under: 13 Suspicious Incidents. Seth, illus. 2016. (All the Wrong Questions Ser.). (ENG.). 288p. (J). (gr. 3-17). pap. 9.99 *(978-0-316-39306-5(1))* Little, Brown Bks. for Young Readers.

—Poison for Breakfast. 2018. (J). *(978-0-316-41987-1(7))* Little Brown & Co.

—"Shouldn't You Be in School?" Seth, illus. (All the Wrong Questions Ser.: 3). (ENG.). 352p. (J). (gr. 3-17). 2015. pap. 9.99 *(978-0-316-38060-7(1))* 2014. 35.99 *(978-0-316-40968-1(5))* Little, Brown Bks. for Young Readers.

—"When Did You See Her Last?" Seth, illus. (All the Wrong Questions Ser.: 2). (ENG.). 304p. (J). (gr. 3-17). 2014. pap. 8.99 *(978-0-316-33684-0(X))* 2013. 33.99 *(978-0-316-23993-6(3))* Little, Brown Bks. for Young Readers.

—"Who Could That Be at This Hour?" Seth, illus. l.t. ed. 2012. (All the Wrong Questions Ser.: 1). (ENG.). 304p. (J). (gr. 3-17). 25.99 *(978-0-316-22425-3(1))* Little, Brown Bks. for Young Readers.

—"Who Could That Be at This Hour?" Also Published As "All the Wrong Questions: Question 1" Seth, illus. (All the Wrong Questions Ser.: 1). (ENG.). (J). (gr. 3-17). 2014. 288p. pap. 9.99 *(978-0-316-33547-8(9))* 2012. 272p. 15.99 *(978-0-316-12308-2(0))* Little, Brown Bks. for Young Readers.

Snicket, Lemony, pseud & Seth. Who Could That Be at This Hour? 2012. *(978-0-316-24771-9(5))* Little Brown & Co.

Snider, Jesse Blaze. Muppet Snow White. Paroline, Shelli, illus. 2010. (Muppet Show Ser.). 112p. (J). (gr. 3-6). pap. 9.99 *(978-1-60886-574-1(6))* BOOM! Studios.

Snyder, Lavinia Branca. The Treasure of Lodian: The Kyss Family Mysteries. 2003. (Illus.). (J). mass mkt. *(978-1-932233-68-1(7))* Aurora Libris Corp.

Snyder, Zilpha Keatley. The Egypt Game. 2014. (ENG.). 240p. (J). (gr. 3-7). 11.24 *(978-1-63245-327-3(4))* Lectorum Pubns., Inc.

—The Egypt Game. Raible, Alton, illus. 2009. (ENG.). 240p. (J). (gr. 3-7). pap. 8.99 *(978-1-4169-9051-2(8)*, Atheneum Bks. for Young Readers) Simon & Schuster Children's Publishing.

—The Egypt Game. Raible, Alton, illus. 2009. 215p. (gr. 5-9). 19.65 *(978-0-8085-5303-8(8))* Turtleback.

Sobol, Donald J. Encyclopedia Brown & His Best Cases Ever. 2013. (Encyclopedia Brown Ser.). (ENG.). 160p. (J). (gr. 3-7). pap. 7.99 *(978-0-14-750871-3(1)*, Puffin Books) Penguin Young Readers Group.

—Encyclopedia Brown & the Case of the Dead Eagles. 2008. (Encyclopedia Brown Ser.: 12). (ENG., Illus.). 96p. (J). (gr. 3-7). 6.99 *(978-0-14-241135-3(3)*, Puffin Books) Penguin Young Readers Group.

—Encyclopedia Brown & the Case of the Jumping Frogs. Papp, Robert, illus. 2005. (Encyclopedia Brown Ser.). 69p. (J). (gr. 3-7). 13.15 *(978-0-7569-5100-9(3))* Perfection Learning Corp.

—Encyclopedia Brown & the Case of the Jumping Frogs. 2005. (Encyclopedia Brown Ser.: 24). (Illus.). 80p. (J). (gr. 3-7). 6.99 *(978-0-553-48758-9(2)*, Yearling) Random Hse. Children's Bks.

—Encyclopedia Brown & the Case of the Midnight Visitor. 2008. (Encyclopedia Brown Ser.: 13). (ENG., Illus.). 96p. (J). (gr. 3-7). 6.99 *(978-0-14-241106-3(X)*, Puffin Books) Penguin Young Readers Group.

—Encyclopedia Brown & the Case of the Secret Pitch. 2007. (Encyclopedia Brown Ser.: 2). (ENG., Illus.). 96p. (J). (gr. 3-7). 5.99 *(978-0-14-240889-6(1)*, Puffin Books) Penguin Young Readers Group.

—Encyclopedia Brown & the Case of the Secret Pitch. 2004. (Encyclopedia Brown Ser.: No. 2). 112p. (J). (gr. 3-7). pap. 17.00 incl. audio *(978-0-8072-1985-0(1)*, Listening Library) Random Hse. Audio Publishing Group.

—Encyclopedia Brown & the Case of the Secret Pitch. 2007. (Encyclopedia Brown Ser.: 2). 14.75 *(978-1-4177-8623-7(X))* Turtleback.

—Encyclopedia Brown & the Case of the Secret UFOs. 2011. (Encyclopedia Brown Ser.: 27). (ENG.). 96p. (J). (gr. 3-7). 5.99 *(978-0-14-241933-5(8)*, Puffin Books) Penguin Young Readers Group.

—Encyclopedia Brown & the Case of the Slippery Salamander. Chang, Warren, illus. 2003. (Encyclopedia Brown Ser.). 87p. (gr. 3-7). 16.00 *(978-0-7569-1619-0(4))* Perfection Learning Corp.

—Encyclopedia Brown & the Case of the Soccer Scheme. Bernadin, James, illus. 2013. (Encyclopedia Brown Ser.: 29). (ENG.). 96p. (J). (gr. 3-7). pap. 5.99 *(978-0-14-242288-5(6)*, Puffin Books) Penguin Young Readers Group.

—Encyclopedia Brown Box Set (4 Books), 4 vols., Set. 2007. (Encyclopedia Brown Ser.). (ENG., Illus.). 384p. (J). (gr. 3-7). 23.96 *(978-0-14-240985-5(5)*, Puffin Books) Penguin Young Readers Group.

—Encyclopedia Brown, Boy Detective. 2007. (Encyclopedia Brown Ser.: 1). (ENG., Illus.). 96p. (J). (gr. 3-7). 6.99 *(978-0-14-240888-9(3)*, Puffin Books) Penguin Young Readers Group.

—Encyclopedia Brown, Boy Detective. Shortall, Leonard W., illus. 2009. (Encyclopedia Brown Ser.). 88p. lib. bdg. 15.00 *(978-1-60686-386-2(X))* Perfection Learning Corp.

—Encyclopedia Brown, Boy Detective. 2004. (Encyclopedia Brown Ser.: No. 1). 128p. (J). (gr. 3-7). pap. 17.00 incl. audio *(978-0-8072-1984-3(3)*, Listening Library) Random Hse. Audio Publishing Group.

—Encyclopedia Brown, Boy Detective. Shortall, Leonard W., illus. 2007. (Encyclopedia Brown Ser.: 1). 88p. (J). (gr. 4-7). 14.75 *(978-1-4177-8622-0(1))* Turtleback.

—Encyclopedia Brown Cracks the Case. 2008. (Encyclopedia Brown Ser.: 25). (ENG.). 96p. (J). (gr. 3-7). 5.99 *(978-0-14-241167-4(1)*, Puffin Books) Penguin Young Readers Group.

—Encyclopedia Brown Finds the Clues. 2007. (Encyclopedia Brown Ser.: 3). (ENG., Illus.). 96p. (J). (gr. 3-7). 5.99 *(978-0-14-240890-2(5)*, Puffin Books) Penguin Young Readers Group.

—Encyclopedia Brown Finds the Clues. Shortall, Leonard W., illus. 2008. (Encyclopedia Brown Ser.). 96p. (gr. 4-7). 15.00 *(978-0-7569-8846-3(2))* Perfection Learning Corp.

—Encyclopedia Brown Finds the Clues. 2007. (Encyclopedia Brown Ser.: 3). 14.75 *(978-1-4177-8624-4(8))* Turtleback.

—Encyclopedia Brown Gets His Man. 2007. (Encyclopedia Brown Ser.: 4). (ENG., Illus.). 96p. (J). (gr. 3-7). 5.99 *(978-0-14-240891-9(3)*, Puffin Books) Penguin Young Readers Group.

—Encyclopedia Brown Gets His Man. Shortall, Leonard W., illus. 2009. (Encyclopedia Brown Ser.). 96p. lib. bdg. 15.00 *(978-1-60686-464-7(5))* Perfection Learning Corp.

—Encyclopedia Brown Gets His Man. 2007. (Encyclopedia Brown Ser.: 4). 14.75 *(978-1-4177-8626-8(4))* Turtleback.

—Encyclopedia Brown Keeps the Peace. 2008. (Encyclopedia Brown Ser.: 6). (ENG., Illus.). 96p. (J). (gr. 3-7). 6.99 *(978-0-14-240950-3(2)*, Puffin Books) Penguin Young Readers Group.

—Encyclopedia Brown Lends a Hand. 2008. (Encyclopedia Brown Ser.: 11). (ENG., Illus.). 96p. (J). (gr. 3-7). 6.99 *(978-0-14-241105-6(1)*, Puffin Books) Penguin Young Readers Group.
—Encyclopedia Brown Saves the Day. 2008. (Encyclopedia Brown Ser.: 7). (ENG., Illus.). 96p. (J). (gr. 3-7). 5.99 *(978-0-14-240921-3(9)*, Puffin Books) Penguin Young Readers Group.
—Encyclopedia Brown Shows the Way. 2008. (Encyclopedia Brown Ser.: 9). (ENG., Illus.). 96p. (J). (gr. 3-7). 6.99 *(978-0-14-241086-8(1)*, Puffin Books) Penguin Young Readers Group.
—Encyclopedia Brown Shows the Way. Shortall, Leonard W., illus. 2008. (Encyclopedia Brown Ser.). 96p. (J). (gr. 2-5). 12.65 *(978-0-7569-8937-8(X))* Perfection Learning Corp.
—Encyclopedia Brown Solves Them All. 2008. (Encyclopedia Brown Ser.: 5). (ENG., Illus.). 96p. (J). (gr. 3-7). 6.99 *(978-0-14-240920-6(0)*, Puffin Books) Penguin Young Readers Group.
—Encyclopedia Brown, Super Sleuth. 2010. (Encyclopedia Brown Ser.: 26). (ENG.). 96p. (J). (gr. 3-7). 4.99 *(978-0-14-241688-4(6)*, Puffin Books) Penguin Young Readers Group.
—Encyclopedia Brown Takes the Case. 2008. (Encyclopedia Brown Ser.: 10). (ENG., Illus.). 96p. (J). (gr. 3-7). 6.99 *(978-0-14-241085-1(3)*, Puffin Books) Penguin Young Readers Group.
—Encyclopedia Brown Takes the Case. Shortall, Leonard W., illus. 2008. (Encyclopedia Brown Ser.). 96p. (J). (gr. 3-7). 12.65 *(978-0-7569-9078-7(5))* Perfection Learning Corp.
—Encyclopedia Brown Tracks Them Down. 2008. (Encyclopedia Brown Ser.: 8). (ENG., Illus.). 96p. (J). (gr. 3-7). 6.99 *(978-0-14-240951-0(0)*, Puffin Books) Penguin Young Readers Group.
Soderberg, Erin. Scooby-Doo & the Dinosaur Ghost, 1 vol. Sur, Duendes del, illus. 2016. (Scooby-Doo Early Reading Adventures Ser.). (ENG.). 24p. (J). (gr. -1-2). lib. bdg. 31.36 *(978-1-61479-464-6(2)*, 21377) Spotlight.
—Scooby-Doo & the Mystery at the Park, 1 vol. Sur, Duendes del, illus. 2016. (Scooby-Doo Early Reading Adventures Ser.). (ENG.). 24p. (J). (gr. -1-2). lib. bdg. 31.36 *(978-1-61479-469-1(3)*, 21382) Spotlight.
Soileau, Hodges, illus. The Black Widow Spider Mystery. 2004. (Boxcar Children Special Ser.). 130p. (gr. 2-7). 15.50 *(978-0-7569-3266-4(1))* Perfection Learning Corp.
—The Comic Book Mystery. 2003. (Boxcar Children Ser.). 106p. (gr. 4-7). 15.00 *(978-0-7569-1611-4(9))* Perfection Learning Corp.
—The Great Shark Mystery. 2003. (Boxcar Children Special Ser.). 130p. (gr. 4-7). 15.50 *(978-0-7569-1616-9(X))* Perfection Learning Corp.
—The Mystery at Skeleton Point. 2003. (Boxcar Children Ser.). 120p. (gr. 4-7). 15.00 *(978-0-7569-1609-1(7))* Perfection Learning Corp.
Somoskey, Rebecca. Summer of the Buckeye Whistle. 2004. (J). 5.00 *(978-0-9768514-0-0(7))* Bearwallow Blessings Ministries.
Sonik, Madeline. Belinda & the Dustbunnys. Bridal, Grania, tr. 2004. (Illus.). 80p. (J). (gr. 4-7). 12.95 *(978-0-9730831-4-9(X))* Hodgepog Bks. CAN. Dist: Fitzhenry & Whiteside, Ltd.
Sonneborn, Scott. The Computer Meltdown. Lozano, Omar, illus. 2015. (North Police Ser.). (ENG.). 32p. (J). (gr. k-2). lib. bdg. 21.32 *(978-1-4795-6485-9(0)*, 128338, Picture Window Bks.) Capstone.
—The Mystery of Santa's Sleigh. Lozano, Omar, illus. 2016. (ENG.). 32p. (J). pap. *(978-1-4747-0031-3(4)*, Picture Window Bks.) Capstone.
—The Reindeer Games. Lozano, Omar, illus. (ENG.). 32p. (J). 2016. pap. *(978-1-4747-0034-4(9))* 2015. lib. bdg. 21.32 *(978-1-4795-6487-3(7)*, 128340) Capstone. (Picture Window Bks.).
Sorrells, W. A. Nairobi Nightmare. Bancroft, Tom & Corley, Rob, illus. 2007. 144p. (J). *(978-0-9792912-1-0(6))* KidsGive, LLC.
Sorrells, Walter. Club Dread. 2007. (Hunted Ser.: 2). (ENG.). 272p. (YA). (gr. 7-18). 8.99 *(978-0-14-240904-6(9)*, Puffin Books) Penguin Young Readers Group.
—Fake ID. 2007. (Hunted Ser.: 1). (ENG.). 336p. (YA). (gr. 7-18). 9.99 *(978-0-14-240762-2(3)*, Puffin Books) Penguin Young Readers Group.
Space Case. 2014. (Moon Base Alpha Ser.). (ENG., Illus.). 352p. (J). (gr. 3-7). 18.99 *(978-1-4424-9486-2(7)*, Simon & Schuster Bks. For Young Readers) Simon & Schuster Bks. For Young Readers.
Spalding, Andrea & Spalding, David. The Silver Boulder. (Adventure Net Ser.). 8p. tchr. ed. 3.95 *(978-1-55285-160-9(5)*, Walrus Bks.) Whitecap Bks., Ltd. CAN. Dist: Graphic Arts Ctr. Publishing Co.
Spangler, Brie, illus. We Both Read-The Mystery of Pirate's Point: Level 3. 2008. (We Both Read Ser.). 40p. (J). (gr. 1-5). per. 5.99 *(978-1-60115-010-3(5))* Treasure Bay, Inc.
Specter, Baron. All in a Night's Work, 1 vol. Kneupper, Setch, illus. 2012. (Graveyard Diaries). (ENG.). 128p. (J). (gr. 2-5). 38.50 *(978-1-61641-903-5(2)*, 9184, Calico Chapter Bks.) ABDO Publishing Co.
—To Werewolf or Not to Werewolf, 1 vol. Kneupper, Setch, illus. 2012. (Graveyard Diaries). (ENG.). 128p. (J). (gr. 2-5). 38.50 *(978-1-61641-901-1(6)*, 9180, Calico Chapter Bks.) ABDO Publishing Co.
—Vampires Are Not Your Friends, 1 vol. Kneupper, Setch, illus. 2012. (Graveyard Diaries). (ENG.). 128p. (J). (gr. 2-5). 38.50 *(978-1-61641-902-8(4)*, 9182, Calico Chapter Bks.) ABDO Publishing Co.
Spector, Baron. Approaching the Undead, 1 vol. Kneupper, Setch, illus. 2012. (Graveyard Diaries). (ENG.). 128p. (J). (gr. 2-5). lib. bdg. 38.50 *(978-1-61641-899-1(0)*, 9176, Calico Chapter Bks.) ABDO Publishing Co.
Spencer, Octavia. The Case of the Time-Capsule Bandit. To, Vivienne, illus. 2013. (Randi Rhodes, Ninja Detective Ser.: 1). (ENG.). 224p. (J). (gr. 3-7). 16.99 *(978-1-4424-7681-3(8)*, Simon & Schuster Bks. For Young Readers) Simon & Schuster Bks. For Young Readers.
Spoor, Mike, illus. Desperate Measures: Units of Measurement in Action, 1 vol. 2010. (Mandrill Mountain Math Mysteries Ser.). (ENG.). 32p. (J). (gr. 2-3). pap. 11.55 *(978-1-60754-925-3(5)*, 0d0a4546-a9aa-44e2-a596-6f85f71671d5); lib. bdg. 27.27 *(978-1-60754-920-8(4)*, 062ce9eb-2d37-4102-905f-f0621291bce6) Rosen Publishing Group, Inc., The. (Windmill Bks.).
—The Emperor's Guards: Concepts of Time, 1 vol. 2010. (Mandrill Mountain Math Mysteries Ser.). (ENG.). 32p. (J). (gr. 2-3). lib. bdg. 27.27 *(978-1-60754-922-2(0)*, 85dd0127-799d-49a7-b02c-a55c0fa8b8a4, Windmill Bks.) Rosen Publishing Group, Inc., The.
—The Emperor's Last Command: Problem-Solving in Action, 1 vol. 2010. (Mandrill Mountain Math Mysteries Ser.). (ENG.). 32p. (J). (gr. 2-3). lib. bdg. 27.27 *(978-1-60754-923-9(9)*, 6cfa914f-78f4-4422-84b7-89ec55697406, Windmill Bks.) Rosen Publishing Group, Inc., The.
—The Hidden Valley: Reasoning in Action, 1 vol. 2010. (Mandrill Mountain Math Mysteries Ser.). (ENG.). 32p. (J). (gr. 2-3). lib. bdg. 27.27 *(978-1-60754-919-2(0)*, aad83b41-3bb8-4a8c-be7f-3ca4a5a6da9c, Windmill Bks.) Rosen Publishing Group, Inc., The.
—Lightning Flash: Probability in Action, 1 vol. 2010. (Mandrill Mountain Math Mysteries Ser.). (ENG.). 32p. (J). (gr. 2-3). pap. 11.55 *(978-1-60754-926-0(3)*, dd74b064-99ba-4c5a-8f94-699cc3a14a7f); lib. bdg. 27.27 *(978-1-60754-921-5(2)*, de03c233-9c49-4baf-a9f9-69cb03855381) Rosen Publishing Group, Inc., The. (Windmill Bks.).
Spratt, R. A. Friday Barnes, Girl Detective. 2017. (Friday Barnes Ser.: 1). (J). lib. bdg. 18.40 *(978-0-606-39603-5(9))* Turtleback.
—No Rules: a Friday Barnes Mystery. Gosier, Phil, illus. 2018. (Friday Barnes Mysteries Ser.). (ENG.). 272p. (J). pap. 12.99 *(978-1-250-15899-4(0)*, 900163944) Square Fish.
Springer, Nancy. Blood Trail. 2006. (ENG.). 164p. (YA). (gr. 8-12). pap. 6.95 *(978-0-8234-2063-6(9))* Holiday Hse., Inc.
—The Case of the Bizarre Bouquets, 3. 2008. (Enola Holmes Mystery Ser.: 3). (ENG.). 176p. (J). (gr. 6-8). 21.19 *(978-0-399-24518-3(9))* Penguin Young Readers Group.
—The Case of the Gypsy Good-Bye, 6 vols., 6. 2012. (Enola Holmes Mystery Ser.: 6). (ENG.). 176p. (J). (gr. 6-8). 18.69 *(978-0-399-25236-5(3))* Penguin Young Readers Group.
—Enola Holmes: the Case of the Bizarre Bouquets. 2009. (Enola Holmes Mystery Ser.: 3). (ENG.). 192p. (J). (gr. 3-7). pap. 8.99 *(978-0-14-241390-6(9)*, Puffin Books) Penguin Young Readers Group.
—Enola Holmes: the Case of the Cryptic Crinoline. 2011. (Enola Holmes Mystery Ser.: 5). (ENG., Illus.). 176p. (J). (gr. 3-7). 8.99 *(978-0-14-241690-7(8)*, Puffin Books) Penguin Young Readers Group.
—Enola Holmes: the Case of the Left-Handed Lady: An Enola Holmes Mystery. 2008. (Enola Holmes Mystery Ser.: 2). (ENG.). 256p. (J). (gr. 3-7). 8.99 *(978-0-14-241190-2(6)*, Puffin Books) Penguin Young Readers Group.
—Enola Holmes: the Case of the Missing Marquess. 2007. (Enola Holmes Mystery Ser.: 1). (ENG.). 240p. (J). (gr. 3-7). 7.99 *(978-0-14-240933-6(2)*, Puffin Books) Penguin Young Readers Group.
—Enola Holmes: the Case of the Peculiar Pink Fan. 2010. (Enola Holmes Mystery Ser.: 4). (ENG.). 192p. (J). (gr. 3-7). 7.99 *(978-0-14-241517-7(0)*, Puffin Books) Penguin Young Readers Group.
Springstubb, Tricia. Cody & the Mysteries of the Universe. Wheeler, Eliza, illus. 2016. (Cody Ser.). (ENG.). 144p. (J). (gr. 2-5). 14.99 *(978-0-7636-5858-8(8))* Candlewick Pr.
The Spy down the Street, 6 vols., Vol. 2. (Woodland Mysteriestm Ser.). 133p. (gr. 3-7). 42.50 *(978-0-7802-7938-4(7))* Wright Group/McGraw-Hill.
St. Antoine, Sara. Three Bird Summer. 2018. (ENG.). 256p. (J). (gr. 5). pap. 6.99 *(978-1-5362-0045-4(X))* Candlewick Pr.
St. George, Victoria. Barnyard Bandits. 2011. (Illus.). 28p. (J). pap. 12.99 *(978-1-4567-3040-6(1))* AuthorHouse.
St John, Lauren. KENTUCKY THRILLER. 2014. (Jóvenes Lectores. Los Misterios de Laura Ser.). (SPA., Illus.). 248p. (J). (gr. 4-7). pap. 8.95 *(978-84-8343-271-6(4)*, Bambu, Editorial) Combel Editorial, S.A. ESP. Dist: Independent Pubs. Group.
St. John, Wylly Folk. The Ghost Next Door. Hyman, Trina Schart, illus. 2019. 184p. (J). pap. *(978-1-948959-08-7(9))* Purple Hse. Pr.
Stamper, Judith Bauer. Rocky Road Trip. Gangloff, Hope, illus. 2004. (Magic School Bus Science Chapter Bks.). 89p. (gr. 2-5). lib. bdg. 15.00 *(978-0-7569-3093-6(6))* Perfection Learning Corp.
Stampler, Ann Redisch. How to Disappear. 2016. (ENG., Illus.). 416p. (YA). (gr. 9). 18.99 *(978-1-4814-4393-7(3)*, Simon Pulse) Simon Pulse.
Stancic, Giselle M. The Paganini Curse. 2013. 166p. 22.95 *(978-1-4759-6161-4(8))*; pap. 12.95 *(978-1-4759-6159-1(6))* iUniverse, Inc.
Standiford, Natalie. The Secret Tree. (J). 2014. (ENG.). 256p. (gr. 3-7). pap. 7.99 *(978-0-545-33480-8(2)*, Scholastic Paperbacks) 2012. 245p. pap. *(978-0-545-48976-8(8)*, Scholastic Pr.) Scholastic, Inc.
Stanek, Mary Beth. The Fire Keepers: Mystery at Manitou Beach. Stanek, Mary Beth, illus. Stanek, Linda, photos by. 2003. (Illus.). (J). pap. 20.00 *(978-0-9747556-0-1(5))* Stanek, Mary Beth.
Stanford, K. B. Sixteen Wishes (paperback) 2008. 188p. pap. 15.47 *(978-1-4357-1773-2(2))* Lulu Pr., Inc.
Stangherlin, Tonia. T-Bird & the Island of Lost Cats. 2006. 116p. pap. 14.99 *(978-1-4116-6697-9(6))* Lulu Pr., Inc.
Stanley, George E. The Case of the Bank-Robbing Bandit. Murdocca, Salvatore, illus. 2004. (Third-Grade Detectives Ser.: 9). (ENG.). 80p. (J). (gr. 1-4). pap. 5.99 *(978-0-689-86489-6(2)*, Aladdin) Simon & Schuster Children's Publishing.
—The Case of the Dirty Clue. Murdocca, Salvatore, illus. 2003. (Third-Grade Detectives Ser.: 7). (ENG.). 80p. (J). (gr. 1-4). pap. 5.99 *(978-0-689-86357-8(8)*, Simon & Schuster/Paula Wiseman Bks.) Simon & Schuster/Paula Wiseman Bks.
—The Clue of the Left-Handed Envelope/the Puzzle of the Pretty Pink Handkerchief: Third-Grade Detectives #1-2. 2004. (Third-Grade Detectives Ser.: Bk. 1). (ENG., Illus.). 144p. (J). (gr. 1-4). pap. 8.99 *(978-0-689-87106-1(6)*, Aladdin) Simon & Schuster Children's Publishing.
—The Mystery of the Stolen Statue, 10. Murdocca, Salvatore, illus. 2004. (Third-Grade Detectives Ser.: 10). (ENG.). 80p. (J). (gr. 1-4). pap. 5.99 *(978-0-689-86491-9(4))* Simon & Schuster, Inc.
—The Riddle of the Stolen Sand. Murdocca, Salvatore, illus. 2003. (Third-Grade Detectives Ser.: 5). (ENG.). 64p. (J). (gr. 1-4). pap. 5.99 *(978-0-689-85376-0(9)*, Aladdin) Simon & Schuster Children's Publishing.
—The Secret of the Wooden Witness, 8. Murdocca, Salvatore, illus. 2004. (Third-Grade Detectives Ser.: 8). (ENG.). 80p. (J). (gr. 1-4). pap. 5.99 *(978-0-689-86487-2(6))* Simon & Schuster, Inc.
Stanley, George Edward. The Case of the Dirty Clue. Murdocca, Sal, illus. 2005. (Ready-for-Chapters Ser.). (J). lib. bdg. 15.00 *(978-1-59054-898-1(1))* Fitzgerald Bks.
—The Secret of the Green Skin. Murdocca, Sal, illus. 2005. (Third-Grade Detectives Ser.: Bk. 6). 62p. (J). lib. bdg. 15.00 *(978-1-59054-916-2(3))* Fitzgerald Bks.
Stanley, Phillip Orin, 2nd. The Castle Rock Critter. Stanley, Christopher Heath & Parsons, Arielle, illus. l.t. ed. 2004. 16p. (J). 8.00 *(978-0-9761355-0-0(7))* Floodgate Publishing.
Stanton, Nicholas Sheridan. KK Undercover Mystery: The Cookie Caper. 2011. 80p. (gr. 4-6). pap. 26.01 *(978-1-4567-6597-2(3))* AuthorHouse.
Star, Nancy. The Case of the April Fool's Frogs. 2006. 77p. *(978-0-439-67266-5(X))* Scholastic, Inc.
—The Case of the Sneaky Strangers. 2006. 77p. pap. *(978-0-439-67267-2(8))* Scholastic, Inc.
—The Case of the Thanksgiving Thief. Bernardin, James, illus. 2004. 79p. (J). *(978-0-439-67261-0(9))* Scholastic, Inc.
—Mystery of the Snow Day Bigfoot. Bernardin, James, illus. 2005. (Calendar Club Mysteries Ser.: Vol. 3). 77p. (J). pap. 3.95 *(978-0-439-67262-7(7))* Scholastic, Inc.
Starinobets, Anna. In the Wolf's Lair: A Beastly Crimes Book. Bugaeva, Jane, tr. 2018. (ENG., Illus.). 112p. (gr. 2-6). 16.99 *(978-0-486-82762-9(3)*, 827623) Dover Pubns., Inc.
—A Predator's Rights: A Beastly Crimes Book (#2) Bugaeva, Jane, tr. 2019. (ENG., Illus.). 112p. (gr. 2-6). 16.99 *(978-0-486-82951-7(0)*, 829510) Dover Pubns., Inc.
Starobinets, Anna. Claws of Rage: A Beastly Crimes Book (#3) Bugaeva, Jane, tr. Muravski, Marie, illus. 2019. (ENG.). 208p. (gr. 2-6). 16.99 *(978-0-486-82952-4(9)*, 829529) Dover Pubns., Inc.
—The Plucker: A Beastly Crimes Book (#4) Bugaeva, Jane, tr. Muravski, Marie, illus. 2019. (ENG.). 304p. (gr. 2-6). 16.99 *(978-0-486-82953-1(7)*, 829537) Dover Pubns., Inc.
Stead, Rebecca & Mass, Wendy. The Lost Library. 2023. (ENG.). 224p. (J). 17.99 ***(978-1-250-83881-0(9)***, 900255029) Feiwel & Friends.
Steele, Michael Anthony. The Case of the Fright Flight. Neely, Scott, illus. 2016. (You Choose Stories: Scooby-Doo Ser.). (ENG.). 112p. (J). (gr. 2-6). lib. bdg. 32.65 *(978-1-4965-2662-5(7)*, 131221, Stone Arch Bks.) Capstone.
—Creepy Cowboy Caper. Jeralds, Scott, illus. 2017. (Scooby-Doo! Beginner Mysteries Ser.). (ENG.). 112p. (J). (gr. 1-3). lib. bdg. 23.99 *(978-1-4965-4768-2(3)*, 135305, Stone Arch Bks.) Capstone.
—Monster Mutt Madness. Jeralds, Scott, illus. 2017. (Scooby-Doo! Beginner Mysteries Ser.). (ENG.). 112p. (J). (gr. 1-3). lib. bdg. 22.65 *(978-1-4965-4767-5(5)*, 135304, Stone Arch Bks.) Capstone.
—Scooby-Doo! Beginner Mysteries. 2017. (Scooby-Doo! Beginner Mysteries Ser.). (ENG.). 112p. (J). (gr. 1-3). 95.96 *(978-1-4965-4796-5(9)*, 26568, Stone Arch Bks.) Capstone.
—Skeleton Crew Showdown. Jeralds, Scott, illus. 2017. (Scooby-Doo! Beginner Mysteries Ser.). (ENG.). 112p. (J). (gr. 1-3). lib. bdg. 22.65 *(978-1-4965-4769-9(1)*, 135306, Stone Arch Bks.) Capstone.
—Vampire Zoo Hullabaloo. Jeralds, Scott, illus. 2017. (Scooby-Doo! Beginner Mysteries Ser.). (ENG.). 112p. (J). (gr. 1-3). lib. bdg. 22.65 *(978-1-4965-4770-5(5)*, 135307, Stone Arch Bks.) Capstone.
Steensland, Mark. Behind the Bookcase. Murphy, Kelly, illus. 2013. 288p. (J). (gr. 3-7). 6.99 *(978-0-385-74072-2(7)*, Yearling) Random Hse. Children's Bks.
Steiner. Murder Takes a Fast Track. (Thumbprint Mysteries Ser.). 32.86 *(978-0-8092-0417-5(7))* McGraw-Hill/Contemporary.
Steiner, Barbara. The Cry of the Loon: A Samantha Mystery. Tibbles, Jean-Paul, illus. 2006. (ENG.). 192p. (gr. 4-18). 10.95 *(978-1-59369-479-1(2))* American Girl Publishing, Inc.
—23 Shadow Street: Deadly Dreams. 2007. (ENG.). 188p. (J). (gr. -1-12). per. 8.95 *(978-1-59687-329-2(9))* IBks., Inc.
Stem, Jacqueline. The Ghosts of Goliad. 2003. iii, 165p. (J). 17.95 *(978-1-57168-785-2(8)*, Eakin Pr.) Eakin Pr.
—Mystery of the Whispering Walls. 2004. (J). 148p. pap. *(978-1-57168-844-6(7))*; (Hollow Tree Mystery Ser.: Bk. 6). (Illus.). v, 142p. *(978-1-57168-850-7(1)*, Eakin Pr.) Eakin Pr.
Stem, Jacqueline C. The Secret of the Dragonfly Pin. 2006. (Hollow Tree Mystery Ser.: 7). 115p. (J). (gr. 3-7). per. 12.95 *(978-1-57168-264-2(3)*, Eakin Pr.) Eakin Pr.
Stemple, Adam & Yolen, Jane. Sanctuary: Book 2. Zangara, Orion, illus. 2018. (Stone Man Mysteries Ser.). (ENG.). 88p. (YA). (gr. 7-12). pap. 8.99 *(978-1-5415-1043-2(7)*, 56cb1424-a16d-418a-a0c5-52e2dda42a46);No. 2. 29.32 *(978-1-4677-4197-2(3)*, 96ca54a0-3352-4fc3-8226-178cee1ddbb1) Lerner Publishing Group. (Graphic Universe™).
—Stone Cold: Book 1, No. 1. Zangara, Orion, illus. 2016. (Stone Man Mysteries Ser.: 1). (ENG.). 80p. (YA). (gr. 7-12). lib. bdg. 29.32 *(978-1-4677-4196-5(5)*, 1ced9530-2931-4585-8c9c-adff2d2724ca, Graphic Universe™) Lerner Publishing Group.
Steps To Literacy Staff, compiled by. Capitol Mysteries: Gen014. 2005. (ENG., Illus.). (J). *(978-1-59564-732-0(5))* Steps To Literacy, LLC.
—Tales for the House of Bunnicula: Lib710. 2005. (ENG., Illus.). (J). pap. *(978-1-59564-678-1(7))* Steps To Literacy, LLC.
Stern, D. G. Disappearing Diamonds: An Upton Charles Adventure. Bartlett, Rebecca, illus. 2008. (ENG.). 126p. (J). pap. 9.99 *(978-0-9754676-9-5(7))* Yeoman Hse.
Sternberg, Libby. Finding the Forger. 2004. (ENG.). 192p. (J). pap. 14.95 *(978-1-890862-37-4(1)*, e345051e-0205-4c39-b601-ae3c052d1093) Bancroft Pr.
—Uncovering Sadie's Secrets. 2003. (ENG.). 196p. pap. 14.95 *(978-1-890862-28-2(2)*, 0c5e7cb4-aecf-4d5b-afba-7d1088710bf8) Bancroft Pr.
Steuerwald, Shannon B. From Scrawny to Brawny. 2006. (J). per. 9.95 *(978-1-931787-19-2(0))* Fundamental Christian Endeavors.
Stevens, B. K. Fighting Chance. 2015. (ENG.). 336p. (YA). pap. 18.99 *(978-1-929345-14-4(3)*, Poisoned Pen Press) Sourcebooks, Inc.
Stevens, Court. The June Boys, 1 vol. 2020. (ENG., Illus.). (YA). 384p. pap. 12.99 *(978-0-7852-2194-4(8))*; 368p. 18.99 *(978-0-7852-2190-6(5))* Nelson, Thomas Inc.
Stevens, Robin. Jolly Foul Play. (Murder Most Unladylike Mystery Ser.). (ENG.). (J). (gr. 5). 2019. 384p. pap. 8.99 *(978-1-4814-8910-2(0))* 2018. (Illus.). 368p. 19.99 *(978-1-4814-8909-6(7))* Simon & Schuster Bks. For Young Readers. (Simon & Schuster Bks. For Young Readers).
—Mistletoe & Murder. (Murder Most Unladylike Mystery Ser.). (ENG., Illus.). (J). (gr. 5). 2019. 368p. pap. 8.99 *(978-1-4814-8913-3(5))* 2018. 352p. 19.99 *(978-1-4814-8912-6(7))* Simon & Schuster Bks. For Young Readers. (Simon & Schuster Bks. For Young Readers).
—Murder Is Bad Manners. 2015. (Murder Most Unladylike Mystery Ser.). (ENG., Illus.). 320p. (J). (gr. 5). 19.99 *(978-1-4814-2212-3(X)*, Simon & Schuster Bks. For Young Readers) Simon & Schuster Bks. For Young Readers.
—Poison Is Not Polite. 2016. (Murder Most Unladylike Mystery Ser.). (ENG., Illus.). 336p. (J). (gr. 5). 19.99 *(978-1-4814-2215-4(4)*, Simon & Schuster Bks. For Young Readers) Simon & Schuster Bks. For Young Readers.
Stevenson-Ringo, Angela. Keith's Shoes. 2009. 28p. pap. 9.95 *(978-1-4327-2344-6(8))* Outskirts Pr., Inc.
Stevenson, Robert Louis. Dr. Jekyll & Mr. Hyde. Gelev, Penko, illus. 2017. (Classic Graphic Fiction Ser.). (ENG.). 48p. (J). (gr. 4). pap. 7.95 *(978-1-912006-01-4(4))* Book Hse. GBR. Dist: Sterling Publishing Co., Inc.
Stevenson, S. Roy. The Magic Act: A Mystery by S. Roy Stevenson. 2008. 108p. 20.95 *(978-0-595-51841-8(9))*; pap. 10.95 *(978-0-595-53062-5(1))* iUniverse, Inc.
Stevenson, Steve. The Crime on the Norwegian Sea. 2016. (Agatha Girl of Mystery Ser.: 10). lib. bdg. 16.00 *(978-0-606-38415-5(4))* Turtleback.
—The Crown of Venice. 2014. (Agatha Girl of Mystery Ser.: 7). lib. bdg. 16.00 *(978-0-606-36164-4(2))* Turtleback.
—The Curse of the Pharaoh. 2013. (Agatha Girl of Mystery Ser.: 1). lib. bdg. 17.20 *(978-0-606-29986-2(6))* Turtleback.
—The Eiffel Tower Incident. 2014. (Agatha Girl of Mystery Ser.: 5). lib. bdg. 16.00 *(978-0-606-34153-0(6))* Turtleback.
—The Heist at Niagara Falls. 2013. (Agatha Girl of Mystery Ser.: 4). lib. bdg. 16.00 *(978-0-606-32128-0(4))* Turtleback.
—The Kenyan Expedition. 2015. (Agatha Girl of Mystery Ser.: 8). lib. bdg. 16.00 *(978-0-606-36763-9(2))* Turtleback.
—The King of Scotland's Sword #3. Turconi, Stefano, illus. 2013. (Agatha: Girl of Mystery Ser.: 3). (ENG.). 144p. (J). (gr. 2-5). pap. 6.99 *(978-0-448-46220-2(6)*, Grosset & Dunlap) Penguin Young Readers Group.
—The Pearl of Bengal. 2013. (Agatha Girl of Mystery Ser.: 2). lib. bdg. 17.20 *(978-0-606-30016-2(3))* Turtleback.
Stewart, Dianne C. Season of the Cold Moon. 2011. (ENG.). 108p. (J). (gr. 2). pap. 8.95 *(978-0-9831032-0-2(8)*, BeanPole Bks.) OH Industries.
Stewart, Jane. The Island Escapade. 2003. 102p. (YA). pap. 9.95 *(978-0-595-27734-6(9))* iUniverse, Inc.
Stewart, Linda. The Great Catsby: A Sam the Cat Mystery. 2013. (ENG.). 152p. (J). pap. 10.95 *(978-0-9675073-6-1(7))* Cheshire House Bks.
Stewart, Paul & Riddell, Chris. Barnaby Grimes: Phantom of Blood Alley. 2013. (Barnaby Grimes Ser.: 4). (ENG.). 208p. (J). (gr. 3-7). 6.99 *(978-0-385-73700-5(9)*, Yearling) Random Hse. Children's Bks.
Stewart, Trenton Lee. The Extraordinary Education of Nicholas Benedict. Sudyka, Diana, illus. (Mysterious Benedict Society Ser.). (ENG.). (J). (gr. 3-7). 2013. 496p. pap. 9.99 *(978-0-316-17620-0(6))* 2012. 480p. 39.99 *(978-0-316-17619-4(2))* Little, Brown Bks. for Young Readers.
—The Extraordinary Education of Nicholas Benedict. 2013. (Mysterious Benedict Society Ser.: 0). (J). lib. bdg. 19.65 *(978-0-606-31743-6(0))* Turtleback.
Stiberth, Elizabeth. Halloween Mystery. 2008. 32p. pap. 14.49 *(978-1-4389-1112-0(2))* AuthorHouse.
Stilton, Gerónimo. Geronimo & the Gold Medal Mystery. 2008. (Geronimo Stilton Ser.). (Illus.). 87p. (J). (gr. 2-5). lib. bdg. 14.65 *(978-0-7569-8803-6(9))* Perfection Learning Corp.
—Geronimo's Valentine. 2009. (Geronimo Stilton Ser.: 36). (Illus.). 103p. (J). 18.40 *(978-1-4364-5051-5(9))* Turtleback.
Stilton, Geronimo. The Golden Statue Plot (Geronimo Stilton #55) 2018. (True Book (Relaunch) Ser.: 55). (ENG.). 128p. (J). (gr. 3-5). E-Book 31.00 *(978-0-545-55681-1(3)*, Scholastic Paperbacks) Scholastic, Inc.
Stilton, Gerónimo. The Karate Mouse. 2010. (Geronimo Stilton Ser.: 40). lib. bdg. 18.40 *(978-0-606-06847-5(3))* Turtleback.
—Meet Me in Horrorwood. 2011. (Geronimo Stilton — Creepella Von Cacklefur Ser.: 2). (Illus.). 112p. (J). lib. bdg. 18.40 *(978-0-606-22947-0(7))* Turtleback.
—The Mona Mousa Code. Wolf, Matt, illus. 2005. (Geronimo Stilton Ser.: No. 15). 113p. (J). lib. bdg. 10.00 *(978-1-4242-0284-3(1))* Fitzgerald Bks.
—The Mysterious Cheese Thief. 2007. (Geronimo Stilton Ser.). (Illus.). 111p. (J). (gr. 2-5). 14.65 *(978-0-7569-8303-1(7))* Perfection Learning Corp.
—The Mysterious Cheese Thief. 2007. (Geronimo Stilton Ser.: 31). (Illus.). 111p. (gr. 4-7). 18.40 *(978-1-4177-9646-5(4))* Turtleback.
Stilton, Geronimo. Mysterious Eye of the Dragon (Geronimo Stilton #78) 2021. (Geronimo Stilton Ser.). (ENG., Illus.). 109p. (J). (gr. 2-3). 18.86 *(978-1-68505-057-3(3))* Penworthy Co., LLC, The.
—Mysterious Eye of the Dragon (Geronimo Stilton #78) 2021. (Geronimo Stilton Ser.: 78). (ENG.). 128p. (J). (gr. 2-5). pap. 7.99 *(978-1-338-68720-0(4)*, Scholastic Paperbacks);78. (gr. 1-4). 22.44 *(978-1-5364-6914-1(9))* Scholastic, Inc.
Stilton, Gerónimo. The Mystery in Venice. 2012. (Geronimo Stilton Ser.: 48). lib. bdg. 18.40 *(978-0-606-23729-1(1))* Turtleback.
—The Phantom of the Subway. Wolf, Matt, illus. 2004. (Geronimo Stilton Ser.: No. 13). 112p. (J). lib. bdg. 10.00 *(978-1-4242-0282-9(5))* Fitzgerald Bks.

—Thea Stilton & the Dragon's Code. 2009. (Geronimo Stilton Special Edition Ser.: No. 1). (Illus.). 158p. 18.00 *(978-1-60686-420-3(3))* Perfection Learning Corp.

—Thea Stilton & the Dragon's Code. 2009. (Thea Stilton Ser.: 1). lib. bdg. 19.65 *(978-0-606-00231-8(6))* Turtleback.

—Thea Stilton & the Niagara Splash, 27. 2019. (Geronimo Stilton Ser.). (ENG.). 164p. (J). (gr. 2-3). 18.36 *(978-1-64310-997-8(9))* Penworthy Co., LLC, The.

Stilton, Gerónimo & Stilton, Thea. Thea Stilton & the Ghost of the Shipwreck. 2010. (Thea Stilton Ser.: 3). lib. bdg. 19.65 *(978-0-606-06843-7(0))* Turtleback.

Stilton, Gerónimo & Tramontozzi, Lidia Morson. The Cheese Experiment. De Negri, Andrea, illus. 2016. 103p. (J). *(978-1-5182-1588-9(2))* Scholastic, Inc.

Stilton, Thea. Thea Stilton & the Dragon's Code (Thea Stilton #1) A Geronimo Stilton Adventure. 2009. (Thea Stilton Ser.: 1). (ENG., Illus.). 176p. (J). (gr. 2-5). pap. 8.99 *(978-0-545-10367-1(3)*, Scholastic Paperbacks) Scholastic, Inc.

—Thea Stilton & the Hollywood Hoax. 2016. (Thea Stilton Ser.: 23). lib. bdg. 18.40 *(978-0-606-38799-6(4))* Turtleback.

—Thea Stilton & the Journey to the Lion's Den. 2013. (Thea Stilton Ser.: 17). lib. bdg. 19.65 *(978-0-606-32382-6(1))* Turtleback.

—Thea Stilton & the Legend of the Fire Flowers. 2013. (Thea Stilton Ser.: 15). lib. bdg. 19.65 *(978-0-606-32000-9(8))* Turtleback.

—Thea Stilton & the Lost Letters. 2015. (Thea Stilton Ser.: 21). (Illus.). 159p. (J). lib. bdg. 18.40 *(978-0-606-37061-5(7))* Turtleback.

—Thea Stilton & the Missing Myth. 2014. (Thea Stilton Ser.: 20). lib. bdg. 19.65 *(978-0-606-36058-6(1))* Turtleback.

—Thea Stilton & the Mountain of Fire (Thea Stilton #2) A Geronimo Stilton Adventure. 2009. (Thea Stilton Ser.: 2). (ENG., Illus.). 176p. (J). (gr. 2-5). pap. 8.99 *(978-0-545-15060-6(4)*, Scholastic Paperbacks) Scholastic, Inc.

—Thea Stilton & the Mystery on the Orient Express. 2012. (Thea Stilton Ser.: 13). lib. bdg. 19.65 *(978-0-606-26757-1(3))* Turtleback.

—Thea Stilton & the Mystery on the Orient Express (Thea Stilton #13) A Geronimo Stilton Adventure. 2012. (Thea Stilton Ser.: 13). (ENG., Illus.). 176p. (J). (gr. 2-5). pap. 8.99 *(978-0-545-34105-9(1)*, Scholastic Paperbacks) Scholastic, Inc.

—Thea Stilton & the Secret of the Old Castle. 2012. (Thea Stilton Ser.: 10). lib. bdg. 19.65 *(978-0-606-23930-1(8))* Turtleback.

—Thea Stilton & the Spanish Dance Mission. 2013. (Thea Stilton Ser.: 16). lib. bdg. 19.65 *(978-0-606-32381-9(3))* Turtleback.

—Thea Stilton & the Spanish Dance Mission (Thea Stilton #16) A Geronimo Stilton Adventure. 2018. (True Book (Relaunch) Ser.: 16). (ENG.). 176p. (J). (gr. 3-5). E-Book 7.95 *(978-0-545-55685-9(6)*, Scholastic Paperbacks) Scholastic, Inc.

—Thea Stilton Mouseford Academy #9: The Mysterious Love Letter. 2016. (Illus.). 128p. (J). *(978-0-545-91796-4(4))* Scholastic, Inc.

Stine, R. L. Frankenstein's Dog. 2013. (Goosebumps Most Wanted Ser.: 4). 136p. (J). lib. bdg. 17.20 *(978-0-606-32006-1(7))* Turtleback.

—Heads, You Lose! (Goosebumps HorrorLand #15) 2010. (Goosebumps Horrorland Ser.: 15). (ENG.). 160p. (J). (gr. 3-7). 6.99 *(978-0-545-16196-1(7)*, Scholastic Paperbacks) Scholastic, Inc.

—Who's Your Mummy? (Goosebumps HorrorLand #6) 2009. (Goosebumps Horrorland Ser.: 6). (ENG., Illus.). 160p. (J). (gr. 3-7). 7.99 *(978-0-439-91874-9(X)*, Scholastic Paperbacks) Scholastic, Inc.

Stinson, Kathy. One More Clue, 1 vol. 2005. (Lorimer Streetlights Ser.). (ENG.). 104p. (J). (gr. 2-5). 7.95 *(978-1-55028-888-9(1)*, 888) James Lorimer & Co. Ltd., Pubs. CAN. Dist: Formac Lorimer Bks. Ltd.

—Seven Clues, 1 vol. 2005. (Lorimer Streetlights Ser.). (ENG.). 104p. (J). (gr. 2-5). 7.95 *(978-1-55028-889-6(X)*, 889) James Lorimer & Co. Ltd., Pubs. CAN. Dist: Formac Lorimer Bks. Ltd.

Stokes, Jonathan W. Addison Cooke & the Tomb of the Khan. 2018. (Addison Cooke Ser.: 2). (Illus.). 464p. (J). (gr. 3-7). 9.99 *(978-0-14-751564-3(5)*, Puffin Books) Penguin Young Readers Group.

—Addison Cooke & the Treasure of the Incas. 2017. (Addison Cooke Ser.: 1). 352p. (J). (gr. 3-7). 9.99 *(978-0-14-751563-6(7)*, Puffin Books) Penguin Young Readers Group.

Stokes, N. L. Mystery of the Missing Teacup. l.t. ed. 2003. (Illus.). 48p. per. 19.95 *(978-0-9729411-1-2(8))* Stylewriter Pubns.

Stokes, Paula. Hidden Pieces: A Novel. 2018. (ENG.). 448p. (YA). (gr. 8). 17.99 *(978-0-06-267362-6(9)*, HarperTeen) HarperCollins Pubs.

—Liars, Inc. 2015. (ENG.). 368p. (YA). (gr. 8). 17.99 *(978-0-06-232328-6(8)*, HarperTeen) HarperCollins Pubs.

Stokes, Roy Eliot. Andy at Yale: Or, the Great Quadrangle Mystery. 2017. (ENG., Illus.). (J). pap. 14.95 *(978-1-374-97264-3(9))* Capital Communications, Inc.

Storck, Patrick. Muppet Sherlock Holmes. Mebberson, Amy, illus. 2011. (Muppet Show Ser.). 128p. pap. 9.99 *(978-1-60886-613-7(0))* BOOM! Studios.

Storer, Megan. Cowbelle - Snow Day. 2005. (Illus.). 54p. (J). per. 6.99 *(978-0-9769856-0-0(8)*, 0-9769856-0-8) Little River Bookshelf.

Storey, Margaret & Storey, Mags. If Only You Knew, 1 vol. 2009. 272p. pap. 15.99 *(978-0-8254-3895-0(0))* Kregel Pubns.

Storm, Michael. Pulp7: A Sweet Deal, a Killer Calling, & a Man Inside. 2nd enl. ed. 2005. (YA). 23.95 *(978-0-9744929-6-4(5))* Leeway Pubs.

Strange, Spencer. Operation Billion Gazillion. 2005. (Spy Five Ser.). 93p. *(978-0-439-70352-9(2))* Scholastic, Inc.

Strangway, Melissa. 56 Water Street. 2008. 156p. pap. 8.95 *(978-1-60528-031-8(3)*, iUniverse Star) iUniverse, Inc.

Strasser, Todd. Blood on My Hands. 2011. (ENG.). 304p. (YA). (gr. 9-12). pap. 8.99 *(978-1-60684-228-7(5)*, fc739d70-6a40-42fa-b8e1-d93dc4d8aac1, Carolrhoda Lab™) Lerner Publishing Group.

Stratford, Jordan. The Case of the Perilous Palace (the Wollstonecraft Detective Agency, Book 4) Murphy, Kelly, illus. 2018. (Wollstonecraft Detective Agency Ser.: 4). 224p. (J). (gr. 3-7). 16.99 *(978-0-553-53644-7(3)*, Knopf Bks. for Young Readers) Random Hse. Children's Bks.

Stromberg, Ronica. A Shadow in the Dark. 2009. (J). pap. *(978-0-88092-751-2(8))*; lib. bdg. *(978-0-88092-750-5(X))* Royal Fireworks Publishing Co.

Stroud, Jonathan. Lockwood & Co.: the Creeping Shadow. 2016. (Lockwood & Co Ser.: 4). (ENG., Illus.). 464p. (J). (gr. 5-9). 16.99 *(978-1-4847-0967-2(5))* Little, Brown Bks. for Young Readers.

—Lockwood & Co.: the Empty Grave. (Lockwood & Co Ser.: 5). (ENG.). (J). (gr. 5-9). 2018. 480p. pap. 8.99 *(978-1-4847-9006-9(5))* 2017. (Illus.). 448p. 16.99 *(978-1-4847-7872-2(3))* Little, Brown Bks. for Young Readers.

—Lockwood & Co.: the Hollow Boy. (Lockwood & Co Ser.: 3). (ENG.). (J). (gr. 5-9). 2016. 416p. pap. 8.99 *(978-1-4847-1189-7(0))* 2015. 400p. 37.99 *(978-1-4847-0968-9(3))* Little, Brown Bks. for Young Readers.

—Lockwood & Co.: the Whispering Skull. (Lockwood & Co Ser.: 2). (ENG.). (J). (gr. 5-9). 2015. 464p. pap. 9.99 *(978-1-4231-9462-0(4))* 2014. 448p. 17.99 *(978-1-4231-6492-0(X))* Little, Brown Bks. for Young Readers.

Strutz, Amuel U. Santa's New Reindeer Team. 2009. (Illus.). 60p. pap. 24.99 *(978-1-4389-6455-3(2))* AuthorHouse.

Stuchner, Joan Betty. Bagels on Board!, 1 vol. Whamond, Dave, illus. 2015. (Orca Echoes Ser.). (ENG.). 80p. (J). (gr. 1-3). pap. 7.95 *(978-1-4598-0695-5(6))* Orca Bk. Pubs. USA.

Sturk, Karl. Movie Star Mystery. 2010. (Scooby Doo Reader Ser.: 24). lib. bdg. 13.55 *(978-0-606-07085-0(0))* Turtleback.

Stute, Lela LaBree. When Pugs Fly! 2011. 36p. pap. 24.95 *(978-1-4489-5484-1(3))* America Star Bks.

Styles, Walker. The Big Bad Woof. Whitehouse, Ben, illus. 2017. (Rider Woofson Ser.: 8). (ENG.). 128p. (J). (gr. k-4). pap. 6.99 *(978-1-4814-9188-4(1)*, Little Simon) Little Simon.

—The Case of the Missing Tiger's Eye. Whitehouse, Ben, illus. 2016. (Rider Woofson Ser.: 1). (ENG.). 128p. (J). (gr. k-4). 16.99 *(978-1-4814-5738-5(1)*, Little Simon) Little Simon.

—Ghosts & Goblins & Ninja, Oh My! Whitehouse, Ben, illus. 2016. (Rider Woofson Ser.: 4). (ENG.). 128p. (J). (gr. k-4). pap. 5.99 *(978-1-4814-6306-5(3)*, Little Simon) Little Simon.

—Labra-Cadabra-dor's Revenge. Whitehouse, Ben, illus. 2017. (Rider Woofson Ser.: 7). (ENG.). 128p. (J). (gr. k-4). 16.99 *(978-1-4814-8593-7(8))*; pap. 5.99 *(978-1-4814-8592-0(X))* Little Simon. (Little Simon).

—Mystery Mountain Getaway. Whitehouse, Ben, illus. 2017. (Rider Woofson Ser.: 9). (ENG.). 128p. (J). (gr. k-4). 16.99 *(978-1-4814-9896-8(7))*; pap. 5.99 *(978-1-4814-9895-1(9))* Little Simon. (Little Simon).

—The Rival Detective. Whitehouse, Ben, illus. 2016. (Rider Woofson Ser.: 5). (ENG.). 128p. (J). (gr. k-4). pap. 6.99 *(978-1-4814-7107-7(4)*, Little Simon) Little Simon.

—The Soccer Ball Monster Mystery. Whitehouse, Ben, illus. 2016. (Rider Woofson Ser.: 6). (ENG.). 128p. (J). (gr. k-4). pap. 5.99 *(978-1-4814-7110-7(4)*, Little Simon) Little Simon.

—Something Smells Fishy. Whitehouse, Ben, illus. 2016. (Rider Woofson Ser.: 2). (ENG.). 128p. (J). (gr. k-4). 16.99 *(978-1-4814-5742-2(X))*; pap. 5.99 *(978-1-4814-5741-5(1))* Little Simon. (Little Simon).

—Undercover in the Bow-Wow Club. Whitehouse, Ben, illus. 2016. (Rider Woofson Ser.: 3). (ENG.). 128p. (J). (gr. k-4). pap. 5.99 *(978-1-4814-6303-4(9)*, Little Simon) Little Simon.

—The Very First Case. Whitehouse, Ben, illus. 2018. (Rider Woofson Ser.: 10). (ENG.). 128p. (J). (gr. k-4). 16.99 *(978-1-5344-1272-9(7))*; pap. 5.99 *(978-1-5344-1271-2(9))* Little Simon. (Little Simon).

Suma, Nova Ren. Dani Noir. 2009. (ENG.). 272p. (J). (gr. 4-9). 15.99 *(978-1-4169-7564-9(0)*, Simon & Schuster/Paula Wiseman Bks.) Simon & Schuster/Paula Wiseman Bks.

—Fade Out. 2012. (ENG.). 288p. (YA). (gr. 7). pap. 9.99 *(978-1-4169-7565-6(9)*, Simon Pulse) Simon Pulse.

Summer of the Secret Squadron. 2005. Orig. Title: Return of the Secret Squadron. (YA). kivar 14.95 *(978-0-9765750-0-9(0))* Ball, Michael.

Summerill, Erin. Ever the Hunted. 2017. (Clash of Kingdoms Novel Ser.: bk.1). (ENG.). 416p. (YA). (gr. 7). pap. 9.99 *(978-1-328-76700-4(0)*, 1680366, Clarion Bks.) HarperCollins Pubs.

Summers, Courtney. Fall for Anything. 2010. (ENG.). 240p. (YA). (gr. 9-12). 15.99 *(978-0-312-65673-7(4)*, 900069752, St. Martin's Griffin) St. Martin's Pr.

—Sadie. 2018. (ENG.). 320p. (YA). 18.99 *(978-1-250-10571-4(4)*, 900164264, Wednesday Bks.) St. Martin's Pr.

—Sadie. 2019. (SPA.). 344p. (YA). pap. 18.99 *(978-607-8614-62-2(2))* V&R Editoras.

—Sadie: A Novel. 2020. (ENG.). 336p. (YA). pap. 11.99 *(978-1-250-26713-9(7)*, 900211700, Wednesday Bks.) St. Martin's Pr.

Summy, Barrie. I So Don't Do Famous. 2012. (I So Don't Do... Ser.). (ENG.). 304p. (J). (gr. 5). 7.99 *(978-0-385-73791-3(2)*, Yearling) Random Hse. Children's Bks.

—I So Don't Do Makeup. 2011. (I So Don't Do... Ser.). (ENG.). 288p. (J). (gr. 3-7). 7.99 *(978-0-385-73789-0(0)*, Yearling) Random Hse. Children's Bks.

—I So Don't Do Mysteries. 2009. (I So Don't Do... Ser.). (ENG.). 288p. (J). (gr. 3-7). 7.99 *(978-0-385-73603-9(7)*, Yearling) Random Hse. Children's Bks.

—I So Don't Do Spooky. (I So Don't Do... Ser.). (ENG.). (J). 2011. 288p. (gr. 6-8). lib. bdg. 21.19 *(978-0-385-90584-8(X))* 2010. 304p. (gr. 3-7). 7.99 *(978-0-385-73605-3(3))* Random Hse. Children's Bks. (Yearling).

Sur, Duendes Del, illus. Scooby-Doo! Picture Clue Books, 3 vols. 2013. (Scooby-Doo! Picture Clue Bks.: 6). (ENG.). 24p. (J). (gr. -1-2). lib. bdg. 94.08 *(978-1-61479-034-1(5)*, 13228) Spotlight.

Surrisi, C. M. The Maypop Kidnapping: A Quinnie Boyd Mystery. (Quinnie Boyd Mysteries Ser.). (ENG.). 304p. (J). (gr. 4-8). 2018. pap. 9.99 *(978-1-5415-1490-4(4)*, c6bfb82b-5feb-4601-a681-edbe24d09c92) 2016. E-Book 26.65 *(978-1-4677-9560-9(7))* Lerner Publishing Group. (Carolrhoda Bks.).

—A Side of Sabotage: A Quinnie Boyd Mystery. (Quinnie Boyd Mysteries Ser.). (ENG.). 280p. (J). (gr. 4-8). 2019. pap. 9.99 *(978-1-5415-7758-9(2)*, df48a301-f493-4867-acd0-7099f5d7865c) 2018. 16.99 *(978-1-5124-4836-8(2)*, 2f2233a9-53da-4efc-ba4d-e5c7d38d2937) Lerner Publishing Group. (Carolrhoda Bks.).

—Vampires on the Run: A Quinnie Boyd Mystery. (Quinnie Boyd Mysteries Ser.). (ENG.). 296p. (J). (gr. 4-8). 2018. pap. 9.99 *(978-1-5415-3847-4(1)*, bcffe0e1-f11d-4184-8f3a-e68d24760d2f) 2017. 16.99 *(978-1-5124-1150-8(7)*, 7aed6910-020c-4ae6-a0b2-d7143911d482) 2017. E-Book 26.65 *(978-1-5124-2692-2(X))* Lerner Publishing Group. (Carolrhoda Bks.).

Sutherland, Tui T. The Menagerie: Krakens & Lies. 2016. (Menagerie Ser.: 3). (ENG.). 368p. (J). (gr. 3-7). pap. 9.99 *(978-0-06-078069-2(X)*, HarperCollins) HarperCollins Pubs.

Sutherland, Tui T. & Sutherland, Kari H. The Menagerie. 2013. (Menagerie Ser.: 1). (ENG., Illus.). 288p. (J). (gr. 3-7). 16.99 *(978-0-06-078064-7(9)*, HarperCollins) HarperCollins Pubs.

—The Menagerie #3: Krakens & Lies. 2015. (Menagerie Ser.: 3). (ENG., Illus.). 368p. (J). (gr. 3-7). 16.99 *(978-0-06-078067-8(3)*, HarperCollins) HarperCollins Pubs.

Sutton, Laurie S. The Curse of Atlantis. Neely, Scott, illus. 2015. (You Choose Stories: Scooby-Doo Ser.). (ENG.). 112p. (J). (gr. 2-6). lib. bdg. 32.65 *(978-1-4965-0477-7(1)*, 128503, Stone Arch Bks.) Capstone.

—The Fright at Zombie Farm. Neely, Scott, illus. 2015. (You Choose Stories: Scooby-Doo Ser.). (ENG.). 112p. (J). (gr. 2-6). lib. bdg. 32.65 *(978-1-4342-9713-6(6)*, 127039, Stone Arch Bks.) Capstone.

—The Ghost of the Bermuda Triangle, 1 vol. Neely, Scott, illus. 2014. (You Choose Stories: Scooby-Doo Ser.). (ENG.). 112p. (J). (gr. 2-6). 32.65 *(978-1-4342-9126-4(X)*, 125571, Stone Arch Bks.) Capstone.

—The House on Spooky Street. Neely, Scott, illus. 2015. (You Choose Stories: Scooby-Doo Ser.). (ENG.). 112p. (J). (gr. 2-6). lib. bdg. 32.65 *(978-1-4342-9714-3(4)*, 127040, Stone Arch Bks.) Capstone.

—Legend of the Gator Man. Neely, Scott, illus. 2016. (Scooby-Doo Comic Chapter Bks.). (ENG.). 88p. (J). (gr. 3-7). lib. bdg. 27.32 *(978-1-4965-3584-9(7)*, 132730, Stone Arch Bks.) Capstone.

—The Mystery of the Aztec Tomb, 1 vol. Neely, Scott, illus. 2014. (You Choose Stories: Scooby-Doo Ser.). (ENG.). 112p. (J). (gr. 2-6). 32.65 *(978-1-4342-9127-1(8)*, 125572, Stone Arch Bks.) Capstone.

—The Secret of the Flying Saucer. Neely, Scott, illus. 2015. (You Choose Stories: Scooby-Doo Ser.). (ENG.). 112p. (J). (gr. 2-6). lib. bdg. 32.65 *(978-1-4965-0478-4(X)*, 128504, Stone Arch Bks.) Capstone.

—The Secret of the Sea Creature, 1 vol. Neely, Scott, illus. 2014. (You Choose Stories: Scooby-Doo Ser.). (ENG.). 112p. (J). (gr. 2-6). pap. 6.95 *(978-1-4342-7925-5(1)*, 124637, Stone Arch Bks.) Capstone.

—The Terror of the Bigfoot Beast, 1 vol. Neely, Scott, illus. 2014. (You Choose Stories: Scooby-Doo Ser.). (ENG.). 112p. (J). (gr. 2-6). pap. 6.95 *(978-1-4342-7926-2(X)*, 124636, Stone Arch Bks.) Capstone.

Sutton, Margaret. Discovery at Dragon's Mouth #31, No. 31. 2008. (Judy Bolton Ser.). (ENG., Illus.). 196p. (gr. 4-7). pap. 14.95 *(978-1-4290-9051-3(0))* Applewood Bks.

—The Discovery at the Dragon's Mouth: A Judy Bolton Mystery. 2011. 192p. 42.95 *(978-1-258-10071-1(1))* Literary Licensing, LLC.

—The Haunted Fountain: A Judy Bolton Mystery. 2011. 192p. 42.95 *(978-1-258-10127-5(0))* Literary Licensing, LLC.

—Hidden Clue #35, No. 35. 2008. (Judy Bolton Ser.). (ENG., Illus.). 184p. (J). (gr. 4-7). pap. 14.95 *(978-1-4290-9055-1(3))* Applewood Bks.

—Phantom Friend #30, No. 30. 2008. (Judy Bolton Ser.). (ENG., Illus.). 188p. (gr. 4-7). pap. 14.95 *(978-1-4290-9050-6(2))* Applewood Bks.

—The Secret Quest: Judy Bolton. 2011. 182p. 42.95 *(978-1-258-10241-8(2))* Literary Licensing, LLC.

—The Trail of the Green Doll: A Judy Bolton Mystery. 2011. 192p. 42.95 *(978-1-258-09886-5(5))* Literary Licensing, LLC.

—Whispered Watchword #32, No. 32. 2008. (Judy Bolton Ser.). (ENG., Illus.). 196p. (gr. 4-7). pap. 14.95 *(978-1-4290-9052-0(9))* Applewood Bks.

—The Yellow Phantom: A Judy Bolton Mystery. Doane, Pelagie, illus. 2011. 222p. 44.95 *(978-1-258-10044-5(4))* Literary Licensing, LLC.

Swann, Stephen. The Blooter Boys. 2009. (ENG.). 42p. pap. 21.50 *(978-1-4452-2665-1(0))* Lulu Pr., Inc.

Swanson, Matthew. The Real Mccoys. Behr, Robbi, illus. 2018. (Real Mccoys Ser.: 1). (ENG.). 352p. (J). pap. 7.99 *(978-1-250-09853-5(X)*, 900161849) Square Fish.

—The Real Mccoys: Wonder Undercover. Behr, Robbi, illus. 2019. (Real Mccoys Ser.: 3). (ENG.). 352p. (J). 16.99 *(978-1-250-30782-8(1)*, 900198140) Imprint IND. Dist: Macmillan.

Swartz, Michael. Bikes & Bullies: A Neil Everheart Mystery. 2003. 163p. pap. 11.95 *(978-0-595-26550-3(2)*, Writers Club Pr.) iUniverse, Inc.

The Sweetest Heist in History. 2015. (Randi Rhodes, Ninja Detective Ser.: 2). (ENG., Illus.). 224p. (J). (gr. 3-7). 16.99 *(978-1-4424-7684-4(2)*, Simon & Schuster Bks. For Young Readers) Simon & Schuster Bks. For Young Readers.

Swift, John. Tea with a Vampire. 2007. pap. 9.00 *(978-0-8059-8963-2(3))* Dorrance Publishing Co., Inc.

Swindells, Robert. The Ghosts of Givenham Keep. 2015. (ENG., Illus.). 108p. (J). pap. 9.99 *(978-1-78270-056-2(0))* Award Pubns. Ltd. GBR. Dist: Parkwest Pubns., Inc.

—Kidnap at Denton Farm. 2015. (ENG., Illus.). 106p. (J). pap. 9.99 *(978-1-78270-055-5(2))* Award Pubns. Ltd. GBR. Dist: Parkwest Pubns., Inc.

—The Secret of the Weeping Woods. Hartas, Leo, illus. 2021. (Outfit Ser.). (ENG.). 120p. (J). (gr. 5-8). 26.65 *(978-1-5415-7906-4(2)*, 6ce5197f-30b9-4976-8e5b-af50fbe38419, Darby Creek) Lerner Publishing Group.

—The Secret of Weeping Wood. 2015. (ENG., Illus.). 117p. (J). pap. 9.99 *(978-1-78270-053-1(6))* Award Pubns. Ltd. GBR. Dist: Parkwest Pubns., Inc.

—The Strange Tale of Ragger Bill. 2015. (ENG., Illus.). 103p. (J). pap. 9.99 *(978-1-78270-058-6(7))* Award Pubns. Ltd. GBR. Dist: Parkwest Pubns., Inc.

—The Strange Tale of Ragger Bill. Hartas, Leo, illus. 2021. (Outfit Ser.). (ENG.). 104p. (J). (gr. 5-8). 26.65 *(978-1-5415-7910-1(0)*, 07dc9564-47d9-4ebc-8d25-7305e12ec24b, Darby Creek) Lerner Publishing Group.

—We Didn't Mean to, Honest! 2015. (ENG., Illus.). 107p. (J). pap. 9.99 *(978-1-78270-054-8(4))* Award Pubns. Ltd. GBR. Dist: Parkwest Pubns., Inc.

Swinford, Betty. The Cry of the Wild. 2003. (Flamingo Fiction 9-13s Ser.). (ENG.). 192p. (J). mass mkt. 6.99 *(978-1-85792-853-2(9)*, c6313a19-c5d7-416d-8c1a-73c650d0dc58) Christian Focus Pubns. GBR. Dist: Baker & Taylor Publisher Services (BTPS).

Syers, Rita Hsu. Mystery of the Crying Ghost. 2007. 155p. 9.95 *(978-0-9779267-1-8(0))* Bronwen Publishing.

Sylvester, Kevin. Neil Flambé & the Aztec Abduction. Sylvester, Kevin, illus. 2014. (Neil Flambe Capers Ser.: 2). (ENG., Illus.). 336p. (J). (gr. 3-7). pap. 9.99 *(978-1-4424-4608-3(0)*, Simon & Schuster Bks. For Young Readers) Simon & Schuster Bks. For Young Readers.

—Neil Flambé & the Bard's Banquet. Sylvester, Kevin, illus. 2015. (Neil Flambe Capers Ser.: 5). (ENG., Illus.). 320p. (J). (gr. 3-7). 12.99 *(978-1-4814-1038-0(5)*, Simon & Schuster Bks. For Young Readers) Simon & Schuster Bks. For Young Readers.

—Neil Flambé & the Crusader's Curse. Sylvester, Kevin, illus. 2014. (Neil Flambe Capers Ser.: 3). (ENG., Illus.). 320p. (J). (gr. 3-7). pap. 7.99 *(978-1-4424-4287-0(5)*, Simon & Schuster Bks. For Young Readers) Simon & Schuster Bks. For Young Readers.

—Neil Flambé & the Duel in the Desert. Sylvester, Kevin, illus. (Neil Flambe Capers Ser.: 6). (ENG., Illus.). 304p. (J). (gr. 3-7). 2017. pap. 8.99 *(978-1-4814-1042-7(3))* 2016. 13.99 *(978-1-4814-1041-0(5))* Simon & Schuster Bks. For Young Readers. (Simon & Schuster Bks. For Young Readers).

—Neil Flambé & the Marco Polo Murders. 2010. (Neil Flambé Capers Ser.: No. 1). (Illus.). 304p. (YA). (gr. 5-9). *(978-1-55470-266-4(6))* Me to We.

—Neil Flambé & the Marco Polo Murders. Sylvester, Kevin, illus. (Neil Flambe Capers Ser.: 1). (ENG., Illus.). (J). (gr. 3-7). 2014. 320p. pap. 8.99 *(978-1-4424-4605-2(6))* 2012. 304p. 14.99 *(978-1-4424-4604-5(8))* Simon & Schuster Bks. For Young Readers. (Simon & Schuster Bks. For Young Readers).

—Neil Flambé & the Tokyo Treasure. Sylvester, Kevin, illus. (Neil Flambe Capers Ser.: 4). (ENG., Illus.). (J). (gr. 3-7). 2014. 368p. pap. 8.99 *(978-1-4424-4289-4(1))* 2012. 352p. 13.99 *(978-1-4424-4288-7(3))* Simon & Schuster Bks. For Young Readers. (Simon & Schuster Bks. For Young Readers).

—The Neil Flambé Capers Collection: Neil Flambé & the Marco Polo Murders; Neil Flambé & the Aztec Abduction; Neil Flambé & the Crusader's Curse; Neil Flambé & the Tokyo Treasure. Sylvester, Kevin, illus. 2014. (Neil Flambe Capers Ser.). (ENG., Illus.). 1344p. (J). (gr. 3-7). pap. 31.99 *(978-1-4814-3238-2(9)*, Simon & Schuster Bks. For Young Readers) Simon & Schuster Bks. For Young Readers.

Sylvester, Kevin, illus. Neil Flambé & the Aztec Abduction. 2010. (Neil Flambé Capers Ser.: No. 2). 304p. (J). (gr. 4-7). *(978-1-55470-329-6(8))* Me to We.

Taddonio, Lea. Welcome to Deadwood Hill: Book 1. Trunfio, Alessia, illus. 2017. (Lucky 8 Ser.). (ENG.). 48p. (J). (gr. 3-7). lib. bdg. 34.21 *(978-1-5321-3053-3(8)*, 27060, Spellbound) Magic Wagon.

Taft, Christopher C. The Witch of Green Spring. 2013. 120p. pap. 11.00 *(978-1-61204-198-8(1)*, Strategic Bk. Publishing) Strategic Book Publishing & Rights Agency (SBPRA).

Tait, Elena. The Day My Peanut Butter Lost Its Stick. Lee, Joe, illus. 2008. 24p. pap. 12.99 *(978-1-4389-1936-2(0))* AuthorHouse.

Tama. Black Cow. 2012. 116p. pap. 14.95 *(978-1-4685-6680-2(6))* AuthorHouse.

Tamura, Mitsuhisa. BakéGyamon, Vol. 1. 2009. (Bakégyamon Ser.: 1). (ENG., Illus.). 200p. (J). pap. 7.99 *(978-1-4215-1793-3(0))* Viz Media.

—BakéGyamon, Vol. 2. 2009. (Bakégyamon Ser.: 2). (ENG., Illus.). 200p. (J). pap. 7.99 *(978-1-4215-1794-0(9))* Viz Media.

Taylor, Cora. Finding Melissa, 1 vol. 2013. (ENG.). 184p. (J). (gr. 6-10). pap. 12.95 *(978-1-55455-274-0(5)*, 270cb0c0-5f1b-47d2-a33e-2aea755f76ae) éditeur, Annika Parance CAN. Dist: Firefly Bks., Ltd.

Taylor, Jo-Ann. The Alchemist's Secret. 2011. 268p. pap. *(978-1-907652-87-5(6))* Grosvenor Hse. Publishing Ltd.

Taylor, Joseph. Allison Investigates. 2009. 202p. pap. 12.95 *(978-0-9815894-1-1(3))* Four Star Publishing.

Taylor, Kara. Prep School Confidential. 2013. (Prep School Confidential Novel Ser.: 1). (ENG.). 336p. (YA). (gr. 7). pap. 22.99 *(978-1-250-01759-8(9)*, 900087397, St. Martin's Griffin) St. Martin's Pr.

—Wicked Little Secrets. 2014. (Prep School Confidential Novel Ser.: 2). (ENG.). 320p. (YA). (gr. 7). pap. 19.99 *(978-1-250-03360-4(8)*, 900120135, St. Martin's Griffin) St. Martin's Pr.

Taylor, L. D. Motive Games. 2012. (ENG.). 183p. pap. *(978-1-921632-25-9(9))* Wombat Bks.

Taylor, Mary Ann. Spies: A Gander's Cove Mystery. Casteel, Kay, illus. 2006. (J). mass mkt. 5.99 *(978-0-9753367-7-9(0))* Onstage Publishing, LLC.

—Traitors: A Gander's Cove Mystery. Casteel, Kay, illus. 2006. (J). mass mkt. 5.99 *(978-0-9753367-9-3(7))* Onstage Publishing, LLC.

Taylor, Phillip J. Brian, His Granddad & the Cup of Ages. 2012. 310p. pap. *(978-1-78003-422-5(9))* Pen Pr. Pubs., Ltd.

Taylor, Theodore. Teetoncey. 2004. (ENG., Illus.). 228p. (J). (gr. 3-7). pap. 13.95 *(978-0-15-205294-2(1)*, 1195951, Clarion Bks.) HarperCollins Pubs.

Tell Me No Lies, 6 vols. (Ragged Island Mysteriestm Ser.). 161p. (gr. 5-7). 42.50 *(978-0-322-01654-5(1))* Wright Group/McGraw-Hill.

Temple, Bob. The Ghost of J. Stokely. Nitzsche, Shane, illus. 2008. (Shade Bks.). (ENG.). 80p. (J). (gr. 5-9). 25.32 *(978-1-4342-0796-8(X)*, 95201, Stone Arch Bks.) Capstone.

—A Nose for Danger: Jimmy Sniffles. Harpster, Steve, illus. 2006. (Graphic Sparks Ser.). (ENG.). 40p. (J). (gr. 2-5). per. 5.95 *(978-1-59889-171-3(5)*, 86495, Stone Arch Bks.) Capstone.
Tenbeth, Kate. Burly & Grum & the Birthday Surprise. Jones, Rob, illus. 2012. 108p. pap. *(978-0-9572119-9-5(6))* Magic Toy Bks.
Terrell, Brandon. The Cursed Stage. Epelbaum, Mariano, illus. 2017. (Snoops, Inc Ser.). (ENG.). 112p. (J). (gr. 4-8). lib. bdg. 27.32 *(978-1-4965-4346-2(7)*, 134263, Stone Arch Bks.) Capstone.
—Phantom of the Library. Epelbaum, Mariano, illus. 2017. (Snoops, Inc Ser.). (ENG.). 112p. (J). (gr. 4-8). lib. bdg. 27.32 *(978-1-4965-5060-6(9)*, 135986, Stone Arch Bks.) Capstone.
—Science Fair Sabotage. Epelbaum, Mariano, illus. 2017. (Snoops, Inc Ser.). (ENG.). 112p. (J). (gr. 4-8). lib. bdg. 27.32 *(978-1-4965-4347-9(5)*, 134264, Stone Arch Bks.) Capstone.
—Tracking Champ. Epelbaum, Mariano, illus. 2017. (Snoops, Inc Ser.). (ENG.). 112p. (J). (gr. 4-8). lib. bdg. 27.32 *(978-1-4965-4348-6(3)*, 134265, Stone Arch Bks.) Capstone.
—The Undercover Cheerleader. Epelbaum, Mariano, illus. 2017. (Snoops, Inc Ser.). (ENG.). 112p. (J). (gr. 4-8). lib. bdg. 27.32 *(978-1-4965-5061-3(7)*, 135988, Stone Arch Bks.) Capstone.
—The Vanishing Treasure. Epelbaum, Mariano, illus. 2017. (Snoops, Inc Ser.). (ENG.). 112p. (J). (gr. 4-8). lib. bdg. 27.32 *(978-1-4965-4345-5(9)*, 134262, Stone Arch Bks.) Capstone.
Thaler, Mike. Hubie Cool: Super Spy. Lee, Jared D., illus. 2016. 64p. (J). *(978-0-545-85076-6(2))* Scholastic, Inc.
Tharp, Tim. Mojo. 2014. (ENG.). 288p. (YA). (gr. 7). pap. 8.99 *(978-0-375-86402-5(4)*, Ember) Random Hse. Children's Bks.
The Story Pirates & West, Jacqueline. The Story Pirates Present. Aly, Hatem, illus. 2019. (Story Pirates Ser.: 2). 288p. (J). (gr. 3-7). 13.99 *(978-1-63565-091-4(7)*, 9781635650914, Random Hse. Bks. for Young Readers) Random Hse. Children's Bks.
Theer, Justine M. The Backwards Town, 1 vol. 2010. 82p. pap. 19.95 *(978-1-4489-5361-5(8))* America Star Bks.
Thielbar, Melinda. The Ancient Formula: A Mystery with Fractions. Pantoja, Maria Kristina Sb., illus. 2011. (Manga Math Mysteries Ser.: 5). (ENG.). 48p. (J). (gr. 3-5). pap. 6.95 *(978-0-7613-8134-1(1)*, 1c74d365-5757-4fe3-8be4-721e1b06585d, Graphic Universe™) Lerner Publishing Group.
—The Book Bandit: A Mystery with Geometry. Chow, Candice & Lee, Jennifer A., illus. 2011. (Manga Math Mysteries Ser.: 7). (ENG.). 48p. (J). (gr. 3-5). pap. 7.99 *(978-0-7613-8136-5(8)*, e0e0aea2-a276-4124-9f9e-f3e70f31022c, Graphic Universe™) Lerner Publishing Group.
—The Fishy Fountain: A Mystery with Multiplication & Division. Lin, Yali, illus. 2011. (Manga Math Mysteries Ser.: 6). (ENG.). 48p. (J). (gr. 3-5). pap. 7.99 *(978-0-7613-8135-8(X)*, 86863ee0-c152-4a00-ae62-5a6fc9a6ebe3, Graphic Universe™) Lerner Publishing Group.
—The Hundred-Dollar Robber: A Mystery with Money. Pantoja, Maria Kristina Sb., illus. 2010. (Manga Math Mysteries Ser.: 2). (ENG.). 48p. (J). (gr. 3-5). pap. 6.99 *(978-0-7613-5243-3(0)*, eb5149e7-387a-4f32-8264-1a6ba34243fa, Graphic Universe™) Lerner Publishing Group.
—The Hundred-Dollar Robber: A Mystery with Money. Pantoja, Maria Kristina, illus. 2009. (Manga Math Mysteries Ser.: 2). (ENG.). 48p. (J). (gr. 3-5). 29.27 *(978-0-7613-3854-3(3))* Lerner Publishing Group.
—The Kung Fu Puzzle: A Mystery with Time & Temperature. Helmer, Der-shing, illus. 2010. (Manga Math Mysteries Ser.: 4). (ENG.). 48p. (J). (gr. 3-5). pap. 7.99 *(978-0-7613-5246-4(5)*, 95692add-0fab-4091-b7e1-e284d00dadc2, Graphic Universe™) Lerner Publishing Group.
—The Kung Fu Puzzle: A Mystery with Time & Temperature. Ota, Yuko & Helmer, Der-shing, illus. 2009. (Manga Math Mysteries Ser.: No. 4). 48p. (J). (gr. 2-5). 29.27 *(978-0-7613-3856-7(X))* Lerner Publishing Group.
—The Lost Key. rev. ed. 2010. pap. 39.62 *(978-0-7613-6942-4(2))* Lerner Publishing Group.
—The Lost Key: A Mystery with Whole Numbers. Pantoja, Maria Kristina Sb., illus. 2010. (Manga Math Mysteries Ser.: 1). (ENG.). 48p. (J). (gr. 3-5). pap. 6.99 *(978-0-7613-5244-0(9)*, db9985c2-e8b5-4556-bfe1-78181351eb7d, Graphic Universe™) Lerner Publishing Group.
—The Secret Ghost. 3rd rev. ed. 2010. pap. 39.62 *(978-0-7613-6944-8(9))* Lerner Publishing Group.
—The Secret Ghost: A Mystery with Distance & Measurement. Ota, Yuko Geneviev, illus. 2010. (Manga Math Mysteries Ser.: 3). (ENG.). 48p. (J). (gr. 3-5). pap. 6.99 *(978-0-7613-5245-7(7)*, af4534ce-d5c6-48f8-a05a-62530c2a5001, Graphic Universe™) Lerner Publishing Group.
—#5 the Ancient Formula: A Mystery with Fractions. Pantoja, Tintin, illus. 2011. (Manga Math Mysteries Set II Ser.). pap. 39.62 *(978-0-7613-8362-8(X)*, Graphic Universe™) Lerner Publishing Group.
—#6 the Fishy Fountain: A Mystery with Multiplication & Division. Lin, Yali, illus. 2011. (Manga Math Mysteries Set II Ser.). pap. 39.62 *(978-0-7613-8363-5(8)*, Graphic Universe™) Lerner Publishing Group.
—#7 the Book Bandit: A Mystery with Geometry. Lee, Jenn Manley & Chow, Candice, illus. 2011. (Manga Math Mysteries Set II Ser.). pap. 39.62 *(978-0-7613-8364-2(6)*, Graphic Universe™) Lerner Publishing Group.
Thomas, Kara. The Cheerleaders. 2019. (ENG.). 400p. (YA). (gr. 9). pap. 12.99 *(978-1-5247-1835-0(1)*, Ember) Random Hse. Children's Bks.
—The Darkest Corners. 2017. 352p. (YA). (gr. 9). pap. 9.99 *(978-0-553-52148-1(9)*, Ember) Random Hse. Children's Bks.
—Little Monsters. 2018. (ENG.). 368p. (YA). (gr. 9). pap. 10.99 *(978-0-553-52152-8(7)*, Ember) Random Hse. Children's Bks.
Thompson, Kate. La Musica del Tiempo. Delgado, Diana, tr. 2nd ed. 2007. (SPA., Illus.). 317p. (J). (gr. 4-7). 18.95 *(978-84-96544-97-0(4))* Roca Editorial ESP. Dist: Spanish Pubs., LLC.
Thomson, Elizabeth & Albert, Sarah. Andros: the Last Villager. 2008. (ENG.). 226p. pap. 17.04 *(978-1-4357-3557-6(9))* Lulu Pr., Inc.
Thornburg, Michael. The Monster Kids' Adventures: The Retur. 2005. pap. 19.95 *(978-1-4137-8556-2(5))* PublishAmerica, Inc.
Thornton, M. H. Kylee & Lexie: Mystery of the Gholdees. 2010. 64p. pap. 10.99 *(978-1-4269-3713-2(X))* Trafford Publishing.
Thornton, Nicki. The Last Chance Hotel. 2019. (ENG.). 336p. (J). (gr. 3-7). 18.99 *(978-1-338-32362-7(8)*, Chicken Hse., The) Scholastic, Inc.
Thorpe, Kiki. Never Girls #10: on the Trail (Disney: the Never Girls) Christy, Jana, illus. 2015. (Never Girls Ser.: 10). (ENG.). 128p. (J). (gr. 1-4). 6.99 *(978-0-7364-3306-8(6)*, RH/Disney) Random Hse. Children's Bks.
Thrash, Maggie. Strange Lies. (Strange Ser.: 2). (ENG.). 336p. (YA). (gr. 9). 2018. pap. 11.99 *(978-1-4814-6204-4(0))* 2017. (Illus.). 17.99 *(978-1-4814-6203-7(2))* Simon Pulse. (Simon Pulse).
—We Know It Was You. 2016. (Strange Ser.). (ENG., Illus.). 352p. (YA). (gr. 9). 17.99 *(978-1-4814-6200-6(8)*, Simon Pulse) Simon Pulse.
Tillworth, Mary, adapted by. Sherlock Gnomes the Deluxe Movie Novelization. 2018. (Sherlock Gnomes Ser.). (ENG., Illus.). 144p. (J). (gr. 3-7). 9.99 *(978-1-5344-2940-6(9)*, Simon Spotlight) Simon Spotlight.
Tims, Laura. Please Don't Tell. 2016. (ENG.). 336p. (YA). (gr. 8). 17.99 *(978-0-06-231732-2(6)*, HarperTeen) HarperCollins Pubs.
Tinker, Rebecca. Who in the World Is Carmen Sandiego? 2019. (Carmen Sandiego Ser.). (ENG.). 208p. (J). (gr. 5-7). 12.99 *(978-1-328-49529-7(9)*, 1717504, Clarion Bks.) HarperCollins Pubs.
Titus, Eve. Basil & the Cave of Cats. Galdone, Paul, illus. 2016. (Great Mouse Detective Ser.: 2). (ENG.). 112p. (J). (gr. 1-4). pap. 6.99 *(978-1-4814-6404-8(3)*, Aladdin) Simon & Schuster Children's Publishing.
—Basil & the Lost Colony. Galdone, Paul, illus. 2017. (Great Mouse Detective Ser.: 5). (ENG.). 96p. (J). (gr. 1-4). pap. 6.99 *(978-1-4814-6413-0(2)*, Aladdin) Simon & Schuster Children's Publishing.
—Basil in Mexico. Galdone, Paul, illus. 2016. (Great Mouse Detective Ser.: 3). (ENG.). 112p. (J). (gr. 1-4). pap. 6.99 *(978-1-4814-6407-9(8)*, Aladdin) Simon & Schuster Children's Publishing.
—Basil in Mexico. Galdone, Paul, illus. 2016. (Great Mouse Detective Ser.: 3). (ENG.). 112p. (J). (gr. 1-4). 16.99 *(978-1-4814-6408-6(6)*, Simon & Schuster/Paula Wiseman Bks.) Simon & Schuster/Paula Wiseman Bks.
—Basil of Baker Street. Galdone, Paul, illus. 2016. (Great Mouse Detective Ser.: 1). (ENG.). 112p. (J). (gr. 1-4). 16.99 *(978-1-4814-6402-4(7)*, Aladdin) Simon & Schuster Children's Publishing.
Todesco, Angelique. The Way of the Pendant. 2007. (ENG.). 196p. pap. 19.95 *(978-1-84753-846-8(0))* Lulu Pr., Inc.
Tolbert-Klein, Wa-Landa. Paladin: A Different Type of Werewolf Story. 2011. 156p. pap. 11.95 *(978-1-4327-6185-1(4))* Outskirts Pr., Inc.
Tomblin, Marian Strong. The Mystery at Hotel Ormond 2004. (Illus.). 142p. (J). per. 9.95 *(978-0-9766620-0-6(0))* Avery Goode-Reid Pubs.
—Where's Capone's Cash? 2005. (Illus.). 232p. (J). per. 9.95 *(978-0-9766620-1-3(9))* Avery Goode-Reid Pubs.
Tooley, S. D. The Skull. 2006. (YA). 178p. 23.00 *(978-0-9785402-1-0(2))*; per. 12.95 *(978-0-9785402-0-3(4))* Full Moon Publishing LLC.
Toombs, Tom. The Mysterious Money Tree: Little Tommy Learns a Lesson in Giving. Smith, Abby, illus. 2012. 28p. (J). pap. 12.95 *(978-1-61314-033-8(9))*, Innovo Pr.) Innovo Publishing, LLC.
Top Ten Clues You're Clueless. 2014. (ENG.). 304p. (YA). (gr. 8). pap. 9.99 *(978-0-06-227242-3(X)*, HarperTeen) HarperCollins Pubs.
Torres, Jennifer. The Battle: The Briny Deep Mysteries Book 3, 1 vol. 2014. (Briny Deep Mysteries Ser.: Bk. 3). (ENG., Illus.). 96p. (J). (gr. 4-6). pap. 13.88 *(978-1-62285-187-4(0)*, 51cf6dd5-1a8a-4473-9858-9caf72f84df1) Enslow Publishing, LLC.
—The Disappearing: The Briny Deep Mysteries Book 1, 1 vol. 2014. (Briny Deep Mysteries Ser.: Bk. 1). (ENG., Illus.). 96p. (J). (gr. 4-6). pap. 13.88 *(978-1-62285-173-7(0)*, 585ba180-2450-4cac-a487-b9bd7d4e81a9) Enslow Publishing, LLC.
—The Return: The Briny Deep Mysteries Book 2, 1 vol. 2014. (Briny Deep Mysteries Ser.: Bk. 2). (ENG., Illus.). 96p. (J). (gr. 4-6). pap. 13.88 *(978-1-62285-182-9(X)*, 469249a8-6de1-4339-a610-4d64bcb9e170) Enslow Publishing, LLC.
Torrey, Michele. The Case of the Gasping Garbage. Torrey, Michele & Newman, Barbara Johansen, illus. 2009. (Doyle & Fossey, Science Detectives Ser.: 1). (ENG.). 96p. (J). (gr. 4-7). pap. 6.99 *(978-1-4027-4960-5(0))* Sterling Publishing Co., Inc.
—The Case of the Graveyard Ghost. Newman, Barbara Johansen, illus. 2009. (Doyle & Fossey, Science Detectives Ser.: 3). (ENG.). 96p. (J). pap. 6.95 *(978-1-4027-4963-6(5))* Sterling Publishing Co., Inc.
—The Case of the Mossy Lake Monster. Torrey, Michele & Newman, Barbara Johansen, illus. 2009. (Doyle & Fossey, Science Detectives Ser.: 2). (ENG.). 96p. (J). (gr. 4-7). pap. 6.99 *(978-1-4027-4962-9(7))* Sterling Publishing Co., Inc.
Toussaint, Simone. Sharing My Shoes. 2010. 28p. pap. 9.95 *(978-1-4327-5701-4(6))* Outskirts Pr., Inc.
Town, Vicky. Mayhem in the Museum. 2013. 74p. pap. 9.99 *(978-1-61720-974-1(0))* Wilder Pubns., Corp.
Townley, Roderick. The Red Thread: A Novel in Three Incarnations. 2012. (ENG.). 304p. (YA). (gr. 7). pap. 14.99 *(978-1-4169-0895-1(1)*, Atheneum Bks. for Young Readers) Simon & Schuster Children's Publishing.
Townsend, John. The Messenger. 2004. (Shades Ser.). 64p. (J). pap. *(978-0-237-52809-6(6))* Evans Brothers, Ltd.
—Never Odd or Even: US Edition. 2018. (ENG.). 100p. (J). (gr. 4-13). pap. 8.99 *(978-1-944589-31-8(7)*, Incorgnito Publishing Pr.) Incorgnito Publishing Pr. LLC.
Trabert, John. Gnome Chronicles. 2007. 172p. pap. 4.99 *(978-1-4343-1950-0(4))* AuthorHouse.
Treacy, Ann. The Search for the Homestead Treasure: A Mystery. 2016. (ENG., Illus.). 160p. 16.95 *(978-0-8166-9956-8(9))* Univ. of Minnesota Pr.
Trees, Annie Mae. The Last Days of Summer: A Mystery of Two Children & Their Grandma Set Out on an Adventure. 2012. 40p. pap. 24.95 *(978-1-4626-6103-9(3))* America Star Bks.
Trenowden, Mark. The Miracle of Bean's Bullion. 2012. 192p. pap. *(978-1-84667-041-1(1))* Derwent Pr., The.
Trevayne, Emma. Spindrift & the Orchid. (ENG.). 256p. (J). (gr. 3-7). 2019. pap. 8.99 *(978-1-4814-6260-0(1))* 2018. (Illus.). 17.99 *(978-1-4814-6259-4(8))* Simon & Schuster Bks. For Young Readers. (Simon & Schuster Bks. For Young Readers).
Trigg, Michael J. Greanwold & the Mystery Cave: Greanwold & the Minosaurs Story Books. 2013. 148p. pap. 12.97 *(978-1-61897-466-2(1)*, Strategic Bk. Publishing) Strategic Book Publishing & Rights Agency (SBPRA).
Trine, Greg. The Stinky Cheese Caper. 2016. lib. bdg. 14.75 *(978-0-606-38490-2(1))* Turtleback.
Trionfo, Nikki. Shatter. 2017. 346p. (YA). pap. 18.99 *(978-1-4621-2013-0(X)*, Horizon Pubs.) Cedar Fort, Inc./CFI Distribution.
Trivas, Tracy. The Wish Stealers. 2010. (ENG.). 288p. (J). (gr. 3-7). 17.99 *(978-1-4169-8725-3(8)*, Aladdin) Simon & Schuster Children's Publishing.
Tromly, Stephanie. Trouble Never Sleeps. 2019. (ENG.). 304p. (YA). (gr. 7). pap. 10.99 *(978-0-14-751545-2(9)*, Penguin Books) Penguin Young Readers Group.
Trope, Nicole. Forgotten: A Completely Gripping Domestic Noir Thriller. 2018. (ENG.). 400p. pap. 19.95 *(978-1-76029-677-3(5))* Allen & Unwin AUS. Dist: Independent Pubs. Group.
Troupe, Thomas Kingsley. Darling Doll. Faber, Rudy, illus. 2016. (Hauntiques Ser.). (ENG.). 128p. (J). (gr. 4-6). lib. bdg. 25.32 *(978-1-4965-3548-1(0)*, 132657, Stone Arch Bks.) Capstone.
—Phantom's Favorite. Faber, Rudy, illus. 2016. (Hauntiques Ser.). (ENG.). 128p. (J). (gr. 4-6). lib. bdg. 25.32 *(978-1-4965-3546-7(4)*, 132655, Stone Arch Bks.) Capstone.
—Wandering Wagon. Faber, Rudy, illus. 2016. (Hauntiques Ser.). (ENG.). 128p. (J). (gr. 4-6). lib. bdg. 25.32 *(978-1-4965-3547-4(2)*, 132656, Stone Arch Bks.) Capstone.
Truckey, Don. The Adventures of Caraway Kim... Southpaw. 2006. (ENG.). 192p. pap. 10.95 *(978-1-894345-90-3(8))* Thistledown Pr., Ltd. CAN. Dist: Univ. of Toronto Pr.
Trueit, Trudi. Explorer Academy: the Falcon's Feather (Book 2) 2019. (Explorer Academy Ser.: 2). (Illus.). 208p. (J). (gr. 3-7). 16.99 *(978-1-4263-3304-0(8))*; (ENG., lib. bdg. 26.90 *(978-1-4263-3305-7(6))* Disney Publishing Worldwide. (Under the Stars).
—Explorer Academy: the Nebula Secret (Book 1) (Explorer Academy Ser.: 1). (Illus.). (J). (gr. 3-7). 2019. 216p. pap. 9.99 *(978-1-4263-3810-6(4))* 2018. 208p. 16.99 *(978-1-4263-3159-6(2))* 2018. (ENG., 208p. lib. bdg. 26.90 *(978-1-4263-3160-2(6))* Disney Publishing Worldwide. (Under the Stars).
Trumbauer, Lisa. Mountain Manor Mystery. Hawkes, Kevin, illus. 2006. 96p. (J). pap. *(978-1-59034-810-9(9))* Mondo Publishing.
Tubb, Kristin O'Donnell. The Story Collector: A New York Public Library Book. Bruno, Iacopo, illus. 2018. (Story Collector Ser.: 1). (ENG.). 256p. (J). 16.99 *(978-1-250-14380-8(2)*, 900180568, Holt, Henry & Co. Bks. For Young Readers) Holt, Henry & Co.
Tucker, Laura. All the Greys on Greene Street. 2019. (ENG., Illus.). 320p. (J). (gr. 3-7). 17.99 *(978-0-451-47953-2(X)*, Viking Books for Young Readers) Penguin Young Readers Group.
Tulip, Jenny, illus. Who's Hiding in the Garden? 2008. 10p. (gr. -1-k). bds. 6.99 *(978-1-57755-785-2(9))* Gardner Pubns.
Turk, Judy Vanslyke, et al. Laughing Thief. 2007. (Clifton Ser.: 2). (Illus.). 48p. (J). (gr. 4-7). per. 11.95 *(978-1-905460-07-6(4))* CineBook GBR. Dist: National Bk. Network.
—My Dear Wilkinson. 2007. (Clifton Ser.: 1). (Illus.). 48p. (J). (gr. 4-7). per. 11.95 *(978-1-905460-06-9(6))* CineBook GBR. Dist: National Bk. Network.
Turnage, Sheila. The Ghosts of Tupelo Landing. 2015. (Mo & Dale Mysteries Ser.). 368p. (J). (gr. 5). 8.99 *(978-0-14-242571-8(0)*, Puffin Books) Penguin Young Readers Group.
—The Law of Finders Keepers. 2019. (Mo & Dale Mysteries Ser.). 368p. (J). (gr. 5). 8.99 *(978-0-14-242617-3(2)*, Puffin Books) Penguin Young Readers Group.
—The Odds of Getting Even. 2017. (Mo & Dale Mystery Ser.: 3). lib. bdg. 19.65 *(978-0-606-39791-9(4))* Turtleback.
—Three Times Lucky. 2013. (Mo & Dale Mysteries Ser.). (Illus.). 336p. (J). (gr. 5). pap. 9.99 *(978-0-14-242605-0(9)*, Puffin Books) Penguin Young Readers Group.
—Three Times Lucky. 2013. (Mo & Dale Mystery Ser.: 1). lib. bdg. 18.40 *(978-0-606-34168-4(4))* Turtleback.
Turner, Henry. Ask the Dark. 2016. (ENG.). 256p. (YA). (gr. 9). pap. 9.99 *(978-0-544-81353-3(7)*, 1641941, Clarion Bks.) HarperCollins Pubs.
Turner, Suzy. The Temporal Stone: A Morgan Sisters Novel. 2013. 288p. pap. *(978-989-98351-0-8(2))* Turner, Suzanne.
Twain, Mark, pseud. No. 44, the Mysterious Stranger. 2004. 160p. pap. 11.95 *(978-1-59540-326-1(4)*, 1st World Library - Literary Society) 1st World Publishing, Inc.
—Tom Sawyer, Detective. (SPA., Illus.). 160p. (YA). 11.95 *(978-84-7281-062-4(3)*, AF0623) Auriga, Ediciones S.A. ESP. Dist: Continental Bk. Co., Inc.
Twintig, Gus. The Clock Without a Face: A Gus Twintig Mystery. 2010. (Illus.). 30p. (J). (gr. 2-18). bds. 19.95 *(978-1-934781-71-5(1)*, 57ce4b2f-3c83-44ed-891c-1ae966831e7a) McSweeney's Publishing.
Tysinger, Dona. The Cheyenne Dragon & the Dragonfly. 2011. 52p. (gr. 4-6). pap. 10.99 *(978-1-4634-3032-0(9))* AuthorHouse.
Ulrich, Ann Carol. The Mystery at Hickory Hill: Annette Vetter Adventure #1. 2006. (Illus.). 196p. (YA). per. 9.95 *(978-0-944851-25-8(8))* Earth Star Pubns.
Uncovering Sadie's Secrets. 2003. (ENG.). 196p. (gr. 5-9). 19.95 *(978-1-890862-23-7(1)*, f1c75eb5-fea9-4aa0-9bdb-5fe9fc5edde7) Bancroft Pr.
Unexpected Treasure, 6 vols. (Ragged Island Mysteriestm Ser.). 161p. (gr. 5-7). 42.50 *(978-0-322-01650-7(9))* Wright Group/McGraw-Hill.
Urrea, Lourdes, et al. Tenebroso. 2005. (Ediciones Castillo Castillo Del Terror Ser.).Tr. of Sinister. (SPA.). (J). (gr. 2-6). pap. 7.95 *(978-970-20-0332-8(6))* Castillo, Ediciones, S. A. de C. V. MEX. Dist: Iaconi, Mariuccia Bk. Imports.
Vaid, Raj. A Case of Cold Feet: The Super Sleuth - Mystery #2. 2011. 68p. pap. 9.99 *(978-1-4520-6981-4(6))* AuthorHouse.
—The Case of the Holi Chocolate: The Super Sleuth - Mystery #1. 2011. 56p. pap. 9.99 *(978-1-4520-6903-6(4))* AuthorHouse.
Vail, Emily Blake. Carla & the Con Men. 2006. (J). per. 8.90 *(978-0-935087-28-4(1))* Wright Publishing, Inc.
Valencia, O. R. Savior in the Blue Mermaid. 2008. 180p. pap. 14.35 *(978-1-4251-2824-1(6))* Trafford Publishing.
Van Draanen, Wendelin. Sammy Keyes & the Art of Deception. 2008. (Sammy Keyes Ser.: Bk. 8). (J). 64.99 *(978-1-60640-640-3(X))* Findaway World, LLC.
—Sammy Keyes & the Art of Deception. Van Draanen, Wendelin, illus. 2004. (Sammy Keyes Ser.: Bk. 8). (Illus.). pap. 54.95 incl. audio compact disk *(978-1-59519-003-1(1))*; pap. 36.95 incl. audio *(978-1-59519-001-7(5))* Live Oak Media.
—Sammy Keyes & the Art of Deception. 2005. (Sammy Keyes Ser.). (Illus.). 272p. (J). (gr. 4-7). 14.15 *(978-0-7569-5069-9(4))* Perfection Learning Corp.
—Sammy Keyes & the Art of Deception. 2005. (Sammy Keyes Ser.: 8). (ENG.). 304p. (J). (gr. 5-7). 7.99 *(978-0-440-41992-1(1)*, Yearling) Random Hse. Children's Bks.
—Sammy Keyes & the Cold Hard Cash. 2010. (Sammy Keyes Ser.: 12). (ENG.). 320p. (J). (gr. 5-7). 7.99 *(978-0-440-42113-9(6)*, Yearling) Random Hse. Children's Bks.
—Sammy Keyes & the Curse of Moustache Mary. 2008. (Sammy Keyes Ser.: Bk. 5). (J). 59.99 *(978-1-60640-638-0(8))* Findaway World, LLC.
—Sammy Keyes & the Dead Giveaway. 2008. (Sammy Keyes Ser.: Bk. 10). (J). 64.99 *(978-1-60640-639-7(6))* Findaway World, LLC.
—Sammy Keyes & the Dead Giveaway. unabr. ed. 2006. (Sammy Keyes Ser.: Bk. 10). (J). (gr. 5-7). pap. 54.95 incl. audio compact disk *(978-1-59519-771-9(0))*; pap. 36.95 incl. audio *(978-1-59519-770-2(2))* Live Oak Media.
—Sammy Keyes & the Dead Giveaway. 2007. (Sammy Keyes Ser.: 10). (ENG., Illus.). 304p. (J). (gr. 5-7). per. 7.99 *(978-0-440-41911-2(5)*, Yearling) Random Hse. Children's Bks.
—Sammy Keyes & the Hollywood Mummy. 2008. (Sammy Keyes Ser.: Bk. 6). (J). 64.99 *(978-1-60640-641-0(8))* Findaway World, LLC.
—Sammy Keyes & the Hotel Thief. 2008. (Sammy Keyes Ser.: Bk. 1). (J). 54.99 *(978-1-60640-642-7(6))* Findaway World, LLC.
—Sammy Keyes & the Kiss Goodbye. 2018. (Sammy Keyes Ser.: 18). (ENG.). 256p. (J). (gr. 5). 9.99 *(978-0-307-93063-7(7)*, Yearling) Random Hse. Children's Bks.
—Sammy Keyes & the Night of Skulls. 2012. (Sammy Keyes Ser.: 14). (ENG.). 336p. (J). (gr. 5-7). 10.99 *(978-0-375-85457-6(6)*, Yearling) Random Hse. Children's Bks.
—Sammy Keyes & the Power of Justice Jack. 2012. (Sammy Keyes Ser.: 15). (ENG.). 320p. (J). (gr. 5-7). 7.99 *(978-0-307-93060-6(2)*, Yearling) Random Hse. Children's Bks.
—Sammy Keyes & the Psycho Kitty Queen. 2008. (Sammy Keyes Ser.: Bk. 9). (J). 64.99 *(978-1-60640-643-4(4))* Findaway World, LLC.
—Sammy Keyes & the Psycho Kitty Queen. 2006. (Sammy Keyes Ser.: Bk. 9). (J). pap. 36.95 incl. audio *(978-1-59519-774-0(5))*; pap. 54.95 incl. audio compact disk *(978-1-59519-775-7(3))* Live Oak Media.
—Sammy Keyes & the Psycho Kitty Queen. 2006. (Sammy Keyes Ser.: 9). (ENG., Illus.). 320p. (J). (gr. 5-7). 7.99 *(978-0-440-41910-5(7)*, Yearling) Random Hse. Children's Bks.
—Sammy Keyes & the Runaway Elf. 2008. (Sammy Keyes Ser.: Bk. 4). (J). 54.99 *(978-1-60640-644-1(2))* Findaway World, LLC.
—Sammy Keyes & the Search for Snake Eyes. 2008. (Sammy Keyes Ser.: Bk. 7). (J). 64.99 *(978-1-60640-645-8(0))* Findaway World, LLC.
—Sammy Keyes & the Search for Snake Eyes. Van Draanen, Wendelin, illus. 2003. (Sammy Keyes Ser.: Bk. 7). (Illus.). pap. 54.95 incl. audio compact disk *(978-1-59112-281-4(3))*; pap. 36.95 incl. audio *(978-1-59112-273-9(2))* Live Oak Media.
—Sammy Keyes & the Search for Snake Eyes. 2003. (Sammy Keyes Ser.: Bk. 7). (Illus.). 277p. (gr. 5-9). 17.00 *(978-0-7569-1445-5(0))* Perfection Learning Corp.
—Sammy Keyes & the Search for Snake Eyes. 2003. (Sammy Keyes Ser.: 7). 320p. (J). (gr. 5-7). 8.99 *(978-0-440-41900-6(X)*, Yearling) Random Hse. Children's Bks.
—Sammy Keyes & the Showdown in Sin City. 2013. (Sammy Keyes Ser.: 16). (ENG.). 304p. (J). (gr. 5). pap. 7.99 *(978-0-307-93061-3(0)*, Yearling) Random Hse. Children's Bks.
—Sammy Keyes & the Sisters of Mercy. 2008. (Sammy Keyes Ser.: Bk. 3). (J). 59.99 *(978-1-60640-646-5(9))* Findaway World, LLC.
—Sammy Keyes & the Wedding Crasher. 2011. (Sammy Keyes Ser.: 13). (ENG.). 320p. (J). (gr. 5). 8.99 *(978-0-375-85456-9(8)*, Yearling) Random Hse. Children's Bks.

—Sammy Keyes & the Wild Things. 2008. (Sammy Keyes Ser.: 11). (ENG., Illus.). 320p. (J). (gr. 5-7). 7.99 *(978-0-440-42112-2(8),* Yearling) Random Hse. Children's Bks.

Van Dyke, Edith. Mary Louise. l.t. ed. 2005. 280p. pap. *(978-1-84637-096-0(5))* Echo Library.

Van Dyne, Edith. Aunt Jane's Nieces & Uncle John. 2005. 26.95 *(978-1-4218-1024-9(7));* 176p. pap. 11.95 *(978-1-4218-1124-6(3))* 1st World Publishing, Inc. (1st World Library - Literary Society).

—Aunt Jane's Nieces at Millville. 2005. 27.95 *(978-1-4218-1026-3(3));* 204p. pap. 12.95 *(978-1-4218-1126-0(X))* 1st World Publishing, Inc. (1st World Library - Literary Society).

—Aunt Jane's Nieces at Millville. 2017. (ENG., Illus.). (J). pap. 13.95 *(978-1-374-89145-6(2))* Capital Communications, Inc.

—Aunt Jane's Nieces at Millville. 2004. reprint ed. pap. 21.95 *(978-1-4191-0823-5(9));* pap. 1.99 *(978-1-4192-0823-2(3))* Kessinger Publishing, LLC.

—Aunt Jane's Nieces at Work. 2005. 204p. pap. 12.95 *(978-1-4218-1523-7(0),* 1st World Library - Literary Society) 1st World Publishing, Inc.

—Aunt Jane's Nieces at Work. 2017. (ENG., Illus.). (J). 23.95 *(978-1-374-94773-3(3));* pap. 13.95 *(978-1-374-94772-6(5))* Capital Communications, Inc.

—Aunt Jane's Nieces in Society. 2005. 28.95 *(978-1-4218-1424-7(2));* 276p. pap. 13.95 *(978-1-4218-1524-4(9))* 1st World Publishing, Inc. (1st World Library - Literary Society).

—Aunt Jane's Nieces in Society. 2004. reprint ed. pap. 20.95 *(978-1-4191-0824-2(7));* pap. 1.99 *(978-1-4192-0824-9(1))* Kessinger Publishing, LLC.

—Aunt Jane's Nieces on Vacation. 2005. 27.95 *(978-1-4218-1027-0(1));* 200p. pap. 12.95 *(978-1-4218-1127-7(8))* 1st World Publishing, Inc. (1st World Library - Literary Society).

—Aunt Jane's Nieces on Vacation. 2017. (ENG., Illus.). (J). pap. 13.95 *(978-1-374-83427-9(0))* Capital Communications, Inc.

—Aunt Jane's Nieces on Vacation. 2004. reprint ed. pap. 1.99 *(978-1-4192-0825-6(X));* pap. 21.95 *(978-1-4191-0825-9(5))* Kessinger Publishing, LLC.

—Aunt Jane's Nieces out West. 2005. 27.95 *(978-1-4218-1425-4(0));* 212p. pap. 12.95 *(978-1-4218-1525-1(7))* 1st World Publishing, Inc. (1st World Library - Literary Society).

—Aunt Jane's Nieces Out West. 2004. reprint ed. pap. 1.99 *(978-1-4192-0826-3(8));* pap. 21.95 *(978-1-4191-0826-6(3))* Kessinger Publishing, LLC.

—Mary Louise. 2007. (ENG.). 148p. pap. 18.99 *(978-1-4264-1952-2(X));* 144p. pap. 19.99 *(978-1-4264-2063-4(3))* Creative Media Partners, LLC.

Van Hamme, Jean. The Curse of the 30 Pieces of Silver, Vol. 14, Pt. 2. Shreder, Etienne & Aubin, Antoine, illus. 2012. (Blake & Mortimer Ser.: 14). 64p. (J). (gr. 5-12). pap. 15.95 *(978-1-84918-130-3(6))* CineBook GBR. Dist: National Bk. Network.

—The Strange Encounter, Vol. 5. 2009. (Blake & Mortimer Ser.: 5). (Illus.). 66p. pap. 15.95 *(978-1-905460-75-5(9))* CineBook GBR. Dist: National Bk. Network.

Van Tol, Alex. Redline, 1 vol. 2011. (Orca Soundings Ser.). (ENG.). 136p. (YA). (gr. 8-12). pap. 9.95 *(978-1-55469-893-6(6));* lib. bdg. 16.95 *(978-1-55469-894-3(4))* Orca Bk. Pubs. USA.

VanArsdale, Anthony, illus. The Mystery at the Calgary Stampede. 2015. 104p. (J). *(978-1-4806-9406-4(1))* Whitman, Albert & Co.

—The Shackleton Sabotage. 2017. (Boxcar Children Great Adventure Ser.: 4). (ENG.). 160p. (J). (gr. 2-5). 12.99 *(978-0-8075-0687-5(7),* 807506877); 6.99 *(978-0-8075-0688-2(5),* 807506885) Random Hse. Children's Bks. (Random Hse. Bks. for Young Readers).

—The Sleepy Hollow Mystery. 2015. 111p. (J). *(978-1-4806-9407-1(X))* Whitman, Albert & Co.

Vande Velde, Vivian. Magic Can Be Murder. 2009. (ENG.). 208p. (YA). (gr. 7). pap. 12.99 *(978-0-547-25872-0(0),* 1402326, Clarion Bks.) HarperCollins Pubs.

—Never Trust a Dead Man. 2008. (ENG., Illus.). 208p. (YA). (gr. 7). pap. 13.95 *(978-0-15-206448-8(6),* 1199267, Clarion Bks.) HarperCollins Pubs.

—Witch Dreams, 0 vols. 2013. (ENG.). 128p. (J). (gr. 5-9). pap. 7.99 *(978-0-7614-5460-1(8),* 9780761454601, Two Lions) Amazon Publishing.

VanDycke, Lilian Claudine. The Mystery Fire. 2012. 56p. pap. *(978-1-77097-382-4(6))* FriesenPress.

Vanished. 64p. (YA). (gr. 6-12). pap. *(978-0-8224-2367-6(7))* Globe Fearon Educational Publishing.

Vanneman, Alan. Sherlock Holmes & the Giant Rat of Sumatra. 2003. (ENG.). 304p. pap. 21.99 *(978-0-7867-1125-3(6),* Westview Pr.) Avalon Publishing.

Varley, Dax. Book 5: Stained. Proctor, Jon, illus. 2017. (Demon Slayer Set 2 Ser.). (ENG.). 48p. (J). (gr. 3-7). lib. bdg. 34.21 *(978-1-5321-3006-9(6),* 25558, Spellbound) Magic Wagon.

—Book 7: Murder of Crows. Proctor, Jon, illus. 2017. (Demon Slayer Set 2 Ser.). (ENG.). 48p. (J). (gr. 3-7). lib. bdg. 34.21 *(978-1-5321-3008-3(2),* 25562, Spellbound) Magic Wagon.

—Book 8: Scarlet Portal. Proctor, Jon, illus. 2017. (Demon Slayer Set 2 Ser.). (ENG.). 48p. (J). (gr. 3-7). lib. bdg. 34.21 *(978-1-5321-3009-0(0),* 25564, Spellbound) Magic Wagon.

—The Crow. Proctor, Jon, illus. 2016. (Demon Slayer Ser.). (ENG.). 48p. (J). (gr. 3-7). lib. bdg. 34.21 *(978-1-62402-160-2(3),* 21567, Spellbound) Magic Wagon.

—Graveyard Dirt. Proctor, Jon, illus. 2016. (Demon Slayer Ser.). (ENG.). 48p. (J). (gr. 3-7). lib. bdg. 34.21 *(978-1-62402-158-9(1),* 21563, Spellbound) Magic Wagon.

—The Locket. Proctor, Jon, illus. 2016. (Demon Slayer Ser.). (ENG.). 48p. (J). (gr. 3-7). lib. bdg. 34.21 *(978-1-62402-159-6(X),* 21565, Spellbound) Magic Wagon.

Vaught, Susan. Footer Davis Probably Is Crazy. Reinhardt, Jennifer Black, illus. 2015. (ENG.). 240p. (J). (gr. 5-9). 16.99 *(978-1-4814-2276-5(6),* Simon & Schuster Bks. For Young Readers) Simon & Schuster Bks. For Young Readers.

—Super Max & the Mystery of Thornwood's Revenge. (ENG.). (J). (gr. 3-7). 2018. 368p. pap. 8.99 *(978-1-4814-8684-2(5))* 2017. (Illus.). 352p. 16.99 *(978-1-4814-8683-5(7))* Simon & Schuster/Paula Wiseman Bks. (Simon & Schuster/Paula Wiseman Bks.).

—Super Max & the Mystery of Thornwood's Revenge. 2018. lib. bdg. 19.65 *(978-0-606-41467-8(3))* Turtleback.

Vegas, Peter. Bones of the Sun God. (Pyramid Hunters Ser.: 2). (ENG.). 416p. (J). (gr. 5-9). 2018. pap. 8.99 *(978-1-4814-4583-2(9))* 2017. (Illus.). 17.99 *(978-1-4814-4582-5(0))* Simon & Schuster Children's Publishing. (Aladdin).

—The Iron Tomb. 2016. (Pyramid Hunters Ser.: 1). (ENG., Illus.). 304p. (J). (gr. 5-9). 16.99 *(978-1-4814-4578-8(2),* Aladdin) Simon & Schuster Children's Publishing.

Venable, Colleen A. F. Raining Cats & Detectives. Yue, Stephanie, illus. 2012. (Guinea Pig, Pet Shop Private Eye Ser.: 5). lib. bdg. 17.15 *(978-0-606-26631-4(3))* Turtleback.

Venable, Colleen AF. And Then There Were Gnomes: Book 2, No. 2. Yue, Stephanie, illus. 2010. (Guinea PIG, Pet Shop Private Eye Ser.: 2). (ENG.). 48p. (J). (gr. 2-5). pap. 8.99 *(978-0-7613-5480-2(8),* 0b200c20-498b-45e1-a567-cacac4e9f290, Graphic Universe™) Lerner Publishing Group.

—The Ferret's a Foot: Book 3, No. 3. Yue, Stephanie, illus. 2011. (Guinea PIG, Pet Shop Private Eye Ser.: 3). (ENG.). 48p. (J). (gr. 2-5). pap. 8.99 *(978-0-7613-5629-5(0),* 35650f73-6bcc-4b17-8613-e1dfc9de7d05, Graphic Universe™) Lerner Publishing Group.

—Fish You Were Here: Book 4, No. 4. Yue, Stephanie, illus. 2011. (Guinea PIG, Pet Shop Private Eye Ser.: 4). (ENG.). 48p. (J). (gr. 2-5). pap. 8.99 *(978-0-7613-5630-1(4),* 3de37407-5944-42df-b82a-a5f57cd4d807); lib. bdg. 27.99 *(978-0-7613-5224-2(4),* 45cde823-2ed7-4fb5-aa4e-1c7336fa0ad1) Lerner Publishing Group. (Graphic Universe™).

—Going, Going, Dragon! Book 6. Yue, Stephanie, illus. 2013. (Guinea PIG, Pet Shop Private Eye Ser.). (ENG.). 48p. (J). (gr. 2-5). E-Book 42.65 *(978-1-4677-0973-6(5),* Graphic Universe™) Lerner Publishing Group.

—Hamster & Cheese: Book 1, No. 1. Yue, Stephanie, illus. 2010. (Guinea PIG, Pet Shop Private Eye Ser.: 1). (ENG.). 48p. (J). (gr. 2-5). pap. 8.99 *(978-0-7613-5479-6(4),* 96fb073b-ac1d-4d8a-9df6-ac54e9100d0e, Graphic Universe™) Lerner Publishing Group.

Ventresca, Yvonne. Black Flowers, White Lies. (ENG.). (J). 2018. 280p. (gr. 8-8). pap. 9.99 *(978-1-5107-2596-6(2))* 2016. 272p. (gr. 6-6). 16.99 *(978-1-5107-0988-1(6))* Skyhorse Publishing Co., Inc. (Sky Pony Pr.).

—Pandemic. 2016. 368p. (J). (gr. 6-6). pap. 9.99 *(978-1-5107-0390-2(X),* Sky Pony Pr.) Skyhorse Publishing Co., Inc.

Verano, M. Diary of a Haunting. (Diary of a Haunting Ser.). (ENG., Illus.). (YA). (gr. 9). 2016. 336p. pap. 10.99 *(978-1-4814-3068-5(8))* 2015. 320p. 17.99 *(978-1-4814-3069-2(6))* Simon Pulse. (Simon Pulse).

Verney, John. Friday's Tunnel. 2019. (ENG., Illus.). 263p. (J). (gr. 4-7). pap. 11.95 *(978-1-58988-137-2(0))* Dry, Paul Bks., Inc.

Vernon, Ursula. Dragonbreath #9: The Case of the Toxic Mutants. 2013. (Dragonbreath Ser.: 9). (ENG., Illus.). 208p. (J). (gr. 3-7). 14.99 *(978-0-8037-3847-8(1),* Dial Bks) Penguin Young Readers Group.

Via, Jennifer Welsh. The Foggy Meadow Discovery. 2007. 216p. per. 14.95 *(978-0-595-44680-3(9))* iUniverse, Inc.

Vicary, Tim. The Hitchhiker, 5. 2014. (Garnet Oracle Readers Ser.). (Illus.). 40p. pap., stu. ed. 4.50 *(978-1-907575-18-1(9))* Garnet Education GBR. Dist: Garnet Publishing, Ltd.

Vicente, Alidis. The Case of the Three Kings / el Caso de Los Reyes Magos: The Flaca Files / Los Expedientes de Flaca. 2016. (Flaca Files / Los Expedientes de Flaca Ser.). (MUL, ENG & SPA., Illus.). 96p. (J). (gr. 3-6). pap. 9.95 *(978-1-55885-822-0(9),* Piñata Books) Arte Publico Pr.

—The Missing Chancleta & Other Top-Secret Cases / la Chancleta Perdida y Otros Casos Secretos. 2013. (SPA & ENG., Illus.). 64p. (J). pap. 9.95 *(978-1-55885-779-7(6),* Piñata Books) Arte Publico Pr.

Villar Liébana, Luisa. El Ladron de Salchichon. 2005. (Investigator Big Ears Ser.). (SPA., Illus.). 62p. (J). (gr. 2-3). 8.95 *(978-84-348-9384-9(3))* SM Ediciones ESP. Dist: Iaconi, Mariuccia Bk. Imports.

Villareal, Ray. Who's Buried in the Garden? 2009. 160p. (YA). (gr. 6-18). pap. 10.95 *(978-1-55885-546-5(7),* Piñata Books) Arte Publico Pr.

Vincent, Cindy. Mystery of the Missing Ming: A Daisy Diamond Detective Novel. 2004. 172p. (YA). 9.97 *(978-1-932169-37-9(7))* Mysteries by Vincent, LLC.

Viney, Peter. The Case of the Dead Batsman, 7. 2013. (Garnet Oracle Readers Ser.). (Illus.). 40p. pap., stu. ed. 4.50 *(978-1-907575-21-1(9))* Garnet Education GBR. Dist: Garnet Publishing, Ltd.

Vize, Bonnie. The Mystery of the Park Pavilion. 2009. pap. 14.22 *(978-1-61584-491-3(0))* Independent Pub.

Voices in the Night. 64p. (YA). (gr. 6-12). pap. *(978-0-8224-2368-3(5))* Globe Fearon Educational Publishing.

Voigt, Cynthia. The Book of Secrets. 2015. (Mister Max Ser.: 2). lib. bdg. 17.20 *(978-0-606-37702-7(6))* Turtleback.

von Ziegesar, Cecily. Dark Horses. 2017. 336p. (YA). (gr. 9). pap. 10.99 *(978-1-61695-816-9(2),* Soho Teen) Soho Pr., Inc.

Vulliamy, Clara. The Lost Puppy (Dotty Detective, Book 4) 2018. (Dotty Detective Ser.: 4). (ENG.). 176p. (J). 4.99 *(978-0-00-826245-5(5),* HarperCollins Children's Bks.) HarperCollins Pubs. Ltd. GBR. Dist: HarperCollins Pubs.

—The Paw Print Puzzle (Dotty Detective, Book 2) 2018. (Dotty Detective Ser.: 2). (ENG.). 176p. (J). 4.99 *(978-0-00-825107-9(X),* HarperCollins Children's Bks.) HarperCollins Pubs. Ltd. GBR. Dist: HarperCollins Pubs.

Wachtel, Shirley Russak. Brad Sureshot — Coach-Detective: The Baffling Case of the Disappearing Dribbler. 2007. 76p. per. 8.95 *(978-0-595-47266-6(4))* iUniverse, Inc.

Wade, Rebecca. The Whispering House. 2012. (ENG.). 272p. (J). (gr. 3-7). 16.99 *(978-0-06-077497-4(5),* Tegen, Katherine Bks) HarperCollins Pubs.

Wagner, J. I. Legend of the Star Runner: A Timmi Tobbson Adventure. Hall, Bradley, ed. Froehlich, Cindy, illus. 2018. 168p. (YA). pap. 12.99 *(978-3-96326-777-2(1))* Upper Room Bks.

Walker, Landry. Secrets & Lies. Takara, Marcio, illus. 2010. (Incredibles Ser.). 112p. (J). (gr. 3-8). pap. 9.99 *(978-1-60886-583-3(5))* BOOM! Studios.

Wall, Billy James. The Mystery of Marcy & the Stony Squirrel. 2009. 40.00 *(978-1-61584-580-4(1))* Independent Pub.

Wallace, James. Tsunami: Ghost Eagle 1. 2003. 149p. (YA). pap. 11.95 *(978-0-595-27372-0(6))* iUniverse, Inc.

Wallace, Karen. The Case of the Howling Armor. 2004. (Illus.). 47p. *(978-0-439-66552-0(3))* Scholastic, Inc.

—Diamond Takers. 2007. (Lady Violet Mysteries Ser.: 3). (ENG.). 240p. (J). (gr. 4-7). pap. 9.95 *(978-1-4169-0100-6(0),* Simon & Schuster Children's) Simon & Schuster, Ltd. GBR. Dist: Simon & Schuster, Inc.

—Flash Harriet & the Loch Ness Monster: Band 13/Topaz (Collins Big Cat) Nayler, Sarah, illus. 2007. (Collins Big Cat Ser.). (ENG.). 32p. (J). (gr. 2-4). pap. 9.99 *(978-0-00-723082-2(6))* HarperCollins Pubs. Ltd. GBR. Dist: Independent Pubs. Group.

Wallace, Sheila Ryan. Diving for the Gold. 2004. 142p. (YA). pap. 15.95 *(978-0-7414-2269-9(7))* Infinity Publishing.

—Miss Abigail's Antique Treasures. 2007. (ENG.). 152p. per. 15.95 *(978-0-7414-3942-0(5))* Infinity Publishing.

Waller, Stephen. Level 1: Run for Your Life. 2nd ed. 2008. (Pearson English Graded Readers Ser.). (ENG., Illus.). 32p. pap. 11.99 *(978-1-4058-6970-6(4),* Pearson ELT) Pearson Education.

Walsh, Alice. Buried Truth, 1 vol. 2013. (ENG.). 100p. (J). (gr. 4-8). pap. *(978-1-77103-009-0(7))* Breakwater Bks., Ltd.

Walsh, Ann. Moses, Me, & Murder: A Barkerville Mystery. 2nd ed. 2013. (Barkerville Mystery Ser.: 1). (ENG., Illus.). 112p. (J). pap. 11.99 *(978-1-4597-0967-6(5))* Dundurn Pr. CAN. Dist: Publishers Group West (PGW).

Walsh, Brendan & Benchmark Education Co., LLC. Hats off to the President: A White House Mystery. McEvenue, Tim, illus. 2014. (Text Connections Ser.). (J). (gr. 3). *(978-1-4509-9660-0(4))* Benchmark Education Co.

Walsh, Ellen Stoll. Dot & Jabber & the Big Bug Mystery. 2017. (Green Light Readers Level 2 Ser.: Vol. 3). (ENG.). (J). (gr. -1-3). lib. bdg. 13.55 *(978-0-606-39827-5(9))* Turtleback.

Walsh, Laurence & Walsh, Suella. In the Middle of the Night. 2006. (J). pap. *(978-0-88092-473-3(X))* Royal Fireworks Publishing Co.

Walters, Eric. The Money Pit Mystery, 1 vol. 2011. (ENG.). 296p. (J). (gr. 4-7). pap. 9.95 *(978-1-55455-123-1(4),* 9e496663-ad54-46fe-9019-3414ed73a752) Fitzhenry & Whiteside, Ltd. CAN. Dist: Firefly Bks., Ltd.

Walters, Eric & Spreekmeester, Kevin. Death by Exposure. 2nd ed. 2006. (ENG., Illus.). 88p. (J). (gr. 4-8). pap. 9.99 *(978-1-55002-632-0(1))* Dundurn Pr. CAN. Dist: Publishers Group West (PGW).

Walton, Rick. Mini Mysteries 2: 20 More Tricky Tales to Untangle. Scheuer, Lauren, illus. 2006. 87p. (J). *(978-1-4156-6869-6(8),* American Girl) American Girl Publishing, Inc.

Waltz, Dan. Kornstalkers: Corn Maze Massacre. Waltz, Dan, illus. l.t. ed. 2005. (Chilled to the Bone! Ser.: No. 1). (Illus.). 120p. (J). per. 6.99 *(978-0-9741774-3-4(1))* D. W. Publishing.

Ward, Ian. Bobby Blah Blah & the Mystery of the U F O in Sniggery Woods. 2009. (Illus.). 84p. pap. 10.49 *(978-1-4389-7963-2(0))* AuthorHouse.

Ward-Showers, Latanya. Could It Be a Monster in the Attic? 2013. 24p. pap. 17.99 *(978-1-4817-0542-4(3))* AuthorHouse.

Ware, Fletcher K. The Empress Conspiracy. 2004. 285p. (YA). per. 14.95 *(978-1-932496-17-8(3))* Penman Publishing, Inc.

Warner, Gertrude Chandler. Blue Bay Mystery, 1 vol. Dubisch, Michael, illus. 2009. (Boxcar Children Graphic Novels Ser.). (ENG.). 32p. (J). (gr. 3-8). 32.79 *(978-1-60270-591-3(7),* 3674, Graphic Planet - Fiction) Magic Wagon.

—The Box-Car Children. Gregory, Dorothy Lake, illus. 2020. (ENG.). 64p. (J). (gr. 2-5). pap. 6.99 *(978-1-4209-6966-5(8))* Digireads.com Publishing.

—The Box-Car Children. 2019. (ENG.). 70p. (J). (gr. 2-5). pap. 5.99 *(978-1-6777-0963-2(4))* Independently Published.

—The Box-Car Children. Gregory, Dorothy Lake, illus. 2019. (ENG.). 88p. (J). (gr. 1-5). 14.99 *(978-1-5154-4203-5(9));* pap. 6.49 *(978-1-5154-4204-2(7))* Jorge Pinto Bks. (Illustrated Bks.).

—The Boxcar Children. Date not set. (Boxcar Children Ser.: No. 1). (J). (gr. 2-5). lib. bdg. 18.95 *(978-0-8488-1712-1(5))* Amereon Ltd.

—The Boxcar Children. (Boxcar Children Ser.: No. 1). 154p. (J). (gr. 2-5). pap. 3.95 *(978-0-8072-1447-3(7),* Listening Library) Random Hse. Audio Publishing Group.

—The Boxcar Children. Deal, L. Kate, illus. 2020. (Boxcar Children Ser.). (ENG.). 160p. (J). (gr. 2-6). lib. bdg. 31.36 *(978-1-5321-4473-8(3),* 35163, Chapter Bks.) Spotlight.

—The Boxcar Children Fully Illustrated Edition. Gilbert, Anne Yvonne & Powers, Gretchen Ellen, illus. 2017. (Boxcar Children Mysteries Ser.). (ENG.). 168p. (J). (gr. 2-5). 34.99 *(978-0-8075-0925-8(6),* 807509256, Random Hse. Bks. for Young Readers) Random Hse. Children's Bks.

—Boxcar Children Graphic Novels, 6 vols., Set 2. Incl. Amusement Park Mystery. Denton, Shannon Eric. Dubisch, Mike, illus. 32.79 *(978-1-60270-718-4(9),* 3679); Castle Mystery. Denton, Shannon Eric. Dubisch, Mike, illus. 32.79 *(978-1-60270-720-7(0),* 3681); Haunted Cabin Mystery. Bloodworth, Mark, illus. 32.79 *(978-1-60270-717-7(0),* 3678); Pizza Mystery. Worley, Rob M. Dubisch, Mike, illus. 32.79 *(978-1-60270-719-1(7),* 3680); Snowbound Mystery. Dubisch, Mike, illus. 32.79 *(978-1-60270-715-3(4),* 3676); Tree House Mystery. Long, Christopher E. Bloodworth, Mark, illus. 32.79 *(978-1-60270-716-0(2),* 3677); (J). (gr. 3-8). (Boxcar Children Graphic Novels Ser.). (ENG.). 32p. 2010. Set lib. bdg. 196.74 *(978-1-60270-714-6(6),* 3675, Graphic Planet - Fiction) Magic Wagon.

—Boxcar Children Graphic Novels, 6 vols., Set 3. Dunn, Ben, illus. Incl. Bk. 13. Woodshed Mystery. Dunn, Joeming. (gr. 3-8). 32.79 *(978-1-61641-121-3(X),* 3683); Bk. 14. Lighthouse Mystery. Dunn, Joeming. (gr. 3-8). 32.79 *(978-1-61641-122-0(8),* 3684); Bk. 15. Mountain Top Mystery. Dunn, Joeming. (gr. 3-8). 32.79 *(978-1-61641-123-7(6),* 3685); Bk. 16. Houseboat Mystery. Dunn, Joeming W., illus. & adapted by. (gr. 3-8). 32.79 *(978-1-61641-124-4(4),* 3686); Bk. 17. Bicycle Mystery. Dunn, Joeming W., illus. & adapted by. (gr. 3-8). 32.79 *(978-1-61641-125-1(2),* 3687); Bk. 18. Mystery in the Sand. Dunn, Joeming. (gr. 3-8). 32.79 *(978-1-61641-126-8(0),* 3688); (J). (Boxcar Children Graphic Novels Ser.). (ENG., Illus.). 32p. 2011. Set lib. bdg. 196.74 *(978-1-61641-120-6(1),* 3682, Graphic Planet - Fiction) Magic Wagon.

—The Boxcar Children Mysteries Boxed Set Books 1-12, 12 bks. 2010. (Boxcar Children Mysteries Ser.: 1). (ENG., Illus.). 1760p. (J). (gr. 2-5). 95.88 *(978-0-8075-0855-8(1),* 807508551, Random Hse. Bks. for Young Readers) Random Hse. Children's Bks.

—The Dog-Gone Mystery. 2009. (First Read-Alone Mysteries Ser.). (Illus.). 120p. (J). (gr. 1-3). lib. bdg. 14.99 *(978-0-8075-1656-0(2))* Whitman, Albert & Co.

—The Lighthouse Mystery. (Boxcar Children Ser.: No. 8). 147p. (J). (gr. 2-5). pap. 3.95 *(978-0-8072-1474-9(4),* Listening Library) Random Hse. Audio Publishing Group.

—Mike's Mystery. (Boxcar Children Ser.: No. 5). 128p. (J). (gr. 2-5). pap. 3.95 *(978-0-8072-1462-6(0),* Listening Library) Random Hse. Audio Publishing Group.

—Mike's Mystery, 1 vol. Dubisch, Michael, illus. 2009. (Boxcar Children Graphic Novels Ser.). (ENG.). 32p. (J). (gr. 3-8). 32.79 *(978-1-60270-590-6(9),* 3673, Graphic Planet - Fiction) Magic Wagon.

—The Mystery of the Runaway Ghost. Soileau, Hodges, illus. 2004. (Boxcar Children Ser.). 135p. (J). 12.65 *(978-0-7569-3264-0(5))* Perfection Learning Corp.

—Mystery Ranch. (Boxcar Children Ser.: No. 4). 128p. (J). (gr. 2-5). pap. 3.95 *(978-0-8072-1450-3(7),* Listening Library) Random Hse. Audio Publishing Group.

—Mystery Ranch, 1 vol. Dubisch, Michael, illus. 2009. (Boxcar Children Graphic Novels Ser.). (ENG.). 32p. (J). (gr. 3-8). 32.79 *(978-1-60270-589-0(5),* 3672, Graphic Planet - Fiction) Magic Wagon.

—The Yellow House Mystery. (Boxcar Children Ser.: No. 3). 191p. (J). (gr. 2-5). pap. 3.95 *(978-0-8072-1449-7(3),* Listening Library) Random Hse. Audio Publishing Group.

—The Yellow House Mystery, 1 vol. Dubisch, Michael, illus. 2009. (Boxcar Children Graphic Novels Ser.). (ENG.). 32p. (J). (gr. 3-8). 32.79 *(978-1-60270-588-3(7),* 3671, Graphic Planet - Fiction) Magic Wagon.

—The Yellow House Mystery, No. 3. Dubisch, Mike, illus. 2009. (Boxcar Children Graphic Novels Ser.). (ENG.). 32p. (J). (gr. 2-5). 6.99 *(978-0-8075-2869-3(2))* Whitman, Albert & Co.

Warner, Gertrude Chandler, creator. The Black Widow Spider Mystery. 2003. (Boxcar Children Mystery & Activities Specials Ser.: 21). (ENG., Illus.). 128p. (J). (gr. 2-5). pap. 5.99 *(978-0-8075-5544-6(4),* 807555444, Random Hse. Bks. for Young Readers) Random Hse. Children's Bks.

—The Box That Watch Found. 2007. (Boxcar Children Mysteries Ser.: 113). (ENG., Illus.). 128p. (J). (gr. 2-5). lib. bdg. 14.99 *(978-0-8075-5568-2(1),* 807555681); per. 6.99 *(978-0-8075-5569-9(X),* 080755569X) Random Hse. Children's Bks. (Random Hse. Bks. for Young Readers).

—The Boxcar Children Guide to Adventure: A How-To for Mystery Solving, Make-It-Yourself Projects, & More. 2014. (Boxcar Children Mysteries Ser.). (ENG., Illus.). 144p. (J). (gr. 2-5). 12.99 *(978-0-8075-0905-0(1),* 807509051, Random Hse. Bks. for Young Readers) Random Hse. Children's Bks.

—The Celebrity Cat Caper. 2016. (Boxcar Children Mysteries Ser.: 143). (ENG., Illus.). 128p. (J). (gr. 2-5). 15.99 *(978-0-8075-0711-7(3),* 807507113, Random Hse. Bks. for Young Readers) Random Hse. Children's Bks.

—The Comic Book Mystery. 2003. (Boxcar Children Mysteries Ser.: 93). (ENG., Illus.). 112p. (J). (gr. 2-5). 5.99 *(978-0-8075-5529-3(0),* 807555290, Random Hse. Bks. for Young Readers) Random Hse. Children's Bks.

—The Creature in Ogopogo Lake. 2006. (Boxcar Children Mysteries Ser.: 108). (ENG., Illus.). 128p. (J). (gr. 2-5). lib. bdg. 14.99 *(978-0-8075-1336-1(9),* 807513369); per. 6.99 *(978-0-8075-1337-8(7),* 807513377) Random Hse. Children's Bks. (Random Hse. Bks. for Young Readers).

—The Game Store Mystery. 2005. (Boxcar Children Mysteries Ser.: 104). (ENG., Illus.). 144p. (J). (gr. 2-5). per. 6.99 *(978-0-8075-2739-9(4),* 807527394, Random Hse. Bks. for Young Readers) Random Hse. Children's Bks.

—The Ghost at the Drive-In Movie. 2008. (Boxcar Children Mysteries Ser.: 116). (ENG., Illus.). 128p. (J). (gr. 2-5). 14.99 *(978-0-8075-5577-4(0),* 807555770, Random Hse. Bks. for Young Readers) Random Hse. Children's Bks.

—The Ghost in the First Row, Vol. 112. 2007. (Boxcar Children Mysteries Ser.: 112). (ENG., Illus.). 128p. (J). (gr. 2-5). per. 5.99 *(978-0-8075-5567-5(3),* 807555673, Random Hse. Bks. for Young Readers) Random Hse. Children's Bks.

—The Ghost of the Chattering Bones. 2005. (Boxcar Children Mysteries Ser.: 102). (ENG., Illus.). 128p. (J). (gr. 2-5). pap. 6.99 *(978-0-8075-0874-9(8),* 807508748, Random Hse. Bks. for Young Readers) Random Hse. Children's Bks.

—The Giant Yo-Yo Mystery. 2006. (Boxcar Children Mysteries Ser.: 107). (ENG., Illus.). 144p. (J). (gr. 2-5). per. 5.99 *(978-0-8075-0879-4(9),* 807508799, Random Hse. Bks. for Young Readers) Random Hse. Children's Bks.

—The Great Shark Mystery. 2003. (Boxcar Children Mystery & Activities Specials Ser.: 20). (ENG., Illus.). 160p. (J). (gr. 2-5). pap. 7.99 *(978-0-8075-5532-3(0),* 807555320, Random Hse. Bks. for Young Readers) Random Hse. Children's Bks.

—Hidden in the Haunted School. 2016. (Boxcar Children Mysteries Ser.: 144). (ENG., Illus.). 128p. (J). (gr. 2-5). 15.99 *(978-0-8075-0718-6(0),* 807507180, Random Hse. Bks. for Young Readers) Random Hse. Children's Bks.

—A Horse Named Dragon. 2008. (Boxcar Children Mysteries Ser.: 114). (ENG., Illus.). 128p. (J). (gr. 2-5). lib. bdg. 14.99 *(978-0-8075-5571-2(1),* 807555711); per. 7.99 *(978-0-8075-5572-9(X),* 080755572X) Random Hse. Children's Bks. (Random Hse. Bks. for Young Readers).

—The Ice Cream Mystery. 2003. (Boxcar Children Mysteries Ser.: 94). (ENG., Illus.). 128p. (J). (gr. 2-5). pap. 6.99 *(978-0-8075-5535-4(5),* 807555355, Random Hse. Bks. for Young Readers) Random Hse. Children's Bks.

—The Legend of the Howling Werewolf. 2018. (Boxcar Children Mysteries Ser.: 148). (ENG., Illus.). 128p. (J). (gr. 2-5). 12.99 *(978-0-8075-0740-7(7),* 807507407); pap. 6.99 *(978-0-8075-0741-4(5),* 807507415) Random Hse. Children's Bks. (Random Hse. Bks. for Young Readers).

—The Legend of the Irish Castle. 2016. (Boxcar Children Mysteries Ser.: 142). (ENG., Illus.). 128p. (J). (gr. 2-5). 15.99 *(978-0-8075-0705-6(9),* 807507059, Random Hse. Bks. for Young Readers) Random Hse. Children's Bks.

—Midnight at the Haunted Hotel. 2018. (Boxcar Children Interactive Mysteries Ser.). (ENG., Illus.). 160p. (J). (gr. 2-5).

pap. 6.99 *(978-0-8075-2850-1(1),* 807528501, Random Hse. Bks. for Young Readers) Random Hse. Children's Bks.
—The Midnight Mystery. 2003. (Boxcar Children Mysteries Ser.: 95). (ENG., Illus.). 128p. (J). (gr. 2-5). pap. 5.99 *(978-0-8075-5538-5(X),* 080755538X, Random Hse. Bks. for Young Readers) Random Hse. Children's Bks.
—The Mystery in the Fortune Cookie. 2003. (Boxcar Children Mysteries Ser.: 96). (ENG., Illus.). 144p. (J). (gr. 2-5). pap. 6.99 *(978-0-8075-5540-8(1),* 807555401, Random Hse. Bks. for Young Readers) Random Hse. Children's Bks.
—The Mystery of the Grinning Gargoyle. 2014. (Boxcar Children Mysteries Ser.: 137). (ENG., Illus.). 128p. (J). (gr. 2-5). pap. 5.99 *(978-0-8075-0893-0(4),* 807508934, Random Hse. Bks. for Young Readers) Random Hse. Children's Bks.
—The Mystery of the Missing Pop Idol. 2015. (Boxcar Children Mysteries Ser.: 138). (ENG., Illus.). 128p. (J). (gr. 2-5). 15.99 *(978-0-8075-5605-4(X),* 080755605X, Random Hse. Bks. for Young Readers) Random Hse. Children's Bks.
—The Mystery of the Orphan Train. 2005. (Boxcar Children Mysteries Ser.: 105). (ENG., Illus.). 128p. (J). (gr. 2-5). lib. bdg. 14.99 *(978-0-8075-5558-3(4),* 807555584); per. 6.99 *(978-0-8075-5559-0(2),* 807555592) Random Hse. Children's Bks. (Random Hse. Bks. for Young Readers).
—The Mystery of the Soccer Snitch. 2014. (Boxcar Children Mysteries Ser.: 136). (ENG., Illus.). 128p. (J). (gr. 2-5). pap. 6.99 *(978-0-8075-0896-1(9),* 807508969, Random Hse. Bks. for Young Readers) Random Hse. Children's Bks.
—The Mystery of the Stolen Dinosaur Bones. 2015. (Boxcar Children Mysteries Ser.: 139). (ENG., Illus.). 128p. (J). (gr. 2-5). 15.99 *(978-0-8075-5608-5(4),* 807556084, Random Hse. Bks. for Young Readers) Random Hse. Children's Bks.
—The Mystery of the Traveling Tomatoes. 2008. (Boxcar Children Mysteries Ser.: 117). (ENG., Illus.). 128p. (J). (gr. 2-5). pap. 6.99 *(978-0-8075-5580-4(0),* 807555800, Random Hse. Bks. for Young Readers) Random Hse. Children's Bks.
—The Radio Mystery. 2003. (Boxcar Children Mysteries Ser.: 97). (ENG., Illus.). 128p. (J). (gr. 2-5). mass mkt. 6.99 *(978-0-8075-5547-7(9),* 807555479, Random Hse. Bks. for Young Readers) Random Hse. Children's Bks.
—The Robot Ransom. 2018. (Boxcar Children Mysteries Ser.: 147). (ENG., Illus.). 128p. (J). (gr. 2-5). 12.99 *(978-0-8075-0734-6(2),* 807507342); pap. 6.99 *(978-0-8075-0735-3(0),* 807507350) Random Hse. Children's Bks. (Random Hse. Bks. for Young Readers).
—The Rock 'n' Roll Mystery. 2006. (Boxcar Children Mysteries Ser.: 109). (ENG., Illus.). 128p. (J). (gr. 2-5). lib. bdg. 14.99 *(978-0-8075-7089-0(3),* 807570893); per. 5.99 *(978-0-8075-7090-6(7),* 807570907) Random Hse. Children's Bks. (Random Hse. Bks. for Young Readers).
—The Seattle Puzzle. 2007. (Boxcar Children Mysteries Ser.: 111). (ENG., Illus.). (J). (gr. 2-5). 128p. lib. bdg. 14.99 *(978-0-8075-5560-6(6),* 807555606); 112p. per. 5.99 *(978-0-8075-5561-3(4),* 807555614) Random Hse. Children's Bks. (Random Hse. Bks. for Young Readers).
—The Secret of the Mask. 2007. (Boxcar Children Mysteries Ser.: 110). (ENG., Illus.). 128p. (J). (gr. 2-5). lib. bdg. 14.99 *(978-0-8075-5564-4(9),* 807555649); per. 5.99 *(978-0-8075-5565-1(7),* 807555657) Random Hse. Children's Bks. (Random Hse. Bks. for Young Readers).
—The Sleepy Hollow Mystery. 2015. (Boxcar Children Mysteries Ser.: 141). (ENG., Illus.). 128p. (J). (gr. 2-5). 15.99 *(978-0-8075-2843-3(9),* 807528439, Random Hse. Bks. for Young Readers) Random Hse. Children's Bks.
—The Sword of the Silver Knight. 2005. (Boxcar Children Mysteries Ser.: 103). (ENG., Illus.). 128p. (J). (gr. 2-5). per. 6.99 *(978-0-8075-0876-3(4),* 807508764, Random Hse. Bks. for Young Readers) Random Hse. Children's Bks.
—The Tattletale Mystery. 2003. (Boxcar Children Mysteries Ser.: 92). (ENG., Illus.). 128p. (J). (gr. 2-5). pap. 5.99 *(978-0-8075-5526-2(6),* 807555266, Random Hse. Bks. for Young Readers) Random Hse. Children's Bks.
—The Vanishing Passenger. 2006. (Boxcar Children Mysteries Ser.: 106). (ENG., Illus.). 112p. (J). (gr. 2-5). per. 7.99 *(978-0-8075-1067-4(X),* 080751067X, Random Hse. Bks. for Young Readers) Random Hse. Children's Bks.
Warner, Penny. The Haunted Lighthouse, No. 2. 2013. (Code Busters Club Ser.). (ENG.). 208p. (J). (gr. 3-6). pap. 6.99 *(978-1-60684-455-7(5),* e0748b7e-7a00-4d4c-93b0-0741ebc6714b, Darby Creek) Lerner Publishing Group.
—The Hunt for the Missing Spy. 2016. (Code Busters Club Ser.: 5). (ENG.). 168p. (J). (gr. 3-6). E-Book 26.65 *(978-1-5124-0305-3(9),* Darby Creek) Lerner Publishing Group.
—The Mystery of the Missing Mustangs. 2012. 107p. (J). *(978-0-88166-411-9(1))* Meadowbrook Pr.
—The Mystery of the Pirate's Treasure. 2013. (Code Busters Club Ser.). (ENG.). 192p. (J). (gr. 4-7). 16.99 *(978-1-60684-457-1(1),* Darby Creek) Lerner Publishing Group.
—The Secret of the Puzzle Box. 2016. (Code Busters Club Ser.: 6). (ENG.). 192p. (J). (gr. 3-6). 16.99 *(978-1-5124-0307-7(5),* 1b2aafc4-0569-4836-a7a2-2217feba338c, Darby Creek) Lerner Publishing Group.
—The Secret of the Skeleton Key. 1. 2012. (Code Busters Club Ser.). (ENG., Illus.). 224p. (J). (gr. 4-6). 21.19 *(978-1-60684-162-4(9),* 9781606841624) Farshore GBR. Dist: Children's Plus, Inc.
—The Secret of the Skeleton Key. 2012. (Code Busters Club Ser.). (ENG.). 240p. (J). (gr. 3-6). pap. 7.99 *(978-1-60684-390-1(7),* 95a9d0c6-d2f1-4940-839e-8b496d8f98a8, Darby Creek) Lerner Publishing Group.
Warren George A. Staff. The Banner Boy Scouts. rev. ed. 2006. 248p. 27.95 *(978-1-4218-1729-3(2));* pap. 12.95 *(978-1-4218-1829-0(9))* 1st World Publishing, Inc. (1st World Library - Literary Society).
Warrington, Dean Grey. Perfiction. 2007. 188p. per. 13.95 *(978-0-595-43758-0(3))* iUniverse, Inc.
Wasserman, Robin. Scooby-Doo & the Snow Monster Scare, 1 vol. Sur, Duendes del, illus. 2016. (Scooby-Doo Early Reading Adventures Ser.). (ENG.). 24p. (J). (gr. -1-2). lib. bdg. 31.36 *(978-1-61479-473-8(1),* 21386) Spotlight.
Wassner, Gary. The Mystery of the Jubilee Emerald. 2006. (J). pap. *(978-1-59336-712-1(0))* Mondo Publishing.
Watching Josh, 6 vols. (Ragged Island Mysteriestm Ser.). 161p. (gr. 5-7). 42.50 *(978-0-322-01651-4(7))* Wright Group/McGraw-Hill.
Waters, Erica-Jane. Penny for Your Thoughts. Waters, Erica-Jane, illus. 2020. (Miss Bunsen's School for Brilliant Girls Ser.: 3). (ENG., Illus.). 128p. (J). (gr. 1-5). 14.99 *(978-0-8075-5159-2(7),* 807551597) Whitman, Albert & Co.
Watkins, Christopher. Exposure. 2012. 212p. pap. 19.99 *(978-1-4797-1599-2(9))* Xlibris Corp.
Watkins, Elaine. Billy Bobbin at Mystery Farm. 2014. (ENG.). 56p. (J). (gr. 3-4). pap. 8.95 *(978-1-84963-823-4(3),* 69c495c4-d32a-49ec-acc3-e032a2925b46) Austin Macauley Pubs. Ltd. GBR. Dist: Baker & Taylor Publisher Services (BTPS).
Watkins, T. a. Joey & the Ancient Horn: A Mystery Revealed. Davis, Marcus, illus. 2007. 333p. (J). (gr. -1). per. 12.95 *(978-0-9762788-0-1(4))* Great I-AM Publishing Co., The.
Watson, Geoff. Edison's Gold. 2010. (ENG.). 320p. (J). (gr. 4-6). 22.44 *(978-1-60684-094-8(0))* Farshore GBR. Dist: Children's Plus, Inc.
Watson, Jude. In Too Deep (the 39 Clues, Book 6), Book 6. 2009. (39 Clues Ser.: 6). (ENG.). 208p. (J). (gr. 3-7). 13.99 *(978-0-545-06046-2(X))* Scholastic, Inc.
Watson, Lena. Noise in My Room: The Adventure of Jane Barnette, the Problem Solver. Kindred, Christopher, illus. 2012. (ENG.). 32p. pap. 19.99 *(978-1-4685-8780-7(3))* AuthorHouse.
Watts, Julia. Free Spirits. 2009. (ENG.). 176p. (J). (gr. 1). pap. 8.95 *(978-0-9667359-2-5(7),* BeanPole Bks.) OH Industries.
—Kindred Spirits. 2008. (ENG.). 147p. (J). (gr. 3-18). pap. 8.95 *(978-0-9667359-9-4(4))* OH Industries.
Waysman, Dvora. Jewish Detective Stories for Kids. 2005. (Jewish Stories for Kids Ser.). (Illus.). 184p. (J). (gr. 5-9). 16.95 *(978-1-930143-14-2(1));* pap. 12.95 *(978-1-930143-15-9(X))* Simcha Media Group. (Devora Publishing).
We Hold These Truths. 2014. (Benjamin Pratt & the Keepers of the School Ser.: 5). (ENG., Illus.). 288p. (J). (gr. 2-5). pap. 8.99 *(978-1-4169-3911-5(3),* Atheneum Bks. for Young Readers) Simon & Schuster Children's Publishing.
Weakland, Mark. The West End Treehouse Mystery, 1 vol. 2018. (ENG., Illus.). 160p. (J). (gr. 3-7). pap. 9.95 *(978-1-4556-2384-6(9),* Pelican Publishing) Arcadia Publishing.
Webb, Holly. The Case of the Stolen Sixpence: The Mysteries of Maisie Hitchins Book 1. Lindsay, Marion, illus. 2015. (Mysteries of Maisie Hitchins Ser.: 1). (ENG.). 176p. (J). (gr. 3-7). pap. 7.99 *(978-0-544-58234-7(9),* 1613663, Clarion Bks.) HarperCollins Pubs.
—The Case of the Vanishing Emerald: The Mysteries of Maisie Hitchins Book 2. Lindsay, Marion, illus. 2016. (Mysteries of Maisie Hitchins Ser.: 2). (ENG.). 176p. (J). (gr. 3-7). pap. 6.99 *(978-0-544-66851-5(0),* 1625474, Clarion Bks.) HarperCollins Pubs.
Weeks, Sarah. Pie (Scholastic Gold) 2013. (ENG.). 192p. (J). (gr. 3-7). pap. 7.99 *(978-0-545-27012-0(X),* Scholastic Paperbacks) Scholastic, Inc.
Wegelius, Jakob & Graves, Peter. The Murderer's Ape. 2017. (Illus.). 588p. (YA). lib. bdg. *(978-1-101-93176-9(0),* Delacorte Pr) Random House Publishing Group.
Wegman, William. The Hardly Boys. Date not set. (J). *(978-0-7868-0195-4(6))* Hyperion Pr.
Weil, Zoe. Claude & Medea: The Hellburn Dogs. 2007. (ENG., Illus.). 112p. (J). (gr. 2-7). per. 12.00 *(978-1-59056-105-8(8))* Lantern Publishing & Media.
Wein, Elizabeth. The Pearl Thief. (ENG.). (YA). (gr. 7-12). 2018. 352p. pap. 10.99 *(978-1-4847-2370-8(8))* 2017. 336p. 18.99 *(978-1-4847-1716-5(3))* Hyperion Bks. for Children.
—The Pearl Thief. 2018. (YA). lib. bdg. 20.85 *(978-0-606-40964-3(5))* Turtleback.
Weiss, Ellen. The Mystery of Microsneezia: A ClueFinders Mystery Adventure. 2004. (Illus.). 96p. (J). pap. *(978-0-7630-7619-1(8))* Magma.
Welch, Jim. Steven Stevens' Killer App. 2012. (ENG.). 196p. pap. 16.50 *(978-1-105-06310-7(0))* Lulu Pr., Inc.
Wells, Charity. The Trouble with the Supernatural, 1 vol. 2010. 84p. pap. 19.95 *(978-1-4489-2117-1(1))* America Star Bks.
Wells, Dan. Active Memory. 2018. (Mirador Ser.: 3). (ENG.). 400p. (YA). (gr. 8). 17.99 *(978-0-06-234793-0(4),* Balzer & Bray) HarperCollins Pubs.
—Ones & Zeroes. 2018. (Mirador Ser.: 2). (ENG.). 432p. (YA). (gr. 8). pap. 9.99 *(978-0-06-234791-6(8),* Balzer & Bray) HarperCollins Pubs.
Wells, Helen. Cherry Ames, Boarding School Nurse. 10th ed. 2007. (Cherry Ames Nurse Stories Ser.). 224p. (YA). (gr. 7-12). 14.95 *(978-0-8261-0413-7(4))* Springer Publishing Co., Inc.
—Cherry Ames Boxed Set: Volumes 17-20. 2007. 896p. (J). 39.95 *(978-0-8261-0439-7(8))* Springer Publishing Co., Inc.
—Cherry Ames, Camp Nurse. 2007. (Cherry Ames Nurse Stories Ser.). 224p. (YA). (gr. 7-12). 14.95 *(978-0-8261-0417-5(7))* Springer Publishing Co., Inc.
—Cherry Ames, Companion Nurse. 2007. (Cherry Ames Nurse Stories Ser.). 224p. (J). (gr. 3-7). 14.95 *(978-0-8261-0431-1(2))* Springer Publishing Co., Inc.
—Cherry Ames, Cruise Nurse. 2007. (Cherry Ames Nurse Stories Ser.). 224p. (YA). (gr. 7-12). 14.95 *(978-0-8261-0411-3(8))* Springer Publishing Co., Inc.
—Cherry Ames, Department Store Nurse. 2007. (Cherry Ames Nurse Stories Ser.). 224p. (YA). (gr. 8-12). 14.95 *(978-0-8261-0415-1(0))* Springer Publishing Co., Inc.
—Cherry Ames, Island Nurse. 2007. (Cherry Ames Nurse Stories Ser.). 200p. (J). (gr. 3-7). 14.95 *(978-0-8261-0423-6(1))* Springer Publishing Co., Inc.
—Cherry Ames Jungle Nurse. 2007. (Cherry Ames Nurse Stories Ser.). 224p. (J). (gr. 3-7). 14.95 *(978-0-8261-0433-5(9))* Springer Publishing Co., Inc.
—Cherry Ames, Ski Nurse Mystery. 2007. (Cherry Ames Nurse Stories Ser.). 224p. (J). (gr. 3-7). 14.95 *(978-0-8261-0437-3(1))* Springer Publishing Co., Inc.
—Cherry Ames, the Mystery in the Doctor's Office. 2007. (Cherry Ames Nurse Stories Ser.). 224p. (J). (gr. 3-7). 14.95 *(978-0-8261-0435-9(5))* Springer Publishing Co., Inc.
—The Silver Ring Mystery: The Vicki Barr Flight Stewardess Series. 2011. 190p. 42.95 *(978-1-258-10005-6(3))* Literary Licensing, LLC.
Wells, Marcia. Doom at Grant's Tomb. Calo, Marcos, illus. 2017. (Eddie Red Undercover Ser.: 3). (ENG.). (J). (gr. 5-7). lib. bdg. 17.20 *(978-0-606-39813-8(9))* Turtleback.
—Eddie Red Undercover: Mystery in Mayan Mexico. Calo, Marcos, illus. 2016. (Eddie Red Undercover Ser.: 2). (ENG.). 224p. (J). (gr. 5-7). pap. 7.99 *(978-0-544-66850-8(2),* 1625472, Clarion Bks.) HarperCollins Pubs.
—Eddie Red Undercover: Mystery on Museum Mile. Calo, Marcos, illus. 2015. (Eddie Red Undercover Ser.). (ENG.). 256p. (J). (gr. 5-7). pap. 7.99 *(978-0-544-43940-5(6),* 1596839, Clarion Bks.) HarperCollins Pubs.
Wenger, Shaunda. The Farm Stand Mystery. 2006. (Early Explorers Ser.). (J). pap. *(978-1-4108-6121-4(X))* Benchmark Education Co.
West, Carly Anne. Missing Pieces: an AFK Book (Hello Neighbor #1), Vol. 1. Heitz, Tim, illus. 2018. (Hello Neighbor Ser.: 1). (ENG.). 208p. (J). (gr. 5-5). pap. 7.99 *(978-1-338-28007-4(4))* Scholastic, Inc.
West, Ella. Rain Fall. 2020. (ENG.). 224p. (J). (gr. 6-9). pap. 14.99 *(978-1-76029-683-4(X),* A&U Children's) Allen & Unwin AUS. Dist: Independent Pubs. Group.
West, Tracey. Ash Ketchum, Pokémon Detective (Pokémon Classic Chapter Book #10) 2018. (Pokémon Chapter Bks.: 10). (ENG.). 96p. (J). (gr. 2-5). pap. 4.99 *(978-1-338-28403-4(7))* Scholastic, Inc.
—The Audio Files. Harrington, Rich, illus. 2006. 96p. (J). pap. *(978-0-439-90719-4(5))* Scholastic, Inc.
—The Clothing Capers. Harrington, Rich, illus. 2007. 96p. (J). pap. *(978-0-439-91452-9(3))* Scholastic, Inc.
—The Fingerprint Files. Harrington, Rich, illus. 2007. 96p. (J). *(978-0-439-91451-2(5))* Scholastic, Inc.
—The Secret Cipher Cases. Harrington, Rich, illus. 2006. 96p. (J). *(978-0-439-91448-2(5))* Scholastic, Inc.
—The Teeny Tiny Cases. Harrington, Rich, illus. 2007. 96p. (J). *(978-0-439-91450-5(7))* Scholastic, Inc.
Westerfeld, Scott. So Yesterday. 2005. (ENG.). 256p. (YA). (gr. 7-12). reprint ed. 8.99 *(978-1-59514-032-6(8),* Razorbill) Penguin Young Readers Group.
Weyn, Suzanne. The Titanic Locket. 2014. (Hauntings: the Haunted Museum Ser.: 1). lib. bdg. 17.20 *(978-0-606-35809-5(9))* Turtleback.
Weyr, Garret. The Language of Spells: (Fantasy Middle Grade Novel, Magic & Wizard Book for Middle School Kids) Harnett, Katie, illus. 2018. (ENG.). 256p. (J). (gr. 5-9). 16.99 *(978-1-4521-5958-4(0))* Chronicle Bks. LLC.
Whalen, Diane. Tales of the Christmas Store. 2011. 92p. pap. 9.99 *(978-1-4567-1783-4(9))* AuthorHouse.
What's in the Suitcase, Grandma? My Solar-Powered History, Book 3. 2013. (Illus.). 116p. pap. 12.99 *(978-1-937848-08-8(6))* Do Life Right, Inc.
Wheeler, Esther. The Loner. 2003. (J). pap. 4.99 *(978-1-58608-614-5(6))* New Concepts Publishing.
Wheeler, Janet D. Billie Bradley & Her Inheritance or the Queer Homestead at Cherry Corners. 2004. reprint ed. pap. 20.95 *(978-1-4191-0995-9(2))* Kessinger Publishing, LLC.
Whelan, Gloria. After the Train. 2009. 160p. (J). lib. bdg. 16.89 *(978-0-06-029597-4(X))* HarperCollins Pubs.
Whild, Katharine. Marlowe the Great Detective. Whild, Katharine, illus. I.t. ed. 2005. (Illus.). 36p. (J). 16.95 *(978-0-9712488-4-7(2))* Deerbrook Editions.
Whitby, Adele. Beth's Story 1914. 2014. (Secrets of the Manor Ser.: 1). (ENG., Illus.). 160p. (J). (gr. 3-7). 16.99 *(978-1-4814-0632-1(9),* Simon Spotlight) Simon Spotlight.
White, J. Scratch & Sniff: The Case of the Stuck Seagull. 2013. 32p. pap. *(978-1-4602-0552-5(9))* FriesenPress.
White, Jan. Mystery of Mingus Mountain. 2012. (ENG., Illus.). 138p. (YA). (gr. 7-13). pap. 9.99 *(978-0-89824-370-3(X))* Royal Fireworks Publishing Co.
White, K. B. Adrianna Angelica Andrea Mystery Stories: The Case of the Missing Bath Towel. 2012. 24p. pap. 17.99 *(978-1-4772-7058-5(2))* AuthorHouse.
White, Ruth. Belle Prater's Boy. unabr. ed. 2004. 196p. (J). (gr. 5-9). pap. 38.00 incl. audio *(978-0-8072-8682-1(6),* YA234SP, Listening Library) Random Hse. Audio Publishing Group.
Whitehorn, Harriet. Violet & the Hidden Treasure. Moor, Becka, illus. 2017. (Violet Investigates Ser.: 2). (ENG.). 208p. (J). pap. 7.99 *(978-1-4711-1897-5(5),* Simon & Schuster Children's) Simon & Schuster, Ltd. GBR. Dist: Simon & Schuster, Inc.
—Violet & the Mummy Mystery. Moor, Becka, illus. 2018. (Violet Investigates Ser.: 4). (ENG.). 224p. (J). pap. 7.99 *(978-1-4711-4719-7(3),* Simon & Schuster Children's) Simon & Schuster, Ltd. GBR. Dist: Simon & Schuster, Inc.
—Violet & the Pearl of the Orient. Moor, Becka, illus. 2017. (Violet Investigates Ser.: 1). (ENG.). 192p. (J). pap. 7.99 *(978-1-4711-1895-1(9),* Simon & Schuster Children's) Simon & Schuster, Ltd. GBR. Dist: Simon & Schuster, Inc.
—Violet & the Smugglers. Moor, Becka, illus. (Violet Investigates Ser.: 3). (ENG.). 208p. (J). 2018. pap. 7.99 *(978-1-4711-1899-9(1))* 2016. 13.00 *(978-1-4711-2263-7(8))* Simon & Schuster, Ltd. GBR. (Simon & Schuster Children's). Dist: Simon & Schuster, Inc.
Whybrow, Ian. Little Wolf, Forest Detective. Ross, Tony, illus. 2005. (Middle Grade Fiction Ser.). 112p. (J). (gr. 3-6). 14.95 *(978-1-57505-413-1(2));* pap. 6.95 *(978-1-57505-829-0(4))* Lerner Publishing Group.
—Little Wolf, Pack Leader. Ross, Tony, illus. 2005. (Little Wolf Adventures Ser.). 126p. (gr. 3-6). 14.95 *(978-1-57505-400-1(0))* Lerner Publishing Group.
Whyte, June. Murder Sucks. 2008. (ENG., Illus.). 192p. (J). pap. 12.99 *(978-1-934841-12-9(9),* Zumaya Thresholds) Zumaya Pubns. LLC.
Wickstrom, Lois June & Darling, Lucrecia. The Orange Forest Rabbit Mysteries: Book One. 2003. (J). per. 13.95 *(978-0-916176-23-5(1))* Gripper Products.
Widmark, Martin. The Diamond Mystery #1, No. 1. Willis, Helena, illus. 2014. (Whodunit Detective Agency Ser.: 1). (ENG.). 80p. (J). (gr. 2-4). 5.99 *(978-0-448-48066-4(2),* Grosset & Dunlap) Penguin Young Readers Group.
—The Movie Theater Mystery, 7. Willis, Helena, illus. 2016. (Whodunit Detective Agency Ser.). (ENG.). 80p. (J). (gr. 2-4). 18.69 *(978-1-4844-6957-6(7))* Penguin Publishing Group.
Wight, Tamra. Mystery of the Bear Cub, 1 vol. DiRocco, Carl, illus. 2017. (Cooper & Packrat Ser.: 4). (ENG.). 176p. (J). 16.95 *(978-1-944762-25-4(6),* d6c0afff-df5c-441d-b712-69203d6e12ea) Islandport Pr., Inc.
—Mystery of the Missing Fox, 1 vol. 2016. (Cooper & Packrat Ser.: 3). (ENG., Illus.). 206p. (J). 16.95 *(978-1-939017-89-5(0),* 6ccdf9e6-7c93-4da4-86f6-95eedc361b45) Islandport Pr., Inc.
—Mystery on Pine Lake: A Cooper & Packrat Mystery, 1 vol. 2015. (Cooper & Packrat Ser.: 1). (ENG., Illus.). 152p. (J). pap. 14.95 *(978-1-939017-02-4(5),* 202c881d-3dfa-4e4f-bc6b-4b781159627d) Islandport Pr., Inc.
Wilcox. The Hidden Men. (Thumbprint Mysteries Ser.). 32.86 *(978-0-8092-0415-1(0))* McGraw-Hill/Contemporary.
Wild, Ailsa. Squishy Taylor, 6 vols. Wood, Ben, illus. 2018. (Squishy Taylor Ser.). (ENG.). 128p. (J). (gr. 2-4). pap., pap., pap. 41.70 *(978-1-5158-1996-7(5),* 27348, Picture Window Bks.) Capstone.
—Squishy Taylor & the Mess Makers. 2018. (Squishy Taylor Ser.). (ENG., Illus.). 128p. (J). (gr. 2-4). pap. 6.95 *(978-1-5158-1973-8(6),* 136645, Picture Window Bks.) Capstone.
—Squishy Taylor & the Vase That Wasn't. 2018. (Squishy Taylor Ser.). (ENG., Illus.). 128p. (J). (gr. 2-4). pap. 6.95 *(978-1-5158-1974-5(4),* 136644, Picture Window Bks.) Capstone.
—Squishy Taylor in Zero Gravity. 2018. (Squishy Taylor Ser.). (ENG., Illus.). 128p. (J). (gr. 2-4). lib. bdg. 25.32 *(978-1-5158-1980-6(9),* 136647, Picture Window Bks.) Capstone.
Wild, Ailsa. Squishy Taylor & the Mess-Makers. Wood, Ben, illus. 2017. (Squishy Taylor Ser.). (ENG.). 128p. (J). (gr. 2-4). lib. bdg. 25.32 *(978-1-5158-1957-8(4),* 136640, Picture Window Bks.) Capstone.
—Squishy Taylor & the Vase That Wasn't. Wood, Ben, illus. 2017. (Squishy Taylor Ser.). (ENG.). 128p. (J). (gr. 2-4). lib. bdg. 25.32 *(978-1-5158-1958-5(2),* 136641, Picture Window Bks.) Capstone.
Wiles, Patricia. Early-Morning Cemetery: A Novel. 2006. 243p. (YA). pap. *(978-1-59811-077-7(2))* Covenant Communications.
Wilkes, Nita. Stalking Bailey. 2010. 185p. pap. 10.95 *(978-1-4327-4862-3(9))* Outskirts Pr., Inc.
Wilkey, David. Through the Black Hole: The Incredible Adventures of Justin Hart. 2003. 154p. pap. 12.95 *(978-0-595-29497-8(9))* iUniverse, Inc.
Willems, Mo. Who Is the Mystery Reader?-An Unlimited Squirrels Book. 2019. (Unlimited Squirrels Ser.). (ENG., Illus.). 96p. (J). (gr. -1-3). 12.99 *(978-1-368-04686-2(X),* Hyperion Books for Children) Disney Publishing Worldwide.
William H. Sadlier Staff. The Yellow Yarn Mystery. 2005. (Emergent Library: Vol. 2). (gr. -1-1). 24.00 net. *(978-0-8215-8938-0(5))* Sadlier, William H. Inc.
Williams, Brenda May. The Shop of Magical Things. 2013. (ENG., Illus.). 44p. pap. 13.50 *(978-1-78035-526-9(2),* Fastprint Publishing) Upfront Publishing Ltd. GBR. Dist: Printondemand-worldwide.com.
Williams, Carol Lynch. The Chosen One: A Novel. 2010. (ENG.). 240p. (YA). (gr. 7). pap. 15.99 *(978-0-312-62775-1(0),* 900065448, St. Martin's Griffin) St. Martin's Pr.
—Messenger. 2017. (ENG.). 288p. (YA). (gr. 7). pap. 10.99 *(978-1-4814-5777-4(2),* Simon & Schuster/Paula Wiseman Bks.) Simon & Schuster/Paula Wiseman Bks.
Williams, Hays. The Tangled Web: A Mother's Secret - a Jenny & Pete Mystery. 2013. 94p. pap. 12.95 *(978-1-62646-673-9(4))* Booklocker.com, Inc.
Williams, Vanessa A. The Missing Penny. 2013. 28p. pap. 9.95 *(978-1-4787-2429-2(3))* Outskirts Pr., Inc.
Wilson, Heather Gemmen. Lydia Barnes & the Escape from Shark Bay. 2008. 160p. (J). 9.99 *(978-0-89827-352-6(8))* Wesleyan Publishing Hse.
—Lydia Barnes & the Mystery of the Broken Cross. 2007. (Global Warning Ser.). 157p. (J). (gr. 3-7). per. 7.99 *(978-0-89827-351-9(X))* Wesleyan Publishing Hse.
Wilson, Jacqui. Little Johnny's Faith Adventures: Creation Curiosity! 2012. 30p. pap. 15.95 *(978-1-4497-5994-0(7),* WestBow Pr.) Author Solutions, LLC.
Wilson, John. Lost. 2016. (Orca Currents Ser.). lib. bdg. 20.80 *(978-0-606-38694-4(7))* Turtleback.
Wilson, W. Shane. War for Ice. 2010. 158p. pap. 13.99 *(978-0-557-23572-8(3))* Lulu Pr., Inc.
Winfield, Arthur M. Putnam Hall Champions or Bound to Win Ou. 2006. pap. 28.95 *(978-1-4286-2346-0(9))* Kessinger Publishing, LLC.
—The Rover Boys on the Plains or the Mystery of Red Rock Ranch. 2004. reprint ed. pap. 27.95 *(978-1-4179-2626-8(0))* Kessinger Publishing, LLC.
—The Rover Boys on the River. 2007. 248p. 26.95 *(978-1-4218-4139-7(8));* per. 11.95 *(978-1-4218-4237-0(8))* 1st World Publishing, Inc. (1st World Library - Literary Society).
Wingo, W. Bruce. There Grows a Crooked Tree. 2003. 188p. 23.95 *(978-0-595-75271-3(3));* pap. 13.95 *(978-0-595-28903-5(7))* iUniverse, Inc.
Winter, Barbara. The Golden Scarab. 2007. (Illus.). 48p. (J). lib. bdg. 15.00 *(978-1-4242-1617-8(6))* Dingles & Co.
Winters, Ben H. The Mystery of the Missing Everything. 2012. (ENG.). 272p. (J). (gr. 3-7). pap. 6.99 *(978-0-06-196546-3(4),* HarperCollins) HarperCollins Pubs.
Wirt, Mildred A. Guilt of the Brass Thieves. 2011. 178p. pap. 9.99 *(978-1-935774-80-8(8),* Resurrected Pr.) Intrepid Ink, LLC.
—Saboteurs on the River. 2011. 174p. pap. 12.99 *(978-1-935774-86-0(7),* Resurrected Pr.) Intrepid Ink, LLC.
—Signal in the Dark. 2011. 170p. pap. 9.99 *(978-1-935774-82-2(4),* Resurrected Pr.) Intrepid Ink, LLC.
—Swamp Island. 2011. 176p. pap. 12.99 *(978-1-935774-85-3(9),* Resurrected Pr.) Intrepid Ink, LLC.
—Voice from the Cave. 2011. 168p. pap. 9.99 *(978-1-935774-81-5(6),* Resurrected Pr.) Intrepid Ink, LLC.
—Whispering Walls. 2011. 174p. pap. 9.99 *(978-1-935774-83-9(2),* Resurrected Pr.) Intrepid Ink, LLC.
Witrago, Jost. The Wooden Dove. 2007. 16p. per. 24.95 *(978-1-4241-9011-9(8))* America Star Bks.
Wofford, Delaney. For Courage. 2010. 229p. pap. 17.98 *(978-0-557-17045-6(1))* Lulu Pr., Inc.
Wolf, Jennifer Shaw. Dead Girls Don't Lie. (ENG.). 2014. 368p. (YA). (gr. 9). pap. 12.99 *(978-0-8027-3753-3(6),* 900135679)

2013. 304p. E-Book 7.99 *(978-0-8027-3450-1(2))* Bloomsbury Publishing USA. (Bloomsbury USA Childrens).

Wolper, Joanna. The Man Who Could Be Santa. 2008. (Illus.). 78p. (J). pap. *(978-0-88092-765-9(8))*; lib. bdg. *(978-0-88092-764-2(X))* Royal Fireworks Publishing Co.

Wood, Audrey. Alphabet Mystery. Wood, Bruce, illus. 2003. (ENG.). 40p. (J). (gr. -1 — 1). 17.99 *(978-0-439-44337-1(7),* Blue Sky Pr., The) Scholastic, Inc.

Wood, Maryrose. The Incorrigible Children of Ashton Place Bk. 5: Book V: the Unmapped Sea. 2015. (Incorrigible Children of Ashton Place Ser.: 5). (ENG., Illus.). 416p. (J). (gr. 3-7). 15.99 *(978-0-06-211041-1(1),* Balzer & Bray) HarperCollins Pubs.

—The Incorrigible Children of Ashton Place: Book IV Bk. IV: The Interrupted Tale. Wheeler, Eliza, illus. 2013. (Incorrigible Children of Ashton Place Ser.: 4). (ENG.). 400p. (J). (gr. 3-7). 16.99 *(978-0-06-179122-2(9),* Balzer & Bray) HarperCollins Pubs.

Woodbury, Mary. The Innocent Polly McDoodle. 2005. (Polly McDoodle Mystery Ser.: Vol. 3). (ENG.). 192p. (J). (gr. 4-7). pap. 6.95 *(978-1-55050-168-1(2))* Coteau Bks. CAN. Dist: Fitzhenry & Whiteside, Ltd.

Woodfine, Katherine. The Mystery of the Clockwork Sparrow. 2017. (Illus.). 320p. (J). pap. 6.99 *(978-1-61067-437-9(5))* Kane Miller.

—The Mystery of the Jeweled Moth. 2017. (Illus.). 352p. (J). pap. 6.99 *(978-1-61067-438-6(3))* Kane Miller.

Woodfine, Katherine, et al. Mystery & Mayhem. 2016. (ENG., Illus.). 320p. (J). (gr. 3-5). pap. 7.99 *(978-1-4052-8264-2(9))* Farshore GBR. Dist: HarperCollins Pubs.

Woodland Mysteries. (gr. 3-7). Set 1. 424.95 *(978-0-7802-7245-3(5))*Set 2. 424.95 *(978-0-7802-8002-1(4))* Wright Group/McGraw-Hill.

Woodland Mysteries: Classroom Library Set. (gr. 3-7). 313.95 *(978-0-322-02628-5(8))* Wright Group/McGraw-Hill.

Woodland Mysteries: Complete Boxed Set. (gr. 3-7). 1238.95 *(978-0-322-02625-4(3))* Wright Group/McGraw-Hill.

Worley, Rob M. & Warner, Gertrude Chandler. Surprise Island, 1 vol. Dubisch, Michael, illus. 2009. (Boxcar Children Graphic Novels Ser.). (ENG.). 32p. (J). (gr. 3-8). 32.79 *(978-1-60270-587-6(9),* 3670, Graphic Planet - Fiction) Magic Wagon.

Wortman, Barbara. Key in the Candle. (Young Hawk Mystery Ser.). 189p. (YA). (gr. 7-18). 9.99 *(978-0-88092-379-8(2))* Royal Fireworks Publishing Co.

Wright, Betty Ren. Christina's Ghost. 2018. 112p. (J). (gr. 3-7). pap. 8.99 *(978-0-8234-3991-1(7))* Holiday Hse., Inc.

—The Dollhouse Murders (35th Anniversary Edition) Nickolls, Leo, illus. 35th ed. 2019. 160p. (J). (gr. 3-7). pap. 8.99 *(978-0-8234-3984-3(4))* Holiday Hse., Inc.

—The Dollhouse Murders (35th Anniversary Edition) 35th ed. 2018. 160p. (J). (gr. 3-7). 17.99 *(978-0-8234-4030-6(3))* Holiday Hse., Inc.

Wright, Deana. The Playground. 2009. 48p. pap. 9.95 *(978-1-60693-680-1(8),* Eloquent Bks.) Strategic Book Publishing & Rights Agency (SBPRA).

Wright, Dee. The Peanut Butter Finger Mystery. 2013. (Little Ruth Ser.). (ENG., Illus.). 38p. (J). pap. *(978-1-59684-606-7(2))* Penman Publishers.

Wright, Elsie. Patty & Jo, Detectives. 2005. reprint ed. pap. 24.95 *(978-1-4179-9752-7(4))* Kessinger Publishing, LLC.

Wright, Harold Bell. The Shepherd of the Hills. 2017. (ENG., Illus.). (J). 24.95 *(978-1-374-93262-3(0))* Capital Communications, Inc.

—The Shepherd of the Hills. 2018. (ENG., Illus.). (J). 190p. 19.95 *(978-1-64439-017-7(5))*; 188p. pap. 10.95 *(978-1-64439-016-0(7))* IndoEuropeanPublishing.com.

—The Shepherd of the Hills. 2018. (ENG., Illus.). 188p. (J). 19.99 *(978-1-5154-2506-9(1))* Wilder Pubns., Corp.

Wright Johnson, Shelli. Falcon in the Nest: A Story of Bes Adventure. 2004. 273p. pap. 27.95 *(978-1-4137-5263-2(2))* America Star Bks.

Wyatt, Merrill. Ernestine, Catastrophe Queen. 2018. (ENG., Illus.). 304p. (J). (gr. 3-7). 13.99 *(978-0-316-47158-9(5),* Jimmy Patterson) Little Brown & Co.

Wynne-Jones, Tim. The Boy in the Burning House. braille ed. 2003. (J). (gr. 2). spiral bd. *(978-0-616-15275-1(2))* Canadian National Institute for the Blind/Institut National Canadien pour les Aveugles.

—The Boy in the Burning House. 2003. (ENG.). 224p. (J). (gr. 5-9). pap. 13.99 *(978-0-374-40887-9(4),* 900021225, Farrar, Straus & Giroux (BYR)) Farrar, Straus & Giroux.

—The Boy in the Burning House, 1 vol. (ENG.). 232p. pap. 8.95 *(978-0-88899-500-1(8))* Groundwood Bks. CAN. Dist: Publishers Group West (PGW).

—The Ruinous Sweep. 400p. (YA). (gr. 9). 2019. pap. 9.99 *(978-1-5362-0879-5(5))* 2018. (ENG.). 18.99 *(978-0-7636-9745-7(1))* Candlewick Pr.

—The Uninvited. (ENG., Illus.). 368p. (YA). (gr. 9). 2010. pap. 8.99 *(978-0-7636-4826-8(4))* 2009. 16.99 *(978-0-7636-3984-6(2))* Candlewick Pr.

Yang, Gene Luen. Robots & Repeats. 2017. (Secret Coders Ser.: 4). (J). lib. bdg. 22.10 *(978-0-606-40541-6(0))* Turtleback.

Yardley, Liz. The Firefly Legacy - Book Vii. Yardley, Liz, illus. 2013. (Illus.). 314p. pap. *(978-0-9872013-2-4(8))* BlueFlower Bks.

Yasuda, Anita. The Beach Bandit, 1 vol. Harpster, Steve, illus. 2013. (Dino Detectives Ser.). (ENG.). 32p. (J). (gr. 1-2). pap. 5.95 *(978-1-4342-4830-5(5),* 121749); lib. bdg. 22.65 *(978-1-4342-4154-2(8),* 119898) Capstone. (Stone Arch Bks.).

—Crazy Clues. Harpster, Steve, illus. 2013. (Dino Detectives Ser.). (ENG.). 32p. (J). (gr. 1-2). pap. 5.95 *(978-1-4342-6200-4(6),* 123494, Stone Arch Bks.) Capstone.

—Ghost Sounds, 1 vol. Harpster, Steve, illus. 2013. (Dino Detectives Ser.). (ENG.). 32p. (J). (gr. 1-2). pap. 5.95 *(978-1-4342-4831-2(3),* 121750); lib. bdg. 22.65 *(978-1-4342-4152-8(1),* 119896) Capstone. (Stone Arch Bks.).

—The Missing Trumpet, 1 vol. Harpster, Steve, illus. 2013. (Dino Detectives Ser.). (ENG.). 32p. (J). (gr. 1-2). pap. 5.95 *(978-1-4342-4832-9(1),* 121751, Stone Arch Bks.) Capstone.

—The Mystery Coins. Harpster, Steve, illus. 2013. (Dino Detectives Ser.). (ENG.). 32p. (J). (gr. 1-2). pap. 5.95 *(978-1-4342-6201-1(4),* 123495); lib. bdg. 22.65 *(978-1-4342-5972-1(2),* 122929) Capstone. (Stone Arch Bks.).

—The Slime Attack, 1 vol. Harpster, Steve, illus. 2013. (Dino Detectives Ser.). (ENG.). 32p. (J). (gr. 1-2). pap. 5.95 *(978-1-4342-4833-6(X),* 121752, Stone Arch Bks.) Capstone.

—The Surprise Prize. Harpster, Steve, illus. 2013. (Dino Detectives Ser.). (ENG.). 32p. (J). (gr. 1-2). pap. 5.95 *(978-1-4342-6198-4(0),* 123492); lib. bdg. 22.65 *(978-1-4342-5969-1(2),* 122926) Capstone. (Stone Arch Bks.).

Yasuda, Anita & Harpster, Steve. The Crazy Clues. 2013. (Dino Detectives Ser.). (ENG.). 32p. (J). (gr. 1-2). pap. 35.70 *(978-1-4342-6226-4(X),* 20031, Stone Arch Bks.) Capstone.

—The Mystery Coins. 2013. (Dino Detectives Ser.). (ENG.). 32p. (J). (gr. 1-2). pap. 35.70 *(978-1-4342-6228-8(6),* 20033, Stone Arch Bks.) Capstone.

—The Surprise Prize. 2013. (Dino Detectives Ser.). (ENG.). 32p. (J). (gr. 1-2). pap. 35.70 *(978-1-4342-6229-5(4),* 20034, Stone Arch Bks.) Capstone.

The Yellow Yarn Mystery: Take-Home Book. 2005. (Emergent Library: Vol. 2). (YA). (gr. -1-1). 12.60 *(978-0-8215-7268-9(7))* Sadlier, William H. Inc.

Ylvisaker, Anne. Button Down. 2013. (ENG.). 192p. (J). (gr. 3-7). pap. 8.99 *(978-0-7636-6463-3(4))* Candlewick Pr.

—The Luck of the Buttons. 2012. (ENG., Illus.). 240p. (J). (gr. 3-7). pap. 8.99 *(978-0-7636-6061-1(2))* Candlewick Pr.

Yoder, Eric & Yoder, Natalie. One Minute Mysteries: 65 Short Mysteries You Solve with Math! 2010. (One Minute Mysteries Ser.). (ENG., Illus.). 192p. (J). (gr. 5-9). pap. 12.95 *(978-0-9678020-0-8(8))* Platypus Media, L.L.C.

Yolen, Jane & Stemple, Heidi E. Y. The Salem Witch Trials: An Unsolved Mystery from History. Roth, Roger, Sr. & Roth, Roger, illus. 2004. (Unsolved Mystery from History Ser.). (ENG.). 32p. (J). (gr. 1-5). 18.99 *(978-0-689-84620-5(7),* Simon & Schuster Bks. For Young Readers) Simon & Schuster Bks. For Young Readers.

Yorke, Malcolm. La Casa de los Sustez. (Raton de Biblioteca Coleccion). (SPA., Illus.). 128p. (J). (gr. 3). 7.95 *(978-84-88061-71-3(4))* Serres, Ediciones, S. L. ESP. Dist: Lectorum Pubns., Inc.

Young, Brigit. Worth a Thousand Words. 2020. (ENG.). 304p. (J). pap. 7.99 *(978-1-250-30875-7(5),* 900177859) Square Fish.

Young, Judy. The Missing Grizzly Cubs. 2016. (Wild World of Buck Bray Ser.). (ENG.). 240p. (J). (gr. 3-6). 16.99 *(978-1-58536-970-6(5),* 204107) Sleeping Bear Pr.

—The Wolves of Slough Creek. 2019. (Wild World of Buck Bray Ser.). (ENG., Illus.). 240p. (J). (gr. 3-6). pap. 9.99 *(978-1-5341-1021-2(6),* 204662):Bk. 3. 16.99 *(978-1-5341-1020-5(8),* 204651) Sleeping Bear Pr.

Young, Karen Romano. A Girl, a Raccoon, & the Midnight Moon: (Juvenile Fiction, Mystery, Young Reader Detective Story, Light Fantasy for Kids) Bagley, Jessixa, illus. 2020. (ENG.). 392p. (J). (gr. 5-9). 16.99 *(978-1-4521-6952-1(7))* Chronicle Bks. LLC.

Young, Ruth. Aunty Marmalade. 2009. 218p. pap. 13.78 *(978-1-60693-893-5(2),* Eloquent Bks.) Strategic Book Publishing & Rights Agency (SBPRA).

Youree, Barbara. Senegal Sleuths. 2006. 56p. 7.75 *(978-0-8341-2226-0(X))* Beacon Hill Pr. of Kansas City.

Yuricich, Jillian Grace, illus. What did Grandma See? 2006. (J). lib. bdg. 15.99 *(978-0-9774696-0-4(3))* Gilboy Publishing.

Zafon, Carlos. Marina. 2011. (FRE.). (YA). (gr. 8-12). pap. *(978-2-266-21302-8(4))* Le Robert.

Zafon, Carlos Ruiz. Marina. 2014. (ENG.). 336p. (YA). (gr. 7-17). 34.99 *(978-0-316-04471-4(7))* Little, Brown Bks. for Young Readers.

Zalonis, C. B. Strangers in the Forest. 2006. (J). pap. 8.00 *(978-0-8059-6820-0(2))* Dorrance Publishing Co., Inc.

Zaugg, Sandra L. Secret of the Desert Lights: A Story about Following God's Laws. 2009. (J). pap. 9.99 *(978-0-8163-2294-7(5))* Pacific Pr. Publishing Assn.

Zaugg, Sandy. Murdock Mystery #2: The Cats of Rome. 2010. 88p. pap. 10.95 *(978-1-4327-5062-6(3))* Outskirts Pr., Inc.

Zindel, Paul. Egyptian Mystery. Date not set. 192p. (YA). (gr. 6-18). lib. bdg. 16.89 *(978-0-06-028509-8(5))* HarperCollins Pubs.

Zusak, Markus. I Am the Messenger. 2009. 10.52 *(978-0-7848-2491-7(6),* Everbind) Marco Bk. Co.

—I Am the Messenger. 2006. 21.00 *(978-0-7569-7034-5(2))* Perfection Learning Corp.

—I Am the Messenger. 368p. (YA). (gr. 7). 2005. (ENG.). 16.95 *(978-0-375-83099-0(5))* 2006. (Illus.). reprint ed. pap. 12.99 *(978-0-375-83667-1(5))* Random Hse. Children's Bks. (Knopf Bks. for Young Readers).

—I Am the Messenger. (J). 2007. 1.25 *(978-1-4281-2308-3(3))* 2007. 77.75 *(978-1-4281-2309-0(1))* 2006. 74.75 *(978-1-4281-2311-3(3))* Recorded Bks., Inc.

4RV Publishing LLC Staff. Case of the Missing Coach. 2007. (Illus.). 144p. (J). per. 18.99 *(978-0-9797513-1-8(4))* 4RV Pub.

MYTHICAL ANIMALS

see Animals, Mythical

MYTHOLOGY

see also Animals, Mythical; Art and Mythology; Folklore; Heroes; Indians of North America—Religion; Totems and Totemism

Alexander, David E. The Myths of the Lechuza. Smith, Duriel, illus. Date not set. 78p. (Orig.). (J). pap. 12.95 *(978-0-9623078-5-0(8))* Alexander Pubns.

Alexander, Heather. A Child's Introduction to Greek Mythology: The Stories of the Gods, Goddesses, Heroes, Monsters, & Other Mythical Creatures. Hamilton, Meredith, illus. 2011. (Child's Introduction Ser.). (ENG.). 96p. (J). (gr. 3-7). 19.99 *(978-1-57912-867-8(X),* 81867, Black Dog & Leventhal Pubs. Inc.) Hachette Bks.

Allan, Tony. Exploring the Life, Myth, & Art of Ancient Rome, 1 vol. 2011. (Civilizations of the World Ser.). (ENG.). 144p. (YA). (gr. 8-8). lib. bdg. 47.80 *(978-1-4488-4831-7(8),* 46841046-c322-44aa-8cf6-b0825a3804bb) Rosen Publishing Group, Inc., The.

Allan, Tony, et al. Exploring the Life, Myth, & Art of the Medieval World, 1 vol. 2016. (Civilizations of the World Ser.). (ENG., Illus.). 144p. (J). (gr. 8-8). lib. bdg. 47.80 *(978-1-4994-6395-8(2),* f46f5467-4047-4cf2-acc8-1ecf2db1727a) Rosen Publishing Group, Inc., The.

Amery, H. Mini Greek Myths. rev. ed. 2013. (Mini Editions Ser.). 128p. (J). ring bd. 7.99 *(978-0-7945-3366-3(3),* Usborne) EDC Publishing.

Apel, Melanie Ann. Art & Religion in Ancient Greece, 1 vol. 2003. (Primary Sources of Ancient Civilizations: Egypt, Greece, & Rome Ser.). (ENG., Illus.). 24p. (gr. 3-4). pap. 8.25 *(978-0-8239-8938-6(0),* 822ab9c7-ff4b-46d1-b1ee-15fdb3f45bda, PowerKids Pr.) Rosen Publishing Group, Inc., The.

Aperlo, Peter. The Unofficial Magnus Chase & the Gods of Asgard Companion: The Norse Heroes, Monsters & Myths Behind the Hit Series. 2015. (Illus.). 242p. (J). *(978-1-5182-0351-0(5))* Ulysses Pr.

Armitage, Kimo. Akua Hawaii: Hawaiian Gods & Their Stories. Enos, Solomon, illus. 2005. 72p. (J). 16.95 *(978-1-58178-042-0(7))* Bishop Museum Pr.

Aronson, Marc & Mayor, Adrienne. The Griffin & the Dinosaur: How Adrienne Mayor Discovered a Fascinating Link Between Myth & Science. 2014. (Illus.). 48p. (J). (gr. 5-9). 18.99 *(978-1-4263-1108-6(7),* National Geographic Kids) Disney Publishing Worldwide.

Arrington, Joseph & Parker, Mike. The World's Most Unusual Humans. 2016. (Making Headlines Ser.). 160p. (J). lib. bdg. 39.93 *(978-0-7660-8380-6(2))* Enslow Publishing, LLC.

Baldwin, James. Old Greek Stories. 2006. (Illus.). pap. *(978-1-4065-0511-5(0))* Dodo Pr.

—Old Greek Stories. 2005. 192p. pap. 11.95 *(978-1-4218-0155-1(8),* 1st World Library - Literary Society) 1st World Publishing, Inc.

—Old Greek Stories. 2004. reprint ed. pap. 1.99 *(978-1-4192-3803-1(5))*; pap. 19.95 *(978-1-4191-3803-4(0))* Kessinger Publishing, LLC.

—Old Greek Stories. 2008. (Illus.). 192p. pap. 9.95 *(978-1-59915-296-7(7))* Yesterday's Classics.

Barker, Geoff. What Is a Myth?, 1 vol., 1. 2013. (Britannica Common Core Library). (ENG., Illus.). 32p. (J). (gr. 2-3). 27.04 *(978-1-62275-195-2(7),* 50dda2c0-d93d-48b6-9c62-70f383cfbaea) Rosen Publishing Group, Inc., The.

Baxter, Nicola. Celtic Tales & Legends. Shuttleworth, Cathie, illus. 2012. 80p. (J). (gr. 2-7). pap. 9.99 *(978-1-84322-950-6(1))* Anness Publishing GBR. Dist: National Bk. Network.

Belinda, Gallagher. Myths & Legends. Kelly, Richard, ed. 2017. (Illus.). 5120p. (J). pap. 23.95 *(978-1-78617-126-9(0))* Miles Kelly Publishing, Ltd. GBR. Dist: Parkwest Pubns., Inc.

Benjamin, Cynthia, adapted by. Hare Rescues the Sun: And Other Sky Myths. 2003. (ENG., Illus.). 56p. (J). (gr. 6-8). pap. 9.00 net. *(978-0-7652-3278-6(2))* Celebration Pr.

Benson, Jodyanne. Medusa, 1 vol. 2019. (Women of Mythology: Goddesses, Warriors, & Hunters Ser.). (ENG.). 32p. (J). (gr. 2-2). pap. 9.22 *(978-1-5026-5140-2(8),* 5f098213-27f8-4887-8324-63e059ad94cf) Cavendish Square Publishing LLC.

—Pandora, 1 vol. 2019. (Women of Mythology: Goddesses, Warriors, & Hunters Ser.). (ENG.). 32p. (gr. 2-2). pap. 9.22 *(978-1-5026-5144-0(0),* 4e9016f3-96ef-4370-a4f6-4e750ee17021) Cavendish Square Publishing LLC.

Bernard, Catherine. Celtic Mythology Rocks!, 1 vol. 2011. (Mythology Rocks! Ser.). (ENG., Illus.). 104p. (gr. 6-7). pap. 13.88 *(978-1-59845-326-3(2),* 67466d3f-fa92-4ac4-804a-613144f703c6) Enslow Publishing, LLC.

Bernard, Evslin. Heroes, Gods & Monsters of the Greek Myths. 2014. (ENG.). 224p. (YA). (gr. 12-12). 11.24 *(978-1-63245-079-1(8))* Lectorum Pubns., Inc.

Besant, Annie W. Legends & Tales Lotus Leaves for the Y. 2006. pap. 19.95 *(978-1-4286-2494-8(5))* Kessinger Publishing, LLC.

Bingham, Jane. Chinese Myths, 1 vol. Kennedy, Graham & Sansom, Fiona, illus. 2009. (Myths from Many Lands Ser.). (ENG.). 48p. (YA). (gr. 5-5). 33.93 *(978-1-60754-218-6(8),* acc54043-a190-42b2-8e8e-427821213f94); pap. 13.85 *(978-1-60754-219-3(6),* e2d91542-b494-48cd-97b8-2e45aee2391e) Rosen Publishing Group, Inc., The. (Windmill Bks.).

Black Ships Before Troy. 2011. 8.80 *(978-0-7848-3649-1(3),* Everbind) Marco Bk. Co.

Blackwood, Gary L. & Siburt, Ruth. Legends or Lies?, 1 vol. 2010. (History's Mysteries Ser.). (ENG.). 32p. (gr. 3-3). 31.21 *(978-0-7614-4359-9(2),* 758c1f57-b9d3-45ba-a68a-7dad885448c2) Cavendish Square Publishing LLC.

Bornemann Spies, Karen. Heroes in Greek Mythology Rock!, 1 vol. 2011. (Mythology Rocks! Ser.). (ENG., Illus.). 128p. (gr. 6-7). pap. 13.88 *(978-1-59845-331-7(9),* 0877ab5a-ce48-4f29-9ec7-43e7a62d6608) Enslow Publishing, LLC.

Boutland, Craig. Gashadokuro the Giant Skeleton & Other Legendary Creatures of Japan, 1 vol. 2018. (Cryptozoologist's Guide to Curious Creatures Ser.). (ENG.). 32p. (gr. 4-5). lib. bdg. 28.27 *(978-1-5382-2714-5(2),* 3ab7138a-4dc7-4e97-ad50-7058e2e26684) Stevens, Gareth Publishing LLLP.

Bowen, Carl. Thor & Loki. Smith, Tod & Lokus, Rex, illus. 2016. (Norse Myths: a Viking Graphic Novel Ser.). (ENG.). 56p. (J). (gr. 4-8). pap. 5.95 *(978-1-4965-3494-1(8),* 132606, Stone Arch Bks.) Capstone.

Braun, Eric. Egyptian Myths. 2018. (Mythology Around the World Ser.). (ENG., Illus.). 32p. (J). (gr. 3-6). lib. bdg. 27.99 *(978-1-5157-9603-9(5),* 136776, Capstone Pr.) Capstone.

—Greek Myths. 2018. (Mythology Around the World Ser.). (ENG., Illus.). 32p. (J). (gr. 3-6). lib. bdg. 27.99 *(978-1-5157-9606-0(X),* 136779, Capstone Pr.) Capstone.

—Loki. 2017. (Gods of Legend Ser.). (ENG.). 32p. (gr. 2-7). 9.95 *(978-1-68072-447-9(9))*; (J). (gr. 4-6). pap. 9.99 *(978-1-64466-178-9(0),* 11404) Black Rabbit Bks. (Bolt).

—Mythology Around the World. 2018. (Mythology Around the World Ser.). (ENG.). 32p. (J). (gr. 3-6). 119.96 *(978-1-5157-9635-0(3),* 27417, Capstone Pr.) Capstone.

—Roman Myths. 2018. (Mythology Around the World Ser.). (ENG., Illus.). 32p. (J). (gr. 3-6). lib. bdg. 27.99 *(978-1-5157-9605-3(1),* 136778, Capstone Pr.) Capstone.

—Zeus. 2017. (Gods of Legend Ser.). (ENG., Illus.). 32p. (J). (gr. 4-6). lib. bdg. *(978-1-68072-141-6(0),* 10466, Bolt) Black Rabbit Bks.

Brezina, Corona. Celtic Mythology. 2009. (Mythology Around the World Ser.). 64p. (gr. 5-5). 58.50 *(978-1-61514-748-9(9),* Rosen Reference) Rosen Publishing Group, Inc., The.

Briggs, Korwin. Gods & Heroes: Mythology Around the World. 2018. (ENG., Illus.). 304p. (J). (gr. 3-7). 22.99 *(978-1-5235-0378-0(5),* 100378) Workman Publishing Co., Inc.

Buckey, A. W. Greek Gods, Heroes, & Mythology. 2018. (Gods, Heroes, & Mythology Ser.). (ENG., Illus.). 48p. (J). (gr. 4-8). lib. bdg. 35.64 *(978-1-5321-1782-4(5),* 30852) ABDO Publishing Co.

Campbell, Trenton, ed. Gods & Goddesses of Ancient China, 1 vol. 2014. (Gods & Goddesses of Mythology Ser.). (ENG.). 128p. (J). (gr. 8-8). 36.49 *(978-1-62275-393-2(3),* 1af79c2d-0327-4b71-a753-f44588107250) Rosen Publishing Group, Inc., The.

Child's Book of Myths & Enchantments. (J). (gr. 4-7). 12.95 *(978-1-56288-395-9(X))* Checkerboard Pr., Inc.

Christopher, Neil. Those That Cause Fear, 1 vol. Amattaujuq (Arnaktauyok), Germaine, illus. 2016. (ENG.). 48p. (J). (gr. 1-3). 16.95 *(978-1-77227-085-3(7))* Inhabit Media Inc. CAN. Dist: Consortium Bk. Sales & Distribution.

Claybourne, Anna. Greek Myths, 1 vol. Sansom, Fiona, illus. 2009. (Myths from Many Lands Ser.). (ENG.). 48p. (YA). (gr. 5-5). 33.93 *(978-1-60754-224-7(2),* 2820da33-ddf7-41b2-9a28-60bfcb3c8edb); pap. 13.85 *(978-1-60754-225-4(0),* 5ebf3cdd-dd6c-4bc7-98ee-7e0fb4a5d08a) Rosen Publishing Group, Inc., The. (Windmill Bks.).

Collier, Irene Dea. Chinese Mythology Rocks!, 1 vol. 2011. (Mythology Rocks! Ser.). (ENG., Illus.). 128p. (gr. 6-7). pap. 13.88 *(978-1-59845-330-0(0),* 02ae1735-93c8-4bd7-b2f6-7db99e9d7dcc); lib. bdg. 35.93 *(978-0-7660-3898-1(X),* 2d6623fb-62af-433c-a686-7ec4b578ce33) Enslow Publishing, LLC.

Colum, Padraic. The Golden Fleece: And the Heroes Who Lived Before Achilles. Pogány, Willy, illus. 2004. 316p. (J). (gr. 5). 17.60 *(978-0-7569-4048-5(6))* Perfection Learning Corp.

—The Golden Fleece: And the Heroes Who Lived Before Achilles. Pogany, Willy, illus. 2019. (ENG.). 320p. (J). (gr. 5-9). 18.99 *(978-1-5344-5036-3(X),* Aladdin) Simon & Schuster Children's Publishing.

Coolidge, Olivia E. Hercules & Other Tales from Greek Myths. Lockhart, David, illus. 2011. 120p. 39.95 *(978-1-258-02308-9(3))* Literary Licensing, LLC.

Cope, Beatrice. Mythical Monsters. 2014. (ENG., Illus.). 32p. (J). lib. bdg. 25.70 *(978-1-62469-003-7(3))* Purple Toad Publishing, Inc.

Cox, Barbara & Forbes, Scott. Beyond the Grave, 1 vol., Vol. 1. 2014. (Creepy Chronicles Ser.). (ENG., Illus.). 32p. (J). (gr. 5-6). 29.27 *(978-1-4824-0226-1(2),* b31805b5-ea17-4efe-9dc3-194774bd20bc) Stevens, Gareth Publishing LLLP.

Crabtree Staff & Hynson, Colin. Understanding Indian Myths, 1 vol. 2012. (ENG., Illus.). 48p. (J). pap. *(978-0-7787-4529-7(5))* Crabtree Publishing Co.

Croy, Anita. Myths & Legends of Ancient Rome. 2015. (Illus.). 64p. (J). *(978-0-7166-2635-0(7))* World Bk., Inc.

—Myths & Legends of Australia, New Zealand, & Pacific Islands. 2015. (Illus.). 64p. (J). *(978-0-7166-2629-9(2))* World Bk., Inc.

Dalal, Anita. Mesoamerican Myths, 1 vol. 2010. (Myths from Around the World Ser.). (ENG.). 48p. (gr. 6-8). (YA). lib. bdg. 33.67 *(978-1-4339-3539-8(2),* f5b2a7b1-80b5-4db5-b7d3-be0d6cea955c); (Illus.). (J). pap. 15.05 *(978-1-4339-3540-4(6),* c60c079f-591b-4f6f-a3a4-df028d331ff0) Stevens, Gareth Publishing LLLP. (Gareth Stevens Secondary Library).

Daning, Tom. Chinese Mythology: The Four Dragons. 2009. (Jr. Graphic Mythologies Ser.). (ENG.). 24p. (J). (gr. 2-3). 47.90 *(978-1-61513-858-6(7),* PowerKids Pr.) Rosen Publishing Group, Inc., The.

—Chinese Mythology: The Four Dragons, 1 vol. 2006. (Jr. Graphic Mythologies Ser.). (ENG., Illus.). 24p. (gr. 2-3). pap. 10.60 *(978-1-4042-2153-6(0),* 3f24e985-65e7-4288-b252-95b87a6a0347, PowerKids Pr.) Rosen Publishing Group, Inc., The.

—Mitología China: Los Cuatro Dragones, 1 vol. 2009. (Historietas Juveniles: Mitologías (Jr. Graphic Mythologies) Ser.). (SPA., Illus.). 24p. (gr. 2-3). pap. 10.60 *(978-1-4358-3326-5(0),* 6d7cffcd-d246-4f3a-b346-cd7d5c1c3776) Rosen Publishing Group, Inc., The.

Demarco, Stacey. Goddesses & Sirens. Manton, Jimmy, illus. 2013. (ENG.). 176p. (YA). (gr. 7). 19.99 *(978-1-58270-381-7(7),* Beyond Words) Simon & Schuster.

—Gods & Titans. Manton, Jimmy, illus. 2013. (ENG.). 160p. (YA). (gr. 7). 19.99 *(978-1-58270-380-0(9),* Beyond Words) Simon & Schuster.

Demi. Shiva. 2020. (Illus.). 36p. (J). (gr. k-3). 17.95 *(978-1-937786-83-0(8),* Wisdom Tales) World Wisdom, Inc.

Dickmann, Nancy. Stars of Mythology: Chinese. (Stars of Mythology Ser.). (ENG.). 32p. (J). (gr. 4-6). 2020. pap. 12.99 *(978-1-4451-5193-9(6))* 2018. (Illus.). 16.99 *(978-1-4451-5192-2(8))* Hachette Children's Group GBR. (Franklin Watts). Dist: Hachette Bk. Group.

—Stars of Mythology: Indian. (Stars of Mythology Ser.). (ENG.). 32p. (J). (gr. 4-6). 2020. pap. 12.99 *(978-1-4451-5195-3(2))* 2018. (Illus.). 16.99 *(978-1-4451-5194-6(4))* Hachette Children's Group GBR. (Franklin Watts). Dist: Hachette Bk. Group.

DK. Children's Book of Mythical Beasts & Magical Monsters. 2018. (DK Children's Book Of Ser.). (ENG.). 144p. (J). (gr. 2-5). pap. 16.99 *(978-1-4654-7462-9(5),* DK Children) Dorling Kindersley Publishing, Inc.

—Eyewitness Mythology: Discover the Amazing Adventures of Gods, Heroes, & Magical Beasts. 2017. (DK Eyewitness Ser.). (ENG., Illus.). 72p. (J). (gr. 3-7). pap. 9.99 *(978-1-4654-6246-6(5))*; lib. bdg. 19.99 *(978-1-4654-6254-1(6))* Dorling Kindersley Publishing, Inc. (DK Children).

D'Ottavi, Francesca, illus. Isis & Osiris, 1 vol. 2012. (Egyptian Myths Ser.). (ENG.). 32p. (J). (gr. 3-5). lib. bdg. 29.32 *(978-1-4048-7148-9(9),* 117143, Picture Window Bks.) Capstone.

Eastwood, Richard. Seven Welsh Folk Tales. 2006. (ENG., Illus.). 96p. (J). pap. 7.50 *(978-1-84323-598-9(6))* Gomer Pr. GBR. Dist: Casemate Pubs. & Bk. Distributors, LLC.

Elgin, Kathy. Roman Myths, 1 vol. Sansom, Fiona, illus. 2009. (Myths from Many Lands Ser.). (ENG.). 48p. (gr. 5-5). (J). 33.93 *(978-1-60754-230-8(7),* 231041ad-daac-4df5-98fe-57117c530659); (YA). pap. 13.85 *(978-1-60754-231-5(5),* 857d196b-1423-4eca-8434-135bb90368d8) Rosen Publishing Group, Inc., The. (Windmill Bks.).

Encyclopaedia Britannica, Inc. Staff, compiled by. Legends, Myths & Folktales. 2003. (Illus.). 64p. 14.95 *(978-1-59339-037-2(8))* Encyclopaedia Britannica, Inc.

Fleischman, Paul. Dateline: Troy. Morrow, Glenn & Frankfeldt, Gwen, illus. 2006. (ENG.). 80p. (J). (gr. 7-10). pap. 8.99 *(978-0-7636-3084-3(5))* Candlewick Pr.

Flynn, Sarah Wassner. Weird but True Know-It-All: Greek Mythology. 2018. (Weird but True Ser.). (ENG., Illus.). 192p. (J). (gr. 3-7). lib. bdg. 22.90 *(978-1-4263-3190-9(8),* National Geographic Kids) Disney Publishing Worldwide.

—Weird but True KnowItAll: Greek Mythology. 2018. (Weird but True Ser.). (Illus.). 192p. (J). (gr. 3-7). pap. 12.99 *(978-1-4263-3189-3(4),* National Geographic Kids) Disney Publishing Worldwide.

Gagne, Tammy. Chinese Gods, Heroes, & Mythology. 2018. (Gods, Heroes, & Mythology Ser.). (ENG., Illus.). 48p. (J). (gr. 4-8). lib. bdg. 35.64 *(978-1-5321-1780-0(9),* 30848) ABDO Publishing Co.

—Indian Gods, Heroes, & Mythology. 2018. (Gods, Heroes, & Mythology Ser.). (ENG.). 48p. (J). (gr. 4-8). lib. bdg. 35.64 *(978-1-5321-1783-1(3),* 30854) ABDO Publishing Co.

—Japanese Gods, Heroes, & Mythology. 2018. (Gods, Heroes, & Mythology Ser.). (ENG., Illus.). 48p. (J). (gr. 4-8). lib. bdg. 35.64 *(978-1-5321-1784-8(1),* 30856) ABDO Publishing Co.

Ganeri, Anita. Mesoamerican Myth: a Treasury of Central American Legends, Art, & History: A Treasury of Central American Legends, Art, & History. 2007. (ENG., Illus.). 96p. (C). (gr. 6-18). lib. bdg. 180.00 *(978-0-7656-8106-5(4),* Y182745) Routledge.

Garcia, Emmett Shkeme. Coyote & the Sky: How the Sun, Moon, & Stars Began. Pringle, Victoria, illus. 2006. (ENG.). 32p. (J). (gr. 6-18). 19.95 *(978-0-8263-3730-6(9),* P121378) Univ. of New Mexico Pr.

Gerstein, Mordicai. I Am Hermes! Mischief-Making Messenger of the Gods. 2019. (ENG., Illus.). 72p. (J). (gr. 3-7). 18.99 *(978-0-8234-3942-3(9))* Holiday Hse., Inc.

Giles, Bridget. West African Myths, 1 vol. 2010. (Myths from Around the World Ser.). (ENG.). 48p. (gr. 6-8). (YA). lib. bdg. 33.67 *(978-1-4339-3536-7(8),* 91a104ec-ce3a-47ef-89ff-616a00cc969a); (Illus.). (J). pap. 15.05 *(978-1-4339-3537-4(6),* 7dfa905b-cdf2-40e6-a227-a21c2e16da01) Stevens, Gareth Publishing LLLP. (Gareth Stevens Secondary Library).

Gill, Shelley. Up on Denali: Alaska's Wild Mountain. Cartwright, Shannon, illus. 2006. (Paws IV Ser.). (ENG.). 32p. (J). (gr. -1-2). pap. 11.99 *(978-1-57061-365-4(6),* Little Bigfoot) Sasquatch Bks.

Gods & Goddesses of Mythology: Set 2, 16 vols. 2014. (Gods & Goddesses of Mythology Ser.). (ENG.). (YA). (gr. 8-8). 120-128p. 291.92 *(978-1-62275-762-6(9),* eb581f2c-a558-4ef7-acc6-e10b46bb92fe); 160p. 145.96 *(978-1-62275-402-1(6),* 32b1461e-2b4e-4213-8898-09feab0734a9) Rosen Publishing Group, Inc., The.

Gods & Goddesses of Mythology: Sets 1-2, 16 vols. 2014. (Gods & Goddesses of Mythology Ser.). (ENG.). 160p. (YA). (gr. 8-8). 291.92 *(978-1-62275-537-0(5),* 5b6eea00-bd00-4f36-8e1a-d9984dbe31ec) Rosen Publishing Group, Inc., The.

Green, Jen. Ancient Greek Myths, 1 vol. 2010. (Myths from Around the World Ser.). (ENG.). 48p. (gr. 6-8). (YA). lib. bdg. 33.67 *(978-1-4339-3524-4(4),* 1e4d0cc8-74d9-4741-92c0-0a40cb90d7f0); (Illus.). (J). pap. 15.05 *(978-1-4339-3525-1(2),* 8e9c8fc7-594e-433d-a5e0-89994838166f) Stevens, Gareth Publishing LLLP. (Gareth Stevens Secondary Library).

—Chinese & Japanese Myths, 1 vol. 2010. (Myths from Around the World Ser.). (ENG.). 48p. (gr. 6-8). (YA). lib. bdg. 33.67 *(978-1-4339-3533-6(3),* 9261b862-cb91-4c9d-afd7-6f52540c9af0); (Illus.). (J). pap. 15.05 *(978-1-4339-3534-3(1),* 52a1970f-5541-4347-8a40-a998dd755ea5) Stevens, Gareth Publishing LLLP. (Gareth Stevens Secondary Library).

Green, Roger Lancelyn. Tales of the Greek Heroes. 2009. (Puffin Classics Ser.). (Illus.). 304p. (J). (gr. 5-7). pap. 8.99 *(978-0-14-132528-6(3),* Puffin Books) Penguin Young Readers Group.

Gregson, Agatha. Myths, 1 vol. 2019. (Cultures Connect Us! Ser.). (ENG.). 24p. (gr. 1-2). pap. 9.15 *(978-1-5382-3846-2(2),* c3c19e64-9616-4c56-ac78-d150643e0ccd) Stevens, Gareth Publishing LLLP.

Griffin, Ingrid. The Story of the Great Bear, 1 vol. 2015. (Stories in the Stars Ser.). (ENG., Illus.). 24p. (J). (gr. 1-2). pap. 9.15 *(978-1-4824-2665-6(X),* 64f75325-a4ef-4a1b-8fad-7e066ca11e17) Stevens, Gareth Publishing LLLP.

Guerlais, Gérald, illus. The Story of Orion: A Roman Constellation Myth, 1 vol. 2012. (Night Sky Stories Ser.). (ENG.). 24p. (J). (gr. 2-4). pap. 8.95 *(978-1-4048-7718-4(5),* 120448, Picture Window Bks.) Capstone.

Guillain, Charlotte. Writing & Staging Myths & Legends. 2016. (Writing & Staging Plays Ser.). (ENG., Illus.). 48p. (J). (gr. 4-6). lib. bdg. 35.99 *(978-1-4846-2772-3(5),* 131331, Heinemann) Capstone.

Gunderson, Jessica. Olympians vs. Titans: An Interactive Mythological Adventure. Aracabascio, Carolyn, illus. 2017. (You Choose: Ancient Greek Myths Ser.). (ENG.). 112p. (J). (gr. 3-7). pap. 6.95 *(978-1-5157-4825-0(1),* 134440, Capstone Pr.) Capstone.

Haaren, John. Famous Men of Greece. 2008. 112p. pap. 12.95 *(978-1-60459-523-9(X))* Wilder Pubns., Corp.

—Famous Men of Rome. 2008. 120p. pap. 12.95 *(978-1-60459-524-6(8))* Wilder Pubns., Corp.

Hale, Vincent, ed. Mesopotamian Gods & Goddesses, 1 vol., 1. 2013. (Gods & Goddesses of Mythology Ser.). (ENG.). 112p. (YA). (gr. 8-8). 36.49 *(978-1-62275-161-7(2),* c3343ce8-5ebb-4b7a-9ee2-6f37fad6c4db) Rosen Publishing Group, Inc., The.

Haus, Estudio, illus. Theseus & the Minotaur: A Graphic Retelling. 2015. (Ancient Myths Ser.). (ENG.). 32p. (J). (gr. 3-9). lib. bdg. 31.32 *(978-1-4914-2075-1(8),* 127553, Capstone Pr.) Capstone.

—The Voyages of Odysseus: A Graphic Retelling. 2015. (Ancient Myths Ser.). (ENG.). 32p. (J). (gr. 3-9). lib. bdg. 31.32 *(978-1-4914-2076-8(6),* 127554, Capstone Pr.) Capstone.

Hawthorne, Nathaniel. Tanglewood Tales for Girls & Boys. 2013. (Notable American Authors Ser.). 425p. reprint ed. lthr. 79.00 *(978-0-7812-3046-9(2))* Reprint Services Corp.

—A Wonder Book for Girls & Boys. 2013. (Notable American Authors Ser.). 425p. reprint ed. lthr. 79.00 *(978-0-7812-3045-2(4))* Reprint Services Corp.

Hayes, Amy. Medusa & Pegasus, 1 vol. 2015. (Creatures of Fantasy Ser.). (ENG.). 64p. (J). (gr. 6-6). 35.93 *(978-1-5026-0506-1(6),* ea69b058-c5b5-4af4-8f13-9615c38fca4a) Cavendish Square Publishing LLC.

Herdling, Glenn. African Mythology: Anansi. 2009. (Jr. Graphic Mythologies Ser.). (ENG.). 24p. (J). (gr. 2-3). 47.90 *(978-1-61513-855-5(2),* PowerKids Pr.) Rosen Publishing Group, Inc., The.

Herdling, Glenn & Obregón, José María. Mitología Griega: Jasón y el Vellocino de Oro, 1 vol. 2009. (Historietas Juveniles: Mitologías (Jr. Graphic Mythologies) Ser.). (SPA., Illus.). 24p. (J). (gr. 2-3). pap. 10.60 *(978-1-4358-3330-2(9),* 9a89a447-7eea-4c01-9a4a-87ae43fd25b3); lib. bdg. 28.93 *(978-1-4358-8568-4(6),* 04812e2d-65dc-43b2-a5af-c61e198852ca) Rosen Publishing Group, Inc., The.

Hibbert, Clare. Beliefs & Ideas That Changed the World. 2017. (Revolutions Ser.). (ENG., Illus.). 64p. (J). (gr. 3-6). 19.99 *(978-0-7123-5680-0(0))* British Library, The GBR. Dist: Independent Pubs. Group.

—Terrible Tales of Africa, 1 vol., Vol. 1. Jantner, Janos, illus. 2013. (Monstrous Myths Ser.). (ENG.). 32p. (J). (gr. 4-5). 29.27 *(978-1-4824-0194-3(0),* 35d3c319-106b-46f1-b027-4b085740679f) Stevens, Gareth Publishing LLLP.

—Terrible Tales of Ancient Greece, 1 vol., Vol. 1. Jantner, Janos, illus. 2014. (Monstrous Myths Ser.). (ENG.). 32p. (J). (gr. 4-5). 29.27 *(978-1-4824-0181-3(9),* 89ee054b-f192-42f2-a7ec-0b7a4c5c8cb9) Stevens, Gareth Publishing LLLP.

Hicks, Peter. Ancient Romans. 2014. (Gods & Goddesses in Daily Life Ser.). (Illus.). 48p. (gr. 3-6). 37.10 *(978-1-908973-84-9(6))* Book Hse. GBR. Dist: Black Rabbit Bks.

Higgins, Nadia. Perseus the Hero: An Interactive Mythological Adventure. 2016. (You Choose: Ancient Greek Myths Ser.). (ENG., Illus.). 112p. (J). (gr. 3-7). lib. bdg. 32.65 *(978-1-4914-8112-7(9),* 130603, Capstone Pr.) Capstone.

Hinds, Kathryn. Mermaids, 1 vol. 2013. (Creatures of Fantasy Ser.). (ENG., Illus.). 64p. (gr. 6-6). 36.93 *(978-0-7614-4924-9(8),* 04dc1bde-4b50-4789-aede-b0df5b5c8032) Cavendish Square Publishing LLC.

—Sphinxes & Centaurs, 1 vol. 2013. (Creatures of Fantasy Ser.). (ENG.). 64p. (gr. 6-6). 36.93 *(978-0-7614-4927-0(2),* 63533d53-3465-41a1-98a2-7cc359f640f9) Cavendish Square Publishing LLC.

Hoena, Blake. Jason, the Argonauts, & the Golden Fleece: An Interactive Mythological Adventure. Nathan, James, illus. 2016. (You Choose: Ancient Greek Myths Ser.). (ENG.). 112p. (J). (gr. 3-7). lib. bdg. 32.65 *(978-1-4914-8113-4(7),* 130604, Capstone Pr.) Capstone.

Hoena, Blake & Field, Jon Eben. National Geographic Kids: Everything Mythology: Begin Your Quest for Facts, Photos, & Fun Fit for Gods & Goddesses. 2014. (National Geographic Kids Everything Ser.). (Illus.). 64p. (J). (gr. 3-7). pap. 12.99 *(978-1-4263-1498-1(1),* National Geographic Kids) Disney Publishing Worldwide.

Homer, illus. Classic Starts(r): the Iliad. 2014. (Classic Starts(r) Ser.). 160p. (J). (gr. 2-4). 7.99 *(978-1-4549-0612-4(X))* Sterling Publishing Co., Inc.

Houle, Michelle M. Gods & Goddesses in Greek Mythology Rock!, 1 vol. 2011. (Mythology Rocks! Ser.). (ENG., Illus.). 128p. (gr. 6-7). pap. 13.88 *(978-1-59845-329-4(7),* f247f20f-b823-436a-8298-6bd2af8d85df) Enslow Publishing, LLC.

Husain, Shahrukh. Indian Myths. Willey, Bee, illus. 2007. (Stories from Ancient Civilisations Ser.). 32p. (J). pap. 10.99 *(978-0-237-53376-2(6))* Evans Brothers, Ltd. GBR. Dist: Independent Pubs. Group.

Hyde, Natalie. Understanding Greek Myths. 2012. (ENG.). 48p. (J). *(978-0-7787-4509-9(0))*; pap. *(978-0-7787-4514-3(7))* Crabtree Publishing Co.

Hynson, Colin. Understanding Indian Myths. 2012. (ENG.). 48p. (J). *(978-0-7787-4524-2(4))* Crabtree Publishing Co.

I Want to Know: Set 2, 12 vols. 2017. (I Want to Know Ser.). (ENG.). (J). (gr. 3-3). lib. bdg. 161.58 *(978-0-7660-9202-0(X),* 35463236-b076-4284-b60a-cebbe9d8cb1b) Enslow Publishing, LLC.

Ingri, D'Aulaire & Parin, D'Aulaire Edgar. D'Aulaires Book of Greek Myths. 2014. (Yearling Special Ser.). (ENG.). 192p. (gr. 8-12). 24.20 *(978-1-63245-092-0(5))* Lectorum Pubns., Inc.

Innes, Brian. Ancient Roman Myths, 1 vol. 2010. (Myths from Around the World Ser.). (ENG.). 48p. (YA). (gr. 6-8). lib. bdg. 33.67 *(978-1-4339-3527-5(9),* 9e91eb08-9824-4bf8-8578-aa4f1cfe7fcc, Gareth Stevens Secondary Library) Stevens, Gareth Publishing LLLP.

Jacobs Altman, Linda. African Mythology Rocks!, 1 vol. 2011. (Mythology Rocks! Ser.). (ENG., Illus.). 112p. (gr. 6-7). pap. 13.88 *(978-1-59845-328-7(9),* 3cbd81ae-448c-42f5-b487-4198fe55de96) Enslow Publishing, LLC.

James Baldwin. Fifty Famous Stories Retold. 2009. (Illus.). 132p. pap. 5.95 *(978-1-60386-206-6(4),* Merchant Bks.) Rough Draft Printing.

Jarvie, Gordon. Irish Folk & Fairy Tales. 2nd rev. ed. 2009. (ENG.). 224p. pap. 12.95 *(978-0-85640-836-6(0))* Colourpoint Bks. GBR. Dist: Casemate Pubs. & Bk. Distributors, LLC.

Jeffrey, Gary. Achilles & the Trojan War, 1 vol. Spender, Nick, illus. 2012. (Graphic Mythical Heroes Ser.). (ENG.). 24p. (J). (gr. 3-3). pap. 9.15 *(978-1-4339-7508-0(4),* 1e5a4b63-0298-444c-9d2a-0e2f5c08d65a); lib. bdg. 26.60 *(978-1-4339-7507-3(6),* c2476a4c-35f1-48e1-8f09-42ee80f389e2) Stevens, Gareth Publishing LLLP.

—African Myths. 2009. (Graphic Mythology Ser.). (ENG.). 48p. (YA). (gr. 4-5). 58.50 *(978-1-61512-976-8(6),* Rosen Reference) Rosen Publishing Group, Inc., The.

—Jason & the Argonauts, 1 vol. Verma, Dheeraj, illus. 2012. (Graphic Mythical Heroes Ser.). (ENG.). 24p. (J). (gr. 3-3). pap. 9.15 *(978-1-4339-7516-5(5),* 81f12069-40fd-4741-92df-f2d5ee9b5d71); lib. bdg. 26.60 *(978-1-4339-7515-8(7),* 25b221b0-6ef6-416f-8d5c-81ca6337a02c) Stevens, Gareth Publishing LLLP.

Jennings, Ken. Greek Mythology. Lowery, Mike, illus. 2014. (Ken Jennings' Junior Genius Guides). (ENG.). 160p. (J). (gr. 3-5). pap. 7.99 *(978-1-4424-7330-0(4),* Little Simon) Little Simon.

Johnson, Robin. Understanding Roman Myths. 2012. (ENG.). 48p. (J). *(978-0-7787-4510-5(4))*; pap. *(978-0-7787-4515-0(5))* Crabtree Publishing Co.

Jr. Graphic American Legends: Sets 1-2. 2014. (Jr. Graphic American Legends Ser.). 24p. (J). (gr. 3-6). pap. 763.20 *(978-1-4777-7263-8(4),* PowerKids Pr.) Rosen Publishing Group, Inc., The.

Jr. Graphic Mythologies, 8 vols., Set. Incl. Egyptian Mythology: Osiris & Isis. Daning, Tom. lib. bdg. 28.93 *(978-1-4042-3399-7(7),* 1ed8b5cf-961d-4992-be0e-a5fea100f312); Greek Mythology: Jason & the Golden Fleece. Herdling, Glenn. lib. bdg. 28.93 *(978-1-4042-3396-6(2),* 225c1f43-e5d9-4fe4-be6d-9330439a4fab); Mesoamerican Mythology: Quetzalcoatl. Daning, Tom. lib. bdg. 28.93 *(978-1-4042-3401-7(2),* 8fd8cb62-7446-41eb-b798-11ec0af510a8); Roman Mythology: Romulus & Remus. Daning, Tom. lib. bdg. 28.93 *(978-1-4042-3397-3(0),* a6131d89-6894-4339-ba74-879c71059bd6); (Illus.). (J). (gr. 2-3). 2006. (Jr. Graphic Mythologies Ser.). (ENG.). 24p. 2006. Set lib. bdg. 115.72 *(978-1-4042-3551-9(5),* 5c248a84-a353-4aef-b1f1-7b60c3c5bc74) Rosen Publishing Group, Inc., The.

Kahukiwa, Robyn. Ngā Atua: Māori Gods. Hammond, Kiwa, tr. Kahukiwa, Robyn, illus. 2017. (Illus.). 32p. (J). 19.00 *(978-0-947506-26-1(8),* 13416, Oratia Bks.) Oratia Media NZL. Dist: Univ. of Hawaii Pr.

Kallen, Stuart A. African Mythology, 1 vol. 2015. (Mythology & Culture Worldwide Ser.). (ENG., Illus.). 104p. (gr. 7-10). lib. bdg. 41.03 *(978-1-4205-1145-1(9),* 09af23d9-4fcc-4690-8be9-5a09db10c9ae, Lucent Pr.) Greenhaven Publishing LLC.

Kelkar, Gauri. Little Monk's Durga. 2011. (ENG., Illus.). 60p. (J). 14.95 *(978-81-8328-190-4(7))* Wisdom Tree IND. Dist: SCB Distributors.

—Little Monk's Lakshmi. 2011. (ENG., Illus.). 60p. (J). 14.95 *(978-81-8328-191-1(5))* Wisdom Tree IND. Dist: SCB Distributors.

—Little Monk's Parvati. 2011. (ENG.). 60p. (J). 14.95 *(978-81-8328-192-8(3))* Wisdom Tree IND. Dist: SCB Distributors.

—Little Monk's Saraswati. 2011. (ENG.). 60p. (J). 14.95 *(978-81-8328-189-8(3))* Wisdom Tree IND. Dist: SCB Distributors.

Kerrigan, Michael, et al. Exploring the Life, Myth, & Art of the Ancient near East, 1 vol. 2016. (Civilizations of the World Ser.). (ENG., Illus.). 144p. (J). (gr. 8-8). lib. bdg. 47.80 *(978-1-4994-6397-2(9),* ee7ecfe9-a717-4268-a7b6-89f663b70dd7) Rosen Publishing Group, Inc., The.

Kingsley, Charles. The Heroes. Robinson, T. H., illus. 2009. 240p. pap. 10.95 *(978-1-59915-291-2(6))* Yesterday's Classics.

—The Heroes: Or Greek Fairy Tales for My Children. 2012. 314p. pap. *(978-1-290-05368-6(5))* HardPr.

—Heroes of Greek Mythology. Squire, M H & Mars, E., illus. 2006. (Dover Children's Classics Ser.). (ENG.). 240p. (YA). (gr. 3-12). per. 10.95 *(978-0-486-44854-1(1),* 448541) Dover Pubns., Inc.

Kopp, Megan. Understanding Chinese Myths. 2012. (ENG.). 48p. (J). *(978-0-7787-4507-5(4))*; pap. *(978-0-7787-4512-9(0))* Crabtree Publishing Co.

Krieg, Katherine. What We Get from Greek Mythology. 2015. (21st Century Skills Library: Mythology & Culture Ser.). (ENG., Illus.). 32p. (gr. 3-6). 32.07 *(978-1-63188-913-4(3),* 205976) Cherry Lake Publishing.

Kuhtz, Cleo & Martell, Hazel. Ancient Greek Civilization, 1 vol. D'Ottavi, Francesca, illus. 2009. (Ancient Civilizations & Their Myths & Legends Ser.). (ENG.). 48p. (YA). (gr. 6-6). lib. bdg. 34.47 *(978-1-4042-8033-5(2),* a4a28111-bebb-4a23-aa33-d14873787eaa) Rosen Publishing Group, Inc., The.

Labrecque, Ellen. The Amazons, 1 vol. 2019. (Women of Mythology: Goddesses, Warriors, & Hunters Ser.). (ENG.). 32p. (gr. 2-2). pap. 9.22 *(978-1-5026-5152-5(1),* 2df3fe58-3fb2-4614-88e5-10cddd774221) Cavendish Square Publishing LLC.

Laflamme, Sonia K. & Delezenne, Christine. Les Hommes de Maïs. (FRE., Illus.). 71p. (J). pap. 9.95 *(978-2-923234-58-8(8))* Editions de l'Isatis CAN. Dist: Crabtree Publishing Co.

Lang, Andrew. Tales of Troy: Ulysses the Sacker of Cities. 2004. reprint ed. pap. 1.99 *(978-1-4192-5072-9(8))* Kessinger Publishing, LLC.

—Tales of Troy & Greece. Ford, H. J., illus. 2006. (Dover Children's Classics Ser.). (ENG.). 336p. (gr. 9-12). per. 9.95 *(978-0-486-44917-3(3))* Dover Pubns., Inc.

LaRoche, Amy. Chimaera. 2010. (Monsters in Myth Ser.). (Illus.). 48p. (J). (gr. 4-7). lib. bdg. 29.95 *(978-1-58415-925-4(1))* Mitchell Lane Pubs.

Lawrence, Sandra. Myths & Legends. Trithart, Emma, illus. 2017. (ENG.). 64p. (J). *(978-1-84857-596-7(3),* 360 Degrees) Tiger Tales.

Leavy, Una. Magical Celtic Tales. O'Connor, Fergal, illus. 2016. (ENG.). 96p. (J). 25.00 *(978-1-84717-546-5(5))* O'Brien Pr., Ltd., The IRL. Dist: Casemate Pubs. & Bk. Distributors, LLC.

Leonard, Scott A. Myths & Legends of Ancient Britain & Ireland. 2015. (Illus.). 64p. (J). *(978-0-7166-2637-4(3))* World Bk., Inc.

—Myths & Legends of China. 2015. (Illus.). 64p. (J). *(978-0-7166-2632-9(2))* World Bk., Inc.

—Myths & Legends of South Asia & Southeast Asia. 2015. (Illus.). 64p. (J). *(978-0-7166-2630-5(6))* World Bk., Inc.

Lindgren, Astrid. The Brothers Lionheart. Morgan, Jill, tr. from SWE. Wikland, Ilon, illus. 2004. 231p. (J). 17.95 *(978-1-930900-24-0(4))* Purple Hse. Pr.

Loewen, Nancy. Cyclops Tells All: The Way EYE See It. Pentney, Ryan, illus. 2014. (Other Side of the Myth Ser.). (ENG.). 32p. (J). (gr. -1-3). pap. 6.95 *(978-1-4795-2937-7(0),* 124535, Picture Window Bks.) Capstone.

—Helen of Troy Tells All: Blame the Boys, 1 vol. Gilpin, Stephen, illus. 2014. (Other Side of the Myth Ser.). (ENG.). 32p. (J). (gr. -1-3). 27.99 *(978-1-4795-2182-1(5),* 123983, Picture Window Bks.) Capstone.

Loh-Hagan, Virginia. Artemis. 2017. (Gods & Goddesses of the Ancient World Ser.). (ENG., Illus.). 32p. (J). (gr. 4-8). 32.07 *(978-1-63472-136-3(5),* 209116, 45th Parallel Press) Cherry Lake Publishing.

—Athena. 2017. (Gods & Goddesses of the Ancient World Ser.). (ENG., Illus.). 32p. (J). (gr. 4-8). 32.07 *(978-1-63472-135-6(7),* 209112, 45th Parallel Press) Cherry Lake Publishing.

—Demeter. 2017. (Gods & Goddesses of the Ancient World Ser.). (ENG., Illus.). 32p. (J). (gr. 4-8). 32.07 *(978-1-63472-138-7(1),* 209124, 45th Parallel Press) Cherry Lake Publishing.

—Genies. 2017. (Magic, Myth, & Mystery Ser.). (ENG., Illus.). 32p. (J). (gr. 4-8). lib. bdg. 32.07 *(978-1-63472-885-0(8),* 209966, 45th Parallel Press) Cherry Lake Publishing.

—Hades. 2017. (Gods & Goddesses of the Ancient World Ser.). (ENG., Illus.). 32p. (J). (gr. 4-8). 32.07 *(978-1-63472-132-5(2),* 209100, 45th Parallel Press) Cherry Lake Publishing.

—Hera. 2017. (Gods & Goddesses of the Ancient World Ser.). (ENG., Illus.). 32p. (J). (gr. 4-8). 32.07 *(978-1-63472-137-0(3),* 209120, 45th Parallel Press) Cherry Lake Publishing.

—Hydra. 2016. (Magic, Myth, & Mystery Ser.). (ENG., Illus.). 32p. (J). (gr. 4-8). 32.07 *(978-1-63471-114-2(9),* 208567, 45th Parallel Press) Cherry Lake Publishing.

—Poseidon. 2017. (Gods & Goddesses of the Ancient World Ser.). (ENG., Illus.). 32p. (J). (gr. 4-8). 32.07 *(978-1-63472-133-2(0),* 209104, 45th Parallel Press) Cherry Lake Publishing.

Looney, Bill, illus. The Flood of Noah: Legends & Lore of Survival. 2014. 24p. (J). 18.99 *(978-0-89051-801-4(7),* Master Books) New Leaf Publishing Group.

Lunge-Larsen, Lise. Gifts from the Gods: Ancient Words & Wisdom from Greek & Roman Mythology. Hinds, Gareth, illus. 2011. (ENG.). 96p. (J). (gr. 5-7). 18.99 *(978-0-547-15229-5(9),* 1051948, Clarion Bks.) HarperCollins Pubs.

Lupton, Hugh & Morden, Daniel. Greek Myths: Three Heroic Tales. Henaff, Carol, illus. 2017. (ENG.). 136p. (J). (gr. 3-5). pap. 12.99 *(978-1-78285-349-7(9))* Barefoot Bks., Inc.

Mabie, Hamilton Wright. Myths That Every Child Should Know. 2007. (ENG.). 270p. pap. 21.99 *(978-1-4346-0177-3(3))* Creative Media Partners, LLC.

Macdonald, Fiona. Celtic Myths & Legends, 1 vol. 2013. (All about Myths Ser.). (ENG.). 48p. (J). (gr. 5-8). pap. 9.25 *(978-1-4109-5472-5(2),* 123404, Raintree) Capstone.

MacKay, Jennifer. Hindu Mythology, 1 vol. 2014. (Mythology & Culture Worldwide Ser.). (ENG., Illus.). 104p. (gr. 7-10). lib. bdg. 41.03 *(978-1-4205-1147-5(5),* 62b517f5-ef08-4b27-a7fa-53877e7c368f, Lucent Pr.) Greenhaven Publishing LLC.

Mandala Publishing, Mandala. Gopal the Infallible: Volume I. 2009. (ENG., Illus.). 38p. (J). (gr. k-4). 9.95 *(978-1-886069-17-6(4),* 1212) Mandala Publishing.

Marshall, James Vance. Stories from the Billabong. Firebrace, Francis, illus. 2010. (ENG.). 64p. (J). (gr. k-3). pap. 9.99 *(978-1-84780-124-1(2),* Frances Lincoln Children's Bks.) Quarto Publishing Group UK GBR. Dist: Hachette Bk. Group.

Marsico, Katie. What We Get from Celtic Mythology. 2015. (21st Century Skills Library: Mythology & Culture Ser.). (ENG., Illus.). 32p. (gr. 3-6). 32.07 *(978-1-63188-910-3(9),* 205964) Cherry Lake Publishing.

Mason, Jennifer. Werewolf Myths, 1 vol. 2017. (Myths Across the Map Ser.). (ENG.). 48p. (J). (gr. 5-6). pap. 15.05 *(978-1-5382-1449-7(0),* e1513221-1bda-43ab-a9c0-2b43982028b8); lib. bdg. 33.60 *(978-1-5382-1376-6(1),* 5899ffed-3c58-4fd0-b7d8-94ceae3671bc) Stevens, Gareth Publishing LLLP.

—Zombie Myths, 1 vol. 2017. (Myths Across the Map Ser.). (ENG.). 48p. (J). (gr. 5-6). pap. 15.05 *(978-1-5382-1450-3(4),* 5635f4f7-2a4d-439f-8cb1-d41cafd5c556); lib. bdg. 33.60 *(978-1-5382-1378-0(8),* 0c098448-3dc0-4dc4-abde-5a07de4b7dda) Stevens, Gareth Publishing LLLP.

Mason, Paul. The Fact or Fiction Behind Urban Myths, 1 vol. 2015. (Fact or Phony? Ser.). (ENG.). 96p. (J). (gr. 5-6). lib. bdg. 34.93 *(978-1-4824-4274-8(4),* b44de6a5-2fbb-478a-bba3-5b418ef27466) Stevens, Gareth Publishing LLLP.

Mattern, Joanne. Atalanta, 1 vol. 2019. (Women of Mythology: Goddesses, Warriors, & Hunters Ser.). (ENG.). 32p. (gr. 2-2). pap. 9.22 *(978-1-5026-5148-8(3),* 4800be4b-8685-4f30-aeba-1f5053a67539) Cavendish Square Publishing LLC.

Matthews, Rupert & Van Pelt, Todd. Ancient Chinese Civilization, 1 vol. D'Ottavi, Francesca, illus. 2009. (Ancient

Civilizations & Their Myths & Legends Ser.). (ENG.). 48p. (J). (gr. 6-6). lib. bdg. 34.47 *(978-1-4042-8035-9(9)*, 21c713e3-2b0e-4709-b14e-e78f8a973d13) Rosen Publishing Group, Inc., The.

McCaughrean, Geraldine. Jason y el Vellocino de Oro: Aracne, la Tejedora. Barroso, Paz, tr. Ross, Tony, illus. 2005. (Mythology Series Collection Mitos Ser.).Tr. of Jason & the Golden Fleece. (SPA.). 48p. (J). (gr. 2-3). 9.95 *(978-84-348-6425-2(8))* SM Ediciones ESP. Dist: Iaconi, Mariuccia Bk. Imports.

—Perseo y la Gorgona Medisa. Barroso, Paz, tr. Ross, Tony, illus. 2005. (Mythology Series Collection Mitos Ser.).Tr. of Perseus & the Gorgon Medusa. (SPA.). 48p. (J). (gr. 2-3). 9.95 *(978-84-348-6430-6(4))* SM Ediciones ESP. Dist: Iaconi, Mariuccia Bk. Imports.

McKinley, Herald P. Myths of the Aztecs, 1 vol. 2015. (World Mythologies Ser.). (ENG., Illus.). 96p. (gr. 6-6). lib. bdg. 44.50 *(978-1-5026-0996-0(7)*, 116dcebe-2c56-4039-af58-32b959b1f0ff) Cavendish Square Publishing LLC.

McMullan, Kate. Get to Work, Hercules! 2003. (Myth-o-Mania Ser.: No. 7). (ENG., Illus.). (J). 9.99 *(978-0-7868-0863-2(2))* Hyperion Bks. for Children.

McNeely, Tom, illus. Isis & the Seven Scorpions, 1 vol. 2012. (Egyptian Myths Ser.). (ENG.). 32p. (J). (gr. 3-5). lib. bdg. 29.32 *(978-1-4048-7150-2(0)*, 117145, Picture Window Bks.) Capstone.

Mellado, Carisa. Mythic Oracle: Wisdom of the Ancient Greek Pantheon. Phelan, Michele-lee, illus. 2012. (ENG.). 160p. (YA). (gr. 7). pap. 24.99 *(978-1-58270-325-1(6))* Simon Pulse/Beyond Words.

Meschini, Leonardo, illus. The Prince & the Sphinx, 1 vol. 2012. (Egyptian Myths Ser.). (ENG.). 32p. (J). (gr. 3-5). pap. 8.95 *(978-1-4048-7242-4(6)*, 118181, Picture Window Bks.) Capstone.

Mhlophe, Gcina. African Tales: A Barefoot Collection. Griffin, Rachel, illus. 96p. (J). 2017. (ENG.). (gr. 2-5). pap. 16.99 *(978-1-78285-359-6(6))* 2015. (gr. 3-6). pap. 14.99 *(978-1-84686-590-9(5))* Barefoot Bks., Inc.

Milbourne, Anna & Stowell, Louie. The Usborne Book of Greek Myths. Brocklehurst, Ruth, ed. Bursi, Simona et al, illus. 2014. (ENG.). 301p. (J). (gr. 4-7). pap. 22.99 *(978-0-7945-2130-1(4)*, Usborne) EDC Publishing.

Miller, Reagan & Walker, Robert. How to Tell a Myth. Crabtree Publishing Staff, ed. 2011. (Text Styles Ser.: No. 4). (ENG.). 32p. (J). (gr. 3-6). pap. *(978-0-7787-1638-9(4))* Crabtree Publishing Co.

Mincks, Margaret. What We Get from Roman Mythology. 2015. (21st Century Skills Library: Mythology & Culture Ser.). (ENG., Illus.). 32p. (J). (gr. 3-6). pap. 14.21 *(978-1-63188-931-8(1)*, 205985) Cherry Lake Publishing.

Mitton, Jacqueline. Once upon a Starry Night: A Book of Constellations. 2009. (ENG., Illus.). 32p. (J). (gr. 1-3). pap. 10.99 *(978-1-4263-0391-3(2)*, National Geographic Kids) Disney Publishing Worldwide.

Monsters in Myth, 8 vols., Set. Incl. Cerberus. Tracy, Kathleen. lib. bdg. 29.95 *(978-1-58415-924-7(3))*; Chimaera. LaRoche, Amy. lib. bdg. 29.95 *(978-1-58415-925-4(1))*; Cyclopes. Roberts, Russell. lib. bdg. 29.95 *(978-1-58415-926-1(X))*; Medusa. Tracy, Kathleen. lib. bdg. 29.95 *(978-1-58415-928-5(6))*; Minotaur. Roberts, Russell. lib. bdg. 29.95 *(978-1-58415-929-2(4))*; Monsters of Hercules. Orr, Tamra. lib. bdg. 29.95 *(978-1-58415-927-8(8))*; Sirens. Orr, Tamra. lib. bdg. 29.95 *(978-1-58415-930-8(8))*; Sphinx. DiPrimio, Pete. lib. bdg. 29.95 *(978-1-58415-931-5(6))*; (Illus.). 48p. (J). (gr. 4-7). 2010. 239.60 *(978-1-58415-932-2(4))* Mitchell Lane Pubs.

Mora, Pat. The Night the Moon Fell: A Maya Myth, 1 vol. Domi, illus. 2009. (ENG.). 32p. (J). (gr. k-k). pap. 6.95 *(978-0-88899-938-2(0))* Groundwood Bks. CAN. Dist: Publishers Group West (PGW).

—La Noche Que Se Cayó la Luna. Domi, illus. 2nd ed. 2009. (SPA.). 32p. (J). (gr. -1-k). pap. 6.95 *(978-0-88899-963-4(1))* Groundwood Bks. CAN. Dist: Publishers Group West (PGW).

Morden, Daniel. Dark Tales from the Woods. 2006. (ENG., Illus.). 102p. (J). (gr. 4-6). 19.99 *(978-1-84323-583-5(8))* Gomer Pr. GBR. Dist: Independent Pubs. Group, Casemate Pubs. & Bk. Distributors, LLC.

Morley, Jacqueline. Greek Myths: Volume 2: Volume 2. 2019. (Myths Ser.). (ENG., Illus.). 96p. (J). (gr. 2). 12.95 *(978-1-912006-70-0(7)*, Scribblers) Book Hse. GBR. Dist: Sterling Publishing Co., Inc.

Morley, Jacqueline & Salariya, David. World of Myths & Legends. Franklin, Carolyn, illus. 2013. (Mythology Ser.). 64p. (gr. 3-6). 41.35 *(978-1-908973-93-1(5))* Book Hse. GBR. Dist: Black Rabbit Bks.

Morris, Neil. African Myths, 1 vol. Kennedy, Graham & Sansom, Fiona, illus. 2009. (Myths from Many Lands Ser.). (ENG.). 48p. (YA). (gr. 5-5). pap. 13.85 *(978-1-60754-216-2(1)*, df4dec55-bdd4-483f-9da5-9337e653e887, Windmill Bks.) Rosen Publishing Group, Inc., The.

Murphy, John, ed. Gods & Goddesses of the Inca, Maya, & Aztec Civilizations, 1 vol. 2014. (Gods & Goddesses of Mythology Ser.). (ENG.). 120p. (J). (gr. 8-8). 36.49 *(978-1-62275-396-3(8)*, fc781c3b-649e-4ac3-aad0-8062e4a7c879) Rosen Publishing Group, Inc., The.

Muten, Burleigh. Goddesses: A World of Myth & Magic. Guay, Rebecca, illus. 2003. (ENG.). 80p. (J). 19.99 *(978-1-84148-075-6(4))* Barefoot Bks., Inc.

Mythology a to Z, 9-Volumes, 9 vols., Set. 2010. (Mythology A to Z Ser.). (ENG.). (gr. 5-8). 405.00 *(978-1-60413-956-3(0)*, P459464, Facts On File) Infobase Holdings, Inc.

Mythology & Legends Around the World, 16 vols. 2017. (Mythology & Legends Around the World Ser.). (ENG., Illus.). (J). (gr. 4-4). lib. bdg. 287.44 *(978-1-5026-3301-9(9)*, e8534701-26e6-4f7b-b4a4-e66bad702d55) Cavendish Square Publishing LLC.

Myths & Legends. pap. *(978-1-84458-374-4(0)*, Pavilion Children's Books) Pavilion Bks.

Myths from Around the World, 12 vols., Set. Incl. Ancient Greek Myths. Green, Jen. lib. bdg. 33.67 *(978-1-4339-3524-4(4)*, 1e4d0cc8-74d9-4741-92c0-0a40cb90d7f0); Ancient Roman Myths. Innes, Brian. lib. bdg. 33.67 *(978-1-4339-3527-5(9)*, 9e91eb08-9824-4bf8-8578-aa4f1cfe7fcc); Chinese & Japanese Myths. Green, Jen. lib. bdg. 33.67 *(978-1-4339-3533-6(3)*, 9261b862-cb91-4c9d-afd7-6f52540c9af0); Mesoamerican Myths. Dalal, Anita. lib. bdg. 33.67 *(978-1-4339-3539-8(2)*, f5b2a7b1-80b5-4db5-b7d3-be0d6cea955c); Native American Myths. Dalal, Anita. lib. bdg. 33.67 *(978-1-4339-3530-5(9)*, c0083934-7d65-40ea-906a-efb36ec8341e); West African Myths. Giles, Bridget. lib. bdg. 33.67 *(978-1-4339-3536-7(8)*, 91a104ec-ce3a-47ef-89ff-616a00cc969a); (YA). (gr. 6-8). (Myths from Around the World Ser.). (ENG.). 48p. 2010. Set lib. bdg. 202.02 *(978-1-4339-3591-6(0)*, 0a0fd9da-79cd-4c9f-a7b6-03e462572fbd, Gareth Stevens Secondary Library) Stevens, Gareth Publishing LLLP.

Nagle, Frances. Medusa, 1 vol. 2016. (Monsters! Ser.). (ENG., Illus.). 32p. (J). (gr. 1-2). pap. 11.50 *(978-1-4824-4867-2(X)*, fd05e48a-b793-4966-aa5e-ca2e81e3df8a) Stevens, Gareth Publishing LLLP.

Namm, Diane. Classic Starts(r): Roman Myths. Freeberg, Eric, illus. 2014. (Classic Starts(r) Ser.). 160p. (J). (gr. 2-4). 6.95 *(978-1-4549-0611-7(1))* Sterling Publishing Co., Inc.

Napoli, Donna Jo. Treasury of Greek Mythology: Classic Stories of Gods, Goddesses, Heroes & Monsters. 2011. (Illus.). 192p. (J). (gr. 3-7). 24.95 *(978-1-4263-0844-4(2))*; (ENG., lib. bdg. 33.90 *(978-1-4263-0845-1(0))* Disney Publishing Worldwide. (National Geographic Kids).

Nardo, Don. Greek Mythology, 1 vol. 2012. (Mythology & Culture Worldwide Ser.). (ENG., Illus.). 112p. (J). (gr. 7-10). lib. bdg. 41.03 *(978-1-4205-0633-4(1)*, 41c35879-ea32-480a-b180-381e7fa7cd5c, Lucent Pr.) Greenhaven Publishing LLC.

—Persian Mythology, 1 vol. 2012. (Mythology & Culture Worldwide Ser.). (ENG., Illus.). 104p. (gr. 7-10). lib. bdg. 41.03 *(978-1-4205-0794-2(X)*, 2b63b356-8a93-4dba-91f1-d8af887ef262, Lucent Pr.) Greenhaven Publishing LLC.

—Roman Mythology, 1 vol. 2012. (Mythology & Culture Worldwide Ser.). (ENG., Illus.). 104p. (gr. 7-10). lib. bdg. 41.03 *(978-1-4205-0746-1(X)*, 3a7595ac-66bf-4bb1-92e0-03324e9f57b0, Lucent Pr.) Greenhaven Publishing LLC.

Nardo, Don & Currie, Stephen. Aztec Mythology, 1 vol. 2014. (Mythology & Culture Worldwide Ser.). (ENG., Illus.). 96p. (gr. 7-10). lib. bdg. 41.03 *(978-1-4205-0922-9(5)*, 2439b3fd-caff-400f-ae73-4dd2e0f6eb38, Lucent Pr.) Greenhaven Publishing LLC.

National Geographic Kids. National Geographic Kids Funny Fill-in: My Mythology Adventure. 2015. (NG Kids Funny Fill In Ser.). 48p. (J). (gr. 3-7). pap. 4.99 *(978-1-4263-2198-6(8)*, National Geographic Kids) Disney Publishing Worldwide.

Nordenstrom, Michael, illus. & adapted by. Hina & the Sea of Stars. Nordenstrom, Michael, adapted by. 2003. 32p. 10.95 *(978-1-57306-167-4(0))* Bess Pr., Inc.

Novel Units. Mythology Novel Units Student Packet. 2019. (ENG.). (YA). pap. 13.99 *(978-1-56137-817-3(8)*, Novel Units, Inc.) Classroom Library Co.

O'Brian, Pliny. Myths of the Ancient Romans, 1 vol. 2015. (World Mythologies Ser.). (ENG., Illus.). 96p. (gr. 6-6). lib. bdg. 44.50 *(978-1-5026-0994-6(0)*, 0ae7e21c-c048-4635-b812-59062b60d2e2) Cavendish Square Publishing LLC.

O'Brien, Cynthia. Fairy Myths, 1 vol. 2017. (Myths Across the Map Ser.). (ENG.). 48p. (J). (gr. 5-6). pap. 15.05 *(978-1-5382-1443-5(1)*, a58b4786-ec82-4368-bc64-2fe70828fd6d); lib. bdg. 33.60 *(978-1-5382-1370-4(2)*, b7aa72ed-f474-4c7f-8296-2ef7d989568e) Stevens, Gareth Publishing LLLP.

O'Connor, George. Apollo: The Brilliant One. 2016. (Olympians Ser.: 8). (ENG., Illus.). 80p. (J). pap. 12.99 *(978-1-62672-015-2(0)*, 900131515, First Second Bks.) Roaring Brook Pr.

—Ares: Bringer of War. 2015. (Olympians Ser.: 7). (ENG., Illus.). 80p. (J). (gr. 4-9). pap. 12.99 *(978-1-62672-013-8(4)*, 900131512, First Second Bks.) Roaring Brook Pr.

Orr, Tamra. The Sirens. 2010. (Monsters in Myth Ser.). (Illus.). 48p. (J). (gr. 4-7). lib. bdg. 29.95 *(978-1-58415-930-8(8))* Mitchell Lane Pubs.

O'Shei, Tim. Bone-Chilling Myths, 1 vol. 2010. (Scary Stories Ser.). (ENG.). 32p. (J). (gr. 3-9). lib. bdg. 28.65 *(978-1-4296-4573-7(3)*, 103055, Capstone Pr.) Capstone.

Pearce, Q. L. Celtic Mythology, 1 vol. 2014. (Mythology & Culture Worldwide Ser.). (ENG., Illus.). 112p. (gr. 7-10). lib. bdg. 41.03 *(978-1-4205-0923-6(3)*, 7a3bc9dc-bb42-4473-9e8b-23c85197c616, Lucent Pr.) Greenhaven Publishing LLC.

Phillipps, Francis, illus. Jason & the Golden Fleece: A Greek Legend. 2004. (ENG.). 24p. (J). (gr. 3-3). pap. 6.47 net. *(978-0-7685-2126-9(2)*, Dominie Elementary) Savvas Learning Co.

Poeschel, Ann. Helen of Troy, 1 vol. 2019. (Women of Mythology: Goddesses, Warriors, & Hunters Ser.). (ENG.). 32p. (gr. 2-2). pap. 9.22 *(978-1-5026-5132-7(7)*, b9316d67-6f00-4511-aa18-365581dde565) Cavendish Square Publishing LLC.

Pommaux, Yvan. Oedipus: Trapped by Destiny. 2016. (TOON Graphic Mythology Ser.). (Illus.). 48p. (J). (gr. 3-7). 16.95 *(978-1-935179-95-5(0)*, TOON Books) Astra Publishing Hse.

—Orpheus in the Underworld: A TOON Graphic. 2015. (TOON Graphic Mythology Ser.). (Illus.). 56p. (J). (gr. 3-7). 16.95 *(978-1-935179-84-9(5)*, TOON Books) Astra Publishing Hse.

Pommaux, Yvan & Kutner, Richard. Orpheus in the Underworld, 1 vol. Pommaux, Yvan, illus. 2016. (Toon Graphics Ser.). (ENG., Illus.). 56p. (J). (gr. 4-7). lib. bdg. 34.21 *(978-1-61479-500-1(2)*, 21436, Graphic Novels) Spotlight.

Posner, Pat. Gods & Goddesses from Greek Myths. 2010. (ENG.). 45p. (J). 19.00 *(978-1-4379-7397-6(3))* DIANE Publishing Co.

Ram-Prasad, Chakravarthi. Exploring the Life, Myth, & Art of India, 1 vol. 2009. (Civilizations of the World Ser.). (ENG.). 144p. (YA). (gr. 8-8). lib. bdg. 47.80 *(978-1-4358-5615-8(5)*, 5dc2e99e-fe03-418e-b134-d33ade1a28b0) Rosen Publishing Group, Inc., The.

Randall, Ron. Psyche & Eros: The Lady & the Monster: A Greek Myth. 2008. (Illus.). 48p. (J). (gr. 4-8). 27.93 *(978-0-8225-7177-3(3)*, Graphic Universe™) Lerner Publishing Group.

Randall, Ronne. Children's Stories from Myths & Legends: Classic Tales from Around the World. Howells, Graham, illus. 2017. 128p. (J). (gr. 3-12). 16.99 *(978-1-86147-852-8(6)*, Armadillo) Anness Publishing GBR. Dist: National Bk. Network.

Randolph, Joanne, ed. Celtic Myths & Legends, 1 vol. 2017. (Mythology & Legends Around the World Ser.). (ENG.). 64p. (gr. 4-4). lib. bdg. 35.93 *(978-1-5026-3281-4(0)*, a6df76b2-f963-43aa-931e-27c2ba0e3d9a) Cavendish Square Publishing LLC.

—The Myths & Legends of India, 1 vol. 2017. (Mythology & Legends Around the World Ser.). (ENG.). 64p. (gr. 4-4). lib. bdg. 35.93 *(978-1-5026-3282-1(9)*, 01a91972-a63e-4fe9-a47f-76e6c99a9b83) Cavendish Square Publishing LLC.

—The Myths & Legends of the Middle East, 1 vol. 2017. (Mythology & Legends Around the World Ser.). (ENG.). 64p. (gr. 4-4). lib. bdg. 35.93 *(978-1-5026-3279-1(9)*, 62d4c7a2-611f-44cf-958a-55c35c0ae4ef) Cavendish Square Publishing LLC.

Redmond, Shirley Raye. Cerberus, 1 vol. 2008. (Monsters Ser.). (ENG., Illus.). 48p. (gr. 4-8). lib. bdg. 36.83 *(978-0-7377-4274-9(7)*, 696999d9-6748-4217-b725-5093134397f4, KidHaven Publishing) Greenhaven Publishing LLC.

Reed, Natasha. Mythical Creatures: Sticker Book. Kincaid, Angela, illus. 2005. (Stickertastic Ser.). 24p. (J). (gr. -1-7). pap. *(978-1-84510-119-0(7))* Top That! Publishing PLC.

Reinhart, Matthew & Sabuda, Robert. Encyclopedia Mythologica: Gods & Heroes Pop-Up. Reinhart, Matthew & Sabuda, Robert, illus. 2010. (Encyclopedia Mythologica Ser.: 2). (ENG., Illus.). 12p. (J). (gr. k-4). 29.99 *(978-0-7636-3171-0(X))* Candlewick Pr.

—Encyclopedia Mythologica: Gods & Heroes Pop-Up Special Edition. Reinhart, Matthew & Sabuda, Robert, illus. 2010. (Encyclopedia Mythologica Ser.). (ENG., Illus.). 12p. (J). (gr. k-4). 250.00 *(978-0-7636-3486-5(7))* Candlewick Pr.

Riordan, Rick. Percy Jackson's Greek Heroes. 2017. (ENG., Illus.). 528p. (J). (gr. 3-7). pap. 12.99 *(978-1-4847-7643-8(7)*, Disney-Hyperion) Disney Publishing Worldwide.

—Percy Jackson's Greek Heroes. 2017. (Percy Jackson & the Olympians Ser.). (J). lib. bdg. 24.50 *(978-0-606-39498-7(2))* Turtleback.

Roberts, Jeremy. Japanese Mythology a to Z. 2nd rev. ed. 2009. (Mythology A to Z Ser.). (ENG., Illus.). 168p. (gr. 5-8). 45.00 *(978-1-60413-435-3(6)*, P173445, Facts On File) Infobase Holdings, Inc.

Roesser, Blanche. The Story of Pegasus, 1 vol. 2015. (Stories in the Stars Ser.). (ENG., Illus.). 24p. (J). (gr. 1-2). pap. 9.15 *(978-1-4824-2677-9(3)*, 36f45a46-54b1-40c7-b1ab-c9b093944a6e) Stevens, Gareth Publishing LLLP.

—The Story of Perseus, 1 vol. 2015. (Stories in the Stars Ser.). (ENG., Illus.). 24p. (J). (gr. 1-2). 24.27 *(978-1-4824-2683-0(8)*, c474c835-92b6-4301-a844-88ac2424fce7) Stevens, Gareth Publishing LLLP.

Román, Pedro Josél. PANDORA -la portadora de todos los Dones- 2005. (SPA.). 32p. *(978-958-30-1924-1(0))* Panamericana Editorial.

Rose, Simon. Orion: The Myth & Science. 2015. (Illus.). 24p. (J). *(978-1-5105-0018-1(9))* SmartBook Media, Inc.

Rosemary, Sutcliff. Black Ships Before Troy: The Story of the Iliad. 2014. (ENG.). 160p. (YA). 11.24 *(978-1-63245-187-3(5))* Lectorum Pubns., Inc.

Rosenberg, Donna & McGraw-Hill Staff. World Mythology. 2005. (Ntc: World Mythology Ser.). (ENG., Illus.). 752p. (gr. 9-12). stu. ed. 82.40 *(978-0-07-872909-6(2)*, 0078729092) McGraw-Hill Higher Education.

Rylant, Cynthia. The Beautiful Stories of Life: Six Greeks Myths, Retold. Ellis, Carson, illus. 2009. (ENG.). 88p. (J). (gr. 3-7). 17.99 *(978-0-15-206184-5(3)*, 1098959, Clarion Bks.) HarperCollins Pubs.

Schlesinger, Emily. Zombie Creatures. 2018. (Red Rhino Nonfiction Ser.). (ENG.). 60p. (J). (gr. 4-7). pap. 11.95 *(978-1-68021-074-3(2))* Saddleback Educational Publishing, Inc.

Schomp, Virginia. The Ancient Chinese, 1 vol. 2010. (Myths of the World Ser.). (ENG.). 96p. (gr. 6-6). 36.93 *(978-0-7614-4216-5(2)*, 3810ed3d-e276-4281-ad98-98c086ae1a14) Cavendish Square Publishing LLC.

—The Ancient Maya, 1 vol. 2010. (Myths of the World Ser.). (ENG.). 96p. (gr. 6-6). 36.93 *(978-0-7614-4217-2(0)*, 1367a57a-3a02-4180-9b7b-770dd65be176) Cavendish Square Publishing LLC.

—The Ancient Mesopotamians, 1 vol. 2009. (Myths of the World Ser.). (ENG.). 96p. (gr. 6-6). lib. bdg. 36.93 *(978-0-7614-3095-7(4)*, 6f2675fe-2cb1-4620-96a9-e218ba29c2e2) Cavendish Square Publishing LLC.

—Myths of the World - Group 2, 8 vols., Set. Incl. Ancient Africans. lib. bdg. 36.93 *(978-0-7614-3099-5(7)*, f1ee9181-ff82-4179-a11c-f3bac093858a); Ancient Mesopotamians. lib. bdg. 36.93 *(978-0-7614-3095-7(4)*, 6f2675fe-2cb1-4620-96a9-e218ba29c2e2); Ancient Romans. (Illus.). lib. bdg. 36.93 *(978-0-7614-3094-0(6)*, 38280b3a-537a-4619-ae81-62db9178a8d5); Aztecs. lib. bdg. 36.93 *(978-0-7614-3096-4(2)*, 9c66dde1-129d-469c-ab2a-50ba7eb57fa5); 96p. (gr. 6-6). (Myths of the World Ser.). (ENG.). 2009. Set lib. bdg. 147.72 *(978-0-7614-3093-3(8)*, 638e5083-3c33-434f-a7a1-0a607c40ee34, Cavendish Square) Cavendish Square Publishing LLC.

Schulte, Mary. The Minotaur, 1 vol. 2008. (Monsters Ser.). (ENG., Illus.). 48p. (gr. 4-8). lib. bdg. 36.83 *(978-0-7377-3590-1(2)*, 9a39ae2f-265c-41b1-bb40-827607cf618f, KidHaven Publishing) Greenhaven Publishing LLC.

Schuman, Michael A. Maya & Aztec Mythology Rocks!, 1 vol. 2011. (Mythology Rocks! Ser.). (ENG., Illus.). 128p. (gr. 6-7). pap. 13.88 *(978-1-59845-327-0(0)*, 89cf0e16-b918-4a1a-a0d8-f55e184ca2cf); lib. bdg. 35.93 *(978-0-7660-3899-8(8)*, 0fd3a344-aef2-489b-87e1-178f2e46e5a2) Enslow Publishing, LLC.

Scurman, Ike & Malam, John. Ancient Roman Civilization, 1 vol. D'Ottavi, Francesca, illus. 2009. (Ancient Civilizations & Their Myths & Legends Ser.). (ENG.). 48p. (YA). (gr. 6-6). lib. bdg. 34.47 *(978-1-4042-8038-0(3)*, 5c68aa67-b50f-4bb2-b357-dcd6a28bf1c6) Rosen Publishing Group, Inc., The.

Shahrukh Husain. Greece. 2004. (Stories from Ancient Civilizations Ser.). (J). lib. bdg. 27.10 *(978-1-58340-619-9(0))* Black Rabbit Bks.

Shea, Therese M. Fables, Myths, & Legends, 1 vol. 2018. (Let's Learn about Literature Ser.). (ENG.). 24p. (gr. 1-2). pap. 10.35 *(978-0-7660-9595-3(9)*, 58fadc45-4efe-420c-82e7-1a011310bf6b) Enslow Publishing, LLC.

Sheppard, Si. Heroes of the Trojan War, 1 vol. 2015. (Heroes & Legends Ser.). (ENG., Illus.). 88p. (J). (gr. 8-8). 38.80 *(978-1-4994-6172-5(0)*, 5add6ebf-2b69-4f6f-a2a3-82ddb2bb0bfe, Rosen Young Adult) Rosen Publishing Group, Inc., The.

Sherman, Patrice. Roman Gods, Heroes, & Mythology. 2018. (Gods, Heroes, & Mythology Ser.). (ENG., Illus.). 48p. (J). (gr. 4-8). lib. bdg. 35.64 *(978-1-5321-1786-2(8)*, 30860) ABDO Publishing Co.

Shone, Rob. Greek Myths, 1 vol. 2006. (Graphic Mythology Ser.). (ENG., Illus.). 48p. (gr. 4-5). (J). lib. bdg. 37.13 *(978-1-4042-0801-8(1)*, 6fe8bb37-416e-4d4c-ab26-5702377e1e15); pap. 14.05 *(978-1-4042-0813-1(5)*, af9012e4-72f1-4389-a3dd-33ffa50d46b1) Rosen Publishing Group, Inc., The.

Silva, Gabriel, adapted by. HERACLES -Doce años tras la Inmortalidad. 2006. (SPA.). 32p. *(978-958-30-2002-5(8))* Panamericana Editorial.

—POSIDÓN -el dios del Mar- 2005. (SPA.). 32p. *(978-958-30-2003-2(6))* Panamericana Editorial.

—ZEUS -el padre de los Dioses. 2006. (SPA.). 32p. *(978-958-30-2000-1(1))* Panamericana Editorial.

Simonson, Louise & Garcia, Eduardo. The Death of Baldur. Garcia, Eduardo, illus. 2016. (Norse Myths: a Viking Graphic Novel Ser.). (ENG., Illus.). 56p. (J). (gr. 4-8). lib. bdg. 27.99 *(978-1-4965-3488-0(3)*, 132600, Stone Arch Bks.) Capstone.

Smalls, June. Celtic Gods, Heroes, & Mythology. 2018. (Gods, Heroes, & Mythology Ser.). (ENG., Illus.). 48p. (J). (gr. 4-8). lib. bdg. 35.64 *(978-1-5321-1779-4(5)*, 30846) ABDO Publishing Co.

Smith, Neil. Jason & the Argonauts, 1 vol. 2014. (Heroes & Legends Ser.). (ENG., Illus.). 88p. (J). (gr. 8-8). 38.80 *(978-1-4777-8138-8(2)*, 3bd305ce-2fe1-454a-ae3e-ab219d528a19, Rosen Young Adult) Rosen Publishing Group, Inc., The.

Steele, Philip. Incredible Quests: Epic Journeys in Myth & Legend. Climpson, Sue, illus. 2006. 48p. (J). (gr. 3-7). pap. 11.99 *(978-1-84476-247-7(5))* Anness Publishing GBR. Dist: National Bk. Network.

Storrie, Paul D. Amaterasu. 2008. pap. 52.95 *(978-0-8225-9459-8(5))* Lerner Publishing Group.

—Amaterasu: Return of the Sun [a Japanese Myth]. Randall, Ron, illus. 2008. (Graphic Myths & Legends Ser.). (ENG.). 48p. (J). (gr. 4-8). per. 10.99 *(978-0-8225-6573-4(0)*, bb3c971f-bc02-40fc-8c66-54931357a695, Graphic Universe™) Lerner Publishing Group.

Sullivan, Laura L. Pallas Athena, 1 vol. 2019. (Women of Mythology: Goddesses, Warriors, & Hunters Ser.). (ENG.). 32p. (gr. 2-2). pap. 9.22 *(978-1-5026-5136-5(X)*, c788f6be-83d0-4645-b80e-8cce040b89fd) Cavendish Square Publishing LLC.

Sutcliff, Rosemary. Black Ships Before Troy: The Story of the Iliad. 2005. (ENG.). 176p. (YA). (gr. 7). mass mkt. 8.99 *(978-0-553-49483-9(X)*, Laurel Leaf) Random Hse. Children's Bks.

Swain, Cynthia & Benchmark Education Co., LLC. Opinions about Odysseus: A Greek Hero. Ramos, Jose, illus. 2014. (Text Connections Ser.). (J). (gr. 3). *(978-1-4509-9669-3(8))* Benchmark Education Co.

Takvorian, Nadine, illus. Jason & the Argonauts, 1 vol. 2011. (Greek Myths Ser.). (ENG.). 32p. (J). (gr. 3-5). lib. bdg. 29.32 *(978-1-4048-6669-0(8)*, 115023, Picture Window Bks.) Capstone.

Temple, Teri. Aphrodite. 2016. (J). *(978-1-4896-4631-6(0))* Weigl Pubs., Inc.

—Apollo. 2016. (J). *(978-1-4896-4633-0(7))* Weigl Pubs., Inc.

—Ares. 2016. (J). *(978-1-4896-4635-4(3))* Weigl Pubs., Inc.

—Artemis. 2016. (J). *(978-1-4896-4637-8(X))* Weigl Pubs., Inc.

—Athena. 2016. (J). *(978-1-4896-4639-2(6))* Weigl Pubs., Inc.

—Eros. 2016. (J). *(978-1-4896-4641-5(8))* Weigl Pubs., Inc.

—Hades. 2016. (J). *(978-1-4896-4643-9(4))* Weigl Pubs., Inc.

—Hephaestus. 2016. (J). *(978-1-4896-4645-3(0))* Weigl Pubs., Inc.

—Hera. 2016. (J). *(978-1-4896-4647-7(7))* Weigl Pubs., Inc.

—Hermes. 2016. (J). *(978-1-4896-4649-1(3))* Weigl Pubs., Inc.

—Jupiter King of the Gods, God of Sky & Storms. 2019. (Gods & Goddesses of Ancient Rome Ser.). (ENG., Illus.). 32p. (J). (gr. 3-6). pap. 13.95 *(978-1-4896-9496-6(X))*; lib. bdg. 29.99 *(978-1-4896-9495-9(1))* Weigl Pubs., Inc.

—Mars God of War. 2019. (Gods & Goddesses of Ancient Rome Ser.). (ENG.). 32p. (J). (gr. 3-6). pap. 13.95 *(978-1-4896-9500-0(1))*; lib. bdg. 29.99 *(978-1-4896-9499-7(4))* Weigl Pubs., Inc.

—Mercury God of Travels & Trade. 2019. (Gods & Goddesses of Ancient Rome Ser.). (ENG., Illus.). 32p. (J). (gr. 3-6). pap. 13.95 *(978-1-4896-9504-8(4))*; lib. bdg. 29.99 *(978-1-4896-9503-1(6))* Weigl Pubs., Inc.

—Neptune God of the Sea & Earthquakes. 2019. (Gods & Goddesses of Ancient Rome Ser.). (ENG., Illus.). 32p. (J). (gr. 3-6). pap. 13.95 *(978-1-4896-9508-6(7))*; lib. bdg. 29.99 *(978-1-4896-9507-9(9))* Weigl Pubs., Inc.

—Pluto God of the Underworld. 2019. (Gods & Goddesses of Ancient Rome Ser.). (ENG., Illus.). 32p. (J). (gr. 3-6). pap. 13.95 *(978-1-4896-9512-3(5))*; lib. bdg. 29.99 *(978-1-4896-9511-6(7))* Weigl Pubs., Inc.

—Poseidon. 2016. (J). *(978-1-4896-4651-4(5))* Weigl Pubs., Inc.

—Venus Goddess of Love & Beauty. 2019. (Gods & Goddesses of Ancient Rome Ser.). (ENG.). 32p. (J). (gr.

3-6). pap. 13.95 *(978-1-4896-9520-8(6))*; lib. bdg. 29.99 *(978-1-4896-9519-2(2))* Weigl Pubs., Inc.
—Zeus. 2016. (J). *(978-1-4896-4653-8(1))* Weigl Pubs., Inc.
Temple, Teri & Temple, Emily. Diana: Goddess of Hunting & Protector of Animals. Young, Eric, illus. 2015. (Roman Mythology Ser.). (ENG.). 32p. (J). (gr. 2-5). 35.64 *(978-1-63143-716-8(X)*, 208559) Child's World, Inc, The.
—Juno: Queen of the Gods, Goddess of Marriage. Young, Eric, illus. 2015. (Roman Mythology Ser.). (ENG.). 32p. (J). (gr. 2-5). 35.64 *(978-1-63143-717-5(8)*, 208560) Child's World, Inc, The.
—Jupiter: King of the Gods, God of Sky & Storms. Young, Eric, illus. 2015. (Roman Mythology Ser.). (ENG.). 32p. (J). (gr. 2-5). 35.64 *(978-1-63143-718-2(6)*, 208561) Child's World, Inc, The.
—Mars: God of War. Young, Eric, illus. 2015. (Roman Mythology Ser.). (ENG.). 32p. (J). (gr. 2-5). 35.64 *(978-1-63143-719-9(4)*, 208562) Child's World, Inc, The.
—Mercury: God of Travels & Trade. Young, Eric, illus. 2015. (Roman Mythology Ser.). (ENG.). 32p. (J). (gr. 2-5). 35.64 *(978-1-63143-720-5(8)*, 208563) Child's World, Inc, The.
—Minerva: Goddess of Wisdom, War, & Crafts. Young, Eric, illus. 2015. (Roman Mythology Ser.). (ENG.). 32p. (J). (gr. 2-5). 35.64 *(978-1-63143-721-2(6)*, 208564) Child's World, Inc, The.
—Neptune: God of the Sea & Earthquakes. Young, Eric, illus. 2015. (Roman Mythology Ser.). 32p. (J). (gr. 2-5). 35.64 *(978-1-63143-722-9(4)*, 208565) Child's World, Inc, The.
—Pluto: God of the Underworld. Young, Eric, illus. 2015. (Roman Mythology Ser.). (ENG.). 32p. (J). (gr. 2-5). 35.64 *(978-1-63143-723-6(2)*, 208566) Child's World, Inc, The.
—Saturn: God of Sowing & Seeds. Young, Eric, illus. 2015. (Roman Mythology Ser.). (ENG.). 32p. (J). (gr. 2-5). 35.64 *(978-1-63143-724-3(0)*, 208567) Child's World, Inc, The.
—Venus: Goddess of Love & Beauty. Young, Eric, illus. 2015. (Roman Mythology Ser.). (ENG.). 32p. (J). (gr. 2-5). 35.64 *(978-1-63143-725-0(9)*, 208568) Child's World, Inc, The.
Tracy, Kathleen. The Life & Times of Homer. 2004. (Biography from Ancient Civilizations Ser.). (Illus.). 48p. (J). (gr. 4-8). lib. bdg. 29.95 *(978-1-58415-260-6(5))* Mitchell Lane Pubs.
—Medusa. 2010. (Monsters in Myth Ser.). (Illus.). 48p. (J). (gr. 4-7). lib. bdg. 29.95 *(978-1-58415-928-5(6))* Mitchell Lane Pubs.
Turnbull, Ann. Greek Myths. Young, Sarah, illus. 2010. (ENG.). 168p. (J). (gr. 5). 24.99 *(978-0-7636-5111-4(7))* Candlewick Pr.
Turner, Tracey & Lenman, Jamie. Hard As Nails in Myths & Legends. 2015. (Hard As Nails in History Ser.). (ENG., Illus.). 64p. (J). (gr. 4-5). lib. bdg. *(978-0-7787-1520-7(5))* Crabtree Publishing Co.
Uschan, Michael V. Chinese Mythology, 1 vol. 2014. (Mythology & Culture Worldwide Ser.). (ENG., Illus.). 104p. (gr. 7-10). lib. bdg. 41.03 *(978-1-4205-1146-8(7)*, 4b1129f8-7ad4-47ca-9917-099470dc7a25, Lucent Pr.) Greenhaven Publishing LLC.
Van Lente, Fred. Hercules, 1 vol. 2014. (Heroes & Legends Ser.). (ENG., Illus.). 88p. (J). (gr. 8-8). 38.80 *(978-1-4777-8137-1(4)*, cbe4c805-da19-4ad9-9864-9266fadf8ca2, Rosen Young Adult) Rosen Publishing Group, Inc., The.
Wargin, Kathy-jo. The Legend of the Petoskey Stone. Frankenhuyzen, Gijsbert van, illus. 2004. (Myths, Legends, Fairy & Folktales Ser.). (ENG.). 40p. (J). (gr. 2-5). 17.95 *(978-1-58536-217-2(4)*, 202047) Sleeping Bear Pr.
Wildwood, Gretchen. Ancient Mesopotamian Civilization, 1 vol. Cantucci, Alessandro & Morandi, Andrea, illus. 2009. (Ancient Civilizations & Their Myths & Legends Ser.). (ENG.). 48p. (YA). (gr. 6-6). lib. bdg. 34.47 *(978-1-4042-8037-3(5)*, d4c1502f-6782-45a0-9920-2a2811f55808) Rosen Publishing Group, Inc., The.
Wilkinson, Philip. Chinese Myth: A Treasury of Legends, Art, & History. 2007. (Myth Ser.). (Illus.). 96p. (J). (gr. 4-7). pap. 7.99 *(978-0-7858-2348-3(4)*, Chartwell) Book Sales, Inc.
—Chinese Myth: a Treasury of Legends, Art, & History: A Treasury of Legends, Art, & History. 2007. (ENG., Illus.). 96p. (C). (gr. 6-18). lib. bdg. 180.00 *(978-0-7656-8103-4(X)*, Y181705) Routledge.
Williams, Marcia. Greek Myths. Williams, Marcia, illus. 2011. (ENG., Illus.). 40p. (J). (gr. k-4). pap. 8.99 *(978-0-7636-5384-2(5))* Candlewick Pr.
Wolfson, Evelyn. Mythology of the Romans, 1 vol. 2014. (Mythology, Myths, & Legends Ser.). (ENG.). 96p. (gr. 6-7). 31.61 *(978-0-7660-6187-3(6)*, 2422bdf8-b6d7-4661-9644-9a14e67bd3e3) Enslow Publishing, LLC.
World Book, Inc. Staff, contrib. by. Myths & Legends of Africa. 2015. (Illus.). 64p. (J). *(978-0-7166-2631-2(4))* World Bk., Inc.
—Tales Through Time: A Supplement to Childcraft-The How & Why Library. 2009. (Illus.). 204p. (J). *(978-0-7166-0622-2(4))* World Bk., Inc.
World Mythology. 2003. 320p. 5.98 *(978-1-4054-0326-9(8))* Parragon, Inc.
World of Mythology (Set), 5 bks., Set. Incl. Celtic Myth: a Treasury of Legends, Art, & History: A Treasury of Legends, Art, & History. Harpur, James. lib. bdg. 180.00 *(978-0-7656-8102-7(1)*, Y181569); Chinese Myth: a Treasury of Legends, Art, & History: A Treasury of Legends, Art, & History. Wilkinson, Philip. lib. bdg. 180.00 *(978-0-7656-8103-4(X)*, Y181705); Classical Myth: a Treasury of Greek & Roman Legends, Art, & History: A Treasury of Greek & Roman Legends, Art, & History. Bingham, Jane. lib. bdg. 165.00 *(978-0-7656-8104-1(8)*, Y181755); Egyptian Myth: a Treasury of Legends, Art, & History: A Treasury of Legends, Art, & History. Kramer, Ann. lib. bdg. 180.00 *(978-0-7656-8105-8(6)*, Y182128); Mesoamerican Myth: a Treasury of Central American Legends, Art, & History: A Treasury of Central American Legends, Art, & History. Ganeri, Anita. lib. bdg. 180.00 *(978-0-7656-8106-5(4)*, Y182745); (C). (gr. 6-18). (ENG., Illus.). 96p. 2007. Set lib. bdg. 180.00 *(978-0-7656-8101-0(3)*, Y184677) Routledge.
Yasuda, Anita. Explore Ancient Chinese Myths! With 25 Great Projects. Casteel, Tom, illus. 2017. (Explore Your World Ser.). (ENG.). 96p. (J). (gr. 3-4). pap. 14.95 *(978-1-61930-611-0(5)*, d9bdc34e-3c81-4911-bed0-b7f120c808b7) Nomad Pr.
—The 12 Most Amazing American Myths & Legends. 2015. (Amazing America Ser.). (ENG., Illus.). 32p. (J). (gr. 3-6). 32.80 *(978-1-63235-010-7(6)*, 11549); pap. 9.95 *(978-1-63235-070-1(X)*, 11555) Bookstaves, LLC. (12-Story Library).
Yomtov, Nel. Dawn of Time: Creation Myths Around the World. Lividini, Dante, illus. 2017. (Universal Myths Ser.). (ENG.). 48p. (J). (gr. 3-9). lib. bdg. 31.32 *(978-1-5157-6629-2(2)*, 135200, Capstone Pr.) Capstone.

MYTHOLOGY, CLASSICAL

Amery, Heather. Greek Myths. 2015. (Stories for Young Children Ser.). (ENG.). 128p. (J). (gr. k-5). 18.99 *(978-0-7945-3466-0(X)*, Usborne) EDC Publishing.
—Greek Myths for Young Children. Edwards, Linda, illus. 2004. (Greek Myths for Young Children Ser.). 128p. (J). (gr. -1-3). lib. bdg. 26.95 *(978-1-58086-261-5(6))*; 7.99 *(978-0-7945-0141-9(9)*, Usborne) EDC Publishing.
Antoniades, Basil. Having Fun with the Gods & Goddesses of the Ancient Greeks. 2008. 108p. pap. 9.94 *(978-0-615-24661-1(3))* Antoniades, Basil.
Bailey, Carolyn Sherwin. Wonder Stories the Best Myths for Boys & Girls. 2004. reprint ed. pap. 31.95 *(978-1-4179-3481-2(6))* Kessinger Publishing, LLC.
Barkow, Henriette. Pandora's Box: English Only. Mayo, Diana, illus. 2004. (ENG.). 32p. (J). pap. *(978-1-84444-380-2(9))* Mantra Lingua.
Bingham, Jane. Classical Myth: A Treasury of Greek & Roman Legends, Art, & History. 2007. (Myth Ser.). (Illus.). 96p. (J). (gr. 4-7). pap. 7.99 *(978-0-7858-2350-6(6))* Book Sales, Inc.
—Classical Myth: a Treasury of Greek & Roman Legends, Art, & History: A Treasury of Greek & Roman Legends, Art, & History. 2007. (ENG., Illus.). 96p. (C). (gr. 6-18). lib. bdg. 165.00 *(978-0-7656-8104-1(8)*, Y181755) Routledge.
Bloom, Harold, ed. Oedipus Rex. 2007. (Bloom's Guides). (ENG.). 118p. (gr. 9-12). 30.00 *(978-0-7910-9360-3(3)*, P125634, Facts On File) Infobase Holdings, Inc.
Bornemann Spies, Karen. Heroes in Greek Mythology Rock!, 1 vol. 2011. (Mythology Rocks! Ser.). (ENG., Illus.). 128p. (gr. 6-7). lib. bdg. 35.93 *(978-0-7660-3900-1(5)*, cd55895f-7245-4d0b-963e-31a33cb6f64c) Enslow Publishing, LLC.
Braun, Eric. Athena. 2017. (Gods of Legend Ser.). (ENG.). 32p. (gr. 2-7). 9.95 *(978-1-68072-445-5(2))*; (J). (gr. 4-6). pap. 9.99 *(978-1-64466-176-5(4)*, 11400); (Illus.). (J). (gr. 4-6). lib. bdg. *(978-1-68072-136-2(4)*, 10456) Black Rabbit Bks. (Bolt).
Calcium Staff, contrib. by. The Monsters & Creatures of Greek Mythology, 1 vol. 2011. (Ancient Greek Mythology Ser.). (ENG.). 64p. (J). (gr. 5-9). lib. bdg. 34.65 *(978-0-7565-4481-2(5)*, 115728, Compass Point Bks.) Capstone.
Catherine, Mary. Classic Myths. 2004. reprint ed. pap. 15.95 *(978-1-4191-1334-5(8))*; pap. 1.99 *(978-1-4192-1334-2(2))* Kessinger Publishing, LLC.
Church, Alfred John. Stories of the Iliad & the Aeneid. 2006. pap. 24.95 *(978-1-4286-0468-1(5))* Kessinger Publishing, LLC.
—The Story of the Iliad. 2005. reprint ed. pap. 31.95 *(978-1-4191-5466-9(4))* Kessinger Publishing, LLC.
Clarke, M. The Story of Troy. 2007. (Illus.). 184p. per. *(978-1-4065-1381-3(4))* Dodo Pr.
Clarke, Michael. The Story of Troy. 2017. (ENG., Illus.). (J). 23.95 *(978-1-374-81990-0(5))*; pap. 13.95 *(978-1-374-81989-4(1))* Capital Communications, Inc.
Clayton, Sally Pomme. Persephone. Lee, Virginia, illus. 2009. (ENG.). 28p. (J). (gr. 2-5). 18.00 *(978-0-8028-5349-3(8)*, Eerdmans Bks For Young Readers) Eerdmans, William B. Publishing Co.
Colum, Padraic. The Golden Fleece & the Heroes Who Lived Before Achilles. Pogány, Willy, illus. 2007. 144p. per. 8.99 *(978-1-4209-3040-5(0))* Digireads.com Publishing.
Craft, Charlotte. King Midas & the Golden Touch. Craft, Kinuko Y., illus. 2003. (ENG.). 32p. (J). (gr. -1-3). pap. 8.99 *(978-0-06-054063-0(X)*, HarperCollins) HarperCollins Pubs.
Curlee, Lynn. Mythological Creatures: A Classical Bestiary. Curlee, Lynn, illus. 2008. (ENG., Illus.). 40p. (J). (gr. 3-7). 19.99 *(978-1-4169-1453-2(6)*, Atheneum Bks. for Young Readers) Simon & Schuster Children's Publishing.
Dakota, Heather. The Complete Guide to Greek Myths. 2015. (Illus.). 144p. (J). *(978-1-4351-6162-7(9))* Barnes & Noble, Inc.
DiPrimio, Pete. The Sphinx. 2010. (Monsters in Myth Ser.). (Illus.). 48p. (J). (gr. 4-7). lib. bdg. 29.95 *(978-1-58415-931-5(6))* Mitchell Lane Pubs.
Evans, C. & Millard, A. Greek Myths & Legends. 2004. (Myths & Legends Ser.). 64p. (J). pap. 10.95 *(978-0-7945-0455-7(8))* EDC Publishing.
Evans, Cheryl & Millard, Anne. Greek Myths & Legends. Matthews, Rodney, illus. 2006. (Myths & Legends Ser.). 64p. (J). (gr. 6). lib. bdg. 18.95 *(978-1-58086-553-1(4))* EDC Publishing.
Evans, Hestia. Mythology. Steer, Dugald A., ed. 2007. (Ologies Ser.). (ENG., Illus.). 32p. (J). (gr. 3-7). 29.99 *(978-0-7636-3403-2(4))* Candlewick Pr.
Fontes, Justine & Fontes, Ron. Atalanta: The Race Against Destiny [a Greek Myth]. Yeates, Thomas, illus. 2008. (Graphic Myths & Legends Ser.). (ENG.). 48p. (J). (gr. 4-8). per. 9.99 *(978-0-8225-6569-7(2)*, e56c756f-428a-4e04-89b3-2ee8a4565245, Graphic Universe™) Lerner Publishing Group.
Fontes, Ron & Fontes, Justine. Demeter & Persephone. 2008. pap. 52.95 *(978-0-8225-9461-1(7))* Lerner Publishing Group.
Francillon, R. E. Gods & Heroes: An Introduction to Greek Mythology (Yesterday's Classics) 2007. 276p. per. 11.95 *(978-1-59915-085-7(9))* Yesterday's Classics.
Freeman, Philip. Heroes of Olympus. Willis, Drew, illus. (ENG.). 352p. (J). (gr. 3-7). 2013. pap. 12.99 *(978-1-4424-1730-4(7))* 2012. 17.99 *(978-1-4424-1729-8(3))* Simon & Schuster Bks. For Young Readers. (Simon & Schuster Bks. For Young Readers).
Geras, Adèle. Troy. 2004. 368p. (J). (gr. 8-18). pap. 48.00 incl. audio *(978-0-8072-2288-1(7)*, Listening Library) Random Hse. Audio Publishing Group.
Guess McKerley, Jennifer. Hydra, 1 vol. 2008. (Monsters Ser.). (ENG., Illus.). 48p. (gr. 4-8). lib. bdg. 36.83 *(978-0-7377-4081-3(7)*, e607b7e0-ad22-4080-a128-4ebc9a4526e1, KidHaven Publishing) Greenhaven Publishing LLC.
Gunderson, Jessica. Olympians vs. Titans: An Interactive Mythological Adventure. Arcabascio, Carolyn, illus. 2017. (ENG.). 112p. (J). pap. *(978-1-4747-3767-8(6))*; (gr. 3-7). lib. bdg. 32.65 *(978-1-5157-4820-5(0)*, 134436, Capstone Pr.) Capstone.
Harris, Nick, illus. The Wooden Horse of Troy, 1 vol. 2011. (Greek Myths Ser.). (ENG.). 32p. (J). (gr. 3-5). lib. bdg. 29.32 *(978-1-4048-6670-6(1)*, 115024, Picture Window Bks.) Capstone.
Haus, Estudio, illus. The 12 Labors of Hercules: A Graphic Retelling. 2015. (Ancient Myths Ser.). (ENG.). 32p. (J). (gr. 3-9). lib. bdg. 31.32 *(978-1-4914-2071-3(5)*, 127549, Capstone Pr.) Capstone.
Hawthorne, Nathanial. Tanglewood Tales. Sterrett, Virginia, illus. 2012. (Calla Editions Ser.). (ENG.). 304p. (gr. 4). 40.00 *(978-0-60660-026-9(5)*, 600265) Dover Pubns., Inc.
—Tanglewood Tales. Pogány, Willy, illus. 2009. 272p. pap. 11.95 *(978-1-59915-091-8(3))* Yesterday's Classics.
—A Wonder Book: Heroes & Monsters of Greek Mythology. 2003. (Dover Children's Evergreen Classics Ser.). (ENG.). 176p. (J). (gr. 3-8). pap. 5.99 *(978-0-486-43209-0(2)*, 432092) Dover Pubns., Inc.
—A Wonder Book & Tanglewood Tales. l.t. ed. 2004. (Large Print Ser.). 563p. 26.00 *(978-1-58287-673-3(8))* North Bks.
Herdling, Glenn. Greek Mythology: Jason & the Golden Fleece. (Jr. Graphic Mythologies Ser.). (ENG.). 24p. (J). (gr. 2-3). 2009. 47.90 *(978-1-61513-864-7(1)*, PowerKids Pr.) 2006. (Illus.). pap. 10.60 *(978-1-4042-2149-9(2)*, 6eedbb3e-d580-4990-84e9-99d0f22f2cb4, PowerKids Pr.) 2006. (Illus.). lib. bdg. 28.93 *(978-1-4042-3396-6(2)*, 225c1f43-e5d9-4fe4-be6d-9330439a4fab) Rosen Publishing Group, Inc., The.
Hibbert, Clare. Terrible Tales of Ancient Greece, 1 vol., Vol. 1. Janther, Janos, illus. 2014. (Monstrous Myths Ser.). (ENG.). 32p. (J). (gr. 4-5). pap. 11.50 *(978-1-4824-0184-4(3)*, 473e82b0-d16f-4d59-8a69-e193576da68d) Stevens, Gareth Publishing LLLP.
Hoena, Blake. Hades & the Underworld: An Interactive Mythological Adventure. Takvorian, Nadine, illus. 2017. (You Choose: Ancient Greek Myths Ser.). (ENG.). 112p. (J). (gr. 3-7). lib. bdg. 32.65 *(978-1-5157-4823-6(5)*, 134439, Capstone Pr.) Capstone.
—The Trojan War: An Interactive Mythological Adventure. Takvorian, Nadine, illus. 2017. (You Choose: Ancient Greek Myths Ser.). (ENG.). 112p. (J). (gr. 3-7). lib. bdg. 32.65 *(978-1-5157-4822-9(7)*, 134438, Capstone Pr.) Capstone.
Hoena, Blake & Gunderson, Jessica. You Choose: Ancient Greek Myths. 2017. (You Choose: Ancient Greek Myths Ser.). (ENG., Illus.). 112p. (J). (gr. 3-7). 277.20 *(978-1-5157-4824-3(3)*, 25963, Capstone Pr.) Capstone.
Houle, Michelle M. Gods & Goddesses in Greek Mythology Rock!, 1 vol. 2011. (Mythology Rocks! Ser.). (ENG., Illus.). 128p. (gr. 6-7). lib. bdg. 35.93 *(978-0-7660-3897-4(1)*, e8297756-6c82-47cb-984d-8e4b312c4ca1) Enslow Publishing, LLC.
Jeffrey, Gary. Centaurs, 1 vol. Poluzzi, Alessandro, illus. 2012. (Graphic Mythical Creatures Ser.). (ENG.). 24p. (J). (gr. 3-3). pap. 9.15 *(978-1-4339-6753-5(7)*, e12305a9-f643-4206-8e3c-4eb0afd783c1); lib. bdg. 26.60 *(978-1-4339-6751-1(0)*, cde53394-7b99-4771-8793-376dd333f420) Stevens, Gareth Publishing LLLP. (Gareth Stevens Learning Library).
Judd, Mary Catherine. Classic Myths. MacDonall, Angus, illus. 2007. 172p. per. *(978-1-4065-4675-0(5))* Dodo Pr.
Katz, Leon. The Greek Myths: Puppet Plays for Children from Ovid's Metamorphoses. 2004. (Applause Bks.). (ENG., Illus.). 160p. pap. 12.95 *(978-1-55783-502-4(0)*, 1557835020, Applause Theatre & Cinema) Leonard, Hal Corp.
Kendree, McLean, illus. Pandora's Vase, 1 vol. 2011. (Greek Myths Ser.). (ENG.). 32p. (J). (gr. 3-5). lib. bdg. 29.32 *(978-1-4048-6668-3(X)*, 115022, Picture Window Bks.) Capstone.
Kimmel, Eric A. The Mcelderry Book of Greek Myths. Montserrat, Pep, illus. 2008. (ENG.). 112p. (J). (gr. 1-5). 21.99 *(978-1-4169-1534-8(6)*, McElderry, Margaret K. Bks.) McElderry, Margaret K. Bks.
Korba, Joanna. Demeter & Persephone: A Myth from Ancient Greece. 2006. (J). pap. *(978-1-4108-7166-4(5))* Benchmark Education Co.
Kovacs, Charles. Ancient Greece, 40 vols. 2004. (Waldorf Education Resources Ser.). 160p. pap. 19.95 *(978-0-86315-429-4(8))* Floris Bks. GBR. Dist: Consortium Bk. Sales & Distribution.
Leonard, Scott A. Myths & Legends of Ancient Greece. 2015. (Illus.). 64p. (J). *(978-0-7166-2634-3(9))* World Bk., Inc.
Lester, Julius. Cupid: A Tale of Love & Desire. 2007. (ENG., Illus.). 208p. (YA). (gr. 7-12). 17.00 *(978-0-15-202056-9(X)*, 1191683, Clarion Bks.) HarperCollins Pubs.
Limke, Jeff. Jason. 2008. pap. 52.95 *(978-0-8225-9462-8(5))* Lerner Publishing Group.
Loewen, Nancy. Cyclops Tells All: The Way EYE See It, 1 vol. Pentney, Ryan, illus. 2014. (Other Side of the Myth Ser.). (ENG.). 32p. (J). (gr. -1-3). lib. bdg. 27.99 *(978-1-4795-2180-7(9)*, 123981, Picture Window Bks.) Capstone.
Loria, Laura. What Is a Constellation?, 1 vol. 2014. (Let's Find Out! Space Science Ser.). (ENG.). 32p. (J). (gr. 2-3). 26.06 *(978-1-62275-476-2(X)*, 7eed2aac-c84c-4391-b199-d071a2a9dca2) Rosen Publishing Group, Inc., The.
Lupton, Hugh. Demeter & Persephone, 1. Hénaff, Carole, illus. 2013. (Greek Myths Ser.: 1). 40p. (J). (gr. 3-6). pap. 22.44 *(978-1-84686-834-4(3))* Barefoot Bks., Ltd. GBR. Dist: Children's Plus, Inc.
—Theseus & the Minotaur, 2. Hénaff, Carole, illus. 2013. (Greek Myths Ser.: 2). 40p. (J). (gr. 3-6). pap. 24.94 *(978-1-84686-782-8(7))* Barefoot Bks., Ltd. GBR. Dist: Children's Plus, Inc.
Lupton, Hugh, et al. The Adventures of Achilles. Henaff, Carole, illus. 2012. (Advanced Readers: Classics Ser.). (J). 128p. (gr. 3-6). pap. 12.99 *(978-1-84686-800-9(9))*; 96p. (gr. 6-9). 23.99 *(978-1-84686-420-9(8))* Barefoot Bks., Inc.
McCaughrean, Geraldine. Los Doce Trabajos de Hércules: Eco y Narciso. Barroso, Paz, tr. Ross, Tony, illus. 2005. (Mythology Series Collection Mitos Ser.). Tr. of Twelve Labours of Heracles. (SPA.). 48p. (J). (gr. 2-3). 9.95 *(978-84-348-6429-0(0))* SM Ediciones ESP. Dist: Iaconi, Mariuccia Bk. Imports.
McCaughrean, Geraldine, retold by. Odysseus. 2004. (Heroes Ser.). (ENG., Illus.). 128p. (J). 17.95 *(978-0-8126-2721-3(0))* Cricket Bks.
Mitchell Lane Publishers Inc. Staff. Profiles in Greek & Roman Mythology, 15 vols., Set. 2010. (J). (gr. 4-8). lib. bdg. 449.25 *(978-1-58415-751-9(8))* Mitchell Lane Pubs.
Oberman, Sheldon. Island of the Minotaur: The Greek Myths of Ancient Crete. Drawson, Blair, illus. 2003. (ENG.). 96p. (J). (gr. 5-8). 19.95 *(978-1-56656-531-8(6)*, Crocodile Bks.) Interlink Publishing Group, Inc.
O'Connor, George. Olympians: Poseidon: Earth Shaker. O'Connor, George, illus. 2013. (Olympians Ser.: 5). (ENG., Illus.). 80p. (J). (gr. 4-9). 21.99 *(978-1-59643-828-6(2)*, 900087634, First Second Bks.) Roaring Brook Pr.
—Poseidon: Earth Shaker. 2013. (Olympians Ser.: 5). (ENG., Illus.). 80p. (J). (gr. 4-9). pap. 12.99 *(978-1-59643-738-8(3)*, 900077385, First Second Bks.) Roaring Brook Pr.
Orr, Tamra. Achilles. 2008. (Profiles in Greek & Roman Mythology Ser.). (Illus.). 48p. (YA). (gr. 4-7). lib. bdg. 29.95 *(978-1-58415-706-9(2))* Mitchell Lane Pubs.
—Apollo. 2008. (Profiles in Greek & Roman Mythology Ser.). (Illus.). 48p. (YA). (gr. 4-7). lib. bdg. 29.95 *(978-1-58415-704-5(6))* Mitchell Lane Pubs.
Osborne, Mary Pope. Mitos Griegos. (Torre de Papel Ser.). (SPA.). (YA). (gr. 6-18). 8.95 *(978-958-04-2863-3(8))* Norma S.A. COL. Dist: Distribuidora Norma, Inc.
Palmer, Erin. Greek Mythology. Forsyth, Matt, illus. 2017. (Mythology Marvels Ser.). (ENG.). 32p. (gr. 3-5). pap. 9.95 *(978-1-68342-892-3(7)*, 9781683428923) Rourke Educational Media.
Pandora's Box. 2004. (J). cd-rom *(978-1-84444-465-6(1))* Mantra Lingua.
The Parthenon Code. 2006. (ENG., Illus.). 29.95 *(978-0-9705438-3-7(2))* Solving Light Bks.
Payment, Simone. Greek Mythology. 2009. (Mythology Around the World Ser.). 64p. (gr. 5-5). 58.50 *(978-1-61514-750-2(0)*, Rosen Reference) Rosen Publishing Group, Inc., The.
Pearce, Q. L. The Furies, 1 vol. 2010. (Monsters Ser.). (ENG., Illus.). 48p. (gr. 4-8). 32.08 *(978-0-7377-5035-5(9)*, 354ea899-c567-40ff-9209-eb461698d736, KidHaven Publishing) Greenhaven Publishing LLC.
Peebles, Alice. Monsters of the Gods. Chilvers, Nigel, illus. 2015. (Mythical Beasts Ser.). (ENG.). 32p. (J). (gr. 3-6). 27.99 *(978-1-4677-6342-4(X)*, f638c111-d1c9-46d2-978f-9226ec1847e8, Hungry Tomato (r)) Lerner Publishing Group.
Pommaux, Yvan. Theseus & the Minotaur (a Toon Graphic) Pommaux, Yvan, illus. 2014. (Toon Ser.). (ENG., Illus.). 56p. (J). (gr. 3-7). 16.95 *(978-1-935179-61-0(6)*, Toon Books) Astra Publishing Hse.
Profiles in Greek & Roman Mythology, 12 vols., Set. Incl. Achilles. Orr, Tamra. (YA). 2008. lib. bdg. 29.95 *(978-1-58415-706-9(2))*; Apollo. Orr, Tamra. (YA). 2008. lib. bdg. 29.95 *(978-1-58415-704-5(6))*; Artemis. O'Neal, Claire. (YA). 2007. lib. bdg. 29.95 *(978-1-58415-555-3(8))*; Athena. Roberts, Russell. (J). 2007. lib. bdg. 29.95 *(978-1-58415-556-0(6))*; Dionysus. Roberts, Russell. (YA). 2007. lib. bdg. 29.95 *(978-1-58415-557-7(4))*; Hercules. Whiting, Jim. (YA). 2007. lib. bdg. 29.95 *(978-1-58415-553-9(1))*; Jason. Whiting, Jim. (J). 2007. lib. bdg. 29.95 *(978-1-58415-552-2(3))*; Odysseus. Tracy, Kathleen. (J). 2008. lib. bdg. 29.95 *(978-1-58415-705-2(4))*; Perseus. Harkins, Susan Sales & Harkins, William H. (J). 2007. lib. bdg. 29.95 *(978-1-58415-558-4(2))*; Poseidon. Roberts, Russell. (J). 2008. lib. bdg. 29.95 *(978-1-58415-707-6(0))*; Theseus. Tracy, Kathleen. (YA). 2007. lib. bdg. 29.95 *(978-1-58415-554-6(X))*; Zeus. Roberts, Russell. (YA). 2007. lib. bdg. 29.95 *(978-1-58415-559-1(0))*; (Illus.). 48p. (gr. 4-7). 2009. Set lib. bdg. 359.40 *(978-1-58415-708-3(9))* Mitchell Lane Pubs.
Randolph, Joanne, ed. The Myths & Legends of Ancient Greece & Rome, 1 vol. 2017. (Mythology & Legends Around the World Ser.). (ENG.). 64p. (gr. 4-4). 35.93 *(978-1-5026-3276-0(4)*, 9262cafa-2b0e-4276-9b4c-d582eff15246); pap. 13.93 *(978-1-5026-3446-7(5)*, 2a39ca45-6749-471d-a36e-329f4df9e260) Cavendish Square Publishing LLC.
Redmond, Diane & Mould, Chris. Hercules: Superhero: Band 11/Lime (Collins Big Cat) 2005. (Collins Big Cat Ser.). (ENG.). 288p. (J). (gr. 1-3). pap. 10.99 *(978-0-00-718638-9(X))* HarperCollins Pubs. Ltd. GBR. Dist: Independent Pubs. Group.
Riordan, James. Jason & the Golden Fleece. Cockcroft, Jason, illus. 2004. 64p. (YA). *(978-1-84507-271-1(5))* ReiseArt Buchhandlung GmbH.
—Jason & the Golden Fleece. Cockcroft, Jason, tr. Cockcroft, Jason, illus. 2003. (ENG.). 64p. (J). *(978-0-7112-2081-2(6))* ReiseArt Buchhandlung GmbH.
Roberts, Russell. Athena. 2007. (Profiles in Greek & Roman Mythology Ser.). (Illus.). 48p. (J). (gr. 4-7). lib. bdg. 29.95 *(978-1-58415-556-0(6))* Mitchell Lane Pubs.
—The Cyclopes. 2010. (Monsters in Myth Ser.). (Illus.). 48p. (J). (gr. 4-7). lib. bdg. 29.95 *(978-1-58415-926-1(X))* Mitchell Lane Pubs.
—Dionysus. 2007. (Profiles in Greek & Roman Mythology Ser.). (Illus.). 48p. (YA). (gr. 4-7). lib. bdg. 29.95 *(978-1-58415-557-7(4))* Mitchell Lane Pubs.
—The Minotaur. 2010. (Monsters in Myth Ser.). (Illus.). 48p. (J). (gr. 4-7). lib. bdg. 29.95 *(978-1-58415-929-2(4))* Mitchell Lane Pubs.
—Poseidon. 2008. (Profiles in Greek & Roman Mythology Ser.). (Illus.). 48p. (J). (gr. 4-7). lib. bdg. 29.95 *(978-1-58415-707-6(0))* Mitchell Lane Pubs.
—Zeus. 2007. (Profiles in Greek & Roman Mythology Ser.). (Illus.). 48p. (YA). (gr. 4-7). lib. bdg. 29.95 *(978-1-58415-559-1(0))* Mitchell Lane Pubs.
Rose, Simon. Orion: The Myth & Science. 2015. (Illus.). 24p. (J). pap. *(978-1-5105-0268-0(8))* SmartBook Media, Inc.
Salariya, David. Ancient Greek Myths. 2013. (Illus.). 168p. (J). *(978-1-4351-5066-9(X))* Barnes & Noble, Inc.

MNO

Schomp, Virginia. The Ancient Greeks, 1 vol. 2008. (Myths of the World Ser.). (ENG., Illus.). 96p. (gr. 6-6). lib. bdg. 36.93 (978-0-7614-2547-2(0), 49d4fc2f-b61c-4bd5-aab2-7081bbef77b0) Cavendish Square Publishing LLC.

—The Ancient Romans, 1 vol. 2009. (Myths of the World Ser.). (ENG., Illus.). 96p. (gr. 6-6). lib. bdg. 36.93 (978-0-7614-3094-0(6), 38280b3a-537a-4619-ae81-62db9178a8d5) Cavendish Square Publishing LLC.

Seeley, Tim & Schulz, Barbara, illus. Jason: Quest for the Golden Fleece. 2006. (Graphic Myths & Legends Ser.). 48p. (J). (gr. 4-7). lib. bdg. 26.60 (978-0-8225-5967-2(6)) Lerner Publishing Group.

Sherman, Patrice. Legendary Creatures. 2015. (Illus.). 64p. (978-1-61900-067-4(9)) Eldorado Ink.

Shone, Rob. Greek Myths. 2009. (Graphic Mythology Ser.). (ENG.). 48p. (YA). (gr. 4-5). 58.50 (978-1-61512-985-0(5), Rosen Reference) Rosen Publishing Group, Inc., The.

Spinner, Stephanie. Atlanta, la Cazadora. Holguin, Magdalena, tr. 2003. (Zona Libre Ser.). (SPA.). 174p. 7.50 (978-958-04-7080-9(4)) Norma S.A. COL. Dist: Lectorum Pubns., Inc.

Spires, Elizabeth. I Am Arachne: Fifteen Greek & Roman Myths. Gerstein, Mordicai, illus. 2009. (ENG.). 112p. (J). (gr. 3-7). pap. 10.99 (978-0-312-56125-3(3), 900058860) Square Fish.

Tracy, Kathleen. Cerberus. 2010. (Monsters in Myth Ser.). (Illus.). 48p. (J). (gr. 4-7). lib. bdg. 29.95 (978-1-58415-924-7(3)) Mitchell Lane Pubs.

Trujillo, Luis Francisco. Mitologia Maravillosa para Ninos. 2018. (Coleccion Literatura Inf. y Juv Ser.). (SPA., Illus.). 160p. (YA). (gr. -1-7). per. 6.95 (978-968-403-926-1(3)) Selector, S.A. de C.V. MEX. Dist: Spanish Pubs., LLC.

Ware, Kay & Sutherland, Lucille. Greek & Roman Myths. Kottmeyer, William, ed. 2011. 146p. 40.95 (978-1-258-02410-9(1)) Literary Licensing, LLC.

West, David. Roman Myths, 1 vol. Watton, Ross, illus. 2006. (Graphic Mythology Ser.). (ENG.). 48p. (J). (gr. 4-5). lib. bdg. 37.13 (978-1-4042-0803-2(8), 96aecbc5-8fe0-4201-abfe-51453aabae76) Rosen Publishing Group, Inc., The.

Whiting, Jim. Jason. 2007. (Profiles in Greek & Roman Mythology Ser.). (Illus.). 48p. (J). (gr. 4-7). lib. bdg. 29.95 (978-1-58415-552-2(3)) Mitchell Lane Pubs.

Wilbur, Helen L. Z Is for Zeus: A Greek Mythology Alphabet. Juhasz, Victor, illus. rev. ed. 2008. (Art & Culture Ser.). (ENG.). 40p. (J). (gr. 1-4). 17.95 (978-1-58536-341-4(3), 202131) Sleeping Bear Pr.

Williams, Rose. The Labors of Aeneas: What a Pain It Was to Found the Roman Race. 2003. (ENG., Illus.). (YA). pap. 18.00 (978-0-86516-556-4(4)) Bolchazy-Carducci Pubs.

MYTHOLOGY, EGYPTIAN

Asselin, Kristine Carlson. Ancient Egyptian Myths. 2012. (Ancient Egyptian Civilization Ser.). (ENG.). 32p. (gr. 3-4). pap. 47.70 (978-1-4296-8402-6(X), Capstone Pr.) Capstone.

Bell, Michael & Quie, Sarah. Ancient Egyptian Civilization, 1 vol. D'Ottavi, Francesca, illus. 2009. (Ancient Civilizations & Their Myths & Legends Ser.). (ENG.). 48p. (YA). (gr. 6-6). lib. bdg. 34.47 (978-1-4042-8034-2(0), e72e435c-7f0c-4fb6-af5c-d2851a1a44eb) Rosen Publishing Group, Inc., The.

Broyles, Janell. Egyptian Mythology, 1 vol. 2006. (Mythology Around the World Ser.). (ENG., Illus.). 64p. (YA). (gr. 5-5). lib. bdg. 37.13 (978-1-4042-0770-7(8), 0bc1c9f8-67d6-4dcd-b062-ae51e89436e2) Rosen Publishing Group, Inc., The.

Casey, Dawn. Isis & Osiris. Mayo, Diana & Mistry, Nilesh, illus. 2004. (ENG & HIN.). 32p. (J). pap. (978-1-84444-433-5(3)); pap. (978-1-84444-330-7(2)); pap. (978-1-84444-315-4(9)); pap. (978-1-84444-323-9(X)); pap. (978-1-84444-434-2(1)); pap. (978-1-84444-435-9(X)) Mantra Lingua.

Daning, Tom. Egyptian Mythology: Osiris & Isis. (Jr. Graphic Mythologies Ser.). (ENG.). 24p. (gr. 2-3). 2009. (J). 47.90 (978-1-61513-861-6(7), PowerKids Pr.) 2006. (Illus.). (J). lib. bdg. 28.93 (978-1-4042-3399-7(7), 1ed6b5cf-961d-4992-be0e-a5fea100f312) 2006. (Illus.). pap. 10.60 (978-1-4042-2152-9(2), e6cf9585-eda0-43ff-824d-4ccf34f3bcd0, PowerKids Pr.) Rosen Publishing Group, Inc., The.

—Mitología Egipcia: Isis y Osiris, 1 vol. 2009. (Historietas Juveniles: Mitologías (Jr. Graphic Mythologies) Ser.). (SPA., Illus.). 24p. (gr. 2-3). pap. 10.60 (978-1-4358-3328-9(7), 2d4727bb-8f2a-4efb-9ae5-3d694c25736b, Editorial Buenas Letras) Rosen Publishing Group, Inc., The.

Dickmann, Nancy. Stars of Mythology: Egyptian. 2020. (Stars of Mythology Ser.). (ENG.). 32p. (J). (gr. 4-6). pap. 12.99 (978-1-4451-5191-5(X), Franklin Watts) Hachette Children's Group GBR. Dist: Hachette Bk. Group.

Doyle, Sheri. Understanding Egyptian Myths. 2012. (ENG.). 48p. (J). (978-0-7787-4508-2(2)); pap. (978-0-7787-4513-6(9)) Crabtree Publishing Co.

EGYPTIAN MYTHOLOGY a to Z, 3RD EDITION. 3rd rev. ed. 2010. (ENG., Illus.). 232p. (gr. 5-8). 45.00 (978-1-60413-926-6(9), P179401, Facts On File) Infobase Holdings, Inc.

Elgin, Kathy. Egyptian Myths, 1 vol. Sansom, Fiona, illus. 2009. (Myths from Many Lands Ser.). (ENG.). 48p. (YA). (gr. 5-5). 33.93 (978-1-60754-221-6(8), 2800d5d8-af62-455c-977f-d2691ff82753); pap. 13.85 (978-1-60754-222-3(6), 831a74df-5767-490f-89cd-c1c6d2764579) Rosen Publishing Group, Inc., The. (Windmill Bks.).

Forest, Christopher. Ancient Egyptian Gods & Goddesses. 2012. (Ancient Egyptian Civilization Ser.). (ENG.). 32p. (gr. 3-4). pap. 47.70 (978-1-4296-8400-2(3), Capstone Pr.); (J). pap. 8.10 (978-1-4296-7970-1(0), 118302); (J). lib. bdg. 27.99 (978-1-4296-7628-1(0), 117225) Capstone.

Gagne, Tammy. Egyptian Gods, Heroes, & Mythology. 2018. (Gods, Heroes, & Mythology Ser.). (ENG., Illus.). 48p. (J). (gr. 4-8). lib. bdg. 35.64 (978-1-5321-1781-7(7), 30850) ABDO Publishing Co.

Green, Roger Lancelyn. Tales of Ancient Egypt. 2011. (Puffin Classics Ser.). (Illus.). 256p. (J). (gr. 5-7). 7.99 (978-0-14-133259-8(X), Puffin Books) Penguin Young Readers Group.

Hibbert, Clare. Terrible Tales of Ancient Egypt, 1 vol., Vol. 1. Jantner, Janos, illus. 2014. (Monstrous Myths Ser.). (ENG.). 32p. (J). (gr. 4-5). 29.27 (978-1-4824-0177-6(0), 48d91e3d-c095-4ac7-9e1d-561923e98a3f) Stevens, Gareth Publishing LLLP.

Hunt, Jilly. Greek Myths & Legends, 1 vol. 2013. (All about Myths Ser.). (ENG., Illus.). 48p. (J). (gr. 5-8). pap. 9.25 (978-1-4109-5474-9(9), 123406, Raintree) Capstone.

Isis & Osiris. 2004. (J). cd-rom (978-1-84444-461-8(9)) Mantra Lingua.

Jacq, Christian. Cuentos y Leyendas de la Epoca de Las Pirámides. Corral, Mercedes, tr. from FRE. 6th ed. 2003. (Fables & Legends Ser.). (SPA., Illus.). 144p. (J). 9.95 (978-84-239-8893-8(7)) Espasa Calpe, S.A. ESP. Dist: Planeta Publishing Corp.

Jeffrey, Gary. Egyptian Myths. 2009. (Graphic Mythology Ser.). (ENG.). 48p. (YA). (gr. 4-5). 58.50 (978-1-61512-982-9(0), Rosen Reference) Rosen Publishing Group, Inc., The.

—Egyptian Myths, 1 vol. Felmang, Romano, illus. 2006. (Graphic Mythology Ser.). (ENG.). 48p. (gr. 4-5). (J). lib. bdg. 37.13 (978-1-4042-0800-1(3), 81499da4-02ab-48cd-938b-78f78ff932ed); pap. 14.05 (978-1-4042-0812-4(7), ac28459b-47ce-41d6-b1d8-42acf7f433c2) Rosen Publishing Group, Inc., The.

Kramer, Ann. Egyptian Myth: A Treasury of Legends, Art, & History. 2007. (Myth Ser.). (Illus.). 96p. (J). (gr. 4-7). pap. 7.99 (978-0-7858-2347-6(6), Chartwell) Book Sales, Inc.

—Egyptian Myth: a Treasury of Legends, Art, & History: A Treasury of Legends, Art, & History. 2007. (ENG., Illus.). 96p. (C). (gr. 6-18). lib. bdg. 180.00 (978-0-7656-8105-8(6), Y182128) Routledge.

Loh-Hagan, Virginia. Anubis. 2019. (Gods & Goddesses of the Ancient World Ser.). (ENG., Illus.). 32p. (J). (gr. 4-8). pap. 14.21 (978-1-5341-5059-1(5), 213543); lib. bdg. 32.07 (978-1-5341-4773-7(X), 213542) Cherry Lake Publishing. (45th Parallel Press).

—Horus. 2019. (Gods & Goddesses of the Ancient World Ser.). (ENG., Illus.). 32p. (J). (gr. 4-8). pap. 14.21 (978-1-5341-5057-7(9), 213535); lib. bdg. 32.07 (978-1-5341-4771-3(3), 213534) Cherry Lake Publishing. (45th Parallel Press).

—Isis. 2019. (Gods & Goddesses of the Ancient World Ser.). (ENG., Illus.). 32p. (J). (gr. 4-8). pap. 14.21 (978-1-5341-5061-4(7), 213551); lib. bdg. 32.07 (978-1-5341-4775-1(6), 213550) Cherry Lake Publishing. (45th Parallel Press).

—Ma'at. 2019. (Gods & Goddesses of the Ancient World Ser.). (ENG., Illus.). 32p. (J). (gr. 4-8). pap. 14.21 (978-1-5341-5064-5(1), 213563); lib. bdg. 32.07 (978-1-5341-4778-2(0), 213562) Cherry Lake Publishing. (45th Parallel Press).

—Ra. 2019. (Gods & Goddesses of the Ancient World Ser.). (ENG., Illus.). 32p. (J). (gr. 4-8). pap. 14.21 (978-1-5341-5058-4(7), 213539); lib. bdg. 32.07 (978-1-5341-4772-0(1), 213538) Cherry Lake Publishing. (45th Parallel Press).

—Sobek. 2019. (Gods & Goddesses of the Ancient World Ser.). (ENG., Illus.). 32p. (J). (gr. 4-8). pap. 14.21 (978-1-5341-5063-8(3), 213559); lib. bdg. 32.07 (978-1-5341-4777-5(2), 213558) Cherry Lake Publishing. (45th Parallel Press).

—Thoth. 2019. (Gods & Goddesses of the Ancient World Ser.). (ENG., Illus.). 32p. (J). (gr. 4-8). pap. 14.21 (978-1-5341-5062-1(5), 213555); lib. bdg. 32.07 (978-1-5341-4776-8(4), 213554) Cherry Lake Publishing. (45th Parallel Press).

Macdonald, Fiona. Egyptian Myths & Legends. 2013. (All about Myths Ser.). (ENG.). 48p. (J). (gr. 4-7). pap. 56.50 (978-1-4109-4982-0(6), 18998, Raintree) Capstone.

Mayo, Diana, illus. Isis & Osiris. 2004. (J). (TAM & ENG.). 27p. (978-1-84444-328-4(0)); (GER.). 30p. (978-1-84444-320-8(5)); (SOM & ENG.). 30p. (978-1-84444-326-0(4)); (SER & ENG.). 30p. (978-1-84444-325-3(6)); (VIE & ENG.). 30p. (978-1-84444-331-4(0)); (POR & ENG.). 30p. (978-1-84444-324-6(8)); (TUR & ENG.). 30p. (978-1-84444-329-1(9)); (ITA & ENG.). 30p. (978-1-84444-322-2(1)); (GUJ & ENG.). 30p. (978-1-84444-321-5(3)); (SPA.). 30p. (978-1-84444-327-7(2)); (ALB & ENG.). 30p. (978-1-84444-313-0(2)); (ARA & ENG.). 30p. (978-1-84444-314-7(0)); (CHI & ENG.). 30p. (978-1-84444-316-1(7)); (PER & ENG.). 30p. (978-1-84444-318-5(3)); (ENG & FRE.). 32p. pap. (978-1-84444-319-2(1)) Mantra Lingua.

Napoli, Donna Jo. Treasury of Egyptian Mythology: Classic Stories of Gods, Goddesses, Monsters & Mortals. 2013. (Illus.). 192p. (J). (gr. 3-7). 24.95 (978-1-4263-1380-6(2)); (ENG., lib. bdg. 33.90 (978-1-4263-1381-3(0)) Disney Publishing Worldwide. (National Geographic Kids).

Nardo, Don. Egyptian Mythology, 1 vol. 2013. (Mythology & Culture Worldwide Ser.). (ENG., Illus.). 104p. (gr. 7-10). lib. bdg. 41.03 (978-1-4205-0745-4(1), 5c7f0d91-238c-4089-bb3a-f7fd229c9ff8, Lucent Pr.) Greenhaven Publishing LLC.

—Mythology of the Egyptians, 1 vol. 2014. (Mythology, Myths, & Legends Ser.). (ENG.). 96p. (gr. 6-7). 31.61 (978-0-7660-6167-5(1), 2b10e957-7954-4fdf-ad88-795c38069ff4) Enslow Publishing, LLC.

Orme, David. Ancient Mysteries. 2010. (Fact to Fiction Grafx Ser.). (Illus.). 36p. (J). lib. bdg. 16.95 (978-1-60686-470-8(X)) Perfection Learning Corp.

Owings, Lisa. What We Get from Eqyptian Mythology. 2015. (21st Century Skills Library: Mythology & Culture Ser.). (ENG., Illus.). 32p. (J). (gr. 3-6). pap. 14.21 (978-1-63188-928-8(1), 205973) Cherry Lake Publishing.

Randolph, Joanne, ed. The Myths & Legends of Ancient Egypt & Africa, 1 vol. 2017. (Mythology & Legends Around the World Ser.). (ENG.). 64p. (gr. 4-4). pap. 13.93 (978-1-5026-3445-0(7), f92e3081-c15c-4af9-a6a3-75e1bb6b1c5d); lib. bdg. 35.93 (978-1-5026-3277-7(2), f7fa4bfc-01d6-4c16-9924-313ae939a233) Cavendish Square Publishing LLC.

Shahrukh Husain & Willey, Bee. Egypt. 2004. (Stories from Ancient Civilizations Ser.). (J). lib. bdg. 27.10 (978-1-58340-618-2(2)) Black Rabbit Bks.

Viegas, Jennifer, ed. Critical Perspectives on Natural Disasters, 1 vol. 2006. (Scientific American Critical Anthologies on Environment & Climate Ser.). (ENG., Illus.). 208p. (J). (gr. 9-9). 42.47 (978-1-4042-0824-7(0), 9ec32f41-0dae-4f18-93f3-30149c489bf8) Rosen Publishing Group, Inc., The.

World Book, Inc. Staff, contrib. by. Myths & Legends of Ancient Egypt. 2015. (Illus.). 64p. (J). (978-0-7166-2633-6(0)) World Bk., Inc.

MYTHOLOGY, INDIAN

see Indian Mythology

MYTHOLOGY, NORSE

Alexander, Heather. A Child's Introduction to Norse Mythology: Odin, Thor, Loki, & Other Viking Gods, Goddesses, Giants, & Monsters. Hamilton, Meredith, illus. 2018. (Child's Introduction Ser.). (ENG.). 96p. (J). (gr. 3-7). 19.99 (978-0-316-48215-8(3), Black Dog & Leventhal Pubs. Inc.) Running Pr.

Allan, Tony. Exploring the Life, Myth, & Art of the Vikings, 1 vol. 2011. (Civilizations of the World Ser.). (ENG.). 144p. (YA). (gr. 8-8). lib. bdg. 47.80 (978-1-4488-4833-1(4), fe20b559-bf95-4076-ba34-53d6e153ad55) Rosen Publishing Group, Inc., The.

Bowen, Carl, et al. Gods & Thunder: A Graphic Novel of Old Norse Myths. Garcia, Eduardo et al, illus. 2017. (ENG.). 208p. (J). (gr. 4-7). pap., pap., pap. 14.95 (978-1-62370-848-1(6), 134753, Capstone Young Readers) Capstone.

Braun, Eric. Loki. 2017. (Gods of Legend Ser.). (ENG., Illus.). 32p. (J). (gr. 4-6). lib. bdg. (978-1-68072-138-6(0), 10460, Bolt) Black Rabbit Bks.

—Norse Myths. 2018. (Mythology Around the World Ser.). (ENG., Illus.). 32p. (J). (gr. 3-6). lib. bdg. 27.99 (978-1-5157-9604-6(3), 136777, Capstone Pr.) Capstone.

—Odin. 2017. (Gods of Legend Ser.). (ENG.). 32p. (J). (gr. 4-6). pap. 9.99 (978-1-64466-179-6(9), 11406); (Illus.). lib. bdg. (978-1-68072-139-3(9), 10462) Black Rabbit Bks. (Bolt).

—Thor. 2017. (Gods of Legend Ser.). (ENG.). 32p. (gr. 2-7). 9.95 (978-1-68072-449-3(5)); (J). (gr. 4-6). pap. 9.99 (978-1-64466-180-2(2), 11408); (Illus.). (J). (gr. 4-6). lib. bdg. (978-1-68072-140-9(2), 10464) Black Rabbit Bks. (Bolt).

—Zeus. 2017. (Gods of Legend Ser.). (ENG.). 32p. (gr. 2-7). 9.95 (978-1-68072-450-9(9)); (J). (gr. 4-6). pap. 9.99 (978-1-64466-181-9(0), 11410) Black Rabbit Bks. (Bolt).

Buckey, A. W. Norse Gods, Heroes, & Mythology. 2018. (Gods, Heroes, & Mythology Ser.). (ENG., Illus.). 48p. (J). (gr. 4-8). lib. bdg. 35.64 (978-1-5321-1785-5(X), 30858) ABDO Publishing Co.

Colum, Padraic. The Children of Odin: The Book of Northern Myths. Pogány, Willy, illus. 2008. 216p. (gr. 5-9). pap. (978-1-4065-9868-1(2)) Dodo Pr.

—The Children of Odin: The Book of Northern Myths. Pogany, Willy, illus. 2004. (ENG.). 288p. (J). (gr. 5-9). pap. 10.99 (978-0-689-86885-6(5), Aladdin) Simon & Schuster Children's Publishing.

—The Children of Odin: The Book of Northern Myths. Pogany, Willy, illus. 2016. (ENG.). (J). pap. 6.95 (978-1-68422-041-0(6)) Martino Fine Bks.

—The Children of Odin: The Book of Northern Myths. Pogany, Willy, illus. 2019. (ENG.). 288p. (J). (gr. 5-9). 18.99 (978-1-5344-5038-7(6), Aladdin) Simon & Schuster Children's Publishing.

Colum, Padraic & Pogány, Willy. The Children of Odin the Book of Northern Myths. 2011. (Illus.). 224p. (978-1-84902-498-3(7)) Benediction Classics.

Crabtree Staff & Williams, Brian. Understanding Norse Myths, 1 vol. 2012. (ENG., Illus.). 48p. (J). pap. (978-0-7787-4532-7(5)) Crabtree Publishing Co.

Daly, Kathleen N. & Rengel, Marian. Norse Mythology a to Z. 3rd rev. ed. 2009. (Mythology A to Z Ser.). (ENG., Illus.). 144p. (gr. 5-8). 45.00 (978-1-60413-411-7(9), P166655, Facts On File) Infobase Holdings, Inc.

Dawson, Patricia A. Myths of the Norsemen, 1 vol. 2015. (World Mythologies Ser.). (ENG., Illus.). 96p. (gr. 6-6). lib. bdg. 44.50 (978-1-5026-0992-2(4), d44cf2ee-4946-4025-b878-92986b0b0e94) Cavendish Square Publishing LLC.

Hopkins, Andrea. Viking Gods & Legends. 2009. (Viking Library). 24p. (gr. 3-3). 42.50 (978-1-60854-258-1(0), PowerKids Pr.) Rosen Publishing Group, Inc., The.

Husain, Shahrukh. The Vikings. 2005. (Stories from Ancient Civilizations Ser.). (Illus.). 32p. (J). (gr. 4-18). lib. bdg. 27.10 (978-1-58340-621-2(2), 1236428) Black Rabbit Bks.

Krieg, Katherine. What We Get from Norse Mythology. 2015. (21st Century Skills Library: Mythology & Culture Ser.). (ENG., Illus.). 32p. (gr. 3-6). 32.07 (978-1-63188-914-1(1), 205980) Cherry Lake Publishing.

Leonard, Scott A. Myths & Legends of Scandinavia. 2015. (Illus.). 63p. (J). (978-0-7166-2636-7(5)) World Bk., Inc.

Limke, Jeff. Thor & Loki. 2008. pap. 52.95 (978-0-8225-9458-1(7)) Lerner Publishing Group.

—Thor Y Loki: En la Tierra de Los Gigantes; Thor & Loki: in the Land of Giants. 2008. pap. 52.95 (978-0-8225-9675-2(X)) Lerner Publishing Group.

Loh-Hagan, Virginia. Baldur. 2018. (Gods & Goddesses of the Ancient World Ser.). (ENG., Illus.). 32p. (J). (gr. 4-8). lib. bdg. 32.07 (978-1-5341-2943-6(X), 211816, 45th Parallel Press) Cherry Lake Publishing.

—Freya. 2018. (Gods & Goddesses of the Ancient World Ser.). (ENG., Illus.). 32p. (J). (gr. 4-8). lib. bdg. 32.07 (978-1-5341-2942-9(1), 211812, 45th Parallel Press) Cherry Lake Publishing.

—Frigg. 2018. (Gods & Goddesses of the Ancient World Ser.). (ENG., Illus.). 32p. (J). (gr. 4-8). lib. bdg. 32.07 (978-1-5341-2947-4(2), 211832, 45th Parallel Press) Cherry Lake Publishing.

—Heimdall. 2018. (Gods & Goddesses of the Ancient World Ser.). (ENG., Illus.). 32p. (J). (gr. 4-8). lib. bdg. 32.07 (978-1-5341-2948-1(0), 211836, 45th Parallel Press) Cherry Lake Publishing.

—Hel. 2018. (Gods & Goddesses of the Ancient World Ser.). (ENG., Illus.). 32p. (J). (gr. 4-8). lib. bdg. 32.07 (978-1-5341-2945-0(6), 211824, 45th Parallel Press) Cherry Lake Publishing.

—Loki. 2018. (Gods & Goddesses of the Ancient World Ser.). (ENG., Illus.). 32p. (J). (gr. 4-8). lib. bdg. 32.07 (978-1-5341-2946-7(4), 211828, 45th Parallel Press) Cherry Lake Publishing.

—Odin. 2018. (Gods & Goddesses of the Ancient World Ser.). (ENG., Illus.). 32p. (J). (gr. 4-8). lib. bdg. 32.07 (978-1-5341-2941-2(3), 211808, 45th Parallel Press) Cherry Lake Publishing.

—Thor. 2018. (Gods & Goddesses of the Ancient World Ser.). (ENG., Illus.). 32p. (J). (gr. 4-8). lib. bdg. 32.07 (978-1-5341-2944-3(8), 211820, 45th Parallel Press) Cherry Lake Publishing.

Mabie, Hamilton Wright. Norse Stories Retold from the Eddas. 2006. (Illus.). pap. 30.95 (978-1-4254-9336-3(X)) Kessinger Publishing, LLC.

Menges, Jeff A. Norse Gods & Goddesses. 2004. (Dover Classic Stories Coloring Book Ser.). (ENG., Illus.). 32p. (J). (gr. 3-8). pap., spiral bd. 3.99 (978-0-486-43337-0(4), 433374) Dover Pubns., Inc.

Napoli, Donna Jo. Treasury of Norse Mythology: Stories of Intrigue, Trickery, Love, & Revenge. 2015. (Illus.). 192p. (J). (gr. 3-7). 24.99 (978-1-4263-2098-9(1), National Geographic Kids) Disney Publishing Worldwide.

Philip, Neil. Myths of the Vikings: Odin's Family & Other Tales of the Norse Gods. Foa, Maryclare, illus. 2018. 128p. (J). (gr. 3-7). 13.99 (978-1-86147-860-3(7), Armadillo) Anness Publishing GBR. Dist: National Bk. Network.

Randolph, Joanne, ed. Norse Myths & Legends, 1 vol. 2017. (Mythology & Legends Around the World Ser.). (ENG.). 64p. (gr. 4-4). lib. bdg. 35.93 (978-1-5026-3278-4(0), 691bd07c-62fc-4bd9-a772-f4b83a3a1458) Cavendish Square Publishing LLC.

Rayner, Olivia, illus. World Book Myths & Legends Series, 8 vols., Vol. 8. 2007. (World Book Myths & Legends Ser.). 64p. (gr. 4-8). 239.00 (978-0-7166-2613-8(6), 31020) World Bk., Inc.

Redmond, Shirley Raye. Norse Mythology, 1 vol. 2012. (Mythology & Culture Worldwide Ser.). (ENG., Illus.). 96p. (gr. 7-10). lib. bdg. 41.03 (978-1-4205-0717-1(6), 39295f41-9889-4683-b972-301bf8cd0e0f, Lucent Pr.) Greenhaven Publishing LLC.

Rydberg, Viktor & Reaves, William P. Our Fathers' Godsaga: Retold for the Young. 2003. 223p. pap. 15.95 (978-0-595-29978-2(4)) iUniverse, Inc.

Rydberg, Viktor & Reeves, William P. Our Fathers' Godsaga: Retold for the Young. Rydberg, Viktor, tr. 2003. (Illus.). 223p. 25.95 (978-0-595-66097-1(5)) iUniverse, Inc.

Schomp, Virginia. The Norsemen, 1 vol. 2008. (Myths of the World Ser.). (ENG., Illus.). 96p. (gr. 6-6). lib. bdg. 36.93 (978-0-7614-2548-9(9), 14d864d0-48a5-4d7c-b061-2c12187c9050) Cavendish Square Publishing LLC.

Williams, Brian. Understanding Norse Myths. 2012. (ENG., Illus.). 48p. (J). (978-0-7787-4527-3(9)) Crabtree Publishing Co.

Yasuda, Anita. Explore Norse Myths! With 25 Great Projects. Stone, Bryan, illus. 2015. (Explore Your World Ser.). (ENG.). 96p. (J). (gr. 1-5). 19.95 (978-1-61930-316-4(7), e49fb609-39c4-4183-a5a6-eb96d5c1a30f) Nomad Pr.

MYTHOLOGY, POLYNESIAN

Croy, Anita. Myths & Legends of Australia, New Zealand, & Pacific Islands. 2015. (Illus.). 64p. (J). (978-0-7166-2629-9(2)) World Bk., Inc.

MYTHOLOGY IN ART

see Art and Mythology

MYTHS

see Mythology

N

NAGASAKI-SHI (JAPAN)

Bodden, Valerie. The Bombing of Hiroshima & Nagasaki. 2007. (Days of Change Ser.). (Illus.). 48p. (J). (gr. 4-7). lib. bdg. 31.35 (978-1-58341-545-0(9), Creative Education) Creative Co., The.

—The Bombing of Hiroshima & Nagasaki: Odysseys in History. 2016. (Odysseys in History Ser.). (ENG., Illus.). 80p. (J). (gr. 7-10). pap. 15.99 (978-1-62832-126-5(1), 20948, Creative Paperbacks) Creative Co., The.

Burgan, Michael. Hiroshima & Nagasaki: The Atomic Bombings That Shook the World. 2019. (Tangled History Ser.). (ENG., Illus.). 112p. (J). (gr. 3-9). pap. 6.95 (978-1-5435-7556-9(0), 141088); lib. bdg. 34.65 (978-1-5435-7256-8(1), 140592) Capstone.

Langley, Andrew. Hiroshima & Nagasaki. 2017. (Eyewitness to World War II Ser.). (ENG., Illus.). 112p. (J). (gr. 5-9). lib. bdg. 38.65 (978-0-7565-5584-9(1), 135469, Compass Point Bks.) Capstone.

Orr, Tamra. The Atom Bomb: Creating & Exploding the First Nuclear Weapon, 1 vol. 2004. (Library of Weapons of Mass Destruction Ser.). (ENG., Illus.). 64p. (J). (gr. 5-5). lib. bdg. 37.13 (978-1-4042-0292-4(7), 65241642-3041-4d65-b2f4-c22a61745108) Rosen Publishing Group, Inc., The.

Peppas, Lynn. Hiroshima & Nagasaki. 2013. (ENG., Illus.). 48p. (J). (978-0-7787-1171-1(4)); pap. (978-0-7787-1179-7(X)) Crabtree Publishing Co.

Stelson, Caren. Sachiko: A Nagasaki Bomb Survivor's Story. 2016. (ENG., Illus.). 144p. (J). (gr. 5-12). E-Book 30.65 (978-1-5124-0893-5(X)); E-Book 9.99 (978-1-5124-1884-2(6), 9781512418842); E-Book 30.65 (978-1-5124-1885-9(4), 9781512418859) Lerner Publishing Group. (Carolrhoda Bks.).

NAMES—FICTION

August, Rachel. Adventures of Libby Nickel: What's your Mommy's First Name? 2011. 25p. (J). pap. 17.95 (978-1-4327-6513-2(2)) Outskirts Pr., Inc.

Belonie, Shannon. Oliver Andrew Ostrich: My Full Name. 2008. 12p. pap. 8.74 *(978-1-4343-5849-3(6))* AuthorHouse.
Blackstone, Stella. Who Are You, Baby Kangaroo? Beaton, Clare, illus. 2004. (ENG.). 32p. (J). 14.99 *(978-1-84148-217-0(X))* Barefoot Bks., Inc.
Choi, Yangsook. The Name Jar. 2003. (gr. k-3). lib. bdg. 18.40 *(978-0-613-82979-3(4))* Turtleback.
Farnsley, Kathleen. This Little Piggy Named Pony. 2008. 24p. pap. 12.99 *(978-1-4389-2659-9(6))* AuthorHouse.
Gunderson, Jessica. Frankly, I'd Rather Spin Myself a New Name! The Story of Rumpelstiltskin As Told by Rumpelstiltskin. Bock, Janna Rose, illus. 2016. (Other Side of the Story Ser.). (ENG.). 24p. (J). (gr. -1-3). lib. bdg. 27.99 *(978-1-4795-8624-0(2)*, 130446, Picture Window Bks.) Capstone.
Hartman, Colleen Kelley. My Grandma Calls Me Lovey. Hammons, Mark, illus. 2011. pap. 19.95 *(978-1-934333-26-6(3))* Eagle Bk. Bindery.
Ivey, Douglas G. The Three Cows. 2010. 28p. pap. 13.99 *(978-1-4520-4272-5(1))* AuthorHouse.
Kappler, Kathleen. Whitney's School Morning. 2004. 38p. pap. 24.95 *(978-1-4137-3711-0(0))* PublishAmerica, Inc.
Kay, Cassandra. A Week in the Life of Mertyle. 2009. 96p. pap. 10.49 *(978-1-4389-4049-6(1))* AuthorHouse.
Little Bear, Shena. How the lone wolf got her Name. 2008. 80p. pap. 9.95 *(978-0-578-00171-5(3))* Stone Castle Publishing.
Mervine, M.A., CCC-SLP, Patricia. How Katie Got a Voice: (and a Cool New Nickname) Acker, Ian, illus. 2012. (ENG.). 40p. pap. 19.57 *(978-1-4269-6649-1(0))* Trafford Publishing.
Millard, Glenda. The Naming of Tishkin Silk. Magerl, Caroline, illus. 2019. (Kingdom of Silk Ser.: 01). 96p. mass mkt. 4.99 *(978-0-7333-1314-1(0))* ABC Bks. AUS. Dist: HarperCollins Pubs.
Neelon, Caleb. Liiman Makes a Name for Himself. 2004. (J). lib. bdg. *(978-0-9745150-0-7(0))* Cantab Publishing.
Raschka, Chris. New York Is English, Chattanooga Is Creek. Raschka, Chris, illus. 2018. (ENG., Illus.). 40p. (J). (gr. -1-2). 11.99 *(978-1-5344-3371-7(6)*, Atheneum Bks. for Young Readers) Simon & Schuster Children's Publishing.
Renard Roach, Marietta. Come, Bless the Baby. 2006. 28p. pap. 21.95 incl. audio compact disk *(978-0-9768626-0-4(3))* Aaduna.
Roddy-Worsham, Clara. Bear Baby & New Baby Forever. 2012. 24p. 24.95 *(978-1-4626-4672-2(7))* America Star Bks.
Russo, Angela B. Beautiful. 2013. 28p. pap. 24.95 *(978-1-62709-040-7(1))* America Star Bks.
Siegel, Rv. A Bee Called Kangaroo. 2005. (ENG.). 81p. pap. 9.16 *(978-1-4116-2890-8(X))* Lulu Pr., Inc.
Swiatkowska, Recorvits -. Me llamo Yoon. 2003. (SPA., Illus.). 32p. (gr. k-2). 18.99 *(978-84-261-3335-9(5))* Juventud, Editorial ESP. Dist: Lectorum Pubns., Inc.
Yolen, Jane. My Father Knows the Names of Things. Jorisch, Stéphane, illus. 2010. (ENG.). 32p. (J). (gr. -1-3). 19.99 *(978-1-4169-4895-7(3)*, Simon & Schuster Bks. For Young Readers) Simon & Schuster Bks. For Young Readers.

NAMES, GEOGRAPHICAL

Herman, Debbie. From Pie Town to Yum Yum: Weird & Wacky Place Names Across the United States. Goldman, Linda Sarah, illus. 2011. (ENG.). 120p. (J). pap. 10.99 *(978-1-935279-79-2(3))* Kane Miller.
MacKinnon, Christopher. Canadian Sports Sites for Kids: Places Named for Speedsters, Scorers, & Other Sportsworld Citizens (Large Print 16pt) 2013. 208p. pap. *(978-1-4596-6305-3(5))* ReadHowYouWant.com, Ltd.
Places in Time: A Kid's Historic Guide to the Changing Names & Places of the World, 6 vols., Set. Incl. Brief Political & Geographic History of Africa: Where Are... Belgian Congo, Rhodesia, & Kush. Davenport, John. (YA). lib. bdg. 37.10 *(978-1-58415-624-6(4))*; Brief Political & Geographic History of Asia: Where Are... Saigon, Kampuchea, & Burma. Dillon, Doug. (YA). lib. bdg. 37.10 *(978-1-58415-623-9(6))*; Brief Political & Geographic History of Europe: Where Are... Prussia, Gaul, & the Holy Roman Empire. Davey, Frances. (YA). lib. bdg. 37.10 *(978-1-58415-625-3(2))*; Brief Political & Geographic History of Latin America: Where Are... Gran Colombia, la Plata, & Dutch Guiana. Rice, Earle, Jr. (J). lib. bdg. 37.10 *(978-1-58415-626-0(0)*, 1270683); Brief Political & Geographic History of North America: Where Are... New France, New Netherland, & New Sweden. Johnston, Lissa. (YA). lib. bdg. 37.10 *(978-1-58415-627-7(9))*; Brief Political & Geographic History of the Middle East: Where Are... Persia, Babylon, & the Ottoman Empire. Davenport, John. (YA). lib. bdg. 37.10 *(978-1-58415-622-2(8))*; 112p. (gr. 5-9). 2007. (Places in Time Ser.). (Illus.). 2007. Set lib. bdg. 222.60 *(978-1-58415-628-4(7))* Mitchell Lane Pubs.

NAMES, PERSONAL

dePaola, Tomie. Andy, That's My Name. dePaola, Tomie, illus. 2019. (ENG., Illus.). 32p. (J). (gr. -1-3). 7.99 *(978-1-5344-3014-3(8)*, Simon & Schuster Bks. For Young Readers) Simon & Schuster Bks. For Young Readers.
EchoHawk, Terry. Call Me Little Echo Hawk. 2005. (Illus.). 22p. (J). 15.99 *(978-1-55517-804-8(9))* Cedar Fort, Inc./CFI Distribution.
Haas, Kristin. The Shape Family Babies, 1 vol. Bersani, Shennen, illus. 2014. (ENG.). 32p. (J). (gr. -1-3). 17.95 *(978-1-62855-211-9(5))* Arbordale Publishing.
—The Shape Family Babies: Spanish, 1 vol. Bersani, Shennen, illus. 2014.Tr. of Shape Family Babies. (SPA.). 32p. (J). (gr. k-1). pap. 11.95 *(978-1-62855-229-4(8)*, 7549eeb9-cd18-4d9e-85a8-4759621d2e4f) Arbordale Publishing.
Hayes, Larry E. My Name Starts with J. Anderson, Airlie, illus. 2004. (My Name Starts With Ser.). 31p. (J). 14.95 *(978-0-9725292-2-8(5))* Inspire Pubns.
—My Name Starts with M. Anderson, Airlie, illus. Hayes, Larry E., photos by. 2004. (My Name Starts With Ser.). 31p. (J). 14.95 *(978-0-9725292-3-5(3)*, 1) Inspire Pubns.
—My Name Starts with S. Anderson, Airlie, illus. Hayes, Larry E., photos by. 2003. (My Name Starts With Ser.). 31p. 14.95 *(978-0-9725292-1-1(7))* Inspire Pubns.
Onuoha-Ezemma, Glory. Don't Make Fun of My Name: My Name Is Special to My Parents & Me. unabr. ed. 2003. (Illus.). 47p. (J). (gr. k-6). pap. 9.95 *(978-0-9661598-6-8(1))* Orange County Publishing.
Onyefulu, Ifeoma. Your Name Is Dede: An African Baby's Naming Ceremony. 2003. (ENG., Illus.). 32p. (J). *(978-0-7112-1938-0(9))* ReiseArt Buchhandlung GmbH.
Phillips, Karen. The Truth about My Name: And What It Reveals about Me! 2010. 50p. (J). (gr. 3-18). 16.99 *(978-1-59174-855-7(0))* Klutz.
Schultz, Sam. Ivan to Make You Laugh: Jokes about Novel, Nifty, & Notorious Names. Gable, Brian, illus. 2005. (Make Me Laugh! Ser.). 32p. (J). (gr. k-3). lib. bdg. 19.93 *(978-1-57505-659-3(3))* Lerner Publishing Group.
Wood, Vanessa, ed. Antique Names: Tried & True & Truly Rare Historical Names. 2003. 92p. per. 11.00 *(978-0-9744281-1-6(6))* Design to Spec LLC.

NAMES, PERSONAL—FICTION

Alderton, Sylvia. A Real Name for Puppy. McCartney, Michael David, illus. 2006. (J). *(978-1-930566-58-3(1)*, WestWind Pr.) Scott, D.& F. Publishing, Inc.
Alexie, Sherman. Thunder Boy Jr. Morales, Yuyi, illus. 2016. (ENG.). 40p. (J). (gr. -1-3). 18.99 *(978-0-316-01372-7(2))* Little, Brown Bks. for Young Readers.
Anderson, Robert Gordon. Seven O'Clock Stories. l.t. ed. 2007. (ENG.). 122p. pap. 19.99 *(978-1-4264-2903-3(7))* Creative Media Partners, LLC.
Angelou, Maya. Cedric of Jamaica. Rockwell, Lizzy, illus. 2005. (Random House Pictureback Book Ser.). (J). *(978-0-375-83269-7(6))* Random Hse., Inc.
Bailey, Jennifer P. I Call Mine Mimi. What Do You Call Your Grandmother?, 1 vol. 2010. 24p. pap. 24.95 *(978-1-4489-7141-1(1))* PublishAmerica, Inc.
Benton, Jim. The Fran That Time Forgot. Benton, Jim, illus. 4th ed. 2005. (Franny K. Stein, Mad Scientist Ser.: 4). (ENG., Illus.). 112p. (J). (gr. 2-5). mass mkt. 6.99 *(978-0-689-86298-4(9))*; 17.99 *(978-0-689-86294-6(6))* Simon & Schuster Bks. For Young Readers. (Simon & Schuster Bks. For Young Readers).
Blasi, Kathleen McAlpin. A Name of Honor. Bowman, Leslie W., illus. 2006. (J). *(978-1-59336-692-6(2))* Mondo Publishing.
Brimmer, Debi & Coleson, Julie. How Six Little Ipu Got Their Names. Coleson, Julie, illus. 2005. (Illus.). 30p. (J). 9.95 incl. audio compact disk *(978-1-57306-186-5(7))* Bess Pr., Inc.
Cassany, Mia & Casal, Mikel. Frankfurt. 2018. (ENG., Illus.). 32p. (J). (gr. -1-k). 14.99 *(978-1-84976-579-4(0)*, 1325401) Tate Publishing, Ltd. GBR. Dist: Abrams, Inc.
Choi, Yangsook. The Name Jar. Choi, Yangsook, illus. 2003. (ENG., Illus.). 40p. (J). (gr. -1-2). pap. 8.99 *(978-0-440-41799-6(6)*, Dragonfly Bks.) Random Hse. Children's Bks.
Do, Anh. Super Weird! (WeirDo #4) 2019. (WeirDo Ser.: 4). (ENG., Illus.). 160p. (J). (gr. 2-5). pap. 5.99 *(978-1-338-30565-4(4))* Scholastic, Inc.
Dunklee, Annika. My Name Is Elizabeth! Forsythe, Matthew, illus. 2011. (ENG.). 24p. (J). (gr. -1-2). 14.95 *(978-1-55453-560-6(3))* Kids Can Pr., Ltd. CAN. Dist: Hachette Bk. Group.
Flood, Pansie Hart. Tiger's Trouble with Donut Head. Wummer, Amy, illus. 2005. 71p. (J). lib. bdg. 19.93 *(978-1-57505-814-6(6)*, Carolrhoda Bks.) Lerner Publishing Group.
Florence, Debbi Michiko. Dorothy & Toto What's YOUR Name? Roe, Monika, illus. 2016. (Dorothy & Toto Ser.). (ENG.). 40p. (J). (gr. k-2). lib. bdg. 21.32 *(978-1-4795-8702-5(8)*, 130945) Capstone.
Gadot, A. S. The First Gift. Lafrance, Marie, illus. 2006. (ENG.). 24p. (J). (gr. -1-3). lib. bdg. 15.95 *(978-1-58013-146-9(8)*, Kar-Ben Publishing) Lerner Publishing Group.
Green, John. Will Grayson, Will Grayson. 2011. lib. bdg. 22.10 *(978-0-606-15358-4(6))* Turtleback.
Green, John & Levithan, David. Will Grayson, Will Grayson. (ENG., (YA). (gr. 9-18). 2011. Illus.). 326p. 12.99 *(978-0-14-241847-5(1)*, Speak) 2010. 320p. 19.99 *(978-0-525-42158-0(0)*, Dutton Books for Young Readers) Penguin Young Readers Group.
—Will Grayson, Will Grayson (Spanish Edition) 2019. (SPA.). 336p. (YA). (gr. 7). pap. 12.95 *(978-607-31-3340-1(5)*, Nube De Tinta) Penguin Random House Grupo Editorial ESP. Dist: Penguin Random Hse. LLC.
Greenspan, Shari Dash. Shemot Muzarim. Katz, Avi, illus. 2005.Tr. of Strange Names. (HEB.). 32p. 14.00 *(978-965-7108-58-1(6))* Urim Pubns. ISR. Dist: Coronet Bks.
Harris, Carol Gahara. My Name is Leona. Fujiwara, Kim, illus. 2013. 24p. (J). 19.95 *(978-0-9860324-0-0(9))* Snowy Night Pub.
Henkes, Kevin. Chrysanthemum. 2004. (Illus.). (J). (gr. k-3). spiral bd. *(978-0-616-14575-3(6))* Canadian National Institute for the Blind/Institut National Canadien pour les Aveugles.
—Chrysanthemum. 2008. (J). (gr. -1-2). lib. bdg. 17.20 *(978-0-613-00459-6(0))* Turtleback.
—Chrysanthemum Big Book: A First Day of School Book for Kids. Henkes, Kevin, illus. 2007. (ENG., Illus.). 32p. (J). (gr. -1-3). pap. 24.99 *(978-0-06-111974-3(1)*, Greenwillow Bks.) HarperCollins Pubs.
—Crisantemo. 2017.Tr. of Chrysanthemum. (SPA., Illus.). 32p. (J). pap. 9.99 *(978-1-63245-664-9(8))* Lectorum Pubns., Inc.
—Crisantemo. Mlawer, Teresa, tr. from ENG. 2006.Tr. of Chrysanthemum. (Illus.). 31p. (gr. 4-7). 19.00 *(978-0-7569-7316-2(3))* Perfection Learning Corp.
—Penny & Her Doll. Henkes, Kevin, illus. 2012. (ENG., Illus.). 32p. (J). (gr. -1-3). 14.99 *(978-0-06-208199-5(3))*; lib. bdg. 15.89 *(978-0-06-208200-8(0))* HarperCollins Pubs. (Greenwillow Bks.).
—Penny & Her Doll. 2013. (I Can Read! Level 1 Ser.). (J). lib. bdg. 13.55 *(978-0-606-27147-9(3))* Turtleback.
Katz, Karen. Princess Baby. Katz, Karen, illus. 2012. (Princess Baby Ser.). (Illus.). 30p. (J). (gr. k-k). 7.99 *(978-0-307-93146-7(3)*, Schwartz & Wade Bks.) Random Hse. Children's Bks.
Kevin, Henkes. Chrysanthemum. 2014. (ENG.). 32p. (J). (gr. k-3). 11.24 *(978-1-63245-281-8(2))* Lectorum Pubns., Inc.
Korngold, Jamie S. Mazel Tov! It's a Boy; Mazel Tov! It's a Girl. Finkelstein, Jeff, illus. Finkelstein, Jeff, photos by. 2015. (J). 6.99 *(978-1-4677-6206-9(7)*, Kar-Ben Publishing) Lerner Publishing Group.
Lafrance, Marie, illus. The First Gift. 2006. (ENG.). 24p. (J). (gr. 2). per. 6.95 *(978-1-58013-149-0(2)*, Kar-Ben Publishing) Lerner Publishing Group.
Laínez, René Colato. I Am Rene, the Boy. Graullera, Fabiola, illus. 2005.Tr. of Yo Soy Rene, el Nino. (ENG & SPA.). 32p. (J). (gr. -1-2). 16.95 *(978-1-55885-378-2(2)*, Piñata Books) Arte Publico Pr.
—René Has Two Last Names/René Tiene Dos Apellidos. Laínez, René Colato & Graullera Ramírez, Fabiola, illus. 2009. (SPA & ENG.). 32p. (J). (gr. -1-3). 16.95 *(978-1-55885-530-4(0))* Arte Publico Pr.
Lester, Helen. A Porcupine Named Fluffy. Munsinger, Lynn, illus. 2013. (Laugh-Along Lessons Ser.). (ENG.). 32p. (J). (gr. -1-3). 8.99 *(978-0-544-00319-4(5)*, 1526352, Clarion Bks.) HarperCollins Pubs.
Martinez-Neal, Juana. Alma & How She Got Her Name. Martinez-Neal, Juana, illus. 2018. (ENG., Illus.). 32p. (J). (gr. -1-3). 17.99 *(978-0-7636-9355-8(3))* Candlewick Pr.
Meyers, Tim. Let's Call Him Lau-Wiliwili-Humuhumu-Nukunuku-Nukunuku-Apua'a-Oi'oi. 2005. (Illus.). 24p. (J). 16.95 incl. audio compact disk *(978-1-57306-252-7(9))* Bess Pr., Inc.
Monk, Isabell. Hope. Porter, Janice Lee, illus. 2004. (Carolrhoda Picture Books Ser.). 32p. (J). (gr. -1-3). 6.95 *(978-1-57505-792-7(1))* Lerner Publishing Group.
Moss, Marissa. The Name Game! Moss, Marissa, illus. 2011. (Daphne's Diary of Daily Disasters Ser.). (ENG., Illus.). 80p. (J). (gr. 2-5). lib. bdg. 9.99 *(978-1-4424-2676-4(4)*, Simon & Schuster/Paula Wiseman Bks.) Simon & Schuster/Paula Wiseman Bks.
Murphy, Stuart J. Carlos Escribe Su Nombre. 2014. (I See I Learn Ser.: 24). (Illus.). 32p. (J). (-k). 14.95 *(978-1-58089-496-8(8))* Charlesbridge Publishing, Inc.
—Write on, Carlos! 2011. (I See I Learn Ser.: 8). (Illus.). 32p. (J). (-k). pap. 6.95 *(978-1-58089-465-4(8))*; (gr. -1-k). 14.95 *(978-1-58089-464-7(X))* Charlesbridge Publishing, Inc.
—Write on, Carlos! ¡Carlos Escribe Su Nombre! Jones, Tim, illus. 2017. (J). pap. *(978-1-63289-030-6(5))* Charlesbridge Publishing, Inc.
Nöstlinger, Christine. Piruleta. Kaufman, Angelika, illus. 2003. (SPA.). 132p. (gr. 3-5). pap. 9.95 *(978-968-19-0983-3(6))* Santillana USA Publishing Co., Inc.
Philip, Simon. I Don't Know What to Call My Cat. Bailey, Ella, illus. 2017. (ENG.). 32p. (J). (gr. -1-3). 16.99 *(978-0-544-97143-1(4)*, 1662675, Clarion Bks.) HarperCollins Pubs.
Primavera, Elise. I'm a Baked Potato! (Funny Children's Book about a Pet Dog, Puppy Story) Medina, Juana, illus. 2019. (ENG.). 32p. (J). (gr. -1-k). 16.99 *(978-1-4521-5592-0(5))* Chronicle Bks. LLC.
Recorvits, Helen. My Name Is Yoon. Swiatkowska, Gabi, illus. 2003. (ENG.). 32p. (J). (gr. -1-3). 18.99 *(978-0-374-35114-4(7)*, 900020207, Farrar, Straus & Giroux (BYR)) Farrar, Straus & Giroux.
—My Name Is Yoon. Swiatkowska, Gabi, illus. 2014. (ENG.). 32p. (J). (gr. -1-3). 8.99 *(978-1-250-05711-2(6)*, 900139124) Square Fish.
Sadu, Itah & Condy, Roy. Christopher Changes His Name. (ENG., Illus.). 32p. (J). pap. 4.99 *(978-0-590-24624-8(0))* Scholastic, Inc.
Sandburg, Carl. Rootabaga Stories. 2009. 128p. (gr. 3-18). pap. 10.95 *(978-1-60664-425-6(4))* Rodgers, Alan Bks.
Schatz, Letta. So Many Henrys, 1 vol. rev. ed. 2013. (Literary Text Ser.). (ENG., Illus.). 28p. (J). (gr. 2-3). pap. 10.99 *(978-1-4333-5602-5(3))*; lib. bdg. 19.96 *(978-1-4807-1724-4(X))* Teacher Created Materials, Inc.
Sharp, Rhonda Winchell. The Nine Most Famous Reindeer of All. Vandewater, Rena, illus. 2004. 40p. (J). pap. 15.99 *(978-0-9748047-8-1(9))* Hickory Bark Productions.
Sheinmel, Courtney. Stella Batts Needs a New Name. Bell, Jennifer A., illus. 2012. (Stella Batts Ser.). (ENG.). 160p. (J). (gr. 1-3). pap. 7.99 *(978-1-58536-183-0(6)*, 202266); 1. lib. bdg. 9.99 *(978-1-58536-185-4(2)*, 202267) Sleeping Bear Pr.
Shurtliff, Liesl. Rump: the (Fairly) True Tale of Rumpelstiltskin. 2014. (ENG.). 288p. (J). (gr. 3-7). pap. 8.99 *(978-0-307-97796-0(X)*, Yearling) Random Hse. Children's Bks.
Stein, Gertrude. To Do: A Book of Alphabets & Birthdays. 2011. (ENG., Illus.). 128p. 30.00 *(978-0-300-17097-9(1))* Yale Univ. Pr.
Stiefel, Chana. My Name Is Wakawakaloch! Sullivan, Mary, illus. 2019. (ENG.). 32p. (J). (gr. -1-3). 17.99 *(978-1-328-73209-5(6)*, 1675985, Clarion Bks.) HarperCollins Pubs.
Williams, Karen & Mohammed, Khadra. My Name Is Sangoel. Stock, Catherine, illus. 2009. (ENG.). 36p. (J). (gr. 1-5). 17.00 *(978-0-8028-5307-3(2)*, Eerdmans Bks For Young Readers) Eerdmans, William B. Publishing Co.
Yangsook, Choi. The Name Jar. 2014. (ENG.). 40p. (J). (gr. k-2). 11.24 *(978-1-63245-313-6(4))* Lectorum Pubns., Inc.

NAMIBIA

Leaf, Christina. Kolmanskop: The Diamond Mine Ghost Town. 2020. (Abandoned Places Ser.). (ENG., Illus.). 24p. (J). (gr. 3-7). lib. bdg. 26.95 *(978-1-64487-161-4(0)*, Torque Bks.) Bellwether Media.
Streissguth, Thomas. Namibia in Pictures. 2008. (Visual Geography Ser.). (YA). (gr. 7-12). lib. bdg. 31.93 *(978-0-8225-8574-9(X))* Twenty First Century Bks.

NANTUCKET ISLAND (MASS.)

Herold, Vickey. Discover A Whaling Community: Nantucket. 2006. (J). pap. *(978-1-4108-6429-1(4))* Benchmark Education Co.
Thompson, Gare. A Whaling Community: New Bedford, Mass: Text Pairs. 2008. (Bridges/Navigators Ser.). (J). (gr. 3). 89.00 *(978-1-4108-8377-3(9))* Benchmark Education Co.

NANTUCKET ISLAND (MASS.)—FICTION

Alderson, Sarah. The Sound: Where Secrets Are Buried. 2014. (ENG.). 320p. (J). pap. *(978-1-4711-1573-8(9)*, Simon Pulse) Simon Pulse.
Angelini, Josephine. Dreamless. 2013. (Starcrossed Trilogy Ser.: 2). (ENG.). 512p. (YA). (gr. 8). pap. 10.99 *(978-0-06-201202-9(9)*, HarperTeen) HarperCollins Pubs.
—Starcrossed. 2012. (Starcrossed Trilogy Ser.: 1). (ENG.). 512p. (YA). (gr. 8). pap. 10.99 *(978-0-06-201200-5(2)*, HarperTeen) HarperCollins Pubs.
Bagley, Conor. Ziggy McFinster's Nantucket Adventure. Bernard Westcott, Nadine, illus. 2008. (ENG.). 40p. (J). (gr. -1-3). 16.95 *(978-1-56625-315-4(2))* Bonus Bks., Inc.
Balliett, Blue. Out of the Wild Night. (ENG.). 320p. (J). (gr. 3-7). 2019. pap. 7.99 *(978-0-545-86757-3(6))* 2018. 17.99 *(978-0-545-86756-6(8))* Scholastic, Inc. (Scholastic Pr.).
Bouton, Warren Hussey. The Captain's Return: A Spooky Tale from Nantucket. Locke, Barbara Kauffmann, illus. 2004. (J). per. 5.95 *(978-0-9700555-4-5(4))* Hither Creek Pr.
Finley, Martha. Elsie at Nantucket. 2018. (ENG., Illus.). 218p. (YA). (gr. 7-12). pap. *(978-93-5297-352-1(6))* Alpha Editions.
—Elsie at Nantucket. 2018. (ENG., Illus.). 240p. (J). 29.98 *(978-0-464-94306-8(X))* Blurb, Inc.
—Elsie at Nantucket. 2017. (ENG., Illus.). (J). 24.95 *(978-1-374-83782-9(2))* Capital Communications, Inc.
Gamble, Adam. Good Night Nantucket. Rosen, Anne, illus. 2007. (Good Night Our World Ser.). (ENG.). 20p. (J). (gr. -1-k). bds. 9.95 *(978-1-60219-013-9(5))* Good Night Bks.
Manley, Molly. Nantucket Nanny. Marshall, Janet, illus. 2005. (Little Limericks Ser.). (ENG.). 24p. (J). (gr. k-3). 12.95 *(978-1-889833-96-5(7)*, Commonwealth Editions) Applewood Bks.
My Time on Nantucket. 2005. (J). cd-rom 11.95 *(978-0-9755078-2-7(6))* Sweet Punkin Pr.
The Phantom of Nantucket. 2014. (Nancy Drew Diaries: 7). (ENG., Illus.). 192p. (J). (gr. 3-7). pap. 7.99 *(978-1-4814-0015-2(0)*, Aladdin) Simon & Schuster Children's Publishing.
Snedeker, Caroline Dale & Barney, Maginel Wright. Downright Dencey. 2003. (Young Adult Library). (ENG., Illus.). 274p. (J). (gr. 4-6). pap. 12.95 *(978-1-883937-79-9(5))* Ignatius Pr.
Stewart, Whitney. Marshall: A Nantucket Sea Rescue. Lyall, Dennis, illus. 2008. (ENG.). 32p. (J). (gr. -1-2). 10.95 *(978-1-59249-857-4(4))*; 2.95 *(978-1-59249-856-7(6))*; 6.95 *(978-1-59249-855-0(8))* Soundprints.
Thorpe, Rochelle O'Neal. Gabe's Nantucket Adventure: Daffodils, Dogs, & Cars. Nakell, Eugenie, ed. Margolis, Al, illus. l.t. ed. 2010. 28p. (YA). pap. 7.95 *(978-1-935706-02-1(0))* Wiggles Pr.
Turkle, Brinton. Obadiah the Bold. 2004. 36p. pap. 7.95 *(978-1-893103-19-1(6))* Beautiful Feet Bks.
—Rachel & Obadiah. 2004. 30p. pap. 7.95 *(978-1-893103-18-4(8))* Beautiful Feet Bks.
Turkle, Brinton, illus. Thy Friend, Obadiah. 2018. (J). pap. *(978-1-893103-69-6(2))* Beautiful Feet Bks.
Turkle, Brinton, illus. & text. Obadiah the Bold. Turkle, Brinton, text. 2018. (J). pap. *(978-1-893103-73-3(0))* Beautiful Feet Bks.

NAPOLEON I, EMPEROR OF THE FRENCH, 1769-1821

Baicker, Karen. Napoleon Complex: A Young General Takes France by Storm. 2011. (J). pap. *(978-0-545-32938-5(8))* Scholastic, Inc.
Boyd, David. Napoleon's Last Stand. Okum, David, illus. 2007. 48p. (J). lib. bdg. 23.08 *(978-1-4242-1639-0(7))* Fitzgerald Bks.
Doyle, William. Napoleon Bonaparte: Emperor, 1 vol. 2016. (History Makers Ser.). (ENG., Illus.). 144p. (YA). (gr. 9-9). 47.36 *(978-1-5026-2447-5(8)*, b7639853-43b4-4b44-beae-186162b5d27f) Cavendish Square Publishing LLC.
du Garde Peach, L. The Story of Nelson. 2016. (Adventure from History Ser.). (ENG., Illus.). 56p. (J). (gr. 3-7). 10.99 *(978-0-7232-9799-4(1))* Penguin Bks., Ltd. GBR. Dist: Independent Pubs. Group.
Foa, Eugenie. Boy Life of Napoleon Afterwards Emperor of the French. 2004. reprint ed. pap. 1.99 *(978-1-4192-5499-4(5))*; pap. 19.95 *(978-1-4191-5499-7(0))* Kessinger Publishing, LLC.
Freedman, Jeri. Strategic Inventions of the Napoleonic Wars, 1 vol. 2016. (Tech in the Trenches Ser.). (ENG., Illus.). 112p. (J). (gr. 9-9). 44.50 *(978-1-5026-2351-5(X)*, 5374cf10-2ca1-427a-a1ee-cf76bcf4c4d8) Cavendish Square Publishing LLC.
Gigliotti, Jim & Who HQ. Who Was Napoleon? Copeland, Gregory, illus. 2018. (Who Was? Ser.). 112p. (J). (gr. 3-7). 5.99 *(978-0-448-48860-8(4)*, Penguin Workshop) Penguin Young Readers Group.
Goldberg, Jan. Napoleon Bonaparte. 2004. (ZB Reads Trio Books). 87p. (gr. 5-7). pap. 5.00 *(978-0-7367-1799-1(4))* Zaner-Bloser, Inc.
Greenblatt, Miriam. Napoleon Bonaparte & Imperial France, 1 vol. 2007. (Rulers & Their Times Ser.). (ENG., Illus.). 80p. (J). (gr. 6-6). lib. bdg. 36.93 *(978-0-7614-1837-5(7)*, e263ac46-7d98-4d74-8dd2-972dc76f7518) Cavendish Square Publishing LLC.
Heuston, Kimberley & Heuston, Kimberley Burton. Napoleon I: Emperor & Conqueror. 2009. (Wicked History Ser.). (ENG., Illus.). 128p. (J). (gr. 5-9). 31.00 *(978-0-531-21277-6(7))* Scholastic Library Publishing.
Landau, Elaine. Jefferson's Louisiana Purchase: Would You Make the Deal of the Century?, 1 vol. 2014. (What Would You Do? Ser.). (ENG.). 48p. (gr. 3-4). 27.93 *(978-0-7660-6305-1(4)*, 4a599c69-5c92-4682-95d0-9a93f9891693); pap. 11.53 *(978-0-7660-6306-8(2)*, 0c240e39-3a16-4732-bbd2-78d7c4c61d18, Enslow Elementary) Enslow Publishing, LLC.
—The Louisiana Purchase: Would You Close the Deal?, 1 vol. 2008. (What Would You Do? Ser.). (ENG., Illus.). 48p. (gr. 3-3). pap. 11.53 *(978-1-59845-196-2(0)*, ba81a5a3-263e-4e3c-99e1-1f0721932655); lib. bdg. 27.93 *(978-0-7660-2902-6(6)*, ab076af9-e6df-4809-afdd-7ab429047f40) Enslow Publishing, LLC. (Enslow Elementary).
—Napoleon Bonaparte. 2006. (Illus.). 112p. (J). 27.93 *(978-0-8225-3420-4(7)*, Twenty-First Century Bks.) Lerner Publishing Group.
Lethbridge, Lucy. Napoleon. 2005. (Illus.). 64p. (J). 8.95 *(978-0-7945-1050-3(7)*, Usborne) EDC Publishing.
Lynette, Rachel. The Louisiana Purchase, 1 vol. 2013. (Pioneer Spirit: the Westward Expansion Ser.). (Illus.). 24p. (J). (ENG.). (gr. 2-3). pap. 9.25 *(978-1-4777-0895-8(2)*, a62ea59e-dc6c-4758-a467-b78fe89be66c); (ENG., (gr. 2-3). lib. bdg. 26.27 *(978-1-4777-0781-4(6)*, acb9c5a6-da9b-41af-a96d-5cc2e728ce70); (gr. 3-6). pap. 49.50 *(978-1-4777-0896-5(0))* Rosen Publishing Group, Inc., The. (PowerKids Pr.).
Mills Hoffman, Megan. Napoleon Bonaparte, 1 vol. 2017. (Great Military Leaders Ser.). (ENG., Illus.). 128p. (J). (gr. 9-9). 47.36 *(978-1-5026-2782-7(5)*,

MNO

98bb5a2a-a196-42e6-8a97-29a738de85e0) Cavendish Square Publishing LLC.

O'Donoghue, Sean. Thomas Jefferson & the Louisiana Purchase, 1 vol. 2016. (Spotlight on American History Ser.). (ENG., Illus.). 24p. (J). (gr. 4-6). 27.93 *(978-1-5081-4948-4(8),* 05df1466-a916-4843-9a6b-54ecd33a7ede, PowerKids Pr.) Rosen Publishing Group, Inc., The.

Roberts, Russell. Battle of Waterloo. 2011. (Technologies & Strategies in Battle Ser.). (Illus.). 48p. (J). (gr. 4-7). lib. bdg. 29.95 *(978-1-61228-076-9(5))* Mitchell Lane Pubs.

Streissguth, Thomas. The Napoleonic Wars: Defeat of the Grand Army. 2003. (History's Great Defeats Ser.). (ENG., Illus.). 112p. (J). 32.10 *(978-1-59018-065-5(8),* Lucent Bks.) Cengage Gale.

Yasuda, Anita. 12 Incredible Facts about the Louisiana Purchase. 2016. (Turning Points in US History Ser.). (ENG., Illus.). 32p. (J). (gr. 3-6). 32.80 *(978-1-63235-131-9(5),* 12003, 12-Story Library) Bookstaves, LLC.

Zamoyski, Adam. Napoleon: A Life. 2018. (ENG., Illus.). 784p. 40.00 *(978-0-465-05593-7(1))* Basic Bks.

NAPOLEON I, EMPEROR OF THE FRENCH, 1769-1821—FICTION

Brighton, Catherine. My Napoleon. Brighton, Catherine, illus. 2005. (Illus.). 26p. (J). (gr. k-4). reprint ed. 17.00 *(978-0-7567-8931-2(1))* DIANE Publishing Co.

Hausman, Gerald & Hausman, Loretta. Farewell, Josephine: The Romance of Josephine & Napoleon. 2013. 248p. pap. 13.95 *(978-1-61720-381-7(5))* Wilder Pubns., Corp.

Henty, George. At Aboukir & Acre: A Story of Napoleon's Invasion of Egypt (Henty Homeschool History Series) 2010. 344p. pap. 19.95 *(978-1-935585-23-7(1))* Fireship Pr.

Marcellino, Fred. Arrivederci, Crocodile: Or See You Later, Alligator. Marcellino, Fred & Puybaret, Eric, illus. 2019. (ENG.). 40p. (J). (gr. -1-3). 17.99 *(978-1-5344-0401-4(5),* Atheneum Bks. for Young Readers) Simon & Schuster Children's Publishing.

Rabin, Staton. Betsy & the Emperor. 2006. (ENG., Illus.). 304p. (YA). (gr. 7). reprint ed. mass mkt. 8.99 *(978-1-4169-1336-8(X),* Simon Pulse) Simon Pulse.

NAPOLEONIC WARS, 1800-1815

Allport, Alan. The Congress of Vienna. 2011. (ENG., Illus.). 126p. (gr. 9). 35.00 *(978-1-60413-497-1(6),* P189855, Facts On File) Infobase Holdings, Inc.

Freedman, Jeri. Strategic Inventions of the Napoleonic Wars, 1 vol. 2016. (Tech in the Trenches Ser.). (ENG., Illus.). 112p. (J). (gr. 9-9). 44.50 *(978-1-5026-2351-5(X),* 5374cf10-2ca1-427a-a1ee-cf76bcf4c4d8) Cavendish Square Publishing LLC.

Roberts, Russell. Battle of Waterloo. 2011. (Technologies & Strategies in Battle Ser.). (Illus.). 48p. (J). (gr. 4-7). lib. bdg. 29.95 *(978-1-61228-076-9(5))* Mitchell Lane Pubs.

Streissguth, Thomas. The Napoleonic Wars: Defeat of the Grand Army. 2003. (History's Great Defeats Ser.). (ENG., Illus.). 112p. (J). 32.10 *(978-1-59018-065-5(8),* Lucent Bks.) Cengage Gale.

NARCOTIC HABIT

see Drug Addiction

NARCOTICS

Cashin, John. The Heroin Crisis. 2017. (Opioids & Opiates: the Silent Epidemic* Ser.: Vol. 5). (ENG., Illus.). 64p. (YA). (gr. 7-12). 23.95 *(978-1-4222-3825-7(3))* Mason Crest.

Ferguson, Grace. Chronic Pain & Prescription Painkillers. 2017. (Opioids & Opiates: the Silent Epidemic* Ser.: Vol. 5). (ENG., Illus.). 64p. (YA). (gr. 7-12). 23.95 *(978-1-4222-3823-3(7))* Mason Crest.

Gleason, Carrie. The Biography of Tobacco. 2006. (How Did That Get Here? Ser.). (ENG., Illus.). 32p. (J). (gr. 4-7). pap. *(978-0-7787-2525-1(1),* 1259497) Crabtree Publishing Co.

Goldsmith, Connie. Addiction & Overdose: Confronting an American Crisis. 2017. (ENG., Illus.). 128p. (YA). (gr. 8-12). 37.32 *(978-1-5124-0953-6(7),* 33aec29b-ac47-4fa7-b324-1ead1dff74fd, Twenty-First Century Bks.) Lerner Publishing Group.

Grinapol, Corinne. Racial Profiling & Discrimination: Your Legal Rights, 1 vol. 2015. (Know Your Rights Ser.). (ENG., Illus.). 64p. (J). (gr. 7-7). 36.47 *(978-1-4777-8020-6(3),* 5ceacb72-a9ca-4d3b-a623-3cccceb4ac46, Rosen Young Adult) Rosen Publishing Group, Inc., The.

Illicit & Misused Drugs, 16 vols., Set. Incl. Addiction in America: Society, Psychology, & Heredity. Walker, Ida. (Illus.). (YA). lib. bdg. 24.95 *(978-1-4222-0151-0(1));* Addiction Treatment: Escaping the Trap. Walker, Ida. (Illus.). (YA). lib. bdg. 24.95 *(978-1-4222-0152-7(X));* Alcohol Addiction: Not Worth the Buzz. Walker, Ida J. (YA). lib. bdg. 24.95 *(978-1-4222-0153-4(8));* Hallucinogens: Unreal Visions. Nelson, Sheila. (Illus.). (YA). lib. bdg. 24.95 *(978-1-4222-0155-8(4));* Inhalants & Solvents: Sniffing Disaster. Flynn, Noa. (Illus.). (YA). lib. bdg. 24.95 *(978-1-4222-0157-2(0));* Marijuana: Mind-Altering Weed. Sanna, E. J. (Illus.). (J). lib. bdg. 24.95 *(978-1-4222-0158-9(9));* Methamphetamines: Unsafe Speed. Etingoff, Kim. (Illus.). (YA). lib. bdg. 24.95 *(978-1-4222-0159-6(7));* Sedatives & Hypnotics: Deadly Downers. Walker, Ida J. (Illus.). (J). lib. bdg. 24.95 *(978-1-4222-0163-3(5));* Tobacco: Through the Smokescreen. Chastain, Zachary. (YA). lib. bdg. 24.95 *(978-1-4222-0165-7(1));* (gr. 7-18). 2009. (Illus.). 128p. 2007. Set lib. bdg. 399.20 *(978-1-4222-0149-7(X))* Mason Crest.

Kerrigan, Michael. The War Against Drugs. 2004. (Crime & Detection Ser.). (Illus.). 96p. (J). (gr. 7-18). lib. bdg. 22.95 *(978-1-59084-368-0(1))* Mason Crest.

LeVert, Suzanne. The Facts about Cocaine, 1 vol. 2007. (Facts about Drugs Ser.). (ENG., Illus.). 128p. (gr. 6-6). 45.50 *(978-0-7614-1973-0(X),* ad8291e8-5622-4d72-80e8-ac3f5b8ea0ba) Cavendish Square Publishing LLC.

Lew, Kristi. The Truth about Oxycodone & Other Narcotics, 1 vol. 2013. (Drugs & Consequences Ser.). (ENG., Illus.). 64p. (J). (gr. 5-5). 37.13 *(978-1-4777-1894-0(X),* 0d8d84eb-c92b-4c24-b8c5-2e00c52084e2) Rosen Publishing Group, Inc., The.

McCoy, Erin L. & Worth, Richard. Illicit Drug Use: Legalization, Treatment, or Punishment?, 1 vol. 2018. (Today's Debates Ser.). (ENG.). 144p. (gr. 7-7). pap. 22.16 *(978-1-5026-4328-5(6),* 8027de93-561c-4c5b-87a8-70b1f8319e1f) Cavendish Square Publishing LLC.

Mirman, Heather Moehn. Issues in Drug Abuse. 2003. (Contemporary Issues Ser.). (ENG., Illus.). 112p. (YA). (gr. 7-10). 30.85 *(978-1-59018-035-8(6),* Lucent Bks.) Cengage Gale.

Olive, M. Foster. Morphine. 2011. (ENG., Illus.). 112p. (gr. 9-12). 34.95 *(978-1-60413-544-2(1),* P189862, Facts On File) Infobase Holdings, Inc.

Paris, Stephanie. Drugs & Alcohol, 1 vol. 2nd rev. ed. 2012. (TIME for KIDS(r): Informational Text Ser.). (ENG., Illus.). 48p. (gr. 4-6). pap. 13.99 *(978-1-4333-4859-4(4))* Teacher Created Materials, Inc.

Petersen, Christine. Vicodin & OxyContin, 1 vol. 2013. (Dangerous Drugs Ser.). (ENG.). 64p. (gr. 6-6). 36.93 *(978-1-60870-827-7(6),* 1388ff47-86a1-4e82-b3ec-37fbbb4f6cf6); pap. 16.28 *(978-1-62712-063-0(7),* 1f4de41a-4f44-42ce-a9a6-984219e9c671) Cavendish Square Publishing LLC.

Quinones, Sam. Dreamland (YA Edition) The True Tale of America's Opiate Epidemic. 2019. (ENG., Illus.). 224p. (YA). 18.99 *(978-1-5476-0131-8(0),* 900199623, Bloomsbury Young Adult) Bloomsbury Publishing USA.

Sanna, E. J. Heroin & Other Opioids: Poppies' Perilous Children. Henningfield, Jack E., ed. 2012. (Illicit & Misused Drugs Ser.). 128p. (J). (gr. 7). 24.95 *(978-1-4222-2433-5(3));* pap. 14.95 *(978-1-4222-2452-6(X))* Mason Crest.

Somerville, Clive. The Drug Enforcement Administration. 2004. (Rescue & Prevention Ser.). (Illus.). 96p. (YA). (gr. 7-18). lib. bdg. 22.95 *(978-1-59084-413-7(0))* Mason Crest.

NARNIA (IMAGINARY PLACE)—FICTION

Baynes, Pauline & Lewis, C. S. Prince Caspian, Bk. 7. Baynes, Pauline, illus. 2008. (Chronicles of Narnia Ser.). (Illus.). 768p. (J). (gr. 3). pap. 99.99 *(978-0-06-076552-1(6))* HarperCollins Pubs.

Beahm, George. Passport to Narnia: A Newcomer's Guide. Kirk, Tim, illus. 2005. (ENG.). 200p. (YA). (gr. 8-12). per. 12.95 *(978-1-57174-465-4(7))* Hampton Roads Publishing Co., Inc.

—Passport to Narnia: The Unofficial Giude. Kirk, Tim, illus. 2005. (J). lib. bdg. 15.95 *(978-1-57174-481-4(9))* Hampton Roads Publishing Co., Inc.

Frantz, Jennifer, adapted by. Narnia: Welcome to Narnia. 2005. (Illus.). 32p. (J). lib. bdg. 13.85 *(978-1-4242-0617-9(0))* Fitzgerald Bks.

Lewis, C. S. L' Armoire Magique. Orig. Title: The Lion, the Witch & the Wardrobe. (FRE.). pap. 12.95 *(978-2-08-161994-4(6))* Flammarion et Cie FRA. Dist: Distribooks, Inc.

—The Chronicles of Narnia: 7 Books in 1 Hardcover. Baynes, Pauline, illus. 2004. (Chronicles of Narnia Ser.). (ENG.). 784p. (J). (gr. 5). 32.99 *(978-0-06-059824-2(7),* HarperCollins) HarperCollins Pubs.

—The Chronicles of Narnia Hardcover 7-Book Box Set: 7 Books in 1 Box Set, Bks. 1 to 7, Set. Baynes, Pauline, illus. rev. ed. 2007. (Chronicles of Narnia Ser.). (ENG.). (J). (gr. 3-18). 120.00 *(978-0-06-024488-0(7),* HarperCollins) HarperCollins Pubs.

—The Horse & His Boy. Baynes, Pauline, illus. (Chronicles of Narnia Ser.: 3). (ENG.). 240p. (J). (gr. 3-18). 2008. pap. 10.99 *(978-0-06-440501-0(X))* 2007. 19.99 *(978-0-06-023488-1(1))* HarperCollins Pubs. (HarperCollins).

—Las Cronicas de Narnia: The Chronicles of Narnia (Spanish Edition), 1 vol. 2006. (Las Cronicas de Narnia Ser.). (SPA., Illus.). 816p. (J). (gr. 3-7). pap. 21.99 *(978-0-06-119900-4(1))* HarperCollins Español.

—The Last Battle. Baynes, Pauline, illus. (Chronicles of Narnia Ser.: 7). (ENG.). 224p. (J). (gr. 3-18). 2008. pap. 10.99 *(978-0-06-440503-4(6))* 2007. 19.99 *(978-0-06-023493-5(8))* HarperCollins Pubs. (HarperCollins).

—El Leon, la Bruja y el Ropero: The Lion, the Witch & the Wardrobe (Spanish Edition), 1 vol. 2005. (Las Cronicas de Narnia Ser.: 2). (SPA.). 208p. (J). (gr. 3). pap. 9.99 *(978-0-06-084253-6(9))* HarperCollins Español.

—The Lion, the Witch & the Wardrobe. Humphries, Tudor, illus. 2004. (Chronicles of Narnia Ser.). 48p. (J). (gr. -1-2). lib. bdg. 17.89 *(978-0-06-055651-8(X))* HarperCollins Pubs.

—The Lion, the Witch & the Wardrobe. Baynes, Pauline, illus. abr. ed. (Chronicles of Narnia Ser.: 2). (ENG.). 208p. (J). (gr. 3-18). 2008. pap. 8.99 *(978-0-06-440499-0(4))* 2007. 19.99 *(978-0-06-023481-2(4))* 2007. lib. bdg. 19.89 *(978-0-06-023482-9(2))* HarperCollins Pubs. (HarperCollins).

—The Lion, the Witch & the Wardrobe. 2008. (Chronicles of Narnia Ser.: 2). (J). 18.40 *(978-0-613-94066-5(0))* Turtleback.

—The Lion, the Witch & the Wardrobe: Picture Book Edition. Humphries, Tudor, illus. 2004. (Chronicles of Narnia Ser.). (ENG.). 48p. (J). (gr. -1-2). 18.99 *(978-0-06-055650-1(1),* HarperCollins) HarperCollins Pubs.

—The Magician's Nephew. Baynes, Pauline, illus. (Chronicles of Narnia Ser.: 1). (ENG.). 208p. (J). (gr. 3-18). 2008. pap. 8.99 *(978-0-06-440505-8(2))* 2007. 19.99 *(978-0-06-023497-3(0))* HarperCollins Pubs. (HarperCollins).

—Prince Caspian: The Return to Narnia. Baynes, Pauline, illus. (Chronicles of Narnia Ser.: 4). (ENG.). 240p. (J). (gr. 3-18). 2008. pap. 10.99 *(978-0-06-440500-3(1))* 2007. 19.99 *(978-0-06-023483-6(0))* HarperCollins Pubs. (HarperCollins).

—The Silver Chair. Baynes, Pauline, illus. (Chronicles of Narnia Ser.: 6). (ENG.). 256p. (J). (gr. 3-18). 2008. pap. 10.99 *(978-0-06-440504-1(4))* 2007. 19.99 *(978-0-06-023495-9(4))* HarperCollins Pubs. (HarperCollins).

—The Voyage of the Dawn Treader. Baynes, Pauline, illus. (Chronicles of Narnia Ser.: 5). (ENG.). 256p. (J). (gr. 3-18). 2008. pap. 10.99 *(978-0-06-440502-7(8))* 2007. 18.99 *(978-0-06-023486-7(5))* HarperCollins Pubs. (HarperCollins).

Novel Units. The Lion Witch & the Wardrobe Novel Units Student Packet. 2019. (Chronicles of Narnia Ser.). (ENG.). (J). (gr. 4-8). pap. 13.99 *(978-1-56137-704-6(X),* Novel Units, Inc.) Classroom Library Co.

—The Lion Witch & the Wardrobe Novel Units Teacher Guide. 2019. (Chronicles of Narnia Ser.). (ENG.). (J). (gr. 4-8). pap. 12.99 *(978-1-56137-243-0(9),* Novel Units, Inc.) Classroom Library Co.

Peacock, Ann & Lewis, C. S. The Chronicles of Narnia. Barbera, Tony et al, illus. Barbera, Tony et al, photos by. 2005. (Chronicles of Narnia Ser.). 64p. (J). *(978-1-4156-3678-7(8))* HarperCollins Pubs.

Prince Caspian Chapter Book #1. 2008. (Chronicles of Narnia Ser.). 96p. (J). pap. 3.99 *(978-0-06-147260-2(3),* Harper Trophy) HarperCollins Pubs.

Prince Caspian Chapter Book #2. 2008. (Chronicles of Narnia Ser.). 96p. (J). pap. 3.99 *(978-0-06-147261-9(1),* Harper Trophy) HarperCollins Pubs.

Prince Caspian Chapter Book #3. 2008. (Chronicles of Narnia Ser.). 96p. (J). pap. 3.99 *(978-0-06-147262-6(X),* Harper Trophy) HarperCollins Pubs.

Prince Caspian Chapter Book #4. 2008. (Chronicles of Narnia Ser.). 96p. (J). pap. 3.99 *(978-0-06-147263-3(8),* Harper Trophy) HarperCollins Pubs.

Wilson, Douglas, reader. What I Learned in Narnia. 2004. cd-rom 35.00 *(978-1-59128-438-3(4))* Canon Pr.

NASCIMENTO, EDSON ARANTES DO, 1940-2022

see Pele, 1940-2022

NATE THE GREAT (FICTITIOUS CHARACTER)—FICTION

Novel Units. Nate the Great & the Sticky Case Novel Units Teacher Guide. 2019. (Nate the Great Ser.). (ENG.). (J). (gr. 1-4). pap. 12.99 *(978-1-56137-263-8(3),* Novel Units, Inc.) Classroom Library Co.

Sharmat, Andrew & Sharmat, Marjorie Weinman. Nate the Great & the Missing Birthday Snake. Wheeler, Jody, illus. 2018. (Nate the Great Ser.). 80p. (J). (gr. 1-4). 5.99 *(978-1-101-93470-8(0),* Yearling) Random Hse. Children's Bks.

Sharmat, Marjorie Weinman. Nate the Great. Simont, Marc, illus. (Nate the Great Ser.: No. 1). 48p. (J). (gr. 1-4). pap. 4.50 *(978-0-8072-1351-3(9),* Listening Library) Random Hse. Audio Publishing Group.

—Nate the Great & the Halloween Hunt. Simont, Marc, illus. (Nate the Great Ser.: No. 12). 48p. (J). (gr. 1-4). pap. 4.50 *(978-0-8072-1283-7(0),* Listening Library) Random Hse. Audio Publishing Group.

—Nate the Great & the Missing Key. Simont, Marc, illus. (Nate the Great Ser.: No. 6). 48p. (J). (gr. 1-4). pap. 4.50 *(978-0-8072-1335-3(7),* Listening Library) Random Hse. Audio Publishing Group.

—Nate the Great Goes Undercover. Simont, Marc, illus. (Nate the Great Ser.: No. 2). 48p. (J). (gr. 1-4). pap. 4.50 *(978-0-8072-1284-4(9));* 2004. pap. 17.00 incl. audio *(978-0-8072-0201-2(0),* FTR172SP) Random Hse. Audio Publishing Group. (Listening Library).

Sharmat, Marjorie Weinman & Sharmat, Andrew. Nate the Great & the Wandering Word. Wheeler, Jody, illus. 2019. (Nate the Great Ser.: Bk. 27). 80p. (J). (gr. 1-4). 6.99 *(978-1-5247-6547-7(3),* Yearling) Random Hse. Children's Bks.

Sharmat, Marjorie Weinman & Sharmat, Mitchell. Nate the Great & the Big Sniff. Weston, Martha, illus. 2003. (Nate the Great Ser.: No. 23). (ENG.). 80p. (J). (gr. 1-4). pap. 5.99 *(978-0-440-41502-2(0),* Yearling) Random Hse. Children's Bks.

—Nate the Great & the Big Sniff. Weston, Martha, illus. 2003. (Nate the Great Ser.: Bk. 23). 47p. (gr. -1-3). lib. bdg. 16.00 *(978-0-613-63966-8(9))* Turtleback.

—Nate the Great, Where Are You? Wheeler, Jody, illus. 2015. (Nate the Great Ser.). 80p. (J). (gr. 1-4). 5.99 *(978-0-449-81078-1(X),* Yearling) Random Hse. Children's Bks.

NATION OF ISLAM (MOVEMENT)

see Black Muslims

NATIONAL ANTHEMS

see National Songs

NATIONAL BASEBALL HALL OF FAME AND MUSEUM

Levit, Joe. Babe Ruth: Super Slugger. 2020. (Epic Sports Bios (Lerner (tm) Sports) Ser.). (ENG., Illus.). 32p. (J). (gr. 2-5). 30.65 *(978-1-5415-9747-1(8),* 356f1bee-8a7f-4e68-a799-9c2fcf7f2802); pap. 9.99 *(978-1-7284-1339-6(7),* 828c0149-0390-4600-b23e-13a8557c31db) Lerner Publishing Group. (Lerner Pubns.).

Nicholson, Lois P. From Maryland to Cooperstown: Seven Maryland Natives in Baseball's Hall of Fame, 1 vol. 2010. (ENG., Illus.). 144p. (gr. 4-8). 19.95 *(978-0-87033-494-8(8),* 3620, Cornell Maritime Pr./Tidewater Pubs.) Schiffer Publishing, Ltd.

NATIONAL BASKETBALL ASSOCIATION

Adamson, Thomas K. Basketball Records. 2018. (Incredible Sports Records Ser.). (ENG., Illus.). 32p. (J). (gr. 3-8). pap. 8.99 *(978-1-61891-312-8(3),* 12107, Blastoff! Discovery) Bellwether Media.

De Medeiros, Michael. The NBA. 2007. (Sporting Championships Ser.). (Illus.). 32p. (J). (gr. 4-6). lib. bdg. 26.00 *(978-1-59036-691-2(3));* per. 9.95 *(978-1-59036-692-9(1))* Weigl Pubs., Inc.

—NBA. 2012. (J). *(978-1-61913-060-9(2));* pap. 28.55 *(978-1-61913-622-9(8))* Weigl Pubs., Inc.

—The NBA Finals. 2017. (J). *(978-1-5105-0846-0(5))* SmartBook Media, Inc.

de Medeiros, Michael. NBA Finals. 2019. (We Are the Champions Ser.). (ENG., Illus.). 32p. (J). (gr. 4-7). pap. 13.95 *(978-1-7911-0579-2(3));* lib. bdg. 29.99 *(978-1-7911-0044-5(9))* Weigl Pubs., Inc.

Doeden, Matt. The NBA Playoffs: In Pursuit of Basketball Glory. 2019. (Spectacular Sports Ser.). (ENG., Illus.). 64p. (J). (gr. 5-8). lib. bdg. 34.65 *(978-1-5415-4153-5(7),* 1001c391-09ab-4e1b-9abd-f09771a439ca, Millbrook Pr.) Lerner Publishing Group.

Donnelly, Patrick. Best NBA Centers of All Time, 1 vol. 2014. (NBA's Best Ever Ser.). (ENG., Illus.). 64p. (J). (gr. 3-6). lib. bdg. 35.64 *(978-1-62403-409-1(8),* 1558, SportsZone) ABDO Publishing Co.

—Best NBA Forwards of All Time, 1 vol. 2014. (NBA's Best Ever Ser.). (ENG.). 64p. (J). (gr. 3-6). lib. bdg. 35.64 *(978-1-62403-411-4(X),* 1562, SportsZone) ABDO Publishing Co.

Fishman, Jon M. Joel Embiid. 2020. (Sports All-Stars (Lerner (tm) Sports) Ser.). (ENG., Illus.). 32p. (J). (gr. 2-5). pap. 9.99 *(978-1-5415-8954-4(8),* 3ebee820-bf9b-4a7e-a8f0-3e7d8ce6f311); lib. bdg. 29.32 *(978-1-5415-7729-9(9),* f4738cc9-7877-4d70-85ed-39dd29d6c72e) Lerner Publishing Group. (Lerner Pubns.).

Gilliam, MicKey. Pro Basketball Upsets. 2020. (Sports' Wildest Upsets (Lerner (tm) Sports) Ser.). (ENG., Illus.). 32p. (J). (gr. 2-5). 29.32 *(978-1-5415-7716-9(7),* 57767a82-0dca-43e6-8a6c-0488c33d440c, Lerner Pubns.) Lerner Publishing Group.

Gitlin, Marty. NBA Underdog Stories. 2018. (Underdog Sports Stories Ser.). (ENG., Illus.). 48p. (J). (gr. 5-8). lib. bdg. 34.21 *(978-1-5321-1762-6(0),* 30812, SportsZone) ABDO Publishing Co.

Graves, Will. Best NBA Guards of All Time, 1 vol. 2014. (NBA's Best Ever Ser.). (ENG., Illus.). 64p. (J). (gr. 3-6). lib. bdg. 35.64 *(978-1-62403-412-1(8),* 1564, SportsZone) ABDO Publishing Co.

—Best NBA Teams of All Time, 1 vol. 2014. (NBA's Best Ever Ser.). (ENG.). 64p. (J). (gr. 3-6). lib. bdg. 35.64 *(978-1-62403-414-5(4),* 1568, SportsZone) ABDO Publishing Co.

Hareas, John. NBA Slam Dunk 3-D. 2006. (J). pap. *(978-0-439-78814-4(5))* Scholastic, Inc.

Hoffman, Mary Ann. Dwayne Wade: Basketball Star. 2009. (Sports Superstars Ser.). 24p. (gr. 1-1). 42.50 *(978-1-60853-176-9(7),* PowerKids Pr.) Rosen Publishing Group, Inc., The.

—Dwayne Wade: Basketball Star/Estrella del Baloncesto. 2009. (Amazing Athletes/Atletas increíbles Ser.). (ENG & SPA.). 24p. (gr. 1-2). 42.50 *(978-1-61511-305-7(3),* Editorial Buenas Letras) Rosen Publishing Group, Inc., The.

LeBoutillier, Nate. The Ultimate Guide to Pro Basketball Teams. 2010. (Ultimate Pro Team Guides (Sports Illustrated for Kids) Ser.). (ENG.). 72p. (J). (gr. 3-4). pap. 53.70 *(978-1-4296-5734-1(0),* 15506); pap. 8.95 *(978-1-4296-5641-2(7),* 114132, Capstone Pr.) Capstone.

McCollum, Sean. Pro Basketball's All-Time Greatest Comebacks. 2019. (Sports Comebacks Ser.). (ENG., Illus.). 32p. (J). (gr. 3-9). lib. bdg. 28.65 *(978-1-5435-5433-5(4),* 139283, Capstone Pr.) Capstone.

Nelson, Kadir, illus. Basket Ball. 2019. (J). *(978-1-4847-7181-5(8))* Disney Publishing Worldwide.

Omoth, Tyler. A Superfan's Guide to Pro Basketball Teams. 2017. (Pro Sports Team Guides). (ENG., Illus.). 72p. (J). (gr. 3-9). lib. bdg. 35.32 *(978-1-5157-8850-8(4),* 136344, Capstone Pr.) Capstone.

Scheff, Matt. NBA & WNBA Finals: Basketball's Biggest Playoffs. 2020. (Big Game (Lerner (tm) Sports) Ser.). (ENG., Illus.). 32p. (J). (gr. 2-5). 30.65 *(978-1-5415-9759-4(1),* c719fbcd-5061-47a9-82df-f5bb99b22ce9, Lerner Pubns.) Lerner Publishing Group.

Segal, Adam Elliott & Segal, Adam Elliott. Basketball Stars. 2017. (ENG., Illus.). 64p. (J). (gr. 4-7). 19.95 *(978-1-77085-827-5(X),* 4d5a977e-a73b-45bb-9927-ad1fb50b93fa); pap. 6.95 *(978-1-77085-772-8(9),* f0ee451a-8e87-41b0-b35f-de2b0513e7da) Firefly Bks., Ltd.

Velasco, Catherine Ann. Behind the Scenes of Pro Basketball. 2019. (Behind the Scenes with the Pros Ser.). (ENG., Illus.). 32p. (J). (gr. 3-9). lib. bdg. 28.65 *(978-1-5435-5424-3(5),* 139279, Capstone Pr.) Capstone.

Wilner, Barry. Best NBA Dunkers of All Time, 1 vol. 2014. (NBA's Best Ever Ser.). (ENG.). 64p. (J). (gr. 3-6). lib. bdg. 35.64 *(978-1-62403-410-7(1),* 1560, SportsZone) ABDO Publishing Co.

—Best NBA Shooters of All Time, 1 vol. 2014. (NBA's Best Ever Ser.). (ENG., Illus.). 64p. (J). (gr. 3-6). lib. bdg. 35.64 *(978-1-62403-413-8(6),* 1566, SportsZone) ABDO Publishing Co.

NATIONAL DANCES

see Folk Dancing

NATIONAL FOOTBALL LEAGUE

Abdo, Kenny. Super Bowl. 2018. (Arena Events Ser.). (ENG., Illus.). 24p. (J). (gr. 2-8). lib. bdg. 31.36 *(978-1-5321-2539-3(9),* 30087, Abdo Zoom-Fly) ABDO Publishing Co.

Bowker, Paul. Best Super Bowl Finishes. 2019. (Best of the Super Bowl Ser.). (ENG., Illus.). 32p. (J). (gr. 3-6). 32.80 *(978-1-63235-543-0(4),* 13933, 12-Story Library) Bookstaves, LLC.

—Biggest Super Bowl Plays. 2019. (Best of the Super Bowl Ser.). (ENG., Illus.). 32p. (J). (gr. 3-6). 32.80 *(978-1-63235-546-1(9),* 13936, 12-Story Library) Bookstaves, LLC.

—Biggest Super Bowl Upsets. 2019. (Best of the Super Bowl Ser.). (ENG., Illus.). 32p. (J). (gr. 3-6). 32.80 *(978-1-63235-547-8(7),* 13937, 12-Story Library) Bookstaves, LLC.

Brock, Ted. Running Pro Football: Commissioner, Owners, Front Office, & More, Vol. 10. 2016. (All about Professional Football Ser.: Vol. 10). (ENG., Illus.). 64p. (J). (gr. 7-12). 23.95 *(978-1-4222-3585-0(8))* Mason Crest.

Ellenport, Craig. NFL 100: The Greatest Moments of the NFL's Century. 2019. (Illus.). 240p. 29.95 *(978-1-62937-745-2(7))* Triumph Bks.

Gigliotti, Jim. The Intense World of a Pro Football Coach, Vol. 10. 2016. (All about Professional Football Ser.). (Illus.). 64p. (J). (gr. 7). 23.95 *(978-1-4222-3582-9(3))* Mason Crest.

—The Pro Football Draft, Vol. 10. 2016. (All about Professional Football Ser.: Vol. 10). (ENG., Illus.). 64p. (J). (gr. 7-12). 23.95 *(978-1-4222-3583-6(1))* Mason Crest.

Gilbert, Sara. The Story of the NFL. 2011. (Built for Success Ser.). (J). (gr. 5-9). (Illus.). 34.25 *(978-1-60818-063-9(8));* (ENG.). 48p. pap. 12.00 *(978-0-89812-661-7(4),* 22120, Creative Paperbacks) Creative Co., The.

Gilliam, MicKey. Pro Football Upsets. 2020. (Sports' Wildest Upsets (Lerner (tm) Sports) Ser.). (ENG., Illus.). 32p. (J). (gr. 2-5). 29.32 *(978-1-5415-7709-1(4),* 8226ceff-2a68-40cb-8636-907b9f0e2ecb, Lerner Pubns.) Lerner Publishing Group.

Glave, Tom. NFL's Top 10 Rookies. 2017. (NFL's Top Ten Ser.). (ENG., Illus.). 32p. (J). (gr. 3-6). lib. bdg. 32.79 *(978-1-5321-1143-3(6),* 25862, SportsZone) ABDO Publishing Co.

Graves, Will. NFL's Top 10 Teams. 2017. (NFL's Top Ten Ser.). (ENG., Illus.). 32p. (J). (gr. 3-6). lib. bdg. 32.79 *(978-1-5321-1144-0(4),* 25864, SportsZone) ABDO Publishing Co.

—NFL's Top 10 Upsets. 2017. (NFL's Top Ten Ser.). (ENG.). 32p. (J). (gr. 3-6). lib. bdg. 32.79 *(978-1-5321-1145-7(2),* 25866, SportsZone) ABDO Publishing Co.

Hall, Brian. NFL's Top 10 Comebacks. 2017. (NFL's Top Ten Ser.). (ENG., Illus.). 32p. (J). (gr. 3-6). lib. bdg. 32.79 *(978-1-5321-1139-6(8)*, 25854, SportsZone) ABDO Publishing Co.

Howell, Brian. NFL's Top 10 Games. 2017. (NFL's Top Ten Ser.). (ENG., Illus.). 32p. (J). (gr. 3-6). lib. bdg. 32.79 *(978-1-5321-1140-2(1)*, 25856, SportsZone) ABDO Publishing Co.

Kelley, K. C. Quarterback Superstars 2015. 2015. (Illus.). 32p. (J). *(978-0-545-88736-6(4))* Scholastic, Inc.

Kortemeier, Todd. Tampa Bay Buccaneers, 1 vol. 2016. (NFL up Close Ser.). (ENG., Illus.). 32p. (J). (gr. 3-9). lib. bdg. 32.79 *(978-1-68078-235-6(5)*, 22071, SportsZone) ABDO Publishing Co.

Kortemeier, Todd & Graves, Will. Pittsburgh Steelers, 1 vol. 2016. (NFL up Close Ser.). (ENG., Illus.). 32p. (J). (gr. 3-9). lib. bdg. 32.79 *(978-1-68078-230-1(4)*, 22063, SportsZone) ABDO Publishing Co.

Kortemeier, Tom. Pro Football by the Numbers. 2016. (Pro Sports by the Numbers Ser.). (ENG., Illus.). 32p. (J). pap. 47.70 *(978-1-4914-9070-9(5)*, 24527); (gr. 3-9). lib. bdg. 28.65 *(978-1-4914-9060-0(8)*, 131635, Capstone Pr.) Capstone.

Lajiness, Katie. Houston Texans. 2016. (NFL's Greatest Teams Set 3 Ser.). (ENG., Illus.). 32p. (J). (gr. 2-5). 51.35 *(978-1-68079-894-4(4)*, 23971, Big Buddy Bks.) ABDO Publishing Co.

Layden, Joseph. Rising Stars, NFL. 2005. (Illus.). 32p. (J). pap. *(978-0-439-80247-5(4))* Scholastic, Inc.

Levit, Joe. Football's G. O. A. T. Jim Brown, Tom Brady, & More. 2019. (Sports' Greatest of All Time (Lerner (tm) Sports) Ser.). (ENG., Illus.). 32p. (J). (gr. 2-5). pap. 9.99 *(978-1-5415-7443-4(5)*, 6431219c-c133-4b57-a5c1-233a432befb3); lib. bdg. 30.65 *(978-1-5415-5602-7(X)*, ce79eb1f-a752-4aed-ba8c-3c3a78ebd31c) Lerner Publishing Group. (Lerner Pubns.).

Lyon, Drew. Pro Football's All-Time Greatest Comebacks. 2019. (Sports Comebacks Ser.). (ENG., Illus.). 32p. (J). (gr. 3-9). lib. bdg. 28.65 *(978-1-5435-5434-2(2)*, 139284, Capstone Pr.) Capstone.

—A Superfan's Guide to Pro Football Teams. 2017. (Pro Sports Team Guides). (ENG., Illus.). 72p. (J). (gr. 3-9). lib. bdg. 35.32 *(978-1-5157-8852-2(0)*, 136346, Capstone Pr.) Capstone.

Monson, James. Behind the Scenes Football. 2019. (Inside the Sport (Lerner (tm) Sports) Ser.). (ENG., Illus.). 32p. (J). (gr. 2-5). 29.32 *(978-1-5415-5605-8(4)*, caf6e762-2e55-4bf3-b855-6b4fd634c6ae, Lerner Pubns.) Lerner Publishing Group.

Morey, Allan & Hoena, Blake. Football Records. 2018. (Incredible Sports Records Ser.). (ENG., Illus.). 32p. (J). (gr. 3-8). pap. 8.99 *(978-1-61891-313-5(1)*, 12108, Blastoff! Discovery) Bellwether Media.

Myers, Dan. NFL's Top 10 Plays. 2017. (NFL's Top Ten Ser.). (ENG., Illus.). 32p. (J). (gr. 3-6). lib. bdg. 32.79 *(978-1-5321-1141-9(X)*, 25858, SportsZone) ABDO Publishing Co.

Myers, Jess. NFL's Top 10 Coaches. 2017. (NFL's Top Ten Ser.). (ENG.). 32p. (J). (gr. 3-6). lib. bdg. 32.79 *(978-1-5321-1138-9(X)*, 25852, SportsZone) ABDO Publishing Co.

NFL up Close: Set, 32 vols. 2016. (NFL up Close Ser.). (ENG.). 32p. (J). (gr. 3-9). lib. bdg. 1049.28 *(978-1-68078-205-9(3)*, 22011, SportsZone) ABDO Publishing Co.

Omoth, Tyler. Pro Football's Championship. 2018. (Major Sports Championships Ser.). (ENG., Illus.). 32p. (J). (gr. 3-9). lib. bdg. 27.32 *(978-1-5435-0479-8(5)*, 137284, Capstone Pr.) Capstone.

Parker, Donald. Alvin Kamara. 2019. (Gridiron Greats: Pro Football's Best Players Ser.). (Illus.). 80p. (J). (gr. 12). lib. bdg. 34.60 *(978-1-4222-4341-1(9))* Mason Crest.

Patrick, James. Football Madness: The Road to Super Bowl XXXVII. 2003. (Illus.). 24p. (J). *(978-0-439-48650-7(5))* Scholastic, Inc.

Rausch, David. National Football League. 2014. (Major League Sports Ser.). (ENG.). 24p. (J). (gr. 3-7). 26.95 *(978-1-62617-136-7(X)*, Epic Bks.) Bellwether Media.

Robinson, Tom. Today's 12 Hottest NFL Superstars. 2015. (Today's Superstars Ser.). (ENG., Illus.). 32p. (J). (gr. 3-6). 32.80 *(978-1-63235-022-0(X)*, 11579, 12-Story Library) Bookstaves, LLC.

Ryan, Mike. Amazing Football: Stars, Stats & Facts. 2016. (ENG., Illus.). 64p. (J). (gr. 5-10). pap. 9.95 *(978-1-77085-777-3(X)*, 76054987-5121-4332-8ff4-a9aadd7c1b43) Firefly Bks., Ltd.

—Football Stars. 2018. (ENG., Illus.). 64p. (J). (gr. 4-7). 19.95 *(978-0-2281-0073-7(9)*, ac03c1e8-c239-46b4-9587-2b70910f1b85); pap. 6.95 *(978-0-2281-0072-0(0)*, bf2759d4-1824-47c6-8e96-3bf5098f6782) Firefly Bks., Ltd.

Scheff, Matt. Amazing NFL Stories: 12 Highlights from NFL History. 2016. (NFL at a Glance Ser.). (ENG., Illus.). 32p. (J). (gr. 3-6). 32.80 *(978-1-63235-151-7(X)*, 11948, 12-Story Library) Bookstaves, LLC.

—Classic NFL Games: 12 Thrillers from NFL History. 2016. (NFL at a Glance Ser.). (ENG., Illus.). 32p. (J). (gr. 3-6). 32.80 *(978-1-63235-154-8(4)*, 11951, 12-Story Library) Bookstaves, LLC.

—Excelling in Football. 2019. (Teen Guide to Sports Ser.). (ENG.). 80p. (YA). (gr. 6-12). 41.27 *(978-1-68282-699-7(6))* ReferencePoint Pr., Inc.

Silverman, Drew. The Super Bowl: 12 Reasons to Love the NFL's Big Game. 2016. (NFL at a Glance Ser.). (ENG., Illus.). 32p. (J). (gr. 3-6). 32.80 *(978-1-63235-157-9(9)*, 11954, 12-Story Library) Bookstaves, LLC.

—Today's NFL: 12 Reasons Fans Follow the Game. 2016. (NFL at a Glance Ser.). (ENG., Illus.). 32p. (J). (gr. 3-6). 32.80 *(978-1-63235-158-6(7)*, 11955, 12-Story Library) Bookstaves, LLC.

Tustison, Matt. Awesome NFL Records: 12 Hard-To-Reach Marks. 2016. (NFL at a Glance Ser.). (ENG., Illus.). 32p. (J). (gr. 3-6). 32.80 *(978-1-63235-156-2(0)*, 11953, 12-Story Library) Bookstaves, LLC.

Tuvey, John. NFL Underdog Stories. 2018. (Underdog Sports Stories Ser.). (ENG.). 48p. (J). (gr. 5-8). lib. bdg. 34.21 *(978-1-5321-1763-3(9)*, 30814, SportsZone) ABDO Publishing Co.

Whiting, Jim. Chicago Bears. 2019. (NFL Today Ser.). (ENG.). 48p. (J). (gr. 3-6). *(978-1-64026-135-8(4)*, 19012, Creative Education) Creative Co., The.

Wilner, Barry. NFL's Top 10 Rivalries. 2017. (NFL's Top Ten Ser.). (ENG., Illus.). 32p. (J). (gr. 3-6). lib. bdg. 32.79 *(978-1-5321-1142-6(8)*, 25860, SportsZone) ABDO Publishing Co.

—Ultimate NFL Road Trip. 2018. (Ultimate Sports Road Trips Ser.). (ENG., Illus.). 48p. (J). (gr. 3-6). lib. bdg. 34.21 *(978-1-5321-1755-8(8)*, 30798, SportsZone) ABDO Publishing Co.

Wyner, Zach. Atlanta Falcons. 2014. (Inside the NFL Ser.). (ENG., Illus.). 32p. (J). (gr. 4-7). lib. bdg. 28.55 *(978-1-4896-0786-7(2)*, AV2 by Weigl) Weigl Pubs., Inc.

—Dallas Cowboys. 2014. (Inside the NFL Ser.). (ENG., Illus.). 32p. (J). (gr. 4-7). lib. bdg. 28.55 *(978-1-4896-0814-7(1)*, AV2 by Weigl) Weigl Pubs., Inc.

—Denver Broncos. 2014. (Inside the NFL Ser.). (ENG., Illus.). 32p. (J). (gr. 4-7). lib. bdg. 28.55 *(978-1-4896-0818-5(4)*, AV2 by Weigl) Weigl Pubs., Inc.

—Philadelphia Eagles. 2014. (Inside the NFL Ser.). (ENG., Illus.). 32p. (J). (gr. 4-7). lib. bdg. 28.55 *(978-1-4896-0874-1(5)*, AV2 by Weigl) Weigl Pubs., Inc.

Zappa, Marcia. NFL's Greatest Teams Set 2, 8 vols. 2015. (NFL's Greatest Teams Ser.: 8). (ENG.). 32p. (J). (gr. 2-5). lib. bdg. 273.76 *(978-1-62403-584-5(1)*, 17195, Big Buddy Bks.) ABDO Publishing Co.

NATIONAL GUARD (UNITED STATES)

see United States—National Guard

NATIONAL HOLIDAYS

see Holidays

NATIONAL HYMNS

see National Songs

NATIONAL MONUMENTS

see Monuments; National Parks and Reserves; Natural Monuments

NATIONAL PARKS AND RESERVES

see also Natural Monuments

also names of national parks, e.g. Yellowstone National park

Adams, Presley. Let's Go to Acadia National Park: Solve Problems Involving the Four Operations, 1 vol. 2014. (InfoMax Math Readers Ser.). (ENG.). 24p. (J). (gr. 3-3). pap. 8.25 *(978-1-4777-4687-5(0)*, 8d710430-dae1-4bfa-bb99-3e94c3e59eb3, Rosen Classroom) Rosen Publishing Group, Inc., The.

Augustin, Byron & Kubena, Jake. Yellowstone National Park, 1 vol. 2010. (Nature's Wonders Ser.). (ENG., Illus.). 96p. (gr. 6-6). 38.36 *(978-0-7614-3936-3(6)*, 10487224-f74e-4a5b-9a08-f39375ed1ed0) Cavendish Square Publishing LLC.

Banting, Erinn. Zion. 2020. (J). *(978-1-7911-1604-0(3)*, AV2 by Weigl) Weigl Pubs., Inc.

Burnham, Brad. Mammoth Cave: The World's Longest Cave System. 2009. (Famous Caves of the World Ser.). 24p. (gr. 3-4). 42.50 *(978-1-61512-498-5(5)*, PowerKids Pr.) Rosen Publishing Group, Inc., The.

Carson, Mary Kay. Park Scientists: Gila Monsters, Geysers, & Grizzly Bears in America's Own Backyard. 2017. (Scientists in the Field Ser.). (ENG., Illus.). 80p. (J). (gr. 5-7). pap. 9.99 *(978-1-328-74090-8(0)*, 1677131, Clarion Bks.) HarperCollins Pubs.

Chapman, Helen. Landmarks of the World: Band 07/Turquoise. 2015. (Collins Big Cat Ser.). (ENG., Illus.). 24p. (J). (gr. 2-2). pap. 8.99 *(978-0-00-759112-1(8))* HarperCollins Pubs. Ltd. GBR. Dist: Independent Pubs. Group.

Connors, Kathleen. Acadia National Park, 1 vol. 2015. (Road Trip: National Parks Ser.). (ENG., Illus.). 24p. (J). (gr. 2-3). lib. bdg. 25.27 *(978-1-4824-1674-9(3)*, 68ff248b-ce52-4f2d-afef-777706e6a9b0) Stevens, Gareth Publishing LLLP.

Davies, Monika. Komodo National Park: Operations with Whole Numbers. 2019. (Mathematics in the Real World Ser.). (ENG., Illus.). 32p. (gr. 5-8). pap. 11.99 *(978-1-4258-5876-6(7))* Teacher Created Materials, Inc.

Defries, Cheryl L. What Are the 7 Natural Wonders of the United States?, 1 vol. 2013. (What Are the Seven Wonders of the World? Ser.). (ENG.). 48p. (gr. 4-6). 27.93 *(978-0-7660-4154-7(9)*, 3eebb45e-2245-4acb-be30-896bc35041ee) Enslow Publishing, LLC.

Doeden, Matt. Gettysburg Battlefield: A Chilling Interactive Adventure. 2017. (You Choose: Haunted Places Ser.). (ENG., Illus.). 112p. (J). (gr. 3-7). lib. bdg. 32.65 *(978-1-5157-3649-3(0)*, 133622, Capstone Pr.) Capstone.

Domeniconi, David. M Is for Majestic: A National Parks Alphabet. Carroll, Pam, illus. (ENG.). 48p. (J). (gr. 1-4). 2007. per. 7.95 *(978-1-58536-333-9(2)*, 202296) 2003. 17.95 *(978-1-58536-138-0(0)*, 201999) Sleeping Bear Pr.

Dunton, Blair. Where the Animals Are King: Ranthambore National Park. Dunton, Blair, illus. 2016. (ENG., Illus.). (J). 12.95 *(978-1-934159-29-3(8))* ThingsAsian Pr.

Establishment of Mount McKinley Park. (Shorey Historical Ser.). (Illus.). 32p. (J). reprint ed. pap. 10.00 *(978-0-8466-0015-2(3)*, S15) Shorey's Bookstore.

Frisch, Nate. Badlands National Park. 2016. (Preserving America Ser.). (ENG.). 48p. (J). (gr. 4-7). pap. 12.00 *(978-1-62832-179-1(2)*, 20999, Creative Paperbacks) Creative Co., The.

—Big Bend National Park. 2016. (Preserving America Ser.). (ENG.). 48p. (J). (gr. 4-7). pap. 12.00 *(978-1-62832-180-7(6)*, 21002, Creative Paperbacks) Creative Co., The.

—Death Valley National Park. 2013. (Preserving America Ser.). (ENG., Illus.). 48p. (J). (gr. 4-7). 35.65 *(978-1-60818-194-0(4)*, 21649, Creative Education) Creative Co., The.

—Everglades National Park. 2013. (Preserving America Ser.). (ENG., Illus.). 48p. (J). (gr. 4-7). 35.65 *(978-1-60818-195-7(2)*, 21652, Creative Education) Creative Co., The.

—Grand Canyon National Park. 2013. (Preserving America Ser.). (ENG., Illus.). 48p. (J). (gr. 4-7). 35.65 *(978-1-60818-196-4(0)*, 21655, Creative Education) Creative Co., The.

—Grand Teton National Park. 2016. (Preserving America Ser.). (ENG.). 48p. (J). (gr. 4-7). pap. 12.00 *(978-1-62832-181-4(4)*, 21005, Creative Paperbacks) Creative Co., The.

—Great Smoky Mountains National Park. 2013. (Preserving America Ser.). (ENG., Illus.). 48p. (J). (gr. 4-7). 35.65 *(978-1-60818-197-1(9)*, 21658, Creative Education) Creative Co., The.

Gish, Melissa. Elephant. 2019. (Spotlight on Nature Ser.). (ENG.). 32p. (J). (gr. 4-7). *(978-1-64026-182-2(6)*, 19184, Creative Education) Creative Co., The.

Hackett, Jennifer. Bryce Canyon (a True Book: National Parks) (Library Edition) 2019. (True Book (Relaunch) Ser.). (ENG., Illus.). 48p. (J). (gr. 3-5). lib. bdg. 31.00 *(978-0-531-12931-9(4)*, Children's Pr.) Scholastic Library Publishing.

—Bryce Canyon National Park (Rookie National Parks) (Library Edition) 2019. (Rookie National Parks Ser.). (ENG., Illus.). 32p. (J). (gr. 1-2). lib. bdg. 25.00 *(978-0-531-13318-7(4)*, Children's Pr.) Scholastic Library Publishing.

Hall, M. C. Welcome to Denali National Park & Preserve. 2018. (National Parks Ser.). (ENG.). 32p. (J). (gr. 2-5). lib. bdg. 35.64 *(978-1-5038-2338-9(5)*, 212173) Child's World, Inc, The.

Hamalainen, Karina. Everglades (a True Book: National Parks) (Library Edition) 2018. (True Book (Relaunch) Ser.). (ENG., Illus.). 48p. (J). (gr. 3-5). lib. bdg. 31.00 *(978-0-531-17592-7(8)*, Children's Pr.) Scholastic Library Publishing.

—Hawai'i Volcanoes National Park (Rookie National Parks) (Library Edition) 2018. (Rookie National Parks Ser.). (ENG., Illus.). 32p. (J). (gr. 1-2). lib. bdg. 25.00 *(978-0-531-13320-0(6)*, Children's Pr.) Scholastic Library Publishing.

Hansen, Grace. Acadia National Park. 2018. (National Parks (Abdo Kids Jumbo) Ser.). (ENG., Illus.). 24p. (J). (gr. -1-2). lib. bdg. 32.79 *(978-1-5321-8205-1(8)*, 29869, Abdo Kids) ABDO Publishing Co.

—Badlands National Park. 2018. (National Parks (Abdo Kids Jumbo) Ser.). (ENG., Illus.). 24p. (J). (gr. -1-2). lib. bdg. 32.79 *(978-1-5321-8206-8(6)*, 29871, Abdo Kids) ABDO Publishing Co.

—Grand Teton National Park. 2018. (National Parks (Abdo Kids Jumbo) Ser.). (ENG., Illus.). 24p. (J). (gr. -1-2). lib. bdg. 32.79 *(978-1-5321-8207-5(4)*, 29873, Abdo Kids) ABDO Publishing Co.

—Hawai'i Volcanoes National Park. 2018. (National Parks (Abdo Kids Jumbo) Ser.). (ENG., Illus.). 24p. (J). (gr. -1-2). lib. bdg. 32.79 *(978-1-5321-8208-2(2)*, 29875, Abdo Kids) ABDO Publishing Co.

—Parque Nacional de Yosemite (Yosemite National Park) 2018. (Parques Nacionales (National Parks) Ser.). (SPA., Illus.). 24p. (J). (gr. -1-2). lib. bdg. 32.79 *(978-1-5321-8048-4(9)*, 28311, Abdo Kids) ABDO Publishing Co.

—Rocky Mountain National Park. 2018. (National Parks (Abdo Kids Jumbo) Ser.). (ENG., Illus.). 24p. (J). (gr. -1-2). lib. bdg. 32.79 *(978-1-5321-8209-9(0)*, 29877, Abdo Kids) ABDO Publishing Co.

—Zion National Park. 2018. (National Parks (Abdo Kids Jumbo) Ser.). (ENG., Illus.). 24p. (J). (gr. -1-2). lib. bdg. 32.79 *(978-1-5321-8210-5(4)*, 29879, Abdo Kids) ABDO Publishing Co.

Hodge, Deborah. West Coast Wild: A Nature Alphabet, 1 vol. Reczuch, Karen, illus. 2015. (West Coast Wild Ser.: 1). (ENG.). 48p. (J). (gr. k-2). 19.99 *(978-1-55498-440-4(8))* Groundwood Bks. CAN. Dist: Publishers Group West (PGW).

Holtz, Monica Stauber. Behind the Zoo: Find Out What the Animals Eat & Do at Irvine Park Zoo, Chippewa Falls, Wisconsin. Opatz, Shane, illus. Opatz, Shane, photos by. 2011. (J). *(978-0-9837617-1-6(X))* Holtz Creative Enterprises.

Hosley, Helen S. Do I Get to Wear That Neat Hat? A National Park Ranger's Story. 2015. (Illus.). iv, 181p. pap. *(978-1-60571-264-2(7)*, Shires Press) Northshire Pr.

Hurtig, Jennifer. Uluru: Sacred Rock of the Australian Desert. 2006. (Natural Wonders Ser.). (Illus.). 32p. (J). (gr. 3-7). pap. 9.95 *(978-1-59036-454-3(6))*; lib. bdg. 26.00 *(978-1-59036-448-2(1))* Weigl Pubs., Inc.

Labrecque, Ellen. Land Trusts & National Parks. 2017. (21st Century Skills Library: Global Citizens: Environmentalism Ser.). (ENG., Illus.). 32p. (J). (gr. 4-7). lib. bdg. 32.07 *(978-1-63472-873-7(4)*, 209918) Cherry Lake Publishing.

Leavitt, Amie Jane. National Parks Volunteer. 2016. (Illus.). 32p. (J). *(978-1-4896-5854-8(9))* Weigl Pubs., Inc.

Lewin, Ted & Lewin, Betsy. Balarama: a Royal Elephant. 2009. (Adventures Around the World Ser.). (ENG., Illus.). 56p. (J). (gr. 1-6). 19.95 *(978-1-60060-265-8(7))* Lee & Low Bks., Inc.

Mattern, Joanne. Cuyahoga Valley (a True Book: National Parks) (Library Edition) 2018. (True Book (Relaunch) Ser.). (ENG., Illus.). 48p. (J). (gr. 3-5). lib. bdg. 31.00 *(978-0-531-17593-4(6)*, Children's Pr.) Scholastic Library Publishing.

—Mount Rainier (a True Book: National Parks) (Library Edition) 2018. (True Book (Relaunch) Ser.). (ENG., Illus.). 48p. (J). (gr. 3-5). lib. bdg. 31.00 *(978-0-531-17594-1(4)*, Children's Pr.) Scholastic Library Publishing.

—Mount Rainier National Park (Rookie National Parks) (Library Edition) 2018. (Rookie National Parks Ser.). (ENG., Illus.). 32p. (J). (gr. 1-2). lib. bdg. 25.00 *(978-0-531-12653-0(6)*, Children's Pr.) Scholastic Library Publishing.

McReynolds, Stacy. San Antonio Zoo. 2009. (Great Zoos of the United States Ser.). 24p. (gr. 3-4). 42.50 *(978-1-61513-223-2(6)*, PowerKids Pr.) Rosen Publishing Group, Inc., The.

National Geographic Kids. National Geographic Kids National Parks Guide USA Centennial Edition: The Most Amazing Sights, Scenes, & Cool Activities from Coast to Coast! 2016. (Illus.). 176p. (J). (gr. 3-7). pap. 14.99 *(978-1-4263-2314-0(X))*; (ENG., lib. bdg. 24.90 *(978-1-4263-2315-7(8))* Disney Publishing Worldwide. (National Geographic Kids).

Ogintz, Eileen. Acadia National Park. 2019. (Kid's Guides Ser.). (Illus.). 144p. (J). (gr. 1-5). pap. 15.95 *(978-1-60893-984-8(7))* Down East Bks.

O'Reilly, Wenda. Amazing places natl Parks. 2007. n/ap. pap. 119.40 *(978-1-59960-014-7(5))* Birdcage Pr.

Orme, David. Weird Places. 2009. (Fact to Fiction Ser.). (Illus.). 36p. (J). pap. 6.95 *(978-0-7891-7897-8(4))* Perfection Learning Corp.

Peabody, Erin. A Weird & Wild Beauty: The Story of Yellowstone, the World's First National Park. 2016. (ENG., Illus.). 192p. (J). (gr. 6-6). 14.99 *(978-1-63450-204-7(3)*, Sky Pony Pr.) Skyhorse Publishing Co., Inc.

Pecorella, Jane. Yellowstone: Our First National Park. 2009. (Reading Room Collection 2 Ser.). 24p. (gr. 3-4). 42.50 *(978-1-60852-004-6(8)*, PowerKids Pr.) Rosen Publishing Group, Inc., The.

Rath, Robert. Go Wild for Puzzles Glacier National Park. Rath, Robert, illus. 2008. (Illus.). 32p. (J). (gr. k-3). pap. 5.95 *(978-1-56037-428-2(4))* Farcountry Pr.

Raum, Elizabeth. The Star Spangled Banner in Translation: What It Really Means. rev. ed. 2016. (Kids' Translations Ser.). (ENG., Illus.). 32p. (J). (gr. 3-6). pap. 8.10 *(978-1-5157-6274-4(2)*, 135072, Capstone Pr.) Capstone.

Road Trip: National Parks. 2015. (Road Trip Ser.). (ENG.). 24p. (J). (gr. 2-3). pap., pap., pap. 293.40 *(978-1-4824-3487-3(3))* Stevens, Gareth Publishing LLLP.

Shepherd, Jodie. Joshua Tree (a True Book: National Parks) (Library Edition) 2018. (True Book (Relaunch) Ser.). (ENG., Illus.). 48p. (J). (gr. 3-5). lib. bdg. 31.00 *(978-0-531-17591-0(X)*, Children's Pr.) Scholastic Library Publishing.

—Joshua Tree National Park (Rookie National Parks) (Library Edition) 2018. (Rookie National Parks Ser.). (ENG., Illus.). 32p. (J). (gr. 1-2). lib. bdg. 25.00 *(978-0-531-12650-9(1)*, Children's Pr.) Scholastic Library Publishing.

Spalding, Maddie. Great Smoky Mountains National Park. 2016. (National Parks (Core Library) Ser.). (ENG., Illus.). 48p. (J). (gr. 4-8). lib. bdg. 35.64 *(978-1-68078-474-9(9)*, 23885) ABDO Publishing Co.

Steck-Vaughn Staff. National Parks. 2003. pap. 4.10 *(978-0-7398-7651-0(1))* Steck-Vaughn.

Temple, Bob & Teri, Bob. Welcome to Grand Canyon National Park. 2018. (National Parks Ser.). (ENG.). 32p. (J). (gr. 2-5). lib. bdg. 35.64 *(978-1-5038-2341-9(5)*, 212176) Child's World, Inc, The.

Teri, Bob & Temple, Teri. Welcome to Badlands National Park. 2018. (National Parks Ser.). (ENG.). 32p. (J). (gr. 2-5). lib. bdg. 35.64 *(978-1-5038-2336-5(9)*, 212171) Child's World, Inc, The.

—Welcome to Hawai'i Volcanoes National Park. 2018. (National Parks Ser.). (ENG.). 32p. (J). (gr. 2-5). lib. bdg. 35.64 *(978-1-5038-2343-3(1)*, 212178) Child's World, Inc, The.

Tornio, Stacy & Keffer, Ken. The National Parks! 2016. (Ranger Rick's Travels Ser.). (Illus.). 144p. (J). (gr. 2-6). pap. 16.95 *(978-1-63076-230-8(X))* Muddy Boots Pr.

Trumbauer, Lisa. National Parks. 2005. (Yellow Umbrella Fluent Level Ser.). (ENG., Illus.). 16p. (gr. k-1). pap. 35.70 *(978-0-7368-5314-9(6)*, Capstone Pr.) Capstone.

Van Valkenburgh, Norman J. America's First Wilderness: New York State's Forest Preserves. 2008. (Illus.). 44p. (J). 6.50 *(978-1-930098-88-6(X))* Purple Mountain Pr., Ltd.

Wallace, Audra. Acadia (a True Book: National Parks) (Library Edition) 2018. (True Book (Relaunch) Ser.). (ENG., Illus.). 48p. (J). (gr. 3-5). lib. bdg. 31.00 *(978-0-531-23505-8(X)*, Children's Pr.) Scholastic Library Publishing.

Weakland, Mark. Scooby-Doo! & the Cliff Dwellings of Mesa Verde: The Ghostly Gaze. Cornia, Christian, illus. 2018. (Unearthing Ancient Civilizations with Scooby-Doo! Ser.). (ENG.). 32p. (J). (gr. 3-6). lib. bdg. 27.99 *(978-1-5157-7511-9(9)*, 135891, Capstone Pr.) Capstone.

Williams, Colleen Madonna Flood. My Adventure at the Safari Park. 2007. 44p. (J). 8.99 *(978-1-59092-577-5(7))* Blue Forge Pr.

Willman, Lisa. Travel Adventures: Kruger National Park: Repeated Addition (Grade 2) rev. ed. 2018. (Mathematics in the Real World Ser.). (ENG., Illus.). 32p. (J). (gr. 2-3). pap. 10.99 *(978-1-4258-5751-6(5))* Teacher Created Materials, Inc.

Winterberg, Jenna. Parks for All: U. S. National Parks (Level 4) 2017. (TIME for KIDS(r): Informational Text Ser.). (ENG., Illus.). 32p. (J). (gr. 3-5). pap. 12.99 *(978-1-4258-4979-5(2))* Teacher Created Materials, Inc.

Woods, Michael & Woods, Mary B. Seven Natural Wonders of North America. 2009. (Seven Wonders Ser.). (ENG., Illus.). 80p. (gr. 5-8). lib. bdg. 33.26 *(978-0-8225-9069-9(7))* Lerner Publishing Group.

World Book, Inc. Staff, contrib. by. Enchanted Landscapes. 2017. (Illus.). 40p. (J). *(978-0-7166-3366-2(3))* World Bk., Inc.

NATIONAL PARKS AND RESERVES—FICTION

Beall, Linda R. We , Four Paws & Me at Yellowstone National Park. 2012. 40p. pap. 24.95 *(978-1-4626-8305-5(3))* America Star Bks.

Beaty, Janice C. Jarod & the Mystery of the Joshua Trees: A National Park Adventure Series Book. 2015. (Illus.). 108p. (J). pap. *(978-1-63293-037-8(4))* Sunstone Pr.

Beaty, Janice J. & Beaty, Lillian C., illus. Jarod & the Mystery of the Utah Arches: A National Park Adventure Series Book. 2016. 118p. (J). pap. *(978-1-63293-122-1(2))* Sunstone Pr.

Bowen, Carl. Back Burn. Lee, Marc, illus. 2016. (Firestormers Ser.). (ENG.). 112p. (J). (gr. 4-8). lib. bdg. 27.32 *(978-1-4965-3305-0(4)*, 132446, Stone Arch Bks.) Capstone.

—Bone Yard. Lee, Marc, illus. 2016. (Firestormers Ser.). (ENG.). 112p. (J). (gr. 4-8). lib. bdg. 27.32 *(978-1-4965-3306-7(2)*, 132447, Stone Arch Bks.) Capstone.

Bush, Laura. Our Great Big Backyard. Rogers, Jacqueline, illus. 2018. (ENG.). 40p. (J). (gr. -1-3). pap. 8.99 *(978-0-06-246841-3(3)*, HarperCollins) HarperCollins Pubs.

Bush, Laura & Hager, Jenna Bush. Our Great Big Backyard. Rogers, Jacqueline, illus. 2016. (ENG.). 40p. (J). (gr. -1-3). 18.99 *(978-0-06-246835-2(9)*, HarperCollins) HarperCollins Pubs.

M
N
O

Chandler, Kristen. Wolves, Boys & Other Things That Might Kill Me. 2011. (ENG.). 283p. (YA). (gr. 7-12). 24.94 *(978-0-670-01142-1(8))* Penguin Young Readers Group.

Chandler, Mitzi. I See Something Grand. 2003. (Illus.). 32p. (J). (gr. -1-1). pap. 8.95 *(978-0-938216-50-6(3))* Grand Canyon Conservancy.

Coyle, Carmela Lavigna. Do Princesses & Super Heroes Hit the Trails? A National Park Adventure. 2016. (Do Princesses Ser.). (Illus.). 32p. (J). (gr. -1-12). 15.95 *(978-1-63076-244-5(X))* Muddy Boots Pr.

Crute, Josh. Oliver: The Second-Largest Living Thing on Earth. Kim, John Taesoo, illus. 2018. (ENG.). 32p. (J). 17.99 *(978-1-62414-577-3(9)*, 900192298) Page Street Publishing Co.

Dunbar, Paula J. Ruby's Rainbow: A Story of Acadia National Park. l.t. ed. 2005. (Illus.). 32p. (J). *(978-1-931207-59-1(3))* Dilligaf Publishing.

Farnsworth, Frances. Cubby in Wonderland. 2005. pap. 20.95 *(978-1-4179-8778-8(2))* Kessinger Publishing, LLC.

Farnsworth, Frances Joyce. Tike & Tiny in the Tetons. 2007. (Illus.). 172p. (J). pap. 14.95 *(978-0-943972-79-4(5))* Homestead Publishing.

Ferguson, Alane. Mysteries in Our National Parks: Deadly Waters: A Mystery in Everglades National Park. 2007. (Mysteries in Our National Park Ser.). (Illus.). 160p. (J). (gr. 3-7). 4.99 *(978-1-4263-0093-6(X)*, National Geographic Kids) Disney Publishing Worldwide.

—Mysteries in Our National Parks: Ghost Horses: A Mystery in Zion National Park. 2007. (Mysteries in Our National Park Ser.). (Illus.). 160p. (J). (gr. 3-7). per. 4.99 *(978-1-4263-0108-7(1)*, National Geographic Kids) Disney Publishing Worldwide.

—Mysteries in Our National Parks: over the Edge: A Mystery in Grand Canyon National Park. 2008. (Mysteries in Our National Park Ser.). (Illus.). 160p. (J). (gr. 3-7). per. 4.99 *(978-1-4263-0177-3(4)*, National Geographic Kids) Disney Publishing Worldwide.

—Mysteries in Our National Parks: the Hunted: A Mystery in Glacier National Park. 2007. (Mysteries in Our National Park Ser.). (Illus.). 160p. (J). (gr. 3-7). per. 4.99 *(978-1-4263-0095-0(6)*, National Geographic Kids) Disney Publishing Worldwide.

—Mysteries in Our National Parks: Valley of Death: A Mystery in Death Valley National Park. 2008. (Mysteries in Our National Park Ser.). (Illus.). 160p. (J). (gr. 3-7). per. 4.99 *(978-1-4263-0178-0(2)*, National Geographic Kids) Disney Publishing Worldwide.

—Night of the Black Bear: A Mystery in Great Smoky Mountains National Park. 2007. (Mysteries in Our National Park Ser.). (Illus.). 160p. (J). (gr. 3-7). 4.99 *(978-1-4263-0094-3(8)*, National Geographic Kids) Disney Publishing Worldwide.

Hill, Carolyn Swan. A Summer to Remember. 2013. 256p. (YA). (gr. 10-12). pap. 17.99 *(978-1-4624-0543-5(6)*, Inspiring Voices) Author Solutions, LLC.

Hoena, Blake. Can You Survive a Supervolcano Eruption? An Interactive Doomsday Adventure. Vanzo, Filippo, illus. 2016. (You Choose: Doomsday Ser.). (ENG.). 112p. (J). (gr. 3-7). lib. bdg. 32.65 *(978-1-4914-8108-0(0)*, 130599, Capstone Pr.) Capstone.

Iverson, Diane. Rascal, the Tassel Eared Squirrel. 2007. 64p. pap. 9.95 *(978-0-932821-64-5(2))* Grand Canyon Conservancy.

Kittredge, James M. The Three Little Explorers, 1 vol. Reyes, Glendalys, illus. 2010. 16p. pap. 24.95 *(978-1-4489-8973-7(6))* PublishAmerica, Inc.

Lamond, Peter. The Rainforest Family & Those Terrible Toads. Purnell, Teresa, illus. 2011. 92p. pap. 27.25 *(978-1-60976-297-1(5)*, Eloquent Bks.) Strategic Book Publishing & Rights Agency (SBPRA).

Marsh, Carole. The Mystery at Cape Cod. 2010. (Real Kids, Real Places Ser.). (Illus.). 158p. (J). pap. 18.99 *(978-0-635-07594-9(6)*, Marsh, Carole Mysteries) Gallopade International.

—The Mystery at Cape Cod. Friedlander, Randolyn, illus. 2010. (Real Kids, Real Places Teacher Guides). 32p. (J). pap. 7.99 *(978-0-635-07600-7(4))* Gallopade International.

—The Mystery at Death Valley. 2010. (Real Kids, Real Places Ser.). (Illus.). 158p. (J). pap. 7.99 *(978-0-635-07596-3(2)*, Marsh, Carole Mysteries) Gallopade International.

—The Mystery at Grizzly Graveyard. 2014. (Real Kids, Real Places Ser.: Vol. 3). (ENG., Illus.). 158p. (J). (gr. 3-5). pap. 7.99 *(978-0-635-11187-6(X)*, Marsh, Carole Mysteries) Gallopade International.

—The Mystery at Yellowstone National Park. 2010. (Real Kids, Real Places Ser.). (Illus.). 158p. (J). 18.99 *(978-0-635-07437-9(0)*, Marsh, Carole Mysteries) Gallopade International.

—The Rip-Roaring Mystery on the African Safari. 2009. (Around the World in 80 Mysteries Ser.). (J). (gr. 2-9). lib. bdg. 18.99 *(978-0-635-06835-4(4))* Gallopade International.

Parks, M. Elizabeth. The Sea Cow. 2013. (Illus.). 44p. pap. 16.95 *(978-0-9824565-2-1(2))* Sibyl Merritt.

Redmon, Jaylyle. Gracie the Lop-Eared Burro. 2008. 17p. pap. 24.95 *(978-1-60672-626-6(9))* America Star Bks.

Schuette, Leslie Elaine. Little Autumn's Adventure in the Smoky Mountains. 2013. 32p. pap. 24.95 *(978-1-4626-9924-7(3))* America Star Bks.

Service, Pamela F. #5 Alien Contact. Gorman, Mike, illus. 2011. (Alien Agent Ser.). pap. 33.92 *(978-0-7613-8347-5(6)*, Darby Creek) Lerner Publishing Group.

Skurzynski, Gloria. Mysteries in Our National Parks: Buried Alive! A Mystery in Denali National Park. 2008. (Mysteries in Our National Park Ser.). (Illus.). 160p. (J). (gr. 3-7). pap. 4.99 *(978-1-4263-0252-7(5)*, National Geographic Kids) Disney Publishing Worldwide.

—Mysteries in Our National Parks: CliffHanger: A Mystery in Mesa Verde National Park. 2007. (Mysteries in Our National Park Ser.). (Illus.). 160p. (J). (gr. 3-7). per. 4.99 *(978-1-4263-0092-9(1)*, National Geographic Kids) Disney Publishing Worldwide.

—Mysteries in Our National Parks: Escape from Fear: A Mystery in Virgin Islands National Park. 2008. (Mysteries in Our National Park Ser.). (Illus.). 160p. (J). (gr. 3-7). mass mkt. 4.99 *(978-1-4263-0181-0(2)*, National Geographic Kids) Disney Publishing Worldwide.

—Mysteries in Our National Parks: Out of the Deep: A Mystery in Acadia National Park. 2008. (Mysteries in Our National Park Ser.). (Illus.). 160p. (J). (gr. 3-7). pap. 4.99 *(978-1-4263-0251-0(7)*, National Geographic Kids) Disney Publishing Worldwide.

—Mysteries in Our National Parks: Wolf Stalker: A Mystery in Yellowstone National Park. 2007. (Mysteries in Our National Park Ser.). (Illus.). 160p. (J). (gr. 3-7). per. 4.99 *(978-1-4263-0096-7(4)*, National Geographic Kids) Disney Publishing Worldwide.

—Running Scared: A Mystery in Carlsbad Caverns National Park. 2008. (Mysteries in Our National Park Ser.). (Illus.). 160p. (J). (gr. 3-7). mass mkt. 4.99 *(978-1-4263-0182-7(0)*, National Geographic Kids) Disney Publishing Worldwide.

Skurzynski, Gloria & Ferguson, Alane. Buried Alive. 2003. (Mysteries in Our National Park Ser.: No. 12). (ENG.). 160p. (J). (gr. 3-7). 15.95 *(978-0-7922-6966-3(7)*, National Geographic Children's Bks.) National Geographic Society.

Wood, Audrey. Bunyans. 2014. 17.00 *(978-1-63419-650-5(3))* Perfection Learning Corp.

Young, Judy. The Missing Grizzly Cubs. 2016. (Wild World of Buck Bray Ser.). (ENG.). 240p. (J). (gr. 3-6). 16.99 *(978-1-58536-970-6(5)*, 204107) Sleeping Bear Pr.

NATIONAL PARKS AND RESERVES—UNITED STATES

Acadia National Park: Eye of the Whale. 2013. (Adventures with the Parkers Ser.: 11). (Illus.). 96p. (J). (gr. -1-12). pap. 12.95 *(978-0-7627-8262-8(5)*, Falcon Guides) Globe Pequot Pr., The.

Acadia National Park Park Pal Booklet: 7 Years or Younger. 2004. (Illus.). 16p. (J). 1.95 *(978-1-59091-031-3(1))* Eastern National.

Adams, Colleen. Exploring the Grand Canyon. 2009. (Reading Room Collection 2 Ser.). 24p. (gr. 3-4). 42.50 *(978-1-60851-963-7(5)*, PowerKids Pr.) Rosen Publishing Group, Inc., The.

Arches & Canyonlands National Parks: In the Land of Standing Rocks. 2012. (Adventures with the Parkers Ser.: 10). (Illus.). 112p. (J). (gr. -1-12). pap. 12.95 *(978-0-7627-7962-8(4)*, Falcon Guides) Globe Pequot Pr., The.

Aretha, David. Denali National Park & Preserve: Adventure, Explore, Discover, 1 vol. 2008. (America's National Parks Ser.). (ENG., Illus.). 128p. (gr. 6-7). lib. bdg. 37.27 *(978-1-59845-089-7(1)*, 0c943e2e-78b8-4203-ad92-86d32e3d3f47) Enslow Publishing, LLC.

Bottone, Ann. My National Parks & Monuments Photo Journal. 2007. (Illus.). (J). (gr. -1-10). spiral bd. 9.95 *(978-1-58071-065-7(4))* Sierra Pr.

Burnham, Brad. Carlsbad Caverns: America's Largest Underground Chamber. 2009. (Famous Caves of the World Ser.). 24p. (gr. 3-4). 42.50 *(978-1-61512-494-7(2)*, PowerKids Pr.) Rosen Publishing Group, Inc., The.

Calkhoven, Laurie. Mount Rushmore's Hidden Room & Other Monumental Secrets: Monuments & Landmarks (Ready-To-Read Level 3) Fabbretti, Valerio, illus. 2018. (Secrets of American History Ser.). (ENG.). 48p. (J). (gr. 1-3). 17.99 *(978-1-5344-2925-3(5))*; pap. 4.99 *(978-1-5344-2924-6(7))* Simon Spotlight. (Simon Spotlight).

Colmenares, Sandra. Natural Parks of Texas, 1 vol. 2018. (Explore Texas Ser.). (ENG.). 24p. (gr. 9-12). 26.27 *(978-1-5081-8663-2(4)*, 2382daef-d401-44c3-8500-c4e195c2052a, Rosen Young Adult) Rosen Publishing Group, Inc., The.

Cosson, M. J. Welcome to Death Valley National Park. 2018. (National Parks Ser.). (ENG.). 32p. (J). (gr. 2-5). lib. bdg. 35.64 *(978-1-5038-2337-2(7)*, 212172) Child's World, Inc, The.

—Welcome to Redwood National & State Parks. 2018. (National Parks Ser.). (ENG.). 32p. (J). (gr. 2-5). lib. bdg. 35.64 *(978-1-5038-2345-7(8)*, 212180) Child's World, Inc, The.

Deffries, Cheryl L. What Are the 7 Natural Wonders of the United States?, 1 vol. 2013. (What Are the Seven Wonders of the World? Ser.). (ENG.). 48p. (gr. 4-6). pap. 11.53 *(978-1-4644-0233-3(7)*, f4fc867d-dfc4-4794-b64d-4fcf503c47c7) Enslow Publishing, LLC.

Dell, Pamela. Welcome to Mount Rainier National Park. 2018. (National Parks Ser.). (ENG.). 32p. (J). (gr. 2-5). lib. bdg. 35.64 *(978-1-5038-2344-0(X)*, 212179) Child's World, Inc, The.

Dyan, Penelope. The Comeback Kids, Book 12, the Redwood Forest. Weigand, John D., photos by. 2013. (Illus.). 34p. pap. 14.95 *(978-1-61477-081-7(6))* Bellissima Publishing, LLC.

Feinstein, Stephen. Hawai'i Volcanoes National Park: Adventure, Explore, Discover, 1 vol. 2008. (America's National Parks Ser.). (ENG., Illus.). 128p. (gr. 6-7). lib. bdg. 37.27 *(978-1-59845-094-1(8)*, 651973a5-ceb7-40f5-af53-361b03e452d0) Enslow Publishing, LLC.

—Yosemite National Park: Adventure, Explore, Discover, 1 vol. 2008. (America's National Parks Ser.). (ENG., Illus.). 128p. (gr. 6-7). lib. bdg. 37.27 *(978-1-59845-095-8(6)*, b9135467-72e1-485a-ba72-5b2f1ca06ad6) Enslow Publishing, LLC.

Friedman, Mel. True Books: the Oregon Trail. 2010. (True Book Ser.). (ENG., Illus.). 48p. (J). (gr. 2-5). 29.00 *(978-0-531-20584-6(3))* Scholastic Library Publishing.

Frisch, Nate. Badlands National Park. 2015. (Preserving America Ser.). (ENG., Illus.). 48p. (J). (gr. 4-7). *(978-1-60818-604-4(0)*, 20998, Creative Education) Creative Co., The.

—Big Bend National Park. 2015. (Preserving America Ser.). (ENG., Illus.). 48p. (J). (gr. 4-7). *(978-1-60818-605-1(9)*, 21001, Creative Education) Creative Co., The.

—Death Valley National Park. 2014. (Preserving America Ser.). (ENG.). 48p. (J). (gr. 4-7). pap. 12.00 *(978-0-89812-877-2(3)*, 21650, Creative Paperbacks) Creative Co., The.

—Grand Canyon National Park. 2014. (Preserving America Ser.). (ENG.). 48p. (J). (gr. 4-7). pap. 12.00 *(978-0-89812-879-6(X)*, 21656, Creative Paperbacks) Creative Co., The.

—Grand Teton National Park. 2015. (Preserving America Ser.). (ENG., Illus.). 48p. (J). (gr. 4-7). *(978-1-60818-606-8(7)*, 21004, Creative Education) Creative Co., The.

—Rocky Mountain National Park. 2015. (Preserving America Ser.). (ENG., Illus.). 48p. (J). (gr. 4-7). *(978-1-60818-607-5(5)*, 21007, Creative Education) Creative Co., The.

Gonzales, Doreen. Rocky Mountain National Park: Adventure, Explore, Discover, 1 vol. 2008. (America's National Parks Ser.). (ENG., Illus.). 128p. (gr. 6-7). lib. bdg. 37.27 *(978-1-59845-096-5(4)*, 5d905d3e-bf5c-4529-91b6-5cd9d0d1b243) Enslow Publishing, LLC.

Graf, Mike. Glacier National Park: Going to the Sun. Leggitt, Marjorie, illus. 2012. (Adventures with the Parkers Ser.: 7). (ENG.). 96p. (J). (gr. -1-12). pap. 12.95 *(978-0-7627-7964-2(0)*, Falcon Guides) Globe Pequot Pr., The.

—Olympic National Park: Touch of the Tide Pool, Crack of the Glacier. Marjorie, Leggitt, illus. 2012. (Adventures with the Parkers Ser.: 5). (ENG.). 96p. (J). (gr. -1-12). pap. 12.95 *(978-0-7627-7969-7(1)*, Falcon Guides) Globe Pequot Pr., The.

Graham, Amy. Acadia National Park: Adventure, Explore, Discover, 1 vol. 2008. (America's National Parks Ser.). (ENG., Illus.). 128p. (gr. 6-7). lib. bdg. 37.27 *(978-1-59845-090-3(5)*, ad138307-609c-4e0e-b8fa-73532753c34b) Enslow Publishing, LLC.

Grand Canyon National Park: Tail of the Scorpion. 2012. (Adventures with the Parkers Ser.: 2). (Illus.). 96p. (J). (gr. -1-12). pap. 14.95 *(978-0-7627-7965-9(9)*, Falcon Guides) Globe Pequot Pr., The.

Great Smokies National Park: Ridge Runner Rescue. 2012. (Adventures with the Parkers Ser.: 6). (Illus.). 96p. (J). (gr. -1-12). pap. 12.95 *(978-0-7627-7966-6(7)*, Falcon Guides) Globe Pequot Pr., The.

Gregory, Josh. Grand Canyon (a True Book: National Parks) (Library Edition) 2017. (True Book (Relaunch) Ser.). (ENG., Illus.). 48p. (J). (gr. 3-5). lib. bdg. 31.00 *(978-0-531-23393-1(6)*, Children's Pr.) Scholastic Library Publishing.

—Grand Teton (a True Book: National Parks) (Library Edition) 2018. (True Book (Relaunch) Ser.). (ENG., Illus.). 48p. (J). (gr. 3-5). lib. bdg. 31.00 *(978-0-531-23507-2(6)*, Children's Pr.) Scholastic Library Publishing.

Hansen, Doug, illus. The Sierra Adventure Coloring Book: Featuring Yosemite National Park. 2013. (ENG.). 24p. (J). (gr. -1-2). pap. 4.95 *(978-1-930238-39-8(8))* Yosemite Conservancy.

Hansen, Grace. Grand Canyon National Park. 2017. (National Parks (Abdo Kids Jumbo) Ser.). (ENG., Illus.). 24p. (J). (gr. -1-2). lib. bdg. 32.79 *(978-1-5321-0434-3(0)*, 26560, Abdo Kids) ABDO Publishing Co.

—Great Smoky Mountains National Park. 2017. (National Parks (Abdo Kids Jumbo) Ser.). (ENG., Illus.). 24p. (J). (gr. -1-2). lib. bdg. 32.79 *(978-1-5321-0435-0(9)*, 26561, Abdo Kids) ABDO Publishing Co.

—Parque Nacional de Yellowstone (Yellowstone National Park) 2018. (Parques Nacionales (National Parks) Ser.). (SPA., Illus.). 24p. (J). (gr. -1-2). lib. bdg. 32.79 *(978-1-5321-8047-7(0)*, 28309, Abdo Kids) ABDO Publishing Co.

Heacox, Kim. National Geographic the National Parks: An Illustrated History. 2015. (Illus.). 384p. 50.00 *(978-1-4262-1559-9(2)*, National Geographic) Disney Publishing Worldwide.

Hunt, Santana. Grand Canyon National Park, 1 vol. 2015. (Road Trip: National Parks Ser.). (ENG., Illus.). 24p. (J). (gr. 2-3). lib. bdg. 25.27 *(978-1-4824-1682-4(4)*, fda42ce3-a012-47d3-b372-3c1f2fa7e241) Stevens, Gareth Publishing LLLP.

Jankowski, Susan. Olympic National Park: Adventure, Explore, Discover, 1 vol. 2008. (America's National Parks Ser.). (ENG., Illus.). 128p. (gr. 6-7). lib. bdg. 37.27 *(978-1-59845-092-7(1)*, 6f22f0f7-6d6a-49f3-97aa-62b0a5617467) Enslow Publishing, LLC.

Lindeen, Mary. Natural States. 2011. (Wonder Readers Fluent Level Ser.). (ENG.). 16p. (gr. -1-2). pap. 35.94 *(978-1-4296-8131-5(4)*, Capstone Pr.) Capstone.

—Parks of the U. S. A. 2011. (Wonder Readers Fluent Level Ser.). (ENG.). 16p. (J). (gr. -1-2). pap. 6.25 *(978-1-4296-7949-7(2)*, 118281, Capstone Pr.) Capstone.

Lorbiecki, Marybeth. Welcome to Grand Teton National Park. 2018. (National Parks Ser.). (ENG.). 32p. (J). (gr. 2-5). lib. bdg. 35.64 *(978-1-5038-2342-6(3)*, 212177) Child's World, Inc, The.

Marsico, Katie. The Everglades. 2013. (Explorer Library: Social Studies Explorer Ser.). (ENG.). 32p. (gr. 4-8). pap. 14.21 *(978-1-62431-041-6(9)*, 202521); (Illus.). lib. bdg. 32.07 *(978-1-62431-017-1(6)*, 202519) Cherry Lake Publishing.

O'Donnell, Kerri. Denali National Park: An Alaskan Ecosystem: Creating Graphical Representations of Data. 2009. (PowerMath: Advanced Proficiency Plus Ser.). 32p. (gr. 5-5). 47.90 *(978-1-60851-353-6(X)*, PowerKids Pr.) Rosen Publishing Group, Inc., The.

—Denali National Park, An Alaskan Ecosystem: Creating Graphical Representations of Data, 1 vol. 2009. (Math for the REAL World Ser.). (ENG., Illus.). 32p. (gr. 5-5). pap. 10.00 *(978-1-4042-6083-2(8)*, 5eb69dd7-73d7-4c44-809a-6b796130770a) Rosen Publishing Group, Inc., The.

—Denali State Park - An Alaskan Ecosystem: Creating Graphical Representation of Data. 2006. (Math Bog Bookstm Ser.). 32p. (gr. 6-7). 47.50 *(978-1-4042-6368-0(3))* Rosen Publishing Group, Inc., The.

Pearce, Claudia. San Diego Zoo. 2009. (Great Zoos of the United States Ser.). 24p. (gr. 3-4). 42.50 *(978-1-61513-224-9(4)*, PowerKids Pr.) Rosen Publishing Group, Inc., The.

Pearson, Carrie A. Stretch to the Sun: From a Tiny Sprout to the Tallest Tree on Earth. Swan, Susan, illus. 2018. 32p. (J). (gr. k-3). 17.99 *(978-1-58089-771-6(1))* Charlesbridge Publishing, Inc.

Prior, Jennifer Overend. America's Natural Landmarks. rev. ed. 2014. (Social Studies: Informational Text Ser.). (ENG., Illus.). 32p. (J). (gr. 2-4). pap. 11.99 *(978-1-4333-7371-8(8))* Teacher Created Materials, Inc.

Purslow, Neil. Redwood National Park: Forest of Giants. 2006. (Natural Wonders Ser.). 32p. (J). (gr. 3-7). pap. 9.95 *(978-1-59036-457-4(0))*; (Illus.). lib. bdg. 26.00 *(978-1-59036-451-2(1))* Weigl Pubs., Inc.

Rice, Dona Herweck. Banff National Park Area. 2019. (Mathematics in the Real World Ser.). (ENG., Illus.). 32p. (gr. 5-8). pap. 11.99 *(978-1-4258-5889-6(9))* Teacher Created Materials, Inc.

—Designing National Parks. rev. ed. 2018. (Smithsonian: Informational Text Ser.). (ENG., Illus.). 32p. (J). (gr. 4-8). pap. 11.99 *(978-1-4938-6711-0(3))* Teacher Created Materials, Inc.

Richter, Bernd & Richter, Susan. Discover Alaskas Denali Park. 2008. (Illus.). 48p. (J). pap. 9.95 *(978-1-931353-37-3(9))* Saddle Pal Creations, Inc.

Road Trip: National Parks. 2015. (Road Trip Ser.). (ENG.). 24p. (J). (gr. 2-3). pap., pap., pap. 48.90 *(978-1-4824-3488-0(1))* Stevens, Gareth Publishing LLLP.

Robson, Gary D. Who Pooped in the Park: Grand Teton. 2004. (Illus.). 48p. (J). pap. 11.95 *(978-1-56037-280-6(X))* Farcountry Pr.

—Who Pooped in the Park? Clark, Elijah Brady, illus. 2006. 48p. (J). pap. 11.95 *(978-1-56037-388-9(1))* Farcountry Pr.

—Who Pooped in the Park? Sequoia & Kings Canyon National Parks: Scats & Tracks for Kids. 2006. (Who Pooped in the Park? Ser.). (Illus.). 48p. (J). (gr. -1-3). pap. 11.95 *(978-1-56037-327-8(X))* Farcountry Pr.

Rocky Mountain National Park: Peril on Long's Peak. 2012. (Adventures with the Parkers Ser.: 8). (Illus.). 96p. (J). (gr. -1-12). pap. 12.95 *(978-0-7627-7970-3(5)*, Falcon Guides) Globe Pequot Pr., The.

Rosenstock, Barb. The Camping Trip That Changed America: Theodore Roosevelt, John Muir, & Our National Parks. Gerstein, Mordecai, illus. 2012. 32p. (J). (gr. 1-3). 18.99 *(978-0-8037-3710-5(6)*, Dial Bks) Penguin Young Readers Group.

Rowell, Rebecca. The 12 Most Amazing American Natural Wonders. 2015. (Amazing America Ser.). (ENG.). 32p. (J). (gr. 3-6). 32.80 *(978-1-63235-011-4(4)*, 11550, 12-Story Library) Bookstaves, LLC.

Selda, Toby. Simply Father: Life with Theodore Roosevelt As Seen through the Eyes of His Children. Roosevelt, Theodore, illus. 2007. 28p. (J). 7.95 *(978-1-59091-030-6(3))* Eastern National.

Siber, Kate. National Parks of the USA. Turnham, Chris, illus. 2018. (National Parks of the USA Ser.: 1). (ENG.). 112p. (J). (gr. 1-4). 30.00 *(978-1-84780-976-6(6)*, 302819, Wide Eyed Editions) Quarto Publishing Group UK GBR. Dist: Hachette UK Distribution.

Tomio, Stacy & Keffer, Ken. Ranger Rick Goes to the National Parks! 2016. (Illus.). 138p. (J). *(978-1-5182-3207-7(8))* Muddy Bks.

Travelers Guide to National Parks 2005: Your Digital Gateway to 467 Vacation Destinations Across America. 2nd ed. 2004. cd-rom 15.00 *(978-0-9747471-5-6(7))* Belknap Digital Archives.

Turk, Evan. You Are Home: An Ode to the National Parks. Turk, Evan, illus. 2019. (ENG., Illus.). 56p. (J). (gr. -1-3). 18.99 *(978-1-5344-3282-6(5)*, Atheneum Bks. for Young Readers) Simon & Schuster Children's Publishing.

Wadsworth, Ginger. Camping with the President. Dugan, Karen, illus. 2009. (ENG.). 32p. (J). (gr. 2-5). 16.99 *(978-1-59078-497-6(9)*, Calkins Creek) Highlights Pr., c/o Highlights for Children, Inc.

Wallace, Audra. Olympic (a True Book: National Parks) (Library Edition) 2018. (True Book (Relaunch) Ser.). (ENG., Illus.). 48p. (J). (gr. 3-5). lib. bdg. 31.00 *(978-0-531-23508-9(4)*, Children's Pr.) Scholastic Library Publishing.

Weintraub, Aileen. Secrets of the National Parks: Weird & Wonderful Facts about America's Natural Wonders. 2016. (ENG., Illus.). 160p. (J). (gr. 1-3). 8.95 *(978-1-4549-2004-5(1))* Sterling Publishing Co., Inc.

Windsor, Wesley. America Wilderness, 1865-1890. 2018. (J). *(978-1-5105-3604-3(3))* SmartBook Media, Inc.

—American Wilderness: Alaska & the National Parks, 1865-1890. 2013. (Illus.). 48p. (J). pap. *(978-1-4222-2419-9(8))* Mason Crest.

—American Wilderness: Alaska & the National Parks (1865-1890) Rakove, Jack N., ed. 2012. (How America Became America Ser.). (Illus.). 48p. (J). (gr. 3-4). 19.95 *(978-1-4222-2405-2(8))* Mason Crest.

Winterberg, Jenna. Parques para Todos: Parques Nacionales de EE.UU. 2019. (SPA.). (J). pap. *(978-1-4938-9048-4(4))* Teacher Created Materials, Inc.

Yanuchi, Lori & Yanuchi, Jeff. Ranger Trails: Jobs of Adventure in America's Parks. Morris, James R., illus. 2005. 64p. (J). per. 12.95 *(978-0-9670177-2-3(6))* Ridge Rock Pr.

Yellowstone National Park: Eye of the Grizzly. 2012. (Adventures with the Parkers Ser.: 4). (Illus.). 96p. (J). (gr. -1-12). pap. 12.95 *(978-0-7627-7972-7(1)*, Falcon Guides) Globe Pequot Pr., The.

NATIONAL PLANNING

see Social Policy

see names of countries with the subdivision Economic Policy; Social Policy; e.g. United States—Economic Policy; United States—Social Policy

NATIONAL RESOURCES

see Natural Resources

see names of countries with the subdivision Economic Conditions, e.g. United States.—Economic Conditions

NATIONAL SECURITY

see also United States—Defenses

Anniss, Matt. Cyber Wars, 1 vol. 2017. (I Witness War Ser.). (ENG.). 48p. (gr. 5-6). pap. 13.93 *(978-1-5026-3434-4(1)*, f9ef625c-abe0-4a00-ac3e-f136ef2b243c); lib. bdg. 33.07 *(978-1-5026-3257-9(8)*, 786739f2-45aa-4dd4-a194-18f1cbdfe7d8) Cavendish Square Publishing LLC.

Beyer, Mark. Homeland Security & Weapons of Mass Destruction: How Prepared Are We? 2009. (Library of Weapons of Mass Destruction Ser.). 64p. (gr. 5-5). 58.50 *(978-1-60853-952-9(0))* Rosen Publishing Group, Inc., The.

Campbell, Geoffrey A. A Vulnerable America: An Overview of National Security. 2007. (Lucent Library of Homeland

Security). (ENG., Illus.). 112p. (J). 30.85 *(978-1-59018-383-0(5)*, Lucent Bks.) Cengage Gale.

Coddington, Andrew. Mass Government Surveillance: Spying on Citizens, 1 vol. 2017. (Spying, Surveillance, & Privacy in the 21st Century Ser.). (ENG.). 112p. (YA). (gr. 8-8). 44.50 *(978-1-5026-2672-1(1)*, ffd99925-2eeb-4b09-9dcb-1df4d331b902) Cavendish Square Publishing LLC.

Doak, Robin S. Homeland Security. 2011. (Cornerstones of Freedom, Third Ser.). (Illus.). 64p. (J). lib. bdg. 30.00 *(978-0-531-25036-5(9)*, Children's Pr.) Scholastic Library Publishing.

Freedman, Jeri. America Debates Privacy Versus Security, 1 vol. 2007. (America Debates Ser.). (ENG., Illus.). 64p. (YA). (gr. 5-6). lib. bdg. 37.13 *(978-1-4042-1929-8(3)*, 2eb69dee-61d6-4b38-aa54-f78f558adcd3) Rosen Publishing Group, Inc., The.

Gerdes, Louise I., ed. How Safe Is America's Infrastructure?, 1 vol. 2009. (At Issue Ser.). (ENG., Illus.). 120p. (gr. 10-12). 41.03 *(978-0-7377-4104-9(X)*, 805ffe96-5e82-4c63-8e77-d36ba36a1075); pap. 28.80 *(978-0-7377-4105-6(8)*, 8880381e-e8ca-421f-bde8-cf53ce753f6c) Greenhaven Publishing LLC. (Greenhaven Publishing).

—Should the U. S. Close Its Borders?, 1 vol. 2014. (At Issue Ser.). (ENG., Illus.). 152p. (gr. 10-12). pap. 28.80 *(978-0-7377-4690-7(4)*, 7ea8647a-c7e4-48e2-beac-c61bb9d493b2, Greenhaven Publishing) Greenhaven Publishing LLC.

Gonzalez, Lissette. The U. S. Military: Defending the Nation. (Dangerous Jobs Ser.). 24p. (gr. 2-3). 2009. 42.50 *(978-1-61512-137-3(4)*, PowerKids Pr.) 2007. (ENG., Illus.). (J). lib. bdg. 26.27 *(978-1-4042-3777-3(1)*, 1824257e-f710-4fc7-b56c-43f1b2c32996) Rosen Publishing Group, Inc., The.

Grant, R. G. Why Did Hiroshima Happen?, 1 vol. 2010. (Moments in History Ser.). (ENG., Illus.). 48p. (YA). (gr. 6-8). pap. 15.05 *(978-1-4339-4164-1(3)*, 4285aa00-25dc-4d29-8457-40bedebcfee9, Gareth Stevens Secondary Library); lib. bdg. 34.60 *(978-1-4339-4163-4(5)*, 2b6ea7b6-a641-4b5e-86c9-252c57d25795) Stevens, Gareth Publishing LLLP.

Grayson, Robert. The FBI & National Security. 2009. (FBI Story Ser.). 64p. (J). (gr. 4-7). lib. bdg. 22.95 *(978-1-4222-0564-8(9))* Mason Crest.

Haugen, David M., ed. National Security, 1 vol. 2008. (At Issue Ser.). (ENG., Illus.). 128p. (gr. 10-12). 41.03 *(978-0-7377-3924-4(X)*, ab6938b5-bf7d-4203-a656-67b782c21cc7); pap. 28.80 *(978-0-7377-3925-1(8)*, a9e96794-a690-4a51-8739-42d006de95dc) Greenhaven Publishing LLC. (Greenhaven Publishing).

Haulley, Fletcher. The Deparment of Homeland Security, 1 vol. 2005. (This Is Your Government Ser.). (ENG., Illus.). 64p. (J). (gr. 4-6). lib. bdg. 37.13 *(978-1-4042-0209-2(9)*, cb6cd31a-5bf6-494c-8fe0-965b27083d84) Rosen Publishing Group, Inc., The.

—The Department of Homeland Security. (This Is Your Government Ser.). 64p. 2009. (gr. 5-6). 58.50 *(978-1-60854-371-7(4)*, Rosen Reference) 2005. (ENG., Illus.). (gr. 4-6). per. 12.95 *(978-1-4042-0662-5(0)*, c66a2c7f-a844-416e-b0cc-f92dbb0022f6) Rosen Publishing Group, Inc., The.

Immell, Myra, ed. Homeland Security, 1 vol. 2009. (At Issue Ser.). (ENG., Illus.). 136p. (gr. 10-12). 41.03 *(978-0-7377-4420-0(0)*, ee6f02cd-66cc-4b74-b372-f168db95e26b); pap. 28.80 *(978-0-7377-4421-7(9)*, 23b6bdf6-26f2-4222-a4a0-7c82f2b1e1ed) Greenhaven Publishing LLC. (Greenhaven Publishing).

Katz, Samuel M. U. S. Counterstrike: American Counterterrorism. 2005. (Terrorist Dossiers Ser.). (Illus.). 72p. (J). (gr. 6-12). 26.60 *(978-0-8225-1569-2(5))* Lerner Publishing Group.

Keeter, Hunter. The U. S. Homeland Security Forces, 1 vol. 2004. (America's Armed Forces Ser.). (ENG., Illus.). 48p. (gr. 5-8). lib. bdg. 33.67 *(978-0-8368-5682-8(1)*, b7c9a2ce-1c39-4fd3-8173-a658ff1f4996, Gareth Stevens Secondary Library) Stevens, Gareth Publishing LLLP.

Kenney, Karen Latchana. The Department of Homeland Security: A Look Behind the Scenes. 2019. (U. S. Government Behind the Scenes Ser.). (ENG., Illus.). 64p. (J). (gr. 7-12). pap. 8.95 *(978-0-7565-5910-6(3)*, 138704); lib. bdg. 35.32 *(978-0-7565-5901-4(4)*, 138700) Capstone. (Compass Point Bks.).

Kerrigan, Michael. The Department of Homeland Security. 2004. (Rescue & Prevention Ser.). (Illus.). 96p. (J). (gr. 7-18). lib. bdg. 22.95 *(978-1-59084-409-0(2))* Mason Crest.

—Homeland Security. 2017. (Illus.). 80p. (J). *(978-1-4222-3767-0(2))* Mason Crest.

Koestler-Grack, Rachel A. The Department of Homeland Security. 2007. (U. Government: How It Works). (ENG., Illus.). 104p. (gr. 5-9). lib. bdg. 30.00 *(978-0-7910-9286-6(0)*, P125636, Facts On File) Infobase Holdings, Inc.

Labov, Steven L., ed. Rescue & Prevention: Defending Our Nation, 15 vols., Set. (Illus.). 96p. (YA). (gr. 7-18). lib. bdg. *(978-1-59084-401-4(7))* Mason Crest.

Mara, Wil. Homeland Security. 2016. (21st Century Skills Library: a Citizen's Guide Ser.). (ENG., Illus.). 32p. (J). (gr. 4-7). 32.07 *(978-1-63471-068-8(1)*, 208351) Cherry Lake Publishing.

Mattern, Joanne. Standing in the First Lady's Shoes, 1 vol. 2017. (My Government Ser.). (ENG.). 32p. (gr. 3-3). pap. 11.58 *(978-1-5026-3070-4(2)*, f5756819-e3f9-43b5-b486-0283dbfb6bc9); lib. bdg. 30.21 *(978-1-5026-3072-8(9)*, 458069a8-b8e0-4843-83ce-a9bc7b6e1412) Cavendish Square Publishing LLC.

Miller, Debra A. The Patriot Act, 1 vol. 2007. (Hot Topics Ser.). (ENG., Illus.). 112p. (gr. 7-7). lib. bdg. 41.03 *(978-1-59018-981-8(7)*, bbc5ead7-8fa1-4ddf-b860-f44969a6dd51, Lucent Pr.) Greenhaven Publishing LLC.

Miller, Debra A., ed. Homeland Security, 1 vol. 2008. (Current Controversies Ser.). (ENG., Illus.). 216p. (gr. 10-12). pap. 33.00 *(978-0-7377-4139-1(2)*, 83428b4a-f082-4982-bb03-5abdae638736); lib. bdg. 48.03 *(978-0-7377-4138-4(4)*, ca810325-cc8c-420c-a3b5-ebfb05b298a0) Greenhaven Publishing LLC. (Greenhaven Publishing).

Mullins, Matt. Homeland Security. 2010. (21st Century Skills Library: Citizens & Their Governments Ser.). (ENG., Illus.). 32p. (gr. 4-8). lib. bdg. 32.07 *(978-1-60279-633-1(5)*, 200338) Cherry Lake Publishing.

parks, peggy j. Cyberterrorism. 2012. (Illus.). 96p. (J). lib. bdg. *(978-1-60152-264-1(9))* ReferencePoint Pr., Inc.

Perritano, John. Border Security, Vol. 12. 2015. (On a Mission Ser.). (Illus.). 48p. (J). (gr. 5). 20.95 *(978-1-4222-3393-1(6))* Mason Crest.

Peters, Jennifer. Inside the Department of Homeland Security, 1 vol. 2018. (Understanding the Executive Branch Ser.). (ENG.). 48p. (gr. 5-5). 29.60 *(978-0-7660-9893-0(1)*, c64646e4-c10f-49cb-8e4b-3f1a23675300) Enslow Publishing, LLC.

Ruffin, David C. The Duties & Responsibilities of the Secretary of Homeland Security. (Your Government in Action Ser.). 32p. (gr. 3-3). 2009. 43.90 *(978-1-60854-918-4(6))* 2004. (ENG., Illus.). (J). lib. bdg. 27.60 *(978-1-4042-2693-7(1)*, 97d96ea1-5d59-451f-b7a8-fb9372cf17c6) Rosen Publishing Group, Inc., The. (PowerKids Pr.).

Scherer, Lauri S., ed. Privacy, 1 vol. 2014. (Introducing Issues with Opposing Viewpoints Ser.). (ENG., Illus.). 120p. (gr. 7-10). lib. bdg. 43.63 *(978-0-7377-6927-2(0)*, 31e9fa16-25a3-43d2-8d9a-3b9bf33d2967, Greenhaven Publishing) Greenhaven Publishing LLC.

Stefoff, Rebecca. Security V. Privacy, 1 vol. 2008. (Open for Debate Ser.). (ENG., Illus.). 144p. (YA). (gr. 8-8). lib. bdg. 45.50 *(978-0-7614-2578-6(0)*, 03769338-a097-45e0-8d15-575f505a8f98) Cavendish Square Publishing LLC.

Stinson, Doug. Protecting the Nation's Borders. 2005. (At Issue Ser.). (ENG.). 80-128p. (gr. 10-12). pap. 24.45 *(978-0-7377-2740-1(3)*, Greenhaven Pr., Inc.) Cengage Gale.

Stinson, Douglass, ed. Protecting America's Borders. 2005. (At Issue Ser.). 94p. (YA). (gr. 10-13). lib. bdg. 29.95 *(978-0-7377-2739-5(X)*, Greenhaven Pr., Inc.) Cengage Gale.

Streissguth, Tom. The Security Agencies of the United States: How the CIA, FBI, NSA, & Homeland Security Keep Us Safe, 1 vol. 2013. (Constitution & the United States Government Ser.). (ENG., Illus.). 104p. (gr. 5-6). 35.93 *(978-0-7660-4064-9(X)*, 3e4b285d-d68a-47f7-a469-2d442178525a) Enslow Publishing, LLC.

Wade, Mary Dodson. Condoleezza Rice: Being the Best. 2003. (Gateway Biography Ser.: 4). 48p. lib. bdg. 23.90 *(978-0-7613-2619-9(7))*; (Illus.). (gr. 2-4). pap. 8.95 *(978-0-7613-1927-6(1))* Lerner Publishing Group. (Millbrook Pr.).

NATIONAL SOCIALISM

see also Socialism

Bartoletti, Susan Campbell. Hitler Youth: Growing up in Hitler's Shadow (Scholastic Focus) 2019. (ENG.). 384p. (YA). (gr. 7-7). pap. 10.99 *(978-1-338-30984-3(6)*, Scholastic Nonfiction) Scholastic, Inc.

Dufner, Annette. The Rise of Adolf Hitler. 2003. (At Issue in History Ser.). (ENG., Illus.). 144p. (YA). 26.70 *(978-0-7377-1519-4(7))*; pap. 35.75 *(978-0-7377-1518-7(9))* Cengage Gale. (Greenhaven Pr., Inc.).

Freeman, Charles. The Rise of the Nazis. 2005. (How Did It Happen? Ser.). (ENG., Illus.). 48p. (gr. 7-10). lib. bdg. 36.70 *(978-1-59018-608-4(7)*, Lucent Bks.) Cengage Gale.

—Why Did the Rise of the Nazis Happen?, 1 vol. 2010. (Moments in History Ser.). (ENG., Illus.). 48p. (gr. 6-8). (J). pap. 15.05 *(978-1-4339-4176-4(7)*, f4af284b-ec1c-4ad4-b4ff-362a5cc5aa21, Gareth Stevens Secondary Library); (YA). lib. bdg. 34.60 *(978-1-4339-4175-7(9)*, 325cb1a1-640f-4027-a952-3ea9ec96c7d3) Stevens, Gareth Publishing LLLP.

Giblin, James Cross. The Life & Death of Adolf Hitler. 2015. (ENG., Illus.). 256p. (J). (gr. 5-7). pap. 11.99 *(978-0-544-45591-7(6)*, 1599316, Clarion Bks.) HarperCollins Pubs.

—The Life & Death of Adolf Hitler. 2015. lib. bdg. 20.85 *(978-0-606-36830-8(2))* Turtleback.

Gottfried, Ted. Nazi Germany: The Face of Tyranny. Alcorn, Stephen, illus. (Holocaust History Ser.). 112p. (YA). (gr. 7-12). 22.95 *(978-1-58013-203-9(0)*, Kar-Ben Publishing) Lerner Publishing Group.

Hitler's Treasure: Nazi Gold. 2004. (YA). cd-rom 1500.00 *(978-0-934269-58-2(0))* UFO Photo Archives.

Jacobs Altman, Linda. Adolf Hitler & the Rise of the Third Reich, 1 vol. 2015. (People & Events That Changed the World Ser.). (ENG., Illus.). 112p. (gr. 7-8). 38.93 *(978-0-7660-7175-9(8)*, 2d85cc23-3dac-444a-8ed1-0b7c2fdb8bd2) Enslow Publishing, LLC.

Knight, Patricia. Mussolini & Fascism. 2003. (Questions & Analysis in History Ser.). (ENG., Illus.). 144p. (C). 130.00 *(978-0-415-27921-5(6)*, RU24353); per. 35.95 *(978-0-415-27922-2(4)*, RU24354) Routledge.

Lowery, Zoe & Norton, James R. The Nazi Regime & the Holocaust, 1 vol. 2016. (Bearing Witness: Genocide & Ethnic Cleansing Ser.). (ENG.). 64p. (J). (gr. 6-6). 36.13 *(978-1-5081-7163-8(7)*, 132e8b78-c8df-4b5e-a24e-c8f857163833) Rosen Publishing Group, Inc., The.

Marcovitz, Hal. Life in Nazi Germany. 2015. (ENG., Illus.). 96p. (J). lib. bdg. *(978-1-60152-776-9(4))* ReferencePoint Pr., Inc.

—The Rise of the Nazis. 2014. (Understanding World History Ser.). (ENG., Illus.). 96p. (J). lib. bdg. *(978-1-60152-654-0(7))* ReferencePoint Pr., Inc.

McIlroy, Michelle. Sophie Scholl: Student Resister & Anti-Nazi Political Activist. 2017. (Spotlight on Civic Courage: Heroes of Conscience Ser.). (Illus.). 48p. (J). (gr. 10-15). 70.50 *(978-1-5383-8108-3(7))* Rosen Publishing Group, Inc., The.

McKay, Jenny. Children of the Holocaust. 2015. (ENG., Illus.). 80p. (J). (gr. 5-12). lib. bdg. *(978-1-60152-838-4(8))* ReferencePoint Pr., Inc.

Oshiro, Beverly & Sachs, Ruth. Adolf Eichmann, 1 vol., 1. 2015. (Holocaust Ser.). (ENG., Illus.). 112p. (J). (gr. 7-7). 38.80 *(978-1-4994-6246-3(8)*, 72e969a8-1c46-4180-b92c-fc9636f96ca3, Rosen Young Adult) Rosen Publishing Group, Inc., The.

Price, Sean Stewart. Adolf Hitler. 2010. (Wicked History Ser.). (ENG., Illus.). 128p. (J). 31.00 *(978-0-531-20757-4(9)*, Watts, Franklin) Scholastic Library Publishing.

—Adolf Hitler (a Wicked History) 2010. (Wicked History Ser.). (ENG.). 136p. (J). (gr. 6-12). pap. 5.95 *(978-0-531-22357-4(4)*, Watts, Franklin) Scholastic Library Publishing.

Rice, Earle. Adolf Hitler & Nazi Germany. 2006. (World Leaders Ser.). (Illus.). 176p. (J). (gr. 3-7). lib. bdg. 28.95 *(978-1-931798-78-5(8))* Reynolds, Morgan Inc.

Saxena, Shalini, ed. Dictatorship, Fascism, & Totalitarianism, 1 vol. 2014. (Political & Economic Systems Ser.). (ENG.). 192p. (YA). (gr. 10-10). 47.59 *(978-1-62275-350-5(X)*, 453bdf07-61a4-41c0-8e04-5f8bc94f07ed) Rosen Publishing Group, Inc., The.

Vander Hook, Sue. Adolf Hitler: German Dictator, 1 vol. 2011. (Essential Lives Set 6 Ser.). (ENG., Illus.). 112p. (J). (gr. 6-12). lib. bdg. 41.36 *(978-1-61714-781-4(8)*, 6727, Essential Library) ABDO Publishing Co.

Woolf, Alex. The Rise of Nazi Germany. 2004. (Questioning History Ser.). (J). lib. bdg. 28.50 *(978-1-58340-442-3(2))* Black Rabbit Bks.

NATIONAL SOCIALISM—FICTION

Stasse, Lisa M. The Forsaken: The Forsaken Trilogy. 2012. (ENG.). 384p. (YA). (gr. 7). 16.99 *(978-1-4424-3265-9(9)*, Simon & Schuster Bks. For Young Readers) Simon & Schuster Bks. For Young Readers.

Van Ryk, Laverne. A Garland of Emeralds. 2006. (Illus.). 305p. 31.50 *(978-1-4122-0156-8(X))* Trafford Publishing.

West Lewis, Amanda. The Pact, 1 vol. 2016. (ENG., Illus.). 352p. (YA). (gr. 7-12). pap. 14.95 *(978-0-88995-544-8(1)*, 996a5f80-c8eb-4176-9d48-0345fa4f947d) Trifolium Bks., Inc. CAN. Dist: Firefly Bks., Ltd.

NATIONAL SONGS

see also Folk Songs

Brannon, Cecelia H. Zoom in on the National Anthem, 1 vol. 2016. (Zoom in on American Symbols Ser.). (ENG., Illus.). 24p. (gr. 2-2). pap. 10.95 *(978-0-7660-8446-9(9)*, 70dcf44c-43c7-46a5-872f-c8dd7f1a1c43) Enslow Publishing, LLC.

Darnanda, Lori. The Story of the "Star-Spangled Banner", 1 vol. (American History Milestones Ser.). (ENG.). 32p. (J). (gr. 5-5). 2009. lib. bdg. 28.93 *(978-1-4358-3015-8(6)*, f2e5f903-40c2-4903-afa4-1d952dbeb193) 2008. (Illus.). pap. 10.00 *(978-1-4358-0205-6(5)*, 4f301343-44f2-47a1-9f74-353cdd17b026) Rosen Publishing Group, Inc., The. (PowerKids Pr.).

—The Story of the Star-Spangled Banner. 2009. (American History Milestones Ser.). 32p. (gr. 5-5). 47.90 *(978-1-61511-375-0(4)*, PowerKids Pr.) Rosen Publishing Group, Inc., The.

Dell, Pamela. The Star-Spangled Banner. 2016. (Spring Forward Ser.). (J). (gr. 1). *(978-1-4900-9383-3(4))* Benchmark Education Co.

Gershenson, Harold P. America the Musical 1776-1899: A Nation's History Through Music. Chesworth, Michael, illus. 2005. 21p. (J). *(978-1-58987-116-8(2))* Kindermusik International.

Harris, Duchess & Carser, A. R. The Story of the Black National Anthem. 2018. (Freedom's Promise Ser.). (ENG., Illus.). 48p. (J). (gr. 4-8). lib. bdg. 35.64 *(978-1-5321-1776-3(0)*, 30840) ABDO Publishing Co.

Harrison, Ted. O Canada. 2004. (J). (gr. k-3). spiral bd. *(978-0-616-03038-7(X))* Canadian National Institute for the Blind/Institut National Canadien pour les Aveugles.

Healy, Nick. The Star-Spangled Banner. 2003. (J). *(978-1-58417-055-6(7))*; pap. *(978-1-58417-118-8(9))* Lake Street Pubs.

Hess, Debra. The Star-Spangled Banner, 1 vol. 2008. (Symbols of America Ser.). (ENG.). 40p. (gr. 3-3). pap. 9.23 *(978-0-7614-3392-7(9)*, 80f9c4eb-419a-487b-9908-119fa761e234) Cavendish Square Publishing LLC.

Kallio, Jamie. 12 Questions about the Star-Spangled Banner. 2017. (Examining Primary Sources Ser.). (ENG., Illus.). 32p. (J). (gr. 3-6). 32.80 *(978-1-63235-288-0(5)*, 11757, 12-Story Library) Bookstaves, LLC.

McKinney, Devon. I Sing the Star-Spangled Banner, 1 vol. 2016. (Symbols of Our Country Ser.). (ENG.). 24p. (J). (gr. 1-1). 25.27 *(978-1-4994-2730-1(1)*, f7f73664-ef3f-4a9b-98f1-e4a91782ea64); pap. 9.25 *(978-1-4994-2729-5(8)*, e5009c40-19e2-45a0-92ba-e158c447fdb0) Rosen Publishing Group, Inc., The. (PowerKids Pr.).

Mills, Nathan & Wesolowski, Harriet. The Songs We Sing: Honoring Our Country, 1 vol. 2012. (Rosen Readers Ser.). (ENG., Illus.). 24p. (J). (gr. 1-2). pap. 8.25 *(978-1-4488-8821-4(2)*, 45c822f8-b9c7-4ecb-af47-3e5ded263e4b, Rosen Classroom) Rosen Publishing Group, Inc., The.

Monroe, Tyler. The Star-Spangled Banner. 2013. (U. S. Symbols Ser.). (ENG.). 24p. (J). (gr. -1-2). 27.32 *(978-1-4765-3087-1(4)*, 123064); pap. 7.95 *(978-1-4765-3536-4(1)*, 123582) Capstone. (Capstone Pr.).

Pingry, Patricia A. O Little Town of Bethlehem. 2008. (ENG., Illus.). 16p. (J). bds. 12.99 *(978-0-8249-6566-2(3)*, Ideals Pubns.) Worthy Publishing.

Raum, Elizabeth. The Star Spangled Banner in Translation: What It Really Means. rev. ed. 2017. (Kids' Translations Ser.). (ENG., Illus.). 32p. (J). (gr. 3-6). lib. bdg. 27.99 *(978-1-5157-9134-8(3)*, 136569, Capstone Pr.) Capstone.

Reed, Jennifer. The Star-Spangled Banner, 1 vol. 2019. (America's Songs Ser.). (ENG.). 32p. (gr. 3-3). pap. 11.58 *(978-1-5026-4857-0(1)*, a6d3a1b6-cd5c-48d9-972e-062d15ba9afe) Cavendish Square Publishing LLC.

Sonneborn, Liz. America the Beautiful: The Story Behind Our National Hymn. 2003. (America in Words & Song Ser.). (Illus.). 32p. (gr. 4-6). 23.00 *(978-0-7910-7332-2(7)*, Facts On File) Infobase Holdings, Inc.

Susienka, Kristen. America the Beautiful, 1 vol. 2019. (America's Songs Ser.). (ENG.). 32p. (J). (gr. 3-3). pap. 11.58 *(978-1-5026-4861-7(X)*, c1e4ca3e-57f6-4f00-8125-4e860a39629d) Cavendish Square Publishing LLC.

Vilsaint, Fequiere. Children Songs from Haiti: Chante Timoun Ayiti. Date not set. 28p. (J). (gr. 1-5). wbk. ed. 25.00 *(978-1-881839-55-2(9))* Educa Vision Inc.

Wesolowski, Harriet. The Songs We Sing: Honoring Our Country, 1 vol. 2012. (I'm an American Citizen Ser.). (ENG., Illus.). 24p. (J). (gr. 1-2). 26.27 *(978-1-4488-8581-7(7)*, d0e84b88-61f5-4cdc-a0e5-8c808b2c9380, PowerKids Pr.) Rosen Publishing Group, Inc., The.

NATIONALITY (CITIZENSHIP)

see Citizenship

NATIONS, LAW OF

see International Law

NATIVE PEOPLES

see Indigenous Peoples

NATIVE RACES

see Indigenous Peoples

NATIVITY OF CHRIST

see Jesus Christ—Nativity

NATO

see North Atlantic Treaty Organization

NATURAL CALAMITIES

see Natural Disasters

NATURAL DISASTERS

see also Earthquakes; Floods; Forest Fires; Storms; Volcanoes

Aboff, Marcie & Gray-Wilburn, Renée. First Graphics: Wild Earth. Sotirovski, Aleksandar, illus. 2012. (First Graphics: Wild Earth Ser.). (ENG.). 24p. (gr. 1-2). pap. 142.80 *(978-1-4296-8375-3(9))* Capstone.

Aboff, Marcie, et al. First Graphics: Wild Earth. Sotirovski, Aleksandar, illus. 2012. (First Graphics: Wild Earth Ser.). (ENG.). 24p. (J). (gr. k-3). pap., pap., pap. 25.16 *(978-1-4296-8374-6(0)*, 17676) Capstone.

Anaxos Inc. Staff, contrib. by. UXL Encyclopedia of Weather & Natural Disasters. 2007. (J). *(978-1-4144-1881-0(7))*; *(978-1-4144-1880-3(9))*; *(978-1-4144-1882-7(5))*; *(978-1-4144-1884-1(1))*; *(978-1-4144-1883-4(3))* Cengage Gale.

Aronin, Miriam. Slammed by a Tsunami! 2010. (Disaster Survivors Ser.). (Illus.). 32p. (YA). (gr. 4-7). lib. bdg. 28.50 *(978-1-936087-48-8(0))* Bearport Publishing Co., Inc.

Augsburger, A. Don. The World Is a Beautiful Place. Ressler-Horst, Lara, illus. 2007. 48p. per. 14.95 *(978-1-934246-44-3(1))* Peppertree Pr., The.

Bailey, Gerry. Fragile Planet, 1 vol. 2011. (Planet SOS Ser.). (ENG., Illus.). 48p. (J). (gr. 4-5). pap. 15.05 *(978-1-4339-4975-3(X)*, f585e2b4-f204-48d9-9792-f5d1ee8d2955); lib. bdg. 34.60 *(978-1-4339-4974-6(1)*, 3ace0f78-ebc2-42b2-8d5f-78d0044e2277) Stevens, Gareth Publishing LLLP. (Gareth Stevens Learning Library).

Bankoff, Greg. Cultures of Disaster: Society & Natural Hazard in the Philippines. 2015. (ENG.). 256p. (C). pap. 56.95 *(978-1-138-87926-3(6)*, Y179793) Routledge.

Barker, Geoff. Hunger. 2010. (Voices Ser.). (YA). (gr. 5-9). 34.25 *(978-1-59920-281-5(6))* Black Rabbit Bks.

Bell, Samantha S. Detecting Hurricanes. 2017. (Detecting Disasters Ser.). (ENG., Illus.). 32p. (J). (gr. 3-5). lib. bdg. 31.35 *(978-1-63517-003-0(6)*, 1635170036, Focus Readers) North Star Editions.

Blackwell, Amy Hackney, ed. U-X-L Encyclopedia of Weather & Natural Disasters, 5 vols. 2nd ed. 2016. (U-X-L Encyclopedia of Weather & Natural Disasters Ser.). (ENG., Illus.). 1200p. (gr. 6-8). 557.00 *(978-1-4103-3290-5(X)*, UXL) Cengage Gale.

Blohm, Craig E. Catastrophic Events of The 2000s. 2013. (YA). lib. bdg. *(978-1-60152-522-2(2))* ReferencePoint Pr., Inc.

Brezina, Corona. Disappearing Forests: Deforestation, Desertification, & Drought. 2009. (Extreme Environmental Threats Ser.). 64p. (gr. 6-6). 58.50 *(978-1-61512-426-8(8))* Rosen Publishing Group, Inc., The.

Bullard, Lisa. Tsunamis. 2009. pap. 40.95 *(978-0-7613-4770-5(4))* Lerner Publishing Group.

Burnie, David. Disasters. 2013. (Illus.). 112p. (J). pap. *(978-1-4071-3653-0(4))* Scholastic, Inc.

Burton, Margie, et al. The Power of Nature. 2011. (Early Connections Ser.). (J). *(978-1-61672-507-5(9))* Benchmark Education Co.

Capaccio, George. Tsunamis: Set Of 6. 2011. (Navigators Ser.). (J). pap. 48.00 net. *(978-1-4108-5081-2(1))* Benchmark Education Co.

—Tsunamis: Text Pairs. 2008. (Bridges/Navigators Ser.). (J). (gr. 5). 89.00 *(978-1-4108-8424-4(4))* Benchmark Education Co.

Challen, Paul C. Environmental Disaster Alert! 2004. (Disaster Alert! Ser.). (ENG., Illus.). 32p. (J). lib. bdg. *(978-0-7787-1581-8(7))* Crabtree Publishing Co.

Challen, Paul C. & Challen, Paul. Environmental Disaster Alert! 2004. (Disaster Alert! Ser.). (ENG., Illus.). 32p. (J). pap. *(978-0-7787-1613-6(9))* Crabtree Publishing Co.

Claybourne, Anna. 100 Deadliest Things on the Planet. 2012. (100 Most... Ser.). lib. bdg. 18.40 *(978-0-606-26744-1(1))* Turtleback.

—100 Most Destructive Natural Disasters Ever. 2014. (100 Most... Ser.). lib. bdg. 18.40 *(978-0-606-36336-5(X))* Turtleback.

Close, Edward. Extreme Weather, 1 vol., 1. 2014. (Discovery Education: Earth & Space Science Ser.). (ENG.). 32p. (gr. 4-5). 28.93 *(978-1-4777-6194-6(2)*, 1b048c95-feb0-48ca-8404-bf5d9bbd0dd1, PowerKids Pr.) Rosen Publishing Group, Inc., The.

Collier Hillstrom, Laurie. Natural Disaster Response, 1 vol. 2015. (Hot Topics Ser.). (ENG., Illus.). 104p. (gr. 7-7). lib. bdg. 41.03 *(978-1-4205-0873-4(3)*, 745ef91c-7e03-4b95-80c1-eb815ded2c51, Lucent Pr.) Greenhaven Publishing LLC.

Corbett, Sean. Heat Waves. 2015. (Illus.). 32p. (J). *(978-1-5105-0078-5(2))* SmartBook Media, Inc.

—Heat Waves. 2014. (J). *(978-1-4896-3272-2(7))* Weigl Pubs., Inc.

Cunningham, Kevin. Surviving Tsunamis, 1 vol. 2011. (Children's True Stories: Natural Disasters Ser.). (ENG.). 32p. (J). (gr. 3-5). 31.32 *(978-1-4109-4095-7(0)*, 114630);

M N O

pap. 8.29 (978-1-4109-4102-2(7), 114636) Capstone. (Raintree).

Currie, Stephen. Escapes from Natural Disasters. 2004. (Great Escapes Ser.). (ENG., Illus.). 112p. (J). 30.85 (978-1-59018-278-9(2), Lucent Bks.) Cengage Gale.

David, Alex. Swept Away: Escalating Storms & Disasters, 1 vol. 2019. (Taking Action on Climate Change Ser.). (ENG.). 64p. (gr. 6-6). pap. 16.28 (978-1-5026-5234-8(X), c9264b2c-3909-4e41-8ad4-3650193a872a) Cavendish Square Publishing LLC.

Disaster Plan: Individual Title Six-Packs. (Bookweb Ser.). 32p. (gr. 5-18). 34.00 (978-0-7635-3794-4(2)) Rigby Education.

Dodge Cummings, Judy. Earth, Wind, Fire, & Rain: Real Tales of Temperamental Elements. 2018. (Mystery & Mayhem Ser.). (ENG., Illus.). 128p. (J). (gr. 5-8). 19.95 (978-1-61930-626-4(3), 7a0fba13-3dd8-4c1a-b8b0-315ee8c168f8) Nomad Pr.

Dodson Wade, Mary. Deadly Waves: Tsunamis, 1 vol. 2013. (Disasters: People in Peril Ser.). (ENG., Illus.). 48p. (gr. 5-7). 27.93 (978-0-7660-4018-2(6), c35ba7f0-bccb-4a78-accd-e3db47217c3f) Enslow Publishing, LLC.

Doudna, Kelly & Craig, Diane. Tidal Wave or Tsunami?, 1 vol. 2015. (This or That? Weather Ser.). (ENG., Illus.). 24p. (J). (gr. k-4). 32.79 (978-1-62403-956-0(1), 19568, Super SandCastle) ABDO Publishing Co.

Dougherty, Terri. The Worst Tsunamis of All Time, 1 vol. 2012. (Epic Disasters Ser.). (ENG.). 32p. (J). (gr. 3-9). lib. bdg. 28.65 (978-1-4296-8416-3(X), 118489, Capstone Pr.) Capstone.

Draper, Allison Stark. Coping with Natural Disasters. 2009. (Coping Ser.). 192p. (gr. 7-12). 63.90 (978-1-61512-006-2(8)) Rosen Publishing Group, Inc., The.

Dunn, Karen Lewit. Technology & Natural Disasters. 2008. (Discovering & Exploring Science Ser.). (Illus.). 16p. (J). (gr. -1-3). lib. bdg. 12.95 (978-0-7569-8435-9(1)) Perfection Learning Corp.

Dwyer, Helen. Tsunamis!, 1 vol. 2011. (Eyewitness Disaster Ser.). (ENG.). 32p. (gr. 3-3). 31.21 (978-1-60870-005-9(4), a1f565c3-042b-4d54-bb49-84546feb14c9) Cavendish Square Publishing LLC.

Earth's Natural Disasters. 2015. (Earth's Natural Disasters Ser.). (ENG.). 32p. (J). (gr. 3-4). pap., pap., pap. 63.12 (978-0-7660-7055-4(7)); pap., pap., pap. 378.72 (978-0-7660-6681-6(9)); lib. bdg. 161.58 (978-0-7660-6680-9(0), 639e357a-001f-4f3b-96b2-68f586d46330) Enslow Publishing, LLC.

Eaton, Gale. A History of Civilization in 50 Disasters, 1 vol. Hoose, Phillip, ed. 2015. (History In 50 Ser.: 0). (ENG., Illus.). (YA). (gr. 6-12). 224p. 24.95 (978-0-88448-383-0(5), 884383); 240p. pap. 16.95 (978-0-88448-489-9(0), 884489) Tilbury Hse. Pubs.

Elkins, Elizabeth. Investigating Floods. 2017. (Investigating Natural Disasters Ser.). (ENG., Illus.). 32p. (J). (gr. 3-9). lib. bdg. 28.65 (978-1-5157-4040-7(4), 133921, Capstone Pr.) Capstone.

—Investigating Tornadoes. 2017. (Investigating Natural Disasters Ser.). (ENG., Illus.). 32p. (J). (gr. 3-9). lib. bdg. 28.65 (978-1-5157-4037-7(4), 133918, Capstone Pr.) Capstone.

Englar, Mary, et al. Epic Disasters. 2012. (Epic Disasters Ser.). (ENG.). 32p. (gr. 3-4). pap. 190.80 (978-1-4296-8512-2(3), Capstone Pr.) Capstone.

Espejo, Roman, ed. Are Natural Disasters Increasing?, 1 vol. 2014. (At Issue Ser.). (ENG.). 104p. (gr. 10-12). lib. bdg. 41.03 (978-0-7377-6822-0(3), 632272e1-6fd9-49ad-8b27-b11f1c3e8499, Greenhaven Publishing) Greenhaven Publishing LLC.

Estigarribia, Diana. Learning about the Effects of Natural Events with Graphic Organizers. (Graphic Organizers in Science Ser.). 24p. 2009. (gr. 3-4). 42.50 (978-1-61513-050-4(0)) 2005. (ENG., Illus.). (gr. 4-5). pap. 8.25 (978-1-4042-5038-3(7), ecf54c72-39c4-48d7-ae3b-54bd4d664985) 2004. (ENG., Illus.). (J). (gr. 4-5). lib. bdg. 26.27 (978-1-4042-2804-7(7), fdb9f1a2-d672-4704-ac9f-145afaac0b37) Rosen Publishing Group, Inc., The. (PowerKids Pr.).

Farndon, John. Extreme Volcanoes. 2017. (When Nature Attacks Ser.). (ENG., Illus.). 32p. (J). (gr. 3-6). 27.99 (978-1-5124-3220-6(2), 184d1b3e-2de1-46be-a0fa-6110c01b4062, Hungry Tomato (r)) Lerner Publishing Group.

Faust, Daniel R. Collision Course: Asteroids & Earth, 1 vol. 2007. (Jr. Graphic Environmental Dangers Ser.). (ENG., Illus.). 24p. (J). (gr. 4-4). lib. bdg. 28.93 (978-1-4042-4228-9(7), 11fc33eb-7a12-4cd5-988c-b2dc198fe7b2) Rosen Publishing Group, Inc., The.

Fecher, Sarah & Oliver, Clare. Freaky Facts about Natural Disasters. Anderson, Jill, ed. Bines, Gary & Boller, Gary, illus. 2006. (Freaky Facts Ser.). (ENG.). 32p. (J). (gr. 2-5). pap. 8.95 (978-1-58728-542-4(8)) Cooper Square Publishing Llc.

Feldman, Sarah. Twisters: Set Of 6. 2010. (Early Connections Ser.). (J). pap. 39.00 net. (978-1-4108-1544-6(7)) Benchmark Education Co.

Fine, Jil. Tsunamis. 2007. (High Interest Books: Natural Disasters Ser.). (ENG., Illus.). 48p. (J). (gr. 7-9). lib. bdg. 21.19 (978-0-531-12444-4(4), Children's Pr.) Scholastic Library Publishing.

Flows & Quakes & Spinning Winds: Individual Title Six-Packs. (gr. k-1). 23.00 (978-0-7635-9043-7(6)) Rigby Education.

Force Of Nature. 3rd ed. 2018. (J). (978-0-7166-9933-0(8)) World Bk., Inc.

Fry, Erin. Earth: Fast Changes: Text Pairs. 2008. (Bridges/Navigators Ser.). (J). (gr. 4). 81.00 (978-1-4108-8382-7(5)) Benchmark Education Co.

Garbe, Suzanne. Threatening Skies: History's Most Dangerous Weather, 1 vol. 2013. (Dangerous History Ser.). (ENG.). 32p. (J). (gr. 3-9). 28.65 (978-1-4765-0128-4(9), 122205, Capstone Pr.) Capstone.

Gardiner, Lisa. Catastrophic Colorado! The History & Science of Our Natural Disasters. 2006. (Illus.). 48p. (J). (gr. 1-8). 14.95 (978-1-56579-549-5(0), Westcliffe Pubs.) Bower Hse.

Gelletly, LeeAnne. Ecological Issues. Ojakorotu, Victor & Rotberg, Robert I., eds. 2013. (Africa: Progress & Problems Ser.: 13). (Illus.). 112p. (J). (gr. 7-18). 24.95 (978-1-4222-2937-8(8)) Mason Crest.

Gibson, Karen Bush. Mudslide in la Conchita, California 2005. 2005. (Natural Disasters Ser.). (Illus.). 32p. (J). (gr. 1-4). lib. bdg. 25.70 (978-1-58415-418-1(7)) Mitchell Lane Pubs.

Goldstein, Natalie. Droughts & Heat Waves: A Practical Survival Guide, 1 vol. 2006. (Library of Emergency Preparedness Ser.). (ENG., Illus.). 64p. (YA). (gr. 6-6). lib. bdg. 37.13 (978-1-4042-0536-9(5), e0d5f9e5-6a9a-4c5d-8a36-2ca056ac7b3b) Rosen Publishing Group, Inc., The.

Goyal, Anuj, ed. Higher Ground. 2006. (Illus.). 160p. (gr. 7-9). per. 8.99 (978-1-84458-581-6(6), Pavilion Children's Books) Pavilion Bks. GBR. Dist: Trafalgar Square Publishing.

Graphic Natural Disasters, 12 vols., Set. Incl. Avalanches & Landslides. Shone, Rob. (J). lib. bdg. 37.13 (978-1-4042-1992-2(7), 4730c481-094c-4ddd-92ad-2ef53b93576f); Earthquakes. Shone, Rob. Spender, Nick, illus. (YA). lib. bdg. 37.13 (978-1-4042-1989-2(7), ef4138bd-88e2-41f5-a34d-ab78306d13c7); Hurricanes. Jeffrey, Gary. Lacey, Mike, illus. (J). lib. bdg. 37.13 (978-1-4042-1991-5(9), 9ef767ce-3b5b-4a27-83d1-f7d52746265b); Tornadoes & Superstorms. Jeffrey, Gary. Riley, Terry, illus. (J). lib. bdg. 37.13 (978-1-4042-1993-9(5), 341abb57-9639-4eda-b52c-cd55d0121d81); Tsunamis & Floods. Jeffrey, Gary, illus. (J). lib. bdg. 37.13 (978-1-4042-1990-8(0), 9439fba3-87de-4545-8c3e-b391962ad03a); Volcanoes. Shone, Rob. Riley, Terry, illus. (J). lib. bdg. 37.13 (978-1-4042-1988-5(9), 574bee2a-b4ca-4b2f-afca-bd7195505561); (gr. 5-5). 2007. (Graphic Natural Disasters Ser.). (ENG.). 48p. 2006. Set lib. bdg. 222.78 (978-1-4042-1064-6(4), 0ef669d1-4605-4cba-b64b-bb1aa108d210) Rosen Publishing Group, Inc., The.

Greve, Tom. Plate Tectonics & Disasters. 2012. (Let's Explore Science Ser.). (ENG.). 48p. (gr. 4-6). pap. 10.95 (978-1-61810-255-3(9), 9781618102553) Rourke Educational Media.

Griffey, Harriet. Earthquakes & Other Natural Disasters. 2010. (DK Readers Level 4 Ser.). (ENG.). 48p. (J). (gr. 2-4). 16.19 (978-0-7566-5933-2(7)) Dorling Kindersley Publishing, Inc.

Gullo, Arthur. Tsunamis. 2015. (J). lib. bdg. (978-1-62713-515-3(4)) Cavendish Square Publishing LLC.

Hackney Blackwell, Amy & Manar, Elizabeth P. U-X-L Encyclopedia of Weather & Natural Disasters. 2016. (Illus.). (J). (978-1-4103-3292-9(6)); (978-1-4103-3291-2(8)) Cengage Gale. (Blackbirch Pr., Inc.).

Hamen, Susan E. The 12 Worst Earthquakes of All Time. 2019. (All-Time Worst Disasters Ser.). (ENG., Illus.). 32p. (J). (gr. 3-6). 14.25 (978-1-63235-599-7(X), 13916); 32.80 (978-1-63235-534-8(5), 13908) Bookstaves, LLC. (12-Story Library).

—The 12 Worst Hurricanes of All Time. 2019. (All-Time Worst Disasters Ser.). (ENG., Illus.). 32p. (J). (gr. 3-6). 14.25 (978-1-63235-603-1(1), 13920); 32.80 (978-1-63235-538-6(8), 13912) Bookstaves, LLC. (12-Story Library).

Hamilton, John. Droughts, 1 vol. 2006. (Nature's Fury Ser.). (ENG., Illus.). 32p. (gr. 3-8). 27.07 (978-1-59679-329-3(5), Abdo & Daughters) ABDO Publishing Co.

—Nature's Fury, Set. 2006. (Nature's Fury Set 2 Ser.). (gr. 3-8). lib. bdg. 162.42 (978-1-59679-327-9(9), Abdo & Daughters) ABDO Publishing Co.

—Tsunamis, 1 vol. 2006. (Nature's Fury Ser.). (ENG., Illus.). 32p. (gr. 4-8). 27.07 (978-1-59679-333-0(3), Abdo & Daughters) ABDO Publishing Co.

Harmon, Daniel E. Tsunamis, 1 vol. 2018. (Nature's Mysteries Ser.). (ENG.). 32p. (gr. 2-3). pap. 13.90 (978-1-5081-0653-1(3), fb4f2b3c-a265-4ef0-8a5d-deea541bb396, Britannica Educational Publishing) Rosen Publishing Group, Inc., The.

Heitzmann, Connie & Koch, Janie. Gulf Coast Memory Scrapbook: A Pictorial Journey of Hope & Healing. 2007. (Illus.). 32p. (J). 16.95 (978-1-883651-30-5(1)) Winters Publishing.

Henry, Claire. The World's Deadliest Man-Made Disasters, 1 vol., 1. 2014. (World's Deadliest Ser.). (ENG.). 32p. (J). (gr. 4-5). pap. 11.00 (978-1-4777-6141-0(1), 1da78edf-9988-4af8-982f-98dbbd80084a, PowerKids Pr.) Rosen Publishing Group, Inc., The.

—The World's Deadliest Natural Disasters, 1 vol., 1. 2014. (World's Deadliest Ser.). (ENG.). 32p. (J). (gr. 4-5). lib. bdg. 28.93 (978-1-4777-6142-7(X), e840ca19-aec2-4215-8917-61a323fc7141, PowerKids Pr.) Rosen Publishing Group, Inc., The.

Higgins, Nadia. Natural Disasters Through Infographics. Sciuto, Alex, illus. 2013. (Super Science Infographics Ser.). (ENG.). 32p. (J). (gr. 3-5). pap. 8.99 (978-1-4677-1593-5(X), 8e5fbd34-cdcd-4003-a245-300d3df47c71); lib. bdg. 26.65 (978-1-4677-1287-3(6), f18f01f3-003e-463b-8726-63570dcde1b2, Lerner Pubns.) Lerner Publishing Group.

Hofer, Charles. Washed Away by Floods, 1 vol. 2017. (Natural Disasters: How People Survive Ser.). (ENG.). 32p. (J). (gr. 4-5). 27.93 (978-1-5383-2569-8(1), 43c66e57-bc9a-4563-b3c8-d5dc0a19ac49, PowerKids Pr.) Rosen Publishing Group, Inc., The.

Hoffman, Mary Ann. Hurricane Katrina. 2009. (Nature in the News Ser.). 32p. (gr. 3-4). 42.50 (978-1-61514-821-9(3), PowerKids Pr.) Rosen Publishing Group, Inc., The.

Hollingsworth, Tamara. Unforgettable Natural Disasters, 1 vol. 2nd rev. ed. 2013. (TIME for KIDS(r): Informational Text Ser.). (ENG.). 64p. (gr. 4-8). pap. 14.99 (978-1-4333-4944-7(2)); (Illus.). (J). lib. bdg. 31.96 (978-1-4333-7443-2(9)) Teacher Created Materials, Inc.

Honders, Christine. Chasing Extreme Weather, 1 vol. 2018. (Spotlight on Weather & Natural Disasters Ser.). (ENG.). 24p. (gr. 4-6). 27.93 (978-1-5081-6876-8(8), 096b4c8a-990e-4504-9cd3-edb0ab25b6ce, PowerKids Pr.) Rosen Publishing Group, Inc., The.

Immell, Myra, ed. Japan's 2011 Natural Disaster & Nuclear Meltdown, 1 vol. 2014. (Perspectives on Modern World History Ser.). (ENG., Illus.). 216p. (gr. 10-12). lib. bdg. 49.43 (978-0-7377-6973-9(4), 7d6f1913-f671-4a0f-a996-00b345ebf852, Greenhaven Publishing) Greenhaven Publishing LLC.

Ingram, Scott. Tsunami! 2018. (X-Treme Disasters That Changed America Ser.). (ENG.). 32p. (J). (gr. 2-7). 7.99 (978-1-64280-095-1(3)) Bearport Publishing Co., Inc.

Isaacs, April. Tornadoes, Hurricanes, & Tsunamis: A Practical Survival Guide. (Library of Emergency Preparedness Ser.). 64p. (gr. 6-6). 2009. 58.50 (978-1-60853-598-9(3), Rosen Reference) 2006. (ENG., Illus.). (YA). 37.13 (978-1-4042-0533-8(0), 50071294-9b86-46a3-914c-08e151042a0f) Rosen Publishing Group, Inc., The.

Jacobs, Elaina & Benchmark Education Co. Staff. The Dust Bowl. 2014. (Text Connections Ser.). (J). (gr. 6). (978-1-4900-1527-9(2)) Benchmark Education Co.

Jeffrey, Gary. Tsunamis & Floods. 2009. (Graphic Natural Disasters Ser.). (ENG.). 48p. (YA). (gr. 5-5). 58.50 (978-1-61513-005-4(5), Rosen Reference) Rosen Publishing Group, Inc., The.

Jennings, Terry J. Earthquakes & Tsunamis. 2009. (Amazing Planet Earth Ser.). 32p. (gr. 4-7). 31.35 (978-1-59920-372-0(3)) Black Rabbit Bks.

Jordan, Shirley. America's Greatest Natural Disaster. 2003. (Cover-to-Cover Informational Ser.). (Illus.). 72p. (J). (gr. 4-7). lib. bdg. 17.95 (978-0-7569-1184-3(2)) Perfection Learning Corp.

—America's Greatest Natural Disasters. 2003. (Cover-To-Cover Books). (Illus.). 72p. pap. 9.00 (978-0-7891-5916-8(3)) Perfection Learning Corp.

Karwoski, Gail Langer. Tsunami: The True Story of an April Fools' Day Disaster. MacDonald, John, illus. 2006. (ENG.). 64p. (J). (gr. 5-12). lib. bdg. 17.95 (978-1-58196-044-0(1), Darby Creek) Lerner Publishing Group.

Katirgis, Jane & Ingber Drohan, Michele. Scary Tsunamis, 1 vol. 2015. (Earth's Natural Disasters Ser.). (ENG.). 32p. (gr. 3-4). pap. 11.52 (978-0-7660-6805-6(6), f1e5b7a7-2f3b-4fa7-9e51-c2c367f4639c); (Illus.). 26.93 (978-0-7660-6807-0(2), 9882d306-2e5a-44df-9d45-1d2f22b427cc) Enslow Publishing, LLC.

Kenah, Katharine. Destruction Earth. 2004. (Extreme Readers Level 2 - Emerging Reader Ser.). (ENG., Illus.). 32p. (gr. k-3). 16.19 (978-0-7696-3185-1(1)) School Specialty, Incorporated.

Kopp, Megan. Avalanches. 2015. (Illus.). 32p. (J). (978-1-5105-0074-7(X)) SmartBook Media, Inc.

—Avalanches. 2014. (J). (978-1-4896-3264-7(6)) Weigl Pubs., Inc.

—Tsunamis. 2016. (Illus.). 32p. (J). (978-1-5105-2079-0(1)) SmartBook Media, Inc.

La Bella, Laura. Not Enough to Drink: Pollution, Drought, & Tainted Water Supplies, 1 vol. 2009. (Extreme Environmental Threats Ser.). (ENG.). 64p. (gr. 6-6). (YA). lib. bdg. 37.13 (978-1-4358-5020-0(3), cf0dacbb-bb36-4473-8051-c316c07cd725); (Illus.). (J). pap. 13.95 (978-1-4358-5376-8(8), 3351956c-73e1-4fab-83f5-891c2435bd86) Rosen Publishing Group, Inc., The.

Lerner, K. Lee, et al. U-X-L Doomed: The Science Behind Disasters. 2015. (Illus.). (J). (978-1-4103-1777-3(3)) Cengage Gale.

Levete, Sarah. Destroying the Oceans. 2010. (Protecting Our Planet Ser.). (ENG., Illus.). 32p. (J). (gr. 3-6). (978-0-7787-5211-0(9)); pap. (978-0-7787-5228-8(3)) Crabtree Publishing Co.

Levy, Janey. World's Worst Tsunamis. (Deadly Disasters Ser.). 24p. (gr. 2-3). 2009. 42.50 (978-1-61512-142-7(0), PowerKids Pr.) 2008. (ENG.). pap. 9.40 (978-1-4042-4538-9(3), 97f9372b-b1ca-46a1-8333-f2a0130d80bc, Rosen Classroom) 2008. (ENG., Illus.). (J). lib. bdg. 26.27 (978-1-4042-4514-3(6), 34c588bb-3824-45cd-bfae-079b8cf4caa6, PowerKids Pr.) Rosen Publishing Group, Inc., The.

Lewis, Mark L. Storm Rescues. 2019. (Rescues in Focus Ser.). (ENG., Illus.). 32p. (J). (gr. 2-3). pap. 9.95 (978-1-64185-843-4(5), 1641858435); lib. bdg. 31.35 (978-1-64185-774-1(9), 1641857749) North Star Editions. (Focus Readers).

Life Nature's Fury. 2008. (Time Inc. Home Entertainment Library-Bound Titles Ser.). (ENG.). 144p. (gr. 5-12). lib. bdg. 39.93 (978-0-7613-4051-5(3), Twenty-First Century Bks.) Lerner Publishing Group.

Linde, Barbara M. Ecological Disasters: Set Of 6. 2011. (Navigators Ser.). (J). pap. 50.00 net. (978-1-4108-5091-1(9)) Benchmark Education Co.

—Ecological Disasters: Text Pairs. 2008. (Bridges/Navigators Ser.). (J). (gr. 6). 81.00 (978-1-4108-8433-6(3)) Benchmark Education Co.

Loeschnig, L. V. Experimentos Sencillos de Quimica. (Juego de la Ciencia Ser.). (SPA.). 124p. (gr. 5-8). (978-84-95456-49-6(4), 87802) Ediciones Oniro S.A.

Malaspina, Ann. Tsunamis. (In the News Ser.). 64p. (gr. 6-6). 2009. 58.50 (978-1-61513-491-5(3)) 2007. (ENG., Illus.). (YA). lib. bdg. 37.13 (978-1-4042-0978-7(6), 0fd850f9-1111-4870-85e1-6b959e09c631) Rosen Publishing Group, Inc., The.

Marrin, Albert. Years of Dust: The Story of the Dust Bowl. 2012. 144p. (J). (gr. 5). mass mkt. 10.99 (978-0-14-242579-4(6), Puffin Books) Penguin Young Readers Group.

Maurer, Tracy Nelson. The World's Worst Avalanches. 2019. (World's Worst Natural Disasters Ser.). (ENG., Illus.). 32p. (J). (gr. 3-9). lib. bdg. 27.32 (978-1-5435-5481-6(4), 139349, Capstone Pr.) Capstone.

—The World's Worst Tsunamis. 2019. (World's Worst Natural Disasters Ser.). (ENG., Illus.). 32p. (J). (gr. 3-9). lib. bdg. 27.32 (978-1-5435-5478-6(4), 139346, Capstone Pr.) Capstone.

—The World's Worst Volcanic Eruptions. 2019. (World's Worst Natural Disasters Ser.). (ENG., Illus.). 32p. (J). (gr. 3-9). lib. bdg. 27.32 (978-1-5435-5480-9(6), 139348, Capstone Pr.) Capstone.

—The World's Worst Wildfires. 2019. (World's Worst Natural Disasters Ser.). (ENG., Illus.). 32p. (J). (gr. 3-9). lib. bdg. 27.32 (978-1-5435-5479-3(2), 139347, Capstone Pr.) Capstone.

McDowell, Pamela. Landslides. 2015. (J). (978-1-5105-0082-2(0)) SmartBook Media, Inc.

—Landslides. 2014. (J). (978-1-4896-3260-9(3)) Weigl Pubs., Inc.

McFadzean, Lesley. Earth in Peril, 1 vol. 2012. (Discovery Education: the Environment Ser.). (ENG., Illus.). 32p. (J). (gr. 4-5). pap. 11.00 (978-1-4488-7977-9(9), 03f6ceed-42b5-4ca8-90df-37d37d11ee80); lib. bdg. 28.93 (978-1-4488-7889-5(6), 38f5a397-f743-4aa4-b5d0-1f2411594b64) Rosen Publishing Group, Inc., The. (PowerKids Pr.).

McNab, Chris. World's Worst Historical Disasters. 2009. (World's Worst: from Innovation to Disaster Ser.). 80p. (gr. 8-8). 61.20 (978-1-60854-859-0(7)) Rosen Publishing Group, Inc., The.

Meinking, Mary. Natural Disasters. 2018. (Weather Watch Ser.). (ENG., Illus.). 24p. (J). (gr. 1-1). pap. 8.95 (978-1-63517-842-5(8), 1635178428) North Star Editions.

—Natural Disasters. 2018. (Weather Watch Ser.). (ENG., Illus.). 24p. (J). (gr. k-3). lib. bdg. 31.36 (978-1-5321-6054-7(2), 28740, Pop! Cody Koala) Pop!

Meister, Cari. Tsunamis. 2015. (Illus.). 24p. (J). lib. bdg. (978-1-62031-226-1(3)) Jump! Inc.

Miller, Connie Colwell. The Deadliest Places on Earth. 2010. (World's Deadliest Ser.). (ENG.). 32p. (J). (gr. 3-9). lib. bdg. 27.32 (978-1-4296-3932-3(6), 102542, Capstone Pr.) Capstone.

Mitchell Lane Publishers Inc. Staff. Natural Disasters, 15 vols., Set. 2007. (Natural Disasters Ser.). (J). (gr. 1-5). lib. bdg. 385.50 (978-1-58415-572-0(8)) Mitchell Lane Pubs.

Morey, Allan. Supervolcano Eruption. 2019. (It's the End of the World! Ser.). (ENG., Illus.). 24p. (J). (gr. 3-7). lib. bdg. 26.95 (978-1-64487-085-3(1), Torque Bks.) Bellwether Media.

Morris, Janel, ed. Disaster Planning, 1 vol. 2008. (At Issue Ser.). (ENG., Illus.). 96p. (gr. 10-12). 41.03 (978-0-7377-4090-5(6), 15763d35-684f-4942-91c3-bf027f8a790e); pap. 28.80 (978-0-7377-4091-2(4), 4645bde3-6d74-4567-8a12-9620a09d5a8d) Greenhaven Publishing LLC. (Greenhaven Publishing).

National Geographic Learning. Reading Expeditions (Social Studies: Voices from America's Past): Dust Bowl Days. 2007. (ENG., Illus.). 40p. (J). pap. 21.95 (978-0-7922-4557-5(1)) CENGAGE Learning.

Natural Disasters. (Eyes on Adventure Ser.). 32p. (J). (gr. 1). pap. (978-1-882210-64-0(6)) Action Publishing, Inc.

Natural Disasters, 3 cass.; set. 2004. (NOVA Ser.). (gr. 7-18). 49.95 incl. VHS (978-1-57807-041-1(4), WG165) WGBH Boston Video.

Natural Disasters, 11 bks., Set. Incl. Ancient Mystery of Easter Island. Torres, John A. (gr. 1-4). 2006. lib. bdg. 25.70 (978-1-58415-495-2(0)); Bermuda Triangle. Whiting, Jim. (gr. 1-4). 2006. lib. bdg. 25.70 (978-1-58415-497-6(7)); Bubonic Plague. Whiting, Jim. (gr. 1-4). 2006. lib. bdg. 25.70 (978-1-58415-494-5(2)); Earthquake in Loma Prieta, California 1989. Harkins, William & Harkins, Susan. (gr. 1-4). 2005. lib. bdg. 25.70 (978-1-58415-417-4(9)); Fury of Hurricane Andrew 1992. Gibson, Karen Bush. (gr. 1-4). 2005. lib. bdg. 25.70 (978-1-58415-416-7(0)); Hurricane Katrina 2005. Torres, John. (gr. 1-4). 2006. lib. bdg. 25.70 (978-1-58415-498-3(5)); Lost Continent of Atlantis. Roberts, Russell. (gr. 3-7). 2006. lib. bdg. 25.70 (978-1-58415-496-9(9)); Mt. Vesuvius & the Destruction of Pompei, A. D. 79. Roberts, Russell. (gr. 1-4). 2005. lib. bdg. 25.70 (978-1-58415-419-8(5)); Mudslide in la Conchita, California 2005. Gibson, Karen Bush. (gr. 1-4). 2005. lib. bdg. 25.70 (978-1-58415-418-1(7)); Tsunami Disaster in Indonesia 2004. Torres, John Albert. (gr. 1-4). 2005. lib. bdg. 25.70 (978-1-58415-415-0(2)); Where Did All the Dinosaurs Go? Roberts, Russell. (gr. 1-4). 2005. lib. bdg. 25.70 (978-1-58415-420-4(9)); (Illus.). 32p. (J). 2007. 186.45 (978-1-58415-499-0(3)) Mitchell Lane Pubs.

Nelson, John. Collision Course: Asteroids & Earth, 1 vol. 2007. (Jr. Graphic Environmental Dangers Ser.). (ENG., Illus.). 24p. (gr. 4-4). pap. 10.60 (978-1-4042-4595-2(2), 5b59406e-0385-4b29-b3b2-ad5659302acc, PowerKids Pr.) Rosen Publishing Group, Inc., The.

Oliver, Clare. Natural Disasters: Atlas in the Round. 2005. (Illus.). 32p. (J). (gr. k-4). 16.00 (978-0-7567-9190-2(1)) DIANE Publishing Co.

Orme, David. Great Disasters. 2009. (Fact to Fiction Ser.). (Illus.). 36p. (J). pap. 6.95 (978-0-7891-7903-6(2)) Perfection Learning Corp.

Orme, David & Orme, David. Great Disasters. 2008. (ENG., Illus.). 36p. pap. (978-1-84167-694-4(2)) Ransom Publishing Ltd.

Orr, Tamra B. Tsunamis. 2012. (21st Century Skills Library: Real World Math Ser.). (ENG.). 32p. (gr. 4-8). (J). pap. 14.21 (978-1-61080-410-3(4), 201342); (Illus.). lib. bdg. 32.07 (978-1-61080-327-4(2), 201306) Cherry Lake Publishing.

Osborne, Mary Pope & Boyce, Natalie Pope. Tsunamis & Other Natural Disasters: A Nonfiction Companion to Magic Tree House #28: High Tide in Hawaii. Murdocca, Sal, illus. 2007. (Magic Tree House (R) Fact Tracker Ser.: 15). 128p. (J). (gr. 2-5). 6.99 (978-0-375-83221-5(1), Random Hse. Bks. for Young Readers) Random Hse. Children's Bks.

Otfinoski, Steven. Major Disasters in U.S. History. 2005. (Illus.). 48p. (J). (978-0-669-51416-2(0)) Great Source Education Group, Inc.

Owings, Lisa. Craco: The Medieval Ghost Town. 2017. (Abandoned Places Ser.). (ENG., Illus.). 24p. (J). (gr. 3-7). lib. bdg. 26.95 (978-1-62617-695-9(7), Torque Bks.) Bellwether Media.

—What Protects Us During Natural Disasters? 2015. (Engineering Keeps Us Safe Ser.). (ENG., Illus.). 32p. (J). (gr. 4-6). E-Book 39.99 (978-1-4677-8649-2(7), Lerner Pubns.) Lerner Publishing Group.

Peacock, L. A. The Truth (and Myths) about Disasters. Davis, Jon, illus. 2014. 96p. (J). pap. (978-0-545-70565-3(7)) Scholastic, Inc.

Perdew, Laura. The 12 Worst Floods of All Time. 2019. (All-Time Worst Disasters Ser.). (ENG., Illus.). 32p. (J). (gr. 3-6). 32.80 (978-1-63235-536-2(1), 13910, 12-Story Library) Bookstaves, LLC.

Perritano, John. The Ultimate Book of Dangerous Weather. 2019. (Ultimate Danger Ser.). (Illus.). 80p. (J). (gr. 12). lib. bdg. 34.60 (978-1-4222-4230-8(7)) Mason Crest.

Pettiford, Rebecca. Droughts. 2020. (Natural Disasters Ser.). (ENG.). 24p. (J). (gr. k-3). lib. bdg. 26.95 *(978-1-64487-150-8(5)*, Blastoff! Readers) Bellwether Media.

—Floods. 2020. (Natural Disasters Ser.). (ENG.). 24p. (J). (gr. k-3). lib. bdg. 26.95 *(978-1-64487-151-5(3)*, Blastoff! Readers) Bellwether Media.

—Ice Storms. 2020. (Natural Disasters Ser.). (ENG.). 24p. (J). (gr. k-3). lib. bdg. 26.95 *(978-1-64487-152-2(1)*, Blastoff! Readers) Bellwether Media.

Poole, Hilary W. The Ultimate Book of Dangerous Places. 2019. (Illus.). 80p. (J). *(978-1-4222-4224-7(2))* Mason Crest.

Rathburn, Betsy. Earthquakes. 2019. (Natural Disasters Ser.). (ENG., Illus.). 24p. (J). (gr. k-3). pap. 7.99 *(978-1-61891-746-1(3)*, 12315, Blastoff! Readers) Bellwether Media.

—Tornadoes. 2019. (Natural Disasters Ser.). (ENG., Illus.). 24p. (J). (gr. k-3). pap. 7.99 *(978-1-61891-748-5(X)*, 12317, Blastoff! Readers) Bellwether Media.

—Tsunamis. 2019. (Natural Disasters Ser.). (ENG., Illus.). 24p. (J). (gr. k-3). pap. 7.99 *(978-1-61891-749-2(8)*, 12318, Blastoff! Readers) Bellwether Media.

—Volcanoes. 2019. (Natural Disasters Ser.). (ENG., Illus.). 24p. (J). (gr. k-3). pap. 7.99 *(978-1-61891-750-8(1)*, 12319, Blastoff! Readers) Bellwether Media.

Rea, Amy C. Perspectives on the Dust Bowl. 2018. (Perspectives on US History Ser.). (ENG., Illus.). 32p. (J). (gr. 3-6). 32.80 *(978-1-63235-399-3(7)*, 13721, 12-Story Library) Bookstaves, LLC.

Reilly, Kathleen M. Natural Disasters: Investigate Earth's Most Destructive Forces with 25 Projects. Casteel, Tom, illus. 2012. (Build It Yourself Ser.). 128p. (J). (gr. 3-7). pap. 15.95 *(978-1-61930-146-7(6)*, 13e35dd8-8e9e-4df9-9b2a-257bfb58d421); (ENG.). 21.95 *(978-1-61930-147-4(4)*, 3cdf9456-5426-4711-b37d-f489395cb17f) Nomad Pr.

The Remarkable World, 16 bks., Set. Incl. Birds of Prey. Penny, Malcolm. (Illus.). 1996. lib. bdg. 18.98 *(978-1-56847-414-4(8))*; Fossils & Bones. Pirotta, Saviour. (Illus.). 1997. lib. bdg. 18.98 *(978-0-8172-4542-9(1))*; Great Journeys. Chrisp, Peter. 1996. lib. bdg. 18.98 *(978-0-8172-4537-5(5))*; Hidden Past. Hicks, Peter. (Illus.). 1997. lib. bdg. 18.98 *(978-0-8172-4541-2(3))*; Land Predators. Stidworthy, John. (Illus.). 1996. lib. bdg. 18.98 *(978-1-56847-416-8(4))*; Mapping the Unknown. Chrisp, Peter. (Illus.). 1996. lib. bdg. 18.98 *(978-0-8172-4535-1(9))*; Monsters of the Deep. Pirotta, Saviour. (Illus.). 1995. lib. bdg. 18.98 *(978-1-56847-367-3(2))*; Night Creatures. Penny, Malcolm. (Illus.). 1996. lib. bdg. 18.98 *(978-1-56847-371-0(0))*; Pirates & Treasure. Pirotta, Saviour. (Illus.). 1997. lib. bdg. 18.98 *(978-0-8172-4820-8(X))*; Search for Riches. Langley, Andrew. (Illus.). 1997. lib. bdg. 18.98 *(978-0-8172-4544-3(8))*; Volcano, Earthquake & Hurricane. Arnold, Nick. (Illus.). 1997. lib. bdg. 18.98 *(978-0-8172-4540-5(5))*; Voyages of Exploration. Arnold, Nick. (Illus.). 1995. lib. bdg. 18.98 *(978-1-56847-368-0(0))*; Whalers. Chrisp, Peter. (Illus.). 1995. lib. bdg. 18.98 *(978-1-56847-421-2(0))*; When Dinosaurs Ruled the Earth. Theodorou, Rod. (Illus.). 1996. lib. bdg. 18.98 *(978-1-56847-415-1(6))*; Wild, Wild West. Pirotta, Saviour. (Illus.). 1997. lib. bdg. 18.98 *(978-0-8172-4536-8(7))*; World's Wild Places. Morgan, Sally. (Illus.). 1997. lib. bdg. 18.98 *(978-0-8172-4538-2(3))*; 48p. (J). (gr. 4-7). (Illus.). Set lib. bdg. 303.68 *(978-0-8172-5397-4(1))* Heinemann-Raintree.

Remson, Billie. Mississippi Autumn on Bluebird Hill: A True Story about our Little Farm in the Hills of Southern Mississippi. 2006. (J). per. 14.95 *(978-1-59571-121-2(X))* Word Association Pubs.

—A Mississippi Autumn on Bluebird Hill: A true story about our little farm in the hills of Southern Mississippi. 2006. (J). 21.95 *(978-1-59571-158-8(9))* Word Association Pubs.

Rissman, Rebecca. Swept Away: The Story of the 2011 Japanese Tsunami. 2017. (Tangled History Ser.). (ENG., Illus.). 112p. (J). (gr. 3-9). lib. bdg. 32.65 *(978-1-5157-3605-9(9)*, 133595, Capstone Pr.) Capstone.

Rivera, Andrea. Droughts. 2017. (Natural Disasters (Launch!) Ser.). (ENG., Illus.). 24p. (J). (gr. -1-2). lib. bdg. 31.36 *(978-1-5321-2036-7(2)*, 25322, Abdo Zoom-Launch) ABDO Publishing Co.

—Tsunamis. 2017. (Natural Disasters (Launch!) Ser.). (ENG., Illus.). 24p. (J). (gr. -1-2). lib. bdg. 31.36 *(978-1-5321-2040-4(0)*, 25330, Abdo Zoom-Launch) ABDO Publishing Co.

Roza, Greg. The Indian Ocean Tsunami. (Nature in the News Ser.). 32p. (gr. 3-4). 2009. 42.50 *(978-1-61514-822-6(1)*, PowerKids Pr.) 2006. (ENG., Illus.). (YA). lib. bdg. 27.60 *(978-1-4042-3538-0(8)*, 0f19653b-3323-4992-a27b-b3e635171d57) Rosen Publishing Group, Inc., The.

Sanna, Ellyn. Nature's Wrath: Surviving Natural Disasters. (Survivors Ser.). 2010. 128p. (YA). (gr. 7-12). 24.95 *(978-1-4222-0454-2(5))* 2009. (J). pap. 24.95 *(978-1-4222-1467-1(2))* Mason Crest.

Searl, Duncan. Trapped! 2005. (Illus.). 48p. (J). *(978-0-669-51413-1(6))* Great Source Education Group, Inc.

Sepahban, Lois. Floods. 2013. (Earth in Action Ser.). (ENG., Illus.). 48p. (J). (gr. 4-8). pap. 18.50 *(978-1-62403-003-1(3)*, 8678) ABDO Publishing Co.

Shea, Therese M. Freaky Weather Stories, 1 vol. 2015. (Freaky True Science Ser.). (ENG.). 32p. (J). (gr. 4-5). pap. 11.50 *(978-1-4824-2968-8(3)*, b3c64bfa-3c3a-417a-9da9-882b0b3dd071) Stevens, Gareth Publishing LLLP.

—Rocked by Earthquakes, 1 vol. 2017. (Natural Disasters: How People Survive Ser.). (ENG.). 32p. (J). (gr. 4-5). 27.93 *(978-1-5383-2563-6(2)*, e15dea7a-b9dd-4b64-8ce8-8bed472221c0, PowerKids Pr.) Rosen Publishing Group, Inc., The.

Shoals, James. Extreme Weather. 2019. (Illus.). 48p. (J). *(978-1-4222-4355-8(9))* Mason Crest.

—What Is Climate Change? 2019. (Climate Change: Problems & Progress Ser.). (Illus.). 48p. (J). (gr. 10). 30.60 *(978-1-4222-4363-3(X))* Mason Crest.

Shofner, Melissa Raé. Weather & Natural Disasters, 1 vol. 2016. (Spotlight on Earth Science Ser.). (ENG.). 24p. (J). (gr. 4-6). pap. 11.00 *(978-1-4994-2547-5(3)*, 26838812-6f83-43bd-b67e-37beffbea773, PowerKids Pr.) Rosen Publishing Group, Inc., The.

Shone, Rob. Avalanches & Landslides. 2009. (Graphic Natural Disasters Ser.). (ENG.). 48p. (YA). (gr. 5-5). 58.50 *(978-1-61512-994-2(4)*, Rosen Reference) Rosen Publishing Group, Inc., The.

Shulman, Mark. Super Storms That Rocked the World: Hurricanes, Tsunamis, & Other Disasters. 2007. (Illus.). 40p. (J). *(978-0-696-23702-7(4))* Meredith Bks.

Sommers, Michael. Tsunami: True Stories of Survival. 2009. (Survivor Stories Ser.). 48p. (gr. 5-5). 53.00 *(978-1-60853-258-2(5)*, Rosen Reference) Rosen Publishing Group, Inc., The.

Spilsbury, Louise. The Science of Avalanches, 1 vol. 2013. (Nature's Wrath: the Science Behind Natural Disasters Ser.). (ENG., Illus.). 48p. (J). (gr. 5-5). 34.60 *(978-1-4339-8651-2(5)*, b5fd5e6a-fdc3-44c3-8b06-0bcae1c836d7); pap. 15.05 *(978-1-4339-8652-9(3)*, a0c373f5-3355-47d6-bd0c-e281257d8f72) Stevens, Gareth Publishing LLLP. (Gareth Stevens Learning Library).

—What Are Natural Disasters?, 1 vol., 1. 2013. (Let's Find Out! Earth Science Ser.). (ENG.). 32p. (gr. 2-3). 27.04 *(978-1-62275-271-3(6)*, 3386ba0f-d5e7-4432-8880-18f1705d1263) Rosen Publishing Group, Inc., The.

Spilsbury, Louise & Spilsbury, Richard. Awesome Forces of Nature, 1 vol., Set. 2nd ed. Incl. Shattering Earthquakes. 2nd ed. (ENG., Illus.). 32p. (J). (gr. 3-6). 2010. pap. 8.29 *(978-1-4329-3791-1(X)*, 102926, Heinemann); (Awesome Forces of Nature Ser.). (ENG.). 32p. 2010. pap., pap., pap. 47.94 o.p. *(978-1-4329-3794-2(4)*, 13967, Heinemann) Capstone.

—Top 10 Worst Tsunamis, 1 vol. 2016. (Nature's Ultimate Disasters Ser.). (ENG.). 32p. (J). (gr. 3-4). pap. 11.00 *(978-1-4994-3081-3(7)*, 157898f4-b5a1-47dd-b739-b32722bcb470, PowerKids Pr.) Rosen Publishing Group, Inc., The.

—Top 10 Worst Volcanic Eruptions, 1 vol. 2016. (Nature's Ultimate Disasters Ser.). (ENG.). 32p. (J). (gr. 3-4). pap. 11.00 *(978-1-4994-3085-1(X)*, 923ab1da-2553-4444-95e7-e3c18df31374, PowerKids Pr.) Rosen Publishing Group, Inc., The.

—Tsunami Crushes Coastline, 1 vol. 2017. (Earth under Attack! Ser.). (ENG.). 48p. (J). (gr. 5-5). pap. 15.05 *(978-1-5382-1315-5(X)*, 160b5b69-9ded-4209-97c8-3a2e34ff517d) Stevens, Gareth Publishing LLLP.

—Tsunami Crushes Coastline, 1 vol. 2017. (Earth under Attack! Ser.). (ENG.). 48p. (J). (gr. 5-5). lib. bdg. 33.60 *(978-1-5382-1317-9(6)*, 634f4ac8-563e-4af6-9692-e475412a988a) Stevens, Gareth Publishing LLLP.

—Tsunamis in Action, 1 vol. 2008. (Natural Disasters in Action Ser.). (ENG., Illus.). 48p. (gr. 5-5). pap. 11.75 *(978-1-4358-5136-8(6)*, df4757fa-c63d-4db1-8d5d-086d90a61ee6, Rosen Classroom) Rosen Publishing Group, Inc., The.

Spilsbury, Richard & Spilsbury, Louise. Tsunamis in Action, 1 vol. 2008. (Natural Disasters in Action Ser.). (ENG., Illus.). 48p. (J). (gr. 5-5). lib. bdg. 34.47 *(978-1-4042-1866-6(1)*, 2c743be8-8b58-400d-b393-2a095ccca55d) Rosen Publishing Group, Inc., The.

Stiefel, Chana. Tsunamis. 2009. (True Book(tm), a — Earth Science Ser.). (ENG., Illus.). 48p. (J). (gr. 2-5). 31.00 *(978-0-531-16885-1(9))* Scholastic Library Publishing.

Swanson, Jennifer. Tsunamis. 2013. (Earth in Action Ser.). (ENG., Illus.). 48p. (J). (gr. 4-8). pap. 18.50 *(978-1-62403-006-2(8)*, 8681) ABDO Publishing Co.

Tarshis, Lauren. Five Epic Disasters (I Survived True Stories #1), 1 vol. 2014. (I Survived True Stories Ser.: 1). (ENG.). 176p. (J). (gr. 2-5). 12.99 *(978-0-545-78224-1(4)*, Scholastic Pr.) Scholastic, Inc.

Thoron, Joe. Kaleidoscope Natural Disasters Group 1, 4 bks., Set. Incl. Earthquakes. lib. bdg. 32.64 *(978-0-7614-2102-3(5)*, 5fcaed5c-46f0-4e11-b281-5264ba038905); Hurricanes. lib. bdg. 32.64 *(978-0-7614-2103-0(3)*, c1a07c2f-7950-4d04-8919-73375cdb80e7); Tornadoes. lib. bdg. 32.64 *(978-0-7614-2104-7(1)*, 4e144da4-5aa7-4d0f-b6b3-7f0abdc14d79); Volcanoes. lib. bdg. 32.64 *(978-0-7614-2105-4(X)*, a9afe808-91dd-44d9-a334-77ac9f454931); (Illus.). 48p. (gr. 4-4). 2007. lib. bdg. *(978-0-7614-2101-6(7)*, Cavendish Square) Cavendish Square Publishing LLC.

Tornadoes. 3rd ed. 2018. (J). *(978-0-7166-9940-8(0))* World Bk., Inc.

Torres, John Albert. Disaster in the Indian Ocean, Tsunami 2004. 2005. (Monumental Milestones Ser.). (Illus.). 48p. (YA). (gr. 4-7). lib. bdg. 29.95 *(978-1-58415-344-3(X))* Mitchell Lane Pubs.

—Threat to Haiti. 2008. (On the Verge of Extinction Ser.). (Illus.). 32p. (YA). (gr. 2-5). lib. bdg. 25.70 *(978-1-58415-686-4(4))* Mitchell Lane Pubs.

—Tsunami Disaster in Indonesia 2004. 2005. (Natural Disasters Ser.). (Illus.). 32p. (J). (gr. 1-4). lib. bdg. 25.70 *(978-1-58415-415-0(2))* Mitchell Lane Pubs.

Tracey, Michele. When Can a Flood Happen? 2012. (Level D Ser.). (ENG., Illus.). 16p. (J). (gr. k-2). pap. 7.95 *(978-1-927136-35-5(0)*, 19428) RiverStream Publishing.

Tsunamis & Seiches. 2nd ed. 2009. (Illus.). 47p. (J). *(978-0-7166-9830-2(7))* World Bk., Inc.

Tyler, Madeline. Surviving a Megatsunami, 1 vol. 2018. (Surviving the Impossible Ser.). (ENG.). 32p. (gr. 4-5). pap. 11.50 *(978-1-5382-3506-5(4)*, 1020e8d5-fbbd-4c5b-bdad-5d447acd68ef) Stevens, Gareth Publishing LLLP.

U X L, ed. UXL Man-Made Disasters, 3 vols. 2015. (U-X-L Man-Made Disasters Ser.). (ENG., Illus.). 348.00 *(978-1-4103-1774-2(9)*, UXL) Cengage Gale.

The Ultimate 10: Natural Disasters, 12 vols., Set. Incl. Blizzards & Winter Storms. Stewart, Mark. (YA). lib. bdg. 33.67 *(978-0-8368-9150-8(3)*, 9550c152-1cbb-4db1-a2f5-7dd71c58b1b2); Earthquakes. Prokos, Anna. (YA). lib. bdg. 33.67 *(978-0-8368-9151-5(1)*, 1c2e79e3-1e02-4d2f-8263-2d1f77313ead); Hurricanes. Ryback, Carol. (YA). lib. bdg. 33.67 *(978-0-8368-9152-2(X)*, 55f359f5-6232-4185-9d36-16148de9ddf9); Tornadoes. Prokos, Anna. (YA). lib. bdg. 33.67 *(978-0-8368-9153-9(8)*, 2731cf19-97f4-44c7-a2ef-bd538de9519f); Tsunamis & Floods. Keedle, Jayne. (Illus.). (J). lib. bdg. 33.67 *(978-0-8368-9154-6(6)*, 6088c08a-5690-4c38-a9f5-9850b59f0aed); Volcanoes. Keedle, Jayne. (YA). lib. bdg. 33.67 *(978-0-8368-9155-3(4)*, e7a5c288-8e4c-4f47-b0bd-47d871c49800); (gr. 3-3). (Ultimate 10: Natural Disasters Ser.). (ENG.). 48p. 2008. Set lib. bdg. 202.02 *(978-0-8368-9186-7(4)*, 772414f2-2008-41e2-b042-5a8146a2f3e6) Stevens, Gareth Publishing LLLP.

Vail, Grace. More Freaky Weather Stories, 1 vol. 2019. (Freaky True Science Ser.). (ENG.). 32p. (gr. 4-5). pap. 11.50 *(978-1-5382-4074-8(2)*, 5b669164-55c7-492b-92c6-e77ac1d84f03) Stevens, Gareth Publishing LLLP.

Veigas, Jennifer, ed. Critical Perspectives on Natural Disasters. 2009. (Scientific American Critical Anthologies on Environment & Climate Ser.). 208p. (gr. 9-9). 63.90 *(978-1-60853-067-0(1))* Rosen Publishing Group, Inc., The.

Ventura, Marne. Detecting Tsunamis. 2017. (Detecting Disasters Ser.). (ENG., Illus.). 32p. (J). (gr. 3-5). lib. bdg. 31.35 *(978-1-63517-005-4(2)*, 1635170052, Focus Readers) North Star Editions.

—Tsunamis. 2018. (J). *(978-1-4896-9793-6(4)*, AV2 by Weigl) Weigl Pubs., Inc.

Walker, Niki. Tsunami Alert!, 1 vol. 2005. (Disaster Alert! Ser.). (ENG., Illus.). 32p. (J). (gr. 4-7). pap. *(978-0-7787-1614-3(7))*; lib. bdg. *(978-0-7787-1582-5(5))* Crabtree Publishing Co.

Wallace, Elise. Saving Culture from Disaster (Grade 3) rev. ed. 2018. (Smithsonian: Informational Text Ser.). (ENG., Illus.). 32p. (J). (gr. 3-4). pap. 11.99 *(978-1-4938-6681-6(8))* Teacher Created Materials, Inc.

Wendorff, Anne. Droughts. 2008. (Extreme Weather Ser.). (ENG., Illus.). 24p. (J). (gr. 2-5). lib. bdg. 26.95 *(978-1-60014-184-3(6))* Bellwether Media.

—Tsunamis. 2008. (Extreme Weather Ser.). (ENG., Illus.). 24p. (J). (gr. 2-5). lib. bdg. 26.95 *(978-1-60014-188-1(9))* Bellwether Media.

West, David & Parker, Steve. Natural Disasters, 1 vol. 2011. (ENG., Illus.). 32p. (J). pap. *(978-0-7787-7581-2(X))*; pap. *(978-0-7787-7579-9(8))*; lib. bdg. *(978-0-7787-7576-8(3))* Crabtree Publishing Co.

Westcott, Jim. Natural Disasters. 2017. (Rank It! Ser.). (ENG.). 32p. (J). (gr. 4-6). pap. 9.99 *(978-1-64466-209-0(4)*, 11472); (Illus.). lib. bdg. *(978-1-68072-175-1(5)*, 10534) Black Rabbit Bks. (Bolt).

Whitmore, Andrew. How to Survive Asteroids & Other Disasters. 2007. 96p. (J). *(978-1-4207-0733-5(7))* Sundance/Newbridge Educational Publishing.

Williams-Noren, Carolyn. Catastrophes in the Twenty-First Century. 2019. (Defining Events of the Twenty-First Century Ser.). (ENG.). 80p. (YA). (gr. 6-12). 41.27 *(978-1-68282-601-0(5))* ReferencePoint Pr., Inc.

Wilson, Patrick. Surviving Natural Disasters. Carney, John, ed. 2014. (Extreme Survival in the Military Ser.: 12). 64p. (J). (gr. 7-18). lib. bdg. 23.95 *(978-1-4222-3091-6(0))* Mason Crest.

Winchester, Simon. The Day the World Exploded: The Earthshaking Catastrophe at Krakatoa. Chin, Jason, illus. 2008. 96p. (J). (gr. 5-9). lib. bdg. 23.89 *(978-0-06-123983-0(6))* HarperCollins Pubs.

Wiseman, Blaine. Blizzards. 2015. (J). *(978-1-5105-0076-1(6))* SmartBook Media, Inc.

—Blizzards. 2014. (J). *(978-1-4896-3268-5(9))* Weigl Pubs., Inc.

—Volcanoes. 2014. (J). *(978-1-4896-3276-0(X))* Weigl Pubs., Inc.

Wood, Alix. Disasters on the Map, 1 vol. 2014. (Fun with Map Skills Ser.). (ENG., Illus.). 32p. (J). (gr. 4-4). lib. bdg. 27.93 *(978-1-4777-6976-8(5)*, 83fbca92-d2f6-48fe-b323-ba803fef9377, PowerKids Pr.) Rosen Publishing Group, Inc., The.

Woods, Michael. Mudflows & Landslides. 2009. pap. 8.95 *(978-0-8225-6861-2(6))* Lerner Publishing Group.

Woods, Michael & Woods, Mary B. Droughts. 2007. (Disasters up Close Ser.). (Illus.). 64p. (J). (gr. 3-7). lib. bdg. 27.93 *(978-0-8225-6576-5(5)*, Lerner Pubns.) Lerner Publishing Group.

—Tsunamis. 2006. (Disasters up Close Ser.). (Illus.). 64p. (J). (gr. 3-7). lib. bdg. 27.93 *(978-0-8225-6054-8(2)*, Lerner Pubns.) Lerner Publishing Group.

Woolf, Alex. The Science of Natural Disasters: the Devastating Truth about Volcanoes, Earthquakes, & Tsunamis (the Science of the Earth) (Library Edition) Rowland, Andy, illus. 2018. (Science Of... Ser.). (ENG.). 32p. (J). (gr. 3-7). lib. bdg. 29.00 *(978-0-531-22766-4(9)*, Watts, Franklin) Scholastic Library Publishing.

World Book, Inc. Staff, contrib. by. Droughts. 2007. (J). *(978-0-7166-9803-6(X))* World Bk., Inc.

—Heat Waves. (J). 2007. *(978-0-7166-9807-4(2))* 2nd ed. 2009. (Illus.). 47p. *(978-0-7166-9823-4(4))* 3rd ed. 2018. *(978-0-7166-9934-7(6))* World Bk., Inc.

—Hurricanes, Typhoons, & Other Tropical Cyclones. 3rd ed. 2018. (J). *(978-0-7166-9935-4(4))* World Bk., Inc.

—Ice Storms. (J). 2007. *(978-0-7166-9809-8(9))* 2nd ed. 2009. (Illus.). 47p. *(978-0-7166-9825-8(0))* 3rd ed. 2018. *(978-0-7166-9936-1(2))* World Bk., Inc.

—Landslides, Mudslides, & Avalanches. 3rd ed. 2018. (J). *(978-0-7166-9937-8(0))* World Bk., Inc.

—Tornadoes. 2nd ed. 2009. (Illus.). 47p. (J). *(978-0-7166-9829-6(3))* World Bk., Inc.

—Tsunamis & Seiches. 2007. (Illus.). 47p. (J). *(978-0-7166-9814-2(5))* World Bk., Inc.

Zuehlke, Jeffrey. Landslides. 2009. pap. 40.95 *(978-0-7613-4769-9(0))* Lerner Publishing Group.

Zullo, Allan. Heroes of Hurricane Katrina (10 True Tales) 2015. (10 True Tales Ser.). (ENG.). 192p. (YA). (gr. 3-7). pap. 5.99 *(978-0-545-83123-9(7))* Scholastic, Inc.

NATURAL DISASTERS—FICTION

Bauer, Marion Dane. Mama for Owen. Butler, John, illus. 2007. (ENG.). 32p. (J). (gr. -1-3). 19.99 *(978-0-689-85787-4(X)*, Simon & Schuster Bks. For Young Readers) Simon & Schuster Bks. For Young Readers.

Bywaters, Mayer. Tempest. (J). 16.95 *(978-1-58717-206-9(2)*, SeaStar Bks.) Chronicle Bks. LLC.

Chim, Wai. Shaozhen: Through My Eyes - Natural Disaster Zones. White, Lyn, ed. 2018. (Through My Eyes Ser.). (ENG.). 208p. (J). (gr. 6-9). pap. 15.99 *(978-1-76011-379-7(4))* Allen & Unwin AUS. Dist: Independent Pubs. Group.

Dashner, James. The Fever Code (Maze Runner, Book Five; Prequel) 2016. (Maze Runner Ser.: 5). (ENG.). 384p. (YA). (gr. 7). 18.99 *(978-0-553-51309-7(5)*, Delacorte Pr.) Random Hse. Children's Bks.

—The Kill Order. 2014. (Maze Runner Ser.: 0). lib. bdg. 20.85 *(978-0-606-35572-8(3))* Turtleback.

—The Kill Order (Maze Runner, Book Four; Origin) Book Four; Origin. 2014. (Maze Runner Ser.: 4). (ENG.). 384p. (YA). (gr. 7). pap. 10.99 *(978-0-385-74289-4(4)*, Delacorte Pr.) Random Hse. Children's Bks.

—The Maze Runner: Virus Letal. 2013. 362p. (YA). pap. 15.99 *(978-987-612-565-9(6))* V&R Editoras.

de la Peña, Matt. The Living. 2015. (Living Ser.). (ENG.). 336p. (YA). (gr. 9). pap. 10.99 *(978-0-385-74121-7(9)*, Ember) Random Hse. Children's Bks.

Diggle, David Mark. Annie: A Small Ant with Some Big Questions. Preuss, Sarah Louise, illus. 2011. 24p. (J). pap. *(978-0-9871658-2-4(8))* Diggle de Doo Productions Pty, Ltd.

Donald, Margaret. Eli the Elephant: A Tsunami Story. Grant, Sophia & Noble, Stuart, illus. 2007. (ENG.). 25p. (gr. 3-7). *(978-81-8386-024-6(9))* India Research Pr. IND. Dist: Independent Pubs. Group.

Ebwelleson, Nelson. The Helpless King. 2012. 24p. pap. 17.99 *(978-1-4772-8262-5(9))* AuthorHouse.

Farmer, Nancy. The Lord of Opium. 2013. (House of the Scorpion Ser.). (ENG., Illus.). 432p. (YA). (gr. 7). 21.99 *(978-1-4424-8254-8(0))* Simon & Schuster Children's Publishing.

Fournier, Kevin Mark. Sandbag Shuffle. 2007. (ENG.). 240p. (gr. 8-13). per. 12.95 *(978-1-897235-22-5(4))* Thistledown Pr., Ltd. CAN. Dist: Univ. of Toronto Pr.

Groth-Fleming, Candace. Professor Fergus Fahrenheit & His Wonderful Weather Machine. Weller, Don, illus. 2009. (ENG.). 36p. (J). (gr. -1-3). pap. 10.99 *(978-1-4424-0220-1(2)*, Simon & Schuster Bks. For Young Readers) Simon & Schuster Bks. For Young Readers.

Hall, Barbara. Dixie Storms. 2006. (ENG., Illus.). 224p. (YA). (gr. 7-12). pap. 12.95 *(978-0-15-205756-5(0)*, 1197300, Clarion Bks.) HarperCollins Pubs.

Kajikawa, Kimiko. Tsunami! Young, Ed, illus. 2009. (ENG.). 32p. (J). (gr. -1-k). 17.99 *(978-0-399-25006-4(9)*, Philomel Bks.) Penguin Young Readers Group.

Kroll, Virginia. Selvakumar Knew Better, 1 vol. Li, Xiaojun, illus. 2009. (ENG.). 32p. (J). (gr. -1-3). pap. 8.95 *(978-1-885008-36-7(8)*, leelowshens, Shen's Bks.) Lee & Low Bks., Inc.

Kropp, Paul. Avalanche. 2012. (HIP Sr Ser.). (ENG., Illus.). 91p. (gr. 7-12). 26.19 *(978-1-897039-07-6(7))* High Interest Publishing (HIP) CAN. Dist: Children's Plus, Inc.

Laiz, Jana. Elephants of the Tsunami. Cafiero, Tara, illus. 2005. (J). 10.00 *(978-0-9771818-3-4(9))* EarthBound Bks.

Lawrence, Kelsey. Rune. 2006. (Illus.). 92p. pap. 13.50 *(978-1-84426-399-8(1))* Upfront Publishing Ltd. GBR. Dist: Printondemand-worldwide.com.

Lawrence, Margaret. Earthshakers, Top Blowers & High Rollers. 2012. 170p. pap. 36.95 *(978-1-937600-74-7(2))* Salem Author Services.

Laybourne, Emmy. Monument 14. 2013. (Monument 14 Ser.: 1). (ENG., Illus.). 352p. (YA). (gr. 8-13). pap. 11.99 *(978-1-250-02738-2(1)*, 900098310) Square Fish.

—Monument 14: Sky on Fire. 2014. (Monument 14 Ser.: 2). (ENG.). 272p. (YA). (gr. 8-13). pap. 12.99 *(978-1-250-04432-7(4)*, 900128326) Square Fish.

—Sky on Fire. 2013. (Monument 14 Ser.: Bk. 2). (ENG.). vi, 217p. (YA). *(978-1-4449-1765-9(X))* Feiwel & Friends.

Lewis, Richard. The Killing Sea. 2008. (ENG., Illus.). 256p. (J). (gr. 7-12). mass mkt. 8.99 *(978-1-4169-5372-2(8)*, Simon Pulse) Simon Pulse.

MacHale, D. J. The Rivers of Zadaa. 2006. (Pendragon Ser.: Bk. 6). 405p. (gr. 5-9). 19.00 *(978-0-7569-7040-6(7))* Perfection Learning Corp.

Martens, J. D. Countdown to Destruction: Book 5. 2017. (Meteor Ser.). (ENG.). 184p. (YA). (gr. 5-12). 31.42 *(978-1-68076-831-2(X)*, 27434, Epic Escape) EPIC Pr.

—Days of Anarchy: Book 2. 2017. (Meteor Ser.). (ENG.). 184p. (YA). (gr. 5-12). 31.42 *(978-1-68076-828-2(X)*, 27431, Epic Escape) EPIC Pr.

—Defeat Judgment Day: Book 3. 2017. (Meteor Ser.). (ENG.). 184p. (YA). (gr. 5-12). 31.42 *(978-1-68076-829-9(8)*, 27432, Epic Escape) EPIC Pr.

—A New World Order: Book 6. 2017. (Meteor Ser.). (ENG.). 184p. (YA). (gr. 5-12). 31.42 *(978-1-68076-832-9(8)*, 27435, Epic Escape) EPIC Pr.

—The Sky Is Falling: Book 1. 2017. (Meteor Ser.). (ENG.). 184p. (YA). (gr. 5-12). 31.42 *(978-1-68076-827-5(1)*, 27430, Epic Escape) EPIC Pr.

—Three-Headed Monster: Book 4. 2017. (Meteor Ser.). (ENG.). 184p. (YA). (gr. 5-12). 31.42 *(978-1-68076-830-5(1)*, 27433, Epic Escape) EPIC Pr.

Ormerod, Jan. Water Witcher. 2008. (ENG., Illus.). 32p. (J). (gr. -1-2). 16.95 *(978-1-921049-51-4(0))* Little Hare Bks. AUS. Dist: Independent Pubs. Group.

Orr, Wendy. Swallow's Dance. 2018. (Minoan Wings Ser.: 2). (ENG., Illus.). 288p. (J). (gr. 4-10). 17.95 *(978-1-77278-062-8(6))* Pajama Pr. CAN. Dist: Publishers Group West (PGW).

Padula, Stacy A. The Aftermath. 2013. 176p. pap. 13.00 *(978-1-62857-057-1(1)*, Strategic Bk. Publishing) Strategic Book Publishing & Rights Agency (SBPRA).

Parker, John. Chaos Mountain. 2007. 96p. (YA). pap. *(978-1-4207-0734-2(5))* Sundance/Newbridge Educational Publishing.

Pfeffer, Susan Beth. The Dead & the Gone. 2010. (Life As We Knew It Ser.: 2). (ENG.). 336p. (YA). (gr. 7-12). pap. 9.99 *(978-0-547-25855-3(0)*, 1402120, Clarion Bks.) HarperCollins Pubs.

—The Dead & the Gone. 2010. (Last Survivors Ser.: 2). 321p. lib. bdg. 19.65 *(978-0-606-14464-3(1))* Turtleback.

—Life As We Knew It. (Life As We Knew It Ser.: 1). (ENG., Illus.). 352p. (YA). (gr. 7-18). 2008. pap. 15.99 *(978-0-15-206154-8(1)*, 1060872) 2006. 18.99 *(978-0-15-205826-5(5)*, 1197505) HarperCollins Pubs. (Clarion Bks.).

—Life As We Knew It. 2008. (Last Survivors Ser.: 1). 347p. (gr. 7-12). lib. bdg. 19.65 *(978-1-4178-1541-8(8))* Turtleback.

—The Life As We Knew It 4-Book Collection. 2015. (Life As We Knew It Ser.). (ENG.). 1252p. (YA). (gr. 7). pap. 29.99 *(978-0-544-54263-1(0)*, 1608921, Clarion Bks.) HarperCollins Pubs.

—The Shade of the Moon. 2014. (Life As We Knew It Ser.: 4). (ENG.). 304p. (YA). (gr. 7). pap. 9.99 *(978-0-544-33615-5(1)*, 1584161, Clarion Bks.) HarperCollins Pubs.

Pratchett, Terry. Nation. 2009. (ENG.). 384p. (YA). (gr. 8-18). pap. 11.99 *(978-0-06-143303-0(9)*, Clarion Bks.) 2008. 504p. (J). pap. 16.99 *(978-0-06-170913-5(1))* 2008. (ENG.). 384p. (YA). (gr. 8-18). 17.99 *(978-0-06-143301-6(2)*, Clarion Bks.) HarperCollins Pubs.

Prentiss, Timothy. A Good Pick. 2006. (Early Explorers Ser.). (J). pap. *(978-1-4108-6111-5(2))* Benchmark Education Co.

Robbins, Sandra. The Earth & Me. 2004. (J). *(978-1-882601-48-6(3))*; 23.95 incl. audio compact disk *(978-1-882601-49-3(1))*; pap. 9.95 *(978-1-882601-47-9(5))*; pap. 16.95 incl. audio *(978-1-882601-52-3(1))* See-More's Workshop.

—The Earth & Me (Hard Cover Book & Tape Set) 2004. (J). mass mkt. 21.95 incl. audio *(978-1-882601-50-9(5))* See-More's Workshop.

Robbins, Sandra, told to. The Earth & Me (Soft Cover Book & CD Set) 2004. (J). pap. 18.95 incl. audio compact disk *(978-1-882601-51-6(3))* See-More's Workshop.

Robison, Dan. Death Chant: Kimo's Battle with the Shamanic Forces. 2006. 194p. (J). pap. *(978-0-922993-52-9(1))* Marquette Bks.

Salkey, Andrew. Drought, 1 vol. 2011. (Caribbean Modern Classics Ser.). (ENG., Illus.). 128p. (J). (gr. 7). pap. 13.95 *(978-1-84523-183-5(X))* Peepal Tree Pr., Ltd. GBR. Dist: Independent Pubs. Group.

Sugg, Nan. Erin & Katrina. Huber, Becca & Pope, Lauren, illus. 2007. 32p. (J). 19.90 *(978-0-9788889-0-9(1))* Acorn Hill Pr.

Tarshis, Lauren. I Survived the Japanese Tsunami 2011. 2013. (I Survived Ser.: No. 8). lib. bdg. 14.75 *(978-0-606-32390-1(2))* Turtleback.

—I Survived the Japanese Tsunami, 2011 (I Survived #8) 2013. (I Survived Ser.: 8). (ENG., Illus.). 112p. (J). (gr. 2-5). pap. 5.99 *(978-0-545-45937-2(0)*, Scholastic Paperbacks) Scholastic, Inc.

NATURAL HISTORY

Here are entered popular works describing animals, plants, minerals and nature in general. Handbooks on the detailed study of birds, flowers, etc. are entered under Nature Study.

see also Aquariums; Biology; Botany; Fossils; Freshwater Biology; Geology; Marine Biology; Mineralogy; Zoology

Aguilera, Rich. Mud: Off-Road Discoveries. 2017. (Illus.). xi, 128p. pap. *(978-0-8163-6252-3(1))* Pacific Pr. Publishing Assn.

Aloian, Molly. The Andes, 1 vol. 2011. (ENG., Illus.). 48p. (J). pap. *(978-0-7787-7567-6(4))*; (gr. 4-7). lib. bdg. *(978-0-7787-7560-7(7))* Crabtree Publishing Co.

Andrews, Jane. The Stories Mother Nature Told Her Child. 2004. reprint ed. pap. 15.95 *(978-1-4191-8357-7(5))* Kessinger Publishing, LLC.

—The Stories Mother Nature Told Her Children. 2004. reprint ed. pap. 1.99 *(978-1-4192-8357-4(X))* Kessinger Publishing, LLC.

Arnold, Jude. The Lipizzan Reunion: A True Story. 2009. 48p. pap. 19.49 *(978-1-4389-7060-8(9))* AuthorHouse.

Atwood, Frederick D. Rocks & Minerals - Pb: A Portrait of the Natural World. 2013. (Portrait of the Natural World Ser.). (Illus.). 72p. pap. 9.95 *(978-1-59764-332-0(7))* New Line Bks.

Augustin, Byron & Kubena, Jake. Yellowstone National Park, 1 vol. 2010. (Nature's Wonders Ser.). (ENG., Illus.). 96p. (gr. 6-6). 38.36 *(978-0-7614-3936-3(6)*, 10487224-f74e-4a5b-9a08-f39375ed1ed0) Cavendish Square Publishing LLC.

Baker, Kate. Highest Mountain, Smallest Star: A Visual Compendium of Wonders. Tsou, Page, illus. 2018. (ENG.). 80p. (J). (gr. 2-5). 22.00 *(978-1-5362-0405-6(6)*, Big Picture Press) Candlewick Pr.

Banting, Erinn. Aconcagua. 2019. (Illus.). 32p. (J). pap. *(978-1-7911-1411-4(3)*, AV2 by Weigl) Weigl Pubs., Inc.

—The Galapagos Islands. 2006. (Natural Wonders Ser.). (Illus.). 32p. (gr. 3-7). 17.95 *(978-0-7569-6994-3(8))* Perfection Learning Corp.

Barlowe, Dot. Rocky Mountains Plants & Animals. 2004. (Dover Nature Coloring Book Ser.). (ENG., Illus.). 32p. (gr. 3-8). pap. 3.99 *(978-0-486-43045-4(6)*, 430456) Dover Pubns., Inc.

Bear Hunt Films Ltd., Bear Hunt. We're Going on a Bear Hunt: My Explorer's Journal. 2017. (We're Going on a Bear Hunt Ser.). (ENG.). 96p. (J). (gr. 1-4). 14.99 *(978-0-7636-9842-3(3)*, Candlewick Entertainment) Candlewick Pr.

Beebe, Katherine & Kingsley, Nellie F. The First Year Nature Reader. 2004. reprint ed. pap. 21.95 *(978-1-4191-3072-4(2))* Kessinger Publishing, LLC.

Benjamin, Tina. Let's Walk in the Woods, 1 vol. 2015. (Let's Go Outdoors! Ser.). (ENG.). 24p. (J). (gr. k-k). lib. bdg. 24.27 *(978-1-4824-2635-9(8)*, 57baae28-3833-466a-81e1-506c135b02a0) Stevens, Gareth Publishing LLLP.

Berenstain, Stan, et al. The Berenstain Bears' Big Book of Science & Nature. 2013. (Dover Science for Kids Ser.). (ENG.). 192p. (J). (gr. k-3). pap. 15.99 *(978-0-486-49834-8(4)*, 498344) Dover Pubns., Inc.

Blythe, Philip. Nature Hunt! Bewildering Puzzles of the Animal Kingdom. Blythe, Philip, illus. 2005. (ENG., Illus.). 32p. pap., act. bk. ed. *(978-1-877003-82-0(4))* Little Hare Bks. AUS. Dist: HarperCollins Pubs. Australia.

Borgert-Spaniol, Megan. Fun with Nature Projects: Bubble Wands, Sunset in a Glass, & More. 2019. (Unplug with Science Buddies (r) Ser.). (ENG., Illus.). 32p. (J). (gr. 2-5). pap. 8.99 *(978-1-5415-7489-2(3)*, ede12981-bd06-4ecf-a6fe-ebf12e168c6a); lib. bdg. 27.99 *(978-1-5415-5496-2(5)*, 9abb24cb-23af-476c-9107-f019c9171f92) Lerner Publishing Group. (Lerner Pubns.).

Brooks, Sheldon. Life in the Arctic. (Life in Extreme Environments Ser.). 64p. (gr. 5-8). 2009. 53.00 *(978-1-61514-270-5(3))* 2003. (ENG., Illus.). lib. bdg. 37.13 *(978-0-8239-3984-8(7)*, e6153ff0-1922-4213-9686-2e4f9cb67299) Rosen Publishing Group, Inc., The. (Rosen Reference).

Brynie, Faith Hickman. Six-Minute Nature Experiments. Whittingham, Kim, illus. 2006. 80p. (J). (gr. 4-8). reprint ed. pap. 11.00 *(978-1-4223-5105-5(X))* DIANE Publishing Co.

Burris, Judy & Richards, Wayne. Nature's Notes: Bite-sized Learning & Projects for All Ages. 2012. (ENG., Illus.). 232p. spiral bd. *(978-1-60755-477-6(1))* Willow Creek Pr., Inc.

Castella, Krystina & Boyl, Brian. Discovering Nature's Alphabet. 2017. (ENG., Illus.). 28p. (J). bds. 8.99 *(978-1-59714-353-0(7))* Heyday.

—Discovering Nature's Hidden Alphabet. 2017. (ENG.). 64p. (J). 16.00 *(978-1-59714-358-5(8))* Heyday.

Chapman, S. I. mon. In the Desert. 2006. (Illus.). 111p. (J). lib. bdg. 20.00 *(978-1-4242-0628-5(6))* Fitzgerald Bks.

Chin, Jason. Island: A Story of the Galápagos. Chin, Jason, illus. 2012. (ENG., Illus.). 40p. (J). (gr. k-3). 18.99 *(978-1-59643-716-6(2)*, 900075227) Roaring Brook Pr.

Cohen, Fiona. Curious Kids Nature Guide: Explore the Amazing Outdoors of the Pacific Northwest. Fylling, Marni, illus. 2017. (Curious Kids Ser.). 96p. (J). (gr. k-4). 19.99 *(978-1-63217-083-5(3)*, Little Bigfoot) Sasquatch Bks.

Connors, Kathleen. Plants & Animals of the Chesapeake Bay, 1 vol. 2013. (Exploring the Chesapeake Bay Ser.). 32p. (J). (gr. 3-4). (ENG.). 29.27 *(978-1-4339-9780-8(0)*, c90dd9f0-6246-4367-9b8c-3b8ff12f1933); (ENG.). pap. 11.50 *(978-1-4339-9781-5(9)*, e24a2ae6-ddf3-4b6f-a605-7ccff7ce0b53); pap. 63.00 *(978-1-4339-9782-2(7))* Stevens, Gareth Publishing LLLP.

Craats, Rennay. Natural Landmarks. 2004. (American Symbols Ser.). (Illus.). 24p. (J). (gr. 4-7). per. 8.95 *(978-1-59036-177-1(6))*; (gr. 1-3). lib. bdg. 24.45 *(978-1-59036-133-7(4))* Weigl Pubs., Inc.

Crewe, Sabrina. In the Backyard. 2010. (Under the Microscope Ser.). 32p. (gr. 2-4). 30.00 *(978-1-60413-822-1(X)*, Chelsea Clubhse.) Infobase Holdings, Inc.

Cuthbert, Megan. Europe. 2014. (J). *(978-1-4896-0950-2(4))* Weigl Pubs., Inc.

Day, Nancy Raines. What in the World? Numbers in Nature. Cyrus, Kurt, illus. 2015. (ENG.). 32p. (J). (gr. -1-3). 17.99 *(978-1-4814-0060-2(6)*, Beach Lane Bks.) Beach Lane Bks.

Dellaccio, Tanya. Aboard HMS Beagle, 1 vol. 2019. (History on the High Seas Ser.). (ENG.). 24p. (gr. 2-3). pap. 9.15 *(978-1-5382-3786-1(5)*, 120f318f-4d11-49fa-9e0d-7509e6f9071c) Stevens, Gareth Publishing LLLP.

Demetrios, Aristides. Life Story. 2009. (ENG., Illus.). 80p. (J). (gr. 3-7). pap. 8.99 *(978-0-547-20359-1(4)*, 1059051, Clarion Bks.) HarperCollins Pubs.

Dyan, Penelope. The Comeback Kids — Book 9 — the Barbary Macaques of Gibraltar. Weigand, John D., photos by. 2012. (Illus.). 36p. pap. 14.95 *(978-1-61477-036-7(0))* Bellissima Publishing, LLC.

Esbaum, Jill. Everything Spring. 2010. (Illus.). 16p. (J). (gr. -1-k). pap. 5.95 *(978-1-4263-0607-5(5)*, National Geographic Kids) Disney Publishing Worldwide.

Fabre, J. Henri. Animal Life in Field & Garden. 2005. pap. 34.95 *(978-1-4179-0762-5(2))* Kessinger Publishing, LLC.

Forte, Imogene. Nature Crafts. 2004. (Fun Things to Make & Do Ser.). (Illus.). 80p. (J). per. 9.95 *(978-0-86530-617-2(6))* Incentive Pubns., Inc.

Ganeri, Anita. Record-Breaking Earth. 2010. (ENG.). 32p. (J). *(978-0-7787-9908-5(5))*; pap. *(978-0-7787-9929-0(8))* Crabtree Publishing Co.

Gatty. Parables from Nature. 2006. 320p. per. *(978-1-4067-9365-9(5)*, Pomona Pr.) Read Bks.

Gatty, Alfred. Parables from Nature. 2009. 248p. (gr. 4-7). pap. 10.35 *(978-1-60459-621-2(X))* Wilder Pubns., Corp.

Goldsworthy, Steve. Antarctica. 2014. (J). *(978-1-4896-0938-0(5))* Weigl Pubs., Inc.

Groskreutz, Rochelle. Elbrus. 2019. (Illus.). 32p. (J). *(978-1-7911-1407-7(5)*, AV2 by Weigl) Weigl Pubs., Inc.

Guin, Valerie. In the Country. 2005. (One World (Smart Apple Media) Ser.). (Illus.). 30p. (J). (gr. 3-6). lib. bdg. 27.10 *(978-1-58340-695-3(6))* Black Rabbit Bks.

Haegele, Katie. Cool Careers Without College for Nature Lovers. 2009. (Cool Careers Without College Ser.). 144p. (gr. 6-6). 66.50 *(978-1-61511-961-5(2))*; 2nd ed. (ENG., Illus.). (J). (gr. 7-7). 41.13 *(978-1-4358-5245-7(1)*, fd88bd8b-26f5-4390-86d5-d7c6a80dbf20) Rosen Publishing Group, Inc., The.

Hansen, Grace. Parque Nacional de Yellowstone (Yellowstone National Park) 2018. (Parques Nacionales (National Parks) Ser.). (SPA., Illus.). 24p. (J). (gr. -1-2). lib. bdg. 32.79 *(978-1-5321-8047-7(0)*, 28309, Abdo Kids) ABDO Publishing Co.

Harkrader, Lisa. Park Naturalist. 2019. (Jobs with Animals Ser.). (ENG., Illus.). 32p. (J). (gr. 4-6). pap. 7.95 *(978-1-5435-6047-3(4)*, 140092); lib. bdg. 28.65 *(978-1-5435-5785-5(6)*, 139741) Capstone.

Head, Honor. Welcome to the Coral Reef. 2017. (Nature's Neighborhoods: All about Ecosystems Ser.). (ENG., Illus.). 32p. (J). (gr. -1-3). lib. bdg. 30.65 *(978-1-911341-91-8(X)*, 55c859f0-12f1-43c4-9fc9-d26902b78c0f) Ruby Tuesday Books Limited GBR. Dist: Lerner Publishing Group.

Helbrough, Emma. Great Planet Earth Search. Jackson, Ian, illus. 2006. 32p. (J). *(978-0-439-83402-5(3))* Scholastic, Inc.

Hoare, Ben. The Wonders of Nature. 2019. (DK Children's Anthologies Ser.). (ENG., Illus.). 224p. (J). (gr. 2-4). 21.99 *(978-1-4654-8536-6(8)*, DK Children) Dorling Kindersley Publishing, Inc.

Holland, Gini. I Live in the Country, 1 vol. 2004. (Where I Live Ser.). (ENG., Illus.). 24p. (gr. k-2). pap. 9.15 *(978-0-8368-4086-5(0)*, b342fec9-6a81-4f56-b669-4866a6c6787f); lib. bdg. 24.67 *(978-0-8368-4079-7(8)*, 4f0cc796-8b6d-4dde-8d65-aacfbb3ea6f5) Stevens, Gareth Publishing LLLP. (Weekly Reader Leveled Readers).

—I Live in the Country / Vivo en el Campo, 1 vol. 2004. (Where I Live / Donde Vivo Ser.). (SPA & ENG., Illus.). 24p. (gr. k-2). lib. bdg. 24.67 *(978-0-8368-4127-5(1)*, 7f949f44-c145-4c4e-a45e-c39e0f60d064) Stevens, Gareth Publishing LLLP.

Hooper, Meredith. The Pebble in My Pocket: A History of Our Earth. Coady, Chris, illus. rev. ed. 2015. (ENG.). 40p. (J). (gr. 2-5). pap. 9.99 *(978-1-84780-768-7(2)*, 315232, Frances Lincoln Children's Bks.) Quarto Publishing Group UK GBR. Dist: Hachette UK Distribution.

Jacobs, Pat. I Wonder Why Penguins Can't Fly. 2014. 32p. pap. 7.00 *(978-1-61003-350-3(7))* Center for the Collaborative Classroom.

—I Wonder Why Penguins Can't Fly: And Other Questions about Polar Lands. 2011. (I Wonder Why Ser.). (ENG., Illus.). 32p. (J). (gr. k-3). pap. 6.99 *(978-0-7534-6530-1(2)*, 900070299, Kingfisher) Roaring Brook Pr.

Johnson, Robin. The Urals, 1 vol. 2011. (ENG., Illus.). 48p. (J). pap. *(978-0-7787-7571-3(2))*; (gr. 4-7). lib. bdg. *(978-0-7787-7564-5(X))* Crabtree Publishing Co.

Kalman, Bobbie. What Is Super Nature?, 1 vol. 2010. (Big Science Ideas Ser.). (ENG.). 32p. (J). (gr. k-3). pap. *(978-0-7787-3307-2(6))*; lib. bdg. *(978-0-7787-3287-7(8))* Crabtree Publishing Co.

—Yellowstone National Park. 2009. (Introducing Habitats Ser.). (ENG., Illus.). 32p. (J). (gr. k-3). pap. *(978-0-7787-2989-1(3))* Crabtree Publishing Co.

Kenison, Misti, illus. The Tiny Traveler: Japan: A Book of Nature. 2016. (ENG.). 24p. (J). (— 1). bds. 5.99 *(978-1-5107-0472-5(8)*, Sky Pony Pr.) Skyhorse Publishing Co., Inc.

Latham, Irene. When the Sun Shines on Antarctica: And Other Poems about the Frozen Continent. Wadham, Anna, illus. 2016. (ENG.). 32p. (J). (gr. 3-6). E-Book 30.65 *(978-1-4677-9729-0(4)*, Millbrook Pr.) Lerner Publishing Group.

Lazor, Stephanie. Life on the Equator. 2009. (Life in Extreme Environments Ser.). 64p. (gr. 5-8). 53.00 *(978-1-61514-275-0(4)*, Rosen Reference) Rosen Publishing Group, Inc., The.

Leavitt, Amie Jane. Vinson Massif. 2019. (J). *(978-1-7911-1419-0(9)*, AV2 by Weigl) Weigl Pubs., Inc.

Lerner Publishing Group Staff, ed. Time Nature's Wonders: The Science & Splendor of Earth's Most Fascinating Places. 2008. (Time Inc. Home Entertainment Library-Bound Titles Ser.). (ENG.). 128p. (gr. 5-12). lib. bdg. 39.93 *(978-0-7613-4228-1(1)*, Twenty-First Century Bks.) Lerner Publishing Group.

LernerClassroom Editors, ed. Teaching Guide for Fsn / Discovering Nature's Cycles. 2010. pap. 5.95 *(978-0-7613-6683-6(0))* Lerner Publishing Group.

Leslie, Clare Walker. The Curious Nature Guide: Explore the Natural Wonders All Around You. 2015. (ENG., Illus.). 144p. pap. 14.99 *(978-1-61212-509-1(3)*, 622509) Storey Publishing, LLC.

Lord, Michelle. Nature Recycles - How about You?, 1 vol. Morrison, Cathy, illus. 2013. (ENG.). 32p. (J). (gr. -1-4). 17.95 *(978-1-60718-615-1(2))*; pap. 9.95 *(978-1-60718-627-4(6))* Arbordale Publishing.

—Nature Recycles - How about You? (Spanish), 1 vol. Morrison, Cathy, illus. 2013. (SPA & ENG.). 32p. (J). (gr. -1-4). 17.95 *(978-1-60718-711-0(6))* Arbordale Publishing.

Lowrie, Paul. Hooray for Minnesota Lakes. 2008. 19.95 *(978-0-9755801-8-9(3))* Questmarc Publishing.

Lucas, Diane & Searle, Ken. Walking with the Seasons in Kakadu. 2005. (ENG., Illus.). 32p. (J). (gr. 2-4). pap. 12.95 *(978-1-74114-471-0(X))* Allen & Unwin AUS. Dist: Independent Pubs. Group.

Mahaney, Ian F. Energy in Action, 4 vols., Set. Incl. Heat. (YA). lib. bdg. 26.27 *(978-1-4042-3477-2(2)*, c7a457ef-db3c-4391-abdf-b561fd4a3278); Light. (YA). lib. bdg. 26.27 *(978-1-4042-3476-5(4)*, 6f958087-0feb-4b4d-865d-94bbf08a35e0); Solar Energy. (J). lib. bdg. 26.27 *(978-1-4042-3479-6(9)*, caa8fd1d-7f50-4d7e-9267-b4708a556374, PowerKids Pr.); (Illus.). 24p. (gr. 3-3). 2007. (Energy in Action Ser.). (ENG.). 2006. Set lib. bdg. 52.54 *(978-1-4042-3504-5(3)*, 888f1685-a313-4558-9910-008b3766a673) Rosen Publishing Group, Inc., The.

Marciniak, Kristin. Incredible Nature. 2018. (Unbelievable Ser.). (ENG., Illus.). 32p. (J). (gr. 3-6). 32.80 *(978-1-63235-421-1(7)*, 13769, 12-Story Library) Bookstaves, LLC.

Martineau, Susan. Bugs in the Garden, 1 vol. Noyes, Leighton, illus. 2011. (Everyday Science Experiments Ser.). (ENG.). 24p. (J). (gr. 3-4). lib. bdg. 29.93 *(978-1-61533-370-7(3)*, 1a14b8c5-5282-4386-a2cf-6d9851c1d833, Windmill Bks.) Rosen Publishing Group, Inc., The.

McGinlay, Richard. My First Encylopedia of British Wildlife: Mammals, Birds, Fish, Bugs, Flowers, Trees. 2020. (ENG., Illus.). 24p. (J). (gr. -1-12). pap. 7.99 *(978-1-86147-849-8(6)*, Armadillo) Anness Publishing GBR. Dist: National Bk. Network.

Miché, Mary. Nature's Patchwork Quilt: Understanding Habitats. Powell, Consie, illus. 2012. (ENG.). 32p. (J). (gr. 1-4). 24.94 *(978-1-58469-169-3(7))* Take Heart Pubns.

Miche, Mary. Nature's Patchwork Quilt: Understanding Habitats, 1 vol. Powell, Consie, illus. 2012. 32p. (J). (gr. k-6). pap. 8.99 *(978-1-58469-170-9(0)*, Dawn Pubns.) Sourcebooks, Inc.

Miles, Liz. Linnaeus Organising Nature: Band 18/Pearl. 2017. (Collins Big Cat Ser.). (ENG., Illus.). 80p. (J). pap. 12.99 *(978-0-00-820897-4(2))* HarperCollins Pubs. Ltd. GBR. Dist: Independent Pubs. Group.

Minsky, Howie. In the Everglades. 2019. (Hello, Everglades! Ser.). (ENG.). 16p. (J). (gr. -1-2). pap. 11.36 *(978-1-5341-5728-6(X)*, 214159, Cherry Blossom Press) Cherry Lake Publishing.

Morgan, Sally. The Incredible Life of Sir David Attenborough: Band 16/Sapphire, Bd. 16. 2017. (Collins Big Cat Ser.). (ENG.). 56p. (J). pap. 12.99 *(978-0-00-820889-9(1))* HarperCollins Pubs. Ltd. GBR. Dist: Independent Pubs. Group.

Morley, Margaret W. Little Wanderers. 2009. (Illus.). 116p. pap. 8.95 *(978-1-59915-317-9(3))* Yesterday's Classics.

Morley, Margaret Warner. A Song of Life 1922. Forsyth, Robert, illus. 2004. reprint ed. pap. 21.95 *(978-1-4179-7842-7(2))* Kessinger Publishing, LLC.

Morris, Sandra. Welcome to New Zealand: a Nature Journal. Morris, Sandra, illus. 2015. (ENG., Illus.). 48p. (J). (gr. 3-7). 16.99 *(978-0-7636-7477-9(X))* Candlewick Pr.

Natural History. (Illus.). (J). (gr. -1-6). pap., act. bk. ed. 2.95 *(978-0-565-00857-4(9))* Natural History Museum Pubns. GBR. Dist: Parkwest Pubns., Inc.

O'Connell, Caitlin & Jackson, Donna M. The Elephant Scientist. Rodwell, Timothy, illus. 2016. (Scientists in the Field Ser.). (ENG.). 80p. (J). (gr. 5-7). 11.99 *(978-0-544-66830-0(8)*, 1625422, Clarion Bks.) HarperCollins Pubs.

Oxlade, Chris. Hands-on Science Projects: Nature. 2008. (ENG., Illus.). 64p. (J). (gr. 4-7). pap. 7.99 *(978-1-84476-532-4(6))* Anness Publishing GBR. Dist: National Bk. Network.

Paquette, Ammi-Joan & Thompson, Laurie Ann. Two Truths & a Lie: It's Alive! Weber, Lisa K., illus. 2018. (ENG.). 176p. (J). (gr. 3-7). pap. 10.99 *(978-0-06-241881-4(5)*, Waldon Pond Pr.) HarperCollins Pubs.

Parker, Francis W. Uncle Robert's Geography (Uncle Robert's Visit, V. 3) 2006. 84p. pap. *(978-1-84702-205-9(7))* Echo Library.

Parker, Steve & Parker, Jane. Show Me How: Nature Projects. 2015. (ENG., Illus.). 48p. (J). (gr. -1-12). 7.99 *(978-1-86147-298-4(6)*, Armadillo) Anness Publishing GBR. Dist: National Bk. Network.

Pecorella, Jane. Yellowstone: Our First National Park. 2009. (Reading Room Collection 2 Ser.). 24p. (gr. 3-4). 42.50 *(978-1-60852-004-6(8)*, PowerKids Pr.) Rosen Publishing Group, Inc., The.

Peppas, Lynn. The Alps, 1 vol. 2011. (ENG., Illus.). 48p. (J). pap. *(978-0-7787-7566-9(6))*; (gr. 4-7). lib. bdg. *(978-0-7787-7559-1(3))* Crabtree Publishing Co.

Percy, J.P. Nature. 2013. (Can You Guess What I Am? Ser.). 24p. (gr. k-3). 28.50 *(978-1-59920-895-4(4))* Black Rabbit Bks.

Pipe, Jim. Wonderful World. 2009. (ENG.). 112p. (J). (gr. 4-7). pap. 12.95 *(978-1-84696-204-2(8)*, TickTock Books) Octopus Publishing Group GBR. Dist: Independent Pubs. Group.

Pollard, Simon. Why Is That Lake So Blue? A Children's Guide to New Zealand's Natural World. 2018. (ENG., Illus.). 112p. pap. 30.95 *(978-0-9941460-1-4(9))* Te Papa Pr. NZL. Dist: Independent Pubs. Group.

Pomeroy, Sarah B. & Kathirithamby, Jeyaraney. Maria Sibylla Merian: Artist, Scientist, Adventurer. (J). 2018. (ENG., Illus.). 96p. (gr. 3-7). 21.95 *(978-1-947440-01-2(2)*, 1317301) 2017. *(978-1-60606-555-6(6)*, J. Paul Getty Museum) Getty Pubns.

Pratt-Serafini, Kristin Joy, illus. Saguaro Moon: A Desert Journal. 2004. (Sharing Nature with Children Book Ser.). 32p. (YA). 16.95 *(978-1-58469-037-5(2))* Take Heart Pubns.

Pyers, Greg. Biodiversity of Polar Regions, 1 vol. 2011. (Biodiversity Ser.). (ENG.). 32p. (gr. 4-4). 31.21 *(978-1-60870-072-1(0)*, 41f2a9a6-5c45-430e-bd96-332dd9ecd761) Cavendish Square Publishing LLC.

Questions & Answers of the Natural World. 2003. (Illus.). 256p. (J). 12.98 *(978-1-4054-1682-5(3))* Parragon, Inc.

Reeves, Diane Lindsey. Food & Natural Resources. 2017. (Bright Futures Press: World of Work Ser.). (ENG., Illus.). 32p. (J). (gr. 4-7). lib. bdg. 32.07 *(978-1-63472-622-1(7)*, 209522) Cherry Lake Publishing.

Rice, David L. Lifetimes. Maydak, Michael S., illus. 2015. 32p. pap. 9.00 *(978-1-61003-549-1(6))* Center for the Collaborative Classroom.

Rice, Dona Herweck. Environment: A World of Change, 1 vol. rev. ed. 2014. (Science: Informational Text Ser.). (ENG.). 32p. (gr. 2-3). pap. 10.99 *(978-1-4807-4602-2(9))* Teacher Created Materials, Inc.

Richards, Jon & Simkins, Ed. The Natural World. 2016. (Mapographica Ser.). 32p. (J). (gr. 3-6). *(978-0-7787-2658-6(4))* Crabtree Publishing Co.

Richardson, Donna. Yellowstone: A Blast from the Past. 2007. (Illus.). 14p. pap. 4.75 *(978-0-15-377369-3(3))* Harcourt Schl. Pubs.

A Ride Around Presque Isle: Natural History along the Roadsides. 2004. (Illus.). spiral bd. 15.00 *(978-0-9747001-1-3(8))* Edinboro Bk. Arts Collective.

Rissman, Rebecca. Living & Nonliving in the Polar Regions, 1 vol. 2013. (Is It Living or Nonliving? Ser.). (ENG.). 24p. (J). (gr. k-2). pap. 6.95 *(978-1-4109-5390-2(4)*, 123330, Raintree) Capstone.

Roth, Susan L. & Trumbore, Cindy. Parrots over Puerto Rico, 1 vol. Roth, Susan L., illus. 2013. (ENG., Illus.). 48p. (J). (gr. 1-6). 20.95 *(978-1-62014-004-8(7)*, leelowbooks) Lee & Low Bks., Inc.

Rustad, Martha E. H. Do Trees Get Hungry? Noticing Plant & Animal Traits. Moran, Mike, illus. 2015. (Cloverleaf Books (tm) — Nature's Patterns Ser.). (ENG.). 24p. (J). (gr. k-2). lib. bdg. 25.32 *(978-1-4677-8559-4(8)*, e8fac711-bc92-49fc-a0b8-45ed7bda81f4, Millbrook Pr.) Lerner Publishing Group.

Sanchez, Anita. Karl, Get Out of the Garden! Carolus Linnaeus & the Naming of Everything. Stock, Catherine, illus. 2017. 48p. (J). (gr. 2-5). lib. bdg. 17.99 *(978-1-58089-606-1(5))* Charlesbridge Publishing, Inc.

Sanchez, Michael. Natural History Collector: Hunt, Discover, Learn! Expert Tips on How to Care for & Display Your Collections & Turn Your Room into a Cabinet of Curiosities. 2017. (ENG.). 128p. (J). (gr. 3-6). pap. 24.99 *(978-1-63159-367-3(6)*, 225166, Quarry Bks.) Quarto Publishing Group USA.

Sayre, April Pulley. Greeting, Asia! The Ultimate Guide to America's 4 Regional Styles of 'Cue. 2003. (Illus.). 32p. lib. bdg. 21.90 *(978-0-7613-2124-8(1)*, Millbrook Pr.) Lerner Publishing Group.

Seton, Ernest Thompson. Woodmyth & Fable. 2005. pap. 22.95 *(978-1-885529-83-1(X))* Stevens Publishing.

Silva Lee, Alfonso. Mi Isla y Yo: La Naturaleza de Puerto Rico. Hayskar, Bonnie J., ed. Lago, Alexis, illus. 2007. (SPA.). 32p. (J). pap. 8.95 *(978-1-929165-19-3(6))* PANGAEA.

—Mi isla y yo/My Island & I: La naturaleza de Puerto Rico/The Nature of Puerto Rico. Hayskar, Bonnie J., ed. Lago, Alexis, illus. 2003. (SPA & ENG.). 32p. (J). pap. 9.95 *(978-1-929165-12-4(9))* PANGAEA.

Slade, Suzanne. Out of School & into Nature: The Anna Comstock Story. Lanan, Jessica, illus. 2017. (ENG.). 32p. (J). (gr. 1-4). 16.99 *(978-1-58536-986-7(1)*, 204225) Sleeping Bear Pr.

Smith, David J. If: A Mind-Bending New Way of Looking at Big Ideas & Numbers. Adams, Steve, illus. 2014. (ENG.). 40p. (J). (gr. 3-7). 19.99 *(978-1-894786-34-8(3))* Kids Can Pr., Ltd. CAN. Dist: Hachette Bk. Group.

Smith, Lynn & Faust Kalscheur, Jann. ABC's Naturally: A Child's Guide to the Alphabet Through Nature. Faust Kalscheur, Jann, photos by. 2003. (Illus.). (J). 16.95 *(978-1-931599-27-6(0),* Trails Bks.) Bower Hse.

Sollinger, Emily. This Is Our World: A Story about Taking Care of the Earth. Brown, Jo, illus. 2010. (Little Green Bks.). (ENG.). 12p. (J). (gr. -1-1). bds. 8.99 *(978-1-4169-7821-3(6),* Little Simon) Little Simon.

St. Antoine, Sara, ed. The North Atlantic Coast: A Literary Field Guide. Nicholson, Trudy & Mirocha, Paul, illus. 2004. (Stories from Where We Live Ser.). (ENG.). 288p. (J). pap., instr.'s gde. ed. 10.95 *(978-1-57131-643-1(4))* Milkweed Editions.

Stienecker, David. Blast Zone: The Eruption & Recovery of Mount St. Helens. 2003. (ENG., Illus.). 32p. (J). (gr. 6-8). pap. 7.97 net. *(978-0-7652-3265-6(0),* Celebration Pr.) Savvas Learning Co.

Suzuki, David. There's a Barnyard in My Bedroom. Fernandes, Eugenie, illus. 2010. (ENG.). 64p. (gr. -1-3). pap. 10.95 *(978-1-55365-532-9(X),* Greystone Books) Greystone Books Ltd. CAN. Dist: Publishers Group West (PGW).

Suzuki, David. & Vanderlinden, Kathy. You Are the Earth: Know Your World So You Can Help Make It Better. Edwards, Wallace, illus. 2nd rev. ed. 2010. 144p. (gr. k-7). pap. 18.95 *(978-1-55365-476-6(5),* Greystone Kids) Greystone Books Ltd. CAN. Dist: Publishers Group West (PGW).

Swinburne, Stephen R. Lots & Lots of Zebra Stripes. 2014. 21.45 *(978-1-63419-671-0(6))* Perfection Learning Corp.

Ticktock Media, Ltd. Staff. Living Planet: Uncovering the Wonders of the Natural World. 2008. (ENG.). 128p. (J). (gr. 4-7). pap. 12.95 *(978-1-84696-816-7(X),* TickTock Books) Octopus Publishing Group GBR. Dist: Independent Pubs. Group.

Trumbauer, Lisa. A Year in the Desert, 6 vols., Set. 2005. (Yellow Umbrella Fluent Level Ser.). (ENG., Illus.). 16p. (gr. k-1). pap. 35.70 *(978-0-7368-5302-6(2),* Capstone Pr.) Capstone.

U. S. National Geographic Society Staff, ed. Books for Young Explorers, 4 vols., Set 6. (J). lib. bdg. 16.95 *(978-0-87044-250-6(3))* National Geographic Society.

Usborne Books Staff, creator. The Young Naturalist Kid Kit. 2007. (Kid Kits Ser.). (Illus.). 32p. (J). pap. 14.99 *(978-1-60130-037-9(9),* Usborne) EDC Publishing.

Variety of Life, 10 vols., 8 Vols. 2004. (Variety of Life Ser.). (ENG.). 32p. (gr. 2-4). lib. bdg. 143.35 *(978-0-8368-4501-3(3),* 3f144a92-c054-47d6-a9a0-926e89d7fb55, Gareth Stevens Learning Library) Stevens, Gareth Publishing LLLP.

Viano, Hannah. B Is for Bear: A Natural Alphabet. Viano, Hannah, illus. 2015. (ENG., Illus.). 32p. (J). (-k). 16.99 *(978-1-63217-039-2(6),* Little Bigfoot) Sasquatch Bks.

Vierow, Wendy. Europe. (Atlas of the Seven Continents Ser.). 24p. (gr. 3-3). 2009. 42.50 *(978-1-61511-480-1(7),* PowerKids Pr.) 2003. (ENG., Illus.). (J). lib. bdg. 26.27 *(978-0-8239-6691-2(7),* 0d677122-4d04-4b07-a468-29c482a00784) Rosen Publishing Group, Inc., The.

Wadsworth, Pamela. Gwahanol Blanhigion AC Anifeiliaid. Owen, Ken & Owen, Siân, illus. 2005. (WEL.). 24p. pap. *(978-1-85596-223-1(3))* Dref Wen.

—Rhagor Am Wahanol Blanhigion Ac Anifeiliaid. 2005. (WEL., Illus.). 24p. pap. *(978-1-85596-224-8(1))* Dref Wen.

Watson, Galadriel Findlay. Kilimanjaro. 2019. (Illus.). 32p. (J). *(978-1-7911-1399-5(0),* AV2 by Weigl) Weigl Pubs., Inc.

Watson, Jane Werner. Wonders of Nature. Wilkin, Eloise, illus. 2010. (Little Golden Book Ser.). 24p. (J). (gr. -1-2). 5.99 *(978-0-375-85486-6(X),* Golden Bks.) Random Hse. Children's Bks.

Williams, Brian. The Natural World. 2010. (What About... Ser.). (Illus.). 40p. (J). (gr. 6-8). lib. bdg. 19.95 *(978-1-4222-1562-3(8))* Mason Crest.

Williams, Zella. Experiments about the Natural World. (Do-It-Yourself Science Ser.). 24p. (gr. 2-3). 2009. 47.90 *(978-1-61512-186-1(2),* PowerKids Pr.) 2007. (ENG., Illus.). (J). lib. bdg. 28.93 *(978-1-4042-3661-5(9),* a5e956c1-e54e-4ed3-8250-9921e544f32d) Rosen Publishing Group, Inc., The.

Wiseman, Blaine. The Midwest. 2014. (Illus.). 32p. (J). *(978-1-4896-1226-7(2))* Weigl Pubs., Inc.

Woods, Michael & Woods, Mary B. Seven Natural Wonders of the Arctic, Antarctica, & the Oceans. 2009. (Seven Wonders Ser.). (ENG., Illus.). 80p. (gr. 5-8). 33.26 *(978-0-8225-9075-0(1))* Lerner Publishing Group.

Woodward, John & Gray, Leon. Backyard. 2007. (Close-up Ser.). (Illus.). 32p. (J). (gr. 4-7). lib. bdg. *(978-1-933834-13-9(7))* Brown Bear Books.

World Book, Inc. Staff, contrib. by. Explore & Learn — The Natural World. 2008. (J). *(978-0-7166-3019-7(2))* World Bk., Inc.

—Icy Worlds. 2011. (J). *(978-0-7166-1788-4(9))* World Bk., Inc.

Young, Caroline & Needham, Kate. Great Wildlife Search: Big Bug Search, Great Animal Search & Great Undersea Search. Jackson, Ian, illus. 2004. (Great Searches Ser.). 112p. (J). pap. 15.99 *(978-0-7945-0892-0(8),* Usborne) EDC Publishing.

NATURAL HISTORY—AFRICA

Aloian, Molly. The Kalahari Desert. 2012. (ENG.). 32p. (J). lib. bdg. *(978-0-7787-0712-7(1));* (Illus.). pap. *(978-0-7787-0720-2(2))* Crabtree Publishing Co.

Cuthbert, Megan. Africa. 2014. (J). *(978-1-4896-0934-2(2))* Weigl Pubs., Inc.

Galvin, Laura Gates. Alphabet of African Animals. Leeper, Christopher J. et al, illus. 2011. (Alphabet Bks.). (ENG.). 40p. (J). (gr. -1-3). 17.95 *(978-1-60727-574-9(0))* Soundprints.

—Alphabet of African Animals. Denman, Michael et al, illus. 2008. (ENG.). 40p. (J). (gr. -1-2). 17.95 *(978-1-59249-854-3(X))* Soundprints.

Rebus, Anna. Victoria Falls: One of the World's Most Spectacular Waterfalls. 2006. (Natural Wonders Ser.). (Illus.). 32p. (J). (gr. 3-7). lib. bdg. 26.00 *(978-1-59036-453-6(8));* per. 9.95 *(978-1-59036-459-8(7))* Weigl Pubs., Inc.

Wojahn, Rebecca Hogue & Wojahn, Donald. A Cloud Forest Food Chain: A Who-Eats-What Adventure in Africa. 2009. (Follow That Food Chain Ser.). (ENG.). 64p. (gr. 3-5). 30.60 *(978-0-8225-7612-9(0))* Lerner Publishing Group.

Woods, Michael & Woods, Mary B. Seven Natural Wonders of Africa. 2009. (Seven Wonders Ser.). (ENG., Illus.). 80p. (gr. 5-8). lib. bdg. 33.26 *(978-0-8225-9071-2(9))* Lerner Publishing Group.

NATURAL HISTORY—ASIA

Aloian, Molly. The Himalayas, 1 vol. 2011. (ENG., Illus.). 48p. (J). pap. *(978-0-7787-7569-0(0));* (gr. 4-7). lib. bdg. *(978-0-7787-7562-1(3))* Crabtree Publishing Co.

Orr, Tamra. Carstensz Pyramid. 2019. (Illus.). 31p. (J). *(978-1-7911-1415-2(6),* AV2 by Weigl) Weigl Pubs., Inc.

Yasuda, Anita. Asia. 2014. (J). *(978-1-4896-0942-7(3))* Weigl Pubs., Inc.

NATURAL HISTORY—AUSTRALIA

Barwood, Lee. Klassic Koalas: Ancient Aboriginal Tales in New Retellings, BW Edition. 2007. (ENG., Illus.). 24p. (J). pap. 14.99 *(978-0-9764698-6-3(5))* Koala Jo Publishing.

Collard, Sneed B., III. One Night in the Coral Sea. Brickman, Robin, illus. 2006. 32p. (gr. 3-7). 17.95 *(978-0-7569-6969-1(7))* Perfection Learning Corp.

Lewin, Ted & Lewin, Betsy. Top to Bottom down Under, 1 vol. 2014. (Adventures Around the World Ser.). (ENG., Illus.). 48p. (J). (gr. 1-6). pap. 11.95 *(978-1-62014-184-7(1),* leelowbooks) Lee & Low Bks., Inc.

Mahoney, Emily. 20 Fun Facts about the Great Barrier Reef, 1 vol. 2019. (Fun Fact File: World Wonders! Ser.). (ENG.). 32p. (J). (gr. 2-3). pap. 11.50 *(978-1-5382-3774-8(1),* 67063623-8d28-456f-b65d-fd019cc845bc) Stevens, Gareth Publishing LLLP.

Myers, Jenna. Australia. 2014. (J). *(978-1-4896-0946-5(6))* Weigl Pubs., Inc.

Woods, Michael & Woods, Mary B. Seven Natural Wonders of Australia & Oceania. 2009. (Seven Wonders Ser.). (ENG., Illus.). 80p. (gr. 5-8). 33.26 *(978-0-8225-9074-3(3))* Lerner Publishing Group.

NATURAL HISTORY, BIBLICAL

see Bible—Natural History

NATURAL HISTORY—CANADA

Daly, Ruth. Denali. (Illus.). (J). 2019. 32p. *(978-1-7911-1403-9(2))* 2014. (ENG., (gr. 4-7). lib. bdg. 28.55 *(978-1-4896-0744-7(7))* Weigl Pubs., Inc. (AV2 by Weigl).

Kitts, Wendy. Sable Island the Wandering Sandbar, 1 vol. 2011. (Compass Ser.). (ENG., Illus.). 90p. (J). (gr. 4-7). pap. 15.95 *(978-1-55109-865-4(2),* 60bc9aec-060e-4f4d-aa76-23ff15d18b5d) Nimbus Publishing, Ltd. CAN. Dist: Baker & Taylor Publisher Services (BTPS).

Matthews, Sheelagh. Canadian Shield. 2010. (Illus.). 32p. *(978-1-55388-628-0(3));* pap. *(978-1-55388-629-7(1))* Weigl Educational Pubs. Ltd.

Morrison, Jessica. Maritimes. 2010. (Illus.). 32p. *(978-1-55388-637-2(2));* pap. *(978-1-55388-638-9(0))* Weigl Educational Pubs. Ltd.

Pratt, Laura. Arctic. 2010. (Illus.). 32p. *(978-1-55388-631-0(3));* pap. *(978-1-55388-632-7(1))* Weigl Educational Pubs. Ltd.

—Plains. 2010. (Illus.). 32p. *(978-1-55388-625-9(9));* pap. *(978-1-55388-626-6(7))* Weigl Educational Pubs. Ltd.

NATURAL HISTORY—DICTIONARIES

Brooks, F. First Encyclopedia of Our World. 2004. (First Encyclopedia Ser.). (ENG., Illus.). 1p. (J). (gr. 3-18). pap. 9.99 *(978-0-7945-0216-4(4),* Usborne) EDC Publishing.

Burnie, David. The Kingfisher Nature Encyclopedia. 2019. (Kingfisher Encyclopedias Ser.). (ENG., Illus.). 320p. (J). 29.99 *(978-0-7534-7502-7(2),* 900198580, Kingfisher) Roaring Brook Pr.

NATURAL HISTORY—FICTION

Andrews, Jane. Stories Mother Nature Told Her Children. 2006. pap. *(978-1-4065-0875-8(6))* Dodo Pr.

—Young Reader's Series: The stories mother nature told her Children. 2009. 156p. pap. 16.95 *(978-1-60444-036-2(8))* IndoEuropeanPublishing.com.

Ballantyne, R. M. Blown to Bits; or, the Lonely Man of Rak. 2006. pap. *(978-1-4065-0515-3(3))* Dodo Pr.

—Red Rooney: Or, the Last of the Crew. 2007. (R. M. Ballantyne Collection). (Illus.). 408p. 22.00 *(978-1-934554-08-1(1))* Vision Forum, Inc., The.

Barnum, P. T. Dick Broadhead: A Story of Perilous Adve. 2006. pap. 30.95 *(978-1-4286-1959-3(3))* Kessinger Publishing, LLC.

Belaney, Archibald Stansfeld. On the Trail: Pages from the Writings of Grey Owl. Reynolds, E. E., ed. 2011. (ENG., Illus.). 130p. pap. 24.99 *(978-1-107-60015-7(4))* Cambridge Univ. Pr.

Delacre, Lulu. Rafi & Rosi. Delacre, Lulu, illus. 2005. (I Can Read Bks.). (Illus.). 64p. (J). (gr. k-3). pap. 3.99 *(978-0-06-009897-1(X),* Rayo) HarperCollins Pubs.

—Rafi & Rosi, 1 vol. Delacre, Lulu, illus. 2016. (Rafi & Rosi Ser.). (ENG., Illus.). 64p. (J). (gr. k-3). pap. 11.95 *(978-0-89239-377-0(7),* leelowcbp) Lee & Low Bks., Inc.

—Rafi y Rosi, 1 vol. Delacre, Lulu, illus. 2016. (Rafi & Rosi Ser.).Tr. of Rafi & Rosi. (SPA., Illus.). 64p. (J). (gr. k-3). pap. 10.95 *(978-0-89239-378-7(5),* leelowcbp) Lee & Low Bks., Inc.

Ganeri, Anita. My Pop-Up World Atlas. Waterhouse, Stephen, illus. 2012. (ENG.). 16p. (J). (gr. k-3). 24.99 *(978-0-7636-6094-9(9),* Templar) Candlewick Pr.

Grant, Robert. Jack in the Bush or A Summer on a Salmon River. 2005. pap. 33.95 *(978-1-4179-5573-2(2))* Kessinger Publishing, LLC.

Hadley, Caroline. Woodside; or, Look, Listen & Learn. 2007. (ENG., Illus.). 80p. per. *(978-1-4065-1557-2(4))* Dodo Pr.

McCabe, James Dabney, Jr. Planting the Wilderness or, the Pioneer Boys: a Story of Frontier Life. 2007. pap. 27.95 *(978-1-4304-8187-4(0))* Kessinger Publishing, LLC.

Meyer, Carolyn. The True Adventures of Charley Darwin. 2011. (ENG., Illus.). 336p. (YA). (gr. 7-12). 24.94 *(978-0-15-206194-4(0))* Harcourt Children's Bks.

—The True Adventures of Charley Darwin. 2011. (ENG., Illus.). 336p. (YA). (gr. 7). pap. 9.99 *(978-0-547-41564-2(8),* 1429780, Clarion Bks.) HarperCollins Pubs.

Miranda, Edward. The Truth about Dragons & Dinosaurs. Cassetta, Andrea, illus. 2007. 32p. per. 10.95 *(978-1-934246-22-1(0))* Peppertree Pr., The.

Stauffer, Sharon. Cornfield Baby: And Other Nature Surprises. 2003. (Illus.). 179p. 8.40 *(978-0-7399-2314-6(5),* 2344) Rod & Staff Pubs., Inc.

Stockton, Frank Richard. Round-about Rambles in Lands of Fact & Fancy. 2006. pap. *(978-1-4068-3083-5(6))* Echo Library.

Thomes, William Henry. The Bushrangers a Yankee's Adventures During His Second Visit to Australia by William H Thomes. 2006. 420p. per. 26.99 *(978-1-4255-4567-3(X))* Michigan Publishing.

Verne, Jules. The English at the North Pole. 2009. 160p. 24.95 *(978-1-60664-684-7(2));* pap. 13.95 *(978-1-60664-313-6(4))* Rodgers, Alan Bks.

Weaver, Anne H. The Voyage of the Beetle: A Journey Around the World with Charles Darwin & the Search for the Solution to the Mystery of Mysteries, As Narrated by Rosie, an Articulate Beetle. Lawrence, George, tr. Lawrence, George, illus. 2004. (Roman Mysteries Ser.). 80p. (J). (gr. 5-8). lib. bdg. 26.90 *(978-0-7613-2923-7(4),* Millbrook Pr.) Lerner Publishing Group.

NATURAL HISTORY—HAWAII

Looye, Juliette, text. I Live on an Island. 2004. (Illus.). 16p. (J). pap. *(978-0-7367-1936-0(9))* Zaner-Bloser, Inc.

NATURAL HISTORY—MIDDLE EAST

Vogel, Carole Garbuny & Leshem, Yossi. The Man Who Flies with Birds. 2009. (Israel Ser.). (ENG., Illus.). 64p. (J). (gr. 5-12). 18.95 *(978-0-8225-7643-3(0),* Kar-Ben Publishing) Lerner Publishing Group.

NATURAL HISTORY—NORTH AMERICA

Aloian, Molly. The Appalachians, 1 vol. 2011. (ENG., Illus.). 48p. (J). pap. *(978-0-7787-7568-3(2));* (gr. 4-7). lib. bdg. *(978-0-7787-7561-4(5))* Crabtree Publishing Co.

—The Rocky Mountains, 1 vol. 2011. (ENG., Illus.). 48p. (J). pap. *(978-0-7787-7570-6(4));* (gr. 4-7). lib. bdg. *(978-0-7787-7563-8(1))* Crabtree Publishing Co.

Bauer, Marion Dane. The Rocky Mountains: Ready-To-Read Level 1. Wallace, John, illus. (Wonders of America Ser.). (ENG.). 32p. (J). (gr. -1-1). 2019. 17.99 *(978-1-5344-4539-0(0))* 2006. pap. 4.99 *(978-0-689-86948-8(7))* Simon Spotlight. (Simon Spotlight).

Berkes, Marianne. Over in a River: Flowing Out to the Sea, 1 vol. Dubin, Jill, illus. 2013. (ENG.). 32p. (J). (gr. -1-3). 16.95 *(978-1-58469-329-1(0),* Dawn Pubns.) Sourcebooks, Inc.

Daly, Ruth. North America. 2014. (J). *(978-1-4896-0954-0(7))* Weigl Pubs., Inc.

Loughran, Donna. Living in the Tundra. (Rookie Read-About Geography Ser.). (ENG., Illus.). 32p. (J). (gr. 1-2). 2004. pap. 5.95 *(978-0-516-27331-0(0))* 2003. 18.69 *(978-0-516-22738-2(6))* Scholastic Library Publishing. (Children's Pr.).

Morrison, Jessica. Cordillera. 2010. (Illus.). 32p. *(978-1-55388-634-1(8));* pap. *(978-1-55388-635-8(6))* Weigl Educational Pubs. Ltd.

National Geographic Learning. Reading Expeditions (World Studies: World Cultures): North America: People & Places. 2007. (ENG., Illus.). 64p. (J). pap. 27.95 *(978-0-7922-4381-6(1))* CENGAGE Learning.

—Reading Expeditions (World Studies: World Regions): North America: Geography & Environments. 2007. (ENG., Illus.). 64p. (J). pap. 27.95 *(978-0-7922-4380-9(3))* CENGAGE Learning.

NATURAL HISTORY—OUTDOOR BOOKS

see Nature Study

NATURAL HISTORY—POETRY

Canetti, Yanitzia. El mundo es una Semilla: Un mundo Mejor. 2010. (SPA.). 32p. (J). 9.99 *(978-1-59835-287-0(3),* BrickHouse Education) Cambridge BrickHouse, Inc.

—Our Great Big World. 2010. 32p. pap. 9.99 *(978-1-59835-288-7(1),* BrickHouse Education) Cambridge BrickHouse, Inc.

Ewing, Susan. Lucky Hares & Itchy Bears: And Other Alaskan Animals. Blessing, Marlene, ed. Zerbetz, Evon, illus. 2012. (ENG.). 32p. (J). 16.95 *(978-0-9858506-0-9(4))* Octopoda Pr.

NATURAL HISTORY—SOUTH AMERICA

Banting, Erinn. The Galapagos Islands. 2006. (Natural Wonders Ser.). (Illus.). 32p. (J). (gr. 3-7). per. 9.95 *(978-1-59036-455-0(4))* Weigl Pubs., Inc.

—The Galapagos Islands: A Unique Ecosystem. 2006. (Natural Wonders Ser.). (Illus.). 32p. (J). (gr. 3-7). lib. bdg. 26.00 *(978-1-59036-449-9(X))* Weigl Pubs., Inc.

Roza, Greg. The Galapagos Islands. 2009. (Reading Room Collection 2 Ser.). 24p. (gr. 3-4). 42.50 *(978-1-60851-993-4(7),* PowerKids Pr.) Rosen Publishing Group, Inc., The.

Seiple, Samantha. Death on the River of Doubt: Theodore Roosevelt's Amazon Adventure. 2017. (Illus.). 214p. (J). *(978-1-338-12771-3(3),* Scholastic Pr.) Scholastic, Inc.

Sirota, Lyn A. South America. 2014. (J). *(978-1-4896-0958-8(X))* Weigl Pubs., Inc.

NATURAL HISTORY—UNITED STATES

Ake, Anne. Everglades: An Ecosystem Facing Choices & Challenges. 2017. 122p. (J). (gr. -1-12). pap. 19.95 *(978-1-68334-032-4(9))* Pineapple Pr., Inc.

America's Great Outdoors. (YA). (gr. 7-12). 39.00 *(978-0-87827-250-1(X))* Encyclopaedia Britannica, Inc.

Augustin, Byron & Kubena, Jake. The Grand Canyon, 1 vol. 2010. (Nature's Wonders Ser.). (ENG.). 96p. (gr. 6-6). 38.36 *(978-0-7614-3935-6(8),* 2a2af76d-3fb9-458d-b7b8-2c0e236fb6c0) Cavendish Square Publishing LLC.

Bakshi, Kelly. The First Americans. Bakshi, Kelly, illus. 2012. (Illus.). 16p. pap. 9.95 *(978-1-61633-278-5(6))* Guardian Angel Publishing, Inc.

Barlowe, Dot. Grand Canyon Plants & Animals. 2010. (Dover Nature Coloring Book Ser.). (ENG., Illus.). 32p. (gr. 3-8). pap. 4.99 *(978-0-486-47294-2(9),* 472949) Dover Pubns., Inc.

Burnham, Brad. Mammoth Cave: The World's Longest Cave System. 2009. (Famous Caves of the World Ser.). 24p. (gr. 3-4). 42.50 *(978-1-61512-498-5(5),* PowerKids Pr.) Rosen Publishing Group, Inc., The.

Chin, Jason. Grand Canyon. 2017. (ENG., Illus.). 54p. (J). 19.99 *(978-1-59643-950-4(5),* 900125249) Roaring Brook Pr.

Clickard, Carrie. Thomas Jefferson & the Mammoth Hunt: The True Story of the Quest for America's Biggest Bones. Carpenter, Nancy, illus. 2019. (ENG.). 40p. (J). (gr. -1-3). 17.99 *(978-1-4814-4268-8(6),* Beach Lane Bks.) Beach Lane Bks.

Dunphy, Madeleine. Here Is the Southwestern Desert. Coe, Anne, illus. 2006. (Web of Life Ser.: 4). (ENG.). 32p. (J). (gr. -1-3). pap. 11.95 *(978-0-9773795-6-9(6))* Web of Life Children's Bks.

Furstinger, Nancy. The Everglades. 2013. (J). *(978-1-62127-473-5(X));* pap. *(978-1-62127-479-7(9))* Weigl Pubs., Inc.

Hale, Wendy & Lantz, Peggy. The Young Naturalist's Guide to Florida. 2nd ed. 2006. (ENG., Illus.). 200p. (J). (gr. -1-12). per. 21.95 *(978-1-56164-377-6(7))* Pineapple Pr., Inc.

Hale, Wendy A. & Lantz, Peggy. The Coastlines of Florida. 2014. (Florida Water Story Ser.). (Illus.). 36p. (J). (gr. -1-12). pap. 6.95 *(978-1-56164-702-6(0))* Pineapple Pr., Inc.

—The Coral Reefs of Florida. 2014. (Florida Water Story Ser.). (Illus.). 36p. (J). (gr. -1-12). pap. 6.95 *(978-1-56164-703-3(9),* 9781561647033) Pineapple Pr., Inc.

—The Oceans of Florida. 2014. (Florida Water Story Ser.). (Illus.). 36p. (J). (gr. -1-12). pap. 6.95 *(978-1-56164-704-0(7))* Pineapple Pr., Inc.

—The Wetlands of Florida. 2014. (Florida Water Story Ser.). (Illus.). 36p. (J). (gr. -1-12). pap. 11.95 *(978-1-56164-705-7(5))* Pineapple Pr., Inc.

Hawley, Linda Gallo. Nature Adventures: A Guidebook of Nature Facts, Songs, & Hikes in San Diego County. 2017. (ENG., Illus.). viii, 56p. (J). (gr. 3-7). pap. 12.95 *(978-1-941384-28-2(5))* Sunbelt Pubns., Inc.

Helman, Andrea. Southwest Colors. Jecan, Gavriel, photos by. 2011. (Illus.). 24p. (J). 12.95 *(978-1-933855-64-6(9))* Rio Nuevo Pubs.

HELMAN, Wolfe Jecan. C Is for Coyote: A Southwest Alphabet Book. 2017. (Illus.). 32p. (J). (gr. k-3). bds. 7.95 *(978-1-63076-300-8(4))* Muddy Boots Pr.

Hubbs, Brian. Mountain Kings: A Collective Natural History of California, Sonoran, Durango & Queretaro Mountain Kingsnakes 2004. (Illus.). 356p. per. 45.00 *(978-0-9754641-0-6(8))* Tricolor Bks.

James, Helen Foster. Midwest. 2017. (21st Century Basic Skills Library: Outdoor Explorers Ser.). (ENG., Illus.). 24p. (J). (gr. k-3). lib. bdg. 30.64 *(978-1-63472-876-8(9),* 209930) Cherry Lake Publishing.

—Northeast. 2017. (21st Century Basic Skills Library: Outdoor Explorers Ser.). (ENG., Illus.). 24p. (J). (gr. k-3). lib. bdg. 30.64 *(978-1-63472-874-4(2),* 209922) Cherry Lake Publishing.

—Southeast. 2017. (21st Century Basic Skills Library: Outdoor Explorers Ser.). (ENG., Illus.). 24p. (J). (gr. k-3). lib. bdg. 30.64 *(978-1-63472-875-1(0),* 209926) Cherry Lake Publishing.

—Southwest. 2017. (21st Century Basic Skills Library: Outdoor Explorers Ser.). (ENG., Illus.). 24p. (J). (gr. k-3). lib. bdg. 30.64 *(978-1-63472-877-5(7),* 209934) Cherry Lake Publishing.

—West. 2017. (21st Century Basic Skills Library: Outdoor Explorers Ser.). (ENG., Illus.). 24p. (J). (gr. k-3). lib. bdg. 30.64 *(978-1-63472-878-2(5),* 209938) Cherry Lake Publishing.

Jankowski, Susan. Everglades National Park: Adventure, Explore, Discover, 1 vol. 2008. (America's National Parks Ser.). (ENG., Illus.). 128p. (gr. 6-7). lib. bdg. 37.27 *(978-1-59845-091-0(3),* db33302c-656c-441a-99b0-9da0ee6bf126) Enslow Publishing, LLC.

Kalman, Bobbie. Everglades National Park. 2009. (Introducing Habitats Ser.). (ENG., Illus.). 32p. (J). (gr. k-3). pap. *(978-0-7787-2988-4(5));* (gr. 1-3). lib. bdg. *(978-0-7787-2960-0(5))* Crabtree Publishing Co.

Larsen, Laurel. One Night in the Everglades. Turley, Joyce Mihran, illus. 2012. (Long Term Ecological Research Ser.). (ENG.). 32p. (J). (gr. 3-7). 15.95 *(978-0-9817700-4-8(5))* Taylor Trade Publishing.

Leotti-Bachem, Janice. Rookie Read-About Geography: the Everglades. 2005. (Rookie Read-About Geography Ser.). (ENG., Illus.). 32p. (J). (gr. 1-2). 20.50 *(978-0-516-22750-4(5),* Children's Pr.) Scholastic Library Publishing.

Lindeen, Mary. Natural States. 2011. (Wonder Readers Fluent Level Ser.). (ENG.). 16p. (J). (gr. -1-2). pap. 35.94 *(978-1-4296-8131-5(4),* Capstone Pr.) Capstone.

—Parks of the U. S. A. 2011. (Wonder Readers Fluent Level Ser.). (ENG.). 16p. (J). (gr. -1-2). pap. 6.25 *(978-1-4296-7949-7(2),* 118281, Capstone Pr.) Capstone.

Lynch, Wayne. Sonoran Desert. 2009. (ENG.). 64p. (J). (gr. 3-7). 16.95 *(978-1-58979-389-7(7))* Taylor Trade Publishing.

Mattern, Joanne. Glacier (a True Book: National Parks) (Library Edition) 2018. (True Book (Relaunch) Ser.). (ENG., Illus.). 48p. (J). (gr. 3-5). lib. bdg. 31.00 *(978-0-531-23506-5(8),* Children's Pr.) Scholastic Library Publishing.

Matthews, Sheelagh. Canadian Shield. 2010. (Illus.). 32p. *(978-1-55388-628-0(3));* pap. *(978-1-55388-629-7(1))* Weigl Educational Pubs. Ltd.

McCurdy, Michael. Walden Then & Now: An Alphabetical Tour of Henry Thoreau's Pond. McCurdy, Michael, illus. 2010. (ENG., Illus.). 32p. (J). (gr. 2-12). 16.95 *(978-1-58089-253-7(1))* Charlesbridge Publishing, Inc.

Mullen, Amy. Colors of New England: Explore the Colors of Nature. Kids Will Love Discovering the Colors of New England with Vivid & Beautiful Art, from the Purple Northern Blazing Star to the Green Mallard Duck. 2017. (Naturally Local Ser.). (ENG., Illus.). 20p. (J). (gr. -1-k). bds. 8.95 *(978-1-938093-99-9(2),* 809399) Duo Pr. LLC.

—Colors of the Southwest: Explore the Colors of Nature. Kids Will Love Discovering the Natural Colors of the Southwest in This Bilingual English-Spanish Book. 2019. (Naturally Local Ser.). (ENG., Illus.). 20p. (J). (gr. -1 — 1). bds. 8.99 *(978-1-947458-51-2(5),* 805851) Duo Pr. LLC.

Putnam, Jeff. National Monuments: Nature. 2004. (ZB Reads Trio Books). (Illus.). iii, 92p. (gr. 4-6). pap. 5.00 *(978-0-7367-1788-5(9))* Zaner-Bloser, Inc.

Rossi, Joe, photos by. Minnesota's Hidden Alphabet. 2010. (ENG., Illus.). 48p. (J). (gr. -1-1). 16.95 *(978-0-87351-808-6(X))* Minnesota Historical Society Pr.

M
N
O

Rowell, Rebecca. The 12 Most Amazing American Natural Wonders. 2015. (Amazing America Ser.). (ENG.). 32p. (J). (gr. 3-6). 32.80 *(978-1-63235-011-4(4),* 11550, 12-Story Library) Bookstaves, LLC.

St. Antoine, Sara, ed. The South Atlantic Coast & Piedmont: A Literary Field Guide. Nicholson, Trudy, illus. 2006. (Stories from Where We Live Ser.). (ENG.). 256p. (J). (gr. 4-7). per. 10.95 *(978-1-57131-664-6(7))* Milkweed Editions.

Viano, Hannah. S Is for Salmon: A Pacific Northwest Alphabet. Viano, Hannah, illus. 2014. (ENG., Illus.). 32p. (J). (-k). 16.99 *(978-1-57061-873-4(9),* Little Bigfoot) Sasquatch Bks.

Wade, Mary Dodson. Texas Plants & Animals. 2003. (Heinemann State Studies). (Illus.). 48p. (J). lib. bdg. 27.07 *(978-1-4034-0690-3(1))* Heinemann-Raintree.

Webb, Sophie. Looking for Seabirds: Journal from an Alaskan Voyage. 2004. (ENG., Illus.). 48p. (J). (gr. 5-7). tchr. ed. 16.00 *(978-0-618-21235-4(3),* 510539, Clarion Bks.) HarperCollins Pubs.

Weintraub, Aileen. The Grand Canyon: The Widest Canyon. 2009. (Great Record Breakers in Nature Ser.). 24p. (gr. 3-4). 42.50 *(978-1-61513-183-9(3),* PowerKids Pr.) Rosen Publishing Group, Inc., The.

Wiseman, Blaine. The Northeast. 2014. (Illus.). 32p. (J). *(978-1-4896-1230-4(0))* Weigl Pubs., Inc.

—The Southeast. 2014. (Illus.). 32p. (J). *(978-1-4896-1234-2(3))* Weigl Pubs., Inc.

—The Southwest. 2014. (Illus.). 32p. (J). *(978-1-4896-1238-0(6))* Weigl Pubs., Inc.

—The West. 2014. (Illus.). 32p. (J). *(978-1-4896-1242-7(4))* Weigl Pubs., Inc.

NATURAL HISTORY MUSEUMS

Lee, Sally. The National Museum of Natural History. 2017. (Smithsonian Field Trips Ser.). (ENG., Illus.). 32p. (J). (gr. 2-5). lib. bdg. 28.65 *(978-1-5157-7978-0(5),* 136048, Capstone Pr.) Capstone.

NATURAL LAW

see Civil Rights; Ethics; International Law; Liberty

NATURAL MONUMENTS

Bateman, Teresa. Red, White, Blue & Uncle Who? The Stories Behind Some of America's Patriotic Symbols. O'Brien, John, illus. 2003. (ENG.). 64p. (J). (gr. 3-7). pap. 8.99 *(978-0-8234-1784-1(0))* Holiday Hse., Inc.

Diemer, Lauren. Natural Landmarks. 2009. (U. S. Sites & Symbols Ser.). (Illus.). 48p. (J). (gr. 3-5). lib. bdg. 29.05 *(978-1-60596-146-0(9))* Weigl Pubs., Inc.

Edison, Erin. National Landmarks. 2018. (National Landmarks Ser.). (ENG.). 24p. (J). (gr. 1-3). 111.96 *(978-1-5435-3142-8(3),* 28584, Capstone Pr.) Capstone.

Freund, Lisa. The Seven Natural Wonders & Las siete maravillas naturales del Mundo: 6 English, 6 Spanish Adaptations. 2011. (ENG & SPA.). (J). 89.00 net. *(978-1-4108-5671-5(2))* Benchmark Education Co.

Graham, Amy. What Are the 7 Wonders of the Natural World?, 1 vol. 2013. (What Are the Seven Wonders of the World? Ser.). (ENG.). 48p. (gr. 4-6). 27.93 *(978-0-7660-4153-0(0),* af6a964e-2dd9-4996-b6ec-350ba4d998dd); pap. 11.53 *(978-1-4644-0232-6(9),* 33939e7a-ef2d-4ea9-a044-7ce3d21da59b) Enslow Publishing, LLC.

Lawrence, Ellen. Famous Rocks. 2015. (Illus.). 24p. (J). lib. bdg. 26.99 *(978-1-62724-297-4(X))* Bearport Publishing Co., Inc.

Lewison, Wendy Cheyette. L is for Liberty. Hines, Laura Freeman, illus. 2003. 24p. (J). (gr. -1-3). mass mkt. 5.99 *(978-0-448-43228-1(5),* Grosset & Dunlap) Penguin Young Readers Group.

Moore, David. National Geographic Science 1-2 (Earth Science: Rocks & Soil): Explore on Your Own: the Old Man of the Mountain. 2009. (Illus.). 12p. (C). pap. 8.95 *(978-0-7362-5581-3(8))* National Geographic School Publishing, Inc.

O'Donnell, Kerri. Natural Wonders of the World: Converting Distance Measurements to Metric Units. 2009. (PowerMath: Proficiency Plus Ser.). 32p. (gr. 4-5). 47.90 *(978-1-60851-414-4(5),* PowerKids Pr.) Rosen Publishing Group, Inc., The.

—Natural Wonders of the World: Converting Measurements to Metric Units, 1 vol. 2004. (PowerMath: Proficiency Plus Ser.). (ENG., Illus.). 32p. (J). (gr. 5-6). lib. bdg. 28.93 *(978-1-4042-2928-0(0),* 5c2ea680-9b31-45fd-bb0d-ac54c677dd07, PowerKids Pr.) Rosen Publishing Group, Inc., The.

—Natural Wonders of the World: Understanding & Representing Numbers in the Billions, 1 vol. 2010. (Math for the REAL World Ser.). (ENG., Illus.). 32p. (gr. 5-6). pap. 10.00 *(978-1-4042-5119-9(7),* 933a3be5-d151-44b2-bc03-c234e2f49077) Rosen Publishing Group, Inc., The.

Woods, Michael & Woods, Mary B. Seven Natural Wonders of North America. 2009. (Seven Wonders Ser.). (ENG., Illus.). 80p. (gr. 5-8). lib. bdg. 33.26 *(978-0-8225-9069-9(7))* Lerner Publishing Group.

NATURAL MONUMENTS—UNITED STATES

Brown Bear Books. Personalities & Places. 2010. (Native North Americans Ser.). (ENG.). 112p. (J). (gr. 9-12). 42.80 *(978-1-933834-81-8(1),* 16770) Brown Bear Bks.

Craats, Rennay. Natural Landmarks. 2004. (American Symbols Ser.). (Illus.). 24p. (J). (gr. 4-7). per. 8.95 *(978-1-59036-177-1(6));* (gr. 1-3). lib. bdg. 24.45 *(978-1-59036-133-7(4))* Weigl Pubs., Inc.

Defries, Cheryl L. What Are the 7 Natural Wonders of the United States?, 1 vol. 2013. (What Are the Seven Wonders of the World? Ser.). (ENG.). 48p. (gr. 4-6). 27.93 *(978-0-7660-4154-7(9),* 3eebb45e-2245-4acb-be30-896bc35041ee); pap. 11.53 *(978-1-4644-0233-3(7),* f4fc867d-dfc4-4794-b64d-4fcf503c47c7) Enslow Publishing, LLC.

Hurtig, Jennifer. Natural Landmarks. 2009. (U. S. Sites & Symbols Ser.). (Illus.). 48p. (J). (gr. 3-5). 10.95 *(978-1-60596-147-7(7))* Weigl Pubs., Inc.

Keppeler, Jill. Betsy Ross Didn't Create the American Flag: Exposing Myths about U. S. Symbols, 1 vol. 2016. (Exposed! Myths about Early American History Ser.). (ENG., Illus.). 32p. (J). (gr. 2-3). pap. 11.50 *(978-1-4824-5717-9(2),* cf9181ec-aaf5-45d6-9da4-23975869c3a7) Stevens, Gareth Publishing LLLP.

Shava, Ryder. Famous American Landmarks, 1 vol., 1. 2015. (Rosen REAL Readers: Social Studies Nonfiction / Fiction: Myself, My Community, My World Ser.). (ENG.). 12p. (J). (gr. k-1). pap. 6.33 *(978-1-5081-1800-8(0),* d0a53e29-9a3a-4ebd-a549-4f6730c760a9, Rosen Classroom) Rosen Publishing Group, Inc., The.

NATURAL RESOURCES

see also Conservation of Natural Resources; Fisheries; Forests and Forestry; Marine Resources; Mines and Mineral Resources; Power Resources; Reclamation of Land; Soil Conservation; Water Power; Water Resources Development; Water-Supply

Aboff, Marcie. The Giving Earth Natural Resources. 2016. (Spring Forward Ser.). (J). (gr. 2). *(978-1-4900-9427-4(X))* Benchmark Education Co.

Anniss, Matt. Planet under Pressure: Too Many People on Earth?, 1 vol. 2013. (Ask the Experts Ser.). (ENG., Illus.). 48p. (gr. 6-8). 34.60 *(978-1-4339-8643-7(4),* ba9a4679-8fc9-481e-89d7-dcd3e08b8840); pap. 15.05 *(978-1-4339-8644-4(2),* 104d6700-c607-4c06-a7c3-f24abfa7f72b) Stevens, Gareth Publishing LLLP. (Gareth Stevens Secondary Library).

Apel, Melanie Ann. Land & Resources of Ancient Greece, 1 vol. 2003. (Primary Sources of Ancient Civilizations: Egypt, Greece, & Rome Ser.). (ENG., Illus.). 24p. (gr. 3-4). pap. 8.25 *(978-0-8239-8937-9(2),* d7fa57df-c79d-45cc-ab13-992234f7e35a, PowerKids Pr.) Rosen Publishing Group, Inc., The.

Bailey, Gerry. Out of Energy, 1 vol. 2011. (Planet SOS Ser.). (ENG., Illus.). 48p. (J). (gr. 4-5). pap. 15.05 *(978-1-4339-4979-1(2),* ca3aae56-c396-4b06-abe1-98ea9e16d790); lib. bdg. 34.60 *(978-1-4339-4978-4(4),* f084b4fd-2536-4f54-8523-1986dc22daf0) Stevens, Gareth Publishing LLLP. (Gareth Stevens Learning Library).

Bard, Mariel. Geothermal Energy: Harnessing the Power of Earth's Heat, 1 vol. 2017. (Powered up! a STEM Approach to Energy Sources Ser.). (ENG.). 24p. (J). (gr. 3-3). 25.27 *(978-1-5081-6428-9(2),* 07634654-6e70-4565-8f3b-ee13fd9c6f0b, PowerKids Pr.) Rosen Publishing Group, Inc., The.

Bauman, Amy. Earth's Natural Resources, 1 vol. 2008. (Planet Earth Ser.). (ENG., Illus.). 32p. (gr. 3-3). pap. 11.50 *(978-0-8368-8924-6(X),* 6e7b5be6-9ff0-428a-84af-c4aa1c849a95) Stevens, Gareth Publishing LLLP.

Bensinger, Henry. Ancient Greek Geography, 1 vol. 2013. (Spotlight on Ancient Civilizations: Greece Ser.). (ENG., Illus.). 24p. (J). (gr. 3-4). pap. 11.00 *(978-1-4777-0879-8(0),* e18fb7e5-2305-4a2e-8411-b39b08ba3cee); lib. bdg. 26.27 *(978-1-4777-0773-9(5),* 2b314858-d4ba-4fc9-8c55-528a76309821) Rosen Publishing Group, Inc., The. (PowerKids Pr.).

Bethune, Helen. Why Do Diamonds Sparkle? All about Earth's Resources. 2010. (Illus.). 24p. (J). 49.50 *(978-1-61531-920-6(4),* PowerKids Pr.) Rosen Publishing Group, Inc., The.

Blankenship, LeeAnn. What Are Community Resources?, 1 vol. 2017. (Let's Find Out! Communities Ser.). (ENG., Illus.). 32p. (J). (gr. 2-3). 26.06 *(978-1-68048-719-0(1),* ba84014b-3d24-487a-941e-4db5e27074ce); pap. 13.90 *(978-1-68048-717-6(5),* a816def0-4548-4b2b-9ae1-c43e0c9fd655) Rosen Publishing Group, Inc., The. (Britannica Educational Publishing).

Bouler, Olivia. Olivia's Birds: Saving the Gulf. 2011. (Illus.). 32p. (J). (gr. -1-4). 17.99 *(978-1-4027-8665-5(4))* Sterling Publishing Co., Inc.

Brearley, Laurie. Geothermal Energy: the Energy Inside Our Planet (a True Book: Alternative Energy) 2018. (True Book (Relaunch) Ser.). (ENG.). 48p. (J). (gr. 3-5). pap. 7.95 *(978-0-531-23942-1(X),* Children's Pr.) Scholastic Library Publishing.

—Geothermal Energy: the Energy Inside Our Planet (a True Book: Alternative Energy) (Library Edition) 2018. (True Book (Relaunch) Ser.). (ENG.). 48p. (J). (gr. 3-5). lib. bdg. 31.00 *(978-0-531-23685-7(4),* Children's Pr.) Scholastic Library Publishing.

Brenner, C. M. The Petoskey & Me: Look & Find. 2016. (Illus.). 24p. (J). 16.95 *(978-0-9980042-0-4(0))* SimplyCMB,LLC.

Burgan, Michael. Polar Politics: Earth's Next Battlegrounds? 2017. (Exploring the Polar Regions Today Ser.: Vol. 8). (ENG., Illus.). 64p. (J). (gr. 7-12). 23.95 *(978-1-4222-3871-4(7))* Mason Crest.

Burton, Margie, et al. Riches from Nature. 2011. (Early Connections Ser.). (J). *(978-1-61672-504-4(4))* Benchmark Education Co.

Cardenas, Ernesto & Saavedra, Patricia. Recursos Naturales. Lt. ed. 2006. (SPA., Illus.). 16p. pap. 4.95 *(978-1-933668-34-5(2))* Milo Educational Bks. & Resources.

Cardenas, Ernesto A. Natural Resources. 2009. pap. 4.95 *(978-1-60698-084-2(X))* Milo Educational Bks. & Resources.

Carr, Aaron. Natural o Hecho Por el Hombre. 2013. (SPA., Illus.). 24p. (J). *(978-1-62127-607-4(4))* Weigl Pubs., Inc.

Cohn, Jessica. What Is Scarcity of Resources? 2008. (Economics in Action Ser.). (ENG., Illus.). 32p. (J). (gr. 3-7). pap. *(978-0-7787-4261-6(X))* Crabtree Publishing Co.

—What is Scarcity of Resources? 2008. (Economics in Action Ser.). (ENG.). 32p. (J). (gr. 3-6). 19.75 *(978-1-5311-7654-9(2))* Perfection Learning Corp.

Davis, Deneena. The 10 Most Essential Natural Resources. 2008. 14.99 *(978-1-55448-549-9(5))* Scholastic Library Publishing.

Doeden, Matt. Finding Out about Geothermal Energy. 2014. (Searchlight Books (tm) — What Are Energy Sources? Ser.). (ENG., Illus.). 40p. (J). (gr. 3-5). lib. bdg. 30.65 *(978-1-4677-3658-9(9),* 8f4ff786-843b-47d5-975f-8184a275845d, Lerner Pubns.) Lerner Publishing Group.

Downing, David. Geography & Resources of the Middle East, 1 vol. 2006. (World Almanac(r) Library of the Middle East Ser.). (ENG., Illus.). 48p. (gr. 5-8). pap. 15.05 *(978-0-8368-7341-2(6),* c35660ba-d711-42b1-bd2b-ea313d3f56f7); lib. bdg. 33.67 *(978-0-8368-7334-4(3),* 6015ec5a-10cb-469b-94db-ce6ade0fec4a) Stevens, Gareth Publishing LLLP. (Gareth Stevens Secondary Library).

Environment & Natural Resources. 2010. (ENG., Illus.). 112p. (gr. 5-8). 35.00 *(978-1-60413-289-2(2),* P178893, Facts On File) Infobase Holdings, Inc.

Explore Natural Resources! With 25 Great Projects. 2014. (Explore Your World Ser.). (ENG., Illus.). 96p. (J). (gr. k-4). pap. 13.95 *(978-1-61930-223-5(3),* d77aea72-75bd-4c5c-ab85-da4f5d6e346d) Nomad Pr.

Fredericks, Carrie, ed. Natural Gas, 1 vol. 2006. (Fueling the Future Ser.). (ENG., Illus.). 128p. (gr. 10-12). lib. bdg. 46.23 *(978-0-7377-3598-7(8),* fe55d9c4-7cf1-4b78-8c9d-67ae417f9dd0, Greenhaven Publishing) Greenhaven Publishing LLC.

From the Earth: How Resources Are Made, 12 vols. 2016. (From the Earth: How Resources Are Made Ser.). 32p. (ENG.). (gr. 3-4). lib. bdg. 169.62 *(978-1-4824-4605-0(7),* 8c7df53c-b798-41ef-ad7f-d3ed418a2fc1); (gr. 4-3). pap. 63.00 *(978-1-4824-5321-8(5))* Stevens, Gareth Publishing LLLP.

Gallant, Roy A. Resources: Nature's Riches, 1 vol. 2003. (EarthWorks Ser.). (ENG.). 80p. (gr. 6-6). 36.93 *(978-0-7614-1369-1(3),* 0dd95c64-fb9a-45cc-92d4-f94e0a8f1b32) Cavendish Square Publishing LLC.

Gedacht, Daniel C. Land & Resources in Ancient Rome, 1 vol. 2003. (Primary Sources of Ancient Civilizations Ser.). (ENG., Illus.). 24p. (J). (gr. 3-4). lib. bdg. 26.27 *(978-0-8239-6775-9(1),* c797989d-47f6-4af1-ae48-73b4cbd9c209, PowerKids Pr.) Rosen Publishing Group, Inc., The.

—Land & Resources of Ancient Rome, 1 vol. 2003. (Primary Sources of Ancient Civilizations: Egypt, Greece, & Rome Ser.). (ENG., Illus.). 24p. (gr. 3-4). pap. 8.25 *(978-0-8239-8943-0(7),* 2b3920d1-1dc8-47d0-a34b-f3d8f57c67d4, PowerKids Pr.) Rosen Publishing Group, Inc., The.

Gillett, Jack & Gillett, Meg. Natural-Resource Maps, 1 vol. 2012. (Maps of the Environmental World Ser.). (ENG., Illus.). 32p. (J). (gr. 5-5). pap. 11.60 *(978-1-4488-8616-6(3),* 649cb9b3-4c6b-4e66-a8ce-954b7092dc15, PowerKids Pr.) Rosen Publishing Group, Inc., The.

—Natural Resource Maps, 1 vol. 2012. (Maps of the Environmental World Ser.). (ENG., Illus.). 32p. (J). (gr. 5-5). lib. bdg. 30.27 *(978-1-4488-8612-8(0),* 8dd39e5b-dce3-4c53-a974-f784e6e1ddb1, PowerKids Pr.) Rosen Publishing Group, Inc., The.

Gleason, Carrie. Geothermal Energy: Using Earth's Furnace. 2008. (Energy Revolution Ser.). (ENG.). 32p. (J). (gr. 3-8). pap. *(978-0-7787-2931-0(1))* Crabtree Publishing Co.

Grady, Colin. Fossil Fuels, 1 vol. 2016. (Saving the Planet Through Green Energy Ser.). (ENG.). 24p. (gr. 3-3). pap. 10.35 *(978-0-7660-8276-2(8),* a2f49025-a1cc-49e5-a00b-747f911c770e) Enslow Publishing, LLC.

—Hydropower, 1 vol. 2016. (Saving the Planet Through Green Energy Ser.). (ENG., Illus.). 24p. (gr. 3-3). pap. 10.35 *(978-0-7660-8284-7(9),* 7d2aeac8-82d3-4230-8e07-415ec3f89ceb) Enslow Publishing, LLC.

—Solar Energy, 1 vol. 2016. (Saving the Planet Through Green Energy Ser.). (ENG.). 24p. (gr. 3-3). pap. 10.35 *(978-0-7660-8292-2(X),* 63428589-9614-420f-bd74-f18d6f17d432) Enslow Publishing, LLC.

—Wind Energy, 1 vol. 2016. (Saving the Planet Through Green Energy Ser.). (ENG.). 24p. (gr. 3-3). pap. 10.35 *(978-0-7660-8296-0(2),* 5ce62c39-a64f-4ac0-954f-1abb8003b926) Enslow Publishing, LLC.

Hansen, Amy. Geothermal Energy: Hot Stuff!, 1 vol. 2010. (Powering Our World Ser.). (ENG.). 24p. (J). (gr. 3-3). pap. 9.25 *(978-1-4358-9748-9(X),* 987c9f8f-0e33-4851-944c-62f92ef522bd, PowerKids Pr.) Rosen Publishing Group, Inc., The.

Hansen, Amy S. Geothermal Energy: Hot Stuff! 2010. (Powering Our World Ser.). 24p. (J). (gr. 2-5). E-Book 42.50 *(978-1-4488-0205-0(9));* (ENG., Illus.). (gr. 3-3). lib. bdg. 26.27 *(978-1-4358-9330-6(1),* 852da467-48ad-40cb-adcb-aa570b4fc4fe, PowerKids Pr.) Rosen Publishing Group, Inc., The.

Haugen, David M., ed. Coal, 1 vol. 2006. (Fueling the Future Ser.). (ENG., Illus.). 120p. (gr. 10-12). lib. bdg. 46.23 *(978-0-7377-3591-8(0),* 937b9193-6ad8-4722-8818-72ee5286d53e, Greenhaven Publishing) Greenhaven Publishing LLC.

Holt, Rinehart and Winston Staff. Environmental Science Chptr. 18: Renewable Energy. 4th ed. Date not set. pap. 11.20 *(978-0-03-068079-3(4))* Holt McDougal.

—Holt Science Spectrum Chptr. 23: Using Natural Resources. 4th ed. Date not set. pap. 11.20 *(978-0-03-068062-5(X))* Holt McDougal.

Howell, Izzi. Earth's Resources Geo Facts. 2018. (Geo Facts Ser.). (Illus.). 32p. (J). (gr. 5-5). *(978-0-7787-4383-5(7))* Crabtree Publishing Co.

—Natural Resources Eco Facts. 2019. (Eco Facts Ser.). (ENG., Illus.). 32p. (J). (gr. 5-5). pap. *(978-0-7787-6363-5(3),* 9dc87f35-1df2-417c-b19c-d6f7e5d71941); lib. bdg. *(978-0-7787-6347-5(1),* b98309aa-4ab7-476f-aab4-f5e2f67278fb) Crabtree Publishing Co.

Johanson, Paula. Making Good Choices about Nonrenewable Resources, 1 vol. 2009. (Green Matters Ser.). (ENG.). 64p. (YA). (gr. 6-6). pap. 13.95 *(978-1-4358-5604-2(X),* fa00a907-c6e1-4ed5-922e-f683c420249c); (Illus.). 37.13 *(978-1-4358-5311-9(3),* 15f3eabb-e491-4ba4-bbb0-97cf3aa2d1c2) Rosen Publishing Group, Inc., The.

Kaplan, Leslie C. Land & Resources in Ancient Egypt, 1 vol. 2003. (Primary Sources of Ancient Civilizations Ser.). (ENG., Illus.). 24p. (J). (gr. 3-4). lib. bdg. 26.27 *(978-0-8239-6781-0(6),* 533f4e71-2dc4-4ed4-b5b5-c75ef52cb58e, PowerKids Pr.) Rosen Publishing Group, Inc., The.

—Land & Resources of Ancient Egypt. (Primary Sources of Ancient Civilizations Ser.). 24p. (gr. 3-3). 2009. 42.50 *(978-1-60851-560-8(5))* 2003. (ENG., Illus.). pap. 8.25 *(978-0-8239-8931-7(3),* f38f6796-2234-4a61-94ec-a4940b7e3c5c) Rosen Publishing Group, Inc., The. (PowerKids Pr.).

Kerrod, Robin. New Materials. 2003. (21st Century Science Ser.). 48p. (J). lib. bdg. 27.10 *(978-1-58340-353-2(1))* Black Rabbit Bks.

Killian, Maryellen. Energy for Earth. 2013. (InfoMax Readers Ser.). (ENG.). 24p. (J). (gr. 2-3). pap. 49.50 *(978-1-4777-2435-4(4));* (Illus.). pap. 8.25 *(978-1-4777-2434-7(6),* 2dc4e581-12d6-4361-a0d1-2da53eaf3a05) Rosen Publishing Group, Inc., The. (Rosen Classroom).

Lachner, Elizabeth. Geothermal Energy, 1 vol. 2018. (Exploring Energy Technology Ser.). (ENG., Illus.). 48p. (J). (gr. 6-6). pap. 15.05 *(978-1-5081-0615-9(0),* 5e33db50-b943-470c-9dc6-568bde12f8c8, Britannica Educational Publishing) Rosen Publishing Group, Inc., The.

Let's Learn about Natural Resources, 14 vols. 2017. (Let's Learn about Natural Resources Ser.). (ENG.). (J). (gr. 1-2). lib. bdg. 169.89 *(978-0-7660-9233-4(X),* 575b98f2-5bec-4db1-b8b2-2e361c88a5db) Enslow Publishing, LLC.

Lewis, Daniel. Agriculture, Food & Natural Resources, Vol. 10. 2018. (Careers in Demand for High School Graduates Ser.). 112p. (J). (gr. 7). lib. bdg. 34.60 *(978-1-4222-4136-3(X))* Mason Crest.

Linde, Barbara M. All about Resource Maps, 1 vol. 2018. (Map Basics Ser.). (ENG.). 24p. (gr. 2-3). lib. bdg. 24.27 *(978-1-5382-2918-7(8),* 5002bfa9-e33f-44bb-8978-edd1de8072f0) Stevens, Gareth Publishing LLLP.

Loria, Laura. What Are Resources? 2016. (Let's Find Out! Ser.). (ENG.). 32p. (J). (gr. 3-7). 23.70 *(978-1-5311-8659-3(9))* Perfection Learning Corp.

—What Are Resources?, 1 vol. 2016. (Let's Find Out! Community Economics Ser.). (ENG.). 32p. (J). (gr. 2-3). lib. bdg. 26.06 *(978-1-68048-404-5(4),* 061ecdd6-1dc0-4f0e-bee7-1fdb23f71350) Rosen Publishing Group, Inc., The.

MacAulay, Kelley. Why Do We Need Soil? 2014. (Natural Resources Close-Up Ser.). (ENG., Illus.). 24p. (J). (gr. 1-1). lib. bdg. *(978-0-7787-0493-5(9))* Crabtree Publishing Co.

Machajewski, Sarah. 20 Fun Facts about Earth's Resources, 1 vol. 2017. (Fun Fact File: Earth Science Ser.). (ENG.). 32p. (J). (gr. 2-3). pap. 11.50 *(978-1-5382-1177-9(7),* c1d72276-a1e0-4d1f-ae22-9281d6a5cf98); lib. bdg. 27.93 *(978-1-5382-1179-3(3),* 98e3db7e-72ff-4b25-9811-e101ac67ec9c) Stevens, Gareth Publishing LLLP.

Mangor, Jodie. Geothermal Energy. 2016. (Alternative Energy Ser.). (ENG., Illus.). 48p. (J). (gr. 4-8). lib. bdg. 35.64 *(978-1-68078-454-1(4),* 23845) ABDO Publishing Co.

Maurer, Tracy Nelson. Using Economic & Resource Maps. 2016. (Searchlight Books (tm) — What Do You Know about Maps? Ser.). (ENG., Illus.). 40p. (J). (gr. 3-5). 30.65 *(978-1-5124-0951-2(0),* 13bcb8a7-1238-4e73-bbee-ce32e6ebde1a, Lerner Pubns.) Lerner Publishing Group.

Montgomery, Anne. Nature Made, 1 vol. rev. ed. 2014. (Science: Informational Text Ser.). (ENG., Illus.). 24p. (J). (gr. k-1). pap. 9.99 *(978-1-4807-4528-6(6))* Teacher Created Materials, Inc.

Morgan, Sally. Natural Resources. 2009. (Illus.). 46p. (J). 32.80 *(978-1-59920-102-3(X),* 1283677) Black Rabbit Bks.

Morrill, Amos. Augusta & Elliott. 2007. (ENG., Illus.). (J). 15.95 *(978-1-892738-36-3(8))* Island Nation Pr., LLC.

Morris, Neil. Geothermal Power. 2009. (Energy Now & in the Future Ser.). (ENG.). 48p. (J). (gr. 6-10). 34.25 *(978-1-59920-340-9(5),* 19269, Smart Apple Media) Black Rabbit Bks.

Nagle, Jeanne. Making Good Choices about Renewable Resources. 2009. (J). 77.70 *(978-1-4358-5603-5(1));* (ENG.). 64p. (YA). (gr. 6-6). pap. 13.95 *(978-1-4358-5602-8(3),* d79d9d0b-48f4-4595-91cf-8442930ad0d1); (ENG., Illus.). 64p. (YA). (gr. 6-6). lib. bdg. 37.13 *(978-1-4358-5310-2(5),* 2cbe5ab7-3998-443d-932b-b56b1dea8327) Rosen Publishing Group, Inc., The.

New Careers for the 21st Century: Finding Your Role in the Global Renewal, 15 vols., Set. Incl. Environmental Science & Protection: Keeping Our Planet Green. Strange, Cordelia. pap. 9.95 *(978-1-4222-2034-4(6));* Freelance & Technical Writers: Words for Sale. Flath, Camden. pap. 9.95 *(978-1-4222-2035-1(4));* Green Construction: Creating Energy-Efficient, Low-Impact Buildings. Miller, Malinda. pap. 9.95 *(978-1-4222-2036-8(2));* Medical Technicians: Health-Care Support for the 21st Century. Strange, Cordelia. pap. 9.95 *(978-1-4222-2038-2(9));* Modern Mechanics: Maintaining Tomorrow's Green Vehicles. Miller, Malinda. pap. 9.95 *(978-1-4222-2039-9(7));* Pharmaceutical Industry: Better Medicine for the 21st Century. Miller, Malinda. pap. 9.95 *(978-1-4222-2040-5(0));* Physicians Assistants & Nurses: New Opportunities in the 21st-Century Health System. Strange, Cordelia. pap. 9.95 *(978-1-4222-2041-2(9));* Social Workers: Finding Solutions for Tomorrow's Society. Flath, Camden. (Illus.). pap. 9.95 *(978-1-4222-2042-9(7));* Therapy Jobs in Educational Settings: Speech, Physical, Occupational & Audiology. Flath, Camden. (Illus.). pap. 9.95 *(978-1-4222-2047-4(8));* Tomorrow's Enterprising Scientists: Computer Software Designers & Specialists. Flath, Camden. pap. 9.95 *(978-1-4222-2043-6(5));* Tomorrow's Teachers: Urban Leadership, Empowering Students & Improving Lives. Miller, Malinda. pap. 9.95 *(978-1-4222-2044-3(3));* Tomorrow's Transportation: Green Solutions for Air, Land, & Sea. Miller, Malinda. pap. 9.95 *(978-1-4222-2045-0(1));* 21st-Century Counselors: New Approaches to Mental Health & Substance Abuse. Flath, Camden. pap. 9.95 *(978-1-4222-2046-7(X));* 64p. (YA). (gr. 7-18). 2010. 2011. Set pap. 149.25 *(978-1-4222-2032-0(X))* Mason Crest.

Paderewski, Elliot. The Natural Resources of My Community, 1 vol. 2016. (Rosen REAL Readers: Social Studies Nonfiction / Fiction: Myself, My Community, My World Ser.). (ENG.). 12p. (gr. k-1). pap. 6.33 *(978-1-5081-2362-0(4),* 78f620bf-3c49-4827-901a-b6550a44e5de, Rosen Classroom) Rosen Publishing Group, Inc., The.

Prior, Jennifer Overend. Our Natural Resources. rev. ed. 2014. (Social Studies: Informational Text Ser.). (ENG., Illus.). 32p. (J). (gr. 3-4). pap. 11.99 (978-1-4333-7373-2(4)) Teacher Created Materials, Inc.

Ravilious, Kate. Power: Ethical Debates about Resources & the Environment. 2009. (Dilemmas in Modern Science Ser.). (YA). (gr. 7-12). 34.25 (978-1-59920-096-5(1)) Black Rabbit Bks.

Reynoldson, Fiona. Understanding Geothermal Energy & Bioenergy, 1 vol. 2010. (World of Energy Ser.). (ENG.). 48p. (J). (gr. 5-6). lib. bdg. 34.60 (978-1-4339-4121-4(X), 86099706-fa9f-428f-886d-c82ef916e319, Gareth Stevens Learning Library) Stevens, Gareth Publishing LLLP.

Rice, William B. Our Resources. 2015. (Science: Informational Text Ser.). (ENG., Illus.). 32p. (J). (gr. 3-5). pap. 11.99 (978-1-4807-4689-3(4)) Teacher Created Materials, Inc.

—The Story of Fossil Fuels. 2015. (Science: Informational Text Ser.). (ENG., Illus.). 32p. (J). (gr. 3-5). pap. 11.99 (978-1-4807-4690-9(8)) Teacher Created Materials, Inc.

Robert, Nolan. What Are Natural Resources?, 1 vol. 2008. (Real Life Readers Ser.). (ENG.). 12p. (gr. 2-3). pap. 5.90 (978-1-4042-7953-7(9), fbab2261-dfe5-49da-b648-ee505550f1d2, Rosen Classroom) Rosen Publishing Group, Inc., The.

Sanchez, Micah. Natural Resource Depletion. 2018. (Earth's Environment in Danger Ser.). (ENG.). 24p. (J). (gr. 2-5). 19.05 (978-1-5311-8668-5(8)) Perfection Learning Corp.

—Natural Resource Depletion, 1 vol. 2017. (Earth's Environment in Danger Ser.). (ENG.). 24p. (J). (gr. 3-3). 25.27 (978-1-5383-2541-4(1), db316b00-8349-4ea0-9a3b-ac48fb859b10); pap. 9.25 (978-1-5383-2611-4(6), 4490c9c3-d1ee-4612-9e03-8566cd88d76c) Rosen Publishing Group, Inc., The. (PowerKids Pr.).

Smith, David J. If: A Mind-Bending New Way of Looking at Big Ideas & Numbers. Adams, Steve, illus. 2014. (ENG.). 40p. (J). (gr. 3-7). 19.99 (978-1-894786-34-8(3)) Kids Can Pr., Ltd. CAN. Dist: Hachette Bk. Group.

Smuskiewicz, Alfred J. Earth's Resources, 1 vol. 2007. (Gareth Stevens Vital Science Library: Earth Science Ser.). (ENG., Illus.). 48p. (gr. 5-8). pap. 15.05 (978-0-8368-7874-5(4), 07354a9e-9007-41dd-84e8-73657a420708, Gareth Stevens Secondary Library) Stevens, Gareth Publishing LLLP.

Spilsbury, Richard & Spilsbury, Louise. Natural Resources, 1 vol. 2018. (Flowchart Smart Ser.). (ENG.). 48p. (gr. 4-5). pap. 15.05 (978-1-5382-3488-4(2), be156216-0d44-46a5-93a7-9833da920256) Stevens, Gareth Publishing LLLP.

Stewart, Audrey. Our Natural Resources, 1 vol. 2013. (InfoMax Readers Ser.). (ENG.). 24p. (J). (gr. 2-2). pap. 8.25 (978-1-4777-2356-2(0), e71e7dff-7c69-4d50-b7c2-4187f305ba5c); pap. 49.50 (978-1-4777-2357-9(9)) Rosen Publishing Group, Inc., The. (Rosen Classroom).

Sundance/Newbridge LLC Staff. Our Natural Resources. 2004. (Reading PowerWorks Ser.). (gr. 1-3). 37.50 (978-0-7608-9221-3(0)); pap. 6.10 (978-0-7608-9222-0(9)) Sundance/Newbridge Educational Publishing.

Tracey, Michele. What Is a Natural Resource? 2012. (Level B Ser.). (ENG., Illus.). 16p. (J). (gr. k-2). pap. 7.95 (978-1-927136-15-7(6), 19423) RiverStream Publishing.

Ventura, Marne. Conserving Resources. 2018. (Community Economics Ser.). (ENG., Illus.). 24p. (J). (gr. 1-1). pap. 8.95 (978-1-63517-796-1(0), 1635177960) North Star Editions.

—Conserving Resources. 2018. (Community Economics Ser.). (ENG., Illus.). 24p. (J). (gr. k-3). lib. bdg. 31.36 (978-1-5321-6001-1(1), 28634, Pop! Cody Koala) Pop!

White, Nancy. Using Earth's Underground Heat. 2009. (Going Green Ser.). (Illus.). 32p. (J). (gr. 3-6). lib. bdg. 28.50 (978-1-59716-963-9(3), 1299203) Bearport Publishing Co., Inc.

Willis, John. Natural Resources. 2018. (J). (978-1-5105-2181-0(X)) SmartBook Media, Inc.

Winters, Adam. Destruction of Earth's Resources: The Need for Sustainable Development. (Extreme Environmental Threats Ser.). 64p. (gr. 6-6). 2009. 58.50 (978-1-61512-425-1(X)) 2006. (ENG., Illus.). (YA). lib. bdg. 37.13 (978-1-4042-0746-2(5), 6e97614f-4fba-4350-b61b-96d281efacaa) Rosen Publishing Group, Inc., The.

Zuchora-Walske, Christine. Energy in the Real World. 2013. (Science in the Real World Ser.). (ENG.). 48p. (J). (gr. 4-8). pap. 18.50 (978-1-61783-789-0(X), 14613) ABDO Publishing Co.

NATURAL RESOURCES—UNITED STATES

Conklin, Wendy. Georgia's Location & Resources. rev. ed. 2016. (Social Studies: Informational Text Ser.). (ENG., Illus.). 32p. (gr. 2-4). pap. 10.99 (978-1-4938-2549-3(6)) Teacher Created Materials, Inc.

Fourment, Tiffany. My Water Comes from the Rocky Mountains. Emerling, Dorothy, illus. 2009. (Long Term Ecological Research Ser.). (ENG.). 32p. (J). (gr. 1-5). pap. 9.95 (978-0-9817700-1-7(0)) Taylor Trade Publishing.

—My Water Comes from the San Juan Mountains. 2009. (ENG.). 32p. (J). (gr. 4-7). 16.95 (978-0-9817700-2-4(9)) Taylor Trade Publishing.

Fourment, Tiffany & Gianniny, Gary. My Water Comes from the San Juan Mountains. Emerling, Dorothy, illus. 2009. (ENG.). 32p. (J). (gr. 4-7). pap. 9.95 (978-0-9817700-3-1(7)) Taylor Trade Publishing.

Marfa, Isabelle. The Land & Resources of Texas: Shaping the Growth of the State, 1 vol. 2010. (Spotlight on Texas Ser.). (ENG., Illus.). 32p. (J). (gr. 3-4). pap. 11.75 (978-1-61532-478-1(X), 37cfdc00-8cea-43d9-ab4c-31e32f0e88bc); lib. bdg. 28.93 (978-1-61532-480-4(1), ccfc673c-de8c-4cc5-a9a7-c32e75942b0e) Rosen Publishing Group, Inc., The.

McAneney, Robert. America's Natural Resources, 1 vol. 2013. (Rosen Readers Ser.). (ENG.). 24p. (J). (gr. 2-2). pap. 8.25 (978-1-4777-2361-6(7), aac0cf63-11a9-4288-a643-98ebdba03762); pap. 49.50 (978-1-4777-2363-0(3)) Rosen Publishing Group, Inc., The. (Rosen Classroom).

Schimel, Kate & Roza, Greg. The Land & Resources of New York. (Illus.). 24p. (J). 2012. 60.00 (978-1-4488-5754-8(6)) 2011. (ENG., (gr. 3-4). pap. 10.00 (978-1-4488-5753-1(8), 564ffb79-14f9-4066-8539-3a5288f7cd18) 2011. (ENG., (gr. 3-4). lib. bdg. 26.27 (978-1-4488-5740-1(6), bbd49960-90e6-47a9-b62c-9107484f67b6) Rosen Publishing Group, Inc., The. (PowerKids Pr.).

NATURAL SELECTION

see also Evolution

Bortz, Fred. Charles Darwin & the Theory of Evolution by Natural Selection, 1 vol. 2013. (Revolutionary Discoveries of Scientific Pioneers Ser.). (ENG., Illus.). 80p. (J). (gr. 6-6). 38.41 (978-1-4777-1802-5(8), b57f63b3-2c59-46d6-b2db-37b21932fa7a) Rosen Publishing Group, Inc., The.

Byrne, Eugene. Darwin: A Graphic Biography. Gurr, Simon, illus. 2013. (ENG.). 100p. (gr. 7). pap. 9.95 (978-1-58834-352-9(9), Smithsonian Bks.) Smithsonian Institution Scholarly Pr.

Darwin, Charles. Charles Darwin's on the Origin of Species. White, Teagan, illus. 2018. 170p. (J). pap. (978-1-4814-6250-1(4), Atheneum Bks. for Young Readers) Simon & Schuster Children's Publishing.

—On the Origin of Species. 2019. (ENG.). (J). 228p. pap. 8.99 (978-1-6975-8223-9(0)); 298p. pap. 20.00 (978-1-0897-3497-0(2)) Independently Published.

Drake, Jane & Love, Ann. Alien Invaders: Species That Threaten Our World. Thurman, Mark, illus. 2013. 56p. (J). (gr. 4-7). pap. 8.95 (978-1-77049-512-8(6), Tundra Bks.) Tundra Bks. CAN. Dist: Penguin Random Hse. LLC.

Gray, Susan H. Australian Spotted Jellyfish. 2010. (21st Century Skills Library: Animal Invaders Ser.). (ENG., Illus.). 32p. (gr. 4-8). lib. bdg. 32.07 (978-1-60279-628-7(9), 200333) Cherry Lake Publishing.

Jackson, Cari. Alien Invasion: Invasive Species Become Major Menaces. 2009. (Current Science Ser.). (ENG.). 48p. (J). (gr. 4-6). pap. 8.95 (978-1-4339-2128-5(6), Gareth Stevens Learning Library) Stevens, Gareth Publishing LLLP.

—Alien Invasion: Invasive Species Become Major Menaces, 1 vol. 2009. (Current Science Ser.). (ENG.). 48p. (C). (gr. 4-6). lib. bdg. 33.67 (978-1-4339-2057-8(3), 2b0ddd7e-122f-45ba-9cda-c11f2e8ea6b7) Stevens, Gareth Publishing LLLP.

Luongo, Charlotte. Evolution, 1 vol. 2010. (Big Ideas in Science Ser.). (ENG., Illus.). 48p. (J). (gr. 5-5). 34.07 (978-0-7614-4393-3(2), 748ea2c0-82ba-46c2-abc8-9a5a1a32dee4) Cavendish Square Publishing LLC.

McCormick, Joyce. Natural Selection, 1 vol. 2016. (Spotlight on Ecology & Life Science Ser.). (ENG.). 24p. (J). (gr. 4-6). pap. 11.00 (978-1-4994-2583-3(X), 22a1d518-4813-45d2-aa6d-6a02767766a8, PowerKids Pr.) Rosen Publishing Group, Inc., The.

O'Connor, Karen. The Threat of Invasive Species. 2013. (Animal 911: Environmental Threats Ser.). 48p. (J). (gr. 3-5). pap. 84.30 (978-1-4339-9724-2(X)); (ENG., Illus.). (gr. 4-4). pap. 15.05 (978-1-4339-9723-5(1), c5676dfc-cca0-461f-82de-babf31c738a2); (ENG., Illus.). (gr. 4-4). lib. bdg. 34.61 (978-1-4339-9722-8(3), 4d5dbd73-bb07-4b99-9192-181857cf2b58) Stevens, Gareth Publishing LLLP.

Ridley, Kimberly. Extreme Survivors: Animals That Time Forgot (How Nature Works), 1 vol. 2017. (How Nature Works: 0). (ENG., Illus.). 48p. (J). (gr. 2-7). 17.95 (978-0-88448-500-1(5), 884500) Tilbury Hse. Pubs.

Stefoff, Rebecca, adapted by. On the Origin of Species: Young Readers Edition. 2018. (ENG., Illus.). 176p. (J). (gr. 5). 25.99 (978-1-4814-6249-5(0), Atheneum Bks. for Young Readers) Simon & Schuster Children's Publishing.

Tweet, Jonathan. Grandmother Fish. Lewis, Karen, illus. 2016. (ENG.). 40p. (J). 18.99 (978-1-250-11323-8(7), 900170789) Feiwel & Friends.

NATURALISTS

Anastasio, Dina. Who Was Steve Irwin? 2015. (Who Was... ? Ser.). lib. bdg. 16.00 (978-0-606-36749-3(7)) Turtleback.

Anderson, Margaret J. Carl Linnaeus: Father of Classification, 1 vol. 2009. (Great Minds of Science Ser.). (ENG., Illus.). 128p. (gr. 5-6). lib. bdg. 35.93 (978-0-7660-3009-1(1), b4a47fe9-85d9-4947-b0ad-cdbcc62f40db) Enslow Publishing, LLC.

—Carl Linnaeus: Genius of Classification, 1 vol. 2014. (Genius Scientists & Their Genius Ideas Ser.). (ENG.). 96p. (gr. 5-5). (J). 29.60 (978-0-7660-6540-6(5), 83c9f646-5d58-49d7-b4fb-cf0e34a75de2); pap. 13.88 (978-0-7660-6541-3(3), f46de9af-6872-45da-aa5e-e0751b90bbce) Enslow Publishing, LLC.

—Charles Darwin: Genius of a Revolutionary Theory, 1 vol. 2014. (Genius Scientists & Their Genius Ideas Ser.). (ENG.). 96p. (gr. 5-5). (J). 29.60 (978-0-7660-6545-1(6), 322fba36-b6dc-45fa-bd0d-759c2b174f83); pap. 13.88 (978-0-7660-6546-8(4), dba8ccd0-f3ad-4640-9cf2-c4c108ae1bc1) Enslow Publishing, LLC.

Bortz, Fred. Charles Darwin & the Theory of Evolution by Natural Selection, 1 vol. 2013. (Revolutionary Discoveries of Scientific Pioneers Ser.). (ENG., Illus.). 80p. (J). (gr. 6-6). 38.41 (978-1-4777-1802-5(8), b57f63b3-2c59-46d6-b2db-37b21932fa7a) Rosen Publishing Group, Inc., The.

Bowler, Peter J. An Interview with Charles Darwin, 1 vol. 2014. (Meet the Masters Ser.). (ENG.). 112p. (YA). (gr. 9-9). lib. bdg. 44.50 (978-1-62712-909-1(X), 0ea5fed2-1157-4273-82fd-9e8d089c1f23) Cavendish Square Publishing LLC.

Burns, Monique. Cool Careers Without College for People Who Love to Make Things Grow. 2009. (Cool Careers Without College Ser.). 144p. (gr. 6-6). 66.50 (978-1-61511-975-2(2)) Rosen Publishing Group, Inc., The.

Carson, Mary Kay. Park Scientists: Gila Monsters, Geysers, & Grizzly Bears in America's Own Backyard. 2017. (Scientists in the Field Ser.). (ENG., Illus.). 80p. (J). (gr. 5-7). pap. 9.99 (978-1-328-74090-8(0), 1677131, Clarion Bks.) HarperCollins Pubs.

Coates, Eileen S. Charles Darwin & the Origin of Species, 1 vol. 2018. (STEM Milestones: Historic Inventions & Discoveries Ser.). (ENG.). 24p. (gr. 3-3). 25.27 (978-1-5383-4355-5(X), eb5c4eda-2b83-4135-9a93-da10d3bd05f9, PowerKids Pr.) Rosen Publishing Group, Inc., The.

Colson, Mary. Charles Darwin & Alfred Russel Wallace. 2014. (Dynamic Duos of Science Ser.). 48p. (YA). (gr. 5-8). pap. 84.30 (978-1-4824-1280-2(2)) Stevens, Gareth Publishing LLLP.

Cook, Diane. Charles Darwin: British Naturalist. 2013. (People of Importance Ser.: 21). (Illus.). 32p. (J). (gr. 4-18). 19.95 (978-1-4222-2844-9(4)) Mason Crest.

Crum, Anna-Maria. Animal Behaviorists & Conductistas de Animales: 6 English, 6 Spanish Adaptations. 2011. (ENG & SPA.). (J). 89.00 net. (978-1-4108-5679-1(8)) Benchmark Education Co.

—Trackers of Dynamic Earth & Rastreadores de nuestra dinámica Tierra: 6 English, 6 Spanish Adaptations. 2011. (ENG & SPA.). (J). 97.00 net. (978-1-4108-5718-7(2)) Benchmark Education Co.

Danneberg, Julie. John Muir Wrestles a Waterfall. Hogan, Jamie, illus. 2015. (ENG.). 32p. (J). (gr. -1-3). lib. bdg. 17.99 (978-1-58089-586-6(7)) Charlesbridge Publishing, Inc.

Devera, Czeena. Charles Darwin. Bane, Jeff, illus. 2018. (My Early Library: My Itty-Bitty Bio Ser.). (ENG.). 24p. (J). (gr. k-1). lib. bdg. 30.64 (978-1-5341-2887-3(5), 211592) Cherry Lake Publishing.

—John Muir. Bane, Jeff, illus. 2017. (My Early Library: My Itty-Bitty Bio Ser.). (ENG.). 24p. (J). (gr. k-1). lib. bdg. 30.64 (978-1-63472-814-0(9), 209682) Cherry Lake Publishing.

Dolz, Jordi Bayarri. Charles Darwin & the Theory of Evolution. Dolz, Jordi Bayarri, illus. 2020. (Graphic Science Biographies Ser.). (ENG., Illus.). 40p. (J). (gr. 5-8). 30.65 (978-1-5415-7822-7(8), 02b64816-f2d2-4c79-b467-760ef0a9a26b, Graphic Universe™) Lerner Publishing Group.

Edwards, Roberta. Who Is Jane Goodall? 2012. (Who Is... ? Ser.). lib. bdg. 16.00 (978-0-606-26651-2(8)) Turtleback.

Eggerling, Kristin J. Breath of Wilderness: The Life of Sigurd Olson. 2014. (ENG., Illus.). 112p. (J). (gr. 4-7). pap. 12.95 (978-1-938486-10-4(2)) Fulcrum Publishing.

Elliot, Henry. John Muir: Protecting & Preserving the Environment. 2009. (Voices for Green Choices Ser.). (ENG., Illus.). 48p. (J). (gr. 5-9). pap. (978-0-7787-4681-2(X)); lib. bdg. (978-0-7787-4668-3(2)) Crabtree Publishing Co.

Ferrara, Cos. Anna Comstock: A Love Affair with Nature. 2004. (Girls Explore, Reach for the Stars Ser.). (Illus.). 112p. (J). 20.00 (978-0-9749456-1-3(7), Girls Explore) Girls Explore LLC.

Gibbons, Alan. Charles Darwin. 2008. (Illus.). 64p. (J). (978-0-7534-1729-4(4), Kingfisher) Roaring Brook Pr.

Gillam, Scott. Rachel Carson: Pioneer of Environmentalism, 1 vol. 2010. (Essential Lives Set 5 Ser.). (ENG.). 112p. (YA). (gr. 6-12). lib. bdg. 41.36 (978-1-61613-511-9(5), 6705, Essential Library) ABDO Publishing Co.

Goldstein, Natalie. John Muir. 2011. (ENG., Illus.). 144p. (gr. 6-12). 35.00 (978-1-60413-945-7(5), P189956, Facts On File) Infobase Holdings, Inc.

Goodridge, Catherine. Jane Goodall & Jane Goodall (Spanish) 6 English, 6 Spanish Adaptations. 2011. (ENG & SPA.). (J). 79.00 net. (978-1-4108-5658-6(5)) Benchmark Education Co.

Green, John. Charles Darwin. 2009. (Dover Nature Coloring Book Ser.). (ENG.). 32p. (J). (gr. 3-8). pap. 3.99 (978-0-486-47282-9(5), 472825) Dover Pubns., Inc.

Hand, Carol. Cool Careers Without College for People Who Love Animals, 1 vol. 2nd ed. 2013. (Cool Careers Without College Ser.). (ENG.). 144p. (YA). (gr. 7-7). 41.12 (978-1-4777-1822-3(2), 76e82eb8-1815-4087-ba91-95ebb2aca1af) Rosen Publishing Group, Inc., The.

Hanson-Harding, Alexandra. Charles Darwin: Naturalist, 1 vol. 2017. (Britannica Beginner Bios Ser.). (ENG., Illus.). 32p. (J). (gr. 2-3). pap. 13.90 (978-1-68048-800-5(7), fb80dc85-949c-4fc3-8f50-6cca5156868c) Rosen Publishing Group, Inc., The.

Harkrader, Lisa. Park Naturalist. 2019. (Jobs with Animals Ser.). (ENG., Illus.). 32p. (J). (gr. 4-6). pap. 7.95 (978-1-5435-6047-3(4), 140092); lib. bdg. 28.65 (978-1-5435-5785-5(6), 139741) Capstone.

Harrison, Troon. The Birdman, 1 vol. Thisdale, François, illus. 2019. (ENG.). 36p. (J). (gr. 1-5). 24.95 (978-0-88995-506-6(9), 4e560030-f5f4-4446-bb89-a8156d970d30) Red Deer Pr. CAN. Dist: Firefly Bks., Ltd.

Hayhurst, Chris. Cool Careers Without College for Animal Lovers. 2009. (Cool Careers Without College Ser.). 144p. (gr. 6-6). 66.50 (978-1-61511-955-4(8)) Rosen Publishing Group, Inc., The.

Heiligman, Deborah. Charles & Emma: The Darwins' Leap of Faith. 2011. (ENG., Illus.). 288p. (YA). (gr. 8-12). pap. 10.99 (978-0-312-66104-5(5), 900070656) Square Fish.

Hile, Lori. Rachel Carson: Environmental Pioneer, 1 vol. 2014. (Women in Conservation Ser.). (ENG., Illus.). 48p. (J). (gr. 3-6). pap. 8.99 (978-1-4846-0476-2(8), 126607, Heinemann) Capstone.

Hopkinson, Deborah & Who HQ. Who Was Charles Darwin? Harrison, Nancy, illus. 2005. (Who Was? Ser.). 112p. (J). (gr. 3-7). pap. 5.99 (978-0-448-43764-4(3), Penguin Workshop) Penguin Young Readers Group.

Howell, Izzi. Why Do We Remember?: Charles Darwin. 2019. (Why Do We Remember? Ser.). (ENG., Illus.). 32p. (J). (gr. 1-5). pap. 11.99 (978-1-4451-4855-7(2), Franklin Watts) Hachette Children's Group GBR. Dist: Hachette Bk. Group.

Hurwitz, Jane. Choosing a Career in Animal Care. 2009. (World of Work Ser.). 64p. (gr. 5-5). 58.50 (978-1-60854-329-8(3)) Rosen Publishing Group, Inc., The.

Hustad, Douglas. Environmentalist Rachel Carson. 2016. (STEM Trailblazer Bios Ser.). (ENG., Illus.). 32p. (J). (gr. 2-5). lib. bdg. 26.65 (978-1-5124-0787-7(9), 71706330-1186-4f5c-b659-d7d68008c0ed, Lerner Pubns.) Lerner Publishing Group.

Kiely Miller, Barbara. John Muir, 1 vol. 2007. (Grandes Personajes (Great Americans) Ser.). 24p. (gr. 2-4). (SPA.). pap. 9.15 (978-0-8368-8339-8(X), 027deba2-1d65-4f22-afdd-b25c74e7ca0c); (ENG.). lib. bdg. 24.67 (978-0-8368-8318-3(7), 86d24b9e-cde3-4ee8-a2b1-a311970c63af); (SPA.). lib. bdg. 24.67 (978-0-8368-8332-9(2), fc2fd432-5fd4-462b-87ac-0011ba6ede2f) Stevens, Gareth Publishing LLLP. (Weekly Reader Leveled Readers).

Knowlton, Laurie Lazzaro. Cowgirl Alphabet, 1 vol. Knowlton, Charlotte & Coates, Kathy, illus. 2011. (ABC Ser.). (ENG.). 32p. (J). (gr. k-3). 16.99 (978-1-58980-669-6(7), Pelican Publishing) Arcadia Publishing.

Krull, Kathleen. Charles Darwin. Kulikov, Boris, illus. 2015. (Giants of Science Ser.). 144p. (J). (gr. 3-7). 7.99 (978-0-14-751463-9(0), Puffin Books) Penguin Young Readers Group.

Kuligowski, Stephanie & Cohn, Jessica. Wild Work! Animal Trainers, 1 vol. 2nd rev. ed. 2013. (TIME for KIDS(r): Informational Text Ser.). (ENG., Illus.). 64p. (J). (gr. 4-8). lib. bdg. 31.96 (978-1-4333-7441-8(2)) Teacher Created Materials, Inc.

Lantier, Patricia. Rachel Carson: Fighting Pesticides & Other Chemical Pollutants, 1 vol. 2009. (Voices for Green Choices Ser.). (ENG., Illus.). 48p. (J). (gr. 5-9). pap. (978-0-7787-4676-8(3)) Crabtree Publishing Co.

Lasky, Kathryn. One Beetle Too Many: Candlewick Biographies: The Extraordinary Adventures of Charles Darwin. Trueman, Matthew, illus. 2014. (Candlewick Biographies Ser.). (ENG.). 48p. (J). (gr. 2-5). 14.99 (978-0-7636-6842-6(7)) Candlewick Pr.

Lawson, Kristan. Darwin & Evolution for Kids: His Life & Ideas with 21 Activities. 2003. (For Kids Ser.: 16). (ENG., Illus.). 160p. (J). (gr. 4). pap. 19.99 (978-1-55652-502-5(8)) Chicago Review Pr., Inc.

Lin, Yoming S. Charles Darwin & Evolution, 1 vol. 2011. (Eureka! Ser.). (ENG., Illus.). 24p. (YA). (gr. 2-3). lib. bdg. 26.27 (978-1-4488-5031-0(2), 1311f1b0-9f65-4b4a-a830-acbd0627a7ac) Rosen Publishing Group, Inc., The.

Locker, Thomas. John Muir: America's Naturalist. 2010. (ENG.). 32p. (J). (gr. -1-3). pap. 12.95 (978-1-55591-705-0(4)) Fulcrum Publishing.

Lorbiecki, Marybeth. Things Natural, Wild, & Free: The Life of Aldo Leopold. 2011. (ENG., Illus.). 112p. (J). (gr. 4-7). pap. 12.95 (978-1-55591-474-5(8)) Fulcrum Publishing.

Magnuson Bell, Karen. What Linnaeus Saw: A Scientist's Quest to Name Every Living Thing. 2019. (ENG., Illus.). 256p. (J). (gr. 5-12). 21.95 (978-1-324-00468-4(1), 340468, Norton Young Readers) Norton, W. W. & Co., Inc.

Malnor, Carol & Malnor, Bruce. Earth Heroes: Champions of Wild Animals, 1 vol. Hovemann, Anisa Claire, illus. 2011. (ENG.). 144p. (J). (gr. 5-8). pap. 12.95 (978-1-58469-123-5(9), Dawn Pubns.) Sourcebooks, Inc.

Matthews, Sheelagh. Steve Irwin. 2007. (Remarkable People Ser.). (Illus.). 24p. (J). (gr. 3-7). pap. 8.95 (978-1-59036-650-9(6)); lib. bdg. 24.45 (978-1-59036-649-3(2)) Weigl Pubs., Inc.

Matthewson, Sarah. On the Lookout: Lives of Naturalists. 2007. (Shockwave: Life Stories Ser.). (ENG., Illus.). 36p. (J). (gr. 4-6). lib. bdg. 25.00 (978-0-531-17772-3(6), Children's Pr.) Scholastic Library Publishing.

Maynard, Charles W. John Muir: Naturalist & Explorer. 2009. (Famous Explorers of the American West Ser.). 24p. (gr. 3-4). 42.50 (978-1-61512-504-3(3), PowerKids Pr.) Rosen Publishing Group, Inc., The.

McDonnell, Patrick. Me ... Jane (Caldecott Honor Book) 2011. (ENG., Illus.). 40p. (J). (gr. -1-3). 18.99 (978-0-316-04546-9(2)) Little, Brown Bks. for Young Readers.

Mcdonnell, Patrick. Me... Jane. 2011. (CHI., Illus.). 40p. (J). (gr. -1-2). (978-986-189-308-2(3)) Grimm Cultural Ent., Co., Ltd.

—Me... Jane. 2011. (J). (978-1-4618-4349-8(9)) Recorded Bks., Inc.

McVey, James. Martha Maxwell: Natural History Pioneer. 2005. (Now You Know Bio Ser.: 4). (Illus.). 84p. (J). pap. (978-0-86541-075-6(5)) Filter Pr., LLC.

Meltzer, Milton. Henry David Thoreau: A Biography. 2007. (Literary Greats Ser.). (ENG., Illus.). 160p. (gr. 7-12). lib. bdg. 33.26 (978-0-8225-5893-4(9), Twenty-First Century Bks.) Lerner Publishing Group.

Miles, Liz. Linnaeus Organising Nature: Band 18/Pearl. 2017. (Collins Big Cat Ser.). (ENG., Illus.). 80p. (J). pap. 12.99 (978-0-00-820897-4(2)) HarperCollins Pubs. Ltd. GBR. Dist: Independent Pubs. Group.

Miller, Derek. Henry David Thoreau: Civil Disobedience, 1 vol. 2017. (Peaceful Protesters Ser.). (ENG.). 112p. (YA). (gr. 9-9). 44.50 (978-1-5026-3112-1(1), 4b717c79-3772-4863-b139-314149e81f94); pap. 20.99 (978-1-5026-3394-1(9), 76a179c1-ef69-4873-9b81-1b0d2136d836) Cavendish Square Publishing LLC.

Morgan, Sally. The Incredible Life of Sir David Attenborough: Band 16/Sapphire, Bd. 16. 2017. (Collins Big Cat Ser.). (ENG.). 56p. (J). pap. 12.99 (978-0-00-820889-9(1)) HarperCollins Pubs. Ltd. GBR. Dist: Independent Pubs. Group.

Morlock, Theresa. HMS Beagle Voyage & the Galápagos Islands, 1 vol. 2018. (Real-Life Scientific Adventures Ser.). (ENG.). 32p. (gr. 4-5). 29.27 (978-1-5081-6846-1(6), 4d01f316-4230-479c-b4cf-5ea0443fc99a, PowerKids Pr.) Rosen Publishing Group, Inc., The.

Moss, Leila & Knox, Linda L. The Storyteller. 2015. (Illus.). xiv, 107p. 24.95 (978-1-935204-53-4(X)) Salem Author Services.

Niver, Heather Moore. Henry David Thoreau: Author of Civil Disobedience. 2017. (Spotlight on Civic Courage: Heroes of Conscience Ser.). 48p. (J). (gr. 10-15). 70.50 (978-1-5383-8113-7(3)); (ENG.). (gr. 6-6). pap. 12.75 (978-1-5383-8112-0(5), 7c10f464-f9db-4f25-8dab-18c09483a071) Rosen Publishing Group, Inc., The. (Rosen Young Adult).

Pomeroy, Sarah B. & Kathirithamby, Jeyaraney. Maria Sibylla Merian: Artist, Scientist, Adventurer. (J). 2018. (ENG., Illus.). 96p. (gr. 3-7). 21.95 (978-1-947440-01-2(2), 1317301) 2017. (978-1-60606-555-6(6), J. Paul Getty Museum) Getty Pubns.

Ritchey, Richard I. True Adventures of the Reptileman. 2007. 60p. per. 10.95 (978-0-595-45020-6(2)) iUniverse, Inc.

Rose, Simon. Animal Caretaker. 2014. (J). (978-1-4896-2982-1(3)) Weigl Pubs., Inc.

Ruurs, Margriet. Robert Bateman: the Boy Who Painted Nature, 1 vol. 2018. (ENG., Illus.). 40p. (J). (gr. 1-3). 29.95 (978-1-4598-1992-4(6)) Orca Bk. Pubs. USA.

Sanchez, Anita. Karl, Get Out of the Garden! Carolus Linnaeus & the Naming of Everything. Stock, Catherine, illus. 2017. 48p. (J). (gr. 2-5). lib. bdg. 17.99 (978-1-58089-606-1(5)) Charlesbridge Publishing, Inc.

Schier, Helga. George Washington Carver: Agricultural Innovator, 1 vol. 2008. (Essential Lives Set 2 Ser.). (ENG., Illus.). 112p. (YA). (gr. 6-12). lib. bdg. 41.36 (978-1-60453-035-3(9), 6651, Essential Library) ABDO Publishing Co.

Sis, Peter. The Tree of Life: Charles Darwin. (Illus.). 22.95 (978-0-88899-564-3(4)) Groundwood Bks. CAN. Dist: Publishers Group West (PGW).

Sis, Peter. The Tree of Life: Charles Darwin. Sis, Peter, illus. 2003. (ENG., Illus.). 44p. (J). (gr. k-3). 24.99 (978-0-374-45628-3(3), 9780374456283, Farrar, Straus & Giroux (BYR)) Farrar, Straus & Giroux.

Slade, Suzanne. Out of School & into Nature: The Anna Comstock Story. Lanan, Jessica, illus. 2017. (ENG.). 32p. (J). (gr. 1-4). 16.99 (978-1-58536-986-7(1), 204225) Sleeping Bear Pr.

Stanley, Phyllis M. Elizabeth Terwilliger - Someone Special: A Biography of the Celebrated Naturalist. 2003. (ENG., Illus.). 110p. (J). (gr. 4-10). pap. 17.95 (978-1-878044-54-9(0)) Mayhaven Publishing, Inc.

Stansfield, John. Enos Mills: Rocky Mountain Naturalist. 2005. (Now You Know Bio Ser.). (Illus.). 103p. (J). pap. 8.95 (978-0-86541-072-5(0)) Filter Pr., LLC.

Thermes, Jennifer. Charles Darwin's Around-The-World Adventure. 2016. (ENG., Illus.). 48p. (J). (gr. k-2). 19.99 (978-1-4197-2120-5(8), 1117901, Abrams Bks. for Young Readers) Abrams, Inc.

Trueit, Trudi Strain. Animal Trainer. 2013. (J). (978-0-7614-8075-4(7)) Marshall Cavendish Corp.

Turner, Amanda. Helping Animals. 2019. (Careers Making a Difference Ser.). (Illus.). 80p. (J). (gr. 12). lib. bdg. 34.60 (978-1-4222-4254-4(4)) Mason Crest.

Walsh, Steve. Enos Mills: Rocky Mountain Conservationist. 2011. (ENG & SPA., Illus.). 64p. (J). pap. 8.95 (978-0-86541-122-7(0)) Filter Pr., LLC.

Waxman, Laura Hamilton. Jane Goodall. Butler, Tad, illus. 2007. (History Maker Biographies Ser.). (ENG.). 48p. (J). (gr. 3-6). lib. bdg. 27.93 (978-0-8225-7610-5(4), Lerner Pubns.) Lerner Publishing Group.

Weaver, Anne H. The Voyage of the Beetle: A Journey Around the World with Charles Darwin & the Search for the Solution to the Mystery of Mysteries, As Narrated by Rosie, an Articulate Beetle. Lawrence, George, illus. 2007. (ENG.). 80p. (J). (gr. 5-8). 19.95 (978-0-8263-4304-8(X), P128170) Univ. of New Mexico Pr.

Webster, Stephen. Charles Darwin: Naturalist, 1 vol. 2016. (History Makers Ser.). (ENG., Illus.). 144p. (J). (gr. 9-9). 47.36 (978-1-5026-1916-7(4), 6291d6e7-0874-4d67-b411-4bf540b5a78d) Cavendish Square Publishing LLC.

Whiting, Jim. Charles Darwin & the Origin of the Species. 2005. (Uncharted, Unexplored, & Unexplained Ser.). (Illus.). 48p. (J). (gr. 3-8). lib. bdg. 29.95 (978-1-58415-364-1(4)) Mitchell Lane Pubs.

NATURE

Adamson, Heather. Blue in Nature. 2013. (ENG., Illus.). 24p. (J). lib. bdg. 25.65 (978-1-62031-040-3(6)) Jump! Inc.

Aguilera, Rich. Mud: Off-Road Discoveries. 2017. (Illus.). xi, 128p. pap. (978-0-8163-6252-3(1)) Pacific Pr. Publishing Assn.

Algarra, Alejandro & Mazali, Gustavo. Nature's Wonders. 2018. (ENG., Illus.). 96p. (J). (gr. 1-6). pap. 9.99 (978-1-4380-1096-0(6)) Sourcebooks, Inc.

All Things Bright And Beautiful. 2006. 16p. (J). pap. 1.99 (978-0-7847-1588-8(2), 22135) Standard Publishing.

Amazing Magnets: Level E. 8p. 20.95 (978-0-322-00353-8(9)) Wright Group/McGraw-Hill.

Animals Hide & Seek: Level E. 8p. 20.95 (978-0-322-00354-5(7)) Wright Group/McGraw-Hill.

AZ Books Staff. Discovering the Savanna. Gorojan, Elena, ed. 2012. (Wild Theater Ser.). (ENG.). 8p. (J). (gr. -1-3). bds. 17.95 (978-1-61889-017-7(4)) AZ Bks. LLC.

Azadi, Azita. Thank You Sun. 2009. 32p. pap. 16.50 (978-1-4269-2197-1(7)) Trafford Publishing.

Barefoot Books. Big & Small. Teckentrup, Britta, illus. 2013. (ENG.). 16p. (J). (gr. -1-k). bds. 7.99 (978-1-84686-951-8(X)) Barefoot Bks., Inc.

Barradas, Michele. Rainbow of Shapes: Learn shapes & Colors. 2008. 20p. pap. 15.95 (978-1-4389-0177-0(1)) AuthorHouse.

Baruzzi, Agnese. Hidden in Nature: Search, Find, & Count! 2018. (ENG., Illus.). 56p. (J). (gr. k). 14.95 (978-1-4549-2937-6(5)) Sterling Publishing Co., Inc.

Baxter, Nicola. My First Words: Nature. Lacome, Susie, illus. 2016. 24p. (J). (gr. -1-12). pap. 7.99 (978-1-86147-770-5(8), Armadillo) Anness Publishing GBR. Dist: National Bk. Network.

Benchmark Education Company, LLC Staff, compiled by. Cactus & Canyons & Ecosystems. 2005. spiral bd. 225.00 (978-1-4108-5806-1(5)) Benchmark Education Co.

—Cactus & Canyons & Regions. 2005. spiral bd. 225.00 (978-1-4108-5805-4(7)) Benchmark Education Co.

Bernath, Stefen. Trees of the Northeast. 2013. (Dover Nature Coloring Book Ser.). (ENG., Illus.). 48p. (J). (gr. 6-12). pap. 4.99 (978-0-486-23734-3(6), 237346) Dover Pubns., Inc.

Bockol, Leslie & Ikids Staff. One Tree. Phillips, Jillian, illus. 2009. (ENG.). 20p. (J). (gr. -1-1). 6.99 (978-1-58476-811-1(8)) Innovative Kids.

Bodden, Valerie. Wildlife in Danger. 2010. (Earth Issues Ser.). (Illus.). 48p. (J). (gr. 5-18). 23.95 (978-1-58341-987-8(X), Creative Education) Creative Co., The.

Bookworms: Nature's Cycles/Los Ciclos de la Naturaleza, 12 vols., Set. 2010. (Los Ciclos de la Naturaleza / Nature's Cycles Ser.). (SPA & ENG.). 32p. (gr. 1-2). lib. bdg. 153.00 (978-0-7614-4785-6(7), 801e2f56-0d9e-49a2-8c18-fcc676d9e46b, Cavendish Square) Cavendish Square Publishing LLC.

Boone, Mary. I Can Care for Nature. 2019. (Helping the Environment Ser.). (ENG., Illus.). 24p. (J). (gr. -1-2). lib. bdg. 27.32 (978-1-9771-0311-6(1), 139312, Capstone Pr.) Capstone.

Bowman, Debbie. The Happy Tree. 2013. 20p. pap. 8.99 (978-1-62509-760-6(3)) Salem Author Services.

Brady, Irene. Illustrating Nature: Right-brain Art in a Left-Brain World. Brady, Irene, illus. 2004. (Illus.). spiral bd. 25.95 (978-0-915965-09-0(7)) Nature Works Press.

Britannica, Learning Library. Science & Nature. 2003. (Illus.). 64p. 14.95 (978-1-59339-033-4(5)) Encyclopaedia Britannica, Inc.

Brookes, Olivia. Uncover Nature, 1 vol. Studio Inklink, Studio, illus. 2009. (Hide-And-Seek Visual Adventures Ser.). (ENG.). 24p. (J). (gr. 2-2). lib. bdg. 27.27 (978-1-60754-655-9(8), 2970f8bd-eab5-4a06-a5ba-07933df674e3, Windmill Bks.) Rosen Publishing Group, Inc., The.

Brown, Laaren. Volcanoes: Run for Your Life! 2013. (Illus.). 32p. (J). (978-0-545-62413-8(4)) Scholastic, Inc.

Brunelle, Lynn. Camp Out! The Ultimate Kids' Guide. 2007. (ENG., Illus.). 256p. (J). (gr. 2-7). pap. 16.95 (978-0-7611-4122-8(7), 14122) Workman Publishing Co., Inc.

Budnick, Madeleine. Outside Todo el Dia: Nature in English y Espanol. 2017. (ArteKids Ser.). (ENG., Illus.). 16p. (J). (gr. -1-k). bds. 7.95 (978-1-59534-830-2(1)) Trinity Univ. Pr.

Burnie, David. The Kingfisher Nature Encyclopedia. 2019. (Kingfisher Encyclopedias Ser.). (ENG., Illus.). 320p. (J). 29.99 (978-0-7534-7502-7(2), 900198580, Kingfisher) Roaring Brook Pr.

Burrill, Richard L. Somewhere Behind the Eyes: Surprise Images in Nature Aha! Date not set. (Somewhere Behind the Eyes Ser.). (Illus.). 96p. (J). (gr. 4-12). pap. 12.95 (978-1-878464-19-4(1)) Anthro Co., The.

—Somewhere Behind the Eyes Vol. 3: Surprise Images in Nature Aha! Date not set. (Illus.). 96p. (J). (gr. 4-12). 10.95 (978-1-878464-18-7(3)) Anthro Co., The.

Canetti, Yanitzia. Colorful Sights Paisajes de Colores: A World of Color. 2010. (SPA & ENG.). 24p. (J). pap. 6.99 (978-1-59835-280-1(6), BrickHouse Education) Cambridge BrickHouse, Inc.

Capstone Press. Natural Wonders, 1 vol. 2010. (Natural Wonders Ser.). (ENG.). 32p. lib. bdg. 143.94 (978-1-4296-5920-8(3), Capstone Pr.) Capstone.

Carr, Aaron. Nature Patterns. 2011. (J). (978-1-61690-592-7(1)) Weigl Pubs., Inc.

Changing Habitats. 2015. (Illus.). 44p. (J). (978-0-7166-2708-1(6)) World Bk., Inc.

Chinery, Michael & Michael, Chinery. Las Costas.Tr. of Seashores. (SPA.). 40p. (J). (gr. 3-5). 12.76 (978-84-241-2053-5(1)) Everest Editora ESP. Dist: Lectorum Pubns., Inc.

—Los Desiertos.Tr. of Desert Animals. (SPA.). 40p. (J). (gr. 3-5). 12.76 (978-84-241-2051-1(5)) Everest Editora ESP. Dist: Lectorum Pubns., Inc.

—Los Lagos y los Rios.Tr. of Lakes & Rivers. (SPA.). 40p. (J). (gr. 3-5). 12.76 (978-84-241-2058-0(2)) Everest Editora ESP. Dist: Lectorum Pubns., Inc.

—Los Oceanos.Tr. of Oceans. (SPA.). 40p. (J). (gr. 3-5). 12.76 (978-84-241-2055-9(8)) Everest Editora ESP. Dist: Lectorum Pubns., Inc.

—Los Polos.Tr. of Polar Lands. (SPA.). 40p. (J). (gr. 3-5). 12.76 (978-84-241-2056-6(6)) Everest Editora ESP. Dist: Lectorum Pubns., Inc.

—Las Sabanas y las Praderas.Tr. of Grassland Animals. (SPA.). (J). (gr. 3-5). 12.76 (978-84-241-2054-2(X)) Everest Editora ESP. Dist: Lectorum Pubns., Inc.

Christelis, Paul. Get Outdoors: A Mindfulness Guide to Noticing Nature. Paganelli, Elisa, illus. 2018. (Everyday Mindfulness Ser.). (ENG.). 32p. (J). (gr. k-4). 16.99 (978-1-63198-333-7(4), 83337) Free Spirit Publishing Inc.

Collins, Sarah Jean. God Made the Rain Forest. Collins, Sarah Jean, illus. 2020. (God Made Ser.). (ENG., Illus.). 20p. (J). bds. 7.99 (978-1-4964-3632-0(6), 20_32354, Tyndale Kids) Tyndale Hse. Pubs.

Colvin, L. Living World Encyclopedia. 2009. pap. 14.99 (978-0-7945-2784-6(1)) EDC Publishing.

Colvin, L. & Speare, E. Living World Encyclopedia. 2004. (Encyclopedias Ser.). (Illus.). 128p. (J). 7.95 (978-0-7945-0005-4(6)) EDC Publishing.

Confluence 2004. 2004. (YA). per. (978-0-9745192-4-1(3)) Little Bay Pr.

Connolly, Randy, et al. Poison Ivy, Pets & People: Scratching the Poison Ivy, Oak & Sumac Itch. 2005. (10thingstoknow about ... Ser.). (Illus.). 104p. pap. 9.95 (978-0-9722400-1-7(2)) 2Lakes Publishing.

Conroy, Jim & Alexander, Basia. Messages from Trees Set 1: A Coloring Book for the Young & Young-At-Heart. 2013. (ENG., Illus.). 32p. (J). pap. 8.00 (978-0-9834114-5-1(X)) Plant Kingdom Communications.

Corcorane, Ann. Patterns Everywhere. 2011. (Wonder Readers Emergent Level Ser.). (ENG.). 8p. (J). (gr. -1-1). pap. 6.25 (978-1-4296-7869-8(0), 118201, Capstone Pr.) Capstone.

Cork, Barbara. Pocket Nature. 2004. (First Nature Ser.). (Illus.). 170p. (J). 8.95 (978-0-7945-0346-8(2), Usborne) EDC Publishing.

Cousteau, Philippe & Hopkinson, Deborah. Follow the Moon Home: A Tale of One Idea, Twenty Kids, & a Hundred Sea Turtles (Children's Story Books, Sea Turtle Gifts, Moon Books for Kids, Children's Environment Books, Kid's Turtle Books) So, Meilo, illus. 2016. (ENG.). 48p. (J). (gr. k-3). 16.99 (978-1-4521-1241-1(X)) Chronicle Bks. LLC.

Cowcher, Helen. Rainforest. (Illus.). 40p. (VIE, ENG, URD, TUR & CHI.). 16.95 (978-1-84059-022-7(X)); (CHI, ENG, URD, TUR & VIE.). 16.95 (978-1-84059-017-3(3)) Milet Publishing.

—Whistling Thorn. (CHI, ENG, URD, TUR & VIE., Illus.). 40p. (J). 16.95 (978-1-84059-033-3(5)) Milet Publishing.

Cromarty, Jim. Great Barrier Reef Adventures. rev. ed. 2005. (Adventure Ser.). (ENG., Illus.). 96p. (J). (gr. 3-7). per. 8.99 (978-1-84550-068-9(7), 564a4e70-1b9b-46b4-9860-25f6b85dfd41) Christian Focus Pubns. GBR. Dist: Baker & Taylor Publisher Services (BTPS).

Curious Nature, 12 vols. 2017. (Curious Nature Ser.). 32p. (ENG.). (gr. 3-3). 167.58 (978-1-4994-3399-9(9), 75a84e70-8317-4b89-a46e-c36ebc127288); (gr. 8-8). pap. 60.00 (978-1-5081-5368-9(X)) Rosen Publishing Group, Inc., The. (PowerKids Pr.).

Cycles in Nature. 2015. (Cycles in Nature Ser.). (ENG.). 24p. (J). (gr. 1-2). pap., pap., pap. 293.40 (978-1-4824-3446-0(6)); pap., pap., pap. 48.90 (978-1-4824-3447-7(4)) Stevens, Gareth Publishing LLLP.

Dalby, Elizabeth. Mysteries & Marvels of Nature. Tatchell, Judy, ed. Whatmore, Candice & Barrance, Reuben, illus. 2008. (Nature Encyclopedias Ser.). 128p. (J). (gr. 4-7). pap. 16.99 (978-0-7945-1738-0(2), Usborne) EDC Publishing.

Dalby, L. Mysteries & Marvels of Nature. 2004. (First Stories Ser.). 128p. (J). 19.95 (978-0-7945-0597-4(X)); lib. bdg. 27.95 (978-1-58086-610-1(7), Usborne) EDC Publishing.

Davidson, Annie. Colour Together: Nature. 2016. (ENG., Illus.). 64p. (J). (gr. k-2). pap. 16.99 (978-1-78344-517-2(3)) Andersen Pr. GBR. Dist: Independent Pubs. Group.

Davies, Gill & Morris, Neil. 365 Awesome Facts & Records about Nature. 2008. (365 Awesome Facts & Records Ser.). (ENG., Illus.). 176p. (J). (gr. 1-18). 19.95 (978-88-6098-112-7(3)) McRae Bks. Srl ITA. Dist: Independent Pubs. Group.

Davis, Bela. Diseños en la Naturaleza. 2018. (¡Diseños Divertidos! (Patterns Are Fun!) Ser.).Tr. of Patterns in Nature. (SPA.). 24p. (J). (gr. -1-2). lib. bdg. 31.36 (978-1-5321-8376-8(3), 29945, Abdo Kids) ABDO Publishing Co.

—Patterns in Nature. 2018. (Patterns Are Fun! Ser.). (ENG., Illus.). 24p. (J). (gr. -1-2). lib. bdg. 31.36 (978-1-5321-0796-2(X), 28153, Abdo Kids) ABDO Publishing Co.

Daynes, Katie. Lift-The-Flap Questions & Answers about Nature IR. 2018. (Lift-The Flap Questions & Answers Ser.). (ENG.). 14p. (J). 14.99 (978-0-7945-4121-7(6), Usborne) EDC Publishing.

De Koning, Lezanne. The Magic of Nature. 2011. (Illus.). 44p. pap. 19.48 (978-1-4520-9231-7(1)) AuthorHouse.

Delano, Marfe Ferguson. Cielo. 2008. (Descubre la Naturaleza Ser.). (Illus.). 60p. (J). 12.95 (978-1-58087-127-3(5)) Stampley, C. D. Enterprises, Inc.

Dempski, Seth. Natalie's Nature Walk: Represent & Interpret Data, 1 vol. 2014. (Math Masters: Measurement & Data Ser.). (ENG.). 24p. (J). (gr. 2-2). 25.27 (978-1-4777-6440-4(2), 09a87ac6-290b-41f7-9077-83d9583a8831); pap. 8.25 (978-1-4777-4828-2(8), 412e89a8-6561-4f46-b5a3-dda4db51d115) Rosen Publishing Group, Inc., The. (Rosen Classroom).

Dickmann, Nancy. Math in Nature. 2018. (Amazing World of Math Ser.). (ENG., Illus.). 32p. (J). (gr. 3-6). 27.99 (978-1-5415-0099-0(7), 057e2314-88ef-4141-98d0-68eb52e22443, Hungry Tomato (r)) Lerner Publishing Group.

Discover Series: Science, Nature, Wildlife, 11 bks. (Illus.). (J). (gr. 3-6). lib. bdg. 175.45 (978-1-56674-935-0(2)) Forest Hse. Publishing Co., Inc.

DK. Explanatorium of Nature. 2017. (DK Explanatorium Ser.). (ENG., Illus.). 360p. (J). (gr. 4-7). 29.99 (978-1-4654-6363-0(1), DK Children) Dorling Kindersley Publishing, Inc.

Donnelly, Karen. Biomes of the Past & the Future. 2009. (Earth's Changing Weather & Climate Ser.). 24p. (gr. 4-4). 42.50 (978-1-61512-243-1(5), PowerKids Pr.) Rosen Publishing Group, Inc., The.

Dowdy, Penny. Nature Math, 1 vol. 2009. (Math Alive! Ser.). (ENG.). 32p. (gr. 4-4). lib. bdg. 31.21 (978-0-7614-3214-2(0), d8d75ca1-dbbf-4d9c-aae0-7f17b28f7fa0) Cavendish Square Publishing LLC.

Durber, Matt & Jones, Stephanie, illus. First Picture Nature. MMStudios, photos by. 2007. (First Picture Board Bks). 16p. (J). (gr. -1-k). bds. 11.99 (978-0-7945-1751-9(X), Usborne) EDC Publishing.

Earth's Treasures. (Eyes on Adventure Ser.). 32p. (J). (gr. 1). pap. (978-1-882210-63-3(8)) Action Publishing, Inc.

EarthWorks, 12 vols., Set. 2003. (EarthWorks Ser.). (ENG.). (gr. 6-6). 221.58 (978-0-7614-1364-6(2), 8234fb55-264b-4116-9779-62152c449390, Cavendish Square) Cavendish Square Publishing LLC.

Editors of Storey Publishing. Backpack Explorer: on the Nature Trail: What Will You Find? 2018. (Backpack Explorer Ser.). (ENG., Illus.). 48p. (J). (gr. -1-3). 12.95 (978-1-63586-197-6(7), 626197) Storey Publishing, LLC.

Education.com. Fun with Nature: A Workbook of Natural Science Topics. 2015. (ENG.). 128p. (J). (gr. 2-2). pap. 7.99 (978-0-486-80265-7(5)) Dover Pubns., Inc.

—Let's Go Outside! A Workbook of Plants, Animals, & the Outdoors. 2015. (ENG.). 128p. (J). (gr. 1-1). pap. 7.99 (978-0-486-80259-6(0)) Dover Pubns., Inc.

Elmore, Amber. Betsy Beansprout Camping Guide. Hickey, Josh, illus. 2013. 50p. pap. 13.99 (978-1-937331-37-5(7)) ShadeTree Publishing, LLC.

Enciclopedia Ilustrada de Ciencia Naturaleza (Understanding Science & Nature), 16 bks. Incl. Comportamiento de los Animales (Animal Behavior) 17.95 (978-0-7835-3358-2(6)); Cuerpo Humano (Human Body) 17.95 (978-0-7835-3350-6(0)); Era de la Computadora. 17.95 (978-0-7835-3375-9(6)); Espacio y Planetas. 17.95 (978-0-7835-3370-4(5)); Estructura de la Materia (Structure of Matter) 17.95 (978-0-7835-3383-4(7)); Evolucion de la Vida. 17.95 (978-0-7835-3354-4(3)); Fuerzas Fisicas (Physical Forces) 17.95 (978-0-7835-3395-7(0)); Geografia. 17.95 (978-0-7835-3387-2(X)); Insectos y Aranas. 17.95 (978-0-7835-3398-8(5)); Maquinas e Inventos (Machines & Inventions) 17.95 (978-0-7835-3400-8(0)); Mundo Submarino (Underwater World) 17.95 (978-0-7835-3397-1(7)); Planeta Tierra (Planet Earth) 17.95 (978-0-7835-3396-4(9)); Plantas (Plant Life) 17.95 (978-0-7835-3399-5(3)); Tiempo y Clima (Weather & Climate) 17.95 (978-0-7835-3366-7(7)); Transporte y la Navegacion (Transportation) 17.95 (978-0-7835-3379-7(9)); 152p. (YA). (gr. 6-18). 1996. (Illus.). Set lib. bdg. 319.20 (978-0-7835-3391-9(8)) Time-Life, Inc.

Encyclopaedia Britannica, Inc. Staff, compiled by. Science & Nature. 2003. (Britannica Learning Library). (Illus.). (gr. 2-5). 14.95 (978-1-59339-002-0(5), 049903-EN-REF) Encyclopaedia Britannica, Inc.

Everett, Jason M. U-X-L Sustainable Living. 2015. (Illus.). (J). (978-1-4103-1784-1(6), UXL) Cengage Gale.

Explora la Naturaleza (Getting into Nature) Set, 12 vols. 2003. (Explora la Naturaleza (Getting into Nature) Ser.). (SPA.). (gr. 3-4). 173.58 (978-1-4042-7552-2(5), 3177eb04-3808-48af-ad12-ba245d7a4068) Rosen Publishing Group, Inc., The.

Eyre, Jane. Creatures of the New Jersey Pine Barrens Coloring Book, 1 vol. Eyre, Jane, illus. 2004. (Illus.). 36p. spiral bd. 6.00 (978-0-9762483-0-9(1)) Fun Fitness Publishing.

Facts on File, Inc. Staff, ed. Nature Walk, 7 Vols., Set. 2006. (Nature Walk Ser.). 80p. (gr. 4-6). 196.00 (978-0-7910-9445-7(6), Chelsea Clubhse.) Infobase Holdings, Inc.

Falchetta, Drew. Is This Living or Non-Living? 2015. (1-3Y Science Ser.). (ENG., Illus.). 24p. (J). pap. 8.00 (978-1-63437-605-1(6)) American Reading Co.

Ferris, Diane J. Weather Watcher. 2009. (Illus.). 20p. pap. 13.00 (978-1-4490-1218-2(3)) AuthorHouse.

First Graphics: Nature Cycles. 2010. (First Graphics: Nature Cycles Ser.). (ENG.). 24p. (J). (gr. 1-2). pap., pap., pap. 25.16 (978-1-4296-6232-1(8), 171164) Capstone.

First Graphics: Nature Cycles Classroom Collection. 2010. (First Graphics: Nature Cycles Ser.). (ENG.). 24p. (J). (gr. 1-2). 154.96 (978-1-4296-6401-1(0), 171202) Capstone.

Fitzsimons, Cecilia. 50 Nature Projects for Kids: Fun-Packed Outdoor & Indoor Things to Do & Make. 2013. (Illus.). 96p. (J). (gr. 2-9). 13.99 (978-1-84322-852-3(1), Armadillo) Anness Publishing GBR. Dist: National Bk. Network.

Flatt, Lizann. Counting on Fall. Barron, Ashley, illus. 2017. (Math in Nature Ser.: 1). (ENG.). 32p. (J). (gr. k-2). pap. 8.95 (978-1-77147-310-1(X)) Owlkids Bks. Inc. CAN. Dist: Publishers Group West (PGW).

—Sizing up Winter. Barron, Ashley, illus. 2018. (Math in Nature Ser.: 3). (ENG.). 32p. (J). (gr. k-3). pap. 8.95 (978-1-77147-339-2(8)) Owlkids Bks. Inc. CAN. Dist: Publishers Group West (PGW).

—Sorting Through Spring. Barron, Ashley, illus. 2018. (Math in Nature Ser.: 2). (ENG.). 32p. (J). (gr. 1-4). pap. 8.95 (978-1-77147-153-4(0)) Owlkids Bks. Inc. CAN. Dist: Publishers Group West (PGW).

French, Felicity. Colour & Frame: Nature. French, Felicity, illus. 2016. (ENG., Illus.). 64p. pap. 12.95 (978-1-78243-584-6(0)) O'Mara, Michael Bks., Ltd. GBR. Dist: Independent Pubs. Group.

Furgang, Kathy. Nature in Focus: Set Of 6. 2011. (Navigators Ser.). (J). pap. 48.00 net. (978-1-4108-0420-4(8)) Benchmark Education Co.

—Nature in Focus & Enfoque en la Naturaleza: 6 English, 6 Spanish Adaptations. 2011. (ENG & SPA.). (J). 97.00 net. (978-1-4108-5690-6(9)) Benchmark Education Co.

La Furia de la Naturaleza: El Poder del Clima. (Colección Ventana Transparente). (SPA., Illus.). (J). (gr. 3-5). (978-950-11-1361-7(2), SG0561) Sigmar ARG. Dist: Lectorum Pubns., Inc.

Galvin, Laura Gates. Peep's Nature. 2006. (ENG., Illus.). 24p. (J). (gr. -1-k). 15.99 (978-1-59249-519-1(2), 1C301) Soundprints.

Ganeri, Anita. Endangered Places, 1 vol. 2017. (Last Chance to Save Ser.). (ENG.). 32p. (J). (gr. 4-5). 27.93 (978-1-5383-2286-4(2), b7a5b881-4af5-4444-8274-8234bce8876c); pap. 11.00 (978-1-5383-2386-1(9), 70188c63-f368-42af-b5c8-9320c1b77ad2) Rosen Publishing Group, Inc., The. (PowerKids Pr.).

—Fearsome Forces of Nature, 1 vol. 2012. (Extreme Nature Ser.). (ENG.). 32p. (gr. 3-5). pap. 8.29 (978-1-4109-4701-7(7), 119202, Raintree) Capstone.

—Tell Me Where Is the Top of the World? And More about Planet Earth. 2004. (Illus.). 32p. (J). pap. (978-1-84458-060-6(1), Pavilion Children's Books) Pavilion Bks.

Gatty, Alfred. Parables from Nature (Yesterday's Classics) 2006. (Illus.). 456p. (J). per. 14.95 (978-1-59915-005-5(0)) Yesterday's Classics.

Gerbracht, Edie. Especially Me! Stoner, Alexis, illus. 2012. 34p. pap. 11.77 (978-0-9843855-5-3(X)) aBASK Publishing.

Getting into Nature, 16 vols. 2003. (Getting into Nature Ser.). (ENG., Illus.). (J). (gr. 3-4). 231.44 (978-0-8239-7668-3(8), fed1e29f-c2a8-44f7-aacf-2b296e153482) Rosen Publishing Group, Inc., The.

Gibson, J. Phil & Gibson, Terri R. Natural Selection. 2009. (Science Foundations Ser.). (ENG., Illus.). 112p. (gr. 7-12). lib. bdg. 35.00 (978-0-7910-9784-7(6), P165525, Facts On File) Infobase Holdings, Inc.

Gifford, Peggy. The Great Big Green. Desimini, Lisa, illus. 2014. (ENG.). 32p. (J). (gr. -1-3). 15.95 (978-1-62091-629-2(0), Astra Young Readers) Astra Publishing Hse.

Glaser, Rebecca. Red in Nature. 2013. (ENG.). 24p. (J). lib. bdg. 25.65 (978-1-62031-036-6(8)) Jump! Inc.

God's Wonders. 3.50 (978-0-8054-5877-0(8)) B&H Publishing Group.

Griffin Llanas, Sheila. Nature Poetry: Make Me a Picture of the Sun, 1 vol. 2014. (Pure Poetry Ser.). (ENG., Illus.). 128p. (gr. 9-10). lib. bdg. 35.93 (978-0-7660-4244-5(8), a5cd3846-7f27-4e73-9ca3-963acb74f09c) Enslow Publishing, LLC.

Guiraud, Florence. Wonders of Nature: Explorations in the World of Birds, Insects & Fish. 2018. (ENG., Illus.). 96p. (J). (gr. k-4). 25.00 (978-3-7913-7365-2(X)) Prestel Verlag GmbH & Co KG. DEU. Dist: Penguin Random Hse. LLC.

Hays, Susan. Nature Friends Creativity Book. 2003. (Illus.). 52p. (J). 11.95 (978-0-9729192-0-3(1)) Art & Soul Expressions.

Hilton, Samantha, et al. Nature's Neighborhoods. Holmes, Steve, illus. 2004. (Interfact Ladders Ser.). (ENG.). 48p. (J). (gr. -1-2). 14.95 (978-1-58728-420-5(0)) Cooper Square Publishing Llc.

Hoare, Ben. The Wonders of Nature. 2019. (DK Children's Anthologies Ser.). (ENG., Illus.). 224p. (J). (gr. 2-4). 21.99 (978-1-4654-8536-6(8), DK Children) Dorling Kindersley Publishing, Inc.

Holden, Pam. Look Outside, 1 vol. 2017. (ENG., Illus.). 23p. (J). pap. (978-1-77654-222-2(3), Red Rocket Readers) Flying Start Bks.

Hooker, Worthington. The Child's Book of Nature. 2005. reprint ed. pap. 37.95 (978-1-4179-3598-7(7)) Kessinger Publishing, LLC.

Houbre, Gilbert & Verdet, Jean-Pierre. Light. Matthews, Sarah, tr. from FRE. Houbre, Gilbert, illus. 2012. (ENG., Illus.). 36p.

(J). (gr. -1-k). 19.99 (978-1-85103-405-5(6)) Moonlight Publishing, Ltd. GBR. Dist: Independent Pubs. Group.

Hunter, William. Nature & Nurture: The Causes of Obesity. Garcia, Victor, ed. 2014. (Understanding Obesity Ser.: 10). 104p. (J). (gr. 7-18). lib. bdg. 24.95 (978-1-4222-3064-0(3)) Mason Crest.

I See You: Level E. 8p. 20.95 (978-0-322-00342-2(3)) Wright Group/McGraw-Hill.

Ikids Staff. The Five Senses. 2009. (ENG., Illus.). 20p. (J). (gr. -1-1). 6.99 (978-1-58476-812-8(6)) Innovative Kids.

In the Rain Forest: Level F. 16p. 31.50 (978-0-322-00376-7(8)) Wright Group/McGraw-Hill.

Ireland, Karin. Wonderful Nature, Wonderful You, 1 vol. Canyon, Christopher, illus. 2017. 32p. (J). (gr. k-3). 16.95 (978-1-58469-582-0(X), Dawn Pubns.) Sourcebooks, Inc.

Jankowski, Matt. Be a Conservationist!, 1 vol. 2018. (Be the Change! Shaping Your Community Ser.). (ENG.). 32p. (gr. 3-4). 28.27 (978-1-5382-2003-0(2), d832120d-c6f0-4674-aac2-6797b2312317) Stevens, Gareth Publishing LLLP.

Jenkins, Pete. Shapes in Nature. 2018. (I Know Ser.). (ENG., Illus.). 16p. (gr. -1-2). pap. 9.95 (978-1-64156-227-0(7), 9781641562270) Rourke Educational Media.

Jenkins, Steve. Just a Second. Jenkins, Steve, illus. 2011. (ENG., Illus.). 40p. (J). (gr. -1-3). 18.99 (978-0-618-70896-3(0), 518919, Clarion Bks.) HarperCollins Pubs.

—Just a Second. Jenkins, Steve, illus. 2017. (ENG., Illus.). 32p. (J). (gr. -1-3). pap. 7.99 (978-1-328-74086-1(2), 1677123, Clarion Bks.) HarperCollins Pubs.

Johnson, Kathy. Let's Take a Walk in the Rain. Peer, Kate, illus. 2012. 28p. pap. 13.54 (978-1-4669-3252-4(X)) Trafford Publishing.

Johnson, Rebecca L. A Walk in the Tundra. Saroff, Phyllis V., illus. Braasch, Gary, photos by. 2005. (Biomes of North America Ser.). 48p. (gr. 3-6). lib. bdg. 23.93 (978-1-57505-157-4(5)) Lerner Publishing Group.

Der Jugend Brockhaus: Natur und Technik. (GER., Illus.). 640p. (YA). (gr. 5-11). (978-3-7653-1851-1(5)) Brockhaus, F. A., GmbH DEU. Dist: International Bk. Import Service, Inc.

Kalman, Bobbie. ¿Cómo se siente al Tocarlo? 2008. (SPA.). 24p. (J). lib. bdg. (978-0-7787-8722-8(2)) Crabtree Publishing Co.

—¿Como Se Siente Al Tocarlo? 2008.Tr. of How Does It Feel? (SPA.). 24p. (J). pap. (978-0-7787-8731-0(1)) Crabtree Publishing Co.

—My Backyard Community. 2010. (My World Ser.). (ENG., Illus.). 24p. (J). (gr. k-2). (978-0-7787-9448-6(2)); pap. (978-0-7787-9492-9(X)) Crabtree Publishing Co.

—What Are Opposites in Nature? 2010. (Looking at Nature Ser.). (ENG.). 24p. (J). (gr. -1-2). pap. (978-0-7787-3346-1(7)); lib. bdg. (978-0-7787-3326-3(2)) Crabtree Publishing Co.

—What Is Super Nature?, 1 vol. 2010. (Big Science Ideas Ser.). (ENG.). 32p. (J). (gr. k-3). pap. (978-0-7787-3307-2(6)); lib. bdg. (978-0-7787-3287-7(8)) Crabtree Publishing Co.

—Where Is It? 2007. (Looking at Nature Ser.). (ENG., Illus.). 24p. (J). (gr. -1-2). pap. (978-0-7787-3341-6(6)); lib. bdg. (978-0-7787-3321-8(1)) Crabtree Publishing Co.

Kalman, Bobbie & Smithyman, Kathryn. El Ciclo de Vida del Arbol. Bedell, Barbara, illus. 2005. (Serie Ciclos de Vida Ser.). (SPA.). 32p. (J). (gr. 1-4). pap. (978-0-7787-8711-2(7)) Crabtree Publishing Co.

Kaplan, Osman. Animal Wonders of the Sky. Kalender, Oznur, illus. 2009. (Amazing Animals Ser.). (ENG.). 56p. (J). (gr. 2-4). 9.95 (978-1-59784-201-3(X), Tughra Bks.) Blue Dome, Inc.

Kauffman, Judy. The Lord God Made Them All. 2003. (Illus.). 40p. 1.90 (978-0-7399-2347-4(1), 2927) Rod & Staff Pubs., Inc.

Kavanagh, James & Waterford Press Staff. In God's Kitchen. Belisle, John, illus. 2004. (ENG.). 32p. (J). 15.95 (978-1-58355-241-4(3)) Western National Parks Assn.

Kids Can Press Staff. This Is Daniel Cook on a Hike. Li, Karen, ed. 2006. (This Is Daniel Cook Ser.). (Illus.). 24p. (J). (gr. -1-1). 4.95 (978-1-55453-080-9(6)) Kids Can Pr., Ltd. CAN. Dist: Hachette Bk. Group.

Knight, M. J. Why Should I Care about Nature? 2009. (One Small Step Ser.). (YA). (gr. 2-5). 27.10 (978-1-59920-266-2(2)) Black Rabbit Bks.

Koniver, Laura. From the Ground Up. Koniver, Laura, illus. 2012. (Illus.). 44p. (J). pap. 16.99 (978-1-937848-03-3(5)) Do Life Right, Inc.

Koontz, Robin. Nature Inspired Contraptions. 2018. (Nature-Inspired Innovations Ser.). (ENG., Illus.). 48p. (gr. 4-8). lib. bdg. 35.64 (978-1-64156-455-7(5), 9781641564557) Rourke Educational Media.

Koontz, Robin Michal. Water Goes Round, 4 vols. Davidson, Chris, illus. Incl. Hide & Seek Moon: The Moon Phases. 24.65 (978-1-4296-5365-7(5), 1321992); Water Goes Round: The Water Cycle. lib. bdg. 24.65 (978-1-4296-5364-0(7), 113792); (Illus.). (J). (gr. 1-3). (First Graphics: Nature Cycles Ser.). (ENG.). 24p. 2010. 49.30 o.p. (978-1-4296-5368-8(X), 170546) Capstone.

Kowalski, Gary. Earth Day: An Alphabet Book. Baviera, Rocco, illus. 2009. (ENG.). 32p. (J). (gr. -1-4). 12.00 (978-1-55896-542-3(4), 1297770, Skinner Hse. Bks.) Unitarian Universalist Assn.

Kranz, Linda. My Nature Book: A Journal & Activity Book for Kids. 2nd ed. 2013. (Illus.). 128p. (J). (gr. -1-12). pap., act. bk. ed. 14.95 (978-1-58979-822-9(8)) Taylor Trade Publishing.

KUBU. Farm Friends: A Visit to the Farm. 2016. (Kubu Ser.: 2). (Illus.). 32p. (J). (gr. -1-2). pap. 5.99 (978-1-57826-475-9(8), Hatherleigh Pr.) Hatherleigh Co., Ltd., The.

Laber-Warren, Emily. A Walk in the Woods: Into the Field Guide. 2013. (ENG.). 112p. (J). (gr. k). 19.99 (978-1-935703-23-5(4)) Downtown Bookworks.

Lambert, Mark John. The 10 Most Incredible Landforms. 2008. (J). 14.99 (978-1-55448-529-1(0)) Scholastic Library Publishing.

Lawler, Jean C. Experience Nature: How Time Outside Makes You Feel. 2018. (Experience Personal Power Ser.). (ENG., Illus.). 24p. (J). (gr. 2-4). pap. 6.99 (978-1-63440-377-1(0), 432aa309-550f-430d-bcda-cee5cd474b67) Red Chair Pr.

Leslie, Clare Walker. The Curious Nature Guide: Explore the Natural Wonders All Around You. 2015. (ENG., Illus.). 144p. pap. 14.99 (978-1-61212-509-1(3), 622509) Storey Publishing, LLC.

Lewis, J. Patrick. Earth & You - A Closer View: Nature's Features. Canyon, Christopher, illus. 2004. (Sharing Nature with Children Book Ser.). 36p. (J). (gr. -1-3). 16.95 (978-1-58469-016-0(X)) Take Heart Pubns.

Lewis, Kelly; Grudzina. From Egg to Butterfly. Grudzina, Rebecca, ed. 2016. (Spring Forward Ser.). (ENG.). (J). (gr. 1). 7.20 net. (978-1-4900-6020-0(0)) Benchmark Education Co.

Lindeen, Mary. Ideas from Nature. 2018. (BeginningtoRead Ser.). (ENG.). 32p. (J). (gr. -1-2). 22.60 (978-1-59953-901-0(2)); (gr. k-2). pap. 13.26 (978-1-68404-148-0(1)) Norwood Hse. Pr.

—Patterns in the Sky. 2018. (BeginningtoRead Ser.). (ENG.). 32p. (J). (gr. -1-2). lib. bdg. 22.60 (978-1-59953-900-3(4)); (gr. k-2). pap. 13.26 (978-1-68404-147-3(3)) Norwood Hse. Pr.

Locker, Thomas. Walking with Henry: The Life & Works of Henry David Thoreau. 2011. (ENG., Illus.). 32p. (J). (gr. -1-5). pap. 21.95 (978-1-55591-016-7(5)) Fulcrum Publishing.

Loh-Hagan, Virginia. Weird Nature. 2017. (Stranger Than Fiction Ser.). (ENG., Illus.). 32p. (J). (gr. 4-8). lib. bdg. 32.07 (978-1-63472-894-2(7), 210002, 45th Parallel Press) Cherry Lake Publishing.

Londt, Claire, et al. English Matters for Zambia Basic Education Grade 3 Pupil's Book. 2nd ed. 2007. (ENG., Illus.). 64p. pap., stu. ed. 5.75 (978-0-521-68755-3(1)) Cambridge Univ. Pr.

Lowcountry A to Z. 2004. (J). 24.95 (978-0-9744035-0-2(4)) Makai Concepts, LLC.

Lunchbox Lessons Staff, creator. The Neighborhood Naturalist. 2009. (Backyard Pioneers Ser.). (ENG., Illus.). 80p. (gr. 1-10). pap., wbk. ed. (978-1-60507-047-6(5)) Lunchbox Lessons.

MacCoon, Nancy. Backyard Wonders. Watkins, Courtney, illus. l.t. ed. 2003. 38p. (J). pap. 14.95 (978-0-9742495-0-6(5)) Vibatorium LLC.

MacKenzie, Catherine. Scottish Highland Adventures. 2007. (Adventure Ser.). (ENG., Illus.). 96p. (J). per. 8.99 (978-1-84550-281-2(7), 790df1fd-063a-4fc3-8fa4-17d4063ada97) Christian Focus Pubns. GBR. Dist: Baker & Taylor Publisher Services (BTPS).

Marciniak, Kristin. Incredible Nature. 2018. (Unbelievable Ser.). (ENG., Illus.). 32p. (J). (gr. 3-6). 32.80 (978-1-63235-421-1(7), 13769, 12-Story Library) Bookstaves, LLC.

Marsico, Katie. The Nature Conservancy. 2016. (Community Connections: How Do They Help? Ser.). (ENG., Illus.). 24p. (J). (gr. 2-5). 29.21 (978-1-63471-051-0(7), 208284) Cherry Lake Publishing.

—World Wildlife Fund. 2016. (Community Connections: How Do They Help? Ser.). (ENG., Illus.). 24p. (J). (gr. 2-5). 29.21 (978-1-63471-055-8(X), 208300) Cherry Lake Publishing.

Martin, Bill, Jr. & Sampson, Michael. I Love Our Earth / Amo Nuestra Tierra. Lipow, Dan, photos by. 2013. (Charlesbridge Bilingual Bks.). (Illus.). 32p. (J). (gr. -1-2). pap. 7.95 (978-1-58089-557-6(3)) Charlesbridge Publishing, Inc.

Mattern, Joanne. Angel Falls: World's Highest Waterfall. 2009. (Nature's Greatest Hits Ser.). 24p. (gr. 2-2). 42.50 (978-1-61514-837-0(X), PowerKids Pr.) Rosen Publishing Group, Inc., The.

Mattern, Joanne & Herndon, Ryan, compiled by. Guinness World Records. 2005. (Illus.). 47p. pap. (978-0-439-71568-3(7)) Scholastic, Inc.

McConnell, Lynn. Grandma's Tree. 2009. 24p. pap. 11.49 (978-1-4389-8069-0(8)) AuthorHouse.

Meachen Rau, Dana. El Arco Iris / Rainbows, 1 vol. 2009. (Maravillas de la Naturaleza / Wonders of Nature Ser.). (ENG & SPA., Illus.). 32p. (gr. 1-2). lib. bdg. 25.50 (978-0-7614-2831-2(3), d2e159e1-1ab4-4bb9-8b5f-9dbb7bd96578) Cavendish Square Publishing LLC.

—El Arco Iris (Rainbows), 1 vol. 2009. (Maravillas de la Naturaleza (Wonders of Nature) Ser.). (SPA., Illus.). 32p. (gr. 1-2). lib. bdg. 25.50 (978-0-7614-2807-7(0), 08fae9c6-ba1b-483d-b51e-baf9ed491d8e) Cavendish Square Publishing LLC.

—Bookworms: Nature's Cycles, 6 vols., Set. Incl. Animals. 25.50 (978-0-7614-4093-2(3), 2e97af87-fb08-4efb-91c0-189ee16d08a9); Day & Night. 25.50 (978-0-7614-4094-9(1), aeecde50-db38-4962-a48a-c2d1818757a6); Food Chains. 25.50 (978-0-7614-4095-6(X), 5162d218-1229-483f-929d-9ae35e85f1f6); Plants. 25.50 (978-0-7614-4097-0(6), db00efba-461a-4a43-86fb-99db11bd8002); Seasons. 25.50 (978-0-7614-4098-7(4), 38183a44-2664-46df-8a69-0808a7042d24); Water. 25.50 (978-0-7614-4099-4(2), 43c76e68-1bd4-4b50-91db-32856615d919); 32p. (gr. 1-2). 2010. (Bookworms: Nature's Cycles Ser.). 2009. Set lib. bdg. 95.70 o.p. (978-0-7614-4092-5(5), Cavendish Square) Cavendish Square Publishing LLC.

—Day & Night, 1 vol. 2010. (Nature's Cycles Ser.). (ENG.). 32p. (gr. 1-2). 25.50 (978-0-7614-4094-9(1), aeecde50-db38-4962-a48a-c2d1818757a6) Cavendish Square Publishing LLC.

—Las Cataratas / Waterfalls, 1 vol. 2009. (Maravillas de la Naturaleza / Wonders of Nature Ser.). (ENG & SPA., Illus.). 32p. (gr. 1-2). lib. bdg. 25.50 (978-0-7614-2833-6(X), 83f446c9-1ea7-4515-a735-6ea225802ccd) Cavendish Square Publishing LLC.

—Las Cataratas (Waterfalls), 1 vol. 2009. (Maravillas de la Naturaleza (Wonders of Nature) Ser.). (SPA., Illus.). 32p. (gr. 1-2). lib. bdg. 25.50 (978-0-7614-2810-7(0), d8bd4814-7ee1-4171-8d36-fdeef15fe221) Cavendish Square Publishing LLC.

—Rainbows, 1 vol. 2008. (Wonders of Nature Ser.). (ENG.). 32p. (gr. 1-2). lib. bdg. 25.50 (978-0-7614-2669-1(8), 00c110df-3d2a-49d6-943f-7f9f3a4b7611) Cavendish Square Publishing LLC.

—Waterfalls, 1 vol. 2008. (Wonders of Nature Ser.). (ENG.). 32p. (gr. 1-2). lib. bdg. 25.50 (978-0-7614-2671-4(X), fe7ad268-3a21-4ed8-b7ac-66b02f18e2f7) Cavendish Square Publishing LLC.

Meredith, Susan & Cullis, Megan. Nature to Color. Cooper, Jenny, illus. 2013. (ENG.). 96p. (J). 9.99 (978-0-7945-1913-1(X), Usborne) EDC Publishing.

Miché, Mary. Nature's Patchwork Quilt: Understanding Habitats. Powell, Consie, illus. 2012. (ENG.). 32p. (J). (gr. 1-4). 24.94 (978-1-58469-169-3(7)) Take Heart Pubns.

Miche, Mary. Nature's Patchwork Quilt: Understanding Habitats, 1 vol. Powell, Consie, illus. 2012. 32p. (J). (gr. k-6). pap. 8.99 (978-1-58469-170-9(0), Dawn Pubns.) Sourcebooks, Inc.

Miles Kelly Staff. Nature. 2003. (Ask Me a Question Ser.). (Illus.). 20p. spiral bd. 7.95 (978-1-84236-125-2(2)) Miles Kelly Publishing, Ltd. GBR. Dist: Independent Pubs. Group.

Molina, M. Isabel. Arco Iris (The Rainbow) (SPA.). (J). 7.95 (978-84-86563-03-5(8)) Nuevas Estructuras Gondomar ESP. Dist: AIMS International Bks., Inc.

Monroe, Colleen. The Wonders of Nature Sketchbook: Learn about Nature & How to Draw It. Monroe, Michael Glenn, illus. 2006. 40p. (J). (gr. 4-7). lib. bdg. 15.00 (978-0-9754942-1-9(X)) Storytime Pr., Inc.

Montgomery, Anne. Nature Made, 1 vol. rev. ed. 2014. (Science: Informational Text Ser.). (ENG., Illus.). 24p. (J). (gr. k-1). pap. 9.99 (978-1-4807-4528-5(6)) Teacher Created Materials, Inc.

Morris, Neil. Our Wonderful World: Fun Finding Out. 2003. (Fun Finding Out Ser.). (Illus.). 48p. (J). pap. 7.95 (978-1-902947-36-5(3)) Miles Kelly Publishing, Ltd. GBR. Dist: Independent Pubs. Group.

El Mundo de la Naturaleza. (Coleccion Lo Sabias?). (SPA., Illus.). 44p. (J). 12.95 (978-950-11-0938-2(0), SGM9380) Sigmar ARG. Dist: Continental Bk. Co., Inc.

Murphy, Julie & Amstutz, Lisa J. Nature Starts. 2012. (Nature Starts Ser.). (ENG.). 32p. (gr. 1-2). pap. 190.80 (978-1-4296-8302-9(3), Capstone Pr.) Capstone.

Muse, Elizabeth St. Cloud. A Child's Garden: Introducing Your Child to the Joys of the Garden. Saull, Eve, illus. 2007. 45p. reprint ed. 15.00 (978-1-4223-6638-7(3)) DIANE Publishing Co.

My First Nature Books, 11 bks., Set. Incl. Air. Benedict, Kitty & Soutter-Perrot, Andrienne. Delessert, Etienne, illus. lib. bdg. 14.60 (978-0-88682-547-8(4)); Ant. Benedict, Kitty. Felix, Monique, illus. lib. bdg. 14.60 (978-0-88682-564-5(4)); Cow. Benedict, Kitty. Wuest, Gerard, illus. lib. bdg. 14.60 (978-0-88682-567-6(9)); Earth. Soutter-Perrot, Andrienne. Delessert, Etienne, illus. lib. bdg. 14.60 (978-0-88682-548-5(2)); Earthworm. Soutter-Perrot, Andrienne. Delessert, Etienne, illus. lib. bdg. 14.60 (978-0-88682-566-9(0)); Fire. Soutter-Perrot, Andrienne. Gaudard, Patrick, illus. lib. bdg. 14.60 (978-0-88682-553-9(9)); Oak. Soutter-Perrot, Andrienne. Schmid, Eleonore, illus. lib. bdg. 14.60 (978-0-88682-550-8(4)); Toad. Felix, Monique, illus. lib. bdg. 14.60 (978-0-88682-568-3(7)); 32p. (J). (gr. 1-5). 1993. o.p. (978-0-88682-570-6(9), Creative Education) Creative Co., The.

My First Reference Book about Nature IR. 2017. (Reference Bks.). (ENG.). (J). 9.99 (978-0-7945-3774-6(X), Usborne) EDC Publishing.

Nadeau, Isaac. Canyons, 1 vol. 2005. (Library of Landforms Ser.). (ENG., Illus.). 24p. (J). (gr. 3-4). lib. bdg. 26.27 (978-1-4042-3123-8(4), 12f6b60c-e86e-4970-b3f6-5467f5297f83) Rosen Publishing Group, Inc., The.

National Geographic Learning. Windows on Literacy Emergent (Science: Life Science): Living Things Need Water. 2007. (ENG., Illus.). 16p. (J). (gr. k-2). pap. 12.95 (978-0-7922-9211-1(1)) CENGAGE Learning.

Naturaleza. 2005. (Coleccion Primeras Imagenes).Tr. of Wind & Weather. (SPA., Illus.). 86p. (J). (gr. -1-18). pap. 7.95 (978-950-11-0989-4(5), SGM9895) Sigmar ARG. Dist: Continental Bk. Co., Inc.

Nature (Gr. PreK-5) 2003. (J). (978-1-58232-023-6(3)) ECS Learning Systems, Inc.

Nature in Focus, 10 vols., Set. Incl. Life in a Backyard. Green, Jen. lib. bdg. 28.67 (978-1-4339-3414-8(0), ef5a3ae1-2788-4916-8fea-43355068fdaf); Life in a Coral Reef. Green, Jen. lib. bdg. 28.67 (978-1-4339-3423-0(X), 780d3128-bd53-47bc-8e3e-c0cbf7135050); Life in a Pond. Hibbert, Adam. lib. bdg. 28.67 (978-1-4339-3411-7(6), ec8318cf-d92b-4a90-9337-e14c2778c78a); Life in a Rain Forest. Kite, Lorien. lib. bdg. 28.67 (978-1-4339-3410-0(8), b2ac692e-f5b0-4eeb-a840-b8d449db10c9); Life in the Desert. Green, Jen. lib. bdg. 28.67 (978-1-4339-3420-9(5), e96502d2-4cdb-423b-bcc4-8d0e5deafcd8); Life on the Tundra. Green, Jen. lib. bdg. 28.67 (978-1-4339-3417-9(5), 1df7e4ca-d7b7-434d-b63e-9e15834d579f); (Illus.). (YA). (gr. 3-4). (Nature in Focus Ser.). (ENG.). 32p. 2010. Set lib. bdg. 143.35 (978-1-4339-3583-1(X), 9823c116-0769-4282-a0a2-2ae3aec90ac9, Gareth Stevens Learning Library) Stevens, Gareth Publishing LLLP.

Nature Riddles [Capstone Sole Source]. 2010. (Nature Riddles Ser.). 32p. lib. bdg. 103.96 (978-1-4296-5873-7(8), Capstone Pr.) Capstone.

Nature Watch. 2004. (Illus.). lib. bdg. 7.95 (978-0-8225-4353-4(2)) 2004. (Illus.). lib. bdg. 7.95 (978-0-8225-4365-7(6))Set. 2007. (J). (gr. 4-8). lib. bdg. 771.40 (978-0-8225-8465-0(4)) Lerner Publishing Group.

Nature's Formations, 12 vols. 2017. (Nature's Formations Ser.). (ENG.). 24p. (gr. 1-1). lib. bdg. 155.58 (978-1-5026-2885-5(6), 4b02ae0a-7599-488b-932b-01cba7dd65fb) Cavendish Square Publishing LLC.

Nature's Got Talent. 2014. (Nature's Got Talent Ser.). 32p. (J). (gr. k-5). pap. 60.00 (978-1-4777-7236-2(7)); (ENG.). (gr. 3-3). 167.58 (978-1-4777-7076-4(3), a1169fc5-2125-43b2-803b-f3de13a813f3) Rosen Publishing Group, Inc., The. (PowerKids Pr.).

Nature's Mysteries, 16 vols. 2016. (Nature's Mysteries Ser.). 32p. (ENG.). (gr. 2-3). 208.48 (978-1-5081-0218-2(X), 8648caf4-a919-49d9-bf23-7d9acdc06f6b); (gr. 3-2). pap. 103.20 (978-1-68048-600-1(4)) Rosen Publishing Group, Inc., The. (Britannica Educational Publishing).

Nature's Wonders, 10 vols., Set. Incl. Galapagos Islands. Kras, Sara Louise. 2009. lib. bdg. 38.36 (978-0-7614-2856-5(9), 83b48911-cf09-4e16-89d9-3f2d485691de); Great Barrier Reef. Kummer, Patricia K. 2009. lib. bdg. 38.36 (978-0-7614-2852-7(6), 13ac5250-935b-4cad-ad63-74b792d5e9a8); Great Lakes. Kummer, Patricia K. 2009. lib. bdg. 38.36 (978-0-7614-2853-4(4), 0140d51f-e6ca-40fc-8646-f34a315a75a9); Nile. Heinrichs, Ann. 2008. lib. bdg. 38.36 (978-0-7614-2854-1(2), 034df8ba-08c1-4a12-8c3e-7e454fa8dbf0); Sahara. Heinrichs, Ann. 2008. lib. bdg. 38.36 (978-0-7614-2855-8(0), c67647b4-e723-4c6a-bec5-65e5ead444f1); 96p. (gr. 6-6). (Nature's Wonders Ser.). (ENG.). 2009. Set lib. bdg. 191.80 (978-0-7614-2851-0(8), 0a2f02c7-0083-4fb7-ad9b-5973b6dc2544, Cavendish Square) Cavendish Square Publishing LLC.

Nuevo Investiguemos 8: Ciencias Naturales y de la Salud. (SPA.). (YA). (gr. 8). (978-958-02-1536-3(7)) Editorial Voluntad S.A. COL. Dist: Distribuidora Norma, Inc.

Nuevo Investiguemos 9: Ciencias Naturales y de la Salud. (SPA.). (YA). (gr. 9). (978-958-02-1537-0(5)) Editorial Voluntad S.A. COL. Dist: Distribuidora Norma, Inc.

Nunn, Daniel. ABCs in Nature, 1 vol. 2012. (Everyday Alphabet Ser.). (ENG.). 32p. (gr. -1-k). pap. 9.95 (978-1-4109-4737-6(8), 119325, Raintree) Capstone.

Olien, Rebecca & Hansen, Amy S. First Graphics: Science Mysteries: A Science Mystery. Scott, Korey & McDermed, Kathryn, illus. 2011. (First Graphics: Science Mysteries Ser.). (ENG.). 24p. (J). (gr. k-3). pap., pap., pap. 25.16 (978-1-4296-7181-1(5), 16735) Capstone.

—First Graphics: Science Mysteries Classroom Collection: A Science Mystery. Scott, Korey & McDermed, Kathryn, illus. 2011. (First Graphics: Science Mysteries Ser.). (ENG.). 24p. (J). (gr. 1-2). 146.80 (978-1-4296-7182-8(3), 16736) Capstone.

Paderewski, Elliot. Animals Help Plants Pollinate, 1 vol. 2016. (Rosen REAL Readers: STEM & STEAM Collection). (ENG.). 12p. (gr. 1-2). pap. 6.33 (978-1-5081-2455-9(8), 592842a5-e12f-41f7-8ba6-8bc23bdac909, Rosen Classroom) Rosen Publishing Group, Inc., The.

Parramón, José María. Mi Calle. Borday, Irene, illus. (Coleccion Estoy En...).Tr. of My Street. (SPA.). 32p. (J). (gr. k-3). 6.36 (978-84-342-1003-5(7)) Parramon Ediciones S.A. ESP. Dist: Lectorum Pubns., Inc.

—Mi Casa. Borday, Irene, illus. (Coleccion Estoy En...).Tr. of My House. (SPA.). 32p. (J). (gr. k-3). 6.36 (978-84-342-1002-8(9)) Parramon Ediciones S.A. ESP. Dist: Lectorum Pubns., Inc.

—Mi Jardin. Borday, Irene, illus. (Coleccion Estoy En...).Tr. of My Garden. (SPA.). 32p. (J). (gr. k-3). 6.36 (978-84-342-1005-9(3)) Parramon Ediciones S.A. ESP. Dist: Lectorum Pubns., Inc.

Parramón, José María & Bordoy, Irene. Mi Calle.Tr. of My Street. (SPA., Illus.). (J). (gr. -1-1). 6.95 (978-958-04-1277-9(4)) Norma S.A. COL. Dist: Distribuidora Norma, Inc.

Percy, J.P. Nature. 2013. (Can You Guess What I Am? Ser.). 24p. (gr. k-3). 28.50 (978-1-59920-895-4(4)) Black Rabbit Bks.

Pèrols, Sylvaine. La Tierra y el Cielo. (Coleccion Mundo Maravilloso). (SPA., Illus.). 24p. (J). (gr. 2-4). (978-84-348-6322-4(7), SM30014) SM Ediciones.

Peters, Katie. Nature Walk. 2019. (Science All Around Me (Pull Ahead Readers — Nonfiction) Ser.). (ENG., Illus.). 16p. (J). (gr. -1-1). pap. 8.99 (978-1-5415-7333-8(1), 5adc289f-d86a-444b-a8c9-19066d04d792); lib. bdg. 27.99 (978-1-5415-5845-8(6), f13c0d01-5d4c-4f4e-944f-cae97a65d1bd) Lerner Publishing Group. (Lerner Pubns.).

Peters, Scott. What We Like. 2011. (Early Connections Ser.). (J). (978-1-61672-339-2(4)) Benchmark Education Co.

Peterson, Jorrien. Seek & Find Biomes: Tundra, Alpine, Forest, Rainforest, Savanna, Grassland, Desert, Freshwater, Marine, 1 vol. 2020. (Illus.). 32p. (J). (gr. k-5). pap. 14.99 (978-1-4236-5403-2(X)) Gibbs Smith, Publisher.

Playhouse Disney Encyclopedia. 2009. (ENG.). 196p. (gr. -1-k). 19.99 (978-1-4231-1921-0(5)) Disney Pr.

Podojil, Catherine. Saving Endangered Species. 2005. (ENG., Illus.). 24p. (J). (gr. 5-5). pap. 5.97 net. (978-0-328-13528-8(3), Scott Foresman) Savvas Learning Co.

Polito, James A. My First Book of Critters. 2004. (Illus.). 24p. (J). spiral bd. 12.95 (978-0-9752842-0-9(7)) Kind Critter Junction.

Portis, Antoinette. A New Green Day. 2020. (ENG., Illus.). 40p. (J). (gr. -1-2). 18.99 (978-0-8234-4488-5(0), Neal Porter Bks) Holiday Hse., Inc.

Potter, Jean. La Naturaleza Explicada A Los Ninos En Pocas Palabras: Mas De 100 Actividades Realizables En 10 Minutos O Menos. 2003. (SPA.). 264p. (978-84-493-0278-7(1)) Ediciones Paidos Iberica, S.A.

Priest, Saira, photos by & des. If We Were... Priest, Saira, des. l.t. ed. 2003. (Illus.). 20p. 12.95 (978-0-9726628-7-1(1)) Niche Publishing & Marketing.

Racanelli, Marie. Crazy Nature, 10 vols., Set. Incl. Albino Animals. (J). lib. bdg. 26.27 (978-1-4358-9381-8(6), 3ffba6f6-c937-41c4-bd06-cf6378052baa); Animal Mimics. (YA). lib. bdg. 26.27 (978-1-4358-9382-5(4), 89fbc4d1-fd1b-479f-82fa-74df54433ceb); Animals with Armor. (J). lib. bdg. 26.27 (978-1-4358-9386-3(7), 8334aa6e-a738-40b3-a38c-20f4387d628f); Animals with Pockets. (J). lib. bdg. 26.27 (978-1-4358-9385-6(9), 304fc356-b80f-4327-8599-d03e8a3c40e5); Camouflaged Creatures. (YA). lib. bdg. 26.27 (978-1-4358-9383-2(2), 8a335866-75e3-44cd-8674-4d4d60af4440); Underground Animals. (J). lib. bdg. 26.27 (978-1-4358-9384-9(0), 9077a117-4bbd-455e-adcd-15663f17b234); (gr. 2-3). (Crazy Nature Ser.). (ENG., Illus.). 24p. 2010. Set lib. bdg. 131.35 (978-1-4358-9411-2(1), 20b44acd-e780-41e9-acf6-bfe2be02a65c, PowerKids Pr.) Rosen Publishing Group, Inc., The.

Randolph, Joanne. All about a Day, 1 vol. 2007. (It's about Time Ser.). (ENG., Illus.). 24p. (J). (gr. 1-1). lib. bdg. 26.27 (978-1-4042-3767-4(4), aa94ace2-544c-4a7f-8b91-ecc04a244d43) Rosen Publishing Group, Inc., The.

Ranger Rick's Naturescope. 2005. (Ranger Rick's Naturescope Ser.). (gr. 5-8). 279.50 (978-0-7910-9168-5(6), Facts On File) Infobase Holdings, Inc.

Ransone, Rob & Ransone Associates Inc Staff. Lit'L Drip: The Life Story of a Drop of Water. 2010. 24p. pap. 14.99 (978-1-4490-8512-4(1)) AuthorHouse.

Rappoport, Bernice. Outside My Window. Johnson, Pamela G., illus. 2004. (Treasure Tree Ser.). 32p. (J). (978-0-7166-1622-1(X)) World Bk., Inc.

Reda, Sheryl A. A Forest Tree House. Barrett, Peter, illus. 2004. (Treasure Tree Ser.). 32p. (J). (978-0-7166-1606-1(8)) World Bk., Inc.

Reeve, Penny. Himalayan Adventures. rev. ed. 2005. (Adventure Ser.). (ENG., Illus.). 96p. (J). (gr. 3-7). per. 8.99 (978-1-84550-080-1(6), 28b208ac-c1c9-4630-8237-5c413980016d, CF4Kids) Christian Focus Pubns. GBR. Dist: Baker & Taylor Publisher Services (BTPS).

Richards, Jon & Simkins, Ed. The Natural World. 2016. (Mapographica Ser.). 32p. (J). (gr. 3-6). (978-0-7787-2658-6(4)) Crabtree Publishing Co.

Ridley, Kimberly. The Secret Bay, 1 vol. Raye, Rebekah, illus. 2019. (Tilbury House Nature Book Ser.: 0). (ENG.). 40p. (J). (gr. 1-6). pap. 8.95 (978-0-88448-751-7(2), 884751) Tilbury Hse. Pubs.

Ross, Michael Elsohn. Nature Art with Chiura Obata. Smith, Wendy, illus. 2005. (Naturalist's Apprentice Biographies Ser.). 48p. (gr. 3-6). lib. bdg. 19.93 (978-1-57505-378-3(0)) Lerner Publishing Group.

—Rolypolyology. 2003. (Backyard Buddies Ser.). 48p. (YA). (gr. 3-5). 6.95 (978-0-87614-901-0(8), Carolrhoda Bks.) Lerner Publishing Group.

Rotner, Shelley & Kreisler, Ken. Nature Spy. Rotner, Shelley, illus. 2014. (ENG., Illus.). 32p. (J). (gr. -1-1). pap. 13.99 (978-1-4814-5042-3(5), Atheneum Bks. for Young Readers) Simon & Schuster Children's Publishing.

Rustad, Martha E. H. Rainbows. 2017. (Amazing Sights of the Sky Ser.). (ENG., Illus.). 24p. (J). (gr. -1-2). lib. bdg. 27.32 (978-1-5157-6750-3(7), 135288, Capstone Pr.) Capstone.

Salzmann, Mary Elizabeth. Know Your Numbers: Nature. 2014. (Numbers 1-20 Ser.). (ENG.). 24p. (J). (gr. -1-3). lib. bdg. 29.93 (978-1-62403-266-0(4), 1594, SandCastle) ABDO Publishing Co.

San Antonio 2004. 2003. (YA). 11.99 (978-0-9721368-0-8(0)) Apollo Pubs.

Sayre, April Pulley. Thank You, Earth: A Love Letter to Our Planet. Sayre, April Pulley, illus. 2018. (ENG., Illus.). 40p. (J). (gr. -1-3). 17.99 (978-0-06-269734-9(X), Greenwillow Bks.) HarperCollins Pubs.

Scholastic Library Publishing. Nature's Children. 2012. (J). 280.00 (978-0-531-24499-9(7)); 560.00 (978-0-531-25950-4(1)) Scholastic Library Publishing. (Children's Pr.).

Schuh, Mari. Crayola (r) World of Blue. 2019. (Crayola (r) World of Color Ser.). (ENG., Illus.). 32p. (J). (gr. k-3). 29.32 (978-1-5415-5465-8(5), 0a6aa2f2-de9c-43d4-9ec5-18a120d5a87f); pap. 7.99 (978-1-5415-7383-3(8), 939bccdb-7d62-46f9-8e2b-516ba04b4759) Lerner Publishing Group. (Lerner Pubns.).

Schuh, Mari C. Compost Basics. 2011. (Science Builders Ser.). (ENG.). 24p. (gr. k-1). pap. 41.70 (978-1-4296-7112-5(2), Capstone Pr.) Capstone.

Schwartz, Heather E. Mimicking Nature. rev. ed. 2019. (Smithsonian: Informational Text Ser.). (ENG., Illus.). 32p. (J). (gr. 2-3). pap. 10.99 (978-1-4938-6675-5(3)) Teacher Created Materials, Inc.

Shand, Jennifer. Why Do Rainbows Have So Many Colors? 2015. (Why Do... ? Ser.). lib. bdg. 19.65 (978-1-4867-0625-9(8)) Turtleback.

Shand, Jennifer & Fabbri, Daniele. Why Do Rainbows Have So Many Colors? Paiva, Johannah Gilman, ed. 2014. (ENG., Illus.). 20p. (J). (gr. k-4). 8.99 (978-1-4867-0383-8(6)) Flowerpot Children's Pr. Inc. CAN. Dist: Cardinal Pubs. Group.

Silva Lee, Alfonso. Mi Isla y Yo: La Naturaleza de Republica Dominicana. Hayskar, Bonnie, ed. Lago, Alexis, illus. 2010. (SPA.). 32p. (J). pap. 9.95 (978-1-929165-25-4(0)) PANGAEA.

—Mon Ile et Moi: La Nature d'Haiti: Lanati an Ayti: Peym Avem. Hayskar, Bonnie, ed. Hilaire, Jean Vilmond, tr. Lago, Alexis, illus. 2010. (FRE & CRP.). 32p. (J). pap. 9.95 (978-1-929165-28-5(5)) PANGAEA.

Singley, Judith M. A B C Trees. 2012. 32p. pap. 17.25 (978-1-4669-4640-8(7)) Trafford Publishing.

Smith, Alastair. Nighttime. 2004. (Lift-the-Flap Learners Ser.). (Illus.). 16p. (J). (gr. 1-18). pap. 8.95 (978-0-7945-0366-6(7), Usborne) EDC Publishing.

Smith, Alastair & Howell, Laura. On the Beach. 2004. (Lift-the-Flap Learners Ser.). (Illus.). 16p. (J). (gr. 1-18). pap. 8.95 (978-0-7945-0213-3(X), Usborne) EDC Publishing.

Smith, Corinne Hosfeld. Henry David Thoreau for Kids: His Life & Ideas, with 21 Activities. 2016. (For Kids Ser.: 64). (ENG., Illus.). 128p. (J). (gr. 4). pap. 16.95 (978-1-61373-146-8(9)) Chicago Review Pr., Inc.

Smith, Laurie Chance. Snapshots: Nature Stories in the Bible. 2012. 128p. (J). pap. 19.99 (978-0-8280-2689-5(0)) Review & Herald Publishing Assn.

Start to Finish, Second Series - Nature's Cycles: Spring 2012 New Releases. 2012. (Start to Finish, Second Series: Nature's Cycles Ser.). (ENG.). 24p. (gr. k-3). lib. bdg. 143.58 (978-0-7613-6559-4(1), Lerner Pubns.) Lerner Publishing Group.

Start to Finish, Second Series, Nature's Cycles. 2012. (Start to Finish, Second Series: Nature's Cycles Ser.). (ENG.). 24p. (gr. k-3). pap. 39.62 (978-0-7613-9297-2(1));Set, Pack. pap. 237.69 (978-0-7613-9298-9(X)) Lerner Publishing Group.

Stewart, Henry. He Created Me. 2007. (Illus.). (J). 28.99 (978-1-59879-345-1(4)); per. 20.99 (978-1-59879-269-0(5)) Lifevest Publishing, Inc.

Story, Dan. Where Wild Things Live: Wildlife Watching Techniques & Adventures. 2009. (J). (978-0-87961-276-4(2)) Naturegraph Pubs., Inc.

Sundance/Newbridge LLC Staff. The Four Seasons. 2007. (Early Science Ser.). (gr. k-3). 18.95 (978-1-4007-6143-2(3)); pap. 6.10 (978-1-4007-6139-5(5)) Sundance/Newbridge Educational Publishing.

Tallarico, Tony. Nature Trivia Mazes. 2007. (Dover Kids Activity Books: Nature Ser.). (ENG., Illus.). 48p. (J). (gr. 3-3). per. 5.99 (978-0-486-45364-4(2), 453642) Dover Pubns., Inc.

Teckentrup, Britta, illus. Grande y Pequeno. 2013. 14p. (J). (gr. -1-k). bds. 6.99 (978-1-78285-034-2(1)) Barefoot Bks., Inc.

Tell Me Why, Tell Me How, 12 vols., Group 3. Incl. How Do Caterpillars Become Butterflies? Bailer, Darice. 32.64 (978-0-7614-3987-5(0), dac13246-c0ec-4976-8304-e12a8660a29c); How Do Mountains Form? Hicks, Terry Allan. 32.64 (978-0-7614-3992-9(7), a8f8a923-b56f-4c40-8251-d52754e27fdd); Why Do Bears Hibernate? Bailer, Darice. 32.64 (978-0-7614-3990-5(0), 9842ecfd-fd64-47d1-88b4-b94c49faa2e6); Why Do Volcanoes Erupt? Mara, Wil. 32.64 (978-0-7614-3989-9(7), 98188da6-bd9e-42b7-9d2c-b6a3f1b18060); Why Does It Rain? Mara, Wil. 32.64 (978-0-7614-3991-2(9), c05579b7-5861-4743-92a1-872870ab1603); Why Does the Sun Set? Hicks, Terry Allan. 32.64 (978-0-7614-3993-6(5), dbac377f-8741-4b5f-b064-c5ae72121529); 32p. (gr. 3-3). (Tell Me Why, Tell Me How Ser.). (ENG.). 2010. Set lib. bdg. 195.84 (978-0-7614-3986-8(2), 137b0a86-f4ea-4e63-b639-2128877586fd); Set lib. bdg. 195.84 (978-0-7614-2106-1(8), 994d3ddb-dad6-4775-81d7-8228aedd4c1e) Cavendish Square Publishing LLC. (Cavendish Square).

Thoreau, Henry D. Walking. Clifton Johnson, illus. 2010. 100p. pap. 3.49 (978-1-60386-305-6(2), Watchmaker Publishing) Wexford College Pr.

Tief im Meer. (GER.). 19.95 (978-3-411-09271-0(8)) Bibliographisches Institut & F. A. Brockhaus AG DEU. Dist: Distribooks, Inc.

Tiere unter der Erde. (GER.). (978-3-411-09251-2(3)) Bibliographisches Institut & F. A. Brockhaus AG DEU. Dist: i. b. d., Ltd.

Tilmont, Amy. Man vs. Animal: Species at Risk. 2011. (Second Nature Ser.). 48p. (J). (gr. 5-8). lib. bdg. 26.60 (978-1-59953-460-2(6)) Norwood Hse. Pr.

Tornio, Stacy & Keffer, Ken. The Kids' Outdoor Adventure Book: 448 Great Things to Do in Nature Before You Grow Up. 2013. (ENG., Illus.). 224p. (J). (gr. -1-4). pap. 18.95 (978-0-7627-8352-6(4), Falcon Guides) Globe Pequot Pr., The.

The Truth about Nature: A Family's Guide to 144 Common Myths about the Great Outdoors. 2014. (Illus.). 224p. (J). (gr. -1-12). pap. 22.95 (978-0-7627-9628-1(6), Falcon Guides) Globe Pequot Pr., The.

Tullet, Hervé & Tullet, Hervé. The Countryside Game. 2013. (ENG., Illus.). 14p. 12.95 (978-0-7148-6074-9(3)) Phaidon Pr., Inc.

Turk, Evan. You Are Home: An Ode to the National Parks. Turk, Evan, illus. 2019. (ENG., Illus.). 56p. (J). (gr. -1-3). 18.99 (978-1-5344-3282-6(5), Atheneum Bks. for Young Readers) Simon & Schuster Children's Publishing.

Tuxworth, Nicola. Nature. 2015. (Illus.). 20p. (J). (gr. -1-12). bds. 6.99 (978-1-86147-411-7(3), Armadillo) Anness Publishing GBR. Dist: National Bk. Network.

Unpredictable Nature: Changing Man's Daily Life, 15 vols., Set. Incl. Archeology. Farndon, John. (Illus.). lib. bdg. 19.95 (978-1-4222-1994-2(1)); Coral Reef. De la Bédoyère, Camilla. (Illus.). lib. bdg. 19.95 (978-1-4222-1995-9(X)); Deadly Creatures. De la Bédoyère, Camilla. (Illus.). lib. bdg. 19.95 (978-1-4222-1996-6(8)); Deep Ocean. De la Bédoyère, Camilla. (Illus.). lib. bdg. 19.95 (978-1-4222-1997-3(6)); Extinction. Parker, Steve. (Illus.). lib. bdg. 19.95 (978-1-4222-1998-0(4)); Extreme Survival. Green, Jen. (Illus.). lib. bdg. 19.95 (978-1-4222-1999-7(2)); Fossils. Parker, Steve. (Illus.). lib. bdg. 19.95 (978-1-4222-2000-9(1)); Magic & Mystery. Scott, Carey. (Illus.). lib. bdg. 19.95 (978-1-4222-2001-6(X)); Prehistoric Life. Matthews, Rupert. (Illus.). lib. bdg. 19.95 (978-1-4222-2003-0(6)); Rainforests. De la Bédoyère, Camilla. (Illus.). lib. bdg. 19.95 (978-1-4222-2004-7(4)); Rocks & Minerals. Callery, Sean. (Illus.). lib. bdg. 19.95 (978-1-4222-2005-4(2)); Seashore. Parker, Steve. (Illus.). lib. bdg. 19.95 (978-1-4222-2006-1(0)); Volcanoes. Oxlade, Chris. (Illus.). lib. bdg. 19.95 (978-1-4222-2007-8(9)); World Wonders. Hibbert, Adam. lib. bdg. 19.95 (978-1-4222-2008-5(7)); 48p. (J). (gr. 3-18). 2010. 2011. Set lib. bdg. 299.25 (978-1-4222-1993-5(3)) Mason Crest.

Usborne Books Staff, creator. 100 Things to Spot in the Night Sky. 2008. (Spotter's Cards Ser.). (Illus.). 52p. (J). 9.99 (978-0-7945-1966-7(0), Usborne) EDC Publishing.

Vann, Donna. Wild West Adventures. 2006. (Adventure Ser.). (ENG., Illus.). 96p. (J). per. 8.99 (978-1-84550-065-8(2), 022fcbc9-e8f2-45c7-a720-4619344ecbc4) Christian Focus Pubns. GBR. Dist: Baker & Taylor Publisher Services (BTPS).

Wadkovsky, Alex. Forces of Mother Nature. 2010. 20p. 13.99 (978-1-4520-5370-7(7)) AuthorHouse.

Walters, Jennifer Marino. Colors in Nature. 2018. (Nature Is All Around Me (LOOK! Books (tm)) Ser.). (ENG., Illus.). 24p. (J). (gr. -1-3). pap. 8.99 (978-1-63440-356-6(8), 7f69606c-1064-485a-9b04-a413997f6f38); lib. bdg. 25.32 (978-1-63440-300-9(2), 765d053f-efd4-431f-9c08-1cc5f0d64e55) Red Chair Pr.

—Numbers in Nature. 2018. (Nature Is All Around Me (LOOK! Books (tm)) Ser.). (ENG., Illus.). 24p. (J). (gr. -1-3). pap. 8.99 (978-1-63440-354-2(1), 605cd85b-c8c3-4b38-9b34-65341b671e0e) Red Chair Pr.

—Shapes in Nature. 2018. (Nature Is All Around Me (LOOK! Books (tm)) Ser.). (ENG., Illus.). 24p. (J). (gr. -1-3). pap. 8.99 (978-1-63440-355-9(X), 23e1da7a-47bd-4e54-b8a9-e8146eb8e12d); lib. bdg. 25.32 (978-1-63440-299-6(5), 9faad1fc-3d85-4088-93d5-716916678805) Red Chair Pr.

—Sizes in Nature. 2018. (Nature Is All Around Me (LOOK! Books (tm)) Ser.). (ENG., Illus.). 24p. (J). (gr. -1-3). lib. bdg. 25.32 (978-1-63440-301-6(0), c07f2b1c-b32f-4fed-a74c-16f478b8baf5) Red Chair Pr.

Walton, Rick. The Sky's the Limit: Naturally Funny Jokes. Gable, Brian, illus. 2005. (Make Me Laugh! Ser.). 32p. (J). (gr. k-3). lib. bdg. 19.93 (978-1-57505-663-0(1)) Lerner Publishing Group.

Wargin, Kathy-jo. K Is for Kite: God's Springtime Alphabet, 1 vol. Gatto, Kim, illus. 2010. (ENG.). 40p. (J). (gr. -1-2). 15.99 (978-0-310-71662-4(4)) Zonderkidz.

Watson, Hannah. 1,000 Things in Nature. 2018. (1,000 Pictures Ser.). (ENG.). 34p. 14.99 (978-0-7945-4119-4(4), Usborne) EDC Publishing.

Watson, Lori Ann. Beginnings. Bersani, Shennen, illus. 2009. 32p. (J). (gr. -1-1). 12.95 (978-0-8198-1172-1(6)) Pauline Bks. & Media.

We Can Read about Nature! (Group 3), 12 vols., Set. 2003. (We Can Read about Nature! Ser.). (ENG.). (gr. 1-2). 153.00 (978-0-7614-1429-2(0), e803902c-42cb-42da-b169-5e3d170684b1, Cavendish Square) Cavendish Square Publishing LLC.

Welsh, Anne Marie. It's Your Planet-Love It! Breathe. 2009. (Girl Scout Journey Books Ser.: Vol. 2). (Illus.). 112p. (YA). pap. (978-0-88441-734-7(4)) Girl Scouts of the USA.

West, Edith. A World Just for Me. 2009. 32p. pap. 13.99 (978-1-4389-7083-7(8)) AuthorHouse.

Weston Woods Staff, creator. Giving Thanks. 2011. 29.95 (978-0-439-73469-1(X)); 38.75 (978-0-439-72676-4(X)); 18.95 (978-0-439-72673-3(5)) Weston Woods Studios, Inc.

World Book, Inc. Staff, contrib. by. Nature's Patterns. 2010. (J). (978-0-7166-7740-6(7)) World Bk., Inc.

—Wildlife & Climate Change. 2015. (Illus.). 44p. (J). (978-0-7166-2709-8(4)) World Bk., Inc.

Wright, Holly. Sky. 2004. (Illus.). (J). (978-0-9743690-9-9(8)) Britt Allcroft Productions.

Zondervan Bibles Staff. Big Bugs, Little Bugs, 1 vol. 2011. (I Can Read! / Made by God Ser.). (ENG., Illus.). 32p. (J). (gr. -1-2). pap. 4.99 (978-0-310-72186-4(5)) Zonderkidz.

Zoobooks, 56 bks., Set. Incl. Animal Champions 2. Shaw, Marjorie B. & Elwood, Ann. 24p. (gr. 1-4). lib. bdg. 19.95 (978-0-88682-774-8(4)); Birds of Prey. Wexo, John Bonnett. 24p. (gr. 2-12). lib. bdg. 19.95 (978-0-88682-332-0(3)); Butterflies. Brust, Beth Wagner. 32p. (gr. 3-12). lib. bdg. 19.95 (978-0-88682-421-1(4)); Cheetahs. Wood, Linda C. & Jenson, Cynthia L. 32p. (gr. 2-12). lib. bdg. 19.95 (978-0-88682-417-4(6)); Deer Family. Biel, Timothy Levi. 24p. (gr. 2-12). lib. bdg. 19.95 (978-0-88682-775-5(2)); Dinosaurs. Wexo, John Bonnett. 24p. (gr. 2-12). lib. bdg. 19.95 (978-0-88682-223-1(8)); Ducks, Geese & Swans. Wexo, John Bonnett. 24p. (gr. 3-12). lib. bdg. 19.95 (978-0-88682-224-8(6)); Endangered Animals. Wexo, John Bonnett. 24p. (gr. 2-12). lib. bdg. 19.95 (978-0-88682-269-9(6)); Giraffes. Wexo, John Bonnett. 24p. (gr. 2-12). lib. bdg. 19.95 (978-0-88682-334-4(X)); Insects 2. Wexo, John Bonnett. 24p. (gr. 2-12). lib. bdg. 19.95 (978-0-88682-776-2(0)); Night Animals. Wexo, John Bonnett. 24p. (gr. 2-12). lib. bdg. 19.95 (978-0-88682-777-9(9)); Ostriches, Emus, Rheas, Kiwis & Cassowaries. Elwood, Ann. 24p. (gr. 2-12). lib. bdg. 19.95 (978-0-88682-338-2(2)); Owls. Biel, Timothy Levi. 24p. (gr. 3-12). lib. bdg. 19.95 (978-0-88682-268-2(8)); Parrots. Wexo, John Bonnett. 32p. (gr. 2-12). lib. bdg. 19.95 (978-0-88682-408-2(7)); Penguins. Wexo, John Bonnett. 24p. (gr. 2-12). lib. bdg. 19.95 (978-0-88682-263-7(7)); Polar Bears. Biel, Timothy Levi. 32p. (gr. 2-12). lib. bdg. 19.95 (978-0-88682-414-3(1)); Rattlesnakes. Brust, Beth Wagner & Dorn, Bob. 32p. (gr. 2-12). lib. bdg. 19.95 (978-0-88682-426-6(5)); Sea Otters. Brust, Beth Wagner. 32p. (gr. 2-12). lib. bdg. 19.95 (978-0-88682-415-0(X)); Seals, Sea Lions & Walruses. Wexo, John Bonnett. 24p. (gr. 2-12). lib. bdg. 19.95 (978-0-88682-271-2(8)); Sharing the World with Animals. Shaw, Marjorie B. & Elwood, Ann. 24p. (gr. 1-4). lib. bdg. 19.95 (978-0-88682-778-6(7)); Sharks. Wexo, John Bonnett. 24p. (gr. 2-12). lib. bdg. 19.95 (978-0-88682-229-3(7)); Skunks & Their Relatives. Biel, Timothy Levi. 24p. (gr. 2-12). lib. bdg. 19.95 (978-0-88682-779-3(5)); Snakes. Wexo, John Bonnett. 24p. (gr. 2-12). lib. bdg. 19.95 (978-0-88682-331-3(5)); Spiders. Biel, Timothy Levi. 32p. (gr. 2-12). lib. bdg. 19.95 (978-0-88682-410-5(9)); Turtles. Biel, Timothy Levi. 32p. (gr. 2-12). lib. bdg. 19.95 (978-0-88682-411-2(7)); Zebras. Wood, Linda C. 32p. (gr. 2-12). lib. bdg. 19.95 (978-0-88682-420-4(6)); (J). 1995. (Illus.). 1157.10 (978-0-88682-238-5(6), Creative Education) Creative Co., The.

NATURE (AESTHETICS)

Baumbusch, Brigitte. Nature in Art, 1 vol. 2004. (What Makes a Masterpiece? Ser.). (ENG., Illus.). 32p. (gr. 2-4). lib. bdg. 25.67 (978-0-8368-4448-1(3), 5400bb61-80cf-479d-8588-6253aa749972, Gareth Stevens Learning Library) Stevens, Gareth Publishing LLLP.

Lebeuf, Darren. My Forest Is Green. Barron, Ashley, illus. 2019. (ENG.). 32p. (J). (gr. -1-2). 19.99 (978-1-77138-930-3(3)) Kids Can Pr., Ltd. CAN. Dist: Hachette Bk. Group.

Noble, Marty, et al. Nature Mandalas. 2012. (Adult Coloring Books: Mandalas Ser.). (ENG., Illus.). 64p. (gr. 3). pap. 6.99 (978-0-486-49137-0(4), 491374) Dover Pubns., Inc.

NATURE CRAFT

Beaton, Clare. Read, Learn & Create — The Nature Craft Book. Beaton, Clare, illus. 2019. (ENG., Illus.). 32p. (J). (gr. 1-4). lib. bdg. 17.99 (978-1-58089-843-0(2)) Charlesbridge Publishing, Inc.

Beaton, Clare & Haig, Rudi. Read, Learn & Create — The Ocean Craft Book. Beaton, Clare, illus. 2019. (ENG., Illus.). 32p. (J). (gr. 1-4). 17.99 (978-1-58089-941-3(2)) Charlesbridge Publishing, Inc.

Bolte, Mari. Amazing Outdoor Art You Can Make & Share. 2015. (Sleepover Girls Crafts Ser.). (ENG., Illus.). 32p. (J). (gr. 2-5). lib. bdg. 28.65 (978-1-4765-0229-8(3), 122239, Capstone Young Readers) Capstone.

—Sleepover Girls Crafts: Amazing Outdoor Art You Can Make & Share. 2015. (Sleepover Girls Crafts Ser.). (ENG., Illus.). 64p. (J). (gr. 2-5). pap. 9.95 (978-1-62370-423-0(5), 129032, Capstone Young Readers) Capstone.

Chapman, Gillian & Robson, Pam. Making Art with Sand & Earth, 1 vol. 2007. (Everyday Art Ser.). (ENG., Illus.). 32p. (YA). (gr. 4-5). lib. bdg. 30.27 (978-1-4042-3723-0(2), 9a877ec4-7e47-44cb-83e4-3cf395ff69d4) Rosen Publishing Group, Inc., The.

—Making Art with Wood, 1 vol. 2007. (Everyday Art Ser.). (ENG., Illus.). 32p. (YA). (gr. 4-5). lib. bdg. 30.27 (978-1-4042-3726-1(7), 96ad20ac-e562-40d6-a4e9-0860f5d558e8) Rosen Publishing Group, Inc., The.

Forte, Imogene. Nature Crafts. 2004. (Fun Things to Make & Do Ser.). (Illus.). 80p. (J). per. 9.95 (978-0-86530-617-2(6)) Incentive Pubns., Inc.

Fossen Brown, Renata. Garden Art: Fun Experiments to Learn, Grow, Harvest, Make, & Play. 2018. (Gardening Lab for Kids Ser.). (ENG., Illus.). 32p. (J). (gr. 3-6). lib. bdg. 27.99 (978-1-63159-451-9(6), d21b0eef-b7bc-457e-a43f-211d975cf772, Quarry Bks.) Quarto Publishing Group USA.

Henry, Sally & Cook, Trevor. Eco Crafts, 1 vol. 2010. (Make Your Own Art Ser.). (ENG., Illus.). 32p. (J). (gr. 3-4). pap. 12.75 (978-1-4488-1611-8(4), 641a56b7-616a-46bb-9a49-1fe78db9cea2); lib. bdg. 30.27 (978-1-4488-1582-1(7), 9954893c-0fed-4f20-854d-2d05e915234b) Rosen Publishing Group, Inc., The. (PowerKids Pr.).

Jones, Jen. Cool Crafts with Flowers, Leaves, & Twigs: Green Projects for Resourceful Kids, 1 vol. 2010. (Green Crafts Ser.). (ENG.). 32p. (J). (gr. 3-9). lib. bdg. 28.65 (978-1-4296-4766-3(3), 103297) Capstone.

Kington, Emily. Make a Nature Sculpture. 2019. (Get Outside! Ser.). (ENG., Illus.). 24p. (J). (gr. 1-3). lib. bdg. 26.65 (978-1-5415-5525-9(2), 03250f4a-79f2-4789-ab1f-aeec0ad8187e, Hungry Tomato (r)) Lerner Publishing Group.

—Make Forest Faces & Mud Monsters. 2019. (Get Outside! Ser.). (ENG., Illus.). 24p. (J). (gr. 1-3). lib. bdg. 26.65 (978-1-5415-5527-3(9), 0a08c9ae-3d67-46b5-a92d-a13500e070ae, Hungry Tomato (r)) Lerner Publishing Group.

Levete, Sarah. Maker Projects for Kids Who Love Exploring the Outdoors. 2016. (Be a Maker! Ser.). (ENG., Illus.). 32p. (J). (gr. 5-9). (978-0-7787-2576-3(6)) Crabtree Publishing Co.

Lim, Annalees. Nature Crafts, 1 vol., Vol. 1. 2013. (Craft Attack! Ser.). (ENG.). 32p. (J). (gr. 3-3). 29.27 (978-1-4824-0203-2(3), 46cd6978-72db-46f2-b80d-3f64ecfc32f6); pap. 11.50 (978-1-4824-0205-6(X), d4eca8ee-9ac0-464b-926f-81fcf3b4d9eb) Stevens, Gareth Publishing LLLP.

Llimós, Anna. Earth-Friendly Crafts with Nuts & Veggies in 5 Easy Steps, 1 vol. 2013. (Earth-Friendly Crafts in 5 Easy Steps Ser.). (ENG., Illus.). 32p. (gr. 3-3). lib. bdg. 26.61 (978-0-7660-4191-2(3), 2f01de9a-ce36-4d45-9788-d2ef04e325a2) Enslow Publishing, LLC.

Llimós, Anna & Llimós, Anna. Earth-Friendly Crafts with Nuts & Veggies in 5 Easy Steps, 1 vol. 2013. (Earth-Friendly Crafts in 5 Easy Steps Ser.). (ENG.). 32p. (gr. 3-3). pap. 10.35 (978-1-4644-0313-2(9), 9c28f5d6-9584-481e-8c30-0e36173ea229, Enslow Elementary) Enslow Publishing, LLC.

Martin, Laura C. Nature's Art Box: From T-Shirts to Twig Baskets, 65 Cool Projects for Crafty Kids to Make with Natural Materials You Can Find Anywhere. Cain, David, illus. 2003. (ENG.). 192p. (J). (gr. 3-7). pap. 16.99 (978-1-58017-490-9(6), 67490) Storey Publishing, LLC.

Paredes, L. Magical Forest Fairy Crafts Through Seas. 2018. (ENG., Illus.). 144p. (J). (gr. 2-6). pap. 21.95 (978-1-61745-661-9(6), FunStitch Studio) C & T Publishing.

Parker, Steve & Parker, Jane. My Giant Book of Nature Projects: Fun & Easy Learning, with Simple Step-By-Step Experiments. 2019. (Illus.). 24p. (J). (gr. -1-12). pap. 10.00 (978-1-86147-861-0(5), Armadillo) Anness Publishing GBR. Dist: National Bk. Network.

Rathburn, Betsy. Stick Crafts. 2020. (Crafting with Nature Ser.). (ENG.). 24p. (J). (gr. 3-8). lib. bdg. 26.95 (978-1-64487-192-8(0), Epic Bks.) Bellwether Media.

Ryall, Jeanette. Nature Art, 1 vol. 2012. (Awesome Art Ser.). (ENG., Illus.). 32p. (J). (gr. 3-3). 31.27 (978-1-4488-8088-1(2), 890025c2-8aae-40a7-9d55-e2e0e313dbd5); pap. 12.75 (978-1-4488-8141-3(2), 22770aec-59cd-4a8f-b689-449332157f77) Rosen Publishing Group, Inc., The. (Windmill Bks.).

—Sand Art, 1 vol. 2012. (Awesome Art Ser.). (ENG., Illus.). 32p. (J). (gr. 3-3). 31.27 (978-1-4488-8090-4(4), 44858311-c61f-4c59-8da3-11e4a05d9fc4); pap. 12.75 (978-1-4488-8143-7(9), d7ac932e-f09a-4d75-96f7-3fb077fa4d59) Rosen Publishing Group, Inc., The. (Windmill Bks.).

Sabelko, Rebecca. Flower Crafts. 2020. (Crafting with Nature Ser.). (ENG., Illus.). 24p. (J). (gr. 3-8). lib. bdg. 26.95 (978-1-64487-187-4(4), Epic Bks.) Bellwether Media.

—Sand Crafts. 2020. (Crafting with Nature Ser.). (ENG.). 24p. (J). (gr. 3-8). lib. bdg. 26.95 (978-1-64487-190-4(4), Epic Bks.) Bellwether Media.

Senisi, Ellen B. Berry Smudges & Leaf Prints: Finding & Making Colors from Nature. Senisi, Ellen B., photos by. 2005. (Illus.). 40p. (J). (gr. 4-8). reprint ed. 17.00 (978-0-7567-9707-2(1)) DIANE Publishing Co.

Staff, Gareth Editorial Staff. Plants & Seeds, 1 vol. 2003. (Let's Create! Ser.). (ENG., Illus.). 32p. (gr. 2-4). lib. bdg. 28.67 (978-0-8368-3748-3(7), affa3c25-6d8e-4769-9740-1ef3d2d75f7a, Gareth Stevens Learning Library) Stevens, Gareth Publishing LLLP.

—Stones & Stuff, 1 vol. 2004. (Let's Create! Ser.). (ENG., Illus.). 32p. (gr. 2-4). lib. bdg. 28.67 (978-0-8368-4019-3(4), f8d0bd01-4d5b-43c8-9730-87de920f993b, Gareth Stevens Learning Library) Stevens, Gareth Publishing LLLP.

NATURE—EFFECT OF HUMAN BEINGS ON

Blake, Kevin. Feral Pigs: Chomp, Chomp! 2015. (They Don't Belong: Tracking Invasive Species Ser.). (ENG., Illus.). 32p. (J). (gr. 2-7). lib. bdg. 28.50 (978-1-62724-829-7(3)) Bearport Publishing Co., Inc.

—Guam's Brown Tree Snakes: Hanging Out. 2015. (They Don't Belong: Tracking Invasive Species Ser.). (ENG., Illus.). 32p. (J). (gr. 2-7). lib. bdg. 28.50 (978-1-62724-830-3(7)) Bearport Publishing Co., Inc.

Bodden, Valerie. Wildlife in Danger. 2010. (Earth Issues Ser.). (Illus.). 48p. (J). (gr. 5-18). 23.95 (978-1-58341-987-8(X), Creative Education) Creative Co., The.

Booth, Edison. Animals & Their Environments, 1 vol. 2016. (Spotlight on Ecology & Life Science Ser.). (ENG.). 24p. (J). (gr. 4-6). 27.93 (978-1-4994-2558-1(9), 2c920445-5d7a-4c13-acbb-61f4fd944263); pap. 11.00 (978-1-4994-2556-7(2), 729a0900-d7a8-4e55-9e30-c8e3090c8418) Rosen Publishing Group, Inc., The. (PowerKids Pr.).

Brainard, Jason. Operating Farms & Logging Companies, 1 vol. 2018. (Impacting Earth: How People Change the Land

Ser.). (ENG.). 24p. (gr. 2-2). pap. 9.25 *(978-1-5383-4196-4(4),* c2c4485d-829c-4e46-8a4b-6aa585861b9f, PowerKids Pr.) Rosen Publishing Group, Inc., The.

Buchanan, Shelly. Shaping Our Environment. rev. ed. 2014. (Social Studies: Informational Text Ser.). (ENG., Illus.). 32p. (J). (gr. 2-4). pap. 11.99 *(978-1-4333-7368-8(8))* Teacher Created Materials, Inc.

Changing Climates. 2010. (ENG., Illus.). 120p. (gr. 5-8). 35.00 *(978-1-60413-291-5(4),* P178894, Facts On File) Infobase Holdings, Inc.

Cherry, Lynne. A River Ran Wild. 2015. 40p. pap. 7.00 *(978-1-61003-490-6(2))* Center for the Collaborative Classroom.

—A River Ran Wild. 2005. 17.00 *(978-0-7569-5231-0(X))* Perfection Learning Corp.

Collard, Sneed B., III. Australia's Cane Toads: Overrun! 2015. (They Don't Belong: Tracking Invasive Species Ser.). (ENG., Illus.). 32p. (J). (gr. 2-7). lib. bdg. 28.50 *(978-1-62724-828-0(5))* Bearport Publishing Co., Inc.

Dal Fuoco, Gina. Spaceship Earth, 1 vol. rev. ed. 2007. (Science: Informational Text Ser.). (ENG., Illus.). 32p. (gr. 4-6). pap. 12.99 *(978-0-7439-0565-7(2))* Teacher Created Materials, Inc.

David, Alex. Dying Off: Endangered Plants & Animals, 1 vol. 2019. (Taking Action on Climate Change Ser.). (ENG.). 64p. (J). (gr. 6-6). pap. 16.28 *(978-1-5026-5231-7(5),* c4398af3-9733-40db-8ab6-30e00844d2a7) Cavendish Square Publishing LLC.

Davies, Nicola. Many: the Diversity of Life on Earth. Sutton, Emily, illus. 2017. (Our Natural World Ser.). (ENG.). 40p. (J). (gr. k-3). 17.99 *(978-0-7636-9483-8(5))* Candlewick Pr.

Dellaccio, Tanya. Changing Rain Forest Environments. 2019. (Human Impact on Earth: Cause & Effect Ser.). (ENG.). 32p. (gr. 4-5). 60.00 *(978-1-7253-0137-5(7),* PowerKids Pr.) Rosen Publishing Group, Inc., The.

Diamond, Jared. The Third Chimpanzee for Young People: On the Evolution & Future of the Human Animal. (For Young People Ser.). (ENG., Illus.). (J). (gr. 7). 2015. 368p. pap. 17.95 *(978-1-60980-611-8(5))* 2014. 352p. 22.95 *(978-1-60980-522-7(4))* Seven Stories Pr. (Triangle Square).

Donnelly, Karen. Rising Temperatures of the Past & Future. 2009. (Earth's Changing Weather & Climate Ser.). 24p. (gr. 4-4). 42.50 *(978-1-61512-249-3(4),* PowerKids Pr.) Rosen Publishing Group, Inc., The.

Downer, Ann. Wild Animal Neighbors: Sharing Our Urban World. 2013. (ENG., Illus.). 64p. (J). (gr. 5-12). E-Book 50.65 *(978-1-4677-1663-5(4),* Twenty-First Century Bks.) Lerner Publishing Group.

Doyle, James. A Young Scientist's Guide to Faulty Freaks of Nature: Including 20 Experiments for the Sink, Bathtub & Backyard (Large Print 16pt) 2013. 200p. pap. *(978-1-4596-5848-6(5))* ReadHowYouWant.com, Ltd.

Eboch, M. M., ed. The Next Mass Extinction, 1 vol. 2017. (Introducing Issues with Opposing Viewpoints Ser.). (ENG.). 120p. (YA). (gr. 7-10). 43.63 *(978-1-5345-0194-2(0),* 20a5dc01-e6b0-4ad8-9454-4bcff459e075); pap. 29.30 *(978-1-5345-0278-9(5),* 7dca3067-6837-4131-8b13-a19b7092adea) Greenhaven Publishing LLC.

Faust, Daniel R. Changing Mountain Environments. 2019. (Human Impact on Earth: Cause & Effect Ser.). (ENG.). 32p. (gr. 4-5). 60.00 *(978-1-7253-0025-5(7),* PowerKids Pr.) Rosen Publishing Group, Inc., The.

Goldsmith, Connie. Pandemic: How Climate, the Environment, & Superbugs Increase the Risk. 2018. (ENG., Illus.). 136p. (YA). (gr. 6-12). 42.65 *(978-1-5124-5215-0(7),* d2fb99bd-fb15-40c2-9fef-5ef48573d314, Twenty-First Century Bks.) Lerner Publishing Group.

Green, Mary. Rivers in Action. 2004. (Earth's Changing Landscape Ser.). (Illus.). 46p. (YA). (gr. 7-12). lib. bdg. 28.50 *(978-1-58340-477-5(5))* Black Rabbit Bks.

Hawley, Ella. Exploring Our Impact on the Environment. 2012. (Let's Explore Life Science (Powerkids) Ser.). (ENG.). 24p. (J). (gr. 2-4). 19.05 *(978-1-5311-8906-8(7))* Perfection Learning Corp.

—Exploring Our Impact on the Environment, 1 vol. 2012. (Let's Explore Life Science Ser.). (ENG., Illus.). 24p. (J). (gr. 2-3). pap. 9.25 *(978-1-4488-6308-2(2),* 63cb2dd7-a88a-4c88-b80a-eece3e6ae48c); lib. bdg. 26.27 *(978-1-4488-6177-4(2),* fb8f9526-1c05-4b1e-a366-a57118cafbac) Rosen Publishing Group, Inc., The. (PowerKids Pr.).

Hudak, Heather C. Climate Change. 2018. (Get Informed — Stay Informed Ser.). (Illus.). 48p. (J). (gr. 5-6). *(978-0-7787-4959-2(2))* Crabtree Publishing Co.

—Epic Migrations by Water. 2019. (Epic Animal Journeys Ser.). (ENG.). 32p. (J). (gr. 4-5). pap. *(978-0-7787-6373-4(0),* 71748963-42f0-4217-aa0a-907b66cf4aa6); lib. bdg. *(978-0-7787-6369-7(2),* 9d38b793-1833-456d-8ed9-78c6048dbd54) Crabtree Publishing Co.

Hyde, Natalie. Epic Migrations by Air. 2019. (Epic Animal Journeys Ser.). (ENG.). 32p. (J). (gr. 4-5). pap. *(978-0-7787-6371-0(4),* 8c79ad3d-4702-4ad9-8a11-a6bb069dea68); lib. bdg. *(978-0-7787-6367-3(6),* bada59cb-ed06-4df9-9b47-beab5aa1bcfe) Crabtree Publishing Co.

—Unusual Animal Journeys. 2019. (Epic Animal Journeys Ser.). (ENG., Illus.). 32p. (J). (gr. 4-5). pap. *(978-0-7787-6378-9(1),* 113bc733-33bd-4590-849c-3d127f75ce67); lib. bdg. *(978-0-7787-6370-3(6),* 89c2121e-60ee-4600-8b80-8b1be588acd8) Crabtree Publishing Co.

Iyengar, Godha. The Stinkiest Day in May: The Story of a Stink. 2010. (Illus.). 22p. (J). pap. 16.95 *(978-1-4327-4825-8(4))* Outskirts Pr., Inc.

Jakab, Cheryl. Ecological Footprints, 1 vol. Lauricella, Domenic, illus. 2011. (Environment in Focus Ser.). (ENG.). 32p. (gr. 4-4). 31.21 *(978-1-60870-088-2(7),* 8017bb6d-cf23-45f5-b8de-84affdea7f21) Cavendish Square Publishing LLC.

Kinsner, Kathy. Relationships in Nature & Relaciones en la Naturaleza: 6 English, 6 Spanish Adaptations. 2011. (ENG & SPA.). (J). 101.00 net. *(978-1-4108-5729-3(8))* Benchmark Education Co.

Kirk, Ellen. Human Footprint: Everything You Will Eat, Use, Wear, Buy, & Throw Out in Your Lifetime. 2011. (Illus.). 32p. (J). (gr. 3-7). pap. 6.95 *(978-1-4263-0767-6(5),* National Geographic Kids) Disney Publishing Worldwide.

Krajnik, Elizabeth. Changing Tundra Environments, 1 vol. 2019. (Human Impact on Earth: Cause & Effect Ser.). (ENG.). 32p. (gr. 4-5). 27.93 *(978-1-7253-0142-9(3),* 67885588-130d-4fc8-9b50-2a7565bb2eff, PowerKids Pr.) Rosen Publishing Group, Inc., The.

—Making Dams & Reservoirs, 1 vol. 2018. (Impacting Earth: How People Change the Land Ser.). (ENG.). 24p. (gr. 2-2). pap. 9.25 *(978-1-5383-4192-6(1),* b5134104-39eb-490d-b137-0a0b74b0efc1, PowerKids Pr.) Rosen Publishing Group, Inc., The.

—Paving Roads & Highways, 1 vol. 2018. (Impacting Earth: How People Change the Land Ser.). (ENG.). 24p. (gr. 2-2). pap. 9.25 *(978-1-5383-4200-8(6),* b11945cd-105f-440b-a355-ab9f367cb846, PowerKids Pr.) Rosen Publishing Group, Inc., The.

Kurtz, Kevin. Climate Change & Rising Temperatures. 2019. (Searchlight Books (tm) — Climate Change Ser.). (ENG., Illus.). 32p. (J). (gr. 3-5). 30.65 *(978-1-5415-3862-7(5),* 7b092650-b1ed-451c-a047-d7b92f22458a, Lerner Pubns.); pap. 9.99 *(978-1-5415-4594-6(X),* c150120d-3477-4c82-b1c5-3c973e76e6f2) Lerner Publishing Group.

Leathers, Dan. The Snows of Kilimanjaro. 2007. (On the Verge of Extinction Ser.). (Illus.). 32p. (YA). (gr. 2-5). lib. bdg. 25.70 *(978-1-58415-584-3(1))* Mitchell Lane Pubs.

Lepetit, Angie. Three Cheers for Trees! A Book about Our Carbon Footprint, 1 vol. 2013. (Earth Matters Ser.). (ENG.). 32p. (J). (gr. -1-2). pap. 8.10 *(978-1-62065-741-6(4),* 121726); (gr. 1-2). pap. 49.60 *(978-1-62065-742-3(2),* 19323) Capstone. (Capstone Pr.).

Lundgren, Julie K. How Do Humans Depend on Earth? 2012. (My Science Library). (ENG., Illus.). 24p. (gr. 4-5). pap. 8.95 *(978-1-61810-238-6(9),* 9781618102386) Rourke Educational Media.

Maloof, Torrey. People & the Planet, 1 vol. 2015. (Science: Informational Text Ser.). (ENG., Illus.). 32p. (gr. 3-4). pap. 11.99 *(978-1-4807-4650-3(9))* Teacher Created Materials, Inc.

McPartland, Lisa A. Changing Desert Environments, 1 vol. 2019. (Human Impact on Earth: Cause & Effect Ser.). (ENG.). 32p. (gr. 4-5). pap. 11.00 *(978-1-7253-0020-0(6),* 1e8cd114-a2ad-462d-8bb6-30c3e9e9f6e5, PowerKids Pr.) Rosen Publishing Group, Inc., The.

Morgan, Anne. The Smallest Carbon Footprint in the Land & Other Eco-Tales. McKinnon, Gay, illus. 2012. (ENG.). 82p. pap. *(978-1-922120-23-6(5),* IP Kidz) Interactive Pubns. Pty, Ltd.

Morrison, Yvonne. Earth Partners: Saving the Planet. 2007. (Shockwave Science Ser.). (Illus.). 36p. (J). (gr. 4-6). pap. 6.95 *(978-0-531-15489-2(0),* Children's Pr.) Scholastic Library Publishing.

—Shockwave Science: Earth Partners. 2007. (Shockwave: History & Politics Ser.). (ENG., Illus.). 36p. (J). (gr. 4-6). lib. bdg. 25.00 *(978-0-531-17753-2(X),* Children's Pr.) Scholastic Library Publishing.

Nardo, Don. Planet under Siege: Climate Change. 2020. (ENG.). 80p. (YA). (gr. 6-12). 41.27 *(978-1-68282-757-4(7))* ReferencePoint Pr., Inc.

National Geographic Learning. Reading Expeditions (Science: Life Science): Protecting the Planet. 2007. (ENG., Illus.). 32p. (J). pap. 18.95 *(978-0-7922-8864-0(5))* CENGAGE Learning.

Nelson, John. Collision Course: Asteroids & Earth, 1 vol. 2007. (Jr. Graphic Environmental Dangers Ser.). (ENG., Illus.). 24p. (gr. 4-4). pap. 10.60 *(978-1-4042-4595-2(2),* 5b59406e-0385-4b29-b3b2-ad5659302acc, PowerKids Pr.) Rosen Publishing Group, Inc., The.

Newland, Sonya. Epic Migrations by Land. 2019. (Epic Animal Journeys Ser.). (ENG.). 32p. (J). (gr. 4-5). pap. *(978-0-7787-6372-7(2),* e3670579-db89-4e64-b7a9-852de4658e16); lib. bdg. *(978-0-7787-6368-0(4),* a5c1835d-4cbf-4ee8-bdc4-5f3d16484567) Crabtree Publishing Co.

Orme, Helen. Habitat Destruction. 2008. (Earth in Danger Ser.). (Illus.). 32p. (YA). (gr. 3-6). lib. bdg. 25.27 *(978-1-59716-725-3(8),* 1284353) Bearport Publishing Co., Inc.

Owings, Lisa. Climate Change. 2019. (It's the End of the World! Ser.). (ENG., Illus.). 24p. (J). (gr. 3-7). lib. bdg. 26.95 *(978-1-64487-080-8(0),* Torque Bks.) Bellwether Media.

Perdew, Laura. The Great Pacific Garbage Patch. 2017. (Ecological Disasters Ser.). (ENG.). 112p. (J). (gr. 6-12). lib. bdg. 41.36 *(978-1-5321-1023-8(5),* 25622, Essential Library) ABDO Publishing Co.

The Power of Nature, 12 vols. 2014. (Power of Nature Ser.). (ENG.). 48p. (J). (gr. 4-4). lib. bdg. 198.42 *(978-1-5026-0306-7(3),* a1e2b921-5777-4ad1-b290-5b68388575b1, Cavendish Square) Cavendish Square Publishing LLC.

Redlin, Janice L. Saving the Natural World. 2006. (Understanding Global Issues Ser.). (Illus.). 56p. per. 11.95 *(978-1-59036-510-6(0),* 1266440) Weigl Pubs., Inc.

Riley, Joelle. Erosion. 2006. (Early Bird Earth Science Ser.). (Illus.). 48p. (J). (gr. 3-7). lib. bdg. 25.26 *(978-0-8225-5949-8(8),* Lerner Pubns.) Lerner Publishing Group.

Rooney, Anne. Reducing the Carbon Footprint. 2009. (World at Risk Ser.). (ENG.). 48p. (J). (gr. 5-9). 34.25 *(978-1-59920-375-1(8),* 19398, Smart Apple Media) Black Rabbit Bks.

Rose, Elizabeth. Human Impact on the Environment. (Life Science Library). 24p. (gr. 3-4). 2009. 42.50 *(978-1-60854-006-8(5),* PowerKids Pr.) 2005. (ENG., Illus.). (YA). lib. bdg. 26.27 *(978-1-4042-2822-1(5),* d53b5a28-5e4c-454c-ba9f-0f9a940f041d) Rosen Publishing Group, Inc., The.

Royston, Angela. The Race to Survive Climate Change, 1 vol. 2014. (World in Crisis Ser.). (ENG.). 48p. (YA). (gr. 5-5). 33.47 *(978-1-4777-7848-7(9),* 2fcc0800-ba38-4b62-97da-9ed0382328a3, Rosen Reference) Rosen Publishing Group, Inc., The.

Sawyer, Ava. Human Environmental Impact: How We Affect Earth. 2017. (Humans & Our Planet Ser.). (ENG., Illus.). 32p. (J). (gr. 3-6). lib. bdg. 27.99 *(978-1-5157-7196-8(2),* 135553, Capstone Pr.) Capstone.

—Humans & Earth's Atmosphere: What's in the Air? 2017. (Humans & Our Planet Ser.). (ENG., Illus.). 32p. (J). (gr. 3-6). lib. bdg. 27.99 *(978-1-5157-7199-9(7),* 135556, Capstone Pr.) Capstone.

—Humans & Other Life on Earth: Sharing the Planet. 2017. (Humans & Our Planet Ser.). (ENG., Illus.). 32p. (J). (gr. 3-6). lib. bdg. 27.99 *(978-1-5157-7197-5(0),* 135554, Capstone Pr.) Capstone.

—Humans & Our Planet. 2017. (Humans & Our Planet Ser.). (ENG., Illus.). 32p. (J). (gr. 3-6). 119.96 *(978-1-5157-7252-1(7),* 26699, Capstone Pr.) Capstone.

—Humans & the Hydrosphere: Protecting Earth's Water Sources. 2017. (Humans & Our Planet Ser.). (ENG., Illus.). 32p. (J). (gr. 3-6). lib. bdg. 27.99 *(978-1-5157-7198-2(9),* 135555, Capstone Pr.) Capstone.

Schafer, Susan. Invasive Mammals, 1 vol. 2016. (Invasive Species Ser.). (ENG.). 48p. (gr. 4-4). 33.07 *(978-1-5026-1832-0(X),* 956ebcc0-c427-44ec-b32a-e8eae0dc4f73) Cavendish Square Publishing LLC.

—Invasive Reptiles & Amphibians, 1 vol. 2016. (Invasive Species Ser.). (ENG.). 48p. (gr. 4-4). 33.07 *(978-1-5026-1830-6(3),* a5a22c0e-46c6-48fa-9125-d71c4d4ce3a1) Cavendish Square Publishing LLC.

Shoals, James. The Future of Biodiversity. 2019. (Climate Change: Problems & Progress Ser.). (Illus.). 48p. (J). (gr. 10). 30.60 *(978-1-4222-4356-5(7))* Mason Crest.

—What Is Climate Change? 2019. (Climate Change: Problems & Progress Ser.). (Illus.). 48p. (J). (gr. 10). 30.60 *(978-1-4222-4363-3(X))* Mason Crest.

Shone, Rob. Avalanches & Landslides. (Graphic Natural Disasters Ser.). (ENG.). 48p. (gr. 5-5). 2009. (YA). 58.50 *(978-1-61512-994-2(4),* Rosen Reference) 2007. (Illus.). (J). lib. bdg. 37.13 *(978-1-4042-1992-2(7),* 4730c481-094c-4ddd-92ad-2ef53b98576f) Rosen Publishing Group, Inc., The.

Shone, Rob, illus. Avalanches & Mudslides, 1 vol. 2007. (Graphic Natural Disasters Ser.). (ENG.). 48p. (gr. 5-5). pap. 14.05 *(978-1-4042-1983-0(8),* a85e0ee8-d141-4f32-926d-dfab07a3994c) Rosen Publishing Group, Inc., The.

Simmons, Jaime. Deforestation & Habitat Loss, 1 vol. 2017. (Earth's Environment in Danger Ser.). (ENG.). 24p. (J). (gr. 3-3). 25.27 *(978-1-5383-2535-3(7),* a4d7cc54-6694-42b3-a775-b8c10b79509c, PowerKids Pr.) Rosen Publishing Group, Inc., The.

Smith, Andrea Claire Harte. The Effects of Farming. 2004. (Earth's Changing Landscape Ser.). (Illus.). 45p. (J). lib. bdg. 28.50 *(978-1-58340-475-1(9))* Black Rabbit Bks.

Smith, Paula. Be the Change for the Environment. 2014. (Be the Change! Ser.). (ENG., Illus.). 24p. (J). (gr. 2-3). *(978-0-7787-0620-5(6)),* pap. *(978-0-7787-0632-8(X))* Crabtree Publishing Co.

Snedden, Robert. The Growth of Cities. 2004. (Earth's Changing Landscape Ser.). (J). lib. bdg. 28.50 *(978-1-58340-474-4(0))* Black Rabbit Bks.

Steele, Phillip W. Changing Coastlines. 2004. (Earth's Changing Landscape Ser.). (Illus.). 46p. (J). lib. bdg. 28.50 *(978-1-58340-476-8(7))* Black Rabbit Bks.

Stein, Paul. Floods of the Future. 2009. (Library of Future Weather & Climate Ser.). 64p. (gr. 5-5). 58.50 *(978-1-60853-645-0(9))* Rosen Publishing Group, Inc., The.

—Ice Ages of the Future. 2009. (Library of Future Weather & Climate Ser.). 64p. (gr. 5-5). 58.50 *(978-1-60853-647-4(5))* Rosen Publishing Group, Inc., The.

Stewart, Melissa. A Place for Frogs, 1 vol. Bond, Higgins, illus. rev. ed. 2016. (Place For... Ser.: 3). 32p. (J). (gr. 2-6). 16.95 *(978-1-56145-901-8(1))* Peachtree Publishing Co. Inc.

Tolli, Jenna. Changing Coastline Environments, 1 vol. 2019. (Human Impact on Earth: Cause & Effect Ser.). (ENG.). 32p. (gr. 4-5). pap. 11.00 *(978-1-7253-0016-3(8),* 4108a758-714f-4003-afdb-5d70bc011315, PowerKids Pr.) Rosen Publishing Group, Inc., The.

Vogel, Carole Garbuny. Human Impact. 2003. (Restless Sea Ser.). (ENG., Illus.). 96p. (J). (gr. 5-8). 30.50 *(978-0-531-12323-2(5),* Watts, Franklin) Scholastic Library Publishing.

Webb, Barbara. Endangered! 2011. (Green Earth Science Discovery Library). (ENG., Illus.). 24p. (gr. k-2). pap. 9.95 *(978-1-61741-974-4(5),* 9781617419744) Rourke Educational Media.

West, David & Parker, Steve. Ecological Disasters. 2011. (ENG., Illus.). 32p. (J). pap. *(978-0-7787-7578-2(X));* lib. bdg. *(978-0-7787-7573-7(9))* Crabtree Publishing Co.

—Human-Made Disasters, 1 vol. 2011. (ENG., Illus.). 32p. (J). pap. *(978-0-7787-7580-5(1));* lib. bdg. *(978-0-7787-7575-1(5))* Crabtree Publishing Co.

Wild Earth. 2007. (Illus.). 32p. (J). *(978-0-696-24002-7(5))* Meredith Bks.

World Book, Inc. Staff, contrib. by. Understanding Climate Change. 2015. (Illus.). 48p. (J). *(978-0-7166-2706-7(X))* World Bk., Inc.

—Weather & Climate Change. 2015. (Illus.). 47p. (J). *(978-0-7166-2707-4(8))* World Bk., Inc.

—Wildlife & Climate Change. 2016. (ENG., Illus.). 44p. (J). E-Book *(978-0-7166-2719-7(1))* World Bk., Inc.

NATURE—EFFECT OF HUMAN BEINGS ON—FICTION

Barkley, Callie. Amy on Park Patrol. Bishop, Tracy, illus. 2017. (Critter Club Ser.: 17). (ENG.). 128p. (J). (gr. k-3). pap. 6.99 *(978-1-4814-9432-8(5),* Little Simon) Little Simon.

Cooper, Susan. Green Boy. 2003. (ENG., Illus.). 208p. (J). (gr. 4-7). pap. 7.99 *(978-0-689-84760-8(2),* McElderry, Margaret K. Bks.) McElderry, Margaret K. Bks.

Gleitzman, Morris. Second Childhood. 2016. 128p. (Orig.). (J). (gr. 4-6). 14.99 *(978-0-14-330877-5(7))* Random Hse. Australia AUS. Dist: Independent Pubs. Group.

Liberto, Lorenzo. Save the Planet / Salva el Planeta. Gomez, Rocio, tr. Torres, Irving, illus. 2005. (Matt the Rat Ser. / La Serie de Ratón Mateo). (ENG & SPA.). 32p. (J). lib. bdg. 20.00 *(978-0-9743668-5-2(4))* Harvest Sun Pr., LLC.

Mon, S. Aka - the Wonder Girl. 2011. (Illus.). 40p. pap. 18.79 *(978-1-4567-8047-0(6))* AuthorHouse.

Oe, Patricia Daly. Where Are My Stripes? Oe, Patricia Daly, illus. 2007. (R. I. C. Story Chest Ser.). (Illus.). 20p. (J). (gr. -1-k). 11.95 incl. audio compact disk *(978-1-74126-438-8(3))* R.I.C. Pubns. AUS. Dist: SCB Distributors.

Patricia Diane Craine, Ma-Lmft. Our Miracle Our Earth. 2009. 56p. pap. 24.49 *(978-1-4389-5918-4(4))* AuthorHouse.

Samos (Amos Amir). Nemo the Mole Rat: Stories from the Woodland. 2011. (Illus.). 52p. pap. 23.51 *(978-1-4567-8187-3(1))* AuthorHouse.

Thomas, Rosemary. The Kiwi Kingdom. 2010. 154p. pap. 18.00 *(978-1-4349-0857-5(7))* Dorrance Publishing Co., Inc.

von Olfers, Sibylle. Mother Earth & Her Children Coloring Book: Color the Wonderful World of Nature As You See It! 24 Magical, Mythical Coloring Scenes. Zipes, Jack, tr. Schoen-Smith, Sieglinde, illus. 2015. (ENG.). 24p. (J). (gr. 2-4). pap. 6.95 *(978-1-933308-54-8(0))* Breckling Pr.

Wood, Douglas. Old Turtle & the Broken Truth. Muth, Jon J., illus. 2003. (ENG.). 64p. (J). (gr. -1-3). 21.99 *(978-0-439-32109-9(3),* Scholastic Pr.) Scholastic, Inc.

—Old Turtle: Questions of the Heart: From the Lessons of Old Turtle #2. Ruth, Greg, illus. 2017. (ENG.). 56p. (J). (gr. -1-3). 19.99 *(978-0-439-32111-2(5),* Scholastic Pr.) Scholastic, Inc.

NATURE—FICTION

Addy, Sharon. In Grandpa's Woods. Akins, Tamlyn, illus. 2004. (J). *(978-1-931599-42-9(4),* Trails Bks.) Bower Hse.

Alexander, John. The Adventures of Thunder & Avalanche: Laws of Nature. Alexander, John, illus. 2013. (Illus.). 46p. 18.99 *(978-0-9887625-0-3(1))* Mountain Thunder Publishing.

Allamand, Maite. Alamito el Largo. (SPA.). (J). (gr. 2-3). pap. *(978-956-13-1428-3(2),* AB3840) Bello, Andres CHL. Dist: Lectorum Pubns., Inc.

Allen, Elaine Ann. Olly Explores 7 Wonders of the Chesapeake Bay, 1 vol. Nash, Kelli, illus. 2015. (ENG.). 32p. (J). (gr. -1-3). 16.99 *(978-0-7643-4938-6(4),* 6693) Schiffer Publishing, Ltd.

Allen, Elise & Stanford, Halle. Jim Henson's Enchanted Sisters: Autumn's Secret Gift. 2014. (Enchanted Sisters Ser.). (ENG., Illus.). 128p. (J). (gr. 2-4). pap. 5.99 *(978-1-61963-254-7(3),* 900131787, Bloomsbury USA Childrens) Bloomsbury Publishing USA.

—Winter's Flurry Adventure. Pooler, Paige, illus. 2014. (Enchanted Sisters Ser.: 2). (YA). lib. bdg. 16.00 *(978-0-606-36217-7(7))* Turtleback.

Allen, Page. Madison's Descent: A Child's Journey. (Illus.). (J). 2006. pap. 25.00 *(978-0-9752516-2-1(7))* 2004. lib. bdg. 60.00 *(978-0-9752516-1-4(9))* Otis & Randolph Pr.

—The Way to Davis: On the River of Stars. collector's ed. 2007. (Illus.). (J). 75.00 *(978-0-9752516-3-8(5))* Otis & Randolph Pr.

Anderson, Henry Morgan. Timmy the Goat: Spelunking Adventure. Falk, Wendy & Makepeace, Jonathan, eds. Funnell, Sonja, illus. 2011. (Adventures of Henry Ser.). 48p. 14.99 *(978-1-936813-00-1(9))* Adventures of Henry, LLC.

Andrews, Jane. Young Reader's Series: The stories mother nature told her Children. 2011. 150p. pap. 11.89 *(978-1-61279-069-5(0))* Publishing in Motion.

Applegate, Katherine. Willodeen. 2023. (SPA.). 220p. (J). (gr. 2-4). pap. 13.95 ***(978-607-557-486-8(7))*** Editorial Oceano de Mexico MEX. Dist: Independent Pubs. Group.

—Willodeen. Santoso, Charles, illus. 2021. (ENG.). 272p. (J). 16.99 *(978-1-250-14740-0(9),* 900181551) Feiwel & Friends.

Archer, Micha. Daniel Finds a Poem. Archer, Micha, illus. 2016. (Illus.). 32p. (J). (gr. k-3). 18.99 *(978-0-399-16913-7(X),* Nancy Paulsen Books) Penguin Young Readers Group.

—Wonder Walkers. Archer, Micha, illus. 2021. (Illus.). 32p. (J). (gr. -1-2). 18.99 *(978-0-593-10964-9(3),* Nancy Paulsen Books) Penguin Young Readers Group.

Arrington, Linda. Purple Time. 2012. 36p. pap. 24.95 *(978-1-4626-9613-0(9))* America Star Bks.

—Ugly Trees. Arrington, Linda, photos by. 2012. (Illus.). 24p. pap. 24.95 *(978-1-4626-8925-5(6))* America Star Bks.

Atteberry, Kevan. Bunnies!!! 2015. (ENG., Illus.). 32p. (J). (gr. -1-3). 12.99 *(978-0-06-230783-5(5),* HarperCollins) HarperCollins Pubs.

Austin, Sarah & Boyle, Eleanor Vere. The Story Without an End. 2015. (ENG., Illus.). 64p. (J). (gr. 2-5). pap. 5.99 *(978-0-486-79495-2(4))* Dover Pubns., Inc.

Avalos, Francisco. Amazon Tale. 2013. 124p. 29.99 *(978-1-4797-6689-5(5));* pap. 19.99 *(978-1-4797-6688-8(7))* Xlibris Corp.

Avignone, June. A Peek into the Secret Little Ones of Turtle Back Island. My Wolf Dog, illus. 2004. 40p. (J). pap. *(978-0-9654628-2-2(X))* Mill Street Forward, The.

Azman, Hacer. God Loves Us All. 2011. (ENG.). 103p. (J). (gr. -1-12). 14.95 *(978-1-59784-233-4(8),* Tughra Bks.) Blue Dome, Inc.

Baby Bear Sees Blue. 2014. (Baby Bear Ser.). (ENG., Illus.). 42p. (J). (gr. -1 — 1). bds. 8.99 *(978-1-4814-1503-3(4),* Little Simon) Little Simon.

Baby Lauren & Theodore, Paperback. 2007. (J). pap. 9.95 *(978-0-9779643-0-7(2))* Healing Tree Arts.

Babypants, Caspar. My Woodland Wish. Endle, Kate, illus. 2011. (ENG.). 32p. (J). (gr. -1-2). 17.99 *(978-1-57061-748-5(1),* Little Bigfoot) Sasquatch Bks.

Bailey, Dawn Wentz. Joey & the Mighty Oak. 2008. 20p. pap. 24.95 *(978-1-60813-377-2(X))* PublishAmerica, Inc.

Bailey, S. D. All While Holding My Ladybug Lunch Pail. 2008. (ENG.). 24p. pap. 11.49 *(978-1-4389-0617-1(X))* AuthorHouse.

Barkley, Callie. Liz at Marigold Lake. Riti, Marsha, illus. 2014. (Critter Club Ser.: 7). (ENG.). 128p. (J). (gr. k-4). pap. 5.99 *(978-1-4424-9525-8(1),* Little Simon) Little Simon.

—Liz at Marigold Lake. 2014. (Critter Club Ser.: 7). lib. bdg. 16.00 *(978-0-606-35445-5(X))* Turtleback.

Baum, L. Frank. Twinkle & Chubbins. 2011. 106p. pap. 9.95 *(978-1-60664-470-6(X))* Rodgers, Alan Bks.

Baum, L. Frank & Bancroft, Laura. Policeman Bluejay. 2009. 116p. pap. 9.95 *(978-1-60664-382-2(7))* Rodgers, Alan Bks.

Bekis, Joanne. Bubble & Butterfly. 2009. 20p. pap. 10.50 *(978-1-60693-696-2(4),* Strategic Bk. Publishing) Strategic Book Publishing & Rights Agency (SBPRA).

Bentley, Dawn. Saber-Tooth Trap. (Smithsonian's Prehistoric Pals Ser.). (ENG., Illus.). 36p. (J). (gr. -1-2). 9.95 *(978-1-59249-457-6(9),* PS2456) Soundprints.

M
N
O

—Saber-Tooth Trap. Reavely, Trever, illus. (Smithsonian's Prehistoric Pals Ser.). (ENG.). 36p. (J). (gr. -1-2). 2.95 *(978-1-59249-456-9(0)*, S2456) Soundprints.

—Saber-Tooth Trap. Reavely, Trevor, illus. 2005. (Smithsonian's Prehistoric Pals Ser.). (ENG.). 36p. (J). (gr. k-2). 14.95 *(978-1-59249-453-8(6)*, H2406); pap. 6.95 *(978-1-59249-454-5(4)*, S2406) Soundprints.

Berry, Ron. Look for the Rainbow! Sharp, Chris, illus. 2009. (ENG.). 18p. bds. 10.99 *(978-0-8249-1428-8(7)*, Ideals Pubns.) Worthy Publishing.

Bird, Jodi Stiriz. Going on a Tree Hunt: A Tree Identification Book for Young Children. 2011. 28p. (gr. 1-2). pap. 14.99 *(978-1-4490-8308-3(0))* AuthorHouse.

Bissonette, Aimee. North Woods Girl. McGehee, Claudia, illus. 2015. (ENG.). 32p. (J). 17.95 *(978-0-87351-966-3(3))* Minnesota Historical Society Pr.

Blaskowsky, Michael, tr. Sato the Rabbit. 2021. (Sato the Rabbit Ser.: 1). (Illus.). 68p. (J). (gr. 1-4). 17.95 *(978-1-59270-318-0(6))* Enchanted Lion Bks., LLC.

—Sato the Rabbit, a Sea of Tea. 2022. (Sato the Rabbit Ser.: 3). (Illus.). 72p. (J). (gr. 1-4). 17.95 *(978-1-59270-355-5(0))* Enchanted Lion Bks., LLC.

Blevins, Wiley. Near or Far. 2019. (Location Words Ser.). (ENG., Illus.). 24p. (J). (gr. -1-2). pap. 6.95 *(978-1-9771-0540-0(8)*, 139943, Pebble) Capstone.

Blume, Rebecca. When the World Was Green! Blume, Rebecca, illus. 2007. (Illus.). 32p. (J). per. 14.00 *(978-0-9785427-1-9(1))* Liberty Artists Management.

Bogart, Jo Ellen. The Big Tree Gang. Griffiths, Dean, illus. 2005. 60p. (J). lib. bdg. 20.00 *(978-1-4242-1251-4(0))* Fitzgerald Bks.

Bond, A. Russell. Scientific American Boy: Or the Camp at Willow Clump Island. 2006. (Applewood Bks.). (ENG., Illus.). 320p. (gr. 4-7). 19.95 *(978-1-55709-185-7(4))* Applewood Bks.

Bonnell, Kris. Look Up! 2007. (J). pap. 5.95 *(978-1-933727-48-6(9))* Reading Reading Bks., LLC.

Brodland, Rita, ed. All Dried Out. Freeman, Troy, illus. l.t. ed. 2006. (WeWrite Kids! Ser.: 50). 68p. (J). pap. 11.95 *(978-1-57635-063-8(0))* WeWrite LLC.

Budbill, David. Snowshoe Trek to Otter River. 2005. (J). pap. *(978-0-9657144-9-5(7))* Onion River Pr.

Bunce, Margaret. Adventures with Nature: A Story about Olivia & Her Little Dog, Jake. 2011. 24p. pap. 12.95 *(978-1-4567-2497-9(5))* AuthorHouse.

Bunting, Eve. Anna's Table. Morley, Taia, illus. 2003. (ENG.). 32p. (J). (gr. 3-6). 16.95 *(978-1-55971-841-7(2))* Cooper Square Publishing Llc.

Burke, Gloreen. Mother Nature Dear. 2008. 16p. pap. 24.95 *(978-1-60672-235-0(2))* America Star Bks.

Busheri, Devora. In the Jerusalem Forest. Kelner, Noa, illus. 2019. (ENG.). 32p. (J). (gr. -1-3). 17.99 *(978-1-5415-3472-8(7)*, 44f7f14e-ddaf-4dfe-9235-7200edce6859, Kar-Ben Publishing) Lerner Publishing Group.

Caglaroglu, Nurefsan. My Sweet Grandparents. 2011. (ENG.). 120p. 14.95 *(978-1-59784-230-3(3)*, Tughra Bks.) Blue Dome, Inc.

Carrie C Yakola. Lucy's Shooting Star. 2009. 32p. pap. 15.99 *(978-1-4343-5276-7(5))* AuthorHouse.

Carson, Penny & Hess, Amy. Simon Goes Camping. 2008. 19p. 10.95 *(978-1-4357-1560-8(8))* Lulu Pr., Inc.

Casanova, Mary. Wake up, Island. Wroblewski, Nick, illus. 2016. (J). 40p. 14.95 *(978-0-8166-8935-4(0))*; pap. *(978-0-8166-8936-1(9))* Univ. of Minnesota Pr.

Chapman, Joan. A Cloud Called Cleo, 1 vol. 2006. (Neighborhood Readers Ser.). (ENG.). 12p. (gr. 1-2). pap. 5.90 *(978-1-4042-7050-3(7)*, 9681a169-6e6d-4385-acb4-4caf92e594ea, Rosen Classroom) Rosen Publishing Group, Inc., The.

Charters, Jane. The General. Foreman, Michael, illus. 2010. (ENG.). 48p. (J). (gr. k-3). 16.99 *(978-0-7636-4875-6(2)*, Templar) Candlewick Pr.

Chatel, Kim. A Talent for Quiet. Chatel, Kim, photos by. 2009. (Illus.). 32p. pap. 10.95 *(978-1-935137-56-6(5))* Guardian Angel Publishing, Inc.

Chen, Julia. On the Way Home. Stewart, Fion, illus. 2009. (J). *(978-0-9787550-6-5(5))* Heryin Publishing Corp.

Chur, R. G. Penny the Pink Cloud. 2012. pap. 9.95 *(978-0-7414-7028-7(4))* Infinity Publishing.

Cole, Henry. Nesting. Cole, Henry, illus. 2020. (ENG., Illus.). 40p. (J). (gr. -1-3). 17.99 *(978-0-06-288592-0(8)*, Tegen, Katherine Bks) HarperCollins Pubs.

—On Meadowview Street. Cole, Henry, illus. 2007. (ENG., Illus.). 32p. (J). (gr. -1-3). 17.99 *(978-0-06-056481-0(4)*, Greenwillow Bks.) HarperCollins Pubs.

Collins, Pat Lowery. The Deer Watch. Slonim, David, illus. 2013. (ENG.). 32p. (J). (gr. -1-2). 15.99 *(978-0-7636-4890-9(6))* Candlewick Pr.

Cook, Sherry & Johnson, Terri. Watery William, 26. Kuhn, Jesse, illus. l.t. ed. 2006. (Quirkles -- Exploring Phonics through Science Ser.: 23). 32p. (J). 7.99 *(978-1-933815-22-0(1)*, Quirkles, The) Creative 3, LLC.

Cooke, Flora J. Nature Myths & Stories for Little Chil. 2006. pap. 19.95 *(978-1-4254-9629-6(6))* Kessinger Publishing, LLC.

Cordery-Maring, Jeanee. Climbing over Rainbows. 2008. 76p. pap. 19.95 *(978-1-4241-6243-7(2))* America Star Bks.

Corso, Joseph. Mother Earth Four. 2012. (ENG.). 39p. (J). pap. 15.95 *(978-1-4327-8041-8(7))* Outskirts Pr., Inc.

Coste, Marion. Wild Beach. Gray, Cissy, illus. 2005. (ENG.). 32p. (J). pap. 8.25 *(978-0-89317-062-2(3)*, WW-623); lib. bdg. 17.95 *(978-0-89317-061-5(5)*, WW-0615) Finney Co., Inc. (Windward Publishing).

Covey, Richard D. & Pappas, Diane H. What Is Global Warming? 2009. (Planet Earth Patrol Ser.). (Illus.). (J). *(978-0-545-06104-9(0))* Scholastic, Inc.

Cox Gray, Marjorie. Bucky's Adventures. Griffin, Marlin, illus. 2008. 100p. pap. 28.99 *(978-1-4389-2645-2(6))* AuthorHouse.

Crawford, Laura. In Arctic Waters, 1 vol. Hodson, Ben, illus. 2007. (ENG.). 32p. (J). (gr. -1-2). 15.95 *(978-0-9768823-4-3(5))* Arbordale Publishing.

Cruz De Jesus, Marta. Chosen: By Nature. 2010. 116p. 21.49 *(978-1-4520-3479-9(6))*; pap. 10.99 *(978-1-4520-3480-5(X))* AuthorHouse.

D. Good Morning World. 2013. 46p. pap. 21.99 *(978-1-4575-2154-6(7))* Dog Ear Publishing, LLC.

Da Puzzo, Allegra & Da Puzzo, Jackson. A Cloudy Day. Gauvin, Matthew, illus. 2012. 24p. pap. *(978-0-9843477-5-9(5))* Roxby Media Ltd.

Dane, Dichira A. Pathway of Pebbles. 2008. 20p. pap. 24.95 *(978-1-60703-801-6(3))* America Star Bks.

Dann, Colin. The Animals of Farthing Wood (Modern Classics) 2016. (Modern Classics Ser.). (ENG., Illus.). 400p. (J). (gr. 2-6). pap. 7.99 *(978-1-4052-8180-5(4))* Farshore GBR. Dist: HarperCollins Pubs.

—The Animals of Farthing Wood: the Adventure Begins. 2017. (Puffin Book Ser.). (Illus.). 272p. (J). (gr. 2-4). pap. 16.99 *(978-0-14-136874-0(8))* Penguin Bks., Ltd. GBR. Dist: Independent Pubs. Group.

Danyi, Barb. The Maker of Heaven & Earth. 2011. 28p. (gr. -1). pap. 11.99 *(978-1-4634-1300-2(9))* AuthorHouse.

Darlison, Aleesah & Hart, James. Awesome Animal Stories for Kids. 2016. (Illus.). 192p. (J). (gr. 1-4). pap. 9.99 *(978-0-85798-968-0(5))* Random Hse. Australia AUS. Dist: Independent Pubs. Group.

Davies, Nicola. The Pond. Fisher, Cathy, illus. 2017. 32p. (J). (gr. k-2). 16.99 *(978-1-912050-70-3(6))* Graffeg Limited GBR. Dist: Independent Pubs. Group.

Dee, Carolyn. The Tree Who Couldn't Choose. 2008. 36p. pap. 15.49 *(978-1-4389-2950-7(1))* AuthorHouse.

Delacre, Lulu. ¿Hasta dónde Me Amas? Delacre, Lulu, illus. 2014. (SPA., Illus.). 32p. (J). (gr. -1-6). pap. 12.95 *(978-1-62014-208-0(2)*, leelowbooks) Lee & Low Bks., Inc.

Demasse-Pottier, Stephanie. My Island. Ratanavanh, Seng Soun, illus. 2019. (ENG.). 25p. (J). (gr. -1-k). 16.95 *(978-1-61689-813-7(5))* Princeton Architectural Pr.

Denver, John. Sunshine on My Shoulders, 1 vol. Canyon, Christopher, illus. 2003. 32p. (J). (gr. -1 — 1). pap. 8.99 *(978-1-58469-050-4(X)*, Dawn Pubns.) Sourcebooks, Inc.

dePaola, Tomie. Michael Bird-Boy. dePaola, Tomie, illus. 2015. (ENG., Illus.). 32p. (J). (gr. -1-3). 16.99 *(978-1-4814-4333-3(X)*, Simon & Schuster Bks. For Young Readers) Simon & Schuster Bks. For Young Readers.

Dubuc, Marianne. Up the Mountain Path. 2018. (ENG., Illus.). (J). (gr. -1-2). 17.95 *(978-1-61689-723-9(6))* Princeton Architectural Pr.

Dundon, Adamarie. Niklas Rogers: The Adventure Begins. 2004. 60p. pap. 13.95 *(978-1-4184-4361-0(1))* AuthorHouse.

Dussling, Jennifer. El Misterio Del Arco Iris (the Rainbow Mystery) Gott, Barry, illus. 2009. (Science Solves It! (r) en Espanol Ser.). (SPA.). (gr. 1-3). pap. 33.92 *(978-0-7613-4798-9(4))* Lerner Publishing Group.

Duvall, Sheila Marie. I See Fun. 2009. 16p. pap. 8.75 *(978-1-4389-4963-5(4))* AuthorHouse.

Earth Coffee Table Book. 2009. 128p. 24.95 *(978-1-4231-2205-0(4)*, Disney Editions) Disney Pr.

Earth Picture Book. 2009. 64p. 8.99 *(978-1-4231-2204-3(6))* Disney Pr.

Edwards, Glenna S. Rainbow Bed: A child's perspective on coping with Grief. 2009. 20p. pap. 17.95 *(978-1-4327-2422-1(3))* Outskirts Pr., Inc.

Edwards, Pamela Duncan. Clara Caterpillar. Cole, Henry, illus. 2004. (ENG.). 40p. (J). (gr. -1-1). reprint ed. pap. 8.99 *(978-0-06-443691-5(8)*, HarperCollins) HarperCollins Pubs.

Ehlert, Lois. In My World. Ehlert, Lois, illus. 2006. (ENG., Illus.). 36p. (J). (gr. -1-3). reprint ed. pap. 9.99 *(978-0-15-205429-8(4)*, 1196338, Clarion Bks.) HarperCollins Pubs.

Ekholm, Jan. The Little Red Rascal. 2011. 88p. pap. 30.28 *(978-1-4567-9501-6(5))* AuthorHouse.

Eleanor, Coalson. Simon Says Run. 2006. (Illus.). (J). 8.95 *(978-1-56167-944-7(5))* American Literary Pr.

Elmore, Amber. Betsy Beansprout Adventure Guide. Short, Kasey, illus. 2011. (J). pap. 15.99 *(978-0-9822632-8-0(7))* ShadeTree Publishing, LLC.

Ergün, Erol & Ergün, Erol. Generous Bestower. 2011. (ENG., Illus.). 160p. (J). (gr. -1-12). pap. 9.95 *(978-1-59784-258-7(3)*, Tughra Bks.) Blue Dome, Inc.

—Supreme Ruler. 2011. (ENG., Illus.). 192p. (J). (gr. -1-12). pap. 9.95 *(978-1-59784-259-4(1)*, Tughra Bks.) Blue Dome, Inc.

Evers, Alf. Treasure of Watchdog Mountain: The Story of a Mountain in the Catskills. Yanow-Schwartz, Jo & Schwartz, Arthur, eds. 2006. 76p. (J). 16.95 *(978-1-879504-19-6(7))* Woodstocker Books/Arthur Schwartz & Company.

Farrell, Alison. The Hike: (Nature Book for Kids, Outdoors-Themed Picture Book for Preschoolers & Kindergarteners) 2019. (ENG., Illus.). 56p. (J). (gr. -1-k). 17.99 *(978-1-4521-7461-7(X))* Chronicle Bks. LLC.

Flatley, Paula Chorman. Olivia's Tree, 1 vol. Palmer, Kimmy, illus. 2010. 16p. pap. 24.95 *(978-1-4489-5870-2(9))* America Star Bks.

Fletcher, Ralph. Hello, Harvest Moon. Kiesler, Kate, illus. 2017. (ENG.). 32p. (J). (gr. -1-3). pap. 8.99 *(978-1-328-74049-6(8)*, 1677015, Clarion Bks.) HarperCollins Pubs.

The Flower Pot Bunnies Return. 2006. (J). *(978-0-9755390-2-6(7))* Fifth Ave Pr.

Fogliano, Julie. If I Was the Sunshine. Long, Loren, illus. 2019. (ENG.). 48p. (J). (gr. -1-3). 17.99 *(978-1-4814-7243-2(7)*, Atheneum Bks. for Young Readers) Simon & Schuster Children's Publishing.

Fontes, Justine. El Dia Que Jordan Se Enfermo: Jordan's Silly Sick Day. Lee, Jared, illus. 2005. (Rookie Reader Español Ser.). 32p. (gr. k-2). 19.50 *(978-0-516-24445-7(0)*, Children's Pr.) Scholastic Library Publishing.

Forbes, J. L. Under the Faithful Watch of the River Hawk. Forbes, Justin, illus. 2013. 20p. pap. 24.95 *(978-1-62709-899-1(2))* America Star Bks.

Foreman, Grindley -. La playa de Pedro. 2003. (SPA., Illus.). 32p. (J). (gr. 1-3). 19.99 *(978-84-261-3314-4(2))* Juventud, Editorial ESP. Dist: Lectorum Pubns., Inc.

Forte, Lauren. Olivia Helps Mother Nature. 2014. (Olivia Ready-To-Read Level 1 Ser.). lib. bdg. 13.55 *(978-0-606-35452-3(2))* Turtleback.

Fox, Paula. Traces. 2011. (ENG., Illus.). 32p. (gr. 2-4). 26.19 *(978-1-932425-43-7(8))* Highlights Pr., c/o Highlights for Children, Inc.

Frasier, Debra. The Incredible Water Show. Frasier, Debra, illus. 2004. (ENG., Illus.). 40p. (J). (gr. -1-3). 16.00 *(978-0-15-216287-0(9)*, 1200556, Clarion Bks.) HarperCollins Pubs.

Frederick Edward Pitts. Tale of the Hummingopotomus: The Flight for Life. 2009. 40p. pap. 18.49 *(978-1-4389-6453-9(6))* AuthorHouse.

Freedman, Deborah. This House, Once. Freedman, Deborah, illus. 2017. (ENG., Illus.). 40p. (J). (gr. -1-3). 17.99 *(978-1-4814-4284-8(8))* Simon & Schuster Children's Publishing.

Frisch, Aaron. The Lonely Pine. Delessert, Etienne, illus. 2011. (ENG.). 32p. (J). (gr. 1-3). 17.99 *(978-1-56846-214-1(X)*, 22066, Creative Editions) Creative Co., The.

Frontiera, Deborah. Eric & the Enchanted Leaf: A Night with Echo. Scott, Korey, illus. 2007. Tr. of Eric y la hojita encantada: una noche con Eco. (SPA.). 32p. (J). *(978-0-9795474-2-3(3))* KAM Publishing.

Frye, Karen. Flake, 1 vol. 2010. 16p. 24.95 *(978-1-4489-4935-9(1))* PublishAmerica, Inc.

Fuhr, Ute & Sautai, Raoul. The Earth's Surface. 2012. (ENG., Illus.). 32p. (J). (gr. k-3). spiral bd. 11.99 *(978-1-85103-362-1(9))* Moonlight Publishing, Ltd. GBR. Dist: Independent Pubs. Group.

Galbraith, Kathryn O. Spring Babies. Pons, Adela, illus. 2019. (Babies in the Park Ser.). 20p. (J). (gr. -1 — 1). bds. 7.99 *(978-1-68263-068-6(4))* Peachtree Publishing Co. Inc.

—Summer Babies, 1 vol. Pons, Adela, illus. 2019. (Babies in the Park Ser.). 20p. (J). (gr. -1 — 1). bds. 6.99 *(978-1-68263-069-3(2))* Peachtree Publishing Co. Inc.

—Winter Babies. Pons, Adela, illus. 2018. (Babies in the Park Ser.). 20p. (J). (gr. -1 — 1). bds. 6.99 *(978-1-68263-067-9(6))* Peachtree Publishing Co. Inc.

Galliez, Roxane Marie. Patience, Miyuki: (intergenerational Picture Book Ages 5-8 Teaches Life Lessons of Learning How to Wait, Japanese Art & Scenery) Ratanavanh, Seng Soun, illus. 2019. (ENG.). 32p. (J). (gr. k-3). 18.95 *(978-1-61689-843-4(7))* Princeton Architectural Pr.

—Time for Bed, Miyuki. Ratanavanh, Seng Soun, illus. 2018. (ENG.). 32p. (J). (gr. k-3). 18.95 *(978-1-61689-705-5(8))* Princeton Architectural Pr.

Gamble, Adam. Good Night World. Kelly, Cooper, illus. 2009. (Good Night Our World Ser.). (ENG.). 28p. (J). (gr. -1-k). bds. 9.95 *(978-1-60219-030-6(5))* Good Night Bks.

Gates, Mysti. Noises in the Night. Steward, Brian, photos by. 2009. (ENG.). 52p. pap. 22.99 *(978-1-4389-4359-6(8))* AuthorHouse.

Gentner, Norma L. & Young, Steve. Save a Tree for Me. (Song Box Ser.). (Illus.). 16p. (gr. 1-2). 31.50 *(978-0-7802-2264-9(4))* Wright Group/McGraw-Hill.

Gershator, Phillis. Listen, Listen. Jay, Alison, illus. (ENG.). 32p. (J). (gr. -1-2). 2008. bds. 14.99 *(978-1-84686-201-4(9))* 2007. 16.99 *(978-1-84686-084-3(9))* Barefoot Bks., Inc.

Getz, Jeanine Behr. Think Green! Nightingale, Jenny, illus. 2008. (ENG.). 32p. (J). 15.50 *(978-0-9797362-0-9(X))* Kids Think Big LLC.

Gingold, Janet. Finch Goes Wild. 2007. 280p. (YA). pap. 14.99 *(978-1-59092-385-6(5))* Blue Forge Pr.

Gisbert, Joan Manuel. El Palacio de los Tres Ojos. 2006. (SPA., Illus.). 127p. (J). (gr. 4-7). pap. 10.99 *(978-84-263-4614-8(6))* Vives, Luis Editorial (Edelvives) ESP. Dist: Lectorum Pubns., Inc.

Golden Books. Eloise Wilkin Stories. Wilkin, Eloise, illus. 2005. 224p. (J). (gr. -1-2). 12.99 *(978-0-375-82928-4(8)*, Golden Bks.) Random Hse. Children's Bks.

Golden Eagle Productions Staff. Grandmother Moon & Sammy the Loon, 36 vols. l.t. ed. 2003. (Illus.). 24p. per. 12.99 *(978-1-932338-24-9(1))* Lifevest Publishing, Inc.

Golden, Robert Charles. Pee Wee: The Blackcapped Chickadee. 2013. 36p. pap. 24.95 *(978-1-62709-101-5(7))* America Star Bks.

González, Xelena. All Around Us, 1 vol. Garcia, Adriana M., illus. 2017. (ENG.). 32p. (J). (gr. -1-4). 19.95 *(978-1-941026-76-2(1)*, 23353382, Cinco Puntos Press) Lee & Low Bks., Inc.

Goodale, E. B. Under the Lilacs. Goodale, E. B., illus. 2020. (ENG., Illus.). 32p. (J). (gr. -1-3). 17.99 *(978-0-358-15393-1(X)*, 1756213, Clarion Bks.) HarperCollins Pubs.

Goodhart, Pippa. Slow Magic. Kelly, John, illus. (Basketball Source Ser.). (J). 2015. (ENG.). 32p. (gr. 3-4). *(978-0-7787-1535-1(3))* 2003. *(978-0-7787-1489-7(6))* Crabtree Publishing Co.

Goodhart, Pippa & Goodheart, Pippa. Slow Magic. Kelly, John, illus. 2003. (Flying Foxes Ser.). (ENG.). 48p. (J). *(978-0-7787-1528-3(0))*; lib. bdg. *(978-0-7787-1482-8(9))* Crabtree Publishing Co.

Grahame, Kenneth. Oxford Bookworms Library: the Wind in the Willows: Level 3: 1000-Word Vocabulary. 3rd ed. 2008. (ENG., Illus.). 80p. 11.00 *(978-0-19-479137-3(8))* Oxford Univ. Pr., Inc.

—The Wind in the Willows. Freeman, Tor, illus. 2017. (Alma Junior Classics Ser.). (ENG.). 192p. (J). pap. 9.99 *(978-1-84749-638-6(5)*, 900184101, Alma Classics) Bloomsbury Publishing USA.

Grahame, Kenneth & Williams, Nicholas. An Gwyns I'n Helyk. Shepard, Ernest H., illus. 2013. (COR.). 202p. pap. *(978-1-78201-029-6(7))* Evertype.

Greig, Louise. A Walk Through the Woods. Musselwhite, Helen, illus. 2018. (ENG.). 20p. (J). (gr. k). 19.99 *(978-1-4549-2988-8(X))* Sterling Publishing Co., Inc.

Griggs, Rosemarie. The Adventures of Donkey Tom Volume 2: Crystal Forest. 2012. 40p. pap. 32.70 *(978-1-4797-0553-5(5))* Xlibris Corp.

Grimes, Nikki. Southwest Sunrise. Minor, Wendell, illus. 2020. (ENG.). 40p. (J). 18.99 *(978-1-5476-0082-3(9)*, 900197954, Bloomsbury Children's Bks.) Bloomsbury Publishing USA.

Hale, Ohara. Be Still;Life. 2018. (ENG., Illus.). 48p. (J). (gr. -1). 17.95 *(978-1-59270-257-2(0))* Enchanted Lion Bks., LLC.

Hall, Hannah C. Sunrise, Easter Surprise! Jatkowska, Ag, illus. 2018. (ENG.). 20p. (J). (gr. -1-k). bds. 6.99 *(978-0-8249-1659-6(X))* Worthy Publishing.

Hallinan, P. K. The Looking Book. Barton, Patrice, illus. (ENG.). (J). (gr. -1-1). 2019. 26p. bds. 7.99 *(978-0-8249-1698-5(0)*, Worthy Kids/Ideals) 2009. 32p. 16.99 *(978-0-8249-5607-3(9)*, Ideals Pubns.) Worthy Publishing.

Hamilton, L. Los Ninos y la Naturaleza. (SPA.). 198p. 12.00 *(978-84-89920-62-0(1)*, 87106) Ediciones Oniro S.A. ESP. Dist: Lectorum Pubns., Inc.

Hannigan, Katherine. Ida B: ... & Her Plans to Maximize Fun, Avoid Disaster, & (Possibly) Save the World. 2004. (ENG.). 256p. (J). (gr. 4-18). 17.99 *(978-0-06-073024-6(2)*, Greenwillow Bks.) HarperCollins Pubs.

—Ida B: ... And Her Plans to Maximize Fun, Avoid Disaster, & (Possibly) Save the World. 2004. 256p. (gr. 4-18). lib. bdg. 16.89 *(978-0-06-073025-3(0))* HarperCollins Pubs.

—Ida B: ... & Her Plans to Maximize Fun, Avoid Disaster, & (Possibly) Save the World. 2011. (ENG.). 272p. (J). (gr. 5-9). reprint ed. pap. 7.99 *(978-0-06-073026-0(9)*, Greenwillow Bks.) HarperCollins Pubs.

Harris, Annaka. I Wonder. Rowe, John, illus. 2013. 32p. (J). 16.95 *(978-1-940051-04-8(5))* Four Elephants Pr.

Hatton, Laura. The Fairy's Garden. 2012. 64p. pap. 26.52 *(978-1-4669-3961-5(3))* Trafford Publishing.

Hayes, Ned. The Eagle Tree: A Novel. 2016. (ENG.). 270p. pap. 14.95 *(978-1-5039-3664-5(3)*, 9781503936645, Little A) Amazon Publishing.

Healy, Reneé. You Are Safe in the Universe. 2011. 28p. pap. 25.00 *(978-1-936688-07-4(7))* AKA:yoLa.

Heather Rose Brabant. The Moon Princess. 2009. 20p. pap. 11.95 *(978-1-4389-2980-4(3))* AuthorHouse.

Heathfield, Lisa. Seed. 2015. (ENG.). 336p. (YA). (gr. 7-17). 25.00 *(978-0-7624-5634-5(5)*, Running Pr. Kids) Running Pr.

Heinz, Brian J. Adirondack Lullaby. Henry, Maggie, illus. 2016. (ENG.). (J). bds. *(978-1-59531-053-8(3))* North Country Bks., Inc.

—A Coming of Winter in the Adirondacks. Healy, Maggie, illus. 2011. (ENG.). 32p. (J). 19.95 *(978-1-59531-038-5(X))* North Country Bks., Inc.

—The Great North Woods. Rothman, Michael, illus. 2016. (ENG.). 32p. (J). (gr. 3-6). 18.99 *(978-1-56846-275-2(1)*, 20817, Creative Editions) Creative Co., The.

Hemery, Kathleen Maresh. Sunflower Promise. Bordelois, Augusto, illus. 2005. (J). *(978-1-56123-188-1(6))* Centering Corp.

Hensley, Sarah M. Water Fun. Crowell, Knox, illus. l.t. ed. 2005. (J). (gr. -1-k). pap. 10.95 *(978-1-57332-342-0(X))*; pap. 10.95 *(978-1-57332-343-7(8))* Carson-Dellosa Publishing, LLC. (HighReach Learning, Incorporated).

Herbauts, Anne, creator. What Color Is the Wind? 2016. (Illus.). 48p. (J). (gr. k). pap. 21.95 *(978-1-59270-221-3(X))* Enchanted Lion Bks., LLC.

Herndon, Susen A. Janie's World: Walk with Me Through Nature's Door. 2013. 36p. pap. 16.46 *(978-1-4669-8057-0(5))* Trafford Publishing.

Hildreth, Ruth Erixon. Fun Lovin' Delanie Jo. Aughe, Roger, illus. 2012. 36p. pap. 24.95 *(978-1-4626-7851-8(3))* America Star Bks.

Hillert, Margaret. ¿Qué Hay en el Estanque, Querido Dragón? Fernandez, Queta, tr. from ENG. Schimmell, David, illus. 2014. (BeginningtoRead Ser.).Tr. of What's in the Pond, Dear Dragon? (ENG & SPA.). 32p. (J). (-2). lib. bdg. 22.60 *(978-1-59953-608-8(0))* Norwood Hse. Pr.

—What's in the Pond, Dear Dragon? Schimmell, David, illus. 2014. (BeginningtoRead Ser.). (ENG.). 32p. (J). (-2). lib. bdg. 22.60 *(978-1-59953-607-1(2))* Norwood Hse. Pr.

—What's in the Pond, Dear Dragon? David Schimmell, illus. 2013. (Beginning-To-Read Ser.). (ENG.). 32p. (J). (gr. k-2). pap. 13.26 *(978-1-60357-601-7(0))* Norwood Hse. Pr.

—What's in the Woods, Dear Dragon? Schimmell, David, illus. 2014. (BeginningtoRead Ser.). (ENG.). 32p. (J). (-2). lib. bdg. 22.60 *(978-1-59953-606-4(4))* Norwood Hse. Pr.

—What's in the Woods, Dear Dragon? David Schimmell, illus. 2013. (Beginning-To-Read Ser.). (ENG.). 32p. (J). (gr. k-2). pap. 13.26 *(978-1-60357-599-7(5))* Norwood Hse. Pr.

Hillert, Margaret & Fernández, Queta. ¿Que Hay en el Bosque, Querido Dragon? Schimmell, David, illus. 2014. (BeginningtoRead Ser.).Tr. of What's in the Woods, Dear Dragon? (ENG & SPA.). 32p. (J). (-2). lib. bdg. 22.60 *(978-1-59953-609-5(9))* Norwood Hse. Pr.

Hines, Anna Grossnickle. Gramma's Walk. Hines, Anna Grossnickle, illus. 2016. (ENG., Illus.). (J). (gr. -1-3). 18.95 *(978-1-930900-66-0(X))* Purple Hse. Pr.

Hochman, Marisa. A Walk in Pirate's Cove, 1 vol. 2012. (ENG., Illus.). 32p. (J). *(978-0-9865679-0-2(6))* Fitzhenry & Whiteside, Ltd.

Hoffelt, Jane. We Share One World. Husted, Marty, illus. 2004. 32p. (J). per. 15.95 *(978-0-9701907-8-9(6))* Illumination Arts Publishing Co., Inc.

Holbrook, Florence. Why the Crocodile Has a Wide Mouth: And Other Nature Myths. 2004. (Dover Children's Classics Ser.). (ENG., Illus.). 128p. (gr. 3-5). pap. 5.95 *(978-0-486-43649-4(7))* Dover Pubns., Inc.

Hougasian, Amy. The Big Foot Sun. 2008. 36p. pap. 16.99 *(978-1-4343-3920-1(3))* AuthorHouse.

Houston, Rebecca. My Butterfly. 2013. 20p. pap. 24.95 *(978-1-62709-079-7(7))* America Star Bks.

Howard, Jim & Welsh-Howard, Paula. Tell Me Tell Me If You Can. 2006. (J). per. 14.95 *(978-1-60002-291-3(X))* Mountain Valley Publishing, LLC.

Howerton-Willis, Deborah. Amos the Aardvark. 2012. 48p. pap. 24.99 *(978-1-62419-623-2(3))* Salem Author Services.

Hughes, Fox Carlton. Rainbow Rhino. Hughes, Fox Carlton, illus. 2007. (ENG., Illus.). 36p. (J). (gr. -1-3). 16.95 *(978-0-9790275-3-6(5))* Ovation Bks.

Hughes-Odgers, Kyle. One Thousand Trees. 2019. 32p. (J). 12.95 *(978-1-925591-78-1(6))* Fremantle Pr. AUS. Dist: Independent Pubs. Group.

Hunter, Erin. Warriors Manga: the Rise of Scourge. Kurkoski, Bettina M., illus. 2008. (Warriors Manga Ser.: No. 3). (ENG.). 112p. (J). (gr. 3-7). pap. 9.99 *(978-0-06-147867-3(9)*, HarperCollins) HarperCollins Pubs.

Hutton, John. Yard: Baby Unplugged. Kang, Andrea, illus. 2011. (Baby Unplugged Ser.). (ENG.). 14p. (J). (— 1). bds. 7.99 *(978-1-936669-01-1(3))* Blue Manatee Press.

Hyde, Katherine Bolger. Everything Tells Us about God. Coloji, Livia, illus. l.t. ed. 2018. (ENG.). 32p. (J). 19.95 *(978-1-944967-29-1(X))* Ancient Faith Publishing.

James, Ian. Why the Sky Is Far Away: A Tale from Nigeria. 2006. (J). pap. *(978-1-4108-6172-6(4))* Benchmark Education Co.

Jameson, Catherine. Zoe & the Fawn. Flett, Julie, illus. 2006. (ENG.). 32p. (J). (gr. -1-k). pap. 12.95 *(978-1-894778-43-5(X))* Theytus Bks., Ltd. CAN. Dist: Orca Bk. Pubs. USA.

Jeanmarie, Michele. Curiosity, Curiosity: Lost in an Array. 2008. 74p. pap. 19.95 *(978-1-60610-169-8(2))* America Star Bks.

Jeffers, Oliver. Here We Are: Notes for Living on Planet Earth. Jeffers, Oliver, illus. 2017. (ENG., Illus.). 48p. (J). (gr. -1-2). 19.99 *(978-0-399-16789-8(7)*, Philomel Bks.) Penguin Young Readers Group.

Jennings, Arleen Naish. God Is in the Rain. 2012. 64p. (gr. 1-2). pap. 8.95 *(978-1-4759-3292-8(8))* iUniverse, Inc.

Johnson, Christine. Deep in Alaska. Johnson, Gary R., illus. 2013. (ENG.). 42p. pap. 13.95 *(978-1-60223-215-0(6))* Univ. of Alaska Pr.

Johnson, D. B. Henry Hikes to Fitchburg. 2006. (Henry Book Ser.). (ENG., Illus.). 32p. (J). (gr. -1-3). reprint ed. 8.99 *(978-0-618-73749-9(9)*, 488706, Clarion Bks.) HarperCollins Pubs.

—Henry Hikes to Fitchburg. Johnson, D. B., illus. 2006. (Illus.). (gr. -1-3). 16.95 *(978-0-7569-6798-7(8))* Perfection Learning Corp.

Johnston, Julie. A Very Fine Line. 2006. 208p. (YA). (gr. 7). 18.95 *(978-0-88776-746-3(X)*, Tundra Bks.) Tundra Bks. CAN. Dist: Penguin Random Hse. LLC.

Jones, Angela. The Bird Lady. Newell, Brian, illus. 2009. 16p. pap. 7.31 *(978-1-4251-8612-8(2))* Trafford Publishing.

Jue, Thea. Remember the Love. Lenz, Mary, illus. 2013. 36p. pap. 13.95 *(978-0-9827753-3-2(4))* Interdimensional Pr.

Kaplan, Madeline. Planet Earth Gets Well. 2008. (ENG.). 24p. pap. 9.99 *(978-1-4196-8986-4(X))* CreateSpace Independent Publishing Platform.

Kaplan, Osman. Animal Wonders of the Water. Kalender, Öznur, illus. 2009. (Amazing Animals Ser.). (ENG.). 56p. (J). (gr. 2-4). 9.95 *(978-1-59784-200-6(1)*, Tughra Bks.) Blue Dome, Inc.

Katz, Susan B. My Mama Earth. Launay, Melissa, illus. 2012. (ENG.). 24p. (J). 16.99 *(978-1-84686-418-6(6))* Barefoot Bks., Inc.

Kelly, Jacqueline. La Evolución de Calpurnia Tate. 2010.Tr. of Evolution of Calpurnia Tate. (SPA.). 272p. (YA). pap. 20.95 *(978-84-9918-103-5(1))* Roca Editorial ESP. Dist: Spanish Pubs., LLC.

—La evolución de Calpurnia Tate, Vol. 2. 2011. (SPA.). 272p. pap. 12.95 *(978-84-92833-15-3(7))* Roca Editorial ESP. Dist: Spanish Pubs., LLC.

—La Evolución de Calpurnia Tate, Vol. 3. 2015.Tr. of Evolution of Calpurnia Tate. (SPA.). 320p. (YA). (gr. 5-8). 19.95 *(978-84-15729-78-5(2))* Roca Editorial ESP. Dist: Spanish Pubs., LLC.

—The Evolution of Calpurnia Tate. 2010. (CHI.). 344p. (J). (gr. 5-9). pap. *(978-986-216-538-6(3))* Commonwealth Publishing Co., Ltd.

—The Evolution of Calpurnia Tate. 2018. (CHI.). (J). (gr. 5-9). pap. *(978-7-221-14182-8(7))* Guizhou People's Publishing Hse.

—The Evolution of Calpurnia Tate. 2011. (JPN.). 412p. (J). (gr. 5-9). *(978-4-593-53474-6(7))* Holp Shuppan, Publishing.

—The Evolution of Calpurnia Tate. 2009. (Calpurnia Tate Ser.: 1). (ENG.). 352p. (J). (gr. 4-7). 19.99 *(978-0-8050-8841-0(5)*, 900051792, Holt, Henry & Co. Bks. For Young Readers) Holt, Henry & Co.

—The Evolution of Calpurnia Tate. 2010. 340p. 18.00 *(978-1-60686-849-2(7))* Perfection Learning Corp.

—The Evolution of Calpurnia Tate. 2011. (Calpurnia Tate Ser.: 1). (ENG.). 368p. (J). (gr. 4-7). pap. 8.99 *(978-0-312-65930-1(X)*, 900070517) Square Fish.

—The Evolution of Calpurnia Tate. 2011. (Calpurnia Tate Ser.: 1). (J). lib. bdg. 18.40 *(978-0-606-20974-8(3))* Turtleback.

Khan, Nafeesa. Pompom's Rainbow Day. 2012. 24p. pap. 28.03 *(978-1-4771-2918-0(9))* Xlibris Corp.

Kirk B. Gradin. Jadhu Ram & the Thirsty Forest. 2012. 36p. 17.95 *(978-1-105-04735-0(0))*; pap. 10.95 *(978-0-9855683-0-6(5))* Banyan Bks.

Kisiel, Soren & Jarock, Dawn. Once upon a Tree. McClure, Jessica, illus. 2017. 40p. (J). (gr. -1-3). 16.95 *(978-1-941529-74-4(7)*, Plum Blossom Bks.) Parallax Pr.

Kitzmiller, Brenda. Muddy Mud — an Easy to Read Beginning Reader Book. 2005. 24p. 7.85 *(978-1-4116-2937-0(X))* Lulu Pr., Inc.

Kleczka, John A. Flick the Butterfly: Flick & Mom Go to Grandma's. 2008. 48p. per. 24.95 *(978-1-60441-290-1(9))* America Star Bks.

Knapp, Artie. Little Otter Learns to Swim. 2018. (ENG., Illus.). 32p. (J). (gr. 1-4). 15.95 *(978-0-8214-2340-0(1))* Ohio Univ. Pr.

Knight, Hilary. A Firefly in a Fir Tree: A Carol for Mice. Knight, Hilary, illus. 2004. (Illus.). 32p. (J). (gr. -1-3). lib. bdg. 15.89 *(978-0-06-000992-2(6)*, Tegen, Katherine Bks) HarperCollins Pubs.

Konkle, Thomas. Red Skies. 2017. (Survive Ser.). (ENG.). 192p. (YA). (gr. 5-12). lib. bdg. 31.42 *(978-1-68076-733-9(X)*, 25400, Epic Escape) EPIC Pr.

Krishnaswami, Uma. Out of the Way! Out of the Way!, 1 vol. Krishnaswamy, Uma, illus. 2012. (ENG.). 28p. (J). (gr. -1-2). 17.95 *(978-1-55498-130-4(1))* Groundwood Bks. CAN. Dist: Publishers Group West (PGW).

—Out of the Way! Out of the Way!, 1 vol. Uma Krishnaswamy, illus. 2022. (ENG.). 24p. (J). (gr. k-2). pap. 11.99 ***(978-81-8146-792-8(2))*** Tulika Pubs. IND. Dist: Independent Pubs. Group.

Krohn, Kathryn T. Sarah's Most Perfect Day. Sage, Trina, illus. 2007. 24p. (J). 13.99 *(978-1-59879-325-3(X)*, Lifevest) Lifevest Publishing, Inc.

Krovatin, Christopher. Gravediggers: Mountain of Bones. 2013. (Gravediggers Ser.: 1). (ENG.). 352p. (J). (gr. 3-7). pap. 6.99 *(978-0-06-207741-7(4)*, Tegen, Katherine Bks) HarperCollins Pubs.

Kurtz, Jane. Lanie, Bk. 1. Hirsch, Jennifer, ed. Papp, Robert, illus. 2010. (American Girl: Lanie Ser.). (ENG.). 112p. (J). (gr. 2-4). pap. 21.19 *(978-1-59369-682-5(5))* American Girl Publishing, Inc.

—Lanie's Real Adventures. Papp, Robert, illus. 2010. (American Girl Today Ser.). (ENG.). 112p. (YA). (gr. 3-18). 12.95 *(978-1-59369-685-6(X))* American Girl Publishing, Inc.

Lacamara, Laura. Dalia's Wondrous Hair / el Maravilloso Cabello de Dalia. Baeza Ventura, Gabriela, tr. from SPA. Lacamara, Laura, illus. 2014. (ENG & SPA., Illus.). (J). 17.95 *(978-1-55885-789-6(3)*, Piñata Books) Arte Publico Pr.

Ladybird, Ladybird. The Wind in the Willows. 2016. (Ladybird Classics Ser.). (Illus.). 72p. (J). (gr. 3-7). 10.99 *(978-1-4093-1356-4(5))* Penguin Bks., Ltd. GBR. Dist: Independent Pubs. Group.

LaMarche, Jim. Pond. LaMarche, Jim, illus. 2016. (ENG., Illus.). 40p. (J). (gr. -1-3). 18.99 *(978-1-4814-4735-5(1)*, Simon & Schuster/Paula Wiseman Bks.) Simon & Schuster/Paula Wiseman Bks.

Lampert, Diane Charlotte. Suite for Human Nature. Puybaret, Eric, illus. 2016. (ENG.). 48p. (J). (gr. -1). 17.99 *(978-1-4169-5373-9(6)*, Atheneum Bks. for Young Readers) Simon & Schuster Children's Publishing.

Lamptey, Belinda N. Little Drops of Water. 2007. (ENG.). 32p. pap. 14.99 *(978-1-4257-3308-7(5))* Xlibris Corp.

Langdale, Mark Roland. Professor Doppelganger & the Fantastical Cloud Factory. 2012. 106p. pap. *(978-1-78003-267-2(6))* Pen Pr. Pubs., Ltd.

Lavin, Christine. Amoeba Hop. Feeney, Betsy Franco, illus. 2003. 36p. (J). (gr. 2-3). 19.95 incl. audio compact disk *(978-0-9726487-4-5(7))* Puddle Jump Pr., Ltd.

Lawrence, Kelsey. Rune. 2006. (Illus.). 92p. pap. 13.50 *(978-1-84426-399-8(1))* Upfront Publishing Ltd. GBR. Dist: Printondemand-worldwide.com.

Leadbetter, Lesley. Harold the Owl Who Couldn't Sleep. Leszek, Cedryll, illus. 2012. 30p. (J). pap. *(978-1-921869-89-1(5)*, Digital Publishing Centre) Interactive Pubns. Pty, Ltd.

Lee, Uk-Bae. When Spring Comes to the DMZ. Lee, Uk-Bae, illus. 2019. (Illus.). 40p. (J). (gr. -1-3). 17.95 *(978-0-87486-972-9(2))* Plough Publishing Hse.

Lehner, Montserrat. The Legend of the Açaí: Retold & Illustrated by Montserrat Lehner. 2010. 30p. pap. 14.00 *(978-1-60911-364-3(0)*, Eloquent Bks.) Strategic Book Publishing & Rights Agency (SBPRA).

Lenart, Claudia, illus. Seasons of Joy: Every Day Is for Outdoor Play. 2017. 27p. (J). pap. *(978-1-61599-317-8(7))* Loving Healing Pr., Inc.

Lewis, Rose. Sweet Dreams. Corace, Jen, illus. 2012. (ENG.). 32p. (J). (gr. -1-2). 16.95 *(978-1-4197-0189-4(4)*, 692701, Abrams Bks. for Young Readers) Abrams, Inc.

Linenthal, Peter. Look Look Outside. 2012. 16p. (J). (gr. -1 — 1). bds. 7.99 *(978-0-8037-3729-7(7)*, Dial Bks) Penguin Young Readers Group.

Little Green Giants. 2008. (Illus.). 28p. (J). 14.95 *(978-0-615-21480-1(0))* Allocca, Christine A.

Livingston, Mary A. & Shufelberger, Amanda. Buddy & the Magic Chicken Tree, 2 bks. Livingston, Tim, illus. 2014th ed. 2014. (ENG.). 34p. (J). 19.99 *(978-0-9635757-3-9(2))* Red Tail Publishing.

Locker, Thomas. Cloud Dance. Locker, Thomas, illus. 2003. (ENG., Illus.). 32p. (J). (gr. -1-3). pap. 7.99 *(978-0-15-204596-8(1)*, 1193840, Clarion Bks.) HarperCollins Pubs.

LoDestro, Christine. The Littlest Cloud. 2005. 15p. (J). 12.01 *(978-1-4116-6377-0(2))* Lulu Pr., Inc.

Loh-Hagan, Virginia. Pourquoi Stories. 2019. (Stone Circle Stories: Culture & Folktales Ser.). (ENG., Illus.). 32p. (J). (gr. 4-8). pap. 14.21 *(978-1-5341-4006-6(9)*, 212853); lib. bdg. 32.07 *(978-1-5341-4350-0(5)*, 212852) Cherry Lake Publishing. (45th Parallel Press).

London, Jack. White Fang. 2005. 28.95 *(978-1-4218-1472-8(2))*; 276p. pap. 13.95 *(978-1-4218-1572-5(9))* 1st World Publishing, Inc. (1st World Library - Literary Society).

—White Fang. 2005. (ENG.). 176p. (gr. 3-7). per. 14.95 *(978-1-59818-531-7(4))* Aegypan.

—White Fang. 2005. 120p. per. 5.95 *(978-1-4209-2246-2(7))* Digireads.com Publishing.

—White Fang. 2004. reprint ed. pap. 1.99 *(978-1-4192-9386-3(9))*; pap. 22.95 *(978-1-4191-9386-6(4))* Kessinger Publishing, LLC.

—White Fang. 2006. (Aladdin Classics Ser.). (ENG., Illus.). 368p. (J). (gr. 4-7). pap. 7.99 *(978-1-4169-1414-3(5)*, Aladdin) Simon & Schuster Children's Publishing.

London, Jonathan. Grizzly Peak. London, Sean, illus. 2017. (Aaron's Wilderness Ser.). (ENG.). 174p. (YA). (gr. 3-7). pap. 12.99 *(978-1-943328-77-2(3)*, West Winds Pr.) West Margin Pr.

Lonsdale, Cathy. Bill the Brush Turkey. 2008. (ENG.). 24p. 13.95 *(978-1-4092-0414-5(6))* Lulu Pr., Inc.

Luby, Brittany. Encounter. Goade, Michaela, illus. 2019. (ENG.). 40p. (J). (gr. -1-3). 18.99 *(978-0-316-44918-2(0))* Little, Brown Bks. for Young Readers.

Luyken, Corinna. The Tree in Me. 2021. (Illus.). 56p. (J). (gr. -1-3). 18.99 *(978-0-593-11259-5(8)*, Dial Bks) Penguin Young Readers Group.

Madison's Descent: A Child's Journey. collector's ed. 2004. (J). 75.00 *(978-0-9752516-0-7(0))* Otis & Randolph Pr.

Mahoney, Liana. Forest Green: A Walk Through the Adirondack Seasons. Henry, Maggie, illus. 2014. (ENG.). (J). *(978-1-59531-047-7(9))* North Country Bks., Inc.

Mair, J. Samia. Amira's Totally Chocolate World. 2010. (ENG., Illus.). 29p. (J). (gr. k-3). 8.95 *(978-0-86037-408-4(4))* Kube Publishing Ltd. GBR. Dist: Consortium Bk. Sales & Distribution.

Margulies, Paul. What Julianna Could See, 1 vol. Zonneveld, Famke, illus. 2004. 32p. (J). 11.95 *(978-0-88010-515-6(1))* SteinerBooks, Inc.

Marino Walters, Jennifer. Wonderful Winter. Nez, John, illus. 2016. (Seasons Ser.). (ENG.). 24p. (J). (gr. -1 — 1). lib. bdg. 25.32 *(978-1-63440-046-6(1)*, 8ddc45ac-25da-4bdf-ab3f-80c90e8aad36, Rocking Chair Kids) Red Chair Pr.

Marsh, Carole. The Voracious Volcano Mystery. 2008. (Masters of Disasters Ser.). (Illus.). 118p. (J). (gr. 3-5). 14.95 *(978-0-635-06466-0(9))*; per. 5.99 *(978-0-635-06463-9(4))* Gallopade International.

Marston, Hope Irvin. My Little Book of Manatees. Mirocha, Stephanie, illus. 2007. (ENG.). 32p. (J). (gr. k-5). pap. 7.95 *(978-0-89317-065-3(8)*, Windward Publishing) Finney Co., Inc.

Mason, David. Davey McGravy. Silverstein, Grant, illus. 2015. (ENG.). 120p. (J). (gr. k). pap. 14.95 *(978-1-58988-099-3(4))* Dry, Paul Bks., Inc.

Mayer, Mercer. It's Earth Day!, No. 5. Mayer, Mercer, illus. 2008. (Little Critter Ser.: No. 5). (ENG., Illus.). 24p. (J). (gr. -1-2). pap. 3.99 *(978-0-06-053959-7(3)*, HarperFestival) HarperCollins Pubs.

McCarthy, Mary. A Closer Look. 2007. (ENG., Illus.). 40p. (J). (gr. -1-k). 17.99 *(978-0-06-124073-7(7)*, Greenwillow Bks.) HarperCollins Pubs.

McCaughren, Tom. Run with the Wind. Sheridan, Bex, illus. 2016. (Run with the Wind Ser.). (ENG.). 208p. (J). 15.00 *(978-1-84717-837-4(5))* O'Brien Pr., Ltd., The IRL. Dist: Casemate Pubs. & Bk. Distributors, LLC.

McFadden, Patricia. Oh No, Wolly Bear!, 1 vol. Coxon, Michele, illus. 2008. (ENG.). 32p. (J). (gr. -1-3). 6.50 *(978-1-59572-149-5(5))* Star Bright Bks., Inc.

McKee, David. Elmer's Walk. McKee, David, illus. 2018. (Elmer Ser.). (ENG., Illus.). 32p. (J). (gr. -1-3). 17.99 *(978-1-5415-3554-1(5)*, 5065be78-503a-4ed9-b0c9-1c9e170daf43) Lerner Publishing Group.

McKelvey, Lonnie. Benny the Brave. Wooten, Neal, illus. 2008. 28p. (J). pap. 7.99 *(978-0-9817521-3-6(6))* Mirror Publishing.

Meachen Rau, Dana. ¡a Flotar! (Floating), 1 vol. 2008. (En Movimiento (on the Move) Ser.). (SPA., Illus.). 32p. (gr. k-1). lib. bdg. 25.50 *(978-0-7614-2420-8(2)*, f3c6d2be-3278-48ea-9712-4152559b992e) Cavendish Square Publishing LLC.

—Floating, 1 vol. 2007. (On the Move Ser.). (ENG., Illus.). 24p. (gr. k-1). lib. bdg. 25.50 *(978-0-7614-2315-7(X)*, a4076c80-2d16-49ca-ae51-436497538529) Cavendish Square Publishing LLC.

Meil, Gabriel & Rylander, Emily. Goodbye Earth Hello Moon. 2008. (ENG.). 32p. (J). (gr. k-2). 16.95 *(978-1-934866-02-3(4))* Warren Machine Co.

Las Mil y una Noches. (Coleccion Estrella). (SPA., Illus.). 64p. (J). 14.95 *(978-950-11-0001-3(4)*, SGM001) Sigmar ARG. Dist: Continental Bk. Co., Inc.

Milbourne, Anna. Sunny Day (Picture Book) 2008. (Picture Bks). 24p. (J). 9.99 *(978-0-7945-2117-2(7)*, Usborne) EDC Publishing.

Mills, Wynette. The Backyard Explorer: The Nana & Me Series. 2010. 36p. pap. 15.49 *(978-1-4520-2483-7(9))* AuthorHouse.

Mjolhus, Joy. Squirrel Babies & Friends. 2008. 16p. pap. 24.95 *(978-1-4241-8562-7(9))* America Star Bks.

Montijo, Rhode. Cloud Boy/Nino Nube. Mlawer, Teresa, tr. from ENG. 2006. (SPA & ENG., Illus.). 24p. (J). (gr. -1-3). 12.99 *(978-1-933032-06-1(5))* Lectorum Pubns., Inc.

Mooney, Ginger. Spirit Elk. 2009. 16p. pap. 9.99 *(978-1-4490-0447-7(4))* AuthorHouse.

Morel, Alicia. Cuentos Araucanos: La Gente de la Tierra. (SPA.). (J). (gr. 4-6). pap. *(978-956-13-1152-7(6)*, AB1252) Bello, Andres CHL. Dist: Lectorum Pubns., Inc.

Morningforest, Chris & Raymond, Rebecca. The Adventures of Nate & Naomi. 2006. 36p. (J). pap. 15.43 *(978-1-4116-9244-2(6))* Lulu Pr., Inc.

Moulton, Erin E. Flutter: The Story of Four Sisters & an Incredible Journey. 2012. (ENG.). 224p. (J). (gr. 3-7). pap. 6.99 *(978-0-14-242133-8(2)*, Puffin Books) Penguin Young Readers Group.

Mundy, Dawn. The Gift: A Woodsong Story. Tigue, Terry & Turner, Diane, illus. 2003. (J). lib. bdg. *(978-1-932139-16-7(8))* DEMDACO.

Murphy & Pimlott. Certain Island. 2014. (ENG.). 240p. (J). (gr. 5-8). pap. 14.95 *(978-1-59077-324-6(1))* Evans, M. & Co., Inc.

Murray, Diana. Summer Color! Persico, Zoe, illus. 2018. (ENG.). 40p. (J). (gr. -1-3). 18.99 *(978-0-316-37094-3(0))* Little, Brown Bks. for Young Readers.

Mwangi, Nyaruai. Argwings & the Lamplighters. 2008. 96p. (YA). pap. 13.95 *(978-0-9796476-8-0(1))* HM Bks.

Myers, Jean Emily. Mickey's Mini Farm. Tanner Voyles, illus. 2009. 32p. pap. 21.99 *(978-1-4389-5544-5(8))* AuthorHouse.

Nellist, Glenys. The Wonder That Is You, 1 vol. Blanz, Aurélie, illus. (ENG.). (J). 2020. 28p. bds. 9.99 *(978-0-310-76659-9(1))* 2019. 32p. 17.99 *(978-0-310-76669-8(9))* Zonderkidz.

Nesbit, E. In Homespun. 2007. 108p. per. *(978-1-4065-3079-7(4))* Dodo Pr.

Neubert, Oliver. Chantel's Quest for the Enchanted Medallion. 2009. (Cozy Classics Ser.). (ENG., Illus.). 224p. (J). (gr. 3-6). 16.95 *(978-1-897476-15-4(9))* Simply Read Bks. CAN. Dist: Ingram Publisher Services.

Nevins, Mary. The Adventures of Molly. 2009. 20p. pap. 14.50 *(978-1-60693-919-2(X)*, Eloquent Bks.) Strategic Book Publishing & Rights Agency (SBPRA).

Nichols, Lori. Maple & Willow Together. Nichols, Lori, illus. 2014. (Illus.). 32p. (J). (gr. -1-k). 17.99 *(978-0-399-16283-1(6)*, Nancy Paulsen Books) Penguin Young Readers Group.

Nigro Heroux, Regina. Grandma's Butterfly Garden. 2009. 28p. pap. 13.99 *(978-1-4490-3054-4(8))* AuthorHouse.

Nolan, Allia Zobel. God's Rainbow. Chung, Chi, illus. 2007. 16p. (J). 12.99 *(978-0-8254-5572-7(5))* Kregel Pubns.

O'Brien, Anne Sibley & Gal, Susan. Abracadabra, It's Spring! 2016. (Seasonal Magic Ser.). (ENG., Illus.). 24p. (J). (gr. -1-k). 15.99 *(978-1-4197-1891-5(6)*, 1121301, Abrams Appleseed) Abrams, Inc.

O'Donnel, Liam. Scout Hits the Trail. Huerta, Catherine, illus. (Pet Tales Ser.). (ENG.). 32p. (J). (gr. -1-3). 2008. 4.95 *(978-1-59249-740-9(3))* 2007. 9.95 *(978-1-59249-742-3(X))* Soundprints.

O'Donnell, Candy. Where Is God, Grandfather. Gillen, Rosemarie, illus. 2008. 28p. pap. 12.95 *(978-0-9814532-1-7(X))* Living Waters Publishing Co.

O'Donnell, Liam. Scout Hits the Trail. Huerta, Catherine, illus. 2007. (ENG.). 32p. (J). 2.95 *(978-1-59249-741-6(1))* Soundprints.

Oppenheim, Shulamith. Where Do I End & You Begin? Felix, Monique, illus. 2015. (ENG.). 32p. (J). (gr. 1-3). 17.99 *(978-1-56846-274-5(3)*, 20831, Creative Editions) Creative Co., The.

Overton, Kim G. Nathan & Father: A Walk of Wonder. 2017. (Illus.). 32p. (J). 17.95 *(978-0-9980141-0-4(9))* Flying Wren Studio.

Pages, Christina. The Mountain Boy. Caruth, Jeannette, illus. 2007. (Nature Children Ser.). 39p. (J). (gr. -1-3). 12.95 *(978-0-9794863-9-5(4))* Summerland Publishing.

Pak, Kenard. Goodbye Autumn, Hello Winter. Pak, Kenard, illus. 2017. (ENG., Illus.). 32p. (J). 18.99 *(978-1-62779-416-9(6)*, 900149958, Holt, Henry & Co. Bks. For Young Readers) Holt, Henry & Co.

—Goodbye Summer, Hello Autumn. Pak, Kenard, illus. 2016. (ENG., Illus.). 32p. (J). 18.99 *(978-1-62779-415-2(8)*, 900149957, Holt, Henry & Co. Bks. For Young Readers) Holt, Henry & Co.

Pandell, Karen. I Love You Sun / I Love You Moon: Te Amo Sol / Te Amo Luna. dePaola, Tomie, illus. 2003.Tr. of I Love You, Sun - I Love You, Moon. 12p. (J). (gr. -1 — 1). bds. 7.99 *(978-0-399-24165-9(5)*, G.P. Putnam's Sons Books for Young Readers) Penguin Young Readers Group.

Paquette, Ammi-Joan. The Tiptoe Guide to Tracking Fairies. LeTourneau, Marie, illus. 2010. (ENG.). 32p. (J). (gr. -1-3). pap. 8.95 *(978-1-933718-50-7(1))* Tanglewood Pr.

—The Tiptoe Guide to Tracking Fairies. Unzner, Christa, illus. 2009. (ENG.). 32p. (J). (gr. k-5). 15.95 *(978-1-933718-20-0(X))* Tanglewood Pr.

Parry, Rosanne. A Wolf Called Wander. 2021. (Voice of the Wilderness (Trade) Ser.). (ENG.). 272p. (gr. 3-6). 22.44 *(978-1-5364-6706-2(5))* HarperCollins Pubs.

—A Wolf Called Wander. Armiño, Mónica, illus. (Voice of the Wilderness Novel Ser.). (ENG.). 256p. (J). (gr. 3-7). 2021. pap. 7.99 *(978-0-06-289594-3(X))* 2019. 16.99 *(978-0-06-289593-6(1))* HarperCollins Pubs. (Greenwillow Bks.).

—A Wolf Called Wander. Armiño, Mónica, illus. 2019. (ENG.). 256p. lib. bdg. 18.80 *(978-1-6636-3081-0(X))* Perfection Learning Corp.

Paterson, John B., Jr. & Paterson, John B., Sr. Roberto's Trip to the Top. Alarcao, Renato, illus. 2009. (ENG.). 40p. (J). (gr. -1-3). 16.99 *(978-0-7636-2708-9(9))* Candlewick Pr.

Paterson, Katherine. Brother Sun, Sister Moon. Dalton, Pamela, illus. 2011. (ENG.). 36p. (J). (gr. -1-1). 17.99 *(978-0-8118-7734-3(5))* Chronicle Bks. LLC.

Patten, William. Animal & Nature Stories Vol. 8: The Junior Classics. 2004. reprint ed. pap. 1.99 *(978-1-4192-6805-2(8))* Kessinger Publishing, LLC.

Patterson, Eric. Nature Boy Nature Strikes Back. Wright, Chris, illus. 2008. 108p. pap. 6.95 *(978-1-935105-15-2(9))* Avid Readers Publishing Group.

Paulsen, Gary. Fishbone's Song. 2016. (ENG., Illus.). 160p. (J). (gr. 5). 18.99 *(978-1-4814-5226-7(6)*, Simon & Schuster Bks. For Young Readers) Simon & Schuster Bks. For Young Readers.

—The Island. 2006. (Point Ser.). 202p. (gr. 7-12). 16.00 *(978-0-7569-6382-8(6))* Perfection Learning Corp.

Penick Phillips-Cermak, Mosetta. The Wishing Flower. 2007. 24p. 16.50 *(978-0-615-15573-9(1))* PM Moon Pub., LLC.

Perry, Rex. illus. All Things Bright & Beautiful. 2004. 24p. (J). lib. bdg. 8.00 *(978-1-4242-0638-4(3))* Fitzgerald Bks.

Pfister, Marcus. Questions, Questions. 2011. (ENG., Illus.). 32p. (J). (gr. -1-2). 18.95 *(978-0-7358-4000-3(8))* North-South Bks., Inc.

Pimot, Karen Hutchins. Rainbows Are the Best. Allen, Sandra Hutchins, illus. 2009. 24p. pap. 12.95 *(978-1-936051-01-4(X))* Peppertree Pr., The.

Pita, Charo. Thank You! Allepuz, Anuska, illus. 2019. (ENG.). 32p. (J). 16.99 *(978-0-8028-5524-4(5)*, Eerdmans Bks For Young Readers) Eerdmans, William B. Publishing Co.

Plum, Amy. Until the Beginning. 2015. (After the End Ser.: 2). (ENG.). 336p. (YA). (gr. 8). 17.99 *(978-0-06-222563-4(4)*, HarperTeen) HarperCollins Pubs.

Polinski, Jo. Minnesota Moon. Webber, Carol, illus. 2007. 20p. per. 12.95 *(978-1-933482-60-6(5))* White Turtle Bks.

Price, Ellen Ann. Gladly's Magic. 2011. 160p. 27.50 *(978-0-557-71561-9(X))*; (ENG.). pap. 18.00 *(978-1-257-10561-8(2))* Lulu Pr., Inc.

Ramsey, Ann Louise. Me, the Tree. Ramsey, Ann Louise, illus. 2006. (ENG., Illus.). 56p. (J). 19.95 *(978-0-9645663-4-7(6))* Crown Peak Publishing.

Raney, Renee Simmons. Hairy, Scary, but Mostly Merry Fairies! Curing Nature Deficiency Through Folklore, Imagination, & Creative Activities. Crowe, Carolyn Walker, illus. 2017. (ENG.). 128p. pap. 15.95 *(978-1-58838-328-0(8)*, 8814, NewSouth Bks.) NewSouth, Inc.

Rawlinson, Julia. Fletcher & the Falling Leaves. 2011. (J). (gr. -1-2). 18.95 *(978-0-545-19705-2(8))*; 29.95 *(978-0-545-19699-4(X))* Weston Woods Studios, Inc.

Rebello, Kevin. Julia & Mckinley's Day at the Beach. 2009. 32p. pap. 12.99 *(978-1-4389-7330-2(6))* AuthorHouse.

Reed-jones, Carol. El arbol del viejo bosque. 2005. (SPA.). 32p. 18.95 *(978-84-7720-789-4(5))* Ediciones Obelisco ESP. Dist: Spanish Pubs., LLC.

Rehm, Carolyn. The Flower Pot Bunnies: Not A Good Place For A Nest. Schanck, Agnes, illus. 2004. 48p. (J). bds. 12.99 *(978-0-9755390-1-9(9))* Fifth Ave Pr.

Richards, Brenda. A Woodland Tale. 2011. 32p. pap. 21.99 *(978-1-4568-5708-0(8))* Xlibris Corp.

Riggs, Kate. Colors of Nature. Paolo, Domeniconi, illus. 2017. (ENG.). 14p. (J). (gr. -1 — 1). bds. 8.99 *(978-1-56846-299-8(9)*, 20160, Creative Education) Creative Co., The.

—Shapes All Around. Devernay, Laëtitia, illus. 2018. (ENG.). 14p. (J). (gr. -1-k). bds. 8.99 *(978-1-56846-317-9(0)*, 19651, Creative Editions) Creative Co., The.

Riley Guertin, Annemarie. Why Evergreens Keep Their Leaves. Garcia, Helena Perez, illus. 2019. (ENG.). 32p. (J). (gr. k-3). 16.99 *(978-1-64170-158-7(7)*, 550158) Familius LLC.

Robinson, Nikki Slade. Anywhere Artist. 2018. (ENG., Illus.). 40p. (J). (gr. -1-3). 18.99 *(978-1-328-70736-9(9)*, 1673035, Clarion Bks.) HarperCollins Pubs.

Rockwell, Anne. My Spring Robin. Rockwell, Harlow, illus. 2015. (ENG.). 24p. (J). (gr. -1-3). 16.99 *(978-1-4814-1137-0(3)*, Aladdin) Simon & Schuster Children's Publishing.

Rodricks, Marie. Razzle the Sunbeam. 2008. 68p. pap. 10.49 *(978-1-4343-9651-8(7))* AuthorHouse.

Rogers, Suzanne J. Cody Meets A Butterfly. 2008. 72p. pap. 19.95 *(978-1-4327-2069-8(4))* Outskirts Pr., Inc.

Ross, Patrick. Joseph & Snowy Joe Blue, 1 vol. Burcham, David, illus. 2009. 25p. pap. 24.95 *(978-1-61582-314-7(X))* PublishAmerica, Inc.

Ross, Thea. Molly Mole Takes a Nature Walk. 2004. (Lift-the-Flap Surprise on Every Spread! Ser.). 12p. (J). 5.99 *(978-1-59384-045-7(4))* Parklane Publishing.

MNO

Rossiter, Nan Parson. The Fo'c'sle: Henry Beston's Outermost House. 2012. (ENG., Illus.). 32p. (J). (gr. 5-18). 17.95 *(978-1-56792-433-6(6))* Godine, David R. Pub.

Ruley, Garrett. Hollin. 2011. (ENG.). 225p. pap. 15.00 *(978-0-557-55873-5(5))* Lulu Pr., Inc.

Russell-Gilmer, Phyllis A. Where Do Crickets Go When Winter Comes? Jones, Chamira, illus. 2009. 32p. (J). 16.95 *(978-1-934363-10-2(3))* Zoe Life Christian Communications.

Russell, Lyndsey & Hanson, Tippi. Rainbow Weaver. Hanson, Tippi, illus. 2007. (ENG., Illus.). 48p. (J). (gr. k-2). 11.95 *(978-1-84243-229-7(X))* Oldcastle Bks., Ltd. GBR. Dist: Independent Pubs. Group.

Ruth, Nick. The Breezes of Inspire. Concannon, Sue, illus. 2005. (Remin Chronicles: 2). (ENG.). 264p. (J). (gr. 3-7). 16.95 *(978-0-9745603-3-5(2))* Imaginator Pr.

Rylant, Cynthia. Life. Wenzel, Brendan, illus. 2017. (ENG.). 48p. (J). (gr. -1). 18.99 *(978-1-4814-5162-8(6)*, Beach Lane Bks.) Beach Lane Bks.

Sage, Cathryn. Destiny's Secret. 2012. 44p. (-18). pap. 21.99 *(978-1-4389-1530-2(6))* AuthorHouse.

Salmieri, Daniel. Bear & Wolf. 2018. (Illus.). 48p. (J). (gr. -1-3). 17.95 *(978-1-59270-238-1(4))* Enchanted Lion Bks., LLC.

Salwey, Kenny. Muskrat for Supper: Exploring the Natural World with the Last River Rat. 2012. (ENG., Illus.). 260p. (J). (gr. 4-9). pap. 12.95 *(978-1-55591-567-4(1))* Fulcrum Publishing.

Sams II, Carl R. & Stoick, Jean, photos by. When Snowflakes Fall. 2009. (ENG., Illus.). 14p. bds. 7.95 *(978-0-9770108-9-9(9))* Sams, II, Carl R. Photography, Inc.

Santos de las Heras, José María. Cachicos. 2007. 176p. pap. 20.95 *(978-1-84799-885-9(2))* Lulu Pr., Inc.

Santos, Penelope. Paula's Pinecone, 1 vol. 2015. (Rosen REAL Readers: STEM & STEAM Collection). (ENG.). 8p. (gr. k-1). pap. 5.46 *(978-1-4994-9545-4(5)*, 0787829b-18bf-4757-9475-002a85da5113, Rosen Classroom) Rosen Publishing Group, Inc., The.

Scanlon, Liz Garton. In the Canyon. Wolff, Ashley, illus. 2015. (ENG.). 40p. (J). (gr. -1-3). 17.99 *(978-1-4814-0348-1(6)*, Beach Lane Bks.) Beach Lane Bks.

Scelsa, Greg. Rainbow of Colors. Faulkner, Stacey, ed. Sexton, Brenda, illus. 2006. (J). pap. 2.99 *(978-1-59198-351-4(7))* Creative Teaching Pr., Inc.

—The World Is a Rainbow. Faulkner, Stacey, ed. Schneider, Christine, illus. 2006. (J). pap. 2.99 *(978-1-59198-319-4(3))* Creative Teaching Pr., Inc.

Schkolnik, Saul. Cuentos Ecologicos. Cardemil, Carmen, illus. 2nd ed. 2003. (la Orilla del Viento Ser.).Tr. of Ecological Tales. (SPA.). 56p. (J). (gr. 3-7). per. *(978-968-16-4757-5(2)*, FC6400) Fondo de Cultura Economica MEX. Dist: Lectorum Pubns., Inc.

Schmidt, Hans-Christian & Bieber, Hartmut. The Wondrous Day. 2004. (Illus.). 18p. (J). 10.99 *(978-1-59384-047-1(0))* Parklane Publishing.

Schwartz, Betty Ann. One to Ten... & Back Again. Shakir, Susie, illus. 2009. 24p. bds. 12.99 *(978-0-8249-1436-3(8)*, Ideals Pubns.) Worthy Publishing.

Schwartz, Tom. How Mother Nature Flowered the Fields. 2006. (Illus.). 120p. (J). per. 14.95 *(978-1-57545-102-2(6)*, Reagent Pr. Echo) RP Media.

Segarra, Angelo M. Coca Finds a Shell. Segarra, Kirstie, ed. Segarra, Angelo M., illus. 2004. (Illus.). 24p. (J). 14.95 *(978-0-9752664-0-3(3))* Segarra, Angelo.

Senir, Mirik & Shubow, Mary Jane. When I First Held You: A Lullaby from Israel. 2009. (J). lib. bdg. 17.95 *(978-0-7613-5096-5(9)*, Kar-Ben Publishing) Lerner Publishing Group.

Seton, Ernest Thompson. The Biography of a Silver Fox. 2005. pap. 24.95 *(978-1-885529-39-8(2))* Stevens Publishing.

Seven, John. Gorilla Gardener: How to Help Nature Take over the World. Christy, Jana, illus. 2017. (Wee Rebel Ser.). (ENG.). 44p. (J). (gr. -1). 16.95 *(978-1-945665-00-4(9))* Manic D Pr.

Shearer, Tony. The Praying Flute: Song of the Earth Mother. rev. ed. 2006. (Illus.). 96p. pap. 16.95 *(978-0-87961-268-9(1))* Naturegraph Pubs., Inc.

Sherrell, Deborah. Baby Lauren & Theodore,hardcover. 2007. (Illus.). (J). bds. 17.95 *(978-0-9779643-5-2(3))* Healing Tree Arts.

Shields, Kathleen J. Hamilton Troll Meets Elwood Woodpecker. Klug, Leigh A. & Bryant, Carol W., illus. 5th ed. 2013. 36p. 14.00 *(978-0-9882745-4-9(X))* Erin Go Bragh Publishing.

Simler, Isabelle. The Blue Hour. 2017. (ENG., Illus.). 42p. (J). 19.00 *(978-0-8028-5488-9(5)*, Eerdmans Bks For Young Readers) Eerdmans, William B. Publishing Co.

Simler, Isabelle, illus. A Web. 2018. (ENG.). 48p. (J). 16.99 *(978-1-4413-2843-4(2)*, a81ee573-86b8-4cb0-9ebc-1e5d399ac580) Peter Pauper Pr. Inc.

Skipper, Cecil. The Deer Lick. 2004. 166p. (YA). pap. 12.95 *(978-0-595-30949-8(6))* iUniverse, Inc.

Smith, Brooke. The Keeper of Wild Words: (Nature for Kids, Exploring Nature with Children) Kloepper, Madeline, illus. 2020. (ENG.). 62p. (J). (gr. k-3). 18.99 *(978-1-4521-7073-2(8))* Chronicle Bks. LLC.

Smith, David. Nature's Garden. 2009. 132p. 22.50 *(978-1-60693-169-1(5)*, Eloquent Bks.) Strategic Book Publishing & Rights Agency (SBPRA).

Sparks, Shanti. Honey & the Sunset. 2008. (Illus.). 38p. (J). pap. 9.00 *(978-0-8059-7553-6(5))* Dorrance Publishing Co., Inc.

Spelvin, Justin. Take a Trip with Trucktown! Shannon, David et al, illus. 2011. (Jon Scieszka's Trucktown Ser.). (ENG.). 24p. (J). (gr. -1-3). pap. 4.99 *(978-1-4169-4181-1(9)*, Simon & Schuster Bks. For Young Readers) Simon & Schuster Bks. For Young Readers.

Stack, Kevin W. The Great Oak Tree. 2008. (Illus.). 32p. pap. 12.99 *(978-1-4389-1856-3(9))* AuthorHouse.

Stauffer, Sharon. Cornfield Baby: And Other Nature Surprises. 2003. (Illus.). 179p. 8.40 *(978-0-7399-2314-6(5)*, 2344) Rod & Staff Pubs., Inc.

Stein, David Ezra. Honey. Stein, David Ezra, illus. 2018. (ENG., Illus.). 32p. (J). (-k). 16.99 *(978-1-5247-3786-3(0)*, Nancy Paulsen Books) Penguin Young Readers Group.

Steinberg, Laya. All Around Me, I See. Arbo, Cris, illus. 2005. (Sharing Nature with Children Book Ser.). 32p. (J). 16.95 *(978-1-58469-068-9(2))*; pap. 8.95 *(978-1-58469-069-6(0))* Take Heart Pubns.

Stiverson, Charlotte L. Nellie's Walk. Aitken, Kati, illus. 2016. (J). *(978-1-935864-62-2(9))* Oncology Nursing Society.

Stone, Jodi. I Want to Catch a Dragonfly. 2008. 28p. per. 24.95 *(978-1-4241-8770-6(2))* America Star Bks.

Stuart, Tara. Trees: A Tara's Tale about Being Yourself. 2006. (Illus.). (J). bds. 15.00 *(978-0-9765060-3-4(3))* TouchSmart Publishing, LLC.

Sudo, Kumiko. Coco-Chan's Kimono. Sudo, Kumiko, illus. 2010. (ENG., Illus.). 32p. (J). (gr. k-2). 16.95 *(978-1-933308-26-5(5))* Breckling Pr.

Sullivan, Silvia. Hip Hip Hurray We Found Teddy: A Book Series to Teach Children Practical Life Skills & Eco-Friendly Skills. 2008. 32p. pap. 15.48 *(978-1-4343-5897-4(6))* AuthorHouse.

Tarsky, Sue. Fall in the Country. Lordon, Claire, illus. 2019. (Taking a Walk Ser.). (ENG.). 32p. (J). (gr. -1-3). 16.99 *(978-0-8075-7729-5(4)*, 807577294) Whitman, Albert & Co.

Tarter, Mildred. Alexis Uses the Elements of Nature. 2011. 24p. pap. 16.49 *(978-1-4389-6879-7(5))* AuthorHouse.

Tate, Suzanne. Skippy Scallop: A Tale of Bright Blue Eyes. Melvin, James, illus. 2003. (Suzanne Tate's Nature Ser.: No. 26). 28p. (J). pap. 4.95 *(978-1-878405-43-2(8))* Nags Head Art, Inc.

Thomas, Isabel. Moth: An Evolution Story. Egneus, Daniel, illus. 2019. (ENG.). 48p. (J). 18.99 *(978-1-5476-0020-5(9)*, 900195004, Bloomsbury Children's Bks.) Bloomsbury Publishing USA.

Thomas, Shelley Moore. From Tree to Sea. Neal, Christopher Silas, illus. 2019. (ENG.). 32p. (J). (gr. -1-3). 18.99 *(978-1-4814-9531-8(3)*, Simon & Schuster/Paula Wiseman Bks.) Simon & Schuster/Paula Wiseman Bks.

Thompson, Lauren. Mouse's First Fall. Erdogan, Buket, illus. 2010. (Classic Board Bks.). (ENG.). 34p. (J). (gr. -1 — 1). bds. 8.99 *(978-1-4169-9477-0(7)*, Little Simon) Little Simon.

—Mouse's First Fall. 2006. (ENG., Illus.). 32p. (J). (gr. -1-1). 18.99 *(978-0-689-85837-6(X)*, Simon & Schuster Bks. For Young Readers) Simon & Schuster Bks. For Young Readers.

—Mouse's First Spring. Erdogan, Buket, illus. 2012. (Classic Board Bks.). (ENG.). 34p. (J). (gr. -1-3). bds. 8.99 *(978-1-4424-3431-8(7)*, Little Simon) Little Simon.

—Mouse's First Spring. Erdogan, Buket, illus. 2005. (ENG.). 32p. (J). (gr. -1-3). 19.99 *(978-0-689-85838-3(8)*, Simon & Schuster Bks. For Young Readers) Simon & Schuster Bks. For Young Readers.

Thorpe, Rochelle O'Neal. Gabe's Nantucket Adventure: Daffodils, Dogs, & Cars. Nakell, Eugenie, ed. Margolis, Al, illus. l.t. ed. 2010. 28p. (YA). pap. 7.95 *(978-1-935706-02-1(0))* Wiggles Pr.

Ticktock Media, Ltd. Staff. Zoom into Space with the Shiny Red Rocket. 2009. (Touch & Feel Fun Ser.). (ENG.). 10p. (J). (gr. k — 1). bds. 5.95 *(978-1-84696-812-9(7)*, TickTock Books) Octopus Publishing Group GBR. Dist: Independent Pubs. Group.

Tietz, Heather. Yes, Jesus Loves You. Miller, Nancy, illus. 2009. 20p. (J). (gr. k-4). 14.95 *(978-0-8091-6743-2(3)*, Ambassador Bks.) Paulist Pr.

Tillman, Nancy. On the Night You Were Born. (ENG., Illus.). 32p. (J). 2017. bds. 9.99 *(978-1-250-16401-8(X)*, 900186655) 2010. bds. 7.99 *(978-0-312-60155-3(7)*, 900064146) Feiwel & Friends.

—On the Night You Were Born, 1 vol., Set. unabr. ed. 2012. (ENG., Illus.). 32p. (J). (— 1). pap. 12.99 *(978-1-4272-2646-4(6)*, 900087155) Macmillan Audio.

Todd, Pamela. The Blind Faith Hotel. 2008. (ENG.). 320p. (YA). (gr. 7-18). 16.99 *(978-1-4169-5494-1(5)*, McElderry, Margaret K. Bks.) McElderry, Margaret K. Bks.

Townsend, Wendy. The Sundown Rule. 2011. (J). (gr. 5-9). 18.95 *(978-1-60898-099-4(5))* namelos llc.

Turnbull, Victoria. Pandora. 2017. (ENG., Illus.). 32p. (J). (gr. -1-3). 17.99 *(978-0-544-94733-7(9)*, 1659597, Clarion Bks.) HarperCollins Pubs.

Twigger, J. Nicci & Her Amazing Adventure. 2008. (Illus.). 40p. pap. 18.49 *(978-1-4389-1295-0(1))* AuthorHouse.

Underwood, Deborah. Outside In: A Caldecott Honor Award Winner. Derby, Cindy, illus. 2020. (ENG.). 40p. (J). (gr. -1-3). 17.99 *(978-1-328-86682-0(3)*, 1695831, Clarion Bks.) HarperCollins Pubs.

Updike, John. A Child's Calendar. Updike, John & Hyman, Trina Schart, illus. 2004. (J). (gr. k-4). 28.95 incl. audio compact disk *(978-1-59112-932-5(X))* Live Oak Media.

—A Child's Calendar. Hyman, Trina Schart, illus. unabr. ed. 2004. (J). (gr. k-4). 25.95 incl. audio *(978-1-59112-472-6(7))* Live Oak Media.

Valverde, Mikel. Paula en Nueva York. 2006. (SPA., Illus.). 32p. (J). (gr. 6-8). 14.99 *(978-1-933032-15-3(4))* Lectorum Pubns., Inc.

Van Pelt, Jason. The Color Wheel. 2013. 28p. pap. 24.95 *(978-1-4626-9697-0(X))* America Star Bks.

Vanalstine, Carrie. Frizzy Izzy Yelp! 2012. 32p. pap. 11.95 *(978-1-4685-4609-5(0))* AuthorHouse.

Vrba, Christina. Good Night Connecticut. Rosen, Anne, illus. 2009. (Good Night Our World Ser.). (ENG.). 20p. (J). (gr. k — 1). bds. 9.95 *(978-1-60219-035-1(6))* Good Night Bks.

Wagner Lloyd, Megan. Finding Wild. Halpin, Abigail, illus. 2016. 32p. (J). (gr. -1-2). 18.99 *(978-1-101-93281-0(3)*, Knopf Bks. for Young Readers) Random Hse. Children's Bks.

Walker, Anna. Florette. Walker, Anna, illus. 2018. (ENG., Illus.). 40p. (J). (gr. -1-3). 17.99 *(978-0-544-87683-5(0)*, 1649580, Clarion Bks.) HarperCollins Pubs.

Walker, Johnny. The Planet Blue: The Adventures of Harry Lee & Bingo. 2011. (ENG.). 24p. pap. 11.32 *(978-1-4567-4879-1(3))* AuthorHouse.

Walrath, Dana. I Am a Bird. Kim, Jaime, illus. 2018. (ENG.). 40p. (J). (gr. -1-3). 17.99 *(978-1-4814-8002-4(2))* Simon & Schuster Children's Publishing.

Walters, Jennifer Marino. Surprising Spring. Nez, John, illus. 2016. (Seasons Ser.). (ENG.). 24p. (J). (gr. -1 — 1). lib. bdg. 25.32 *(978-1-63440-047-3(X)*, 3ce02d63-4297-4c10-b965-f130b6cfd455, Rocking Chair Kids) Red Chair Pr.

Ward, Terri & Ward, Tom. Aunt Tami's Strawberry Farm. Kindt, Rita, illus. 2010. 38p. pap. 14.50 *(978-1-60693-935-2(1)*, Eloquent Bks.) Strategic Book Publishing & Rights Agency (SBPRA).

Welles, Lee. Gaia Girls Way of Water. Coogan, Carol, illus. 2007. (Gaia Girls Ser.: 2). (ENG.). 336p. (YA). (gr. 4-7). pap. 24.95 *(978-1-933609-03-4(6))* Chelsea Green Publishing.

—Gaia Girls: Way of Water. Coogan, Carol, illus. 2007. (Gaia Girls Ser.). (ENG.). 336p. (J). (gr. 4-7). 18.95 *(978-1-933609-02-7(8))* Chelsea Green Publishing.

Wenzel, Brendan, illus. A Stone Sat Still. 2019. (ENG.). 56p. (J). (gr. -1-k). 17.99 *(978-1-4521-7318-4(4))* Chronicle Bks. LLC.

Weston Woods Staff, creator. Fletcher & the Falling Leaves. 2011. 38.75 *(978-0-545-19710-6(4))* Weston Woods Studios, Inc.

—Henry Hikes to Fitchburg. 2011. 38.75 *(978-0-439-90698-2(9))*; 18.95 *(978-0-439-90696-8(2))* Weston Woods Studios, Inc.

Whincup, Sara. The St John's Cross Spider. Yapsangco, Kenn, illus. 2015. (ENG.). 28p. (J). pap. 28.22 *(978-1-5035-0985-6(0))* Xlibris Corp.

Wilke, Cheryl Weibye. At the Cabin: In the Woods by the Lake up North. Stouffer, Rebecca, illus. 2017. (J). pap. *(978-0-9835189-7-6(1))* Raven Productions, Inc.

Williams, Mavis E. A Cricket. 2009. 24p. pap. 11.99 *(978-1-4389-7714-0(X))* AuthorHouse.

Williams, S. L. Polka-Dot Maddy's Birthday Fun: Colors of the Rainbow. 2008. 36p. pap. 24.95 *(978-1-60672-908-3(X))* America Star Bks.

Wilshire, Florence. All from the Skies. 2005. 82p. pap. 18.08 *(978-1-4116-3114-4(5))* Lulu Pr., Inc.

Wilson, Jacqui. Little Johnny's Faith Adventures: Creation Curiosity! 2012. 30p. pap. 15.95 *(978-1-4497-5994-0(7)*, WestBow Pr.) Author Solutions, LLC.

Winnie the Pooh. The Close-up Day. 2010. 16p. 5.99 *(978-1-4231-3096-3(0))* Disney Pr.

Wisdom, Eileen Mary. Harry Meets Mathilda, 5 bks., Bk.1. Saunders, M. D., illus. 2007. 36p. (J). pap. 20.00 *(978-0-9771102-2-3(2))* Pelican Pr. Pensacola.

Wissinger, Tamera Will. Gone Camping: A Novel in Verse. Cordell, Matthew, illus. 2017. (ENG.). 112p. (J). (gr. 1-4). 15.99 *(978-0-544-63873-0(5)*, 1620560, Clarion Bks.) HarperCollins Pubs.

Wolff, Ashley. Baby Bear Sees Blue. Wolff, Ashley, illus. 2012. (Baby Bear Ser.). (ENG., Illus.). 40p. (J). (gr. -1-1). 18.99 *(978-1-4424-1306-1(9)*, Beach Lane Bks.) Beach Lane Bks.

Wood, Douglas. Grandad's Prayers of the Earth. Lynch, P. J., illus. 2009. 32p. pap. 6.99 *(978-0-7636-1865-0(9))*; (ENG.). (J). (gr. 1-4). pap. 8.99 *(978-0-7636-4675-2(X))* Candlewick Pr.

—Where the Sunrise Begins. Popp, K. Wendy, illus. 2010. (ENG.). 32p. (J). (gr. -1-3). 17.99 *(978-0-689-86172-7(9)*, Simon & Schuster Bks. For Young Readers) Simon & Schuster Bks. For Young Readers.

Woods, Shirley & Wood, Muriel. Tooga: Story of a Polar Bear, 1 vol. 2004. (ENG., Illus.). 32p. (J). (gr. 3-4). pap. 7.95 *(978-1-55041-900-9(5)*, e6c34d50-a508-4bd7-a89a-c4051840ab4d) Clockwise Pr. CAN. Dist: Firefly Bks., Ltd.

Wuehr, Tina L. Field Dance. Brown, Mari, illus. 2005. 18p. (J). (gr. -1-3). *(978-0-9739962-0-3(X))* Wuehr, Tina.

Yang, Angela. Out of the Dark. 2012. 166p. pap. 12.85 *(978-0-578-09356-7(1))* Yang, Jennifer.

Yee, Wong Herbert. Abracadabra! Magic with Mouse & Mole (Reader) 2010. (Mouse & Mole Story Ser.). (ENG., Illus.). 48p. (J). (gr. -1-3). pap. 4.99 *(978-0-547-40621-3(5)*, 1428499, Clarion Bks.) HarperCollins Pubs.

Yerushalmi, Miriam. Let's Go Camping & Discover Our Nature. Perez, Esther Ido, illus. 2007. 28p. (J). (gr. 2-4). 16.50 *(978-0-911643-38-1(9))* Aura Printing, Inc.

—Let's Go Camping & Discover Our Nature. Perez, Esther Ido, illus. 2017. (ENG.). 30p. (J). (gr. 2-4). 22.00 *(978-1-934152-56-0(0))* Sane.

Yost, B. L. Have You Ever Seen a Wild Bird Dance? Perkins, Chelsea, illus. 2008. 16p. pap. 24.95 *(978-1-60703-127-7(2))* America Star Bks.

Young, Sunshine. Mother Earth's ABC. 2007. (J). spiral bd. 14.95 *(978-0-9796180-2-4(9))* Williams, Benjamin Publishing.

Zaidi, Nadeem, illus. Baby Mozart: Musica Por Todas Partes. 2005. (Baby Einstein: Libros de Carton Ser.). (SPA.). 16p. (J). (gr. -1). bds. *(978-970-718-309-4(8)*, Silver Dolphin en Español) Advanced Marketing, S. de R. L. de C. V.

NATURE IN LITERATURE

see also Nature—Poetry

Collins, Carolyn Strom & Eriksson, Christina Wyss. Inside the Secret Garden: A Treasury of Crafts, Recipes, & Activities. Tudor, Tasha, illus. 2004. 130p. (J). (gr. 2-8). reprint ed. 25.00 *(978-0-7567-7630-5(9))* DIANE Publishing Co.

Griffin Llanas, Sheila. Nature Poetry: Make Me a Picture of the Sun, 1 vol. 2014. (Pure Poetry Ser.). (ENG., Illus.). 128p. (gr. 9-10). lib. bdg. 35.93 *(978-0-7660-4244-5(8)*, a5cd3846-7f27-4e73-9ca3-963acb74f09c) Enslow Publishing, LLC.

NATURE IN ORNAMENT

see Design, Decorative

NATURE PHOTOGRAPHY

see also Photography of Animals

Fielder, John, photos by. Do You See What I See? 2006. (Illus.). (J). 14.99 *(978-1-56579-554-9(7))* Fielder, John Publishing.

Martin, Jacqueline Briggs. Snowflake Bentley. 2004. (Illus.). (J). (gr. -1-3). spiral bd. *(978-0-616-01714-2(6))* Canadian National Institute for the Blind/Institut National Canadien pour les Aveugles.

—Snowflake Bentley: A Caldecott Award Winner. Azarian, Mary, illus. 2009. (ENG.). 32p. (J). (gr. -1-3). pap. 8.99 *(978-0-547-24829-5(6)*, 1100744, Clarion Bks.) HarperCollins Pubs.

McAdam, Claudia Cangilla. Do You See What I See? Texas. 2007. (Illus.). (J). (gr. 3-7). 14.95 *(978-1-56579-589-1(X)*, Westcliffe Pubs.) Bower Hse.

Swinow, Linda. Take on Alaska! a Photophonics Reader. 2009. 28p. pap. 12.99 *(978-1-4389-1394-0(X))* AuthorHouse.

Weston Woods Staff, creator. Snowflake Bentley. 2011. 18.95 *(978-0-545-31414-5(3))*; 38.75 *(978-0-545-31415-2(1))* Weston Woods Studios, Inc.

NATURE—POETRY

Alexander, Cecil F. All Things Bright & Beautiful. Bryan, Ashley, illus. 2010. (ENG.). 40p. (J). (gr. -1-3). 19.99 *(978-1-4169-8939-4(0)*, Atheneum Bks. for Young Readers) Simon & Schuster Children's Publishing.

Brown, Margaret Wise. Nibble Nibble: An Easter & Springtime Book for Kids. Minor, Wendell, illus. 2007. (ENG.). 32p. (J). (gr. -1-3). 17.99 *(978-0-06-059208-0(7)*, HarperCollins) HarperCollins Pubs.

Camden, Marian Louise. An Earth Child's Book of Verse. Wright, Diane Beem, illus. 2011. 32p. pap. *(978-1-77067-695-4(3))* FriesenPress.

Canetti, Yanitzia. Imagine a Better World. 2010. (Illus.). 32p. (J). pap. 9.99 *(978-1-59835-284-9(9)*, BrickHouse Education) Cambridge BrickHouse, Inc.

Davies, Nicola. Outside Your Window: A First Book of Nature. Hearld, Mark, illus. 2012. (ENG.). 108p. (J). (gr. -1-2). 22.00 *(978-0-7636-5549-5(X))* Candlewick Pr.

Frost, Helen. Step Gently Out. Lieder, Rick, illus. 2018. (ENG.). 32p. (J). (-k). 8.99 *(978-0-7636-9517-0(3))* Candlewick Pr.

—Sweep up the Sun. Lieder, Rick, illus. 2015. (ENG.). 32p. (J). (-k). 15.99 *(978-0-7636-6904-1(0))* Candlewick Pr.

—Sweep up the Sun. Lieder, Rick, illus. 2018. (ENG.). 32p. (J). (-k). 6.99 *(978-0-7636-9673-3(0))* Candlewick Pr.

Giovanni, Nikki. The Sun Is So Quiet. Bryan, Ashley, illus. 2014. (ENG.). 32p. (J). (gr. -1-3). 8.99 *(978-1-250-04669-7(6)*, 900131698) Square Fish.

Lewis, J. Patrick. National Geographic Book of Nature Poetry: More Than 200 Poems with Photographs That Float, Zoom, & Bloom! 2015. (Illus.). 192p. (J). (gr. -1-k). 24.99 *(978-1-4263-2094-1(9)*, National Geographic Kids) Disney Publishing Worldwide.

Nash, Myrna Lee. Spinman, Katydid & Bump: A Spider Vane Collection. Johnson, Sharon, illus. 2003. 48p. (YA). (gr. 4-10). 11.95 *(978-0-9724549-0-2(X))* Chapter & Verse Pr.

Paolilli, Paul & Brewer, Dan. Silver Seeds. 2014. 32p. pap. 7.00 *(978-1-61003-311-4(6))* Center for the Collaborative Classroom.

Randolph, Joanne, ed. Poems about Nature, 1 vol. 2018. (Poet's Journal: Exploring Nature & the Seasons Ser.). (ENG.). 24p. (gr. 2-4). 26.27 *(978-1-5081-9701-0(6)*, 87164b80-e37a-47d0-89b4-5d886ca7e01b); pap. 9.25 *(978-1-5081-9702-7(4)*, 20417174-75d9-467d-b8bd-969cea2ddd9a) Rosen Publishing Group, Inc., The. (Windmill Bks.).

Robbins, Karen. Care for Our World. Ball, Alexandra, illus. 2012. (ENG.). 36p. (J). (gr. -1-3). 16.95 *(978-1-935414-61-2(5))* Compendium, Inc., Publishing & Communications.

Scanlon, Liz Garton. All the World. Frazee, Marla, illus. 2009. (ENG.). 40p. (J). (gr. -1-3). 18.99 *(978-1-4169-8580-8(8)*, Beach Lane Bks.) Beach Lane Bks.

—All the World. Frazee, Marla, illus. 2015. (Classic Board Bks.). (ENG.). 44p. (J). (gr. -1-k). bds. 7.99 *(978-1-4814-3121-7(8)*, Little Simon) Little Simon.

—All the World. Frazee, Marla, illus. 2011. (J). (gr. -1-2). 29.95 *(978-0-545-32716-9(4))* Weston Woods Studios, Inc.

Sidman, Joyce. Ubiquitous: Celebrating Nature's Survivors. Prange, Beckie, illus. 2010. (ENG.). 40p. (J). (gr. 1-4). 17.99 *(978-0-618-71719-4(6)*, 515198, Clarion Bks.) HarperCollins Pubs.

White, Mandy. Imagine with Me. 2012. 24p. pap. 12.45 *(978-1-4525-0714-9(7))* Balboa Pr.

Yolen, Jane. Shape Me a Rhyme: Nature's Forms in Poetry. Stemple, Jason, photos by. 2015. (ENG., Illus.). 32p. (J). (gr. 1-4). 7.99 *(978-1-62091-791-6(2)*, Wordsong) Highlights Pr., c/o Highlights for Children, Inc.

NATURE POETRY

see Nature—Poetry

NATURE STUDY

see also Animals—Habits and Behavior; Botany; Nature Photography; Zoology

Ahrens, Niki. Hack Your Backyard: Discover a World of Outside Fun with Science Buddies (r). Ahrens, Niki, photos by. 2019. (ENG., Illus.). 32p. (J). (gr. 2-5). pap. 8.99 *(978-1-5415-5717-8(4)*, cd54a986-bf19-4a32-8f1c-71d6c1192ce8); 27.99 *(978-1-5415-3915-0(X)*, 4aa57832-bbc6-4429-a592-ec16090159e1) Lerner Publishing Group. (Lerner Pubns.).

Baggott, Stella, illus. Baby's Very First Outdoors Book. 2009. (Baby Board Bks). 10p. (J). bds. 6.99 *(978-0-7945-2468-5(0)*, Usborne) EDC Publishing.

Bauer, Cheryl. Our Visit to the Nature Center: Nuestra Visita Al Centro Ecologico. 2003. (SPA.). (J). lib. bdg. 22.00 *(978-1-59298-013-0(9))* Beaver's Pond Pr., Inc.

Beaton, Clare. Read, Learn & Create — The Nature Craft Book. Beaton, Clare, illus. 2019. (ENG., Illus.). 32p. (J). (gr. 1-4). lib. bdg. 17.99 *(978-1-58089-843-0(2))* Charlesbridge Publishing, Inc.

Beaton, Clare & Haig, Rudi. Read, Learn & Create — The Ocean Craft Book. Beaton, Clare, illus. 2019. (ENG., Illus.). 32p. (J). (gr. 1-4). 17.99 *(978-1-58089-941-3(2))* Charlesbridge Publishing, Inc.

Buckley, Arabella. Plant Life in Field & Garden. 2008. 88p. pap. 11.95 *(978-1-59915-273-8(8))* Yesterday's Classics.

Buckley, Arabella B. By Pond & River. 2008. (Illus.). 60p. pap. 9.95 *(978-1-59915-272-1(X))* Yesterday's Classics.

—Insect Life. 2008. (Illus.). 88p. pap. 11.95 *(978-1-59915-276-9(2))* Yesterday's Classics.

—Wild Life in Woods & Fields (Yesterday's Classics) 2008. (Illus.). 60p. pap. 9.95 *(978-1-59915-271-4(1))* Yesterday's Classics.

Burris, Judy & Richards, Wayne. Nature's Notes: Bite-sized Learning & Projects for All Ages. 2012. (ENG., Illus.). 232p. spiral bd. *(978-1-60755-477-6(1))* Willow Creek Pr., Inc.

Burroughs, John. Fresh Fields. Fuert, L. A. & Woodbury et al, Charles H., illus. 2008. 196p. pap. *(978-1-4099-2065-6(8))* Dodo Pr.

—Fresh Fields. 2008. 348p. 32.95 *(978-1-4344-9784-0(4))*; per. 19.95 *(978-1-4344-9783-3(6))* Wildside Pr., LLC.

Cornell, Kari. Nature up Close. 2016. (Illus.). 24p. (J). pap. *(978-0-87659-703-3(7))* Gryphon Hse., Inc.

Cycles in Nature, 12 vols. 2015. (Cycles in Nature Ser.). (ENG.). 24p. (J). (gr. 1-2). lib. bdg. 145.62 (978-1-4824-1636-7(0), 884ce7ec-ee28-4870-bdac-4df6da5ec292) Stevens, Gareth Publishing LLLP.

Dael, Do Van. An Earthly Walk: A Season-ing Story. 2012. (Illus.). 20p. pap. 19.82 (978-1-4685-8629-9(7)) AuthorHouse.

Ferrara, Cos. Anna Comstock: A Love Affair with Nature. 2004. (Girls Explore, Reach for the Stars Ser.). (Illus.). 112p. (J). 20.00 (978-0-9749456-1-3(7), Girls Explore) Girls Explore LLC.

Fitzsimmons, Kakie. Anna Goes Hiking: Discover Hiking & Explore Nature. l.t. ed. 2007. (Bur Bur & Friends Ser.). (Illus.). 40p. (J). (gr. 3-7). lib. bdg. 14.95 (978-0-9777121-7-5(6)) IGI Pr.

Fleischman, Paul. Eyes Wide Open: Going Behind the Environmental Headlines. 2014. (ENG., Illus.). 208p. (YA). (gr. 9). 17.99 (978-0-7636-7102-0(9)); pap. 12.99 (978-0-7636-7545-5(8)) Candlewick Pr.

Franklin, Devin. Put on Your Owl Eyes: Open Your Senses & Discover Nature's Secrets; Mapping, Tracking & Journaling Activities. 2019. (ENG., Illus.). 160p. (J). (gr. 3-8). pap. 16.95 (978-1-63586-022-1(9), 626022) Storey Publishing, LLC.

Fredericks, Anthony D. Simple Nature Experiments with Everyday Materials. Zweifel, Frances, illus. 2004. 128p. (J). (gr. 4-8). reprint ed. pap. 6.00 (978-0-7567-7727-2(5)) DIANE Publishing Co.

Ganeri, Anita. Hunt for Food. (Illus.). 32p. (YA). (gr. 4-18). lib. bdg. 27.10 (978-1-931983-88-4(7)) Chrysalis Education.

Glassman, Michael. Kinder Gardens: Games & Adventures, 1 vol. 2011. (ENG., Illus.). 64p. pap. 12.99 (978-0-7643-3811-3(0), 4145, Schiffer Publishing Ltd) Schiffer Publishing, Ltd.

Hands-On Nature. 2004. (Illus.). 96p. (J). (gr. -1-k). 11.95 (978-1-885358-65-3(2)); (gr. 1-2). 11.95 (978-1-885358-66-0(0)); (gr. 3-4). 11.95 (978-1-885358-67-7(9)) Rainbow Pubs. & Legacy Pr.

Harris, Nicholas & Joanna, Turner. El Porque de las Cosas: Naturaleza y Ciencia. (Coleccion Enciclopedia Ilustrada del Conocimiento).Tr. of Why Things Occur: Nature & Science. (SPA., Illus.). 64p. (J). (gr. 3-5). 7.96 (978-84-7630-749-6(7)) Editorial Libsa, S.A. ESP. Dist: Lectorum Pubns., Inc.

Hewitt, Ben. The Young Adventurer's Guide to (Almost) Everything: Build a Fort, Camp Like a Champ, Poop in the Woods — 45 Action-Packed Outdoor Act Ivities. Boushee, Luke, illus. 2019. 208p. (J). (gr. 3-7). 19.95 (978-1-61180-594-9(5), Roost Books) Shambhala Pubns., Inc.

Hickman, Pamela & Federation of Ontario Naturalists. Naturaleza Divertida. Shore, Judie, illus. (SPA.). 92p. (978-84-9754-095-7(6), 87821) Ediciones Oniro S.A.

—La Naturaleza y Tú. Shore, Judie, illus. (SPA.). 63p. (978-84-9754-106-0(5), 87822) Ediciones Oniro S.A.

Hoena, Blake A. If You Plant a Seed... & Other Nature Predictions. 2012. (If Bks.). (ENG.). 32p. (J). (gr. 1-2). pap. 48.60 (978-1-4296-9252-6(9), 18505, Capstone Pr.) Capstone.

Holt, Rinehart and Winston Staff. Holt Science & Technology Chapter 19: Life Science: Cycles in Nature. 5th ed. 2004. (Illus.). pap. 12.86 (978-0-03-030229-9(3)) Holt McDougal.

Jennings, Terry J. Wildlife Watcher. 2014. (Illus.). 128p. (J). pap. (978-1-4351-5923-5(3)) Barnes & Noble, Inc.

Kochanoff, Peggy. You Can Be a Nature Detective, 1 vol. 2009. (ENG.). 64p. (J). pap. 14.00 (978-0-87842-556-3(X)) Mountain Pr. Publishing Co., Inc.

Larsen, Laurel. One Night in the Everglades. Turley, Joyce Mihran, illus. 2012. (Long Term Ecological Research Ser.). (ENG.). 32p. (J). (gr. 3-7). 15.95 (978-0-9817700-4-8(5)) Taylor Trade Publishing.

LernerClassroom Editors, ed. Teaching Guide for Fsn / Discovering Nature's Cycles. 2010. pap. 5.95 (978-0-7613-6683-6(0)) Lerner Publishing Group.

Levy, Duncan. Happy about Animals: An 8-Year-Old's View (Now 11) on Sharing the Earth. 2010. 48p. pap. 14.95 (978-1-60005-177-7(4)) Happy About.

Maynard, Christopher. Why Do Sunflowers Face the Sun? Questions Children Ask about Nature. (Why Bks.). (Illus.). 24p. (J). pap. 10.99 (978-0-590-24954-6(1)) Scholastic, Inc.

Miché, Mary. Nature's Patchwork Quilt: Understanding Habitats. Powell, Consie, illus. 2012. (ENG.). 32p. (J). (gr. 1-4). 24.94 (978-1-58469-169-3(7)) Take Heart Pubns.

Miche, Mary. Nature's Patchwork Quilt: Understanding Habitats, 1 vol. Powell, Consie, illus. 2012. 32p. (J). (gr. k-6). pap. 8.99 (978-1-58469-170-9(0), Dawn Pubns.) Sourcebooks, Inc.

Mitchell, Andrew. The Young Naturalist. Jacquemier, Sue & Bramwell, Martyn, eds. Jackson, Ian, illus. 2008. (Hobby Guides Ser.). 32p. (J). (gr. 5-9). pap. 6.99 (978-0-7945-2219-3(X), Usborne) EDC Publishing.

Nadeau, Isaac. Learning about Earth's Cycles with Graphic Organizers. (Graphic Organizers in Science Ser.). 24p. 2009. (gr. 3-4). 42.50 (978-1-61513-029-0(2)) 2005. (ENG., Illus.). (J). (gr. 4-5). lib. bdg. 26.27 (978-1-4042-2807-8(1), ada0811a-5be4-4a76-9321-4e8ca97250a0) 2005. (ENG., Illus.). (gr. 4-5). pap. 8.25 (978-1-4042-5044-4(1), 57687033-db1f-42ec-8e67-7ab5242f6329) Rosen Publishing Group, Inc., The. (PowerKids Pr.).

Orr, Richard. Richard Orr's Nature Cross-Sections. (Illus.). 30p. (J). pap. 22.99 (978-0-590-24633-0(X)) Scholastic, Inc.

Owen, Ruth. Science & Craft Projects with Insects, Spiders, & Other Minibeasts, 1 vol. 2013. (Get Crafty Outdoors Ser.). (ENG., Illus.). 32p. (J). (gr. 2-3). 30.27 (978-1-4777-0245-1(8), b38403ee-8fe0-4313-aa33-cf81a4f5796a); pap. 12.75 (978-1-4777-0253-6(9), 322fcfd3-8985-46ba-ba68-fb515ce013f5) Rosen Publishing Group, Inc., The. (PowerKids Pr.).

—Science & Craft Projects with Plants & Seeds, 1 vol. 2013. (Get Crafty Outdoors Ser.). (ENG., Illus.). 32p. (J). (gr. 2-3). 30.27 (978-1-4777-0247-5(4), 7d5a3b0c-ada1-4af8-a0f7-023eb105439d); pap. 12.75 (978-1-4777-0257-4(1), 145185e6-8bb6-44f9-9b9f-db3c07dde47a) Rosen Publishing Group, Inc., The. (PowerKids Pr.).

—Science & Craft Projects with Rocks & Soil, 1 vol. 2013. (Get Crafty Outdoors Ser.). (ENG., Illus.). 32p. (J). (gr. 2-3). 30.27 (978-1-4777-0246-8(6), f2a967f2-9843-4ea9-bb1c-19b48ee2cca2); pap. 12.75 (978-1-4777-0255-0(5), d0be45d2-a926-4418-bc9e-b297f565040d) Rosen Publishing Group, Inc., The. (PowerKids Pr.).

—Science & Craft Projects with Trees & Leaves, 1 vol. 2013. (Get Crafty Outdoors Ser.). (ENG., Illus.). 32p. (J). (gr. 2-3). 30.27 (978-1-4777-0248-2(2), 4ec901d9-4d27-4a64-8507-e1ed446eed8f); pap. 12.75 (978-1-4777-0259-8(8), be0f4e5a-740f-4a00-8387-bffd8afc2443) Rosen Publishing Group, Inc., The. (PowerKids Pr.).

—Science & Craft Projects with Weather, 1 vol. 2013. (Get Crafty Outdoors Ser.). (ENG., Illus.). 32p. (J). (gr. 2-3). 30.27 (978-1-4777-0244-4(X), e641b76d-7079-4d7f-be39-794b3ed78831); pap. 12.75 (978-1-4777-0251-2(2), 9a0898fe-fbdf-42c2-be9a-3d6c6a53639c) Rosen Publishing Group, Inc., The. (PowerKids Pr.).

—Science & Craft Projects with Wildlife, 1 vol. 2013. (Get Crafty Outdoors Ser.). (ENG., Illus.). 32p. (J). (gr. 2-3). 30.27 (978-1-4777-0243-7(1), 60790642-1f33-44c6-81b3-18daf481f743, PowerKids Pr.) Rosen Publishing Group, Inc., The.

Schwartz, David M. Animal Noses. Kuhn, Dwight, photos by. (Plants & Animals Ser.). (Illus.). 16p. (J). (gr. 1-3). pap. 2.99 (978-1-57471-321-3(3), 3030) Creative Teaching Pr., Inc.

Spilsbury, Louise & Spilsbury, Richard. A Nature Walk on the Farm, 1 vol. 2014. (Nature Walks Ser.). (ENG., Illus.). 24p. (J). (gr. -1-2). 25.99 (978-1-4846-0402-1(4), 126577, Heinemann) Capstone.

Stevens, Sky. Looking Close: Teaching Kids to Love the Earth. 2012. 32p. pap. 24.95 (978-1-4772-8446-9(X)) AuthorHouse.

Usborne Books Staff, creator. The Young Naturalist Kid Kit. 2007. (Kid Kits Ser.). (Illus.). 32p. (J). pap. 14.99 (978-1-60130-037-9(9), Usborne) EDC Publishing.

White, Nancy. Why Polar Bears Like Snow... & Flamingos Don't & Por qué hay osos polares en la nieve ... y no hay Flamencos: 6 English, 6 Spanish Adaptations, 122 vols., Vol. 2. 2011. (SPA.). (J). instr.'s gde. ed. 89.00 net. (978-1-4108-2222-2(2), 2222-2) Benchmark Education Co.

Williams, Brian. What about the Natural World. 2008. 40p. pap. (978-1-84810-071-8(X)) Miles Kelly Publishing, Ltd.

Woodward, John & Gray, Leon. Backyard. 2007. (Close-up Ser.). (Illus.). 32p. (J). (gr. 4-7). lib. bdg. (978-1-933834-13-9(7)) Brown Bear Books.

World Book, Inc. Staff, contrib. by. World Book's Science & Nature Guides, 12 vols. 2004. (World Book's Science & Nature Guides Ser.). (Illus.). 80p. (gr. 5-9). 319.00 (978-0-7166-4208-4(5), SKU 30119) World Bk., Inc.

NATURE STUDY—DICTIONARIES

Enciclopedia Juvenil de la Naturaleza. rev. ed. (SPA., Illus.). 256p. (J). 39.95 (978-84-272-5930-0(1), MO500) Molino, Editorial ESP. Dist: Continental Bk. Co., Inc.

NATURE STUDY—FICTION

Below, Halina. Chestnut Dreams, 1 vol. 2003. (ENG., Illus.). 40p. (J). (gr. -1-2). pap. 5.95 (978-1-55041-690-9(1), 4cc85dad-60ec-42a1-8cce-6eb02c85b388) Clockwise Pr. CAN. Dist: Firefly Bks., Ltd.

Blunt, Michele. A Walk Through Time. 2011. 36p. pap. 21.99 (978-1-4653-6182-0(0)) Xlibris Corp.

Burgess, Thornton W. Old Mother West Wind. (J). 16.95 (978-0-8488-0385-8(X)) Amereon Ltd.

Corwin, Jeff. Your Backyard Is Wild: Junior Explorer Series Book 1. 2009. 96p. (J). (gr. 1-3). 4.99 (978-0-14-241404-0(2), Puffin Books) Penguin Young Readers Group.

Donaldson, Julia. The Wrong Kind of Bark. Parsons, Garry, illus. 2005. (Red Bananas Ser.). (ENG.). 48p. (J). lib. bdg. (978-0-7787-1073-8(4)); (gr. 1-3). (978-0-7787-1089-9(0)) Crabtree Publishing Co.

Glaser, Linda. It's Spring! Swan, Susan, illus. 2003. (Celebrate the Seasons Ser.). (ENG.). 32p. (J). (gr. k-3). pap. 7.95 (978-0-7613-1345-8(1), 7b76d9d0-459e-4c2b-9c59-c0392071e43e, First Avenue Editions) Lerner Publishing Group.

Lewis, J. Patrick. Earth & Me, Our Family Tree: Nature's Creatures. Canyon, Christopher, illus. 2004. (Sharing Nature with Children Book Ser.). 36p. (J). (gr. -1-5). 16.95 (978-1-58469-031-3(3)); pap. 7.95 (978-1-58469-030-6(5)) Take Heart Pubns.

Li, Judith L. Ellie's Log: Exploring the Forest Where the Great Tree Fell. Herring, M. L., illus. 2013. (ENG.). 112p. (J). (gr. 3-6). pap. 17.95 (978-0-87071-696-6(4)) Oregon State Univ. Pr.

Li, Judith L. & Herring, M. L. Ricky's Atlas: Mapping a Land on Fire. 2016. (ENG., Illus.). 128p. (J). (gr. 3-6). pap. 17.95 (978-0-87071-842-7(8)) Oregon State Univ. Pr.

Mohler, Marie. Hearts of Trees. 2008. 32p. pap. 18.95 (978-1-4357-4614-5(7)) Lulu Pr., Inc.

—Little Bird's Earth Nest. 2008. 32p. 18.95 (978-1-4357-1711-4(2)) Lulu Pr., Inc.

Parish, Herman. Amelia Bedelia Hits the Trail. Avril, Lynne, illus. 2013. (I Can Read Level 1 Ser.). (ENG.). 32p. (J). (gr. -1-3). 16.99 (978-0-06-209527-5(7), Greenwillow Bks.) HarperCollins Pubs.

—Amelia Bedelia Hits the Trail. 2013. (Amelia Bedelia: I Can Read! Ser.). (J). lib. bdg. 13.55 (978-0-606-27135-6(X)) Turtleback.

Reader's Digest Staff. Let's Help the Earth. Brannon, Tom, illus. 2008. (Sesame Street Ser.). (ENG.). 12p. (J). (gr. -1-k). bds. 12.99 (978-0-7944-1696-6(9)) Reader's Digest Assn., Inc., The.

Wasson, Dawn K. T. Kuu Tutu. 2008. (ENG & HAW., Illus.). (J). lib. bdg. (978-0-9773495-8-6(6)) Na Kamalei Koolauloa Early Education Program.

Weber, Jen Funk. Been There, Done That: Reading Animal Signs, 1 vol. Gabriel, Andrea, illus. 2016. 39p. (J). (gr. k-1). (SPA.). pap. 11.95 (978-1-62855-741-1(9), f6f671b2-08d6-44d4-b97e-238d1d7afb41); (ENG.). 17.95 (978-1-62855-727-5(3)) Arbordale Publishing.

Yep, Laurence. Sweetwater. Noonan, Julia, illus. 2004. 191p. (J). pap. 5.99 (978-0-06-056029-4(0)) HarperCollins Pubs.

NAVAL ADMINISTRATION

see Naval Art and Science

see names of countries with the subhead Navy, e.g. United States—Navy

NAVAL AERONAUTICS

see Aeronautics, Military

NAVAL AIR BASES

see Air Bases

NAVAL AIRPLANES

see Airplanes, Military

NAVAL ART AND SCIENCE

see also Military Art and Science; Navigation; Sea Power; Shipbuilding; Signals and Signaling; Submarine Warfare; Submarines (Ships); Warships

Bolitho, Mark. Fold Your Own Origami Navy, 1 vol. 2013. (Origami Army Ser.). (ENG.). 32p. (J). (gr. 4-5). 30.17 (978-1-4777-1318-1(2), bf7d4de7-f93a-46c8-91c4-ba2855630374); pap. 12.75 (978-1-4777-1467-6(7), 27357e93-155b-4e06-aea9-a429de38b1ea) Rosen Publishing Group, Inc., The. (PowerKids Pr.).

Dougherty, Martin J. Sea Warfare, 1 vol. 2010. (Modern Warfare Ser.). (ENG., Illus.). 32p. (J). (gr. 3-5). lib. bdg. 28.67 (978-1-4339-2734-8(9), 45af19c0-ebb4-47bd-acbf-dcc391772edf) Stevens, Gareth Publishing LLLP.

Fold Your Own Origami Navy. 2013. (Origami Army Ser.). 32p. (J). (gr. 3-6). pap. 70.50 (978-1-4777-1468-3(5), PowerKids Pr.) Rosen Publishing Group, Inc., The.

Hobbs, Richard R. Naval Science 2 2: Maritime History, Leadership & Nautical Sciences for the NJROTC Student. 2nd ed. 2006. (ENG., Illus.). 360p. 36.95 (978-1-59114-366-6(7), P221125) Naval Institute Pr.

—Naval Science 3: Naval Knowledge & Skills for the NJROTC Student. 2003. (Illus.). 252p. 27.95 (978-1-55750-319-0(2)) Naval Institute Pr.

NAVAL BIOGRAPHY

see also Admirals; Sailors

also names of navies with the subdivision Biography, e.g. United States—Navy—Biography

Cawthorne, Nigel. Military Commanders: The 100 Greatest Throughout History. 2004. (Illus.). 208p. 18.95 (978-1-59270-029-5(2)) Enchanted Lion Bks., LLC.

—Victory: 100 Great Military Commanders. 2012. (Illus.). 208p. (J). (978-1-4351-4242-8(X)) Metro Bks.

NAVAL HISTORY

see also Military History; Naval Biography; Pirates

also names of countries with the subhead Navy or the subdivision History, Naval, e.g. United States—Navy; United States—History, Naval

Barrington, Richard. The History of Navies Around the World, 1 vol., 1. Saxena, Shalini, ed. 2013. (World's Armed Forces Ser.). (ENG.). 136p. (YA). (gr. 8-8). 38.84 (978-1-62275-142-6(6), a9b39e7c-9222-472b-a442-a0f9205bee36) Rosen Publishing Group, Inc., The.

Cawthorne, Nigel. Military Commanders: The 100 Greatest Throughout History. 2004. (Illus.). 208p. 18.95 (978-1-59270-029-5(2)) Enchanted Lion Bks., LLC.

—Victory: 100 Great Military Commanders. 2012. (Illus.). 208p. (J). (978-1-4351-4242-8(X)) Metro Bks.

Hobbs, Richard R. Naval Science 2 2: Maritime History, Leadership & Nautical Sciences for the NJROTC Student. 2nd ed. 2006. (ENG., Illus.). 360p. 36.95 (978-1-59114-366-6(7), P221125) Naval Institute Pr.

Hull, Robert. Trade & Warfare. 2007. (World of Ancient Greece Ser.). (Illus.). 32p. (YA). (gr. 3-6). lib. bdg. 27.10 (978-1-59771-062-6(8)) Sea-To-Sea Pubns.

Marsico, Katie. A a True Book - Engineering Wonders (NEW SUBSET): Warships. 2016. (True Book(tm) — Engineering Wonders Ser.). (ENG., Illus.). 48p. (J). pap. 6.95 (978-0-531-22274-4(8), Children's Pr.) Scholastic Library Publishing.

NAVAL SCIENCE

see Naval Art and Science

NAVAL SIGNALING

see Signals and Signaling

NAVAL UNIFORMS

see Military Uniforms

NAVAL WARFARE

see Naval Art and Science; Submarine Warfare

NAVIGATION

see also Harbors; Knots and Splices; Lighthouses; Naval Art and Science; Pilots and Pilotage; Radar; Shipwrecks; Signals and Signaling; Tides; Winds

Champion, Neil. Orienteering, 1 vol. 2009. (Get Outdoors Ser.). (ENG., Illus.). 32p. (gr. 4-4). (J). pap. 11.00 (978-1-4358-3052-3(0), da1e10ed-7078-4bfb-bdac-0a6d3bfd8e37, PowerKids Pr.); (YA). lib. bdg. 28.93 (978-1-4358-3044-8(X), ea7e2e27-062f-4bd6-b3f0-35dab72c488f) Rosen Publishing Group, Inc., The.

Faulkner, Nicholas. A Visual History of Ships & Navigation, 1 vol. 2016. (Visual History of the World Ser.). (ENG., Illus.). 96p. (J). (gr. 8-8). 38.80 (978-1-4994-6594-5(7), 6100f876-8ced-48ff-b09a-6b0a423d36a9) Rosen Publishing Group, Inc., The.

Gagne, Tammy. GPS Technology. 2018. (21st Century Inventions Ser.). (ENG.). 24p. (J). (gr. 1-1). pap. 8.95 (978-1-63517-792-3(8), 1635177928) North Star Editions.

—GPS Technology. 2018. (21st Century Inventions Ser.). (ENG., Illus.). 24p. (J). (gr. k-3). lib. bdg. 31.36 (978-1-5321-6041-7(0), 28714, Pop! Cody Koala) Pop!

Grack, Rachel. Navigation from Then to Now. 2019. (Sequence Developments in Technology Ser.). (ENG.). 32p. (J). (gr. 2-5). (978-1-68151-683-7(7), 10815); pap. 9.99 (978-1-68152-469-6(4), 11055) Amicus.

Gray, Leon. How Does GPS Work?, 1 vol., Vol. 1. 2013. (High-Tech Science Ser.). (ENG., Illus.). 48p. (J). (gr. 4-5). 34.61 (978-1-4824-0393-0(5), 473ae997-b585-4db2-b3d5-fcc53676cb7b) Stevens, Gareth Publishing LLLP.

Green, Cathy, et al. Great Ships on the Great Lakes: A Maritime History. 2013. (ENG., Illus.). 144p. (J). pap. 18.95 (978-0-87020-582-8(X)) Wisconsin Historical Society.

—Great Ships on the Great Lakes Teacher's Guide: A Maritime History. 2013. (ENG., Illus.). cd-rom 49.95 (978-0-87020-583-5(8)) Wisconsin Historical Society.

Krebs, Laurie. A Day in the Life of a Colonial Lighthouse Keeper, 1 vol. 2003. (Library of Living & Working in Colonial Times Ser.). (ENG., Illus.). 24p. (J). (gr. 3-3). lib. bdg. 26.27 (978-0-8239-6226-6(1), 41475366-8539-435f-8390-3e2e08bc9bcf) Rosen Publishing Group, Inc., The.

Macdonald, Fiona. You Wouldn't Want to Sail with Christopher Columbus! 2014. (You Wouldn't Want to... Ser.). (ENG.). 32p. (J). lib. bdg. 29.00 (978-0-531-21177-9(0), Watts, Franklin) Scholastic Library Publishing.

McNab, Chris. Survival in the Wilderness. 2015. (Illus.). 64p. (J). (978-1-4222-3081-7(3)) Mason Crest.

Nagelhout, Ryan. The Problem with Early Navigation Tools, 1 vol. 2015. (Bloopers of Invention Ser.). (ENG., Illus.). 24p. (J). (gr. 2-3). pap. 9.15 (978-1-4824-2776-9(1), 80932cce-a098-4f6e-9a32-5a9321dcd742) Stevens, Gareth Publishing LLLP.

Pritchard, Herman S. The Nautical Road: A Straight Forward Approach to Learning the Navigation Rules. Helwig, Teresa L., ed. Sink, Cynthia, illus. 2nd rev. l.t. ed. 2004. 176p. (YA). 29.95 (978-0-9716479-3-0(3)) Selby Dean Ventures, Inc.

Quinlan, Julia J. GPS & Computer Maps, 1 vol. 2012. (How to Use Maps Ser.). (ENG.). 24p. (J). (gr. 2-3). pap. 9.25 (978-1-4488-6276-4(0), 0d7364db-83f3-45fb-892c-9850d024d03e, PowerKids Pr.); lib. bdg. 26.27 (978-1-4488-6159-0(4), 664e37b5-ea25-4624-b23d-5b073d3b411e) Rosen Publishing Group, Inc., The.

Rice, Dona Herweck. Navigating at Sea (Grade 3) rev. ed. 2018. (Smithsonian: Informational Text Ser.). (ENG., Illus.). 32p. (J). (gr. 3-4). pap. 11.99 (978-1-4938-6680-9(X)) Teacher Created Materials, Inc.

Richardson, Gillian. 10 Ships That Rocked the World. Rosen, Kim, illus. 2015. (World of Tens Ser.). (ENG.). 176p. (J). (gr. 4-7). pap. 14.95 (978-1-55451-781-7(8), 9781554517817) Annick Pr., Ltd. CAN. Dist: Publishers Group West (PGW).

Sipe, Roger. Guided by Stars (Grade 5) rev. ed. 2018. (Smithsonian: Informational Text Ser.). (ENG., Illus.). 32p. (gr. 4-8). pap. 11.99 (978-1-4938-6718-9(0)) Teacher Created Materials, Inc.

Williams, Linda D. Navigational Aids, 1 vol. 2008. (Great Inventions Ser.). (ENG., Illus.). 144p. (YA). (gr. 8-8). lib. bdg. 45.50 (978-0-7614-2599-1(3), 4fc1ac96-ac12-4dff-9cee-ec355d570514) Cavendish Square Publishing LLC.

Wilson, Patrick. Surviving with Navigation & Signaling. Carney, John, ed. 2014. (Extreme Survival in the Military Ser.: 12). 64p. (J). (gr. 7-18). lib. bdg. 23.95 (978-1-4222-3093-0(7)) Mason Crest.

Wood, Alix. Pirates on the Map, 1 vol. 2014. (Fun with Map Skills Ser.). (ENG.). 32p. (J). (gr. 4-4). lib. bdg. 27.93 (978-1-4777-6964-5(1), fec8c55f-d565-4b07-9de6-666ba09f7e0d, PowerKids Pr.) Rosen Publishing Group, Inc., The.

NAVIGATORS

see Explorers

NAVY

see Naval Art and Science; Sea Power

see names of countries with the subhead Navy, e.g. United States—Navy

NAZI MOVEMENT

see National Socialism

NEAR EAST

see Asia; Middle East

NEBRASKA

Bjorklund, Ruth. Nebraska, 1 vol. 2003. (Celebrate the States (First Edition) Ser.). (ENG., Illus.). 144p. (gr. 6-6). lib. bdg. 39.79 (978-0-7614-1311-0(1), ec28e9ce-8c1b-44fb-8eed-5f7c385b8fa7) Cavendish Square Publishing LLC.

Brown, Jonatha A. Nebraska, 1 vol. 2006. (Portraits of the States Ser.). (ENG.). 32p. (gr. 3-5). pap. 11.50 (978-0-8368-4720-8(2), 13d20138-dcb1-48e7-8843-639e6f2fc48b); (Illus.). lib. bdg. 28.67 (978-0-8368-4703-1(2), 08038ee4-4b5c-4a91-a14f-dd012db38089) Stevens, Gareth Publishing LLLP. (Gareth Stevens Learning Library).

Galiano, Dean. Nebraska, 1 vol. Brusca, Maria Cristina, tr. 2005. (Bilingual Library of the United States of America Ser.: Set 2). (ENG & SPA., Illus.). 32p. (J). (gr. 2-2). lib. bdg. 28.93 (978-1-4042-3092-7(0), 1b0c67e0-14b5-4e93-a1c6-91fb50e9d7a1) Rosen Publishing Group, Inc., The.

Heinrichs, Ann. America the Beautiful, Third Series: Nebraska (Revised Edition) rev. ed. 2014. (America the Beautiful Ser.: 3). (ENG.). 144p. (J). lib. bdg. 40.00 (978-0-531-24892-8(5)) Scholastic Library Publishing.

—Nebraska. Kania, Matt, illus. 2017. (U. S. A. Travel Guides). (ENG.). 40p. (J). (gr. 2-5). lib. bdg. 38.50 (978-1-5038-1967-2(1), 211604) Child's World, Inc, The.

Marsh, Carole. Nebraska Current Events Projects: 30 Cool, Activities, Crafts, Experiments & More for Kids to Do to Learn about Your State! 2003. (Nebraska Experience Ser.). 32p. (gr. k-8). pap. 5.95 (978-0-635-02046-8(7), Marsh, Carole Bks.) Gallopade International.

—Nebraska Government Projects: 30 Cool, Activities, Crafts, Experiments & More for Kids to Do to Learn about Your State! 2003. (Nebraska Experience Ser.). 32p. (gr. k-5). pap. 5.95 (978-0-635-01946-2(9), Marsh, Carole Bks.) Gallopade International.

—Nebraska People Projects: 30 Cool, Activities, Crafts, Experiments & More for Kids to Do to Learn about Your State! 2003. (Nebraska Experience Ser.). 32p. (gr. k-5). pap. 5.95 (978-0-635-01996-7(5), Marsh, Carole Bks.) Gallopade International.

—Nebraska Symbols & Facts Projects: 30 Cool, Activities, Crafts, Experiments & More for Kids to Do to Learn about Your State! 2003. (Nebraska Experience Ser.). 32p. (gr. k-5). pap. 5.95 (978-0-635-01896-0(9), Marsh, Carole Bks.) Gallopade International.

McNamara, Connie. My First Nebraska Words. 2004. (J). 0.00 (978-0-9759703-0-0(5)) Shamrock Publishing, Inc.

M N O

Murray, Julie. Nebraska, 1 vol. 2006. (Buddy Book Ser.). (ENG., Illus.). 32p. (gr. 2-4). 27.07 *(978-1-59197-686-8(3),* Buddy Bks.) ABDO Publishing Co.

Porter, A. P. Nebraska. (J). 2012. lib. bdg. 25.26 *(978-0-7613-4543-5(4))* 2nd exp. rev. ed. 2003. (Illus.). 84p. (gr. 3-6). 25.26 *(978-0-8225-4093-9(2))* Lerner Publishing Group. (Lerner Pubns.).

Sanders, Doug. Nebraska, 1 vol. Santoro, Christopher, illus. 2006. (It's My State! (First Edition)(r) Ser.). (ENG.). 80p. (gr. 4-4). lib. bdg. 34.07 *(978-0-7614-1911-2(X),* 140162ce-d800-41e1-9a86-db7d657a9bed) Cavendish Square Publishing LLC.

Shepherd, Rajean Luebs. C Is for Cornhusker: A Nebraska Alphabet. Appleoff, Sandy, illus. 2004. (Discover America State by State Ser.). (ENG.). 40p. (J). (gr. 1-3). 18.99 *(978-1-58536-147-2(X),* 202007) Sleeping Bear Pr.

—Little Nebraska. Urban, Helle, illus. 2015. (Little State Ser.). (ENG.). 22p. (J). (gr. -1-k). bds. 9.95 *(978-1-58536-928-7(4),* 203819) Sleeping Bear Pr.

Weatherly, Myra S. Nebraska. 2003. (From Sea to Shining Sea Ser.: 2). (ENG., Illus.). 80p. (J). 30.50 *(978-0-516-22396-4(8),* Children's Pr.) Scholastic Library Publishing.

Weintraub, A. How to Draw Nebraska's Sights & Symbols. 2009. (Kid's Guide to Drawing America Ser.). 32p. (gr. k-k). 50.50 *(978-1-61511-076-6(3),* PowerKids Pr.) Rosen Publishing Group, Inc., The.

Zeiger, Jennifer. Nebraska (a True Book: My United States) 2018. (True Book (Relaunch) Ser.). (ENG., Illus.). 48p. (J). (gr. 3-5). pap. 7.95 *(978-0-531-25083-9(0),* Children's Pr.) Scholastic Library Publishing.

—Nebraska (a True Book: My United States) (Library Edition) 2018. (True Book (Relaunch) Ser.). (ENG., Illus.). 48p. (J). (gr. 3-5). 31.00 *(978-0-531-23564-5(5),* Children's Pr.) Scholastic Library Publishing.

Zollman, Pam. Nebraska. 2007. (Rookie Read-About Geography Ser.). (Illus.). 31p. (J). (gr. 1-2). 20.50 *(978-0-516-25466-1(9),* Children's Pr.) Scholastic Library Publishing.

NEBRASKA—FICTION

Clements, Andrew. Room One: A Mystery or Two. Elliott, Mark, illus. (ENG.). (J). (gr. 3-7). 2008. 192p. pap. 7.99 *(978-0-689-86687-6(9))* 2006. 176p. 19.99 *(978-0-689-86686-9(0))* Simon & Schuster Children's Publishing. (Atheneum Bks. for Young Readers).

Connor, Leslie. All Rise for the Honorable Perry T. Cook. (ENG.). (J). (gr. 3-7). 2017. 416p. pap. 9.99 *(978-0-06-233347-6(X))* 2016. 400p. 16.99 *(978-0-06-233346-9(1))* HarperCollins Pubs. (Tegen, Katherine Bks).

Gray, Dianne. Holding up the Earth. 2006. (ENG.). 210p. (J). (gr. 5-7). pap. 12.95 *(978-0-618-73747-5(2),* 486718, Clarion Bks.) HarperCollins Pubs.

House, E. A. Deep Waters #4. 2017. (Treasure Hunters Ser.). (ENG.). 184p. (YA). (gr. 5-12). 32.84 *(978-1-68076-879-4(4),* 27447, Epic Escape) EPIC Pr.

Jacobs, Lily. The Littlest Bunny in Nebraska: An Easter Adventure. Dunn, Robert, illus. 2015. (Littlest Bunny Ser.). (ENG.). 32p. (J). (gr. -1-3). 9.99 *(978-1-4926-1132-5(8),* Hometown World) Sourcebooks, Inc.

—The Littlest Bunny in Omaha: An Easter Adventure. Dunn, Robert, illus. 2015. (Littlest Bunny Ser.). (ENG.). 32p. (J). (gr. -1-3). 9.99 *(978-1-4926-1168-4(9),* Hometown World) Sourcebooks, Inc.

Jacoby, Sue. The Sneakies in Las Vegas: A Coby Jay Adventure. 2012. 128p. (gr. 4-6). 22.60 *(978-1-4669-6672-7(6));* pap. 12.60 *(978-1-4669-6670-3(X))* Trafford Publishing.

James, Eric. Santa's Sleigh Is on Its Way to Nebraska: A Christmas Adventure. Dunn, Robert, illus. 2016. (Santa's Sleigh Is on Its Way Ser.). (ENG.). 32p. (J). (gr. k-2). 12.99 *(978-1-4926-4339-5(4),* 9781492643395, Hometown World) Sourcebooks, Inc.

—Santa's Sleigh Is on Its Way to Omaha: A Christmas Adventure. Dunn, Robert, illus. 2016. (Santa's Sleigh Is on Its Way Ser.). (ENG.). 32p. (J). (gr. k-2). 12.99 *(978-1-4926-4347-0(5),* 9781492643470, Hometown World) Sourcebooks, Inc.

—The Spooky Express Nebraska. Piwowarski, Marcin, illus. 2017. (Spooky Express Ser.). (ENG.). 32p. (J). (gr. k-6). 9.99 *(978-1-4926-5376-9(4),* Hometown World) Sourcebooks, Inc.

—Tiny the Nebraska Easter Bunny. 2018. (Tiny the Easter Bunny Ser.). (ENG.). 40p. (J). (gr. k-3). 9.99 *(978-1-4926-5942-6(8),* Hometown World) Sourcebooks, Inc.

LaFaye, A. Worth. unabr. ed. 2006. (Live Oak Histories Ser.). (J). (gr. 3-6). pap. 24.95 incl. audio *(978-1-59519-766-5(4))* Live Oak Media.

—Worth. 2006. (ENG.). 160p. (J). (gr. 4-7). reprint ed. pap. 8.99 *(978-1-4169-1624-6(5),* Simon & Schuster Bks. For Young Readers) Simon & Schuster Bks. For Young Readers.

Lieb, Josh. I Am a Genius of Unspeakable Evil & I Want to Be Your Class President. 2010. (J). (ENG.). 272p. (gr. 7-12). 24.94 *(978-1-59514-240-5(1));* 304p. (gr. 5-7). 9.99 *(978-1-59514-354-9(8))* Penguin Young Readers Group. (Razorbill).

Liess, Claudia Schmidt. But Where Is Dad? 2007. 96p. per. 19.95 *(978-1-4241-6912-2(7))* America Star Bks.

McGaa, Ed. Spirit Horse: An Adventure in Crazy Horse Country. 2007. 80p. (YA). pap. *(978-1-57579-360-3(1))* Pine Hill Pr.

Merrill, Karen Grill. Oh, What a State I'm In: The USA in Rhyme & Riddle, 1 vol. Grill, Gerald, illus. 2010. 48p. pap. 24.95 *(978-1-4489-7979-0(X))* PublishAmerica, Inc.

Miller, Scott E. Prairie Sunsets. 2008. 103p. pap. 19.95 *(978-1-60441-763-0(3))* America Star Bks.

Moskowitz, Hannah. Not Otherwise Specified. 2015. (ENG., Illus.). 304p. (YA). (gr. 9). pap. 12.99 *(978-1-4814-0595-9(0),* Simon Pulse) Simon Pulse.

Myers, Jason. Dead End. 2011. (ENG.). 384p. (YA). (gr. 10-18). pap. 9.99 *(978-1-4424-1430-3(8),* Simon Pulse) Simon Pulse.

Polk, Douglas. Marie's Home, 1 vol. 2009. 48p. pap. 16.95 *(978-1-60749-454-6(X))* America Star Bks.

Pyrtle Second Graders & Writers' Circle. Poetry & a Fifth Grade Cinderell: An Anthology from Nebraska. 2009. 60p. pap. 8.95 *(978-0-595-53233-9(0))* iUniverse, Inc.

Reed, Amy. Over You. (ENG., Illus.). (YA). (gr. 9). 2014. 336p. pap. 9.99 *(978-1-4424-5697-6(3))* 2013. 320p. 16.99 *(978-1-4424-5696-9(5))* Simon Pulse. (Simon Pulse).

Richardson, Arleta. Whistle Stop West. 2003. (Orphans' Journey Ser.: Vol. 2). 144p. (J). (gr. 3-7). pap., pap. 5.99 *(978-0-7814-3537-6(4),* 0781435374) Cook, David C.

—Whistle-Stop West. 2016. (Beyond the Orphan Train Ser.: 2). (ENG.). 192p. (J). pap. 7.99 *(978-1-4347-0956-1(6),* 136203) Cook, David C.

Sandburg, Carl. The Huckabuck Family: And How They Raised Popcorn in Nebraska & Quit & Came Back. Small, David, illus. 2006. 30p. (J). (gr. k-4). reprint ed. 16.00 *(978-1-4223-5854-2(2))* DIANE Publishing Co.

Silverman, Laura. Girl Out of Water. 2017. (ENG.). 368p. (YA). (gr. 8-12). pap. 15.99 *(978-1-4926-4686-0(5),* 9781492646860) Sourcebooks, Inc.

Sully, Katherine. Night-Night Nebraska. Poole, Helen, illus. 2017. (Night-Night Ser.). (ENG.). 20p. (J). (gr. -1-1). bds. 9.99 *(978-1-4926-5482-7(5),* Hometown World) Sourcebooks, Inc.

Trueblood, Amy. Nothing but Sky. 2018. (ENG.). 288p. (YA). (gr. 9-12). pap. 11.99 *(978-1-63583-016-3(8),* 1635830168, Flux) North Star Editions.

—Nothing but Sky. 2018. lib. bdg. 23.30 *(978-0-606-41246-9(8))* Turtleback.

Valente, Catherynne M. The Girl Who Circumnavigated Fairyland in a Ship of Her Own Making. 2012. (CHI & ENG., Illus.). 304p. (J). (gr. 5-8). pap. *(978-986-6026-24-9(8))* Muses Publishing Hse.

—The Girl Who Circumnavigated Fairyland in a Ship of Her Own Making. Juan, Ana, illus. 2012. (Fairyland Ser.: 1). (ENG.). 288p. (YA). (gr. 5-9). pap. 9.99 *(978-1-250-01019-3(5),* 900084756) Square Fish.

Walker, Lane. The Hunt for Scarface. 2014. (ENG.). 161p. (YA). (gr. 7-13). pap. 9.99 *(978-1-58169-518-2(7),* Evergreen Pr.) Genesis Communications, Inc.

Warne, Jude. Landlocked. 2017. (Crushing Ser.). (ENG.). 192p. (YA). (gr. 5-12). lib. bdg. 31.42 *(978-1-68076-720-9(8),* 25388, Epic Escape) EPIC Pr.

NEBRASKA—HISTORY

Abraham Lincoln's Shining Star: The Inspiring Story of Abraham Lincoln & Nebraska. 2010. (Illus.). 64p. 18.95 *(978-0-615-34265-8(5))* America's Great Stories.

Bailer, Darice. What's Great about Nebraska? 2015. (Our Great States Ser.). (ENG., Illus.). 32p. (J). (gr. 2-5). pap. 7.95 *(978-1-4677-6094-2(3),* 68d4a50d-6914-4355-8eb3-4b3e95d49b6c); lib. bdg. 26.65 *(978-1-4677-3870-5(0),* 5510998e-a921-4318-a75d-2fbceb81f46b, Lerner Pubns.) Lerner Publishing Group.

Bjorklund, Ruth & Richards, Marlee. Nebraska, 1 vol. 2nd rev. ed. 2010. (Celebrate the States (Second Edition) Ser.). (ENG.). 144p. (gr. 6-6). 39.79 *(978-0-7614-4732-0(6),* f1826c7d-3353-4cab-abbe-caf76e8b4ca1) Cavendish Square Publishing LLC.

Bringle, Jennifer. Nebraska: Past & Present, 1 vol. 2010. (United States: Past & Present Ser.). (ENG.). 48p. (YA). (gr. 5-5). pap. 12.75 *(978-1-4358-9514-0(2),* 2e1eac68-b08c-464c-8ffd-663b04f38513); lib. bdg. 34.47 *(978-1-4358-9487-7(1),* dd33f541-a8db-42d4-a6a4-1ff317515b11) Rosen Publishing Group, Inc., The. (Rosen Reference).

Coleman, Miriam. Nebraska: The Cornhusker State, 1 vol. 2010. (Our Amazing States Ser.). (ENG.). 24p. (J). (gr. 3-3). pap. 9.25 *(978-1-4488-0744-4(1),* fe8e0cf6-a49d-48f9-97d1-75162a496962); lib. bdg. 26.27 *(978-1-4488-0656-0(9),* 6e8bbef6-628f-4130-97bb-d857852fcddb) Rosen Publishing Group, Inc., The. (PowerKids Pr.).

Foran, Jill. Nebraska. 2011. (Guide to American States Ser.). (Illus.). 48p. (YA). (gr. 3-6). 29.99 *(978-1-61690-799-0(1));* (J). *(978-1-61690-475-3(5))* Weigl Pubs., Inc.

—Nebraska: The Cornhusker State. 2016. (J). *(978-1-4896-4896-9(8))* Weigl Pubs., Inc.

Gamble, Adam & Jasper, Mark. Good Night Nebraska. 2015. (Good Night Our World Ser.). (ENG., Illus.). 20p. (J). (— 1). bds. 9.95 *(978-1-60219-087-0(9))* Good Night Bks.

Hamilton, John. Nebraska, 1 vol. 2016. (United States of America Ser.). (ENG., Illus.). 48p. (J). (gr. 5-9). 34.21 *(978-1-68078-329-2(7),* 21643, Abdo & Daughters) ABDO Publishing Co.

Hanel, Rachael. Nebraska. 2009. (This Land Called America Ser.). (Illus.). 32p. (YA). (gr. 3-6). 19.95 *(978-1-58341-780-5(X))* Creative Co., The.

Herschbach, Elisabeth. Lower Plains: Kansas, Nebraska, Vol. 19. 2015. (Let's Explore the States Ser.). (Illus.). 64p. (J). (gr. 5). 23.95 *(978-1-4222-3326-9(X))* Mason Crest.

Kopp, Megan. Nebraska: The Cornhusker State. 2012. (J). *(978-1-61913-373-0(3));* pap. *(978-1-61913-374-7(1))* Weigl Pubs., Inc.

Lukesh, Jean A. Sky Rider: Story of Evelyn Sharp, World War II WASP. 2011. (Noteworthy Americans Young Readers Biography Book Ser.). (ENG., Illus.). 161p. (J). pap. 14.95 *(978-0-9647586-3-6(6))* Field Mouse Productions.

Marsh, Carole. Exploring Nebraska Through Project-Based Learning: Geography, History, Government, Economics & More. 2016. (Nebraska Experience Ser.). (ENG.). (J). pap. 9.99 *(978-0-635-12351-0(7))* Gallopade International.

—I'm Reading about Nebraska. 2014. (Nebraska Experience Ser.). (ENG., Illus.). (J). pap., pap. 8.99 *(978-0-635-11302-3(3))* Gallopade International.

—Nebraska History Projects: 30 Cool, Activities, Crafts, Experiments & More for Kids to Do to Learn about Your State! 2003. (Nebraska Experience Ser.). 32p. (gr. k-5). pap. 5.95 *(978-0-635-01796-3(2),* Marsh, Carole Bks.) Gallopade International.

Mills, Jordan & Parker, Bridget. Nebraska. 2016. (States Ser.). (ENG., Illus.). 32p. (J). (gr. 3-6). lib. bdg. 27.99 *(978-1-5157-0414-0(9),* 132025, Capstone Pr.) Capstone.

The Nebraska Adventure Program Kit: All program components for the Nebraska Adventure, 1 vol. 2009. 99.95 *(978-1-4236-0722-9(8))* Gibbs Smith, Publisher.

Plain, Nancy. Light on the Prairie: Solomon D. Butcher, Photographer of Nebraska's Pioneer Days. 2012. (ENG., Illus.). 128p. (YA). pap. 16.95 *(978-0-8032-3520-5(8),* Bison Bks.) Univ. of Nebraska Pr.

Sanders, Doug. Nebraska, 1 vol. 2nd rev. ed. 2014. (It's My State! (Second Edition)(r) Ser.). (ENG.). 80p. (gr. 4-4). pap. 18.64 *(978-1-62712-498-0(5),* fa0118ed-bfe9-48b4-8deb-9c3908235e8b); (Illus.). 35.93 *(978-1-62712-241-2(9),* 137670ce-8c7c-43ca-8560-fc043cf7f778) Cavendish Square Publishing LLC.

Sanders, Doug & Schauer, Pete. Nebraska: The Cornhusker State, 1 vol. 3rd rev. ed. 2016. (It's My State! (Third Edition)(r) Ser.). (ENG., Illus.). 80p. (gr. 4-4). 35.93 *(978-1-62713-247-3(3),* 739f9d37-3795-4025-999e-24bd79a7f10b) Cavendish Square Publishing LLC.

Warren, Andrea. Pioneer Girl: A True Story of Growing up on the Prairie. 2009. (ENG., Illus.). 104p. pap. 16.95 *(978-0-8032-2526-8(1),* WARPIX, Bison Bks.) Univ. of Nebraska Pr.

Weatherly, Myra S. From Sea to Shining Sea: Nebraska. 2009. (From Sea to Shining Sea, Second Ser.). (ENG.). 80p. (J). pap. 7.95 *(978-0-531-21136-6(3),* Children's Pr.) Scholastic Library Publishing.

NEBRASKA—HISTORY—FICTION

Blanc, Esther Silverstein & Eagle, Godeane. Long Johns for a Small Chicken. Dixon, Tennessee, illus. 2003. (J). 16.95 *(978-1-884244-23-0(8))* volcano pr.

Figley, Marty Rhodes. The Prairie Adventure of Sarah & Annie, Blizzard Survivors. Hammond, Ted & Carbajal, Richard Pimentel, illus. 2011. (History's Kid Heroes Set III Ser.). pap. 51.02 *(978-0-7613-8621-6(1),* Graphic Universe™) Lerner Publishing Group.

—The Prairie Adventure of Sarah & Annie, Blizzard Survivors. Carbajal, Richard & Hammond, Ted, illus. 2011. (History's Kid Heroes Ser.). (ENG.). 32p. (J). (gr. 3-5). pap. 9.99 *(978-0-7613-7808-2(1),* d4c7e7ff-1ce6-47c5-8250-3453ef99ba72, Graphic Universe™) Lerner Publishing Group.

—The Schoolchildren's Blizzard. Haas, Shelly O., illus. 2004. (On My Own History Ser.). (ENG.). 48p. (J). (gr. 2-4). pap. 8.99 *(978-1-57505-619-7(4),* a675f403-7243-488e-ad5b-fbd615d20ef5, First Avenue Editions) Lerner Publishing Group.

Hart, Alison. Anna's Blizzard, 1 vol. Bachem, Paul, illus. 2017. 176p. (J). (gr. 2-5). pap. 7.95 *(978-1-68263-002-0(1))* Peachtree Publishing Co. Inc.

Hoffman, Emily Allen. A Friend of the Enemy. 2003. 108p. (J). pap. 7.95 *(978-1-57249-312-4(7),* White Mane Kids) White Mane Publishing Co., Inc.

LaFaye, A. Worth. unabr. ed. 2006. (Live Oak Histories Ser.). (J). (gr. 3-6). pap. 28.95 incl. audio compact disk *(978-1-59519-767-2(2))* Live Oak Media.

—Worth. 2006. 144p. (J). (gr. 4-7). 13.65 *(978-0-7569-6614-0(0))* Perfection Learning Corp.

Levinson, Nancy Smiler. Prairie Friends. Schuett, Stacey, illus. 2003. (I Can Read Bks.). 64p. (J). (gr. k-3). 15.99 *(978-0-06-028001-7(8))* HarperCollins Pubs.

McGaa Tonemah, Paula & McGaa, Ed. The Animals Talk. 2009. 72p. (J). pap. *(978-1-57579-373-3(3))* Pine Hill Pr.

Riege, Cheryl. Tracks Rivers Roads: Across Nebraska on the Meridian Highway. 2012. (ENG.). 184p. pap. 12.95 *(978-1-4327-8573-4(7))* Outskirts Pr., Inc.

NECROMANCY

see Divination; Witchcraft

NEEDLEWORK

see also names of needlework; e.g. Dressmaking; Embroidery; Sewing; Tapestry

Akass, Susan. My First Sewing Book: 35 Easy & Fun Projects for Children Aged 7 Years + 2011. (ENG., Illus.). 128p. (J). (gr. 7-11). pap. 14.95 *(978-1-907563-71-3(7),* 1907563717, CICO Books) Ryland Peters & Small GBR. Dist: WIPRO.

Kuskowski, Alex. Cool Needle Felting for Kids: A Fun & Creative Introduction to Fiber Art. 2014. (Cool Fiber Art Ser.). (ENG.). 32p. (J). (gr. 3-6). lib. bdg. 34.21 *(978-1-62403-309-4(1),* 1280, Checkerboard Library) ABDO Publishing Co.

—Cool Punch Needle for Kids: A Fun & Creative Introduction to Fiber Art. 2014. (Cool Fiber Art Ser.). (ENG.). 32p. (J). (gr. 3-6). lib. bdg. 34.21 *(978-1-62403-310-0(5),* 1282, Checkerboard Library) ABDO Publishing Co.

NEFERTITI, QUEEN OF EGYPT, ACTIVE 14TH CENTURY B.C.

Spirn, Michele Sobel. Mysterious People. 2006. (True Tales: A Chapter Book Ser.). (ENG., Illus.). 48p. (J). (gr. 2-4). per. 4.95 *(978-0-516-25454-8(5),* Children's Pr.) Scholastic Library Publishing.

NEFERTITI, QUEEN OF EGYPT, ACTIVE 14TH CENTURY B.C.—FICTION

Friesner, Esther. Sphinx's Princess. 2010. (Princesses of Myth Ser.). (ENG.). 400p. (YA). (gr. 7). pap. 9.99 *(978-0-375-85655-6(2),* Random Hse. Bks. for Young Readers) Random Hse. Children's Bks.

—Sphinx's Queen. 2011. (Princesses of Myth Ser.). (ENG., Illus.). 368p. (YA). (gr. 7). pap. 9.99 *(978-0-375-85658-7(7),* Ember) Random Hse. Children's Bks.

Hofmeyr, Dianne. Eye of the Sun. 2011. (ENG.). 336p. (J). (gr. 3-7). pap. 6.99 *(978-1-4424-1186-9(4),* Aladdin) Simon & Schuster Children's Publishing.

NEGROES

see African Americans; Blacks

NEGRO RACE

see Blacks

NEIGHBORHOOD

see Community Life

NEIGHBORHOOD CENTERS

see Social Settlements

NEIGHBORHOOD SCHOOLS

see Schools

NEIGHBORS

Bullard, Lisa. This Is My Neighborhood. Conger, Holli, illus. 2016. (Cloverleaf Books (tm) — Where I Live Ser.). (ENG.). 24p. (J). (gr. k-2). 25.32 *(978-1-4677-9521-0(6),* 1cd189fa-76eb-4767-a614-4c905623e009, Millbrook Pr.) Lerner Publishing Group.

Donner, Candie. Apologia Worldview: Assembled: 'Who Is My Neighbor? Lapbook. Kinney, Cyndi, ed. 2013. (J). pap. 35.99 *(978-1-61625-531-2(5))* Knowledge Box Central.

—Apologia Worldview: 'Who Is My Neighbor? Lapbook. Kinney, Cyndi, ed. 2013. (J). pap. 25.99 *(978-1-61625-529-9(3));* cd-rom 19.99 *(978-1-61625-528-2(5))* Knowledge Box Central.

Holko, Suzanne L. Grampy & Me. 2012. 34p. pap. 13.95 *(978-1-4624-0080-5(9),* Inspiring Voices) Author Solutions, LLC.

Holland, Trish. Neighborhood Song. 2010. (J). *(978-1-60617-143-1(7))* Teaching Strategies, LLC.

Lyons, Shelly. People in My Neighborhood. 2013. (My Neighborhood Ser.). (ENG.). 24p. (J). (gr. k-1). pap. 44.74 *(978-1-62065-884-0(4),* 19441, Capstone Pr.); (Illus.). (gr. -1-2). pap. 7.29 *(978-1-62065-883-3(6),* 121802); (Illus.). (gr. -1-2). lib. bdg. 27.32 *(978-1-62065-099-8(1),* 120796) Capstone.

—Places in My Neighborhood. 2013. (My Neighborhood Ser.). (ENG.). 24p. (J). (gr. k-1). pap. 43.74 *(978-1-62065-886-4(0),* 19442, Capstone Pr.) Capstone.

Mason, Paul. 25 Fun Things to Do for Your Neighbors. Sassin, Eva, illus. 2019. (100 Fun Things to Do to Unplug Ser.). (ENG.). 32p. (J). (gr. 3-6). lib. bdg. 27.99 *(978-1-5415-0136-2(5),* e1c3cd8f-d0a5-48df-a1e2-13a8fc09a671, Hungry Tomato (r)) Lerner Publishing Group.

Summers, Portia. My Neighborhood, 1 vol. 2016. (Zoom in on Communities Ser.). (ENG.). 24p. (gr. 2-2). pap. 10.95 *(978-0-7660-7800-0(0),* deb65ad4-f11d-4adc-b504-9245bbd3b407) Enslow Publishing, LLC.

NEIGHBORS—FICTION

Abrahams, Peter. The Outlaws of Sherwood Street: Stealing from the Rich. 2013. 320p. (J). (gr. 5). 7.99 *(978-0-14-242438-4(2),* Puffin Books) Penguin Young Readers Group.

Adderson, Caroline. Middle of Nowhere. 2013. 212p. pap. *(978-1-4596-6452-4(3))* ReadHowYouWant.com, Ltd.

Adler, David A. Andy Russell, Not Wanted by the Police. Franson, Leanne, illus. 2005. (Andy Russell Ser.: Bk. 5). (ENG.). 128p. (J). (gr. 1-4). pap. 7.99 *(978-0-15-216719-6(6),* 1201719, Clarion Bks.) HarperCollins Pubs.

Alter, Anna. Sprout Street Neighbors: Bon Voyage. 2017. (Sprout Street Neighbors Ser.: 3). (ENG., Illus.). 96p. (J). (gr. 1-4). pap. 6.99 *(978-1-5247-0053-9(3),* Yearling) Random Hse. Children's Bks.

Anderson, Alice. Danny Be Good! 2012. 24p. pap. 17.99 *(978-1-4685-6433-4(1))* AuthorHouse.

Archer, Micha. Daniel's Good Day. Archer, Micha, illus. 2019. (Illus.). 32p. (J). (-k). 18.99 *(978-0-399-54672-3(3),* Nancy Paulsen Books) Penguin Young Readers Group.

Arnold, Marsha Diane. May I Come In? Poh, Jennie, illus. 2018. (ENG.). 32p. (J). (gr. k-3). 16.99 *(978-1-58536-394-0(4),* 204396) Sleeping Bear Pr.

Arsenault, Isabelle. Albert's Quiet Quest. 2019. (ENG., Illus.). 48p. (J). (gr. -1-3). lib. bdg. 20.99 *(978-0-553-53657-7(5),* Random Hse. Bks. for Young Readers) Random Hse. Children's Bks.

—Albert's Quiet Quest. 2019. (Mile End Kids Story Ser.: 2). (ENG., Illus.). 48p. (J). (gr. -1-3). 16.99 ***(978-1-101-91762-6(8),*** Tundra Bks.) Tundra Bks. CAN. Dist: Penguin Random Hse. LLC.

Ashman, Linda. Outside My Window. Christoph, Jamey, illus. 2018. (ENG.). 40p. (J). 17.00 *(978-0-8028-5465-0(6),* Eerdmans Bks For Young Readers) Eerdmans, William B. Publishing Co.

—Rain! Calvo, Carlos, tr. Robinson, Christian, illus. 2013. (ENG.). 32p. (J). (gr. -1-3). 18.99 *(978-0-547-73395-1(X),* 1484490, Clarion Bks.) HarperCollins Pubs.

—Rain! Board Book. Calvo, Carlos, tr. Robinson, Christian, illus. 2017. (ENG.). 30p. (J). (— 1). bds. 7.99 *(978-0-544-88037-5(4),* 1651189, Clarion Bks.) HarperCollins Pubs.

Atchison, David C. The Adventures of Black Bart: an Encounter with Regret. 2008. 84p. pap. 7.94 *(978-0-615-23723-7(1))* Black Bart Bks.

Atkinson, Elizabeth. From Alice to Zen & Everyone in Between. 2008. (Exceptional Reading & Language Arts Titles for Intermediate Grades Ser.). 247p. (YA). (gr. 4-7). 16.95 *(978-0-8225-7271-8(0))* Lerner Publishing Group.

Atwell, A. Erika Laura. 2008. 157p. pap. 24.95 *(978-1-60703-006-5(3))* PublishAmerica, Inc.

Auerbach, Annie. Naughty Nautical Neighbors, Vol. 2. 2004. 64p. (J). (gr. 2-5). pap. 17.00 incl. audio *(978-0-8072-1987-4(8),* Listening Library) Random Hse. Audio Publishing Group.

Babineaux, Jim. Cody Cottontail Makes a Wise Choice! Babineaux, Jim, illus. l.t. ed. 2005. (Illus.). 18p. (J). *(978-0-9769769-0-5(0))* ALCAPS, LLC.

Baker, Jeannie. Home. Baker, Jeannie, illus. 2004. (ENG., Illus.). 32p. (J). (gr. k-5). 16.99 *(978-0-06-623935-4(4),* Greenwillow Bks.) HarperCollins Pubs.

Banks, Robin Washington. Big Boy. Morgan, Vincent, illus. 2011. 20p. pap. 24.95 *(978-1-4560-7068-7(1))* PublishAmerica, Inc.

Banks, Steven. The Song That Never Ends. DePorter, Vince, illus. 2004. (Spongebob Squarepants Ser.). 32p. (J). (gr. k-2). 11.65 *(978-0-7569-5374-4(X))* Perfection Learning Corp.

Baraou, Anne & Sardon, Vincent. The Skeleton Family: The Neighbors from Elsewhere. 2005. (Illus.). 64p. *(978-1-59687-825-9(8),* ipicturebooks) ibooks, Inc.

Barbo, Maria S. & Preller, James. The Case of the Four-Leaf Clover. Smith, Jamie, illus. 2008. 104p. (J). pap. *(978-0-545-03837-9(5))* Scholastic, Inc.

Barkow, Henriette. Don't Cry, Sly! Johnson, Richard, illus. 2004. 32p. (J). (ENG & GUJ.). pap. *(978-1-85269-656-6(7));* (GER & ENG.). pap. *(978-1-85269-655-9(9));* (ENG & CZE.). pap. *(978-1-85269-652-8(4));* (ENG & CHI.). pap. *(978-1-85269-651-1(6));* (ENG & BEN.). pap. *(978-1-85269-650-4(8));* (ENG & ITA.). pap. *(978-1-85269-657-3(5));* (ENG & PAN.). pap. *(978-1-85269-658-0(3));* (ENG.). pap. *(978-1-85269-660-3(5));* (ENG & SOM.). pap. *(978-1-85269-661-0(3));* (ENG & TAM.). pap. *(978-1-85269-663-4(X));* (ENG & URD.). pap.

(978-1-85269-671-9(0)); (ENG & TUR.). pap. (978-1-85269-670-2(2)); (ENG & POL.). pap. (978-1-85269-813-3(6)) Mantra Lingua.

Barnes, Ben. Don't Eat My Garden. Barnes, Page, illus. 2007. 28p. per. 24.95 (978-1-4241-8964-9(0)) America Star Bks.

Barrett, Ms S. Moe. Mangoe & Marlie: Mangoe Takes Care of Marlie. 2013. 56p. pap. 11.93 (978-0-9701289-5-9(9)) Moselle Productions, Inc.

Barrows, Annie. Bound to Be Bad. 2009. (Ivy & Bean Ser.: 5). (J). lib. bdg. 16.00 (978-0-606-14473-5(0)) Turtleback.

—Ivy + Bean. Blackall, Sophie, illus. 2007. (Ivy & Bean Ser.: Bk. 1). 120p. (gr. 1-5). 16.00 (978-0-7569-8142-6(5)) Perfection Learning Corp.

—Ivy + Bean. Blackall, Sophie, illus. 2007. (Ivy & Bean Ser.: 1). (J). lib. bdg. 16.00 (978-1-4177-7972-7(1)) Turtleback.

—Ivy + Bean - No News Is Good News. Blackall, Sophie, illus. 2012. (Ivy & Bean Ser.: 8). (J). lib. bdg. 16.00 (978-0-606-26950-6(9)) Turtleback.

—Ivy & Bean - Book 5, Book 5. Blackall, Sophie, illus. 2008. (Ivy & Bean Ser.: IVYB). (ENG.). 124p. (J). (gr. 1-5). 14.99 (978-0-8118-6265-3(8)) Chronicle Bks. LLC.

—Ivy & Bean - Book 6, Book 6. Blackall, Sophie, illus. 2009. (Ivy & Bean Ser.: IVYB). (ENG.). 136p. (J). (gr. 1-5). 14.99 (978-0-8118-6266-0(6)) Chronicle Bks. LLC.

—Ivy & Bean 1, Volume 1. 2007. (Ivy & Bean Ser.: IVYB). (ENG., Illus.). 120p. (J). (gr. 1-5). pap. 5.99 (978-0-8118-4909-8(0)) Chronicle Bks. LLC.

—Ivy & Bean #5: Bound to Be Bad, Volume 5. Blackall, Sophie, illus. 2009. (Ivy & Bean Ser.: IVYB). (ENG.). 128p. (J). (gr. 1-5). pap. 5.99 (978-0-8118-6857-0(5)) Chronicle Bks. LLC.

—Ivy & Bean Book 1, Bk. 1. Blackall, Sophie, illus. 2006. (Ivy & Bean Ser.: IVYB). (ENG.). 120p. (J). (gr. 1-5). 14.99 (978-0-8118-4903-6(1)) Chronicle Bks. LLC.

—Ivy & Bean Boxed Set: Books 7- 9, 1 vol. Blackall, Sophie, illus. 2013. (Ivy & Bean Ser.). (ENG.). 428p. (J). (gr. 1-4). 17.97 (978-1-4521-1732-4(2)) Chronicle Bks. LLC.

—Ivy & Bean: Break the Fossil Record - Book 3. Blackall, Sophie, illus. 2007. (Ivy & Bean Ser.: IVYB). (ENG.). 132p. (J). (gr. 1-5). 14.99 (978-0-8118-5683-6(6)) Chronicle Bks. LLC.

—Ivy & Bean No News Is Good News (Book 8) Blackall, Sophie, illus. 2011. (Ivy & Bean Ser.: IVYB). (ENG.). 128p. (J). (gr. 1-5). 14.99 (978-0-8118-6693-4(9)) Chronicle Bks. LLC.

—Ivy & Bean No News Is Good News (Book 8) (Best Friends Books for Kids, Elementary School Books, Early Chapter Books), Volume 8. Blackall, Sophie, illus. 2012. (Ivy & Bean Ser.). (ENG.). 144p. (J). (gr. 1-5). pap. 5.99 (978-1-4521-0781-3(5)) Chronicle Bks. LLC.

Barrows, Annie & Blackall, Sophie. Ivy + Bean. 2011. (Ivy & Bean Ser.). (ENG., Illus.). 120p. (J). (gr. 2-5). 31.36 (978-1-59961-928-6(8), 10108, Chapter Bks.) Spotlight.

—Ivy + Bean Bound to Be Bad. 2011. (Ivy & Bean Ser.). (ENG., Illus.). 128p. (J). (gr. 2-5). 31.36 (978-1-59961-932-3(6), 10112, Chapter Bks.) Spotlight.

Behar, Ruth. Lucky Broken Girl. (ENG.). (J). (gr. 5). 2018. 272p. 8.99 (978-0-399-54645-7(6), Puffin Books) 2017. 256p. 17.99 (978-0-399-54644-0(8), Nancy Paulsen Books) Penguin Young Readers Group.

Benchmark Education Co., LLC. Guess Who Lives on My Street Big Book. 2014. (Shared Reading Foundations Ser.). (J). (gr. -1). (978-1-4509-9428-6(8)) Benchmark Education Co.

Berenda, M. J. Helping with Pocket Change. 2011. 24p. pap. 12.95 (978-1-4567-5836-3(5)) AuthorHouse.

Berenstain, Mike. The Berenstain Bears Go Christmas Caroling, 1 vol. 2019. (Berenstain Bears/Living Lights: a Faith Story Ser.). (ENG., Illus.). 24p. (J). pap. 6.99 (978-0-310-76363-5(0)) Zonderkidz.

Bessler, edward. A Smile for Billy. 2008. 175p. pap. 13.95 (978-1-4357-4439-4(X)) Lulu Pr., Inc.

Birney, Betty G. The Seven Wonders of Sassafras Springs. Phelan, Matt, illus. 2007. 210p. 17.00 (978-0-7569-8075-7(5)) Perfection Learning Corp.

—The Seven Wonders of Sassafras Springs. Phelan, Matt, illus. 2007. (ENG.). 224p. (J). (gr. 3-7). pap. 7.99 (978-1-4169-3489-9(8), Atheneum Bks. for Young Readers) Simon & Schuster Children's Publishing.

Blackford, Andy. The Three Little Pigs & the New Neighbor. Zlatic, Tomislav, illus. 2014. (Tadpoles: Fairytale Twists Ser.). (ENG.). 32p. (J). (gr. 1-2). (978-0-7787-0447-8(5)); pap. (978-0-7787-0482-9(3)) Crabtree Publishing Co.

Blackwood, Gary L. The Just-So Woman. Manning, Jane K., illus. 2006. (I Can Read Bks.). 48p. (J). (gr. -1-3). lib. bdg. 16.89 (978-0-06-057728-5(2)) HarperCollins Pubs.

Bluemle, Elizabeth. How Do You Wokka-Wokka? Cecil, Randy, illus. 2012. (ENG.). 32p. (J). (gr. -1-2). pap. 7.99 (978-0-7636-6085-7(X)) Candlewick Pr.

Blume, Lesley M. M. Cornelia & the Audacious Escapades of the Somerset Sisters. 2008. 272p. (J). (gr. 3-7). 8.99 (978-0-440-42110-8(1), Yearling) Random Hse. Children's Bks.

Blyton, Enid. Those Dreadful Children: Family Adventure. 2013. 224p. (J). pap. 9.99 (978-1-84135-646-4(8)) Award Pubns. Ltd. GBR. Dist: Parkwest Pubns., Inc.

Borsky, Mary. Benny Bensky & the Parrot-Napper. Hendry, Linda, illus. 2008. 128p. (J). (gr. 4-7). pap. 9.95 (978-0-88776-840-8(7), Tundra Bks.) Tundra Bks. CAN. Dist: Penguin Random Hse. LLC.

Bourgeois, Paulette. Neighborhood. 2004. (Illus.). (J). (gr. k-3). spiral bd. (978-0-616-01588-9(7)); spiral bd. (978-0-616-01589-6(5)) Canadian National Institute for the Blind/Institut National Canadien pour les Aveugles.

Branam, Lucy. Roof Octopus. Coelho, Rogério, illus. 2018. (ENG.). 32p. (J). (gr. k-3). 17.99 (978-1-58536-997-3(7), 204327) Sleeping Bear Pr.

Brennan-Nelson, Denise. Willow & the Snow Day Dance. Moore, Cyd, illus. 2010. (ENG.). 32p. (J). (gr. 1-4). lib. bdg. 16.95 (978-1-58536-522-7(X), 202210) Sleeping Bear Pr.

Broach, Elise. Shakespeare's Secret. 2007. (Illus.). 258p. (gr. 4-9). 17.00 (978-0-7569-8204-1(9)) Perfection Learning Corp.

—Shakespeare's Secret. 2007. (ENG.). 272p. (YA). (gr. 6-8). pap. 8.99 (978-0-312-37132-6(2), 900044660) Square Fish.

—Shakespeare's Secret. l.t. ed. 2006. (Thorndike Literacy Bridge Ser.). (Illus.). 263p. (J). (gr. 5-10). 22.95 (978-0-7862-8735-2(7)) Thorndike Pr.

Brookins, Cara. Doris Free. Barrow, Ann, illus. 2006. 127p. (J). pap. (978-1-59336-333-8(8)) Mondo Publishing.

Burket, Shelia. Silver & Gold: Sissy Stringbean Meets Morris Norris. 2012. 28p. 24.95 (978-1-4626-3591-7(1)) America Star Bks.

Butler, Dori Hillestad. King & Kayla & the Case of the Unhappy Neighbor. Meyers, Nancy, illus. 2020. (King & Kayla Ser.: 6). 48p. (J). (gr. 2-4). 14.99 (978-1-68263-055-6(2)) Peachtree Publishing Co. Inc.

Cali, Davide & Dek, Maria. Good Morning, Neighbor: (Picture Book on Sharing, Kindness, & Working As a Team, Ages 4-8) 2018. (ENG., Illus.). 48p. (J). (gr. -1-2). 18.95 (978-1-61689-699-7(X)) Princeton Architectural Pr.

Campoy, F. Isabel & Howell, Theresa. Quizás Algo Hermoso: Cómo el Arte Transformó un Barrio (Maybe Something Beautiful Spanish Edition) López, Rafael, illus. 2018. (SPA.). 40p. (J). (gr. -1-3). 19.99 (978-1-328-90406-5(7), 1700744, Clarion Bks.) HarperCollins Pubs.

Capucilli, Alyssa Satin. Katy Duck Makes a Friend: Ready-To-Read Level 1. Cole, Henry, illus. 2012. (Katy Duck Ser.). (ENG.). 24p. (J). (gr. -1-1). 16.99 (978-1-4424-1977-3(6)); pap. 4.99 (978-1-4424-1976-6(8)) Simon Spotlight. (Simon Spotlight).

Carney, Larry, adapted by. Silly Neighborhood. 2010. (ENG., Illus.). 24p. (J). pap. 6.95 (978-1-60072-157-1(5)) PC Treasures, Inc.

Cartaya, Pablo. The Epic Fail of Arturo Zamora. (ENG.). (J). (gr. 5). 2018. 272p. 8.99 (978-1-101-99725-3(7), Puffin Books) 2017. 256p. 17.99 (978-1-101-99723-9(0), Viking Books for Young Readers) Penguin Young Readers Group.

Cepeda, Joe. The Swing. 2006. (Illus.). (J). 15.99 (978-0-439-14261-8(X), Levine, Arthur A. Bks.) Scholastic, Inc.

Cheaney, J. B. My Friend the Enemy. 2007. 266p. (gr. 4-7). 16.50 (978-0-7569-7946-1(3)) Perfection Learning Corp.

Clark, Chris Elliott. Hazel's Secret. 2008. 64p. pap. 19.95 (978-1-60474-500-9(2)) America Star Bks.

Clary, Julian. The Bolds. Roberts, David, illus. 2017. (Bolds Ser.). (ENG.). 288p. (J). (gr. 3-6). pap. 9.99 (978-1-5124-8174-7(2), 0d6da9d3-74f5-4236-ac56-c272446de989, Carolrhoda Bks.) Lerner Publishing Group.

Clough, Lisa. Missing Molly. 2005. (ENG., Illus.). 32p. (J). (gr. -1-3). reprint ed. 5.95 (978-0-618-55562-8(5), 488681, Clarion Bks.) HarperCollins Pubs.

Cormier, Robert. Frenchtown Summer. unabr. ed. 2004. 128p. (J). (gr. 7-18). pap. 29.00 incl. audio (978-0-8072-0663-8(6), Listening Library) Random Hse. Audio Publishing Group.

Couloumbis, Audrey. Jake. 2011. (ENG.). 176p. (J). (gr. 3-7). pap. 6.99 (978-0-375-85631-0(5), Yearling) Random Hse. Children's Bks.

Creech, Sharon. Moo. 2018. (Penworthy Picks Middle School Ser.). (ENG.). 278p. (J). (gr. 5-7). 17.96 (978-1-64310-363-1(6)) Penworthy Co., LLC, The.

—Moo. 2017. (J). lib. bdg. 17.20 (978-0-606-40402-0(3)) Turtleback.

—Moo: A Novel. (ENG.). 288p. (J). (gr. 3-7). 2017. pap. 9.99 (978-0-06-241526-4(3)) 2016. 16.99 (978-0-06-241524-0(7)) 2016. lib. bdg. 17.89 (978-0-06-241525-7(5)) HarperCollins Pubs. (HarperCollins).

Crimi, Carolyn. The Louds Move In!, 1 vol. Dunnick, Regan, illus. 2006. (ENG.). 32p. (J). (gr. -1-3). 14.95 (978-0-7614-5221-8(4)) Marshall Cavendish Corp.

Cumpiano, Ina. Quinito's Neighborhood (El Vecindario de Quinito) Ramirez, Jose, illus. 2005. (ENG & SPA.). 24p. (J). (gr. -1-1). 16.95 (978-0-89239-209-4(6)) Lee & Low Bks., Inc.

—Quinito's Neighborhood/el Vecindario de Quinito, 1 vol. Ramírez, José, illus. 2013. (Quinito Ser.). (ENG.). 24p. (J). (gr. k-2). pap. 11.95 (978-0-89239-229-2(0), leelowcbp) Lee & Low Bks., Inc.

Dallas, Sandra. Hardscrabble. 2018. (ENG.). 264p. (J). (gr. 3-6). pap. 9.99 (978-1-58536-376-6(6), 204412); 15.95 (978-1-58536-375-9(8), 204400) Sleeping Bear Pr.

Davick, Linda. It's Not Easy Being Mimi. Davick, Linda, illus. (Mimi's World Ser.: 1). (ENG., Illus.). (J). (gr. 1-4). 2019. 192p. pap. 7.99 (978-1-4424-5890-1(9)) 2018. 176p. 13.99 (978-1-4424-5889-5(5)) Beach Lane Bks. (Beach Lane Bks.).

De Marco, Clare. The Mad Scientist Next Door. 2014. (Race Ahead with Reading Ser.). (ENG., Illus.). 32p. (J). (gr. 2-2). (978-0-7787-1305-0(9)) Crabtree Publishing Co.

de Sève, Randall & de Sève, Randall. Zola's Elephant. Zagarenski, Pamela, illus. 2018. (ENG.). 40p. (J). (gr. -1-3). 17.99 (978-1-328-88629-3(8), 1698512, Clarion Bks.) HarperCollins Pubs.

Denton, P. J. Girls Against Boys. Denos, Julia, illus. 2013. (Sleepover Squad Ser.: 7). (ENG.). 96p. (J). (gr. 1-4). pap. 4.99 (978-1-4169-5933-5(5), Simon & Schuster/Paula Wiseman Bks.) Simon & Schuster/Paula Wiseman Bks.

Deveze, Winky. Hewitch. Neate, Andy, illus. 2006. (J). (978-0-9787174-0-7(6)) Love Bug Bks.

DiCamillo, Kate. Mercy Watson to the Rescue. Van Dusen, Chris, illus. (Mercy Watson Ser.: 1). (ENG.). 80p. (J). (gr. k-3). 2009. pap. 6.99 (978-0-7636-4504-5(4)) 2005. 15.99 (978-0-7636-2270-1(2)) Candlewick Pr.

Dicamillo, Kate. Mercy Watson to the Rescue. 2009. (Mercy Watson Ser.: Bk. 1). lib. bdg. 16.00 (978-0-606-06704-1(3)) Turtleback.

Diehl, J. H. Tiny Infinities. 2018. (ENG., Illus.). 352p. (J). (gr. 5-9). 16.99 (978-1-4521-6335-2(9)) Chronicle Bks. LLC.

Doerrfeld, Cori. The Welcome Wagon: A Cubby Hill Tale. 2020. (Cubby Hill Tale Ser.). (ENG., Illus.). 40p. (J). (gr. -1-2). 17.99 (978-1-4197-4417-4(8), 1688701, Abrams Bks. for Young Readers) Abrams, Inc.

Donnelly, Rebecca. How to Stage a Catastrophe. 2017. (ENG., Illus.). 256p. (J). (gr. 4-7). 12.95 (978-1-62370-807-8(9), 133357, Capstone Young Readers) Capstone.

Dooley, Norah. Everybody Brings Noodles. Thornton, Peter J., illus. 40p. (J). 2005. (ENG.). (gr. k-3). pap. 7.99 (978-1-57505-916-7(9), 67d3f290-0d43-43e1-922d-5168d9080e37, First Avenue Editions) 2003. (gr. -1-3). 15.95 (978-0-87614-455-8(5), Carolrhoda Bks.) Lerner Publishing Group.

Duddle, Jonny. The Pirates Next Door. 2012. (ENG., Illus.). 44p. (J). (gr. -1-2). 17.99 (978-0-7636-5842-7(1), Templar) Candlewick Pr.

Durango, Julia. The One Day House. Diaz, Bianca, illus. 2017. 32p. (J). (gr. -1-2). lib. bdg. 17.99 (978-1-58089-709-9(6)) Charlesbridge Publishing, Inc.

Ecton, Emily. Project Jackalope. 2012. (ENG., Illus.). 256p. (J). (gr. 3-7). 15.99 (978-1-4521-0155-2(8)) Chronicle Bks. LLC.

Edwards, Michelle. A Hat for Mrs. Goldman: A Story about Knitting & Love. Karas, G. Brian, illus. 2016. 40p. (J). (gr. -1-3). 18.99 (978-0-553-49710-6(3), Schwartz & Wade Bks.) Random Hse. Children's Bks.

Ellis, Ann Dee. You May Already Be a Winner. 2018. lib. bdg. 19.65 (978-0-606-41307-7(3)) Turtleback.

Ellis, Julie. The New Neighbors. Lewis, Naomi C., illus. 2009. (Rigby PM Stars Bridge Bks.). (ENG.). 16p. (gr. 2-3). pap. 8.70 (978-1-4190-5507-2(0)) Rigby Education.

English, Karen. Nikki & Deja: the Newsy News Newsletter: Nikki & Deja, Book Three, Bk. 3. Freeman, Laura, illus. 2011. (Nikki & Deja Ser.: 3). (ENG.). 96p. (J). (gr. 1-4). pap. 6.99 (978-0-547-40626-8(6), 1428504, Clarion Bks.) HarperCollins Pubs.

—Trouble Next Door: The Carver Chronicles, Book Four. Freeman, Laura, illus. 2018. (Carver Chronicles Ser.). (ENG.). 144p. (J). (gr. 1-4). pap. 6.99 (978-1-328-90011-1(8), 1700039, Clarion Bks.) HarperCollins Pubs.

Fagan, Cary. Mr. Tempkin Climbs a Tree. Arbat, Carles, illus. 2019. (ENG.). 32p. (J). (gr. -1-2). 17.99 (978-1-5415-2173-5(0), 91d22d39-8a82-48ce-a5d1-699b688c7999, Kar-Ben Publishing) Lerner Publishing Group.

Faruqi, Saadia. Yasmin la Superheroína. Aparicio Publishing LLC, Aparicio Publishing, tr. from ENG. Aly, Hatem, illus. 2020. (Yasmin en Español Ser.).Tr. of Yasmin the Superhero. (SPA.). 32p. (J). (gr. k-2). pap. 5.95 (978-1-5158-5733-4(6), 142099); lib. bdg. 20.65 (978-1-5158-5729-7(8), 142094) Capstone. (Picture Window Bks.).

—Yasmin the Superhero. Aly, Hatem, illus. 2019. (Yasmin Ser.). (ENG.). 32p. (J). (gr. k-2). pap. 5.95 (978-1-5158-4579-9(6), 141179); lib. bdg. 22.65 (978-1-5158-3783-1(1), 139365) Capstone. (Picture Window Bks.).

Felix, Monique. The Rumor. Felix, Monique, illus. 2011. (ENG., Illus.). 24p. (J). (gr. 1-3). 19.99 (978-1-56846-219-6(0), 22700, Creative Editions) Creative Co., The.

Fields, Terri. One Good Deed. Melmon, Deborah, illus. 2015. (ENG.). 24p. (J). (gr. -1-3). pap. 7.99 (978-1-4677-3479-0(9), 426fe59e-11b7-4c68-b6d5-5def82f3b7cc, Kar-Ben Publishing) Lerner Publishing Group.

Foston, Desirae. The Hawaiian Hiatus of Herkimer Street. Foston, Desirae, illus. 2013. (Illus.). 24p. 24.00 (978-1-940021-00-3(6)) Bliss Group.

Frank, Lucy. Just Ask Iris. 2003. (ENG., Illus.). 224p. (J). (gr. 5-9). pap. 10.99 (978-0-689-84454-6(9), Atheneum Bks. for Young Readers) Simon & Schuster Children's Publishing.

Friedman, Becky. Nighttime in the Neighborhood. 2015. (Daniel Tiger's Neighborhood 8X8 Ser.). lib. bdg. 13.55 (978-0-606-37876-5(6)) Turtleback.

—Welcome to the Neighborhood! Garwood, Gord, illus. 2014. (Daniel Tiger's Neighborhood Ser.). (ENG.). 24p. (J). (gr. -1-1). pap. 4.99 (978-1-4424-9741-2(6), Simon Spotlight) Simon Spotlight.

Frost, Helen. Blue Daisy. Shepperson, Rob, illus. 2020. 96p. (J). (gr. 2-5). 15.99 (978-0-8234-4414-4(7), Margaret Ferguson Books) Holiday Hse., Inc.

Fruchter, Jason, illus. Daniel's New Friend. 2015. (Daniel Tiger's Neighborhood Ser.). (ENG.). 24p. (J). (gr. -1-2). pap. 4.99 (978-1-4814-3543-7(4), Simon Spotlight) Simon Spotlight.

—Friends Help Each Other: Ready-To-Read Pre-Level 1. 2014. (Daniel Tiger's Neighborhood Ser.). (ENG.). 32p. (J). (gr. -1-k). pap. 4.99 (978-1-4814-0366-5(4), Simon Spotlight) Simon Spotlight.

Gal, Susan. Day by Day. 2012. (ENG., Illus.). 40p. (J). (gr. k-4). E-Book (978-0-375-98433-4(X), Knopf Bks. for Young Readers) Random Hse. Children's Bks.

Gale, Emily. My Super-Spy Diary. Dreidemy, Joëlle & Dreidemy, Joëlle, illus. 2014. (Eliza Boom Ser.: 2). (ENG.). 128p. (J). (gr. 1-4). pap. 5.99 (978-1-4814-0652-9(3), Aladdin) Simon & Schuster Children's Publishing.

Gellock, Ed. The Top Dog Lives Indoors & My Neighbors Live Outside. 2013. 32p. pap. 24.95 (978-1-63000-511-5(8)) America Star Bks.

Gilbert, Michael T., et al. Walt Disney's Comics & Stories #693. Clark, John, ed. 2008. (ENG., Illus.). 64p. pap. 7.99 (978-1-60360-038-5(8), 9781603600385) Gemstone Publishing, Inc.

Gilmore, Rachna. Roses for Gita. Priestley, Alice, illus. 2004. 24p. (J). (TUR & ENG.). (978-1-85269-369-5(X)); (978-1-85269-367-1(3)) Mantra Lingua.

Glaser, Karina Yan. The Vanderbeekers & the Hidden Garden. (Vanderbeekers Ser.: 2). (ENG., Illus.). (J). (gr. 3-7). 2019. 352p. pap. 8.99 (978-0-358-11734-6(8), 1750649) 2018. 336p. 16.99 (978-1-328-77002-8(8), 1681000) HarperCollins Pubs. (Clarion Bks.).

Glines, Abbi. Bad for You. 2015. (Sea Breeze Ser.). (ENG., Illus.). 320p. (YA). (gr. 11). pap. 12.99 (978-1-4814-2074-7(7), Simon Pulse) Simon Pulse.

Grant, Jennifer. Maybe I Can Love My Neighbor Too. Schipper, Benjamin, illus. 2019. 32p. (J). (gr. k-3). 16.99 (978-1-5064-5201-2(9), Beaming Books) 1517 Media.

Gray, Shelly. A Cat Called Spot. 2011. 24p. pap. 24.95 (978-1-4626-0346-6(7)) America Star Bks.

Green, Ruth. Noisy Neighbors. 2011. (ENG., Illus.). 32p. (J). (gr. -1-3). 14.95 (978-1-85437-994-8(1)) Tate Publishing, Ltd. GBR. Dist: Abrams, Inc.

Green, Shari. Macy Mcmillan & the Rainbow Goddess. 2017. (ENG.). 240p. (J). (gr. 3-7). pap. 12.95 (978-1-77278-017-8(0)) Pajama Pr. CAN. Dist: Publishers Group West (PGW).

Grimes, Shaunta. The Astonishing Maybe. 2020. (ENG.). 256p. (J). pap. 20.99 (978-1-250-23363-9(1), 900192879) Square Fish.

Gunderson, Jessica. Olivia Bitter, Spooked-Out Sitter! 2016. (Babysitter Chronicles Ser.). (ENG.). 160p. (J). (gr. 4-7). pap. 6.95 (978-1-4914-8862-1(X), 131487, Stone Arch Bks.) Capstone.

Hahn, Mary Downing. Closed for the Season. 2010. (ENG.). 192p. (J). (gr. 5-7). pap. 7.99 (978-0-547-39853-2(0), 1427651, Clarion Bks.) HarperCollins Pubs.

Hamilton, Martha & Weiss, Mitch. The Stolen Smell. Wrenn, Tom, illus. 2007. (Story Cove Ser.). (ENG.). 32p. (J). (gr. -1-3). 4.95 (978-0-87483-838-1(X)) August Hse. Pubs., Inc.

Hamilton, Pat. Peaches the Private Eye Poodle: The Missing Muffin Caper. 2008. 32p. pap. 13.50 (978-1-60693-277-3(2), Eloquent Bks.) Strategic Book Publishing & Rights Agency (SBPRA).

Harnett, Katie, illus. Archie Snufflekins Oliver Valentine Cupcake Tiberius Cat. 2016. (ENG.). 32p. (J). (gr. -1-k). 16.95 (978-1-909263-37-6(0)) Flying Eye Bks. GBR. Dist: Penguin Random Hse. LLC.

Harper, Charise Mericle. Just Grace. 2008. (Just Grace Ser.: 1). (ENG., Illus.). 144p. (J). (gr. 1-4). pap. 7.99 (978-0-547-01440-1(6), 1030987, Clarion Bks.) HarperCollins Pubs.

Harris, Meena. Kamala & Maya's Big Idea. González, Ana Ramírez, illus. 2020. (ENG.). 32p. (J). (gr. -1-3). 18.99 (978-0-06-293740-7(5), Balzer & Bray) HarperCollins Pubs.

Havill, Juanita. Grow: A Novel in Verse, 1 vol. Kodman, Stanislawa, illus. 160p. (J). (gr. 3-7). 2011. pap. 7.99 (978-1-56145-575-1(X)) 2008. 14.95 (978-1-56145-441-9(9)) Peachtree Publishing Co. Inc.

Hayes, Geoffrey. Benny & Penny in Just Pretend. 2013. (Toon Books Level 2 Ser.). lib. bdg. 14.75 (978-0-606-31597-5(7)) Turtleback.

—Benny & Penny in the Big No-No! Toon Books Level 2. Hayes, Geoffrey, illus. 2009. (Toon Ser.). (ENG., Illus.). 32p. (J). (gr. -1-3). 12.99 (978-0-9799238-9-0(1), TOON Books) Astra Publishing Hse.

Herman, Michael. The Cholent Brigade. Harmer, Sharon, illus. 2017. (ENG.). 24p. (J). (gr. -1-2). 17.99 (978-1-5124-0844-7(1), b722c6c0-cad2-413d-b91b-0dc341c18f8f, Kar-Ben Publishing) Lerner Publishing Group.

Hest, Amy. On the Night of the Shooting Star. Desmond, Jenni, illus. 2017. (ENG.). 32p. (J). (-k). 16.99 (978-0-7636-9154-7(2)) Candlewick Pr.

Hicks, Benjamin. Byron's Tie. Hicks, Benjamin & Hicks, Rosetta, eds. 2013. (Illus.). 35p. pap. 10.00 (978-1-929883-08-0(0)) Ingleside Pr.

Higgins, Nadia. The Zombie Next Door: Zombie Zappers Book 3, 1 vol. 2014. (Zombie Zappers Ser.). (ENG.). 64p. (J). (gr. 5-7). 30.60 (978-1-62285-010-5(6), 95f6a3f4-cb6e-419d-a80d-c1689695a711); pap. 12.71 (978-1-62285-011-2(4), 58a00cf5-5c38-40c1-9132-f56f3c0e0c5c) Enslow Publishing, LLC.

Horvath, Polly. The Pepins & Their Problems, 1 vol. Hafner, Marylin, illus. (ENG.). 192p. pap. 13.95 (978-0-88899-633-6(0)) Groundwood Bks. CAN. Dist: Publishers Group West (PGW).

—The Pepins & Their Problems. Hafner, Marylin, illus. 2008. (ENG.). 208p. (J). (gr. 3-7). per. 9.99 (978-0-312-37751-9(7), 900049141) Square Fish.

Hughes, Melissa. Myles & Otis: A Story of Friendship. 2009. (Illus.). 30p. (J). pap. 14.95 (978-1-4327-5182-1(4)) Outskirts Pr., Inc.

Hulst, W. G. van de & Hulst, Willem G. van de, illus. Kittens, Kittens Everywhere. 2014. (J). (978-1-928136-20-0(6)) Inheritance Pubns.

—The Rockity Rowboat. 2014. (J). (978-1-928136-18-7(4)) Inheritance Pubns.

Hurwitz, Michele Weber. The Summer I Saved the World ... in 65 Days. 2015. (ENG.). 272p. (J). (gr. 5). pap. 9.99 (978-0-385-37109-4(8), Ember) Random Hse. Children's Bks.

Isadora, Rachel. Say Hello! Isadora, Rachel, illus. (Illus.). (J). 2017. 30p. (-k). bds. 8.99 (978-0-399-25632-5(6), Nancy Paulsen Books) 2010. (ENG., 32p. (gr. -1-k). 17.99 (978-0-399-25230-3(4), G.P. Putnam's Sons Books for Young Readers) Penguin Young Readers Group.

Jakubowski, Michele. Third Grade Mix-Up, 1 vol. Montalto, Luisa, illus. 2013. (Sidney & Sydney Ser.). (ENG.). 128p. (J). (gr. 1-3). 8.95 (978-1-4048-8104-4(2), 121876, Picture Window Bks.) Capstone.

James, Kristopher. Lyrian. 2009. (Illus.). 171p. pap. 16.95 (978-1-4092-8986-9(9)) Lulu Pr., Inc.

Jenkins, Emily. The Little Bit Scary People. Boiger, Alexandra, illus. 2008. (ENG.). 32p. (gr. -1-1). 16.99 (978-1-4231-0075-1(1)) Hyperion Pr.

John, Jory. Goodnight Already! Davies, Benji, illus. 2014. (ENG.). 32p. (J). (gr. -1-3). 19.99 (978-0-06-228620-8(X), HarperCollins) HarperCollins Pubs.

Johnson, DeAnna. Blarron Creek Chronicles. 2009. 108p. 23.49 (978-1-4389-5580-3(4)) AuthorHouse.

Johnson, Regan. Little Bunny Kung Fu. Johnson, Regan, illus. 2005. (ENG., Illus.). 32p. (J). (gr. -1 — 1). 14.95 (978-0-9769417-8-1(3)) Blooming Tree Pr.

Johnson, Richard, illus. Don't Cry, Sly! 2004. 32p. (J). (ENG, ARA & BEN.). pap. (978-1-85269-649-8(4)); (ENG & PER.). pap. (978-1-85269-653-5(2)); (ENG & POR.). pap. (978-1-85269-659-7(1)); (SPA & ENG.). pap. (978-1-85269-662-7(1)) Mantra Lingua.

Jun, Nie. My Beijing: Four Stories of Everyday Wonder. 2018. (ENG., Illus.). 128p. (J). (gr. 2-5). pap. 15.99 (978-1-5415-2642-6(2), eb6ccd5f-a831-48d5-9325-cec88d5d3470); 30.65 (978-1-5124-4590-9(8), f9e5accf-7aeb-4c2a-88bb-5a21312d4a9a) Lerner Publishing Group. (Graphic Universe™).

Kaiser, Lori. Florence Flamingo Gets the Flu. Kaiser, Lori, illus. 2012. (Illus.). 30p. pap. (978-0-9836651-5-1(X)) Roxby Media Ltd.

Kane, Kim. The Next Door Friend. 2018. (Ginger Green, Playdate Queen Ser.). (ENG., Illus.). 64p. (J). (gr. 1-3). pap. 5.95 (978-1-5158-2011-6(4), 136658, Picture Window Bks.) Capstone.

—The Next Door Friend. Davis, Jon, illus. 2017. (Ginger Green, Playdate Queen Ser.). (ENG.). 64p. (J). (gr. 1-3). lib.

MNO

bdg. 23.32 *(978-1-5158-1949-3(3)*, 136632, Picture Window Bks.) Capstone.

Karsten, Margo & Karsten, Steven. The Story of Sugar Cookie. 2010. 36p. 18.99 *(978-1-4520-8177-9(8))* AuthorHouse.

Keller, Laurie. Do unto Otters: A Book about Manners. Keller, Laurie, illus. 2007. (ENG., Illus.). 40p. (J). (gr. k-3). 21.99 *(978-0-8050-7996-8(3)*, 900034600, Holt, Henry & Co. Bks. For Young Readers) Holt, Henry & Co.

—Do unto Otters: A Book about Manners. Keller, Laurie, illus. 2009. (ENG., Illus.). 40p. (J). (gr. k-3). pap. 9.99 *(978-0-312-58140-4(8)*, 900061994) Square Fish.

Kimmel, Haven. Kaline Klattermaster's Tree House. Brown, Peter, illus. 2008. (ENG.). 152p. (J). (gr. 4-6). 18.69 *(978-0-689-87402-4(2))* Simon & Schuster, Inc.

Kittinger, Jo S. The House on Dirty-Third Street, 1 vol. Gonzalez, Thomas, illus. 2012. 32p. (J). (gr. -1-3). 16.95 *(978-1-56145-619-2(5))* Peachtree Publishing Co. Inc.

Ko, Hannah. Jonny's Neighborhood. de Polonia, Nina, illus. 2017. (All about Me Ser.). (ENG.). 24p. (gr. -1-2). pap. 9.95 *(978-1-68342-778-0(5)*, 9781683427780) Rourke Educational Media.

Konigsburg, E. L. The Mysterious Edge of the Heroic World. 2007. (ENG., Illus.). 256p. (J). (gr. 4-8). 16.99 *(978-1-4169-4972-5(0))* Simon & Schuster, Inc.

Kroll, Steven. Stuff! Reduce, Reuse, Recycle: Reduce, Reuse, Recycle, 0 vols. Cox, Steve, illus. 2012. (ENG.). 32p. (J). (gr. -1-3). pap. 9.99 *(978-0-7614-6237-8(6)*, 9780761462378, Two Lions) Amazon Publishing.

Kroll, Virginia. Makayla Cares about Others. Cote, Nancy, illus. 2007. (Way I Act Bks.). (ENG.). 24p. (J). (gr. -1-3). lib. bdg. 15.99 *(978-0-8075-4945-2(2)*, 807549452) Whitman, Albert & Co.

Krulik, Nancy. Doggone It! #8. John and Wendy, illus. 8th ed. 2006. (Katie Kazoo, Switcheroo Ser.: 8). (ENG.). 80p. (J). (gr. 2-4). 6.99 *(978-0-448-43172-7(6)*, Grosset & Dunlap) Penguin Young Readers Group.

Lachtman, Ofelia Dumas. Pepita on Pepper Street/Pepita en la Calle Pepper. Monsivais, Maria Estela, tr. from ENG. Delange, Alex Pardo, illus. 2008. (SPA & ENG.). 32p. (J). (gr. -1-3). 16.95 *(978-1-55885-443-7(6)*, Piñata Books) Arte Publico Pr.

—Pepita Packs Up: Pepita Empaca. Ventura, Gabriela Baeza, tr. from ENG. Delange, Alex Pardo, illus. 2005. 48p. (J). (gr. -1-k). lib. bdg. 16.95 *(978-1-55885-431-4(2)*, Piñata Books) Arte Publico Pr.

—The Trouble with Tessa. 2005. 122p. (J). (gr. 3-7). per. 9.95 *(978-1-55885-448-2(7)*, Piñata Books) Arte Publico Pr.

Lange, Willem. Favor Johnson: A Christmas Story. Dodson, Bert, illus. 2009. (ENG.). 32p. (J). (gr. 1-3). 16.95 *(978-1-59373-082-6(9))* Bunker Hill Publishing, Inc.

Lasky, Kathryn. Chasing Orion. 2010. (ENG., Illus.). 368p. (J). (gr. 5-18). 17.99 *(978-0-7636-3982-2(6))* Candlewick Pr.

Lawlor, Laurie. Big Tree Down! Gordon, David, illus. 2018. (ENG.). 32p. (J). (gr. -1-3). 17.95 *(978-0-8234-3661-3(6))* Holiday Hse., Inc.

Leoni, Gail. Chalk Dust. 2008. 36p. pap. 24.95 *(978-1-60474-881-9(8))* America Star Bks.

Levy, Dana Alison. The Family Fletcher Takes Rock Island. 2017. (Family Fletcher Ser.: 2). (ENG.). 272p. (J). (gr. 4-7). 7.99 *(978-0-553-52133-7(0)*, Yearling) Random Hse. Children's Bks.

Liphardt, Linda. Secret in the Old Barn. 2008. 116p. pap. 19.95 *(978-1-60703-615-9(0))* America Star Bks.

Lisle, Janet Taylor. Afternoon of the Elves. 2017. (ENG., Illus.). 128p. (J). (gr. 3-7). 19.99 *(978-1-4814-9308-8(4)*, Atheneum Bks. for Young Readers) Simon & Schuster Children's Publishing.

Littman, Sarah Darer. Backlash. 2015. (ENG.). 336p. (YA). (gr. 7). 17.99 *(978-0-545-65126-4(3)*, Scholastic Pr.) Scholastic, Inc.

Lloyd, Sam R. Yummy Yummy! Food for My Tummy. Tickle, Jack, illus. 2004. 32p. (J). tchr. ed. 15.95 *(978-1-58925-035-2(4))* Tiger Tales.

Loney, Andrea J. Double Bass Blues. Gutierrez, Rudy, illus. 2019. 32p. (J). (gr. -1-3). 18.99 *(978-1-5247-1852-7(1)*, Knopf Bks. for Young Readers) Random Hse. Children's Bks.

Look, Lenore. Ruby Lu, Brave & True. 2004. (Illus.). 104p. (J). lib. bdg. 15.00 *(978-1-4242-0914-9(5))* Fitzgerald Bks.

—Ruby Lu, Brave & True. Wilsdorf, Anne, illus. 2006. (Ruby Lu Ser.). (ENG.). 112p. (J). (gr. 1-5). pap. 6.99 *(978-1-4169-1389-4(0)*, Atheneum Bks. for Young Readers) Simon & Schuster Children's Publishing.

Lopez-Alt, J. Kenji & Ruggiero, Gianna. Every Night Is Pizza Night. 2020. (ENG., Illus.). 48p. (J). (gr. -1-2). 17.95 *(978-1-324-00525-4(4)*, 340525, Norton Young Readers) Norton, W. W. & Co., Inc.

Lottridge, Celia. The Listening Tree, 1 vol. 2010. (ENG.). 154p. (J). (gr. 4-6). pap. 11.95 *(978-1-55455-052-4(1)*, 9f0bfe2e-3d5f-41a8-a347-4a63232b6e17) Trifolium Bks., Inc. CAN. Dist: Firefly Bks., Ltd.

Lowe, Natasha. Lucy Castor Finds Her Sparkle. 2018. (ENG., Illus.). 240p. (J). (gr. 3-7). 16.99 *(978-1-5344-0196-9(2)*, Simon & Schuster/Paula Wiseman Bks.) Simon & Schuster/Paula Wiseman Bks.

Macomber, Debbie. The Yippy, Yappy Yorkie in the Green Doggy Sweater. Lambert, Sally Anne, illus. 2011. (ENG.). 32p. (J). (gr. -1-2). 17.99 *(978-0-06-165096-3(X)*, HarperCollins) HarperCollins Pubs.

Maithya, Susan M. Struffel Cares: Struffel's New Pet. 2012. 40p. pap. 20.99 *(978-1-4772-3323-8(7))* AuthorHouse.

Manning, Maurie J. Laundry Day. Manning, Maurie J., illus. 2012. (ENG., Illus.). 40p. (J). (gr. -1-3). 16.99 *(978-0-547-24196-8(8)*, 1099085, Clarion Bks.) HarperCollins Pubs.

Mannone, Christine. Flowers for Pudding Street. Carolan, Christine, illus. 2009. (ENG.). 32p. (J). 15.95 *(978-1-934860-02-1(6))* Shenanigan Bks.

Mansfield, Creina. My Nutty Neighbours. 2006. (ENG., Illus.). 192p. (J). pap. 12.95 *(978-0-86278-788-2(2))* O'Brien Pr., Ltd., The IRL. Dist: Dufour Editions, Inc.

Manushkin, Fran. Katie Saves Thanksgiving, 1 vol. Lyon, Tammie, illus. 2010. (Katie Woo Ser.). (ENG.). 32p. (J). (gr. k-2). pap. 5.95 *(978-1-4048-6367-5(2)*, 114019); lib. bdg. 21.32 *(978-1-4048-5988-3(8)*, 102656) Capstone. (Picture Window Bks.).

Manzano, Sonia. Miracle on 133rd Street. Priceman, Marjorie, illus. 2015. (ENG.). 48p. (J). (gr. -1-3). 17.99 *(978-0-689-87887-9(7))* Simon & Schuster Children's Publishing.

Marsh, Carole. The Puzzle of the Shark Surfer Girl. 2006. (Criss Cross Applesauce Ser.). (Illus.). 54p. (J). (gr. 1-3). 14.95 *(978-0-635-06204-8(6))* Gallopade International.

Marston, Elsa. The Olive Tree. Ewart, Claire, illus. 2014. 32p. (J). (gr. -1-2). 16.95 *(978-1-937786-29-8(3)*, Wisdom Tales) World Wisdom, Inc.

Martin, Ann M. Keeping Secrets, 7. 2009. (Main Street Ser.: 7). (ENG.). 208p. (J). (gr. 4-6). 21.19 *(978-0-439-86885-3(8))* Scholastic, Inc.

Martinez, Claudia Guadalupe. Pig Park, 1 vol. 2014. (ENG.). 248p. (J). (gr. 9-12). 15.95 *(978-1-935955-76-4(4)*, 23353382, Cinco Puntos Press) Lee & Low Bks., Inc.

Massie, Elizabeth. Ameri-Scares: Virginia. 2013. 150p. (J). pap. 12.99 *(978-1-937530-52-5(3)*, Wonderstruck Bks.) Crossroad Pr.

May, Kyla. Coco: My Delicious Life. 2013. (Lotus Lane Ser.: 2). lib. bdg. 14.75 *(978-0-606-31978-2(6))* Turtleback.

—Lulu: My Glamorous Life: a Branches Book (Lotus Lane #3) 2013. (Lotus Lane Ser.: 3). (ENG.). 96p. (J). (gr. 1-3). E-Book *(978-0-545-49682-7(9))* Scholastic, Inc.

—My Glamorous Life. 2013. (Lotus Lane Ser.: 3). lib. bdg. 14.75 *(978-0-606-32364-2(3))* Turtleback.

—Pug's Snow Day: a Branches Book (Diary of a Pug #2) (Library Edition) May, Kyla, illus. 2019. (Diary of a Pug Ser.: 2). (ENG., Illus.). 80p. (J). (gr. k-2). 24.99 *(978-1-338-53007-0(0))* Scholastic, Inc.

McBay, Bruce. Angels Inc, 1 vol. LaFave, Kim, illus. 2008. (ENG.). 71p. (J). (gr. 1-3). pap. 7.95 *(978-1-896580-30-2(0))* Tradewind Bks. CAN. Dist: Orca Bk. Pubs. USA.

McIntyre, Sarah. The New Neighbors. 2019. (ENG., Illus.). 32p. (J). (gr. -1-2). 17.99 *(978-1-5247-8996-1(8)*, Penguin Workshop) Penguin Young Readers Group.

McKay, Hilary. Binny Bewitched. Ross, Tony, illus. 2017. (ENG.). 240p. (J). (gr. 3-7). 17.99 *(978-1-4814-9102-0(4)*, McElderry, Margaret K. Bks.) McElderry, Margaret K. Bks.

—Lulu & the Rabbit Next Door. 2014. (Lulu Ser.: 4). (J). lib. bdg. 14.75 *(978-0-606-41566-8(1))* Turtleback.

—Lulu & the Rabbit Next Door. Lamont, Priscilla, illus. 2014. (Lulu Ser.: 4). (ENG.). 112p. (J). (gr. 1-5). 13.99 *(978-0-8075-4816-5(2)*, 807548162) Whitman, Albert & Co.

Meltzer, Amy. A Mezuzah on the Door. Fried, Janice, illus. 2007. (Jewish Identity Ser.). 32p. (J). (gr. -1-3). 17.95 *(978-1-58013-249-7(9)*, Kar-Ben Publishing) Lerner Publishing Group.

Michelin, Linda. Zuzu's Wishing Cake. Johnson, D. B., illus. 2006. (ENG.). 32p. (J). (gr. -1-3). 16.00 *(978-0-618-64640-1(X)*, 518747, Clarion Bks.) HarperCollins Pubs.

Miller, Tiwana Mutch. Praying Time. 2008. (YA). per. 10.00 *(978-0-9788937-8-1(6))* Amani Publishing, LLC.

Mills, Claudia. Mason Dixon: Basketball Disasters. Francis, Guy, illus. 2013. (Mason Dixon Ser.: 3). 176p. (J). (gr. 2-5). pap. 6.99 *(978-0-375-87276-1(0)*, Yearling) Random Hse. Children's Bks.

Mills, Nathan & Nolan, Mary. Mike's Busy Neighborhood, 1 vol. 2012. (Rosen Readers Ser.). (ENG., Illus.). 16p. (J). (gr. k-k). pap. 7.00 *(978-1-4488-8758-3(5)*, c12d1007-788c-4d55-a78e-56f3fe2881c2, Rosen Classroom) Rosen Publishing Group, Inc., The.

Mincks, Margaret. Payback on Poplar Lane. 2019. (Poplar Kids Ser.: 1). 336p. (J). (gr. 3-7). 10.99 *(978-0-425-29091-0(3)*, Puffin Books) Penguin Young Readers Group.

Miyares, Daniel. That Neighbor Kid. Miyares, Daniel, illus. 2017. (ENG., Illus.). 32p. (J). (gr. -1-3). 19.99 *(978-1-4814-4979-3(6)*, Simon & Schuster Bks. For Young Readers) Simon & Schuster Bks. For Young Readers.

Mora, Oge. Thank You, Omu! (Caldecott Honor Book) 2018. (ENG., Illus.). 40p. (J). (gr. -1-3). 18.99 *(978-0-316-43124-8(9))* Little, Brown Bks. for Young Readers.

Muir, Leslie. C. R. Mudgeon. Hector, Julian, illus. 2012. (ENG.). 32p. (J). (gr. -1-3). 15.99 *(978-1-4169-7906-7(9)*, Atheneum Bks. for Young Readers) Simon & Schuster Children's Publishing.

Mullaly Hunt, Lynda. Shouting at the Rain. 2019. 288p. (J). (gr. 5). 17.99 *(978-0-399-17515-2(6)*, Nancy Paulsen Books) Penguin Young Readers Group.

Mullican, Judy. Someone New in the Neighborhood. Storch, Ellen N. & Gillen, Lisa P., illus. l.t. ed. 2005. 20p. (J). (gr. -1-k). pap. 10.95 *(978-1-57332-356-7(X)*, HighReach Learning, Incorporated) Carson-Dellosa Publishing, LLC.

Munsell, Jill. What a Day for a Parade. 2010. 48p. pap. 19.95 *(978-1-4389-9080-4(4))* AuthorHouse.

Murphy, Stuart J. Emma's Friendwich. 2010. (I See I Learn Ser.: 1). (Illus.). 32p. (J). (gr. -1-k). pap. 6.95 *(978-1-58089-451-7(8))* Charlesbridge Publishing, Inc.

Muth, Jon J. Zen Ties (a Stillwater & Friends Book) Muth, Jon J., illus. 2008. (ENG., Illus.). 40p. (J). (gr. -1-3). 18.99 *(978-0-439-63425-0(3)*, Scholastic Pr.) Scholastic, Inc.

Naumann-Villemin, Christine. When a Wolf Is Hungry. Di Giacomo, Kris, illus. 2017. (ENG.). 34p. (J). 16.00 *(978-0-8028-5482-7(6)*, Eerdmans Bks For Young Readers) Eerdmans, William B. Publishing Co.

Naylor, Phyllis Reynolds. Cuckoo Feathers, 0 vols. Ramsey, Marcy, illus. 2012. (Simply Sarah Ser.: 2). (ENG.). 96p. (J). (gr. 1-4). pap. 7.99 *(978-0-7614-5541-7(8)*, 9780761455417, Two Lions) Amazon Publishing.

—Patches & Scratches, 0 vols. Ramsey, Marcy, illus. 2012. (Simply Sarah Ser.: 3). (ENG.). 80p. (J). (gr. 1-3). pap. 7.99 *(978-0-7614-5731-2(3)*, 9780761457312, Two Lions) Amazon Publishing.

Norfleet, Mary Crockett. Hand Me down House. Mallory, Edgar, illus. 2011. 98p. 38.95 *(978-1-258-07946-8(1))* Literary Licensing, LLC.

O'Coyne, James. Gravelle's Land of Horror. Whispering Pine Press International, Inc. Staff, ed. Baer, Brian, illus. 2007. (ENG.). 120p. (J). per. 9.95 *(978-1-59649-604-0(5))* Whispering Pine Pr. International, Inc.

Oldcorne, Michelle. Landy Saves the Day. 2009. (Illus.). 32p. pap. 12.49 *(978-1-4490-0574-0(8))* AuthorHouse.

Olson, Norah. Twisted Fate. 2016. (ENG.). 288p. (YA). (gr. 8). pap. 9.99 *(978-0-06-227206-5(3)*, Tegen, Katherine Bks) HarperCollins Pubs.

Packer, Rachel Orenstein. Sky High Sukkah. Zemke, Deborah, illus. 2016. (ENG.). 32p. (J). 17.95 *(978-1-68115-513-5(3)*, fa1eb525-090c-42a2-b44c-b9fecdbdcf77) Behrman Hse., Inc.

Parish, Herman. Amelia Bedelia Makes a Friend. Avril, Lynne, illus. 2011. (I Can Read Level 1 Ser.). (ENG.). 32p. (J). (gr. k-3). 16.99 *(978-0-06-207516-1(0))*; pap. 4.99 *(978-0-06-207515-4(2))* HarperCollins Pubs. (Greenwillow Bks.).

Parker, Deborah. In the Garden (Cj) 2008. 24p. 7.95 *(978-1-60231-000-1(9)*, Cub Bks.) Global Business Information Strategies, Inc.

Paschkis, Julie. Kalinka & Grakkle, 1 vol. 2018. (Illus.). 32p. (J). (gr. -1-3). 17.95 *(978-1-68263-030-3(7))* Peachtree Publishing Co. Inc.

Patch, Lisa. Tales of the Lush Green Woods. Patch, Michael, illus. 2012. 42p. 16.50 *(978-0-9852501-5-7(1))* Inkwell Books LLC.

Paulsen, Gary. Notes from the Dog. 2011. (ENG.). 144p. (YA). (gr. 7). pap. 8.99 *(978-0-375-85542-9(4)*, Ember) Random Hse. Children's Bks.

Payne, C. C. Something to Sing About. 2008. (ENG.). 167p. (J). (gr. 4-7). pap. 8.50 *(978-0-8028-5344-8(7))* Eerdmans, William B. Publishing Co.

Peck, Richard. A Season of Gifts. 2010. (ENG.). 208p. (J). (gr. 5-18). 8.99 *(978-0-14-241729-4(7)*, Puffin Books) Penguin Young Readers Group.

Perkins, Stephanie. Lola & the Boy Next Door. 2013. 368p. (YA). (gr. 9). pap. 12.99 *(978-0-14-242201-4(0)*, Speak) Penguin Young Readers Group.

Peterson, Esther Allen. The House That Cared. 2010. (J). pap. *(978-0-88092-505-1(1))* Royal Fireworks Publishing Co.

—Will Spring Come? 2009. (Illus.). 157p. (J). *(978-0-88092-768-0(2))* Royal Fireworks Publishing Co.

Pierro, Rita. No Veggies for Me. Iukel, Onur, illus. 2011. 32p. pap. 24.95 *(978-1-4626-4554-1(2))* America Star Bks.

Platt, Cynthia. Grow. Holden, Olivia, illus. 2018. (ENG.). 32p. (J). (gr. 1-3). 17.99 *(978-1-68152-239-5(X)*, 14937) Amicus.

Polk, James. Mr. & Mrs. Love & the Neighborhood Children. 2003. pap. 11.00 *(978-0-8059-9232-8(4)*, RoseDog Bks.) Dorrance Publishing Co., Inc.

Powell, Alma. America's Promise. Winborn, Marsha, illus. 2003. 32p. (J). (gr. -1-2). 16.89 *(978-0-06-052173-8(2))* HarperCollins Pubs.

Powell, Lenora Y. Ardo: The Mysterious New House. 2008. 105p. pap. 19.95 *(978-1-60672-133-9(X))* America Star Bks.

Publications International Ltd. Staff, ed. Elmo's Neighborhood Lights & Music Treasury. 2009. 160p. (J). bds. 17.98 *(978-1-4127-2388-6(4)*, PIL Kids) Publications International, Ltd.

Ran, Gila. The Lemonheads, the Crown of Wisdom. 2011. (ENG.). 20p. 11.00 *(978-1-257-12995-9(3))* Lulu Pr., Inc.

Reich, Dale. Noah's Neighbor. 2015. (ENG., Illus.). 34p. (J). pap. 9.95 *(978-1-55571-799-5(3)*, Grid Pr.) L & R Publishing, LLC.

Reiner, Carl. Tell Me A Scary Story... but Not Too Scary. 2009. (ENG.). (J). (gr. 1-3). 18.95 incl. lp *(978-1-59687-926-3(2))* IBks., Inc.

Reynolds, Alison. A New Friend for Marmalade. McKenzie, Heath, illus. 2014. (ENG.). 40p. (J). (gr. -1-1). 15.99 *(978-1-4814-2046-4(1)*, Little Simon) Little Simon.

Reynolds Naylor, Phyllis. Boys Rock! 2007. (Boy/Girl Battle Ser.: 11). (ENG.). 144p. (J). (gr. 3-7). 5.99 *(978-0-440-41990-7(5)*, Yearling) Random Hse. Children's Bks.

—The Girls Take Over. 2004. (Boys Against Girls Ser.: No. 8). 146p. (J). (gr. 4-7). 13.65 *(978-0-7569-2804-9(4))* Perfection Learning Corp.

—The Girls Take Over. 2004. (Boy/Girl Battle Ser.: 8). 160p. (J). (gr. 3-7). 6.99 *(978-0-440-41678-4(7)*, Yearling) Random Hse. Children's Bks.

—Who Won the War? 2008. (Boy/Girl Battle Ser.: 12). (ENG.). 160p. (J). (gr. 3-7). 5.99 *(978-0-440-41991-4(3)*, Yearling) Random Hse. Children's Bks.

Richler, Mordecai. Jacob Two-Two's First Spy Case. Petricic, Dusan, illus. 2009. (Jacob Two-Two Ser.). (ENG.). 176p. (J). (gr. 4-7). 10.95 *(978-0-88776-927-6(6))* Tundra Bks. CAN. Dist: Random Hse., Inc.

Rigby Education Staff. Jacko of Baker Street. (Sails Literacy Ser.). (Illus.). 16p. (gr. 1-2). 27.00 *(978-0-7635-9931-7(X)*, 699319C99) Rigby Education.

Roberts, Emma Perry. Mrs. Murphy's Marvelous Mansion. Rogalski, Robert, illus. 2006. 32p. (J). (gr. -1-3). 15.95 *(978-0-9740190-4-8(6)*, 888-210-8216) Illumination Arts Publishing Co., Inc.

Roberts, Willo Davis. Hostage. 2016. (ENG., Illus.). 176p. (J). (gr. 3-7). pap. 7.99 *(978-1-4814-5788-0(8)*, Aladdin) Simon & Schuster Children's Publishing.

—Hostage. 2016. (ENG., Illus.). 176p. (J). (gr. 3-7). 17.99 *(978-1-4814-5789-7(6)*, Simon & Schuster/Paula Wiseman Bks.) Simon & Schuster/Paula Wiseman Bks.

Robey, Katharine Crawford. Hare & the Big Green Lawn. MacDougall, Larry, illus. 2006. (ENG.). 32p. (J). (gr. -1-3). 15.95 *(978-0-87358-889-8(4))* Cooper Square Publishing Llc.

Rockliff, Mara. Chik Chak Shabbat. Brooker, Kyrsten, illus. (ENG.). 32p. (J). (gr. -1-2). 2016. 7.99 *(978-0-7636-8895-0(9))* 2014. 16.99 *(978-0-7636-5528-0(7))* Candlewick Pr.

Rocklin, Joanne. One Day & One Amazing Morning on Orange Street. 2012. (ENG., Illus.). 224p. (J). (gr. 3-7). pap. 8.95 *(978-1-4197-0181-8(9)*, 690103, Amulet Bks.) Abrams, Inc.

Rowe, Vicki J. Yellow Roses. 2012. 64p. pap. 15.99 *(978-1-4771-2636-3(8))* Xlibris Corp.

Roy, Ron. Calendar Mysteries #11: November Night. Gurney, John Steven, illus. 2014. (Calendar Mysteries Ser.: 11). 80p. (J). (gr. 1-4). 7.99 *(978-0-385-37165-0(9)*, Random Hse. Bks. for Young Readers) Random Hse. Children's Bks.

Rozelaar, Angie. The Great Pumpkin Contest. Rozelaar, Angie, illus. 2019. (ENG., Illus.). 40p. (J). (gr. -1-3). 17.99 *(978-0-06-274137-0(3)*, Tegen, Katherine Bks) HarperCollins Pubs.

Rubin, Adam. Those Darn Squirrels! Salmieri, Daniel, illus. 2011. (ENG.). 32p. (J). (gr. -1-3). pap. 7.99 *(978-0-547-57681-7(1)*, 1458442, Clarion Bks.) HarperCollins Pubs.

—Those Darn Squirrels & the Cat Next Door. Salmieri, Daniel, illus. 2011. (ENG.). 32p. (J). (gr. -1-3). 16.99 *(978-0-547-42922-9(3)*, 1432155, Clarion Bks.) HarperCollins Pubs.

Rykken, John. Bloodwood: The Chronicles of Max Mayhem. 2011. 264p. (gr. 10-12). 26.95 *(978-1-4620-0656-4(6))*; pap. 16.95 *(978-1-4620-0657-1(4))* iUniverse, Inc.

Rylant, Cynthia. Annie & Snowball & the Thankful Friends: Ready-To-Read Level 2. Stevenson, Suçie & Stevenson, Suçie, illus. 2011. (Annie & Snowball Ser.: 10). (ENG.). 40p. (J). (gr. k-2). 15.99 *(978-1-4169-7200-6(5)*, Simon Spotlight) Simon Spotlight.

—Mr. Putter & Tabby Clear the Decks. Howard, Arthur, illus. alt. ed. 2011. (Mr. Putter & Tabby Ser.). (ENG.). 44p. (J). (gr. 1-4). pap. 5.99 *(978-0-547-57695-4(1)*, 1458450, Clarion Bks.) HarperCollins Pubs.

—Mr. Putter & Tabby Dance the Dance. Howard, Arthur, illus. 2013. (Mr. Putter & Tabby Ser.). (ENG.). 40p. (J). (gr. 1-4). pap. 5.99 *(978-0-544-10496-9(X)*, 1540802, Clarion Bks.) HarperCollins Pubs.

—Mr. Putter & Tabby Dance the Dance. 2013. (Mr. Putter & Tabby Ser.). lib. bdg. 16.00 *(978-0-606-32338-3(4))* Turtleback.

—Mr. Putter & Tabby Hit the Slope. Howard, Arthur, illus. (Mr. Putter & Tabby Ser.). (ENG.). 40p. (J). (gr. 1-4). 2017. pap. 5.99 *(978-1-328-74060-1(9)*, 1677037) 2016. 14.99 *(978-0-15-206427-3(3)*, 1199224) HarperCollins Pubs. (Clarion Bks.).

—Mr. Putter & Tabby Make a Wish. Howard, Arthur, illus. 2006. (Mr. Putter & Tabby Ser.). (ENG.). 44p. (J). (gr. -1-3). pap. 5.99 *(978-0-15-205443-4(X)*, 1196381, Clarion Bks.) HarperCollins Pubs.

—Mr. Putter & Tabby Make a Wish. Howard, Arthur, illus. 2006. (Mr. Putter & Tabby Ser.). (gr. 1-4). 16.00 *(978-0-7569-6892-2(5))* Perfection Learning Corp.

—Mr. Putter & Tabby Ring the Bell. Howard, Arthur, illus. 2012. (Mr. Putter & Tabby Ser.). (ENG.). 44p. (J). (gr. 1-4). pap. 5.99 *(978-0-547-85075-7(1)*, 1501053, Clarion Bks.) HarperCollins Pubs.

—Mr. Putter & Tabby Ring the Bell. Howard, Arthur, illus. 2012. (Mr. Putter & Tabby Ser.). lib. bdg. 16.00 *(978-0-606-26614-7(3))* Turtleback.

—Mr. Putter & Tabby See the Stars. Howard, Arthur, illus. 2008. (Mr. Putter & Tabby Ser.). (ENG.). 44p. (J). (gr. 1-4). pap. 6.99 *(978-0-15-206366-5(8)*, 1199066, Clarion Bks.) HarperCollins Pubs.

—Mr. Putter & Tabby Spill the Beans. Howard, Arthur, illus. 2010. (Mr. Putter & Tabby Ser.). (ENG.). 44p. (J). (gr. 1-4). pap. 5.99 *(978-0-547-41433-1(1)*, 1429464, Clarion Bks.) HarperCollins Pubs.

—Mr. Putter & Tabby Spin the Yarn. Howard, Arthur, illus. 2007. (Mr. Putter & Tabby Ser.). (ENG.). 44p. (J). (gr. 1-4). pap. 5.99 *(978-0-15-206095-4(2)*, 1198308, Clarion Bks.) HarperCollins Pubs.

—Mr. Putter & Tabby Spin the Yarn. Howard, Arthur, illus. 2007. (Mr. Putter & Tabby Ser.). (gr. 1-4). lib. bdg. 16.00 *(978-0-7569-8062-7(3))* Perfection Learning Corp.

—Mr. Putter & Tabby Stir the Soup. Howard, Arthur, illus. 2004. (Mr. Putter & Tabby Ser.). (ENG.). 44p. (J). (gr. 1-4). pap. 5.99 *(978-0-15-205058-0(2)*, 1195275, Clarion Bks.) HarperCollins Pubs.

—Mr. Putter & Tabby Stir the Soup. Howard, Arthur, illus. 2004. (Mr. Putter & Tabby Ser.). (gr. 1-4). 16.00 *(978-0-7569-3915-1(1))* Perfection Learning Corp.

Scarry, Richard. Richard Scarry's Postman Pig & His Busy Neighbors. 2015. lib. bdg. 14.75 *(978-0-606-36401-0(3))* Turtleback.

Schaefer, Laura. Littler Women: A Modern Retelling. 2017. (ENG., Illus.). 224p. (J). (gr. 3-7). 16.99 *(978-1-4814-8761-0(2)*, Simon & Schuster/Paula Wiseman Bks.) Simon & Schuster/Paula Wiseman Bks.

Schulman, Janet. 10 Trim-The-Tree'ers. Davick, Linda, illus. 2011. (ENG.). 32p. (J). (gr. -1 — 1). bds. 6.99 *(978-0-375-87302-7(3)*, Knopf Bks. for Young Readers) Random Hse. Children's Bks.

Sharp, N. L. Effie's Image. 2008. (ENG., Illus.). 29p. pap. 8.95 *(978-0-9759829-2-1(3))* Prairieland Pr.

Silvey, Craig. The Amber Amulet. 2018. (ENG., Illus.). 96p. (J). (gr. 5-5). 14.99 *(978-1-5107-2189-0(4)*, Sky Pony Pr.) Skyhorse Publishing Co., Inc.

Smalley, Ruth Ann. Sheila Thinks We're Weird, 1 vol. Emery, Jennifer, illus. 2011. (ENG.). 32p. (J). 16.95 *(978-0-88448-326-7(6))* Tilbury Hse. Pubs.

Smallman, Jeff. Stump's in the Cellar. 2008. 100p. pap. 13.95 *(978-0-557-03091-0(9))* Lulu Pr., Inc.

Sobol, John. Friend or Foe?, 1 vol. Tolstikova, Dasha, illus. 2016. (ENG.). 32p. (J). (gr. -1-2). 18.95 *(978-1-55498-407-7(6))* Groundwood Bks. CAN. Dist: Publishers Group West (PGW).

Soileau, Hodges, illus. The Black Widow Spider Mystery. 2004. (Boxcar Children Special Ser.). 130p. (gr. 2-7). 15.50 *(978-0-7569-3266-4(1))* Perfection Learning Corp.

Springstubb, Tricia. Mo Wren, Lost & Found. Ross, Heather, illus. 2011. (Fox Street Ser.: 2). (ENG.). 256p. (J). (gr. 3-7). 15.99 *(978-0-06-199039-7(6)*, Balzer & Bray) HarperCollins Pubs.

—What Happened on Fox Street. Ross, Heather, illus. 2011. (Fox Street Ser.: 1). (ENG.). 240p. (J). (gr. 3-7). pap. 7.99 *(978-0-06-198636-9(4)*, Balzer & Bray) HarperCollins Pubs.

Stine, R. L. Zombie Halloween. 2014. (Goosebumps Most Wanted Ser.). lib. bdg. 18.40 *(978-0-606-35855-2(2))* Turtleback.

Stinson, Kathy. One More Clue, 1 vol. 2005. (Lorimer Streetlights Ser.). (ENG.). 104p. (J). (gr. 2-5). 7.95 *(978-1-55028-888-9(1)*, 888) James Lorimer & Co. Ltd., Pubs. CAN. Dist: Formac Lorimer Bks. Ltd.

Stroud, Scott. Baby Kong. Hunt, Jim, illus. 2006. (J). 8.95 *(978-1-60131-001-9(3)*, Castlebridge Bks.) Big Tent Bks.

—Grumpy Mr. Grady. Hunt, Jim, illus. 2007. 24p. (J). 8.95 *(978-1-60131-008-8(0)*, Castlebridge Bks.) Big Tent Bks.

Sullivan, Kate. On Linden Square. Sullivan, Kate, illus. 2013. (ENG., Illus.). 40p. (J). (gr. 1-3). 15.99 *(978-1-58536-832-7(6)*, 202894) Sleeping Bear Pr.

Summers, Natalie. The Noweos: Neighbors One with Each Other. 2009. 20p. pap. 12.99 *(978-1-4490-3710-9(0))* AuthorHouse.

Sutton, Katisha Barner. Caring & Sharing. 2011. 26p. pap. 12.50 *(978-1-60976-177-6(4)*, Strategic Bk. Publishing) Strategic Book Publishing & Rights Agency (SBPRA).

Tamaki, Jillian. Our Little Kitchen. (ENG., Illus.). (J). (gr. -1 — 1). 2022. 36p. bds. 9.99 *(978-1-4197-4656-7(1)*, 1289810) 2020. 48p. 17.99 *(978-1-4197-4655-0(3)*, 1289801) Abrams, Inc. (Abrams Bks. for Young Readers).

Thayer, Jane. Part-Time Dog. Barasch, Lynne & McCue, Lisa, illus. 2004. (ENG.). 32p. (J). (gr. -1-3). 14.99 *(978-0-06-029693-3(3))* HarperCollins Pubs.

Thiel, Annie. Danny Is Moving. Edwards, William M., illus. 2006. (Playdate Kids Ser.). 32p. (J). (gr. -1-3). 14.95 *(978-1-933721-02-6(2))* Playdate Kids Publishing.

Thomas, Mary Ann. The New Neighbors, 1 vol. 2006. (Neighborhood Readers Ser.). (ENG.). 8p. (gr. k-1). pap. 5.15 *(978-1-4042-6694-0(1)*, eaf74479-570f-4568-8f7d-95bdf3d1b983, Rosen Classroom) Rosen Publishing Group, Inc., The.

Thompson, Colin. Good Neighbors. Scrambly, Crab, illus. 2008. (Floods Ser.: No. 1). 214p. (J). (gr. 3-7). 15.99 *(978-0-06-113196-7(2))* HarperCollins Pubs.

Thompson, Lisa. The Goldfish Boy. 2018. (ENG.). 320p. (J). (gr. 3-7). pap. 7.99 *(978-1-338-05393-7(0))* Scholastic, Inc.

Thong, Roseanne. Round Is a Mooncake: A Book of Shapes. Lin, Grace, illus. 2014. (ENG.). 40p. (J). (gr. -1-k). 7.99 *(978-1-4521-3644-8(0))* Chronicle Bks. LLC.

Toon Books, 6 vols., Set. 2013. (Toon Bks.: 10). (ENG.). 36p. (J). (gr. k-3). lib. bdg. 196.74 *(978-1-61479-147-8(3)*, 14839) Spotlight.

Trowbridge, Terri. Tulowly the Possum. McConkey, Barbara, illus. l.t. ed. 2005. 24p. (J). 9.95 *(978-0-9766418-0-3(1))* Sidewalk Publishing.

Truchan - Schulte, Carol. Arizona Lucy. Tadema-Wielandt, Rebecca, illus. 2007. (ENG.). 34p. per. 14.99 *(978-1-4257-7368-7(0))* Xlibris Corp.

Tsarfati, Einat. The Neighbors. Appel, Annette, tr. 2019. (ENG., Illus.). 40p. (J). (gr. -1-3). 16.99 *(978-1-4197-3168-6(8)*, 1243101, Abrams Bks. for Young Readers) Abrams, Inc.

Tyler-Vaughn, Savanna. Flour Sack Wear. 2006. (ENG.). 48p. per. 16.95 *(978-1-4241-2501-2(4))* America Star Bks.

Upperman, Katy. Kissing Max Holden. 2018. (ENG.). 320p. (YA). pap. 17.99 *(978-1-250-15896-3(6)*, 900185542) Square Fish.

USCCB Department of Justice, Peace, and Human Development. Green Street Park. 2015. (ENG., Illus.). 32p. (J). (gr. k-3). pap. 7.95 *(978-0-8294-4099-7(2))* Loyola Pr.

Venable, Colleen A. F. Katie the Catsitter: (a Graphic Novel) Yue, Stephanie, illus. 2021. (Katie the Catsitter Ser.: 1). 224p. (J). (gr. 3-7). 20.99 *(978-0-593-30632-1(5))* Penguin Random Hse. LLC.

Venable, Colleen AF. Katie the Catsitter: (a Graphic Novel) Yue, Stephanie, illus. 2021. (Katie the Catsitter Ser.: 1). 224p. (J). (gr. 3-7). pap. 13.99 *(978-1-9848-9563-9(X))* Penguin Random Hse. LLC.

Viau, Nancy. First Snow. Shipman, Talitha, illus. 2018. (ENG.). 32p. (J). (gr. -1-3). 16.99 *(978-0-8075-2440-4(9)*, 807524409) Whitman, Albert & Co.

Vickery-Bharadwaj, Janice. Valentino & His Friends: It's Magic! 2012. 28p. pap. 12.99 *(978-1-4691-7709-0(9))* Xlibris Corp.

Wahl, Jan. Candy Shop. Wong, Nicole, illus. 2005. (ENG.). 32p. (J). (gr. -1-3). pap. 7.95 *(978-1-57091-668-7(3))* Charlesbridge Publishing, Inc.

Walters, Eric. The Rule of Three: Fight for Power. 2015. (Rule of Three Ser.: 2). (ENG.). 352p. (YA). (gr. 7). 27.99 *(978-0-374-30179-8(4)*, 900140944, Farrar, Straus & Giroux (BYR)) Farrar, Straus & Giroux.

Weeks, Sarah. Oggie Cooder, Party Animal, 2. 2011. (ENG.). 176p. (J). (gr. 2-5). pap. 6.99 *(978-0-439-92796-3(X)*, Scholastic Paperbacks) Scholastic, Inc.

Weitzman, Jacqueline Preiss. Superhero Joe & the Creature Next Door. Barrett, Ron, illus. 2013. (ENG.). 32p. (J). (gr. -1-3). 16.99 *(978-1-4424-1268-2(2)*, Simon & Schuster Bks. For Young Readers) Simon & Schuster Bks. For Young Readers.

Weller, Frances Ward. The Day the Animals Came: A Story of Saint Francis Day. Long, Loren, illus. 2006. 35p. (J). (gr. k-4). reprint ed. 17.00 *(978-1-4223-5396-7(6))* DIANE Publishing Co.

Wildsmith, Brian. The Owl & the Woodpecker, 1 vol. Wildsmith, Brian, illus. 2006. (ENG., Illus.). 32p. (J). (gr. -1-3). 16.95 *(978-1-59572-043-6(X))* Star Bright Bks., Inc.

Wolk, Lauren. Echo Mountain. 2020. (ENG.). 368p. (J). (gr. 5). 17.99 *(978-0-525-55556-8(0)*, Dutton Books for Young Readers) Penguin Young Readers Group.

Wood, Deanna Plummer. Whenever Monkeys Move Next Door, 1 volume. 2005. (Illus.). 24p. (J). pap. 8.50 *(978-0-9762935-1-4(X))* Perkins Crawford.

Wright, Lynda. Flowers for Addison. 2012. 24p. pap. 24.95 *(978-1-4626-5787-2(7))* America Star Bks.

Wuest, Marcia. Twelve Things to Do at Age 12. 2009. (Readers for Teens Ser.). (ENG.). 26p. pap. 14.75 *(978-0-521-73733-3(8))* Cambridge Univ. Pr.

Yee, Wong Herbert. Upstairs Mouse, Downstairs Mole (Reader) 12th ed. 2007. (Mouse & Mole Story Ser.). (ENG., Illus.). 48p. (J). (gr. -1-3). 4.99 *(978-0-618-91586-6(9)*, 1014891, Clarion Bks.) HarperCollins Pubs.

Yim, Natasha. Goldy Luck & the Three Pandas. Zong, Grace, illus. 32p. (J). (gr. -1-3). 2015. (ENG.). pap. 7.95 *(978-1-58089-653-5(7))* 2014. lib. bdg. 17.99 *(978-1-58089-652-8(9))* Charlesbridge Publishing, Inc.

Yost, B. L. Have You Ever Seen a Wild Bird Dance? Perkins, Chelsea, illus. 2008. 16p. pap. 24.95 *(978-1-60703-127-7(2))* America Star Bks.

Zemke, Deborah. Tale of a Scaredy-Dog. 2018. (Bea Garcia Ser.: 3). (Illus.). 160p. (J). (gr. 1-4). pap. 7.99 *(978-0-7352-2939-6(2)*, Puffin Books) Penguin Young Readers Group.

—Tale of a Scaredy-Dog. 2018. (Bea Garcia Ser.: 3). lib. bdg. 18.40 *(978-0-606-41327-5(8))* Turtleback.

Zoboi, Ibi. Pride: A Pride & Prejudice Remix. (ENG.). 304p. (YA). (gr. 8). 2019. pap. 11.99 *(978-0-06-256405-4(6))* 2018. 17.99 *(978-0-06-256404-7(8))* 2018. E-Book *(978-0-06-256407-8(2)*, 9780062564078) HarperCollins Pubs. (Balzer & Bray).

NELSON, HORATIO NELSON, VISCOUNT, 1758-1805

Lacey, Minna. Nelson. Cuzik, David, illus. 2006. (Usborne Famous Lives Gift Bks.). 64p. (J). 8.95 *(978-0-7945-1121-0(X)*, Usborne) EDC Publishing.

NELSON, HORATIO NELSON, VISCOUNT, 1758-1805—FICTION

Henty, George. By Conduct & Courage: A Story of the Days of Nelson. 2011. 364p. pap. 19.95 *(978-1-61179-089-4(1))* Fireship Pr.

NEO-IMPRESSIONISM (ART)

see Impressionism (Art)

NEOLITHIC PERIOD

see Stone Age

NEPAL

Adhikary, Anita. N Is for Nepal. Mundy, Jen, illus. 2011. (J). 14.95 *(978-1-936319-52-7(7))* Amplify Publishing Group.

Athans, Sandra K. Secrets of the Sky Caves: Danger & Discovery on Nepal's Mustang Cliffs. 2014. (ENG., Illus.). 64p. (J). (gr. 4-8). lib. bdg. 33.32 *(978-1-4677-0016-0(9)*, 72d8d6df-062d-4285-a9a5-05b384d9a7cb, Millbrook Pr.) Lerner Publishing Group.

Bailey, Diane & Chhetri, Purneema. My Teenage Life in Nepal. 2017. (Customs & Cultures of the World Ser.). (Illus.). 128p. (J). *(978-1-4222-3909-4(8))* Mason Crest.

Burbank, Jon. Nepal, 1 vol. 2nd rev. ed. 2003. (Cultures of the World (First Edition)(r) Ser.). (ENG., Illus.). 144p. (gr. 5-5). lib. bdg. 49.79 *(978-0-7614-1476-6(2)*, eb2a5032-77b0-4100-886c-058b890c5778) Cavendish Square Publishing LLC.

Chick, Chloe. Mighty Mira Based on the Story. 2016. (ENG., Illus.). 35p. (J). *(978-981-320-254-2(8))* World Scientific Publishing Co. Pte Ltd.

Glaser, Chaya. Nepal. 2019. (Countries We Come From Ser.). (ENG., Illus.). 32p. (J). (gr. k-3). 19.95 *(978-1-64280-197-2(6))* Bearport Publishing Co., Inc.

Mattern, Joanne. Nepal, 1 vol. 2017. (Exploring World Cultures (First Edition) Ser.). (ENG., Illus.). 32p. (gr. 3-3). pap. 12.16 *(978-1-5026-2500-7(8)*, eba9e581-3214-4f0b-8bba-32bf0ab6cbb5) Cavendish Square Publishing LLC.

Orr, Tamra. Nepali Heritage. 2018. (21st Century Junior Library: Celebrating Diversity in My Classroom Ser.). (ENG., Illus.). 24p. (J). (gr. 2-4). lib. bdg. 30.64 *(978-1-5341-2904-7(9)*, 211660) Cherry Lake Publishing.

Owings, Lisa. Nepal. 2014. (Exploring Countries Ser.). (ENG., Illus.). 32p. (J). (gr. 3-7). lib. bdg. 27.95 *(978-1-62617-069-8(X)*, Blastoff! Readers) Bellwether Media.

Trussell-Cullen, Alan. Edmund Hillary. 2009. pap. 13.25 *(978-1-60559-058-5(4))* Hameray Publishing Group, Inc.

Yomtov, Nel. Nepal (Enchantment of the World) (Library Edition) 2018. (Enchantment of the World. Second Ser.). (ENG., Illus.). 144p. (J). (gr. 5-9). lib. bdg. 40.00 *(978-0-531-13049-0(5)*, Children's Pr.) Scholastic Library Publishing.

Zuchora-Walske, Christine. Nepal in Pictures. 2008. (Visual Geography Ser.). (YA). (gr. 7-12). lib. bdg. 31.93 *(978-0-8225-8578-7(2))* Twenty First Century Bks.

NEPAL—FICTION

Asnong, Jocey, illus. Nuptse & Lhotse Go to the Rockies, 1 vol. 2014. 40p. (J). (gr. k). pap. 12.00 *(978-1-77160-019-4(5))* Rocky Mountain Bks.

Cohn, Diana. Namaste!, 1 vol. Cordova, Amy, illus. 2012. 32p. (J). pap. 9.95 *(978-1-62148-005-1(4))* SteinerBooks, Inc.

Engle, Margarita, et al. A Dog Named Haku: A Holiday Story from Nepal. Jeyaveeran, Ruth, illus. 2018. (ENG.). 32p. (J). (gr. k-3). 19.99 *(978-1-5124-3205-3(9)*, f7c55141-c8b7-4e5c-bd93-eb25853b9290, Millbrook Pr.) Lerner Publishing Group.

Heine, Theresa & Barefoot Books Staff. Chandra's Magic Light. Gueyfier, Judith, illus. 2013. (J). 16.99 *(978-1-84686-493-3(3))* Barefoot Bks., Inc.

Hunt, Elizabeth Singer. Secret Agent Jack Stalwart: Book 13: the Hunt for the Yeti Skull: Nepal. 2011. (Secret Agent Jack Stalwart Ser.: 13). (ENG.). 128p. (J). (gr. 1-4). pap. 5.99 *(978-1-60286-151-0(X)*, Running Pr. Kids) Running Pr.

Jeffrey, Rosemary. Allio, Are you Free. 2010. (ENG.). 176p. pap. 12.00 *(978-0-557-75342-0(2))* Lulu Pr., Inc.

Korman, Gordon. The Summit. 2012. (Everest Ser.: 3). lib. bdg. 17.20 *(978-0-606-23935-6(9))* Turtleback.

Lumry, Amanda & Hurwitz, Laura. Tigers in Terai. McIntyre, Sarah, illus. 2003. (Adventures of Riley Ser.). 36p. 15.95 *(978-0-9662257-7-8(5))* Eaglemont Pr.

McCormick, Patricia. Sold. 2011. 10.36 *(978-0-7848-3420-6(2)*, Everbind) Marco Bk. Co.

—Sold. 2008. 263p. (J). (gr. 7-12). 19.65 *(978-1-4178-1810-5(7))* Turtleback.

—Sold (National Book Award Finalist) 2008. (ENG.). 272p. (J). (gr. 5-9). pap. 11.99 *(978-0-7868-5172-0(4))* Little, Brown Bks. for Young Readers.

Pelletier, Cynthia L. & Rabin, Shri. She Who Walks with Tigers, 1 vol. 2010. 80p. pap. 19.95 *(978-1-4512-8767-7(4))* America Star Bks.

Stewart, Jennifer J. Close Encounters of a Third World Kind. 2004. (ENG.). 128p. (J). (gr. 4-6). tchr. ed. 16.95 *(978-0-8234-1850-3(2))* Holiday Hse., Inc.

—Close Encounters of a Third-World Kind. 2008. (ENG., Illus.). 181p. (J). (gr. 3-7). 6.95 *(978-0-8234-2161-9(9))* Holiday Hse., Inc.

NEPTUNE (PLANET)

Adamson, Thomas K. Neptune [Scholastic]: Revised Edition. 2010. (Exploring the Galaxy Ser.). (ENG.). 24p. pap. 0.49 *(978-1-4296-5813-3(4)*, Capstone Pr.) Capstone.

—The Secrets of Neptune. 2015. (Planets Ser.). (ENG., Illus.). 32p. (J). (gr. 2-4). lib. bdg. 32.65 *(978-1-4914-5867-9(4)*, 128830) Capstone.

Bloom, J. P. Neptune, 1 vol. 2015. (Planets Ser.). (ENG., Illus.). 24p. (J). (gr. -1-2). lib. bdg. 32.79 *(978-1-62970-719-8(8)*, 17237, Abdo Kids) ABDO Publishing Co.

—Neptune. 2017. (Planets Ser.). (ENG.). 24p. (J). (gr. -1-2). pap. 7.95 *(978-1-4966-1284-7(1)*, 135016, Capstone Classroom) Capstone.

—Neptuno (Neptune), 1 vol. 2016. (Planetas (Planets) Ser.). (SPA., Illus.). 24p. (J). (gr. -1-2). lib. bdg. 32.79 *(978-1-68080-756-1(0)*, 22674, Abdo Kids) ABDO Publishing Co.

Brockman, Noah. Journey to Neptune, 1 vol. 2014. (Spotlight on Space Science Ser.). (ENG.). 32p. (J). (gr. 5-5). pap. 12.75 *(978-1-4994-0374-9(7)*, 6434d72e-16cf-4df5-b1e7-027c0d15c494, PowerKids Pr.) Rosen Publishing Group, Inc., The.

Carson, Mary Kay. Far-Out Guide to Neptune, 1 vol. 2010. (Far-Out Guide to the Solar System Ser.). (ENG., Illus.). 48p. (gr. 4-6). 27.93 *(978-0-7660-3186-9(1)*, 425d9053-44bb-4ac5-93c6-9be12d72702f); pap. 11.53 *(978-1-59845-189-4(8)*, 441e756c-3661-4b0f-8ee9-89f36210b720, Enslow Elementary) Enslow Publishing, LLC.

Chrismer, Melanie. Neptune. 2007. (Scholastic News Nonfiction Readers Ser.). (ENG., Illus.). 24p. (J). (gr. 1-2). 22.00 *(978-0-531-14750-4(9))* Scholastic Library Publishing.

Fleisher, Paul. Neptune. 2009. (Early Bird Astronomy Ser.). (ENG.). 48p. (gr. 2-5). lib. bdg. 26.60 *(978-0-7613-4155-0(2))* Lerner Publishing Group.

Goldstein, Margaret J. Discover Neptune. 2018. (Searchlight Books (tm) — Discover Planets Ser.). (ENG., Illus.). 32p. (J). (gr. 3-5). pap. 9.99 *(978-1-5415-2788-1(7)*, 51eaaec4-6c34-42cc-95ff-4bd895393f6a); lib. bdg. 30.65 *(978-1-5415-2341-8(5)*, 28554a92-9db5-4a55-b638-6e179704d878, Lerner Pubns.) Lerner Publishing Group.

Hantula, Richard & Asimov, Isaac. Neptuno (Neptune), 1 vol. 2003. (Isaac Asimov's Biblioteca Del Universo Del Siglo XXI (Isaac Asimov's 21st Century Library of the Universe) Ser.).Tr. of Neptune: The Farthest Giant. (SPA., Illus.). 32p. (gr. 3-5). lib. bdg. 28.67 *(978-0-8368-3858-9(0)*, c23dcb68-cd60-4e2d-b4f2-f06c3c7f3c3e, Gareth Stevens Learning Library) Stevens, Gareth Publishing LLLP.

Hayhurst, Chris. Neptune. (Library of Planets Ser.). 48p. (gr. 5-8). 2009. 55.90 *(978-1-60853-819-5(2)*, Rosen Reference) 2007. (ENG.). 34.47 *(978-1-4042-1966-3(8)*, e89cfe2e-505d-4a47-b4cc-55e3214bface) Rosen Publishing Group, Inc., The.

Jefferis, David. Gas Giants: Huge Far off Worlds. 2008. (ENG., Illus.). 32p. (J). (gr. 3-7). pap. *(978-0-7787-3750-6(0))* Crabtree Publishing Co.

Jones, Emma. Exploring Neptune. 2017. (Journey Through Our Solar System Ser.). 24p. (gr. 1-2). 49.50 *(978-1-5345-2257-2(3)*, KidHaven Publishing) Greenhaven Publishing LLC.

Kazunas, Ariel. Neptune. 2011. (21st Century Junior Library: Solar System Ser.). (ENG., Illus.). 24p. (gr. 2-5). lib. bdg. 29.21 *(978-1-61080-083-9(4)*, 201076) Cherry Lake Publishing.

Markovics, Joyce. Neptuno: Muy, Muy Lejos. 2015. (Fuera de Este Mundo Ser.). (SPA., Illus.). 24p. (J). (gr. -1-3). lib. bdg. 26.99 *(978-1-62724-593-7(6))* Bearport Publishing Co., Inc.

Markovics, Joyce L. Neptune: Far, Far Away. 2015. (Out of This World Ser.). (ENG.). 24p. (J). (gr. -1-3). lib. bdg. 26.99 *(978-1-62724-568-5(5))* Bearport Publishing Co., Inc.

Murray, Julie. Neptune. 2018. (Planets (Dash!) Ser.). (ENG., Illus.). 24p. (J). (gr. k-4). lib. bdg. 31.36 *(978-1-5321-2530-0(5)*, 30069, Abdo Zoom-Dash) ABDO Publishing Co.

Neptune. 2nd rev. ed. 2009. (New Solar System Ser.). (ENG.). 32p. (gr. 3-6). 23.00 *(978-1-60413-215-1(9)*, P166423, Facts On File) Infobase Holdings, Inc.

Owen, Ruth. Neptune, 1 vol. 2013. (Explore Outer Space Ser.). (ENG.). 32p. (J). (gr. 2-3). 29.93 *(978-1-61533-729-3(6)*, 53cc8e8c-31d3-4e3b-aa61-658f524bcaac); pap. 11.00 *(978-1-61533-775-0(X)*, c14aad5b-52f2-4cc9-8a1d-7c1278dc668c) Rosen Publishing Group, Inc., The. (Windmill Bks.).

—Neptune. 2013. (Explore Outer Space Ser.). 32p. (J). (gr. 3-6). pap. 60.00 *(978-1-61533-776-7(8))* Windmill Bks.

Riggs, Kate. Neptune. 2018. (Seedlings Ser.). (Illus.). 24p. (J). (ENG.). (gr. -1-1). pap. 7.99 *(978-1-62832-533-1(X)*, 19620, Creative Paperbacks); (FRE.). *(978-1-77092-409-3(4)*, 19698); (ENG.). (gr. -1-k). *(978-1-60818-917-5(1)*, 19622, Creative Education) Creative Co., The.

Ring, Susan. Neptune. (J). 2013. 27.13 *(978-1-62127-267-0(2))* 2013. pap. 12.95 *(978-1-62127-276-2(1))* 2004. pap. 8.95 *(978-1-59036-229-7(2))* 2004. (Illus.). 24p. (gr. 4-7). lib. bdg. 24.45 *(978-1-59036-102-3(4))* Weigl Pubs., Inc.

Ring, Susan & Roumanis, Alexis. Neptune. 2016. (Illus.). 24p. (J). *(978-1-5105-0986-3(0))* SmartBook Media, Inc.

Roumanis, Alexis. Neptune. 2016. (J). *(978-1-5105-2053-0(8))* SmartBook Media, Inc.

—Neptune. 2015. (Illus.). 24p. (J). *(978-1-4896-3296-8(4))* Weigl Pubs., Inc.

Roza, Greg. Neptune, 1 vol. 2010. (Our Solar System Ser.). (ENG.). 24p. (J). (gr. k-2). pap. 9.15 *(978-1-4339-3834-4(0)*, 5836b9b0-5c4a-49a3-b669-110776997034); (Illus.). lib. bdg. 25.27 *(978-1-4339-3833-7(2)*, c9acc356-3fea-4d9c-a656-3e8153d626db) Stevens, Gareth Publishing LLLP.

Sherman, Josepha. Neptune, 1 vol. 2010. (Space! Ser.). (ENG.). 64p. (gr. 5-5). lib. bdg. 35.50 *(978-0-7614-4246-2(4)*, d91b43d2-82d9-4db3-a383-ed6a607b5085) Cavendish Square Publishing LLC.

Slade, Suzanne. A Look at Neptune. 2009. (Astronomy Now! Ser.). 24p. (gr. 2-3). 42.50 *(978-1-61511-471-9(8)*, PowerKids Pr.) Rosen Publishing Group, Inc., The.

Sommer, Nathan. Neptune. 2019. (Space Science Ser.). (ENG., Illus.). 24p. (J). (gr. 3-7). lib. bdg. 26.95 *(978-1-62617-976-9(X)*, Torque Bks.) Bellwether Media.

Sparrow, Giles. Destination Uranus, Neptune, & Pluto, 1 vol. 2009. (Destination Solar System Ser.). (ENG., Illus.). 32p. (J). (gr. 3-4). 28.93 *(978-1-4358-3446-0(1)*, 05e1d277-a173-4544-8294-068018bd164f); pap. 11.00 *(978-1-4358-3463-7(1)*, da375e81-83d8-47ac-b022-097405e0edbb) Rosen Publishing Group, Inc., The. (PowerKids Pr.).

Squire, Ann O. Planet Neptune. 2014. (True Book — Space (Revised Edition) Ser.). (ENG.). 48p. (J). lib. bdg. 29.00 *(978-0-531-21155-7(X))* Scholastic Library Publishing.

Thompson, Luke. Neptune. 2009. (Library of the Planets Ser.). 24p. (gr. 3-3). 42.50 *(978-1-60853-919-2(9)*, PowerKids Pr.) Rosen Publishing Group, Inc., The.

Waxman, Laura Hamilton. Neptune. 2005. (Pull Ahead Bks.). (Illus.). 32p. (gr. 2-4). lib. bdg. 22.60 *(978-0-8225-4655-9(8))* Lerner Publishing Group.

Wimmer, Teresa. Neptune. 2007. (My First Look at: Planets Ser.). (Illus.). 24p. (J). (gr. -1-3). lib. bdg. 24.25 *(978-1-58341-520-7(3)*, Creative Education) Creative Co., The.

World Book, Inc. Staff, contrib. by. Neptune & Pluto. 2006. (World Book's Solar System & Space Exploration Library). (Illus.). 63p. (J). *(978-0-7166-9507-3(3))* World Bk., Inc.

—Neptune & the Distant Dwarf Planets. 2nd ed. 2006. (World Book's Solar System & Space Exploration Library). (Illus.). 64p. (J). *(978-0-7166-9518-9(9))* World Bk., Inc.

—Neptune, Comets, & Dwarf Planets. 2010. (J). *(978-0-7166-9538-7(3))* World Bk., Inc.

Zobel, Derek. Neptune. 2010. (Exploring Space Ser.). (ENG., Illus.). 24p. (J). (gr. k-3). lib. bdg. 26.95 *(978-1-60014-409-7(8)*, Blastoff! Readers) Bellwether Media.

NERO, EMPEROR OF ROME, 37-68

Abbott, Jacob. Nero. 2009. 202p. (J). pap. 12.00 *(978-1-59128-057-6(5))* Canon Pr.

Lowery, Zoe & Morgan, Julian. Nero, 1 vol. 2016. (Leaders of the Ancient World Ser.). (ENG.). 112p. (J). (gr. 6-6). 38.80 *(978-1-5081-7256-7(0)*, 167c953e-c1d8-49b3-986f-90c2c3e781f3) Rosen Publishing Group, Inc., The.

Morgan, Julian. Nero: Destroyer of Rome. 2009. (Ancient Leaders Ser.). 112p. (gr. 5-8). 66.50 *(978-1-61511-426-9(2)*, Rosen Reference) Rosen Publishing Group, Inc., The.

Saxena, Shalini. Nero: Ruthless Roman Emperor, 1 vol. 2016. (History's Most Murderous Villains Ser.). (ENG., Illus.). 32p. (J). (gr. 4-5). pap. 11.50 *(978-1-4824-4799-6(1)*, b3b131ea-2cca-45bf-ad07-d0fb72992d7d) Stevens, Gareth Publishing LLLP.

Whiting, Jim. The Life & Times of Nero. 2005. (Biography from Ancient Civilizations Ser.). (Illus.). 48p. (J). (gr. 5-8). lib. bdg. 29.95 *(978-1-58415-349-8(0))* Mitchell Lane Pubs.

NERO, EMPEROR OF ROME, 37-68—FICTION

Weerstand, R. Quintus: A Story about the Persecution of Christians at the Time of Emperor Nero. 2006. (Illus.). 135p. (J). *(978-1-894666-70-1(4))* Inheritance Pubns.

NERVOUS SYSTEM

see also Brain; Psychology, Pathological

Andrews, Barbara. Discover the Nervous & Digestive Systems. 2006. (J). pap. *(978-1-4108-6515-1(0))* Benchmark Education Co.

—The Nervous & Digestive Systems. 2006. (J). pap. *(978-1-4108-6512-0(6))* Benchmark Education Co.

Becker, Jack & Hayhurst, Chris. The Brain & Spinal Cord in 3D, 1 vol. 2015. (Human Body In 3D Ser.). (ENG., Illus.). 64p. (J). (gr. 5-6). 36.13 *(978-1-4994-3581-8(9)*, aeb2c884-806d-4658-b194-a377963d7e19, Rosen Central) Rosen Publishing Group, Inc., The.

Brett, Flora. Your Nervous System Works! 2015. (Your Body Systems Ser.). (ENG., Illus.). 24p. (J). (gr. 1-3). lib. bdg. 27.99 *(978-1-4914-2066-9(9)*, 127544, Capstone Pr.) Capstone.

Brinkerhoff, Shirley. Attention — Deficit/Hyperactivity Disorder. 2014. (Illus.). 128p. (J). *(978-1-4222-3027-5(9))* Mason Crest.

Burstein, John. The Astounding Nervous System: How Does My Brain Work?, 1 vol. 2009. (Slim Goodbody's Body Buddies Ser.). (ENG., Illus.). 32p. (J). (gr. 3-5). pap. *(978-0-7787-4428-3(0))*; lib. bdg. *(978-0-7787-4414-6(0))* Crabtree Publishing Co.

Canavan, Thomas. Sensing the World: The Nervous System, 1 vol. 2015. (How Your Body Works). (ENG.). 32p. (J). (gr. 4-4). pap. 11.00 *(978-1-4994-1232-1(0)*, 79005b7e-5147-42e3-bab7-bcf86a1adf6d, PowerKids Pr.) Rosen Publishing Group, Inc., The.

Canetti, Yanitzia. La Adaptación, ¡qué Sensación! 2010. (SPA.). (J). *(978-1-59835-170-5(2))* Cambridge BrickHouse, Inc.

Capaccio, George. Nervous System, 1 vol. 2010. (Amazing Human Body Ser.). (ENG.). 80p. (gr. 6-6). 36.93 *(978-0-7614-4039-0(9)*, d46b7fb1-0bc7-4cbb-94e5-a78454bd2b83) Cavendish Square Publishing LLC.

Chudler, Eric H., ed. Gray Matter Set, 19 vols., Set. 2007. (Gray Matter Ser.). (ENG.). (gr. 9). 665.00 *(978-0-7910-9659-8(9)*, P179174, Facts On File) Infobase Holdings, Inc.

DeSalle, Rob. Brain: A 21st Century Look at a 400 Million Year Old Organ. Wynne, Patricia, illus. 2010. (Wallace & Darwin Ser.: 2). (ENG.). 40p. (gr. 3-7). 18.95 *(978-1-59373-085-7(3))* Bunker Hill Publishing, Inc.

Duke, Shirley. The Nervous System. 2012. (Let's Explore Science Ser.). (ENG.). 48p. (gr. 4-6). pap. 10.95 *(978-1-61810-254-6(0)*, 9781618102546) Rourke Educational Media.

Einspruch, Andrew. Brain Works, 1 vol., 1. 2014. (Discovery Education: How It Works). (ENG.). 32p. (gr. 4-5). 28.93 *(978-1-4777-6305-6(8)*, 3ba88cd7-6fde-41b5-a540-206225f91d95, PowerKids Pr.) Rosen Publishing Group, Inc., The.

Engdahl, Sylvia, ed. Meningitis, 1 vol. 2010. (Perspectives on Diseases & Disorders Ser.). (ENG., Illus.). 144p. (gr. 10-12). 45.93 *(978-0-7377-4790-4(0)*, 023e3956-bced-43b3-a548-0e7f7d7d1544, Greenhaven Publishing) Greenhaven Publishing LLC.

—Neurodegenerative Disorders, 1 vol. 2013. (Perspectives on Diseases & Disorders Ser.). (ENG., Illus.). 160p. (gr. 10-12). lib. bdg. 45.93 *(978-0-7377-6357-7(4)*, 7ea78616-7a42-4570-aadd-8c32dea9bb38, Greenhaven Publishing) Greenhaven Publishing LLC.

Farndon, John. Stickmen's Guide to Your Brilliant Brain. Dean, Venitia, illus. 2017. (Stickmen's Guides to Your Awesome Body Ser.). (ENG.). 32p. (J). (gr. 3-6). 27.99 *(978-1-5124-3213-8(X)*, 64319f2f-57f9-4d90-a986-883c311327e5, Hungry Tomato (r)) Lerner Publishing Group.

Farris Naff, Clay, ed. Huntington's Disease, 1 vol. 2012. (Perspectives on Diseases & Disorders Ser.). (ENG., Illus.). 120p. (gr. 10-12). lib. bdg. 45.93 *(978-0-7377-5775-0(2)*, 695925b3-203f-4a80-8065-24f6ff115137, Greenhaven Publishing) Greenhaven Publishing LLC.

M N O

Faulk, Michelle. The Case of the Rusty Nail: Annie Biotica Solves Nervous System Disease Crimes, 1 vol. 2013. (Body System Disease Investigations Ser.). (ENG.). 48p. (gr. 5-6). pap. 11.53 *(978-1-4644-0227-2(2),* 295a9ff0-efa9-4f11-8563-12db1201d1e7); lib. bdg. 27.93 *(978-0-7660-3949-0(8),* cbf8437d-e4cb-479d-8085-7f8e3b86eb5d) Enslow Publishing, LLC.

French, Kathy. Your Nervous System: Set Of 6. 2010. (Early Connections Ser.). (J). pap. 39.00 net. *(978-1-4108-1538-5(2))* Benchmark Education Co.

Gold, Martha V. Learning about the Nervous System, 1 vol. 2013. (Learning about the Human Body Systems Ser.). (ENG.). 48p. (gr. 5-6). 27.93 *(978-0-7660-4160-8(3),* 1a1859fd-3da3-43db-9cd3-b97242e66266); pap. 11.53 *(978-1-4644-0241-8(8),* 91724858-7732-4d4b-8db3-67108ad7695d) Enslow Publishing, LLC.

Goldsmith, Connie. Meningitis. 2007. (Twenty-First Century Medical Library). (Illus.). 128p. (YA). (gr. 7-12). lib. bdg. 30.60 *(978-0-8225-7034-9(3))* Twenty First Century Bks.

Gray-Wilburn, Renée & Gray-Wilburn, Renée. What You Need to Know about Meningitis. 2015. (Focus on Health Ser.). (ENG., Illus.). 32p. (J). (gr. 3-6). pap. 7.95 *(978-1-4914-4900-4(4),* 128735, Capstone Pr.) Capstone.

Green, Emily & Manolis, Kay. The Nervous System. 2009. (Body Systems Ser.). (ENG., Illus.). 24p. (J). (gr. 2-5). lib. bdg. 26.95 *(978-1-60014-245-1(1))* Bellwether Media.

Hansen, Grace. Nervous System. 2018. (Beginning Science: Body Systems Ser.). (ENG., Illus.). 24p. (J). (gr. -1-2). lib. bdg. 32.79 *(978-1-5321-8187-0(6),* 29847, Abdo Kids) ABDO Publishing Co.

Harding, Jennie. Ellie Bean the Drama Queen: How Ellie Learned to Keep Calm & Not Overreact. 2011. (ENG., Illus.). 48p. (gr. -1-3). pap. 9.95 *(978-1-935567-27-1(6),* P186847) Future Horizons, Inc.

Harrold, Kimberly. Sometimes, MS Is Yucky. Whitfield, Eric, illus. 2005. (ENG.). 40p. (J). pap. 12.95 *(978-1-59630-006-4(X),* 1-59630-006-X) Science & Humanities Pr.

Holt, Rinehart and Winston Staff. Holt Science & Technology Chapter 25: Life Science: Communication & Control. 5th ed. 2004. (Illus.). pap. 12.86 *(978-0-03-030246-6(3))* Holt McDougal.

Houghton, Gillian. The Nervous System, 1 vol. 2006. (Human Body: a Closer Look Ser.). (ENG., Illus.). 24p. (gr. 2-3). pap. 9.25 *(978-1-4042-2183-3(2),* 5617dc3c-ebf6-4b69-bff2-194b1f6a5bd0, PowerKids Pr.) Rosen Publishing Group, Inc., The.

Kneib, Martha. Meningitis. 2009. (Epidemics Ser.). 64p. (gr. 5-5). 58.50 *(978-1-61512-297-4(4))* Rosen Publishing Group, Inc., The.

Knowles, Johanna. Huntington's Disease. 2009. (Genetic Diseases & Disorders Ser.). 64p. (gr. 6-6). 58.50 *(978-1-61512-668-2(6))* Rosen Publishing Group, Inc., The.

Laird, Chynna T. I'm Not Weird, I Have Sensory Processing Disorder (SPD) Alexandra's Journey. 2nd ed. 2012. (J). 24p. 29.95 *(978-1-61599-159-4(X));* (Illus.). 22p. pap. *(978-1-61599-158-7(1))* Loving Healing Pr., Inc.

Libra, Anna. Why Does My Head Hurt? An Inside Look at the Nervous System. 2003. (J). pap. *(978-1-58417-065-5(4));* lib. bdg. *(978-1-58417-002-0(6))* Lake Street Pubs.

Mahoney, Emily. 20 Fun Facts about the Nervous System, 1 vol. 2018. (Fun Fact File: Body Systems Ser.). (ENG.). 32p. (gr. 2-3). lib. bdg. 27.93 *(978-1-5382-2924-8(2),* e2ae22a9-d413-4ab7-9efc-e7b01cec5b75) Stevens, Gareth Publishing LLLP.

Manolis, Kay. The Nervous System. 2009. (Blastoff! Readers Ser.). (ENG., Illus.). 24p. (J). (gr. k-3). 20.00 *(978-0-531-21704-7(3),* Children's Pr.) Scholastic Library Publishing.

Mason, Paul. Your Mind-Bending Brain & Networking Nervous System. 2015. (Your Brilliant Body! Ser.). (ENG., Illus.). 32p. (J). (gr. 4-5). *(978-0-7787-2199-4(X))* Crabtree Publishing Co.

Meachen Rau, Dana. El Cerebro / My Brain, 1 vol. 2008. (Qué Hay Dentro de Mí? / What's Inside Me? Ser.). (ENG & SPA., Illus.). 32p. (gr. 1-2). lib. bdg. 25.50 *(978-0-7614-2480-2(6),* ad7c82b1-76ab-4a72-a02a-7f76a87bef2a) Cavendish Square Publishing LLC.

—El Cerebro (My Brain), 1 vol. 2008. (Qué Hay Dentro de Mí? (What's Inside Me?) Ser.). (SPA., Illus.). 32p. (gr. 1-2). lib. bdg. 25.50 *(978-0-7614-2402-4(4),* d5184882-263d-4f4f-b06c-4dc8332e9e34) Cavendish Square Publishing LLC.

—My Brain, 1 vol. (Bookworms: My Body Ser.). (ENG.). 2013. 24p. (gr. 2-2). pap. 9.23 *(978-1-62712-033-3(5),* 9904ea40-e038-4448-97c8-537992edc68cb) 2006. (Illus.). 32p. (gr. 1-2). 25.50 *(978-0-7614-1781-1(8),* 15d3112e-161a-4ed9-b4a0-3bc7cc723251, Cavendish Square) Cavendish Square Publishing LLC.

Moe, Barbara. Coping with Tourette's Syndrome & Other Tic Disorders. 2009. (Coping Ser.). 192p. (gr. 7-12). 63.90 *(978-1-61512-016-1(5))* Rosen Publishing Group, Inc., The.

Moore Niver, Heather. The Nervous System, 1 vol. 2012. (Human Body Ser.). (ENG., Illus.). 32p. (J). (gr. 4-5). pap. 11.50 *(978-1-4339-6590-6(9),* 9e7f7751-3dc4-452b-ba11-b27fb497414, Gareth Stevens Learning Library); lib. bdg. 29.27 *(978-1-4339-6588-3(7),* 1d3ad9ad-8b98-402b-8c98-6ff78560b3f9) Stevens, Gareth Publishing LLLP.

Morgan, Philip. Sending Messages. 2010. (How Your Body Works). (ENG.). 32p. (J). (gr. 4-7). lib. bdg. 28.50 *(978-1-60753-055-8(4),* 17209) Amicus.

—Sending Messages. 2012. (ENG., Illus.). 32p. (gr. 4-7). pap. 8.95 *(978-1-926722-65-8(5))* Saunders Bk. Co. CAN. Dist: RiverStream Publishing.

Morgan, Philip & Turnbull, Stephanie. Sending Messages. 2011. (Secrets of Magic Ser.). 32p. (gr. 4-7). lib. bdg. 31.35 *(978-1-59920-496-3(7))* Black Rabbit Bks.

National Geographic Learning. Reading Expeditions (Science: the Human Body): Understanding the Brain. 2007. (Nonfiction Reading & Writing Workshops Ser.). (ENG., Illus.). 32p. (J). pap. 18.95 *(978-0-7922-8859-6(9))* CENGAGE Learning.

Nervensystem und Sinnesorgane: Fachliche Inhalte und Uebungsaufgaben. 2nd ed. (Duden Abiturhilfen Ser.). (GER.). 112p. (YA). (gr. 12-13). *(978-3-411-04152-7(8))* Bibliographisches Institut & F. A. Brockhaus AG DEU. Dist: International Bk. Import Service, Inc.

The Nervous System/The Senses/The Skin. 2006. (World Book's Human Body Works). (Illus.). 48p. (J). *(978-0-7166-4430-9(4))* World Bk., Inc.

Pettiford, Rebecca. The Nervous System. 2019. (Your Body Systems Ser.). (ENG., Illus.). 24p. (J). (gr. k-3). pap. 7.99 *(978-1-61891-754-6(4),* 12311, Blastoff! Readers) Bellwether Media.

Porterfield, Jason. Downers: Depressant Abuse. (Incredibly Disgusting Drugs Ser.). 48p. (gr. 5-8). 2009. 53.00 *(978-1-61513-496-0(4),* Rosen Reference) 2007. (ENG., Illus.). (YA). lib. bdg. 34.47 *(978-1-4042-1957-1(9),* 141ccedf-db2d-4917-ac32-7f493f5cc77a) Rosen Publishing Group, Inc., The.

Riley, Joelle. The Nervous System. (Early Bird Body Systems Ser.). (Illus.). 48p. (J). 2005. (gr. 2-4). lib. bdg. 25.26 *(978-0-8225-1249-3(1))* 2004. pap. 8.95 *(978-0-8225-2521-9(6))* Lerner Publishing Group.

—El Sistema Nervioso. Translations.com Staff, tr. 2006. (Libros Sobre el Cuerpo Humano para Madrugadores Ser.). (ENG & SPA., Illus.). 48p. (gr. 2-4). lib. bdg. 26.60 *(978-0-8225-6255-9(3))* Lerner Publishing Group.

—El sistema nervioso (the Nervous System) 2006. (Libros Sobre el Cuerpo Humano para Madrugadores Ser.). (Illus.). 48p. (J). (gr. -1-3). per. 8.95 *(978-0-8225-6651-9(6),* Ediciones Lerner) Lerner Publishing Group.

—Your Nervous System. 2012. (Searchlight Books (tm) — How Does Your Body Work? Ser.). (ENG., Illus.). 40p. (J). (gr. 3-5). lib. bdg. 30.65 *(978-0-7613-7450-3(7),* 813206d8-e999-41f0-b2c3-06cd3b730f07, Lerner Pubns.) Lerner Publishing Group.

Rooney, Anne. The History of Neuroscience, 1 vol. 2017. (History of Science Ser.). (ENG.). 216p. (YA). (gr. 7-7). 47.80 *(978-1-5081-7705-0(8),* 8b1f17ce-c868-44cd-8954-ce0d0bf73a66, Rosen Young Adult) Rosen Publishing Group, Inc., The.

Rose, Simon. The Brain: All about the Nervous System. 2017. (Illus.). 32p. (J). *(978-1-5105-0893-4(7))* SmartBook Media, Inc.

—Nervous System. (J). 2018. (Illus.). 32p. pap. *(978-1-4896-9915-2(5),* AV2 by Weigl) 2014. *(978-1-4896-1174-1(6))* Weigl Pubs., Inc.

Rustad, Martha E. H. My Nervous System: A 4D Book. 2018. (My Body Systems Ser.). (ENG., Illus.). 24p. (J). (gr. -1-2). lib. bdg. 29.32 *(978-1-9771-0022-1(8),* 138175, Capstone Pr.) Capstone.

Simon, Seymour. The Brain: All about Our Nervous System & More! 2006. (ENG., Illus.). 32p. (J). (gr. k-4). pap. 7.99 *(978-0-06-087719-4(7),* HarperCollins) HarperCollins Pubs.

—The Brain: Our Nervous System. 2006. (Illus.). 30p. (gr. k-4). 17.00 *(978-0-7569-6740-6(6))* Perfection Learning Corp.

El Sistema Nervioso, Nuestro Proceso de Datos. (Coleccion Mundo Invisible).Tr. of Nervous System & the Brain. (SPA.). (YA). (gr. 5-8). pap. 8.00 *(978-958-04-3226-5(0))* Norma S.A. COL. Dist: Distribuidora Norma, Inc.

El Sistema Nervioso Nuestro Proceso de Datos. (SPA.). (J). 10.00 *(978-84-342-1907-6(7))* Parramon Ediciones S.A. ESP. Dist: Distribuidora Norma, Inc.

Snedden, Robert. Understanding the Brain & the Nervous System, 1 vol. 2009. (Understanding the Human Body Ser.). (ENG., Illus.). 48p. (YA). (gr. 7-7) pap. 12.75 *(978-1-4358-9691-8(2),* 7bbc560b-7e13-4847-b7d0-60e84cd51907); lib. bdg. 34.47 *(978-1-4358-9685-7(8),* 8a94ea28-7c5f-485e-b63a-2c2f521f87cf) Rosen Publishing Group, Inc., The. (Rosen Reference).

Stewart, Melissa. You've Got Nerve! The Secrets of the Brain & Nerves, 1 vol. Hamlin, Janet, illus. 2011. (Gross & Goofy Body Ser.). (ENG.). 48p. (gr. 3-3). 32.64 *(978-0-7614-4157-1(3),* 5c638822-01f2-4100-8986-fb7f368f0c1f) Cavendish Square Publishing LLC.

Viegas, Jennifer. The Revolution in Healing the Brain. 2009. (Library of Future Medicine Ser.). 64p. (gr. 5-5). 58.50 *(978-1-60853-633-7(5))* Rosen Publishing Group, Inc., The.

Williams, Mary E., ed. Tourette Syndrome, 1 vol. 2012. (Perspectives on Diseases & Disorders Ser.). (ENG., Illus.). 136p. (gr. 10-12). lib. bdg. 45.93 *(978-0-7377-6360-7(4),* e902ecf9-37bc-409b-ba57-23702b382c1e, Greenhaven Publishing) Greenhaven Publishing LLC.

World Book, Inc. Staff, contrib. by. The Nervous System. 2013. (J). *(978-0-7166-1846-1(X))* World Bk., Inc.

NESS, LOCH (SCOTLAND)

Brassey, Richard. Nessie the Loch Ness Monster. 2010. (ENG., Illus.). 24p. (gr. k-2). pap. 9.99 *(978-1-4440-0056-6(X),* Orion Children's Bks.) Hachette Children's Group GBR. Dist: Hachette Bk. Group.

DeMolay, Jack. The Loch Ness Monster: Scotland's Mystery Beast. 2009. (Jr. Graphic Mysteries Ser.). (ENG.). 24p. (J). (gr. 2-3). 47.90 *(978-1-61513-849-4(8),* PowerKids Pr.) Rosen Publishing Group, Inc., The.

NETHERLANDS

Abramson, Ann. Who Was Anne Frank? Harrison, Nancy, illus. 2007. (Who Was...? Ser.). 103p. (J). (gr. 4-7). 16.00 *(978-1-4177-6854-7(1))* Turtleback.

Ainsley, Dominic J. Netherlands, Vol. 16. 2018. (European Countries Today Ser.). (Illus.). 96p. (J). (gr. 7). 34.60 *(978-1-4222-3988-9(8))* Mason Crest.

Bowen, Richard. Vincent Van Gogh: Modern Artist. 2013. (People of Importance Ser.: 21). (Illus.). 32p. (J). (gr. 4-18). 19.95 *(978-1-4222-2858-6(4))* Mason Crest.

Britton, Tamara L. The Netherlands. 2003. (Countries Set 4 Ser.). 40p. (gr. k-6). 27.07 *(978-1-57765-755-2(1),* Checkerboard Library) ABDO Publishing Co.

Docalavich, Heather & Indovino, Shaina C. The Netherlands. Bruton, John, ed. 2012. (Major European Union Nations Ser.). 64p. (J). (gr. 7). 22.95 *(978-1-4222-2253-9(5))* Mason Crest.

Kaltenhauser, Bettina & van Swol-Ulbrich, Hilly. When Abroad - Do As the Local Children Do: Ori's Guide for Young Expats. 2004. (ENG., Illus.). 112p. (J). pap. *(978-90-5594-262-6(6))* Cyan Communications GBR. Dist: Independent Pubs. Group.

Lomberg, Michelle & Gillespie, Katie. The Diary of a Young Girl. 2018. (J). *(978-1-5105-3706-4(6))* SmartBook Media, Inc.

Lossani, Chiara. Vincent Van Gogh & the Colors of the Wind. Monaco, Octavia, illus. 2011. (ENG.). 40p. (YA). (gr. 2). 19.00 *(978-0-8028-5390-5(0),* Eerdmans Bks For Young Readers) Eerdmans, William B. Publishing Co.

Seward, Pat & Lal, Sunandini Arora. Netherlands, 1 vol. 2nd rev. ed. 2006. (Cultures of the World (Second Edition)(r) Ser.). (ENG., Illus.). 144p. (gr. 5-5). lib. bdg. 49.79 *(978-0-7614-2052-1(5),* 1151ead3-5ade-484d-b351-4e421109da98) Cavendish Square Publishing LLC.

Van Maarsen, Jacqueline. A Friend Called Anne: One Girl's Story of War, Peace, & a Unique Friendship with Anne Frank. 2007. (Illus.). 163p. (J). (gr. 5-9). 14.65 *(978-0-7569-8146-4(8))* Perfection Learning Corp.

Yount, Lisa. Antoni Van Leeuwenhoek: Genius Discoverer of Microscopic Life, 1 vol. 2014. (Genius Scientists & Their Genius Ideas Ser.). (ENG.). 96p. (gr. 5-5). pap. 13.88 *(978-0-7660-6526-0(X),* db072058-a2a3-416c-a7e1-619e9409190f) Enslow Publishing, LLC.

NETHERLANDS—FICTION

Abbott, Jacob. Rollo in Holland. 2008. 108p. 23.95 *(978-1-60664-820-9(9));* pap. 9.95 *(978-1-60664-065-4(8))* Aegypan.

Borden, Louise. The Greatest Skating Race: A World War II Story from the Netherlands. Daly, Niki, illus. 2004. (ENG.). 48p. (J). (gr. 4-7). 19.99 *(978-0-689-84502-4(2),* McElderry, Margaret K. Bks.) McElderry, Margaret K. Bks.

Brandeis, Madeline. The Little Dutch Tulip Girl. 2011. 194p. 42.95 *(978-1-258-09813-1(X))* Literary Licensing, LLC.

Brown, Jeffrey. Lucy & Andy Neanderthal: the Stone Cold Age. 2018. (Lucy & Andy Neanderthal Ser.: 2). (Illus.). 224p. (J). (gr. 3-7). pap. 7.99 *(978-0-525-64398-2(2),* Yearling) Random Hse. Children's Bks.

Brust, Beth Wagner. The Great Tulip Trade. Mattheson, Jenny, illus. 2005. (Step into Reading Ser.). 48p. (J). (gr. 1-3). 11.65 *(978-0-7569-5160-3(7))* Perfection Learning Corp.

—The Great Tulip Trade. 2005. (Step into Reading Ser.: Vol. 3). (ENG., Illus.). 48p. (J). (gr. k-3). pap. 5.99 *(978-0-375-82573-6(8),* Random Hse. Bks. for Young Readers) Random Hse. Children's Bks.

Chambers, Aidan. Postcards from No Man's Land. 2004. (ENG.). 320p. (YA). (gr. 9-18). reprint ed. 8.99 *(978-0-14-240145-3(5),* Speak) Penguin Young Readers Group.

Cinema, Bobby. Princess School. 2012. 68p. 18.66 *(978-1-4669-3968-4(0));* 18p. pap. 8.66 *(978-1-4669-3967-7(2))* Trafford Publishing.

Comora, Madeleine. Rembrandt & Titus: Artist & Son. 2005. (ENG., Illus.). 32p. (J). (gr. 3-5). 17.95 *(978-1-55591-490-5(X))* Fulcrum Publishing.

Crain, Kira. SEK Statton. 2009. (GER.). 136p. 29.95 *(978-1-4092-6127-8(1))* Lulu Pr., Inc.

Cullen, Lyn. I Am Rembrandt's Daughter. 2011. 8.88 *(978-0-7848-3491-6(1),* Everbind) Marco Bk. Co.

De Vries, Maggie. Hunger Journeys: A Novel. 2012. (ENG.). 288p. (J). mass mkt. 7.99 *(978-1-55468-580-6(X),* Harper Trophy) HarperCollins Pubs.

di Vries, Maggie. Hunger Journeys. 2014. 240p. (YA). (gr. 8). pap. 8.99 *(978-0-06-231351-5(7))* HarperCollins Pubs.

Dodge, Mary Mapes. Hans Brinker, or the Silver Skates. 2007. 308p. (gr. 3-7). 32.95 *(978-1-4344-9309-5(1));* per. 19.95 *(978-1-4344-9308-8(3))* Wildside Pr., LLC.

—Hans Brinker or the Silver Skates A Story of Life in Holland. Doggett, Allen B., illus. 2004. reprint ed. pap. 34.95 *(978-1-4179-4127-8(8))* Kessinger Publishing, LLC.

—Hans Brinker; or, the Silver Skates (Dod. 2006. pap. *(978-1-4065-0961-8(2))* Dodo Pr.

—The Silver Skates. Bailey, Peter, illus. 2019. (Alma Junior Classics Ser.). (ENG.). 320p. (J). pap. 11.00 *(978-1-84749-720-8(9),* 900200636, Alma Classics) Bloomsbury Publishing USA.

Duble, Kathleen Benner. Quest. 2008. (ENG.). 256p. (J). (gr. 5-9). 19.99 *(978-1-4169-3386-1(7),* McElderry, Margaret K. Bks.) McElderry, Margaret K. Bks.

Fleming, Candace. Boxes for Katje. Dressen-McQueen, Stacey, illus. 2003. (ENG.). 40p. (J). (gr. -1-3). 19.99 *(978-0-374-30922-0(1),* 900021221, Farrar, Straus & Giroux (BYR)) Farrar, Straus & Giroux.

—Boxes for Katje. Dressen-McQueen, Stacey, illus. 2004. (YA). 27.95 incl. audio *(978-0-8045-6930-9(4),* SAC6930) Spoken Arts, Inc.

Garlick, Nicholas. Storm Horse. 2017. 242p. (J). pap. *(978-0-545-90415-5(3))* Scholastic, Inc.

Griffis, William. Dutch Fairy Tales for Young Folks. 2005. pap. 15.95 *(978-1-59605-348-9(8),* Cosimo Classics) Cosimo, Inc.

Griffis, William Elliot. Dutch Fairy Tales for Young Folks. 2004. reprint ed. pap. 1.99 *(978-1-4192-1705-0(4))* Kessinger Publishing, LLC.

Hapka, Catherine, pseud. Luna. 2015. (Horse Diaries: 12). lib. bdg. 18.40 *(978-0-606-37711-9(5))* Turtleback.

Henty, George. By Pike & Dyke: A Tale of the Rise of the Dutch Republic. 2017. (ENG., Illus.). (J). 26.95 *(978-1-374-91444-5(4));* pap. 16.95 *(978-1-374-91443-8(6))* Capital Communications, Inc.

Hering, Marianne & Younger, Marshal. Escape to the Hiding Place. 2012. (AIO Imagination Station Bks.: 9). (ENG., Illus.). 128p. (J). pap. 5.99 *(978-1-58997-693-1(2),* 4609384) Focus on the Family Publishing.

Hesse, Monica. Girl in the Blue Coat. (ENG.). 320p. (YA). (gr. 7-17). 2017. pap. 11.99 *(978-0-316-26063-3(0))* 2016. E-Book 45.00 *(978-0-316-26064-0(9))* Little, Brown Bks. for Young Readers.

—Girl in the Blue Coat. 2017. (YA). lib. bdg. 20.85 *(978-0-606-39918-0(6))* Turtleback.

Heuvel, Eric. A Family Secret. Miller, Lorraine T., tr. Heuvel, Eric, illus. 2009. (ENG., Illus.). 64p. (J). (gr. 5-8). pap. 11.99 *(978-0-374-42265-3(6),* 900057558) Square Fish.

Kuijer, Guus & Nieuwenhuizen, John. The Book of Everything. 2006. ix, 101p. (J). 16.99 *(978-0-439-74919-0(0),* Levine, Arthur A. Bks.) Scholastic, Inc.

Lindelauf, Benny. Nine Open Arms. Nieuwenhuizen, John, tr. 2014. (ENG., Illus.). 264p. (J). (gr. 3). 16.95 *(978-1-59270-146-9(9))* Enchanted Lion Bks., LLC.

Lucy Fitch Perkins. The Dutch Twins. 2005. pap. *(978-1-905432-05-9(4))* Dodo Pr.

Miller, David Lee & Rubin, Steven Jay. The Cat Who Lived with Anne Frank. Baddeley, Elizabeth, illus. 2019. (ENG.). 40p. (J). (gr. -1-3). 18.99 *(978-1-5247-4150-1(7),* Philomel Bks.) Penguin Young Readers Group.

Miller, Jennifer. Run, Rasputin, Run! Trials & Friendships (Book 2) 2006. (ENG., Illus.). 172p. per. 14.85 *(978-1-4120-8494-9(6))* Trafford Publishing.

Peet, Mal. Tamar: A Novel of Espionage, Passion, & Betrayal. (ENG.). 432p. (YA). (gr. 9). 2018. pap. 10.99 *(978-1-5362-0030-0(1))* 2007. (Illus.). 17.99 *(978-0-7636-3488-9(3))* Candlewick Pr.

Perkins, Lucy Fitch. The Dutch Twins. 2004. reprint ed. pap. 1.99 *(978-1-4192-6040-7(5))* Kessinger Publishing, LLC.

Priestley, Chris. Through Dead Eyes. 2014. (ENG.). 240p. (J). (gr. 7). pap. *(978-1-4088-1107-8(3),* 31012, Bloomsbury Children's Bks.) Bloomsbury Publishing Plc.

Prins, Piet. The Flying Phantom. 2006. (Illus.). 142p. (J). pap. *(978-1-894666-45-9(3))* Inheritance Pubns.

—The Grim Reaper. 2006. (Illus.). 130p. (J). pap. *(978-1-894666-74-9(7))* Inheritance Pubns.

—The Haunted Castle. 2006. (Illus.). 139p. (J). pap. *(978-1-894666-44-2(5))* Inheritance Pubns.

—Hideout in the Swamp. 2006. (Illus.). 136p. (J). pap. *(978-1-894666-73-2(9))* Inheritance Pubns.

—The Lonely Sentinel. 2006. (Illus.). 140p. (J). pap. *(978-1-894666-72-5(0))* Inheritance Pubns.

—The Mystery of the Abandoned Mill. Kramer, Jaap, illus. 2006. 127p. (J). pap. *(978-1-894666-48-0(8))* Inheritance Pubns.

—The Sailing Sleuths. Kramer, Jaap, illus. 2006. 137p. (J). pap. *(978-1-894666-46-6(1))* Inheritance Pubns.

—Scout's Distant Journey. 2006. (Illus.). 141p. (J). pap. *(978-1-894666-49-7(6))* Inheritance Pubns.

—The Search for Sheltie. Kramer, Jaap, illus. 2006. 137p. (J). pap. *(978-1-894666-43-5(7))* Inheritance Pubns.

—Stefan Derksen's Polar Adventure. 2004. (Illus.). 237p. (J). pap. *(978-1-894666-67-1(4))* Inheritance Pubns.

—The Treasure of Rodensteyn Castle. Kramer, Jaap, illus. 2006. 132p. (J). pap. *(978-1-894666-47-3(X))* Inheritance Pubns.

Prins, Piet & McAdam, Fraser. The Beggars Victory: The Sequel to Dispelling the Tyranny. 2006. (Illus.). 173p. (J). pap. *(978-0-921100-53-9(1))* Inheritance Pubns.

—For the Heart of Holland. 2008. (J). *(978-1-894666-20-6(8))* Inheritance Pubns.

Propp, Vera W. When the Soldiers Were Gone: A Novel. 2006. 101p. (J). (gr. 4-8). reprint ed. 15.00 *(978-1-4223-5310-3(9))* DIANE Publishing Co.

Robb, Jackie & Stringle, Berny. The Story of Pea Brain. Duncan, Karen & Stringle, Sam, illus. 2004. (Bang on the Door Ser.). 32p. (YA). pap. *(978-1-85602-383-2(4),* Pavilion Children's Books) Pavilion Bks.

Smet, Margaret. Exploring Amsterdam from A to Z. 2008. (ENG.). 32p. 18.50 *(978-1-4092-0577-7(0))* Lulu Pr., Inc.

Spring, Debbie. The Righteous Smuggler, 1 vol. 2005. (Holocaust Remembrance Series for Young Readers Ser.: 6). (ENG., Illus.). 162p. (J). (gr. 4-7). pap. 9.95 *(978-1-896764-97-9(5))* Second Story Pr. CAN. Dist: Orca Bk. Pubs. USA.

Stilton, Thea. Thea Stilton & the Great Tulip Heist. 2014. (Thea Stilton Ser.: 18). lib. bdg. 19.65 *(978-0-606-35386-1(0))* Turtleback.

Van Ryk, Laverne. A Garland of Emeralds. 2006. (Illus.). 305p. 31.50 *(978-1-4122-0156-8(X))* Trafford Publishing.

Van Stockum, Hilda. The Borrowed House. 2016. 203p. (J). pap. *(978-1-930900-89-9(9))* Purple Hse. Pr.

—A Day on Skates: The Story of a Dutch Picnic. Van Stockum, Hilda, illus. 2007. (Illus.). 40p. (J). (gr. 1). 19.95 *(978-1-932350-18-0(7))* Bethlehem Bks.

William Elliot, Griffis. Dutch Fairy Tales for Young Folks. 2007. (ENG.). 140p. pap. 18.99 *(978-1-4264-3924-7(5))* Creative Media Partners, LLC.

Wilson, Martha. Latin Primer II - Student. 3rd ed. 2003. (ENG & LAT.). 138p. (gr. 3-6). spiral bd. 17.00 *(978-1-885767-52-3(8))* Canon Pr.

NETHERLANDS—HISTORY

Brown, Jonatha A. Anne Frank, 1 vol. 2004. (Gente Que Hay Que Conocer (People We Should Know) Ser.). (SPA., Illus.). 24p. (gr. 2-4). lib. bdg. 24.67 *(978-0-8368-4351-4(7),* 7fe331d8-2239-48d7-b26a-bd97a16a9e3e, Weekly Reader Leveled Readers) Stevens, Gareth Publishing LLLP.

Docalavich, Heather. The Netherlands. 2007. (European Union Ser.). (Illus.). 88p. (YA). (gr. 4-7). lib. bdg. 21.95 *(978-1-4222-0057-5(4))* Mason Crest.

Docalavich, Heather & Indovino, Shaina Carmel. The Netherlands. 2012. (J). pap. *(978-1-4222-2284-3(5))* Mason Crest.

Gibson, Karen Bush. New Netherland: The Dutch Settle the Hudson Valley. 2006. (Building America Ser.). (Illus.). 48p. (J). (gr. 3-7). lib. bdg. 29.95 *(978-1-58415-461-7(6))* Mitchell Lane Pubs.

Hintz, Martin. The Netherlands (Enchantment of the World) (Library Edition) 2015. (Enchantment of the World. Second Ser.). (ENG., Illus.). 144p. (J). (gr. 5-9). lib. bdg. 40.00 *(978-0-531-21697-2(7),* Children's Pr.) Scholastic Library Publishing.

Landau, Jennifer. Vincent Van Gogh: Master of Post-Impressionist Painting, 1 vol. 2015. (Britannica Beginner Bios Ser.). (ENG., Illus.). 32p. (J). (gr. 2-3). 26.06 *(978-1-62275-946-0(X),* 061286c9-3523-4bc2-88dd-fa4ae70dd02d, Britannica Educational Publishing) Rosen Publishing Group, Inc., The.

McDowell, Pamela. Anne Frank. 2014. (Illus.). 24p. (J). *(978-1-4896-2456-7(2))* Weigl Pubs., Inc.

Miner Huey, Lois. American Archaeology Uncovers the Dutch Colonies, 1 vol. 2010. (American Archaeology Ser.). (ENG.). 64p. (gr. 5-5). 34.07 *(978-0-7614-4263-9(4),* 1f8072ff-8845-4639-93ba-34d02d7acbc3) Cavendish Square Publishing LLC.

Murray, Julie. Netherlands. 2017. (Explore the Countries Set 4 Ser.). (ENG., Illus.). 40p. (J). (gr. 2-5). lib. bdg. 35.64

(978-1-5321-1050-4(2), 25676, Big Buddy Bks.) ABDO Publishing Co.

Owings, Lisa. The Netherlands. 2012. (Exploring Countries Ser.). (ENG., Illus.). 32p. (J). (gr. 3-7). lib. bdg. 27.95 *(978-1-60014-766-1(6),* Blastoff! Readers) Bellwether Media.

Parker, Lewis K. Dutch Colonies in the Americas. 2009. (European Colonies in the Americas Ser.). 24p. (gr. 2-2). 42.50 *(978-1-61512-316-2(4),* PowerKids Pr.) Rosen Publishing Group, Inc., The.

Seward, Pat, et al. The Netherlands, 1 vol. 3rd rev. ed. 2016. (Cultures of the World (Third Edition)(r) Ser.). (ENG., Illus.). 144p. (gr. 5-5). 48.79 *(978-1-5026-1695-1(5),* 10fc9ac4-8598-43cd-ba56-a1ee8befaef9) Cavendish Square Publishing LLC.

Shoup, Kate. From New Amsterdam to New York: Dutch Settlement of America, 1 vol. 2017. (Primary Sources of Colonial America Ser.). (ENG.). 64p. (gr. 6-6). 35.93 *(978-1-5026-3136-7(9),* 519b4b31-6af0-4f2e-996c-352933d1b1b9); pap. 16.28 *(978-1-5026-3458-0(9),* dd842f9b-a997-4986-a7bf-b102d7428422) Cavendish Square Publishing LLC.

Slier, Deborah. Hidden Letters, 1 vol. Shine, Ian, illus. 2008. (ENG.). 32p. (YA). (gr. 7-18). 35.00 *(978-1-887734-88-2(0))* Star Bright Bks., Inc.

Spence, Kelly. Cultural Traditions in the Netherlands. 2016. (ENG., Illus.). 32p. (J). *(978-0-7787-8089-2(9))* Crabtree Publishing Co.

Thomson, Ruth. Vincent Van Gogh, 1 vol., 1. 2015. (Inspiring Artists Ser.). (ENG.). 48p. (J). (gr. 7-7). 33.47 *(978-1-5081-7056-3(8),* 16e5c66d-9659-44f1-91ff-52e7b68922cb, Rosen Young Adult) Rosen Publishing Group, Inc., The.

Waxman, Laura Hamilton. Anne Frank. 2009. (History Maker Biographies Ser.). (ENG.). 48p. (gr. 3-6). 27.93 *(978-0-7613-4221-2(4),* Lerner Pubns.) Lerner Publishing Group.

Whitehurst, Susan. The Pilgrims Before the Mayflower. 2009. (Library of the Pilgrims Ser.). 24p. (gr. 3-4). 42.50 *(978-1-60853-915-4(6),* PowerKids Pr.) Rosen Publishing Group, Inc., The.

Wood, Alix. Johannes Vermeer, 1 vol. 2013. (Artists Through the Ages Ser.). (ENG., Illus.). 32p. (J). (gr. 2-3). pap. 11.00 *(978-1-61533-633-3(8),* 0b49d21b-ed88-4285-babf-044a5a73f5b9); lib. bdg. 29.93 *(978-1-61533-623-4(0),* fcf77482-fd27-4f4c-8bba-2c5d8413185d) Rosen Publishing Group, Inc., The. (Windmill Bks.).

—Vincent Van Gogh, 1 vol. 2013. (Artists Through the Ages Ser.). (ENG., Illus.). 32p. (gr. 2-3). 29.93 *(978-1-61533-622-7(2),* cb601fd8-ed7e-42e5-b696-68547669498e); pap. 11.00 *(978-1-61533-631-9(1),* 122108d6-6d93-42d7-a5d9-7afc23e6b28c) Rosen Publishing Group, Inc., The. (Windmill Bks.).

Yount, Lisa. Antoni Van Leeuwenhoek: Genius Discoverer of Microscopic Life, 1 vol. 2014. (Genius Scientists & Their Genius Ideas Ser.). (ENG.). 96p. (gr. 5-5). 29.60 *(978-0-7660-6525-3(1),* e5734917-5b05-43e7-9909-c0835f58d414) Enslow Publishing, LLC.

Zaczek, Iain. Vincent Van Gogh. 2014. (Great Artists Ser.). 32p. (J). (gr. 3-6). pap. 63.00 *(978-1-4824-1249-9(7))* Stevens, Gareth Publishing LLLP.

NEUMANN, JOHN, SAINT, 1811-1860

Brown, Laura Rhoderica. Saint John Neumann: Missionary to Immigrants. Esquinaldo, Virginia, illus. 2016. 144p. (J). pap. *(978-0-8198-9066-5(9))* Pauline Bks. & Media.

NEUMANN, JOHN NEPOMUCENE, SAINT, 1811-1860

see Neumann, John, Saint, 1811-1860

NEUROLOGY

see Nervous System

NEUTRINOS

Bortz, Fred. The Neutrino. 2009. (Library of Subatomic Particles Ser.). 64p. (gr. 6-6). 58.50 *(978-1-60853-879-9(6))* Rosen Publishing Group, Inc., The.

NEUTRON, JIMMY (FICTITIOUS CHARACTER)—FICTION

Banks, Steven. Thanks a Lot, Robo-Turkey! LaPadula, Tom, illus. 2005. (Adventures of Jimmy Neutron Ser.: 10). 24p. (J). lib. bdg. 15.00 *(978-1-59054-787-8(X))* Fitzgerald Bks.

Mattern, Joanne. Dino Disaster! Spaziante, Patrick & Giles, Mike, illus. 2005. (Adventures of Jimmy Neutron Ser.: 9). 24p. (J). lib. bdg. 15.00 *(978-1-59054-782-3(9))* Fitzgerald Bks.

McCann, Jesse Leon. The Science Project. Fruchter, Jason, illus. 2003. 61p. (J). *(978-0-439-56271-3(6))* Scholastic, Inc.

NEVADA

Brown, Jonatha A. Nevada, 1 vol. 2005. (Portraits of the States Ser.). (ENG., Illus.). 32p. (gr. 3-5). pap. 11.50 *(978-0-8368-4690-4(7),* 3e15be7b-3935-4510-af29-a1566e452a72); lib. bdg. 28.67 *(978-0-8368-4671-3(0),* 05d58434-5961-4def-a4bf-641faecff094) Stevens, Gareth Publishing LLLP. (Gareth Stevens Learning Library).

Coerr, Eleanor. S Is for Silver: A Nevada Alphabet. Park, Darcie, illus. 2004. (Discover America State by State Ser.). (ENG.). 40p. (J). (gr. 1-3). 18.99 *(978-1-58536-117-5(8),* 201984) Sleeping Bear Pr.

Craig, Janet. Nevada, 1 vol. 2003. (World Almanac(r) Library of the States Ser.). (ENG., Illus.). 48p. (gr. 4-6). pap. 15.05 *(978-0-8368-5325-4(3),* 7948e980-8a12-41da-b66d-e1ac7fd65d81); lib. bdg. 33.67 *(978-0-8368-5154-0(4),* 1f08b073-0e01-4396-bc97-3dc96107b99d) Stevens, Gareth Publishing LLLP. (Gareth Stevens Learning Library).

Fein, E. How to Draw Nevada's Sights & Symbols. 2009. (Kid's Guide to Drawing America Ser.). 32p. (gr. k-k). 50.50 *(978-1-61511-077-3(1),* PowerKids Pr.) Rosen Publishing Group, Inc., The.

Heinrichs, Ann. America the Beautiful, Third Series: Nevada (Revised Edition) 2014. (America the Beautiful Ser.: 3). (ENG.). 144p. (J). lib. bdg. 40.00 *(978-0-531-24893-5(3))* Scholastic Library Publishing.

—Nevada. Kania, Matt, illus. 2017. (U. S. A. Travel Guides). (ENG.). 40p. (J). (gr. 2-5). lib. bdg. 38.50 *(978-1-5038-1968-9(X),* 211605) Child's World, Inc, The.

Hicks, Terry Allan. Nevada, 1 vol. Santoro, Christopher, illus. 2005. (It's My State! (First Edition)(r) Ser.). (ENG.). 80p. (gr. 4-4). lib. bdg. 34.07 *(978-0-7614-1860-3(1),* 5122d465-0b42-447f-8d17-ca24fa1547aa) Cavendish Square Publishing LLC.

—Nevada, 1 vol. 2nd rev. ed. 2013. (It's My State! (Second Edition)(r) Ser.). (ENG.). 80p. (gr. 4-4). pap. 18.64 *(978-1-62712-101-9(3),* ef5b61c8-18bc-4ee5-aad3-b6f3b39f9493) Cavendish Square Publishing LLC.

Labella, Susan. Nevada. 2007. (Rookie Read-About Geography Ser.). (Illus.). 31p. (J). (gr. 1-2). 20.50 *(978-0-516-25467-8(7),* Children's Pr.) Scholastic Library Publishing.

Marsh, Carole. Nevada Current Events Projects: 30 Cool, Activities, Crafts, Experiments & More for Kids to Do to Learn about Your State! 2003. (Nevada Experience Ser.). 32p. (gr. k-5). pap. 5.95 *(978-0-635-02047-5(5),* Marsh, Carole Bks.) Gallopade International.

—Nevada Geography Projects: 30 Cool, Activities, Crafts, Experiments & More for Kids to Do to Learn about Your State! 2003. (Nevada Experience Ser.). 32p. (gr. k-5). pap. 5.95 *(978-0-635-01847-2(0),* Marsh, Carole Bks.) Gallopade International.

—Nevada Government Projects: 30 Cool, Activities, Crafts, Experiments & More for Kids to Do to Learn about Your State! 2003. (Nevada Experience Ser.). 32p. (gr. k-5). pap. 5.95 *(978-0-635-01947-9(7),* Marsh, Carole Bks.) Gallopade International.

—Nevada People Projects: 30 Cool, Activities, Crafts, Experiments & More for Kids to Do to Learn about Your State! 2003. (Nevada Experience Ser.). 32p. (gr. k-5). pap. 5.95 *(978-0-635-01997-4(3),* Marsh, Carole Bks.) Gallopade International.

—Nevada Symbols & Facts Projects: 30 Cool, Activities, Crafts, Experiments & More for Kids to Do to Learn about Your State! 2003. (Nevada Experience Ser.). 32p. (gr. k-5). pap. 5.95 *(978-0-635-01897-7(7),* Marsh, Carole Bks.) Gallopade International.

Mills, Jordan & Parker, Bridget. Nevada. 2016. (States Ser.). (ENG., Illus.). 32p. (J). (gr. 3-6). lib. bdg. 27.99 *(978-1-5157-0415-7(7),* 132026, Capstone Pr.) Capstone.

Murray, Julie. Nevada, 1 vol. 2006. (United States Ser.). (ENG., Illus.). 32p. (gr. 2-4). 27.07 *(978-1-59197-687-5(1),* Buddy Bks.) ABDO Publishing Co.

Obregon, Jose Maria. Nevada, 1 vol. Brusca, Maria Cristina, tr. 2005. (Bilingual Library of the United States of America Ser.: Set 2). (ENG & SPA., Illus.). 32p. (J). (gr. 2-2). lib. bdg. 28.93 *(978-1-4042-3093-4(9),* d378eb63-0dbf-41f3-ae86-fb2400022a75) Rosen Publishing Group, Inc., The.

Obregón, José María. Nevada. 2009. (Bilingual Library of the United States of America Ser.). (ENG & SPA.). 32p. (gr. 2-2). 47.90 *(978-1-60853-372-5(7),* Editorial Buenas Letras) Rosen Publishing Group, Inc., The.

Sirvaitis, Karen. Nevada. 2012. (J). lib. bdg. 25.26 *(978-0-7613-4544-2(2),* Lerner Pubns.) Lerner Publishing Group.

Stewart, Gail B. Area 51, 1 vol. 2009. (Mysterious Encounters Ser.). (ENG., Illus.). 48p. (gr. 4-8). lib. bdg. 30.63 *(978-0-7377-4410-1(3),* a066f5ef-d734-45b3-bc2d-a683dcf87f15, KidHaven Publishing) Greenhaven Publishing LLC.

Voz, Samuel. Exploring the Great Basin, 1 vol. 2013. (InfoMax Readers Ser.). (ENG.). 24p. (J). (gr. 3-3). pap. 8.25 *(978-1-4777-2491-0(5),* bd0fe216-f39e-4d85-b9bc-a8c0ec4794c9); pap. 49.50 *(978-1-4777-2492-7(3))* Rosen Publishing Group, Inc., The. (Rosen Classroom).

NEVADA—FICTION

Acton, Vanessa. Backfire. 2017. (Day of Disaster Ser.). (ENG.). 112p. (YA). (gr. 6-12). 26.65 *(978-1-5124-2775-2(6),* 65f1861b-fdfc-4ecb-ac4a-beb3f6360b27); E-Book 39.99 *(978-1-5124-3503-0(1),* 9781512435030); E-Book 6.99 *(978-1-5124-3504-7(X),* 9781512435047) Lerner Publishing Group. (Darby Creek).

Bond, Gwenda. Girl in the Shadows, 0 vols. 2016. (Cirque American Ser.: 2). (ENG.). 380p. (YA). (gr. 9-13). pap. 9.99 *(978-1-5039-5393-2(9),* 9781503953932, Skyscape) Amazon Publishing.

Bowman, Akemi Dawn. Harley in the Sky. 2020. (ENG.). 416p. (YA). (gr. 7). 19.99 *(978-1-5344-3712-8(6),* Simon Pulse) Simon Pulse.

Brand, Mary. Aspen Cat: Adventurer Extraordinaire. Roberts, Tempie, illus. 2009. 44p. pap. 24.95 *(978-1-60749-165-1(6))* America Star Bks.

Carlson, Melody. Lost in Las Vegas, 1 vol. 2014. (Carter House Girls Ser.: 5). (ENG.). 208p. (YA). pap. 9.99 *(978-0-310-74716-1(3))* Zondervan.

Cheng, Jack. See You in the Cosmos. 2018. lib. bdg. 19.65 *(978-0-606-41314-5(6))* Turtleback.

Farley, Terri. Heartbreak Bronco. 2004. 227p. (J). lib. bdg. 16.92 *(978-1-4242-0830-2(0))* Fitzgerald Bks.

—Rain Forest Rose Bk. 3. 2007. (Phantom Stallion: Wild Horse Island Ser.: 3). (ENG.). 224p. (J). (gr. 5-18). pap. 4.99 *(978-0-06-088616-5(1))* HarperCollins Pubs.

Ferguson, Alane. Mysteries in Our National Parks: Valley of Death: A Mystery in Death Valley National Park. 2008. (Mysteries in Our National Park Ser.). (Illus.). 160p. (J). (gr. 3-7). per. 4.99 *(978-1-4263-0178-0(2),* National Geographic Kids) Disney Publishing Worldwide.

Fields, Jan. Tame Tahoe Tessie, 1 vol. Brundage, Scott, illus. 2014. (Monster Hunters Ser.). (ENG.). 80p. (J). (gr. 2-5). 35.64 *(978-1-62402-047-6(X),* 1529, Calico Chapter Bks.) ABDO Publishing Co.

Gamble, Adam & Jasper, Mark. Good Night Nevada. Veno, Joe, illus. 2012. (Good Night Our World Ser.). (ENG.). 20p. (J). (gr. -1 — 1). bds. 9.95 *(978-1-60219-060-3(7))* Good Night Bks.

Giles, Lamar. Overturned. (ENG.). 352p. (YA). (gr. 7-7). 2019. pap. 12.99 *(978-1-338-31284-3(7),* Scholastic Paperbacks) 2017. 17.99 *(978-0-545-81250-4(X),* Scholastic Pr.) Scholastic, Inc.

Grimes, Shaunta. The Astonishing Maybe. 2020. (ENG.). 256p. (J). pap. 20.99 *(978-1-250-23363-9(1),* 900192879) Square Fish.

Hancock, H. Irving. The Young Engineers in Nevada. rev. ed. 2006. 220p. 27.95 *(978-1-4218-1754-5(3));* pap. 12.95 *(978-1-4218-1854-2(X))* 1st World Publishing, Inc. (1st World Library - Literary Society).

—The Young Engineers in Nevada. 2007. 188p. per. *(978-1-4065-1995-2(2))* Dodo Pr.

—Young Engineers in Nevada: Or, Seeking Fortune on the Turn of a Pick. 2017. (ENG., Illus.). (J). 23.95 *(978-1-374-93148-0(9))* Capital Communications, Inc.

Hautman, Pete. All-In. 2012. (ENG.). 208p. (YA). (gr. 7). pap. 8.99 *(978-1-4424-3335-9(3),* Simon & Schuster Bks. For Young Readers) Simon & Schuster Bks. For Young Readers.

—All-In. 2008. (ENG., Illus.). 208p. (YA). (gr. 7). mass mkt. 5.99 *(978-1-4169-1326-9(2),* Simon Pulse) Simon Pulse.

Hemphill, Helen. Long Gone Daddy. 2014. (ENG.). 176p. (YA). (gr. 7). pap. 8.95 *(978-1-62091-737-4(8),* Astra Young Readers) Astra Publishing Hse.

Hendershot, Eric. A Horse for Christmas. 2012. (Illus.). 87p. (J). pap. 8.99 *(978-1-4621-1078-0(9))* Cedar Fort, Inc./CFI Distribution.

Hermes, Patricia. Black Cloud. 2012. (Horse Diaries: 8). lib. bdg. 18.40 *(978-0-606-26553-9(8))* Turtleback.

—Horse Diaries #8: Black Cloud, No. 8. Sheckels, Astrid, illus. 2012. (Horse Diaries: 8). 176p. (J). (gr. 3-7). pap. 7.99 *(978-0-375-86881-8(X),* Random Hse. Bks. for Young Readers) Random Hse. Children's Bks.

Hopkins, Ellen. Burned. 2013. (ENG., Illus.). 560p. (YA). (gr. 9). pap. 14.99 *(978-1-4424-9461-9(1),* McElderry, Margaret K. Bks.) McElderry, Margaret K. Bks.

—Perfect. (ENG., (YA). (gr. 9). 2013. Illus.). 656p. pap. 14.99 *(978-1-4169-8325-5(2))* 2011. 640p. 18.99 *(978-1-4169-8324-8(4))* McElderry, Margaret K. Bks. (McElderry, Margaret K. Bks.).

—Tilt. (ENG., (YA). (gr. 9). 2014. Illus.). 624p. pap. 13.99 *(978-1-4169-8331-6(7))* 2012. 608p. 18.99 *(978-1-4169-8330-9(9))* McElderry, Margaret K. Bks. (McElderry, Margaret K. Bks.).

Horvath, Polly. Northward to the Moon. 2012. (My One Hundred Adventures Ser.). (ENG.). 256p. (J). (gr. 6-8). lib. bdg. 22.44 *(978-0-375-96110-6(0))* Random House Publishing Group.

—Northward to the Moon. 2012. (My One Hundred Adventures Ser.: 2). 256p. (J). (gr. 5-8). 7.99 *(978-0-307-92980-8(9),* Yearling) Random Hse. Children's Bks.

Howe, Norma. Angel in Vegas: The Chronicles of Noah Sark. 2009. (ENG., Illus.). 256p. (YA). (gr. 7-18). 16.99 *(978-0-7636-3985-3(0))* Candlewick Pr.

Inagaki, Riichiro. Eyeshield 21, Vol. 12. 2007. (Eyeshield 21 Ser.: 12). (ENG., Illus.). 208p. pap. 9.99 *(978-1-4215-1061-3(8))* Viz Media.

—Eyeshield 21, Vol. 13. 2007. (Eyeshield 21 Ser.: 13). (ENG., Illus.). 216p. pap. 9.99 *(978-1-4215-1062-0(6))* Viz Media.

Ius, Dawn. Overdrive. (ENG.). (YA). (gr. 9). 2017. 368p. pap. 10.99 *(978-1-4814-3945-9(6))* 2016. (Illus.). 352p. 17.99 *(978-1-4814-3944-2(8))* Simon Pulse. (Simon Pulse).

Jacobs, Lily. The Littlest Bunny in Las Vegas: An Easter Adventure. Dunn, Robert, illus. 2015. (Littlest Bunny Ser.). (ENG.). 32p. (J). (gr. -1-3). 9.99 *(978-1-4926-1099-1(2),* Hometown World) Sourcebooks, Inc.

—The Littlest Bunny in Nevada: An Easter Adventure. Dunn, Robert, illus. 2015. (Littlest Bunny Ser.). (ENG.). 32p. (J). (gr. -1-3). 9.99 *(978-1-4926-1135-6(2),* Hometown World) Sourcebooks, Inc.

Jaffe, Michele. Bad Kitty. 2006. (Bad Kitty Ser.: Bk. 1). (ENG., Illus.). 288p. (YA). (gr. 7-12). 16.99 *(978-0-06-078108-8(4))* HarperCollins Pubs.

—Kitty Kitty. 2008. (Bad Kitty Ser.: Bk. 2). 320p. (YA). (gr. 7-18). lib. bdg. 17.89 *(978-0-06-078114-9(9),* HarperTeen) HarperCollins Pubs.

James, Eric. Santa's Sleigh Is on Its Way to Las Vegas: A Christmas Adventure. Dunn, Robert, illus. 2016. (Santa's Sleigh Is on Its Way Ser.). (ENG.). 32p. (J). (gr. k-2). 12.99 *(978-1-4926-4332-6(7),* 9781492643326, Hometown World) Sourcebooks, Inc.

—Santa's Sleigh Is on Its Way to Nevada: A Christmas Adventure. Dunn, Robert, illus. 2016. (Santa's Sleigh Is on Its Way Ser.). (ENG.). 32p. (J). (gr. k-2). 12.99 *(978-1-4926-4340-1(8),* 9781492643401, Hometown World) Sourcebooks, Inc.

—The Spooky Express Las Vegas. Piwowarski, Marcin, illus. 2017. (Spooky Express Ser.). (ENG.). 32p. (J). (gr. k-6). 9.99 *(978-1-4926-5365-3(9),* Hometown World) Sourcebooks, Inc.

—The Spooky Express Nevada. Piwowarski, Marcin, illus. 2017. (Spooky Express Ser.). (ENG.). 32p. (J). (gr. k-6). 9.99 *(978-1-4926-5377-6(2),* Hometown World) Sourcebooks, Inc.

—Tiny the Las Vegas Easter Bunny. 2018. (Tiny the Easter Bunny Ser.). (ENG.). 40p. (J). (gr. k-3). 9.99 *(978-1-4926-5931-0(2),* Hometown World) Sourcebooks, Inc.

Jan, Young. Starting the Colt. 2014. (ENG.). 174p. (J). pap. 12.00 *(978-1-937849-10-8(4))* Raven Publishing Inc. of Montana.

Kelso, Mary Jean. Andy & Spirit in the Big Rescue. Snider, K. C., illus. 2009. 24p. pap. 10.95 *(978-1-935137-67-2(0))* Guardian Angel Publishing, Inc.

—Andy & Spirit Meet the Rodeo Queen. Snider, K. C., illus. 2010. 24p. pap. 10.95 *(978-1-61633-031-6(7))* Guardian Angel Publishing, Inc.

Kirov, Erica. Magickeepers: The Eternal Hourglass. Fortune, Eric, illus. 2010. 256p. (J). (gr. 4-7). pap. 10.99 *(978-1-4022-3855-0(X))* Sourcebooks, Inc.

Kristina Simmons. Winter Beauty. 2010. 192p. pap. 13.95 *(978-1-4401-4449-3(4))* iUniverse, Inc.

Lawrence, Caroline. The Case of the Deadly Desperados, 1. 2013. (P. K. Pinkerton Novels Ser.: 1). (ENG.). 272p. (J). (gr. 4-6). 21.19 *(978-0-399-25633-2(4))* Penguin Young Readers Group.

—P. K. Pinkerton & the Case of the Deadly Desperados. 2013. (P. K. Pinkerton Ser.: 1). (ENG.). 304p. (J). (gr. 3-7). pap. 8.99 *(978-0-14-242381-3(5),* Puffin Books) Penguin Young Readers Group.

—P. K. Pinkerton & the Pistol-Packing Widows. 2015. (P. K. Pinkerton Ser.: 3). (ENG.). 320p. (J). (gr. 3-7). 7.99 *(978-0-14-751130-0(5),* Puffin Books) Penguin Young Readers Group.

Leavitt, Lindsey. The Chapel Wars. 2014. (ENG.). 304p. (YA). (gr. 7). 17.99 *(978-1-59990-788-8(7),* 9781599907888, Bloomsbury USA Childrens) Bloomsbury Publishing USA.

Lee, Sharon Alberta. Mickey of Las Vegas. 2009. 32p. (J). 31.99 *(978-1-4363-4642-9(8))* Xlibris Corp.

Lu, Marie. Prodigy: The Graphic Novel. 2016. (Legend Graphic Novels Ser.: 2). lib. bdg. 26.95 *(978-0-606-38425-4(1))* Turtleback.

Magoon, Kekla. Camo Girl. 2012. (ENG.). 224p. (J). (gr. 3-9). pap. 8.99 *(978-1-4169-7805-3(4),* Aladdin) Simon & Schuster Children's Publishing.

—Camo Girl. 2011. (ENG., Illus.). 224p. (J). (gr. 3-9). 19.99 *(978-1-4169-7804-6(6),* Simon & Schuster/Paula Wiseman Bks.) Simon & Schuster/Paula Wiseman Bks.

Marsh, Carole. The Mystery at Area 51. Friedlander, Randolyn, illus. 2011. (Carole Marsh Mysteries Ser.). 32p. pap. 7.99 *(978-0-635-07961-9(5),* Marsh, Carole Mysteries) Gallopade International.

—The Mystery in Las Vegas. 2009. (Real Kids, Real Places Ser.). (Illus.). 145p. (J). lib. bdg. 18.99 *(978-0-635-07045-6(6),* Marsh, Carole Mysteries) Gallopade International.

Michael Batdorf. Pair of Jacks: A Novel. 2009. 332p. 29.95 *(978-1-4401-4482-0(6));* pap. 19.95 *(978-1-4401-4479-0(6))* iUniverse, Inc.

O'Neill, Elizabeth. Alfred Visits Nevada. 2007. (ENG., Illus.). 24p. (J). pap. 12.00 *(978-0-9799121-1-5(3))* Funny Bone Bks.

Ostow, Micol. Gettin' Lucky. 2012. (Romantic Comedies Ser.). (ENG.). 256p. (YA). (gr. 9). pap. 12.99 *(978-1-4424-8568-6(X),* Simon Pulse) Simon Pulse.

Otis, James. Dick in the Desert. 2005. reprint ed. pap. 15.95 *(978-1-4179-0335-1(X))* Kessinger Publishing, LLC.

Pierson, Jan. The Haunted Horse of Gold Hill. 2005. (Ghostowners Ser.: Vol. 4). (Illus.). 109p. (J). per. 9.95 *(978-0-9721800-3-0(6))* WildWest Publishing.

Ralphson, G. Harvey. Boy Scouts in Death Valley. 2005. pap. 27.95 *(978-1-885529-51-0(1))* Stevens Publishing.

Romito, Dee. No Place Like Home. 2017. (Mix Ser.). (ENG.). 256p. (J). (gr. 4-8). 17.99 *(978-1-4814-9109-9(1));* (Illus.). pap. 7.99 *(978-1-4814-9108-2(3))* Simon & Schuster Children's Publishing. (Aladdin).

Salter, Sydney. My Big Nose & Other Natural Disasters. 2009. (ENG., Illus.). 352p. (YA). (gr. 7-18). pap. 19.95 *(978-0-15-206643-7(8),* 1099023, Clarion Bks.) HarperCollins Pubs.

Sargent, Dave & Sargent, Pat. Gus: (Slate Grullo) Be Thankful, 30 vols., Vol. 32. Lenoir, Jane, illus. 2003. (Saddle up Ser.: Vol. 32). 42p. (J). lib. bdg. 23.60 *(978-1-56763-693-2(4));* pap. 10.95 *(978-1-56763-694-9(2))* Ozark Publishing.

Sedoti, Chelsea. As You Wish. 2018. 432p. (YA). (gr. 7-12). 17.99 *(978-1-4926-4231-2(2))* Sourcebooks, Inc.

Smith, Roland. Zach's Lie. 2003. (ENG.). 224p. (J). (gr. 5-9). pap. 8.99 *(978-0-7868-1440-4(3))* Little, Brown Bks. for Young Readers.

—Zach's Lie. 2003. (J). (gr. 5-8). lib. bdg. 17.20 *(978-0-613-63491-5(8))* Turtleback.

Van Draanen, Wendelin. Sammy Keyes & the Showdown in Sin City. 2013. (Sammy Keyes Ser.: 16). (ENG.). 304p. (J). (gr. 5). pap. 7.99 *(978-0-307-93061-3(0),* Yearling) Random Hse. Children's Bks.

Warner, Penny. The Mystery of the Missing Mustangs. 2012. 107p. (J). *(978-0-88166-411-9(1))* Meadowbrook Pr.

Weiss, Sonya. Rising. 2017. (ENG., Illus.). (YA). pap. 15.00 *(978-1-5161-0028-6(X))* Kensington Publishing Corp.

Wells, Rosemary. Ivy Takes Care. LaMarche, Jim, illus. (ENG.). 208p. (J). (gr. 3-7). 2015. pap. 6.99 *(978-0-7636-7660-5(8))* 2013. 15.99 *(978-0-7636-5352-1(7))* Candlewick Pr.

Young, Jan. Starting the Colt. 2014. 173p. (J). *(978-1-937849-11-5(2))* Raven Publishing Inc. of Montana.

NEVADA—HISTORY

Felix, Rebecca. What's Great about Nevada? 2015. (Our Great States Ser.). (ENG., Illus.). 32p. (J). (gr. 2-5). 26.65 *(978-1-4677-3880-4(8),* b96b7c17-ab8e-40f2-9e4d-cbe0d9fa8a83, Lerner Pubns.) Lerner Publishing Group.

Gregory, Josh. Nevada (a True Book: My United States) (Library Edition) 2018. (True Book (Relaunch) Ser.). (ENG., Illus.). 48p. (J). (gr. 3-5). 31.00 *(978-0-531-23168-5(2),* Children's Pr.) Scholastic Library Publishing.

Hamilton, John. Nevada, 1 vol. 2016. (United States of America Ser.). (ENG., Illus.). 48p. (J). (gr. 5-9). 34.21 *(978-1-68078-330-8(0),* 21645, Abdo & Daughters) ABDO Publishing Co.

Hanel, Rachael. Nevada. 2009. (This Land Called America Ser.). (Illus.). 32p. (YA). (gr. 3-6). 19.95 *(978-1-58341-781-2(8))* Creative Co., The.

Haney, Jill. Area 51. 2015. (Red Rhino Nonfiction Ser.). (J). lib. bdg. 20.80 *(978-0-606-37198-8(2))* Turtleback.

Hicks, Terry Allan. Nevada, 1 vol. 2nd rev. ed. 2013. (It's My State! (Second Edition)(r) Ser.). (ENG.). 80p. (gr. 4-4). 35.93 *(978-0-7614-8000-6(5),* 7e263c61-3e72-451c-a29c-81144bb19fd0) Cavendish Square Publishing LLC.

Hicks, Terry Allan, et al. Nevada, 1 vol. 3rd rev. ed. 2015. (It's My State! (Third Edition)(r) Ser.). (ENG., Illus.). 80p. (gr. 4-4). 35.93 *(978-1-62713-207-7(4),* f191a43b-57f0-4e9a-a1da-efc109b0641c) Cavendish Square Publishing LLC.

Higgins, Nadia. Area 51. 2014. (Unexplained Mysteries Ser.). (ENG., Illus.). 24p. (J). (gr. 3-7). lib. bdg. 26.95 *(978-1-62617-101-5(7),* Epic Bks.) Bellwether Media.

Jerome, Kate B. Lucky to Live in Nevada. 2017. (Arcadia Kids Ser.). (ENG., Illus.). 32p. (J). 16.99 *(978-0-7385-2802-1(1))* Arcadia Publishing.

—The Wise Animal Handbook Nevada. 2017. (Arcadia Kids Ser.). (ENG., Illus.). 32p. (J). 16.99 *(978-0-7385-2831-1(5))* Arcadia Publishing.

Karst, Ken. Area 51. 2014. (Enduring Mysteries Ser.). (ENG.). 48p. (J). (gr. 5-8). pap. 12.00 *(978-1-62832-070-1(2),* 21319, Creative Paperbacks) Creative Co., The.

Kopp, Megan. Nevada: The Silver State. 2012. (J). *(978-1-61913-375-4(X));* pap. *(978-1-61913-376-1(8))* Weigl Pubs., Inc.

M
N
O

Larson, Kirsten W. The West: Arizona, California, Nevada. 2015. (Let's Explore the States Ser.). (Illus.). 64p. (J). (gr. 5). 23.95 *(978-1-4222-3337-5(5))* Mason Crest.

Linde, Barbara M. What Happened at Area 51?, 1 vol. 2014. (History's Mysteries Ser.). (ENG., Illus.). 32p. (J). (gr. 4-5). pap. 11.50 *(978-1-4824-2102-6(X),* 51d26442-184d-4b30-aab3-931487150fc8) Stevens, Gareth Publishing LLLP.

Lusted, Marcia Amidon. Nevada: The Silver State, 1 vol. 2010. (Our Amazing States Ser.). (ENG.). 24p. (J). (gr. 3-3). pap. 9.25 *(978-1-4488-0750-5(6),* 91db01b8-6347-4547-b80f-804c12dbec7c); lib. bdg. 26.27 *(978-1-4488-0659-1(3),* 93b5ad28-d780-47ed-8a8e-cd6200f12497) Rosen Publishing Group, Inc., The. (PowerKids Pr.).

Marsh, Carole. Exploring Nevada Through Project-Based Learning: Geography, History, Government, Economics & More. 2016. (Nevada Experience Ser.). (ENG.). (J). pap. 9.99 *(978-0-635-12352-7(5))* Gallopade International.

—I'm Reading about Nevada. 2014. (Nevada Experience Ser.). (ENG., Illus.). (J). pap., pap. 8.99 *(978-0-635-11303-0(1))* Gallopade International.

—Nevada History Projects: 30 Cool, Activities, Crafts, Experiments & More for Kids to Do to Learn about Your State! 2003. (Nevada Experience Ser.). 32p. (gr. k-5). pap. 5.95 *(978-0-635-01797-0(0),* Marsh, Carole Bks.) Gallopade International.

McLuskey, Krista. Nevada. 2011. (Guide to American States Ser.). (Illus.). 48p. (YA). (gr. 3-6). 29.99 *(978-1-61690-800-3(9))* Weigl Pubs., Inc.

—Nevada: The Silver State. 2016. (J). *(978-1-4896-4899-0(2))* Weigl Pubs., Inc.

Nevada, Our Home Program Kit: All program components for Nevada, Our Home, 1 vol. 2009. 99.95 *(978-1-4236-0723-6(6))* Gibbs Smith, Publisher.

Roza, Greg. Nevada: Past & Present, 1 vol. 2010. (United States: Past & Present Ser.). (ENG.). 48p. (YA). (gr. 5-5). pap. 12.75 *(978-1-4358-9515-7(0),* 93f93e5b-7f11-4e8e-a5fb-f4cc96538e9b); lib. bdg. 34.47 *(978-1-4358-9488-4(X),* 9d0af66c-53af-4df9-9079-edade078263b) Rosen Publishing Group, Inc., The. (Rosen Reference).

Stefoff, Rebecca. Nevada, 1 vol. 2nd rev. ed. 2010. (Celebrate the States (Second Edition) Ser.). (ENG.). 144p. (gr. 6-6). 39.79 *(978-0-7614-4728-3(8),* 89b560f4-3cdf-4c61-8b24-4ca3af03937a) Cavendish Square Publishing LLC.

Steinkraus, Kyla. Area 51. 2017. (Strange ... but True? Ser.). (ENG., Illus.). 32p. (J). (gr. 4-6). lib. bdg. *(978-1-68072-180-5(1),* 10544, Bolt) Black Rabbit Bks.

Williams, Suzanne. Nevada. 2009. (From Sea to Shining Sea, Second Ser.). (ENG.). 80p. (J). pap. 7.95 *(978-0-531-21137-3(1),* Children's Pr.) Scholastic Library Publishing.

Zalewski, Aubrey. Area 51 Alien & UFO Mysteries. 2019. (Aliens Ser.). (ENG., Illus.). 32p. (J). (gr. 4-6). 28.65 *(978-1-5435-7106-6(9),* 140398) Capstone.

NEVER-NEVER LAND (IMAGINARY PLACE)—FICTION

Barrie, J. M. Peter Pan. Bedford, Francis Donkin & Rackham, Arthur, illus. 2015. (Word Cloud Classics Ser.). (ENG.). 272p. pap. 14.99 *(978-1-62686-392-7(X),* Canterbury Classics) Printers Row Publishing Group.

—Peter Pan. 2013. (Puffin Chalk Ser.). 224p. (J). (gr. 3-7). pap. 7.99 *(978-0-14-750865-2(7),* Puffin Books) Penguin Young Readers Group.

—Peter Pan, 1 vol. Tenney, Shawna J. C., illus. 2010. (Calico Illustrated Classics Ser.: No. 1). (ENG.). 112p. (J). (gr. 2-5). 38.50 *(978-1-60270-710-8(3),* 3973, Calico Chapter Bks.) ABDO Publishing Co.

—Peter Pan (MinaLima Edition) (Illustrated with Interactive Elements) MinaLima Ltd., MinaLima, illus. 2015. (ENG.). 256p. 32.50 *(978-0-06-236222-3(4),* Harper) HarperCollins Pubs.

Barrie, J. M. & Barrie, J. M. Peter Pan. 2009. (Puffin Classics Ser.). (Illus.). 240p. (J). (gr. 5-7). 7.99 *(978-0-14-132257-5(8),* Puffin Books) Penguin Young Readers Group.

Barrie, James Matthew. Peter Pan. 2008. 124p. (gr. 5-18). 23.95 *(978-1-60664-889-6(6));* pap. 10.95 *(978-1-60664-007-4(0))* Aegypan.

—Peter Pan. 2005. 112p. per. 6.95 *(978-1-933652-07-8(1))* Bed Bks.

—Peter Pan. Date not set. (C). pap. *(978-0-7593-9877-1(1),* Cengage Learning) CENGAGE Learning.

—Peter Pan. Cowley, Joy, ed. Jang, Yeong-seon, illus. 2015. (World Classics Ser.). (ENG.). 32p. (gr. k-4). 26.65 *(978-1-925246-19-3(1));* 7.99 *(978-1-925246-71-1(X));* 26.65 *(978-1-925246-45-2(0))* ChoiceMaker Pty. Ltd., The AUS. (Big and SMALL). Dist: Lerner Publishing Group.

—Peter Pan. Jang, Yeong-seon, illus. 2015. (World Classics Ser.). (ENG.). 32p. (J). (gr. k-4). 27.99 *(978-1-925186-71-0(7),* 68033772-4b22-4594-b508-2cc9c61895ea); pap. 7.99 *(978-1-925186-65-9(2),* 76d77fd9-e2f3-40ca-9ebe-3ef0b02658a5) ChoiceMaker Pty. Ltd., The AUS. (Big and SMALL). Dist: Lerner Publishing Group.

—Peter Pan. 2005. 96p. per. 4.95 *(978-1-4209-2538-8(5))* Digireads.com Publishing.

—Peter Pan. 2006. pap. *(978-1-4065-0949-6(3))* Dodo Pr.

—Peter Pan. 2009. 276p. (gr. 3-7). pap. *(978-1-4068-9291-8(2))* Echo Library.

—Peter Pan. Bustelo, Gabriela, tr. Vicente, Fernando, illus. 2006. (Alfaguara Infantil y Juvenil Ser.). 229p. (J). (gr. 4-7). pap. *(978-970-770-677-4(5))* Ediciones Alfaguara.

—Peter Pan. pap. 16.95 *(978-2-07-051627-8(X))* Gallimard, Editions FRA. Dist: Distribooks, Inc.

—Peter Pan. 160p. pap. *(978-1-85471-231-8(4))* Penguin Bks., Ltd.

—Peter Pan. 2013. (Vintage Children's Classics Ser.). (Illus.). 256p. (J). (gr. 4-7). pap. 10.99 *(978-0-09-957304-3(0))* Penguin Random Hse. GBR. Dist: Independent Pubs. Group.

—Peter Pan: The Original Tale of Neverland. Jaramillo, Raquel, illus. Jaramillo, Raquel, photos by. unabr. ed. 2003. 135p. (YA). (gr. 5-8). reprint ed. 25.00 *(978-0-7567-6883-6(7))* DIANE Publishing Co.

—Peter Pan - the Original Classic Edition. 2011. pap. *(978-1-74244-781-0(3),* Tebbo) Emereo Pty Ltd.

—Peter Pan & Wendy. 2013. (ENG.). 172p. (YA). 14.95 *(978-1-940849-05-8(5))* Murine Pubns.

—Peter Pan & Wendy. Foreman, Michael, illus. 2003. (Chrysalis Childrens Classics Ser.). 176p. (YA). pap. *(978-1-84365-039-3(8),* Pavilion Children's Books) Pavilion Bks.

—Peter Pan & Wendy: Centenary Edition. Ingpen, Robert R., illus. 2004. (ENG.). 216p. (J). *(978-1-897035-12-2(8),* Blue Heron Bks.) Raincoast Bk. Distribution.

—Peter Pan, by J. M. Barrie - the Original Classic Edition. 2011. mass mkt. *(978-1-74244-961-6(1),* Tebbo) Emereo Pty Ltd.

—Peter Pan in Kensington Gardens. (J). 18.95 *(978-0-8488-0427-5(9))* Amereon Ltd.

—Peter Pan in Kensington Gardens. 2013. 123p. reprint ed. lthr. 69.00 *(978-0-7426-2518-1(4))* Classic Bks.

—Peter Pan in Kensington Gardens. unabr. ed. 2012. (Illus.). 147p. 39.99 *(978-1-4622-8152-7(4))* Repressed Publishing LLC.

—Peter Pan in Kensington Gardens. 2009. 108p. (gr. -1-18). pap. 9.95 *(978-1-60664-381-5(9))* Rodgers, Alan Bks.

—Peter Pan in Kensington Gardens & Peter & Wendy. 2009. 120p. pap. 7.99 *(978-1-4209-3191-4(1))* Digireads.com Publishing.

Braswell, Liz. Straight on till Morning-A Twisted Tale. 2020. (Twisted Tale Ser.). (ENG.). 496p. (YA). (gr. 7-12). 17.99 *(978-1-4847-8130-2(9),* Disney-Hyperion) Disney Publishing Worldwide.

Disney Storybook Art Team. Jake & the Neverland Pirates: Playful Pirates: Play-A-Sound Book. Publications International Ltd. Staff, ed. 2013. (Play-A-Sound Ser.). (ENG.). 10p. (J). (gr. k-3). bds. *(978-1-4508-6772-6(3),* d1399e5b-b94b-4ab0-91ab-a035f527d2af) Phoenix International Publications, Inc.

Jenny Press Staff. Peter Pan. 2016. (Illus.). 24p. (J). (gr. -1-12). pap. 7.99 *(978-1-86147-815-3(1),* Armadillo) Anness Publishing GBR. Dist: National Bk. Network.

Levine, Gail Carson. Fairy Haven & the Quest for the Wand. Christiana, David, illus. 2007. 191p. (J). *(978-1-4287-6391-3(0))* Disney Pr.

RH Disney. Peter Pan Step into Reading (Disney Peter Pan) RH Disney, illus. 2013. (Step into Reading Ser.). (ENG., Illus.). 32p. (J). (gr. -1-1). 5.99 *(978-0-7364-3114-9(4),* RH/Disney) Random Hse. Children's Bks.

Sabuda, Robert, illus. Peter Pan: Peter Pan. 2008. (ENG.). 16p. (J). 39.99 *(978-0-689-85364-7(5),* Little Simon) Little Simon.

Sterne, Laurence. The Life & Opinions of Tristram Shandy, Gentleman. 2015. (Vintage Classics Ser.). 624p. pap. 13.95 *(978-0-09-951915-7(1))* Penguin Random Hse. GBR. Dist: Independent Pubs. Group.

Thorpe, Kiki. A Dandelion Wish. Christy, Jana, illus. 2013. (Never Girls Ser.: 3). lib. bdg. 16.00 *(978-0-606-32199-0(3))* Turtleback.

—Never Girls #2: the Space Between (Disney: the Never Girls) Christy, Jana, illus. 2013. (Never Girls Ser.: 2). (ENG.). 128p. (J). (gr. 1-4). 6.99 *(978-0-7364-2795-1(3),* RH/Disney) Random Hse. Children's Bks.

—Never Girls #3: a Dandelion Wish (Disney: the Never Girls) Christy, Jana, illus. 2013. (Never Girls Ser.: 3). (ENG.). 128p. (J). (gr. 1-4). 6.99 *(978-0-7364-2796-8(1),* RH/Disney) Random Hse. Children's Bks.

—Never Girls #7: a Pinch of Magic (Disney: the Never Girls) Christy, Jana, illus. 2014. (Never Girls Ser.: 7). (ENG.). 128p. (J). (gr. 1-4). 6.99 *(978-0-7364-3097-5(0),* RH/Disney) Random Hse. Children's Bks.

—A Pinch of Magic. 2014. (Never Girls Ser.: 7). lib. bdg. 16.00 *(978-0-606-36008-1(5))* Turtleback.

—The Space Between. Christy, Jana, illus. 2013. (Never Girls Ser.: 2). lib. bdg. 16.00 *(978-0-606-26974-2(6))* Turtleback.

NEW DELHI (INDIA)

Khemka, Nitya. Good Night Delhi. Kale, Kavita Singh, illus. 2017. (Good Night Our World Ser.). 20p. (J). (— 1). bds. 9.95 *(978-1-60219-481-6(5))* Good Night Bks.

NEW ENGLAND

Connery-Boyd, Peg. Totally New England! 2016. (Hawk's Nest Activity Bks.: 0). (ENG.). 64p. (J). pap. 12.99 *(978-1-4926-3379-2(8),* 9781492633792) Sourcebooks, Inc.

Koestler-Grack, Rachel A. Northern Colonial Town: Plymouth. 2003. (J). pap. *(978-1-58417-079-2(4))* Lake Street Pubs.

NEW ENGLAND—FICTION

Adams, James D. Creepy Campfire Tales: Halloween Campout, Vol. 1. 2008. 132p. (J). per. 12.95 *(978-1-60404-103-3(X))* Owl Creek Media Ltd.

—Creepy Campfire Tales Vol. 1: Halloween Campout. 2008. 132p. (YA). 26.95 *(978-1-60404-104-0(8))* Owl Creek Media Ltd.

Alcott, Louisa. Jack & Jill. Date not set. 352p. (YA). 25.95 *(978-0-8488-2671-0(X))* Amereon Ltd.

—Jack & Jill. 2013. (Works of Louisa May Alcott). 425p. reprint ed. lthr. 79.00 *(978-0-7812-1638-8(9))* Reprint Services Corp.

—Jo's Boys. l.t. ed. 2007. (ENG.). 288p. pap. 23.99 *(978-1-4346-0451-4(9))* Creative Media Partners, LLC.

—Jo's Boys. 2005. pap. *(978-1-4065-0107-0(7))* Dodo Pr.

—Jo's Boys. l.t. ed. 2005. 424p. pap. *(978-1-84637-067-0(1))* Echo Library.

—Jo's Boys. 2013. (Works of Louisa May Alcott). 366p. reprint ed. lthr. 79.00 *(978-0-7812-1642-5(7))* Reprint Services Corp.

—Little Men. rev. ed. 2006. 352p. 31.95 *(978-1-4218-1800-9(0));* pap. 15.95 *(978-1-4218-1900-6(7))* 1st World Publishing, Inc. (1st World Library - Literary Society).

—Little Men. (ENG.). (J). 2020. 300p. pap. 12.98 *(978-1-714-79319-8(2))* 2017. (Illus.). pap. 11.99 *(978-1-366-58954-5(8))* Blurb, Inc.

—Little Men. (ENG.). (J). 2018. 380p. 46.95 *(978-0-343-77916-0(1))* 2018. 380p. pap. 29.95 *(978-0-343-77915-3(3))* 2017. (Illus.). pap. 17.95 *(978-1-375-47932-5(6))* 2015. (Illus.). 27.95 *(978-1-298-78052-2(7))* 2015. (Illus.). 27.95 *(978-1-296-65257-9(2))* Creative Media Partners, LLC.

—Little Men. l.t. ed. 2005. 564p. pap. *(978-1-84637-068-7(X))* Echo Library.

—Little Men. 2019. (ENG.). (J). (gr. 3-7). 606p. pap. 38.99 *(978-1-6925-3269-7(3));* 448p. pap. 25.99 *(978-1-0899-8038-4(8));* 310p. pap. 21.99 *(978-1-0803-8276-7(3));* 448p. pap. 25.99 *(978-1-0859-0181-9(5));* 482p. pap. 26.99 *(978-1-0756-8767-9(5));* 634p. pap. 42.99 *(978-1-0753-6849-3(9));* 482p. pap. 26.99 *(978-1-0730-0563-5(1));* 310p. pap. 21.99 *(978-1-0706-0670-5(7));* 666p. pap. 36.99 *(978-1-0985-5102-5(8));* 636p. pap. 36.99 *(978-1-0971-3721-3(X))* Independently Published.

—Little Men. 2012. (Signet Classics Ser.). (ENG.). (J). (gr. 12). lib. bdg. 16.55 *(978-1-61383-896-9(4))* Perfection Learning Corp.

—Little Men: Life at Plumfield with Jo's Boys. 2013. (Early Best Sellers Ser.). 425p. reprint ed. lthr. 69.00 *(978-0-7426-1004-0(7))* Classic Bks.

—Little Men: Life at Plumfield with Jo's Boys. 2013. (Works of Louisa May Alcott). 292p. reprint ed. lthr. 79.00 *(978-0-7812-1629-6(X))* Reprint Services Corp.

—Little Women. Dunn, Robert, illus. 2013. 46p. (J). *(978-1-4351-4813-0(4))* Barnes & Noble, Inc.

—Little Women. 2007. 264p. (YA). 11.95 *(978-1-933486-01-7(5))* Core Knowledge Foundation.

—Little Women. unabr. ed. 2004. (Chrysalis Childrens Classics Ser.). (Illus.). 190p. (YA). pap. *(978-1-84365-049-2(5),* Pavilion Children's Books) Pavilion Bks.

—Little Women. 2013. (Works of Louisa May Alcott). 451p. reprint ed. lthr. 79.00 *(978-0-7812-1627-2(3))* Reprint Services Corp.

—Little Women. 2008. (Puffin Classics Ser.). (gr. k-3). lib. bdg. 19.65 *(978-0-613-86261-5(9))* Turtleback.

—Little Women: Bring the Classics to Life. 2008. (Bring the Classics to Life Ser.). (Illus.). 72p. (gr. 1-12). pap., act. bk. ed. 10.95 *(978-1-55576-047-2(3),* EDCTR-103B) EDCON Publishing Group.

—Little Women: With a Discussion of Family. Lauter, Richard, illus. 2003. (Values in Action Illustrated Classics Ser.). 191p. (J). *(978-1-59203-032-3(7))* Learning Challenge, Inc.

—Mujercitas.Tr. of Little Women. (SPA., Illus.). 192p. (YA). 11.95 *(978-84-7281-101-0(8),* AF1101) Auriga, Ediciones S.A. ESP. Dist: Continental Bk. Co., Inc.

—Mujercitas. 2004.Tr. of Little Women. (SPA.). lib. bdg. *(978-1-4135-2067-5(7))* El Cid Editor Incorporated.

—Mujercitas. (Coleccion Estrella).Tr. of Little Women. (SPA., Illus.). 64p. (J). 14.95 *(978-950-11-0010-5(3),* SGM010) Sigmar ARG. Dist: Continental Bk. Co., Inc.

—An Old-Fashioned Girl. 2013. (Works of Louisa May Alcott). 409p. reprint ed. lthr. 79.00 *(978-0-7812-1628-9(1))* Reprint Services Corp.

—An Old-Fashioned Thanksgiving. Wheeler, Jody, illus. 2010. 40p. (J). (gr. -1-3). 14.99 *(978-0-8249-5620-2(6),* Ideals Pubns.) Worthy Publishing.

Alcott, Louisa & Lacey, Mike. Little Women, 1 vol. 2011. (Calico Illustrated Classics Ser.: No. 4). (ENG., Illus.). 112p. (J). (gr. 2-5). 38.50 *(978-1-61641-617-1(3),* 4049, Calico Chapter Bks.) ABDO Publishing Co.

Alcott, Louisa May. The Annotated Little Women. 2015. (Annotated Bks.: 0). (ENG., Illus.). 744p. (gr. 11-17). 39.95 *(978-0-393-07219-8(3),* 7219) Norton, W. W. & Co., Inc.

—Classic Starts(r): Little Women. Corvino, Lucy, illus. 2005. (Classic Starts(r) Ser.). 160p. (J). (gr. 2-4). 6.95 *(978-1-4027-1236-4(7))* Sterling Publishing Co., Inc.

—Little Men. 2019. (Little Women Series,Virago Modern Classi Ser.). (ENG.). 400p. (J). (gr. 3-7). 15.99 *(978-0-349-01184-4(2),* Virago Press) Little, Brown Book Group Ltd. GBR. Dist: Hachette Bk. Group.

—Little Men. 2019. (Little Women Collection: 3). (ENG.). 400p. (J). (gr. 3). 17.99 *(978-1-5344-6224-3(4));* pap. 7.99 *(978-1-5344-6223-6(6))* Simon & Schuster Children's Publishing. (Aladdin).

—Little Women. 2013. (Vintage Children's Classics Ser.). (Illus.). 432p. (J). (gr. 4-7). pap. 10.99 *(978-0-09-957296-1(6))* Penguin Random Hse. GBR. Dist: Independent Pubs. Group.

Alcott, Louisa May & Barbarese, J. T. Little Men. 2012. (Little Women Ser.). 368p. (gr. 12). mass mkt. 5.95 *(978-0-451-53223-7(6),* Signet) Penguin Publishing Group.

Aldrich, Thomas Bailey. The Story of a Bad Boy. 2006. pap. *(978-1-4065-0613-6(3))* Dodo Pr.

—The Story of a Bad Boy. 2005. pap. 26.95 *(978-1-885529-78-7(3))* Stevens Publishing.

Alger, Horatio. Struggling Upward: Or, Luke Larkin's Luck. 2006. pap. *(978-1-4065-0723-2(7))* Dodo Pr.

—Struggling Upward; or, Luck Larkin's Luck. 2008. 104p. pap. 7.99 *(978-1-4209-3044-3(3))* Digireads.com Publishing.

Allbritton, Stacy Demoran. The Diary of Marie Landry, Acadian Exile, 1 vol. Haynes, Joyce, illus. 2012. (ENG.). 160p. (J). (gr. 3-7). pap. 14.95 *(978-1-58980-865-2(7),* Pelican Publishing) Arcadia Publishing.

Atwood, Megan. A Fall for Friendship. Andrewson, Natalie, illus. 2018. (Orchard Novel Ser.: 3). (ENG.). 240p. (J). (gr. 2-6). 12.99 *(978-1-4814-9051-1(6),* Aladdin) Simon & Schuster Children's Publishing.

—Ice Cream Summer. Andrewson, Natalie, illus. 2017. (Orchard Novel Ser.: 1). (ENG.). 272p. (J). (gr. 2-6). 12.99 *(978-1-4814-9047-4(8),* Aladdin) Simon & Schuster Children's Publishing.

—Once upon a Winter. Andrewson, Natalie, illus. 2017. (Orchard Novel Ser.: 2). (ENG.). 240p. (J). (gr. 2-6). 12.99 *(978-1-4814-9049-8(4),* Aladdin) Simon & Schuster Children's Publishing.

Bardsley-Sirois, Lois. Katherine's Winter Garden. 2012. 24p. pap. 12.99 *(978-1-4525-6269-8(5))* Balboa Pr.

Bass, Ruth. Sarah's Daughter. 2007. 389p. (YA). (gr. 8-12). per. 14.95 *(978-0-9774053-4-3(6))* North River Pr. Publishing Corp., The.

Cathie & Jessie's Noisy New England Adventure. 2006. (Illus.). 32p. (J). cd-rom 12.99 *(978-0-9773526-1-6(7))* Diversified A+ Pubns.

Coatsworth, Elizabeth & Sewell, Helen. Away Goes Sally. 2003. (ENG., Illus.). 118p. (J). (gr. 3-9). pap. 10.95 *(978-1-883937-83-6(3))* Ignatius Pr.

Collins, Pat Lowery. Schooner. Collins, Pat Lowery, illus. 2003. (ENG., Illus.). 32p. (J). (gr. 2-5). 14.95 *(978-1-889833-35-4(5),* Commonwealth Editions) Applewood Bks.

Cooper, Blayne. Blind Side of the Moon. 2016. (ENG.). 240p. (J). (gr. 7). pap. 16.95 *(978-1-59493-531-2(9))* Bella Bks., Inc.

Cornelia Meigs. Master Simon's Garden. 2010. (Illus.). 244p. pap. 6.95 *(978-1-60386-299-8(4),* Watchmaker Publishing) Wexford College Pr.

Dalton, Linda J. The Mystery of the Broomstick Horse. 2012. 116p. 29.99 *(978-1-4797-4781-8(5));* pap. 19.99 *(978-1-4797-4780-1(7))* Xlibris Corp.

Daly, Mariah. James Has Diabetes. 2009. (ENG.). 56p. pap. 21.99 *(978-1-4389-3188-3(3))* AuthorHouse.

DeMitchell, Terri A. You Will Come Back - the First in the Olde Locke Beach Mysteries. 2004. (ENG., Illus.). 176p. 14.95 *(978-1-932278-02-6(8))* Mayhaven Publishing, Inc.

Devlin, Wende. Old Black Witch! Devlin, Harry, illus. 2012. (ENG.). 32p. (J). (gr. -1-3). 18.95 *(978-1-930900-62-2(7))* Purple Hse. Pr.

Digby Tracks a Catamount. 2008. (Illus.). 36p. (J). per. *(978-0-9745931-1-1(7))* Vermont Bookworks.

Dixon, Franklin W. Killer Connections: Book Three in the Killer Mystery Trilogy. 2010. (Hardy Boys (All New) Undercover Brothers Ser.: 33). (ENG.). 176p. (J). (gr. 3-7). pap. 7.99 *(978-1-4169-8696-6(0),* Aladdin) Simon & Schuster Children's Publishing.

Dzidrums, Christine. Fair Youth: Emylee of Forest Springs. Lopez, Lyle & Dzidrums, Joseph, illus. 2012. (ENG.). 120p. (YA). pap. 9.99 *(978-1-938438-05-9(1))* Creative Media Publishing.

Ehrenhaft, Daniel. Drawing a Blank: Or How I Tried to Solve a Mystery, End a Feud, & Land the Girl of My Dreams. Ristow, Trevor, illus. 2009. (ENG.). 352p. (J). pap. 8.99 *(978-0-06-075254-5(8),* HarperTeen) HarperCollins Pubs.

Eiselein, Gregory, et al. Little Women. 2003. (Norton Critical Editions Ser.: 0). (ENG., Illus.). 688p. (C). pap. 13.00 *(978-0-393-97614-4(9),* 97614) Norton, W. W. & Co., Inc.

Frederick, Heather Vogel. A Little Women Christmas. Ibatoulline, Bagram, illus. 2014. (ENG.). 32p. (J). (gr. -1-3). 19.99 *(978-1-4424-1359-7(X),* Simon & Schuster Bks. For Young Readers) Simon & Schuster Bks. For Young Readers.

Freeberg, Jane. The Scallop Christmas. Sheckels, Astrid, illus. 2011. (ENG.). 36p. (J). 17.95 *(978-1-934031-25-4(9),* e2c69617-3a60-43d3-82d0-b5a01bf93ade) Islandport Pr., Inc.

Hatch, Richard W. The Curious Lobster. Wakeman, Marion Freeman, illus. 2018. 400p. (J). (gr. 2-5). 14.99 *(978-1-68137-288-4(6),* NYRB Kids) New York Review of Bks., Inc., The.

Hathaway, Lucinda Churchman. 'Round the World: Takashi Sails Home. 2008. (Illus.). 135p. (J). 12.95 *(978-1-59322-034-1(0))* Down The Shore Publishing.

Hawthorne, Nathanial. The House of the Seven Gables, 1 vol. Fisher, Scott, illus. 2010. (Calico Illustrated Classics Ser.). (ENG.). 112p. (J). (gr. 2-5). 38.50 *(978-1-60270-746-7(4),* 3993, Calico Chapter Bks.) ABDO Publishing Co.

Hemphill, Stephanie. Wicked Girls: A Novel of the Salem Witch Trials. 2010. 336p. (YA). (gr. 7-18). lib. bdg. 17.89 *(978-0-06-185329-6(1))* HarperCollins Pubs.

Holdman, Shirley Terrill. The Adventures of Giggles & Owen: A True Story. Riecks Goss, Carol, illus. 2010. 26p. pap. 14.95 *(978-1-60844-490-8(2))* Dog Ear Publishing, LLC.

Huntington, Geoffrey. Blood Moon: The Ravenscliff Series - Book Three. 2013. (Ravenscliff Ser.: 3). (ENG.). 260p. (YA). pap. 17.99 *(978-1-62681-169-0(5),* Diversion Bks.) Diversion Publishing Corp.

Irving, Washington. The Devil & Tom Walker. 2007. (Tale Blazers: American Literature Ser.). 37p. (J). (gr. 4-7). pap. 3.30 *(978-0-89598-665-8(5))* Perfection Learning Corp.

Isenhoff, Michelle. The Quill Pen. 2011. (ENG.). 168p. pap. 9.98 *(978-1-4664-9691-0(6))* CreateSpace Independent Publishing Platform.

Jacobs, Lily. The Littlest Bunny in New England: An Easter Adventure. Dunn, Robert, illus. 2015. (Littlest Bunny Ser.). (ENG.). 32p. (J). (gr. -1-3). 9.99 *(978-1-4926-1138-7(7),* Hometown World) Sourcebooks, Inc.

James, Eric. Santa's Sleigh Is on Its Way to New England: A Christmas Adventure. Dunn, Robert, illus. 2016. (Santa's Sleigh Is on Its Way Ser.). (ENG.). 32p. (J). (gr. k-2). 12.99 *(978-1-4926-4341-8(6),* 9781492643418, Hometown World) Sourcebooks, Inc.

—The Spooky Express New England. Piwowarski, Marcin, illus. 2017. (Spooky Express Ser.). (ENG.). 32p. (J). (gr. k-6). 9.99 *(978-1-4926-5378-3(0),* Hometown World) Sourcebooks, Inc.

Kimmel, Elizabeth Cody. ParaNormaN. 2012. (ENG.). (J). (gr. 4-7). 64.99 *(978-1-61969-450-7(6))* Findaway World, LLC.

Kinkade, Thomas. Katherine's Story. 2004. (Girls of Lighthouse Lane Ser.). 176p. (J). (gr. 5-18). 13.89 *(978-0-06-054342-6(6))* HarperCollins Pubs.

Kinkade, Thomas & Tamar, Erika. Rose's Story. 2004. (Girls of Lighthouse Lane Ser.: No. 2). (Illus.). 192p. (J). (gr. 5-18). 12.99 *(978-0-06-054344-0(2))* HarperCollins Pubs.

Lauter, Richard, illus. Little Women. (Young Collector's Illustrated Classics Ser.). 192p. (J). 9.95 *(978-1-56156-371-5(4))* Kidsbooks, LLC.

Levin, Betty. Shoddy Cove. 2003. 208p. (J). (gr. 5-18). 15.99 *(978-0-06-052271-1(2))* HarperCollins Pubs.

Lindskoog, Kathryn, ed. Little Women. Chitouras, Barbara, illus. 2003. (Classics for Young Readers Ser.). 432p. (J). per. 12.99 *(978-0-87552-734-5(5))* P & R Publishing.

Litrel, Suzanne M. Jackie Tempo & the Emperor's Seal. 2007. 172p. (YA). per. 13.95 *(978-0-595-46822-5(5))* iUniverse, Inc.

MacLachlan, Patricia. Your Moon, My Moon: A Grandmother's Words to a Faraway Child. Collier, Bryan, illus. 2011. (ENG.). 32p. (J). (gr. -1-3). 16.99 *(978-1-4169-7950-0(6),* Simon & Schuster Bks. For Young Readers) Simon & Schuster Bks. For Young Readers.

Martin, Ann M. Needle & Thread. 2007. (Main Street Ser.). (Illus.). 205p. (J). (gr. 4-7). 14.65 *(978-0-7569-8328-4(2))* Perfection Learning Corp.

—Needle & Thread. Andreasen, Dan, illus. 2007. 205p. (J). pap. *(978-0-545-03660-3(7))* Scholastic, Inc.

—The Secret Book Club. 2008. (Main Street Ser.). (Illus.). 212p. (J). (gr. 4-7). 14.65 *(978-0-7569-8823-4(3))* Perfection Learning Corp.
—Tis the Season. 2007. (Main Street Ser.). (Illus.). 195p. (J). (gr. 4-7). 14.65 *(978-0-7569-8327-7(4))* Perfection Learning Corp.
Mckenzie, Riford. The Witches of Dredmoore Hollow, 0 vols. unabr. ed. 2013. (ENG.). 274p. (J). (gr. 5-7). pap. 9.99 *(978-1-4778-1702-5(6),* 9781477817025, Two Lions) Amazon Publishing.
Meigs, Cornelia. Clearing Weather. 2018. (ENG., Illus.). 320p. (YA). (gr. 2-6). pap. 8.99 *(978-0-486-81742-2(3),* 817423) Dover Pubns., Inc.
Ohlin, Nancy. Always, Forever. 2014. (ENG., Illus.). 320p. (YA). (gr. 9). pap. 9.99 *(978-1-4424-6487-2(9),* Simon Pulse) Simon Pulse.
—Thorn Abbey. 2013. (ENG.). 304p. (YA). (gr. 9). 16.99 *(978-1-4424-6486-5(0),* Simon Pulse) Simon Pulse.
Papp, Robert, illus. The Pumpkin Head Mystery. 2010. (Boxcar Children Mysteries Ser.: 124). (ENG.). 128p. (J). (gr. 2-5). 14.99 *(978-0-8075-6668-8(3),* 807566683);No. 124. pap. 5.99 *(978-0-8075-6669-5(1),* 807566691) Random Hse. Children's Bks. (Random Hse. Bks. for Young Readers).
Parker, John. Chaos Mountain. 2007. 96p. (YA). pap. *(978-1-4207-0734-2(5))* Sundance/Newbridge Educational Publishing.
Parramore, Helen. The Fragments of Fern Valley. 2009. 112p. pap. 10.95 *(978-1-4401-2943-8(6))* iUniverse, Inc.
Penrose, Margaret. The Motor Girls Through New England: Or Held by the Gypsies. 2007. (ENG.). 154p. pap. 19.99 *(978-1-4346-5805-0(8));* 172p. pap. 21.99 *(978-1-4346-5806-7(6))* Creative Media Partners, LLC.
Ritter, William. Beastly Bones. 2016. (Jackaby Ser.: 2). lib. bdg. 20.80 *(978-0-606-39017-0(0))* Turtleback.
Rodriguez, Jason, ed. Colonial Comics: New England, 1620 ¿ 1750. 2014. (Colonial Comics Ser.). (ENG., Illus.). 208p. (gr. 4). pap. 29.95 *(978-1-938486-30-2(7))* Fulcrum Publishing.
Sales, Leila. Past Perfect. 2012. (ENG.). 336p. (YA). (gr. 9). pap. 10.99 *(978-1-4424-0683-4(6),* Simon Pulse) Simon Pulse.
Santaniello, Shelly W. Tommy's Needham Rocket. 2011. 53p. pap. 10.95 *(978-1-4327-7000-6(4))* Outskirts Pr., Inc.
Schaefer, Laura. Littler Women: A Modern Retelling. 2017. (ENG., Illus.). 224p. (J). (gr. 3-7). 16.99 *(978-1-4814-8761-0(2),* Simon & Schuster/Paula Wiseman Bks.) Simon & Schuster/Paula Wiseman Bks.
Schmidt, Gary D. Trouble. 2010. (ENG.). 304p. (YA). (gr. 7). pap. 15.99 *(978-0-547-33133-1(9),* 1417365, Clarion Bks.) HarperCollins Pubs.
Seidler, Tor. The Dulcimer Boy. Selznick, Brian, illus. 2003. 160p. (J). (gr. 3-7). lib. bdg. 16.89 *(978-0-06-623610-0(X))* HarperCollins Pubs.
—The Dulcimer Boy. Selznick, Brian, illus. 2004. 153p. (gr. 5-7). 17.00 *(978-0-7569-3520-7(2))* Perfection Learning Corp.
Sewell, Anna. Black Beauty. 2006. (My First Classics Ser.). 112p. (J). (gr. k-3). pap. 4.99 *(978-0-06-079148-3(9),* HarperFestival) HarperCollins Pubs.
Shasha, Mark. Night of the Moonjellies: 15th Anniversary Edition. 2007. (Illus.). 32p. (J). (gr. -1-2). 12.95 *(978-1-930900-34-9(1))* Purple Hse. Pr.
Sheckels, Astrid, illus. Nic & Nellie, 1 vol. 2013. (ENG.). 36p. (J). (gr. 1-4). 17.95 *(978-1-934031-52-0(6),* d981927c-4686-4ef6-bbee-9d134ce68c96) Islandport Pr., Inc.
Shute, Henry. Sequil or Things Whitch Aint Finished in The. 2007. 108p. per. 14.99 *(978-0-9773040-3-5(5))* Wilder Pubns., Corp.
Sidney, Margaret. Five Little Peppers & How They Grew. 2017. (ENG., Illus.). (J). 24.95 *(978-1-374-93472-6(0));* pap. 14.95 *(978-1-374-93471-9(2))* Capital Communications, Inc.
—Five Little Peppers & How They Grew. 2006. (Dover Children's Classics Ser.). (ENG., Illus.). 224p. (J). (gr. 3-5). per. 9.95 *(978-0-486-45267-8(0),* 452670) Dover Pubns., Inc.
Smith, Cynthia Leitich. Diabolical. 2012. (Tantalize Ser.: 4). (ENG., Illus.). 368p. (YA). (gr. 9-12). 17.99 *(978-0-7636-5118-3(4))* Candlewick Pr.
Solod, Margo. Coyote Summer: A Summerhood Island Book. 2014. (Illus.). 118p. (J). pap. 15.00 *(978-1-939930-18-7(9))* Brandylane Pubs., Inc.
Spotswood, Jessica. Born Wicked. 2013. (Cahill Witch Chronicles Ser.: 1). (ENG.). 352p. (YA). (gr. 7). pap. 10.99 *(978-0-14-242187-1(1),* Speak) Penguin Young Readers Group.
—Born Wicked. 2013. lib. bdg. 22.10 *(978-0-606-26729-8(8))* Turtleback.
Stowe, Harriet. Betty's Bright Idea. 2006. pap. *(978-1-4068-3093-4(3))* Echo Library.
Sully, Katherine. Night-Night New England. Poole, Helen, illus. 2017. (Night-Night Ser.). (ENG.). 20p. (J). (gr. -1-1). bds. 9.99 *(978-1-4926-4772-0(1),* 9781492647720, Hometown World) Sourcebooks, Inc.
Swegles, Maryanne. Digging for Bottles. 2005. (Illus.). 28p. (J). 15.00 *(978-0-9768418-0-7(0))* Hydrangea Pr.
Terrill Holdman, Shirley. The Adventures of Giggles & Owen: Adventure Three - Unlimited Pawsibilities. Leeds, Marjorie M., illus. 2013. 50p. pap. 17.95 *(978-1-4575-2175-1(X))* Dog Ear Publishing, LLC.
Thorson, Kristine & Thorson, Robert M. Stone Wall Secrets. Moore, Gustav, illus. 2010. (ENG.). 40p. (J). (gr. 3-7). 16.95 *(978-0-88448-195-9(6))* Tilbury Hse. Pubs.
Tuthill, Louisa C. Hurrah for New England! or the Virginia Boy's Vacation. 2004. reprint ed. pap. 15.95 *(978-1-4191-2504-1(4));* pap. 1.99 *(978-1-4192-2504-8(9))* Kessinger Publishing, LLC.
Wall, Patricia Q. Child Out of Place: A Story for New England. Ronnquist, Debby, illus. 2003. 116p. (J). (gr. 6-9). pap. 15.00 *(978-0-9742185-0-2(2))* Fall Rose Bks.
Wallace, Carey. The Ghost in the Glass House. 2014. (ENG.). 240p. (YA). (gr. 7). pap. 13.99 *(978-0-544-33618-6(6),* 1584164, Clarion Bks.) HarperCollins Pubs.
Wiggin, Kate Douglas. Rebecca of Sunnybrook Farm. (J). 23.95 *(978-0-8488-0854-9(1))* Amereon Ltd.
—Rebecca of Sunnybrook Farm. 2016. (ENG., Illus.). (J). 27.95 *(978-1-358-96338-4(X))* Creative Media Partners, LLC.
—Rebecca of Sunnybrook Farm. 2003. (Dover Children's Evergreen Classics Ser.). (ENG.). 208p. (J). (gr. 3-8). pap. 5.99 *(978-0-486-42845-1(1),* 428451) Dover Pubns., Inc.
—Rebecca of Sunnybrook Farm. 2005. pap. 30.95 *(978-1-4179-1457-9(2))* Kessinger Publishing, LLC.
—Rebecca of Sunnybrook Farm. 2003. (Aladdin Classics Ser.). (ENG.). 368p. (J). pap. 7.99 *(978-0-689-86001-0(3),* Aladdin) Simon & Schuster Children's Publishing.
—Rebecca of Sunnybrook Farm. Akib, Jamel, illus. 2007. (Classic Starts(r) Ser.). (ENG.). 160p. (J). (gr. 2-4). 6.95 *(978-1-4027-3693-3(2))* Sterling Publishing Co., Inc.
—Rebecca of Sunnybrook Farm. Warren, Eliza Gatewood, ed. Tadiello, Ed, illus. 2006. 240p. (YA). (gr. 4-8). reprint ed. 10.00 *(978-0-7567-9830-7(2))* DIANE Publishing Co.
—Rebecca of Sunnybrook Farm. 2004. reprint ed. pap. 19.95 *(978-1-4179-9996-5(9));* pap. 1.99 *(978-1-4179-9946-0(2))* Kessinger Publishing, LLC.
Wiggin, Kate Douglas & Fisher, Eric Scott. Rebecca of Sunnybrook Farms, 1 vol. 2011. (Calico Illustrated Classics Ser.: No. 4). (ENG., Illus.). 112p. (J). (gr. 2-5). 38.50 *(978-1-61641-620-1(3),* 4055, Calico Chapter Bks.) ABDO Publishing Co.
Winfield, Arthur M. The Rover Boys down East or the Struggle for the Stanhope Fortune. 2006. (ENG.). 316p. per. 30.95 *(978-1-4286-4113-6(0))* Kessinger Publishing, LLC.
Yancey, Rick. The Monstrumologist. 2010. (Monstrumologist Ser.: 1). (ENG.). 464p. (YA). (gr. 9). pap. 13.99 *(978-1-4169-8449-8(6),* Simon & Schuster Bks. For Young Readers) Simon & Schuster Bks. For Young Readers.

NEW ENGLAND—HISTORY

Arenstam, Peter, et al. MayFlower 1620: A New Look at a Pilgrim Voyage. 2004. (Illus.). 47p. (J). (gr. k-4). 18.00 *(978-0-7567-7967-2(7))* DIANE Publishing Co.
Baker, Allison. New England a to Z. Coffey, Kevin, illus. 2012. 38p. (J). 14.95 *(978-1-62086-065-6(1))* Amplify Publishing Group.
Bartley, Niccole. New England, 1 vol. 2014. (Land That I Love: Regions of the United States Ser.). (ENG., Illus.). 32p. (J). (gr. 3-3). 27.93 *(978-1-4777-6849-5(1),* ec7dc212-65a3-4828-94b0-1203b2ce1a2c, PowerKids Pr.) Rosen Publishing Group, Inc., The.
Bell, Samantha S. Exploring New England. 2017. (Exploring America's Regions Ser.). (ENG., Illus.). 48p. (J). (gr. 4-8). lib. bdg. 35.64 *(978-1-5321-1380-2(3),* 27678) ABDO Publishing Co.
Carole Marsh. New England Coloring. 2004. (City Bks.). 24p. (gr. k-5). pap., act. bk. ed. 3.95 *(978-0-635-02233-2(8))* Gallopade International.
Cowan, Mary Morton. Timberrr! A History of Logging in New England. 2003. (Women at War Ser.). (Illus.). 128p. (gr. 5-18). lib. bdg. 25.90 *(978-0-7613-1866-8(6),* Twenty-First Century Bks.) Lerner Publishing Group.
Ferguson, Isabel & Frederick, Heather Vogel. A World More Bright: The Life of Mary Baker Eddy. 2013. (Illus.). vi, 279p. *(978-0-87510-494-2(0),* Christian Science Publishing Society, The) Christian Science Publishing Society.
Jameson, W. C. Buried Treasures of New England. 2005. (Buried Treasure Ser.). (ENG.). 192p. (J). (gr. 4-17). pap. 11.95 *(978-0-87483-485-7(6))* August Hse. Pubs., Inc.
Koestler-Grack, Rachel A. Northern Colonial Town: Plymouth. 2003. (J). *(978-1-58417-016-7(6))* Lake Street Pubs.
Magsamen, Sandra. I Love New England: An ABC Adventure. 2016. (ABC Adventure Ser.). (ENG., Illus.). 40p. (J). (gr. -1-5). 12.99 *(978-1-4926-2841-5(7),* Hometown World) Sourcebooks, Inc.
Rajczak Nelson, Kristen. The Mayflower Compact, 1 vol. 2013. (Documents That Shaped America Ser.). (Illus.). 32p. (J). (gr. 4-5). (ENG.). pap. 11.50 *(978-1-4339-9006-9(7),* d09f0491-5854-40b8-accf-ceccd2ad1e89); (ENG., lib. bdg. 29.27 *(978-1-4339-9005-2(9),* 9fa5d6d6-0346-4074-ba27-f3727b38e89c); pap. 63.00 *(978-1-4339-9007-6(5))* Stevens, Gareth Publishing LLLP.
Seguin, Marilyn. No Ordinary Lives: Four 19th Century Teenage Diaries. 2009. (J). pap. *(978-0-8283-2158-7(2))* Branden Bks.

NEW ENGLAND PATRIOTS (FOOTBALL TEAM)

Barrington, Richard. Tom Brady: Super Bowl Champion, 1 vol. 2015. (Living Legends of Sports Ser.). (ENG., Illus.). 48p. (J). (gr. 5-6). 28.41 *(978-1-68048-119-8(3),* 021cd15f-9752-4f8d-9c05-99a3b51a85f8, Britannica Educational Publishing) Rosen Publishing Group, Inc., The.
Bell, Lonnie. The History of the New England Patriots. 2004. (NFL Today Ser.). (Illus.). 32p. (YA). (gr. 5-9). 18.95 *(978-1-58341-304-3(9))* Creative Co., The.
Buckley, James, Jr. Tom Brady & the New England Patriots: Super Bowl XLIX. 2015. (Super Bowl Superstars Ser.). (ENG., Illus.). 24p. (J). (gr. 1-3). lib. bdg. 26.99 *(978-1-62724-869-3(2))* Bearport Publishing Co., Inc.
Burgess, Zack. Meet the New England Patriots. 2016. (Big Picture Sports Ser.). (ENG., Illus.). 24p. (J). (gr. k-3). lib. bdg. 22.60 *(978-1-59953-742-9(7))* Norwood Hse. Pr.
Epstein, Brad M. New England Patriots 101. 2010. (Illus.). 24p. (J). bds. *(978-1-60730-118-9(0),* 101 Bk.) Michaelson Entertainment.
Ervin, Phil & Scheff, Matt. New England Patriots, 1 vol. 2016. (NFL up Close Ser.). (ENG., Illus.). 32p. (J). (gr. 3-9). lib. bdg. 32.79 *(978-1-68078-224-0(X),* 22051, SportsZone) ABDO Publishing Co.
Evans, John Fredric. Bill Belichick, 1 vol. 2019. (Championship Coaches Ser.). (ENG.). 112p. (gr. 7-7). 40.27 *(978-0-7660-9794-0(3),* e0483d96-2fe2-4e1c-a902-b3bd80e452a1) Enslow Publishing, LLC.
Frisch, Aaron. New England Patriots. 2014. (Super Bowl Champions Ser.). (ENG., Illus.). 24p. (J). (gr. 1-4). *(978-1-60818-380-7(7),* 21565, Creative Education) Creative Co., The.
Kelley, K. C. Tom Brady. 2018. (Amazing Americans: Football Stars Ser.). (ENG.). 24p. (J). (gr. -1-3). lib. bdg. 17.95 *(978-1-68402-452-0(8))* Bearport Publishing Co., Inc.
Leboutillier, Nate. New England Patriots. 2005. (Super Bowl Champions Ser.). (Illus.). 24p. (J). (gr. 1-4). lib. bdg. 16.95 *(978-1-58341-386-9(3),* Creative Education) Creative Co., The.
MacRae, Sloan. The New England Patriots, 1 vol. 2011. (America's Greatest Teams Ser.). (ENG., Illus.). 24p. (J). (gr. 2-3). pap. 9.25 *(978-1-4488-2739-8(6),* b1549861-0b9d-4310-a879-97ecaa456f90); lib. bdg. 26.27 *(978-1-4488-2575-2(X),* b54c09a4-781f-46f1-98b6-05125d3b87c2) Rosen Publishing Group, Inc., The. (PowerKids Pr.).
Morgan, Joe L. Rob Gronkowski, Vol. 9. 2018. (Gridiron Greats: Pro Football's Best Players Ser.). 80p. (J). (gr. 7). lib. bdg. 33.27 *(978-1-4222-4074-8(6))* Mason Crest.
O'Hearn, Michael. The Story of the New England Patriots. 2009. (NFL Today Ser.). (Illus.). 48p. (YA). (gr. 5-9). 22.95 *(978-1-58341-763-8(X))* Creative Co., The.
Osborne, M. K. Superstars of the New England Patriots. 2018. (Pro Sports Superstars - NFL Ser.). (ENG.). 24p. (J). (gr. 1-4). pap. 8.99 *(978-1-68152-328-6(0),* 15085) Amicus.
Publications International Ltd. Staff. Yesterday & Today Nfl New England Patriots. 2009. 160p. 24.98 *(978-1-4127-9828-0(0))* Publications International, Ltd.
Storm, Marysa. Highlights of the New England Patriots. 2018. (Team Stats — Football Edition Ser.). (ENG.). 32p. (J). (gr. 4-6). pap. 9.99 *(978-1-64466-282-3(5),* 12381); (Illus.). lib. bdg. *(978-1-68072-435-6(5),* 12380) Black Rabbit Bks. (Bolt).
Whiting, Jim. New England Patriots. rev. ed. 2019. (NFL Today Ser.). (ENG.). 48p. (J). (gr. 4-7). pap. 12.00 *(978-1-62832-713-7(8),* 19058, Creative Paperbacks) Creative Co., The.
—The Story of the New England Patriots. (NFL Today Ser.). (J). 2019. (ENG.). 48p. (gr. 3-6). *(978-1-64026-150-1(8),* 19060) 2013. 35.65 *(978-1-60818-310-4(6))* Creative Co., The. (Creative Education).
Wyner, Zach. New England Patriots. (Illus.). 32p. (J). 2015. pap. *(978-1-4896-0855-0(9))* 2014. (ENG., (gr. 4-7). lib. bdg. 28.55 *(978-1-4896-0854-3(0),* AV2 by Weigl) Weigl Pubs., Inc.
Zappa, Marcia. New England Patriots, 1 vol. 2014. (NFL's Greatest Teams Ser.). (ENG.). 32p. (J). (gr. 2-5). lib. bdg. 34.21 *(978-1-62403-363-6(6),* 1580, Big Buddy Bks.) ABDO Publishing Co.

NEW FRANCE—HISTORY

see Canada—History—To 1763 (New France); Mississippi River Valley—History

NEW GUINEA—FICTION

Nighthawk, Tori. Don't Judge a Bird by Its Feathers. Nighthawk, Tori, illus. 2013. (ENG., Illus.). 60p. (J). (gr. -1-3). 17.99 *(978-0-9858811-9-1(4))* Stone, Anne Publishing.

NEW HAMPSHIRE

Brown, Dottie. New Hampshire. 2012. (J). lib. bdg. 25.26 *(978-0-7613-4545-9(0),* Lerner Pubns.) Lerner Publishing Group.
Harris, Marie. Primary Numbers: A New Hampshire Number Book. Holman, Karen Busch, illus. 2004. (America by the Numbers Ser.). (ENG.). 40p. (J). (gr. 1-3). 16.95 *(978-1-58536-192-2(5),* 202036) Sleeping Bear Pr.
Heinrichs, Ann. New Hampshire. Kania, Matt, illus. 2017. (U. S. A. Travel Guides). (ENG.). 40p. (J). (gr. 2-5). lib. bdg. 38.50 *(978-1-5038-1969-6(8),* 211606) Child's World, Inc, The.
Hicks, Terry Allan. New Hampshire, 1 vol. Santoro, Christopher, illus. 2006. (It's My State! (First Edition)(r) Ser.). (ENG.). 80p. (J). (gr. 4-4). lib. bdg. 34.07 *(978-0-7614-1825-2(3),* 6a3fc930-f49f-45f5-abdd-69a91d221882) Cavendish Square Publishing LLC.
Marsh, Carole. New Hampshire Geography Projects: 30 Cool, Activities, Crafts, Experiments & More for Kids to Do to Learn about Your State! 2003. (New Hampshire Experience Ser.). 32p. (gr. k-5). pap. 5.95 *(978-0-635-01848-9(9),* Marsh, Carole Bks.) Gallopade International.
—New Hampshire Government Projects: 30 Cool, Activities, Crafts, Experiments & More for Kids to Do to Learn about Your State! 2003. (New Hampshire Experience Ser.). 32p. (gr. k-5). pap. 5.95 *(978-0-635-01948-6(5),* Marsh, Carole Bks.) Gallopade International.
—New Hampshire People Projects: 30 Cool, Activities, Crafts, Experiments & More for Kids to Do to Learn about Your State! 2003. (New Hampshire Experience Ser.). 32p. (gr. k-5). pap. 5.95 *(978-0-635-01998-1(1),* Marsh, Carole Bks.) Gallopade International.
—New Hampshire Symbols & Facts Projects: 30 Cool, Activities, Crafts, Experiments & More for Kids to Do to Learn about Your State! 2003. (New Hampshire Experience Ser.). 32p. (gr. k-8). pap. 5.95 *(978-0-635-01898-4(5),* Marsh, Carole Bks.) Gallopade International.
Mattern, Joanne. New Hampshire, 1 vol. 2003. (World Almanac(r) Library of the States Ser.). (ENG., Illus.). 48p. (gr. 4-6). lib. bdg. 33.67 *(978-0-8368-5155-7(2),* e1f41f93-790b-4af0-a793-aac2bfb5f300, Gareth Stevens Learning Library) Stevens, Gareth Publishing LLLP.
Mills, Jordan & Parker, Bridget. New Hampshire. 2016. (States Ser.). (ENG., Illus.). 32p. (J). (gr. 3-6). lib. bdg. 27.99 *(978-1-5157-0416-4(5),* 132027, Capstone Pr.) Capstone.
Murray, Julie. New Hampshire, 1 vol. 2006. (United States Ser.). (ENG., Illus.). 32p. (gr. 2-4). 27.07 *(978-1-59197-688-2(X),* Buddy Bks.) ABDO Publishing Co.
Otfinoski, Steven. New Hampshire, 1 vol. 2nd rev. ed. 2008. (Celebrate the States (Second Edition) Ser.). (ENG.). 144p. (gr. 6-6). lib. bdg. 39.79 *(978-0-7614-2718-6(X),* d4b8d275-783a-437d-847e-8c8889d4f813) Cavendish Square Publishing LLC.
Peters, S. True. How to Draw New Hampshire's Sights & Symbols. 2009. (Kid's Guide to Drawing America Ser.). 32p. (gr. k-k). 50.50 *(978-1-61511-078-0(X),* PowerKids Pr.) Rosen Publishing Group, Inc., The.
Thomas, William David. New Hampshire, 1 vol. 2006. (Portraits of the States Ser.). (ENG.). 32p. (gr. 3-5). pap. 11.50 *(978-0-8368-4721-5(0),* eb32f11c-3897-4a14-82b6-00bf0b0187bf, Gareth Stevens Learning Library) Stevens, Gareth Publishing LLLP.
—New Hampshire, 1 vol. 2006. (Portraits of the States Ser.). (ENG., Illus.). 32p. (gr. 3-5). lib. bdg. 28.67 *(978-0-8368-4704-8(0),* b60823e3-0381-45fa-866a-918bde971388, Gareth Stevens Learning Library) Stevens, Gareth Publishing LLLP.
Way, Jennifer. New Hampshire. 2009. (Bilingual Library of the United States of America Ser.). (ENG & SPA.). 32p. (gr. 2-2). 47.90 *(978-1-60853-373-2(5),* Editorial Buenas Letras) Rosen Publishing Group, Inc., The.
—New Hampshire/Nuevo Hampshire, 1 vol. Brusca, Maria Cristina, tr. 2005. (Bilingual Library of the United States of America Ser.: Set 2). (ENG & SPA., Illus.). 32p. (J). (gr. 2-2). lib. bdg. 28.93 *(978-1-4042-3094-1(7),* ff231793-0bed-47f8-837d-fb542c2db773) Rosen Publishing Group, Inc., The.

NEW HAMPSHIRE—FICTION

Absolutely Truly. 2014. (Pumpkin Falls Mystery Ser.). (ENG., Illus.). 368p. (J). (gr. 3-7). 19.99 *(978-1-4424-2972-7(0),* Simon & Schuster Bks. For Young Readers) Simon & Schuster Bks. For Young Readers.
Aldridge, Janet. The Meadow-Brook Girls in the Hills: Or the Missing Pilot of the White Mountains. 2006. pap. *(978-1-4065-0694-5(X))* Dodo Pr.
Alger, Horatio. Risen from the Ranks: Or, Harry Walton's Success. 2006. pap. *(978-1-4065-0721-8(0))* Dodo Pr.
Arenstam, Peter. Nicholas: a New Hampshire Tale. Holman, Karen Busch, illus. 2009. (Nicholas Northeastern Ser.: 3). 144p. (J). (gr. k-7). 14.95 *(978-1-58726-521-1(4),* Mitten Pr.) Ann Arbor Editions LLC.
Banks, Kate. Dillon Dillon. 2005. 149p. (gr. 3-7). 18.00 *(978-0-7569-5767-4(2))* Perfection Learning Corp.
Bruchac, Joseph. The Heart of a Chief. 2007. 153p. (gr. 4-7). 17.00 *(978-0-7569-7805-1(X))* Perfection Learning Corp.
—Night Wings. Comport, Sally Wern, illus. 2018. (ENG.). 224p. (J). (gr. 3-7). pap. 7.99 *(978-0-06-112321-4(8),* HarperCollins) HarperCollins Pubs.
Cornwell, Betsy. Tides. 2014. (ENG.). 304p. (YA). (gr. 7). pap. 8.99 *(978-0-544-30296-9(6),* 1578441, Clarion Bks.) HarperCollins Pubs.
DeMitchell, Terri A. The Portsmouth Alarm. 2013. 161p. pap. 16.95 *(978-1-932278-92-7(3))* Mayhaven Publishing, Inc.
Douglass, E. The Squirrel Friends Adventures: The Monster & the Great Storm. 2013. 100p. 19.95 *(978-1-4759-6640-4(7));* pap. 9.95 *(978-1-4759-6638-1(5))* iUniverse, Inc.
Eaton, Walter Prichard. Boy Scouts in the White Mountains: the Story of a Long Hike. Merrill, Frank T., illus. 2006. (ENG.). 316p. per. 30.95 *(978-1-4286-4117-4(3))* Kessinger Publishing, LLC.
Emerson, Kevin. Carlos Is Gonna Get It. 2008. (J). pap. *(978-0-439-93526-5(1),* Levine, Arthur A. Bks.) Scholastic, Inc.
Farish, Terry. Either the Beginning or the End of the World. 2015. (ENG.). 200p. (YA). (gr. 8-12). 18.99 *(978-1-4677-7483-3(9),* b2cbce4f-14d6-4326-9b41-74047d9506c0); E-Book 29.32 *(978-1-4677-8813-7(9))* Lerner Publishing Group. (Carolrhoda Lab™).
Frederick, Heather Vogel. Absolutely Truly. 2015. (Pumpkin Falls Mystery Ser.). (ENG., Illus.). 368p. (J). (gr. 3-7). pap. 8.99 *(978-1-4424-2973-4(9),* Simon & Schuster Bks. For Young Readers) Simon & Schuster Bks. For Young Readers.
—Mother-Daughter Book Camp. 2016. (Mother-Daughter Book Club Ser.). (ENG., Illus.). 336p. (J). (gr. 5-9). 19.99 *(978-1-4424-7183-2(2),* Simon & Schuster Bks. For Young Readers) Simon & Schuster Bks. For Young Readers.
Frizzell, Sally Parker. The Adventures in the Secret Valley. 2007. 40p. pap. 9.00 *(978-0-8059-7615-1(9))* Dorrance Publishing Co., Inc.
Gamble, Adam. Good Night New Hampshire. Rosen, Anne, illus. 2009. (Good Night Our World Ser.). (ENG.). 20p. (J). (gr. -1 — 1). bds. 9.95 *(978-1-60219-037-5(2))* Good Night Bks.
Hall, Donald. Lucy's Summer. McCurdy, Michael, illus. 2015. (ENG.). 40p. (J). (gr. 1-18). pap. 14.95 *(978-1-56792-348-3(8))* Godine, David R. Pub.
Harrar, George. The Trouble with Jeremy Chance. 2007. (Historical Fiction for Young Readers Ser.). (ENG., Illus.). 168p. (J). (gr. 2-8). per. 6.95 *(978-1-57131-669-1(8))* Milkweed Editions.
Hendrickson, David H. Cracking the Ice. 2018. (ENG., Illus.). 256p. (YA). 24.99 *(978-1-948134-02-6(0));* pap. 12.99 *(978-1-948134-07-1(1))* Pentucket Publishing.
—Cracking the Ice. 2011. (YA). 365p. (gr. 9-18). 16.95 *(978-1-934813-55-3(9));* 366p. *(978-1-934813-56-0(7))* Westside Bks.
Hilton, Marilyn. Found Things. (ENG.). 240p. (J). (gr. 4-7). 2015. pap. 7.99 *(978-1-4424-6088-1(1))* 2014. 16.99 *(978-1-4424-6087-4(3))* Simon & Schuster Children's Publishing.
Jacobs, Lily. The Littlest Bunny in New Hampshire: An Easter Adventure. Dunn, Robert, illus. 2015. (Littlest Bunny Ser.). (ENG.). 32p. (J). (gr. -1-3). 9.99 *(978-1-4926-1141-7(7),* Hometown World) Sourcebooks, Inc.
Jacobson, Jennifer Richard. Stained. (ENG.). 208p. (YA). (gr. 8). 2012. pap. 10.99 *(978-1-4424-8565-5(5),* Atheneum Bks. for Young Readers) 2005. (Illus.). 16.95 *(978-0-689-86745-3(X),* Atheneum/Richard Jackson Bks.) Simon & Schuster Children's Publishing.
James, Eric. Santa's Sleigh Is on Its Way to New Hampshire: A Christmas Adventure. Dunn, Robert, illus. 2016. (Santa's Sleigh Is on Its Way Ser.). (ENG.). 32p. (J). (gr. k-2). 12.99 *(978-1-4926-4342-5(4),* 9781492643425, Hometown World) Sourcebooks, Inc.
—The Spooky Express New Hampshire. Piwowarski, Marcin, illus. 2017. (Spooky Express Ser.). (ENG.). 32p. (J). (gr. k-6). 9.99 *(978-1-4926-5379-0(9),* Hometown World) Sourcebooks, Inc.
—Tiny the New Hampshire Easter Bunny. 2018. (Tiny the Easter Bunny Ser.). (ENG.). 40p. (J). (gr. k-3). 9.99 *(978-1-4926-5945-7(2),* Hometown World) Sourcebooks, Inc.
Janelle, Dick. Salmon Falls 1956. 2012. (ENG.). (YA). pap. 15.00 *(978-0-9856073-7-1(8))* RIVERRUN BOOKSTORE INC.
Jensen, Dorothea. A Buss from Lafayette. 2016. (ENG.). 266p. (YA). (gr. 7-12). pap. 16.95 *(978-1-939371-90-4(2))* Boutique of Quality Books Publishing Co., Inc.
Koncerak, Veronica. The Bubble That Never Popped. 2010. 24p. 11.49 *(978-1-4520-3935-0(6))* AuthorHouse.
Logue, C. Robert & Logue, Michael. From the Top of the Mountain. 2013. (ENG.). 50p. (J). pap. 12.99 *(978-1-936172-74-0(7))* Elfrig Publishing.
Monninger, Joseph. Game Change. 2019. (ENG.). 240p. (YA). (gr. 9). pap. 15.99 *(978-1-328-59586-7(2),* 1730760, Clarion Bks.) HarperCollins Pubs.

MNO

—Whippoorwill. 2016. (ENG.). 288p. (YA). (gr. 7). pap. 9.99 *(978-0-544-81356-4(1)*, 1641957, Clarion Bks.) HarperCollins Pubs.

Opel, Andrew. The Bobhouse: A Winnipesaukee Christmas. Hayes, Karel & Gorey, John, illus. 2017. (ENG.). 32p. (J). 19.95 *(978-1-937721-45-9(0)*, Jetty Hse.) Randall, Peter E. Pub.

Opel, Andy. The Witches: A Winnipesaukee Adventure. Hayes, Karel, illus. 2011. (ENG.). 32p. (J). 19.95 *(978-0-9828236-6-8(5)*, Jetty Hse.) Randall, Peter E. Pub.

Philbrick, Rodman. The Big Dark. 2019. (Penworthy Picks Middle School Ser.). (ENG.). 178p. (J). (gr. 4-5). 17.96 *(978-1-64310-933-6(2))* Penworthy Co., LLC, The.

—The Big Dark. 2017. (ENG.). 192p. (J). (gr. 3-7). pap. 6.99 *(978-0-545-78976-9(1)*, Blue Sky Pr., The) Scholastic, Inc.

Rand, Johnathan. American Chillers #24 Haunting in New Hampshire. 2008. 208p. (J). pap. 5.99 *(978-1-893699-96-0(X))* AudioCraft Publishing, Inc.

Rowland, Wickie. Good Morning, Strawbery Banke. 2010. (ENG.). 40p. (J). (gr. -1-5). pap. 12.95 *(978-1-935557-62-3(9))* PublishingWorks.

Schmidt, Gary D. First Boy. 2007. (ENG.). 224p. (YA). (gr. 5-9). pap. 14.99 *(978-0-312-37149-4(7)*, 900044687) Square Fish.

Schoen, Robin. Grandmother's Guest: The Blue Lady of Wilton. Hoar, Gail, illus. 2013. 32p. 16.95 *(978-0-615-89154-5(3))* Hobby Horse Publishing, LLC.

Tomaszewski, Suzanne Lyon. Samuel's Exeter Walkabout. Dionne, Nina, illus. 2003. 37p. (J). *(978-0-9744855-0-8(0))* Gold Charm Publishing, LLC.

Townley, Roderick. The Red Thread: A Novel in Three Incarnations. 2012. (ENG.). 304p. (YA). (gr. 7). pap. 14.99 *(978-1-4169-0895-1(1)*, Atheneum Bks. for Young Readers) Simon & Schuster Children's Publishing.

Tregay, Sarah. Love & Leftovers. (ENG.). (YA). (gr. 8). 2014. 464p. pap. 9.99 *(978-0-06-202360-5(8))* 2011. 448p. 17.99 *(978-0-06-202358-2(6))* HarperCollins Pubs. (Tegen, Katherine Bks).

Urban, Linda. The Center of Everything. 2015. (ENG.). 208p. (J). (gr. 5-7). pap. 7.99 *(978-0-544-34069-5(8)*, 1584793, Clarion Bks.) HarperCollins Pubs.

NEW HAMPSHIRE—HISTORY

Bowman, Chris. The Betty & Barney Hill Alien Abduction. 2019. (Paranormal Mysteries Ser.). (ENG., Illus.). 24p. (J). (gr. 3-8). pap. 8.99 *(978-1-61891-731-7(5)*, 12333, Black Sheep) Bellwether Media.

—The Betty & Barney Hill Alien Abduction. Brady, D., illus. 2019. (Paranormal Mysteries Ser.). (ENG.). 24p. (J). (gr. 3-8). lib. bdg. 29.95 *(978-1-64487-093-8(2)*, Black Sheep) Bellwether Media.

Cherry, Lynne. A River Ran Wild. 2005. 17.00 *(978-0-7569-5231-0(X))* Perfection Learning Corp.

Ciarleglio, Lauren. New Hampshire: Past & Present, 1 vol. 2010. (United States: Past & Present Ser.). (ENG.). 48p. (YA). (gr. 5-5). pap. 12.75 *(978-1-4358-9516-4(9)*, 08492468-7d45-4899-8470-7a935c5a1ee8); lib. bdg. 34.47 *(978-1-4358-9489-1(8)*, 95c5d87c-031c-4416-821c-e7398374f78b) Rosen Publishing Group, Inc., The. (Rosen Reference).

Craats, Rennay. New Hampshire. 2011. (Guide to American States Ser.). (Illus.). 48p. (YA). (gr. 3-6). 29.99 *(978-1-61690-801-0(7))* Weigl Pubs., Inc.

—New Hampshire: The Granite State. 2016. (J). *(978-1-4896-4902-7(6))* Weigl Pubs., Inc.

Cunningham, Kevin. The New Hampshire Colony. 2011. (True Bk Ser.). (ENG., Illus.). 48p. (J). pap. 6.95 *(978-0-531-26605-2(2))*; lib. bdg. 29.00 *(978-0-531-25392-2(9))* Scholastic Library Publishing. (Children's Pr.).

Gagnon, Lauren. An Exeter Alphabet: Learning about Exeter from A to Z. 2005. (Illus.). 44p. (J). (gr. 3-7). per. *(978-1-933002-05-7(0))* PublishingWorks.

Haulley, Fletcher. A Primary Source History of the Colony of New Hampshire. (Primary Sources of the Thirteen Colonies & the Lost Colony Ser.). 64p. 2009. (gr. 5-8). 58.50 *(978-1-60851-881-4(7))* 2005. (ENG., Illus.). (gr. 4-6). per. 12.95 *(978-1-4042-0676-2(0)*, fb84cc5b-c579-4c2d-a7ad-88501982f00b) 2005. (ENG., Illus.). (YA). (gr. 4-6). lib. bdg. 37.13 *(978-1-4042-0429-4(6)*, d57bbeab-7b55-4199-81a9-c31eeab771a9) Rosen Publishing Group, Inc., The.

Hicks, Terry Allan & McGeveran, William. New Hampshire, 1 vol. 2nd rev. ed. 2012. (It's My State! (Second Edition)(r) Ser.). (ENG.). 80p. (gr. 4-4). 34.07 *(978-1-60870-658-7(3)*, 02605eab-3bc1-466c-b822-135ac03b16f5) Cavendish Square Publishing LLC.

Hicks, Terry Allan, et al. New Hampshire, 1 vol. 3rd rev. ed. 2015. (It's My State! (Third Edition)(r) Ser.). (ENG., Illus.). 80p. (gr. 4-4). 35.93 *(978-1-62713-166-7(3)*, 5b135525-77e9-4e04-8c5c-cb4558d577fa) Cavendish Square Publishing LLC.

Kent, Deborah. America the Beautiful: New Hampshire (Revised Edition) 2014. (America the Beautiful, Third Ser. (Revised Edition) Ser.). (ENG., Illus.). 144p. (J). lib. bdg. 40.00 *(978-0-531-28284-7(8))* Scholastic Library Publishing.

Koontz, Robin Michal. New Hampshire: The Granite State, 1 vol. 2010. (Our Amazing States Ser.). (ENG., Illus.). 24p. (J). (gr. 3-3). pap. 9.25 *(978-1-4488-0728-4(X)*, b0720e7a-fbe9-41da-b792-2dff449edab8); lib. bdg. 26.27 *(978-1-4488-0648-5(8)*, 0cfe6d4b-05ab-4132-a220-1a8e59297257) Rosen Publishing Group, Inc., The. (PowerKids Pr.).

Kopp, Megan. New Hampshire: The Granite State. 2012. (J). *(978-1-61913-377-8(6))*; pap. *(978-1-61913-378-5(4))* Weigl Pubs., Inc.

Marsh, Carole. Exploring New Hampshire Through Project-Based Learning: Geography, History, Government, Economics & More. 2016. (New Hampshire Experience Ser.). (ENG.). (J). pap. 9.99 *(978-0-635-12353-4(3))* Gallopade International.

—I'm Reading about New Hampshire. 2014. (New Hampshire Experience Ser.). (ENG., Illus.). (J). pap., pap. 8.99 *(978-0-635-11304-7(X))* Gallopade International.

—New Hampshire History Projects: 30 Cool, Activities, Crafts, Experiments & More for Kids to Do to Learn about Your State! 2003. (New Hampshire Experience Ser.). 32p. (gr. k-5). pap. 5.95 *(978-0-635-01798-7(9)*, Marsh, Carole Bks.) Gallopade International.

Mis, Melody S. The Colony of New Hampshire: A Primary Source History. (Primary Source Library of the Thirteen Colonies & the Lost Colony Ser.). 24p. (gr. 3-4). 2009. 42.50 *(978-1-60854-143-0(6))* 2006. (ENG., Illus.). (J). lib. bdg. 26.27 *(978-1-4042-3435-2(7)*, d7e99ce5-3875-471a-aae5-0bea2cd4375d) Rosen Publishing Group, Inc., The. (PowerKids Pr.).

Moore, David. National Geographic Science 1-2 (Earth Science: Rocks & Soil): Explore on Your Own: the Old Man of the Mountain. 2009. (Illus.). 12p. (C). pap. 8.95 *(978-0-7362-5581-3(8))* National Geographic School Publishing, Inc.

Raum, Elizabeth. Exploring the New Hampshire Colony. 2016. (Exploring the 13 Colonies Ser.). (ENG., Illus.). 48p. (J). (gr. 3-6). lib. bdg. 34.65 *(978-1-5157-2236-6(8)*, 132760) Capstone.

Rissman, Rebecca. What's Great about New Hampshire? 2015. (Our Great States Ser.). (ENG., Illus.). 32p. (J). (gr. 2-5). lib. bdg. 26.65 *(978-1-4677-3853-3(1)*, 7ae5d58b-52b9-45d3-9f99-be7c4a8d2f2f, Lerner Pubns.) Lerner Publishing Group.

Rule, Rebecca. N Is for New Hampshire. Snyder, Scott, photos by. 2016. (ENG., Illus.). 32p. (J). 17.95 *(978-1-934031-68-1(2)*, ec28e695-5308-4df6-9abd-a9641174713f) Islandport Pr., Inc.

Shannon, Terry Miller. From Sea to Shining Sea: New Hampshire. 2009. (From Sea to Shining Sea, Second Ser.). (ENG.). 80p. (J). pap. 7.95 *(978-0-531-21138-0(X)*, Children's Pr.) Scholastic Library Publishing.

Wimmer, Teresa. New Hampshire. 2009. (This Land Called America Ser.). (Illus.). 32p. (YA). (gr. 3-6). 19.95 *(978-1-58341-782-9(6))* Creative Co., The.

Wyborny, Sheila. New Hampshire. 2003. (Seeds of a Nation Ser.). (Illus.). 48p. (J). (gr. 3-5). 23.70 *(978-0-7377-1448-7(4)*, Kidhaven) Cengage Gale.

Yomtov, Nel. New Hampshire (a True Book: My United States) (Library Edition) 2018. (True Book (Relaunch) Ser.). (ENG., Illus.). 48p. (J). (gr. 3-5). 31.00 *(978-0-531-23565-2(3)*, Children's Pr.) Scholastic Library Publishing.

Ziff, John. Northern New England: Maine, New Hampshire, Vermont, Vol. 19. 2015. (Let's Explore the States Ser.). (Illus.). 64p. (J). (gr. 5). 23.95 *(978-1-4222-3330-6(8))* Mason Crest.

NEW JERSEY

Brown, Vanessa. New Jersey. 2009. (Bilingual Library of the United States of America Ser.). (ENG & SPA.). 32p. (gr. 2-2). 47.90 *(978-1-60853-374-9(3)*, Editorial Buenas Letras) Rosen Publishing Group, Inc., The.

—New Jersey/Nueva Jersey, 1 vol. Brusca, Maria Cristina, tr. 2005. (Bilingual Library of the United States of America Ser.: Set 2). (ENG & SPA., Illus.). 32p. (J). (gr. 2-2). lib. bdg. 28.93 *(978-1-4042-3095-8(5)*, d190b957-c07f-4797-be16-5ab537843919) Rosen Publishing Group, Inc., The.

Cameron, Eileen. G Is for Garden State: A New Jersey Alphabet. Ettlinger, Doris, illus. 2004. (Discover America State by State Ser.). (ENG.). 40p. (J). (gr. 1-3). 17.95 *(978-1-58536-152-6(6)*, 202012) Sleeping Bear Pr.

Clark, Dennis. Good Night New Jersey. Veno, Joe, illus. 2008. (Good Night Our World Ser.). (ENG.). 20p. (J). (gr. k — 1). bds. 9.95 *(978-1-60219-025-2(9))* Good Night Bks.

Evento, Susan. Nueva Jersey. Hamilton, Harriet, tr. 2005. (Rookie Español Geografía Ser.). (SPA., Illus.). 32p. (J). (gr. k-2). lib. bdg. 19.50 *(978-0-516-25246-9(1)*, Children's Pr.) Scholastic Library Publishing.

Evento, Susan & Vargus, Nanci Reginelli. New Jersey. 2004. (Rookie Read-About Geography Ser.). (J). 20.50 *(978-0-516-22754-2(8)*, Children's Pr.) Scholastic Library Publishing.

Fredeen, Charles. New Jersey. (J). 2012. lib. bdg. 25.26 *(978-0-7613-4546-6(9)*, Lerner Pubns.) 2nd exp. rev. ed. 2003. (Illus.). 84p. (gr. 3-6). pap. 6.95 *(978-0-8225-4148-6(3))* Lerner Publishing Group.

Herman, Gail & Who HQ. Who Is Derek Jeter? Thomson, Andrew, illus. 2015. (Who Was? Ser.). 112p. (J). (gr. 3-7). 6.99 *(978-0-448-48697-0(0)*, Penguin Workshop) Penguin Young Readers Group.

Kent, Deborah. America the Beautiful, Third Series: New Jersey (Revised Edition) rev. ed. 2014. (America the Beautiful Ser.: 3). (ENG.). 144p. (J). lib. bdg. 40.00 *(978-0-531-24894-2(1))* Scholastic Library Publishing.

—New Jersey. 2011. (America the Beautiful, Third Ser.). 144p. (J). pap. 12.95 *(978-0-531-22921-7(1)*, Children's Pr.) Scholastic Library Publishing.

King, David C. New Jersey, 1 vol. Santoro, Christopher, illus. 2005. (It's My State! (First Edition)(r) Ser.). (ENG.). 80p. (gr. 4-4). lib. bdg. 34.07 *(978-0-7614-1529-9(7)*, 88182afb-f4f8-4f5a-82fe-ef351ba695ff) Cavendish Square Publishing LLC.

Lohnes, Marilyn. F Is for Fiddlehead: A New Brunswick Alphabet. Tooke, Susan, illus. rev. ed. 2007. (Discover Canada Province by Province Ser.). (ENG.). 40p. (J). (gr. 1-3). 17.95 *(978-1-58536-318-6(9)*, 202122) Sleeping Bear Pr.

Malaspina, Ann. New Jersey, 1 vol. 2005. (Portraits of the States Ser.). (ENG., Illus.). 32p. (gr. 3-5). pap. 11.50 *(978-0-8368-4648-5(6)*, f9cd3469-cded-4a6e-a079-3e2f25af49d0, Gareth Stevens Learning Library) Stevens, Gareth Publishing LLLP.

Marsh, Carole. My First Book about New Jersey. 2004. (New Jersey Experience! Ser.). (Illus.). 32p. (J). (gr. k-4). pap. 7.95 *(978-0-7933-9521-7(6))* Gallopade International.

—My First Pocket Guide New Jersey. 2004. (New Jersey Experience! Ser.). (Illus.). 96p. (J). (gr. 3-8). pap. 6.95 *(978-0-7933-9453-1(8))* Gallopade International.

—New Jersey Current Events Projects: 30 Cool, Activities, Crafts, Experiments & More for Kids to Do to Learn about Your State! 2003. (New Jersey Experience Ser.). 32p. (gr. k-8). pap. 5.95 *(978-0-635-02049-9(1)*, Marsh, Carole Bks.) Gallopade International.

—New Jersey Geography Projects: 30 Cool, Activities, Crafts, Experiments & More for Kids to Do to Learn about Your State! 2003. (New Jersey Experience Ser.). 32p. (gr. k-5). pap. 5.95 *(978-0-635-01849-6(7)*, Marsh, Carole Bks.) Gallopade International.

—New Jersey Government Projects: 30 Cool, Activities, Crafts, Experiments & More for Kids to Do to Learn about Your State! 2003. (New Jersey Experience Ser.). 32p. (gr. k-5). pap. 5.95 *(978-0-635-01949-3(3)*, Marsh, Carole Bks.) Gallopade International.

—New Jersey Jeopardy! Answers & Questions about Our State! 2004. (New Jersey Experience! Ser.). (Illus.). 32p. (J). (gr. 3-8). pap. 7.95 *(978-0-7933-9522-4(4))* Gallopade International.

—New Jersey "Jography" A Fun Run Thru Our State! 2004. (New Jersey Experience! Ser.). (Illus.). 32p. (J). (gr. 3-8). pap. 7.95 *(978-0-7933-9523-1(2))* Gallopade International.

—New Jersey People Projects: 30 Cool, Activities, Crafts, Experiments & More for Kids to Do to Learn about Your State! 2003. (New Jersey Experience Ser.). 32p. (gr. k-5). pap. 5.95 *(978-0-635-01999-8(X)*, Marsh, Carole Bks.) Gallopade International.

—New Jersey Symbols & Facts Projects: 30 Cool, Activities, Crafts, Experiments & More for Kids to Do to Learn about Your State! 2003. (New Jersey Experience Ser.). 32p. (gr. k-5). pap. 5.95 *(978-0-635-01899-1(3)*, Marsh, Carole Bks.) Gallopade International.

—The Nifty New Jersey Coloring Book. 2004. (New Jersey Experience! Ser.). (Illus.). 32p. (J). (gr. k-2). pap. 3.95 *(978-0-7933-9473-9(2))* Gallopade International.

Mis, M. S. How to Draw New Jersey's Sights & Symbols. 2009. (Kid's Guide to Drawing America Ser.). 32p. (gr. k-k). 50.50 *(978-1-61511-079-7(8)*, PowerKids Pr.) Rosen Publishing Group, Inc., The.

Murray, Julie. New Jersey, 1 vol. 2006. (Buddy Book Ser.). (ENG., Illus.). 32p. (gr. 2-4). 27.07 *(978-1-59197-689-9(8)*, Buddy Bks.) ABDO Publishing Co.

Nagelhout, Ryan. The Hindenburg Disaster, 1 vol. 2015. (Doomed! Ser.). (ENG., Illus.). 32p. (J). (gr. 4-5). 28.27 *(978-1-4824-2938-1(1)*, b98d41c8-6424-4a95-b11e-a6c7c1205fd5) Stevens, Gareth Publishing LLLP.

New Jersey. 2003. (Switched on Schoolhouse Ser.). cd-rom 24.95 *(978-0-7403-0654-9(5))* Alpha Omega Pubns., Inc.

Otfinoski, Steven. The Hindenburg Explosion: Core Events of a Disaster in the Air, 1 vol. 2014. (What Went Wrong? Ser.). (ENG., Illus.). 32p. (J). (gr. 3-6). lib. bdg. 27.99 *(978-1-4765-4184-6(1)*, 124289) Capstone.

Scholl, Elizabeth J. From Sea to Shining Sea: New Jersey. 2008. (From Sea to Shining Sea, Second Ser.). (ENG., Illus.). 80p. (J). (gr. 3-5). pap. 7.95 *(978-0-531-18806-4(X)*, Children's Pr.) Scholastic Library Publishing.

Siegfried Holtz, Eric. Nueva Jersey (New Jersey), 1 vol. 2003. (World Almanac(r) Biblioteca de Los Estados (World Almanac(r) Library of the States) Ser.). (SPA., Illus.). 48p. (gr. 4-6). lib. bdg. 33.67 *(978-0-8368-5545-6(0)*, 8c071da2-729d-42cd-a71d-b6d374be725b, Gareth Stevens Learning Library) Stevens, Gareth Publishing LLLP.

Webber, Diane. Celebrity's Son Snatched: Can Handwriting Help Nab the Perp? 2011. (J). pap. *(978-0-545-32810-4(1))* Scholastic, Inc.

You, New jersey & the World. 2004. lib. bdg. *(978-0-89359-121-2(1))* Afton Publishing.

NEW JERSEY—FICTION

Amato, Anne McCoy. Moving Shelly: A Novel. 2010. 148p. (gr. 4-6). pap. 12.95 *(978-1-4502-2584-7(5))* iUniverse, Inc.

Arnold, David. Kids of Appetite. 2017. (ENG.). 368p. (YA). (gr. 9). pap. 10.99 *(978-0-14-751366-3(9)*, Speak) Penguin Young Readers Group.

—Kids of Appetite. 2017. lib. bdg. 22.10 *(978-0-606-40491-4(0))* Turtleback.

Ashford, Rachel. My First Santa's Coming to New Jersey. Dunn, Robert, illus. 2015. (Santa Claus Is on His Way Ser.). (ENG.). 18p. (J). (gr. -1-k). bds. 9.99 *(978-1-4926-2882-8(4)*, Hometown World) Sourcebooks, Inc.

Bauman, Beth Ann. Rosie & Skate. 2011. (ENG.). 224p. (YA). (gr. 9). pap. 8.99 *(978-0-385-73736-4(X)*, Ember) Random Hse. Children's Bks.

Blake-Garrett, Andrea. Las Aventuras de Izzy y Juju: Gemelos Detectives Investigadores (G. D. I.) 2012. 28p. pap. 19.99 *(978-1-4772-2523-3(4))* AuthorHouse.

Blume, Judy. Superfudge. 2007. (Fudge Bks.: 3).Tr. of Superfudge. lib. bdg. 18.40 *(978-1-4177-8843-9(7))* Turtleback.

—Then Again, Maybe I Won't. (J). 125p. pap. 3.99 *(978-0-8072-1445-9(0))*; 2004. 164p. (gr. 5-9). pap. 29.00 incl. audio *(978-0-8072-0796-3(9)*, LYA 354 SP) Random Hse. Audio Publishing Group. (Listening Library).

Bryant, Jen. Kaleidoscope Eyes. 2010. 272p. (J). (gr. 3-7). 7.99 *(978-0-440-42190-0(X)*, Yearling) Random Hse. Children's Bks.

—The Trial. 2005. (Illus.). 176p. (J). (gr. 3-7). 7.99 *(978-0-440-41986-0(7)*, Yearling) Random Hse. Children's Bks.

Budhos, Marina. Tell Us We're Home. 2011. (ENG.). 320p. (YA). (gr. 7). pap. 12.99 *(978-1-4424-2128-8(2)*, Atheneum Bks. for Young Readers) Simon & Schuster Children's Publishing.

Campbell, Angella. Angel & Turkish. 2011. 32p. pap. 14.99 *(978-1-4634-0372-0(0))* AuthorHouse.

Carestio, Michael A. Black Jack Jetty: A Boy's Journey Through Grief. 2010. (Illus.). 64p. (J). (gr. 3-8). (ENG.). 14.95 *(978-1-4338-0784-8(X))*; pap. 9.95 *(978-1-4338-0786-2(6))* American Psychological Assn. (Magination Pr.).

Charles, Tami. Becoming Beatriz. 2019. 272p. (YA). (gr. 7). 17.99 *(978-1-58089-778-5(9)*, Charlesbridge Teen) Charlesbridge Publishing, Inc.

—Daphne Definitely Doesn't Do Dances. Calo, Marcos, illus. 2018. (Daphne, Secret Vlogger Ser.). (ENG.). 96p. (J). (gr. 4-7). pap. 4.95 *(978-1-4965-6301-9(8)*, 138030); lib. bdg. 24.65 *(978-1-4965-6297-5(6)*, 138024) Capstone. (Stone Arch Bks.).

—Daphne Definitely Doesn't Do Drama. Calo, Marcos, illus. 2018. (Daphne, Secret Vlogger Ser.). (ENG.). 96p. (J). (gr. 4-7). pap. 4.95 *(978-1-4965-6299-9(2)*, 138029); lib. bdg. 24.65 *(978-1-4965-6295-1(X)*, 138021) Capstone. (Stone Arch Bks.).

—Daphne Definitely Doesn't Do Fashion. Calo, Marcos, illus. 2018. (Daphne, Secret Vlogger Ser.). (ENG.). 96p. (J). (gr. 4-7). pap. 4.95 *(978-1-4965-6300-2(X)*, 138031, Stone Arch Bks.) Capstone.

—Daphne Definitely Doesn't Do Sports. Calo, Marcos, illus. 2018. (Daphne, Secret Vlogger Ser.). (ENG.). 96p. (J). (gr. 4-7). lib. bdg. 24.65 *(978-1-4965-6294-4(1)*, 138020, Stone Arch Bks.) Capstone.

—Like Vanessa. Brantley-Newton, Vanessa, illus. (J). (gr. 5). 2019. 304p. pap. 8.99 *(978-1-58089-899-7(8))* 2018. 288p. 16.99 *(978-1-58089-777-8(0))* Charlesbridge Publishing, Inc.

Cofer, Judith Ortiz. An Island Like You: Stories of the Barrio. 2009. 243p. 17.00 *(978-1-60686-446-3(7))* Perfection Learning Corp.

Constantine, Robin. The Promise of Amazing. 2015. (ENG.). 400p. (YA). (gr. 9). pap. 9.99 *(978-0-06-227949-1(1)*, Balzer & Bray) HarperCollins Pubs.

Danziger, Paula. Amber Brown Is Green with Envy. 2014. (Amber Brown Ser.: 9). (ENG., Illus.). 176p. (J). (gr. 2-5). pap. 7.99 *(978-0-14-242699-9(7)*, Puffin Books) Penguin Young Readers Group.

Díaz, Junot. Drown. 2014. (ENG.). 1p. (gr. 1-4). 20.25 *(978-1-63245-053-1(4))* Lectorum Pubns., Inc.

—Drown. 2011. 14.45 *(978-0-7848-3380-3(X))*; 14.45 *(978-0-7848-3428-2(8))* Marco Bk. Co. (Everbind).

Doktorski, Jennifer. August & Everything After. 2018. 320p. (YA). (gr. 8-12). pap. 10.99 *(978-1-4926-5715-6(8))* Sourcebooks, Inc.

—The Summer after You & Me. 2015. 304p. (YA). (gr. 8-12). pap. 12.99 *(978-1-4926-1903-1(5))* Sourcebooks, Inc.

Dorisann. Blasting Ogres. 2012. 108p. (gr. 4-6). 20.95 *(978-1-4759-2900-3(5))*; pap. 10.95 *(978-1-4759-2899-0(8))* iUniverse, Inc.

Durst, Sarah Beth. Enchanted Ivy. (ENG.). (YA). (gr. 7). 2011. 336p. pap. 9.99 *(978-1-4169-8646-1(4))* 2010. 320p. 16.99 *(978-1-4169-8645-4(6))* McElderry, Margaret K. Bks. (McElderry, Margaret K. Bks.).

Freeman, Martha. Zap! 2018. (ENG., Illus.). 304p. (J). (gr. 3-7). 18.99 *(978-1-5344-0557-8(7)*, Simon & Schuster/Paula Wiseman Bks.) Simon & Schuster/Paula Wiseman Bks.

Funari Willever, Lisa. Nicky Fifth on 32 Dandelion Court. 2003. 160p. pap. 5.95 *(978-0-9679227-7-5(1)*, 329-008) Franklin Mason Pr.

Grandpa Dennis, as told by. George Washington's Smallest Army: The Miracle Before Trenton. 2009. 216p. (J). pap. 17.49 *(978-1-4389-3147-0(6))* AuthorHouse.

Green, Tim. Football Hero. (Football Genius Ser.: 2). (ENG.). (J). (gr. 3-7). 2009. 320p. pap. 9.99 *(978-0-06-112276-7(9))* 2008. (Illus.). 304p. 16.99 *(978-0-06-112274-3(2))* HarperCollins Pubs. (HarperCollins).

—Football Hero. l.t. ed. 2008. (YA). 23.95 *(978-1-4104-1116-7(8))* Thorndike Pr.

Gutman, Dan. Flashback Four #4: the Hamilton-Burr Duel. 2019. (Flashback Four Ser.: 4). (ENG., Illus.). 240p. (J). (gr. 3-7). 16.99 *(978-0-06-237447-9(8)*, HarperCollins) HarperCollins Pubs.

Holm, Jennifer L. Penny from Heaven. 2007. 265p. (gr. 3-7). 17.00 *(978-0-7569-8206-5(5))* Perfection Learning Corp.

—Penny from Heaven. 2007. (ENG., Illus.). 304p. (J). (gr. 3-7). 7.99 *(978-0-375-83689-3(6)*, Yearling) Random Hse. Children's Bks.

—Penny from Heaven. l.t. ed. 2007. (Literacy Bridge Middle Reader Ser.). (Illus.). 285p. (J). (gr. 5-7). 23.95 *(978-0-7862-9698-9(4))* Thorndike Pr.

Hull, Norman. Robin's Big Brother. 2011. 56p. (gr. 4-6). pap. 9.99 *(978-1-4634-3691-9(2))* AuthorHouse.

Jacobs, Lily. The Littlest Bunny in New Jersey: An Easter Adventure. Dunn, Robert, illus. 2015. (Littlest Bunny Ser.). (ENG.). 32p. (J). (gr. -1-3). 9.99 *(978-1-4926-1144-8(1)*, Hometown World) Sourcebooks, Inc.

James, Eric. Santa's Sleigh Is on Its Way to New Jersey: A Christmas Adventure. Dunn, Robert, illus. 2015. (Santa's Sleigh Is on Its Way Ser.). (ENG.). 32p. (J). (gr. k-2). 12.99 *(978-1-4926-2758-6(5)*, Hometown World) Sourcebooks, Inc.

—The Spooky Express New Jersey. Piwowarski, Marcin, illus. 2017. (Spooky Express Ser.). (ENG.). 32p. (J). (gr. k-6). 9.99 *(978-1-4926-5380-6(2)*, Hometown World) Sourcebooks, Inc.

—Tiny the New Jersey Easter Bunny. 2018. (Tiny the Easter Bunny Ser.). (ENG.). 40p. (J). (gr. k-3). 9.99 *(978-1-4926-5946-4(0)*, Hometown World) Sourcebooks, Inc.

Jessell, Tim, illus. The Boardwalk Mystery. 2013. (Boxcar Children Mysteries Ser.: 131). (ENG.). 144p. (J). (gr. 2-5). pap. 6.99 *(978-0-8075-0803-9(9)*, 807508039);131. 15.99 *(978-0-8075-0802-2(0)*, 807508020) Random Hse. Children's Bks. (Random Hse. Bks. for Young Readers).

Jeter, Derek. Curveball. (Jeter Publishing Ser.). (ENG.). (J). (gr. 3-7). 2019. 192p. pap. 7.99 *(978-1-5344-0990-3(4))* 2018. (Illus.). 176p. 16.99 *(978-1-5344-0989-7(0))* Simon & Schuster/Paula Wiseman Bks. (Simon & Schuster/Paula Wiseman Bks.).

Jonas. Three's a Crowd. 6th ed. 2010. 128p. pap. 4.99 *(978-1-4231-2282-1(8))* Disney Pr.

Kephart, Beth. This Is the Story of You. 2016. (ENG., Illus.). 264p. (YA). (gr. 7-12). 17.99 *(978-1-4521-4284-5(X))* Chronicle Bks. LLC.

Kingsley Troupe, Thomas. Phantom of the Tracks. Ivy, Maggie, illus. 2019. (Haunted States of America Set 2 Ser.). (ENG.). 136p. (J). (gr. 3-4). pap. 7.99 *(978-1-63163-352-2(X)*, 163163352X); lib. bdg. 27.13 *(978-1-63163-351-5(1)*, 1631633511) North Star Editions. (Jolly Fish Pr.).

Knights, David. Stumpy the Tree. 2013. 28p. pap. 24.95 *(978-1-62709-375-0(3))* America Star Bks.

Kramer, Stacy & Thomas, Valerie. Karma Bites. 2010. (ENG.). 348p. (J). (gr. 5-7). pap. 18.99 *(978-0-547-36301-1(X)*, 1422027, Clarion Bks.) HarperCollins Pubs.

Larsen, Elizabeth. Buster Hardings: Buster Makes New Friends. 2008. 104p. pap. 19.95 *(978-1-60563-951-2(6))* America Star Bks.

Lascurain, Anna. Apollo in the Moon House. 2006. Orig. Title: The Moonboy. (J). per. 7.99 *(978-0-9769612-3-9(7))* Darker Intentions Pr.

Lewis, Anne Margaret. What Am I? New Jersey. DeWildt, Jim, illus. 2007. 32p. (J). 9.95 *(978-1-934133-19-4(1)*, Mackinac Island Press, Inc.) Charlesbridge Publishing, Inc.

Lipsyte, Robert. Center Field. 2010. (ENG.). 288p. (YA). (gr. 8-18). 17.99 *(978-0-06-055704-1(4)*, HarperTeen) HarperCollins Pubs.

Litzenberg, Corinne M. The Sand Lady: A Cape May Tale, 1 vol. 2006. (ENG., Illus.). 32p. (gr. 3-6). 14.95 *(978-0-7643-2479-6(9)*, 2676) Schiffer Publishing, Ltd.

Lowthert, Carrie. Minkie & Emily. 2007. 66p. pap. 11.95 *(978-1-4303-2576-5(3))* Lulu Pr., Inc.

Lubar, David. Dunk. 2004. (ENG.). 272p. (YA). (gr. 7-18). reprint ed. pap. 9.99 *(978-0-618-43909-6(9)*, 490005, Clarion Bks.) HarperCollins Pubs.

Many Ways to Be a Soldier. 2009. (On My Own History Ser.). (gr. 2-4). pap. 6.95 *(978-0-8225-9021-7(2)*, First Avenue Editions) Lerner Publishing Group.

Martin, Ann M. Sea City, Here We Come! (the Baby-Sitters Club: Super Special #10) 2014. (Fly Guy Ser.: 10). (ENG.). 240p. (J). (gr. -1-3). E-Book 16.99 *(978-0-545-63322-2(2))* Scholastic, Inc.

Martino, Alfred C. Pinned. 2006. (ENG., Illus.). 320p. (YA). (gr. 7-12). reprint ed. pap. 8.99 *(978-0-15-205631-5(9)*, 1196935, Clarion Bks.) HarperCollins Pubs.

Maxwell, Ruth H. Eighteen Roses Red: A Young Girl's Heroic Mission in the Revolutionary War. 2006. (American Revolution Adventures Ser.). 126p. (J). (gr. 3-7). per. 8.95 *(978-1-57249-380-3(1)*, White Mane Kids) White Mane Publishing Co., Inc.

McDonald, Joyce. Shades of Simon Gray. 2003. (Readers Circle Ser.). 245p. (YA). 14.15 *(978-0-7569-1880-4(4))* Perfection Learning Corp.

Messner, Kate. Night of Soldiers & Spies (Ranger in Time #10) (Library Edition) McMorris, Kelley, illus. 2019. (Ranger in Time Ser.: 10). (ENG.). 160p. (J). (gr. 2-5). lib. bdg. 17.99 *(978-1-338-13402-5(7)*, Scholastic Pr.) Scholastic, Inc.

Miller, Patricia Maida. Carlos the Sailor Visits Atlantic City. 2005. (Illus.). 16p. (J). pap. 12.95 *(978-0-9766889-0-7(5))* ComteQ Publishing.

Moldover, Joseph. Every Moment After. 2019. (ENG.). 368p. (YA). (gr. 9). 17.99 *(978-1-328-54727-9(2)*, 1724070, Clarion Bks.) HarperCollins Pubs.

Moses, Jennifer Anne. Tales from My Closet. 2014. 298p. (J). pap. *(978-0-545-66811-8(5)*, Scholastic Pr.) Scholastic, Inc.

Myers, Walter Dean & Workman, Ross. Kick. 2012. (ENG.). 224p. (YA). (gr. 9). pap. 10.99 *(978-0-06-200491-8(3)*, HarperTeen) HarperCollins Pubs.

Noble, Trinka Hakes. The Legend of the Jersey Devil. Kelley, Gerald, illus. 2013. (ENG.). 32p. (J). (gr. 2-5). 16.99 *(978-1-58536-837-2(7)*, 202886) Sleeping Bear Pr.

O'Neill, Elizabeth. Alfred Visits New Jersey. 2007. 24p. (J). pap. 12.00 *(978-0-9790240-7-8(2))* Funny Bone Bks.

Patterson, James & Grabenstein, Chris. Jacky Ha-Ha: My Life Is a Joke. Kerascoët, illus. 2017. (Jacky Ha-Ha Ser.: 2). (ENG.). 352p. (J). (gr. 3-7). 13.99 *(978-0-316-43376-1(4)*, Jimmy Patterson) Little Brown & Co.

—Jacky Ha-Ha: My Life Is a Joke. Kerascoët, illus. 2023. (Jacky Ha-Ha Ser.: 2). (ENG.). 368p. (J). (gr. 3-7). pap. 8.99 *(978-0-316-50837-7(3)*, Jimmy Patterson) Little Brown & Co.

Patterson, Nancy. May the Magnificent Lighthouse. Patterson, Nancy, illus. 2012. (Illus.). 24p. 18.95 *(978-0-615-61021-4(8))* Bayberry Cottage Gallery.

Pearce, Arline June. Sunrise the Barnegat Pony. Pearce, Arline June, illus. 2011. (ENG., Illus.). 26p. pap. 15.99 *(978-1-4628-8601-2(9))* Xlibris Corp.

Pinkwater, Daniel M. Four Hoboken Stories. 2017. (ENG.). 240p. pap. 16.95 *(978-0-486-81571-8(4)*, 815714) Dover Pubns., Inc.

Plum-Ucci, Carol. Fire Will Fall. 2011. (ENG.). 492p. (YA). (gr. 9). pap. 25.99 *(978-0-547-55007-7(3)*, 1450217, Clarion Bks.) HarperCollins Pubs.

—Fire Will Fall. 2011. (ENG.). 496p. (YA). (gr. 9-12). 24.94 *(978-0-15-216562-8(2))* Houghton Mifflin Harcourt Publishing Co.

Prose, Francine. Bullyville. 2007. 260p. (YA). (gr. 7-12). 16.99 *(978-0-06-057497-0(6))*; lib. bdg. 17.89 *(978-0-06-057498-7(4))* HarperCollins Pubs. (HarperTeen).

—Bullyville. 2011. 10.36 *(978-0-7848-3625-5(6)*, Everbind) Marco Bk. Co.

Rand, Johnathan. American Chillers #22 Nuclear Jelly Fish of New Jersey. 2007. 208p. (J). pap. 5.99 *(978-1-893699-93-9(5))* AudioCraft Publishing, Inc.

Raskin, Joyce. My Misadventures As a Teenage Rock Star. Chu, Carol, illus. 2011. (ENG.). 112p. (YA). (gr. 7-18). pap. 8.99 *(978-0-547-39311-7(3)*, 1426898, Clarion Bks.) HarperCollins Pubs.

Rigaud, Debbie. Truly Madly Royally. 2019. (ENG.). 304p. (YA). (gr. 7-7). pap. 9.99 *(978-1-338-33272-8(4))* Scholastic, Inc.

Rinaldi, Ann. Keep Smiling Through. 2005. (ENG.). 208p. (J). (gr. 3-7). pap. 13.95 *(978-0-15-205399-4(9)*, 1196254, Clarion Bks.) HarperCollins Pubs.

—A Ride into Morning: The Story of Tempe Wick. 2003. (Great Episodes Ser.). (ENG.). 368p. (YA). (gr. 5-7). pap. 21.95 *(978-0-15-204683-5(6)*, Clarion Bks.) HarperCollins Pubs.

Rivers, Phoebe. Ghost Town. 1. 2012. (Saranormal Ser.: 1). (ENG.). 160p. (J). (gr. 4-6). 18.69 *(978-1-4424-5378-4(8)*, Simon Spotlight) Simon & Schuster Children's Publishing.

—Ghost Town. 2012. (Saranormal Ser.: 1). (ENG.). 160p. (J). (gr. 3-7). pap. 5.99 *(978-1-4424-4038-8(4)*, Simon Spotlight) Simon Spotlight.

—Haunted Memories. 2. 2012. (Saranormal Ser.: 2). (ENG.). 176p. (J). (gr. 3-7). 15.99 *(978-1-4424-5381-4(8)*, Simon Spotlight) Simon & Schuster Children's Publishing.

—Haunted Memories. 2012. (Saranormal Ser.: 2). (ENG.). 176p. (J). (gr. 3-7). pap. 6.99 *(978-1-4424-4040-1(6)*, Simon Spotlight) Simon Spotlight.

—A Perfect Storm. 2013. (Saranormal Ser.: 10). (ENG., Illus.). 160p. (J). (gr. 3-7). 15.99 *(978-1-4424-8959-2(6))*; pap. 5.99 *(978-1-4424-8958-5(8))* Simon Spotlight. (Simon Spotlight).

—The Secrets Within. 2013. (Saranormal Ser.: 7). (ENG.). 160p. (J). (gr. 3-7). pap. 5.99 *(978-1-4424-6849-8(1)*, Simon Spotlight) Simon Spotlight.

Robertson, Keith. Henry Reed, Inc. abr. ed. (J). (gr. 4-7). pap. 15.95 incl. audio *(978-0-670-36801-3(6))* Live Oak Media.

—Henry Reed, Inc., Set. McCloskey, Robert, illus. abr. ed. (J). (gr. 4-7). 24.95 incl. audio *(978-0-670-36800-6(8))* Live Oak Media.

Ruby, Laura. Lily's Ghosts. 2005. (Illus.). 258p. (J). (gr. 5-9). 13.65 *(978-0-7569-5115-3(1))* Perfection Learning Corp.

Schumacher, Julie. The Book of One Hundred Truths. 2008. (ENG.). 192p. (J). (gr. 3-7). 6.99 *(978-0-440-42085-9(7)*, Yearling) Random Hse. Children's Bks.

Scott, Kieran. He's So Not Worth It. (He's So/She's So Trilogy Ser.). (ENG.). (YA). (gr. 7). 2012. 384p. pap. 12.99 *(978-1-4169-9954-6(X))* 2011. 368p. 17.99 *(978-1-4169-9953-9(1))* Simon & Schuster Bks. For Young Readers. (Simon & Schuster Bks. For Young Readers).

—She's So Dead to Us. (He's So/She's So Trilogy Ser.). (ENG.). (YA). (gr. 7). 2011. 304p. pap. 11.99 *(978-1-4169-9952-2(3))* 2010. 288p. 16.99 *(978-1-4169-9951-5(5))* Simon & Schuster Bks. For Young Readers. (Simon & Schuster Bks. For Young Readers).

—This Is So Not Happening. (He's So/She's So Trilogy Ser.). (ENG.). 320p. (YA). (gr. 7). 2013. Illus.). pap. 9.99 *(978-1-4169-9956-0(6))* 2012. 16.99 *(978-1-4169-9955-3(8))* Simon & Schuster Bks. For Young Readers. (Simon & Schuster Bks. For Young Readers).

Seuling, Barbara. Robert Finds a Way. 2005. (Robert Bks.). (ENG., Illus.). 150p. (J). 15.95 *(978-0-8126-2734-3(2))* Cricket Bks.

Sharenow, Robert. The Girl in the Torch. 2015. (ENG.). 304p. (J). (gr. 3-7). 16.99 *(978-0-06-222795-9(5)*, Balzer & Bray) HarperCollins Pubs.

Skinner, Tina. The Story of Story Book Land, 1 vol. 2008. (ENG., Illus.). 96p. pap. 20.00 *(978-0-7643-2957-9(X)*, 7305) Schiffer Publishing, Ltd.

Smallman, Steve. Santa Is Coming to New Jersey. Dunn, Robert, illus. 2013. (ENG.). 32p. (J). (-3). 9.99 *(978-1-4022-8797-8(6)*, Sourcebooks Jabberwocky) Sourcebooks, Inc.

Sonnenblick, Jordan. After Ever After. 2014. (ENG.). 272p. (YA). (gr. 7-7). pap. 10.99 *(978-0-545-72287-2(X))* Scholastic, Inc.

Sparling, Eric. Tantramar. 2012. (ENG.). 144p. pap. *(978-1-55081-257-2(2))* Breakwater Bks., Ltd.

Strasser, Todd & Thacker, Nola. The Shore: Shirt & Shoes Not Required; LB (Laguna Beach) 2011. (ENG.). 480p. (YA). (gr. 9). pap. 9.99 *(978-1-4424-1970-4(9)*, Simon Pulse) Simon Pulse.

Sully, Katherine. Night-Night New Jersey. Poole, Helen, illus. 2016. (Night-Night Ser.). (ENG.). 20p. (J). (gr. -1-1). bds. 9.99 *(978-1-4926-3933-6(8)*, 9781492639336, Hometown World) Sourcebooks, Inc.

Suma, Nova Ren. Imaginary Girls. 2012. (ENG.). 352p. (YA). (gr. 9-18). pap. 8.99 *(978-0-14-242143-7(X)*, Speak) Penguin Young Readers Group.

Tarshis, Lauren. I Survived the Shark Attacks of 1916. 2010. (I Survived Ser.: No. 2). lib. bdg. 14.75 *(978-0-606-23742-0(9))* Turtleback.

—I Survived the Shark Attacks of 1916 (I Survived #2) Dawson, Scott, illus. 2010. (I Survived Ser.: 2). (ENG.). 112p. (J). (gr. 2-5). pap. 5.99 *(978-0-545-20695-2(2)*, Scholastic Paperbacks) Scholastic, Inc.

Telmosse, Gerard. The Curse of the Sourlands. 2008. 132p. pap. 14.51 *(978-1-4357-0169-4(0))* Lulu Pr., Inc.

Vernick, Audrey. After the Worst Thing Happens. 2020. 224p. (J). (gr. 4-7). 17.99 *(978-0-8234-4490-8(2)*, Margaret Ferguson Books) Holiday Hse., Inc.

Vivian, Siobhan. Same Difference. 2014. (ENG.). 304p. (YA). (gr. 7-7). pap. 10.99 *(978-0-545-75802-4(5))* Scholastic, Inc.

Voltaire, Aurelio. Call of the Jersey Devil. 2013. (ENG.). 331p. pap. 7.95 *(978-1-939392-00-8(4)*, Spence City) Spencer Hill Pr.

Wallace, Rich. Roar of the Crowd. 2004. 101p. (J). lib. bdg. 15.38 *(978-1-4242-2165-3(X))* Fitzgerald Bks.

Warstler, Mary Lu. Michael's Angel, 1 vol. 2009. 227p. pap. 24.95 *(978-1-61546-723-5(8))* PublishAmerica, Inc.

Wasserman, Sand. The Sun's Special Blessing: Happens Only Once in 28 Years - French Flap. Koffsky, Ann, illus. 2009. 36p. 12.95 *(978-1-934440-76-6(0)*, Pitspopany Pr.) Simcha Media Group.

—The Sun's Special Blessing: Happens Only Once in 28 Years - HC. Koffsky, Ann, illus. 2009. 36p. 17.95 *(978-1-934440-92-6(2)*, Pitspopany Pr.) Simcha Media Group.

NEW JERSEY—HISTORY

ABC Atlantic City: An Alphabet Book, Travel Guide & Souvenir for Kids! 2006. (J). 8.95 *(978-0-9760047-1-4(2))* Rosenberger, Matthew.

Barth, Linda J. Hidden New Jersey. Mitchell, Hazel, illus. 2012. 32p. (J). (gr. 1-4). 17.95 *(978-1-934133-23-1(X)*, Mackinac Island Press, Inc.) Charlesbridge Publishing, Inc.

Benoit, Peter. The Hindenburg Disaster. 2011. (Illus.). 48p. (J). pap. *(978-0-531-29025-5(5))* Children's Pr., Ltd.

—True Book: the Hindenburg Disaster. 2011. (True Book(tm), A — Disasters Ser.). (ENG.). 48p. (J). (gr. 3-5). lib. bdg. 31.00 *(978-0-531-20626-3(2)*, Children's Pr.) Scholastic Library Publishing.

Clinton, Greg, et al. New Jersey, 1 vol. 3rd rev. ed. 2014. (It's My State! (Third Edition)(r) Ser.). (ENG., Illus.). 80p. (gr. 4-4). 35.93 *(978-1-5026-0013-4(7)*, 5cf3e34d-8791-46e2-aaa1-1d9cf1dea377) Cavendish Square Publishing LLC.

The Colors of the Lighthouse: A Children's History of Absecon Lighthouse. 2006. (J). 8.95 *(978-0-9779988-0-7(0))* Absecon Lighthouse.

Cunningham, Kevin. The New Jersey Colony. 2011. (True Bk Ser.). (ENG., Illus.). 48p. (J). pap. 6.95 *(978-0-531-26606-9(0))*; lib. bdg. 29.00 *(978-0-531-25393-9(7))* Scholastic Library Publishing. (Children's Pr.).

Davis, Lynn. Thomas Edison, 1 vol. 2015. (Amazing Inventors & Innovators Ser.). (ENG., Illus.). 24p. (J). (gr. k-3). 32.79 *(978-1-62403-723-8(2)*, 17952, Super SandCastle) ABDO Publishing Co.

Downey, Tika. New Jersey: The Garden State, 1 vol. 2010. (Our Amazing States Ser.). (ENG., Illus.). 24p. (J). (gr. 3-3). pap. 9.25 *(978-1-4358-9806-6(0)*, 51d2ca48-08fe-4662-88f1-a16cab9ce806); lib. bdg. 26.27 *(978-1-4358-9355-9(7)*, 1815a012-9104-4289-87ea-8881f7107ea8) Rosen Publishing Group, Inc., The. (PowerKids Pr.).

Dzidrums, Christine. Mike Trout: Baseball Sensation. Dzidrums, Joseph, photos by. 2013. (Illus.). 64p. pap. 9.99 *(978-1-938438-28-8(0))* Creative Media Publishing.

Hamilton, John. New Jersey, 1 vol. 2016. (United States of America Ser.). (ENG., Illus.). 48p. (J). (gr. 5-9). 34.21 *(978-1-68078-332-2(7)*, 21649, Abdo & Daughters) ABDO Publishing Co.

Heinrichs, Ann. New Jersey. Kania, Matt, illus. 2017. (U. S. A. Travel Guides). (ENG.). 40p. (J). (gr. 2-5). lib. bdg. 38.50 *(978-1-5038-1970-2(1)*, 211607) Child's World, Inc, The.

Jerome, Kate B. Lucky to Live in New Jersey. 2017. (Arcadia Kids Ser.). (ENG., Illus.). 32p. (J). 16.99 *(978-0-7385-2782-6(3))* Arcadia Publishing.

—The Wise Animal Handbook New Jersey. 2017. (Arcadia Kids Ser.). (ENG., Illus.). 32p. (J). 16.99 *(978-0-7385-2832-8(3))* Arcadia Publishing.

Jordan, Joe. Cape May Point: The Illustrated History from 1875 to the Present, 1 vol. 2003. (ENG., Illus.). 144p. (gr. 10-13). 24.95 *(978-0-7643-1830-6(6)*, 2206) Schiffer Publishing, Ltd.

King, David C. & McGeveran, William. New Jersey, 1 vol. 2nd rev. ed. 2011. (It's My State! (Second Edition)(r) Ser.). (ENG.). 80p. (gr. 4-4). lib. bdg. 34.07 *(978-1-60870-055-4(0)*, 7ed34966-1ff2-4a8a-9359-a61ffd712fa1) Cavendish Square Publishing LLC.

King, David C., et al. New Jersey. 2015. (J). lib. bdg. *(978-1-62712-505-5(1))* Cavendish Square Publishing LLC.

Kopp, Megan. New Jersey: The Garden State. 2012. (J). *(978-1-61913-379-2(2))*; pap. *(978-1-61913-380-8(6))* Weigl Pubs., Inc.

Kopp, Megan & Nault, Jennifer. New Jersey. 2018. (Illus.). 24p. (J). *(978-1-4896-7461-6(6)*, AV2 by Weigl) Weigl Pubs., Inc.

Landau, Elaine. General Washington Crosses the Delaware: Would You Join the American Revolution?, 1 vol. 2014. (What Would You Do? Ser.). (ENG.). 48p. (gr. 3-4). 27.93 *(978-0-7660-6315-0(1)*, c1b912c5-4351-47ec-a62e-2ca9aed546a5) Enslow Publishing, LLC.

—George Washington Crosses the Delaware: Would You Risk the Revolution?, 1 vol. 2009. (What Would You Do? Ser.). (ENG., Illus.). 48p. (gr. 3-3). lib. bdg. 27.93 *(978-0-7660-2904-0(2)*, 842b7348-ded7-40fe-9d38-b4aee15fa2cd, Enslow Elementary) Enslow Publishing, LLC.

Marsh, Carole. Exploring New Jersey Through Project-Based Learning: Geography, History, Government, Economics & More. 2016. (New Jersey Experience Ser.). (ENG.). (J). pap. 9.99 *(978-0-635-12354-1(1))* Gallopade International.

—I'm Reading about New Jersey. 2014. (New Jersey Experience Ser.). (ENG., Illus.). (J). pap., pap. 8.99 *(978-0-635-11305-4(8))* Gallopade International.

—New Jersey History Projects: 30 Cool, Activities, Crafts, Experiments & More for Kids to Do to Learn about Your State! 2003. (New Jersey Experience Ser.). 32p. (gr. k-5). pap. 5.95 *(978-0-635-01799-4(7)*, Marsh, Carole Bks.) Gallopade International.

McCloy, James F., et al. The Jersey Devil. 2005. (Illus.). 121p. (J). (gr. 5). per. *(978-0-912608-11-2(0))* Middle Atlantic Pr.

McGrath, Brian. Aaron Burr: More Than a Villain (Alexander Hamilton) rev. ed. 2017. (Social Studies: Informational Text Ser.). (ENG., Illus.). 32p. (gr. 4-8). pap. 11.99 *(978-1-4258-6355-5(8))* Teacher Created Materials, Inc.

McMahon, William. Pine Barrens Legends & Lore. 2005. (Illus.). 149p. (J). (gr. 6). per. *(978-0-912608-19-8(6))* Middle Atlantic Pr.

Meinking, Mary. What's Great about New Jersey? 2015. (Our Great States Ser.). (ENG., Illus.). 32p. (J). (gr. 2-5). 26.65 *(978-1-4677-3873-6(5)*, edaf1ff0-61ac-4f8e-890e-6d92dd9ba6be, Lerner Pubns.) Lerner Publishing Group.

Micklos, John & Micklos, John, Jr. Washington's Crossing the Delaware & the Winter at Valley Forge: Through Primary Sources, 1 vol. 2013. (American Revolution Through Primary Sources Ser.). (ENG., Illus.). 48p. (J). (gr. 4-6). pap. 11.53 *(978-1-4644-0190-9(X)*, c759c386-064d-4048-9796-e54bc92199cf) Enslow Publishing, LLC.

Miller, Derek, et al. New Jersey: The Garden State, 1 vol. 2019. (It's My State! (Fourth Edition)(r) Ser.). (ENG.). 80p. (gr. 4-4). 35.93 *(978-1-5026-4236-3(0)*, c5799676-4b95-49de-b1e0-6fb398222770) Cavendish Square Publishing LLC.

Miller, Jake. The Colony of New Jersey: A Primary Source History. (Primary Source Library of the Thirteen Colonies & the Lost Colony Ser.). 24p. (gr. 3-4). 2009. 42.50 *(978-1-60854-146-1(0))* 2005. (ENG., Illus.). (J). lib. bdg. 26.27 *(978-1-4042-3031-6(9)*, e34434a2-7c63-4d96-b3ea-ad406b7c6693) Rosen Publishing Group, Inc., The. (PowerKids Pr.).

Moragne, Wendy, et al. New Jersey, 1 vol. 2nd rev. ed. 2009. (Celebrate the States (Second Edition) Ser.). (ENG.). 144p. (gr. 6-6). lib. bdg. 39.79 *(978-0-7614-3006-3(7)*, 9e599e6f-f25f-48d3-965e-92c07a7f7d35) Cavendish Square Publishing LLC.

Nault, Jennifer. New Jersey. 2011. (Guide to American States Ser.). (Illus.). 48p. (YA). (gr. 3-6). 29.99 *(978-1-61690-802-7(5))* Weigl Pubs., Inc.

—New Jersey: The Garden State. 2016. (J). *(978-1-4896-4905-8(0))* Weigl Pubs., Inc.

The New Jersey Adventure Program Kit: All program components for the New Jersey Adventure, 1 vol. 2009. 99.95 *(978-1-4236-0725-0(2))* Gibbs Smith, Publisher.

Noble, Trinka Hakes. Little New Jersey. Brett, Jeannie, illus. 2012. (Little State Ser.). (ENG.). 20p. (J). (gr. -1-1). bds. 9.95 *(978-1-58536-786-3(9)*, 202349) Sleeping Bear Pr.

Orr, Tamra. A Primary Source History of the Colony of New Jersey. 2009. (Primary Sources of the Thirteen Colonies & the Lost Colony Ser.). 64p. (gr. 5-8). 58.50 *(978-1-60851-882-1(5))* Rosen Publishing Group, Inc., The.

Orr, Tamra B. A Primary Source History of the Colony of New Jersey, 1 vol. 2005. (Primary Sources of the Thirteen Colonies & the Lost Colony Ser.). (ENG., Illus.). 64p. (gr. 4-6). per. 12.95 *(978-1-4042-0668-7(X)*, 26c1c4a4-330a-4bc8-abb4-b2b412bf180a); (YA). lib. bdg. 37.13 *(978-1-4042-0430-0(X)*, 45432235-f3eb-4d11-b637-b97034182289) Rosen Publishing Group, Inc., The.

Otfinoski, Steven. The Hindenburg Explosion: Core Events of a Disaster in the Air, 1 vol. 2014. (What Went Wrong? Ser.). (ENG., Illus.). 32p. (J). (gr. 3-6). pap. 7.95 *(978-1-4765-5133-3(2)*, 124452) Capstone.

Pfeffer, Wendy. Many Ways to Be a Soldier. Verstraete, Elaine, illus. 2008. (On My Own History Ser.). (ENG.). 48p. (gr. 2-4). lib. bdg. 25.26 *(978-0-8225-7279-4(6)*, Millbrook Pr.) Lerner Publishing Group.

—Many Ways to Be A Soldier. 2009. pap. 40.95 *(978-0-7613-4795-8(X))* Lerner Publishing Group.

Rameck, Hunt, et al. We Beat the Street: How a Friendship Pact Led to Success. 2014. (ENG.). 208p. (J). 12.24 *(978-1-63245-093-7(3))* Lectorum Pubns., Inc.

Wimmer, Teresa. New Jersey. 2009. (This Land Called America Ser.). (Illus.). 32p. (YA). (gr. 3-6). 19.95 *(978-1-58341-783-6(4))* Creative Co., The.

Words for All Time: Students Letters to Holocaust Survivors. 2008. (YA). mass mkt. 19.95 *(978-0-9793771-6-7(1))* ComteQ Publishing.

Ziff, John. Northeast: New Jersey, New York, Pennsylvania, Vol. 19. 2015. (Let's Explore the States Ser.). (Illus.). 64p. (J). (gr. 5). 23.95 *(978-1-4222-3329-0(4))* Mason Crest.

NEW MEXICO

Barco, Kathy. READiscover New Mexico: A Tri-Lingual Adventure in Literacy. 2007. (ENG, SPA & NAV.). 192p. (J). per. 24.95 *(978-0-86534-544-7(9))* Sunstone Pr.

Baxter, Roberta. Battles for Gold & Glory: Civil War Skirmishes in New Mexico Territory. 2012. (ENG.). 81p. pap. 11.95 *(978-1-4327-8643-4(1))* Outskirts Pr., Inc.

Bjorklund, Ruth. New Mexico, 1 vol. Santoro, Christopher, illus. 2003. (It's My State! (First Edition)(r) Ser.). (ENG.). 80p. (gr. 4-4). 34.07 *(978-0-7614-1526-8(2)*, e81d63c8-b61d-4c4b-bc1b-58ec039e5733) Cavendish Square Publishing LLC.

—New Mexico, 1 vol. 2nd rev. ed. 2013. (It's My State! (Second Edition)(r) Ser.). (ENG.). 80p. (gr. 4-4). pap. 18.64 *(978-1-62712-095-1(5)*, 8813e503-3a1c-4d90-bb2e-30debc507370) Cavendish Square Publishing LLC.

Burgan, Michael. New Mexico, 1 vol. 2003. (World Almanac(r) Library of the States Ser.). (ENG., Illus.). 48p. (gr. 4-6). pap. 15.05 *(978-0-8368-5327-8(X)*, cc16d741-3033-4620-b802-b76770051493); lib. bdg. 33.67 *(978-0-8368-5156-4(0)*, 7a2e5d7c-c10b-4bac-9cbf-ae91758c5e63) Stevens, Gareth Publishing LLLP. (Gareth Stevens Learning Library).

—Nuevo México (New Mexico), 1 vol. 2003. (World Almanac(r) Biblioteca de Los Estados (World Almanac(r) Library of the States) Ser.). (SPA.). 48p. (gr. 4-6). lib. bdg. 33.67 *(978-0-8368-5725-2(9)*, cc339016-7362-40d8-8489-e33d67d7d613, Gareth Stevens Learning Library) Stevens, Gareth Publishing LLLP.

Cash, Marie Romero. Santos: A Coloring Book of New Mexican Saints. 2008. 80p. (J). pap. 10.95 *(978-0-86534-701-4(8))* Sunstone Pr.

Early, Theresa S. New Mexico. 2012. (J). lib. bdg. 25.26 *(978-0-7613-4547-3(7)*, Lerner Pubns.) Lerner Publishing Group.

Finley, Toiya Kristen. Russell Simmons. 2007. (Sharing the American Dream Ser.). 64p. (YA). (gr. 7-18). pap. 9.95 *(978-1-4222-0762-8(5))* Mason Crest.

Grace, N. B. UFO Lands in USA! Was a Spacecraft Crash Covered Up? 2011. (J). pap. *(978-0-545-32947-7(7))* Scholastic, Inc.

Hernández, Roger E. & Hernández, Roger E. 1898 to World War II, 1 vol. 2010. (Hispanic America Ser.). (ENG.). 80p. (gr. 5-5). 36.93 *(978-0-7614-4176-2(X)*, cd22c781-913c-43d9-a0ab-9cc0282583ea) Cavendish Square Publishing LLC.

James, Helen Foster. E Is for Enchantment: A New Mexico Alphabet. Twinem, Neecy, illus. 2004. (Discover America State by State Ser.). (ENG.). 40p. (J). (gr. 1-3). 18.99 *(978-1-58536-153-3(4)*, 202013) Sleeping Bear Pr.

Lavash, Donald R. A Journey Through New Mexico History: The Land of Enchantment. 3rd rev. ed. 2006. (Illus.). 208p. (YA). (gr. 8-12). pap. 26.95 *(978-0-86534-194-4(X))* Sunstone Pr.

Maine, Tyler & Parker, Bridget. New Mexico. 2016. (States Ser.). (ENG., Illus.). 32p. (J). (gr. 3-6). lib. bdg. 27.99 *(978-1-5157-0418-8(1)*, 132029, Capstone Pr.) Capstone.

Marsh, Carole. New Mexico Current Events Projects: 30 Cool, Activities, Crafts, Experiments & More for Kids to Do to Learn about Your State! 2003. (New Mexico Experience Ser.). 32p. (gr. k-8). pap. 5.95 *(978-0-635-02050-5(5)*, Marsh, Carole Bks.) Gallopade International.

—New Mexico Geography Projects: 30 Cool, Activities, Crafts, Experiments & More for Kids to Do to Learn about Your State! 2003. (New Mexico Experience Ser.). 32p. (gr. k-5). pap. 5.95 *(978-0-635-01850-2(0)*, Marsh, Carole Bks.) Gallopade International.

—New Mexico Government Projects: 30 Cool, Activities, Crafts, Experiments & More for Kids to Do to Learn about Your State! 2003. (New Mexico Experience Ser.). 32p. (gr. k-5). pap. 5.95 *(978-0-635-01950-9(7)*, Marsh, Carole Bks.) Gallopade International.

—New Mexico People Projects: 30 Cool, Activities, Crafts, Experiments & More for Kids to Do to Learn about Your State! 2003. (New Mexico Experience Ser.). 32p. (gr. k-5). pap. 5.95 *(978-0-635-02000-0(9)*, Marsh, Carole Bks.) Gallopade International.

—New Mexico Symbols & Facts Projects: 30 Cool, Activities, Crafts, Experiments & More for Kids to Do to Learn about Your State! 2003. (New Mexico Experience Ser.). 32p. (gr. k-5). pap. 5.95 *(978-0-635-01900-4(0)*, Marsh, Carole Bks.) Gallopade International.

Mcdaniel, Melissa, et al. New Mexico, 1 vol. 2nd rev. ed. 2008. (Celebrate the States (Second Edition) Ser.). (ENG.). 144p. (gr. 6-6). lib. bdg. 39.79 *(978-0-7614-2719-3(8)*, 7a72205b-adec-4f29-a429-fa58f8b9a73f) Cavendish Square Publishing LLC.

Moskal, Greg. An Apache Indian Community. 2009. (Reading Room Collection 2 Ser.). 24p. (gr. 3-4). 42.50 *(978-1-60851-956-9(2)*, PowerKids Pr.) Rosen Publishing Group, Inc., The.

Murray, Julie. New Mexico, 1 vol. 2006. (Buddy Book Ser.). (ENG., Illus.). 32p. (gr. 2-4). 27.07 *(978-1-59197-690-5(1)*, Buddy Bks.) ABDO Publishing Co.

Obregón, José María. New Mexico. 2009. (Bilingual Library of the United States of America Ser.). (ENG & SPA.). 32p. (gr.

MNO

2-2). 47.90 (978-1-60853-375-6(1), Editorial Buenas Letras) Rosen Publishing Group, Inc., The.

Obregon, Jose Maria. New Mexico/Nuevo Mexico, 1 vol. Brusca, Maria Cristina, tr. 2005. (Bilingual Library of the United States of America Ser.: Set 2). (ENG & SPA., illus.). 32p. (J). (gr. 2-2). lib. bdg. 28.93 (978-1-4042-3096-5(3), 2f73be2c-991c-4c03-91e4-2029b122902c) Rosen Publishing Group, Inc., The.

Phillips, Larissa. Cochise: Apache Chief / Cochise: Jefe Apache. 2009. (Famous People in American History/Grandes personajes en la historia de los Estados Unidos Ser.). (ENG & SPA.). 32p. (gr. 2-3). 47.90 (978-1-61512-540-1(X), Editorial Buenas Letras) Rosen Publishing Group, Inc., The.

Rice, Liz. Bill Richardson. 2009. (Sharing the American Dream Ser.). (Illus.). 64p. (J). (gr. 7-12). 22.95 (978-1-4222-0589-1(4)) Mason Crest.

Walker, Cynthia. Nuevo Mexico. 2005. (Rookie Español Geografía Ser.). (SPA., Illus.). 32p. (J). (gr. k-2). lib. bdg. 19.50 (978-0-516-25247-6(X), Children's Pr.) Scholastic Library Publishing.

Walker, Cynthia & Vargus, Nanci Reginelli. New Mexico. 2004. (Rookie Read-About Geography Ser.). (Illus.). 31p. (J). 20.50 (978-0-516-22755-9(6), Children's Pr.) Scholastic Library Publishing.

Weintraub, A. How to Draw New Mexico's Sights & Symbols. 2009. (Kid's Guide to Drawing America Ser.). 32p. (gr. k-k). 50.50 (978-1-61511-080-3(1), PowerKids Pr.) Rosen Publishing Group, Inc., The.

Weiss-Malik, Linda. New Mexico, 1 vol. 2006. (Portraits of the States Ser.). (ENG.). 32p. (gr. 3-5). pap. 11.50 (978-0-8368-4722-2(9), 801e509e-45cb-4c79-ba65-f7e5e8e44ae1); (Illus.). lib. bdg. 28.67 (978-0-8368-4705-5(9), e314164d-5583-4c01-a9ba-3c3a724421c3) Stevens, Gareth Publishing LLLP. (Gareth Stevens Learning Library).

NEW MEXICO—FICTION

Abruzzo, Nancy. Pop Flop's Great Balloon Ride. 2005. (ENG., Illus.). 32p. (J). (gr. k-17). bds. 12.95 (978-0-89013-475-7(8)) Museum of New Mexico Pr.

Alarid, Carilyn & Markel, Marilyn. Talks All Day Has the Courage to Speak: Mimbres Children Learn Citizenship. Alarid, Carilyn & Markel, Marilyn, illus. 2006. (Illus.). 125p. (J). pap. 16.95 (978-0-86534-470-9(1)) Sunstone Pr.

Alarid, Carilyn & Markel, Marilyn, illus. Runs Like the Wind Stops in Her Tracks: Mimbres Children Learn about Trustworthiness. 2016. 95p. (J). pap. (978-1-63293-099-6(4)) Sunstone Pr.

Amato, Carol J. The Lost Treasure of the Golden Sun. 2005. 172p. (J). (978-0-9713756-3-5(1)) Stargazer Publishing Co.

Anaya, Rudolfo. ChupaCabra & the Roswell UFO. 2008. (ENG.). 144p. (YA). (gr. 9-18). 9.95 (978-0-8263-4469-4(0), P154251) Univ. of New Mexico Pr.

—How Hollyhocks Came to New Mexico. Garcia, Nasario, tr. from ENG. Otéro, Nicolas, illus. 2012. (SPA & ENG.). 48p. (J). 24.95 (978-1-936744-12-1(0), Rio Grande Bks.) LPD Pr.

—How Hollyhocks Came to New Mexico. Garcia, Nasario, tr. Otero, Nicolas, illus. 2018. (ENG.). 48p. (J). (gr. 1-3). pap. 17.95 (978-1-943681-22-8(8)) Nuevo Bks.

—Santero's Miracle: A Bilingual Story. Lamadrid, Enrique R., tr. Córdova, Amy, illus. 2004. (ENG.). 32p. (J). 19.95 (978-0-8263-2847-2(4), P123068) Univ. of New Mexico Pr.

Aragón, Carla, et al. Dance of the Eggshells: Baile de Los Cascarones. Aragon, Socorro, tr. Saville, Kathy Dee, illus. 2010. (ENG.). 32p. (J). (gr. 1). 18.95 (978-0-8263-4770-1(3), P174638) Univ. of New Mexico Pr.

Beaty, Janice J. Jarod & the Mystery of the Petroglyphs: A National Park Adventure Series Book. Beaty, Lillian C., illus. 2015. 118p. (J). pap. (978-1-63293-071-2(4)) Sunstone Pr.

Bell, Juliet. Kepler's Dream. 2013. 256p. (J). (gr. 5-8). 6.99 (978-0-14-242648-7(2), Puffin Books) Penguin Young Readers Group.

Blume, Judy. Tiger Eyes. 2014. (ENG., Illus.). 256p. (YA). (gr. 7). pap. 11.99 (978-1-4814-1387-9(2), Atheneum Bks. for Young Readers) Simon & Schuster Children's Publishing.

Bostick, B. k. Huber Hill & the Golden Staff of Cibola. 2013. (J). pap. 14.99 (978-1-4621-1098-8(3), Horizon Pubs.) Cedar Fort, Inc./CFI Distribution.

Bradley, Timothy J. Infestation. Bradley, Timothy J., illus. 2013. (ENG., Illus.). 192p. (J). (gr. 3-7). pap. 5.99 (978-0-545-45904-4(4)) Scholastic, Inc.

Bronson, Wilfrid S. Pinto's Journey. 2007. (ENG.). 64p. (J). per. 14.95 (978-0-86534-557-7(0)) Sunstone Pr.

Caban, Connie. Don't Be Afraid of the Storm. Page, illus. 2011. 32p. pap. 12.95 (978-1-936343-97-3(5)) Peppertree Pr., The.

Cash, Marie Romero. The Saint Maker's Daughter: A Christmas Dream Fulfilled. 2019. (J). (978-1-63293-261-7(X)) Sunstone Pr.

Cervantes, Jennifer. Tortilla Sun. 2014. (ENG.). 224p. (J). (gr. 3-7). pap. 8.99 (978-1-4521-3150-4(3)) Chronicle Bks. LLC.

Cheng, Jack. See You in the Cosmos. 2018. lib. bdg. 19.65 (978-0-606-41314-5(6)) Turtleback.

Church, Peggy Pond. The Burro of Angelitos. 2013. 52p. pap. 18.95 (978-0-86534-965-0(7)) Sunstone Pr.

—Shoes for the Santo Niño. Carrillo, Charles M., illus. 2013. 64p. 25.95 (978-1-936744-23-7(6), Rio Grande Bks.) LPD Pr.

—Shoes for the Santo Niño: Zapitillos para el Santo Niño: A Bilingual Tale. Carrillo, Charles M., illus. 2009. (SPA & ENG.). 61p. (J). pap. (978-1-890689-64-3(5), Rio Grande Bks.) LPD Pr.

Cole, Steve. Z. Rex. (ENG.). (J). 2010. 256p. (gr. 5-18). 8.99 (978-0-14-241712-6(2), Puffin Books)1. 2009. 276p. (gr. 6-8). 22.44 (978-0-399-25253-2(3)) Penguin Young Readers Group.

Conticelli, Lori Martinez. Red or Green: The Colors of a Family Tradition. Laemmle, Bobbie, illus. 2008. (ENG.). 30p. pap. 13.99 (978-1-4257-3320-9(4)) Xlibris Corp.

Crane, Phyllis F. Anything but the Most Boring Place on Earth. 2011. 174p. pap. 24.95 (978-1-4560-6802-8(4)) America Star Bks.

Creel, Ann Howard. Under a Stand Still Moon. 2005. 183p. (YA). (gr. 7-12). per. 8.95 (978-0-9746481-8-7(3)) Brown Barn Bks.

Dahlstrom, S. J. The Elk Hunt: the Adventures of Wilder Good #1. 2013. (Adventures of Wilder Good Ser.: 1). (ENG., Illus.). 110p. (J). (gr. 3). pap. 9.95 (978-1-58988-087-0(0)) Dry, Paul Bks., Inc.

Deal, Paul. Lighting Candles. 2003. 122p. (YA). 20.95 (978-0-595-65804-6(0)); pap. 10.95 (978-0-595-28457-3(4)) iUniverse, Inc.

Dix, Catherine R. Rosetta Stones. 2009. (ENG.). 213p. (J). pap. 14.95 (978-0-9798452-2-2(X), 9780979845222) Central Ave. Pr.

Duncan, Lois. Summer of Fear. 2011. (ENG.). 256p. (YA). (gr. 7-17). pap., pap. 14.99 (978-0-316-09907-3(4)) Little, Brown Bks. for Young Readers.

Eagar, Lindsay. Hour of the Bees. 368p. (J). (gr. 5-9). 2017. (ENG.). pap. 9.99 (978-0-7636-9120-2(8)) 2016. 16.99 (978-0-7636-7922-4(4)) Candlewick Pr.

Eschberger, Beverly. The Elephants in the Land of Enchantment. Gower, Jim, illus. 2009. (Elephant Family Adventure Ser.: 3). (ENG.). 96p. (J). (-1). pap. 3.99 (978-1-932926-02-6(X)) Artemesia Publishing, LLC.

A First Clay Gathering (Review Multiple Meanings), Level C. 2003. ("Plaid" Phonics & Stories Libraries). 43.50 (978-0-8136-9234-0(2)) Modern Curriculum Pr.

Foard, Sheila Wood. Harvey Girl. 2006. (ENG., Illus.). 176p. (J). (gr. 7-12). per. 18.95 (978-0-89672-570-6(7), P171685) Texas Tech Univ. Pr.

Foster, Darlene. Amanda in New Mexico: Ghosts in the Wind. 2017. (Amanda Travels Adventure Ser.: 6). (ENG.). 128p. (J). (gr. 2-1). pap. 12.99 (978-1-77168-120-9(9)) Central Avenue Publishing CAN. Dist: Independent Pubs. Group.

Garcia, Nasario. Grandma Lale's Magic Adobe Oven: El Horno Magico de Abuelita Lale. Aragon, Dolores, illus. 2018. (SPA & ENG.). (J). pap. (978-1-943681-64-8(3), Rio Grande Bks.) LPD Pr.

—Grandpa Lolo & Trampa: A Story of Surprise & Mystery = Abuelito Lolo y Trampa: Un Cuento de Sorpresa y Misterio. Montoya, Jeremy, illus. 2014. (SPA & ENG.). 41p. (J). 9.99 (978-1-936744-30-5(9)) LPD Pr.

—Grandpa Lolo's Navajo Saddle Blanket: La Tilma de Abuelito Lolo. Moeller, Richard, illus. Moeller, Richard, photos by. 2012. (J). (978-0-8263-5078-7(X)) Univ. of New Mexico Pr.

—Grandpa Lolo's Navajo Saddle Blanket: La Tilma de Abuelito Lolo. 2012. (ENG., Illus.). 72p. (J). E-Book (978-0-8263-5080-0(1)) Univ. of New Mexico Pr.

—Rattling Chains & Other Stories for Children/Ruido de Cadenas y Otros Cuentos para Ninos. Mora, Giovanni, illus. 2009. (SPA & ENG.). 160p. (J). (gr. 3-7). pap. 9.95 (978-1-55885-544-1(0), Piñata Books) Arte Publico Pr.

García, Nasario & Aragon, Dolores, illus. Grandpa Lolo's Matanza: A New Mexican Tradition = la Matanza de Abuelito Lolo: Una Tradición Nuevo Mexicana. 2015. (SPA & ENG.). 70p. (J). (978-1-936744-47-3(3), Rio Grande Bks.) LPD Pr.

García, Nasario & Moeller, Richard. Grandpa Lolo's Navajo Saddle Blanket: La Tilma de Abuelito Lolo. 2012. (ENG & SPA., Illus.). 72p. (J). pap. 19.95 (978-0-8263-5079-4(8), P203507) Univ. of New Mexico Pr.

Gillman, Melanie. Stage Dreams. Gillman, Melanie, illus. 2019. (ENG., Illus.). 104p. (YA). (gr. 8-12). 29.32 (978-1-5124-4000-3(0), 3f3783d0-fdab-4aa6-813e-16633529cda8, Graphic Universe™) Lerner Publishing Group.

Gonzales, Felipe C. Little Folk Stories & Tales by Don Pablo: Bilingual Stories in Spanish & English = Chistes y Cuentos de Don Pablo: Cuentos Bilingües en Español e Inglés. 2010. (SPA & ENG.). (J). pap. 24.95 (978-0-86534-772-4(7)) Sunstone Pr.

Grill, William, illus. The Wolves of Currumpaw. 2016. (ENG.). 80p. (J). (gr. 2-9). 24.00 (978-1-909263-83-3(4)) Flying Eye Bks. GBR. Dist: Penguin Random Hse. LLC.

Grimes, Nikki. Southwest Sunrise. Minor, Wendell, illus. 2020. (ENG.). 40p. (J). 18.99 (978-1-5476-0082-3(9), 900197954, Bloomsbury Children's Bks.) Bloomsbury Publishing USA.

Haas, Jessie. Saige Paints the Sky. Davis, Sarah, illus. 2012. (American Girl Today Ser.: Bk. 2). lib. bdg. 17.15 (978-0-606-31569-2(1)) Turtleback.

Haston, Meg. Paperweight. 2015. (ENG.). 304p. (YA). (gr. 9). 17.99 (978-0-06-233574-6(X), HarperTeen) HarperCollins Pubs.

Hayes, Joe. The Coyote under the Table: El Coyote Debajo de la Mesa, 1 vol. Castro L., Antonio, illus. 2022.Tr. of Folk Tales Told in Spanish & English. (ENG.). 136p. (J). (gr. 1-7). pap. 15.95 (978-1-935955-06-1(3), 23353382, Cinco Puntos Press) Lee & Low Bks., Inc.

—The Day It Snowed Tortillas - El DÃ a que Nevaron Tortillas: Folktales Told in Spanish & English, 1 vol. Castro L., Antonio, illus. 2003. (SPA & ENG.). 144p. (J). (gr. 3-6). pap. 14.95 (978-0-938317-76-0(8), 3488840c-6617-4886-98d7-0a90d3b6bce5, Cinco Puntos Press) Lee & Low Bks., Inc.

Hays, Anna Jane. The Secret of the Circle-K Cave. Smath, Jerry, illus. 2006. (Science Solves It! Ser.). (ENG.). 32p. (J). (gr. k-2). pap. 5.99 (978-1-57565-189-7(0), 3c159770-6a2b-4f79-b62b-9bd5318deb31, Kane Press) Astra Publishing Hse.

Heller, Marcy. Loco Dog in the Santa Fe Rail Yard, 1 vol. 2nd rev. ed. 2015. (Historical New Mexico for Children Ser.: Volume 1). (ENG., Illus.). 48p. (J). pap. 16.95 (978-0-9912516-1-2(X)) Rock Point Pr.

Hobbs, Will. Kokopelli's Flute. 2005. 148p. (gr. 5-9). 17.00 (978-0-7569-5503-8(3)) Perfection Learning Corp.

—Kokopelli's Flute. 2005. (ENG.). 160p. (J). (gr. 5-9). pap. 7.99 (978-1-4169-0250-8(3), Simon & Schuster/Paula Wiseman Bks.) Simon & Schuster/Paula Wiseman Bks.

Hodder, Beth. The Ghost of Schafer Meadows. 2007. (J). per. 7.99 (978-0-9793963-0-4(1)) Grizzly Ridge Publishing.

Hulme, Joy N. Climbing the Rainbow. 2004. 224p. (J). 15.99 (978-0-380-81572-2(9)) HarperCollins Pubs.

Istenes, Wanda. Manuel: A Novel. 2016. (ENG.). 138p. (J). pap. 13.00 (978-1-4809-2442-0(3)) Dorrance Publishing Co., Inc.

Jacobs, Lily. The Littlest Bunny in Albuquerque: An Easter Adventure. Dunn, Robert, illus. 2015. (Littlest Bunny Ser.). (ENG.). 32p. (J). (gr. -1-3). 9.99 (978-1-4926-1021-2(6), Hometown World) Sourcebooks, Inc.

—The Littlest Bunny in New Mexico: An Easter Adventure. Dunn, Robert, illus. 2015. (Littlest Bunny Ser.). (ENG.). 32p. (J). (gr. -1-3). 9.99 (978-1-4926-1147-9(6), Hometown World) Sourcebooks, Inc.

James, Eric. Santa's Sleigh Is on Its Way to Albuquerque: A Christmas Adventure. Dunn, Robert, illus. 2016. (Santa's Sleigh Is on Its Way Ser.). (ENG.). 32p. (J). (gr. k-2). 12.99 (978-1-4926-4315-9(7), 9781492643159, Hometown World) Sourcebooks, Inc.

—Santa's Sleigh Is on Its Way to New Mexico: A Christmas Adventure. Dunn, Robert, illus. 2016. (Santa's Sleigh Is on Its Way Ser.). (ENG.). 32p. (J). (gr. k-2). 12.99 (978-1-4926-4343-2(2), 9781492643432, Hometown World) Sourcebooks, Inc.

—The Spooky Express Albuquerque. Piwowarski, Marcin, illus. 2017. (Spooky Express Ser.). (ENG.). 32p. (J). (gr. k-6). 9.99 (978-1-4926-5339-4(X), Hometown World) Sourcebooks, Inc.

—The Spooky Express New Mexico. Piwowarski, Marcin, illus. 2017. (Spooky Express Ser.). (ENG.). 32p. (J). (gr. k-6). 9.99 (978-1-4926-5381-3(0), Hometown World) Sourcebooks, Inc.

—Tiny the Albuquerque Easter Bunny. 2018. (Tiny the Easter Bunny Ser.). (ENG.). 40p. (J). (gr. k-3). 9.99 (978-1-4926-5905-1(3), Hometown World) Sourcebooks, Inc.

—Tiny the New Mexico Easter Bunny. 2018. (Tiny the Easter Bunny Ser.). (ENG.). 40p. (J). (gr. k-3). 9.99 (978-1-4926-5947-1(9), Hometown World) Sourcebooks, Inc.

James, Jenni. Pride & Popularity. 2011. (Jane Austen Diaries). (ENG.). 238p. (YA). (gr. 8-12). pap. 11.99 (978-0-9838293-0-0(6)) Inkberry Pr.

Johnson, LouAnne. Muchacho: a Novel. 2011. (ENG.). 208p. (YA). (gr. 7). pap. 9.99 (978-0-375-85903-8(9), Ember) Random Hse. Children's Bks.

Kellerman, Faye & Kellerman, Aliza. Prism. 2009. 272p. (YA). (gr. 7-18). lib. bdg. 17.89 (978-0-06-168722-8(7), HarperTeen) HarperCollins Pubs.

King, Wesley. A World Below. (ENG., Illus.). (J). (gr. 3-7). 2019. 288p. pap. 8.99 (978-1-4814-7823-6(0)) 2018. 272p. 17.99 (978-1-4814-7822-9(2)) Simon & Schuster/Paula Wiseman Bks. (Simon & Schuster/Paula Wiseman Bks.).

Klages, Ellen. White Sands, Red Menace. 2010. (Gordon Family Saga Ser.: 2). 352p. (J). (gr. 5-18). 9.99 (978-0-14-241518-4(9), Puffin Books) Penguin Young Readers Group.

Lasky, Kathryn. A Voice in the Wind: A Starbuck Twins Mystery, Book Three. 2008. (ENG., Illus.). 272p. (J). (gr. 3-7). pap. 15.95 (978-0-15-205875-3(3), 1197642, Clarion Bks.) HarperCollins Pubs.

Leonard, Julia Platt. Cold Case. (ENG.). 288p. (J). (gr. 3-7). 2012. pap. 5.99 (978-1-4424-2010-6(3)) 2011. (Illus.). 15.99 (978-1-4424-2009-0(X)) Simon & Schuster/Paula Wiseman Bks. (Simon & Schuster/Paula Wiseman Bks.).

Little, Kimberley Griffiths. The Last Snake Runner. 2006. 201p. (YA). (gr. 7-10). reprint ed. 16.00 (978-1-4223-5838-2(0)) DIANE Publishing Co.

Martinez, Mario X. Abran & Isabella's Hidden Faith. 2015. 103p. (J). pap. (978-1-935604-73-0(2)) Gaon Bks.

Mazzio, Joann. Leaving Eldorado. 2014. (ENG.). 176p. (YA). (gr. 7). pap. 10.99 (978-0-544-33613-1(5), 1584159, Clarion Bks.) HarperCollins Pubs.

McCormick, Wilfred. Eagle Scout: A Bronc Burnett Story. 2011. 192p. 42.95 (978-1-258-07309-1(9)) Literary Licensing, LLC.

—Quick Kick: A Bronc Burnett Story. 2011. 192p. 42.95 (978-1-258-10149-7(1)) Literary Licensing, LLC.

McKann, Anna. Chavos: The Kids of Distrito Federal. 2006. (Illus.). 261p. (J). per. (978-0-9554438-0-0(6)) Sharon Hse. Publishing, Ltd.

Meyer, Carolyn. Diary of a Waitress: The Not-So-Glamorous Life of a Harvey Girl. 2015. (ENG., Illus.). 288p. (J). (gr. 5-9). 17.95 (978-1-62091-652-0(5), Calkins Creek) Highlights Pr., c/o Highlights for Children, Inc.

Mora, Pat & Carling, Amelia Lau. Abuelos, 1 vol. 2011. (ENG., Illus.). 32p. (J). (gr. -1-2). pap. 9.95 (978-1-55498-101-4(8)) Groundwood Bks. CAN. Dist: Publishers Group West (PGW).

Murphy, Barbara Beasley. Ace Flies Like an Eagle. 2003. (Can't Stop Ace Ser.: No. 3). 180p. (J). pap. 16.95 (978-0-86534-409-9(4)) Sunstone Pr.

Nesbit, Troy. Diamond Cave Mystery. 2013. (Wilderness Mystery Ser.). (ENG., Illus.). 280p. (J). (gr. 3-7). pap. 12.95 (978-1-58979-809-0(0)) Taylor Trade Publishing.

New Mexico Night Before Christmas. 2006. (YA). per. 19.99 (978-0-9710675-5-4(4)) 2020 Vision Pr.

Nickell, Judy. A New Mexico Dictionary for Young People. 2012. (J). pap. (978-1-890689-93-3(9), Rio Grande Bks.) LPD Pr.

Noel, Alyson. Echo. 2012. (Soul Seekers Ser.: 2). (ENG.). 352p. (YA). (gr. 7). pap. 13.99 (978-0-312-57566-3(1), 900075090, St. Martin's Griffin) St. Martin's Pr.

—Fated. 2012. (Soul Seekers Ser.: 1). (ENG.). 368p. (YA). (gr. 7). pap. 27.00 (978-0-312-57565-6(3), 900075089, St. Martin's Griffin) St. Martin's Pr.

—Mystic. 2013. (Soul Seekers Ser.: 3). (ENG.). 320p. (YA). (gr. 7). pap. 24.00 (978-0-312-57567-0(X), 900075091, St. Martin's Griffin) St. Martin's Pr.

Orona-Ramirez, Kristy. Kiki's Journey, 1 vol. Warm Day, Jonathan, illus. 2017. (ENG.). 32p. (J). (gr. 2-5). pap. 10.95 (978-0-89239-410-4(2), leelowcbp, Children's Book Press) Lee & Low Bks., Inc.

Orona-Ramirez, Kristy. Kiki's Journey. 2013. (ENG., Illus.). 32p. (J). (gr. k-3). 16.95 (978-0-89239-214-8(2)) Lee & Low Bks., Inc.

Ortega, Cristina. Eyes of the Weaver: Los Ojos Del Tejedor. Garcia, Patricio E., illus. 2006. (ENG.). 64p. (J). 19.95 (978-0-8263-3990-4(5), P123378) Univ. of New Mexico Pr.

Palma, B. El Dorado: A Palo Alto Adventure. 2012. 136p. (gr. -1). 23.99 (978-1-4634-3110-5(4)); pap. 13.99 (978-1-4634-3111-2(2)) AuthorHouse.

Patchin, Frank Gee. The Pony Rider Boys in New Mexico. 2005. 28.95 (978-1-4218-1429-2(3)); 252p. pap. 13.95 (978-1-4218-1529-9(X)) 1st World Publishing, Inc. (1st World Library - Literary Society).

Plum, Amy. Until the Beginning. 2016. (After the End Ser.: 2). (ENG.). 352p. (YA). (gr. 8). pap. 9.99 (978-0-06-222564-1(2), HarperTeen) HarperCollins Pubs.

Podos, Rebecca. Like Water. 2017. (ENG.). 320p. (YA). (gr. 9). 17.99 (978-0-06-237337-3(4), Balzer & Bray) HarperCollins Pubs.

Poulsen, David A. No Time Like the Past. 3rd rev. ed. 2007. (Salt & Pepper Chronicles). (ENG., Illus.). 160p. (J). (gr. 4-7). 6.95 (978-1-55263-807-1(3)) Leaf Storm Pr.

Reeder, Carolyn. The Secret Project Notebook. 2005. 247p. (J). 15.00 (978-0-941232-33-3(6)) Bathtub Row Pr.

Roanhorse, Rebecca. Race to the Sun. 2021. (ENG.). 256p. (gr. 3-6). 22.44 (978-1-5364-6679-9(4), Riordan, Rick) Disney Pr.

—Race to the Sun. 2021. (Penworthy Picks YA Fiction Ser.). (ENG., Illus.). 298p. (J). (gr. 4-5). 19.46 (978-1-68505-027-6(1)) Penworthy Co., LLC, The.

—Rick Riordan Presents Race to the Sun. (J). (gr. 3-7). 2021. 48p. pap. 7.99 (978-1-368-02482-2(3)) 2020. 12p. 16.99 (978-1-368-02466-2(1)) Disney Publishing Worldwide. (Riordan, Rick).

Romero-Anderson, Emerita. Milagro of the Spanish Bean Pot. Pijoan, Randall, illus. 2011. (ENG.). 128p. (J). (gr. 4-6). 18.95 (978-0-89672-681-9(9), P200877) Texas Tech Univ. Pr.

Rowe, Anne Burgess, illus. The Newest Angel. 2015. 47p. (J). pap. (978-1-63293-039-2(0)) Sunstone Pr.

Ruiz, Joseph J. Angel on Daniel's Shoulder. 2004. (SPA & ENG., Illus.). 108p. (J). pap. 12.95 (978-0-86534-402-0(7)) Sunstone Pr.

—Manuel & the Magic Ring. 2003. (SPA & ENG., Illus.). 108p. (J). pap. 12.95 (978-0-86534-399-3(3)) Sunstone Pr.

Sandoval, John. The Witches of Ruidoso. 2013. (ENG.). 120p. (YA). pap. 12.95 (978-1-55885-766-7(4), Piñata Books) Arte Publico Pr.

Service, Pamela F. Alien Encounter. Gorman, Mike, illus. 2010. (Alien Agent Ser.: 4). (ENG.). 152p. (J). (gr. 4-6). 16.95 (978-0-8225-8873-3(0), 07e31f3f-08b4-4f75-89d0-8685b56dd365, Darby Creek) Lerner Publishing Group.

—#4 Alien Encounter. Gorman, Mike, illus. 2011. (Alien Agent Ser.). 152p. (J). pap. 33.92 (978-0-7613-7608-8(9), Darby Creek) Lerner Publishing Group.

Skurzynski, Gloria. Running Scared: A Mystery in Carlsbad Caverns National Park. 2008. (Mysteries in Our National Park Ser.). (Illus.). 160p. (J). (gr. 3-7). mass mkt. 4.99 (978-1-4263-0182-7(0), National Geographic Kids) Disney Publishing Worldwide.

Slate, Joseph. The Secret Stars, 1 vol. Dávalos, Felipe, illus. 2005. (ENG.). 32p. (J). pap. 5.95 (978-0-7614-5152-5(8)) Marshall Cavendish Corp.

Smith, Lane. Return to Augie Hobble. 2017. (J). lib. bdg. 18.40 (978-0-606-38550-3(9)) Turtleback.

Stanley, Diane. Saving Sky. 2012. (ENG.). 208p. (J). (gr. 3-7). pap. 6.99 (978-0-06-123907-6(0), HarperCollins) HarperCollins Pubs.

Steinlage, Ben. Bird Boy. 2011. 290p. pap. 17.95 (978-1-4327-6667-2(8)) Outskirts Pr., Inc.

Steinsiek, Sabra Brown. The Tale of the Pronghorned Cantaloupe. Chilton, Noel Dora, illus. 2013. 48p. 24.95 (978-1-936744-11-4(2), Rio Grande Bks.) LPD Pr.

—The Tale of the Pronghorned Cantaloupe. Chilton, Noel, illus. 2009. (SPA & ENG.). 48p. (J). (gr. -1-3). pap. 17.95 (978-1-890689-85-8(8), Rio Grande Bks.) LPD Pr.

Stern, Jacqueline. Mystery of the Whispering Walls. 2004. (J). 148p. pap. (978-1-57168-844-6(7)); (Hollow Tree Mystery Ser.: Bk. 6). (Illus.). v, 142p. (978-1-57168-850-7(1), Eakin Pr.) Eakin Pr.

Stork, Francisco X. The Last Summer of the Death Warriors. 2012. (ENG.). 352p. (J). (gr. 9-12). 26.19 (978-0-545-15134-4(1), Levine, Arthur A. Bks.) Scholastic, Inc.

Strickland, Deborah. Mary Reeder, Prairie Girl. 2007. 68p. per. 8.95 (978-0-595-44514-1(4)) iUniverse, Inc.

Taschek, Karen. Horse of Seven Moons. 2005. (ENG., Illus.). 192p. (YA). pap. 14.95 (978-0-8263-3215-8(3), P123190) Univ. of New Mexico Pr.

—The the Risen Horse. 2010. (ENG.). 248p. (YA). (gr. 7-18). pap. 15.95 (978-0-8263-4837-1(8), P198426) Univ. of New Mexico Pr.

Tingle, Tim. Danny Blackgoat, Rugged Road to Freedom. 2014. (Danny Blackgoat Ser.: 2). (ENG.). 144p. (YA). (gr. 8-12). pap. 9.95 (978-1-939053-05-3(6), 7th Generation) BPC.

Tripp, Valerie. Josefina Story Collection. Tibbles, Jean-Paul, illus. 2008. 420p. pap. 29.95 (978-1-59369-453-1(9)) American Girl Publishing, Inc.

Valdes, Alisa. Perdition: A Kindred Novel. 2013. (YA). pap. (978-0-06-202421-3(3), HarperTeen) HarperCollins Pubs.

Voorhees, Coert. The Brothers Torres. 2009. (ENG.). 336p. (J). (gr. 7-12). 24.94 (978-1-4231-0306-6(8)) Hyperion Bks. for Children.

Williams Hall, Kathy. Kay Kay's Adventures on Ojo Caliente: The Old Aspen Tree & the Posi Ouinge. 2012. 32p. pap. 19.99 (978-1-4772-7667-9(X)) AuthorHouse.

Yeager, Graham. Diablo: The Third Millersburg Novel. 2006. 145p. (YA). per. 7.99 (978-0-9765478-4-6(8)) Stone Acres Publishing Co.

Zindel, Paul. The Gadget. 2003. (ENG., Illus.). 192p. (YA). (gr. 7). mass mkt. 7.99 (978-0-440-22951-3(0), Laurel Leaf) Random Hse. Children's Bks.

NEW MEXICO—HISTORY

The Art Illustrations & Brief History of Padre Antonio Jose Martinez de Taos: New Mexico 1793-1867. 2003. pap. 10.00 (978-0-9748002-0-2(1)) Martinez, Leroy F.

Art Illustrations & Brief History of Padre Antonio Jose Martinez de Taos: New Mexico 1793-1867 Version: Color. 2003. pap. (978-0-9748002-1-9(X)) Martinez, Leroy F.

Bjorklund, Ruth. New Mexico, 1 vol. 2nd rev. ed. 2013. (It's My State! (Second Edition)(r) Ser.). (ENG.). 80p. (gr. 4-4). 35.93 (978-1-60870-882-6(9), 8c0f4ad4-8bec-40d2-8291-0ed3fd73cc62) Cavendish Square Publishing LLC.

Bjorklund, Ruth, et al. New Mexico, 1 vol. 3rd rev. ed. 2015. (It's My State! (Third Edition)(r) Ser.). (ENG., Illus.). 80p. (gr. 4-4). 35.93 (978-1-62713-210-7(4), ab961c74-7b66-4367-984d-d276b5571984) Cavendish Square Publishing LLC.

Bodden, Valerie. New Mexico. 2009. (This Land Called America Ser.). 32p. (YA). (gr. 3-6). 19.95 (978-1-58341-784-3(2)) Creative Co., The.

Brezina, Corona. New Mexico: Past & Present, 1 vol. 2010. (United States: Past & Present Ser.). (ENG.). 48p. (YA). (gr. 5-5). pap. 12.75 (978-1-4358-9517-1(7),

db50006e-9ddc-4d16-9aee-3252d00d63a5); lib. bdg. 34.47 *(978-1-4358-9490-7(1),* 109324d1-a4e5-44bf-8b8d-823bf88db334) Rosen Publishing Group, Inc., The. (Rosen Reference).
Brown, Rachel K. Santa Fe: Daily Life in a Western Trading Center. 2003. (J). pap. *(978-1-58417-074-7(3))* Lake Street Pubs.
Burgan, Michael. America the Beautiful: New Mexico (Revised Edition) 2014. (America the Beautiful, Third Ser. (Revised Edition) Ser.). (ENG.). 144p. (J). lib. bdg. 40.00 *(978-0-531-28285-4(6))* Scholastic Library Publishing.
—New Mexico (a True Book: My United States) (Library Edition) 2018. (True Book (Relaunch) Ser.). (ENG., Illus.). 48p. (J). (gr. 3-5). 31.00 *(978-0-531-23566-9(1),* Children's Pr.) Scholastic Library Publishing.
Coleman, Miriam. New Mexico: Land of Enchantment, 1 vol. 2010. (Our Amazing States Ser.). (ENG.). 24p. (J). (gr. 3-3). pap. 9.25 *(978-1-4488-0748-2(4),* 5b8ca145-eb0d-4b4e-ad0f-96e9099892ae); lib. bdg. 26.27 *(978-1-4488-0658-4(5),* bc04348f-6d4c-4e14-969b-02ddac1dc676) Rosen Publishing Group, Inc., The. (PowerKids Pr.).
Craats, Rennay. New Mexico. 2011. (Guide to American States Ser.). (Illus.). 48p. (YA). (gr. 3-6). 29.99 *(978-1-61690-803-4(3))* Weigl Pubs., Inc.
—New Mexico: The Land of Enchantment. 2016. (J). *(978-1-4896-4908-9(5))* Weigl Pubs., Inc.
Daugherty, Sharleen, ed. Young Voices of Silver City. 2013. 40p. pap. 10.99 *(978-1-936744-16-9(3),* Rio Grande Bks.) LPD Pr.
DeAngelis, Therese. From Sea to Shining Sea: New Mexico. 2009. (From Sea to Shining Sea, Second Ser.). (ENG.). 80p. (J). pap. 7.95 *(978-0-531-21139-7(8),* Children's Pr.) Scholastic Library Publishing.
DeMolay, Jack. Ovnis: El Caso Roswell, 1 vol. Obregón, José María, tr. 2008. (Historietas Juveniles: Misterios (Jr. Graphic Mysteries) Ser.). (SPA., Illus.). 24p. (J). (gr. 2-3). lib. bdg. 28.93 *(978-1-4358-2539-0(X),* e886f791-ad7e-41a6-8ea3-d30606fff3be) Rosen Publishing Group, Inc., The.
Eboch, Chris. Chaco Canyon, 1 vol. 2014. (Digging up the Past Ser.). (ENG.). 112p. (YA). (gr. 6-12). lib. bdg. 41.36 *(978-1-62403-231-8(1),* 1294, Essential Library) ABDO Publishing Co.
Gamble, Adam & Jasper, Mark. Good Night New Mexico. Palmer, Ruth, illus. 2014. (Good Night Our World Ser.). (ENG.). 20p. (J). (— 1). bds. 9.95 *(978-1-60219-088-7(7))* Good Night Bks.
Hamilton, John. New Mexico, 1 vol. 2016. (United States of America Ser.). (ENG., Illus.). 48p. (J). (gr. 5-9). 34.21 *(978-1-68078-333-9(5),* 21651, Abdo & Daughters) ABDO Publishing Co.
Heinrichs, Ann. New Mexico. Kania, Matt, illus. 2017. (U. S. A. Travel Guides). (ENG.). 40p. (J). (gr. 2-5). lib. bdg. 38.50 *(978-1-5038-1971-9(X),* 211608) Child's World, Inc, The.
Hoena, Blake. The Roswell UFO Incident. Yotter, Tate, illus. 2019. (Paranormal Mysteries Ser.). (ENG.). 24p. (J). (gr. 3-8). lib. bdg. 29.95 *(978-1-64487-097-6(5),* Black Sheep) Bellwether Media.
Jerome, Kate B. Lucky to Live in New Mexico. 2017. (Arcadia Kids Ser.). (ENG., Illus.). 32p. (J). 16.99 *(978-0-7385-2804-5(8))* Arcadia Publishing.
—The Wise Animal Handbook New Mexico. 2017. (Arcadia Kids Ser.). (ENG., Illus.). 32p. (J). 16.99 *(978-0-7385-2833-5(1))* Arcadia Publishing.
Laird, Johnna M. Southwest: New Mexico, Oklahoma, Texas, Vol. 19. 2015. (Let's Explore the States Ser.). (Illus.). 64p. (J). (gr. 5). 23.95 *(978-1-4222-3334-4(0))* Mason Crest.
Lavash, Donald. Journey Through New Mexico History Hardc. 2006. 300p. 34.95 *(978-0-86534-541-6(4))* Sunstone Pr.
Lyon, Robin. A True Book: Spanish Missions of New Mexico. 2010. (True Book Ser.). (ENG.). 48p. (J). pap. 6.95 *(978-0-531-21242-4(4),* Children's Pr.) Scholastic Library Publishing.
—True Books: the Spanish Missions of New Mexico. 2010. (True Book: Spanish Missions Ser.). (ENG.). 48p. (J). (gr. 3-5). 21.19 *(978-0-531-20579-2(7),* Children's Pr.) Scholastic Library Publishing.
Marsh, Carole. Exploring New Mexico Through Project-Based Learning: Geography, History, Government, Economics & More. 2016. (New Mexico Experience Ser.). (ENG.). (J). pap. 9.99 *(978-0-635-12355-8(X))* Gallopade International.
—I'm Reading about New Mexico. 2014. (New Mexico Experience Ser.). (ENG., Illus.). (J). pap., pap. 8.99 *(978-0-635-11306-1(6))* Gallopade International.
—New Mexico History Projects: 30 Cool, Activities, Crafts, Experiments & More for Kids to Do to Learn about Your State! 2003. (New Mexico Experience Ser.). 32p. (gr. k-5). pap. 5.95 *(978-0-635-01800-7(4),* Marsh, Carole Bks.) Gallopade International.
Martinez Martinez, Deborah. Trade on the Taos Mountain Trail. Pacheco, Robert, illus. 2010. (ENG.). 48p. (J). pap. 15.00 *(978-0-9823445-0-7(3))* Vanishing Horizons.
Moss, Leila & Knox, Linda L. The Storyteller. 2015. (Illus.). xiv, 107p. 24.95 *(978-1-935204-53-4(X))* Salem Author Services.
O'Neill, Elizabeth. Alfred Visits New Mexico. 2009. (ENG.). 24p. (J). pap. 12.00 *(978-0-9822288-7-6(2))* Funny Bone Bks.
Rodriguez, Cindy. New Mexico: The Land of Enchantment. 2012. (Illus.). 24p. (J). *(978-1-61913-381-5(4));* pap. *(978-1-61913-382-2(2))* Weigl Pubs., Inc.
Winter, Jonah. The Secret Project. Winter, Jeanette, illus. 2017. (ENG.). 40p. (J). (gr. k-3). 17.99 *(978-1-4814-6913-5(4),* Beach Lane Bks.) Beach Lane Bks.

NEW ORLEANS (LA.)

Benoit, Peter. Hurricane Katrina. 2011. (True Book-Disasters Ser.). (ENG., Illus.). 48p. (J). (gr. 3-5). lib. bdg. 29.00 *(978-0-531-25421-9(6),* Children's Pr.) Scholastic Library Publishing.
—Hurricane Katrina (a True Book: Disasters) 2011. (True Book (Relaunch) Ser.). (ENG., Illus.). 48p. (J). (gr. 3-5). pap. 6.95 *(978-0-531-26626-7(5),* Children's Pr.) Scholastic Library Publishing.
Bloom Fradin, Judith & Brindell Fradin, Dennis. Hurricane Katrina, 1 vol. 2010. (Turning Points in U. S. History Ser.). (ENG.). 48p. (gr. 4-4). 34.07 *(978-0-7614-4261-5(8),* 516d2f6d-7f79-4ec9-b419-2220b5bdeb93) Cavendish Square Publishing LLC.
Brian, marion. Rolling down the Avenue, 1 vol. Lindsley, Jennifer, illus. 2016. (ENG.). 32p. (J). pap. 9.95 *(978-1-4556-2179-8(X),* Pelican Publishing) Arcadia Publishing.
Bridges, Ruby. Ruby Bridges Goes to School: My True Story. 2009. (Scholastic Reader, Level 2 Ser.). (ENG., Illus.). 32p. (J). (gr. -1-3). pap. 3.99 *(978-0-545-10855-3(1))* Scholastic, Inc.
Bridges, Ruby & Maccarone, Grace. Let's Read About — Ruby Bridges. Van Wright, Cornelius & Hu, Ying-Hwa, illus. 2003. (Scholastic First Biographies Ser.). (J). *(978-0-439-51362-3(6))* Scholastic, Inc.
Friesen, Helen Lepp. New Orleans. 2020. (J). *(978-1-7911-1590-6(X),* AV2 by Weigl) Weigl Pubs., Inc.
Goodman, Steve. The Train They Call the City of New Orleans. McCurdy, Michael, illus. 2003. 16.99 *(978-3-00-100280-8(8),* Putnam Juvenile) Penguin Publishing Group.
Hedlund, Stephanie F. New Orleans, 1 vol. 2007. (Cities Set 2 Ser.). (Illus.). 32p. (gr. -1-3). 27.07 *(978-1-59679-721-5(5),* Checkerboard Library) ABDO Publishing Co.
Koontz, Robin & Who HQ. What Was Hurricane Katrina? Hinderliter, John, illus. 2015. (What Was? Ser.). 112p. (J). (gr. 3-7). 5.99 *(978-0-448-48662-8(8),* Penguin Workshop) Penguin Young Readers Group.
Looye, Juliette. Ruby Bridges. (Voices Reading Ser.). (Illus.). 16p. (J). pap. *(978-0-7367-2913-0(5))* Zaner-Bloser, Inc.
Lundy, Kathleen Gould. In a Class of Her Own. Alward, Jeff, illus. 2007. 48p. (J). lib. bdg. 23.08 *(978-1-4242-1629-1(X))* Fitzgerald Bks.
Prior, Jennifer. Art & Culture: Mardi Gras: Subtraction (Grade 2) rev. ed. 2018. (Mathematics in the Real World Ser.). (ENG., Illus.). 32p. (J). (gr. 2-3). pap. 10.99 *(978-1-4258-5748-6(5))* Teacher Created Materials, Inc.
Prior, Jennifer Overend. Arte y Cultura: Mardi Gras: Resta. rev. ed. 2018. (Mathematics in the Real World Ser.). (SPA., Illus.). 32p. (J). (gr. 2-3). pap. 10.99 *(978-1-4258-2865-3(5))* Teacher Created Materials, Inc.
Zullo, Allan. Heroes of Hurricane Katrina. 2015. xii, 180p. (J). *(978-1-4806-8729-5(4))* Scholastic, Inc.

NEW ORLEANS (LA.)—FICTION

Ades, Audrey. Judah Touro Didn't Want to Be Famous. Mildenberger, Vivien, illus. 2020. (ENG.). 32p. (J). (gr. k-3). 17.99 *(978-1-5415-4561-8(3),* 35256b85-1e87-4c96-b654-f9cca58b6dcc, Kar-Ben Publishing) Lerner Publishing Group.
Agresti, Aimee. Illuminate: A Gilded Wings Novel, Book One. 2013. (ENG.). 544p. (YA). (gr. 7). pap. 28.99 *(978-0-544-02222-5(X),* 1528480, Clarion Bks.) HarperCollins Pubs.
—Infatuate: A Gilded Wings Novel, Book Two. 2013. (ENG.). 416p. (YA). (gr. 7). 17.99 *(978-0-547-62615-4(0),* 1466666, Clarion Bks.) HarperCollins Pubs.
Ahdieh, Renée. The Beautiful. (Beautiful Quartet Ser.: 1). (ENG.). (YA). (gr. 7). 2021. 480p. pap. 5.99 *(978-1-5247-3819-8(0),* Penguin Books) 2021. 480p. pap. 12.99 *(978-0-593-46266-9(1),* G.P. Putnam's Sons Books for Young Readers) 2019. 448p. 18.99 *(978-1-5247-3817-4(4),* G.P. Putnam's Sons Books for Young Readers) Penguin Young Readers Group.
Amoss, Berthe. Secret Lives. 2014. (ENG., Illus.). 184p. (gr. 4). pap. 12.95 *(978-1-939601-05-6(3))* Ig Publishing, Inc.
Applewood Books. Little Maid of New Orleans. 2011. (Little Maid Ser.). (ENG.). 236p. pap. 12.95 *(978-1-4290-9746-8(9))* Applewood Bks.
Arden, Alys. The Casquette Girls: A Novel, 0 vols. 2015. (Casquette Girls Ser.: 1). (ENG., Illus.). 574p. (YA). (gr. 8-13). pap. 9.99 *(978-1-5039-4654-5(1),* 9781503946545, Skyscape) Amazon Publishing.
Asher, Sally. Mermaids of New Orleans. Vandiver, Melissa, illus. 2018. (J). *(978-1-946160-28-7(8))* Univ. of Louisiana at Lafayette Pr.
Bildner, Phil. Marvelous Cornelius: Hurricane Katrina & the Spirit of New Orleans. Parra, John, illus. 2015. (ENG.). 44p. (J). (gr. k-3). 16.99 *(978-1-4521-2578-7(3))* Chronicle Bks. LLC.
Blume, Lesley M. M. Tennyson. 2008. (ENG.). 240p. (J). (gr. 6-8). lib. bdg. 21.19 *(978-0-375-94703-2(5))* Random House Publishing Group.
Boston Weatherford, Carole. Freedom in Congo Square. Christie, R. Gregory, illus. 2016. (ENG.). 40p. (J). (gr. -1-3). 17.99 *(978-1-4998-0103-3(3))* Little Bee Books Inc.
Brezenoff, Steve. The Zombie Who Visited New Orleans, 1 vol. Canga, Chris, illus. 2010. (Field Trip Mysteries Ser.). (ENG.). 88p. (J). (gr. 3-6). 25.32 *(978-1-4342-2141-4(5),* 102871); pap. 5.95 *(978-1-4342-2773-7(1),* 114040) Capstone. (Stone Arch Bks.).
Burk, Rachelle. Tree House in a Storm. Schneider, Rex, illus. 2009. (ENG.). 42p. (J). (gr. k-4). 16.95 *(978-0-916144-23-4(2))* Stemmer Hse. Pubs.
Camp, Bryan. The City of Lost Fortunes. 2018. (Crescent City Novel Ser.). (ENG., Illus.). 384p. 24.00 *(978-1-328-81079-3(8),* 1687328, Harper Voyager) HarperCollins Pubs.
Chopin, Kate. The Awakening. 2014. (American Classics Ser.). (ENG., Illus.). 64p. pap. 7.95 *(978-1-906230-78-4(1))* Real Reads Ltd. GBR. Dist: Casemate Pubs. & Bk. Distributors, LLC.
Cole, Henry. A Nest for Celeste: A Story about Art, Inspiration, & the Meaning of Home. 2012. (Nest for Celeste Ser.: 1). (ENG., Illus.). 352p. (J). (gr. 3-7). pap. 9.99 *(978-0-06-170412-3(1),* Tegen, Katherine Bks) HarperCollins Pubs.
—A Nest for Celeste: A Story about Art, Inspiration, & the Meaning of Home. Cole, Henry, illus. 2010. (Nest for Celeste Ser.: 1). (ENG., Illus.). 352p. (J). (gr. 3-7). 16.99 *(978-0-06-170410-9(5),* Tegen, Katherine Bks) HarperCollins Pubs.
Coleman, Evelyn. The Cameo Necklace: A Cecile Mystery. Giovine, Sergio, illus. 2012. (American Girl Mysteries Ser.). (ENG.). 192p. (J). (gr. 4-6). pap. 18.69 *(978-1-59369-900-0(X))* American Girl Publishing, Inc.
Courage, Nick. Storm Blown. 2019. (ENG.). 352p. (J). (gr. 4-7). 16.99 *(978-0-525-64596-2(9),* Delacorte Bks. for Young Readers) Random Hse. Children's Bks.
Dartez, Cecilia. Jenny Giraffe's Mardi Gras Ride, 1 vol. Dartez, Cecilia & Green, Andy, illus. 2018. (Jenny Giraffe Ser.). (ENG.). 32p. (gr. -1-3). 8.99 *(978-1-4556-2387-7(3),* Pelican Publishing) Arcadia Publishing.
Dawson, Keila. The King Cake Baby, 1 vol. Smith, Vernon, illus. 2015. (ENG.). 32p. (J). (gr. k-3). 8.99 *(978-1-4556-2013-5(0),* Pelican Publishing) Arcadia Publishing.
de Las Casas, Dianne. Dinosaur Mardi Gras, 1 vol. Gentry, Marita, illus. 2011. (ENG.). 32p. (J). (gr. k-3). 17.99 *(978-1-58980-966-6(1),* Pelican Publishing) Arcadia Publishing.
Decker, Jeni. Far from Happy. 2014. 200p. pap. 14.99 *(978-1-62798-407-2(0))* Dreamspinner Pr.
Dixon, Franklin W. & Keene, Carolyn. Bonfire Masquerade. 2011. (Nancy Drew/Hardy Boys Ser.: 5). (ENG.). 176p. (J). (gr. 3-7). pap. 6.99 *(978-1-4424-0328-4(4),* Aladdin) Simon & Schuster Children's Publishing.
Downing, Johnette. Spooky Second Line, 1 vol. 2019. (ENG., Illus.). 32p. (J). pap. 9.95 *(978-1-4556-2505-5(1),* Pelican Publishing) Arcadia Publishing.
Dragon, Laura. Hurricane Boy, 1 vol. 2014. (ENG., Illus.). 160p. (J). (gr. 3-7). pap. 14.95 *(978-1-4556-1916-0(7),* Pelican Publishing) Arcadia Publishing.
Eldredge, Jan. Evangeline of the Bayou. Kuefler, Joseph, illus. 2018. (ENG.). 320p. (J). (gr. 3-7). 16.99 *(978-0-06-268034-1(X),* Balzer & Bray) HarperCollins Pubs.
Falter, Laury. Residue. 2013. (Residue Ser.: bk.1). 306p. pap. 12.99 *(978-0-9855110-0-5(1))* William & William Publishing.
Friedmann, Patty. Taken Away. 2010. (ENG.). 427p. (J). (gr. 6). pap. 18.95 *(978-0-9845318-2-0(3))* Tiny Stachel Pr.
Gallagher, Denise, illus. A Tip Tap Tale. 2017. (J). *(978-1-946160-09-6(1))* Univ. of Louisiana at Lafayette Pr.
Gamble, Adam & Jasper, Mark. Good Night New Orleans. Stevenson, Harvey, illus. 2012. (Good Night Our World Ser.). (ENG.). 20p. (J). (gr. k — 1). bds. 9.95 *(978-1-60219-061-0(5))* Good Night Bks.
Gerowin, Sean. Catte au Lait & the Big Hurricane. 2005. 36p. (J). 8.99 *(978-1-4116-5157-9(X))* Lulu Pr., Inc.
Gumbo Goes Downtown - Evaluation Guide: Evaluation Guide. 2006. (J). *(978-1-55942-407-3(9))* Witcher Productions.
Guzman, Lila & Guzman, Rick. Lorenzo & the Turncoat. 2006. 183p. (J). (gr. 5). per. 9.95 *(978-1-55885-471-0(1),* Piñata Books) Arte Publico Pr.
Harrison, Daisy. My Grandmother Lives in a Shotgun House, 1 vol. Henriquez, Emile, illus. 2018. (ENG.). 32p. (J). (gr. -1-3). 16.99 *(978-1-4556-2302-0(4),* Pelican Publishing) Arcadia Publishing.
Hawthorne, Rachel. One Perfect Summer: Labor of Love & Thrill Ride. 2015. (ENG.). 544p. (YA). (gr. 9). pap. 9.99 *(978-0-06-232134-3(X),* HarperTeen) HarperCollins Pubs.
Herlong, M. H. Buddy. 2013. 320p. (J). (gr. 5). pap. 8.99 *(978-0-14-242544-2(3),* Puffin Books) Penguin Young Readers Group.
Jackson, Nellie O. The Worst Day of My Life. 2008. 24p. pap. 24.95 *(978-1-60474-524-5(X))* America Star Bks.
Jacobs, Lily. The Littlest Bunny in New Orleans. Dunn, Robert, illus. 2016. (Littlest Bunny Ser.). (ENG.). 32p. (J). (gr. -1-3). 9.99 *(978-1-4926-3350-1(X),* 9781492633501, Hometown World) Sourcebooks, Inc.
Jennings, Carol E. Marshall & Satchmo. 2008. 40p. pap. 21.32 *(978-1-4363-7117-9(1))* Xlibris Corp.
Karwoski, Gail Langer. When Hurricane Katrina Hit Home. Marshall, Julia, illus. 2013. Orig. Title: When Hurricane Katrina Hit Home. (ENG.). 192p. (gr. 4-7). 29.99 *(978-1-62619-083-2(6),* History Pr., The) Arcadia Publishing.
Keaton, Kelly. A Beautiful Evil. (ENG.). (YA). (gr. 9). 2013. 320p. pap. 11.99 *(978-1-4424-0928-6(2))*2. 2012. 304p. 17.99 *(978-1-4424-0927-9(4))* Simon Pulse. (Simon Pulse).
—Darkness Becomes Her. (ENG.). (YA). (gr. 9). 2012. 320p. pap. 12.99 *(978-1-4424-0925-5(8))* 2011. 288p. 16.99 *(978-1-4424-0924-8(X))* Simon Pulse. (Simon Pulse).
—The Wicked Within. (ENG., Illus.). 288p. (YA). (gr. 9). 2014. pap. 9.99 *(978-1-4424-9316-2(X))* 2013. 17.99 *(978-1-4424-9315-5(1))* Simon Pulse. (Simon Pulse).
Kenyon, Sherrilyn. The Dark-Hunters: Infinity, Vol. 1, Vol. 1. 2013. (Dark-Hunters Ser.: 1). (ENG., Illus.). 240p. (gr. 11-17). 13.00 *(978-0-316-19053-4(5),* Yen Pr.) Yen Pr. LLC.
—Inferno: Chronicles of Nick. 2014. (Chronicles of Nick Ser.: 4). (ENG.). 464p. (YA). (gr. 7). pap. 14.99 *(978-1-250-00286-0(9),* 900079522, St. Martin's Griffin) St. Martin's Pr.
—Infinity: Chronicles of Nick. 2011. (Chronicles of Nick Ser.: 1). (ENG.). 480p. (YA). (gr. 7-18). pap. 14.00 *(978-0-312-60304-5(5),* 900064333, St. Martin's Griffin) St. Martin's Pr.
—Invincible: The Chronicles of Nick. (Chronicles of Nick Ser.: 2). (ENG.). 432p. (YA). (gr. 7). 2012. pap. 15.00 *(978-0-312-60327-4(4),* 900064304) 2011. 27.99 *(978-0-312-59906-5(4),* 900063529) St. Martin's Pr. (St. Martin's Griffin).
—Invision: Chronicles of Nick. 2017. (Chronicles of Nick Ser.: 7). (ENG.). 400p. (YA). pap. 14.99 *(978-1-250-06390-8(6),* 900143383, Wednesday Bks.) St. Martin's Pr.
Lamana, Julie T. Upside down in the Middle of Nowhere. 2015. (ENG.). 328p. (J). (gr. 4-7). pap. 7.99 *(978-1-4521-2880-1(4))* Chronicle Bks. LLC.
Larson, Hope. Compass South. 2017. (Four Points Ser.: 1). (J). lib. bdg. 24.50 *(978-0-606-39953-1(4))* Turtleback.
Larson, Kirby. Liberty. 2018. (Dogs of World War II Ser.). lib. bdg. 18.40 *(978-0-606-41133-2(X))* Turtleback.
Lee, Chris. Becoming a Sant: A Guidebook for Parents & Santa's Helpers. 2008. 48p. pap. 16.95 *(978-1-60563-449-4(2))* America Star Bks.
Littell, William Adams. Guillaume. 2008. 74p. pap. 10.00 *(978-0-8059-7757-8(0))* Dorrance Publishing Co., Inc.
Long, Loren & Bildner, Phil. Blastin' the Blues. Long, Loren, illus. 2011. (Sluggers Ser.: 5). (ENG., Illus.). 448p. (J). (gr. 3-7). pap. 8.99 *(978-1-4169-1891-2(4),* Simon & Schuster Bks. For Young Readers) Simon & Schuster Bks. For Young Readers.
Mack, Iris Marie. Mama Says, Money Doesn't Grow on Trees! 2004. (World of Dr. Mackamatix Mathematics Edutainment Book Ser.). (Illus.). 48p. (J). per. 18.99 *(978-1-4134-0891-1(5))* Xlibris Corp.
Mahin, Michael. Stalebread Charlie & the Razzy Dazzy Spasm Band. Tate, Don, illus. 2018. (ENG.). 40p. (J). (gr. -1-3). 17.99 *(978-0-547-94201-8(X),* 1517145, Clarion Bks.) HarperCollins Pubs.
Maria, Miss Yvonne. Beautiful Black Mermaids of the Bayou, 1 vol. 2009. 48p. pap. 16.95 *(978-1-60836-236-3(1))* America Star Bks.
Marsh, Carole. The Mystery on the Mighty Mississippi. 2009. (Real Kids, Real Places Ser.). (Illus.). 146p. (J). lib. bdg. 18.99 *(978-0-635-07001-2(4),* Marsh, Carole Mysteries) Gallopade International.
Miller, William. Rent Party Jazz, 1 vol. Riley-Webb, Charlotte, illus. 2005. (ENG.). 32p. (J). pap. 7.95 *(978-1-55041-972-6(2),* 3ca9646f-756c-41ec-94eb-4f013485a6b1) Fitzhenry & Whiteside, Ltd. CAN. Dist: Firefly Bks., Ltd.
—Rent Party Jazz. Riley-Webb, Charlotte, illus. (ENG.). 32p. (J). (gr. 1-5). 2013. 16.95 *(978-1-58430-025-0(6))* 2011. pap. 10.95 *(978-1-60060-344-0(0),* leelowbooks) Lee & Low Bks., Inc.
Osborne, Mary Pope. A Good Night for Ghosts. 2010. (Magic Tree House Merlin Missions Ser.: No. 14). (Illus.). 157p. (J). pap. *(978-4-8401-3411-8(1))* Fukuinkan Shoten.
—A Good Night for Ghosts. Murdocca, Sal, illus. 2011. (Magic Tree House (R) Merlin Mission Ser.: 14). 144p. (J). (gr. 2-5). 5.99 *(978-0-375-85649-5(8),* Random Hse. Bks. for Young Readers) Random Hse. Children's Bks.
Owen, Rob. Spy Boy, Cheyenne, & Ninety-Six Crayons: A "Mardi Gras" Indian's Story, 1 vol. Owen, Rob, illus. 2013. (ENG., Illus.). 32p. (J). (gr. k-3). 16.99 *(978-1-4556-1799-9(7),* Pelican Publishing) Arcadia Publishing.
Parcus, Stephanie, illus. Jupiter Storm. gif. ltd. ed. 2017. 256p. (J). (gr. 3-6). pap. 14.99 *(978-1-943169-31-3(4))* Plum Street Press.
Pardo, Juan. When the Morning Comes: A Mardi Gras Indian Story, 1 vol. Smith, Vernon, illus. 2019. (ENG.). 32p. (gr. -1-3). 19.99 *(978-1-4556-2439-3(X),* Pelican Publishing) Arcadia Publishing.
Patrick, Denise Lewis. Finding Someplace. 2016. (ENG.). 224p. (J). pap. 8.99 *(978-1-250-07982-4(9),* 900154630) Square Fish.
—Finding Someplace. 2016. (J). lib. bdg. 17.20 *(978-0-606-38560-2(6))* Turtleback.
Perelman, Helen. Tiana: The Grand Opening. Studio IBOIX Staff, illus. 2011. (Disney Princess Ser.). (ENG.). 96p. (J). (gr. 2-6). 31.36 *(978-1-59961-880-7(X),* 5180, Chapter Bks.) Spotlight.
Philbrick, Rodman. Zane & the Hurricane: a Story of Katrina. 2015. (ENG.). 192p. (J). (gr. 5-9). pap. 8.99 *(978-0-545-34239-1(2),* Blue Sky Pr., The) Scholastic, Inc.
Pogo the Clown. A Taste of Shrimp: Harley's Great Adventures. Miller, Richard D., illus. 2005. (J). 12.95 *(978-0-9755253-4-0(4))* Chilinic Pubns.
Preble, Laura. Lica's Angel. 2003. 142p. (YA). 21.95 *(978-0-595-74914-0(3));* pap. 11.95 *(978-0-595-28253-1(9))* iUniverse, Inc.
Priest, Cherie. The Agony House. O'Connor, Tara, illus. (ENG.). 272p. (gr. 7-7). 2020. (J). pap. 10.99 *(978-1-338-58217-8(8))* 2018. (YA). 18.99 *(978-0-545-93429-9(X))* Scholastic, Inc. (Levine, Arthur A. Bks.).
RH Disney. The Princess & the Frog Little Golden Book (Disney Princess & the Frog) RH Disney, illus. 2009. (Little Golden Book Ser.). (ENG., Illus.). 24p. (J). (gr. -1-2). 5.99 *(978-0-7364-2628-2(0),* Golden/Disney) Random Hse. Children's Bks.
Rhodes, Jewell Parker. Ninth Ward. 2012. (J). lib. bdg. 18.40 *(978-0-606-26158-6(3))* Turtleback.
Rowley, Julie P. The Little Purple Mardi Gras Bead, 1 vol. Paquette, John R., illus. 2016. (ENG.). 32p. pap. 9.99 *(978-1-4556-2344-0(X),* Pelican Publishing) Arcadia Publishing.
Roy, Ron. A to Z Mysteries: the Zombie Zone. Gurney, John Steven, illus. 2005. (to Z Mysteries Ser.: 26). 96p. (J). (gr. 1-4). pap. 6.99 *(978-0-375-82483-8(9),* Random Hse. Bks. for Young Readers) Random Hse. Children's Bks.
Scheffler, Stephanie. Elizabeth & the War of 1812. 2010. 292p. (YA). 28.95 *(978-1-4502-3539-6(5));* (ENG.). pap. 18.95 *(978-1-4502-3540-2(9))* iUniverse, Inc.
Shankman, Ed. The Bourbon Street Band Is Back. O'Neill, Dave, illus. 2011. (Shankman & O'Neill Ser.). (ENG.). 32p. (J). (gr. -1-3). 14.95 *(978-1-933212-79-1(9),* Commonwealth Editions) Applewood Bks.
Sharenow, Robert. My Mother the Cheerleader. 2009. (ENG.). 320p. (YA). (gr. 8). pap. 10.99 *(978-0-06-114898-9(9),* Balzer & Bray) 2007. 304p. (J). (gr. 7-18). 16.99 *(978-0-06-114896-5(2),* Geringer, Laura Book) 2007. 304p. (J). (gr. 7-18). lib. bdg. 17.89 *(978-0-06-114897-2(0),* Geringer, Laura Book) HarperCollins Pubs.
Smith, L. J. & Kevin Williamson & Julie Plec, Kevin Williamson. The Vampire Diaries: Stefan's Diaries #1: Origins No. 5. 2010. (Vampire Diaries: Stefan's Diaries: 1). (ENG.). 256p. (YA). (gr. 9-18). pap. 11.99 *(978-0-06-200393-5(3),* HarperTeen) HarperCollins Pubs.
Sobel, Sheila. Color Blind. 2016. (ENG.). 253p. (YA). 17.99 *(978-1-4405-9746-6(4),* Simon Pulse) Simon Pulse.
Stewart, Emma. The Adventures of Fillmore the Gerbil. 2008. 24p. pap. 13.50 *(978-1-60693-033-5(8),* Eloquent Bks.) Strategic Book Publishing & Rights Agency (SBPRA).
Sutton, Laurie S. The House on Spooky Street. Neely, Scott, illus. 2015. (You Choose Stories: Scooby-Doo Ser.). (ENG.). 112p. (J). (gr. 2-6). lib. bdg. 32.65 *(978-1-4342-9714-3(4),* 127040, Stone Arch Bks.) Capstone.
Tangerine, Tracey. Buddy Zooka: In the French Quarter & Beyond. 2010. (ENG.). 201p. (J). (gr. 7-12). pap. 16.00 *(978-0-9741995-8-0(3))* Chin Music Pr.
Tarshis, Lauren. I Survived Hurricane Katrina 2005. 2011. (I Survived Ser.: No. 3). lib. bdg. 14.75 *(978-0-606-23743-7(7))* Turtleback.
—I Survived Hurricane Katrina, 2005 (I Survived #3) Dawson, Scott, illus. 2011. (I Survived Ser.: 3). (ENG.). 112p. (J). (gr. 2-5). pap. 5.99 *(978-0-545-20696-9(0),* Scholastic Paperbacks) Scholastic, Inc.
Thomas, Deborah Kadiar. Cemetery Jamboree, 1 vol. Thomas, Deborah Kadiar, illus. 2016. (ENG., Illus.). 32p. (J).

M
N
O

(gr. k-5). pap. 9.95 *(978-1-4556-2239-9(7)*, Pelican Publishing) Arcadia Publishing.

Tubb, Kristin O'Donnell. The 13th Sign. 2014. (ENG.). 288p. (J). (gr. 5-9). pap. 21.99 *(978-1-250-05059-5(6)*, 900134114) Square Fish.

Uhlberg, Myron. A Storm Called Katrina, 1 vol. Bootman, Colin, illus. 2015. 40p. (J). (gr. 2-5). pap. 8.99 *(978-1-56145-887-5(2))* Peachtree Publishing Co. Inc.

—A Storm Called Katrina. 2015. lib. bdg. 19.60 *(978-0-606-37467-5(1))* Turtleback.

Watson, Renée. A Place Where Hurricanes Happen. Stickland, Shadra, illus. 2014. 40p. (J). (gr. k-4). 7.99 *(978-0-385-37668-6(5)*, Dragonfly Bks.) Random Hse. Children's Bks.

Webber, Jake. Lafitte's Black Box: Bolt Noir. 2009. 228p. 32.95 *(978-1-60594-361-9(4))*; pap. 14.95 *(978-1-60594-360-2(6))* Aeon Publishing Inc. (Lumina Pr.).

Westerfeld, Scott, et al. Nexus. 2018. (Zeroes Ser.: 3). (ENG.). 496p. (YA). (gr. 9). 19.99 *(978-1-4814-4342-5(9)*, Simon Pulse) Simon Pulse.

Woods, Brenda. Saint Louis Armstrong Beach. 2012. 160p. (J). (gr. 5). pap. 6.99 *(978-0-14-242186-4(3)*, Puffin Books) Penguin Young Readers Group.

—Saint Louis Armstrong Beach. 2012. lib. bdg. 16.00 *(978-0-606-26661-1(5))* Turtleback.

Zschock, Martha. Hello, New Orleans! 2011. (Hello Ser.). (ENG., Illus.). 16p. (J). (gr. -1-k). bds. 9.99 *(978-1-933212-63-0(2)*, Commonwealth Editions) Applewood Bks.

NEW ORLEANS (LA.)—HISTORY

Alberti, Frances C. Finding Rover. Gremillion, Barry, illus. 2006. (J). per. *(978-0-9785937-1-1(5))* Open Pages Publishing.

Bridges, Ruby. This Is Your Time. 2020. (ENG., Illus.). 64p. (J). (gr. 5). lib. bdg. 18.99 *(978-0-593-37853-3(9))*; 15.99 *(978-0-593-37852-6(0))* Random Hse. Children's Bks. (Delacorte Bks. for Young Readers).

Brown, Don. Drowned City: Hurricane Katrina & New Orleans. 2015. (ENG., Illus.). 96p. (J). (gr. 7). 18.99 *(978-0-544-15777-4(X)*, 1550232, Clarion Bks.) HarperCollins Pubs.

—Drowned City: Hurricane Katrina & New Orleans. 2017. (ENG.). (YA). (gr. 7). lib. bdg. 20.85 *(978-0-606-39819-0(8))* Turtleback.

Cohen-Janca, Irène. Ruby, Head High: Ruby Bridge's First Day of School. 2019. (ENG., Illus.). 32p. (J). (gr. 1-3). 19.99 *(978-1-56846-341-4(3)*, 18671, Creative Editions) Creative Co., The.

Coles, Robert. The Story of Ruby Bridges. 2009. 8.44 *(978-0-7848-3016-1(9)*, Everbind) Marco Bk. Co.

—The Story of Ruby Bridges. 2011. 17.00 *(978-1-61383-173-1(0))* Perfection Learning Corp.

—The Story of Ruby Bridges. Ford, George, illus. 50th anniv. ed. 2010. (ENG.). 32p. (J). (gr. -1-3). pap. 7.99 *(978-0-439-47226-5(1)*, Scholastic Paperbacks) Scholastic, Inc.

—The Story of Ruby Bridges. 2010. lib. bdg. 17.20 *(978-0-606-23189-3(7))* Turtleback.

Derosier, M. Michelle. Ruby Bridges: Get to Know the Girl Who Took a Stand for Education. 2019. (People You Should Know Ser.). (ENG., Illus.). 32p. (J). (gr. 3-6). lib. bdg. 27.99 *(978-1-5435-5527-1(6)*, 139387, Capstone Pr.) Capstone.

Epstein, Brad M. New Orleans Saints 101. 2010. (Illus.). 24p. (J). bds. *(978-1-60730-119-6(9)*, 101 Bk.) Michaelson Entertainment.

Evans, Freddi Williams. Come Sunday: A Young Reader's History of Congo Square. 2017. (J). *(978-1-946160-10-2(5))* Univ. of Louisiana at Lafayette Pr.

Everin, Gretchen. Dreaming of New Orleans: Counting down Around the Town. 2019. (Dreaming Of Ser.). (ENG., Illus.). 16p. (J). bds. 9.99 *(978-1-64194-132-7(4)*, Commonwealth Editions) Applewood Bks.

Ferut, Michael. St. Louis Cemetery No. 1. 2014. (Scariest Places on Earth Ser.). (ENG., Illus.). 24p. (J). (gr. 3-7). lib. bdg. 26.95 *(978-1-60014-997-9(9)*, Torque Bks.) Bellwether Media.

Finch, Fletcher C. Hurricane Katrina, 1 vol. 2018. (History Just Before You Were Born Ser.). (ENG.). 32p. (gr. 4-5). 28.27 *(978-1-5382-3029-9(1)*, 0c1f284c-cf5e-49a6-831e-fb296a3bb589) Stevens, Gareth Publishing LLLP.

Foran, Jill. Mardi Gras. 2003. (Celebrating Cultures Ser.). (Illus.). 24p. (J). lib. bdg. 24.45 *(978-1-59036-093-4(1))* Weigl Pubs., Inc.

Hoffman, Mary Ann. Hurricane Katrina. 2009. (Nature in the News Ser.). 32p. (gr. 3-4). 42.50 *(978-1-61514-821-9(3)*, PowerKids Pr.) Rosen Publishing Group, Inc., The.

McGee, Randel. Paper Crafts for Mardi Gras, 1 vol. 2012. (Paper Craft Fun for Holidays Ser.). (ENG., Illus.). 48p. (gr. 3-3). pap. 11.53 *(978-1-59845-334-8(3)*, 5fe996d3-ac5d-43f9-a146-3501ac646298, Enslow Elementary) Enslow Publishing, LLC.

Orr, Tamra B. Hurricane Katrina & America's Response. 2017. (Perspectives Library: Modern Perspectives Ser.). (ENG., Illus.). 32p. (J). (gr. 4-7). lib. bdg. 32.07 *(978-1-63472-859-1(9)*, 209862) Cherry Lake Publishing.

Person, Stephen. Voodoo in New Orleans. 2010. (HorrorScapes Ser.). 32p. (YA). (gr. 4-7). lib. bdg. 28.50 *(978-1-936087-99-0(5))* Bearport Publishing Co., Inc.

Rathié, Simone & Lee, Tania. Topsy Turvy History of New Orleans & Ten Tiny Turtles: 300 Years & Slowly Counting... Lee, Tania, illus. 2018. (ENG., Illus.). 35p. (J). 16.95 *(978-0-692-98877-0(7))* simoneink, llc.

Strom, Laura Layton. Shockwave: Built below Sea Level. 2007. (Shockwave: People & Communities Ser.). (ENG., Illus.). 36p. (J). (gr. 3-5). 25.00 *(978-0-531-17746-4(7)*, Children's Pr.) Scholastic Library Publishing.

Vierow, Wendy. The Capture of New Orleans: Union Fleet Takes Control of the Lower Mississippi River, 1 vol. 2004. (Headlines from History Ser.). (ENG., Illus.). 24p. (YA). (gr. 3-3). lib. bdg. 26.27 *(978-0-8239-6222-8(9)*, 775c6083-abd6-4be8-90fc-56df6867eda4) Rosen Publishing Group, Inc., The.

Zullo, Allan. Heroes of Hurricane Katrina (10 True Tales) 2015. (10 True Tales Ser.). (ENG.). 192p. (YA). (gr. 3-7). pap. 5.99 *(978-0-545-83123-9(7))* Scholastic, Inc.

NEW ORLEANS, BATTLE OF, NEW ORLEANS, LA., 1815

Weintraub, Aileen. Jean Lafitte: Pirate Hero of the War Of 1812. 2009. (Library of Pirates Ser.). 24p. (gr. 3-3). 42.50 *(978-1-60853-813-3(3)*, PowerKids Pr.) Rosen Publishing Group, Inc., The.

NEW ORLEANS, BATTLE OF, NEW ORLEANS, LA., 1815—FICTION

Evans, Freddi Williams. The Battle of New Orleans: The Drummer's Story, 1 vol. 2005. (ENG., Illus.). 32p. (gr. k-3). 16.99 *(978-1-58980-300-8(0)*, Pelican Publishing) Arcadia Publishing.

Lane, Frederick A. A Flag for Lafitte: Story of the Battle of New Orleans. Vosburgh, Leonard, illus. 2011. 192p. 42.95 *(978-1-258-06624-6(6))* Literary Licensing, LLC.

NEW TESTAMENT

see Bible—New Testament

NEW YEAR

Allard, Mario, illus. Caillou: Chinese New Year: Dragon Mask & Mosaic Stickers Included. 2018. (Playtime Ser.). (ENG.). 24p. (J). (gr. -1-1). 4.99 *(978-2-89718-498-8(1))* Caillouet, Gerry.

Appleby, Alex. Happy New Year!, 1 vol., Vol. 1. 2014. (Happy Holidays! Ser.). (ENG.). 24p. (J). (gr. k-k). 25.27 *(978-1-4339-9943-7(9)*, f4869f9b-a32c-4007-a91f-6fc2981bce54) Stevens, Gareth Publishing LLLP.

Bledsoe, Karen E. Fun Chinese New Year Crafts, 1 vol. 2014. (Kid Fun Holiday Crafts! Ser.). (ENG.). 32p. (gr. 3-4). 25.60 *(978-0-7660-6240-5(6)*, f41e9bbd-44b6-4aee-a0e6-556f7890fa15) Enslow Publishing, LLC.

Bullard, Lisa. Chelsea's Chinese New Year. Saunders, Katie, illus. 2012. (Cloverleaf Books (tm) — Holidays & Special Days Ser.). 24p. (J). (gr. k-2). (ENG.). pap. 8.99 *(978-0-7613-8579-0(7)*, 6d2e5b1b-e9b4-4293-9afa-0c34ee933125); pap. 39.62 *(978-0-7613-9247-7(5))* Lerner Publishing Group. (Millbrook Pr.).

Carr, Aaron. Chinese New Year. 2016. (Illus.). 24p. (J). *(978-1-5105-1002-9(8))* Lightbox, The.

Chinese New Year's Dragon. (J). 48.95 *(978-0-8136-2242-2(5))* Modern Curriculum Pr.

Coleman, Clara O. Happy New Year!, 1 vol. 2016. (Celebrations Ser.). (ENG.). 24p. (J). (gr. 1-1). pap. 9.25 *(978-1-4994-2671-7(2)*, 1334b96c-2d12-4dd0-aa93-e2534b5fdffa, PowerKids Pr.) Rosen Publishing Group, Inc., The.

Compestine, Ying Chang. D Is for Dragon Dance. Xuan, YongSheng, illus. 2018. 32p. (J). (gr. -1-3). 18.99 *(978-0-8234-4029-0(X))* Holiday Hse., Inc.

DK. Baby's First Chinese New Year. 2018. (Baby's First Holidays Ser.). (Illus.). 14p. (J). (— 1). bds. 6.99 *(978-1-4654-8401-7(9)*, DK Children) Dorling Kindersley Publishing, Inc.

Gleason, Carrie. Chinese New Year, 1 vol. 2008. (Celebrations in My World Ser.). (ENG., Illus.). 32p. (J). (gr. k-3). pap. *(978-0-7787-4298-2(9))*; lib. bdg. *(978-0-7787-4280-7(6))* Crabtree Publishing Co.

Grack, Rachel. Chinese New Year. 2017. (Celebrating Holidays Ser.). (ENG., Illus.). 24p. (J). (gr. k-3). pap. 7.99 *(978-1-61891-270-1(4)*, 12059, Blastoff! Readers) Bellwether Media.

Jalali, Yassaman. Celebrating Norouz (Persian New Year) Zamanian, Marjan, illus. 2003. 28p. (J). (gr. -1-6). pap. 12.99 *(978-0-9728020-0-0(2))* Saman Publishing.

Johnson, Robin. New Year Celebrations in Different Places. (Illus.). 24p. (J). 2018. *(978-1-4271-1966-7(X))* 2017. (gr. 2-2). *(978-0-7787-3655-4(5))* 2017. (gr. 2-2). pap. *(978-0-7787-3664-6(4))* Crabtree Publishing Co.

Jones, Grace. Chinese New Year. 2019. (Festivals Around the World Ser.). (ENG.). 24p. (J). (gr. k-2). pap. 9.99 *(978-1-78637-819-4(1))* BookLife Publishing Ltd. GBR. Dist: Independent Pubs. Group.

Kaplan, Leslie C. Chinese New Year. 2009. (Library of Holidays Ser.). 24p. (gr. 2-3). 42.50 *(978-1-60853-707-5(2)*, PowerKids Pr.) Rosen Publishing Group, Inc., The.

Lee, Jen Sookfong. The Animals of Chinese New Year / 中国农历新年动物生肖, 1 vol. Wong, Kileasa Che Wan, tr. 2019. (ENG & CHI., Illus.). 28p. (J). (gr. -1 — 1). bds. 9.95 *(978-1-4598-1902-3(0))* Orca Bk. Pubs. USA.

Lee, Michelle. Chinese New Year. 2016. (World's Greatest Celebrations Ser.). (ENG., Illus.). 32p. (gr. 3-8). 27.99 *(978-1-62920-566-3(4))* Scobre Pr. Corp.

Linde, Barbara. Celebrating the Chinese New Year, 1 vol. 2019. (History of Our Holidays Ser.). (ENG.). 24p. (gr. 1-2). 24.27 *(978-1-5382-3864-6(0)*, b761220b-9fff-4169-9476-4b596b43d210) Stevens, Gareth Publishing LLLP.

McGee, Randel. Celebrate Chinese New Year with Paper Crafts, 1 vol. 2014. (Celebrate Holidays with Paper Crafts Ser.). (ENG.). 48p. (gr. 3-4). 26.93 *(978-0-7660-6350-1(X)*, f7b1992c-23e1-4c92-a9f7-53ef7ac0ddc0) Enslow Publishing, LLC.

McNeil, Niki, et al. HOCPP1022 New Years. 2004. spiral bd. 17.50 *(978-1-60308-022-4(8))* In the Hands of a Child.

Mercer, Abbie. Happy New Year. (Holiday Fun Ser.). 24p. (gr. 2-3). 2009. 42.50 *(978-1-61513-376-5(3)*, PowerKids Pr.) 2007. (ENG., Illus.). (J). lib. bdg. 26.27 *(978-1-4042-3808-4(5)*, a1afa796-119a-4fe6-86bb-4f6b2c83c583) Rosen Publishing Group, Inc., The.

MoonRattles. Heritage Holiday Activity Guide: Chinese New Year 2007, 1 vol. 2006. (Illus.). 52p. (J). spiral bd. *(978-0-9790920-0-8(0))* MoonRattles.

Morrill, Ann. Religious New Year's Celebrations. 2009. (ENG., Illus.). 112p. (gr. 5-8). 40.00 *(978-1-60413-094-2(6)*, P163108, Facts On File) Infobase Holdings, Inc.

National Geographic Learning. World Windows 3 (Social Studies): New Year Celebrations: Content Literacy, Nonfiction Reading, Language & Literacy. 2011. (World Windows Ser.). (ENG., Illus.). 16p. (J). stu. ed. 10.95 *(978-1-133-49269-6(X))* Cengage Heinle.

Peppas, Lynn. New Year's Day. 2010. (ENG., Illus.). 32p. (J). *(978-0-7787-4762-8(X))*; pap. *(978-0-7787-4780-2(8))* Crabtree Publishing Co.

Peter, Val J., creator. Reflections for a Happy New Year: From the Kids at Boys Town. 2004. 121p. pap. 5.95 *(978-1-889322-40-7(7)*, 19-016) Boys Town Pr.

Pettiford, Rebecca. Chinese New Year. 2015. (Illus.). 24p. (J). (gr. k-3). lib. bdg. *(978-1-62031-184-4(4)*, Bullfrog Bks.) Jump! Inc.

Richardson, Betsy. Marking the Religious New Year, Vol. 10. 2018. (Celebrating Holidays & Festivals Around the World Ser.). (Illus.). 96p. (J). (gr. 7). lib. bdg. 34.60 *(978-1-4222-4151-6(3))* Mason Crest.

—Ringing in the Western & Chinese New Year, Vol. 10. 2018. (Celebrating Holidays & Festivals Around the World Ser.). (Illus.). 112p. (J). (gr. 7). lib. bdg. 34.60 *(978-1-4222-4153-0(X))* Mason Crest.

Sanmu, Tang. Celebrating the Chinese New Year. Ying, Wu, tr. Tang, Sanmu, illus. 2010. 32p. (gr. -1-3). pap. 4.95 *(978-1-60220-958-9(8))* Shanghai Pr.

Schuh, Mari. Crayola (r) Chinese New Year Colors. 2018. (Crayola (r) Holiday Colors Ser.). (ENG., Illus.). 32p. (J). (gr. -1-3). 29.32 *(978-1-5415-1091-3(7)*, 06f1cdc0-2f92-46c8-9303-1989feadc6f4, Lerner Pubns.) Lerner Publishing Group.

Sebra, Richard. It's Chinese New Year! 2016. (Bumba Books (r) — It's a Holiday! Ser.). (ENG., Illus.). 24p. (J). (gr. -1-1). 26.65 *(978-1-5124-1425-7(5)*, 237470de-fe3e-4800-8131-f70fccbec532, Lerner Pubns.) Lerner Publishing Group.

—It's New Year's Day! 2017. (Bumba Books (r) — It's a Holiday! Ser.). (ENG., Illus.). 24p. (J). (gr. -1-1). E-Book 4.99 *(978-1-5124-3702-7(6)*, 9781512437027); E-Book 39.99 *(978-1-5124-2744-8(6))*; E-Book 39.99 *(978-1-5124-3701-0(8)*, 9781512437010) Lerner Publishing Group. (Lerner Pubns.).

Trumbore, Cindy. New Year's Around the World. 2012. (ENG., Illus.). 48p. (J). (gr. 2-3). pap. 9.50 *(978-0-7652-0885-9(7)*, Modern Curriculum Pr.) Savvas Learning Co.

Walker, Sylvia. Happy New Year Around the World. 2012. (Dover Holiday Coloring Book Ser.). (ENG., Illus.). 32p. (J). (gr. -1-3). pap. 3.99 *(978-0-486-48988-9(4)*, 489884) Dover Pubns., Inc.

Williams, Colleen Madonna Flood. My Adventure on New Year's Day. 2006. 44p. (J). 8.99 *(978-1-59092-554-6(8))* Blue Forge Pr.

World Book, Inc. Staff, contrib. by. New Year's Celebrations. 2009. (Illus.). 46p. (J). *(978-0-7166-5040-9(1))* World Bk., Inc.

Yasuda, Anita. Chinese New Year. 2011. (J). (gr. 3-5). pap. 12.95 *(978-1-61690-683-2(9)*, AV2 by Weigl); (Illus.). 24p. (YA). (gr. 2-5). 27.13 *(978-1-61690-677-1(4))* Weigl Pubs., Inc.

Zocchi, Judy. Number 1 What Grows in the Sun? Wallis, Rebecca, illus. 2005. (Holiday Happenings Ser.). 32p. (J). per. 10.95 *(978-1-59646-273-1(6))* Dingles & Co.

—On Chinese New Year. Wallis, Rebecca, illus. 2005. (Holiday Happenings Ser.). 32p. (J). per. 10.95 *(978-1-59646-189-5(6))* Dingles & Co.

—On Chinese New Year/el Año Nuevo Chino. Wallis, Rebecca, illus. 2005. (Holiday Happenings Ser.).Tr. of Año Nuevo Chino. (ENG & SPA.). 32p. (J). per. 10.95 *(978-1-59646-191-8(8))* Dingles & Co.

—On New Year's Eve. Wallis, Rebecca, illus. 2005. (Holiday Happenings Ser.). 32p. (J). pap. 10.95 *(978-1-59646-216-8(7))*; lib. bdg. 21.65 *(978-1-891997-51-8(3))*; per. 10.95 *(978-1-59646-217-5(5))* Dingles & Co.

—On New Year's Eve/la Nochevieja. Wallis, Rebecca, illus. 2005. (Holiday Happenings Ser.).Tr. of Nochevieja. (ENG & SPA.). 32p. (J). pap. 10.95 *(978-1-59646-218-2(3))*; lib. bdg. 21.65 *(978-1-891997-52-5(1))*; per. 10.95 *(978-1-59646-219-9(1))* Dingles & Co.

NEW YEAR—FICTION

Bunting, Eve. Frog & Friends Celebrate Thanksgiving, Christmas, & New Year's Eve. Masse, Josée, illus. 2015. (I AM a READER!: Frog & Friends Ser.). (ENG.). 40p. (J). (gr. 1-2). 9.99 *(978-1-58536-897-6(0)*, 203949) Sleeping Bear Pr.

Charles, Tami. Freedom Soup. Alcántara, Jacqueline, illus. 2019. (ENG.). 32p. (J). (gr. k-4). 17.99 *(978-0-7636-8977-3(7))* Candlewick Pr.

Chen, Yong. A Gift. 2011. (ENG.). 32p. (J). (gr. k-2). pap. 9.99 *(978-1-59078-898-1(2)*, Astra Young Readers) Astra Publishing Hse.

Compestine, Ying Chang. The Runaway Wok: A Chinese New Year Tale. Serra, Sebastia, illus. 2011. 32p. (J). (gr. 1-3). 17.99 *(978-0-525-42068-2(1)*, Dutton Books for Young Readers) Penguin Young Readers Group.

Crompton, Lee. 12 Months. 2006. 230p. pap. 9.14 *(978-1-4116-2196-1(4))* Lulu Pr., Inc.

Di Luzio-Poitras, Linda & Poitras, Bruno. Kitchi's New Year's Resolution. 2011. 44p. (gr. -1). pap. 16.59 *(978-1-4520-2152-2(X))* AuthorHouse.

Downing, Johnette. Mademoiselle Grands Doigts: A Cajun New Year's Eve Tale, 1 vol. Stanley, Heather, illus. 2018. (ENG.). 32p. (gr. -1-3). 16.99 *(978-1-4556-2393-8(8)*, Pelican Publishing) Arcadia Publishing.

England, Nora. The Witches of Dorkdom. 2013. 180p. pap. 9.95 *(978-0-9676344-4-9(X))* Penury Pr.

Erickson, John. The Case of the Three Rings. Holmes, Gerald L., illus. 2014. 124p. (J). pap. *(978-1-59188-164-3(1))* Maverick Bks., Inc.

Flor Ada, Alma. Celebra el Ano Nuevo Chino con la Familia Fong. 2006. (Cuentos para Celebrar / Stories to Celebrate Ser.). (Illus.). 30p. (gr. k-6). per. 11.95 *(978-1-59820-114-7(X)*, Alfaguara) Santillana USA Publishing Co., Inc.

—Celebrate Chinese New Year with the Fong Family. Castro, Mima, illus. 2006. (Cuentos para Celebrar / Stories to Celebrate Ser.). 30p. (gr. k-6). per. 11.95 *(978-1-59820-126-0(3))* Santillana USA Publishing Co., Inc.

Friedman, Laurie. Happy New Year, Mallory! Kalis, Jennifer, illus. 2010. (Mallory Ser.: 12). (ENG.). 176p. (J). (gr. 2-5). pap. 7.99 *(978-0-7613-3947-2(7)*, c930191f-8192-4d65-a9fd-492ff472642f, Darby Creek) Lerner Publishing Group.

Haugaard, Kay. The Day the Dragon Danced, 1 vol. Barritt, Carolyn Reed, illus. 2006. (ENG.). 32p. (J). (gr. 2-4). 17.95 *(978-1-885008-30-5(9)*, leelowshens, Shen's Bks.) Lee & Low Bks., Inc.

Hill, Eric. Happy New Year, Spot! 2016. (Spot Ser.). (ENG., Illus.). 10p. (J). (-k). bds. 6.99 *(978-0-14-137009-5(2)*, Warne) Penguin Young Readers Group.

Katz, Karen. My First Chinese New Year. Katz, Karen, illus. 2012. (My First Holiday Ser.). (ENG., Illus.). 32p. (J). (gr. -1-k). 6.99 *(978-1-250-01868-7(4)*, 900087705) Square Fish.

Lee, Vickie. Ruby's Chinese New Year. Chou, Joey, illus. 2017. (ENG.). 40p. (J). 17.99 *(978-1-250-13338-0(6)*, 900177279, Holt, Henry & Co. Bks. For Young Readers) Holt, Henry & Co.

Li-Qiong, Yu. A New Year's Reunion: A Chinese Story. Cheng-Liang, Zhu, illus. 2013. (ENG.). 40p. (J). (gr. -1-2). 7.99 *(978-0-7636-6748-1(X))* Candlewick Pr.

Lin, Grace. Bringing in the New Year. (Illus.). (J). 2013. 28p. (— 1). bds. 7.99 *(978-0-385-75365-4(9)*, Knopf Bks. for Young Readers) 2010. 34p. (gr. -1-2). pap. 8.99 *(978-0-375-86605-0(1)*, Dragonfly Bks.) 2008. 34p. (gr. -1-2). 18.99 *(978-0-375-83745-6(0)*, Knopf Bks. for Young Readers) Random Hse. Children's Bks.

—The Year of the Dog. 2007. (Pacy Lin Novel Ser.: 1). (ENG., Illus.). 160p. (J). (gr. 3-7). per. 8.99 *(978-0-316-06002-8(X))* Little, Brown Bks. for Young Readers.

Lo, Rich. New Year. 2016. (ENG., Illus.). 40p. (J). (gr. -1-k). 16.99 *(978-1-5107-0723-8(9)*, Sky Pony Pr.) Skyhorse Publishing Co., Inc.

Mcdonald, Megan. Happy New Year, Julie, Bk. 3. McAliley, Susan & Hunt, Robert, illus. 2007. (American Girl Ser.). (ENG.). 88p. (J). (gr. 3-7). 12.95 *(978-1-59369-292-6(7))* American Girl Publishing, Inc.

Miller, Pat. Squirrel's New Year's Resolution. Ember, Kathi, illus. 2012. (J). 34.28 *(978-1-61913-135-4(8))* Weigl Pubs., Inc.

—Squirrel's New Year's Resolution. Ember, Kathi, illus. 2017. (ENG.). 32p. (J). (gr. -1-3). pap. 8.99 *(978-0-8075-7592-5(5)*, 807575925) Whitman, Albert & Co.

Mitsui Brown, Janet, illus. Oshogatsu with Obaachan. 2005. (J). *(978-1-879965-24-9(0))* Polychrome Publishing Corp.

Neely, Kirk H. Santa Almost Got Caught: Stories for Thanksgiving, Christmas, & the New Year. Cash, Emory, illus. 2011. 152p. pap. 14.99 *(978-1-4575-0477-8(4))* Dog Ear Publishing, LLC.

Night, P. J. The House Next Door. 2013. (Creepover Ser.: 16). lib. bdg. 17.20 *(978-0-606-32323-9(6))* Turtleback.

—Your Worst Nightmare. 2013. (Creepover Ser.: 17). lib. bdg. 17.20 *(978-0-606-32324-6(4))* Turtleback.

Piernas-Davenport, Gail. Shante Keys & the New Year's Peas. Eldridge, Marion, illus. 2017. (ENG.). 32p. (J). (gr. -1-3). pap. 8.99 *(978-0-8075-7331-0(0)*, 807573310) Whitman, Albert & Co.

Rolleston-Cummins, Toni. The Seven Stars of Matariki. Slade-Robinson, Nikki, illus. 2009. (ENG.). 28p. pap. 12.00 *(978-1-86969-327-5(2)*, 4346) Huia Pubs. NZL. Dist: Univ. of Hawaii Pr.

Roy, Ron. Calendar Mysteries #13: New Year's Eve Thieves. Gurney, John Steven, illus. 2014. (Calendar Mysteries Ser.: 13). 80p. (J). (gr. 1-4). 5.99 *(978-0-385-37171-1(3)*, Random Hse. Bks. for Young Readers) Random Hse. Children's Bks.

Roy, Ronald. New Year's Eve Thieves. 2014. (Calendar Mysteries Ser.: 13). lib. bdg. 14.75 *(978-0-606-36020-3(4))* Turtleback.

Roza, Greg. Happy New Year!, 1 vol. 2006. (Neighborhood Readers Ser.). (ENG., Illus.). 16p. (gr. 1-2). pap. 6.50 *(978-1-4042-7026-8(4)*, 8687ac4d-c67d-467d-9fa8-bc57916e13bb, Rosen Classroom) Rosen Publishing Group, Inc., The.

Ruelle, Karen Gray. Just in Time for New Year's! 2004. (ENG., Illus.). 32p. (J). tchr. ed. 14.95 *(978-0-8234-1841-1(3))* Holiday Hse., Inc.

Shields, Carrie. Sweet Dreams. 2012. 32p. pap. 19.99 *(978-1-4772-9321-8(3))* AuthorHouse.

Stuart, Carrie. Chinese New Year, 1 vol. 2006. (Neighborhood Readers Ser.). (ENG.). 12p. (gr. k-1). pap. 5.90 *(978-1-4042-6461-8(2)*, 1c3397a3-2927-432e-96c5-ee9af0868bca, Rosen Classroom) Rosen Publishing Group, Inc., The.

Thong, Roseanne Greenfield. The Wishing Tree, 1 vol. McLennan, Connie, illus. 2006. (ENG.). 32p. (J). (gr. k-3). 16.95 *(978-1-885008-26-8(0)*, c82554ab-4650-4b7f-b9af-6b4cf0912984, Shen's Bks.) Lee & Low Bks., Inc.

Tran, Quoc. The Tet Pole/Su Tich Cay Neu Ngay Tet: The Story of Tet Festival. Smith, William, tr. from VIE. Nguyen, Bich, illus. 2006. (ENG & VIE.). 32p. (J). (gr. 1-4). 16.95 *(978-0-9701654-5-9(5))* East West Discovery Pr.

Van Draanen, Wendelin. Sammy Keyes & the Curse of Moustache Mary. 2008. (Sammy Keyes Ser.: Bk. 5). (J). 59.99 *(978-1-60640-638-0(8))* Findaway World, LLC.

Wayland, April Halprin. New Year at the Pier: A Rosh Hashanah Story. Jorisch, Stéphane, illus. 2009. 352p. (J). *(978-0-8037-3110-3(8)*, Dial) Penguin Publishing Group.

Yep, Laurence. When the Circus Came to Town. Wang, Suling, illus. 2004. 112p. (J). (gr. 3-5). 13.65 *(978-0-7569-2969-5(5))* Perfection Learning Corp.

Yim, Natasha. Goldy Luck & the Three Pandas. Zong, Grace, illus. 32p. (J). (gr. -1-3). 2015. (ENG.). pap. 7.95 *(978-1-58089-653-5(7))* 2014. lib. bdg. 17.99 *(978-1-58089-652-8(9))* Charlesbridge Publishing, Inc.

NEW YORK (N.Y.)

Ball, Jacqueline A. Blizzard! The 1888 Whiteout. 2005. (X-Treme Disasters That Changed America Ser.). (Illus.). 32p. (J). (gr. 2-5). lib. bdg. 25.27 *(978-1-59716-006-3(7))* Bearport Publishing Co., Inc.

Ball, Jacqueline A. & Behrens, Kristen. Nueva York (New York), 1 vol. 2003. (World Almanac(r) Biblioteca de Los Estados (World Almanac(r) Library of the States) Ser.). (SPA., Illus.). 48p. (gr. 4-6). pap. 15.05 *(978-0-8368-5553-1(1)*, 35cd6582-5039-44ea-857b-3d18206a1889, Gareth Stevens Learning Library) Stevens, Gareth Publishing LLLP.

De Capua, Sarah. Nueva York. 2004. (Rookie Readers Spanish Ser.). 19.50 *(978-0-516-25109-7(0)*, Watts, Franklin) Scholastic Library Publishing.

—Nueva York: New York. 2005. (Rookie Espanol: Geografia Ser.). (SPA., Illus.). 32p. (J). (gr. k-2). pap. 5.95

(978-0-516-25515-6(0), Children's Pr.) Scholastic Library Publishing.

Eldridge, Alison & Eldridge, Stephen. The Statue of Liberty: An American Symbol, 1 vol. 2012. (All about American Symbols Ser.). (ENG.). 24p. (gr. -1-1). 25.27 (978-0-7660-4061-8(5), 4fcc892a-fb93-4d2e-bf2b-d218cf8205b1, Enslow Publishing) Enslow Publishing, LLC.

Evans, Colin. New York Police Department. 2011. (ENG., Illus.). 120p. (gr. 6-12). 35.00 (978-1-60413-614-2(6), P189867, Facts On File) Infobase Holdings, Inc.

Garrington, Sally. New York. 2006. (ENG., Illus.). 61p. (gr. 5-8). lib. bdg. 30.00 (978-0-7910-8853-1(7), P119689, Facts On File) Infobase Holdings, Inc.

Gerstein, Mordicai. The Man Who Walked Between the Towers. 2007. (J). 18.40 (978-1-4177-7491-3(6)) Turtleback.

Grabowski, John F. Bobby Flay. 2012. (J). (978-1-61900-010-0(5)); pap. (978-1-61900-011-7(3)) Eldorado Ink.

Gutman, Anne. Lisa a New York. (FRE.). pap. 17.95 (978-2-01-224058-2(5)) Hachette Groupe Livre FRA. Dist: Distribooks, Inc.

Halpern, Monica. Three Immigrant Communities: New York City In 1900: Text Pairs. 2008. (Bridges/Navigators Ser.). (J). (gr. 3). 89.00 (978-1-4108-8376-6(0)) Benchmark Education Co.

Heinrichs, Ann. New York. Kania, Matt, illus. 2017. (U. S. A. Travel Guides). (ENG.). 40p. (J). (gr. 2-5). lib. bdg. 38.50 (978-1-5038-1972-6(8), 211577) Child's World, Inc, The.

Hicer, Nancy. Maps & New York City, 1 vol. 2011. (My Community Ser.). (ENG.). 12p. (gr. 2-2). pap. 6.95 (978-1-4488-5732-6(5), 9a11f075-0ce3-4587-9ceb-882143a5d414) Rosen Publishing Group, Inc., The.

—New York City's Five Boroughs, 1 vol. 2011. (My Community Ser.). (ENG.). 12p. (gr. 2-2). pap. 6.95 (978-1-4488-5730-2(9), 1a09c7ca-af43-4a54-a4af-cdbb0e163e3f) Rosen Publishing Group, Inc., The.

Jakobsen, Kathy. My New York. Jakobsen, Kathy, illus. anniv. rev. ed. 2005. (Illus.). 54p. (J). (gr. k-4). 19.00 (978-0-7567-8588-8(X)) DIANE Publishing Co.

—My New York. anniv. ed. 2003. (ENG., Illus.). 48p. (J). (gr. -1-3). 20.99 (978-0-316-92711-6(2)) Little, Brown Bks. for Young Readers.

Johnson, Stephen T. & Johnson, Stephen. City by Numbers. 2003. (gr. k-3). lib. bdg. 18.40 (978-0-613-67534-5(7)) Turtleback.

Kavanagh, James & Waterford Press Staff. Pennsylvania Birds: A Folding Pocket Guide to Familiar Species in the Metropolitan Area. Leung, Raymond, illus. 2017. (Wildlife & Nature Identification Ser.). (ENG.). 12p. 7.95 (978-1-58355-012-0(7)) Waterford Pr., Inc.

Kenney, Karen Latchana. David Karp: The Mastermind Behind Tumblr. 2015. (Gateway Biographies Ser.). (ENG., Illus.). 48p. (J). (gr. 4-8). E-Book 46.65 (978-1-4677-5975-5(9), 9781467759755, Lerner Digital) Lerner Publishing Group.

Ketchum, Ron, illus. Rochestrivia: 2,000 Amazing questions & answers all about Rochester NY, it's people & surrounding Towns. l.t. ed. 2005. 250p. per. 19.95 (978-0-930249-01-4(1)) LL Cameron Group, LLC.

Kirkpatrick, Robert. Bob Cousy. 2009. (Basketball Hall of Famers Ser.). 112p. (gr. 5-8). 63.90 (978-1-61511-531-0(5), Rosen Reference) Rosen Publishing Group, Inc., The.

Markovics, Joyce L. New York City. 2017. (Citified! Ser.). (ENG., Illus.). 24p. (J). (gr. k-3). 17.95 (978-1-68402-230-4(4)) Bearport Publishing Co., Inc.

Mattern, Joanne. New York City, 1 vol. 2007. (Cities Set 2 Ser.). (Illus.). 32p. (gr. -1-3). 27.07 (978-1-59679-719-2(3), Checkerboard Library) ABDO Publishing Co.

Melmed, Laura Krauss. New York, New York! The Big Apple from a to Z. Lessac, Frane, illus. 2008. (ENG.). 48p. (J). (gr. 1-6). pap. 8.99 (978-0-06-054877-3(0), HarperCollins) HarperCollins Pubs.

Melmoth, Jonathan. See Inside New York. 2017. (See Inside Board Bks.). (ENG.). 16p. 14.99 (978-0-7945-4021-0(X), Usborne) EDC Publishing.

Munro, Roxie. The Inside-Outside Book of New York City. Munro, Roxie, illus. 2005. (Illus.). 44p. (J). (gr. 4-8). reprint ed. 16.00 (978-0-7567-9455-2(2)) DIANE Publishing Co.

Neumann, Dietrich. Joe & the Skyscraper: The Empire State Building in New York City. Heritage, Anne, tr. 2005. (GER., Illus.). 28p. (J). (gr. 4-8). 17.00 (978-0-7567-9380-7(7)) DIANE Publishing Co.

Obregón, José María. New York / Nueva York. 2009. (Bilingual Library of the United States of America Ser.). (ENG & SPA.). 32p. (gr. 2-2). 47.90 (978-1-60853-376-3(X), Editorial Buenas Letras) Rosen Publishing Group, Inc., The.

O'Dell, Kathryn. Bright Lights on Broadway, 1 vol. 2014. (ENG., Illus.). 28p. (J). pap., E-Book 9.50 (978-1-107-65022-0(4)) Cambridge Univ. Pr.

Paradis, Anne. New York Monsters: A Search-And-Find Book. Danis Drouot, Lucile, illus. 2017. (ENG.). 22p. (J). bds. 9.99 (978-2-924734-02-5(9)) City Monsters Bks. CAN. Dist: Publishers Group West (PGW).

Puck. New York Baby: A Fun & Engaging Book for Babies & Toddlers That Explores NYC, the Big Apple, with Delightful Illustrations. Incudes Activities & Reading Tips. Great Gift. Lemay, Violet, illus. 2012. (Local Baby Bks.). (ENG.). 22p. (J). (gr. k — 1). bds. 9.99 (978-0-9838121-4-2(4), 801214) Duo Pr. LLC.

—123 New York: A Cool Counting Book. 2008. (Cool Counting Bks.). (ENG., Illus.). 22p. (J). (gr. -1 — 1). bds. 8.99 (978-0-9796213-0-7(5), 802130) Duo Pr. LLC.

Randall, Marisa. The Geographic Features of New York City, 1 vol. 2011. (My Community Ser.). (ENG.). 12p. (gr. 2-2). pap. 6.95 (978-1-4488-5733-3(3), ee1120a5-af23-4cfd-9c9e-c26d4688dcf6) Rosen Publishing Group, Inc., The.

Rauf, Don. Bobby Flay, 1 vol. 2015. (Celebrity Chefs Ser.). (ENG., Illus.). 128p. (gr. 7-8). 38.93 (978-0-7660-7172-8(3), dd790b63-823a-4eb4-9117-da9d49f8b1f2) Enslow Publishing, LLC.

Rochester, Boys & Girls Clubs of. N Is for New York: Written by Kids for Kids. 2011. (See-My-State Alphabet Book Ser.). (ENG., Illus.). 32p. (J). (gr. -1-3). 13.95 (978-0-88240-777-7(5), West Winds Pr.) West Margin Pr.

Romanek, Trudee. Life in a Commercial City, 1 vol. 2010. (Learn about Urban Life Ser.). (ENG., Illus.). 32p. (J). (gr. 4-9). pap. (978-0-7787-7401-3(5)); lib. bdg. (978-0-7787-7391-7(4)) Crabtree Publishing Co.

Rubbino, Salvatore. A Walk in New York. Rubbino, Salvatore, illus. 2017. (ENG., Illus.). 40p. (J). (gr. -1-3). 8.99 (978-0-7636-9510-1(6)) Candlewick Pr.

Sasek, Miroslav. This Is New York. 2003. (This Is ... Ser.). (ENG., Illus.). 64p. (J). (gr. 2-12). 17.95 (978-0-7893-0884-9(3)) Universe Publishing.

Tan, Richard. The Bridges & Tunnels of New York City, 1 vol. 2011. (My Community Ser.). (ENG., Illus.). 12p. (gr. 2-2). pap. 6.95 (978-1-4488-5717-3(1), eadfb852-7d71-42eb-8d5d-e46d36f2c213, Rosen Classroom) Rosen Publishing Group, Inc., The.

Von La Valette, Desiree, ed. Cool Shops New York. 2005. (ENG, SPA, FRE, ITA & GER., Illus.). 135p. pap., pap. 16.95 (978-3-8327-9021-9(7)) teNeues Publishing Co.

Wade, Angela. New York City. 2006. (Illus.). 8p. (J). pap. (978-0-439-74035-7(5)) Scholastic, Inc.

Walsh, Francis. New York City, 1 vol. 2003. (Great Cities of the World Ser.). (ENG., Illus.). 48p. (gr. 5-8). lib. bdg. 33.67 (978-0-8368-5025-3(4), 40521900-641f-41ca-b1e1-aad82fe9b6ce, Gareth Stevens Secondary Library) Stevens, Gareth Publishing LLLP.

NEW YORK (N.Y.)—ANTIQUITIES

Goodman, Susan. On This Spot: An Expedition Back Through Time. Christiansen, Lee, illus. 2004. (ENG.). 32p. (J). (gr. k-5). 17.99 (978-0-688-16913-8(9), Greenwillow Bks.) HarperCollins Pubs.

Murphy, Jim. The Giant & How He Humbugged America. 2012. (ENG.). 112p. (J). (gr. 4-7). 20.99 (978-0-439-69184-0(2), Scholastic Pr.) Scholastic, Inc.

Reis, Ronald A. The Empire State Building. 2009. (Building America Ser.). (Illus.). 144p. (gr. 5-8). 35.00 (978-1-60413-045-4(8), Facts On File) Infobase Holdings, Inc.

Shea, Therese M. The African Burial Ground, 1 vol. 2016. (Hidden History Ser.). (ENG., Illus.). 32p. (J). (gr. 4-5). pap. 11.50 (978-1-4824-5787-2(3), 819cc515-201f-4a11-9ab1-b6c2dbbb160a) Stevens, Gareth Publishing LLLP.

NEW YORK (N.Y.)—BRIDGES

Stine, Megan. Where Is the Brooklyn Bridge? 2016. (Where Is... ? Ser.). lib. bdg. 16.00 (978-0-606-38411-7(1)) Turtleback.

NEW YORK (N.Y.)—DESCRIPTION AND TRAVEL

Adams, Jennifer. My Little Cities: New York: (Travel Books for Toddlers, City Board Books) Pizzoli, Greg, illus. 2017. (My Little Cities Ser.). (ENG.). 22p. (J). (gr. -1-k). bds. 9.99 (978-1-4521-5388-9(4)) Chronicle Bks. LLC.

Ayo's Awesome Adventures in New York City: The Big Apple. 2018. (J). (978-0-7166-3642-7(5)) World Bk., Inc.

Banting, Erinn. Empire State Building. 2007. (Structural Wonders Ser.). (Illus.). 32p. (J). (gr. 4-7). lib. bdg. 26.00 (978-1-59036-721-6(9)); per. 9.95 (978-1-59036-722-3(7)) Weigl Pubs., Inc.

Blake, Kevin. Grand Central Terminal. 2018. (American Places: from Vision to Reality Ser.). (ENG.). 32p. (J). (gr. 2-7). lib. bdg. 19.95 (978-1-68402-436-0(6)) Bearport Publishing Co., Inc.

Boehm Jerome, Kate. Buffalo, NY: Cool Stuff Every Kid Should Know. 2010. (Arcadia Kids Ser.). (ENG., Illus.). 48p. (J). (gr. 3-6). pap. 11.99 (978-1-4396-0069-6(4)) Arcadia Publishing.

Bolt Simons, Lisa M. Niagara Falls. 2018. (Natural Wonders of the World Ser.). (ENG., Illus.). 32p. (J). (gr. 3-5). pap. 9.95 (978-1-63517-588-2(7), 1635175887); lib. bdg. 31.35 (978-1-63517-516-5(X), 163517516X) North Star Editions. (Focus Readers).

Britton, Tamara L. The Empire State Building. 2005. (Symbols, Landmarks, & Monuments Set 3 Ser.: Set III). (Illus.). 32p. (gr. k-6). 27.07 (978-1-59197-834-3(3), Checkerboard Library) ABDO Publishing Co.

Bullard, Lisa. The Empire State Building. 2009. (Lightning Bolt Books (r) — Famous Places Ser.). (ENG., Illus.). 32p. (J). (gr. 1-3). 30.65 (978-0-8225-9404-8(8), 8c2ca64f-d960-4383-871a-b5472e0846ea, Lerner Pubns.) Lerner Publishing Group.

Cochran, Josh. Inside & Out: New York. Cochran, Josh, illus. 2014. (ENG., Illus.). 16p. (J). (gr. 2-5). 17.99 (978-0-7636-7520-2(2), Big Picture Press) Candlewick Pr.

Cordier, Claire. Candy Apple. 2009. (JPN & ENG.). 32p. pap. 19.50 (978-0-557-08498-2(9)) Lulu Pr., Inc.

—Candy Apple; Dolce Mela. 2009. 32p. pap. 19.50 (978-0-557-08531-6(4)) Lulu Pr., Inc.

—Candy Apple; Maçã do Amor. 2009. 32p. pap. 19.50 (978-0-557-08439-5(3)) Lulu Pr., Inc.

—Candy Apple; Manzana de Dulce. 2009. 32p. pap. 19.50 (978-0-557-08530-9(6)) Lulu Pr., Inc.

—Candy Apple; Pomme d'Amour. 2009. (ENG.). 32p. pap. 19.50 (978-0-557-08454-8(7)) Lulu Pr., Inc.

—Candy Apple; Ponm-madousiwo. 2009. (ENG.). 32p. pap. 19.50 (978-0-557-08539-2(X)) Lulu Pr., Inc.

duopress labs. Go, New York, Go! Cleland, Josh, illus. 2018. (ENG.). 22p. (J). (gr. -1-k). bds. 9.99 (978-1-946064-97-4(1), 806497) Duo Pr. LLC.

Dyan, Penelope. New York! New York! a Kid's Guide to New York City. Weigand, John D., photos by. 2009. (Illus.). 44p. pap. 11.95 (978-1-935118-79-4(X)) Bellissima Publishing, LLC.

Epstein, Brad M. New York 101. l.t. ed. 2009. (My First City Ser.). (Illus.). 24p. (J). (gr. -1-k). bds. (978-1-60730-003-8(6), 101 Bk.) Michaelson Entertainment.

Evanson, Ashley. New York: A Book of Colors. Evanson, Ashley, illus. 2015. (Hello, World Ser.). (Illus.). 16p. (J). (— 1). bds. 7.99 (978-0-448-48913-1(9), Penguin Workshop) Penguin Young Readers Group.

Fowler, Gloria. Come with Me to New York. 2015. (ENG., Illus.). 56p. 16.95 (978-1-62326-050-7(7)) AMMO Bks., LLC.

Franceschelli, Christopher. Hello, New York! Cosneau, Géraldine, illus. 2018. (Hello, Big City! Ser.). (ENG.). 46p. (J). (gr. -1 — 1). bds. 12.99 (978-1-4197-2829-7(6), 1184410) Abrams, Inc.

Fuka, V. New York a Mod Portrait of the City. 2014. (ENG., Illus.). 128p. 24.95 (978-0-7893-2727-7(9)) Universe Publishing.

Gamble, Adam. Good Night New York City. Veno, Joe, illus. 2006. (Good Night Our World Ser.). (ENG.). 24p. (J). (gr. k — 1). bds. 9.95 (978-0-9777979-3-6(7)) Good Night Bks.

Gamble, Adam & Jasper, Mark. Good Night Brooklyn. 2013. (Good Night Our World Ser.). (ENG., Illus.). 20p. (J). (— 1). bds. 9.95 (978-1-60219-094-8(1)) Good Night Bks.

Gloor, Elizabeth. The Cultural Institutions of New York City, 1 vol. 2011. (My Community Ser.). (ENG., Illus.). 12p. (gr. 2-2). pap. 6.95 (978-1-4488-5716-6(3), 3beefc8a-3df4-4e55-b576-8f98f7f37532, Rosen Classroom) Rosen Publishing Group, Inc., The.

—New York City: An Urban Community, 1 vol. 2011. (My Community Ser.). (ENG., Illus.). 12p. (gr. 2-2). pap. 6.95 (978-1-4488-5720-3(1), 33ec7264-c682-43c5-a32c-e071a0f045dc, Rosen Classroom) Rosen Publishing Group, Inc., The.

Goode, Teresa. Wildcat Adventures: A Vacation in the Big Apple. Kotrous, Chad, illus. 2006. 31p. (J). pap. 5.95 (978-1-890622-13-8(3)) Leathers Publishing.

Gregory, Joy. The Metropolitan Museum of Art. 2014. (Illus.). 24p. (J). (978-1-4896-1194-9(0)) Weigl Pubs., Inc.

Hayn, Carter. New York City: Old & New, 1 vol. 2011. (My Community Ser.). (ENG., Illus.). 12p. (gr. 2-2). pap. 6.95 (978-1-4488-5723-4(6), 5cf95efd-e88a-4dda-bcc9-b974d139068a, Rosen Classroom) Rosen Publishing Group, Inc., The.

Holub, Joan & Who HQ. What Is the Statue of Liberty? Hinderliter, John, illus. 2014. (What Was? Ser.). 112p. (J). (gr. 3-7). 5.99 (978-0-448-47917-0(6), Penguin Workshop) Penguin Young Readers Group.

Hurtig, Jennifer. Statue of Liberty. 2019. (Structural Wonders of the World Ser.). (ENG., Illus.). 24p. (J). (gr. 2-5). pap. 12.95 (978-1-4896-9944-2(9)); lib. bdg. 28.55 (978-1-4896-9943-5(0)) Weigl Pubs., Inc.

Hurtig, Jennifer & Kissock, Heather. The Statue of Liberty. 2014. (J). (978-1-4896-1966-2(6)) Weigl Pubs., Inc.

Kallen, Stuart A. A Travel Guide to Harlem Renaissance. 2003. (Travel Guide To Ser.). (ENG.). (J). 30.85 (978-1-59018-358-8(4), Lucent Bks.) Cengage Gale.

Mahoney, Emily. 20 Fun Facts about the Empire State Building, 1 vol. 2019. (Fun Fact File: World Wonders! Ser.). (ENG.). 32p. (gr. 2-3). pap. 11.50 (978-1-5382-3766-3(0), 23a9d88a-b207-4e04-a8f7-7898ed9a0bd5) Stevens, Gareth Publishing LLLP.

Maizels, Jennie. Pop-Up New York. Maizels, Jennie, illus. 2014. (ENG., Illus.). 12p. (J). (gr. k-4). 19.99 (978-0-7636-7162-4(2)) Candlewick Pr.

Marcovitz, Hal. Statue of Liberty: A Beacon of Welcome & Hope. Moreno, Barry, ed. 2014. (Patriotic Symbols of America Ser.: 20). 48p. (J). (gr. 4-18). 20.95 (978-1-4222-3130-2(5)) Mason Crest.

Markovics, Joyce. Green & Spiky: What Am I? 2018. (American Place Puzzlers Ser.). (ENG.). 24p. (J). (gr. -1-3). E-Book 41.36 (978-1-68402-536-7(2)) Bearport Publishing Co., Inc.

Markovics, Joyce L. Grand & Busy: What Am I? 2018. (American Place Puzzlers Ser.). (ENG.). 24p. (J). (gr. -1-3). lib. bdg. 17.95 (978-1-68402-484-1(6)) Bearport Publishing Co., Inc.

—Green & Spiky: What Am I? 2018. (American Place Puzzlers Ser.). (ENG.). 24p. (J). (gr. -1-3). lib. bdg. 26.99 (978-1-68402-478-0(1)) Bearport Publishing Co., Inc.

—Haunted Gotham. 2016. (Scary Places Ser.). (ENG., Illus.). 32p. (J). (gr. 4-8). 28.50 (978-1-68402-020-1(4)) Bearport Publishing Co., Inc.

—Tall & Sleek: What Am I? 2018. (American Place Puzzlers Ser.). (ENG.). 24p. (J). (gr. -1-3). lib. bdg. 17.95 (978-1-68402-479-7(X)) Bearport Publishing Co., Inc.

Mason Crest. New York, Vol. 8. 2016. (Major World Cities Ser.: Vol. 8). (ENG., Illus.). 48p. (J). (gr. 5-8). 20.95 (978-1-4222-3543-0(2)) Mason Crest.

McMenemy, Sarah. New York: Panorama Pops. 2011. (Panorama Pops Ser.). (ENG., Illus.). 20p. (J). (gr. k-4). 8.99 (978-0-7636-5483-2(3)) Candlewick Pr.

Melmed, Laura Krauss. New York, New York! The Big Apple from a to Z. Lessac, Frane, illus. 2005. (ENG.). 48p. (J). (gr. 1-6). 17.99 (978-0-06-054874-2(6), HarperCollins) HarperCollins Pubs.

Metropolitan Museum of Art, compiled by. Nyc ABC. 2011. (ENG., Illus.). 60p. (J). (gr. -1-3). 15.95 (978-0-8478-3701-4(7), Skira) Rizzoli International Pubns., Inc.

Meyers, Haily & Meyers, Kevin. All Aboard! New York: A City Primer, 1 vol. 2015. (Lucy Darling Ser.). (ENG., Illus.). 22p. (J). (— 1). bds. 9.99 (978-1-4236-4074-5(8)) Gibbs Smith, Publisher.

Moore, Andrew. Traveling in New York City, 1 vol. 2011. (My Community Ser.). (ENG., Illus.). 12p. (gr. 2-2). pap. 6.95 (978-1-4488-5719-7(8), 981569f2-163d-44c2-8621-fa202567b4a1, Rosen Classroom) Rosen Publishing Group, Inc., The.

New York Russian Language Restaurant Guide. 2005. (RUS.). per. (978-0-9764633-0-6(X)) Press Release Group Corp.

Plenty: The Ultimate Guide to Life & Leisure in Clinton Hill/Fort Greene. 2003. (Illus.). (YA). pap. 20.00 (978-0-9721708-0-2(4), PCHFG01) RedMEDIA.

RJF Publishing Staff & Staton, Hilarie. The Statue of Liberty. 2009. (Symbols of American Freedom Ser.). 48p. (gr. 4-6). 30.00 (978-1-60413-516-9(6), Chelsea Clubhse.) Infobase Holdings, Inc.

Roydhouse, Sally. Find & Seek New York. 2017. (ENG.). 36p. (gr. k-5). 19.95 (978-1-940743-28-8(1), Goff Bks.) ORO Editions.

Rudd, Brandon Kyle. Cooper's Pack — New York City: New York City, Vol. 1. McCann, Martin, illus. 2007. 72p. (J). per. 14.95 (978-0-9794882-0-7(6)) Cooper's Pack.

Scholl, Elizabeth. New York City. 2009. (Class Trip Ser.). (Illus.). 48p. (J). (gr. 2-5). lib. bdg. 29.95 (978-1-58415-808-0(5)) Mitchell Lane Pubs.

Shoup, Kate. Lady Liberty: Symbol of a Nation, 1 vol. Gennari, Joel, illus. 2018. (American Legends & Folktales Ser.). (ENG.). 32p. (J). (gr. 3-3). 30.21 (978-1-5026-3686-7(7), ffa5b6b2-bf0c-4b51-948a-9d56aa08b0b4) Cavendish Square Publishing LLC.

Skewes, John. Larry Loves New York City! A Larry Gets Lost Book. Skewes, John, illus. 2014. (Larry Gets Lost Ser.). (ENG., Illus.). 20p. (J). (— 1). bds. 10.99 (978-1-57061-936-6(0), Little Bigfoot) Sasquatch Bks.

Skewes, John & Mullin, Michael. Larry Gets Lost in New York City. Skewes, John, illus. 2010. (Larry Gets Lost Ser.). (ENG., Illus.). 32p. (J). (gr. -1-2). 17.99 (978-1-57061-620-4(5), Little Bigfoot) Sasquatch Bks.

Sullivan, Laura L. Building the Empire State Building, 1 vol. 2017. (Engineering North America's Landmarks Ser.). (ENG.). 32p. (gr. 3-3). pap. 11.58 (978-1-5026-2956-2(9), de4b4570-878e-4008-adcc-eaf6e89e5163) Cavendish Square Publishing LLC.

Thompson, Elissa. Drawing New York's Sights & Symbols, 1 vol. 2018. (Drawing Our States Ser.). (ENG.). 32p. (gr. 3-3). 26.93 (978-1-9785-0321-2(0), 5959a786-b464-4916-afe5-34338e023b3a) Enslow Publishing, LLC.

NEW YORK (N.Y.)—FICTION

Ackerman, Pauline. Three Busy Boys Plus One. 2006. (ENG.). 28p. per. 22.49 (978-1-4259-1293-2(1)) AuthorHouse.

Ackerman, Peter. The Lonely Phone Booth. Dalton, Max, illus. 2010. (ENG.). 32p. (J). (gr. k-2). 16.95 (978-1-56792-414-5(X)) Godine, David R. Pub.

Adams, Jennifer. My Little Cities: New York City Skyline Playset: (Travel Books for Toddlers, City Board Books) Pizzoli, Greg, illus. 2017. (My Little Cities Ser.). (ENG.). 8p. (J). (gr. -1-k). 14.99 (978-1-4521-5389-6(2)) Chronicle Bks. LLC.

Airgood, Ellen. Prairie Evers. 2014. 224p. (J). (gr. 3-7). pap. 7.99 (978-0-14-242668-5(7), Puffin Books) Penguin Young Readers Group.

Albertalli, Becky & Silvera, Adam. What If It's Us. (YA). 2020. (ENG.). 480p. (gr. 9). pap. 12.99 (978-0-06-279523-6(6), HarperTeen) 2018. (ENG.). 448p. (gr. 9). 18.99 (978-0-06-279525-0(2), HarperTeen) 2018. 437p. (978-0-06-287050-6(5)) 2018. 437p. (978-0-06-288930-0(3)) HarperCollins Pubs.

Alderson, Sarah. Out of Control. 2015. (ENG., Illus.). 320p. (YA). (gr. 9). 17.99 (978-1-4814-2716-6(4), Simon Pulse) Simon Pulse.

Alger, Horatio. Jack's Ward. 2005. 28.95 (978-1-4218-1454-4(4), 1st World Library - Literary Society) 1st World Publishing, Inc.

Alger Jr. Horatio Staff. Struggling Upward. rev. ed. 2006. 284p. 28.95 (978-1-4218-1760-6(8)); pap. 13.95 (978-1-4218-1860-3(4)) 1st World Publishing, Inc. (1st World Library - Literary Society).

Allen, Eleanor. Mouse Monk in a Christmas Adventure. 2009. 36p. pap. 15.49 (978-1-4490-2197-9(2)) AuthorHouse.

Altreche, Jeanine. Talula Goes to New York. 2007. 32p. per. 12.95 (978-1-4327-0538-1(5)) Outskirts Pr., Inc.

Anastos, Ernie. Ernie & the Big Newz. 2007. 32p. pap. 15.95 (978-0-9705100-5-1(5)) NK Pubns.

Andrews, Julie & Hamilton, Emma Walton. The Great American Mousical. Walton, Tony, illus. 2006. (Julie Andrews Collection). (J). (gr. k-4). 160p. 15.99 (978-0-06-057918-0(8), Julie Andrews Collection); 147p. lib. bdg. 16.89 (978-0-06-057919-7(6)) HarperCollins Pubs.

Angel, Ido. Vipo in New York: Uncle Florence. 2015. (AV2 Animated Storytime Ser.). (ENG.). (J). lib. bdg. 29.99 (978-1-4896-3917-2(9), AV2 by Weigl) Weigl Pubs., Inc.

Arato, Rona. Ice Cream Town, 1 vol. 2006. (ENG.). 192p. (J). (gr. 3-4). pap. 12.95 (978-1-55041-591-9(3), 3011cf3e-87a3-4d4e-9031-5a5ffd95d187) Trifolium Bks., Inc. CAN. Dist: Firefly Bks., Ltd.

Archibald, Laura. The Cats of Grand Central. Beckett, Garner, illus. 2004. 30p. 16.95 (978-0-9730951-0-4(5)) Solomon's Signature CAN. Dist: Hushion Hse. Publishing, Ltd.

Arena, Jen. Lady Liberty's Holiday. Hunt, Matt, illus. 2016. (ENG.). 40p. (J). (gr. k-3). 17.99 (978-0-553-52067-5(9), Knopf Bks. for Young Readers) Random Hse. Children's Bks.

Armistead, Cal. Being Henry David. (ENG.). 312p. (YA). (gr. 8-12). 2014. pap. 9.99 (978-0-8075-0616-5(8), 807506168) 2013. 16.99 (978-0-8075-0615-8(X), 080750615X) Whitman, Albert & Co.

Armstrong, Kim. Petunia in Manhattan. 2009. 50p. pap. 12.99 (978-1-935436-97-3(X)) Rodaian Pr.

Arnold, George "Speedy". What's an Elephant Doing in the Ausable River?!! Arnold, George "Speedy", illus. 2012. (ENG., Illus.). 64p. (J). 20.00 (978-0-9836925-5-3(6)) Bloated Toe Publishing.

Aronskind, Ofer. Escape from Sunday School. 2009. 152p. pap. 12.95 (978-1-4401-3217-9(8)) iUniverse, Inc.

Aronson, Marc & Smith Jr., Charles R., eds. Pick-Up Game: A Full Day of Full Court. Smith Jr., Charles R., illus. 2012. (ENG., Illus.). 176p. (YA). (gr. 9). pap. 7.99 (978-0-7636-6068-0(X));1. 18.69 (978-0-7636-4562-5(1)) Candlewick Pr.

Arruzza, Rick. El Paseo de Sparky. Newton, Pilar, illus. 2003. (SPA.). 24p. mass mkt. 7.95 (978-0-9744509-1-9(X)) Three Spots Productions.

—Sparky's Walk. Newton, Pilar, illus. 2003. 24p. (J). mass mkt. 7.95 (978-0-9744509-0-2(1)) Three Spots Productions.

Ashton, Victoria. Confessions of a Teen Nanny. (Confessions of a Teen Nanny Ser.). (ENG.). 208p. 2005. (J). (gr. 8-18). 15.99 (978-0-06-073173-1(7)) 2006. (YA). (gr. 9-12). reprint ed. pap. 8.99 (978-0-06-073178-6(8), HarperCollins) HarperCollins Pubs.

At Your Service. 2014. (Mix Ser.). (ENG., Illus.). 272p. (J). (gr. 4-8). pap. 7.99 (978-1-4814-0283-5(8), Aladdin) Simon & Schuster Children's Publishing.

Atwood, Megan. Molly Discovers Magic (Then Wants to Un-Discover It) Fleming, Lucy, illus. 2017. (Dear Molly, Dear Olive Ser.). (ENG.). 96p. (J). (gr. 1-3). pap. 5.95 (978-1-62370-616-6(5), 130934, Capstone Young Readers) Capstone.

—Molly Gets a Goat (and Wants to Give It Back) Llewhellin, Gareth, illus. 2018. (Dear Molly, Dear Olive Ser.). (ENG.). 96p. (J). (gr. 1-3). lib. bdg. 21.99 (978-1-5158-2921-8(9), 138457, Picture Window Bks.) Capstone.

—Molly Meets Trouble (Whose Real Name Is Jenna) Fleming, Lucy, illus. 2016. (Dear Molly, Dear Olive Ser.). (ENG.). 96p. (J). (gr. 1-3). lib. bdg. 21.99 (978-1-4795-8696-7(X), 130933, Picture Window Bks.) Capstone.

—Olive Finds Treasure (of the Most Precious Kind) Fleming, Lucy, illus. (Dear Molly, Dear Olive Ser.). (ENG.). 96p. (J). (gr. 1-3). 2017. pap. 5.95 (978-1-62370-615-9(7), 130932,

Capstone Young Readers) 2016. lib. bdg. 21.99 (978-1-4795-8693-6(5), 130929, Picture Window Bks.) Capstone.

—Olive Spins a Tale (and It's a Doozy!) Fleming, Lucy, illus. 2016. (Dear Molly, Dear Olive Ser.). (ENG.). 96p. (J). (gr. 1-3). lib. bdg. 21.99 (978-1-4795-8695-0(1), 130931, Picture Window Bks.) Capstone.

Auch, Mary Jane. Ashes of Roses. 2004. 250p. (YA). (gr. 8-12). 14.15 (978-0-7569-4069-0(9)) Perfection Learning Corp.

Augenstein, Marianne R. The Quest for Kair, 1 vol. 2009. 152p. pap. 24.95 (978-1-60813-899-9(2)) America Star Bks.

Aureliani, Franco, illus. Dino-Mike & the Museum Mayhem. 2015. (J). lib. bdg. (978-1-4062-9391-3(1), Stone Arch Bks.) Capstone.

Averill, Esther. Jenny's Birthday Book. Averill, Esther, illus. 2005. (Jenny's Cat Club Ser.). (Illus.). 44p. (J). (gr. -1-2). reprint ed. 16.95 (978-1-59017-154-7(3), NYR Children's Collection) New York Review of Bks., Inc., The.

Avi. Don't You Know There's a War On? 2003. (ENG.). 208p. (J). (gr. 3-7). pap. 7.99 (978-0-380-81544-9(3), HarperCollins) HarperCollins Pubs.

—Silent Movie. Mordan, C. B., illus. 2003. (ENG.). 48p. (J). (gr. -1-3). 19.99 (978-0-689-84145-3(0), Atheneum Bks. for Young Readers) Simon & Schuster Children's Publishing.

Avi & Vail, Rachel. Never Mind! 2005. (Twin Novels Ser.). 200p. (gr. 5-9). 16.00 (978-0-7569-5667-7(6)) Perfection Learning Corp.

—Never Mind! A Twin Novel. 2005. (ENG.). 208p. (J). (gr. 5-18). reprint ed. pap. 6.99 (978-0-06-054316-7(7), HarperCollins) HarperCollins Pubs.

Axelsson, Carina. Model Undercover: New York. 2015. (Model Undercover Ser.: 2). (ENG.). 320p. (J). (gr. 4-8). pap. 10.99 (978-1-4926-0785-4(1)) Sourcebooks, Inc.

Baccalario, P. d. Century #2: Star of Stone. Janeczko, Leah D., tr. 2011. (Century Ser.: 2). 336p. (J). (gr. 3-7). 8.99 (978-0-375-85796-6(6), Yearling) Random Hse. Children's Bks.

Baccalario, Pierdomenico. Star of Stone, 2. Janeczko, Leah D., tr. Bruno, Iacopo, illus. 2012. (Century Quartet Ser.). (ENG.). 304p. (J). (gr. 6-8). lib. bdg. 22.44 (978-0-375-95896-0(7)) Random House Publishing Group.

Bailey's Birthday - Evaluation Guide: Evaluation Guide. 2006. (J). (978-1-55942-399-1(4)) Witcher Productions.

Bancks, Tristan. Mac Slater vs. the City. 2011. (Mac Slater Hunts the Cool Ser.). (ENG.). 192p. (J). (gr. 3-7). 15.99 (978-1-4169-8576-1(X), Simon & Schuster Bks. For Young Readers) Simon & Schuster Bks. For Young Readers.

Barbour, Ralph Henry. The Half-Back. 2007. 132p. per. (978-1-4068-3665-3(6)) Echo Library.

Bartone, Elisa. Peppe the Lamplighter. Lewin, Ted, illus. 2015. 32p. pap. 7.00 (978-1-61003-612-2(3)) Center for the Collaborative Classroom.

Behar, Ruth. Lucky Broken Girl. (ENG.). (J). (gr. 5). 2018. 272p. 8.99 (978-0-399-54645-7(6), Puffin Books) 2017. 256p. 17.99 (978-0-399-54644-0(8), Nancy Paulsen Books) Penguin Young Readers Group.

—Lucky Broken Girl. 2018. lib. bdg. 19.65 (978-0-606-40874-5(6)) Turtleback.

Benincasa, Sara. Great. 2014. (ENG.). 272p. (YA). (gr. 9). 17.99 (978-0-06-222269-5(4), HarperTeen) HarperCollins Pubs.

Bennardo, Charlotte & Zaman, Natalie. Sirenz. 2011. (ENG.). 270p. (YA). (gr. 9-12). E-Book 29.97 (978-0-7387-2968-8(X), B01L7QUIH0, Flux) North Star Editions.

Berk, Sheryl & Berk, Carrie. Designer Drama. 2016. (Fashion Academy Ser.: 3). 192p. (J). (gr. 5-8). pap. 10.99 (978-1-4926-1353-4(3), 9781492613534) Sourcebooks, Inc.

—Fashion Academy. 2015. (Fashion Academy Ser.: 1). 160p. (J). (gr. 5-8). pap. 10.99 (978-1-4926-0162-3(4)) Sourcebooks, Inc.

—Fashion Academy: Model Madness. 2017. (Fashion Academy Ser.: 4). 192p. (J). (gr. 5-8). pap. 10.99 (978-1-4926-4496-5(X), 9781492644965) Sourcebooks, Inc.

Berman, Valerie & Berman, Neil. Bubba Goes to New York: Bubba Travel Series. 2009. 44p. pap. 16.99 (978-1-4389-6860-5(4)) AuthorHouse.

Berry, Andrea. Goalie: The Dynamite Diaries. 2003. 144p. (YA). pap. 11.95 (978-0-595-27678-3(4)) iUniverse, Inc.

Bhakta, Sanjini. My Life as a Dollar Bill. 2010. 28p. pap. 12.95 (978-1-4520-6152-8(1)) AuthorHouse.

Bildner, Phil. Derek Jeter Presents Night at the Stadium. Booth, Tom, illus. 2016. (Jeter Publishing Ser.). (ENG.). 32p. (J). (gr. -1-3). 19.99 (978-1-4814-2655-8(9), Aladdin) Simon & Schuster Children's Publishing.

Black, Holly. Valiant: A Modern Faerie Tale. 2020. (Modern Faerie Tales Ser.). (ENG.). 256p. (YA). (gr. 9). 19.99 (978-1-5344-8453-5(1)); pap. 11.99 (978-1-5344-8452-8(3)) McElderry, Margaret K. Bks. (McElderry, Margaret K. Bks.).

Black, Yelena. Dance of Shadows. 2014. (Dance of Shadows Ser.). (ENG., Illus.). 384p. (YA). (gr. 7). pap. 9.99 (978-1-61963-185-4(7), 900125810, Bloomsbury USA Childrens) Bloomsbury Publishing USA.

Bliss, Harry. Luke on the Loose. 2014. (Toon Books Level 2 Ser.). lib. bdg. 14.75 (978-0-606-32101-3(2)) Turtleback.

—Luke on the Loose: Toon Books Level 2. Bliss, Harry, illus. (Toon Ser.). (ENG., Illus.). 32p. (J). (gr. -1-3). 2014. pap. 7.99 (978-1-935179-36-8(5), 9781935179368, Toon Books) 2009. 12.99 (978-1-935179-00-9(4), TOON Books) Astra Publishing Hse.

Blue Moon. 2014. (Dead City Ser.: 2). (ENG., Illus.). 336p. (J). (gr. 4-8). pap. 8.99 (978-1-4424-4132-3(1), Aladdin) Simon & Schuster Children's Publishing.

Bluemle, Elizabeth. Tap Tap Boom Boom. Karas, G. Brian, illus. 2014. (ENG.). 32p. (J). (gr. -1-2). 17.99 (978-0-7636-5696-6(8)) Candlewick Pr.

Blume-D'Ausilio, Carole Ed. D. The Bronx Bully. 2011. 28p. pap. 15.99 (978-1-4628-5235-2(1)) Xlibris Corp.

Blume, Judy. Otherwise Known As Sheila the Great. 2007. (ENG.). 176p. (J). (gr. 3-7). 8.99 (978-0-14-240879-7(4), Puffin Books) Penguin Young Readers Group.

—Otherwise Known as Sheila the Great. 2007. 154p. (gr. 4-7). 16.00 (978-0-7569-7915-7(3)) Perfection Learning Corp.

—Otherwise Known as Sheila the Great. 2007. (Fudge Bks.: 2). 138p. (gr. 4-7). lib. bdg. 18.40 (978-1-4177-8370-0(2)) Turtleback.

Bonk, John J. Madhattan Mystery. 2012. (ENG., Illus.). 304p. (J). (gr. 4-6). 22.44 (978-0-8027-2349-9(7), 9780802723499) Walker & Co.

Booth, Coe. Bronxwood. 2013. (ENG.). 336p. (YA). (gr. 9). pap. 12.99 (978-0-439-92535-8(5), PUSH) Scholastic, Inc.

—Kendra. 2010. (Push Fiction Ser.). (ENG.). 304p. (J). (gr. 9-12). 22.44 (978-0-439-92537-2(1)) Scholastic, Inc.

—Tyrell. 2011. 9.04 (978-0-7848-3385-8(0), Everbind) Marco Bk. Co.

Boss, S. Up in the Leaves. 2018. (ENG., Illus.). 40p. (J). (gr. k-3). 18.99 (978-1-4549-2071-7(8)) Sterling Publishing Co., Inc.

Bowden, Roger. Tales from Wild Westernville. 2007. 52p. per. 16.95 (978-1-4241-6923-8(2)) America Star Bks.

Brashares, Ann. The Here & Now. 2014. 242p. (YA). (978-0-385-39008-8(4), Delacorte Pr) Random House Publishing Group.

—The Here & Now. 2015. (ENG.). 256p. (YA). (gr. 7). pap. 10.99 (978-0-385-73683-1(5), Ember) Random Hse. Children's Bks.

Brege, K. B. Champ... A Wave of Terror! Five Ways to Finish. 2006. (Mick Morris Myth Solver Ser.: No. 3). (J). mass mkt. 6.99 (978-0-9774119-2-4(3)) Team B Creative LLC.

Brennan, Sarah Rees. Tell the Wind & Fire. 2017. (ENG.). 368p. (YA). (gr. 7). pap. 9.99 (978-0-544-93887-8(9), 1658467, Clarion Bks.) HarperCollins Pubs.

Brezenoff, Steve. Field Trip Mysteries: the Burglar Who Bit the Big Apple. Canga, Chris, illus. 2010. (Field Trip Mysteries Ser.). (ENG.). 88p. (J). (gr. 3-6). 25.32 (978-1-4342-2139-1(3), 102869); pap. 5.95 (978-1-4342-2771-3(5), 114038) Capstone. (Stone Arch Bks.).

Broach, Elise. Masterpiece. 2010. 18.00 (978-1-60686-888-1(8)) Perfection Learning Corp.

—Masterpiece. Murphy, Kelly, illus. 2010. (Masterpiece Adventures Ser.). (ENG.). 320p. (J). (gr. 4-6). pap. 8.99 (978-0-312-60870-5(5), 900065170) Square Fish.

—Masterpiece. 2010. (J). lib. bdg. 18.40 (978-0-606-14604-3(0)) Turtleback.

Brown, Anne. The Dumari Chronicles: Year One: Year One. 2007. 376p. (YA). per. 20.95 (978-0-595-45725-0(8)) iUniverse, Inc.

Brown, Marc. Arthur in New York. 2008. (Step into Reading Ser.). (ENG., Illus.). 24p. (J). (gr. k-3). pap. 5.99 (978-0-375-82976-5(8), Random Hse. Bks. for Young Readers) Random Hse. Children's Bks.

Bryant, Annie. Fashion Frenzy. 2006. (Beacon Street Girls Ser.: No. 9). (Illus.). 203p. (J). (gr. 4-8). per. 7.99 (978-1-933566-02-3(7), Beacon Street Girls); (978-1-4156-9393-3(5)) B*tween Productions, Inc.

Buckley, Michael. Undertow. (Undertow Trilogy Ser.). (ENG.). (YA). (gr. 7). 2016. 400p. pap. 10.99 (978-0-544-81319-9(7), 1641921) 2015. 384p. 18.99 (978-0-544-34825-7(7), 1585834) HarperCollins Pubs. (Clarion Bks.).

Budhos, Marina. Ask Me No Questions. 2007. 159p. (gr. 7-12). 20.00 (978-0-7569-8114-3(X)) Perfection Learning Corp.

—Ask Me No Questions. 2007. (ENG.). 192p. (YA). (gr. 7-12). pap. 11.99 (978-1-4169-4920-6(8), Atheneum Bks. for Young Readers) Simon & Schuster Children's Publishing.

—The Long Ride. 2019. (Illus.). 208p. (J). (gr. 5). 16.99 (978-0-553-53422-1(X), Lamb, Wendy Bks.) Random Hse. Children's Bks.

Bukiet, Melvin. Undertown. 2013. (ENG.). 304p. (J). (gr. 3-7). 17.95 (978-1-4197-0589-2(X), 1045901, Amulet Bks.) Abrams, Inc.

Burgos, Hilda Eunice. Ana Maria Reyes Does Not Live in a Castle, 1 vol. 2018. (ENG.). 288p. (J). (gr. 4-7). 18.95 (978-1-62014-362-9(3), leelowtu, Tu Bks.) Lee & Low Bks., Inc.

Burkhart, Jessica. Jealousy. 2013. (Canterwood Crest Ser.: 17). (ENG.). 208p. (J). (gr. 4-7). pap. 7.99 (978-1-4424-3657-2(3), Aladdin) Simon & Schuster Children's Publishing.

—Jealousy. 2013. (Canterwood Crest Ser.: 17). lib. bdg. 17.20 (978-0-606-27032-8(9)) Turtleback.

Burleigh, Robert. Zoom! Zoom! Sounds of Things That Go in the City. Carpenter, Tad, illus. 2014. (ENG.). 32p. (J). (gr. -1-3). 18.99 (978-1-4424-8315-6(6), Simon & Schuster Bks. For Young Readers) Simon & Schuster Bks. For Young Readers.

Burns, Catherine Lloyd. The Half-True Lies of Cricket Cohen. 2018. (J). lib. bdg. 18.40 (978-0-606-41096-0(1)) Turtleback.

Bushnell, Candace. Summer & the City. 2012. (Carrie Diaries: 2). (ENG.). 416p. (YA). (gr. 9). pap. 10.99 (978-0-06-172900-3(0), Balzer & Bray) HarperCollins Pubs.

—Summer & the City TV Tie-In Edition. movie tie-in ed. 2013. (Carrie Diaries: 2). (ENG.). 416p. (YA). (gr. 9). pap. 10.99 (978-0-06-223686-9(5), Balzer & Bray) HarperCollins Pubs.

Buxbaum, Julie. Hope & Other Punch Lines. 2019. (ENG.). 320p. (YA). (gr. 7). 18.99 (978-1-5247-6677-1(1), Delacorte Pr.) Random Hse. Children's Bks.

Byng, Georgia. Molly Moon y el Increible Libro. 2003. (SPA.). 349p. (J). 18.99 (978-84-348-9076-3(3)) SM Ediciones ESP. Dist: Lectorum Pubns., Inc.

—Molly Moon's Incredible Book of Hypnotism. 2003. 135.92 (978-0-06-057217-4(5)) 2003. (Molly Moon Ser.: 1). (ENG., Illus.). 384p. (J). (gr. 3-7). 17.99 (978-0-06-051406-8(X), HarperCollins) 2004. (Molly Moon Ser.: 1). (ENG., Illus.). 384p. (J). (gr. 3-7). reprint ed. pap. 7.99 (978-0-06-051409-9(4), HarperCollins) HarperCollins Pubs.

—Molly Moon's Incredible Book of Hypnotism. 2004. (Molly Moon Ser.). 371p. (gr. 3-7). 18.00 (978-0-7569-3484-2(2)) Perfection Learning Corp.

Cabot, Meg. Jinx. 2009. (ENG.). 288p. (YA). (gr. 8-12). pap. 9.99 (978-0-06-083766-2(7)) 2007. 262p. (YA). (gr. 7-12). lib. bdg. 17.89 (978-0-06-083765-5(9)) 2007. (ENG.). 272p. (J). (gr. 7-18). 16.99 (978-0-06-083764-8(0)) HarperCollins Pubs. (HarperTeen).

—Journal d'une Princesse.Tr. of Princess Diaries. pap. 13.95 (978-2-01-321853-5(2)) Hachette Groupe Livre FRA. Dist: Distribooks, Inc.

—The Princess Diaries. 2008. (Princess Diaries: 1). (ENG.). 256p. (YA). (gr. 8). pap. 10.99 (978-0-06-147993-9(4))Vols. 1-3, Set. 2006. (Princess Diaries: Vol. I). (J). pap., pap. 19.99 (978-0-06-115389-1(3)) HarperCollins Pubs. (HarperTeen).

—The Princess Diaries. 2008. 20.00 (978-0-7569-8793-0(8)) Perfection Learning Corp.

—The Princess Diaries. unabr. ed. 2004. (Princess Diaries: Vol. I). 240p. (J). (gr. 7-18). pap. 38.00 incl. audio (978-0-8072-0669-0(5), Listening Library) Random Hse. Audio Publishing Group.

—The Princess Diaries. 2008. (Princess Diaries: 1). (YA). lib. bdg. 20.85 (978-1-4178-2328-4(3)) Turtleback.

—The Princess Diaries Box Set: The Princess Diaries; Princess in the Spotlight; Princess in Love. 2003. (Princess Diaries). 304p. (gr. 7-18). pap. 19.99 (978-0-06-058745-1(8)) HarperCollins Pubs.

—The Princess Diaries: Volume 7 & 3/4: Valentine Princess. 2006. (Princess Diaries: 7.75). (ENG.). 96p. (YA). (gr. 8-12). 13.99 (978-0-06-084718-0(2), HarperTeen) HarperCollins Pubs.

—The Princess Diaries, Volume II: Princess in the Spotlight Vol. 2. 2008. (Princess Diaries: 2). (ENG.). 256p. (YA). (gr. 8-12). pap. 11.99 (978-0-06-147994-6(2), HarperTeen) HarperCollins Pubs.

—The Princess Diaries, Volume III: Princess in Love, Vol. 3. 2008. (Princess Diaries: 3). (ENG.). 256p. (YA). (gr. 8-12). pap. 10.99 (978-0-06-147995-3(0), HarperTeen) HarperCollins Pubs.

—The Princess Diaries, Volume IV: Princess in Waiting. 2008. (Princess Diaries: 4). (ENG.). 256p. (YA). (gr. 8). pap. 10.99 (978-0-06-154364-7(0), HarperTeen) HarperCollins Pubs.

—The Princess Diaries, Volume IX: Princess Mia, Vol. 9. 2009. (Princess Diaries: 9). (ENG.). 304p. (YA). (gr. 8). pap. 10.99 (978-0-06-072463-4(3), HarperTeen) HarperCollins Pubs.

—The Princess Diaries, Volume V: Princess in Pink. 2008. (Princess Diaries: 5). (ENG.). 288p. (YA). (gr. 8). pap. 10.99 (978-0-06-154363-0(2), HarperTeen) HarperCollins Pubs.

—The Princess Diaries, Volume VI: Princess in Training, Vol. VI. 2008. (Princess Diaries: 6). (ENG.). 304p. (YA). (gr. 8). pap. 10.99 (978-0-06-154365-4(9), HarperTeen) HarperCollins Pubs.

—The Princess Diaries, Volume VIII: Princess on the Brink. 2007. (Princess Diaries: 8). (ENG.). 272p. (YA). (gr. 8). pap. 10.99 (978-0-06-072460-3(9), HarperTeen) HarperCollins Pubs.

—Princess in Love. 2004. (Princess Diaries: Vol. 3). 288p. (J). (gr. 7-18). pap. 38.00 incl. audio (978-0-8072-2284-3(4), Listening Library) Random Hse. Audio Publishing Group.

—Princess in Pink. 2004. (Princess Diaries: Vol. 5). (ENG., Illus.). 272p. (J). (gr. 7-18). 15.99 (978-0-06-009610-6(1)) HarperCollins Pubs.

—Princess in the Spotlight. 2008. (Princess Diaries). 222p. (gr. 7-12). 19.00 (978-0-7569-8794-7(6)) Perfection Learning Corp.

—Princess in the Spotlight, unabr. ed. 2004. (Princess Diaries: Vol. 2). 272p. (J). (gr. 7-18). pap. 38.00 incl. audio (978-0-8072-1197-7(4), S YA 332 SP, Listening Library) Random Hse. Audio Publishing Group.

—Princess in Training. 2005. (Princess Diaries: Vol. 6). (ENG., Illus.). 288p. (J). (gr. 7-18). 16.99 (978-0-06-009613-7(6)) HarperCollins Pubs.

—Princess Mia. 2008. (Princess Diaries: Vol. 9). (ENG.). 256p. (J). (gr. 7-18). 16.99 (978-0-06-072461-0(7)) HarperCollins Pubs.

—Princess Mia. 2009. (Princess Diaries: 9). (YA). lib. bdg. 20.85 (978-0-606-02178-4(7)) Turtleback.

—Princess on the Brink. 2007. (Princess Diaries: Vol. 8). (ENG.). 256p. (J). 16.99 (978-0-06-072456-6(0)) HarperCollins Pubs.

Callen, Sharon. This Is the Tower That Frank Built, 1 vol. rev. ed. 2013. (Literary Text Ser.). (ENG., Illus.). 24p. (gr. 2-3). pap. 8.99 (978-1-4333-5535-6(3)) Teacher Created Materials, Inc.

Calonita, Jen. Summer State of Mind. 2014. (ENG.). 256p. (YA). (gr. 7-17). pap. 10.00 (978-0-316-09115-2(4), Poppy) Little, Brown Bks. for Young Readers.

—Turn It Up! 2018. (ENG.). 272p. (YA). (gr. 7). 17.99 (978-1-338-16115-1(6), Scholastic Pr.) Scholastic, Inc.

Cameron, Peter. Someday This Pain Will Be Useful to You: A Novel. 2009. (ENG.). 240p. (YA). (gr. 9-13). pap. 18.00 (978-0-312-42816-7(2), 900054659) Picador.

Caraballo, Samuel & Torrecilla, Pablo. Estrellita in the Big City/Estrellita en la Ciudad Grande. Caraballo, Samuel & Torrecilla, Pablo, illus. 2008. (SPA & ENG., Illus.). 32p. (J). (gr. -1-4). 16.95 (978-1-55885-498-7(3), Piñata Books) Arte Publico Pr.

Carey, Anna. Deadfall. 2015. (Blackbird Ser.: 2). (ENG.). 256p. (YA). (gr. 9). 17.99 (978-0-06-229976-5(X), HarperTeen) HarperCollins Pubs.

Carlson, Melody. Catwalk, 1 vol. 2014. (On the Runway Ser.: 2). (ENG.). 224p. (YA). pap. 9.99 (978-0-310-74810-6(0)) Zondervan.

—Ciao, 1 vol. 2014. (On the Runway Ser.: 6). (ENG.). 208p. (YA). pap. 9.99 (978-0-310-74843-4(7)) Zondervan.

—Rendezvous, 1 vol. 2014. (On the Runway Ser.: 3). (ENG.). 224p. (YA). pap. 9.99 (978-0-310-74861-8(5)) Zondervan.

Casciano, Christie & Moziak, Rose Mary Casciano, illus. Haunted Hockey in Lake Placid. 2012. (ENG.). 72p. (J). pap. (978-1-59531-040-8(1)) North Country Bks., Inc.

Castillo, Lauren. Nana in the City: A Caldecott Honor Award Winner. Castillo, Lauren, illus. 2014. (ENG., Illus.). 40p. (J). (gr. -1-3). 19.99 (978-0-544-10443-3(9), 1540055, Clarion Bks.) HarperCollins Pubs.

Castle, Jennifer. Together at Midnight. 2018. (ENG.). 352p. (YA). (gr. 9). 17.99 (978-0-06-225051-3(5), HarperTeen) HarperCollins Pubs.

Cataneo, D. M. Eggplant Alley. 2013. (ENG.). 352p. (YA). (gr. 7-14). 17.95 (978-1-59373-146-5(9)) Bunker Hill Publishing, Inc.

Chace, Rebecca. June Sparrow & the Million-Dollar Penny. Schwartz, Kacey, illus. 2017. (ENG.). 352p. (J). (gr. 3-7). 16.99 (978-0-06-246498-9(1), Balzer & Bray) HarperCollins Pubs.

Chan, Marty. Demon Gate, 1 vol. 2013. (Ehrich Weisz Chronicles Ser.). (ENG.). 262p. (YA). (gr. 7-10). pap. 12.95 (978-1-55455-306-8(7), ea320d17-ce0b-4bdd-ad87-d1058c095c34) Trifolium Bks., Inc. CAN. Dist: Firefly Bks., Ltd.

Chance, Megan. The Web, 0 vols. 2015. (Fianna Trilogy Ser.: 2). (ENG.). 384p. (YA). (gr. 7-12). pap. 9.99 (978-1-4778-2708-6(0), 9781477827086, Skyscape) Amazon Publishing.

Chang, Ifay, as told by. Outopians. 2007. (Illus.). 27p. (YA). pap. (978-0-9771594-1-3(8)) TLC Information Services.

Chari, Sheela. Finding Mighty. 2019. (ENG.). 336p. (J). (gr. 5-9). pap. 9.99 (978-1-4197-3479-3(2), 1144603, Amulet Bks.) Abrams, Inc.

Chibbaro, Julie. Deadly. Sovak, Jean-Marc Superville, illus. 2012. (ENG.). 304p. (YA). (gr. 7). pap. 11.99 (978-0-689-85739-3(X), Atheneum Bks. for Young Readers) Simon & Schuster Children's Publishing.

Choi, Mary H. K. Permanent Record. (ENG.). (YA). (gr. 9). 2020. 448p. pap. 11.99 (978-1-5344-4598-7(6)) 2019. (Illus.). 432p. 18.99 (978-1-5344-4597-0(8)) Simon & Schuster Bks. For Young Readers. (Simon & Schuster Bks. For Young Readers).

—Permanent Record. l.t. ed. 2020. (ENG.). lib. bdg. 22.99 (978-1-4328-7743-9(7)) Thorndike Pr.

Christopher, Matt. Fairway Phenom. 2003. (ENG.). 144p. (J). (gr. 5-8). pap. 10.99 (978-0-316-07551-0(5)) Little, Brown Bks. for Young Readers.

Clare, Cassandra. City of Ashes. 2008. (Mortal Instruments Ser.: Bk. 2). (YA). (gr. 9). 64.99 (978-1-60640-964-0(6)) Findaway World, LLC.

—City of Ashes. 2008. (YA). (Mortal Instruments Ser.: 2). (ENG.). 464p. (gr. 9-12). 24.99 (978-1-4169-1429-7(3)); 416p. pap. (978-1-4063-1849-4(3)) McElderry, Margaret K. Bks. (McElderry, Margaret K. Bks.).

—City of Bones. (Mortal Instruments Ser.: 1). (ENG., Illus.). (YA). (gr. 9). 2015. 544p. pap. 14.99 (978-1-4814-5592-3(3)) 2007. 496p. 24.99 (978-1-4169-1428-0(5)) McElderry, Margaret K. Bks. (McElderry, Margaret K. Bks.).

—City of Bones. 2008. (Mortal Instruments Ser.: Bk. 1). 485p. (gr. 9-12). 23.00 (978-1-60686-361-9(4)) Perfection Learning Corp.

—City of Bones, 12 vols. 2007. (Mortal Instruments Ser.: 1). (YA). 131.75 (978-1-4281-5454-4(X)); 133.75 (978-1-4281-5452-0(3)); 286.75 (978-1-4281-5449-0(3)); 1.25 (978-1-4281-5445-2(0)); 122.75 (978-1-4281-5448-3(5)); 120.75 (978-1-4281-5450-6(7)) Recorded Bks., Inc.

—City of Bones. 2013. (The Mortal Instruments Ser.: Bk. 1). pap. (978-1-4424-9306-3(2)) Simon & Schuster, Inc.

—City of Bones. l.t. ed. 2008. (Mortal Instruments Ser.: 1). (ENG.). 503p. (YA). 31.95 (978-1-4104-0958-4(9)) Thorndike Pr.

—City of Bones. 2015. (Mortal Instruments Ser.: Bk. 1). (Illus.). 544p. (YA). lib. bdg. 25.75 (978-0-606-37731-7(X)) Turtleback.

—City of Fallen Angels. 2011. (Mortal Instruments Ser.: 4). (ENG.). 432p. (YA). (gr. 9-18). 24.99 (978-1-4424-0354-3(3), McElderry, Margaret K. Bks.) McElderry, Margaret K. Bks.

—City of Fallen Angels, 11 vols. (Mortal Instruments Ser.: 4). (YA). 2012. 133.75 (978-1-4618-0638-7(0)) 2011. 135.75 (978-1-4618-0637-0(2)) 2011. 1.25 (978-1-4640-2483-2(9)) 2011. 317.75 (978-1-4618-0642-4(9)) 2011. 133.75 (978-1-4618-0641-7(0)) Recorded Bks., Inc.

—City of Glass. (Mortal Instruments Ser.: 3). (ENG., (YA). (gr. 9). 2015. Illus.). 592p. pap. 14.99 (978-1-4814-5598-5(2)) 2009. 560p. 24.99 (978-1-4169-1430-3(7)) McElderry, Margaret K. Bks. (McElderry, Margaret K. Bks.).

—City of Glass. 2010. 23.00 (978-1-60686-827-0(6)) Perfection Learning Corp.

—City of Glass. 2009. pap. (978-1-4424-9308-7(9)) Simon & Schuster.

—City of Glass. 2015. (Mortal Instruments Ser.: Bk. 3). (Illus.). 592p. (J). lib. bdg. 25.75 (978-0-606-37733-1(6)) Turtleback.

—City of Heavenly Fire. 2014. (Mortal Instruments Ser.: 6). (ENG., Illus.). 752p. (YA). (gr. 9). 24.99 (978-1-4424-1689-5(0), McElderry, Margaret K. Bks.) McElderry, Margaret K. Bks.

—City of Lost Souls. (Mortal Instruments Ser.: 5). (ENG., (YA). (gr. 9). 2015. Illus.). 592p. pap. 14.99 (978-1-4814-5600-5(8)) 2012. 544p. 24.99 (978-1-4424-1686-4(6)) McElderry, Margaret K. Bks. (McElderry, Margaret K. Bks.).

—City of Lost Souls, 16 vols. 2012. (Mortal Instruments Ser.: Bk. 5). (YA). 135.75 (978-1-4640-3948-5(8)); 133.75 (978-1-4640-3951-5(8)); 317.75 (978-1-4640-3949-2(6)); 133.75 (978-1-4640-3952-2(6)) Recorded Bks., Inc.

—City of Lost Souls. 2015. (Mortal Instruments Ser.: Bk. 5). 592p. (YA). lib. bdg. 25.75 (978-0-606-37736-2(0)) Turtleback.

—City of Lost Souls. 2012. 512p. pap. (978-1-4063-3760-0(9)) Walker Bks., Ltd.

Clawson, David. My Fairy Godmother Is a Drag Queen. 2017. (ENG.). 336p. (J). (gr. 8-8). 17.99 (978-1-5107-1411-3(1), Sky Pony Pr.) Skyhorse Publishing Co., Inc.

Clements, Andrew. Things Hoped For. 2008. (ENG.). 176p. (J). (gr. 5-18). 7.99 (978-0-14-241073-8(X), Puffin Books) Penguin Young Readers Group.

—Things Hoped For. 2008. 167p. (gr. 5-9). 17.00 (978-0-7569-8933-0(7)) Perfection Learning Corp.

—Things Hoped For. l.t. ed. 2008. (Thorndike Literacy Bridge Ser.). 207p. 23.95 (978-1-4104-0500-5(1)) Thorndike Pr.

Clough, Lisa. Country Girl, City Girl. 2009. (ENG.). 192p. (YA). (gr. 7). pap. 12.95 (978-0-547-22322-3(6), 1061786, Clarion Bks.) HarperCollins Pubs.

Coburn, Jake. Prep. 2005. 192p. (YA). (gr. 7-7). 6.99 (978-0-14-240307-5(5), Speak) Penguin Young Readers Group.

Cochrane, Mick. The Girl Who Threw Butterflies. 2010. (ENG.). 192p. (J). (gr. 3-7). 7.99 (978-0-375-84610-6(7), Yearling) Random Hse. Children's Bks.

Cody, Matthew. The Dead Gentleman. 2012. 288p. (J). (gr. 5). 7.99 (978-0-375-84490-4(2), Yearling) Random Hse. Children's Bks.

Cohen, Miriam. Down in the Subway, 1 vol. Hope Greenberg, Melanie, illus. 2003. (ENG.). 32p. (J). (gr. k-3). pap. 6.99 (978-1-932065-24-4(5)); 16.99 (978-1-932065-08-4(3)) Star Bright Bks., Inc.

Cohen, Neil. American Gargoyles. 2019. (ENG., Illus.). 48p. (J). 20.00 (978-1-64428-011-9(6), Vireo Bk., A) Rare Bird Bks.

Cohn, Rachel & Levithan, David. Dash & Lily's Book of Dares. 2011. (Dash & Lily Ser.: 1). (ENG.). 288p. (YA). (gr. 7). pap. 9.99 (978-0-375-85955-7(1), Ember) Random Hse. Children's Bks.

—Nick & Norah's Infinite Playlist. 2009. 10.54 *(978-0-7848-2769-7(9),* Everbind) Marco Bk. Co.
—Nick & Norah's Infinite Playlist. 2007. 183p. (gr. 9-12). 19.00 *(978-0-7569-7949-2(8))* Perfection Learning Corp.
—Nick & Norah's Infinite Playlist. 2007. (ENG.). 208p. (YA). (gr. 9-12). pap. 9.99 *(978-0-375-83533-9(4),* Ember) Random Hse. Children's Bks.
—The Twelve Days of Dash & Lily. (Dash & Lily Ser.: 2). (ENG.). (YA). (gr. 7). 2017. 240p. pap. 10.99 *(978-0-399-55383-7(5),* Ember) 2016. (Illus.). 224p. 17.99 *(978-0-399-55380-6(0),* Knopf Bks. for Young Readers) Random Hse. Children's Bks.
Colasanti, Susane. Forever in Love. 2018. (City Love Ser.: 3). (ENG.). 320p. (YA). (gr. 9). pap. 9.99 *(978-0-06-230777-4(0),* Tegen, Katherine Bks) HarperCollins Pubs.
—Take Me There. 2009. 320p. (YA). (gr. 7-18). 9.99 *(978-0-14-241435-4(2),* Speak) Penguin Young Readers Group.
Colfer, Chris. The Land of Stories: Worlds Collide. 2018. (Land of Stories Ser.: 6). (ENG.). 464p. (J). (gr. 3-7). pap. 9.99 *(978-0-316-35588-9(7))* Little, Brown Bks. for Young Readers.
—Worlds Collide. Dorman, Brandon, illus. 2017. 434p. (J). *(978-0-316-43920-6(7))* Little Brown & Co.
Collins, Nancy A. Vamps. 2008. (Vamps Ser.: 1). (ENG.). 256p. (YA). (gr. 9-18). pap. 8.99 *(978-0-06-134917-1(8),* HarperTeen) HarperCollins Pubs.
Colon, Edie. Good-Bye, Havana! Hola, New York! ón, Raúl, illus. 2011. (ENG.). 32p. (J). (gr. -1-3). 19.99 *(978-1-4424-0674-2(7),* Simon & Schuster/Paula Wiseman Bks.) Simon & Schuster/Paula Wiseman Bks.
Connor, Leslie. Waiting for Normal. 2008. (ENG.). 304p. (J). (gr. 5-18). 16.99 *(978-0-06-089088-9(6),* Tegen, Katherine Bks) HarperCollins Pubs.
Cooney, Caroline B. Code Orange. 2007. 200p. (gr. 7-12). 17.00 *(978-0-7569-8210-2(3))* Perfection Learning Corp.
—Code Orange. 2007. (ENG.). 224p. (YA). (gr. 7-12). mass mkt. 8.99 *(978-0-385-73260-4(0),* Laurel Leaf) Random Hse. Children's Bks.
—Code Orange. 2007. lib. bdg. 17.20 *(978-1-4177-7788-4(5))* Turtleback.
Cooper, Elisha. River. Cooper, Elisha, illus. 2019. (ENG., Illus.). 48p. (J). (gr. -1-3). 18.99 *(978-1-338-31226-3(X),* Orchard Bks.) Scholastic, Inc.
Cordier, Claire. The POLAR BEAR in CENTRAL PARK. 2009. (ENG.). 32p. pap. 23.50 *(978-0-557-08167-7(X))* Lulu Pr., Inc.
Corey, Shana. Milly & the Macy's Parade. Helquist, Brett, illus. 2006. 38p. (J). (gr. 4-8). reprint ed. 17.00 *(978-1-4223-5174-1(2))* DIANE Publishing Co.
Corris, Charles R. Donald Ditz & the Red Tiger, 1 vol. 2010. 64p. pap. 19.95 *(978-1-4512-2193-0(2))* America Star Bks.
Corwin, Jeff. Your Backyard Is Wild: Junior Explorer Series Book 1. 2009. 96p. (J). (gr. 1-3). 4.99 *(978-0-14-241404-0(2),* Puffin Books) Penguin Young Readers Group.
Cosson, Kip. Ned Visits New York. 2006. (ENG., Illus.). 40p. (J). 16.95 *(978-0-9789384-0-6(2))* Kip Kids of New York.
Cotter, Natasha. Pj Is Special. 2011. 20p. pap. 24.95 *(978-1-4560-6564-5(5))* America Star Bks.
Cox, Suzy. The Dead Girls Detective Agency. 2012. (ENG.). 368p. (YA). (gr. 9). pap. 9.99 *(978-0-06-202064-2(1),* HarperTeen) HarperCollins Pubs.
Creek, Silent. All the Ice of Afric. 2009. 160p. 22.95 *(978-1-4401-2118-0(4))* iUniverse, Inc.
Cross, Julie & Perini, Mark. You Before Anyone Else. 2016. 400p. (YA). (gr. 8-12). pap. 10.99 *(978-1-4926-0492-1(5),* 9781492604921) Sourcebooks, Inc.
Curry, Don, ed. The Crate Escape No. 2. 2008. (I Can Find It Ser.). 22p. (J). 7.99 *(978-0-696-23490-3(4))* Meredith Bks.
—Esape Africa. 2008. 22p. (J). 15.95 *(978-0-696-23488-0(2))* Meredith Bks.
Curtis, Alice Turner. A Frontier Girl of New York. Snyder, Harold E., illus. 2011. 282p. 48.95 *(978-1-258-01096-6(8))* Literary Licensing, LLC.
Czerw, Nancy Carpenter. Itty & Bitty - On the Road. Berlin, Rose Mary, illus. 2008. (Itty & Bitty Ser.: 3). (ENG.). 32p. (J). (gr. -1-3). 16.95 *(978-0-9755618-4-3(7))* McWitty Pr., Inc.
The Daisy Bug Kids Say Hello New York. 2004. (J). *(978-0-9712349-2-5(2))* Univ. At Buffalo, Child Care Ctr.
La Dama de Cobre (the Copper Lady) 2006. (J). pap. 6.95 *(978-0-8225-6616-8(8),* Ediciones Lerner) Lerner Publishing Group.
Danziger, Paula. Amber Brown Wants Extra Credit. Ross, Tony, illus. 2008. (Amber Brown Ser.: 4). (ENG.). 144p. (J). (gr. 2-5). 6.99 *(978-0-14-241049-3(7),* Puffin Books) Penguin Young Readers Group.
—Remember Me to Harold Square. (Remember Me to Harold Square Ser.: No. 1). 139p. (YA). (gr. 6-18). pap. 3.99 *(978-0-8072-1472-5(8),* Listening Library) Random Hse. Audio Publishing Group.
Davies, Jocelyn. The Odds of Lightning. (ENG.). 384p. (YA). (gr. 9). 2017. pap. 10.99 *(978-1-4814-4054-7(3))* 2016. (Illus.). 17.99 *(978-1-4814-4053-0(5))* Simon Pulse. (Simon Pulse).
Davies, Valentine. Miracle on 34th Street: [Facsimile Edition]. fac. ed. 2010. (ENG., Illus.). 136p. (J). (gr. 2-4). 22.44 *(978-0-15-216377-8(8))* Houghton Mifflin Harcourt Publishing Co.
Davis, Cynthia. Drink the Rain. 2007. (Illus.). 256p. (YA). per. 12.95 *(978-0-9712163-1-0(2))* Greenroom Bks.
de la Cruz, Melissa. Beach Lane. 2013. (Beach Lane Ser.: 1). (ENG., Illus.). 320p. (YA). (gr. 9). pap. 9.99 *(978-1-4424-7409-3(2),* Simon & Schuster Bks. For Young Readers) Simon & Schuster Bks. For Young Readers.
De la Cruz, Melissa. Blue Bloods. 2007. (Blue Bloods Ser.: 1). (J). lib. bdg. 20.85 *(978-1-4178-2375-8(5))* Turtleback.
de la Cruz, Melissa. Blue Bloods 3-Book Boxed Set, 3 bks., Set. 2009. (Blue Bloods Ser.). (ENG.). 944p. (J). (gr. 5-9). pap. 24.99 *(978-1-4231-2595-2(9),* Disney-Hyperion) Disney Publishing Worldwide.
—Blue Bloods-Blue Bloods, Vol. 1. 2007. (Blue Bloods Ser.: 1). (ENG.). 336p. (J). (gr. 5-9). pap. 9.99 *(978-1-4231-0126-0(X),* Disney-Hyperion) Disney Publishing Worldwide.
—Gates of Paradise-A Blue Bloods Novel, Book 7. 2013. (Blue Bloods Ser.: 7). (ENG.). 368p. (J). (gr. 5-9). pap. 9.99 *(978-1-4231-6110-3(6),* Disney-Hyperion) Disney Publishing Worldwide.
De la Cruz, Melissa. Skinny-Dipping. 2006. (Au Pairs Ser.: 2). (ENG.). 304p. (YA). (gr. 9-18). reprint ed. pap. 8.99 *(978-1-4169-0383-3(6),* Simon & Schuster Bks. For Young Readers) Simon & Schuster Bks. For Young Readers.
—Sun-Kissed. (Au Pairs Ser.: 3). (ENG.). 320p. (YA). (gr. 9-12). 2007. pap. 8.99 *(978-1-4169-1747-2(0))* 2006. 15.95 *(978-1-4169-1746-5(2))* Simon & Schuster Bks. For Young Readers. (Simon & Schuster Bks. For Young Readers).
De Los Heros, Luis & Wilson, Elizabeth. Chifa Chi's Little Adventure in New York City. 2011. (ENG.). 44p. pap. 21.99 *(978-0-557-91842-3(1))* Lulu Pr., Inc.
Dean, Myers Walter. Fast Sam, Cool Clyde, & Stuff. 2014. (ENG.). 192p. (J). (gr. 12-12). 11.24 *(978-1-63245-241-2(3))* Lectorum Pubns., Inc.
Decker, Jeni. Far from Happy. 2014. 200p. pap. 14.99 *(978-1-62798-407-2(0))* Dreamspinner Pr.
Dee, Carolyn. The Tree Who Couldn't Choose. 2008. 36p. pap. 15.49 *(978-1-4389-2950-7(1))* AuthorHouse.
DeFelice, Cynthia. Under the Same Sky. 2005. (ENG.). 224p. (J). (gr. 5-9). pap. 18.99 *(978-0-374-48065-3(6),* 900028273) Square Fish.
DEKELB-RITTENHOUSE, Diane. Immortal Longings. 2012. (ENG.). 340p. (J). (gr. 7). pap. 14.95 *(978-0-9845318-4-4(X))* Tiny Stachel Pr.
DeKeyser, Stacy. Jump the Cracks. 2008. (ENG.). 216p. (YA). (gr. 9-12). per. 9.95 *(978-0-7387-1274-1(4),* 0738712744, Flux) North Star Editions.
DeLand, M. Maitland. Baby Santa & the Gift of Giving. Wilson, Phil, illus. 2014. (ENG.). 36p. (J). (gr. -1-2). 14.95 *(978-1-62634-086-2(2),* Greenleaf Book Group Pr.) Greenleaf Book Group.
Dempsey, Kristy. A Dance Like Starlight: One Ballerina's Dream. Cooper, Floyd, illus. 2014. 32p. (J). (gr. k-3). 17.99 *(978-0-399-25284-6(3),* Philomel Bks.) Penguin Young Readers Group.
DeVillers, Julia & Roy, Jennifer. Double Feature. 2012. (Mix Ser.). (ENG.). 288p. (J). (gr. 4-8). pap. 7.99 *(978-1-4424-3403-5(1),* Aladdin) Simon & Schuster Children's Publishing.
—Times Squared. 2011. (Mix Ser.). (ENG.). (J). (gr. 4-8). 272p. pap. 8.99 *(978-1-4169-6732-3(X));* 240p. 16.99 *(978-1-4169-7532-8(2))* Simon & Schuster Children's Publishing. (Aladdin).
deVos, Kelly. Fat Girl on a Plane. 2018. (ENG.). 384p. (YA). 18.99 *(978-0-373-21253-8(4),* Harlequin Teen) Harlequin Enterprises ULC CAN. Dist: HarperCollins Pubs.
Diallo, Elishia Shelene. Boogalou: A Boogie down Bronx Tale. 2015. (ENG.). 272p. (YA). pap. 14.99 *(978-1-4951-7655-5(X))* Independent Pub.
DiCerto, Joseph J. The Wall People: In Search of a Home. 2014. (Illus.). 128p. (J). pap. 14.00 *(978-0-87842-633-1(7))* Mountain Pr. Publishing Co., Inc.
Disney Press Staff. School's Out. 2010. 128p. pap. 4.99 *(978-1-4231-2677-5(7))* Disney Pr.
Dixon, Amy. Marathon Mouse. Denlinger, Sam, illus. 2012. (ENG.). 32p. (J). (gr. -1-k). 16.95 *(978-1-61608-966-5(0),* 608966, Sky Pony Pr.) Skyhorse Publishing Co., Inc.
Dorismond, Joanne R. A Day in New York with Beatrice & Duke. 2010. 37p. pap. 17.95 *(978-0-557-23850-7(1))* Lulu Pr., Inc.
Doyle McQuerry, Maureen. Between Before & After, 1 vol. 2019. (ENG., Illus.). 304p. (YA). pap. 9.99 *(978-0-310-76728-2(8))* Blink.
Dreyer, Ellen. Speechless in New York. Huerta, Catherine, illus. 2nd rev. ed. 2003. (Going to Ser.). (ENG.). 129p. (J). (gr. 4-8). pap. 6.95 *(978-1-893577-09-1(0))* Four Corners Publishing Co., Inc.
Driftin' Aarong. Claude Henry, the Iditarod Mouse ~3: The Great Castaway Adventure. 2009. 92p. pap. 9.95 *(978-1-4401-1949-1(X))* iUniverse, Inc.
Druvert, Hélène & Druvert, Hélène. New York Melody. 2018. (ENG., Illus.). 36p. (J). (gr. k-3). 24.95 *(978-0-500-65173-5(6),* 565173) Thames & Hudson.
D'shindia, Albert. The Fable Musical. 2012. 56p. (gr. -1). pap. 10.95 *(978-1-4567-9978-6(9))* AuthorHouse.
Dubrule, Jackie. Kelli, God & New York. Baker, David, illus. 2013. 28p. pap. 24.95 *(978-1-4560-0969-4(9))* America Star Bks.
Dunshee, Gloria. Will & the Red Ball. 2010. 32p. pap. 11.95 *(978-0-9828231-0-1(X))* WillGo Pr.
Egan, Tim. Dodsworth in New York. 2009. (Dodsworth Book Ser.). (ENG., Illus.). 48p. (J). (gr. 1-4). pap. 4.99 *(978-0-547-24831-8(8),* 1100746, Clarion Bks.) HarperCollins Pubs.
—Dodsworth in New York. Egan, Tim, illus. 2007. (Dodsworth Ser.). (ENG., Illus.). 48p. (J). (gr. 1-3). 17.44 *(978-0-618-77708-2(3))* Houghton Mifflin Harcourt Publishing Co.
Eldridge, Courtney. Ghost Time. 2016. (ENG.). 418p. (YA). (gr. 7-12). pap. 9.99 *(978-1-4778-1697-4(6),* 9781477816974, Skyscape) Amazon Publishing.
Elish, Dan. The Attack of the Frozen Woodchucks. Call, Greg, illus. 2008. (ENG.). 256p. (J). (gr. 3-7). 16.99 *(978-0-06-113870-6(3),* Geringer, Laura Book) HarperCollins Pubs.
Enright, Elizabeth. The Saturdays. Enright, Elizabeth, illus. 3rd ed. 2008. (Melendy Quartet Ser.: 1). (ENG., Illus.). 192p. (J). (gr. 3-7). per. 8.99 *(978-0-312-37598-0(0),* 900048317) Square Fish.
Eulberg, Elizabeth. The Great Shelby Holmes Meets Her Match. 2017. (ENG., Illus.). 240p. (J). 16.99 *(978-1-68119-054-9(0),* 900157431, Bloomsbury USA Childrens) Bloomsbury Publishing USA.
Falk, Barbara Bustetter & Hyman, Helen Kandel. Don't Park on the Roof. 2007. 36p. per. 21.32 *(978-1-4257-7096-9(7))* Xlibris Corp.
Famularo, Joe. Chiara's Bite of the Big Apple: A Happy Book. 2013. 28p. pap. 16.09 *(978-1-4669-5274-4(1))* Trafford Publishing.
Farnol, Jeffery. Money Moon. 2006. pap. 13.95 *(978-1-4218-3066-7(3))* 1st World Publishing, Inc.
Federle, Tim. Better Nate Than Ever. 2014. (ENG.). (J). (gr. 4-8). lib. bdg. 18.60 *(978-1-62765-461-6(5))* Perfection Learning Corp.
—Better Nate Than Ever. (Nate Ser.). (ENG.). (J). (gr. 4-8). 2018. 304p. pap. 8.99 *(978-1-5344-2913-0(1))* 2013. (Illus.). 288p. 18.99 *(978-1-4424-4689-2(7))* Simon & Schuster Bks. For Young Readers. (Simon & Schuster Bks. For Young Readers).
—Five, Six, Seven, Nate! (Nate Ser.). (ENG.). (J). (gr. 5). 2018. 336p. pap. 7.99 *(978-1-5344-2914-7(X))* 2014. (Illus.). 298p. 19.99 *(978-1-4424-4693-9(5))* Simon & Schuster Bks. For Young Readers. (Simon & Schuster Bks. For Young Readers).
Feldman, Thea, et al. Harry Cat & Tucker Mouse: Harry to the Rescue! 2011. (My Readers: Level 2 Ser.). (ENG., Illus.). 48p. (J). (gr. k-2). 16.19 *(978-0-312-62507-8(3))* Square Fish.
Ferrari, Vincent. Blogosfear. 2005. 143p. (YA). pap. 15.00 *(978-1-4116-6814-0(6))* Lulu Pr., Inc.
Fiedler, Lisa. Mouseheart. To, Vivienne, illus. 2014. (Mouseheart Ser.: 1). (ENG.). 320p. (J). (gr. 3-7). 18.99 *(978-1-4424-8781-9(X),* McElderry, Margaret K. Bks.) McElderry, Margaret K. Bks.
Fields, Jan. Hunt for Sewer Gators, 1 vol. Brundage, Scott, illus. 2014. (Monster Hunters Ser.). (ENG.). 80p. (J). (gr. 2-5). 35.64 *(978-1-62402-045-2(3),* 1525, Calico Chapter Bks.) ABDO Publishing Co.
Finley, Leah. The One & Only Mr C. 2009. 82p. pap. 8.95 *(978-1-935118-75-6(7))* Bellissima Publishing, LLC.
Firestone, Carrie. The Unlikelies. (ENG.). (YA). (gr. 9-17). 2018. 352p. pap. 10.99 *(978-0-316-38289-2(2))* 2017. 336p. 17.99 *(978-0-316-38286-1(8))* Little, Brown Bks. for Young Readers.
Fitzgerald, Laura Marx. Under the Egg. 2015. 272p. (J). (gr. 3-7). 8.99 *(978-0-14-242765-1(9),* Puffin Books) Penguin Young Readers Group.
Fitzhugh, Louise. Harriet the Spy. 298p. (J). (gr. 3-5). pap. 5.95 *(978-0-8072-1535-7(X),* Listening Library) Random Hse. Audio Publishing Group.
—Harriet the Spy: 50th Anniversary Edition. 50th anniv. ed. 2014. (Harriet the Spy Ser.). (ENG., Illus.). 336p. (J). (gr. 3-7). 18.99 *(978-0-385-37610-5(3),* Delacorte Bks. for Young Readers) Random Hse. Children's Bks.
Fitzhugh, Louise & Gold, Maya. Harriet the Spy, Double Agent. 2007. (ENG.). 160p. (J). (gr. 3-7). 6.99 *(978-0-440-41691-3(4),* Yearling) Random Hse. Children's Bks.
Fitzhugh, Percy K. Pee-Wee Harris. 2004. reprint ed. pap. 1.99 *(978-1-4192-4057-7(9));* pap. 15.95 *(978-1-4191-4057-0(4))* Kessinger Publishing, LLC.
Flack, Sophie. Bunheads. 2012. (ENG.). 320p. (YA). (gr. 7-17). pap. 10.99 *(978-0-316-12654-0(3),* Poppy) Little, Brown Bks. for Young Readers.
Fleming, Anne. The Goat, 1 vol. 2019. (ENG.). 120p. (J). (gr. 4-6). 9.95 *(978-1-77306-299-0(9))* Groundwood Bks. CAN. Dist: Publishers Group West (PGW).
Flinn, Alex. Beastly. (Kendra Chronicles Ser.: 1). (ENG.). (YA). (gr. 9). 2009. 336p. pap. 11.99 *(978-0-06-199866-9(4))* 2007. 320p. 17.99 *(978-0-06-087416-2(3))* HarperCollins Pubs. (HarperTeen).
—Beastly Movie Tie In. movie tie-in ed. 2011. (Kendra Chronicles Ser.: 1). (ENG.). 336p. (YA). (gr. 9-18). pap. 9.99 *(978-0-06-196328-5(3),* HarperTeen) HarperCollins Pubs.
Forman, Gayle. I Have Lost My Way. (ENG.). (YA). (gr. 9). 2019. 304p. pap. 10.99 *(978-0-425-29078-1(6),* Penguin Books) 2018. 272p. 18.99 *(978-0-425-29077-4(8),* Viking Books for Young Readers) Penguin Young Readers Group.
—I Have Lost My Way. 2018. (ENG.). 272p. (YA). (gr. 9). pap. *(978-0-451-48074-3(0))* Topaz.
—Where She Went. l.t. ed. 2015. (If I Stay Ser.: BK.2). (ENG.). 288p. (YA). 23.99 *(978-1-4104-7562-6(X))* Cengage Gale.
—Where She Went. (ENG.). (YA). (gr. 9-18). 2012. 304p. 10.99 *(978-0-14-242089-8(1),* Speak) 2011. 272p. 17.99 *(978-0-525-42294-5(3),* Dutton Books for Young Readers) Penguin Young Readers Group.
—Where She Went. 2012. (If I Stay Ser.: BK.2). (YA). 21.00 *(978-1-61383-394-0(6))* Perfection Learning Corp.
—Where She Went. l.t. ed. 2015. (If I Stay Ser.: BK.2). (ENG.). 286p. (YA). pap. 12.99 *(978-1-59413-855-3(9),* Large Print Pr.) Thorndike Pr.
—Where She Went. 2012. (If I Stay Ser.: BK.2). (YA). lib. bdg. 22.10 *(978-0-606-23644-7(9))* Turtleback.
Forsberg, Victoria. Little Irma Shirley & the Wand of Better: City Adventures. 2013. (ENG.). 23p. (J). pap. 10.95 *(978-1-4327-9671-6(2))* Outskirts Pr., Inc.
Fox, Erin. A Butterfly's Dream. 2012. 16p. pap. 12.68 *(978-1-4669-2066-8(1))* Trafford Publishing.
Fox, Janet. Sirens. 2012. 384p. (YA). (gr. 7). pap. 9.99 *(978-0-14-242430-8(7),* Speak) Penguin Young Readers Group.
Frank, Lucy. Just Ask Iris. 2003. (ENG., Illus.). 224p. (J). (gr. 5-9). pap. 10.99 *(978-0-689-84454-6(9),* Atheneum Bks. for Young Readers) Simon & Schuster Children's Publishing.
—Lucky Stars. 2014. (ENG.). 304p. (J). (gr. 5-9). pap. 14.99 *(978-1-4814-2901-6(9),* Atheneum Bks. for Young Readers) Simon & Schuster Children's Publishing.
Fredericks, Mariah. Life. Watkins, Liselotte, illus. 2009. (In the Cards Ser.: No. 3). (ENG.). 272p. (J). pap. 5.99 *(978-0-689-87659-2(9),* Simon & Schuster/Paula Wiseman Bks.) Simon & Schuster/Paula Wiseman Bks.
Freedman, Nancy Price. Isak & the Oranges: The Half-Orphans of HOA (Hebrew Orphan Asylum, NY) 2015. (ENG., Illus.). 107p. (J). pap. 10.95 *(978-1-4787-5564-7(4))* Outskirts Pr., Inc.
Freeman, Blake. Haibu Lost in New York. 2018. (Haibu Ser.). (ENG., Illus.). 144p. (J). (gr. 1-4). 18.99 *(978-1-5132-6221-5(1));* pap. 7.99 *(978-1-5132-6220-8(3))* West Margin Pr. (Graphic Arts Bks.).
Frenette, Liza. Dead End. Gillis, Jane, illus. 2005. (ENG.). x, 65p. (J). pap. *(978-1-59531-001-9(0))* North Country Bks., Inc.
Freymann-Weyr, Garret. Stay with Me. 2007. (ENG.). 320p. (YA). (gr. 9-12). pap. 17.99 *(978-0-618-88404-9(1),* 487146, Clarion Bks.) HarperCollins Pubs.
Friedman, Aimee. Two Summers. 2016. (ENG.). 368p. (YA). (gr. 7). 17.99 *(978-0-545-51807-9(5))* Scholastic, Inc.
Friedman, Laurie. Mallory & Mary Ann Take New York, No. 19. Kalis, Jennifer, illus. 2014. (Mallory Ser.: 19). (ENG.). 160p. (J). (gr. 2-5). pap. 7.99 *(978-1-4677-0935-4(2),* 613566c1-b9c7-4f65-bf8d-e99fe344eb41, Darby Creek) Lerner Publishing Group.
Frossard, Claire, illus. Emma's Journey. Frossard, Etienne, photos by. 2010. (ENG.). 56p. (J). (gr. -1-3). 17.95 *(978-1-59270-099-8(3))* Enchanted Lion Bks., LLC.
Funk, Josh. Lost in the Library: A Story of Patience & Fortitude. Lewis, Stevie, illus. 2018. (New York Public Library Book Ser.). (ENG.). 40p. (J). 18.99 *(978-1-250-15501-6(0),* 900184517, Holt, Henry & Co. Bks. For Young Readers) Holt, Henry & Co.
Fyne, Olga M. Be Satisfied with Who You Are. Mathis, Leslie, illus. 2013. 24p. pap. 9.99 *(978-1-61286-142-5(3))* Avid Readers Publishing Group.
Galvin, Larry J. The Pythagoras Solution. 2008. 102p. pap. 19.95 *(978-1-60441-990-0(3))* America Star Bks.
Gamble, Adam. Buenas Noches, Nueva York. Veno, Joe, illus. 2013. (Buenas Noches Ser.). (SPA.). 24p. (J). (— 1). bds. 9.95 *(978-1-60219-091-7(7))* Good Night Bks.
Ganeshram, Ramin. Stir It Up! 2011. (J). *(978-0-545-16583-9(0))* Scholastic, Inc.
George, Jean Craighead. Frightful's Mountain. 2014. (ENG.). 272p. (J). (gr. 4-8). 11.24 *(978-1-63245-351-8(7))* Lectorum Pubns., Inc.
Gilbert, Julie. Lucy Fights the Flames: A Triangle Shirtwaist Factory Survival Story. Trunfio, Alessia, illus. 2019. (Girls Survive Ser.). (ENG.). 112p. (J). (gr. 3-7). pap. 7.95 *(978-1-4965-8448-9(1),* 140973); lib. bdg. 26.65 *(978-1-4965-8386-4(8),* 140682) Capstone. (Stone Arch Bks.).
Glaser, Karina Yan. The Vanderbeekers & the Hidden Garden. (Vanderbeekers Ser.: 2). (ENG., Illus.). (J). (gr. 3-7). 2019. 352p. pap. 8.99 *(978-0-358-11734-6(8),* 1750649) 2018. 336p. 16.99 *(978-1-328-77002-8(8),* 1681000) HarperCollins Pubs. (Clarion Bks.).
—The Vanderbeekers of 141st Street. (Vanderbeekers Ser.: 1). (ENG., Illus.). (J). (gr. 3-7). 2018. 320p. pap. 7.99 *(978-1-328-49921-9(9),* 1718015) 2017. 304p. 16.99 *(978-0-544-87639-2(3),* 1649655) HarperCollins Pubs. (Clarion Bks.).
Glasthal, Jacqueline B. Liberty on 23rd Street. Reingold, Alan, illus. 2006. (Adventures in America Ser.). (gr. 4). 14.95 net. *(978-1-893110-45-8(1))* Silver Moon Pr.
Godbersen, Anna. The Lucky Ones. 2013. (Bright Young Things Ser.: 3). (ENG.). 400p. (YA). (gr. 9). pap. 10.99 *(978-0-06-196271-4(6),* HarperCollins) HarperCollins Pubs.
—The Luxe, Rumors, & Envy, Set, Bks. 1-3. 2009. (Luxe Ser.). (YA). (gr. 9). pap. 24.99 *(978-0-06-192118-6(1))* HarperCollins Pubs.
Going, K. L. Fat Kid Rules the World. 2004. (ENG.). 224p. (YA). (gr. 7-18). reprint ed. pap. 10.99 *(978-0-14-240208-5(7),* Penguin Books) Penguin Young Readers Group.
Goldman, Leslie. Night at the Museum: A Junior Novelization. 2006. (Illus.). 144p. (J). (gr. 4-6). per. 4.99 *(978-0-7641-3576-7(7))* Sourcebooks, Inc.
González, Lucía. The Storyteller's Candle: La Velita de Los Cuentos, 1 vol. Delacre, Lulu, illus. 2013. (ENG.). 32p. (J). (gr. 1-6). pap. 11.95 *(978-0-89239-237-7(1),* leelowcbp, Children's Book Press) Lee & Low Bks., Inc.
Gonzalez, Lucia M. & Delacre, Lulu. The Storyteller's Candle. 2008.Tr. of La Velita de los Cuentos. (SPA & ENG., Illus.). 32p. (J). (gr. k-4). 16.95 *(978-0-89239-222-3(3))* Lee & Low Bks., Inc.
Gownley, Jimmy. Amelia in Joy & Wonder, 1 vol. Gownley, Jimmy, illus. 2013. (Amelia Rules! Ser.). (ENG., Illus.). 36p. (J). (gr. 2-6). 31.36 *(978-1-61479-072-3(8),* 2391, Graphic Novels) Spotlight.
Grace, N. B. Rev It Up! 9th ed. 2010. (Wizards of Waverly Place Ser.: No. 9). 128p. (J). (gr. 3-7). pap. 4.99 *(978-1-4231-2676-8(9))* Disney Pr.
Graff, Lisa. A Tangle of Knots. 2013. (ENG.). 240p. (J). (gr. 3-7). 17.99 *(978-0-399-25517-5(6),* Philomel Bks.) Penguin Young Readers Group.
Grambling, Lois G. Can I Bring Saber to New York, Ms. Mayor? Love, Judy, illus. 2014. (Prehistoric Pets Ser.: 3). 32p. (J). (gr. k-3). 17.95 *(978-1-58089-570-5(0))* Charlesbridge Publishing, Inc.
Grant, Natalie. Light up New York, 1 vol. 2017. (Faithgirlz / Glimmer Girls Ser.: 4). (ENG., Illus.). 208p. (J). pap. 8.99 *(978-0-310-75274-5(4))* Zonderkidz.
Green, Tim. Football Hero. (Football Genius Ser.: 2). (ENG.). (J). (gr. 3-7). 2009. 320p. pap. 9.99 *(978-0-06-112276-7(9))* 2008. (Illus.). 304p. 16.99 *(978-0-06-112274-3(2))* HarperCollins Pubs. (HarperCollins).
—Football Hero. l.t. ed. 2008. (YA). 23.95 *(978-1-4104-1116-7(8))* Thorndike Pr.
—Rivals. (Baseball Great Ser.: 2). (ENG.). (J). (gr. 3-7). 2011. 288p. pap. 9.99 *(978-0-06-162694-4(5))* 2010. 272p. 16.99 *(978-0-06-162692-0(9))* HarperCollins Pubs. (HarperCollins).
Greenburg, Dan. How I Went from Bad to Verse. Davis, Jack E., illus. 2004. (Zack Files Ser.). 59p. lib. bdg. 15.00 *(978-0-7569-2235-1(6))* Perfection Learning Corp.
Griffin, Adele. The Knaveheart's Curse: A Vampire Island Book. 2009. (Vampire Island Ser.: 2). (ENG.). 160p. (J). (gr. 3-7). 6.99 *(978-0-14-241407-1(7),* Puffin Books) Penguin Young Readers Group.
—The Unfinished Life of Addison Stone: a Novel. 2016. (Illus.). 256p. (YA). (gr. 9). pap. 11.99 *(978-1-61695-596-0(1),* Soho Teen) Soho Pr., Inc.
Griffin, Paul. The Orange Houses. 2011. (ENG.). 160p. (YA). (gr. 9-12). 22.44 *(978-0-8037-3346-6(1),* Dial) Penguin Publishing Group.
—The Orange Houses. 2011. 176p. (YA). (gr. 9-18). 8.99 *(978-0-14-241982-3(6),* Speak) Penguin Young Readers Group.
—Ten Mile River. 2011. (ENG.). 208p. (YA). (gr. 7-18). 7.99 *(978-0-14-241983-0(4),* Speak) Penguin Young Readers Group.
Grimes, Nikki. Bronx Masquerade. 2017. (ENG.). 192p. (YA). (gr. 7). pap. 10.99 *(978-0-425-28976-1(1),* Speak) Penguin Young Readers Group.
—Bronx Masquerade. 2003. (gr. 7-12). lib. bdg. 17.20 *(978-0-613-81701-1(X))* Turtleback.
Gromosiak, Paul. Owahonton: Maid of the Mist. 2012. (ENG.). (J). pap. 12.95 *(978-1-4675-4107-7(9))* Independent Pub.
Grossinger, Tania. Jackie & Me: A Very Special Friendship. Esperanza, Charles George, illus. (ENG.). 32p. (J). (gr. -1-k).

M N O

2017. 6.99 *(978-1-5107-1270-6(4))* 2013. 16.95 *(978-1-62087-683-1(3)*, 620683) Skyhorse Publishing Co., Inc. (Sky Pony Pr.).

Gulledge, Laura Lee. Page by Paige. 2011. (ENG., Illus.). 192p. (YA). (gr. 8-17). pap. 11.99 *(978-0-8109-9722-6(3)*, 681001, Amulet Bks.) Abrams, Inc.

Gunther, Joseph. The Bluff, 1. Sabiston, Susan, illus. l.t. ed. 2006. 28p. (J). 14.95 *(978-0-9789525-0-1(2))* Young Readers Publications.

Gurevich, Margaret. Chloe by Design: Balancing Act. Hagel, Brooke, illus. 2015. (Chloe by Design Ser.). (ENG.). 384p. (J). (gr. 4-8). 14.95 *(978-1-62370-258-8(5)*, 128580, Capstone Young Readers) Capstone.

—Design Destiny, 1 vol. Hagel, Brooke, illus. 2014. (Chloe by Design Ser.). (ENG.). 96p. (J). (gr. 5-8). 25.32 *(978-1-4342-9180-6(4)*, 125654, Stone Arch Bks.) Capstone.

—Design Disaster. Hagel, Brooke, illus. 2015. (Chloe by Design Ser.). (ENG.). 96p. (J). (gr. 5-8). 25.32 *(978-1-4965-0505-7(0)*, 128577, Stone Arch Bks.) Capstone.

—Fashion Week Finale. Hagel, Brooke, illus. 2015. (Chloe by Design Ser.). (ENG.). 96p. (J). (gr. 5-8). 25.32 *(978-1-4965-0507-1(7)*, 128579, Stone Arch Bks.) Capstone.

—Runway Rundown. Hagel, Brooke, illus. 2015. (Chloe by Design Ser.). (ENG.). 96p. (J). (gr. 5-8). 25.32 *(978-1-4965-0506-4(9)*, 128578, Stone Arch Bks.) Capstone.

—Unraveling, 1 vol. Hagel, Brooke, illus. 2014. (Chloe by Design Ser.). (ENG.). 96p. (J). (gr. 5-8). 25.32 *(978-1-4342-9179-0(0)*, 125653, Stone Arch Bks.) Capstone.

Gutknecht, Allison. Spring Break Mistake. 2017. (Mix Ser.). (ENG., Illus.). 240p. (J). (gr. 4-8). pap. 7.99 *(978-1-4814-7153-4(8)*, Simon & Schuster/Paula Wiseman Bks.) Simon & Schuster/Paula Wiseman Bks.

Gutman, Dan. Houdini & Me. 2021. (ENG., Illus.). 224p. (J). (gr. 3-7). 16.99 *(978-0-8234-4515-8(1))* Holiday Hse., Inc.

—Willie & Me. 2015. (Baseball Card Adventures Ser.: 12). (ENG.). 176p. (J). (gr. 3-7). 16.99 *(978-0-06-170404-8(0)*, HarperCollins) HarperCollins Pubs.

Hall, Bruce Edward. Henry & the Kite Dragon. Low, William, illus. 2004. 40p. (J). (gr. 1-4). 18.99 *(978-0-399-23727-0(5)*, Philomel Bks.) Penguin Young Readers Group.

Hansen, Joyce. One True Friend. 2005. (ENG.). 160p. (J). (gr. 5-7). pap. 11.95 *(978-0-618-60991-8(1)*, 100443, Clarion Bks.) HarperCollins Pubs.

Harden, Perry Lee. The Percy Hargrove Stories: It's All Elementary. 2012. 160p. pap. 14.95 *(978-1-4772-2438-0(6))* AuthorHouse.

Harkins, Philip. Knockout. 2011. 250p. 46.95 *(978-1-258-08794-4(4))* Literary Licensing, LLC.

Harper, Suzanne. The Secret Life of Sparrow Delaney. (YA). 2008. (ENG.). 368p. (gr. 8-12). pap. 9.99 *(978-0-06-113160-8(1)*, Greenwillow Bks.) 2007. 224p. (gr. 7-12). 16.99 *(978-0-06-113158-5(X))* 2007. 362p. (gr. 7-12). lib. bdg. 17.89 *(978-0-06-113159-2(8))* HarperCollins Pubs.

Harris, Isobel. Little Boy Brown. Francois, Andre, illus. 2013. 48p. (J). (gr. -1-3). 15.95 *(978-1-59270-135-3(3))* Enchanted Lion Bks., LLC.

Harrison, Lisi. Bratfest at Tiffany's, No. 9. 2008. (Clique Ser.: 9). (ENG., Illus.). 256p. (J). (gr. 7-17). per. 9.99 *(978-0-316-00680-4(7)*, Poppy) Little, Brown Bks. for Young Readers.

—Charmed & Dangerous: The Clique Prequel. 2012. (Clique Ser.). (ENG.). 208p. (YA). (gr. 7-17). pap. 8.99 *(978-0-316-05536-9(0)*, Poppy) Little, Brown Bks. for Young Readers.

—Dial L for Loser. 2008. (Clique Novels Ser.). 268p. 20.00 *(978-1-60686-291-9(X))* Perfection Learning Corp.

—Dial l for Loser. 2006. (Clique Ser.: 6). (ENG.). 272p. (J). (gr. 7-17). per. 9.99 *(978-0-316-11504-9(5)*, Poppy) Little, Brown Bks. for Young Readers.

—It's Not Easy Being Mean, No. 7. rev. ed. 2007. (Clique Ser.: 7). (ENG.). 224p. (YA). (gr. 7-17). per. 13.99 *(978-0-316-11505-6(3)*, Poppy) Little, Brown Bks. for Young Readers.

—It's Not Easy Being Mean. 2008. (Clique Ser.). 193p. 20.00 *(978-1-60686-330-5(4))* Perfection Learning Corp.

—The Pretty Committee Strikes Back, No. 5. 2006. (Clique Ser.: 5). (ENG.). 272p. (J). (gr. 7-17). per. 9.99 *(978-0-316-11500-1(2)*, Poppy) Little, Brown Bks. for Young Readers.

—Sealed with a Diss. 2008. (Clique Novels Ser.). 248p. 20.00 *(978-1-60686-345-9(2))* Perfection Learning Corp.

—Sealed with a Diss: A Clique Novel. 2007. (Clique Ser.: 8). (ENG.). 272p. (YA). (gr. 7-17). pap. 15.99 *(978-0-316-11506-3(1)*, Poppy) Little, Brown Bks. for Young Readers.

—A Tale of Two Pretties. 2011. (Clique Ser.: 14). (ENG.). 224p. (J). (gr. 7-17). pap. 13.99 *(978-0-316-08442-0(5)*, Poppy) Little, Brown Bks. for Young Readers.

—These Boots Are Made for Stalking. 12th ed. 2010. (Clique Ser.: 12). (ENG.). 256p. (J). (gr. 7-17). pap. 9.99 *(978-0-316-00683-5(1)*, Poppy) Little, Brown Bks. for Young Readers.

Hazen, Lynn E. The Amazing Trail of Seymour Snail. Cushman, Doug, illus. 2009. (ENG.). 64p. (J). (gr. 1-4). 17.99 *(978-0-8050-8698-0(6)*, 900048258, Holt, Henry & Co. Bks. For Young Readers) Holt, Henry & Co.

Henry, O. & Escott, John. Oxford Bookworms Playscripts: One Thousand Dollars & Other Plays: Level 2: 700-Word Vocabulary. 2nd ed. 2008. (ENG., Illus.). 64p. 11.00 *(978-0-19-423520-4(3))* Oxford Univ. Pr., Inc.

Hepler, Heather. We Were Beautiful, 1 vol. 2019. (ENG.). 304p. (YA). pap. 12.99 *(978-0-310-76643-8(5))* Blink.

Herren, Greg. Lake Thirteen. 2013. (ENG.). 264p. (gr. 7). pap. 11.95 *(978-1-60282-894-0(6))* Bold Strokes Bks.

Hesse, Karen. Brooklyn Bridge: A Novel. Sheban, Chris, illus. 2011. (ENG.). 256p. (J). (gr. 6-8). pap. 11.99 *(978-0-312-67428-1(7)*, 900072843) Square Fish.

Hest, Amy. Remembering Mrs. Rossi. Maione, Heather, illus. 2007. (ENG.). 192p. (J). (gr. 3-7). 14.99 *(978-0-7636-2163-6(3))* Candlewick Pr.

—Remembering Mrs. Rossi. Maione, Heather, illus. 2010. (ENG.). 192p. (J). (gr. 3-7). 6.99 *(978-0-7636-4089-7(1))* Candlewick Pr.

Hieber, Leanna Renee. Darker Still. 2011. (Magic Most Foul Ser.: 1). (ENG.). 336p. (YA). (gr. 7-12). pap. 8.99 *(978-1-4022-6052-0(0))* Sourcebooks, Inc.

Holm, M. S. How Mohammed Saved Miss Liberty: The Story of a Good Muslim Boy. 2008. (ENG., Illus.). 270p. (YA). (gr. 7-12). pap. 12.00 *(978-0-9796199-0-8(4)*, Sentry Bks.) Great West Publishing.

Hope, Laura Lee. The Bobbsey Twins in a Great City. 2005. 27.95 *(978-1-4218-1482-7(X))*; 204p. pap. 12.95 *(978-1-4218-1582-4(6))* 1st World Publishing, Inc. (1st World Library - Literary Society).

—The Outdoor Girls of Deepdale. 2005. 180p. pap. 11.95 *(978-1-4218-1164-2(2)*, 1st World Library - Literary Society) 1st World Publishing, Inc.

Hopkinson, Deborah. A Bandit's Tale: The Muddled Misadventures. 2018. lib. bdg. 18.40 *(978-0-606-40940-7(8))* Turtleback.

—Sky Boys: How They Built the Empire State Building. Ransome, James E., illus. 2012. 48p. (J). (gr. -1-3). pap. 8.99 *(978-0-375-86541-1(1)*, Dragonfly Bks.) Random Hse. Children's Bks.

Howard, J. J. That Time I Joined the Circus. 2013. (ENG.). 272p. (YA). (gr. 7). 17.99 *(978-0-545-43381-5(9))* Scholastic, Inc.

Howe, Peter. Waggit Forever. Rayyan, Omar, illus. 2011. (Waggit Ser.: 3). (ENG.). 288p. (J). (gr. 5). pap. 7.99 *(978-0-06-176516-2(3)*, HarperCollins) HarperCollins Pubs.

Howells, Amanda. The Summer of Skinny Dipping. (YA). 2019. 320p. (gr. 8-12). pap. 10.99 *(978-1-4926-9671-1(4))* 2010. (ENG.). 304p. (gr. 7-12). pap. 9.99 *(978-1-4022-3862-8(2))* Sourcebooks, Inc.

Hughes, Cheryl. Jackson, the Pigeon Who Was Afraid of Heights. 2008. 44p. pap. 16.99 *(978-1-4389-2143-3(8))* AuthorHouse.

Hull, Norman. Robin's Big Brother. 2011. 56p. (gr. 4-6). pap. 9.99 *(978-1-4634-3691-9(2))* AuthorHouse.

Hyde, Catherine Ryan. Becoming Chloe. 2008. 224p. (YA). (gr. 9). pap. 8.99 *(978-0-375-83260-4(2)*, Knopf Bks. for Young Readers) Random Hse. Children's Bks.

Hyde, Heidi Smith. Feivel's Flying Horses. van der Sterre, Johanna, illus. 2010. (ENG.). 32p. (J). (gr. k-4). lib. bdg. 17.95 *(978-0-7613-3957-1(4)*, Kar-Ben Publishing) Lerner Publishing Group.

Iacovone, Lauren Marie. Here Lies Thomas Crawford, 1 vol. 2010. 252p. pap. 27.95 *(978-1-61582-690-2(4))* America Star Bks.

Jablonski, Carla. Book One of the Travelers, Bk. 1. 2009. (Pendragon: Before the War Ser.: 1). (ENG., Illus.). 256p. (J). (gr. 5-9). pap. 8.99 *(978-1-4169-6522-0(X)*, Aladdin) Simon & Schuster Children's Publishing.

Jackson, Tiffany D. Let Me Hear a Rhyme. (ENG.). (YA). (gr. 8). 2020. 400p. pap. 11.99 *(978-0-06-284033-2(9))* 2019. 384p. 19.99 *(978-0-06-284032-5(0))* HarperCollins Pubs. (Tegen, Katherine Bks).

Jacobs, Lily. The Littlest Bunny in Buffalo. Dunn, Robert, illus. 2016. (Littlest Bunny Ser.). (ENG.). 32p. (J). (gr. -1-3). 9.99 *(978-1-4926-3346-4(1)*, 9781492633464, Hometown World) Sourcebooks, Inc.

—The Littlest Bunny in New York: An Easter Adventure. Dunn, Robert, illus. 2015. (Littlest Bunny Ser.). (ENG.). 32p. (J). (gr. -1-3). 9.99 *(978-1-4926-1150-9(6)*, Hometown World) Sourcebooks, Inc.

—The Littlest Bunny in New York City: An Easter Adventure. Dunn, Robert, illus. 2015. (Littlest Bunny Ser.). (ENG.). 32p. (J). (gr. -1-3). 9.99 *(978-1-4926-1153-0(0)*, Hometown World) Sourcebooks, Inc.

James, Eric. Santa's Sleigh Is on Its Way to New York: A Christmas Adventure. Dunn, Robert, illus. 2015. (Santa's Sleigh Is on Its Way Ser.). (ENG.). 32p. (J). (gr. k-2). 12.99 *(978-1-4926-2751-7(8)*, Hometown World) Sourcebooks, Inc.

—Santa's Sleigh Is on Its Way to New York City: A Christmas Adventure. Dunn, Robert, illus. 2016. (Santa's Sleigh Is on Its Way Ser.). (ENG.). 32p. (J). (gr. k-2). 12.99 *(978-1-4926-4344-9(0)*, 9781492643449, Hometown World) Sourcebooks, Inc.

—The Spooky Express New York. Piwowarski, Marcin, illus. 2017. (Spooky Express Ser.). (ENG.). 32p. (J). (gr. k-6). 9.99 *(978-1-4926-5382-0(9)*, Hometown World) Sourcebooks, Inc.

—The Spooky Express New York City. Piwowarski, Marcin, illus. 2017. (Spooky Express Ser.). (ENG.). 32p. (J). (gr. k-6). 9.99 *(978-1-4926-5383-7(7)*, Hometown World) Sourcebooks, Inc.

—Tiny the New York City Easter Bunny. 2018. (Tiny the Easter Bunny Ser.). (ENG.). 40p. (J). (gr. k-3). 9.99 *(978-1-4926-5949-5(5)*, Hometown World) Sourcebooks, Inc.

—Tiny the New York Easter Bunny. 2018. (Tiny the Easter Bunny Ser.). (ENG.). 40p. (J). (gr. k-3). 9.99 *(978-1-4926-5948-8(7)*, Hometown World) Sourcebooks, Inc.

James, Henry. Washington Square. 2004. (gr. 7-12). reprint ed. pap. *(978-0-87720-743-6(7)*. N387ALS) AMSCO Schl. Pubns., Inc.

Jane, Pamela. Winky Blue Goes Wild! Tilley, Debbie, illus. 2003. 64p. (J). 13.95 *(978-1-59034-588-7(6))*; pap. *(978-1-59034-589-4(4))* Mondo Publishing.

Jean, April. A Little Dachshund's Tale. Cross, Kevin, illus. 2012. 36p. pap. 9.95 *(978-1-61897-367-2(3)*, Strategic Bk. Publishing) Strategic Book Publishing & Rights Agency (SBPRA).

Jean, Sagine. Darkness. 2017. (Survive Ser.). (ENG.). 192p. (YA). (gr. 5-12). lib. bdg. 31.42 *(978-1-68076-731-5(3)*, 25396, Epic Escape) EPIC Pr.

Jenkins, Emily. All-Of-a-Kind Family Hanukkah. Zelinsky, Paul O., illus. 2018. 40p. (J). (gr. -1-2). 18.99 *(978-0-399-55419-3(X)*, Schwartz & Wade Bks.) Random Hse. Children's Bks.

Jenkins, Ward, illus. New York, Baby! 2012. (ENG.). 24p. (J). (gr. -1 — 1). 12.99 *(978-1-4521-0619-9(3))* Chronicle Bks. LLC.

Jennings, Rashad. Arcade & the Triple T Token, 1 vol. 2019. (Coin Slot Chronicles Ser.). (ENG., Illus.). 256p. (J). 16.99 *(978-0-310-76741-1(5))* Zonderkidz.

Jeremiah, Omari. Paper Boy Four: L. O. E. P. S. Worst Nightmare. Rollins, Berni, illus. 2007. 96p. (YA). (gr. 7-12). pap. 12.99 *(978-1-929188-15-4(3))* Morton Bks.

Johnson, Harvell. What about Johnson? Howard, Vanetta, ed. Clark, Donna Osborn, illus. 2013. 132p. pap. 11.95 *(978-0-9885056-0-5(6))* Word on Da Street Publishing.

Joseph, Lynn. Flowers in the Sky. 2013. (ENG.). 240p. (YA). (gr. 8). 17.99 *(978-0-06-029794-7(8)*, HarperTeen) HarperCollins Pubs.

Jules, Jacqueline. Freddie Ramos Rules New York. Benítez, Miguel, illus. 2016. (Zapato Power Ser.: 6). (ENG.). 96p. (J). (gr. 1-5). 14.99 *(978-0-8075-9497-1(0)*, 807594970) Whitman, Albert & Co.

June, Christina. Everywhere You Want to Be, 1 vol. 2018. (ENG.). 288p. (YA). pap. 12.99 *(978-0-310-76333-8(9))* Blink.

Kalda, Sam, illus. The Great Gatsby. adapted ed. 2014. (American Classics Ser.). (ENG.). 64p. pap. 7.95 *(978-1-906230-74-6(9))* Real Reads Ltd. GBR. Dist: Casemate Pubs. & Bk. Distributors, LLC.

Kaldor, Connie. A Duck in New York City. Fil & Julie, Connie, illus. 2005. (ENG.). 36p. (J). (gr. -1-2). 16.95 *(978-2-923163-02-4(8))* La Montagne Secrete CAN. Dist: Independent Pubs. Group.

Kalman, Maira. Max Makes a Million. 2017. (Illus.). 48p. (J). (gr. k-3). 18.95 *(978-1-68137-170-2(7)*, NYR Children's Collection) New York Review of Bks., Inc., The.

Kantor, Melissa. If I Have a Wicked Stepmother, Where's My Prince? 2005. 283p. (YA). *(978-1-4156-2763-1(0))* Hyperion Pr.

Karasyov, Carrie & Kargman, Jill. Summer Intern. 2007. 184p. (YA). (gr. 7-18). lib. bdg. 17.89 *(978-0-06-115376-1(1)*, HarperTeen) HarperCollins Pubs.

Kargman, Jill & Karasyov, Carrie. Bittersweet Sixteen. 2006. (YA). (gr. 7-12). (ENG.). 240p. 15.99 *(978-0-06-077844-6(X))*; 230p. lib. bdg. 16.89 *(978-0-06-077845-3(8))* HarperCollins Pubs.

Kearney, Meg. When You Never Said Goodbye: An Adoptee's Search for Her Birth Mother: a Novel in Poems & Journal Entries. 2017. (ENG.). 224p. (YA). (gr. 9-17). 17.95 *(978-0-89255-479-9(7)*, 255479) Persea Bks., Inc.

Kebbi, Yann. Americanine: A Haute Dog in New York. 2015. (ENG., Illus.). 72p. (J). 19.95 *(978-1-59270-172-8(8))* Enchanted Lion Bks., LLC.

Kelman, Jennifer. Mrs Pinkelmeyer & Moopus Mcglinden Prance into New York City. 2011. 44p. pap. 15.99 *(978-1-4575-0497-6(9))* Dog Ear Publishing, LLC.

Kennedy, C. Omorphi. Girault, Bénédicte, tr. 2016. (ENG., Illus.). (J). 34.99 *(978-1-63533-055-7(6)*, Harmony Ink Pr.) Dreamspinner Pr.

Kent, Rose. Rocky Road. 2012. (ENG.). 304p. (J). (gr. 4-6). 21.19 *(978-0-375-86344-8(3)*, Knopf Bks. for Young Readers); (gr. 3-7). 7.99 *(978-0-375-86345-5(1)*, Yearling) Random Hse. Children's Bks.

Kern, Peggy. Little Peach. 2015. (ENG.). 208p. (YA). (gr. 9). 17.99 *(978-0-06-226695-8(0)*, Balzer & Bray) HarperCollins Pubs.

Keyes, Joseph W. The Sparrows of Saint Thomas. 2007. (ENG.). 92p. pap. 14.95 *(978-1-4303-1410-3(9))* Lulu Pr., Inc.

Kheiriyeh, Rashin. Saffron Ice Cream. Kheiriyeh, Rashin, illus. 2018. (ENG., Illus.). 40p. (J). (gr. -1-3). 18.99 *(978-1-338-15052-0(9)*, Levine, Arthur A. Bks.) Scholastic, Inc.

Kiem, Elizabeth. Hider, Seeker, Secret Keeper. 2017. (Bolshoi Saga Ser.: 2). (Illus.). 288p. (YA). (gr. 9). pap. 10.99 *(978-1-61695-569-4(4)*, Soho Teen) Soho Pr., Inc.

Kingsley, Kate. Pretty on the Outside. 2010. (Young, Loaded, & Fabulous Ser.: 1). (ENG.). 320p. (YA). (gr. 9-18). pap. 9.99 *(978-1-4169-9399-5(1)*, Simon Pulse) Simon Pulse.

Kirk, Connie Ann. Sky Dancers, 1 vol. Hale, Christy, illus. 2013. (ENG.). 32p. (J). (gr. 2-4). pap. 11.95 *(978-1-62014-147-2(7)*, leelowbooks) Lee & Low Bks., Inc.

Konen, Leah. Happy Messy Scary Love. 2019. (ENG., Illus.). 336p. (YA). (gr. 8-17). 18.99 *(978-1-4197-3489-2(X)*, 1149101, Amulet Bks.) Abrams, Inc.

Konigsburg, E. L. From the Mixed-up Files of Mrs. Basil E. Frankweiler. 2007. (Illus.). 74p. (J). pap. *(978-0-545-04173-7(2))* Scholastic, Inc.

—From the Mixed-up Files of Mrs. Basil E. Frankweiler. l.t. ed. 2005. 186p. pap. 10.95 *(978-0-7862-7358-4(5)*, Large Print Pr.) Thorndike Pr.

Korman, Gordon. The Hypnotists. 2014. (Hypnotists Ser.: 1). lib. bdg. 17.20 *(978-0-606-35808-8(0))* Turtleback.

—The Hypnotists (the Hypnotists, Book 1), Bk. 1. 2014. (Hypnotists Ser.: 1). (ENG.). 240p. (J). (gr. 3-7). pap. 7.99 *(978-0-545-50325-9(6)*, Scholastic Paperbacks) Scholastic, Inc.

Kroll, Steven. Pooch on the Loose: A Christmas Adventure, 0 vols. Garland, Michael, illus. 2013. (ENG.). 40p. (J). (gr. -1-3). pap. 9.99 *(978-0-7614-5443-4(8)*, 9780761454434, Two Lions) Amazon Publishing.

—When I Dream of Heaven: Angelina's Story. 2004. 156p. (J). lib. bdg. 16.92 *(978-1-4242-0770-1(3))* Fitzgerald Bks.

Kroll, Steven & Droll. Pooch on the Loose: A Christmas Adventure, 1 vol. Garland, Michael, illus. 2005. (ENG.). 32p. (J). (gr. -1-3). 14.95 *(978-0-7614-5239-3(7))* Marshall Cavendish Corp.

Krovatin, Christopher. Venomous. Yates, Kelly, illus. 2011. (ENG.). 336p. (YA). (gr. 8). pap. 8.99 *(978-1-4424-1298-9(4)*, Atheneum Bks. for Young Readers) Simon & Schuster Children's Publishing.

Krulik, Nancy. Broadway Doggie. 2016. (Magic Bone Ser.: 10). lib. bdg. 14.75 *(978-0-606-38416-2(2))* Turtleback.

—Ripped at the Seams. 2004. (Romantic Comedies Ser.). (ENG.). 336p. (YA). (gr. 9). mass mkt. 6.99 *(978-0-689-86771-2(9)*, Simon Pulse) Simon Pulse.

Kuhlman, Evan. Brother from a Box. Bruno, Iacopo, illus. 2013. (ENG.). 288p. (J). (gr. 4-7). pap. 6.99 *(978-1-4424-2659-7(4)*, Atheneum Bks. for Young Readers) Simon & Schuster Children's Publishing.

—Brother from a Box. Bruno, Iacopo, illus. 2012. (ENG.). 288p. (J). (gr. 4-7). 16.99 *(978-1-4424-2658-0(6))* Simon & Schuster, Inc.

Laberje, Reji. Max Explores New York. Fenech, Liza, illus. 2014. (Max Explores Ser.). (ENG.). 20p. (J). (— 1). bds. 9.95 *(978-1-62937-004-0(5))* Triumph Bks.

LaBrot, Matthew & Daniel, Hale. Green Streak. 2004. (Zeke Armstrong Mysteries Ser.: 2). 236p. (J). per. 8.95 *(978-1-929976-28-7(3))* Top Pubns., Ltd.

Lane, Dakota. The Orpheus Obsession. 2008. (ENG., Illus.). 288p. (YA). (gr. 9). pap. 8.99 *(978-0-06-074175-4(9)*, HarperTeen) HarperCollins Pubs.

Lane, Nathan & Elliott, Devlin. Naughty Mabel Sees It All. Krall, Dan, illus. 2016. (Naughty Mabel Ser.). (ENG.). 48p. (J). (gr. -1-3). 17.99 *(978-1-4814-3024-1(6)*, Simon & Schuster Bks. For Young Readers) Simon & Schuster Bks. For Young Readers.

Larbalestier, Justine. Magic's Child. 2007. (Magic or Madness Trilogy). 291p. (YA). *(978-1-4287-3603-0(4)*, Razorbill) Penguin Publishing Group.

Law, Jerel. Spirit Fighter, 1 vol. 2012. (Son of Angels, Jonah Stone Ser.). (ENG.). 256p. (J). pap. 9.99 *(978-1-4003-1843-8(2)*, Tommy Nelson) Nelson, Thomas Inc.

Lawson, Brandi. The Soap Bubble Frog. Kinra, Richa, illus. 2012. 32p. pap. 14.50 *(978-1-61897-784-7(9)*, Strategic Bk. Publishing) Strategic Book Publishing & Rights Agency (SBPRA).

Lee, Mary Ellen. Danny & Life on Bluff Point: Blizzard of '95 revised Edition. 2009. 160p. (gr. 4-7). 22.95 *(978-1-4401-1383-3(1))*; pap. 12.95 *(978-0-595-53308-4(6))* iUniverse, Inc.

—Danny & Life on Bluff Point: Lost in the Dark. 2009. 160p. (gr. 4-7). 22.95 *(978-1-4401-4607-7(1))*; pap. 12.95 *(978-1-4401-4608-4(X))* iUniverse, Inc.

Lee, Thomas. The Battle at Otter Lake. 2007. 167p. pap. 24.95 *(978-1-60441-488-2(X))* America Star Bks.

L'Engle, Madeleine. Camilla. 2009. (ENG.). 272p. (YA). (gr. 7-12). pap. 18.99 *(978-0-312-56132-1(6)*, 900058867) Square Fish.

—The Young Unicorns: Book Three of the Austin Family Chronicles. 2008. (Austin Family Ser.: 3). (ENG.). 304p. (J). (gr. 7-12). pap. 12.99 *(978-0-312-37933-9(1)*, 900050196) Square Fish.

Lenzi, Danielle E. My Search for Prince Charming's Normal Brother. 2011. 136p. pap. 25.70 *(978-1-4634-0446-8(8))*; (gr. 10-12). 33.70 *(978-1-4634-0445-1(X))* AuthorHouse.

Lerangis, Peter. Wtf. (ENG., (YA). (gr. 9). 2013. Illus.). 288p. 17.99 *(978-1-4424-9369-8(0))* 2013. (Illus.). 288p. pap. 9.99 *(978-1-4424-9368-1(2))* 2009. 272p. pap. 8.99 *(978-1-4169-1360-3(2))* Simon Pulse. (Simon Pulse).

Levine, Rhoda. Arthur. Aison, Everett, illus. 2015. 48p. (J). (gr. -1-2). 15.95 *(978-1-59017-935-2(8)*, NYR Children's Collection) New York Review of Bks., Inc., The.

Levis, Caron. Ida, Always. Santoso, Charles, illus. 2016. (ENG.). 40p. (J). (gr. -1-3). 19.99 *(978-1-4814-2640-4(0))* Simon & Schuster Children's Publishing.

Levithan, David. Love Is the Higher Law. 2010. 176p. (YA). (gr. 7). pap. 9.99 *(978-0-375-83469-1(9)*, Knopf Bks. for Young Readers) Random Hse. Children's Bks.

Levoy, Myron. Alan & Naomi. 2011. 14.12 *(978-0-7848-3566-1(7)*, Everbind) Marco Bk. Co.

Lewis, Linda. All for the Love of That Boy. 2007. (ENG.). 224p. (YA). (gr. 7). pap. 12.95 *(978-1-4169-6142-0(9)*, Simon Pulse) Simon Pulse.

Lewis, Stewart. You Have Seven Messages. 2012. (ENG.). 304p. (YA). (gr. 7). pap. 11.99 *(978-0-385-74029-6(8)*, Ember) Random Hse. Children's Bks.

Lewman, David. Out of the Shadows Junior Novelization. 2016. lib. bdg. 17.20 *(978-0-606-38886-3(9))* Turtleback.

Light, Steve. Have You Seen My Dragon? Light, Steve, illus. 2014. (ENG., Illus.). 48p. (J). (-k). 16.99 *(978-0-7636-6648-4(3))* Candlewick Pr.

Lindner, April. Catherine. 2014. (ENG.). 336p. (YA). (gr. 10-17). pap. 10.00 *(978-0-316-19693-2(2)*, Poppy) Little, Brown Bks. for Young Readers.

Lipsyte, Robert. The Brave. 2003. (ENG.). 240p. (J). (gr. 8-18). pap. 6.99 *(978-0-06-447079-7(2)*, HarperCollins) HarperCollins Pubs.

Littlefield, Holly. The Rooftop Adventure of Minnie & Tessa, Factory Fire Survivors. Hammond, Ted & Carbajal, Richard, illus. 2011. (History's Kid Heroes Ser.). 32p. pap. 51.02 *(978-0-7613-7639-2(9)*, Graphic Universe™) Lerner Publishing Group.

Littman, Sarah Darer. Life, After. 2010. (ENG.). 288p. (J). (gr. 7-18). 17.99 *(978-0-545-15144-3(9)*, Scholastic Pr.) Scholastic, Inc.

—Taming of the Shoe. 2019. (ENG.). 240p. (J). (gr. 3-7). 17.99 *(978-1-5344-3157-7(8))*; (Illus.). pap. 7.99 *(978-1-5344-3156-0(X))* Simon & Schuster Children's Publishing. (Aladdin).

Livingston, Lesley. Transcendent. 2014. (Starling Trilogy Ser.: 3). (ENG.). 352p. (YA). (gr. 8). 17.99 *(978-0-06-206313-7(8)*, HarperTeen) HarperCollins Pubs.

Lockhart, E. Fly on the Wall. 2007. (ENG., Illus.). 192p. (YA). (gr. 7-12). pap. 8.99 *(978-0-385-73282-6(1)*, Delacorte Pr.) Random Hse. Children's Bks.

Lombard, Jenny. Drita, My Homegirl. 2008. 144p. (J). (gr. 3-7). 6.99 *(978-0-14-240905-3(7)*, Puffin Books) Penguin Young Readers Group.

—Drita, My Homegirl. 2008. 135p. (J). (gr. 4-6). 13.65 *(978-0-7569-8919-4(1))* Perfection Learning Corp.

Lovascio, Jane. Casey & Bella Go to New York. Jasuna, Aija, illus. 2008. 24p. (J). 14.95 *(978-1-60131-007-1(2))* Big Tent Bks.

Low, William. Chinatown. 2014. 32p. pap. 9.00 *(978-1-61003-224-7(1))* Center for the Collaborative Classroom.

Luciano, Sonia. Mr. I Forgot. 2009. 48p. pap. 16.95 *(978-1-61582-765-7(X))* America Star Bks.

Lupica, Mike. Hero. 2011. (ENG.). 304p. (J). (gr. 5-18). 8.99 *(978-0-14-241960-1(5)*, Puffin Books) Penguin Young Readers Group.

Lyga, Barry. Blood of My Blood. 2014. (I Hunt Killers Ser.: 3). (ENG.). 480p. (YA). (gr. 10-17). 18.00 *(978-0-316-19870-7(6))* Little, Brown Bks. for Young Readers.

Lyon, Tammie, illus. Eloise at the Wedding/Ready-To-Read: Ready-To-Read Level 1. 2006. (Eloise Ser.). (ENG.). 32p.

(J). (gr. -1-1). pap. 4.99 *(978-0-689-87449-9(9)*, Simon Spotlight) Simon Spotlight.

Lyttleton, Kay. Jean Craig in New York. 2005. pap. 24.95 *(978-1-4179-9293-5(X))* Kessinger Publishing, LLC.

Mac. Anna Smudge: Professional Shrink: Professional Shrink. 2008. (Professionals Ser.: 1). (ENG., Illus.). 256p. (J). (gr. 4-18). pap. 9.99 *(978-1-934906-00-2(X))* Toasted Coconut Media LLC.

Macaraeg, Diane. Last Meal. 2008. 132p. pap. *(978-3-639-03548-3(8))* AV Akademikerverlag GmbH & Co. KG.

Maccoll, Michaela & Nichols, Rosemary. Rory's Promise. 2014. (Hidden Histories Ser.). (ENG.). 288p. (J). (gr. 4-7). 16.95 *(978-1-62091-623-0(1)*, Calkins Creek) Highlights Pr., c/o Highlights for Children, Inc.

MacCullough, Carolyn. Once a Witch. 2010. (ENG.). 320p. (YA). (gr. 7). pap. 17.99 *(978-0-547-41730-1(6)*, 1430229, Clarion Bks.) HarperCollins Pubs.

—Once a Witch. 2009. (ENG.). 304p. (YA). (gr. 7-12). 24.94 *(978-0-547-22399-5(4))* Houghton Mifflin Harcourt Publishing Co.

Mackler, Carolyn. The Earth, My Butt, & Other Big Round Things. 2018. (ENG.). 288p. (YA). pap. 11.99 *(978-1-68119-798-2(7)*, 900187324, Bloomsbury USA Childrens) Bloomsbury Publishing USA.

—The Earth, My Butt, & Other Big Round Things, 1. 2012. (Earth, My Butt, & Other Big Round Things Ser.). (ENG., Illus.). 246p. (YA). (gr. 9). 24.94 *(978-0-7636-1958-9(2))* Candlewick Pr.

—Not If I Can Help It (Scholastic Gold) 2019. (ENG.). 240p. (J). (gr. 3-7). 16.99 *(978-0-545-70948-4(2)*, Scholastic Pr.) Scholastic, Inc.

—The Universe Is Expanding & So Am I. 2019. (ENG.). 304p. (YA). pap. 10.99 *(978-1-68119-982-5(3)*, 900194721, Bloomsbury Young Adult) Bloomsbury Publishing USA.

Mak, Kam. My Chinatown: One Year in Poems. Mak, Kam, illus. 2016. (ENG., Illus.). 32p. (J). (gr. -1-3). pap. 8.99 *(978-0-06-443732-5(9)*, HarperCollins) HarperCollins Pubs.

Manning, Dennis & Crisalli, Joseph. The Emeritus Peabody Mysteries. 2008. 212p. pap. 13.98 *(978-1-4303-2186-6(5))* Lulu Pr., Inc.

Manning, Matthew K. Greener on the Other Side. Sommariva, Jon, illus. 2018. (Batman / Teenage Mutant Ninja Turtles Adventures Ser.). (ENG.). 32p. (J). (gr. 2-6). lib. bdg. 28.95 *(978-1-4965-7383-4(8)*, 138941, Stone Arch Bks.) Capstone.

—Through the Looking Glass. Sommariva, Jon, illus. 2018. (Batman / Teenage Mutant Ninja Turtles Adventures Ser.). (ENG.). 32p. (J). (gr. 2-6). lib. bdg. 28.95 *(978-1-4965-7386-5(2)*, 138943, Stone Arch Bks.) Capstone.

Manzano, Sonia. No Dogs Allowed! Muth, Jon J., illus. 2005. (J). 27.95 incl. audio *(978-0-8045-6927-9(4)*, SAC6927); 29.95 incl. audio compact disk *(978-0-8045-4101-5(9)*, SACD4101) Spoken Arts, Inc.

—The Revolution of Evelyn Serrano. 2014. (ENG.). 224p. (YA). (gr. 9). pap. 10.99 *(978-0-545-32506-6(4))* Scholastic, Inc.

Manzo, Christopher. Oliver Brightside: You Don't Want That Penny. Adams, Lisa, illus. 2016. (ENG.). 36p. (J). 16.95 *(978-0-9963756-4-1(3))* All About Kids Publishing.

Marina, Budhos. Ask Me No Questions. 2014. (ENG.). 176p. (YA). (gr. 7-12). 14.24 *(978-1-63245-300-6(2))* Lectorum Pubns., Inc.

Marsh, Carole. The Behemoth Blizzard Mystery. (Masters of Disasters Ser.). (Illus.). 118p. (J). (gr. 3-5). 2008. per. 5.99 *(978-0-635-06464-6(2))* 2007. 14.95 *(978-0-635-06467-7(7))* Gallopade International.

—The Mystery in New York City. (Real Kids, Real Places Ser.). 146p. (J). 2009. (Illus.). lib. bdg. 18.99 *(978-0-635-06998-6(9)*, Marsh, Carole Mysteries)10. 2003. (ENG.). (gr. 4-6). 22.44 *(978-0-635-02099-4(8))* Gallopade International.

Marsh, Laura F. Steps to Liberty. Wright, John R., illus. 2007. 32p. (J). 17.95 *(978-0-615-16563-9(X))* Junior League of Central Westchester.

Marsh, Scott. Hannah & the Golden Swan. 2011. 216p. pap. 24.95 *(978-1-4626-1084-6(6))* America Star Bks.

Martin, Ann M. Ten Good & Bad Things about My Life (So Far) 2013. (ENG.). 288p. (J). (gr. 4-7). pap. 8.99 *(978-1-250-03413-7(2)*, 900120583) Square Fish.

—Ten Rules for Living with My Sister. 2012. (ENG.). 256p. (J). (gr. 4-7). pap. 11.99 *(978-1-250-01021-6(7)*, 900084758) Square Fish.

Marz, Ron. Witchblade Redemption, Vol. 4. 2012. (ENG., Illus.). 160p. pap. 19.99 *(978-1-60706-424-4(3)*, 12a49951-f938-438c-9d58-a3c76bfa591f) Image Comics.

Maskame, Estelle. Did I Mention I Need You? 2016. (Did I Mention I Love You (DIMILY) Ser.: 2). (ENG.). 384p. (YA). (gr. 8-12). pap. 10.99 *(978-1-4926-3218-4(X)*, 9781492632184) Sourcebooks, Inc.

Massie, Elizabeth. Ameri-Scares: New York. 2013. 148p. pap. 12.99 *(978-1-937530-55-6(8))* Crossroad Pr.

Matas, Carol. Rosie in New York City: Gotcha! 2003. (ENG., Illus.). 128p. (J). (gr. 4-7). pap. 9.95 *(978-0-689-85714-0(4)*, Simon & Schuster/Paula Wiseman Bks.) Simon & Schuster/Paula Wiseman Bks.

Matti, Truus. Mister Orange. 2013. (ENG., Illus.). 156p. (J). (gr. 3). 16.95 *(978-1-59270-123-0(X))* Enchanted Lion Bks., LLC.

Maxwell, Lisa. The Devil's Thief. 2018. (Last Magician Ser.: 2). (ENG., Illus.). 704p. (YA). (gr. 9). 18.99 *(978-1-4814-9445-8(7)*, Simon Pulse) Simon Pulse.

McClatchy, Lisa. Eloise & the Dinosaurs: Ready-To-Read Level 1. Lyon, Tammie, illus. 2007. (Eloise Ser.). (ENG.). 32p. (J). (gr. -1-1). pap. 4.99 *(978-0-689-87453-6(7)*, Simon Spotlight) Simon Spotlight.

—Eloise & the Snowman, 1 vol. Lyon, Tammie, illus. 2015. (Kay Thompson's Eloise Ser.). (ENG.). 32p. (J). (gr. -1-2). 31.36 *(978-1-61479-402-8(2)*, 18187) Spotlight.

—Eloise & the Snowman: Ready-To-Read Level 1. Lyon, Tammie, illus. 2006. (Eloise Ser.). (ENG.). 32p. (J). (gr. -1-1). pap. 4.99 *(978-0-689-87451-2(0)*, Simon Spotlight) Simon Spotlight.

—Eloise's New Bonnet: Ready-To-Read Level 1. Lyon, Tammie, illus. 2007. (Eloise Ser.). (ENG.). 32p. (J). (gr. -1-1). pap. 3.99 *(978-0-689-87452-9(9)*, Simon Spotlight) Simon Spotlight.

McGee, Katharine. The Dazzling Heights. 2017. (Thousandth Floor Ser.: 2). (ENG.). 432p. (YA). (gr. 8). 18.99 *(978-0-06-241862-3(9)*, HarperCollins) HarperCollins Pubs.

—The Thousandth Floor. (Thousandth Floor Ser.: 1). (ENG.). (YA). (gr. 8). 2017. 496p. pap. 11.99 *(978-0-06-241860-9(2))* 2016. 448p. 18.99 *(978-0-06-241859-3(9))* HarperCollins Pubs. (HarperCollins).

—The Towering Sky. (Thousandth Floor Ser.: 3). (ENG.). 464p. (YA). (gr. 8). 2019. pap. 11.99 *(978-0-06-241866-1(1))* 2018. 18.99 *(978-0-06-241865-4(3))* HarperCollins Pubs. (HarperCollins).

McGee, Ron. Ryan Quinn & the Rebel's Escape. 2016. (Ryan Quinn Ser.: 1). (ENG., Illus.). 368p. (J). (gr. 3-7). 16.99 *(978-0-06-242164-7(6)*, HarperCollins) HarperCollins Pubs.

McGhee, Patti Gray. Ducky Bill's Great Race. Vermillion, Danny, illus. 2013. 46p. 24.95 *(978-1-63000-424-8(3))*; 48p. pap. 24.95 *(978-1-62709-522-8(5))* America Star Bks.

McNally, Janet. Girls in the Moon. (ENG.). (YA). (gr. 8). 2018. 368p. pap. 9.99 *(978-0-06-243625-2(2))* 2016. 352p. 17.99 *(978-0-06-243624-5(4))* HarperCollins Pubs. (HarperTeen).

Mebus, Scott. Gods of Manhattan 2: Spirits in the Park, Vol. 2. 2010. (ENG.). 400p. (J). (gr. 3-7). 8.99 *(978-0-14-241645-7(2)*, Puffin Books) Penguin Young Readers Group.

—Spirits in the Park. 2009. (Gods of Manhattan Ser.: No. 2). (J). *(978-0-525-47963-5(5)*, Dutton Juvenile) Penguin Publishing Group.

Mechling, Lauren & Moser, Laura. All Q, No A: More Tales of a 10th-Grade Social Climber. 2006. (ENG.). 288p. (YA). (gr. 7-12). pap. 15.95 *(978-0-618-66378-1(9)*, 419818, Clarion Bks.) HarperCollins Pubs.

Medina, Meg. Burn Baby Burn. (ENG.). 320p. (YA). (gr. 9). 2018. pap. 8.99 *(978-1-5362-0027-0(1))* 2016. 17.99 *(978-0-7636-7467-0(2))* Candlewick Pr.

Medina, Tony. I Am Alfonso Jones, 1 vol. Jennings, John & Robinson, Stacey, illus. 2017. (I Am Alfonso Jones Ser.: 1). (ENG.). 176p. (YA). (gr. 6-12). pap. 18.95 *(978-1-62014-263-9(5)*, leelowtu, Tu Bks.) Lee & Low Bks., Inc.

Mendle, Jane. My Ultimate Sister Disaster: A Novel. 2010. (ENG.). 208p. (YA). (gr. 7-18). pap. 18.99 *(978-0-312-36904-0(2)*, 900042729, St. Martin's Griffin) St. Martin's Pr.

Merrill, Jean. The Pushcart War. 2006. (J). 1.25 *(978-1-4193-8348-9(5))* Recorded Bks., Inc.

—The Pushcart War. Solbert, Ronni, illus. 50th ed. 2015. 232p. (J). (gr. 3-7). pap. 12.99 *(978-1-59017-936-9(6)*, NYRB Kids) New York Review of Bks., Inc., The.

Messner, Kate. Escape from the Twin Towers (Ranger in Time #11) McMorris, Kelley, illus. 2020. (Ranger in Time Ser.: 11). (ENG.). 144p. (J). (gr. 2-5). pap. 5.99 *(978-1-338-53794-9(6)*, Scholastic Pr.) Scholastic, Inc.

—Night of Soldiers & Spies (Ranger in Time #10) (Library Edition) McMorris, Kelley, illus. 2019. (Ranger in Time Ser.: 10). (ENG.). 160p. (J). (gr. 2-5). lib. bdg. 17.99 *(978-1-338-13402-5(7)*, Scholastic Pr.) Scholastic, Inc.

—Spitfire. 2007. (ENG.). (J). pap. *(978-1-59531-018-7(5))* North Country Bks., Inc.

Metzger, Steve. Dancing Clock. Nez, John Abbott, illus. 2011. (ENG.). 32p. 12.95 *(978-1-58925-100-7(8))*; (J). pap. 7.95 *(978-1-58925-429-9(5))* Tiger Tales.

Midler, Bette. The Tale of the Mandarin Duck: A Modern Fable. Kakutani, Michiko, photos by. 2021. (ENG., Illus.). 40p. (J). (gr. -1-2). 18.99 *(978-0-593-17676-4(6))*; lib. bdg. 21.99 *(978-0-593-17677-1(4))* Random Hse. Children's Bks. (Random Hse. Bks. for Young Readers).

Mihaley, James. You Can't Have My Planet: But Take My Brother, Please. 2013. (ENG.). 272p. (J). (gr. 4-7). pap. 13.99 *(978-1-250-01667-6(3)*, 900087081) Square Fish.

Milanes, Janelle. The Victoria in My Head. (ENG.). (YA). (gr. 7). 2018. 416p. pap. 12.99 *(978-1-4814-8090-1(1))* 2017. (Illus.). 400p. 17.99 *(978-1-4814-8089-5(8))* Simon Pulse. (Simon Pulse).

Miller, Barnabas, et al. 7 Souls. 2011. (ENG.). 384p. (J). (gr. 9-12). 26.19 *(978-0-385-73673-2(8)*, Delacorte Pr.) Random Hse. Children's Bks.

Miller-Stehr, Felicia. Are You Chanukah or Christmas? Block, Rosalinde, illus. 2008. (ENG.). 32p. pap. 17.99 *(978-1-4343-9517-7(0))* AuthorHouse.

Millner, Denene. Miss You, Mina. 2010. 163p. (J). pap. *(978-0-545-25106-8(0))* Scholastic, Inc.

Millner, Robert W. The Chicken Coop Gang. 2011. 130p. 29.99 *(978-1-4568-5517-8(4))*; pap. 19.99 *(978-1-4568-5516-1(6))* Xlibris Corp.

Mitchell, Dennis. First Day of School: A Day in the Life of Noah. 2009. 36p. pap. 16.99 *(978-1-4389-9198-6(3))* AuthorHouse.

Mlynowski, Sarah. Frogs & French Kisses. 2007. (Magic in Manhattan Ser.: 2). (ENG.). 304p. (YA). (gr. 7). pap. 8.99 *(978-0-385-73185-0(X)*, Delacorte Pr.) Random Hse. Children's Bks.

—Magic in Manhattan: Bras & Broomsticks & Frogs & French Kisses. 2012. (Magic in Manhattan Ser.). (ENG.). 608p. (YA). (gr. 7). pap. 11.99 *(978-0-385-74232-0(0)*, Ember) Random Hse. Children's Bks.

—Parties & Potions. 2010. (Magic in Manhattan Ser.: 4). (ENG., Illus.). 368p. (YA). (gr. 7). pap. 10.99 *(978-0-385-73646-6(0)*, Ember) Random Hse. Children's Bks.

Moldavsky, Goldy. Kill the Boy Band. 2017. lib. bdg. 20.85 *(978-0-606-39701-8(9))* Turtleback.

Moon, Sarah. Sparrow. 2019. (ENG.). 272p. (YA). (gr. 7-7). pap. 10.99 *(978-1-338-31286-7(3)*, Levine, Arthur A. Bks.) Scholastic, Inc.

Moore, David Barclay. The Stars Beneath Our Feet. l.t. ed. 2018. (ENG.). 340p. 22.99 *(978-1-4328-4916-0(6))* Cengage Gale.

—The Stars Beneath Our Feet. 2019. (Penworthy Picks Middle School Ser.). (ENG.). 294p. (J). (gr. 6-8). 20.49 *(978-1-64310-932-9(4))* Penworthy Co., LLC, The.

—The Stars Beneath Our Feet. 2019. 304p. (J). (gr. 5). 8.99 *(978-1-5247-0127-7(0)*, Yearling) Random Hse. Children's Bks.

Moore, Ted. Eagle Eye & the Fall of Creek Canyon. 2007. 112p. per. 10.95 *(978-0-595-43133-5(X))* iUniverse, Inc.

Morgan, Melissa J. Rsvp #6, 6. 2005. (Camp Confidential Ser.: 6). (ENG., Illus.). 160p. (J). (gr. 3-7). 4.99 *(978-0-448-43962-4(X)*, Grosset & Dunlap) Penguin Young Readers Group.

Mosier, Paul. Echo's Sister. 2018. (ENG., Illus.). 240p. (J). (gr. 3-7). 16.99 *(978-0-06-245567-3(2)*, HarperCollins) HarperCollins Pubs.

Murphy, Barbara Beasley & Wolkoff, Judie. Ace Hits Rock Bottom. 2003. (Can't Stop Ace Ser.: No. 2). 204p. (J). pap. 16.95 *(978-0-86534-408-2(6))* Sunstone Pr.

—Ace Hits the Big Time. 2003. (Can't Stop Ace Ser.: No. 1). 184p. (J). pap. 16.95 *(978-0-86534-407-5(8))* Sunstone Pr.

Musselwhite, Harry. Martin - The Guitar. 2012. (ENG.). 32p. 19.99 incl. audio compact disk *(978-1-57424-280-5(6)*, 00001601) Centerstream Publishing.

Muszynski, Julie. Henley on Safari. 2012. (Illus.). 48p. (J). (gr. -1-12). 20.00 *(978-0-9832702-3-2(6))* G Arts LLC.

My Day in New York City. 2004. (J). ring bd. 4.50 *(978-0-9762740-1-8(9)*, Flat Kids) Smart Smiles Co., The.

Myers, Walter Dean. All the Right Stuff. 2013. (ENG.). 240p. (YA). (gr. 8). pap. 9.99 *(978-0-06-196089-5(6)*, Amistad) HarperCollins Pubs.

—Darius & Twig. 2013. (ENG.). 208p. (YA). (gr. 8). 17.99 *(978-0-06-172823-5(3))*; lib. bdg. 18.89 *(978-0-06-172824-2(1))* HarperCollins Pubs. (Amistad).

—Juba! A Novel. 2015. (ENG., Illus.). 208p. (YA). (gr. 8-12). 17.99 *(978-0-06-211271-2(6)*, Amistad) HarperCollins Pubs.

—Riot. 2011. (ENG., Illus.). 192p. (YA). (gr. 7-12). pap. 9.99 *(978-1-60684-209-6(9)*, b7b06363-c232-442b-80cf-700d0f5a9b7b, Carolrhoda Lab™) Lerner Publishing Group.

—145th Street: Short Stories. 2012. 208p. (YA). (gr. 7). pap. 11.99 *(978-0-307-97610-9(6)*, Ember) Random Hse. Children's Bks.

Nastro, Caroline. The Bear Who Couldn't Sleep. Nastanlieva, Vanya, illus. (ENG.). 32p. (J). 2018. (gr. -1-2). pap. 9.95 *(978-0-7358-4333-2(3))* 2016. 17.95 *(978-0-7358-4268-7(X))* North-South Bks., Inc.

Nazemian, Abdi. Like a Love Story. (ENG.). 432p. (YA). (gr. 8). 2020. pap. 15.99 *(978-0-06-283937-4(3))* 2019. 17.99 *(978-0-06-283936-7(5))* HarperCollins Pubs. (Balzer & Bray).

Nelson, Vaunda Micheaux. The Book Itch: Freedom, Truth & Harlem's Greatest Bookstore. Christie, R. Gregory, illus. 2015. (ENG.). 32p. (J). (gr. 2-4). E-Book 27.99 *(978-1-4677-4618-2(5)*, Carolrhoda Bks.) Lerner Publishing Group.

—No Crystal Stair: A Documentary Novel of the Life & Work of Lewis Michaux, Harlem Bookseller. Christie, R. Gregory, illus. 2018. (ENG.). 192p. (YA). (gr. 7-12). pap. 14.99 *(978-1-5415-1491-1(2)*, 127a1175-2803-48df-bdbe-bea624f07578, Carolrhoda Lab™) Lerner Publishing Group.

Neville, Emily. It's Like This, Cat. Weiss, Emil, illus. 2017. (ENG.). 192p. (gr. 2-6). pap. 5.95 *(978-0-486-81478-0(5)*, 814785) Dover Pubns., Inc.

Neville, Emily Cheney. It's Like This, Cat: A Newbery Award Winner. Weiss, Emil, illus. 2019. (ENG.). 176p. (J). (gr. 5-9). pap. 7.99 *(978-0-06-440073-2(5)*, HarperCollins) HarperCollins Pubs.

Nicholasa, Mohr. El Bronx Remembered. 2014. (Trophy Keypoint Bks). (ENG.). 272p. (J). (gr. 8-12). 13.24 *(978-1-63245-280-1(4))* Lectorum Pubns., Inc.

Nicholson, Simon. The Magician's Fire. 2015. (Young Houdini Ser.: 1). (ENG.). 272p. (J). (gr. 4-7). pap. 7.99 *(978-1-4926-0949-0(8))* Sourcebooks, Inc.

Nikki, Grimes. Bronx Masquerade. 2014. (ENG.). 176p. (YA). 11.24 *(978-1-63245-077-7(1))* Lectorum Pubns., Inc.

Noble, Trinka Hakes. Rettie & the Ragamuffin Parade: A Thanksgiving Story. Gardner, David C., illus. 2017. (Tales of Young Americans Ser.). (ENG.). 32p. (J). (gr. 1-4). 17.95 *(978-1-58536-960-7(8)*, 204322) Sleeping Bear Pr.

Nolan, Han. When We Were Saints. 2005. (ENG.). 312p. (YA). (gr. 7-12). pap. 15.95 *(978-0-15-205322-2(0)*, 1196035, Clarion Bks.) HarperCollins Pubs.

North, Julian. State of Order. 2017. (ENG.). 344p. (YA). pap. *(978-0-9992658-0-2(6))* Plebeian Media.

Northrop, Michael. Book of the Dead. 2015. (TombQuest Ser.: Bk. 1). (J). 197p. *(978-1-76015-315-1(X))*; 208p. pap. *(978-1-74362-924-6(9))* Scholastic, Inc.

—Book of the Dead (TombQuest, Book 1) 2015. (TombQuest Ser.: 1). (ENG.). 208p. (J). (gr. 3-7). 12.99 *(978-0-545-72338-1(8)*, Scholastic Pr.) Scholastic, Inc.

Novel Units. The Cricket in Times Square Novel Units Teacher Guide. 2019. (Chester Cricket Ser.). (ENG.). (J). (gr. 3-6). pap. 12.99 *(978-1-56137-396-3(6)*, Novel Units, Inc.) Classroom Library Co.

—It's Like This, Cat Novel Units Teacher Guide. 2019. (ENG.). (J). pap. 12.99 *(978-1-56137-101-3(7)*, Novel Units, Inc.) Classroom Library Co.

O'Hearn, Kate. Olympus at War. 2013. (Pegasus Ser.: 2). (ENG.). 400p. (J). (gr. 3-7). 19.99 *(978-1-4424-4412-6(6)*, Simon & Schuster/Paula Wiseman Bks.) Simon & Schuster/Paula Wiseman Bks.

Older, Daniel José. Shadowhouse Fall (the Shadowshaper Cypher, Book 2) 2017. (Shadowshaper Cypher Ser.: 2). (ENG., Illus.). 368p. (YA). (gr. 9-9). 18.99 *(978-0-545-95282-8(4)*, Levine, Arthur A. Bks.) Scholastic, Inc.

—Shadowshaper (the Shadowshaper Cypher, Book 1) 2016. (Shadowshaper Cypher Ser.: 1). (ENG.). 320p. (YA). (gr. 9-9). pap. 12.99 *(978-1-338-03247-5(X))* Scholastic, Inc.

Olsen, Nora. Swans & Klons. 2013. (ENG.). 192p. (gr. 7). pap. 11.95 *(978-1-60282-874-2(1))* Bold Strokes Bks.

Olswanger, Anna. Greenhorn. Nerlove, Miriam, illus. 2012. (ENG.). (J). 48p. 17.95 *(978-1-58838-235-1(4)*, 8806); E-Book 9.99 *(978-1-60306-159-9(2)*, 8807) NewSouth, Inc. (NewSouth Bks.).

O'Neill, Elizabeth & McPherson, Missie. Alfred Visits New York City. 2003. (Illus.). 24p. (J). pap. 12.00 *(978-1-4120-1338-3(0))* Funny Bone Bks.

Osborne, Mary Pope. New York's Bravest. Johnson, Steve & Fancher, Lou, illus. 2006. (ENG.). 32p. (J). (gr. -1-2). 7.99 *(978-0-375-83841-5(4)*, Dragonfly Bks.) Random Hse. Children's Bks.

O'Shea, M.J. Cold Moon. 2nd ed. 2016. (ENG., Illus.). (J). 24.99 *(978-1-63477-954-8(1)*, Harmony Ink Pr.) Dreamspinner Pr.

—Hunter's Moon. 3rd ed. 2016. (ENG., Illus.). (J). 27.99 *(978-1-63533-032-8(7)*, Harmony Ink Pr.) Dreamspinner Pr.

Otis, James. Peter of New Amsterdam: A story of Old New York. 2007. 136p. per. 9.95 *(978-0-9790876-2-2(7))* Living Bks. Pr.

Paley, Jane. Hooper Finds a Family: A Hurricane Katrina Dog's Survival Tale. 2018. (ENG.). 144p. (J). (gr. 3-7). pap. 6.99 *(978-0-06-201105-3(7)*, HarperCollins) HarperCollins Pubs.

Papademetriou, Lisa. Apartment 1986. 2017. (ENG.). 272p. (J). (gr. 3-7). 16.99 *(978-0-06-237108-9(8)*, HarperCollins) HarperCollins Pubs.

Pascucci, Adele. Duck on a Dock. 2011. (ENG.). 19p. 13.95 *(978-1-105-40403-0(X))* Lulu Pr., Inc.

Pataki, Allison & Myers, Marya. Nelly Takes New York: A Little Girl's Adventures in the Big Apple. Valiant, Kristi, illus. 2019. (Big City Adventures Ser.). (ENG.). 48p. (J). (gr. -1-3). 18.99 *(978-1-5344-2504-0(7)*, Simon & Schuster Bks. For Young Readers) Simon & Schuster Bks. For Young Readers.

Patterson, James & Grabenstein, Chris. I Totally Funniest: A Middle School Story. Park, Laura, illus. 2015. 320p. (J). *(978-0-316-26161-6(0))* Little Brown & Co.

—Treasure Hunters. Neufeld, Juliana, illus. (Treasure Hunters Ser.: 1). (ENG.). 480p. (J). (gr. 3-7). 2015. pap. 9.99 *(978-0-316-20757-7(8))* 2013. 14.99 *(978-0-316-20756-0(X))* Little Brown & Co. (Jimmy Patterson).

—Treasure Hunters. 2015. (Treasure Hunters Ser.: 1). (J). lib. bdg. 18.45 *(978-0-606-37305-0(5))* Turtleback.

Patterson, James & Paetro, Maxine. Confessions of a Murder Suspect. (YA). 2013. (Confessions Ser.: 1). (ENG.). 400p. (gr. 7-17). pap. 10.99 *(978-0-316-20700-3(4)*, Jimmy Patterson) 2012. (Confessions Ser.: 1). (ENG.). 384p. (gr. 7-17). 19.99 *(978-0-316-20698-3(9)*, Jimmy Patterson) 2012. 372p. 11.99 *(978-0-316-22641-7(6))* 2012. (Confessions Ser.: 1). (ENG.). 400p. (gr. 7-17). 36.99 *(978-0-316-22418-5(9)*, Jimmy Patterson) Little Brown & Co.

—Confessions of a Murder Suspect. 2013. (Confessions Ser.: 1). lib. bdg. 20.85 *(978-0-606-32278-2(7))* Turtleback.

—Confessions: the Murder of an Angel. 2016. (Confessions Ser.: 4). (ENG.). 304p. (YA). (gr. 7-17). pap. 9.99 *(978-0-316-39218-1(9)*, Jimmy Patterson) Little Brown & Co.

—The Private School Murders. 2014. (Confessions Ser.: 2). (YA). lib. bdg. 20.85 *(978-0-606-35945-0(1))* Turtleback.

Patterson, James, et al. Treasure Hunters. Neufeld, Juliana, illus. 2013. 451p. (J). *(978-0-316-24262-2(4))* Little Brown & Co.

Paul, John. Copters. Young, Bill, illus. 2012. 36p. 24.95 *(978-1-4626-9458-7(6))* America Star Bks.

Pavlicin, Karen. Perch, Mrs. Sackets, & Crow's Nest. 2007. (J). pap. *(978-1-934617-01-4(6)*, Alma Little) Elva Resa Publishing, LLC.

Peer, H. Der Feyerdiger Shabes: An Emese Ertseylung. Kohen, Avigayil, illus. 2018. (YID.). 86p. (J). *(978-1-68091-256-2(9))* Kinder Shpiel USA, Inc.

Penafior, Lygia Day. All of This Is True: a Novel. 2018. (ENG.). 432p. (YA). (gr. 8). 17.99 *(978-0-06-267365-7(3)*, HarperTeen) HarperCollins Pubs.

Penn, Astor. All the Devils Here. 2016. (ENG., Illus.). (YA). (gr. 8-12). 24.99 *(978-1-63477-933-3(9)*, Harmony Ink Pr.) Dreamspinner Pr.

Perelman, Helen. Heart to Heart. 2007. (High School Musical Stories from East High Ser.). 125p. (J). (gr. 3-7). 12.65 *(978-0-7569-8340-6(1))* Perfection Learning Corp.

Perkins, Mitali. You Bring the Distant Near. l.t. ed. 2018. (ENG.). 340p. (J). lib. bdg. 22.99 *(978-1-4328-4928-3(X))* Cengage Gale.

Perl, Lila. Isabel's War. 2014. (ENG.). 224p. (J). (gr. 2-7). pap. 12.95 *(978-1-939601-27-8(4))* Ig Publishing, Inc.

Peschke, Marci. Vacation Queen. Mourning, Tuesday, illus. 2016. (Kylie Jean Ser.). (ENG.). 112p. (J). (gr. 1-3). lib. bdg. 22.65 *(978-1-5158-0058-3(X)*, 131864, Picture Window Bks.) Capstone.

Peterson, Kathryn. Reilly's Leap of Faith, 1 vol. 2010. 48p. pap. 16.95 *(978-1-4512-0154-3(0))* America Star Bks.

Phelan, James. Survivor, 2. 2013. (Alone Ser.). (ENG.). 256p. (YA). (gr. 9-12). 26.19 *(978-0-7582-8068-8(8))* Kensington Publishing Corp.

Philbin, Joanna. The Daughters. 2010. (Daughters Ser.: 1). (ENG.). 304p. (YA). (gr. 7-17). pap. 16.99 *(978-0-316-04901-6(8)*, Poppy) Little, Brown Bks. for Young Readers.

—The Daughters Break the Rules. 2011. (Daughters Ser.: 2). (ENG.). 304p. (YA). (gr. 7-17). pap. 16.99 *(978-0-316-04905-4(0)*, Poppy) Little, Brown Bks. for Young Readers.

—The Daughters Take the Stage. 2011. (Daughters Ser.: 3). (ENG.). 304p. (YA). (gr. 7-17). pap. 16.99 *(978-0-316-04908-5(5)*, Poppy) Little, Brown Bks. for Young Readers.

—Rules of Summer. 2014. (Rules of Summer Ser.: 1). (ENG.). 368p. (YA). (gr. 10-17). pap. 18.99 *(978-0-316-21204-5(0)*, Poppy) Little, Brown Bks. for Young Readers.

Phillips, Ruby Ann. Pet Psychic. Isik, Semur, illus. 2015. (Krystal Ball Ser.). (ENG.). 112p. (J). (gr. 1-3). lib. bdg. 25.32 *(978-1-4795-5875-9(3)*, 126919, Picture Window Bks.) Capstone.

Pirzada, Nefes & Simeone, Angelique. Young Equestrian: Something in Common. 2012. 386p. (gr. 4-18). pap. 21.14 *(978-1-4669-5242-3(3))* Trafford Publishing.

Platt, Kin. The Blue Man. 3rd collector's ed. 2005. (YA). 125.00 *(978-1-59885-000-0(8))*; 192p. 24.95 *(978-1-59885-001-7(6))* Two Lakes Pr., Inc.

Polisner, Gae. The Pull of Gravity. 2013. (ENG.). 224p. (YA). (gr. 7). pap. 10.99 *(978-1-250-01933-2(8)*, 900087944) Square Fish.

Ponti, James. Blue Moon. 2013. (Dead City Ser.: 2). (ENG., Illus.). 336p. (J). (gr. 4-8). 19.99 *(978-1-4424-4131-6(3)*, Aladdin) Simon & Schuster Children's Publishing.

—Dark Days. 2015. (Dead City Ser.: 3). (ENG., Illus.). 304p. (J). (gr. 4-8). 18.99 *(978-1-4814-3636-6(8)*, Aladdin) Simon & Schuster Children's Publishing.

—Dead City. 2013. (Dead City Ser.: 1). (ENG., Illus.). 304p. (J). (gr. 4-8). pap. 8.99 *(978-1-4424-4130-9(5)*, Aladdin) Simon & Schuster Children's Publishing.

Potter, Ellen. Olivia Kidney Secret Beneath City. 2009. (ENG.). 336p. (J). (gr. 3-7). 9.99 *(978-0-14-241263-3(5)*, Puffin Books) Penguin Young Readers Group.

MNO

—Pish Posh. 2011. (ENG.). 176p. (J). (gr. 3-7). 7.99 (978-0-14-241906-9(0), Puffin Books) Penguin Young Readers Group.

Power, Michael. The Zoo. 2009. 201p. pap. 13.75 (978-1-60695-075-3(4)) Cacoethes Publishing Hse., LLC.

Primavera, Elise. Auntie Claus, Home for the Holidays. Primavera, Elise, illus. 2009. (ENG., Illus.). 40p. (J). (gr. -1-3). 19.99 (978-1-4169-5485-9(6), Simon & Schuster/Paula Wiseman Bks.) Simon & Schuster/Paula Wiseman Bks.

Publications International Ltd. Staff, ed. The Smurfs Large Play a Sound. 2011. 24p. (J). 14.98 (978-1-60553-403-9(X)) Phoenix International Publications, Inc.

Punter, Russell. Kitty Kat, Kitty Kat Where Have You Been - New York. 2018. (Picture Bks.). (ENG.). 24p. (J). 9.99 (978-0-7945-3975-7(0), Usborne) EDC Publishing.

Quintero, Sofia. Efrain's Secret. 2011. (ENG.). 272p. (YA). (gr. 9). pap. 8.99 (978-0-440-24062-4(X), Ember) Random Hse. Children's Bks.

Raab, Ralph. The Dewey Deception: The First Adventure from the Biblio Files. 2009. (ENG.). 248p. 26.95 (978-1-4401-4687-9(X)); pap. 16.95 (978-1-4401-4685-5(3)) iUniverse, Inc.

Rabley, Stephen. Easystart: Flying Home. 2nd ed. 2008. (Pearson English Graded Readers Ser.). (ENG.). 20p. pap. 11.99 (978-1-4058-6946-1(1), Pearson ELT) Pearson Education.

Ramsey, Charmaine J. Frollica & Frenzi: New York City Friends. Steinlage, Kelly, illus. 2009. 36p. pap. 15.49 (978-1-4490-0487-3(3)) AuthorHouse.

Random House. Pizza Party! (Teenage Mutant Ninja Turtles) Random House, illus. 2017. (Step into Reading Ser.). (ENG., Illus.). 24p. (J). (gr. -1-1). pap. 5.99 (978-1-5247-6982-6(7), Random Hse. Bks. for Young Readers) Random Hse. Children's Bks.

Ray, Anna Chapin. Half a Dozen Girls. 2007. 148p. (gr. 4-7). per. (978-1-4068-3752-0(0)) Echo Library.

Redding, LaTisha. Calling the Water Drum, 1 vol. Boyd, Aaron, illus. 2016. (ENG.). 32p. (J). (gr. -1-5). 17.95 (978-1-62014-194-6(9), 1dbccc72-9d38-4d4a-8811-50b865e16029) Lee & Low Bks., Inc.

Reisenauer, Cynthia Mauro. Emerita. Reisenauer, Cynthia Mauro, illus. 2007. (Illus.). 48p. (J). 18.95 (978-0-9726487-5-2(5)) Puddle Jump Pr., Ltd.

Resnicoff, Stan. The BIG Parade: New York. 2012. (ENG.). (J). pap. (978-1-4675-1538-2(8)) Independent Pub.

Reyes, Nikki. An Unexpected Guest: It Started with a fish. It ended with a Friend. 2009. 48p. pap. 17.49 (978-1-4363-9133-7(4)) Xlibris Corp.

Reynolds, Jason. When I Was the Greatest. 2014. (ENG., Illus.). 240p. (YA). (gr. 7). 19.99 (978-1-4424-5947-2(6), Atheneum Bks. for Young Readers) Simon & Schuster Children's Publishing.

Riazi, Karuna. The Gauntlet. 2018. (ENG., Illus.). 304p. (J). (gr. 3-7). pap. 8.99 (978-1-4814-8697-2(7), Salaam Reads) Simon & Schuster Bks. For Young Readers.

Ringgold, Faith. Cassie's Word Quilt. Ringgold, Faith, illus. 2004. (Illus.). 32p. (J). (gr. -1-2). pap. 8.99 (978-0-553-11233-7(3), Dragonfly Bks.) Random Hse. Children's Bks.

Rivera, Lilliam. The Education of Margot Sanchez. 2017. (ENG., Illus.). 304p. (YA). (gr. 9). 19.99 (978-1-4814-7211-1(9), Simon & Schuster Bks. For Young Readers) Simon & Schuster Bks. For Young Readers.

Roberts, Willo Davis. The Kidnappers. 2016. (ENG., Illus.). 208p. (J). (gr. 3-7). pap. 7.99 (978-1-4814-4904-5(4), Aladdin) Simon & Schuster Children's Publishing.

Robertson, Jacob Ryan. Far Away. 2012. 50p. (-18). pap. 15.99 (978-1-4797-4679-8(7)) Xlibris Corp.

Robinson, Gwen. The Renshaw Diversion. 2007. (Illus.). 204p. per. (978-0-7552-0275-1(9)) Authors OnLine, Ltd.

Robinson, Sharon. Safe at Home. 2007. (ENG.). 150p. (J). (gr. 6-8). 17.44 (978-0-439-67198-9(1)) Scholastic, Inc.

Rockliff, Mara. Around America to Win the Vote: Two Suffragists, a Kitten, & 10,000 Miles. Hooper, Hadley, illus. 2019. (ENG.). 40p. (J). (gr. k-3). 8.99 (978-1-5362-0836-8(1)) Candlewick Pr.

—Me & Momma & Big John. Low, William, illus. 2012. (ENG.). 32p. (J). (gr. -1-2). 16.99 (978-0-7636-4359-1(9)) Candlewick Pr.

Rodkey, Geoff. The Tapper Twins Go to War (with Each Other) 2016. (Tapper Twins Ser.: 1). (ENG., Illus.). 240p. (J). (gr. 3-7). pap. 7.99 (978-0-316-31597-5(4)) Little, Brown Bks. for Young Readers.

—The Tapper Twins Go Viral. 2017. (Tapper Twins Ser.: 4). (ENG., Illus.). 256p. (J). (gr. 3-7). 13.99 (978-0-316-29784-4(4)) Little, Brown Bks. for Young Readers.

—The Tapper Twins Go Viral. 2018. (Tapper Twins Ser.: 4). (J). lib. bdg. 17.20 (978-0-606-40992-6(0)) Turtleback.

—The Tapper Twins Run for President. 2016. (Tapper Twins Ser.: 3). (ENG., Illus.). 304p. (J). (gr. 3-7). 13.99 (978-0-316-29785-1(2)) Little, Brown Bks. for Young Readers.

—The Tapper Twins Tear up New York. 2016. (Tapper Twins Ser.: 2). (ENG., Illus.). 288p. (J). (gr. 3-7). pap. 8.99 (978-0-316-31601-9(6)) Little, Brown Bks. for Young Readers.

Rodriguez, Cindy L. Heroes Were Made On 9/11, 1 vol. Elliott, Joyce L., illus. 2010. 26p. 24.95 (978-1-4489-6070-5(3)) PublishAmerica, Inc.

Ross, Alice & Ross, Kent. La Dama de Cobre. Bowman, Leslie, illus. 2006. (Yo Solo - Historia (on My Own - History) Ser.). (SPA.). 48p. (gr. 2-4). lib. bdg. 25.26 (978-0-8225-6262-7(6)) Lerner Publishing Group.

Rothenberger, Suzanne. Mattie: Life at Paddock Mansion. 2013. 136p. pap. 9.95 (978-0-9890509-4-4(7)) Garland City Bks. of Watertown.

Roy, Lillian Elizabeth. Polly in New York. Barbour, H. S., illus. 2004. reprint ed. pap. 28.95 (978-1-4179-0068-8(7)) Kessinger Publishing, LLC.

Roy, Ron. Sleepy Hollow Sleepover. 4th ed. 2010. (to Z Mysteries Ser.: 30). lib. bdg. 16.00 (978-0-606-14007-2(7)) Turtleback.

—A to Z Mysteries Super Edition #4: Sleepy Hollow Sleepover. Gurney, John Steven, illus. 4th ed. 2010. (to Z Mysteries Ser.: 4). 144p. (J). (gr. 1-4). pap. 6.99 (978-0-375-86669-2(8), Random Hse. Bks. for Young Readers) Random Hse. Children's Bks.

Rubel, David. The Carpenter's Gift: A Christmas Tale about the Rockefeller Center Tree. LaMarche, Jim, illus. 2011. (ENG.). 48p. (J). (gr. k-4). 18.99 (978-0-375-86922-8(0), Random Hse. Bks. for Young Readers) Random Hse. Children's Bks.

Rubin, Sarah. Someday Dancer. 2012. (J). (978-0-545-39379-9(5)) Scholastic, Inc.

Ruby, Laura. The Shadow Cipher. 2018. (York Ser.: 1). (J). lib. bdg. 18.40 (978-0-606-41390-9(1)) Turtleback.

—York: The Clockwork Ghost. 2019. (Illus.). 464p. (YA). (978-0-06-293755-1(3), Waldon Pond Pr.) HarperCollins Pubs.

—York: The Shadow Cipher. Stevenson, Dave, illus. 2018. (York Ser.: 1). (ENG.). 496p. (J). (gr. 3-7). pap. 9.99 (978-0-06-230694-4(4), Waldon Pond Pr.) HarperCollins Pubs.

—York: the Clockwork Ghost. 2019. (York Ser.: 2). (ENG., Illus.). 464p. (J). (gr. 3-7). 17.99 (978-0-06-230696-8(0), Waldon Pond Pr.) HarperCollins Pubs.

Russell, David. Who'z Who at the Zoo. 2012. (Illus.). 26p. pap. 12.95 (978-1-4575-1395-4(1)) Dog Ear Publishing, LLC.

Russell, Paul. Immaculate Blue: A Beautiful & Captivating Novel about Love, Friendship & the Passing of Time. 2015. (ENG., Illus.). 340p. pap. 16.95 (978-1-62778-095-7(5), Cleis Pr.) Start Publishing LLC.

Rutledge, Eddie. Amani's World: Amani & Friends Go to New York City. 2012. 24p. pap. 17.99 (978-1-4772-9554-0(2)) AuthorHouse.

Saldana, Theresa. The Almost Murder & Other Stories. 2008. (ENG.). 144p. (YA). (gr. 6-18). pap. 10.95 (978-1-55885-507-6(6), Piñata Books) Arte Publico Pr.

Salerni, Dianne K. Eleanor, Alice, & the Roosevelt Ghosts. 2020. (ENG., Illus.). 240p. (J). (gr. 4-7). 17.99 (978-0-8234-4697-1(2)) Holiday Hse., Inc.

Scarrow, Alex & Bale, Tim. TimeRiders, 1. 2011. (TimeRiders Ser.). (ENG.). 416p. (YA). (gr. 7-12). 26.19 (978-0-8027-2172-3(9), 9780802721723) Walker & Co.

Schmidt, Gary D. Okay for Now. 2011. (Playaway Children Ser.). (J). (gr. 5-9). 54.99 (978-1-61707-313-7(X)) Random Hse., Inc.

Schroeder, Lisa. Keys to the City. 2017. (ENG.). 240p. (J). (gr. 3-7). 16.99 (978-0-545-90738-5(1), Scholastic Pr.) Scholastic, Inc.

Schroff, Laura & Tresniowski, Alex. An Invisible Thread: A Young Readers' Edition. 2019. (ENG., Illus.). 224p. (J). (gr. 5). 17.99 (978-1-5344-3727-2(4), Simon & Schuster Bks. For Young Readers) Simon & Schuster Bks. For Young Readers.

Scieszka, Jon. Hey Kid, Want to Buy a Bridge? McCauley, Adam, illus. 2005. (Time Warp Trio Ser.: No. 11). 74p. (gr. 4-7). 15.00 (978-0-7569-5988-3(8)) Perfection Learning Corp.

—Hey Kid, Want to Buy a Bridge? #11. McCauley, Adam, illus. 2004. (Time Warp Trio Ser.: 11). 80p. (J). (gr. 2-4). pap. 5.99 (978-0-14-240089-0(0), Puffin Books) Penguin Young Readers Group.

—SPHDZ Book #1! Prigmore, Shane, illus. 2010. (Spaceheadz Ser.: 1). (ENG.). 176p. (J). (gr. 2-5). 14.99 (978-1-4169-7951-7(4), Simon & Schuster Bks. For Young Readers) Simon & Schuster Bks. For Young Readers.

—2095. Smith, Lane, illus. 2005. (Time Warp Trio Ser.: No. 5). 72p. (gr. 4-7). 15.00 (978-0-7569-5989-0(6)) Perfection Learning Corp.

—2095 #5. Smith, Lane, illus. 2004. (Time Warp Trio Ser.: 5). 80p. (J). (gr. 2-4). pap. 6.99 (978-0-14-240044-9(0), Puffin Books) Penguin Young Readers Group.

Scott, D. P. The Christmas Elf. Hayward, Roy, illus. 2013. 86p. pap. (978-0-9880635-2-5(2)) Scott, Daren.

Seabrooke, Brenda. The Bridges of Summer. 2007. (ENG.). 160p. per. 12.95 (978-0-595-43720-7(6), Backinprint.com) iUniverse, Inc.

Seidler, Tor. Oh, Rats! Evans, Gabriel, illus. 2020. (ENG.). 336p. (J). (gr. 3-7). pap. 8.99 (978-1-5344-2685-6(X), Atheneum Bks. for Young Readers) Simon & Schuster Children's Publishing.

Selden, George. The Cricket in Times Square. Williams, Garth, illus. (Chester Cricket Ser.). 151p. (J). (gr. 3-6). pap. 5.50 (978-0-8072-8311-0(8), Listening Library) Random Hse. Audio Publishing Group.

—The Cricket in Times Square. unabr. ed. 2004. (Chester Cricket Ser.). 151p. (J). (gr. 3-7). pap. 29.00 incl. audio (978-0-8072-8310-3(X), S YA 158 SP, Listening Library) Random Hse. Audio Publishing Group.

—Harry Kitten & Tucker Mouse / Chester Cricket's Pigeon Ride: Two Books in One. Williams, Garth, illus. 2009. (Chester Cricket & His Friends Ser.). (ENG.). 144p. (J). (gr. 1-4). pap. 8.99 (978-0-312-58248-7(X), 900062061) Square Fish.

Sharenow, Robert. The Girl in the Torch. 2015. (ENG.). 304p. (J). (gr. 3-7). 16.99 (978-0-06-222795-9(5), Balzer & Bray) HarperCollins Pubs.

Shaw, Tucker. Oh Yeah, Audrey! 2014. (ENG., Illus.). 256p. (YA). (gr. 8-17). 16.95 (978-1-4197-1223-4(3), 1077501, Amulet Bks.) Abrams, Inc.

Sheinmel, Alyssa B. The Lucky Kind. 2012. (ENG.). 208p. (J). (gr. 7-12). lib. bdg. 22.44 (978-0-375-96785-6(0)) Random House Publishing Group.

Sheinmel, Courtney. All the Things You Are. 2011. (ENG.). 256p. (J). (gr. 4-8). 15.99 (978-1-4169-9717-7(2), Simon & Schuster Bks. For Young Readers) Simon & Schuster Bks. For Young Readers.

—Sincerely: Sincerely, Sophie; Sincerely, Katie. 2010. (ENG.). 400p. (J). (gr. 3-7). 15.99 (978-1-4169-4010-4(3), Simon & Schuster Bks. For Young Readers) Simon & Schuster Bks. For Young Readers.

—Sincerely: Sincerely, Sophie, Sincerely, Katie. 2011. (ENG.). 416p. (J). (gr. 3-7). pap. 8.99 (978-1-4169-4022-7(7), Simon & Schuster Bks. For Young Readers) Simon & Schuster Bks. For Young Readers.

Sheinmel, Courtney & Turetsky, Bianca. Magic on the Map #2: the Show Must Go On. Lewis, Stevie, illus. 2019. (Magic on the Map Ser.: 2). 128p. (J). (gr. 2-5). 5.99 (978-1-63565-169-0(7), Random Hse. Bks. for Young Readers) Random Hse. Children's Bks.

Sherman, Delia. Changeling. 2008. (ENG.). 304p. (J). (gr. 6-8). 24.94 (978-0-14-241188-9(4)) Penguin Young Readers Group.

Sherry, Maureen. Walls Within Walls. 2012. (ENG., Illus.). 368p. (J). (gr. 3-7). pap. 9.99 (978-0-06-176703-6(4), Tegen, Katherine Bks) HarperCollins Pubs.

—Walls Within Walls. Stower, Adam, illus. 2010. (ENG.). 368p. (J). (gr. 3-7). 16.99 (978-0-06-176700-5(X), Tegen, Katherine Bks) HarperCollins Pubs.

Shin, Ami. Mice in the City: New York. 2018. (Mice in the City Ser.: 0). (Illus.). 32p. (J). (gr. k-5). 19.95 (978-0-500-65128-5(0), 565128) Thames & Hudson.

Shortt, Yvonne. A New York City Public School Goes Green. 2009. 44p. pap. 19.95 (978-0-557-07182-1(8)) Lulu Pr., Inc.

Shrum, Brianna R. How to Make Out. (ENG.). (gr. 6-12). 2018. 296p. (YA). pap. 9.99 (978-1-5107-3204-9(7)) 2016. 284p. (J). 16.99 (978-1-5107-0167-0(2)) Skyhorse Publishing Co., Inc. (Sky Pony Pr.).

Shulman, Polly. The Grimm Legacy. 2011. (ENG.). (J). 352p. (gr. 5-18). 8.99 (978-0-14-241904-5(4), Puffin Books);1. (Illus.). 336p. (gr. 6-8). 24.94 (978-0-399-25096-5(4)) Penguin Young Readers Group.

Shusterman, Neal. Downsiders. 2009. (ENG.). 272p. (YA). (gr. 7). pap. 12.99 (978-1-4169-9747-4(4), Simon & Schuster Bks. For Young Readers) Simon & Schuster Bks. For Young Readers.

—The Schwa Was Here. (Antsy Bonano Novels Ser.). 2004. (ENG.). 228p. (J). (gr. 6-8). 21.19 (978-0-525-47182-0(0)) 2006. 240p. (YA). (gr. 7-18). reprint ed. 10.99 (978-0-14-240577-2(9), Puffin Books) Penguin Young Readers Group.

Silvera, Adam. They Both Die at the End. l.t. ed. 2022. (ENG.). 516p. lib. bdg. 24.99 Cengage Gale.

—They Both Die at the End. (YA). 2018. (ENG.). 416p. (gr. 8). pap. 12.99 (978-0-06-245780-6(2), Quill Tree Bks.) 2017. (ENG.). 384p. (gr. 8). 21.99 (978-0-06-245779-0(9), Quill Tree Bks.) 2017. 373p. (978-0-06-268851-4(0), HarperTeen) HarperCollins Pubs.

—They Both Die at the End. 2019. (YA). lib. bdg. 22.10 (978-0-606-41431-9(2)) Turtleback.

Smale, Holly. Geek Girl: Picture Perfect. 2016. (Geek Girl Ser.: 3). (ENG.). 416p. (YA). (gr. 8). 17.99 (978-0-06-233363-6(1), HarperTeen) HarperCollins Pubs.

Smallman, Steve. Santa Is Coming to New York. Dunn, Robert, illus. 2nd ed. 2019. (Santa Is Coming... Ser.). (ENG.). 40p. (J). (gr. -1-3). 12.99 (978-1-7282-0083-5(0), Hometown World) Sourcebooks, Inc.

—Santa Is Coming to New York City. Dunn, Robert, illus. 2nd ed. 2019. (Santa Is Coming... Ser.). (ENG.). 40p. (J). (gr. -1-3). 12.99 (978-1-7282-0084-2(9), Hometown World) Sourcebooks, Inc.

Smiley, Jess Smart. 10 Little Monsters Visit New York City, Volume 5. Hardyman, Nathan, illus. 2016. (10 Little Monsters Ser.: 5). (ENG.). 32p. (J). (gr. k-3). 16.95 (978-1-942934-67-7(X), 553467) Familius LLC.

Smith, Alexander Gordon. The Devil's Engine: Hellraisers: (Book 1) 2015. (Devil's Engine Ser.: 1). (ENG.). 352p. (YA). (gr. 7). 29.99 (978-0-374-30169-9(7), 900140530, Farrar, Straus & Giroux (BYR)) Farrar, Straus & Giroux.

—Hellraisers. 2016. (Devil's Engine Ser.: 1). (ENG.). 368p. (YA). (gr. 7). 22.10 (978-0-606-39284-6(X)) Turtleback.

Smith, Roland. Beneath. 2015. (ENG., Illus.). 272p. (J). (gr. 4-7). 16.99 (978-0-545-56486-1(7), Scholastic Pr.) Scholastic, Inc.

Snow, Susie. The Old Cookie Jar. Motz, Mike, illus. 2012. 34p. pap. 19.99 (978-1-61996-595-9(X)) Salem Author Services.

Snyder, Marilyn. A Second Chance for Tina. Shiffman, Lena, illus. 2003. (Hello Reader! Ser.). (J). (978-0-439-44154-4(4)) Scholastic, Inc.

Sobel, Deane. Philip the Sea Lion. 2012. (ENG.). (J). pap. (978-1-4675-2347-9(X)) Independent Pub.

Sollano, Carolyn. Tree Top Angels. 2010. 56p. (gr. 4-6). pap. 8.95 (978-1-4502-2276-1(5)) iUniverse, Inc.

Sonneborn, Scott. A Pain in the Butt. Banks, Timothy, illus. 2015. (Frankenstein Journals). (ENG.). 80p. (J). (gr. 2-4). 22.65 (978-1-4965-0222-3(1), 128036, Stone Arch Bks.) Capstone.

Sorrells, Walter. Book Two of the Travelers, Bk. 2. 2009. (Pendragon: Before the War Ser.: 2). (ENG.). 240p. (J). (gr. 5-9). pap. 8.99 (978-1-4169-6523-7(8), Aladdin) Simon & Schuster Children's Publishing.

Spiegelman, Nadja. Lost in NYC: A Subway Adventure. Sánchez, Sergio García, illus. 2016. (Toon Graphics Ser.). (ENG.). 52p. (J). (gr. 3-6). lib. bdg. 34.21 (978-1-61479-499-8(5), 21435, Graphic Novels) Spotlight.

—Lost in NYC: a Subway Adventure: A TOON Graphic. Garcia Sanchez, Sergio, illus. 2015. 52p. (J). (gr. 3-7). 16.99 (978-1-935179-81-8(0), TOON Books) Astra Publishing Hse.

Spizman, Robyn Freedman & Johnston, Mark. Secret Agent. 2006. (ENG.). 240p. (J). (gr. 4-7). pap. 11.99 (978-1-4169-1862-2(0), Atheneum Bks. for Young Readers) Simon & Schuster Children's Publishing.

St Jean, Catherine Avery. A Staten Island Ferry Tale. Frahm, Paul, illus. 2006. 32p. (J). per. 26.99 (978-1-4134-0262-9(3)) Xlibris Corp.

Staake, Bob. Bluebird. Staake, Bob, illus. 2013. (Illus.). 40p. (J). (gr. -1-3). 17.99 (978-0-375-87037-8(7), Schwartz & Wade Bks.) Random Hse. Children's Bks.

Stampler, Laura. Little Black Dresses, Little White Lies. 2016. (ENG., Illus.). 352p. (YA). (gr. 9). 17.99 (978-1-4814-5989-1(9), Simon Pulse) Simon Pulse.

Stancic, Giselle M. The Paganini Curse. 2013. 166p. 22.95 (978-1-4759-6161-4(8)); pap. 12.95 (978-1-4759-6159-1(6)) iUniverse, Inc.

Staub, Rusty. Hello, Mr. Met. Moore, Danny, illus. 2006. 24p. (J). lib. bdg. 17.95 (978-1-932888-82-9(9)) Amplify Publishing Group.

Stead, Rebecca. Goodbye Stranger. 2017. (ENG.). 320p. (J). (gr. 5). 8.99 (978-0-307-98086-1(3), Yearling) Random Hse. Children's Bks.

Sternin, Joshua & Ventimilia, Jeffrey. Teenage Mutant Ninja Turtles: Pizza Party! 2014. (Step into Reading Level 2 Ser.). lib. bdg. 13.55 (978-0-606-36282-5(7)) Turtleback.

Stevenson, James. Runaway Horse! Date not set. (J). 15.99 (978-0-06-051978-0(9)); 16.89 (978-0-06-051979-7(7)) HarperCollins Pubs.

Stevenson, Steve. The Heist at Niagara Falls. 2013. (Agatha Girl of Mystery Ser.: 4). lib. bdg. 16.00 (978-0-606-32128-0(4)) Turtleback.

Stilton, Geronimo. A Very Merry Christmas (Geronimo Stilton #35), Vol. 35. 2008. (Geronimo Stilton Ser.: 35). (ENG.). 128p. (J). (gr. 2-5). 7.99 (978-0-545-02135-7(9), Scholastic Paperbacks) Scholastic, Inc.

Stilton, Thea. Thea Stilton: Big Trouble in the Big Apple (Thea Stilton #8) A Geronimo Stilton Adventure, Volume 8. 2011. (Thea Stilton Ser.: 8). (ENG., Illus.). 176p. (J). (gr. 2-5). pap. 8.99 (978-0-545-22775-9(5), Scholastic Paperbacks) Scholastic, Inc.

Stoddard, Lindsey. Right As Rain. 2019. (ENG.). 304p. (J). (gr. 3-7). 16.99 (978-0-06-265294-2(X), HarperCollins) HarperCollins Pubs.

Stoddard, William O. Dab Kinzer A Story of A Growing Boy. 2004. reprint ed. pap. 24.95 (978-1-4191-1488-5(3)); pap. 1.99 (978-1-4192-1488-2(8)) Kessinger Publishing, LLC.

Strasser, Todd. Can't Get There from Here. 2012. (ENG.). 224p. (YA). (gr. 7). pap. 11.99 (978-1-4424-3357-1(4), Simon & Schuster Bks. For Young Readers) Simon & Schuster Bks. For Young Readers.

Sullivan, Maureen. Cabbages & Queens. Ferrando, Carol, illus. 2010. 57p. (J). pap. (978-0-9820381-3-0(5)) MoJo InkWorks.

Sullivan, Maureen & Josephs, Alison. Ankle Soup: A Thanksgiving Story. Josephs, Alison, illus. 2008. (Illus.). 32p. 17.95 (978-0-9820381-0-9(0)) MoJo InkWorks.

Sully, Katherine. Night-Night Buffalo. Poole, Helen, illus. 2017. (Night-Night Ser.). (ENG.). 20p. (J). (gr. -1-1). bds. 9.99 (978-1-4926-5492-6(2), Hometown World) Sourcebooks, Inc.

—Night-Night New York. Poole, Helen, illus. 2017. (Night-Night Ser.). (ENG.). 20p. (J). (gr. -1-1). bds. 9.99 (978-1-4926-5318-9(7), Hometown World) Sourcebooks, Inc.

—Night-Night New York City. Poole, Helen, illus. 2016. (Night-Night Ser.). (ENG.). 20p. (J). (gr. -1-1). bds. 9.99 (978-1-4926-3932-9(X), 9781492639329, Hometown World) Sourcebooks, Inc.

Suma, Nova Ren. Imaginary Girls. 2012. (ENG.). 352p. (YA). (gr. 9-18). pap. 8.99 (978-0-14-242143-7(X), Speak) Penguin Young Readers Group.

Sutherland, Tui T. Shadow Falling. 2007. (Avatars Ser.: Bk.2). 356p. (YA). (gr. 7-12). lib. bdg. 17.89 (978-0-06-085147-7(3), Eos) HarperCollins Pubs.

Swift, Hildegarde H. The Little Red Lighthouse & the Great Gray Bridge: Restored Edition. Ward, Lynd, illus. 2003. (ENG.). 64p. (J). (gr. -1-3). pap. 9.99 (978-0-15-204573-9(2), 1193768, Clarion Bks.) HarperCollins Pubs.

Takabayashi, Mari. I Live in Brooklyn. 2004. (ENG., Illus.). 32p. (J). (gr. -1-3). tchr. ed. 17.99 (978-0-618-30899-6(7), 590016, Clarion Bks.) HarperCollins Pubs.

Tan, Sheri. Follow That Map!, 1 vol. Ng-Benitez, Shirley, illus. 2019. (Confetti Kids Ser.: 7). (ENG.). 32p. (J). (gr. k-2). 14.95 (978-1-62014-569-2(3), leelowbooks); pap. 10.95 (978-1-62014-570-8(7), leelowbooks) Lee & Low Bks., Inc.

Tarshis, Lauren. I Survived the Attacks of September 11, 2001. 2012. (I Survived Ser.: No. 6). lib. bdg. 14.75 (978-0-606-26205-7(9)) Turtleback.

—I Survived the Attacks of September 11th, 2001 (I Survived #6) Dawson, Scott, illus. 2012. (I Survived Ser.: 6). (ENG.). 112p. (J). (gr. 3-7). pap. 5.99 (978-0-545-20700-3(2), Scholastic Paperbacks) Scholastic, Inc.

Taylor, Janet B. Sparks of Light. 2018. (ENG.). 448p. (YA). (gr. 9). pap. 9.99 (978-1-328-91526-9(3), 1701811, Clarion Bks.) HarperCollins Pubs.

Taylor, Kara. Deadly Little Sins: A Prep School Confidential Novel. 2014. (Prep School Confidential Novel Ser.: 3). (ENG.). 288p. (YA). (gr. 7). pap. 19.99 (978-1-250-03363-5(2), 900120137, St. Martin's Griffin) St. Martin's Pr.

Taylor, Sydney. All-Of-a-Kind Family Uptown. 2014. (ENG.). 200p. (J). (gr. 3). pap. 12.95 (978-1-939601-17-9(7)) Ig Publishing, Inc.

Tesler, Ellen. Zeke in Central Park. 2010. 32p. pap. 12.99 (978-1-4490-7211-7(9)) AuthorHouse.

Testa, Maria. Becoming Joe Dimaggio. Hunt, Scott, illus. 2005. (ENG.). 64p. (J). (gr. 5-9). reprint ed. pap. 7.99 (978-0-7636-2444-6(6)) Candlewick Pr.

Theule, Larissa. Born to Ride: A Story about Bicycle Face. Garrity-Riley, Kelsey, illus. 2019. (ENG.). 32p. (J). (gr. -1-3). 18.99 (978-1-4197-3412-0(1), 1207001, Abrams Bks. for Young Readers) Abrams, Inc.

Thomas, Rich. The Amazing Spider-Man. Clark, Jeff, illus. 2012. (Marvel Origins Ser.). (ENG.). 48p. (J). (gr. k-5). lib. bdg. 31.36 (978-1-61479-007-5(8), 11335, Marvel Age) Spotlight.

Thompson, Kay. Eloise & the Very Secret Room: Ready-To-Read Level 1. 2006. (Eloise Ser.). (ENG., Illus.). 32p. (J). (gr. -1-1). pap. 4.99 (978-0-689-87450-5(2), Simon Spotlight) Simon Spotlight.

—Eloise at the Plaza. Knight, Hilary, illus. 2015. (Eloise Ser.). (ENG.). 26p. (J). (gr. -1-2). bds. 8.99 (978-1-4814-5159-8(6), Little Simon) Little Simon.

Thompson, Robbie. Spidey #1. Bradshaw, Nick & Campbell, Jim, illus. 2016. (Spidey Ser.). (ENG.). 24p. (J). (gr. 2-8). lib. bdg. 31.36 (978-1-61479-593-3(2), 24374, Marvel Age) Spotlight.

—Spidey #2. Bradshaw, Nick & Campbell, Jim, illus. 2016. (Spidey Ser.). (ENG.). 24p. (J). (gr. 2-8). lib. bdg. 31.36 (978-1-61479-594-0(0), 24375, Marvel Age) Spotlight.

—Spidey #3. Bradshaw, Nick & Campbell, Jim, illus. 2016. (Spidey Ser.). (ENG.). 24p. (J). (gr. 2-8). lib. bdg. 31.36 (978-1-61479-595-7(9), 24376, Marvel Age) Spotlight.

—Spidey #4. Araujo, Andre Lima & Rosenberg, Rachelle, illus. 2016. (Spidey Ser.). (ENG.). 24p. (J). (gr. 2-8). lib. bdg. 31.36 (978-1-61479-596-4(7), 24377, Marvel Age) Spotlight.

—Spidey #5. Araujo, Andre Lima & Campbell, Jim, illus. 2016. (Spidey Ser.). (ENG.). 24p. (J). (gr. 2-8). lib. bdg. 31.36 (978-1-61479-597-1(5), 24378, Marvel Age) Spotlight.

—Spidey #6. Araujo, Andre Lima & Campbell, Jim, illus. 2016. (Spidey Ser.). (ENG.). 24p. (J). (gr. 2-8). lib. bdg. 31.36 (978-1-61479-598-8(3), 24379, Marvel Age) Spotlight.

Thompson, Roger E., II. A Sister's Love: A Novel. 2007. 80p. per. 8.95 (978-0-595-44549-3(7)) iUniverse, Inc.

Thomson, Sarah L. The Ring of Honor. 2018. (Secrets of the Seven Ser.). (ENG.). 224p. (J). 17.99 (978-1-61963-735-1(9), 900146561, Bloomsbury USA Childrens) Bloomsbury Publishing USA.
Thome, Jenn Marie. Night Music. 2019. 400p. (YA). (gr. 9). 17.99 (978-0-7352-2877-1(9), Dial Bks) Penguin Young Readers Group.
Tome. Spirou & Fantasio in New York. Janry, illus. 2011. (Spirou & Fantasio Ser.: 2). 48p. (J). (gr. 3-17). pap. 11.95 (978-1-84918-054-2(7)) CineBook GBR. Dist: National Bk. Network.
Tonatiuh, Duncan. Dear Primo: A Letter to My Cousin. 2010. (ENG., Illus.). 32p. (J). (gr. k-2). 18.99 (978-0-8109-3872-4(3), 661901, Abrams Bks. for Young Readers) Abrams, Inc.
Topol, Carolyn LeVine. Run for It All. (ENG., Illus.). (YA). 2017. 25.99 (978-1-64080-361-9(0)) 2016. 200p. pap. 14.99 (978-1-63477-065-1(X)) Dreamspinner Pr. (Harmony Ink Pr.).
Townsend, Wendy. Lizard Love. 2013. 198p. 18.95 (978-1-60898-151-9(7)) namelos llc.
Treggiari, Jo. Ashes, Ashes. (ENG.). 352p. (YA). (gr. 7). 2013. pap. 9.99 (978-0-545-25564-6(3), Scholastic Paperbacks) 2011. 17.99 (978-0-545-25563-9(5), Scholastic Pr.) Scholastic, Inc.
Trooboff, Rhoda. Ben, the Bells & the Peacocks. Bucher, Cecile, illus. 2006. (ENG.). 36p. (J). per. 15.00 (978-0-9773536-0-6(5)) Tenley Circle Pr.
Tubb, Kristin O'Donnell. The Story Collector: A New York Public Library Book. Bruno, Iacopo, illus. 2018. (Story Collector Ser.: 1). (ENG.). 256p. (J). 16.99 (978-1-250-14380-8(2), 900180568, Holt, Henry & Co. Bks. For Young Readers) Holt, Henry & Co.
Uhlberg, Myron. The Sound of All Things, 1 vol. Papoulas, Ted, illus. 2016. 36p. (J). (gr. 1-4). 17.95 (978-1-56145-833-2(3)) Peachtree Publishing Co. Inc.
Vail, Rachel. Well, That Was Awkward. 2018. 336p. (J). (gr. 5). 8.99 (978-0-14-751398-4(7), Puffin Books) Penguin Young Readers Group.
—Well, That Was Awkward. 2018. lib. bdg. 19.65 (978-0-606-40876-9(2)) Turtleback.
Valentine, Sally. The Ghost of the Charlotte Lighthouse. 2006. (ENG.). (J). pap. (978-1-59531-013-2(4)) North Country Bks., Inc.
van Diepen, Allison. Raven. 2010. (ENG.). 304p. (YA). (gr. 9). pap. 12.99 (978-1-4169-7468-0(7), Simon Pulse) Simon Pulse.
Van Dyne, Edith. Aunt Jane's Nieces & Uncle John. 2005. 26.95 (978-1-4218-1024-9(7), 1st World Library - Literary Society) 1st World Publishing, Inc.
—Aunt Jane's Nieces in Society. 2005. 28.95 (978-1-4218-1424-7(2)); 276p. pap. 13.95 (978-1-4218-1524-4(9)) 1st World Publishing, Inc. (1st World Library - Literary Society).
—Aunt Jane's Nieces in Society. 2004. reprint ed. pap. 1.99 (978-1-4192-0824-9(1)); pap. 20.95 (978-1-4191-0824-2(7)) Kessinger Publishing, LLC.
—Aunt Jane's Nieces out West. 2005. 27.95 (978-1-4218-1425-4(0)); 212p. pap. 12.95 (978-1-4218-1525-1(7)) 1st World Publishing, Inc. (1st World Library - Literary Society).
Vanasse, Patricia. Resilient. Shalaby, Asharaf, illus. 2013. (ENG.). 328p. (YA). pap. 13.99 (978-0-9860373-2-0(X)) Pants On Fire Pr.
Vardamaskos, Angela. Everlasting Truth. Bournakis, Maria, illus. 2008. 48p. pap. 24.95 (978-1-60610-950-2(2)) America Star Bks.
Velasquez, Eric. Grandma's Gift. Velasquez, Eric, illus. 2013. (ENG., Illus.). 32p. (J). (gr. k-1). pap. 9.99 (978-0-8027-3536-2(3), 900120816, Bloomsbury USA Childrens) Bloomsbury Publishing USA.
Verday, Jessica. The Hidden. (ENG.). 400p. (YA). (gr. 9). 2012. pap. 14.99 (978-1-4169-7898-5(4)) 2011. 17.99 (978-1-4169-7897-8(6)) Simon Pulse. (Simon Pulse).
—The Hollow. (ENG.). (YA). (gr. 7). 2010. 528p. pap. 14.99 (978-1-4169-7894-7(1))No. 1. 2009. 544p. 17.99 (978-1-4169-7893-0(3)) Simon Pulse. (Simon Pulse).
Viva, Frank. Outstanding in the Rain. 2015. (Illus.). 32p. (J). (gr. -1-3). 18.00 (978-0-316-36627-4(7)) Little, Brown Bks. for Young Readers.
Vizzini, Ned. It's Kind of a Funny Story. 2007. (ENG.). 464p. (J). (gr. 7-12). per. 10.99 (978-0-7868-5197-3(X), Disney-Hyperion) Disney Publishing Worldwide.
—It's Kind of a Funny Story. 2011. 11.04 (978-0-7848-3383-4(4), Everbind) Marco Bk. Co.
—It's Kind of a Funny Story. 2007. (YA). lib. bdg. 20.85 (978-1-4178-1818-1(2)) Turtleback.
Volponi, Paul. Rooftop. 2007. 199p. 17.00 (978-0-7569-7958-4(7)) Perfection Learning Corp.
von Ziegesar, Cecily. Gossip Girl #10: Would I Lie to You: A Gossip Girl Novel. 2006. (Gossip Girl Ser.: 10). (ENG.). 224p. (YA). (gr. 10-17). per. 13.99 (978-0-316-01183-9(5), Poppy) Little, Brown Bks. for Young Readers.
—Gossip Girl: Don't You Forget about Me: A Gossip Girl Novel. 2007. (Gossip Girl Ser.: 11). (ENG.). 304p. (YA). (gr. 10-17). per. 16.99 (978-0-316-01184-6(3), Poppy) Little, Brown Bks. for Young Readers.
—Gossip Girl: I Like It Like That: A Gossip Girl Novel, 5. 2004. (Gossip Girl Ser.: 5). (ENG.). 224p. (YA). (gr. 10-17). pap. 12.99 (978-0-316-73518-6(3), Poppy) Little, Brown Bks. for Young Readers.
—Gossip Girl: I Will Always Love You: A Gossip Girl Novel. 2010. (Gossip Girl Ser.: 12). (ENG.). 400p. (YA). (gr. 10-17). pap. 19.99 (978-0-316-04359-5(1), Poppy) Little, Brown Bks. for Young Readers.
—Gossip Girl: It Had to Be You: The Gossip Girl Prequel. 2009. (Gossip Girl Ser.). (ENG.). 432p. (YA). (gr. 10-17). pap. 10.99 (978-0-316-01769-5(8), Poppy) Little, Brown Bks. for Young Readers.
—Gossip Girl: Nobody Does It Better: A Gossip Girl Novel, 7. 7th ed. 2005. (Gossip Girl Ser.: 7). (ENG.). 256p. (YA). (gr. 10-17). pap. 13.99 (978-0-316-73512-4(4), Poppy) Little, Brown Bks. for Young Readers.
—Gossip Girl: Only in Your Dreams: A Gossip Girl Novel. 2006. (Gossip Girl Ser.: 9). (ENG.). 256p. (YA). (gr. 10-17). per. 14.99 (978-0-316-01182-2(7), Poppy) Little, Brown Bks. for Young Readers.
—Gossip Girl: the Carlyles, Vol. 1. 2008. (Gossip Girl: the Carlyles Ser.: 1). (ENG.). 256p. (YA). (gr. 10-17). pap. 14.99 (978-0-316-02064-0(8), Poppy) Little, Brown Bks. for Young Readers.
—Gossip Girl: You're the One That I Want: A Gossip Girl Novel, 6. 2004. (Gossip Girl Ser.: 6). (ENG.). 256p. (YA). (gr. 10-17). pap. 14.99 (978-0-316-73516-2(7), Poppy) Little, Brown Bks. for Young Readers.
Vrettos, Adrienne Maria. Burnout. (ENG., 208p. (YA). (gr. 7). 2012. Illus.). pap. 8.99 (978-1-4169-9470-1(X)) 2011. 16.99 (978-1-4169-9469-5(6)) McElderry, Margaret K. Bks. (McElderry, Margaret K. Bks.).
Walters, Eric. I've Got an Idea, 1 vol. 2011. (ENG.). 208p. (J). (gr. 3-7). pap. 9.95 (978-1-55455-119-4(6), acf1ba12-ea60-48c1-809a-ecb21c9233ed) Fitzhenry & Whiteside, Ltd. CAN. Dist: Firefly Bks., Ltd.
—I've Got an Idea. 2004. 166p. (J). pap. (978-0-00-639196-8(6), HarperTrophy) HarperCollins Canada, Ltd.
Warnes, Tim. Chalk & Cheese. Warnes, Tim, illus. 2008. (ENG., Illus.). 32p. (J). (gr. -1-3). 19.99 (978-1-4169-1378-8(5), Simon & Schuster Bks. For Young Readers) Simon & Schuster Bks. For Young Readers.
Warwick, J. M. An Open Vein. 2007. (YA). per. 12.95 (978-1-933963-96-9(4)) Grove Creek Publishing, LLC.
Watson, Renee & Hagan, Ellen. Watch Us Rise. (ENG.). 368p. (YA). 2020. pap. 11.99 (978-1-5476-0311-4(9), 900211274) 2019. 18.99 (978-1-5476-0008-3(X), 900194808) Bloomsbury Publishing USA. (Bloomsbury Young Adult).
Weil, Zoe. Claude & Medea: The Hellburn Dogs. 2007. (ENG., Illus.). 112p. (J). (gr. 2-7). per. 12.00 (978-1-59056-105-8(8)) Lantern Publishing & Media.
Weiner, Jennifer. Little Bigfoot, Big City. (Littlest Bigfoot Ser.: 2). (ENG.). 336p. (J). (gr. 3-7). 2018. pap. 8.99 (978-1-4814-7078-0(7)) 2017. (Illus.). 17.99 (978-1-4814-7077-3(9)) Simon & Schuster Children's Publishing. (Aladdin).
—Little Bigfoot, Big City. 2018. (Littlest Bigfoot Ser.: 2). lib. bdg. 19.65 (978-0-606-41343-5(X)) Turtleback.
Weiss, Ellen. Eloise & the Very Secret Room, 1 vol. Lyon, Tammie, illus. 2015. (Kay Thompson's Eloise Ser.). (ENG.). 32p. (J). (gr. -1-2). 31.36 (978-1-61479-403-5(0), 18188) Spotlight.
Weitz, Chris. The Revival. 2016. (Young World Ser.: 3). (ENG.). 272p. (YA). (gr. 10-17). 18.99 (978-0-316-22634-9(3)) Little, Brown Bks. for Young Readers.
—The Young World. 2015. (Young World Ser.: 1). (ENG.). 400p. (YA). (gr. 10-17). pap. 19.99 (978-0-316-22628-8(9)) Little, Brown Bks. for Young Readers.
Weller, Frances Ward. The Day the Animals Came: A Story of Saint Francis Day. Long, Loren, illus. 2006. 35p. (J). (gr. k-4). reprint ed. 17.00 (978-1-4223-5396-7(6)) DIANE Publishing Co.
Wells, Carolyn & E. C. CASWELL. Two Little Women on a Holiday. l.t. ed. 2006. 178p. pap. 21.99 (978-1-4264-2807-4(3)) Creative Media Partners, LLC.
Wells, Helen. Cherry Ames, the Mystery in the Doctor's Office. 2007. (Cherry Ames Nurse Stories Ser.). 224p. (J). (gr. 3-7). 14.95 (978-0-8261-0435-9(5)) Springer Publishing Co., Inc.
Wells, Marcia. Doom at Grant's Tomb. Calo, Marcos, illus. 2017. (Eddie Red Undercover Ser.: 3). (ENG.). (J). (gr. 5-7). lib. bdg. 17.20 (978-0-606-39813-8(9)) Turtleback.
—Eddie Red Undercover: Mystery on Museum Mile. Calo, Marcos, illus. 2015. (Eddie Red Undercover Ser.). (ENG.). 256p. (J). (gr. 5-7). pap. 7.99 (978-0-544-43940-5(6), 1596839, Clarion Bks.) HarperCollins Pubs.
Westerfeld, Scott. Afterworlds. 2014. (ENG., Illus.). 608p. (YA). (gr. 9). 19.99 (978-1-4814-2234-5(0), Simon Pulse) Simon Pulse.
—So Yesterday. 2005. (ENG.). 256p. (YA). (gr. 7-12). reprint ed. 8.99 (978-1-59514-032-6(8), Razorbill) Penguin Young Readers Group.
—Spill Zone Book 2: The Broken Vow. Puvilland, Alex, illus. 2019. (Spill Zone Ser.: 2). (ENG.). 240p. (YA). pap. 17.99 (978-1-250-30942-6(5), 900198487, First Second Bks.) Roaring Brook Pr.
Weston, Carol. Speed of Life. (ENG.). 352p. (J). (gr. 6-8). 2018. pap. 9.99 (978-1-4926-6083-5(3)) 2017. 16.99 (978-1-4926-5449-0(3)) Sourcebooks, Inc.
Wetterer, Margaret K. & Wetterer, Charles M. The Snowshoeing Adventure of Milton Daub, Blizzard Trekker. 2010. pap. 51.02 (978-0-7613-6921-9(X)) Lerner Publishing Group.
Wheeler-Cribb, Peggy. Madeline Becomes a Star. Bensch, April, illus. 2013. 50p. 29.95 (978-0-9886194-1-8(5)) ProsePress.
Wilbur, Helen L. Finnegan & Fox: The Ten-Foot Cop. Manders, John, illus. 2013. (ENG.). 32p. (J). (gr. 1-4). 19.99 (978-1-58536-784-9(2), 202354) Sleeping Bear Pr.
Wilcox, Brian & David, Lawrence. Full Moon. Wilcox, Brian, illus. 2004. (Illus.). 30p. (J). (gr. k-4). reprint ed. 16.00 (978-0-7567-7762-3(3)) DIANE Publishing Co.
Wilsdon, Christina. A New York Sailing Adventure. Hockerman, Dennis, illus. 2006. 26p. (J). 7.99 (978-1-59939-014-7(0)) Cornerstone Pr.
Winfield, Arthur M. The Rover Boys in Business or the Search for the Missing Bonds. 2006. (ENG.). 316p. per. 30.95 (978-1-4286-4098-6(3)) Kessinger Publishing, LLC.
—The Rover Boys in New York. 2007. 268p. 26.95 (978-1-4218-4133-5(9)); per. 11.95 (978-1-4218-4231-8(9)) 1st World Publishing, Inc. (1st World Library - Literary Society).
—The Rover Boys in New York or Saving the. 2004. reprint ed. pap. 22.95 (978-1-4191-8117-7(3)) Kessinger Publishing, LLC.
—The Rover Boys in New York or Saving Their Father's Honor. 2004. reprint ed. pap. 1.99 (978-1-4192-8117-4(8)) Kessinger Publishing, LLC.
Winston, Sherri. Jada Sly, Artist & Spy. 2019. (ENG., Illus.). 272p. (J). (gr. 3-7). 32.99 (978-0-316-50536-9(6)) Little, Brown Bks. for Young Readers.
Witherow, Wendy. Bridget's Blog. Pulley, Kelly, illus. 2007. 95p. (J). pap. (978-1-934306-09-3(6)) Mission City Pr., Inc.
Wolff, Ferida. Rachel's Roses. Lucas, Margeaux, illus. 2019. (ENG.). 112p. (J). (gr. 2-5). 15.99 (978-0-8234-4365-9(5)) Holiday Hse., Inc.
Woodruff, Stephen B. Among Friends: A Quaker Boy at the Battle of Plattsburgh. 2013. (ENG.). x, 155p. (J). pap. (978-1-59531-044-6(4)) North Country Bks., Inc.
Woodson, Jacqueline. After Tupac & d Foster. 2008. (ENG.). 160p. (J). (gr. 5-18). 18.99 (978-0-399-24654-8(1), Nancy Paulsen Books) Penguin Young Readers Group.
—After Tupac & D Foster. 2010. lib. bdg. 18.40 (978-0-606-10720-4(7)) Turtleback.
—Behind You. (ENG.). 176p. (YA). 2010. (gr. 7-18). 8.99 (978-0-14-241554-2(5), Puffin Books) 2004. (gr. 5-12). 22.44 (978-0-399-23988-5(X)) Penguin Young Readers Group.
—If You Come Softly: Twentieth Anniversary Edition. 20th ed. 2018. (ENG.). 192p. (YA). (gr. 7). 17.99 (978-0-525-51548-7(8), Nancy Paulsen Books) Penguin Young Readers Group.
Woodward, J. Howland. A Moment in Time. 2006. 55p. pap. 16.95 (978-1-4241-1334-7(2)) America Star Bks.
Wright, Bil. Putting Makeup on the Fat Boy. (ENG., 240p. (YA). (gr. 7). 2012. Illus.). pap. 12.99 (978-1-4169-4004-3(9)) 2011. 19.99 (978-1-4169-3996-2(2)) Simon & Schuster Bks. For Young Readers. (Simon & Schuster Bks. For Young Readers).
Wurge, B. B. Billy & the Birdfrogs. 2008. (ENG.). 178p. (J). (gr. 3-8). pap. 9.95 (978-0-9815148-2-6(0)) Leapfrog Pr.
—Squiggle. 2009. (LeapKids Ser.). (ENG., Illus.). 152p. (J). (gr. 2-7). pap. 9.95 (978-0-9815148-9-5(8)) Leapfrog Pr.
Yael Mermelstein. The Face in the Mirror. 2012. (ENG.). 285p. (J). pap. (978-1-4226-1292-7(9), Shaar Pr.) Mesorah Pubns., Ltd.
Yoo, Paula. Lily's New Home (Confetti Kids), 1 vol. 2016. (Confetti Kids Ser.: 1). (ENG., Illus.). 32p. (J). (gr. k-2). 14.95 (978-1-62014-249-3(X), leelowbooks) Lee & Low Bks., Inc.
Zadoff, Allen. I Am the Weapon. 2014. (Unknown Assassin Ser.: 1). (ENG.). 368p. (YA). (gr. 10-17). pap. 11.99 (978-0-316-19967-4(2)) Little, Brown Bks. for Young Readers.
Zalben, Jane Breskin. A Moon for Moe & Mo. Amini, Mehrdokht, illus. 2018. 48p. (J). (gr. -1-2). lib. bdg. 17.99 (978-1-58089-727-3(4)) Charlesbridge Publishing, Inc.
Zarin, Cynthia. Albert, the Dog Who Liked to Ride in Taxis. Pratt, Pierre, illus. 2004. (ENG.). 32p. (J). (gr. -1-3). 19.99 (978-0-689-84762-2(9), Atheneum/Richard Jackson Bks.) Simon & Schuster Children's Publishing.
Zevin, Gabrielle. Because It Is My Blood: A Novel. 2013. (Birthright Ser.: 2). (ENG.). 384p. (YA). (gr. 7). pap. 19.99 (978-1-250-03422-9(1), 900120595) Square Fish.
—In the Age of Love & Chocolate: A Novel. 2014. (Birthright Ser.: 3). (ENG.). 320p. (YA). (gr. 7). pap. 15.99 (978-1-250-05071-7(5), 900134142) Square Fish.

NEW YORK (N.Y.)—FIRES AND FIRE PREVENTION

Broyles, Janell. The Triangle Shirtwaist Factory Fire of 1911, 1 vol. 2003. (Tragic Fires Throughout History Ser.). (ENG., Illus.). 48p. (gr. 5-8). lib. bdg. 34.47 (978-0-8239-4489-7(1), 3eb57009-3236-44fb-8ac7-d8777e213104, Rosen Reference) Rosen Publishing Group, Inc., The.

NEW YORK (N.Y.)—HISTORY

Adams, Alison. The Geography of New York City. 2017. (Text Connections Guided Close Reading Ser.). (J). (gr. 1). (978-1-4900-1823-2(9)) Benchmark Education Co.
Alko, Selina. B Is for Brooklyn. Alko, Selina, illus. 2012. (ENG., Illus.). 40p. (J). (gr. -1-1). 19.99 (978-0-8050-9213-4(7), 900066076, Holt, Henry & Co. Bks. For Young Readers) Holt, Henry & Co.
Bailey, Rachel A. The Triangle Shirtwaist Factory Fire: A History Perspectives Book. 2014. (Perspectives Library). (ENG., Illus.). 32p. (J). (gr. 4-8). 32.07 (978-1-63137-620-7(9), 205263) Cherry Lake Publishing.
Banting, Erinn. Empire State Building. 2019. (Structural Wonders of the World Ser.). (ENG., Illus.). 24p. (J). (gr. 2-5). pap. 12.95 (978-1-4896-9940-4(6)); lib. bdg. 28.55 (978-1-4896-9939-8(2)) Weigl Pubs., Inc.
Barter, James. Colonial New York. 2003. (Travel Guide To Ser.). (ENG., Illus.). 112p. (J). 30.85 (978-1-59018-250-5(2), Lucent Bks.) Cengage Gale.
Bartoletti, Susan Campbell. Terrible Typhoid Mary: A True Story of the Deadliest Cook in America. 2015. (ENG., Illus.). 240p. (YA). (gr. 8-7). 18.99 (978-0-544-31367-5(4), 1581808, Clarion Bks.) HarperCollins Pubs.
Bauer, Marion Dane. The Statue of Liberty: Ready-To-Read Level 1. Wallace, John, illus. 2018. (Wonders of America Ser.). (ENG.). 32p. (J). (gr. -1-1). 17.99 (978-1-5344-3031-0(8), Simon Spotlight) Simon Spotlight.
Belovitch, Jeanne & Bonnevie, Bonnie. New York City Firsts: A Coloring Book for Families about New York History & America's. Belovitch, Jeanne, ed. 2004. 19p. (J). (gr. -1-6). pap. 3.00 (978-0-9722969-1-5(3)) CMB Publishing Co.
Birle, Pete. On the Hardwood: New York Knicks. 2013. (On the Hardwood Ser.). (ENG., Illus.). 48p. (gr. 3-8). pap. 8.95 (978-1-61570-834-5(0)) Scobre Pr. Corp.
Boehm Jerome, Kate. Buffalo, NY: Cool Stuff Every Kid Should Know. 2010. (Arcadia Kids Ser.). (ENG., Illus.). 48p. (J). (gr. 3-6). pap. 11.99 (978-1-4396-0069-6(4)) Arcadia Publishing.
Bolden, Tonya. Maritcha: A Nineteenth-Century American Girl. 2015. (ENG., Illus.). 56p. (J). (gr. 3-7). 9.95 (978-1-4197-1626-3(3), 533803, Abrams Bks. for Young Readers) Abrams, Inc.
Branscomb, Leslie Wolf. Marc Jacobs. 2011. (Profiles in Fashion Ser.). (Illus.). 112p. 28.95 (978-1-59935-153-7(6), 1320457) Reynolds, Morgan Inc.
Brezina, Corona. America's Political Scandals in the Late 1800s: Boss Tweed & Tammany Hall. 2009. (America's Industrial Society in the 19th Century Ser.). 32p. (gr. 4-4). 47.90 (978-1-61511-336-1(3)) Rosen Publishing Group, Inc., The.
Britton, Tamara L. The World Trade Center. 2003. (Symbols, Landmarks & Monuments Set 1 Ser.). 32p. (gr. k-6). 27.07 (978-1-57765-850-4(7), Checkerboard Library) ABDO Publishing Co.
Broyles, Janell. The Triangle Shirtwaist Factory Fire of 1911, 1 vol. 2003. (Tragic Fires Throughout History Ser.). (ENG., Illus.). 48p. (gr. 5-8). lib. bdg. 34.47 (978-0-8239-4489-7(1), 3eb57009-3236-44fb-8ac7-d8777e213104, Rosen Reference) Rosen Publishing Group, Inc., The.
—The Triangle Shirtwaist Factory Fire Of 1911. 2009. (Tragic Fires Throughout History Ser.). 48p. (gr. 5-8). 53.00 (978-1-60854-584-1(9), Rosen Reference) Rosen Publishing Group, Inc., The.
Carole Marsh. New York City Coloring & Activity Book. 2004. (City Bks.). 24p. (gr. k-5). pap. 3.95 (978-0-635-02226-4(5)) Gallopade International.
Copeland, Peter F. Scenes of Olde New York Coloring Book. 2009. (Dover American History Coloring Bks.). (ENG.). 48p. (gr. 3-8). pap. 5.99 (978-0-486-47494-6(1), 474941) Dover Pubns., Inc.
Crewe, Sabrina & Schaefer, Adam. The Triangle Shirtwaist Factory Fire, 1 vol. 2004. (Events That Shaped America Ser.). (ENG., Illus.). 32p. (gr. 3-5). lib. bdg. 28.67 (978-0-8368-3402-4(X), aefb702f-ab39-4955-b21f-908dd17b92d9, Gareth Stevens Learning Library) Stevens, Gareth Publishing LLLP.
Cunningham, Kevin. The New York Colony. 2011. (True Book-the Thirteen Colonies Ser.). (ENG., Illus.). 48p. (J). (gr. 3-5). lib. bdg. 29.00 (978-0-531-25394-6(5), Children's Pr.) Scholastic Library Publishing.
—The New York Colony (a True Book: the Thirteen Colonies) 2011. (True Book (Relaunch) Ser.). (ENG., Illus.). 48p. (J). (gr. 3-5). pap. 6.95 (978-0-531-26607-6(9), Children's Pr.) Scholastic Library Publishing.
Curtiss, A. B. The Little Chapel That Stood Golino, Mirto, illus. l.t. ed. 2005. (ENG.). 36p. (J). (gr. -1-3). 18.95 (978-0-932529-77-0(1)) Oldcastle Publishing.
Derezinski, Amelia. Star Turns: Dancing on Broadway. 2009. (Curtain Call Library of Dance Ser.). 48p. (gr. 5-8). 53.00 (978-1-60853-422-7(7), Rosen Reference) Rosen Publishing Group, Inc., The.
Doman, Mary Kate. Tragedy at the Triangle: Friendship in the Tenements & the Shirtwaist Factory Fire. 2015. (ENG., Illus.). 96p. 29.99 (978-1-62619-645-2(1), History Pr., The) Arcadia Publishing.
Francis, Isabelle. New York City: Yesterday & Today: Understand Properties of Multiplication, 1 vol. 2014. (InfoMax Math Readers Ser.). (ENG.). 24p. (J). (gr. 3-3). pap. 8.25 (978-1-4777-4699-8(4), ef462daa-3867-4c21-bc3c-2ce7fad2c299, Rosen Classroom) Rosen Publishing Group, Inc., The.
Furgang, Kathy. The Declaration of Independence & Robert Livingston of New York. 2009. (Framers of the Declaration of Independence Ser.). 24p. (gr. 3-3). 42.50 (978-1-61512-631-6(7), PowerKids Pr.) Rosen Publishing Group, Inc., The.
George, Lynn & Schimel, Kate. New York's Early Explorers, 1 vol. 2011. (Spotlight on New York Ser.). (ENG., Illus.). 24p. (J). (gr. 3-4). lib. bdg. 26.27 (978-1-4488-5749-4(X), 7dac17cf-d2fe-4f7b-85e5-95d5260f17dd, PowerKids Pr.) Rosen Publishing Group, Inc., The.
Gloor, Elizabeth. New York City: An Urban Community, 1 vol. 2011. (My Community Ser.). (ENG., Illus.). 12p. (gr. 2-2). pap. 6.95 (978-1-4488-5720-3(1), 33ec7264-c682-43c5-a32c-e071a0f045dc, Rosen Classroom) Rosen Publishing Group, Inc., The.
Goldish, Meish. The Empire State Building. 2016. (American Places: from Vision to Reality Ser.). (ENG., Illus.). 32p. (J). (gr. 2-7). 28.50 (978-1-944102-43-2(4)) Bearport Publishing Co., Inc.
—Ground Zero Dogs. 2012. (Dog Heroes Ser.). 32p. (J). (gr. 2-7). lib. bdg. 28.50 (978-1-61772-576-0(5)) Bearport Publishing Co., Inc.
Goldsworthy, Steve. Estatua de la Libertad. 2013. (SPA.). (J). (978-1-62127-623-4(6)) Weigl Pubs., Inc.
—Statue of Liberty with Code. 2012. (AV2 American Icons Ser.). (ENG., Illus.). 24p. (J). (gr. -1-3). pap. 12.95 (978-1-61913-303-7(2), AV2 by Weigl) Weigl Pubs., Inc.
Goodman, Susan. On This Spot: An Expedition Back Through Time. Christiansen, Lee, illus. 2004. (ENG.). 32p. (J). (gr. k-5). 17.99 (978-0-688-16913-8(9), Greenwillow Bks.) HarperCollins Pubs.
Greene, Jacqueline Dembar. The Triangle Shirtwaist Factory Fire. 2007. (Code Red Ser.). (Illus.). 32p. (YA). (gr. 2-5). lib. bdg. 28.50 (978-1-59716-359-0(7)) Bearport Publishing Co., Inc.
Gregory, Joy. St. Patrick's Cathedral. 2014. (Illus.). 24p. (J). (978-1-4896-2610-3(7)) Weigl Pubs., Inc.
Gunderson, Jessica. The Triangle Shirtwaist Factory Fire. Miller, Phil & Barnett III, Charles, illus. 2006. (Disasters in History Ser.). (ENG.). 32p. (J). (gr. 3-9). per. 8.10 (978-0-7368-6878-5(X), 91581); pap. 48.60 (978-0-7368-6999-7(9), 5667) Capstone. (Capstone Pr.).
Hamilton, John. New York, 1 vol. 2016. (United States of America Ser.). (ENG., Illus.). 48p. (J). (gr. 5-9). 34.21 (978-1-68078-334-6(3), 21653, Abdo & Daughters) ABDO Publishing Co.
Hannigan, Paula. New York City. Chandler, Shannon, illus. 2012. (ENG.). 12p. (J). bds. 14.99 (978-1-4494-1876-2(7)) Andrews McMeel Publishing.
Hart Beckman, Wendy. Harlem Renaissance Artists & Writers, 1 vol. 2013. (Inspiring Collective Biographies Ser.). (ENG.). 112p. (gr. 5-6). pap. 13.88 (978-1-4644-0269-2(8), ea6b960a-62ad-4c33-91d5-2d86cb75d3d2) Enslow Publishing, LLC.
Hayn, Carter. New York City: Old & New, 1 vol. 2011. (My Community Ser.). (ENG., Illus.). 12p. (gr. 2-2). pap. 6.95 (978-1-4488-5723-4(6), 5cf95efd-e88a-4dda-bcc9-b974d139068a, Rosen Classroom) Rosen Publishing Group, Inc., The.
—New York City's Historical Heritage, 1 vol. 2011. (My Community Ser.). (ENG., Illus.). 12p. (gr. 2-2). pap. 6.95 (978-1-4488-5722-7(8), ba49466a-84fc-456b-b602-b96e4d736e71, Rosen Classroom) Rosen Publishing Group, Inc., The.
Hintz, Martin. The New York Colony. rev. ed. 2016. (American Colonies Ser.). (ENG.). 32p. (J). (gr. 3-6). pap. 8.10 (978-1-5157-4220-3(2), 133983, Capstone Pr.) Capstone.
The History of New York City: Understand Properties of Multiplication, 1 vol. 2014. (Rosen Math Readers Ser.). (ENG., Illus.). 24p. (J). (gr. 3-3). pap. 8.25 (978-1-4777-4958-6(6), fb507ace-3628-4951-9cde-39e6057ceb5a, PowerKids Pr.) Rosen Publishing Group, Inc., The.
Hopkinson, Deborah. Shutting Out the Sky: Life in the Tenements of New York, 1880-1924 (Scholastic Focus) 2003. (ENG., Illus.). 144p. (J). (gr. 4-7). 19.99 (978-0-439-37590-0(8)) Scholastic, Inc.
Humphrey, Jeff & O'Donnell, Kerri. The American Revolution in New York. (Illus.). 24p. (J). 2012. 60.00

(978-1-4488-5756-2(2)) 2011. (ENG., (gr. 3-4). pap. 10.00 (978-1-4488-5755-5(4), 4cada24e-0557-4210-a1ad-a42288ccb8b2) 2011. (ENG., (gr. 3-4). lib. bdg. 26.27 (978-1-4488-5741-8(4), 7b72a5b9-5589-4d4e-9f5b-6b9d863789ed) Rosen Publishing Group, Inc., The. (PowerKids Pr.).

Jerome, Kate B. Lucky to Live in New York. 2017. (Arcadia Kids Ser.). (ENG., Illus.). 32p. (J). 16.99 (978-0-7385-2778-9(5)) Arcadia Publishing.

—The Wise Animal Handbook New York. 2017. (Arcadia Kids Ser.). (ENG., Illus.). 32p. (J). 16.99 (978-0-7385-2834-2(X)) Arcadia Publishing.

Kallen, Stuart A. The Harlem Renaissance, 1 vol. 2009. (American History Ser.). (ENG.). 104p. (gr. 7-7). 41.03 (978-1-4205-0104-9(6), 39e1b90e-6c9d-4132-9a91-a517f9e95be1, Lucent Pr.) Greenhaven Publishing LLC.

Kaur, Ramandeep. One World Trade Center. 2015. (How Did They Build That? Ser.). (ENG., Illus.). 32p. (gr. 3-8). 27.99 (978-1-62920-554-0(0)) Scobre Pr. Corp.

Kent, Deborah. The Great Civil War Draft Riots. 2005. (Cornerstones of Freedom Ser.). (ENG., Illus.). 48p. (YA). (gr. 4-7). lib. bdg. 26.00 (978-0-516-23632-2(6)) Scholastic Library Publishing.

Landau, Elaine. The Triangle Shirtwaist Factory Fire. 2005. (Cornerstones of Freedom Ser.). (ENG., Illus.). 48p. (YA). (gr. 4-7). 26.00 (978-0-516-23626-1(1)) Scholastic Library Publishing.

Lange, Brenda. The Triangle Shirtwaist Factory Fire. 2008. (Great Historic Disasters Ser.). (ENG., Illus.). 112p. (gr. 5-8). lib. bdg. 35.00 (978-0-7910-9641-3(6), P150893, Facts On File) Infobase Holdings, Inc.

LaPlante, Walter. The Erie Canal, 1 vol. 2016. (Road Trip: Famous Routes Ser.). (ENG., Illus.). 24p. (J). (gr. 2-3). pap. 9.15 (978-1-4824-4674-6(X), e1849b3f-c692-4714-bbe9-b74124e85cf5) Stevens, Gareth Publishing LLLP.

Lassieur, Allison. Building the Empire State Building: An Interactive Engineering Adventure, 1 vol. 2014. (You Choose: Engineering Marvels Ser.). (ENG., Illus.). 112p. (J). (gr. 3-7). 32.65 (978-1-4914-0400-3(0), 125866, Capstone Pr.) Capstone.

Leoni, Cristiana. New York in the 1930s with la Guardia, 1 vol. Cappon, Manuela, illus. 2009. (Come See My City Ser.). (ENG.). 48p. (gr. 4-4). 31.21 (978-0-7614-4336-0(3), 8018822b-c09d-4855-b1fe-9641b91bec49) Cavendish Square Publishing LLC.

Libretto, Ellen V. The General Slocum Steamboat Fire Of 1904. 2009. (Tragic Fires Throughout History Ser.). 48p. (gr. 5-8). 53.00 (978-1-60854-581-0(4), Rosen Reference) Rosen Publishing Group, Inc., The.

Loewen, Nancy. Scarlett the Cat to the Rescue: Fire Hero, 1 vol. Sorra, Kristin, illus. 2014. (Animal Heroes Ser.). (ENG.). 32p. (J). (gr. k-2). 29.32 (978-1-4795-5464-5(2), 126114, Picture Window Bks.) Capstone.

Lonely Planet. Mi Primera Lonely Planet Nueva York, 1 vol. 2012. (Lonely Planet Kids Ser.).Tr. of New York Not for Parents. (SPA., Illus.). 96p. (J). pap. 14.99 (978-84-08-10916-7(2), 103549) Lonely Planet Pubns.

Mansfield, Andy. Lonely Planet Kids Pop-Up New York 1. Mansfield, Andy, illus. 2016. (Lonely Planet Kids Ser.). (ENG., Illus.). 8p. (J). (gr. -1-k). 9.99 (978-1-76034-337-8(4), 5337) Lonely Planet Global Ltd. IRL. Dist: Hachette Bk. Group.

Markel, Michelle. Brave Girl: Clara & the Shirtwaist Makers' Strike Of 1909. Sweet, Melissa, illus. 2013. (ENG.). 32p. (J). (gr. -1-3). 18.99 (978-0-06-180442-7(8), Balzer & Bray) HarperCollins Pubs.

Marsh, Carole. Exploring New York Through Project-Based Learning: Geography, History, Government, Economics & More. 2016. (New York Experience Ser.). (ENG.). (J). pap. 9.99 (978-0-635-12356-5(8)) Gallopade International.

—I'm Reading about New York. 2014. (New York Experience Ser.). (ENG., Illus.). (J). pap., pap. 8.99 (978-0-635-11307-8(4)) Gallopade International.

—The NYC-5 Boroughs: Activity Book. Baker, Janice, ed. 2005. (Illus.). 24p. (gr. k-8). pap. 8.95 (978-0-635-03080-1(2)) Gallopade International.

Marsico, Katie. The Triangle Shirtwaist Factory Fire: Its Legacy of Labor Rights, 1 vol. 2010. (Perspectives On Ser.). (ENG.). 112p. (YA). (gr. 8-8). 42.64 (978-0-7614-4027-7(5), 7ef29bbe-25f8-4d7e-910d-080aa67757ce) Cavendish Square Publishing LLC.

Maynard, Charles W. Fort Ticonderoga. 2009. (Famous Forts Throughout American History Ser.). 24p. (gr. 3-4). 42.50 (978-1-61512-521-0(3), PowerKids Pr.) Rosen Publishing Group, Inc., The.

Medina, Nico & Who HQ. What Was Stonewall? Murray, Jake, illus. 2019. (What Was? Ser.). 112p. (J). (gr. 3-7). 7.99 (978-1-5247-8600-7(4)); lib. bdg. 15.99 (978-1-5247-8602-1(0)) Penguin Young Readers Group. (Penguin Workshop).

Morley, Jacqueline. You Wouldn't Want to Meet Typhoid Mary! A Deadly Cook You'd Rather Not Know. Antram, David, illus. 2013. (You Wouldn't Want To... Ser.). (ENG.). 32p. (J). (gr. 4-6). 26.19 (978-0-531-25944-3(7), Watts, Franklin) Scholastic Library Publishing.

Nau, Myrna. Questions & Answers about Ellis Island, 1 vol. 2018. (Eye on Historical Sources Ser.). (ENG.). 32p. (gr. 4-4). 27.93 (978-1-5383-4111-7(5), 65f028bf-13d2-49a4-bbe1-c9107d451c8f, PowerKids Pr.) Rosen Publishing Group, Inc., The.

Nelson, Vaunda Micheaux. The Book Itch: Freedom, Truth & Harlem's Greatest Bookstore. Christie, R. Gregory, illus. 2015. (ENG.). 32p. (J). (gr. 2-4). lib. bdg. 17.99 (978-0-7613-3943-4(4), 03a7c337-69d2-46b1-8a7d-9c24dc64cf05, Carolrhoda Bks.) Lerner Publishing Group.

Panchyk, Richard. New York City History for Kids: From New Amsterdam to the Big Apple with 21 Activities. 2012. (For Kids Ser.: 44). (ENG., Illus.). 144p. (J). (gr. 4). pap. 18.99 (978-1-883052-93-5(9)) Chicago Review Pr., Inc.

Pascal, Janet. Where Is the Empire State Building? 2015. (Where Is... ? Ser.). lib. bdg. 16.00 (978-0-606-36758-5(6)) Turtleback.

Pascal, Janet B. & Who HQ. Where Is the Empire State Building? Colon, Daniel, illus. 2015. (Where Is? Ser.). 112p. (J). (gr. 3-7). 6.99 (978-0-448-48426-6(9), Penguin Workshop) Penguin Young Readers Group.

Peterson, Sheryl. Empire State Building. 2006. (Modern Wonders of the World Ser.). (Illus.). 32p. (J). 18.95 (978-1-58341-439-2(8), Creative Education) Creative Co., The.

Publications International Ltd. Staff. Yesterday & Today New York. 2009. 192p. 24.95 (978-1-4127-4294-8(3)) Publications International, Ltd.

Regan, Lisa. Broadway Star, 1 vol. 2012. (Stage School Ser.). (ENG., Illus.). 32p. (J). (gr. 2-3). 29.93 (978-1-4488-8092-8(0), 9df4b6dd-cedd-48fa-be1e-7b61fc5eb5f0); pap. 11.00 (978-1-4488-8151-2(X), 584ddf15-0ccf-49eb-83b4-e0023dfeee41) Rosen Publishing Group, Inc., The. (Windmill Bks.).

Riggs, Kate. Empire State Building. 2009. (Now That's Big Ser.). 24p. (J). (gr. 1-5). lib. bdg. 24.25 (978-1-58341-703-4(6), Creative Education) Creative Co., The.

Ringgold, Faith. We Came to America. 2016. (Illus.). 32p. (J). (gr. k-3). 18.99 (978-0-517-70947-4(3)); (ENG., lib. bdg. 20.99 (978-0-517-70948-1(1)) Random Hse. Children's Bks. (Knopf Bks. for Young Readers).

Rubinstein, Robert E. Zishe the Strongman. Miller, Woody, illus. 2010. (Kar-Ben Favorites Ser.). (ENG.). 32p. (J). (gr. k-3). lib. bdg. 17.95 (978-0-7613-3958-8(2), Kar-Ben Publishing) Lerner Publishing Group.

Rudd, Brandon Kyle. Cooper's Pack Travel Guide to New York City. McCann, Martin, illus. rev. ed. 2012. (ENG.). 72p. (J). (gr. 1-6). pap. 12.95 (978-0-9794882-5-2(7)) Cooper's Pack.

Sanderson, Jeanette. A Visit to the New Amsterdam. 2005. (J). pap. (978-1-4108-4229-9(0)) Benchmark Education Co.

Shipton, Vicky & Lerner, Alan. Level 3: New York Book & MP3 Pack: Industrial Ecology. 2nd ed. 2012. (ENG.). (C). pap., pap. 14.65 incl. cd-rom (978-1-4479-2569-9(6)) Pearson Education.

Spotlight on New York, 196 vols. 2014. (Spotlight on New York Ser.). (ENG.). 24p. (J). (gr. 4-4). 367.78 (978-1-4777-7345-1(2), a8de6de6-e3d0-43e1-bca2-b720b47e00ce); pap. 140.00 (978-1-4777-7346-8(0)) Rosen Publishing Group, Inc., The. (Rosen Classroom).

Stanley, Ed. Grand Central Terminal: Gateway to New York City. 2003. (Illus.). 48p. (J). 16.95 (978-1-59034-491-0(X)); pap. (978-1-59034-492-7(8)) Mondo Publishing.

Sweet, Melissa. Balloons over Broadway: The True Story of the Puppeteer of Macy's Parade. Sweet, Melissa, illus. 2011. (ENG., Illus.). 40p. (J). (gr. -1-3). 17.99 (978-0-547-19945-0(7), 1058458, Clarion Bks.) HarperCollins Pubs.

Tan, Richard. Dutch New Amsterdam & English New York, 1 vol. 2011. (My Community Ser.). (ENG., Illus.). 12p. (gr. 2-2). pap. 6.95 (978-1-4488-5726-5(0), f10435d0-1a97-45ac-917e-0753eb68eeca, Rosen Classroom) Rosen Publishing Group, Inc., The.

—The Famous Explorers of New York City, 1 vol. 2011. (My Community Ser.). (ENG., Illus.). 12p. (gr. 2-2). pap. 6.95 (978-1-4488-5725-8(2), a37d9d07-f919-4854-a2df-acabb6019846, Rosen Classroom) Rosen Publishing Group, Inc., The.

—The Native American Peoples of New York City, 1 vol. 2011. (My Community Ser.). (ENG., Illus.). 12p. (gr. 2-2). pap. 6.95 (978-1-4488-5724-1(4), 6600b219-ec4d-450c-b714-5b6d4e6e58b0, Rosen Classroom) Rosen Publishing Group, Inc., The.

Tani, Branca. New York in The 1700s, 1 vol. 2011. (My Community Ser.). (ENG., Illus.). 12p. (gr. 2-2). pap. 6.95 (978-1-4488-5727-2(9), dee69975-adeb-4515-9766-6091e3c3995e, Rosen Classroom) Rosen Publishing Group, Inc., The.

—New York in The 1800s, 1 vol. 2011. (My Community Ser.). (ENG., Illus.). 12p. (gr. 2-2). pap. 6.95 (978-1-4488-5728-9(7), 785e724a-ad0a-4f33-a38d-9599b4fd1f35, Rosen Classroom) Rosen Publishing Group, Inc., The.

—New York in The 1900s, 1 vol. 2011. (My Community Ser.). (ENG., Illus.). 12p. (gr. 2-2). pap. 6.95 (978-1-4488-5729-6(5), 0fc48cc6-17e6-4fcd-89aa-eabe90ab7ca8, Rosen Classroom) Rosen Publishing Group, Inc., The.

Thermes, Jennifer. Manhattan: Mapping the Story of an Island. 2019. (ENG., Illus.). 64p. (J). (gr. 3-7). 19.99 (978-1-4197-3655-1(8), 1219101, Abrams Bks. for Young Readers) Abrams, Inc.

Thornton, Jeremy. The History of Early New York. 2009. (Building America's Democracy Ser.). 24p. (gr. 3-3). 42.50 (978-1-61511-767-3(9), PowerKids Pr.) Rosen Publishing Group, Inc., The.

Van Valkenburgh, Norman J. America's First Wilderness: New York State's Forest Preserves. 2008. (Illus.). 44p. (J). 6.50 (978-1-930098-88-6(X)) Purple Mountain Pr., Ltd.

Watson, Renée. Harlem's Little Blackbird: The Story of Florence Mills. Robinson, Christian, illus. 2012. 40p. (J). (gr. -1-2). 17.99 (978-0-375-86973-0(5), Random Hse. Bks. for Young Readers) Random Hse. Children's Bks.

Weston Woods Staff, creator. Man Who Walked Between the Towers. 2011. 18.95 (978-0-545-14930-3(4)); 38.75 (978-0-545-14931-0(2)) Weston Woods Studios, Inc.

—The Man Who Walked Between the Towers. 2011. 29.95 (978-0-439-76703-3(2)) Weston Woods Studios, Inc.

Wetterer, Margaret K. & Wetterer, Charles M. Caminando Bajo la Nieve. Young, Mary O'Keefe, illus. 2007. (Yo Solo Historia Ser.). 48p. (J). (gr. 4-7). per. 6.95 (978-0-8225-7789-8(5)) Lerner Publishing Group.

—Caminando Bajo la Nieve. Young, Mary, illus. 2007. (Yo Solo - Historia (on My Own - History) Ser.). (SPA.). 48p. (gr. 2-4). lib. bdg. 25.26 (978-0-8225-7786-7(0)) Lerner Publishing Group.

—Caminando Bajo la Nieve; the Snow Walker. 2008. pap. 40.95 (978-0-8225-9699-8(7)) Lerner Publishing Group.

Wishinsky, Frieda. How Emily Saved the Bridge: The Story of Emily Warren Roebling & the Building of the Brooklyn Bridge, 1 vol. Nelson, Natalie, illus. 2019. (ENG.). 32p. (J). (gr. 2-5). 19.99 (978-1-77306-104-7(6)) Groundwood Bks. CAN. Dist: Publishers Group West (PGW).

Woodland, Faith. New York. 2017. (Illus.). 24p. (J). (978-1-4896-7305-3(9), AV2 by Weigl) Weigl Pubs., Inc.

Worth, Richard. Black Culture in Bloom: The Harlem Renaissance. 2020. (J). pap. (978-1-9785-1518-5(9)) Enslow Publishing, LLC.

Yacka, Douglas, et al. Where Is Broadway? Hinderliter, John, illus. 2019. (Where Is? Ser.). 112p. (J). (gr. 3-7). 7.99 (978-1-5247-8650-2(0)); 15.99 (978-1-5247-8651-9(9)) Penguin Young Readers Group. (Penguin Workshop).

Yazdani, Ashley Benham. A Green Place to Be: the Creation of Central Park. Yazdani, Ashley Benham, illus. 2019. (ENG., Illus.). 40p. (J). (gr. 2-5). 18.99 (978-0-7636-9695-5(1)) Candlewick Pr.

Ziff, John. Northeast: New Jersey, New York, Pennsylvania, Vol. 19. 2015. (Let's Explore the States Ser.). (Illus.). 64p. (J). (gr. 5). 23.95 (978-1-4222-3329-0(4)) Mason Crest.

NEW YORK (N.Y.)—HISTORY—FICTION

Adler, David A. The Babe & I. Widener, Terry, illus. 2004. (ENG.). 32p. (J). (gr. -1-3). reprint ed. pap. 7.99 (978-0-15-205026-9(4), 1195179, Clarion Bks.) HarperCollins Pubs.

—The Babe & I. Widener, Terry, illus. 2006. 28p. (gr. 1-4). 18.00 (978-0-7569-6560-0(8)) Perfection Learning Corp.

Alger, Horatio. Fame & Fortune: Or: the Progress of Richard Hunter. 2007. (ENG.). 160p. per. 19.99 (978-1-4346-5061-0(8)) Creative Media Partners, LLC.

—Helping Himself. 2006. 180p. pap. 19.99 (978-1-4264-0881-6(1)); (ENG.). 168p. pap. 21.99 (978-1-4264-0862-5(5)) Creative Media Partners, LLC.

—Helping Himself. 2006. pap. (978-1-4065-0709-6(1)) Dodo Pr.

—Jack's Ward. 2005. 260p. pap. 13.95 (978-1-4218-1554-1(0), 1st World Library - Literary Society) 1st World Publishing, Inc.

—Jack's Ward. 2006. pap. (978-1-4065-0711-9(3)) Dodo Pr.

—Jack's Ward: Or, The Boy Guardian. 2006. 176p. pap. 19.99 (978-1-4264-0882-3(X)); (ENG.). 168p. pap. 21.99 (978-1-4264-0863-2(3)) Creative Media Partners, LLC.

—Phil the Fiddler. 2006. pap. (978-1-4068-0667-0(6)) Echo Library.

—The Store Boy. 2005. 256p. 28.95 (978-1-4218-0954-0(0), 1st World Library - Literary Society) 1st World Publishing, Inc.

—The Store Boy. 2007. (ENG.). 170p. pap. 19.99 (978-1-4264-4359-6(5)) Creative Media Partners, LLC.

—The Store Boy. 2006. pap. (978-1-4065-0722-5(9)) Dodo Pr.

—The Store Boy. 2007. 116p. per. (978-1-4068-1617-4(5)) Echo Library.

—Timothy Crump's Ward. 2005. 27.95 (978-1-4218-1451-3(X)); 220p. pap. 12.95 (978-1-4218-1551-0(6)) 1st World Publishing, Inc. (1st World Library - Literary Society).

—Tom Temple's Career. reprint ed. pap. 79.00 (978-1-4047-3611-5(5)) Classic Textbooks.

—The Young Outlaw: Or, Adrift in the Streets. 2004. (Illus.). 15.90 (978-1-4145-0294-6(X)) Pavilion Pr., Inc.

Anderson, Laurie Halse. Chains. (Seeds of America Trilogy Ser.). (ENG., Illus.). (J). (gr. 5-9). 2010. 336p. pap. 8.99 (978-1-4169-0586-8(3)) 2008. 320p. 19.99 (978-1-4169-0585-1(5)) Simon & Schuster Children's Publishing. (Atheneum Bks. for Young Readers).

Arato, Rona. Mrs. Kaputnik's Pool Hall & Matzo Ball Emporium. 2010. (Illus.). 192p. (J). (gr. 4-7). pap. 9.95 (978-0-88776-967-2(5), Tundra Bks.) Tundra Bks. CAN. Dist: Penguin Random Hse. LLC.

Auch, Mary Jane. One-Handed Catch. 2009. 272p. (J). (gr. 5-9). pap. 6.99 (978-0-312-58002-5(9)) Square Fish.

Avi. City of Orphans. Ruth, Greg, illus. 2012. (ENG.). 368p. (J). (gr. 5-9). pap. 8.99 (978-1-4169-7108-5(4), Atheneum Bks. for Young Readers) Simon & Schuster Children's Publishing.

—The Mayor of Central Park. Floca, Brian, illus. 2003. (ENG.). 208p. (J). (gr. 3-6). 15.99 (978-0-06-000682-2(X)) HarperCollins Pubs.

—The Mayor of Central Park. Floca, Brian, illus. 2005. 193p. (J). (gr. 3-7). 13.65 (978-0-7569-5125-2(9)) Perfection Learning Corp.

—The Seer of Shadows. 2009. (ENG.). 224p. (J). (gr. 4-7). pap. 7.99 (978-0-06-000017-2(1), HarperCollins) HarperCollins Pubs.

—Sophia's War: A Tale of the Revolution. 2012. (ENG., Illus.). 320p. (J). (gr. 3-7). 19.99 (978-1-4424-1441-9(3), Beach Lane Bks.) Beach Lane Bks.

—Sophia's War: A Tale of the Revolution. 2013. (ENG., Illus.). 336p. (J). (gr. 3-7). pap. 8.99 (978-1-4424-1442-6(1)) Simon & Schuster Children's Publishing.

Bennett, Carolyn Hart. Seven Sisters: The Voyage. 2008. 232p. 25.95 (978-0-595-51213-3(5)); pap. 15.95 (978-0-595-52242-2(4)) iUniverse, Inc.

Bernardin, James & Plehal, Christopher J. Yes, Virginia: There Is a Santa Claus. 2010. (ENG., Illus.). 32p. (J). (gr. -1-2). 17.99 (978-0-06-200173-3(6), HarperCollins) HarperCollins Pubs.

Bildner, Phil. Twenty-One Elephants. Pham, LeUyen, illus. 2004. (ENG.). 40p. (J). (gr. -1-3). 19.99 (978-0-689-87011-8(6), Simon & Schuster Bks. For Young Readers) Simon & Schuster Bks. For Young Readers.

Blundell, Judy. Strings Attached (Unabridged Edition), 2 vols. unabr. ed. 2011. (ENG.). 2p. (YA). (gr. 8-8). audio compact disk 29.99 (978-0-545-28280-2(2)) Scholastic, Inc.

Bray, Libba. Before the Devil Breaks You. 2017. (Diviners Ser.: 3). (ENG.). 560p. (YA). (gr. 10-17). 21.99 (978-0-316-12606-9(3)) Little, Brown Bks. for Young Readers.

—The Diviners. 2012. 578p. (YA). 9.99 (978-0-316-23242-5(4)) Little Brown & Co.

—The Diviners. (Diviners Ser.: 1). (ENG.). (YA). (gr. 10-17). 2013. 496p. pap. 16.99 (978-0-316-12610-6(1)) 2012. 800p. 52.99 (978-0-316-22426-0(X)) Little, Brown Bks. for Young Readers.

—The Diviners. 2013. (Diviners Ser.: 1). 468p. (YA). lib. bdg. 24.50 (978-0-606-32284-3(1)) Turtleback.

—Lair of Dreams: A Diviners Novel. (Diviners Ser.: 2). (ENG.). (YA). 2017. 592p. (gr. 10-17). pap. 15.99 (978-0-316-12603-8(9)) 2015. 624p. (gr. 7-17). E-Book 45.00 (978-0-316-36488-1(6)) Little, Brown Bks. for Young Readers.

Brown, Teri. Born of Illusion. 2013. (ENG.). 384p. (YA). pap. 9.99 (978-0-06-227720-6(0)) HarperCollins Pubs.

Carter, Rachel. Find Me Where the Water Ends. 2014. (ENG.). 352p. (YA). (gr. 9). 17.99 (978-0-06-208111-7(X), HarperTeen) HarperCollins Pubs.

—This Strange & Familiar Place. 2013. (ENG.). 272p. (YA). (gr. 9). 17.99 (978-0-06-208108-7(X), HarperTeen) HarperCollins Pubs.

Clark, Clara Gillow. Hattie on Her Way. Thompson, John, illus. 2005. (Trials of Hattie Belle Basket Ser.). (ENG.). 208p. (J). (gr. 5-18). 15.99 (978-0-7636-2286-2(9)) Candlewick Pr.

Donnelly, Jennifer. These Shallow Graves. 2016. (ENG.). 512p. (YA). (gr. 7). pap. 11.99 (978-0-385-73766-1(1), Ember) Random Hse. Children's Bks.

—These Shallow Graves. 2016. (ENG.). 496p. (YA). (gr. 7). 22.10 (978-0-606-39341-6(2)) Turtleback.

Godbersen, Anna. The Luxe. (ENG.). (YA). (gr. 9). 2018. (Luxe Ser.: 1). 480p. pap. 9.99 (978-0-06-285216-8(7), HarperTeen) 2008. (Luxe Ser.: 1). 464p. pap. 9.99 (978-0-06-134568-5(7)) 2007. (Luxe Ser.: No. 1). 448p. 17.99 (978-0-06-134566-1(0), HarperTeen) HarperCollins Pubs.

—Rumors. 2018. (Luxe Ser.: 2). (ENG.). 464p. (YA). (gr. 9). pap. 9.99 (978-0-06-285217-5(5), HarperTeen) 2009. (Luxe Ser.: 2). (ENG.). 448p. (YA). (gr. 9). pap. 9.99 (978-0-06-134571-5(7)) 2008. (Luxe Ser.: No. 2). 456p. (J). pap. 17.99 (978-0-06-170950-0(6)) HarperCollins Pubs.

—Splendor. (Luxe Ser.: 4). (ENG.). (YA). (gr. 9). 2018. 432p. pap. 9.99 (978-0-06-285219-9(1), HarperTeen) 2010. 416p. pap. 9.99 (978-0-06-162633-3(3)) HarperCollins Pubs.

Gratz, Alan. Ground Zero, 1 vol. 2021. (ENG., Illus.). 336p. (J). (gr. 4-7). 17.99 (978-1-338-24575-2(9), Scholastic Pr.) Scholastic, Inc.

Greene, Jacqueline. Rebecca Story Collection. Hirsch, Jennifer, ed. Hunt, Robert, illus. 2009. (ENG.). 456p. (YA). (gr. 3-18). 29.95 (978-1-59369-626-9(4)) American Girl Publishing, Inc.

Haddix, Margaret Peterson. Uprising. (ENG.). 352p. (YA). (gr. 7). 2011. pap. 12.99 (978-1-4169-1172-2(3)) 2007. 19.99 (978-1-4169-1171-5(5)) Simon & Schuster Bks. For Young Readers. (Simon & Schuster Bks. For Young Readers).

Halse Anderson, Laurie. Chains. l.t. ed. 2017. (Seeds of America Ser.). (ENG.). 442p. 22.99 (978-1-4104-9917-2(0)) Cengage Gale.

—Chains. 2014. (Seeds of America Trilogy). (ENG.). 336p. (J). 12.24 (978-1-63245-094-4(1)) Lectorum Pubns., Inc.

—Chains. 2009. 9.00 (978-0-7848-3678-1(7), Everbind) Marco Bk. Co.

—Chains. l.t. ed. 2009. (ENG.). 390p. (YA). 23.95 (978-1-4104-1425-0(6)) Thorndike Pr.

—Chains. 2010. (Seeds of America Trilogy Ser.: 1). lib. bdg. 19.65 (978-0-606-14520-6(6)) Turtleback.

Healy, Christopher. A Perilous Journey of Danger & Mayhem #1: a Dastardly Plot. 2018. (Perilous Journey of Danger & Mayhem Ser.: 1). (ENG.). (J). (gr. 3-7). 384p. 16.99 (978-0-06-234197-6(9)); 400p. E-Book (978-0-06-234199-0(5), 9780062341990) HarperCollins Pubs. (Waldon Pond Pr.).

High, Linda Oatman. Tenth Avenue Cowboy. Farnsworth, Bill, illus. 2008. 32p. (J). (gr. 4-7). 17.00 (978-0-8028-5330-1(7), Eerdmans Bks For Young Readers) Eerdmans, William B. Publishing Co.

Hopkinson, Deborah. A Bandit's Tale: the Muddled Misadventures of a Pickpocket. 2018. 304p. (J). (gr. 3-7). 8.99 (978-0-385-75502-3(3), Yearling) Random Hse. Children's Bks.

—Sky Boys: How They Built the Empire State Building. Ransome, James E., illus. 2012. lib. bdg. 18.40 (978-0-606-23847-2(6)) Turtleback.

Kerr, M. E., pseud. If I Love You, Am I Trapped Forever?, 0 vols. 2012. (ENG.). 192p. (YA). (gr. 7-12). pap. 9.99 (978-0-7614-5839-5(5), 9780761458395, Skyscape) Amazon Publishing.

Kirkpatrick, Katherine. Escape Across the Wide Sea. 2004. (ENG., Illus.). 224p. (J). (gr. 4-6). tchr. ed. 17.95 (978-0-8234-1854-1(5)) Holiday Hse., Inc.

Krensky, Stephen. The Great Moon Hoax. Bisaillon, Josée, illus. 2011. (Carolrhoda Picture Bks.). (ENG.). 32p. (J). (gr. 2-5). lib. bdg. 16.95 (978-0-7613-5110-8(8)) Lerner Publishing Group.

Kroll, Steven. Sweet America: An Immigrant's Story. 2004. 172p. (J). lib. bdg. 16.92 (978-1-4242-0773-2(8)) Fitzgerald Bks.

Larkin, Jillian. Diva. 2013. (Flappers Ser.: 3). (ENG.). 320p. (YA). (gr. 7). pap. 10.99 (978-0-385-74042-5(5), Ember) Random Hse. Children's Bks.

Lieurance, Suzanne. The Locket: Surviving the Triangle Shirtwaist Fire, 1 vol. 2008. (Historical Fiction Adventures Ser.). (ENG., Illus.). 160p. (J). (gr. 3-5). lib. bdg. 31.93 (978-0-7660-2928-6(X), 22662cfe-5ae4-4ede-affa-913d7a92d0d5) Enslow Publishing, LLC.

Lunievicz, Joe. Open Wounds. 2011. 352p. (YA). (gr. 9-18). 16.95 (978-1-934813-51-5(6)) Westside Bks.

Manning, Maurie J. Laundry Day. Manning, Maurie J., illus. 2012. (ENG., Illus.). 40p. (J). (gr. -1-3). 16.99 (978-0-547-24196-8(8), 1099085, Clarion Bks.) HarperCollins Pubs.

Maxwell, Lisa. The Last Magician. (Last Magician Ser.: 1). (ENG., Illus.). (YA). (gr. 9). 2018. 528p. pap. 13.99 (978-1-4814-3208-5(7)) 2017. 512p. 21.99 (978-1-4814-3207-8(9)) Simon Pulse. (Simon Pulse).

McDonough, Yona Zeldis. The Cats in the Doll Shop. Maione, Heather, illus. 2012. (ENG.). 128p. (J). (gr. 2-4). 18.69 (978-0-670-01279-4(3)) Penguin Young Readers Group.

McMorrow, T. E. The Nutcracker in Harlem. Ransome, James, illus. 2017. (ENG.). 32p. (J). (gr. -1-3). lib. bdg. 18.89 (978-0-06-117599-2(4), HarperCollins) HarperCollins Pubs.

—The Nutcracker in Harlem: A Christmas Holiday Book for Kids. Ransome, James, illus. 2017. (ENG.). 32p. (J). (gr. -1-3). 17.99 (978-0-06-117598-5(6), HarperCollins) HarperCollins Pubs.

Mebus, Scott. Gods of Manhattan, 1 vol. 2009. (ENG.). 368p. (J). (gr. 3-7). 9.99 (978-0-14-241307-4(0), Puffin Books) Penguin Young Readers Group.

—Gods of Manhattan 3: Sorcerer's Secret, Bk. 3. 2011. 384p. (J). (gr. 5-18). 8.99 *(978-0-14-241878-9(1)*, Puffin Books) Penguin Young Readers Group.

—Spirits in the Park. 2009. (Gods of Manhattan Ser.: No. 2). (J). *(978-0-525-47963-5(5)*, Dutton Juvenile) Penguin Publishing Group.

Mendelsohn, Martha. Bromley Girls. 2015. (ENG.). 192p. (YA). pap. 14.95 *(978-0-89672-922-3(2))* Texas Tech Univ. Pr.

Milford, Kate. The Broken Lands. Offermann, Andrea, illus. 2015. (ENG.). 464p. (J). (gr. 5-7). pap. 9.99 *(978-0-544-43942-9(2)*, 1596841, Clarion Bks.) HarperCollins Pubs.

Monir, Alexandra. Timekeeper. 2014. (Timeless Ser.). (ENG.). 304p. (YA). (gr. 7). pap. 9.99 *(978-0-385-73841-5(2)*, Ember) Random Hse. Children's Bks.

Morpurgo, Michael. Kaspar the Titanic Cat. Foreman, Michael, illus. 2012. (ENG.). 208p. (J). (gr. 3-7). 16.99 *(978-0-06-200618-9(5)*, Balzer & Bray) HarperCollins Pubs.

Myers, Walter Dean. Juba!: A Novel. 2016. (ENG., Illus.). 208p. (YA). (gr. 8). pap. 10.99 *(978-0-06-211273-6(2)*, Quill Tree Bks.) HarperCollins Pubs.

Napoli, Donna Jo. The King of Mulberry Street. 2007. (ENG.). 256p. (J). (gr. 3-7). 8.99 *(978-0-553-49416-7(3)*, Yearling) Random Hse. Children's Bks.

Nolan, Han. A Summer of Kings. 2006. 334p. (J). *(978-1-4156-7340-9(3))* Harcourt Trade Pubs.

—A Summer of Kings. 2006. (ENG., Illus.). 352p. (YA). (gr. 7-8). 17.00 *(978-0-15-205108-2(2)*, 1195424, Clarion Bks.) HarperCollins Pubs.

Older, Daniel José. Dactyl Hill Squad (Dactyl Hill Squad #1) (Dactyl Hill Squad Ser.: 1). (ENG.). (J). (gr. 3-7). 2019. 288p. pap. 6.99 *(978-1-338-26882-9(1))* 2018. (Illus.). 272p. 16.99 *(978-1-338-26881-2(3))* Scholastic, Inc. (Levine, Arthur A. Bks.).

Oppenheim, Joanne. The Knish War on Rivington Street. Davis, Jon, illus. 2017. (ENG.). 32p. (J). (gr. -1-3). 16.99 *(978-0-8075-4182-1(6)*, 807541826) Whitman, Albert & Co.

Osborne, Mary Pope. Blizzard of the Blue Moon. Murdocca, Sal, illus. 2007. (Magic Tree House (R) Merlin Mission Ser.: 8). 144p. (J). (gr. 2-5). 5.99 *(978-0-375-83038-9(3)*, Random Hse. Bks. for Young Readers) Random Hse. Children's Bks.

Osborne, Mary Pope, et al. A Time to Dance: Virginia's Civil War Diary. 2003. (My America Ser.). (ENG.). 112p. (J). 12.95 *(978-0-439-44341-8(5))* Scholastic, Inc.

—Tormenta de Nieve en Luna Azul. Murdocca, Sal, illus. 2016. (SPA.). (J). (gr. 2-4). pap. 6.99 *(978-1-63245-646-5(X))* Lectorum Pubns., Inc.

Petrucha, Stefan. Ripper. (ENG.). 432p. (YA). (gr. 7). 2013. pap. 9.99 *(978-0-14-242418-6(8)*, Speak) 2012. 26.19 *(978-0-399-25524-3(9))* Penguin Young Readers Group.

Pollack, Jenny. Klepto. 2008. (ENG.). 288p. (YA). (gr. 7-18). 8.99 *(978-0-14-241072-1(1)*, Speak) Penguin Young Readers Group.

Prince, April Jones. Twenty-One Elephants & Still Standing. 2005. (ENG., Illus.). 32p. (J). (gr. -1-3). 17.99 *(978-0-618-44887-6(X)*, 593934, Clarion Bks.) HarperCollins Pubs.

Rebecca, Stead. When You Reach Me. 2014. (ENG.). 208p. (J). (gr. 12-12). 11.24 *(978-1-63245-235-1(9))* Lectorum Pubns., Inc.

Reiss, Kathryn. A Bundle of Trouble: A Rebecca Mystery. Giovine, Sergio, illus. 2011. (American Girl Mysteries Ser.). (ENG.). 192p. (YA). (gr. 4-6). pap. 21.19 *(978-1-59369-754-9(6))* American Girl Publishing, Inc.

Saxena, Shalini. The Legend of Sleepy Hollow, 1 vol. 2015. (Famous Legends Ser.). (ENG., Illus.). 32p. (J). (gr. 2-3). pap. 11.50 *(978-1-4824-2752-3(4)*, e011c932-b402-4821-b653-2788a1c3e395) Stevens, Gareth Publishing LLLP.

Selznick, Brian. Wonderstruck, 1 vol. Selznick, Brian, illus. 2011. (ENG., Illus.). 640p. (J). (gr. 4-7). 29.99 *(978-0-545-02789-2(6)*, Scholastic Pr.) Scholastic, Inc.

Smith, Sasha Peyton. The Witch Haven. 2022. (ENG., Illus.). 464p. (YA). (gr. 9). pap. 13.99 *(978-1-5344-5439-2(X)*, Simon & Schuster Bks. For Young Readers) Simon & Schuster Bks. For Young Readers.

Stead, Rebecca. Cuando Me Alcances. 2011.Tr. of When You Reach Me. (SPA.). 294p. pap. *(978-958-45-3215-2(4))* Norma S.A.

—When You Reach Me. 2010. lib. bdg. 18.40 *(978-0-606-15179-5(6))* Turtleback.

—When You Reach Me: (Newbery Medal Winner) (ENG.). (J). (gr. 3-7). 2010. 240p. 8.99 *(978-0-375-85086-8(4)*, Yearling) 2009. 208p. 16.99 *(978-0-385-73742-5(4)*, Lamb, Wendy Bks.) Random Hse. Children's Bks.

Stephens, John. The Fire Chronicle. 2012. (Illus.). 437p. (J). *(978-0-449-81015-6(1))* Knopf, Alfred A. Inc.

—The Fire Chronicle. 2013. (Books of Beginning Ser.: 2). (ENG., Illus.). 464p. (J). (gr. 3-7). 9.99 *(978-0-375-87272-3(8)*, Yearling) Random Hse. Children's Bks.

Townley, Roderick. Sky. 2010. (ENG.). 272p. (YA). (gr. 7). pap. 12.99 *(978-1-4423-3973-6(X)*, Atheneum Bks. for Young Readers) Simon & Schuster Children's Publishing.

Tucker, Laura. All the Greys on Greene Street. 2019. (ENG., Illus.). 320p. (J). (gr. 3-7). 17.99 *(978-0-451-47953-2(X)*, Viking Books for Young Readers) Penguin Young Readers Group.

Weatherford, Carole Boston. Sugar Hill: Harlem's Historic Neighborhood. Christie, R. Gregory, illus. 2014. (ENG.). 32p. (J). (gr. -1-3). 16.99 *(978-0-8075-7650-2(6)*, 807576506) Whitman, Albert & Co.

Wells, Helen. Cherry Ames, Visiting Nurse. 2006. (Cherry Ames Nurse Stories Ser.). 224p. (J). (gr. 3-7). 14.95 *(978-0-8261-0399-4(5))* Springer Publishing Co., Inc.

Zoboi, Ibi. My Life As an Ice Cream Sandwich. (Illus.). 256p. (J). (gr. 5). 2020. 8.99 *(978-0-399-18736-0(7)*, Puffin Books) 2019. 17.99 *(978-0-399-18735-3(9)*, Dutton Books for Young Readers) Penguin Young Readers Group.

—My Life As an Ice Cream Sandwich. l.t. ed. 2020. (ENG.). lib. bdg. 22.99 *(978-1-4328-7709-5(7))* Thorndike Pr.

NEW YORK (N.Y.)—POLITICS AND GOVERNMENT

Bankston, John. Rudy Giuliani. l.t. ed. 2003. (Blue Banner Biography Ser.). (Illus.). 32p. (J). (gr. 3-8). lib. bdg. 25.70 *(978-1-58415-194-4(3))* Mitchell Lane Pubs.

Brezina, Corona. America's Political Scandals in the Late 1800s: Boss Tweed & Tammany Hall. 2009. (America's Industrial Society in the 19th Century Ser.). 32p. (gr. 4-4). 47.90 *(978-1-61511-336-1(3))* Rosen Publishing Group, Inc., The.

Shichtman, Sandra H. Michael Bloomberg. 2010. (Political Profiles Ser.). 112p. (J). 28.95 *(978-1-59935-135-3(8))* Reynolds, Morgan Inc.

NEW YORK (N.Y.)—SOCIAL CONDITIONS

Arora, Sabina G. The Great Migration & the Harlem Renaissance, 1 vol. 2015. (African American Experience: from Slavery to the Presidency Ser.). (ENG., Illus.). 80p. (J). (gr. 7-8). 35.47 *(978-1-68048-045-0(6)*, 71b04636-5dec-41b5-807f-cef61bb5872a, Britannica Educational Publishing) Rosen Publishing Group, Inc., The.

Bolden, Tonya. Maritcha: A Nineteenth-Century American Girl. 2005. (ENG., Illus.). 48p. (J). (gr. k-4). 19.95 *(978-0-8109-5045-0(6))* Abrams, Inc.

Halpern, Monica. Three Immigrant Communities New York City In 1900: Set Of 6. 2011. (Navigators Ser.). (J). pap. 44.00 net. *(978-1-4108-6249-5(6))* Benchmark Education Co.

Hearth, Amy Hill. Streetcar to Justice: How Elizabeth Jennings Won the Right to Ride in New York. 2018. (ENG., Illus.). 160p. (J). (gr. 3-7). 19.99 *(978-0-06-267360-2(2)*, Greenwillow Bks.) HarperCollins Pubs.

Hopkinson, Deborah. Shutting Out the Sky: Life in the Tenements of New York, 1880-1924 (Scholastic Focus) 2003. (ENG., Illus.). 144p. (J). (gr. 4-7). 19.99 *(978-0-439-37590-0(8))* Scholastic, Inc.

Johnson, Linda Carlson & Johnson, Keri. 9.11 Helping the Heroes: A Salvation Army Story. 2011. (Illus.). (J). *(978-0-89216-130-0(2))* Salvation Army.

Mattern, Joanne. It's Great to Be a Fan in New York. 2018. (Sports Nation Ser.). (ENG., Illus.). 48p. (J). (gr. 5-6). pap. 11.95 *(978-1-64185-035-3(3)*, 1641850353); lib. bdg. 34.21 *(978-1-63517-933-0(5)*, 1635179335) North Star Editions. (Focus Readers).

Moore, Andrew. New York City's Industries: Jobs for People, 1 vol. 2011. (My Community Ser.). (ENG., Illus.). 12p. (gr. 2-2). pap. 6.95 *(978-1-4488-5721-0(X)*, 70d9d4e8-b9fa-43cf-b428-78888f000662, Rosen Classroom) Rosen Publishing Group, Inc., The.

Puck. One to Ten NYC. Pettingill, Charla, illus. 2013. (ENG.). 22p. (J). (— 1). bds. 9.99 *(978-1-938093-19-7(4)*, 809319) Duo Pr. LLC.

Schimel, Kate & Levy, Janey. New York: The Dutch Colony of New Amsterdam. (Illus.). 24p. (J). 2012. 60.00 *(978-1-4488-5758-6(9))* 2011. (ENG., (gr. 3-4). pap. 10.00 *(978-1-4488-5757-9(0)*, 3de932b2-e68e-48d3-a443-b2a878c61a0c) 2011. (ENG., (gr. 3-4). lib. bdg. 26.27 *(978-1-4488-5742-5(2)*, fff08119-669d-4b5b-982a-7abba7bfcc7f) Rosen Publishing Group, Inc., The. (PowerKids Pr.).

Tan, Richard. New York City's Neighborhoods, 1 vol. 2011. (My Community Ser.). (ENG., Illus.). 12p. (gr. 2-2). pap. 6.95 *(978-1-4488-5718-0(X)*, d4de6b49-6b68-4fa1-aef8-7cdef1142f91, Rosen Classroom) Rosen Publishing Group, Inc., The.

Thomas, Zachary & Wilson, Natashya. The Melting Pot: The People & Cultures of New York. (Illus.). 24p. (J). 2012. 60.00 *(978-1-4488-5768-5(6))* 2011. (ENG., (gr. 3-4). lib. bdg. 26.27 *(978-1-4488-5747-0(3)*, 25a1b07b-b474-4a01-aca9-a0a7371381f7) Rosen Publishing Group, Inc., The. (PowerKids Pr.).

Thomas, Zachary, et al. The Melting Pot: The People & Cultures of New York, 1 vol. 2011. (Spotlight on New York Ser.). (ENG., Illus.). 24p. (J). (gr. 3-4). pap. 10.00 *(978-1-4488-5767-8(8)*, 49e46d01-80be-4899-a626-e696ca9d48be, PowerKids Pr.) Rosen Publishing Group, Inc., The.

NEW YORK (STATE)

Bodden, Valerie. New York. 2010. (Let's Explore America Ser.). 24p. (J). (gr. k-2). 19.95 *(978-1-58341-835-2(0))* Creative Co., The.

Burg, Ann E. E Is for Empire: A New York Alphabet. Brookfield, Maureen K., illus. 2003. (Discover America State by State Ser.). (ENG.). 40p. (J). (gr. 1-3). 17.95 *(978-1-58536-113-7(5)*, 201982) Sleeping Bear Pr.

—The New York Reader. Darnell, K. L., illus. 2008. (State/Country Readers Ser.). (ENG.). 96p. (J). (gr. 1-4). pap. 5.95 *(978-1-58536-349-0(9)*, 202136) Sleeping Bear Pr.

—Times Square: A New York Number Book. Brookfield, Maureen K., illus. 2005. (America by the Numbers Ser.). (ENG.). 40p. (J). (gr. 1-3). 16.95 *(978-1-58536-195-3(X)*, 202037) Sleeping Bear Pr.

DeMolay, Jack. Amitiville: La casa encantada (Ghosts in Amityville:the Haunted House) 2009. (Historietas Juveniles: Misterios (Jr. Graphic Mysteries) Ser.). (SPA.). 24p. (gr. 2-3). 47.90 *(978-1-61513-344-4(5)*, Editorial Buenas Letras) Rosen Publishing Group, Inc., The.

Dunn, Mary. My Adventure in a Mohawk Village. 2006. 44p. (J). 8.99 *(978-1-59092-419-8(3))* Blue Forge Pr.

Dunn, Mary R. I Want to Be in Musicals. 2009. (Dream Jobs Ser.). 24p. (gr. 2-3). 42.50 *(978-1-61512-215-8(X)*, PowerKids Pr.) Rosen Publishing Group, Inc., The.

Elish, Dan. New York, 1 vol. Santoro, Christopher, illus. 2003. (It's My State! (First Edition)(r) Ser.). (ENG.). 80p. (gr. 4-4). 34.07 *(978-0-7614-1419-3(3)*, f097f344-c9b2-4587-b2a2-c960df0e4813) Cavendish Square Publishing LLC.

Fein, E. How to Draw New York's Sights & Symbols. 2009. (Kid's Guide to Drawing America Ser.). 32p. (gr. k-k). 50.50 *(978-1-61511-081-0(X)*, PowerKids Pr.) Rosen Publishing Group, Inc., The.

Gelman, Amy. New York. (J). 2012. lib. bdg. 25.26 *(978-0-7613-4548-0(5)*, Lerner Pubns.) 2nd rev. exp. ed. 2003. (Illus.). 84p. (gr. 3-6). pap. 6.95 *(978-0-8225-4151-6(3))* Lerner Publishing Group.

Glaser, Linda. Emma's Poem: The Voice of the Statue of Liberty. Nivola, Claire A., illus. 2010. (ENG.). 32p. (J). (gr. -1-3). 17.99 *(978-0-547-17184-5(6)*, 1054295, Clarion Bks.) HarperCollins Pubs.

Johnston, Marianne. New York: Nueva York, 1 vol. 2007. (Conflict Resolution Library). (ENG.). (J). E-Book 25.27 *(978-1-4042-3138-2(2)*, 03a72018-daa6-49f9-9b6d-3d5608000656, PowerKids Pr.) Rosen Publishing Group, Inc., The.

Lawton, Val. New York: The Empire State. 2016. (Illus.). 48p. (J). *(978-1-5105-2089-9(9))* SmartBook Media, Inc.

Lawton, Val & Rodriguez, Cindy. New York. 2018. (Illus.). 24p. (J). *(978-1-4896-7465-4(9)*, AV2 by Weigl) Weigl Pubs., Inc.

Maine, Tyler & Parker, Bridget. New York. 2016. (States Ser.). (ENG., Illus.). 32p. (J). (gr. 3-6). lib. bdg. 27.99 *(978-1-5157-0419-5(X)*, 132030, Capstone Pr.) Capstone.

Malaspina, Ann. Heart on Fire: Susan B. Anthony Votes for President. James, Steve, illus. 2012. (ENG.). 32p. (J). (gr. 1-3). 17.99 *(978-0-8075-3188-4(X)*, 080753188X) Whitman, Albert & Co.

Marsh, Carole. The Big New York Activity Book! 2004. (New York Experience! Ser.). (Illus.). 96p. (gr. 2-6). per. 9.95 *(978-0-635-00165-8(9))* Gallopade International.

—Jography. 2004. (New York Experience! Ser.). 32p. (J). (gr. 3-8). pap. 7.95 *(978-0-635-00162-7(4))* Gallopade International.

—New York Current Events Projects: 30 Cool, Activities, Crafts, Experiments & More for Kids to Do to Learn about Your State! 2003. (New York Experience Ser.). 32p. (gr. k-8). pap. 5.95 *(978-0-635-02051-2(3)*, Marsh, Carole Bks.) Gallopade International.

—New York Geography Projects: 30 Cool, Activities, Crafts, Experiments & More for Kids to Do to Learn about Your State! 2003. (New York Experience Ser.). 32p. (gr. k-5). pap. 5.95 *(978-0-635-01851-9(9)*, Marsh, Carole Bks.) Gallopade International.

—New York People Projects: 30 Cool, Activities, Crafts, Experiments & More for Kids to Do to Learn about Your State! 2003. (New York Experience Ser.). 32p. (gr. k-5). pap. 5.95 *(978-0-635-02001-7(7)*, Marsh, Carole Bks.) Gallopade International.

—New York Pocket Guide. 2004. (New York Experience! Ser.). 96p. (J). (gr. 3-8). pap. 6.95 *(978-0-635-00163-4(2))* Gallopade International.

—New York Symbols & Facts Projects: 30 Cool, Activities, Crafts, Experiments & More for Kids to Do to Learn about Your State! 2003. (New York Experience Ser.). 32p. (gr. k-5). pap. 5.95 *(978-0-635-01901-1(9)*, Marsh, Carole Bks.) Gallopade International.

Mills, J. Elizabeth. New York: Past & Present. 2009. (Illus.). 48p. (J). 70.50 *(978-1-4358-5569-4(8))*; (ENG., (gr. 5-5). pap. 12.75 *(978-1-4358-5568-7(X)*, ad3d1e02-d961-4e21-919b-e2fe26e6dd59); (ENG., (gr. 5-5). lib. bdg. 34.47 *(978-1-4358-5285-3(0)*, d288db11-a0ae-443e-aebc-cfa1ceaeaeb6) Rosen Publishing Group, Inc., The. (Rosen Reference).

Murray, Julie. New York, 1 vol. 2006. (Buddy Book Ser.). (ENG., Illus.). 32p. (gr. 2-4). 27.07 *(978-1-59197-691-2(X)*, Buddy Bks.) ABDO Publishing Co.

Oestreicher, David M. The Algonquian of New York. 2009. (Library of Native Americans Ser.). 64p. (gr. 4-4). 58.50 *(978-1-60853-742-6(0)*, PowerKids Pr.) Rosen Publishing Group, Inc., The.

Orr, Tamra B. New York, 1 vol. 2005. (Portraits of the States Ser.). (ENG., Illus.). 32p. (gr. 3-5). lib. bdg. 28.67 *(978-0-8368-4630-0(3)*, 58481c3d-7f5d-4c6f-827a-2d5fab4fb613, Gareth Stevens Learning Library) Stevens, Gareth Publishing LLLP.

Schomp, Virginia. New York, 1 vol. 2nd rev. ed. 2007. (Celebrate the States (Second Edition) Ser.). (ENG., Illus.). 144p. (gr. 6-6). lib. bdg. 39.79 *(978-0-7614-1738-5(9)*, 6ecf009c-cfc1-4790-974b-3b4c33050477) Cavendish Square Publishing LLC.

Somervill, Barbara A. America the Beautiful, Third Series: New York (Revised Edition) 2014. (America the Beautiful Ser.: 3). (ENG.). 144p. (J). lib. bdg. 40.00 *(978-0-531-24895-9(X))* Scholastic Library Publishing.

—New York. 2011. (America the Beautiful, Third Ser.). 144p. (J). pap. 12.95 *(978-0-531-22919-4(X)*, Children's Pr.) Scholastic Library Publishing.

Von La Valette, Desiree, ed. Cool Shops New York. 2005. (ENG, SPA, FRE, ITA & GER., Illus.). 135p. pap., pap. 16.95 *(978-3-8327-9021-9(7))* teNeues Publishing Co.

NEW YORK (STATE)—FICTION

Altsheler, Joseph A. The French & Indian War Novels: The Lords of the Wild & The Sun of Quebec, Vol. 3. 2008. (J). reprint ed. 428p. *(978-1-84677-590-1(6))*; 424p. pap. *(978-1-84677-589-5(2))* Leonaur Ltd.

—The French & Indian War Novels: The Rulers of the Lakes & The Masters of the Peaks, Vol. 2. 2008. 416p. (J). reprint ed. *(978-1-84677-588-8(4))*; pap. *(978-1-84677-587-1(6))* Leonaur Ltd.

—The Lords of the Wild: A Story of the Old New York Border. rev. ed. 2006. (French & Indian War Ser.). 264p. (J). 28.95 *(978-1-4218-2335-5(7))*; pap. 13.95 *(978-1-4218-2435-2(3))* 1st World Publishing, Inc. (1st World Library - Literary Society).

—The Lords of the Wild: A Story of the Old New York Border. (French & Indian War Ser.: Vol. 1). (J). reprint ed. 24.95 *(978-0-8488-0905-8(X))* Amereon Ltd.

—The Lords of the Wild: A Story of the Old New York Border. 2006. (French & Indian War Ser.). (J). pap. *(978-1-4065-0816-1(0))* Dodo Pr.

—The Lords of the Wild: A Story of the Old New York Border. 2007. (French & Indian War Ser.). 156p. (J). per. *(978-1-4068-1681-5(7))* Echo Library.

—The Lords of the Wild: A Story of the Old New York Border. 2010. (French & Indian War Ser.: Vol. 5). (Illus.). 138p. (J). (gr. 4-7). reprint ed. pap. 19.99 *(978-1-153-71020-6(X))* General Bks. LLC.

—The Lords of the Wild: A Story of the Old New York Border. (French & Indian War Ser.: Vol. 5). (J). reprint ed. 2010. 208p. (gr. 4-7). 31.96 *(978-1-169-28834-8(0))* 2010. 208p. (gr. 4-7). pap. 19.96 *(978-1-162-70072-4(6))* 2010. 39.95 *(978-1-161-46937-0(0))* 2004. pap. 1.99 *(978-1-4192-7070-3(2))* 2004. pap. 24.95 *(978-1-4191-7070-6(8))* Kessinger Publishing, LLC.

—The Lords of the Wild: A Story of the Old New York Border. 2011. (French & Indian War Ser.: Vol. 5). 236p. (J). reprint ed. pap. *(978-3-8424-4395-2(1))* tredition Verlag.

—The Scouts of the Valley: A Story of Wyoming & the Chemung. 2010. (Young Trailers Ser.: Vol. 7). (Illus.). 184p. (J). (gr. 4-7). reprint ed. pap. 19.99 *(978-1-153-72010-6(8))* General Bks. LLC.

—The Scouts of the Valley: A Story of Wyoming & the Chemung. 2010. (Young Trailers Ser.: Vol. 7). 250p. (J). pap. *(978-1-4076-0985-0(8))* HardPr.

—The Scouts of the Valley: A Story of Wyoming & the Chemung. 2010. (Young Trailers Ser.: Vol. 7). (J). reprint ed. 268p. (gr. 4-7). 34.36 *(978-1-169-30757-5(4))*; 42.95 *(978-1-161-47633-0(4))* Kessinger Publishing, LLC.

—The Shadow of the North: A Story of Old New York & a Lost Campaign. 2006. (French & Indian War Ser.: Vol. 2). (J). reprint ed. pap. *(978-1-4065-0823-9(3))* Dodo Pr.

Auch, M. J. Guitar Boy. 2012. (ENG.). 288p. (J). (gr. 5-9). pap. 15.99 *(978-0-312-64124-5(9)*, 900077675) Square Fish.

—One-Handed Catch. 2009. (ENG.). 272p. (J). (gr. 5-9). pap. 12.99 *(978-0-312-53575-9(9)*, 900054755) Square Fish.

Auch, Mary Jane. Journey to Nowhere. 2004. (Illus.). 202p. (gr. 5-9). 16.00 *(978-0-7569-4144-4(X))* Perfection Learning Corp.

Bauer, Joan. Backwater. rev. ed. 2005. (ENG.). 192p. (YA). (gr. 7-12). pap. 7.99 *(978-0-14-240434-8(9)*, Speak) Penguin Young Readers Group.

—Peeled. 2009. (ENG.). 256p. (YA). (gr. 7-18). 10.99 *(978-0-14-241430-9(1)*, Speak) Penguin Young Readers Group.

Bennese, Ray & Bennese, Kristian. Till the Train Runs Out of Track. 2007. 76p. per. 19.95 *(978-1-4241-7567-3(4))* America Star Bks.

Bruchac, Joseph. The Legend of Skeleton Man: Skeleton Man & the Return of Skeleton Man. 2019. (ENG.). 288p. (J). (gr. 3-7). pap. 7.99 *(978-0-06-274768-6(1)*, HarperCollins) HarperCollins Pubs.

—The Return of Skeleton Man. Comport, Sally Wern, illus. 2006. 144p. (J). (gr. 5-9). lib. bdg. 16.89 *(978-0-06-058091-9(7))* HarperCollins Pubs.

—The Return of Skeleton Man. 2. 2008. (Skeleton Man Ser.: 2). (ENG., Illus.). 144p. (J). (gr. 3-8). pap. 7.99 *(978-0-06-058092-6(5)*, HarperCollins) HarperCollins Pubs.

—Walking Two Worlds. Fadden, David Kanietakeron, illus. 2015. (PathFinders Ser.). (ENG.). 120p. (YA). (gr. 8-12). pap. 9.95 *(978-1-939053-10-7(2)*, 7th Generation) BPC.

Calonita, Jen. Sleepaway Girls. 1. 2009. (Sleepaway Girls Ser.). (ENG.). 304p. (J). (gr. 7-12). 22.44 *(978-0-316-01717-6(5))* Little Brown & Co.

Carter, Ally. Heist Society. 2011. (Heist Society Novel Ser.: 1). (ENG.). 304p. (YA). (gr. 7-17). pap. 10.99 *(978-1-4231-1661-5(5))* Hyperion Pr.

—Uncommon Criminals. 2012. (Heist Society Novel Ser.: 2). (ENG.). 304p. (YA). (gr. 7-17). pap. 16.99 *(978-1-4231-4807-4(X))* Hyperion Pr.

—Uncommon Criminals: A Heist Society Novel. 2011. (Playaway Children Ser.). (YA). (gr. 7-12). 69.99 *(978-1-4558-2483-0(6))* Findaway World, LLC.

Coleman, Alice Scovell. The Spirit of Chatsworth Mansion. 2006. 176p. (J). (gr. 4-7). pap. 6.99 *(978-0-9729846-1-4(5))* Tiara Bks. LLC.

Connor, Leslie. Waiting for Normal. 2010. (ENG.). 320p. (J). (gr. 5). pap. 7.99 *(978-0-06-089090-2(8)*, Tegen, Katherine Bks) HarperCollins Pubs.

Cook, Kristi. Haven. 2012. (ENG.). 448p. (YA). (gr. 9). pap. 12.99 *(978-1-4424-0761-9(1)*, Simon Pulse) Simon Pulse.

—Mirage. (ENG., (YA). (gr. 9). 2013. Illus.). 416p. pap. 12.99 *(978-1-4424-4300-6(6))* 2012. 384p. 16.99 *(978-1-4424-4299-3(9))* Simon Pulse. (Simon Pulse).

De Baun, Hillary Hall. The Last Stop Before Heaven. Cooper, Floyd, illus. 2012. (ENG.). 236p. (J). pap. 9.00 *(978-0-8028-5398-1(6)*, Eerdmans Bks For Young Readers) Eerdmans, William B. Publishing Co.

De la Cruz, Melissa. Crazy Hot. 2008. (Au Pairs Ser.: 4). (ENG.). 320p. (YA). (gr. 9-12). pap. 9.99 *(978-1-4169-4808-7(2)*, Simon & Schuster Bks. For Young Readers) Simon & Schuster Bks. For Young Readers.

de la Cruz, Melissa. Crazy Hot. 2013. (Beach Lane Ser.: 4). (ENG., Illus.). 288p. (YA). (gr. 9). pap. 9.99 *(978-1-4424-7412-3(2)*, Simon & Schuster Bks. For Young Readers) Simon & Schuster Bks. For Young Readers.

—Skinny-Dipping. 2013. (Beach Lane Ser.: 2). (ENG., Illus.). 320p. (YA). (gr. 9). pap. 9.99 *(978-1-4424-7410-9(6)*, Simon & Schuster Bks. For Young Readers) Simon & Schuster Bks. For Young Readers.

—Sun-Kissed. 2013. (Beach Lane Ser.: 3). (ENG., Illus.). 336p. (YA). (gr. 9). pap. 9.99 *(978-1-4424-7411-6(4)*, Simon & Schuster Bks. For Young Readers) Simon & Schuster Bks. For Young Readers.

Emery, Joanna. Brothers of the Falls. Erickson, David, illus. 2004. (Adventures in America Ser.). (gr. 4). 14.95 *(978-1-893110-37-3(0))* Silver Moon Pr.

Felin, M. Sindy. Touching Snow. (ENG., Illus.). 240p. (YA). (gr. 7). 2011. pap. 11.99 *(978-1-4424-1735-9(8))* 2007. 16.99 *(978-1-4169-1795-3(0))* Simon & Schuster Children's Publishing. (Atheneum Bks. for Young Readers).

Gansworth, Eric. Give Me Some Truth. (ENG.). 432p. (gr. 9-9). 2022. (J). pap. 12.99 *(978-1-338-58216-1(X))* 2018. (Illus.). (YA). 18.99 *(978-1-338-14354-6(9))* Scholastic, Inc. (Levine, Arthur A. Bks.).

George, Jean Craighead. My Side of the Mountain. l.t. ed. 2005. (ENG.). 211p. (J). (gr. 4-7). pap. 15.99 *(978-0-7862-7359-1(3))* Cengage Gale.

Giff, Patricia Reilly. Eleven. (ENG.). (J). 2009. 176p. (gr. 3-7). 7.99 *(978-0-440-23802-7(1)*, Yearling) 2008. 164p. (gr. 4-6). lib. bdg. 21.19 *(978-0-385-90098-0(8)*, Lamb, Wendy Bks.) Random Hse. Children's Bks.

—Pictures of Hollis Woods. 2014. (ENG.). 176p. (J). (gr. 3-7). 11.24 *(978-1-63245-318-1(5))* Lectorum Pubns., Inc.

—Pictures of Hollis Woods. 2004. (ENG.). 176p. (J). (gr. 3-7). 8.99 *(978-0-440-41578-7(0)*, Yearling) Random Hse. Children's Bks.

—Wild Girl. 2011. (ENG.). 160p. (J). (gr. 4-6). lib. bdg. 21.19 *(978-0-375-93890-0(7)*, Lamb, Wendy Bks.); (gr. 3-7). pap. 7.99 *(978-0-440-42177-1(2)*, Yearling) Random Hse. Children's Bks.

Going, K. L. The Garden of Eve. 2009. (ENG., Illus.). 240p. (J). (gr. 3-7). pap. 14.95 *(978-0-15-206614-7(4)*, 1099005, Clarion Bks.) HarperCollins Pubs.

Grab, Daphne. Alive & Well in Prague, New York. 2008. (Laura Geringer Bks.). 247p. (YA). (gr. 7-18). lib. bdg. 17.89 *(978-0-06-125671-4(4)*, Geringer, Laura Book) HarperCollins Pubs.

Hagar, Erin. Doing Her Bit: A Story about the Women's Land Army of America. Hill, Jen, illus. 2016. 32p. (J). (gr. 1-4). lib. bdg. 16.95 *(978-1-58089-646-7(4))* Charlesbridge Publishing, Inc.

Harrison, Lisi. Best Friends for Never: A Clique Novel. 2004. (Clique Ser.: 2). (ENG.). 208p. (J). (gr. 7-17). pap. 13.99 *(978-0-316-70131-0(9)*, Poppy) Little, Brown Bks. for Young Readers.

—The Revenge of the Wannabes. 2005. (Clique Ser.: 3). (ENG.). 304p. (J). (gr. 7-17). pap. 16.99 *(978-0-316-70133-4(5)*, Poppy) Little, Brown Bks. for Young Readers.

Harrison, Lisi, creator. Massie. 2008. (Clique Summer Collection: 1). (ENG.). 144p. (YA). (gr. 7-17). pap. 6.99 *(978-0-316-02751-9(0)*, Poppy) Little, Brown Bks. for Young Readers.

Hepler, Heather. The Cupcake Queen. 2010. (ENG.). 256p. (YA). (gr. 7-18). 7.99 *(978-0-14-241668-6(1)*, Speak) Penguin Young Readers Group.

Hope, Laura Lee. Bunny Brown & His Sister Sue at Aunt Lu's City Home. 2007. 184p. 25.96 *(978-1-4218-3886-1(9)*, 1st World Library - Literary Society) 1st World Publishing, Inc.

Irving, Washington. The Legend of Sleepy Hollow. 2008. 48p. (gr. -1-4). pap. 6.45 *(978-1-60597-509-2(5)*, Bk. Jungle) Standard Publications, Inc.

—The Legend of Sleepy Hollow. Van Nutt, Robert, illus. 2005. (Rabbit Ears Ser.). 36p. (J). (gr. k-5). 25.65 *(978-1-59679-225-8(6))* Spotlight.

—Rip Van Winkle. 2010. (Creative Short Stories Ser.). (ENG., Illus.). 48p. (J). (gr. 5-8). 19.95 *(978-1-58341-923-6(3)*, 22125, Creative Education) Creative Co., The.

—Rip Van Winkle: The Mountaintop Edition. Wyeth, N. C., illus. 2016. 96p. pap. 13.95 *(978-1-883789-85-5(0))* Black Dome Pr. Corp.

Irving, Washington. & Busch, Jeffrey. Rip Van Winkle. (Classics Illustrated Ser.). (Illus.). 52p. (YA). pap. 4.95 *(978-1-57209-009-5(X))* Classics International Entertainment, Inc.

Kerr, M. E., pseud. Your Eyes in Stars. 2006. (YA). (gr. 7-12). (ENG.). 240p. 16.99 *(978-0-06-075682-6(9))*; 229p. lib. bdg. 17.89 *(978-0-06-075683-3(7))* HarperCollins Pubs.

Konen, Leah. Love & Other Train Wrecks. 2018. (ENG.). 368p. (YA). (gr. 8). 17.99 *(978-0-06-240250-9(1)*, Tegen, Katherine Bks) HarperCollins Pubs.

Laura Lee Hope. Bunny Brown & His Sister Sue at Aunt Lu's City Home. 2007. 184p. per. 11.95 *(978-1-4218-3986-8(5)*, 1st World Library - Literary Society) 1st World Publishing, Inc.

Lesczynski, Jim. The Walton Street Tycoons. 2007. 269p. (YA). pap. 9.95 *(978-0-9791283-0-1(7))* East River Pr.

Lin, Grace. The Year of the Dog. 2007. (Illus.). 134p. (gr. 3-7). 16.00 *(978-0-7569-8143-3(3))* Perfection Learning Corp.

Lincoln, Dallas Ford. The Sawmill Sant. 2011. 36p. pap. 16.95 *(978-1-4626-4335-6(3))* America Star Bks.

Mackler, Carolyn. Tangled. 2011. (ENG.). 336p. (YA). (gr. 9-12). pap. 10.99 *(978-0-06-173106-8(4)*, HarperTeen) HarperCollins Pubs.

Mann, J. Albert. What Every Girl Should Know: Margaret Sanger's Journey. (ENG.). (YA). (gr. 9). 2020. 256p. pap. 11.99 *(978-1-5344-1933-9(0))* 2019. (Illus.). 240p. 18.99 *(978-1-5344-1932-2(2))* Simon & Schuster Children's Publishing. (Atheneum Bks. for Young Readers).

Martin, Ann M. Here Today. 2005. 308p. (gr. 5-9). 18.00 *(978-0-7569-5104-7(6))* Perfection Learning Corp.

Maurer, Shari. Change of Heart. 2010. 290p. (YA). 16.95 *(978-1-934813-36-2(2))* Westside Bks.

Mazer, Norma Fox. The Missing Girl. 2010. (ENG.). 304p. (YA). (gr. 8-12). pap. 9.99 *(978-0-06-447365-1(1)*, HarperTeen) HarperCollins Pubs.

—Ten Ways to Make My Sister Disappear. (ENG.). 160p. (J). (gr. 4-6). 2012. 21.19 *(978-0-439-83984-6(X))* 2007. 16.99 *(978-0-439-83983-9(1))* Scholastic, Inc. (Levine, Arthur A. Bks.).

—Ten Ways to Make My Sister Disappear. l.t. ed. 2008. (Thorndike Literacy Bridge Ser.). 207p. (J). (gr. 4-7). 22.95 *(978-1-4104-0510-4(9))* Thorndike Pr.

McDonough, Yona Zeldis. The Doll Shop Downstairs. Maione, Heather, illus. 2011. 144p. (J). (gr. 2-5). 5.99 *(978-0-14-241691-4(6)*, Puffin Books) Penguin Young Readers Group.

Mebus, Scott. Gods of Manhattan. 2008. (Gods of Manhattan Ser.). (ENG., Illus.). 256p. (J). (gr. 6-8). 24.94 *(978-0-525-47955-0(4))* Penguin Young Readers Group.

Moldavsky, Goldy. No Good Deed. (ENG.). 352p. (YA). (gr. 9-9). 2018. pap. 9.99 *(978-0-545-86754-2(1))* 2017. 17.99 *(978-0-545-86751-1(7))* Scholastic, Inc.

Ockler, Sarah. Bittersweet. 2012. (ENG.). (YA). (gr. 9). 400p. pap. 9.99 *(978-1-4424-3036-5(2))*; 384p. 16.99 *(978-1-4424-3035-8(4))* Simon Pulse. (Simon Pulse).

Oliver, Lauren. Panic. 2015. (ENG.). 432p. (gr. 9-12). 28.69 *(978-1-4844-5031-4(0))* 2015. (ENG.). 432p. (YA). (gr. 9). pap. 10.99 *(978-0-06-201456-6(0)*, HarperCollins) 2014. (J). 137.91 *(978-0-06-230092-8(X))* 2014. (ENG.). 416p. (YA). (gr. 9). 18.99 *(978-0-06-201455-9(2)*, HarperCollins) HarperCollins Pubs.

—Panic. 2015. (YA). lib. bdg. 20.85 *(978-0-606-36509-3(5))* Turtleback.

Osborne, Mary Pope. My Secret War: The World War II Diary of Madeline Beck, Long Island, New York 1941. 2008. (Dear America Ser.). (J). (gr. 3-7). 39.95 incl. audio compact disk *(978-1-4301-0359-2(0))* Live Oak Media.

Russo, Richard. Bridge of Sighs: A Novel. 2007. (ENG.). pap. *(978-0-7393-2751-7(8))* Random Hse. Large Print.

Rycroft, Frederick. Young World: Book Two - Friends 'Til the End. 2012. 568p. pap. 23.99 *(978-1-4797-1311-0(2))* Xlibris Corp.

Schneeberger, Thomas M. Catch the Wind & Spin, Spin, Spin, 1 vol. 2008. (ENG.). 23p. 24.95 *(978-1-4241-8874-1(1))* America Star Bks.

Shen, E. L. The Comeback: A Figure Skating Novel. 2021. (ENG., Illus.). 272p. (J). 16.99 *(978-0-374-31379-1(2)*, 900221649, Farrar, Straus & Giroux (BYR)) Farrar, Straus & Giroux.

Small, Cathleen. The Legend of Sleepy Hollow: the Headless Horseman, 1 vol. Antal, Lara, illus. 2016. (American Legends & Folktales Ser.). (ENG.). 32p. (J). (gr. 3-3). pap. 11.58 *(978-1-5026-2206-8(8)*, d0c99fc1-08b8-423b-9dc3-e640db0d6901) Cavendish Square Publishing LLC.

Starmer, Aaron. The Riverman. 2015. (Riverman Trilogy Ser.: 1). (ENG.). 336p. (YA). (gr. 5-9). pap. 12.99 *(978-1-250-05685-6(3)*, 900139058) Square Fish.

Stern, A. J. Fashion Frenzy. Marts, Doreen Mulryan, illus. 2011. (Frankly, Frannie Ser.: 6). 128p. (J). (gr. 1-3). pap. 6.99 *(978-0-448-45544-0(7)*, Grosset & Dunlap) Penguin Young Readers Group.

Stilton, Gerónimo. Field Trip to Niagara Falls. Keys, Larry et al, illus. 2005. (Geronimo Stilton Ser.: No. 24). 121p. (J). lib. bdg. 18.46 *(978-1-4242-0293-5(0))* Fitzgerald Bks.

Strasser, Todd. Wish You Were Dead. (ENG.). 240p. (gr. 9-12). 2010. (YA). pap. 9.99 *(978-1-60684-138-9(6)*, 83351663-102d-409d-ba04-349ec33baab2) 2009. 16.99 *(978-1-60684-007-8(X))* Lerner Publishing Group. (Carolrhoda Lab™).

Stratemeyer, Edward. Richard Dare's Venture. 2007. 232p. 26.95 *(978-1-4218-4146-5(0))*; per. 11.95 *(978-1-4218-4244-8(0))* 1st World Publishing, Inc. (1st World Library - Literary Society).

Taylor, Gaylia. George Crum & the Saratoga Chip, 1 vol. Morrison, Frank, illus. 2006. (ENG.). 32p. (J). (gr. 1-5). pap. 11.95 *(978-1-60060-656-4(3)*, leelowbooks); 16.95 *(978-1-58430-255-1(0))* Lee & Low Bks., Inc.

Tocher, Timothy. Bill Pennant, Babe Ruth, & Me. 2009. (ENG.). 184p. (J). (gr. 3-7). 17.95 *(978-0-8126-2755-8(5))* Cricket Bks.

Tooke, Wes. Lucky: Maris, Mantle, & My Best Summer Ever. 2011. (ENG.). 192p. (J). (gr. 3-7). pap. 6.99 *(978-1-4169-8664-5(2)*, Simon & Schuster Bks. For Young Readers) Simon & Schuster Bks. For Young Readers.

Vail, Rachel. Gorgeous. 2009. (Avery Sisters Trilogy Ser.: 2). (ENG.). 288p. (YA). (gr. 8-18). 16.99 *(978-0-06-089046-9(0)*, HarperTeen) HarperCollins Pubs.

Van Dyne, Edith. Aunt Jane's Nieces & Uncle John. 2005. 176p. pap. 11.95 *(978-1-4218-1124-6(3)*, 1st World Library - Literary Society) 1st World Publishing, Inc.

—Aunt Jane's Nieces at Millville. 2005. 27.95 *(978-1-4218-1026-3(3))*; 204p. pap. 12.95 *(978-1-4218-1126-0(X))* 1st World Publishing, Inc. (1st World Library - Literary Society).

—Aunt Jane's Nieces at Work. 2005. 204p. pap. 12.95 *(978-1-4218-1523-7(0)*, 1st World Library - Literary Society) 1st World Publishing, Inc.

—Aunt Jane's Nieces at Work. 2017. (ENG., Illus.). (J). 23.95 *(978-1-374-94773-3(3))*; pap. 13.95 *(978-1-374-94772-6(5))* Capital Communications, Inc.

Vande Velde, Vivian. There's a Dead Person Following My Sister Around. 2008. (ENG., Illus.). 160p. (J). (gr. 5-7). pap. 11.95 *(978-0-15-206467-9(2)*, 1199316, Clarion Bks.) HarperCollins Pubs.

Vega, Danielle. The Haunted. 2019. (Haunted Ser.). (ENG.). 256p. (YA). (gr. 9). 17.99 *(978-0-451-48146-7(1)*, Razorbill) Penguin Young Readers Group.

Verday, Jessica. The Haunted. (ENG.). (YA). (gr. 9). 2011. 496p. pap. 14.99 *(978-1-4169-7896-1(8))* 2010. 480p. 17.99 *(978-1-4169-7895-4(X))* Simon Pulse. (Simon Pulse).

Vlahos, Len. The Scar Boys. 2014. (ENG.). 256p. (YA). (gr. 9-12). 17.99 *(978-1-60684-439-7(3)*, 7c28d344-7e6b-4861-86a8-26702e69f318, Carolrhoda Lab™) Lerner Publishing Group.

Volponi, Paul. Rikers High. 2011. (ENG.). 272p. (YA). (gr. 7-18). 9.99 *(978-0-14-241778-2(5)*, Speak) Penguin Young Readers Group.

von Ziegesar, Cecily. Adored. 2009. (It Girl Ser.: 8). (ENG.). 240p. (YA). (gr. 10-17). pap. 14.99 *(978-0-316-02509-6(7)*, Poppy) Little, Brown Bks. for Young Readers.

—The It Girl. 2005. (It Girl Ser.: 1). (ENG.). 272p. (YA). (gr. 10-17). per. 15.99 *(978-0-316-01185-3(1)*, Poppy) Little, Brown Bks. for Young Readers.

—Reckless: An It Girl Novel. 2006. (It Girl Ser.: 3). (ENG.). 288p. (YA). (gr. 10-17). per. 14.99 *(978-0-316-01187-7(8)*, Poppy) Little, Brown Bks. for Young Readers.

Ward, Kaitlin. Where She Fell. 2018. (ENG., Illus.). 304p. (YA). (gr. 7-7). 18.99 *(978-1-338-23007-9(7))* Scholastic, Inc.

Weeks, Sarah. As Simple As It Seems. 2010. (ENG.). 192p. (J). (gr. 3-7). 15.99 *(978-0-06-084663-3(1)*, HarperCollins) HarperCollins Pubs.

Wilder, Laura Ingalls. Farmer Boy. Williams, Garth, illus. 2008. (Little House Ser.: 2). (ENG.). 384p. (J). (gr. 3-7). pap. 8.99 *(978-0-06-440003-9(4)*, HarperCollins) HarperCollins Pubs.

—Farmer Boy: Full Color Edition. Williams, Garth, illus. 2004. (Little House Ser.: 2). (ENG.). 384p. (J). (gr. 3-7). pap. 9.99 *(978-0-06-058182-4(4)*, HarperCollins) HarperCollins Pubs.

Winfield, Arthur M. Putnam Hall Champions or Bound to Win Ou. 2006. pap. 28.95 *(978-1-4286-2346-0(9))* Kessinger Publishing, LLC.

—The Rover Boys on the Ocean. 2007. 232p. 26.95 *(978-1-4218-4138-0(X))*; per. 11.95 *(978-1-4218-4236-3(X))* 1st World Publishing, Inc. (1st World Library - Literary Society).

NEW YORK (STATE)—HISTORY

Ball, Jacqueline A. & Behrens, Kristen. Nueva York (New York), 1 vol. 2003. (World Almanac(r) Biblioteca de Los Estados (World Almanac(r) Library of the States) Ser.). (SPA., Illus.). 48p. (gr. 4-6). lib. bdg. 33.67 *(978-0-8368-5546-3(9)*, b6aa876c-c6d2-4c46-8bdd-9471adbb3186, Gareth Stevens Learning Library) Stevens, Gareth Publishing LLLP.

Bauer, Marion Dane. Celebrating New York: 50 States to Celebrate. Canga, C. B., illus. 2013. (ENG.). 40p. (J). (gr. 1-4). pap. 4.99 *(978-0-547-89781-3(2)*, 1509706, Clarion Bks.) HarperCollins Pubs.

Boehm Jerome, Kate. Rochester & the State of New York: Cool Stuff Every Kid Should Know. 2011. (Arcadia Kids Ser.). (ENG., Illus.). 48p. (J). (gr. 3-6). pap. 11.99 *(978-1-4396-0093-1(7))* Arcadia Publishing.

Bolden, Tonya. Maritcha: A Nineteenth-Century American Girl. 2005. (ENG., Illus.). 48p. (J). (gr. k-4). 19.95 *(978-0-8109-5045-0(6))* Abrams, Inc.

Brill, Marlene Targ. Annie Shapiro & the Clothing Workers' Strike. 2010. pap. 56.72 *(978-0-7613-6924-0(4))* Lerner Publishing Group.

Cunningham, Kevin. The New York Colony. 2011. (True Book-the Thirteen Colonies Ser.). (ENG., Illus.). 48p. (J). (gr. 3-5). lib. bdg. 29.00 *(978-0-531-25394-6(5)*, Children's Pr.) Scholastic Library Publishing.

—The New York Colony (a True Book: the Thirteen Colonies) 2011. (True Book (Relaunch) Ser.). (ENG., Illus.). 48p. (J). (gr. 3-5). pap. 6.95 *(978-0-531-26607-6(9)*, Children's Pr.) Scholastic Library Publishing.

Downey, Tika. New York: The Empire State, 1 vol. 2009. (Our Amazing States Ser.). (ENG., Illus.). 24p. (J). (gr. 3-3). pap. 9.25 *(978-1-4358-3336-4(8)*, 0a949cea-150f-41b6-87f2-a94cb529311a); lib. bdg. 26.27 *(978-1-4042-8108-0(8)*, 5a8b8669-1307-4819-8e51-efc3152e0dad) Rosen Publishing Group, Inc., The. (PowerKids Pr.).

Dunn, Mary R. & Alamán, Eduardo. Quiero Trabajar en Los Musicales, 1 vol. 2009. (Trabajos de Ensueño (Dream Jobs) Ser.). (SPA., Illus.). 24p. (J). (gr. 2-3). lib. bdg. 26.27 *(978-1-4042-8153-0(3)*, e9477ed8-5664-4202-83cd-a73a13cf47a8) Rosen Publishing Group, Inc., The.

Elish, Dan & Fitzgerald, Stephanie. New York, 1 vol. 2nd rev. ed. 2011. (It's My State! (Second Edition)(r) Ser.). (ENG.). 80p. (gr. 4-4). lib. bdg. 34.07 *(978-1-60870-056-1(9)*, 09295635-a487-47bb-b479-872716533eef) Cavendish Square Publishing LLC.

Fitzgerald, Stephanie & Elish, Dan. New York, 1 vol. 3rd rev. ed. 2014. (It's My State! (Third Edition)(r) Ser.). (ENG., Illus.). 80p. (gr. 4-4). lib. bdg. 35.93 *(978-1-62712-752-3(6)*, c6c09ec1-f3b6-4879-bc4e-1362dfc30d6d) Cavendish Square Publishing LLC.

Flynn, Andy. New York State's Mountain Heritage: Adirondack Attic 2. 2005. (Illus.). 240p. per. 18.00 *(978-0-9754007-1-5(1))* Hungry Bear Publishing.

—New York State's Mountain Heritage Vol. 1: Adirondack Attic 1. 2004. (Illus.). 184p. per. 16.95 *(978-0-9754007-0-8(3))* Hungry Bear Publishing.

Gamble, Adam & Jasper, Mark. Good Night New York State. 2012. (Good Night Our World Ser.). (ENG., Illus.). 20p. (J). (gr. k — 1). bds. 9.95 *(978-1-60219-063-4(1))* Good Night Bks.

George, Lynn & Schimel, Kate. New York's Early Explorers. (Illus.). 24p. (J). 2012. 60.00 *(978-1-4488-5772-2(4))* 2011. (ENG., (gr. 3-4). pap. 10.00 *(978-1-4488-5771-5(6)*, 0097a284-3567-4d8b-b7e3-5a29e8617926) Rosen Publishing Group, Inc., The. (PowerKids Pr.).

Goodman, Michael E. The Story of the New York Knicks. 2010. (NBA — A History of Hoops Ser.). 48p. (YA). (gr. 5-18). 23.95 *(978-1-58341-955-7(1)*, Creative Education) Creative Co., The.

Holub, Joan. What Was Woodstock? 2016. (What Was... Ser.). (Illus.). 108p. (J). lib. bdg. 16.00 *(978-0-606-38414-8(6))* Turtleback.

Holub, Joan & Who HQ. What Was Woodstock? Copeland, Gregory, illus. 2016. (What Was? Ser.). 112p. (J). (gr. 3-7). 5.99 *(978-0-448-48696-3(2)*, Penguin Workshop) Penguin Young Readers Group.

Houghton, Gillian. The Oneida of Wisconsin. 2009. (Library of Native Americans Ser.). 64p. (gr. 4-4). 58.50 *(978-1-60853-759-4(5)*, PowerKids Pr.) Rosen Publishing Group, Inc., The.

Ingram, Scott. The Battle of Valcour Bay. 2003. (Triangle Histories of the American Revolution Ser.). (Illus.). 32p. (J). 22.45 *(978-1-56711-778-3(3)*, Blackbirch Pr., Inc.) Cengage Gale.

Keranen, Rachel, et al. New York: The Empire State, 1 vol. 2018. (It's My State! (Fourth Edition)(r) Ser.). (ENG.). 80p. (gr. 4-4). 35.93 *(978-1-5026-2624-0(1)*, 786605b1-95b3-41b0-bc26-f15ddb8b98f3); pap. 18.64 *(978-1-5026-4439-8(8)*, d287d336-0e63-4442-9f5a-4f464377b8df) Cavendish Square Publishing LLC.

Krizner, L. J. Peter Stuyvesant: New Amsterdam, & the Origins of New York. 2009. (Library of American Lives & Times Ser.). 112p. (gr. 5-5). 69.20 *(978-1-60853-498-2(7))* Rosen Publishing Group, Inc., The.

Kupperberg, Paul. A Primary Source History of the Colony of New York, 1 vol. 2005. (Primary Sources of the Thirteen Colonies & the Lost Colony Ser.). (ENG., illus.). 64p. (gr. 4-6). per. 12.95 *(978-1-4042-0677-9(9)*, dbbffb46-1638-4765-ab0f-14e129e078ae) Rosen Publishing Group, Inc., The.

Lawton, Val. New York. 2011. (Guide to American States Ser.). (Illus.). 48p. (YA). (gr. 3-6). 29.99 *(978-1-61690-804-1(1))*; (J). 29.99 *(978-1-61690-480-7(1))* Weigl Pubs., Inc.

—New York: The Empire State. 2016. (J). *(978-1-4896-4911-9(5))* Weigl Pubs., Inc.

Marsh, Carole. My First Book. 2004. (New York Experience! Ser.). 32p. (J). (gr. k-4). pap. 7.95 *(978-0-635-00160-3(8))* Gallopade International.

—New York History Projects: 30 Cool, Activities, Crafts, Experiments & More for Kids to Do to Learn about Your State! 2003. (New York Experience Ser.). 32p. (gr. k-5). pap. 5.95 *(978-0-635-01801-4(2)*, Marsh, Carole Bks.) Gallopade International.

McCarthy, Meghan. All That Trash: The Story of the 1987 Garbage Barge & Our Problem with Stuff. McCarthy, Meghan, illus. 2018. (ENG., Illus.). 48p. (J). (gr. -1-3). 19.99 *(978-1-4814-7752-9(8)*, Simon & Schuster/Paula Wiseman Bks.) Simon & Schuster/Paula Wiseman Bks.

McNeese, Tim. New Amsterdam. 2007. (ENG., Illus.). 109p. (gr. 5-9). lib. bdg. 30.00 *(978-0-7910-9334-4(4)*, P124708, Facts On File) Infobase Holdings, Inc.

Mis, Melody S. The Colony of New York: A Primary Source History. (Primary Source Library of the Thirteen Colonies & the Lost Colony Ser.). 24p. (gr. 3-4). 2009. 42.50 *(978-1-60854-147-8(9))* 2006. (ENG., Illus.). (J). lib. bdg. 26.27 *(978-1-4042-3432-1(2)*, 42405f1d-ae56-452f-bbbc-2f80c6e75a41) Rosen Publishing Group, Inc., The. (PowerKids Pr.).

National Geographic Learning. Reading Expeditions (Social Studies: American Communities Across Time): a Suburban Community of The 1950s. 2007. (ENG., Illus.). 24p. (J). pap. 15.95 *(978-0-7922-8691-2(X))* CENGAGE Learning.

Orr, Tamra B. New York, 1 vol. 2005. (Portraits of the States Ser.). (ENG., Illus.). 32p. (gr. 3-5). pap. 11.50 *(978-0-8368-4649-2(4)*, f5796b80-791c-4e78-bbaa-2597d3c87e32, Gareth Stevens Learning Library) Stevens, Gareth Publishing LLLP.

Reis, Ronald A. The New York City Subway System. 2009. (ENG., Illus.). 144p. (gr. 5-8). 35.00 *(978-1-60413-046-1(6)*, P162091, Facts On File) Infobase Holdings, Inc.

Rodriguez, Cindy. New York: The Empire State. 2012. (J). *(978-1-61913-383-9(0))*; pap. *(978-1-61913-384-6(9))* Weigl Pubs., Inc.

Schimel, Kate & Adams, Colleen. Colonial Leaders in New York. 24p. (J). 2012. 60.00 *(978-1-4488-5762-3(7))* 2011. (ENG.). (gr. 3-4). pap. 10.00 *(978-1-4488-5761-6(9)*, c3f3508b-4fc5-4b02-a1e2-4f4c8967198d) Rosen Publishing Group, Inc., The. (PowerKids Pr.).

Schimel, Kate & Cefrey, Holly. New York's Industrial Growth. (Illus.). 24p. (J). 2012. 60.00 *(978-1-4488-5774-6(0))* 2011. (ENG., (gr. 3-4). pap. 10.00 *(978-1-4488-5773-9(2)*, 60ab915f-b9e0-489e-90d9-f418c92a9148) 2011. (ENG., (gr. 3-4). lib. bdg. 26.27 *(978-1-4488-5750-0(3)*, e1b3794d-734c-465a-a98d-71b3ac02d62d) Rosen Publishing Group, Inc., The. (PowerKids Pr.).

Schimel, Kate & Khu, Jannell. The British Colony of New York. (Illus.). 24p. (J). 2012. 60.00 *(978-1-4488-5760-9(0))* 2011. (ENG., (gr. 3-4). pap. 10.00 *(978-1-4488-5759-3(7)*, d3aaf699-8fbd-4ed1-b5d4-1f4338214b05) 2011. (ENG., (gr. 3-4). lib. bdg. 26.27 *(978-1-4488-5743-2(0)*, 749aab06-30a5-4f5b-863e-95497248d0ea) Rosen Publishing Group, Inc., The. (PowerKids Pr.).

Schimel, Kate & Levy, Janey. New York: The Dutch Colony of New Amsterdam. (Illus.). 24p. (J). 2012. 60.00 *(978-1-4488-5758-6(9))* 2011. (ENG., (gr. 3-4). pap. 10.00 *(978-1-4488-5757-9(0)*, 3de932b2-e68e-48d3-a443-b2a878c61a0c) 2011. (ENG., (gr. 3-4). lib. bdg. 26.27 *(978-1-4488-5742-5(2)*, fff08119-669d-4b5b-982a-7abba7bfcc7f) Rosen Publishing Group, Inc., The. (PowerKids Pr.).

Schimel, Kate & Zuravicky, Orli. New York's Role in the New Nation. (Illus.). 24p. (J). 2012. 60.00 *(978-1-4488-5770-8(8))* 2011. (ENG., (gr. 3-4). pap. 10.00 *(978-1-4488-5769-2(4)*, e7d45694-dddd-4d68-9529-edf724ab7909) 2011. (ENG., (gr. 3-4). lib. bdg. 26.27 *(978-1-4488-5748-7(1)*, 0063ca98-74ab-4d90-8fa8-c7c357919d68) Rosen Publishing Group, Inc., The. (PowerKids Pr.).

Schimel, Kate, et al. Colonial Leaders in New York, 1 vol. 2011. (Spotlight on New York Ser.). (ENG.). 24p. (J). (gr. 3-4). lib. bdg. 26.27 *(978-1-4488-5744-9(9)*, f3214a71-3e52-417f-bf18-4e9ca02e5077, PowerKids Pr.) Rosen Publishing Group, Inc., The.

Schnobrich, Emily. New York. 2013. (Exploring the States Ser.). (ENG., Illus.). 32p. (J). (gr. 3-7). lib. bdg. 27.95 *(978-1-62617-031-5(2)*, Blastoff! Readers) Bellwether Media.

Tougas, Joe. New York. 2009. (This Land Called America Ser.). (Illus.). 32p. (YA). (gr. 3-6). 19.95 *(978-1-58341-785-0(0))* Creative Co., The.

Wilbur, Helen L. Little New York. Brett, Jeannie, illus. 2010. (Little State Ser.). (ENG.). 20p. (J). (gr. -1-1). bds. 9.95 *(978-1-58536-491-6(6)*, 202244) Sleeping Bear Pr.

Wyner, Zach. On the Hardwood: Brooklyn Nets. 2013. (On the Hardwood Ser.). (ENG., Illus.). 48p. (gr. 3-8). pap. 8.95 *(978-1-61570-835-2(9))* Scobre Pr. Corp.

NEW YORK (STATE)—HISTORY—FICTION

Alger, Horatio. Hector's Inheritance: Or, The Boys of Smith Institute. 2006. pap. *(978-1-4065-0708-9(3))* Dodo Pr.

—Herbert Carter's Legacy. 2006. pap. *(978-1-4065-0710-2(5))* Dodo Pr.

Alger Jr. Horatio Staff. Hector's Inheritance. rev. ed. 2006. 276p. 28.95 *(978-1-4218-1758-3(6))*; pap. 13.95 *(978-1-4218-1858-0(2))* 1st World Publishing, Inc. (1st World Library - Literary Society).

Altsheler, Joseph A. The Hunters of the Hills: A Story of the Great French & Indian War. rev. ed. 2006. (French & Indian War Ser.). 316p. (J). 29.95 *(978-1-4218-2334-8(9))*; pap. 14.95 *(978-1-4218-2434-5(5))* 1st World Publishing, Inc. (1st World Library - Literary Society).

—The Hunters of the Hills: A Story of the Great French & Indian War. (French & Indian War Ser.: Vol. 1). (J). reprint ed. 26.95 *(978-0-8488-0904-1(1))* Amereon Ltd.

—The Hunters of the Hills: A Story of the Great French & Indian War. 2009. (French & Indian War Ser.: Vol. 1). 200p. (J). reprint ed. pap. *(978-0-217-62835-8(4))* Books LLC.

—The Hunters of the Hills: A Story of the Great French & Indian War. 2012. 392p. reprint ed. pap. 33.75 *(978-1-277-16849-5(0))* Creative Media Partners, LLC.

—The Hunters of the Hills: A Story of the Great French & Indian War. 2006. (French & Indian War Ser.). (J). pap. *(978-1-4065-0815-4(2))* Dodo Pr.

—The Hunters of the Hills: A Story of the Great French & Indian War. 2007. (French & Indian War Ser.). 188p. (J). per. *(978-1-4068-1680-8(9))* Echo Library.

—The Hunters of the Hills: A Story of the Great French & Indian War. 2010. (French & Indian War Ser.: Vol. 1). (Illus.). 168p. (J). (gr. 4-7). reprint ed. pap. 19.99 *(978-1-153-70670-4(9))* General Bks. LLC.

—The Hunters of the Hills: A Story of the Great French & Indian War. (French & Indian War Ser.: Vol. 1). (J). reprint ed. 2011. 372p. (gr. 4-7). 48.95 *(978-1-169-83864-2(2))* 2010. 372p. (gr. 4-7). 39.16 *(978-1-163-20015-5(8))* 2010. 372p. (gr. 4-7). pap. 27.16 *(978-1-162-64218-5(1))* 2004. pap. 33.95 *(978-1-4179-1500-2(5))* Kessinger Publishing, LLC.

—The Hunters of the Hills: A Story of the Great French & Indian War. 2011. (French & Indian War Ser.: Vol. 1). 284p. (J). (gr. 4-7). reprint ed. pap. *(978-3-8424-7700-1(7))* tredition Verlag.

—The Shadow of the North: A Story of Old New York & a Lost Campaign. 2010. (French & Indian War Ser.: Vol. 2). (ENG.). 378p. (J). (gr. 4-7). reprint ed. pap. 33.75 *(978-1-176-98060-0(2))* Creative Media Partners, LLC.

—The Shadow of the North: A Story of Old New York & a Lost Campaign. 2007. (French & Indian War Ser.: Vol. 2). 188p. (J). reprint ed. per. *(978-1-4068-1687-7(6))* Echo Library.

—The Shadow of the North: A Story of Old New York & a Lost Campaign. 2010. (French & Indian War Ser.: Vol. 2). (Illus.). 170p. (J). (gr. 4-7). reprint ed. pap. 19.99 *(978-1-153-72063-2(9))* General Bks. LLC.

—The Shadow of the North: A Story of Old New York & a Lost Campaign. (French & Indian War Ser.: Vol. 2). (J). reprint ed. 2010. 256p. (gr. 4-7). 34.36 *(978-1-169-30396-6(X))* 2010. 256p. (gr. 4-7). pap. 22.36 *(978-1-162-70813-3(1))* 2010. 42.95 *(978-1-161-47677-4(6))* 2004. pap. 27.95

(978-1-4191-8225-9(0)) 2004. pap. 1.99 *(978-1-4192-8225-6(5))* Kessinger Publishing, LLC.

—The Shadow of the North: A Story of Old New York & a Lost Campaign. 2011. (French & Indian War Ser.: Vol. 2). 286p. (J). reprint ed. pap. *(978-3-8424-4397-6(8))* tredition Verlag.

Brummel Crook, Connie. Flight, 1 vol. 2011. (ENG.). 293p. (YA). (gr. 6-10). pap. 9.95 *(978-1-55455-190-3(0),* f4bc05c9-a7cc-42a4-8b5f-834778d0190d) Fitzhenry & Whiteside, Ltd. CAN. Dist: Firefly Bks., Ltd.

Clark, Clara Gillow. Secrets of Greymoor. 2009. (Trials of Hattie Belle Basket Ser.). (Illus.). 176p. (J). (gr. 5). 15.99 *(978-0-7636-3249-6(X))* Candlewick Pr.

Cremer, Andrea. The Inventor's Secret. 2015. (Inventor's Secret Ser.: 1). (ENG.). 416p. (YA). (gr. 7). pap. 10.99 *(978-0-14-751438-7(X),* Speak) Penguin Young Readers Group.

Donnelly, Jennifer. A Northern Light. 2004. 396p. (gr. 9-12). 20.00 *(978-0-7569-3614-3(4))* Perfection Learning Corp.

Ernst, Kathleen. A Surprise for Caroline, 3. 2012. (American Girls Collection: Caroline Stories Ser.). (ENG., Illus.). 96p. (J). (gr. 2-4). pap. 21.19 *(978-1-59369-886-7(0))* American Girl Publishing, Inc.

Falk, Elizabeth Sullivan. Lettie's North Star. Wolf, Elizabeth, illus. 2006. (J). *(978-1-59336-694-0(9))* Mondo Publishing.

Gansworth, Eric. If I Ever Get Out of Here. (ENG.). 368p. (YA). 2015. (gr. 6-11). pap. 12.99 *(978-0-545-41731-0(7))* 2013. (gr. 7). 19.99 *(978-0-545-41730-3(9))* Scholastic, Inc. (Levine, Arthur A. Bks.).

Giff, Patricia Reilly. Gingersnap. 2014. (ENG.). 160p. (J). (gr. 3-7). 6.99 *(978-0-440-42178-8(0),* Yearling) Random Hse. Children's Bks.

Griffith, A. J. America's Child. 2008. (J). pap. 9.99 *(978-0-88092-493-1(4))* Royal Fireworks Publishing Co.

Irving, Washington. The Legend of Sleepy Hollow & Rip Van Winkle, 1 vol. McWilliam, Howard, illus. 2010. (Calico Illustrated Classics Ser.). (ENG.). 112p. (J). (gr. 2-5). 38.50 *(978-1-60270-747-4(2),* 3995, Calico Chapter Bks.) ABDO Publishing Co.

Johnson, J. J. Believarexic. 1 vol. 2017. 464p. (YA). (gr. 9-11). pap. 9.95 *(978-1-68263-007-5(2))* Peachtree Publishing Co. Inc.

Napoli, Donna Jo. The King of Mulberry Street. 2007. 245p. (gr. 3-7). 17.00 *(978-0-7569-7945-4(5))* Perfection Learning Corp.

Neale, Cynthia. Hope in New York City: The Continuing Story of the Irish Dresser. 2008. (ENG.). 176p. (J). pap. 7.95 *(978-1-57249-387-2(9),* White Mane Kids) White Mane Publishing Co., Inc.

Ostrom, Melissa. The Beloved Wild. 2018. (ENG.). 320p. (YA). 29.99 *(978-1-250-13279-6(7),* 900177171) Feiwel & Friends.

Peterson, Mike. Freehand: A Young Boy's Adventures in the War Of 1812. Baldwin, Christopher, illus. 2012. (ENG.). 44p. (J). pap. 6.95 *(978-1-938384-03-5(2))* Baldwin, Christopher John.

Pinkney, Andrea Davis. Bird in a Box. Qualls, Sean, illus. 2012. (J). lib. bdg. 18.45 *(978-0-606-26157-9(5))* Turtleback.

Stafford, Gerry. Young Canaller. Wanecski, Erica Joan, illus. 2012. 60p. (J). pap. *(978-0-9667989-7-5(X))* Carlisle Pr.- Walnut Creek.

Tarshis, Lauren. I Survived the American Revolution, 1776 (I Survived #15), Vol .15. 2017. (I Survived Ser.: 15). (ENG., Illus.). 144p. (J). (gr. 2-5). pap. 4.99 *(978-0-545-91973-9(8),* Scholastic Paperbacks) Scholastic, Inc.

Tooke, Wes. Lucky: Maris, Mantle, & My Best Summer Ever. 2010. (ENG.). 192p. (J). (gr. 3-7). 15.99 *(978-1-4169-8663-8(4),* Simon & Schuster Bks. For Young Readers) Simon & Schuster Bks. For Young Readers.

Vernick, Shirley Reva. The Blood Lie. (ENG.). 144p. (YA). (gr. 9-12). 2015. pap. 16.95 *(978-1-941026-09-0(5),* 23353382) 2011. 15.95 *(978-1-933693-84-2(3),* 23353382) Lee & Low Bks., Inc. (Cinco Puntos Press).

Villani, Donna. The Capture of Art. 2008. 244p. pap. 14.95 *(978-1-60693-104-2(0),* Eloquent Bks.) Strategic Book Publishing & Rights Agency (SBPRA).

Walvoord, Linda. Rosetta, Rosetta, Sit by Me!, 0 vols. Velasquez, Eric, illus. 2012. (ENG.). 98p. (J). (gr. 1-3). 14.95 *(978-0-7614-5171-6(4),* 9780761451716, Two Lions) Amazon Publishing.

Zink, Michelle. Prophecy of the Sisters. 2010. (Prophecy of the Sisters Ser.: 1). (ENG.). 368p. (YA). (gr. 7-17). pap. 18.99 *(978-0-316-02741-0(3))* Little, Brown Bks. for Young Readers.

NEW YORK (STATE)—POLITICS AND GOVERNMENT

Schimel, Kate & Alagna, Magdalena. New York's Government. (Illus.). 24p. (J). 2012. 60.00 *(978-1-4488-5764-7(3))* 2011. (ENG., (gr. 3-4). pap. 10.00 *(978-1-4488-5763-0(5),* 2e6e2681-7fb3-4ab9-bedb-d4b74527807e) 2011. (ENG., (gr. 3-4). lib. bdg. 26.27 *(978-1-4488-5745-6(7),* d7d8ef1a-3b1e-441d-a74f-952b92f63ec4) Rosen Publishing Group, Inc., The. (PowerKids Pr.).

White, Casey. John Jay: Diplomat of the American Experiment. (Library of American Thinkers Ser.). 112p. (gr. 6-6). 2009. 66.50 *(978-1-60853-515-6(0),* Rosen Reference) 2006. (ENG., Illus.). (YA). lib. bdg. 39.80 *(978-1-4042-0507-9(1),* d02aee73-ee35-409b-89c1-7c009ebf0d42) Rosen Publishing Group, Inc., The.

NEW YORK GIANTS (FOOTBALL TEAM)

Blumberg, Saulie. New York Giants, 1 vol. 2016. (NFL up Close Ser.). (ENG.). 32p. (J). (gr. 3-9). lib. bdg. 32.79 *(978-1-68078-226-4(6),* 22055, SportsZone) ABDO Publishing Co.

Burgess, Zack. Meet the New York Giants. 2016. (Big Picture Sports Ser.). (ENG., Illus.). 24p. (J). (gr. k-3). lib. bdg. 22.60 *(978-1-59953-736-8(2))* Norwood Hse. Pr.

Epstein, Brad. New York Giants 101. 2010. (Illus.). 24p. (J). bds. *(978-1-60730-120-2(2),* 101 Bk.) Michaelson Entertainment.

Frisch, Aaron. New York Giants. 2011. (Super Bowl Champions Ser.). (J). (gr. 1-3). 24.25 *(978-1-60818-023-3(9))* Creative Co., The.

—New York Giants. 2014. (Super Bowl Champions Ser.). (ENG., Illus.). 24p. (J). (gr. 1-4). *(978-1-60818-382-1(3),* 21571, Creative Education) Creative Co., The.

Gigliotti, Jim. Odell Beckham Jr. 2018. (Amazing Americans: Football Stars Ser.). (ENG.). 24p. (J). (gr. -1-3). lib. bdg. 17.95 *(978-1-68402-451-3(X))* Bearport Publishing Co., Inc.

Goodman, Michael E. The History of the New York Giants. 2004. (NFL Today Ser.). (Illus.). 32p. (YA). (gr. 5-9). 18.95 *(978-1-58341-306-7(5))* Creative Co., The.

—The Story of the New York Giants. 2009. (NFL Today Ser.). 48p. (YA). (gr. 5-9). 22.95 *(978-1-58341-804-8(0))* Creative Co., The.

Grayson, Robert. Plaxico Burress. 2009. (Superstars of Pro Football Ser.). (Illus.). 64p. (YA). (gr. 7-12). lib. bdg. 22.95 *(978-1-4222-0552-5(5))* Mason Crest.

Leboutillier, Nate. New York Giants. 2005. (Super Bowl Champions Ser.). (Illus.). 24p. (J). (gr. 1-4). lib. bdg. 16.95 *(978-1-58341-387-6(1),* Creative Education) Creative Co., The.

Mack, Larry. The New York Giants Story. 2016. (NFL Teams Ser.). (ENG., Illus.). 32p. (J). (gr. 3-7). lib. bdg. 26.95 *(978-1-62617-375-0(3),* Torque Bks.) Bellwether Media.

MacRae, Sloan. The New York Giants, 1 vol. 2011. (America's Greatest Teams Ser.). (ENG., Illus.). 24p. (J). (gr. 2-3). pap. 9.25 *(978-1-4488-2741-1(8),* 49c587df-95f2-40bb-928a-d96d424b4bf1); lib. bdg. 26.27 *(978-1-4488-2576-9(8),* 1c626256-f05b-4602-b0a2-1c16c9c52a4d) Rosen Publishing Group, Inc., The. (PowerKids Pr.).

Nagelhout, Ryan. Odell Beckham Jr: Pro Bowl Wide Receiver, 1 vol. 2018. (Living Legends of Sports Ser.). (ENG.). 48p. (gr. 5-6). pap. 15.05 *(978-1-5383-0209-5(8),* 9d26d803-9636-4b77-8c92-980fe7d90303, Britannica Educational Publishing) Rosen Publishing Group, Inc., The.

New York Giants, 1 vol. 2014. (NFL's Greatest Teams Ser.). (ENG.). 32p. (J). (gr. 2-5). 34.21 *(978-1-62403-364-3(4),* 1582, Big Buddy Bks.) ABDO Publishing Co.

Osborne, M. K. Superstars of the New York Giants. 2018. (Pro Sports Superstars - NFL Ser.). (ENG.). 24p. (J). (gr. 1-4). pap. 8.99 *(978-1-68152-329-3(9),* 15086); lib. bdg. *(978-1-68151-409-3(5),* 15076) Amicus.

Publications International Ltd. Staff. Yesterday & Today Nfl New York Giants. 2010. 160p. 24.95 *(978-1-4127-9829-7(9))* Publications International, Ltd.

Sandler, Michael. Eli Manning & the New York Giants: Super Bowl Xlvi. 2012. (Super Bowl Superstars Ser.). (Illus.). 24p. (J). (gr. 1-6). lib. bdg. 26.99 *(978-1-61772-578-4(1))* Bearport Publishing Co., Inc.

Storm, Marysa. Highlights of the New York Giants. 2018. (Team Stats — Football Edition Ser.). (ENG.). 32p. (J). (gr. 4-6). pap. 9.99 *(978-1-64466-283-0(3),* 12385); lib. bdg. *(978-1-68072-436-3(3),* 12384) Black Rabbit Bks. (Bolt).

Whiting, Jim. New York Giants. rev. ed. 2019. (NFL Today Ser.). (ENG.). 48p. (J). (gr. 4-7). pap. 12.00 *(978-1-62832-715-1(4),* 19064, Creative Paperbacks) Creative Co., The.

—The Story of the New York Giants. (NFL Today Ser.). (J). 2019. (ENG.). 48p. (gr. 3-6). *(978-1-64026-152-5(4),* 19066) 2013. 35.65 *(978-1-60818-312-8(2))* Creative Co., The. (Creative Education).

Wyner, Zach. New York Giants. 2014. (Inside the NFL Ser.). (ENG., Illus.). 32p. (J). (gr. 4-7). lib. bdg. 28.55 *(978-1-4896-0862-8(1),* AV2 by Weigl) Weigl Pubs., Inc.

NEW YORK JETS (FOOTBALL TEAM)

Burgess, Zack. Meet the New York Jets. 2016. (Big Picture Sports Ser.). (ENG., Illus.). 24p. (J). (gr. k-3). lib. bdg. 22.60 *(978-1-59953-738-2(9))* Norwood Hse. Pr.

Cohn, Nate. Newyork Jets. 2018. (Illus.). 24p. (J). *(978-1-4896-5537-0(9),* AV2 by Weigl) Weigl Pubs., Inc.

Epstein, Brad. New York Jets 101. 2010. (ENG., Illus.). 24p. (J). bds. *(978-1-60730-121-9(0),* 101 Bk.) Michaelson Entertainment.

Frisch, Aaron. New York Jets. 2011. (Super Bowl Champions Ser.). (J). (gr. 1-3). 24.25 *(978-1-60818-024-0(7))* Creative Co., The.

—New York Jets. 2014. (Super Bowl Champions Ser.). (ENG., Illus.). 24p. (J). (gr. 1-4). *(978-1-60818-383-8(1),* 21574, Creative Education) Creative Co., The.

Goodman, Michael E. The History of the New York Jets. 2004. (NFL Today Ser.). (Illus.). 32p. (YA). (gr. 5-9). 18.95 *(978-1-58341-307-4(3))* Creative Co., The.

—The Story of the New York Jets. 2009. (NFL Today Ser.). 48p. (YA). (gr. 5-9). 22.95 *(978-1-58341-805-5(9))* Creative Co., The.

Kelley, Patrick & Blumberg, Saulie. New York Jets, 1 vol. 2016. (NFL up Close Ser.). (ENG., Illus.). 32p. (J). (gr. 3-9). lib. bdg. 32.79 *(978-1-68078-227-1(4),* 22057, SportsZone) ABDO Publishing Co.

Temple, Ramey. New York Jets. 2014. (Inside the NFL Ser.). (ENG., Illus.). 32p. (J). (gr. 4-7). lib. bdg. 28.55 *(978-1-4896-0866-6(4),* AV2 by Weigl) Weigl Pubs., Inc.

Whiting, Jim. New York Jets. rev. ed. 2019. (NFL Today Ser.). (ENG.). 48p. (J). (gr. 4-7). pap. 12.00 *(978-1-62832-716-8(2),* 19067, Creative Paperbacks) Creative Co., The.

—The Story of the New York Jets. (NFL Today Ser.). (J). 2019. (ENG.). 48p. (gr. 3-6). *(978-1-64026-153-2(2),* 19069) 2013. 35.65 *(978-1-60818-313-5(0))* Creative Co., The. (Creative Education).

Wyner, Zach. New York Jets. 2015. (Illus.). 32p. (J). pap. *(978-1-4896-0867-3(2))* Weigl Pubs., Inc.

Zappa, Marcia. New York Jets, 1 vol. 2015. (NFL's Greatest Teams Ser.). (ENG., Illus.). 32p. (J). (gr. 2-5). 34.21 *(978-1-62403-589-0(2),* 17205, Big Buddy Bks.) ABDO Publishing Co.

NEW YORK METS (BASEBALL TEAM)

Boone, Mary. David Wright. 2010. (Blue Banner Biography Ser.). (Illus.). 32p. (YA). (gr. 4-7). lib. bdg. 25.70 *(978-1-58415-910-0(3))* Mitchell Lane Pubs.

Epstein, Brad. New York Mets 101. 2013. (My First Team-Board-Book Ser.). (ENG., Illus.). 24p. (J). bds. *(978-1-60730-285-8(3),* 101 Bk.) Michaelson Entertainment.

—New York Mets ABC. 2013. (My First Alphabet Books (Michaelson Entertainment) Ser.). (ENG., Illus.). 28p. (J). bds. *(978-1-60730-208-7(X),* ABC Bk.) Michaelson Entertainment.

Gilbert, Sara. New York Mets. 2013. (World Series Champions Ser.). (ENG.). 24p. (J). (gr. 1-4). pap. 7.99 *(978-0-89812-819-2(6),* 21852, Creative Paperbacks); (Illus.). 25.65 *(978-1-60818-268-8(1),* 21851, Creative Education) Creative Co., The.

Goodman, Michael E. The Story of the New York Mets. 2011. (J). 35.65 *(978-1-60818-048-6(4),* Creative Education) 2007. (Illus.). 48p. (YA). (gr. 4-7). lib. bdg. 32.80 *(978-1-58341-494-1(0))* Creative Co., The.

Knobel, Andy. New York Mets, 1 vol. 2015. (Inside MLB Ser.). (ENG., Illus.). 48p. (J). (gr. 3-6). lib. bdg. 34.21 *(978-1-62403-477-0(2),* 17117, SportsZone) ABDO Publishing Co.

MacRae, Sloan. The New York Mets. (Illus.). 24p. (J). 2012. 49.50 *(978-1-4488-5154-6(8),* 1329148) 2011. (ENG., (gr. 2-3). pap. 9.25 *(978-1-4488-5153-9(X),* c0bcfbac-0d81-4726-96ff-b224521d0725) 2011. (ENG., (gr. 2-3). lib. bdg. 26.27 *(978-1-4488-5010-5(X),* fc6142cd-60a0-42b3-bd41-6c7df0e1d476) Rosen Publishing Group, Inc., The. (PowerKids Pr.).

Noble, Marty. Mike Piazza: Mike & the Mets. Rains, Rob, ed. 2003. (Superstar Ser.). (Illus.). 96p. (J). (gr. 4-7). pap. 4.95 *(978-1-58261-051-1(7))* Sports Publishing, LLC.

Sauver, Dennis St. New York Mets. 2018. (MLB's Greatest Teams Ser.). (ENG., Illus.). 32p. (J). (gr. 2-5). lib. bdg. 34.21 *(978-1-5321-1811-1(2),* 30668, Big Buddy Bks.) ABDO Publishing Co.

Stewart, Mark. The New York Mets. 2012. (Team Spirit Ser.). 48p. (J). (gr. 3-6). lib. bdg. 29.27 *(978-1-59953-489-3(4))* Norwood Hse. Pr.

NEW YORK STOCK EXCHANGE

Ingram, Scott. The Stock Market Crash Of 1929, 1 vol. 2004. (Landmark Events in American History Ser.). (ENG., Illus.). 48p. (gr. 5-8). pap. 15.05 *(978-0-8368-5425-1(X),* 6e01ff38-f8fc-4247-8464-817c4a13cd62, Gareth Stevens Secondary Library) Stevens, Gareth Publishing LLLP.

—Stock Market Crash Of 1929. 2004. (Landmark Events in American History Ser.). (ENG.). 48p. (J). (gr. 3-6). 24.85 *(978-1-5311-8646-3(7))* Perfection Learning Corp.

NEW YORK TIMES

Dudley Gold, Susan. The Pentagon Papers: National Security or the Right to Know, 1 vol. 2006. (Supreme Court Milestones Ser.). (ENG., Illus.). 128p. (YA). (gr. 8-8). 45.50 *(978-0-7614-1843-6(1),* f905cf70-6773-479d-8840-68679c7e7d7a) Cavendish Square Publishing LLC.

Herda, D. J. New York Times V. United States: National Security & Censorship, 1 vol. rev. ed. 2010. (Landmark Supreme Court Cases, Gold Edition Ser.). (ENG., Illus.). 112p. (gr. 6-7). 35.93 *(978-0-7660-3429-7(1),* c23a6da6-70e0-436a-bdde-50c5500824b2) Enslow Publishing, LLC.

NEW YORK YANKEES (BASEBALL TEAM)

Appel, Marty. Pinstripe Pride: The Inside Story of the New York Yankees. 2016. (ENG.). 352p. (J). (gr. 3-7). pap. 15.99 *(978-1-4814-1603-0(0),* Simon & Schuster Bks. For Young Readers) Simon & Schuster Bks. For Young Readers.

Bates, Greg. Aaron Judge: Baseball Star. 2018. (Biggest Names in Sports Set 3 Ser.). (ENG., Illus.). 32p. (J). (gr. 3-5). pap. 9.95 *(978-1-63517-968-2(8),* 1635179688); lib. bdg. 31.35 *(978-1-63517-867-8(3),* 1635178673) North Star Editions. (Focus Readers).

Boothroyd, Jennifer. Lou Gehrig. 2008. pap. 40.95 *(978-0-8225-9473-4(0))* Lerner Publishing Group.

—Lou Gehrig: A Life of Dedication. 2008. (Pull Ahead Bks.). (Illus.). 32p. (J). (gr. -1-3). lib. bdg. 22.60 *(978-0-8225-8587-9(1),* Lerner Pubns.) Lerner Publishing Group.

Christopher, Matt. The New York Yankees: Legendary Sports Teams. 2008. (ENG., Illus.). 128p. (J). (gr. 3-7). pap. 10.99 *(978-0-316-01115-0(0))* Little, Brown Bks. for Young Readers.

Frisch, Aaron. New York Yankees. 2009. (World Series Champions Ser.). (Illus.). 23p. (J). (gr. 2-3). 24.25 *(978-1-58341-697-6(8),* Creative Education) Creative Co., The.

Gilbert, Sara. New York Yankees. 2013. (World Series Champions Ser.). (ENG.). 24p. (J). (gr. 1-4). pap. 7.99 *(978-0-89812-820-8(X),* 21855, Creative Paperbacks); (Illus.). 25.65 *(978-1-60818-269-5(X),* 21854, Creative Education) Creative Co., The.

Glueckstein, Fred. Mickey Mantle: Rookie in Pinstripes. 2008. (ENG.). 170p. 25.95 *(978-0-595-70936-6(2));* pap. 15.95 *(978-0-595-46921-5(3))* iUniverse, Inc.

Goodman, Michael E. The Story of the New York Yankees. 2011. (J). 35.65 *(978-1-60818-049-3(2),* Creative Education) 2007. (Illus.). 48p. (YA). (gr. 4-7). lib. bdg. 32.80 *(978-1-58341-495-8(9))* Creative Co., The.

Greenberg, Keith Elliot. Derek Jeter. 2005. (Sports Heroes & Legends Ser.). (Illus.). 106p. (J). (gr. 3-7). lib. bdg. 27.93 *(978-0-8225-3068-8(6),* Lerner Pubns.) Lerner Publishing Group.

Herman, Gail. Who Is Derek Jeter? 2015. (Who Is...? Ser.). lib. bdg. 16.00 *(978-0-606-37552-8(X))* Turtleback.

Herman, Gail & Who HQ. Who Is Derek Jeter? Thomson, Andrew, illus. 2015. (Who Was? Ser.). 112p. (J). (gr. 3-7). 6.99 *(978-0-448-48697-0(0),* Penguin Workshop) Penguin Young Readers Group.

Howell, Brian. New York Yankees, 1 vol. 2015. (Inside MLB Ser.). (ENG.). 48p. (J). (gr. 3-6). lib. bdg. 34.21 *(978-1-62403-478-7(0),* 17119, SportsZone) ABDO Publishing Co.

Karpovich, Todd. Derek Jeter & the New York Yankees. 2018. (Sports Dynasties Ser.). (ENG., 48p. (J). Illus.). (gr. 4-4). pap. 11.95 *(978-1-64185-281-4(X),* 164185281X); (gr. 3-6). lib. bdg. 34.21 *(978-1-5321-1432-8(X),* 29074) ABDO Publishing Co. (SportsZone).

Kelley, K. C. New York Yankees. 2016. (Illus.). 32p. (J). *(978-1-4896-5941-5(2),* AV2 by Weigl) Weigl Pubs., Inc.

Kelly, David A. Babe Ruth & the Baseball Curse (Totally True Adventures) How the Red Sox Curse Became a Legend ... Jessell, Tim, illus. 2009. (Totally True Adventures Ser.). (ENG.). 112p. (J). (gr. 2-5). 5.99 *(978-0-375-85603-7(X),* Random Hse. Bks. for Young Readers) Random Hse. Children's Bks.

Kennedy, Mike & Stewart, Mark. Meet the Yankees. 2010. (Smart about Sports Ser.). (Illus.). 24p. (J). (gr. k-3). lib. bdg. 22.60 *(978-1-59953-372-8(3),* 1309057) Norwood Hse. Pr.

Klein, Fredrick C. For the Love of the Yankees: An A-to-Z Primer for Yankees Fans of All Ages. Anderson, Mark, illus. 2003. 48p. (J). 19.95 *(978-1-57243-579-7(8))* Triumph Bks.

Lajiness, Katie. New York Yankees. 2018. (MLB's Greatest Teams Ser.). (ENG., Illus.). 32p. (J). (gr. 2-5). lib. bdg. 34.21 *(978-1-5321-1518-9(0),* 28872, Big Buddy Bks.) ABDO Publishing Co.

Levit, Joe. Babe Ruth: Super Slugger. 2020. (Epic Sports Bios (Lerner (tm) Sports) Ser.). (ENG., Illus.). 32p. (J). (gr. 2-5). 30.65 *(978-1-5415-9747-1(8),* 356f1bee-8a7f-4e68-a799-9c2fcf7f2802); pap. 9.99 *(978-1-7284-1339-6(7),* 828c0149-0390-4600-b23e-13a8557c31db) Lerner Publishing Group. (Lerner Pubns.).

MacRae, Sloan. The New York Yankees, 1 vol. 2009. (America's Greatest Teams Ser.). (ENG., Illus.). 24p. (J). (gr. 2-3). pap. 9.25 *(978-1-4358-3390-6(2),* 90a54e60-a5d2-47a0-9329-4a70c2738994); lib. bdg. 26.27 *(978-1-4042-8129-5(0),* 7061f3c9-1659-40d5-8d05-c57cdfc2ee68) Rosen Publishing Group, Inc., The. (PowerKids Pr.).

Marlin, John. Mickey Mantle. 2004. (Sports Heroes & Legends Ser.). (ENG., Illus.). 112p. (gr. 5-12). lib. bdg. 30.60 *(978-0-8225-1796-2(5))* Lerner Publishing Group.

Morey, Allan. Aaron Judge. 2019. (ENG.). 24p. (J). (gr. 1-3). pap. 10.99 *(978-1-68152-448-1(1),* 11034) Amicus.

O'Connell, Jack. Derek Jeter: The Yankee Kid. Rains, Rob, ed. 2003. (Super Star Ser.). 96p. (J). pap. 4.95 *(978-1-58261-043-6(6))* Sports Publishing, LLC.

Reis, Ronald A. Lou Gehrig. 2007. (ENG., Illus.). 130p. (gr. 7-12). lib. bdg. 30.00 *(978-0-7910-9423-5(5),* P126612, Facts On File) Infobase Holdings, Inc.

Rivera, Mariano. The Closer: Young Readers Edition. l.t. ed. 2014. (ENG.). 432p. (J). (gr. 3-7). 38.99 *(978-0-316-40962-9(6))* Little, Brown Bks. for Young Readers.

Sandler, Michael. Derek Jeter & the New York Yankees: 2000 World Series. 2008. (World Series Superstars). (Illus.). 24p. (J). (gr. 1-4). lib. bdg. 26.99 *(978-1-59716-641-6(3))* Bearport Publishing Co., Inc.

Shaughnessy, Dan. The Legend of the Curse of the Bambino. Payne, C. F., illus. 2005. (ENG.). 32p. (J). (gr. k-3). 16.95 *(978-0-689-87235-8(6),* Simon & Schuster/Paula Wiseman Bks.) Simon & Schuster/Paula Wiseman Bks.

Skinner, J. E. 2001 New York Yankees. 2018. (21st Century Skills Library: Sports Unite Us Ser.). (ENG., Illus.). 32p. (J). (gr. 3-6). lib. bdg. 32.07 *(978-1-5341-2963-4(4),* 211896) Cherry Lake Publishing.

Terrell, Brandon. Calling His Shot: Babe Ruth's Legendary Home Run. Garcia, Eduardo, illus. 2018. (Greatest Sports Moments Ser.). (ENG.). 32p. (J). (gr. 3-9). lib. bdg. 31.32 *(978-1-5435-2868-8(6),* 138371, Capstone Pr.) Capstone.

Tometich, Annabelle. Superstars of the New York Yankees. 2014. (Pro Sports Superstars Ser.). 24p. (J). 27.10 *(978-1-60753-594-2(7))* Amicus Learning.

Viola, Kevin. Lou Gehrig. (Sports Heroes & Legends Ser.). (J). 2005. (Illus.). 112p. (gr. 6-12). lib. bdg. 27.93 *(978-0-8225-1794-8(9))* 2004. pap. 9.95 *(978-0-8225-5311-3(2))* Lerner Publishing Group.

Weinstein, Howard. Mickey Mantle. 2009. (Baseball Hall of Famers Ser.). 112p. (gr. 5-8). 63.90 *(978-1-61511-513-6(7),* Rosen Reference) Rosen Publishing Group, Inc., The.

Wilner, Barry. Pinstripes & Pennants: The Ultimate New York Yankees Fan Guide. 2019. (Season Ticket: Teams Ser.). (ENG., Illus.). 112p. (J). (gr. 3-9). pap. 9.99 *(978-1-63494-059-7(8),* 1634940598) Pr. Room Editions LLC.

Winter, Jonah. You Never Heard of Casey Stengel?! Blitt, Barry, illus. 2016. 40p. (J). (gr. -1-3). 17.99 *(978-0-375-87013-2(X),* Schwartz & Wade Bks.) Random Hse. Children's Bks.

NEW ZEALAND

Beech, Terry. Design, Graphics & Visual Communication for New Zealand, Years 9 & 10. 2013. (ENG.). pap., stu. ed. *(978-1-107-61205-1(5))* Cambridge Univ. Pr.

Boom, Rosie. Where Lions Roar at Night. 2nd ed. 2013. (Illus.). 240p. *(978-1-921161-18-6(3))* Boom Tree Publishing.

Britton, Tamara L. New Zealand. 2004. (Countries Set 5 Ser.). 40p. (gr. k-6). 27.07 *(978-1-59197-294-5(9),* Checkerboard Library) ABDO Publishing Co.

Comire, S. Joshua & Porter, Malcolm. Atlas of Australia & the Pacific, 1 vol. 2010. (Atlases of the World Ser.). (ENG., Illus.). 48p. (YA). (gr. 5-5). 34.47 *(978-1-4358-8456-4(6),* 1671208c-0c67-4fc3-99fb-590f6130c402, Rosen Reference) Rosen Publishing Group, Inc., The.

DiPiazza, Francesca Davis. New Zealand in Pictures. 2nd ed. 2005. (Visual Geography Series, Second Ser.). (ENG., Illus.). 80p. (gr. 5-12). lib. bdg. 31.93 *(978-0-8225-2550-9(X))* Lerner Publishing Group.

Encyclopaedia Britannica, Inc. Staff, compiled by. My First Britannica: Asia, Australia, & New Zealand. 2008. (gr. 7-12). *(978-1-59339-407-3(1))* Encyclopaedia Britannica, Inc.

Frazel, Ellen. New Zealand. 2013. (Exploring Countries Ser.). (ENG., Illus.). 32p. (J). (gr. 3-7). lib. bdg. 27.95 *(978-1-60014-862-0(X))* Bellwether Media.

Grace, Patricia. Haka. 2015. (ENG., Illus.). 32p. pap. 18.00 *(978-1-77550-207-4(4),* 5701) Huia Pubs. NZL. Dist: Univ. of Hawaii Pr.

Hill, Bartha. Kiwi Adventures. rev. ed. 2007. (Adventure Ser.). (ENG., Illus.). 96p. (J). per. 8.99 *(978-1-84550-282-9(5),* 176d859b-368f-4c04-9cb3-6bf1432efe9c) Christian Focus Pubns. GBR. Dist: Baker & Taylor Publisher Services (BTPS).

Hill, Valerie. New Zealand. 2004. (Ask about Asia Ser.). (Illus.). 48p. (J). (gr. 4-18). lib. bdg. 19.95 *(978-1-59084-207-2(3))* Mason Crest.

Hirsch, Rebecca. New Zealand, 1 vol. 2013. (Countries of the World Set 2 Ser.). (ENG.). 144p. (YA). (gr. 6-12). lib. bdg. 42.79 *(978-1-61783-631-2(1),* 4886, Essential Library) ABDO Publishing Co.

Kopp, Megan. New Zealand. 2016. (Illus.). 32p. (J). *(978-1-4896-5421-2(6))* Weigl Pubs., Inc.

Krumenauer, Heidi. Lorde. 2015. (ENG., Illus.). 32p. (J). 26.50 *(978-1-62469-122-5(6))* Purple Toad Publishing, Inc.

Larson, Lyn. New Zealand. 2011. (Country Explorers Ser.). 48p. pap. 51.02 *(978-0-7613-7626-2(7));* (ENG., Illus.). (J). (gr. 2-4). pap. 9.99 *(978-0-7613-7083-3(8),* e1083bf2-54be-473f-b7db-cfd3f8c78da2) Lerner Publishing Group.

Lindop, Christine. Oxford Bookworms Factfiles: Australia & New Zealand: Level 3: 1000-Word Vocabulary. 3rd ed.

M N O

2008. (ENG., Illus.). 80p. 11.00 *(978-0-19-423390-3(1))* Oxford Univ. Pr., Inc.
Mara, Wil. Peter Jackson, 1 vol. 2014. (Great Filmmakers Ser.). (ENG., Illus.). 80p. (YA). (gr. 7-7). lib. bdg. 37.36 *(978-1-62712-942-8(1),* 22307fb1-f1e8-4fa0-9d66-ca9558e19a87) Cavendish Square Publishing LLC.
Meredith, Courtney Sina. The Adventures of Tupaia. Tait, Mat, illus. 2019. (ENG.). 64p. (J). (gr. 3-7). 22.99 *(978-1-988547-14-5(8))* Allen & Unwin AUS. Dist: Independent Pubs. Group.
Murray, Julie. New Zealand, 1 vol. 2014. (Explore the Countries Ser.). (ENG.). 40p. (J). (gr. 2-5). lib. bdg. 35.64 *(978-1-62403-344-5(X),* 1364, Big Buddy Bks.) ABDO Publishing Co.
O'Brien, Gregory. Back & Beyond: New Zealand in Painting for the Young & Curious. 2008. (ENG., Illus.). 104p. 24.95 *(978-1-86940-404-8(1))* Auckland Univ. Pr. NZL. Dist: Independent Pubs. Group.
Schroeder, Holly. New Zealand ABCs: A Book about the People & Places of New Zealand. Wolf, Claudia, illus. 2004. (Country ABCs Ser.). (ENG.). 32p. (J). (gr. k-5). 28.65 *(978-1-4048-0178-3(2),* 93250, Picture Window Bks.) Capstone.
Smelt, Roselynn. New Zealand, 1 vol. 2nd rev. ed. 2009. (Cultures of the World (Second Edition)(r) Ser.). (ENG.). 144p. (gr. 5-5). lib. bdg. 49.79 *(978-0-7614-3415-3(1),* 038c29eb-0a44-4d86-b3f3-9264fc2ebd88) Cavendish Square Publishing LLC.
Smelt, Roselynn, et al. New Zealand, 1 vol. 2018. (Cultures of the World (Third Edition)(r) Ser.). (ENG.). 144p. (gr. 5-5). lib. bdg. 48.79 *(978-1-5026-3628-7(X),* 92606fc8-0e9c-423e-8c2e-7b9d926af45c) Cavendish Square Publishing LLC.
Trussell-Cullen, Alan. Edmund Hillary. 2009. pap. 13.25 *(978-1-60559-058-5(4))* Hameray Publishing Group, Inc.
Weil, Ann. Meet Our New Student from New Zealand. 2008. (Meet Our New Student Ser.). (Illus.). 48p. (J). (gr. 2-5). lib. bdg. 29.95 *(978-1-58415-657-4(2))* Mitchell Lane Pubs.
World Book, Inc. Staff, contrib. by. Endangered Animals of Australia, New Zealand, & Pacific Islands. 2014. *(978-0-7166-5623-4(X))* World Bk., Inc.
Zappa, Marcia. Kakapos, 1 vol. 2015. (World's Weirdest Animals Ser.). (ENG., Illus.). 32p. (J). (gr. 2-5). 34.21 *(978-1-62403-776-4(3),* 17854, Big Buddy Bks.) ABDO Publishing Co.

NEW ZEALAND—FICTION

Beale, Fleur. Lyla: Through My Eyes - Natural Disaster Zones. White, Lyn, ed. 2018. (Through My Eyes Ser.). (ENG., Illus.). 208p. (J). (gr. 6-9). pap. 15.99 *(978-1-76011-378-0(6))* Allen & Unwin AUS. Dist: Independent Pubs. Group.
Bixley, Donovan. Double Cross. 2019. (Flying Furballs Ser.: 6). (Illus.). 112p. (J). (gr. 2-4). pap. 9.99 *(978-1-988516-17-2(X))* Upstart Pr. NZL. Dist: Independent Pubs. Group.
Boock, Paula. Dare Truth or Promise. 2009. (ENG.). 176p. (YA). (gr. 9). pap. 10.99 *(978-0-547-07617-1(7),* 1042007, Clarion Bks.) HarperCollins Pubs.
Brammer, Deb. Two Sides to Everything. 2003. (Illus.). 151p. (J). *(978-1-59166-166-5(8))* BJU Pr.
Bridges, Grace. Earthcore Book 1: Rotovegas. 2017. (ENG., Illus.). (J). pap. *(978-1-927154-50-2(2))* Splashdown Bks.
Brocker, Susan. Restless Spirit. 2007. (ENG.). 178p. *(978-1-86950-623-0(5))* HarperCollins Pubs. Australia.
Catran, Ken. Dawn Hawk. 96p. pap. *(978-0-7344-0468-8(9),* Lothian Children's Bks.) Hachette Australia.
Cowley, Joy. The Hungry Giant's Shoe Big Book. 2010. 48.25 *(978-1-60559-250-3(1))* Hameray Publishing Group, Inc.
—Meanies in the House Big Book. 2010. 48.25 *(978-1-60559-251-0(X))* Hameray Publishing Group, Inc.
—Mrs. WishyWashy & the Big Wash Big Book. 2010. 48.25 *(978-1-60559-247-3(1))* Hameray Publishing Group, Inc.
—Smarty Pants at the Circus Big Book. 2010. 48.25 *(978-1-60559-249-7(8))* Hameray Publishing Group, Inc.
—Song of the River. Andrews, Kimberly, illus. 2019. (ENG.). 32p. (J). (gr. k-2). 17.99 *(978-1-77657-253-3(X),* 79bc1618-5da9-4d6e-bc66-c53f1dc2c0a2) Gecko Pr. NZL. Dist: Lerner Publishing Group.
Dauphin, Vaya. The Greenstone Garden: The Elementals of Aotearoa, Vol. 2. 2013. viii, 297p. pap. *(978-1-74284-346-9(8))* ReadOnTime.
Dixon, Pamela. A Windy Day Walk. Horner, Maree, illus. 2016. (ENG.). 32p. (J). (gr. 1-4). *(978-0-473-34486-3(6))* Lizzy Web Bks.
Falkner, Brian. The Tomorrow Code. 2008. (ENG.). 368p. (J). (gr. 6-8). lib. bdg. 26.19 *(978-0-375-93923-5(7))* Random House Publishing Group.
—The Tomorrow Code. 2009. (ENG.). 372p. (YA). (gr. 7). pap. 9.99 *(978-0-375-84365-5(5),* Ember) Random Hse. Children's Bks.
Friedman, J. S. In the Beginning. Beatrice, Chris, illus. 2013. (Maurice's Valises Ser.: Vol. 1). (ENG.). 45p. (J). (gr. k-4). 16.95 *(978-94-91613-03-6(0))* Mouse Prints Pr. NLD. Dist: Ingram Publisher Services.
Gee, Maurice. The Fire Raiser. 2007. (ENG.). 176p. (J). (gr. 5-7). pap. 11.95 *(978-0-618-75041-2(X),* 486378, Clarion Bks.) HarperCollins Pubs.
Gibbs, Jephson. Rata & the Waka: A Tale from New Zealand. Williamson, Fraser, illus. 2016. 24p. (J). pap. 9.95 *(978-1-927244-55-5(2))* Flying Start Bks. NZL. Dist: Flying Start Bks.
—Rata & the Waka (Big Book Edition) A Tale from New Zealand. Williamson, Fraser, illus. 2016. 24p. (J). pap. *(978-1-927244-65-4(X))* Flying Start Bks.
Gregg, Stacy. The Thunderbolt Pony. 2018. (ENG.). 256p. (J). 6.99 *(978-0-00-825700-2(0),* HarperCollins Children's Bks.) HarperCollins Pubs. Ltd. GBR. Dist: HarperCollins Pubs.
Hall, Barbara. That is Choice! 2009. 192p. pap. *(978-1-84748-314-0(3))* Athena Pr.
Healey, Karen. The Shattering. 2013. (ENG.). 336p. (YA). (gr. 7-17). pap. 8.99 *(978-0-316-12573-4(3))* Little, Brown Bks. for Young Readers.
Ireland, Kenneth. Noises in the Night. 2004. 126p. (J). 5.00 *(978-1-84161-031-3(3))* Ravette Publishing, Ltd. GBR. Dist: Parkwest Pubns., Inc.
Knox, Elizabeth. Dreamquake. 2007. (Dreamhunter Duet Ser.: No. 2). (ENG.). 530p. *(978-0-7322-8194-6(6),* Fourth Estate) HarperCollins Pubs. Australia.
Lindop, Christine, retold by. Oxford Bookworms Library: the Long White Cloud: Stories from New Zealand: Level 3: 1000-Word Vocabulary. 3rd ed. 2008. (ENG., Illus.). 80p. 11.00 *(978-0-19-479139-7(4))* Oxford Univ. Pr., Inc.
Locke, Elsie. A Canoe in the Mist. 2005. (ENG.). 224p. *(978-1-86950-568-4(9))* HarperCollins Pubs. Australia.
MacAndrewRichard. The Black Pearls Starter/Beginner. 2008. (Cambridge English Readers Ser.). (ENG.). 32p. pap. 14.75 *(978-0-521-73289-5(1))* Cambridge Univ. Pr.
Mahy, Margaret. Great Piratical Rumbustification & the Librarian & the Robbers. Blake, Quentin, illus. 2013. (ENG.). 64p. (J). pap. 8.95 *(978-1-56792-169-4(8))* Godine, David R. Pub.
McConchie, Lyn. Autumn of the Wild Poney. 2012. (ENG.). 126p. (YA). pap. 12.00 *(978-1-936021-40-6(4),* Banana Oil Bks.) Cyberwizard Productions.
—Winter of Waiting. 2015. (YA). (gr. 5-18). pap. 15.00 *(978-1-936021-55-0(2),* Banana Oil Bks.) Cyberwizard Productions.
Millton, Jane. Moo & Moo & the Little Calf Too. Hinde, Deborah, illus. 2017. (ENG.). 32p. (J). (-3). pap. 14.99 *(978-1-877505-92-8(7))* Allen & Unwin AUS. Dist: Independent Pubs. Group.
Nooks, Nanny. Nina in the Forest of Faces. 2011. 46p. pap. 16.00 *(978-1-61204-606-8(1),* Strategic Bk. Publishing) Strategic Book Publishing & Rights Agency (SBPRA).
Owen, Sarah. The Enchanted Tales. 2009. 39p. pap. 26.50 *(978-1-4452-5948-2(6))* Lulu Pr., Inc.
Russell, Ann. Little Truff & the Siamese Cat. Morris, Adrienne, ed. 2nd ed. 2013. 144p. pap. *(978-0-473-26077-4(8))* AM Publishing New Zealand.
Summer of Dreaming. 2010. (Illus.). 157p. (YA). pap. *(978-1-936021-22-2(6),* Banana Oil Bks.) Cyberwizard Productions.
Sutcliffe, Kathy. When Romeo Kissed Mercutio. 2012. (ENG.). 242p. pap. *(978-1-922120-28-1(6),* IP Digital) Interactive Pubns. Pty, Ltd.
Thomas, Rosemary. The Kiwi Kingdom. 2010. 154p. pap. 18.00 *(978-1-4349-0857-5(7))* Dorrance Publishing Co., Inc.
Tipene, Tim. Māui: Sun Catcher. Ruha, Rob, tr. Waipara, Zak, illus. 2016. 32p. (J). 19.00 *(978-0-947506-14-8(4),* 13417, Oratia Bks.) Oratia Media NZL. Dist: Univ. of Hawaii Pr.
Tulloch, Scott. Willy's Mum. 2008. (Illus.). 32p. pap. *(978-1-86950-682-7(0))* HarperCollins Pubs. Australia.
Vaughn, Richard. Rowena & the Magic Hawk, the First Adventure. 2009. 224p. pap. 14.95 *(978-1-60860-157-8(9),* Eloquent Bks.) Strategic Book Publishing & Rights Agency (SBPRA).
Vyvyan, Taylor. A Dragon's Odyssey. 2012. 120p. pap. *(978-1-78281-021-6(8))* Athena Pr.
West, Ella. Rain Fall. 2020. (ENG.). 224p. (J). (gr. 6-9). pap. 14.99 *(978-1-76029-683-4(X),* A&U Children's) Allen & Unwin AUS. Dist: Independent Pubs. Group.
West, Joyce. The Drovers Road Collection: Three New Zealand Adventures, 3 vols. West, Joyce, illus. 2003. (Bethlehem Budget Bks). (ENG., Illus.). 448p. (J). (gr. 7-9). pap. 16.95 *(978-1-883937-69-0(3))* Ignatius Pr.

NEWBERY, JOHN, 1713-1767

Markel, Michelle. Balderdash! John Newbery & the Boisterous Birth of Children's Books (Nonfiction Books for Kids, Early Elementary History Books) Carpenter, Nancy, illus. 2017. (ENG.). 44p. (J). (gr. 1-3). 17.99 *(978-0-8118-7922-4(4))* Chronicle Bks. LLC.
Roberts, Russell. John Newbery & the Story of the Newbery Medal. 2003. (Great Achiever Awards Ser.). (Illus.). 48p. (J). (gr. 4-8). lib. bdg. 29.95 *(978-1-58415-201-9(X))* Mitchell Lane Pubs.

NEWBERY MEDAL BOOKS

Roberts, Russell. John Newbery & the Story of the Newbery Medal. 2003. (Great Achiever Awards Ser.). (Illus.). 48p. (J). (gr. 4-8). lib. bdg. 29.95 *(978-1-58415-201-9(X))* Mitchell Lane Pubs.

NEWFOUNDLAND

see Newfoundland and Labrador

NEWFOUNDLAND AND LABRADOR

Beckett, Harry. Newfoundland & Labrador. 2003. (Eye on Canada Ser.). (Illus.). 32p. (J). pap. 9.95 *(978-1-894705-03-5(3))* Weigl Pubs., Inc.
Keating, Nancy & Keating, Laurel. Find Scruncheon & Touton 2: All Around Newfoundland, 1 vol. 2012. (ENG., Illus.). 32p. (J). (gr. k-3). pap. *(978-1-897174-89-0(6))* Breakwater Bks., Ltd.
—Search for Scruncheon & Touton, 1 vol. 2012. (ENG., Illus.). 26p. (J). (gr. -1-3). *(978-1-897174-69-2(1))* Breakwater Bks., Ltd.
Miner Huey, Lois. American Archaeology Uncovers the Vikings, 1 vol. 2010. (American Archaeology Ser.). (ENG.). 64p. (gr. 5-5). 34.07 *(978-0-7614-4270-7(7),* 8037f8b4-0c8b-4e94-831a-85cc50743cb4) Cavendish Square Publishing LLC.
Skirving, Janet. P is for Puffin: A Newfoundland & Labrador Alphabet. Archibald, Odell, illus. rev. ed. 2006. (Discover Canada Province by Province Ser.). (ENG.). 40p. (J). (gr. 1-3). 17.95 *(978-1-58536-287-5(5),* 202098) Sleeping Bear Pr.

NEWFOUNDLAND AND LABRADOR—FICTION

Ballantyne, R. M. The Crew of the Water Wagtail. 2011. 146p. 24.95 *(978-1-4638-9596-9(8))* Rodgers, Alan Bks.
Chalker Browne, Susan. The Land of a Thousand Whales, 1 vol. Keating, Nancy, illus. 2007. (ENG.). 32p. (J). (gr. 3-7). pap. *(978-1-897174-08-1(X))* Breakwater Bks., Ltd.
Choyce, Lesley. Refuge Cove. 2004. (Orca Soundings Ser.). 89p. 19.95 *(978-0-7569-4325-7(6))* Perfection Learning Corp.
Cotter, Charis. The Ghost Road. 368p. (J). (gr. 4-7). 2019. (ENG.). pap. 9.99 *(978-0-7352-6325-3(6))* 2018. (Illus.). 16.99 *(978-1-101-91889-0(6))* Tundra Bks. CAN. (Tundra Bks.). Dist: Penguin Random Hse. LLC.
Davidge, Bud. The Mummer's Song, 1 vol. Wallace, Ian, illus. 2009. (ENG.). 32p. (J). (gr. k-k). pap. 16.95 *(978-0-88899-960-3(7))* Groundwood Bks. CAN. Dist: Publishers Group West (PGW).
Eubank, Patricia Reeder. Seaman's Journal. 2010. (ENG.). 40p. (J). (gr. -1-3). pap. 9.99 *(978-0-8249-5619-6(2),* Ideals Pubns.) Worthy Publishing.
Harlow, Joan Hiatt. Secret of the Night Ponies. 2009. (ENG.). 336p. (J). (gr. 3-7). 16.99 *(978-1-4169-0783-1(1))* Simon & Schuster, Inc.
—Thunder from the Sea. 2004. (ENG., Illus.). 208p. (J). (gr. 3-7). 17.99 *(978-0-689-86403-2(5),* McElderry, Margaret K. Bks.) McElderry, Margaret K. Bks.
Jacobs, Lily. The Littlest Bunny in Newfoundland. Dunn, Robert, illus. 2016. (Littlest Bunny Ser.). (ENG.). 32p. (J). (gr. -1-3). 9.99 *(978-1-4926-3352-5(6),* 9781492633525, Hometown World) Sourcebooks, Inc.
James, Eric. Santa's Sleigh Is on It's Way to Newfoundland: A Christmas Adventure. Dunn, Robert, illus. 2016. (Santa's Sleigh Is on Its Way Ser.). (ENG.). 32p. (J). (gr. k-2). 12.99 *(978-1-4926-4505-4(2),* 9781492645054, Hometown World) Sourcebooks, Inc.
—The Spooky Express Newfoundland. Piwowarski, Marcin, illus. 2017. (Spooky Express Ser.). (ENG.). 32p. (J). (gr. k-6). 9.99 *(978-1-4926-5384-4(5),* Hometown World) Sourcebooks, Inc.
Lane, Lori & Winsor, Kathy. Nana's Quilt: Stitched in St. John'S, Newfoundland & Labrador, 1 vol. Costello, Jim, illus. 2007. (ENG.). 32p. (J). (gr. -1-4). per. *(978-1-894294-82-9(3))* Breakwater Bks., Ltd.
—Poppy & Allie: Hooked on St. John's, Newfoundland, 1 vol. Costello, Jim, photos by. 2009. (ENG., Illus.). 32p. (J). (gr. 1-8). pap. *(978-1-897174-22-7(5))* Breakwater Bks., Ltd.
Mahoney, Jan. Moose Tales. 2010. 12p. 9.99 *(978-1-4520-6950-0(6))* AuthorHouse.
Malone, Beni & White, Marian Frances. The Sights Before Christmas, 1 vol. 2007. (ENG., Illus.). 32p. (J). (gr. -1-2). per. *(978-1-894294-94-2(7))* Breakwater Bks., Ltd.
McGrath, Robin. Livyers World. 2007. (ENG.). 150p. (J). (gr. 4-7). per. *(978-1-897174-15-9(2))* Breakwater Bks., Ltd.
McMurchy-Barber, Gina. A Bone to Pick: A Peggy Henderson Adventure. 2015. (Peggy Henderson Adventure Ser.: 4). (ENG.). 168p. (J). pap. 12.99 *(978-1-4597-3072-4(0))* Dundurn Pr. CAN. Dist: Publishers Group West (PGW).
Mowat, Farley. The Black Joke. 2009. (ENG.). 192p. pap. 9.95 *(978-0-7710-6469-2(1),* Emblem Editions) McClelland & Stewart CAN. Dist: Random Hse., Inc.
Pryse-Phillips, William. Free Flight. 2013. 24p. pap. *(978-1-4602-0671-3(1))* FriesenPress.
Simons, Alan L. The Incredible Adventures of Captain Cameron MacDuddyfunk in Cuggermuggerland. Boggelen-Heutink, Ellen van, illus. 2013. 98p. pap. *(978-0-9877503-8-9(0))* Baronel Bks.
Smallman, Steve. Santa is Coming to Newfoundland. Dunn, Robert, illus. 2nd ed. 2019. (Santa Is Coming... Ser.). (ENG.). 40p. (J). (gr. -1-3). 12.99 *(978-1-7282-0085-9(7),* Hometown World) Sourcebooks, Inc.
Smith, Heather. Baygirl, 1 vol. 2013. (ENG.). 288p. (YA). (gr. 8-12). pap. 12.95 *(978-1-4598-0274-2(8))* Orca Bk. Pubs. USA.
Sullivan-Fraser, Deannie. Johnny & the Gypsy Moth, 1 vol. Rose, Hilda, illus. 2009. (ENG.). 32p. (J). (gr. k-5). *(978-1-897174-40-1(3))* Breakwater Bks., Ltd.
Walsh, Alice. Buried Truth, 1 vol. 2013. (ENG.). 100p. (J). (gr. 4-8). pap. *(978-1-77103-009-0(7))* Breakwater Bks., Ltd.
—Heroes of Isle aux Morts. 2004. (J). (gr. k-3). spiral bd. *(978-0-616-11139-0(8));* spiral bd. *(978-0-616-11138-3(X))* Canadian National Institute for the Blind/Institut National Canadien pour les Aveugles.
—A Sky Black with Crows, 1 vol. 2006. (ENG.). 224p. (YA). (gr. 9-12). per. 9.95 *(978-0-88995-368-0(6),* ecf60828-ccee-4bec-a54f-875ea02f2f74) Red Deer Pr. CAN. Dist: Firefly Bks., Ltd.
Wells, Helen. Cherry Ames, Island Nurse. 2007. (Cherry Ames Nurse Stories Ser.). 200p. (J). (gr. 3-7). 14.95 *(978-0-8261-0423-6(1))* Springer Publishing Co., Inc.

NEWMAN, JOHN HENRY, 1801-1890

Schmid, Evan. Cardinal from Oxford: A Story of John Henry Newman. 2011. 142p. 40.95 *(978-1-258-06803-5(6))* Literary Licensing, LLC.

NEWS BROADCASTS

see Radio Broadcasting; Television Broadcasting

NEWS PHOTOGRAPHY

see Photojournalism

NEWSPAPER WORK

see Journalism; Reporters and Reporting

NEWSPAPERS

see also Periodicals; Reporters and Reporting

Emmer, Rae. School Newspaper. 2009. (School Activities Ser.). 24p. (gr. 1-1). 42.50 *(978-1-60852-999-5(1),* PowerKids Pr.) Rosen Publishing Group, Inc., The.
—School Newspaper: Periodico Escolar, 1 vol. 2003. (School Activities / Actividades Escolares Ser.). (SPA & ENG., Illus.). 24p. (J). (gr. 1-2). lib. bdg. 26.27 *(978-0-8239-6901-2(0),* b886277e-7281-44cf-b082-49dadaecc818) Rosen Publishing Group, Inc., The.
—School Newspaper / Periódico Escolar. 2009. (School Activities / Actividades escolares Ser.). (ENG & SPA.). 24p. (gr. 1-2). 42.50 *(978-1-60853-005-2(1),* Editorial Buenas Letras) Rosen Publishing Group, Inc., The.
Engdahl, Sylvia, ed. Free Press, 1 vol. 2011. (Teen Rights & Freedoms Ser.). (ENG., Illus.). 184p. (gr. 10-12). 43.63 *(978-0-7377-5827-6(9),* d9784d40-9b05-483a-92d1-105d1463f01e, Greenhaven Publishing) Greenhaven Publishing LLC.
Fandel, Jennifer. You Can Write a Terrific Opinion Piece, 1 vol. 2012. (You Can Write Ser.). (ENG., Illus.). 24p. (J). (gr. 1-3). pap. 7.29 *(978-1-4296-9316-5(9),* 120368, Capstone Pr.) Capstone.
—You Can Write a Terrific Opinion Piece. 2012. (You Can Write Ser.). (ENG.). 24p. (J). (gr. 1-2). pap. 43.74 *(978-1-4296-9317-2(7),* 18548, Capstone Pr.) Capstone.
Fromowitz, Lori. 12 Great Moments That Changed Newspaper History. 2015. (Great Moments in Media Ser.). (ENG., Illus.). 32p. (J). (gr. 3-6). 32.80 *(978-1-63235-025-1(4),* 11595); pap. 9.95 *(978-1-63235-085-5(8),* 11599) Bookstaves, LLC. (12-Story Library).
Gish, Melissa. A Newspaper Publisher. 2003. 24p. (J). lib. bdg. 21.35 *(978-1-58340-324-2(8))* Black Rabbit Bks.
Hamilton, John. Newspapers, 1 vol. 2005. (Straight to the Source Ser.). (ENG., Illus.). 32p. (gr. k-6). 27.07 *(978-1-59197-547-2(6),* Checkerboard Library) ABDO Publishing Co.
Hunt, Jilly. Beyond the Headlines! 2017. (Beyond the Headlines! Ser.). (ENG., Illus.). 48p. (J). (gr. 4-8). 143.96 *(978-1-4846-4160-6(4),* 27026, Heinemann) Capstone.
Levin, Mark. Kids in Print: Publishing A School Newspaper. 2nd ed. 2004. 80p. (J). (gr. 3-9). pap. 15.00 *(978-0-9676409-2-1(X))* Mind - Stretch.
Pascual Marquina, Cira. Newspapers: A Project by Siemon Allen. 2000th ed. 2004. (Illus.). 60p. per. 20.00 *(978-0-9749296-1-3(1))* Drake Univ., Anderson Gallery.
Pelleschi, Andrea. Olivia & Oscar Build an Opinion Piece. Hu, Caroline, illus. 2014. (Writing Builders Ser.). (ENG.). 32p. (J). (gr. 2-4). pap. 11.94 *(978-1-60357-556-0(1));* lib. bdg. 25.27 *(978-1-59953-582-1(3))* Norwood Hse. Pr.
Pelusey, Michael & Pelusey, Jane. Newspapers. 2005. (Media Ser.). (ENG., Illus.). 32p. (gr. 5-8). lib. bdg. 21.95 *(978-0-7910-8800-5(6),* P114421, Facts On File) Infobase Holdings, Inc.
Petley, Julian. Newspapers & Magazines. 2003. (Media Wise Ser.). (Illus.). 64p. (J). lib. bdg. 28.50 *(978-1-58340-258-0(6))* Black Rabbit Bks.
Whitelaw, Nancy. Joseph Pulitzer: And the New York World. 2004. (Makers of the Media Ser.). (Illus.). 112p. (YA). (gr. 6-12). 21.95 *(978-1-883846-44-2(7),* First Biographies) Reynolds, Morgan Inc.
—William Randolph Hearst & the American Century. rev. exp. ed. 2004. (Makers of the Media Ser.). (Illus.). 128p. (gr. 6-12). 28.95 *(978-1-931798-35-8(4))* Reynolds, Morgan Inc.

NEWSPAPERS—FICTION

Alger Jr. Horatio Staff. Herbert Carter's Legacy. rev. ed. 2006. 264p. 28.95 *(978-1-4218-1756-9(X));* pap. 13.95 *(978-1-4218-1856-6(6))* 1st World Publishing, Inc. (1st World Library - Literary Society).
Banks, Steven. Stop the Presses! DePorter, Vince, illus. 2005. 22p. (J). lib. bdg. 15.00 *(978-1-4242-0973-6(0))* Fitzgerald Bks.
Barrows, Annie. Ivy + Bean - No News Is Good News. Blackall, Sophie, illus. 2012. (Ivy & Bean Ser.: 8). (J). lib. bdg. 16.00 *(978-0-606-26950-6(9))* Turtleback.
—Ivy & Bean No News Is Good News (Book 8) Blackall, Sophie, illus. 2011. (Ivy & Bean Ser.: IVYB). (ENG.). 128p. (J). (gr. 1-5). 14.99 *(978-0-8118-6693-4(9))* Chronicle Bks. LLC.
—Ivy & Bean No News Is Good News (Book 8) (Best Friends Books for Kids, Elementary School Books, Early Chapter Books), Volume 8. Blackall, Sophie, illus. 2012. (Ivy & Bean Ser.). (ENG.). 144p. (J). (gr. 1-5). pap. 5.99 *(978-1-4521-0781-3(5))* Chronicle Bks. LLC.
Barrows, Annie & Blackall, Sophie. Ivy + Bean. 2011. (Ivy & Bean Ser.). (ENG., Illus.). 120p. (J). (gr. 2-5). 31.36 *(978-1-59961-928-6(8),* 10108, Chapter Bks.) Spotlight.
Breault, Christie Merriman. Logan West, Printer's Devil. Archambault, Matthew, illus. 2006. 142p. (J). pap. *(978-1-59336-762-6(7))* Mondo Publishing.
Butler, Dori Hillestad. The Truth about Truman School, 1 vol. 2009. (ENG.). 176p. (J). (gr. 3-7). pap. 8.99 *(978-0-8075-8096-7(1),* 807580961) Whitman, Albert & Co.
Clements, Andrew. Head of the Class (Boxed Set) Frindle; the Landry News; the Janitor's Boy. Selznick, Brian, illus. 2007. (ENG.). 416p. (J). (gr. 3-7). pap. 23.99 *(978-1-4169-4974-9(7),* Atheneum Bks. for Young Readers) Simon & Schuster Children's Publishing.
—El Periodico Landry. Selznick, Brian, illus. 2004.Tr. of Landry News. (SPA.). (YA). pap. 9.99 *(978-84-241-7886-4(6))* Everest Editora ESP. Dist: Lectorum Pubns., Inc.
Corbett, Sue. The Last Newspaper Boy in America. 2010. (ENG.). 176p. (J). (gr. 6-8). 21.19 *(978-0-525-42205-1(6))* Penguin Young Readers Group.
Devlin, Calla. Right Where You Left Me. 2017. (ENG., Illus.). 256p. (YA). (gr. 9). 17.99 *(978-1-4814-8699-6(3),* Atheneum Bks. for Young Readers) Simon & Schuster Children's Publishing.
El diario de mis Abejas: Individual Title, 6 packs. (Literatura 2000 Ser.). (SPA.). (gr. 2-3). 33.00 *(978-0-7635-1647-5(3))* Rigby Education.
Elmore, Barbara. Saviors of the Bugle. 2003. 208p. (YA). per. 6.99 *(978-0-9714941-0-7(X))* Mud Pie Pr.
English, Karen. Nikki & Deja: the Newsy News Newsletter: Nikki & Deja, Book Three, Bk. 3. Freeman, Laura, illus. 2011. (Nikki & Deja Ser.: 3). (ENG.). 96p. (J). (gr. 1-4). pap. 6.99 *(978-0-547-40626-8(6),* 1428504, Clarion Bks.) HarperCollins Pubs.
Fantaskey, Beth. Isabel Feeney, Star Reporter. 2017. (ENG.). (J). (gr. 5-7). lib. bdg. 18.40 *(978-0-606-39809-1(0))* Turtleback.
Frampton, David. Beastie ABC. Frampton, David, illus. Date not set. (Illus.). 32p. (J). (gr. -1-1). pap. 5.99 *(978-0-06-443653-3(5))* HarperCollins Pubs.
Goo, Maurene. Since You Asked... 2013. (YA). 262p. pap. *(978-0-545-44822-2(0));* (ENG.). 272p. (gr. 7). 17.99 *(978-0-545-44821-5(2))* Scholastic, Inc. (Scholastic Pr.).
Hoena, Blake A. Swamp Sting!, 1 vol. Facio, Sebastian, illus. 2011. (Graphic Sparks Ser.). (ENG.). 40p. (J). (gr. 2-4). pap. 5.95 *(978-1-4342-3065-2(1),* 114681, Stone Arch Bks.) Capstone.
Kerr, M. E., pseud. If I Love You, Am I Trapped Forever?, 0 vols. 2012. (ENG.). 192p. (YA). (gr. 7-12). pap. 9.99 *(978-0-7614-5839-5(5),* 9780761458395, Skyscape) Amazon Publishing.
Khan, Hena. More to the Story. 2019. (ENG., Illus.). 272p. (J). (gr. 3-7). 17.99 *(978-1-4814-9209-6(8),* Salaam Reads) Simon & Schuster Bks. For Young Readers.
Krensky, Stephen. The Great Moon Hoax. Bisaillon, Josée, illus. 2011. (Carolrhoda Picture Bks.). (ENG.). 32p. (J). (gr. 2-5). lib. bdg. 16.95 *(978-0-7613-5110-8(8))* Lerner Publishing Group.
Meddaugh, Susan. Martha Speaks: Martha's Nose for News (chapter Book) 2013. (Martha Speaks Ser.). (ENG., Illus.). 96p. (J). (gr. 1-4). 14.99 *(978-0-544-13567-3(9))* Houghton Mifflin Harcourt Publishing Co.
—Nose for News. 2013. (Martha Speaks Ser.). (ENG., Illus.). 96p. (J). (gr. 1-4). pap. 5.99 *(978-0-544-08572-5(8))* Houghton Mifflin Harcourt Publishing Co.
Mercer, Sienna. My Sister the Vampire #2: Fangtastic! 2007. (My Sister the Vampire Ser.: 2). (ENG.). 208p. (J). (gr. 3-7). per. 6.99 *(978-0-06-087115-4(6),* HarperCollins) HarperCollins Pubs.

Meyers, Dolores. Herbie's New Home. 2011. 20p. pap. 24.95 *(978-1-60749-665-6(8))* America Star Bks.

Nelson, Blake. The New Rules of High School. 2004. (ENG.). 240p. (YA). (gr. 7-18). reprint ed. 7.99 *(978-0-14-240242-9(7),* Speak) Penguin Young Readers Group.

Nixon, Joan Lowery. Maria's Story, 1773. 2004. (J). *(978-0-87935-227-1(2))* Colonial Williamsburg Foundation.

O'Connor, Jane. Fancy Nancy: Nancy Clancy, Late-Breaking News! Glasser, Robin Preiss, illus. 2018. (Nancy Clancy Ser.: 8). (ENG.). 144p. (J). (gr. 1-5). pap. 5.99 *(978-0-06-226972-0(0),* HarperCollins) HarperCollins Pubs.

Pounder, Sibéal. Bad Mermaids Make Waves. Cockcroft, Jason, illus. 2018. (Bad Mermaids Ser.). (ENG.). 256p. (J). 13.99 *(978-1-68119-792-0(8),* 900187211, Bloomsbury Children's Bks.) Bloomsbury Publishing USA.

Reynolds Naylor, Phyllis. Boys Rock! 2007. (Boy/Girl Battle Ser.: 11). (ENG.). 144p. (J). (gr. 3-7). 5.99 *(978-0-440-41990-7(5),* Yearling) Random Hse. Children's Bks.

Robinson, A. M. Vampire Crush. 2010. (ENG.). 416p. (YA). (gr. 8-18). pap. 8.99 *(978-0-06-198971-1(1),* HarperTeen) HarperCollins Pubs.

Stewart, Paul. Far-Flung Adventures: Hugo Pepper. 2012. (Far-Flung Adventures Ser.). (ENG.). 272p. (J). (gr. 3-7). 7.99 *(978-0-385-75223-7(7),* Yearling) Random Hse. Children's Bks.

Stilton, Gerónimo. The Stone of Fire. 2013. (Geronimo Stilton Cavemice Ser.: 1). lib. bdg. 18.40 *(978-0-606-31526-5(8))* Turtleback.

Stilton, Geronimo. The Stone of Fire (Geronimo Stilton Cavemice #1) 2004. (Geronimo Stilton Ser.: 1). (ENG.). 128p. (J). (gr. 2-5). E-Book 7.99 *(978-0-545-52048-5(7),* Scholastic Paperbacks) Scholastic, Inc.

Stilton, Thea. A Fashionable Mystery (Thea Stilton Mouseford Academy #8) Stilton, Thea, illus. 2019. (Thea Stilton Mouseford Academy Ser.: 8). (ENG., Illus.). 128p. (J). (gr. 2-5). pap. 7.99 *(978-0-545-87096-2(8),* Scholastic Paperbacks) Scholastic, Inc.

Whittemore, Jo. Brooke's Bad Luck, 5. 2017. (Confidentially Yours Ser.). (ENG.). 288p. (J). (gr. 4-7). 21.19 *(978-1-5364-0247-6(8))* HarperCollins Pubs.

Winerip, Michael. Adam Canfield of the Slash. (Adam Canfield of the Slash Ser.: 1). (ENG., Illus.). 336p. (J). (gr. 3-7). 2007. per. 8.99 *(978-0-7636-2794-2(1))* 2005. 15.99 *(978-0-7636-2340-1(7))* Candlewick Pr.

—Adam Canfield: the Last Reporter. 2010. (Adam Canfield of the Slash Ser.: 3). (ENG., Illus.). 384p. (J). (gr. 3-7). 7.99 *(978-0-7636-4838-1(8))* Candlewick Pr.

—Adam Canfield, Watch Your Back! 2009. (Adam Canfield of the Slash Ser.: 2). (ENG., Illus.). 352p. (J). (gr. 3-7). 8.99 *(978-0-7636-4412-3(9))* Candlewick Pr.

Wise, Rachel. Black & White & Gray All Over, 7. 2013. (Dear Know-It-All Ser.: 7). (ENG.). 160p. (J). (gr. 3-7). 15.99 *(978-1-4424-7517-5(X),* Simon Spotlight) Simon & Schuster Children's Publishing.

—Black & White & Gray All Over. 2013. (Dear Know-It-All Ser.: 7). (ENG., Illus.). 160p. (J). (gr. 3-7). pap. 5.99 *(978-1-4424-7515-1(3),* Simon Spotlight) Simon Spotlight.

—Digital Disaster!, 6. 2013. (Dear Know-It-All Ser.: 6). (ENG.). 160p. (J). (gr. 3-7). 15.99 *(978-1-4424-7218-1(9),* Simon Spotlight) Simon & Schuster Children's Publishing.

—Digital Disaster! 2013. (Dear Know-It-All Ser.: 6). (ENG.). 160p. (J). (gr. 3-7). pap. 6.99 *(978-1-4424-7217-4(0),* Simon Spotlight) Simon Spotlight.

—Stop the Presses! 2014. (Dear Know-It-All Ser.: 12). (ENG., Illus.). 160p. (J). (gr. 3-7). pap. 5.99 *(978-1-4424-9797-9(1),* Simon Spotlight) Simon Spotlight.

Yeh, Kat. The Way to Bea. 2018. (ENG.). 368p. (J). (gr. 3-7). pap. 7.99 *(978-0-316-23669-0(1))* Little, Brown Bks. for Young Readers.

NEWTON, ISAAC, SIR, 1642-1727

Anderson, Margaret J. Isaac Newton: Greatest Genius of Science, 1 vol. 2014. (Genius Scientists & Their Genius Ideas Ser.). (ENG.). 96p. (gr. 5-5). (J). 29.60 *(978-0-7660-6570-3(7),* c024e73b-77b0-49dd-8539-2348f721f97e); pap. 13.88 *(978-0-7660-6571-0(5),* f7079f7b-165a-4d7b-8a01-007b93f6769d) Enslow Publishing, LLC.

Benchmark Education Company. Newton & His Laws (Teacher Guide) 2005. *(978-1-4108-4670-9(9))* Benchmark Education Co.

Bortz, Fred. Laws of Motion & Isaac Newton, 1 vol. 2013. (Revolutionary Discoveries of Scientific Pioneers Ser.). (ENG., Illus.). 80p. (J). (gr. 6-6). 38.41 *(978-1-4777-1808-7(7),* 874ae16c-2d37-4d79-a8df-bb2a415e1f52) Rosen Publishing Group, Inc., The.

Brannon, Barbara. Discover Sir Isaac Newton. 2005. (J). pap. *(978-1-4108-5127-7(3))* Benchmark Education Co.

Chiang, Mona. Isaac Newton & His Laws of Motion: Set Of 6. 2011. (Navigators Ser.). (J). pap. 50.00 net. *(978-1-4108-5089-8(7))* Benchmark Education Co.

—Isaac Newton & His Laws of Motion: Text Pairs. 2008. (Bridges/Navigators Ser.). (J). (gr. 6). 94.00 *(978-1-4108-8442-8(2))* Benchmark Education Co.

Dolz, Jordi Bayarri. Isaac Newton & the Laws of Motion. Dolz, Jordi Bayarri, illus. 2020. (Graphic Science Biographies Ser.). (ENG., Illus.). 40p. (J). (gr. 5-8). 30.65 *(978-1-5415-7824-1(4),* f4e739d4-966f-428f-b673-126f76a0245c, Graphic Universe™) Lerner Publishing Group.

Ferrie, Chris. Newtonian Physics for Babies. 2017. (Baby University Ser.: 0). (Illus.). 24p. (J). (gr. -1-k). bds. 9.99 *(978-1-4926-5620-3(8))* Sourcebooks, Inc.

Funk, Tara. Newton & His Laws. 2005. (J). pap. *(978-1-4108-4622-8(9))* Benchmark Education Co.

Gianopoulos, Andrea & Barnett, Charles, III. Isaac Newton & the Laws of Motion, 1 vol. Miller, Phil, illus. 2007. (Inventions & Discovery Ser.). (ENG.). 32p. (J). (gr. 3-9). pap. 8.10 *(978-0-7368-7899-9(8),* 93895, Capstone Pr.) Capstone.

Graham, Ian. You Wouldn't Want to Be Sir Isaac Newton! A Lonely Life You'd Rather Not Lead. 2013. (You Wouldn't Want To Ser.). lib. bdg. 20.80 *(978-0-606-31632-3(9))* Turtleback.

Hollihan, Kerrie Logan. Isaac Newton & Physics for Kids: His Life & Ideas with 21 Activities. 2009. (For Kids Ser.: 30). (Illus.). 144p. (J). (gr. 4-7). pap. 20.99 *(978-1-55652-778-4(0))* Chicago Review Pr., Inc.

Isaac Newton: Organizing the Universe. 2004. (Great Scientists Ser.). (Illus.). 144p. (YA). (gr. 6-12). 26.95 *(978-1-931798-01-3(X))* Reynolds, Morgan Inc.

Kramer, Alan & Kramer, Candice. Isaac Newton: The World in Motion. 2005. (J). pap. *(978-1-4108-4222-0(3))* Benchmark Education Co.

Krull, Kathleen. Isaac Newton. Kulikov, Boris, illus. 2008. (Giants of Science Ser.). 128p. (J). (gr. 3-7). 7.99 *(978-0-14-240820-9(4),* Puffin Books) Penguin Young Readers Group.

Lasky, Kathryn. Newton's Rainbow: The Revolutionary Discoveries of a Young Scientist. Hawkes, Kevin, illus. 2017. (ENG.). 48p. (J). 17.99 *(978-0-374-35513-5(4),* 900074251, Farrar, Straus & Giroux (BYR)) Farrar, Straus & Giroux.

Lin, Yoming S. Isaac Newton & Gravity, 1 vol. 2011. (Eureka! Ser.). (ENG., Illus.). 24p. (YA). (gr. 2-3). lib. bdg. 26.27 *(978-1-4488-5032-7(0),* 045846db-34e4-4764-b472-196b83ca9a9e) Rosen Publishing Group, Inc., The.

Losure, Mary. Isaac the Alchemist: Secrets of Isaac Newton, Reveal'd. 2018. (ENG.). 176p. (J). (gr. 5). pap. 12.99 *(978-1-5362-0363-9(7))* Candlewick Pr.

McNeil, Niki, et al. HOCPP 1059 Isaac Newton. 2006. spiral bd. 18.50 *(978-1-60308-059-0(7))* In the Hands of a Child.

Meyer, Susan. Isaac Newton, 1 vol. 2017. (Leaders of the Scientific Revolution Ser.). (ENG., Illus.). 112p. (J). (gr. 8-8). 38.80 *(978-1-5081-7470-7(9),* 66a1cb61-49f7-483d-9294-4756e72496bc, Rosen Young Adult) Rosen Publishing Group, Inc., The.

National Geographic Learning. Reading Expeditions (Science: Physical Science): Newton's Laws. 2007. (ENG., Illus.). 32p. (J). pap. 18.95 *(978-0-7922-4584-1(9))* CENGAGE Learning.

Nittany, Paul M. Isaac Newton, Vol. 11. 2018. (Scientists & Their Discoveries Ser.). (Illus.). 96p. (J). (gr. 7). lib. bdg. 34.60 *(978-1-4222-4031-1(2))* Mason Crest.

Novelli, Luca. Newton & the Antigravity Formula. 2017. (Flashes of Genius Ser.). (ENG., Illus.). 112p. (J). (gr. 2). pap. 9.99 *(978-1-61373-861-0(7))* Chicago Review Pr., Inc.

O'Donnell, Kerri. Sir Isaac Newton: Using the Laws of Motion to Solve Problems, 1 vol. (Math for the REAL World Ser.). 32p. (gr. 5-5). 2009. (ENG., Illus.). pap. 10.00 *(978-1-4042-6079-5(X),* ce33957a-c41c-4955-bcc4-d67057e0f665) 2009. 47.90 *(978-1-60851-366-6(1),* PowerKids Pr.) 2006. (ENG., Illus.). (YA). lib. bdg. 28.93 *(978-1-4042-3363-8(6),* f0654ff1-b3f5-49ff-b288-9b7bdf626c27) Rosen Publishing Group, Inc., The.

O'Leary, Denyse. What Are Newton's Laws of Motion? 2010. (Shaping Modern Science Ser.). (ENG.). 64p. (J). (gr. 5-8). pap. *(978-0-7787-7207-1(1));* (Illus.). (gr. 6-6). lib. bdg. *(978-0-7787-7200-2(4))* Crabtree Publishing Co.

Pascal, Janet. Who Was Isaac Newton? 2014. (Who Was... ? Ser.). (Illus.). 104p. (J). lib. bdg. 16.00 *(978-0-606-36174-3(X))* Turtleback.

Pascal, Janet B. Who Was Isaac Newton? 2019. (Who HQ Ser.). (ENG., Illus.). 112p. (J). (gr. 2-4). 16.36 *(978-1-64310-815-5(8))* Penworthy Co., LLC, The.

Pascal, Janet B. & Who HQ. Who Was Isaac Newton? Foley, Tim, illus. 2014. (Who Was? Ser.). 112p. (J). (gr. 3-7). pap. 5.99 *(978-0-448-47913-2(3),* Penguin Workshop) Penguin Young Readers Group.

Petersen, Kristen. Understanding the Laws of Motion. 2015. (J). lib. bdg. *(978-1-62713-427-9(1))* Cavendish Square Publishing LLC.

Royston, Angela. Sir Isaac Newton: Overlord of Gravity, 1 vol. 2015. (Superheroes of Science Ser.). (ENG., Illus.). 48p. (J). (gr. 6-6). pap. 15.05 *(978-1-4824-3153-7(X),* 94ec08bd-56b2-4aeb-8ee9-a40af70d4c7a) Stevens, Gareth Publishing LLLP.

Sullivan, Anne Marie. Sir Isaac Newton: Famous English Scientist. (Illus.). 32p. (J). 2013. (People of Importance Ser.: 21). (gr. 4-18). 19.95 *(978-1-4222-2856-2(8))* 2004. (Great Names Ser.). (gr. 3-18). lib. bdg. 19.95 *(978-1-59084-139-6(5))* Mason Crest.

Tolish, Alexander. Gravity Explained, 1 vol. 2018. (Mysteries of Space Ser.). (ENG.). 80p. (gr. 7-7). 38.93 *(978-0-7660-9950-0(4),* 6f687c8e-4426-49a7-88d1-24013624ca22) Enslow Publishing, LLC.

Weir, Jane. Isaac Newton & the Laws of the Universe, 1 vol. rev. ed. 2007. (Science: Informational Text Ser.). (ENG.). 32p. (gr. 3-6). pap. 12.99 *(978-0-7439-0574-9(1))* Teacher Created Materials, Inc.

NEWTS

Goldish, Meish. Little Newts. 2010. (Amphibiana Ser.). (Illus.). 24p. (YA). (gr. k-3). lib. bdg. 26.99 *(978-1-936087-38-9(3))* Bearport Publishing Co., Inc.

Hansen, Grace. Becoming a Newt. 2018. (Changing Animals Ser.). (ENG., Illus.). 24p. (J). (gr. -1-2). lib. bdg. 32.79 *(978-1-5321-0818-1(4),* 28197, Abdo Kids) ABDO Publishing Co.

NIAGARA FALLS (N.Y. AND ONT.)

Bauer, Marion Dane. Niagara Falls: Ready-To-Read Level 1. Wallace, John, illus. (Wonders of America Ser.). (ENG.). 32p. (J). (gr. -1-1). 2019. 17.99 *(978-1-5344-4540-6(4))* 2006. pap. 4.99 *(978-0-689-86944-0(4))* Simon Spotlight. (Simon Spotlight).

Bolt Simons, Lisa M. Niagara Falls. 2018. (Natural Wonders of the World Ser.). (ENG., Illus.). 32p. (J). (gr. 3-5). pap. 9.95 *(978-1-63517-588-2(7),* 1635175887); lib. bdg. 31.35 *(978-1-63517-516-5(X),* 163517516X) North Star Editions. (Focus Readers).

Bowman, Donna Janell. King of the Tightrope: When the Great Blondin Ruled Niagara, 1 vol. Gustavson, Adam, illus. 2019. 48p. (J). (gr. 1-4). 17.95 *(978-1-56145-937-7(2))* Peachtree Publishing Co. Inc.

Butcher, Timothy. ABACA Flows over Niagara Falls: An Illustrated History. 2006. (Illus.). 48p. (J). lib. bdg. 16.95 *(978-0-9786473-0-8(0))* Amoeba Bks.

Marsh, Carole. The Wild Water Mystery of Niagra Falls. 2009. (Real Kids, Real Places Ser.). (J). (gr. 2-9). lib. bdg. 18.99 *(978-0-635-06831-6(1))* Gallopade International.

Sisk, Siobhan. Would You Dare Walk Across Niagara Falls?, 1 vol. 2016. (Would You Dare?. Ser.). (ENG.). 32p. (J). (gr. 1-2). pap. 11.50 *(978-1-4824-5830-5(6),* 3f0a6757-b152-4d89-8e75-92b7abbd6315); lib. bdg. 28.27 *(978-1-4824-5832-9(2),* 3aec7f27-5555-4a99-8e1f-3c0d0ca058ca) Stevens, Gareth Publishing LLLP.

Stine, Megan. Where Is Niagara Falls? 2015. (Where Is... ? Ser.). lib. bdg. 16.00 *(978-0-606-37548-1(1))* Turtleback.

Stine, Megan & Who HQ. Where Is Niagara Falls? Foley, Tim, illus. 2015. (Where Is? Ser.). 112p. (J). (gr. 3-7). 5.99 *(978-0-448-48425-9(0),* Penguin Workshop) Penguin Young Readers Group.

Tokunaga, Wendy. Niagara Falls. 2003. (Illus.). 48p. (J). 26.20 *(978-0-7377-2056-3(5),* Greenhaven Pr., Inc.) Cengage Gale.

Van Allsburg, Chris. Queen of the Falls. Van Allsburg, Chris, illus. 2011. (ENG., Illus.). 40p. (J). (gr. 1-4). 18.99 *(978-0-547-31581-2(3),* 1415337, Clarion Bks.) HarperCollins Pubs.

NICARAGUA

Kallen, Stuart A. The Aftermath of the Sandinista Revolution. 2009. (Aftermath of History Ser.). 160p. (YA). (gr. 7-12). 38.60 *(978-0-8225-9091-0(3))* Twenty First Century Bks.

Klepeis, Alicia Z. Nicaragua, 1 vol. 2020. (Exploring World Cultures (First Edition) Ser.). (ENG.). 32p. (J). (gr. 3-3). pap. 12.16 *(978-1-5026-5685-8(X),* 845768c5-333f-41c0-b6d8-adbb6b340d02) Cavendish Square Publishing LLC.

Kott, Jennifer & Streiffert, Kristi. Nicaragua, 1 vol. 2nd rev. ed. 2007. (Cultures of the World (Second Edition)(r) Ser.). (ENG., Illus.). 144p. (gr. 5-5). lib. bdg. 49.79 *(978-0-7614-1969-3(1),* 973c827e-6a5a-4f9f-a339-95137c9e887f) Cavendish Square Publishing LLC.

Mundera, Kristina. A Day in Pueblo Nuevo. 2012. 40p. pap. 9.75 *(978-1-937314-36-1(7))* ABREN (A Bk. to Read Empowers Nicaraguans).

Owings, Lisa. Nicaragua. 2014. (Exploring Countries Ser.). (ENG., Illus.). 32p. (J). (gr. 3-7). lib. bdg. 27.95 *(978-1-60014-985-6(5),* Blastoff! Readers) Bellwether Media.

Peason, Sweetie. Nicaragua. 2018. (Countries We Come From Ser.). (ENG., Illus.). 32p. (J). (gr. k-3). 19.95 *(978-1-68402-686-9(5))* Bearport Publishing Co., Inc.

Shields, Charles J. Nicaragua. 2010. (Central America Today Ser.). 63p. (YA). (gr. 7-18). pap. 9.95 *(978-1-4222-0717-8(X));* (Illus.). (gr. 9-12). 21.95 *(978-1-4222-0650-8(5))* Mason Crest.

—Nicaragua, Vol. 8. Henderson, James D., ed. 2015. (Discovering Central America: History, Politics, & Culture Ser.). (Illus.). 64p. (J). (gr. 7). lib. bdg. 22.95 *(978-1-4222-3291-0(3))* Mason Crest.

Torres, John Albert. Meet Our New Student from Nicaragua. 2009. (Meet Our New Student Ser.). 48p. (J). (gr. 2-5). 29.95 *(978-1-58415-834-9(4))* Mitchell Lane Pubs.

NICHOLAS, SAINT, BISHOP OF MYRA

Collins, Janet Ann. Secret Service Saint. Ruble, Eugene, illus. 2009. 16p. pap. 9.95 *(978-1-935137-98-6(0))* Guardian Angel Publishing, Inc.

Demi. The Legend of Saint Nicholas. 2003. (ENG., Illus.). 40p. (J). (gr. k-5). 21.99 *(978-0-689-84681-6(9),* McElderry, Margaret K. Bks.) McElderry, Margaret K. Bks.

Forest, Jim. Saint Nicholas & the Nine Gold Coins. Andrejev, Vladislav, illus. 2015. (J). *(978-0-88141-511-7(1))* St. Vladimir's Seminary Pr.

Grun, Anselm. The Legend of Saint Nicholas. Ferri, Giuliano, illus. 2014. (ENG.). 26p. (J). 16.00 *(978-0-8028-5434-6(6),* Eerdmans Bks For Young Readers) Eerdmans, William B. Publishing Co.

Stiegemeyer, Julie. Saint Nicholas: The Real Story of the Christmas Legend. Ellison, Chris, illus. (J). 2005. 16p. (gr. -1-17). bds. 7.49 *(978-0-7586-0688-4(5))* 2003. 32p. 13.49 *(978-0-7586-0376-0(2))* Concordia Publishing Hse.

NICHOLAS, SAINT, BISHOP OF MYRA—FICTION

Mackall, Dandi Daley. The Legend of St. Nicholas: A Story of Christmas Giving, 1 vol. Cowdrey, Richard, illus. 2014. (ENG.). 32p. (J). 16.99 *(978-0-310-73115-3(1))* Zonderkidz.

Stiegemeyer, Julie. Saint Nicholas: The Real Story of the Christmas Legend. Ellison, Chris, illus. 2007. 32p. (J). (gr. -1). per. 7.49 *(978-0-7586-1341-7(5))* Concordia Publishing Hse.

NICHOLAS II, EMPEROR OF RUSSIA, 1868-1918

Fleming, Candace. The Family Romanov: Murder, Rebellion, & the Fall of Imperial Russia. 2014. (ENG., Illus.). 304p. (YA). (gr. 7). 19.99 *(978-0-375-86782-8(1),* Schwartz & Wade Bks.) Random Hse. Children's Bks.

NICKLAUS, JACK, 1940-

Glave, Tom. Tiger Woods vs. Jack Nicklaus. 2017. (Versus Ser.). (ENG., Illus.). 32p. (J). (gr. 3-6). lib. bdg. 32.79 *(978-1-5321-1359-8(5),* 27657, SportsZone) ABDO Publishing Co.

NIGER RIVER

Behnke, Alison. Niger in Pictures. 2008. (Visual Geography (Lerner) Ser.). (Illus.). 80p. (YA). (gr. 7-12). lib. bdg. 31.93 *(978-0-8225-7147-6(1))* Twenty First Century Bks.

Seffal, Rabah & Spilling, Jo-Ann. Niger, 1 vol. 2nd rev. ed. 2011. (Cultures of the World (Second Edition)(r) Ser.). (ENG.). 144p. (gr. 5-5). 49.79 *(978-1-60870-026-4(7),* 48e7f69a-1903-4d0b-af6e-c4824e710684) Cavendish Square Publishing LLC.

NIGERIA

Barber, Nicola & Brownlie Bojang, Ali. Focus on Nigeria, 1 vol. 2005. (World in Focus Ser.). (ENG., Illus.). 64p. (gr. 5-8). pap. 15.05 *(978-0-8368-6239-3(2),* 424ed6e6-0f5b-4739-ab46-2e3d344cca3f); lib. bdg. 36.67 *(978-0-8368-6230-1(1),* f9a22221-9a42-4548-a5e6-dd85a7a67614) Stevens, Gareth Publishing LLLP. (Gareth Stevens Secondary Library).

Brownlie Bojang, Ali. Discover Nigeria, 1 vol. 2011. (Discover Countries Ser.). (ENG., Illus.). 32p. (YA). (gr. 4-4). lib. bdg. 30.27 *(978-1-4488-5270-3(6),* b35ac17d-6759-4ef7-816b-2024a6999396) Rosen Publishing Group, Inc., The.

Cantor, Rachel Anne. Nigeria. 2018. (Countries We Come From Ser.). (ENG.). 32p. (J). (gr. k-3). 19.95 *(978-1-68402-469-8(2))* Bearport Publishing Co., Inc.

Gibson, Karen. We Visit Nigeria. 2012. (J). lib. bdg. 33.95 *(978-1-61228-309-8(8))* Mitchell Lane Pubs.

Graham, Ian. Nigeria. 2004. (Country File Ser.). (J). lib. bdg. 27.10 *(978-1-58340-498-0(8))* Black Rabbit Bks.

Hamilton, Janice. Nigeria in Pictures. 2nd ed. 2003. (Visual Geography Series, Second Ser.). (ENG., Illus.). 80p. (gr. 5-12). 31.93 *(978-0-8225-0373-6(5))* Lerner Publishing Group.

Heinrichs, Ann. Nigeria. 2009. (Enchantment of the World Ser.). (ENG.). 144p. (J). (gr. 5-9). 40.00 *(978-0-531-20653-9(X))* Scholastic Library Publishing.

Jay, Ruth Johnson. Mary Slessor: Missionary to Calabar. 2006. (Illus.). 143p. (J). *(978-1-56265-077-3(7))* Accelerated Christian Education, Inc.

Levy, Patricia. Nigeria, 1 vol. 2nd rev. ed. 2004. (Cultures of the World (Second Edition)(r) Ser.). (ENG., Illus.). 144p. (gr. 5-5). lib. bdg. 49.79 *(978-0-7614-1703-3(6),* 1ccf5db5-e4f7-4ae3-b91b-0dafa4385f80) Cavendish Square Publishing LLC.

Murphy, Patricia J. Nigeria, 1 vol. 2006. (Discovering Cultures Ser.). (ENG.). 48p. (gr. 3-4). 31.21 *(978-0-7614-1795-8(8),* 89f943e3-66b8-461c-9a95-c2b0d7f1ce69) Cavendish Square Publishing LLC.

Ogunnaike, Anna M. Meet Our New Student from Nigeria. 2008. (Meet Our New Student Ser.). (Illus.). 47p. (YA). (gr. 2-5). lib. bdg. 29.95 *(978-1-58415-655-0(4))* Mitchell Lane Pubs.

Oluonye, Mary. Nigeria. 2008. pap. 40.95 *(978-0-8225-9306-5(8))* Lerner Publishing Group.

Oluonye, Mary N. Nigeria. 2007. (Country Explorers Ser.). (Illus.). 48p. (J). (gr. 4-8). lib. bdg. 27.93 *(978-0-8225-7131-5(5),* Lerner Pubns.) Lerner Publishing Group.

Orr, Tamra. Nigeria. 2006. (A to Z Ser.). (ENG., Illus.). 40p. (J). (gr. 2-4). pap. 6.95 *(978-0-516-24954-4(1),* Children's Pr.) Scholastic Library Publishing.

Powell, Jillian. Looking at Nigeria, 1 vol. 2007. (Looking at Countries Ser.). (ENG., Illus.). 32p. (gr. 2-4). pap. 11.50 *(978-0-8368-7678-9(4),* 7b77c911-8f12-4fd4-afe8-2db0a26c791d); lib. bdg. 28.67 *(978-0-8368-7671-0(7),* 1e10282c-2be5-42bb-9896-062c9e4d8ed8) Stevens, Gareth Publishing LLLP. (Gareth Stevens Learning Library).

Rau, Dana Meachen. It's Cool to Learn about Countries: Nigeria. 2010. (Explorer Library: Social Studies Explorer Ser.). (ENG., Illus.). 48p. (gr. 4-8). lib. bdg. 34.93 *(978-1-60279-830-4(3),* 200526) Cherry Lake Publishing.

Rodger, Ellen. A Refugee's Journey from Nigeria. 2018. (Leaving My Homeland Ser.). (Illus.). 32p. (J). (gr. 4-4). *(978-0-7787-4688-1(7))* Crabtree Publishing Co.

Walker, Ida. Nigeria. Rotberg, Robert I., ed. 2012. (Evolution of Africa's Major Nations Ser.). (Illus.). 80p. (J). (gr. 7). 22.95 *(978-1-4222-2200-3(4))* Mason Crest.

—Nigeria. 2011. (J). pap. *(978-1-4222-2228-7(4))* Mason Crest.

Zocchi, Judy. In Nigeria. Brodie, Neale, illus. 2005. (Global Adventures II Ser.). 32p. (J). per. 10.95 *(978-1-59646-144-4(6))* Dingles & Co.

—In Nigeria/en Nigeria. Brodie, Neale, illus. 2005. (Global Adventures II Ser.).Tr. of En Nigeria. (ENG & SPA.). 32p. (J). per. 10.95 *(978-1-59646-146-8(2))* Dingles & Co.

NIGERIA—FICTION

Achebe, Chinua. Chike & the River. 2011. (ENG., Illus.). 96p. (YA). (gr. 4-6). pap. 14.00 *(978-0-307-47386-8(4),* Penguin Bks.) Penguin Publishing Group.

Alakija, Polly. Catch That Goat! Alakija, Polly, illus. 2007. (ENG., Illus.). 40p. (J). (gr. -1-3). pap. 9.99 *(978-1-84686-057-7(1))* Barefoot Bks., Inc.

Bodden, Michelle, adapted by. Obara the Gatekeeper. 2007. (J). 14.95 *(978-0-9753089-1-2(2))* Water Daughter Publishing.

Holman, Nedra. Beautiful Queen. Velitchenko, Olga, illus. 2008. 40p. (J). *(978-1-4363-5461-5(7))* Xlibris Corp.

Nwaubani, Adaobi Tricia & Mazza, Viviana. Buried Beneath the Baobab Tree. 2018. (ENG.). 336p. (YA). (gr. 8). 17.99 *(978-0-06-269672-4(6),* Tegen, Katherine Bks) HarperCollins Pubs.

Okorafor, Nnedi. Akata Warrior. 2018. (Nsibidi Scripts Ser.: 2). (ENG.). 512p. (YA). (gr. 7). pap. 12.99 *(978-0-14-242585-5(0),* Speak) Penguin Young Readers Group.

—Akata Witch. (Nsibidi Scripts Ser.: 1). (ENG.). (YA). (gr. 7). 2017. 384p. pap. 11.99 *(978-0-14-242091-1(3),* Speak) 2011. 368p. 18.99 *(978-0-670-01196-4(7),* Viking Books for Young Readers) Penguin Young Readers Group.

—Akata Witch. 2017. (Akata Witch Ser.: 1). lib. bdg. 22.10 *(978-0-606-40101-2(6))* Turtleback.

—Akata Woman. 2022. (Nsibidi Scripts Ser.: 3). (Illus.). 416p. (J). (gr. 7). 18.99 *(978-0-451-48058-3(9),* Viking Books for Young Readers) Penguin Young Readers Group.

—Ikenga. 2020. 240p. (J). (gr. 5). 16.99 *(978-0-593-11352-3(7),* Viking Books for Young Readers) Penguin Young Readers Group.

Onyebuchi, Tochi. War Girls. 2019. (ENG.). 464p. (YA). (gr. 7). 18.99 *(978-0-451-48167-2(4),* Razorbill) Penguin Young Readers Group.

Unobagha, Uzo. Grandma, How Do You Say I Love You? Krassa, Victoria, illus. 2007. 28p. (J). 16.95 *(978-0-9773180-0-1(1))* Adonoke Inc.

NIGERIA—HISTORY

Hudak, Heather C. Hoping for a Home after Nigeria, 1 vol. 2019. (Leaving My Homeland: after the Journey Ser.). (ENG., Illus.). 32p. (J). (gr. 4-4). pap. *(978-0-7787-6502-8(4),* 289deecd-ae47-424d-961e-d0d40467ced1); lib. bdg. *(978-0-7787-6496-0(6),* 2e7d411b-dda2-4747-b81d-b0dc7b0b6833) Crabtree Publishing Co.

Kelly, Terri B. Mary Slessor: Missionary Mother. 2014. (Illus.). 164p. (J). *(978-1-60682-630-0(1))* BJU Pr.

Leavitt, Amie Jane. Discovering the Kingdom of Benin, 1 vol. 2013. (Exploring African Civilizations Ser.). (ENG.). 64p. (J). (gr. 6-6). 37.12 *(978-1-4777-1884-1(2),* 5fe5f798-c5dc-4b26-ab48-43c2e5a1c7ff, Rosen Reference) Rosen Publishing Group, Inc., The.

M
N
O

Newland, Sonya. The Genius of the Benin Kingdom. 2019. (Genius of the Ancients Ser.). (ENG.). 32p. (J). (gr. 4-5). lib. bdg. (978-0-7787-6574-5(1), 7c8a3dad-f3b9-4f00-ac11-4c4d928bdbf0) Crabtree Publishing Co.

Owings, Lisa. Nigeria. 2011. (Exploring Countries Ser.). (ENG., Illus.). 32p. (J). (gr. 3-7). lib. bdg. 27.95 (978-1-60014-619-0(8), Blastoff! Readers) Bellwether Media.

Wiseman, Blaine. Nigeria. 2014. (J). (978-1-4896-3058-2(9)) Weigl Pubs., Inc.

Zocchi, Judy. In Nigeria. Brodie, Neale, illus. 2005. (Global Adventures I Ser.). 32p. (J). pap. 10.95 (978-1-59646-143-7(8)); lib. bdg. 21.65 (978-1-59646-010-2(5)) Dingles & Co.

—In Nigeria/en Nigeria. Brodie, Neale, illus. 2005. (Global Adventures I Ser.).Tr. of En Nigeria. (ENG & SPA.). 32p. (J). pap. 10.95 (978-1-59646-145-1(4)); lib. bdg. 21.65 (978-1-59646-011-9(3)) Dingles & Co.

NIGHT

Banks, Rosie. I Know Day & Night, 1 vol. 2018. (What I Know Ser.). (ENG.). 24p. (J). (gr. k-k). 24.27 (978-1-5382-1730-6(9), ad014099-0b7d-4fe2-949a-522d95184baf) Stevens, Gareth Publishing LLLP.

Branley, Franklyn M. What Makes Day & Night? 2015. (Let's-Read-And-Find-Out Science: Stage 2 Ser.). (J). lib. bdg. 17.20 (978-0-606-37738-6(7)) Turtleback.

Eggers, Dave. The Lights & Types of Ships at Night. Dills, Annie, illus. 2020. 32p. (J). 18.99 (978-1-952119-07-1(3), d4bd153f-5743-440f-87b9-47476f71591b) McSweeney's Publishing.

Evans, Shira. National Geographic Readers: Day & Night. 2016. (Readers Ser.). (Illus.). 48p. (J). (gr. -1-k). pap. 4.99 (978-1-4263-2470-3(7), National Geographic Kids) Disney Publishing Worldwide.

Green, Jen. Day & Night, 1 vol. 2007. (Our Earth Ser.). (ENG., Illus.). 24p. (J). (gr. 2-3). lib. bdg. 26.27 (978-1-4042-4275-3(9), f2032ba1-e9d0-4d33-acd8-a1f74f1c4c7d) Rosen Publishing Group, Inc., The.

Havener, Katherine. Nursies When the Sun Shines: A Little Book on Night Weaning. Burrier, Sara, illus. 2nd ed. 2013. 20p. (J). pap. 9.99 (978-0-615-75642-4(5)) Elea Pr.

Hughes, Tom. Day & Night, 1 vol. 2016. (All about Opposites Ser.). (ENG., Illus.). 24p. (gr. k-1). pap. 10.35 (978-0-7660-8082-9(X), 292b3005-29c3-461d-9170-d94e89a5faae) Enslow Publishing, LLC.

Katirgis, Jane. Day & Night, 1 vol. 2011. (All about Opposites Ser.). (ENG., Illus.). 24p. (gr. -1-1). (J). lib. bdg. 25.27 (978-0-7660-3915-5(3), 485378d7-4d0d-477e-9ae7-f50d300be7c8); pap. 10.35 (978-1-59845-262-4(2), 41142589-e229-47b1-8f2d-4e5d40470dad) Enslow Publishing, LLC. (Enslow Publishing).

Kochanoff, Peggy. Be a Night Detective: Solving the Mysteries of Twilight, Dusk, & Nightfall, 1 vol. 2017. (Be a Nature Detective Ser.). (ENG., Illus.). 56p. (J). (gr. 1-3). pap. 14.95 (978-1-77108-464-2(2), 07ce4bca-bf65-4861-ba4a-7b0455a42c90) Nimbus Publishing, Ltd. CAN. Dist: Baker & Taylor Publisher Services (BTPS).

Llewellyn, Claire. Day & Night. 2006. (I Know That, Cycles of Nature Set Ser.). (Illus.). 24p. (J). (gr. -1-3). lib. bdg. 22.80 (978-1-59771-018-3(0)) Sea-To-Sea Pubns.

Llyfr Lliwio Dydd a Nos. 2005. (WEL., Illus.). 26p. pap. (978-1-870222-48-8(2)) Mudiad Ysgolion Meithrin.

Murphy, Stuart J. It's about Time! Speirs, John, illus. 2005. (MathStart Ser.). 40p. (J). 16.99 (978-0-06-055768-3(0)); (ENG.). (gr. -1). pap. 6.99 (978-0-06-055769-0(9), HarperCollins) HarperCollins Pubs.

—It's about Time! Speirs, John, illus. 2005. (Mathstart Ser.). 33p. (gr. -1-3). 16.00 (978-0-7569-5224-2(7)) Perfection Learning Corp.

Neumeyer, Peter F. & Gorey, Edward. Why We Have Day & Night. 2011. (Illus.). 36p. (J). (gr. -1-1). 12.95 (978-0-7649-5886-1(0)) Pomegranate Communications, Inc.

O'DellKathryn. THE SCIENCE OF DARKNESS LOW INTERMEDIATE BOOK WITH ONLINE ACCESS, 1 vol. 2014. (ENG., Illus.). 28p. (J). pap., E-Book 9.50 (978-1-107-65493-8(9)) Cambridge Univ. Pr.

¿Por Que Es Oscura la Noche? (Coleccion Primeros Pasos en la Ciencia). (SPA., Illus.). (J). (gr. 1-3). pap. (978-950-724-112-3(4), LMA8218) Lumen ARG. Dist: Lectorum Pubns., Inc.

Rice, Dona Herweck. Living in Sunlight: Extremes. rev. ed. 2019. (Smithsonian: Informational Text Ser.). (ENG.). 32p. (J). (gr. 2-3). pap. 10.99 (978-1-4938-6666-3(4)) Teacher Created Materials, Inc.

Sasso, Sandy Eisenberg. Adam & Eve's New Day. Rothenberg, Joani Keller, illus. 2006. (ENG.). 24p. (gr. -1). bds. 7.99 (978-1-59473-205-8(1), 316f8644-7638-4472-b248-c71e33b4d423, Skylight Paths Publishing) LongHill Partners, Inc.

Smith, Alastair. Nighttime. 2004. (Lift-the-Flap Learners Ser.). (Illus.). 16p. (J). (gr. 1-18). pap. 8.95 (978-0-7945-0366-6(7), Usborne) EDC Publishing.

Smith, Sian. Night & Day, 1 vol. 2014. (Opposites Ser.). (ENG.). 24p. (J). (gr. -1-1). pap. 5.99 (978-1-4846-0336-9(2), 126425, Heinemann) Capstone.

Tagholm, Sally. The Complete Book of the Night. 2006. (Illus.). 96p. (J). (gr. 4-8). reprint ed. 19.00 (978-1-4223-5329-5(X)) DIANE Publishing Co.

NIGHT—FICTION

Abrahams, Peter, et al. Up All Night: A Short Story Collection. 2008. (Illus.). 240p. (J). (gr. 7). lib. bdg. 17.89 (978-0-06-137077-9(0)); 16.99 (978-0-06-137076-2(2)) HarperCollins Pubs. (Geringer, Laura Book).

Achurch, Holly. Tennessee Breeze. Schneider, Leighanne, illus. 2018. (ENG.). (J). 15.00 (978-0-9970690-1-3(5), Academy Park Pr.) Williamson County Public Library.

Allgood, Jean. Come Follow Me Bk. 1: Understanding One's Worth: Color Orange. Smith, Sandra, illus. l.t. ed. 2004. 23p. (J). 14.95 (978-0-9741627-3-7(6)) PricePoint+Publications.

Anderson, Sara. Noisy City Night (2015 Board Book) Anderson, Sara, illus. 2015. (ENG., Illus.). 12p. (J). (gr. -1-1). bds. 10.95 (978-1-943459-01-8(0)) Sara Anderson Children's Bks.

Ashman, Linda. How to Make a Night. Tusa, Tricia, illus. Date not set. 32p. (J). (gr. -1-3). pap. 5.99 (978-0-06-443699-1(3)) HarperCollins Pubs.

Awdry, W. Thomas & Friends: Blue Train, Green Train (Thomas & Friends) Stubbs, Tommy, illus. 2006. (Bright & Early Books(R) Ser.). (ENG.). 36p. (J). (gr. k-k). 9.99 (978-0-375-83463-9(X), Random Hse. Bks. for Young Readers) Random Hse. Children's Bks.

—Thomas & Friends: Blue Train, Green Train (Thomas & Friends) Stubbs, Tommy, illus. 2007. (Bright & Early Board Books(TM) Ser.). (ENG.). 24p. (J). (— 1). bds. 4.99 (978-0-375-83984-9(4), Random Hse. Bks. for Young Readers) Random Hse. Children's Bks.

Babbitt, Natalie. The Something. 40p. (J). (gr. k-2). pap. 2.95 (978-0-8072-1333-9(0), Listening Library) Random Hse. Audio Publishing Group.

Baldwin, Christy. Nine Things Nathan Noticed at Night. Barnes, Sarah, illus. 2005. 24p. (J). per. 13.00 (978-0-9765072-1-5(8)) Tribute Bks.

Ban Breathnach, Sarah. The Best Part of the Day. Edelson, Wendy, illus. 2014. (ENG.). 40p. (J). (-k). 16.99 (978-1-62157-252-7(8), Regnery Kids) Regnery Publishing.

Banks, Kate. The Night Worker. Hallensleben, Georg, illus. 2007. (ENG.). 40p. (J). (gr. -1-1). 9.99 (978-0-374-40000-2(8), 900038843) Square Fish.

—Night Worker. 2014. 19.00 (978-1-63419-674-1(0)) Perfection Learning Corp.

Barlics, Brian. Brady Needs a Nightlight. Jones, Gregory Burgess, illus. 2013. (ENG.). 32p. (J). pap. 18.95 (978-1-61296-195-8(9)) Black Rose Writing.

Bartoletti, Susan Campbell. Naamah & the Ark at Night. Meade, Holly, illus. 2011. (ENG.). 32p. (J). (gr. -1-3). 16.99 (978-0-7636-4242-6(8)) Candlewick Pr.

Bell, Taj. The Little Night Fairy: Written & illustrated by Taj Bell graphic design & co-illustration by Lisa. 2008. 40p. pap. 20.99 (978-1-4389-2602-5(2)) AuthorHouse.

Bentley, Dawn. Goodnight Bear: A Book & Night Light. Couri, Kathryn A., illus. 2005. (Stories to Share Ser.). 12p. (J). 12.95 (978-1-58117-034-4(3), Intervisual/Piggy Toes) Bendon, Inc.

Berenstain, Jan. Berenstain Bears Go Out to Eat. 2009. (Berenstain Bears Ser.). (ENG., Illus.). 32p. (J). (gr. -1-2). pap. 4.99 (978-0-06-057393-5(7), HarperFestival) HarperCollins Pubs.

Biggs, Mac Barnett; pictures by Brian. Noisy Night. 2017. (ENG., Illus.). 32p. (J). 18.99 (978-1-59643-967-2(X), 900126272) Roaring Brook Pr.

Bond, Felicia. Poinsettia & the Firefighters. Bond, Felicia, illus. 2003. (Illus.). (J). (978-0-06-056871-9(2)) HarperCollins Pubs.

Boyd, Lizi. Flashlight: (Picture Books, Wordless Books for Kids, Camping Books for Kids, Bedtime Story Books, Children's Activity Books, Children's Nature Books) 2014. (ENG., Illus.). 40p. (J). (gr. -1-1). 16.99 (978-1-4521-1894-9(9)) Chronicle Bks. LLC.

Boynton, Sandra. The Going to Bed Book. Boynton, Sandra, illus. 2006. (ENG., Illus.). 14p. (J). bds. 12.95 (978-1-4169-2794-5(8), Little Simon) Little Simon.

Bradbury, Ray. Switch on the Night. Dillon, Leo & Dillon, Diane, illus. 2004. 40p. (J). (gr. -1-2). reprint ed. pap. 7.99 (978-0-553-11244-3(9), Dragonfly Bks.) Random Hse. Children's Bks.

Brand, Brandon. Lily Is... Wide Awake. 2008. 32p. (J). 16.00 (978-0-9802329-0-5(2)) Upside Down Tree Publishing.

Brown, Marc. Good Night, D. W. Brown, Marc, illus. 2004. (ENG., Illus.). 24p. (J). (gr. -1-1). pap. 3.99 (978-0-316-73385-4(7)) Little, Brown Bks. for Young Readers.

Brown, Margaret Wise. Buenas Noches, Luna: Goodnight Moon (Spanish Edition), 1 vol. Hurd, Clement, illus. 2006.Tr. of Goodnight Moon. (SPA.). 32p. (J). (gr. -1-3). 18.99 (978-0-06-026214-3(1), HC0528) HarperCollins Español.

—Goodnight Moon 123 Board Book: A Counting Book. Hurd, Clement, illus. 2008. (ENG.). 30p. (J). (gr. -1-k). bds. 8.99 (978-0-06-112597-3(0), HarperFestival) HarperCollins Pubs.

Buchanan, Nelda. The Hall Closet Light. 2009. 36p. (J). pap. 13.95 (978-1-4327-4584-4(0)) Outskirts Pr., Inc.

Burleigh, Robert. Night Train, Night Train. Minor, Wendell, illus. 2018. 32p. (J). (-k). lib. bdg. 16.99 (978-1-58089-717-4(7)) Charlesbridge Publishing, Inc.

Butler, M. Christina & Pedler, Caroline. Don't Be Afraid Little Ones. 2018. (ENG.). 32p. (J). (gr. -1-1). bds. 9.99 (978-1-68099-425-4(5), Good Bks.) Skyhorse Publishing Co., Inc.

—Don't Be Afraid Little Ones - Choice Edition. 2018. (ENG.). 32p. (J). (gr. -1-1). bds. 9.99 (978-1-68099-428-5(X), Good Bks.) Skyhorse Publishing Co., Inc.

Butterworth, Nick. One Snowy Night. Butterworth, Nick, illus. 2007. (ENG., Illus.). 32p. (J). 24.00 (978-0-00-725942-7(5)) HarperCollins Pubs. Ltd. GBR. Dist: Independent Pubs. Group.

Carroll, James Christopher. The Boy & the Moon. Carroll, James Christopher, illus. 2010. (ENG., Illus.). 32p. (J). (gr. 1-4). 19.99 (978-1-58536-521-0(1), 202209) Sleeping Bear Pr.

Castro, Edmund Lee. Crystal & the Not-So-Scary Night. 2008. 36p. pap. 24.95 (978-1-60672-236-7(0)) America Star Bks.

Catran, Ken. Tomorrow the Dark. 2005. 208p. pap. (978-0-7344-0417-6(4), Lothian Children's Bks.) Hachette Australia.

Cinderfella's Big Night: Individual Title Six-Packs. (Action Packs Ser.). 104p. (gr. 3-5). 44.00 (978-0-7635-2984-0(2)) Rigby Education.

Condon, Tom. The Sandman: Stories to Read to Children. 2003. 136p. (J). pap. 11.95 (978-0-595-27291-4(6)) iUniverse, Inc.

Costales, Amy. Hello Night: Hola Noche. McDonald, Mercedes, illus. 2007. (ENG.). 24p. (J). (gr. -1 — 1). 14.95 (978-0-87358-927-7(0)) Cooper Square Publishing Llc.

Crawford, Deborah. Tyler the Turtle Is Afraid of the Dark. Balzer, Jeremy, illus. 2006. 32p. (J). 14.95 (978-0-9770516-1-8(7)) Laffin Minor Pr.

Crimi, Carolyn. Where's My Mummy? Manders, John, illus. 2009. (ENG.). 32p. (J). (gr. -1-3). 7.99 (978-0-7636-4337-9(8)) Candlewick Pr.

Crowther, Kitty, creator. Scritch Scratch Scraww Plop. 2015. (ENG., Illus.). 40p. (J). (gr. -1-3). 16.95 (978-1-59270-179-7(5)) Enchanted Lion Bks., LLC.

Crummel, Susan Stevens. All in One Hour, 0 vols. Donohue, Dorothy, illus. 2012. (ENG.). 40p. (J). (gr. k-3). pap. 9.99 (978-0-7614-5537-0(X), 9780761455370, Two Lions) Amazon Publishing.

Deneen, Brendan. Night Night, Groot. 2018. (ENG., Illus.). 30p. (J). (gr. -1-k). bds. 8.99 (978-1-4847-8765-6(X)) Marvel Worldwide, Inc.

Denos, Julia. Windows. Goodale, E. B., illus. 2017. (ENG.). 32p. (J). (gr. -1-2). 17.99 (978-0-7636-9035-9(X)) Candlewick Pr.

dePaola, Tomie. When Everyone Was Fast Asleep. 2019. (Illus.). (J). (— 1). 28p. bds. 7.99 (978-0-8234-4336-9(1)); 32p. 17.99 (978-0-8234-4281-2(0)) Holiday Hse., Inc.

Disney Publishing Staff. Piglet's Night Lights, 15 vols. 2003. (It's Fun to Learn Ser.). (Illus.). 32p. (J). (gr. -1-3). 3.99 (978-1-57973-127-4(9)) Advance Pubs. LLC.

Esenwine, Matt Forrest. Flashlight Night. Koehler, Fred, illus. 2017. (ENG.). 32p. (J). (gr. -1-3). 16.95 (978-1-62979-493-8(7), Astra Young Readers) Astra Publishing Hse.

Feder, Sandra V. The Moon Inside, 1 vol. Sicuro, Aimée, illus. 2016. (ENG.). 32p. (J). (gr. -1-k). 17.95 (978-1-55498-823-5(3)) Groundwood Bks. CAN. Dist: Publishers Group West (PGW).

Feiffer, Kate. No Go Sleep! Feiffer, Jules, illus. 2012. (ENG.). 32p. (J). (gr. -1-2). 16.99 (978-1-4424-1683-3(1), Simon & Schuster/Paula Wiseman Bks.) Simon & Schuster/Paula Wiseman Bks.

Ford, Bernette. First Snow. Braun, Sébastien, illus. 2018. (ENG.). 28p. (J). (gr. -1-1). bds. 7.95 (978-1-910716-63-2(4)) Boxer Bks., Ltd. GBR. Dist: Sterling Publishing Co., Inc.

Fox, Sabrina. Who Can Help Me Sleep? Rothan, Ann, illus. 2004. 32p. (gr. -1-3). 16.95 (978-1-885394-36-1(5)) Bluestar Communications Corp.

Fraley, Patty. Fear at Night: To Matthew. 2011. 24p. (gr. -1). pap. 12.79 (978-1-4567-5555-3(2)) AuthorHouse.

Freeman, B. A. The Night of My Birth. Lett, M., illus. 2010. (ENG.). 28p. (YA). pap. 21.99 (978-1-4500-1028-3(8)) Xlibris Corp.

Gerstein, Mordicai. The Night World. 2015. (ENG., Illus.). 40p. (J). (gr. -1-3). 18.99 (978-0-316-18822-7(0)) Little, Brown Bks. for Young Readers.

Grover, Neha Lamba. Shaurya's Adventures. 2010. 43p. pap. 17.40 (978-0-557-12636-1(3)) Lulu Pr., Inc.

Guilloppé, Antoine. One Scary Night. 2007. (ENG., Illus.). 32p. (J). (gr. 4-7). 15.95 (978-1-59687-185-4(7)) IBks., Inc.

Gutierrez, Lorna. Hello, Mr. Moon. Watkins, Laura, illus. 2016. (J). (978-1-4351-6412-3(1)) Barnes & Noble, Inc.

Hadland, W. Into the Night. 2010. 312p. (gr. 4-6). pap. 19.13 (978-1-4251-4187-5(0)) Trafford Publishing.

Harris, Sally M. Rainbow Nights. Grady, Kit, illus. 2009. 20p. pap. 9.95 (978-1-61633-002-6(3)) Guardian Angel Publishing, Inc.

—Rainbow Nights. Grady, Kit, illus. 2018. (ENG.). 26p. (J). pap. 9.95 (978-0-9660839-8-9(9)) Top Cat Publishing.

Harshman, Marc. All the Way to Morning. Dávalos, Felipe, illus. 2006. (J). per. 7.95 (978-1-891852-49-7(3)) Quarrier Pr.

Harwood, Beth. One Snowy Night. Ronchi, Susanna, illus. 2005. 12p. (J). (978-1-84011-627-4(7)) Templar Publishing.

Hawkins, Jacqui. Snap! Snap! 2005. (ENG., Illus.). 32p. (J). pap. 7.99 (978-1-4052-1099-7(0)) Farshore GBR. Dist: Trafalgar Square Publishing.

Heine, Helme. El Maravilloso Viaje a Traves de la Noche. 3rd ed. 2003. (SPA., Illus.). 250p. (978-84-85334-62-9(0)) Lóguez Ediciones ESP. Dist: Lectorum Pubns., Inc.

—Wunderbare Reise Durch Die Na. 12.95 (978-3-7876-9528-7(1)) Middelhauve Verlags GmbH DEU. Dist: Distribooks, Inc.

Heo, Yumi. Sun & Moon Have a Tea Party. Stoop, Naoko, illus. 2020. 40p. (J). (gr. -1-2). 17.99 (978-0-385-39033-0(5), Schwartz & Wade Bks.) Random Hse. Children's Bks.

Hodge, Rosamund. Crimson Bound. 2016. (ENG.). 464p. (YA). (gr. 8). pap. 9.99 (978-0-06-222477-4(8), Balzer & Bray) HarperCollins Pubs.

Hood, Karen Jean Matsko. Goodnight, I Wish You Goodnight, Bilingual English & Icelandic, Vol. 1. Whispering Pine Press International, ed. Hatakeyama, Hiroshi, illus. 2015. (Hood Picture Book Ser.). (ENG & ICE.). 60p. (J). 34.95 (978-1-59649-920-1(6)); pap. 29.95 (978-1-59649-919-5(2)) Whispering Pine Pr. International, Inc.

Hornsby, Ashley. Pretty Little Lilly & the Magical Light. Couch, Greg, illus. 2007. 32p. (J). 15.95 (978-0-9777241-0-9(7)) Cepia LLC.

Hornsby, Ashley Brooke. Pretty Little Lilly & the Magical Night (paperback) 2006. (Illus.). (J). (978-0-9777241-1-6(5)) Cepia LLC.

Horwitz, Elinor Lander. When the Sky Is Like Lace: Barbara Cooney Reissue, 1 vol. Cooney, Barbara, illus. 2015. (ENG.). 32p. (J). 18.95 (978-1-939017-47-5(5), e9145bcd-2e3f-43cd-a54e-f8a299e3df30) Islandport Pr., Inc.

Hosta, Dar. I Love the Night. Hosta, Dar, illus. l.t. ed. 2003. (Illus.). 32p. (J). (gr. k-3). 16.95 (978-0-9721967-0-3(6)) Brown Dog Bks.

Iriyama, Satoshi. Good Night, Chirp. 2015. (Chirp the Chick Ser.). (ENG., Illus.). 36p. (J). (— 1). 8.99 (978-0-544-35994-9(1), 1587557, Clarion Bks.) HarperCollins Pubs.

Jenkins, Martin. Fox Explores the Night: a First Science Storybook. Smythe, Richard, illus. 2018. (Science Storybooks Ser.). (ENG.). 32p. (J). (-k). 16.99 (978-0-7636-9883-6(0)) Candlewick Pr.

Johnson, Mariana Ruiz. While You Are Sleeping: (Bedtime Books for Kids, Wordless Bedtime Stories for Kids) 2018. (ENG., Illus.). 36p. (J). (gr. -1-k). 16.99 (978-1-4521-6599-8(8)) Chronicle Bks. LLC.

Juan, Ana. The Night Eater. 2004. (Illus.). (J). (978-0-439-48892-1(3), Levine, Arthur A. Bks.) Scholastic, Inc.

Kemble, Mai S. The Moon & the Night Sweeper. Kemble, Mai S., illus. 2008. (Illus.). (J). pap. 6.95 (978-1-60108-023-3(9)) Red Cygnet Pr.

Kemble, Mai S., illus. The Moon & the Night Sweeper. 2007. 30p. (J). (gr. -1-2). 15.95 (978-1-60108-013-4(1)) Red Cygnet Pr.

Krensky, Stephen. Fraidy Cats. Lewin, Betsy, illus. 2015. (Scholastic Reader, Level 2 Ser.). (ENG.). 32p. (J). (gr. -1-3). pap. 3.99 (978-0-545-79966-9(X), Cartwheel Bks.) Scholastic, Inc.

Lacoursiere, Patrick. Dream Songs Night Songs: From China to Senegal. Bourbonnière, Sylvie, illus. 2006. (ENG.). 36p. (J). (gr. -1-2). 16.95 (978-2-923163-24-6(9)) La Montagne Secrete CAN. Dist: Independent Pubs. Group.

Lewis, Rose. Sweet Dreams. Corace, Jen, illus. 2012. (ENG.). 32p. (J). (gr. -1-2). 16.95 (978-1-4197-0189-4(4), 692701, Abrams Bks. for Young Readers) Abrams, Inc.

Liniers. Buenas Noches, Planeta: TOON Level 2. 2017. (SPA., Illus.). 36p. (J). (gr. k-1). 12.99 (978-1-943145-21-8(0), 9781943145218, TOON Books) Astra Publishing Hse.

—Buenas Noches, Planeta: TOON Level 2. 2017. (SPA., Illus.). 36p. (J). (gr. k-1). pap. 7.99 (978-1-943145-19-5(9), 9781943145195, Toon Books) Candlewick Pr.

—Good Night, Planet: TOON Level 2. 2017. (ENG., Illus.). 36p. (J). (gr. k-2). 12.99 (978-1-943145-20-1(2), 9781943145201, TOON Books) Astra Publishing Hse.

Listening with Zachary. (J). pap. 13.75 (978-0-8136-4655-8(3)) Modern Curriculum Pr.

Low, J. H. Night in the Gardens. 2017. (ENG.). 40p. (J). 14.99 (978-981-4751-42-1(1)) Marshall Cavendish International (Asia) Private Ltd. SGP. Dist: Independent Pubs. Group.

MacLachlan, Patricia & Charest, Emily MacLachlan. Before You Came. Diaz, David, illus. 2011. (ENG.). 32p. (J). (gr. -1-3). 16.99 (978-0-06-051234-7(2)); lib. bdg. 17.89 (978-0-06-051235-4(0)) HarperCollins Pubs. (Tegen, Katherine Bks).

Marlar, Debra L. Morgan's Sleepover at Grandma's. 2010. 36p. 16.99 (978-1-4520-6496-3(2)) AuthorHouse.

Matheson, Christie. Touch the Brightest Star. 2015. (ENG., Illus.). 40p. (J). (gr. -1-3). 15.99 (978-0-06-227447-2(3), Greenwillow Bks.) HarperCollins Pubs.

—Touch the Brightest Star Board Book. Matheson, Christie, illus. 2017. (ENG., Illus.). 42p. (J). (gr. -1-3). bds. 9.99 (978-0-06-227448-9(1), Greenwillow Bks.) HarperCollins Pubs.

McKay, Amanda S. The New Night Sky. 2012. 28p. pap. 19.99 (978-1-4685-2517-5(4)) AuthorHouse.

McMillan, Dawn. Awake in the Dark! Fino, Roberto, illus. 2009. (Rigby PM Stars Bridge Bks.). (ENG.). 24p. (gr. 2-3). pap. 8.70 (978-1-4190-5527-0(5)) Rigby Education.

Miller, Jules, illus. When Night Became Day. 2015. (ENG.). 32p. (J). (gr. -1-k). 16.95 (978-1-62914-632-4(3), Sky Pony Pr.) Skyhorse Publishing Co., Inc.

Montardre, Hélène. Night & Day. 2003. (Illus.). 8p. (J). bds. 7.95 (978-1-58728-481-6(2), Two-Can Publishing) T&N Children's Publishing.

Morales, Yuyi. Little Night / Nochecita. 2016. (SPA.). (J). lib. bdg. 18.40 (978-0-606-38443-8(X)) Turtleback.

Moulton, Mark Kimball. The Visit. Winget, Susan, tr. Winget, Susan, illus. 2003. (ENG.). 56p. (J). 14.95 (978-0-8249-5859-6(4), Ideals Pubns.) Worthy Publishing.

Padur, Simone. Things That Go Bump in the Night. 2012. 20p. pap. 19.99 (978-0-9847831-7-5(2)) Big Country Publishing, LLC.

Paolilli, Paul & Brewer, Dan. Nightlights. Brereton, Alice, illus. 2017. (ENG.). 32p. (J). (gr. -1-3). 16.99 (978-0-8075-5622-1(X), 080755622X) Whitman, Albert & Co.

Paraskevas, Michael. Mr. Moon. 2017. (Illus.). 34p. (J). (gr. -1-2). bds. 7.99 (978-0-399-54995-3(1), Crown Books For Young Readers) Random Hse. Children's Bks.

Parker, Amy. Night Night, Train, 1 vol. Allyn, Virginia, illus. 2017. (Night Night Ser.). (ENG.). 20p. (J). bds. 9.99 (978-0-7180-8932-0(4), Tommy Nelson) Nelson, Thomas Inc.

Pearson, Anthony. Baby Bear Eats the Night, 0 vols. Leick, Bonnie, illus. 2012. (ENG.). 32p. (J). (gr. -1-1). 16.99 (978-0-7614-6103-6(5), 9780761461036, Two Lions) Amazon Publishing.

Pendziwol, Jean E. Once upon a Northern Night, 1 vol. Arsenault, Isabelle, illus. 2013. (ENG.). 36p. (J). (gr. k-2). 17.95 (978-1-55498-138-0(7)) Groundwood Bks. CAN. Dist: Publishers Group West (PGW).

Pilkey, Dav. The Paperboy. 2015. 32p. pap. 7.00 (978-1-61003-556-9(9)) Center for the Collaborative Classroom.

Priddy, Roger. Night Night Farm. 2017. (Night Night Bks.). (ENG., Illus.). 20p. (J). bds. 9.99 (978-0-312-52163-9(4), 900170061) St. Martin's Pr.

Reilly, Carmel & Ashforth, Kate. A Night Out. 2008. (Rigby Focus Forward: Level E Ser.). (Illus.). 24p. (J). (gr. 4-7). pap. (978-1-4190-3678-1(5), Rigby) Pearson Education Australia.

Rey, H. A. Curious George a Winter's Nap: A Winter & Holiday Book for Kids. 2010. (Curious George TV Ser.). (ENG., Illus.). 24p. (J). (gr. -1-3). pap. 4.99 (978-0-547-23590-5(9), 1083308, Clarion Bks.) HarperCollins Pubs.

Ricci, Christine. Buenas Noches, Dora! Cuento Para Levantar la Tapita. Hall, Susan, illus. 2004. (Dora the Explorer Ser.).Tr. of Good Night, Dora! (SPA.). 16p. (J). pap. 5.99 (978-0-689-86648-7(8), Libros Para Ninos) Libros Para Ninos.

Rimland, Mark, illus. The Secret Night World of Cats. 2008. 32p. (YA). 15.00 (978-0-9740360-6-9(4)) Autism Research Institute.

Rodgers, Frank. Ruidos en la Noche. (SPA.). 64p. (J). (gr. 3). 7.95 (978-84-88061-85-0(4)) Serres, Ediciones, S. L. ESP. Dist: Lectorum Pubns., Inc.

Runton, Andy. Owly & Wormy, Bright Lights & Starry Nights. Runton, Andy, illus. 2012. (ENG., Illus.). 40p. (J). (gr. -1-3). 19.99 (978-1-4169-5775-1(8), Atheneum Bks. for Young Readers) Simon & Schuster Children's Publishing.

Rylant, Cynthia. Mr. Putter & Tabby See the Stars. Howard, Arthur, illus. 2008. (Mr. Putter & Tabby Ser.). (ENG.). 44p. (J). (gr. 1-4). pap. 6.99 (978-0-15-206366-5(8), 1199066, Clarion Bks.) HarperCollins Pubs.

—Night in the Country. Szilagyi, Mary, illus. 2014. 32p. pap. 7.00 (978-1-61003-359-6(0)) Center for the Collaborative Classroom.

Sanroman, Susana. Senora Reganona: A Mexican Bedtime Story. Domi, illus. 2006. 20p. (J). (gr. k-4). reprint ed. 15.00 (978-1-4223-5466-7(0)) DIANE Publishing Co.

Sendak, Maurice. La Cocina de Noche. Sendak, Maurice, illus. 2003. (Picture Books Collection). (SPA., Illus.). 40p. (J). (gr.

k-3). 10.95 (978-84-204-4570-0(3)) Ediciones Alfaguara ESP. Dist: Santillana USA Publishing Co., Inc.
Sergeant, Kate. It's a Very Good Night. 2005. (J). (978-0-9770158-5-6(8)) BeachWalk Bks. Inc.
Shulevitz, Uri. Dusk. Shulevitz, Uri, illus. 2013. (ENG., Illus.). 32p. (J). (gr. -1-3). 19.99 (978-0-374-31903-8(0), 900083618, Farrar, Straus & Giroux (BYR)) Farrar, Straus & Giroux.
Snider, Grant. What Color Is Night? 2019. (ENG., Illus.). 44p. (J). (gr. -1 — 1). 15.99 (978-1-4521-7992-6(1)) Chronicle Bks. LLC.
Sparks, Fredda. One October Night. 2012. 20p. pap. 17.99 (978-1-4772-5656-5(3)) AuthorHouse.
Spider Night! (Early Intervention Levels Ser.). 28.38 (978-0-7362-0411-8(3)) CENGAGE Learning.
Srinivasan, Divya. Little Owl's 1-2-3. Srinivasan, Divya, illus. 2015. (Little Owl Ser.). (Illus.). 18p. (J). (— 1). bds. 6.99 (978-0-451-47454-4(6), Viking Books for Young Readers) Penguin Young Readers Group.
—Little Owl's Night. (Little Owl Ser.). (Illus.). (J). 2013. 34p. (— 1). bds. 6.99 (978-0-670-01579-5(2)) 2011. 40p. (gr. -1-k). 18.99 (978-0-670-01295-4(5)) Penguin Young Readers Group. (Viking Books for Young Readers).
Swanson, Susan Marie. The House in the Night: A Caldecott Award Winner. Krommes, Beth, illus. 2008. (ENG.). 40p. (J). (gr. -1-3). 18.99 (978-0-618-86244-3(7), 513213, Clarion Bks.) HarperCollins Pubs.
—The House in the Night Board Book. Krommes, Beth, illus. 2011. (ENG.). 36p. (J). (gr. -1-k). bds. 7.99 (978-0-547-57769-2(9), 1458661, Clarion Bks.) HarperCollins Pubs.
Teckentrup, Britta. Moon: a Peek-Through Picture Book. 2018. (ENG., Illus.). 32p. (J). (gr. -1-2). 17.99 (978-1-5247-6966-6(5), Doubleday Bks. for Young Readers) Random Hse. Children's Bks.
Thompson, Lauren. Little Quack's Bedtime. Anderson, Derek, illus. 2005. (ENG.). 32p. (J). (gr. -1-3). 18.99 (978-0-689-86894-8(4), Simon & Schuster Bks. For Young Readers) Simon & Schuster Bks. For Young Readers.
—Polar Bear Night. Savage, Stephen, illus. 2004. (ENG.). 32p. (J). (gr. -1-k). 18.99 (978-0-439-49524-0(5), Scholastic Pr.) Scholastic, Inc.
Thomson, Sarah L. Imagine a Night. Gonsalves, Rob, illus. 2003. (Imagine A... Ser.). (ENG.). 40p. (J). (gr. -1-3). 19.99 (978-0-689-85218-3(5), Atheneum Bks. for Young Readers) Simon & Schuster Children's Publishing.
Tibo, Gilles. Le Voyage du Funambule. 2004. (Mon Roman Ser.). (FRE., Illus.). 64p. (J). (gr. 2). pap. (978-2-89021-701-0(9)) Diffusion du livre Mirabel (DLM).
Tremblay, Carole. Floop in the Dark, 1 vol. Beshwaty, Steve, illus. 2009. (Floop Ser.). (ENG.). 24p. (J). (gr. -1-k). 27.27 (978-1-60754-341-1(9), f9f994d3-11e5-46ab-b443-f75e57a42e33, Windmill Bks.) Rosen Publishing Group, Inc., The.
Wargin, Kathy-jo. Frank & Beans, 1 vol. Lewis, Anthony, illus. 2010. (I Can Read! / Frank & Beans Ser.). (ENG.). 32p. (J). pap. 4.99 (978-0-310-71847-5(3)) Zondervan.
Waring, Geoff. Oscar & the Moth: A Book about Light & Dark. Waring, Geoff, illus. 2008. (Start with Science Ser.). (ENG., Illus.). 32p. (J). (gr. -1-3). pap. 7.99 (978-0-7636-4031-6(X)) Candlewick Pr.
Warner, Gertrude Chandler, creator. The Midnight Mystery. 2003. (Boxcar Children Mysteries Ser.: 95). (ENG., Illus.). 128p. (J). (gr. 2-5). pap. 5.99 (978-0-8075-5538-5(X), 080755538X, Random Hse. Bks. for Young Readers) Random Hse. Children's Bks.
Watson, Clyde. Midnight Moon. Natti, Susanna, illus. 2006. (ENG.). 24p. (J). (gr. -1-k). (978-1-59692-162-7(5)) MacAdam/Cage Publishing, Inc.
Willis, Jeanne. Mayfly Day. Ross, Tony, illus. 2012. (ENG.). 32p. (J). (gr. -1-k). pap. 10.99 (978-1-84270-606-0(3)) Andersen Pr. GBR. Dist: Independent Pubs. Group.
Willson, Sarah & Thompson Bros. Estrellita. Thompson Brothers Studio Staff, illus. 2003. (Dora la Exploradora Ser.).Tr. of Little Star. (SPA.). 24p. (J). pap. 3.99 (978-0-689-86307-3(1), Libros Para Ninos) Libros Para Ninos.
Wilson, Karma. Mama, Why? Mendez, Simon, illus. 2011. (ENG.). 40p. (J). (gr. -1-2). 16.99 (978-1-4169-4205-4(X), McElderry, Margaret K. Bks.) McElderry, Margaret K. Bks.
Yee, Wong Herbert. Summer Days & Nights. Yee, Wong Herbert, illus. 2012. (ENG., Illus.). 32p. (J). (gr. -1-1). 19.99 (978-0-8050-9078-9(9), 900061501, Holt, Henry & Co. Bks. For Young Readers) Holt, Henry & Co.
Zachariah, Abdul-Razak. The Night Is Yours. Bobo, Keturah A., illus. 2019. 32p. (J). (gr. -1-2). 17.99 (978-0-525-55271-0(5), Dial Bks) Penguin Young Readers Group.
Zschock, Heather. Whoo's There? A Bedtime Shadow Book. Zschock, Martha Day, illus. 2005. (Bedtime Shadow Bks.). (ENG.). 7p. (J). (gr. -1-4). spiral bd. 12.99 (978-1-59359-904-1(8), 73a51dd1-93f6-4ff1-8a98-79fc4b06d109) Peter Pauper Pr. Inc.

NIGHT—POETRY

Andrew, Moira, et al, selected by. Night Poems & Ghost Poems. 2008. (Illus.). 32p. (J). pap. 10.95 (978-1-59646-623-4(5)) Dingles & Co.
Andrew, Moira, et al. Night Poems & Ghost Poems. 2008. (Illus.). 32p. (J). lib. bdg. 23.65 (978-1-59646-622-7(7)) Dingles & Co.
Sidman, Joyce. Dark Emperor & Other Poems of the Night: A Newbery Honor Award Winner. Allen, Rick, illus. 2010. (ENG.). 32p. (J). (gr. 1-4). 17.99 (978-0-547-15228-8(0), 1051947, Clarion Bks.) HarperCollins Pubs.

NIGHTINGALE, FLORENCE, 1820-1910

Adler, David A. A Picture Book of Florence Nightingale. Wallner, John & Wallner, Alexandra, illus. 2019. (Picture Book Biography Ser.). 32p. (J). (gr. -1-3). pap. 7.99 (978-0-8234-4271-3(3)) Holiday Hse., Inc.
Alexander, Carol. Florence Nightingale. 2005. (Rookie Biographies Ser.). (ENG., Illus.). 32p. (J). (gr. 1-2). pap. 4.95 (978-0-516-25828-7(1), Children's Pr.) Scholastic Library Publishing.
Alexander, Carol & Vargus, Nanci Reginelli. Florence Nightingale. 2004. (Rookie Biography Ser.). (J). 20.50 (978-0-516-24406-8(X)) Scholastic Library Publishing.
Aller, Susan Bivin. Florence Nightingale. 2008. pap. 52.95 (978-0-8225-9389-8(0)) Lerner Publishing Group.
—Florence Nightingale. Butler, Tad, illus. 2007. (History Maker Biographies Ser.). (ENG.). 48p. (gr. 3-6). lib. bdg. 27.93 (978-0-8225-7609-9(0), Lerner Pubns.) Lerner Publishing Group.
Connors, Kathleen. The Life of Florence Nightingale, 1 vol., Vol. 1. 2013. (Famous Lives Ser.). (ENG., Illus.). 24p. (J). (gr. 1-2). 25.27 (978-1-4824-0405-0(2), a4ee7e1d-f389-4e59-acd6-f6658e980946) Stevens, Gareth Publishing LLLP.
Cooke, Tim. Florence Nightingale, 1 vol. 2016. (Meet the Greats Ser.). (ENG.). 48p. (J). (gr. 5-5). pap. 15.65 (978-1-4824-5948-7(5), c2083cbd-472c-4525-b6e1-081162ca31d8) Stevens, Gareth Publishing LLLP.
Dorling Kindersley Publishing Staff. Florence Nightingale: DK Life Stories. 2019. (Illus.). 128p. (J). (978-0-241-35631-9(8)) Dorling Kindersley Publishing, Inc.
Edison, Erin. Florence Nightingale, 1 vol. 2014. (Great Women in History Ser.). (ENG., Illus.). 24p. (J). (gr. -1-2). lib. bdg. 24.65 (978-1-4765-4214-0(7), 124312) Capstone.
Garnett, Emmeline & Jauss, Anne Marie. Florence Nightingale's Nuns. 2009. (Vision Bks.). (ENG.). 158p. (J). (gr. 4-10). pap. 12.95 (978-1-58617-297-8(2)) Ignatius Pr.
Hinman, Bonnie. Florence Nightingale & the Advancement of Nursing. 2004. (Uncharted, Unexplored, & Unexplained Ser.). (Illus.). 48p. (J). (gr. 4-8). lib. bdg. 29.95 (978-1-58415-257-6(5)) Mitchell Lane Pubs.
Jazynka, Kitson. DK Life Stories: Florence Nightingale. Ager, Charlotte, illus. 2019. (DK Life Stories Ser.). (ENG.). 128p. (J). (gr. 3-7). pap. 5.99 (978-1-4654-7843-6(4), DK Children) Dorling Kindersley Publishing, Inc.
Reef, Catherine. Florence Nightingale: The Courageous Life of the Legendary Nurse. 2016. (ENG., Illus.). 192p. (YA). (gr. 7). 18.99 (978-0-544-53580-0(4), 1608187, Clarion Bks.) HarperCollins Pubs.
Richter, Sandy. The Life of Florence Nightingale, 1 vol. 2008. (Real Life Readers Ser.). (ENG.). 16p. (gr. 2-3). pap. 7.05 (978-1-4358-0225-4(X), 39f032ec-baec-4ef8-a950-6d7640b3e2f9, Rosen Classroom) Rosen Publishing Group, Inc., The.
Robbins, Trina. Florence Nightingale: Lady with the Lamp, 1 vol. Timmons, Anne, illus. 2007. (Graphic Biographies Ser.). (ENG.). 32p. (J). (gr. 3-9). per. 8.10 (978-0-7368-7902-6(1), 93899, Capstone Pr.) Capstone.
Ross, Stewart. Don't Say No to Flo: The Story of Florence Nightingale. Shields, Susan, illus. (ENG.). 32p. (J). pap. (978-0-7502-3273-9(0), Wayland) Hachette Children's Group.
Webb, Robert N. The How & Why Wonder Book of Florence Nightingale. Vosburgh, Leonard, illus. 2011. 50p. 35.95 (978-1-258-09107-1(0)) Literary Licensing, LLC.
Wood, Jill G. Florence Nightingale: Called to Serve with Buffalo Biff & Farley's Raiders. Cox, Brian T., illus. 2006. (Time Traveler's Adventure Ser.). 56p. (J). 13.50 incl. audio compact disk (978-1-932332-29-2(4)) Toy Box Productions.
Zemlicka, Shannon. Florence Nightingale. Debon, Nicolas, illus. (On My Own Biographies Ser.). 48p. (gr. 2-5). 2005. 23.93 (978-0-87614-917-1(4)) 2003. (ENG.). (J). pap. 8.99 (978-0-87614-102-1(5), 10848be9-6bec-4f56-bb10-2039b051f907, First Avenue Editions) Lerner Publishing Group.

NIGHTINGALE, FLORENCE, 1820-1910—FICTION

Osborne, Mary Pope. High Time for Heroes. Murdocca, Sal, illus. 2016. (Magic Tree House (R) Merlin Mission Ser.: 23). 144p. (J). (gr. 2-5). 6.99 (978-0-307-98052-6(9), Random Hse. Bks. for Young Readers) Random Hse. Children's Bks.
—High Time for Heroes. 2016. (Magic Tree House Merlin Missions Ser.: 23). lib. bdg. 16.00 (978-0-606-38464-3(2)) Turtleback.
Springer, Nancy. Enola Holmes: the Case of the Cryptic Crinoline. 2011. (Enola Holmes Mystery Ser.: 5). (ENG., Illus.). 176p. (J). (gr. 3-7). 8.99 (978-0-14-241690-7(8), Puffin Books) Penguin Young Readers Group.

NIGHTMARES

Apel, Melanie Ann. Let's Talk about Nightmares. 2009. (Let's Talk Library). 24p. (gr. 2-3). 42.50 (978-1-60853-446-3(4), PowerKids Pr.) Rosen Publishing Group, Inc., The.

NIGHTMARES—FICTION

Adams, Mark Wayne. Good NightMare. 2007. (ENG.). 32p. (J). (gr. -1-1). lib. bdg. 12.99 (978-1-59616-001-9(2), SYP Kids) Southern Yellow Pine (SYP) Publishing LLC.
Arnold, Tedd. Fly Guy & the Frankenfly. 2013. (Fly Guy Ser.: 13). lib. bdg. 17.20 (978-0-606-32440-3(2)) Turtleback.
—Fly Guy & the Frankenfly (Fly Guy #13) Arnold, Tedd, illus. 2013. (Fly Guy Ser.: 13). (ENG., Illus.). 32p. (J). (gr. -1-3). 6.99 (978-0-545-49328-4(5), Cartwheel Bks.) Scholastic, Inc.
Baker, Monica S. Freestyle, 1 vol. 2010. (ENG., Illus.). 160p. (gr. 3-6). 14.99 (978-0-7643-3538-9(3), 3791) Schiffer Publishing, Ltd.
Balzola, Asun. Munia y el Cocolilo Naranja. (SPA.). 32p. (J). (978-84-233-1335-8(2)) Ediciones Destino ESP. Dist: Lectorum Pubns., Inc.
Begler, Pete. The Fearless Travelers' Guide to Wicked Places. 2017. (ENG., Illus.). 384p. (J). (gr. 4-8). 14.95 (978-1-62370-799-6(4), 133339, Capstone Young Readers) Capstone.
Bellisario, Gina. Super Spooked. von Innerebner, Jessika, illus. 2018. (Ellie Ultra Ser.). (ENG.). 128p. (J). (gr. 1-3). lib. bdg. 25.99 (978-1-4965-6512-9(6), 138517, Stone Arch Bks.) Capstone.
Berenstain, Stan & Berenstain, Jan. The Berenstain Bears & the Bad Dream. 2004. (Berenstain Bears First Time Bks.). (J). (gr. -1-2). spiral bd. (978-0-616-01555-1(0)); spiral bd. (978-0-616-01556-8(9)) Canadian National Institute for the Blind/Institut National Canadien pour les Aveugles.
Bour, Daniele. Petit ours brun fait un Cauche. pap. 12.95 (978-2-227-70921-8(9)) Bayard Editions FRA. Dist: Distribooks, Inc.
Bray, Libba. Lair of Dreams: A Diviners Novel. 2017. (Diviners Ser.: 2). (ENG.). 592p. (YA). (gr. 10-17). pap. 15.99 (978-0-316-12603-8(9)) Little, Brown Bks. for Young Readers.
Butler, Darren J. The Secret of Crybaby Hollow. 2004. (YA). mass mkt. 6.99 (978-0-9753367-5-5(4)) Onstage Publishing, LLC.
Cach, Lisa. Wake unto Me. 2011. 320p. (YA). (gr. 7-18). 8.99 (978-0-14-241436-1(0), Speak) Penguin Young Readers Group.
Carnevale, Michael. The Hotel Coolidge. 2007. 91p. pap. 10.95 (978-0-7414-3752-5(X)) Infinity Publishing.
Carter, Rebecca. Moonlit Daydreams. 2010. (ENG.). 71p. pap. 11.99 (978-0-557-35588-4(5)) Lulu Pr., Inc.
Chalmers, Jason. Fall Nightmares 101: A Parody. 2011. 72p. pap. 19.95 (978-1-4626-2883-4(4)) America Star Bks.
Chee, Traci. The Speaker. 2018. (Reader Ser.: 2). 512p. (YA). (gr. 7). pap. 10.99 (978-0-14-751806-4(7), Speak) Penguin Young Readers Group.
Christenson, Debra. Hairy Harry, 1 vol. 2010. 38p. pap. 24.95 (978-1-4489-2549-0(5)) PublishAmerica, Inc.
Cordero, Silvia Jaeger & Cordero, Silvia Jaegar. El Huevo Azul. Sunset Producciones & Producciones, Sunset, illus. rev. ed. 2005. (Castillo de la Lectura Verde Ser.). (SPA & ENG.). 136p. (J). (gr. -1-7). pap. 7.95 (978-970-20-0127-0(7)) Castillo, Ediciones, S. A. de C. V. MEX. Dist: Macmillan.
Corentin, Philippe. Papa! (SPA.). 32p. (978-84-95150-38-7(7)) Corimbo, Editorial S.L.
—Papa. 2003. (SPA.). (J). (gr. -1-k). 19.99 (978-84-8470-094-4(1)) Corimbo, Editorial S.L. ESP. Dist: Lectorum Pubns., Inc.
Darke, J. A. The Grin in the Dark. Evergreen, Nelson, illus. 2015. (Spine Shivers Ser.). (ENG.). 128p. (J). (gr. 4-6). lib. bdg. 27.32 (978-1-4965-0217-9(5), 128031, Stone Arch Bks.) Capstone.
Drouin, Véronique. L' Île D'Aurélie. 2004. (Mon Roman Ser.). (FRE.). 304p. (J). (gr. 2). pap. (978-2-89021-690-7(X)) Diffusion du livre Mirabel (DLM).
Dunbar, Joyce. Tell Me Something Happy Before I Go to Sleep Padded Board Book. Gliori, Debi, illus. 2018. (Lullaby Lights Ser.). (ENG.). 24p. (J). (— 1). bds. 8.99 (978-1-328-91068-4(7), 1701812, Clarion Bks.) HarperCollins Pubs.
Gutierrez, Debbi Miller. Cactus Factory. 2007. (J). pap. 5.99 (978-0-9740173-4-1(5)) Prints By Mail.
Hill, Andrew G. The Song of the Seraphim. 2009. 196p. pap. 13.95 (978-1-60860-194-3(3), Strategic Bk. Publishing) Strategic Book Publishing & Rights Agency (SBPRA).
Hinchcliffe, L. T. For the Love of Prudence Possum. 2008. 76p. pap. 15.50 (978-1-60693-136-3(9), Eloquent Bks.) Strategic Book Publishing & Rights Agency (SBPRA).
The Iris House. 2006. (YA). per. 12.95 (978-0-9677047-7-7(4)) Marble Hse. Editions.
Johnson, Linda & Hodges, Quae. 21st Century Parables: A Child's Book. 2006. 48p. pap. 14.95 (978-1-60145-071-5(0)) Booklocker.com, Inc.
Joseph, Curtis. Fairy Tales of the Forbidden & Untold. 2011. 24p. pap. 24.95 (978-1-4626-3485-9(0)) America Star Bks.
Joy, Judith Bourassa. A Doorway Through Space: Winner of Mayhaven Award for Children's Fiction. 2008. (ENG.). 224p. (YA). 14.95 (978-1-932278-17-0(6)) Mayhaven Publishing, Inc.
Joyce, William. E. Aster Bunnymund & the Warrior Eggs at the Earth's Core! Joyce, William, illus. (Guardians Ser.: 2). (ENG., Illus.). (J). (gr. 2-6). 2018. 288p. pap. 8.99 (978-1-4424-3051-8(6))Bk. 2. 2012. 272p. 18.99 (978-1-4424-3050-1(8)) Simon & Schuster Children's Publishing. (Atheneum Bks. for Young Readers).
Joyce, William & Geringer, Laura. Nicholas St. North & the Battle of the Nightmare King. Joyce, William, illus. 2018. (Guardians Ser.: 1). (ENG., Illus.). 256p. (J). (gr. 2-6). pap. 8.99 (978-1-4424-3049-5(4), Atheneum Bks. for Young Readers) Simon & Schuster Children's Publishing.
Kaufman, Kathleen. The Lairdbalor. 2017. (ENG.). 288p. (YA). 29.99 (978-1-68336-588-4(7)); pap. 15.99 (978-1-68336-587-7(9)) Turner Publishing Co.
Kitami, Yoko. Cactus. 2005. (Los Especiales de A la Orilla del Viento Ser.).Tr. of Cactus. (SPA., Illus.). 36p. (J). (gr. 2-4). (978-968-16-7386-4(7), FC15223) Fondo de Cultura Economica.
Klavan, Andrew. Nightmare City, 1 vol. 2013. (ENG.). 320p. (YA). 14.99 (978-1-59554-797-2(5)) Nelson, Thomas Inc.
Klein, Abby. Ready, Freddy! #6: Help! a Vampire's Coming! Help! a Vampire's Coming! McKinley, John, illus. 2005. (Ready, Freddy! Ser.: 6). (ENG.). 96p. (J). (gr. -1-3). 5.99 (978-0-439-55606-4(6), Blue Sky Pr., The) Scholastic, Inc.
Lawrence, Dionne L. The Story of Her?! 2012. 28p. (-18). pap. 16.95 (978-1-62709-253-1(6)) America Star Bks.
Lowry, Lois. Gossamer. 2008. (ENG.). 176p. (J). (gr. 3-7). 6.99 (978-0-385-73416-5(6), Yearling) Random Hse. Children's Bks.
MacKenzie, Ross. Zac & the Dream Stealers. 2013. 297p. (J). (978-0-545-40107-4(0), Chicken Hse., The) Scholastic, Inc.
Mayer, Jeffrey J. Il y a Cauchemar dans Mon Placard.Tr. of There's a Nightmare in My Cupboard. (FRE.). (J). pap. 10.95 (978-2-07-050611-8(8)) Gallimard, Editions FRA. Dist: Distribooks, Inc.
McMann, Lisa. Don't Close Your Eyes: Wake; Fade; Gone. 2013. (ENG., Illus.). 720p. (YA). (gr. 9). pap. 14.99 (978-1-4424-9913-3(3), Simon Pulse) Simon Pulse.
Moffett, Rodney. The Eighth Crest. 2006. (ENG.). 228p. per. 24.95 (978-1-4241-3907-1(4)) PublishAmerica, Inc.
Nero, Molly. Smarty Pig & the Test Taking Terror. Turchan, Monique, illus. 2012. 28p. pap. 12.95 (978-1-61244-055-2(X)) Halo Publishing International.
Night, P. J. Together Forever. 2012. (Creepover Ser.: 8). lib. bdg. 16.00 (978-0-606-26339-9(X)) Turtleback.
—Your Worst Nightmare. 2013. (You're Invited to a Creepover Ser.: 17). (ENG., Illus.). 160p. (J). (gr. 3-7). pap. 6.99 (978-1-4424-8235-7(4), Simon Spotlight) Simon Spotlight.
Nixon, Joan Lowery. Nightmare. 2005. 166p. (gr. 5-7). 17.00 (978-0-7569-5239-6(5)) Perfection Learning Corp.
Perez, Marlene. Dead Is Just a Dream. 2014. (Dead Is Ser.: 8). lib. bdg. 18.40 (978-0-606-35990-0(7)) Turtleback.
Peters, Robert. Da Goodie Monsta: Chase Dem Nightmares Away. Peters, Robert, illus. 2009. (Illus.). 28p. (YA). lib. bdg. (978-0-9823906-7-2(X)) Wiggles Pr.
Piggy Toes Press Staff. All the Way's I Love You Mini. Downing, Julie, illus. 2005. (ENG.). 10p. (J). 4.95 (978-1-58117-437-3(3), Intervisual/Piggy Toes) Bendon, Inc.
Plum, Amy. Dreamfall. (Dreamfall Ser.: 1). (ENG.). (YA). (gr. 9). 2018. 304p. pap. 10.99 (978-0-06-242988-9(4)) 2017. 288p. 17.99 (978-0-06-242987-2(6)) HarperCollins Pubs. (HarperTeen).
Richardson, Tracy. The Field. unabr. ed. 2013. (ENG.). 200p. (YA). (gr. 7-12). pap. 11.95 (978-1-935462-82-8(2)) Luminis Bks., Inc.
Rippin, Sally. The Night Fright. Fukuoka, Aki, illus. 2015. (Billie B. Brown Ser.). (ENG.). 43p. (J). (978-1-61067-451-5(0)) Kane Miller.
—The Night Fright: Billie B Brown. Fukuoka, Aki, illus. 2016. (ENG.). 48p. (J). pap. 4.99 (978-1-61067-391-4(3)) Kane Miller.
Roe, D. J. The Impossible Dream. 2008. 59p. pap. 16.95 (978-1-60610-173-5(0)) America Star Bks.
Roman, Stacey. Some of Us Want Wrinkles. Wurster, Laurie, illus. 2005. (J). per. 16.95 (978-1-59858-033-4(7)) Dog Ear Publishing, LLC.
Schroeder, Lisa. Chasing Brooklyn. (ENG.). (YA). (gr. 9). 2011. 432p. pap. 12.99 (978-1-4169-9174-8(3)) 2010. 320p. 24.94 (978-1-4169-9168-7(9)) Simon Pulse. (Simon Pulse).
Segel, Jason & Miller, Kirsten. Nightmares! Kwasny, Karl, illus. 2015. (Nightmares! Ser.: 1). (ENG.). 400p. (J). (gr. 3-7). 8.99 (978-0-385-74426-3(9), Yearling) Random Hse. Children's Bks.
—Nightmares! the Lost Lullaby. Kwasny, Karl, illus. 2017. (Nightmares! Ser.: 3). (ENG.). 352p. (J). (gr. 3-7). pap. 8.99 (978-0-385-74430-0(7), Yearling) Random Hse. Children's Bks.
—The Sleepwalker Tonic. Kwasny, Karl, illus. 2016. (Nightmares! Ser.: 2). (ENG.). 384p. (J). (gr. 3-7). 18.40 (978-0-606-39350-8(1)) Turtleback.
Sewell, Byron W. Alix's Adventures in Wonderland: Lewis Carroll's Nightmare. 2011. (Illus.). 130p. pap. (978-1-904808-72-5(7)) Evertype.
Shepherd, Kat. Babysitting Nightmares: the Shadow Hand. Vieira, Rayanne, illus. 2018. (Babysitting Nightmares Ser.: 1). (ENG.). 208p. (J). 13.99 (978-1-250-15696-9(3), 900185121) Imprint IND. Dist: Macmillan.
Spring, Manda. Emerald & the Withered Willow. 2007. 148p. pap. 18.00 (978-1-4303-1353-3(6)) Lulu Pr., Inc.
Stine, R. L. Fear Street Super Thriller. 2015. (Fear Street Ser.). (ENG.). 592p. (YA). (gr. 7-12). pap. 12.99 (978-1-250-07693-9(5), 900152585, St. Martin's Griffin) St. Martin's Pr.
—Welcome to Camp Nightmare (Classic Goosebumps #14) 2010. (Classic Goosebumps Ser.: 14). (ENG.). 160p. (J). (gr. 3-7). 7.99 (978-0-545-15889-3(3), Scholastic Paperbacks) Scholastic, Inc.
Stolarz, Laurie Faria. Red Is for Remembrance. l.t. ed. 2008. (Blue Is for Nightmares Ser.: Bk. 4). 385p. (YA). (gr. 7). 22.95 (978-1-4104-0339-1(4)) Thorndike Pr.
Sweet Dreams, Curious George. 2013. (Curious George Ser.). (ENG., Illus.). 24p. (J). (gr. -1-3). 9.99 (978-0-544-03880-6(0), 1531375, Clarion Bks.) HarperCollins Pubs.
Taft, Christopher C. The Witch of Green Spring. 2013. 120p. pap. 11.00 (978-1-61204-198-8(1), Strategic Bk. Publishing) Strategic Book Publishing & Rights Agency (SBPRA).
Teare, Nellie. Celia & the Witches. Senkel, Nicholas, illus. 2008. 24p. (J). 13.95 (978-0-9820852-0-2(6)) Harmon Creek Pr.
Tetri, Emily. Tiger vs. Nightmare. Tetri, Emily, illus. 2018. (ENG., Illus.). 64p. (J). 18.99 (978-1-62672-535-5(7), 900160471, First Second Bks.) Roaring Brook Pr.
Tibo, Gilles. Le Gardien du Sommeil. Jorisch, Stéphane, illus. 2004. (Mon Roman Ser.). (FRE.). 64p. (J). (gr. 2). pap. (978-2-89021-691-4(8)) Diffusion du livre Mirabel (DLM).
Timroth, Stephen. Dreamhawk. 2009. 24p. pap. 12.00 (978-1-60860-501-9(9), Strategic Bk. Publishing) Strategic Book Publishing & Rights Agency (SBPRA).
Van Zant, Dawn. No More Night Mares: A Dream of Freedom. McElroy, Kim, illus. 2005. (J). pap. 9.99 (978-0-9761768-1-7(5)) Wild Heart Ranch, Inc.
Vernon, Ursula. Dragonbreath #8: Nightmare of the Iguana. 2013. (Dragonbreath Ser.: 8). (ENG., Illus.). 208p. (J). (gr. 3-7). 14.99 (978-0-8037-3846-1(3), Dial Bks) Penguin Young Readers Group.
Villoro, Carmen & Perez, Federico. Amarina y el Viejo Pesadilla y Otros Cuentos. (Torre de Papel Ser.). (SPA.). (J). (gr. 2). 7.95 (978-958-04-3650-8(9)) Norma S.A. COL. Dist: Distribuidora Norma, Inc.
Walsh, Ann. The Doctor's Apprentice. 2005. 160p. (YA). (gr. 3-8). pap., tchr. ed. 8.95 (978-0-88878-389-9(2)) Beach Holme Pubs., Ltd. CAN. Dist: Literary Pr. Group of Canada.
—The Doctor's Apprentice: A Barkerville Mystery. 2007. (Barkerville Mystery Ser.: 2). (ENG.). 148p. (J). pap. 11.99 (978-1-55002-633-7(X)) Dundurn Pr. CAN. Dist: Publishers Group West (PGW).
Weston, Paula. Shadows. 2013. (Rephaim Ser.: 1). (ENG.). 400p. (YA). (gr. 9). 17.99 (978-1-77049-547-0(9), Tundra Bks.) Tundra Bks. CAN. Dist: Penguin Random Hse. LLC.
Williams, Harland, illus. The Kid with Too Many Nightmares. 2004. (J). (978-0-8431-1582-6(3), Price Stern Sloan) Penguin Publishing Group.
Wynne-Jones, Tim. Stephen Fair. (J). pap. 6.95 (978-0-88899-360-1(9)) Groundwood Bks. CAN. Dist: Publishers Group West (PGW).

NIKOLAEVA, VALENTINA VLADIMIROVNA TERESHKOVA, 1937-

Feldman, Heather. Valentina Tereshkova: The First Woman in Space. 2009. (Space Firsts Ser.). 24p. (gr. 3-4). 42.50 (978-1-60853-114-1(7), PowerKids Pr.) Rosen Publishing Group, Inc., The.

NILE RIVER AND VALLEY

Aloian, Molly. The Nile: River in the Sand, 1 vol. 2010. (Rivers Around the World Ser.). (ENG., Illus.). 32p. (J). (gr. 5-8). pap. (978-0-7787-7468-6(6)); lib. bdg. (978-0-7787-7445-7(7)) Crabtree Publishing Co.
Banting, Erinn. The Nile River. (Natural Wonders Ser.). (Illus.). 32p. (J). 2007. per. 8.95 (978-1-59036-275-4(6)) 2005. (gr. 4-6). lib. bdg. 26.00 (978-1-59036-269-3(1)) Weigl Pubs., Inc.
Gagne, Tammy. The Nile River. 2012. (Illus.). 47p. (J). lib. bdg. 29.95 (978-1-61228-294-7(6)) Mitchell Lane Pubs.
Gregory, Stefan. Life along the Nile, 1 vol. 2008. (Real Life Readers Ser.). (ENG.). 16p. (gr. 2-4). pap. 7.05

(978-1-4358-0226-1(8), 13e7ee15-5296-4dd5-8c75-88c298c2a183, Rosen Classroom) Rosen Publishing Group, Inc., The.

Heinrichs, Ann. The Nile, 1 vol. 2008. (Nature's Wonders Ser.). (ENG.). 96p. (gr. 6-6). lib. bdg. 38.36 *(978-0-7614-2854-1(2),* 034df8ba-08c1-4a12-8c3e-7e454fa8dbf0) Cavendish Square Publishing LLC.

Manning, Paul. Nile River. 2014. (River Adventures Ser.). (J). lib. bdg. 31.35 *(978-1-59920-917-3(9))* Black Rabbit Bks.

The Nile. 2011. (River Journey Ser.). (ENG.). 48p. (YA). (gr. 5-8). 27.95 *(978-1-4488-6012-8(1),* Rosen Reference) Rosen Publishing Group, Inc., The.

Parks, Peggy J. Aswan High Dam. (Building World Landmarks Ser.). (J). 2004. 26.19 *(978-1-4103-0204-5(0))* 2003. (Illus.). 48p. 24.95 *(978-1-56711-329-7(X))* Cengage Gale. (Blackbirch Pr., Inc.).

Spradlin, Michael P. Nile Chaos: A 4D Book. Karkavelas, Spiros, illus. 2018. (Pararescue Corps Ser.). (ENG.). 128p. (J). (gr. 4-8). lib. bdg. 27.32 *(978-1-4965-5201-3(6),* 136212, Stone Arch Bks.) Capstone.

Weintraub, Aileen. The Nile: The Longest River. 2009. (Great Record Breakers in Nature Ser.). 24p. (gr. 3-4). 42.50 *(978-1-61513-184-6(1),* PowerKids Pr.) Rosen Publishing Group, Inc., The.

NINO CURRENT

see El Nino Current

NIXON, RICHARD M. (RICHARD MILHOUS), 1913-1994

Archer, Jules. Watergate: A Story of Richard Nixon & the Shocking 1972 Scandal. rev. ed. 2015. (Jules Archer History for Young Readers Ser.). (ENG., Illus.). 344p. (J). (gr. 6-6). 16.99 *(978-1-63220-606-0(4),* Sky Pony Pr.) Skyhorse Publishing Co., Inc.

Aronson, Billy. Richard M. Nixon, 1 vol. 2008. (Presidents & Their Times Ser.). (ENG., Illus.). 96p. (gr. 6-6). lib. bdg. 36.93 *(978-0-7614-2428-4(8),* 7d1fb918-7384-47cb-80e3-91d437f81f88) Cavendish Square Publishing LLC.

Barron, Rachel Stiffler. Richard Nixon: American Politician. rev. exp. ed. 2003. (Notable Americans Ser.). (Illus.). 128p. (J). (gr. 6-12). 23.95 *(978-1-931798-30-3(3))* Reynolds, Morgan Inc.

Britton, Tamara L. Richard Nixon, 1 vol. 2016. (United States Presidents *2017 Ser.). (ENG., Illus.). 40p. (J). (gr. 2-5). lib. bdg. 35.64 *(978-1-68078-110-6(3),* 21837, Big Buddy Bks.) ABDO Publishing Co.

Burgan, Michael. TV Shapes Presidential Politics in the Kennedy-Nixon Debates: 4D an Augmented Reading Experience. 2018. (Captured Television History 4D Ser.). (ENG., Illus.). 64p. (J). (gr. 5-9). pap. 8.99 *(978-0-7565-5827-7(1),* 138352, Compass Point Bks.) Capstone.

Donaldson, Madeline. Richard Nixon. 2009. pap. 52.95 *(978-0-7613-4956-3(1))* 2008. (ENG.). 48p. (gr. 3-6). 27.93 *(978-0-8225-8896-2(X),* Lerner Pubns.) Lerner Publishing Group.

Elish, Dan. The Watergate Scandal. 2004. (Cornerstones of Freedom Ser.). (ENG., Illus.). 48p. (J). 26.00 *(978-0-516-24239-2(3),* Children's Pr.) Scholastic Library Publishing.

Fremon, David K. The Watergate Scandal in United States History, 1 vol. 2014. (In United States History Ser.). (ENG., Illus.). 96p. (gr. 5-6). (J). pap. 13.88 *(978-0-7660-6108-8(6),* 620b45c8-e671-4b5c-b7d8-6d22b4045811); 31.61 *(978-0-7660-6107-1(8),* 7733f69b-38ff-41c5-8ffe-24a281bb7dcc) Enslow Publishing, LLC.

Hasselius, Michelle M. Richard M. Nixon, 1 vol. 2014. (Presidential Biographies Ser.). (ENG.). 24p. (J). (gr. -1-2). lib. bdg. 27.32 *(978-1-4765-9612-9(3),* 125418, Capstone Pr.) Capstone.

Honders, Christine. Watergate & the Resignation of President Nixon, 1 vol. 2018. (American History Ser.). (ENG.). 104p. (gr. 7-7). 41.03 *(978-1-5345-6427-5(6),* 09e66a89-585c-4750-b227-8241dc49ea84, Lucent Pr.) Greenhaven Publishing LLC.

Lewis K., Parker. How to Draw the Life & Times of Richard M. Nixon, 1 vol. 2005. (Kid's Guide to Drawing the Presidents of the United States of America Ser.). (ENG., Illus.). 32p. (YA). (gr. 4-4). 30.27 *(978-1-4042-3013-2(0),* 1f1b6ca4-e13a-40d6-9ca7-bc451b930ad4) Rosen Publishing Group, Inc., The.

Marquez, Heron. Richard M. Nixon. 2003. (Presidential Leaders Ser.). (Illus.). 112p. (J). 29.27 *(978-0-8225-0098-8(1),* Lerner Pubns.) Lerner Publishing Group.

Meter, Larry A. Van. United States V. Nixon. 2007. (Great Supreme Court Decisions Ser.). (ENG., Illus.). 112p. (gr. 5-9). lib. bdg. 32.95 *(978-0-7910-9381-8(6),* P124639, Facts On File) Infobase Holdings, Inc.

Parker, Lewis. How to Draw the Life & Times of Richard M. Nixon. 2009. (Kid's Guide to Drawing the Presidents of the United States of America Ser.). 32p. (gr. 4-4). 50.50 *(978-1-61511-157-2(3),* PowerKids Pr.) Rosen Publishing Group, Inc., The.

Stine, Megan & Who HQ. Who Was Richard Nixon? Gutierrez, Manuel, IV & Gutierrez, Manuel, illus. 2020. (Who Was? Ser.). 112p. (J). (gr. 3-7). 5.99 *(978-1-5247-8980-0(1),* Penguin Workshop) Penguin Young Readers Group.

Tracy, Kathleen. The Watergate Scandal. 2006. (Monumental Milestones Ser.). (Illus.). 48p. (YA). (gr. 4-7). lib. bdg. 29.95 *(978-1-58415-470-9(5))* Mitchell Lane Pubs.

Uschan, Michael V. Watergate, 1 vol. 2009. (American History Ser.). (ENG., Illus.). 104p. (gr. 7-7). 41.03 *(978-1-4205-0135-3(6),* 25c4e805-a3e4-4787-8933-293ffb81b51e, Lucent Pr.) Greenhaven Publishing LLC.

Venezia, Mike. Getting to Know the U. S. Presidents: Richard M. Nixon. Venezia, Mike, illus. 2007. (Getting to Know the U. S. Presidents Ser.). (ENG., Illus.). 32p. (J). (gr. 3-4). pap. 7.95 *(978-0-531-17949-9(4),* Children's Pr.) Scholastic Library Publishing.

—Richard M. Nixon: Thirty-Seventh President, 1969-1974. Venezia, Mike, illus. 2007. (Getting to Know the U. S. Presidents Ser.). (Illus.). 32p. (J). (gr. 3-4). 28.00 *(978-0-516-22641-5(X),* Children's Pr.) Scholastic Library Publishing.

NOAH'S ARK

Amery, H. Noah's Ark. rev. ed. 2004. (Bible Tales Readers Ser.). (Illus.). 16p. (J). pap. 4.95 *(978-0-7945-0416-8(7));* lib. bdg. 12.95 *(978-1-58086-542-5(9))* EDC Publishing.

Ark (J). bds. 9.95 *(978-0-87162-415-4(X))* Warner Pr., Inc.

Bagley, Val Chadwick. Seek & Find Noah's Ark. 2017. (Illus.). (J). *(978-1-5244-0292-1(3))* Covenant Communications, Inc.

Barry, Bruce. The Roach Approach, Noah's Journey of Faith. 2003. (Illus.). (J). per. 16.99 *(978-0-9742997-0-9(7))* Wacky World Studios LLC.

Beaton, Clare. Make Your Own Noah's Ark. Beaton, Clare, illus. 2007. (Illus.). (J). (gr. k-3). 9.95 *(978-0-8198-4862-8(X))* Pauline Bks. & Media.

Blyton, Enid. Noah & the Ark: See the Picture & Say the Word. 2012. 24p. (J). 9.95 *(978-1-84135-746-1(4))* Award Pubns. Ltd. GBR. Dist: Parkwest Pubns., Inc.

Box, Su. The First Rainbow Sparkle & Squidge: The Story of Noah's Ark. Poole, Susie, illus. 2008. (ENG.). 28p. (J). (gr. -1-k). bds. 7.99 *(978-0-7459-6904-6(6),* c51495d3-0205-4911-b628-d080a26e8859, Lion Children's) Lion Hudson PLC GBR. Dist: Baker & Taylor Publisher Services (BTPS).

Brayley, Genevieve. Noah Saves the Tigers. 2010. 28p. pap. 28.03 *(978-1-4500-3077-9(7))* Xlibris Corp.

Carlson, Melody. Noah & the Incredible Flood, 5 vols. Francisco, Wendy, illus. 2003. (Bible Adventure Club Ser.). 36p. wbk. ed. 19.99 incl. audio, cd-rom *(978-1-58134-336-6(1))* Crossway.

Coburn, Claudia. Did the Aardvarks Say "No Ark"? Hoard, Angela, illus. 2004. 32p. (J). *(978-0-9759343-1-9(7))* Purfect Promises.

Dalmatian Press Staff. Noah's Ark. 2004. (ENG., Illus.). 24p. (J). 2.99 *(978-1-4037-0968-4(8),* Spirit Pr.) Bendon, Inc.

David, Juliet. All Aboard with Noah, 1 vol. Canuso, Jackie & Canuso, Jackie, illus. 2016. (ENG.). 12p. (J). (gr. -1-k). 11.99 *(978-1-78128-249-6(8),* b8b47fdf-710b-4ba4-850d-be9857166e82, Candle Bks.) Lion Hudson PLC GBR. Dist: Baker & Taylor Publisher Services (BTPS).

—The Great Flood, 1 vol. Parry, Jo, illus. 2014. 12p. (J). bds. 3.99 *(978-1-85985-991-9(7),* Candle Bks.) Lion Hudson PLC GBR. Dist: Kregel Pubns.

David, R. Noahs Ark. 2010. 12p. *(978-965-91286-1-7(4))* Sifrei Bet Shearim Ltd.

Davidson, Alice Joyce. The Story of Noah. Guile, Gill, illus. 2016. (ENG.). (J). 9.95 *(978-0-87029-706-9(6))* Abbey Pr.

De Graaf, A. M. Noe y el Arca. (Divertidas Historias Biblicas para Ninos Ser.). (SPA.). (J). 3.49 *(978-0-7899-0524-6(8),* 496641) Editorial Unilit.

DK. Noah's Ark. Di Lernia, Giuseppe, illus. 2018. (Bible Bedtime Stories Ser.). (ENG.). 30p. (J). (-k). bds. 12.99 *(978-1-4654-6999-1(0),* DK Children) Dorling Kindersley Publishing, Inc.

Dowley, Tim. Noah & His Big Boat. 2005. (Magnetic Adventures Ser.). (Illus.). 10p. (J). (gr. -1-3). 15.99 *(978-0-8254-7294-7(6),* Candle Bks.) Lion Hudson PLC GBR. Dist: Kregel Pubns.

Dudley, Becki. Inside Noah's Ark 4 Kids. Looney, Bill, illus. 2017. (ENG.). 12p. (J). bds. 12.99 *(978-1-68344-072-7(2),* Master Books) New Leaf Publishing Group.

—Remarkable Rescue: Saved on Noah's Ark. Albrecht, Jeff, illus. 2016. (ENG.). 12p. (J). bds. 8.99 *(978-0-89051-976-9(5),* Master Books) New Leaf Publishing Group.

Embleton-Hall, Chris. Noah's Amazing Ark: A Lift-The-Flap Adventure, 1 vol. 2017. (ENG., Illus.). 12p. (J). (gr. -1-k). 10.99 *(978-1-78128-317-2(6),* 42def216-dbb4-4fac-bddb-9605966ab6b3, Candle Bks.) Lion Hudson PLC GBR. Dist: Baker & Taylor Publisher Services (BTPS).

Froeb, Lori C. Noah's Ark, 1 vol. Rinaldo, Luana, illus. 2008. 12p. (J). bds. 7.99 *(978-0-8254-5546-9(4))* Kregel Pubns.

Golden, William Lee. Noah, Didn't It Rain. Looney, Bill, illus. 2008. 29p. (J). (gr. -1-3). 13.99 incl. audio compact disk *(978-0-89221-683-3(2))* New Leaf Publishing Group.

Ham, Ken & Malott, Cindy. The Answers Book for Kids Volume 2: 22 Questions from Kids on Dinosaurs & the Flood of Noah. 2008. 2. (Illus.). 48p. (J). (gr. 4-6). pap. 7.99 *(978-0-89051-527-3(1),* Master Books) New Leaf Publishing Group.

Hawksley, Gerald. Amazing Journey of Noah & His Incredible Ark. 2004. 20p. pap. 11.99 *(978-0-8254-7275-6(X))* Kregel Pubns.

Hazen, Barbara Shook. Noah's Ark. Catusanu, Mircea, illus. 2003. (Little Golden Book Ser.). 32p. (J). (gr. -1-2). 5.99 *(978-0-307-10440-3(0),* Golden Bks.) Random Hse. Children's Bks.

James, Annabelle. Noah's Ark: Story in a Box. 2003. (J). bds. 8.99 *(978-1-883043-51-3(4))* Straight Edge Pr., The.

Janisch, Heinz. Noah's Ark. Zwerger, Lisbeth, illus. 2018. 96p. (J). (gr. k-2). 17.99 *(978-988-8341-70-2(7),* Minedition) Penguin Young Readers Group.

Josephs, Mary. All Aboard Noah's Ark! Bratun, Katy, illus. 2007. (Chunky Book(R) Ser.). 22p. (J). (— 1). 3.99 *(978-0-679-86054-9(1),* Golden Inspirational) Random Hse. Children's Bks.

Karr, Lily. Noah's Ark. Berg, Michelle, illus. 2007. (ENG.). 6p. (J). (gr. -1). bds. 12.99 *(978-0-439-86396-4(1))* Scholastic, Inc.

Kneen, Maggie. Two by Two: The Story of Noah & the Ark. 2008. (ENG., Illus.). 12p. (J). *(978-1-55168-324-9(5))* Fenn, H. B. & Co., Ltd.

Knudsen, Michelle. Noah's Ark. Santoro, Christopher, illus. 2016. (Lift-The-Flap Ser.). 14p. (J). (gr. -1 — 1). bds. 6.99 *(978-0-553-53537-2(4),* Random Hse. Bks. for Young Readers) Random Hse. Children's Bks.

Ladybird Books Staff. Noah's Ark. (Bible Stories Ser.: No. S846-2). (Illus.). (J). (gr. -1-2). pap. 3.95 *(978-0-7214-5065-0(2),* Dutton Juvenile) Penguin Publishing Group.

Larcombe, Jennifer Rees. The Best Boat Ever Built. Björkman, Steve, illus. 2004. (Best Bible Stories Ser.). 24p. (gr. -1-3). pap. 2.99 *(978-1-58134-148-5(2))* Crossway.

Macdonald, Mindy. Noah's Crew Came 2 By 2. 2004. (GodCounts Ser.). (ENG.). 24p. (J). bds. 16.99 *(978-1-59052-409-1(8),* Multnomah Bks.) Crown Publishing Group, The.

MacKenzie, Carine. Bible Heroes Noah. 2013. (Bible Art Ser.). (ENG.). 16p. (J). pap., act. bk. ed. 2.50 *(978-1-85792-823-5(7),* 5e6657dc-d365-4f5b-9cf3-766ec0113496) Christian Focus Pubns. GBR. Dist: Baker & Taylor Publisher Services (BTPS).

Make Believe Ideas. Noah. 2006. (Illus.). 32p. (J). (gr. -1-3). 8.97 *(978-1-59145-526-4(X))* Nelson, Thomas Inc.

Martin, Jr., Bill & Sampson, Michael. Noah, Noah, What Do You See?, 1 vol. 2017. (ENG., Illus.). 30p. (J). bds. 7.99 *(978-0-7180-8949-8(9),* Tommy Nelson) Nelson, Thomas Inc.

Martin, Oscar, Jr., creator. Noah l.t. ed. 2003. (Illus.). 25p. (J). E-Book 19.95 incl. cd-rom *(978-0-9748416-1-8(7))* Build Your Story.

McCombs, Margi. Noah's Ark. Fox, Lisa, illus. 2014. (ENG.). 10p. (J). (gr. -1-k). bds. 7.99 *(978-0-545-60557-1(1),* Little Shepherd) Scholastic, Inc.

Miller, Sharon J. Noah. Adona, Nomer, illus. 2016. (ENG.). 26p. (J). pap. 9.97 *(978-0-9774756-4-3(6))* Miller, Sharon.

Mitter, Matt. Guess Who Noah's Boat, 1 vol. Jarzabek, Ela, illus. 2014. 10p. (J). 11.99 *(978-0-8254-4205-6(2))* Kregel Pubns.

Nilsen, Lenie. The Elephant & the Dove. 2013. (Illus.). 42p. (J). 18.99 *(978-1-940473-04-8(7))* Rise Up.

Noah & the Ark. 2004. 5.95 *(978-1-57264-240-9(8))* Parsons Technology.

Noah & the Ark. Date not set. (J). 8.95 *(978-0-88271-533-9(X),* 10521) Regina Pr., Malhame & Co.

Noah's Ark. Date not set. (Illus.). (J). bds. 9.98 *(978-1-4054-2048-8(0))* Parragon, Inc.

Noah's Ark: A Bible Story to Color. (Illus.). 16p. (J). pap. 1.50 *(978-0-87162-823-7(6),* E6017) Warner Pr., Inc.

Noah's Ark Bible Sticker Book. 2003. (Illus.). 16p. (J). 2.98 *(978-1-4054-1558-3(4))* Parragon, Inc.

Noah's Ark Fun Book. (Illus.). 16p. (J). pap. 1.50 *(978-0-87162-977-7(1),* E4982) Warner Pr., Inc.

Noble, Marty. Fun with Noah's Ark Stencils. 2006. (Dover Stencils Ser.). (ENG., Illus.). 6p. (J). (gr. -1-5). pap. 1.50 *(978-0-486-44881-7(9))* Dover Pubns., Inc.

Page, Nick & Claire. Noah & the Ark. 2006. (Read with Me (Make Believe Ideas) Ser.). (Illus.). 32p. (J). (gr. k-2). *(978-1-84610-168-7(9))* Make Believe Ideas.

Pinkney, Jerry. Noah's Ark. 2004. (J). (gr. k-3). 29.95 *(978-1-55592-533-8(2))* Weston Woods Studios, Inc.

Prestofillopo, Mary Nazarene, tr. The Story of Noah's Ark. Flamini, Lorella, illus. 2003. 38p. (J). 9.95 *(978-0-8198-7084-1(6),* 332-380) Pauline Bks. & Media.

Publications International Ltd. Staff, ed. Look & Find - Noah's Arc & Other Bible Stories. 2011. 24p. (J). 3.75 net. *(978-1-4508-1554-3(5))* Phoenix International Publications, Inc.

Pulley, Kelly & Zondervan Staff. Noah & the Ark, 1 vol. Pulley, Kelly, illus. 2009. (I Can Read! / the Beginner's Bible / ¡Yo Sé Leer! Ser.). (SPA., Illus.). 32p. (J). pap. 4.99 *(978-0-310-71886-4(4))* Zonderkidz.

Reinhart, Matthew. The Ark: A Pop-up Book. Reinhart, Matthew, illus. 2006. (Illus.). 12p. (J). (gr. k-4). reprint ed. 17.00 *(978-1-4223-5673-9(6))* DIANE Publishing Co.

Rivadeneira, Caryn Dahlstrand. The Story of Noah's Ark: A Spark Bible Story. Grosshauser, Peter, illus. 2016. (Spark Story Bibles Ser.). (ENG.). 32p. (J). (gr. -1-3). 12.99 *(978-1-5064-1767-7(1))* 1517 Media.

Rowlands, Avril. All the Tales from the Ark. 2003. (Illus.). 446p. pap. 13.99 *(978-0-7459-4835-5(9),* Lion Books) Lion Hudson PLC GBR. Dist: Trafalgar Square Publishing.

Rutherford, Peter, illus. Noah's Ark. 2015. 24p. (J). (gr. -1-k). bds. 6.99 *(978-1-86147-644-9(2),* Armadillo) Anness Publishing GBR. Dist: National Bk. Network.

Simon, Mary Mans. Noah's Ark: Read & Learn the Bible. 2005. (ENG., Illus.). 24p. (J). pap. 2.99 *(978-1-4037-1157-1(7),* Spirit Pr.) Bendon, Inc.

Smart Kids Publishing Staff. Noah's Ark Story of Being Thankful. 2007. (ENG.). 16p. (J). 19.99 *(978-0-8249-6703-1(8),* Ideals Pubns.) Worthy Publishing.

Smart Kids Publishing Staff, creator. Noah & the Ark: A Story about Being Thankful. 2005. (I Can Read the Bible Ser.). (Illus.). 12p. (J). (gr. -1-3). 19.95 *(978-0-8249-6658-4(9),* Ideals Pubns.) Worthy Publishing.

Smith, Brendan Powell. Noah's Ark: The Brick Bible for Kids. (Brick Bible for Kids Ser.). (ENG., Illus.). 32p. (J). (gr. -1-k). 2015. 3.99 *(978-1-63450-054-8(7))* 2012. 12.95 *(978-1-61608-737-1(4),* 608737) Skyhorse Publishing Co., Inc. (Sky Pony Pr.).

Smith, Dororthy. Noah's Ark Coloring Book. 2007. (Illus.). 16p. (J). pap. 1.89 *(978-1-59317-188-9(9))* Warner Pr., Inc.

Snellenberger, Earl & Snellenberger, Bonita. Noah's Ark Pre-School Activity Book. Snellenberger, Earl & Snellenberger, Bonita, illus. 2014. (ENG., Illus.). 98p. (J). (gr. -1-3). pap. 8.99 *(978-0-89051-832-8(7),* Master Books) New Leaf Publishing Group.

Suter, Janine. Noah's Floating Animal Park. Gunther, Richard, illus. 2009. 32p. (J). 10.99 *(978-0-89051-576-1(X),* Master Books) New Leaf Publishing Group.

Taib, Saadah. Prophet Nuh & the Great Ark Activity Book. Rosli, Shazana, illus. 2020. (Prophets of Islam Activity Bks.). 16p. (J). pap. 3.95 *(978-0-86037-644-6(3))* Kube Publishing Ltd. GBR. Dist: Consortium Bk. Sales & Distribution.

Tebbs, Victoria. Noah's Ark Story, 1 vol. Mitchell, Melanie, illus. 2009. (See & Say! Ser.). 24p. (J). 6.99 *(978-0-8254-7885-7(5),* Lion Children's) Lion Hudson PLC GBR. Dist: Kregel Pubns.

Turgeon, Stephane, illus. Noah's Ark. 2007. 16p. (J). (gr. -1-3). *(978-2-7641-0340-1(9))* Tormont Pubns.

Tyndale House Publisher Staff, creator. El Arca. 2019. Orig. Title: The Ark. (SPA., Illus.). 112p. 14.99 *(978-1-4964-3665-8(2),* 20_32400) Tyndale Hse. Pubs.

Umansky, Kaye. Noah's Ark, Vol. 7. 2nd ed. 2003. (Curtain Up Ser.: Vol. 7). (Illus.). 48p. (J). (gr. 1-4). pap. *(978-0-7136-4340-4(4),* A&C Black) Bloomsbury Publishing Plc.

Wedeven, Carol. El arca de Noé (Noah's 2-by-2 Adventure) - Bilingual. 2011. 16p. pap. 2.99 *(978-0-7586-3072-8(7))* Concordia Publishing Hse.

Winkler, Jude. Noah & the Flood (Puzzle Book) St. Joseph Puzzle Book: Book Contains 5 Exciting Jigsaw Puzzles. 2004. (ENG., Illus.). 12p. bds. 9.95 *(978-0-89942-718-8(9),* 972/97) Catholic Bk. Publishing Corp.

Zondervan Bibles Staff. Noah's Voyage, 1 vol. Miles, David, illus. 2015. (I Can Read! / Adventure Bible Ser.). (ENG.). 32p. (J). pap. 4.99 *(978-0-310-74683-6(3))* Zonderkidz.

NOAH'S ARK—FICTION

Amoss, Berthe. Draw Yourself into the Ark with Noah & His Family. 2003. 32p. (J). spiral bd. 12.95 *(978-1-59325-003-4(7))* Word Among Us Pr.

Auerbach, Annie. Traveling in Two's: The Journey to Noah's Ark. Dillard, Sarah, illus. 2005. 8p. (J). 10.95 *(978-1-58117-236-2(2),* Intervisual/Piggy Toes) Bendon, Inc.

Bartoletti, Susan Campbell. Naamah & the Ark at Night. Meade, Holly, illus. 2011. (ENG.). 32p. (J). (gr. -1-3). 16.99 *(978-0-7636-4242-6(8))* Candlewick Pr.

Bell, Bill. Noah: The Incredible Voyager. Bell, Bill, illus. 2004. (Illus.). 48p. (J). (gr. -1-3). per. 14.99 *(978-0-88092-801-4(8))* Royal Fireworks Publishing Co.

Booth, Bradley. Noah: The End of the World. 2010. (J). pap. 19.99 *(978-0-8163-2407-1(7))* Pacific Pr. Publishing Assn.

Brett, Jan. On Noah's Ark. Brett, Jan, illus. (Illus.). (J). (gr. -1 — 1). 2009. 36p. bds. 7.99 *(978-0-399-25220-4(7))* 2003. 32p. 18.99 *(978-0-399-24028-7(4))* Penguin Young Readers Group. (G.P. Putnam's Sons Books for Young Readers).

Brooks, Felicity. Noisy Noah's Ark. 2013. (Noisy Bks). 10p. (J). ring bd. 19.99 *(978-0-7945-3347-2(7),* Usborne) EDC Publishing.

Corman, Dick. Noah Knows. 2006. 183p. (YA). pap. 12.95 *(978-0-9655749-3-8(8))* Corman Productions.

Cote, Jenny. The Ark, the Reed & the Fire Cloud: The Amazing Tales of Max & Liz Book One, 2 bks, Bk 1. 2008. (Amazing Tales of Max & Liz Ser.: 1). (ENG., Illus.). 432p. (J). (gr. 5-11). pap. 16.99 *(978-0-89957-198-0(0),* Living Ink Bks.) AMG Pubs.

Curry, Kenneth. Mandu & Minka. 2007. (Illus.). 22p. (J). 10.95 *(978-0-9798364-7-3(6))* Curry Brothers Publishing Group.

David, Juliet. Noah & His Boat, 1 vol. Denham, Gemma, illus. 2008. (Candle Playbook Ser.). 18p. (J). bds. 7.99 *(978-0-8254-7378-4(0),* Candle Bks.) Lion Hudson PLC GBR. Dist: Kregel Pubns.

Emberley, Barbara. One Wide River to Cross. 2015. (ENG., Illus.). 32p. 17.95 *(978-1-62326-059-0(0))* AMMO Bks., LLC.

Falewee, Samantha. The Stowaway aboard Noah's Ark. 2004. (YA). per. 8.95 *(978-1-59712-001-2(4))* Catawba Publishing Co.

Farrer, Vashti & Curtis, Neil. Mr. Noah & the Cats. 2005. (Illus.). 62p. (J). (gr. -1 — 1). pap. *(978-0-7344-0630-9(4),* Lothian Children's Bks.) Hachette Australia.

Goodwin, John. An Arkful of Animal Stories. Macnaughton, Tina, illus. 2008. 32p. (J). (gr. k-3). 13.95 *(978-0-8198-0782-3(6))* Pauline Bks. & Media.

Ham, Ken & Ham, Mally. N Is for Noah Coloring Book. 2016. (ENG., Illus.). 32p. (J). pap. 4.99 *(978-1-68344-016-1(1),* Master Books) New Leaf Publishing Group.

Harrah, Judith. Come Inside the Ark. Foster, Jack, illus. 2012. (J). pap. 17.99 *(978-1-937331-12-2(1))* ShadeTree Publishing, LLC.

Hub, Ulrich. Meet at the Ark at Eight. Mühle, Jörg & Mühle, Jörg, illus. 2012. (ENG.). 68p. (J). 12.00 *(978-0-8028-5410-0(9),* Eerdmans Bks For Young Readers) Eerdmans, William B. Publishing Co.

Jennings, Arleen Naish. God Is in the Rain. 2012. 64p. (gr. 1-2). pap. 8.95 *(978-1-4759-3292-8(8))* iUniverse, Inc.

Jones, Liz. Noah's Bed. Copplestone, Jim, illus. 2004. 32p. (J). *(978-1-84507-002-1(X))* ReiseArt Buchhandlung GmbH.

Kiffel-Alcheh, Jamie. Can You Hear a Coo, Coo? Lumer, Marc, illus. 2018. (ENG.). 12p. (J). (gr. -1 — 1). bds. 5.99 *(978-1-5124-4443-8(X),* 943a2e0b-1e25-486b-a196-9b5299a360f8, Kar-Ben Publishing) Lerner Publishing Group.

Lane, W. Seth. Riley Rabbit's Quest to the Ark. 2011. 32p. (gr. -1 — 1). pap. 17.25 *(978-1-4269-6178-6(2))* Trafford Publishing.

L'Engle, Madeleine. Many Waters. 2007. (Wrinkle in Time Quintet Ser.: 3). (ENG.). 368p. (J). (gr. 5-9). per. 7.99 *(978-0-312-36857-9(7),* 900042674) Square Fish.

Lodge, Yvette. Noah's Ark: Baby's First Pop-up! Lodge, Ali, illus. gif. ed. 2006. 8p. (J). 19.95 *(978-1-57791-217-0(9))* Brighter Minds Children's Publishing.

Marks, Allison & Marks, Wayne. Og's Ark. Peluso, Martina, illus. 2016. (ENG.). 32p. (J). (gr. -1-3). 17.99 *(978-1-4677-6149-9(4),* 2b0d9617-d05e-45c2-82e3-1faaa703679e, Kar-Ben Publishing) Lerner Publishing Group.

McCardell, Ken. BibleRhymes' Noah & the Ark, bk. 2. Chirco, Antonella, illus. 2007. (BibleRhymes Ser.: 2). 28p. (J). 17.95 *(978-0-9790605-1-9(6),* BibleRhymes) BibleRhymes Publishing, L.L.C.

McCaughrean, Geraldine. Not the End of the World. 2005. 256p. (YA). (gr. 5-8). (ENG.). 16.99 *(978-0-06-076030-4(3));* lib. bdg. 17.89 *(978-0-06-076031-1(1))* HarperCollins Pubs. (HarperTeen).

Monroe, Colleen. A Is for Ark: Noah's Journey. Monroe, Michael Glenn, illus. 2004. 38p. (gr. -1-1). pap. 17.95 *(978-0-9754942-0-2(1))* Storytime Pr., Inc.

Munter, June. Noah's Ark: The Animals Story. 2011. 20p. pap. 10.03 *(978-1-4634-4992-6(5))* AuthorHouse.

Napoli, Donna Jo. Storm. 2014. (ENG., Illus.). 368p. (YA). (gr. 9). 17.99 *(978-1-4814-0302-3(8),* Simon & Schuster/Paula Wiseman Bks.) Simon & Schuster/Paula Wiseman Bks.

Noah & the Ark. 2012. (ENG., Illus.). 24p. (J). pap. 6.50 *(978-1-84135-603-7(4))* Award Pubns. Ltd. GBR. Dist: Parkwest Pubns., Inc.

Nolan, Allia Zobel. God's Rainbow. Chung, Chi, illus. 2007. 16p. (J). 12.99 *(978-0-8254-5537-7(5))* Kregel Pubns.

Okrant, Mark. Judson's Island. 2006. per. 10.95 *(978-0-9791757-2-5(0))* Oak Manor Publishing, Inc.

Olitzky, Kerry. Where's the Potty on This Ark? Tompkins, Abigail, illus. 2018. (ENG.). 24p. (J). (gr. -1 — 1). 12.99 *(978-1-5124-8370-3(2),* f1073f5f-4f95-4a5a-b01d-4ba62f2f5d09, Kar-Ben Publishing) Lerner Publishing Group.

Parry, Jo. Under the Rainbow. 2009. (Wow! Bks.). (Illus.). (J). bds. 12.99 *(978-1-934650-04-2(8))* Just For Kids Pr., LLC.

Peters, E. G. The Voyage of Noah's Ark. 2011. 166p. 29.99 *(978-1-4653-4080-1(7));* pap. 19.99 *(978-1-4653-4079-5(3))* Xlibris Corp.

Price, Olivia. All Aboard Noah's Ark: A Touch & Feel Book. Mitchell, Melanie, illus. 2008. (ENG.). 12p. (J). (gr. -1). 12.95 *(978-1-58117-778-7(X)*, Intervisual/Piggy Toes) Bendon, Inc.
Racklin-Siegel, Carol, illus. Noah's Ark. 2003. 32p. (J). per. 11.95 *(978-0-939144-42-6(5))* EKS Publishing Co.
Rangel, Graciela. Anthony's Journey to God's Ark. 2007. 84p. pap. 8.95 *(978-1-59526-907-2(X)*, Llumina Christian Bks.) Aeon Publishing Inc.
Ranson, Erin. The Story of Noah's Ark. Petrlik, Andrea, illus. 2007. (Interactive Magnetic Book Ser.). 10p. (J). (gr. -1). *(978-1-84666-359-8(8)*, Tide Mill Pr.) Top That! Publishing PLC.
Reynolds, Loralyn & Caldwell, Christiana Marie Melvin. Animals of the Ark: (for a boy named Clay) Foster, Trista, photos by. 2011. (Illus.). 36p. pap. 15.14 *(978-1-4634-3328-4(X))* AuthorHouse.
Richardson, Robert. Twin Hicks Noah's Ark. Hicks, Alan and Aaron, illus. 2008. 36p. pap. 16.95 *(978-1-4389-1809-9(7))* AuthorHouse.
Rouss, Sylvia. The Littlest Pair. Hannon, Holly, illus. 2015. (ENG.). 32p. (J). pap. 9.95 *(978-1-68115-505-0(2)*, b8306127-883e-4b5b-92a7-d5a9df4fb77f, Apples & Honey Pr.) Behrman Hse., Inc.
Rouss, Sylvia A. The Littlest Pair. Hannon, Holly, illus. 2005. 32p. (J). (gr. -1-1). 14.95 *(978-1-930143-17-3(6)*, Devora Publishing) Simcha Media Group.
Rowlands, Avril. All the Tales from the Ark, 1 vol. Rowlands, Avril & Moran, Rosslyn, illus. 2nd ed. 2016. (ENG.). 400p. (J). (gr. 2-4). pap. 10.99 *(978-0-7459-7682-2(4)*, 3390e080-339c-4d8b-919d-ce0ff1bb67a5, Lion Books) Lion Hudson PLC GBR. Dist: Baker & Taylor Publisher Services (BTPS).
Santore, Charles. Stowaway on Noah's Ark Oversized Padded Board Book: The Classic Edition. 2018. (Oversized Padded Board Bks.). (ENG., Illus.). 24p. (J). (gr. -1). bds. 12.95 *(978-1-60433-801-0(6)*, Applesauce Pr.) Cider Mill Pr. Bk. Pubs., LLC.
Sassi, Laura. Goodnight, Ark, 1 vol. Chapman, Jane, illus. (ENG.). (J). 2015. 24p. bds. 8.99 *(978-0-310-74938-7(7))* 2014. 32p. bds. 16.99 *(978-0-310-73784-1(2))* Zonderkidz.
Saxon, Terrill. Baby's Noah's Ark. 2006. (Baby Blessings Ser.). (Illus.). 6p. 15.99 *(978-0-7847-1430-0(4)*, 04013) Standard Publishing.
Schultz, Doreen. The Days of Noah. 2013. 26p. pap. 9.99 *(978-1-62697-228-5(1))* Salem Author Services.
Singer, Isaac Bashevis. Why Noah Chose the Dove. 2013. (J). lib. bdg. 19.65 *(978-0-606-28425-7(7))* Turtleback.
Stauffer, Lisa Lowe. Two by Two, 1 vol. Scudamore, Angelika, illus. 2018. (ENG.). 18p. (J). bds. 8.99 *(978-0-310-76273-7(1))* Zonderkidz.
Stewart, Dorothy. It's Hard to Hurry When You're a Snail, 1 vol. Taylor, Thomas, illus. 2009. 32p. (J). 14.95 *(978-0-8254-7838-3(3)*, Lion Children's) Lion Hudson PLC GBR. Dist: Kregel Pubns.
Swinson, Joyce Ann. Noah's Boat. Clark, Casey, illus. 2007. 32p. per. 24.95 *(978-1-4241-9012-6(6))* America Star Bks.
Thomas, Leigh Maria. Ray & the Rainbow. 2003. (ENG., Illus.). 24p. pap. 11.00 *(978-1-4120-1490-8(5))* Trafford Publishing.
Torseter, Oyvind & Steven, Kenneth. Why Dogs Have Wet Noses. 2015. (ENG., Illus.). 40p. (J). (gr. -1-3). 17.95 *(978-1-59270-173-5(6))* Enchanted Lion Bks., LLC.
Townsend, Stephanie Z. Not Too Small at All: A Mouse Tale. Looney, Bill, illus. 2008. (ENG.). 30p. (J). (gr. -1). 13.99 *(978-0-89051-524-2(7)*, Master Books) New Leaf Publishing Group.
Travis, Lucille. Timna. 2009. (ENG.). 168p. (J). (gr. 3-9). pap. 9.99 *(978-0-8361-9484-5(5))* Herald Pr.
Wells, Janet F. For Petey's Sake! 2013. 24p. pap. 10.99 *(978-1-4525-8297-9(1)*, Balboa Pr.) Author Solutions, LLC.
Whyte, Hugh, illus. Rock Steady: A Story of Noah's Ark. 2006. 28p. (J). (gr. k-4). reprint ed. 17.00 *(978-1-4223-5556-5(X))* DIANE Publishing Co.
Widner, Jan. Then Came the Rains. 2013. 28p. pap. 16.95 *(978-1-4497-9456-9(4)*, WestBow Pr.) Author Solutions, LLC.
Wildsmith, Brian. Professor Noah's Spaceship, 1 vol. 2008. (ENG., Illus.). 32p. (J). 16.95 *(978-1-59572-124-2(X))* Star Bright Bks., Inc.
Wilkinson, Simon. Noah's Ark Black & White Visual Development Book for Babies. 2008. 34p. pap. 17.95 *(978-1-4092-4702-9(3))* Lulu Pr., Inc.
Zondervan Staff. Noah & God's Great Promise, 1 vol. Jones, Dennis, illus. 2010. (I Can Read! / Dennis Jones Ser.). (ENG.). 32p. (J). (gr. -1-2). pap. 4.99 *(978-0-310-71884-0(8))* Zonderkidz.

NOBEL, ALFRED BERNHARD, 1833-1896

Devera, Czeena. Alfred Nobel. Bane, Jeff, illus. 2018. (My Early Library: My Itty-Bitty Bio Ser.). (ENG.). 24p. (J). (gr. k-1). lib. bdg. 30.64 *(978-1-5341-2885-9(9)*, 211584) Cherry Lake Publishing.
Wargin, Kathy-jo. Alfred Nobel: The Man Behind the Peace Prize. Pullen, Zachary, illus. 2009. (ENG.). 32p. (J). (gr. 1-4). 17.95 *(978-1-58536-281-3(6)*, 202092) Sleeping Bear Pr.
Warner, Timmy. Alfred Nobel, Vol. 11. 2018. (Scientists & Their Discoveries Ser.). (Illus.). 96p. (J). (gr. 7). lib. bdg. 34.60 *(978-1-4222-4026-7(6))* Mason Crest.

NOBEL PRIZES

Alagna, Magdalena. Anwar Sadat, 1 vol. 2003. (Middle East Leaders Ser.). (ENG., Illus.). 112p. (J). (gr. 5-8). lib. bdg. 39.80 *(978-0-8239-4464-4(6)*, 4c4dbcaf-7d24-4dbf-98ac-1bb5a29fa445, Rosen Reference) Rosen Publishing Group, Inc., The.
Anderson, Dale. Al Gore: A Wake-Up Call to Global Warming. 2009. (Voices for Green Choices Ser.). (ENG., Illus.). 48p. (J). (gr. 5-9). pap. *(978-0-7787-4679-9(8))* Crabtree Publishing Co.
Benjamin, Michelle & Mooney, Maggie. Nobel's Women of Peace, 1 vol. 2008. (Women's Hall of Fame Ser.: 13). (ENG., Illus.). 146p. (J). (gr. 4-8). pap. 10.95 *(978-1-897187-38-8(6))* Second Story Pr. CAN. Dist: Orca Bk. Pubs. USA.
Brexel, Bernadette. Yasser Arafat. 2009. (Middle East Leaders Ser.). 112p. (gr. 5-8). 66.50 *(978-1-61514-649-9(0)*, Rosen Reference) Rosen Publishing Group, Inc., The.
Cefery, Holly. Yasser Arafat, 1 vol. 2003. (Middle East Leaders Ser.). (ENG., Illus.). 112p. (J). (gr. 5-8). lib. bdg. 39.80 *(978-0-8239-4469-9(7)*, b6f139c6-f41f-49bf-a31a-60d4f1b04fbc, Rosen Reference) Rosen Publishing Group, Inc., The.
Cullerton Johnson, Jen. Seeds of Change: Wangari's Gift to the World, 1 vol. Sadler, Sonia Lynn, illus. 2013. (ENG.). 32p. (J). (gr. 1-6). 19.95 *(978-1-60060-367-9(X)*, leelowbooks) Lee & Low Bks., Inc.
Darraj, Susan Muaddi. Mairead Corrigan & Betty Williams. 2006. (ENG., Illus.). 106p. (gr. 9-12). lib. bdg. 30.00 *(978-0-7910-9001-5(9)*, P114508, Facts On File) Infobase Holdings, Inc.
Frisch, Aaron. Albert Einstein. 2005. (Genius Ser.). (Illus.). 48p. (J). (gr. 5-9). lib. bdg. 21.95 *(978-1-58341-328-9(6)*, Creative Education) Creative Co., The.
Houghton, Sarah. Elie Wiesel: A Holocaust Survivor Cries Out for Peace. 2003. (High Five Reading - Green Ser.). (ENG., Illus.). 48p. (J). (gr. 3-4). per. 9.00 *(978-0-7368-2833-8(8))* Capstone.
—Elie Wiesel Set: A Holocaust Survivor Cries Out for Peace, 6. 2003. (High Five Reading - Green Ser.). (ENG.). 48p. (gr. 3-4). pap. 54.00 *(978-0-7368-2843-7(5))* Capstone.
Kepnes, Caroline. Stephen Crane. 2004. (Classic Storytellers Ser.). (Illus.). 48p. (J). (gr. 4-8). lib. bdg. 29.95 *(978-1-58415-272-9(9))* Mitchell Lane Pubs.
Labrecque, Ellen. Gertrude B. Elion & Pharmacology. 2017. (21st Century Junior Library: Women Innovators Ser.). (ENG., Illus.). 24p. (J). (gr. 2-5). pap. 12.79 *(978-1-63472-314-5(7)*, 209301) Cherry Lake Publishing.
MacBain, Jennifer. Gertrude Elion: Nobel Prize Winner in Physiology & Medicine. 2009. (Women Hall of Famers in Mathematics & Science Ser.). 112p. (gr. 5-8). 63.90 *(978-1-60854-811-8(2)*, Rosen Reference) Rosen Publishing Group, Inc., The.
Rusch, Elizabeth. Mario y el Agujero en el Cielo / Mario & the Hole in the Sky: Cómo un Químico Salvó Nuestro Planeta. Calvo, Carlos E., tr. Martinez, Teresa, illus. 2019.Tr. of Mario & the Hole in the Sky. 40p. (J). (gr. 1-4). lib. bdg. 16.99 *(978-1-58089-582-8(4))* Charlesbridge Publishing, Inc.
Stiekel, Bettina, ed. The Nobel Book of Answers: A the Dalai Lama, Mikhail Gorbachev, Shimon Peres. 2010. (ENG.). 272p. (J). (gr. 5-9). pap. 12.99 *(978-1-4424-2193-6(2)*, Atheneum Bks. for Young Readers) Simon & Schuster Children's Publishing.
Stiekel, Bettina, et al. The Nobel Book of Answers: The Dalai Lama, Mikhail Gorbachev, Shimon Peres, & Other Nobel Prize Winners Answer Some of Life's Most Intriguing Questions for Young People. Stiekel, Bettina, ed. 2003. (ENG., Illus.). 255p. (J). 16.00 *(978-0-689-86310-3(1))* Chemical Heritage Foundation.
Tracy, Kathleen. John Steinbeck. 2004. (Classic Storytellers Ser.). (Illus.). 48p. (J). (gr. 4-8). lib. bdg. 29.95 *(978-1-58415-271-2(0))* Mitchell Lane Pubs.
—Robert Koch & the Study of Anthrax. 2004. (Uncharted, Unexplored, & Unexplained Ser.). (Illus.). 48p. (J). (gr. 4-8). lib. bdg. 29.95 *(978-1-58415-261-3(3))* Mitchell Lane Pubs.
Wargin, Kathy-jo. Alfred Nobel: The Man Behind the Peace Prize. Pullen, Zachary, illus. 2009. (ENG.). 32p. (J). (gr. 1-4). 17.95 *(978-1-58536-281-3(6)*, 202092) Sleeping Bear Pr.
Whiting, Jim. Otto Hahn & the Story of Nuclear Fission. 2003. (Unlocking the Secrets of Science Ser.). (Illus.). 56p. (J). (gr. 4-10). lib. bdg. 25.70 *(978-1-58415-204-0(4))* Mitchell Lane Pubs.

NOCTURNAL ANIMALS

Animals of the Night. 2015. (Animals of the Night Ser.). (ENG.). 32p. (J). (gr. 3-4). pap., pap., pap. 63.12 *(978-0-7660-7053-0(0))* Enslow Publishing, LLC.
Arnold, Quinn M. Aye-Ayes. 2019. (Creatures of the Night Ser.). (ENG.). 24p. (J). (gr. 1-4). *(978-1-64026-116-7(8)*, 18933, Creative Education); pap. 8.99 *(978-1-62832-679-6(4)*, 18934, Creative Paperbacks) Creative Co., The.
—Barn Owls. 2019. (Creatures of the Night Ser.). (ENG.). 24p. (J). (gr. 1-4). *(978-1-64026-117-4(6)*, 18937, Creative Education); pap. 8.99 *(978-1-62832-680-2(8)*, 18938, Creative Paperbacks) Creative Co., The.
—Flying Foxes. 2019. (Creatures of the Night Ser.). (ENG.). 24p. (J). (gr. 1-4). *(978-1-64026-118-1(4)*, 18941, Creative Education); pap. 8.99 *(978-1-62832-681-9(6)*, 18942, Creative Paperbacks) Creative Co., The.
—Luna Moths. 2019. (Creatures of the Night Ser.). (ENG.). 24p. (J). (gr. 1-4). pap. 8.99 *(978-1-62832-682-6(4)*, 18946, Creative Paperbacks) Creative Co., The.
—Slow Lorises. 2019. (Creatures of the Night Ser.). (ENG.). 24p. (J). (gr. 1-4). *(978-1-64026-120-4(6)*, 18949, Creative Education); pap. 8.99 *(978-1-62832-683-3(2)*, 18950, Creative Paperbacks) Creative Co., The.
—Tasmanian Devils. 2019. (Creatures of the Night Ser.). (ENG.). 24p. (J). (gr. 1-4). *(978-1-64026-121-1(4)*, 18953, Creative Education); pap. 8.99 *(978-1-62832-684-0(0)*, 18954, Creative Paperbacks) Creative Co., The.
Bedoyere, Camilla. Creatures of the Night. 2014. (ENG., Illus.). 80p. (J). (gr. 3-6). pap. 9.95 *(978-1-77085-459-8(2)*, 403d1c35-cd6f-4f43-9cb9-c00bc3918d5c) Firefly Bks., Ltd.
Clarke, Ginjer L. Black Out!: Animals That Live in the Dark: Animals That Live in the Dark. Mueller, Pete, illus. 2008. (Penguin Young Readers, Level 3 Ser.). 48p. (J). (gr. 1-3). mass mkt. 4.99 *(978-0-448-44824-4(6)*, Penguin Young Readers) Penguin Young Readers Group.
De la Bédoyère, Camilla. Nocturnal Animals. 2010. (100 Things You Should Know About Ser.). 48p. (YA). (gr. 4-6). lib. bdg. 19.95 *(978-1-4222-1523-4(7))* Mason Crest.
Dunn, Mary R. Nocturnal Animals, 8 vols., Set. Incl. Owls. (ENG.). 24p. (J). (gr. -1-2). 2011. lib. bdg. 27.32 *(978-1-4296-5997-0(1)*, 114928, Capstone Pr.); (Nocturnal Animals Ser.). (ENG.). 24p. 2011. 81.96 o.p. *(978-1-4296-6651-0(X)*, 16373, Capstone Pr.) Capstone.
Dunne, Abbie. Nocturnal Animals. 2016. (Life Science Ser.). (ENG., Illus.). 24p. (J). (gr. -1-2). lib. bdg. 27.32 *(978-1-5157-0946-6(9)*, 132260, Capstone Pr.) Capstone.
Esbaum, Jill. Explore My World Nighttime. 2015. (Explore My World Ser.). 32p. (J). (gr. -1-k). pap. 4.99 *(978-1-4263-2048-4(5)*, National Geographic Kids) Disney Publishing Worldwide.
Golding, Elizabeth. Moonlight Ocean. Lodge, Ali, illus. 2012. (ENG.). 12p. (J). (gr. -1-3). 14.99 *(978-0-7624-4486-1(X)*, Running Pr. Kids) Running Pr.
Gonzales, Doreen. Raccoons in the Dark, 1 vol. 2009. (Creatures of the Night Ser.). (ENG.). 24p. (gr. 2-3). (YA). pap. 9.25 *(978-1-4358-3259-6(0)*, c6a93620-ed7d-4814-86b5-b5aab5874745); (Illus.). (J). 26.27 *(978-1-4042-8101-1(0)*, 6c1de3d2-d0b1-49cd-8e23-165dbfcdaa60) Rosen Publishing Group, Inc., The.
—Scorpions in the Dark, 1 vol. 2009. (Creatures of the Night Ser.). (ENG.). 24p. (gr. 2-3). (YA). pap. 9.25 *(978-1-4358-3257-2(4)*, 8c962ee3-f6c1-4d97-a1f7-c7c1499fa95d); (Illus.). (J). 26.27 *(978-1-4042-8100-4(2)*, e123172f-5292-45cb-987c-62c52b26ad5b) Rosen Publishing Group, Inc., The.
Harasymiw, Teppo. Hedgehogs in the Dark, 1 vol. 2012. (Creatures of the Night Ser.). (ENG., Illus.). 24p. (J). (gr. 1-2). pap. 9.15 *(978-1-4339-6374-2(4)*, 27f3bfce-0243-40a3-a72f-eae3bae3fe50) Stevens, Gareth Publishing LLLP.
Heliadore & Delafosse, Claude. Animals at Night. Best, Clare, tr. Heliadore, illus. 2013. (ENG., Illus.). 38p. (J). (gr. -1-k). 13.99 *(978-1-85103-413-0(7))* Moonlight Publishing, Ltd. GBR. Dist: Independent Pubs. Group.
Hirschmann, Kris. Owls, Bats, Wolves & Other Nocturnal Animals. 2003. (World Discovery Science Readers Ser.). (Illus.). 32p. (J). *(978-0-439-56628-5(2))* Scholastic, Inc.
Hoff, Mary. Life at Night. 2003. (Illus.). 32p. (J). lib. bdg. *(978-1-58341-267-1(0)*, Creative Education) Creative Co., The.
Honders, Christine. How Cats & Other Animals See at Night, 1 vol. 2015. (Superior Animal Senses Ser.). (ENG., Illus.). 24p. (J). (gr. 3-4). pap. 9.25 *(978-1-4994-0989-5(3)*, 0a4ad4c6-6684-4d26-901c-b656f62fa1be, PowerKids Pr.) Rosen Publishing Group, Inc., The.
Kalman, Bobbie. Night Animals. 2011. (ENG.). 16p. (J). lib. bdg. *(978-0-7787-9558-2(6))*; pap. *(978-0-7787-9583-4(7))* Crabtree Publishing Co.
Klepeis, Alicia Z. Nocturnal & Diurnal Animals Explained, 1 vol. 2016. (Distinctions in Nature Ser.). (ENG., Illus.). 32p. (gr. 3-3). pap. 11.58 *(978-1-5026-2173-3(8)*, ea61367a-e56c-46d5-85c4-0c243bada899) Cavendish Square Publishing LLC.
Kochanoff, Peggy. Be a Night Detective: Solving the Mysteries of Twilight, Dusk, & Nightfall, 1 vol. 2017. (Be a Nature Detective Ser.). (ENG., Illus.). 56p. (J). (gr. 1-3). pap. 14.95 *(978-1-77108-464-2(2)*, 07ce4bca-bf65-4861-ba4a-7b0455a42c90) Nimbus Publishing, Ltd. CAN. Dist: Baker & Taylor Publisher Services (BTPS).
Kratt, Chris & Kratt, Martin. Glow Wild! (Wild Kratts) 2018. (Pictureback(R) Ser.). (Illus.). 16p. (J). (gr. -1-2). pap. 5.99 *(978-0-525-57783-6(1)*, Random Hse. Bks. for Young Readers) Random Hse. Children's Bks.
Kudlinski, Kathleen V. The Sunset Switch. Burnett, Lindy, illus. 2005. (Picture Book Ser.). (ENG.). 32p. (J). (gr. k-3). 15.95 *(978-1-55971-916-2(8))* Cooper Square Publishing Llc.
Landau, Elaine. Hunters of the Night, 1 vol. 2012. (Animals after Dark Ser.). (ENG., Illus.). 96p. (gr. 3-3). pap. 13.88 *(978-1-4644-0033-9(4)*, 0b31e8b6-cc75-469d-8926-466aefa2bb72) Enslow Publishing, LLC.
Lang, Diane. Daytime Nighttime, All Through the Year, 1 vol. Gabriel, Andrea, illus. 2017. 32p. (J). (gr. -1-3). pap. 8.99 *(978-1-58469-607-0(9)*, Dawn Pubns.) Sourcebooks, Inc.
Lewis, Kelly. Animals by Day, Animals by Night. 2016. (Spring Forward Ser.). (J). (gr. 1). *(978-1-4900-3727-1(6))* Benchmark Education Co.
Lockerd, Jodi. Nocturnal Animals: Represent & Solve Problems Involving Multiplication. 2014. (Rosen Math Readers Ser.). (ENG.). 24p. (J). (gr. 3-4). pap. 49.50 *(978-1-4777-4969-2(1)*, Rosen Classroom); (Illus.). pap. 8.25 *(978-1-4777-4968-5(3)*, ab2c62c8-5022-4622-bef0-875403ae5ee2, PowerKids Pr.); (Illus.). lib. bdg. 25.27 *(978-1-4777-6447-3(X)*, aae32665-9dc9-43d1-a470-3c22e71b5ec0, PowerKids Pr.) Rosen Publishing Group, Inc., The.
Maximus, Sofia. Badgers in the Dark, 1 vol. 2012. (Creatures of the Night Ser.). (ENG., Illus.). 24p. (J). (gr. 1-2). pap. 9.15 *(978-1-4339-6362-9(0)*, bb425622-336d-4b47-b264-b10850b8e4cd); lib. bdg. 25.27 *(978-1-4339-6480-0(5)*, d89bf113-70ec-449c-8fee-93aa41e4ee74) Stevens, Gareth Publishing LLLP.
Meredith, S. Night Animals. 2004. (Beginners Ser.). (ENG.). 32p. (J). (gr. 1-18). pap. 4.95 *(978-0-7945-0383-3(7))* EDC Publishing.
Meredith, Sue. Night Animals: Level 1. Donaera, Patrizia & Larkum, Adam, illus. 2007. (Beginners Ser.). 32p. (J). 4.99 *(978-0-7945-1656-7(4)*, Usborne) EDC Publishing.
Moore Niver, Heather. Bull Sharks after Dark, 1 vol. 2016. (Animals of the Night Ser.). (ENG., Illus.). 32p. (gr. 3-3). 26.93 *(978-0-7660-7712-6(8)*, 37b70ea2-7eaf-4763-91d7-ec6eb1fa44e1) Enslow Publishing, LLC.
Murray, Julie. Aye-Ayes. 2017. (Nocturnal Animals (Abdo Kids Junior) Ser.). (ENG., Illus.). 24p. (J). (gr. -1-2). lib. bdg. 31.36 *(978-1-5321-0404-6(9)*, 26530, Abdo Kids) ABDO Publishing Co.
—Sugar Gliders. 2017. (Nocturnal Animals (Abdo Kids Junior) Ser.). (ENG.). 24p. (J). (gr. -1-2). lib. bdg. 31.36 *(978-1-5321-0407-7(3)*, 26533, Abdo Kids) ABDO Publishing Co.
—Tarsiers. 2017. (Nocturnal Animals (Abdo Kids Junior) Ser.). (ENG., Illus.). 24p. (J). (gr. -1-2). lib. bdg. 31.36 *(978-1-5321-0408-4(1)*, 26534, Abdo Kids) ABDO Publishing Co.
Night Animals, 10 vols. 2007. (Night Animals Ser.). (ENG.). 24p. (gr. 1-3). lib. bdg. 123.35 *(978-0-8368-7844-8(2)*, fdc19e83-6557-4404-9316-3d40ac0d7c2f, Weekly Reader Leveled Readers) Stevens, Gareth Publishing LLLP.
Night Animals (Animales Nocturnos), 12 vols. 2007. (Night Animals / Animales Nocturnos Ser.). (SPA & ENG.). 24p. (gr. 1-3). lib. bdg. 148.02 *(978-0-8368-8041-0(2)*, fefda260-50ea-420a-89ab-85d6a1a4e75f, Weekly Reader Leveled Readers) Stevens, Gareth Publishing LLLP.
O'Mara, Jack. Raccoons in the Dark, 1 vol. 2012. (Creatures of the Night Ser.). (ENG., Illus.). 24p. (J). (gr. 1-2). pap. 9.15 *(978-1-4339-6378-0(7)*, 2112addc-e565-41ac-b97b-d5431a57f3ec); lib. bdg. 25.27 *(978-1-4339-6376-6(0)*, 9162e3c7-bfd1-4428-a910-9748da4e6137) Stevens, Gareth Publishing LLLP.
O'Shaughnessy, Ruth. Bats after Dark, 1 vol. 2015. (Animals of the Night Ser.). (ENG., Illus.). 32p. (gr. 3-4). 26.93 *(978-0-7660-6752-3(1)*, 594646e5-78a8-479b-87ae-f227226b359f) Enslow Publishing, LLC.
—Big Cats after Dark, 1 vol. 2015. (Animals of the Night Ser.). (ENG.). 32p. (gr. 3-4). pap. 11.52 *(978-0-7660-7044-8(1)*, 2bbfa41f-2774-48cf-acb2-70061186dd07); (Illus.). 26.93 *(978-0-7660-7046-2(8)*, e65b2934-9168-43b9-874b-0d20b061aa73) Enslow Publishing, LLC.
—Crocodiles & Alligators after Dark, 1 vol. 2015. (Animals of the Night Ser.). (ENG.). 32p. (gr. 3-4). pap. 11.52 *(978-0-7660-6754-7(8)*, 6a06ccd4-10e6-46c8-a39f-2ac8c8e4c8ff); (Illus.). 26.93 *(978-0-7660-6756-1(4)*, 93c0f189-4bac-42c6-b518-76312d6a2ef2) Enslow Publishing, LLC.
—Raccoons after Dark, 1 vol. 2015. (Animals of the Night Ser.). (ENG.). 32p. (gr. 3-4). pap. 11.52 *(978-0-7660-6762-2(9)*, ce787fe7-43fb-4c4a-b119-e3e9e668d904); (Illus.). 26.93 *(978-0-7660-6764-6(5)*, 680d43ce-0b3d-41cb-a5e0-df1e2f62ebee) Enslow Publishing, LLC.
—Snakes after Dark, 1 vol. 2015. (Animals of the Night Ser.). (ENG.). 32p. (gr. 3-4). pap. 11.52 *(978-0-7660-6766-0(1)*, ba5a2650-d6f9-49cd-9c02-8d21b49d54c4); (Illus.). 26.93 *(978-0-7660-6768-4(8)*, 43c9ee6d-d368-49a5-9dcf-9bf4e029386b) Enslow Publishing, LLC.
Pearson, Jane & Bryan, Philip. Creatures of the Dark. 2007. (Literacy 2000 Satellites: Stage 6 Ser.). (Illus.). 24p. (J). (gr. -1-3). pap. *(978-0-7327-1731-5(0)*, Rigby) Pearson Education Australia.
Rissman, Rebecca. Red Foxes: Nocturnal Predators, 1 vol. 2014. (Night Safari Ser.). (ENG., Illus.). 24p. (J). (gr. -1-2). 25.99 *(978-1-4846-0312-3(5)*, 126402, Heinemann) Capstone.
SANCHEZ, Anita. Wait till It Gets Dark. 2017. (Illus.). 64p. (J). (gr. 3-7). 14.95 *(978-1-63076-318-3(7))* Muddy Boots Pr.
Shea, Mary Molly. Poisonous Slow Lorises, 1 vol. 2017. (Cutest Animals... That Could Kill You! Ser.). (ENG.). 24p. (J). (gr. 2-3). pap. 9.15 *(978-1-5382-1095-6(9)*, 8e91732f-3508-4521-b988-4f0dbd0c8d66) Stevens, Gareth Publishing LLLP.
Shea, Therese M. Bobcats in the Dark, 1 vol. 2012. (Creatures of the Night Ser.). (ENG., Illus.). 24p. (J). (gr. 1-2). pap. 9.15 *(978-1-4339-6366-7(3)*, 09101bf1-eb47-49bf-b2d1-09561653a91b); lib. bdg. 25.27 *(978-1-4339-6364-3(7)*, fd1972ee-c32c-4ee3-858c-2c10d990bf83) Stevens, Gareth Publishing LLLP.
Stanek, Linda. Night Creepers. Bersani, Shennen, illus. 2011. (ENG.). 32p. (J). 23.10 *(978-1-60718-323-5(4))*; 29.80 *(978-1-60718-322-8(6))* Arbordale Publishing.
—Sigilosos de la Noche. 2017. (SPA., Illus.). 32p. (J). (gr. -1-3). pap. 11.95 *(978-1-60718-325-9(0)*, 9d65d387-4995-4fdd-9529-174de72e3c3b) Arbordale Publishing.
Thompson, Holly. Twilight Chant. Betton, Jen, illus. 2018. (ENG.). 32p. (J). (gr. -1-3). 17.99 *(978-0-544-58648-2(4)*, 1614141, Clarion Bks.) HarperCollins Pubs.
Van Eck, Thomas. Tarsiers in the Dark, 1 vol. 2012. (Creatures of the Night Ser.). (ENG., Illus.). 24p. (J). (gr. 1-2). pap. 9.15 *(978-1-4339-6382-7(5)*, 58f95b4a-65c9-453a-a379-6fbed62dcff9); lib. bdg. 25.27 *(978-1-4339-6380-3(9)*, fc350b8f-6f9b-4c8d-9cd6-6e9d954043c7) Stevens, Gareth Publishing LLLP.
Ward, Jennifer. Forest Bright, Forest Night, 1 vol. Henterly, Jamichael, illus. 2005. (J). (gr. -1 — 1). 32p. pap. 8.99 *(978-1-58469-067-2(4))*; 26p. bds. 7.95 *(978-1-58469-089-4(5))* Sourcebooks, Inc. (Dawn Pubns.).
—Forest Bright, Forest Night. Henterly, Jamichael, illus. 2005. (Sharing Nature with Children Book Ser.). 32p. (J). (gr. k-3). 16.95 *(978-1-58469-066-5(6))* Take Heart Pubns.
Wood, Alix. Amazing Animals at Night, 1 vol. 2012. (Wow! Wildlife Ser.). (ENG., Illus.). 24p. (J). (gr. 2-3). 27.27 *(978-1-4488-8102-4(1)*, 8f33b2fd-c45c-48f4-b0bf-fac914f6104c); pap. 9.25 *(978-1-4488-8165-9(X)*, 52ff3760-19f3-4b1e-b583-99778df1cfc9) Rosen Publishing Group, Inc., The. (Windmill Bks.).
Wren, Jenny, illus. Night Animals. 2017. (First Explorers Ser.). (ENG.). 10p. (J). (— 1). bds. 8.95 *(978-1-4549-2657-3(0))* Sterling Publishing Co., Inc.

NOISE

Brasch, Nicolas. Why Does Sound Travel? All about Sound. 2010. (Illus.). 24p. (J). 49.50 *(978-1-61531-909-1(3)*, 1307169, PowerKids Pr.) Rosen Publishing Group, Inc., The.
—Why Is It So Loud?, 1 vol. 2010. (Solving Science Mysteries Ser.). (ENG., Illus.). 24p. (gr. 4-5). (J). pap. 9.25 *(978-1-61531-908-4(5)*, 04161079-3e60-46ab-b5fb-88e85aacaf0e, PowerKids Pr.); (YA). lib. bdg. 26.27 *(978-1-61531-888-9(7)*, be0e23e3-0ff9-4975-91cf-320daa17e939) Rosen Publishing Group, Inc., The.
Johnson, Marion. Caillou, What's That Noise. CINAR Corporation Staff, illus. 2004. (Clubhouse Usa Ser.). (ENG.). 24p. (J). pap. 3.95 *(978-2-89450-489-5(6))* Ellipsis Pr.
Jordan, Apple. Noisy / Quiet, 1 vol. 2nd rev. ed. 2012. (Opposites Ser.). (ENG.). 16p. (gr. k-1). 24.07 *(978-1-60870-421-7(1)*, 4b235804-e819-4282-8b39-840ebcb00bda) Cavendish Square Publishing LLC.
Phillips, Jessica, illus. Zoom Along. 2018. (Zoom Along Ser.). (ENG.). 16p. (J). (gr. -1 — 1). bds. 15.99 *(978-1-77138-797-2(1))* Kids Can Pr., Ltd. CAN. Dist: Hachette Bk. Group.
The something Noise: Individual Title Six-Packs. (gr. 1-2). 25.00 *(978-0-7635-9130-4(0))* Rigby Education.

M N O

Thomson, Ruth. Ruidos. (Coleccion Mi Primer Libro). (SPA.). 32p. (J). 13.95 *(978-84-207-3779-9(8)*, ANY872) Grupo Anaya, S.A. ESP. Dist: Continental Bk. Co., Inc.

NOISE—FICTION

Alizadeh, Kip. Quiet! Alizadeh, Kip, illus. 2017. (Child's Play Library). (Illus.). 32p. (J). pap. *(978-1-84643-888-2(8))* Child's Play International Ltd.

Anderson, Sara. Noisy City Night (2015 Board Book) Anderson, Sara, illus. 2015. (ENG., Illus.). 12p. (J). (gr. -1-1). bds. 10.95 *(978-1-943459-01-8(0))* Sara Anderson Children's Bks.

Banks, Steven. The Song That Never Ends. DePorter, Vince, illus. 2004. (Spongebob Squarepants Ser.). 32p. (J). (gr. k-2). 11.65 *(978-0-7569-5374-4(X))* Perfection Learning Corp.

Beckstrand, Karl. Sounds in the House! A Mystery. Jones, Channing, illus. 2004.Tr. of Sonidos en la Casa. (ENG.). 24p. (J). per. 4.00 *(978-0-9672012-5-2(X))* Premio Publishing & Gozo Bks., LLC.

Bernstein, Galia. Leyla. 2019. (ENG., Illus.). 32p. (J). (gr. -1-3). 16.99 *(978-1-4197-3543-1(8)*, 1268901, Abrams Bks. for Young Readers) Abrams, Inc.

Burleigh, Robert. Clang! Clang! Beep! Beep! Listen to the City. Giacobbe, Beppe, illus. 2009. (ENG.). 32p. (J). (gr. -1-2). 19.99 *(978-1-4169-4052-4(9)*, Simon & Schuster/Paula Wiseman Bks.) Simon & Schuster/Paula Wiseman Bks.

—Zoom! Zoom! Sounds of Things That Go in the City. Carpenter, Tad, illus. 2014. (ENG.). 32p. (J). (gr. -1-3). 18.99 *(978-1-4424-8315-6(6)*, Simon & Schuster Bks. For Young Readers) Simon & Schuster Bks. For Young Readers.

Cameron, Kristy. Behind the Door of Timothy Moore. Schickle, Ian, illus. 2013. 28p. pap. *(978-0-9859790-1-0(1))* LP Publishing.

Crimi, Carolyn. The Louds Move In!, 1 vol. Dunnick, Regan, illus. 2006. (ENG.). 32p. (J). (gr. -1-3). 14.95 *(978-0-7614-5221-8(4))* Marshall Cavendish Corp.

Desautels, Jodi. There Were Always Noises. 2012. 20p. pap. 24.95 *(978-1-4626-8628-5(1))* PublishAmerica, Inc.

Donegan, Noel & Donegan, Luz. The Noisy Blue Drum. 2013. (Magical Mozart & His Musical Ser.). (ENG.). 32p. (J). pap. 8.95 *(978-1-84730-391-2(9))* Veritas Pubns. IRL. Dist: Casemate Pubs. & Bk. Distributors, LLC.

Doyle, Malachy. Too Noisy! Vere, Ed, illus. 2012. (ENG.). 32p. (J). (gr. -1-2). 15.99 *(978-0-7636-6226-4(7))* Candlewick Pr.

Garcia, Emma. Toot Toot Beep Beep. 2013. (All about Sounds Ser.). (ENG., Illus.). 26p. (J). (— 1). bds. 7.99 *(978-1-906250-84-3(7))* Boxer Bks., Ltd. GBR. Dist: Sterling Publishing Co., Inc.

Gibson, Ginger Foglesong. Tiptoe Joe. Rankin, Laura, illus. 2013. (ENG.). 32p. (J). (gr. -1-k). 17.99 *(978-0-06-177203-0(8)*, Greenwillow Bks.) HarperCollins Pubs.

Gonzalez, Julie. How Could a Bear Sleep Here? Laberis, Stephanie, illus. 2018. 32p. (J). (gr. -1-3). 17.99 *(978-0-8234-3679-8(9))* Holiday Hse., Inc.

Goss, Leon. By the Light of the Moon. Luo, Shiyin Sean, illus. 2005. (J). pap. *(978-1-933156-12-5(0))*; per. 16.99 *(978-1-933156-05-7(8))* GSVQ Publishing. (VisionQuest Kids).

Harris, Robie H. When Lions Roar. Raschka, Chris, illus. 2013. (ENG.). 32p. (J). (gr. -1-k). 16.99 *(978-0-545-11283-3(4)*, Orchard Bks.) Scholastic, Inc.

Herbauts, Anne. Prince Silencio. 2006. (ENG., Illus.). 32p. (J). (gr. -1-3). 14.95 *(978-1-59270-055-4(1))* Enchanted Lion Bks., LLC.

Holden, Pam. The Long, Long Ride, 1 vol. Storey, Jim, illus. 2009. (Red Rocket Readers Ser.). (ENG.). 22p. (gr. 2-2). pap. *(978-1-877363-76-4(6))* Flying Start Bks.

Keep, Richard. A Thump from Upstairs: Starring Mr. Boo & Max, 1 vol. 2005. (ENG., Illus.). 36p. (J). (gr. -1-3). 15.95 *(978-1-56145-348-1(X))* Peachtree Publishing Co. Inc.

Kohuth, Jane. Ducks Go Vroom. Garofoli, Viviana, illus. 2011. (Step into Reading Ser.). 32p. (J). (gr. -1-1). pap. 4.99 *(978-0-375-86560-2(8)*, Random Hse. Bks. for Young Readers) Random Hse. Children's Bks.

Kramer, Alan & Kramer, Candice. Brer Rabbit Hears a Big Noise in the Woods: An African /American Folktale. 2006. (J). pap. *(978-1-4108-7163-3(0))* Benchmark Education Co.

Lemniscates. Silence. 2012. (Illus.). (J). 32p. 14.95 *(978-1-4338-1137-1(5))*; 29p. pap. 9.95 *(978-1-4338-1136-4(7))* American Psychological Assn. (Magination Pr.).

Light, Steve. Diggers Go. 2013. (Vehicles Go! Ser.). (ENG., Illus.). 16p. (J). (gr. -1 — 1). bds. 9.99 *(978-1-4521-1864-2(7))* Chronicle Bks. LLC.

Long, Ethan. One Drowsy Dragon. 2010. (Illus.). (J). *(978-0-545-23412-2(3)*, Orchard Bks.) Scholastic, Inc.

Lord, Jill Roman. Noisy Silent Night. 2018. (J). *(978-0-8198-5188-8(4))* Pauline Bks. & Media.

MacLeod, Jennifer Tzivia. Fast Asleep in a Little Village in Israel. Beeke, Tiphanie, illus. 2018. (ENG.). 32p. (J). 17.95 *(978-1-68115-539-5(7)*, 73160a0c-1e6a-4190-81ea-4157ce5b2e5a, Apples & Honey Pr.) Behrman Hse., Inc.

Maier, Inger. When Fuzzy Was Afraid of Big & Loud Things. Candon, Jennifer, illus. 2005. (Fuzzy the Little Sheep Ser.). 32p. (J). (gr. -1-3). 14.95 *(978-1-59147-322-0(5)*, Magination Pr.) American Psychological Assn.

Maier, Inger M. When Fuzzy Was Afraid of Big & Loud Things. Candon, Jennifer, illus. 2005. 32p. (J). (gr. -1-3). per. 9.95 *(978-1-59147-323-7(3)*, Magination Pr.) American Psychological Assn.

Mandy and Ness Staff, et al. Hattie's House: A First Book about Sound. 2005. (Senses Ser.). (URD, ENG, VIE, CHI & BEN., Illus.). 16p. (J). pap. 9.95 *(978-1-84059-156-9(0))* Milet Publishing.

McGovern, Ann. Too Much Noise. 2014. 16.95 *(978-1-63419-746-5(1))* Perfection Learning Corp.

Medearis, Angela Shelf. Lucy's Quiet Book. Ernst, Lisa Campbell, illus. 2004. (ENG.). 24p. (J). (gr. -1-3). pap. 5.99 *(978-0-15-205143-3(0)*, 1195521, Clarion Bks.) HarperCollins Pubs.

—Lucy's Quiet Book. Ernst, Lisa Campbell, illus. 2004. (Green Light Readers Level 2 Ser.). (gr. k-2). 13.95 *(978-0-7569-4310-3(8))* Perfection Learning Corp.

Molitoris, Cathy. I've Got Music! McConnell, Sarah, illus. 2006. (J). *(978-0-439-88620-8(1))* Scholastic, Inc.

Moore, Nicholas & Murton, Gareth. Princess Lydia & the wailing Monster. 2008. (ENG.). 32p. pap. 18.95 *(978-1-4092-4993-1(X))* Lulu Pr., Inc.

Morris, Eileen. The Original "Shnoozles" Starring in "and Next Came a Roar" 2005. (ENG.). 16p. pap. 3.99 *(978-0-9768852-0-7(4))* Shnoozles, LLC.

Mortimer, Rachael. The Three Billy Goats Fluff. Pichon, Liz, illus. 2013. (ENG.). 32p. (J). (gr. -1-2). pap. 7.95 *(978-1-58925-439-8(2))* Tiger Tales.

Morton, Christine. No Te Preocupes, Guille. McMullen, Nigel, illus. (Buenas Noches Ser.). (SPA.). 26p. (J). (gr. k-3). 8.95 *(978-958-04-5088-7(9))* Norma S.A. COL. Dist: Distribuidora Norma, Inc.

Newton, Jill, illus. Crash Bang Donkey! 2015. 32p. (J). *(978-1-4896-3858-8(X))* Weigl Pubs., Inc.

Niner, Holly L. No More Noisy Nights. 2017. (ENG., Illus.). (J). (gr. k-2). 7.99 *(978-1-936261-96-3(0))* Flashlight Pr.

—No More Noisy Nights. Wolek, Guy, illus. 2017. (ENG.). 32p. (J). (gr. k-2). 17.95 *(978-1-936261-93-2(6))* Flashlight Pr.

Pennypacker, Sara. Sparrow Girl. Tanaka, Yoko, illus. 2009. (ENG.). 40p. (J). (gr. -1-3). 17.99 *(978-1-4231-1187-0(7))* Little, Brown Bks. for Young Readers.

Rauss, Ron. Can I Just Take a Nap? Shepperson, Rob, illus. 2012. (ENG.). 32p. (J). (gr. -1-1). 15.99 *(978-1-4424-3497-4(X)*, Simon & Schuster/Paula Wiseman Bks.) Simon & Schuster/Paula Wiseman Bks.

Rosen, Robert. It's Too Noisy! Piworski, Marcin, illus. 2017. (All about Me Ser.). (ENG.). 24p. (gr. -1-2). pap. 9.95 *(978-1-68342-770-4(X)*, 9781683427704) Rourke Educational Media.

Schotter, Roni. When the Wizzy Foot Goes Walking. Wohnoutka, Mike, illus. 2007. (J). *(978-5-525-47791-9(2)*, Dutton Juvenile) Penguin Publishing Group.

Sosin, Deborah. Charlotte & the Quiet Place. Woolley, Sara, illus. 2015. 40p. (J). (gr. -1-2). 16.95 *(978-1-941529-02-7(X)*, Plum Blossom Bks.) Parallax Pr.

Sullivan-Ringe, Laurie. Noise in the Night. Matiuzzo, Nick, illus. 2008. 37p. pap. 24.95 *(978-1-60672-476-7(2))* America Star Bks.

Teal, Val. The Little Woman Wanted Noise. Lawson, Robert, illus. 2013. (ENG.). 48p. (J). (gr. -1-2). 14.95 *(978-1-59017-711-2(8)*, NYR Children's Collection) New York Review of Bks., Inc., The.

Tyler, Jenny & Hawthorn, Phillip. Who's Making That Noise? 2008. (Luxury Flap Bks). 16p. (J). 9.99 *(978-0-7945-1695-6(5)*, Usborne) EDC Publishing.

Underwood, Deborah. The Loud Book! Liwska, Renata, illus. 2018. (ENG.). 32p. (J). (gr. -1-3). pap. 7.99 *(978-1-328-86929-6(6)*, 1696691, Clarion Bks.) HarperCollins Pubs.

—The Loud Book! 2018. lib. bdg. 18.40 *(978-0-606-41007-6(4))* Turtleback.

Urey, Gary. Super Schnoz Boxed Set #1-3. Long, Ethan & Frawley, Keith, illus. 2017. (Super Schnoz Ser.). (ENG.). 480p. (J). (gr. 3-7). pap., pap., pap. 19.99 *(978-0-8075-9989-1(1)*, 807599891) Whitman, Albert & Co.

Van Biesen, Koen. Roger Is Reading a Book. 2015. (ENG., Illus.). 42p. (J). 16.00 *(978-0-8028-5442-1(7)*, Eerdmans Bks For Young Readers) Eerdmans, William B. Publishing Co.

Williams, Rozanne. Mr. Noisy. 2017. (Learn-To-Read Ser.). (ENG., Illus.). (J). pap. 3.49 *(978-1-68310-208-3(8))* Pacific Learning, Inc.

Willson, Sarah. Do Not Wake Jake. Johnson, Meredith, illus. 2006. (Step-By-Step Readers Ser.). (J). *(978-1-59939-059-8(0)*, Reader's Digest Young Families, Inc.) Studio Fun International.

Wilson, Karma. Who Goes There? Currey, Anna, illus. 2013. (ENG.). 40p. (J). (gr. -1-3). 19.99 *(978-1-4169-8002-5(4)*, McElderry, Margaret K. Bks.) McElderry, Margaret K. Bks.

NOMADS

Eggleton, Jill. Nomads. 2007. (Connectors Ser.). (gr. 2-5). pap. *(978-1-877453-12-0(9))* Global Education Systems Ltd.

Hinds, Kathryn. Huns, 1 vol. 2010. (Barbarians! Ser.). (ENG.). 80p. (gr. 6-6). 38.36 *(978-0-7614-4066-6(6)*, dc36f0e8-1c42-4638-9bda-8aed62c62065) Cavendish Square Publishing LLC.

—Scythians & Sarmatians, 1 vol. 2010. (Barbarians! Ser.). (ENG.). 80p. (gr. 6-6). 38.36 *(978-0-7614-4072-7(0)*, 0fc68840-e2ef-4b12-8f44-79b63b02a60f) Cavendish Square Publishing LLC.

Jadhava, Hukumacanda. Ghumantu- Lokajivana Ki Samskrti Ke Vividha Ayama. 2016. (HIN.). 336p. *(978-93-83862-18-4(1))* Mittal & Sons.

Kocienda, Genevieve. On the Move: The Lives of Nomads, 1 vol. 2014. (ENG., Illus.). 28p. pap., E-Book, E-Book 9.50 *(978-1-107-63293-6(5))* Cambridge Univ. Pr.

Rice, Earle. The Life & Times of Attila the Hun. 2009. (Biography from Ancient Civilizations Ser.). (Illus.). 48p. (J). (gr. 4-8). 29.95 *(978-1-58415-741-0(0))* Mitchell Lane Pubs.

NONOBJECTIVE ART

see Art, Abstract

NONSENSE VERSES

see also Limericks

Adams, Pam, illus. There Was an Old Lady Who Swallowed a Fly. 2003. (Classic Books with Holes 8x8 Ser.). (ENG.). 16p. (J). pap. *(978-0-85953-134-4(1))* Child's Play International Ltd.

Barrett, Judi. I Knew Two Who Said Moo: A Counting & Rhyming Book. Moreton, Daniel, illus. 2003. (ENG.). 32p. (J). (gr. -1-3). 8.99 *(978-0-689-85935-9(X)*, Atheneum Bks. for Young Readers) Simon & Schuster Children's Publishing.

Baxter, Nicola & Shuttleworth, Cathie. Silly Rhymes & Limericks. 2013. (ENG., Illus.). 64p. (J). (gr. -1-12). pap. 8.99 *(978-1-84322-866-0(1)*, Armadillo) Anness Publishing GBR. Dist: National Bk. Network.

Belloc, Hilaire. A Moral Alphabet: In Words of from One T. 2006. (Illus.). pap. 16.95 *(978-1-4286-1934-0(8))* Kessinger Publishing, LLC.

—More Beasts for Worse Children. B. T. B., illus. 2008. 48p. pap. *(978-1-4099-1329-0(5))* Dodo Pr.

Canetti, Yanitzia. Trabalenguas Científicos. 2010. 32p. (J). pap. 6.99 *(978-1-59835-264-1(4)*, BrickHouse Education) Cambridge BrickHouse, Inc.

Carroll, Lewis, pseud. The Hunting of the Snark. Peake, Mervyn, illus. 2004. 64p. *(978-0-413-74380-0(2))* Methuen Publishing Ltd.

—The Hunting of the Snark: An Agony in Eight Fits. Lipchenko, Oleg, illus. 2012. 48p. (J). (gr. 5-12). 17.95 *(978-1-77049-407-7(3)*, Tundra Bks.) Tundra Bks. CAN. Dist: Penguin Random Hse. LLC.

Chaudet, Annette. The Nose Book. 2007. (Illus.). 56p. (J). pap. 16.95 *(978-1-932636-36-9(6))* Pronghorn Pr.

Colandro, Lucille. There Was an Old Lady Who Swallowed a Clover! Lee, Jared, illus. 2012. (ENG.). 32p. (J). (gr. -1-k). pap. 6.99 *(978-0-545-35222-2(3)*, Cartwheel Bks.) Scholastic, Inc.

—There Was an Old Lady Who Swallowed a Rose! Lee, Jared, illus. 2012. (ENG.). 32p. (J). (gr. -1-k). pap. 6.99 *(978-0-545-35223-9(1))* Scholastic, Inc.

—There Was an Old Lady Who Swallowed Some Books! Lee, Jared, illus. 2012. (ENG.). 32p. (J). (gr. -1-k). 6.99 *(978-0-545-40287-3(5)*, Cartwheel Bks.) Scholastic, Inc.

—There Was an Old Mermaid Who Swallowed a Shark! Lee, Jared, illus. 2018. (ENG.). 64p. (J). (gr. -1-3). 8.99 *(978-1-338-12993-9(7)*, Cartwheel Bks.) Scholastic, Inc.

Dalmatian Press Staff. I Know an Old Lady Who Swallow. 2008. (ENG.). 12p. (J). bds. 4.95 *(978-1-58117-710-7(0)*, Intervisual/Piggy Toes) Bendon, Inc.

Dowell, Ruth I. Move over, Mother Goose! Finger Plays, Action Verses & Funny Rhymes. Charner, Kathleen, ed. Scott, Concetta C., illus. 2004. 126p. (Orig.). (gr. -1-1). pap. 12.95 *(978-0-87659-113-0(6)*, 10006) Gryphon Hse., Inc.

Downing, Johnette, illus. & adapted by. There Was an Old Lady Who Swallowed Some Bugs, 1 vol. Downing, Johnette, adapted by. 2010. (ENG.). 32p. (J). (gr. k-3). 16.99 *(978-1-58980-858-4(4)*, Pelican Publishing) Arcadia Publishing.

Foster, John, ed. Completely Crazy Poems. 2011. (ENG., Illus.). 96p. (gr. k-4). pap. 5.99 *(978-0-00-714802-8(X)*, HarperCollins Children's Bks.) HarperCollins Pubs. Ltd. GBR. Dist: HarperCollins Pubs.

—Seriously Scary Poems. 2011. (ENG., Illus.). 96p. (gr. k-4). pap. 5.99 *(978-0-00-714801-1(1)*, HarperCollins Children's Bks.) HarperCollins Pubs. Ltd. GBR. Dist: HarperCollins Pubs.

Fyleman, Rose & Philip, Neil. Mary Middling & Other Silly Folk: Nursery Rhymes & Nonsense Poems. Bandlow, Katja, illus. 2004. (ENG.). 32p. (J). (gr. -1-3). tchr. ed. 16.00 *(978-0-618-38141-8(4)*, 100334, Clarion Bks.) HarperCollins Pubs.

Gorey, Edward & Lear, Edward, illus. The Dong with the Luminous Nose. 2010. 48p. 14.95 *(978-0-7649-5427-6(X))* Pomegranate Communications, Inc.

—Jumblies. 2010. 48p. 14.95 *(978-0-7649-5426-9(1))* Pomegranate Communications, Inc.

Guarino, Deborah & Kellogg, Steven. Ta Maman Est-Elle un Lama? (FRE., Illus.). (J). pap. 7.99 *(978-0-590-74555-0(7))* Scholastic, Inc.

Guinness, Louise, ed. The Everyman Book of Nonsense Verse: Written & Introduced by Louise Guinness; Illustrated by Mervyn Peake. Peake, Mervyn, illus. 2005. (Everyman's Library Children's Classics Ser.). (ENG.). 256p. (gr. -1-17). 16.95 *(978-1-4000-4425-2(1)*, Everyman's Library) Knopf Doubleday Publishing Group.

Harris, Chris. I'm Just No Good at Rhyming: And Other Nonsense for Mischievous Kids & Immature Grown-Ups. Smith, Lane, illus. 2020. (Mischievous Nonsense Ser.: 1). (ENG.). 192p. (J). (gr. 1-17). 19.99 *(978-0-316-42710-4(1))* Little, Brown Bks. for Young Readers.

Harris, Tony. There's a Wombat in My Bed. 2nd rev. ed. 2012. (Illus.). 32p. (J). *(978-1-875763-00-9(7))* ThinkSoft.

Hoena, Blake, et al. Tickles, Pickles, & Floofing Persnickles: Reading & Writing Nonsense Poems, 1 vol. Smith, Simon et al, illus. 2014. (Poet in You Ser.). (ENG.). 32p. (J). (gr. 2-4). lib. bdg. 27.99 *(978-1-4795-2198-2(1)*, 124034, Picture Window Bks.) Capstone.

Ingersoll, Donna. Ten Tempting Tongue Twisters. 2012. 28p. 24.95 *(978-1-4626-8217-1(0))* America Star Bks.

Kralovansky, Susan. There Was a Tall Texan Who Swallowed a Flea, 1 vol. Kadair, Deborah, illus. 2013. (ENG.). 32p. (J). (gr. -1-3). 17.99 *(978-1-4556-1717-3(2)*, Pelican Publishing) Arcadia Publishing.

Lear, Edward. Nonsense Poems. 2011. (Dover Children's Thrift Classics Ser.). (ENG., Illus.). 96p. (Orig.). (J). (gr. 3-8). reprint ed. pap. 4.00 *(978-0-486-28031-8(4)*, 280314) Dover Pubns., Inc.

—Nonsense Song. l.t. ed. 2006. 108p. pap. *(978-1-84637-276-6(3))* Echo Library.

—The Pelican Chorus: And Other Nonsense. Marcellino, Fred, illus. 2017. (ENG.). 40p. (J). (gr. -1-3). 17.99 *(978-1-4814-7049-0(3)*, Atheneum/Caitlyn Dlouhy Books) Simon & Schuster Children's Publishing.

Lee, Dennis. Garbage Delight. 2014. (ENG., Illus.). 64p. (J). 17.99 *(978-0-06-231350-8(9)*, HarperCollins) HarperCollins Pubs.

Rice, Dona Herweck. Communicate! Tongue Twisters (Level 2) 2017. (TIME for KIDS(r): Informational Text Ser.). (ENG., Illus.). 28p. (gr. 2-3). pap. 10.99 *(978-1-4258-4965-8(2))* Teacher Created Materials, Inc.

Rosen, Michael. Nonsense. Mackie, Clare, illus. 2003. (ENG.). 48p. pap. *(978-0-7500-2671-0(5)*, Wayland) Hachette Children's Group.

Seuss. Huevos Verdes con Jamón (Green Eggs & Ham Spanish Edition) 2019. (Beginner Books(R) Ser.). (SPA., Illus.). 72p. (J). (gr. -1-2). 9.99 *(978-0-525-70723-3(9)*, Random Hse. Bks. for Young Readers) Random Hse. Children's Bks.

Twin Sisters(r) Staff. Down by the Bay. 2010. (J). (gr. k-2). pap. 4.99 *(978-1-59922-505-0(0))* Twin Sisters IP, LLC.

Walrus Books. Children's Treasure Chest: Fairy Tales, Nursery Rhymes, & Nonsense Verse. 2004. (ENG., Illus.). 386p. (J). (gr. k-12). 29.95 *(978-1-55285-579-9(1))* Whitecap Bks., Ltd. CAN. Dist: Graphic Arts Ctr. Publishing Co.

Ward, Jennifer. There Was an Odd Princess Who Swallowed a Pea, 0 vols. Calderon, Lee, illus. 2012. (ENG.). 32p. (J). (gr. -1-3). 16.99 *(978-0-7614-5822-7(0)*, 9780761458227, Two Lions) Amazon Publishing.

—There Was an Old Monkey Who Swallowed a Frog, 0 vols. Gray, Steve, illus. 2012. (ENG.). 40p. (J). (gr. k-3). 16.99 *(978-0-7614-5580-6(9)*, 9780761455806, Two Lions) Amazon Publishing.

Winn, Whee. Lots of Tongue Twisters for Kids, 1 vol. 2019. (ENG., Illus.). 128p. (J). pap. 4.99 *(978-0-310-76708-4(3))* Zonderkidz.

NONVIOLENCE

Gandhi, Mahatma. My Experiments with Truth. Chougule, Shailja Jain, illus. 2016. (ENG.). 64p. pap. 7.95 *(978-1-906230-88-3(9))* Real Reads Ltd. GBR. Dist: Casemate Pubs. & Bk. Distributors, LLC.

Haldy, Emma E. Martin Luther King, Jr. Bane, Jeff, illus. 2016. (My Early Library: My Itty-Bitty Bio Ser.). (ENG.). 24p. (J). (gr. k-1). 30.64 *(978-1-63470-477-9(0)*, 207639) Cherry Lake Publishing.

—Martin Luther King, Jr. SP. Bane, Jeff, illus. 2018. (My Early Library: Mi Mini Biografía (My Itty-Bitty Bio) Ser.). (SPA.). 24p. (J). (gr. k-1). lib. bdg. 30.64 *(978-1-5341-2998-6(7)*, 212040) Cherry Lake Publishing.

Kuhn, Betsy. The Force Born of Truth: Mohandas Gandhi & the Salt March, India 1930. 2010. (Civil Rights Struggles Around the World Ser.). (ENG., Illus.). 160p. (YA). (gr. 6-12). lib. bdg. 38.65 *(978-0-8225-8968-6(0)*, deaff85b-8573-436b-a823-e0da6015bbfa, Twenty-First Century Bks.) Lerner Publishing Group.

Meltzer, Brad. I Am Martin Luther King, Jr. Eliopoulos, Christopher, illus. 2016. (Ordinary People Change the World Ser.). 32p. (J). (gr. k-4). 15.99 *(978-0-525-42852-7(6)*, Dial Bks) Penguin Young Readers Group.

O'Brien, Anne Sibley & O'Brien, Perry Edmond. After Gandhi: One Hundred Years of Nonviolent Resistance. 2018. (Illus.). 224p. (J). (gr. 5). pap. 11.99 *(978-1-58089-130-1(6))* Charlesbridge Publishing, Inc.

Vander Hook, Sue. Mahatma Gandhi: Proponent of Peace, 1 vol. 2010. (Essential Lives Set 5 Ser.). (ENG.). 112p. (YA). (gr. 6-12). lib. bdg. 41.36 *(978-1-61613-515-7(8)*, 6713, Essential Library) ABDO Publishing Co.

NONVIOLENT NONCOOPERATION

see Passive Resistance

NORMANDY (FRANCE)—FICTION

Myers, Walter Dean. Invasion. (ENG.). 224p. (YA). 2015. (gr. 7). pap. 12.99 *(978-0-545-38429-2(X))* 2013. E-Book *(978-0-545-57659-8(8))* Scholastic, Inc. (Scholastic Pr.).

Stein, Evaleen. Our Little Norman Cousin of Long Ago. Goss, John, illus. 2007. 112p. per. 8.95 *(978-1-59915-245-5(2))* Yesterday's Classics.

Yonge, Charlotte M. The Little Duke. 2005. 26.95 *(978-1-4218-0318-0(6))*; 164p. pap. 11.95 *(978-1-4218-0418-7(2))* 1st World Publishing, Inc. (1st World Library - Literary Society).

—The Little Duke. 2004. reprint ed. pap. 1.99 *(978-1-4179-9908-8(X))*; pap. 15.95 *(978-1-4179-9958-3(6))* Kessinger Publishing, LLC.

—The Little Duke. 2008. 112p. pap. 9.05 *(978-1-60459-557-4(4))* Wilder Pubns., Corp.

Zafon, Carlos Ruiz. The Watcher in the Shadows. (ENG.). (YA). (gr. 7-17). 2014. 288p. pap. 15.99 *(978-0-316-04475-2(X))* 2013. 272p. 18.00 *(978-0-316-04476-9(8))* Little, Brown Bks. for Young Readers.

NORMANS

see also Northmen

Abbott, Jacob. History of William the Conqueror. 2003. 291p. 89.00 *(978-0-7950-4508-0(5))* New Library Press LLC.

—William the Conqueror. 2019. (J). pap. *(978-1-947644-15-1(7))* Canon Pr.

Hamilton, Janice. The Norman Conquest of England. 2007. (Pivotal Moments in History Ser.). (ENG., Illus.). 160p. (J). (gr. 9-12). lib. bdg. 38.60 *(978-0-8225-5902-3(1))* Lerner Publishing Group.

Harkins, Susan Sales & Harkins, William H. The Life & Times of William the Conqueror. 2008. (Biography from Ancient Civilizations Ser.). (Illus.). 48p. (J). (gr. 4-8). lib. bdg. 29.95 *(978-1-58415-700-7(3))* Mitchell Lane Pubs.

Hilliam, Paul. William the Conqueror: First Norman King of England. 2009. (Leaders of the Middle Ages Ser.). 112p. (gr. 5-8). 66.50 *(978-1-61513-903-3(6)*, Rosen Reference) Rosen Publishing Group, Inc., The.

HOCPP 1101 the Norman Conquest. 2006. spiral bd. 23.50 *(978-1-60308-101-6(1))* In the Hands of a Child.

NORMANS—FICTION

Henty, George. Wulf the Saxon: A Story of the Norman Conquest. Peacock, Ralph, illus. 2010. (Dover Children's Classics Ser.). (ENG.). 352p. (YA). (gr. 3-8). pap. 14.95 *(978-0-486-47595-0(6)*, 475956) Dover Pubns., Inc.

Leighton-Porter, Wendy. The Shadow of the Norman Arrow. 2013. 270p. pap. *(978-1-909411-07-4(8))* Mauve Square Publishing.

Welch, Ronald. The Gauntlet. 2017. (ENG., Illus.). (J). (gr. 5-6). pap. 16.95 *(978-0-9976647-1-3(1))* Hillside Education.

NORSEMEN

see Northmen

NORTH AFRICA

see Africa, North

NORTH AMERICA

Adasiewicz, Sue. Shockwave: Your Papers, Please. 2007. (Shockwave: People & Communities Ser.). (ENG., Illus.). 36p. (J). (gr. 3-5). 25.00 *(978-0-531-17572-9(3)*, Children's Pr.) Scholastic Library Publishing.

Allgor, Marie. Endangered Animals of North America, 1 vol. 2011. (Save Earth's Animals! Ser.). (ENG., Illus.). 24p. (J). (gr. 2-3). 26.27 *(978-1-4488-2532-5(6)*, 17080219-fb7e-41bb-872b-1a3a96820527); pap. 9.25 *(978-1-4488-2648-3(9)*, b923a14f-9fc4-4cb5-97dd-6a807ac18db8) Rosen Publishing Group, Inc., The. (PowerKids Pr.).

Aloian, Molly & Kalman, Bobbie. Explore North America. 2007. (Explore the Continents Ser.). (ENG., Illus.). 32p. (J). (gr. 4-7). lib. bdg. *(978-0-7787-3075-0(1))*; (gr. 2-3). pap. *(978-0-7787-3089-7(1))* Crabtree Publishing Co.

Animals of North America, 6 vols. 2015. (Animals of North America Ser.: 6). (ENG.). 24p. (J). (gr. -1-2). lib. bdg. 196.74 *(978-1-68080-106-4(6)*, 18987, Abdo Kids) ABDO Publishing Co.

Banting, Erinn. North America. (Illus.). 32p. (J). 2016. *(978-1-4896-5725-1(8))* 2005. (gr. -1-7). pap. 9.95 *(978-1-59036-328-7(0))* 2005. (gr. 4-6). lib. bdg. 26.00 *(978-1-59036-321-8(3))* Weigl Pubs., Inc.

The check digit for ISBN-10 appears in parentheses after the full ISBN-13

Benchmark Education Co., LLC. Ancient Cultures of North America. 2014. (PRIME Ser.). (J). (gr. 6-8). pap. *(978-1-4509-9483-5(0))* Benchmark Education Co.

—The Geography of North & South America. 2014. (PRIME Ser.). (J). (gr. 6-8). pap. *(978-1-4509-9505-4(5))* Benchmark Education Co.

Branden, Claire Vanden. North America. 2018. (Continents (Cody Koala) Ser.). (ENG., Illus.). 24p. (J). (gr. k-3). lib. bdg. 31.36 *(978-1-5321-6174-2(3)*, 30131, Pop! Cody Koala) Pop!

Catt, Thessaly. Migrating with the Caribou, 1 vol. 2011. (Animal Journeys Ser.). (ENG., Illus.). 24p. (gr. 2-3). (J). pap. 9.25 *(978-1-4488-2666-7(7)*, 8ea0b4d8-5fd4-441d-99f4-bef587e56aac, PowerKids Pr.); (YA). 26.27 *(978-1-4488-2541-7(5)*, 64d852e8-3d3d-41f9-9342-2e68974cd586) Rosen Publishing Group, Inc., The.

Dahl, Michael. Wolves, 1 vol. 2012. (North American Animals Ser.). (ENG.). 24p. (J). (gr. -1-2). lib. bdg. 27.32 *(978-1-4296-7701-1(5)*, 117298) Capstone.

Donaldson, Madeline. North America. 2005. (Pull Ahead Books — Continents Ser.). (Illus.). 32p. (J). (gr. k-3). (ENG.). pap. 7.99 *(978-0-8225-2494-6(5)*, 124cd68a-7e57-4c03-914d-ebf0caae823a); lib. bdg. 22.60 *(978-0-8225-4722-8(8))* Lerner Publishing Group.

Dutcher, Jim. National Geographic Kids Chapters: Living with Wolves! True Stories of Adventures with Animals. 2016. (NGK Chapters Ser.). (Illus.). 112p. (J). (gr. 3-7). pap. 5.99 *(978-1-4263-2563-2(0)*, National Geographic Kids) Disney Publishing Worldwide.

Ellis, Deborah. Looks Like Daylight: Voices of Indigenous Kids, 1 vol. 2018. (ENG., Illus.). 256p. (J). (gr. 7). pap. 12.99 *(978-1-55498-121-2(2))* Groundwood Bks. CAN. Dist: Publishers Group West (PGW).

Encyclopaedia Britannica, Inc. Staff, compiled by. My First Britannica: The Americas. 2008. (gr. 7-12). *(978-1-59339-409-7(8))* Encyclopaedia Britannica, Inc.

Encyclopaedia Britannica Publishers, Inc. Staff. Views of the Americas. 2003. (Britannica Learning Library). (Illus.). 14.95 *(978-1-59339-012-9(2))* Encyclopaedia Britannica, Inc.

Esbensen, Barbara Juster. Playful Slider: The North American River Otter. Brown, Mary Barrett, illus. 2011. (Fesler-Lampert Minnesota Heritage Ser.). (ENG.). 32p. pap. 11.95 *(978-0-8166-7765-8(4))* Univ. of Minnesota Pr.

Gamble, Adam. Good Night Lake. Stevenson, Harvey, illus. 2008. (Good Night Our World Ser.). (ENG.). 28p. (J). (gr. k — 1). bds. 9.95 *(978-1-60219-028-3(3))* Good Night Bks.

Gardner, Jane P. Timber & Forest Products, Vol. 12. 2015. (North American Natural Resources Ser.). (Illus.). 64p. (J). (gr. 7). 23.95 *(978-1-4222-3389-4(8))* Mason Crest.

Hovanec, Erin M. An Online Visit to North America. 2009. (Internet Field Trips Ser.). 24p. (gr. 3-3). 45.00 *(978-1-61513-606-3(1)*, PowerKids Pr.) Rosen Publishing Group, Inc., The.

Johnson, Jinny. Brown Bear. 2014. (North American Mammals Ser.). (ENG.). 24p. (J). (gr. 1-4). 28.50 *(978-1-62588-032-1(4)*, 17370) Black Rabbit Bks.

King, Colin, illus. Jigsaw Atlas of North America. 2006. (Usborne Jigsaw Bks.). 14p. (J). (gr. k-3). bds. 14.99 *(978-0-7945-1242-2(9)*, Usborne) EDC Publishing.

Lindeen, Mary. Welcome to North America, 1 vol. 2011. (Wonder Readers Fluent Level Ser.). (ENG.). 16p. (J). (gr. -1-2). pap. 6.25 *(978-1-4296-7974-9(3)*, 118306, Capstone Pr.) Capstone.

Mattern, Joanne, et al. North American Animals. 2012. (North American Animals Ser.). (ENG.). 24p. (gr. k-1). pap. 250.20 *(978-1-4296-8363-0(5)*, Capstone Pr.) Capstone.

Max And Steven Oscherwitz. Gilbert's Adventure. 2008. 56p. pap. 27.99 *(978-1-4257-4577-6(6))* Xlibris Corp.

McAneney, Caitlin. North American Birds: Represent & Solve Problems Involving Multiplication, 1 vol. 2014. (Rosen Math Readers Ser.). (ENG., Illus.). 24p. (J). (gr. 3-3). pap. 8.25 *(978-1-4777-4971-5(3)*, 20d66ff6-9866-48af-be2e-8884ab8c615a); lib. bdg. 25.27 *(978-1-4777-6445-9(3)*, 6e82c6fd-ade5-4fe9-b5a6-7d09069015ad) Rosen Publishing Group, Inc., The. (PowerKids Pr.).

McNeil, Niki, et al. North America. 2007. (In the Hands of a Child: Project Pack Continent Study Ser.). (Illus.). 104p. spiral bd. 24.00 *(978-1-60308-076-7(7))* In the Hands of a Child.

Nagle, Garrett. North America, 1 vol. 2005. (Continents of the World Ser.). (ENG.). 64p. (gr. 5-8). pap. 15.05 *(978-0-8368-5921-8(9)*, 81e76f44-57a3-4297-9749-32fd9b423ea9); (Illus.). lib. bdg. 36.67 *(978-0-8368-5914-0(6)*, 1d24571b-825b-4c7e-81e3-62256f0ddb2d) Stevens, Gareth Publishing LLLP. (Gareth Stevens Secondary Library).

North American Historical Atlases (Group 2), 10 vols., Set. 2003. (North American Historical Atlases Ser.). (ENG.). (gr. 5-5). 163.20 *(978-0-7614-1344-8(8)*, ae05733d-7bdd-4147-bf90-10c42b4d337e, Cavendish Square) Cavendish Square Publishing LLC.

Parker, Steve. Coal, Vol. 12. 2015. (North American Natural Resources Ser.). 64p. (J). (gr. 7). 23.95 *(978-1-4222-3379-5(0))* Mason Crest.

Proudfit, Benjamin. The Pan-American Highway, 1 vol. 2016. (Road Trip: Famous Routes Ser.). (ENG., Illus.). 24p. (J). (gr. 2-3). 25.27 *(978-1-4824-4669-2(3)*, 4b03770c-476b-44ef-bca0-90ea4c6c5e26) Stevens, Gareth Publishing LLLP.

Ring, Susan. We Live in North America. 2005. (Yellow Umbrella Fluent Level Ser.). (ENG.). 16p. (gr. k-1). pap. 35.70 *(978-0-7368-5311-8(1)*, Capstone Pr.) Capstone.

Sabelko, Rebecca. Rocky Mountain Elk. 2018. (North American Animals Ser.). (ENG., Illus.). 24p. (J). (gr. k-3). lib. bdg. 26.95 *(978-1-62617-800-7(3)*, Blastoff! Readers) Bellwether Media.

Sayre, April Pulley. Welcome to North America! 2003. 32p. (J). (gr. 2-5). pap. 7.95 *(978-0-7613-1988-7(3))*; (Illus.). lib. bdg. 21.90 *(978-0-7613-2150-7(0))* Lerner Publishing Group. (Millbrook Pr.).

Strauss, Bob. A Field Guide to Dinosaurs of North America: And Prehistoric Megafauna. 2015. (Illus.). 224p. (YA). (gr. 8-17). pap. 22.95 *(978-1-4930-0925-1(7))* Globe Pequot Pr., The.

Tarbox, A. D. A Prairie Food Chain: Nature's Bounty. 2015. (Odysseys in Nature Ser.). (ENG., Illus.). 80p. (J). (gr. 7-10). *(978-1-60818-542-9(7)*, 20974, Creative Education) Creative Co., The.

The Library of the Western Hemisphere: Set 2, 8 vols. 2004. (Library of the Western Hemisphere Ser.). (ENG.). (J). (gr. 4-4). 105.08 *(978-1-4042-2964-8(7)*, fde7c6d7-7fa8-46df-ab9a-e8c45db0f4ec) Rosen Publishing Group, Inc., The.

The Libray of the Western Hemisphere: Set 1, 8 vols. 2004. (Library of the Western Hemisphere Ser.). (ENG.). (J). (gr. 4-4). 105.08 *(978-1-4042-2963-1(9)*, 9e4d3bdc-ec44-4267-baa8-a92197cb5390) Rosen Publishing Group, Inc., The.

Vanden Branden, Claire. North America. 2019. (Continents Ser.). (ENG., Illus.). 24p. (J). (gr. 1-1). pap. 8.95 *(978-1-64185-545-7(2)*, 1641855452) North Star Editions.

Vierow, Wendy. North America. (Atlas of the Seven Continents Ser.). 24p. (gr. 3-3). 2009. 42.50 *(978-1-61511-481-8(5)*, PowerKids Pr.) 2003. (ENG., Illus.). (J). lib. bdg. 26.27 *(978-0-8239-6692-9(5)*, 53307848-1e84-4d4d-bf60-52cde8844566) Rosen Publishing Group, Inc., The.

Williams, Heather DiLorenzo & Rylands, Warren. North America. 2019. (Illus.). 24p. (J). *(978-1-4896-8325-0(9)*, AV2 by Weigl) Weigl Pubs., Inc.

Wojahn, Rebecca Hogue & Wojahn, Donald. A Desert Food Chain: A Who-Eats-What Adventure in North America. 2009. (Follow That Food Chain Ser.). (ENG.). 64p. (gr. 3-5). 30.60 *(978-0-8225-7501-6(9))* Lerner Publishing Group.

—A Temperate Forest Food Chain: A Who-Eats-What Adventure in North America. 2009. (Follow That Food Chain Ser.). (ENG., Illus.). 64p. (J). (gr. 3-5). 30.60 *(978-0-8225-7496-5(9))* Lerner Publishing Group.

Wolny, Philip. Muslims Around the World Today. 2009. (Understanding Islam Ser.). 64p. (gr. 6-6). 58.50 *(978-1-60854-626-8(8))* Rosen Publishing Group, Inc., The.

Woods, Michael & Woods, Mary B. Seven Natural Wonders of North America. 2009. (Seven Wonders Ser.). (ENG., Illus.). 80p. (gr. 5-8). lib. bdg. 33.26 *(978-0-8225-9069-9(7))* Lerner Publishing Group.

NORTH AMERICA—ANTIQUITIES

Harrison, David L. Mammoth Bones & Broken Stones: The Mystery of North America's First People. Hilliard, Richard, illus. 2010. (ENG.). 48p. (J). (gr. 4-7). 18.95 *(978-1-59078-561-4(4)*, Astra Young Readers) Astra Publishing Hse.

Woods, Mary B. & Woods, Michael. Seven Wonders of Ancient North America. 2008. (Seven Wonders Ser.). (ENG., Illus.). 80p. (gr. 5-8). lib. bdg. 33.26 *(978-0-8225-7572-6(8))* Lerner Publishing Group.

NORTH AMERICA—DISCOVERY AND EXPLORATION

see America—Discovery and Exploration

NORTH AMERICA—HISTORY

Alderfer, Jonathan. National Geographic Backyard Guide to the Birds of North America, 2nd Edition. 2nd ed. 2019. (Illus.). 256p. pap. 21.99 *(978-1-4262-2062-3(6)*, National Geographic Books) Disney Publishing Worldwide.

Aloian, Molly & Kalman, Bobbie. Explora America del Norte. 2007. (Explora Los Continentes Ser.). (SPA & ENG., Illus.). 32p. (J). (gr. 4-7). pap. *(978-0-7787-8300-8(6))* Crabtree Publishing Co.

Banting, Erinn. North America. 2012. (J). pap. 13.95 *(978-1-61913-452-2(7))*; 28.55 *(978-1-61913-451-5(9))* Weigl Pubs., Inc.

Benchmark Education Company, LLC Staff, compiled by. Historical Communities: Theme Set. 2006. (J). 121.00 *(978-1-4108-7097-1(9))* Benchmark Education Co.

Boyd, Judy. North America, Vol. 10. 2016. (Social Progress & Sustainability Ser.). (Illus.). 80p. (J). (gr. 7). 24.95 *(978-1-4222-3498-3(3))* Mason Crest.

Brown Bear Books. North America. 2008. (Countries Ser.). (ENG., Illus.). 64p. (J). (gr. 8-11). lib. bdg. 39.95 *(978-1-933834-07-8(2)*, 16480) Brown Bear Bks.

Chandler, Matt. Famous Ghost Stories of North America. 2018. (Haunted World Ser.). (ENG., Illus.). 32p. (J). (gr. 3-9). lib. bdg. 28.65 *(978-1-5435-2595-3(4)*, 138074, Capstone Pr.) Capstone.

Coletti, Sharon. Everything You Need to Teach North America. 2005. (YA). ring bd. 149.95 *(978-1-933558-05-9(9))* InspirEd Educators.

Daly, Ruth. North America. 2014. (J). *(978-1-4896-0954-0(7))* Weigl Pubs., Inc.

Exploring North America, 1800-1900. 2nd rev. ed. 2010. (ENG., Illus.). 152p. (gr. 7-12). 35.00 *(978-1-60413-194-9(2)*, P174277, Facts On File) Infobase Holdings, Inc.

Fox, Mary Virginia. North America. 2nd rev. ed. 2016. (Continents Ser.). (ENG.). 32p. (J). (gr. 1-3). pap. 8.29 *(978-1-4846-3821-7(2)*, 134720, Heinemann) Capstone.

In North & South America. (J). (gr. 5). 3.80 *(978-0-8374-1454-6(7)*, 405) Weekly Reader Corp.

Jankowski, Emily. Mapping North America, 1 vol. 2013. (Mapping the World Ser.). 24p. (J). (gr. 2-3). (ENG.). 25.27 *(978-1-4339-9114-1(4)*, cf9da6ff-1825-4714-82ae-f6f5667184d9); pap. 48.90 *(978-1-4339-9116-5(0))*; (ENG., Illus.). pap. 9.15 *(978-1-4339-9115-8(2)*, f75e6964-aa70-4551-9a24-71eb75d5a1ac) Stevens, Gareth Publishing LLLP.

Johnston, Lissa. A Brief Political & Geographic History of North America: Where Are... New France, New Netherland, & New Sweden. 2007. (Places in Time Ser.). (Illus.). 112p. (YA). (gr. 5-9). lib. bdg. 37.10 *(978-1-58415-627-7(9))* Mitchell Lane Pubs.

Juarez, Christine. North America: A 4D Book. 2018. (Investigating Continents Ser.). (ENG., Illus.). 24p. (J). (gr. 1-3). lib. bdg. 27.99 *(978-1-5435-2799-5(X)*, 138242, Capstone Pr.) Capstone.

Kalman, Bobbie. L'Amérique du Nord. 2012. (FRE.). 32p. (J). pap. 9.95 *(978-2-89579-460-8(X))* Bayard Canada CAN. Dist: Crabtree Publishing Co.

Kellaher, Karen. North America (a True Book: the Seven Continents) (Library Edition) 2019. (True Book (Relaunch) Ser.). (ENG., Illus.). 48p. (J). (gr. 3-5). lib. bdg. 31.00 *(978-0-531-12809-1(1)*, Children's Pr.) Scholastic Library Publishing.

Kjelle, Marylou Morano. Pre-Columbian America. 2009. (How'd They Do That? Ser.). (Illus.). 64p. (J). (gr. 4-8). lib. bdg. 33.95 *(978-1-58415-826-4(3))* Mitchell Lane Pubs.

Koenig, Emily C. North America, 1 vol. 2013. (Continents Ser.). (ENG.). 48p. (J). (gr. 4-8). lib. bdg. 35.64 *(978-1-61783-933-7(7)*, 4568) ABDO Publishing Co.

Koponen, Libby. North America. 2008. (True Book(tm), A — Continents Ser.). (ENG., Illus.). 48p. (J). (gr. 2-5). 31.00 *(978-0-531-16868-4(9))* Scholastic Library Publishing.

Lindeen, Mary. North America. 2018. (Continents of the World Ser.). (ENG.). 24p. (J). (gr. -1-2). lib. bdg. 32.79 *(978-1-5038-2498-0(5)*, 212322) Child's World, Inc, The.

—Welcome to North America, 1 vol. (Wonder Readers: Social Studies). (ENG.). (gr. -1-2). 2012. 20p. (J). lib. bdg. 25.32 *(978-1-4296-9617-3(6)*, 120533) 2011. 16p. pap. 35.94 *(978-1-4296-8204-6(3))* Capstone. (Capstone Pr.).

Looye, Juliette, text. I Live on the Earth. 2004. (Illus.). 16p. (J). pap. *(978-0-7367-1931-5(8))* Zaner-Bloser, Inc.

Lucas, Bruce. North America on the Map. 2013. (InfoMax Readers Ser.). (ENG.). 24p. (J). (gr. 2-3). pap. 49.50 *(978-1-4777-2432-3(X))*; (Illus.). pap. 8.25 *(978-1-4777-2431-6(1)*, d802f550-008c-47c9-b3d8-c309294f6d41) Rosen Publishing Group, Inc., The. (Rosen Classroom).

MacLeod, Elizabeth. Secrets Underground: North America's Buried Past. 2014. (ENG., Illus.). 96p. (YA). (gr. 5-12). pap. 14.95 *(978-1-55451-630-8(7)*, 9781554516308) Annick Pr., Ltd. CAN. Dist: Publishers Group West (PGW).

—Secrets Underground: North America's Buried Past. Martchenko, Michael, illus. 2014. (ENG.). 96p. (YA). (gr. 5-12). 24.95 *(978-1-55451-631-5(5)*, 9781554516315) Annick Pr., Ltd. CAN. Dist: Publishers Group West (PGW).

McClish, Bruce. New World Continents & Land Bridges: North & South America. rev. ed. 2016. (Continents Ser.). (ENG.). 32p. (J). (gr. 4-6). pap. 8.99 *(978-1-4846-3639-8(2)*, 134035, Heinemann) Capstone.

North America: Regions of the World. 2003. spiral bd. 16.95 *(978-1-56004-160-3(9))* Social Studies Schl. Service.

North American Historical Atlases (Group 2), 10 vols., Set. 2003. (North American Historical Atlases Ser.). (ENG.). (gr. 5-5). 163.20 *(978-0-7614-1344-8(8)*, ae05733d-7bdd-4147-bf90-10c42b4d337e, Cavendish Square) Cavendish Square Publishing LLC.

Oachs, Emily Rose. North America. 2016. (Discover the Continents Ser.). (ENG., Illus.). 24p. (J). (gr. k-3). pap. 7.99 *(978-1-61891-259-6(3)*, 12043); lib. bdg. 26.95 *(978-1-62617-328-6(1))* Bellwether Media. (Blastoff! Readers).

O'Brien, Cynthia. Explore with Sieur de la Salle. 2014. (Travel with the Great Explorers Ser.). (ENG., Illus.). 32p. (J). (gr. 4-5). *(978-0-7787-1430-9(6))* Crabtree Publishing Co.

Oxlade, Chris. Introducing North America, 1 vol. 2013. (Introducing Continents Ser.). (ENG.). 32p. (J). (gr. 1-3). pap. 8.95 *(978-1-4329-8051-1(3)*, 123214, Heinemann) Capstone.

Petersen, Christine. Learning about North America. 2015. (Searchlight Books (tm) — Do You Know the Continents? Ser.). (ENG., Illus.). 40p. (J). (gr. 3-5). 30.65 *(978-1-4677-8020-9(0)*, b15d679b-8470-4721-9937-c95516535a22, Lerner Pubns.) Lerner Publishing Group.

Phelps, Bonnie. Map Facts: North America, 1 vol. 2013. (Rosen Readers Ser.). (ENG.). 24p. (J). (gr. 2-2). pap. 8.25 *(978-1-4777-2281-7(5)*, c240b699-4d72-417d-b696-b4d1d8d6906a); pap. 49.50 *(978-1-4777-2282-4(3))* Rosen Publishing Group, Inc., The. (Rosen Classroom).

Rockett, Paul. Mapping North America. 2016. (Mapping the Continents Ser.). (Illus.). 32p. (J). (gr. 3-6). *(978-0-7787-2616-6(9))* Crabtree Publishing Co.

Roumanis, Alexis. North America. 2014. (Illus.). 24p. (J). *(978-1-4896-3042-1(2))* Weigl Pubs., Inc.

Stanley, George E. The European Settlement of North America (1492-1763), 1 vol. 2004. (Primary Source History of the United States Ser.). (ENG., Illus.). 48p. (gr. 5-8). pap. 15.05 *(978-0-8368-5833-4(6)*, 3a40b780-1d7f-4821-ab02-8bb37c6319da); lib. bdg. 33.67 *(978-0-8368-5824-2(7)*, d81a23d2-645d-46fa-8e2e-f7e74414d24f) Stevens, Gareth Publishing LLLP. (Gareth Stevens Secondary Library).

Stefoff, Rebecca. Cities & Towns. 2007. (ENG., Illus.). 96p. (C). (gr. 6-18). lib. bdg. 165.00 *(978-0-7656-8109-6(9)*, Y181735) Routledge.

Weird America: Set 2. 2016. (Weird America Ser.). 00032p. (J). pap. 63.00 *(978-1-4824-5835-0(7))* Stevens, Gareth Publishing LLLP.

Wingate, Philippa & Reid, Struan. Who Were the First North Americans? 2004. (Starting Point History Ser.). (Illus.). 32p. (J). pap. 4.99 *(978-0-7945-0397-0(7)*, Usborne); lib. bdg. 12.95 *(978-1-58086-512-8(7))* EDC Publishing.

NORTH AMERICAN INDIANS

see Indians of North America

NORTH ATLANTIC TREATY ORGANIZATION

Richardson, Erik. NATO, the Warsaw Pact, & the Iron Curtain, 1 vol. 2017. (Cold War Chronicles Ser.). (ENG., Illus.). 112p. (YA). (gr. 9-9). 44.50 *(978-1-5026-2727-8(2)*, 37fd8157-5916-41d7-9852-9f26364cd4c6) Cavendish Square Publishing LLC.

NORTH CAROLINA

Alex, Nan. From Sea to Shining Sea: North Carolina. 2008. (From Sea to Shining Sea, Second Ser.). (ENG., Illus.). 80p. (J). (gr. 3-5). pap. 7.95 *(978-0-531-18808-8(6)*, Children's Pr.) Scholastic Library Publishing.

Bird, Janice W. Freddy in the City: Center City Sites. Bird, Richard E., photos by. Date not set. (Illus.). 32p. (J). (gr. 2-5). pap. 5.95 *(978-0-9710071-1-6(X))* JFW, Ltd.

Browning, Wilt, ed. Nothing Finer: North Carolina's Sports History & the People Who Made It. 2014. (ENG.). 416p. pap. 35.00 *(978-1-61163-608-6(6))* Carolina Academic Pr.

Crane, Carol. T Is for Tar Heel: A North Carolina Alphabet. Palmer, Gary, illus. 2003. (Discover America State by State Ser.). (ENG.). 40p. (J). (gr. 1-3). 18.99 *(978-1-58536-082-6(1)*, 201972) Sleeping Bear Pr.

—Wright Numbers: A North Carolina Number Book. Palmer, Gary, illus. 2005. (America by the Numbers Ser.). (ENG.). 40p. (J). (gr. 1-3). 19.99 *(978-1-58536-196-0(8)*, 202038) Sleeping Bear Pr.

Galiano, Dean. North Carolina. 2009. (Bilingual Library of the United States of America Ser.). (ENG & SPA.). 32p. (gr. 2-2). 47.90 *(978-1-60853-377-0(8)*, Editorial Buenas Letras) Rosen Publishing Group, Inc., The.

—North Carolina/Carolina del Norte, 1 vol. Brusca, Maria Cristina, tr. 2005. (Bilingual Library of the United States of America Ser.: Set 2). (ENG & SPA., Illus.). 32p. (J). (gr. 2-2). lib. bdg. 28.93 *(978-1-4042-3098-9(X)*, b6fc87d9-b54e-46eb-9cd0-92fa4e9f100f) Rosen Publishing Group, Inc., The.

George, Pamela. The North Carolina Alphabet Book. Brown, Walter, ed. 2005. (ENG., Illus.). 64p. (J). (gr. 5-12). pap. 16.95 *(978-0-932112-50-7(1))* Carolina Wren Pr.

Graham Gaines, Ann. North Carolina, 1 vol. Santoro, Christopher, illus. 2005. (It's My State! (First Edition)(r) Ser.). (ENG.). 80p. (gr. 4-4). lib. bdg. 34.07 *(978-0-7614-1533-6(5)*, f06ae3a2-8fae-4c4c-9ed6-11f0e72a833b) Cavendish Square Publishing LLC.

Greene, Melanie W., et al. Goodnight, Boone. Marlowe, Susan B., illus. 2012. (J). *(978-1-933251-80-6(8))* Parkway Pubs., Inc.

Heinrichs, Ann. America the Beautiful, Third Series: North Carolina (Revised Edition) 2014. (America the Beautiful Ser.: 3). (ENG.). 144p. (J). lib. bdg. 40.00 *(978-0-531-24896-6(8))* Scholastic Library Publishing.

—North Carolina. Kania, Matt, illus. 2017. (U. S. A. Travel Guides). (ENG.). 40p. (J). (gr. 2-5). lib. bdg. 38.50 *(978-1-5038-1973-3(6)*, 211609) Child's World, Inc, The.

—North Carolina. 2011. (America the Beautiful, Third Ser.). 144p. (J). pap. 12.95 *(978-0-531-22917-0(3)*, Children's Pr.) Scholastic Library Publishing.

Hyman, Teresa L. North Carolina. 2003. (Seeds of a Nation Ser.). (Illus.). 48p. (J). 23.70 *(978-0-7377-1420-3(4))* Cengage Gale.

Jerome, Kate Boehm. North Carolina: What's So Great about This State? 2011. (Arcadia Kids Ser.). (ENG.). 48p. (J). pap. 9.99 *(978-1-58973-017-5(8))* Arcadia Publishing.

Marsh, Carole. My First Book about North Carolina. 2004. (North Carolina Experience! Ser.). 32p. (J). (gr. k-4). pap. 7.95 *(978-0-7933-9518-7(6))* Gallopade International.

—The Nifty North Carolina Coloring Book. 2004. (North Carolina Experience! Ser.). (Illus.). 32p. (J). (gr. k-2). pap. 3.95 *(978-0-7933-9472-2(4))* Gallopade International.

—North Carolina Current Events Projects: 30 Cool, Activities, Crafts, Experiments & More for Kids to Do to Learn about Your State! 2003. (North Carolina Experience Ser.). 32p. (gr. k-8). pap. 5.95 *(978-0-635-02052-9(1)*, Marsh, Carole Bks.) Gallopade International.

—The North Carolina Experience Pocket Guide. 2004. (North Carolina Experience! Ser.). (Illus.). 96p. (J). (gr. 3-8). pap. 6.95 *(978-0-7933-9452-4(X))* Gallopade International.

—North Carolina Geography Projects: 30 Cool, Activities, Crafts, Experiments & More for Kids to Do to Learn about Your State! 2003. (North Carolina Experience Ser.). 32p. (gr. k-5). pap. 5.95 *(978-0-635-01852-6(7)*, Marsh, Carole Bks.) Gallopade International.

—North Carolina Government Projects: 30 Cool, Activities, Crafts, Experiments & More for Kids to Do to Learn about Your State! 2003. (North Carolina Experience Ser.). 32p. (gr. k-5). pap. 5.95 *(978-0-635-01952-3(3)*, Marsh, Carole Bks.) Gallopade International.

—North Carolina Jeopardy! Answers & Questions about Our State! 2004. (North Carolina Experience! Ser.). (Illus.). 32p. (J). (gr. 3-8). pap. 7.95 *(978-0-7933-9519-4(4))* Gallopade International.

—North Carolina "Jography" A Fun Run Through the Tarheel State! 2004. (North Carolina Experience! Ser.). (Illus.). 32p. (J). (gr. 3-8). pap. 7.95 *(978-0-7933-9520-0(8))* Gallopade International.

—North Carolina People Projects: 30 Cool, Activities, Crafts, Experiments & More for Kids to Do to Learn about Your State! 2003. (North Carolina Experience Ser.). 32p. (gr. k-5). pap. 5.95 *(978-0-635-02002-4(5)*, Marsh, Carole Bks.) Gallopade International.

—North Carolina Symbols & Facts Projects: 30 Cool, Activities, Crafts, Experiments & More for Kids to Do to Learn about Your State! 2003. (North Carolina Experience Ser.). 32p. (gr. k-8). pap. 5.95 *(978-0-635-01902-8(7)*, Marsh, Carole Bks.) Gallopade International.

—North Carolina's Big Activity Book. 2004. (North Carolina Experience! Ser.). (Illus.). 96p. (J). (gr. 2-6). pap. 9.95 *(978-0-7933-9462-3(7))* Gallopade International.

McNeil, Niki, et al. HOCPP 1080 North Carolina. 2006. spiral bd. 24.00 *(978-1-60308-080-4(5))* In the Hands of a Child.

Meyer, John H. Wilmington Today: A Guide to Cape Fear Leisure. 2003. Orig. Title: A Guide to Cape Fear Leisure. (Illus.). 60p. 13.95 *(978-0-9729573-0-4(8))* Wilmington Today LLC.

Murray, Julie. North Carolina, 1 vol. 2006. (Buddy Book Ser.). (ENG., Illus.). 32p. (gr. 2-4). 27.07 *(978-1-59197-692-9(8)*, Buddy Bks.) ABDO Publishing Co.

Peters, S. True. How to Draw North Carolina's Sights & Symbols. 2009. (Kid's Guide to Drawing America Ser.). 32p. (gr. k-k). 50.50 *(978-1-61511-084-1(4)*, PowerKids Pr.) Rosen Publishing Group, Inc., The.

Schulz, Andrea. North Carolina. (J). 2012. lib. bdg. 25.26 *(978-0-7613-4549-7(3)*, Lerner Pubns.) 2nd exp. rev. ed. 2003. (Illus.). 84p. (gr. 3-6). pap. 6.95 *(978-0-8225-4137-0(8))* Lerner Publishing Group.

Sermons, Faye. My Granma Lives at the Airport. 2012. 20p. pap. 12.00 *(978-1-4490-1893-1(9))* AuthorHouse.

Shirley, David & Hart, Joyce. North Carolina, 1 vol. 2nd rev. ed. 2010. (Celebrate the States (Second Edition) Ser.). (ENG.). 144p. (gr. 6-6). 39.79 *(978-0-7614-4729-0(6)*, c2a73bde-98a5-438d-806e-e1b43af036b8) Cavendish Square Publishing LLC.

Sullivan, E. J. N is for North Carolina. Eldredge, Ernie, illus. 2007. (State Alphabet Bks.). 20p. *(978-1-58173-625-0(8))* Sweetwater Pr.

NORTH CAROLINA—FICTION

Asim, Jabari. The Road to Freedom: A Story of the Reconstruction. 2004. 131p. (J). lib. bdg. 16.92 *(978-1-4242-0765-7(7))* Fitzgerald Bks.

M
N
O

Averette, Sonya M. Aunt Ruby's Kisses, 1 vol. Proulx, Denis, illus. 2009. 35p. pap. 24.95 *(978-1-60749-045-6(5))* America Star Bks.
Baker, Mary. Amy's Apple Butter Granny. 2009. 48p. pap. 16.95 *(978-1-61582-032-0(9))* America Star Bks.
Baldwin, Cindy. Where the Watermelons Grow. (ENG.). (J). (gr. 3-7). 2020. 272p. pap. 9.99 *(978-0-06-266587-4(1))* 2018. 256p. 16.99 *(978-0-06-266586-7(3))* HarperCollins Pubs. (Quill Tree Bks.).
Bare, Bart. Girl. 2010. 188p. (YA). pap. 11.95 *(978-0-9825396-4-4(9))* Canterbury Hse. Publishing, Ltd.
Beatty, Robert. Serafina & the Black Cloak. 2016. (Serafina Ser.: 1). (J). lib. bdg. 18.40 *(978-0-606-38336-3(0))* Turtleback.
—Serafina & the Black Cloak-The Serafina Series Book 1. (ENG.). (J). (gr. 3-7). 2016. (Serafina Ser.: 1). 320p. pap. 8.99 *(978-1-4847-1187-3(4))* 2015. 304p. 16.99 *(978-1-4847-0901-6(2))* Disney Publishing Worldwide. (Disney-Hyperion).
—Serafina & the Seven Stars-The Serafina Series Book 4. 2019. (Serafina Ser.: 4). (ENG., Illus.). 352p. (J). (gr. 3-7). 16.99 *(978-1-368-00759-7(7)*, Disney-Hyperion) Disney Publishing Worldwide.
—Serafina & the Splintered Heart. 2018. (Serafina Ser.: 3). (J). lib. bdg. 18.40 *(978-0-606-40962-9(9))* Turtleback.
—Serafina & the Splintered Heart-The Serafina Series Book 3. (Serafina Ser.: 3). (ENG.). (J). (gr. 3-7). 2018. 384p. pap. 8.99 *(978-1-4847-7805-0(7))* 2017. 368p. 16.99 *(978-1-4847-7504-2(X))* Disney Publishing Worldwide. (Disney-Hyperion).
—Serafina & the Twisted Staff. 2017. (Serafina Ser.: 2). (J). lib. bdg. 18.40 *(978-0-606-39977-7(1))* Turtleback.
—Serafina & the Twisted Staff-The Serafina Series Book 2. (Serafina Ser.: 2). (ENG.). (J). (gr. 3-7). 2017. 400p. pap. 8.99 *(978-1-4847-7806-7(5))* 2016. 384p. 16.99 *(978-1-4847-7503-5(1))* Disney Publishing Worldwide. (Disney-Hyperion).
Bennett, Amy Culbertson. The Little Donkey & the Shadow of the Cross. 2008. 15p. pap. 24.95 *(978-1-60563-545-3(6))* America Star Bks.
Bird, Janie. Freddy in the City: Memorable Monday. Treffeisen, Brian, photos by. 2nd rev. ed. 2005.Tr. of Freddy en la Ciudad un Lunes Memorble. (SPA., Illus.). 32p. (J). 10.95 *(978-1-59494-005-7(3))* CPCC Pr.
Bond, Gwenda. Strange Alchemy. 2017. (ENG., Illus.). 336p. (YA). (gr. 9-12). 17.95 *(978-1-63079-076-9(1)*, 134212, Switch Pr.) Capstone.
Bradfield, Carl. The Sullivans of Little Horsepen Creek: A Tale of Colonial North Carolina's Regulator Era, Circa: 1760s. (Illus.). 350p. (YA). (gr. 8-12). *(978-0-9632319-2-5(8))* ASDA Publishing, Inc.
Burnell, Pamela H. The Light Keeper: An Epps Kids Mystery. 2008. 76p. pap. 19.95 *(978-1-60474-847-5(8))* America Star Bks.
Calonita, Jen. Belles. 2012. (Belles Ser.: 1). (ENG.). 384p. (YA). (gr. 7-17). pap. 19.99 *(978-0-316-09112-1(X)*, Poppy) Little, Brown Bks. for Young Readers.
—The Grass Is Always Greener. 2014. (Belles Ser.: 3). (ENG.). 320p. (YA). (gr. 7-17). pap. 10.00 *(978-0-316-09109-1(X)*, Poppy) Little, Brown Bks. for Young Readers.
—Winter White. 2013. (Belles Ser.: 2). (ENG.). 384p. (YA). (gr. 7-17). pap. 19.99 *(978-0-316-09118-3(9)*, Poppy) Little, Brown Bks. for Young Readers.
Carmichael, Clay. Brother, Brother. 2013. (ENG.). 320p. (YA). (gr. 7). 22.99 *(978-1-59643-743-2(X)*, 900077700) Roaring Brook Pr.
Carris, Joan D. A Ghost of a Chance. 2003. (Legends of the Carolinas Ser.). 155p. (J). 8.95 *(978-1-928556-40-4(X))* Coastal Carolina Pr.
Church, Bryan. The Dreamcatcher Bowl. 2009. (ENG.). 54p. pap. 9.99 *(978-0-557-07517-1(3))* Lulu Pr., Inc.
Collins, Yozette Yogi & Jennings, Marlis. Goodnight, Boone. Ziolkowski, Ania, illus. 2012. 24p. pap. 11.95 *(978-1-937376-18-5(4))* All Star Pr.
Doherty, Patrick. Waves of Grace. Ordaz, Frank, illus. 2007. (ENG.). 160p. (YA). (gr. 9-12). pap. 11.95 *(978-0-9744446-6-6(9))* All About Kids Publishing.
Dowell, Frances O'Roark. Anybody Shining. (ENG., Illus.). (J). (gr. 5-7). 2015. 256p. pap. 8.99 *(978-1-4424-3293-2(4))* 2014. 240p. 16.99 *(978-1-4424-3292-5(6))* Simon & Schuster Children's Publishing. (Atheneum Bks. for Young Readers).
—Ten Miles Past Normal. (ENG., 224p. (YA). (gr. 7). 2012. Illus.). pap. 10.99 *(978-1-4169-9586-9(2))* 2011. 16.99 *(978-1-4169-9585-2(4))* Simon & Schuster Children's Publishing. (Atheneum Bks. for Young Readers).
Draper, Sharon M. Stella by Starlight. (ENG., Illus.). (J). (gr. 4-8). 2016. 352p. pap. 9.99 *(978-1-4424-9498-5(0))* 2015. 336p. 19.99 *(978-1-4424-9497-8(2)*, Atheneum Bks. for Young Readers) Simon & Schuster Children's Publishing.
—Stella by Starlight. 2016. lib. bdg. 18.40 *(978-0-606-38255-7(0))* Turtleback.
Edgerton, Martha. Civility Matters: Anna Moves to the Big City. 2011. 38p. pap. 16.95 *(978-1-4626-4211-3(X))* America Star Bks.
Edward, J. P. Truckin with Rocky, 1 vol. 2010. 22p. 24.95 *(978-1-4512-9082-0(9))* PublishAmerica, Inc.
Ernst, Kathleen. Highland Fling. 2006. (ENG.). 192p. (J). (gr. 3-8). 15.95 *(978-0-8126-2742-8(3))* Cricket Bks.
Flowers, Fran. Rosita: The Journey Home. 2012. 108p. (gr. 4-6). 28.95 *(978-1-4497-3505-0(3))*; pap. 11.95 *(978-1-4497-3503-6(7))* Author Solutions, LLC. (WestBow Pr.).
Franklin, Miriam Spitzer. Call Me Sunflower. (ENG.). (J). (gr. 2-7). 2019. 256p. pap. 8.99 *(978-1-5107-3914-7(9))* 2017. 272p. 15.99 *(978-1-5107-1179-2(1))* Skyhorse Publishing Co., Inc. (Sky Pony Pr.).
Furman, Ben. Sam's Quest. 2008. 240p. pap. 8.95 *(978-0-9778731-4-2(5))* Black Hawk Pr., Inc., The.
—Sam's Quest for the Crimson Crystal. 2007. 189p. (J). per. 8.95 *(978-0-9778731-8-0(8))* Black Hawk Pr., Inc., The.
Gamble, Adam. Good Night North Carolina. Rosen, Anne, illus. 2009. (Good Night Our World Ser.). (ENG.). 20p. (J). (gr. k — 1). bds. 9.95 *(978-1-60219-033-7(X))* Good Night Bks.
Garza, Amy Ammons. Sterlen: And a Mosaic of Mountain Women. Ammons, David F. & Ammons, Sherilyn, eds. Cain, Doreyl Ammons, illus. 2005. 308p. (YA). per. 16.00 *(978-0-9753023-2-3(9)*, Catch the Spirit of Appalachia) Ammons Communications, Ltd.
Griffin, Kitty. The Ride: The Legend of Betsy Dowdy. Priceman, Marjorie, illus. 2010. (ENG.). 40p. (J). (gr. -1-3). 17.99 *(978-1-4169-2816-4(2)*, Atheneum Bks. for Young Readers) Simon & Schuster Children's Publishing.
Griffith, Gretchen. When Christmas Feels Like Home. Farias, Carolina, illus. 2014. (AV2 Fiction Readalong Ser.: Vol. 119). (ENG.). 32p. (J). (gr. k-3). lib. bdg. 34.28 *(978-1-4896-2392-8(2)*, AV2 by Weigl) Weigl Pubs., Inc.
Guo, Amy. Vhonk. 2012. 588p. pap. 34.95 *(978-1-4626-9981-0(2))* America Star Bks.
Gutenberg, S. R. Abby Longbotham & the Quilt. 2008. 28p. pap. 24.95 *(978-1-4241-9428-5(8))* America Star Bks.
Gutman, Dan. Race for the Sky: The Kitty Hawk Diaries of Johnny Moore. 2003. (ENG., Illus.). 192p. (J). (gr. 5-9). 19.99 *(978-0-689-84554-3(5)*, Simon & Schuster Bks. For Young Readers) Simon & Schuster Bks. For Young Readers.
Haddix, Margaret Peterson. Sabotaged. (Missing Ser.: 3). (ENG.). (J). (gr. 3-7). 2011. 400p. pap. 8.99 *(978-1-4169-5425-5(2))* 2010. 384p. 17.99 *(978-1-4169-5424-8(4))* Simon & Schuster Bks. For Young Readers. (Simon & Schuster Bks. For Young Readers).
Hall, Terri L. Denny & Denise: A Story of Two Ducks: Introducing Pretty Boy & Fella, 1 vol. Hall, Terri L. & Babeaux, Dennis, photos by. 2009. (Illus.). 42p. pap. 24.95 *(978-1-60749-609-0(7))* America Star Bks.
Hall, Tessa Emily. Purple Moon. 2013. 328p. pap. 13.95 *(978-1-938499-87-6(5))* LPC.
Hallinan, Annie. Brinkley Boyd of Weymouth. Preveza, Amy, illus. 2017. 46p. (J). *(978-0-9971477-4-2(1))* Turnberry Pr.
Harvell, Richard Brian. Adventures of the Book Battling Kids: The Carson Corners Chronicles. 2006. (J). per. 5.99 *(978-0-9769044-7-2(0))* Waterwood Publishing Group.
Harvey, Jeanne Walker. My Hands Sing the Blues: Romare Bearden's Childhood Journey, 0 vols. Zunon, Elizabeth, illus. 2012. (ENG.). 40p. (J). (gr. 1-3). 17.99 *(978-0-7614-5810-4(7)*, 9780761458104, Two Lions) Amazon Publishing.
Hemingway, Edith M. Road to Tater Hill. 2011. 224p. (J). (gr. 3-7). 8.99 *(978-0-375-84544-4(5)*, Yearling) Random Hse. Children's Bks.
Hitchcock, Shannon. One True Way. (ENG.). 224p. (J). (gr. 4-7). 2019. pap. 8.99 *(978-1-338-18174-6(2))* 2018. (Illus.). 17.99 *(978-1-338-18172-2(6))* Scholastic, Inc. (Scholastic Pr.).
Hostetter, Joyce Moyer. Aim. (Bakers Mountain Stories Ser.). 288p. (J). (gr. 4-7). 2019. pap. 9.95 *(978-1-68437-276-8(3))* 2016. (ENG.). 17.95 *(978-1-62979-673-4(5))* Highlights Pr., c/o Highlights for Children, Inc. (Calkins Creek).
—Comfort, 2. 2011. (Bakers Mountain Stories Ser.: 2). (ENG.). 312p. (J). (gr. 4-7). pap. 9.99 *(978-1-59078-895-0(8)*, Calkins Creek) Highlights Pr., c/o Highlights for Children, Inc.
Hutton, John. Flowers for Mr. President. 2012. (Illus.). (J). *(978-0-9789608-3-4(1))* Salem Academy & College.
Jacobs, Lily. The Littlest Bunny in North Carolina: An Easter Adventure. Dunn, Robert, illus. 2015. (Littlest Bunny Ser.). (ENG.). 32p. (J). (gr. -1-3). 9.99 *(978-1-4926-1156-1(5)*, Hometown World) Sourcebooks, Inc.
James, Eric. Santa's Sleigh Is on Its Way to North Carolina: A Christmas Adventure. Dunn, Robert, illus. 2015. (Santa's Sleigh Is on Its Way Ser.). (ENG.). 32p. (J). (gr. k-2). 12.99 *(978-1-4926-2750-0(X)*, Hometown World) Sourcebooks, Inc.
—The Spooky Express North Carolina. Piwowarski, Marcin, illus. 2017. (Spooky Express Ser.). (ENG.). 32p. (J). (gr. k-6). 9.99 *(978-1-4926-5385-1(3)*, Hometown World) Sourcebooks, Inc.
—Tiny the North Carolina Easter Bunny. 2018. (Tiny the Easter Bunny Ser.). (ENG.). 40p. (J). (gr. k-3). 9.99 *(978-1-4926-5950-1(9)*, Hometown World) Sourcebooks, Inc.
Johnson, Denise Donna. The Veridical Circle. 2011. 78p. pap. 19.95 *(978-1-4626-0472-2(2))* America Star Bks.
Johnson, Harriet McBryde. Accidents of Nature. rev. ed. 2006. (ENG.). 240p. (YA). (gr. 7-12). 21.99 *(978-0-8050-7634-9(4)*, 900024489, Holt, Henry & Co. Bks. For Young Readers) Holt, Henry & Co.
—Accidents of Nature. rev. l.t. ed. 2007. (Thorndike Literacy Bridge Ser.). 273p. (YA). (gr. 7-12). 22.95 *(978-0-7862-9182-3(6))* Thorndike Pr.
Johnson, T. The Beach Club: Magic Beach, Vol. 1. 2012. (ENG.). 131p. pap. 11.95 *(978-1-4327-9316-6(0))* Outskirts Pr., Inc.
Lau, Barbara & Nesbitt, Kris. Sokita Celebrates the New Year: A Cambodian American Holiday. Chatterley, Cedric N., photos by. 2004. (Illus.). 32p. (J). per. 9.95 *(978-0-9747456-0-2(X))* Greensboro Historical Museum, Inc.
Lawrence, Donna. Susie's Tale Hand with Paw We Changed the Law. Coble, Lynn Berner, ed. Cappoen, Jennifer Tipton, illus. 2012. 64p. 24.95 *(978-0-9846724-1-7(9))* Paws and Claws Publishing, LLC.
Lawrenson, Judith. Petunia the Pirate of Port Royal Sound. 2007. (Illus.). (J). 14.95 *(978-0-9767278-0-4(3))* Mrs. L's Reading Room.
LeBrun, Barbie. Porter Horse Finds Blackbeard's Treasure. 2013. (ENG.). 24p. (J). pap. 21.95 *(978-1-4787-1604-4(5))* Outskirts Pr., Inc.
Leppard, Lois Gladys. The Mandie Collection. (ENG.). (J). (gr. 3-8). 2011. 366p. pap. 16.00 *(978-0-7642-0932-1(9))* 2011. 382p. pap. 16.00 *(978-0-7642-0878-2(0))* 2011. 368p. pap. 16.00 *(978-0-7642-0689-4(3))* 2011. 368p. pap. 16.00 *(978-0-7642-0877-5(2))* Vol. 1. 2007. 544p. pap. 16.99 *(978-0-7642-0446-3(7))* Vol. 2. 2008. (Illus.). 576p. pap. 17.99 *(978-0-7642-0538-5(2))* Bethany Hse. Pubs.
—Mandie Collection, Vol. 3. 2008. (ENG.). 608p. (J). pap. 18.99 *(978-0-7642-0593-4(5))* Bethany Hse. Pubs.
Lipsyte, Robert. Yellow Flag. 2009. (ENG.). 256p. (YA). (gr. 8). pap. 10.99 *(978-0-06-055709-6(5)*, HarperCollins) HarperCollins Pubs.
Looper, Grace W. Molasses Making Time. l.t. ed. 2004. 152p. (YA). pap. 8.95 *(978-0-9747685-5-7(3))* Bella Rosa Bks.
Madden, Kerry. Gentle's Holler. 2007. (Maggie Valley Ser.). 237p. (gr. 4-7). 17.00 *(978-0-7569-8090-0(9))* Perfection Learning Corp.
Marsh, Carole. The Mystery at Kill Devil Hills. 2009. (Real Kids, Real Places Ser.). (Illus.). 145p. (J). lib. bdg. 18.99 *(978-0-635-06999-3(7)*, Marsh, Carole Mysteries) Gallopade International.
—The Mystery of Blackbeard the Pirate. Marsh, Carole, photos by. 2009. (Real Kids, Real Places Ser.). (Illus.). 150p. (J). 18.99 *(978-0-635-06992-4(X)*, Marsh, Carole Mysteries) Gallopade International.
—The Mystery of the Biltmore House. 25th ed. 2009. (Real Kids, Real Places Ser.). 148p. (J). 18.99 *(978-0-635-06989-4(X)*, Marsh, Carole Mysteries) Gallopade International.
—The Mystery of the Lost Colony. 2010. (Real Kids, Real Places Ser.). (Illus.). 158p. (J). 24.99 *(978-0-635-07607-6(1)*, Marsh, Carole Mysteries);36. (ENG., (gr. 4-6). 22.44 *(978-0-635-07595-6(4))* Gallopade International.
The Marsh Runners. 2004. (J). per. 14.95 *(978-0-9761178-0-3(0))* Maritime Kids Quest Pr.
Martin, Amy. As You Wake. 2013. 294p. pap. 10.93 *(978-0-9882051-2-3(2))* Martin, Amy.
Martone, Ginny. Trapped in Dead Man's Cave. 2007. 61p. pap. 19.95 *(978-1-60474-227-5(5))* America Star Bks.
McDonald, Megan. Judy Moody & Stink: la Loca, Loca Búsqueda Del Tesoro / JM & Stink: the Mad, Mad, Mad, Mad Treasure Hunt. 2011. (Judy Moody & Stink Ser.). (SPA., Illus.). 144p. (J). (gr. 2-5). pap. 14.95 *(978-1-61605-137-2(X)*, Alfaguara) Penguin Random House Grupo Editorial ESP. Dist: Penguin Random Hse. LLC.
—Judy Moody & Stink: the Mad, Mad, Mad, Mad Treasure Hunt. Reynolds, Peter H., illus. 2010. (Judy Moody & Stink Ser.: 2). (ENG.). 128p. (J). (gr. 1-4). pap. 7.99 *(978-0-7636-4351-5(3))* Candlewick Pr.
Mcdonald, Megan. The Mad, Mad, Mad, Mad Treasure Hunt. 2010. (Judy Moody & Stink Ser.: 2). lib. bdg. 18.40 *(978-0-606-01311-6(3))* Turtleback.
McDowell, Marilyn Taylor. Carolina Harmony. 2010. (ENG.). 336p. (J). (gr. 4-6). 22.44 *(978-0-440-42285-3(X))* Random House Publishing Group.
McDunn, Gillian. Caterpillar Summer. (ENG.). (J). 2020. 320p. pap. 7.99 *(978-1-5476-0314-5(3)*, 900211246) 2019. (Illus.). 304p. 16.99 *(978-1-68119-743-2(X)*, 900184196) Bloomsbury Publishing USA. (Bloomsbury Children's Bks.).
McGougan, Kathy. Fixin' Buddy's Little Red Wagon. Hale, Sally, illus. 2009. (ENG.). 24p. pap. 9.95 *(978-1-4251-8975-4(X))* Trafford Publishing.
McKay, Laurie. The Last Dragon Charmer #1: Villain Keeper. 2016. (Last Dragon Charmer Ser.: 1). (ENG.). 368p. (J). (gr. 3-7). pap. 6.99 *(978-0-06-230844-3(0)*, HarperCollins) HarperCollins Pubs.
Michaels, Craig. Blackbeard's Treasure. 2008. (J). *(978-0-936389-99-8(0))* Tudor Pubs., Inc.
Milburn, Trish. White Witch. 2012. 188p. pap. 12.95 *(978-1-61194-083-1(4)*, Bell Bridge Bks.) BelleBks., Inc.
Moses, Shelia P. The Baptism. 2008. (ENG., Illus.). 144p. (J). (gr. 5-9). pap. 7.99 *(978-1-4169-5833-8(9)*, McElderry, Margaret K. Bks.) McElderry, Margaret K. Bks.
—The Legend of Buddy Bush. 2005. (Illus.). 211p. (gr. 7-12). 17.00 *(978-0-7569-5459-8(2))* Perfection Learning Corp.
—The Legend of Buddy Bush, 3 vols. unabr. ed. 2005. (YA). (gr. 3-7). 54.75 *(978-1-4193-3575-4(8)*, 42043) Recorded Bks., Inc.
Mr. Bud's Country Store: A Story of Family & Community. 2003. (J). per. 18.95 *(978-0-9711534-1-7(8))* Hidden Path Pubn., Inc.
Novel Units. The Weirdo Novel Units Student Packet. 2019. (ENG.). (J). pap., stu. ed. 13.99 *(978-1-56137-815-9(1)*, Novel Units, Inc.) Classroom Library Co.
O'Connor, Barbara. How to Steal a Dog: A Novel. 2009. (ENG.). 208p. (J). (gr. 3-7). pap. 7.99 *(978-0-312-56112-3(1)*, 900058842) Square Fish.
Patterson, Nancy Ruth. A Simple Gift. 2009. 128p. (gr. 3-7). pap. 10.95 *(978-1-4401-1206-5(1))* iUniverse, Inc.
Pearson, Joanna. The Rites & Wrongs of Janice Wills. 2011. (YA). pap. *(978-0-545-19774-8(0)*, Levine, Arthur A. Bks.) Scholastic, Inc.
Penn, Audrey. Blackbeard & the Gift of Silence. 2009. (ENG.). 350p. (J). (gr. 2-7). pap. 8.95 *(978-1-933718-32-3(3))* Tanglewood Pr.
—Blackbeard & the Sandstone Pillar: When Lightning Strikes. 2009. (ENG.). 350p. (J). (gr. 2-7). pap. 8.95 *(978-1-933718-31-6(5))* Tanglewood Pr.
—The Whistling Tree. Gibson, Barbara, illus. 2003. 32p. 16.95 *(978-0-87868-852-4(8)*, 8528, Child & Family Pr.) Child Welfare League of America, Inc.
—The Whistling Tree. Gibson, Barbara, illus. 2006. (ENG.). 32p. (J). (gr. -1-4). 16.95 *(978-0-9749303-9-8(3))* Tanglewood Pr.
Pfaff, Eugene E. Guns at Guilford Court House. 2008. 132p. (YA). (gr. 6-9). pap. 14.95 *(978-0-936389-97-4(4))* Tudor Pubs., Inc.
Pickett, Anola. Whisper Island. 2013. (ENG.). 235p. (J). (gr. 3-7). pap. 14.99 *(978-1-4621-1167-1(X)*, Sweetwater Bks.) Cedar Fort, Inc./CFI Distribution.
Poehler, S. Applecheeks & the Pop E. Tree. 2012. 12p. pap. 15.99 *(978-1-4772-8180-2(0))* AuthorHouse.
Posey, S. A. M. The Last Station Master: A Boy, a Terroist, a Secret, & Trouble. 2013. (ENG.). 200p. (J). (-12). pap. 19.99 *(978-1-926780-22-1(1)*, b7dd1daf-5356-4491-b008-913c73ef1a54) Key Publishing Hse., Inc., The CAN. Dist: Baker & Taylor Publisher Services (BTPS).
Propst, Milam McGraw. The Further Adventures of Ociee Nash. 2009. 146p. pap. 14.95 *(978-0-9841258-0-7(9)*, Bell Bridge Bks.) BelleBks., Inc.
Pyron, Bobbie. A Dog's Way Home. 2012. (ENG.). 336p. (J). (gr. 3-7). pap. 6.99 *(978-0-06-198672-7(0)*, Tegen, Katherine Bks) HarperCollins Pubs.
Ransom, Candice. The Life-Saving Adventure of Sam Deal, Shipwreck Rescuer. 2010. pap. 51.02 *(978-0-7613-6918-9(X))* Lerner Publishing Group.
Ridley, R. W. Banshee Worm King. 2012. 242p. pap. 9.99 *(978-0-9792067-5-7(8))* Middleburry Hse. Publishing.
Ritch, Catherine. Zipper Finds a Job. Trexler, Jennifer Suther, illus. 2014. (White Squirrel Parables Ser.: Vol. 2). (ENG.). 32p. (J). (gr. -1-3). 13.95 *(978-1-933341-40-8(8))* CRM.
Salter, Kay. Fifteenth Summer: The Sarah Bowers Series. 2011. 188p. (gr. -1). 24.99 *(978-1-4567-6380-0(6))*; pap. 15.99 *(978-1-4567-6381-7(4))* AuthorHouse.
—Fourteenth Summer: So begins the search for a suitable Bride. Noe, Amy, ed. 2009. 287p. pap. 14.95 *(978-0-9842517-2-8(3))* Bara Publishing.
—Thirteenth Summer: More fun & adventure on the Carolina Coast. Noe, Amy, ed. 2009. 293p. pap. 14.95 *(978-0-9842517-1-1(5))* Bara Publishing.
—Twelfth Summer: Coming of age in a time of War. Noe, Amy, ed. 2009. 297p. pap. 14.95 *(978-0-9842517-0-4(7))* Bara Publishing.
Scott, Lisa Ann. Back on the Map. 2017. (ENG.). 320p. (J). (gr. 2-7). 15.99 *(978-1-5107-1353-6(0)*, Sky Pony Pr.) Skyhorse Publishing Co., Inc.
—School of Charm. 2014. (ENG.). 304p. (J). (gr. 3-7). 16.99 *(978-0-06-220758-6(X)*, Tegen, Katherine Bks) HarperCollins Pubs.
Self, Jeffery. A Very, Very Bad Thing. 2017. (ENG.). 240p. (YA). (gr. 9). 17.99 *(978-1-338-11840-7(4)*, PUSH) Scholastic, Inc.
Sharpe, Stella Gentry. Tobe: a Critical Edition: New Views on a Children's Classic. Filene, Benjamin, ed. 2019. (ENG., Illus.). 184p. 99.00 *(978-1-4696-5416-4(4)*, 01PODHC) Univ. of North Carolina Pr.
Simpson, N. J. Not So Random. 2011. 200p. pap. 13.67 *(978-0-557-83059-6(1))* Lulu Pr., Inc.
Smith, Donna Campbell. An Independent Spirit: The Tale of Betsy Dowdy & Black Bess. 2006. (Illus.). 182p. (J). per. 11.95 *(978-0-9779889-0-7(2))* Faithful Publishing.
Smith, Roland. Kitty Hawk. 2012. (I, Q Ser.: Bk. 3). (ENG., Illus.). 240p. (YA). (gr. 6-8). pap. 9.99 *(978-1-58536-604-0(8)*, 202326);Bk. 3. lib. bdg. 16.99 *(978-1-58536-605-7(6)*, 202327) Sleeping Bear Pr.
Solomon, Jef. Right in My Own Neighborhood. 2008. (ENG.). 53p. pap. 15.50 *(978-0-557-05790-0(6))* Lulu Pr., Inc.
Stead, Judy, illus. The Twelve Days of Christmas in North Carolina. 2017. (Twelve Days of Christmas in America Ser.). (ENG.). 22p. (J). (-k). bds. 7.95 *(978-1-4549-2285-8(0))* Sterling Publishing Co., Inc.
Sully, Katherine. Night-Night North Carolina. Poole, Helen, illus. 2017. (Night-Night Ser.). (ENG.). 20p. (J). (gr. -1-1). bds. 9.99 *(978-1-4926-4778-2(0)*, 9781492647782, Hometown World) Sourcebooks, Inc.
Surviving the Applewhites. (J). tchr. ed. *(978-0-06-058369-9(X))* HarperCollins Pubs.
Taylor, Theodore. The Odyssey of Ben O'neal. 2004. (ENG., Illus.). 264p. (J). (gr. 3-7). pap. 15.95 *(978-0-15-205295-9(X)*, 1195954, Clarion Bks.) HarperCollins Pubs.
—Teetoncey. 2004. (ENG., Illus.). 228p. (J). (gr. 3-7). pap. 13.95 *(978-0-15-205294-2(1)*, 1195951, Clarion Bks.) HarperCollins Pubs.
—Teetoncey & Ben O'neal. 2004. (ENG., Illus.). 240p. (J). (gr. 3-7). pap. 15.95 *(978-0-15-205297-3(6)*, 1195960, Clarion Bks.) HarperCollins Pubs.
—The Weirdo. 2006. (Illus.). 292p. (gr. 7-12). 18.00 *(978-0-7569-6752-9(X))* Perfection Learning Corp.
Thomas, Blair L. The Sabatini Prophecy. 2008. (ENG.). 496p. (YA). 8.99 *(978-0-9760237-4-6(1))* Axiom Hse.
Tolan, Stephanie S. Applewhites at Wit's End. 2013. (Applewhites Ser.: 2). (ENG.). 288p. (J). (gr. 5). pap. 7.99 *(978-0-06-057940-1(4)*, HarperCollins) HarperCollins Pubs.
Tuck, Pamela M. As Fast As Words Could Fly?, 1 vol. Velasquez, Eric, illus. 2013. (ENG.). 40p. (J). 18.95 *(978-1-60060-348-8(3))* Lee & Low Bks., Inc.
Tucker, Valerie Nell. The Hermit's Box. 2009. 36p. pap. 15.49 *(978-1-4490-2285-3(5))* AuthorHouse.
Turnage, Sheila. The Ghosts of Tupelo Landing. 2015. (Mo & Dale Mysteries Ser.). 368p. (J). (gr. 5). 8.99 *(978-0-14-242571-8(0)*, Puffin Books) Penguin Young Readers Group.
—The Ghosts of Tupelo Landing. 2015. lib. bdg. 18.40 *(978-0-606-36773-8(X))* Turtleback.
—The Law of Finders Keepers. 2019. (Mo & Dale Mysteries Ser.). 368p. (J). (gr. 5). 8.99 *(978-0-14-242617-3(2)*, Puffin Books) Penguin Young Readers Group.
—Three Times Lucky. 2013. (Mo & Dale Mysteries Ser.). (Illus.). 336p. (J). (gr. 5). pap. 9.99 *(978-0-14-242605-0(9)*, Puffin Books) Penguin Young Readers Group.
—Three Times Lucky. 2013. (Mo & Dale Mystery Ser.: 1). lib. bdg. 18.40 *(978-0-606-34168-4(4))* Turtleback.
Waddell, Barbara. If I Could Catch a Train. 2009. 20p. pap. 9.15 *(978-1-4251-8667-8(X))* Trafford Publishing.
Walker, Melissa. Let's Pretend We Never Met. 2018. (ENG.). 256p. (J). (gr. 3-7). pap. 6.99 *(978-0-06-256717-8(9)*, HarperCollins) HarperCollins Pubs.
Watson, J. A. Hatchling Hero: A Sea Turtle Defender's Journal. Olbey, Arpad, illus. 2018. (Science Squad Ser.). (ENG.). 192p. (J). (gr. 3-4). 28.50 *(978-1-63163-160-3(8)*, 1631631608); pap. 9.99 *(978-1-63163-161-0(6)*, 1631631616) North Star Editions. (Jolly Fish Pr.).
Weatherford, Carole Boston. Freedom on the Menu: The Greensboro Sit-Ins. Lagarrigue, Jerome Lagarrigue, illus. 2007. 32p. (J). (gr. -1-3). pap. 8.99 *(978-0-14-240894-0(8)*, Puffin Books) Penguin Young Readers Group.
—Freedom on the Menu: The Greensboro Sit-Ins. Lagarrigue, Jerome, illus. 2004. (ENG.). 32p. (J). (gr. 1-3). 21.19 *(978-0-8037-2860-8(3))* Penguin Young Readers Group.
—Freedom on the Menu: The Greensboro Sit-Ins. Lagarrigue, Jerome, illus. 2007. (gr. 4-7). 16.00 *(978-0-7569-8160-0(3))* Perfection Learning Corp.
Wright, Barbara. Crow. 2013. (ENG.). 320p. (J). (gr. 5-7). pap. 9.99 *(978-0-375-87367-6(8)*, Yearling) Random Hse. Children's Bks.

NORTH CAROLINA—HISTORY

Bartram, Pat. Guide to New Bern NC History. 2009. (ENG., Illus.). 56p. (J). pap. 7.50 *(978-0-615-31220-0(9))* Bartram Team, The.
Boehm Jerome, Kate. Charlotte & the State of North Carolina: Cool Stuff Every Kid Should. 2011. (Arcadia Kids Ser.). (ENG., Illus.). 48p. (J). (gr. 3-6). pap. 11.99 *(978-1-4396-0097-9(X))* Arcadia Publishing.
—Raleigh & the State of North Carolina: Cool Stuff Every Kid Should Know. 2011. (Arcadia Kids Ser.). (ENG., Illus.). 48p. (J). (gr. 3-6). pap. 11.99 *(978-1-4396-0096-2(1))* Arcadia Publishing.

Brickey, Peter, creator. Coastal Impressions... A photographic journey along the North Carolina Coast. 2004. (Illus.). 186p. cd-rom *(978-0-9758964-1-9(5))* Brickey E-Publishing.

—From Currituck to Oak Island... A Photo Tour of North Carolina's Lighthouses. 2004. (Illus.). 88p. cd-rom 10.00 net. *(978-0-9758964-0-2(7))* Brickey E-Publishing.

Crane, Carol. Little North Carolina. Brett, Jeannie, illus. 2011. (Little State Ser.). (ENG.). 20p. (J). (gr. -1-1). bds. 9.95 *(978-1-58536-545-6(9),* 202245) Sleeping Bear Pr.

Cunningham, Kevin. The North Carolina Colony. 2011. (True Book-the Thirteen Colonies Ser.). (ENG., Illus.). 48p. (J). lib. bdg. 29.00 *(978-0-531-25395-3(3),* Children's Pr.) Scholastic Library Publishing.

Daly, Ruth. Biltmore Estate. 2015. (Illus.). 24p. (J). *(978-1-4896-3388-0(X))* Weigl Pubs., Inc.

Davidson, Tish. Atlantic: North Carolina, Virginia, West Virginia, Vol. 19. 2015. (Let's Explore the States Ser.). (Illus.). 64p. (J). (gr. 5). 23.95 *(978-1-4222-3320-7(0))* Mason Crest.

Englar, Xavier & Niz, Xavier W. The Mystery of the Roanoke Colony, 1 vol. Denton, Shannon E., illus. 2006. (Graphic History Ser.). (ENG.). 32p. (J). (gr. 3-9). per. 8.10 *(978-0-7368-9657-3(0),* 93442) Capstone.

Ervin, C. H. Hummingbird,Hummingbird. 2012. 20p. pap. 13.77 *(978-1-4669-5912-5(6))* Trafford Publishing.

Foran, Jill. North Carolina. 2011. (Guide to American States Ser.). (Illus.). 48p. (YA). (gr. 3-6). 29.99 *(978-1-61690-805-8(X));* (J). 29.99 *(978-1-61690-481-4(X))* Weigl Pubs., Inc.

—North Carolina: The Tar Heel State. 2016. (J). *(978-1-4896-4914-0(X))* Weigl Pubs., Inc.

Gunderson, Jessica. Exploring the North Carolina Colony. 2016. (Exploring the 13 Colonies Ser.). (ENG., Illus.). 48p. (J). (gr. 3-6). lib. bdg. 34.65 *(978-1-5157-2233-5(3),* 132757) Capstone.

Hamilton, John. North Carolina, 1 vol. 2016. (United States of America Ser.). (ENG., Illus.). 48p. (J). (gr. 5-9). 34.21 *(978-1-68078-335-3(1),* 21655, Abdo & Daughters) ABDO Publishing Co.

Harcourt School Publishers Staff. Horizons: North Carolina Edition. 3rd ed. 2003. (Illus.). (gr. 4). 73.50 *(978-0-15-321347-2(7))* Harcourt Schl. Pubs.

Harkins, Susan. The Carolinas: Sir George Carteret & Sir Anthony Ashley Cooper. 2006. (J). lib. bdg. *(978-1-58415-464-8(0))* Mitchell Lane Pubs.

Jerome, Kate B. Lucky to Live in North Carolina. 2017. (Arcadia Kids Ser.). (ENG., Illus.). 32p. (J). 16.99 *(978-0-7385-2783-3(1))* Arcadia Publishing.

—The Wise Animal Handbook North Carolina. 2017. (Arcadia Kids Ser.). (ENG., Illus.). 32p. (J). 16.99 *(978-0-7385-2835-9(8))* Arcadia Publishing.

Johnson, Anna Maria, et al. North Carolina: The Tarheel State, 1 vol. 2018. (It's My State! (Fourth Edition)(r) Ser.). (ENG.). 80p. (gr. 4-4). 35.93 *(978-1-5026-2632-5(2),* ecaeb295-5353-4f58-bba2-10ff3895ead9); pap. 18.64 *(978-1-5026-4441-1(X),* 0ad4bdf1-f570-42bb-a045-469de337bf2e) Cavendish Square Publishing LLC.

Knoke, Paul. The Storm on Godfather Mountain: A True Story. 2010. 24p. pap. 14.99 *(978-1-4490-5773-2(X))* AuthorHouse.

Lew, Kristi. North Carolina: Past & Present, 1 vol. 2010. (United States: Past & Present Ser.). (ENG.). 48p. (YA). (gr. 5-5). pap. 12.75 *(978-1-4358-9518-8(5),* baced1aa-6071-4791-9da6-c2f3ce3bc16e); lib. bdg. 34.47 *(978-1-4358-9491-4(X),* 297b8bbc-1abb-440b-a4ea-b03f78c1e7c7) Rosen Publishing Group, Inc., The. (Rosen Reference).

Living in Our World, Grade 5: Its Land & People, 2 vols. 2nd ed. 2003. 586p. (J). tchr. ed., spiral bd. *(978-1-885647-42-9(5))* North Carolina State Univ. Humanities Extension Pubns./Program.

Margulies, Philip. A Primary Source History of the Colony of North Carolina, 1 vol. 2005. (Primary Sources of the Thirteen Colonies & the Lost Colony Ser.). (ENG., Illus.). 64p. (YA). (gr. 4-6). lib. bdg. 37.13 *(978-1-4042-0432-4(6),* 1bfccb8a-ebce-4efb-ab55-cb30b5135f82) Rosen Publishing Group, Inc., The.

Margulies, Phillip. The Colony of North Carolina, 1 vol. 2005. (Primary Sources of the Thirteen Colonies & the Lost Colony Ser.). (ENG., Illus.). 64p. (gr. 4-6). per. 12.95 *(978-1-4042-0666-3(3),* 9343c985-8450-4a47-924e-e07f918094b2) Rosen Publishing Group, Inc., The.

—A Primary Source History of the Colony of North Carolina. 2009. (Primary Sources of the Thirteen Colonies & the Lost Colony Ser.). 64p. (gr. 5-8). 58.50 *(978-1-60851-886-9(8))* Rosen Publishing Group, Inc., The.

Marsh, Carole. Exploring North Carolina Through Project-Based Learning: Geography, History, Government, Economics & More. 2016. (North Carolina Experience Ser.). (ENG.). (J). pap. 9.99 *(978-0-635-12357-2(6))* Gallopade International.

—North Carolina History Projects: 30 Cool, Activities, Crafts, Experiments & More for Kids to Do to Learn about Your State! 2003. (North Carolina Experience Ser.). 32p. (gr. k-5). pap. 5.95 *(978-0-635-01802-1(0),* Marsh, Carole Bks.) Gallopade International.

Mayr, Diane. North Carolina, 1 vol. 2005. (Portraits of the States Ser.). (ENG., Illus.). 32p. (gr. 3-5). pap. 11.50 *(978-0-8368-4650-8(8),* eb77bbea-f194-41ce-becb-a174c1a2b31c); lib. bdg. 28.67 *(978-0-8368-4631-7(1),* acad9fde-30fb-4b9c-986b-4286b8d5df1b) Stevens, Gareth Publishing LLLP. (Gareth Stevens Learning Library).

McKinney, Donna B. It's Great to Be a Fan in North Carolina. 2018. (Sports Nation Ser.). (ENG., Illus.). 48p. (J). (gr. 5-6). pap. 11.95 *(978-1-64185-036-0(1),* 1641850361); lib. bdg. 34.21 *(978-1-63517-934-7(3),* 1635179343) North Star Editions. (Focus Readers).

—It's Great to Be a Fan in North Carolina. 2019. (Illus.). 48p. (J). *(978-1-64185-137-4(6),* Focus Readers) North Star Editions.

Mis, Melody S. The Colony of North Carolina: A Primary Source History. 2009. (Primary Source Library of the Thirteen Colonies & the Lost Colony Ser.). 24p. (gr. 3-4). 42.50 *(978-1-60854-150-8(9),* PowerKids Pr.) Rosen Publishing Group, Inc., The.

Phipps, Shane. The Carter Journals: Time Travels in Early U.S. History. 2015. (Illus.). xii, 189p. (J). pap. *(978-0-87195-364-3(1))* Indiana Historical Society.

Reed, Jennifer. Cape Hatteras National Seashore: Adventure, Explore, Discover, 1 vol. 2008. (America's National Parks Ser.). (ENG., Illus.). 128p. (gr. 6-7). lib. bdg. 37.27 *(978-1-59845-086-6(7),* 5232229c-0e1a-410c-bf8d-3f9abcdab042) Enslow Publishing, LLC.

Rodriguez, Cindy. North Carolina: The Tar Heel State. 2012. (J). *(978-1-61913-385-3(7));* pap. *(978-1-61913-386-0(5))* Weigl Pubs., Inc.

Silcox, Diane. A Light to Keep. Moates, Carol Meetze, illus. 2013. 30p. pap. 14.95 *(978-1-938101-36-6(7))* Indigo Sea Pr., LLC.

Smith-Llera, Danielle. Lunch Counter Sit-Ins: How Photographs Helped Foster Peaceful Civil Rights Protests. 2018. (Captured History Ser.). (ENG., Illus.). 64p. (J). (gr. 5-9). pap. 8.95 *(978-0-7565-5880-2(8),* 138648, Compass Point Bks.) Capstone.

Squire, Ann O. North Carolina (a True Book: My United States) (Library Edition) 2018. (True Book (Relaunch) Ser.). (ENG., Illus.). 48p. (J). (gr. 3-5). 31.00 *(978-0-531-23169-2(0),* Children's Pr.) Scholastic Library Publishing.

Steinitz, Andy & Graham Gaines, Ann. North Carolina, 1 vol. (It's My State! (Second Edition)(r) Ser.). (ENG.). 80p. (gr. 4-4). 2nd rev. ed. 2011. lib. bdg. 34.07 *(978-1-60870-057-8(7),* ff33e2dd-3df2-459d-aabc-42904fd41252) 3rd rev. ed. 2014. lib. bdg. 35.93 *(978-1-62712-754-7(2),* 06dd5519-2fbc-4c92-bba6-eb5ea312bc12) Cavendish Square Publishing LLC.

Taylor, Michaelle. Singing Across the Old North State: Story-Songs of North Carolina. 2004. 44p. (J). pap. *(978-1-880970-89-8(9))* Aerial Photography Services, Inc.

Traylor, Waverley. Indian Legends of the Great Dismal Swamp. Traylor, Margaret, ed. Hancock, Stefanie, illus. 2004. 72p. (gr. 8-18). pap. 9.95 *(978-0-9715068-3-1(3))* Traylor, Waverley Publishing.

Truette, Charlotte. Adam's Adventure: Walking in the Footsteps of History in His Hometown. 2012. 224p. pap. 24.95 *(978-1-4626-7630-9(8))* America Star Bks.

Wagner, Tricia & Wagner, Tricia Martineau. North Carolina, the First Golden State, 1 vol. Camling, Candace, illus. 2017. (ENG.). 32p. (J). (gr. -1-3). 16.99 *(978-1-4556-2273-3(7),* Pelican Publishing) Arcadia Publishing.

Walser, Richard. North Carolina Parade: Stories of History & People. 2012. (ENG., Illus.). 216p. pap. 50.00 *(978-0-8078-3708-5(3),* 01PODPB) Univ. of North Carolina Pr.

Wimmer, Teresa. North Carolina. 2009. (This Land Called America Ser.). (Illus.). 32p. (YA). (gr. 3-6). 19.95 *(978-1-58341-786-7(9))* Creative Co., The.

Zepke, Terrance. Pirates of the Carolinas for Kids. 2009. (Carolinas for Kids Ser.). (ENG.). 72p. (J). (gr. -1-12). pap. 12.95 *(978-1-56164-459-5(5))* Pineapple Pr., Inc.

NORTH CENTRAL STATES

see Middle West

NORTH DAKOTA

Brown, Vanessa. North Dakota. 2009. (Bilingual Library of the United States of America Ser.). (ENG & SPA.). 32p. (gr. 2-2). 47.90 *(978-1-60853-378-7(6),* Editorial Buenas Letras) Rosen Publishing Group, Inc., The.

—North Dakota/Dakota del Norte, 1 vol. Brusca, Maria Cristina, tr. 2005. (Bilingual Library of the United States of America Ser.: Set 2). (ENG & SPA., Illus.). 32p. (J). (gr. 2-2). lib. bdg. 28.93 *(978-1-4042-3099-6(8),* 8c0b1a61-8c88-4452-9cc3-93b3eaf7f479) Rosen Publishing Group, Inc., The.

Heinrichs, Ann. North Dakota. Kania, Matt, illus. 2017. (U. S. A. Travel Guides). (ENG.). 40p. (J). (gr. 2-5). lib. bdg. 38.50 *(978-1-5038-1974-0(4),* 211610) Child's World, Inc, The.

Hoena, Blake. North Dakota. 2013. (Exploring the States Ser.). (ENG., Illus.). 32p. (J). (gr. 3-7). lib. bdg. 27.95 *(978-1-62617-033-9(9),* Blastoff! Readers) Bellwether Media.

Hoover Severin, E. North Dakota, 1 vol. 2006. (Portraits of the States Ser.). (ENG.). 32p. (gr. 3-5). pap. 11.50 *(978-0-8368-4723-9(7),* 8c5756e5-4995-4d85-84f7-11123ab5b999); (Illus.). lib. bdg. 28.67 *(978-0-8368-4706-2(7),* 74e03b7c-674c-474c-af38-a5471505763c) Stevens, Gareth Publishing LLLP. (Gareth Stevens Learning Library).

Maine, Tyler & Parker, Bridget. North Dakota. 2016. (States Ser.). (ENG., Illus.). 32p. (J). (gr. 3-6). lib. bdg. 27.99 *(978-1-5157-0421-8(1),* 132032, Capstone Pr.) Capstone.

Marsh, Carole. North Dakota Current Events Projects: 30 Cool, Activities, Crafts, Experiments & More for Kids to Do to Learn about Your State! 2003. (North Dakota Experience Ser.). 32p. (gr. k-8). pap. 5.95 *(978-0-635-02053-6(X),* Marsh, Carole Bks.) Gallopade International.

—North Dakota Geography Projects: 30 Cool, Activities, Crafts, Experiments & More for Kids to Do to Learn about Your State! 2003. (North Dakota Experience Ser.). 32p. (gr. k-5). pap. 5.95 *(978-0-635-01853-3(5),* Marsh, Carole Bks.) Gallopade International.

—North Dakota Government Projects: 30 Cool, Activities, Crafts, Experiments & More for Kids to Do to Learn about Your State! 2003. (North Dakota Experience Ser.). 32p. (gr. k-5). pap. 5.95 *(978-0-635-01953-0(1),* Marsh, Carole Bks.) Gallopade International.

—North Dakota People Projects: 30 Cool, Activities, Crafts, Experiments & More for Kids to Do to Learn about Your State! 2003. (North Dakota Experience Ser.). 32p. (gr. k-5). pap. 5.95 *(978-0-635-02003-1(3),* Marsh, Carole Bks.) Gallopade International.

Mcdaniel, Melissa. North Dakota, 1 vol. 2003. (Celebrate the States (First Edition) Ser.). (ENG., Illus.). 144p. (gr. 6-6). lib. bdg. 39.79 *(978-0-7614-1314-1(6),* b203a4f7-a516-4df0-b483-d05db2a4e979) Cavendish Square Publishing LLC.

Mcdaniel, Melissa & Kras, Sara Louise. North Dakota, 1 vol. 2nd rev. ed. 2010. (Celebrate the States (Second Edition) Ser.). (ENG.). 144p. (gr. 6-6). 39.79 *(978-0-7614-4733-7(4),* 1e58e1bc-e22a-4dee-b804-f685e6b05fbe) Cavendish Square Publishing LLC.

Mis, M. S. How to Draw North Dakota's Sights & Symbols. 2009. (Kid's Guide to Drawing America Ser.). 32p. (gr. k-k). 50.50 *(978-1-61511-087-2(9),* PowerKids Pr.) Rosen Publishing Group, Inc., The.

Murray, Julie. North Dakota, 1 vol. 2006. (Buddy Book Ser.). (ENG., Illus.). 32p. (gr. 2-4). 27.07 *(978-1-59197-693-6(6),* Buddy Bks.) ABDO Publishing Co.

Salonen, Roxane B. P Is for Peace Garden: A North Dakota Alphabet. Yardley, Joanna, illus. 2005. (Discover America State by State Ser.). (ENG.). 40p. (J). (gr. 1-3). 17.95 *(978-1-58536-142-7(9),* 202002) Sleeping Bear Pr.

Sanders, Doug. North Dakota, 1 vol. Santoro, Christopher, illus. 2004. (It's My State! (First Edition)(r) Ser.). (ENG.). 80p. (gr. 4-4). lib. bdg. 34.07 *(978-0-7614-1687-6(0),* 233d0f1f-913b-475b-bcf3-e1b37bd17867) Cavendish Square Publishing LLC.

Silverman, Robin Landew. North Dakota. 2003. (From Sea to Shining Sea Ser.: 2). (ENG., Illus.). 80p. (J). 30.50 *(978-0-516-22385-8(2),* Children's Pr.) Scholastic Library Publishing.

Squire, Ann O. North Dakota (a True Book: My United States) (Library Edition) 2018. (True Book (Relaunch) Ser.). (ENG., Illus.). 48p. (J). (gr. 3-5). 31.00 *(978-0-531-23567-6(X),* Children's Pr.) Scholastic Library Publishing.

Verba, Joan Marie. North Dakota. 2012. (J). lib. bdg. 25.26 *(978-0-7613-4189-5(7),* Lerner Pubns.) Lerner Publishing Group.

Zollman, Pam. North Dakota. 2005. (Rookie Read-About Geography Ser.). (ENG., Illus.). 32p. (J). (gr. 1-2). lib. bdg. 20.50 *(978-0-516-25259-9(3),* Children's Pr.) Scholastic Library Publishing.

NORTH DAKOTA—FICTION

Baum, L. Frank & Bancroft, Laura. Twinkle & Chubbins. 2011. 106p. 22.95 *(978-1-4638-9604-1(2))* Rodgers, Alan Bks.

Bergstrom, Candace. People of the Prairie. 2008. 12.95 *(978-0-9787648-1-4(1))* Bergstrom Bks.

Byler, Linda. The Homestead: The Dakota Series, Book 1. 2017. (Dakota Ser.: 1). (ENG.). 368p. pap. 14.99 *(978-1-68099-213-7(9),* Good Bks.) Skyhorse Publishing Co., Inc.

DeFelice, Cynthia. Wild Life. 2013. (ENG.). 208p. (J). (gr. 3-7). pap. 8.99 *(978-1-250-03407-6(8),* 900120577) Square Fish.

Fournier, Kevin Mark. Sandbag Shuffle. 2007. (ENG.). 240p. (gr. 8-13). per. 12.95 *(978-1-897235-22-5(4))* Thistledown Pr., Ltd. CAN. Dist: Univ. of Toronto Pr.

Gunderson, Jessica. Emma's New Beginning. Foti, Anthony J., illus. 2015. (U. S. Immigration in The 1900s Ser.). (ENG.). 96p. (J). (gr. 3-6). pap. 7.95 *(978-1-4965-0501-9(8),* 128573, Stone Arch Bks.) Capstone.

Jacobs, Lily. The Littlest Bunny in North Dakota: An Easter Adventure. Dunn, Robert, illus. 2015. (Littlest Bunny Ser.). (ENG.). 32p. (J). (gr. -1-3). 9.99 *(978-1-4926-1159-2(X),* Hometown World) Sourcebooks, Inc.

James, Eric. Santa's Sleigh Is on Its Way to North Dakota: A Christmas Adventure. Dunn, Robert, illus. 2016. (Santa's Sleigh Is on Its Way Ser.). (ENG.). 32p. (J). (gr. k-2). 12.99 *(978-1-4926-4345-6(9),* 9781492643456, Hometown World) Sourcebooks, Inc.

—The Spooky Express North Dakota. Piwowarski, Marcin, illus. 2017. (Spooky Express Ser.). (ENG.). 32p. (J). (gr. k-6). 9.99 *(978-1-4926-5386-8(1),* Hometown World) Sourcebooks, Inc.

—Tiny the North Dakota Easter Bunny. 2018. (Tiny the Easter Bunny Ser.). (ENG.). 40p. (J). (gr. k-3). 9.99 *(978-1-4926-5951-8(7),* Hometown World) Sourcebooks, Inc.

Kurtz, Jane. River Friendly, River Wild. Brennan, Neil, illus. 2007. (ENG.). 40p. (J). (gr. -1-3). 8.99 *(978-1-4169-3487-5(1),* Simon & Schuster/Paula Wiseman Bks.) Simon & Schuster/Paula Wiseman Bks.

Martin, Rebecca. Blossoms on the Roof. 2015. (Amish Frontier Ser.). (ENG.). 160p. (J). (gr. 2-6). pap. 10.99 *(978-0-7369-6367-1(7),* 6963671) Harvest Hse. Pubs.

Peterson, Esther Allen. Will Spring Come? 2009. (Illus.). 157p. (J). pap. *(978-0-88092-768-0(2))* Royal Fireworks Publishing Co.

Pyke, Helen Godfrey. Julia. 2012. (J). pap. *(978-0-8163-3400-1(5))* Pacific Pr. Publishing Assn.

Rylander, Chris. Codename Zero. 2015. (Codename Conspiracy Ser.: 1). (ENG.). 384p. (J). (gr. 3-7). pap. 6.99 *(978-0-06-212009-0(3),* Walden Pond Pr.) HarperCollins Pubs.

Salonen, Roxane Beauclair. The Twelve Days of Christmas in North Dakota. Golden, Jessica, illus. 2017. (Twelve Days of Christmas in America Ser.). (ENG.). 40p. (J). (gr. k). 12.95 *(978-1-4549-2008-3(4))* Sterling Publishing Co., Inc.

Sigafus, Kim. Nowhere to Hide. 2019. (Autumn's Dawn Trilogy Ser.: 1). (ENG.). 112p. (YA). (gr. 8-12). pap. 9.95 *(978-1-939053-21-3(8),* 7th Generation) BPC.

Sully, Katherine. Night-Night North Dakota. Poole, Helen, illus. 2017. (Night-Night Ser.). (ENG.). 20p. (J). (gr. -1-1). bds. 9.99 *(978-1-4926-5478-0(7),* Hometown World) Sourcebooks, Inc.

Tooke, Wes. King of the Mound: My Summer with Satchel Paige. (ENG.). 160p. (J). (gr. 3-7). 2013. pap. 7.99 *(978-1-4424-3347-2(7))* 2012. (Illus.). 17.99 *(978-1-4424-3346-5(9))* Simon & Schuster Bks. For Young Readers. (Simon & Schuster Bks. For Young Readers).

Wilder, Laura Ingalls. By the Shores of Silver Lake. (Little House Ser.). (J). (gr. 3-6). lib. bdg. 23.95 *(978-0-8488-2117-3(3))* Amereon Ltd.

—By the Shores of Silver Lake: Full Color Edition: A Newbery Honor Award Winner. Williams, Garth, illus. 2004. (Little House Ser.: 5). (ENG.). 304p. (J). (gr. 3-7). pap. 9.99 *(978-0-06-058184-8(0),* HarperCollins) HarperCollins Pubs.

NORTH DAKOTA—HISTORY

Blauvelt, Marie. Sacajawea. 2011. (Early Connections Ser.). (J). *(978-1-61672-616-4(4))* Benchmark Education Co.

Edwards, Sue Bradford. The Dakota Access Pipeline. 2017. (Special Reports Set 3 Ser.). (ENG., Illus.). 112p. (J). (gr. 6-12). lib. bdg. 41.36 *(978-1-5321-1332-1(3),* 27540, Essential Library) ABDO Publishing Co.

Hamilton, John. North Dakota, 1 vol. 2016. (United States of America Ser.). (ENG., Illus.). 48p. (J). (gr. 5-9). 34.21 *(978-1-68078-336-0(X),* 21657, Abdo & Daughters) ABDO Publishing Co.

Lewis, Mark J. North Dakota: Past & Present, 1 vol. 2010. (United States: Past & Present Ser.). (ENG.). 48p. (YA). (gr. 5-5). pap. 12.75 *(978-1-4358-9519-5(3),* ac13ed8b-7cda-4edb-b602-13f93b421715); lib. bdg. 34.47 *(978-1-4358-9492-1(8),* 1f81537e-4389-4e50-aba6-995bf4de2138) Rosen Publishing Group, Inc., The. (Rosen Reference).

Lusted, Marcia Amidon. North Dakota: The Peace Garden State, 1 vol. 2010. (Our Amazing States Ser.). (ENG.). 24p. (J). (gr. 3-3). pap. 9.25 *(978-1-4488-0764-2(6),* 663f4663-8a21-40aa-96e9-42fe96c34aa7); lib. bdg. 26.27 *(978-1-4488-0664-5(X),* 721d74d7-64c1-4f75-ac3a-04ee43352628) Rosen Publishing Group, Inc., The. (PowerKids Pr.).

Marsh, Carole. Exploring North Dakota Through Project-Based Learning: Geography, History, Government, Economics & More. 2016. (North Dakota Experience Ser.). (ENG.). (J). pap. 9.99 *(978-0-635-12358-9(4))* Gallopade International.

—I'm Reading about North Dakota. 2014. (North Dakota Experience Ser.). (ENG., Illus.). (J). pap., pap. 8.99 *(978-0-635-11309-2(0))* Gallopade International.

—North Dakota History Projects: 30 Cool, Activities, Crafts, Experiments & More for Kids to Do to Learn about Your State! 2003. (North Dakota Experience Ser.). 32p. (gr. k-5). pap. 5.95 *(978-0-635-01803-8(9),* Marsh, Carole Bks.) Gallopade International.

Peterson, Sheryl. North Dakota. 2009. (This Land Called America Ser.). (Illus.). 32p. (YA). (gr. 3-6). 19.95 *(978-1-58341-787-4(7))* Creative Co., The.

Rodriguez, Cindy. North Dakota: The Peach Garden State. 2012. (J). *(978-1-61913-387-7(3));* pap. *(978-1-61913-388-4(1))* Weigl Pubs., Inc.

Sanders, Doug. North Dakota, 1 vol. 2nd rev. ed. 2014. (It's My State! (Second Edition)(r) Ser.). (ENG.). 80p. (gr. 4-4). pap. 18.64 *(978-1-62712-483-6(7),* 38338739-3180-4cd2-9e24-241bea8a9a57); (Illus.). 35.93 *(978-1-62712-223-8(0),* acae2a3e-e459-4e57-aae4-157f22a78e95) Cavendish Square Publishing LLC.

Sanders, Doug & Bjorklund, Ruth. North Dakota: The Peace Garden State, 1 vol. 3rd rev. ed. 2016. (It's My State! (Third Edition)(r) Ser.). (ENG.). 80p. (gr. 4-4). 35.93 *(978-1-62713-250-3(3),* f7de9795-8584-4393-8270-30bccc300869) Cavendish Square Publishing LLC.

Silverman, Robin Landew. North Dakota. 2009. (From Sea to Shining Sea, Second Ser.). (ENG.). 80p. (J). pap. 7.95 *(978-0-531-21140-3(1),* Children's Pr.) Scholastic Library Publishing.

Stille, Darlene R. America the Beautiful: North Dakota (Revised Edition) 2014. (America the Beautiful, Third Ser. (Revised Edition) Ser.). (ENG.). 144p. (J). lib. bdg. 40.00 *(978-0-531-28286-1(4))* Scholastic Library Publishing.

Watson, Galadriel Findlay. North Dakota. 2011. (Guide to American States Ser.). (Illus.). 48p. (YA). (gr. 3-6). 29.99 *(978-1-61690-806-5(8))* Weigl Pubs., Inc.

—North Dakota: The Peace Garden State. 2016. (J). *(978-1-4896-4917-1(4))* Weigl Pubs., Inc.

Westcott, Jim. Upper Plains: Montana, North Dakota, South Dakota, Vol. 19. 2015. (Let's Explore the States Ser.). (Illus.). 64p. (J). (gr. 5). 23.95 *(978-1-4222-3336-8(7))* Mason Crest.

NORTH POLE

see also Arctic Regions

Aboff, Marcie. Do You Really Want to Meet a Polar Bear? Fabbri, Daniele, illus. 2014. (Do You Really Want to Meet ... ? Ser.). (ENG.). 24p. (J). (gr. 1-4). 27.10 *(978-1-60753-455-6(X),* 15899) Amicus.

Bedesky, Baron. Peary & Henson: The Race to the North Pole, 1 vol. 2006. (In the Footsteps of Explorers Ser.). (ENG., Illus.). 32p. (J). (gr. 4-7). pap. *(978-0-7787-2462-9(X));* lib. bdg. *(978-0-7787-2426-1(3))* Crabtree Publishing Co.

Blaisdell, Molly. If You Were a Comma [LTD Commodities]. Gray, Sara, illus. 2010. (Word Fun Ser.). 24p. pap. 3.50 *(978-1-4048-6251-7(X),* Picture Window Bks.) Capstone.

Bluthenthal, Todd. The North Pole, 1 vol. 2017. (Where on Earth? Mapping Parts of the World Ser.). (ENG.). 24p. (gr. 1-2). pap. 9.15 *(978-1-4824-6429-0(2),* 6231b5db-707c-4654-a710-2c5a57ec785b) Stevens, Gareth Publishing LLLP.

Chapman, Simon. At the North Pole. 2005. (Illus.). 115p. (J). lib. bdg. 20.00 *(978-1-4242-0629-2(4))* Fitzgerald Bks.

Cooke, Tim. The Exploration of the North & South Poles, 1 vol. 2013. (Explorers Discovering the World Ser.). (ENG., Illus.). 48p. (J). (gr. 4-5). 34.60 *(978-1-4339-8631-4(0),* 2313c10c-11d4-4c82-bda1-79ec3d5d0908); pap. 15.05 *(978-1-4339-8632-1(9),* 2c8796b4-bddb-4528-b8fe-758db89089b2) Stevens, Gareth Publishing LLLP. (Gareth Stevens Learning Library).

Dodson Wade, Mary. Amazing Arctic Explorer Matthew Henson, 1 vol. 2009. (Amazing Americans Ser.). (ENG., Illus.). 24p. (gr. k-2). pap. 10.35 *(978-0-7660-5974-0(X),* 74989fbd-6c8f-4f19-aa83-5c26fc272c04, Enslow Elementary); lib. bdg. 25.27 *(978-0-7660-3286-6(8),* 3ec5bedd-aa9e-42df-9d7b-7d3253166845) Enslow Publishing, LLC.

DuBose, Judy. Santa's Count down 'Til Christmas. 2011. 36p. (gr. -1). pap. 16.00 *(978-1-4269-6545-6(1))* Trafford Publishing.

Dunn, Joeming W. Reaching the North Pole, 1 vol. Espinosa, Rod, illus. 2008. (Graphic History Ser.). (ENG.). 32p. (J). (gr. 3-8). 32.79 *(978-1-60270-185-4(7),* 9062, Graphic Planet - Fiction) Magic Wagon.

Hopkinson, Deborah. Keep On! The Story of Matthew Henson, Co-Discoverer of the North Pole, 1 vol. Alcorn, Stephen, illus. 2015. 36p. (J). (gr. 1-4). pap. 8.99 *(978-1-56145-886-8(4))* Peachtree Publishing Co. Inc.

Hyde, Natalie. Expedition to the Arctic. 2013. (ENG., Illus.). 48p. (J). *(978-0-7787-1169-8(2));* pap. *(978-0-7787-1177-3(3))* Crabtree Publishing Co.

Isaacs, Sally, Helen Thayer's Arctic Adventure: A Woman & a Dog Walk to the North Pole. Sasheva, Iva, illus. 2016. (Encounter: Narrative Nonfiction Picture Bks.). (ENG.). 32p. (J). (gr. 4-5). lib. bdg. 29.32 *(978-1-4914-8044-1(0),* 130548, Capstone Young Readers) Capstone.

Isaacs, Sally Senzell. Helen Thayer's Arctic Adventure: A Woman & a Dog Walk to the North Pole. Sasheva, Iva, illus. 2017. (Encounter: Narrative Nonfiction Picture Bks.). (ENG.). 32p. (J). (gr. 4-5). pap. 7.95 *(978-1-4914-8045-8(9),* 130549, Capstone Young Readers) Capstone.

Rajczak Nelson, Kristen. All about the North Pole, 1 vol. 2019. (It's Christmas! Ser.). (ENG.). 24p. (J). (gr. 2-2). 25.27

MNO

(978-1-7253-0090-3(7), 98fc8430-c7c9-45c8-8594-0496b65f25d1); pap. 9.25 (978-1-7253-0088-0(5), 41dcba67-c371-4686-af5f-1ca8ffcf208b) Rosen Publishing Group, Inc., The. (PowerKids Pr.).

Roxburgh, Ellis. Robert Peary vs. Frederick Cook: Race to the North Pole, 1 vol. 2015. (History's Greatest Rivals Ser.). (ENG., Illus.). 48p. (J). (gr. 6-8). pap. 15.05 (978-1-4824-4231-1(0), 83dfe8bc-2ced-4f42-8c42-d7674bdb08e4) Stevens, Gareth Publishing LLLP.

Scraper, Katherine. Matthew Henson. 2011. (Early Connections Ser.). (J). (978-1-61672-563-1(X)) Benchmark Education Co.

Weidt, Maryann N. Matthew Henson. 2003. (History Maker Bios Ser.). (Illus.). 48p. (J). (gr. 2-4). 26.60 (978-0-8225-0397-2(2), Lerner Pubns.) Lerner Publishing Group.

Worth, Bonnie. Ice Is Nice! All about the North & South Poles. Ruiz, Aristides & Mathieu, Joe, illus. 2010. (Cat in the Hat's Learning Library). (ENG.). 48p. (J). (gr. -1-3). 9.99 (978-0-375-82885-0(0), Random Hse. Bks. for Young Readers) Random Hse. Children's Bks.

NORTH POLE—FICTION

Adair, Dick. The Story of Aloha Bear. Britt, Stephanie, illus. 2008. 24p. (J). 12.95 (978-1-59700-492-3(8)) Island Heritage Publishing.

Bamford, Desmond Nicholas. Beekemose. 2012. (Illus.). 54p. (gr. 2-4). pap. 13.66 (978-1-4685-7773-0(5)) AuthorHouse.

Bigalow, Stephen W. Who Is Santa? And How Did He Get to the North Pole? Megenhardt, Bill, illus. 2013. (ENG.). 144p. (J). (gr. 4-7). 19.95 (978-0-9773757-3-8(0)) Profit Publishing.

Brinkley, Lonnie. I Believe: Lost at the North Pole. 2008. (Illus.). 450p. (J). 29.95 (978-0-9801215-3-7(1)) Big Bear Publishing U.S.

Dineen, Kaite. What Santa Wants You to Know: A Story of Santa's Love for Jesus, 1 vol. 2010. 34p. pap. 24.95 (978-1-4489-7071-1(7)) PublishAmerica, Inc.

Eaton, Kay A. Gleason, the Christmas Giraffe. 2009. 28p. pap. 12.50 (978-1-4389-3010-7(0)) AuthorHouse.

Fearne, Peter. My Week with Father Christmas. 2006. 176p. per. (978-1-84667-021-3(7)) Derwent Pr., The.

Hansen, Eric. Ian, Ceo, North Pole. 2008. 108p. pap. 9.95 (978-1-60693-554-5(2), Eloquent Bks.) Strategic Book Publishing & Rights Agency (SBPRA).

Hatfield, Kara. The Real Story of Sant. 2011. 30p. pap. 16.95 (978-1-4626-1022-8(6)) America Star Bks.

Head, Jean. Andrew's Christmas Dream. 2012. 28p. pap. 5.00 (978-1-937260-19-4(4)) Sleepytown Pr.

Higginson, Sheila Sweeny. A Very McStuffins Christmas. 2014. (Doc Mcstuffins 8X8 Ser.). (J). lib. bdg. 16.00 (978-0-606-35908-5(7)) Turtleback.

Hurst, Joshua. One Day at the North Pole. Johnson, Jared, illus. 2008. 44p. pap. 24.95 (978-1-60703-327-1(5)) America Star Bks.

Ianieri, Tom. Polar Pals. 2011. 28p. pap. 15.99 (978-1-4628-5403-5(6)) Xlibris Corp.

Jones, Carl. Rudy the Rangifer & Why Her Nose Turned Orange. 2007. 64p. pap. 14.99 (978-0-9748266-3-9(4)) Grampa Jones's Publishing Co.

Judge, Chris. The Great Explorer. 2012. (ENG., Illus.). 32p. (J). (gr. -1-2). pap. 13.99 (978-1-84939-401-7(6)) Andersen Pr. GBR. Dist: Independent Pubs. Group.

King, Lisa. The Gingerbread Baby in Search of a Family. 2013. 28p. pap. 24.95 (978-1-63004-147-2(5)) America Star Bks.

Kramer, Candice. Matthew Henson en el Polo Norte & Matthew Henson at the North Pole. 2005. spiral bd. 76.00 (978-1-4108-5790-3(5)) Benchmark Education Co.

Kurtz, John. Claus Kids Christmas Coloring Book. 2011. (Dover Holiday Coloring Book Ser.). (ENG.). 32p. (J). (gr. k-5). pap. 3.99 (978-0-486-48292-7(3)) Dover Pubns., Inc.

La Porte, Mary Ellen. The Almost Christmas Story. 2011. 44p. pap. 18.99 (978-1-4520-9946-0(4)) AuthorHouse.

LePage, Michaele L. & Lovass-Nagy, Nicole. A Year at the North Pole. 2009. 31p. 16.95 (978-0-557-06430-4(9)) Lulu Pr., Inc.

Macy, Carolyn. Who Can Save the North Pole? 2017. (ENG., Illus.). (J). 29.99 (978-0-9988838-7-8(5)); pap. 19.99 (978-0-9988838-6-1(7)) Macy, Carolyn.

Mitcham Davis, Zipporah. The Fox & Emily's Long Migration. 2008. 28p. pap. 13.99 (978-1-4389-0326-2(X)) AuthorHouse.

Palmer, Slim. Albert & the Christmas Elf. 2005. (ENG.). 88p. pap. 11.55 (978-1-4116-4503-5(0)) Lulu Pr., Inc.

Primavera, Elise. Auntie Claus & the Key to Christmas: A Christmas Holiday Book for Kids. Primavera, Elise, illus. 2011. (ENG., Illus.). 40p. (J). (gr. -1-3). pap. 7.99 (978-0-547-57679-4(X), 1458441, Clarion Bks.) HarperCollins Pubs.

—Auntie Claus Deluxe Edition: A Christmas Holiday Book for Kids. Primavera, Elise, illus. 2015. (ENG., Illus.). 40p. (J). (gr. -1-3). 18.99 (978-0-544-53872-6(2), 1608615, Clarion Bks.) HarperCollins Pubs.

Schomer-Wendel, Gretchen & Schomer, Adam Anthony. Becka Goes to the North Pole, 1 vol. Renthrope, Damon, illus. 2009. (Becka & the Big Bubble Ser.). (ENG.). 32p. (J). (gr. 1-2). pap. 11.55 (978-1-60754-117-2(3), c00b48e1-07cf-4ffd-b439-e3a8068d929d); lib. bdg. 27.27 (978-1-60754-116-5(5), dc207ff7-b36b-4fc4-8048-4f53104e6923) Rosen Publishing Group, Inc., The. (Windmill Bks.).

Shepherd, Anita. The Santa Genie. 2012. 50p. pap. 7.95 (978-0-9882368-0-6(X)) New Eden Publishing.

Smallman, Steve. Santa Is Coming to My House. Dunn, Robert, illus. 2nd ed. 2019. (Santa Is Coming... Ser.). (ENG.). 40p. (J). (gr. -1-3). 12.99 (978-1-7282-0076-7(8), Hometown World) Sourcebooks, Inc.

Snedeker, Erin. The Littlest Elf: Marvin Mcgee & the Candle of Fate. Drotleff, David J., illus. 2010. 44p. pap. 15.50 (978-1-60911-194-6(X), Eloquent Bks.) Strategic Book Publishing & Rights Agency (SBPRA).

Soderberg, Erin. Puppy Pirates Super Special #3: Race to the North Pole. 2018. (Puppy Pirates Ser.: 3). (Illus.). 144p. (J). (gr. 1-4). 5.99 (978-0-525-57920-5(6), Random Hse. Bks. for Young Readers) Random Hse. Children's Bks.

Sonneborn, Scott. The Computer Meltdown. Lozano, Omar, illus. 2015. (North Police Ser.). (ENG.). 32p. (J). (gr. k-2). lib. bdg. 21.32 (978-1-4795-6485-9(0), 128338, Picture Window Bks.) Capstone.

—Meet the South Police. Lozano, Omar, illus. 2015. (North Police Ser.). (ENG.). 32p. (J). (gr. k-2). lib. bdg. 21.32 (978-1-4795-6486-6(9), 128339, Picture Window Bks.) Capstone.

—The Reindeer Games. Lozano, Omar, illus. 2015. (North Police Ser.). (ENG.). 32p. (J). (gr. k-2). lib. bdg. 21.32 (978-1-4795-6487-3(7), 128340, Picture Window Bks.) Capstone.

Sullivan, E. J. Bubba the Redneck Reindeer. Eldredge, Ernie, illus. 2007. 32p. (J). (gr. 4-7). 12.95 (978-1-60261-008-8(8)) Cliff Road Bks.

Van Allsburg, Chris. The Polar Express: Sam's Edition. annot. ed. 2006. (J). (gr. k-3). 35.00 (978-0-618-83659-8(4)) Houghton Mifflin Harcourt Trade & Reference Pubs.

—Polar Express 30th Anniversary Edition: A Christmas Holiday Book for Kids. Van Allsburg, Chris, illus. 30th anniv. ed. 2015. (ENG., Illus.). 32p. (J). (gr. -1-3). 21.99 (978-0-544-58014-5(1), 1613461, Clarion Bks.) HarperCollins Pubs.

—The Polar Express Big Book: A Caldecott Award Winner. Van Allsburg, Chris, illus. 2014. (ENG., Illus.). 32p. (J). (gr. -1-3). pap. 29.99 (978-0-544-45798-0(6), 1599870, Clarion Bks.) HarperCollins Pubs.

Vern, Jules. The English at the North Pole. 2009. 160p. 24.95 (978-1-60664-684-7(2)); pap. 13.95 (978-1-60664-313-6(4)) Rodgers, Alan Bks.

Yoon, Salina. Penguin's Big Adventure. 2015. (Penguin Ser.). (ENG., Illus.). 40p. (J). (gr. -1-1). 14.99 (978-0-8027-3828-8(1), 900141990, Bloomsbury USA Childrens) Bloomsbury Publishing USA.

Zurcher, Corina. Growing up Claus. 2007. 188p. 21.99 (978-1-60477-046-9(5)); per. 13.99 (978-1-60266-917-8(1)) Salem Author Services.

NORTHMEN

Here are entered works on the inhabitants of Scandinavia prior to the 10th century. Works on the Scandinavian sea-warriors who plundered the northern and western coasts of Europe from the 8th to the 10th centuries are entered under Vikings. Works on the inhabitants of Scandinavia since the 10th century are entered under Scandinavians.

see also Normans; Vikings

Dowling, Lucy. Why Why Why... Were Vikings So Fierce? 2010. (Why Why Why Ser.). 32p. (YA). (gr. 1-3). lib. bdg. 18.95 (978-1-4222-1591-3(1)) Mason Crest.

Grant, Neil. Vikings. 2017. (ENG.) (J). pap. 7.99 (978-1-78121-225-7(2)) Brown Bear Bks.

Hindley, Judy, et al. Time Traveler: Visit Medieval Times, the Viking Age, the Roman World & Ancient Egypt. rev. ed. 2004. (Time Travelers Bks.). (Illus.). 130p. (J). (gr. 3-6). 22.95 (978-0-7460-3365-4(6)) EDC Publishing.

Hinds, Kathryn. Vikings, 1 vol. 2010. (Barbarians! Ser.). (ENG.). 80p. (gr. 6-6). 38.36 (978-0-7614-4074-1(7), 099ce436-f8bc-407e-924a-e48d46d1f27d) Cavendish Square Publishing LLC.

Hopkins, Andrea. Viking Families & Farms. 2009. (Viking Library). 24p. (gr. 3-3). 42.50 (978-1-60854-257-4(2), PowerKids Pr.) Rosen Publishing Group, Inc., The.

—Viking Raiders & Traders. 2009. (Viking Library). 24p. (gr. 3-3). 42.50 (978-1-60854-260-4(2), PowerKids Pr.) Rosen Publishing Group, Inc., The.

Macdonald, Fiona. The Medieval Chronicles: Vikings, Knights, & Castles. Antram, David, illus. 2013. 92p. (J). (978-1-4351-5067-6(8)) Barnes & Noble, Inc.

—Vikings. 2010. (Remarkable Man & Beast Ser.). (Illus.). 48p. (J). (gr. 3-18). lib. bdg. 19.95 (978-1-4222-1977-5(1)) Mason Crest.

MacDonald, Fiona. Vikings: Dress, Eat, Write & Play Just Like the Vikings. 2008. (Hands-on History Ser.). (ENG., Illus.). 32p. (J). (gr. 3-7). pap. (978-0-7787-4072-8(2)) Crabtree Publishing Co.

McLeese, Don. Vikings. 2009. 32p. pap. 7.99 (978-0-8249-1445-5(7), Ideals Pubns.) Worthy Publishing.

Nardo, Don. The Vikings, 1 vol. 2010. (World History Ser.). (ENG.). 112p. (gr. 7-7). 41.53 (978-1-4205-0316-6(2), 4ff27f54-92a7-4acb-aa69-8ad20b4fdfa7, Lucent Pr.) Greenhaven Publishing LLC.

Strain Trueit, Trudi. The Vikings, 1 vol. 2012. (Technology of the Ancients Ser.). (ENG.). 64p. (gr. 6-6). 35.50 (978-1-60870-769-0(5), bfde65a9-f39b-43d0-98ff-f355d9f71ac8) Cavendish Square Publishing LLC.

Toth, Henrietta. Viking Explorers, 1 vol. 2016. (Spotlight on Explorers & Colonization Ser.). (ENG., Illus.). 48p. (J). (gr. 6-6). pap. 12.75 (978-1-4777-8832-5(8), 99e43bde-33d5-4e4a-91be-d92fdad36ed7) Rosen Publishing Group, Inc., The.

NORTHMEN—FICTION

Brown, Abbie Farwell. In the Days of Giants. Smith, E. Boyd, illus. 2008. 204p. per. 9.95 (978-1-59915-044-4(1)) Yesterday's Classics.

NORTHWEST, OLD

see also Middle West

O'Maley, Elizabeth. Bones on the Ground. 2014. (J). (978-0-87195-362-9(5)) Indiana Historical Society.

NORTHWEST, PACIFIC

Benchmark Education Company. The Pacific Northwest Region (Teacher Guide). 2005. (978-1-4108-4646-4(6)) Benchmark Education Co.

Blomgren, Jennifer. Why Do I Sing? Animal Songs of the Pacific Northwest. Gabriel, Andrea, illus. 2013. 32p. (J). (gr. -1-2). 16.99 (978-1-57061-845-1(3), Little Bigfoot) Sasquatch Bks.

Brannon, Barbara. Discover the Pacific Northwest Region. 2005. (J). pap. (978-1-4108-5150-5(8)) Benchmark Education Co.

Connery-Boyd, Peg. Totally Pacific Northwest! 2016. (Hawk's Nest Activity Bks.: 0). (ENG.). 64p. (J). (gr. k-3). pap. 8.99 (978-1-4926-3969-5(9), 9781492639695) Sourcebooks, Inc.

Goddu, Krystyna Poray. Native Peoples of the Northwest. 2016. (North American Indian Nations Ser.). (ENG., Illus.). 48p. (J). (gr. 3-5). 33.32 (978-1-4677-7939-5(3), a2d93c0d-94f5-4f6f-b041-3ec2dadac0ee, Lerner Pubns.) Lerner Publishing Group.

Johnson, Marlys & Clarke, Duncan. Native Tribes of the Great Basin & Plateau, 1 vol. 2004. (Native Tribes of North America Ser.). (ENG., Illus.). 64p. (J). (gr. 5-8). lib. bdg. 36.67 (978-0-8368-5610-1(4), 3e81fe87-615f-4224-aa78-8b2b6fc38e48, Gareth Stevens Secondary Library) Stevens, Gareth Publishing LLLP.

Leonardo, Victoria. The Pacific Northwest Region. 2005. (J). pap. (978-1-4108-4598-6(2)) Benchmark Education Co.

Mullen, Amy. Colors of the Pacific Northwest: Explore the Colors of Nature. Kids Will Love Discovering the Amazing Natural Colors in the Pacific Northwest, from the Red Sapsucker to the Green Douglas Fir. 2017. (Naturally Local Ser.). (ENG., Illus.). 20p. (J). (gr. -1 — 1). bds. 8.99 (978-1-938093-80-7(1), 809380) Duo Pr. LLC.

O'Dell, Kathryn L., et al. My Coast Is Better Than Yours! 2017. (Text Connections Guided Close Reading Ser.). (J). (gr. 2). (978-1-4900-1852-2(2)) Benchmark Education Co.

Shallop, Laura. The Pacific Northwest: Set Of 6. 2011. (Navigators Ser.). (J). pap. 48.00 net. (978-1-4108-6255-6(0)) Benchmark Education Co.

—The Pacific Northwest: Text Pairs. 2008. (Bridges/Navigators Ser.). (J). (gr. 4). 89.00 (978-1-4108-8395-7(7)) Benchmark Education Co.

Smith, Emma Bland. To Live on an Island. Person, Elizabeth, illus. 2019. 32p. (J). (gr. -1-1). 17.99 (978-1-63217-181-8(3), Little Bigfoot) Sasquatch Bks.

NORTHWEST, PACIFIC—FICTION

Allen, Quinc. The Outdoor Chums after Big Game (Illust. 2006. pap. (978-1-4065-0780-5(6)) Dodo Pr.

Anderson, Margaret J. Olla-Piska: Tales of David Douglas. 2006. (ENG., Illus.). 144p. (J). 19.95 (978-0-87595-297-0(6)) Univ. of Washington Pr.

Blomgren, Jennifer. The Tale of Alice's Quilt. 2008. (That Patchwork Place Ser.). (ENG., Illus.). 95p. (YA). (gr. 8-12). per. 14.95 (978-1-56477-833-8(9), That Patchwork Place) Martingale & Co.

Challenger, Robert James. Eagle's Reflection: And Other Northwest Coast Stories, 1 vol. 2009. (ENG., Illus.). 48p. (J). (gr. 1-3). pap. 9.95 (978-1-895811-07-0(4)) Heritage Hse. CAN. Dist: Orca Bk. Pubs. USA.

Condie, Ally & Reichs, Brendan. The Beast. 2019. (Darkdeep Ser.). (ENG.). 336p. (J). 16.99 (978-1-5476-0203-2(1), 900203288, Bloomsbury Children's Bks.) Bloomsbury Publishing USA.

—The Darkdeep. (Darkdeep Ser.). (ENG.). (J). 2019. 288p. pap. 7.99 (978-1-5476-0248-3(1), 900207570) 2018. 272p. 16.99 (978-1-5476-0046-5(2), 900196366) Bloomsbury Publishing USA. (Bloomsbury Children's Bks.).

Condie, Allyson Braithwaite & Reichs, Brendan. The Darkdeep. 2018. 261p. (J). (978-1-5476-0215-5(5)) Bloomsbury Publishing USA.

Crews, Marcia. Little Red Riding Hood of the Pacific Northwest. Trammell, Jeremiah, illus. 2018. (Pacific Northwest Fairy Tales Ser.). 32p. (J). (gr. -1-3). 17.99 (978-1-63217-183-2(X), Little Bigfoot) Sasquatch Bks.

Fernandez, Joy C. Rockman. 2010. 36p. pap. 16.45 (978-1-4520-6751-3(1)) AuthorHouse.

LaCour, Nina. The Disenchantments. 2013. (ENG.). 336p. (YA). (gr. 9). pap. 10.99 (978-0-14-242391-2(2), Speak) Penguin Young Readers Group.

London, Jonathan. Bella Bella. London, Sean, illus. 2016. (Aaron's Wilderness Ser.: 2). (ENG.). 180p. (gr. 3-5). (J). pap. 12.99 (978-0-88240-923-8(9)); (YA). 23.99 (978-1-943328-33-8(1)) West Margin Pr. (West Winds Pr.).

Meyers, Haily & Meyers, Kevin. All Aboard Pacific Northwest: A Recreation Primer, 1 vol. 2017. (Lucy Darling Ser.). (ENG., Illus.). 22p. (J). (— 1). bds. 9.99 (978-1-4236-4601-3(0)) Gibbs Smith, Publisher.

Nickerson, Sara. How to Disappear Completely & Never Be Found. Comport, Sally Wern, illus. 2003. (ENG.). 288p. (J). (gr. 5-18). pap. 5.99 (978-0-06-441027-4(7)) HarperCollins Pubs.

Norris, David A. The CBARCs of Cannon Bay: Storm Clouds over Cannon Bay, 5 bks, Bk.3. Norris, Judy-Jo Harris, illus. 2012. 128p. (YA). pap. 16.95 (978-1-937493-30-1(X)) Dancing Moon Pr.

Parry, Rosanne. Written in Stone. 2014. (Illus.). 208p. (J). (gr. 4-7). pap. 7.99 (978-0-375-87135-1(7), Yearling) Random Hse. Children's Bks.

Richmond, Blair. The Last Mile: The Lithia Trilogy, Book 3. 2018. (ENG.). 244p. (YA). 27.95 (978-1-61822-079-0(9), Ashland Creek Pr.) Byte Level Research.

Sanderson, Whitney. Horse Diaries #5: Golden Sun. Sanderson, Ruth, illus. 2010. (Horse Diaries: 5). 160p. (J). (gr. 3-7). pap. 7.99 (978-0-375-86194-9(7), Random Hse. Bks. for Young Readers) Random Hse. Children's Bks.

Spalding, Andrea & Scow, Alfred. Secret of the Dance, 1 vol. Gait, Darlene, illus. 2009. (ENG.). 32p. (J). (gr. -1-k). 10.95 (978-1-55469-129-6(X)) Orca Bk. Pubs. USA.

Suzuki, David. & Ellis, Sarah. Salmon Forest. Lott, Sheena, illus. 2006. (David Suzuki Institute Ser.). (ENG.). 32p. (J). (gr. k-3). pap. 9.95 (978-1-55365-163-5(4), Greystone Kids) Greystone Books Ltd. CAN. Dist: Publishers Group West (PGW).

Vanasse, Patricia. Resilient. Shalaby, Asharaf, illus. 2013. (ENG.). 328p. (YA). pap. 13.99 (978-0-9860373-2-0(X)) Pants On Fire Pr.

Vaughan, Richard Lee. Eagle Boy: A Pacific Northwest Native Tale. Christiansen, Lee, illus. 2008. 32p. (J). (gr. -1-3). pap. 10.99 (978-1-57061-592-4(6), Little Bigfoot) Sasquatch Bks.

NORTHWEST PASSAGE

Berton, Pierre. Exploring the Frozen North: Pierre Berton's History for Young Canadians, 1 vol. 2006. (ENG., Illus.). 176p. (YA). (gr. 5-10). pap. 16.95 (978-1-894856-93-5(7), 802e7667-6490-4340-b835-b99a43d4d983) Fifth Hse. Pubs. CAN. Dist: Firefly Bks., Ltd.

Connelly, Jack. Henry Hudson: Exploring the Northwest Passage, 1 vol. 2014. (Incredible Explorers Ser.). (ENG., Illus.). 64p. (YA). (gr. 7-7). 35.93 (978-1-5026-0127-8(3), 08dad433-7221-402d-8d8a-14ac592f6816) Cavendish Square Publishing LLC.

Cooke, Tim. Explore with Henry Hudson. 2014. (Travel with the Great Explorers Ser.). (ENG., Illus.). 32p. (J). (gr. 4-5). (978-0-7787-1246-6(X)); pap. (978-0-7787-1258-9(3)) Crabtree Publishing Co.

Donohue, Moira Rose. Jacques Cartier. 2013. (Illus.). 24p. (J). (978-1-938813-03-0(0)) State Standards Publishing, LLC.

Foran, Jill. Search for the Northwest Passage. 2004. (Great Journeys Ser.). (Illus.). 32p. (J). lib. bdg. 26.00 (978-1-59036-205-1(5)) Weigl Pubs., Inc.

—The Search for the Northwest Passage. 2005. (Great Journeys Ser.). (Illus.). 32p. (J). (gr. -1-3). per. 9.95 (978-1-59036-259-4(4)) Weigl Pubs., Inc.

Gleason, Carrie. Henry Hudson: Seeking the Northwest Passage, 1 vol. 2005. (In the Footsteps of Explorers Ser.). (ENG., Illus.). 32p. (J). (gr. -1-9). pap. (978-0-7787-2444-5(1)) Crabtree Publishing Co.

Hyde, Natalie. Expedition to the Arctic. 2013. (ENG., Illus.). 48p. (J). (978-0-7787-1169-8(2)); pap. (978-0-7787-1177-3(3)) Crabtree Publishing Co.

—Search for the Northwest Passage. 2018. (Uncovering the Past: Analyzing Primary Sources Ser.). 48p. (J). (gr. 5-6). (978-0-7787-4799-4(9)) Crabtree Publishing Co.

Keranen, Rachel. The Northwest Passage, 1 vol. 2017. (Routes of Cross-Cultural Exchange Ser.). (ENG.). 96p. (YA). (gr. 8-8). 44.50 (978-1-5026-2695-0(0), af06c108-6b9b-46b8-a7b4-b40a85c938fd) Cavendish Square Publishing LLC.

Knudsen, Anders. Sir John Franklin: The Search for the Northwest Passage. 2007. (In the Footsteps of Explorers Ser.). (ENG., Illus.). 32p. (J). (gr. 4-7). lib. bdg. (978-0-7787-2420-9(4)); pap. (978-0-7787-2456-8(5)) Crabtree Publishing Co.

O'Brien, Cynthia. Explore with John Franklin. 2015. (Travel with the Great Explorers Ser.). (ENG., Illus.). 32p. (J). (gr. 4-5). (978-0-7787-1703-4(8)) Crabtree Publishing Co.

Rogers, Stan. Northwest Passage, 1 vol. James, Matt, illus. 2013. (ENG.). 56p. (J). (gr. 1). 24.95 (978-1-55498-153-3(0)) Groundwood Bks. CAN. Dist: Publishers Group West (PGW).

Sherman, Josepha. Henry Hudson: English Explorer of the Northwest Passage. 2009. (Library of Explorers & Exploration Ser.). 112p. (gr. 5-8). 66.50 (978-1-60853-605-4(X), Rosen Reference) Rosen Publishing Group, Inc., The.

NORTHWEST TERRITORIES

Andre, Julie-Ann & Willett, Mindy. Comme on Se Sent Bien Ici!, 1 vol. Macintosh, Tessa, photos by. 2011. (Land Is Our Storybook Ser.). (FRE., Illus.). 32p. (J). 19.95 (978-1-897252-85-7(4), 0a1ceeee-c240-4715-8827-659a4a8b1073) Fifth Hse. Pubs. CAN. Dist: Firefly Bks., Ltd.

Laws, Gordon D. & Laws, Lauren M. The Northwest Territories. 2003. (Exploring Canada Ser.). (ENG., Illus.). 112p. (J). 30.85 (978-1-59018-049-5(6), Lucent Bks.) Cengage Gale.

McLeod, Tom & Willett, Mindy. Le Delta, C'est Mon Chez Moi, 1 vol. Macintosh, Tessa, photos by. 2011. (Land Is Our Storybook Ser.). (FRE., Illus.). 32p. (J). 19.95 (978-1-897252-84-0(6), e9dd5f27-4ef0-443b-aa8b-a81a3f324858) Fifth Hse. Pubs. CAN. Dist: Firefly Bks., Ltd.

—The Delta Is My Home, 1 vol. Macintosh, Tessa, photos by. 2008. (Land Is Our Storybook Ser.). (ENG., Illus.). 32p. (J). (gr. 5-8). 16.95 (978-1-897252-32-1(3), 16be51b4-8247-4cd7-aaad-b92486f0ed59) Fifth Hse. Pubs. CAN. Dist: Firefly Bks., Ltd.

Stephenson, Wendy. Idaa Trail: In the Steps of Our Ancestors, 1 vol. Downey, Autumn, illus. 2005. (ENG.). 64p. (J). (gr. 2-5). 18.95 (978-0-88899-576-6(8)) Groundwood Bks. CAN. Dist: Publishers Group West (PGW).

Willett, Mindy. Viens Avec Moi: Nous Apprendrons Ensemble!, 1 vol. Macintosh, Tessa, photos by. 2011. (Land Is Our Storybook Ser.). (FRE., Illus.). 32p. (J). (gr. 1-2). 19.95 (978-1-897252-98-7(6), 968f188a-c95b-4311-9346-95e22c36e451) Fifth Hse. Pubs. CAN. Dist: Firefly Bks., Ltd.

Willett, Mindy & Enzoe, Peter. Le Caribou Nourrit Notre âme: The Caribou Feed Our Soul (French), 1 vol. Benoit, France, tr. Macintosh, Tessa, photos by. 2012. (Land Is Our Storybook Ser.: 6). (FRE., Illus.). 32p. (J). 19.95 (978-1-927083-05-5(2), ce593b32-8f5b-4c51-873d-3c1ffbba5b75) Fifth Hse. Pubs. CAN. Dist: Firefly Bks., Ltd.

NORTHWEST TERRITORIES—FICTION

Fletcher, Archibald Lee. Boy Scouts in Northern Wilds. 2018. (ENG., Illus.). 132p. (YA). (gr. 7-12). pap. (978-93-5297-269-2(4)) Alpha Editions.

—Boy Scouts in Northern Wilds. 2017. (ENG., Illus.). (J). 22.95 (978-1-374-94345-2(2)) Capital Communications, Inc.

Football, Virginia. How the Fox Saved the People. Wedzin, James, illus. 2009. (Fox Ser.). (ENG & DGR.). 56p. (gr. k-6). 26.95 (978-1-894778-75-6(8)) Theytus Bks., Ltd. CAN. Dist: Univ. of Toronto Pr.

Wilson, John. The Alchemist's Dream. 2009. (ENG.). 248p. (YA). (gr. 7-18). pap. (978-1-55470-101-8(5)) Me to We.

NORTHWESTERN STATES

Here are entered works on the northern part of the United States between the Great Lakes or Mississippi River and the Pacific Ocean.

Holmes, Parker. Amazing Snakes of the Northwest, 1 vol. 2014. (Amazing Snakes Ser.). (ENG., Illus.). 24p. (J). (gr. 3-3). 25.27 (978-1-4777-6507-4(7), 9f49225d-95e9-4043-9f95-c82c66d72424, PowerKids Pr.) Rosen Publishing Group, Inc., The.

NORWAY

Bodden, Valerie. To the South Pole. 2011. (Great Expeditions Ser.). (ENG.). 48p. (J). (gr. 5-8). pap. 12.00 (978-0-89812-667-9(3), 22161, Creative Paperbacks) Creative Co., The.

Bowman, Chris. Norway. 2020. (Country Profiles Ser.). (ENG., Illus.). 32p. (J). (gr. 3-8). lib. bdg. 27.95 (978-1-64487-171-3(8), Blastoff! Discovery) Bellwether Media.

Discover Norway. 2012. (Discover Countries Ser.). (ENG., Illus.). 32p. (J). (gr. 3-5). 25.25 (978-1-4488-6623-6(5), PowerKids Pr.) Rosen Publishing Group, Inc., The.

Fouberg, Erin & Hogan, Edward. Norway. 2003. (Modern World Nations Ser.). (ENG., Illus.). 150p. (gr. 6-12). 35.00 (978-0-7910-7479-4(X), P113859, Facts On File) Infobase Holdings, Inc.

Ganeri, Anita. How to Live Like a Viking Warrior. Epelbaum, Mariano, illus. 2015. (How to Live Like ... Ser.). (ENG.). 32p. (J). (gr. 3-6). lib. bdg. 27.99 (978-1-4677-6354-7(3), b777eb9b-1d65-475c-8f9c-8cd0579a0a5b, Hungry Tomato (r)) Lerner Publishing Group.

Hand, Carol. Norway, 1 vol. 2013. (Countries of the World Set 2 Ser.). (ENG.). 144p. (YA). (gr. 6-12). lib. bdg. 42.79 *(978-1-61783-633-6(8)*, 4890, Essential Library) ABDO Publishing Co.

—Norway, 1 vol. 2020. (Exploring World Cultures (First Edition) Ser.). (ENG.). 32p. (gr. 3-3). pap. 12.16 *(978-1-5026-5689-6(2)*, ae7068b8-3038-4590-9844-f2836cd0cab6) Cavendish Square Publishing LLC.

Kagda, Sakina & Cooke, Barbara. Norway, 1 vol. 2nd rev. ed. 2007. (Cultures of the World (Second Edition)(r) Ser.). (ENG., Illus.). 144p. (gr. 5-5). lib. bdg. 49.79 *(978-0-7614-2067-5(3)*, 83c806b9-8a5a-444a-a789-31a3f4ec077c) Cavendish Square Publishing LLC.

Kagda, Sakina, et al. Norway, 1 vol. 3rd rev. ed. 2016. (Cultures of the World (Third Edition)(r) Ser.). (ENG.). 144p. (gr. 5-5). lib. bdg. 48.79 *(978-1-5026-1848-1(6)*, 0bf37022-9043-4f2c-9c25-8c2b72e5ac86) Cavendish Square Publishing LLC.

Llewellyn, Claire. A Dark Winter Turquoise Band. 2017. (Cambridge Reading Adventures Ser.). (ENG., Illus.). 24p. pap. 7.35 *(978-1-108-43978-7(0))* Cambridge Univ. Pr.

Lunge-Larsen, Lise. The Race of the Birkebeiners. Azarian, Mary, illus. 2007. (ENG.). 32p. (J). (gr. k — 1). 7.99 *(978-0-618-91599-6(0)*, 1014894, Clarion Bks.) HarperCollins Pubs.

Manning, Jack. Christmas in Norway, 1 vol. 2013. (Christmas Around the World Ser.). (ENG.). 24p. (J). (gr. 1-3). 27.99 *(978-1-4765-3101-4(3)*, 123083, Capstone Pr.) Capstone.

Mis, Melody S. How to Draw Norway's Sights & Symbols. 2009. (Kid's Guide to Drawing the Countries of the World Ser.). 48p. (gr. 4-4). 53.00 *(978-1-61511-119-0(0)*, PowerKids Pr.) Rosen Publishing Group, Inc., The.

Murray, Julie. Norway, 1 vol. 2014. (Explore the Countries Ser.). (ENG.). 40p. (J). (gr. 2-5). lib. bdg. 35.64 *(978-1-62403-345-2(8)*, 1366, Big Buddy Bks.) ABDO Publishing Co.

Rose, Elizabeth. A Primary Source Guide to Norway. (Countries of the World). 24p. (gr. 2-3). 2009. 42.50 *(978-1-61512-041-3(6))* 2003. (ENG., Illus.). (J). lib. bdg. 26.27 *(978-0-8239-6732-2(8)*, 0abcf0e7-a7c4-478e-b791-d8a6a1f3618e) Rosen Publishing Group, Inc., The. (PowerKids Pr.).

Undset, Sigrid, ed. True & Untrue & Other Norse Tales. Chapman, Frederick T., illus. 2013. (ENG.). 264p. pap. 16.95 *(978-0-8166-7828-0(6))* Univ. of Minnesota Pr.

Wan, Vanessa. Welcome to Norway, 1 vol. 2004. (Welcome to My Country Ser.). (ENG., Illus.). 48p. (J). (gr. 2-4). lib. bdg. 29.67 *(978-0-8368-2562-6(4)*, 30e8fcdd-edbf-4c41-94bb-d4ea431b28d5, Gareth Stevens Learning Library) Stevens, Gareth Publishing LLLP.

Yomtov, Nel. Roald Amundsen Explores the South Pole. 2015. (Extraordinary Explorers Ser.). (ENG., Illus.). 24p. (J). (gr. 3-8). lib. bdg. 29.95 *(978-1-62617-295-1(1)*, Black Sheep) Bellwether Media.

Zobel, Derek. Norway. 2011. (Exploring Countries Ser.). (ENG., Illus.). 32p. (J). (gr. 3-7). lib. bdg. 27.95 *(978-1-60014-620-6(1)*, Blastoff! Readers) Bellwether Media.

NORWAY—FICTION

Asbjørnsen, Peter Christen. The Three Billy Goats Gruff. Vohra, Sibi, illus. 2010. (J). *(978-1-60617-149-3(6))* Teaching Strategies, LLC.

Bentley, Sue. Snowy Wishes. 2013. (Magic Puppy Ser.). lib. bdg. 16.00 *(978-0-606-32124-2(1))* Turtleback.

d'Aulaire, Ingri & d'Aulaire, Edgar. The Terrible Troll-Bird. 2007. (ENG., Illus.). 52p. (J). (gr. k-4). 15.95 *(978-1-59017-252-0(3)*, NYR Children's Collection) New York Review of Bks., Inc., The.

d'Aulaire, Ingri & d'Aulaire, Edgar Parin. Ola. 2013. (ENG., Illus.). 56p. 16.95 *(978-0-8166-9017-6(0))* Univ. of Minnesota Pr.

Daykin, Chloe. The Boy Who Hit Play, Bk. 2. 2018. (ENG.). 336p. (J). pap. 9.95 *(978-0-571-32678-5(1)*, Faber & Faber Children's Bks.) Faber & Faber, Inc.

Endicott, Megan. In the Hall of the Mountain King. 2013. 48p. pap. 20.95 *(978-1-4582-0789-0(7)*, Abbott Pr.) Author Solutions, LLC.

A Foal Is Born. 2007. (J). *(978-1-933343-46-4(X)*, PONY) Stabenfeldt Inc.

Gulliksen, Anne. A Boy from Nøtterøy. 2009. 108p. pap. 13.00 *(978-1-59858-939-9(3))* Dog Ear Publishing, LLC.

Haig, Matt. Shadow Forest. 2009. pap. 1.00 *(978-1-4074-4391-1(7))* Recorded Bks., Inc.

Halse, Leif. The Boys from Vangen: Vangsgutane. Huntrods, Alexander Knud, tr. Nilssen, Jens R., illus. 2009. (ENG & NNO.). 176p. (J). 19.95 *(978-0-9760541-5-3(9))* Astri My Astri Publishing.

Haugaard, Erik Christian. Hakon of Rogen's Saga. Dillon, Leo & Dillon, Diane, illus. 2013. 144p. pap. 11.95 *(978-0-8166-8127-3(9))* Univ. of Minnesota Pr.

Hayes, Tracey J. Bartina in Trouble Again. 2009. 64p. pap. 15.99 *(978-1-4415-2050-0(3))* Xlibris Corp.

Hole, Stian. Garmann's Secret. 2011. (ENG., Illus.). 56p. (J). 17.00 *(978-0-8028-5400-1(1)*, Eerdmans Bks For Young Readers) Eerdmans, William B. Publishing Co.

Ingemundsen, Linni. The Unpredictability of Being Human. 2018. (ENG.). 285p. (YA). (gr. 6-9). pap. 12.95 *(978-1-944589-36-3(8)*, Incorgnito Publishing Pr.) Incorgnito Publishing Pr. LLC.

Inger's Promise: Evaluation Guide. 2006. (J). *(978-1-55942-409-7(5))* Witcher Productions.

Jacobsen, Annie. The Terrible Troll Cat. Hanson, Susan Jo, illus. 2012. 32p. (J). 9.98 *(978-0-9778276-4-0(X))* Pickled Herring Pr.

Jennewein, James & Parker, Tom S. RuneWarriors. 2008. (RuneWarriors Ser.). 320p. (J). (gr. 3-7). lib. bdg. 17.89 *(978-0-06-144937-6(7)*, Geringer, Laura Book) HarperCollins Pubs.

Johnson, Lois Walfrid. The Raider's Promise. 2006. (Viking Quest Ser.: 5). (ENG., Illus.). 304p. (J). (gr. 3-3). per. 10.99 *(978-0-8024-3116-5(X))* Moody Pubs.

Louise, Martha. Why Kings & Queens Don't Wear Crowns. Sevig-Fajardo, Mari Elise, tr. from NOR. Nyhus, Svein, illus. 2005. Orig. Title: Hvorfor de kongelige ikke har krone på Hodet. 32p. (J). 17.95 *(978-1-57534-037-1(2)*, CSC 100) Skandisk, Inc.

Lund, Celia. Square Sails & Dragons. 2006. 284p. per. 19.95 *(978-1-4120-5758-5(2))* Trafford Publishing.

Nesbo, Jo. Doctor Proctor's Fart Powder. Chace, Tara F., tr. Lowery, Mike, illus. 2010. (Doctor Proctor's Fart Powder Ser.). (ENG.). 288p. (J). (gr. 3-7). pap. 8.99 *(978-1-4169-7973-9(5)*, Aladdin) Simon & Schuster Children's Publishing.

Nesbø, Jo. Doctor Proctor's Fart Powder. 2010. (Dr. Proctor's Fart Powder Ser.: 1). lib. bdg. 18.40 *(978-0-606-15419-2(1))* Turtleback.

Nesbo, Jo. Doctor Proctor's Fart Powder, 1. Chace, Tara F., tr. from NOR. Lowery, Mike, illus. 2009. (Doctor Proctor's Fart Powder Ser.). (ENG.). 272p. (J). (gr. 3-7). 17.99 *(978-1-4169-7972-2(7)*, Aladdin) Simon & Schuster Children's Publishing.

—Silent (but Deadly) Night. Lowery, Mike, illus. 2017. (Doctor Proctor's Fart Powder Ser.). (ENG.). 368p. (J). (gr. 3-7). 17.99 *(978-1-5344-0999-6(8)*, Aladdin) Simon & Schuster Children's Publishing.

—Silent (but Deadly) Night. Lowery, Mike, illus. 2018. (Doctor Proctor's Fart Powder Ser.). (ENG.). 368p. (J). (gr. 3-7). pap. 8.99 *(978-1-5344-1000-8(7)*, Simon & Schuster/Paula Wiseman Bks.) Simon & Schuster/Paula Wiseman Bks.

—Who Cut the Cheese? Chace, Tara F., tr. Lowery, Mike, illus. 2012. (Doctor Proctor's Fart Powder Ser.). (ENG.). 464p. (J). (gr. 3-7). pap. 8.99 *(978-1-4424-3308-3(6))*; 17.99 *(978-1-4424-3307-6(8))* Simon & Schuster Children's Publishing. (Aladdin).

Ovreas, Hakon. Brown. Torseter, Oyvind, illus. 2019. (My Alter Ego Is a Superhero Ser.: 1). 136p. (J). (gr. k-5). pap. 9.95 *(978-1-59270-251-0(1))* Enchanted Lion Bks., LLC.

Parr, Maria. Astrid the Unstoppable. 2018. (ENG., Illus.). 320p. (J). (gr. 2-5). 16.99 *(978-1-5362-0017-1(4))* Candlewick Pr.

Paulson, Ingrid. Valkyrie Rising. 2012. (ENG.). 352p. (YA). (gr. 8). 17.99 *(978-0-06-202572-2(4)*, HarperTeen) HarperCollins Pubs.

Peers, Bobbie. William Wenton & the Impossible Puzzle. Chace, Tara F., tr. (William Wenton Ser.: 1). (ENG.). (J). (gr. 3-7). 2018. 288p. pap. 7.99 *(978-1-4814-7826-7(5))* 2017. (Illus.). 272p. 16.99 *(978-1-4814-7825-0(7))* Simon & Schuster Children's Publishing. (Aladdin).

Preus, Margi. West of the Moon. 2014. (ENG., Illus.). 224p. (J). (gr. 5-9). 16.95 *(978-1-4197-0896-1(1)*, 1062301, Amulet Bks.) Abrams, Inc.

Rossing, Nina. Fjord Blue. 2016. (ENG., Illus.). (YA). 27.99 *(978-1-63533-016-8(5))*; 256p. pap. 16.99 *(978-1-63476-385-1(8))* Dreamspinner Pr. (Harmony Ink Pr.).

Røssland, Ingelin & Røssland, Ingelin. Minus Me. 2015. (ENG.). 288p. (YA). (gr. 4-9). pap. 10.99 *(978-1-78074-694-4(6)*, 1780746946, Rock the Boat) Oneworld Pubns. GBR. Dist: Grantham Bk. Services.

Sharp, Margery. The Rescuers. Williams, Garth, illus. 2016. (ENG.). 160p. (J). (gr. 4-7). pap. 11.99 *(978-1-68137-007-1(7)*, NYRB Kids) New York Review of Bks., Inc., The.

Thorne-Thomsen, Gudrun. East O' the Sun & West O' the Moon. Richardson, Frederick, illus. 2009. 148p. pap. 8.95 *(978-1-59915-337-7(8))* Yesterday's Classics.

—East o' the Sun & West o' the Moon: With Other Norwegian Folk Tales. 2017. (ENG., Illus.). (J). pap. 12.95 *(978-1-374-81425-7(3))* Capital Communications, Inc.

Undset, Sigrid. Sigurd & His Brave Companions: A Tale of Medieval Norway. Bull Teilman, Gunvor, illus. 2013. (ENG.). 152p. pap. 16.95 *(978-0-8166-7826-6(X))* Univ. of Minnesota Pr.

NORWAY—HISTORY—FICTION

Casanova, Mary. The Klipfish Code. 2012. (ENG.). 240p. (J). (gr. 5-7). pap. 7.99 *(978-0-547-74447-6(1)*, 1485490, Clarion Bks.) HarperCollins Pubs.

McSwigan, Marie. Snow Treasure. 2006. (Illus.). 208p. (J). (gr. 3-7). 7.99 *(978-0-14-240224-5(9)*, Puffin Books) Penguin Young Readers Group.

Preus, Margi. Shadow on the Mountain. 2014. (ENG., Illus.). 320p. (YA). (gr. 3-7). pap. 9.99 *(978-1-4197-1159-6(8)*, 1006603) Abrams, Inc.

NORWEGIAN LANGUAGE

Hippocrene Books Staff, ed. Norwegian Children's Picture Dictionary: English-Norwegian/Norwegian-English. 2006. (ENG., Illus.). 114p. pap. 14.95 *(978-0-7818-1164-4(3))* Hippocrene Bks., Inc.

Modéré, Armelle. My First English/Norwegian Dictionary of Sentences. 2008. (NOR & ENG., Illus.). 128p. (J). *(978-1-57534-048-7(8))* Skandisk, Inc.

NORWEGIANS—UNITED STATES—FICTION

Laybourne, Emmy. Berserker. 2018. (Berserker Ser.: 1). (ENG.). 352p. (YA). pap. 10.99 *(978-1-250-18076-6(7)*, 900190256) Square Fish.

Peterson, Esther Allen. Coming of Age. 2010. (J). pap. *(978-0-88092-485-6(3))* Royal Fireworks Publishing Co.

—The House That Cared. 2010. (J). pap. *(978-0-88092-505-1(1))* Royal Fireworks Publishing Co.

—A Long Journey to a New Home. 2006. (J). pap. *(978-0-88092-470-2(5))*; lib. bdg. *(978-0-88092-469-6(1))* Royal Fireworks Publishing Co.

—Will Spring Come? 2009. (Illus.). 157p. (J). *(978-0-88092-768-0(2))* Royal Fireworks Publishing Co.

Push to the West (Norwegians) 76p. (YA). (gr. 6-12). pap. 9.95 *(978-0-8224-3678-2(7))* Globe Fearon Educational Publishing.

NOTATION, MUSICAL

see Musical Notation

NOVA SCOTIA

Beckett, Harry. Nova Scotia. 2003. (Eye on Canada Ser.). (Illus.). 32p. (J). pap. 9.95 *(978-1-894705-05-9(X))* Weigl Pubs., Inc.

Boudreau, Hélène. Life in a Fishing Community. 2009. (Learn about Rural Life Ser.). (ENG., Illus.). 32p. (J). (gr. 3-4). pap. *(978-0-7787-5085-7(X))* Crabtree Publishing Co.

Bowles, Stella. My River: Cleaning up the Lahave River. 2018. (ENG.). 96p. (J). (gr. 3-6). pap. 8.99 *(978-1-4595-0551-3(4)*, a5c560da-b2bc-49df-80f9-c4b26c017a7e) Formac Publishing Co., Ltd. CAN. Dist: Lerner Publishing Group.

Grant, Vicki. The Dreadful Truth: the Halifax Citadel. Pilsworth, Graham, illus. 2003. (Dreadful Truth Ser.). (ENG.). 80p. (J). (gr. 3-8). *(978-0-88780-599-8(X))* Formac Publishing Co., Ltd.

Joyce, Jaime. A Fatal Fall: Was It an Accident or Murder? 2011. (J). pap. *(978-0-545-32809-8(8))* Scholastic, Inc.

Lamb, Lee. Oak Island Family: The Restall Hunt for Buried Treasure. 2012. (ENG., Illus.). 136p. (YA). pap. 19.99 *(978-1-4597-0342-1(1))* Dundurn Pr. CAN. Dist: Publishers Group West (PGW).

—Oak Island Family: The Restall Hunt for Buried Treasure (Large Print 16pt) 2013. 204p. pap. *(978-1-4596-6324-4(1))* ReadHowYouWant.com, Ltd.

Redmond, Shirley Raye. Oak Island Treasure Pit, 1 vol. 2011. (Mysterious Encounters Ser.). (ENG.). 48p. (gr. 4-8). lib. bdg. 35.23 *(978-0-7377-5140-6(1)*, be1c3ddf-05ba-4628-b9c1-7d9d43c3e88f, KidHaven Publishing) Greenhaven Publishing LLC.

Stanbridge, Joanne. Maurice Ruddick: Un Survivant. 2004. (FRE., Illus.). (J). *(978-2-7650-0744-9(6))* Les Editions de la Cheneliere, Inc.

Tooke, Susan. B Is for Bluenose: A Nova Scotia Alphabet. Tooke, Susan, illus. 2008. (Discover Canada Province by Province Ser.). (ENG., Illus.). 40p. (J). (gr. 1-3). 19.99 *(978-1-58536-362-9(6)*, 202147) Sleeping Bear Pr.

Walker, Sally M. Blizzard of Glass: The Halifax Explosion Of 1917. 2014. (ENG., Illus.). 160p. (YA). (gr. 5-9). pap. 16.99 *(978-1-250-04008-4(6)*, 900123711) Square Fish.

Watson, Joan & Creed, Murray. The Accidental Farmer: The Story of Ross Farm, 1 vol. 2017. (Stories of Our Past Ser.). (ENG., Illus.). 128p. pap. 15.95 *(978-1-77108-527-4(4)*, 39e531ec-2366-4499-a968-326aa3a282c6) Nimbus Publishing, Ltd. CAN. Dist: Baker & Taylor Publisher Services (BTPS).

NOVA SCOTIA—FICTION

Aker, Don. The Fifth Rule. 2014. (ENG.). 256p. (YA). (gr. 8). pap. 8.99 *(978-0-06-231348-5(7)*, HarperCollins) HarperCollins Pubs.

—The First Stone. 2004. (ENG.). 304p. (J). mass mkt. 6.50 *(978-0-00-639286-6(5)*, Harper Trophy) HarperCollins Pubs.

Ashby, Freya Katrina. Summer at the Dunes: A Deirdre Carlisle Mystery. 2007. 108p. per. 9.95 *(978-0-595-43663-7(3))* iUniverse, Inc.

Barkhouse, Joyce & Barkhouse, Janet. Pit Pony: The Picture Book. Smith, Sydney, illus. 2012. (ENG.). 32p. (J). (gr. -1-2). 14.95 *(978-1-4595-0143-0(8)*, 0143) Formac Publishing Co., Ltd. CAN. Dist: Formac Lorimer Bks. Ltd.

Barkhouse, Joyce & Lucas, Zoe. Pit Pony, 1 vol. 2nd ed. 2010. (ENG., Illus.). 136p. (J). (gr. 3-5). 12.95 *(978-0-88780-924-8(3)*, e8068c4f-3b80-4f50-94f2-76c6f29c1921) Formac Publishing Co., Ltd. CAN. Dist: Lerner Publishing Group.

Bass, Karen. Two Times a Traitor. 2017. (ENG., Illus.). 288p. (J). (gr. 4-8). 15.95 *(978-1-77278-031-4(6))*; pap. 10.95 *(978-1-77278-024-6(3))* Pajama Pr. CAN. Dist: Publishers Group West (PGW).

Bastedo, Jamie. Free As the Wind, 1 vol. Tooke, Susan, illus. 2010. (ENG.). 32p. (J). (gr. 2-4). pap. 10.95 *(978-0-88995-446-5(1)*, f48a8b3c-4e9a-4203-ade3-d7446e3c4f11) Trifolium Bks., Inc. CAN. Dist: Firefly Bks., Ltd.

Bawtree, Michael. Joe Howe to the Rescue, 1 vol. 2004. (ENG., Illus.). 152p. (J). (gr. 4-7). pap. 12.95 *(978-1-55109-495-3(9)*, 6abc5d4c-fffd-41f0-afc2-40b817af61ce) Nimbus Publishing, Ltd. CAN. Dist: Baker & Taylor Publisher Services (BTPS).

Bieber Domm, Kristin. Hatchling's Journey, 1 vol. Domm, Jeffrey, illus. 2003. (ENG.). 40p. (J). (gr. -1-3). pap. 10.95 *(978-1-55109-438-0(X)*, f57d42de-ae15-4d0b-b10c-3384cc83a12d) Nimbus Publishing, Ltd. CAN. Dist: Baker & Taylor Publisher Services (BTPS).

Choyce, Lesley. Hell's Hotel, 1 vol. rev. ed. 2008. (Lorimer SideStreets Ser.). (ENG.). 224p. (YA). (gr. 9-12). 8.99 *(978-1-55277-022-1(2)*, 82130189-e9e2-4997-9190-40a0d07205e1); 26.19 *(978-1-55277-038-2(9)*, 038) James Lorimer & Co. Ltd., Pubs. CAN. Dist: Lerner Publishing Group, Children's Plus, Inc.

Coates, Jan. King of Keji, 1 vol. MacKinnon, Patsy, illus. 2015. (ENG.). 32p. (J). (gr. 1-3). pap. 12.95 *(978-1-77108-281-5(X)*, c3c6c62e-8fd5-4e3b-b25d-d7005121e3ed) Nimbus Publishing, Ltd. CAN. Dist: Baker & Taylor Publisher Services (BTPS).

Coates, Jan L. The Power of Harmony: A Novel, 1 vol. 2013. (ENG., Illus.). 260p. (J). (gr. 4-6). pap. 12.95 *(978-0-88995-495-3(X)*, a4cef73e-02a1-4ae9-89d1-04f54f86ad9d) Red Deer Pr. CAN. Dist: Firefly Bks., Ltd.

Cook, Lyn. Flight from the Fortress, 1 vol. 2006. (ENG.). 156p. (J). (gr. 5-8). per. 7.95 *(978-1-55041-792-0(4)*, 92ef756c-8e41-4829-b659-cf8fe5b05d66) Trifolium Bks., Inc. CAN. Dist: Firefly Bks., Ltd.

Dale, Mitzi. The Great & Awful Summer, 1 vol. 2007. (ENG.). 192p. (YA). (gr. 8-12). pap. 9.95 *(978-1-55109-614-8(5))* Nimbus Publishing, Ltd. CAN. Dist: Orca Bk. Pubs. USA.

Dinsdale, Christopher. Betrayed: The Legend of Oak Island. 2009. (Stories of Canada Ser.). (ENG., Illus.). 304p. (J). (gr. 6-8). pap. 10.95 *(978-1-894917-91-9(X)*, Napoleon & Co.) Dundurn Pr. CAN. Dist: Publishers Group West (PGW).

Fraser, Ivan. Peggy of the Cove: Secrets. 2008. (ENG.). 182p. (J). pap. 15.00 *(978-0-9736872-6-2(6)*, ec4e87eb-e8d2-4197-a60f-1136aac623d9) Nimbus Publishing, Ltd. CAN. Dist: Baker & Taylor Publisher Services (BTPS).

Grant, Shauntay. Africville, 1 vol. Campbell, Eva, illus. 2018. (ENG.). 32p. (J). (gr. k-2). 19.99 *(978-1-77306-043-9(0))* Groundwood Bks. CAN. Dist: Publishers Group West (PGW).

Gunnery, Sylvia. Personal Best, 1 vol. 2005. (Lorimer Sports Stories Ser.). (ENG.). 112p. (J). (gr. 3-7). 17.44 *(978-1-55028-897-1(0)*, 897) James Lorimer & Co. Ltd., Pubs. CAN. Dist: Children's Plus, Inc.

Halsey, Jacqueline. Explosion Newsie. Migani, Loretta, illus. 2015. (ENG.). 32p. (J). (gr. -1-4). 16.95 *(978-1-4595-0401-1(1)*, 0401) Formac Publishing Co., Ltd. CAN. Dist: Formac Lorimer Bks. Ltd.

Hull, Maureen. View from a Kite, 1 vol. 2006. (ENG., Illus.). 320p. (J). (gr. 8-12). pap. 15.95 *(978-1-55109-591-2(2)*, 6f32f5b9-f6a2-4631-b4f2-24c39c9047b3, Vagrant Pr.) Nimbus Publishing, Ltd. CAN. Dist: Baker & Taylor Publisher Services (BTPS).

James, Eric. The Spooky Express Nova Scotia. Piwowarski, Marcin, illus. 2017. (Spooky Express Ser.). (ENG.). 32p. (J). (gr. k-6). 9.99 *(978-1-4926-5387-5(X)*, Hometown World) Sourcebooks, Inc.

Larson, Hope. Mercury. Larson, Hope, illus. 2010. (ENG., Illus.). 240p. (YA). (gr. 7-18). pap. 17.99 *(978-1-4169-3588-9(6)*, Atheneum Bks. for Young Readers) Simon & Schuster Children's Publishing.

Lawson, Julie. A Blinding Light, 1 vol. 2017. (ENG.). 264p. (J). (gr. 4-7). pap. 14.95 *(978-1-77108-541-0(X)*, ba0f87d3-0c6b-482f-98c1-0175b91b0487) Nimbus Publishing, Ltd. CAN. Dist: Baker & Taylor Publisher Services (BTPS).

Lightburn, Sandra. Pumpkin People, 1 vol. Lightburn, Ron, illus. 2008. (ENG.). 32p. (J). (gr. -1-k). 17.95 *(978-1-55109-681-0(1)*, 13b97ce6-9128-4c3d-bb24-cd1b6efa4608) Nimbus Publishing, Ltd. CAN. Dist: Baker & Taylor Publisher Services (BTPS).

May, Maggie. Pilot, Swaydy & Friends. Larade, April, illus. 2011. 30p. pap. 24.95 *(978-1-4560-8499-8(2))* America Star Bks.

Montgomery, L. M. Anne of the Island. 2006. (ENG.). pap. *(978-1-4068-2171-0(3))*; pap. *(978-1-4068-3175-7(1))* Echo Library.

—Anne of the Island. 2004. reprint ed. pap. 1.99 *(978-1-4192-0718-1(0))*; pap. 30.95 *(978-1-4179-0885-1(8))* Kessinger Publishing, LLC.

—Anne of the Island. l.t. ed. 2004. 396p. 26.00 *(978-1-58287-640-5(1))* North Bks.

—Anne of the Island. 2010. (Puffin Classics Ser.). (ENG.). 368p. (J). (gr. 5-7). pap. 7.99 *(978-0-14-132736-5(7)*, Puffin Books) Penguin Young Readers Group.

Nervelle, Rosemarie. The Witch of Beaver Creek Mine. 2007. (ENG.). 160p. (J). (gr. 3-7). 14.95 *(978-0-89272-741-4(1))*; 2nd ed. pap. 9.95 *(978-0-89272-763-6(2))* Down East Bks.

Payzant, Joan M. Who's a Scaredy Cat! A Story of the Halifax Explosion, 1 vol. Simons, Marijke, tr. Simons, Marijke, illus. 2005. (ENG.). 85p. (J). (gr. 4-7). pap. 11.95 *(978-1-55109-456-4(8)*, 3b1c6d2a-645b-45bf-aff6-2fa80e2e8b53) Nimbus Publishing, Ltd. CAN. Dist: Baker & Taylor Publisher Services (BTPS).

Perkyns, Dorothy. Last Days in Africville. 2005. (Illus.). 144p. (YA). pap., tchr. ed. *(978-0-88878-446-9(5)*, Sandcastle Bks.) Dundurn Pr.

—Last Days in Africville. 2006. (ENG.). 120p. (J). (gr. 4-7). pap. 10.99 *(978-1-55002-630-6(5))* Dundurn Pr. CAN. Dist: Publishers Group West (PGW).

Poplawska, Yolanda, illus. Halifax Harbour 123 (BB), 1 vol. 2014. (ENG.). 10p. (J). (gr. -1 — 1). bds. 9.95 *(978-1-77108-002-6(7)*, 3395fa8b-2301-459b-8f7f-95ffb90185a7) Nimbus Publishing, Ltd. CAN. Dist: Baker & Taylor Publisher Services (BTPS).

Ryan, Tom. A Giant Man from a Tiny Town: A Story of Angus MacAskill, 1 vol. Hoyt, Christopher, illus. 2018. (ENG.). 32p. (J). (gr. -1-k). 22.95 *(978-1-77108-654-7(8)*, 30748773-4b07-43a8-a6e7-b868399e986e) Nimbus Publishing, Ltd. CAN. Dist: Baker & Taylor Publisher Services (BTPS).

Schwarzkopf, Tom. Danger at Mason's Island, 1 vol. 2006. (ENG.). 127p. (J). (gr. 4-7). pap. 10.95 *(978-1-55109-562-2(9)*, 6c93e895-88d1-4aaa-ba25-534b2c668e92) Nimbus Publishing, Ltd. CAN. Dist: Baker & Taylor Publisher Services (BTPS).

Smallman, Steve. Santa Is Coming to Nova Scotia. Dunn, Robert, illus. 2nd ed. 2019. (Santa Is Coming... Ser.). (ENG.). 40p. (J). (gr. -1-3). 12.99 *(978-1-7282-0088-0(1)*, Hometown World) Sourcebooks, Inc.

Thompson, Lisa. Search for the Lost Cavern. 2007. (Illus.). 56p. (J). pap. *(978-1-4207-0718-2(3))* Sundance/Newbridge Educational Publishing.

Trenowden, Mark. The Miracle of Bean's Bullion. 2012. 192p. pap. *(978-1-84667-041-1(1))* Derwent Pr., The.

Vaughan, Garth. Tommy's New Block Skates PB, 1 vol. Smith, David Preston, illus. 2007. (ENG.). 36p. (J). (gr. 1-3). pap. 12.95 *(978-1-55109-620-9(X)*, 1d8ca434-d869-49ba-aaa1-01edef613a79) Nimbus Publishing, Ltd. CAN. Dist: Baker & Taylor Publisher Services (BTPS).

Viva, Frank. Sea Change: A TOON Graphic. 2016. (Illus.). 120p. (J). (gr. 3-7). 18.95 *(978-1-935179-92-4(6)*, Toon Books) Astra Publishing Hse.

Wesley, Gloria Ann. Abigail's Wish, 1 vol. Rudnicki, Richard, illus. 2016. (ENG.). 32p. (J). (gr. 1-3). 22.95 *(978-1-77108-439-0(1)*, defd3a5e-1b53-4362-8bd4-703fa1483fd1) Nimbus Publishing, Ltd. CAN. Dist: Baker & Taylor Publisher Services (BTPS).

Wilson, Budge. The Leaving, 1 vol. (ENG.). 176p. (J). mass mkt. 6.95 *(978-0-7736-7363-2(6))* Stoddart Kids CAN. Dist: Fitzhenry & Whiteside, Ltd.

NOVELISTS

see Authors

NUCLEAR ENERGY

Bailey, Diane. Nuclear Power. 2014. (Harnessing Energy Ser.). (ENG.). 48p. (J). (gr. 5-8). pap. 12.00 *(978-0-89812-997-7(4)*, 21359, Creative Paperbacks) Creative Co., The.

Benduhn, Tea. Energía Nuclear (Nuclear Power), 1 vol. 2008. (Energía para el Presente (Energy for Today) Ser.). (SPA.). 24p. (gr. 3-3). (J). lib. bdg. 24.67 *(978-0-8368-9268-0(2)*, efaf551b-2983-49ac-91f8-85da85139b69); pap. 9.15 *(978-0-8368-9367-0(0)*, f512ad48-12cd-4a1b-b228-fbda174fcb38) Stevens, Gareth Publishing LLLP. (Weekly Reader Leveled Readers).

—Nuclear Power, 1 vol. 2008. (Energy for Today Ser.). (ENG.). 24p. (gr. 3-3). (J). lib. bdg. 24.67 *(978-0-8368-9262-8(3)*, 75a03bf9-9898-4309-8a58-3c22a49f5885); pap. 9.15 *(978-0-8368-9361-8(1)*,

M N O

f64e8880-b818-4658-940c-68162d4b8694) Stevens, Gareth Publishing LLLP. (Weekly Reader Leveled Readers).

Benoit, Peter. Cornerstones of Freedom, Third Series: the Nuclear Age. 2012. (Cornerstones of Freedom, Third Ser.). (ENG., Illus.). 64p. (J). pap. 8.95 *(978-0-531-28162-8(0)*, Children's Pr.) Scholastic Library Publishing.

—True Book - Disasters: Nuclear Meltdowns. 2011. (True Bk Ser.). (ENG., Illus.). 48p. (J). pap. 6.95 *(978-0-531-26627-4(3)*, Children's Pr.) Scholastic Library Publishing.

Carson, Jill. Nuclear Power. 2010. (Compact Research Ser.). (YA). (gr. 7-12). 41.27 *(978-1-60152-123-1(5))* ReferencePoint Pr., Inc.

Cunningham, Anne C., ed. Revisiting Nuclear Power, 1 vol. 2017. (Global Viewpoints Ser.). (ENG.). 256p. (gr. 10-12). pap. 32.70 *(978-1-5345-0127-0(4)*, 4b981fe4-ece3-470f-9735-7f0384df1301); lib. bdg. 47.83 *(978-1-5345-0129-4(0)*, 9c57ee34-27d3-4a55-b553-162d1c67c94b) Greenhaven Publishing LLC.

Derkins, Susie. The Meltdown at Three Mile Island. 2009. (When Disaster Strikes! Ser.). 48p. (gr. 5-8). 53.00 *(978-1-60854-781-4(7)*, Rosen Reference) Rosen Publishing Group, Inc., The.

Dickmann, Nancy. Energy from Nuclear Fission: Splitting the Atom. 2015. (Next Generation Energy Ser.). (ENG., Illus.). 32p. (J). (gr. 5-5). *(978-0-7787-1981-6(2))* Crabtree Publishing Co.

Doeden, Matt. Finding Out about Nuclear Energy. 2014. (Searchlight Books (tm) — What Are Energy Sources? Ser.). (ENG., Illus.). 40p. (J). (gr. 3-5). pap. 9.99 *(978-1-4677-4556-7(1)*, 6e7b6aef-cf2c-4e53-8df4-fbc922019d56) Lerner Publishing Group.

Duke, Shirley Smith. Nuclear Power. 2013. (Explorer Library: Language Arts Explorer Ser.). (ENG.). 32p. (gr. 4-8). pap. 14.21 *(978-1-61080-921-4(1)*, 202565); (Illus.). 32.07 *(978-1-61080-896-5(7)*, 202563); (Illus.). E-Book 49.21 *(978-1-61080-971-9(8)*, 202566) Cherry Lake Publishing.

Follett, Katherine. Energy Sources for the 21st Century. 2011. (Readers' & Writers' Genre Workshop Ser.). (J). pap. *(978-1-4509-3029-1(8))* Benchmark Education Co.

Friedman, Lauri S., ed. Nuclear Power, 1 vol. 2009. (Introducing Issues with Opposing Viewpoints Ser.). (ENG., Illus.). 144p. (gr. 7-10). 43.63 *(978-0-7377-4482-8(0)*, 882707e8-089a-4c94-bcb6-df1312a9a5f6, Greenhaven Publishing) Greenhaven Publishing LLC.

Grady, Colin. Nuclear Energy, 1 vol. 2016. (Saving the Planet Through Green Energy Ser.). (ENG.). 24p. (gr. 3-3). pap. 10.35 *(978-0-7660-8288-5(1)*, 6644e703-140c-48d5-9acc-1e7209c77c69) Enslow Publishing, LLC.

Haney, Johannah. Nuclear Energy, 1 vol. 2012. (Debating the Issues Ser.). (ENG.). 64p. (gr. 6-6). 35.50 *(978-0-7614-4976-8(0)*, 14c1b944-f69c-414a-a2b2-cd5de14e3cc1) Cavendish Square Publishing LLC.

Hansen, Amy. Nuclear Energy: Amazing Atoms, 1 vol. 2010. (Powering Our World Ser.). (ENG.). 24p. (J). (gr. 3-3). pap. 9.25 *(978-1-4358-9744-1(7)*, 3884d1a8-1c0f-4d57-a61b-557b7ebb701e, PowerKids Pr.) Rosen Publishing Group, Inc., The.

Hansen, Amy S. Nuclear Energy: Amazing Atoms. 2010. (Powering Our World Ser.). 24p. (J). (gr. 2-5). E-Book 42.50 *(978-1-4488-0201-2(6))*; (ENG., Illus.). (gr. 3-3). lib. bdg. 26.27 *(978-1-4358-9328-3(X)*, e1ea66a5-0bc5-4d20-a877-28ca166c7190, PowerKids Pr.) Rosen Publishing Group, Inc., The.

Harrison Adams, Troon & Adams, Troon Harrison. Nuclear Energy: Power from the Atom, 1 vol. 2010. (ENG., Illus.). 32p. (J). pap. *(978-0-7787-2935-8(4))*; lib. bdg. *(978-0-7787-2921-1(4))* Crabtree Publishing Co.

Hillstrom, Kevin. Nuclear Energy, 1 vol. 2013. (Hot Topics Ser.). (ENG., Illus.). 96p. (gr. 7-7). lib. bdg. 41.03 *(978-1-4205-0874-1(1)*, 18a439b1-0684-429d-ae44-f8fb49c35902, Lucent Pr.) Greenhaven Publishing LLC.

Holt, Rinehart and Winston Staff. Holt Science & Technology Chapter 16: Physical Science: Atomic Energy. 5th ed. 2004. (Illus.). pap. 12.86 *(978-0-03-030413-2(X))* Holt McDougal.

Hulick, Kathryn. Real-World STEM: Develop Fusion Energy. 2017. (ENG.). 80p. (YA). (gr. 5-12). *(978-1-68282-245-6(1))* ReferencePoint Pr., Inc.

Loh-Hagan, Virginia. Nuclear Explosion Hacks. 2019. (Could You Survive? Ser.). (ENG.). 32p. (J). (gr. 4-8). pap. 14.21 *(978-1-5341-5071-3(4)*, 213591); (Illus.). lib. bdg. 32.07 *(978-1-5341-4785-0(3)*, 213590) Cherry Lake Publishing. (45th Parallel Press).

Manatt, Kathleen. Nuclear Energy. 2007. (21st Century Skills Library: Power Up! Ser.). (ENG.). 32p. (gr. 4-8). pap. 14.21 *(978-1-60279-099-5(X)*, 200660) Cherry Lake Publishing.

Mara, Wil & Bredeson, Carmen. The Chernobyl Disaster: Legacy & Impact on the Future of Nuclear Energy, 1 vol. 2011. (Perspectives On Ser.). (ENG.). 112p. (YA). (gr. 8-8). 42.64 *(978-0-7614-4984-3(1)*, 06c8c4c1-aad7-47bd-8039-4f9679c22535) Cavendish Square Publishing LLC.

Marquardt, Meg. Nuclear Energy. 2016. (Alternative Energy Ser.). (ENG., Illus.). 48p. (J). (gr. 4-8). lib. bdg. 35.64 *(978-1-68078-457-2(9)*, 23851) ABDO Publishing Co.

McLean, Adam. What Is Atomic Theory? 2010. (Shaping Modern Science Ser.). (ENG.). 64p. (J). (gr. 5-8). lib. bdg. *(978-0-7787-7197-5(0))* Crabtree Publishing Co.

McLeish, Ewan. The Pros & Cons of Nuclear Power, 1 vol. 2007. (Energy Debate Ser.). (ENG., Illus.). 48p. (YA). (gr. 6-6). lib. bdg. 34.47 *(978-1-4042-3740-7(2)*, 92fd774d-8329-46f9-a926-b15eae0be97e) Rosen Publishing Group, Inc., The.

Miller, Debra A., ed. Nuclear Energy, 1 vol. 2010. (Current Controversies Ser.). (ENG.). 240p. (gr. 10-12). 48.03 *(978-0-7377-4917-5(2)*, 9a00a626-afd9-4256-8ff8-967069f78c9b); pap. 33.00 *(978-0-7377-4918-2(0)*, deef9864-6780-47e5-aa0b-a27f0b2ae70d) Greenhaven Publishing LLC. (Greenhaven Publishing).

Morris, Neil. Nuclear Power. 2010. (J). 34.25 *(978-1-59920-341-6(3))* 2007. (Illus.). 32p. (YA). (gr. 4-7). lib. bdg. 28.50 *(978-1-58340-907-7(6))* Black Rabbit Bks.

Owen, Ruth. Energy from Atoms: Nuclear Power, 1 vol. 2013. (Power: Yesterday, Today, Tomorrow Ser.). (ENG., Illus.). 32p. (J). (gr. 4-5). 28.93 *(978-1-4777-0272-7(5)*, 049cbe88-1870-4752-906d-d6fc3d7efaa1); pap. 12.75 *(978-1-4777-0283-3(0)*, 0d40f056-5988-4c24-87cf-e7fc1f40d0ac) Rosen Publishing Group, Inc., The. (PowerKids Pr.).

Oxlade, Chris. Nuclear Power. 2010. (J). 34.25 *(978-1-59920-320-1(0))* Black Rabbit Bks.

Paley, Caitlyn. The Pros & Cons of Nuclear Power, 1 vol. 2015. (Economics of Energy Ser.). (ENG., Illus.). 80p. (YA). (gr. 7-7). 37.36 *(978-1-5026-0950-2(9)*, df2acd90-df6a-4242-96fc-9de4307a1fbe) Cavendish Square Publishing LLC.

Parker, Steve. Nuclear Energy, 1 vol. 2004. (Science Files: Energy Ser.). (ENG., Illus.). 32p. (gr. 3-5). lib. bdg. 28.67 *(978-0-8368-4030-8(5)*, 674b9e34-0664-4120-b8e2-72ae6ac29612, Gareth Stevens Learning Library) Stevens, Gareth Publishing LLLP.

Pipe, Jim. Nuclear Power. 2010. (J). 28.50 *(978-1-59604-210-0(9))* Black Rabbit Bks.

Reynoldson, Fiona. Understanding Nuclear Power, 1 vol. 2010. (World of Energy Ser.). (ENG.). 48p. (J). (gr. 5-6). lib. bdg. 34.60 *(978-1-4339-4124-5(4)*, 0d6ff821-30cf-4320-9e7e-52647b062921, Gareth Stevens Learning Library) Stevens, Gareth Publishing LLLP.

Richards, Julie. Nuclear Energy, 1 vol. 2010. (Energy Choices Ser.). (ENG.). 32p. (gr. 3-3). 31.21 *(978-0-7614-4433-6(5)*, 1e2867cb-a8f9-4d64-99b4-c91266fa639c) Cavendish Square Publishing LLC.

Spilsbury, Richard & Spilsbury, Louise. Nuclear Power, 1 vol. 2011. (Let's Discuss Energy Resources Ser.). (ENG., Illus.). 32p. (YA). (gr. 4-5). lib. bdg. 30.27 *(978-1-4488-5291-8(9)*, fbaad005-1d88-4f88-9967-c87bf9389d1b) Rosen Publishing Group, Inc., The.

Tiner, John Hudson. Uranium & Plutonium Make Nuclear Power. 2003. (From Resource to Energy Source Ser.). (J). *(978-1-58417-288-8(6))*; pap. *(978-1-58417-289-5(4))* Lake Street Pubs.

Venezia, Mike. Getting to Know the World's Greatest Inventors & Scientists: Lise Meitner. Venezia, Mike, illus. 2010. (Getting to Know the World's Greatest Inventors & Scientists Ser.). (ENG., Illus.). 32p. (J). (gr. 3-4). pap. 6.95 *(978-0-531-20776-5(5)*, Children's Pr.) Scholastic Library Publishing.

Young-Brown, Fiona. Nuclear Fusion & Fission, 1 vol. 2016. (Great Discoveries in Science Ser.). (ENG., Illus.). 128p. (J). (gr. 9-9). 47.36 *(978-1-5026-1949-5(0)*, 408b7774-5ea4-4236-b498-05d142996130) Cavendish Square Publishing LLC.

Zott, Lynn M. & Schier, Helga, eds. Nuclear Power, 1 vol. 2012. (Opposing Viewpoints Ser.). (ENG., Illus.). 256p. (gr. 10-12). pap. 34.80 *(978-0-7377-6063-7(X)*, fe5d3b87-18e3-4e97-8d6d-83545c866747); lib. bdg. 50.43 *(978-0-7377-6062-0(1)*, f1000adc-ba51-49d9-b0ad-f71699260ee3) Greenhaven Publishing LLC. (Greenhaven Publishing).

NUCLEAR ENGINEERING

see also Nuclear Reactors

Bailey, Diane. Nuclear Power. 2014. (Harnessing Energy Ser.). (ENG.). 48p. (J). (gr. 5-8). pap. 12.00 *(978-0-89812-997-7(4)*, 21359, Creative Paperbacks) Creative Co., The.

Friedman, Lauri S., ed. Nuclear Power, 1 vol. 2009. (Introducing Issues with Opposing Viewpoints Ser.). (ENG., Illus.). 144p. (gr. 7-10). 43.63 *(978-0-7377-4482-8(0)*, 882707e8-089a-4c94-bcb6-df1312a9a5f6, Greenhaven Publishing) Greenhaven Publishing LLC.

Honders, Christine. Nuclear Power Plants: Harnessing the Power of Nuclear Energy, 1 vol. 2017. (Powered up! a STEM Approach to Energy Sources Ser.). (ENG.). 24p. (J). (gr. 3-3). 25.27 *(978-1-5081-6426-5(6)*, 86dcb20d-7fb5-4d2f-a9ae-7abe90b025e3, PowerKids Pr.) Rosen Publishing Group, Inc., The.

Jakubiak, David J. What Can We Do about Nuclear Waste? (Illus.). 24p. 2012. (J). 49.50 *(978-1-4488-5115-7(7)*, PowerKids Pr.) 2011. (ENG., (J). (gr. 2-3). pap. 9.25 *(978-1-4488-5114-0(9)*, 66ed02f8-fae5-4874-b22b-50a219072878, PowerKids Pr.) 2011. (ENG., (YA). (gr. 2-3). lib. bdg. 26.27 *(978-1-4488-4983-3(7)*, 739b604f-73c0-45f5-a6b2-4f54858a6513) Rosen Publishing Group, Inc., The.

Morris, Neil. Nuclear Power. 2007. (Energy Sources Ser.). (Illus.). 32p. (YA). (gr. 4-7). lib. bdg. 28.50 *(978-1-58340-907-7(6))* Black Rabbit Bks.

Oxlade, Chris. Nuclear Power. 2010. (J). 34.25 *(978-1-59920-320-1(0))* Black Rabbit Bks.

Paley, Caitlyn. The Pros & Cons of Nuclear Power, 1 vol. 2015. (Economics of Energy Ser.). (ENG., Illus.). 80p. (YA). (gr. 7-7). 37.36 *(978-1-5026-0950-2(9)*, df2acd90-df6a-4242-96fc-9de4307a1fbe) Cavendish Square Publishing LLC.

Richards, Julie. Nuclear Energy, 1 vol. 2010. (Energy Choices Ser.). (ENG.). 32p. (gr. 3-3). 31.21 *(978-0-7614-4433-6(5)*, 1e2867cb-a8f9-4d64-99b4-c91266fa639c) Cavendish Square Publishing LLC.

NUCLEAR PHYSICS

see also Chemistry, Physical and Theoretical; Electrons; Nuclear Engineering; Nuclear Reactors; Radioactivity

Barron, Rachel Stiffler. Lise Meitner: Discoverer of Nuclear Fission. 2004. (Profiles in Science Ser.). (Illus.). 112p. (YA). (gr. 6-12). lib. bdg. 23.95 *(978-1-883846-52-7(8)*, First Biographies) Reynolds, Morgan Inc.

Bortz, Fred. Understanding the Large Hadron Collider, 1 vol. 2015. (Exploring the Subatomic World Ser.). (ENG., Illus.). 64p. (YA). (gr. 8-8). lib. bdg. 35.93 *(978-1-5026-0552-8(X)*, 62f40d12-e2b2-4af0-908c-324fbcab8975) Cavendish Square Publishing LLC.

Conkling, Winifred. Radioactive! How Irène Curie & Lise Meitner Revolutionized Science & Changed the World. 2018. (ENG., Illus.). 240p. (YA). (gr. 5-9). pap. 10.95 *(978-1-61620-641-3(1)*, 73641) Algonquin Young Readers.

Cooper, Christopher. The Basics of Nuclear Physics, 1 vol. 2014. (Core Concepts Ser.). (ENG.). 96p. (YA). (gr. 7-7). 39.77 *(978-1-4777-7770-1(9)*, 2580579a-088a-47c1-add5-db4448c389b1) Rosen Publishing Group, Inc., The.

Ferrie, Chris & Florance, Cara. Nuclear Physics for Babies. 2018. (Baby University Ser.: 0). (Illus.). 24p. (J). (gr. -1-k). bds. 9.99 *(978-1-4926-7117-6(7))* Sourcebooks, Inc.

Jackson, Tom. The Basics of Atoms & Molecules, 1 vol. 2013. (Core Concepts Ser.). (ENG.). 96p. (YA). (gr. 7-7). 39.77 *(978-1-4777-2715-7(9)*, 3ef6df4b-f2ba-4735-8783-0dee38507838) Rosen Publishing Group, Inc., The.

Morris, Neil. Nuclear Power. 2010. (J). 34.25 *(978-1-59920-341-6(3))* Black Rabbit Bks.

Oxlade, Chris. Nuclear Power. 2010. (J). 34.25 *(978-1-59920-320-1(0))* Black Rabbit Bks.

Parker, Katie. Splitting the Atom, 1 vol. 2010. (Big Ideas in Science Ser.). (ENG., Illus.). 48p. (gr. 5-5). 34.07 *(978-0-7614-4399-5(1)*, 3e72849f-adbc-48ac-aa8d-a21c77989462) Cavendish Square Publishing LLC.

Rock, Meghan. String Theory, 1 vol. 2016. (Great Discoveries in Science Ser.). (ENG.). 128p. (YA). (gr. 9-9). 47.36 *(978-1-5026-1961-7(X)*, 56ce0d62-8075-4ee3-99b8-80ffe5401ca2) Cavendish Square Publishing LLC.

Singer, Neal. Wonders of Nuclear Fusion: Creating an Ultimate Energy Source. 2011. (Barbara Guth Worlds of Wonder Science Series for Young Readers Ser.). (ENG., Illus.). 130p. (J). (gr. 4-18). 34.95 *(978-0-8263-4778-7(9)*, P187535) Univ. of New Mexico Pr.

Slade, Suzanne. The Structure of Atoms. (Library of Physical Science Ser.). 24p. (gr. 4-4). 2009. 42.50 *(978-1-60853-795-2(1))* 2006. (ENG., Illus.). pap. 7.05 *(978-1-4042-2161-1(1)*, ccbf09dd-9ec1-408d-926f-2ab8bc98b454) Rosen Publishing Group, Inc., The. (PowerKids Pr.).

Spiro, Ruth. ¡Al Bebé le Encantan Los Quarks! / Baby Loves Quarks! Chan, Irene, illus. 2019. (Baby Loves Science Ser.). 20p. (J). (— 1). bds. 8.99 *(978-1-58089-984-0(6))* Charlesbridge Publishing, Inc.

—Baby Loves Quarks! Chan, Irene, illus. 2016. (Baby Loves Science Ser.: 2). 20p. (J). (— 1). bds. 8.99 *(978-1-58089-540-8(9))* Charlesbridge Publishing, Inc.

Venezia, Mike. Lise Meitner: Had the Right Vision about Nuclear Fission. Venezia, Mike, illus. 2009. (Getting to Know the World's Greatest Inventors & Scientists Ser.). (ENG., Illus.). 32p. (J). (gr. 2-5). 28.00 *(978-0-531-23702-1(8))* Scholastic Library Publishing.

Walliman, Dominic. Professor Astro Cat's Atomic Adventure. Newman, Ben, illus. 2016. (Professor Astro Cat Ser.). (ENG.). 56p. (J). (gr. 2-5). 19.99 *(978-1-909263-60-4(5))* Flying Eye Bks. GBR. Dist: Penguin Random Hse. LLC.

Young-Brown, Fiona. Nuclear Fusion & Fission, 1 vol. 2016. (Great Discoveries in Science Ser.). (ENG., Illus.). 128p. (J). (gr. 9-9). 47.36 *(978-1-5026-1949-5(0)*, 408b7774-5ea4-4236-b498-05d142996130) Cavendish Square Publishing LLC.

NUCLEAR POWER

see also Atomic Bomb; Nuclear Engineering; Nuclear Reactors

Bailey, Diane. Nuclear Power. 2014. (Harnessing Energy Ser.). (ENG.). 48p. (J). (gr. 5-8). 35.65 *(978-1-60818-411-8(0)*, 21358) Creative Co., The.

Gillard, Arthur, ed. Nuclear Power, 1 vol. 2011. (Issues That Concern You Ser.). (ENG., Illus.). 136p. (gr. 7-10). 43.63 *(978-0-7377-5696-8(9)*, 76609b5a-d733-4f5f-9d59-b9dc0089c0bc, Greenhaven Publishing) Greenhaven Publishing LLC.

Lopatka, Michael. Nuclear Power Facility Virtual Field Trip. 2003. (YA). cd-rom 15.95 *(978-0-9723218-8-4(8))* Awesome Guides, Inc.

Metcalf, Tom & Metcalf, Gena, eds. Nuclear Power, 1 vol. 2006. (Fueling the Future Ser.). (ENG., Illus.). 128p. (gr. 10-12). lib. bdg. 46.23 *(978-0-7377-3587-1(2)*, 0ffe4312-10f8-44d8-8e81-1c9dee828a52, Greenhaven Publishing) Greenhaven Publishing LLC.

Parker, Steve. Nuclear Energy, 1 vol. 2004. (Science Files: Energy Ser.). (ENG., Illus.). 32p. (gr. 3-5). lib. bdg. 28.67 *(978-0-8368-4030-8(5)*, 674b9e34-0664-4120-b8e2-72ae6ac29612, Gareth Stevens Learning Library) Stevens, Gareth Publishing LLLP.

NUCLEAR POWER—FICTION

Beard, Linda P. Remember ... Remember Your Name. 2011. 24p. (gr. 4-6). pap. 14.99 *(978-1-4269-6859-4(0))* Trafford Publishing.

Hesse, Karen. Phoenix Rising. 2009. (ENG.). 208p. (J). (gr. 6-11). pap. 14.99 *(978-0-312-53562-9(7)*, 900054738) Square Fish.

Tulien, Sean. Meltdown Town. 2016. (Tartan House Ser.). (ENG.). 96p. (J). (gr. 3-6). *(978-1-63235-165-4(X)*, 11896, 12-Story Library) Bookstaves, LLC.

NUCLEAR POWER PLANTS

Arato, Rona. Fukushima Nuclear Disaster. 2013. (ENG., Illus.). 32p. (J). *(978-0-7787-1192-6(7))*; pap. *(978-0-7787-1194-0(3))* Crabtree Publishing Co.

Benoit, Peter. True Book - Disasters: Nuclear Meltdowns. 2011. (True Bk Ser.). (ENG., Illus.). 48p. (J). pap. 6.95 *(978-0-531-26627-4(3)*, Children's Pr.) Scholastic Library Publishing.

Burgan, Michael. Chernobyl Explosion: How a Deadly Nuclear Accident Frightened the World. 2018. (Captured Science History Ser.). (ENG., Illus.). 64p. (J). (gr. 5-9). lib. bdg. 35.32 *(978-0-7565-5744-7(5)*, 137540, Compass Point Bks.) Capstone.

Derkins, Susie. The Meltdown at Three Mile Island. 2009. (When Disaster Strikes! Ser.). 48p. (gr. 5-8). 53.00 *(978-1-60854-781-4(7)*, Rosen Reference) Rosen Publishing Group, Inc., The.

Feigenbaum, Aaron. Emergency at Three Mile Island. 2007. (Code Red Ser.). (Illus.). 32p. (YA). (gr. 2-5). lib. bdg. 28.50 *(978-1-59716-364-4(3))* Bearport Publishing Co., Inc.

Greeley, August. Fallout: Nuclear Disasters in Our World. 2009. (Man-Made Disasters Ser.). 24p. (gr. 3-3). 42.50 *(978-1-61514-348-1(3)*, PowerKids Pr.) Rosen Publishing Group, Inc., The.

Haney, Johannah. Nuclear Energy, 1 vol. 2012. (Debating the Issues Ser.). (ENG.). 64p. (gr. 6-6). 35.50 *(978-0-7614-4976-8(0)*, 14c1b944-f69c-414a-a2b2-cd5de14e3cc1) Cavendish Square Publishing LLC.

Honders, Christine. Nuclear Power Plants: Harnessing the Power of Nuclear Energy, 1 vol. 2017. (Powered up! a STEM Approach to Energy Sources Ser.). (ENG.). 24p. (J). (gr. 3-3). 25.27 *(978-1-5081-6426-5(6)*, 86dcb20d-7fb5-4d2f-a9ae-7abe90b025e3, PowerKids Pr.) Rosen Publishing Group, Inc., The.

Hulick, Kathryn. Real-World STEM: Develop Fusion Energy. 2017. (ENG.). 80p. (YA). (gr. 5-12). *(978-1-68282-245-6(1))* ReferencePoint Pr., Inc.

Larson, Kirsten. Nuclear Meltdowns. 2015. (Devastating Disasters Ser.). (ENG.). 48p. (gr. 4-8). 35.64 *(978-1-63430-428-3(4)*, 9781634304283) Rourke Educational Media.

Lusted, Greg & Lusted, Marcia Amidon. A Nuclear Power Plant. 2005. (Building History Ser.). (ENG., Illus.). 112p. (YA). (gr. 7-12). lib. bdg. 32.45 *(978-1-59018-392-2(4))* Cengage Gale.

Marquardt, Meg. The Science of a Nuclear Plant Explosion. 2015. (21st Century Skills Library: Disaster Science Ser.). (ENG., Illus.). 32p. (J). (gr. 4-8). 32.07 *(978-1-63362-480-1(3)*, 206828) Cherry Lake Publishing.

Rissman, Rebecca. Chernobyl Disaster, 1 vol. 2013. (History's Greatest Disasters Ser.). (ENG.). 48p. (J). (gr. 4-8). lib. bdg. 35.64 *(978-1-61783-955-9(8)*, 9481) ABDO Publishing Co.

—Chernobyl Disaster Paperback. 2013. (History's Greatest Disasters Ser.). (ENG.). (J). (gr. 4-8). pap. 18.50 *(978-1-62403-020-8(3)*, 10769) ABDO Publishing Co.

Smith, Jim & Beresford, Nicholas A. Chernobyl: Catastrophe & Consequences, 1 vol. 2005. (Springer Praxis Bks.). (ENG., Illus.). xxvi, 310p. 169.99 *(978-3-540-23866-9(2)*, 978-3-540-23866-9, Springer) Springer Berlin / Heidelberg.

Woods, Michael & Woods, Mary B. Environmental Disasters. 2008. (Disasters up Close Ser.). (ENG., Illus.). 64p. (gr. 4-8). lib. bdg. 27.93 *(978-0-8225-6774-5(1)*, Lerner Pubns.) Lerner Publishing Group.

NUCLEAR REACTORS

Cruise, Robin. The Nuclear Disaster at Chernobyl. Taylor, Marjorie, illus. rev. ed. 2003. (Take Ten Ser.). 46p. (J). (gr. 4-18). pap. 4.95 *(978-1-58659-022-2(7))* Artesian Pr.

NUCLEAR SUBMARINES

Amato, William. Nuclear Submarines. 2009. (High-Tech Vehicles Ser.). 24p. (gr. 2-3). 42.50 *(978-1-61513-306-2(2)*, PowerKids Pr.) Rosen Publishing Group, Inc., The.

—Submarinos Nucleares, 1 vol. 2003. (Vehículos de Alta Tecnología (High-Tech Vehicles) Ser.). (SPA., Illus.). 24p. (J). (gr. 2-2). lib. bdg. 26.27 *(978-0-8239-6882-4(0)*, 944b2d8c-1c0e-41bc-ac52-3f6f3a47b201) Rosen Publishing Group, Inc., The.

—Submarinos nucleares (Nuclear Submarines) 2009. (Vehículos de alta tecnología (High-Tech Vehicles) Ser.). (SPA.). 24p. (gr. 2-3). 42.50 *(978-1-60854-720-3(5)*, Editorial Buenas Letras) Rosen Publishing Group, Inc., The.

Loveless, Antony. Nuclear Submariners. 2009. (World's Most Dangerous Jobs Ser.). (ENG., Illus.). 32p. (J). (gr. 3-6). pap. *(978-0-7787-5111-3(2))*; lib. bdg. *(978-0-7787-5097-0(3))* Crabtree Publishing Co.

NUCLEAR TEST BAN

see Disarmament

NUCLEAR WARFARE

Beyer, Mark. Nuclear Weapons & the Cold War. (Library of Weapons of Mass Destruction Ser.). 64p. (gr. 5-5). 2009. 58.50 *(978-1-60853-953-6(9))* 2004. (ENG., Illus.). (J). lib. bdg. 37.13 *(978-1-4042-0290-0(0)*, 0a80bba8-6f1b-4ad3-a8af-407d12a0d36d) Rosen Publishing Group, Inc., The.

Bougie, Matt. Strategic Inventions of the Cold War, 1 vol. 2015. (Tech in the Trenches Ser.). (ENG., Illus.). 112p. (YA). (gr. 9-9). 44.50 *(978-1-5026-1022-5(1)*, ade1ae44-2ff8-4dfe-9a9e-61a6b84a0bca) Cavendish Square Publishing LLC.

Gerdes, Louise I., ed. Nuclear Weapons, 1 vol. 2009. (At Issue Ser.). (ENG.). 120p. (gr. 10-12). 41.03 *(978-0-7377-4308-1(5)*, 8bc86dfd-eddf-4869-bd78-772dde9f55e7); pap. 28.80 *(978-0-7377-4307-4(7)*, bec9bcdb-ce50-4436-aa9e-fd0e3db7b6ef) Greenhaven Publishing LLC. (Greenhaven Publishing).

Hudak, Heather C. Nuclear Weapons & the Arms Race. 2018. (Uncovering the Past: Analyzing Primary Sources Ser.). (Illus.). 48p. (J). (gr. 5-6). *(978-0-7787-4801-4(4))* Crabtree Publishing Co.

Maus, Derek C., ed. Living under the Threat of Nuclear War. 2005. (Living Through the Cold War Ser.). (ENG., Illus.). 143p. (YA). (gr. 10-12). lib. bdg. 37.90 *(978-0-7377-2130-0(8)*, Greenhaven Pr., Inc.) Cengage Gale.

McCoy, Erin L. Nuclear Confrontation, 1 vol. 2018. (Top Six Threats to Civilization Ser.). (ENG.). 64p. (J). (gr. 5-5). pap. 16.28 *(978-1-5026-4134-2(8)*, 340b1cb1-b023-4572-ba8f-1b3cae9e9b5d) Cavendish Square Publishing LLC.

Minneus, Steve. Nukes: The Spread of Nuclear Weapons, 1 vol. 2007. (In the News Ser.). (ENG., Illus.). 64p. (YA). (gr. 6-6). lib. bdg. 37.13 *(978-1-4042-1916-8(1)*, ba946ed1-9ee7-406e-b6ca-7ffd9b6ca863) Rosen Publishing Group, Inc., The.

Morey, Allan. Nuclear War. 2019. (It's the End of the World! Ser.). (ENG., Illus.). 24p. (J). (gr. 3-7). lib. bdg. 26.95 *(978-1-64487-082-2(7)*, Torque Bks.) Bellwether Media.

Orr, Tamra. The Hydrogen Bomb: Unleashing the Nuclear Age & Arms Race. 2009. (Library of Weapons of Mass Destruction Ser.). 64p. (gr. 5-5). 58.50 *(978-1-60853-956-7(3))* Rosen Publishing Group, Inc., The.

—The Hydrogen Bomb: Unleashing the Nuclear & Arms Race, 1 vol. 2004. (Library of Weapons of Mass Destruction Ser.). (ENG., Illus.). 64p. (J). (gr. 5-5). lib. bdg. 37.13 *(978-1-4042-0293-1(5)*, 8a321fdb-9cc0-4839-a0d7-89d339d20184) Rosen Publishing Group, Inc., The.

Spalding, Frank. Nuclear Annihilation. 2010. (Doomsday Scenarios: Separating Fact from Fiction Ser.). 64p. (YA). (gr. 5-8). E-Book 58.50 *(978-1-4488-1208-0(9))*; (ENG.). (gr. 7-7). pap. 13.95 *(978-1-4358-8522-6(8)*, cdd04e17-bb4e-47ca-9b69-ab27f237dd09, Rosen Reference); (ENG., Illus.). (gr. 7-7). lib. bdg. 37.13 *(978-1-4358-3560-3(3)*, 26e39103-8f17-433b-9c0b-5cee1e78350f, Rosen Reference) Rosen Publishing Group, Inc., The.

Tyler, Michael. Surviving a Nuclear War, 1 vol. 2018. (Surviving the Impossible Ser.). (ENG.). 32p. (gr. 4-5). pap. 11.50 *(978-1-5382-3510-2(2)*, 61d325dc-6886-4f9f-a63d-709305d07e0e) Stevens, Gareth Publishing LLLP.

NUCLEAR WARFARE—FICTION

Higgins, Jack & Richards, Justin. First Strike. 2011. (Chance Twins Ser.: Bk. 4). (ENG.). 240p. (YA). (gr. 7-12). 24.94 *(978-0-399-25240-2(1))* Penguin Young Readers Group.

O'Brien, Robert C. Z for Zachariah. 2007. (ENG.). 240p. (YA). (gr. 7-12). pap. 11.99 *(978-1-4169-3921-4(0)*, Simon Pulse) Simon Pulse.

Zorn, Claire. The Sky So Heavy. 2014. 304p. (gr. 7). 16.00 *(978-0-7022-4976-1(9))* Univ. of Queensland Pr. AUS. Dist: Independent Pubs. Group.

NUCLEAR WEAPONS AND DISARMAMENT

see Disarmament

NUMBER CONCEPT

Aboff, Marcie. If You Were an Even Number, 1 vol. Dillard, Sarah, illus. 2008. (Math Fun Ser.). (ENG.). 24p. (J). (gr. 2-4). 28.65 *(978-1-4048-4796-5(0)*, 95275, Picture Window Bks.) Capstone.

Accord Publishing, Accord. Numbers: A Caterpillar-Shaped Book. 2012. (ENG.). 24p. (J). 11.99 *(978-1-4494-1736-9(1))* Andrews McMeel Publishing.

Ackland, Nick. Numbers. 2015. (Bright Beginnings Ser.). (ENG., Illus.). 20p. (J). (gr. -1 — 1). bds. 7.99 *(978-0-7641-6744-7(8))* Sourcebooks, Inc.

Adamson, Thomas K. and Heather. Fun with Numbers. 2012. (Fun with Numbers Ser.). (ENG.). 32p. (gr. 1-2). pap. 190.80 *(978-1-4296-8454-5(2)*, Capstone Pr.) Capstone.

Adler, David A. Millions, Billions, & Trillions: Understanding Big Numbers. Miller, Edward, illus. (ENG.). 32p. (J). (gr. 1-4). 2014. 7.99 *(978-0-8234-3049-9(9))* 2013. 18.99 *(978-0-8234-2403-0(0))* Holiday Hse., Inc.

Allen, Susan & Lindaman, Jane. Used Any Numbers Lately? Enright, Vicky, illus. 2008. 32p. (J). (gr. k-4). 16.95 *(978-0-8225-8658-6(4)*, Millbrook Pr.) Lerner Publishing Group.

Alvarez, Lourdes M. Mi Primer Libro Numeros. Brooks, David, illus. 2005. (Mi primer libro Ser.). (SPA.). 9p. (J). (gr. -1 — 1). bds. 3.95 *(978-1-933050-00-3(4))* Sweetwater Pr.

—My First Book Numbers. Brooks, David, illus. 2005. (My First Book Ser.). 9p. (J). (gr. -1-1). bds. 3.95 *(978-1-933050-06-5(3))* Sweetwater Pr.

Anastasio, Dina. Number Games: Set Of 6. 2011. (Early Connections Ser.). (J). pap. 37.00 net. *(978-1-4108-1082-3(8))* Benchmark Education Co.

Anderson, Joanna. Cooking with My Dad: Number Names & Count Sequence. 2013. (InfoMax Math Readers Ser.). (ENG.). 16p. (J). (gr. k-1). pap. 42.00 *(978-1-4777-1998-5(9))*; (Illus.). pap. 7.00 *(978-1-4777-1997-8(0)*, 7ef9d8bc-8b49-4e41-9e80-00f6b86d8c01) Rosen Publishing Group, Inc., The. (Rosen Classroom).

Anthony, Susan C. Casting Nines Quick Check For. 2004. pap. 8.00 *(978-1-879478-09-1(9))* Instructional Resources Co.

Aryai, Sia, photos by. 1 2 3s. (Baby Bright Board Bks.). (Illus.). 10p. (J). (gr. -1). 5.95 *(978-1-56565-824-0(8)*, 08248W, Roxbury Park Juvenile) Lowell Hse. Juvenile.

Aufbau des Zahlensystems, Vollstaendige Induktion. (Duden-Schuelerhilfen Ser.). (GER.). 80p. (YA). (gr. 7-10). *(978-3-411-02625-8(1))* Bibliographisches Institut & F. A. Brockhaus AG DEU. Dist: International Bk. Import Service, Inc.

Austen, Amy. Endangered Animals: Develop Understanding of Fractions & Numbers, 1 vol. 2014. (Rosen Math Readers Ser.). (ENG.). 24p. (J). (gr. 3-3). pap. 8.25 *(978-1-4777-4921-0(7)*, a66416c3-294e-4aa8-ba9c-a5eb362e09a2, PowerKids Pr.) Rosen Publishing Group, Inc., The.

AWARD & Award, Anna. Bumper Dot to Dot. 2015. (ENG.). 64p. (J). pap. 7.99 *(978-1-78270-158-3(3))* Award Pubns. Ltd. GBR. Dist: Parkwest Pubns., Inc.

Award, Anna. 123. 2017. (ENG., Illus.). 24p. (J). pap. 5.99 *(978-1-78270-066-1(8))* Award Pubns Ltd. GBR. Dist: Parkwest Pubns., Inc.

Bambi727 & Bambi727. Having Fun with Colors' & Numbers' I wrote this book in hopes our younger children would enjoy & have fun learning their colors' & Numbers' 2009. 32p. pap. 14.49 *(978-1-4389-6226-9(6))* AuthorHouse.

Believe It Or Not!, Ripleys, compiled by. Ripley's Believe It or Not! Wacky 1-2-3. 2017. (Little Bks.: 1). (ENG., Illus.). 26p. (J). bds. 6.99 *(978-1-60991-181-2(4))* Ripley Entertainment, Inc.

Berenstain, Jan, et al. The Berenstain Bears' Count on Numbers Coloring Book. 2014. (Dover Kids Coloring Bks.). (ENG.). 48p. (J). (gr. -1). pap. 5.99 *(978-0-486-49469-2(1)*, 494691) Dover Pubns., Inc.

Beveridge, Dorothy. Counting Belize Frogs & Toads. Beveridge, Jim, photos by. 2012. (Illus.). 26p. pap. *(978-976-8142-47-4(2))* Producciones de la Hamaca.

Blechman, R. O. The One & Only 1, 2, 3 Book. 2013. (ENG., Illus.). 24p. (J). (gr. -1-k). 15.99 *(978-1-56846-245-5(X)*, 22703, Creative Editions) Creative Co., The.

Boye, B. D. Easy As 1, 2, 3. Boye, B. D., illus. l.t. ed. 2005. (Illus.). 22p. (J). per. 4.99 *(978-0-9768078-0-3(7))* Innerchild Publishing, Inc.

Brainy Baby Quad Book. 2005. (Brainy Baby Ser.). 40p. (J). bds. 10.39 *(978-1-59394-240-3(0))* Bendon, Inc.

Brallier, Max. The Numbers Field Guide. 2012. (ENG.). (J). pap. *(978-0-8118-7771-8(X))* Chronicle Bks. LLC.

Brighter Child, compiled by. Numbers 1 to 100 (Numeros del 1 al 100) 2006. (ENG., Illus.). 54p. (gr. k-3). 2.99 *(978-0-7696-4799-9(5)*, 0769647995, Brighter Child) Carson-Dellosa Publishing, LLC.

Brinker, Spencer. Odd or Even in a Monstrous Season. 2015. (Illus.). 32p. (J). lib. bdg. 28.50 *(978-1-62724-331-5(3))* Bearport Publishing Co., Inc.

Brocket, Jane. 1 Cookie, 2 Chairs, 3 Pears: Numbers Everywhere. Brocket, Jane, photos by. 2013. (Jane Brocket's Clever Concepts Ser.). (ENG., Illus.). 32p. (J). (gr. -1-2). lib. bdg. 26.65 *(978-1-4677-0232-4(3)*, b820777b-0684-42b8-b656-11e39b5f80d3); E-Book 39.99 *(978-1-4677-1702-1(9))* Lerner Publishing Group. (Millbrook Pr.).

Brooks, F. & Litchfield, J. Primeros Numeros. 2004.Tr. of First Numbers. (SPA., Illus.). 48p. (J). (gr. -1-18). lib. bdg. 20.95 *(978-1-58086-352-0(3))* EDC Publishing.

Burnett, James & Irons, Calvin. The Flower Pot Hen: A Book about Representing Data. 2012. (J). *(978-1-921358-60-9(2))* Origo Education.

—Scaredy Cats: A Book about Combinations of Ten. 2012. (J). *(978-1-921358-98-2(X))* Origo Education.

—Stella's Store: Book about Skip Counting by Five. 2012. (J). *(978-1-921358-61-6(0))* Origo Education.

—Sweet Dreams: A Book about Counting Quantities to Ten. 2012. (J). *(978-1-921358-96-8(3))* Origo Education.

Burstein, John. Number Conservation: Planting Monster Melons, 1 vol. 2003. (Math Monsters(tm) Ser.). (ENG., Illus.). 24p. (J). (gr. k-3). pap. 9.15 *(978-0-8368-3829-9(7)*, 541c92ac-93a6-4d7c-80ea-cc3c4a3871bc, Weekly Reader Leveled Readers) Stevens, Gareth Publishing LLLP.

Burton, Margie, et al. We Use Numbers. 2011. (Early Connections Ser.). (J). *(978-1-61672-511-2(7))* Benchmark Education Co.

Bussiere, Desireé. Tennis by the Numbers, 1 vol. 2013. (Sports by the Numbers Ser.). (ENG.). 24p. (J). (gr. k-3). lib. bdg. 29.93 *(978-1-61783-847-7(0)*, 13708, SandCastle) ABDO Publishing Co.

Butler, Nathalie. Numbers Parade, 1 vol. 2017. (Learning with Stories Ser.). (ENG.). 24p. (gr. 1-1). pap. 9.25 *(978-1-5081-6233-9(6)*, c09ee474-9dee-4e62-8298-25128bb346b8, PowerKids Pr.) Rosen Publishing Group, Inc., The.

Cameron, Antonia & Fosnot, Catherine Twomey. Games for Early Number Sense: A Yearlong Resource. 2008. (ENG.). 96p. (gr. k-1). pap. 31.25 *(978-0-325-01009-0(9)*, E01009, Firsthand) Heinemann.

Capote, Lori. Monster Knows More Than, Less Than, 1 vol. Wass, Chip, illus. 2013. (Monster Knows Math Ser.). (ENG.). 24p. (J). (gr. -1-3). lib. bdg. 25.32 *(978-1-4048-7947-8(1)*, 120698, Picture Window Bks.) Capstone.

Carroll, Danielle. Place Value. 2005. (Yellow Umbrella Fluent Level Ser.). (ENG., Illus.). 16p. (gr. k-1). pap. 35.70 *(978-0-7368-5324-8(3)*, Capstone Pr.) Capstone.

Carter, David A. The Glittery Crittery Pop-up Counting Book. 2007. (ENG., Illus.). 10p. (gr. -1). bds. 16.95 *(978-1-58117-651-3(1)*, Intervisual/Piggy Toes) Bendon, Inc.

Cernek, Kim & Williams, Rozanne Lanczak. Build-a-Skill Instant Books Color, Shape & Number Words. Shiotsu, Vicky & Faulkner, Stacey, eds. Campbell, Jenny & Tom, Darcy, illus. 2007. (J). 4.99 *(978-1-59198-411-5(4))* Creative Teaching Pr., Inc.

Chapman, Joan. Count the Ways to Get Around: Learning to Count To 5, 1 vol. 2010. (Math for the REAL World Ser.). (ENG., Illus.). 8p. (gr. k-1). pap. 5.15 *(978-0-8239-8841-9(4)*, 5bfeaf78-b854-461d-aa34-927d1d10d0fe) Rosen Publishing Group, Inc., The.

Coe, Layla. At the Art Store: Compare Numbers. 2013. (Rosen Math Readers Ser.). (ENG.). 16p. (J). (gr. k-1). pap. 42.00 *(978-1-4777-1663-2(7))*; (Illus.). pap. 7.00 *(978-1-4777-1662-5(9)*, c6dd105f-557c-499e-abf2-33df39b29e3c) Rosen Publishing Group, Inc., The. (Rosen Classroom).

Collins Easy Learning. Numbers Flashcards: Ideal for Home Learning. 2017. (Collins Easy Learning Preschool Ser.). (ENG.). 52p. (J). (gr. -1). 8.99 *(978-0-00-820106-7(4))* HarperCollins Pubs. Ltd. GBR. Dist: Independent Pubs. Group.

Corcorane, Ann. Numbers Are Everywhere, 1 vol. 2011. (Wonder Readers Emergent Level Ser.). (ENG.). 8p. (gr. -1-1). (J). pap. 6.25 *(978-1-4296-7846-9(1)*, 118159); pap. 35.94 *(978-1-4296-8233-6(7)*, Capstone Pr.) Capstone.

Craig, Diane & Doudna, Kelly. No One Slumbers When We Use Numbers!, 1 vol. 2007. (Science Made Simple Ser.). (Illus.). 24p. (J). (gr. k-3). lib. bdg. 24.21 *(978-1-59928-612-9(2)*, SandCastle) ABDO Publishing Co.

Crane, Carol. Net Numbers: A South Carolina Numbers Book. Palmer, Gary, illus. 2006. (America by the Numbers Ser.). (ENG.). 40p. (J). (gr. 1-3). 17.95 *(978-1-58536-202-8(6)*, 202040) Sleeping Bear Pr.

Crews, G. Ellen G Goes Fishing. marion, designs & proctor, brian, illus. 2007. 28p. pap. 4.99 *(978-0-9795236-0-1(5))* Crews Pubns., LLC.

Crisp, Dan, illus. Five Little Men in a Flying Saucer. 2006. (Classic Books with Holes Big Book Ser.). 16p. (J). spiral bd. *(978-1-84643-007-7(0))* Child's Play International Ltd.

Dahl, Michael. From the Garden: A Counting Book about Growing Food, 1 vol. Ouren, Todd, illus. 2004. (Know Your Numbers Ser.). (ENG.). 24p. (J). (gr. -1-2). per. 8.95 *(978-1-4048-1116-4(8)*, 92617, Picture Window Bks.) Capstone.

Daybell, Chad. Book of Mormon Numbers. Bonham, Bob, illus. 2004. (J). bds. 8.95 *(978-1-55517-755-3(7)*, 77557) Cedar Fort, Inc./CFI Distribution.

Deen, Marilyn. Odd & Even. 2011. (Wonder Readers Fluent Level Ser.). (ENG.). 16p. (gr. -1-2). pap. 35.94 *(978-1-4296-8133-9(0)*, Capstone Pr.) Capstone.

Dennison, Matt. Building with Blocks: Work with 11-19 to Gain Foundations for Place Value. 2013. (InfoMax Math Readers Ser.). (ENG.). 16p. (J). (gr. k-1). pap. 42.00 *(978-1-4777-1962-6(8))*; (Illus.). pap. 7.00 *(978-1-4777-1961-9(X)*, dab57707-6cc7-4119-868d-ebe48734fd8b) Rosen Publishing Group, Inc., The. (Rosen Classroom).

Diaz, James & Gerth, Melanie, illus. Numbers: Learning Fun for Little Ones! 2007. 10p. (J). reprint ed. *(978-1-4223-6683-7(9))* DIANE Publishing Co.

Dingles, Molly. Number 1 What Grows in the Sun?/Número 1 Qué crece en el Sol? Wallis, Rebecca, illus. 2005. (Community of Counting Ser.).Tr. of Número 1 Qué crece en el Sol?. (ENG & SPA.). 32p. (J). per. 10.95 *(978-1-59646-275-5(2))* Dingles & Co.

—Number 10 Where Is the Hen? Wallis, Rebecca, illus. 2005. (Community of Counting Ser.). 32p. (J). per. 10.95 *(978-1-59646-309-7(0))* Dingles & Co.

—Number 10 Where Is the Hen?/Número 10 en dónde está la Gallina? Wallis, Rebecca, illus. 2005. (Community of Counting Ser.). (ENG & SPA.). 32p. (J). per. 10.95 *(978-1-59646-311-0(2))* Dingles & Co.

—Number 2 Let's Go to the Zoo! Wallis, Rebecca, illus. 2005. (Community of Counting Ser.). 32p. (J). 10.95 *(978-1-59646-277-9(9))* Dingles & Co.

—Number 2 Let's Go to the Zoo!/Número 2 Vamos al Zoologico! Wallis, Rebecca, illus. 2005. (Community of Counting Ser.).Tr. of Número 2 Vamos al Zoologico! (ENG & SPA.). 32p. (J). per. 10.95 *(978-1-59646-279-3(5))* Dingles & Co.

—Number 3 What's in the Sea? Wallis, Rebecca, illus. 2005. (Community of Counting Ser.). 32p. (J). per. 10.95 *(978-1-59646-281-6(7))* Dingles & Co.

—Number 3 What's in the Sea?/Número 3 Qué hay en el Mar? Wallis, Rebecca, illus. 2005. (Community of Counting Ser.).Tr. of Número 3 Qué hay en el Mar? (ENG & SPA.). 32p. (J). pap. 10.95 *(978-1-59646-282-3(5))*; per. 10.95 *(978-1-59646-283-0(3))* Dingles & Co.

—Number 4 Shop at the Store! Wallis, Rebecca, illus. 2005. (Community of Counting Ser.). 32p. (J). per. 10.95 *(978-1-59646-285-4(X))* Dingles & Co.

—Number 4 Shop at the Store!/Número 4 Vamos de compras a la Tienda! Wallis, Rebecca, illus. 2005. (Community of Counting Ser.).Tr. of Número 4 Vamos de compras a la Tienda! (ENG & SPA.). 32p. (J). per. 10.95 *(978-1-59646-287-8(6))* Dingles & Co.

—Number 5 Let's Go for a Drive! Wallis, Rebecca, illus. 2005. (Community of Counting Ser.). 32p. (J). per. 10.95 *(978-1-59646-289-2(2))* Dingles & Co.

—Number 5 Let's Go for a Drive!/Número 5 Vamos a viajar en Coche! Wallis, Rebecca, illus. 2005. (Community of Counting Ser.).Tr. of Número 5 Vamos a viajar en Coche! (ENG & SPA.). 32p. (J). per. 10.95 *(978-1-59646-291-5(4))* Dingles & Co.

—Number 6 What Can We Mix? Wallis, Rebecca, illus. 2005. (Community of Counting Ser.). 32p. (J). per. 10.95 *(978-1-59646-293-9(0))* Dingles & Co.

—Number 6 What Can We Mix?/Número 6 Qué podemos Mezclar? Wallis, Rebecca, illus. 2005. (Community of Counting Ser.).Tr. of Número 6 Qué podemos Mezclar? (ENG & SPA.). 32p. (J). per. 10.95 *(978-1-59646-295-3(7))* Dingles & Co.

—Number 7 Stars in the Heaven. Wallis, Rebecca, illus. 2005. (Community of Counting Ser.). 32p. (J). per. 10.95 *(978-1-59646-297-7(3))* Dingles & Co.

—Number 7 Stars in the Heaven/Número 7 Estrellas en el Cielo. Wallis, Rebecca, illus. (Community of Counting Ser.).Tr. of Número 7 Estrellas en el Cielo. (ENG & SPA.). 32p. (J). 2005. per. 10.95 *(978-1-59646-299-1(X))* 2004. lib. bdg. 21.65 *(978-1-891997-83-9(1))* Dingles & Co.

—Number 8 Let's Stay up Late! Wallis, Rebecca, illus. 2005. (Community of Counting Ser.). 32p. (J). per. 10.95 *(978-1-59646-301-1(5))* Dingles & Co.

—Number 8 Let's Stay up Late!/Número 8 Vamos a quedarnos en vela hasta muy Noche! Wallis, Rebecca, illus. (Community of Counting Ser.).Tr. of Número 8 Vamos a quedarnos en vela hasta muy Noche! (ENG & SPA.). 32p. (J). 2005. per. 10.95 *(978-1-59646-303-5(1))* 2004. lib. bdg. 21.65 *(978-1-891997-82-2(3))* Dingles & Co.

—Number 9 Dress up to Dine! Wallis, Rebecca, illus. 2005. (Community of Counting Ser.). 32p. (J). per. 10.95 *(978-1-59646-305-9(8))* Dingles & Co.

—Number 9 Dress up to Dine!/Número 9 Vestirse con elegancia para Cenar! Wallis, Rebecca, illus. 2005. (Community of Counting Ser.).Tr. of Número 9 Vestirse con elegancia para Cenar! (ENG & SPA.). 32p. (J). per. 10.95 *(978-1-59646-307-3(4))* Dingles & Co.

DK. Baby Touch & Feel Counting. 2013. (Baby Touch & Feel Ser.). (ENG.). 14p. (J). (gr. -1 — 1). bds. 7.99 *(978-1-4654-1432-8(0)*, DK Children) Dorling Kindersley Publishing, Inc.

—Pop-Up Peekaboo! Numbers. 2018. (Pop-Up Peekaboo! Ser.). (ENG., Illus.). 12p. (J). (— 1). bds. 12.99 *(978-1-4654-6840-6(4)*, DK Children) Dorling Kindersley Publishing, Inc.

—Tabbed Board Books: My First Numbers: Let's Get Counting! 2008. (My First Tabbed Board Book Ser.). (ENG.). 28p. (J). (gr. -1-k). bds. 12.99 *(978-0-7566-3604-3(3)*, DK Children) Dorling Kindersley Publishing, Inc.

Donahue, Peter. Build a Poster Coloring Book — ABC & 123. 2010. (Dover Alphabet Coloring Bks.). (ENG., Illus.). 48p. (J). (gr. 3-5). pap. 4.99 *(978-0-486-47946-0(3)*, 479463) Dover Pubns., Inc.

Dot-to-Dot Numbers 1-100 (Gr. 1-2) 2003. (J). *(978-1-58232-069-4(1))* ECS Learning Systems, Inc.

Dot-to-Dot Numbers 1-25 (Gr. K-1) 2003. (J). *(978-1-58232-068-7(3))* ECS Learning Systems, Inc.

Dowdy, Penny. Money, 1 vol. 2008. (My Path to Math Ser.). (ENG., Illus.). 24p. (J). (gr. k-3). pap. *(978-0-7787-4360-6(8))*; lib. bdg. *(978-0-7787-4342-2(X))* Crabtree Publishing Co.

—Place Value, 1 vol. 2008. (My Path to Math Ser.). (ENG., Illus.). 24p. (J). (gr. k-3). pap. *(978-0-7787-4361-3(6))* Crabtree Publishing Co.

Editorial Staff, Gareth. I Know Numbers, 1 vol. 2005. (I'm Ready for Math Ser.). (ENG., Illus.). 16p. (gr. k-1). pap. 6.30 *(978-0-8368-6480-9(8)*, ce350bc6-8632-42b1-8d00-ea4254d1698f, Weekly Reader Leveled Readers) Stevens, Gareth Publishing LLLP.

—I Know Numbers / Los Números, 1 vol. 2005. (I'm Ready for Math / Ya Puedo Aprender Matemáticas Ser.). (ENG & SPA., Illus.). 16p. (gr. k-1). pap. 6.30 *(978-0-8368-6490-8(5)*, 74759b1f-9eb0-489d-b553-ec56e7abf470, Weekly Reader Leveled Readers) Stevens, Gareth Publishing LLLP.

Ekeland, Ivar. The Cat in Numberland. O'Brien, John, illus. 2006. 56p. (J). (gr. 3-9). 19.95 *(978-0-8126-2744-2(X))* Cricket Bks.

Encycbrita. Revisiting Numbers Mic 2006 G. 6th ed. 2005. pap. 10.60 *(978-0-03-038568-1(7))* Harcourt Schl. Pubs.

Encyclopaedia Britannica Publishers, Inc. Staff. Math in Context: Picturing Numbers. 6th ed. 2005. (Math in Context Ser.). (gr. 6). pap. 10.60 *(978-0-03-042402-1(X))* Harcourt Schl. Pubs.

Etringer, Kathy. Mrs. E's Extraordinary Number Activities. Mitchell, Judy & Sussman, Ellen, eds. Rojas, Mary Galan, illus. 2006. 128p. (J). pap. 13.95 *(978-1-57310-506-4(6))* Teaching & Learning Co.

Feldman, Jean. Highway Letters, Numbers & Shapes: PreK-1. 2010. 80p. pap. 22.99 *(978-1-61601-036-2(3))* Creative Teaching Pr., Inc.

First Number Skills (Gr. K-1) 2003. (J). *(978-1-58232-081-6(0))* ECS Learning Systems, Inc.

Fisher, Valorie. Everything I Need to Know Before I'm Five. Fisher, Valorie, illus. 2011. (Illus.). 40p. (J). (gr. k-k). 17.99 *(978-0-375-86865-8(8)*, Schwartz & Wade Bks.) Random Hse. Children's Bks.

Flash Kids Editors, ed. Place Value: Grade 1 (Flash Skills) 2010. (Flash Skills Ser.). (ENG.). 64p. (J). pap. 3.95 *(978-1-4114-3455-4(2)*, Spark Publishing Group) Sterling Publishing Co., Inc.

—Place Value: Grade 2 (Flash Skills) 2010. (Flash Skills Ser.). (ENG.). 64p. (J). pap. 3.95 *(978-1-4114-3459-2(5)*, Spark Publishing Group) Sterling Publishing Co., Inc.

Freeman, Marcia S. My Sister Is in Third Grade: Putting Numbers in Order. 2007. (Math Focal Points (Discovery Library) Ser.). (Illus.). 24p. (J). (gr. 3-7). lib. bdg. 22.79 *(978-1-60044-638-2(8))* Rourke Educational Media.

Gagliano, Eugene. Four Wheels West: A Wyoming Number Book. Guy, Susan, illus. 2006. (America by the Numbers Ser.). (ENG.). 40p. (J). (gr. 1-3). 17.95 *(978-1-58536-210-3(7)*, 202041) Sleeping Bear Pr.

Galvin, Laura Gates. Tracing 123s. rev. ed. 2005. (Trace & Learn Ser.). (ENG., Illus.). 28p. (J). (gr. -1-3). 16.49 *(978-1-59069-446-6(5)*, 1A601) Studio Mouse LLC.

Goldstone, Bruce. 100 Ways to Celebrate 100 Days. Goldstone, Bruce, illus. 2013. (ENG., Illus.). 48p. (J). (gr. -1-3). 8.99 *(978-1-250-03369-7(1)*, 900120168) Square Fish.

Granger, Ronald. A Day at the Zoo: Compare Numbers. 2013. (InfoMax Math Readers Ser.). (ENG.). 16p. (J). (gr. k-1). pap. 42.00 *(978-1-4777-1986-2(5))*; (Illus.). pap. 7.00 *(978-1-4777-1985-5(7)*, ad81376c-a2f4-4fb9-b7ed-f9900ee916a9) Rosen Publishing Group, Inc., The. (Rosen Classroom).

Guille-Marrett, Emily & Raby, Charlotte. Collins Big Cat Phonics for Letters & Sounds - Number Fun: Band 00/Lilac. Gonzales, Laura, illus. 2018. (Collins Big Cat Phonics Ser.). (ENG.). 16p. (J). (gr. -1-k). pap. 6.99 *(978-0-00-825122-2(3))* HarperCollins Pubs. Ltd. GBR. Dist: Independent Pubs. Group.

Hammelef, Danielle S. Numbers Big & Small. 2006. (Early Explorers Ser.). (J). pap. *(978-1-4108-6130-6(9))* Benchmark Education Co.

Harcourt, creator. I Know Numbers: Math Concept Reader. 2007. (Illus.). (J). pap. 31.53 *(978-0-15-379893-1(9))* Houghton Mifflin Harcourt School Pubs.

Harcourt School Publishers Staff. Math Program Development, Grades K-2: Number Sense Binder Package. 3rd ed. 2003. ring bd. 355.40 *(978-0-15-340574-7(0))* Harcourt Schl. Pubs.

Harris, Nancy. Sticky Fingers: Exploring the Number 5. 2007. (Math Focal Points (Discovery Library) Ser.). (Illus.). 24p. (J). (gr. 3-7). lib. bdg. 22.79 *(978-1-60044-639-9(6))* Rourke Educational Media.

Harris, Trudy. Splitting the Herd: A Corral of Odds & Evens. Julian, Russell, illus. 2008. (Math Is Fun! Ser.). (ENG.). 32p. (gr. k-2). 16.95 *(978-0-8225-7466-8(7)*, Millbrook Pr.) Lerner Publishing Group.

Hawley, Ella. The Number 1. 2010. (Numbers in My World Ser.). (ENG.). 16p. (J). bds. 11.95 *(978-1-4358-9319-1(0)*, PowerKids Pr.) Rosen Publishing Group, Inc., The.

—The Number 2. 2010. (Numbers in My World Ser.). (ENG.). 16p. (J). bds. 11.95 *(978-1-4358-9320-7(4)*, PowerKids Pr.) Rosen Publishing Group, Inc., The.

—The Number 3. 2010. (Numbers in My World Ser.). (ENG.). 16p. (J). bds. 11.95 *(978-1-4358-9321-4(2)*, PowerKids Pr.) Rosen Publishing Group, Inc., The.

—The Number 4. 2010. (Numbers in My World Ser.). (ENG.). 16p. (J). bds. 11.95 *(978-1-4358-9322-1(0)*, PowerKids Pr.) Rosen Publishing Group, Inc., The.

—The Number 5. 2010. (Numbers in My World Ser.). (ENG.). 16p. (J). bds. 11.95 *(978-1-4358-9323-8(9)*, PowerKids Pr.) Rosen Publishing Group, Inc., The.

—Numbers 1, 2, 3, 4, 5. 2010. (Numbers in My World Ser.). (ENG.). 16p. (J). bds. 11.95 *(978-1-4358-9324-5(7)*, PowerKids Pr.) Rosen Publishing Group, Inc., The.

Head, Debby & Pollett, Libby. Bby Practice Pages: 02-Modeling Numbers 0-100. 2004. (ENG., Illus.). spiral bd. 37.00 *(978-1-885775-19-1(9))* bby Publications at The University of West Alabama.

—Bby Practice Pages: 06-Numbers & Words 0-10. 2004. (ENG., Illus.). spiral bd. 37.00 *(978-1-885775-22-1(9))* bby Publications at The University of West Alabama.

—Bby Practice Pages: 07-Making Ten. 2004. (ENG., Illus.). spiral bd. 37.00 *(978-1-885775-23-8(7))* bby Publications at The University of West Alabama.

—Bby Practice Pages: 09-Numbers & Words 11-20. 2004. (ENG., Illus.). spiral bd. 37.00 *(978-1-885775-25-2(3))* bby Publications at The University of West Alabama.

Heinst, Marie. My First Number Book. (Illus.). (J). pap. 16.95 *(978-0-590-74282-5(5))* Scholastic, Inc.

—My First Number Book. Scholastic, Inc. Staff, ed. (FRE., Illus.). 48p. (J). 19.99 *(978-0-590-74416-4(X))* Scholastic, Inc.

Hickman, Debbie. The Exasperated Clock. Taylor, Adam, illus. 2013. 40p. pap. *(978-1-4602-1811-2(6))* FriesenPress.

Hill, Eric. S. S. Happiness Crew: Book of Numbers. (Illus.). 11p. (J). (gr. -1). *(978-0-915696-65-9(7))* Determined Productions, Inc.

Hinkler Books Staff. 1 2 3. rev. ed. 2006. (ENG., Illus.). 12p. (J). (gr. -1-1). bds. 7.95 *(978-1-74157-603-0(2))* Hinkler Bks. Pty, Ltd. AUS. Dist: Penton Overseas, Inc.

Hoffman, Joan. Nursery Rhymes. 2019. (ENG.). 32p. (J). (gr. -1-k). pap. 4.49 *(978-1-60159-115-9(2)*, bc300fd1-1047-40c3-92d7-ba873f82a7f0) School Zone Publishing Co.

Holden, Pam. Name the Numbers, 1 vol. 2015. (ENG., Illus.). 16p. (-1). pap. *(978-1-77654-117-1(0)*, Red Rocket Readers) Flying Start Bks.

HOP, LLC. Hooked on Numbers. 2006. 24.99 *(978-1-60143-034-2(5))* HOP, LLC.

In Step with the Standards - Number Sense. 2005. (J). spiral bd. 15.95 *(978-1-58123-375-9(2))* Larson Learning, Inc.

It's Counting Time. 2004. (J). per. 15.99 *(978-0-9744205-2-3(2))* Golden Eagle Publishing Hse., Inc.

Kelly, Jodi. At the Race: Count to Tell the Number of Objects. 2013. (InfoMax Math Readers Ser.). (ENG.). 16p. (J). (gr. k-1). pap. 42.00 *(978-1-4777-1971-8(7))*; (Illus.). pap. 7.00 *(978-1-4777-1970-1(9),* 96e1e351-7901-4811-96ef-51e14cb79659) Rosen Publishing Group, Inc., The. (Rosen Classroom).

Kenyon, Dolores. The History of Complex Numbers - A Genealogy. 2007. spiral bd. 8.95 net. *(978-1-60402-110-3(1))* Independent Pub.

Kernan, Elizabeth. Counting at the Store: Learning to Count from 6 To 10, 1 vol. 2010. (Math for the REAL World Ser.). (ENG., Illus.). 8p. (gr. k-1). pap. 5.15 *(978-0-8239-8842-6(2),* bc4a3c61-c19d-44fd-bb24-d507c8eb2f1f) Rosen Publishing Group, Inc., The.

King, Zelda. The Story of Our Numbers: The History of Arabic Numerals, 1 vol. 2010. (Math for the REAL World Ser.). (ENG., Illus.). 24p. (gr. 3-4). pap. 8.25 *(978-0-8239-8870-9(8),* d80752d6-c164-4f90-88ac-3eadecc1a2df, PowerKids Pr.) Rosen Publishing Group, Inc., The.

La Jars, David. One, Two, Red & Blue. rev. ed. 2004. (Talk Together Ser.). (ENG., Illus.). 24p. (J). (gr. -1-k). pap. 5.95 *(978-1-58728-019-1(1),* Two-Can Publishing) T&N Children's Publishing.

Lamb, Stacey, illus. Wipe Clean 123 Book. 2011. (Wipe-Clean Bks). 20p. (J). pap. 7.99 *(978-0-7945-3075-4(3),* Usborne) EDC Publishing.

Larousse Color ABC y 123 (Amarillo), Vol. 1. 2003. (SPA., Illus.). 6p. (J). 2.98 *(978-970-22-0163-2(2))* Larousse, Ediciones, S. A. de C. V. MEX. Dist: Giron Bks.

Learn Your Numbers. 2003. (Illus.). 10p. (J). bds. *(978-1-74047-003-2(6))* Book Co. Publishing Pty, Ltd., The.

Let's Say Our Numbers. 2007. (Simple First Words Ser.). (Illus.). 14p. (J). *(978-1-84332-520-8(9))* Priddy Bks.

El Libro de Contar de los Chocolates M & M's Brand. 2004. 32p. (J). pap. 6.95 *(978-1-57091-370-9(6))* Charlesbridge Publishing, Inc.

Linda, Winder. Glitter: My First Book of Shapes Numbers Colors & the Alphabet Gods Way. 2003. *(978-1-892354-85-3(3))* Educational Publishing Concepts, Inc.

Litchfield, Felicity. Primeros Numeros. 2004.Tr. of First Numbers. (SPA., Illus.). 48p. (J). (gr. -1-18). 12.95 *(978-0-7460-4508-4(5))* EDC Publishing.

Litchfield, Jo, illus. First Picture 123. 2005. (First Picture Board Books Ser.). 16p. (J). 11.95 *(978-0-7945-0939-2(8),* Usborne) EDC Publishing.

Little, Richard. I Know Halves & Wholes, 1 vol. 2018. (What I Know Ser.). (ENG.). 24p. (gr. k-k). 24.27 *(978-1-5382-1738-2(4),* 9403776d-7608-4061-9314-11102c1ec140) Stevens, Gareth Publishing LLLP.

Lluch, Alex A. I Like to Learn Numbers: Hungry Chameleon. 2011. 32p. (J). (gr. -1-k). bds. 4.95 *(978-1-934386-01-9(4))* WS Publishing.

—Let's Leap Ahead Numbers. 2012. 80p. (J). (gr. -1). spiral bd. 9.95 *(978-1-936061-60-0(0))* WS Publishing.

—Trace & Learn The 123s. 2014. (Illus.). 28p. (J). (-k). bds. 8.95 *(978-1-61351-088-9(8))* WS Publishing.

LoPresti, Angeline Sparagna. A Place for Zero. Hornung, Phyllis, illus. alt. ed. 2003. (Charlesbridge Math Adventures Ser.). 32p. (J). (gr. 1-4). pap. 7.95 *(978-1-57091-196-5(7))* Charlesbridge Publishing, Inc.

Lucy Ladybug Learns Numbers. (Board Bks.). (Illus.). 6p. (J). (gr. -1-k). 4.99 *(978-0-7847-1119-4(4),* 03529, Bean Sprouts) Standard Publishing.

Lundie, Isobel. The Amicus Book Of 123. 2019. (ENG.). 10p. (J). (gr. -1-1). bds. 8.99 *(978-1-68152-569-3(0),* 10870) Amicus.

Madden, Jean Griffing. Digger Digs Digits. 2011. 36p. pap. *(978-1-4269-9587-3(3))* Trafford Publishing (UK) Ltd.

Makeeff, Cyndi Sue. Inky Winky Spider 1,2,3,4. Riley, Kevin, illus. 2006. 32p. (J). pap. 7.99 *(978-0-9778310-1-2(9))* New Vision Entertainment, LLC.

Mattern, Joanne. At the Football Game: Learning the Symbols , And =, 1 vol. 2010. (Math for the REAL World Ser.). (ENG.). 16p. (gr. 2-3). pap. 7.05 *(978-0-8239-8875-4(9),* 75a3d101-e531-4df0-bad7-8190e0af2c8f, Rosen Classroom) Rosen Publishing Group, Inc., The.

McDonnell, Rory. Odd & Even with Otters, 1 vol. 2017. (Animal Math Ser.). (ENG.). 24p. (J). (gr. 1-2). pap. 9.15 *(978-1-5382-0852-6(0),* d3db3c5f-a581-4da2-937b-b2a516f99b12) Stevens, Gareth Publishing LLLP.

Meachen Rau, Dana. Cinco / Five, 1 vol. 2010. (¡Cuenta con Ello! / Count on It! Ser.). (ENG & SPA.). 24p. (gr. k-1). lib. bdg. 25.50 *(978-0-7614-3477-1(1),* 9217f5b0-80e0-4f12-b670-380bd4ea4e26) Cavendish Square Publishing LLC.

—Cinco (Five), 1 vol. 2010. (¡Cuenta con Ello! (Count on It!) Ser.). (SPA.). 24p. (gr. k-1). lib. bdg. 25.50 *(978-0-7614-3449-8(6),* cbaf1b48-075c-4f9b-b1ad-24a288269bef) Cavendish Square Publishing LLC.

—Cuatro / Four, 1 vol. 2010. (¡Cuenta con Ello! / Count on It! Ser.). (ENG & SPA.). 24p. (gr. k-1). lib. bdg. 25.50 *(978-0-7614-3476-4(3),* f86b75e1-9ed0-42a4-94ca-eec7ddf95666) Cavendish Square Publishing LLC.

—Cuatro (Four), 1 vol. 2010. (¡Cuenta con Ello! (Count on It!) Ser.). (SPA.). 24p. (gr. k-1). lib. bdg. 25.50 *(978-0-7614-3448-1(8),* 9957861d-3f82-4364-b812-4b2e42dfaf2b) Cavendish Square Publishing LLC.

—Diez / Ten, 1 vol. 2010. (¡Cuenta con Ello! / Count on It! Ser.). (ENG & SPA.). 24p. (gr. k-1). lib. bdg. 25.50 *(978-0-7614-3478-8(X),* b2374705-efa4-4627-9101-0e05b905898c) Cavendish Square Publishing LLC.

—Diez (Ten), 1 vol. 2010. (¡Cuenta con Ello! (Count on It!) Ser.). (SPA.). 24p. (gr. k-1). lib. bdg. 25.50 *(978-0-7614-3452-8(6),* 9a75949b-3a49-49bb-8bc4-ed4054751e49) Cavendish Square Publishing LLC.

—Dos / Two, 1 vol. 2010. (¡Cuenta con Ello! / Count on It! Ser.). (ENG & SPA.). 24p. (gr. k-1). lib. bdg. 25.50 *(978-0-7614-3474-0(7),* 8cb8a9eb-f91f-4818-8f25-d207b47dc58a) Cavendish Square Publishing LLC.

—Dos (Two), 1 vol. 2010. (¡Cuenta con Ello! (Count on It!) Ser.). (SPA.). 24p. (gr. k-1). lib. bdg. 25.50 *(978-0-7614-3445-0(3),* 0726e9b4-da53-47e3-a2ef-66ce4473590a) Cavendish Square Publishing LLC.

—Five, 1 vol. 2009. (Count on It! Ser.). (ENG.). 24p. (gr. k-1). lib. bdg. 25.50 *(978-0-7614-2970-8(0),* 713f8ffa-9145-4399-91cd-379220e02bb4) Cavendish Square Publishing LLC.

—Four, 1 vol. 2009. (Count on It! Ser.). (ENG.). 24p. (gr. k-1). lib. bdg. 25.50 *(978-0-7614-2969-2(7),* 06d325d6-245f-4970-94ed-cec008c1eab7) Cavendish Square Publishing LLC.

—One, 1 vol. 2009. (Count on It! Ser.). (ENG.). 24p. (gr. k-1). lib. bdg. 25.50 *(978-0-7614-2966-1(2),* df6e6dca-e254-4e1d-aa74-169c26b1588f) Cavendish Square Publishing LLC.

—Uno / One, 1 vol. 2010. (¡Cuenta con Ello! / Count on It! Ser.). (ENG & SPA.). 24p. (gr. k-1). lib. bdg. 25.50 *(978-0-7614-3472-6(0),* 10e0d891-c780-4423-aa62-d9038782bf17) Cavendish Square Publishing LLC.

—Uno (One), 1 vol. 2010. (¡Cuenta con Ello! (Count on It!) Ser.). (SPA.). 24p. (gr. k-1). lib. bdg. *(978-0-7614-3444-3(5),* afc6c8ae-aa8e-4033-8f50-b3dc9454446a) Cavendish Square Publishing LLC.

—Ten, 1 vol. 2009. (Count on It! Ser.). (ENG.). 24p. (gr. k-1). lib. bdg. 25.50 *(978-0-7614-2971-5(9),* ff0ebf7f-58c2-4638-baf2-7901a586b320) Cavendish Square Publishing LLC.

—Three, 1 vol. 2009. (Count on It! Ser.). (ENG.). 24p. (gr. k-1). lib. bdg. 25.50 *(978-0-7614-2968-5(9),* 7e068de5-fd49-43b6-beba-1da5a59cc7a9) Cavendish Square Publishing LLC.

—Tres / Three, 1 vol. 2010. (¡Cuenta con Ello! / Count on It! Ser.). (ENG & SPA.). 24p. (gr. k-1). lib. bdg. 25.50 *(978-0-7614-3475-7(5),* 7bc66dd1-aea9-41e3-989c-9621b4495e2c) Cavendish Square Publishing LLC.

—Tres (Three), 1 vol. 2010. (¡Cuenta con Ello! (Count on It!) Ser.). (SPA.). 24p. (gr. k-1). lib. bdg. 25.50 *(978-0-7614-3446-7(1),* 1746f546-853f-4516-96de-6a5fa26344d7) Cavendish Square Publishing LLC.

—Two, 1 vol. 2009. (Count on It! Ser.). (ENG.). 24p. (gr. k-1). lib. bdg. 25.50 *(978-0-7614-2967-8(0),* db55df7c-e239-43d2-be15-90e815e48ba3) Cavendish Square Publishing LLC.

Mega Jumbo ABC And 123. 2006. (J). per. 9.95 *(978-1-885920-13-3(X))* Pyramid Publishing, Inc.

Meredith, Susan. Half or Whole? 2010. (Little World Math Ser.). (ENG., Illus.). 24p. (gr. k-2). pap. 9.95 *(978-1-61590-532-4(4),* 9781615905324) Rourke Educational Media.

Miles Kelly Staff & Nilsen, Anna. Numbers: Let's Learn. 2003. (Let's Learn Ser.). (Illus.). 20p. (J). 7.95 *(978-1-84236-018-7(3))* Miles Kelly Publishing, Ltd. GBR. Dist: Independent Pubs. Group.

Moon, Jo, illus. Making Numbers. 2006. (Making... Ser.). 14p. (J). (gr. -1-3). bds. 7.95 *(978-1-57791-249-1(7))* Brighter Minds Children's Publishing.

Morris, Charlie. Avery's Art Supplies: Compare Numbers. 2013. (InfoMax Math Readers Ser.). (ENG.). 16p. (J). (gr. k-1). pap. 42.00 *(978-1-4777-1953-4(9))*; (Illus.). pap. 7.00 *(978-1-4777-1952-7(0),* 3e72faaf-9f59-4cfb-89b7-32f9bc2dd1e2) Rosen Publishing Group, Inc., The. (Rosen Classroom).

Napier, Matt. Hat Tricks Count: A Hockey Number Book. Rose, Melanie, illus. rev. ed. 2005. (Sports Ser.). (ENG.). 40p. (J). (gr. 1-4). 16.95 *(978-1-58536-163-2(1),* 202259) Sleeping Bear Pr.

—Hockey Numbers. Rose, Melanie, illus. (Numbers & Counting Ser.). (ENG.). 28p. (J). (gr. -1-1). 2009. bds. 11.75 *(978-1-58536-495-4(9),* 202304) 2007. bds. 7.99 *(978-1-58536-346-9(4),* 203001) Sleeping Bear Pr.

National Geographic Learning. Reading Expeditions (Science: Math Behind the Science): Number Know-How. 2007. (ENG., Illus.). 24p. (J). pap. 15.95 *(978-0-7922-4591-9(1))* CENGAGE Learning.

Nickelodeon Staff, ed. 1-2-3 - Go Diego Go! 2010. (Write, Slide & Learn Ser.). 14p. (J). (gr. -1-1). 9.99 *(978-1-74184-521-1(1))* Hinkler Bks. Pty. Ltd. AUS. Dist: Ideals Pubns.

Nimble with Numbers: Student Practice Book. 2003. (Nimble with Numbers Ser.). 11.95 *(978-0-7690-2824-8(1))*; 11.95 *(978-0-7690-2823-1(3))*; (J). (gr. 4). 11.95 *(978-0-7690-2821-7(7))*; (J). (gr. 5). 11.95 *(978-0-7690-2820-0(9))*; (J). (gr. 6). 11.95 *(978-0-7690-2819-4(5))* Seymour, Dale Pubns.

Norton, Grace R. Count Us in Too. 2005. (Illus.). 32p. (J). (gr. -1-4). 14.95 *(978-1-889506-03-6(6))* Kendar Publishing, Inc.

Novick, Mary & Hale, Jenny. Numbers. Harlin, Sybel, illus. 2010. (Double Delight Ser.). (ENG.). 24p. (J). (gr. -1 — 1). pap. 11.99 *(978-1-877003-57-8(3))* Little Hare Bks. AUS. Dist: Independent Pubs. Group.

Number Facts To 10 (Gr. 1-2) 2003. (J). *(978-1-58232-083-0(7))* ECS Learning Systems, Inc.

Number Facts to 10 Spanish Version. 2007. (J). per. *(978-1-58232-152-3(3))* ECS Learning Systems, Inc.

Number Fun. 2005. (Little Celebrations Thematic Packages Ser.). (J). (gr. k-3). 133.50 *(978-0-673-75381-6(6))* Celebration Pr.

Numbers. 2003. (J). per. *(978-1-884907-43-2(1))*; per. *(978-1-884907-47-0(4))* Paradise Pr., Inc.

Numbers. 2004. (Early Days Ser.). (Illus.). 18p. (J). bds. *(978-1-84229-973-9(5))* Top That! Publishing PLC.

Numbers - Book 2. 2005. (J). per. 8.95 *(978-1-59566-158-6(1))* QEB Publishing Inc.

Numbers: English & Spanish Book 3. 2006. (SPA.). (J). bds. *(978-0-9785744-3-7(5))* LTL Media LLC.

Numbers 1-20, 6 vols. 2014. (Numbers 1-20 Ser.: 6). (ENG.). 24p. (J). (gr. -1-3). lib. bdg. 179.58 *(978-1-62403-263-9(X),* 1588, SandCastle) ABDO Publishing Co.

Numbers & More. 2005. (J). bds. *(978-1-4194-0051-3(7))* Paradise Pr., Inc.

Numbers Book 1. 2005. (J). per. 8.95 *(978-1-59566-154-8(9))* QEB Publishing Inc.

Numbers Count. 2003. (J). per. *(978-1-57657-951-0(4))* Paradise Pr., Inc.

Numeracy Through Spreadsheets. (Illus.). 48p. (J). (gr. 4-6). pap. *(978-1-876367-63-3(6))* Wizard Bks.

O'Donnell, Kerri. Numbers & Operations, 1 vol. 2003. (BrainBuilders Ser.). (ENG.). 48p. (J). (gr. k-4). pap. 5.25 *(978-1-4042-8536-1(9),* 882423ab-cd90-4109-aa82-b36778a3ed3c) Rosen Publishing Group, Inc., The.

Oquendo, Lisa, illus. Números - Numbers. 2006. (ENG & SPA.). (J). bds. 5.99 *(978-1-934113-01-1(8))* Little Cubans, LLC.

Penn, M. W. Comparing Numbers! 2012. (Pebble Math Ser.). (ENG.). 24p. (gr. k-1). pap. 35.70 *(978-1-4296-8307-4(4),* Pebble) Capstone.

Phillips, Dee. Colors. 2009. (Christmas Lift the Flap Ser.). (ENG.). 10p. (J). (gr. -1-k). bds. 5.95 *(978-1-84696-966-9(2),* TickTock Books) Octopus Publishing Group GBR. Dist: Independent Pubs. Group.

—First Addition. 2009. (Christmas Lift the Flap Ser.). (ENG.). 10p. (J). (gr. -1-k). bds. 5.95 *(978-1-84696-967-6(0),* TickTock Books) Octopus Publishing Group GBR. Dist: Independent Pubs. Group.

—Numbers. 2009. (Christmas Lift the Flap Ser.). (ENG.). 10p. (J). (gr. -1-k). bds. 5.95 *(978-1-84696-969-0(7),* TickTock Books) Octopus Publishing Group GBR. Dist: Independent Pubs. Group.

Phillips, Sarah & Tattam, Mark. Numbers. 2005. (Baby See a Shape Ser.). (Illus.). 12p. (gr. -1-k). per., bds. *(978-1-905051-91-5(3))* Make Believe Ideas.

Priddy Books Staff. First Concepts: Numbers. 2003. (Illus.). (J). bds. *(978-0-312-49232-8(4),* Priddy Bks.) St. Martin's Pr.

Professor Q's Chinese-English Language Books: Shu' Zi' - Numbers. 2006. (J). *(978-0-9743359-6-4(7))* Murdock Publishing Co.

Publications International Ltd. Staff, ed. Eric Carle Counting Write & Erase Sound. 2011. 16p. (J). bds. 16.98 *(978-1-4508-1373-0(9),* 89ea66b2-f0ff-4240-b53e-290c676c9925) Phoenix International Publications, Inc.

—My Numbers Book. 2011. 32p. (J). bds. *(978-1-4508-1021-0(7))* Publications International, Ltd.

—Numbers Learning Board. 2011. 1p. (J). bds. *(978-1-4508-1431-7(X))* Publications International, Ltd.

—Numbers (Listen & Learn Sound Book) 2011. 19p. (J). bds. 11.98 *(978-1-4508-1705-9(X))* Phoenix International Publications, Inc.

Publishing, Arcturus. Color by Numbers Animals. 2017. (ENG.). 96p. (J). (gr. 1-7). pap. 9.99 *(978-1-78428-473-2(4),* 302eb4f8-5a96-4ef0-ae97-e61fcd04a33e) Arcturus Publishing GBR. Dist: Baker & Taylor Publisher Services (BTPS).

QEB Maths Club National Book Stores Edition: Using Numbers Book 1. 2006. (J). per. *(978-1-59566-286-6(3))* QEB Publishing Inc.

QEB Maths Club National Book Stores Edition: Using Numbers Book 2. 2006. (J). per. *(978-1-59566-290-3(1))* QEB Publishing Inc.

QEB Start Math Book National Book Stores Edition: Numbers - Book 1. 2006. (J). per. *(978-1-59566-272-9(3))* QEB Publishing Inc.

QEB Start Math Book Stores Edition: Numbers - Book 2. 2006. (J). per. *(978-1-59566-276-7(6))* QEB Publishing Inc.

Really Big Numbers. 2014. (ENG., Illus.). 192p. pap. 27.00 *(978-1-4704-1425-2(2),* P233118) American Mathematical Society.

Rebman, Nick. What Comes First? A Book about Sequences. 2016. (Concept Fun Ser.). (ENG.). 16p. (J). (gr. -1-2). 29.93 *(978-1-5038-0763-1(0),* 210611) Child's World, Inc, The.

—Which One Is Not Like the Others? A Book about Differences. 2016. (Concept Fun Ser.). (ENG.). 16p. (J). (gr. -1-2). 29.93 *(978-1-5038-0768-6(1),* 210616) Child's World, Inc, The.

Reynolds, Cynthia Furlong. Fishing for Numbers: A Maine Number Book. Brett, Jeannie, illus. 2005. (America by the Numbers Ser.). (ENG.). 40p. (J). (gr. 1-3). 19.99 *(978-1-58536-035-2(X),* 201953) Sleeping Bear Pr.

Rhodes, Immacula A. Little Learners Packets: Numbers. 2018. (Little Learner Packets Ser.). (ENG.). 96p. (gr. -1-k). pap. 12.99 *(978-1-338-22829-8(3))* Scholastic, Inc.

Rigol, Francesc, illus. Dan & Din Learn Numbers. 2009. (Learning with Dan & Din Ser.). 12p. (J). (gr. -1-k). bds. 11.40 *(978-1-60754-402-9(4))* Windmill Bks.

Robinson, C. L. MATH1on1 Numbers & Operations. 2006. (YA). per. 9.99 *(978-0-9786767-0-4(X))* Robinson, Consuelo.

Robleda, Margarita. Los Numeros Tragaldabas. Gurovich, Natalia, illus. 2004. (SPA.). 24p. (J). 12.95 *(978-970-690-807-0(2))* Planeta Mexicana Editorial S. A. de C. V. MEX. Dist: Lectorum Pubns., Inc.

Rosa-Mendoza, Gladys. Numbers. Cifuentes, Carolina, ed. Noiset, Michele, illus. 2004. (English-Spanish Foundations Ser.).Tr. of Los Numeros. (ENG & SPA.). 20p. (J). bds. 6.95 *(978-0-9679748-2-8(8))* Me+Mi Publishing.

Rosario, Sherwin, illus. Meet the Numbers Lift the Flap Book. 2005. 12p. (J). bds. 9.99 *(978-0-9767008-1-4(6))* Preschool Prep Co.

—Meet the Numbers One to Ten. 2005. 10p. (J). bds. 7.99 *(978-0-9767008-3-8(2))* Preschool Prep Co.

Rosen, Michael J. Mind-Boggling Numbers. Patton, Julia, illus. 2016. (ENG.). 32p. (J). (gr. 2-5). 19.99 *(978-1-4677-3489-9(6),* 4baa6444-7e37-4a76-8734-e8b558533462, Millbrook Pr.) Lerner Publishing Group.

—Mind-Boggling Numbers. Patton, Julia, illus. 2016. (ENG.). 32p. (J). (gr. 2-5). E-Book 30.65 *(978-1-5124-1108-9(6),* Millbrook Pr.) Lerner Publishing Group.

Rosenberg, Pam. Is It Still a Number? 2006. (Rookie Read-About Math Ser.). (ENG., Illus.). 32p. (J). (gr. 1-2). lib. bdg. 20.50 *(978-0-516-25443-2(X))* Scholastic Library Publishing.

Roza, Greg. The Hubble Space Telescope: Understanding & Representing Numbers in the Billions, 1 vol. 2004. (PowerMath: Proficiency Plus Ser.). (ENG., Illus.). 32p. (J). (gr. 5-6). lib. bdg. 28.93 *(978-1-4042-2931-0(0),* 7af2f6d7-2234-4b48-ae6e-bc071138672d, PowerKids Pr.) Rosen Publishing Group, Inc., The.

—The Hubble Space Telescope: Understanding & Representing Numbers up to 1 Billion, 1 vol. 2010. (Math for the REAL World Ser.). (ENG., Illus.). 32p. (gr. 5-6). pap. 10.00 *(978-1-4042-5129-8(4),* 881be7c6-f2f5-4e5e-bf41-3aab27d0b7a2) Rosen Publishing Group, Inc., The.

Rozines Roy, Jennifer & Roy, Gregory. Numbers on the Street, 1 vol. (Math All Around Ser.). (ENG.). 32p. (gr. 2-2). 2008. pap. 9.23 *(978-0-7614-3406-1(2),* 0af6003d-01c5-40d9-9769-3a6d138a78a9) 2007. (Illus.). lib. bdg. 32.64 *(978-0-7614-2002-6(9),* cb3bfc0b-d11f-4c11-96fb-29017df3202b) Cavendish Square Publishing LLC.

Santillana & Dorling Kindersley Publishing Staff. Numeros. (Show Me Ser.). (SPA., Illus.). 16p. (J). (gr. -1-k). bds. 6.95 *(978-1-58986-326-2(7))* Santillana USA Publishing Co., Inc.

Sargent, Daina. Colors & the Number 1, 11 vols. Lenoir, Jane, illus. 2005. (Learn to Read Ser.: 11). 24p. (J). pap. 10.95 *(978-1-59381-031-3(8))* Ozark Publishing.

—Colors & the Number 10/Los Colores y el Número 10, 11 vols. Lenoir, Jane, illus. 2005. (Learn to Read Ser.: 11). (ENG & SPA.). 24p. (J). pap. 10.95 *(978-1-59381-147-1(0))*; lib. bdg. 20.95 *(978-1-59381-146-4(2))* Ozark Publishing.

—Colors & the Number 2, 11 vols. Lenoir, Jane, illus. l.t. ed. 2004. (Learn to Read Ser.). 24p. (J). lib. bdg. 20.95 *(978-1-59381-032-0(6))* Ozark Publishing.

—Colors & the Number 4, 11 vols. Lenoir, Jane, illus. 2005. (Learn to Read Ser.). 24p. (J). pap. 10.95 *(978-1-59381-037-5(7))* Ozark Publishing.

—Colors & the Number 6, 11 vols. Lenoir, Jane, illus. l.t. ed. 2004. (Learn to Read Ser.). 24p. (J). lib. bdg. 20.95 *(978-1-59381-040-5(7))* Ozark Publishing.

—Colors & the Number 6/Los Colores y el Número 6, 11 vols. Lenoir, Jane, illus. 2005. (Learn to Read Ser.: 11). (ENG & SPA.). 24p. (J). pap. 10.95 *(978-1-59381-139-6(X))* Ozark Publishing.

—Colors & the Number 7, 11 vols. Lenoir, Jane, illus. l.t. ed. 2004. (Learn to Read Ser.). 24p. (J). lib. bdg. 20.95 *(978-1-59381-042-9(3))* Ozark Publishing.

—Colors & the Number 8, 11 vols. Lenoir, Jane, illus. l.t. ed. 2004. (Learn to Read Ser.). 24p. (J). lib. bdg. 20.95 *(978-1-59381-044-3(X))* Ozark Publishing.

—Colors & the Number 9, 11 vols. Lenoir, Jane, illus. l.t. ed. 2004. (Learn to Read Ser.). 24p. (J). lib. bdg. 20.95 *(978-1-59381-046-7(6))* Ozark Publishing.

—Introduction to Colors & Numbers, 11 vols. Lenoir, Jane, illus. l.t. ed. 2004. (Learn to Read Ser.: 11). 24p. (J). lib. bdg. 20.95 *(978-1-59381-050-4(4))* Ozark Publishing.

—Introduction to Colors & Numbers/Introducción a los Colores Numeros, 11 vols. Lenoir, Jane, illus. l.t. ed. 2005. (Learn to Read Ser.: 11). (SPA & ENG.). 24p. (J). pap. 10.95 *(978-1-59381-149-5(7))* Ozark Publishing.

Sargent, Daina & Lenoir, Jane. Colors & the Number 6/Los colores y el Número 6, 11 vols. 2005. (Learn to Read Ser.).Tr. of Los colores y el Número 6. (ENG & SPA., Illus.). 24p. (J). lib. bdg. 20.95 *(978-1-59381-138-9(1))* Ozark Publishing.

School Zone Publishing Company Staff. Bilingual 1-25 Dot to Dots. rev. ed. 2007. (ENG.). 64p. (J). (gr. k). pap. 3.99 *(978-1-58947-971-5(8))* School Zone Publishing Co.

—Numbers & Shapes. 2008. (ENG.). (J). 5.99 *(978-1-60159-102-9(0))* School Zone Publishing Co.

School Zone Staff. Bilingual Numbers 1-100. 2004. (ENG.). (J). 2.99 *(978-1-58947-983-8(1))* School Zone Publishing Co.

—Numbers 0-25, 56 vols. rev. ed. 2019. (ENG.). (J). (gr. -1-k). 3.49 *(978-1-58947-478-9(3),* 7da579c2-506b-4ebd-b03d-65687002aa3f) School Zone Publishing Co.

Schrier, Allyson Valentine. First in Line. 2008. (Discovering & Exploring Science Ser.). (Illus.). 16p. (J). (gr. -1-3). lib. bdg. 12.95 *(978-0-7569-8437-3(8))* Perfection Learning Corp.

Schwartz, David M. How Much Is a Million? Kellogg, Steven, illus. 20th anniv. ed. 2004. (ENG.). 40p. (J). (gr. -1-3). pap. 7.99 *(978-0-688-09933-6(5),* HarperCollins) HarperCollins Pubs.

—How Much Is a Million? 2004. (J). (gr. k-3). 18.40 *(978-0-8085-7914-4(2))* Turtleback.

Schwartz, Richard Evan. Gallery of the Infinite. 2016. (ENG., Illus.). 187p. pap. 29.00 *(978-1-4704-2557-9(2),* P508593) American Mathematical Society.

—Life on the Infinite Farm. 2018. (Monograph Bks.). (ENG., Illus.). 176p. pap. 25.00 *(978-1-4704-4736-6(3),* P590691) American Mathematical Society.

—You Can Count on Monsters: The First 100 Numbers & Their Characters. 2015. (Monograph Bks.). (ENG., Illus.). 242p. pap. 27.00 *(978-1-4704-2209-7(3),* P470408) American Mathematical Society.

Shea. Working with Numbers. 2004. (Steck-Vaughn Working with Numbers Ser.). (ENG., Illus.). 160p. (gr. 5-5). pap. 18.85 *(978-0-7398-9160-5(X))*;Level D. (gr. 4-4). pap. 18.85 *(978-0-7398-9159-9(6))*;Level F. (gr. 6-6). pap. 18.85 *(978-0-7398-9161-2(8))* Houghton Mifflin Harcourt Publishing Co.

Silver Dolphin en Español Editors. Disney Tesoro de libros de Calcomanias: Disney Sticker Book Treasury, Spanish-Language Edition. 2007. (Illus.). 48p. (J). *(978-970-718-447-3(7),* Silver Dolphin en Español) Advanced Marketing, S. de R. L. de C. V.

Slaughter, Tom. 1 2 3. 2005. (SPA.). (J). (gr. k-18). pap. 7.95 *(978-968-7381-54-1(X))* Tecolote, Ediciones, S.A. de C.V. MEX. Dist: Iaconi, Mariuccia Bk. Imports.

Staff, Gareth Editorial Staff. I Know Numbers, 1 vol. 2005. (I'm Ready for Math Ser.). (ENG., Illus.). 16p. (gr. k-1). lib. bdg. 21.67 *(978-0-8368-6475-5(1),* 64d07ae2-372d-41bf-a66d-2b4866f0ca9d, Weekly Reader Leveled Readers) Stevens, Gareth Publishing LLLP.

—I Know Numbers / Los Números, 1 vol. 2005. (I'm Ready for Math / Ya Puedo Aprender Matemáticas Ser.). (ENG & SPA., Illus.). 16p. (gr. k-1). lib. bdg. 21.67

(978-0-8368-6485-4(9), cc2b38ae-3072-4ca8-9059-0912e16e52a3, Weekly Reader Leveled Readers) Stevens, Gareth Publishing LLLP.
Steck-Vaughn Staff. At-Home Workbooks: Numbers. 2004. (Illus.). pap., wbk. ed. (978-0-7398-8529-1(4)) Steck-Vaughn.
—Early Math: Number Sense, 10 Pack. 2005. pap. 29.95 (978-1-4190-0343-1(7)); pap. 2.99 (978-1-4190-0319-6(4)) Steck-Vaughn.
—How Much Is 100? 2003. pap. 4.10 (978-0-7398-7661-9(9)) Steck-Vaughn.
—Math Remediation: Number Concepts. 2005. pap. 5.49 (978-1-4190-0366-0(6)) Harcourt Schl. Pubs.
Studio Mouse Staff, creator. Write-with-Me Numbers. rev. ed. 2008. (ENG., Illus.). 28p. (J). 14.99 (978-1-59069-617-0(4)) Studio Mouse LLC.
Tabletop Pocket Chart Counting & Numbers Card Set. 2004. (J). pap. 8.95 (978-1-56911-169-7(3)) Learning Resources, Inc.
TBD. Doodles 123. 2012. (ENG., Illus.). 64p. (gr. k-5). pap. 7.95 (978-1-61608-664-0(5), 608664, Sky Pony Pr.) Skyhorse Publishing Co., Inc.
Teach-Me-Bears Learn Numbers. 2003. (J). per. (978-1-884907-62-3(8)) Paradise Pr., Inc.
TestSMART Plus Whole Numbers, Level B-1. 2004. (J). (978-1-57022-489-8(7)) ECS Learning Systems, Inc.
TestSMART Plus Whole Numbers, Level B-2. 2004. (J). (978-1-57022-490-4(0)) ECS Learning Systems, Inc.
TestSMART Plus Whole Numbers, Level C-1. 2004. (J). (978-1-57022-491-1(9)) ECS Learning Systems, Inc.
TestSMART Plus Whole Numbers, Level C-2. 2004. (J). (978-1-57022-492-8(7)) ECS Learning Systems, Inc.
TestSMART Plus Whole Numbers, Level D-1. 2004. (J). (978-1-57022-493-5(5)) ECS Learning Systems, Inc.
TestSMART Plus Whole Numbers, Level D-2. 2004. (J). (978-1-57022-494-2(3)) ECS Learning Systems, Inc.
TestSMART Plus Whole Numbers, Level E. 2004. (J). (978-1-57022-495-9(1)) ECS Learning Systems, Inc.
TestSMART Plus Whole Numbers, Level F. 2004. (J). (978-1-57022-496-6(X)) ECS Learning Systems, Inc.
TestSMART Plus Whole Numbers, Level G. 2004. (J). (978-1-57022-497-3(8)) ECS Learning Systems, Inc.
TestSMART Plus Whole Numbers, Level H. 2004. (J). (978-1-57022-498-0(6)) ECS Learning Systems, Inc.
TestSMART Plus Whole Numbers, Level I. 2004. (YA). (978-1-57022-499-7(4)) ECS Learning Systems, Inc.
Thomas, Sheeba P. Fun with Numbers. 2011. 28p. pap. 24.95 (978-1-4560-7923-9(9)) America Star Bks.
Thomson, Ruth. 1, 2, 3. (Coleccion Mi Primer Libro). (SPA., Illus.). 32p. (J). 13.95 (978-84-207-3777-5(1), ANY876) Grupo Anaya, S.A. ESP. Dist: Continental Bk. Co., Inc.
The TI Math Mate Calculator. 2004. suppl. ed. 265.50 (978-0-201-25341-2(0)); suppl. ed. 91.50 (978-0-201-25340-5(2)) Addison-Wesley Educational Pubs., Inc. (Scott Foresman).
Tipton, Stacey. The Complete Musical Spanish: With New Bonus Verbs Learning CD, 1. 2nd ed. 2005. (SPA., Illus.). 112p. 49.99 (978-0-9706829-7-0(2)) Musical Linguist, The.
Twine, Alice. My Favorite Book of Numbers. 2008. (Board Bks.). (Illus.). 14p. (J). (gr. -1-k). bds. 11.95 (978-1-4042-4256-2(2)) Rosen Publishing Group, Inc., The.
Van, Muon Thi. One Is a Lot (Except When It's Not) Pratt, Pierre, illus. 2019. (ENG.). 32p. (J). (gr. -1-2). 16.99 (978-1-5253-0013-4(X)) Kids Can Pr., Ltd. CAN. Dist: Hachette Bk. Group.
Watson, Craig. Maddie Counts Marbles: Number Names & Count Sequence. 2013. (InfoMax Math Readers Ser.). (ENG.). 16p. (J). (gr. k-1). pap. 42.00 (978-1-4777-1950-3(4)); (Illus.). pap. 7.00 (978-1-4777-1949-7(0), fded4ee4-f85e-4dd2-9e91-0aac8c8aff3f) Rosen Publishing Group, Inc., The. (Rosen Classroom).
Watt, Fiona & Wells, Rachel. Adding II. 2004. (Usborne Sticker Math Ser.). (ENG., Illus.). 1p. (J). (gr. 1-2). pap., act. bk. ed. 6.95 (978-0-7460-4080-5(6)) EDC Publishing.
Weakland, Mark. Scooby-Doo! a Number Comparisons Mystery: The Case of the Lunchroom Gobbler, 1 vol. Gross, Scott, illus. 2014. (Solve It with Scooby-Doo!: Math Ser.). (ENG.). 24p. (J). (gr. k-2). lib. bdg. 28.65 (978-1-4914-1542-9(8), 126796, Capstone Pr.) Capstone.
—Scooby-Doo! an Even or Odd Mystery: The Case of the Oddzilla, 1 vol. Gross, Scott, illus. 2014. (Solve It with Scooby-Doo!: Math Ser.). (ENG.). 24p. (J). (gr. k-2). lib. bdg. 28.65 (978-1-4914-1541-2(X), 126795, Capstone Pr.) Capstone.
Weatherly. Working with Numbers. 2004. (Steck-Vaughn Working with Numbers Ser.). (ENG., Illus.). Level D. 160p. (gr. 3-3). pap. 18.85 (978-0-7398-9158-2(8))Level A. 144p. (gr. 1-1). pap., stu. ed. 18.85 (978-0-7398-9156-8(1))Level B. 144p. (gr. 2-2). pap. 18.85 (978-0-7398-9157-5(X)) Houghton Mifflin Harcourt Publishing Co.
Weston Woods Staff, creator. How Much Is a Million? 2011. 38.75 (978-0-439-84576-2(9)) 2004. 18.95 (978-1-55592-106-4(X)) 2004. 29.95 (978-1-55592-124-8(8)) Weston Woods Studios, Inc.
White, Ella. I Can Write Numbers! Number Names & Count Sequence, 1 vol. 2013. (Rosen Math Readers Ser.). (ENG., Illus.). 16p. (J). (gr. k-k). pap. 7.00 (978-1-4777-1590-1(8), f583bdc1-7ac0-4495-aa56-3c13464fd367, Rosen Classroom) Rosen Publishing Group, Inc., The.
White, Ella & White, Emma. I Can Write Numbers! Number Names & Count Sequence. 2013. (Rosen Math Readers Ser.). (ENG.). 16p. (J). (gr. k-1). pap. 42.00 (978-1-4777-1591-8(6), Rosen Classroom) Rosen Publishing Group, Inc., The.
World Book, Inc. Staff, contrib. by. Numbers. 2012. (J). (978-0-7166-1436-4(7)); pap. (978-0-7166-1477-7(4)) World Bk., Inc.
The World of Eric Carle My Numbers Activity Kit. 2007. (J). 16.99 (978-0-9794445-1-7(9)) Loew-Cornell, Inc.
Yates, Gene. The Giraffe Numbers Book. 2003. (Illus.). 18p. (J). (978-1-58865-107-5(X)) Kidsbooks, LLC.
Yegoryan, Kristina & Yegoryan, Rubik. I Know Digits & Shapes. 2009. 108p. pap. 33.49 (978-1-4389-5444-8(1)) AuthorHouse.
Yoyo Books Staff. Numbers: Mini Baby's First Library. 2005. 42p. bds. (978-90-5843-804-1(X)) YoYo Bks.
Zakiyyah & Zakiyyah. Chatterworld My Numbers in Spanish/My Numbers in French: MIS Numeros en Espanol/Mes Mombres en Francais. 2006. (Illus.). 40p. (J). (gr. -1-3). 14.99 (978-0-9777085-0-5(0)) Little Linguists Press.
Zinsmeister, Elke, illus. Ten Fat Sausages. 2006. (Classic Books with Holes Big Book Ser.). 16p. (J). (gr. -1-3). spiral bd. (978-1-84643-008-4(9)) Child's Play International Ltd.
1-2-3. (Coleccion Picaros Peluchines). (SPA.). (J). 5.50 (978-950-11-0399-1(4), SGM399); (Illus.). 10p. pap. 5.50 (978-950-11-0791-3(4), SGM914) Sigmar ARG. Dist: Continental Bk. Co., Inc.

NUMBER THEORY

Adams, Colleen. Magic Squares: Learning the Inverse Relationships Between Addition & Subtraction, 1 vol. (Math for the REAL World Ser.). 16p. (gr. 2-3). 2010. (ENG.). pap. 7.05 (978-0-8239-8907-2(0), 801cf11e-a846-44bb-a8fe-817907dd7268, Rosen Classroom) 2009. 37.50 (978-1-60851-374-1(2), PowerKids Pr.) Rosen Publishing Group, Inc., The.
Andreescu, Titu & Tetiva, Marian. Sums & Products. 2018. (ENG.). 340p. 54.95 (978-0-9993428-1-7(9), P586376) XYZ Pr.
Burns, Kylie. Roman Numerals & Ordinals. 2010. (ENG., Illus.). 24p. (J). (978-0-7787-5250-9(X)); pap. (978-0-7787-5297-4(6)) Crabtree Publishing Co.
Carson-Dellosa Publishing Staff. Numbers 0-30, Grades K - 1. 2010. (Home Workbooks Ser.: 10). (ENG.). 64p. (gr. k-1). pap. 4.49 (978-1-60418-783-0(2), 104352) Carson-Dellosa Publishing, LLC.
Downey, Tika. The History of Zero: Exploring Our Place-Value Number System, 1 vol. 2010. (Math for the REAL World Ser.). (ENG., Illus.). 32p. (gr. 4-5). pap. 10.00 (978-0-8239-8869-3(4), ad095911-1b31-428b-a0ed-063ed2535e8c, PowerKids Pr.) Rosen Publishing Group, Inc., The.
Emerson-Stonnell, Sharon. Number Systems. 2006. 372p. pap. 35.95 (978-1-59800-658-2(4)) Outskirts Pr., Inc.
Faulkner, Nicholas & Hosch, William L., eds. Numbers & Measurements, 1 vol. 2017. (Foundations of Math Ser.). (ENG., Illus.). 344p. (J). (gr. 10-10). lib. bdg. 55.59 (978-1-68048-778-7(7), ece40e52-ceb4-4c2e-8148-9f355a3a74ed, Britannica Educational Publishing) Rosen Publishing Group, Inc., The.
Lundy, Miranda. Sacred Number: The Secret Quality of Quantities. 2005. (Wooden Bks.). (ENG., Illus.). 64p. 14.00 (978-0-8027-1456-5(0), 900034405) Bloomsbury Publishing USA.
Numbers. 2004. (J). 12p. bds. 3.99 (978-1-85997-813-9(4)); 24p. 4.99 (978-1-85997-979-2(3)) Byeway Bks.
Numbers. (People's Bible Commentary Ser.). 264p. 14.99 (978-0-7586-0418-7(1)) Concordia Publishing Hse.
Numbers. 2003. (J). per. (978-1-57657-918-3(2)) Paradise Pr., Inc.
Numbers. (Rainbow Ryhmes Ser.). (J). 12p. bds. (978-2-7643-0175-3(8)); 8p. bds. (978-2-7643-0184-5(7)) Phidal Publishing, Inc./Editions Phidal, Inc.
Phidal Publishing Staff, ed. Numbers. (Turn & Learn Ser.). 12p. (J). (978-2-7643-0139-5(1)) Phidal Publishing, Inc./Editions Phidal, Inc.
Prather, Michelle. On the Job: Underwater Investigators: Plotting Rational Numbers (Grade 6) 2019. (Mathematics in the Real World Ser.). (ENG., Illus.). 32p. (gr. 5-8). pap. 11.99 (978-1-4258-5884-1(8)) Teacher Created Materials, Inc.
Scholastic. Write-And-Learn Number Practice Pages: Help Kids Recognize, Write, & Really Learn the Numbers 1-30. 2003. (ENG.). 72p. (gr. -1-1). pap., tchr. ed. 12.99 (978-0-439-45865-8(X), Teaching Resources) Scholastic, Inc.
School Zone Publishing Co. Numbers Bingo Game. 2006. (ENG.). (J). (gr. -1-k). 5.99 (978-1-58947-495-6(3)) School Zone Publishing Co.
Sterling, Kristin. Ordinal Numbers. 2008. pap. 22.95 (978-0-8225-9362-1(9)); (ENG., Illus.). 8p. (J). pap. 5.99 (978-0-8225-8846-7(3), be3c4354-12f9-4da4-844e-42ca962ae364) Lerner Publishing Group.
TestSMART Plus Number Theory, Level A/B. 2004. (J). (978-1-57022-482-9(X)) ECS Learning Systems, Inc.
TestSMART Plus Number Theory, Level C/D. 2004. (J). (978-1-57022-483-6(8)) ECS Learning Systems, Inc.
TestSMART Plus Number Theory, Level E/F. 2004. (J). (978-1-57022-484-3(6)) ECS Learning Systems, Inc.
TestSMART Plus Number Theory, Level G. 2004. (J). (978-1-57022-485-0(4)) ECS Learning Systems, Inc.
TestSMART Plus Number Theory, Level H. 2004. (J). (978-1-57022-486-7(2)) ECS Learning Systems, Inc.
TestSMART Plus Number Theory, Level I. 2004. (YA). (978-1-57022-487-4(0)) ECS Learning Systems, Inc.
Wipe-Clean Writing Numbers. 2017. (Wipe-Clean Bks.). (ENG.). (J). pap. 7.99 (978-0-7945-3697-8(2), Usborne) EDC Publishing.

NUMISMATICS

see also Coins

Bekkering, Annalise. Seals. 2008. (U. S. Sites & Symbols Ser.). (Illus.). 48p. (J). (gr. 3-5). pap. 10.95 (978-1-59036-893-0(2)); lib. bdg. 29.05 (978-1-59036-892-3(4)) Weigl Pubs., Inc.
Whitman Publishing, ed. Adventure Across the States: Collecting State Quarters & Other Coins. 2006. (Official Whitman Guidebook Ser.). (Illus.). 92p. (J). per. 4.99 (978-0-7948-2050-3(6)) Whitman Publishing LLC.
Yeoman, R. S. The Official Blue Book(r) Handbook of United States CoinsTM: With Premium List. Bressett, Ken, ed. 62nd ed. 2004. (Illus.). 224p. pap. 9.95 (978-0-7948-1787-9(4)) Whitman Publishing LLC.

NUNEZ CABEZA DE VACA, ALVAR, ACTIVE 16TH CENTURY

Colmenares, Sandra. Alvar Núñez Cabeza de Vaca: Explorer of the American Southwest, 1 vol. 2019. (Our Voices: Spanish & Latino Figures of American History Ser.). (ENG.). 48p. (gr. 6-6). pap. 12.75 (978-1-5081-8426-3(7), cb28067a-7585-4541-8e45-0537b51cab95, Rosen Reference) Rosen Publishing Group, Inc., The.
Marsh, Carole. Alvar Nunez Cabeza de Vaca:Explorer & Survivor: Explorer & Survivor. 2003. 12p. (gr. k-4). 2.95 (978-0-635-02135-9(8)) Gallopade International.
Peppas, Lynn. Why Cabeza de Vaca Matters to Texas, 1 vol. 2013. (Texas Perspectives Ser.). (ENG., Illus.). 32p. (J). (gr. 4-4). lib. bdg. 28.93 (978-1-4777-0913-9(4), 99187d06-5c9b-4171-8e2d-abd99916f04f) Rosen Publishing Group, Inc., The.

NUNS

Fitzpatrick, Anne. Mother Teresa. 2005. (Genius Ser.). (Illus.). 48p. (J). (gr. 5-9). lib. bdg. 21.95 (978-1-58341-330-2(8), Creative Education) Creative Co., The.
Ganeri, Anita. Mother Teresa's Alms Bowl. Radford, Karen & Noyes, Leighton, illus. 2008. (Stories of Great People Ser.). (ENG.). 40p. (J). (gr. 3-8). pap. (978-0-7787-3712-4(8)) Crabtree Publishing Co.
Ganeri, Anita & Bailey, Gerry. Mother Teresa's Alms Bowl. 2008. (Stories of Great People Ser.). (ENG., Illus.). 40p. (J). (gr. 3-8). lib. bdg. (978-0-7787-3690-5(3)) Crabtree Publishing Co.
Gigliotti, Jim & Who HQ. Who Was Mother Teresa? Groff, David, illus. 2015. (Who Was? Ser.). 112p. (J). (gr. 3-7). 5.99 (978-0-448-48299-6(1), Penguin Workshop) Penguin Young Readers Group.
Glavich, Mary Kathleen. Blessed Teresa of Calcutta: Missionary of Charity. Kiwak, Barbara, tr. Kiwak, Barbara, illus. 2003. (Encounter the Saints Ser.: Vol. 17). 136p. (J). pap. 7.95 (978-0-8198-1160-8(2), 332-024) Pauline Bks. & Media.
Jones, Brenn. Learning about Love from the Life of Mother Teresa. 2009. (Character Building Book Ser.). 24p. (gr. 2-3). 42.50 (978-1-61511-001-8(1), PowerKids Pr.) Rosen Publishing Group, Inc., The.
Lazaro, Georgina. Juana Ines. Preza, Bruno Gonzalez, illus. 2007. (SPA.). 32p. (J). (gr. 3-5). 14.99 (978-1-930332-57-7(2)) Lectorum Pubns., Inc.
Martinez, Elsie & Stelly, Colette. Henriette Delille: Rebellious Saint, 1 vol. Reppel, Phyllis, illus. 2010. (ENG.). 200p. (J). (gr. 3-7). 19.95 (978-1-58980-839-3(8), Pelican Publishing) Arcadia Publishing.
Mora, Pat. Una Biblioteca para Juana: El Mundo de Sor Juana InésThe World of Sor Juana Inés, 1 vol. Vidal, Beatriz, illus. 2019. Orig. Title: A Library for Juana. (SPA.). 32p. (J). (gr. k-3). pap. 12.95 (978-1-64379-059-6(5), leelowcbp) Lee & Low Bks., Inc.
—A Library for Juana: The World of Sor Juana Inés, 1 vol. Vidal, Beatriz, illus. 2019. (ENG.). 32p. (J). (gr. k-3). pap. 11.95 (978-1-64379-058-9(7), leelowcbp) Lee & Low Bks., Inc.
Nelson, Robin. Mother Teresa: A Life of Caring. (Pull Ahead Books — Biographies Ser.). (Illus.). 32p. (J). 2007. (ENG.). (gr. k-3). pap. 7.99 (978-0-8225-6433-1(5), d3ca9c7a-8cce-4f0e-ba3c-b256c4dc2ba9) 2006. (gr. 3-7). lib. bdg. 22.60 (978-0-8225-6384-6(3), Lerner Pubns.) Lerner Publishing Group.
Price, Sean & Price, Sean Stewart. Wicked History: Attila the Hun. 2009. (Wicked History Ser.). (ENG., Illus.). 128p. (J). (gr. 6-12). 31.00 (978-0-531-21801-3(5), Watts, Franklin) Scholastic Library Publishing.
Slavicek, Louise Chipley. Mother Teresa. 2007. (Modern Peacemakers Ser.). (ENG., Illus.). 113p. (gr. 9-12). lib. bdg. 30.00 (978-0-7910-9433-4(2), P124650, Facts On File) Infobase Holdings, Inc.
Sullivan, Anne Marie. Mother Theresa: Religious Humanitarian. 2004. (Great Names Ser.). (Illus.). 32p. (J). (gr. 3-18). lib. bdg. 19.95 (978-1-59084-142-6(5)) Mason Crest.
Trussell-Cullen, Alan. Mother Teresa. 2009. pap. 13.25 (978-1-60559-066-0(5)) Hameray Publishing Group, Inc.
Valentine, Emily. Mother Teresa: With a Discussion of Compassion. 2004. (Values in Action Ser.). (J). (978-1-59203-070-5(X)) Learning Challenge, Inc.

NUNS—FICTION

Ahern, Dianne. Curse of the Coins: Adventures with Sister Philomena, Special Agent to the Pope. 2007. (J). pap. 11.95 (978-0-9679437-7-0(9)) En Route Bks. & Media.
Anand, Manisha. Assassin Nuns of Pistachio. 2015. (ENG.). 200p. (J). pap. 19.99 (978-0-14-333365-4(8), Puffin) Penguin Bks. India PVT, Ltd IND. Dist: Independent Pubs. Group.
Blagden, Scott. Dear Life, You Suck. 2015. (ENG.). 320p. (YA). (gr. 9). pap. 9.99 (978-0-544-33621-6(6), 1584167, Clarion Bks.) HarperCollins Pubs.
Carville, Declan. The Incredible Sister Brigid. Black, Kieron, illus. 29p. pap. 7.95 (978-0-9538222-2-5(2)) Discovery Pubns. GBR. Dist: Irish Bks. & Media, Inc.
Clark, Kathy. Guardian Angel House, 1 vol. 2009. (Holocaust Remembrance Series for Young Readers Ser.: 10). (ENG., Illus.). 228p. (J). (gr. 4-8). pap. 14.95 (978-1-897187-58-6(0)) Second Story Pr. CAN. Dist: Orca Bk. Pubs. USA.
Coats, J. Anderson. R Is for Rebel. 2018. (ENG., Illus.). 256p. (J). (gr. 5). 16.99 (978-1-4814-9667-4(0), Atheneum Bks. for Young Readers) Simon & Schuster Children's Publishing.
Hooper, Mary. Round the Rainbow. Harker, Lesley, illus. 2008. (Two Naughty Angels Ser.). 96p. (J). (gr. 2-4). pap. 11.95 (978-0-7475-9062-0(1)) Bloomsbury Publishing Plc GBR. Dist: Independent Pubs. Group.
Kamachi, Kazuma. A Certain Magical Index, Vol. 14 (light Novel) Haimura, Kiyotaka, illus. 2018. (Certain Magical Index Ser.: 14). (ENG.). 192p. (gr. 8-17). pap. 14.00 (978-0-316-44270-1(4), Yen Pr.) Yen Pr. LLC.
Keffer, Ann. The Seventh Chair. 2007. 76p. (J). per. 8.95 (978-0-595-45917-9(X)) iUniverse, Inc.
Marie, Cynthia. Sister Aggie Goes Surfing. 2012. 50p. pap. 20.95 (978-1-4497-5404-4(X), WestBow Pr.) Author Solutions, LLC.
McClure, Nikki. The Great Chicken Escape. 2018. (ENG., Illus.). 40p. (J). (gr. -1-3). 16.95 (978-1-944903-22-0(4), 1313201, Cameron Kids) Cameron + Co.
Nogar, Anna M. & Lamadrid, Enrique R. Sisters in Blue/Hermanas de Azul: Sor María de Ágreda Comes to New Mexico/Sor María de Ágreda Viene a Nuevo México. 2017. (Querencias Ser.). (ENG., Illus.). 88p. (J). 19.95 (978-0-8263-5821-9(7), P532838) Univ. of New Mexico Pr.
Shofner, Corabel. Almost Paradise. 2018. (ENG.). 304p. (J). pap. 19.99 (978-1-250-15858-1(3), 900157543) Square Fish.
—Almost Paradise. 2018. (J). lib. bdg. 18.40 (978-0-606-41107-3(0)) Turtleback.
Uss, Christina. The Adventures of a Girl Called Bicycle. 2018. (Illus.). 320p. (J). (gr. 3-7). 16.99 (978-0-8234-4007-8(9), Margaret Ferguson Books) Holiday Hse., Inc.
The Year We Sailed the Sun. 2015. (ENG., Illus.). 432p. (J). (gr. 3-7). 17.99 (978-0-689-85827-7(2), Atheneum/Richard Jackson Bks.) Simon & Schuster Children's Publishing.

NUREMBERG TRIAL OF MAJOR GERMAN WAR CRIMINALS, NUREMBERG, GERMANY, 1945-1946

DiPalma, Emilio & Chetkowski, Emily DiPalma. Just a Kid: A Guard at the Nuremberg Trials. 2004. (Illus.). 69p. per. 9.95 (978-0-9744803-3-6(9)) PublishingWorks.

NUREYEV, RUDOLF, 1939-1993

Fandel, Jennifer. Rudolf Nureyev. 2005. (Extraordinary Artists Ser.). (Illus.). 48p. (J). (gr. 5-9). lib. bdg. 21.95 (978-1-58341-380-7(4), Creative Education) Creative Co., The.

NURSERY RHYMES

Ada, Alma Flor & Campoy, F. Isabel. Muu, Moo! Rimas de Animales/Animal Nursery Rhymes: Bilingual English-Spanish. Escriva, Vivi, illus. 2010. (ENG.). 48p. (J). (gr. -1-3). 16.99 (978-0-06-134613-2(6)); lib. bdg. 17.89 (978-0-06-134614-9(4)) HarperCollins Español.
Ada, Alma Flor & Wensell, Ulises. Ten Little Puppies/Diez Perritos. 2011. (ENG., Illus.). 32p. (J). (gr. -1-3). 16.99 (978-0-06-147043-1(0)) HarperCollins Español.
Ada, Alma Flor, et al. Pio Peep! Traditional Spanish Nursery Rhymes: Bilingual English-Spanish. Escriva, Vivi, illus. 2003. (ENG.). 64p. (J). (gr. -1-1). 16.99 (978-0-688-16019-7(0)) HarperCollins Español.
Ahlberg, Allan. Everybody Was a Baby Once: And Other Poems. Ingman, Bruce, illus. 2010. (ENG.). 64p. (J). (gr. -1-k). 15.99 (978-0-7636-4682-0(2)) Candlewick Pr.
Aizen, Marina. Mary Had a Little Lamb. 2015. (Classic Books with Holes Ser.). (Illus.). 16p. (J). (978-1-84643-679-6(6)) Child's Play International Ltd.
Aizen, Marina, illus. Mary Had a Little Lamb. 2014. (Classic Books with Holes Big Book Ser.). 16p. (J). spiral bd. (978-1-84643-669-7(9)) Child's Play International Ltd.
Alvarez, Mrinali, illus. Pon, Pon: ¡A Jugar con el Bebé! 2005. (SPA.). 28p. (J). 8.95 (978-0-8477-1550-3(7)) Univ. of Puerto Rico Pr.
Anderson, Airlie, illus. Cows in the Kitchen. (Classic Books with Holes 8x8 with CD Ser.). (J). 2013. (ENG.). 16p. (gr. -1). (978-1-84643-625-3(7)) 2007. 14p. (gr. -1-1). spiral bd. (978-1-84643-110-4(7)) 2007. 16p. (gr. 1-1). pap. (978-1-84643-106-7(9)) Child's Play International Ltd.
Andrews, Jackie. Old Macdonald on His Farm. Bennett, John, illus. 2012. (ENG.). 32p. pap. 6.50 (978-1-84135-195-7(4)) Award Pubns. Ltd. GBR. Dist: Parkwest Pubns., Inc.
Anness Publishing Ltd., Staff. Nursery Rhymes for Little Ones: Mother Goose Collection, 3 vols. 2013. (Illus.). 72p. (J). (gr. -1-1). bds. 9.99 (978-1-86147-318-9(4), Armadillo) Anness Publishing GBR. Dist: National Bk. Network.
Archer, Dosh. Urgency Emergency! Boxed Set #1-4, 4, Set. Archer, Dosh, illus. 2016. (Urgency Emergency! Ser.). (ENG., Illus.). 192p. (J). (gr. k-2). pap. 19.99 (978-0-8075-9991-4(3), 807599913) Whitman, Albert & Co.
Arenson, Roberta. One, Two, Skip a Few! First Number Rhymes. Arenson, Roberta, illus. 2005. (Illus.). 32p. (J). pap. 6.99 (978-1-84148-130-2(0)) Barefoot Bks., Inc.
Armadillo & Anon. My Mother Goose Collection: Nursery Rhymes for Little Ones, 3 vols. 2018. (Illus.). 72p. (J). (gr. -1-12). 9.99 (978-1-78214-140-2(5), Armadillo) Anness Publishing GBR. Dist: National Bk. Network.
Armadillo Publishing Staff. This Little Pig. Lewis, Jan, illus. 2015. 24p. (J). (gr. -1-12). bds. 6.99 (978-1-86147-486-5(5), Armadillo) Anness Publishing GBR. Dist: National Bk. Network.
Atkins, Alison, illus. Humpty Dumpty & Friends. 2005. 10p. bds. (978-1-84510-767-3(5)) Top That! Publishing PLC.
—Incy Wincy Spider & Friends. 2005. 10p. bds. (978-1-84510-768-0(3)) Top That! Publishing PLC.
Atkinson, Ruth & Atkinson, Brett. Rhyme Templates. Atkinson, Ruth & Atkinson, Brett, illus. (Illus.). (J). (gr. k-2). pap. (978-1-875739-74-5(2)) Wizard Bks.
—Traditional Rhyme Templates. Atkinson, Ruth & Atkinson, Brett, illus. (Illus.). (J). (gr. k-2). pap. (978-1-875739-94-3(7)) Wizard Bks.
Award, Anna. My First Nursery Rhymes. 2012. (ENG., Illus.). 10p. (J). bds. 6.50 (978-1-84135-569-6(0)) Award Pubns. Ltd. GBR. Dist: Parkwest Pubns., Inc.
Baby Jamz Color & Fun Book: Posters of Solange & Beyonce' Inside. 2008. (J). per. 2.57 (978-0-9796536-2-9(2), EPI Kid Bks.) EPI Bks.
Baek, Gina. Classic Collection of Mother Goose Nursery Rhymes: Over 100 Cherished Poems & Rhymes for Kids & Families. 2018. (Classic Edition Ser.: 12). (ENG., Illus.). 128p. (J). (gr. -1). 19.95 (978-1-60433-745-7(1), Applesauce Pr.) Cider Mill Pr. Bk. Pubs., LLC.
Baggott, Stella. Baby's Very First Noisy Nursery Rhymes. 2013. (Baby's Very First Noisy Book Ser.). 10p. (J). ring bd. 14.99 (978-0-7945-3317-5(5), Usborne) EDC Publishing.
Baker, Keith. Big Fat Hen/la Gallina Grande: Bilingual English-Spanish. Baker, Keith, illus. 2014. (ENG., Illus.). 30p. (J). (— 1). bds. 5.99 (978-0-544-17398-9(8), 1552214, Clarion Bks.) HarperCollins Pubs.
—¡Mamá Clo-Cló! 2007. (SPA., Illus.). 30p. (J). (gr. k — 1). bds. 6.95 (978-0-15-205890-6(7), 1197684, Clarion Bks.) HarperCollins Pubs.
Balmer, Paul. Big Nursery Rhyme Songbook. 2009. pap. 12.95 (978-1-84772-579-0(1), AM993828) Wise Pubns. GBR. Dist: Music Sales Corp.
Barefoot Books. The House That Jack Built. Mayo, Diana, illus. 2006. (ENG.). 24p. (J). (gr. -1-1). pap. 8.99 (978-1-84686-051-5(2)) Barefoot Bks., Inc.
—Over in the Meadow. McDonald, Jill, illus. 2012. (Barefoot Singalongs Ser.). (ENG.). 24p. (J). (gr. -1-2). pap. 10.99 (978-1-84686-747-7(9)) Barefoot Bks., Inc.
Baring-Gould, Sabine. A Book of Nursery Songs & Rhymes. 2009. 216p. pap. (978-1-4099-5663-1(6)) Dodo Pr.
Baxter, Nicola. Head, Shoulders, Knees & Toes & Other Action Rhymes. Buckingham, Gabriella, illus. 2013. 16p. (J). (gr. -1-6). bds. 7.99 (978-1-84322-829-5(7), Armadillo) Anness Publishing GBR. Dist: National Bk. Network.

MNO

—Rhymes for Playtime Fun. Shuttleworth, Cathie, illus. 2013. (ENG.). 80p. (J). (gr. -1-k). pap. 9.99 (978-1-84322-921-6(8)) Anness Publishing GBR. Dist: National Bk. Network.
Beall, Mary Kay. Sleep Tight with Angels Tonight. 2008. (ENG.). 84p. pap. 17.95 incl. audio compact disk (978-1-59235-230-2(8), 35020647) Shawnee Pr., Inc.
Beall, Pamela Conn & Nipp, Susan Hagen. Wee Sing Nursery Rhymes & Lullabies, 1 vol. 2005. (Wee Sing Ser.). (ENG.). 64p. (J). (gr. -1-2). 10.99 (978-0-8431-1360-0(X), Price Stern Sloan) Penguin Young Readers Group.
Beaton, Clare. Clare Beaton's Animal Rhymes. Beaton, Clare, illus. 2014. (ENG., Illus.). 16p. (J). (gr. -1-k). bds. 7.99 (978-1-78285-080-9(5)) Barefoot Bks., Inc.
—Clare Beaton's Bedtime Rhymes. Beaton, Clare, illus. 2012. (ENG., Illus.). 16p. (J). (gr. -1-k). bds. 7.99 (978-1-84686-737-8(1)) Barefoot Bks., Inc.
—Clare Beaton's Garden Rhymes. Beaton, Clare, illus. 2014. (ENG., Illus.). 16p. (J). (gr. -1-k). bds. 7.99 (978-1-78285-081-6(3)) Barefoot Bks., Inc.
—Playtime Rhymes for Little People. 2008. (Illus.). 64p. (J). (gr. -1-k). 19.99 (978-1-84686-156-7(X)) Barefoot Bks., Inc.
Benchmark Education Company, LLC Staff, compiled by. Reader's Theater Nursery Rhymes & Songs Big Books. 2009. (Reader's Theater Nursery Rhymes & Songs Ser.). (J). (gr. k-1). 665.00 (978-1-4108-8454-1(6)) Benchmark Education Co.
Bentley, Dawn, et al. Rhyme Time: Rhyme-and-Learn. Schwaeber, Barbie H. & Williams, Tracee, eds. 2008. (ENG., Illus.). 24p. (J). (gr. -1). 4.99 (978-1-59069-653-8(0)) Studio Mouse LLC.
Bixley, Donovan. Te Pamu o Koro Meketanara (Old Macdonald's Farm Maori Edition) 2022. (ENG., Illus.). 24p. (J). (gr. -1-k). pap. 17.99 (978-1-86971-358-4(3)) Hachette Australia AUS. Dist: Hachette Bk. Group.
Bixley, Donovan, illus. Pussycat, Pussycat: Purrfect Nursery Rhymes. 2016. 24p. (J). (— 1). pap. 9.99 (978-1-927262-28-3(3)) Upstart Pr. NZL. Dist: Independent Pubs. Group.
Blake, Quentin. Quentin Blake's Nursery Rhyme Book. 2013. (Illus.). 32p. (J). (gr. k-2). pap. 12.99 (978-1-84941-690-0(7), Red Fox) Random House Children's Books GBR. Dist: Independent Pubs. Group.
—Quentin Blake's Nursery Rhyme Book. 2013. (Illus.). 32p. lib. bdg. 24.50 (978-0-606-31771-9(6)) Turtleback.
Blyton, Enid. Mother Goose: Treasury of Favourite Rhymes. Barnes-Murphy, Rowan, illus. 2012. 160p. 24.95 (978-1-84135-591-7(7)) Award Pubns. Ltd. GBR. Dist: Parkwest Pubns., Inc.
Blyton, Enid, et al. Magical Creatures. 2013. 10p. (J). bds. 9.95 (978-1-84135-725-6(1)) Award Pubns. Ltd. GBR. Dist: Parkwest Pubns., Inc.
Bodden, Valerie. Poetry Basics - Nursery Rhymes. 2009. (Poetry Basics Ser.). (ENG.). 32p. (J). (gr. 5-8). 19.95 (978-1-58341-778-2(8), 22278, Creative Education) Creative Co., The.
Bonnet, Rosalinde, illus. Fold-Out Nursery Rhymes. 2018. (Fold-Out Board Bks.). (ENG.). 12p. (J). 7.99 (978-0-7945-4196-5(8), Usborne) EDC Publishing.
Bonnet, Rosaline. Very First Nursery Rhymes. Bonnet, Rosaline, illus. 2010. (Very First Words Board Bks). (Illus.). 12p. (J). bds. 6.99 (978-0-7945-2723-5(X), Usborne) EDC Publishing.
Borreguita Negra: Poems, Rhymes, & Songs Listening Packs. 2003. 34.50 (978-0-673-58629-2(4)) Celebration Pr.
Bourdeau, Marje. Baby's 1st Times, Baby's 1st Rhymes. 2011. 56p. pap. 15.99 (978-1-4628-4641-2(6)) Xlibris Corp.
Bousquet, Anthea. Lucy's St. Lucian Alphabet: The ABCs of Caribbean Culture in Upbeat Rhyming Verse. Sandiford, Ted, illus. 2012. 20p. (J). pap. (978-976-8238-02-3(X)) Maryli Pubs.
Briggs, Raymond, illus. The Puffin Book of Nursery Rhymes. 2016. 160p. (J). (gr. -1-k). 24.99 (978-0-14-137016-3(5)) Penguin Bks., Ltd. GBR. Dist: Independent Pubs. Group.
Brilla, Brilla Estrellita: Poems, Rhymes & Songs Listening Packs. 2003. 34.50 (978-0-673-58608-7(1)) Celebration Pr.
Britton, April Spring. Alphabet Rhymes. 2011. 24p. pap. 15.99 (978-1-4653-4897-5(2)) Xlibris Corp.
Brooke, L. Leslie. Ring o' Roses, a Nursery Rhyme Picture Book. Brooke, L. Leslie, illus. 2012. (Illus.). 102p. pap. 9.99 (978-1-61720-438-8(2)) Wilder Pubns., Corp.
—The Ring o' Roses Treasury: Nursery Rhymes & Stories. 2015. (Calla Editions Ser.). (ENG., Illus.). 232p. (J). (gr. -1-6). 30.00 (978-1-60660-074-0(5), 600745) Dover Pubns., Inc.
Brooks, Felicity. Animal Rhymes. 2010. (Look & Say Board Bks). (Illus.). 12p. (J). bds. 8.99 (978-0-7945-2817-1(1), Usborne) EDC Publishing.
—Counting Rhymes. Gregorio, Giuliana, illus. 2010. (Look & Say Board Bks). 12p. (J). bds. 8.99 (978-0-7945-2779-2(5), Usborne) EDC Publishing.
—Finger Rhymes. Gregorio, Giuliana, illus. 2010. (Rhyming Look & Say Ser.). 12p. (J). bds. 8.99 (978-0-7945-2780-8(9), Usborne) EDC Publishing.
Brown, Jean. My Treasure Book of Nursery Rhymes & Hymns. 2007. (Illus.). 56p. per. (978-1-84748-087-3(X)) Athena Pr.
Brown, Marc, illus. Read-Aloud Rhymes for the Very Young. 2016. (ENG.). 112p. (J). (gr. -1-2). 15.99 (978-0-399-55357-8(6), Dragonfly Bks.) Random Hse. Children's Bks.
Bruriah, D. Around the Yamim Tovim. 14p. 13.99 (978-1-58330-620-8(X)) Feldheim Pubs.
—Let's Welcome Shabbos. 24p. 12.99 (978-1-58330-591-1(2)) Feldheim Pubs.
Bunton, M. Catherine. The Fairy Tale Keeper. 2012. 134p. pap. 8.95 (978-1-60594-783-9(0)) Aeon Publishing Inc.
Bush, Timothy, illus. Teddy Bear, Teddy Bear: A Traditional Rhyme. 2005. 32p. (J). 14.99 (978-0-06-057835-0(1)); (gr. -1 — 1). lib. bdg. 15.89 (978-0-06-057836-7(X)) HarperCollins Pubs.
Butler, John. Ten in the Den, 1 vol. 2016. (ENG., Illus.). 32p. (J). (gr. -1-k). pap. 7.95 (978-1-56145-965-0(8)) Peachtree Publishing Co. Inc.
Byeway Books, creator. Rhymes. 2011. (My First Picture Fun Bks.). (ENG., Illus.). 24p. (J). (gr. -1). bds. 5.99 (978-1-60176-022-7(1)) Byeway Bks.
Byrne, Mike, illus. Twinkle, Twinkle, Little Star; and, Spaceship, Spaceship, Zooming, 1 vol. 2013. (ENG.). 24p. (J). pap. (978-0-7787-1150-6(1)) Crabtree Publishing Co.
—Twinkle, Twinkle, Little Star; and, Spaceship, Spaceship, Zooming High. 2013. (ENG.). 24p. (J). (978-0-7787-1132-2(3)) Crabtree Publishing Co.
Cabrera, Jane. One, Two, Buckle My Shoe. 2019. (Jane Cabrera's Story Time Ser.). (Illus.). (J). (ENG.). 32p. (-k). 18.99 (978-0-8234-4467-0(8)); 24p. (gr. -1 — 1). bds. 7.99 (978-0-8234-4466-3(X)) Holiday Hse., Inc.
Caldecott, Randolph. Come Lasses & Lads. 2006. pap. (978-1-4065-1220-5(6)) Dodo Pr.
—The Farmer's Boy. 2006. (Illus.). pap. (978-1-4065-1223-6(0)) Dodo Pr.
—Hey Diddle Diddle & Baby Bunting. 2006. pap. (978-1-4065-1226-7(5)) Dodo Pr.
—The House That Jack Built. 2006. pap. (978-1-4065-1227-4(3)) Dodo Pr.
—The Queen of Hearts, & Sing a Song for Sixpence. 2006. pap. (978-1-4065-1228-1(1)) Dodo Pr.
—Ride a Cock-Horse to Banbury Cross, & a Farmer Went Trotting upon His Grey Mare. 2006. pap. (978-1-4065-1229-8(X)) Dodo Pr.
—The Three Jovial Huntsmen. 2007. pap. (978-1-4065-1230-4(3)) Dodo Pr.
Carleton, Will. Rhymes of Our Planet, by Will Carleton. 2006. 216p. per. 20.99 (978-1-4255-1746-5(3)) Michigan Publishing.
Carpenter, Stephen, illus. Mary Had a Little Jam: And Other Silly Rhymes. 2017. (Giggle Poetry Ser.). (ENG.). 80p. (J). (gr. -1-2). pap. 8.99 (978-1-4814-9278-2(0), Running Pr.) Running Pr.
—Mary Had a Little Jam, & Other Silly Rhymes. 2004. 32p. (J). (978-0-88166-470-6(7)) Meadowbrook Pr.
—Mary Had a Little Jam & Other Silly Rhymes: Expanded with Twice As Many Rhymes. 2016. 80p. (J). (978-0-88166-597-0(5)) Meadowbrook Pr.
Caswell, Kelly, illus. Hickory Dickory Dock. 2012. (Classic Books with Holes Board Book Ser.). (J). 14p. spiral bd. (978-1-84643-510-2(2)); 16p. pap. (978-1-84643-499-0(8)) Child's Play International Ltd.
Caviezel, Giovanni. Humpty Dumpty's Nursery Rhymes. Pagnoni, Roberta, illus. 2010. 10p. (J). (gr. -1-k). bds. 7.99 (978-0-7641-6278-7(0)) Sourcebooks, Inc.
Chambers, Mark, illus. Five Little Monkeys; and, Five Little Penguins. 2013. (ENG.). 24p. (J). (978-0-7787-1133-9(1)) Crabtree Publishing Co.
—Five Little Monkeys; Five Little Penguins. 2013. (ENG.). 24p. (J). pap. (978-0-7787-1151-3(X)) Crabtree Publishing Co.
Chiesa, Lynn. Guess What? 2011. 20p. pap. 10.03 (978-1-4634-8754-6(1)) AuthorHouse.
Christelow, Eileen. Cinco Monitos Brincando en la Cama/Five Little Monkeys Jumping on the Bed: Bilingual Spanish-English. Christelow, Eileen, illus. 2014. (Five Little Monkeys Story Ser.). (ENG., Illus.). 30p. (J). (— 1). bds. 9.99 (978-0-544-08900-6(6), 1537638, Clarion Bks.) HarperCollins Pubs.
—Five Little Monkeys Jumping on the Bed Deluxe Edition. Christelow, Eileen, illus. 25th ed. 2014. (Five Little Monkeys Story Ser.). (ENG., Illus.). 40p. (J). (gr. -1-3). 19.99 (978-0-544-28329-9(5), 1571237, Clarion Bks.) HarperCollins Pubs.
Chronicle Books Staff. Nick Jr. Nursery Rhyme Time: A Touch-and-See Activity Book. (J). 15.95 (978-0-8118-4726-1(8)) Chronicle Bks. LLC.
Church, Caroline Jayne. Twinkle, Twinkle, Little Star. Church, Caroline Jayne, illus. 2014. (ENG., Illus.). 12p. (J). (— 1). bds. 6.99 (978-0-545-51806-2(7), Cartwheel Bks.) Scholastic, Inc.
Cleary, Brian P. Pre- & Re-, Mis- & Dis- What is a Prefix? Goneau, Martin, illus. 2015. (Words Are CATegorical (r) Ser.). (ENG.). 32p. (J). (gr. 2-5). pap. 7.99 (978-1-4677-9383-4(3), 6f6a3bec-953a-40db-8b48-fdba9a4e4e05, Millbrook Pr.) Lerner Publishing Group.
Cloke, Rene, illus. My First Picture Book of Nursery Rhymes. 2012. (ENG.). 24p. 9.95 (978-1-84135-581-8(X)) Award Pubns. Ltd. GBR. Dist: Parkwest Pubns., Inc.
Codell, Esmé Raji & Codell, Esmé Raji. Maybe Mother Goose. Chavarri, Elisa, illus. 2016. (ENG.). 32p. (J). (gr. -1-3). 17.99 (978-1-4814-4036-3(5), Aladdin) Simon & Schuster Children's Publishing.
Cole, Joanna & Calmenson, Stephanie, eds. Tons of Fun: Over 300 Action Rhymes, Old & New Riddles, Tongue Twisters, & Play Rhymes. Tiegren, Alan, illus. 2004. 229p. (J). (gr. k-4). reprint ed. pap. 15.00 (978-0-7567-8222-1(8)) DIANE Publishing Co.
Collins, Heather, illus. Jack & Jill. 2003. (Traditional Nursery Rhymes Ser.). (ENG.). 12p. (J). (gr. -1 — 1). bds. 3.95 (978-1-55337-075-8(9)) Kids Can Pr., Ltd. CAN. Dist: Hachette Bk. Group.
—Little Miss Muffet. 2003. (Traditional Nursery Rhymes Ser.). (ENG.). 12p. (J). (gr. -1 — 1). bds. 3.95 (978-1-55337-076-5(7)) Kids Can Pr., Ltd. CAN. Dist: Hachette Bk. Group.
Conway, David. The Great Nursery Rhyme Disaster. Williamson, Melanie, illus. 2009. (ENG.). 32p. (J). (gr. -1-1). 22.44 (978-1-58925-080-2(X)) Tiger Tales.
Cowle, Ken. Harold Can't Stand to Be Alone. Dorland, Andrew, illus. 2006. 24p. per. (978-0-9781338-3-2(8)) Soul Asylum Poetry.
Crews, Nina. The Neighborhood Mother Goose. Crews, Nina, illus. 2003. (ENG., Illus.). 64p. (J). (gr. -1-3). 18.99 (978-0-06-051573-7(2), Greenwillow Bks.) HarperCollins Pubs.
Crisp, Dan, illus. The Ants Go Marching. (Classic Books with Holes 8x8 Ser.). (J). 2013. (ENG.). 16p. (gr. -1). pap. (978-1-84643-618-5(4)) 2007. 14p. spiral bd. (978-1-84643-109-8(3)) 2007. 16p. (gr. 1-2). pap. (978-1-84643-105-0(0)) Child's Play International Ltd.
Currey, Anna, illus. Hush-a-Bye, Baby: And Other Nursery Rhymes. 2003. (ENG.). 14p. (J). bds. 8.99 (978-0-333-78086-2(8)) Macmillan Pubs., Ltd. GBR. Dist: Trafalgar Square Publishing.
—Pat-a-Cake: And Other Nursery Rhymes. 2003. (ENG.). 14p. (J). bds. 6.95 (978-0-333-78083-1(3)) Macmillan Pubs., Ltd. GBR. Dist: Trafalgar Square Publishing.
—Ring-a-Ring O' Roses: And Other Nursery Rhymes. 2003. (ENG.). 14p. (J). bds. 6.95 (978-0-333-78084-8(1)) Macmillan Pubs., Ltd. GBR. Dist: Trafalgar Square Publishing.
Dalmatian Press Staff. My First Nursery Rhymes. 2008. (ENG.). 5p. bds. 4.95 (978-1-58117-716-9(X), Intervisual/Piggy Toes) Bendon, Inc.
David C. Cook Publishing Company Staff. Nursery Rhymes. 2003. (My Jesus Pocket Bks.). (Illus.). 32p. (J). pap., pap. 8.90 (978-1-55513-102-9(6), 1555131026) Cook, David C.
Davidson, Susanna. Baby & Toddler Treasury. Furukawa, Masumi et al, illus. 2007. (Baby & Toddler Treasury Ser.). 95p. (J). (gr. -1-k). 19.99 (978-0-7945-1150-0(3), Usborne) EDC Publishing.
—Nursery Rhyme Treasury. Kolanovic, Dubravka, illus. 2006. 96p. (J). 19.99 (978-0-7945-1281-1(X), Usborne) EDC Publishing.
Davies, Caroline, tr. & illus. Hey, Diddle Diddle. Davies, Caroline, illus. 2004. (Baby's First Nursery Rhymes Ser.). 12p. (J). bds. 3.99 (978-1-85854-622-3(2)) Brimax Books Ltd. GBR. Dist: Byeway Bks.
—Humpty Dumpty. Davies, Caroline, illus. 2004. (Baby's First Nursery Rhymes Ser.). 12p. (J). bds. 3.99 (978-1-85854-610-0(9)) Brimax Books Ltd. GBR. Dist: Byeway Bks.
—Little Miss Muffet. Davies, Caroline, illus. 2004. (Baby's First Nursery Rhymes Ser.). 12p. (J). bds. 3.99 (978-1-85854-623-0(0)) Brimax Books Ltd. GBR. Dist: Byeway Bks.
—Pat-A-Cake. Davies, Caroline, illus. 2004. (Baby's First Nursery Rhymes Ser.). 12p. (J). bds. 3.99 (978-1-85854-611-7(7)) Brimax Books Ltd. GBR. Dist: Byeway Bks.
Davies, Gill. My Nursery Rhyme Pop-up Book. Guile, Gill, illus. 2005. 20p. (J). (gr. k-4). reprint ed. 20.00 (978-0-7567-8704-2(1)) DIANE Publishing Co.
Davis, Jimmie. You Are My Sunshine. Church, Caroline Jayne, illus. 2011. (ENG.). 12p. (J). (gr. -1 — 1). bds. 6.99 (978-0-545-07552-7(1), Cartwheel Bks.) Scholastic, Inc.
DAVIS**DECEASED**, David. Texas Mother Goose, 1 vol. 2006. (ENG., Illus.). 40p. (gr. k-3). 18.99 (978-1-58980-369-5(8), Pelican Publishing) Arcadia Publishing.
de La Cour, Gary, et al, illus. Twinkle Twinkle: And Other Sleepy-Time Rhymes. 2005. (Mother Goose Ser.). (ENG.). 36p. (J). (gr. -1-k). 12.95 (978-1-59249-464-4(1), 1D016) Soundprints.
Deacon, Melissa. I Have a Monkey in My Tub! 2011. 32p. pap. 24.95 (978-1-4626-2001-2(9)) America Star Bks.
Dean, James. Twinkle, Twinkle, Little Star. 2014. (Pete the Cat Ser.). (ENG.). 32p. (J). (978-0-06-235967-4(3)) Harper & Row Ltd.
Delacre, Lulu. Arrorro, Mi Nino: Latino Lullabies & Gentle Games, 1 vol. 2004. (ENG., Illus.). 32p. (J). 16.95 (978-1-58430-159-2(7)) Lee & Low Bks., Inc.
Dellas, Melanie & Woodworth, John. Pat-A-Cake, Pat-a-Cake... We Made a Mistake! Sun, Antuanette, illus. 2012. 24p. pap. 9.95 (978-0-9830163-2-8(1)) Dellas, Melanie.
Denslow, W. W. Denslow's Mother Goose. 2011. (Dover Children's Classics Ser.). (ENG., Illus.). 96p. (J). (gr. k-3). 20.00 (978-0-486-48466-2(1)) Dover Pubns., Inc.
Denton, Kady MacDonald. A Child's Treasury of Nursery Rhymes. 2004. (J). (gr. -1-2). spiral bd. (978-0-616-01640-4(9)) Canadian National Institute for the Blind/Institut National Canadien pour les Aveugles.
—A Child's Treasury of Nursery Rhymes. 2018. (ENG.). 96p. (J). 14.99 (978-0-7534-7490-7(5), 900197793, Kingfisher) Roaring Brook Pr.
Denton, Kady MacDonald, illus. A Child's Treasury of Nursery Rhymes. 2004. (J). (gr. k). audio compact disk 12.95 (978-0-618-49306-7(9)) Houghton Mifflin Harcourt Trade & Reference Pubs.
dePaola, Tomie. More Mother Goose Favorites. dePaola, Tomie, illus. 2007. (Illus.). (gr. -1-3). 14.00 (978-0-7569-8138-9(7)) Perfection Learning Corp.
Disney Books. Disney Nursery Rhymes ReadAlong Storybook & CD. 2011. (Read-Along Storybook & CD Ser.). (ENG., Illus.). 32p. (J). (gr. -1-k). 10.99 (978-1-4231-3743-6(4), Disney Press Books) Disney Publishing Worldwide.
Dodge, Mary Mapes. Rhymes & Jingles. 2006. 288p. per. 23.99 (978-1-4255-2592-7(X)) Michigan Publishing.
Dolby, Karen. Oranges & Lemons: Rhymes from Past Times. 2013. (ENG., Illus.). 192p. 15.95 (978-1-84317-959-7(8)) O'Mara, Michael Bks., Ltd. GBR. Dist: Independent Pubs. Group.
Dovidija-Budney, Elizabeth. My Little Red Mittens. 2011. 32p. pap. 16.39 (978-1-4634-3735-0(8)) AuthorHouse.
Dowell, Ruth I. Move over, Mother Goose! Finger Plays, Action Verses & Funny Rhymes. Charner, Kathleen, ed. Scott, Concetta C., illus. 2004. 126p. (Orig.). (gr. -1-1). pap. 12.95 (978-0-87659-113-0(6), 10006) Gryphon Hse., Inc.
Doyle, Mick & Doyle, Laura. My Rhyming Abc. 2011. (Illus.). 32p. pap. (978-0-7552-0656-8(8)) Authors OnLine, Ltd.
Dunn, Opal. Un Deux Trois (Dual Language French/English) Aggs, Patrice, illus. 2006. (ENG.). 24p. (J). (gr. k-3). pap. 9.99 (978-1-84507-623-8(0), Frances Lincoln Children's Bks.) Quarto Publishing Group UK GBR. Dist: Hachette Bk. Group.
Eagle, Kin. Humpty Dumpty. 2004. (Illus.). (J). (gr. 1-18). spiral bd., bds. (978-0-616-14612-5(4)) Canadian National Institute for the Blind/Institut National Canadien pour les Aveugles.
Early Macken, JoAnn. Read, Recite, & Write Nursery Rhymes. 2014. (Poet's Workshop Ser.). (ENG., Illus.). 32p. (J). (gr. 4-4). (978-0-7787-0411-9(4)) Crabtree Publishing Co.
East, Jacqueline, et al, illus. Hickory Dickory Dock: And Other Silly-Time Rhymes. 2005. (Mother Goose Rhymes Ser.). (ENG.). 36p. (J). (gr. -1-k). 12.95 (978-1-59249-463-7(3), 1D019) Soundprints.
Education.com. Nursery Rhymes & More: A Workbook of Letter Tracing, Letter Recognition, & Rhymes. 2015. (ENG.). 128p. (J). (gr. -1-k). pap. 7.99 (978-0-486-80255-8(8)) Dover Pubns., Inc.
Ellwand, David. Twinkle Twinkle Little Star: David Ellwand's Bears. Ellwand, David, illus. 2018. (ENG., Illus.). 14p. (J). (— 1). bds. 6.99 (978-1-5362-0220-5(7)) Candlewick Pr.
Elya, Susan Middleton. La Madre Goose: Nursery Rhymes for Los Niños. Martinez-Neal, Juana, illus. 2016. 32p. (J). (gr. k-3). 16.99 (978-0-399-25157-3(X), G.P. Putnam's Sons Books for Young Readers) Penguin Young Readers Group.
Engel, Christiane. Knick Knack Paddy Whack. 2009. (ENG., Illus.). (J). pap. 9.99 (978-1-84686-304-2(X)) Barefoot Bks., Inc.
—Knick Knack Paddy Whack. Songs, Steve, illus. 2009. 24p. (J). pap. 6.99 (978-1-84686-305-9(8)) Barefoot Bks., Inc.
Engelbreit, Mary. Mary Engelbreit's Mother Goose Board Book. Engelbreit, Mary, illus. 2018. (ENG., Illus.). 36p. (J). (gr. -1-3). bds. 8.99 (978-0-06-274223-0(X), HarperFestival) HarperCollins Pubs.
Esparz, Esther LaMadrid. Rocking Horse Rhymes. 3rd ed. 2003.Tr. of Rimas Del Caballo Mecedor, Edicion 3. (SPA & ENG.). (J). lib. bdg. 24.95 (978-1-879817-32-6(2)) Star Light Pr.
Esparza, Thomas, Jr., prod. Esther's Playhouse, Disk G. 2004. (Illus.). (J). cd-rom (978-1-879817-48-7(9), Children) Star Light Pr.
Everett, Melissa. Baa, Baa, Black Sheep. Imodraj, illus. 2013. (ENG.). 20p. (J). (gr. -1-3). bds. 8.99 (978-1-77093-537-2(1)) Flowerpot Children's Pr. Inc. CAN. Dist: Cardinal Pubs. Group.
—Diddle, Diddle, Dumpling. Imodraj, illus. 2013. (ENG.). 20p. (J). (gr. -1-1). bds. 8.99 (978-1-77093-522-8(3)) Flowerpot Children's Pr. Inc. CAN. Dist: Cardinal Pubs. Group.
—Hey Diddle Diddle. Manning, Mary, illus. 2017. (ENG.). 24p. (J). (gr. -1-3). (978-1-4867-1258-8(4)) Flowerpot Children's Pr. Inc.
—Hey Diddle Diddle. Manning, Mary, illus. 2013. (ENG.). 20p. (J). (gr. -1-3). 8.99 (978-1-77093-536-5(3)) Flowerpot Children's Pr. Inc. CAN. Dist: Cardinal Pubs. Group.
—I Wish I Was a Little. Paiva, Johannah Gilman, ed. Manning, Mary, illus. 2014. (ENG.). 20p. (J). 8.99 (978-1-77093-844-1(3)) Flowerpot Children's Pr. Inc. CAN. Dist: Cardinal Pubs. Group.
—Jack & Jill. Imodraj, illus. 2014. (ENG.). 20p. (J). (gr. -1-1). 8.99 (978-1-77093-843-4(5)) Flowerpot Children's Pr. Inc. CAN. Dist: Cardinal Pubs. Group.
—One, Two, Buckle My Shoe. Morgan, Christopher, illus. 2013. (ENG.). 20p. (J). 8.99 (978-1-77093-523-5(1)) Flowerpot Children's Pr. Inc. CAN. Dist: Cardinal Pubs. Group.
—Pat-A-Cake. Kummer, Mark, illus. 2013. (ENG.). 20p. (J). (gr. -1-1). 8.99 (978-1-77093-521-1(5)) Flowerpot Children's Pr. Inc. CAN. Dist: Cardinal Pubs. Group.
—Rain, Rain, Go Away. 2017. (ENG.). 20p. (J). (gr. -1-1). bds. (978-1-4867-1247-2(9)) Flowerpot Children's Pr. Inc.
—Rain, Rain, Go Away. 2013. (ENG., Illus.). 20p. (J). (gr. -1-1). 8.99 (978-1-77093-524-2(X)) Flowerpot Children's Pr. Inc. CAN. Dist: Cardinal Pubs. Group.
—Rock-A-Bye Baby. Wendel, Carrie, illus. 2013. (Record-A-Story Ser.). (ENG.). 18p. (J). (gr. -1). bds. (978-1-77093-464-1(2)) Flowerpot Children's Pr. Inc.
—Rock-A-Bye Baby. Wendel, Carrie, illus. 2013. (ENG.). 20p. (J). (gr. -1-3). 8.99 (978-1-77093-668-3(8)) Flowerpot Children's Pr. Inc. CAN. Dist: Cardinal Pubs. Group.
—Twinkle, Twinkle, Little Star. Pasishnychenko, Oksana, illus. 2013. (ENG.). 20p. (J). (gr. -1-3). 8.99 (978-1-77093-534-1(7)) Flowerpot Children's Pr. Inc. CAN. Dist: Cardinal Pubs. Group.
Everitt, Anne. Hush Little Baby. Flowerpot Press, ed. 2012. (Illus.). 18p. (J). (978-1-77093-463-4(4)) Flowerpot Children's Pr. Inc.
Ezozo, Wanda. According to the Book of Genesis Nursery Rhyme. 2005. (Illus.). 24p. (J). 13.50 (978-1-4120-4425-7(1)) Trafford Publishing.
Factor, June, ed. Roll over, Pavlova. 2017. (Far Out! Ser.). (ENG.). 104p. (J). (gr. -1-k). pap. 8.99 (978-1-925386-10-3(4), Brolly Bks.) Borghesi & Adam Pubs. Pty Ltd AUS. Dist: Independent Pubs. Group.
Farmer in Dell. 2005. (Mother Goose Ser.). (ENG., Illus.). 32p. (J). 15.95 (978-1-59249-387-6(4), 1D006) Soundprints.
Faundez, Anne. One, Two, Buckle My Shoe. 2004. (QEB Start Talking Ser.). (Illus.). 24p. (J). lib. bdg. 15.95 (978-1-59566-007-7(0)) QEB Publishing Inc.
Faurot, Kimberly. Mother Goose Rhyme Time Animals. Cox, Steve, illus. 2006. 68p. (gr. -1-1). pap. 16.95 (978-1-932146-66-0(0), Upstart Bks.) Highsmith Inc.
—Mother Goose Rhyme Time Night. Cox, Steve, illus. 2006. 72p. (gr. -1-1). pap. 16.95 (978-1-932146-65-3(2), Upstart Bks.) Highsmith Inc.
—Mother Goose Rhyme Time People. Cox, Steve, illus. 2006. 66p. (gr. -1-1). pap. 16.95 (978-1-932146-67-7(9), Upstart Bks.) Highsmith Inc.
Favret, Hafida & Lerasle, Magdeleine. Songs In the Shade of the Olive Tree. Novi, Nathalie, illus. 2012. (ENG.). 52p. (J). (gr. -1-k). 16.95 (978-2-923163-84-0(2)) La Montagne Secrete CAN. Dist: Independent Pubs. Group.
Figueroia & Alonso. Sal, Caracol. 2005. (SPA.). 8p. 5.99 (978-84-263-4739-8(8)) Juventud, Editorial ESP. Dist: Lectorum Pubns., Inc.
—Tengo Tres Ovejas. 2005. (SPA.). 8p. 5.99 (978-84-263-4735-0(5)) Vives, Luis Editorial (Edelvives) ESP. Dist: Lectorum Pubns., Inc.
First Nursery Rhymes. 2004. (Baby's First Nursery Rhymes Gift Set Ser.). 12p. (J). bds. 12.99 (978-1-85854-693-3(1)) Brimax Books Ltd. GBR. Dist: Byeway Bks.
Fisher Wright, Blanche. The Real Mother Goose. 2007.Tr. of 160. 160p. per. 11.45 (978-1-59462-888-7(2), Bk. Jungle) Standard Publications, Inc.
Flying Frog Pub, creator. Hey Diddle Diddle. 2011. (Read along with Elmo Bks.). (ENG., Illus.). 14p. (gr. -1-k). bds. 3.99 (978-1-60745-083-2(6)) Flying Frog Publishing.
—Mary Had a Little Lamb. 2011. (Read along with Elmo Bks.). (ENG., Illus.). 14p. (J). (gr. -1-3). bds. 3.99 (978-1-60745-080-1(1)) Flying Frog Publishing.
—Rock-A-Bye, Baby. 2011. (Read along with Elmo Bks.). (ENG., Illus.). 14p. (J). (gr. -1-k). bds. 3.99 (978-1-60745-081-8(X)) Flying Frog Publishing.
—This Little Piggy. 2011. (Read along with Elmo Bks.). (ENG., Illus.). 14p. (gr. -1-k). bds. 3.99 (978-1-60745-082-5(8)) Flying Frog Publishing.
—Twinkle, Twinkle, Little Star. 2011. (Read along with Elmo Bks.). (ENG., Illus.). 14p. (J). (gr. -1-3). bds. 3.99 (978-1-60745-079-5(8)) Flying Frog Publishing.
Fontanez, Edwin. Hadas, Sirenas y Sapos: Un ramito de poemas Encantados. Fontanez, Edwin, illus. 2008. (SPA.,

Illus.). 32p. (J). lib. bdg. 19.99 *(978-0-9640868-8-3(3))* Exit Studio.

Foote, Samuel. Great Panjandrum Himself. 2006. (Illus.). pap. *(978-1-4065-1225-0(7))* Dodo Pr.

Fox, Mem. Ten Little Fingers & Ten Little Toes. Oxenbury, Helen, illus. (ENG.). 40p. (J). 2018. (— 1). pap. 26.99 *(978-1-328-85225-0(3)*, 1694584) 2008. (gr. -1 — 1). 17.99 *(978-0-15-206057-2(X)*, 1198193) HarperCollins Pubs. (Clarion Bks.).

—Ten Little Fingers & Ten Little Toes Lap Board Book. Oxenbury, Helen, illus. 2011. (ENG.). 38p. (J). (gr. k — 1). bds. 14.99 *(978-0-547-58103-3(3)*, 1459676, Clarion Bks.) HarperCollins Pubs.

—Ten Little Fingers & Ten Little Toes Padded Board Book. Oxenbury, Helen, illus. 2010. (ENG.). 38p. (J). (gr. k — 1). bds. 8.99 *(978-0-547-36620-3(5)*, 1422523, Clarion Bks.) HarperCollins Pubs.

Franck, Charlotte. Little Rhymes for Quiet Times. Garvin, Sheri, illus. 2006. 29p. per. 15.95 *(978-1-60002-116-9(6)*, 4029) Mountain Valley Publishing, LLC.

Freed, Herb. Sing & Learn Spanish. 2004. 271p. (J). pap. 14.95 *(978-0-9760472-0-9(9))* Global Village Kids, LLC.

Fuentes, Jose. Paisaje del eco/EchoLandscape. 2008. 16p. pap. *(978-84-934160-0-3(2))* Atalante.

—Paisaje infantil/Children Landscape. 2008. 16p. pap. *(978-84-934160-1-0(0))* Atalante.

Fujikawa, Gyo, illus. Mother Goose. 2007. (ENG.). 130p. (J). (gr. -1-2). 12.95 *(978-1-4027-5064-9(1))* Sterling Publishing Co., Inc.

Fyleman, Rose & Philip, Neil. Mary Middling & Other Silly Folk: Nursery Rhymes & Nonsense Poems. Bandlow, Katja, illus. 2004. (ENG.). 32p. (J). (gr. -1-3). tchr. ed. 16.00 *(978-0-618-38141-8(4)*, 100334, Clarion Bks.) HarperCollins Pubs.

Gache, Stephen Vance. The Real Mother Goose Coloring Book. Wright, Blanche Fisher, illus. 2009. (Dover Classic Stories Coloring Book Ser.). (ENG.). 32p. (J). (gr. k-5). pap. 3.99 *(978-0-486-46991-1(3)*, 469913) Dover Pubns., Inc.

Galdone, Paul. Three Little Kittens. Galdone, Paul, illus. (Paul Galdone Nursery Classic Ser.). (ENG., Illus.). (J). (gr. -1-3). 2013. 32p. pap. 26.99 *(978-0-547-99480-2(X)*, 1525235) 2011. 40p. 9.99 *(978-0-547-57575-9(0)*, 1457871) HarperCollins Pubs. (Clarion Bks.).

Gallagher, Belinda & Maccuish, Isla, eds. 100 Best-Loved Nursery Rhymes. 2007. (Illus.). 128p. (J). (gr. -1-3). *(978-1-84236-123-8(6))* Miles Kelly Publishing, Ltd.

Gentry, J. Richard & Craddock, Richard S. Nursery Rhyme Time. 2005. (ENG.). 6.95 *(978-1-931181-98-3(5))* Universal Publishing.

Gerlings, Rebecca, ed. Hey, Diddle, Diddle & Other Best-Loved Rhymes, 1 vol. 2009. (Nursery Rhymes Ser.). (ENG., Illus.). 32p. (J). (gr. 1-2). lib. bdg. 27.27 *(978-1-60754-125-7(4)*, ad6d3609-aedd-4e83-867f-0979c27784a7, Windmill Bks.) Rosen Publishing Group, Inc., The.

—Itsy Bitsy Spider: and Other Best-Loved Rhymes, 1 vol. 2009. (Nursery Rhymes Ser.). (ENG., Illus.). 32p. (J). (gr. 1-2). pap. 11.55 *(978-1-60754-129-5(7)*, f8c0f912-2fc6-408b-9c2b-4986f65b10d1, Windmill Bks.) Rosen Publishing Group, Inc., The.

—Itsy Bitsy Spider & Other Best-Loved Rhymes, 1 vol. 2009. (Nursery Rhymes Ser.). (ENG., Illus.). 32p. (J). (gr. 1-2). lib. bdg. 27.27 *(978-1-60754-128-8(9)*, a4aac0fc-b197-4c06-86dc-77015d73f41e, Windmill Bks.) Rosen Publishing Group, Inc., The.

—Little Miss Muffet: and Other Best-Loved Rhymes, 1 vol. 2009. (Nursery Rhymes Ser.). (ENG., Illus.). 32p. (J). (gr. 1-2). pap. 11.55 *(978-1-60754-132-5(7)*, 261da9a7-b022-48fa-8356-a175959ba801, Windmill Bks.) Rosen Publishing Group, Inc., The.

—Little Miss Muffet & Other Best-Loved Rhymes, 1 vol. 2009. (Nursery Rhymes Ser.). (ENG., Illus.). 32p. (J). (gr. 1-2). lib. bdg. 27.27 *(978-1-60754-131-8(9)*, a27f9abe-7716-4ecf-ad9f-f0890c2fd72b, Windmill Bks.) Rosen Publishing Group, Inc., The.

—Mary Had a Little Lamb and Other Best-Loved Rhymes, 1 vol. 2009. (Nursery Rhymes Ser.). (ENG., Illus.). 32p. (J). (gr. 1-2). pap. 11.55 *(978-1-60754-135-6(1)*, a307e0b0-36fe-4584-9d66-f82745a5ad63, Windmill Bks.) Rosen Publishing Group, Inc., The.

—Mary Had a Little Lamb & Other Best-Loved Rhymes, 1 vol. 2009. (Nursery Rhymes Ser.). (ENG., Illus.). 32p. (J). (gr. 1-2). lib. bdg. 27.27 *(978-1-60754-134-9(3)*, b974b175-f70c-475f-89a6-352e99f38a36, Windmill Bks.) Rosen Publishing Group, Inc., The.

—Wee Willie Winkie: and Other Best-Loved Rhymes, 1 vol. 2009. (Nursery Rhymes Ser.). (ENG., Illus.). 32p. (J). (gr. 1-2). pap. 11.55 *(978-1-60754-138-7(6)*, 07e67333-9264-4d23-ac2a-23f18a1c12bb, Windmill Bks.) Rosen Publishing Group, Inc., The.

—Wee Willie Winkie & Other Best-Loved Rhymes, 1 vol. 2009. (Nursery Rhymes Ser.). (ENG., Illus.). 32p. (J). (gr. 1-2). lib. bdg. 27.27 *(978-1-60754-137-0(8)*, 3ebff4e3-d980-40cc-b2d1-c9b6c4318122, Windmill Bks.) Rosen Publishing Group, Inc., The.

—Yankee Doodle: and Other Best-Loved Rhymes, 1 vol. 2009. (Nursery Rhymes Ser.). (ENG., Illus.). 32p. (J). (gr. 1-2). pap. 11.55 *(978-1-60754-123-3(8)*, 93591563-2fd1-4a9e-b71d-d893c8a372cd, Windmill Bks.) Rosen Publishing Group, Inc., The.

—Yankee Doodle & Other Best-Loved Rhymes, 1 vol. 2009. (Nursery Rhymes Ser.). (ENG., Illus.). 32p. (J). (gr. 1-2). lib. bdg. 27.27 *(978-1-60754-122-6(X)*, 2128fdd0-27df-4dcf-b039-3957c0cc1d08, Windmill Bks.) Rosen Publishing Group, Inc., The.

Gilbert, John. Mother Goose's Nursery Rhymes. Tenniel, John & Weir, Harrison, illus. 2010. (Applewood Bks.). (ENG.). 324p. (gr. -1-k). pap. 19.95 *(978-1-4290-9005-6(7))* Applewood Bks.

Giles, Sophie. My First... Nursery Rhymes. 2012. (ENG., Illus.). 10p. (J). bds. 9.95 *(978-1-84135-570-2(4))* Award Pubns. Ltd. GBR. Dist: Parkwest Pubns., Inc.

Giuffre, Mary & Clark, Paul L. Scribble & Grin: 53 Rhymes for Inspiring Times. Sullivan, Troy, illus. 2013. 142p. *(978-0-9919101-0-6(9))* inspirtainment ink.

Goembel, Ponder. Animal Fair, 0 vols. Goembel, Ponder, illus. 2012. (ENG., Illus.). 24p. (J). (gr. -1 — 1). bds. 7.99 *(978-0-7614-6205-7(8)*, 9780761462057, Two Lions) Amazon Publishing.

Goldsmith, Oliver. Elegy on the Death of A Mad Dog. 2006. (Illus.). pap. *(978-1-4065-1221-2(4))* Dodo Pr.

—Elegy on the Glory of Her Sex Mrs Mary B. 2006. (Illus.). pap. *(978-1-4065-1222-9(2))* Dodo Pr.

Goodnight, Rosemary. Dear Old Granny's Nursery Rymes for the 21st Century. Turner, Michael W., illus. 2009. 64p. (J). 14.99 *(978-0-9816282-7-1(3))* Recipe Pubs.

—Dear Old Granny's Nursery Rymes for the 21st Century. 2010. (ENG.). (J). 9.95 *(978-0-9826424-3-6(1))* Recipe Pubs.

Govier, Katherine. Half for You & Half for Me: Best-Loved Nursery Rhymes & the Stories Behind Them, 1 vol. Clement, Sarah, illus. 2014. (ENG.). 176p. (J). (gr. -1-3). 22.95 *(978-1-77050-212-3(2)*, b3525536-b321-4a8b-b85a-40778d9bb0ac) Whitecap Bks., Ltd. CAN. Dist: Firefly Bks., Ltd.

Gowar, Mick. Baa Baa, Black Sheep & Baa Baa, Pink Sheep, 1 vol. 2012. (ENG., Illus.). 24p. (J). pap. *(978-0-7787-7895-0(9))* Crabtree Publishing Co.

Gray, E. Travis. Ridalin Phymes: Poetry for the ADHD Generation. 2012. (ENG.). pap. 10.95 *(978-1-4675-1962-5(6))* Independent Pub.

Green, Alison. Mother Goose's Nursery Rhymes: And How She Came to Tell Them. Scheffler, Axel, illus. 2006. (ENG.). 128p. *(978-0-333-96136-0(6)*, Macmillan Children's Bks.) Pan Macmillan.

Grimly, Gris. Gris Grimly's Wicked Nursery Rhymes III. 2017. (ENG., Illus.). 32p. 16.95 *(978-1-61404-014-9(1))* Baby Tattoo Bks.

Grimly, Gris & Last, First. Gris Grimly's Wicked Nursery Rhymes. Grimly, Gris, illus. 2003. (ENG., Illus.). 32p. pap. 16.95 *(978-0-9729388-7-7(7))* Baby Tattoo Bks.

Grosléziat, Chantal. Songs in the Shade of the Flamboyant Tree: French Creole Lullabies & Nursery Rhymes, 1 vol. Corvaisier, Laurent, illus. 2012. (ENG.). 52p. (J). (gr. -1-k). 16.95 *(978-2-923163-82-6(6))* La Montagne Secrete CAN. Dist: Independent Pubs. Group.

Grosset & Dunlap. Wheels on the Bus. Smath, Jerry, illus. 2016. (Pudgy Board Bks.). 18p. (J). (— 1). bds. 5.99 *(978-0-451-53270-1(8)*, Grosset & Dunlap) Penguin Young Readers Group.

Group, Cricket Magazine. Favorite Mother Goose Rhymes. 2007. (ENG., Illus.). 20p. (J). (gr. k-k). bds. 7.95 *(978-0-8126-7935-9(0))* Cricket Bks.

Grudzina, Rebecca. Mary, Mary, Quite Contrary. Harrington, David, illus. 2010. (Rising Readers Ser.). (J). 3.49 *(978-1-60719-704-1(9))* Newmark Learning LLC.

Guile, Gill, illus. In My Garden. 20p. (J). *(978-1-932209-38-9(7))* Bendon, Inc.

—My Nursery Rhyme Pop-up Book. 20p. (J). *(978-1-59394-119-2(6))* Bendon, Inc.

Gustafson, Scott. Classic Bedtime Stories. 2016. (ENG., Illus.). 84p. (J). (gr. k-3). 20.00 *(978-1-57965-760-4(5)*, 85760) Artisan.

—Favorite Nursery Rhymes from Mother Goose. 2016. (ENG., Illus.). 100p. (J). 20.00 *(978-1-57965-698-0(6)*, 85698) Artisan.

Hal Leonard Corp. Staff, creator. John Thompson's First Nursery Rhymes: Early to Mid-Elementary Level. 2005. (ENG.). 32p. pap. 8.99 *(978-0-87718-022-7(9)*, 00406229) Willis Music Co.

—211. the Big Book of Nursery Rhymes & Children's Songs. 2012. (ENG.). 236p. pap. 19.99 *(978-1-4584-4071-6(0)*, 14041777) Music Sales Corp.

Hall, Dee. Can You Imagine? Hall, Dee & Hesselbein, Kent, illus. 2013. 64p. pap. 8.95 *(978-1-935786-59-7(8))* St. Clair Pubns.

Hall, Pamela. Rena & Rio Build a Rhyme. Pilo, Cary, illus. 2011. (Poetry Builders Ser.). 32p. (J). (gr. 2-4). lib. bdg. 25.27 *(978-1-59953-439-8(8))* Norwood Hse. Pr.

Halverson, Lydia, illus. Nursery Rhymes. 2004. (Elements of Reading: Phonics Ser.). 24p. pap. 40.00 *(978-0-7398-9014-1(X))* Houghton Mifflin Harcourt Supplemental Pubs.

Harbo, Christopher. Humpty Dumpty Flip-Side Rhymes. Chatzikonstantinou, Danny, illus. 2015. (Flip-Side Nursery Rhymes Ser.). (ENG.). 24p. (J). (gr. -1-2). lib. bdg. 27.99 *(978-1-4795-5986-2(5)*, 127227, Picture Window Bks.) Capstone.

Harcourt School Publishers Staff. Big Book of Rhymes. 3rd ed. 2003. (Trophies Reading Program Ser.). (gr. -1). pap. 70.10 *(978-0-15-340344-6(6))* Harcourt Schl. Pubs.

—Trophies Reading Program: Nursery Rhymes Anthology. 3rd ed. 2003. (Illus.). (gr. k). pap. 47.70 *(978-0-15-340345-3(4))* Harcourt Schl. Pubs.

Harris, Brooke. Twinkle, Twinkle, Little Star. Harrington, David, illus. 2010. (Rising Readers Ser.). (J). 3.49 *(978-1-60719-697-6(2))* Newmark Learning LLC.

Harvey, Barbara. Inner City Nursery Rhymes. 2004. 48p. (J). per. 11.95 *(978-1-56167-863-1(5))* American Literary Pr.

Havener, Katherine. Nursies When the Sun Shines: A Little Book on Night Weaning. Burrier, Sara, illus. 2nd ed. 2013. 20p. (J). pap. 9.99 *(978-0-615-75642-4(5))* Elea Pr.

Head Shoulders Knees & Toes. 2005. (Mother Goose Ser.). (ENG., Illus.). 36p. (J). 12.95 *(978-1-59249-381-4(5)*, 1D007) Soundprints.

Hefferan, Rob, illus. My Pop-up Nursery Rhymes. 2006. (ENG.). 10p. (J). (gr. -1-3). 4.95 *(978-1-58117-439-7(X)*, Intervisual/Piggy Toes) Bendon, Inc.

—My Sparkling Nursery Rhymes. 2005. (ENG.). 10p. (J). 8.95 *(978-1-58117-295-9(8)*, Intervisual/Piggy Toes) Bendon, Inc.

Henley, Ralph. Action Rhymes & Active Games: Over 200 Bible Story Activities for Ages 2 To 5. 2004. (J). tchr. ed., per. 19.99 *(978-1-933803-02-9(9))* Child Sensitive Communication, LLC.

Hentley, Sheila Rose. Nursery Rhymes & Nursery Riddles for All Ages. 2007. 28p. per. 21.99 *(978-1-4257-9011-0(9))* Xlibris Corp.

Heras, Theo. What Will We Do with the Baby-O? Herbert, Jennifer, illus. 2004. 32p. (J). (gr. k-k). 12.95 *(978-0-88776-689-3(7)*, Tundra Bks.) Tundra Bks. CAN. Dist: Penguin Random Hse. LLC.

Hey Diddle Diddle. 2004. (J). per. *(978-1-57657-428-7(8))* Paradise Pr., Inc.

Hilb, Nora, illus. Itsy Bitsy Spider. (Classic Books with Holes 8x8 Ser.). 16p. (J). 2017. (ENG.). pap. *(978-1-84643-974-2(4))* 2014. spiral bd. *(978-1-84643-666-6(4))* Child's Play International Ltd.

Hillenbrand, Will. Mother Goose Picture Puzzles, 0 vols. Hillenbrand, Will, illus. 2012. (ENG., Illus.). 40p. (J). (gr. 1-3). 17.99 *(978-0-7614-5808-1(5)*, 9780761458081, Two Lions) Amazon Publishing.

Hoberman, Mary Ann. Miss Mary Mack. Westcott, Nadine Bernard, illus. (ENG.). (J). (gr. -1-1). 2003. 32p. pap. 7.99 *(978-0-316-07614-2(7))* 2019. 24p. bds. 7.99 *(978-0-316-53734-6(9))* Little, Brown Bks. for Young Readers.

—You Read to Me, I'll Read to You: Very Short Mother Goose Tales to Read Together. 2012. (J). lib. bdg. 18.40 *(978-0-606-26684-0(4))* Turtleback.

Hone, Brettell. My African Bedtime Rhymes. 2009. (ENG., Illus.). 32p. *(978-0-620-40992-6(4))* Shamwari Publishing.

Hooper, Caroline & Danes, Emma. Little Book of Nursery Rhymes. 2005. 64p. (J). 6.99 *(978-0-7945-0954-5(1)*, Usborne) EDC Publishing.

Hopkins, Lee Bennett. The Lee Bennett Hopkins Mother Goose. 2005. (Poetry Ser.). (gr. -1-2). 270.00 *(978-0-8215-0459-8(2))* Sadlier, William H. Inc.

—Mother Goose Through the Seasons. Fehlau, Dagmar et al, illus. 2005. (Lee Bennett Hopkins Mother Goose Ser.). (YA). (gr. -1-1). 76.50 *(978-0-8215-0480-2(0))* Sadlier, William H. Inc.

Howard, Jennie & Howard, Akime. Creepy Colored Creatures. 2007. 28p. per. 15.95 *(978-1-4327-0723-1(X))* Outskirts Pr., Inc.

Humpty Dumpty: 6 Small Books. (gr. k-2). 23.00 *(978-0-7635-8498-6(3))* Rigby Education.

Humpty Dumpty at Sea. 2003. (J). per. *(978-1-57657-800-1(3))* Paradise Pr., Inc.

Hunter, Emily. The Bible-Time Nursery Rhyme Book. 2013. (ENG.). 98p. pap. 30.95 *(978-1-4787-1182-7(5))* Outskirts Pr., Inc.

Iglesias González, Natalia. Nursery rhymes for the English Classroom. 2009. (ENG.). 51p. pap. 28.50 *(978-1-4092-6513-9(7))* Lulu Pr., Inc.

Itchyka-Dana. Asian Nursery Rhymes. 2004. (J). *(978-1-85269-701-3(6))* Mantra Lingua.

Ives, Penny, illus. Five Little Ducks. (Classic Books with Holes 8x8 with CD Ser.). (ENG.). 16p. (J). 2007. *(978-1-84643-137-1(9))* 2005. pap. *(978-0-85953-447-5(2))* Child's Play International Ltd.

Izuora, Ikechukwu. Dazzle-Kids Book of Nursery Rhymes & Poems: Book of Nursery Rhymes & Poems. 2012. (Illus.). 40p. pap. 21.99 *(978-1-4653-0366-0(9))* Xlibris Corp.

Jack & Jill. 2003. (J). per. *(978-1-57657-801-8(1))* Paradise Pr., Inc.

Jack & Jill: 6 Small Books. (gr. k-2). 23.00 *(978-0-7635-8492-4(4))* Rigby Education.

Jackson, Marilyn Malloy, ed. Mother Goose on the Loose in Guam A Chamorro Adaptation of Traditional Nursery Rhymes. Tayama, Thomas, illus. 2006. (J). 6.50 net. *(978-0-9790111-5-3(9))* M-m-mauleg Publishing.

James, Diane. Baa, Baa, Black Sheep. 2004. (Jigsaw Nursery Rhymes Ser.). (ENG., Illus.). 12p. (J). (gr. -1-k). 9.95 *(978-1-58728-625-4(4)*, Two-Can Publishing) T&N Children's Publishing.

—Pat-a-Cake. 2004. (Jigsaw Nursery Rhymes Ser.). (ENG., Illus.). 12p. (J). (gr. -1-k). 9.95 *(978-1-58728-623-0(8)*, Two-Can Publishing) T&N Children's Publishing.

—Three Blind Mice. 2004. (Jigsaw Nursery Rhymes Ser.). (ENG., Illus.). 12p. (J). (gr. -1-k). 9.95 *(978-1-58728-626-1(2)*, Two-Can Publishing) T&N Children's Publishing.

Jerrold, Walter, ed. The Big Book of Nursery Rhymes. Robinson, Charles, illus. 2012. (Calla Editions Ser.). (ENG.). 352p. (gr. -1). 40.00 *(978-1-60660-030-6(3)*, 600303) Dover Pubns., Inc.

Jigsaw Nursery Rhymes. Blow, Wind, Blow. 2003. (Jigsaw Nursery Rhymes Ser.). 12p. (J). (gr. -1). bds. 9.95 *(978-1-58728-640-7(8)*, Two-Can Publishing) T&N Children's Publishing.

—Jack & Jill. 2003. (Jigsaw Nursery Rhymes Ser.). 12p. (J). (gr. -1). bds. 9.95 *(978-1-58728-641-4(6)*, Two-Can Publishing) T&N Children's Publishing.

—Old King Cole. 2003. (Jigsaw Nursery Rhymes Ser.). 12p. (J). (gr. -1). bds. 9.95 *(978-1-58728-642-1(4)*, Two-Can Publishing) T&N Children's Publishing.

—Rub-a-Dub-Dub. 2003. (Jigsaw Nursery Rhymes Ser.). 12p. (J). bds. 9.95 *(978-1-58728-643-8(2)*, Two-Can Publishing) T&N Children's Publishing.

John Knapp, Ii. A Pillar of Pepper & Other Bible Rhymes. Turner-Deckert, Dianne, illus. 2012. 130p. 29.99 *(978-0-912290-34-8(X))* Ephemeron Pr.

Jones, LaToya. My Learning Rhythms: Book 1. 2012. 20p. pap. 13.77 *(978-1-4669-3267-8(8))* Trafford Publishing.

—My Learning Rhythms: Book 3. 2012. 20p. pap. 13.77 *(978-1-4669-3599-0(5))* Trafford Publishing.

—My Learning Rhythms: Book 4. 2012. 20p. pap. 13.77 *(978-1-4669-3602-7(9))* Trafford Publishing.

Kays, Judy. ABC Rhymes by Grammy. 2010. 36p. pap. 19.95 *(978-1-4520-5154-3(2))* AuthorHouse.

Keith, Barbara Benson, illus. & compiled by. The Girls & Boys of Mother Goose. Keith, Barbara Benson, compiled by. 2006. 32p. (J). per. 7.99 *(978-0-9789688-0-9(8))* Brownian Bee Pr.

Kessey, K.O. Rhythms of African Drums: Rhymes & Lyrics for School Children & Youngsters. 2011. 232p. (gr. -1). pap. 22.87 *(978-1-4567-8610-6(5))* AuthorHouse.

Kolar, Rachel. Mother Ghost: Nursery Rhymes for Little Monsters. Garrigue, Roland, illus. 2018. (ENG.). 32p. (J). (gr. k-2). 16.99 *(978-1-58536-392-6(8)*, 204588) Sleeping Bear Pr.

Kole, Ted & Genet, John, eds. Katoufs in Nursery Rhymes Chapbook: Mother Goose. (Illus.). 48p. (Orig.). (J). (gr. 1-4). pap. 3.95 *(978-0-9641381-0-0(7))* Kreative Character Kreations, Inc.

Krumwiede, Lana. Just Itzy. Pizzoli, Greg, illus. 2015. (ENG.). 40p. (J). (-k). 15.99 *(978-0-7636-5811-3(1))* Candlewick Pr.

Kubler, Annie. Baa, Baa, Black Sheep! 2005. (Illus.). 12p. (J). spiral bd. *(978-1-904550-01-3(0))* Child's Play International Ltd.

—Head, Shoulders, Knees & Toes. (Illus.). 10p. (J). 2004. (ENG & PAN.). bds. *(978-1-84444-151-8(2))* 2004. (ENG & POR., bds. *(978-1-84444-152-5(0))* 2004. (ENG & SOM., bds. *(978-1-84444-153-2(9))* 2004. (ENG & SPA., bds. *(978-1-84444-154-9(7))* 2004. (ENG & TAM., bds. *(978-1-84444-155-6(5))* 2004. (ENG & GUJ., bds. *(978-1-84444-150-1(4))* 2004. (FRE & ENG., bds. *(978-1-84444-149-5(0))* 2004. (ENG & PER., bds. *(978-1-84444-148-8(2))* 2004. (ENG & CHI., bds. *(978-1-84444-147-1(4))* 2004. (ENG & ARA., bds. *(978-1-84444-145-7(8))* 2004. (ENG & ALB., bds. *(978-1-84444-144-0(X))* 2004. (ENG & TUR., bds. *(978-1-84444-156-3(3))* 2003. (BEN & ENG., bds. *(978-1-84444-146-4(6))* Mantra Lingua.

—Twinkle, Twinkle, Little Star. 2005. (Illus.). 12p. (J). spiral bd. *(978-1-904550-02-0(9))* Child's Play International Ltd.

Kubler, Annie, illus. Baa, Baa, Black Sheep! American Sign Language. 2005. (Sign & Singalong Ser.). (ENG.). 12p. (J). (gr. k-1). bds. *(978-1-904550-41-9(X))* Child's Play International Ltd.

—I'm a Little Teapot. 2007. (Baby Board Bks.). 12p. (J). (gr. k-1). bds. *(978-1-84643-122-7(0))* Child's Play International Ltd.

—Itsy, Bitsy Spider: American Sign Language. 2005. (Sign & Singalong Ser.). (ENG.). 12p. (J). (gr. k-k). bds. *(978-1-904550-43-3(6))* Child's Play International Ltd.

—Pussy Cat, Pussy Cat. 2010. (Baby Board Bks.). 12p. (J). bds. *(978-1-84643-340-5(1))* Child's Play International Ltd.

—Row, Row, Row Your Boat. 2003. (Baby Board Bks.). 12p. (J). bds. *(978-0-85953-658-5(0))* Child's Play International Ltd.

—Teddy Bear, Teddy Bear: American Sign Language. 2005. (Sign & Singalong Ser.). (ENG.). 12p. (J). (gr. k-1). bds. *(978-1-904550-40-2(1))* Child's Play International Ltd.

—This Little Piggy / Este Cochinito. 2009. (Baby Board Bks.). (ENG.). 12p. (J). bds. *(978-1-84643-313-9(4))* Child's Play International Ltd.

—Twinkle, Twinkle, Little Star: American Sign Language. 2005. (Sign & Singalong Ser.). (ENG.). 12p. (J). (gr. k-k). bds. *(978-1-904550-42-6(8))* Child's Play International Ltd.

—The Wheels on the Bus. 2019. (Baby Rhyme Time Ser.). 12p. (J). bds. *(978-1-78628-196-8(1))* Child's Play International Ltd.

—The Wheels on the Bus Go Round & Round. (Classic Books with Holes 8x8 with CD Ser.). (ENG.). 16p. (J). 2007. (gr. -1-1). *(978-1-904550-66-2(5))* 2003. *(978-0-85953-136-8(8))* Child's Play International Ltd.

Kumon. My Book of Rhyming Words & Phrases. 2004. (ENG., Illus.). 80p. (J). per. 7.95 *(978-4-7743-0762-6(9))* Kumon Publishing North America, Inc.

Kumon Publishing North America, ed. My Book of Rhyming Words. Kumon Publishing North America, . 2004. (ENG., Illus.). 80p. (J). per. 7.95 *(978-4-7743-0761-9(0))* Kumon Publishing North America, Inc.

Lacome, Julie. Walking Through the Jungle Big Book. Lacome, Julie, illus. 2004. (ENG., Illus.). 32p. (J). (gr. k-k). pap. 27.99 *(978-0-7636-2471-2(3))* Candlewick Pr.

Ladybird. Ladybird I'm Ready to Sing! 2018. (Ladybird I'm Ready Ser.). (ENG., Illus.). 48p. (J). (— 1). pap. 10.99 *(978-0-241-21595-1(1))* Penguin Bks., Ltd. GBR. Dist: Independent Pubs. Group.

Ladybird Books Staff. Nursery Rhymes. (First Bks.: No. S808-5). (Illus.). (J). (gr. -1). pap. 3.95 *(978-0-7214-5056-8(3)*, Dutton Juvenile) Penguin Publishing Group.

Landon, Angela. What Is Freedom? How Does It Ring? 2011. 40p. (gr. 1-2). 16.59 *(978-1-4567-4538-7(7))* AuthorHouse.

Language Works Rhyme Time. 8p. (J). *(978-0-8136-3519-4(5))* Modern Curriculum Pr.

Le Ray, Marina, illus. Row, Row, Row Your Boat; and, Ride, Ride, Ride Your Bike. 2013. (ENG.). 24p. (J). *(978-0-7787-1149-0(8))* Crabtree Publishing Co.

Leonard, Barry, ed. Humpty Dumpty & Other Rhymes. 2003. (Illus.). 12p. (J). (gr. k-5). reprint ed. 17.00 *(978-0-7567-6855-3(1))* DIANE Publishing Co.

—Mary Had a Little Lamb & Other Rhymes. 2003. (Illus.). 12p. (J). (gr. k-4). reprint ed. 17.00 *(978-0-7567-6861-4(6))* DIANE Publishing Co.

—Mary, Mary, Quite Contrary & Other Rhymes. 2003. (Illus.). 12p. (J). (gr. k-5). reprint ed. 17.00 *(978-0-7567-6857-7(8))* DIANE Publishing Co.

—Rock-a-Bye, Baby & Other Rhymes. 2003. (Illus.). 12p. (J). (gr. k-4). reprint ed. 17.00 *(978-0-7567-6863-8(2))* DIANE Publishing Co.

—See-Saw Margery Daw & Other Rhymes. 2003. (Illus.). 12p. (J). (gr. k-5). reprint ed. 17.00 *(978-0-7567-6866-9(7))* DIANE Publishing Co.

—Wee Willie Winkie & Other Rhymes. 2003. (Illus.). 12p. (J). (gr. k-4). reprint ed. 17.00 *(978-0-7567-6859-1(4))* DIANE Publishing Co.

Lewis, Anthony, illus. Five Little Ducks: American Sign Language. 2013. (Hands-On Songs Ser.). (ENG.). 12p. (J). (gr. -1). bds. *(978-1-84643-630-7(3))* Child's Play International Ltd.

—Jack & Jill: American Sign Language. 2013. (Hands-On Songs Ser.). (ENG.). 12p. (J). (gr. -1). bds. *(978-1-84643-629-1(X))* Child's Play International Ltd.

—Old Macdonald: American Sign Language. 2013. (Hands-On Songs Ser.). (ENG.). 12p. (J). (gr. -1). bds. *(978-1-84643-628-4(1))* Child's Play International Ltd.

—The Wheels on the Bus: American Sign Language. 2013. (Hands-On Songs Ser.). (ENG.). 12p. (J). bds. *(978-1-84643-626-0(5))* Child's Play International Ltd.

Lewis, Jan. Best-Ever Rhymes. 2015. (Illus.). 24p. (J). (gr. -1-12). bds. 6.99 *(978-1-86147-499-5(7)*, Armadillo) Anness Publishing GBR. Dist: National Bk. Network.

—Mother Goose Nursery Rhymes. 2015. (Illus.). 48p. (J). (gr. -1-12). bds. 9.99 *(978-1-86147-649-4(3)*, Armadillo) Anness Publishing GBR. Dist: National Bk. Network.

Lewis, Jan, illus. Mother Goose Action Rhymes: Old MacDonald Had a Farm; One, Two, Buckle My Shoe; Round & Round the Garden; This Little Pig. 2004. 90p. (J). vinyl bd. *(978-1-902272-32-0(3))* Tucker Slingsby, Ltd.

—Mother Goose Rhymes: One, Two, Buckle My Shoe. 2015. 24p. (J). (gr. -1-12). bds. 6.99 *(978-1-86147-637-1(X)*, Armadillo) Anness Publishing GBR. Dist: National Bk. Network.

—My Favourite Nursery Rhyme Collection, Set. 2017. (ENG.). 1p. (J). (gr. -1-12). bds. 14.99 *(978-1-86147-740-8(6),* Armadillo) Anness Publishing GBR. Dist: National Bk. Network.

—Old MacDonald Had a Farm. 2015. 24p. (J). (gr. -1-12). bds. 6.99 *(978-1-86147-468-1(7),* Armadillo) Anness Publishing GBR. Dist: National Bk. Network.

—Playtime Rhymes: My Mother Goose Collection. 2018. 24p. (J). (gr. -1-12). bds. 6.99 *(978-1-86147-694-4(9),* Armadillo) Anness Publishing GBR. Dist: National Bk. Network.

—Round & Round the Garden. 2015. 24p. (J). (gr. -1-12). bds. 6.99 *(978-1-86147-636-4(1),* Armadillo) Anness Publishing GBR. Dist: National Bk. Network.

Linder, Dorothy Perillo. A Vegetable Collection: Recipes & Rhymes to Conquer Kids of All Ages. 2008. (Illus.). (J). 35.00 *(978-0-9753334-2-6(9))* Sanctuary Bks.

Lipchenko, Oleg, selected by. Humpty Dumpty & Friends: Nursery Rhymes for the Young at Heart. 2010. 24p. (J). (gr. -1-2). 17.95 *(978-1-77049-205-9(4),* Tundra Bks.) Tundra Bks. CAN. Dist: Penguin Random Hse. LLC.

Listen! Listen! Letter Sounds in Rhyme: Blends & Digraphs Set. (gr. k-1). 89.95 *(978-0-322-02639-1(3))* Wright Group/McGraw-Hill.

Listen! Listen! Letter Sounds in Rhyme: Consonants Set. (gr. k-1). 84.95 *(978-0-322-02637-7(7))* Wright Group/McGraw-Hill.

Listen! Listen! Letter Sounds in Rhyme: Vowels Set. (gr. k-1). 52.95 *(978-0-322-02638-4(5))* Wright Group/McGraw-Hill.

Litchfield, Jo, illus. First Picture Nursery Rhymes. 2005. (Usborne First Book Ser.). 16p. (J). (gr. -1-k). per. 11.99 *(978-0-7945-1014-5(0),* Usborne) EDC Publishing.

Litchfield, Jo & Allen, Francesca, illus. First Picture Nursery Rhymes With. 2006. 18p. (J). bds. 18.99 *(978-0-7945-1489-1(8),* Usborne) EDC Publishing.

Little Jack Horner. 6 Small Books. (gr. k-2). 23.00 *(978-0-7635-8500-6(9))* Rigby Education.

Locatelli, Ellen, illus. Filastrocche Italiane- Italian Nursery Rhymes. 2013. 54p. *(978-1-938712-08-1(0))* Roxby Media Ltd.

Long, Sylvia, illus. Sylvia Long's Big Book for Small Children. 2018. (Family Treasure Nature Encylopedias Ser.). (ENG.). 112p. (J). (gr. -1 — 1). 22.99 *(978-0-8118-3441-4(7))* Chronicle Bks. LLC.

Loper, Kathleen. Angelina Katrina: Builds Troy Snowman. Waltz, Dan, illus. l.t. ed. 2004. 36p. (J). 17.95 *(978-0-9741774-5-8(8))* D. W. Publishing.

Low, Elizabeth Cothen. Big Book of Seasons, Holidays, & Weather: Rhymes, Fingerplays, & Songs for Children. 2011. (ENG., Illus.). 168p. E-Book 45.00 *(978-1-59884-624-9(8),* A3162E, Libraries Unlimited) ABC-CLIO, LLC.

Mabie, Hamilton Wright, et al, eds. Childhood's Favorites & Fairy Stories. 2007. (Illus.). 660p. per. *(978-1-4065-2960-9(5))* Dodo Pr.

Maccarone, Grace, ed. The Real Mother Goose: Anniversary Edition. Wright, Blanche Fisher, illus. anniv. ed. 2006. (ENG.). 144p. (J). (gr. 3-7). 10.99 *(978-0-439-85875-5(5),* Cartwheel Bks.) Scholastic, Inc.

Magee, Wes. Itsy Bitsy Spider & Itsy Bitsy Beetle. 2012. (ENG., Illus.). 24p. (J). *(978-0-7787-7886-8(X));* pap. *(978-0-7787-7898-1(3))* Crabtree Publishing Co.

Make Believe Ideas. Hey Diddle Diddle & Other Nursery Rhymes. Machell, Dawn, illus. 2015. (ENG.). 24p. (J). (— 1). bds. 7.99 *(978-1-78393-436-2(0))* Make Believe Ideas GBR. Dist: Scholastic, Inc.

—My Awesome Nursery Rhymes Book, 1 vol. Machell, Dawn, illus. 2018. (ENG.). 30p. (J). (gr. -1 — 1). bds. 9.99 *(978-1-78692-905-1(8))* Make Believe Ideas GBR. Dist: Scholastic, Inc.

Malley, Barbara. Read Me A Rhyme Please. 2006. (Illus.). 236p. per. 19.95 *(978-0-89334-414-6(1),* Humanics Learning) Green Dragon Bks.

Manousos, Dave. Life Is Good & Other Reasons for Rhyme. Manousos, Dave, illus. 2008. (Illus.). 36p. pap. 16.95 *(978-1-59858-590-2(8))* Dog Ear Publishing, LLC.

MansBach, Sara. Round & Round the Garden, Finger Games in English & Spanish. Arroyave, Heidy, tr. Landau, Donna, illus. 2007. 42p. spiral bd. *(978-0-9785477-2-1(1))* BladeRunner Publishing.

Marinaro, Stacy. Nap Time. 2009. 34p. pap. 16.50 *(978-0-557-06881-4(9))* Lulu Pr., Inc.

Marks, Alan. The People of the Town: Nursery-Rhyme Friends for You & Me. Marks, Alan, illus. 2016. (Illus.). 40p. (J). (-k). lib. bdg. 16.95 *(978-1-58089-726-6(6))* Charlesbridge Publishing, Inc.

Marshall, Natalie. Five Little Monkeys: a Fingers & Toes Nursery Rhyme Book. Marshall, Natalie, illus. 2015. (Fingers & Toes Nursery Rhymes Ser.). (ENG.). 12p. (J). (— 1). bds. 6.99 *(978-0-545-76762-0(8),* Cartwheel Bks.) Scholastic, Inc.

Mathers, Petra, compiled by. McElderry Book of Mother Goose: McElderry Book of Mother Goose. 2012. (ENG., Illus.). 96p. (J). (gr. k-5). 21.99 *(978-0-689-85605-1(9),* McElderry, Margaret K. Bks.) McElderry, Margaret K. Bks.

Mavor, Salley. Pocketful of Posies: A Treasury of Nursery Rhymes. 2010. (ENG., Illus.). 72p. (J). (gr. -1-k). 21.99 *(978-0-618-73740-6(5),* 521918, Clarion Bks.) HarperCollins Pubs.

Mayo, Diana. House That Jack Built. 2007. (ENG., Illus.). 24p. (J). pap. 9.99 *(978-1-84686-076-8(8))* Barefoot Bks., Inc.

McDermott, Mustafa Yusuf. Muslim Nursery Rhymes. rev. ed. 2015. (ENG., Illus.). 29p. (J). 14.95 *(978-0-86037-563-0(3))* Kube Publishing Ltd. GBR. Dist: Consortium Bk. Sales & Distribution.

McDonald, Jill. Over in the Meadow. 2011. (J). *(978-1-84686-542-8(5))* Barefoot Bks., Inc.

McKay-Lawton, Toni. In Bloom. Manning, Eddie, illus. 2007. (Just in Rhyme Ser.). (ENG.). 12p. (J). (gr. -1-3). pap. *(978-1-84167-030-0(8))* Ransom Publishing Ltd.

McLoughlin Brothers, McLoughlin Brothers. Baby's Opera (HC) A Book of Old Rhymes with New Dresses. 2012. (Applewood Bks.). (ENG., Illus.). 64p. (J). (gr. k-1). 14.95 *(978-1-4290-8033-0(7))* Applewood Bks.

Mendicino, Valentina, illus. Dinosaur Rhyme Time. 2014. (ENG.). 32p. (J). 13.00 *(978-0-571-30833-0(3),* Faber & Faber Children's Bks.) Faber & Faber, Inc.

Mendonca, Angela. Nursery Rhymes Island Style. Mendonca, Angela, illus. 2013. (Illus.). 24p. pap. 9.99 *(978-0-9843125-6-6(0))* Wealth of Wisdom LLC, A.

Miles, Kelly. Big Book of Fairy Tales. Kelly, Richard, ed. 2017. (Illus.). 96p. (J). pap. 17.95 *(978-1-78209-659-7(0))* Miles Kelly Publishing, Ltd. GBR. Dist: Parkwest Pubns., Inc.

Miller, J. P., illus. Little Golden Book Nursery Tales. 2017. 80p. (J). (gr. -1-2). 7.99 *(978-0-553-53667-6(2),* Golden Bks.) Random Hse. Children's Bks.

Mills, Liz. African Nursery Rhymes. 2017. (ENG., Illus.). pap. 11.00 *(978-1-4323-0790-5(8))* Penguin Random House Grupo Editorial ESP. Dist: Casemate Pubs. & Bk. Distributors, LLC.

Monreal, Violeta & Violeta, Monreal. Mio, Mio! el Huevo Es Mio. 2003. (Coleccion Pictogramas Pictograms Ser.). (SPA.). 36p. (J). (gr. k-3). pap. 8.50 *(978-84-241-8102-4(6))* Everest Editora ESP. Dist: Lectorum Pubns., Inc.

Moore, Colin. Modern Nursery Rhymes: For Grown-Ups. 2012. (Illus.). 100p. pap. 13.95 *(978-1-4678-9029-8(4))* AuthorHouse.

Moran, Erin. Colorful Spring. Pickett, Danny, illus. 2005. 32p. (J). mass mkt. 15.95 *(978-0-9763778-0-1(2))* Seal Rock Publishing, LLC.

Moreillon, Judi. Vamos a Leer. Mercado, Mary M., tr. from ENG. Teis, Kyra, illus.Tr. of Read to Me. (SPA.). 12p. (J). 2005. bds. 6.95 *(978-1-59572-015-3(4))* 2004. 6.95 *(978-1-932065-50-3(4))* Star Bright Bks., Inc.

Morgan, Richard, illus. The Wheels on the Bus - The Boat on the Waves. 2013. (ENG.). 24p. (J). *(978-0-7787-1148-3(X))* Crabtree Publishing Co.

—The Wheels on the Bus; The Boat on the Waves, 1 vol. 2013. (ENG.). 24p. (J). pap. *(978-0-7787-1152-0(8))* Crabtree Publishing Co.

Moroney, Trace, creator. Baa, Baa, Black Sheep. 2008. (Illus.). 10p. (gr. -1-1). bds. 4.99 *(978-1-74178-526-5(X))* Gardner Pubns.

Moses, Brian. Hey Diddle Diddle & Hey Diddle Doodle, 1 vol. 2012. (ENG., Illus.). 24p. (J). pap. *(978-0-7787-7896-7(7))* Crabtree Publishing Co.

—Humpty Dumpty & Humpty Dumpty at Sea. 2012. (ENG., Illus.). 24p. (J). *(978-0-7787-7885-1(1));* pap. *(978-0-7787-7897-4(5))* Crabtree Publishing Co.

Mother Goose, ed. Nursery Rhyme Classics. 2006. (ENG., Illus.). 12p. (J). 17.95 *(978-1-59069-472-5(4))* Soundprints.

—Nursery Rhyme Songs. 2006. (ENG., Illus.). 12p. 17.95 *(978-1-59069-473-2(2))* Soundprints.

La Muneca Azul: Poems, Rhymes, & Songs Listening Packs. 2003. 34.50 *(978-0-673-58631-5(6))* Celebration Pr.

Music Sales. The Nursery Rhyme Songbook. 2009. (ENG.). 104p. (J). 9.95 *(978-1-84772-580-6(5),* AM993839) Wise Pubns. GBR. Dist: Music Sales Corp.

Nascimbeni, Barbara. Little Miss Muffet. 2015. (Classic Books with Holes Ser.). (Illus.). 16p. (J). *(978-1-84643-678-9(8))* Child's Play International Ltd.

Nascimbeni, Barbara, illus. Little Miss Muffet. (Classic Books with Holes Big Book Ser.). (J). 2014. 16p. spiral bd. *(978-1-84643-668-0(0))* 2012. 14p. spiral bd. *(978-1-84643-511-9(0))* 2012. 16p. pap. *(978-1-84643-500-3(5))* Child's Play International Ltd.

Newman, Leslea. Daddy, Papa, & Me. Thompson, Carol, illus. 2009. 20p. (J). (gr. -1 — 1). 8.99 *(978-1-58246-262-2(3),* Tricycle Pr.) Random Hse. Children's Bks.

—Mommy, Mama, & Me. Thompson, Carol, illus. 2009. 20p. (J). (gr. -1-2). 8.99 *(978-1-58246-263-9(1),* Tricycle Pr.) Random Hse. Children's Bks.

Nippert, Brenda & Nippert, George. An Alphabet of Catholic Saints. bks. 13000. Nippert, Brenda & Nippert, George, illus. 3rd ed. 2006. (ENG., Illus.). 64p. (J). pap. 11.95 *(978-0-9787035-1-6(0))* Joseph's Heartprint.

—An Alphabet of Mary. bks. 3000. Nippert, Brenda & Nippert, George, illus. 2012. (ENG., Illus.). 64p. (J). pap. 12.95 *(978-0-9787035-0-9(2))* Joseph's Heartprint.

Noe, David C. Tres Mures Caeci. Thoburn, Michelle, illus. 2005. (LAT.). 48p. (J). (gr. k-12). 11.99 *(978-0-9714458-1-9(8))* Patrick Henry College Pr.

Novick, Mary. Nursery Songs. Hale, Jenny, illus. 2003. (ENG.). 16p. (Orig.). pap. *(978-1-877003-33-2(6))* Little Hare Bks. AUS. Dist: HarperCollins Pubs. Australia.

Nursery Rhymes. (My First Sing-Alongs Ser.). (J). 7.99 incl. audio *(978-1-55723-603-6(8))* Walt Disney Records.

Nursery Rhymes - Jack & Jill. 2005. (J). bds. *(978-1-4194-0077-3(0))* Paradise Pr., Inc.

Nursery Rhymes - Old Mcdonald. 2005. (J). bds. *(978-1-4194-0076-6(2))* Paradise Pr., Inc.

Nursery Rhymes - One, Two, Buckle my Shoe. 2005. (J). bds. *(978-1-4194-0078-0(9))* Paradise Pr., Inc.

NUrsery rhymes- Bah,Bah black Sheep. 2005. (J). bds. *(978-1-4194-0079-7(7))* Paradise Pr., Inc.

Nursery Rhymes Set 800783, 5. 2005. (J). bds. *(978-1-59794-018-4(6))* Environments, Inc.

Nursery Rymes Book. 2005. (J). bds. *(978-1-4194-0070-4(3))* Paradise Pr., Inc.

Nursery Songs & Rhyms Gift Book. 2006. (J). 9.99 *(978-1-934004-03-6(0))* Byeway Bks.

O'Brien, Eileen. This Little Piggy. Tyler, Jenny, ed. Edward, Linda, illus. 2004. (Carry-Me Bks.). 16p. (J). 5.95 *(978-0-7945-0125-9(7),* Usborne) EDC Publishing.

Olowoyeye, Ola. Rhythm & Motion: Volume 2. 2011. 28p. pap. 12.03 *(978-1-4634-3256-0(9))* AuthorHouse.

Opie, Iain, ed. My Very First Mother Goose. Wells, Rosemary, illus. 2004. 107p. (J). reprint ed. 17.00 *(978-0-7567-8384-6(4))* DIANE Publishing Co.

Opie, Iona. My Very First Mother Goose. Wells, Rosemary, illus. 2016. (My Very First Mother Goose Ser.). (ENG.). 108p. (J). (gr. k-k). 24.99 *(978-0-7636-8891-2(6))* Candlewick Pr.

Osborne, Nancy. Rhyming Words: Cut & Paste. l.t. ed. 2007. (Illus.). 52p. ring bd. 9.95 *(978-1-928856-07-8(1))* Osborne Pr.

Oscar: Poems, Rhymes, & Songs Listening Packs. 2003. 34.50 *(978-0-673-58622-3(7))* Celebration Pr.

Parekh, R. Nursery Rhymes. 2004. (Flashcards Ser.). (ENG., Illus.). 48p. (J). pap. 8.95 *(978-0-7945-0530-1(9))* EDC Publishing.

Passchier, Anne, illus. She'll Be Coming 'Round the Mountain. (Classic Books with Holes 8x8 Ser.). (ENG.). (J). 2019. 16p. pap. *(978-1-78628-211-8(9))* 2019. 14p. bds. *(978-1-78628-216-3(X))* 2018. 16p. *(978-1-78628-232-3(1))* 2018. 16p. *(978-1-78628-228-6(3))* 2018. 16p. pap. *(978-1-78628-141-8(4))* Child's Play International Ltd.

Pat-a-Cake. 2003. (J). per. *(978-1-57657-802-5(X))* Paradise Pr., Inc.

Pedro, Pedrito: Poems, Rhymes, & Songs Listening Packs. 2003. 34.50 *(978-0-673-58632-2(4))* Celebration Pr.

Penner, Fred. Here We Go Round the Mulberry Bush. Fatus, Sophie, illus. 2008. (ENG.). 24p. (J). 6.99 *(978-1-84686-189-5(6))* Barefoot Bks., Inc.

Pernice, Clare. The Real Mother Goose: Hard-Boiled Humpty & More Scrambled Rhymes. 2022. (ENG., Illus.). 40p. (gr. 1-3). pap. 17.95 *(978-1-927018-83-5(8))* Simply Read Bks. CAN. Dist: Ingram Publisher Services.

Phonics Songs & Rhymes Flip Chart. 2004. (gr. k-18). suppl. ed. 109.15 *(978-0-328-02213-7(6));* (gr. 1-18). suppl. ed. 109.15 *(978-0-673-59716-8(4));* (gr. 3-18). suppl. ed. 109.50 *(978-0-673-59718-2(0))* Addison-Wesley Educational Pubs., Inc.

PI Kids. The World of Eric Carle: Froggie Went Hopping a Pop-Up Songbook. 2014. (ENG., Illus.). 10p. (J). (gr. k-4). bds. 15.99 *(978-1-4508-6821-1(5),* 1549, PI Kids) Phoenix International Publications, Inc.

Pi Kids, creator. Mother Goose. 2007. (My First Treasury Ser.). (Illus.). 38p. (J). bds. 7.98 *(978-1-4127-8713-0(0),* PIL Kids) Publications International, Ltd.

Pinkney, Jerry. Three Little Kittens. Pinkney, Jerry, illus. 2010. (ENG., Illus.). 40p. (J). (gr. -1-k). 18.99 *(978-0-8037-3533-0(2),* Dial Bks) Penguin Young Readers Group.

Poplin, Isaac E. A-Z's of Ancient Rome: A Rhyming Introduction to Roman History. 2011. 60p. (gr. 1-2). pap. 9.99 *(978-1-4567-6931-4(6))* AuthorHouse.

Potter, Beatrix. Beatrix Potter's Nursery Rhyme Book R/I. 2007. (Peter Rabbit Ser.). (ENG., Illus.). 80p. (J). (gr. -1-2). 14.99 *(978-0-7232-5771-4(X),* Warne) Penguin Young Readers Group.

Potter, Debra, illus. I Am the Music Man. 2005. (Classic Books with Holes Board Book Ser.). (J). 14p. spiral bd. *(978-1-904550-60-0(6));* 16p. pap. *(978-1-904550-34-1(7))* Child's Play International Ltd.

Power, Eloise. The Apple Tree Inside of Me. 2012. 36p. pap. 16.95 *(978-1-4525-5522-5(2))* Balboa Pr.

Priddy Books Staff. My Bedtime Book of Favorite Nursery Rhymes: Including Ladybug, Baa Baa Black Sheep, I Had a Nut Tree, Plus Many More... 2003. (Illus.). (J). bds. *(978-0-312-49174-1(3),* Priddy Bks.) St. Martin's Pr.

Priddy, Roger. Nursery Rhymes: With a Sing-Along Music CD. 2006. (Sing-Along Ser.). (ENG., Illus.). 28p. (J). (gr. -1 — 1). 12.95 *(978-0-312-49808-5(X),* 900041009) St. Martin's Pr.

La Primavera: Poems, Rhymes, & Songs Listening Packs. 2003. 34.50 *(978-0-673-58633-9(2))* Celebration Pr.

Profiri, Charline. Rain, Rain, Stay Today: Southwestern Nursery Rhymes. Watson, Laura, illus. 2014. (J). *(978-1-933855-85-1(1))* Rio Nuevo Pubs.

Public Domain, Public. The Tall Book of Mother Goose. Ivanov, Aleksey & Ivanov, Olga, illus. 2006. (ENG.). 80p. (J). (gr. -1-2). pap. 7.99 *(978-0-06-054373-0(6),* HarperCollins) HarperCollins Pubs.

Publications International Ltd. Staff. Mother Goose. 2009. 320p. (J). lib. bdg. 19.98 *(978-1-4127-4528-4(4))* Phoenix International Publications, Inc.

Publications International Ltd. Staff, creator. Mother Goose. 2006. (Keepsake Collection). (Illus.). 96p. (J). (gr. -1-3). 12.98 *(978-1-4127-6061-4(5),* PIL Kids) Publications International, Ltd.

Publications International Ltd. Staff, ed. Happy Baby. 2011. 8p. (J). bds. 7.98 *(978-1-4508-1243-6(0))* Publications International, Ltd.

Railes, H. J. Looking Out My Window. 2013. (Illus.). 38p. (J). lib. bdg. 16.00 *(978-1-935722-80-9(8),* TOP) Top Pubns., Ltd.

Read along Nursery Rhymes - Student Books. 2005. (J). pap. 19.95 *(978-1-58970-701-6(X))* Lakeshore Learning Materials.

Read along Nursery Rhymes Big Book. 2005. (J). pap. 16.95 *(978-1-58970-700-9(1))* Lakeshore Learning Materials.

Reading 2000 Phonics Songs & Rhymes Flip Chart. 2004. (gr. 2-18). suppl. ed. 109.15 *(978-0-673-59717-5(2))* Addison-Wesley Educational Pubs., Inc.

Reasoner, Charles. Hey, Diddle, Diddle, 1 vol. Le Ray, Marina, illus. 2014. (Charles Reasoner Nursery Rhymes Ser.). (ENG.). 10p. (J). (gr. -1 — 1). bds. 4.99 *(978-1-4795-3807-2(8),* 124649, Picture Window Bks.) Capstone.

—Hickory, Dickory, Dock. Le Ray, Marina, illus. 2014. (Charles Reasoner Nursery Rhymes Ser.). (ENG.). 10p. (J). (gr. -1 — 1). bds. 4.99 *(978-1-4795-3805-8(1),* 124647, Picture Window Bks.) Capstone.

—Itsy Bitsy Spider, 1 vol. Le Ray, Marina. 2013. (Charles Reasoner Nursery Rhymes Ser.). (ENG.). 10p. (J). (gr. -1 — 1). bds. 4.99 *(978-1-4795-1691-9(0),* 123217, Picture Window Bks.) Capstone.

Reasoner, Charles & Borgert-Spaniol, Megan. Twinkle, Twinkle, Little Star, 1 vol. Le Ray, Marina & McNicholas, Shelagh, illus. 2013. (Charles Reasoner Nursery Rhymes Ser.). (ENG.). 10p. (J). (gr. -1 — 1). bds. 4.99 *(978-1-4795-1693-3(7),* 123219, Picture Window Bks.) Capstone.

Reinhart, Matthew. A Pop-Up Book of Nursery Rhymes: A Classic Collectible Pop-Up. Reinhart, Matthew, illus. 2009. (ENG., Illus.). 12p. (J). (gr. -1-3). 34.99 *(978-1-4169-1825-7(6),* Little Simon) Little Simon.

Rescek, Sanja, illus. One Elephant Went Out to Play. 2007. (Classic Books with Holes Board Book Ser.). 14p. (J). (gr. -1-1). spiral bd. *(978-1-84643-111-1(5))* Child's Play International Ltd.

Rhyme Time. 2006. (J). bds. *(978-1-4194-0144-2(0))* Paradise Pr., Inc.

Richardson, Frederick, illus. Mother Goose: A Classic Collection of Children's Nursery Rhymes. 2008. (ENG.). 24p. (J). 19.95 *(978-1-58117-687-2(2),* Intervisual/Piggy Toes) Bendon, Inc.

Rigby Education Staff. Humpty Dumpty Bigbook: Rhyme 2. (gr. k-2). 21.00 *(978-0-7635-2410-4(7))* Rigby Education.

—Jack & Jill Big Book: Rhyme 1. (gr. k-2). 21.00 *(978-0-7635-2404-3(2))* Rigby Education.

—Little Jack. (gr. k-2). 21.00 *(978-0-7635-2412-8(3))* Rigby Education.

—Mary Big Book: Rhyme 2. (gr. k-2). 21.00 *(978-0-7635-2411-1(5))* Rigby Education.

—Old King: Rhyme 1. (gr. k-2). 21.00 *(978-0-7635-2405-0(0))* Rigby Education.

Riley, James Whitcomb. Riley Child-Rhymes. 2007. 64p. per. *(978-1-4068-3909-8(4))* Echo Library.

—Riley Farm-Rhymes. 2007. 60p. per. *(978-1-4068-3912-8(4))* Echo Library.

Ritter-Henley, Sharlene. 123 Count Drive Nursery Rhyme, 1 vol. 2010. 20p. pap. 24.95 *(978-1-4489-8141-0(7))* PublishAmerica, Inc.

Robleda, Margarita. Rebeca. Suarez, Maribel, illus. (Rana, Rema, Rimas Ser.).Tr. of Rebecca. (SPA.). 16p. (J). (gr. k-3). 7.95 *(978-1-59437-819-5(3))* Santillana USA Publishing Co., Inc.

—Suenos. Suarez, Maribel, illus. (Rana, Rema, Rimas Ser.). (SPA.). 16p. (J). (gr. k-3). 7.95 *(978-1-59437-821-8(5))* Santillana USA Publishing Co., Inc.

Rossetti, Christina. Blooming Beneath the Sun. Bryan, Ashley, illus. 2019. (ENG.). 40p. (J). (gr. -1-3). 17.99 *(978-1-5344-4092-0(5),* Atheneum/Caitlyn Dlouhy Books) Simon & Schuster Children's Publishing.

Rossetti, Christina Georgina. Speaking Likenesses / by Christina Rossetti; with Pictures Thereof by Arthur Hughes. 2006. 112p. per. 16.99 *(978-1-4255-0744-2(1))* Michigan Publishing.

Rossitter, Derek. The Greedy Pigeon & the Hungry Porcupine & Friends. 2008. (Illus.). 60p. (J). (gr. 4-7). pap. *(978-0-7552-0406-9(9))* Authors OnLine, Ltd.

—Greedy Pigeon the Hungry Porcupine & Friends. Horne, Grace, illus. 2004. 60p. pap. *(978-0-7552-0142-6(6))* Authors OnLine, Ltd.

Rudisill, J. J. Hickory Dickory Dock. 2012. (Early Literacy Ser.). (ENG.). 16p. (gr. -1-1). 19.99 *(978-1-4333-3494-8(1));* 6.99 *(978-1-4333-3493-1(3))* Teacher Created Materials, Inc.

Sacred Friends. I Found the Answer. 2013. (Illus.). 16p. (J). pap. 7.95 *(978-1-4525-8515-4(6),* Balboa Pr.) Author Solutions, LLC.

Salgado, Tono. Versos y Rimas para Ninos.Tr. of Verses & Ryhmes for Children. (SPA.). (J). 7.98 *(978-968-403-880-6(1))* Selector, S.A. de C.V. MEX. Dist: Spanish Pubs., LLC.

Salzmann, Ann. Rainbow Rhymes. 2012. (ENG.). pap. *(978-1-4675-1531-3(0))* Independent Pub.

Scheffler, Axel & Green, Alison. Mother Goose's Storytime Nursery Rhymes. 2007. (J). *(978-0-439-90307-3(6),* Levine, Arthur A. Bks.) Scholastic, Inc.

Scholastic. Knees & Toes! (Rookie Toddler) 2009. (Rookie Toddler Ser.). (ENG., Illus.). 14p. (J). (gr. -1 — 1). bds. 6.95 *(978-0-531-24546-0(2),* Children's Pr.) Scholastic Library Publishing.

Scieszka, Jon. Truckery Rhymes. 2009. (ENG., Illus.). 24p. (J). (gr. k-k). pap. 6.25 *(978-0-328-50050-5(X),* Scott Foresman) Savvas Learning Co.

—Truckery Rhymes. Shannon, David et al, illus. 2009. (Jon Scieszka's Trucktown Ser.). (ENG.). 64p. (J). (gr. -1-3). 19.99 *(978-1-4169-4135-4(5),* Simon & Schuster Bks. For Young Readers) Simon & Schuster Bks. For Young Readers.

Sellers, Amy. Miss Amy's: Hurray for Rhyme It's Story Time: Contemporary Rhyming Stories for Children of All Ages. 2007. 32p. (J). pap. 19.95 *(978-0-9787632-0-6(3))* Sellers, Amy.

Senor Cascaron: Poems, Rhymes, & Songs Listening Packs. 2003. (SPA.). 34.50 *(978-0-673-58623-0(5))* Celebration Pr.

Settel, Jim. The Things I See & the Things I Do. Han, Mylene, illus. 2013. 52p. pap. 19.95 *(978-1-4787-0879-7(4))* Outskirts Pr., Inc.

Shearer, Susan. Wacky Rhymes: Three-Letter A, E, I, O & U Words. 2007. 141p. pap. 24.95 *(978-1-60441-498-1(7))* America Star Bks.

Sickler, Jonas, illus. Indestructibles: Hickory Dickory Dock: Chew Proof · Rip Proof · Nontoxic · 100% Washable (Book for Babies, Newborn Books, Safe to Chew) 2011. (Indestructibles Ser.). (ENG.). 12p. (J). (gr. -1 — 1). pap. 5.95 *(978-0-7611-5921-6(5),* 15921) Workman Publishing Co., Inc.

Smart Kidz, creator. I'm a Little Teapot. 2013. (Sing N Play Songs Ser.). (ENG., Illus.). 12p. (J). bds. 12.99 *(978-1-891100-07-9(6),* Smart Kids) Penton Overseas, Inc.

Smee, Nicola. Sleepyhead. 2004. (ENG & PAN., Illus.). 10p. (J). bds. *(978-1-85269-096-0(8))* Mantra Lingua.

—Sleepyhead. Smee, Nicola, illus. 2004. (ENG & URD., Illus.). 10p. (J). bds. *(978-1-85269-097-7(6));* bds. *(978-1-85269-095-3(X))* Mantra Lingua.

Smith, Eric, et al, illus. This Little Piggy: And Other Favorite Rhymes. 2005. (Mother Goose Rhymes Ser.). (ENG.). 36p. (J). (gr. -1-k). 12.95 *(978-1-59249-466-8(8),* 1D013) Soundprints.

Smith, L. & Mcgee, B. Clappity clap all through the Town. 2009. (J). pap. 9.95 *(978-1-61584-680-1(8))* Independent Pub.

Smith, Lesley, illus. My Big Book of Rhymes. 2012. (ENG.). 96p. (J). 13.50 *(978-1-84135-134-6(2))* Award Pubns. Ltd. GBR. Dist: Parkwest Pubns., Inc.

Smith, Roland & Smith, Marie. T Is for Time. Graef, Renée, illus. 2015. (ENG.). 40p. (J). (gr. 2-5). 16.99 *(978-1-58536-512-8(2),* 203809) Sleeping Bear Pr.

Snyder, Susan E. Grandma's Crazy Chickens. Richardson, Mike, illus. 2012. 34p. (J). 14.95 *(978-0-9846428-8-5(9))* FireFly Publishings & Entertainment LLC.

Sommers, Faith & Burkholder, Diane. Helping Mama. 2003. (Illus.). 24p. (J). *(978-0-87813-608-7(8))* Christian Light Pubns., Inc.

Soundprints Staff. Farmer in Dell. 2005. (Mother Goose Ser.). (ENG., Illus.). 32p. (J). 12.95 *(978-1-59249-380-7(7),* 1D005) Soundprints.

—Hey Diddle Diddle & Other Favorites. (Mother Goose Nursery Rhymes Ser.). (ENG., Illus.). 36p. (J). 14.95 *(978-1-59069-221-9(7),* MPD1110) Studio Mouse LLC.

—Hey Diddle Diddle & Other Favorites. (Mother Goose Nursery Rhymes Ser.). (Illus.). 36p. (J). 10.95 *(978-1-59069-219-6(5),* MD1110); 2003. bds. 8.95 *(978-1-59069-218-9(7))* Studio Mouse LLC.

—I'm a Little Teapot & Other Favorites. 2003. (Nursery Sing-a-Longs Ser.). (Illus.). 36p. (J). 8.95 *(978-1-59069-202-8(0))* Studio Mouse LLC.

—I've Been Workin on Railroad. 2005. (Mother Goose Ser.). (ENG., Illus.). 36p. (J). 12.95 *(978-1-59249-379-1(3)*, 1D003) Soundprints.
—Mother Goose Bitsy Board Book Travel Pack, Vol. 2. 2005. (Studio Mouse Ser.). (ENG., Illus.). 10p. (J). 9.95 *(978-1-59069-360-5(4))* Studio Mouse LLC.
—Mother Goose's Hide n' Seek Book. 2005. (Studio Mouse Ser.). (ENG., Illus.). 24p. (J). 12.95 *(978-1-59069-376-6(0))* Studio Mouse LLC.
—Nursery Rhymes: Story Time Treasury. 2005. (Studio Mouse Ser.). (Illus.). 256p. (J). (gr. -1-2). 14.95 *(978-1-59069-228-8(4)*, MT1001) Studio Mouse LLC.
Soundprints Staff, creator. Head, Shoulders, Knees & Toes: And Other Move-along Rhymes. 2004. (Mother Goose Ser.). (ENG., Illus.). 34p. (J). 15.95 *(978-1-59249-386-9(6)*, 1D008) Soundprints.
Soy La Cafetera: Poems, Rhymes, & Songs Listening Packs. 2003. 34.50 *(978-0-673-58634-6(0))* Celebration Pr.
Spenceley, Annabel. The Faber Book of Nursery Rhymes. 2003. (Faber Edition Ser.). (ENG., Illus.). 999p. pap. 11.99 *(978-0-571-10099-6(6))* Faber & Faber, Ltd. GBR. Dist: Alfred Publishing Co., Inc.
Spengler, Margaret, illus. One, Two, Buckle My Shoe. 2004. (J). bds. 6.99 *(978-1-890647-12-4(8))* TOMY International, Inc.
Spicer, Maggee & Thompson, Richard. When They Are Up, 1 vol. Wakelin, Kirsti Anne, illus. 2007. (ENG.). 36p. (J). (gr. -1-k). per. 5.95 *(978-1-55041-709-8(6)*, 57612e99-3900-4438-9247-91b280f7d2c1) Trifolium Bks., Inc. CAN. Dist: Firefly Bks., Ltd.
—When They Are Up..., 1 vol. Wakelin, Kirsti Anne, illus. 2003. (ENG.). 36p. (J). (gr. -1-k). 9.95 *(978-1-55041-707-4(X)*, 6deb1948-567d-430a-ba26-b75805e12a2c) Trifolium Bks., Inc. CAN. Dist: Firefly Bks., Ltd.
Spradlin, Michael P. Jack & Jill Went up to Kill: A Book of Zombie Nursery Rhymes. Weigel, Jeff, illus. 2011. (ENG.). 96p. pap. 9.99 *(978-0-06-208359-3(7)*, William Morrow Paperbacks) HarperCollins Pubs.
Squillace, Elisa, illus. Down in the Jungle. (Classic Books with Holes 8x8 with CD Ser.). 16p. (J). 2013. (ENG.). (gr. -1). *(978-1-84643-623-9(0))* 2005. pap. *(978-1-904550-32-7(0))* Child's Play International Ltd.
Stanley, Mandy, illus. Jack & Jill & Other Nursery Favourites. 2010. (Time for a Rhyme Ser.). (ENG.). 24p. (J). (gr. k — 1). 6.99 *(978-0-00-731564-2(3))* HarperCollins Pubs. Ltd. GBR. Dist: Independent Pubs. Group.
Strevens-Marzo, Bridget. Bridget's Book of Nursery Rhymes. 2008. (ENG., Illus.). 24p. (J). (gr. -1-k). pap. 7.95 *(978-1-921272-12-7(0))* Little Hare Bks. AUS. Dist: Independent Pubs. Group.
Studio Mouse. Nursery Rhymes. 2003. (ENG., Illus.). 22p. (J). 16.95 *(978-1-59069-392-6(2))* Studio Mouse LLC.
—Sesame Street Abby Cadabby's Nursery Rhymes. 2008. (ENG.). 20p. (J). 9.99 *(978-1-59069-658-3(1))* Studio Mouse LLC.
Studio Mouse, creator. Let's Listen: Nursery Rhymes for Listening & Learning. 2005. (Mother Goose Ser.). (ENG., Illus.). 36p. (J). (gr. -1-k). 7.95 *(978-1-59249-533-7(8)*, 1D203) Soundprints.
Studio Mouse Staff. Five Little Monkeys: And Other Counting Rhymes. Elliott, Rebecca et al, illus. rev. ed. 2007. (ENG.). 24p. (J). (gr. -1-k). 4.99 *(978-1-59069-608-8(5))* Studio Mouse LLC.
—Let's Listen: Nursery Rhymes for Listening & Learning. 2008. (Mother Goose Ser.). (ENG., Illus.). 36p. (gr. -1-k). 7.99 *(978-1-59249-795-9(0))* Studio Mouse LLC.
—Let's Move: Nursery Rhymes for Moving & Learning. 2008. (ENG., Illus.). 36p. (gr. -1-k). 7.99 *(978-1-59249-796-6(9))* Studio Mouse LLC.
—Let's Play: Nursery Rhymes for Playing & Learning. 2008. (Mother Goose Ser.). (ENG.). 36p. (gr. -1-k). 7.99 *(978-1-59249-797-3(7))* Studio Mouse LLC.
—Princess Rhyme Time. 2006. (Learn-Aloud Bks.). (ENG., Illus.). 36p. (gr. -1). 12.99 *(978-1-59069-495-4(3)*, 1A802) Studio Mouse LLC.
Sullivan, Cheryl. The New Nursery Rhymes. 2011. 24p. pap. *(978-1-4269-7332-1(2))* Trafford Publishing (UK) Ltd.
Sullivan, Kevin. The Best Hawaiian Style Mother Goose Ever! Aoki, Deb, illus. 2006. 40p. 16.95 incl. cd-rom *(978-0-9644149-6-9(1))* Hawaya, Inc.
Taback, Simms. This Is the House That Jack Built. 2004. (Illus.). 32p. (J). (gr. k-3). reprint ed. 8.99 *(978-0-14-240200-9(1)*, Puffin Books) Penguin Young Readers Group.
Taggart, Katy, et al, illus. Workin' on the Railroad: And Other Favorite Rhymes. 2004. (Mother Goose Ser.). (ENG.). 32p. (J). 15.95 *(978-1-59249-385-2(8)*, 1D004) Soundprints.
Tanner, Suzy-Jane, illus. Nursery Rhymes. 2012. 24p. (J). 9.95 *(978-1-84135-743-0(X))* Award Pubns. Ltd. GBR. Dist: Parkwest Pubns., Inc.
Taplin, Sam. The Usborne Book of Bedtime Rhymes. Luraschi, Anna, illus. 2008. (Usborne Book Of... Ser.). 12p. (J). (gr. -1-3). bds. 12.99 *(978-0-7945-1898-1(2)*, Usborne) EDC Publishing.
Taylor, Jane. Twinkle, Twinkle Little Star. Duffy, Katherine, illus. 2016. (ENG.). 32p. (J). (gr. -1-k). pap. 9.99 *(978-1-5324-0073-5(X))* Xist Publishing.
Teel, Karen. Robot Rhymes. Teets, Ashley, illus. 2013. (ENG.). 31p. (J). (gr. -1-3). 16.95 *(978-0-938467-79-3(4))* Headline Bks., Inc.
Thienes-Schunemann, Mary. Lavender's Blue Dilly Dilly, 1 bk, 1 CD. 2004. (J). spiral bd. 21.95 incl. audio compact disk *(978-0-9708397-7-0(4))* Naturally You Can Sing.
Thomson, Sarah L. Around the Neighborhood: A Counting Lullaby, 0 vols. Christy, Jana, illus. 2012. (ENG.). 32p. (J). (gr. -1-3). 16.99 *(978-0-7614-6164-7(7)*, 9780761461647, Two Lions) Amazon Publishing.
Three Little Kittens Book & Cd, 1 vol. 2007. (Paul Galdone Nursery Classic Ser.). (ENG., Illus.). 32p. (J). (gr. -1-3). audio 10.99 *(978-0-618-85285-7(9)*, 416198, Clarion Bks.) HarperCollins Pubs.
Tian, Elli. Silly nursery Rhymes. Tian, Elli, illus. 2007. (Illus.). 12p. (J). 9.49 *(978-0-9798611-5-4(2))* Byte Me! Inc.
Tiger Tales Staff. 5 Minute Nursery Rhymes. 2013. (ENG.). 292p. (J). 14.95 *(978-1-58925-506-7(2))* Tiger Tales Pubns.
Tildes, Phyllis Limbacher. Will You Be Mine? A Nursery Rhyme Romance. Tildes, Phyllis Limbacher, illus. 2011. (Illus.). 32p. (J). (gr. -1-2). pap. 7.95 *(978-1-58089-245-2(0))* Charlesbridge Publishing, Inc.
Traditional & Cloke, Rene. My Book of Favourite Tales & Rhymes. 2013. (ENG., Illus.). 93p. (J). 16.50 *(978-1-84135-812-3(6))* Award Pubns. Ltd. GBR. Dist: Parkwest Pubns., Inc.
Trapani, Iza. Jingle Bells. Trapani, Iza, illus. 2007. (Illus.). 32p. (J). (gr. -1-k). 7.95 *(978-1-58089-096-0(2))* Charlesbridge Publishing, Inc.
—Little Miss Muffet. 2013. (ENG., Illus.). 32p. (J). (gr. -1-1). 16.95 *(978-1-62087-986-3(7)*, 620986, Sky Pony Pr.) Skyhorse Publishing Co., Inc.
—Old King Cole. Trapani, Iza, illus. 2015. (Iza Trapani's Extended Nursery Rhymes Ser.). (Illus.). 32p. (J). (-k). lib. bdg. 15.95 *(978-1-58089-632-0(4))* Charlesbridge Publishing, Inc.
—Rufus & Friends: Rhyme Time. Trapani, Iza, illus. 2008. (Illus.). 40p. (J). (gr. -1-3). pap. 7.95 *(978-1-58089-207-0(8))* Charlesbridge Publishing, Inc.
—Rufus & Friends: School Days. Trapani, Iza, illus. 2010. (Illus.). 36p. (J). (gr. -1-3). 16.95 *(978-1-58089-248-3(5))*; pap. 7.95 *(978-1-58089-249-0(3))* Charlesbridge Publishing, Inc.
Trapani, Iza, illus. Little Miss Muffet. 2015. (ENG.). 32p. (J). (gr. -1-k). 6.95 *(978-1-62914-616-4(1)*, Sky Pony Pr.) Skyhorse Publishing Co., Inc.
Twin Sister Productions & Galvin, Laura Gates. Sesame Street Abby Cadabby's Nursery Rhymes. 2010. (J). (gr. k-2). 14.99 *(978-1-59922-636-1(7))* Twin Sisters IP, LLC.
Twin Sisters(r) Staff. Abc Nursery Rhymes. 2010. (J). (gr. k-2). pap. 4.99 *(978-1-59922-507-4(7))* Twin Sisters IP, LLC.
—Humpty Dumpty & More. 2010. (J). (gr. k-2). pap. 4.99 *(978-1-59922-506-7(9))* Twin Sisters IP, LLC.
—30 Nursery Rhymes Songs CD. 2008. 6.99 *(978-1-59922-156-4(X))* Twin Sisters IP, LLC.
Twin Sisters(r) Staff, et al. Five Little Bunnies. 2010. (J). (gr. k-1). 14.99 *(978-1-59922-421-3(6))*; 14.99 *(978-1-59922-629-3(4))* Twin Sisters IP, LLC.
Twinkle Twinkle Little Star. 2012. (Nursery Rhymes (Little Birdie) Ser.). 10p. (J). (gr. -1-k). bds. 6.99 *(978-1-61236-979-2(0))* Rourke Educational Media.
Various Authors. Nursery Rhyme Comics: 50 Timeless Rhymes from 50 Celebrated Cartoonists. Duffy, Chris, ed. 2011. (ENG., Illus.). 128p. (J). (gr. -1-3). 22.99 *(978-1-59643-600-8(X)*, 900065610, First Second Bks.) Roaring Brook Pr.
Verrett, Michael. The Rhymes of the Gray Beard Tree. 2010. (ENG.). 186p. pap. 15.95 *(978-0-557-57957-0(0))* Lulu Pr., Inc.
Wadsworth, Olive A. Over in the Meadow. Vojtech, Anna, illus. 2003. (Cheshire Studio Book Ser.). (ENG.). 32p. (J). (gr. -1-2). pap. 8.95 *(978-0-7358-1871-2(1))* North-South Bks., Inc.
Walrus Books. Children's Treasure Chest: Fairy Tales, Nursery Rhymes, & Nonsense Verse. 2004. (ENG., Illus.). 386p. (J). (gr. k-12). 29.95 *(978-1-55285-579-9(1))* Whitecap Bks., Ltd. CAN. Dist: Graphic Arts Ctr. Publishing Co.
Watt, Fiona. Nursery Rhymes Touchy-Feely Board Book. Meyer, Kerry, illus. 2010. (Luxury Touchy-Feely Board Bks). 10p. (J). bds. 15.99 *(978-0-7945-2662-7(4)*, Usborne) EDC Publishing.
—Sing-along Nursery Rhymes. Bordoni, Chiara, illus. 2009. (Baby Board Books w/CD Ser.). 12p. (J). (gr. -1). bds. 15.99 *(978-0-7945-2351-0(X)*, Usborne) EDC Publishing.
Weaver, Joyce Mckissick. Little Rhymes for Little Minds, 1 vol. 2010. 38p. 24.95 *(978-1-4489-9622-3(8))* PublishAmerica, Inc.
Webb, Sarah & Ranson, Claire. Sally Go Round the Stars: Favourite Rhymes from an Irish Childhood. McCarthy, Steve, illus. (ENG.). 64p. (J). 2014. pap. 17.00 *(978-1-84717-675-2(5))* 2011. 26.00 *(978-1-84717-211-2(3))* O'Brien Pr., Ltd., The IRL. Dist: Casemate Pubs. & Bk. Distributors, LLC.
White, Jill & White, Robbin. Can Starfish Make A Wish. 2nd ed. 2008. (Illus.). 26p. (J). 4.95 *(978-0-9746613-1-5(7))* Starfish Aquatics Institute.
White, Larisa. Teacup Rhymes for Teacup Humans. 2012. 24p. pap. 17.99 *(978-1-4685-5784-8(X))* AuthorHouse.
Williams, Shannon. Songs of Science: Physics in the Bathtub. 2012. 20p. pap. 13.77 *(978-1-4669-3021-6(7))* Trafford Publishing.
—Songs of Science: Physics in the Car. 2012. 20p. pap. 13.77 *(978-1-4669-4967-6(8))* Trafford Publishing.
Wohnoutka, Mike, illus. This Little Piggy. 2005. (J). *(978-1-58987-106-9(5))* Kindermusik International.
Wong, JoyLynn Charity. Carried Away: A Collection of Wrapscapes & Nursery Rhymes. 2014. (Illus.). 40p. pap. *(978-1-4600-0406-7(X))* Essence Publishing.
Wright, Blanche Fisher, illus. The Real Mother Goose. 2017. (J). pap. *(978-1-5124-2602-1(4))* Lerner Publishing Group.
—Real Mother Goose Clock Book. 22p. (J). (gr. -1-2). 6.95 *(978-1-56288-095-8(0))* Checkerboard Pr., Inc.
Wright, Danielle. Korean & English Nursery Rhymes: Wild Geese, Land of Goblins & Other Favorite Songs & Rhymes (Audio Recordings in Korean & English Included) Acraman, Helen, illus. 2018. 32p. (J). (gr. -1-3). 12.99 *(978-0-8048-4998-2(6))* Tuttle Publishing.
Wu, Faye-Lynn. Chinese & English Nursery Rhymes: Little Mouse & Other Charming Chinese Rhymes (Audio Disc in Chinese & English Included) Dutcher, Kieren, illus. 2018. 32p. (J). (gr. -1-3). 12.99 *(978-0-8048-4999-9(4))* Tuttle Publishing.
Yolen, Jane. Wee Rhymes: Baby's First Poetry Book. Dyer, Jane, illus. 2013. (ENG.). 112p. (J). (gr. -1-3). 19.99 *(978-1-4169-4898-8(8)*, Simon & Schuster/Paula Wiseman Bks.) Simon & Schuster/Paula Wiseman Bks.
Young, Judy. Sleepy Snoozy Coozy Coozy: A Book of Animal Beds. Monroe, Michael Glenn, illus. 2015. (ENG.). 32p. (J). (gr. 1-3). 15.99 *(978-1-58536-908-9(X)*, 203808) Sleeping Bear Pr.

NURSERY SCHOOLS

see also Kindergarten

Anderson, Pamela. My New School: Blonde Girl. Lee, Han & Wu, Stacie, illus. 2004. (J). 12.95 *(978-1-932555-04-2(8))* Watch Me Grow Kids.
Bridges, Doreen. Music, Young Children & You: A Parent-Teacher Guide to Music for 0-5 Year-Olds. (Illus.). 160p. (J). (gr. -1-k). pap. *(978-0-86806-530-4(7)*, Hale & Iremonger) GHR Pr., The.
Bunnett, Rochelle. Friends at School: Spanish, 1 vol. Brown, Matt, illus. 2007.Tr. of Friends at School. (SPA.). 32p. (J). (gr. -1). pap. 6.99 *(978-1-59572-041-2(3))* Star Bright Bks., Inc.
Burton, Marilee R. Kindergarten Scholar. Boyer, Robin, illus. 2004. (ENG.). 32p. (J). pap. 2.99 *(978-1-58947-455-0(4))* School Zone Publishing Co.
Cleveland, Alexandra, et al. Camino al Primer Grado. Franco, Sharon, tr. from ENG. Koeller, Carol, illus. 2004. (SPA.). 128p. (Orig.). (J). pap. 14.95 *(978-0-943452-35-7(X))* Building Blocks, LLC.
Codell, Esmé Raji. It's Time for Preschool! Rama, Sue, illus. 2012. (ENG.). 40p. (J). (gr. -1-k). 15.99 *(978-0-06-145518-6(0)*, Greenwillow Bks.) HarperCollins Pubs.
Contando. 2005. (SPA.). (J). (gr. -1-18). pap. 6.95 *(978-950-11-0903-0(8))* Sigmar ARG. Dist: Lectorum Pubns., Inc., Iaconi, Mariuccia Bk. Imports.
Equipo Staff. La Escuela Infantil. (Coleccion Mundo Maravilloso). (SPA., Illus.). 36p. (J). (gr. 2-4). *(978-84-348-7228-8(5)*, SM31363) SM Ediciones ESP. Dist: Lectorum Pubns., Inc.
Guckian, Mara. 1-2-3 Learn Ages 3-4. Kelly, McMahon, illus. 2016. (ENG.). 128p. pap. 14.99 *(978-1-4206-8002-7(1))* Teacher Created Resources, Inc.
Haley, Amanda. 3-2-1 School Is Fun! 2009. (Rookie Preschool Ser.). (ENG.). 24p. (J). (gr. -1). 23.00 *(978-0-531-24405-0(9))* Scholastic Library Publishing.
Heinemann Educational Ltd. Publishing Staff. Minbeasts Up Close Package. 2004. pap. 243.00 *(978-1-4109-1386-9(4))* Harcourt Schl. Pubs.
Hoffman, Joan. Kindergarten Basics. Boyer, Robin, illus. 2004. (ENG.). 32p. (J). pap. 2.99 *(978-1-58947-436-9(8))* School Zone Publishing Co.
—Nursery Rhymes. 2019. (ENG.). 32p. (J). (gr. -1-k). pap. 4.49 *(978-1-60159-115-9(2)*, bc300fd1-1047-40c3-92d7-ba873f82a7f0) School Zone Publishing Co.
—Preschool Practice. 2019. (ENG.). 30p. (J). (gr. -1-k). pap. 4.49 *(978-1-60159-116-6(0)*, f7002a79-da67-4b8e-b45a-0dd46e69721b) School Zone Publishing Co.
—Preschool Scholar: Scholar Series Workbooks. 2008. (ENG.). 32p. (J). pap. 2.99 *(978-1-58947-454-3(6))* School Zone Publishing Co.
Kannenberg, Stacey. Let's Get Ready for Kindergarten! rev. ed. 2006. (Let's Get Ready Ser.). (Illus.). 30p. (J). (gr. -1-1). per. 19.00 *(978-1-933476-00-1(1))* Cedar Valley Publishing.
Key Porter Books, creator. Face Painting: Enchanting Designs for Faces & Bodies. rev. ed. 2007. (Gymboree Play & Music Ser.). (ENG., Illus.). 36p. (J). (gr. -1-2). bds. *(978-1-55263-962-7(2))* Magma.
—Music Play: Inspired Ways to Explore Music. rev. ed. 2007. (Gymboree Play & Music Ser.). (ENG., Illus.). 36p. (J). (gr. -1-2). bds. *(978-1-55263-964-1(9))* Magma.
Key Porter Books Staff. Gymboree in a Princess Castle. rev. ed. 2007. (ENG., Illus.). 1p. (J). *(978-1-55263-923-8(1))* Magma.
—Gymboree on a Pirate Ship. rev. ed. 2007. (ENG., Illus.). 1p. (J). *(978-1-55263-921-4(5))* Magma.
Kilodavis, Cheryl. My Princess Boy. DeSimone, Suzanne, illus. 2010. (ENG.). 36p. (J). (gr. -1-3). 17.99 *(978-1-4424-2988-8(7)*, Aladdin) Simon & Schuster Children's Publishing.
Mason, Jane B. & Stephens, Sarah Hines. Gymboree Dance Play. rev. ed. 2007. (ENG., Illus.). 36p. (J). (gr. -1-2). bds. *(978-1-55263-960-3(6))* Magma.
School Zone Interactive Staff. Kindergarten. 2006. (ENG.). (J). cd-rom 24.99 *(978-1-58947-682-0(4))* School Zone Publishing Co.
Stella, Heather. Get Ready for Kindergarten: On-The-Go. 2018. (Get Ready for School Ser.). (ENG.). 160p. (J). spiral bd. 13.99 *(978-0-316-48243-1(9)*, Black Dog & Leventhal Pubs. Inc.) Running Pr.
The Mailbox Books Staff. Totally for Twos: Art Age 2. 2010. (Illus.). 128p. (J). 18.95 *(978-1-56234-934-9(1)*, Mailbox Bks., The) Education Ctr., Inc.

NURSERY SCHOOLS—FICTION

Ashdown, Rebecca. Bob & Flo. Ashdown, Rebecca, illus. 2015. (ENG., Illus.). 32p. (J). (gr. -1-3). 16.99 *(978-0-544-44430-0(2)*, 1597717, Clarion Bks.) HarperCollins Pubs.
Brignaud, Pierre, illus. Caillou Goes to Day Care. 2019. (Caillou's Essentials Ser.). (ENG.). 24p. (J). (gr. -1-k). bds. 7.99 *(978-2-89718-490-2(6))* Caillouet, Gerry.
Cousins, Lucy. Maisy Goes to Preschool: A Maisy First Experiences Book. Cousins, Lucy, illus. 2010. (Maisy Ser.). (ENG., Illus.). 32p. (J). (gr. k-k). pap. 7.99 *(978-0-7636-5086-5(2))* Candlewick Pr.
Dewdney, Anna. Llama Llama Misses Mama. (Llama Llama Ser.). (Illus.). (J). 2019. (ENG.). 36p. (— 1). bds. 9.99 *(978-0-593-11671-5(2))* 2009. 40p. (gr. -1-k). 18.99 *(978-0-670-06198-3(0))* Penguin Young Readers Group. (Viking Books for Young Readers).
Dorsey, Maggie. My Hero, My Dad, the Nurse. 2008. (ENG.). 36p. pap. 16.99 *(978-1-4196-9476-9(6))* CreateSpace Independent Publishing Platform.
Edwards, Becky. My First Day at Nursery School. Flintoft, Anthony, illus. 2004. (ENG.). 32p. (J). (gr. -1-1). pap. 7.99 *(978-1-58234-909-1(6)*, 900024733, Bloomsbury USA Childrens) Bloomsbury Publishing USA.
Henkes, Kevin. Prudencia Se Preocupa. 2017.Tr. of Wemberly Worried. (SPA.). (J). pap. 9.99 *(978-1-63245-666-3(4))* Lectorum Pubns., Inc.
—Wemberly Worried. Henkes, Kevin, illus. 2010. (ENG., Illus.). 32p. (J). (gr. -1-4). pap. 9.99 *(978-0-06-185776-8(9)*, Greenwillow Bks.) HarperCollins Pubs.
—Wemberly Worried. Henkes, Kevin, illus. (Illus.). pap. 39.95 incl. audio compact disk *(978-1-59112-561-7(8))*; pap. 18.95 incl. audio compact disk *(978-1-59112-359-0(3))*; pap. incl. audio *(978-0-87499-808-5(5))*; pap. 16.95 incl. audio *(978-0-87499-806-1(9))* Live Oak Media.
Huber, Mike. All in One Day. Cowman, Joseph, illus. 2014. (ENG.). 32p. (gr. -1-k). 15.95 *(978-1-60554-207-2(5))* Redleaf Pr.
Hudson, Wade. Puddin', Jeffrey & Leah. 2008. (Illus.). 16p. (gr. -1). 6.95 *(978-1-60349-006-1(X)*, Marimba Bks.) Just Us Bks., Inc.
Kehret, Peg. Race to Disaster. 2008. (ENG.). 128p. (J). (gr. 3-7). pap. 7.99 *(978-1-4169-9108-3(5)*, Simon & Schuster/Paula Wiseman Bks.) Simon & Schuster/Paula Wiseman Bks.
PI Kids. Sesame Street: Let's Go to School! First Look & Find. Berry, Bob, illus. 2012. (ENG.). 16p. (J). bds. 12.99 *(978-1-4508-2933-5(3)*, 1448, PI Kids) Phoenix International Publications, Inc.
Rockwell, Anne. My Preschool. Rockwell, Anne, illus. 2008. (ENG., Illus.). 32p. (J). (gr. -1-k). 18.99 *(978-0-8050-7955-5(6)*, 900031917, Holt, Henry & Co. Bks. For Young Readers) Holt, Henry & Co.
Wing, Natasha. The Night Before Preschool. Wummer, Amy, illus. (Night Before Ser.). 32p. (J). (gr. -1-k). 2014. (ENG.). 12.99 *(978-0-448-48254-5(1))* 2011. pap. 4.99 *(978-0-448-45451-1(3))* Penguin Young Readers Group. (Grosset & Dunlap).

NURSES

see also Children—Health and Hygiene; First Aid; Hospitals; School Nursing

Alexander, Carol. Florence Nightingale. 2005. (Rookie Biographies Ser.). (ENG., Illus.). 32p. (J). (gr. 1-2). pap. 4.95 *(978-0-516-25828-7(1)*, Children's Pr.) Scholastic Library Publishing.
Alexander, Carol & Vargus, Nanci Reginelli. Florence Nightingale. 2004. (Rookie Biography Ser.). (J). 20.50 *(978-0-516-24406-8(X))* Scholastic Library Publishing.
Aller, Susan Bivin. Florence Nightingale. 2008. pap. 52.95 *(978-0-8225-9389-8(0))* Lerner Publishing Group.
—Florence Nightingale. Butler, Tad, illus. 2007. (History Maker Biographies Ser.). (ENG.). 48p. (gr. 3-6). lib. bdg. 27.93 *(978-0-8225-7609-9(0)*, Lerner Pubns.) Lerner Publishing Group.
Arnold, Quinn M. Nurses. 2017. (Seedlings Ser.). (ENG., Illus.). 24p. (J). (gr. -1-k). *(978-1-60818-874-1(4)*, 20357, Creative Education) Creative Co., The.
Bell, Samantha. Nurse. Bane, Jeff, illus. 2017. (My Early Library: My Friendly Neighborhood Ser.). (ENG.). 24p. (J). (gr. k-1). lib. bdg. 30.64 *(978-1-63472-831-7(9)*, 209750) Cherry Lake Publishing.
Bickerstaff, Linda. What Degree Do I Need to Pursue a Career in Nursing?, 1 vol. 2014. (Right Degree for Me Ser.). (ENG., Illus.). 80p. (J). (gr. 7-7). 37.80 *(978-1-4777-7857-9(8)*, 96004254-caea-4fa7-b4fa-61aab2bee73a, Rosen Young Adult) Rosen Publishing Group, Inc., The.
Braun, Eric. Trapped Behind Enemy Lines: The Story of the U. S. Army Air Force 807th Medical Evacuation Squadron. 2016. (Encounter: Narrative Nonfiction Stories Ser.). (ENG., Illus.). 224p. (J). (gr. 4-5). lib. bdg. 33.32 *(978-1-4914-8042-7(4)*, 130545, Capstone Young Readers) Capstone.
—Trapped Behind Nazi Lines: The Story of the U. S. Army Air Force 807th Medical Evacuation Squadron. 2016. (Encounter: Narrative Nonfiction Stories Ser.). (ENG., Illus.). 224p. (J). (gr. 4-5). 14.95 *(978-1-62370-605-0(X)*, 130547, Capstone Young Readers) Capstone.
Brill, Marlene Targ. Nurses. 2005. (Pull Ahead Bks.). (Illus.). 32p. (J). (gr. 3-7). lib. bdg. 22.60 *(978-0-8225-1692-7(6))* Lerner Publishing Group.
Campbell, Candy. My Mom Is A Nurse, 1 vol. 2010. (ENG.). 208p. pap., pap. 27.95 *(978-0-578-02360-1(1))* New Year Publishing.
—My Mom Is a Nurse. Imura, Toshiyoshi, tr. Fusco, Michael Vincent, illus. 2017. (JPN.). (J). pap. 14.95 *(978-0-9842385-4-5(9))* Peripatetic Productions, LLC.
Clark, Sarah Kartchner. Nurses Then & Now, 1 vol. rev. ed. 2006. (Social Studies: Informational Text Ser.). (ENG.). 32p. (gr. 2-3). pap. 11.99 *(978-0-7439-9374-6(8))* Teacher Created Materials, Inc.
Connors, Kathleen. The Life of Clara Barton, 1 vol., Vol. 1. 2013. (Famous Lives Ser.). (ENG.). 24p. (J). (gr. 1-2). 25.27 *(978-1-4824-0375-6(7)*, bd50ae70-bc7a-454f-bf50-af09015618a2) Stevens, Gareth Publishing LLLP.
—The Life of Florence Nightingale, 1 vol., Vol. 1. 2013. (Famous Lives Ser.). (ENG., Illus.). 24p. (J). (gr. 1-2). 25.27 *(978-1-4824-0405-0(2)*, a4ee7e1d-f389-4e59-acd6-f6658e980946) Stevens, Gareth Publishing LLLP.
Cunningham, Kevin. Nurse. (21st Century Skills Library: Cool STEAM Careers Ser.). (ENG., Illus.). 32p. (gr. 4-7). 2015. (J). 32.07 *(978-1-63362-561-7(3)*, 206428) 2008. lib. bdg. 32.07 *(978-1-60279-299-9(2)*, 200138) Cherry Lake Publishing.
Dell, Pamela. Memoir of Susie King Taylor: A Civil War Nurse. 2017. (First-Person Histories Ser.). (ENG.). 32p. (J). (gr. 3-6). pap. 8.95 *(978-1-5157-3356-0(4)*, 133348); (Illus.). lib. bdg. 27.99 *(978-1-5157-3354-6(8)*, 133346) Capstone. (Capstone Pr.).
Ditchfield, Christin. Clara Barton: Founder of the American Red Cross. 2004. (Great Life Stories Ser.). (ENG., Illus.). 112p. (J). 30.50 *(978-0-531-12276-1(X)*, Watts, Franklin) Scholastic Library Publishing.
Dodson Wade, Mary. Amazing Civil War Nurse Clara Barton, 1 vol. 2009. (Amazing Americans Ser.). (ENG., Illus.). 24p. (gr. k-2). pap. 10.35 *(978-0-7660-5977-1(4)*, da71448e-d5c8-4686-ab68-3b6b544e50f3, Enslow Elementary); lib. bdg. 25.27 *(978-0-7660-3281-1(7)*, 710aaf69-7e45-4d56-ba1b-eac58e3c9ebc) Enslow Publishing, LLC.
Dorling Kindersley Publishing Staff. Florence Nightingale: DK Life Stories. 2019. (Illus.). 128p. (J). *(978-0-241-35631-9(8))* Dorling Kindersley Publishing, Inc.
Early Macken, JoAnn. Nurses, 1 vol. 2010. (People in My Community (Second Edition) Ser.). (ENG.). 24p. (J). (gr. k-2). pap. 9.15 *(978-1-4339-3807-8(3)*, d0cb1a99-b557-44f9-873a-333cc79d4d50); lib. bdg. 25.27 *(978-1-4339-3806-1(5)*, a0549847-2aab-4bf0-b7d8-de47a7d7ee11) Stevens, Gareth Publishing LLLP.
Edison, Erin. Clara Barton, 1 vol. 2013. (Great Women in History Ser.). (ENG.). 24p. (J). (gr. -1-2). pap. 6.29 *(978-1-62065-857-4(7)*, 121791); (gr. k-1). pap. 37.74 *(978-1-62065-858-1(5)*, 19426); (Illus.). (gr. -1-2). lib. bdg. 24.65 *(978-1-62065-076-9(2)*, 120778) Capstone. (Pebble).

M N O

—Florence Nightingale, 1 vol. 2014. (Great Women in History Ser.). (ENG., Illus.). 24p. (J). (gr. -1-2). lib. bdg. 24.65 *(978-1-4765-4214-0(7),* 124312) Capstone.

Favor, Lesli J. Women Doctors & Nurses of the Civil War. 2009. (American Women at War Ser.). 112p. (gr. 8-8). 63.90 *(978-1-61511-404-7(1))* Rosen Publishing Group, Inc., The.

Favor, Leslie. Women Doctors & Nurses of the Civil War, 1 vol. 2004. (American Women at War Ser.). (ENG.). 112p. (YA). (gr. 8-8). pap. 13.95 *(978-1-4358-3273-2(6),* d5d1a2e9-429e-42e8-b242-5f13ee7d9c16) Rosen Publishing Group, Inc., The.

Ferguson, Amanda. American Women of the Vietnam War, 1 vol. 2004. (American Women at War Ser.). (ENG., Illus.). 112p. (YA). (gr. 8-8). lib. bdg. 39.80 *(978-0-8239-4448-4(4),* 1e969f8c-b989-41bb-a39e-09010cf3e2b8) Rosen Publishing Group, Inc., The.

Fields, J. Choosing a Career as a Nurse-Midwife. 2009. (World of Work Ser.). 64p. (gr. 5-5). 58.50 *(978-1-60854-323-6(4))* Rosen Publishing Group, Inc., The.

Gaertner, Meg. Nurses. 2018. (Community Workers Ser.). (ENG., Illus.). 24p. (J). (gr. 1-1). pap. 8.95 *(978-1-63517-808-1(8),* 1635178088) North Star Editions.

—Nurses. 2018. (Community Workers Ser.). (ENG., Illus.). 24p. (J). (gr. k-3). lib. bdg. 31.36 *(978-1-5321-6013-4(5),* 28658, Pop! Cody Koala) Pop!

Garnett, Emmeline & Jauss, Anne Marie. Florence Nightingale's Nuns. 2009. (Vision Bks.). (ENG.). 158p. (J). (gr. 4-10). pap. 12.95 *(978-1-58617-297-8(2))* Ignatius Pr.

Garrett, Winston. What Does the School Nurse Do? (¿Qué Hace la Enfermera de la Escuela?), 1 vol. de la Vega, Eida, ed. 2014. (Oficios en Mi Escuela / Jobs in My School Ser.). (SPA & ENG.). 24p. (J). (gr. 1-2). lib. bdg. 25.27 *(978-1-4777-6801-3(7),* 6af04b39-7ce2-42c5-917a-6a30ed97d7bc, PowerKids Pr.) Rosen Publishing Group, Inc., The.

Glasscock, Sarah & Stewart, Rhea A. How Nurses Use Math. 2009. (Math in the Real World Ser.). (ENG.). 32p. (gr. 4-6). 28.00 *(978-1-60413-607-4(3),* P466916, Chelsea Clubhse.) Infobase Holdings, Inc.

Greenwood, Nancy. I Can Be a Nurse, 1 vol. 2020. (I Can Be Anything! Ser.). (ENG.). 24p. (gr. k-k). pap. 9.15 *(978-1-5382-5550-6(2),* 149e1c9d-49fe-48bc-9a96-f8af66091b94) Stevens, Gareth Publishing LLLP.

Guillain, Charlotte. Brave Nurses: Mary Seacole & Edith Cavell: Band 10/White. 2015. (Collins Big Cat Ser.). (ENG.). 32p. (J). (gr. 2-2). pap. 9.95 *(978-0-00-759124-4(1))* HarperCollins Pubs. Ltd. GBR. Dist: Independent Pubs. Group.

Harkins, Susan Sales & Harkins, William H. The Life & Times of Clara Barton. 2008. (Profiles in American History Ser.). (Illus.). 48p. (J). (gr. 4-8). lib. bdg. 29.95 *(978-1-58415-667-3(8))* Mitchell Lane Pubs.

Hinman, Bonnie. Florence Nightingale & the Advancement of Nursing. 2004. (Uncharted, Unexplored, & Unexplained Ser.). (Illus.). 48p. (J). (gr. 4-8). lib. bdg. 29.95 *(978-1-58415-257-6(5))* Mitchell Lane Pubs.

Jazynka, Kitson. DK Life Stories: Florence Nightingale. Ager, Charlotte, illus. 2019. (DK Life Stories Ser.). (ENG.). 128p. (J). (gr. 3-7). pap. 5.99 *(978-1-4654-7843-6(4),* DK Children) Dorling Kindersley Publishing, Inc.

Jeffries, Joyce. Meet the Nurse, 1 vol. 2012. (People Around Town Ser.). (Illus.). 24p. (J). (gr. k-k). (ENG.). (J). 25.27 *(978-1-4339-7332-1(4),* 3a9f846a-b797-4912-8532-b252f78829de); (ENG., (J). pap. 9.15 *(978-1-4339-7333-8(2),* 312578d9-d9dd-4208-83c6-e2dcb5228ced); 69.20 *(978-1-4339-8061-9(4))* Stevens, Gareth Publishing LLLP.

—Meet the Nurse / Te Presento a Los Enfermeros, 1 vol. 2012. (People Around Town / Gente de Mi Ciudad Ser.). (SPA & ENG., Illus.). 24p. (J). (gr. k-k). 25.27 *(978-1-4339-7388-8(X),* c6976847-d812-4e74-b759-334323544250) Stevens, Gareth Publishing LLLP.

Kaplan, Paul. Lillian Wald: America's Great Social & Healthcare Reformer, 1 vol. 2018. (ENG., Illus.). 112p. (gr. 6-7). 14.95 *(978-1-4556-2349-5(0),* Pelican Publishing) Arcadia Publishing.

Lakin, Patricia. Clara Barton: Spirit of the American Red Cross (Ready-To-Read Level 3) Sullivan, Simon, illus. 2004. (Ready-To-Read Stories of Famous Americans Ser.). (ENG.). 48p. (J). (gr. 1-3). pap. 4.99 *(978-0-689-86513-8(9),* Simon Spotlight) Simon Spotlight.

Leaf, Christina. Nurses. 2018. (Community Helpers Ser.). (ENG., Illus.). 24p. (J). (gr. k-3). lib. bdg. 26.95 *(978-1-62617-748-2(1),* Blastoff! Readers) Bellwether Media.

Less, Emma. Nurses. 2018. (Real-Life Superheroes Ser.). (ENG.). 16p. (J). (gr. k-2). pap. 7.99 *(978-1-68152-279-1(9),* 14919) Amicus.

Liebman, Dan. Je Veux Etre Infirmiere. Lior, Tsipora, tr. 2006. (Je Veux Etre Ser.). (FRE., Illus.). 24p. (J). (gr. -1-2). pap. 5.95 *(978-1-55407-107-4(0),* b85ed4b6-3fe3-4cb5-9a97-14895c208e63) Firefly Bks., Ltd.

Marko, Eve. Clara Barton & the American Red Cross. Marcos, Pablo, illus. 2005. (Heroes of America Ser.). 237p. (gr. 3-8). 27.07 *(978-1-59679-255-5(8),* Abdo & Daughters) ABDO Publishing Co.

Marsh, Carole. Clara Barton. 2003. 12p. (gr. k-4). 2.95 *(978-0-635-02353-7(9))* Gallopade International.

McDoniel, Estelle. Registered Nurse to Rear Admiral: A First for Navy Women. 2003. (Illus.). viii, 81p. (J). 16.95 *(978-1-57168-766-1(1),* Eakin Pr.) Eakin Pr.

Mills, Nathan & Machajewski, Sarah. Nurses Are There to Help, 1 vol. 2012. (Rosen Readers Ser.). (ENG., Illus.). 24p. (J). (gr. 1-1). pap. 8.25 *(978-1-4488-8782-8(8),* 612fbee7-4ddd-4a38-ad7f-377beeca67bf, Rosen Classroom) Rosen Publishing Group, Inc., The.

Morris, Ann. That's Our Nurse! Linenthal, Peter, illus. Linenthal, Peter, photos by. 2003. (That's Our School Ser.). (ENG.). 32p. (gr. k-3). lib. bdg. 22.60 *(978-0-7613-2402-7(X),* Millbrook Pr.) Lerner Publishing Group.

Moss, Marissa. Nurse, Soldier, Spy: The Story of Sarah Edmonds, a Civil War Hero. Hendrix, John, illus. 2011. (ENG.). 48p. (J). (gr. 3-7). 19.95 *(978-0-8109-9735-6(5),* 658701, Abrams Bks. for Young Readers) Abrams, Inc.

Murphy, Frank. Brave Clara Barton. Green, Sarah, illus. 2018. (Step into Reading Ser.). 48p. (J). (gr. k-3). pap. 4.99 *(978-1-5247-1557-1(3),* Random Hse. Bks. for Young Readers) Random Hse. Children's Bks.

Murray, Aaron R. Nurses Help Us, 1 vol. 2012. (All about Community Helpers Ser.). (ENG., Illus.). 24p. (gr. -1-1). 25.27 *(978-0-7660-4044-1(5),* d54f115c-04ac-4683-b693-962e0feeea67, Enslow Publishing) Enslow Publishing, LLC.

Murray, Hallie. The Role of Female Doctors & Nurses in the Civil War, 1 vol. 2019. (Warrior Women in American History Ser.). (ENG.). 104p. (gr. 7-7). pap. 21.00 *(978-1-5026-5543-1(8),* 1d4603e4-36a5-404a-8032-14ce1cb0311f); lib. bdg. 44.50 *(978-1-5026-5544-8(6),* a5c3b949-3c8d-40e5-8e7a-8277fd0a565b) Cavendish Square Publishing LLC.

—The Role of Female Doctors & Nurses in the Civil War. 2019. pap. *(978-1-9785-1407-2(7))* Enslow Publishing, LLC.

Nardo, Don. Clara Barton: Face Danger, but Never Fear It, 1 vol. 2008. (Americans: the Spirit of a Nation Ser.). (ENG., Illus.). 128p. (gr. 5-6). lib. bdg. 35.93 *(978-0-7660-3024-4(5),* f74588c9-3549-43cd-a5ea-6edce16e2b14) Enslow Publishing, LLC.

Parkes, Elle. Hooray for Nurses! 2016. (Bumba Books (r) — Hooray for Community Helpers! Ser.). (ENG., Illus.). 24p. (J). (gr. -1-1). lib. bdg. 26.65 *(978-1-5124-1444-8(1),* 9b046fa2-a419-4678-8522-56ab4ab4892b, Lerner Pubns.) Lerner Publishing Group.

Polacco, Patricia. Clara & Davie. Polacco, Patricia, illus. 2014. (ENG.). 40p. (J). (gr. -1-k). 18.99 *(978-0-545-35477-6(3),* Scholastic Pr.) Scholastic, Inc.

Ransom, Candice. Clara Barton. 2003. (History Maker Bios Ser.). (Illus.). 48p. (J). (gr. 3-5). lib. bdg. 26.60 *(978-0-8225-4677-1(9))* Lerner Publishing Group.

Ready, Dee. Nurses Help. 2013. (Our Community Helpers Ser.). (ENG.). 24p. (J). (gr. k-1). pap. 37.74 *(978-1-62065-850-5(X),* 19421, Pebble) Capstone.

Ready, Dee & Ready, Dee. Nurses Help, 1 vol. 2013. (Our Community Helpers Ser.). (ENG.). 24p. (J). (gr. -1-2). pap. 6.29 *(978-1-62065-849-9(6),* 121789); lib. bdg. 24.65 *(978-1-62065-080-6(0),* 120780) Capstone. (Pebble).

Reef, Catherine. Florence Nightingale: The Courageous Life of the Legendary Nurse. 2016. (ENG., Illus.). 192p. (YA). (gr. 7). 18.99 *(978-0-544-53580-0(4),* 1608187, Clarion Bks.) HarperCollins Pubs.

Richter, Sandy. The Life of Florence Nightingale, 1 vol. 2008. (Real Life Readers Ser.). (ENG.). 16p. (gr. 2-3). pap. 7.05 *(978-1-4358-0225-4(X),* 39f032ec-baec-4ef8-a950-6d7640b3e2f9, Rosen Classroom) Rosen Publishing Group, Inc., The.

Riggs, Kate. Seedlings: Nurses. 2017. (Seedlings Ser.). (ENG., Illus.). 24p. (J). (gr. -1-1). pap. 8.99 *(978-1-62832-489-1(9),* 20358, Creative Paperbacks) Creative Co., The.

Rivera, Sheila. Nurse. 2007. (First Step Nonfiction — Work People Do Ser.). (ENG., Illus.). 8p. (J). (gr. k-2). pap. 5.99 *(978-0-8225-6846-9(2),* 607e34c0-4726-4e54-9c41-5eb77f46965f) Lerner Publishing Group.

Robbins, Trina. Florence Nightingale: Lady with the Lamp, 1 vol. Timmons, Anne, illus. 2007. (Graphic Biographies Ser.). (ENG.). 32p. (J). (gr. 3-9). per. 8.10 *(978-0-7368-7902-6(1),* 93899, Capstone Pr.) Capstone.

Rose, Mary Catherine. Clara Barton: Soldier of Mercy. Johnson, E. Harper, illus. 2011. 80p. 37.95 *(978-1-258-07364-0(1))* Literary Licensing, LLC.

Ross, Stewart. Don't Say No to Flo: The Story of Florence Nightingale. Shields, Susan, illus. (ENG.). 32p. (J). pap. *(978-0-7502-3273-9(0),* Wayland) Hachette Children's Group.

Simon, Samantha. Nurses. 2017. (Careers in Healthcare Ser.: Vol. 13). (ENG., Illus.). 64p. (YA). (gr. 7-12). 23.95 *(978-1-4222-3800-4(8))* Mason Crest.

Simons, Rae & Gommer, Viola Ruelke. Nurse. Riggs, Ernestine G. & Gholar, Cheryl, eds. 2013. (Careers with Character Ser.: 18). 96p. (J). (gr. 7-18). 22.95 *(978-1-4222-2761-9(8))* Mason Crest.

Spinner, Stephanie. Who Was Clara Barton? Groff, David, illus. 2014. (Who Was-? Chapters Ser.). (ENG.). 112p. (J). (gr. 3-6). lib. bdg. 18.69 *(978-1-4844-3355-3(6),* Penguin Workshop) Penguin Young Readers Group.

Spinner, Stephanie & Who HQ. Who Was Clara Barton? Groff, David, illus. 2014. (Who Was? Ser.). 112p. (J). (gr. 3-7). 5.99 *(978-0-448-47953-8(2),* Penguin Workshop) Penguin Young Readers Group.

Strange, Cordelia. Physicians Assistants & Nurses: New Opportunities in the 21st-Century Health System. 2010. (New Careers for the 21st Century Ser.). 64p. (YA). (gr. 7-18). pap. 9.95 *(978-1-4222-2041-2(9))*; lib. bdg. 22.95 *(978-1-4222-1820-4(1))* Mason Crest.

Stratton, Connor. Working at a Hospital. 2020. (People at Work Ser.). (ENG., Illus.). 16p. (J). (gr. k-1). pap. 7.95 *(978-1-64493-094-6(3),* 1644930943); lib. bdg. 25.64 *(978-1-64493-015-1(3),* 1644930153) North Star Editions. (Focus Readers).

—Working at a School. 2020. (People at Work Ser.). (ENG.). 16p. (J). (gr. k-1). pap. 7.95 *(978-1-64493-095-3(1),* 1644930951); lib. bdg. 25.64 *(978-1-64493-016-8(1),* 1644930161) North Star Editions. (Focus Readers).

Time-Magazine. Time for Kids: Clara Barton. 2008. (Time for Kids Ser.). (ENG., Illus.). 48p. (J). (gr. 2-4). pap. 3.99 *(978-0-06-057622-6(7),* Collins) HarperCollins Pubs.

Vogel, Elizabeth. Meet the School Nurse. 2009. (My School Ser.). 24p. (gr. 1-2). 37.50 *(978-1-61514-708-3(X),* PowerKids Pr.) Rosen Publishing Group, Inc., The.

Waxman, Laura Hamilton. Nurse Tools. 2019. (Bumba Books (r) — Community Helpers Tools of the Trade Ser.). (ENG., Illus.). 24p. (J). (gr. -1-1). 26.65 *(978-1-5415-5732-1(8),* a84260dc-221a-48c5-af55-32eb5a1c23e6); pap. 8.99 *(978-1-5415-7353-6(6),* c96f1f53-d31c-446f-9c11-944e15aaceb3) Lerner Publishing Group. (Lerner Pubns.).

Wohlrabe, Sarah C. Helping You Heal: A Book about Nurses, 1 vol. Thomas, Eric, illus. 2003. (Community Workers Ser.). (ENG.). 24p. (J). (gr. -1-3). per. 8.95 *(978-1-4048-0480-7(3),* 92512, Picture Window Bks.) Capstone.

Zeiger, Jennifer. What Do They Do? Nurses. 2010. (Community Connections: What Do They Do? Ser.). (ENG., Illus.). 24p. (gr. 2-5). lib. bdg. 29.21 *(978-1-60279-808-3(7),* 200506) Cherry Lake Publishing.

Zemlicka, Shannon. Florence Nightingale. Debon, Nicolas, illus. 2003. (On My Own Biography Ser.). (ENG.). 48p. (J). (gr. 2-4). pap. 8.99 *(978-0-87614-102-1(5),* 10848be9-6bec-4f56-bb10-2039b051f907, First Avenue Editions) Lerner Publishing Group.

NURSES—FICTION

Binger, Christine. Show Me Some Urgency, I'm an Emergency: A trip to the ER. 2010. 16p. 8.49 *(978-1-4490-9318-1(3))* AuthorHouse.

Bloch, Robert. The Crowded Earth. 2009. 112p. 22.95 *(978-1-60664-648-9(6))*; pap. 9.95 *(978-1-60664-273-3(1))* Rodgers, Alan Bks.

Brand, Christianna. Nurse Matilda Goes to Hospital. Ardizzone, Edward, illus. 128p. *(978-0-7475-7678-5(5))* Bloomsbury Publishing Plc GBR. Dist: Macmillan.

Daley, Robert. What Color Are You? 2007. (Illus.). 34p. (J). pap. 8.75 *(978-0-9800839-1-0(5))* Daley, Robert.

Davidson, Michele R. Stowaways to Smith Island: Hayden & Chloe's Enchanted Journey with the Nurses to Maryland's Mysterious Smith Island. Watjen, Lauren, illus. 2004. 128p. (J). pap. 8.95 *(978-0-9754170-1-0(0))* Smith Island Foundation.

Farenhorst, Christine. A Cup of Cold Water: The Compassion of Nurse Edith Cavell. 2007. 222p. (J). (gr. 3-7). per. 11.99 *(978-1-59638-026-4(8))* P & R Publishing.

Gutman, Dan. My Weird School #7: Mrs. Cooney Is Loony! Paillot, Jim, illus. 2005. (My Weird School Ser.: 7). (ENG.). 112p. (J). (gr. 1-5). pap. 5.99 *(978-0-06-074522-6(3),* HarperCollins) HarperCollins Pubs.

Hammock, Mary B. Msn Cpnp. Princess Reagan & the Paci Fairy. 2012. 24p. pap. 15.99 *(978-1-4797-1074-4(1))* Xlibris Corp.

Hendry, Frances. Quest for a Queen: The Falcon. 2006. pap. *(978-1-905665-06-8(7))* Pollinger In Print.

Hill, Maree. Nurse Nerid. 2011. 28p. pap. 28.03 *(978-1-4568-5419-5(4))* Xlibris Corp.

Howat, Irene. Helen Roseveare: On His Majesty's Service. rev. ed. 2008. (Trail Blazers Ser.). (ENG.). 176p. (J). (gr. 4-9). per. 8.99 *(978-1-84550-259-1(0),* e13685db-3248-44b9-b6e0-24f841ba2e10) Christian Focus Pubns. GBR. Dist: Baker & Taylor Publisher Services (BTPS).

Jackson, Kathryn. Nurse Nancy. Malvern, Corinne, illus. 2005. (Little Golden Book Ser.). (ENG.). 24p. (J). (gr. -1-2). 5.99 *(978-0-375-83262-8(9),* Golden Bks.) Random Hse. Children's Bks.

Jacobs, Evan. FatherSonFather, 1 vol. 2015. (Gravel Road Ser.). (ENG.). 216p. (YA). (gr. 9-12). pap. 11.95 *(978-1-68021-038-5(6))* Saddleback Educational Publishing, Inc.

—Fathersonfather. 2015. (Gravel Road Ser.). (YA). lib. bdg. 20.80 *(978-0-606-37959-5(2))* Turtleback.

Juslin, Lee. Nurse Frosty & the Four Paws Retirement Home. 2009. 36p. pap. 20.00 *(978-1-4357-5568-0(5))* Lulu Pr., Inc.

Kemnitz, Dianna. Mia, Jack & Nurse Olivi. 2012. 40p. pap. 24.95 *(978-1-4626-8795-4(4))* America Star Bks.

Ladd, Debbie. Nurse Robin's Hats. Nakasone, Shaun, illus. 2006. 52p. (J). 16.95 *(978-0-9727615-3-6(5))* Deb on Air Bks.

LeSourd, Nancy. Secrets of Civil War Spies, 1 vol. 2008. (Liberty Letters Ser.). (ENG.). 224p. (J). pap. 7.99 *(978-0-310-71390-6(0))* Zonderkidz.

Machajewski, Sarah. My Dad Is a Nurse, 1 vol. 2012. (InfoMax Readers Ser.). (ENG., Illus.). 24p. (J). (gr. 1-1). pap. 8.25 *(978-1-4488-9001-9(2),* c0518bd3-67d8-42d8-a8af-5c116ab858e9, Rosen Classroom) Rosen Publishing Group, Inc., The.

Nancy St. Paul-Martin. Go to the Nurse: Peanut Puffs & Snicker-Doodles. 2009. 28p. pap. 15.49 *(978-1-4389-7653-2(4))* AuthorHouse.

Norman, Thelma G. A Wife Called Tommie. 2005. 226p. per. 14.95 *(978-1-57258-295-8(2))* TEACH Services, Inc.

Nurse, B. A. Outrageously Cool Nurses. 2007. 84p. per. 8.95 *(978-0-595-43530-2(0))* iUniverse, Inc.

Osborne, Mary Pope. High Time for Heroes. Murdocca, Sal, illus. 2016. (Magic Tree House (R) Merlin Mission Ser.: 23). 144p. (J). (gr. 2-5). 6.99 *(978-0-307-98052-6(9),* Random Hse. Bks. for Young Readers) Random Hse. Children's Bks.

Paul, Bette. Nurses: Claire's Conquests & Jan's Journey. 2007. 312p. per. *(978-1-905665-43-3(1))* Pollinger In Print.

—Nurses: Katie Goes to College (Large Pri. 2006. pap. *(978-1-905665-09-9(1))* Pollinger In Print.

—Nurses: Nikki, Barbara & Nick. 2007. 488p. per. *(978-1-905665-44-0(X))* Pollinger In Print.

Rothstein, Evelyn. My Great Grandpa Dave. 2007. (J). per. 12.95 *(978-0-9786745-1-9(0))* Marble Hse. Editions.

Sawyer, Ruth. The Primrose Ring. 2007. 104p. per. *(978-1-4065-3881-6(7))* Dodo Pr.

Siebold, Jan. Doing Time Online. 2004. 88p. (gr. 4-7). 17.50 *(978-0-7569-3612-9(8))* Perfection Learning Corp.

Spanyol, Jessica. Clive Is a Nurse. Spanyol, Jessica, illus. 2017. (Clive's Jobs Ser.: 4). (Illus.). 14p. (J). spiral bd. *(978-1-84643-991-9(4))* Child's Play International Ltd.

Stevens, Serita. The Adventure Begins. 2004. (Illus.). 182p. *(978-0-9753548-1-0(7))* Palm Publishing LLC.

Thaler, Mike. The School Nurse from the Black Lagoon, 1 vol. Lee, Jared, illus. 2011. (Black Lagoon Ser.: No. 1). (ENG.). 32p. (J). (gr. k-4). lib. bdg. 31.36 *(978-1-59961-798-5(6),* 3624, Picture Bk.) Spotlight.

Van Dyne, Edith. Aunt Jane's Nieces in the Red Cross. rev. ed. 2006. 180p. 26.95 *(978-1-4218-1724-8(1))*; pap. 11.95 *(978-1-4218-1824-5(8))* 1st World Publishing, Inc. (1st World Library - Literary Society).

—Aunt Jane's Nieces in the Red Cross. 2017. (ENG., Illus.). (J). 22.95 *(978-1-374-81524-7(1))* Capital Communications, Inc.

—Aunt Jane's Nieces in the Red Cross. 2018. (ENG.). 294p. (J). pap. 12.25 *(978-1-63391-657-9(X))* Westphalia Press.

Wells, Helen. Cherry Ames, Army Nurse. 2005. (Cherry Ames Nurse Stories Ser.: Bk. 3). 224p. (J). (gr. 4-7). 14.95 *(978-0-9771597-2-7(8))* Springer Publishing Co., Inc.

—Cherry Ames at Hilton Hospital: Book 13. 2007. (Cherry Ames Nurse Stories Ser.). 200p. (J). (gr. 3-7). 14.95 *(978-0-8261-0421-2(5))* Springer Publishing Co., Inc.

—Cherry Ames, Boarding School Nurse. 10th ed. 2007. (Cherry Ames Nurse Stories Ser.). 224p. (YA). (gr. 7-12). 14.95 *(978-0-8261-0413-7(4))* Springer Publishing Co., Inc.

—Cherry Ames Boxed Set Volumes 17-20. 2007. 896p. (J). 39.95 *(978-0-8261-0439-7(8))* Springer Publishing Co., Inc.

—Cherry Ames, Camp Nurse. 2007. (Cherry Ames Nurse Stories Ser.). 224p. (YA). (gr. 7-12). 14.95 *(978-0-8261-0417-5(7))* Springer Publishing Co., Inc.

—Cherry Ames, Chief Nurse. 2005. (Cherry Ames Nurse Stories Ser.: Bk. 4). 224p. (YA). (gr. 8-12). 14.95 *(978-0-9771597-3-4(6))* Springer Publishing Co., Inc.

—Cherry Ames, Companion Nurse. 2007. (Cherry Ames Nurse Stories Ser.). 224p. (J). (gr. 3-7). 14.95 *(978-0-8261-0431-1(2))* Springer Publishing Co., Inc.

—Cherry Ames, Cruise Nurse. 2007. (Cherry Ames Nurse Stories Ser.). 224p. (YA). (gr. 7-12). 14.95 *(978-0-8261-0411-3(8))* Springer Publishing Co., Inc.

—Cherry Ames, Department Store Nurse. 2007. (Cherry Ames Nurse Stories Ser.). 224p. (YA). (gr. 8-12). 14.95 *(978-0-8261-0415-1(0))* Springer Publishing Co., Inc.

—Cherry Ames, Flight Nurse. 2006. (Cherry Ames Nurse Stories Ser.). 224p. (J). (gr. 3-7). 14.95 *(978-0-8261-0397-0(9))* Springer Publishing Co., Inc.

—Cherry Ames, Island Nurse. 2007. (Cherry Ames Nurse Stories Ser.). 200p. (J). (gr. 3-7). 14.95 *(978-0-8261-0423-6(1))* Springer Publishing Co., Inc.

—Cherry Ames Jungle Nurse. 2007. (Cherry Ames Nurse Stories Ser.). 224p. (J). (gr. 3-7). 14.95 *(978-0-8261-0433-5(9))* Springer Publishing Co., Inc.

—Cherry Ames, Private Duty Nurse. 2006. (Cherry Ames Nurse Stories Ser.). 224p. (J). (gr. 3-7). 14.95 *(978-0-8261-0398-7(7))* Springer Publishing Co., Inc.

—Cherry Ames, Rural Nurse. 2007. (Cherry Ames Nurse Stories Ser.). 224p. (J). (gr. 3-7). 14.95 *(978-0-8261-0425-0(8))* Springer Publishing Co., Inc.

—Cherry Ames, Senior Nurse. 2005. (Cherry Ames Nurse Stories Ser.: Bk. 2). 224p. (J). (gr. 4-7). 14.95 *(978-0-9771597-1-0(X))* Springer Publishing Co., Inc.

—Cherry Ames, Ski Nurse Mystery. 2007. (Cherry Ames Nurse Stories Ser.). 224p. (J). (gr. 3-7). 14.95 *(978-0-8261-0437-3(1))* Springer Publishing Co., Inc.

—Cherry Ames, Staff Nurse. 2007. (Cherry Ames Nurse Stories Ser.). 200p. (J). (gr. 3-7). 14.95 *(978-0-8261-0427-4(4))* Springer Publishing Co., Inc.

—Cherry Ames, Student Nurse. 2005. (Cherry Ames Nurse Stories Ser.: Bk. 1). 224p. (J). (gr. 4-7). 14.95 *(978-0-9771597-0-3(1))* Springer Publishing Co., Inc.

—Cherry Ames, the Mystery in the Doctor's Office. 2007. (Cherry Ames Nurse Stories Ser.). 224p. (J). (gr. 3-7). 14.95 *(978-0-8261-0435-9(5))* Springer Publishing Co., Inc.

—Cherry Ames Veteran's Nurse. 2006. (Cherry Ames Nurse Stories Ser.). 224p. (J). (gr. 3-7). 14.95 *(978-0-8261-0400-7(2))* Springer Publishing Co., Inc.

—Cherry Ames, Visiting Nurse. 2006. (Cherry Ames Nurse Stories Ser.). 224p. (J). (gr. 3-7). 14.95 *(978-0-8261-0399-4(5))* Springer Publishing Co., Inc.

Wick, Elaine. It's MY Future: Should I Be a Nurse Practitioner? Tremaine, Michele, illus. 2004. 64p. (J). lib. bdg. 12.95 *(978-0-9749769-0-7(3))* NAPNAP.

Woolf, Virginia. Nurse Lugton's Curtain. Vivas, Julie, illus. 2004. (ENG.). 32p. 16.00 *(978-0-15-205048-1(5),* 1195248, Clarion Bks.) HarperCollins Pubs.

Yonge, Charlotte M. Little Lucy's Wonderful Globe. 2007. 52p. per. *(978-1-4065-5529-5(0))* Dodo Pr.

—Little Lucy's Wonderful Globe. 2007. 156p. per. 21.95 *(978-0-548-67542-7(2))* 2004. reprint ed. pap. 15.95 *(978-1-4191-3079-3(X))* Kessinger Publishing, LLC.

NURSES AND NURSING

see Nurses; Nursing

NURSING

Arnold, Quinn M. Les Infirmiers. 2017. (Graines de Savoir Ser.). (FRE., Illus.). 24p. (J). (gr. -1-k). *(978-1-77092-388-1(8),* 20428) Creative Co., The.

—Nurses. 2017. (Seedlings Ser.). (ENG., Illus.). 24p. (J). (gr. -1-k). *(978-1-60818-874-1(4),* 20357, Creative Education) Creative Co., The.

Bickerstaff, Linda. What Degree Do I Need to Pursue a Career in Nursing?, 1 vol. 2014. (Right Degree for Me Ser.). (ENG., Illus.). 80p. (J). (gr. 7-7). 37.80 *(978-1-4777-7857-9(8),* 96004254-caea-4fa7-b4fa-61aab2bee73a, Rosen Young Adult) Rosen Publishing Group, Inc., The.

Craig, Lizabeth. The History of Nursing, 1 vol. 2013. (World History Ser.). (ENG., Illus.). 104p. (gr. 7-7). lib. bdg. 41.53 *(978-1-4205-0823-9(7),* 91edbe73-559e-4c90-9f13-9e672274088d, Lucent Pr.) Greenhaven Publishing LLC.

Cunningham, Kevin. Nurse. 2015. (21st Century Skills Library: Cool STEAM Careers Ser.). (ENG., Illus.). 32p. (J). (gr. 4-7). 32.07 *(978-1-63362-561-7(3),* 206428) Cherry Lake Publishing.

Greenwood, Nancy. I Can Be a Nurse, 1 vol. 2020. (I Can Be Anything! Ser.). (ENG.). 24p. (gr. k-k). pap. 9.15 *(978-1-5382-5550-6(2),* 149e1c9d-49fe-48bc-9a96-f8af66091b94) Stevens, Gareth Publishing LLLP.

Jeffries, Joyce. Meet the Nurse, 1 vol. 2012. (People Around Town Ser.). (Illus.). 24p. (gr. k-k). (ENG.). (J). 25.27 *(978-1-4339-7332-1(4),* 3a9f846a-b797-4912-8532-b252f78829de); (ENG., (J). pap. 9.15 *(978-1-4339-7333-8(2),* 312578d9-d9dd-4208-83c6-e2dcb5228ced); 69.20 *(978-1-4339-8061-9(4))* Stevens, Gareth Publishing LLLP.

—Meet the Nurse / Te Presento a Los Enfermeros, 1 vol. 2012. (People Around Town / Gente de Mi Ciudad Ser.). (SPA & ENG., Illus.). 24p. (J). (gr. k-k). 25.27 *(978-1-4339-7388-8(X),* c6976847-d812-4e74-b759-334323544250) Stevens, Gareth Publishing LLLP.

Leaf, Christina. Nurses. 2018. (Community Helpers Ser.). (ENG., Illus.). 24p. (J). (gr. k-3). lib. bdg. 26.95 *(978-1-62617-748-2(1),* Blastoff! Readers) Bellwether Media.

Less, Emma. Nurses. 2018. (Real-Life Superheroes Ser.). (ENG.). 16p. (J). (gr. k-2). pap. 7.99 *(978-1-68152-279-1(9),* 14919) Amicus.

Liebman, Dan & Liebman, Dan. I Want to Be a Nurse. 2nd rev. ed. 2018. (I Want to Be Ser.). (ENG., Illus.). 24p. (J). (gr.

-1-2). pap. 3.99 *(978-0-2281-0099-7(2),* c7a162ee-b3ec-4cc1-9c70-54da00d9fda2) Firefly Bks., Ltd.
Murray, Aaron R. Nurses Help Us, 1 vol. 2012. (All about Community Helpers Ser.). (ENG., Illus.). 24p. (gr. -1-1). 25.27 *(978-0-7660-4044-1(5),* d54f115c-04ac-4683-b693-962e0feeea67, Enslow Publishing) Enslow Publishing, LLC.
Parkes, Elle. Hooray for Nurses! 2016. (Bumba Books (r) — Hooray for Community Helpers! Ser.). (ENG., Illus.). 24p. (J). (gr. -1-1). lib. bdg. 26.65 *(978-1-5124-1444-8(1),* 9b046fa2-a419-4678-8522-56ab4ab4892b, Lerner Pubns.) Lerner Publishing Group.
Riggs, Kate. Seedlings: Nurses. 2017. (Seedlings Ser.). (ENG., Illus.). 24p. (J). (gr. -1-1). pap. 8.99 *(978-1-62832-489-1(9),* 20358, Creative Paperbacks) Creative Co., The.
Simons, Rae & Gommer, Viola Ruelke. Nurse. Riggs, Ernestine G. & Gholar, Cheryl, eds. 2013. (Careers with Character Ser.: 18). 96p. (J). (gr. 7-18). 22.95 *(978-1-4222-2761-9(8))* Mason Crest.
Wasson, E. & Strausser, A. Mommies & Daddies Are Nurses. Ebert, Roey, illus. 2011. 32p. pap. 15.99 *(978-1-4634-3451-9(0))* AuthorHouse.
Waxman, Laura Hamilton. Nurse Tools. 2019. (Bumba Books (r) — Community Helpers Tools of the Trade Ser.). (ENG., Illus.). 24p. (J). (gr. -1-1). 26.65 *(978-1-5415-5732-1(8),* a84260dc-221a-48c5-af55-32eb5a1c23e6); pap. 8.99 *(978-1-5415-7353-6(6),* c96f1f53-d31c-446f-9c11-944e15aaceb3) Lerner Publishing Group. (Lerner Pubns.).

NURSING—FICTION

Battista, Brianna. I Want to Be a Nurse, 1 vol. 2018. (What Do I Want to Be? Ser.). (ENG.). 24p. (gr. 1-1). 25.27 *(978-1-5383-2995-5(6),* 67fe0d03-2c05-4625-805d-cc5ece17d35f); pap. 9.25 *(978-1-5383-2997-9(2),* 805c4ed2-caf9-4001-aa1c-495fc840fdfe) Rosen Publishing Group, Inc., The. (PowerKids Pr.).
Repkin, Mark. Mommy Breastfeeds My Baby Brother/ Mama Amamanta A Mi Hermanito. Moneysmith, David, illus. 2011.Tr. of Mama Amamanta A Mi Hermanito. (SPA & ENG.). 24p. (J). pap. 9.99 *(978-0-9816538-1-5(2))* Istoria Hse.
Stier, Catherine. What's Bugging Nurse Penny? A Story about Lice. Beaky, Suzanne, illus. 2013. (ENG.). 32p. (J). (gr. -1-3). 16.99 *(978-0-8075-8803-1(2),* 807588032) Whitman, Albert & Co.
Wakem, Samantha. Milly's Magic Play House: The Hospital, 1 vol. Herridge, Debbie, illus. 2010. 20p. 24.95 *(978-1-4489-5114-7(3))* PublishAmerica, Inc.

NUTRITION

see also Diet; Digestion; Food; Metabolism; Vitamins

ABDO Publishing Company Staff & Rondeau, Amanda. What Should I Eat? 2003. (What Should I Eat? Ser.: 6). (Illus.). 24p. (J). (gr. k-3). 145.26 *(978-1-57765-831-3(0),* SandCastle) ABDO Publishing Co.
Adams, Julia. Proteins, 1 vol. 2011. (Good Food Ser.). (ENG.). 24p. (J). (gr. 1-1). lib. bdg. 26.27 *(978-1-4488-3272-9(1),* 3c6d70e9-cdd7-448a-a41e-33c87959daa9, PowerKids Pr.) Rosen Publishing Group, Inc., The.
Alexander's Enrichment Activities. 2006. (J). pap. 5.95 *(978-0-9742806-6-0(6))* Heart to Heart Publishing, Inc.
Allsop, Marcus. We Like to Help Cook: Nos Gusta Ayudar a Cocinar. Iverson, Diane, illus. (We Like To Ser.). (ENG.). 32p. 2011. (J). pap. 10.95 *(978-1-935826-00-2(X))* 2007. (gr. -1-1). pap. 9.95 *(978-1-890772-70-3(4))* 2nd alt. ed. 2012. (J). pap. 9.95 *(978-1-935826-05-7(0))* Kalindi Pr.
Allsop, Marcus & Iverson, Diane. Nos Gusta Ayudar a Cocinar: We Like to Help Cook. Iverson, Diane, illus. 2009. (SPA & ENG., Illus.). (J). pap. *(978-1-890772-97-0(6))* Hohm Pr.
Aloian, Molly. Why We Need Carbohydrates. 2011. (Science of Nutrition Ser.). (ENG.). 48p. (J). (gr. 5-9). lib. bdg. *(978-0-7787-1686-0(4));* pap. *(978-0-7787-1693-8(7))* Crabtree Publishing Co.
—Why We Need Fats. 2011. (Science of Nutrition Ser.). (ENG.). 48p. (J). (gr. 5-9). *(978-0-7787-1687-7(2));* pap. *(978-0-7787-1694-5(5))* Crabtree Publishing Co.
Anthony, Mark, et al. Gut Instinct: Diet's Missing Link. 2003. (Illus.). 216p. per. 19.95 *(978-0-9743664-0-1(4))* Leap Forward Pubns.
Antill, Sara. 10 Ways I Can Live A Healthy Life, 1 vol. 2012. (I Can Make a Difference Ser.). (ENG., Illus.). 24p. (J). (gr. 2-3). 26.27 *(978-1-4488-6207-8(8),* 827c537d-2573-4e81-aa14-98cef262626f); pap. 9.25 *(978-1-4488-6373-0(2),* 5b39282f-aab6-416d-9950-aff26a49e951) Rosen Publishing Group, Inc., The. (PowerKids Pr.).
April, Elyse. We Like to Eat Well. Agrell, Lewis, illus. 2nd rev. ed. 2013. (We Like To Ser.). (ENG.). 32p. (J). pap. 9.95 *(978-1-935826-04-0(2))* Kalindi Pr.
—We Like to Eat Well-Nos Gusta Comer Bien. Agrell, Lewis, illus. 2nd ed. 2011. (We Like To Ser.). (ENG.). 32p. (J). pap. 10.95 *(978-1-935826-01-9(8))* Kalindi Pr.
Ayer, Paula & Banyard, Antonia. Eat Up! An Infographic Exploration of Food. Wuthrich, Belle, illus. 2017. (Visual Exploration Ser.). (ENG.). 72p. (gr. 3-7). 22.95 *(978-1-55451-884-5(9))* Annick Pr., Ltd. CAN. Dist: Publishers Group West (PGW).
—Eat Up! An Infographic Exploration of Food. Wuthrich, Belle, illus. 2017. (Visual Exploration Ser.). (ENG.). 72p. (gr. 3-7). pap. 12.95 *(978-1-55451-883-8(0))* Annick Pr., Ltd. CAN. Dist: Publishers Group West (PGW).
Barraclough, Sue & Lanz, Helen. Eat & Drink. 2012. (Healthy Habits Ser.). (ENG.). 24p. (gr. 1-3). lib. bdg. 24.25 *(978-1-59771-307-8(4))* Sea-To-Sea Pubns.
Bauer, Joy. Yummy Yoga: Playful Poses & Tasty Treats. Stephens, Bonnie, illus. 2019. (ENG.). 24p. (J). (gr. -1-17). 14.99 *(978-1-4197-3824-1(0),* 1284101, Abrams Bks. for Young Readers) Abrams, Inc.
Benchmark Education Company, LLC Staff, compiled by. Nutrition & Exercise. 2006. (J). 91.00 *(978-1-4108-7036-0(7))* Benchmark Education Co.
Benduhn, Tea. Fruit / Fruta, 1 vol. 2007. (Find Out about Food / Conoce la Comida Ser.). (SPA & ENG.). 24p. (gr. k-2). pap. 9.15 *(978-0-8368-8462-3(0),* cda69f67-6693-4b46-a1d6-dd01bbc532b8); (Illus.). lib. bdg. 24.67 *(978-0-8368-8455-5(8),* 2fd0e8c1-8530-41bd-a720-db127f7320d7) Stevens, Gareth Publishing LLLP. (Weekly Reader Leveled Readers).
Berger, Melvin & Berger, Gilda. Healthy Eating. 2007. (Now I Know Ser.). (Illus.). 32p. (J). *(978-0-439-02446-4(3))* Scholastic, Inc.
Bickerstaff, Linda. Careers in Nutrition. 2009. (Careers in the New Economy Ser.). 144p. (gr. 7-7). 63.90 *(978-1-61511-818-2(7))* Rosen Publishing Group, Inc., The.
Bodden, Valerie. Eating Healthy. 2015. (Healthy Plates Ser.). (ENG.). 24p. (J). (gr. 1-4). pap. 9.99 *(978-1-62832-107-4(5),* 21204, Creative Paperbacks); *(978-1-60818-507-8(9),* 21203, Creative Education) Creative Co., The.
—Fruits. 2015. (Healthy Plates Ser.). (ENG.). 24p. (J). (gr. 1-4). pap. 9.99 *(978-1-62832-109-8(1),* 21210, Creative Paperbacks) Creative Co., The.
—Grains. 2015. (Healthy Plates Ser.). (ENG.). 24p. (J). (gr. 1-4). pap. 9.99 *(978-1-62832-110-4(5),* 21213, Creative Paperbacks); *(978-1-60818-510-8(9),* 21212, Creative Education) Creative Co., The.
—Proteins. 2015. (Healthy Plates Ser.). (ENG.). 24p. (J). (gr. 1-4). pap. 9.99 *(978-1-62832-111-1(3),* 21216, Creative Paperbacks) Creative Co., The.
—Vegetables. 2015. (Healthy Plates Ser.). (ENG.). 24p. (J). (gr. 1-4). pap. 9.99 *(978-1-62832-112-8(1),* 21219, Creative Paperbacks) Creative Co., The.
Boothroyd, Jennifer. Taste Something New! Giving Different Foods a Try. 2016. (Lightning Bolt Books (r) — Healthy Eating Ser.). (ENG., Illus.). 32p. (J). (gr. 1-3). 29.32 *(978-1-4677-9472-5(4),* 74d0e26c-7ed4-4971-b19c-a8d1cb0d7ce0, Lerner Pubns.) Lerner Publishing Group.
—What's on My Plate? Choosing from the Five Food Groups. 2016. (Lightning Bolt Books — Healthy Eating Ser.). (ENG., Illus.). 32p. (gr. 1-3). 39.99 *(978-1-5124-1669-5(X),* Lerner Digital); (J). 29.32 *(978-1-4677-9470-1(8),* cc68da85-aa73-40bf-8a03-466a76f35016, Lerner Pubns.); (J). E-Book 42.65 *(978-1-4677-9672-9(7),* 9781467796729, Lerner Pubns.) Lerner Publishing Group.
Borgert-Spaniol, Megan. Dairy Group. 2012. (Eating Right with Myplate Ser.). (ENG., Illus.). 24p. (J). (gr. k-3). lib. bdg. 26.95 *(978-1-60014-754-8(2),* Blastoff! Readers) Bellwether Media.
—Fruit Group. 2012. (Eating Right with Myplate Ser.). (ENG., Illus.). 24p. (J). (gr. k-3). lib. bdg. 26.95 *(978-1-60014-755-5(0),* Blastoff! Readers) Bellwether Media.
—Healthy Eating. 2012. (Eating Right with Myplate Ser.). (ENG., Illus.). 24p. (J). (gr. k-3). lib. bdg. 26.95 *(978-1-60014-757-9(7),* Blastoff! Readers) Bellwether Media.
—Vegetable Group. 2012. (Eating Right with Myplate Ser.). (ENG., Illus.). 24p. (J). (gr. k-3). lib. bdg. 26.95 *(978-1-60014-760-9(7),* 11402, Blastoff! Readers) Bellwether Media.
Bow, James. Why We Need Minerals. 2011. (Science of Nutrition Ser.). (ENG.). 48p. (J). (gr. 5-9). lib. bdg. *(978-0-7787-1688-4(0));* pap. *(978-0-7787-1695-2(3))* Crabtree Publishing Co.
Brancato, Robin F. Food Choices: The Ultimate Teen Guide. 2010. (It Happened to Me Ser.: 28). (ENG., Illus.). 240p. (gr. 7-10). 62.00 *(978-0-8108-6109-1(7))* Scarecrow Pr., Inc.
Brew Ed.D., Ranelle L. Healthy Days. 2013. 24p. pap. 10.96 *(978-1-4669-6005-3(1))* Trafford Publishing.
Brezina, Corona. What Are Minerals?, 1 vol. 2018. (Let's Find Out! Good Health Ser.). (ENG.). 32p. (gr. 2-3). 26.06 *(978-1-5383-0302-3(7),* 6bd32c1c-d3ff-434b-9c61-741ecf772524, Britannica Educational Publishing) Rosen Publishing Group, Inc., The.
—What Are Vitamins?, 1 vol. 2018. (Let's Find Out! Good Health Ser.). (ENG.). 32p. (gr. 2-3). lib. bdg. 26.06 *(978-1-5383-0306-1(X),* da385eb7-a27b-4c8e-8f65-7aa72f5e36b9, Britannica Educational Publishing) Rosen Publishing Group, Inc., The.
Brown, Holly. We Are What We Eat: Understanding Diet & Disease, 1 vol. annot. ed. 2019. (Nutrition & Health Ser.). (ENG.). 104p. (gr. 7-7). pap. 20.99 *(978-1-5345-6884-6(0),* 7b4be668-68d7-40a4-9a50-01a3def61bfc); lib. bdg. 41.03 *(978-1-5345-6875-4(1),* 44f9f67b-8701-42f4-a8bf-5a365b3461a7) Greenhaven Publishing LLC. (Lucent Pr.).
Burstein, John. Delicious Dairy, 1 vol. 2009. (Slim Goodbody's Nutrition Edition Ser.). (ENG., Illus.). 24p. (J). (gr. k-3). pap. *(978-0-7787-5056-7(6));* lib. bdg. *(978-0-7787-5041-3(8))* Crabtree Publishing Co.
—Fabulous Fruits, 1 vol. 2009. (Slim Goodbody's Nutrition Edition Ser.). (ENG., Illus.). 24p. (J). (gr. k-3). pap. *(978-0-7787-5057-4(4));* lib. bdg. *(978-0-7787-5042-0(6))* Crabtree Publishing Co.
—Glorious Grains, 1 vol. 2009. (Slim Goodbody's Nutrition Edition Ser.). (ENG., Illus.). 24p. (J). (gr. k-3). pap. *(978-0-7787-5058-1(2));* lib. bdg. *(978-0-7787-5043-7(4))* Crabtree Publishing Co.
—Marvelous Meats & More, 1 vol. 2009. (Slim Goodbody's Nutrition Edition Ser.). (ENG., Illus.). 24p. (J). (gr. k-3). pap. *(978-0-7787-5059-8(0));* lib. bdg. *(978-0-7787-5044-4(2))* Crabtree Publishing Co.
—Outstanding Oils & Wonderful Water. 2009. (Slim Goodbody's Nutrition Edition Ser.). (ENG., Illus.). 24p. (J). (gr. k-3). pap. *(978-0-7787-5061-1(2));* lib. bdg. *(978-0-7787-5046-8(9))* Crabtree Publishing Co.
—Vital Vegetables, 1 vol. 2009. (Slim Goodbody's Nutrition Edition Ser.). (ENG., Illus.). 24p. (J). (gr. k-3). pap. *(978-0-7787-5060-4(4));* lib. bdg. *(978-0-7787-5045-1(0))* Crabtree Publishing Co.
Burton, Margie, et al. Your Body. 2011. (Early Connections Ser.). (J). *(978-1-61672-549-5(4))* Benchmark Education Co.
Butterworth, Chris. How Did That Get in My Lunchbox? The Story of Food. Gaggiotti, Lucia, illus. 2011. (Exploring the Everyday Ser.). (ENG.). 32p. (J). (gr. k-3). 14.99 *(978-0-7636-5005-6(6))* Candlewick Pr.
Byrd, Tracy. Fruits & Vegetables & How They Grow: A to Z. 2012. 60p. pap. 24.99 *(978-1-4772-4897-3(8))* AuthorHouse.
Canavan, Thomas. Fueling the Body: Digestion & Nutrition, 1 vol. 2015. (How Your Body Works). (ENG.). 32p. (J). (gr. 4-4). pap. 11.00 *(978-1-4994-1227-7(4),* 9fc692c4-1638-43ed-9c1b-eac464db5ed5, PowerKids Pr.) Rosen Publishing Group, Inc., The.
Candlewick Press. Fizzy's Lunch Lab: Super Supper Throwdown. Lunch Lab, LLC., illus. 2014. (Fizzy's Lunch Lab Ser.). (ENG.). 64p. (J). (gr. 1-4). pap. 5.99 *(978-0-7636-6883-9(4),* Candlewick Entertainment) Candlewick Pr.
Carroll, Molly. Chomp & Chew, to a Healthy You! 2008. (My First Science Discovery Library). (ENG., Illus.). 24p. (gr. -1-k). bds. 5.99 *(978-1-60472-436-3(6),* 9781604724363) Rourke Educational Media.
CATTCH Kids Club Nutrition. 2005. per. *(978-1-932032-19-2(3))* Flaghouse, Inc.
Centore, Michael. Fiber. 2017. (Illus.). 64p. (J). *(978-1-4222-3735-9(4))* Mason Crest.
—Salt. 2017. 64p. (J). *(978-1-4222-3742-7(7))* Mason Crest.
Chancellor, Deborah. Healthy Eating. 2009. (Now We Know About... Ser.). (ENG., Illus.). 24p. (J). (gr. k-3). pap. *(978-0-7787-4737-6(9));* lib. bdg. *(978-0-7787-4720-8(4))* Crabtree Publishing Co.
Chastain, Zachary. Nutrition & Society. 2014. (ENG., Illus.). 112p. 42.79 *(978-1-62524-073-6(2),* Village Earth Pr.) Harding Hse. Publishing Sebice Inc.
Chilson, Martin. Carmen Cooks Healthy! Represent & Solve Problems Involving Division, 1 vol. 2014. (Math Masters: Operations & Algebraic Thinking Ser.). (ENG.). 24p. (J). (gr. 3-3). 25.27 *(978-1-4777-6410-7(0),* 30978d13-6971-4be8-938d-fdfceab3c4c3); pap. 8.25 *(978-1-4777-4965-4(9),* e8da09b2-f71e-4394-956e-d555e06ccd20) Rosen Publishing Group, Inc., The. (Rosen Classroom).
Clark, Rosalyn. Why We Eat Healthy Foods. 2018. (Bumba Books (r) — Health Matters Ser.). (ENG., Illus.). 24p. (J). (gr. -1-1). 26.65 *(978-1-5124-8293-5(5),* efb286fe-0d65-46b4-b56b-eec742a203cf, Lerner Pubns.) Lerner Publishing Group.
Cleary, Brian P. & Goneau, Martin. Macaroni & Rice & Bread by the Slice: What Is in the Grains Group? 2011. (Food Is CATegorical Ser.). pap. 45.32 *(978-0-7613-8351-2(4),* Millbrook Pr.) Lerner Publishing Group.
Coan, Sharon. Bueno para Mí - Comida Saludable. 2nd rev. ed. 2016. (TIME for KIDS(r): Informational Text Ser.). (SPA.). 12p. (gr. -1-k). 7.99 *(978-1-4938-3032-9(5))* Teacher Created Materials, Inc.
—Good for Me: Healthy Food. 2nd rev. ed. 2015. (TIME for KIDS(r): Informational Text Ser.). (ENG., Illus.). 12p. (J). (gr. -1-k). 7.99 *(978-1-4938-2151-8(2))* Teacher Created Materials, Inc.
Cohen, Marina. Why We Need Vitamins. 2011. (Science of Nutrition Ser.). (ENG.). 48p. (J). (gr. 5-9). lib. bdg. *(978-0-7787-1690-7(2));* pap. *(978-0-7787-1697-6(X))* Crabtree Publishing Co.
Colored Nuts about Nutrition: Ages 7-11, 12 activity books. 2005. (J). 9.95 *(978-1-57175-176-8(9),* 6508-C) Visualz.
Colored Nuts about Nutrition Activity Books: Ages 2-6, 12 activity books. 2005. (J). 9.95 *(978-1-57175-174-4(2),* 6507-C) Visualz.
Colored Snack Attack Activity Books: Ages 2-6, 12 activity books. 2005. (J). 9.95 *(978-1-57175-169-0(6),* 6503-C) Visualz.
Colored Snack Attack Activity Books: Ages 7-11, 12 activity books. 2005. (J). 9.95 *(978-1-57175-171-3(8),* 6504-C) Visualz.
Conklin, Wendy. Safe & Sound: Our Health. 2nd rev. ed. 2017. (TIME(r): Informational Text Ser.). (ENG., Illus.). 48p. (gr. 6-8). pap. 13.99 *(978-1-4938-3629-1(3))* Teacher Created Materials, Inc.
Crabtree Publishing, creator. Slim Goodbody's Lighten Up. 2008. (ENG.). 32p. (J). pap. *(978-0-7787-3929-6(5))* Crabtree Publishing Co.
Crawford, Greg. Super Hero Foods & the Abc's of Nutrition. 2013. 108p. pap. 21.95 *(978-0-9890227-0-5(6))* It's a Lifestyle Fitness.
Creighton, Judith Matlock, et al. Health Education Primer. 2nd ed. 2006. (Illus.). 76p. (J). spiral bd. 29.95 *(978-0-9773228-0-0(7))* WHA Publishing.
—Nutrition Lessons for Kids: (and Their Parents) 2006. (J). spiral bd. 19.95 *(978-0-9773228-3-1(1))* WHA Publishing.
Crest, Mason. Food & Nutrition. 2019. (Health & Nutrition Ser.). (Illus.). 80p. (J). (gr. 12). lib. bdg. 34.60 *(978-1-4222-4219-3(6))* Mason Crest.
—Healthy Diet. 2019. (Health & Nutrition Ser.). (Illus.). 80p. (J). (gr. 12). lib. bdg. 34.60 *(978-1-4222-4222-3(6))* Mason Crest.
—Malnutrition. 2019. (Health & Nutrition Ser.). (Illus.). 80p. (J). (gr. 12). lib. bdg. 34.60 *(978-1-4222-4223-0(4))* Mason Crest.
Crockett, Kyle A. Managing Your Weight with Nutrition. Borus, Joshua, ed. 2013. (Understanding Nutrition: a Gateway to Physical & Mental Health Ser.: 11). (Illus.). 48p. (J). (gr. 5-18). 19.95 *(978-1-4222-2881-4(9))* Mason Crest.
—Navigating Your School Cafeteria & Convenience Store. Borus, Joshua, ed. 2013. (Understanding Nutrition: a Gateway to Physical & Mental Health Ser.: 11). (Illus.). 48p. (J). (gr. 5-18). 19.95 *(978-1-4222-2882-1(7))* Mason Crest.
—Nutrition & Your Future. Borus, Joshua, ed. 2013. (Understanding Nutrition: a Gateway to Physical & Mental Health Ser.: 11). (Illus.). 48p. (J). (gr. 5-18). 19.95 *(978-1-4222-2885-2(1))* Mason Crest.
—Nutrition for Achievement in Sports & Academics. Borus, Joshua, ed. 2013. (Understanding Nutrition: a Gateway to Physical & Mental Health Ser.). (Illus.). 48p. (J). (gr. 5-18). pap. 9.95 *(978-1-4222-2990-3(4));* 19.95 *(978-1-4222-2884-5(3))* Mason Crest.
Danger Zone: Dieting & Eating Disorders, 12 vols., Set. Incl. Anorexia. Watson, Stephanie. lib. bdg. 37.13 *(978-1-4042-1996-0(X),* 179a64fb-59a6-4f27-97e9-cd1ef28bdafa); Binge Eating. Watson, Stephanie. lib. bdg. 37.13 *(978-1-4042-1998-4(6),* 14aac3b2-7c07-42d9-a54f-e5fb25cea6d); Bulimia. Watson, Stephanie. lib. bdg. 37.13 *(978-1-4042-1997-7(8),* 82cadd7c-6fc2-4639-92f6-9b595c73e301); Diet Drugs. Williams, Kara. lib. bdg. 37.13 *(978-1-4042-1994-6(3),* 491527cc-5c75-4d55-9285-96cd954254a4); Diet Fads. Zahensky, Barbara A. lib. bdg. 37.13 *(978-1-4042-1999-1(4),* 320c05d7-afce-4006-a5e1-995188bacd97); Negative Body Image. Willett, Edward. lib. bdg. 37.13 *(978-1-4042-1995-3(1),* f6b5288b-4dd7-49d8-9ab5-76419a56a291); (Illus.). 64p. (YA). (gr. 5-6). 2007. (Danger Zone: Dieting & Eating Disorders Ser.). (ENG.). 2006. Set lib. bdg. 222.78 *(978-1-4042-1061-5(X),* 9637c9d8-bc4b-4069-ac9f-91d5e817c615) Rosen Publishing Group, Inc., The.
Davis, Sheila & Williams, Nadia. Claudia & Grammy Lose Weight: A Mississippi Grammy & California Granddaughter Lose Weight. 2012. 48p. (-18). pap. 31.99 *(978-1-4771-3594-5(4))* Xlibris Corp.
Deal, Darlene. Play with Your Food & Learn How to Eat Right: Nutritional Book about Fruits & Vegetables. 2004. (ENG & SPA., Illus.). 22p. (J). (gr. 1-4). pap. 9.95 *(978-0-9747299-0-9(6))* Deal, Darlene.
Dell, Helen Sue. The Thinker's Pizza Cookbook. 2003. (Illus.). 64p. (J). pap. 5.99 *(978-0-9747247-0-6(X))* Food Enhancement Enterprises.
DK. Are You What You Eat? 2015. (ENG.). 96p. (J). (gr. 3-7). 16.99 *(978-1-4654-2944-5(1),* DK Children) Dorling Kindersley Publishing, Inc.
Doeden, Matt. Eat Right! How You Can Make Good Food Choices. 2009. pap. 52.95 *(978-0-7613-4684-5(8))* Lerner Publishing Group.
—Eat Right! How You Can Make Good Food Choices. Desrocher, Jack, illus. 2008. (Health Zone Ser.). (ENG.). 64p. (gr. 4-7). lib. bdg. 30.60 *(978-0-8225-7552-8(3))* Lerner Publishing Group.
dupress labs & Margie & Jimbo. My Fridge: My First Book of Food. 2017. (Illus.). 20p. (J). (gr. -1-k). bds. 7.95 *(978-1-946064-00-4(9),* 806400) Duo Pr. LLC.
Durrie, Karen. Health. 2011. (J). 27.13 *(978-1-61690-950-5(1))* Weigl Pubs., Inc.
—Health: Arabic-English Bilingual Edition. 2016. (Community Helpers Ser.). (ENG.). (J). (gr. -1-3). 29.99 *(978-1-61913-903-9(0))* Weigl Pubs., Inc.
—Salud. 2012. (SPA.). (J). *(978-1-61913-210-8(9))* Weigl Pubs., Inc.
Dyer, Janice. Get into Smart Snacks. 2017. (Get-Into-It Guides). (Illus.). 32p. (J). (gr. 4-5). *(978-0-7787-3642-4(3))* Crabtree Publishing Co.
Eating Your Colors. 2010. (Eat Your Colors Ser.). 32p. lib. bdg. 155.94 *(978-1-4296-5196-7(2),* Capstone Pr.) Capstone.
Edwards, Hazel & Alexander, Goldie. Talking about What You Eat, 1 vol. 2010. (Healthy Living Ser.). (ENG., Illus.). 32p. (YA). (gr. 3-4). lib. bdg. 28.67 *(978-1-4339-3656-2(9),* cc24bdc7-7a45-4b00-8506-1dba8abdab01) Stevens, Gareth Publishing LLLP.
Esbaum, Jill. National Geographic Kids: Apples for Everyone. 2009. (Picture the Seasons Ser.). (Illus.). 16p. (J). (gr. -1-k). pap. 5.95 *(978-1-4263-0523-8(0),* National Geographic Kids) Disney Publishing Worldwide.
Espejo, Roman, ed. What Should We Eat?, 1 vol. 2016. (At Issue Ser.). (ENG.). 104p. (gr. 10-12). 41.03 *(978-0-7377-7390-3(1),* 02ffb43d-0b05-4bf1-bab0-bd2d6152cc87, Greenhaven Publishing) Greenhaven Publishing LLC.
Etingoff, Kim. Diet Myths: Sorting Through the Hype. Borus, Joshua, ed. 2013. (Understanding Nutrition: a Gateway to Physical & Mental Health Ser.: 11). (Illus.). 48p. (J). (gr. 5-18). 19.95 *(978-1-4222-2876-0(2))* Mason Crest.
—Eating Out: How to Order in Restaurants. Borus, Joshua, ed. 2013. (Understanding Nutrition: a Gateway to Physical & Mental Health Ser.: 11). (Illus.). 48p. (J). (gr. 5-18). 19.95 *(978-1-4222-2877-7(0))* Mason Crest.
—Healthy Alternatives to Sweets & Snacks. Borus, Joshua, ed. 2013. (Understanding Nutrition: a Gateway to Physical & Mental Health Ser.). (Illus.). 48p. (J). (gr. 5-18). pap. 9.95 *(978-1-4222-2992-7(0));* 19.95 *(978-1-4222-2878-4(9))* Mason Crest.
—Healthy Fast Foods. Borus, Joshua, ed. 2013. (Understanding Nutrition: a Gateway to Physical & Mental Health Ser.). (Illus.). 48p. (J). (gr. 5-18). pap. 9.95 *(978-1-4222-2988-0(2));* 19.95 *(978-1-4222-2879-1(7))* Mason Crest.
—How to Read Food Product Labels. Borus, Joshua, ed. 2013. (Illus.). 48p. (J). (gr. 5-18). pap. 9.95 *(978-1-4222-2993-4(9));* (Understanding Nutrition: a Gateway to Physical & Mental Health Ser.: 11). 19.95 *(978-1-4222-2880-7(0))* Mason Crest.
—Understanding Nutrition: A Gateway to Physical & Mental Health, 11 vols. 2014. (Illus.). 11p. (J). *(978-1-4222-2874-6(6))* Mason Crest.
Favor, Lesli J. & Freed, Kira. Food As Foe: Nutrition & Eating Disorders, 1 vol. 2010. (Food & You Ser.). (ENG.). 32p. (gr. 5-5). 31.21 *(978-0-7614-4364-3(9),* b5b1c437-9cd4-40b9-80eb-3dd2154ecb05) Cavendish Square Publishing LLC.
Favor, Lesli J. & Massie, Elizabeth. Weighing In: Nutrition & Weight Management, 1 vol. 2010. (Food & You Ser.). (ENG.). 32p. (gr. 5-5). 31.21 *(978-0-7614-4367-4(3),* 8bcc9d94-97c1-4fc7-8954-1f45ff54c7a6) Cavendish Square Publishing LLC.
Feeding the Baby: Individual Title Six-Packs. (gr. -1-2). 23.00 *(978-0-7635-8790-1(7))* Rigby Education.
Feldman, Julie, creator. The No Diet Diet: Healthy Meals in 5 Minutes. 2003. (YA). spiral bd. 19.95 *(978-0-615-12437-7(2))* Creative Nutrition & Wellness.
Figtree, Dale. Eat Smarter: The Smarter Choice for Healthier Kids. 2006. (Illus.). 120p. (YA). (gr. 7-12). 19.95 *(978-0-8329-7001-6(8),* Z Health Bks.) New Win Publishing.
Fisher, Beverly. Mental Toughness for Weight Management: Workbook for Life. 2004. (Illus.). 60p. pap. 10.99 *(978-0-9745066-1-6(3))* Sports In Mind.
Food Friends: How to Make Friends Out of Food. 2016. (J). *(978-0-87659-713-2(4))* Gryphon Hse., Inc.
Fordham, Henrietta. Healthy Food for Young Children Inernet-Referenced. 2010. (Parent's Guides). 128p. (J). pap. 12.99 *(978-0-7945-1925-4(3),* Usborne) EDC Publishing.
Frederick, Shane, et al. Sports Training Zone. 2012. (Sports Training Zone Ser.). (ENG.). 48p. (J). (gr. 5-9). pap., pap., pap. 24.57 *(978-1-4296-8491-0(7),* 17771) Capstone.
Friddle-Ponder, Alma. Chile Pepper Unit Study Comprehensive Edition. 2007. (Illus.). 93p. spiral bd. 19.95 *(978-1-934627-00-6(3))* Fish Head Pubns., LLC.
—Chile Pepper Unit Study Graphic Edition. 2007. (Illus.). 63p. spiral bd. 14.95 *(978-1-934627-01-3(1))* Fish Head Pubns., LLC.
—Chile Pepper Unit Study Reading Enhanced Edition. 2007. (Illus.). 68p. spiral bd. 14.95 *(978-1-934627-02-0(X))* Fish Head Pubns., LLC.

M N O

Furgang, Kathy. Having Healthful Habits & Tener hábitos Sanos: 6 English, 6 Spanish Adaptations. 2011. (ENG & SPA.). (J). 97.00 net. *(978-1-4108-5710-1(7))* Benchmark Education Co.

Gardner, Robert, et al. Ace Your Exercise & Nutrition Science Project: Great Science Fair Ideas, 1 vol. 2009. (Ace Your Biology Science Project Ser.). (ENG., Illus.). 128p. (gr. 5-6). lib. bdg. 35.93 *(978-0-7660-3218-7(3),* 89019949-f036-4c97-8705-b72bdc5a442d) Enslow Publishing, LLC.

Gay, Kathlyn. Do You Know What to Eat?, 1 vol. 2015. (Got Issues? Ser.). (ENG., Illus.). 128p. (gr. 7-7). 38.93 *(978-0-7660-6987-9(7),* cf7df775-dba4-4875-9619-8c16ea63285f) Enslow Publishing, LLC.

—The Scoop on What to Eat: What You Should Know about Diet & Nutrition, 1 vol. 2009. (Issues in Focus Today Ser.). (ENG., Illus.). 112p. (gr. 6-7). lib. bdg. 35.93 *(978-0-7660-3066-4(0),* c3c70a93-39e6-460e-b8f4-070a4504a6e7) Enslow Publishing, LLC.

Giddens, Sandra. Making Smart Choices about Food, Nutrition, & Lifestyle. 2009. (Making Smart Choices Ser.). 48p. (gr. 5-5). 53.00 *(978-1-61514-339-9(4),* Rosen Reference) Rosen Publishing Group, Inc., The.

Giddens, Sandra & Giddens, Owen. Making Smart Choices about Food, Nutrition, & Lifestyle, 1 vol. 2008. (Making Smart Choices Ser.). (ENG., Illus.). 48p. (YA). (gr. 5-5). lib. bdg. 34.47 *(978-1-4042-1389-0(9),* 0256e2cb-afdb-4d45-9e25-95585751d1d4) Rosen Publishing Group, Inc., The.

Gilpin, Rebecca. 30 Healthy Things to Cook & Eat. 2010. (Children's Cooking Ser.). (ENG., Illus.). 30p. (J). (gr. 1). 9.99 *(978-0-7945-2396-1(X),* Usborne) EDC Publishing.

Gleisner, Jenna Lee. My Body Needs Food. 2014. (Healthy Me Ser.). (ENG., Illus.). 24p. (J). (gr. 1-4). lib. bdg. 27.10 *(978-1-60753-587-4(4),* 15962) Amicus.

Gogerly, Liz. Eating Well. Gordon, Mike, illus. 2008. (Looking after Me Ser.). (ENG.). 32p. (J). (gr. -1-3). pap. *(978-0-7787-4117-6(6))* Crabtree Publishing Co.

Goldsmith, Connie. Dietary Supplements: Harmless, Helpful, or Hurtful? 2015. (ENG., Illus.). 96p. (YA). (gr. 6-12). lib. bdg. 34.65 *(978-1-4677-3848-4(4),* 9cc05dfa-3dec-4b47-a991-3ccb99b402de, Twenty-First Century Bks.) Lerner Publishing Group.

Good Times with Good Foods Activity Books: Ages 2-6, 12 vols. 2005. (J). 9.95 *(978-1-57175-172-0(6),* 6505-C) Visualz.

Good Times with Good Foods Activity Books: Ages 7-11, 12 vols. 2005. (J). 9.95 *(978-1-57175-173-7(4),* 6506-C) Visualz.

Goodacre, Sonia, et al. Cambridge VCE Health & Human Development Units 3 & 4 Bundle. 2nd ed. 2013. (ENG.). *(978-1-107-68809-4(4))* Cambridge Univ. Pr.

Goodbody, Slim. Eating Right, 1 vol. 2007. (Slim Goodbody's Good Health Guides). (ENG., Illus.). 32p. (J). (gr. 3-5). lib. bdg. 28.67 *(978-0-8368-7740-3(3),* 06f952fa-ae2d-4c56-ac2e-0a5c8abb154c, Gareth Stevens Learning Library) Stevens, Gareth Publishing LLLP.

Goodbody, Slim & Burstein, John. Energy in, Energy Out: Food As Fuel. 2008. (Slim Goodbody's Lighten Up! Ser.). (ENG., Illus.). 32p. (J). (gr. 3-7). lib. bdg *(978-0-7787-3914-2(7))* Crabtree Publishing Co.

—Fast Food: Slowing Us All Down. 2008. (Slim Goodbody's Lighten Up! Ser.). (ENG., Illus.). 32p. (J). (gr. 3-7). pap. *(978-0-7787-3933-3(3));* lib. bdg. *(978-0-7787-3915-9(5))* Crabtree Publishing Co.

—Grocery Shopping: It's in the Bag. 2008. (Slim Goodbody's Lighten Up! Ser.). (ENG., Illus.). 32p. (J). (gr. 3-7). pap. *(978-0-7787-3934-0(1));* lib. bdg. *(978-0-7787-3916-6(3))* Crabtree Publishing Co.

—Looking at Labels: The Inside Story. 2008. (Slim Goodbody's Lighten Up! Ser.). (ENG., Illus.). 32p. (J). (gr. 3-7). pap. *(978-0-7787-3935-7(X));* lib. bdg. *(978-0-7787-3917-3(1))* Crabtree Publishing Co.

—The Shape of Good Nutrition: The Food Pyramid, 1 vol. 2008. (Slim Goodbody's Lighten Up! Ser.). (ENG., Illus.). 32p. (J). (gr. 3-7). pap. *(978-0-7787-3937-1(6));* lib. bdg. *(978-0-7787-3919-7(8))* Crabtree Publishing Co.

—Snack Attack: Unhealthy Treats. 2008. (Slim Goodbody's Lighten Up! Ser.). (ENG., Illus.). 32p. (J). (gr. 3-7). pap. *(978-0-7787-3936-4(8));* lib. bdg. *(978-0-7787-3918-0(X))* Crabtree Publishing Co.

Gordon, Sharon. You Are What You Eat. 2003. (Rookie Read-About Health Ser.). (ENG., Illus.). 32p. (J). (gr. k-2). pap. 5.95 *(978-0-516-26952-8(6),* Children's Pr.) Scholastic Library Publishing.

Graham, Gillian. The Rainbow Cookbook for Kids. 2011. 64p. pap. 26.49 *(978-1-4567-5209-5(X))* AuthorHouse.

Graimes, Nicola. Kids' Fun & Healthy Cookbook. Shooter, Howard, photos by. 2007. (ENG., Illus.). 128p. (J). (gr. 2-5). 18.99 *(978-0-7566-2916-8(0),* DK Children) Dorling Kindersley Publishing, Inc.

Greathouse, Lisa. Eat Healthy, 1 vol. 2011. (Science: Informational Text Ser.). (ENG., Illus.). 32p. (gr. 3-4). pap. 11.99 *(978-1-4333-3087-2(3))* Teacher Created Materials, Inc.

—Make It Healthy, 1 vol. 2011. (Science: Informational Text Ser.). (ENG.). 32p. (gr. 3-4). pap. 11.99 *(978-1-4333-3088-9(1))* Teacher Created Materials, Inc.

Green, Emily K. Fruits. 2006. (Blastoff! Readers Ser.). (ENG., Illus.). 24p. (J). (gr. k-3). lib. bdg. 24.95 *(978-1-60014-005-1(X),* Blastoff! Readers) Bellwether Media.

—Fruits. 2011. (Blastoff! Readers: New Food Guide Pyramid Ser.). (Illus.). 24p. (J). pap. 5.95 *(978-0-531-25850-7(5),* Children's Pr.) Scholastic Library Publishing.

—Grains. 2006. (Blastoff! Readers Ser.). (ENG., Illus.). 24p. (J). (gr. k-3). lib. bdg. 24.95 *(978-1-60014-003-7(3),* Blastoff! Readers) Bellwether Media.

—Grains. 2011. (Blastoff! Readers Ser.). (Illus.). 24p. (J). pap. 5.95 *(978-0-531-25851-4(3),* Children's Pr.) Scholastic Library Publishing.

—Healthy Eating. 2006. (Blastoff! Readers Ser.). (ENG., Illus.). 24p. (J). (gr. k-3). lib. bdg. 24.95 *(978-1-60014-007-5(6))* Bellwether Media.

—Meat & Beans. 2006. (Blastoff! Readers Ser.). (ENG., Illus.). 24p. (J). (gr. k-3). lib. bdg. 24.95 *(978-1-60014-004-4(1),* Blastoff! Readers) Bellwether Media.

—Meat & Beans. 2011. (Blastoff! Readers: New Food Guide Pyramid Ser.). (Illus.). 24p. (J). pap. 5.95 *(978-0-531-25854-5(8),* Children's Pr.) Scholastic Library Publishing.

—Milk, Yogurt, & Cheese. 2006. (Blastoff! Readers Ser.). (ENG., Illus.). 24p. (J). (gr. k-3). lib. bdg. 24.95 *(978-1-60014-000-6(9),* Blastoff! Readers) Bellwether Media.

—Milk, Yogurt, & Cheese. 2011. (Blastoff! Readers Ser.). (Illus.). 24p. (J). pap. 5.95 *(978-0-531-25855-2(6),* Children's Pr.) Scholastic Library Publishing.

—Oils. 2006. (Blastoff! Readers Ser.). (ENG., Illus.). 24p. (J). (gr. k-3). lib. bdg. 24.95 *(978-1-60014-001-3(7),* Blastoff! Readers) Bellwether Media.

—Oils. 2011. (Blastoff! Readers: New Food Guide Pyramid Ser.). (Illus.). 24p. (J). pap. 5.95 *(978-0-531-25856-9(4),* Children's Pr.) Scholastic Library Publishing.

—Vegetables. 2006. (Blastoff! Readers Ser.). (ENG., Illus.). 24p. (J). (gr. k-3). lib. bdg. 24.95 *(978-1-60014-002-0(5),* Blastoff! Readers) Bellwether Media.

—Vegetables. 2011. (Blastoff! Readers Ser.). (Illus.). 24p. (J). pap. 5.95 *(978-0-531-25857-6(2),* Children's Pr.) Scholastic Library Publishing.

Gregory, Helen. Healthy Eating, 1 vol. (Wonder Readers Next Steps: Science Ser.). (ENG.). (gr. -1-1). 2013. 20p. (J). lib. bdg. 25.32 *(978-1-4765-0036-2(3),* 121954) 2011. 16p. (J). pap. 6.25 *(978-1-4296-7828-5(3),* 118115) 2011. 16p. pap. 35.94 *(978-1-4296-8094-3(6))* Capstone. (Capstone Pr.).

Hamilton, Bethany. Body & Soul, 1 vol. 2014. (ENG.). 160p. (J). pap. 19.99 *(978-0-310-73105-4(4))* Zondervan.

Hardyman, Robyn. Eating Well, 1 vol. 2011. (Healthy & Happy Ser.). (ENG., Illus.). 32p. (J). (gr. 2-2). lib. bdg. 30.27 *(978-1-4488-5273-4(0),* fc689051-56bb-4a4a-a715-afed9ed68ae2) Rosen Publishing Group, Inc., The.

Harmon, Daniel E. What Are Calories?, 1 vol. 2018. (Let's Find Out! Good Health Ser.). (ENG.). 32p. (gr. 2-3). lib. bdg. 26.06 *(978-1-5383-0310-8(8),* 3df28c2b-d61b-4904-ba21-226f7df04d97, Britannica Educational Publishing) Rosen Publishing Group, Inc., The.

—What Are Carbohydrates?, 1 vol. 2018. (Let's Find Out! Good Health Ser.). (ENG., Illus.). 32p. (J). (gr. 2-3). 26.06 *(978-1-5383-0290-3(X),* 74b3a452-568c-49d9-a6d5-fd3665eba53f, Britannica Educational Publishing) Rosen Publishing Group, Inc., The.

—What Are Fats?, 1 vol. 2018. (Let's Find Out! Good Health Ser.). (ENG.). 32p. (gr. 2-3). 26.06 *(978-1-5383-0294-1(2),* 16652c32-e147-4700-b9f4-38d76a636cc8, Britannica Educational Publishing) Rosen Publishing Group, Inc., The.

Harris, Pj. Fat, Fat, What's Wrong with That? The Importance of Diet & Exercise. 2009. 36p. pap. 15.49 *(978-1-4490-2345-4(2))* AuthorHouse.

Hasler, Doris, et al. Nutrition & Wellness, Student Edition, 2 vols. 7th l.t. ed. 2003. (NUTRITION & WELLNESS Ser.). (ENG., Illus.). 576p. (gr. 5-8). stu. ed. 86.88 *(978-0-07-846332-7(7),* 0078463327) McGraw-Hill Education.

Hassan, Masood. Madeline & Friends: Fruits & Veggies vs Candy. Lady Josephine, illus. 2010. *(978-0-9812600-6-8(3))* Sapphira Pubns.

Hau, Stephanie. I Can Live To 100! Secrets Just for Kids. Hau, Joseph, illus. 2005. 60p. (J). per. 9.95 *(978-0-9767324-0-2(8),* Kids Can) Proactive Publishing.

Haugen, David M. & Musser, Susan, eds. Nutrition, 1 vol. 2011. (Opposing Viewpoints Ser.). (ENG., Illus.). 240p. (gr. 10-12). 50.43 *(978-0-7377-5751-4(5),* 07c7b114-9b6c-44e3-a671-536cd7c051c3); pap. 34.80 *(978-0-7377-5752-1(3),* b30ee04d-8b16-4faa-a472-6d962b0ce83d) Greenhaven Publishing LLC. (Greenhaven Publishing).

Having a Healthy Baby - Diet & Nutrition. 2004. (YA). pap. 4.00 net. *(978-1-930996-57-1(8))* Planned Parenthood Federation of America, Inc.

Hawley, Ella. Exploring Food & Nutrition, 1 vol. 2012. (Let's Explore Life Science Ser.). (ENG., Illus.). 24p. (J). (gr. 2-3). pap. 9.25 *(978-1-4488-6310-5(4),* 28354bd2-e8e1-4be5-ae52-b61f9cc72979); lib. bdg. 26.27 *(978-1-4488-6176-7(4),* 8c994979-2e24-42d8-ab4d-246f9379cfe9) Rosen Publishing Group, Inc., The. (PowerKids Pr.).

Head, Honor. Healthy Eating. 2013. (Let's Read & Talk about Ser.). (ENG., Illus.). 32p. (gr. 2-5). 28.50 *(978-1-59771-394-8(5))* Sea-To-Sea Pubns.

Health & Your Body. 2010. (Health & Your Body Ser.). (ENG.). 24p. (gr. k-1). lib. bdg. 109.28 *(978-1-4296-5926-0(2),* Capstone Pr.) Capstone.

Healthy Eating with Mypyramid [US Toy]. 2010. (Healthy Eating with Mypyramid Ser.). pap. 34.75 *(978-1-4296-5566-8(6),* Capstone Pr.) Capstone.

Heavenrich, Sue. Food As Fuel. 2018. (Human Machine Ser.). (ENG., Illus.). 32p. (gr. 3-6). lib. bdg. 32.79 *(978-1-64156-436-6(9),* 9781641564366) Rourke Educational Media.

Hendricks, Jamal. Dinner Is Delicious, 1 vol. 2018. (Let's Eat Healthy! Ser.). (ENG.). 24p. (gr. 1-1). 25.27 *(978-1-5081-6798-3(2),* f3640ec6-f069-473b-800f-89cd5b03630c); pap. 9.25 *(978-1-5081-6800-3(8),* 9e8caca9-7c9c-44db-8343-39be5216be42) Rosen Publishing Group, Inc., The. (PowerKids Pr.).

Hidalgo-Robert, Alberto. Fat No More: A Teenager's Victory over Obesity. 2012. (J). pap. 16.95 *(978-1-55885-745-2(1),* Piñata Books) Arte Publico Pr.

Hovius, Christopher. Fitness & Nutrition. McDonnell, Mary Ann & Forman, Sara, eds. 2013. (Young Adult's Guide to the Science of Health Ser.: 15). 128p. (J). (gr. 7-18). 24.95 *(978-1-4222-2809-8(6))* Mason Crest.

Hulme, Janet A. Bladder & Bowel Issues for Kids: A Handy Guide for Kids Ages 4-12. 2003. (Illus.). 92p. pap. 14.95 *(978-1-928812-05-0(8),* 4000-07) Phoenix Publishing.

Incredibly Disgusting Food, 8 vols., Set. Incl. Carbonated Beverages: The Incredibly Disgusting Story. Furgang, Adam. (YA). lib. bdg. 34.47 *(978-1-4488-1266-0(6),* c0fcce05-4248-4419-8bab-46623bd01854); Fake Foods: Fried, Fast, & Processed: The Incredibly Disgusting Story. Johanson, Paula. (YA). lib. bdg. 34.47 *(978-1-4488-1269-1(0),* 6a036b2b-966d-4ba3-9a69-561d26844963); Mystery Meat: Hot Dogs, Sausages, & Lunch Meats. Watson, Stephanie. (J). lib. bdg. 34.47 *(978-1-4488-1268-4(2),* e646c131-08ce-42a9-aa74-cef761287444); Salty & Sugary Snacks: The Incredibly Disgusting Story. Furgang, Adam. (YA). lib. bdg. 34.47 *(978-1-4488-1267-7(4),* d5bb4c7d-9142-436e-8f91-6cb697ad4aa8); (gr. 5-8). 2011. (Incredibly Disgusting Food Ser.). (ENG., Illus.). 48p. 2010. Set lib. bdg. 137.88 *(978-1-4488-1390-2(5),* eb80863f-13f3-4b51-9e7b-93175ab8a36b, Rosen Reference) Rosen Publishing Group, Inc., The.

Ingredients for a Healthy Life. 2014. (Ingredients for a Healthy Life Ser.). 24p. (J). (gr. 2-5). pap. 48.90 *(978-1-4824-1543-8(7))* Stevens, Gareth Publishing LLLP.

Innovative Kids Staff. In the Garden. Phillips, Jillian, illus. 2009. (ENG.). 20p. (J). (gr. -1-1). 8.99 *(978-1-58476-810-4(X))* Innovative Kids.

Johnson, Katherine. Nutrition Education for Kids: Health Science Series. 2013. 62p. pap. 24.99 *(978-1-4817-0099-3(5))* AuthorHouse.

Jones, Susan Smith & Warren, Dianne. Vegetable Soup - The Fruit Bowl. Lindman, Amy Sorvaag, illus. rev. ed. 2006. 64p. (J). (gr. -1-3). per. 14.95 *(978-0-9652736-0-2(1))* Oasis Pubns.

Jones, Tammy. I Am Active. 2009. (Sight Word Readers Set A Ser.). (J). *(978-1-60719-139-1(3))* Newmark Learning LLC.

Jukes, Mavis, et al. Be Healthy! It's a Girl Thing: Food, Fitness, & Feeling Great. Ziss, Debra, illus. 2003. (ENG.). 128p. (J). (gr. 3-7). pap. 12.99 *(978-0-679-89029-4(7),* Knopf Bks. for Young Readers) Random Hse. Children's Bks.

Kalman, Bobbie. I Eat a Rainbow. 2010. (ENG., Illus.). 16p. (J). (gr. k-2). *(978-0-7787-9412-7(1));* pap. *(978-0-7787-9456-1(3))* Crabtree Publishing Co.

—I Eat a Rainbow: Me Como un Arco Iris. 2010. (SPA, ENG & MUL.). 16p. (J). pap. *(978-0-7787-8263-6(8));* lib. bdg. *(978-0-7787-8270-4(0))* Crabtree Publishing Co.

—Me Como un Arco Iris. 2010. (SPA.). 16p. (J). pap. *(978-0-7787-8578-1(5));* lib. bdg. *(978-0-7787-8552-1(1))* Crabtree Publishing Co.

Kalz, Jill. Fruits. 2003. 24p. (J). lib. bdg. 21.35 *(978-1-58340-299-3(3))* Black Rabbit Bks.

—Grains. 2003. 24p. (J). lib. bdg. 21.35 *(978-1-58340-301-3(9))* Black Rabbit Bks.

—Meats & Protein. 2003. 24p. (J). lib. bdg. 21.35 *(978-1-58340-298-6(5))* Black Rabbit Bks.

—Vegetables. 2003. 24p. (J). lib. bdg. 21.35 *(978-1-58340-300-6(0))* Black Rabbit Bks.

Kelly, Sheila M. & Rotner, Shelley. Yummy! Good Food Makes Me Strong! 2018. (ENG.). 32p. (J). (gr. -1-k). 7.99 *(978-0-8234-3996-6(8))* Holiday Hse., Inc.

Kesselman, Robin & Kesselman, Marc. Nerdel's ABC Book. Martinez, Natali, illus. 2009. 38p. (J). 16.99 *(978-0-9823357-2-7(5))* Nerdel Co., The.

Kids Mypyramid Tablet. 2005. (J). pap. 9.95 *(978-1-57175-091-4(6),* 4275-T) Visualz.

Kingston, Anna. What Are Proteins?, 1 vol. 2018. (Let's Find Out! Good Health Ser.). (ENG., Illus.). 32p. (J). (gr. 2-3). 26.06 *(978-1-5383-0298-9(5),* b796bebe-7ca0-4be9-9d22-88167c21fb7e) Rosen Publishing Group, Inc., The.

Knighton, Kate. Why Shouldn't I Eat Junk Food? Larkum, Adam, illus. 2008. (Usborne Ser.). 48p. (J). (gr. 4-7). pap. 6.99 *(978-0-7945-1953-7(9),* Usborne) EDC Publishing.

Koellhoffer, Tara, ed. Food & Nutrition. 2006. (Science News for Kids Ser.). (Illus.). 128p. (gr. 4-6). lib. bdg. 30.00 *(978-0-7910-9121-0(X),* Chelsea Clubhse.) Infobase Holdings, Inc.

Landau, Elaine. Watts Library: a Healthy Diet. 2003. (Watts Library). (ENG., Illus.). 64p. (J). 25.50 *(978-0-531-12027-9(9),* Watts, Franklin) Scholastic Library Publishing.

Lawler, Jean C. Experience Nutrition: How the Food You Eat Makes You Feel. 2018. (Experience Personal Power Ser.). (ENG., Illus.). 24p. (J). (gr. 2-4). pap. 6.99 *(978-1-63440-378-8(9),* 09b077ca-214c-468e-9d2c-5d2ab8ff42b3) Red Chair Pr.

Lee, Sally. Healthy Snacks, Healthy You! [Scholastic]. Swift, Gary, illus. 2013. (First Graphics: Myplate & Healthy Eating Ser.). (ENG.). 24p. (gr. 1-2). pap. 0.50 *(978-1-4765-3129-8(3))* Capstone.

Lin, Grace. Our Food. 2019. (ENG.). 40p. (J). (gr. k-1). 18.96 *(978-1-64310-947-3(2))* Penworthy Co., LLC, The.

Lin, Grace & McKneally, Ranida T. Our Food: A Healthy Serving of Science & Poems. Zong, Grace, illus. 2018. 40p. (J). (gr. k-3). pap. 7.99 *(978-1-58089-591-0(3))* Charlesbridge Publishing, Inc.

Llewellyn, Claire. Your Food. 2008. (Look after Yourself Ser.). (Illus.). 30p. (J). (gr. 1-4). lib. bdg. 28.50 *(978-1-59771-098-5(9))* Sea-To-Sea Pubns.

Love. Why Do I Take Vitamins? a Book for Children with Autism. 2010. 20p. pap. 9.99 *(978-1-60911-169-4(9),* Eloquent Bks.) Strategic Book Publishing & Rights Agency (SBPRA).

Maile, Ruby. Why Should I Eat Fruit? 2012. (Level A Ser.). (ENG., Illus.). 16p. (J). (gr. k-2). pap. 7.95 *(978-1-927136-03-4(2),* 19467) RiverStream Publishing.

Manolis, Kay. Blastoff! Readers - Body Systems, 6 vols., Set. Incl. Circulatory System. 20.00 *(978-0-531-21701-6(9));* Digestive System. 20.00 *(978-0-531-21702-3(7));* Muscular System. 20.00 *(978-0-531-21703-0(5));* Nervous System. 20.00 *(978-0-531-21704-7(3));* Respiratory System. 20.00 *(978-0-531-21705-4(1));* Skeletal System. 20.00 *(978-0-531-21706-1(X));* (Illus.). 24p. (J). (gr. k-3). 2009. 2009. Set lib. bdg. 120.00 *(978-0-531-27900-7(6),* Children's Pr.) Scholastic Library Publishing.

Mansbach, Adam. Seriously, You Have to Eat: Fixed Layout Edition. Brozman, Owen, illus. 2015. 32p. (J). 15.95 *(978-1-61775-408-1(0))* Akashic Bks.

Marsico, Katie. Eat a Balanced Diet! 2015. (21st Century Junior Library: Your Healthy Body Ser.). (ENG., Illus.). 24p. (gr. 2-5). 29.21 *(978-1-63188-983-7(4),* 205844) Cherry Lake Publishing.

—Eat Healthy Foods! Bane, Jeff, illus. 2019. (My Early Library: My Healthy Habits Ser.). (ENG.). 24p. (J). (gr. k-1). pap. 12.79 *(978-1-5341-3934-3(6),* 212565); lib. bdg. 30.64 *(978-1-5341-4278-7(9),* 212564) Cherry Lake Publishing.

—Your Healthy Plate: Dairy. 2012. (21st Century Basic Skills Library: Your Healthy Plate Ser.). (ENG.). 24p. (gr. k-3). pap. 12.79 *(978-1-61080-398-4(1),* 201333); (Illus.). lib. bdg. 26.35 *(978-1-61080-350-2(7),* 201288) Cherry Lake Publishing.

—Your Healthy Plate: Fruits. 2012. (21st Century Basic Skills Library: Your Healthy Plate Ser.). (ENG., Illus.). 24p. (J). (gr. k-3). pap. 12.79 *(978-1-61080-400-4(7),* 201335) Cherry Lake Publishing.

—Your Healthy Plate: Grains. 2012. (21st Century Basic Skills Library: Your Healthy Plate Ser.). (ENG.). 24p. (gr. k-3). (J). pap. 12.79 *(978-1-61080-401-1(5),* 201336); (Illus.). lib. bdg. 26.35 *(978-1-61080-348-9(5),* 201294) Cherry Lake Publishing.

—Your Healthy Plate: Oils & Fats. 2012. (21st Century Basic Skills Library: Your Healthy Plate Ser.). (ENG., Illus.). 24p. (gr. k-3). (J). pap. 12.79 *(978-1-61080-402-8(3),* 201337); lib. bdg. 26.35 *(978-1-61080-351-9(5),* 201296) Cherry Lake Publishing.

—Your Healthy Plate: Protein. 2012. (21st Century Basic Skills Library: Your Healthy Plate Ser.). (ENG., Illus.). 24p. (gr. k-3). (J). pap. 12.79 *(978-1-61080-403-5(1),* 201338); lib. bdg. 26.35 *(978-1-61080-349-6(3),* 201298) Cherry Lake Publishing.

—Your Healthy Plate: Vegetables. 2012. (21st Century Basic Skills Library: Your Healthy Plate Ser.). (ENG.). 24p. (gr. k-3). pap. 12.79 *(978-1-61080-399-1(X),* 201334); (Illus.). lib. bdg. 26.35 *(978-1-61080-347-2(7),* 201290) Cherry Lake Publishing.

Mason Crest Publishers Staff, contrib. by. Malnutrition. 2019. (Illus.). 80p. (J). *(978-1-4222-4217-9(X))* Mason Crest.

Mayo Clinic. The Mayo Clinic Kids' Cookbook: 50 Favorite Recipes for Fun & Healthy Eating. 2012. (ENG., Illus.). 128p. (J). (gr. -1-7). spiral bd. 19.95 *(978-1-56148-751-6(1),* Da Capo Lifelong) Hachette Bks.

Mayo Clinic Staff, contrib. by. Eating Out: Your Pocket Guide to Healthy Dining. 2004. (Mayo Clinic on Health Ser.). (Illus.). 36,52p. (YA). (gr. 8-18). lib. bdg. 15.95 *(978-1-59084-249-2(9))* Mason Crest.

—Healthy Meals for Hurried Lives. 2004. (Mayo Clinic on Health Ser.). (Illus.). 36,52p. (YA). (gr. 8-18). lib. bdg. 15.95 *(978-1-59084-252-2(9))* Mason Crest.

McCarthy, Rose. Food Labels: Using Nutrition Information to Create a Healthy Diet, 1 vol. (Library of Nutrition Ser.). (ENG., Illus.). 48p. (gr. 5-8). 2008. (YA). lib. bdg. 34.47 *(978-1-4042-1869-7(6),* dd5f7b2c-f711-414b-8554-0a37d5587fe6, Rosen Reference) 2007. per. 12.75 *(978-1-4042-1633-4(2),* 6065dce0-ce72-4aa5-807a-b4b349226751) Rosen Publishing Group, Inc., The.

—Food Labels: Using Nutritional Information to Create a Healthy Diet. 2004. (Library of Nutrition). (Illus.). 48p. (J). lib. bdg. 26.50 *(978-1-4042-0300-6(1))* Rosen Publishing Group, Inc., The.

Meiners, Cheri J. Grow Strong! A Book about Healthy Habits. Allen, Elizabeth, illus. 2016. (Being the Best Me(r) Ser.). (ENG.). 40p. (J). (gr. -1-2). pap. 11.99 *(978-1-63198-085-5(8))* Free Spirit Publishing Inc.

Miller, Edward. The Monster Health Book: A Guide to Eating Healthy, Being Active & Feeling Great for Monsters & Kids! 2008. (ENG., Illus.). 40p. (J). (gr. 1-4). 8.99 *(978-0-8234-2139-8(2))* Holiday Hse., Inc.

Minden, Cecilia. Cooking by the Numbers. 2007. (21st Century Skills Library: Real World Math Ser.). (ENG., Illus.). 32p. (gr. 4-8). lib. bdg. 32.07 *(978-1-60279-007-0(8),* 200061) Cherry Lake Publishing.

Mooney, Carla. Healthy Weight for Teens, 1 vol. 2013. (Nutrition & Health Ser.). (ENG., Illus.). 104p. (gr. 7-10). lib. bdg. 37.33 *(978-1-4205-1021-8(5),* 7855ef43-1ee0-49c2-9b85-f577a6b2468c, Lucent Pr.) Greenhaven Publishing LLC.

MyPyramid for Kids Tablet. 2005. (J). pap. 9.95 *(978-1-57175-179-9(3),* 4281-T) Visualz.

Nardo, Don. Vegan Diets, 1 vol. 2014. (Nutrition & Health Ser.). (ENG., Illus.). 104p. (gr. 7-10). lib. bdg. 37.33 *(978-1-4205-1151-2(3),* 147be79d-d719-41fc-9652-4f75938f99e9, Lucent Pr.) Greenhaven Publishing LLC.

Needham, Kate. Why Do People Eat? Spenceley, Annabel & Chen, Kuo Kang, illus. rev. ed. 2007. (Starting Point Science Ser.). 24p. (J). (gr. 1-4). pap. 4.99 *(978-0-7945-1623-9(8),* Usborne) EDC Publishing.

Nelson, Robin. Dairy. 2003. (First Step Nonfiction - Food Groups Ser.). (ENG., Illus.). 24p. (gr. k-2). lib. bdg. 23.93 *(978-0-8225-4632-0(9))* Lerner Publishing Group.

—Fruits. 2003. (First Step Nonfiction Ser.). (Illus.). 24p. (J). (gr. k-2). lib. bdg. 18.60 *(978-0-8225-4624-5(8))* Lerner Publishing Group.

—Grains. 2003. (First Step Nonfiction — Food Groups Ser.). (ENG., Illus.). 24p. (J). (gr. k-2). lib. bdg. 23.99 *(978-0-8225-4628-3(0),* 0d0eabab-2f7f-4854-89ab-6c7316bf6b0d, Lerner Pubns.) Lerner Publishing Group.

—Vegetables. 2003. (First Step Nonfiction - Food Groups Ser.). (ENG., Illus.). 24p. (gr. k-2). lib. bdg. 23.93 *(978-0-8225-4626-9(4))* Lerner Publishing Group.

The Nutraceutical Reference Guide. 2005. (YA). per. 14.95 *(978-1-59872-184-3(4))* Instant Pub.

O'Donnell, Sallie. Animals, Vegetables & Minerals from A to Z. Plumley, Alea, illus. l.t. ed. 2005. 60p. pap. 9.95 *(978-0-9764982-5-4(1))* Legacy Publishing Services, Inc.

Olmstead, Lucinda. But Not on My Ice Cream, Please. 2008. (Illus.). 20p. pap. 13.99 *(978-1-4389-0917-2(9))* AuthorHouse.

Olson, Gillia M. MyPlate & You, 1 vol. 2011. (Health & Your Body Ser.). (ENG.). 24p. (J). (gr. -1-2). pap. 7.29 *(978-1-4296-7129-3(7),* 116777); (gr. k-1). pap. 43.74 *(978-1-4296-7135-4(1),* 16708) Capstone. (Capstone Pr.).

Oramasionwu, Angela. Sammy the Cell & the Healthy 1s: Let's Learn about Nutrition. 2004. 33p. pap. 24.95 *(978-1-4137-3449-2(9))* PublishAmerica, Inc.

Orme, Helen. Healthy Eating. 2010. (Science Everywhere! Ser.). 24p. 24.25 *(978-1-84898-289-5(5))* Black Rabbit Bks.

Orr, Tamra. Growing Nutritious Food. 2018. (J). *(978-1-5105-3714-9(7))* SmartBook Media, Inc.

Orr, Tamra B. Growing Nutritious Food. 2015. (Explorer Library: Science Explorer Ser.). (ENG., Illus.). 32p. (J). (gr. 4-8). 32.07 *(978-1-63362-392-7(0),* 206988) Cherry Lake Publishing.

Pappas, Diane H. & Covey, Richard D. I'm a Healthy Eater. Estrada, Ric, illus. 2007. (J). *(978-0-545-01424-3(7))* Scholastic, Inc.

—My Healthy Food Pyramid. Estrada, Ric, illus. 2007. (J). pap. *(978-0-545-01429-8(8))* Scholastic, Inc.

Paris, Stephanie. Straight Talk: The Truth about Food, 1 vol. 2nd rev. ed. 2013. (TIME for KIDS(r): Informational Text Ser.). (ENG., Illus.). 48p. (J). (gr. 4-5). lib. bdg. 29.96 *(978-1-4807-1109-9(8))* Teacher Created Materials, Inc.

—Straight Talk - The Truth about Food , 1 vol. 2nd rev. ed. 2012. (TIME for KIDS(r): Informational Text Ser.). (ENG.). 48p. (gr. 4-5). pap. 13.99 *(978-1-4333-4857-0(8))* Teacher Created Materials, Inc.

Parker, Chance. Nutrition & Science. 2014. (ENG., Illus.). 112p. 42.79 *(978-1-62524-072-9(4),* Village Earth Pr.) Harding Hse. Publishing Sebice Inc.

Parsons, William B., Jr. Tough Talk about Fat! How to Reach & Maintain Your Ideal Weight. 2003. 134p. per. 12.95 *(978-0-9662568-9-5(1))* Lilac Pr.

Perritano, John. Fats & Cholesterol. 2017. 64p. (J). *(978-1-4222-3734-2(6))* Mason Crest.

—Sugar & Sweeteners. 2017. (Illus.). 64p. (J). *(978-1-4222-3744-1(3))* Mason Crest.

Peters, Celeste A. Food. 2009. (Science Q & A Ser.). (Illus.). 48p. (YA). (gr. 5-8). pap. 10.95 *(978-1-60596-075-3(6));* lib. bdg. 29.05 *(978-1-60596-074-6(8))* Weigl Pubs., Inc.

—Food Q & A. 2014. (Science Discovery Ser.). (ENG., Illus.). 48p. (J). (gr. 5-8). pap. 13.95 *(978-1-4896-0689-1(0),* AV2 by Weigl) Weigl Pubs., Inc.

Petrie, Kristin. The Food Pyramid. 2004. (Nutrition Ser.). (Illus.). 32p. (J). (gr. k-6). lib. bdg. 22.78 *(978-1-59197-403-1(8))* ABDO Publishing Co.

Priest, Bonnie. Nancy & the Nutrition Tree. 2008. 28p. pap. 12.95 *(978-1-934925-86-7(1),* Strategic Bk. Publishing) Strategic Book Publishing & Rights Agency (SBPRA).

Que Debo Comer Hoy? 2005. (SPA.). (J). 10.99 *(978-0-9770756-1-4(3))* Family Nutrition Ctr. P.C.

Quinlan, Julia J. & Furgang, Adam. The Truth Behind Soft Drinks, 1 vol. 2017. (From Factory to Table: What You're Really Eating Ser.). (ENG., Illus.). 48p. (J). (gr. 6-6). 33.47 *(978-1-4777-8992-6(8),* 234540d0-4a36-44cd-ac23-bc79c0bac841) Rosen Publishing Group, Inc., The.

Randall, Ronne & Orme, Helen. Healthy Eating: The Best Start in Science. 2013. (Little Science Stars Ser.). (ENG.). 24p. (J). (gr. k-3). 18.69 *(978-1-84696-193-9(9),* TickTock Books) Octopus Publishing Group GBR. Dist: Children's Plus, Inc.

Rau, Dana Meachen. Going Vegetarian: A Healthy Guide to Making the Switch, 1 vol. 2012. (Food Revolution Ser.). (ENG., Illus.). 64p. (J). (gr. 6-9). 35.32 *(978-0-7565-4522-2(6),* 117115); pap. 9.10 *(978-0-7565-4530-7(7),* 118363) Capstone. (Compass Point Bks.).

—Sports Nutrition for Teen Athletes: Eat Right to Take Your Game to the Next Level. 2012. (Sports Training Zone Ser.). (ENG.). 48p. (gr. 4-5). pap. 47.70 *(978-1-4296-8488-0(7))* Capstone.

Rau, Dana Meachen, et al. Sports Training Zone. 2012. (Sports Training Zone Ser.). (ENG.). 48p. (gr. 4-5). pap. 190.80 *(978-1-4296-8492-7(5))* Capstone.

Reese, Brandon. Draw Me Healthy! Reese, Brandon, illus. 2012. (Illus.). 32p. (J). 7.99 *(978-0-8280-2680-2(7))* Review & Herald Publishing Assn.

Reinke, Beth Bence. Healthy Eating Habits. 2018. (Bumba Books (r) — Nutrition Matters Ser.). (ENG., Illus.). 24p. (J). (gr. -1-1). 26.65 *(978-1-5415-0342-7(2),* ab8d0c99-a37a-40c7-b47f-b0e0814b403e, Lerner Pubns.) Lerner Publishing Group.

—Healthy Foods Around the World. 2018. (Bumba Books (r) — Nutrition Matters Ser.). (ENG., Illus.). 24p. (J). (gr. -1-1). 26.65 *(978-1-5415-0341-0(4),* 643aefaa-475c-4480-b212-f27bcb695133, Lerner Pubns.) Lerner Publishing Group.

—Why We Eat Dairy. 2018. (Bumba Books (r) — Nutrition Matters Ser.). (ENG., Illus.). 24p. (J). (gr. -1-1). 26.65 *(978-1-5415-0337-3(6),* 0c5c46d5-8c77-4399-94c8-dd5e3c78be4a, Lerner Pubns.) Lerner Publishing Group.

—Why We Eat Fruits. 2018. (Bumba Books (r) — Nutrition Matters Ser.). (ENG., Illus.). 24p. (J). (gr. -1-1). 26.65 *(978-1-5415-0335-9(X),* 78b31136-e1f3-4e13-b624-5036d16b3632, Lerner Pubns.) Lerner Publishing Group.

—Why We Eat Grains. 2018. (Bumba Books (r) — Nutrition Matters Ser.). (ENG., Illus.). 24p. (J). (gr. -1-1). pap. 8.99 *(978-1-5415-2684-6(8),* 7b86b80d-ae48-444e-aa05-5b28ea2a64d5); lib. bdg. 26.65 *(978-1-5415-0338-0(4),* 175fa0ef-a454-424b-838b-4ab0c9727ac9, Lerner Pubns.) Lerner Publishing Group.

—Why We Eat Protein. 2018. (Bumba Books (r) — Nutrition Matters Ser.). (ENG., Illus.). 24p. (J). (gr. -1-1). 26.65 *(978-1-5415-0339-7(2),* e9f3de4d-1cb7-46f2-980e-03da6e193fe1, Lerner Pubns.) Lerner Publishing Group.

Rice, Dona Herweck. Comer Bien. 2nd rev. ed. 2012. (TIME for KIDS(r): Informational Text Ser.). (SPA.). 20p. (gr. 1-2). 8.99 *(978-1-4333-4430-5(0))* Teacher Created Materials, Inc.

—Delicious & Nutritious. 2011. (Early Literacy Ser.). (ENG.). 16p. (gr. k-1). 19.99 *(978-1-4333-2370-6(2));* 6.99 *(978-1-4333-2369-0(9))* Teacher Created Materials, Inc.

—Eating Right, 1 vol. 2nd rev. ed. 2014. (TIME for KIDS(r): Informational Text Ser.). (ENG., Illus.). 20p. (J). (gr. 1-2). lib. bdg. 19.96 *(978-1-4807-1030-6(X))* Teacher Created Materials, Inc.

Rice, Dona Herwick. Eating Right, 1 vol. 2nd rev. ed. 2011. (TIME for KIDS(r): Informational Text Ser.). (ENG.). 20p. (gr. 1-2). 8.99 *(978-1-4333-3597-6(2))* Teacher Created Materials, Inc.

Ritchie, Scot. See What We Eat! A First Book of Healthy Eating. Ritchie, Scot, illus. 2017. (ENG., Illus.). 32p. (J). (gr. -1-2). 16.99 *(978-1-77138-618-0(5))* Kids Can Pr., Ltd. CAN. Dist: Hachette Bk. Group.

Rizzo, Nicholas. Championship Nutrition & Performance: The Wrestler's Guide to Lifestyle, Diet & Healthy Weight Control. rev. ed. 2004. (Illus.). 114p. 15.95 *(978-0-9748220-1-3(9),* Executive Performances Publishing) Nicholas Rizzo.

Rondeau, Amanda. Food Pyramid, 1 vol. Marx, Monica, ed. 2003. (What Should I Eat? Ser.). (Illus.). 24p. (J). (gr. k-3). lib. bdg. 24.21 *(978-1-57765-832-0(9),* SandCastle) ABDO Publishing Co.

—Grains Are Good, 1 vol. 2003. (What Should I Eat? Ser.). (Illus.). 24p. (J). (gr. k-3). lib. bdg. 24.21 *(978-1-57765-833-7(7),* SandCastle) ABDO Publishing Co.

—Milk Is Magnificent, 1 vol. 2003. (What Should I Eat? Ser.). (Illus.). 24p. (J). (gr. k-3). lib. bdg. 24.21 *(978-1-57765-837-5(X),* SandCastle) ABDO Publishing Co.

—Proteins Are Powerful, 1 vol. 2003. (What Should I Eat? Ser.). (Illus.). 24p. (J). (gr. k-3). lib. bdg. 24.21 *(978-1-57765-836-8(1),* SandCastle) ABDO Publishing Co.

—Vegetables Are Vital, 1 vol. 2003. (What Should I Eat? Ser.). (Illus.). 24p. (J). (gr. k-3). lib. bdg. 24.21 *(978-1-57765-835-1(3),* SandCastle) ABDO Publishing Co.

Rose, Elizabeth. Food & Nutrition. (Life Science Library). 24p. (gr. 3-4). 2009. 42.50 *(978-1-60854-001-3(4))* 2005. (ENG., Illus.). (J). pap. 9.25 *(978-1-4358-3264-0(7),* 7d146c1b-172b-400a-a4c2-cb8ec37562c0) 2005. (ENG., Illus.). (J). lib. bdg. 26.27 *(978-1-4042-2821-4(7),* 9eada094-7f76-4249-9901-dc64aed47c9c) Rosen Publishing Group, Inc., The. (PowerKids Pr.).

Rothenberg, Annye. I Like to Eat Treats. Wenzel, David T., illus. 2010. 48p. (J). pap. 9.95 *(978-0-9790420-2-7(X))* Perfecting Parenting Pr.

Royston, Angela. Diet, 1 vol. 2010. (Being Healthy, Feeling Great Ser.). (ENG.). 32p. (gr. 3-4). (J). pap. 11.60 *(978-1-61532-372-2(4),* 2b630cbc-a0ec-4914-9bc6-969bfb7539b0, PowerKids Pr.); (YA). lib. bdg. 30.27 *(978-1-61532-367-8(8),* 9dd5fd5d-3d04-4598-8e91-dba20f6bc8de) Rosen Publishing Group, Inc., The.

—Why We Need Proteins. 2011. (Science of Nutrition Ser.: No. 4). (ENG., Illus.). 48p. (J). (gr. 5-8). pap. *(978-0-7787-1696-9(1))* Crabtree Publishing Co.

—Why We Need Water & Fiber, 1 vol. 2011. (Science of Nutrition Ser.: No. 6). (ENG., Illus.). 48p. (J). (gr. 5-8). pap. *(978-0-7787-1698-3(8))* Crabtree Publishing Co.

Rustad, Martha E. H. I Eat Well. 2017. (Healthy Me Ser.). (ENG., Illus.). 24p. (J). (gr. -1-2). lib. bdg. 22.65 *(978-1-5157-3983-8(X),* 133882, Pebble) Capstone.

Samson, Tess. Snack Time. 2010. (Sight Word Readers Ser.). (J). 3.49 *(978-1-60719-618-1(2))* Newmark Learning LLC.

Sayer, Melissa & Naik, Anita. Too Fat? Too Thin? The Healthy Eating Handbook. 2009. (Really Useful Handbooks Ser.). (ENG., Illus.). 48p. (J). (gr. 5-11). pap. *(978-0-7787-4405-4(1));* lib. bdg. *(978-0-7787-4392-7(6))* Crabtree Publishing Co.

Scherer, Lauri S., ed. Artificial Ingredients, 1 vol. 2013. (Issues That Concern You Ser.). (ENG., Illus.). 120p. (gr. 7-10). lib. bdg. 43.63 *(978-0-7377-6284-6(5),* 8514c080-849f-4e5d-b7f0-ac6edac7f68c, Greenhaven Publishing) Greenhaven Publishing LLC.

Schrier, Allyson Valentine. Eat Right: Your Guide to Maintaining a Healthy Diet, 1 vol. 2011. (Healthy Me Ser.). (ENG.). 32p. (J). (gr. 3-9). lib. bdg. 28.65 *(978-1-4296-6544-5(0),* 115647) Capstone.

Schuh, Mari. Dairy on Myplate, 1 vol. 2012. (What's on Myplate? Ser.). (ENG., Illus.). 24p. (J). (gr. -1-2). pap. 7.29 *(978-1-4296-9410-0(6),* 120401); lib. bdg. 27.32 *(978-1-4296-8744-7(4),* 119543) Capstone. (Capstone Pr.).

—Healthy Snacks on Myplate. 2012. (What's on Myplate? Ser.). (ENG.). 24p. (J). (gr. k-1). pap. 43.74 *(978-1-4296-9419-3(X),* 18614); (Illus.). (gr. -1-2). pap. 7.29 *(978-1-4296-9418-6(1),* 120404) Capstone. (Capstone Pr.).

—Protein on Myplate. 2012. (What's on Myplate? Ser.). (ENG.). 24p. (J). (gr. k-1). pap. 43.74 *(978-1-4296-9421-6(1),* 18615); (Illus.). (gr. -1-2). pap. 7.29 *(978-1-4296-9420-9(3),* 120405) Capstone. (Capstone Pr.).

—Snacks for Healthy Teeth, 1 vol. 2008. (Healthy Teeth Ser.). (ENG., Illus.). 24p. (J). (gr. -1-2). pap. 7.29 *(978-1-4296-1765-7(3),* 94832, Capstone Pr.) Capstone.

—Sugars & Fats. 2012. (What's on Myplate? Ser.). (ENG.). 24p. (J). (gr. k-1). pap. 43.74 *(978-1-4296-9423-0(8),* 18616); (Illus.). (gr. -1-2). pap. 7.29 *(978-1-4296-9422-3(X),* 120406); (Illus.). (gr. -1-2). lib. bdg. 27.32 *(978-1-4296-8746-1(0),* 119546) Capstone. (Capstone Pr.).

—Vegetables on Myplate. 2012. (What's on Myplate? Ser.). (ENG.). 24p. (J). (gr. k-1). pap. 43.74 *(978-1-4296-9425-4(4),* 18617); (Illus.). (gr. -1-2). pap. 7.29 *(978-1-4296-9424-7(6),* 120407) Capstone. (Capstone Pr.).

—What's on Myplate? 2012. (What's on Myplate? Ser.). (ENG.). 24p. (J). (gr. -1-2). pap., pap., pap. 58.32 *(978-1-4296-9426-1(2),* 18618, Capstone Pr.) Capstone.

—What's on Myplate? Classroom Collection. 2012. (What's on Myplate? Ser.). (ENG.). 24p. (J). (gr. k-1). pap., pap., pap. 333.60 *(978-1-4296-9427-8(0),* 18620, Capstone Pr.) Capstone.

Science stories foss spanish food & nutrition ea Cr05. 2005. (J). *(978-1-59242-596-9(8))* Delta Education, LLC.

Scott, Celicia. My Daily Diet: Proteins. Prock, Lisa Albers, ed. 2014. (On My Plate Ser.: 6). 48p. (J). (gr. 5-18). 20.95 *(978-1-4222-3099-2(6))* Mason Crest.

—My Daily Diet: Vegetables. Prock, Lisa Albers, ed. 2014. (On My Plate Ser.: 6). 48p. (J). (gr. 5-18). 20.95 *(978-1-4222-3100-5(3))* Mason Crest.

Seaborn, Ron. The Children's Health Food Book. rev. ed. 2006. 40p. 16.95 *(978-0-9647089-2-1(2))* Life Line, Inc.

Senker, Cath. Healthy Eating, 1 vol. 2007. (Healthy Choices Ser.). (ENG., Illus.). 24p. (J). (gr. 1-2). lib. bdg. 26.27 *(978-1-4042-4303-3(8),* 0b928006-ad59-485e-b276-56323f62cd19, PowerKids Pr.) Rosen Publishing Group, Inc., The.

Sertori, Trisha. Body Fuel for Healthy Bodies, 12 vols., Set. Incl. Dairy Foods. lib. bdg. 21.27 *(978-0-7614-3797-0(5),* 1e63ab58-2941-467f-ad8d-5623406c7ab7); Fats & Oils. lib. bdg. 21.27 *(978-0-7614-3798-7(3),* 93bae1c8-72c0-4460-9697-1375cfd3c563); Fruits, Vegetables, & Legumes. lib. bdg. 21.27 *(978-0-7614-3799-4(1),* a4f68649-4180-456d-afc7-6e24625cd1e6); Grains, Bread, Cereal, & Pasta. lib. bdg. 21.27 *(978-0-7614-3800-7(9),* 9c91b622-6806-4aa7-b7c6-9f7c70a368ef); Meats, Fish, Eggs, Nuts, & Beans. lib. bdg. 21.27 *(978-0-7614-3801-4(7),* 8a778b33-a803-4692-9ae6-57a54fecf046); Vitamins & Minerals. lib. bdg. 21.27 *(978-0-7614-3802-1(5),* 81531297-13ee-4209-8dd5-6c30be8089c2); 32p. (gr. 4-4). (Body Fuel for Healthy Bodies Ser.). (ENG.). 2009. Set lib. bdg. 127.62 *(978-0-7614-3796-3(7),* 8a16698d-6963-4bac-be52-5f6f892517e1, Cavendish Square) Cavendish Square Publishing LLC.

—Dairy Foods, 1 vol. 2009. (Body Fuel for Healthy Bodies Ser.). (ENG.). 32p. (gr. 4-4). lib. bdg. 21.27 *(978-0-7614-3797-0(5),* 1e63ab58-2941-467f-ad8d-5623406c7ab7) Cavendish Square Publishing LLC.

—Fats & Oils, 1 vol. 2009. (Body Fuel for Healthy Bodies Ser.). (ENG.). 32p. (gr. 4-4). lib. bdg. 21.27 *(978-0-7614-3798-7(3),* 93bae1c8-72c0-4460-9697-1375cfd3c563) Cavendish Square Publishing LLC.

—Fruits, Vegetables, & Legumes, 1 vol. 2009. (Body Fuel for Healthy Bodies Ser.). (ENG.). 32p. (gr. 4-4). lib. bdg. 21.27 *(978-0-7614-3799-4(1),* a4f68649-4180-456d-afc7-6e24625cd1e6) Cavendish Square Publishing LLC.

—Grains, Bread, Cereal, & Pasta, 1 vol. 2009. (Body Fuel for Healthy Bodies Ser.). (ENG.). 32p. (gr. 4-4). lib. bdg. 21.27 *(978-0-7614-3800-7(9),* 9c91b622-6806-4aa7-b7c6-9f7c70a368ef) Cavendish Square Publishing LLC.

—Meats, Fish, Eggs, Nuts, & Beans, 1 vol. 2009. (Body Fuel for Healthy Bodies Ser.). (ENG.). 32p. (gr. 4-4). lib. bdg. 21.27 *(978-0-7614-3801-4(7),* 8a778b33-a803-4692-9ae6-57a54fecf046) Cavendish Square Publishing LLC.

—Vitamins & Minerals, 1 vol. 2009. (Body Fuel for Healthy Bodies Ser.). (ENG.). 32p. (gr. 4-4). lib. bdg. 21.27 *(978-0-7614-3802-1(5),* 81531297-13ee-4209-8dd5-6c30be8089c2) Cavendish Square Publishing LLC.

Sesame's: A Giant Coloring Book that teaches Healthy Eating Habits. 2006. (J). 6.99 *(978-1-59949-499-9(X))* Food Marketing Consultants, Inc.

Shryer, Donna. Body Fuel: A Guide to Good Nutrition, 1 vol. 2008. (Food & Fitness Ser.). (ENG., Illus.). 128p. (YA). (gr. 7-7). lib. bdg. 41.21 *(978-0-7614-2552-6(7),* 4576a223-73c6-46b3-9fe2-6bc73b005989) Cavendish Square Publishing LLC.

Shryer, Donna & Dawson, Stephen. Body Fuel: A Guide to Good Nutrition, 1 vol. 2010. (Food & You Ser.). (ENG.). 32p. (gr. 5-5). 31.21 *(978-0-7614-4362-9(2),* 1ffd2eaa-c91a-42a8-abc2-b0f0e03257ea) Cavendish Square Publishing LLC.

Shryer, Donna & Forschmiedt, Jodi. Peak Performance: Sports Nutrition, 1 vol. 2010. (Food & You Ser.). (ENG.). 32p. (gr. 5-5). 31.21 *(978-0-7614-4366-7(5),* ded32e69-994c-4789-a057-5cd5acf06a56) Cavendish Square Publishing LLC.

Silate, Jennifer. Planning & Preparing Healthy Meals & Snacks: A Day-to-Day Guide to a Healthier Diet. (Library of Nutrition Ser.). 48p. 2009. (gr. 5-8). 53.00 *(978-1-60853-776-1(5),* Rosen Reference) 2007. (ENG., Illus.). (gr. 5-8). per. 12.75 *(978-1-4042-1634-1(0),* 0ef2d217-9d00-4fa8-b55f-5f29767e2608) 2004. (Illus.). (J). lib. bdg. 26.50 *(978-1-4042-0302-0(8))* Rosen Publishing Group, Inc., The.

Simone, Jacquelyn. Nutrition & Politics. 2014. (ENG., Illus.). 112p. (J). 42.79 *(978-1-62524-070-5(8),* Village Earth Pr.) Harding Hse. Publishing Sebice Inc.

Sjonger, Rebecca. How to Choose Foods Your Body Will Use. 2016. (ENG.). 24p. (J). *(978-0-7787-2350-9(X))* Crabtree Publishing Co.

—On a Mission for Good Nutrition! 2015. (Healthy Habits for a Lifetime Ser.). (ENG., Illus.). 24p. (J). (gr. 2-2). *(978-0-7787-1880-2(8))* Crabtree Publishing Co.

Slim Goodbody Corp. What's on Myplate? A Guide to Good Nutrition. 2011. (Illus.). 40p. (J). 14.95 *(978-1-887028-63-9(3))* Slim Goodbody Corp.

Slim Goodbody Corp., creator. What's on Myplate? A Guide to Good Nutrition. 2011. (Illus.). 40p. (J). pap. 9.95 *(978-1-887028-62-2(5))* Slim Goodbody Corp.

Sly, Stacey. What Should I Eat? Gentry, Susana, photos by. 2010. (Illus.). 26p. pap. 12.95 *(978-1-60911-432-9(9),* Eloquent Bks.) Strategic Book Publishing & Rights Agency (SBPRA).

Smalley, Carol Parenzan. Fats, Oils, & Sweets. 2005. (Rookie Read-About Health Ser.). (ENG., Illus.). 32p. (J). (gr. k-2). lib. bdg. 20.50 *(978-0-516-25289-6(5),* Children's Pr.) Scholastic Library Publishing.

—Rookie Read-About Health: Fats, Oils, & Sweets. 2006. (Rookie Read-About Health Ser.). (ENG., Illus.). 32p. (J). (gr. k-2). pap. 5.95 *(978-0-516-24759-5(X),* Children's Pr.) Scholastic Library Publishing.

Smith, Alastair. What Happens to Your Food. Wheatley, Maria, illus. 2003. 16p. (J). (gr. 2-18). pap. 7.95 *(978-0-7945-0643-8(7),* Usborne) EDC Publishing.

Smolin, Lori A. & Grosvenor, Mary B. Nutrition & Eating Disorders. 2nd rev. ed. 2010. (Healthy Eating: a Guide to Nutrition Ser.). (ENG.). 136p. (gr. 9). 35.00 *(978-1-60413-802-3(5),* P459466, Facts On File) Infobase Holdings, Inc.

Snow, Todd. You Are Healthy (PB) Strong, Melodee, illus. 2008. (ENG.). 24p. (J). pap. 8.99 *(978-1-934277-22-5(3))* Mam Green Publishing, Inc.

Sohn, Emily. Food & Nutrition. 2019. (iScience Ser.). (ENG., Illus.). 48p. (J). (gr. 5-6). 23.94 *(978-1-68450-951-5(3));* pap. 13.26 *(978-1-68404-401-6(4))* Norwood Hse. Pr.

Solway, Andrew. Food & Digestion. 2011. (Your Body Inside & Out Ser.). (Illus.). 32p. (J). (gr. 3-6). lib. bdg. 28.50 *(978-1-59771-264-4(7))* Sea-To-Sea Pubns.

Star Bright Books. Eating the Rainbow: English, 1 vol. 2009. (ENG.). 32p. (J). (gr. -1). bds. 6.95 *(978-1-59572-174-7(6))* Star Bright Bks., Inc.

Storper, Barbara. Janey Junkfood's Fresh Adventure! Making Good Eating Great Fun! Schneid, Frances E., illus. 2008. 32p. (J). (gr. 3-7). 15.95 *(978-0-9642858-5-9(1))* FoodPlay Productions.

Sullivan, Jaclyn. What's in Your Soda?, 1 vol. 2012. (What's in Your Fast Food? Ser.). (ENG., Illus.). 24p. (J). (gr. 2-3). pap. 9.25 *(978-1-4488-6379-2(1),* 926f83d4-5d93-49cb-aad9-ff6b9bcd9888, PowerKids Pr.); lib. bdg. 26.27 *(978-1-4488-6210-8(8),* 4e07dbd1-14f4-4398-9329-b08912283b24) Rosen Publishing Group, Inc., The.

Sundance/Newbridge LLC Staff. You Are What You Eat. 2007. (Early Science Ser.). (gr. k-3). 18.95 *(978-1-4007-6432-7(7));* pap. 6.10 *(978-1-4007-6428-0(9))* Sundance/Newbridge Educational Publishing.

Tabletop Pocket Chart Nutrition Card Set. 2004. (J). 8.95 *(978-1-56911-171-0(5))* Learning Resources, Inc.

Tecco, Betsy Dru. Food for Fuel: The Connection Between Food & Physical Activity. (Library of Nutrition Ser.). 48p. 2009. (gr. 5-8). 53.00 *(978-1-60853-766-2(8),* Rosen Reference) 2007. (ENG., Illus.). (gr. 5-8). per. 12.75 *(978-1-4042-1635-8(9),* 030297f5-d816-480a-aa89-080d24465e77) 2004. (Illus.). (J). lib. bdg. 26.50 *(978-1-4042-0303-7(6))* Rosen Publishing Group, Inc., The.

Thomas, Patsy E. A Camp Carrot Cheer for Good Nutrition. 2011. 16p. (gr. 2-4). pap. 10.67 *(978-1-4269-6200-4(2))* Trafford Publishing.

Thompson, Helen. Cookies or Carrots? You Are What You Eat. 2010. (Kids & Obesity Ser.). (Illus.). 48p. (YA). lib. bdg. 19.95 *(978-1-4222-1707-8(8))* Mason Crest.

Thomson, Sarah L. What's for Lunch? Aye, Nila, illus. 2016. (Let's-Read-And-Find-Out Science 1 Ser.). (ENG.). 40p. (J). (gr. -1-3). pap. 6.99 *(978-0-06-233137-3(X),* HarperCollins) HarperCollins Pubs.

Turnbull, Stephanie. Why Do We Eat? Haggerty, Tim, illus. 2006. (Usborne Beginners Ser.). 32p. (J). (gr. 4-7). lib. bdg. 12.99 *(978-1-58086-933-1(5),* Usborne) EDC Publishing.

Ureel, Jessica Mary. Allergy Express: Food Allergy Coloring & Activity Book. 2007. (J). per. 6.95 *(978-0-9745033-1-8(2))* Main Street Pubns.

Ventura, Marne. Nutrition Myths, Busted! 2017. (Science Myths, Busted! Ser.). (ENG., Illus.). 32p. (J). (gr. 3-6). 32.80 *(978-1-63235-304-7(0),* 11809, 12-Story Library) Bookstaves, LLC.

—12 Tips for a Healthy Diet. 2017. (Healthy Living Ser.). (ENG., Illus.). 32p. (J). (gr. 3-6). pap. 9.95 *(978-1-63235-383-2(0),* 11851, 12-Story Library) Bookstaves, LLC.

—12 Tips for a Healthy Diet. 2017. (J). *(978-1-62143-507-5(5))* Pr. Room Editions LLC.

Village Earth. Nutrition: a Global View (5-Volume Series) 2nd ed. 2014. (ENG., Illus.). 112p. (J). 213.95 *(978-1-62524-069-9(4),* Village Earth Pr.) Harding Hse. Publishing Sebice Inc.

Vogel, Elizabeth. ¡A comer sanamente! (Eating Right) 2009. (Limpieza y salud todo el día (Clean & Healthy All Day Long) Ser.). (SPA.). 24p. (gr. 1-1). 37.50 *(978-1-61514-290-3(8),* Editorial Buenas Letras) Rosen Publishing Group, Inc., The.

—A Comer Sanamente!, 1 vol. 2003. (Limpieza y Salud Todo el día (Clean & Healthy All Day Long) Ser.). (SPA., Illus.). 24p. (J). (gr. 1-1). lib. bdg. 22.27 *(978-0-8239-6612-7(7),* da6647c8-3546-4a3b-b224-273efbb37bda) Rosen Publishing Group, Inc., The.

—Eating Right. 2009. (Clean & Healthy All Day Long Ser.). 24p. (gr. 1-1). 37.50 *(978-1-61511-865-6(9),* PowerKids Pr.) Rosen Publishing Group, Inc., The.

Walker, Ida. Nutrition & You. 2014. (ENG., Illus.). 112p. (J). 42.79 *(978-1-62524-074-3(0),* Village Earth Pr.) Harding Hse. Publishing Sebice Inc.

Wallach, Joel Dennis & Ma, Ian. Hell's Kitchen. 2005. 386p. (YA). pap. 19.95 *(978-0-9748581-1-1(0))* Wellness Pubn.

Waters, Rosa. My Daily Diet: Fruits. Prock, Lisa Albers, ed. 2014. (On My Plate Ser.: 6). 48p. (J). (gr. 5-18). 20.95 *(978-1-4222-3097-8(X))* Mason Crest.

—My Daily Diet: Grains. Prock, Lisa Albers, ed. 2014. (On My Plate Ser.: 6). 48p. (J). (gr. 5-18). 20.95 *(978-1-4222-3098-5(8))* Mason Crest.

Where Does My Food Go. 2005. (J). 6.95 *(978-0-9776850-0-4(4))* Sundback, Ruth.

Williams, Kara. Frequently Asked Questions about My Pyramid: Eating Right. 2009. (FAQ: Teen Life Ser.). 64p. (gr. 5-6). 58.50 *(978-1-61512-583-8(3))* Rosen Publishing Group, Inc., The.

—Mypyramid: Eating Right, 1 vol. 2007. (FAQ: Teen Life Ser.). (ENG., Illus.). 64p. (YA). (gr. 5-6). lib. bdg. 37.13 *(978-1-4042-1974-8(9),* b7bb2fde-ad8a-46ee-bf69-b8bd5f8f5a53) Rosen Publishing Group, Inc., The.

Wilson, Scott & Wilkinson, Jody. Eating Healthy, Eating Right. 2004. 200p. 18.99 *(978-0-8307-3022-3(2),* Gospel Light) Gospel Light Pubns.

World Book, Inc. Staff, contrib. by. Good Food for You. 2010. (J). *(978-0-7166-7739-0(3))* World Bk., Inc.

NUTS

Benduhn, Tea. Meat & Beans / Carne y Frijoles, 1 vol. 2007. (Find Out about Food / Conoce la Comida Ser.). (SPA & ENG.). 24p. (gr. k-2). pap. 9.15 *(978-0-8368-8463-0(9),* 74421674-a836-4487-ac7d-ec4c27c8a8c9); (Illus.). lib. bdg. 24.67 *(978-0-8368-8456-2(6),* ccb7da50-548a-4267-8811-a8b2ebd1aeb7) Stevens, Gareth Publishing LLLP. (Weekly Reader Leveled Readers).

Dilkes, D. H. Beans, Nuts, & Oils, 1 vol. 2011. (All about Good Foods We Eat Ser.). (ENG., Illus.). 24p. (gr. -1-1). pap. 10.35 *(978-1-59845-256-3(8),* 1333a1ab-74ba-4448-97ee-77cbdc5f82ca); lib. bdg. 25.27 *(978-0-7660-3928-5(5),* b501cdeb-215b-4f28-9675-4d7cc2eb258d) Enslow Publishing, LLC. (Enslow Publishing).

Head, Honor. Beans & Nuts: On Your Plate. 2010. (J). 24.25 *(978-1-59920-336-2(7))* Black Rabbit Bks.

Hughes, Meredith Sayles. Hard to Crack: Nut Trees. 2005. (Plants We Eat Ser.). (Illus.). 104p. (gr. 6-9). 26.60 *(978-0-8225-2838-8(X))* Lerner Publishing Group.

LaPlante, Walter. I'm Allergic to Tree Nuts, 1 vol. 2018. (I'm Allergic Ser.). (ENG.). 24p. (gr. 1-2). 24.27 *(978-1-5382-2908-8(0),* bcea5ed0-e6a9-4a06-8c41-aad42b2bd2cd) Stevens, Gareth Publishing LLLP.

Sayre, April Pulley. Let's Go Nuts! Seeds We Eat. Sayre, April Pulley, illus. 2013. (ENG., Illus.). 32p. (J). (gr. -1-3). 17.99 *(978-1-4424-6728-6(2),* Beach Lane Bks.) Beach Lane Bks.

M N O

Sertori, Trisha. Meats, Fish, Eggs, Nuts, & Beans, 1 vol. 2009. (Body Fuel for Healthy Bodies Ser.). (ENG.). 32p. (gr. 4-4). lib. bdg. 21.27 *(978-0-7614-3801-4(7),* 8a778b33-a803-4692-9ae6-57a54fecf046) Cavendish Square Publishing LLC.

NUVOLARI, TAZIO, 1892-1953

Briggs, Raymond. Nuvolari & the Alfa Romeo. 2006. (Illus.). (J). *(978-0-9766683-1-2(9))* Racemaker Pr. LLC.

NYERERE, JULIUS K. (JULIUS KAMBARAGE), 1922-1999

Maillu, David G. Julius Nyerere: Father of Ujamaa. 2005. (Lion Book Ser.). (Illus.). ix, 81p. (J). *(978-9966-951-32-8(6))* Sasa Sema Publications Ltd.

O

OAK

Cain, Marie Mowery. Tiny Acorns, Majestic Oaks. 2013. (Big Books, Red Ser.). (ENG & SPA., Illus.). 16p. pap. 33.00 *(978-1-59246-218-6(9))* Big Books, by George!

Carlson-Berne, Emma. From Acorn to Oak Tree. 2017. (Start to Finish, Second Ser.). (ENG., Illus.). 24p. (J). (gr. k-3). pap. 7.99 *(978-1-5124-5621-9(7),* f3f487d7-f792-4502-b80d-6043a6d6e4ea) Lerner Publishing Group.

De la Bédoyère, Camilla. Acorn to Oak Tree. 2013. (Illus.). 24p. (J). *(978-1-4351-4711-9(1))* Barnes & Noble, Inc.

Glaser, Rebecca. Oak Trees. 2012. (ENG., Illus.). 24p. (J). lib. bdg. 25.65 *(978-1-62031-027-4(9))* Jump! Inc.

Herrington, Lisa M. Acorn to Oak Tree. 2014. (Rookie Read-About(r) Science - Life Cycles Ser.). (ENG.). 32p. (J). lib. bdg. 23.00 *(978-0-531-21054-3(5))* Scholastic Library Publishing.

Hipp, Andrew. Oak, 1 vol. 2004. (Getting into Nature Ser.). (ENG., Illus.). 32p. (J). (gr. 3-4). lib. bdg. 28.93 *(978-0-8239-4206-0(6),* ce5f4eec-5093-43f9-9f90-94d8b1908bf1) Rosen Publishing Group, Inc., The.

—Oak Trees: Inside & Out. 2009. (Getting into Nature Ser.). 32p. (gr. 3-4). 47.90 *(978-1-61512-722-1(4),* PowerKids Pr.) Rosen Publishing Group, Inc., The.

—El Roble: Por dentro y por fuera (Oak Tree: Inside & Out) 2009. (Explora la Naturaleza (Getting into Nature) Ser.). (SPA.). 32p. (gr. 3-4). 47.90 *(978-1-61512-338-4(5),* Editorial Buenas Letras) Rosen Publishing Group, Inc., The.

Huseby, Victoria. Oak Tree. 2008. (J). 25.65 *(978-1-59920-178-8(X))* Black Rabbit Bks.

Johnson, Jinny. Oak Tree. Rosewarne, Graham, illus. 2010. (J). 28.50 *(978-1-59920-356-0(1))* Black Rabbit Bks.

Lowery, Lawrence F. Our Very Own Tree. 2015. (I Wonder Why Ser.). (ENG., Illus.). 36p. (J). (gr. k-3). pap. 13.99 *(978-1-941316-24-5(7))* National Science Teachers Assn.

Markovics, Joyce L. Oak Tree. 2015. (See It Grow Ser.). (ENG.). 24p. (J). (gr. -1-3). lib. bdg. 26.99 *(978-1-62724-844-0(7))* Bearport Publishing Co., Inc.

Mitchell, Melanie S. Oak Trees. (First Step Nonfiction Ser.). (Illus.). (gr. k-2). 2005. 24p. lib. bdg. 17.27 *(978-0-8225-4610-8(8))* 2003. 23p. (J). pap. 5.95 *(978-0-8225-4611-5(6),* Lerner Pubns.) Lerner Publishing Group.

Pfeffer, Wendy. A Log's Life. Brickman, Robin, illus. 2007. (ENG.). 32p. (J). (gr. -1-3). 7.99 *(978-1-4169-3483-7(9),* Aladdin) Simon & Schuster Children's Publishing.

Pugliano-Martin, Carol. Discover the Life Cycle of Oak Trees. 2006. (English Explorers Ser.). (J). pap. *(978-1-4108-6472-7(3))* Benchmark Education Co.

—The Life Cycle of Oak Trees. 2006. (English Explorers Ser.). (J). pap. *(978-1-4108-6469-7(3))* Benchmark Education Co.

Reid, Barbara. Acorn to Oak Tree. braille ed. 2004. (J). (gr. 1). spiral bd., bds. *(978-0-616-03085-1(1))* Canadian National Institute for the Blind/Institut National Canadien pour les Aveugles.

Schaefer, Lola M. & Schaefer, Adam. Because of an Acorn: (Nature Autumn Books for Children, Picture Books about Acorn Trees) Preston-Gannon, Frann. illus. 2016. (ENG.). 36p. (J). (gr. -1-k). 16.99 *(978-1-4521-1242-8(8))* Chronicle Bks. LLC.

Thomson, Ruth. The Life Cycle of an Oak Tree, 1 vol. 2009. (Learning about Life Cycles Ser.). (ENG.). 24p. (J). (gr. 2-2). pap. 9.25 *(978-1-4358-2888-9(7),* 001582be-17de-4423-80ff-81ef8b6ff73c, PowerKids Pr.); lib. bdg. 26.27 *(978-1-4358-2838-4(0),* 2ba7d856-6bf6-462e-b14d-c2bfc7dad898) Rosen Publishing Group, Inc., The.

Tonkin, Rachel. Acorn to Oak Tree. Fizer Coleman, Stephanie, illus. 2019. (Follow the Life Cycle Ser.). (ENG.). 24p. (J). (gr. 2-2). pap. *(978-0-7787-6387-1(0),* 22aed180-f6c3-48a2-bb06-864c1a75e594); lib. bdg. *(978-0-7787-6379-6(X),* 06b16217-d63a-45d9-8e8e-0f2fa8128f8d) Crabtree Publishing Co.

OAK—FICTION

Albam, Jessica. The Boy in the Oak. 2010. (ENG., Illus.). 40p. (J). (gr. k-4). 17.95 *(978-1-897476-52-9(3))* Simply Read Bks. CAN. Dist: Ingram Publisher Services.

Barry, Debra R. The Loneliest Leaf. Baker, David, illus. 2011. 28p. pap. 24.95 *(978-1-4560-1002-7(6))* America Star Bks.

Beausoleil, Dana. The Elf in the Oak Tree. 2010. 32p. pap. 17.99 *(978-1-4251-1572-2(1))* Trafford Publishing.

Bedford, Vanessa Jane. Olivia Oak Tree & Friends. 2018. (ENG., Illus.). 40p. (J). (gr. 1-2). *(978-1-5289-2472-6(X))*; pap. *(978-1-5289-2473-3(8))* Austin Macauley Pubs. Ltd.

Clauson, Marilyn & Drake, Lana. Woody Acorn. Drake, Lana, illus. 2012. (Illus.). 48p. pap. 24.95 *(978-1-4626-7946-1(3))* America Star Bks.

George, Lindsay Barrett. That Pup! George, Lindsay Barrett, illus. 2011. (ENG., Illus.). 32p. (J). (gr. -1-k). 16.99 *(978-0-06-200413-0(1),* Greenwillow Bks.) HarperCollins Pubs.

Hansen, Jeff. Alibriana Visits the Branch Office. 2009. 36p. pap. 16.99 *(978-1-4389-4534-7(5))* AuthorHouse.

Hellier, Lorraine. The Wayward Wagon. 2010. 114p. pap. 10.99 *(978-1-4520-3232-0(7))* AuthorHouse.

Hilgendorf, L. B. Orville Oak & Friends. Dow, S. B., illus. 2005. 26p. (gr. -1-1). bds. 11.95 *(978-1-58275-149-8(8))* Black Forest Pr.

Karas, G. Brian. As an Oak Tree Grows. Karas, G. Brian, illus. 2014. (Illus.). 32p. (J). (gr. k-3). 19.99 *(978-0-399-25233-4(9),* Nancy Paulsen Books) Penguin Young Readers Group.

Kimball, Lucy; Grudzina. Big Oak, Little Oak. Grudzina, Rebecca, ed. 2016. (Spring Forward Ser.). (ENG.). (J). (gr. k). 7.02 net. *(978-1-4900-6019-4(7))* Benchmark Education Co.

La Flamme Beighey, Carole. The Waddodles of Hollow Lake: The Mighty Oak. 2009. 344p. 28.49 *(978-1-4389-4037-3(8))* 2008. 340p. pap. 17.99 *(978-1-4343-8201-6(X))* AuthorHouse.

Lough, Erin & Duke, Mave Lough. The Spirit Tree at Toomer's Corner. 2012. (J). 19.95 *(978-1-62086-122-6(4))* Amplify Publishing Group.

Lucado, Max. Oak Inside the Acorn The, 1 vol. 2006. (ENG., Illus.). 48p. (J). 16.99 *(978-1-4003-0601-5(9),* Tommy Nelson) Nelson, Thomas Inc.

Mitchell, Laurence. The Mean Root of Crowteal Pond: Inside a Hollow Oak Tree, Book #4. 2009. 28p. pap. 12.49 *(978-1-4389-5406-6(9))* AuthorHouse.

Mollis Lindquist, Melody Rose. Oak Tree. 2009. 16p. pap. 10.99 *(978-1-4490-0859-8(3))* AuthorHouse.

Parker, Lucy. Acorn Meadow has a Secret. 2010. (ENG., Illus.). 80p. pap. *(978-1-84748-600-4(2))* Athena Pr.

Pride, Wallace. The Mighty Christmas Oak. 2008. 19p. pap. 24.95 *(978-1-60672-752-2(4))* PublishAmerica, Inc.

Taylor, Alice. Secrets of the Oak. Barnett, Russell, illus. (ENG.). 30p. 4.99 *(978-0-86322-138-5(6))* Penguin Publishing Group.

Violet Mackerel's Pocket Protest. 2014. (Violet Mackerel Ser.). (ENG., Illus.). 128p. (J). (gr. 1-5). 17.99 *(978-1-4424-9458-9(1),* Atheneum Bks. for Young Readers) Simon & Schuster Children's Publishing.

OAKLAND ATHLETICS (BASEBALL TEAM)

Gilbert, Sara. The Story of the Oakland Athletics. 2011. (Baseball: the Great American Game Ser.). (Illus.). 48p. (J). (gr. 5-8). lib. bdg. 34.25 *(978-1-60818-050-9(6),* Creative Education) Creative Co., The.

Pueschner, Gordon. The Story of the Oakland Athletics. 2007. (Baseball, the Great American Game Ser.). (Illus.). 48p. (YA). (gr. 4-7). lib. bdg. 32.80 *(978-1-58341-496-5(7))* Creative Co., The.

Sauver, Dennis St. Oakland Athletics. 2018. (MLB's Greatest Teams Ser.). (ENG., Illus.). 32p. (J). (gr. 2-5). lib. bdg. 34.21 *(978-1-5321-1812-8(0),* 30670, Big Buddy Bks.) ABDO Publishing Co.

Stewart, Mark. The Oakland Athletics. 2012. (Team Spirit Ser.). 48p. (J). (gr. 3-6). lib. bdg. 29.27 *(978-1-59953-491-6(6))* Norwood Hse. Pr.

OAKLAND RAIDERS (FOOTBALL TEAM)

Caffrey, Scott. The Story of the Oakland Raiders. 2009. (NFL Today Ser.). (Illus.). 48p. (YA). (gr. 5-9). 22.95 *(978-1-58341-765-2(6))* Creative Co., The.

Frisch, Aaron. The History of the Oakland Raiders. 2003. (NFL Today Ser.). (Illus.). 32p. (YA). (gr. 5-9). 18.95 *(978-1-58341-308-1(1))* Creative Co., The.

—Oakland Raiders. (Super Bowl Champions Ser.). (J). (gr. 1-3). 2011. 24.25 *(978-1-60818-025-7(5))* 2005. (Illus.). 24p. lib. bdg. 16.95 *(978-1-58341-388-3(X),* Creative Education) Creative Co., The.

—Oakland Raiders. 2014. (Super Bowl Champions Ser.). (ENG., Illus.). 24p. (J). (gr. 1-4). *(978-1-60818-384-5(X),* 21577, Creative Education) Creative Co., The.

Frisch, Nate. The Story of the Oakland Raiders. 2013. (J). 35.65 *(978-1-60818-314-2(9),* Creative Education) Creative Co., The.

Graves, Will & Kelley, Patrick. Oakland Raiders, 1 vol. 2016. (NFL up Close Ser.). (ENG., Illus.). 32p. (J). (gr. 3-9). lib. bdg. 32.79 *(978-1-68078-228-8(2),* 22059, SportsZone) ABDO Publishing Co.

Morey, Allan. The Oakland Raiders Story. 2016. (NFL Teams Ser.). (ENG., Illus.). 32p. (J). (gr. 3-7). lib. bdg. 26.95 *(978-1-62617-377-4(X),* Torque Bks.) Bellwether Media.

Whiting, Jim. Oakland Raiders. rev. ed. 2019. (NFL Today Ser.). (ENG.). 48p. (J). (gr. 4-7). pap. 12.00 *(978-1-62832-717-5(0),* 19073, Creative Paperbacks) Creative Co., The.

—The Story of the Oakland Raiders. 2019. (NFL Today Ser.). (ENG.). 48p. (J). (gr. 3-6). *(978-1-64026-154-9(0),* 19096, Creative Education) Creative Co., The.

Wyner, Zach. Oakland Raiders. (Illus.). 32p. (J). 2015. pap. *(978-1-4896-0871-0(0))* 2014. (ENG., (gr. 4-7). lib. bdg. 28.55 *(978-1-4896-0870-3(2),* AV2 by Weigl) Weigl Pubs., Inc.

Zappa, Marcia. Oakland Raiders, 1 vol. 2015. (NFL's Greatest Teams Ser.). (ENG.). 32p. (J). (gr. 2-5). 34.21 *(978-1-62403-590-6(6),* 17207, Big Buddy Bks.) ABDO Publishing Co.

OAKLEY, ANNIE, 1860-1926

Annie Oakley. 2009. 48p. pap. 8.95 *(978-0-8225-5788-3(6))* Lerner Publishing Group.

DiVito, Anna. Annie Oakley Saves the Day: Ready-To-Read Level 2. DiVito, Anna, illus. 2004. (Ready-To-Read Childhood of Famous Americans Ser.). (ENG., Illus.). 32p. (J). (gr. k-2). pap. 4.99 *(978-0-689-86520-6(1),* Simon Spotlight) Simon Spotlight.

Foran, Jill. Annie Oakley. 2018. (J). *(978-1-4896-9568-0(0),* AV2 by Weigl) Weigl Pubs., Inc.

Gilbert, Sara. Annie Oakley. 2005. (Legends of the West (Creative Education) Ser.). (Illus.). 48p. (J). (gr. 5-9). lib. bdg. 21.95 *(978-1-58341-334-0(0),* Creative Education) Creative Co., The.

Graves, Charles P. Annie Oakley: The Shooting Star. Cary, illus. 2011. 80p. (gr. 4-7). 37.95 *(978-1-258-01390-5(8))* Literary Licensing, LLC.

Herwick Rice, Dona & Greathouse, Lisa. Annie Oakley, 1 vol. rev. ed. 2009. (Reader's Theater Ser.). (ENG.). 24p. (gr. 2-4). pap. 8.99 *(978-1-4333-0997-7(1))* Teacher Created Materials, Inc.

Link, Theodore. Annie Oakley: Wild West Sharpshooter, 1 vol. 2003. (Primary Sources of Famous People in American History Ser.). (ENG., Illus.). 32p. (gr. 3-4). pap. 10.00 *(978-0-8239-4174-2(4),* 7d238026-4b5e-4c63-ad77-49a60c6e23ae); (J). lib. bdg. 29.13 *(978-0-8239-4102-5(7),* 2c5e7fe0-03dc-4bad-9f37-1927c5ce3dde) Rosen Publishing Group, Inc., The.

—Annie Oakley: Wild West Sharpshooter = Pistolera Del Lejano Oeste, 1 vol. 2003. (Famous People in American History / Grandes Personajes en la Historia de Los Estados Unidos Ser.). (SPA & ENG., Illus.). 32p. (J). (gr. 2-3). lib. bdg. 29.13 *(978-0-8239-4150-6(7),* c9bf44a4-8733-4b7d-9fe7-c08803ad5713) Rosen Publishing Group, Inc., The.

Macy, Sue. Bull's Eye: A Photobiography of Annie Oakley. 2015. (Photobiographies Ser.). 64p. (J). (gr. 5-9). pap. 7.99 *(978-1-4263-2218-1(6),* National Geographic Kids) Disney Publishing Worldwide.

Porterfield, Jason. Annie Oakley: Pistolera del Oeste Americano, 1 vol. 2003. (Grandes Personajes en la Historia de Los Estados Unidos (Famous People in American History) Ser.). (SPA., Illus.). 32p. (gr. 3-4). lib. bdg. 29.13 *(978-0-8239-4126-1(4),* 39142650-a87f-4054-81e2-0de1f5320e33, Editorial Buenas Letras) Rosen Publishing Group, Inc., The.

—Annie Oakley: Tiradora del Lejano Oeste (Annie Oakley: Wild West Sharpshooter) 2009. (Grandes personajes en la historia de los Estados Unidos (Famous People in American History) Ser.). 32p. (gr. 2-3). 47.90 *(978-1-61512-789-4(5),* Editorial Buenas Letras) Rosen Publishing Group, Inc., The.

—Annie Oakley: Wild West Sharpshooter. 2009. (Primary Sources of Famous People in American History Ser.). 32p. (gr. 2-3). 47.90 *(978-1-60851-651-3(2))* Rosen Publishing Group, Inc., The.

—Annie Oakley: Wild West Sharpshooter / Tiradora del Lejano Oeste. 2009. (Famous People in American History/Grandes personajes en la historia de los Estados Unidos Ser.). 32p. (gr. 2-3). 47.90 *(978-1-61512-537-1(X),* Editorial Buenas Letras) Rosen Publishing Group, Inc., The.

Rose, Katherine. Annie Oakley: the Woman Who Never Missed a Shot, 1 vol. 2014. (American Legends & Folktales Ser.). (ENG., Illus.). 32p. (gr. 3-3). 31.21 *(978-1-62712-286-3(9),* 24b81b1d-1100-458e-bc67-2be07559c2f1); pap. 11.58 *(978-1-62712-287-0(7),* 2ea8bd50-5ade-44e7-ac8d-01ec12f139f7) Cavendish Square Publishing LLC.

Silate, Jennifer. Little Sure Shot: Annie Oakley & Buffalo Bill's Wild West Show. (Great Moments in American History Ser.). 32p. (gr. 3-3). 2009. 47.90 *(978-1-61513-147-1(7))* 2003. (ENG., Illus.). (J). lib. bdg. 29.13 *(978-0-8239-4329-6(1),* fbe363ae-6b6f-45f8-abef-37d0c5da64eb, Rosen Reference) Rosen Publishing Group, Inc., The.

Spinner, Stephanie. Who Was Annie Oakley? Day, Larry, illus. 2003. (Who Was... ? Ser.). 109p. (gr. 4-7). 15.00 *(978-0-7569-1588-9(0))* Perfection Learning Corp.

Wadsworth, Ginger. Annie Oakley. 2005. (History Maker Bios Ser.). (Illus.). 48p. (J). (gr. 3-7). lib. bdg. 26.60 *(978-0-8225-2940-8(8),* Lerner Pubns.) Lerner Publishing Group.

Whiting, Jim. Annie Oakley. 2006. (What's So Great About... ? Ser.). (Illus.). 32p. (J). (gr. 2-4). lib. bdg. 25.70 *(978-1-58415-477-8(2))* Mitchell Lane Pubs.

OAKLEY, ANNIE, 1860-1926—FICTION

Verral, Charles Spain. Annie Oakley, Sharpshooter. Dreany, E. Joseph, illus. 2011. 28p. pap. 35.95 *(978-1-258-06762-5(5))* Literary Licensing, LLC.

OBAMA, BARACK, 1961-

Amédékanya, Ben-Kofi. Pillars of Pride. 2011. 32p. pap. 15.99 *(978-1-4567-3458-9(X))* AuthorHouse.

B. Yes I Can for Kids. 2009. 36p. pap. 17.95 *(978-1-4490-1585-5(9))* AuthorHouse.

Bahadur, Gaiutra. Family Ties. 2011. (J). pap. *(978-0-531-22554-7(2))* Scholastic, Inc.

Barack Obama. 2007. (Political Profiles Ser.). (Illus.). 128p. (YA). (gr. 5-9). lib. bdg. 27.95 *(978-1-59935-045-5(9))* Reynolds, Morgan Inc.

Bartlett, Melissa. Meet President Obama, 1 vol. 2012. (InfoMax Readers Ser.). (ENG., Illus.). 24p. (J). (gr. 1-1). pap. 8.25 *(978-1-4488-9058-3(6),* 3b21bce9-0ef2-415b-963c-861164ba3644, Rosen Classroom) Rosen Publishing Group, Inc., The.

Benjamin, Jenny. Barack Obama. 2019. (Influential People Ser.). (ENG., Illus.). 32p. (J). (gr. 4-6). pap. 7.95 *(978-1-5435-6040-4(7),* 140086); lib. bdg. 28.65 *(978-1-5435-5795-4(3),* 139751) Capstone.

Biskup, Agnieszka. Obama: The Historic Election of America's 44th President, 1 vol. Hayden, Seitu, illus. 2011. (American Graphic Ser.). (ENG.). 32p. (J). (gr. 3-9). pap. 8.10 *(978-1-4296-7339-6(7),* 116882) Capstone.

—Obama: The Historic Election of America's 44th President. Hayden, William, illus. 2011. (American Graphic Ser.). (ENG.). 32p. (J). (gr. 3-4). pap. 49.60 *(978-1-4296-7340-2(0),* 16837, Capstone Pr.) Capstone.

Bourcier, Cammy S. Barack Obama. 2009. (Sharing the American Dream Ser.). (Illus.). 64p. (J). (gr. 7-12). 22.95 *(978-1-4222-0574-7(6))* Mason Crest.

Brill, Marlene Targ. Barack Obama: Working to Make a Difference. 2006. (J). pap. 6.95 *(978-0-8225-6056-2(9),* First Avenue Editions); (Illus.). 48p. 23.93 *(978-0-8225-3417-4(7))* Lerner Publishing Group.

—Barack Obama (Revised Edition) 2009. pap. 52.95 *(978-0-7613-5031-6(4))* Lerner Publishing Group.

Britton, Tamara L. Barack Obama, 1 vol. 2016. (United States Presidents *2017 Ser.). (ENG., Illus.). 40p. (J). (gr. 2-5). lib. bdg. 35.64 *(978-1-68078-111-3(1),* 21839, Big Buddy Bks.) ABDO Publishing Co.

Brophy, David B. Michelle Obama: Meet the First Lady. 2008. 128p. (J). pap. 6.99 *(978-0-06-177990-9(3))* HarperCollins Pubs.

Burgan, Michael. Barack Obama. rev. ed. 2016. (Front-Page Lives Ser.). (ENG.). 112p. (J). (gr. 6-9). pap. 11.99 *(978-1-4846-3813-2(1),* 134676, Heinemann) Capstone.

Carolan, Joanna & Carolan, Terry. A President from Hawaii. Zunon, Elizabeth, illus. 2012. 24p. (J). (gr. 2-5). (ENG.). pap. 7.99 *(978-0-7636-6282-0(8))*; pap. 15.99 *(978-0-7636-5230-2(X))* Candlewick Pr.

Conklin, Blane. Barack Obama: President of the United States. rev. ed. 2011. (Social Studies: Informational Text Ser.). (ENG.). 32p. (gr. 4-8). pap. 11.99 *(978-1-4333-1522-0(X))* Teacher Created Materials, Inc.

Cooke, Tim. Barack Obama, 1 vol. 2018. (Meet the Greats Ser.). (ENG.). 48p. (gr. 5-5). lib. bdg. 34.93 *(978-1-5382-2572-1(7),* 32de5d34-63e6-413d-9b69-938769585584) Stevens, Gareth Publishing LLLP.

Corey, Shana. Barack Obama: Out of Many, One. 2009. (Step into Reading Ser.). (Illus.). 48p. (J). (gr. k-3). pap. 4.99 *(978-0-375-86339-4(7),* Random Hse. Bks. for Young Readers) Random Hse. Children's Bks.

Davis, William Michael. Barack Obama: The Politics of Hope. 2007. (Illus.). 168p. (J). (gr. 10-18). lib. bdg. 25.95 *(978-1-59556-024-7(6),* 1291988); (gr. 8-18). pap. 16.99 *(978-1-59556-032-2(7),* 1291988) OTTN Publishing.

De Medeiros, Michael. Barack Obama. (J). 2013. *(978-1-62127-388-2(1))* 2008. (Illus.). 24p. (gr. 4-6). pap. 8.95 *(978-1-59036-989-0(0))* 2008. (Illus.). 24p. (gr. 4-6). lib. bdg. 24.45 *(978-1-59036-988-3(2))* Weigl Pubs., Inc.

Dillon, Molly, compiled by. Yes She Can: 10 Stories of Hope & Change from Young Female Staffers of the Obama White House. 2019. (Illus.). 288p. (YA). (gr. 7). 18.99 *(978-1-9848-4845-1(3),* Schwartz & Wade Bks.) Random Hse. Children's Bks.

Doak, Robin S. Barack Obama. 2013. (True Book(tm), A — Biographies Ser.). (ENG., Illus.). 48p. (J). lib. bdg. 31.00 *(978-0-531-21904-1(6))*; pap. 6.95 *(978-0-531-23875-2(X))* Scholastic Library Publishing.

Edwards, Roberta. Barack Obama: Presidente de Estados Unidos. Call, Ken, illus. 2009.Tr. of Barack Obama: United States President. (SPA.). 64p. (J). (gr. 2-5). pap. 9.99 *(978-1-63113-956-7(8),* Loqueleo) Santillana USA Publishing Co., Inc.

—Michelle Obama: Primera Dama y Primera Mama. Call, Ken, illus. 2010. (SPA.). 48p. (gr. 3-5). pap. 9.99 *(978-1-60396-946-8(2))* Santillana USA Publishing Co., Inc.

Edwards, Roberta & Who HQ. Who Is Barack Obama? O'Brien, John, illus. 2009. (Who Was? Ser.). 112p. (J). (gr. 3-7). pap. 5.99 *(978-0-448-45330-9(4),* Penguin Workshop) Penguin Young Readers Group.

Epstein, Brad M. Barack Obama 101. Lt. ed. 2009. (My First Presidential Board Book Ser.). (Illus.). 28p. (J). (gr. -1-1). bds. *(978-1-60730-044-1(3),* 101 Bk.) Michaelson Entertainment.

Falk, Laine. Meet President Barack Obama. 2009. (Scholastic News Nonfiction Readers Ser.). (ENG., Illus.). 24p. (J). (gr. k-3). 21.19 *(978-0-531-23403-7(7),* Children's Pr.) Scholastic Library Publishing.

—Scholastic News Nonfiction Reader: Meet President Barack Obama. 2009. (Scholastic News Nonfiction Readers Ser.). (ENG., Illus.). 24p. (J). (gr. 1-2). pap. 6.95 *(978-0-531-23524-9(6),* Children's Pr.) Scholastic Library Publishing.

Feinstein, Stephen. Barack Obama, 1 vol. 2008. (African-American Heroes Ser.). (ENG., Illus.). 24p. (gr. k-2). lib. bdg. 25.27 *(978-0-7660-2893-7(3),* 69df780e-533b-4c3f-82e5-c16548d680f1, Enslow Elementary) Enslow Publishing, LLC.

Feinstein, Stephen & Taylor, Charlotte. Barack Obama: First African-American President, 1 vol. 2015. (Exceptional African Americans Ser.). (ENG.). 24p. (gr. 3-4). pap. 10.35 *(978-0-7660-7122-3(7),* 6d9583a1-f228-4f6b-a009-bf3345f11287); (Illus.). 24.27 *(978-0-7660-7124-7(3),* 30bf2328-d3e3-4cc0-a789-bb42085be796) Enslow Publishing, LLC.

Garner, Lama. A Children's Book of Barack Obama Our 44th President. Garner, Essex, illus. 2009.Tr. of Children's Book of Barack Obama Our 44th President. 24p. pap. 7.95 *(978-0-615-31464-8(3))* Art Of Essex Fine Art, The.

Gibson, Karen Bush. The Historic Fight for the 2008 Democratic Presidential Nomination: The Obama View. 2009. (Monumental Milestones Ser.). (Illus.). 48p. (YA). (gr. 4-7). lib. bdg. 29.95 *(978-1-58415-732-8(1))* Mitchell Lane Pubs.

Gilpin, Caroline Crosson. National Geographic Readers: Barack Obama. 2014. (Readers Bios Ser.). 32p. (J). (gr. 1-3). pap. 4.99 *(978-1-4263-1759-0(X),* National Geographic Kids) Disney Publishing Worldwide.

Gormley, Beatrice. Barack Obama: Our Forty-Fourth President. 2015. (Real-Life Story Ser.). (ENG., Illus.). 272p. (J). (gr. 3-7). 17.99 *(978-1-4814-4648-8(7),* Aladdin) Simon & Schuster Children's Publishing.

Grimes, Nikki. Barack Obama: Son of Promise, Child of Hope. Collier, Bryan, illus. (ENG.). 48p. (J). (gr. k-3). 2012. 9.99 *(978-1-4424-4092-0(9))* 2008. pap. 19.99 *(978-1-4169-7144-3(0))* Simon & Schuster Bks. For Young Readers. (Simon & Schuster Bks. For Young Readers).

Hansen, Grace. Barack Obama, 1 vol. 2014. (United States President Biographies (Abdo Kids Jumbo) Ser.). (ENG.). 24p. (J). (gr. -1-2). lib. bdg. 32.79 *(978-1-62970-086-1(X),* 1717, Abdo Kids) ABDO Publishing Co.

—Barack Obama. 2015. (Biografías de Los Presidentes de Los Estados Unidos Ser.). (SPA., Illus.). 24p. (J). (gr. -1-2). pap. 7.95 *(978-1-4966-0403-3(2),* 130251, Capstone Classroom) Capstone.

Harkness, Karen. Obama, Our Hero. 2008. (Illus.). 32p. (J). lib. bdg. 12.99 *(978-0-9800934-1-4(4))* H&W Publishing Inc.

Hoe, Susan. Rosa Parks. 2007. (Sharing the American Dream Ser.). 64p. (YA). (gr. 7-18). pap. 9.95 *(978-1-4222-0760-4(9))* Mason Crest.

Hollar, Sherman, contrib. by. Barack Obama, 1 vol. 2012. (Pivotal Presidents: Profiles in Leadership Ser.). (ENG.). 80p. (gr. 8-8). (J). lib. bdg. 36.47 *(978-1-61530-945-0(4),* 89b6f3bd-1123-481f-8f7c-3208d4fdadaa); (Illus.). (YA). 72.94 *(978-1-61530-955-9(1),* 302b40ce-9005-4894-bfe5-8b13bde0bbc1) Rosen Publishing Group, Inc., The.

Hoppe, Ludwig Augustin. Die Epiklesis Der Griechischen Und Orientalischen Liturgieen Und Der Römische Consekrationskanon (German Edition) 2010. 350p. pap.

32.75 (978-1-142-96440-5(X)) Creative Media Partners, LLC.

Horn, Geoffrey M. Barack Obama, 1 vol. 2009. (People We Should Know (Second Series) Ser.). (ENG.). 32p. (gr. 3-5). (J). lib. bdg. 33.67 (978-1-4339-0017-4(3), 67cd19d1-ac5a-48d1-b01c-6564e5d14bce); pap. 11.50 (978-1-4339-0157-7(9), 609ef1ad-b3f7-4d65-9a25-ab39a47b7759) Stevens, Gareth Publishing LLLP. (Gareth Stevens Learning Library).

Jd, Duchess Harris. Barack Obama Is Elected President. 2018. (Perspectives on American Progress Ser.). (ENG., Illus.). 48p. (J). (gr. 4-8). lib. bdg. 35.64 (978-1-5321-1487-8(7), 29106) ABDO Publishing Co.

Katirgis, Jane. Celebrating President Barack Obama in Pictures, 1 vol. 2009. (Obama Family Photo Album Ser.). (ENG., Illus.). 32p. (gr. 3-3). lib. bdg. 26.60 (978-0-7660-3651-2(0), 652e8ba5-dae8-470c-b17d-906ca29eb724) Enslow Publishing, LLC.

—Celebrating the Inauguration of Barack Obama in Pictures, 1 vol. 2009. (Obama Family Photo Album Ser.). (ENG., Illus.). 32p. (J). (gr. 3-3). lib. bdg. 26.60 (978-0-7660-3650-5(2), 8b888db6-15cf-407a-93aa-b8ec85653170) Enslow Publishing, LLC.

—Celebrating the Obama Family in Pictures, 1 vol. 2009. (Obama Family Photo Album Ser.). (ENG., Illus.). 32p. (gr. 3-3). lib. bdg. 26.60 (978-0-7660-3653-6(7), ba36c440-f581-4b87-aec2-7c703937a9ed) Enslow Publishing, LLC.

Kawa, Katie. Barack Obama: First African American President, 1 vol. 2012. (Beginning Biographies Ser.). (ENG., Illus.). 24p. (J). (gr. 1-2). 26.27 (978-1-4488-8595-4(7), cf17b6d8-b99a-452b-8894-50f2af33c147, PowerKids Pr.) Rosen Publishing Group, Inc., The.

Klein, Adria F. Barack Obama. 2009. pap. 13.25 (978-1-60559-055-4(X)) Hameray Publishing Group, Inc.

Krensky, Stephen. DK Biography: Barack Obama. 2009. (DK Biography Ser.). (ENG.). 128p. (J). (gr. 5-12). 6.99 (978-0-7566-5805-2(5), DK Children) Dorling Kindersley Publishing, Inc.

Lee, T. S. The Obama Story: The Boy with the Biggest Dream! Shin, Janet Jaywan, tr. from KOR. 2009. 207p. (J). (gr. 6-18). pap. 14.95 (978-0-9819542-0-2(0)) DASANBOOKS.

Lemay, Violet, illus. The Obamas: A Lift-The-Flap Book. 2019. 22p. (J). (gr. -1-k). bds. 9.95 (978-1-947458-82-6(5), 805882) Duo Pr. LLC.

Lowery, Zoe, ed. Barack Obama & the Idea of a Postracial Society, 4 vols. 2015. (African American Experience: from Slavery to the Presidency Ser.). (ENG.). 80p. (YA). (gr. 7-8). 70.94 (978-1-68048-052-8(9), 9ad714e7-60ff-4038-a0fe-ed102443e9a5, Britannica Educational Publishing) Rosen Publishing Group, Inc., The.

Marcovitz, Hal. Barack. 2007. (Obamas Ser.). (Illus.). 64p. (YA). (gr. 3-6). pap. 9.95 (978-1-4222-1484-8(2)); (gr. 4-7). lib. bdg. 19.95 (978-1-4222-1477-0(X)) Mason Crest.

—The Obama Family Tree. 2007. (Obamas Ser.). (Illus.). 64p. (YA). (gr. 3-6). pap. 9.95 (978-1-4222-1488-6(5)); (gr. 4-7). lib. bdg. 19.95 (978-1-4222-1481-7(8)) Mason Crest.

—Obama Mania. 2007. (Obamas Ser.). (Illus.). 64p. (YA). (gr. 3-6). pap. 9.95 (978-1-4222-1489-3(3)); (gr. 4-7). lib. bdg. 19.95 (978-1-4222-1482-4(6)) Mason Crest.

Marsh, Carole. Barack Obama: Biography FunBook. 2009. (J). (gr. 2-9). pap. 3.99 (978-0-635-07053-1(7)) Gallopade International.

—Barack Obama - America's 44th President. 2009. (Here & Now Ser.). 40p. (J). (gr. 2-9). 29.99 (978-0-635-06983-2(0)) Gallopade International.

—Barack Obama Presidential Coloring Book! 2008. (Here & Now Ser.). (J). 5.99 (978-0-635-07050-0(2)) Gallopade International.

—Michelle Obama: Biography FunBook. 2009. (J). (gr. 2-9). pap. 3.99 (978-0-635-07054-8(5)) Gallopade International.

—The Obama Family - Life in the White House: President Barack Obama, First Lady Michelle Obama, First Children Malia & Sasha. 2008. (Here & Now Ser.). 32p. (J). (gr. 2-9). pap. 8.99 (978-0-635-07051-7(0)) Gallopade International.

Mattern, Joanne. Barack Obama. 2013. (Rookie Biographies(r) Ser.). (ENG.). 32p. (J). pap. 5.95 (978-0-531-24701-3(5)); lib. bdg. 23.00 (978-0-531-24735-8(X)) Scholastic Library Publishing.

McDonnell, Julia. Before Barack Obama Was President, 1 vol. 2018. (Before They Were President Ser.). (ENG.). 24p. (gr. 2-3). 24.27 (978-1-5382-2909-5(9), 4cbd92b9-440c-41b5-8bd3-7af73085d418) Stevens, Gareth Publishing LLLP.

Mendell, David & Thomson, Sarah L. Obama: A Promise of Change. 2008. (ENG., Illus.). 192p. (J). (gr. 3-7). pap. 6.99 (978-0-06-169700-5(1), Amistad) HarperCollins Pubs.

Michelle Obama. 2009. (Political Profiles Ser.). 112p. (YA). (gr. 5-9). lib. bdg. 28.95 (978-1-59935-090-5(4)) Reynolds, Morgan Inc.

Miller, Moses. The Barack in Me: An Inspirational Novel for Young African American Males. 2009. 116p. pap. 10.99 (978-0-9786929-2-6(6)) Mind Candy, LLC.

Mills, Nathan & Kawa, Katie. Barack Obama: First African American President, 1 vol. 2012. (Rosen Readers Ser.). (ENG., Illus.). 24p. (J). (gr. 1-2). pap. 8.25 (978-1-4488-8845-0(X), ea0c8872-d080-4456-9eee-8359b89c1646, Rosen Classroom) Rosen Publishing Group, Inc., The.

"Miss Nancy" Sorensen. President Barack Obam. 2009. 16p. pap. 8.50 (978-1-4389-4604-7(X)) AuthorHouse.

Morlock, Rachael. Barack Obama: A Life of Leadership, 1 vol. annot. ed. 2019. (People in the News Ser.). (ENG.). 104p. (gr. 7-7). pap. 20.99 (978-1-5345-6840-2(9), 1dbae1b7-6a06-489e-8227-e56a3ac990bb); lib. bdg. 41.03 (978-1-5345-6841-9(7), ca00a648-b9d2-4f3f-ae82-795d317aa70f) Greenhaven Publishing LLC. (Lucent Pr.).

Obama, Barack. Our Enduring Spirit: President Barack Obama's First Words to America. Ruth, Greg, illus. 2009. 48p. (J). lib. bdg. 18.89 (978-0-06-183456-1(4)) HarperCollins Pubs.

Obama, Barack. & Nelson, Kadir. Change Has Come: An Artist Celebrates Our American Spirit. Nelson, Kadir, illus. 2009. (ENG., Illus.). 64p. (J). (gr. 1). 12.99 (978-1-4169-8955-4(2), Simon & Schuster Bks. For Young Readers) Simon & Schuster Bks. For Young Readers.

O'Neal, Claire. What's So Great about Barack Obama. 2009. (What's So Great About... ? Ser.). 32p. (J). (gr. 2-4). lib. bdg. 25.70 (978-1-58415-830-1(1)) Mitchell Lane Pubs.

Orr, Tamra B. Obama vs. Mccain & the Historic Election. 2017. (Perspectives Library: Modern Perspectives Ser.). (ENG., Illus.). 32p. (J). (gr. 4-7). lib. bdg. 32.07 (978-1-63472-860-7(2), 209866) Cherry Lake Publishing.

Phillips, Alonzo. Follow the Course! an Action Book. 2010. 50p. pap. 15.99 (978-1-4535-3702-2(3)) Xlibris Corp.

Robinson, Tom. Barack Obama: 44th U. S. President. 2009. (J). lib. bdg. 32.79 (978-1-60453-528-0(8), Essential Library) ABDO Publishing Co.

Schuetz, Rachael Law. The Long Road to Change: An American Story of Civil Rights & Barack Obama's Journey to the White House. 2009. (Illus.). 36p. (J). 16.00 (978-0-615-27983-1(X)) NRS Enterprises.

Schuman, Michael A. Barack Obama: We Are One People, 1 vol. rev. ed. 2008. (African-American Biography Library). (ENG., Illus.). 160p. (gr. 6-7). lib. bdg. 35.93 (978-0-7660-3649-9(9), 38ae7d97-e2eb-4050-b3ef-e12048222213) Enslow Publishing, LLC.

Schwartz, Heather E. Michelle Obama: Political Icon. 2020. (Boss Lady Bios (Alternator Books (r)) Ser.). (ENG., Illus.). 32p. (J). (gr. 3-6). 30.65 (978-1-5415-9707-5(9), 4af4e01e-075b-4761-8eac-25b4a12854ed, Lerner Pubns.) Lerner Publishing Group.

Shepherd, Jodie. Barack Obama: Groundbreaking President. 2016. (Rookie Biographies(tm) Ser.). (ENG., Illus.). 32p. (J). lib. bdg. 25.00 (978-0-531-21681-1(0), Children's Pr.) Scholastic Library Publishing.

Sherman, Patrice. What It's Like to Be President Barack Obama? Vega, Eida de la, tr. 2009. (What It's Like to Be/Que se Siente al Ser Ser.). (SPA & ENG., Illus.). 32p. (J). (gr. -1-2). 25.70 (978-1-58415-843-1(3)) Mitchell Lane Pubs.

Snyder, Gail. Malia. 2007. (Obamas Ser.). 64p. (YA). (gr. 3-6). pap. 9.95 (978-1-4222-1486-2(9)); (gr. 4-7). lib. bdg. 19.95 (978-1-4222-1479-4(6)) Mason Crest.

—Sasha. 2007. (Obamas Ser.). (Illus.). 64p. (YA). (gr. 3-6). pap. 9.95 (978-1-4222-1487-9(7)); (gr. 4-7). lib. bdg. 19.95 (978-1-4222-1480-0(X)) Mason Crest.

Souza, Pete. Dream Big Dreams: Photographs from Barack Obama's Inspiring & Historic Presidency (Young Readers) 2017. (ENG., Illus.). 96p. (J). (gr. 5-17). 21.99 (978-0-316-51439-2(X)) Little, Brown Bks. for Young Readers.

Stoltman, Joan. Barack Obama, 1 vol. 2018. (Little Biographies of Big People Ser.). (ENG.). 24p. (gr. 1-2). 24.27 (978-1-5382-1828-0(3), b0e73cd7-4e09-465f-9319-78ac635335da) Stevens, Gareth Publishing LLLP.

Strand, Jennifer. Barack Obama. 2016. (Legendary Leaders Ser.). (ENG.). 24p. (J). (gr. -1-2). 49.94 (978-1-68079-403-8(5), 23024, Abdo Zoom-Launch) ABDO Publishing Co.

Sutcliffe, Jane. Barack Obama. 2010. (History Maker Biographies Ser.). (ENG.). 48p. (gr. 3-6). lib. bdg. 27.93 (978-0-7613-5205-1(8), Lerner Pubns.) Lerner Publishing Group.

Thomas, Garen. Yes We Can: A Biography of President Barack Obama. 2nd rev. ed. 2008. (ENG., Illus.). 256p. (J). (gr. 3-6). 12.99 (978-0-312-58639-3(6), 900062157) Feiwel & Friends.

Torres, John A. How Barack Obama Fought the War on Terrorism, 1 vol. 2017. (Presidents at War Ser.). (ENG.). 128p. (gr. 8-8). lib. bdg. 38.93 (978-0-7660-8535-0(X), 6808ab9c-609c-4f7e-b33b-789b6476f7fb) Enslow Publishing, LLC.

Uschan, Michael V. & Devaney, Sherri. Barack Obama, 1 vol. 2009. (People in the News Ser.). (ENG.). 104p. (gr. 7-7). lib. bdg. 41.03 (978-1-4205-0206-0(9), 0f599642-cdf7-4910-bdbf-993a8537a06a, Lucent Pr.) Greenhaven Publishing LLC.

Wagner, Heather Lehr. Barack Obama. 2008. (Black Americans of Achievement Legacy Edition Ser.). 104p. (gr. 6-12). pap. 11.95 (978-1-60413-324-0(4), Checkmark Bks.) Infobase Holdings, Inc.

Winter, Jonah. Barack. Ford, A. G., illus. 32p. (J). (gr. -1-2). 2010. (ENG.). pap. 8.99 (978-0-06-170396-6(6), Tegen, Katherine Bks) 2008. lib. bdg. 18.89 (978-0-06-170393-5(1)) HarperCollins Pubs.

—Barack, 2 vols. 2009. (J). 38.75 (978-1-4407-3624-7(3)); 40.75 (978-1-4407-3622-3(7)); 38.75 (978-1-4407-3620-9(0)); 40.75 (978-1-4407-3618-6(9)); 1.25 (978-1-4407-3625-4(1)); 222.75 (978-1-4407-3619-3(7)) Recorded Bks., Inc.

Wong, Angi Ma. Barack Obama: Historymaker. 2009. (Illus.). 104p. (J). (978-1-928753-86-5(8)) Pacific Heritage Bks.

Wong, Angi Ma, illus. Meet President Obama: America's 44th President. 2009. 32p. (J). (978-1-928753-28-5(0)) Pacific Heritage Bks.

Zaboly, Gary & Gardner, Martin. Barack Obama Coloring Book. 2009. (Dover American History Coloring Bks.). (ENG., Illus.). 32p. (J). (gr. 3-6). pap. 4.99 (978-0-486-47320-8(1), 473201) Dover Pubns., Inc.

Zeiger, Jennifer. Cornerstones of Freedom, Third Series: Barack Obama. 2012. (Cornerstones of Freedom, Third Ser.). (ENG.). 64p. (J). (gr. 4-6). lib. bdg. 30.00 (978-0-531-23050-3(3), Children's Pr.) Scholastic Library Publishing.

Zumbusch, Amelie von. Barack Obama: Man of Destiny, 1 vol. 2010. (Making History: the Obamas Ser.). (ENG., Illus.). 24p. (J). (gr. 2-3). pap. 9.25 (978-1-4358-9866-0(4), e200cb41-050a-4dda-87d4-a9846743869d); lib. bdg. 26.27 (978-1-4358-9387-0(5), 3e3364d2-8945-4a03-bc46-b5f5f79e1823) Rosen Publishing Group, Inc., The. (PowerKids Pr.).

—Barack Obama's Family Tree: Roots of Achievement, 1 vol. 2010. (Making History: the Obamas Ser.). (ENG., Illus.). 24p. (J). (gr. 2-3). pap. 9.25 (978-1-4358-9872-1(9), 699fd69a-374d-485e-9674-bd8fd2dbac80); lib. bdg. 26.27 (978-1-4358-9390-0(5), c4826398-32e9-4a8a-be59-60f8cdd62981) Rosen Publishing Group, Inc., The. (PowerKids Pr.).

—First Family: The Obamas in the White House, 1 vol. 2010. (Making History: the Obamas Ser.). (ENG., Illus.). 24p. (J). (gr. 2-3). pap. 9.25 (978-1-4358-9870-7(2), 3b0d7460-ff6f-422c-9b8d-54dffd4e98f1); lib. bdg. 26.27 (978-1-4358-9389-4(1), 2248e056-c7f7-4e7f-b083-bcbee019cd64) Rosen Publishing Group, Inc., The. (PowerKids Pr.).

—Making History: The Obamas, 8 vols. Incl. Barack Obama: Man of Destiny. lib. bdg. 26.27 (978-1-4358-9387-0(5), 3e3364d2-8945-4a03-bc46-b5f5f79e1823); Barack Obama's Family Tree: Roots of Achievement. lib. bdg. 26.27 (978-1-4358-9390-0(5), c4826398-32e9-4a8a-be59-60f8cdd62981); First Family: The Obamas in the White House. lib. bdg. 26.27 (978-1-4358-9389-4(1), 2248e056-c7f7-4e7f-b083-bcbee019cd64); Michelle Obama: Our First Lady. lib. bdg. 26.27 (978-1-4358-9388-7(3), 62b0413a-3e96-4376-9e00-b445bdcb7d73); (J). (gr. 2-3). (Making History: the Obamas Ser.). (ENG., Illus.). 24p. 2010. Set lib. bdg. 105.08 (978-1-4358-9407-5(3), 36d46a30-a7a4-4bff-beb4-bdb093b45c13, PowerKids Pr.) Rosen Publishing Group, Inc., The.

OBAMA, MICHELLE, 1964-

Bodden, Valerie. Michelle Obama: First Lady & Role Model, 1 vol. 2009. (Essential Lives Set 4 Ser.). (ENG., Illus.). 112p. (YA). (gr. 6-12). lib. bdg. 41.36 (978-1-60453-703-1(5), 6697, Essential Library) ABDO Publishing Co.

Brill, Marlene Targ. Michelle Obama. 2009. (Illus.). 48p. (J). pap. 8.95 (978-0-7613-5053-8(5)) Lerner Publishing Group.

—Michelle Obama: From Chicago's South Side to the White House. 2009. (Gateway Biographies Ser.). (ENG., Illus.). 48p. (gr. 4-8). 26.60 (978-0-7613-5033-0(0)) Lerner Publishing Group.

Brophy, David B. Michelle Obama: Meet the First Lady. 2008. 128p. (J). pap. 6.99 (978-0-06-177990-9(3)) HarperCollins Pubs.

Colbert, David. Michelle Obama: An American Story. 2008. (ENG., Illus.). 160p. (J). (gr. 3-7). pap. 7.99 (978-0-547-24770-0(2), 1100646, Clarion Bks.) HarperCollins Pubs.

Corey, Shana. Michelle Obama: First Lady, Going Higher. Bernardin, James, illus. 2018. (Step into Reading Ser.). 48p. (J). (gr. k-3). pap. 5.99 (978-1-5247-7229-1(1), Random Hse. Bks. for Young Readers) Random Hse. Children's Bks.

Edwards, Roberta. Michelle Obama: Primera Dama y Primera Mama. Call, Ken, illus. 2010. (SPA.). 48p. (gr. 3-5). pap. 9.99 (978-1-60396-946-8(2)) Santillana USA Publishing Co., Inc.

Endsley, Kezia. Michelle Obama: 44th First Lady & Health & Education Advocate, 1 vol. 2014. (Leading Women Ser.). (ENG.). 112p. (YA). (gr. 7-7). lib. bdg. 41.64 (978-1-62712-975-6(8), 424f474b-768b-42a2-be45-b14edf9bfe03) Cavendish Square Publishing LLC.

Hansen, Grace. Michelle Obama: Former First Lady & Role Model. 2017. (History Maker Biographies (Abdo Kids Jumbo) Ser.). (ENG., Illus.). 24p. (J). (gr. -1-2). lib. bdg. 32.79 (978-1-5321-0427-5(8), 26553, Abdo Kids) ABDO Publishing Co.

Hopkinson, Deborah. Michelle. Ford, A. G., illus. 2009. 32p. (J). (gr. -1-2). 17.99 (978-0-06-182739-6(8)) HarperCollins Pubs.

Hudson, Amanda. Michelle Obama, 1 vol. 2009. (People We Should Know (Second Series) Ser.). (ENG.). 48p. (J). (gr. 3-5). pap. 11.50 (978-1-4339-2192-6(8), 52e0e14d-5612-4f8c-b7d3-6032009fc9db); lib. bdg. 33.67 (978-1-4339-2187-2(1), 39091c59-0022-40d8-9376-30ac82a88229) Stevens, Gareth Publishing LLLP. (Gareth Stevens Learning Library).

Katirgis, Jane. Celebrating First Lady Michelle Obama in Pictures, 1 vol. 2009. (Obama Family Photo Album Ser.). (ENG., Illus.). 32p. (gr. 3-3). lib. bdg. 26.60 (978-0-7660-3652-9(9), d9e0b307-d964-40e1-94b0-d84e91fa5515) Enslow Publishing, LLC.

Leaf, Christina. Michelle Obama: Health Advocate. 2019. (Women Leading the Way Ser.). (ENG., Illus.). 24p. (J). (gr. k-3). lib. bdg. 26.95 (978-1-62617-942-4(5), Blastoff! Readers) Bellwether Media.

—Michelle Obama: Health Advocate. 2019. (Women Leading the Way Ser.). (ENG., Illus.). 24p. (J). (gr. k-3). pap. 7.99 (978-1-61891-502-3(9), 12153, Blastoff! Readers) Bellwether Media.

Machajewski, Sarah. Michelle Obama, 1 vol. 2016. (Superwomen Role Models Ser.). (ENG., Illus.). 32p. (J). (gr. 3-4). 27.93 (978-1-5081-4812-8(0), 8d67cc38-9de9-4c10-90bc-efee1f99a1f6, PowerKids Pr.) Rosen Publishing Group, Inc., The.

Marcovitz, Hal. Michelle. 2007. (Obamas Ser.). 64p. (YA). (gr. 3-6). pap. 9.95 (978-1-4222-1485-5(0)); (gr. 4-7). lib. bdg. 19.95 (978-1-4222-1478-7(8)) Mason Crest.

Marsh, Carole. Michelle Obama: Biography FunBook. 2009. (J). (gr. 2-9). pap. 3.99 (978-0-635-07054-8(5)) Gallopade International.

—The Obama Family - Life in the White House: President Barack Obama, First Lady Michelle Obama, First Children Malia & Sasha. 2008. (Here & Now Ser.). 32p. (J). (gr. 2-9). pap. 8.99 (978-0-635-07051-7(0)) Gallopade International.

Mattern, Joanne. What's So Great about Michelle Obama. 2009. (What's So Great About... ? Ser.). 32p. (J). (gr. 2-4). lib. bdg. 25.70 (978-1-58415-833-2(6)) Mitchell Lane Pubs.

Membrino, Anna. I Look up to... Michelle Obama. Burke, Fatti, illus. 2018. 22p. (J). (— 1). bds. 7.99 (978-0-525-57954-0(0), Random Hse. Bks. for Young Readers) Random Hse. Children's Bks.

Michelle Obama. 2009. (Political Profiles Ser.). 112p. (YA). (gr. 5-9). lib. bdg. 28.95 (978-1-59935-090-5(4)) Reynolds, Morgan Inc.

Nault, Jennifer. Michelle Obama. 2009. (Remarkable People Ser.). (Illus.). 24p. (J). (gr. 4-6). pap. 8.95 (978-1-60596-666-3(5)); lib. bdg. 24.45 (978-1-60596-665-6(7)) Weigl Pubs., Inc.

Obama, Michelle. Becoming: Adapted for Young Readers. 2021. (ENG., Illus.). 432p. (J). (gr. 5). 18.99 (978-0-593-30374-0(1)); lib. bdg. 21.99 (978-0-593-30375-7(X)) Random Hse. Children's Bks. (Delacorte Bks. for Young Readers).

Oliver, Alison. Be Bold, Baby: Michelle Obama. Oliver, Alison, illus. 2018. (Be Bold, Baby Ser.). (ENG., Illus.). 20p. (J). (— 1). bds. 9.99 (978-1-328-51989-4(9), 1720769, Clarion Bks.) HarperCollins Pubs.

Stine, Megan. Who Is Michelle Obama? 2013. (Who Is... ? Ser.). lib. bdg. 14.75 (978-0-606-32131-0(4)) Turtleback.

Stine, Megan & Who HQ. Who Is Michelle Obama? O'Brien, John, illus. 2013. (Who Was? Ser.). 112p. (J). (gr. 3-7). 5.99 (978-0-448-47863-0(3), Penguin Workshop) Penguin Young Readers Group.

Stoltman, Joan. Michelle Obama, 1 vol. 2017. (Little Biographies of Big People Ser.). (ENG.). 24p. (J). (gr. 1-2). pap. 9.15 (978-1-5382-0929-5(2), fbc15435-d338-4ce0-8dfa-22308002b351) Stevens, Gareth Publishing LLLP.

—Michelle Obama, 1 vol. Garcia, Ana Maria, tr. 2017. (Pequeñas Biografías de Grandes Personajes (Little Biographies of Big People) Ser.). (SPA.). 24p. (J). (gr. 1-2). pap. 9.15 (978-1-5382-1555-5(1), 827c2c46-0ae9-4e2d-82a1-1ea660a36de8); lib. bdg. 24.27 (978-1-5382-1528-9(4), 72bafb7a-6a09-4f74-becc-105367d5c6c9) Stevens, Gareth Publishing LLLP.

Strand, Jennifer. Michelle Obama. 2017. (First Ladies (Launch!) Ser.). (ENG., Illus.). 24p. (J). (gr. -1-2). lib. bdg. 31.36 (978-1-5321-2017-6(6), 25284, Abdo Zoom-Launch) ABDO Publishing Co.

Taylor-Butler, Christine. Michelle Obama. 2015. (ENG.). 48p. (J). pap. 6.95 (978-0-531-21206-6(8), Orchard Bks.) Scholastic Library Publishing.

Uschan, Michael V. Michelle Obama, 1 vol. 2010. (People in the News Ser.). (ENG., Illus.). 112p. (gr. 7-7). 41.03 (978-1-4205-0209-1(3), a36bfb24-c866-43d1-b0fe-08faaaaf913e, Lucent Pr.) Greenhaven Publishing LLC.

Zumbusch, Amelie von. First Family: The Obamas in the White House, 1 vol. 2010. (Making History: the Obamas Ser.). (ENG., Illus.). 24p. (J). (gr. 2-3). pap. 9.25 (978-1-4358-9870-7(2), 3b0d7460-ff6f-422c-9b8d-54dffd4e98f1); lib. bdg. 26.27 (978-1-4358-9389-4(1), 2248e056-c7f7-4e7f-b083-bcbee019cd64) Rosen Publishing Group, Inc., The. (PowerKids Pr.).

—Making History: The Obamas, 8 vols. Incl. Barack Obama: Man of Destiny. lib. bdg. 26.27 (978-1-4358-9387-0(5), 3e3364d2-8945-4a03-bc46-b5f5f79e1823); Barack Obama's Family Tree: Roots of Achievement. lib. bdg. 26.27 (978-1-4358-9390-0(5), c4826398-32e9-4a8a-be59-60f8cdd62981); First Family: The Obamas in the White House. lib. bdg. 26.27 (978-1-4358-9389-4(1), 2248e056-c7f7-4e7f-b083-bcbee019cd64); Michelle Obama: Our First Lady. lib. bdg. 26.27 (978-1-4358-9388-7(3), 62b0413a-3e96-4376-9e00-b445bdcb7d73); (J). (gr. 2-3). (Making History: the Obamas Ser.). (ENG., Illus.). 24p. 2010. Set lib. bdg. 105.08 (978-1-4358-9407-5(3), 36d46a30-a7a4-4bff-beb4-bdb093b45c13, PowerKids Pr.) Rosen Publishing Group, Inc., The.

—Michelle Obama: Our First Lady, 1 vol. 2010. (Making History: the Obamas Ser.). (ENG., Illus.). 24p. (J). (gr. 2-3). pap. 9.25 (978-1-4358-9868-4(0), 468c9a7f-e11e-4215-9610-71d2c13860bd); lib. bdg. 26.27 (978-1-4358-9388-7(3), 62b0413a-3e96-4376-9e00-b445bdcb7d73) Rosen Publishing Group, Inc., The. (PowerKids Pr.).

OBEDIENCE

Berry, Joy. Help Me Be Good Disobeying. Bartholomew, illus. 2010. (Help Me Be Good Ser.). (ENG.). 32p. (J). (gr. -1-2). pap. 4.99 (978-1-60577-137-3(6)) Berry, Joy Enterprises.

Berry, Joy Wilt. A Children's Book about Disobeying. 2005. (Illus.). (J). (978-0-7172-8593-8(6)) Scholastic, Inc.

Bloom, Paul. Rules in the Classroom, 1 vol. 2015. (School Rules Ser.). (ENG., Illus.). 24p. (J). (gr. k-k). pap. 9.15 (978-1-4824-2641-0(2), 536733b2-bfaf-4efb-96bb-bc254b3a9015) Stevens, Gareth Publishing LLLP.

—Rules in the Gym, 1 vol. 2015. (School Rules Ser.). (ENG., Illus.). 24p. (J). (gr. k-k). pap. 9.15 (978-1-4824-2645-8(5), 3c827ece-e30a-4f54-b2dc-39089dd24228) Stevens, Gareth Publishing LLLP.

Honders, Christine. Why Should I Listen to My Parents?, 1 vol. 2019. (Listening to Leaders Ser.). (ENG.). 24p. (gr. 2-2). pap. 9.25 (978-1-5383-4168-1(9), 8270b24a-00f6-49d6-8e73-bdfe04395f89, PowerKids Pr.) Rosen Publishing Group, Inc., The.

Leventhal-Belfer, Laurie. Why Do I Have To? A Book for Children Who Find Themselves Frustrated by Everyday Rules. Montaini-Klovdahl, Luisa, illus. 2008. 80p. (C). pap. 11.95 (978-1-84310-891-7(7), 696051) Kingsley, Jessica Pubs. GBR. Dist: Hachette UK Distribution.

Lindeen, Mary. Rules Rule at School! 2019. (BeginningtoRead Ser.). (ENG., Illus.). 32p. (J). (gr. -1-2). 22.60 (978-1-68450-941-6(6)) Norwood Hse. Pr.

MacKenzie, Carine. Glorifying God: Obedient Lives from the Bible. 2013. (ENG., Illus.). 96p. (J). pap. 7.99 (978-1-78191-124-2(X), 243c4181-2a30-44b0-a577-904557174952) Christian Focus Pubns. GBR. Dist: Baker & Taylor Publisher Services (BTPS).

Mayer, Cassie. Following Rules, 1 vol. Beech, Mark, illus. 2007. (Citizenship Ser.). (ENG.). 24p. (J). (gr. -1-1). pap. 6.29 (978-1-4034-9495-5(9), 96163, Heinemann) Capstone.

—Seguir Las Reglas. 2007. (Civismo Ser.). (SPA., Illus.). 24p. (J). (gr. -1-1). pap. 6.29 (978-1-4329-0410-4(8), 97247, Heinemann) Capstone.

Meiners, Cheri J. Know & Follow Rules. Johnson, Meredith, illus. 2005. (Learning to Get Along(r) Ser.). (ENG.). 40p. (J). (gr. -1-3). pap. 11.99 (978-1-57542-130-8(5), 953) Free Spirit Publishing Inc.

—Know & Follow Rules / Saber y Seguir Las Reglas. Johnson, Meredith, illus. 2015. (Learning to Get Along(r) Ser.). (ENG.). 48p. (J). (gr. -1-3). pap. 12.99 (978-1-57542-498-9(3)) Free Spirit Publishing Inc.

Nelson, Robin. Following Rules. 2003. (First Step Nonfiction — Citizenship Ser.). (ENG., Illus.). 24p. (gr. k-2). (J). pap. 6.99 (978-0-8225-1321-6(8),

c14b1c6d-30d0-41fa-ac11-d86c5fe64a81); lib. bdg. 23.93 *(978-0-8225-1284-4(X))* Lerner Publishing Group.
Ricciuti, Edward R. Respetamos Las Reglas / We Follow the Rules, 1 vol. 2008. (Listos para Ir a la Escuela / Ready for School Ser.). (ENG & SPA., Illus.). 24p. (gr. k-1). lib. bdg. 25.50 *(978-0-7614-2438-3(5),* 264eb2e7-181b-469e-8f19-280524b8e4bc) Cavendish Square Publishing LLC.
—Respetamos Las Reglas (We Follow the Rules), 1 vol. 2008. (Listos para Ir a la Escuela (Ready for School) Ser.). (SPA., Illus.). 24p. (gr. k-1). lib. bdg. 25.50 *(978-0-7614-2358-4(3),* 6b193d7d-bfd1-4c5d-a96e-e53ab0cd5173) Cavendish Square Publishing LLC.
—We Follow the Rules, 1 vol. (Ready for School Ser.). (ENG., Illus.). 24p. (gr. k-1). 2008. pap. 9.23 *(978-0-7614-3273-9(6),* 28ec1dc5-cdea-4a9a-a72f-98c359bde0f0) 2007. lib. bdg. 25.50 *(978-0-7614-1995-2(0),* a6ef864a-ff65-4903-a765-9045b52cf979) Cavendish Square Publishing LLC.
Robak, Raelinda. Herbie the Hippo. 2007. (J). *(978-0-8127-0465-5(7))* Autumn Hse. Publishing Co.
Taylor, Charlotte. I Follow the Rules, 1 vol. 2020. (We've Got Character! Ser.). (ENG.). 24p. (J). (gr. 1-2). pap. 9.15 *(978-1-5382-5643-5(6),* bd4c3dad-2b7e-448c-b765-9b75be7dd371) Stevens, Gareth Publishing LLLP.

OBEDIENCE—FICTION

A. L. O. E. The Triumph over Midian. 2006. 344p. per. 23.99 *(978-1-4255-3466-0(X))* Michigan Publishing.
Adbage, Lisen. Koko & Bo. Prime, Annie, tr. 2018. (Koko & Bo Ser.: 1). (ENG., Illus.). (J). 16.95 *(978-1-59270-258-9(9))* Enchanted Lion Bks., LLC.
Aimwell, Walter. Oscar: Or, the Boy Who Had His Own Way. 2017. (ENG., Illus.). (J). 23.95 *(978-1-374-90362-3(0));* pap. 13.95 *(978-1-374-90361-6(2))* Capital Communications, Inc.
Bacigalupi, Paolo. Tool of War. (Ship Breaker Ser.). (ENG.). 384p. (YA). 2018. (gr. 9-17). pap. 19.99 *(978-0-316-22081-1(7))* 2017. (gr. 10-17). 17.99 *(978-0-316-22083-5(3))* Little, Brown Bks. for Young Readers.
Bauer, Marion Dane. On My Honor. 2012. lib. bdg. 18.40 *(978-0-606-24717-7(3))* Turtleback.
Bolton, Robin. Sunny Goes Out to Play. 2011. 28p. pap. 12.03 *(978-1-4634-2530-2(9))* AuthorHouse.
Childs Howard, Betsy. Arlo & the Great Big Cover-Up. Hardy, Samara, illus. 2020. (TGC Kids Ser.). (ENG.). 40p. 14.99 *(978-1-4335-6852-7(7))* Crossway.
Clara Mulholland. Naughty Miss Bunny. 2007. 128p. per. 10.95 *(978-1-4218-3938-7(5),* 1st World Library - Literary Society) 1st World Publishing, Inc.
Cook, Julia. I Just Don't Like the Sound of No! My Story about Accepting No for an Answer & Disagreeing the Right Way. De Weerd, Kelsey, illus. 2011. (ENG.). 32p. (J). *(978-1-934490-26-6(1))* Boys Town Pr.
—I Just Don't Like the Sound of No! My Story about Accepting 'No' for an Answer & Disagreeing the Right Way!: My Story about Accepting 'No' for an Answer & Disagreeing... the Right Way!, Volume 2. De Weerd, Kelsey, illus. 2011. (Best Me I Can Be Ser.). (ENG.). 31p. (J). (gr. k-6). pap. 10.95 *(978-1-934490-25-9(3))* Boys Town Pr.
Crouch, Cheryl. Troo's Big Climb, 1 vol. Zimmer, Kevin, illus. 2011. (I Can Read! / Rainforest Friends Ser.). (ENG.). 32p. (J). (gr. -1-2). pap. 4.99 *(978-0-310-71808-6(2))* Zonderkidz.
Dean, Walter. How Leo the Lion Learned to Roar. 2013. 44p. pap. 12.95 *(978-0-9844342-6-8(7))* C&K Publishing Co.
Feiffer, Jules. I'm Not Bobby! Feiffer, Jules, illus. 2006. (Illus.). 28p. (J). (gr. k-4). reprint ed. 16.00 *(978-0-7567-9853-6(1))* DIANE Publishing Co.
Finley, Martha. Elsie at Nantucket. 2018. (ENG., Illus.). 218p. (YA). (gr. 7-12). pap. *(978-93-5297-352-1(6))* Alpha Editions.
—Elsie at Nantucket. 2018. (ENG., Illus.). 240p. (J). 29.98 *(978-0-464-94306-8(X))* Blurb, Inc.
—Elsie at Nantucket. 2017. (ENG., Illus.). (J). 24.95 *(978-1-374-83782-9(2))* Capital Communications, Inc.
Frye, Timea Csonka. Wishing Star: Lost in the Woods. 2013. 32p. pap. 24.95 *(978-1-63000-931-1(8))* America Star Bks.
Gaichies, Sarah. Mirabelle the Lost Kitten. 2010. (Illus.). 76p. pap. 24.99 *(978-1-4490-5593-6(1))* AuthorHouse.
Gallegos, Eligio Stephen. Nothing Is Nothing. 2013. 144p. pap. 6.99 *(978-0-944164-24-2(2))* Moon Bear Pr.
Hamilton, Elizabeth L. Little Zoh's Submissive Trunk. 2003. (Character Critters Ser.: No. 3). (Illus.). 32p. (J). (gr. -1-3). per. 5.95 *(978-0-9713749-9-7(6),* Character-in-Action) Quiet Impact, Inc.
Jacqueline, Thomas. Birthday Picnic. 2010. 24p. pap. 9.99 *(978-0-88144-493-3(6))* Yorkshire Publishing Group.
Knudsen, Michelle. Library Lion. Hawkes, Kevin, illus. (ENG.). 48p. (J). (gr. -1-3). 2009. pap. 7.99 *(978-0-7636-3784-2(X))* 2006. 18.99 *(978-0-7636-2262-6(1))* Candlewick Pr.
—Library Lion. 2009. lib. bdg. 17.20 *(978-0-606-06666-2(7))* Turtleback.
Laboy, Gloria J. Freddie Learns Obedience. 2008. 24p. pap. 13.95 *(978-1-4327-1906-7(8))* Outskirts Pr., Inc.
Larosa, Marjanita. Mosquit: The Very Disobedient Mosquito. 2012. 36p. pap. 16.95 *(978-1-4497-3283-7(6),* WestBow Pr.) Author Solutions, LLC.
Mulholland, Clara. Naughty Miss Bunny. 2007. 128p. 25.95 *(978-1-4218-3838-0(9),* 1st World Library - Literary Society) 1st World Publishing, Inc.
Richards, Christine. Bobby the Busy Body Boy. 2011. 24p. pap. 14.93 *(978-1-4269-5913-4(3))* Trafford Publishing.
Ries, Lori. Good Dog, Aggie. Dormer, Frank W., illus. 2009. (Aggie & Ben Ser.). (ENG.). 48p. (J). (gr. -1-3). 12.95 *(978-1-57091-645-8(4))* Charlesbridge Publishing, Inc.
Rutland, J. I Love You No Matter What: A Prince Chirpio Story, 1 vol. 2013. (ENG., Illus.). 32p. (J). 9.99 *(978-1-4003-2195-7(6),* Tommy Nelson) Nelson, Thomas Inc.
Snowballs & Coconuts. 2006. 56p. pap. 7.75 *(978-0-8341-2295-6(2),* 083-412-2952) Beacon Hill Pr. of Kansas City.
Sonberg, Caryn. Six Dogs & a Police Officer. Dorenkamp, Michelle, illus. 2006. 31p. pap. 8.40 *(978-1-55501-776-7(2))* Ballard & Tighe Pubs.
Sorenson, Toni. I Will Go, I Will Do: A Book of Mormon Story. 2008. (Illus.). (J). *(978-1-59811-627-4(4))* Covenant Communications.
Tamburri, Pasqualino. Alex & the Trampoline. 2008. 32p. (J). (gr. -1-2). 14.95 *(978-1-60227-473-0(8))* Above the Clouds Publishing.
Weston Woods Staff, creator. Goldilocks & the Three Bears. 2011. 18.95 *(978-0-439-72679-5(4));* 38.75 *(978-0-439-72682-5(4));* 29.95 *(978-0-439-73471-4(1))* Weston Woods Studios, Inc.

OBESITY

see Weight Control

OBI-WAN KENOBI (FICTITIOUS CHARACTER)—FICTION

see Kenobi, Obi-Wan (Fictitious Character)—Fiction

OBSCENITY (LAW)

Axelrod-Contrada, Joan. Reno V. Aclu: Internet Censorship, 1 vol. 2007. (Supreme Court Milestones Ser.). (ENG., Illus.). 128p. (YA). (gr. 8-8). lib. bdg. 45.50 *(978-0-7614-2144-3(0),* b8cb54ba-eff9-4bc1-a337-1ce93d2d0e3b) Cavendish Square Publishing LLC.

OBSERVATORIES, ASTRONOMICAL

see Astronomical Observatories

OBSTETRICS

see Childbirth

OCCULT SCIENCES

see Occultism

OCCULTISM

see also Alchemy; Astrology; Clairvoyance; Divination; Fortune-Telling; Magic; Superstition; Witchcraft

Acer, David. Gotcha! 18 Amazing Ways to Freak Out Your Friends. MacEachern, Stephen, illus. 2008. (ENG.). 48p. (J). (gr. 3-7). 16.95 *(978-1-55453-194-3(2))* Kids Can Pr., Ltd. CAN. Dist: Hachette Bk. Group.
Atwood, Megan. Numerology. 2019. (Psychic Arts Ser.). (ENG., Illus.). 48p. (J). (gr. 4-8). lib. bdg. 31.99 *(978-0-7565-6103-1(5),* 139301, Compass Point Bks.) Capstone.
Belanger, Jeff. Real-Life Ghost Encounters, 1 vol. 2013. (Haunted: Ghosts & the Paranormal Ser.). (ENG.). 208p. (YA). (gr. 8-8). 42.47 *(978-1-4777-0678-7(X),* f126576b-86b6-4317-8026-5fcc5bb657c4) Rosen Publishing Group, Inc., The.
Blohm, Craig E. The Possessed, 1 vol. 2007. (Mysterious Encounters Ser.). (ENG., Illus.). 48p. (gr. 4-8). lib. bdg. 35.23 *(978-0-7377-3781-3(6),* c7b8bc52-51ae-429e-b819-d6346804b67e, KidHaven Publishing) Greenhaven Publishing LLC.
Chandler, Matt. The World's Most Haunted Places, 1 vol. 2011. (Ghost Files Ser.). (ENG.). 32p. (J). (gr. 3-9). lib. bdg. 28.65 *(978-1-4296-6518-6(1),* 115630, Capstone Pr.) Capstone.
Claybourne, Anna. Don't Read This Book Before Bed: Thrills, Chills, & Hauntingly True Stories. 2017. (Illus.). 144p. (J). (gr. 5-9). pap. 14.99 *(978-1-4263-2841-1(9));* (ENG., lib. bdg. 24.90 *(978-1-4263-2842-8(7))* Disney Publishing Worldwide. (National Geographic Kids).
Coronet Instructional Media (Firm) Staff, contrib. by. Counterpoint Reader: Myth, Magic & Mystery. (Illus.). (J). *(978-0-388-30353-5(0))* Steck-Vaughn.
Cox, Barbara & Forbes, Scott. Haunted Homes, 1 vol., Vol. 1. 2014. (Creepy Chronicles Ser.). (ENG.). 32p. (J). (gr. 5-6). 29.27 *(978-1-4824-0230-8(0),* 952cdd42-eb59-4040-a3bf-aa99b37b42b8) Stevens, Gareth Publishing LLLP.
Ellis, Carol. New Orleans Voodoo. 2015. (J). *(978-1-61900-068-1(7))* Eldorado Ink.
Guiley, Rosemary ellen. Ghosts & Haunted Places. 2008. (ENG., Illus.). 144p. (gr. 7-12). 29.95 *(978-0-7910-9392-4(1),* P145799, Facts On File) Infobase Holdings, Inc.
—Spirit Communications. 2009. (Mysteries, Legends, & Unexplained Phenomena Ser.). (ENG., Illus.). 128p. (gr. 7-12). 29.95 *(978-0-7910-9391-7(3),* P171279, Facts On File) Infobase Holdings, Inc.
Hart, Chris. Manga Mania Romance: Drawing Shojo Girls & Bishie Boys. 2008. (Manga Mania(tm) Ser.). (ENG., Illus.). 144p. (gr. 5-18). pap. 19.95 *(978-1-933027-43-2(6),* Hart, Chris Bks.) Sixth&Spring Bks.
Haunted: Ghosts & the Paranormal: Set 3, 8 vols. 2013. (Haunted: Ghosts & the Paranormal Ser.). (ENG.). 208p. (YA). (gr. 8-8). 169.88 *(978-1-4777-0686-2(0),* 9ce296b4-aef7-4e2f-a9e7-ac4033d1070f) Rosen Publishing Group, Inc., The.
Haunted: Ghosts & the Paranormal: Sets 1 - 3, 22 vols. 2013. (Haunted: Ghosts & the Paranormal Ser.). (ENG.). 208p. (YA). (gr. 8-8). 467.17 *(978-1-4777-0734-0(4),* 6cdcc515-54d2-4097-8e69-4ce50ee94fa5) Rosen Publishing Group, Inc., The.
Herbst, Judith. Hoaxes. 2004. (Unexplained Ser.). (Illus.). 48p. (J). pap. 7.95 *(978-0-8225-2406-9(6),* Lerner Pubns.); (ENG., (gr. 5-12). lib. bdg. 26.60 *(978-0-8225-1629-3(2))* Lerner Publishing Group.
Kolpin, Molly. Eerie Haunted Places, 1 vol. 2013. (Scared! Ser.). (ENG.). 32p. (J). (gr. 3-9). 28.65 *(978-1-4296-9980-8(9),* 120681) Capstone.
Krull, Kathleen. They Saw the Future: Oracles, Psychics, Scientists, Great Thinkers, & Pretty Good Guessers. Brooker, Kyrsten, illus. 2014. (ENG.). 112p. (J). (gr. -1-3). pap. 45.99 *(978-1-4814-3623-6(6),* Atheneum Bks. for Young Readers) Simon & Schuster Children's Publishing.
Lynette, Rachel. Curses, 1 vol. 2011. (Mysterious Encounters Ser.). (ENG.). 48p. (gr. 4-8). lib. bdg. 33.58 *(978-0-7377-5422-3(2),* 3f3eeb6d-5fda-4ab3-bb58-6d9f53c7a951, KidHaven Publishing) Greenhaven Publishing LLC.
Main, Sami. How to Deal: Tarot for Everyday Life. de la Pena, Marisa, illus. 2018. (ENG.). 240p. (YA). (gr. 8). pap. 15.99 *(978-0-06-266217-0(1),* HarperCollins) HarperCollins Pubs.
Markovics, Joyce L. Morgues Mortíferas. 2018. (De Puntillas en Lugares Escalofriantes/Tiptoe into Scary Places Ser.). (SPA.). 24p. (J). (gr. k-3). 18.95 *(978-1-68402-614-2(8))* Bearport Publishing Co., Inc.
Mattern, Joanne. Mystics & Psychics. 2011. (World Religions & Beliefs Ser.). 128p. (gr. 7-12). 28.95 *(978-1-59935-148-3(X))* Reynolds, Morgan Inc.
McIntosh, Kenneth. Prophecies & End-Time Speculations: The Shape of Things to Come. 2007. (Religion & Modern Culture Ser.). (Illus.). 112p. (YA). (gr. 3-7). lib. bdg. 22.95 *(978-1-59084-979-8(5),* 1248068) Mason Crest.
Peterson, Megan Cooley. Super Scary Stories. 2016. (Super Scary Stuff Ser.). (ENG., Illus.). 24p. (J). (gr. 3-5). lib. bdg. 27.99 *(978-1-5157-0279-5(0),* 131924, Capstone Pr.) Capstone.
Place, Robert Michael. Astrology & Divination. 2008. (ENG., Illus.). 136p. (gr. 7-12). lib. bdg. 29.95 *(978-0-7910-9385-6(9),* P145801, Facts On File) Infobase Holdings, Inc.
Reed, Ellis M. Ghost Hunting. 2018. (Ghosts & Hauntings Ser.). (ENG., Illus.). 32p. (J). (gr. 4-6). lib. bdg. 28.65 *(978-1-5435-4154-0(2),* 139108, Capstone Pr.) Capstone.
Shecter, Vicky Alvear. Anubis Speaks! A Guide to the Afterlife by the Egyptian God of the Dead. Revoy, Antoine, illus. 2013. (Secrets of the Ancient Gods Ser.). (ENG.). 128p. (J). (gr. 4-7). 16.95 *(978-1-59078-995-7(4),* Astra Young Readers) Astra Publishing Hse.
Stern, Steven L. Cursed Grounds. 2011. (Scary Places Ser.). 32p. (YA). (gr. 4-7). lib. bdg. 28.50 *(978-1-61772-147-2(6))* Bearport Publishing Co., Inc.
Understanding the Paranormal: Set 1, 12 vols. 2014. (Understanding the Paranormal Ser.). (ENG.). 48p. (YA). (gr. 5-5). lib. bdg. 170.46 *(978-1-62275-813-5(7),* 61ff232f-1255-4118-a1f1-575d6f04fa73, Britannica Educational Publishing) Rosen Publishing Group, Inc., The.
Understanding the Paranormal: Set 2, 12 vols. 2016. (Understanding the Paranormal Ser.). 48p. (gr. 5-5). (ENG.). 170.46 *(978-1-5081-0219-9(8),* 092d66ca-f03a-46d0-8de5-fd207de7dadd); pap. 84.30 *(978-1-68048-602-5(0))* Rosen Publishing Group, Inc., The. (Britannica Educational Publishing).
Walker, Kathryn. Mysterious Predictions. 2009. (Unsolved! Ser.). (ENG., Illus.). 32p. (J). (gr. 3-5). pap. *(978-0-7787-4164-0(8));* (gr. 4-6). *(978-0-7787-4151-0(6))* Crabtree Publishing Co.
Walton, Leslye. The Price Guide to the Occult. 2018. 288p. (YA). (gr. 9). 18.99 *(978-0-7636-9110-3(0))* Candlewick Pr.
Williams, Dinah. Monstrous Morgues of the Past. 2011. (Scary Places Ser.). 32p. (YA). (gr. 4-7). lib. bdg. 25.27 *(978-1-61772-149-6(2))* Bearport Publishing Co., Inc.

OCCULTISM—FICTION

Aguirre, Ann. Public Enemies. 2015. (ENG.). 384p. (YA). *(978-1-250-07420-1(7))* St. Martin's Pr.
Amowitz, Lisa. Until Beth. 2015. (ENG.). 260p. (YA). (gr. 10-12). pap. 9.95 *(978-1-63392-033-0(X),* 1400080) Spencer Hill Pr.
Anderson, Laura Ellen. Amelia Fang & the Barbaric Ball. 2019. (Amelia Fang Ser.: 1). (ENG., Illus.). 224p. (J). (gr. 2). 12.99 *(978-1-9848-4839-0(9),* Delacorte Bks. for Young Readers) Random Hse. Children's Bks.
Anonymous. Jay's Journal. Sparks, Beatrice, ed. (Anonymous Diaries). (ENG.). 240p. (YA). 2012. (gr. 9). 17.99 *(978-1-4424-8094-0(7))* 2010. (gr. 7). pap. 11.99 *(978-1-4424-1993-3(8))* Simon Pulse. (Simon Pulse).
Anthony, Horowitz. Evil Star. 2006. (ENG.). 320p. (YA). (gr. 4-7). 26.87 *(978-1-4156-7833-6(2),* Follettbound) Follett School Solutions.
—Necropolis, 9 vols. 2009. (Gatekeepers Ser.: 4). (J). 92.75 *(978-1-4407-0430-7(9));* 122.75 *(978-1-4407-0434-5(1));* 120.75 *(978-1-4407-0436-9(8));* 90.75 *(978-1-4407-0432-1(5));* 254.75 *(978-1-4407-0431-4(7));* 1.25 *(978-1-4407-0439-0(2))* Recorded Bks., Inc.
—Necropolis. 2009. 400p. pap. *(978-1-4063-2108-1(7))* Walker Bks., Ltd.
—Oblivion. 2014. (Gatekeepers Ser.: 5). lib. bdg. 20.85 *(978-0-606-36035-7(2))* Turtleback.
Argyle, Amber. Winter Queen. 2013. 256p. 21.99 *(978-0-9857394-4-7(4))* Starling Publishing.
Armentrout, Jennifer L. Stone Cold Touch. 2019. (Dark Elements Ser.: 2). (ENG.). 480p. (YA). pap. 15.99 *(978-1-335-00920-3(5))* Harlequin Enterprises ULC CAN. Dist: HarperCollins Pubs.
—White Hot Kiss. 2019. (Dark Elements Ser.: 1). (ENG.). 400p. (YA). pap. 10.99 *(978-1-335-00919-7(1))* Harlequin Enterprises ULC CAN. Dist: HarperCollins Pubs.
Barrowman, John & Barrowman, Carole. Inquisitor. 2018. (Orion Chronicles Ser.: 3). (ENG.). 320p. (YA). (gr. 7). 19.99 *(978-1-78185-645-1(1))* Head of Zeus GBR. Dist: Independent Pubs. Group.
Bitterman, Albert. Fortune Cookies. Raschka, Chris, illus. 2011. (ENG.). 28p. (J). (gr. -1-k). 14.99 *(978-1-4169-6814-6(8),* Beach Lane Bks.) Beach Lane Bks.
Black, Teri Bailey. Girl at the Grave. 2019. (ENG.). 336p. (YA). pap. 9.99 *(978-0-7653-9949-6(0),* 900185196, Tor Teen) Doherty, Tom Assocs., LLC.
Black, Yelena. Dance of Shadows. 2014. (Dance of Shadows Ser.). (ENG., Illus.). 384p. (YA). (gr. 7). pap. 9.99 *(978-1-61963-185-4(7),* 900125810, Bloomsbury USA Childrens) Bloomsbury Publishing USA.
Buckingham, Royce. Demonkeeper. 2007. 216p. (J). *(978-1-4287-4608-4(0))* Penguin Publishing Group.
Byars, Betsy. Tarot Says Beware. (Herculeah Jones Mystery Ser.). 160p. (J). (gr. 4-6). pap. 3.99 *(978-0-8072-1498-5(1),* Listening Library) Random Hse. Audio Publishing Group.
Cajoleas, Jimmy. The Good Demon. (ENG.). 2019. 336p. (YA). (gr. 8-17). pap. 10.99 *(978-1-4197-3899-2(2),* 1195803) 2018. (Illus.). 320p. (gr. 9-17). 18.99 *(978-1-4197-3127-3(0),* 1195801) Abrams, Inc. (Amulet Bks.).
Cast, P. C. & Cast, Kristin. Betrayed: A House of Night Novel. 2009. (House of Night Novels Ser.: 2). (ENG.). 320p. (YA). (gr. 7-12). 21.99 *(978-0-312-59629-3(4),* 900063091) St. Martin's Pr.
—Chosen. 2010. (House of Night Novels (Quality) Ser.). (CHI.). 367p. pap. *(978-957-0316-42-1(X))* Locus Publishing Co.
—Chosen: A House of Night Novel. (House of Night Novels Ser.: 3). (ENG.). 320p. (YA). (gr. 8-12). 2009. 21.99 *(978-0-312-36029-0(0),* 900039880) 2008. pap. 11.99 *(978-0-312-36030-6(4),* 900039883, St. Martin's Griffin) St. Martin's Pr.
—Destined: A House of Night Novel. 2013. (House of Night Novels Ser.: 9). (ENG.). 336p. (YA). (gr. 7-12). pap. 12.99 *(978-0-312-38798-3(9),* 900054121, St. Martin's Griffin) St. Martin's Pr.
—Hunted. l.t. ed. 2010. (House of Night Ser.: Bk. 5). (ENG.). 548p. 23.95 *(978-1-4104-1951-4(7))* Thorndike Pr.
—Hunted: A House of Night Novel. (House of Night Novels Ser.: 5). (ENG.). 336p. (YA). (gr. 7-12). 2010. pap. 13.00 *(978-0-312-57799-5(0),* 900061613) 2009. 21.99 *(978-0-312-37982-7(X),* 900050335) St. Martin's Pr. (St. Martin's Griffin).
—Marked. l.t. ed. 2008. (House of Night Ser.: No. 1). (ENG.). 442p. (YA). 23.95 *(978-1-4104-1021-4(8))* Thorndike Pr.
—Marked. 2007. (House of Night Ser.: 1). 306p. (YA). lib. bdg. 22.10 *(978-1-4178-0853-3(5))* Turtleback.
—Marked: A House of Night Novel. (House of Night Novels Ser.: 1). (ENG.). 320p. (YA). (gr. 8-12). 2009. 21.99 *(978-0-312-36025-2(8),* 900039877) 2007. pap. 13.00 *(978-0-312-36026-9(6),* 900039881, St. Martin's Griffin) St. Martin's Pr.
—Tempted: A House of Night Novel. (House of Night Novels Ser.: 6). (ENG.). 336p. (YA). (gr. 7-12). 2011. pap. 12.99 *(978-0-312-60938-2(8),* 900065238) 2009. 19.99 *(978-0-312-56748-4(0),* 900059355) St. Martin's Pr. (St. Martin's Griffin).
Cast, P. C. & Kristin. Awakened. l.t. ed. 2011. (House of Night Ser.). (ENG.). 436p. 23.99 *(978-1-4104-3776-1(0))* Thorndike Pr.
—Burned. l.t. ed. 2011. (House of Night Ser.). (ENG.). 552p. 23.99 *(978-1-4104-3440-1(0))* Thorndike Pr.
—Chosen. l.t. ed. 2009. (House of Night Ser.: Bk. 3). (ENG.). 406p. (YA). 23.95 *(978-1-4104-1608-7(9))* Thorndike Pr.
—Tempted. l.t. ed. 2010. (House of Night Novel Ser.). (ENG.). 552p. 23.99 *(978-1-4104-3141-7(X))* Thorndike Pr.
Cast, P.c. & Cast, Kristin. Awakened: A House of Night Novel. (House of Night Novels Ser.: 8). (ENG.). 304p. (YA). (gr. 7-12). 2012. pap. 12.99 *(978-0-312-38797-6(0),* 900054120) 2011. 21.99 *(978-0-312-65024-7(8),* 900059357) St. Martin's Pr. (St. Martin's Griffin).
DeAngelis, Camille. The Boy from Tomorrow. 2018. (ENG., Illus.). 268p. (J). (gr. 4-7). 15.99 *(978-1-944995-61-4(7))* Amberjack Publishing Co.
DeSpain, Pleasant. Tales of Enchantment. 2016. (ENG., Illus.). 80p. (J). (gr. 3-4). pap. 9.95 *(978-1-941460-37-5(2))* August Hse. Pubs., Inc.
Dunning, John Harris & Singh, Nikhil. Salem Brownstone: All along the Watchtowers. Singh, Nikhil, illus. 2010. (ENG., Illus.). 96p. (YA). (gr. 7-18). 18.99 *(978-0-7636-4735-3(7))* Candlewick Pr.
Ende, Michael. The Night of Wishes: Or the Satanarchaeolidealcohellish Notion Potion. Schwarzbauer, Heike & Takvorian, Rick, trs. Kehn, Regina, illus. 2017. 216p. (J). (gr. 3-7). 16.95 *(978-1-68137-188-7(X),* NYR Children's Collection) New York Review of Bks., Inc., The.
Feasey, Steve. Dark Moon: A Wereling Novel. 2011. (Wereling Ser.: 2). (ENG.). 336p. (YA). (gr. 7-18). pap. 19.99 *(978-0-312-64643-1(7),* 900068714) Feiwel & Friends.
Fleischman, Paul. Graven Images. Ibatoulline, Bagram, illus. 2005. (ENG.). 128p. (YA). (gr. 5-9). per. 8.99 *(978-0-7636-2984-7(7))* Candlewick Pr.
Gayle, Emi. Night & Day. 2014. 132p. (YA). *(978-1-937744-55-7(8))* J. Taylor Publishing.
Giles, Jeff. The Edge of Everything. 2018. (YA). lib. bdg. 22.10 *(978-0-606-41079-3(1))* Turtleback.
Glanville, K. L. The Realm: The Awakening Begins, bk. 1. 2008. (ENG.). 314p. (YA). pap. 12.99 *(978-0-9821199-1-4(7))* Luminations Media Group, Inc.
Gohmann, Johanna. Book 1: the Howler. Sorrentino, Flavia, illus. 2017. (Ursula's Funland Ser.). (ENG.). 48p. (J). (gr. 3-7). lib. bdg. 34.21 *(978-1-5321-3011-3(2),* 25568, Spellbound) Magic Wagon.
—Book 2: the Face in the Photo. Sorrentino, Flavia, illus. 2017. (Ursula's Funland Ser.). (ENG.). 48p. (J). (gr. 3-7). lib. bdg. 34.21 *(978-1-5321-3012-0(0),* 25570, Spellbound) Magic Wagon.
Hamel-Mcevoy, Kristen & Chin, Jonathan L. My Little Leo. 2011. 28p. pap. 12.50 *(978-1-61204-104-9(3),* Strategic Bk. Publishing) Strategic Book Publishing & Rights Agency (SBPRA).
Hansen, Tevin. C. K. & the Worm of Wisdom. 2016. (ENG.). 128p. (YA). pap. 6.99 *(978-1-941429-35-8(1))* Handersen Publishing.
—The Complete Saga One: Evil Mouse Chronicles. 2016. (ENG., Illus.). 346p. (YA). pap. 12.99 *(978-1-941429-39-6(4))* Handersen Publishing.
—An Evening of Temptation & the Ultimate Sacrifice. 2017. 231p. (YA). 19.99 *(978-1-941429-68-6(8))* Handersen Publishing.
—Mr. B Presents: An Evening of Temptation & the Ultimate Sacrifice. 2014. (ENG.). 231p. (YA). pap. 8.95 *(978-1-941429-01-3(7))* Handersen Publishing.
—Mummy Mouse: A Tail of Evil. 2015. (ENG.). 78p. pap. 8.95 *(978-1-941429-19-8(X))* Handersen Publishing.
—Psycho Kim. 2016. (ENG.). 70p. pap. 5.99 *(978-1-941429-30-3(0))* Handersen Publishing.
—Rhomby the Skater Zombie. Hansen, Tevin, illus. 2016. (ENG., Illus.). 134p. (J). pap. 7.99 *(978-1-941429-32-7(7))* Handersen Publishing.
—Rhomby the Skater Zombie & Me. Hansen, Tevin, illus. 2nd ed. 2018. (Illus.). (J). pap. 8.99 *(978-1-947854-19-2(4))* Handersen Publishing.
—Snickers. 2015. (ENG.). 76p. pap. 7.95 *(978-1-941429-20-4(3))* Handersen Publishing.
—A Sunday Demon Drive & a Gathering of Friends. 2014. (ENG.). 210p. (YA). pap. 8.95 *(978-1-941429-08-2(4))* Handersen Publishing.
Hatton, L. J. Sing down the Stars, 0 vols. 2015. (Celestine Ser.: 1). (ENG.). 380p. (YA). (gr. 8-13). pap. 9.99 *(978-1-5039-4656-9(8),* 9781503946569, Skyscape) Amazon Publishing.
Havard, Amanda. The Survivors. 2011. (ENG.). (YA). 294p. 21.99 *(978-0-9833190-0-9(6));* 300p. pap. 11.99 *(978-0-9833190-2-3(2))* Chafie Pr., LLC.
Hunter, C. C. Unspoken: Shadow Falls: after Dark. 2015. (Shadow Falls: after Dark Ser.: 3). (ENG.). 416p. (YA). (gr. 7-12). pap. 14.99 *(978-1-250-06709-8(X),* 900146131, St. Martin's Griffin) St. Martin's Pr.
Hunter, Erin. Warriors: Omen of the Stars #6: the Last Hope. 2012. (Warriors: Omen of the Stars Ser.: 6). (ENG., Illus.). 384p. (J). (gr. 3-7). 16.99 *(978-0-06-155527-5(4),* HarperCollins) HarperCollins Pubs.
Kahler, A. R. Echoes of Memory. 2017. (Ravenborn Ser.: 2). (ENG.). 336p. (YA). (gr. 9). pap. 11.99 *(978-1-4814-3261-0(3));* (Illus.). 17.99 *(978-1-4814-3260-3(5))* Simon Pulse. (Simon Pulse).

—Shades of Darkness. 2016. (Ravenborn Ser.: 1). (ENG., Illus.). 304p. (YA). (gr. 9). 17.99 (978-1-4814-3257-3(5), Simon Pulse) Simon Pulse.

Keay, Ben. Perfect Solution. Hsu, Florence, illus. 2009. (YA). (978-1-933791-09-8(8)) Finial Publishing.

Kress, Adrienne. Outcast: A Novel. 2013. (ENG.). 326p. (YA). pap. 18.99 (978-1-62681-092-1(3), Diversion Bks.) Diversion Publishing Corp.

LaFevers, R. L. Theodosia & the Serpents of Chaos. Tanaka, Yoko, illus. 2008. (Theodosia Ser.: 1). (ENG.). 352p. (J). (gr. 3-7). pap. 8.99 (978-0-618-99976-7(0), 1027887, Clarion Bks.) HarperCollins Pubs.

Lancaster, Susan. The Diamond Talisman. 2004. 168p. pap. (978-0-9730350-0-1(5)) Snosrap Publishing.

Larcombe, Jennifer Rees. Stone of Evil. (ENG.). 173p. pap. (978-0-340-58754-6(7)) Hodder & Stoughton.

Laurie, Victoria. Oracles of Delphi Keep. 2010. (Oracles of Delphi Keep Ser.: 1). 576p. (J). (gr. 3-7). 8.99 (978-0-440-42258-7(2), Yearling) Random Hse. Children's Bks.

Lilleland, Ingrid. A Demon's Touch. 2017. (ENG.). 124p. pap. 11.95 (978-1-78554-775-1(5), 2b1f80e0-2296-4676-9c22-f11b45f3c707) Austin Macauley Pubs. Ltd. GBR. Dist: Baker & Taylor Publisher Services (BTPS).

Maguire, Eden. Arizona. 2010. (Beautiful Dead Ser.: 2). (ENG.). 288p. (YA). (gr. 8-12). pap. 11.99 (978-1-4022-3945-8(9)) Sourcebooks, Inc.

Mak, Olha. Stones under the Scythe. Kaczmarskyj, Vera, tr. from UKR. 2011. 184p. 23.95 (978-1-4620-1038-7(5)); pap. 13.95 (978-1-4620-1037-0(7)) iUniverse, Inc.

McKenzie, Paige. The Sacrifice of Sunshine Girl. 2017. (Haunting of Sunshine Girl Ser.: 3). (ENG.). 336p. (YA). (gr. 7-17). 17.99 (978-1-60286-298-2(2)) Hachette Bk. Group.

Murphy, Shirley Rousseau. The Cat, the Devil, the Last Escape. 2015. (ENG., Illus.). 320p. 24.99 (978-0-06-226910-2(0), Morrow, William & Co.) HarperCollins Pubs.

Myers, Bill. Invisible Terror Collection, 1 vol., Vol. 2. 2011. (Forbidden Doors Ser.: 2). (ENG.). 368p. (YA). pap. 12.99 (978-0-310-72904-4(1)) Zondervan.

—My Life as a Haunted Hamburger, Hold the Pickles, 1 vol., 27. 2006. (Incredible Worlds of Wally Mcdoogle Ser.: 27). (ENG., Illus.). 128p. (J). (gr. 3-7). per. 6.99 (978-1-4003-0636-7(1), Tommy Nelson) Nelson, Thomas Inc.

Noel, Alyson. Fated. 2012. (Soul Seekers Ser.: 1). (ENG.). 368p. (YA). (gr. 7). pap. 27.00 (978-0-312-57565-6(3), 900075089, St. Martin's Griffin) St. Martin's Pr.

O'Connor, Jane. Fancy Nancy: Nancy Clancy Sees the Future. Glasser, Robin Preiss, illus. 2014. (Nancy Clancy Ser.: 3). (ENG.). 144p. (J). (gr. 1-5). pap. 5.99 (978-0-06-208421-7(6), HarperCollins) HarperCollins Pubs.

Odentz, Howard. Dead. 2013. 272p. pap. 14.95 (978-1-61194-299-6(3), Bell Bridge Bks.) BelleBks., Inc.

Oh, Ellen. Warrior. 2015. (Prophecy Ser.: 2). (ENG.). 352p. (YA). (gr. 8). pap. 9.99 (978-0-06-209113-0(1), HarperTeen) HarperCollins Pubs.

Older, Daniel José. Shadowhouse Fall (the Shadowshaper Cypher, Book 2) 2017. (Shadowshaper Cypher Ser.: 2). (ENG., Illus.). 368p. (YA). (gr. 9-9). 18.99 (978-0-545-95282-8(4), Levine, Arthur A. Bks.) Scholastic, Inc.

Ormand, Kate. The Wanderers. 2015. (ENG.). 320p. (J). (gr. 6-6). 16.99 (978-1-63450-201-6(9), Sky Pony Pr.) Skyhorse Publishing Co., Inc.

Osborne, Mary Pope. Haunted Castle on Hallows Eve. 2010. (Magic Tree House Merlin Missions Ser.: 2). lib. bdg. 16.00 (978-0-606-13992-2(3)) Turtleback.

Parker, Daniel. December. 2014. (Countdown Ser.: 12). (ENG.). 144p. (YA). (gr. 7). pap. 13.99 (978-1-4814-2597-1(8), Simon Pulse) Simon Pulse.

Payne, Mary Jennifer. Finding Jade: Daughters of Light. 2017. (Daughters of Light Ser.: 1). (ENG.). 216p. (YA). pap. 12.99 (978-1-4597-3500-2(5)) Dundurn Pr. CAN. Dist: Publishers Group West (PGW).

Plante, Raymond. Marilou Forecasts the Future, 1 vol. Cummins, Sarah, tr. Favreau, Marie-Claude, illus. 2003. (Formac First Novels Ser.: 49). (ENG.). 64p. (J). (gr. 1-5). 4.95 (978-0-88780-614-8(7), 614); (gr. 2-5). 14.95 (978-0-88780-615-5(5), 615) Formac Publishing Co., Ltd. CAN. Dist: Formac Lorimer Bks. Ltd.

Poole, Gabriella. Darke Academy 02: Blood Ties. 2010. (Darke Academy Ser.). (ENG.). 304p. (YA). (gr. 7-17). pap. 9.99 (978-0-340-98925-8(4)) Hachette Children's Group GBR. Dist: Hachette Bk. Group.

Powers, J. L. & Powers, M. A. Broken Circle. 2017. (ENG.). 320p. (J). (gr. 6). pap. 14.95 (978-1-61775-580-4(X), Black Sheep) Akashic Bks.

Preussler, Otfried. Krabat & the Sorcerer's Mill. Bell, Anthea, tr. 2014. (ENG.). 264p. (J). (gr. 3-7). 17.95 (978-1-59017-778-5(9), NYR Children's Collection) New York Review of Bks., Inc., The.

Richardson, Sharde. Watched. 2011. (ENG.). 290p. (YA). pap. 12.99 (978-0-9831498-0-4(1)) Jolt.

Rinehart, J. D. Crown of Three. 2016. (Crown of Three Ser.: 1). (ENG., Illus.). 432p. (J). (gr. 4-8). pap. 8.99 (978-1-4814-2444-8(0), Aladdin) Simon & Schuster Children's Publishing.

Roberts, Rachel. Circles in the Stream. 2007. (Avalon Ser.: Bk. 1). 175p. (J). 9.99 (978-1-933164-64-9(6)) Seven Seas Entertainment, LLC.

Scott, Michael. The Alchemyst. 2009. (ENG., Illus.). 375p. (gr. 6-10). 19.00 (978-1-60686-514-9(5)) Perfection Learning Corp.

—The Alchemyst. (Secrets of the Immortal Nicholas Flamel Ser.: 1). (ENG.). 400p. (YA). (gr. 7). 2008. pap. 11.99 (978-0-385-73600-8(2), Ember) 2007. (Illus.). 18.99 (978-0-385-73357-1(7), Delacorte Bks. for Young Readers) Random Hse. Children's Bks.

Shouoto, Aya. He's My Only Vampire, Vol. 10. 2017. (He's My Only Vampire Ser.: 10). (ENG., Illus.). 176p. (gr. 11-17). pap. 13.00 (978-0-316-39912-8(4), Yen Pr.) Yen Pr. LLC.

Smith, L. J. The Secret Circle: The Initiation & the Captive Part I TV Tie-In Edition. movie tie-in ed. 2011. (Secret Circle Ser.). (ENG.). 416p. (YA). (gr. 8). pap. 9.99 (978-0-06-211900-1(1), HarperTeen) HarperCollins Pubs.

Smith, L. J. & Kevin Williamson & Julie Plec, Kevin Williamson. The Vampire Diaries: Stefan's Diaries #6: the Compelled. 2012. (Vampire Diaries: Stefan's Diaries: 6). (ENG.). 256p. (YA). (gr. 9). pap. 11.99 (978-0-06-211398-6(4), HarperTeen) HarperCollins Pubs.

Smith, Ronald L. The Mesmerist. 2019. (ENG., Illus.). 288p. (J). (gr. 5-7). pap. 9.99 (978-1-328-49800-7(X), 1717857, Clarion Bks.) HarperCollins Pubs.

Snyder, Maria V., et al. Spirited. 2012. (Illus.). 332p. (J). (gr. 8-12). pap. 16.99 (978-1-61603-020-9(8)) Leap Bks.

Stiefvater, Maggie. Blue Lily, Lily Blue. 2015. (Raven Cycle Ser.: 3). lib. bdg. 20.85 (978-0-606-38004-1(3)) Turtleback.

—Blue Lily, Lily Blue (the Raven Cycle, Book 3) (Raven Cycle Ser.: 3). (ENG.). 400p. (YA). (gr. 9-9). 2015. pap. 12.99 (978-0-545-42497-4(6)) 2014. 21.99 (978-0-545-42496-7(8)) Scholastic, Inc. (Scholastic Pr.).

—Blue Lily, Lily Blue (the Raven Cycle, Book 3) (Unabridged Edition), 1 vol. unabr. ed. 2014. (Raven Cycle Ser.: 3). (ENG.). 2p. (YA). (gr. 7). audio compact disk 39.99 (978-0-545-64907-0(2)) Scholastic, Inc.

—The Dream Thieves. 2014. (Raven Cycle Ser.: 2). lib. bdg. 20.85 (978-0-606-36029-6(8)) Turtleback.

—The Dream Thieves (the Raven Cycle, Book 2) (Raven Cycle Ser.: 2). (ENG.). 448p. (YA). (gr. 9). 2014. pap. 12.99 (978-0-545-42495-0(X), Scholastic Paperbacks) 2013. 19.99 (978-0-545-42494-3(1), Scholastic Pr.) Scholastic, Inc.

—The Dream Thieves (the Raven Cycle, Book 2) (Unabridged Edition), 1 vol. unabr. ed. 2013. (Raven Cycle Ser.: 2). (ENG.). 2p. (YA). (gr. 9). audio compact disk 39.99 (978-0-545-60039-2(1)) Scholastic, Inc.

—The Raven Boys. 2015. 50.87 (978-1-320-56337-6(6)) Blurb, Inc.

—The Raven Boys. 2013. (Raven Cycle Ser.: 1). 20.00 (978-1-62765-119-6(5)) Perfection Learning Corp.

—The Raven Boys. 2016. (CHI.). 448p. (YA). (gr. 7). pap. (978-986-361-180-6(8)) Sitak Group Holding, Ltd.

—The Raven Boys. 2013. (Raven Cycle Ser.: 1). lib. bdg. 20.85 (978-0-606-32028-3(8)) Turtleback.

—The Raven Boys (the Raven Cycle, Book 1), 1 vol. (Raven Cycle Ser.: 1). (ENG.). 416p. (gr. 9-9). 2013. (YA). pap. 12.99 (978-0-545-42493-6(3), Scholastic Paperbacks) 2012. (J). E-Book (978-0-545-46979-1(1)) 2012. (J). 21.99 (978-0-545-42492-9(5), Scholastic Pr.) Scholastic, Inc.

—The Raven Boys (the Raven Cycle, Book 1) (Unabridged Edition), 2 vols. unabr. ed. 2012. (Raven Cycle Ser.: 1). (ENG.). (J). (gr. 8). 2p. audio compact disk 39.99 (978-0-545-46593-9(1)); 5p. audio compact disk 79.99 (978-0-545-46594-6(X)) Scholastic, Inc.

Stilton, Geronimo. The Hunt for the Colosseum Ghost (Geronimo Stilton Special Edition) 2018. (Geronimo Stilton Special Edition Ser.). (ENG., Illus.). 208p. (J). (gr. 2-5). 14.99 (978-1-338-21522-9(1), Scholastic Paperbacks) Scholastic, Inc.

Stine, R. L. Nightmare Hour TV Tie-In Edition. movie tie-in ed. 2011. (ENG.). 160p. (J). (gr. 3). pap. 7.99 (978-0-06-210692-6(9), HarperCollins) HarperCollins Pubs.

Sutherland, Tui T. The Dragonet Prophecy. 2018. (Wings of Fire Graphic Novel Ser.: 1). lib. bdg. 24.50 (978-0-606-41053-3(8)) Turtleback.

Tanabe, Yellow. Kekkaishi, Vol. 22. 2010. (Kekkaishi Ser.: 22). (ENG., Illus.). 192p. pap. 9.99 (978-1-4215-3069-7(4)) Viz Media.

—Kekkaishi, Vol. 23. 2010. (Kekkaishi Ser.: 23). (ENG., Illus.). 192p. pap. 9.99 (978-1-4215-3200-4(X)) Viz Media.

Tiernan, Cate. Immortal Beloved. 2012. (Immortal Beloved Ser.: 1). (ENG.). 432p. (YA). (gr. 7-17). pap. 9.99 (978-0-316-03591-0(2), Poppy) Little, Brown Bks. for Young Readers.

—Sweep: Book of Shadows, the Coven, & Blood Witch: Volume 1. 2010. (Sweep Ser.: 1). (ENG.). 592p. (YA). (gr. 7-18). 12.99 (978-0-14-241717-1(3), Speak) Penguin Young Readers Group.

Troupe, Thomas Kingsley. Wandering Wagon. Faber, Rudy, illus. 2016. (Hauntiques Ser.). (ENG.). 128p. (J). (gr. 4-6). lib. bdg. 25.32 (978-1-4965-3547-4(2), 132656, Stone Arch Bks.) Capstone.

Vajda, Tibor Timothy. The End of the World. 2008. 96p. pap. 9.95 (978-0-595-52914-8(3)) iUniverse, Inc.

Voelkel, J&p. The Lost City. 2015. (Jaguar Stones Ser.: 4). (ENG., Illus.). 368p. (J). (gr. 5-12). E-Book 25.49 (978-1-5124-0184-4(6), Darby Creek) Lerner Publishing Group.

Ward, John. Le Secret de l'Alchimiste. Guitard, Agnes & Pineau, Severine, trs. from ENG. 2004. (FRE., Illus.). 336p. (J). pap. (978-2-89021-672-3(1)) Diffusion du livre Mirabel (DLM).

Wass, Eliza. The Life & Death Parade. 2019. (ENG.). 256p. (YA). (gr. 9-17). pap. 9.99 (978-1-4847-8752-6(8)) Hyperion Bks. for Children.

Whyman, Matt. Street Runners. 2008. (ENG.). 272p. (J). (gr. 4-7). pap. 11.95 (978-1-84738-282-5(7)) Simon & Schuster, Ltd. GBR. Dist: Simon & Schuster, Inc.

Wilson, Dianne J. Resonance. 2019. (Spirit Walker Ser.). (ENG.). 338p. (YA). (gr. 6). pap. 15.99 (978-1-5223-0026-7(0)) Pelican Ventures, LLC.

OCCUPATION, CHOICE OF

see Vocational Guidance

OCCUPATIONAL THERAPY—VOCATIONAL GUIDANCE

Amidon Lusted, Marcia. Jump-Starting a Career in Physical Therapy & Rehabilitation, 1 vol. 2013. (Health Care Careers in 2 Years Ser.). (ENG.). 80p. (YA). (gr. 7-7). 38.41 (978-1-4777-1695-3(5), a6197c57-317a-4168-a682-f79c8038b5d5) Rosen Publishing Group, Inc., The.

Flath, Camden. Therapy Jobs in Educational Settings: Speech, Physical, Occupational & Audiology. 2010. (New Careers for the 21st Century Ser.). (Illus.). 64p. (YA). (gr. 7-18). pap. 9.95 (978-1-4222-2047-4(8)); lib. bdg. 22.95 (978-1-4222-1826-6(0)) Mason Crest.

Hunsaker, Jennifer. Occupational Therapists. 2017. (Careers in Healthcare Ser.: Vol. 13). (ENG., Illus.). 64p. (YA). (gr. 7-12). 23.95 (978-1-4222-3801-1(6)) Mason Crest.

OCCUPATIONS

see also Professions; Vocational Guidance

also names of countries, cities, etc. with the subdivision Occupations (e.g. U. S.—Occupations); also such headings as Law—Vocational Guidance

Adamson, Heather. A Day in the Life of a Farmer. 2007. (Community Helpers at Work Ser.). (ENG.). 24p. (gr. 1-2). pap. 41.70 (978-1-4296-0382-9(8), Capstone Pr.) Capstone.

—A Day in the Life of a Police Officer, 1 vol. 2003. (Community Helpers at Work Ser.). (ENG., Illus.). 24p. (J). (gr. 1-3). 25.99 (978-0-7368-2285-5(2), 89393) Capstone.

Aksomitis, Linda, ed. Choosing a Career, 1 vol. 2008. (Issues That Concern You Ser.). (ENG., Illus.). 120p. (gr. 7-10). lib. bdg. 43.63 (978-0-7377-4184-1(8), b5a6a37b-4057-433d-b9aa-43d48e862bc1, Greenhaven Publishing) Greenhaven Publishing LLC.

Alexander, richard. Zoo Workers, 1 vol., 1. 2015. (Hands-On Jobs Ser.). (ENG., Illus.). 24p. (J). (gr. 3-4). pap. 9.25 (978-1-5081-4375-8(7), 5e955f54-ef72-4d75-820a-81c44e572685, PowerKids Pr.) Rosen Publishing Group, Inc., The.

Animal Watch. 2003. (ENG., Illus.). 32p. (gr. 2-4). 23.00 (978-0-7910-7409-1(9), P179933, Facts On File) Infobase Holdings, Inc.

Antill, Sara. 10 Ways I Can Help My Community, 1 vol. 2012. (I Can Make a Difference Ser.). (ENG., Illus.). 24p. (J). (gr. 2-3). pap. 9.25 (978-1-4488-6363-1(5), a06fb6f8-f55a-474b-b499-fe8ab15e6296); lib. bdg. 26.27 (978-1-4488-6202-3(7), e3028fb1-b729-409f-9274-57aeff84d52f) Rosen Publishing Group, Inc., The. (PowerKids Pr.).

Antram, David, illus. You Wouldn't Want To..., 4 vols., Set. Incl. Be in the Forbidden City! A Sheltered Life You'd Rather Avoid. Morley, Jacqueline. (gr. 4-7). 29.00 (978-0-531-18749-4(7), Children's Pr.); Live in Pompeii! A Volcanic Eruption You'd Rather Avoid. Malam, John. (gr. 2-5). 29.00 (978-0-531-18748-7(9)); Sail on an Irish Famine Ship! A Trip Across Teh Atlantic You'd Rather Not Make. Pipe, Jim. (gr. 4-6). 26.19 (978-0-531-13913-4(1), Watts, Franklin); You Wouldn't Want to Be Mary Queen of Scots: A Ruler Who Really Lost Her Head. MacDonald, Fiona. (gr. 4-7). 29.00 (978-0-531-13912-7(3)); (Illus.). 32p. (J). 2008. Set lib. bdg. 116.00 o.p. (978-0-531-24349-7(4), Watts, Franklin) Scholastic Library Publishing.

Anyabwele, Talitha. Black Girls, Brown Girls, What Could You Be? Updegraff, Nicole, illus. 2018. (ENG.). 30p. (J). pap. 12.99 (978-0-9972861-0-6(5)) BGS Productions, Inc.

Appleby, Alex. I Can Be a Ballerina, 1 vol. 2014. (When I Grow Up Ser.). (ENG., Illus.). 24p. (J). (gr. k-k). 24.27 (978-1-4824-0745-7(0), 433d39a6-4a4c-4480-b234-3ce4974bd8ed) Stevens, Gareth Publishing LLLP.

—Puedo Ser Presidente / I Can Be the President, 1 vol. 2014. (Cuando Sea Grande / When I Grow Up Ser.). (SPA & ENG.). 24p. (J). (gr. k-k). 24.27 (978-1-4824-0867-6(8), 4af76403-0e0b-48ae-bbb9-b4e58771e109) Stevens, Gareth Publishing LLLP.

—Puedo Ser un Artista / I Can Be an Artist, 1 vol. 2014. (Cuando Sea Grande / When I Grow Up Ser.). (SPA & ENG.). 24p. (J). (gr. k-k). 24.27 (978-1-4824-0861-4(9), 15d99615-d0a0-4e8e-be8c-7f118c1f0d49) Stevens, Gareth Publishing LLLP.

—Puedo Ser una Cantante / I Can Be a Singer, 1 vol. 2014. (Cuando Sea Grande / When I Grow Up Ser.). (SPA & ENG.). 24p. (J). (gr. k-k). 24.27 (978-1-4824-0865-2(1), e3727007-26fe-44f3-aeb2-089908983b35) Stevens, Gareth Publishing LLLP.

Barber, Nicola. Ancient Roman Jobs, 1 vol. 2010. (Ancient Communities: Roman Life Ser.). (ENG., Illus.). 32p. (J). (gr. 4-4). pap. 11.60 (978-1-61532-317-3(1), ef772b05-c222-4fcc-9411-cc42272ebd3d); lib. bdg. 30.27 (978-1-61532-307-4(4), d0ccd0fd-8bd5-4d66-b590-b7da4e773aef) Rosen Publishing Group, Inc., The. (PowerKids Pr.).

Baxter, Roberta. Bomb Squad Technicians in Action. 2017. (Dangerous Jobs in Action Ser.). (ENG.). 32p. (J). (gr. 3-6). lib. bdg. 35.64 (978-1-5038-1627-5(3), 211143) Child's World, Inc, The.

Beaver, Simon. Dangerous & Dirty Jobs Low Intermediate Book with Online Access, 1 vol. 2014. (ENG., Illus.). 28p. pap., E-Book, E-Book 9.50 (978-1-107-64567-7(0)) Cambridge Univ. Pr.

Benchmark Education Company, LLC Staff, compiled by. Jobs. 2006. (J). 118.00 (978-1-4108-7041-4(3)) Benchmark Education Co.

The Best Job Ever, 12 vols. 2014. (Best Job Ever Ser.). (ENG.). 24p. (J). (gr. 3-3). lib. bdg. 151.62 (978-1-4777-5737-6(6), 6e73c036-6fe2-421c-b26a-8d633ecb9f77, PowerKids Pr.) Rosen Publishing Group, Inc., The.

Blohm, Craig E. Great Jobs in Business. 2019. (Great Jobs Ser.). (ENG.). 80p. (YA). (gr. 6-12). (978-1-68282-517-4(5)) ReferencePoint Pr., Inc.

Boothroyd, Jennifer. From Assembly Lines to Home Offices: How Work Has Changed. 2011. (Comparing Past & Present Ser.). pap. 45.32 (978-0-7613-8389-5(1)); pap. 7.95 (978-0-7613-7842-6(1)); (ENG., Illus.). 32p. lib. bdg. 26.60 (978-0-7613-6748-2(9)) Lerner Publishing Group.

Bowman-Kruhm, Mary. A Day in the Life of a Firefighter. 2009. (Kids' Career Library). 24p. (gr. 3-3). 42.50 (978-1-60853-437-1(5), PowerKids Pr.) Rosen Publishing Group, Inc., The.

Boyd, Nicole. A Doctor's Busy Day. 2009. (Reading Room Collection 2 Ser.). 24p. (gr. 3-4). 42.50 (978-1-60851-952-1(X), PowerKids Pr.) Rosen Publishing Group, Inc., The.

Bozak, Kristin & Cohen, Judith Love. You Can Be a Woman Botanist. Katz, David Arthur, illus. Date not set. 40p. (J). (gr. 3-6). 13.95 (978-1-880599-41-9(4)) Cascade Pass, Inc.

Brezina, Corona. Getting a Job in Health Care, 1 vol. 2013. (Job Basics: Getting the Job You Need Ser.). (ENG.). 80p. (YA). (gr. 8-8). 38.41 (978-1-4488-9610-3(X), f876c137-b5ba-4a0f-b756-134cd7407a1a) Rosen Publishing Group, Inc., The.

Brill, Marlene Targ. Doctors. 2005. (Pull Ahead Bks.). (Illus.). 32p. (J). lib. bdg. 22.60 (978-0-8225-1689-7(6)) Lerner Publishing Group.

Brooks, Felicity. Daisy Doctor. Litchfield, Jo, illus. 2005. 24p. (J). pap. 6.95 (978-0-7945-0724-4(7), Usborne) EDC Publishing.

—Frank the Farmer. Litchfield, Jo, illus. 2005. (Jobs People Do Ser.). 23p. (J). (gr. -1-7). pap. 6.95 (978-0-7945-0723-7(9), Usborne) EDC Publishing.

—Vicky the Vet. Litchfield, Jo, illus. 2004. (Jobs People Do Ser.). 24p. (J). pap. 6.95 (978-0-7945-0726-8(3), Usborne) EDC Publishing.

Brooks, Shunda K. What Should I Be? It's All up to Me! The Opportunities Are Endless! 2013. 48p. 28.99 (978-1-4582-0906-1(7)); pap. 20.99 (978-1-4582-0907-8(5)) Author Solutions, LLC. (Abbott Pr.).

Brown, Janet Allison. My First Book of Jobs. 2004. (Early Learning Ser.). (Illus.). 18p. (J). bds. 5.99 (978-1-85854-429-8(7)) Brimax Books Ltd. GBR. Dist: Byeway Bks.

Bruno, Nikki. Gross Jobs in Science: 4D an Augmented Reading Experience. 2019. (Gross Jobs 4D Ser.). (ENG., Illus.). 32p. (J). (gr. 3-9). lib. bdg. 31.99 (978-1-5435-5490-8(3), 139361, Capstone Pr.) Capstone.

—Gross Jobs Working with Animals: 4D an Augmented Reading Experience. 2019. (Gross Jobs 4D Ser.). (ENG., Illus.). 32p. (J). (gr. 3-9). lib. bdg. 31.99 (978-1-5435-5489-2(X), 139360, Capstone Pr.) Capstone.

Burchett. When I Grow Up: Level A. 2004. (Illus.). (J). pap. 6.00 (978-0-7398-8154-5(X)) Steck-Vaughn.

Burton, Margie, et al. Doing My Job. 2011. (Early Connections Ser.). (J). (978-1-61672-521-1(4)) Benchmark Education Co.

—What Will I Be? 2011. (Early Connections Ser.). (J). (978-1-61672-315-6(7)) Benchmark Education Co.

Butz, Christopher. I Go to Work as a Letter Carrier. 2003. (I Go to Work As Ser.). (Illus.). (J). pap. (978-1-58417-104-1(9)); lib. bdg. (978-1-58417-041-9(7)) Lake Street Pubs.

Byrd-Hill, Ida. Me & My Big Career, Hill, Karen, ed. Hill, Kevin, illus. 2010. (ENG.). 24p. (J). 14.95 (978-0-9829610-0-1(6)) Upheaval Media, Inc.

Calling All Innovators: A Career for You (Fall 2014 Set Of 4) 2014. (Calling All Innovators: a Career for You Ser.). (J). lib. bdg. 120.00 (978-0-531-24352-7(4)) Scholastic Library Publishing.

Calling All Innovators: A Career for You (Fall 2016 Set Of 4) 2016. (Calling All Innovators: a Career for You Ser.). (J). lib. bdg. 120.00 (978-0-531-22057-3(5), Children's Pr.) Scholastic Library Publishing.

Cannon, Shannon. The Letter Uu Set: Jobs, 6. 2004. (Letter Bks.). (ENG.). 8p. (gr. k-1). pap. 29.70 (978-0-7368-4120-7(2)) Capstone.

Careers in Focus: Politics. 2nd rev. ed. 2011. (ENG., Illus.). 194p. (gr. 6-12). 32.95 (978-0-8160-8035-9(6), P189791, Ferguson Publishing Company) Infobase Holdings, Inc.

Careers (Set), 16 vols. 2011. (21st Century Junior Library: Careers Ser.). (ENG., Illus.). 24p. (gr. 2-5). 467.36 (978-1-61080-000-6(1), 200934) Cherry Lake Publishing.

Carson, J. You Can Do It! Learning the Y Sound. 2009. (PowerPhonics Ser.). 24p. (gr. 1-1). 39.90 (978-1-60851-481-6(1), PowerKids Pr.) Rosen Publishing Group, Inc., The.

Cefrey, Holly & Brexel, Bernadette. Your Governor: State Government in Action, 1 vol. 2003. (Primary Source Library of American Citizenship Ser.). (ENG., Illus.). 32p. (YA). (gr. 5-5). lib. bdg. 29.13 (978-0-8239-4480-4(8), de1303fb-e2e3-4478-bbb1-06f11d055284, Rosen Reference) Rosen Publishing Group, Inc., The.

Christopher, Nick. Que Hacen Los Carteros? / What Do Mail Carriers Do?, 1 vol. 2015. (Ayudantes de la Comunidad / Helping the Community Ser.). (ENG & SPA.). 24p. (J). (gr. 1-1). 25.27 (978-1-4994-0633-7(9), 50fcb7d2-e699-44f8-9069-dca7510fdadc, PowerKids Pr.) Rosen Publishing Group, Inc., The.

Christy, Lee Louis. I Go to Work as a Firefighter. 2003. (I Go to Work As Ser.). (Illus.). (J). (978-1-58417-039-6(5)) Lake Street Pubs.

—I Go to Work as a Police Officer. 2003. (I Go to Work As Ser.). (Illus.). (J). (978-1-58417-040-2(9)); pap. (978-1-58417-103-4(0)) Lake Street Pubs.

Coan, Sharon. Trabajadores de Mi Ciudad. 2nd rev. ed. 2016. (TIME for KIDS(r): Informational Text Ser.). (SPA.). 12p. (gr. -1-k). 7.99 (978-1-4938-3027-5(9)) Teacher Created Materials, Inc.

—Workers at My School (Foundations Plus) 2nd rev. ed. 2015. (TIME for KIDS(r): Informational Text Ser.). (ENG., Illus.). 12p. (gr. -1-k). 7.99 (978-1-4938-2145-7(8)) Teacher Created Materials, Inc.

—Workers in My City (Foundations Plus) 2nd rev. ed. 2015. (TIME for KIDS(r): Informational Text Ser.). (ENG., Illus.). 12p. (gr. -1-k). 7.99 (978-1-4938-2146-4(6)) Teacher Created Materials, Inc.

—Workers Who Take Care of Me (Foundations Plus) 2nd rev. ed. 2015. (TIME for KIDS(r): Informational Text Ser.). (ENG., Illus.). 12p. (gr. -1-k). 7.99 (978-1-4938-2147-1(4)) Teacher Created Materials, Inc.

Cohn, Jessica. Pest Control Worker, 1 vol. 2011. (Dirty & Dangerous Jobs Ser.). (ENG.). 32p. (gr. 3-3). 31.21 (978-1-60870-176-6(X), f08e28ce-b446-4066-9f4f-e957d491c226) Cavendish Square Publishing LLC.

Coldfeather, Suzanne D. Places to Work. 2011. (Wonder Readers Early Level Ser.). (ENG.). 16p. (gr. -1-1). pap. 35.94 (978-1-4296-8198-8(5), Capstone Pr.) Capstone.

Community Helpers & Their Tools. 2015. (Community Helpers & Their Tools Ser.). (ENG.). 24p. (J). (gr. 2-3). pap., pap., pap. 297.00 (978-1-4994-1278-9(9), PowerKids Pr.) Rosen Publishing Group, Inc., The.

Cool Arts Careers (Set), 8 vols., Set. Incl. Actor. Somervill, Barbara A. lib. bdg. 32.07 (978-1-61080-129-4(6), 201136); Choreographer. Marsico, Katie. lib. bdg. 32.07 (978-1-61080-136-2(9), 201150); Dancer. Marsico, Katie. lib. bdg. 32.07 (978-1-61080-130-0(X), 201138); Fashion Designer. Wooster, Patricia. lib. bdg. 32.07 (978-1-61080-131-7(8), 201140); Music Producer. Wooster, Patricia. lib. bdg. 32.07 (978-1-61080-133-1(4), 201144); Musician. Somervill, Barbara A. lib. bdg. 32.07 (978-1-61080-132-4(6), 201142); Scriptwriter. Mullins, Matt. lib. bdg. 32.07 (978-1-61080-135-5(0), 201148); Special Effects Technician. Mullins, Matt. lib. bdg. 32.07 (978-1-61080-134-8(2), 201146); (gr. 4-8). (21st Century

Skills Library: Cool Arts Careers Ser.). (ENG., Illus.). 32p. 2011. 256.56 *(978-1-61080-150-8(4)*, 201018) Cherry Lake Publishing.

Cool Careers: On the Go, 12 vols., Set. Incl. Archaeologist. Thomas, William David. (YA). lib. bdg. 28.67 *(978-1-4339-0000-6(9)*, c8cf6e48-4640-4b18-b268-ceef98c3f695); Camera Operator. Horn, Geoffrey M. (YA). lib. bdg. 28.67 *(978-1-4339-0001-3(7)*, 49af9276-9a7b-4d38-a456-1ded60ea920d); Fashion Buyer. Cohn, Jessica. (YA). lib. bdg. 28.67 *(978-1-4339-0002-0(5)*, 46fd3cff-e78c-41c4-9057-cd4a91aa9dec); Flight Attendant. Thomas, William David. (YA). lib. bdg. 28.67 *(978-1-4339-0003-7(3)*, 576f4580-ab5d-415e-814f-92e101b05985); Journalist. Thomas, William David. (Illus.). (J). lib. bdg. 28.67 *(978-1-4339-0004-4(1)*, bf374be7-c0dc-4aa8-9064-fec3f0c7c3dc); Truck Driver. Thomas, William David. (YA). lib. bdg. 28.67 *(978-1-4339-0005-1(X)*, 434a477c-42f6-4db9-ab65-a1739d0970c4); (gr. 3-3). (Cool Careers: on the Go Ser.). (ENG.). 32p. 2009. Set lib. bdg. 172.02 *(978-1-4339-0006-8(8)*, 8c1a36d1-382f-4eb2-a44f-aea0277668dc) Stevens, Gareth Publishing LLLP.

Cool Careers (Set), 24 vols. 2011. (21st Century Skills Library: Cool Careers Ser.). (ENG., Illus.). 32p. (gr. 4-8). 769.68 *(978-1-60279-998-1(9)*, 200936) Cherry Lake Publishing.

Craats, Rennay. The Blacksmith: Pioneers of Canada. 2011. 24p. (YA). (gr. 2-4). *(978-1-77071-681-0(5))*; pap. *(978-1-77071-685-8(8))* Weigl Educational Pubs. Ltd.

—Le Forgeron: Le Début de la Colonie. Karvonen, Tanjah, tr. from ENG. 2011. (FRE., Illus.). 24p. (gr. 3-6). *(978-1-77071-418-2(9))* Weigl Educational Pubs. Ltd.

Crane, Natalie. I Go to Work as a Teacher. 2003. (I Go to Work As Ser.). (Illus.). (J). pap. *(978-1-58417-106-5(5))*; lib. bdg. *(978-1-58417-043-3(3))*; lib. bdg. *(978-1-58417-044-0(1))* Lake Street Pubs.

Crowson, Andrew. Flip Flap People. 2003. (Illus.). 12p. bds. *(978-1-85602-443-3(1)*, Pavilion Children's Books) Pavilion Bks.

Currie, Stephen. Teen Guide to Jobs & Taxes. 2016. (ENG.). 64p. (J). (gr. 5-12). lib. bdg. *(978-1-68282-082-7(3))* ReferencePoint Pr., Inc.

Cutcher, Jenai. Gotta Dance! The Rhythms of Jazz & Tap. (Curtain Call Library of Dance Ser.). 48p. (gr. 5-8). 2009. 53.00 *(978-1-60853-421-0(9))* 2003. (ENG., Illus.). (J). lib. bdg. 34.47 *(978-0-8239-4554-2(5)*, fce23dc8-fd81-40a0-91b5-1349b58bd4f6) Rosen Publishing Group, Inc., The. (Rosen Reference).

Dahlman, Tricia, ed. MnCareers 2005. 2004. (Illus.). 112p. (YA). per. 12.95 *(978-0-9670505-7-7(X)*, ES-90508-09) Minnesota Dept. Employment & Economic Development.

Dalton, Sarah, et al, eds. Encyclopedia of Careers & Vocational Guidance, 5 vols., Set. 15th rev. ed. 2010. 4128p. (C). (gr. 9). 249.95 *(978-0-8160-8313-8(4)*, Ferguson Publishing Company) Infobase Holdings, Inc.

Dunn, Mary R. I Want to Be a Chef. 2009. (Dream Jobs Ser.). 24p. (gr. 2-3). 42.50 *(978-1-61512-205-9(2)*, PowerKids Pr.) Rosen Publishing Group, Inc., The.

—I want to be a Fashion Designer: Set 2, 12 vols. Incl. I Want to Be a Ballet Dancer. lib. bdg. 26.27 *(978-1-4042-4469-6(7)*, b1f6a0a6-19fb-47e8-ad84-ff0d09bb6789); I Want to Be a Chef. lib. bdg. 26.27 *(978-1-4042-4471-9(9)*, 24cafc67-d185-40bd-8f10-81bdeb18eafd); I Want to Be a Fashion Designer. lib. bdg. 26.27 *(978-1-4042-4472-6(7)*, cf88f9c8-b343-4412-830b-79789ccbff65); I Want to Be in Musicals. lib. bdg. 26.27 *(978-1-4042-4470-2(0)*, 4dbd29f9-d7a0-4843-b694-02ce7f7ec6f8); I Want to Make Movies. lib. bdg. 26.27 *(978-1-4042-4473-3(5)*, 83cc834f-3f81-4abb-895f-2dcb536fd764); I Want to Write Books. lib. bdg. 26.27 *(978-1-4042-4474-0(3)*, 89f029e4-2349-43a7-aeba-ca7986f7d6d8); (Illus.). 24p. (YA). (gr. 2-3). (Dream Jobs Ser.). (ENG.). 2008. Set lib. bdg. 157.62 *(978-1-4358-2551-2(9)*, b8b5310f-6b1a-4070-9f4e-2a5d55d5959d, PowerKids Pr.) Rosen Publishing Group, Inc., The.

—Quiero Ser Chef, 1 vol. 2009. (Trabajos de Ensueño (Dream Jobs) Ser.).Tr. of I Want to Be a Chef. (SPA., Illus.). 24p. (gr. 2-3). pap. 8.25 *(978-1-4358-3427-9(5)*, f6e05842-ade1-4e18-b687-9830bda7fc29, Editorial Buenas Letras) Rosen Publishing Group, Inc., The.

—Quiero Ser Diseñador de Modas, 1 vol. 2009. (Trabajos de Ensueño (Dream Jobs) Ser.).Tr. of I Want to Be a Fashion Designer. (SPA., Illus.). 24p. (gr. 2-3). (J). lib. bdg. 26.27 *(978-1-4042-8154-7(1)*, 0fe2bc84-5d75-4610-9b9b-06beaed5252c); pap. 8.25 *(978-1-4358-3433-0(X)*, 92f680d4-2889-4c2c-9c7c-88aa6aaf8c8d, Editorial Buenas Letras) Rosen Publishing Group, Inc., The.

Early Macken, JoAnn. Mail Carriers, 1 vol. 2010. (People in My Community (Second Edition) Ser.). (ENG., Illus.). 24p. (gr. k-2). pap. 9.15 *(978-1-4339-3345-5(4)*, a15a20a5-f602-4614-96dd-7cbd8ed78626) Stevens, Gareth Publishing LLLP.

—Mail Carriers / Carteros, 1 vol. 2010. (People in My Community / Mi Comunidad Ser.). (SPA & ENG., Illus.). 24p. (gr. k-2). pap. 9.15 *(978-1-4339-3763-7(8)*, 9e6c44c4-7613-4698-a386-a15aa3d4fa78) Stevens, Gareth Publishing LLLP.

—Teachers, 1 vol. 2010. (People in My Community (Second Edition) Ser.). (ENG., Illus.). 24p. (gr. k-2). pap. 9.15 *(978-1-4339-3348-6(9)*, e00cd7cc-f89d-4484-9310-c7e273b27d86); (J). 25.27 *(978-1-4339-3347-9(0)*, 67197f32-ddc4-4201-934c-84344cf39571) Stevens, Gareth Publishing LLLP.

—Teachers / Maestros, 1 vol. 2010. (People in My Community / Mi Comunidad Ser.). (SPA & ENG., Illus.). 24p. (gr. k-2). pap. 9.15 *(978-1-4339-3766-8(2)*, 96dde7f4-8a3e-4bdf-a3b9-7bd2ea7a44b6) Stevens, Gareth Publishing LLLP.

EDITORS AT JIST. Young Person's Occupational Outlook Handbook. 7th rev. ed. 2010. (ENG.). 336p. 25.95 *(978-1-59357-743-8(5))* Kendall Hunt Publishing Co.

English, Melissa. Caution: Why You Need to Think about Careers NOW! 2004. (YA). per. 12.95 *(978-0-9754148-0-4(1))* Caution Bks.

Essential Careers: Set 3, 12 vols. 2013. (Essential Careers Ser.). (ENG.). 80p. (YA). (gr. 6-6). 224.82 *(978-1-4488-9485-7(9)*, fa82d95b-6e92-4d9b-a86d-62863d2c5a1d) Rosen Publishing Group, Inc., The.

Essential Careers: Set 4, 10 vols. 2013. (Essential Careers Ser.). (ENG.). 80p. (YA). (gr. 6-6). 187.35 *(978-1-4777-1800-1(1)*, fd163d87-3342-42ab-9fc4-5fe051aedcf9) Rosen Publishing Group, Inc., The.

Essential Careers: Sets 1 - 3. 2013. (Essential Careers Ser.). 80p. (YA). (gr. 7-12). 731.50 *(978-1-4777-0615-2(1))* Rosen Publishing Group, Inc., The.

Extreme Careers: Set 5, 10 vols. Incl. Disaster Relief Workers. Roza, Greg. (J). lib. bdg. 37.13 *(978-1-4042-0943-5(3)*, fb4ff919-eae7-40cf-b092-e3d9e21d9307); Homeland Security Officers. Meyer, Jared. (J). lib. bdg. 37.13 *(978-1-4042-0945-9(X)*, 03f95474-3eae-4225-b097-7fb2f15f714d); Hostage Rescuers. Poolos, Jamie. lib. bdg. 37.13 *(978-1-4042-0941-1(7)*, 8fdbb894-9a6f-4d83-8a1f-c316f0c58f69); Refugee Workers. Levy, Janey. (J). lib. bdg. 37.13 *(978-1-4042-0960-2(3)*, c9b984c3-3155-45c9-8a2a-4ac15e17c4a0); U. S. Air Marshals. Broyles, Matthew. (J). lib. bdg. 37.13 *(978-1-4042-0942-8(5)*, 8fa8bfbc-9017-41d4-90ce-81c18389abc5); Working in a War Zone: Military Contractors. Meyer, Jared. (J). lib. bdg. 37.13 *(978-1-4042-0959-6(X)*, 579b800a-d325-4845-83e2-959efa60b94c); (Illus.). 64p. (gr. 5-5). 2007. (Extreme Careers Ser.). (ENG.). 2006. Set lib. bdg. 185.65 *(978-1-4042-1042-4(3)*, 52dd5a5a-2793-44c2-ac2d-afd67b8d2c91) Rosen Publishing Group, Inc., The.

Extreme Careers: Set 6, 8 vols. Incl. Brain Surgeons. Bailey, Diane. lib. bdg. 37.13 *(978-1-4042-1787-4(8)*, e4fe0185-1f69-45a1-9420-c425ffa8649f); High Risk Construction Work: Life Building Skyscrapers, Bridges, & Tunnels. Wolny, Philip. lib. bdg. 37.13 *(978-1-4042-1789-8(4)*, 0960af74-fa6b-4f71-aea5-51c5e2f3c888); Manga Artists. Orr, Tamra. lib. bdg. 37.13 *(978-1-4042-1854-3(8)*, 8a8c8523-e4a9-4ccb-bcf8-f42c836e6f49); Search & Rescue Swimmers. La Bella, Laura. lib. bdg. 37.13 *(978-1-4042-1786-7(X)*, a630f377-e969-4dc6-9f5e-797f8f893314); Treasure Hunters. Brezina, Corona. lib. bdg. 37.13 *(978-1-4042-1788-1(6)*, b160e510-43ee-4db9-a042-6ddb1f25070a); (Illus.). 64p. (YA). (gr. 5-5). 2008. (Extreme Careers Ser.). (ENG.). 2008. Set lib. bdg. 148.52 *(978-1-4042-1875-8(0)*, d41bdf65-5315-44a0-99cd-8c0ff5ed5e62, Rosen Reference) Rosen Publishing Group, Inc., The.

Ferguson Publishing. Encyclopedia of Careers & Vocational Guidance, 6. 17th ed. 2018. (ENG., Illus.). 6344p. (gr. 9). 299.95 *(978-0-8160-8514-9(5)*, P560536) Ferguson Publishing.

Ferry, Francis. Job-O E: Elementary. Ellis, Amy, illus. 3rd ed. 2003. (Job-O Ser.). (J). *(978-1-887481-43-4(5))* CFKR Career Materials, Inc.

Fields, J. Choosing a Career as a Nurse-Midwife. 2009. (World of Work Ser.). 64p. (gr. 5-5). 58.50 *(978-1-60854-323-6(4))* Rosen Publishing Group, Inc., The.

Flath, Camden. 21st-Century Counselors: New Approaches to Mental Health & Substance Abuse. 2010. (New Careers for the 21st Century Ser.). 64p. (YA). (gr. 7-18). pap. 9.95 *(978-1-4222-2046-7(X))*; (Illus.). lib. bdg. 22.95 *(978-1-4222-1825-9(2))* Mason Crest.

Francis, Amy, ed. Manufacturing Jobs in the U. S., 1 vol. 2015. (At Issue Ser.). (ENG.). 120p. (gr. 10-12). lib. bdg. 41.03 *(978-0-7377-7173-2(9)*, 9d32692f-9c07-4b45-8ed3-158f6c5daaa3, Greenhaven Publishing) Greenhaven Publishing LLC.

Franks, Katie. Dream Jobs: Set 1. 8 vols. Incl. I Want to Be a Baseball Player. (J). lib. bdg. 26.27 *(978-1-4042-3622-6(8)*, 164646bb-2da3-4e4f-92d5-798a0f66589f); I Want to Be a Basketball Player. (J). lib. bdg. 26.27 *(978-1-4042-3621-9(X)*, a4f8b420-cda0-45fa-a2e2-5e45d03a75d6); I Want to Be a Movie Star. (YA). lib. bdg. 26.27 *(978-1-4042-3619-6(8)*, 173dd864-0ee6-4483-b772-e364699a0208); I Want to Be a Race Car Driver. (J). lib. bdg. 26.27 *(978-1-4042-3623-3(6)*, 87391c97-8ca6-46cb-9cd5-ea5e17a97521); (Illus.). 24p. (gr. 2-3). (Dream Jobs Ser.). (ENG.). 2006. Set lib. bdg. 105.08 *(978-1-4042-3598-4(1)*, 75a959c7-dddc-45f9-bf28-32d74732aa6c) Rosen Publishing Group, Inc., The.

Freed, Kira. Making Things, Doing Things. 2017. (Text Connections Guided Close Reading Ser.). (J). (gr. k). *(978-1-4900-1779-2(8))* Benchmark Education Co.

Fremont, Elenor. Odd Jobs: The Wackiest Jobs You've Never Heard Of. 2012. (ENG., Illus.). 80p. (J). (gr. 2-5). pap. 33.99 *(978-0-689-82934-5(5)*, Simon & Schuster/Paula Wiseman Bks.) Simon & Schuster/Paula Wiseman Bks.

French, Cathy. Jobs up High. 2011. (Early Connections Ser.). (J). *(978-1-61672-231-9(2))* Benchmark Education Co.

—Using Numbers at Work. 2011. (Early Connections Ser.). (J). *(978-1-61672-242-5(8))* Benchmark Education Co.

Fronczak, Emerson. Who Works at My School?, 1 vol. 2012. (InfoMax Readers Ser.). (ENG., Illus.). 16p. (J). (gr. k-k). pap. 7.00 *(978-1-4488-8938-9(3)*, 54544a14-d39c-4416-a1a2-b51c2f334d14, Rosen Classroom) Rosen Publishing Group, Inc., The.

Gardiner, Lisa. Big Dreams. Flowerpot Press, ed. 2012. (Illus.). 20p. (J). *(978-1-926988-04-7(3))* Flowerpot Children's Pr. Inc.

—People. Flowerpot Press, ed. 2012. (Illus.). 20p. (J). *(978-1-926988-06-1(X))* Flowerpot Children's Pr. Inc.

Gerry, Lisa M. 100 Things to Be When You Grow Up. 2017. (Illus.). 256p. (J). (gr. 3-7). pap. 9.99 *(978-1-4263-2711-7(0)*, National Geographic Kids) Disney Publishing Worldwide.

Giacobello, John. Bodyguards: Life Protecting Others. 2009. (Extreme Careers Ser.). 64p. (gr. 5-5). 58.50 *(978-1-61512-385-8(7)*, Rosen Reference) Rosen Publishing Group, Inc., The.

Gillis, Jennifer B. Jobs on Wheels. 2006. (My Neighborhood Ser.). (Illus.). 24p. (J). (gr. -1-3). 16.15 *(978-0-7569-6928-8(X))* Perfection Learning Corp.

Gonzalez, Lissette. Bomb Squads in Action. 2009. (Dangerous Jobs Ser.). 24p. (gr. 2-3). 42.50 *(978-1-61512-133-5(1)*, PowerKids Pr.) Rosen Publishing Group, Inc., The.

Graphic Careers, 12 vols., Set. Incl. Astronauts. West, David. Robins, Jim, illus. (YA). lib. bdg. 37.13 *(978-1-4042-1461-3(5)*, 3933503d-1e94-4ba0-88c5-cd4b12cc4d70); Fighter Pilots. West, David. Field, James, illus. (YA). lib. bdg. 37.13 *(978-1-4042-1455-2(0)*, 02066b9c-d906-4cbe-8bfc-7bb784fe0d92); Hurricane Hunters & Tornado Chasers. Jeffrey, Gary. Garofalo, Gianluca, illus. (YA). lib. bdg. 37.13 *(978-1-4042-1458-3(5)*, 3486897e-4cf0-4e1a-83f8-3b59a796e2cf); Secret Agents. Jeffrey, Gary. Riley, Terry, illus. (YA). lib. bdg. 37.13 *(978-1-4042-1464-4(X)*, 600bda56-1c6c-4364-94ee-8b17ceb3fea4); War Correspondents. Shone, Rob. Forsey, Chris, illus. (J). lib. bdg. 37.13 *(978-1-4042-1449-1(6)*, a6d745c4-f2f5-41b5-82e5-d10e71cb82f6); (gr. 5-5). 2008. (Graphic Careers Ser.). (ENG.). 48p. 2007. Set lib. bdg. 222.78 *(978-1-4042-1479-8(8)*, f3eb7c67-3b68-4b4c-bbbf-db2cff62c5cb) Rosen Publishing Group, Inc., The.

Gray, Leon. Horrible Jobs of the Industrial Revolution, 1 vol., Vol. 1. 2013. (History's Most Horrible Jobs Ser.). (ENG.). 48p. (J). (gr. 5-6). 34.61 *(978-1-4824-0343-5(9)*, f7ddfa05-4ca1-4625-8a92-25f41a49422c) Stevens, Gareth Publishing LLLP.

Green Careers, 6 vols., Set. 2010. (Green Careers Ser.). (C). (gr. 9). 197.70 *(978-0-8160-8291-9(X)*, Ferguson Publishing Company) Infobase Holdings, Inc.

Gregory, Helen. Places to Work, 1 vol. (Wonder Readers Next Steps: Social Studies). (ENG.). (J). (gr. -1-1). 2013. 20p. lib. bdg. 25.32 *(978-1-4765-0043-0(6)*, 121961) 2011. 16p. pap. 6.25 *(978-1-4296-7806-3(2)*, 117978) Capstone.

—Where Do People Work?, 1 vol. 2011. (Wonder Readers Early Level Ser.). (ENG.). 16p. (J). (gr. -1-1). pap. 6.25 *(978-1-4296-7879-7(8)*, 118211, Capstone Pr.) Capstone.

Guerrero, Pablo. Mi Laberinto. Urberuaga, Emilio, illus. 2004.Tr. of My Labyrinth. (SPA.). (J). 21.99 *(978-84-88342-42-3(X))* S.A. Kokinos ESP. Dist: Lectorum Pubns., Inc.

Harcourt School Publishers Staff. Jobs People Do, No. 6. 2nd ed. 2003. (Illus.). pap. 139.70 *(978-0-15-337561-3(2))* Harcourt Schl. Pubs.

Harea, Maria. Who Does That? Jobs in Your Community, 1 vol. 2008. (Real Life Readers Ser.). (ENG.). 16p. (gr. 2-3). pap. 7.05 *(978-1-4358-0115-8(6)*, ed89e62f-6e92-442c-8cef-c8a5e145b97a, Rosen Classroom) Rosen Publishing Group, Inc., The.

Harms, Julia. Recipe & Craft Guide to Italy. 2011. (World Crafts & Recipes Ser.). (ENG., Illus.). 64p. (J). (gr. 4-7). lib. bdg. 33.95 *(978-1-61228-083-7(8))* Mitchell Lane Pubs.

Hatanaka, Kellen. Work: An Occupational ABC, 1 vol. 2014. (ENG., Illus.). 40p. (J). (gr. -1-3). 16.95 *(978-1-55498-409-1(2))* Groundwood Bks. CAN. Dist: Publishers Group West (PGW).

Heiman, Diane & Suneby, Liz. See What You Can Be: Explore Careers That Could Be for You! Wood, Tracey, illus. 2009. (ENG.). 108p. (gr. 4-7). spiral bd. 9.95 *(978-1-59369-277-3(3))* American Girl Publishing, Inc.

Heling, Kathryn. Clothesline Clues to Jobs People Do. 2014. 17.95 *(978-1-63419-654-3(6))* Perfection Learning Corp.

Heling, Kathryn & Hembrook, Deborah. Clothesline Clues to Jobs People Do. Davies, Andy Robert, illus. (ENG.). 40p. (J). (gr. -1-2). 2014. pap. 7.95 *(978-1-58089-252-0(3))* 2012. 15.99 *(978-1-58089-251-3(5))* Charlesbridge Publishing, Inc.

Henry, Claire. The World's Deadliest Jobs, 1 vol., 1. 2014. (World's Deadliest Ser.). (ENG.). 32p. (J). (gr. 4-5). 28.93 *(978-1-4777-6161-8(6)*, cb94b5cb-cc17-4af9-96ff-88f04432fd31, PowerKids Pr.) Rosen Publishing Group, Inc., The.

Heos, Bridget. Getting a Job in Hair Care & Makeup, 1 vol. 2013. (Job Basics: Getting the Job You Need Ser.). (ENG.). 80p. (YA). (gr. 8-8). 38.41 *(978-1-4488-9611-0(8)*, f6d350aa-abe0-4544-82fe-3890223f733a) Rosen Publishing Group, Inc., The.

—Make Money! Be a Pet Sitter. Fabbri, Daniele, illus. 2013. (Make Money! Ser.). (ENG.). 24p. (J). (gr. 1-4). lib. bdg. 27.10 *(978-1-60753-362-7(6)*, 16279) Amicus.

Higgins, Melissa. Edward Snowden: Nsa Whistle-Blower. 2016. (Essential Lives Set 10 Ser.). (ENG., Illus.). 112p. (J). (gr. 8-12). lib. bdg. 41.36 *(978-1-68078-300-1(9)*, 21737, Essential Library) ABDO Publishing Co.

High-Tech Jobs, 12 vols. 2014. (High-Tech Jobs Ser.). (ENG.). 96p. (J). (gr. 8-8). lib. bdg. 267.00 *(978-1-5026-0295-4(4)*, 9a777a93-f2c7-436b-a3c2-60df83309800, Cavendish Square) Cavendish Square Publishing LLC.

Hill, Christina. Community Leaders Then & Now, 1 vol. rev. ed. 2006. (Social Studies: Informational Text Ser.). (ENG., Illus.). 32p. (J). (gr. 2-3). pap. 11.99 *(978-0-7439-9385-2(3))* Teacher Created Materials, Inc.

Holden, Pam. Jobs People Do Big Book Edition, 1 vol. 2014. (ENG.). 16p. (gr. 1-1). pap. *(978-1-77654-046-4(8)*, Red Rocket Readers) Flying Start Bks.

—When I Grow Up, 1 vol. East, Jacqueline, illus. 2009. (Red Rocket Readers Ser.). (ENG.). 16p. (gr. -1-1). pap. *(978-1-877363-06-1(5)*, Red Rocket Readers) Flying Start Bks.

I Can Be Anything! 2017. (I Can Be Anything! Ser.). 24p. (gr. k-k). pap. 48.90 *(978-1-5382-0241-8(7))*; (ENG.). lib. bdg. 145.62 *(978-1-5382-0240-1(9)*, 483c8ba2-92d7-45a4-b152-d1b8b9cffe8d) Stevens, Gareth Publishing LLLP.

I Can Be Anything!: Set 2, 12 vols. 2018. (I Can Be Anything! Ser.). (ENG.). 24p. (gr. k-k). lib. bdg. 145.62 *(978-1-5382-1844-0(5)*, e71fe808-42ba-4cda-833d-a9c2813b4d0c) Stevens, Gareth Publishing LLLP.

Ingalls, Ann. Isabella & Ivan Build an Interview. Siegel, Melanie, illus. 2012. (Writing Builders Ser.). 32p. (J). (gr. 2-4). pap. 11.94 *(978-1-60357-389-4(5))*; lib. bdg. 25.27 *(978-1-59953-509-8(2))* Norwood Hse. Pr.

Ivy, Darlene Sigda. Working in Sports. 2018. (Career Files Ser.). (ENG., Illus.). 32p. (J). (gr. 3-6). 32.80 *(978-1-63235-449-5(7)*, 13842, 12-Story Library) Bookstaves, LLC.

Jango-Cohen, Judith. Librarians. 2005. (Pull Ahead Bks.). (Illus.). 32p. (J). lib. bdg. 22.60 *(978-0-8225-1691-0(8))* Lerner Publishing Group.

Jarrell, Jane & Saathoff, Deborah. Off to Work We Go. 2004. 50p. (gr. -1-18). pap., act. bk. ed. 6.99 *(978-0-8054-0823-2(1))* B&H Publishing Group.

Jeffries, Joyce. Meet the Construction Worker, 1 vol. 2013. (People Around Town Ser.). 24p. (J). (gr. k-k). (ENG.). 25.27 *(978-1-4339-9364-0(3)*, c4468dfc-80dd-4203-8bdb-55794a7a97b3); (ENG.). pap. 9.15 *(978-1-4339-9362-6(7)*, 370b2cad-9a66-48b8-a5a2-1c95d43cc002); pap. 48.90 *(978-1-4339-9363-3(5))* Stevens, Gareth Publishing LLLP.

—Meet the Construction Worker / Conoce a Los Trabajadores de la Construcción, 1 vol. 2013. (People Around Town / Gente de Mi Ciudad Ser.). (SPA & ENG., Illus.). 24p. (J). (gr. k-k). 25.27 *(978-1-4339-9464-7(X)*, 4e759752-983f-4b22-bcba-defd5b009694) Stevens, Gareth Publishing LLLP.

—Meet the Farmer, 1 vol. 2013. (People Around Town Ser.). (Illus.). 24p. (J). (gr. k-k). (ENG.). pap. 9.15 *(978-1-4339-9368-8(6)*, a6d2d647-1b85-489e-a7eb-b270cb73de16); (ENG., lib. bdg. 25.27 *(978-1-4339-9367-1(8)*, 066200bc-5770-47f0-9de4-259841e7bf93); pap. 48.90 *(978-1-4339-9369-5(4))* Stevens, Gareth Publishing LLLP.

—Meet the Farmer / Conoce a Los Granjeros, 1 vol. 2013. (People Around Town / Gente de Mi Ciudad Ser.). (SPA & ENG., Illus.). 24p. (J). (gr. k-k). 25.27 *(978-1-4339-9466-1(6)*, 58fc0ec5-5cc2-4023-8c3f-6b0efef29a0a) Stevens, Gareth Publishing LLLP.

—Meet the Mayor, 1 vol. 2013. (People Around Town Ser.). (Illus.). 24p. (J). (gr. k-k). (ENG.). pap. 9.15 *(978-1-4339-9378-7(3)*, 7294b4f3-b9d1-48cb-a7c5-31942839224f); (ENG., lib. bdg. 25.27 *(978-1-4339-9377-0(5)*, f19cff44-3a21-4ac1-bc41-deb0d5c64ea4); pap. 48.90 *(978-1-4339-9379-4(1))* Stevens, Gareth Publishing LLLP.

—Meet the Mayor / Conoce a Los Alcaldes, 1 vol. 2013. (People Around Town / Gente de Mi Ciudad Ser.). (SPA & ENG., Illus.). 24p. (J). (gr. k-k). 25.27 *(978-1-4339-9470-8(4)*, b2aa7e90-b2d6-4cc0-aadb-29ceb8786c8f) Stevens, Gareth Publishing LLLP.

JIST Publishing Staff, creator. Young Person's Career Skills Handbook. 2006. (JIST's Young Person's Handbook Ser.). (Illus.). 250p. per. 19.95 *(978-1-59357-243-3(3)*, J2433, JIST Works) JIST Publishing.

JIST Works. People at Work! Second Edition: A Student's A-Z Guide to 350 Jobs. 2nd ed. 2005. (Early Start Career Ser.). (Illus.). 432p. (J). 27.95 *(978-1-59357-078-1(3)*, 1237657, JIST Works) JIST Publishing.

—Young Person's Occupational Outlook Handbook, Fifth Edition. 5th ed. 2004. (Illus.). 336p. pap. 19.95 *(978-1-59357-125-2(9)*, J1259, JIST Works) JIST Publishing.

Job Basics: Getting the Job You Need, 16 vols. 2013. (Job Basics: Getting the Job You Need Ser.). (ENG.). 80p. (YA). (gr. 8-8). 307.28 *(978-1-4488-9621-9(5)*, 705bbd1f-ba55-49d5-8727-a5385f21b558) Rosen Publishing Group, Inc., The.

Job Basics: Getting the Job You Need: Set 2, 14 vols. 2016. (Job Basics: Getting the Job You Need Ser.). (ENG.). 80p. (gr. 8-8). 268.87 *(978-1-4777-8550-8(7)*, 37a23a4b-df95-4f2b-a562-77b01fb5fb9a, Rosen Young Adult) Rosen Publishing Group, Inc., The.

Jobs in My School. 2014. (Jobs in My School Ser.). 24p. (J). (gr. k-2). pap. 49.50 *(978-1-4777-7226-3(X)*, PowerKids Pr.) Rosen Publishing Group, Inc., The.

Jobs to Do. 2017. (J). *(978-0-7166-7949-3(3))* World Bk., Inc.

Johnson, Jeremy. Unusual & Awesome Jobs in Sports: Pro Team Mascot, Pit Crew Member, & More. 2015. (You Get Paid for THAT? Ser.). (ENG., Illus.). 32p. (J). (gr. 3-9). lib. bdg. 28.65 *(978-1-4914-2032-4(4)*, 127510, Capstone Pr.) Capstone.

Jones, Molly. Top 10 Tips for Planning for a Career, 1 vol. 2012. (Tips for Success Ser.). (ENG., Illus.). 64p. (J). (gr. 6-6). 37.13 *(978-1-4488-6863-6(7)*, a6f4d3f9-3d08-4a8c-a2a6-de2c5c2e61a5) Rosen Publishing Group, Inc., The.

Jones, Tammy. Jobs Around Town. 2009. (Sight Word Readers Set A Ser.). (J). 3.49 net. *(978-1-60719-158-2(X))* Newmark Learning LLC.

Jump-Starting a Career in Medical Technology, 14 vols. 2013. (Health Care Careers in 2 Years Ser.). (ENG.). 80p. (YA). (gr. 7-7). 268.87 *(978-1-4777-1705-9(6)*, 9ebe27c5-d9a0-4d79-b7ab-5a92c4584d9c) Rosen Publishing Group, Inc., The.

Kalman, Bobbie. Community Helpers Then & Now. 2013. (ENG., Illus.). 24p. (J). *(978-0-7787-0115-6(8))*; pap. *(978-0-7787-0143-9(3))* Crabtree Publishing Co.

—Community Helpers Then & Now. 2014. (From Olden Days to Modern Ways in Your Community Ser.). (ENG.). 24p. (J). (gr. 1-4). 18.75 *(978-1-5311-8585-5(1))* Perfection Learning Corp.

Kamberg, Mary-Lane. Getting a Job in Law Enforcement, Security, & Corrections, 1 vol. 2013. (Job Basics: Getting the Job You Need Ser.). (ENG.). 80p. (YA). (gr. 8-8). 38.41 *(978-1-4488-9605-9(3)*, 041d2734-ea1d-4cde-b641-fe4af6b54775) Rosen Publishing Group, Inc., The.

Kidde, Rita. What Does a Janitor Do?, 1 vol. 2014. (Jobs in My School Ser.). (ENG., Illus.). 24p. (J). (gr. 1-2). pap. 9.25 *(978-1-4777-6544-9(1)*, 463c153c-7477-4dbd-988f-cfa1432bc1c4, PowerKids Pr.) Rosen Publishing Group, Inc., The.

Koh, Frederick. Danger at Work. 2007. (Steck-Vaughn BOLDPRINT Anthologies Ser.). (ENG., Illus.). 48p. (gr. 6-9). pap. 16.90 *(978-1-4190-4027-6(8))* Houghton Mifflin Harcourt Publishing Co.

Koosmann, Melissa. Recipe & Craft Guide to South Africa. 2011. (World Crafts & Recipes Ser.). (ENG., Illus.). 64p. (J). (gr. 4-7). lib. bdg. 33.95 *(978-1-61228-080-6(3))* Mitchell Lane Pubs.

Krasinski, Jay. Who Works at the Store?, 1 vol. 2012. (InfoMax Readers Ser.). (ENG., Illus.). 16p. (J). (gr. k-k). pap. 7.00 *(978-1-4488-8956-3(1)*, 292373a8-2d7c-4579-b543-bfa8528b4c24, Rosen Classroom) Rosen Publishing Group, Inc., The.

Laks Gorman, Jacqueline. Bus Drivers, 1 vol. 2010. (People in My Community (Second Edition) Ser.). (ENG., Illus.). 24p. (gr. k-2). pap. 9.15 *(978-1-4339-3336-3(5)*, a2d0d608-38cc-4677-aee6-5010d4e0d356) Stevens, Gareth Publishing LLLP.

—Bus Drivers / Conductores de Autobuses, 1 vol. 2010. (People in My Community / Mi Comunidad Ser.). (SPA & ENG., Illus.). 24p. (gr. k-2). pap. 9.15 *(978-1-4339-3754-5(9)*, 106c6f2b-bfb9-42a0-ac14-f4f6d270b35b) Stevens, Gareth Publishing LLLP.

—Firefighters, 1 vol. 2010. (People in My Community (Second Edition) Ser.). (ENG., Illus.). 24p. (gr. k-2). 25.27 *(978-1-4339-3338-7(1)*, 53173227-d870-43da-8a73-df3f79729066) Stevens, Gareth Publishing LLLP.

—Firefighters / Bomberos, 1 vol. 2010. (People in My Community / Mi Comunidad Ser.). (SPA & ENG., Illus.). 24p. (gr. k-2). pap. 9.15 *(978-1-4339-3757-6(3)*, fcacb159-358b-442d-b94f-237e72fed0db) Stevens, Gareth Publishing LLLP.

—Librarians, 1 vol. 2010. (People in My Community (Second Edition) Ser.). (ENG., Illus.). 24p. (gr. k-2). pap. 9.15 *(978-1-4339-3342-4(X)*, adbc6c35-689b-4232-8a6b-41706b67d7b6) Stevens, Gareth Publishing LLLP.

—Librarians / Bibliotecarios, 1 vol. 2010. (People in My Community / Mi Comunidad Ser.). (SPA & ENG., Illus.). 24p. (gr. k-2). pap. 9.15 *(978-1-4339-3760-6(3)*, fd6b829c-d7b8-4ad7-8816-1751339176f2) Stevens, Gareth Publishing LLLP.

—Police Officers, 1 vol. 2010. (People in My Community (Second Edition) Ser.). (ENG., Illus.). 24p. (gr. k-2). 25.27 *(978-1-4339-3350-9(0)*, 5ac21996-3d00-48ba-a5f4-79634e190ea6); pap. 9.15 *(978-1-4339-3351-6(9)*, cb580bad-1d18-42b1-8380-9f0ff8e7a313) Stevens, Gareth Publishing LLLP.

—Police Officers / Policías, 1 vol. 2010. (People in My Community / Mi Comunidad Ser.). (SPA & ENG., Illus.). 24p. (gr. k-2). pap. 9.15 *(978-1-4339-3769-9(7)*, 1c7c1d4d-bf2c-4f74-8982-decb89af60cd) Stevens, Gareth Publishing LLLP.

Larocque, Katharine. Helping Seniors. 2019. (Careers Making a Difference Ser.). (Illus.). 80p. (J). (gr. 12). lib. bdg. 34.60 *(978-1-4222-4257-5(9))* Mason Crest.

Latour, Pierre. Who Works Here? 2012. (Level C Ser.). (ENG., Illus.). 16p. (J). (gr. k-2). pap. 7.95 *(978-1-927136-22-5(9)*, 19457) RiverStream Publishing.

Leake, Diyan. People in the Community, 6 bks., Set. Incl. Teachers. (ENG., Illus.). 24p. (gr. -1-1). 2008. 21.99 *(978-1-4329-1191-1(0)*, Heinemann); (People in the Community Ser.). (ENG.). 24p. 2008. Set lib. bdg. 21.99 o.p. *(978-1-4329-1193-5(7))* Acorn Pr., The CAN. Dist: Capstone.

LeBoutillier, Linda. Unusual & Awesome Jobs Using Technology: Roller Coaster Designer, Space Robotics Engineer, & More. 2015. (You Get Paid for THAT? Ser.). (ENG., Illus.). 32p. (J). (gr. 3-9). 28.65 *(978-1-4914-2029-4(4)*, 127507, Capstone Pr.) Capstone.

Lerner Publishing Group Staff. Work People Do: Classroom Set. 2005. (Illus.). (J). (gr. -1-1). 24.95 *(978-0-8225-5356-4(2))* Lerner Publishing Group.

LernerClassroom Editors. First Step Nonfiction-Work People Do Set I Teaching Guide. 2009. pap. 7.95 *(978-0-8225-5398-4(8))* Lerner Publishing Group.

—First Step Nonfiction-Work People Do Set Ii Teaching Guide. 2009. pap. 7.95 *(978-0-8225-3858-5(X))* Lerner Publishing Group.

Lindeen, Mary. Earning Money. 2019. (BeginningtoRead Ser.). (ENG., Illus.). 32p. (J). (gr. -1-2). 22.60 *(978-1-68450-934-8(3))*; (gr. k-2). pap. 13.26 *(978-1-68404-434-4(0))* Norwood Hse. Pr.

Litchfield, Jo. Jobs. Litchfield, Jo & Allen, Francesca, illus. 2006. (Usborne Look & Say Ser.). 10p. (J). (gr. -1-k). bds. 7.99 *(978-0-7945-1353-5(0)*, Usborne) EDC Publishing.

Loh-Hagan, Virginia. Odd Jobs. 2018. (Stranger Than Fiction Ser.). (ENG.). 32p. (J). (gr. 4-8). pap. 14.21 *(978-1-5341-0858-5(0)*, 210796); (Illus.). lib. bdg. 32.07 *(978-1-5341-0759-5(2)*, 210795) Cherry Lake Publishing. (45th Parallel Press).

Lopez, Eduardo. 20 Great Career-Building Activities Using Instagram & Snapchat, 1 vol. 2016. (Social Media Career Building Ser.). (ENG., Illus.). 64p. (J). (gr. 7-7). 36.13 *(978-1-5081-7272-7(2)*, 4a14a3a8-7a30-46ed-936a-85dbed0b8860) Rosen Publishing Group, Inc., The.

Lost Jobs: Individual Title Six-Packs. (Bookweb Ser.). 32p. (gr. 6-18). 34.00 *(978-0-7578-0909-5(X))* Rigby Education.

Luebke, Gayle M. When I Grow Up. 2005. 19p. 9.88 *(978-1-4116-2790-1(3))* Lulu Pr., Inc.

Lüsted, Marcia Amidon. What Are Jobs & Earnings?, 1 vol. 2016. (Let's Find Out! Community Economics Ser.). (ENG., Illus.). 32p. (J). (gr. 2-3). lib. bdg. 26.06 *(978-1-68048-401-4(X)*, 9fc89135-4732-402e-a4cc-07abd89e2e95) Rosen Publishing Group, Inc., The.

MacDonald, Margaret. Working as a Team. 2011. (Learn-Abouts Ser.). (Illus.). 16p. (J). pap. 7.95 *(978-1-59920-648-6(X))* Black Rabbit Bks.

Mahaney, Ian F. The Best Job Ever, 1 vol. 2015. (Best Job Ever Ser.). (ENG.). 24p. (J). 49.50 *(978-1-4994-0302-2(X)*, PowerKids Pr.) Rosen Publishing Group, Inc., The.

Maile, Ruby. Why Do You Live Here? 2012. (Level C Ser.). (ENG., Illus.). 16p. (J). (gr. k-2). pap. 7.95 *(978-1-927136-25-6(3)*, 19463) RiverStream Publishing.

Mangrum, Allison. Jobs from A to Z. Capaldi, Gina, illus. 2006. 28p. pap. 9.50 *(978-1-55501-675-3(8))* Ballard & Tighe Pubs.

Marsh, Carole. Job Tracks: 60 Great Careers & How to Get from Where You Are... to Where You Want to Go! 2012. (Carole Marsh's Careers Curriculum Ser.). (ENG., Illus.). 130p. (J). pap. 19.99 *(978-0-635-10552-3(7))* Gallopade International.

—Work Words: Job/Business/Career Words & Terms You Need to Know! 2012. (Carole Marsh's Careers Curriculum Ser.). (ENG., Illus.). 58p. (J). pap. 19.99 *(978-0-635-10556-1(X))* Gallopade International.

—Would You Hire This Person? A Look at Getting Hired (or Not!)... from the Point of View of Your (Possible!) Future Employer. 2012. (Carole Marsh's Careers Curriculum Ser.). (ENG., Illus.). 82p. (J). pap. 19.99 *(978-0-635-10553-0(5))* Gallopade International.

Martin, Bobi. Working As an Electrician in Your Community, 1 vol. 2015. (Careers in Your Community Ser.). (ENG., Illus.). 80p. (YA). (gr. 7-8). 37.47 *(978-1-4994-6111-4(9)*, af409923-852a-4860-b789-8740a5e65cf4, Rosen Young Adult) Rosen Publishing Group, Inc., The.

Mattern, Joanne. Astronauts. 2009. (Working Together Ser.). 24p. (gr. 1-2). 42.50 *(978-1-60854-828-6(7)*, PowerKids Pr.) Rosen Publishing Group, Inc., The.

—Chefs. 2009. (Working Together Ser.). 24p. (gr. 1-2). 42.50 *(978-1-60854-829-3(5)*, PowerKids Pr.) Rosen Publishing Group, Inc., The.

—Cocineros (Chefs) 2009. (Trabajo en grupo (Working Together) Ser.). (SPA.). 24p. (gr. 1-2). 42.50 *(978-1-60854-576-6(8)*, Editorial Buenas Letras) Rosen Publishing Group, Inc., The.

—Emt. 2009. (Working Together Ser.). 24p. (gr. 1-2). 42.50 *(978-1-60854-830-9(9)*, PowerKids Pr.) Rosen Publishing Group, Inc., The.

—Pilotos (Pilots) 2009. (Trabajo en grupo (Working Together) Ser.). (SPA.). 24p. (gr. 1-2). 42.50 *(978-1-60854-577-3(6)*, Editorial Buenas Letras) Rosen Publishing Group, Inc., The.

—Pilots. 2009. (Working Together Ser.). 24p. (gr. 1-2). 42.50 *(978-1-60854-832-3(5)*, PowerKids Pr.) Rosen Publishing Group, Inc., The.

—Técnicos en emergencias Médicas (EMT) 2009. (Trabajo en grupo (Working Together) Ser.). (SPA.). 24p. (gr. 1-2). 42.50 *(978-1-60854-579-7(2)*, Editorial Buenas Letras) Rosen Publishing Group, Inc., The.

Matthews, Sheelagh. Canadian Shield. 2010. (Illus.). 32p. *(978-1-55388-628-0(3))*; pap. *(978-1-55388-629-7(1))* Weigl Educational Pubs. Ltd.

Meister, Cari. Chefs. 2014. (Illus.). 24p. (J). lib. bdg. 25.65 *(978-1-62031-089-2(9)*, Bullfrog Bks.) Jump! Inc.

—Construction Workers. 2014. (Illus.). 24p. (J). lib. bdg. 25.65 *(978-1-62031-090-8(2)*, Bullfrog Bks.) Jump! Inc.

—Farmers. 2014. (Illus.). 24p. (J). lib. bdg. 25.65 *(978-1-62031-092-2(9)*, Bullfrog Bks.) Jump! Inc.

—Mechanics. 2014. (Illus.). 24p. (J). lib. bdg. 25.65 *(978-1-62031-093-9(7)*, Bullfrog Bks.) Jump! Inc.

—Nurses. 2014. (Illus.). 24p. (J). lib. bdg. 25.65 *(978-1-62031-094-6(5)*, Bullfrog Bks.) Jump! Inc.

—Veterinarians. 2014. (Illus.). 24p. (J). lib. bdg. 25.65 *(978-1-62031-096-0(1)*, Bullfrog Bks.) Jump! Inc.

Metz, L. On the Job: Learning the O Sound. 2009. (PowerPhonics Ser.). 24p. (gr. 1-1). 39.90 *(978-1-60851-466-3(8)*, PowerKids Pr.) Rosen Publishing Group, Inc., The.

Meyer, Susan. Getting a Job in Sanitation, 1 vol. 2013. (Job Basics: Getting the Job You Need Ser.). (ENG.). 80p. (YA). (gr. 8-8). 38.41 *(978-1-4488-9607-3(X)*, 87cd22c7-97c7-4370-ac86-06b9c117dfb6) Rosen Publishing Group, Inc., The.

Milet Publishing. My First Bilingual Book-Jobs (English-Spanish), 1 vol. 2012. (My First Bilingual Book Ser.). (ENG & SPA., Illus.). 24p. (J). (gr. k — 1). bds. 7.99 *(978-1-84059-712-7(7))* Milet Publishing.

Milet Publishing Staff. Jobs, 1 vol. 2012. (My First Bilingual Book Ser.). (ENG & ITA., Illus.). 24p. (J). (gr. k — 1). bds. 7.99 *(978-1-84059-706-6(2))*; bds. 7.99 *(978-1-84059-711-0(9))*; bds. 7.99 *(978-1-84059-704-2(6))* Milet Publishing.

—Jobs - Berufe, 1 vol. 2012. (My First Bilingual Book Ser.). (ENG & GER., Illus.). 24p. (J). (gr. k — 1). bds. 7.99 *(978-1-84059-705-9(4))* Milet Publishing.

—Jobs - My First Bilingual Book, 1 vol. 2012. (My First Bilingual Book Ser.). (ENG., Illus.). 24p. (J). (gr. k — 1). bds. 7.99 *(978-1-84059-701-1(1))* Milet Publishing.

—Jobs Empregos, 1 vol. 2012. (My First Bilingual Book Ser.). (ENG., Illus.). 24p. (J). (gr. k — 1). bds. 7.99 *(978-1-84059-709-7(7))* Milet Publishing.

—My First Bilingual Book - Jobs, 1 vol. 2012. (My First Bilingual Book Ser.). (ENG & POR., Illus.). 24p. (J). (gr. k — 1). bds. 7.99 *(978-1-84059-708-0(9))* Milet Publishing.

—My First Bilingual Book-Jobs, 1 vol. 2012. (My First Bilingual Book Ser.). (ENG., Illus.). 24p. (J). (gr. k — 1). bds. 7.99 *(978-1-84059-703-5(8))*; bds. 7.99 *(978-1-84059-700-4(3))* Milet Publishing.

—My First Bilingual Book-Jobs (English-Korean), 1 vol. 2012. (My First Bilingual Book Ser.). (ENG., Illus.). 24p. (J). (gr. k — 1). bds. 7.99 *(978-1-84059-707-3(0))* Milet Publishing.

—My First Bilingual Book-Jobs (English-Russian), 1 vol. 2012. (My First Bilingual Book Ser.). (ENG., Illus.). 24p. (J). (gr. k — 1). bds. 7.99 *(978-1-84059-710-3(0))* Milet Publishing.

—My First Bilingual Book-Jobs (English-Turkish), 1 vol. 2012. (My First Bilingual Book Ser.). (ENG., Illus.). 24p. (J). (gr. k — 1). bds. 7.99 *(978-1-84059-713-4(5))* Milet Publishing.

—My First Bilingual Book-Jobs (English-Urdu), 1 vol. 2012. (My First Bilingual Book Ser.). (ENG., Illus.). 24p. (J). (gr. k — 1). bds. 7.99 *(978-1-84059-714-1(3))* Milet Publishing.

—My First Bilingual Book-Jobs (English-Vietnamese), 1 vol. 2012. (My First Bilingual Book Ser.). (ENG., Illus.). 24p. (J). (gr. k — 1). bds. 7.99 *(978-1-84059-715-8(1))* Milet Publishing.

Miller, Connie Colwell. The Deadliest Jobs on Earth. 2010. (World's Deadliest Ser.). (ENG.). 32p. (J). (gr. 3-9). lib. bdg. 27.32 *(978-1-4296-3931-6(8)*, 102541, Capstone Pr.) Capstone.

—Disgusting Jobs. rev. ed. 2016. (That's Disgusting! Ser.). (ENG.). 32p. (J). (gr. 3-9). pap. 7.95 *(978-1-5157-6268-3(8)*, 135071, Capstone Pr.) Capstone.

Mitchell, Melanie. Principals. (Pull Ahead Bks.). (J). 2005. (Illus.). 32p. lib. bdg. 22.60 *(978-0-8225-1694-1(2))* 2004. pap. 6.95 *(978-0-8225-2535-6(6)*, Lerner Pubns.) Lerner Publishing Group.

—Teachers. 2005. (Pull Ahead Bks.). (Illus.). 32p. (J). lib. bdg. 22.60 *(978-0-8225-1696-5(9))* Lerner Publishing Group.

Mitchell, Missy. Ballet: Pointe by Pointe. (Curtain Call Library of Dance Ser.). 48p. (gr. 5-8). 2009. 53.00 *(978-1-60853-418-0(9)*, Rosen Reference) 2003. (ENG., Illus.). (YA). lib. bdg. 34.47 *(978-0-8239-4555-9(3)*, dd043e4b-b420-451c-88fd-bff87dcd2606) Rosen Publishing Group, Inc., The.

Moening, Kate. Custodians. 2019. (Community Helpers Ser.). (ENG., Illus.). 24p. (J). (gr. k-3). lib. bdg. 26.95 *(978-1-62617-902-8(6)*, Blastoff! Readers) Bellwether Media.

—Plumbers. 2019. (Community Helpers Ser.). (ENG., Illus.). 24p. (J). (gr. k-3). lib. bdg. 26.95 *(978-1-62617-904-2(2)*, Blastoff! Readers) Bellwether Media.

Monroe, Judy. A Day in the Life of a Librarian, 1 vol. 2004. (Community Helpers at Work Ser.). (ENG., Illus.). 24p. (J). (gr. 1-3). 25.99 *(978-0-7368-2630-3(0)*, 89748, Capstone Pr.) Capstone.

Moore, Elizabeth. Keeping Us Safe, 1 vol. 2011. (Wonder Readers Emergent Level Ser.). (ENG.). 8p. (gr. -1-1). (J). pap. 6.25 *(978-1-4296-7845-2(3)*, 118158); pap. 35.94 *(978-1-4296-8232-9(9)*, Capstone Pr.) Capstone.

Moore, Phillip. How Can You Use a Computer? 2012. (Level D Ser.). (ENG., Illus.). 16p. (J). (gr. k-2). pap. 7.95 *(978-1-927136-32-4(6)*, 19412) RiverStream Publishing.

Morkes, Andrew. Flooring Installer, Vol. 10. 2018. (Careers in the Building Trades: a Growing Demand Ser.). 80p. (J). (gr. 7). lib. bdg. 33.27 *(978-1-4222-4115-8(7))* Mason Crest.

—Heating & Cooling Technician, Vol. 10. 2018. (Careers in the Building Trades: a Growing Demand Ser.). 80p. (J). (gr. 7). lib. bdg. 33.27 *(978-1-4222-4116-5(5))* Mason Crest.

—Roofer, Vol. 10. 2018. (Careers in the Building Trades: a Growing Demand Ser.). 80p. (J). (gr. 7). lib. bdg. 33.27 *(978-1-4222-4119-6(X))* Mason Crest.

Morris, Ann. That's Our Custodian! Linenthal, Peter, illus. Linenthal, Peter, photos by. 2003. (That's Our School Ser.). (ENG.). 32p. (gr. k-3). lib. bdg. 22.60 *(978-0-7613-2401-0(1)*, Millbrook Pr.) Lerner Publishing Group.

—That's Our Gym Teacher! Linenthal, Peter, illus. Linenthal, Peter, photos by. 2003. (That's Our School Ser.). (ENG.). 32p. (gr. k-3). lib. bdg. 22.60 *(978-0-7613-2403-4(8)*, Millbrook Pr.) Lerner Publishing Group.

—That's Our Nurse! Linenthal, Peter, illus. Linenthal, Peter, photos by. 2003. (That's Our School Ser.). (ENG.). 32p. (gr. k-3). lib. bdg. 22.60 *(978-0-7613-2402-7(X)*, Millbrook Pr.) Lerner Publishing Group.

Mullins, Matt. Surgical Technologist. 2010. (21st Century Skills Library: Cool Careers Ser.). (ENG., Illus.). 32p. (gr. 4-8). lib. bdg. 32.07 *(978-1-60279-939-4(3)*, 200623) Cherry Lake Publishing.

Murdico, Suzanne J. Bomb Squad Experts: Life Defusing Explosive Devices. 2009. (Extreme Careers Ser.). 64p. (gr. 5-5). 58.50 *(978-1-61512-386-5(5)*, Rosen Reference) Rosen Publishing Group, Inc., The.

Murray, Amy R. The Character & Career Connection. 2005. (ENG., Illus.). 78p. (gr. k-5). per. 19.95 *(978-1-931636-45-2(1))* National Ctr. For Youth Issues.

Nelson, Robin. Coaches. 2005. (Pull Ahead Bks.). (Illus.). 32p. (J). (gr. 3-7). lib. bdg. 22.60 *(978-0-8225-1686-6(1))* Lerner Publishing Group.

—Custodians. 2005. (Pull Ahead Bks.). (Illus.). 32p. (J). 22.60 *(978-0-8225-1687-3(X))* Lerner Publishing Group.

—Jobs. 2004. (First Step Nonfiction — Basic Human Needs Ser.). (ENG., Illus.). 8p. (J). (gr. k-2). pap. 5.99 *(978-0-8225-3929-2(2)*, 1e0dc3ad-f246-4c33-8f26-757a0f0575e2) Lerner Publishing Group.

—Working Then & Now. 2008. pap. 34.95 *(978-0-8225-9486-4(2))* Lerner Publishing Group.

Olson, Elsie. Exploring Fossils: Paleontologists at Work! 2017. (Earth Detectives Ser.). (ENG., Illus.). 24p. (J). (gr. k-4). lib. bdg. 32.79 *(978-1-5321-1230-0(0)*, 27617, Super SandCastle) ABDO Publishing Co.

—Exploring Minerals: Mineralogists at Work! 2017. (Earth Detectives Ser.). (ENG., Illus.). 24p. (J). (gr. k-4). lib. bdg. 32.79 *(978-1-5321-1231-7(9)*, 27618, Super SandCastle) ABDO Publishing Co.

—Exploring Weather: Meteorologists at Work! 2017. (Earth Detectives Ser.). (ENG., Illus.). 24p. (J). (gr. k-4). lib. bdg. 32.79 *(978-1-5321-1234-8(3)*, 27621, Super SandCastle) ABDO Publishing Co.

On the Edge: Individual Title Six-Packs. (Action Packs Ser.). 104p. (gr. 3-5). 44.00 *(978-0-7635-2995-6(8))* Rigby Education.

Owaki, Takashi. Dreams Around the World. 2012. (ENG., Illus.). 32p. (J). 16.95 *(978-1-935548-11-9(5))* One Peace Bks., Inc.

Owen, Ann & National Geographic Learning Staff. Delivering Your Mail: A Book about Mail Carriers. Thomas, Eric, illus. 2003. (Community Workers Ser.). (ENG.). 24p. (J). (gr. -1-3). per. 8.95 *(978-1-4048-0485-2(4)*, 92624, Picture Window Bks.) Capstone.

Paige, Joy. Cool Careers Without College for People Who Love to Build Things. 2009. (Cool Careers Without College Ser.). 144p. (gr. 6-6). 66.50 *(978-1-61511-970-7(1))* Rosen Publishing Group, Inc., The.

Parks, Peggy J. Doctor. 2003. (Exploring Careers Ser.). (ENG., Illus.). 48p. (J). (gr. 3-5). 27.50 *(978-0-7377-1484-5(0)*, Kidhaven) Cengage Gale.

—Firefighter. 2004. (EXPLORING CAREERS Ser.). (ENG., Illus.). 48p. (J). 27.50 *(978-0-7377-2066-2(2)*, Greenhaven Pr., Inc.) Cengage Gale.

Paul, Miranda. Whose Hands Are These? A Community Helper Guessing Book. Powell, Luciana Navarro, illus. 2016. (ENG.). 32p. (J). (gr. -1-3). 19.99 *(978-1-4677-5214-5(2)*, c85dbecc-5d3d-4a35-ad3a-0c5448d5ab75); E-Book 30.65 *(978-1-4677-9726-9(X))*; E-Book 30.65 *(978-1-5124-0738-9(0)*, 9781512407389) Lerner Publishing Group. (Millbrook Pr.).

Pavolino, Amy. When I Grow Up. 2010. (ENG., Illus.). 30p. (J). pap. 16.00 *(978-1-4349-9917-7(3)*, RoseDog Bks.) Dorrance Publishing Co., Inc.

Pelos, Rebecca & Greenberger, Robert. Cool Careers Without College for People Who Love Planning & Organizing, 1 vol. 2017. (Cool Careers Without College Ser.). (ENG., Illus.). 112p. (J). (gr. 7-7). 41.12 *(978-1-5081-7540-7(3)*, 72ed9db2-9f2f-4731-aea6-ec0e04b8b59c, Rosen Young Adult) Rosen Publishing Group, Inc., The.

Perish, Patrick. Disgusting Jobs. 2014. (Totally Disgusting Ser.). (ENG., Illus.). 24p. (J). (gr. 3-7). 26.95 *(978-1-62617-131-2(9)*, Epic Bks.) Bellwether Media.

Perritano, John. The Most Disgusting Jobs on the Planet, 1 vol. 2012. (Disgusting Stuff Ser.). (ENG., Illus.). 48p. (J). (gr. 5-9). lib. bdg. 32.65 *(978-1-4296-7532-1(2)*, 117106) Capstone.

—The Ultimate Book of Dangerous Jobs. 2019. (Ultimate Danger Ser.). (Illus.). 80p. (J). (gr. 12). lib. bdg. 34.60 *(978-1-4222-4227-8(7))* Mason Crest.

Pratt, Laura. Plains. 2010. (Illus.). 32p. *(978-1-55388-625-9(9))*; pap. *(978-1-55388-626-6(7))* Weigl Educational Pubs. Ltd.

Price-Wright, Heather. Life in Numbers: Choose Your Career (Level 5) 2017. (TIME for KIDS(r): Informational Text Ser.). (ENG., Illus.). 48p. (gr. 4-8). pap. 13.99 *(978-1-4258-4985-6(7))* Teacher Created Materials, Inc.

Priddy Books Staff. I Want to Be a Builder & Firefighter, 2 bks. (Illus.). (J). bds. *(978-0-312-49163-5(8)*, Priddy Bks.) St. Martin's Pr.

Raij, Emily. Earn Money. 2019. (Earn It, Save It, Spend It! Ser.). (ENG., Illus.). 24p. (J). (gr. 1-3). pap. 7.95 *(978-1-9771-1002-2(9)*, 140945); lib. bdg. 25.99 *(978-1-9771-0831-9(8)*, 140452) Capstone. (Pebble).

Ready, Dee. Nurses Help. 2013. (Our Community Helpers Ser.). (ENG.). 24p. (J). (gr. k-1). pap. 37.74 *(978-1-62065-850-5(X)*, 19421, Pebble) Capstone.

Ready, Dee & Ready, Dee. Nurses Help, 1 vol. 2013. (Our Community Helpers Ser.). (ENG.). 24p. (J). (gr. -1-2). pap. 6.29 *(978-1-62065-849-9(6)*, 121789); lib. bdg. 24.65 *(978-1-62065-080-6(0)*, 120780) Capstone. (Pebble).

Reeves, Diane Lindsey. Career Ideas for Teens Set. 2005. (Career Ideas for Teens Ser.). 192p. (gr. 6-12). 120.00 *(978-0-8160-5287-5(5)*, Ferguson Publishing Company) Infobase Holdings, Inc.

—Glamorous Jobs. 2009. (Way Out Work Ser.). (ENG., Illus.). 48p. (gr. 3-5). 29.95 *(978-1-60413-129-1(2)*, P173467, Ferguson Publishing Company) Infobase Holdings, Inc.

—Goofy Jobs. 2009. (Way Out Work Ser.). (ENG., Illus.). 48p. (gr. 3-5). 29.95 *(978-1-60413-130-7(6)*, P173466, Ferguson Publishing Company) Infobase Holdings, Inc.

—Gross Jobs. 2009. (Way Out Work Ser.). (ENG., Illus.). 48p. (gr. 3-5). 29.95 *(978-1-60413-131-4(4)*, P173470, Ferguson Publishing Company) Infobase Holdings, Inc.

—Gutsy Jobs. 2009. (Way Out Work Ser.). (ENG., Illus.). 48p. (gr. 3-5). 29.95 *(978-1-60413-133-8(0)*, P173469, Ferguson Publishing Company) Infobase Holdings, Inc.

—Manufacturing. 2017. (Bright Futures Press: World of Work Ser.). (ENG., Illus.). 32p. (J). (gr. 4-7). lib. bdg. 32.07 *(978-1-63472-627-6(8)*, 209542) Cherry Lake Publishing.

—Way Out Work Set, 6-Volumes. 2009. (Way Out Work Ser.). (gr. 3-5). 179.70 *(978-1-60413-831-3(9)*, Ferguson Publishing Company) Infobase Holdings, Inc.

Reina, Mary. Earn Money. 2015. (Money & You Ser.). (ENG., Illus.). 24p. (J). (gr. -1-2). pap. 5.95 *(978-1-4914-2299-1(8)*, 127761) Capstone.

Rhodes, Sam. STEAM Jobs. 2018. (STEAM Jobs Ser.). (ENG.). 32p. (J). (gr. 3-9). 122.60 *(978-1-5435-3104-6(0)*, 28542, Capstone Pr.) Capstone.

—STEAM Jobs for Thrill Seekers. 2018. (STEAM Jobs Ser.). (ENG., Illus.). 32p. (J). (gr. 3-9). lib. bdg. 28.65 *(978-1-5435-3092-6(3)*, 138671, Capstone Pr.) Capstone.

—STEAM Jobs for Workers Willing to Get Dirty. 2018. (STEAM Jobs Ser.). (ENG., Illus.). 32p. (J). (gr. 3-9). lib. bdg. 28.65 *(978-1-5435-3095-7(8)*, 138674, Capstone Pr.) Capstone.

Rice, Dona Herweck. Trabajadores. 2nd rev. ed. 2011. (TIME for KIDS(r): Informational Text Ser.). (SPA.). 12p. (gr. k-1). 7.99 *(978-1-4333-4411-4(4))* Teacher Created Materials, Inc.

—Workers, 1 vol. 2nd rev. ed. (TIME for KIDS(r): Informational Text Ser.). (ENG., 12p. (gr. k-1). 2013. Illus.). (J). lib. bdg. 15.96 *(978-1-4807-1011-5(3))* 2011. 7.99 *(978-1-4333-3572-3(7))* Teacher Created Materials, Inc.

Rosa-Mendoza, Gladys. Jobs Around My Neighborhood/Oficios en Mi Vecindario. Iosa, Ann, illus. 2007. (English Spanish Foundations Ser.). 20p. (gr. -1-k). pap. 19.95 *(978-1-931398-81-7(X))* Me+Mi Publishing.

—Jobs in My Neighborhood, 1 vol. Iosa, Ann, illus. 2010. (My World Ser.). (ENG.). 24p. (J). (gr. k-1). pap. 9.15 *(978-1-61533-037-9(2)*, 3bbf2bf5-a3bf-41d2-8d88-87eb780357e5, Windmill Bks.) Rosen Publishing Group, Inc., The.

Rosa-Mendoza, Gladys, creator. Jobs Around My Neighborhood. 2004. (English-Spanish Foundations Ser.: Vol. 9).Tr. of Officios en Mi Vecindario. (SPA & ENG., Illus.). 20p. (J). bds. 6.95 *(978-1-931398-09-1(7))* Me+Mi Publishing.

Rosenberg, Aaron. Cryptologists: Life Making & Breaking Codes. 2009. (Extreme Careers Ser.). 64p. (gr. 5-5). 58.50 *(978-1-61512-388-9(1)*, Rosen Reference) Rosen Publishing Group, Inc., The.

Ross, Kathy. Community Workers. Barger, Jan, illus. 2005. (Crafts for Kids Who Are Learning about Ser.). (ENG.). 48p. (J). (gr. k-3). lib. bdg., tchr. ed. 26.60 *(978-0-7613-2743-1(6))* Lerner Publishing Group.

Sanders, Michael J. Preteen Challenges: Hurdling to Your Success. 2010. 64p. pap. 12.50 *(978-1-60911-113-7(3)*, Eloquent Bks.) Strategic Book Publishing & Rights Agency (SBPRA).

Saul, Laya. Recipe & Craft Guide to Israel. 2011. (World Crafts & Recipes Ser.). (ENG., Illus.). 64p. (J). (gr. 4-7). lib. bdg. 33.95 *(978-1-61228-081-3(1))* Mitchell Lane Pubs.

Scarry, Richard. Richard Scarry's What Do People Do All Day? 2015. (Illus.). 96p. (J). (gr. -1-2). 17.99 *(978-0-553-52059-0(8)*, Golden Bks.) Random Hse. Children's Bks.

Schuh, Mari. Community Helpers at a Fire. 2016. (Community Helpers on the Scene Ser.). (ENG., Illus.). 24p. (J). (gr. -1-2). lib. bdg. 22.65 *(978-1-5157-2399-8(2)*, 132808, Pebble) Capstone.

Scraper, Katherine. Kids Can Have Jobs. 2006. (Early Explorers Ser.). (J). pap. *(978-1-4108-6034-7(5))* Benchmark Education Co.

Selwyn, Josephine. Who Uses This Machine? 2012. (Level C Ser.). (ENG., Illus.). 16p. (J). (gr. k-2). pap. 7.95 *(978-1-927136-29-4(6)*, 19456) RiverStream Publishing.

Seuss. Maybe You Should Fly a Jet! Maybe You Should Be a Vet! Kennedy, Kelly, illus. 2020. (Beginner Books(R) Ser.). (ENG.). 48p. (J). (gr. -1-2). 9.99 *(978-1-9848-9406-9(4))*; lib.

bdg. 12.99 *(978-1-9848-9407-6(2))* Random Hse. Children's Bks. (Random Hse. Bks. for Young Readers).

Shone, Rob. Crime Scene Investigators. 2009. (Graphic Forensic Science Ser.). (ENG.). 48p. (YA). (gr. 5-5). 58.50 *(978-1-61512-947-8(2)*, Rosen Reference) Rosen Publishing Group, Inc., The.

Siemens, Jared. Construction Worker. 2015. 24p. (J). *(978-1-4896-4217-2(X))* Weigl Pubs., Inc.

—Police Officers. 2015. (Illus.). 24p. (J). *(978-1-4896-3653-9(6))* Weigl Pubs., Inc.

Silate, Jennifer. Your Mayor: Local Government in Action. (Primary Source Library of American Citizenship Ser.). 32p. (gr. 5-5). 2009. 47.90 *(978-1-61511-237-1(5))* 2003. (ENG., Illus.). lib. bdg. 29.13 *(978-0-8239-4481-1(6)*, 85072cd8-c6b7-4740-b7b5-1bdeadb5b181) Rosen Publishing Group, Inc., The. (Rosen Reference).

Simons, Lisa M. Bolt. Unusual & Awesome Jobs Using Math: Stunt Coordinator, Cryptologist, & More. 2015. (You Get Paid for THAT? Ser.). (ENG., Illus.). 32p. (J). (gr. 3-9). 28.65 *(978-1-4914-2030-0(8)*, 127508, Capstone Pr.) Capstone.

Skills for Success, 10 vols. 2017. (Skills for Success Ser.). (ENG.). 64p. (gr. 7-7). 180.65 *(978-1-4994-6636-2(6)*, 475cfaa2-b41e-4d3a-afcf-9e1eefa227b2, Rosen Young Adult) Rosen Publishing Group, Inc., The.

Small, Cathleen. 20 Great Career-Building Activities Using Facebook, 1 vol. 2016. (Social Media Career Building Ser.). (ENG., Illus.). 64p. (J). (gr. 7-7). 36.13 *(978-1-5081-7262-8(5)*, f0a74abf-9abb-4f64-ad67-3efb54f39238) Rosen Publishing Group, Inc., The.

Smith, Ben. Who Listens to the Weather Forecast? 2012. (Level D Ser.). (ENG., Illus.). 16p. (J). (gr. k-2). pap. 7.95 *(978-1-927136-36-2(9)*, 19452) RiverStream Publishing.

Smith, Carrie. Jobs at School. 2006. (Early Explorers Ser.). (J). pap. *(978-1-4108-6032-3(9))* Benchmark Education Co.

St. Clair, Noel. The Unofficial Divergent Aptitude Test: Discover Your True Faction! 2015. (ENG.). 208p. pap. 16.99 *(978-1-4405-8514-2(8))* Adams Media Corp.

Suen, Anastasia. Getting a Job in Child Care, 1 vol. 2013. (Job Basics: Getting the Job You Need Ser.). (ENG.). 80p. (YA). (gr. 8-8). 38.41 *(978-1-4488-9612-7(6)*, 99214e95-1951-4602-b5e3-7492ae6d04cf) Rosen Publishing Group, Inc., The.

Sundance/Newbridge LLC Staff. World of Work. 2004. (Reading PowerWorks Ser.). (gr. 1-3). 37.50 *(978-0-7608-9269-5(5))*; pap. 6.10 *(978-0-7608-9270-1(9))* Sundance/Newbridge Educational Publishing.

Tech Track: Building Your Career in IT, 16 vols. 2017. (Tech Track: Building Your Career in IT Ser.). (ENG.). 80p. (gr. 7-7). 299.76 *(978-1-4994-6637-9(4)*, 4c903528-3d5d-42a2-b1ba-db509acc3b44, Rosen Young Adult) Rosen Publishing Group, Inc., The.

Thomas, William David. Mountain Rescuer, 1 vol. 2008. (Cool Careers: Helping Careers Ser.). (ENG.). 32p. (gr. 3-3). pap. 11.50 *(978-0-8368-9328-1(X)*, 0564e2d3-24a3-4549-ab7d-a94967e1b592); lib. bdg. 28.67 *(978-0-8368-9195-9(3)*, bd25c45f-06de-4de4-bd70-2c6a4c8dc77a) Stevens, Gareth Publishing LLLP.

Trumbauer, Lisa. Lo Que Hacen Los Carteros / What Mail Carriers Do, 1 vol. 2008. (¿Qué Hace un Ayudante de la Comunidad? / What Does a Community Helper Do? Ser.).Tr. of What Mail Carriers Do. (ENG & SPA., Illus.). 24p. (gr. k-2). lib. bdg. 24.27 *(978-0-7660-2827-2(5)*, 3d0e0474-7dc9-42a7-a52c-72dde7b83855, Enslow Elementary) Enslow Publishing, LLC.

Turner, Amanda. Helping Children. 2019. (Careers Making a Difference Ser.). (Illus.). 80p. (J). (gr. 12). lib. bdg. 34.60 *(978-1-4222-4255-1(2))* Mason Crest.

—Helping Those in Poverty. 2019. (Careers Making a Difference Ser.). 80p. (J). (gr. 12). lib. bdg. 34.60 *(978-1-4222-4261-2(7))* Mason Crest.

—Helping Those with Addictions. 2019. (Careers Making a Difference Ser.). (Illus.). 80p. (J). (gr. 12). lib. bdg. 34.60 *(978-1-4222-4258-2(7))* Mason Crest.

—Helping Those with Disabilities. 2019. (Careers Making a Difference Ser.). (Illus.). 80p. (J). (gr. 12). lib. bdg. 34.60 *(978-1-4222-4259-9(5))* Mason Crest.

—Helping Victims. 2019. (Careers Making a Difference Ser.). (Illus.). 80p. (J). (gr. 12). lib. bdg. 34.60 *(978-1-4222-4262-9(5))* Mason Crest.

Vastola, P. What I Think: Learning the TH Sound. 2009. (PowerPhonics Ser.). 24p. (gr. 1-1). 39.90 *(978-1-60851-479-3(X)*, PowerKids Pr.) Rosen Publishing Group, Inc., The.

Verderosa, Laura. When I Grow Up. 2010. (Sight Word Readers Ser.). (J). 3.49 *(978-1-60719-608-2(5))* Newmark Learning LLC.

Vogel, Elizabeth. Meet My Teacher. 2009. (My School Ser.). 24p. (gr. 1-2). 37.50 *(978-1-61514-704-5(7)*, PowerKids Pr.) Rosen Publishing Group, Inc., The.

—Meet the Cafeteria Workers. 2009. (My School Ser.). 24p. (gr. 1-2). 37.50 *(978-1-61514-705-2(5)*, PowerKids Pr.) Rosen Publishing Group, Inc., The.

—Meet the Librarian. 2009. (My School Ser.). 24p. (gr. 1-2). 37.50 *(978-1-61514-706-9(3)*, PowerKids Pr.) Rosen Publishing Group, Inc., The.

—Meet the Principal. 2009. (My School Ser.). 24p. (gr. 1-2). 37.50 *(978-1-61514-707-6(1)*, PowerKids Pr.) Rosen Publishing Group, Inc., The.

Waxman, Laura Hamilton. Let's Explore Earning Money. 2019. (Bumba Books (r) — a First Look at Money Ser.). (ENG., Illus.). 24p. (J). (gr. -1-1). 26.65 *(978-1-5415-3855-9(2)*, e69ee47e-2f23-4cba-b63d-5a7ad086d5dc, Lerner Pubns.) Lerner Publishing Group.

Wendinger, Jennifer. Unusual & Awesome Jobs Using Science: Food Taster, Human Lie Detector, & More. 2015. (You Get Paid for THAT? Ser.). (ENG., Illus.). 32p. (J). (gr. 3-9). 28.65 *(978-1-4914-2031-7(6)*, 127509, Capstone Pr.) Capstone.

When I Grow Up. 2003. (J). per. *(978-1-884907-56-2(3))*; per. *(978-1-884907-75-3(X))* Paradise Pr., Inc.

When I Grow Up, 12 vols. 2014. (When I Grow Up Ser.). (ENG.). 24p. (J). (gr. k-k). 145.62 *(978-1-4824-1035-8(4)*, d0d13b2e-889b-4458-8af5-ced212564834) Stevens, Gareth Publishing LLLP.

Where People Work, 32 vols. 2006. (Where People Work Ser.). (ENG., Illus.). 24p. (J). (gr. k-2). lib. bdg. 394.72 *(978-1-4339-0076-1(9)*, 776700c3-699f-4e9b-bb8b-4c6227f86ddd, Weekly Reader Leveled Readers) Stevens, Gareth Publishing LLLP.

White, Nancy. Paramedics to the Rescue. 2011. (Work of Heroes: First Responders in Action Ser.). (Illus.). 32p. (J). (gr. 1-4). lib. bdg. 28.50 *(978-1-61772-282-0(0))* Bearport Publishing Co., Inc.

Wigu Publishing. When I Grow up I Want to Be... a Teacher! Carlee Learns a Surprising Lesson! 2013. (When I Grow Up I Want To Be....Ser.). (Illus.). 62p. pap. 12.95 *(978-1-939973-08-5(2)*, Wigu Publishing) Wigu Publishing.

Willett, Edward. Careers in Outer Space: New Business Opportunities. 2009. (Career Resource Library). 192p. (gr. 7-12). 63.90 *(978-1-60853-401-2(4))* Rosen Publishing Group, Inc., The.

Williams, Heather DiLorenzo & Reynolds, Warren. People in My Community. 2019. (Illus.). 24p. (J). *(978-1-4896-8051-8(9)*, AV2 by Weigl) Weigl Pubs., Inc.

Williams, Jack S. Sailors, Merchants, & Muleteers of the California Mission Frontier. 2009. (People of the California Missions Ser.). 64p. (gr. 4-4). 58.50 *(978-1-60851-159-4(6)*, PowerKids Pr.) Rosen Publishing Group, Inc., The.

Williams, Jack S. & Davis, Thomas L. Sailors, Merchants, & Muleteers, 1 vol. 2003. (People of the California Missions Ser.). (ENG., Illus.). 64p. (J). (gr. 4-4). lib. bdg. 32.93 *(978-0-8239-6282-2(2)*, 3eeb749c-10fc-4bd8-a9c8-2b60777dd94d) Rosen Publishing Group, Inc., The.

Williams, Rozanne. When I Grow Up. 2017. (Learn-To-Read Ser.). (ENG., Illus.). (J). pap. 3.49 *(978-1-68310-339-4(4))* Pacific Learning, Inc.

Winning at Work Readiness. 2014. (Winning at Work Readiness Ser.). 64p. (YA). (gr. 9-12). pap. 64.75 *(978-1-4777-8116-6(1))* Rosen Publishing Group, Inc., The.

Wood, Alexander. Our Jobs, 1 vol. 2008. (Real Life Readers Ser.). (ENG.). 8p. (gr. k-1). pap. 5.15 *(978-1-4042-8011-3(1)*, d78ff607-a695-4028-82a3-483fd12c5bca, Rosen Classroom) Rosen Publishing Group, Inc., The.

Wood, Alix. Test Pilot, 1 vol., 1. 2014. (World's Coolest Jobs Ser.). (ENG.). 32p. (J). (gr. 4-4). 28.93 *(978-1-4777-6019-2(9)*, f11fb146-5882-471b-940c-625e1ca1b18e, PowerKids Pr.) Rosen Publishing Group, Inc., The.

Wunderlich, Richard. Math on the Job. 2016. (ENG., Illus.). 32p. (J). lib. bdg. *(978-0-7787-2360-8(7))* Crabtree Publishing Co.

Yanuchi, Lori & Yanuchi, Jeff. Ranger Trails: Jobs of Adventure in America's Parks. Morris, James R., illus. 2005. 64p. (J). per. 12.95 *(978-0-9670177-2-3(6))* Ridge Rock Pr.

You Wouldn't Want To..., 4 vols., Set. Incl. Be a Salem Witch! Bizarre Accusations You'd Rather Not Face. Pipe, Jim. (gr. 3-18). 29.00 *(978-0-531-20821-2(4))*; Meet a Body Snatcher! Criminals & Murderers You'D Rather Avoid. MacDonald, Fiona. (gr. 4-6). 26.19 *(978-0-531-20822-9(2))*; (Illus.). 32p. (J). 2009. 2009. Set lib. bdg. 116.00 *(978-0-531-26141-5(7)*, Watts, Franklin) Scholastic Library Publishing.

8-deck Careers for Kids Box Set. (Careers for Kids Ser.). 7.00 *(978-1-57281-409-7(8)*, CFKS8) U.S. Games Systems, Inc.

OCCUPATIONS—FICTION

Abbott, Victoria. What I Want to Be. Curzon, Brett, illus. 2017. (All about Me Ser.). (ENG.). 24p. (J). (gr. -1-2). pap. 9.95 *(978-1-68342-793-3(9)*, 9781683427933) Rourke Educational Media.

Aiken, Zora & David. A to Z: Pick What You'll Be: Pick What You'll Be, 1 vol. 2011. (ENG., Illus.). 32p. (J). 14.99 *(978-0-7643-3701-7(7)*, 4063, Schiffer Publishing Ltd) Schiffer Publishing, Ltd.

Auerbach, Annie. I Can Be Anything! (Peppa Pig) EOne, illus. 2018. (ENG.). 16p. (J). (gr. -1-k). bds. 7.99 *(978-1-338-22883-0(8))* Scholastic, Inc.

Aunt Judy. Chickens in the Know! Chickens of Different Occupations. Aunt Judy, illus. 2007. (Illus.). 40p. (J). pap. 7.00 *(978-0-9780693-1-5(5))* McEwen, Judith A.

Baker, Keith. LMNO Pea-Quel. Baker, Keith, illus. 2017. (Peas Ser.). (ENG., Illus.). 40p. (J). (gr. -1-3). 18.99 *(978-1-4814-5856-6(6)*, Beach Lane Bks.) Beach Lane Bks.

—LMNO Peas. Baker, Keith, illus. 2010. (Peas Ser.). (ENG., Illus.). 40p. (J). (gr. -1-3). 18.99 *(978-1-4169-9141-0(7)*, Beach Lane Bks.) Beach Lane Bks.

—LMNO Peas. Baker, Keith, illus. 2014. (Peas Ser.). (ENG., Illus.). 36p. (J). (gr. -1-k). bds. 8.99 *(978-1-4424-8978-3(2)*, Little Simon) Little Simon.

Berenstain, Mike. The Berenstain Bears: When I Grow Up. Berenstain, Mike, illus. 2015. (Berenstain Bears Ser.). (ENG., Illus.). 24p. (J). (gr. -1-3). pap. 5.99 *(978-0-06-235005-3(6)*, HarperFestival) HarperCollins Pubs.

—When I Grow Up. 2015. (Berenstain Bears Ser.). (J). lib. bdg. 13.55 *(978-0-606-37606-8(2))* Turtleback.

Berenstain, Stan, et al. Jobs Around Town, 1 vol. 2011. (Berenstain Bears/Living Lights: a Faith Story Ser.). (ENG., Illus.). 32p. (J). (gr. -1-2). pap. 4.99 *(978-0-310-72286-1(1))* Zonderkidz.

Birney, Betty G. Humphrey's Mixed-Up Magic Trick. Burris, Priscilla, illus. 2016. (Humphrey's Tiny Tales Ser.: 5). (ENG.). 96p. (J). (gr. k-3). 6.99 *(978-0-14-751461-5(4)*, Puffin Books) Penguin Young Readers Group.

Blackstone, Stella. Bear at Work. Harter, Debbie, illus. (ENG & SPA.). 24p. (J). (gr. -1-k). 2011. pap. 6.99 *(978-1-84686-554-1(9))* 2008. pap. 8.99 *(978-1-84686-110-9(1))* Barefoot Bks., Inc.

—Bear at Work (Oso en el Trabajo) 2012. (ENG & SPA., Illus.). 24p. (J). pap. 7.99 *(978-1-84686-769-9(X))* Barefoot Bks., Inc.

—L'Ours au Travail. 2012.Tr. of Bear at Work. (FRE & ENG.). (J). 6.99 *(978-1-84686-770-5(3))* Barefoot Bks., Inc.

Blance, Ellen & Cook, Tony. Monster Gets a Job. Date not set. (Illus.). 40p. pap. 129.15 *(978-0-582-19307-9(9))* Addison-Wesley Longman, Ltd. GBR. Dist: Trans-Atlantic Pubns., Inc.

Blexbolex, creator. People. 2011. (ENG., Illus.). 208p. (J). (gr. -1). 22.95 *(978-1-59270-110-0(8))* Enchanted Lion Bks., LLC.

Blyton, Enid, et al. The Fairies' Shoemaker & Other Stories. 2013. (ENG., Illus.). 192p. (J). 9.99 *(978-1-84135-458-3(9))* Award Pubns. Ltd. GBR. Dist: Parkwest Pubns., Inc.

Brooks, Felicity. Jobs People Do. Litchfield, Jo, illus. 2008. (Jobs People Do Ser.). 143p. (J). (gr. -1-3). 22.99 *(978-0-7945-1998-8(9)*, Usborne) EDC Publishing.

Brown, Ruby. I Want to Be ... an Astronaut. Coburn, Alisa, illus. 2016. (ENG.). 22p. (J). bds. 8.99 *(978-1-61067-406-5(5))* Kane Miller.

Bunting, Eve. Girls a to Z. Bloom, Suzanne, illus. 2013. (ENG.). 32p. (J). (gr. k-2). pap. 7.95 *(978-1-62091-028-3(4)*, Astra Young Readers) Astra Publishing Hse.

Caletti, Deb. The Fortunes of Indigo Skye. 2009. (ENG.). 320p. (YA). (gr. 7). pap. 9.99 *(978-1-4169-1008-4(5)*, Simon Pulse) Simon Pulse.

Candlewick Press. Peppa Pig & the Career Day. 2018. (Peppa Pig Ser.). (ENG., Illus.). 32p. (J). (-k). 12.99 *(978-1-5362-0344-8(0)*, Candlewick Entertainment) Candlewick Pr.

Canetti, Yanitzia. Abecedario de Profesiones y Oficios. 2009. (SPA.). 40p. (J). pap. 8.99 *(978-1-59835-122-4(2)*, BrickHouse Education) Cambridge BrickHouse, Inc.

Carpenter, Tad. When I Grow Up. 2015. (Who's That? Ser.). (Illus.). 16p. (J). (— 1). bds. 7.95 *(978-1-4549-1228-6(6))* Sterling Publishing Co., Inc.

Catalanotto, Peter. Kitten Red, Yellow, Blue. Catalanotto, Peter, illus. 2005. (ENG., Illus.). 32p. (J). (gr. -1-k). 19.99 *(978-0-689-86562-6(7)*, Atheneum/Richard Jackson Bks.) Simon & Schuster Children's Publishing.

Chen, Julie. When I Grow Up. Goode, Diane, illus. 2018. (ENG.). 32p. (J). (gr. -1-3). 17.99 *(978-1-4814-9719-0(7)*, Simon & Schuster/Paula Wiseman Bks.) Simon & Schuster/Paula Wiseman Bks.

Clark, Carol. Eternity Express. 2009. 32p. pap. 10.95 *(978-0-9818488-6-0(9))* Ajoyin Publishing, Inc.

Cohn, Diana. ¡Sí, Se Puede!, 1 vol. Delgado, Francisco, illus. 2009.Tr. of Yes, We Can! (ENG.). 32p. (J). (gr. k-4). pap. 11.95 *(978-0-938317-89-0(X)*, 23353382, Cinco Puntos Press) Lee & Low Bks., Inc.

Coyle, Carmela Lavigna. Do Princesses Become Astronauts? Gordon, Mike, illus. 2019. (Do Princesses Ser.). 32p. (J). (gr. -1-2). 15.95 *(978-1-63076-347-3(0))* Muddy Boots Pr.

Crow, Sara. Even Superheroes Have to Sleep. Record, Adam, illus. (J). (— 1). 2018. 26p. bds. 6.99 *(978-0-399-55809-2(8))* 2017. 32p. 16.99 *(978-0-399-55806-1(3))* Random Hse. Children's Bks. (Doubleday Bks. for Young Readers).

Cunliffe, John. Postman Pat & the Beast of Greendale, Bk. 12. (ENG., Illus.). 32p. (J). *(978-0-340-67816-9(X))* Hodder & Stoughton.

—Postman Pat Has Too Many Parcels, Pt. 8. (ENG., Illus.). 32p. (J). *(978-0-340-67812-1(7))* Hodder & Stoughton.

Curious George Takes a Job Book & CD. 2007. (Curious George Ser.). (ENG., Illus.). 48p. (J). (gr. -1-3). audio 10.99 *(978-0-618-72406-2(0)*, 462918, Clarion Bks.) HarperCollins Pubs.

DeLand, M. Maitland. Busy Bees at Work & Play. 2010. (Illus.). 32p. (J). 14.95 *(978-1-60832-028-8(6)*, Greenleaf Book Group Pr.) Greenleaf Book Group.

Derrick, David G., Jr. Sid the Squid: And the Search for the Perfect Job. 2010. (ENG., Illus.). 36p. (J). (gr. -1-3). 15.95 *(978-1-59702-021-3(4))* Immedium.

Dillon, Diane. I Can Be Anything! Don't Tell Me I Can't. Dillon, Diane, illus. 2018. (ENG., Illus.). 32p. (J). (gr. -1-3). 18.99 *(978-1-338-16690-3(5)*, Blue Sky Pr., The) Scholastic, Inc.

DiPucchio, Kelly. Dress-Up Mess-up. Ross, Heather, illus. 2013. (Crafty Chloe Ser.). (ENG.). 40p. (J). (gr. -1-3). 16.99 *(978-1-4424-2124-0(X))* Simon & Schuster Children's Publishing.

Dorsey, Maggie. My Hero, My Dad, the Nurse. 2008. (ENG.). 36p. pap. 16.99 *(978-1-4196-9476-9(6))* CreateSpace Independent Publishing Platform.

Edwards, Michelle. Chicken Man. (ENG.). 32p. (J). 2009. pap. 10.95 *(978-1-58838-237-5(0)*, 8701) 3rd ed. 2007. (Illus.). 16.95 *(978-1-58838-223-8(0)*, 8700) NewSouth, Inc. (NewSouth Bks.).

Ferguson, Sally. What Will I Be When I Grow Up? 2005. (J). pap. 1.69 *(978-1-59317-118-6(8))* Warner Pr., Inc.

Friedman, Laurie. Honestly, Mallory! 2009. pap. 34.95 *(978-0-7613-4788-0(7))* Lerner Publishing Group.

—Honestly, Mallory! Pollak, Barbara, illus. (Mallory Ser.: 8). (ENG.). 160p. (J). (gr. 2-5). 2008. pap. 7.99 *(978-1-58013-840-6(3)*, cbae7cde-0701-4e69-b123-1da3c7067db3, Darby Creek) 2007. 15.95 *(978-0-8225-6193-4(X)*, Carolrhoda Bks.) Lerner Publishing Group.

Garton, Sam. Otter: the Best Job Ever! Garton, Sam, illus. 2016. (My First I Can Read Ser.). (ENG., Illus.). 32p. (J). (gr. -1-3). pap. 5.99 *(978-0-06-236654-2(8)*, Balzer & Bray) HarperCollins Pubs.

Grant, Rick S. When I Grow Up. Alfonso, Anabel, illus. 2017. (J). pap. *(978-1-934370-67-4(3))* Editorial Campana.

Gregorowski, Christopher. Fly, Eagle, Fly: An African Tale. Daly, Niki, illus. 2008. (ENG.). 36p. (J). (gr. -1-3). 12.99 *(978-1-4169-7599-1(3)*, Aladdin) Simon & Schuster Children's Publishing.

Guggenheim, Jaenet. Next Week When I'm Big. Verelst, Suana, illus. I.t. ed. 2005. 32p. (J). (gr. -1-2). 19.95i *(978-1-929115-13-6(X))* Azro Pr., Inc.

Hallinan, P. K. When I Grow Up. 24p. (J). 7.95 *(978-0-8249-5392-8(4)*, Ideals Pubns.) Worthy Publishing.

Handy, Libby & Newnham, Jack. Boss for a Week.Tr. of C'Est Moi Qui Mene. (FRE., Illus.). (J). 13.99 incl. audio *(978-0-590-73908-5(5))* Scholastic, Inc.

Hannigan, Paula & Kirkova, Milena. When I'm Big: A Silly Slider Book. 2010. (ENG.). 12p. (J). (gr. -1-1). bds. 14.99 *(978-0-7407-9727-9(1))* Andrews McMeel Publishing.

Harley, Bill. Charlie Bumpers vs. His Big Blabby Mouth. Gustavson, Adam, illus. 2018. (Charlie Bumpers Ser.: 6). 192p. (J). (gr. 2-5). pap. 7.99 *(978-1-68263-064-8(1))* Peachtree Publishing Co. Inc.

Horn, Peter. When I Grow Up... Kadmon, Cristina, illus. 2014. 32p. pap. 8.00 *(978-1-61003-370-1(1))* Center for the Collaborative Classroom.

K. Maurice Strickland. I Want to Be a Bucket. 2009. 32p. pap. 15.99 *(978-1-4389-7015-8(3))* AuthorHouse.

Kittinger, Jo S. Cuando Sea Grande. Lucas, Margeaux, illus. 2005. (Rookie Reader Español Ser.). (SPA.). 23p. (J). (gr. k-2). per. 4.95 *(978-0-516-24692-5(5)*, Children's Pr.) Scholastic Library Publishing.

Kleinhenz, Sydnie Meltzer. Trabajar y Jugar. Reasor, Mick, illus. 2006. (Rookie Reader Español Ser.). (SPA.). 23p. (J). (gr. k-2). lib. bdg. 19.50 *(978-0-516-25306-0(9))* Scholastic Library Publishing.

Krulik, Nancy. Lice Check. 2014. (George Brown, Class Clown Ser.: 12). (Illus.). 121p. (J). lib. bdg. 14.75 *(978-0-606-34144-8(7))* Turtleback.

—Lice Check #12, No. 12. Blecha, Aaron, illus. 2014. (George Brown, Class Clown Ser.: 12). 128p. (J). (gr. 2-4). 6.99 *(978-0-448-46112-0(9)*, Grosset & Dunlap) Penguin Young Readers Group.

Krulik, Nancy E. Lice Check, 12. Blecha, Aaron, illus. 2014. (George Brown, Class Clown Ser.). (ENG.). 128p. (J). (gr. 2-4). 21.19 *(978-1-4844-2140-6(X))* Penguin Young Readers Group.

Kupchella, Rick. Girls Can! Make it Happen. Brown, Marilyn, illus. 2004. (ENG.). 40p. (J). 16.95 *(978-0-9726504-3-4(1))* TRISTAN Publishing, Inc.

Kusmierski, Janet & Colin, Paul. Snowman's Big Job. 2004. (Illus.). (J). *(978-0-439-58392-3(6))* Scholastic, Inc.

Kviat, Hindy & Lefkowitz, Chaya. Yes I Can. Epstein, Len, illus. 2018. (ENG.). 28p. (J). 11.95 *(978-1-945560-05-7(3))* Hachai Publishing.

LaFleur, John & Dubin, Shawn. Dreary & Naughty: the ABCs of Being Dead: The ABCs of Being Dead, 1 vol. 2013. (ENG., Illus.). 72p. (YA). (gr. 8-12). 14.99 *(978-0-7643-4496-1(X)*, 4931) Schiffer Publishing, Ltd.

Lang, Sheri. My Mom Can Code: Careers in Computers, 1 vol. 2017. (Computer Science for the Real World Ser.). (ENG.). 16p. (gr. 2-3). pap. *(978-1-5383-5226-7(5)*, 5bb3d785-691a-4f1e-9f62-ea4036670821, Rosen Classroom) Rosen Publishing Group, Inc., The.

Liberto, Lorenzo. Matt the Rat & His Sister Maggie (Raton Mateo y Su Hermana Maggie) When I Grow Up (Cuando Yo Crezca) Gomez, Rocio, ed. Torres, Irving, illus. 2003. (Matt the Rat Ser. / La Serie de Ratón Mateo). (SPA & ENG.). 40p. (J). lib. bdg. 20.00 *(978-0-9743668-1-4(1))* Harvest Sun Pr., LLC.

Manushkin, Fran. Katie Finds a Job, 1 vol. Lyon, Tammie, illus. 2011. (Katie Woo Ser.). (ENG.). 32p. (J). (gr. k-2). pap. 5.95 *(978-1-4048-6614-0(0)*, 114675); lib. bdg. 21.32 *(978-1-4048-6513-6(6)*, 114209) Capstone. (Picture Window Bks.).

Marrero-Martinez, Gloria. Darling Daughter: What Will You Be? Kozak, Maria, illus. 2006. (ENG.). 44p. per. 26.90 *(978-1-4259-4235-9(0))* AuthorHouse.

Marsh, Carole. The Adventure Diaries of Felipe, the Fearless Firefighter!, 12 vols. 2003. 48p. (J). (gr. 1-4). pap. 5.95 *(978-0-635-01096-4(8))* Gallopade International.

—The Adventure Diaries of Hannah, the Humanitarian Aid Worker!, 6 vols. 2003. 48p. (J). (gr. 1-4). pap. 5.95 *(978-0-635-01153-4(0))* Gallopade International.

—The Adventure Diaries of Haz Matt, the Hazardous Materials Worker!, 11 vols. 2003. 48p. (J). (gr. 1-4). pap. 5.95 *(978-0-635-01152-7(2))* Gallopade International.

—The Adventure Diaries of Li, the Excellent EMT!, 7 vols. 2004. 48p. (J). (gr. 1-4). pap. 5.95 *(978-0-635-01145-9(X))* Gallopade International.

—The Adventure Diaries of P. J., the Photo-Journalist!, 10 vols. 2003. 48p. (J). (gr. 1-4). pap. 5.95 *(978-0-635-01154-1(9))* Gallopade International.

—The Adventure Diaries of Vicki, the Volunteer!, 12 vols. 2003. 48p. (J). (gr. 1-4). pap. 5.95 *(978-0-635-01158-9(1))* Gallopade International.

Mayer, Mercer. Little Critter: Going to the Firehouse. Mayer, Mercer, illus. 2008. (My First I Can Read Ser.). (ENG., Illus.). 32p. (J). (gr. -1-3). 16.99 *(978-0-06-083546-0(X))*; pap. 4.99 *(978-0-06-083545-3(1))* HarperCollins Pubs. (HarperCollins).

—When I Grow Up. 2003. (Little Critter Ser.). (gr. -1-2). lib. bdg. 13.55 *(978-0-613-82737-9(6))* Turtleback.

—When I Grow up (Little Critter) 2003. (Look-Look Ser.). (Illus.). 24p. (J). (gr. -1-k). pap. 5.99 *(978-0-375-82632-0(7)*, Random Hse. Bks. for Young Readers) Random Hse. Children's Bks.

McDonagh, Caitlin. The ABCs of What I Can Be. 2018. (Illus.). 40p. (J). (gr. -1-2). 17.99 *(978-0-8234-3782-5(5))* Holiday Hse., Inc.

McGill, Erin. I Do Not Like Al's Hat. McGill, Erin, illus. 2017. (ENG., Illus.). 32p. (J). (gr. -1-3). 17.99 *(978-0-06-245576-5(1)*, Greenwillow Bks.) HarperCollins Pubs.

McMullan, Kate. Bulldog's Big Day. Lemaître, Pascal, illus. 2011. (J). *(978-0-545-17156-4(3)*, Orchard Bks.) Scholastic, Inc.

—I'm Dirty! McMullan, Jim, illus. 2006. (ENG.). 40p. (J). (gr. -1-3). 18.99 *(978-0-06-009293-1(9)*, HarperCollins) HarperCollins Pubs.

McNamara, Margaret. Dad Goes to School: Ready-To-Read Level 1. Gordon, Mike, illus. 2007. (Robin Hill School Ser.). (ENG.). 32p. (J). (gr. -1-1). pap. 4.99 *(978-1-4169-1541-6(9)*, Simon Spotlight) Simon Spotlight.

Meltzer Kleinhenz, Sydnie. Work & Play. Reasor, Mick, illus. 2011. (Rookie Ready to Learn Ser.). (ENG.). 32p. (J). pap. 5.95 *(978-0-531-26829-2(2)*, Children's Pr.) Scholastic Library Publishing.

Miller, Sibley. A Horse, of Course! A Sumatra Story. 2009. (Wind Dancers Ser.: 7). (ENG., Illus.). 80p. (J). (gr. 1-4). pap. 16.99 *(978-0-312-56402-5(3)*, 900059061) Feiwel & Friends.

Miller, Suzanne. You Can Be... 2010. 24p. pap. 12.99 *(978-1-4520-4697-6(2))* AuthorHouse.

Morris, Bridgette. I Wish I Was All Grown-up. 2004. 20p. pap. 8.99 *(978-1-4116-1719-3(3))* Lulu Pr., Inc.

Nikola-Lisa, W. My Teacher Can Teach... Anyone! Galindo, Felipe, illus. 2004. (ENG.). 32p. (J). (gr. -1-2). 16.95 *(978-1-58430-163-9(5))* Lee & Low Bks., Inc.

O'Donnell, Kerri. Whose Hat Is That?, 1 vol. 2006. (Neighborhood Readers Ser.). (ENG.). 8p. (gr. k-1). pap. 5.15 *(978-1-4042-5647-7(4)*, 8e1b8c15-95f3-4558-ae09-f2e9bd841039, Rosen Classroom) Rosen Publishing Group, Inc., The.

Olsen, Jan Z. Mat Man Hats. Delaney, Molly, illus. 2008. (ENG.). 36p. stu. ed. 13.75 *(978-1-891627-93-4(7))* Handwriting Without Tears.

Parish, Herman. Amelia Bedelia Chapter Book #9: Amelia Bedelia on the Job. Avril, Lynne, illus. 2016. (Amelia Bedelia Ser.). (ENG.). 160p. (J). (gr. 1-5). pap. 6.99

(978-0-06-233412-1(3), Greenwillow Bks.) HarperCollins Pubs.
Patrick, Wendy. When Passion Wins. 2012. 186p. (gr. 4-6). pap. 14.50 (978-1-4669-7131-8(2)) Trafford Publishing.
Pedersen, Laura. Wanda's Better Way. Weber, Penny, illus. 2017. (ENG.). 36p. (J). (gr. k-2). 17.95 (978-1-68275-014-8(0)) Fulcrum Publishing.
Phillips, Dee. What Can I Be? 2010. (Look at Me! Ser.). (ENG.). 5p. (J). (gr. -1-k). bds. 6.95 (978-1-84696-199-1(8), TickTock Books) Octopus Publishing Group GBR. Dist: Independent Pubs. Group.
—Who Can I Be? 2010. (Look at Me! Ser.). (ENG.). 5p. (J). (gr. -1-k). bds. 6.95 (978-1-84696-200-4(5), TickTock Books) Octopus Publishing Group GBR. Dist: Independent Pubs. Group.
Phoenix International Publications, ed. All in a Day's Work: Sound Book. 2013. (ENG.). 6p. (J). bds. 7.99 (978-1-4127-3708-1(7), 1356) Phoenix International Publications, Inc.
Pierce, Heather Vowell. What Does Your Daddy Do? Price, Dana, illus. 2010. 32p. pap. 16.49 (978-1-4520-1723-5(9)) AuthorHouse.
Rey, H. A. Curious George Neighborhood Friends (CGTV Pull Tab Board Book) 2010. (Curious George Ser.). (ENG., Illus.). 12p. (J). (gr. -1 — 1). bds. 6.99 (978-0-547-23875-3(4), 1084264, Clarion Bks.) HarperCollins Pubs.
Roach, Sandra & Torowski, Dave. Alina's Options: Careers from A to Z. 2008. (ENG., Illus.). 52p. pap. 12.99 (978-0-9801426-0-0(1)) Options Galore.
Rosenstiehl, Agnès. Silly Lilly in What Will I Be Today?, 1 vol. Rosenstiehl, Agnès, illus. 2013. (Toon Bks.). (ENG., Illus.). 36p. (J). (gr. -1-1). lib. bdg. 32.79 (978-1-61479-156-0(2), 14848) Spotlight.
Rosenstiehl, Agnes. Silly Lilly in What Will I Be Today? Toon Books Level 1. 2011. (ENG., Illus.). 32p. (J). (gr. -1-3). 12.95 (978-1-935179-08-5(X), Toon Books) Astra Publishing Hse.
Scarry, Patsy. Richard Scarry's the Bunny Book. Scarry, Richard, illus. 2015. (Big Golden Book Ser.). 32p. (J). (-k). 9.99 (978-0-385-39090-3(4), Golden Bks.) Random Hse. Children's Bks.
Scarry, Richard. Richard Scarry's Postman Pig & His Busy Neighbors. Scarry, Richard, illus. 2015. (Pictureback(R) Ser.). (Illus.). 24p. (J). (gr. -1-2). pap. 4.99 (978-0-385-38419-3(X), Random Hse. Bks. for Young Readers) Random Hse. Children's Bks.
Shaw, Natalie. I Can Do Anything! 2016. (Illus.). (J). (978-1-5182-0411-1(2)) Simon & Schuster Children's Publishing.
Shea, Therese. The Summer Job, 1 vol. 2006. (Neighborhood Readers Ser.). (ENG., Illus.). 12p. (gr. 1-2). pap. 5.90 (978-1-4042-6855-5(3), 33e5bd16-1ab9-472f-953c-3aaccbc60d6d, Rosen Classroom) Rosen Publishing Group, Inc., The.
Slade, Suzanne. Astronaut Annie, 1 vol. Tadgell, Nicole, illus. 2018. (ENG.). 36p. (J). (gr. k-3). 17.95 (978-0-88448-523-0(4), 884523) Tilbury Hse. Pubs.
Snyder, Betsy, illus. I Can Dream: (Baby Board Book, Book for Learning, Toddler Book. 2018. (I Can Ser.). (ENG.). 14p. (J). (gr. -1 — 1). bds. 8.99 (978-1-4521-6214-0(X)) Chronicle Bks. LLC.
Sommer, Carl. Your Job Is Easy. James, Kennon, illus. 2003. (Another Sommer-Time Story Ser.). (ENG.). 48p. (J). (gr. -1-4). 9.95 (978-1-57537-018-7(2)); (gr. 1-4). 16.95 incl. audio compact disk (978-1-57537-517-5(6)); (gr. 2-4). lib. bdg. 16.95 (978-1-57537-067-5(0)) Advance Publishing, Inc.
—Your Job Is Easy. 2003. (Another Sommer-Time Story Ser.). (Illus.). 48p. (J). (gr. 1-4). 16.95 incl. audio (978-1-57537-566-3(4)) Advance Publishing, Inc.
Standish, Burt L. Frank Merriwell's First Job. Rudman, Jack, ed. 2003. (Frank Merriwell Ser.). 29.95 (978-0-8373-9330-8(2)); (YA). (gr. 9-18). pap. 9.95 (978-0-8373-9030-7(3)) Merriwell, Frank Inc.
Tong, Kevin. The Earth Machine. Tong, Kevin, illus. 2007. (Illus.). 32p. (J). (gr. -1-3). 15.95 (978-1-60108-001-1(8)) Red Cygnet Pr.
Traylor, Marci. What Will I Be? 2008. 40p. pap. 19.50 (978-1-4389-0247-0(6)) AuthorHouse.
Wang, Margaret C. When I Grow Up: A Touch & Feel Book. Gévry, Claudine, illus. 2005. (ENG.). 12p. (J). bds. 10.95 (978-1-58117-423-6(3), Intervisual/Piggy Toes) Bendon, Inc.
Wess, Robert, illus. & photos by. Friends at Work & Play. Wess, Robert, photos by. Bunnett, Rochelle, photos by. 2003. 32p. (J). 14.95 (978-0-9660884-2-7(5)); pap. (978-0-9660884-1-0(7)) Our Kids Pr.
Wright, Kenneth. Lola Dutch When I Grow Up. Wright, Sarah Jane, illus. 2019. (Lola Dutch Ser.). (ENG.). 40p. (J). 17.99 (978-1-68119-554-4(2), 900177318, Bloomsbury Children's Bks.) Bloomsbury Publishing USA.
Yankovic, Al, pseud. When I Grow Up. Hargis, Wes, illus. 2011. (ENG.). 32p. (J). (gr. -1-3). 19.99 (978-0-06-192691-4(4), HarperCollins) HarperCollins Pubs.
Zoboli, Giovanna. Professional Crocodile: (Wordless Kids Books, Alligator Children's Books, Early Elemetary Story Books) Di Giorgio, Mariachiara, illus. 2017. (ENG.). 32p. (J). (gr. k-3). 17.99 (978-1-4521-6506-6(8)) Chronicle Bks. LLC.

OCEAN

see also Icebergs; Oceanography; Seashore; Storms; Tides

Aitken, Stephen. Ocean Life, 1 vol. 2013. (Climate Crisis Ser.). (ENG., Illus.). 64p. (gr. 5-5). 34.07 (978-1-60870-460-6(2), 02bc06a1-ccb0-42ae-bde1-78be054a8e51); pap. 16.28 (978-1-62712-040-1(8), d6a34bb5-7ab0-4582-9527-17f543de7cb1) Cavendish Square Publishing LLC.
Arnov Jr., Boris. Oceans of the World. 2011. 190p. 42.95 (978-1-258-08168-3(7)) Literary Licensing, LLC.
Austen, Amy. Earth's Oceans, 1 vol. 2016. (Spotlight on Earth Science Ser.). (ENG., Illus.). 24p. (J). (gr. 4-6). pap. 11.00 (978-1-4994-2501-7(5), 33b12f8d-0891-4abf-a344-77b22ec39e94, PowerKids Pr.) Rosen Publishing Group, Inc., The.
AZ Books Staff. Exploring the Ocean. Vasilkova, Elena, ed. 2012. (Wild Theater Ser.). (ENG.). 8p. (J). (gr. -1-3). bds. 17.95 (978-1-61889-020-7(4)) AZ Bks. LLC.
—Living Book of the Ocean. Aksinovich, Natalia, ed. 2012. (Our Amazing World Ser.). (ENG.). 12p. (J). (gr. 1-3). bds. 19.95 (978-1-61889-021-4(2)) AZ Bks. LLC.
—Visiting the Ocean. Lukjanenko, Anna, ed. 2012. (Lively Pictures Ser.). (ENG.). 10p. (J). (gr. -1-1). bds. 9.95 (978-1-61889-180-8(4)) AZ Bks. LLC.
Banks, Christopher. Oceans of the World, 1 vol. 2008. (Real Life Readers Ser.). (ENG.). 16p. (gr. 2-3). pap. 7.05 (978-1-4358-0061-8(3), 97bbf2e6-2ec6-46bb-bb1a-17541d6aaeed, Rosen Classroom) Rosen Publishing Group, Inc., The.
Barnes, J. Lou. 101 Facts about Oceans, 1 vol. 2003. (101 Facts about Our World Ser.). (ENG., Illus.). 32p. (gr. 2-4). lib. bdg. 28.67 (978-0-8368-3709-4(6), 37dd5d85-5ee7-4d60-9ada-0def74dd4ab7, Gareth Stevens Learning Library) Stevens, Gareth Publishing LLLP.
Bayrock, Fiona. The Ocean Explorer's Handbook. 2005. (Undersea University Ser.). (Illus.). 48p. (J). pap. (978-0-439-71184-5(3)) Scholastic, Inc.
Beaton, Clare & Haig, Rudi. Read, Learn & Create — The Ocean Craft Book. Beaton, Clare, illus. 2019. (ENG., Illus.). 32p. (J). (gr. 1-4). 17.99 (978-1-58089-941-3(2)) Charlesbridge Publishing, Inc.
Believe It Or Not!, Ripleys, compiled by. Ripley Twists PB: Oceans. 2018. (Twist Ser.: 8). (ENG.). 48p. (J). pap. 7.99 (978-1-60991-230-7(6)) Ripley Entertainment, Inc.
Benchmark Education Company. Ocean Pollution (Teacher Guide) 2005. (978-1-4108-4678-5(4)) Benchmark Education Co.
Benoit, Peter. Oceans. 2011. (True Bk Ser.). 48p. (J). (ENG.). pap. 6.95 (978-0-531-28105-5(1)); (gr. 3-5). 29.00 (978-0-531-20556-3(8)) Scholastic Library Publishing. (Children's Pr.).
—The Titanic Disaster. 2011. (J). pap. (978-0-531-29026-2(3)) Children's Pr., Ltd.
—The Titanic Disaster. 2011. (True Bks.). 48p. (J). (gr. 3-5). 29.00 (978-0-531-20627-0(0), Children's Pr.) Scholastic Library Publishing.
Beringer Mckissack, Lisa. Counting in the Oceans, 1 vol. 2009. (Counting in the Biomes Ser.). (ENG., Illus.). 32p. (gr. k-2). lib. bdg. 26.60 (978-0-7660-2994-1(8), b0e6b41e-3eaf-4b3a-9a39-27bd997cf58a, Enslow Elementary) Enslow Publishing, LLC.
Bessesen, Brooke. Look Who Lives in the Ocean: Splashing & Dashing, Nibbling & Quibbling, Blending & Fending. 2009. (Illus.). 48p. (J). (gr. k-4). 19.95 (978-1-932082-82-1(4)) Arizona Highways.
Best, Arthur. Oceans, 1 vol. 2017. (Our World of Water Ser.). (ENG.). 24p. (gr. 1-1). pap. 9.22 (978-1-5026-3094-0(X), 65cac6a8-c2e7-4674-9e3d-dcbc4be39956) Cavendish Square Publishing LLC.
Boatner, Kay. National Geographic Kids Funny Fill-in: My Ocean Adventure. 2013. (Illus.). 48p. (J). (gr. 3-7). pap. 4.99 (978-1-4263-1643-2(7), National Geographic Kids) Disney Publishing Worldwide.
Bodden, Valerie. Oceans. 2006. (Our World Ser.). (Illus.). 24p. (J). (gr. -1-3). 16.95 (978-1-58341-464-4(9), Creative Education) Creative Co., The.
Bonder, Dianna. A, B, Sea: A Deep Sea Symphony, 1 vol. 2013. (ENG.). 32p. (J). (gr. k-2). 19.95 (978-1-77050-043-3(X), 196e154e-659c-422c-8103-43f70eec5c9d) Whitecap Bks., Ltd. CAN. Dist: Firefly Bks., Ltd.
Boothroyd, Jennifer. Let's Visit the Ocean. 2016. (Lightning Bolt Books (r) — Biome Explorers Ser.). (ENG., Illus.). 32p. (J). (gr. 1-3). 29.32 (978-1-5124-1194-2(9), cdf4ca2e-6b12-4d4d-bfb5-04b8aebf1395, Lerner Pubns.) Lerner Publishing Group.
Boughton, Samantha. Under the Sea Adventure Coloring Book. 2013. (Dover Sea Life Coloring Bks.). (ENG., Illus.). 48p. (J). (gr. k-5). pap. 4.99 (978-0-486-49166-0(8), 491668) Dover Pubns., Inc.
Brannon, Barbara. Discover Ocean Pollution. 2005. (J). pap. (978-1-4108-5140-6(0)) Benchmark Education Co.
Britton, Tamara L. Red Sea. 2003. (Oceans & Seas Ser.). 24p. (gr. k-6). 25.65 (978-1-57765-990-7(2), Checkerboard Library) ABDO Publishing Co.
Buchanan, Shelly. The Powerful Ocean. 2015. (Science: Informational Text Ser.). (ENG., Illus.). 32p. (gr. 4-8). pap. 11.99 (978-1-4807-4726-5(2)) Teacher Created Materials, Inc.
Bulletpoints Oceans & Rivers. 2005. (Illus.). (J). per. 4.99 (978-1-933581-01-9(8)) Byeway Bks.
Burlingame, Jeff. The Titanic Tragedy: The Price of Prosperity in a Gilded Age, 1 vol. 2012. (Perspectives On Ser.). (ENG.). 112p. (YA). (gr. 8-8). 42.64 (978-1-60870-450-7(5), a919bc2c-906f-4261-970b-44a50982ee01) Cavendish Square Publishing LLC.
Casado, Dami. El Mar. 2005. (Yo Te Hablare De... Ser.). (SPA., Illus.). 14p. (J). per., bds. 8.99 (978-84-272-7298-9(7)) Molino, Editorial ESP. Dist: Santillana USA Publishing Co., Inc.
Cecchini, Marie E. Under the Sea: A Cross-Curricular Unit for Grades 1-3. Mitchell, Judy & Lindeen, Mary, eds. Armbrust, Janet & Skiles, Janet, illus. 2007. 32p. (J). pap. 6.95 (978-1-57310-529-3(5)) Teaching & Learning Co.
Cefrey, Holly. Oceans. 2009. (Biomes Ser.). 24p. (gr. 2-3). 42.50 (978-1-61511-592-1(7), PowerKids Pr.) Rosen Publishing Group, Inc., The.
Channing, Margot. Seas & Oceans. 2014. (Closer Look At... Ser.). (Illus.). 32p. (gr. 3-6). 31.35 (978-1-905087-07-5(1)) Book Hse. GBR. Dist: Black Rabbit Bks.
Clarke, Phillip. Seas & Oceans Sticker Atlas. Le Rolland, Leonard, illus. 2006. 24p. (J). pap. 8.95 (978-0-7945-1218-7(6), Usborne) EDC Publishing.
Cole, Joanna & Carson, Mary Kay. Ocean Adventure. 2014. (Magic School Bus Scholastic Readers Ser.). lib. bdg. 13.55 (978-0-606-36040-1(9)) Turtleback.
Collins Kids. Oceans (Collins Fascinating Facts) 2016. (Collins Fascinating Facts Ser.). (ENG.). 72p. (J). (gr. 1-3). pap. 10.99 (978-0-00-816924-4(1)) HarperCollins Pubs. Ltd. GBR. Dist: Independent Pubs. Group.
Collins, Sarah Jean. God Made the Ocean. Collins, Sarah Jean, illus. 2019. (God Made Ser.). (ENG., Illus.). 22p. (J). bds. 7.99 (978-1-4964-3633-7(4), 20_32104, Tyndale Kids) Tyndale Hse. Pubs.
Cramp, Jessica. Captain Aquatica. 2019. (Illus.). 128p. (J). (gr. 3-7). 17.99 (978-1-4263-3292-0(0), National Geographic Kids) Disney Publishing Worldwide.
Dale, Jay. Taking Care of the Ocean. 2012. (Engage Literacy Blue Ser.). (ENG.). 16p. (gr. k-2). (J). pap. 36.94 (978-1-4296-8845-1(9), 18317); pap. 5.99 (978-1-4296-8837-6(8), 119893) Capstone. (Capstone Pr.).
Davies, Nicola. A First Book of the Sea. Sutton, Emily, illus. 2018. (ENG.). 104p. (J). (gr. -1-2). 22.00 (978-0-7636-9882-9(2)) Candlewick Pr.
—Oceans & Seas. 2014. 48p. pap. 7.00 (978-1-61003-360-2(4)) Center for the Collaborative Classroom.
De la Bédoyère, Camilla. Deep Ocean. 2010. (Unpredictable Nature Ser.). (Illus.). 48p. (J). (gr. 3-18). lib. bdg. 19.95 (978-1-4222-1997-3(6)) Mason Crest.
—Oceans. 2010. (Ripley Twists Ser.). (Illus.). 48p. (J). (gr. 3-18). lib. bdg. 19.95 (978-1-4222-1832-7(5)) Mason Crest.
Denne, B. First Encyclopedia of Seas & Oceans. 2004. (First Encyclopedias Ser.). (Illus.). 64p. (J). (gr. 3-18). lib. bdg. 17.95 (978-1-58086-380-3(9)) EDC Publishing.
—First Encyclopedia of Seas & Oceans II. rev. ed. 2011. (First Encyclopedias Ser.). 64p. (J). pap. 9.99 (978-0-7945-3048-8(6), Usborne) EDC Publishing.
Denne, Ben. First Encyclopedia of Seas & Oceans. 2004. (First Encyclopedias Ser.). (ENG., Illus.). 1p. (J). (gr. 3-18). pap. 9.99 (978-0-7945-0111-2(7), Usborne) EDC Publishing.
Dipper, F. D. & Dipper, Frances. Misterios de los Océanos. (Coleccion Misterios De). (SPA., Illus.). 48p. (YA). (gr. 5-8). 19.95 (978-84-348-5691-2(3), SM6117) SM Ediciones ESP. Dist: AIMS International Bks., Inc., Lectorum Pubns., Inc.
DK. Sticker Encyclopedia: Ocean. 2010. (Sticker Encyclopedias Ser.). (ENG.). 96p. (J). (gr. k-4). pap. 12.99 (978-0-7566-6304-9(0), DK Children) Dorling Kindersley Publishing, Inc.
—Ultimate Sticker Book: Ocean: More Than 250 Reusable Stickers. 2016. (Ultimate Sticker Book Ser.). (ENG.). 32p. (J). (gr. k-3). pap. 6.99 (978-1-4654-4882-8(9), DK Children) Dorling Kindersley Publishing, Inc.
DK & Woodward, John. Ocean: a Visual Encyclopedia. 2015. (DK Children's Visual Encyclopedias Ser.). (ENG.). 256p. (J). (gr. 3-7). pap. 19.99 (978-1-4654-3594-1(8), DK Children) Dorling Kindersley Publishing, Inc.
Duhig, Holly. Life by the Ocean. 2019. (Human Habitats Ser.). (ENG.). 24p. (J). (gr. 2-2). pap. (978-0-7787-6484-7(2), 8a6f0d44-3f95-48a2-aaac-5e8980d0369f); lib. bdg. (978-0-7787-6478-6(8), a336ad18-ce6d-4ef2-be27-1bb6c171daa9) Crabtree Publishing Co.
Endres, Hollie J. The Letter Ww Set: The Ocean, 6 vols. 2004. (Letter Bks.). (ENG.). 8p. (gr. k-1). pap. 29.70 (978-0-7368-4122-1(9)) Capstone.
Eriksson, Ann. Dive In! Exploring Our Connection with the Ocean, 1 vol. 2018. (Orca Footprints Ser.: 14). (ENG., Illus.). 48p. (J). (gr. 4-7). 19.95 (978-1-4598-1586-5(6)) Orca Bk. Pubs. USA.
Feroze, Jen. Lonely Planet Kids Let's Explore... Ocean 1. Cumick, Pippa, illus. 2016. (Lonely Planet Kids Ser.). (ENG.). 48p. (J). (gr. 1-3). pap. 9.99 (978-1-76034-040-7(5), 5146) Lonely Planet Global Ltd. IRL. Dist: Hachette Bk. Group.
Ferri, Francesca, illus. Sea: A Soft Book & Mirror for Baby! 2017. 6p. (J). (gr. -1 — 1). 10.99 (978-1-4380-7761-1(0)) Sourcebooks, Inc.
Fishman, Seth. The Ocean in Your Bathtub. Greenberg, Isabel, illus. 2020. (ENG.). 40p. (J). (gr. -1-3). 17.99 (978-0-06-295336-0(2), Greenwillow Bks.) HarperCollins Pubs.
Foxxe, Ellen. The Rising Seas: Shorelines under Threat, 1 vol. 2006. (Extreme Environmental Threats Ser.). (ENG., Illus.). 64p. (YA). (gr. 6-6). lib. bdg. 37.13 (978-1-4042-0742-4(2), 9ee61077-f555-4f36-9d80-a817106910de) Rosen Publishing Group, Inc., The.
Franklin, Yvonne. Los Océanos. rev. ed. 2010. (Science: Informational Text Ser.). (SPA., Illus.). 32p. (gr. 2-4). pap. 11.99 (978-1-4333-2142-9(4)) Teacher Created Materials, Inc.
Friedman, Lauri S., ed. Oceans, 1 vol. 2011. (Introducing Issues with Opposing Viewpoints Ser.). (ENG.). 144p. (gr. 7-10). lib. bdg. 43.63 (978-0-7377-5200-7(9), 4a57f9a8-4cd2-45d9-8c0e-d9a6f4f51e29, Greenhaven Publishing) Greenhaven Publishing LLC.
Friesen, Helen Lepp. Indian Ocean. 2016. (Illus.). 32p. (J). (978-1-4896-4737-5(6)) Weigl Pubs., Inc.
Froman, Craig, ed. Elementary Science: Soil, Sea, & Sky (Teacher Guide) 2017. (ENG.). 150p. (gr. 4-6). pap. 24.99 (978-1-68344-025-3(0), Master Books) New Leaf Publishing Group.
Furlong, Kate A. Southern Ocean. 2003. (Oceans & Seas Ser.). 24p. (gr. k-6). 25.65 (978-1-57765-991-4(0), Checkerboard Library) ABDO Publishing Co.
Gabbi & Somaschini. Los Oceanos. (SPA.). 242p. (YA). (gr. 5-8). (978-84-7131-935-7(7)) Editex, Editorial S.A. ESP. Dist: Lectorum Pubns., Inc.
Gallagher, Belinda. Why Why Why... Are There Schools in the Sea? 2010. (Why Why Why Ser.). (Illus.). 32p. (J). (gr. 1-3). lib. bdg. 18.95 (978-1-4222-1572-2(5)) Mason Crest.
Ganeri, Anita. Esos Inmensos Oceanos. (Coleccion Esa Horrible Geografia).Tr. of Odious Oceans. (SPA., Illus.). 160p. (YA). (gr. 5-8). (978-84-272-2152-9(5), ML3927) Molino, Editorial ESP. Dist: Lectorum Pubns., Inc.
—I Wonder Why the Sea Is Salty. 2014. 32p. pap. 7.00 (978-1-61003-352-7(3)) Center for the Collaborative Classroom.
—I Wonder Why the Sea Is Salty: And Other Questions about the Oceans. 2011. (I Wonder Why Ser.). (ENG., Illus.). 32p. (J). (gr. k-3). pap. 6.99 (978-0-7534-6521-9(3), 900070301, Kingfisher) Roaring Brook Pr.
—Protecting Ocean Habitats, 1 vol. 2005. (Protecting Habitats Ser.). (ENG., Illus.). 32p. (gr. 4-6). lib. bdg. 28.67 (978-0-8368-4992-9(2), 82d0090f-bada-4da2-846f-0b7f0cceefa6, Gareth Stevens Learning Library) Stevens, Gareth Publishing LLLP.
Gardeski, Christina Mia. All about Oceans. 2017. (Habitats Ser.). (ENG., Illus.). 24p. (J). (gr. -1-2). lib. bdg. 22.65 (978-1-5157-7644-4(1), 135929, Pebble) Capstone.
Goldsack, Gaby. Ocean Animals. Bampton, Bob, illus. (J). (978-1-57755-508-7(2)) Flying Frog Publishing, Inc.
Goldstein, Natalie. How Do We Know the Nature of the Ocean?, 1 vol. 2004. (Great Scientific Questions & the Scientists Who Answered Them Ser.). (ENG., Illus.). 112p. (J). (gr. 7-12). lib. bdg. 39.80 (978-1-4042-0079-1(7), 7efc12bd-b89c-4d89-b2f8-033e824aaef5) Rosen Publishing Group, Inc., The.
—How Do We Know the Nature of the Ocean. 2009. (Great Scientific Questions & the Scientists Who Answered Them Ser.). 112p. (gr. 7-12). 63.90 (978-1-61513-204-1(X)) Rosen Publishing Group, Inc., The.
Gonzales, Doreen. The Mighty Atlantic Ocean, 1 vol. 2013. (Our Earth's Oceans Ser.). (ENG.). 48p. (gr. 3-3). pap. 11.53 (978-1-4644-0152-7(7), a7356a6f-f9c4-4dfc-b569-61f43e82f3d8, Enslow Elementary) Enslow Publishing, LLC.
—The Tropical Indian Ocean, 1 vol. 2013. (Our Earth's Oceans Ser.). (ENG.). 48p. (gr. 3-3). 27.93 (978-0-7660-4089-2(5), d202059b-6a08-4385-bf71-9a8575dc32f9); pap. 11.53 (978-1-4644-0150-3(0), 3a6e2f5d-f0c6-492e-b02b-12c5769e0fda, Enslow Elementary) Enslow Publishing, LLC.
Gordon, Sharon. At Home by the Ocean, 1 vol. (At Home Ser.). (ENG.). 32p. (gr. k-2). 2008. pap. 9.23 (978-0-7614-3312-5(0), fa57719d-3a1d-4c55-95c8-c288b9648842) 2007. (Illus.). lib. bdg. 25.50 (978-0-7614-1959-4(4), b15cc6b0-6fd4-44ee-b6db-e091ea9212a1) Cavendish Square Publishing LLC.
Gosman, Gillian. What Do You Know about Earth's Oceans?, 1 vol. 2013. (20 Questions: Earth Science Ser.). 24p. (J). (ENG.). (gr. 2-3). lib. bdg. 26.27 (978-1-4488-9700-1(9), 4ae8ff16-9cbc-4802-aa80-ce7110cd91ec); (gr. 3-6). pap. 49.50 (978-1-4488-9859-6(5)); (ENG., Illus.). (gr. 2-3). pap. 9.25 (978-1-4488-9858-9(7), 868e7377-0bbb-471b-8641-1af26f642fd8) Rosen Publishing Group, Inc., The. (PowerKids Pr.).
Gould, Jane H. The Flying Dutchman, 1 vol. 2014. (Jr. Graphic Ghost Stories Ser.). (ENG.). 24p. (J). (gr. 2-3). lib. bdg. 28.93 (978-1-4777-7088-7(7), e31f6beb-0403-42bb-8ca8-0c573e342a41, PowerKids Pr.) Rosen Publishing Group, Inc., The.
Gray, Leon. Oceans. 2015. (Amazing Biomes Ser.). (ENG., Illus.). 32p. (J). (gr. 3-6). 31.35 (978-1-78121-243-1(0), 16390) Brown Bear Bks.
Green, Emily K. Oceans. 2006. (Learning about the Earth Ser.). (ENG., Illus.). 24p. (J). (gr. k-3). lib. bdg. 26.95 (978-1-60014-039-6(4)) Bellwether Media.
Green, Jen. Arctic Ocean, 1 vol. 2005. (Oceans & Seas Ser.). (ENG., Illus.). 48p. (gr. 5-8). pap. 15.05 (978-0-8368-6278-2(3), a26bc2dd-564a-4296-b914-ee45376a837c); lib. bdg. 33.67 (978-0-8368-6270-6(8), a676d97b-7acd-4f65-a0ed-09fc5a0e3361) Stevens, Gareth Publishing LLLP. (Gareth Stevens Secondary Library).
—Atlantic Ocean, 1 vol. 2005. (Oceans & Seas Ser.). (ENG., Illus.). 48p. (gr. 5-8). pap. 15.05 (978-0-8368-6279-9(1), b82162b1-1766-4f59-a5aa-758ca08be3f4); lib. bdg. 33.67 (978-0-8368-6271-3(6), 875c7599-eeec-46f0-8838-e45b6ca2051f) Stevens, Gareth Publishing LLLP. (Gareth Stevens Secondary Library).
—Indian Ocean, 1 vol. 2005. (Oceans & Seas Ser.). (ENG., Illus.). 48p. (gr. 5-8). pap. 15.05 (978-0-8368-6281-2(3), 44096eb5-8057-4701-a6ca-302ddba8462b); lib. bdg. 33.67 (978-0-8368-6273-7(2), c8dc6f83-8f3f-4087-aa19-9fe2a856e94a) Stevens, Gareth Publishing LLLP. (Gareth Stevens Secondary Library).
—Mediterranean Sea, 1 vol. 2005. (Oceans & Seas Ser.). (ENG., Illus.). 48p. (gr. 5-8). pap. 15.05 (978-0-8368-6282-9(1), 302df165-48d8-4f8f-8bb5-ea142071e5ad); lib. bdg. 33.67 (978-0-8368-6274-4(0), a0267d04-8e8b-464d-abe2-6e2c6c8d29ff) Stevens, Gareth Publishing LLLP. (Gareth Stevens Secondary Library).
—The World's Oceans. 2009. (Amazing Planet Earth Ser.). 32p. (gr. 4-7). 31.35 (978-1-59920-373-7(1)) Black Rabbit Bks.
Gregory, Joy. Atlantic Ocean. 2016. (Illus.). 32p. (J). (978-1-4896-4735-1(X)) Weigl Pubs., Inc.
Group/McGraw-Hill, Wright. Our World's Oceans, 6 vols. (Book2WebTM Ser.). (gr. 4-8). 36.50 (978-0-322-04447-0(2)) Wright Group/McGraw-Hill.
Hall, Stephen. Exploring the Oceans. 2012. (ENG., Illus.). 48p. (J). 15.00 (978-1-899762-79-8(5)) Award Pubns. Ltd. GBR. Dist: Parkwest Pubns., Inc.
Hansen, Grace. Ocean Life, 6 vols. 2015. (Ocean Life Ser.: 6). (ENG.). 24p. (J). (gr. -1-2). lib. bdg. 196.74 (978-1-62970-707-5(4), 17213, Abdo Kids) ABDO Publishing Co.
Harris, Nicholas, text. Panoramas: Ocean Life. 2006. (Illus.). 23p. (J). (978-0-7607-8156-2(7)) backpackbook.
Hasselfeldt, Lori. The under the Ocean Alphabet Book. Hasselfeldt, Lori, illus. 2013. (Illus.). 32p. 24.95 (978-1-61493-155-3(0)); pap. 14.95 (978-1-61493-154-6(2)) Peppertree Pr., The.
Heinrichs, Ann. Oceans. 2009. (21st Century Skills Library: Real World Math Ser.). (ENG.). 32p. (gr. 4-8). lib. bdg. 32.07 (978-1-60279-496-2(0), 200317) Cherry Lake Publishing.
Henriques, Ricardo. Ocean: A Visual Miscellany. Letria, Andre, illus. 2018. (ENG.). 48p. (J). (gr. 3-7). 18.99 (978-1-4521-5526-5(7)) Chronicle Bks. LLC.
Holland, Gini. I Live near the Ocean, 1 vol. 2004. (Where I Live Ser.). (ENG., Illus.). 24p. (gr. k-2). pap. 9.15 (978-0-8368-4089-6(5), d3ef8710-e9a9-45c7-8479-de3b7fddc8b4, Weekly Reader Leveled Readers) Stevens, Gareth Publishing LLLP.
—I Live near the Ocean / Vivo Cerca Del Mar, 1 vol. 2004. (Where I Live / Donde Vivo Ser.). (SPA & ENG., Illus.). 24p. (gr. k-2). lib. bdg. 24.67 (978-0-8368-4130-5(1), 06abee9a-6c92-4cdf-95ed-03ab6c52a049) Stevens, Gareth Publishing LLLP.
Horning, Nicole. Let's Explore the Ocean!, 1 vol. 2020. (Earth Science Explorers Ser.). (ENG.). 24p. (gr. 1-2). pap. 9.22 (978-1-5026-5625-4(6), cebf5f4c-07a8-43af-8bad-d5d3033d73a3) Cavendish Square Publishing LLC.
Hudak, Heather C. Oceans. (Illus.). 32p. (J). 2017. (978-1-5105-0878-1(3)) 2016. (978-1-5105-0876-7(7)) SmartBook Media, Inc.

M
N
O

—Oceans. 2013. (Illus.). 32p. (J). 28.55 (978-1-61913-074-6(2)); 13.95 (978-1-61913-237-5(0)) Weigl Pubs., Inc.

Hughes, Catherine D. National Geographic Kids: Little Kids First Big Book of the Ocean. 2013. (National Geographic Little Kids First Big Bks.). (Illus.). 128p. (J). (gr. -1-k). 14.95 (978-1-4263-1368-4(3), National Geographic Kids) Disney Publishing Worldwide.

—National Geographic Little Kids First Big Book of the Ocean. 2013. (National Geographic Little Kids First Big Bks.). (ENG., Illus.). 128p. (J). (gr. -1-k). lib. bdg. 23.90 (978-1-4263-1369-1(1), National Geographic Children's Bks.) Disney Publishing Worldwide.

Hunter, Nick. Seas: An Explorer Travel Guide. 2013. (Explorer Travel Guides). (ENG., Illus.). 48p. (J). (gr. 3-6). pap. 8.95 (978-1-4109-5440-4(4), 123374, Raintree) Capstone.

Ishak, Lauren. Map & Track Oceans. 2019. (Map & Track Biomes & Animals Ser.). (Illus.). 32p. (J). (gr. 4-5). (978-0-7787-5369-8(7)); pap. (978-0-7787-5381-0(6)) Crabtree Publishing Co.

James, Ian, ed. Oceans. (Illus.). 32p. (978-0-7540-9031-1(0)) Cherrytree Bks.

Jedicke, Peter. Exploring the Ocean Depths. 2003. (Hot Science Ser.). (J). lib. bdg. 28.50 (978-1-58340-367-9(1)) Black Rabbit Bks.

Johnson, Rebecca L. A Journey into the Ocean. Saroff, Phyllis V., illus. 2004. (Biomes of North America Ser.). (ENG.). 48p. (gr. 3-6). lib. bdg. 23.93 (978-1-57505-591-6(0)) Lerner Publishing Group.

Johnson, Robin. Oceans Inside Out. 2014. (Ecosystems Inside Out Ser.). (ENG., Illus.). 32p. (J). (gr. 4-5). (978-0-7787-0635-9(4)) Crabtree Publishing Co.

Jordano, Kimberly & Corcoran, Tebra. Oceans of Fun. Fisch, Teri L., ed. Campbell, Jenny, illus. 2003. (Stepping into Standards Theme Ser.). 64p. (J). (gr. k-2). pap. 10.99 (978-1-57471-946-8(7), 2474) Creative Teaching Pr., Inc.

K/H (Pathways). Pathways: Grade 4 Where the Waves Break: Life at the Edge of the Sea Trade Book. rev. ed. 2011. (ENG.). 48p. pap. 10.50 (978-0-7575-4072-1(4)) Kendall Hunt Publishing Co.

Kalman, Bobbie. The ABCs of Oceans. 2007. (ABCs of the Natural World Ser.). (ENG., Illus.). 32p. (J). (gr. 1-4). lib. bdg. (978-0-7787-3412-3(9)); pap. (978-0-7787-3432-1(3)) Crabtree Publishing Co.

—Explore Earth's Five Oceans. 2010. (Explore the Continents Ser.). (ENG., Illus.). 32p. (J). (gr. 1-5). lib. bdg. (978-0-7787-3077-4(8)) Crabtree Publishing Co.

—Los Océanos de la Tierra. 2009. (SPA.). 32p. (J). (978-0-7787-8243-8(3)); pap. (978-0-7787-8260-5(3)) Crabtree Publishing Co.

—What Is an Ocean? 2010. (My World Ser.). (ENG.). 24p. (J). (gr. k-3). (978-0-7787-9515-5(2)); pap. (978-0-7787-9540-7(3)) Crabtree Publishing Co.

Kalman, Bobbie & MacAulay, Kelley. Earth's Oceans, 1 vol. 2008. (Looking at Earth Ser.). (ENG., Illus.). 32p. (J). (gr. 3-7). pap. (978-0-7787-3214-3(2)); lib. bdg. (978-0-7787-3204-4(5)) Crabtree Publishing Co.

Kalman, Bobbie & Macaulay, Kelly. Les Mers Tropicales. Briere, Marie-Josee, tr. from ENG. 2008. (Petit Monde Vivant Ser.). (FRE., Illus.). 32p. (J). (gr. 3-7). pap. 9.95 (978-2-89579-182-9(1)) Bayard Canada Livres CAN. Dist: Crabtree Publishing Co.

Karas, G. Brian. Atlantic. Karas, G. Brian, illus. 2004. (Illus.). 32p. (J). (gr. -1-3). reprint ed. pap. 8.99 (978-0-14-240027-2(0), Puffin Books) Penguin Young Readers Group.

Kelley, K. C. Oceans. 2018. (Spot Awesome Nature Ser.). (ENG.). 16p. (J). (gr. -1-2). pap. 7.99 (978-1-68152-248-7(9), 14823) Amicus.

Kelly, Richard. Ultimate Guide - Ocean: Contains 5 See-Through Feature Pages. 2017. 69p. (J). 24.95 (978-1-78209-991-8(3)) Miles Kelly Publishing, Ltd. GBR. Dist: Parkwest Pubns., Inc.

Kerrod, Robin. Find Out about the Sea: With 20 Projects & More Than 260 Pictures. 2013. (ENG., Illus.). 64p. (J). (gr. 3-7). 9.99 (978-1-84322-896-7(3)) Anness Publishing GBR. Dist: National Bk. Network.

Kids: Explore Oceans & Activity Booklet. 2003. (J). 1.00 (978-1-888631-26-5(0)) Project WET Foundation.

Kids, National Geographic. National Geographic Kids Little Kids First Board Book: Ocean. 2019. (First Board Bks.). (Illus.). 26p. (J). (gr. -1 — 1). bds. 7.99 (978-1-4263-3468-9(0), National Geographic Kids) Disney Publishing Worldwide.

Koll, Hilary & Mills, Steve. A Math Journey under the Ocean. 2016. (ENG., Illus.). 32p. (J). (978-0-7787-2315-8(1)) Crabtree Publishing Co.

Kortemeier, Todd. Exploring the Depths of the Ocean. 2017. (Science Frontiers Ser.). (ENG., Illus.). 32p. (J). (gr. 3-6). 32.80 (978-1-63235-377-1(6), 11871); pap. 9.95 (978-1-63235-394-8(6), 11879) Bookstaves, LLC. (12-Story Library).

Leardi, Jeanette. Protecting Our Oceans: Set Of 6. 2011. (Navigators Ser.). (J). pap. 50.00 net. (978-1-4108-5092-8(7)) Benchmark Education Co.

—Protecting Our Oceans: Text Pairs. 2008. (Bridges/Navigators Ser.). (J). (gr. 6). 89.00 (978-1-4108-8447-3(3)) Benchmark Education Co.

Leonhardt, Alice. Why the Ocean Is Salty. 2009. (Steck-Vaughn Pair-It Books Proficiency Stage 5 Ser.). (ENG.). 40p. (gr. 4-4). pap. 9.10 (978-0-7398-0868-9(0)) Steck-Vaughn.

Levete, Sarah. Save the Oceans. 2011. (ENG.). 24p. (J). pap. (978-0-7787-7879-0(7)); (gr. 3-6). (978-0-7787-7857-8(6)) Crabtree Publishing Co.

Lindeen, Carol K. Life in an Ocean. rev. ed. 2016. (Living in a Biome Ser.). (ENG.). 24p. (J). (gr. -1-2). pap. 7.29 (978-1-5157-3693-6(8), 133657) Capstone.

Lindeen, Mary. Crayola (r) Ocean Colors. 2020. (Crayola (r) Colorful Biomes Ser.). (ENG., Illus.). 32p. (J). (gr. k-3). 29.32 (978-1-5415-7754-1(X), f088d48b-7ab5-4854-826b-91151e2194eb, Lerner Pubns.) Lerner Publishing Group.

Llewellyn, Claire. Oceans, 1 vol. 2012. (Habitat Survival Ser.). (ENG.). 32p. (J). (gr. 2-4). pap. 8.29 (978-1-4109-4607-2(X), 119111, Raintree) Capstone.

—The Sea. 2003. (Starters Ser.). 24p. (J). lib. bdg. 21.35 (978-1-58340-262-7(4)) Black Rabbit Bks.

Look Who's Popping Up: Under the Sea. 2003. (J). (gr. -1-k). 4.98 (978-0-7525-8904-6(0)) Parragon, Inc.

Lynch, Seth. There's an Ocean in My Backyard!, 1 vol. 2016. (Backyard Biomes Ser.). (ENG., Illus.). 24p. (J). (gr. 1-2). pap. 9.15 (978-1-4824-5567-0(6), d5ba91f5-a394-4037-8095-1e9ef18bce59) Stevens, Gareth Publishing LLLP.

MacAulay, Kelley & Kalman, Bobbie. Tropical Oceans. 2005. (Living Ocean Ser.). (ENG., Illus.). 32p. (J). (gr. 3-4). lib. bdg. (978-0-7787-1300-5(8)) Crabtree Publishing Co.

Macdonald, Fiona. The Science of Oceans: the Watery Truth about 72 Percent of Our Planet's Surface (the Science of the Earth) (Library Edition) Beach, Bryan, illus. 2018. (Science Of... Ser.). (ENG.). 32p. (J). (gr. 3-7). lib. bdg. 29.00 (978-0-531-22767-1(7), Watts, Franklin) Scholastic Library Publishing.

Make It Work Geography, 4 vol. set. 2003. (gr. 4-8). 59.00 (978-0-7166-5124-6(6)) World Bk., Inc.

Mara, Wil. Deep-Sea Exploration: Science, Technology, Engineering (Calling All Innovators: a Career for You) 2015. (Calling All Innovators: a Career for You Ser.). (ENG., Illus.). 64p. (J). (gr. 5-8). pap. 8.95 (978-0-531-21173-1(8), Children's Pr.) Scholastic Library Publishing.

Martin, Claudia. Complete Guides Ocean Life. 2012. (ENG.). 144p. (J). (978-1-4351-4408-8(2)) Barnes & Noble, Inc.

Marx, Christy. Life in the Ocean Depths. (Life in Extreme Environments Ser.). 64p. (gr. 5-8). 2009. 53.00 (978-1-61514-272-9(X)) 2003. (ENG.). (YA). pap. 13.95 (978-1-4358-3265-7(5), cf7d2f7a-5334-4406-9410-309b306f5853) Rosen Publishing Group, Inc., The. (Rosen Reference).

Mason, Paul. Oceans under Threat. rev. ed. 2016. (World in Peril Ser.). (ENG.). 32p. (J). (gr. 3-5). pap. 7.99 (978-1-4846-4023-4(3), 135094, Heinemann) Capstone.

McCune, Jamie. First Look at Ocean Animals. 2010. (First Look At Ser.). (ENG.). 16p. (J). (gr. -1). 6.95 (978-1-60727-138-3(9)) Soundprints.

McFadzean, Lesley. Ocean Habitats. 2013. (Discovery Education: Habitats Ser.). 32p. (J). (gr. 3-6). pap. 60.00 (978-1-4777-1480-5(4)); (ENG.). (gr. 4-5). 28.93 (978-1-4777-1322-8(0), 96a1a577-3ee1-4511-b2c7-a29335e5ae0c); (ENG.). (gr. 4-5). pap. 11.00 (978-1-4777-1479-9(0), 11a44e58-1dd0-4334-8886-5422085dc012) Rosen Publishing Group, Inc., The. (PowerKids Pr.).

McMillan, Beverly & Musick, John A. Oceans. 2007. (Insiders Ser.). (ENG., Illus.). 64p. (J). (gr. 3-7). 19.99 (978-1-4169-3859-0(1), Simon & Schuster Bks. For Young Readers) Simon & Schuster Bks. For Young Readers.

Meachen Rau, Dana. Los Océanos / Oceans, 1 vol. 2010. (Nuestro Planeta Es Importante / Earth Matters Ser.). (ENG & SPA.). 32p. (gr. 1-2). lib. bdg. 25.50 (978-0-7614-3494-8(1), 816c53bf-0161-48f7-aa6e-a5818d0777bf) Cavendish Square Publishing LLC.

—Los Océanos (Oceans), 1 vol. 2010. (Nuestro Planeta Es Importante (Earth Matters) Ser.). (SPA.). 32p. (gr. 1-2). lib. bdg. 25.50 (978-0-7614-3469-6(0), 904cc289-001e-4110-8e59-1b18d71ce72b) Cavendish Square Publishing LLC.

—Oceans, 1 vol. 2009. (Earth Matters Ser.). (ENG.). 32p. (gr. 1-2). lib. bdg. 25.50 (978-0-7614-3048-3(2), 91011cae-96a6-483d-9bf7-0defd75371b5, Cavendish Square) Cavendish Square Publishing LLC.

Milbourne, Anna. Peek Inside the Sea. 2018. (Peek Inside Board Bks.). (ENG.). 14p. (J). 11.99 (978-0-7945-4038-8(4), Usborne) EDC Publishing.

Moore, Elizabeth. Oceans, 1 vol. 2011. (Wonder Readers Early Level Ser.). (ENG.). 16p. (gr. -1-1). (J). pap. 6.25 (978-1-4296-7829-2(1), 118116); pap. 35.94 (978-1-4296-8132-2(2), Capstone Pr.) Capstone.

Morey, Allan. Ocean Food Chains. 2003. (What Eats What? Ser.). (J). pap. (978-1-58417-219-2(3)); lib. bdg. (978-1-58417-218-5(5)) Lake Street Pubs.

Nadeau, Isaac. Water in Oceans. 2009. (Water Cycle Ser.). 24p. (gr. 4-4). 42.50 (978-1-60854-269-7(6), PowerKids Pr.) Rosen Publishing Group, Inc., The.

National Geographic Learning. Language, Literacy & Vocabulary - Reading Expeditions (Earth Science): Ocean Exploration. 2007. (Avenues Ser.). (ENG., Illus.). 36p. (J). pap. 20.95 (978-0-7922-5430-0(9)) CENGAGE Learning.

Natural History Museum Staff. Ocean Sticker Book. 2013. (ENG.). 14p. (J). (gr. -1-1). pap. 9.99 (978-0-565-09257-3(X)) Natural History Museum Pubns. GBR. Dist: Independent Pubs. Group.

Nelson, Robin. From Sea to Salt. 2003. (Start to Finish Ser.). (ENG., Illus.). 24p. (gr. k-3). 19.93 (978-0-8225-0946-2(6), Lerner Pubns.) Lerner Publishing Group.

Nemeth, Jason D. Rivers, Lakes, & Oceans, 1 vol. 2012. (Our Changing Earth Ser.). (ENG.). 24p. (J). (gr. 2-3). pap. 9.25 (978-1-4488-6300-6(7), ce8cfc52-b506-4397-90b6-e5ca09c737b4, PowerKids Pr.); lib. bdg. 26.27 (978-1-4488-6171-2(3), 3cd615a4-4e19-4b57-bc6c-a637bda1fb22) Rosen Publishing Group, Inc., The.

Nugent, Samantha. Arctic Ocean. 2016. (Illus.). 32p. (J). (978-1-4896-4733-7(3)) Weigl Pubs., Inc.

Oachs, Emily Rose. Arctic Ocean. 2016. (Discover the Oceans Ser.). (ENG., Illus.). 24p. (J). (gr. k-3). pap. 7.99 (978-1-61891-261-9(5), 12045, Blastoff! Readers) Bellwether Media.

—Atlantic Ocean. 2016. (Discover the Oceans Ser.). (ENG., Illus.). 24p. (J). (gr. k-3). pap. 7.99 (978-1-61891-262-6(3), 12046, Blastoff! Readers) Bellwether Media.

—Indian Ocean. 2016. (Discover the Oceans Ser.). (ENG., Illus.). 24p. (J). (gr. k-3). pap. 7.99 (978-1-61891-263-3(1), 12047); lib. bdg. 26.95 (978-1-62617-332-3(X)) Bellwether Media. (Blastoff! Readers).

—Southern Ocean. 2016. (Discover the Oceans Ser.). (ENG., Illus.). 24p. (J). (gr. k-3). pap. 7.99 (978-1-61891-279-4(8), 12049, Blastoff! Readers) Bellwether Media.

Ocean. 2003. (J). per. (978-1-57657-886-5(0)) Paradise Pr., Inc.

The Ocean. 2004. (Illus.). lib. bdg. 7.95 (978-0-8225-4535-4(7)) Lerner Publishing Group.

Ocean (Gr. PreK-5) 2003. (J). (978-1-58232-024-3(1)) ECS Learning Systems, Inc.

El Océano. 2016.Tr. of Ocean. (SPA., Illus.). 64p. (J). (978-0-545-93223-3(8)) Scholastic, Inc.

Oceans Instructional Guide. 2009. (Grade 8: Science Exit Project Kits Ser.). spiral bd. (978-1-4042-4025-4(X), Rosen Classroom) Rosen Publishing Group, Inc., The.

O'Neill, Michael Patrick, photos by. Ocean Magic. O'Neill, Michael Patrick, . 2008. (Illus.). 48p. (J). (gr. 1-4). 19.95 (978-0-9728653-5-7(7)) Batfish Bks.

Orme, David. Sea Killers. 2009. (Fact to Fiction Ser.). (Illus.). 36p. (J). pap. 6.95 (978-0-7891-7905-0(9)) Perfection Learning Corp.

Orr, Tamra B. Ocean Discoveries. 2018. (Marvelous Discoveries Ser.). (ENG., Illus.). 32p. (J). (gr. 2-5). lib. bdg. 28.65 (978-1-5435-2617-2(9), 138088, Capstone Pr.) Capstone.

Ostopowich, Melanie. Oceans, Lakes, & Rivers. 2015. (Illus.). 24p. (J). (978-1-5105-0052-5(9)) SmartBook Media, Inc.

—Oceans, Lakes, & Rivers. 2010. (Water Science Ser.). (Illus.). 24p. (gr. 3-5). (J). pap. 11.95 (978-1-61690-007-6(5)); (YA). lib. bdg. 25.70 (978-1-61690-001-4(6)) Weigl Pubs., Inc.

—Oceans, Rivers, & Lakes. 2005. (Science Matters Ser.). (Illus.). 24p. (J). (gr. 3-7). lib. bdg. 24.45 (978-1-59036-304-1(3)) Weigl Pubs., Inc.

Parker, Steve. Ocean & Sea. 2012. (J). lib. bdg. (978-0-531-22959-0(9)) Scholastic, Inc.

Parsons, Michelle Hyde. Ocean Pollution. 2005. (J). pap. (978-1-4108-4630-3(X)) Benchmark Education Co.

Patchett, Fiona. Under the Sea. Kushii, Tetsuo & Wray, Zoe, illus. 2006. (Beginners Nature: Level 1 Ser.). 32p. (J). (gr. k-2). 4.99 (978-0-7945-1336-8(0), Usborne) EDC Publishing.

—Under the Sea. Kushii, Tetsuo, illus. 2006. (Usborne Beginners Ser.). 32p. (J). (gr. 1). lib. bdg. 12.99 (978-1-58086-931-7(9), Usborne) EDC Publishing.

Penguin Books Staff, ed. The Sea. (Information Activity Ser.). 24p. (J). 3.50 (978-0-7214-3442-1(8), Dutton Juvenile) Penguin Publishing Group.

Phalen, Glen. Extreme Ocean: Amazing Animals, High-Tech Gear, Record-Breaking Depths, & More. 2020. (Illus.). 112p. (J). (gr. 3-7). pap. 12.99 (978-1-4263-3685-0(3), National Geographic Kids) Disney Publishing Worldwide.

Plisson, Phillip. Mar Explicado a los ninos. 2005. 80p. (978-970-651-911-5(4)) Editorial Oceano De Mexico, S.A. DE C.V.

¿Que Hay Debajo del Mar? (Coleccion Primeros Pasos en la Ciencia). (SPA., Illus.). (J). (gr. 1-3). pap. (978-950-724-419-3(0), LMA8226) Lumen ARG. Dist: Lectorum Pubns., Inc.

Rabe, Tish. Clam-I-Am! All about the Beach. Ruiz, Aristides, illus. 2005. (Cat in the Hat's Learning Library). (ENG.). 48p. (J). (gr. -1-3). 9.99 (978-0-375-82280-3(1), Random Hse. Bks. for Young Readers) Random Hse. Children's Bks.

Rake, Jody S. Endangered Oceans: Investigating Oceans in Crisis. 2015. (Endangered Earth Ser.). (ENG., Illus.). 32p. (J). (gr. 3-6). lib. bdg. 27.99 (978-1-4914-2038-6(3), 127516, Capstone Pr.) Capstone.

Rice, Bill & Rice, William, 5th. Survival! Ocean, 1 vol. 2nd rev. ed. 2013. (TIME for KIDS(r): Informational Text Ser.). (ENG., Illus.). 48p. (J). (gr. 4-5). lib. bdg. 29.96 (978-1-4807-1095-5(4)) Teacher Created Materials, Inc.

Rice, Dona Herweck. La Vida Marina. 2nd rev. ed. 2012. (TIME for KIDS(r): Informational Text Ser.). (SPA.). 20p. (gr. 1-2). 6.99 (978-1-4333-4423-7(8)) Teacher Created Materials, Inc.

Rice, William & Franklin, Yvonne. Oceans, 1 vol. rev. ed. 2009. (Science: Informational Text Ser.). (ENG.). 32p. (gr. 2-4). pap. 11.99 (978-1-4333-0320-3(5)) Teacher Created Materials, Inc.

Rice, William B. Survival! Ocean, 1 vol. 2nd rev. ed. 2012. (TIME for KIDS(r): Informational Text Ser.). (ENG., Illus.). 48p. (gr. 4-5). pap. 13.99 (978-1-4333-4819-8(5)) Teacher Created Materials, Inc.

Richmond, Ben. Why Is the Sea Salty? And Other Questions about Oceans. Azhderian, Cecelia, illus. 2014. (Good Question! Ser.). 32p. (J). (gr. 1). pap. 5.95 (978-1-4549-0677-3(4)) Sterling Publishing Co., Inc.

Richter, A. By the Ocean: Learning the Long O Sound. 2009. (PowerPhonics Ser.). 24p. (gr. 1-1). 39.90 (978-1-60851-436-6(6), PowerKids Pr.) Rosen Publishing Group, Inc., The.

Riggs, Kate. Oceans. (Seedlings Ser.). (ENG., Illus.). 24p. (J). 2017. (gr. k-2). pap. 9.99 (978-1-62832-339-9(6), 20737, Creative Paperbacks) 2016. (gr. -1-k). (978-1-60818-743-0(8), 20739, Creative Education) Creative Co., The.

Ring, Susan. The Ocean, 6 vols., Set. 2003. (Yellow Umbrella Early Level Ser.). (ENG.). 16p. (gr. k-1). pap. 35.70 (978-0-7368-2997-7(0), Capstone Pr.) Capstone.

Ripley's Believe It Or Not! Ripley Twists: Oceans: Fun, Facts, & Fish..., 4 vols. 2010. (Twist Ser.: 6). (ENG., Illus.). 48p. (J). 12.95 (978-1-893951-81-5(2)) Ripley Entertainment, Inc.

Rivers Lakes & Oceans. 2009. (ENG.). 112p. (gr. 5-9). 35.00 (978-0-7910-9797-7(8), P159148, Facts On File) Infobase Holdings, Inc.

Rizzo, Johnna. Oceans: Dolphins, Sharks, Penguins, & More! 2010. (Illus.). 64p. (J). (gr. 3-7). 14.95 (978-1-4263-0686-0(5), National Geographic Kids) Disney Publishing Worldwide.

Rodríguez, Ana María. Leatherback Turtles, Giant Squids, & Other Mysterious Animals of the Deepest Seas, 1 vol. 2012. (Extreme Animals in Extreme Environments Ser.). (ENG., Illus.). 48p. (gr. 5-7). pap. 11.53 (978-1-4644-0019-3(9), 32a9cba7-04ad-4d2f-b562-47e58e0090de) Enslow Publishing, LLC.

Rodríguez, Ana María & Rodríguez, Ana María. Leatherback Turtles, Giant Squids, & Other Mysterious Animals of the Deepest Seas, 1 vol. 2012. (Extreme Animals in Extreme Environments Ser.). (ENG., Illus.). 48p. (gr. 5-7). 27.93 (978-0-7660-3696-3(0), 7e31be71-5b07-42a4-b871-9470224cb3d3) Enslow Publishing, LLC.

Rogers, Juniata. The Arctic Ocean. 2018. (Oceans of the World Ser.). (ENG.). 24p. (J). (gr. -1-2). lib. bdg. 32.79 (978-1-5038-2501-7(9), 212362) Child's World, Inc, The.

—The Atlantic Ocean. 2018. (Oceans of the World Ser.). (ENG.). 24p. (J). (gr. -1-2). lib. bdg. 32.79 (978-1-5038-2502-4(7), 212363) Child's World, Inc, The.

—The Indian Ocean. 2018. (Oceans of the World Ser.). (ENG.). 24p. (J). (gr. -1-2). lib. bdg. 32.79 (978-1-5038-2503-1(5), 212364) Child's World, Inc, The.

—The Southern Ocean. 2018. (Oceans of the World Ser.). (ENG.). 24p. (J). (gr. -1-2). lib. bdg. 32.79 (978-1-5038-2500-0(0), 212361) Child's World, Inc, The.

Romaine, Claire. Oceans, 1 vol. 2017. (Our Exciting Earth! Ser.). (ENG.). 24p. (J). (gr. k-k). pap. 9.15 (978-1-5382-0969-1(1), 9bdb52c8-e293-4795-8870-46f30feaa8ea) Stevens, Gareth Publishing LLLP.

Rosa-Mendoza, Gladys. Who Lives in the Sea?/Qui'n Vive en el Mar? O'Neil, Sharron, illus. 2007. (English Spanish Foundations Ser.). (ENG & SPA.). 20p. (J). (gr. -1-k). bds. 6.95 (978-1-931398-24-4(0)) Me+Mi Publishing.

Roumanis, Alexis. Oceans. 2014. (Illus.). 24p. (J). (978-1-4896-3014-8(7)) Weigl Pubs., Inc.

Roydhouse, Sandy. Oceans of the World, 1 vol. 2009. (Our Planet Ser.). (ENG.). 32p. (YA). (gr. 4-4). lib. bdg. 28.93 (978-1-4358-2814-8(3), 26b4363d-9ad5-47c1-8209-b7b75fb91dd6) Rosen Publishing Group, Inc., The.

Royston, Angela. Ocean - It's My Home! 2011. (ENG., Illus.). 24p. (J). pap. (978-0-7787-7873-8(8)) Crabtree Publishing Co.

—Ocean Explorer! 2011. (ENG., Illus.). 24p. (J). pap. (978-0-7787-7864-6(9)); (gr. 3-6). (978-0-7787-7842-4(8)) Crabtree Publishing Co.

—Ocean It's My Home! 2011. (Crabtree Connections Ser.). (ENG., Illus.). 24p. (J). (gr. 3-6). (978-0-7787-7851-6(7)) Crabtree Publishing Co.

—Oceans. 2015. (Research on the Edge Ser.). (ENG., Illus.). 32p. (J). (gr. 3-8). 31.35 (978-1-62588-157-1(6), 19353, Smart Apple Media) Black Rabbit Bks.

Running Press, ed. Posters to Color: Oceans. Running Press, . 2016. (ENG., Illus.). 24p. (J). (gr. -1-17). pap. 9.95 (978-0-7624-5998-8(0), Running Pr. Kids) Running Pr.

Salas, Laura Purdie. Colors of the Ocean. 2011. (Colors All Around Ser.). (ENG.). 32p. (gr. 1-2). pap. 47.70 (978-1-4296-6156-0(9), Capstone Pr.) Capstone.

Schier, Helga & Zott, Lynn M., eds. Endangered Oceans, 1 vol. 2014. (Opposing Viewpoints Ser.). (ENG., Illus.). 232p. (gr. 10-12). lib. bdg. 50.43 (978-0-7377-6052-1(4), 516ffb25-0b31-4cf0-890b-8149bc5a6ac9, Greenhaven Publishing) Greenhaven Publishing LLC.

Scott, Mathew. Lots to Spot: Ocean. 2018. (ENG.). 48p. (J). 9.99 (978-1-78428-931-7(0), 8b9d521d-bb2b-4af4-aea5-4bc073bd6a12) Arcturus Publishing GBR. Dist: Baker & Taylor Publisher Services (BTPS).

The Sea. (Eyes on Adventure Ser.). 32p. (J). (gr. 1). pap. (978-1-882210-81-7(6)) Action Publishing, Inc.

The Sea & its Marvels. (Action Bks.). 64p. (J). (gr. 3-7). pap. (978-1-882210-66-4(2)) Action Publishing, Inc.

Sea into the Sea: Tidal Zone. 2007. (Illus.). 16p. (J). 3.99 (978-0-9792820-1-0(2)) Toe The Line.

Shackleton, Caroline. Deep Blue: Discovering the Sea Intermediate Book with Online Access, 1 vol. 2014. (ENG., Illus.). 28p. (J). pap., E-Book, E-Book 9.50 (978-1-107-69705-8(0)) Cambridge Univ. Pr.

Shea, Therese M. The Dead Sea, 1 vol. 2014. (Scariest Places on Earth Ser.). (ENG.). 24p. (J). (gr. 2-3). 24.27 (978-1-4824-1166-9(0), f2691d62-e626-41cf-9e0c-ff619bde2bba) Stevens, Gareth Publishing LLLP.

Sidabras, Kimberly. Oceans, Vol. 5. 2018. (World's Biomes Ser.). (Illus.). 80p. (J). (gr. 7). 33.27 (978-1-4222-4038-0(X)) Mason Crest.

Sill, Cathryn. About Habitats: Oceans, 1 vol. Sill, John, illus. (About Habitats Ser.: 5). 48p. (J). (gr. -1-2). 2016. pap. 8.99 (978-1-56145-960-5(7)) 2012. 16.95 (978-1-56145-618-5(7)) Peachtree Publishing Co. Inc.

Simon, Seymour. Oceans. 2006. (ENG., Illus.). 40p. (J). (gr. k-4). 7.99 (978-0-06-088999-9(3), HarperCollins) HarperCollins Pubs.

—Oceans. 2006. (Illus.). 31p. (gr. k-4). 17.00 (978-0-7569-6749-9(X)) Perfection Learning Corp.

Sloan, Andy & Benchmark Education Co., LLC. Opinions about Ocean Health. 2014. (Text Connections Ser.). (J). (gr. 3). (978-1-4509-9653-2(1)) Benchmark Education Co.

Smith, Ben. How Are Oceans & Lakes Alike? 2012. (Level F Ser.). (ENG., Illus.). 16p. (J). (gr. k-2). pap. 7.95 (978-1-927136-55-3(5), 19408) RiverStream Publishing.

Smith, Grace Hill. Captain Aquatica. 2019. (ENG., Illus.). 128p. (J). (gr. 3-7). lib. bdg. 27.90 (978-1-4263-3293-7(9), National Geographic Kids) Disney Publishing Worldwide.

Smith, Roland & Smith, Marie. W Is for Waves: An Ocean Alphabet. Megahan, John, illus. 2008. (Science Alphabet Ser.). (ENG.). 40p. (J). (gr. 1-4). 17.95 (978-1-58536-254-7(9), 202070) Sleeping Bear Pr.

Smithyman, Kathryn & Kalman, Bobbie. El Bioma Marino. 2006. (Libro de Bobbie Kalman Ser.). (SPA., Illus.). 32p. (J). (gr. 3-7). pap. (978-0-7787-8414-2(2)); lib. bdg. (978-0-7787-8400-5(2)) Crabtree Publishing Co.

Spilsbury, Louise. Surviving the Sea, 1 vol. 2016. (Sole Survivor Ser.). (ENG.). 48p. (gr. 4-5). pap. 15.05 (978-1-4824-5071-2(2), c00e5327-c5a8-44e2-86cb-8a565c51186d) Stevens, Gareth Publishing LLLP.

Staff, Gareth Editorial Staff. Oceans, 1 vol. 2004. (Discovery Channel School Science: Our Planet Earth Ser.). (ENG., Illus.). 32p. (gr. 5-7). lib. bdg. 28.67 (978-0-8368-3383-6(X), 3d5033a6-811e-4cdc-9b6e-470b5d10a76d, Gareth Stevens Learning Library) Stevens, Gareth Publishing LLLP.

Stone, Lynn M. Oceans. 2003. (Illus.). 24p. (J). 20.64 (978-1-58952-686-0(4)) Rourke Educational Media.

Sullivan, Laura. 24 Hours in the Ocean, 1 vol. 2017. (Day in an Ecosystem Ser.). (ENG., Illus.). 48p. (J). (gr. 4-4). 33.07 (978-1-5026-2478-9(8), 37e3cff0-09b5-49ba-9b0b-260fde1298f2) Cavendish Square Publishing LLC.

Szymanski, Jennifer. National Geographic Readers: in the Ocean (L1/Co-Reader) 2018. (Readers Ser.). (ENG., Illus.).

48p. (J). (gr. -1-k). lib. bdg. 14.90 *(978-1-4263-3236-4(X)*, National Geographic Kids) Disney Publishing Worldwide.
Tahta, Sophie. What's under the Sea? Trotter, Stuart, illus. rev. ed. 2006. (Starting Point Science Ser.). 24p. (J). (gr. 4-7). pap. 4.99 *(978-0-7945-1409-9(X)*, Usborne) EDC Publishing.
Tallarico, Tony. Ultimate Hidden Pictures: Under the Sea. 2003. (Ultimate Hidden Pictures Ser.). (Illus.). 48p. (J). (gr. -1-3). mass mkt. 5.99 *(978-0-8431-0266-6(7)*, Price Stern Sloan) Penguin Young Readers Group.
Taylor, Barbara. Oceans. 2004. (Make It Work! Geography Ser.). (Illus.). 48p. (J). (gr. 3-6). 12.95 *(978-1-58728-255-3(0)*, Two-Can Publishing) T&N Children's Publishing.
Taylor, Trace & Zorzi, Gina. This Is an Ocean. 2011. (Power 100 - Ecosystems Ser.). 28p. pap. 45.32 *(978-1-61541-241-9(7))* American Reading Co.
Taylor, Trace, et al. In the Ocean. Reese, Jonathan, illus. 2012. (1-3Y Ecosystems Ser.). (ENG.). 16p. (J). (gr. k-1). pap. 8.00 *(978-1-59301-438-4(4))* American Reading Co.
—This Is an Ocean. Washington, Joi, illus. 2010. (2G Ecosystems Ser.). (SPA & ENG.). 28p. (J). (gr. k-2). pap. 9.60 *(978-1-61541-224-2(7))* American Reading Co.
Tocci, Salvatore. Marine Habitats: Life in Saltwater. 2004. (Watts Library). (ENG.). (J). 25.50 *(978-0-531-12306-5(5)*, Watts, Franklin) Scholastic Library Publishing.
Twist, Clint. 1000 Things You Should Know about Oceans. 2008. (1000 Things You Should Know about (Miles Kelley) Ser.). (Illus.). 61p. (J). pap. *(978-1-84236-852-7(4))* Miles Kelly Publishing, Ltd.
Vallière, Nathalie. Ocean Life Fun Box: Includes a Storybook & a 2-In-1 Puzzle. Miller, Jonathan, illus. 2018. 24p. (J). (gr. -1). 7.99 *(978-2-924786-23-9(1)*, CrackBoom! Bks.) Chouette Publishing CAN. Dist: Publishers Group West (PGW).
Vilardi, Debbie. Why Is the Ocean Salty? 2019. (Science Questions Ser.). (ENG., Illus.). 24p. (J). (gr. 1-1). pap. 8.95 *(978-1-64185-590-7(8)*, 1641855908) North Star Editions.
—Why Is the Ocean Salty? 2018. (Science Questions Ser.). (ENG., Illus.). 24p. (J). (gr. k-3). lib. bdg. 31.36 *(978-1-5321-6219-0(7)*, 30221, Pop! Cody Koala) Pop!
Wade, Laura. Sea & Sealife. 2003. (Knowledge Masters Ser.). (Illus.). 32p. (YA). pap. incl. cd-rom *(978-1-903954-10-2(X)*, Pavilion Children's Books) Pavilion Bks.
Walden, Libby. Hidden World: Ocean. Coleman, Stephanie Fizer, illus. 2018. (ENG.). 18p. (J). (gr. -1-2). 14.99 *(978-1-944530-15-0(0)*, 360 Degrees) Tiger Tales.
Walker, Rachel. Help Our Oceans, 1 vol. 2015. (ENG., Illus.). 16p. (-2). pap. *(978-1-77654-138-6(3)*, Red Rocket Readers) Flying Start Bks.
West, Krista, ed. Critical Perspectives on the Oceans. (Scientific American Critical Anthologies on Environment & Climate Ser.). 208p. (gr. 9-9). 2009. 63.90 *(978-1-60853-070-0(1))* 2006. (ENG., Illus.). (J). 42.47 *(978-1-4042-0692-2(2)*, a8a33de8-d2a0-460c-bd0e-765d504b6865) Rosen Publishing Group, Inc., The.
Williams, Brenda. Home for a Penguin, Home for a Whale. Beghelli, Annalisa, illus. 2019. (ENG.). 32p. (J). (gr. -1-3). 16.99 *(978-1-78285-743-3(5))* Barefoot Bks., Inc.
Wisdon, Christina. Ultimate Oceanpedia: The Most Complete Ocean Reference Ever. 2016. (Illus.). 272p. (J). (gr. 3-7). 24.99 *(978-1-4263-2550-2(9)*, National Geographic Kids) Disney Publishing Worldwide.
Woods, Michael & Woods, Mary B. Seven Natural Wonders of the Arctic, Antarctica, & the Oceans. 2009. (Seven Wonders Ser.). (ENG., Illus.). 80p. (gr. 5-8). 33.26 *(978-0-8225-9075-0(1))* Lerner Publishing Group.
Woodward, John. Oceans. 2004. (Geography Fact Files Ser.). (J). lib. bdg. 28.50 *(978-1-58340-427-0(9))* Black Rabbit Bks.
—Oceans. (Illus.). 64p. (YA). (gr. 4-18). lib. bdg. 29.95 *(978-1-59389-125-1(3))* Chrysalis Education.
World Book, Inc. Staff, contrib. by. Oceans & Climate Change. 2015. (Illus.). 44p. (J). *(978-0-7166-2710-4(8))* World Bk., Inc.
—Treasures of the Ocean. 2017. (Illus.). 40p. (J). *(978-0-7166-3370-9(1))* World Bk., Inc.
—Treasures of the Oceans. 2017. (Illus.). 40p. (J). *(978-7-01-663363-7(2))* World Bk., Inc.
Wynne, Patricia J. & Silver, Donald M. My First Book about the Oceans. 2018. (Dover Science for Kids Coloring Bks.). (ENG.). 48p. (gr. 3-6). pap. 5.99 *(978-0-486-82171-9(4)*, 821714) Dover Pubns., Inc.
Yasuda, Anita. Oceans & Seas! With 25 Science Projects for Kids. Casteel, Tom, illus. 2018. (Explore Your World Ser.). (ENG.). 96p. (J). (gr. 3-4). 19.95 *(978-1-61930-696-7(4)*, b4b88235-a5a5-43cc-bff0-576376e10876) Nomad Pr.
Zoehfeld, Kathleen Weidner. How Deep Is the Ocean? Puybaret, Eric, illus. 2016. (Let's-Read-And-Find-Out Science 2 Ser.). (ENG.). 40p. (J). (gr. -1-3). pap. 6.99 *(978-0-06-232819-9(0)*, HarperCollins) HarperCollins Pubs.
Zorzi, Gina & Sanchez, Lucia M. OcÉAnos: This is an Ocean. 2011. (poder de 100 - Ecosistemas (Power 100 - Ecosystems) Ser.). (SPA.). 28p. (J). pap. 7.95 *(978-1-61541-428-4(2))* American Reading Co.

OCEAN—ECONOMIC ASPECTS

see Marine Resources

OCEAN—FICTION

Anderson, Carolyn. Water Queen & the Sea of Kings. 2013. 28p. pap. 24.95 *(978-1-63000-446-0(4))* America Star Bks.
Appelt, Kathi. Keeper. Hall, August, illus. (ENG.). (J). (gr. 3-7). 2012. 432p. pap. 9.99 *(978-1-4169-5061-5(3))* 2010. 416p. 17.99 *(978-1-4169-5060-8(5))* Simon & Schuster Children's Publishing. (Atheneum Bks. for Young Readers).
Arrhenius, Ingela P. Pop-Up Ocean. Arrhenius, Ingela P., illus. 2018. (ENG., Illus.). 30p. (J). (— 1). 14.00 *(978-1-5362-0119-2(7))* Candlewick Pr.
Averill, Esther. Jenny Goes to Sea. Averill, Esther, illus. 2005. (Jenny's Cat Club Ser.). (Illus.). 140p. (J). (gr. k-4). reprint ed. 18.95 *(978-1-59017-155-4(1)*, NYR Children's Collection) New York Review of Bks., Inc., The.
Bardhan-Quallen, Sudipta. Purrmaids #6: Quest for Clean Water. Wu, Vivien, illus. 2019. (Purrmaids Ser.: 6). (ENG.). 96p. (J). (gr. 1-4). pap. 6.99 *(978-0-525-64637-2(X)*, Random Hse. Bks. for Young Readers) Random Hse. Children's Bks.
Bozanich, Tony L. & Wight, Joe. Nazi Zombies. Isaksen, Patricia, ed. Isaksen, Lisa A., illus. 2013. (ENG.). 112p. (gr. -1-4). pap. 14.95 *(978-0-930655-00-6(1)*, a9bd196d-051a-4ba3-b0e6-4144539ed51d) Antarctic Pr., Inc.
Bradford, Chris. Bodyguard: Hijack (Book 3), Bk. 3. 2017. (Bodyguard Ser.: 3). (ENG.). 272p. (J). (gr. 5). pap. 8.99 *(978-1-5247-3701-6(1)*, Philomel Bks.) Penguin Young Readers Group.
Brezenoff, Steve. Time Voyage, 1 vol. Murphy, Scott, illus. 2012. (Return to Titanic Ser.). (ENG.). 112p. (J). (gr. 3-6). pap. 6.95 *(978-1-4342-3909-9(8)*, 118094, Stone Arch Bks.) Capstone.
Brouillette, Kathy. What Makes me Smile. 2010. 16p. 8.99 *(978-1-4520-1112-7(5))* AuthorHouse.
Buckingham, Matt. Bright Stanley. 2006. (Illus.). 32p. (J). (gr. -1-3). 15.95 *(978-1-58925-059-8(1))* Tiger Tales.
Cassano, Carol E. A Journey to the Bottom of the Ocean: Heavenly Adventures Volume 2. 2011. 20p. pap. *(978-1-4269-7335-2(7))* Trafford Publishing (UK) Ltd.
Corwin, Katherine A. R. Greg the Bearded Dragon & Thomas the Sea Turtle: A Tale of Adventure, Discovery, & Friendship. 2012. 28p. pap. 19.99 *(978-1-4685-7958-1(4))* AuthorHouse.
Cowan, Catherine. My Life with the Wave. 2004. (Illus.). (J). (gr. k-3). spiral bd. *(978-0-616-01621-3(2))* Canadian National Institute for the Blind/Institut National Canadien pour les Aveugles.
—My Life with the Wave. Buehner, Mark, illus. 2004. (ENG.). 32p. (J). (gr. -1-3). reprint ed. pap. 7.99 *(978-0-06-056200-7(5)*, HarperCollins) HarperCollins Pubs.
Cowley, Joy. Song of the River. Andrews, Kimberly, illus. 2019. (ENG.). 32p. (J). (gr. k-2). 17.99 *(978-1-77657-253-3(X)*, 79bc1618-5da9-4d6e-bc66-c53f1dc2c0a2) Gecko Pr. NZL. Dist: Lerner Publishing Group.
Croteau, Marie-Danielle & St. Aubin, Bruno. Des Fantomes Sous la Mer. 2003. (Roman Jeunesse Ser.). (FRE., Illus.). 96p. (J). (gr. 4-7). pap. *(978-2-89021-610-5(1))* Diffusion du livre Mirabel (DLM).
Curious George Discovers the Ocean. 2015. (Curious George Ser.). (ENG., Illus.). 32p. (J). (gr. -1-3). 6.99 *(978-0-544-43065-5(4)*, 1595740, Clarion Bks.) HarperCollins Pubs.
Davidson, Danica. Clash in the Underwater World. 2018. (Unofficial Overworld Heroes Adventure Ser.: 4). lib. bdg. 18.40 *(978-0-606-41300-8(6))* Turtleback.
Davis, Caroline. Sparkly Ocean. Davis, Caroline, illus. 2008. (Tiger Tales Ser.). (Illus.). 8p. (J). (gr. -1). bds. 6.95 *(978-1-58925-832-7(0))* Tiger Tales.
Diesen, Deborah. The Pout-Pout Fish Cleans up the Ocean. Hanna, Dan, illus. 2019. (Pout-Pout Fish Adventure Ser.: 4). (ENG.). 32p. (J). 18.99 *(978-0-374-30934-3(5)*, 900189997, Farrar, Straus & Giroux (BYR)) Farrar, Straus & Giroux.
Disney Editors. Ocean of Color. 2016. (Step into Reading - Level 1 Ser.). lib. bdg. 14.75 *(978-0-606-38890-0(7))* Turtleback.
DK. Pop-Up Peekaboo: under the Sea. 2018. (Pop-Up Peekaboo! Ser.). (ENG.). 12p. (J). (— 1). bds. 12.99 *(978-1-4654-7316-5(5)*, DK Children) Dorling Kindersley Publishing, Inc.
Duey, Kathleen & Bale, Karen A. Titanic: April 1912. 2014. (Survivors Ser.). (ENG., Illus.). 192p. (J). (gr. 3-7). pap. 7.99 *(978-1-4424-9051-2(9)*, Aladdin) Simon & Schuster Children's Publishing.
Engler, Zoe. The Lonely Starfish, 1 vol. 2010. 26p. 24.95 *(978-1-4489-2929-0(6))* PublishAmerica, Inc.
Fan, Terry & Fan, Eric. Ocean Meets Sky. Fan, Terry & Fan, Eric, illus. 2018. (ENG., Illus.). 48p. (J). (gr. -1-3). 17.99 *(978-1-4814-7037-7(X)*, Simon & Schuster Bks. For Young Readers) Simon & Schuster Bks. For Young Readers.
Fejeran, Tony. Moana. Sastrawinata-Lemay, Griselda, illus. 2016. (J). *(978-1-5182-2105-7(X)*, Golden Bks.) Random Hse. Children's Bks.
Flahive, Jean. The Old Mainer & the Sea. Dieumegard, Mari, illus. 2017. (ENG.). 32p. (J). 17.95 *(978-1-944762-27-8(2)*, 042e941e-dcd1-4698-ad4b-e36abe7edda1) Islandport Pr., Inc.
Floerchinger, Lori Liddic. Ocean of Dreams. Floerchinger, Jeremy, illus. 2008. 36p. pap. 24.95 *(978-1-60703-003-4(9))* America Star Bks.
Flynn, Pat. To the Light. Stewart, Chantal, illus. 2005. 120p. (Orig.). (YA). pap. *(978-0-7022-3492-7(3))* Univ. of Queensland Pr.
Fontes, Justine & Fontes, Ron. Casebook: The Bermuda Triangle, 1 vol. 2009. (Top Secret Graphica Mysteries Ser.). (ENG., Illus.). 48p. (YA). (gr. 4-4). 33.93 *(978-1-60754-591-0(8)*, ce4dd6aa-44d7-47ea-affe-dfbfb2c434ae); pap. 12.75 *(978-1-60754-592-7(6)*, 6f4cc6c9-b1ce-4460-aa2c-bd98329ba34e) Rosen Publishing Group, Inc., The. (Windmill Bks.).
Fuson, Robin Densmore. Rosita Valdez: And the Giant Sea Turtle. 2012. 108p. 28.99 *(978-1-4497-6487-6(8))*; pap. 11.99 *(978-1-4497-6486-9(X))* Author Solutions, LLC. (WestBow Pr.).
Garton, Sam, illus. Otter: Let's Go Swimming! 2017. 32p. (J). *(978-1-5182-4207-6(3)*, Balzer & Bray) HarperCollins Pubs.
Glennon, Michelle. My Big Green Teacher: Don't Rock the Boat: Saving Our Oceans. Glennon, Michelle, illus. 2008. (Illus.). 32p. (J). 19.95 *(978-0-9796625-2-2(4))* GDG Publishing.
Gohmann, Johanna. A Spooky Day at Sea. Innerebner, Jessika von, illus. 2017. (Pirate Kids Ser.). (ENG.). 32p. (J). (gr. -1-3). lib. bdg. 32.79 *(978-1-5321-3040-3(6)*, 27042, Calico Chapter Bks) Magic Wagon.
Groves. Bee & the Sea, Bk. 9. Date not set. (Illus.). 32p. (J). pap. 129.15 *(978-0-582-18770-2(2))* Addison-Wesley Longman, Ltd. GBR. Dist: Trans-Atlantic Pubns., Inc.
Hanton, Sophie. Colors by the Sea. 2009. (Mag-NUT-Tics! Ser.). (Illus.). (J). bds. 9.99 *(978-1-934650-73-8(0))* Just For Kids Pr., LLC.
Hare, John. Field Trip to the Ocean Deep. 2020. (Field Trip Adventures Ser.). (ENG., Illus.). 40p. (J). (gr. -1-3). 17.99 *(978-0-8234-4630-8(1)*, Margaret Ferguson Books) Holiday Hse., Inc.
Hayes, Karel. The Amazing Journey of Lucky the Lobster Buoy. 2009. (ENG.). 32p. (J). (gr. -1-3). 16.95 *(978-0-89272-791-9(8))* Down East Bks.
Hogan, Barbora. How Ryan & Aiden Saved the Ocean. 2013. 36p. pap. 16.99 *(978-1-4525-7776-0(5)*, Balboa Pr.) Author Solutions, LLC.
Holloway, Christina. Irish Selkie. 2008. 12p. pap. 24.95 *(978-1-60610-693-8(7))* America Star Bks.
Holub, Joan & Williams, Suzanne. Poseidon & the Sea of Fury. 2012. (Heroes in Training Ser.: 2). lib. bdg. 16.00 *(978-0-606-26904-9(5))* Turtleback.
Homberg, Ruth. Across the Sea. 2016. (Disney Princess Step into Reading Ser.). lib. bdg. 14.75 *(978-0-606-38472-8(3))* Turtleback.
Houts, Michelle. Sea Glass Summer. Ibatoulline, Bagram, illus. 2019. 32p. (J). (gr. -1-3). 16.99 *(978-0-7636-8443-3(0))* Candlewick Pr.
Howells, Amanda. The Summer of Skinny Dipping. (YA). 2019. 320p. (gr. 8-12). pap. 10.99 *(978-1-4926-9671-1(4))* 2010. (ENG.). 304p. (gr. 7-12). pap. 9.99 *(978-1-4022-3862-8(2))* Sourcebooks, Inc.
Inches, Alison. I Can Save the Ocean! The Little Green Monster Cleans up the Beach. Garofoli, Viviana, illus. 2010. (Little Green Bks.). (ENG.). 24p. (J). (gr. -1-1). 9.99 *(978-1-4169-9514-2(5)*, Little Simon) Little Simon.
Isabel, Michelle. Murtle the Sea Turtle. Isabel, Michelle & Thomas, Franselica, illus. 2011. 24p. pap. 24.95 *(978-1-4626-0114-1(6))* America Star Bks.
Jasper, Mark. Good Night Ocean. Stevenson, Harvey, illus. 2009. (Good Night Our World Ser.). (ENG.). 24p. (gr. k — 1). bds. 9.95 *(978-1-60219-036-8(4))* Good Night Bks.
Joy, Linda. Little Wave & the Mission of Laura Hawksbill. 2012. 24p. pap. 15.99 *(978-1-4691-9178-2(4))* Xlibris Corp.
Jupin, David Perez, illus. Love. 2013. 20p. pap. 11.95 *(978-1-937504-67-0(0))* Worthy Shorts.
Karas, G. Brian. Atlantic. 2014. 32p. pap. 7.00 *(978-1-61003-315-2(9))* Center for the Collaborative Classroom.
Kerr, Gordon. Story of Robinson Crusoe. 2006. 100p. per. *(978-1-4067-2131-7(X)*, Hesperides Pr.) Read Bks.
Kruse, Robyn A. Sammy the Sea Turtle, 1 vol. Litteral, Christopher, illus. 2010. 18p. 24.95 *(978-1-4489-4020-2(6))* PublishAmerica, Inc.
Laden, Nina. Yellow Kayak. Castrillon, Melissa, illus. 2018. (ENG.). 32p. (J). (gr. -1-3). 18.99 *(978-1-5344-0194-5(6)*, Simon & Schuster/Paula Wiseman Bks.) Simon & Schuster/Paula Wiseman Bks.
Maclear, Kyo. The Specific Ocean. Maurey, Katty, illus. 2015. (ENG.). 32p. (J). (gr. -1-3). 17.95 *(978-1-894786-35-5(1))* Kids Can Pr., Ltd. CAN. Dist: Hachette Bk. Group.
Mae, Darcie. Sammy & Robert. 2008. 24p. pap. 24.95 *(978-1-60474-811-6(7))* America Star Bks.
—Sammy & Robert Discover the Ocean, 1 vol. 2009. 39p. pap. 24.95 *(978-1-61546-827-0(7))* America Star Bks.
Maine, Margarita. Un Mar Muy Mojado. (SPA.). pap. 8.95 *(978-950-07-1985-8(1))* Editorial Sudamericana S.A. ARG. Dist: Distribooks, Inc.
Marsh, Carole. The Mystery of the Graveyard of the Atlantic. 2009. (Real Kids, Real Places Ser.). (Illus.). 144p. (J). lib. bdg. 18.99 *(978-0-635-07046-3(4)*, Marsh, Carole Mysteries) Gallopade International.
Marshall, Edward & Marshall, James. Three by the Sea. 48p. (J). (gr. k-3). pap. 3.99 *(978-0-8072-1342-1(X)*, Listening Library) Random Hse. Audio Publishing Group.
Mayer, Mercer. Little Critter: Just an Adventure at Sea. Mayer, Mercer, illus. 2017. (My First I Can Read Ser.). (ENG., Illus.). 32p. (J). (gr. -1-3). pap. 4.99 *(978-0-06-243140-0(4)*, HarperCollins) HarperCollins Pubs.
McCanna, Tim. Bitty Bot's Big Beach Getaway. Carpenter, Tad, illus. 2018. (Bitty Bot Ser.). (ENG.). 32p. (J). (gr. -1-3). 17.99 *(978-1-4814-4931-1(1)*, Simon & Schuster/Paula Wiseman Bks.) Simon & Schuster/Paula Wiseman Bks.
McCarthy, Jenna & Evans, Carolyn. Maggie Malone Makes a Splash. 2015. (Maggie Malone Ser.: 3). (ENG.). 192p. (J). (gr. 4-7). pap. 8.99 *(978-1-4022-9312-2(7))* Sourcebooks, Inc.
McCurdie, Trevor. A Dolphin's Wish: How You Can Help Make a Difference & Save Our Oceans. Battistel, Cinzia, illus. 2020. (ENG.). 32p. (J). (gr. -1-3). 17.99 *(978-1-7282-0522-9(0))* Sourcebooks, Inc.
Meadows, Daisy. Ally the Dolphin Fairy. 2011. (Illus.). 63p. (J). *(978-0-545-28871-2(1))* Scholastic, Inc.
—Courtney the Clownfish Fairy. 2011. (Illus.). 62p. (J). *(978-0-545-28877-4(0))* Scholastic, Inc.
Meister, Cari. Ocean Tales. Harpster, Steve, illus. 2013. (Ocean Tales Ser.). (ENG.). 32p. (J). (gr. -1-3). 158.55 *(978-1-4342-8844-8(7)*, 21118, Stone Arch Bks.) Capstone.
Milbourne, Anna. How Deep Is the Sea? Riglietti, Serena, illus. 2010. (Picture Bks). 24p. (J). 10.99 *(978-0-7945-2311-4(0))* EDC Publishing.
Miller, Jay. Sal & Sally. 2008. 52p. pap. 20.49 *(978-1-935028-13-0(8))* AuthorHouse.
Morgan, G. A. Chantarelle, 1 vol. 2015. (Five Stones Trilogy Ser.: 2). (ENG.). 300p. (J). 18.95 *(978-1-939017-63-5(7)*, d13ddfd9-69e5-436d-8734-e893acab42f3) Islandport Pr., Inc.
Moriarty, Ros. Who Saw Turtle? 2019. (ENG., Illus.). 24p. (J). (gr. -1-k). pap. 9.99 *(978-1-76029-780-0(1))* Allen & Unwin AUS. Dist: Independent Pubs. Group.
O'Neill, Michael Patrick. Fishy Friends: A Journey Through the Coral Kingdom. O'Neill, Michael Patrick, photos by. 2003. (Illus.). 64p. (J). 19.95 *(978-0-9728653-0-2(6))* Batfish Bks.
Osborne, Mary Pope. Dia Negro en el Fondo Del Mar (Dark Day in the Deep Sea) 2018. (Magic Tree House Merlin Missions Ser.: 11). lib. bdg. 16.00 *(978-0-606-41281-0(6))* Turtleback.
Owen, Rena. Moana: Read-Along Storybook & CD. 2016. (Illus.). (J). *(978-1-5182-2280-1(3))* Disney Publishing Worldwide.
Pallotta, Jerry. Dory Story. Biedrzycki, David, illus. 2006. 32p. (J). (gr. -1-3). pap. 7.95 *(978-0-88106-076-8(3))* Charlesbridge Publishing, Inc.
Pearce, Jackson. Fathomless. 2013. (Fairy Tale Retelling Ser.). (ENG.). 320p. (YA). (gr. 10-17). pap. 8.99 *(978-0-316-20777-5(2))* Little, Brown Bks. for Young Readers.
Peck, Jan. Way down Deep in the Deep Blue Sea. 2004. (ENG., Illus.). 32p. (J). (gr. -1-3). 18.99 *(978-0-689-85110-0(3)*, Simon & Schuster Bks. For Young Readers) Simon & Schuster Bks. For Young Readers.
Pelosi, Vincent L. The Magical Underwater Kingdom of Balenarium. 2012. 200p. 46.72 *(978-1-4797-1951-8(X))*; pap. 28.03 *(978-1-4797-1950-1(1))* Xlibris Corp.
Piano, Maureen. When Flamingos Fly: Discovering the Wonders of the World. 2006. (Illus.). 44p. (J). (gr. -1-3). pap. 12.99 incl. audio compact disk *(978-1-59092-362-7(6))* Blue Forge Pr.
Pitt, Sarah. Peek a Boo! Ocean. 2009. (Little Peek a Boo Bks.). (Illus.). (J). bds. 9.99 *(978-1-934650-58-5(7))* Just For Kids Pr., LLC.
Porta, Bill K. Adventures of Henry the Little Boat. 2011. 24p. (gr. -1). pap. 11.32 *(978-1-4520-4448-4(1))* AuthorHouse.
Pratt-Serafini, Kristin Joy. A Swim Through the Sea, 1 vol. 2006. (Illus.). 44p. (J). (gr. k-6). pap. 8.95 *(978-1-883220-04-4(1)*, Dawn Pubns.) Sourcebooks, Inc.
Presley, Loren. The Anastasia Project. 2007. (ENG.). 296p. 34.47 *(978-0-615-18136-3(8))* Presley, Loren John.
The Quest for Courage. 2006. (Amazing Travels of Wannabeb Ser.). (Illus.). 32p. (J). (gr. -1-3). 8.99 *(978-0-7847-1801-8(6)*, 04127) Standard Publishing.
Rash, Ron, et al. The Shark's Tooth. 2015. (Young Palmetto Bks.). (ENG., Illus.). 40p. pap. 12.99 *(978-1-61117-527-1(5)*, P450702) Univ. of South Carolina Pr.
Reasoner, Charles. Numbers under the Sea. Pitt, Sarah, illus. 2009. (3D Board Bks.). 12p. (J). (gr. -1-k). bds. 9.99 *(978-1-934650-37-0(4))* Just For Kids Pr., LLC.
Ryan, Pam Muñoz. Hello Ocean. Astrella, Mark, illus. 2014. 32p. pap. 8.00 *(978-1-61003-319-0(1))* Center for the Collaborative Classroom.
—Hola Mar / Hello Ocean. Astrella, Mark, illus. 2003. (Charlesbridge Bilingual Bks.). Tr. of Hello Ocean (Bilingual). 32p. (J). (gr. -1-2). pap. 7.95 *(978-1-57091-372-3(2))* Charlesbridge Publishing, Inc.
Santillo, LuAnn. Flap. Santillo, LuAnn, ed. 2003. (Half-Pint Kids Readers Ser.). (Illus.). 7p. (J). (gr. -1-1). pap. 1.00 *(978-1-59256-096-7(2))* Half-Pint Kids, Inc.
Santoro, Lucio & Santoro, Meera. Wild Oceans: A Pop-Up Book with Revolutionary Technology. 2010. (ENG.). 12p. (J). (gr. 1-5). 32.99 *(978-1-4169-8467-2(4)*, Little Simon) Little Simon.
Sconyers, Jennifer. John Bunny Goes on Vacation. 2010. 20p. pap. 12.99 *(978-1-4490-7774-7(9))* AuthorHouse.
Scott, Jeff. The Discovery of Monkey Island. 2008. 64p. pap. 19.95 *(978-1-60610-921-2(9))* America Star Bks.
Shasha, Mark. Night of the Moonjellies: 15th Anniversary Edition. 2007. (Illus.). 32p. (J). (gr. -1-2). 12.95 *(978-1-930900-34-9(1))* Purple Hse. Pr.
Simmons, Derek. Flash of Life. 2006. 85p. pap. 16.95 *(978-1-4241-3890-6(6))* PublishAmerica, Inc.
Simpson, Dorothy. Visitors from the Sea. Date not set. 188p. (J). 20.95 *(978-0-8488-2632-1(9))* Amereon Ltd.
Smith, Sindy. Dadu the Dolphin. Smith, Sindy, illus. 2012. (Illus.). 24p. 29.95 *(978-1-4626-9862-2(X))* America Star Bks.
Sollinger, Emily. Diego's Ocean Adventure: A Book of Facts about Ocean Animals. Mawhinney, Art, illus. 2008. (Go, Diego, Go! Ser.). (ENG.). 16p. (J). (gr. -1-2). pap. 6.99 *(978-1-4169-4781-3(7)*, Simon Spotlight/Nickelodeon) Simon Spotlight/Nickelodeon.
Spradlin, Michael P. Into the Killing Seas. 2015. (ENG.). 224p. (J). (gr. 3-7). 16.99 *(978-0-545-72602-3(6)*, Scholastic Pr.) Scholastic, Inc.
Stevenson, William. Ricky's Dream Trip under the Sea. 2013. 38p. (J). pap. 12.99 *(978-1-936517-85-5(X))* Micro Publishing Media, Inc.
Stratemeyer, Edward. The Rover Boys on the Ocean: Or, a Chase for a Fortune. 2007. (ENG.). 158p. pap. 19.99 *(978-1-4264-2766-4(2))*; 170p. pap. 21.99 *(978-1-4264-2804-3(9))* Creative Media Partners, LLC.
ToyBox Innovations, creator. Disney's the Little Mermaid. abr. ed. 2006. (Disney's Read along Collection). (ENG.). (J). (gr. -1-3). pap. *(978-0-7634-2184-7(7))* Walt Disney Records.
Tsarfati, Einat. Sandcastle. Tsarfati, Einat, illus. 2020. (ENG., Illus.). 48p. (J). (gr. -1-1). 17.99 *(978-1-5362-1143-6(5))* Candlewick Pr.
Tsurumi, Andrea. Crab Cake: Turning the Tide Together. 2019. (ENG., Illus.). 48p. (J). (gr. -1-3). 18.99 *(978-0-544-95900-2(0)*, 1661279, Clarion Bks.) HarperCollins Pubs.
Twins, Pope, illus. Poke-A-Dot!: Who's in the Ocean? (30 Poke-able Poppin' Dots) 2012. (ENG.). 1p. (J). (gr. -1-1). 14.99 *(978-1-60169-270-2(6))* Innovative Kids.
Under the Sea Magic Painting Book. 2017. (Magic Painting Bks.). (ENG.). (J). pap. 9.99 *(978-0-7945-3958-0(0)*, Usborne) EDC Publishing.
Van Tassel, Mary. Beach Ball's Journey, 1 vol. 2010. 18p. pap. 24.95 *(978-1-4489-9618-6(X))* America Star Bks.
What's under the Sea? 2003. (J). per. *(978-1-57657-934-3(4))* Paradise Pr., Inc.
Wild, Ailsa, et al. Zobi & the Zoox: A Story of Coral Bleaching. 2018. (Stories of Partnership & Cooperation in Nature Ser.: 1). (Illus.). 44p. (J). (gr. 3-7). 19.95 *(978-1-4863-0960-3(7))* CSIRO Publishing AUS. Dist: Stylus Publishing, LLC.
Williams, Greg. Salty the Sea Gull. 2011. 38p. pap. 19.00 *(978-1-60746-205-7(2))* FastPrncil, Inc.
Worthington, Michelle. Start of the Ocean. Finn, Ann-Marie, illus. 2013. 32p. pap. *(978-0-9874160-1-8(4))* Wybble Publishing.
Wright, Mary. Co-Man & Poppa Meet Kanka. Dewitt, Levi, illus. 2013. 24p. pap. 24.95 *(978-1-62709-328-6(1))* America Star Bks.
Yee, Paul. The Jade Necklace. Lin, Grace, illus. 2006. 29p. (J). (gr. 4-8). reprint ed. 16.00 *(978-1-4223-5135-2(1))* DIANE Publishing Co.

OCEAN BOTTOM

Cole, Joanna. The Magic School Bus on the Ocean Floor, 1 vol. Degen, Bruce, illus. 2010. (Magic School Bus Ser.). (ENG.). (J). (gr. 2-5). pap. 10.99 *(978-0-545-22751-3(8))* Scholastic, Inc.
Early Macken, JoAnn. Ocean Floors, 1 vol. 2005. (Water Habitats Ser.). (ENG., Illus.). 24p. (gr. k-2). lib. bdg. 24.67 *(978-0-8368-4885-4(3)*, 82e30be5-cd4e-4921-8dca-cd425de878cf, Weekly Reader Leveled Readers) Stevens, Gareth Publishing LLLP.
—Ocean Floors / Fondos Oceánicos, 1 vol. 2005. (Water Habitats / Hábitats Acuáticos Ser.). (SPA & ENG., Illus.). 24p. (gr. k-2). pap. 9.15 *(978-0-8368-6037-5(3)*,

MNO

e210bb71-3431-496d-8147-b29b5ea5e054); lib. bdg. 24.67 *(978-0-8368-6030-6(6)*, 774619e7-0791-45c7-9f47-8942856e4db9) Stevens, Gareth Publishing LLLP. (Weekly Reader Leveled Readers).

Martínez, Clarissa G. & Seagraves, Erin. Sand Dwellers: From Desert to Sea. 2016. (Illus.). 18p. (J). pap. *(978-1-60617-723-5(0))* Teaching Strategies, LLC.

Orr, Tamra B. Ocean Discoveries. 2018. (Marvelous Discoveries Ser.). (ENG., Illus.). 32p. (J). (gr. 2-5). lib. bdg. 28.65 *(978-1-5435-2617-2(9)*, 138088, Capstone Pr.) Capstone.

Vallière, Nathalie. Ocean Life Fun Box: Includes a Storybook & a 2-In-1 Puzzle. Miller, Jonathan, illus. 2018. 24p. (J). (gr. -1). 7.99 *(978-2-924786-23-9(1)*, CrackBoom! Bks.) Chouette Publishing CAN. Dist: Publishers Group West (PGW).

Woodward, John. On the Seabed. 2010. (Oceans Alive! Ser.). (ENG.). 32p. (J). (gr. 4-7). lib. bdg. 28.50 *(978-1-933834-64-1(1)*, 16772) Brown Bear Bks.

OCEAN LIFE

see Marine Biology

OCEAN ROUTES

see Trade Routes

OCEAN TRAVEL

Amato, William. Cruceros, 1 vol. 2003. (Vehículos de Alta Tecnología (High-Tech Vehicles) Ser.). (SPA., Illus.). 24p. (J). (gr. 2-2). lib. bdg. 26.27 *(978-0-8239-6884-8(7)*, bf7e0ddf-2b6f-46cd-8b7b-3464eb219baf) Rosen Publishing Group, Inc., The.

Bailey, Gerry. Sea Transportation, 1 vol. 2008. (Simply Science Ser.). (ENG., Illus.). 32p. (YA). (gr. 3-5). lib. bdg. 28.67 *(978-0-8368-9230-7(5)*, efd3f887-3ce4-4750-ada8-9feaef58a5b7) Stevens, Gareth Publishing LLLP.

Brook, Henry. True Sea Stories. 2005. (True Adventure Stories Ser.). (Illus.). 154p. (J). (gr. 5). lib. bdg. 12.95 *(978-1-58086-693-4(X))* EDC Publishing.

Disney Editions, creator. Birnbaum's Disney Cruise Line. 2006. (Birnbaum's Disney Cruise Line Ser.). (ENG., Illus.). 224p. (gr. -1-17). per. 13.95 *(978-1-4231-0052-2(2)*, Disney Editions) Disney Pr.

Macdonald, Fiona. You Wouldn't Want to Sail with Christopher Columbus! 2014. (You Wouldn't Want to... Ser.). (ENG.). 32p. (J). lib. bdg. 29.00 *(978-0-531-21177-9(0)*, Watts, Franklin) Scholastic Library Publishing.

Parker, Steve. On Water, 1 vol. West, David, illus. 2012. (Future Transport Ser.). (ENG.). 32p. (gr. 5-5). 31.21 *(978-1-60870-780-5(6)*, b9062f54-e70d-448a-ad76-b3f9c7785aef) Cavendish Square Publishing LLC.

Paulsen, Gary. Caught by the Sea. 2003. (ENG., Illus.). 112p. (YA). (gr. 7). mass mkt. 5.99 *(978-0-440-40716-4(8)*, Laurel Leaf) Random Hse. Children's Bks.

—Caught by the Sea: My Life on Boats. 2003. (Illus.). 103p. (gr. 7). 16.00 *(978-0-7569-1635-0(6))* Perfection Learning Corp.

Rice, Dona Herweck. Navigating at Sea (Grade 3) rev. ed. 2018. (Smithsonian: Informational Text Ser.). (ENG., Illus.). 32p. (J). (gr. 3-4). pap. 11.99 *(978-1-4938-6680-9(X))* Teacher Created Materials, Inc.

Shoup, Kate. Life As a Passenger on the Titanic, 1 vol. 2017. (Life As... Ser.). (ENG.). 32p. (gr. 3-3). pap. 11.58 *(978-1-5026-3043-8(5)*, 4c85f115-5377-4a78-978e-48067446bb7c) Cavendish Square Publishing LLC.

West, David. Ten of the Best Adventures on the Seas. 2015. (Ten of the Best: Stories of Exploration & Adventure Ser.). (ENG., Illus.). 24p. (J). (gr. 3-4). *(978-0-7787-1839-0(5))* Crabtree Publishing Co.

OCEAN TRAVEL—FICTION

Abbott, Jacob. Rollo on the Atlantic. 2008. 116p. 23.95 *(978-1-60664-822-3(5))*; pap. 9.95 *(978-1-60664-067-8(4))* Aegypan.

Alger, Horatio. Brave & Bold. 2005. 28.95 *(978-1-4218-1452-0(8))*; 280p. pap. 13.95 *(978-1-4218-1552-7(4))* 1st World Publishing, Inc. (1st World Library - Literary Society).

—Brave & Bold. 2006. 152p. per. 12.95 *(978-1-59818-652-9(3))*; 24.95 *(978-1-59818-570-6(5))* Aegypan.

Aromshtam, Marina. The Real Boat. Semykina, Victoria, illus. 2019. (ENG.). 64p. (J). (gr. k-3). 17.99 *(978-1-5362-0277-9(0)*, Templar) Candlewick Pr.

Boisrobert, Anouck & Rigaud, Louis. Under the Ocean. 2014. (ENG., Illus.). 10p. (gr. -1-17). 19.95 *(978-1-84976-159-8(0))* Tate Publishing, Ltd. GBR. Dist: Abrams, Inc.

Bright, Anna. The Beholder. (Beholder Ser.: 1). (ENG.). (YA). (gr. 9). 2020. 464p. pap. 10.99 *(978-0-06-284543-6(8))* 2019. 448p. 17.99 *(978-0-06-284542-9(X))* HarperCollins Pubs. (HarperTeen).

Buckey, Sarah Masters. The Stolen Sapphire. 2007. (American Girl Mysteries Ser.). (Illus.). 181p. (gr. 4-7). 17.45 *(978-0-7569-8278-2(2))* Perfection Learning Corp.

Bunting, Eve. S. O. S. Titanic. 2012. (ENG.). 256p. (YA). (gr. 7-12). pap. 7.99 *(978-0-15-201305-9(9)*, 1189458, Clarion Bks.) HarperCollins Pubs.

Coatsworth, Elizabeth Jane & Sewell, Helen. The Fair American. 2005. (ENG., Illus.). 137p. (J). (gr. 3-4). pap. 11.95 *(978-1-883937-85-0(X))* Ignatius Pr.

Deutsch, Neil. Rose & the Pelican. 2013. 32p. pap. 19.99 *(978-1-4817-0947-7(X))* AuthorHouse.

Hood, Susan. Lifeboat 12. 2018. (ENG., Illus.). 336p. (J). (gr. 3-8). 17.99 *(978-1-4814-6883-1(9)*, Simon & Schuster Bks. For Young Readers) Simon & Schuster Bks. For Young Readers.

Jennings, Paul. A Different Boy. 2019. (Different Ser.). (ENG., Illus.). 112p. (J). (gr. 5-9). pap. 11.99 *(978-1-76052-350-3(X))* Allen & Unwin AUS. Dist: Independent Pubs. Group.

Jorgensen, Norman. Smuggler's Curse. 2017. 356p. (J). (gr. 4-7). 8.95 *(978-1-925164-19-0(5))* Fremantle Pr. AUS. Dist: Independent Pubs. Group.

Keene, Carolyn. Curse of the Arctic Star. 2013. (Nancy Drew Diaries: 1). (ENG.). 208p. (J). (gr. 3-7). 16.99 *(978-1-4424-6610-4(3)*, Aladdin) Simon & Schuster Children's Publishing.

—Nancy Drew Diaries (Boxed Set) Curse of the Arctic Star; Strangers on a Train; Mystery of the Midnight Rider; Once upon a Thriller. 2013. (Nancy Drew Diaries). (ENG., Illus.). 768p. (J). (gr. 3-7). pap. 31.99 *(978-1-4424-8896-0(4)*, Aladdin) Simon & Schuster Children's Publishing.

—Once upon a Thriller. 2013. (Nancy Drew Diaries: 4). (ENG., Illus.). 144p. (J). (gr. 3-7). 17.99 *(978-1-4424-6612-8(X))*; pap. 7.99 *(978-1-4169-9074-1(7))* Simon & Schuster Children's Publishing. (Aladdin).

Kehret, Peg. Secret Journey. 2008. (ENG.). 144p. (J). (gr. 3-7). pap. 8.99 *(978-1-4169-9112-0(3)*, Simon & Schuster/Paula Wiseman Bks.) Simon & Schuster/Paula Wiseman Bks.

Kisko, Stephen. Sailing the Puddles. 2013. 36p. pap. 12.95 *(978-1-62838-002-6(0))* Page Publishing Inc.

Lalicki, Tom. Shots at Sea: A Houdini & Nate Mystery. 2011. (Houdini & Nate Mysteries Ser.). 224p. (J). pap. 6.99 *(978-0-312-65920-2(2))* Square Fish.

Lawrence, Iain. The Convicts. 2006. 15.10 *(978-0-7569-6901-1(8))* Random House Children's Books GBR. Dist: Perfection Learning Corp.

Maniscalco, Kerri. Escaping from Houdini. (Stalking Jack the Ripper Ser.: 3). (ENG., Illus.). (YA). (gr. 10-17). 2019. 480p. pap. 12.99 *(978-0-316-55172-4(4))* 2018. 448p. 19.99 *(978-0-316-55170-0(8))* Little Brown & Co. (Jimmy Patterson).

Manus, Willard. A Dog Called Leka. 2007. (ENG.). 122p. pap. 7.99 *(978-0-9740551-3-8(1))* Smith, Viveca Publishing.

Mumford, Carole. Caribbean Cruise Summer Vacation: A Magnificent Six Adventure, 1 vol. 2009. 96p. pap. 16.95 *(978-1-61546-760-0(2))* PublishAmerica, Inc.

Neale, Cynthia G. The Irish Dresser: A Story of Hope During the Great Hunger (an Gorta Mor, 1845-1850) 2003. 148p. (J). pap. 7.95 *(978-1-57249-344-5(5)*, White Mane Kids) White Mane Publishing Co., Inc.

Peck, Richard. Secrets at Sea. 2012. (ENG.). 272p. (J). (gr. 3-7). pap. 8.99 *(978-0-14-242183-3(9)*, Puffin Books) Penguin Young Readers Group.

Penn, Audrey. Blackbeard & the Gift of Silence. 2009. (ENG.). 350p. (J). (gr. 2-7). pap. 8.95 *(978-1-933718-32-3(3))* Tanglewood Pr.

Redbank, Tennant. Treasure: Ariel's Curious Kitten. 2015. (Disney Princess Palace Pets Ser.). lib. bdg. 16.00 *(978-0-606-36392-1(0))* Turtleback.

Rodda, Emily. The Hungry Isle. 2017. 170p. (J). lib. bdg. *(978-1-61067-638-0(6))* Kane Miller.

—The Hungry Isle: Star of Deltora. 2017. 176p. (J). pap. 5.99 *(978-1-61067-528-4(2))* Kane Miller.

—The Towers of Illica. 2017. 170p. (J). *(978-1-61067-637-3(8))* Kane Miller.

—The Towers of Illica: Star of Deltora. 2017. 176p. (J). pap. 5.99 *(978-1-61067-527-7(4))* Kane Miller.

Roy, Lillian Elizabeth. Polly's Southern Cruise: The Polly Brewster Series. Barbour, H. S., illus. 2011. 294p. 48.95 *(978-1-258-10514-3(4))* Literary Licensing, LLC.

Schliewen, Richard. Paulina's Teddy Bear Journey. Visaya, Artemio, illus. 2012. 104p. 24.95 *(978-1-62709-055-1(X))* America Star Bks.

Shusterman, Neal. Challenger Deep. 2016. (YA). lib. bdg. 20.85 *(978-0-606-38734-7(X))* Turtleback.

Slater, Dashka. The Antlered Ship. Fan, Terry & Fan, Eric, illus. 2017. (ENG.). 48p. (J). (gr. -1-3). 17.99 *(978-1-4814-5160-4(X)*, Beach Lane Bks.) Beach Lane Bks.

Smithwick, John W. Drift. 2012. 36p. pap. 13.95 *(978-1-61897-972-8(8)*, Strategic Bk. Publishing) Strategic Book Publishing & Rights Agency (SBPRA).

Snider, Jesse Blaze. Toy Story: Toy Overboard. Watson, Nathan, illus. 2011. 128p. (J). pap. 9.99 *(978-1-60886-605-2(X))* BOOM! Studios.

Snow, Alan. Worse Things Happen at Sea! A Tale of Pirates, Poison, & Monsters. Snow, Alan, illus. 2013. (Ratbridge Chronicles Ser.: 2). (ENG., Illus.). 352p. (J). (gr. 3-9). 17.99 *(978-0-689-87049-1(3)*, Atheneum Bks. for Young Readers) Simon & Schuster Children's Publishing.

Staniszewski, Anna. Once upon a Cruise: a Wish Novel. 2016. (Wish Ser.). (ENG.). 256p. (J). (gr. 3-7). pap. 6.99 *(978-0-545-87986-6(8)*, Scholastic Paperbacks) Scholastic, Inc.

Stewart, Paul & Riddell, Chris. Far-Flung Adventures: Corby Flood. 2012. (Far-Flung Adventures Ser.). (ENG.). 256p. (J). (gr. 3-7). 7.99 *(978-0-385-75097-4(8)*, Yearling) Random Hse. Children's Bks.

Stier, Catherine. Welcome to America, Champ. Ettlinger, Doris, illus. 2013. (Tales of the World Ser.). (ENG.). 32p. (J). (gr. 1-4). 17.95 *(978-1-58536-606-4(4)*, 202360) Sleeping Bear Pr.

Tanner, Lian. Sunker's Deep. 2016. (Icebreaker Trilogy Ser.: 2). (ENG.). 304p. (J). 27.99 *(978-1-250-05217-9(3)*, 900135665) Feiwel & Friends.

Tarshis, Lauren. I Survived the Sinking of the Titanic 1912. 2010. (I Survived Ser.: No. 1). lib. bdg. 14.75 *(978-0-606-23741-3(0))* Turtleback.

—I Survived the Sinking of the Titanic, 1912 (I Survived #1) Dawson, Scott, illus. 2010. (I Survived Ser.: 1). (ENG.). 112p. (J). (gr. 2-5). 4.99 *(978-0-545-20694-5(4)*, Scholastic Paperbacks) Scholastic, Inc.

Winfield, Arthur M. The Rover Boys on Land & Sea or the Crusoes of Seven Islands. 2006. (ENG.). 284p. per. 28.95 *(978-1-4286-4097-9(5))* Kessinger Publishing, LLC.

Yin. Coolies. Soentpiet, Chris, illus. 2003. 40p. (J). (gr. 2-5). 8.99 *(978-0-14-250055-2(0)*, Puffin Books) Penguin Young Readers Group.

Zaugg, Sandra L. Hidden Notes & High Seas. 2005. (Illus.). 95p. (J). *(978-0-8163-2052-3(7))* Pacific Pr. Pubns.

OCEAN WAVES

Dougherty, Terri. The Worst Tsunamis of All Time, 1 vol. 2012. (Epic Disasters Ser.). (ENG.). 32p. (J). (gr. 3-9). lib. bdg. 28.65 *(978-1-4296-8416-3(X)*, 118489, Capstone Pr.) Capstone.

Ingram, Scott. Tsunami! The 1946 Hilo Wave of Terror. 2005. (X-Treme Disasters That Changed America Ser.). (Illus.). 32p. (J). lib. bdg. 28.50 *(978-1-59716-010-0(5))* Bearport Publishing Co., Inc.

Keedle, Jayne. Tsunamis & Floods, 1 vol. 2008. (Ultimate 10: Natural Disasters Ser.). (ENG., Illus.). 48p. (J). (gr. 3-3). lib. bdg. 33.67 *(978-0-8368-9154-6(6)*, 6088c08a-5690-4c38-a9f5-9850b59f0aed) Stevens, Gareth Publishing LLLP.

MacDonald, Steele Lisa. The Science of Waves & Surfboards. rev. ed. 2018. (Smithsonian: Informational Text Ser.). (ENG., Illus.). 32p. (J). (gr. 3-5). pap. 11.99 *(978-1-4938-6705-9(9))* Teacher Created Materials, Inc.

Peppas, Lynn. Ocean, Tidal & Wave Energy: Power from the Sea, 1 vol. 2008. (Energy Revolution Ser.). (ENG., Illus.). 32p. (J). (gr. 3-8). pap. *(978-0-7787-2933-4(8))*; lib. bdg. *(978-0-7787-2919-8(2))* Crabtree Publishing Co.

Vogel, Carole Garbuny. Shifting Shores. 2003. (Restless Sea Ser.). (ENG., Illus.). 80p. (J). (gr. 5-8). 30.50 *(978-0-531-12322-5(7)*, Watts, Franklin) Scholastic Library Publishing.

Wendorff, Anne. Tsunamis. 2008. (Extreme Weather Ser.). (ENG., Illus.). 24p. (J). (gr. 2-5). lib. bdg. 26.95 *(978-1-60014-188-1(9))* Bellwether Media.

OCEANIA

see Islands of the Pacific

OCEANOGRAPHY

see also Marine Biology; Marine Resources; Navigation; Ocean Waves; Submarine Geology

Anderson, Michael. Investigating Earth's Oceans, 1 vol. 2011. (Introduction to Earth Science Ser.). (ENG., Illus.). 88p. (J). (gr. 8-8). lib. bdg. 35.29 *(978-1-61530-497-4(5)*, dfad9fa3-2d58-476e-8033-9e691f7081ae) Rosen Publishing Group, Inc., The.

Austen, Amy. Earth's Oceans, 1 vol. 2016. (Spotlight on Earth Science Ser.). (ENG., Illus.). 24p. (J). (gr. 4-6). pap. 11.00 *(978-1-4994-2501-7(5)*, 33b12f8d-0891-4abf-a344-77b22ec39e94, PowerKids Pr.) Rosen Publishing Group, Inc., The.

Bailey, Gerry. Swept Away by the Storm. Noyes, Leighton, illus. 2014. (Science to the Rescue Ser.). (ENG.). 32p. (J). (gr. 4-4). *(978-0-7787-0431-7(9))* Crabtree Publishing Co.

Barnes, J. Lou. 101 Facts about Oceans, 1 vol. 2003. (101 Facts about Our World Ser.). (ENG., Illus.). 32p. (gr. 2-4). lib. bdg. 28.67 *(978-0-8368-3709-4(6)*, 37dd5d85-5ee7-4d60-9ada-0def74dd4ab7, Gareth Stevens Learning Library) Stevens, Gareth Publishing LLLP.

Basher, Simon & Green, Dan. Oceans: Making Waves! Basher, Simon, illus. 2012. (Basher Science Ser.). (ENG., Illus.). 128p. (J). (gr. 5-9). pap. 9.99 *(978-0-7534-6822-7(0)*, 900081821, Kingfisher) Roaring Brook Pr.

Bayrock, Fiona. The Ocean Explorer's Handbook. 2005. (Undersea University Ser.). (Illus.). 48p. (J). pap. *(978-0-439-71184-5(3))* Scholastic, Inc.

Belcher, Angie. Oceans Alive: Band 14/Ruby (Collins Big Cat) Belcher, Angie, illus. 2007. (Collins Big Cat Ser.). (ENG., Illus.). 48p. (J). (gr. 3-4). pap. 12.99 *(978-0-00-723092-1(3))* HarperCollins Pubs. Ltd. GBR. Dist: Independent Pubs. Group.

Benoit, Peter. Oceans. 2011. (True Bk Ser.). 48p. (J). (ENG.). pap. 6.95 *(978-0-531-28105-5(1))*; (gr. 3-5). 29.00 *(978-0-531-20556-3(8))* Scholastic Library Publishing. (Children's Pr.).

Best, Arthur. Oceans, 1 vol. 2017. (Our World of Water Ser.). (ENG.). 24p. (gr. 1-1). pap. 9.22 *(978-1-5026-3094-0(X)*, 65cac6a8-c2e7-4674-9e3d-dcbc4be39956) Cavendish Square Publishing LLC.

Buchanan, Shelly. The Powerful Ocean. 2015. (Science: Informational Text Ser.). (ENG., Illus.). 32p. (gr. 4-8). pap. 11.99 *(978-1-4807-4726-5(2))* Teacher Created Materials, Inc.

Burns, Loree Griffin. Tracking Trash: Flotsam, Jetsam, & the Science of Ocean Motion. 2007. (Scientists in the Field Ser.). (ENG., Illus.). 64p. (J). (gr. 6-8). 26.19 *(978-0-618-58131-3(6))* Houghton Mifflin Harcourt Publishing Co.

Cardenas, Ernesto A. Oceans. 2009. pap. 4.95 *(978-1-60698-086-6(5))* Milo Educational Bks. & Resources.

Collard, Sneed B., III. The Deep-Sea Floor. Wenzel, Gregory, illus. 2003. 32p. (J). (gr. 1-4). pap. 7.95 *(978-1-57091-403-4(6))* Charlesbridge Publishing, Inc.

La Conservacion del Mar. (Colección Biblioteca Juvenil de Ecología). (SPA., Illus.). (YA). (gr. 5-8). pap. *(978-958-04-2405-5(5)*, 80424055) Norma S.A. COL. Dist: Lectorum Pubns., Inc.

Croce, Nicholas, ed. Oceanography & Hydrology, 4 vols. 2016. (Study of Science Ser.). (ENG.). 128p. (gr. 8-8). 75.64 *(978-1-68048-234-8(3)*, 96d12eab-a568-4566-9eb3-2548ddcc99d2);1. (Illus.). (J). 37.82 *(978-1-68048-235-5(1)*, 25fc15e1-5523-4168-b9fe-063e7abbf388) Rosen Publishing Group, Inc., The. (Britannica Educational Publishing).

Davies, Monika. How Deep in the Ocean? Ocean Animal Habitats. Martí, Romina, illus. 2018. (Animals Measure Up Ser.). (ENG.). 24p. (J). (gr. 1-4). pap. 9.99 *(978-1-68152-304-0(3)*, 15018); lib. bdg. *(978-1-68151-384-3(6)*, 15012) Amicus.

Diamond, Claudia. What's under the Sea? 2009. (Reading Room Collection 2 Ser.). 24p. (gr. 3-4). 42.50 *(978-1-60852-002-2(1)*, PowerKids Pr.) Rosen Publishing Group, Inc., The.

Douglas. Reading Explorer 4 with Student CD-ROM. 4th ed. 2010. (ENG., Illus.). 224p. (J). pap., stu. ed. incl. cd-rom *(978-1-4240-2939-6(2))* Cengage Heinle.

Eriksson, Ann. Dive In! Exploring Our Connection with the Ocean, 1 vol. 2018. (Orca Footprints Ser.: 14). (ENG., Illus.). 48p. (J). (gr. 4-7). 19.95 *(978-1-4598-1586-5(6))* Orca Bk. Pubs. USA.

Franks, Sharon E. & Cohen, Judith Love. You Can Be A Woman Oceanographer. Katz, David Arthur, illus. 2004. (J). 40p. 19.95 incl. DVD *(978-1-880599-67-9(8))*; pap. 13.95 incl. DVD *(978-1-880599-66-2(X))* Cascade Pass, Inc.

Gallagher, Belinda. Why Why Why... Are There Schools in the Sea? 2010. (Why Why Why Ser.). (Illus.). 32p. (J). (gr. 1-3). lib. bdg. 18.95 *(978-1-4222-1572-2(5))* Mason Crest.

Garbe, Suzanne. The Science Behind Wonders of the Water: Exploding Lakes, Ice Circles, & Brinicles. 2016. (Science Behind Natural Phenomena Ser.). (ENG., Illus.). 32p. (J). (gr. 3-9). lib. bdg. 28.65 *(978-1-5157-0776-9(8)*, 132116, Capstone Pr.) Capstone.

Goldstein, Natalie. How Do We Know the Nature of the Ocean?, 1 vol. 2004. (Great Scientific Questions & the Scientists Who Answered Them Ser.). (ENG., Illus.). 112p. (J). (gr. 7-12). lib. bdg. 39.80 *(978-1-4042-0079-1(7)*, 7efc12bd-b89c-4d89-b2f8-033e824aaef5) Rosen Publishing Group, Inc., The.

—How Do We Know the Nature of the Ocean. 2009. (Great Scientific Questions & the Scientists Who Answered Them Ser.). 112p. (gr. 7-12). 63.90 *(978-1-61513-204-1(X))* Rosen Publishing Group, Inc., The.

Gordon, Sharon. At Home by the Ocean, 1 vol. 2007. (At Home Ser.). (ENG., Illus.). 32p. (gr. k-2). lib. bdg. 25.50 *(978-0-7614-1959-4(4)*, b15cc6b0-6fd4-44ee-b6db-e091ea9212a1) Cavendish Square Publishing LLC.

—Mi Casa Junto Al Mar / at Home by the Ocean, 1 vol. 2008. (Mi Casa / at Home Ser.). (ENG & SPA., Illus.). 32p. (gr. k-2). lib. bdg. 25.50 *(978-0-7614-2456-7(3)*, 8adb9cd5-03ba-4bd0-ba32-d3cafebd86af) Cavendish Square Publishing LLC.

—Mi Casa Junto Al Mar (at Home by the Ocean), 1 vol. 2008. (Mi Casa (at Home) Ser.). (SPA., Illus.). 32p. (gr. k-2). lib. bdg. 25.50 *(978-0-7614-2377-5(X)*, 484828e8-fece-446c-8a10-a0b4d25f52a8) Cavendish Square Publishing LLC.

Gray, Susan Heinrichs. Oceanography: The Study of Oceans. 2012. (True Book Ser.). (ENG., Illus.). 48p. (J). lib. bdg. 29.00 *(978-0-531-24679-5(5)*, Children's Pr.) Scholastic Library Publishing.

Griffin Burns, Loree. Tracking Trash: Flotsam, Jetsam, & the Science of Ocean Motion. 2010. (Scientists in the Field Ser.). (ENG., Illus.). 64p. (J). (gr. 5-7). pap. 10.99 *(978-0-547-32860-7(5)*, 1416942, Clarion Bks.) HarperCollins Pubs.

Hall, Stephen. Exploring the Oceans. 2012. (ENG., Illus.). 48p. (J). 15.00 *(978-1-899762-79-8(5))* Award Pubns. Ltd. GBR. Dist: Parkwest Pubns., Inc.

Heinrichs, Ann. Oceans. 2009. (21st Century Skills Library: Real World Math Ser.). (ENG.). 32p. (gr. 4-8). lib. bdg. 32.07 *(978-1-60279-496-2(0)*, 200317) Cherry Lake Publishing.

Holmes, Parker. Oceanographers, 1 vol., 1. 2015. (Out of the Lab: Extreme Jobs in Science Ser.). (ENG., Illus.). 32p. (J). (gr. 4-5). pap. 11.00 *(978-1-5081-4517-2(2)*, ecf50f7a-d5ae-42c1-81ad-c02d34f36257, PowerKids Pr.) Rosen Publishing Group, Inc., The.

Holt, Rinehart and Winston Staff. Holt Science & Technology Chapter 13: Earth Science: Exploring the Oceans. 5th ed. 2004. (Illus.). pap. 12.86 *(978-0-03-030319-7(2))* Holt McDougal.

—Holt Science & Technology Chapter 14: Earth Science: Movement of the Ocean. 5th ed. 2004. (Illus.). pap. 12.86 *(978-0-03-030321-0(4))* Holt McDougal.

Hudak, Heather C. Oceans. (Illus.). 32p. (J). 2017. *(978-1-5105-0878-1(3))* 2016. *(978-1-5105-0876-7(7))* SmartBook Media, Inc.

Jakubiak, David J. Protecting Our Planet: What Can We Do about Oil Spills & Ocean Pollution?, 1 vol. 2011. (Protecting Our Planet Ser.). (ENG., Illus.). 24p. (J). (gr. 2-3). lib. bdg. 26.27 *(978-1-4488-4982-6(9)*, 43bf3457-3384-4dc2-a1af-7370a4015eb0) Rosen Publishing Group, Inc., The.

Jedicke, Peter. Exploring the Ocean Depths. 2003. (Hot Science Ser.). (J). lib. bdg. 28.50 *(978-1-58340-367-9(1))* Black Rabbit Bks.

Johnson, Robin. Oceans Inside Out. 2014. (Ecosystems Inside Out Ser.). (ENG., Illus.). 32p. (J). (gr. 4-5). *(978-0-7787-0635-9(4))* Crabtree Publishing Co.

Kalman, Bobbie. Explore Earth's Five Oceans. 2010. (Explore the Continents Ser.). (ENG., Illus.). 32p. (J). (gr. 1-5). lib. bdg. *(978-0-7787-3077-4(8))*; (gr. 2-3). pap. *(978-0-7787-3091-0(3))* Crabtree Publishing Co.

—What Is an Ocean? 2010. (My World Ser.). (ENG.). 24p. (J). (gr. k-3). *(978-0-7787-9515-5(2))*; pap. *(978-0-7787-9540-7(3))* Crabtree Publishing Co.

Kerrod, Robin. Find Out about the Sea: With 20 Projects & More Than 260 Pictures. 2013. (ENG., Illus.). 64p. (J). (gr. 3-7). 9.99 *(978-1-84322-896-7(3))* Anness Publishing GBR. Dist: National Bk. Network.

Koll, Hilary & Mills, Steve. A Math Journey under the Ocean. 2016. (ENG., Illus.). 32p. (J). *(978-0-7787-2315-8(1))* Crabtree Publishing Co.

Kranking, Kathy & Carrano, Matthew T. Swimming with Saurs. 2006. 32p. (J). *(978-0-439-83875-7(4))* Scholastic, Inc.

Levete, Sarah. Save the Oceans. 2011. (ENG.). 24p. (J). pap. *(978-0-7787-7879-0(7))*; (gr. 3-6). *(978-0-7787-7857-8(6))* Crabtree Publishing Co.

Life on an Ocean Planet Laboratory & Activity Manual. 2005. (YA). spiral bd. *(978-1-878663-35-1(6))* Current Publishing Corp.

Llewellyn, Claire. The Sea. 2003. (Starters Ser.). 24p. (J). lib. bdg. 21.35 *(978-1-58340-262-7(4))* Black Rabbit Bks.

Macdonald, Fiona. The Science of Oceans: the Watery Truth about 72 Percent of Our Planet's Surface (the Science of the Earth) (Library Edition) Beach, Bryan, illus. 2018. (Science Of... Ser.). (ENG.). 32p. (J). (gr. 3-7). lib. bdg. 29.00 *(978-0-531-22767-1(7)*, Watts, Franklin) Scholastic Library Publishing.

Make It Work Geography, 4 vol. set. 2003. (gr. 4-8). 59.00 *(978-0-7166-5124-6(6))* World Bk., Inc.

Mara, Wil. The Four Oceans. 2005. (Rookie Read-About Geography Ser.). (ENG., Illus.). 32p. (J). (gr. 1-2). per. 5.95 *(978-0-516-25817-1(6)*, Children's Pr.) Scholastic Library Publishing.

McAneney, Caitie. Freaky Stories from Beneath the Sea, 1 vol. 2015. (Freaky True Science Ser.). (ENG.). 32p. (J). (gr. 4-5). pap. 11.50 *(978-1-4824-2964-0(0)*, f93ef275-ee93-4a0d-948f-7987ea744a4e); lib. bdg. 28.27 *(978-1-4824-2966-4(7)*, 1be3a7af-3193-476a-adb1-8aea41b3e5ab) Stevens, Gareth Publishing LLLP.

Meachen Rau, Dana. Oceans, 1 vol. 2009. (Earth Matters Ser.). (ENG.). 32p. (gr. 1-2). pap. 9.23 *(978-0-7614-3572-3(7)*, 9917d336-6497-45ec-b40b-e80de8d5b877) Cavendish Square Publishing LLC.

Montgomery, Sy. The Octopus Scientists. Ellenbogen, Keith, illus. 2015. (Scientists in the Field Ser.). (ENG.). 80p. (J). (gr. 5-7). 18.99 *(978-0-544-23270-9(4)*, 1564095, Clarion Bks.) HarperCollins Pubs.

Myers, Janet Nuzum. Water Wonders of the World: From Killer Waves to Monsters of the Deep. 2006. (Illus.). 96p. (J). pap. *(978-1-59336-729-9(5))* Mondo Publishing.

National Geographic Learning. Language, Literacy & Vocabulary - Reading Expeditions (Earth Science): Ocean

Exploration. 2007. (Avenues Ser.). (ENG., Illus.). 36p. (J). pap. 20.95 *(978-0-7922-5430-0(9))* CENGAGE Learning.

Nelson, John. Polar Ice Caps in Danger: Expedition to Antarctica. (Jr. Graphic Environmental Dangers Ser.). (ENG.). 24p. (J). 2008. 47.90 *(978-1-61532-097-4(0))* 2007. (Illus.). (gr. 4-4). lib. bdg. 28.93 *(978-1-4042-4227-2(9),* ac33ec7f-2b80-47c4-8b97-183a208ca330) Rosen Publishing Group, Inc., The. (PowerKids Pr.).

Nelson, John & Obregón, José María. Casquetes Polares en Riesgo: Expedición a la Antártida, 1 vol. 2009. (Historietas Juveniles: Peligros Del Medioambiente (Jr. Graphic Environmental Dangers) Ser.). (SPA., Illus.). 24p. (gr. 4-4). pap. 10.60 *(978-1-4358-8475-5(2),* c74f3921-6cd2-4472-a45a-e67eb6168d38); (YA). lib. bdg. 28.93 *(978-1-4358-8474-8(4),* d42799de-cdae-4607-b338-bee86145a376) Rosen Publishing Group, Inc., The.

Nivola, Claire A. Life in the Ocean: The Story of Oceanographer Sylvia Earle, 1 vol. Nivola, Claire A., illus. 2012. (ENG., Illus.). 32p. (J). (gr. -1-3). 19.99 *(978-0-374-38068-7(6),* 900068269, Farrar, Straus & Giroux (BYR)) Farrar, Straus & Giroux.

Ostopowich, Melanie. Oceans, Lakes, & Rivers. 2016. *(978-1-4896-5794-7(0))* Weigl Pubs., Inc.

Padilla-Gamino, Jacqueline L. Kupe & the Corals. Leggitt, Marjorie, illus. 2014. (Long Term Ecological Research Ser.). 32p. (J). (gr. 3-7). 15.95 *(978-1-58979-753-6(1))* Taylor Trade Publishing.

Richmond, Ben. Why Is the Sea Salty? And Other Questions about Oceans. Azhderian, Cecelia, illus. 2014. (Good Question! Ser.). 32p. (J). (gr. 1). pap. 5.95 *(978-1-4549-0677-3(4))* Sterling Publishing Co., Inc.

Riggs, Kate. Oceans. 2016. (Seedlings Ser.). (ENG., Illus.). 24p. (J). (gr. -1-k). *(978-1-60818-743-0(8),* 20739, Creative Education) Creative Co., The.

Romaine, Claire. Oceans, 1 vol. 2017. (Our Exciting Earth! Ser.). (ENG.). 24p. (J). (gr. k-k). pap. 9.15 *(978-1-5382-0969-1(1),* 9bdb52c8-e293-4795-8870-46f30feaa8ea) Stevens, Gareth Publishing LLLP.

Royston, Angela. Ocean Explorer! 2011. (ENG., Illus.). 24p. (J). pap. *(978-0-7787-7864-6(9));* (gr. 3-6). *(978-0-7787-7842-4(8))* Crabtree Publishing Co.

Sheehan, Robert. The Undersea Lab: Exploring the Oceans, 1 vol., 1. 2014. (Discovery Education: Earth & Space Science Ser.). (ENG.). 32p. (gr. 4-5). 28.93 *(978-1-4777-6166-3(7),* 6a769a12-03d4-48cc-a641-d87d763751bd, PowerKids Pr.) Rosen Publishing Group, Inc., The.

Sherwin, Frank. The Ocean Book. 2006. (Wonders of Creation Ser.). 72p. pap. 3.99 *(978-1-893345-62-1(9))* Answers in Genesis.

—The Ocean Book. 2004. (Wonders of Creation Ser.). (Illus.). 80p. (J). 15.99 *(978-0-89051-401-6(1),* Master Books) New Leaf Publishing Group.

Sjonger, Rebecca. Ocean Engineering & Designing for the Deep Sea. 2016. (Engineering in Action Ser.). (ENG., Illus.). 32p. (J). (gr. 5-9). *(978-0-7787-7536-2(4))* Crabtree Publishing Co.

Spilsbury, Louise. What Are Rivers, Lakes, & Oceans?, 1 vol., 1. 2013. (Let's Find Out! Earth Science Ser.). (ENG.). 32p. (gr. 2-3). 27.04 *(978-1-62275-281-2(3),* a6c9cc56-3a58-4842-9d8e-5982216028d9) Rosen Publishing Group, Inc., The.

Staff, Gareth Editorial Staff. Oceans, 1 vol. 2004. (Discovery Channel School Science: Our Planet Earth Ser.). (ENG., Illus.). 32p. (gr. 5-7). lib. bdg. 28.67 *(978-0-8368-3383-6(X),* 3d5033a6-811e-4cdc-9b6e-470b5d10a76d, Gareth Stevens Learning Library) Stevens, Gareth Publishing LLLP.

Sundance/Newbridge LLC Staff. Exploring Our Oceans. 2004. (Reading PowerWorks Ser.). (gr. 1-3). 37.50 *(978-0-7608-9759-1(X));* pap. 6.10 *(978-0-7608-9760-7(3))* Sundance/Newbridge Educational Publishing.

Thompson, Lisa. Wild Waves. 2003. (Real Deal Ser.). (Illus.). 32p. (J). pap. *(978-0-7608-6690-0(2))* Sundance/Newbridge Educational Publishing.

Vogel, Carole Garbuny. Savage Waters. 2003. (Restless Sea Ser.). (ENG., Illus.). 80p. (J). 30.50 *(978-0-531-12321-8(9),* Watts, Franklin) Scholastic Library Publishing.

West, Krista. Hands-on Projects about Oceans. 2009. (Great Earth Science Projects Ser.). 24p. (gr. 3-3). 42.50 *(978-1-61513-112-9(4),* PowerKids Pr.) Rosen Publishing Group, Inc., The.

Wilsdon, Christina. Ultimate Oceanpedia: The Most Complete Ocean Reference Ever. 2016. (ENG., Illus.). 272p. (J). (gr. 3-7). lib. bdg. 34.90 *(978-1-4263-2551-9(7),* National Geographic Children's Bks.) Disney Publishing Worldwide.

Wohlers, Bob. Life on an Ocean Planet Student Text Book. 2005. (Illus.). lib. bdg. *(978-1-878663-34-4(8))* Current Publishing Corp.

Wood, Lisa. Marine Science, Vol. 3. 2005. (ENG.). 80p. 12.95 *(978-1-59363-098-0(0))* Prufrock Pr.

Woodward, John. The Deep, Deep Ocean. 2010. (Oceans Alive! Ser.). (ENG.). 32p. (J). (gr. 4-7). lib. bdg. 28.50 *(978-1-933834-63-4(3),* 16773) Brown Bear Bks.

—Oceans. 2004. (Geography Fact Files Ser.). (J). lib. bdg. 28.50 *(978-1-58340-427-0(9))* Black Rabbit Bks.

—Oceans. (Illus.). 64p. (YA). (gr. 4-18). lib. bdg. 29.95 *(978-1-59389-125-1(3))* Chrysalis Education.

—Under the Waves. 2010. (Oceans Alive! Ser.). (ENG.). 32p. (J). (gr. 4-7). lib. bdg. 28.50 *(978-1-933834-62-7(5),* 16774) Brown Bear Bks.

World Book, Inc. Staff, contrib. by. The Sea & Its Marvels. 2011. (Illus.). 64p. (J). *(978-0-7166-1791-4(9))* World Bk., Inc.

Yomtov, Nelson. Polar Ice Caps in Danger: Expedition to Antarctica, 1 vol. 2007. (Jr. Graphic Environmental Dangers Ser.). (ENG., Illus.). 24p. (gr. 4-4). pap. 10.60 *(978-1-4042-4594-5(4),* 2e1f3a08-4e95-453e-a8e8-627d55881d9f, PowerKids Pr.) Rosen Publishing Group, Inc., The.

Zoehfeld, Kathleen Weidner. How Deep Is the Ocean? Puybaret, Eric, illus. 2016. (Let's-Read-And-Find-Out Science 2 Ser.). (ENG.). 40p. (J). (gr. -1-3). pap. 6.99 *(978-0-06-232819-9(0),* HarperCollins) HarperCollins Pubs.

OCEANOGRAPHY—BIOGRAPHY

Hodgkins, Fran. Earth Heroes: Champions of the Ocean, 1 vol. Arbo, Cris, illus. 2011. 144p. (J). (gr. 5-8). pap. 12.95 *(978-1-58469-119-8(0),* Dawn Pubns.) Sourcebooks, Inc.

Zronik, John Paul & Zronik, John. Jacques Cousteau: Conserving Underwater Worlds. 2007. (In the Footsteps of Explorers Ser.). (ENG., Illus.). 32p. (J). (gr. 3-7). lib. bdg. *(978-0-7787-2419-3(0));* pap. *(978-0-7787-2455-1(7))* Crabtree Publishing Co.

OCEANOGRAPHY—FICTION

Gehl, Laura. Baby Oceanographer. Wiseman, Daniel, illus. 2019. (Baby Scientist Ser.: 1). (ENG.). 22p. (J). (gr. -1 — 1). bds. 8.99 *(978-0-06-284133-9(5),* HarperFestival) HarperCollins Pubs.

Hatton, Libby. Pete Puffin's Wild Ride Cruising Alaska's Currents. Hatton, Libby, illus. 2008. (Illus.). (J). pap. 16.95 *(978-0-930931-92-6(0))* Alaska Geographic Assn.

Osborne, Mary Pope. Dark Day in the Deep Sea. Murdocca, Sal, illus. 2009. (Magic Tree House (R) Merlin Mission Ser.: 11). 144p. (J). (gr. 2-5). 6.99 *(978-0-375-83732-6(9),* Random Hse. Bks. for Young Readers) Random Hse. Children's Bks.

—Dark Day in the Deep Sea. 2009. (Magic Tree House Merlin Missions Ser.: 11). lib. bdg. 16.00 *(978-0-606-01778-7(X))* Turtleback.

Osborne, Mary Pope, et al. Día Negro en el Fondo Del Mar. Murdocca, Sal, illus. 2018. (SPA.). 118p. (J). (gr. 2-4). pap. 6.99 *(978-1-63245-682-3(6))* Lectorum Pubns., Inc.

Ricci, Christine. Dora in the Deep Sea. Roper, Robert, illus. 2003. (Dora the Explorer Ser.: Vol. 3). (ENG.). 24p. (J). pap. 3.99 *(978-0-689-85845-1(0),* Simon Spotlight/Nickelodeon) Simon Spotlight/Nickelodeon.

OCEANOGRAPHY—VOCATIONAL GUIDANCE

Mara, Wil. Deep-Sea Exploration: Science, Technology, Engineering (Calling All Innovators: a Career for You) 2015. (Calling All Innovators: a Career for You Ser.). (ENG., Illus.). 64p. (J). (gr. 5-8). pap. 8.95 *(978-0-531-21173-1(8),* Children's Pr.) Scholastic Library Publishing.

OCEANOLOGY

see Oceanography

OCELOT

Randall, Henry. Ocelots, 1 vol. 2011. (Cats of the Wild Ser.). (ENG.). 24p. (J). (gr. 1-2). pap. 9.25 *(978-1-4488-2623-0(3),* 7d6457dc-2128-4aa9-b69b-c52bdb951d55); lib. bdg. 26.27 *(978-1-4488-2519-6(9),* 9aa2d977-ab2f-4d00-81e0-26ffddb5d4f4) Rosen Publishing Group, Inc., The. (PowerKids Pr.).

—Ocelots: Ocelotes, 1 vol. 2011. (Cats of the Wild / Felinos Salvajes Ser.). (SPA & ENG., Illus.). 24p. (gr. 1-2). lib. bdg. 26.27 *(978-1-4488-3131-9(8),* 1962cd39-79a9-4432-88b7-49c1bac7f1b4) Rosen Publishing Group, Inc., The.

OCELOT—FICTION

Appelt, Kathi. Angel Thieves. (ENG.). 336p. (YA). (gr. 9). 2020. pap. 11.99 *(978-1-4423-3966-8(7),* Atheneum Bks. for Young Readers) 2019. 18.99 *(978-1-4424-2109-7(6),* Atheneum/Caitlyn Dlouhy Books) Simon & Schuster Children's Publishing.

OCTOPUSES

Allyn, Daisy. Deadly Blue-Ringed Octopuses, 1 vol. 2011. (Small but Deadly Ser.). (ENG., Illus.). 24p. (J). (gr. 2-3). pap. 9.15 *(978-1-4339-5736-9(1),* 21824685-f308-4531-8edf-076d62737f94); lib. bdg. 25.27 *(978-1-4339-5734-5(5),* 7388734f-3b0c-4edf-ac39-37f8172b4650) Stevens, Gareth Publishing LLLP. (Gareth Stevens Learning Library).

Andover, Max. Octopuses & Squid. 2011. (Illus.). 16p. (J). pap. *(978-0-545-24792-4(6))* Scholastic, Inc.

Berger, Melvin & Berger, Gilda. Octopus. 2003. (Scholastic Reader Ser.). (Illus.). (J). pap. *(978-0-439-47391-0(8))* Scholastic, Inc.

Blaine, John. The Wailing Octopus: A Rick Brant Science Adventure Story. 2011. 218p. 44.95 *(978-1-258-10006-3(1))* Literary Licensing, LLC.

Claybourne, Anna. Octopuses, 1 vol. 2013. (Animal Abilities Ser.). (ENG.). 32p. (J). (gr. 2-4). pap. 8.95 *(978-1-4109-5247-9(X),* 122583, Raintree) Capstone.

Dixon, Norma. In Deep with the Octopus, 1 vol. 2013. (Up Close with Animals Ser.). (ENG.). 40p. (J). (gr. 5-8). 19.95 *(978-1-55455-270-2(2),* 5db56385-3b02-4aff-8057-bc5b8b55f514) Trifolium Bks., Inc. CAN. Dist: Firefly Bks., Ltd.

Duhaime, Darla. Octopuses. 2017. (Ocean Animals Ser.). (ENG.). 24p. (gr. k-2). pap. 9.95 *(978-1-68342-423-9(9),* 9781683424239) Rourke Educational Media.

Gaertner, Meg. Mimic Octopus. 2019. (Unique Animal Adaptations Ser.). (ENG., Illus.). 32p. (J). (gr. 4-6). 28.65 *(978-1-5435-7160-8(3),* 140427) Capstone.

Gish, Melissa. Living Wild: Octopuses. 2014. (Living Wild Ser.). (ENG., Illus.). 48p. (J). (gr. 4-7). pap. 12.00 *(978-0-89812-842-0(0),* 21640, Creative Paperbacks) Creative Co., The.

—Octopuses. 2013. (Living Wild Ser.). (ENG., Illus.). 48p. (J). (gr. 4-7). 35.65 *(978-1-60818-289-3(4),* 21639, Creative Education) Creative Co., The.

Gray, Leon. Giant Pacific Octopus: The World's Largest Octopus. 2013. (Even More SuperSized! Ser.). 24p. (J). (gr. k-3). lib. bdg. 26.99 *(978-1-61772-730-6(X))* Bearport Publishing Co., Inc.

The Greedy Gray Octopus: 6 Small Books. (gr. k-3). 24.00 *(978-0-7635-6235-9(1))* Rigby Education.

Greenburg, Nicki. An Octopus Has Deadly Spit. Greenburg, Nicki, illus. 2007. (It's True! Ser.). (ENG., Illus.). 96p. (J). (gr. 3-6). 18.69 *(978-1-55451-078-8(3),* 9781554510788) Annick Pr., Ltd. CAN. Dist: Children's Plus, Inc.

Gross, Miriam J. The Octopus. (Weird Sea Creatures Ser.). 24p. (gr. 3-3). 2009. 42.50 *(978-1-60854-755-5(8))* 2005. (ENG., Illus.). (J). lib. bdg. 26.27 *(978-1-4042-3188-7(9),* 930cefed-0443-46bb-a119-22d927628be2) Rosen Publishing Group, Inc., The. (PowerKids Pr.).

Grunbaum, Mara. Octopuses: Clever Ocean Creatures (Nature's Children) (Library Edition) 2019. (Nature's Children, Fourth Ser.). (ENG., Illus.). 48p. (J). (gr. 3-5). lib. bdg. 30.00 *(978-0-531-22992-7(0),* Children's Pr.) Scholastic Library Publishing.

Hansen, Grace. Octopuses, 1 vol. 2015. (Ocean Life Ser.). (ENG.). 24p. (J). (gr. -1-2). lib. bdg. 32.79 *(978-1-62970-710-5(4),* 17219, Abdo Kids) ABDO Publishing Co.

—Octopuses. 2017. (Ocean Life Ser.). (ENG.). 24p. (J). (gr. -1-2). pap. 7.95 *(978-1-4966-1254-0(X),* 135002, Capstone Classroom) Capstone.

—Pulpos (Octopuses), 1 vol. 2016. (Vida en el Océano (Ocean Life) Ser.). (SPA., Illus.). 24p. (J). (gr. -1-2). lib. bdg. 32.79 *(978-1-68080-747-9(1),* 22656, Abdo Kids) ABDO Publishing Co.

Herriges, Ann. Octopuses. 2006. (Oceans Alive Ser.). (ENG., Illus.). 24p. (J). (gr. k-3). lib. bdg. 26.95 *(978-1-60014-019-8(X))* Bellwether Media.

Jackson, Ellen. Octopuses One to Ten. Page, Robin, illus. 2016. (ENG.). 32p. (J). (gr. -1-3). 18.99 *(978-1-4814-3182-8(X),* Beach Lane Bks.) Beach Lane Bks.

James, Helen Foster. Discover Octopuses. 2015. (21st Century Basic Skills Library: Splash! Ser.). (ENG., Illus.). 24p. (J). (gr. 2-4). pap. 12.79 *(978-1-63362-692-8(X),* 206593) Cherry Lake Publishing.

Jango-Cohen, Judith. Octopuses, 1 vol. 2005. (Animals, Animals Ser.). (ENG., Illus.). 48p. (gr. 5-5). lib. bdg. 32.64 *(978-0-7614-1614-2(5),* abe2b7ad-04fa-4606-b033-c5ce7fc9a733) Cavendish Square Publishing LLC.

John, Gee. The Octopus. 2011. (Power 100 - Marine Life Ser.). 20p. pap. 39.62 *(978-1-61541-238-9(7))* American Reading Co.

Johnson, Gee. The Octopus. Johnson, Gee, illus. 2010. (2G Marine Life Ser.). (ENG., Illus.). 20p. (J). (gr. k-2). pap. 9.60 *(978-1-61541-221-1(2))* American Reading Co.

Johnson, Gee & Sánchez, Lucia M. El Pulpo. 2013. (2G Vida Marina Ser.). (SPA., Illus.). 20p. (J). (gr. k-2). pap. 9.60 *(978-1-61541-452-9(5))* American Reading Co.

Kalman, Bobbie & Sjonger, Rebecca. The Amazing Octopus. 2003. (Living Ocean Ser.). (ENG., Illus.). 32p. (J). (gr. 2-9). pap. *(978-0-7787-1321-0(0))* Crabtree Publishing Co.

Kalman, Bobbie, et al. Les Pieuvres. 2009. (FRE., Illus.). 32p. (J). pap. 9.95 *(978-2-89579-247-5(X))* Bayard Canada Livres CAN. Dist: Crabtree Publishing Co.

LaPlante, Walter. Octopuses, 1 vol. 2019. (Ocean Animals Ser.). (ENG.). 24p. (gr. k-k). pap. 9.15 *(978-1-5382-4461-6(6),* cf6cadad-304f-46f3-94d0-a6936c56f016) Stevens, Gareth Publishing LLLP.

Laughlin, Kara L. Octopuses. 2017. (In the Deep Blue Sea Ser.). (ENG.). 24p. (J). (gr. k-3). lib. bdg. 32.79 *(978-1-5038-1687-9(7),* 211521) Child's World, Inc, The.

Leaf, Christina. Octopuses. 2016. (Ocean Life up Close Ser.). (ENG., Illus.). 24p. (J). (gr. k-3). 26.95 *(978-1-62617-419-1(9),* Blastoff! Readers) Bellwether Media.

Lunis, Natalie. Blue-Ringed Octopus: Small but Deadly. (Afraid of the Water Ser.). 24p. 2016. (ENG.). (J). (gr. 1-6). pap. 7.99 *(978-1-944998-61-5(6))* 2009. (Illus.). (YA). (gr. 2-5). lib. bdg. 26.99 *(978-1-59716-944-8(7))* Bearport Publishing Co., Inc.

Macheske, Felicia. Awesome Arms: Octopus. 2016. (Guess What Ser.). (ENG., Illus.). 24p. (J). (gr. k-2). 30.64 *(978-1-63470-718-3(4),* 207583) Cherry Lake Publishing.

Markle, Sandra. Los Pulpos. Translations.com Staff, tr. from ENG. 2008. (Animales Presa (Animal Prey) Ser.). (SPA.). 40p. (gr. 3-6). 25.26 *(978-0-7613-3898-7(5))* Lerner Publishing Group.

—Los Pulpos (Octopuses) 2009. (SPA.). pap. 46.95 *(978-0-7613-4721-7(6))* Lerner Publishing Group.

—Octopuses. 2008. pap. 46.95 *(978-0-8225-9321-8(1))* 2008. (ENG., Illus.). 40p. (gr. 3-6). per. 7.95 *(978-0-8225-6066-1(6),* First Avenue Editions) 2007. (Illus.). 40p. (J). (gr. 4-7). lib. bdg. 25.26 *(978-0-8225-6063-0(1))* Lerner Publishing Group.

Meachen Rau, Dana. Guess Who Grabs, 1 vol. 2008. (Guess Who? Ser.). (ENG., Illus.). 32p. (gr. k-1). pap. 9.23 *(978-0-7614-3320-0(1),* 2b963369-b816-4192-a8be-5087ee146898) Cavendish Square Publishing LLC.

Meister, Cari. Do You Really Want to Meet an Octopus? Fabbri, Daniele, illus. 2018. (Do You Really Want to Meet ... ? Ser.). (ENG.). 24p. (J). (gr. 1-4). pap. 9.99 *(978-1-68152-315-6(9),* 15042); lib. bdg. *(978-1-68151-395-9(1),* 15036) Amicus.

—Octopuses. 2012. (Illus.). 24p. (J). lib. bdg. 25.65 *(978-1-62031-010-6(4))* Jump! Inc.

Miller, Tori. Octopuses & Squid. 2009. (Freaky Fish Ser.). 24p. (gr. 2-3). 42.50 *(978-1-61512-640-8(6),* PowerKids Pr.); (ENG.). (J). lib. bdg. 26.27 *(978-1-4358-2757-8(0),* a2123354-0798-4fe4-961e-b248ded374cc); (ENG., Illus.). (J). pap. 9.25 *(978-1-4358-3174-2(8),* 875067de-e53e-4298-8a91-c0363376e20e, PowerKids Pr.) Rosen Publishing Group, Inc., The.

Mitchell, Susan K. Biggest vs. Smallest Sea Creatures, 1 vol. 2010. (Biggest vs. Smallest Animals Ser.). (ENG., Illus.). 24p. (gr. k-2). 25.27 *(978-0-7660-3580-5(8),* b870c237-3a34-4d45-82c2-5f3439953602, Enslow Elementary) Enslow Publishing, LLC.

Montgomery, Sy. Inky's Amazing Escape: How a Very Smart Octopus Found His Way Home. Schimler-Safford, Amy, illus. 2018. (ENG.). 32p. (J). (gr. -1-3). 18.99 *(978-1-5344-0191-4(1),* Simon & Schuster/Paula Wiseman Bks.) Simon & Schuster/Paula Wiseman Bks.

—The Octopus Scientists. Ellenbogen, Keith, illus. 2015. (Scientists in the Field Ser.). (ENG.). 80p. (J). (gr. 5-7). 18.99 *(978-0-544-23270-9(4),* 1564095, Clarion Bks.) HarperCollins Pubs.

Octopus. 2004. (J). 5.99 *(978-0-7566-0251-2(3))* Dorling Kindersley Publishing, Inc.

Olsen, Alana. Look Out for the Blue-Ringed Octopus!, 1 vol. 2015. (Surprisingly Scary! Ser.). (ENG., Illus.). 24p. (J). (gr. 2-3). pap. 9.25 *(978-1-4994-0877-5(3),* 2ae52ae4-513f-4695-9c04-a134a487fd80, PowerKids Pr.) Rosen Publishing Group, Inc., The.

Owen, Ruth. Giant Squid & Octopuses, 1 vol., 1. 2014. (Real Life Sea Monsters Ser.). (ENG.). 32p. (J). (gr. 3-3). 28.93 *(978-1-4777-6261-5(2),* afeff637-d0e2-4d3d-bba5-adc88f143e64, PowerKids Pr.) Rosen Publishing Group, Inc., The.

—Octopuses, 1 vol. 2011. (World's Smartest Animals Ser.). (ENG., Illus.). 32p. (J). (gr. 2-3). pap. 12.75 *(978-1-61533-412-4(2),* 71c884d1-235c-412b-bcbb-f744c181c6f8); lib. bdg. 31.27 *(978-1-61533-374-5(6),* c66efec1-fd41-460f-a860-50ea9fba44fe) Rosen Publishing Group, Inc., The. (Windmill Bks.).

Pearce, Kevin. Being an Octopus, 1 vol. 2013. (Can You Imagine? Ser.). (ENG., Illus.). 32p. (J). (gr. 2-3). pap. 11.50 *(978-1-4824-3281-7(1),* 63f20709-31ff-4ff7-8b54-57cd3491c91a) Rosen Publishing Group, Inc., The.

—Being an Octopus, 1 vol., Vol. 1. 2013. (Can You Imagine? Ser.). (ENG., Illus.). 32p. (J). (gr. 2-3). 27.92 *(978-1-4824-0136-3(3),* 5fcc4ee8-7e92-4d98-a5d2-e2c487666c5a) Stevens, Gareth Publishing LLLP.

Phillips, Jillian. What to Doodle? At the Aquarium. 2011. (Dover Doodle Bks.). (ENG., Illus.). 64p. (J). (gr. k-3). pap. 2.50 *(978-0-486-47819-7(X),* 47819X) Dover Pubns., Inc.

Pringle, Laurence. Octopuses! Strange & Wonderful. Henderson, Meryl Learnihan, illus. 2015. (Strange & Wonderful Ser.). (ENG.). 32p. (J). (gr. 2-5). 17.99 *(978-1-59078-928-5(8),* Astra Young Readers) Astra Publishing Hse.

Raum, Elizabeth. Blue-Ringed Octopuses. 2015. (Poisonous Animals Ser.). (ENG., Illus.). 32p. (J). (gr. 2-5). lib. bdg. 19.95 *(978-1-60753-785-4(0),* 15301) Amicus.

Ricciuti, Edward R. Adivina Quién Atrapa / Guess Who Grabs, 1 vol. 2008. (Adivina Quién / Guess Who? Ser.). (ENG & SPA., Illus.). 32p. (gr. k-2). lib. bdg. 25.50 *(978-0-7614-2464-2(4),* 806d2516-de0b-499c-911b-e90f1b239fb8) Cavendish Square Publishing LLC.

—Adivina Quién Atrapa (Guess Who Grabs), 1 vol. 2008. (Adivina Quién (Guess Who?) Ser.). (SPA., Illus.). 32p. (gr. k-2). lib. bdg. 25.50 *(978-0-7614-2383-6(4),* 2432c2fa-766a-48e6-9509-f541a0032e4e) Cavendish Square Publishing LLC.

—Guess Who Grabs, 1 vol. 2005. (Guess Who? Ser.). (ENG., Illus.). 32p. (gr. k-1). lib. bdg. 25.50 *(978-0-7614-1557-2(2),* c8c0cffb-d2f0-4f3e-b153-f490768ac3a2) Cavendish Square Publishing LLC.

Riggs, Kate. Octopuses. (Seedlings Ser.). (ENG., Illus.). 24p. (J). 2017. (gr. -1-k). *(978-1-60818-779-9(9),* 20149, Creative Education) 2016. (gr. 1-3). pap. 10.99 *(978-1-62832-219-4(5),* 20438, Creative Paperbacks) 2016. (gr. 1-4). 28.95 *(978-1-60818-613-6(X),* 20440, Creative Education) Creative Co., The.

—Seedlings: Octopuses. 2017. (Seedlings Ser.). (ENG., Illus.). 24p. (J). (gr. -1-1). pap. 10.99 *(978-1-62832-399-3(X),* 20147, Creative Paperbacks) Creative Co., The.

Roumanis, Alexis. Giant Octopus. 2014. (J). *(978-1-4896-1070-6(7))* Weigl Pubs., Inc.

Schuh, Mari. Octopuses. 2018. (Spot Ocean Animals Ser.). (ENG.). 16p. (J). (gr. -1-2). pap. 7.99 *(978-1-68152-301-9(9),* 15003); lib. bdg. *(978-1-68151-381-2(1),* 14997) Amicus.

Shaffer, Lindsay. Octopuses. 2020. (Animals of the Coral Reef Ser.). (ENG.). 24p. (J). (gr. k-3). lib. bdg. 26.95 *(978-1-64487-133-1(5),* Blastoff! Readers) Bellwether Media.

Shea, Therese M. The Bizarre Life Cycle of an Octopus, 1 vol. 2012. (Strange Life Cycles Ser.). (ENG., Illus.). 24p. (J). (gr. 2-3). 25.27 *(978-1-4339-7055-9(4),* 163b9713-495c-44cb-8e7d-efdcfdd13b33); pap. 9.15 *(978-1-4339-7056-6(2),* 6dcb43f8-5afc-49e9-934a-d60d4f7ac22d) Stevens, Gareth Publishing LLLP. (Gareth Stevens Learning Library).

Shoemaker, Kate. Octopus Ink, 1 vol. 2014. (Nature's Grossest Ser.). (ENG.). 24p. (J). (gr. 1-2). pap. 9.15 *(978-1-4824-1846-0(0),* 4f4cfe3f-6b39-46e7-b6ab-9386d9a435af); (Illus.). 24.27 *(978-1-4824-1845-3(2),* 9dcf7eb5-6d16-4964-b73e-cdadb809a65a) Stevens, Gareth Publishing LLLP.

Siemens, Jared. Octopus. 2017. (Illus.). 24p. (J). *(978-1-5105-0590-2(3))* SmartBook Media, Inc.

Spirn, Michele. Octopuses. 2006. (Smart Animals! Ser.). (Illus.). 32p. (YA). (gr. 2-5). lib. bdg. 28.50 *(978-1-59716-250-0(7))* Bearport Publishing Co., Inc.

Statts, Leo. Octopuses. 2016. (Ocean Animals Ser.). (ENG., Illus.). 24p. (J). (gr. -1-2). lib. bdg. 31.36 *(978-1-68079-913-2(4),* 24130, Abdo Zoom-Launch) ABDO Publishing Co.

Stone, Tanya Lee. Octopuses. 2003. (Wild Wild World Ser.). 24p. (YA). 24.94 *(978-1-56711-817-9(8),* Blackbirch Pr., Inc.) Cengage Gale.

Strain Trueit, Trudi. Octopuses, 1 vol. 2011. (Ocean Life Ser.). (ENG.). 24p. (gr. k-1). 25.50 *(978-0-7614-4892-1(6),* f1b466d4-f1b6-4c17-b2eb-6ad8d124a56b) Cavendish Square Publishing LLC.

Sullivan, Laura L. Blue-Ringed Octopus. 2017. (Toxic Creatures Ser.). (Illus.). 32p. (J). (gr. 3-3). pap. 63.48 *(978-1-5026-2580-9(6),* Cavendish Square) Cavendish Square Publishing LLC.

Terp, Gail. Octopuses. 2022. (Super Sea Creatures Ser.). (ENG.). 32p. (J). (gr. 4-6). *(978-1-62310-283-8(9),* 13460, Bolt) Black Rabbit Bks.

Thomas, Elizabeth. Octopuses. 2014. (21st Century Skills Library: Exploring Our Oceans Ser.). (ENG., Illus.). 32p. (J). (gr. 3-6). 32.07 *(978-1-62431-601-2(8),* 203188) Cherry Lake Publishing.

Wearing, Judy. Octopuses. 2011. (J). (gr. 2-4). pap. 12.95 *(978-1-61690-693-1(6),* AV2 by Weigl); (Illus.). 24p. (gr. 3-6). 27.13 *(978-1-61690-689-4(8))* Weigl Pubs., Inc.

Weber, Valerie J. Octopuses & Squids, 1 vol. 2008. (Animals That Live in the Ocean Ser.). (ENG., Illus.). 24p. (J). (gr. 1-1). lib. bdg. 25.27 *(978-0-8368-9242-0(9),* 4b2b859f-1912-446c-a41a-50ed9e5ab7f3, Weekly Reader Leveled Readers) Stevens, Gareth Publishing LLLP.

—Octopuses & Squids / Pulpos y Calamares, 1 vol. 2008. (Animals That Live in the Ocean / Animales Que Viven en el Océano Ser.). (SPA & ENG.). 24p. (gr. 1-1). (J). lib. bdg. 25.27 *(978-0-8368-9248-2(8),* f7699b10-e49f-41af-b08b-444ac4153781); pap. 9.15 *(978-0-8368-9347-2(6),* ccd18598-1f8a-43f0-866c-53589950c13d) Stevens, Gareth Publishing LLLP. (Weekly Reader Leveled Readers).

M
N
O

OCTOPUSES—FICTION

Aldrich, Sandra D. Trouble in the Park. 2012. 28p. 19.95 (978-1-4626-8818-0(7)) America Star Bks.

—Willie's Lesson. 2012. 28p. 19.95 (978-1-4626-9663-5(5)) America Star Bks.

Anton, Amy Way. Ina the Octopus & Her Shipwreck Adventure. Way, MaryFaye, illus. 2008. 28p. pap. 13.99 (978-1-4389-2177-8(2)) AuthorHouse.

Arroyo, Yvonne. How the Octopus Got Eight Arms: Two Arms Are Never Enough. 2013. (ENG., Illus.). 45p. (J). pap. 23.95 (978-1-4327-9369-2(1)); pap. 31.95 (978-1-4327-9644-0(5)) Outskirts Pr., Inc.

Baker, Keith. My Octopus Arms. Baker, Keith, illus. 2013. (ENG., Illus.). 40p. (J). (gr. -1-3). 18.99 (978-1-4424-5843-7(7), Beach Lane Bks.) Beach Lane Bks.

Baron, Andrew, illus. The Adventures of Octopus Rex. 2003. (J). per. 17.95 (978-0-9760348-0-3(8)) Bh Pubns.

Branam, Lucy. Roof Octopus. Coelho, Rogério, illus. 2018. (ENG.). 32p. (J). (gr. k-3). 17.99 (978-1-58536-997-3(7), 204327) Sleeping Bear Pr.

Brett, Jan. The Mermaid. Brett, Jan, illus. 2017. (Illus.). 32p. (J). (gr. -1 — 1). 19.99 (978-0-399-17072-0(3), G.P. Putnam's Sons Books for Young Readers) Penguin Young Readers Group.

Burroughs, Caleb. Good Night Octopus. Cottage Door Press, ed. Randall, Emma, illus. 2017. (ENG.). 11p. (J). (gr. -1-k). bds. 6.99 (978-1-68052-239-6(6), 1002250) Cottage Door Pr.

—Good Night, Octopus (down Spc'd) An I Can Do It Book. Randall, Emma, illus. 2016. (J). bds. 0.00 (978-1-68052-104-7(7)) Cottage Door Pr.

Calfee, Pat. Issy Books Set 2, 5 bks. Gee, Isybilla, illus. 2013. 60p. (J). pap. 24.95 (978-1-938406-14-0(1), Compass) Raphel Marketing, Inc.

Cazet, Denys. Grandpa Spanielson's Chicken Pox Stories No. 1: The Octopus. Cazet, Denys, illus. 2005. (I Can Read Bks.). (Illus.). 48p. (J). (gr. -1-3). lib. bdg. 16.89 (978-0-06-051089-3(7)) HarperCollins Pubs.

—The Octopus. Cazet, Denys, illus. 2008. (Grandpa Spanielson's Chicken Pox Stories Ser.). (Illus.). (J). (gr. -1-3). pap. 16.95 incl. audio (978-1-4301-0455-1(4));Set. pap. 31.95 incl. audio compact disk (978-1-4301-0460-5(0));Set. pap. 29.95 incl. audio (978-1-4301-0457-5(0)) Live Oak Media.

Cox, Amy. Odetta the Octopus Teacher. 2013. 28p. pap. 24.95 (978-1-63000-491-0(X)) America Star Bks.

Dahl, Michael. The Night Octopus: And Other Scary Tales. Bonet, Xavier, illus. 2017. (Michael Dahl's Really Scary Stories Ser.). (ENG.). 72p. (J). (gr. 1-3). lib. bdg. 25.32 (978-1-4965-4899-3(X), 135651, Stone Arch Bks.) Capstone.

Daniels, Lucy. Oscar's Best Friends. 2005. 57p. (978-0-439-68199-5(5)) Scholastic, Inc.

DeLorge, Jaqueline. Gilfinton under the Sea. 2005. (Illus.). 28p. (J). per. 7.99 (978-1-932338-97-3(7)) Lifevest Publishing, Inc.

Diller, Kevin & Lowe, Justin. Hello, My Name Is Octicorn. Talib, Binny, illus. 2016. (ENG.). 48p. (J). (gr. -1-3). 17.99 (978-0-06-238793-6(6), Balzer & Bray) HarperCollins Pubs.

Douglas, Babette. Oscarpus. Rockwell, Barry, illus. 2006. (Kiss a Me Teacher Creature Stories Ser.). (J). (gr. -1-3). 9.99 (978-1-890343-30-9(7)) Kiss A Me Productions, Inc.

Flaherty, Kathleen Marion. An Octopus Named Mom. Donehey, Jennifer Caulfield, illus. 2012. (ENG.). 32p. (J). 16.95 (978-0-9767276-8-2(4)) Three Bean Pr.

Fraioli, James O. Polar Ice Expedition: With Jean-Michel Cousteau. 2009. (J). (gr. 4-7). (978-1-4236-0550-8(0)) Gibbs Smith, Publisher.

Friendly Octopus. 2004. (J). per. (978-1-57657-373-0(7)) Paradise Pr., Inc.

Gaffney, K. Ollie the Octopus. 2012. 12p. pap. 12.68 (978-1-4669-7023-6(5)) Trafford Publishing.

Gaines, Pat. O. O. Octopus: Sheriff of Blue Ribbon Sound. 2008. (Illus.). 24p. (J). lib. bdg. (978-0-9801376-4-4(0)); per. (978-0-9801376-5-1(9)) Dragonfly Publishing, Inc.

Galloway, Ruth. Clumsy Crab. Galloway, Ruth, illus. 2005. (Illus.). 32p. (J). (gr. -1-2). 15.95 (978-1-58925-050-5(8)) Tiger Tales.

—Tickly Octopus. Galloway, Ruth, illus. 2007. (Illus.). 15.95 (978-1-58925-064-2(8)) Tiger Tales.

Green, Judy. The Little Blue Octopus. 2009. 28p. pap. 21.99 (978-1-4415-3393-7(1)) Xlibris Corp.

Hart, J. Tristan. The Adventures of Friendly & Barnackel: Book 3 Ollie the Octopus. 2011. (ENG.). 32p. pap. 12.77 (978-1-4567-2602-7(1)) AuthorHouse.

Holmes, Steve, illus. Animales Marinos: Mezcla y Diviertete. 2005. (Mezcla y Diviertete Ser.). (SPA.). 5p. (J). (gr. -1-7). (978-970-718-291-2(1), Silver Dolphin en Español) Advanced Marketing, S. de R. L. de C. V.

Kagan, Dale A. Trip into Space. 2004. (ENG.). 30p. per. 13.99 (978-1-4134-5159-7(4)) Xlibris Corp.

Kesinger, Brian. Coloring with Your Octopus: A Coloring Book for Domesticated Cephalopods. 2014. (ENG., Illus.). 48p. pap. 12.00 (978-1-61404-010-1(9)) Baby Tattoo Bks.

Knox, Dahk. Zander, Friend of the Se. 2008. 32p. pap. 7.95 (978-1-58275-229-7(X)) Black Forest Pr.

Lachenmeyer, Nathaniel. Octopus Escapes! Dormer, Frank W., illus. 2018. 32p. (J). (-k). lib. bdg. 16.99 (978-1-58089-795-2(9)) Charlesbridge Publishing, Inc.

Latham, Irene. Love, Agnes: Postcards from an Octopus. Baker, Thea, illus. 2018. (ENG.). 32p. (J). (gr. k-3). 19.99 (978-1-5124-3993-9(2), 6f85c822-9167-442d-b494-39920b7b3efd, Millbrook Pr.) Lerner Publishing Group.

Lee, Shari. Mandie's & Mindie's Adventure under the Sea, 1 vol. 2009. 63p. pap. 19.95 (978-1-4489-9977-4(4)) America Star Bks.

Making Waves. 2004. (J). per. (978-1-57657-460-7(1)) Paradise Pr., Inc.

Mayer, Mercer. Octopus Soup, 0 vols. Mayer, Mercer, illus. 2012. (ENG., Illus.). 24p. (J). (gr. -1-2). 16.99 (978-0-7614-5812-8(3), 9780761458128, Two Lions) Amazon Publishing.

Mcintyre Brister, Mary. Ollie the Orange Octopus. 2009. 24p. pap. 12.99 (978-1-4389-8372-1(7)) AuthorHouse.

Meister, Cari. The Fancy Octopus, 1 vol. Harpster, Steve, illus. 2011. (Ocean Tales Ser.). (ENG.). 32p. (J). (gr. 2-3). lib. bdg. 22.65 (978-1-4342-3201-4(8), 114965, Stone Arch Bks.) Capstone.

Menard, Lucille. The Top of the Bottom: Inky to the Rescue, Volume 1. 2013. 38p. pap. 12.50 (978-0-9887969-6-6(1)) Four Menards, The.

Michie, Brandon J. Ollie the Octopus: Animal Lessons. 2011. 20p. 13.49 (978-1-4567-4782-4(7)) AuthorHouse.

Morano, John. Makoona. 2nd rev. ed. 2005. (Morano Eco-Adventure Ser.: 2). 236p. (YA). (gr. 8-12). per. 14.99 (978-1-59092-111-1(9)) Blue Forge Pr.

—Makoona. Anderson, Sarah, illus. 2017. (John Morano Eco-Adventure Ser.: Vol. 2). (ENG.). (YA). (gr. 8-12). pap. 9.99 (978-1-945760-04-4(4)) Grey Gecko Pr.

October the Octopus: A Huggable Concept Book about the Months of the Year. 2014. (ENG., Illus.). 28p. (J). (gr. -1-k). 24.99 (978-1-4814-2047-1(X), Simon & Schuster/Paula Wiseman Bks.) Simon & Schuster/Paula Wiseman Bks.

Pichard, Alexandra. Pen Pals. Pichard, Alexandra, illus. 2017. (ENG., Illus.). 48p. (J). (gr. -1-2). 17.99 (978-1-4814-7247-0(X), Simon & Schuster/Paula Wiseman Bks.) Simon & Schuster/Paula Wiseman Bks.

Pitcher, Caroline. Nico's Octopus. Mistry, Nilesh, illus. 2003. (ENG.). 32p. (J). (gr. k-3). 15.95 (978-1-56656-483-0(2), Crocodile Bks.) Interlink Publishing Group, Inc.

Pollard, Mary Jean. Octrina the Octopus. 2011. 28p. pap. 15.99 (978-1-4568-4778-4(3)) Xlibris Corp.

Puckett, A. J., creator. If I Had a Pet Octopus. 2005. (Illus.). 24p. (J). (978-0-9764938-0-8(2)) Puckett Publishing, Inc.

Ramos, Angelica. If My Mommy Was an Octopus. 2008. 12p. pap. 24.95 (978-1-60563-821-8(8)) PublishAmerica, Inc.

Random House. Sea Patrol to the Rescue! (PAW Patrol) Lovett, Nate, illus. 2018. (Pictureback(R) Ser.). (ENG.). 24p. (J). (gr. -1-2). pap. 5.99 (978-1-5247-6875-1(8), Random Hse. Bks. for Young Readers) Random Hse. Children's Bks.

Rathmell, Donna & Rathmell, Doreen. Octavia & Her Purple Ink Cloud, 1 vol. McLennan, Connie, illus. 2006. (ENG.). 32p. (J). (gr. -1-2). 15.95 (978-0-9764943-5-5(3)); pap. 9.95 (978-1-60718-586-4(5)) Arbordale Publishing.

Reed, Lynn Rowe. Shark Kiss, Octopus Hug. Cornell, Kevin, illus. 2014. (ENG.). 32p. (J). (gr. -1-3). 14.99 (978-0-06-220320-5(7), Balzer & Bray) HarperCollins Pubs.

Rinker, Sherri Duskey. How to Put an Octopus to Bed: (Going to Bed Book, Read-Aloud Bedtime Book for Kids) Schwarz, Viviane, illus. 2020. (ENG.). 40p. (J). (gr. -1-k). 17.99 (978-1-4521-4010-0(3)) Chronicle Bks. LLC.

Roby, Ian. Surface Diver Tommy & the Sea Critters, 1 vol. 2010. 40p. 24.95 (978-1-4489-6161-0(0)) PublishAmerica, Inc.

Rouss, Sylvia & Avalone, C. The Littlest Fish. 2008. 32p. 12.95 (978-1-934440-53-7(1), Pitspopany Pr.) Simcha Media Group.

Rylant, Cynthia. The Octopus. McDaniels, Preston, illus. 2005. (Lighthouse Family Ser.: 5). (ENG.). 64p. (J). (gr. 1-5). 17.99 (978-0-689-86246-5(6), Simon & Schuster Bks. For Young Readers) Simon & Schuster Bks. For Young Readers.

Shernock, Judith. Sammi the Seahorse. 2012. 28p. pap. 15.99 (978-1-4691-3293-8(1)) Xlibris Corp.

Srinivasan, Divya. Octopus Alone. 2013. (Illus.). 40p. (J). (gr. -1-k). 18.99 (978-0-670-78515-5(6), Viking Books for Young Readers) Penguin Young Readers Group.

Starr, Ringo, pseud. Octopus's Garden. Cort, Ben, illus. 2014. (ENG.). 32p. (J). (gr. -1-3). 19.99 (978-1-4814-0362-7(1), Aladdin) Simon & Schuster Children's Publishing.

Steele, Michael Anthony. Hunt for the Octo-Shark: A 4D Book. Reeves, Pauline, illus. 2018. (Nearly Fearless Monkey Pirates Ser.). (ENG.). 48p. (J). (gr. k-2). lib. bdg. 23.99 (978-1-5158-2680-4(5), 137835, Picture Window Bks.) Capstone.

Strub, Scott Richard. Otto the Outerspace Octopus. 2007. (J). per. 10.00 (978-1-59872-782-1(6)) Instant Pub.

Tauiliili, Pemerika L. The Rat & the Bat: And Other Short Stories. 2009. 88p. pap. 16.99 (978-1-4490-4389-6(5)); pap. 32.49 (978-1-4389-2700-8(2)) AuthorHouse.

Tillworth, Mary. Up in the Air!/under the Waves! (PAW Patrol) Random House, illus. 2018. (Step into Reading Ser.). (ENG.). 48p. (J). (gr. -1-2). pap. 5.99 (978-1-5247-7279-6(8), Random Hse. Bks. for Young Readers) Random Hse. Children's Bks.

Tokuda-Hall, Maggie. Also an Octopus. Davies, Benji, illus. 2016. (ENG.). 32p. (J). (gr. -1-2). 16.99 (978-0-7636-7084-9(7)) Candlewick Pr.

Trimble, Marcia. The Adventure of Pushy Octopus & His Friends. Sprague, Dean, illus. 2005. 18p. (J). (gr. k-2). 4.95 (978-1-891577-61-1(1), SAN2994844) Images Pr.

Ungerer, Tomi. Emile: The Helpful Octopus. 2019. (ENG., Illus.). 32p. (gr. -1-3). 18.95 (978-0-7148-4973-7(1)) Phaidon Pr., Inc.

Velasquez, Eric. Octopus Stew. 2019. (Illus.). 40p. (J). (gr. -1-3). 17.99 (978-0-8234-3754-2(X)) Holiday Hse., Inc.

Voake, Charlotte. Melissa's Octopus & Other Unsuitable Pets. Voake, Charlotte, illus. 2015. (ENG., Illus.). 32p. (J). (gr. -1-2). 16.99 (978-0-7636-7481-6(8)) Candlewick Pr.

Vosailagi, Jo, illus. Pentapus. 2006. 120p. per. 12.56 (978-1-4120-9272-2(8)) Trafford Publishing.

Wrecks, Billy. Crime Wave! 2012. (Step into Reading Level 2 Ser.). lib. bdg. 13.55 (978-0-606-23739-0(9)) Turtleback.

ODYSSEUS (GREEK MYTHOLOGY)

Bornemann Spies, Karen. Mythology of the Iliad & the Odyssey, 1 vol. 2014. (Mythology, Myths, & Legends Ser.). (ENG.). 96p. (gr. 6-7). 31.61 (978-0-7660-6172-9(8), d2f57f38-2bed-4654-ba55-2672efdd2dc9) Enslow Publishing, LLC.

Capaldi, Mario, illus. Odysseus & the Wooden Horse: A Greek Legend. 2003. (Dominie Collection of Myths & Legends). (SPA.). 20p. (J). lib. bdg. (978-0-7685-2425-3(3)) Dominie Pr., Inc.

—Odysseus & the Wooden Horse: A Greek Legend. 2004. (ENG.). 20p. (J). (gr. 3-3). pap. 6.47 net. (978-0-7685-2128-3(9), Dominie Elementary) Savvas Learning Co.

Church, Alfred J. The Story of the Odyssey. 2007. 128p. per. (978-1-4065-1370-7(9)) Dodo Pr.

Church, Alfred John. The Story of the Odyssey. 2004. reprint ed. pap. 19.95 (978-1-4191-8412-3(1)); pap. 1.99 (978-1-4192-8412-0(6)) Kessinger Publishing, LLC.

Claybourne, A. & Khanduri, K. Greek Myths: Ulysses & the Trojan War: Mini-Edition. 2004. (Spotter's Guides). 160p. (J). 8.95 (978-0-7945-0535-6(X)) EDC Publishing.

Colum, Padraic. The Adventures of Odysseus & the Tale of Troy. Pogány, Willy, illus. 2008. 164p. pap. (978-1-4068-2730-9(4)) Echo Library.

—The Adventures of Odysseus & the Tales of Troy. l.t. ed. 2007. (ENG.). 220p. pap. 22.99 (978-1-4346-0648-8(1)) Creative Media Partners, LLC.

—The Children's Homer: The Adventures of Odysseus & the Tale of Troy. 2015. (ENG., Illus.). (J). 25.95 (978-1-298-49026-1(X)) Creative Media Partners, LLC.

—The Children's Homer: The Adventures of Odysseus & the Tale of Troy. 2018. (ENG., Illus.). 176p. (J). 24.68 (978-1-7317-0502-0(6)) 2018. (ENG., Illus.). 176p. (J). pap. 12.62 (978-1-7317-0503-7(4)) 2018. (ENG., Illus.). 176p. (J). 12.64 (978-1-7317-0085-8(7)) 2018. (ENG., Illus.). 176p. (J). pap. 5.85 (978-1-7317-0086-5(5)) 2012. (ENG., Illus.). 176p. (J). pap. 8.50 (978-1-61382-346-0(0)) 2011. 144p. pap. 7.95 (978-1-61382-004-9(6)) Simon & Brown.

—The Children's Homer: The Adventures of Odysseus & the Tale of Troy. Pogany, Willy, illus. 2019. (ENG.). 256p. (J). (gr. 5-9). 18.99 (978-1-5344-5037-0(8), Aladdin) Simon & Schuster Children's Publishing.

Freeberg, Eric, illus. Classic Starts(r): Greek Myths. 2011. (Classic Starts(r) Ser.). 160p. (J). (gr. 2-4). 6.95 (978-1-4027-7312-9(9)) Sterling Publishing Co., Inc.

Haus, Estudio, illus. The Voyages of Odysseus: A Graphic Retelling. 2015. (Ancient Myths Ser.). (ENG.). 32p. (J). (gr. 3-9). lib. bdg. 31.32 (978-1-4914-2076-8(6), 127554, Capstone Pr.) Capstone.

Hoena, Blake. The Epic Adventures of Odysseus: An Interactive Mythological Adventure. Azzalin, Stefano, illus. 2016. (You Choose: Ancient Greek Myths Ser.). (ENG.). 112p. (J). (gr. 3-7). lib. bdg. 32.65 (978-1-4914-8114-1(5), 130605, Capstone Pr.) Capstone.

Homer. The Odyssey. Gelev, Penko & Sidong, Li, illus. 2009. (Barron's Graphic Classics Ser.). (ENG.). (J). (gr. 5-11). lib. bdg. 21.10 (978-1-62765-645-0(6)) Perfection Learning Corp.

Homer & Homer. The Odyssey. Tsilis, Thanos, illus. 2013. (Greek Classics Ser.). (ENG.). 64p. pap. 7.95 (978-1-906230-54-8(4)) Real Reads Ltd. GBR. Dist: Casemate Pubs. & Bk. Distributors, LLC.

Jeffrey, Gary. Odysseus & the Odyssey, 1 vol. Poluzzi, Allesandro, illus. 2012. (Graphic Mythical Heroes Ser.). (ENG.). 24p. (J). (gr. 3-3). pap. 9.15 (978-1-4339-7520-2(3), 7b6f769b-e4a2-4cce-96c5-11d490fca57d); lib. bdg. 26.60 (978-1-4339-7519-6(X), 1a28523a-66aa-4bd7-b045-f657242ee2d6) Stevens, Gareth Publishing LLLP.

Jolley, Dan. Odysseus: Escaping Poseidon's Curse. 2009. pap. 52.95 (978-0-7613-4759-0(3)) Lerner Publishing Group.

—Odysseus: Escaping Poseidon's Curse [a Greek Legend]. Yeates, Thomas, illus. (Graphic Myths & Legends Ser.). (ENG.). 48p. (gr. 4-8). 2015. 21.32 (978-1-4677-5983-0(X), Lerner Digital) 2008. (J). pap. 9.99 (978-0-8225-8515-2(4), 505ea96b-5bd2-457e-96cd-7f6601714bc8, Graphic Universe™) 2007. (J). lib. bdg. 27.99 (978-0-8225-6208-5(1), 25c9157e-a22e-4ccc-a1df-2f21d7df7585, Graphic Universe™) Lerner Publishing Group.

Jonas, Anne. Ulises y Casimiro. (SPA.). 32p. (J). (gr. 2-4). (978-84-8418-043-2(3)) Zendrera Zariquiey, Editorial ESP. Dist: Lectorum Pubns., Inc.

LaFontaine, Bruce. The Adventures of Ulysses. 2014. (Dover Classic Stories Coloring Book Ser.). (ENG., Illus.). 32p. (J). (gr. 4-6). pap. 3.99 (978-0-486-43328-8(5)) Dover Pubns., Inc.

Lamb, Charles. Adventures of Ulysses. 2006. pap. (978-1-4068-1416-3(4)) Echo Library.

Lupton, Hugh & Morden, Daniel. The Adventures of Odysseus. Balit, Christina, illus. 2012. 96p. (J). 23.99 (978-1-84686-703-3(7)) Barefoot Bks., Inc.

Lupton, Hugh, et al. The Adventures of Odysseus. 2006. (ENG., Illus.). 96p. (J). (gr. 3-7). 19.99 (978-1-84148-800-4(3)) Barefoot Bks., Inc.

Osborne, Mary Pope. Tales from the Odyssey, Part 1, 3 vols., Pt. 1. 2010. (Tales from the Odyssey Ser.: 1). (ENG., Illus.). 288p. (J). (gr. 3-7). pap. 8.99 (978-1-4231-2864-9(8)) Little, Brown Bks. for Young Readers.

—Tales from the Odyssey, Part 2, Pt. 2. 2010. (Tales from the Odyssey Ser.: 2). (ENG., Illus.). 304p. (J). (gr. 3-7). pap. 7.99 (978-1-4231-2610-2(6)) Disney Pr.

Pober, Arthur & Freeberg, Eric, illus. Classic Starts(r): the Odyssey. 2011. (Classic Starts(r) Ser.). 160p. (J). (gr. 2-4). 7.99 (978-1-4027-7334-1(X)) Sterling Publishing Co., Inc.

Sutcliff, Rosemary. The Wanderings of Odysseus: The Story of the Odyssey. 2005. (ENG.). 160p. (YA). (gr. 7-8). mass mkt. 8.99 (978-0-553-49482-2(1), Laurel Leaf) Random Hse. Children's Bks.

Takvorian, Nadine, illus. Odysseus & the Cyclops, 1 vol. 2011. (Greek Myths Ser.). (ENG.). 32p. (J). (gr. 3-5). lib. bdg. 29.32 (978-1-4048-6666-9(3), 115020, Picture Window Bks.) Capstone.

Tracy, Kathleen. Odysseus. 2008. (Profiles in Greek & Roman Mythology Ser.). (Illus.). 48p. (J). (gr. 4-7). lib. bdg. 29.95 (978-1-58415-705-2(4)) Mitchell Lane Pubs.

Weiss, Lynne. The Voyage of Odysseus, 1 vol., 1. 2013. (Jr. Graphic Myths: Greek Heroes Ser.). (ENG., Illus.). 24p. (J). (gr. 2-3). 28.93 (978-1-4777-6244-8(2), 3f8ca8c1-a334-42f6-9ebd-99ec51362d09, PowerKids Pr.) Rosen Publishing Group, Inc., The.

OFFICE WORK—TRAINING

see Business Education

OFFICIALS

see Civil Service

see names of countries, cities, etc. and organizations with subdivision Officials and Employees, e.g. United States—Officials and Employees

OGLETHORPE, JAMES EDWARD, 1696-1785

Bennett, Doraine. Tomochichi. 2008. (Illus.). 23p. (J). (978-1-935077-06-0(6)); pap. (978-1-935077-13-8(9)) State Standards Publishing, LLC.

Blackburn, Joyce. James Edward Oglethorpe: Foreword by Eugenia Price. 2004. (ENG., Illus.). 192p. (J). per. 15.95 (978-1-57736-332-3(9)) Turner Publishing Co.

Schwartz, Heather E. Tomochichi: A Chief & a Friend. rev. ed. 2016. (Social Studies: Informational Text Ser.). (ENG., Illus.). 32p. (gr. 2-4). pap. 10.99 (978-1-4938-2556-1(9)) Teacher Created Materials, Inc.

OHIO

Barker, Charles Ferguson. Under Ohio: The Story of Ohio's Rocks & Fossils. 2007. (ENG., Illus.). 56p. (J). (gr. 3-7). 34.95 (978-0-8214-1755-3(X)) Ohio Univ. Pr.

Birle, Pete. On the Hardwood: Cleveland Cavaliers. 2014. (On the Hardwood Ser.). (ENG.). 48p. (gr. 3-8). pap. 8.95 (978-1-61570-901-4(0)) Scobre Pr. Corp.

Birle, Peter. Cleveland Cavaliers. 2014. (On the Hardwood Ser.). 48p. (gr. 3-8). 27.93 (978-1-61570-902-1(9)) Scobre Pr. Corp.

Brown, Dottie. Ohio. (J). 2012. lib. bdg. 25.26 (978-0-7613-4550-3(7), Lerner Pubns.) 2nd exp. rev. ed. 2003. (Illus.). 84p. (gr. 3-6). pap. 6.95 (978-0-8225-4134-9(3)) Lerner Publishing Group.

Hart, Joyce. Ohio, 1 vol. Santoro, Christopher, illus. 2006. (It's My State! (First Edition)(r) Ser.). (ENG.). 80p. (gr. 4-4). lib. bdg. 34.07 (978-0-7614-1907-5(1), dcefea6f-bbb3-4726-9801-f9a319f5c01f) Cavendish Square Publishing LLC.

Houghton, Gillian. Mildred Taylor, 1 vol. 2004. (Library of Author Biographies Ser.). (ENG., Illus.). 112p. (YA). (gr. 5-8). 39.80 (978-1-4042-0330-3(3), c1c82d6d-d91e-46c4-bb72-3f8d342b93b0) Rosen Publishing Group, Inc., The.

Lew, Kristi. Ohio: Past & Present. 2009. (J). 70.50 (978-1-4358-5571-7(X)); (ENG.). 48p. (J). (gr. 5-5). pap. 12.75 (978-1-4358-5570-0(1), c84846d4-a547-42df-8067-3d937723b382); (ENG., Illus.). 48p. (YA). (gr. 5-5). lib. bdg. 34.47 (978-1-4358-5286-0(9), af4b976b-3b7e-48cc-9401-0c0f96406194) Rosen Publishing Group, Inc., The. (Rosen Reference).

Lusted, Marcia Amidon. Ohio: The Buckeye State, 1 vol. 2009. (Our Amazing States Ser.). (ENG., Illus.). 24p. (J). (gr. 3-3). pap. 9.25 (978-1-4358-3370-8(8), e15d2f76-7937-4b58-beba-ae604f69f143); lib. bdg. 26.27 (978-1-4042-8122-6(3), a4b902e6-bd09-4822-ab70-da559c654f0b) Rosen Publishing Group, Inc., The. (PowerKids Pr.).

Marsh, Carole. Ohio Current Events Projects: 30 Cool, Activities, Crafts, Experiments & More for Kids to Do to Learn about Your State! 2003. (Ohio Experience Ser.). 32p. (gr. k-5). pap. 5.95 (978-0-635-02054-3(8), Marsh, Carole Bks.) Gallopade International.

—Ohio Experience Book (HC) 2004. 64p. 29.95 (978-0-635-02505-0(1)) Gallopade International.

—Ohio Experience Book (PB) 2004. 64p. pap. 14.95 (978-0-635-02504-3(3)) Gallopade International.

—Ohio Geography Projects: 30 Cool, Activities, Crafts, Experiments & More for Kids to Do to Learn about Your State! 2003. (Ohio Experience Ser.). 32p. (gr. k-5). pap. 5.95 (978-0-635-01854-0(3), Marsh, Carole Bks.) Gallopade International.

—Ohio Government Projects: 30 Cool, Activities, Crafts, Experiments & More for Kids to Do to Learn about Your State! 2003. (Ohio Experience Ser.). 32p. (gr. k-5). pap. 5.95 (978-0-635-01954-7(X), Marsh, Carole Bks.) Gallopade International.

—Ohio History Projects: 30 Cool, Activities, Crafts, Experiments & More for Kids to Do to Learn about Your State! 2003. (Ohio Experience Ser.). 32p. (gr. k-5). pap. 5.95 (978-0-635-01804-5(7), Marsh, Carole Bks.) Gallopade International.

—Ohio People Projects: 30 Cool, Activities, Crafts, Experiments & More for Kids to Do to Learn about Your State! 2003. (Ohio Experience Ser.). 32p. (gr. k-5). pap. 5.95 (978-0-635-02004-8(1), Marsh, Carole Bks.) Gallopade International.

—Ohio Symbols & Facts Projects: 30 Cool, Activities, Crafts, Experiments & More for Kids to Do to Learn about Your State! 2003. (Ohio Experience Ser.). 32p. (gr. k-5). pap. 5.95 (978-0-635-01904-2(3), Marsh, Carole Bks.) Gallopade International.

—Ohio's Big Activity Book. 2004. (Ohio Experience! Ser.). (Illus.). 96p. (J). (gr. 2-6). pap. 9.95 (978-0-7933-9464-7(3)) Gallopade International.

Mattern, Joanne. Cuyahoga Valley National Park (Rookie National Parks) (Library Edition) 2018. (Rookie National Parks Ser.). (ENG., Illus.). 32p. (J). (gr. 1-2). lib. bdg. 25.00 (978-0-531-12652-3(8), Children's Pr.) Scholastic Library Publishing.

Murray, Julie. Ohio, 1 vol. 2006. (Buddy Book Ser.). (ENG., Illus.). 32p. (gr. 2-4). 27.07 (978-1-59197-694-3(4), Buddy Bks.) ABDO Publishing Co.

Rexroth, Sharon. Ohio from the Sky. 2006. (ENG., Illus.). (J). 9.95 (978-1-57166-420-4(3)) Quixote Pr.

Roe-Pimm, Nancy. Colo's Story. 2011. (ENG.). 80p. (gr. 4-8). 18.95 (978-0-9841554-4-6(9)); pap. 8.95 (978-0-9841554-5-3(7)) Columbus Zoo & Aquarium, The.

Schonberg, Marcia. The Ohio Reader. Darnell, K. L., illus. rev. ed. 2007. (State/Country Readers Ser.). (ENG.). 96p. (J). (gr. 1-4). 12.95 (978-1-58536-321-6(9), 202125) Sleeping Bear Pr.

Sherrow, Victoria. Ohio, 1 vol. 2nd rev. ed. 2008. (Celebrate the States (Second Edition) Ser.). (ENG.). 144p. (gr. 6-6). lib. bdg. 39.79 (978-0-7614-2558-8(6), 27bd0007-e74c-4e9a-82c9-7f3cbbf2db2e) Cavendish Square Publishing LLC.

Swainston, Jeani. Grandma Stuff: ... it's what love Is made Of. 2006. (J). (978-0-9791384-0-9(X)) Rock Cliff Media.

Taylor-Butler, Christine. Ohio. 2007. (Rookie Read-About Geography Ser.). (Illus.). 31p. (J). (gr. 1-2). 20.50 (978-0-531-12573-1(4), Children's Pr.) Scholastic Library Publishing.

Way, Jennifer. Ohio. 2009. (Bilingual Library of the United States of America Ser.). (ENG & SPA.). 32p. (gr. 2-2). 47.90 (978-1-60853-379-4(4), Editorial Buenas Letras) Rosen Publishing Group, Inc., The.

—Ohio, 1 vol. Brusca, Maria Cristina, tr. 2005. (Bilingual Library of the United States of America Ser.: Set 2). (ENG & SPA., Illus.). 32p. (J). (gr. 2-2). lib. bdg. 28.93

(978-1-4042-3100-9(5), d2d20a18-9b16-41f6-9789-6f47ca668b0e) Rosen Publishing Group, Inc., The.

Weintraub, A. How to Draw Ohio's Sights & Symbols. 2009. (Kid's Guide to Drawing America Ser.). 32p. (gr. k-k). 50.50 *(978-1-61511-088-9(7),* PowerKids Pr.) Rosen Publishing Group, Inc., The.

Woodyard, Chris. Haunted Ohio V: 200 Years of Ghosts. 2003. (Illus.). 240p. pap. *(978-0-9628472-8-8(3))* Kestrel Pubns.

OHIO—BIOGRAPHY

Georgiady, Nicholas P., et al. Ohio Men, Vol. 2. Collins, Julia B., illus. 2nd rev. ed. Date not set. 44p. (J). (gr. 4-8). pap. 4.50 *(978-0-917961-04-5(8))* Argee Pubs.

Huey, Lois Miner. Floodwaters & Flames: The 1913 Disaster in Dayton, Ohio. 2016. (ENG., Illus.). 56p. (J). (gr. 4-8). E-Book 50.65 *(978-1-4677-9728-3(6),* Millbrook Pr.) Lerner Publishing Group.

Mangal, Mélina. Mildred Taylor. 2004. (Classic Storytellers Ser.). (Illus.). 48p. (J). (gr. 4-8). lib. bdg. 29.95 *(978-1-58415-311-5(3))* Mitchell Lane Pubs.

Sims, Rudine. Bishop Daniel A. Payne: Great Black Leader. 2009. (Illus.). 70p. (J). (gr. 3-7). pap. 12.95 *(978-1-933491-15-8(9))* Just Us Bks., Inc.

Sowash, Rick. Heroes of Ohio: 23 True Tales of Courage & Character. 2003. (J). 19.95 *(978-0-9762412-5-6(0))*; pap. 11.95 *(978-0-9762412-4-9(2))* Sowash, Rick Publishing Co.

—Heroes of Ohio Coloring Book. 2003. (J). 5.95 *(978-0-9762412-6-3(9))* Sowash, Rick Publishing Co.

Tait, Leia. Emi the Sumatran Rhino. 2008. (Inspiring Animals Ser.). (Illus.). 24p. (J). (gr. 2-4). pap. 8.95 *(978-1-59036-857-2(6))*; lib. bdg. 24.45 *(978-1-59036-856-5(8))* Weigl Pubs., Inc.

Williams, Dave. Windgalore Farm. 2005. (Illus.). 182p. pap. 21.95 *(978-0-937921-56-2(4))* Acorn Publishing.

OHIO—FICTION

Adams, James D. Creepy Campfire Tales: Halloween Campout, Vol. 1. 2008. 132p. (J). per. 12.95 *(978-1-60404-103-3(X))* Owl Creek Media Ltd.

—Creepy Campfire Tales Vol. 1: Halloween Campout. 2008. 132p. (YA). 26.95 *(978-1-60404-104-0(8))* Owl Creek Media Ltd.

Alpine, Rachele. A Void the Size of the World. 2017. (ENG., Illus.). 368p. (YA). (gr. 9). 17.99 *(978-1-4814-8571-5(7),* Simon Pulse) Simon Pulse.

Altsheler, Joseph A. The Border Watch: A Story of the Great Chief's Last Stand. 2008. 320p. pap. *(978-1-4099-0579-0(9))* Dodo Pr.

—The Border Watch: A Story of the Great Chief's Last Stand. 2008. 232p. pap. *(978-1-84830-132-0(4))* Echo Library.

—The Border Watch: A Story of the Great Chief's Last Stand. 2010. (Young Trailers Ser.: Vol. 8). (Illus.). 206p. (J). (gr. 4-7). reprint ed. pap. 20.31 *(978-1-153-78841-0(1))* General Bks. LLC.

—The Border Watch: A Story of the Great Chief's Last Stand. 2012. (Young Trailers Ser.: Vol. 8). 340p. (J). (gr. 4-7). reprint ed. pap. *(978-3-8472-2486-0(7))* tredition Verlag.

Anderson, Jennifer. Honey Creek Royalty. 2013. 246p. pap. 12.99 *(978-1-62237-148-8(8))* Turquoise Morning Pr.

Anderson, Laurie Halse. Twisted. 2008. (ENG.). 304p. (YA). (gr. 7-18). 10.99 *(978-0-14-241184-1(1),* Penguin Books) Penguin Young Readers Group.

Aryal, Aimee. Hello, Brutus! De Angel, Miguel & Moore, D., illus. 2006. 24p. (J). lib. bdg. 14.95 *(978-1-932888-51-5(9))* Amplify Publishing Group.

Ashford, Rachel. My First Santa's Coming to Ohio. Dunn, Robert, illus. 2015. (Santa Claus Is on His Way Ser.). (ENG.). 18p. (J). (gr. -1-k). bds. 9.99 *(978-1-4926-2876-7(X),* Hometown World) Sourcebooks, Inc.

Barker, Charles Ferguson. Under Ohio: The Story of Ohio's Rocks & Fossils. 2016. (ENG.). 56p. (J). (gr. 3-8). pap. 17.95 *(978-0-8214-2195-6(6))* Ohio Univ. Pr.

Barnes, John. Tales of the Madman Underground. 2011. (ENG.). 544p. (YA). (gr. 9-18). pap. 9.99 *(978-0-14-241702-7(5),* Speak) Penguin Young Readers Group.

Basham, Tom. Accidental Evie. Calvert, Lissa, illus. 2012. 120p. *(978-1-77097-373-2(7))*; pap. *(978-1-77097-374-9(5))* FriesenPress.

Beil, Michael D. Summer at Forsaken Lake. Kneen, Maggie, illus. 2013. (ENG.). 336p. (J). (gr. 5). pap. 10.99 *(978-0-375-86496-4(2),* Yearling) Random Hse. Children's Bks.

Berten, Jinny Powers & Holt, Norah. Littsie of Cincinnati. 2003. (Illus.). 125p. (J). per. 9.95 *(978-0-9724421-0-7(3))* Fountain Square Publishing.

Bogel, Rachel Anne. A Ride on the Monster's Back. Greenfelder, Jill, illus. 2008. 28p. pap. 15.99 *(978-1-59858-752-4(8))* Dog Ear Publishing, LLC.

Borntrager, Mary Christner. Andy. 2015. (Ellie's People Ser.: Vol. 6). (ENG.). 200p. (YA). (gr. 7-18). pap. 9.99 *(978-0-8361-3633-3(0))* Herald Pr.

—Ellie. 2014. (Ellie's People, Book One Ser.: Vol. 1). (ENG.). 193p. (J). (gr. 3-7). pap. 9.99 *(978-0-8361-3468-1(0))* Herald Pr.

—Rebecca. 2014. (Ellie's People, Book Two Ser.: Vol. 2). (ENG.). 234p. (J). (gr. 4-7). pap. 9.99 *(978-0-8361-3500-8(8))* Herald Pr.

Bowditch, Eden Unger. The Atomic Weight of Secrets or the Arrival of the Mysterious Men in Black. 2011. (Young Inventors Guild Ser.: 1). (ENG.). 320p. (YA). 19.95 *(978-1-61088-002-2(1),* 3affde56-4139-4a62-9c5d-612313bb8c2d) Bancroft Pr.

Brenner, Vida. The Magic Music Shop. Sharp, Mary, ed. Sharpnack, Joe, illus. 2013. 102p. pap. 12.95 *(978-1-57216-094-1(2))* Penfield Bks.

Brunstetter, Wanda E. Humble Pie. Madden, Colleen M., illus. 2014. 158p. (J). *(978-1-63058-967-7(5))* Barbour Publishing, Inc.

Charlton-Trujillo, E. E. Fat Angie. 2013. (ENG.). 272p. (YA). (gr. 9). 16.99 *(978-0-7636-6119-9(8))* Candlewick Pr.

Clements, Andrew. Lost & Found. Elliott, Mark, illus. 2010. (ENG.). 192p. (J). (gr. 3-7). pap. 7.99 *(978-1-4169-0986-6(9),* Atheneum Bks. for Young Readers) Simon & Schuster Children's Publishing.

Cohen-Spence, Susan. An Amazing Adventure Back in Time. Scott, Susan, illus. 2013. 32p. pap. 14.99 *(978-0-9886360-4-0(2))* Kids At Heart Publishing, LLC.

Coolidge, Susan. What Katy Did. 2012. 246p. pap. *(978-1-78139-262-1(5))* Benediction Classics.

—What Katy Did. 2012. 302p. pap. 29.75 *(978-1-286-07372-8(3))* 2012. 300p. pap. 29.75 *(978-1-286-00091-5(2))* 2011. 290p. (gr. 3-7). pap. 28.75 *(978-1-179-65265-8(7))* 2010. (ENG.). 282p. (gr. 3-7). pap. 28.75 *(978-1-177-27477-7(9))* 2010. 302p. pap. 29.75 *(978-1-145-74830-9(9))* 2008. 164p. (gr. 4-7). 25.99 *(978-0-554-28634-1(3))* 2007. (ENG.). 144p. pap. 18.99 *(978-1-4346-5943-9(7))* 2007. (ENG.). 160p. pap. 21.99 *(978-1-4346-5944-6(5))* Creative Media Partners, LLC.

—What Katy Did. 2007. (ENG.). 148p. per. *(978-1-4065-1527-5(2))* Dodo Pr.

—What Katy Did. 2006. (Dover Children's Classics Ser.). (ENG., Illus.). 160p. (J). (gr. 3-8). per. 6.95 *(978-0-486-44760-5(X))* Dover Pubns., Inc.

—What Katy Did. 2007. (ENG.). 104p. per. *(978-1-4068-4855-7(7))* Echo Library.

—What Katy Did. 2010. (Illus.). 92p. (gr. 3-7). pap. 19.99 *(978-1-153-74507-9(0))* 2009. 104p. pap. 6.40 *(978-0-217-53637-0(9))* General Bks. LLC.

—What Katy Did. 2010. 132p. pap. *(978-1-4076-5115-6(3))* HardPr.

—What Katy Did. Ledyard, Addie, illus. 284p. 2010. 35.16 *(978-1-163-85079-4(9))* 2010. pap. 23.16 *(978-1-163-77965-1(2))* 2007. 43.95 *(978-0-548-53870-8(0))* 2007. per. 28.95 *(978-0-548-48700-6(6))* Kessinger Publishing, LLC.

—What Katy Did. 2013. (Vintage Children's Classics Ser.). (Illus.). 256p. (J). (gr. 4-7). pap. 12.99 *(978-0-09-957312-8(1))* Penguin Random Hse. GBR. Dist: Independent Pubs. Group.

—What Katy Did. 2007. (ENG.). 192p. pap. 12.45 *(978-1-60424-403-8(8),* Bk. Jungle) Standard Publications, Inc.

—What Katy Did. 2010. 144p. pap. 4.99 *(978-1-61720-100-4(6))* Wilder Pubns., Corp.

—What Katy Did. 2011. 162p. (gr. 3-7). pap. *(978-3-8424-6664-7(1))* tredition Verlag.

Coolidge, Susan & Ledyard, Addie. What Katy Did. 2010. (ENG.). 292p. pap. 28.75 *(978-1-172-34659-2(3))* Creative Media Partners, LLC.

Cooper, Jennifer. Guardian Angel. 2009. 155p. pap. 12.87 *(978-0-557-09330-4(9))* Lulu Pr., Inc.

Cvetkovic, Judith. Mandy & Star's Sheep Ranch Getaway, 1 vol. 2010. 108p. pap. 19.95 *(978-1-4489-5673-9(0))* America Star Bks.

DeSio, Delores. Annie's Journey Through the Golden Door, 1 vol. 2009. 114p. pap. 19.95 *(978-1-4489-8470-1(X))* America Star Bks.

Draper, Sharon M. Blended. (ENG.). 320p. (J). (gr. 3-7). 2020. pap. 8.99 *(978-1-4424-9501-2(4),* Atheneum Bks. for Young Readers) 2018. (Illus.). 17.99 *(978-1-4424-9500-5(6),* Atheneum/Caitlyn Dlouhy Books) Simon & Schuster Children's Publishing.

—Double Dutch. 2004. 183p. (gr. 6-9). 17.00 *(978-0-7569-2934-3(2))* Perfection Learning Corp.

—Double Dutch. 2004. (ENG.). 192p. (J). (gr. 5-9). pap. 7.99 *(978-0-689-84231-3(7),* Atheneum Bks. for Young Readers) Simon & Schuster Children's Publishing.

Evatt, Harriet. The Secret of the Old Coach Inn. Stone, David, illus. 2011. 190p. 42.95 *(978-1-258-08239-0(X))* Literary Licensing, LLC.

Farquhar, Polly. Itch. 2020. (ENG.). 256p. (J). (gr. 3-7). 17.99 *(978-0-8234-4552-3(6))* Holiday Hse., Inc.

FitzGerald, Dawn. Getting in the Game. 2007. (ENG.). 144p. (J). (gr. 4-8). pap. 16.99 *(978-0-312-37753-3(3),* 900049148) Square Fish.

—Soccer Chick Rules. 2007. (ENG.). 160p. (J). (gr. 5-9). per. 16.99 *(978-0-312-37662-8(6),* 900048593) Square Fish.

Gabel, Stacey. The New Blue Tractor. Neuman, Richard, illus. 2007. 24p. per. 13.95 *(978-1-59858-424-0(3))* Dog Ear Publishing, LLC.

Garrott, Dawn E. How Riley Tamed the Invisible Monster. Mazibuko, Luthando, illus. 2009. (How Riley Ser.). (ENG.). 65p. (J). (gr. 2-7). pap. 9.95 *(978-0-87743-709-3(2))* Baha'i Publishing.

Goon, Geraldine. Grandma Tells Dozens of Stories. 2008. 64p. pap. *(978-1-84748-515-1(4))* Athena Pr.

Greenburg, Dan. Secrets of Dripping Fang, Book Six: Attack of the Giant Octopus. Fischer, Scott M., illus. 2007. (Secrets of Dripping Fang Ser.: Bk. 6). (ENG.). 160p. (J). (gr. 3-7). 12.99 *(978-0-15-206041-1(3),* 1198144, Clarion Bks.) HarperCollins Pubs.

—Secrets of Dripping Fang, Book Three: The Vampire's Curse, Bk. 3. Fischer, Scott M., illus. 2006. (Secrets of Dripping Fang Ser.: Bk. 3). (ENG.). 144p. (J). (gr. 3-7). 12.99 *(978-0-15-205469-4(3),* 1196455, Clarion Bks.) HarperCollins Pubs.

—Secrets of Dripping Fang, Book Two: Treachery & Betrayal at Jolly Days. Fischer, Scott M., illus. 2006. (Secrets of Dripping Fang Ser.: Bk. 2). (ENG.). 144p. (J). (gr. 3-7). 12.99 *(978-0-15-205463-2(4),* 1196437, Clarion Bks.) HarperCollins Pubs.

Haddix, Margaret Peterson. Full Ride. 2014. (ENG.). 368p. (YA). (gr. 7). pap. 12.99 *(978-1-4424-4279-5(4),* Simon & Schuster Bks. For Young Readers) Simon & Schuster Bks. For Young Readers.

—Takeoffs & Landings. 2004. 201p. (gr. 5-9). 17.00 *(978-0-7569-4255-7(1))* Perfection Learning Corp.

Halse Anderson, Laurie. Twisted. 2014. (ENG.). 288p. (YA). (gr. 7-12). 14.24 *(978-1-63245-343-3(6))* Lectorum Pubns., Inc.

—Twisted. 2011. 11.04 *(978-0-7848-3388-9(5),* Everbind) Marco Bk. Co.

—Twisted. l.t. ed. 2007. (Literacy Bridge Young Adult Ser.). 299p. (YA). (gr. 7-12). 23.95 *(978-0-7862-9885-3(5))* Thorndike Pr.

Hamilton, Virginia. The House of Dies Drear. 8.97 *(978-0-13-437491-8(6))* Prentice Hall PTR.

—M. C. Higgins, the Great. 2006. 271p. (gr. 8-12). 18.00 *(978-0-7569-6809-0(7))* Perfection Learning Corp.

—M. C. Higgins, the Great. 3rd ed. (J). pap. 3.95 *(978-0-13-800137-7(5))*; pap. 23.70 *(978-0-13-620220-2(9))* Prentice Hall (Schl. Div.).

—M. C. Higgins, the Great. 2006. (ENG., Illus.). 288p. (J). (gr. 3-7). pap. 7.99 *(978-1-4169-1407-5(2),* Aladdin) Simon & Schuster Children's Publishing.

Harwood, Kelsey. Still Alive. 2012. 144p. pap. 9.99 *(978-1-60820-746-6(3))* MLR Pr., LLC.

Hayes, Christine. Mothman's Curse. 2016. (J). lib. bdg. 18.40 *(978-0-606-39560-1(1))* Turtleback.

Holm, M. S. How Mohammed Saved Miss Liberty: The Story of a Good Muslim Boy. 2008. (ENG., Illus.). 270p. (YA). (gr. 7-12). pap. 12.00 *(978-0-9796199-0-8(4),* Sentry Bks.) Great West Publishing.

Horvath, Polly. Very Rich. 2018. 304p. (J). (gr. 3-7). 17.99 *(978-0-8234-4028-3(1),* Margaret Ferguson Books) Holiday Hse., Inc.

Jacobs, Lily. The Littlest Bunny in Cincinnati: An Easter Adventure. Dunn, Robert, illus. 2015. (Littlest Bunny Ser.). (ENG.). 32p. (J). (gr. -1-3). 9.99 *(978-1-4926-1054-0(2),* Hometown World) Sourcebooks, Inc.

—The Littlest Bunny in Ohio: An Easter Adventure. Dunn, Robert, illus. 2015. (Littlest Bunny Ser.). (ENG.). 32p. (J). (gr. -1-3). 9.99 *(978-1-4926-1162-2(X),* Hometown World) Sourcebooks, Inc.

James, Eric. Santa's Sleigh Is on Its Way to Cincinnati: A Christmas Adventure. Dunn, Robert, illus. 2016. (Santa's Sleigh Is on Its Way Ser.). (ENG.). 32p. (J). (gr. k-2). 12.99 *(978-1-4926-4324-1(6),* 9781492643241, Hometown World) Sourcebooks, Inc.

—Santa's Sleigh Is on Its Way to Ohio: A Christmas Adventure. Dunn, Robert, illus. 2015. (Santa's Sleigh Is on Its Way Ser.). (ENG.). 32p. (J). (gr. k-2). 12.99 *(978-1-4926-2742-5(9),* Hometown World) Sourcebooks, Inc.

—The Spooky Express Cincinnati. Piwowarski, Marcin, illus. 2017. (Spooky Express Ser.). (ENG.). 32p. (J). (gr. k-6). 9.99 *(978-1-4926-5349-3(7),* Hometown World) Sourcebooks, Inc.

—The Spooky Express Ohio. Piwowarski, Marcin, illus. 2017. (Spooky Express Ser.). (ENG.). 32p. (J). (gr. k-6). 9.99 *(978-1-4926-5388-2(8),* Hometown World) Sourcebooks, Inc.

—Tiny the Cincinnati Easter Bunny. 2018. (Tiny the Easter Bunny Ser.). (ENG.). 40p. (J). (gr. k-3). 9.99 *(978-1-4926-5916-7(9),* Hometown World) Sourcebooks, Inc.

—Tiny the Ohio Easter Bunny. 2018. (Tiny the Easter Bunny Ser.). (ENG.). 40p. (J). (gr. k-3). 9.99 *(978-1-4926-5952-5(5),* Hometown World) Sourcebooks, Inc.

Jones, Patrick. Out of the Tunnel, No. 1. 2014. (Red Zone Ser.: 1). (ENG.). 104p. (YA). (gr. 6-12). lib. bdg. 27.99 *(978-1-4677-2126-4(3),* 4476b74e-4129-497a-8de3-332d949ef3ba, Darby Creek) Lerner Publishing Group.

Keenan-Bolger, Andrew & Wetherhead, Kate. Act 3. 2018. (Jack & Louisa Ser.: 3). (Illus.). 256p. (J). (gr. 3-7). 8.99 *(978-1-5247-8497-3(4),* Penguin Workshop) Penguin Young Readers Group.

Kennedy, Marlane. Me & the Pumpkin Queen. 2009. (ENG.). 192p. (J). (gr. 3-7). pap. 5.99 *(978-0-06-114024-2(4),* Greenwillow Bks.) HarperCollins Pubs.

Kuhlman, Evan. The Last Invisible Boy. Coovert, J. P., illus. (ENG.). 240p. (J). (gr. 5-9). 2010. pap. 7.99 *(978-1-4169-6089-8(9))* 2008. 16.99 *(978-1-4169-5797-3(9))* Simon & Schuster Children's Publishing. (Atheneum Bks. for Young Readers).

Levine, Phyllis. At the Skylight with Matilda. 2007. (ENG.). 160p. per. 12.95 *(978-1-60047-089-9(0))* Wasteland Pr.

Levine, Susan Sachs. Harriett's Homecoming: A High-Flying Tour of Cincinnati. Burchwell, Erin, illus. 2012. (ENG.). 32p. (J). (gr. -1-3). 19.95 *(978-1-933197-97-5(8))* Orange Frazer Pr.

Lore, Pittacus. I Am Number Four. (Lorien Legacies Ser.: 1). (ENG.). (YA). (gr. 9). 2011. 496p. pap. 15.99 *(978-0-06-196957-7(5))* 2010. 448p. 18.99 *(978-0-06-196955-3(9))* HarperCollins Pubs. (HarperCollins).

—I Am Number Four. 2009. (Lorien Legacies Ser.: Bk. 1). 11.04 *(978-0-7848-3715-3(5),* Everbind) Marco Bk. Co.

—I Am Number Four. 2011. (I Am Number Four Ser.: Vol. 1). (ENG.). 440p. (gr. 9-12). 20.00 *(978-1-61383-207-3(9))* Perfection Learning Corp.

—I Am Number Four. 2011. (Lorien Legacies Ser.: 1). (YA). lib. bdg. 20.85 *(978-0-606-23545-7(0))* Turtleback.

—I Am Number Four Movie Tie-In Edition. movie tie-in ed. 2011. (Lorien Legacies Ser.: 1). (ENG.). (YA). (gr. 9). 496p. pap. 9.99 *(978-0-06-211655-0(X))*; 480p. 17.99 *(978-0-06-202624-8(0))* HarperCollins Pubs. (HarperCollins).

—I Am Number Four: the Lost Files: Rebel Allies. 2015. (Lorien Legacies: the Lost Files Ser.). (ENG.). 416p. (YA). (gr. 9). pap. 10.99 *(978-0-06-236404-3(9),* HarperCollins) HarperCollins Pubs.

—I Am Number Four: the Lost Files: Secret Histories. 2013. (Lorien Legacies: the Lost Files Ser.). (ENG.). 416p. (YA). (gr. 9). pap. 10.99 *(978-0-06-222367-8(4),* HarperCollins) HarperCollins Pubs.

—I Am Number Four: the Lost Files: Zero Hour. 2016. (Lorien Legacies: the Lost Files Ser.). (ENG.). 416p. (YA). (gr. 9). pap. 11.99 *(978-0-06-238771-4(5),* HarperCollins) HarperCollins Pubs.

—Secret Histories. 2013. (Lorien Legacies: the Lost Files Ser.). (YA). lib. bdg. 20.85 *(978-0-606-31823-5(2))* Turtleback.

Marie, Leann. The Ghost of Oberlin. 2008. pap. 16.95 *(978-1-4241-9597-8(7))* America Star Bks.

Marquez, Sofia. Pepe Perez Mexican Mouse: Pepe Perez Comes to the United States: Book 1, 1 vol. Marquez, Sofia, illus. 2009. (Illus.). 20p. pap. 24.95 *(978-1-61546-496-8(4))* America Star Bks.

—Pepe Perez Mexican Mouse: Pepe Perez Comes to the United States: Book 1, 1 vol. 2010. 20p. 24.95 *(978-1-4489-6600-4(0))* PublishAmerica, Inc.

Martin, Rebecca. Joanna's Journey. Yoder, Laura & Weaver, Lisa, illus. 2006. 168p. (YA). pap. 9.99 *(978-1-933753-01-0(3))* Carlisle Pr.- Walnut Creek.

McBride, Kristina. One Moment. 2017. (ENG.). 272p. (YA). (gr. 8-8). pap. 9.99 *(978-1-5107-1455-7(3),* Sky Pony Pr.) Skyhorse Publishing Co., Inc.

Meyer, Karen Ruth. The Tiara Mystery. 2016. (ENG., Illus.). 154p. (J). pap. 10.99 *(978-0-9974953-2-4(4))* Sable Creek Pr. LLC.

Mullen, Paul Michael. The Day I Hit a Home Run at Great American Ball Park. 2007. 146p. (J). *(978-1-933197-30-2(7))* Orange Frazer Pr.

Murphy, Buelina. Boke. 2003. 32p. pap. 8.00 *(978-0-8059-5524-8(0))* Dorrance Publishing Co., Inc.

Novel Units. The House of Dies Drear Novel Units Teacher Guide. 2019. (ENG.). (J). pap. 12.99 *(978-1-56137-516-5(0),* NU5168, Novel Units, Inc.) Classroom Library Co.

Oneill, Elizabeth. Alfred Visits Ohio. 2006. 24p. pap. 12.00 *(978-0-9771836-4-7(5))* Funny Bone Bks.

Osorio, Rick. The Great Adventure of Sally Rock & the Cretaceous Chicken. 2006. 65p. pap. 16.95 *(978-1-4241-0971-5(X))* PublishAmerica, Inc.

Ottman, Frank. Not Wanted: The Memories of Cain Mann. 2005. 194p. pap. 24.95 *(978-1-4241-0163-4(8))* PublishAmerica, Inc.

Pearsall, Shelley. Crooked River. 2007. (ENG.). 272p. (J). (gr. 3-7). 8.99 *(978-0-440-42101-6(2),* Yearling) Random Hse. Children's Bks.

Phillips, Raelene. Towpath to Truth: Finding Family on the Miami & Erie Canal. 2009. (Illus.). 112p. (J). pap. *(978-0-7880-2229-6(6),* Fairway Pr.) CSS Publishing Co.

Polatin, Daria. Devil in Ohio. 2018. (ENG.). 336p. (YA). pap. 12.99 *(978-1-250-18077-3(5),* 900170879) Square Fish.

Price, Roxanne M. Buckeyes Bow Ties & Sweater Vests. 2010. (Illus.). 20p. pap. *(978-1-4251-8537-4(1))* Trafford Publishing (UK) Ltd.

Revenge of the Bully. 2014. (How to Beat the Bully Ser.). (ENG., Illus.). 288p. (J). (gr. 3-7). 17.99 *(978-1-4424-5677-8(9),* Simon & Schuster/Paula Wiseman Bks.) Simon & Schuster/Paula Wiseman Bks.

Rexroth, Sharon. Ohio. 2006. (ENG., Illus.). (J). per. 19.95 *(978-1-57166-421-1(1))* Quixote Pr.

Rininger, Alyce. Ka-Boom. Lucas, Diane, illus. 2012. 46p. pap. 13.95 *(978-1-61244-069-9(X))* Halo Publishing International.

Roos, Stephen. Recycling George. 2010. (ENG.). 144p. (J). (gr. 3-7). pap. 8.99 *(978-1-4424-2941-3(0),* Simon & Schuster Bks. For Young Readers) Simon & Schuster Bks. For Young Readers.

Rosen, Michael J. Don't Shoot! Chase R.'s Top Ten Reasons NOT to Move to the Country. 2007. (ENG., Illus.). 160p. (YA). (gr. 7). per. 6.99 *(978-0-7636-2088-2(2))* Candlewick Pr.

Sanders, Scott Russell. Warm as Wool. Cogancherry, Helen, illus. 2007. (J). lib. bdg. 18.00 *(978-1-59098-421-5(8))* Wooster Bk. Co., The.

Saturen, Myra. Journey to a New World: Mystic River of the West. 2006. (J). pap. *(978-0-88092-495-5(0))* Royal Fireworks Publishing Co.

Shoup, Andrew J. Andy & Elmer's Apple Dumpling Adventure. 2nd ed. 2007. (J). 16.95 *(978-0-9720436-3-2(2))* TokoBooks, LLC.

—Andy & Elmer's Apple Dumpling Adventure Coloring & Activity Book. Shoup, Andrew J., illus. 2007. (Illus.). 36p. (J). 3.95 *(978-0-9720436-2-5(4))* TokoBooks, LLC.

Skovron, Jon. Struts & Frets. 2011. (ENG.). 288p. (YA). (gr. 8-17). pap. 7.95 *(978-1-4197-0028-6(6),* 657403, Amulet Bks.) Abrams, Inc.

Smallman, Steve. Santa Is Coming to Ohio. Dunn, Robert, illus. 2nd ed. 2019. (Santa Is Coming... Ser.). (ENG.). 40p. (J). (gr. -1-3). 12.99 *(978-1-7282-0089-7(X),* Hometown World) Sourcebooks, Inc.

Sowach, Rick. Critters, Flitters & Spitters: 24 Amazing Ohio Animal Tales. 2003. (J). 19.95 *(978-0-9762412-3-2(4))* Sowash, Rick Publishing Co.

Sowash, Rick. Critters, Flitters & Spitters: 24 Amazing Ohio Animal Tales. 2003. (J). pap. 11.95 *(978-0-9762412-2-5(6))* Sowash, Rick Publishing Co.

—Ripsnorting Whoppers! A Book of Ohio Tall Tales. 2003. (J). 19.95 *(978-0-9762412-1-8(8))*; pap. 11.95 *(978-0-9762412-0-1(X))* Sowash, Rick Publishing Co.

Springstubb, Tricia. What Happened on Fox Street. Ross, Heather, illus. 2011. (Fox Street Ser.: 1). (ENG.). 240p. (J). (gr. 3-7). pap. 7.99 *(978-0-06-198636-9(4),* Balzer & Bray) HarperCollins Pubs.

Starkey, Scott. How to Beat the Bully Without Really Trying. (How to Beat the Bully Ser.). (ENG.). 272p. (J). (gr. 3-7). 2013. pap. 8.99 *(978-1-4424-8473-3(X))* 2012. 15.99 *(978-1-4424-1685-7(8))* Simon & Schuster/Paula Wiseman Bks. (Simon & Schuster/Paula Wiseman Bks.).

Stilton, Thea. Thea Stilton & the Dragon's Code (Thea Stilton #1) A Geronimo Stilton Adventure. 2009. (Thea Stilton Ser.: 1). (ENG., Illus.). 176p. (J). (gr. 2-5). pap. 8.99 *(978-0-545-10367-1(3),* Scholastic Paperbacks) Scholastic, Inc.

Stratemeyer, Edward. On the Trail of Pontiac: Or, the Pioneer Boys of the Ohio. 2017. (ENG., Illus.). (J). 24.95 *(978-1-374-85742-1(4))*; pap. 14.95 *(978-1-374-85741-4(6))* Capital Communications, Inc.

Sully, Katherine. Night-Night Ohio. Poole, Helen, illus. 2016. (Night-Night Ser.). (ENG.). 20p. (J). (gr. -1-1). bds. 9.99 *(978-1-4926-4220-6(7),* 9781492642206, Hometown World) Sourcebooks, Inc.

Tama. Black Cow. 2012. 116p. pap. 14.95 *(978-1-4685-6680-2(6))* AuthorHouse.

Wiechman, Kathy Cannon. Not on Fifth Street. 2017. (ENG.). 240p. (J). (gr. 4-7). 17.95 *(978-1-62979-804-2(5),* Calkins Creek) Highlights Pr., c/o Highlights for Children, Inc.

Wilsdon, Christina. An Amusement Park Mystery in Ohio. Ebert, Len, illus. 2006. 26p. (J). 7.99 *(978-1-59939-013-0(2))* Cornerstone Pr.

Wisehart, Randall. Luke's Summer Secret. 2017. 135p. (YA). pap. 12.00 *(978-0-913408-45-2(X))* Friends United Pr.

Wood, David. A Year in the Life of the Kingwood Bunnies. Floeter, Neil, illus. 2010. 54p. pap. 15.95 *(978-1-936343-07-2(X))* Peppertree Pr., The.

Zimmer, Tracie Vaughn. 42 Miles. 2008. (ENG., Illus.). 80p. (J). (gr. 5-7). 16.00 *(978-0-618-61867-5(8),* 100453, Clarion Bks.) HarperCollins Pubs.

OHIO—HISTORY

Bailer, Darice. What's Great about Ohio? 2015. (Our Great States Ser.). (ENG., Illus.). 32p. (J). (gr. 2-5). 26.65 *(978-1-4677-3885-9(9),* d4e13df3-76f5-4473-8ff4-dad50ee01670, Lerner Pubns.) Lerner Publishing Group.

Beckman, Wendy. 8 Wonders of Cincinnati. 2017. (ENG., Illus.). 176p. pap. 21.99 *(978-1-62585-898-6(1),* History Pr., The) Arcadia Publishing.

MNO

Boehm Jerome, Kate. Columbus & the State of Ohio: Cool Stuff Every Kid Should Know. 2011. (Arcadia Kids Ser.). (ENG., Illus.). 48p. (J). (gr. 3-6). pap. 9.99 *(978-1-4396-0087-0(2))* Arcadia Publishing.
Caffmeyer, Judy. Ready, Set, Show What You Know(r) on the Ohio Acheivement Test for Gr. 3: Student Edition. 2004. (J). per. 10.95 *(978-1-59230-062-4(6))* Englefield & Assocs., Inc.
Dalton, Curt. Dayton Inventions: Fact & Fiction. 2003. (Illus.). 74p. per. 12.95 *(978-0-9720965-1-5(5))* Montgomery County Historical Society.
Deady, Kathleen W. Ohio, 1 vol. 2005. (Portraits of the States Ser.). (ENG., Illus.). 32p. (gr. 3-5). pap. 11.50 *(978-0-8368-4651-5(6),* 35128258-b2bf-4f70-8a49-bb0700d3aa54); lib. bdg. 28.67 *(978-0-8368-4632-4(X),* aacd7d61-27f9-441a-b052-bf4eaf9f8cce) Stevens, Gareth Publishing LLLP. (Gareth Stevens Learning Library).
Gamble, Adam. Good Night Ohio. Jasper, Mark, illus. 2013. (Good Night Our World Ser.). (ENG.). 20p. (J). (— 1). bds. 9.95 *(978-1-60219-076-4(3))* Good Night Bks.
Gitlin, Martin. Ohio (a True Book: My United States) (Library Edition) 2018. (True Book (Relaunch) Ser.). (ENG., Illus.). 48p. (J). (gr. 3-5). 31.00 *(978-0-531-23568-3(8),* Children's Pr.) Scholastic Library Publishing.
Gray, Susan. All Across Ohio: A Bird's Eye View with Worthington Cardinal, 7 bks. Messer, Celia, illus. 2003. 24p. (J). 7.95 *(978-0-9742862-0-4(6))* Two's Company.
—Colorful Ohio! A Bird's Eye View with Worthington Cardinal, 7 bks. Gray, Susan & Messer, Celia, illus. 2003. 28p. (J). 4.95 *(978-0-9742862-5-9(7))* Two's Company.
—Plain & Simple: A Bird's Eye View with Worthington Cardinal, 7 bks. Messer, Celia, illus. 2003. 24p. (J). 7.95 *(978-0-9742862-4-2(9))* Two's Company.
—A River Ride: A Bird's Eye View with Worthington Cardinal, 7 bks. Messer, Celia, illus. 2003. 24p. (J). 7.95 *(978-0-9742862-3-5(0))* Two's Company.
—Wagon-O! A Bird's Eye View with Worthington Cardinal, 7 bks. Messer, Celia, illus. 2003. 24p. (J). 7.95 *(978-0-9742862-2-8(2))* Two's Company.
—We Can Fly! A Bird's Eye View with Worthington Cardinal, 7 bks. Messer, Celia, illus. 2003. 24p. (J). 7.95 *(978-0-9742862-1-1(4))* Two's Company.
Gunderson, Jessica. Ohio. 2009. (This Land Called America Ser.). 32p. (YA). (gr. 3-6). 19.95 *(978-1-58341-788-1(5))* Creative Co., The.
Hamilton, John. Ohio, 1 vol. 2016. (United States of America Ser.). (ENG., Illus.). 48p. (J). (gr. 5-9). 34.21 *(978-1-68078-337-7(8),* 21659, Abdo & Daughters) ABDO Publishing Co.
Hart, Joyce & Herrington, Lisa M. Ohio, 1 vol. 2nd rev. ed. 2012. (It's My State! (Second Edition)(r) Ser.). (ENG.). 80p. (gr. 4-4). 34.07 *(978-1-60870-524-5(2),* 36dae9e2-3173-476d-b496-8368aaf9d738) Cavendish Square Publishing LLC.
Hart, Joyce, et al. Ohio: The Buckeye State, 1 vol. 3rd rev. ed. 2016. (It's My State! (Third Edition)(r) Ser.). (ENG., Illus.). 80p. (gr. 4-4). 35.93 *(978-1-62713-169-8(8),* a5ce7fcd-f5ce-4d73-a0bf-894b848e9d6a) Cavendish Square Publishing LLC.
Helweg, Laura. Eastern Great Lakes: Indiana, Michigan, Ohio, Vol. 19. 2015. (Let's Explore the States Ser.). 64p. (J). (gr. 5). 23.95 *(978-1-4222-3323-8(5))* Mason Crest.
Jerome, Kate B. Lucky to Live in Ohio. 2017. (Arcadia Kids Ser.). (ENG., Illus.). 32p. (J). 16.99 *(978-0-7385-2773-4(4))* Arcadia Publishing.
—The Wise Animal Handbook Ohio. 2017. (Arcadia Kids Ser.). (ENG., Illus.). 32p. (J). 16.99 *(978-0-7385-2837-3(4))* Arcadia Publishing.
Jerome, Kate Boehm. Cincinnati, Oh: Cool Stuff Every Kid Should Know. 2010. (Arcadia Kids Ser.). (ENG., Illus.). 48p. (J). (gr. 3-6). pap. 9.99 *(978-1-4396-0068-9(6))* Arcadia Publishing.
Kandel, Megan. Let's Celebrate Ohio. 2003. pap. 10.95 *(978-1-931334-20-4(X),* CLC0287) Pieces of Learning.
Kline, Nancy. Ohio. 2009. (From Sea to Shining Sea, Second Ser.). (ENG.). 80p. (J). pap. 7.95 *(978-0-531-21141-0(X),* Children's Pr.) Scholastic Library Publishing.
Lawton, Val. Ohio. 2011. (Guide to American States Ser.). (Illus.). 48p. (YA). (gr. 3-6). 29.99 *(978-1-61690-807-2(6))* Weigl Pubs., Inc.
—Ohio: The Buckeye State. 2016. (Illus.). 48p. (J). *(978-1-5105-2091-2(0))* SmartBook Media, Inc.
—Ohio: The Buckeye State. 2016. (J). *(978-1-4896-4920-1(4))* Weigl Pubs., Inc.
Levine, Susan Sachs. Packard Takes Flight: A Bird's-Eye View of Columbus, Ohio. Burchwell, Erin McCauley, illus. 2010. (ENG.). 32p. (J). 17.99 *(978-1-60949-051-5(7),* History Pr., The) Arcadia Publishing.
Lucht, Susan & Wilson, Mollie. Olden Days of Medina: A Children's Guide to Medina History. Allman, Cynthia, illus. 2013. iii, 30p. (J). pap. *(978-0-578-10958-9(1))* History Gal's Publishing.
Marsh, Carole. Exploring Ohio Through Project-Based Learning: Geography, History, Government, Economics & More. 2016. (Ohio Experience Ser.). (ENG.). (J). pap. 9.99 *(978-0-635-12359-6(2))* Gallopade International.
McNeese, Tim. The Ohio River. 2004. (Rivers in American Life & Times Ser.). (ENG., Illus.). 120p. (gr. 9-13). 32.50 *(978-0-7910-7725-2(X),* P113990, Facts On File) Infobase Holdings, Inc.
Ohio Historical Society Staff. Ohio, A Sentimental Journey Study Guide, 1 CD. 2004. (Illus.). 102p. (YA). cd-rom *(978-0-9747666-1-4(5))* American Retrospects, LLC.
Raizk, Mary Ann. Happy Birthday, Ohio: Celebrating Ohio's Bicentennial 1803-2003, 1. Raizk, Leyla Marie, illus. 2003. 32p. (J). pap. 14.95 *(978-1-882203-97-0(6))* Orange Frazer Pr.
Rodriguez, Cindy. Ohio: The Buckeye State. 2012. (J). *(978-1-61913-389-1(X));* pap. *(978-1-61913-390-7(3))* Weigl Pubs., Inc.
Schonberg, Marcia. Little Ohio. Monroe, Michael Glenn, illus. 2011. (Little State Ser.). (ENG.). 20p. (J). (gr. -1-1). bds. 9.95 *(978-1-58536-527-2(0),* 202246) Sleeping Bear Pr.
Sipp, Leora Janson. Nathan & Tori Visit Ohio: And Learn about Wild Animals. 2012. 40p. pap. 14.50 *(978-1-4669-3822-9(6))* Trafford Publishing.
Sleeping Bear Press. Diary of a Ohio Kid. Moore, Cyd, illus. 2010. (State Journal Ser.). (ENG.). 128p. (J). (gr. 4-8). pap. 9.95 *(978-1-58536-540-1(8),* 202218) Sleeping Bear Pr.
Snyder, Sally. Hold the Fort. Snyder, Sally, illus. 2003. (Illus.). 45p. (J). 20.00 *(978-1-882203-99-4(2))* Orange Frazer Pr.
Stille, Darlene R. America the Beautiful: Ohio (Revised Edition) 2014. (America the Beautiful, Third Ser. (Revised Edition) Ser.). (ENG.). 144p. (J). lib. bdg. 40.00 *(978-0-531-28287-8(2))* Scholastic Library Publishing.
Weymouth Seguin, Marilyn. The Freedom Stairs: The Story of Adam Lowry Rankin, Underground Railroad Conductor. 2004. (ENG., Illus.). 93p. (J). (gr. 3-7). per. 12.95 net. *(978-0-8283-2084-9(5))* Branden Bks.

OHIO—HISTORY—FICTION

Clark, Henry. The Book That Proves Time Travel Happens. 2015. (ENG., Illus.). 416p. (J). (gr. 3-7). 17.00 *(978-0-316-40617-8(1))* Little, Brown Bks. for Young Readers.
Hulme, Lucy V. Passages, 1 bk. Redpath, Dale, illus. 2005. 40p. (J). 7.95 *(978-0-9769854-0-2(3),* 001) Combs-Hulme Publishing.
Long, Loren & Bildner, Phil. Magic in the Outfield. Long, Loren, illus. 2009. (Sluggers Ser.: 1). (ENG., Illus.). 160p. (J). (gr. 3-7). pap. 9.99 *(978-1-4169-1884-4(1),* Simon & Schuster Bks. For Young Readers) Simon & Schuster Bks. For Young Readers.
McGinnis, Mindy. A Madness So Discreet. 2015. (ENG.). 384p. (YA). (gr. 9). 17.99 *(978-0-06-232086-5(6),* Tegen, Katherine Bks) HarperCollins Pubs.
Pearsall, Shelley. Crooked River. 2007. 249p. (gr. 5-9). 17.00 *(978-0-7569-7771-9(1))* Perfection Learning Corp.
Raven, Margot Theis. Night Boat to Freedom. Lewis, E. B., illus. 2008. (ENG.). 40p. (J). (gr. 1-4). pap. 10.99 *(978-0-312-55018-9(9),* 900055951) Square Fish.
Reed, Stephanie. The Light Across the River, 1 vol. 2008. (Illus.). 216p. (J). (gr. 4-7). pap. 10.99 *(978-0-8254-3574-4(9))* Kregel Pubns.
Saturen, Myra. Journey to a New World: Mystic River of the West. 2006. (J). pap. *(978-0-88092-495-5(0))* Royal Fireworks Publishing Co.
Van Leeuwen, Jean. Cabin on Trouble Creek. 2008. (ENG.). 224p. (J). (gr. 3-7). 7.99 *(978-0-14-241164-3(7),* Puffin Books) Penguin Young Readers Group.

OHIO RIVER AND VALLEY—FICTION

Hemphill, Kris. Ambush in the Wilderness. 2003. (Adventures in America Ser.). (Illus.). 90p. (gr. 4). 14.95 *(978-1-893110-34-2(6))* Silver Moon Pr.
Rush, Barbara & Stratton, Jane. The Boat in the Attic. 2012. (ENG.). 30p. pap. 15.00 *(978-1-938002-02-1(4),* Hummingbird World Media) Double Edge Pr.
Shoemaker, E. W. Mother Nature & the Tales of North Fork. 2009. 220p. pap. 18.75 *(978-1-4389-8604-3(1))* AuthorHouse.
Winfield, Arthur M. The Rover Boys on the River or the Search for the Missing. 2006. (ENG.). 272p. per. 27.95 *(978-1-4286-4115-0(7))* Kessinger Publishing, LLC.

OIL

see Petroleum

OIL FUEL

see Petroleum As Fuel

OIL SPILLS

Beech, Linda Ward. The Exxon Valdez's Deadly Oil Spill. 2007. (Code Red Ser.). (Illus.). 32p. (YA). (gr. 2-5). lib. bdg. 28.50 *(978-1-59716-366-8(X))* Bearport Publishing Co., Inc.
Benchmark Education Company. Oil Spills (Teacher Guide) 2005. *(978-1-4108-4671-6(7))* Benchmark Education Co.
Benoit, Peter. The BP Oil Spill. 2011. (J). pap. *(978-0-531-29029-3(8))* Children's Pr., Ltd.
—The BP Oil Spill. 2011. (True Bks.). 48p. (J). (gr. 3-5). lib. bdg. 29.00 *(978-0-531-20630-0(0),* Children's Pr.) Scholastic Library Publishing.
—The Exxon Valdez Oil Spill. 2011. (J). pap. *(978-0-531-29028-6(X))* Children's Pr., Ltd.
—The Exxon Valdez Oil Spill. 2011. (True Bks.). 48p. (J). (gr. 3-5). 29.00 *(978-0-531-20629-4(7),* Children's Pr.) Scholastic Library Publishing.
—The EXXON Valdez Oil Spill. 2011. (True Bk Ser.). (ENG., Illus.). 48p. (J). pap. 6.95 *(978-0-531-28998-3(2),* Children's Pr.) Scholastic Library Publishing.
Bodden, Valerie. The Deepwater Horizon Oil Spill. 2018. (Disasters for All Time Ser.). (ENG.). 48p. (J). (gr. 4-7). pap. 12.00 *(978-1-62832-548-5(8),* 19725, Creative Paperbacks) Creative Co., The.
Bogart, Jon. Animals & Oil Spills. 2013. (Animal 911: Environmental Threats Ser.). 48p. (J). (gr. 3-5). pap. 84.30 *(978-1-4339-9712-9(6));* (ENG.). (gr. 4-4). pap. 15.05 *(978-1-4339-9711-2(8),* a9fb0983-e7f6-445e-9620-1e6910cb794f); (ENG., Illus.). (gr. 4-4). lib. bdg. 34.61 *(978-1-4339-9710-5(X),* c940cba8-bd8b-4cf9-bc5c-14d61076aa2c) Stevens, Gareth Publishing LLLP.
Brannon, Barbara. Discover Oil Spills. 2005. (J). pap. *(978-1-4108-5139-0(7))* Benchmark Education Co.
Brennan, Linda Crotta. Gulf Oil Spill, 1 vol. 2013. (History's Greatest Disasters Ser.). (ENG.). 48p. (J). (gr. 4-8). lib. bdg. 35.64 *(978-1-61783-957-3(4),* 9485) ABDO Publishing Co.
—Gulf Oil Spill Paperback. 2013. (History's Greatest Disasters Ser.). (ENG.). (J). (gr. 4-8). pap. 18.50 *(978-1-62403-022-2(X),* 10771) ABDO Publishing Co.
Burgan, Michael. Exxon Valdez: How a Massive Oil Spill Triggered an Environmental Catastrophe. 2018. (Captured Science History Ser.). (ENG., Illus.). 64p. (J). (gr. 5-9). lib. bdg. 35.32 *(978-0-7565-5743-0(7),* 137539, Compass Point Bks.) Capstone.
Chiang, Mona. Oil Spill: Disaster in the Gulf. 2010. (Illus.). 32p. (J). pap. *(978-0-545-31128-1(4))* Scholastic, Inc.
Curtis, Jennifer Keats & Yee, Tammy. Rescate en el Río: (River Rescue) [Spanish Edition]. Yee, Tammy, illus. 2019. (SPA., Illus.). 32p. (J). pap. 11.95 *(978-1-60718-875-9(9))* Arbordale Publishing.
Dalton, Anna. Examining Oil Spills. 2015. (ENG., Illus.). 48p. (J). lib. bdg. 24.95 net. *(978-1-934545-65-2(1))* Oliver Pr., Inc.
Dils, Tracey E. Oil Spill Cleaner, 1 vol. 2011. (Dirty & Dangerous Jobs Ser.). (ENG.). 32p. (gr. 3-3). 31.21 *(978-1-60870-174-2(3),* 5ab2f13a-7910-49a4-8948-b685255c6dae) Cavendish Square Publishing LLC.
Faust, Daniel R. Desastres Ecológicos: los Derrames de Petróleo y el MedioAmbiente, 1 vol. 2009. (Historietas Juveniles: Peligros Del Medioambiente (Jr. Graphic Environmental Dangers) Ser.). (SPA., Illus.). 24p. (gr. 4-4). pap. 10.60 *(978-1-4358-8469-4(8),* 45598d3b-0bc0-4b0d-be3b-50c9905819ef, PowerKids Pr.) Rosen Publishing Group, Inc., The.
—Desastres Ecológicos: Los Derrames de Petróleo y el Medio Ambiente = Sinister Sludge: Oil Spills & the Environment, 1 vol. 2009. (Historietas Juveniles: Peligros Del Medioambiente (Jr. Graphic Environmental Dangers) Ser.). (SPA., Illus.). 24p. (YA). (gr. 4-4). lib. bdg. 28.93 *(978-1-4358-8468-7(X),* bbf3bb69-9c5a-4ed8-8ad3-cadb2e6e85ed) Rosen Publishing Group, Inc., The.
—Sinister Sludge: Oil Spills & the Environment. (Jr. Graphic Environmental Dangers Ser.). (ENG.). 24p. 2008. (J). 47.90 *(978-1-61532-100-1(4))* 2007. (Illus.). (J). (gr. 4-4). lib. bdg. 28.93 *(978-1-4042-4230-2(9),* 90f6b70c-8c3d-4b5c-b49e-ec5997b8e911) 2007. (Illus.). (gr. 4-4). pap. 10.60 *(978-1-4042-4597-6(9),* 722b8fb3-1af5-4900-a363-76fbc65aae6a) Rosen Publishing Group, Inc., The. (PowerKids Pr.).
Goldish, Meish. Oil Spill: Deepwater Horizon. 2017. (Eco-Disasters Ser.). (ENG.). 32p. (J). (gr. 2-7). 19.95 *(978-1-68402-226-7(6))* Bearport Publishing Co., Inc.
Greeley, August. Sludge & Slime: Oil Spills in Our World. 2009. (Man-Made Disasters Ser.). 24p. (gr. 3-3). 42.50 *(978-1-61514-352-8(1),* PowerKids Pr.) Rosen Publishing Group, Inc., The.
Haugen, David M., ed. The B. P. Oil Spill, 1 vol. 2011. (At Issue Ser.). (ENG.). 112p. (gr. 10-12). 41.03 *(978-0-7377-5568-8(7),* b39fe2f5-3de5-4f21-8e33-2b07156ca183); pap. 28.80 *(978-0-7377-5569-5(5),* 6d1a6d21-c7c8-4a54-a75a-5409c71f3a64) Greenhaven Publishing LLC. (Greenhaven Publishing).
Jakubiak, David J. Protecting Our Planet: What Can We Do about Oil Spills & Ocean Pollution? (Illus.). 24p. (J). 2012. 49.50 *(978-1-4488-5113-3(0),* PowerKids Pr.) 2011. (ENG., (gr. 2-3). pap. 9.25 *(978-1-4488-5112-6(2),* e582d72d-2ae2-40b9-a71c-d78af4772444, PowerKids Pr.) 2011. (ENG., (gr. 2-3). lib. bdg. 26.27 *(978-1-4488-4982-6(9),* 43bf3457-3384-4dc2-a1af-7370a4015eb0) Rosen Publishing Group, Inc., The.
Keats Curtis, Jennifer. River Rescue. Yee, Tammy, illus. 2019. (ENG & SPA.). 32p. (J). (gr. 2-3). 9.95 *(978-1-60718-835-3(X),* 9781607188353); 17.95 *(978-1-60718-823-0(6),* 9781607188230) Arbordale Publishing.
Landau, Elaine. Oil Spill! Disaster in the Gulf of Mexico. 2011. (Exceptional Science Titles for Intermediate Grades Ser.). (ENG.). 32p. (gr. 3-5). 25.26 *(978-0-7613-7485-5(X),* Millbrook Pr.) Lerner Publishing Group.
Margulies, Phillip. The Exxon Valdez Oil Spill. 2009. (When Disaster Strikes! Ser.). 48p. (gr. 5-8). 53.00 *(978-1-60854-780-7(9),* Rosen Reference) Rosen Publishing Group, Inc., The.
Markle, Sandra. The Great Penguin Rescue: Saving the African Penguins. 2017. (Sandra Markle's Science Discoveries Ser.). (ENG., Illus.). 48p. (J). (gr. 4-6). 33.32 *(978-1-5124-1315-1(1),* 13d008ae-882e-42e2-932f-9f3333384b00, Millbrook Pr.) Lerner Publishing Group.
Nardo, Don. Oil Spills, 1 vol. 2011. (Hot Topics Ser.). (ENG., Illus.). 112p. (gr. 7-7). lib. bdg. 41.03 *(978-1-4205-0624-2(2),* abb2f866-355c-4e28-92b1-5e0064d1e24e, Lucent Pr.) Greenhaven Publishing LLC.
Orr, Tamra B. BP Oil Spill & Energy Policy. 2017. (Perspectives Library: Modern Perspectives Ser.). (ENG., Illus.). 32p. (J). (gr. 4-7). lib. bdg. 32.07 *(978-1-63472-864-5(5),* 209882) Cherry Lake Publishing.
Parsons, Michelle Hyde. Oil Spills. 2005. (J). pap. *(978-1-4108-4623-5(7))* Benchmark Education Co.
Peppas, Lynn. Gulf Oil Spill. 2011. (ENG., Illus.). 32p. (J). *(978-0-7787-1592-4(2),* 1325405); (Disaster Alert! Ser.: No. 20). (gr. 3-6). pap. *(978-0-7787-1625-9(2),* 1325405) Crabtree Publishing Co.
Person, Stephen. Saving Animals from Oil Spills. 2011. (Rescuing Animals from Disasters Ser.). 32p. (YA). (gr. 2-5). lib. bdg. 28.50 *(978-1-61772-288-2(X))* Bearport Publishing Co., Inc.
The Science of an Oil Spill. 2014. (21st Century Skills Library: Disaster Science Ser.). (ENG., Illus.). 32p. (J). (gr. 4-8). 32.07 *(978-1-63137-630-6(6),* 205303) Cherry Lake Publishing.
Smith, Steven Michael. New Carissa: The Ship That Refused to Die. 2010. 52p. pap. 22.99 *(978-1-4520-6612-7(4))* AuthorHouse.
Stone, Adam. The Deepwater Horizon Oil Spill. 2014. (Disaster Stories Ser.). (ENG., Illus.). 24p. (J). (gr. 3-8). 29.95 *(978-1-62617-152-7(1),* Black Sheep) Bellwether Media.
Thompson, Tamara, ed. Oil Spills, 1 vol. 2014. (Current Controversies Ser.). (ENG., Illus.). 168p. (gr. 10-12). pap. 33.00 *(978-0-7377-6881-7(9),* 00569fa8-b41c-4eec-8a51-eabc50dff923); lib. bdg. 48.03 *(978-0-7377-6880-0(0),* b17bc9ff-9843-4701-93f4-a261bf8c22ec) Greenhaven Publishing LLC. (Greenhaven Publishing).

OIL WELLS

see Petroleum

OKEFENOKEE SWAMP (GA. AND FLA.)

Bateman, Donna M. Deep in the Swamp. Lies, Brian, illus. 2007. (ENG.). 32p. (J). (gr. -1-3). pap. 7.95 *(978-1-57091-597-0(0))* Charlesbridge Publishing, Inc.

OKEFENOKEE SWAMP (GA. AND FLA.)—FICTION

Cavanaugh, Nancy J. Elsie Mae Has Something to Say. 2017. (ENG.). 320p. (J). (gr. 3-7). 16.99 *(978-1-4926-4022-6(0))* Sourcebooks, Inc.
Jackson's Plan: Evaluation Guide. 2006. (J). *(978-1-55942-410-3(9))* Witcher Productions.
Marsh, Carole. The Secret of Skullcracker Swamp. 2009. (Pretty Darn Scary Mysteries Ser.). (Illus.). 113p. (YA). lib. bdg. 18.99 *(978-0-635-07020-3(0),* Marsh, Carole Mysteries) Gallopade International.
Smith, Emma Bland. Book 3: Saving the Alligators. Ortega, Mirelle, illus. 2019. (Gavin Mcnally's Year Off Ser.). (ENG.). 48p. (J). (gr. 3-7). lib. bdg. 34.21 *(978-1-5321-3508-8(4),* 31935, Spellbound) Magic Wagon.

OKINAWA ISLAND (JAPAN)—FICTION

Gratz, Alan. Grenade. (ENG.). 288p. E-Book 17.99 *(978-1-338-24571-4(6));* 2018. (Illus.). (J). (gr. 4-7). 17.99 *(978-1-338-24569-1(4))* Scholastic, Inc. (Scholastic Pr.).
—Grenade. Lt. ed. 2020. (ENG.). lib. bdg. 22.99 *(978-1-4328-7747-7(X))* Thorndike Pr.
Mazer, Harry. Heroes Don't Run. 2007. (Aladdin Historical Fiction Ser.). 113p. (gr. 3-7). 16.00 *(978-0-7569-8111-2(5))* Perfection Learning Corp.

OKLAHOMA

Baldwin, Guy & Hart, Joyce. Oklahoma, 1 vol. 2nd rev. ed. 2010. (Celebrate the States (Second Edition) Ser.). (ENG.). 144p. (gr. 6-6). 39.79 *(978-0-7614-4032-1(1),* 5096c608-ae02-489d-af66-6fd853503c63) Cavendish Square Publishing LLC.
Brown, Jonatha A. Oklahoma, 1 vol. 2005. (Portraits of the States Ser.). (ENG., Illus.). 32p. (gr. 3-5). pap. 11.50 *(978-0-8368-4691-1(5),* e2a30d4b-7561-4217-ae4e-6f014dc6d3a1); lib. bdg. 28.67 *(978-0-8368-4672-0(9),* 156c0025-841c-46a5-9ddd-60999b5af5e3) Stevens, Gareth Publishing LLLP. (Gareth Stevens Learning Library).
Brown, Vanessa. Oklahoma. 2009. (Bilingual Library of the United States of America Ser.). (ENG & SPA.). 32p. (gr. 2-2). 47.90 *(978-1-60853-380-0(8),* Editorial Buenas Letras) Rosen Publishing Group, Inc., The.
—Oklahoma, 1 vol. Brusca, María Cristina, tr. 2005. (Bilingual Library of the United States of America Ser.: Set 2). (ENG & SPA., Illus.). 32p. (J). (gr. 2-2). lib. bdg. 28.93 *(978-1-4042-3101-6(3),* 399e4c2b-71c1-4685-8f5b-1e11c85b2400) Rosen Publishing Group, Inc., The.
Brownell, Richard. The Oklahoma City Bombing, 1 vol. 2007. (Crime Scene Investigations Ser.). (ENG., Illus.). 104p. (gr. 7-7). lib. bdg. 42.03 *(978-1-59018-843-9(8),* dcc533b6-e6ce-4b0d-a16c-86ba5c4170a2, Lucent Pr.) Greenhaven Publishing LLC.
Fein, E. How to Draw Oklahoma's Sights & Symbols. 2009. (Kid's Guide to Drawing America Ser.). 32p. (gr. k-k). 50.50 *(978-1-61511-089-6(5),* PowerKids Pr.) Rosen Publishing Group, Inc., The.
Giordano, Geraldine. The Oklahoma City Bombing. 2009. (Terrorist Attacks Ser.). 64p. (gr. 5-5). 58.50 *(978-1-60853-318-3(2))* Rosen Publishing Group, Inc., The.
Heinrichs, Ann. Oklahoma. Kania, Matt, illus. 2017. (U. S. A. Travel Guides). (ENG.). 40p. (J). (gr. 2-5). lib. bdg. 38.50 *(978-1-5038-1976-4(0),* 211612) Child's World, Inc, The.
Kavanagh, James & Waterford Press Staff. Oklahoma Birds: A Folding Pocket Guide to Familiar Species. Leung, Raymond, illus. 2017. (Wildlife & Nature Identification Ser.). (ENG.). 12p. (gr. 9). 7.95 *(978-1-58355-008-3(9))* Waterford Pr., Inc.
Labella, Susan. Oklahoma. 2007. (Rookie Read-About Geography Ser.). (Illus.). 31p. (J). (gr. 1-2). 20.50 *(978-0-516-25468-5(5),* Children's Pr.) Scholastic Library Publishing.
LaDoux, Rita. Oklahoma. 2012. (J). lib. bdg. 25.26 *(978-0-7613-4551-0(5),* Lerner Pubns.) Lerner Publishing Group.
Maine, Tyler & Parker, Bridget. Oklahoma. 2016. (States Ser.). (ENG., Illus.). 32p. (J). (gr. 3-6). lib. bdg. 27.99 *(978-1-5157-0423-2(8),* 132034, Capstone Pr.) Capstone.
Marsh, Carole. My First Book about Oklahoma. 2004. (Oklahoma Experience! Ser.). (Illus.). 32p. (J). (gr. k-4). pap. 7.95 *(978-0-7933-9595-8(X))* Gallopade International.
—My First Pocket Guide: Oklahoma. 2004. (Oklahoma Experience! Ser.). (Illus.). 96p. (J). (gr. 3-8). per. 6.95 *(978-0-7933-9594-1(1))* Gallopade International.
—Oklahoma Current Events Projects: 30 Cool, Activities, Crafts, Experiments & More for Kids to Do to Learn about Your State! 2003. (Oklahoma Experience Ser.). 32p. (gr. k-8). pap. 5.95 *(978-0-635-02055-0(6),* Marsh, Carole Bks.) Gallopade International.
—Oklahoma Geography Projects: 30 Cool, Activities, Crafts, Experiments & More for Kids to Do to Learn about Your State! 2003. (Oklahoma Experience Ser.). 32p. (gr. k-5). pap. 5.95 *(978-0-635-01855-7(1),* Marsh, Carole Bks.) Gallopade International.
—Oklahoma Government Projects: 30 Cool, Activities, Crafts, Experiments & More for Kids to Do to Learn about Your State! 2003. (Oklahoma Experience Ser.). 32p. (gr. k-5). pap. 5.95 *(978-0-635-01955-4(8),* Marsh, Carole Bks.) Gallopade International.
—Oklahoma History Projects: 30 Cool, Activities, Crafts, Experiments & More for Kids to Do to Learn about Your State! 2003. (Oklahoma Experience Ser.). 32p. (gr. k-5). pap. 5.95 *(978-0-635-01805-2(5),* Marsh, Carole Bks.) Gallopade International.
—Oklahoma Jeopardy! Answers & Questions about Our State. 2004. (Oklahoma Experience! Ser.). (Illus.). 32p. (J). (gr. 3-12). pap. 7.95 *(978-0-7933-9596-5(8))* Gallopade International.
—Oklahoma Jography! A Fun Run Thru Our State. 2004. (Oklahoma Experience! Ser.). (Illus.). 32p. (J). (gr. 3-8). pap. 7.95 *(978-0-7933-9597-2(6))* Gallopade International.
—Oklahoma People Projects: 30 Cool, Activities, Crafts, Experiments & More for Kids to Do to Learn about Your State! 2003. (Oklahoma Experience Ser.). 32p. (gr. k-5). pap. 5.95 *(978-0-635-02005-5(X),* Marsh, Carole Bks.) Gallopade International.
—Oklahoma Symbols Projects: 30 Cool Activities, Crafts, Experiments & More for Kids to Do! 2003. (Oklahoma Experience Ser.). (Illus.). 32p. (J). (gr. k-5). pap. 5.95 *(978-0-635-01905-9(1),* Marsh, Carole Bks.) Gallopade International.
—The Out-of-This-World Oklahoma Coloring Book! 2004. (Oklahoma Experience! Ser.). (Illus.). 32p. (J). (gr. k-2). 3.95 *(978-0-7933-9599-6(2))* Gallopade International.
Murray, Julie. Oklahoma, 1 vol. 2006. (Buddy Book Ser.). (ENG., Illus.). 32p. (gr. 2-4). 27.07 *(978-1-59197-695-0(2),* Buddy Bks.) ABDO Publishing Co.

Orr, Tamra B. America the Beautiful, Third Series: Oklahoma (Revised Edition) 2014. (America the Beautiful Ser.: 3). (ENG.). 144p. (J). lib. bdg. 40.00 *(978-0-531-24897-3(6))* Scholastic Library Publishing.

Sanders, Doug. Oklahoma, 1 vol. Santoro, Christopher, illus. 2006. (It's My State! (First Edition)(r) Ser.). (ENG.). 80p. (gr. 4-4). lib. bdg. 34.07 *(978-0-7614-1906-8(3),* 1284273b-2775-434f-babd-b63a5b50d8eb) Cavendish Square Publishing LLC.

—Oklahoma, 1 vol. 2nd rev. ed. 2013. (It's My State! (Second Edition)(r) Ser.). (ENG.). 80p. (gr. 4-4). pap. 18.64 *(978-1-62712-102-6(1),* c4ed02e6-0328-4c70-b73e-b7053fbacdcf) Cavendish Square Publishing LLC.

Savage, Jeff. Kevin Durant. 2011. (Amazing Athletes Set VIII Ser.). pap. 45.32 *(978-0-7613-8602-5(5));* (ENG., Illus.). 32p. (J). (gr. 2-5). pap. 7.95 *(978-0-7613-7819-8(7),* 8cbabad0-9c09-40c2-bb02-618a6080df8a) Lerner Publishing Group.

Saylor-Marchant, Linda. From Sea to Shining Sea: Oklahoma. 2008. (ENG.). 80p. (J). pap. 7.95 *(978-0-531-20810-6(9),* Children's Pr.) Scholastic Library Publishing.

—Oklahoma. 2003. (From Sea to Shining Sea Ser.: 2). (ENG., Illus.). 80p. (J). 30.50 *(978-0-516-22393-3(3),* Children's Pr.) Scholastic Library Publishing.

Scillian, Devin. S Is for Sooner: An Oklahoma Alphabet. Radzinski, Kandy, illus. 2003. (Discover America State by State Ser.). (ENG.). 40p. (J). (gr. 1-3). 18.99 *(978-1-58536-062-8(7),* 201963) Sleeping Bear Pr.

OKLAHOMA—FICTION

Angelique, A. J. Rose Petals & Ash: Curse of the Red Rose Killer, 1 vol. 2010. 94p. pap. 19.95 *(978-1-4489-5316-5(2))* America Star Bks.

Beard, Darleen Bailey. The Flimflam Man. Christelow, Eileen, illus. 2003. (ENG.). 96p. (J). (gr. 2-5). per. 11.99 *(978-0-374-42345-2(8),* 900021220, Farrar, Straus & Giroux (BYR)) Farrar, Straus & Giroux.

Blom, Jen K. Possum Summer. Rayyan, Omar, illus. 2011. (ENG.). 256p. (J). (gr. 3-7). 17.95 *(978-0-8234-2331-6(X))* Holiday Hse., Inc.

Bonner, Gayle. Life on Peavine Creek: Sam's Story. Johnson, Brandon, illus. 2008. 33p. pap. 24.95 *(978-1-60610-624-2(4))* America Star Bks.

Daly, Jerald James. An Early Snow (the Visions Come) 2008. 180p. pap. 24.95 *(978-1-60703-610-4(X))* America Star Bks.

Fazenbaker, Jo Ann. Daisy & Duke, 1 vol. 2010. 18p. 24.95 *(978-1-4512-1483-3(9))* PublishAmerica, Inc.

Foster, Gary Wayne. Launching Motor: A Summer's Tale of Adventure & Exploration. 2017. (ENG., Illus.). (J). pap. 12.95 *(978-1-55571-873-2(6),* Grid Pr.) L & R Publishing, LLC.

Gensler, Sonia. The Revenant. 2013. 352p. (YA). (gr. 7). pap. 9.99 *(978-0-375-86139-0(4),* Ember) Random Hse. Children's Bks.

Griffis, Molly Levite. The Rachel Resistance. 224p. 8.95 *(978-1-57168-553-7(7))* Eakin Pr.

Hartgraves, Richard. Little Cedar. 2006. 130p. pap. 24.95 *(978-1-4241-4603-1(8))* PublishAmerica, Inc.

Hay, Barbara. Lesson of the White Eagle. Hay, Peter, illus. 2012. (ENG.). 144p. (YA). pap. 11.99 *(978-1-937054-01-4(2))* RoadRunner Pr.

Hesse, Karen. Out of the Dust. 240p. (YA). (gr. 5-18). pap. 4.99 *(978-0-8072-1526-5(0),* Listening Library) Random Hse. Audio Publishing Group.

—Out of the Dust. 2009. (gr. 5-8). 18.40 *(978-0-613-11953-5(3))* Turtleback.

Honderich, Lou. Ricki. 2013. 170p. pap. 10.99 *(978-0-9856906-6-3(6))* Mockingbird Lane Pr.

Hudson, Marilyn A. Annie Oklahoma: Tales of the Plains. 2007. (YA). per. *(978-0-9778850-3-9(8))* Whorl Bks.

—Elephant Hips Are Expensive! A Tale of the Sooner State. Fulco, Haley, illus. 2007. 50p. (J). per. *(978-0-9778850-2-2(X),* WhorlBooks Thumbprints) Whorl Bks.

Hudson, Tara. Arise. 2013. (Hereafter Trilogy Ser.: 2). (ENG.). 432p. (YA). (gr. 8). pap. 9.99 *(978-0-06-202680-4(1),* HarperTeen) HarperCollins Pubs.

—Elegy. 2013. (Hereafter Trilogy Ser.: 3). (ENG.). 400p. (YA). (gr. 8). 17.99 *(978-0-06-202681-1(X),* HarperTeen) HarperCollins Pubs.

—Hereafter. 2012. (Hereafter Trilogy Ser.: 1). (ENG.). 432p. (YA). (gr. 8). pap. 9.99 *(978-0-06-202678-1(X),* HarperTeen) HarperCollins Pubs.

I'm Not Afraid of Needles. 2004. (J). 4.99 *(978-0-9776144-0-0(9))* Kidstalk, LLC.

Jacobs, Lily. The Littlest Bunny in Oklahoma: An Easter Adventure. Dunn, Robert, illus. 2015. (Littlest Bunny Ser.). (ENG.). 32p. (J). (gr. -1-3). 9.99 *(978-1-4926-1165-3(4),* Hometown World) Sourcebooks, Inc.

—The Littlest Bunny in Tulsa: An Easter Adventure. Dunn, Robert, illus. 2015. (Littlest Bunny Ser.). (ENG.). 32p. (J). (gr. -1-3). 9.99 *(978-1-4926-1216-2(2),* Hometown World) Sourcebooks, Inc.

James, Eric. Santa's Sleigh Is on Its Way to Oklahoma: A Christmas Adventure. Dunn, Robert, illus. 2016. (Santa's Sleigh Is on Its Way Ser.). (ENG.). 32p. (J). (gr. k-2). 12.99 *(978-1-4926-4346-3(7),* 9781492643463, Hometown World) Sourcebooks, Inc.

—Santa's Sleigh Is on Its Way to Tulsa: A Christmas Adventure. Dunn, Robert, illus. 2016. (Santa's Sleigh Is on Its Way Ser.). (ENG.). 32p. (J). (gr. k-2). 12.99 *(978-1-4926-4359-3(9),* 9781492643593, Hometown World) Sourcebooks, Inc.

—The Spooky Express Oklahoma. Piwowarski, Marcin, illus. 2017. (Spooky Express Ser.). (ENG.). 32p. (J). (gr. k-6). 9.99 *(978-1-4926-5389-9(6),* Hometown World) Sourcebooks, Inc.

—Tiny the Oklahoma Easter Bunny. 2018. (Tiny the Easter Bunny Ser.). (ENG.). 40p. (J). (gr. k-3). 9.99 *(978-1-4926-5953-2(3),* Hometown World) Sourcebooks, Inc.

Kennedy, Marlane. Tornado Alley. 2014. (Disaster Strikes Ser.: 2). lib. bdg. 14.75 *(978-0-606-35828-6(5))* Turtleback.

Krueger, Kathryn L. Road to Grandma's House. 2005. 128p. pap. 13.95 *(978-1-59800-366-6(6))* Outskirts Pr., Inc.

Lansdale, Joe R. All the Earth, Thrown to the Sky. 2012. (ENG.). 256p. (YA). (gr. 7). pap. 8.99 *(978-0-385-73932-0(X),* Ember) Random Hse. Children's Bks.

Latham, Jennifer. Dreamland Burning. 2018.Tr. of s. (ENG.). 400p. (YA). (gr. 9-17). pap. 11.99 *(978-0-316-38490-2(9))* Little, Brown Bks. for Young Readers.

—Dreamland Burning. 2018.Tr. of s. (YA). lib. bdg. 22.10 *(978-0-606-40637-6(9))* Turtleback.

Leech, Richard W. Adventures of Button Broken Tail, Bk. II. 2011. 249p. (J). 29.99 *(978-1-4535-5219-3(7));* pap. 19.99 *(978-1-4535-5218-6(9))* Xlibris Corp.

Macy, Carolyn. Oklahoma Night Before Christmas. 2017. (ENG., Illus.). (J). pap. 11.99 *(978-0-9989127-2-1(7));* (gr. -1-3). 29.99 *(978-0-9989127-3-8(5))* Macy, Carolyn.

Mary, Agnes. The Story of Sammie. 2011. 28p. pap. 15.99 *(978-1-4568-7771-2(2))* Xlibris Corp.

Mills, Timothy. The Mystery Kids: the Phantom Camper. 2010. 88p. pap. 14.95 *(978-0-557-55089-0(0))* Lulu Pr., Inc.

Morrow, John. Ostrich Egg Omelets. 2017. (ENG., Illus.). (J). 19.99 *(978-0-9790832-1-1(4))* 405 Pubns.

Nayeri, Daniel. Everything Sad Is Untrue: (a True Story) 2020. (ENG., Illus.). 368p. (J). (gr. 7-12). 18.99 *(978-1-64614-000-8(1))* Levine Querido.

Oklahoma Energy Resoures Board, creator. The Road to Petroville: Petro Pete's Adventure. 2008. 15.00 *(978-0-615-19844-6(9))* Oklahoma Energy Resources Board.

Onley, Sandra. Halley the Sheepdog. 2011. (Illus.). 28p. pap. 12.50 *(978-1-61204-237-4(6),* Strategic Bk. Publishing) Strategic Book Publishing & Rights Agency (SBPRA).

Paulsen, Gary. The Legend of Bass Reeves. 2008. (ENG., Illus.). 160p. (YA). (gr. 7-9). mass mkt. 7.99 *(978-0-553-49429-7(5),* Laurel Leaf) Random Hse. Children's Bks.

Penn, Linda M. Is Kentucky in the Sky? 2012. 36p. pap. 9.95 *(978-0-9852488-0-2(7))* Linda M. Penn Author.

Rand, Johnathan. American Chillers #26 Oklahoma Outbreak. 2009. 208p. (J). pap. 5.99 *(978-1-893699-99-1(4))* AudioCraft Publishing, Inc.

Robinson, Gary. Billy Buckhorn Abnormal. 2014. (Billy Buckhorn Ser.: 1). (ENG.). 172p. (YA). (gr. 8-12). pap. 9.95 *(978-1-939053-07-7(2),* 7th Generation) BPC.

—Billy Buckhorn Paranormal. 2015. (Billy Buckhorn Ser.: 2). (ENG.). 120p. (YA). (gr. 8-12). pap. 9.95 *(978-1-939053-08-4(0),* 7th Generation) BPC.

—Billy Buckhorn Supranormal. 2015. (Billy Buckhorn Ser.: 3). (ENG.). 128p. (YA). (gr. 8-12). pap. 9.95 *(978-1-939053-12-1(9),* 7th Generation) BPC.

Sala, Sharon. Lunatic Detective. 2011. 164p. (ENG., Illus.). (J). 21.95 *(978-1-61194-915-5(7));* (YA). pap. 11.95 *(978-1-61194-043-5(5))* BelleBks., Inc.

Schabram, Dennis W. Sugar & Me, 1 vol. 2010. 92p. pap. 19.95 *(978-1-4489-2761-6(7))* America Star Bks.

Schuck, Philip. A Ricochet from Circumstance. 2005. (YA). 19.95 *(978-0-9764670-0-7(3))* Smithfield Capital Corp.

Singh, Navneet. The Key to Light & Darkness: Everything Can Feel Like a Dream... 2013. 344p. pap. 19.92 *(978-1-4907-0948-2(7))* Trafford Publishing.

Sisco, Joann Ellen. Midnight at Faraway Farm. 2008. 79p. pap. 19.95 *(978-1-60474-777-5(3))* America Star Bks.

Skye, Obert. The Eyes of the Want. Sowards, Ben, illus. 2008. (Leven Thumps Ser.: 3). (ENG.). 464p. (J). (gr. 3-7). pap. 10.99 *(978-1-4169-4719-6(1),* Aladdin) Simon & Schuster Children's Publishing.

Smith, Darshiel & Haddi, Javon. Introducing the Rollies. 2013. 28p. pap. 24.95 *(978-1-63000-582-5(7))* America Star Bks.

Sully, Katherine. Night-Night Oklahoma. Poole, Helen, illus. 2017. (Night-Night Ser.). (ENG.). 20p. (J). (gr. -1-1). bds. 9.99 *(978-1-4926-5473-5(6),* Hometown World) Sourcebooks, Inc.

Sumner, Jamie. Roll with It. 2019. (Roll with It Ser.). (ENG., Illus.). 256p. (J). (gr. 5). 19.99 *(978-1-5344-4255-9(3),* Atheneum Bks. for Young Readers) Simon & Schuster Children's Publishing.

Tharp, Tim. Knights of the Hill Country. 2013. (ENG.). 240p. (YA). (gr. 7). pap. 8.99 *(978-0-449-81287-7(1),* Ember) Random Hse. Children's Bks.

—The Spectacular Now. 2010. (ENG.). 304p. (YA). (gr. 9). pap. 9.99 *(978-0-375-86502-2(0),* Knopf Bks. for Young Readers) Random Hse. Children's Bks.

Tingle, Tim. How I Became a Ghost: A Choctaw Trail of Tears Story, 1 vol. l.t. ed. 2013. (ENG., Illus.). 160p. (J). 18.95 *(978-1-937054-53-3(5))* RoadRunner Pr.

—No More No Name. 2017. (PathFinders Ser.: 2). (ENG.). 120p. (YA). (gr. 8-12). pap. 9.95 *(978-1-939053-17-6(X),* 7th Generation) BPC.

—No Name. 2014. (No Name Ser.: 1). (ENG.). 168p. (YA). (gr. 8-12). pap. 9.95 *(978-1-939053-06-0(4),* 7th Generation) BPC.

—Trust Your Name. 2018. (PathFinders Ser.: 4). (ENG.). 144p. (YA). (gr. 8-12). pap. 9.95 *(978-1-939053-19-0(6),* 7th Generation) BPC.

Townsend, Una Belle. Toby & the Secret Code. Coleman Lester, Gwen, illus. 2016. (ENG.). 36p. (J). (gr. k-3). 18.99 *(978-0-9966205-9-8(1))* Doodle and Peck Publishing.

Wallace, Sharolyn. The Adventures of Bruce, Ben & Gerry: Bruce's Dream. 2012. 28p. pap. 17.99 *(978-1-4772-0249-4(8))* AuthorHouse.

Worley, Carla. Freedom Choice: A Book that Allows You to Consider Your Options. 2010. 76p. pap. 23.50 *(978-1-60860-624-5(4),* Strategic Bk. Publishing) Strategic Book Publishing & Rights Agency (SBPRA).

OKLAHOMA—HISTORY

Bolden, Tonya. Searching for Sarah Rector: The Richest Black Girl in America. 2014. (ENG., Illus.). 80p. (J). (gr. 3-7). 24.99 *(978-1-4197-0846-6(5),* 672501, Abrams Bks. for Young Readers) Abrams, Inc.

Brean, Alta. Dear Grandchildren: Growing up on the Frontier. 2003. (Illus.). 144p. 18.95 *(978-0-9726360-0-1(5),* (408) 718-5654) Alta Omnimedia.

Calhoun, Sharon Cooper & English, Billie Joan. Oklahoma Adventure. 2007. (Illus.). 444p. (J). *(978-1-934397-00-8(8))* Apple Corps Pubs.

Coleman, Miriam. Oklahoma: The Sooner State, 1 vol. 2010. (Our Amazing States Ser.). (ENG.). 24p. (J). (gr. 3-3). pap. 9.25 *(978-1-4488-0746-8(8),* 1139e8db-4f8e-4cd6-8f2f-beffb99b9292); lib. bdg. 26.27 *(978-1-4488-0657-7(7),* 0b3241e3-e64d-46e4-8607-54685c25d052) Rosen Publishing Group, Inc., The. (PowerKids Pr.).

Dorman, Robert L. Oklahoma: Past & Present, 1 vol. 2010. (United States: Past & Present Ser.). (ENG.). 48p. (YA). (gr. 5-5). pap. 12.75 *(978-1-4358-9520-1(7),* 8e3b7872-0687-471c-a895-a9fa5fbabf0f); lib. bdg. 34.47 *(978-1-4358-9493-8(6),* fedc5209-04f0-4538-ab5e-861fb310327b) Rosen Publishing Group, Inc., The. (Rosen Reference).

Douglas, Bettye. Portrait of a People: The Bettye Douglas Forum, Inc. Multicultural Resource Book. Douglas, Bettye, ed. Douglas, Ana & Douglas, Garbrielle, illus. 222p. (YA). (gr. 5-13). 100.00 *(978-0-9703183-1-2(6))* Douglas, Bettye Forum, Inc., The.

—Safari Oklahoma Presents: God Bless America Historical. Douglas, Garbrielle, illus. 2003. 22p. (J). (gr. 2-7). wbk. ed. 19.95 *(978-0-9703183-6-7(7))* Douglas, Bettye Forum, Inc., The.

Durrett, Deanne. Oklahoma. 2003. (Seeds of a Nation Ser.). (Illus.). 48p. (J). (gr. 3-5). 23.70 *(978-0-7377-1479-1(4),* Kidhaven) Cengage Gale.

Friesen, Helen Lepp. Oklahoma: The Sooner State. 2012. (Illus.). 24p. (J). *(978-1-61913-391-4(1));* pap. *(978-1-61913-392-1(X))* Weigl Pubs., Inc.

Gish, Melissa. Oklahoma. 2009. (This Land Called America Ser.). 32p. (YA). (gr. 3-6). 19.95 *(978-1-58341-789-8(3))* Creative Co., The.

Hamilton, John. Oklahoma, 1 vol. 2016. (United States of America Ser.). (ENG., Illus.). 48p. (J). (gr. 5-9). 34.21 *(978-1-68078-338-4(6),* 21661, Abdo & Daughters) ABDO Publishing Co.

Horn, Geoffrey M., et al. Oklahoma, 1 vol. 3rd rev. ed. 2015. (It's My State! (Third Edition)(r) Ser.). (ENG., Illus.). 80p. (gr. 4-4). 35.93 *(978-1-62713-213-8(9),* 9fd67ea5-8040-4889-b54a-05be1965bd3b) Cavendish Square Publishing LLC.

Jerome, Kate B. Lucky to Live in Oklahoma. 2017. (Arcadia Kids Ser.). (ENG., Illus.). 32p. (J). 16.99 *(978-0-7385-2799-4(8))* Arcadia Publishing.

—The Wise Animal Handbook Oklahoma. 2017. (Arcadia Kids Ser.). (ENG., Illus.). 32p. (J). 16.99 *(978-0-7385-2838-0(2))* Arcadia Publishing.

Laird, Johnna M. Southwest: New Mexico, Oklahoma, Texas, Vol. 19. 2015. (Let's Explore the States Ser.). (Illus.). 64p. (J). (gr. 5). 23.95 *(978-1-4222-3334-4(0))* Mason Crest.

LeBoutillier, Nate. The Story of the Oklahoma City Thunder. 2010. (NBA — A History of Hoops Ser.). 48p. (YA). (gr. 5-18). 23.95 *(978-1-58341-962-5(4),* Creative Education) Creative Co., The.

Marsh, Carole. Exploring Oklahoma Through Project-Based Learning: Geography, History, Government, Economics & More. 2016. (Oklahoma Experience Ser.). (ENG.). (J). pap. 9.99 *(978-0-635-12360-2(6))* Gallopade International.

Nelson, Vaunda Micheaux. Bad News for Outlaws: The Remarkable Life of Bass Reeves, Deputy U. S. Marshal. Christie, R. Gregory, illus. 2009. (ENG.). 40p. (J). (gr. 3-6). lib. bdg. 19.99 *(978-0-8225-6764-6(4),* 8c280ef7-9537-47d5-9cb7-1dc0fc1aa019, Carolrhoda Bks.) Lerner Publishing Group.

Orr, Tamra B. Oklahoma (a True Book: My United States) (Library Edition) 4th ed. 2018. (True Book (Relaunch) Ser.). (ENG., Illus.). 48p. (J). (gr. 3-5). 31.00 *(978-0-531-23170-8(4),* Children's Pr.) Scholastic Library Publishing.

Paul, Michael. Oklahoma City & Anti-Government Terrorism, 1 vol. 2005. (Terrorism in Today's World Ser.). (ENG., Illus.). 48p. (gr. 5-8). pap. 15.05 *(978-0-8368-6565-3(0),* 7990c4ff-3f07-439c-b53a-4704ddb1d829); lib. bdg. 33.67 *(978-0-8368-6558-5(8),* 12f01c40-96b4-488e-ba9d-a0b1ae68b75a) Stevens, Gareth Publishing LLLP. (Gareth Stevens Secondary Library).

Rigby. When Day Turned to Night. 2014. (Rigby Literacy Ser.). (ENG.). 32p. (gr. 4-4). pap. 12.55 *(978-0-7578-2002-1(6))* Rigby Education.

Sanders, Doug. Oklahoma, 1 vol. 2nd rev. ed. 2013. (It's My State! (Second Edition)(r) Ser.). (ENG.). 80p. (gr. 4-4). 35.93 *(978-0-7614-8001-3(3),* e300e1d3-fbdb-48a9-b6b6-62abc15a315c) Cavendish Square Publishing LLC.

Sleeping Bear Press. Little Oklahoma. Urban, Helle, illus. 2015. (Little State Ser.). (ENG.). 22p. (J). (gr. -1-k). bds. 9.95 *(978-1-58536-927-0(6),* 203817) Sleeping Bear Pr.

Spradlin, Michael P. Jack Montgomery: World War II: Gallantry at Anzio. 2019. (Medal of Honor Ser.: 1). (ENG., Illus.). 112p. (J). pap. 8.99 *(978-1-250-15707-2(2),* 900185139, Farrar, Straus & Giroux (BYR)) Farrar, Straus & Giroux.

Strudwick, Leslie. Oklahoma. 2011. (Guide to American States Ser.). (Illus.). 48p. (YA). (gr. 3-6). 29.99 *(978-1-61690-808-9(4));* (J). 29.99 *(978-1-61690-484-5(4))* Weigl Pubs., Inc.

—Oklahoma: The Sooner State. 2016. (J). *(978-1-4896-4923-2(9))* Weigl Pubs., Inc.

Weatherford, Carole Boston. Unspeakable: The Tulsa Race Massacre. Cooper, Floyd, illus. 2021. (ENG.). 32p. (J). (gr. 3-6). 17.99 *(978-1-5415-8120-3(2),* 6b87db4d-4f0f-40cd-b33b-220fb2aea4ae, Carolrhoda Bks.) Lerner Publishing Group.

Zuchora-Walske, Christine. The Dust Bowl: A History Perspectives Book. 2013. (Perspectives Library). (ENG., Illus.). 32p. (J). (gr. 4-8). 32.07 *(978-1-62431-417-9(1),* 202788); pap. 14.21 *(978-1-62431-493-3(7),* 202790) Cherry Lake Publishing.

OKLAHOMA—HISTORY—FICTION

Davis, Russell G. & Ashabranner, Brent. The Choctaw Code. 2006. 121p. (J). (gr. 3-7). per. 8.99 *(978-1-59166-621-9(X))* BJU Pr.

Griffis, Molly Levite. Simon Says. 2004. vi, 263p. (J). 22.95 *(978-1-57168-836-1(6));* pap. *(978-1-57168-847-7(1))* Eakin Pr. (Eakin Pr.).

Kirby, Susan E. A No-Fuss Christmas. 2010. (J). *(978-1-60682-059-9(1))* BJU Pr.

Love, D. Anne. Semiprecious. (ENG.). 304p. (J). (gr. 5-9). 2009. pap. 6.99 *(978-0-689-87389-8(1))* 2006. (Illus.). 17.99 *(978-0-689-85638-9(5))* McElderry, Margaret K. Bks. (McElderry, Margaret K. Bks.).

McCaughrean, Geraldine. Stop the Train! 2003. (ENG.). 304p. (J). (gr. 5-18). 16.99 *(978-0-06-050749-7(7))* HarperCollins Pubs.

Mitchell, Saundra. The Springsweet. 2013. (ENG.). 304p. (YA). (gr. 7). pap. 16.99 *(978-0-544-00327-9(6),* 1526369, Clarion Bks.) HarperCollins Pubs.

Myers, Anna. Tulsa Burning. 2004. (Illus.). 184p. (J). (gr. 3-7). 16.95 *(978-0-8027-8829-0(7))* Walker & Co.

Scillian, Devin. Pappy's Handkerchief. Ellison, Chris, illus. rev. ed. 2007. (Tales of Young Americans Ser.). (ENG.). 40p. (J). (gr. 1-4). 17.95 *(978-1-58536-316-2(2),* 202120) Sleeping Bear Pr.

Sowards, Ben. Asleep on the Hay: A Dust Bowl Christmas. Sowards, Ben, illus. 2015. (ENG., Illus.). 32p. (J). (gr. 3). 17.99 *(978-1-62972-067-8(4),* 5136478, Ensign Peak) Shadow Mountain Publishing.

Stanley, George E. Night Fires. 2009. (ENG.). 192p. (J). (gr. 3-7). 15.99 *(978-1-4169-7559-5(4),* Aladdin) Simon & Schuster Children's Publishing.

—Night Fires. 2011. (ENG.). 192p. (J). (gr. 3-7). pap. 6.99 *(978-1-4169-1250-7(9),* Simon & Schuster/Paula Wiseman Bks.) Simon & Schuster/Paula Wiseman Bks.

Townsend, Una Belle. The Oklahoma Land Run, 1 vol. Henriquez, Emile, illus. 2008. (ENG.). 32p. (J). (gr. k-3). 16.99 *(978-1-58980-566-8(6),* Pelican Publishing) Arcadia Publishing.

Wallace, Bill. The Dog Who Thought He Was Santa. 2008. (ENG.). 192p. (J). (gr. 3-7). pap. 7.99 *(978-1-4169-4816-2(3),* Aladdin) Simon & Schuster Children's Publishing.

Young, Judy & Scillian, Devin. Westward Journeys. Farnsworth, Bill et al, illus. 2013. (American Adventures Ser.). (ENG.). 96p. (J). (gr. 3-6). pap. 6.99 *(978-1-58536-860-0(1),* 202367) Sleeping Bear Pr.

OLD AGE

see also Older People

Bregoli, Jane. The Goat Lady. Bregoli, Jane, illus. 2008. (ENG., Illus.). 32p. (J). (gr. 2-6). pap. 8.95 *(978-0-88448-309-0(6),* 884309) Tilbury Hse. Pubs.

Kenney, Karen Latchana. Extreme Longevity: Discovering Earth's Oldest Organisms. 2018. (ENG., Illus.). 104p. (YA). (gr. 6-12). 37.32 *(978-1-5124-8372-7(9),* b3b547fc-4921-45c2-a6e2-72a8d836f162, Twenty-First Century Bks.) Lerner Publishing Group.

Naughton, Diane. Secrets to a Long Life Intermediate Book with Online Access, 1 vol. 2014. (ENG., Illus.). 28p. (J). pap., E-Book, E-Book 9.50 *(978-1-107-68378-5(5))* Cambridge Univ. Pr.

Thompson, Tamara, ed. Extending the Human Lifespan, 1 vol. 2013. (At Issue Ser.). (ENG.). 128p. (gr. 10-12). 41.03 *(978-0-7377-6836-7(3),* 09160969-d0ff-489b-9614-fddcc25a5d9d, Greenhaven Publishing) Greenhaven Publishing LLC.

OLD AGE—FICTION

Almond, David. Kit's Wilderness. unabr. ed. 2004. 240p. (J). (gr. 7-18). pap. 36.00 incl. audio *(978-0-8072-8216-8(2),* Listening Library) Random Hse. Audio Publishing Group.

Auch, M. J. Wing Nut. 2008. (ENG.). 256p. (J). (gr. 6-8). pap. 15.99 *(978-0-312-38420-3(3),* 900053321) Square Fish.

Baker, Matthew. If You Find This. 2017. (ENG.). 368p. (J). (gr. 3-7). pap. 18.99 *(978-0-316-24009-3(5))* Little, Brown Bks. for Young Readers.

Bauer, Joan. Best Foot Forward. 2006. (ENG.). 192p. (YA). (gr. 7-18). reprint ed. 7.99 *(978-0-14-240690-8(2),* Speak) Penguin Young Readers Group.

—Best Foot Forward. 2006. 183p. (gr. 7-12). 18.00 *(978-0-7569-6767-3(8))* Perfection Learning Corp.

—Rules of the Road. 2005. (ENG.). 208p. (YA). (gr. 7-7). pap. 9.99 *(978-0-14-240425-6(X),* Speak) Penguin Young Readers Group.

Boné, Thomas H., illus. The Teacher Who Would Not Retire Retires. 2017. (J). *(978-0-9885295-7-1(2))* Blue Marlin Pubns.

Bosak, Susan V. Something to Remember Me By. 2015. 32p. pap. 8.00 *(978-1-61003-553-8(4))* Center for the Collaborative Classroom.

Brooks, Mel & Reiner, Carl. The 2000 Year Old Man Goes to School. Bennett, James, illus. 2006. 32p. (J). (gr. 4-8). reprint ed. 18.00 *(978-1-4223-5622-7(1))* DIANE Publishing Co.

—The 2000 Year Old Man Goes to School. Bennett, James, illus. 2005. (ENG.). 40p. (J). (gr. -1-3). 17.99 *(978-0-06-076676-4(X))* HarperCollins Pubs.

Buckley-Archer, Linda. The Many Lives of John Stone. 2015. (ENG., Illus.). 544p. (YA). (gr. 7). 17.99 *(978-1-4814-2637-4(0))* Simon & Schuster Children's Publishing.

Bundy, Tamara. Walking with Miss Millie. 2018. 240p. (J). (gr. 5). 8.99 *(978-0-399-54457-6(7),* Puffin Books) Penguin Young Readers Group.

Burns, Catherine Lloyd. The Half-True Lies of Cricket Cohen. 2018. (J). lib. bdg. 18.40 *(978-0-606-41096-0(1))* Turtleback.

Caletti, Deb. Honey, Baby, Sweetheart. 2008. (ENG.). 336p. (YA). (gr. 7-12). pap. 9.99 *(978-1-4169-5783-6(9),* Simon Pulse) Simon Pulse.

Cannon. VERDI - català. 2003. (SPA., Illus.). 48p. (J). (gr. 1-3). *(978-84-261-3042-6(9),* JV7591) Juventud, Editorial ESP. Dist: Lectorum Pubns., Inc.

Cannon, Janell. Verdi. pap. 24.95 *(978-85-325-1343-4(3))* Rocco, Editora, Ltda BRA. Dist: Distribooks, Inc.

Cascone, Annette & Cascone, Gina. Deadtime Stories: Grave Secrets. 2014. (Deadtime Stories Ser.). (ENG.). 192p. (J). (gr. 3-7). pap. 14.99 *(978-0-7653-3071-0(7),* 900078490, Starscape) Doherty, Tom Assocs., LLC.

Cherry, Alison. The Classy Crooks Club. 2016. (ENG., Illus.). 336p. (J). (gr. 3-7). 16.99 *(978-1-4814-4637-2(1),* Aladdin) Simon & Schuster Children's Publishing.

Christiansen, Candace. The Mitten Tree. Elaine, Greenstein, illus. 2009. (ENG.). 32p. (J). (gr. -1-1). pap. 13.95 *(978-1-55591-733-3(X))* Fulcrum Publishing.

Cooney, Caroline B. Hit the Road. rev. l.t. ed. 2007. (Thorndike Literacy Bridge Ser.). 259p. (YA). (gr. 7-12). 23.95 *(978-0-7862-9429-9(9))* Thorndike Pr.

Corlell, Shelley. Welcome, Caller, This Is Chloe. 2013. (ENG.). 320p. (YA). (gr. 8-17). pap. 7.95 *(978-1-4197-0545-8(8),* 1003903, Amulet Bks.) Abrams, Inc.

M N O

Currim, Nazli. Grandma Lives with Us. Tung, Kadhima Ren, illus. 2010. 46p. (J). 16.95 *(978-0-9814629-5-0(2))* Acacia Publishing, Inc.

De Baun, Hillary Hall. The Last Stop Before Heaven. Cooper, Floyd, illus. 2012. (ENG.). 236p. (J). pap. 9.00 *(978-0-8028-5398-1(6),* Eerdmans Bks For Young Readers) Eerdmans, William B. Publishing Co.

dePaola, Tomie. Nana Upstairs & Nana Downstairs. unabr. ed. 2006. (J). (gr. k-3). pap. 17.95 incl. audio *(978-0-8045-6943-9(6));* pap. 19.95 incl. audio compact disk *(978-0-8045-4157-2(4))* Spoken Arts, Inc.

Drillon, Anne-Fleur. Cloud Chaser. Puybaret, Eric, illus. (ENG.). 32p. (J). (gr. k-5). 2019. pap. 9.99 *(978-1-78285-412-8(6))* 2018. 17.99 *(978-1-78285-411-1(8))* Barefoot Bks., Inc.

—Cloud Chaser. 2019. (ENG.). 32p. (J). (gr. k-2). 20.49 *(978-1-64310-833-9(6))* Penworthy Co., LLC, The.

Dyan, Penelope. Great Grandma Is Getting Old. Dyan, Penelope, illus. 2010. (Illus.). 42p. pap. 11.95 *(978-1-935118-97-8(8))* Bellissima Publishing, LLC.

Edwards, Michelle. A Hat for Mrs. Goldman: A Story about Knitting & Love. Karas, G. Brian, illus. 2016. 40p. (J). (gr. -1-3). 18.99 *(978-0-553-49710-6(3),* Schwartz & Wade Bks.) Random Hse. Children's Bks.

Ellis, Elina. The Truth about Grandparents. 2019. (ENG., Illus.). 32p. (J). (gr. -1-3). 17.99 *(978-0-316-42472-1(2))* Little, Brown Bks. for Young Readers.

Fagan, Cary. Mr. Tempkin Climbs a Tree. Arbat, Carles, illus. 2019. (ENG.). 32p. (J). (gr. -1-2). 17.99 *(978-1-5415-2173-5(0),* 91d22d39-8a82-48ce-a5d1-699b688c7999, Kar-Ben Publishing) Lerner Publishing Group.

Flood, Pansie Hart. Sometimey Friend. Marshall, Felicia, illus. 2005. 124p. (J). (gr. 3-7). 15.95 *(978-1-57505-866-5(9))* Lerner Publishing Group.

—Sylvia & Miz Lula Maye. Marshall, Felicia, illus. 2003. (Middle Grade Fiction Ser.). 120p. (J). (gr. 3-6). 15.95 *(978-0-87614-204-2(8),* Carolrhoda Bks.) Lerner Publishing Group.

Gantos, Jack. Dead End in Norvelt. 2011. (Norvelt Ser.: 1). (ENG., Illus.). 352p. (J). (gr. 5-9). 19.99 *(978-0-374-37993-3(9),* 900041629, Farrar, Straus & Giroux (BYR)) Farrar, Straus & Giroux.

—Dead End in Norvelt. 2013. (Norvelt Ser.: 1). (ENG., Illus.). 384p. (J). (gr. 5-9). pap. 9.99 *(978-1-250-01023-0(3),* 900084760) Square Fish.

—Dead End in Norvelt. 2013. (J). lib. bdg. 18.40 *(978-0-606-31901-0(8))* Turtleback.

—From Norvelt to Nowhere. 2015. (J). lib. bdg. 18.40 *(978-0-606-37280-0(6))* Turtleback.

Giff, Patricia Reilly. Pictures of Hollis Woods. 2014. (ENG.). 176p. (J). (gr. 3-7). 11.24 *(978-1-63245-318-1(5))* Lectorum Pubns., Inc.

—Pictures of Hollis Woods. 2004. (ENG.). 176p. (J). (gr. 3-7). 8.99 *(978-0-440-41578-7(0),* Yearling) Random Hse. Children's Bks.

Henson, Heather. Grumpy Grandpa. MacDonald, Ross, illus. 2009. (ENG.). 40p. (J). (gr. -1-3). 19.99 *(978-1-4169-0811-1(0),* Atheneum Bks. for Young Readers) Simon & Schuster Children's Publishing.

Hest, Amy. Mr. George Baker. Muth, Jon J., illus. 2007. (ENG.). 32p. (J). (gr. k-3). 7.99 *(978-0-7636-3308-0(9))* Candlewick Pr.

—Mr. George Baker. 2007. lib. bdg. 17.20 *(978-1-4177-9067-8(9))* Turtleback.

Holt, Kimberly Willis. Dancing in Cadillac Light. 2003. 176p. (J). (gr. 5-9). 5.99 *(978-0-698-11970-3(3),* Puffin Books) Penguin Young Readers Group.

—Dancing in Cadillac Light. 2004. 176p. (J). (gr. 4-7). pap. 36.00 incl. audio *(978-0-8072-2095-5(7),* Listening Library) Random Hse. Audio Publishing Group.

Howland, Naomi. The Better-Than-Best Purim, 0 vols. 2012. (ENG.). 32p. (J). (gr. -1-2). 16.99 *(978-0-7614-6203-3(1),* 9780761462033, Two Lions) Amazon Publishing.

Joyce, William. The Leaf Men: And the Brave Good Bugs. Joyce, William, illus. 2017. (World of William Joyce Ser.). (ENG., Illus.). 40p. (J). (gr. -1-3). 17.99 *(978-1-4814-8955-3(0),* Atheneum/Caitlyn Dlouhy Books) Simon & Schuster Children's Publishing.

Kennedy, Marlane. The Dog Days of Charlotte Hayes. 2009. (ENG., Illus.). 240p. (J). (gr. 3-7). 16.99 *(978-0-06-145241-3(6),* Greenwillow Bks.) HarperCollins Pubs.

Kimmel, Eric A. Hanukkah Bear. Wohnoutka, Mike, illus. (ENG.). 32p. (J). (gr. -1-3). 2014. 7.99 *(978-0-8234-3169-4(X))* 2013. 17.99 *(978-0-8234-2855-7(9))* Holiday Hse., Inc.

Lakritz, Deborah. Say Hello, Lily. Avilés, Martha, illus. 2010. (Jewish Identity Ser.). 32p. (J). (gr. -1-3). lib. bdg. 17.95 *(978-0-7613-4511-4(6),* Kar-Ben Publishing) Lerner Publishing Group.

Laminack, Lester L. The Sunsets of Miss Olivia Wiggins, 1 vol. Bergum, Constance R., illus. rev. ed. 2018. 32p. (J). (gr. 1-4). pap. 8.95 *(978-1-68263-063-1(3))* Peachtree Publishing Co. Inc.

Levine, Arthur & Kath, Katie. What a Beautiful Morning. 2016. (ENG., Illus.). 40p. (J). (gr. -1-1). 16.95 *(978-0-7624-5906-3(9),* Running Pr. Kids) Running Pr.

Lynch, Chris. Kill Switch. 2013. (ENG., Illus.). 192p. (YA). (gr. 7). pap. 9.99 *(978-1-4424-5442-2(3),* Simon & Schuster Bks. For Young Readers) Simon & Schuster Bks. For Young Readers.

—Kill Switch. 2012. (ENG.). 176p. (YA). (gr. 7-12). 16.99 *(978-1-4169-2702-0(6))* Simon & Schuster, Inc.

MacLachlan, Patricia. Kindred Souls. (ENG.). (J). (gr. 1-5). 2013. 144p. pap. 6.99 *(978-0-06-052299-5(2))* 2012. 128p. 16.99 *(978-0-06-052297-1(6))* HarperCollins Pubs. (Tegen, Katherine Bks).

Maddox, Jake. Hoop Hustle. Aburto, Jesus, illus. 2015. (Jake Maddox Sports Stories Ser.). (ENG.). 72p. (J). (gr. 3-6). lib. bdg. 25.99 *(978-1-4965-0494-4(1),* 128566, Stone Arch Bks.) Capstone.

Mazer, Norma Fox. Ten Ways to Make My Sister Disappear. (ENG.). 160p. (J). (gr. 4-6). 2012. 21.19 *(978-0-439-83984-6(X))* 2007. 16.99 *(978-0-439-83983-9(1))* Scholastic, Inc. (Levine, Arthur A. Bks.).

Messner, Kate. The Brilliant Fall of Gianna Z. 2017. (ENG.). 224p. (J). pap. 8.99 *(978-1-68119-547-6(X),* 900177249, Bloomsbury USA Childrens) Bloomsbury Publishing USA.

—The Brilliant Fall of Gianna Z. 2017. (J). lib. bdg. 19.65 *(978-0-606-40595-9(X))* Turtleback.

—The Brilliant Fall of Gianna Z. 2010. (ENG.). 208p. (YA). (gr. 4-6). 24.94 *(978-0-8027-9842-8(X),* 9780802798428) Walker & Co.

Mikaelsen, Ben. Petey. 2010. (ENG.). 256p. (J). (gr. 3-7). pap. 7.99 *(978-1-4231-3174-8(6))* Hyperion Bks. for Children.

—Petey. 2011. 8.32 *(978-0-7848-3604-0(3),* Everbind) Marco Bk. Co.

Millard, Glenda. Layla, Queen of Hearts. King, Stephen Michael, illus. 2019. (Kingdom of Silk Ser.: 02). 112p. (Orig.). mass mkt. 4.99 *(978-0-7333-1842-9(8))* ABC Bks. AUS. Dist: HarperCollins Pubs.

Murphy, Barbara Beasley & Wolkoff, Judie. Ace Hits Rock Bottom. 2003. (Can't Stop Ace Ser.: No. 2). 204p. (J). pap. 16.95 *(978-0-86534-408-2(6))* Sunstone Pr.

Myers, Walter Dean. Lockdown. (ENG.). (YA). (gr. 8). 2011. 272p. pap. 10.99 *(978-0-06-121482-0(5))* 2010. 256p. 16.99 *(978-0-06-121480-6(9))* HarperCollins Pubs. (Amistad).

Nelson, Vaunda Micheaux. Don't Call Me Grandma. Zunon, Elizabeth, illus. 2016. (ENG.). 32p. (J). (gr. k-3). E-Book 30.65 *(978-1-4677-9559-3(3));* E-Book 30.65 *(978-1-5124-0661-0(9),* 9781512406610) Lerner Publishing Group. (Carolrhoda Bks.).

Newman, Jeff. The Boys. Newman, Jeff, illus. 2010. (ENG., Illus.). 40p. (J). (gr. -1-2). 19.99 *(978-1-4169-5012-7(5),* Simon & Schuster Bks. For Young Readers) Simon & Schuster Bks. For Young Readers.

Oboh, Rolic. Treasure Hunt. 2006. 108p. pap. 7.99 *(978-1-84426-318-9(5))* Upfront Publishing Ltd. GBR. Dist: Printondemand-worldwide.com.

Oliveros, Jessie. The Remember Balloons. Wulfekotte, Dana, illus. 2018. (ENG.). 48p. (J). (gr. k-4). 18.99 *(978-1-4814-8915-7(1),* Simon & Schuster Bks. For Young Readers) Simon & Schuster Bks. For Young Readers.

Orbeck-Nilssen, Constance. I'm Right Here. Düzakin, Akin, illus. 2015. (ENG.). 28p. (J). 16.00 *(978-0-8028-5455-1(9),* Eerdmans Bks For Young Readers) Eerdmans, William B. Publishing Co.

Paulsen, Gary. Fishbone's Song. 2016. (ENG., Illus.). 160p. (J). (gr. 5). 18.99 *(978-1-4814-5226-7(6),* Simon & Schuster Bks. For Young Readers) Simon & Schuster Bks. For Young Readers.

Pearsall, Shelley. Trouble Don't Last. 2003. (ENG.). 256p. (J). (gr. 3-7). reprint ed. 7.99 *(978-0-440-41811-5(9),* Yearling) Random Hse. Children's Bks.

Reynolds, Cynthia Furlong. Across the Reach. 2007. 269p. (J). (gr. 3-7). 16.95 *(978-1-58726-518-1(4),* Mitten Pr.) Ann Arbor Editions LLC.

Rubin, Adam. Those Darn Squirrels! Salmieri, Daniel, illus. 2008. (ENG.). 32p. (J). (gr. -1-3). 17.99 *(978-0-547-00703-8(5),* 1029826, Clarion Bks.) HarperCollins Pubs.

—Those Darn Squirrels Fly South. Salmieri, Daniel, illus. 2012. (ENG.). 32p. (J). (gr. -1-3). 17.99 *(978-0-547-67823-8(1),* 1475037, Clarion Bks.) HarperCollins Pubs.

Rylant, Cynthia. Henry & Mudge & the Great Grandpas. Stevenson, Suçie, illus. 2006. (Henry & Mudge Ser.). 40p. (gr. k-2). 14.00 *(978-0-7569-6793-2(7))* Perfection Learning Corp.

—Henry & Mudge & the Great Grandpas: Ready-To-Read Level 2. Stevenson, Suçie & Stevenson, Suçie, illus. 2006. (Henry & Mudge Ser.: 26). (ENG.). 40p. (J). (gr. k-2). pap. 4.99 *(978-0-689-83447-9(0),* Simon Spotlight) Simon Spotlight.

—Henry & Mudge & the Great Grandpas: Ready-To-Read Level 2. Stevenson, Suçie et al, illus. 2005. (Henry & Mudge Ser.: 26). (ENG.). 40p. (J). (gr. k-2). 17.99 *(978-0-689-81170-8(5),* Simon Spotlight) Simon Spotlight.

—Mr. Putter & Tabby Clear the Decks. Howard, Arthur, illus. alt. ed. 2011. (Mr. Putter & Tabby Ser.). (ENG.). 44p. (J). (gr. 1-4). pap. 5.99 *(978-0-547-57695-4(1),* 1458450, Clarion Bks.) HarperCollins Pubs.

—Mr. Putter & Tabby Dance the Dance. Howard, Arthur, illus. 2013. (Mr. Putter & Tabby Ser.). (ENG.). 40p. (J). (gr. 1-4). pap. 5.99 *(978-0-544-10496-9(X),* 1540802, Clarion Bks.) HarperCollins Pubs.

—Mr. Putter & Tabby Dance the Dance. 2013. (Mr. Putter & Tabby Ser.). lib. bdg. 16.00 *(978-0-606-32338-3(4))* Turtleback.

—Mr. Putter & Tabby Drop the Ball. Howard, Arthur, illus. 2014. (Mr. Putter & Tabby Ser.). (ENG.). 44p. (J). (gr. 1-4). pap. 5.99 *(978-0-544-34115-9(5),* 1584856, Clarion Bks.) HarperCollins Pubs.

—Mr. Putter & Tabby Drop the Ball. 2014. (Mr. Putter & Tabby Ser.). lib. bdg. 16.00 *(978-0-606-35985-6(0))* Turtleback.

—Mr. Putter & Tabby Hit the Slope. Howard, Arthur, illus. (Mr. Putter & Tabby Ser.). (ENG.). 40p. (J). (gr. 1-4). 2017. pap. 5.99 *(978-1-328-74060-1(9),* 1677037) 2016. 14.99 *(978-0-15-206427-3(3),* 1199224) HarperCollins Pubs. (Clarion Bks.).

—Mr. Putter & Tabby Make a Wish. Howard, Arthur, illus. 2006. (Mr. Putter & Tabby Ser.). (ENG.). 44p. (J). (gr. -1-3). pap. 5.99 *(978-0-15-205443-4(X),* 1196381, Clarion Bks.) HarperCollins Pubs.

—Mr. Putter & Tabby Make a Wish. Howard, Arthur, illus. 2006. (Mr. Putter & Tabby Ser.). (J). (gr. 1-4). 16.00 *(978-0-7569-6892-2(5))* Perfection Learning Corp.

—Mr. Putter & Tabby Ring the Bell. Howard, Arthur, illus. 2012. (Mr. Putter & Tabby Ser.). (ENG.). 44p. (J). (gr. 1-4). pap. 5.99 *(978-0-547-85075-7(1),* 1501053, Clarion Bks.) HarperCollins Pubs.

—Mr. Putter & Tabby Ring the Bell. Howard, Arthur, illus. 2012. (Mr. Putter & Tabby Ser.). lib. bdg. 16.00 *(978-0-606-26614-7(3))* Turtleback.

—Mr. Putter & Tabby Spill the Beans. Howard, Arthur, illus. 2010. (Mr. Putter & Tabby Ser.). (ENG.). 44p. (J). (gr. 1-4). pap. 5.99 *(978-0-547-41433-1(1),* 1429464, Clarion Bks.) HarperCollins Pubs.

—Mr. Putter & Tabby Walk the Dog. Howard, Arthur, illus. 2007. (Mr. Putter & Tabby Ser.). pap. 7.93 *(978-1-4189-5209-9(5))* Houghton Mifflin Harcourt Trade & Reference Pubs.

—The Old Woman Who Named Things. Brown, Kathryn, illus. 2015. 32p. pap. 7.00 *(978-1-61003-498-2(8))* Center for the Collaborative Classroom.

—The Old Woman Who Named Things. Brown, Kathryn, illus. 2004. (gr. -1-3). 17.00 *(978-0-7569-4204-5(7))* Perfection Learning Corp.

Shanker, Myrna Gelman. Lazar, the Good Deed Dog. Robinson, Linda, illus. 2010. (J). *(978-0-9829273-0-4(4))* IGI Pr.

Siebold, Jan. Doing Time Online. 2004. 88p. (gr. 4-7). 17.50 *(978-0-7569-3612-9(8))* Perfection Learning Corp.

Smelcer, John. The Trap. 2007. (ENG.). 176p. (YA). (gr. 7-9). per. 10.99 *(978-0-312-37755-7(X),* 900049151) Square Fish.

Smith, Brian. Memory. 2014. (ENG.). 216p. (C). pap. 14.95 *(978-1-138-87117-5(6),* Y178984, Routledge) Taylor & Francis Group.

Smith, Catharine Bowman, illus. General Butterfingers. 2007. (ENG.). 96p. (J). (gr. 5-7). 7.95 *(978-0-618-75922-4(0),* 486370, Clarion Bks.) HarperCollins Pubs.

Steinhöfel, Andreas. If My Moon Was Your Sun: With CD Audiobook & Music. Palmtag, Nele, illus. 2017. (ENG.). 80p. (gr. 8-12). 19.00 *(978-0-87486-079-5(2))* Plough Publishing Hse.

Steinkellner, Elisabeth. My New Granny. Roher, Michael, illus. 2012. 32p. (J). (gr. -1-3). 16.95 *(978-1-62087-223-9(4),* 620223, Sky Pony Pr.) Skyhorse Publishing Co., Inc.

Stevens, Carla & Stevens, Chapman. Who's Knocking at the Door?, 1 vol. Chapman, Lee, illus. 2004. (ENG.). 32p. (J). 16.95 *(978-0-7614-5168-6(4))* Marshall Cavendish Corp.

Tapia, Jeff. Hippomobile! 2013. (ENG., Illus.). 240p. (J). (gr. 5-7). 16.99 *(978-0-547-99548-9(2),* 1525383, Clarion Bks.) HarperCollins Pubs.

Velásquez, Gloria. Rudy's Memory Walk. 2009. (Roosevelt High School Ser.). 140p. (YA). (gr. 6-18). pap. 9.95 *(978-1-55885-593-9(9))* Arte Publico Pr.

Weakland, Mark. The West End Treehouse Mystery, 1 vol. 2018. (ENG., Illus.). 160p. (J). (gr. 3-7). pap. 9.95 *(978-1-4556-2384-6(9),* Pelican Publishing) Arcadia Publishing.

Weston Woods Staff, creator. Wilfrid Gordon Mcdonald Partridge. 2011. 18.95 *(978-0-439-72916-1(5));* 38.75 *(978-0-439-72917-8(3));* 29.95 *(978-0-439-73530-8(0))* Weston Woods Studios, Inc.

Wojciechowska, Maia. A Kingdom in a Horse. 2012. (ENG.). 160p. (J). (gr. 2-7). pap. 9.95 *(978-1-61608-481-3(2),* 608481, Sky Pony Pr.) Skyhorse Publishing Co., Inc.

Woods, Brenda. Saint Louis Armstrong Beach. 2012. lib. bdg. 16.00 *(978-0-606-26661-1(5))* Turtleback.

Yep, Laurence. The Magic Paintbrush. Wang, Suling, illus. 2003. (ENG.). 96p. (J). (gr. 3-7). pap. 6.99 *(978-0-06-440852-3(3),* HarperCollins) HarperCollins Pubs.

—The Magic Paintbrush. Wang, Suling, illus. 2003. 89p. (J). (gr. 3-7). 12.65 *(978-0-7569-1444-8(2))* Perfection Learning Corp.

OLD TESTAMENT

see Bible—Old Testament

OLDER PEOPLE

Engdahl, Sylvia, ed. The Elderly, 1 vol. 2011. (Current Controversies Ser.). (ENG.). 200p. (gr. 10-12). pap. 33.00 *(978-0-7377-5180-2(0),* c86272fe-a70f-45c3-aa25-b992de7a88df); lib. bdg. 48.03 *(978-0-7377-5179-6(7),* 7caa31d3-38a6-4271-a723-e4c260e0e8a7) Greenhaven Publishing LLC. (Greenhaven Publishing).

Haerens, Margaret, ed. The Aging Population, 1 vol. 2014. (Opposing Viewpoints Ser.). (ENG., Illus.). 256p. (gr. 10-12). pap. 34.80 *(978-0-7377-6944-9(0),* c52b2f38-a894-4f4f-9d72-72b3c7f42ea7); lib. bdg. 50.43 *(978-0-7377-6943-2(2),* dbc4e411-bfb1-4c74-b47e-b0c1bd9dc1d3) Greenhaven Publishing LLC. (Greenhaven Publishing).

Holko, Suzanne L. Grampy & Me. 2012. 34p. pap. 13.95 *(978-1-4624-0080-5(9),* Inspiring Voices) Author Solutions, LLC.

Larocque, Katharine. Helping Seniors. 2019. (Careers Making a Difference Ser.). (Illus.). 80p. (J). (gr. 12). lib. bdg. 34.60 *(978-1-4222-4257-5(9))* Mason Crest.

Lüsted, Marcia Amidon. Supporting the Elderly Through Service Learning, 1 vol. 2014. (Service Learning for Teens Ser.). (ENG.). 80p. (YA). (gr. 7-7). 37.80 *(978-1-4777-7957-6(4),* 14cd395b-dc75-405d-9047-4c57c5993a79, Rosen Young Adult) Rosen Publishing Group, Inc., The.

Martz, Sandra, ed. When I Am an Old Woman I Shall Wear Purple: Petite Version. 2nd gif. rev. ed. 2006. (Illus.). 64p. (C). pap. 47.70 *(978-1-57601-093-8(7))* Nodin Pr.

Orr, Tamra. Ways to Help the Elderly: A Guide to Giving Back. 2010. (How to Help Ser.). (Illus.). 48p. (J). (gr. 4-8). lib. bdg. 29.95 *(978-1-58415-915-5(4))* Mitchell Lane Pubs.

Stranaghan, Crystal J. & Bzymek, Izabela. Safety Superheroes: Preventing Grandparents from Falling. 2010. *(978-0-9867103-0-8(X))* Feldman, Fabio.

OLDER PEOPLE—FICTION

Adams, Pam, illus. There Was an Old Lady Who Swallowed a Fly. 2005. (Classic Books with Holes Ser.). (ENG.). 20p. (J). (gr. -1-1). bds. *(978-0-85953-314-0(X))* Child's Play International Ltd.

Adderson, Caroline. Middle of Nowhere. 2013. 212p. pap. *(978-1-4596-6452-4(3))* ReadHowYouWant.com, Ltd.

Amon, Ras Ran. Gerald Fish of the Spirit! Activity Book. 2006. (J). act. bk. ed. 3.99 *(978-0-9776603-2-2(X))* One Love Assn. Bks.

Atkinson, Ruth & Atkinson, Brett. Story Templates. Atkinson, Ruth & Atkinson, Brett, illus. (Illus.). (J). (gr. k-2). pap. *(978-1-875739-73-8(4))* Wizard Bks.

Babbitt, Natalie. Tuck Everlasting. 2007. (ENG.). 160p. (J). (gr. 5-7). per. 8.99 *(978-0-312-36981-1(6),* 900044325) Square Fish.

Byars, Betsy. The Black Tower. 2007. (Herculeah Jones Mystery Ser.: 7). 144p. (J). (gr. 3-7). 6.99 *(978-0-14-240937-4(5),* Puffin Books) Penguin Young Readers Group.

Colandro, Lucille. There Was an Old Lady Who Swallowed a Bell! Lee, Jared, illus. 2008. (ENG.). 32p. (J). (gr. -1-3). pap. 6.99 *(978-0-545-04361-8(1),* Cartwheel Bks.) Scholastic, Inc.

—There Was an Old Lady Who Swallowed a Chick! Lee, Jared, illus. 2010. (ENG.). 32p. (J). (gr. -1-k). pap. 6.99 *(978-0-545-16181-7(9),* Cartwheel Bks.) Scholastic, Inc.

—There Was an Old Lady Who Swallowed a Chick! 2009. (Illus.). (J). *(978-0-545-06059-2(1))* Scholastic, Inc.

—There Was an Old Lady Who Swallowed a Chick! Lee, Jared, illus. 2010. (There Was an Old Lady... Ser.). lib. bdg. 17.20 *(978-0-606-06821-5(X))* Turtleback.

—There Was an Old Lady Who Swallowed a Clover! 2012. (There Was an Old Lady... Ser.). lib. bdg. 17.20 *(978-0-606-23937-0(5))* Turtleback.

—There Was an Old Lady Who Swallowed Some Books! Lee, Jared, illus. 2012. (There Was an Old Lady... Ser.). lib. bdg. 17.20 *(978-0-606-26208-8(3))* Turtleback.

—There Was an Old Lady Who Swallowed Some Leaves! 2010. (There Was an Old Lady... Ser.). lib. bdg. 17.20 *(978-0-606-15050-7(1))* Turtleback.

Diane Lair, Lair & Lair, Diane. Miss Muggles: The Comical Dog. 2010. 28p. pap. 16.09 *(978-1-4269-2844-4(0))* Trafford Publishing.

Elkeles, Simone. Leaving Paradise. 2007. 23.30 *(978-1-4177-8393-9(1))* Turtleback.

Fuerst, Jeffrey B. The Old Woman Who Lived in a Shoe. Greenhead, Bill, illus. 2010. (Rising Readers Ser.). (J). 3.49 *(978-1-60719-703-4(0))* Newmark Learning LLC.

Gaylord, Laurel Porter. Quiero a Mi Mamá Porque (I Love My Mommy Because Eng/Span Ed) Wolff, Ashley, illus. 2004. Tr. of I Love My Mommy Because. 22p. (J). (gr. -1 — 1). bds. 7.99 *(978-0-525-47248-3(7),* Dutton Books for Young Readers) Penguin Young Readers Group.

Hawkins, June Morris. When Tony Caught a Fish. 2011. 28p. (gr. 1-2). 12.03 *(978-1-4567-5249-1(9))* AuthorHouse.

Howell, Ches Lee. The Old Lady's Story. 2010. 24p. pap. 12.99 *(978-1-4490-0715-7(5))* AuthorHouse.

Hughes, Alison. Kasey & Ivy, 1 vol. 2018. (ENG.). 192p. (J). (gr. 4-7). pap. 10.95 *(978-1-4598-1574-2(2))* Orca Bk. Pubs. USA.

Huser, Glen. Skinnybones & the Wrinkle Queen. 2013. 232p. pap. *(978-1-4596-6507-1(4))* ReadHowYouWant.com, Ltd.

Jeffs, Dixie. The Old Man. 2013. 20p. pap. 24.95 *(978-1-62709-344-6(3))* America Star Bks.

Kiernan, Tim. Liams Luck & Finnegans Fortune. 2009. (ENG.). 144p. pap. 10.95 *(978-1-933916-48-4(6),* Ferne Pr.) Nelson Publishing & Marketing.

Lancett, Peter. The Dark Dreams, 1 vol. unabr. ed. 2010. (Dark Man Ser.). (ENG.). 36p. (YA). (gr. 5-12). pap. 8.75 *(978-1-61651-017-6(X))* Saddleback Educational Publishing, Inc.

Lane, Bruce Courand. The Friendly Little Martian. hasegawa, Juli, illus. 2011. (ENG.). 26p. pap. 15.99 *(978-1-4568-6638-9(9))* Xlibris Corp.

Leedahl, Shelley A. The Bone Talker, 1 vol. Slavin, Bill, illus. 2005. (ENG.). 32p. (J). (gr. 1-3). pap. 8.95 *(978-1-55041-350-2(3),* 52f6412d-7212-456f-8556-ff53a5a017c3) Trifolium Bks., Inc. CAN. Dist: Firefly Bks., Ltd.

Lloyd, Patricia. I Love Me 2! 2012. 20p. pap. 9.95 *(978-0-9771160-5-8(0),* Vaughanworks) Vaughanworks Publishing.

Lovato, David C. The Little Old Man. 2013. (ENG.). 24p. pap. 12.68 *(978-1-4669-8292-5(6))* Trafford Publishing.

Malley, Gemma. The Declaration. 2008. (Declaration Ser.). (ENG., Illus.). 320p. (YA). (gr. 7). 10.99 *(978-1-59990-295-1(8),* 900053613, Bloomsbury USA Childrens) Bloomsbury Publishing USA.

—The Declaration, 7 vols. (YA). 2008. 119.75 *(978-1-4281-7284-5(X))* 2007. 1.25 *(978-1-4281-7275-3(0))* 2007. 121.75 *(978-1-4281-7282-1(3))* 2007. 245.75 *(978-1-4281-7279-1(3))* 2007. 89.75 *(978-1-4281-7280-7(7))* 2007. 91.75 *(978-1-4281-7278-4(5))* Recorded Bks., Inc.

McCumbers, Jaime. Don't Step on the Flowers! 2008. 12p. per. 24.95 *(978-1-4241-9092-8(4))* America Star Bks.

Mejuto Rial, Eva. RUN PUMPKIN, RUN. 2007. (ENG., Illus.). 36p. (J). 17.95 *(978-84-96788-88-6(1))* OQO, Editora ESP. Dist: Baker & Taylor Bks.

Nuñez Alvarez, Maria Luisa. BABY WHISKERS. 2007. (ENG., Illus.). 36p. (J). 17.95 *(978-84-96788-90-9(3))* OQO, Editora ESP. Dist: Baker & Taylor Bks.

The Old Woman in a Shoe: 6 Small Books. (gr. k-2). 23.00 *(978-0-7635-8501-3(7))* Rigby Education.

Peyo. Benny Breakiron #2: Madame Adolphine. Maltaite, illus. 2013. (Benny Breakiron Ser.: 2). (ENG.). 64p. (J). (gr. 2-12). 11.99 *(978-1-59707-436-0(5),* 900123323, Papercutz) Mad Cave Studios.

Pitcher, Caroline. Mariana & the Merchild: A Folk Tale from Chile. Morris, Jackie, illus. 2006. 24p. (J). (gr. k-4). reprint ed. 17.00 *(978-1-4223-5136-9(X))* DIANE Publishing Co.

Porter, Rhonda. Brody Learns about Strangers, 1 vol. 2009. 29p. pap. 19.95 *(978-1-61546-699-3(1))* PublishAmerica, Inc.

Rigby Education Staff. Jumble Tumble Old Woman. (gr. k-2). 21.00 *(978-0-7635-2413-5(1))* Rigby Education.

Shawver, Margaret. What's Wrong with Grandma? A Family's Experience with Alzheimer's. Bagby, Jeffrey K., illus. 2003. 62p. (J). (gr. -1-12). pap. 16.99 *(978-1-59102-174-2(X))* Prometheus Bks., Pubs.

Stark, Ulf. Can You Whistle, Johanna? A Boy's Search for a Grandfather. Segerberg, Ebba, tr. from SWE. Hoglund, Anna, illus. 2004. 48p. (J). (gr. 2-5). 16.95 *(978-1-57143-057-1(1))* RDR Bks.

Stevens, Mitchell. The Village of Lights. Pritchett, Emily, illus. 2018. (ENG.). 32p. (J). (gr. 2-5). 14.99 *(978-1-4621-2275-2(2))* Cedar Fort, Inc./CFI Distribution.

Sullivan, Michael. Escapade Johnson & the Witches of Belknap County. Kolitsky, Joy, illus. 2008. (Escapade Johnson Ser.). (ENG.). 99p. (J). (gr. 2-4). pap. 3.95 *(978-1-929945-90-0(6))* Big Guy Bks., Inc.

Thompson, Kim. Eldritch Manor. 2013. 212p. pap. *(978-1-4596-6312-1(8))* ReadHowYouWant.com, Ltd.

Vanoosting, James. Walking Mary. 2005. 144p. (J). (gr. 7-18). lib. bdg. 16.89 *(978-0-06-028472-5(2))* HarperCollins Pubs.

Walters, Celeste. The Glass Mountain. 2003. 280p. (YA). pap. *(978-0-7022-3297-8(1))* Univ. of Queensland Pr.

Ward, Helen. Moon Dog. 2005. (Illus.). 40p. (J). *(978-1-84011-864-3(4))* Templar Publishing.

Watson, Anne-Marie. The Old Lady in the Woods. 2010. 24p. pap. 14.49 *(978-1-4520-5971-6(3))* AuthorHouse.

Weston Woods Staff, creator. The Little Old Lady Who Was Not Afraid of Anything. 2011. 38.75 *(978-0-545-37497-2(9))*; 18.95 *(978-0-545-37419-4(7))* Weston Woods Studios, Inc.
Wilson, Mark A. The Old Man's Secret Friend, 1 vol. 2009. 19p. pap. 19.95 *(978-1-61582-315-4(8))* PublishAmerica, Inc.

OLIVIA (FICTITIOUS CHARACTER: FALCONER)—FICTION

Considine-Johnson, Joan. Olivia Makes Memories. Spaziante, Patrick, illus. 2015. (J). *(978-1-4806-9185-8(2)*, Simon Spotlight) Simon Spotlight.
Evans, Cordelia. Olivia & the Easter Egg Hunt. 2013. (Olivia 8x8 Ser.). lib. bdg. 14.75 *(978-0-606-27062-5(0))* Turtleback.
—Olivia & the Fancy Party. 2014. (Olivia 8x8 Ser.). lib. bdg. 13.55 *(978-0-606-35762-3(9))* Turtleback.
Falconer, Ian. Olivia. 2004. (Olivia Ser.). (J). (gr. k-3). (FRE., Illus.). spiral bd. *(978-0-616-14599-9(3))*; spiral bd. *(978-0-616-07232-5(5))*; spiral bd. *(978-0-616-07233-2(3))* Canadian National Institute for the Blind/Institut National Canadien pour les Aveugles.
—Olivia. (Olivia Ser.). (FRE.). pap. 29.95 *(978-2-02-041087-8(7))* Editions du Seuil FRA. Dist: Distribooks, Inc.
—Olivia. 2009. (Los Especiales de A la Orilla del Viento Ser.). (SPA.). 32p. (J). 13.99 *(978-968-16-6346-9(2))* Fondo de Cultura Económica.
—Olivia. (Olivia Ser.). pap. 27.95 *(978-85-250-3380-2(4))* Globo, Editora SA BRA. Dist: Distribooks, Inc.
—Olivia. Mlawer, Teresa, tr. 2004. (Olivia Ser.). (SPA., Illus.). (J). (gr. k-2). 16.00 *(978-1-930332-20-1(3)*, LC5675) Lectorum Pubns., Inc.
—Olivia. (Olivia Ser.). *(978-3-7891-6504-7(2))* Oetinger, Friedrich GmbH Verlag.
—Olivia: Book & CD. Falconer, Ian, illus. 2009. (ENG., Illus.). 40p. (J). (gr. -1-3). 15.99 *(978-1-4169-8034-6(2)*, Atheneum Bks. for Young Readers) Simon & Schuster Children's Publishing.
—Olivia ... & the Missing Toy. Falconer, Ian, illus. 2003. (ENG., Illus.). 42p. (J). (gr. -1-3). 19.99 *(978-0-689-85291-6(6)*, Atheneum Bks. for Young Readers) Simon & Schuster Children's Publishing.
—Olivia & the Fairy Princesses. 2013. (CHI.). 40p. (J). (gr. -1-2). *(978-986-189-389-1(X))* Grimm Cultural Ent., Co., Ltd.
—Olivia & the Fairy Princesses. Falconer, Ian, illus. 2012. (ENG., Illus.). 40p. (J). (gr. -1-3). 19.99 *(978-1-4424-5027-1(4)*, Atheneum Bks. for Young Readers) Simon & Schuster Children's Publishing.
—Olivia Forms a Band: Book & CD. Falconer, Ian, illus. 2009. (ENG., Illus.). 50p. (J). (gr. -1-3). 14.99 *(978-1-4169-8037-7(7)*, Atheneum Bks. for Young Readers) Simon & Schuster Children's Publishing.
—Olivia Helps with Christmas. Falconer, Ian, illus. 2007. (ENG., Illus.). 58p. (J). (gr. -1-3). 19.99 *(978-1-4169-0786-2(6)*, Atheneum Bks. for Young Readers) Simon & Schuster Children's Publishing.
—Olivia Saves the Circus. 2004. (Olivia Ser.). (J). (gr. k-2). spiral bd. *(978-0-616-11110-9(X))*; spiral bd. *(978-0-616-11111-6(8))* Canadian National Institute for the Blind/Institut National Canadien pour les Aveugles.
—Olivia Saves the Circus. Falconer, Ian, illus. 2010. (Classic Board Bks.). (ENG., Illus.). 36p. (J). (gr. -1-2). bds. 8.99 *(978-1-4424-1287-3(9)*, Atheneum Bks. for Young Readers) Simon & Schuster Children's Publishing.
—Olivia y Las Princesas. 2012. (SPA., Illus.). 32p. (J). (gr. -1-1). 17.99 *(978-1-933032-82-5(0))* Lectorum Pubns., Inc.
Falconer, Ian, et al. Olivia & Her Great Adventures. Osterhold, Jared & Johnson, Shane L., illus. 2012. (J). *(978-1-4351-4316-6(7)*, Simon Spotlight) Simon Spotlight.
Forte, Lauren. Olivia Goes to the Library. 2013. (Olivia Ready-To-Read Level 1 Ser.). lib. bdg. 13.55 *(978-0-606-35186-7(8))* Turtleback.
Gallo, Tina. Olivia Plays Soccer. 2013. (Olivia Ready-To-Read Level 1 Ser.). lib. bdg. 13.55 *(978-0-606-32060-3(1))* Turtleback.
—Olivia Wishes on a Star. 2014. (Olivia 8x8 Ser.). lib. bdg. 13.55 *(978-0-606-36118-7(9))* Turtleback.
Harvey, Alex. Olivia & the Kite Party. Spaziante, Patrick, illus. 2012. (Olivia Ready-To-Read Level 1 Ser.). lib. bdg. 13.55 *(978-0-606-26360-3(8))* Turtleback.
Mcdoogle, Farrah. Olivia Says Good Night. 2016. (Olivia 8x8 Ser.). lib. bdg. 13.55 *(978-0-606-39244-0(0))* Turtleback.
Oliver, Ilanit. Olivia & the Best Teacher Ever. 2012. (Olivia 8x8 Ser.). lib. bdg. 13.55 *(978-0-606-26367-2(5))* Turtleback.
Shaw, Natalie. A Guide to Being a Big Sister. 2014. (Olivia 8x8 Ser.). lib. bdg. 16.00 *(978-0-606-35761-6(0))* Turtleback.
—A Guide to Being a Friend. 2014. (Olivia 8x8 Ser.). lib. bdg. 16.00 *(978-0-606-36117-0(0))* Turtleback.
—Olivia & the Perfect Valentine. 2013. (Olivia 8x8 Ser.). lib. bdg. 14.75 *(978-0-606-35200-0(7))* Turtleback.
—Olivia Leaps! Osterhold, Jared, illus. 2010. (Olivia TV Ser.). (ENG.). 12p. (J). bds. 8.99 *(978-1-84738-612-0(1))* Simon & Schuster Children's Publishing.
Spinner, Cala. There You Are, Olivia! 2018. (Ready-To-Read Ser.). (ENG.). 32p. (J). (gr. -1-1). 13.89 *(978-1-64310-755-4(0))* Penworthy Co., LLC, The.
—There You Are, Olivia! 2017. (Illus.). (J). *(978-1-5182-5137-5(4)*, Simon Spotlight) Simon Spotlight.
Testa, Maggie. Olivia & the Rain Dance. 2012. (Olivia Ready-To-Read Level 1 Ser.). lib. bdg. 13.55 *(978-0-606-23688-1(0))* Turtleback.

OLMSTED, FREDERICK LAW, 1822-1903

Dunlap, Julie & Olmsted, Frederick Law. Parks for the People: The Life of Frederick Law Olmsted. 2011. (ENG., Illus.). 112p. (J). (gr. 4-7). pap. 12.95 *(978-1-55591-470-7(5))* Fulcrum Publishing.
Wishinsky, Frieda. The Man Who Made Parks: The Story of Parkbuilder Frederick Law Olmsted. Zhang, Song Nan, illus. 2009. 32p. (J). (gr. k-4). pap. 10.95 *(978-0-88776-902-3(0)*, Tundra Bks.) Tundra Bks. CAN. Dist: Penguin Random Hse. LLC.

OLSEN TWINS (FICTITIOUS CHARACTERS)—FICTION

Butcher, Nancy, et al. It's Snow Problem, 3 vols. 2003. (ENG., Illus.). 112p. *(978-0-00-714466-2(0)*, HarperCollins Children's Bks.) HarperCollins Pubs. Ltd.
—Two for the Road. 2003. (ENG., Illus.). 112p. *(978-0-00-714463-1(6)*, HarperCollins Children's Bks.) HarperCollins Pubs. Ltd.
Katschke, Judy, et al. Shore Thing. 2003. (ENG., Illus.). 112p. *(978-0-00-714464-8(4)*, HarperCollins Children's Bks.) HarperCollins Pubs. Ltd.
Olsen, Mary-Kate & Olsen, Ashley. Calling All Boys. 2003. (ENG., Illus.). 112p. *(978-0-00-714472-3(5)*, HarperCollins Children's Bks.) HarperCollins Pubs. Ltd.
—The Cool Club. 2003. (ENG., Illus.). 112p. *(978-0-00-714469-3(5)*, HarperCollins Children's Bks.) HarperCollins Pubs. Ltd.
—Dare to Scare. 2005. (ENG., Illus.). 112p. *(978-0-00-715887-4(5))* HarperCollins Pubs. Australia.
—Dating Game, 2 vols. 2003. (ENG., Illus.). 128p. *(978-0-00-714447-1(4)*, HarperCollins Children's Bks.) HarperCollins Pubs. Ltd.
—A Girl's Guide to Guys. 2003. (ENG., Illus.). 128p. *(978-0-00-714455-6(5)*, HarperCollins Children's Bks.) HarperCollins Pubs. Ltd.
—Let's Party, 3 vols. 2003. (ENG., Illus.). 112p. *(978-0-00-714473-0(3))* HarperCollins Pubs. Australia.
—Love-Set-Match. 2005. (ENG., Illus.). 112p. *(978-0-00-715885-0(8))* HarperCollins Pubs. Australia.
—P. S Wish You Were Here. 2003. (ENG., Illus.). 112p. *(978-0-00-714470-9(9)*, HarperCollins Children's Bks.) HarperCollins Pubs. Ltd.
—Santa Girls, 3 vols. 2005. (ENG., Illus.). 112p. *(978-0-00-715888-1(2))* HarperCollins Pubs. Australia.
—Winner Take All. 2003. (ENG., Illus.). 112p. *(978-0-00-714471-6(7)*, HarperCollins Children's Bks.) HarperCollins Pubs. Ltd.
Stine, Megan, et al. Girl Talk. 2003. (ENG., Illus.). 128p. *(978-0-00-714453-2(9)*, HarperCollins Children's Bks.) HarperCollins Pubs. Ltd.
—Likes Me, Likes Me Not. 2003. (ENG., Illus.). 112p. *(978-0-00-714465-5(2)*, HarperCollins Children's Bks.) HarperCollins Pubs. Ltd.
—War of the Wardrobes. 2003. (ENG., Illus.). 112p. *(978-0-00-714468-6(7)*, HarperCollins Children's Bks.) HarperCollins Pubs. Ltd.

OLYMPICS

Adamson, Thomas K. Olympic Records. 2018. (Incredible Sports Records Ser.). (ENG., Illus.). 32p. (J). (gr. 3-8). pap. 8.99 *(978-1-61891-315-9(8)*, 12110, Blastoff! Discovery) Bellwether Media.
Amstutz, Lisa J. The Science Behind Track & Field. 2016. (Science of the Summer Olympics Ser.). (ENG., Illus.). 32p. (J). (gr. 3-9). lib. bdg. 28.65 *(978-1-4914-8158-5(7)*, 130637, Capstone Pr.) Capstone.
Bach, Greg. The Summer Olympics: On the World Stage. 2020. (J). *(978-1-4222-4446-3(6))* Mason Crest.
Bailey, Linda. Game on in Ancient Greece. Slavin, Bill, illus. 2019. (ENG.). 56p. (J). (gr. 3-7). pap. 11.99 *(978-1-77138-988-4(5))* Kids Can Pr., Ltd. CAN. Dist: Hachette Bk. Group.
Bailey, Tom. Jennifer Chandler: Olympic Champion Diver. 2005. (Alabama Roots Biography Ser.). (Illus.). 112p. (J). pap. *(978-1-59421-014-3(4))* Seacoast Publishing, Inc.
Belval, Brian. Olympic Track & Field. (Great Moments in Olympic History Ser.). 2009. 48p. (gr. 5-6). 53.00 *(978-1-61513-163-1(9)*, Rosen Reference) 2007. (Illus.). 52p. (gr. 3-7). pap. 26.50 *(978-1-4358-3779-9(7))* 2007. (ENG., Illus.). 48p. (YA). (gr. 5-6). lib. bdg. 34.47 *(978-1-4042-0971-8(9)*, 9b4d562c-aa63-4cc1-bcbd-172e30c50573) Rosen Publishing Group, Inc., The.
Brown, Daniel James. The Boys in the Boat (Young Readers Adaptation) The True Story of an American Team's Epic Journey to Win Gold at the 1936 Olympics. (ENG., Illus.). (J). (gr. 5). 2016. 256p. 11.99 *(978-0-14-751685-5(4)*, Puffin Books) 2015. 240p. 19.99 *(978-0-451-47592-3(5)*, Viking Books for Young Readers) Penguin Young Readers Group.
—The Boys in the Boat (Young Readers Adaptation) The True Story of an American Team's Epic Journey to Win Gold at the 1936 Olympics. 2016. lib. bdg. 22.10 *(978-0-606-39312-6(9))* Turtleback.
Burgan, Michael. Miracle on Ice: How a Stunning Upset United a Country. 2016. (Captured History Sports Ser.). (ENG., Illus.). 64p. (J). (gr. 5-9). pap. 8.95 *(978-0-7565-5294-7(X)*, 131254, Compass Point Bks.) Capstone.
Butterfield, Moira. The Olympics - History. 2011. (Olympics Ser.). (ENG.). 32p. (YA). (gr. 4-7). lib. bdg. 28.50 *(978-1-59771-319-1(8))* Sea-To-Sea Pubns.
Butterfield, Moira & Hachette Children's Group. The Olympics Events. 2011. (Olympics Ser.). (ENG.). 32p. (YA). (gr. 4-7). 28.50 *(978-1-59771-321-4(X))* Sea-To-Sea Pubns.
—The Olympics Scandals. 2011. (Olympics Ser.). (ENG.). 32p. (YA). (gr. 4-7). 28.50 *(978-1-59771-320-7(1))* Sea-To-Sea Pubns.
Butterfield, Moira, et al. The Olympics Records. 2011. (Olympics Ser.). (ENG.). 32p. (YA). (gr. 4-7). 28.50 *(978-1-59771-322-1(8))* Sea-To-Sea Pubns.
Carmichael, L. E. The Science Behind Gymnastics. 2016. (ENG., Illus.). 32p. (J). *(978-1-4747-1142-5(1))* Capstone.
Carothers, Thomas. Great Moments in Olympic Soccer. (Super Soccer Ser.). (ENG., Illus.). 32p. (J). 2019. (gr. 4-4). pap. 9.95 *(978-1-64185-626-3(2)*, 1641856262) 2018. (gr. 3-9). lib. bdg. 32.79 *(978-1-5321-1744-2(2)*, 30776) ABDO Publishing Co. (SportsZone).
Christopher, Matt. Great Moments in the Summer Olympics. 2012. (ENG., Illus.). 128p. (J). (gr. 3-7). pap. 9.99 *(978-0-316-19579-9(0))* Little, Brown Bks. for Young Readers.
—The Olympics: Legendary Sports Events. 2008. (ENG., Illus.). 112p. (J). (gr. 3-7). pap. 9.99 *(978-0-316-01118-1(5))* Little, Brown Bks. for Young Readers.
Christopher, Matt & Peters, Stephanie. Great Moments in the Summer Olympics. 2012. (J). lib. bdg. 16.00 *(978-0-606-26159-3(1))* Turtleback.
Clinton, Chelsea. She Persisted in Sports: American Olympians Who Changed the Game. Boiger, Alexandra, illus. (She Persisted Ser.). (J). 2022. 30p. (— 1). bds. 9.99 *(978-0-593-35341-7(2))* 2020. 32p. (gr. -1-3). 17.99 *(978-0-593-11454-4(X))* Penguin Young Readers Group. (Philomel Bks.).
Conway, Hollis. Grasshopper: The Hollis Conway Story. 2004. 30p. (J). per. *(978-1-59196-584-8(5))* Instant Pub.
Crabtree Publishing, compiled by. The Olympic Sports. 2008. (ENG.). 32p. (J). (gr. -1-3). *(978-0-7787-4011-7(0))* Crabtree Publishing Co.
D'Addona, Dan & Sandeno, Kaitlin. Golden Glow: How Kaitlin Sandeno Achieved Gold in the Pool & in Life. 2019. (Illus.). 160p. 38.00 *(978-1-5381-1703-3(7))* Rowman & Littlefield Publishers, Inc.
Doeden, Matt. Combat Sports. 2015. (Summer Olympic Sports Ser.). (ENG., Illus.). 32p. (J). (gr. 2-4). 19.95 *(978-1-60753-807-3(5))* Amicus Learning.
—Track & Field. 2015. (Summer Olympic Sports Ser.). (ENG., Illus.). 32p. (J). (gr. 2-4). 19.95 *(978-1-60753-810-3(5))* Amicus Learning.
—Volleyball. 2015. (Summer Olympic Sports Ser.). (ENG., Illus.). 32p. (J). (gr. 2-4). 19.95 *(978-1-60753-811-0(3))* Amicus Learning.
Dublin, Anne. Bobbie Rosenfeld: The Olympian Who Could Do Everything, 1 vol. 2004. (ENG., Illus.). 152p. (J). (gr. 4-8). pap. 14.95 *(978-1-896764-82-5(7))* Second Story Pr. CAN. Dist: Orca Bk. Pubs. USA.
Dunn, Joe. Miracle on Ice, 1 vol. Dunn, Ben, illus. 2007. (Graphic History Ser.). (ENG.). 32p. (J). (gr. 3-8). 32.79 *(978-1-60270-077-2(X)*, 9040, Graphic Planet - Fiction) Magic Wagon.
Dyan, Penelope. The Rain in Spain — -A Kid's Guide to Barcelona, Spain. Weigand, John D., photos by. 2011. (Illus.). 38p. pap. 12.95 *(978-1-935630-56-2(3))* Bellissima Publishing, LLC.
—The Squeaky Wheel Gets to Greece — -A Kid's Guide to Athens, Greece. Weigand, John D., photos by. 2011. (Illus.). 36p. pap. 11.95 *(978-1-935630-58-6(X))* Bellissima Publishing, LLC.
Dzidrums, Christine. Yuna Kim: Ice Queen. Rendon, Leah, ed. Dzidrums, Joseph et al, photos by. 2011. (Skate Stars Ser.: Vol. 2). (Illus.). 72p. (YA). pap. 10.99 *(978-0-9826435-9-4(4))* Creative Media Publishing.
Dzidrums, Christine & Rendon, Leah. Joannie Rochette: Canadian Ice Princess. Allison, Elizabeth, ed. Adeff, Jay & Mittan, J. Barry, photos by. 2nd exp. rev. ed. 2010. (Skate Stars Ser.: Vol. 1). (Illus.). 100p. (YA). pap. 12.99 *(978-0-9826435-0-1(0))* Creative Media Publishing.
Farbs, C. Olympic Ice Skating. 2009. (Great Moments in Olympic History Ser.). 48p. (gr. 5-6). 53.00 *(978-1-61513-161-7(2)*, Rosen Reference) Rosen Publishing Group, Inc., The.
Faster, Higher, Stronger: The Olympics, 6 vols. (Book2WebTM Ser.). (gr. 4-8). 36.50 *(978-0-322-02984-2(8))* Wright Group/McGraw-Hill.
Fishman, Jon M. Michael Phelps. 2017. (Sports All-Stars Ser.). (ENG.). 32p. (J). (gr. 2-5). 12.99 *(978-1-5124-5400-0(1)*, Lerner Pubns.); 39.99 *(978-1-5124-5398-0(6)*, Lerner Pubns.); (Illus.). pap. 9.99 *(978-1-5124-5401-7(X)*, c7692f5e-3c98-491b-9751-34f1c4f6d4dd); (Illus.). lib. bdg. 29.32 *(978-1-5124-5396-6(X)*, c4231634-53a0-4a1e-af58-63f53e4c480a, Lerner Pubns.); (Illus.). E-Book 42.65 *(978-1-5124-5397-3(8)*, Lerner Pubns.) Lerner Publishing Group.
Ford, Jeanne Marie. The 12 Most Influential Athletes of All Time. 2018. (Most Influential Ser.). (ENG., Illus.). 32p. (J). (gr. 3-6). 32.80 *(978-1-63235-407-5(1)*, 13744, 12-Story Library) Bookstaves, LLC.
Ford, Michael. You Wouldn't Want to Be A Greek Athlete! 2014. (You Wouldn't Want to... Ser.). (ENG.). 32p. (J). lib. bdg. 29.00 *(978-0-531-21175-5(4)*, Watts, Franklin) Scholastic Library Publishing.
Ford, Michael & Salariya, David. You Wouldn't Want to Be a Greek Athlete! Races You'd Rather Not Run. Antram, David, illus. 2004. (You Wouldn't Want to Ser.). (ENG.). 32p. (J). 29.00 *(978-0-531-12352-2(9))* Scholastic Library Publishing.
Frederick, Shane. Boxing. 2012. (Illus.). 48p. (J). 35.65 *(978-1-60818-209-1(6)*, Creative Education) Creative Co., The.
—Track & Field. 2012. (Illus.). 48p. (J). 35.65 *(978-1-60818-212-1(6)*, Creative Education) Creative Co., The.
Gifford, Clive. Ball Sports. 2011. (Olympic Sports Ser.). 32p. (YA). (gr. 4-7). 19.95 *(978-1-60753-188-3(7))* Amicus Learning.
—Basketball & Other Ball Sports. 2011. (ENG., Illus.). 32p. (J). pap. 10.95 *(978-1-77092-035-4(8))* Saunders Bk. Co. CAN. Dist: RiverStream Publishing.
—Combat Sports. 2011. (ENG., Illus.). 32p. (J). pap. 10.95 *(978-1-77092-036-1(6))* Saunders Bk. Co. CAN. Dist: RiverStream Publishing.
—Cycling. 2011. (Olympic Sports Ser.). (ENG.). 32p. (J). (gr. 4-8). lib. bdg. 28.50 *(978-1-60753-190-6(9)*, 17105) Amicus.
—Cycling. 2011. (ENG., Illus.). 32p. (J). pap. 10.95 *(978-1-77092-037-8(4))* Saunders Bk. Co. CAN. Dist: RiverStream Publishing.
—Gymnastics. 2011. (Olympic Sports Ser.). (ENG.). 32p. (J). (gr. 4-8). lib. bdg. 28.50 *(978-1-60753-191-3(7)*, 17106) Amicus.
—Gymnastics. 2011. (ENG., Illus.). 32p. (J). pap. 10.95 *(978-1-77092-038-5(2))* Saunders Bk. Co. CAN. Dist: RiverStream Publishing.
—Swimming & Diving. 2011. (Olympic Sports Ser.). (ENG.). 32p. (J). (gr. 4-8). lib. bdg. 19.95 *(978-1-60753-192-0(5)*, 17107) Amicus.
—Swimming & Diving. 2011. (ENG., Illus.). 32p. (J). pap. 10.95 *(978-1-77092-039-2(0))* Saunders Bk. Co. CAN. Dist: RiverStream Publishing.
—Track & Field. 2011. (Olympic Sports Ser.). (ENG.). 32p. (J). (gr. 4-8). lib. bdg. 28.50 *(978-1-60753-187-6(9)*, 17108) Amicus.
—Track & Field. 2011. (ENG., Illus.). 32p. (J). pap. 10.95 *(978-1-77092-040-8(4))* Saunders Bk. Co. CAN. Dist: RiverStream Publishing.
Gitlin, Martin. The 1980 U. S. Olympic Boycott: A History Perspectives Book. 2014. (Perspectives Library). (ENG., Illus.). 32p. (J). (gr. 4-8). 32.07 *(978-1-62431-663-0(8)*, 203216) Cherry Lake Publishing.
Gitlin, Marty. Lindsey Vonn: Olympic Ski Champion, 1 vol. 2018. (Living Legends of Sports Ser.). (ENG.). 48p. (gr. 5-6). pap. 15.05 *(978-1-5081-0639-5(8)*, 1480639d-17cf-43f2-8718-18dd65e04b3d, Britannica Educational Publishing) Rosen Publishing Group, Inc., The.
Goldish, Meish. Michael Phelps: Anything Is Possible! 2009. (Defining Moments Ser.). (Illus.). 32p. (YA). (gr. 2-5). lib. bdg. 28.50 *(978-1-59716-855-7(6))* Bearport Publishing Co., Inc.
Great Moments in Olympic History, 10 vols., Set. Incl. Olympic Basketball. Hofstetter, Adam B. (YA). lib. bdg. 34.47 *(978-1-4042-0967-1(0)*, 1306d162-405e-489c-b4e2-b1a95f5e69ec); Olympic Gymnastics. Hofstetter, Adam B. (J). lib. bdg. 34.47 *(978-1-4042-0968-8(9)*, 798df64e-e4dc-4583-9f17-1d448c33c199, Rosen Reference); Olympic Swimming & Diving. Kehm, Greg. (YA). lib. bdg. 34.47 *(978-1-4042-0970-1(0)*, f230c654-7ef6-4adb-bc81-9080dc33cd67); Olympic Track & Field. Belval, Brian. (YA). lib. bdg. 34.47 *(978-1-4042-0971-8(9)*, 9b4d562c-aa63-4cc1-bcbd-172e30c50573); Olympic Wrestling. Linde, Barbara M. (YA). lib. bdg. 34.47 *(978-1-4042-0972-5(7)*, ee6cb8eb-6a82-4f4b-98eb-35a4a88d2322); (Illus.). 48p. (gr. 5-6). 2007. (Great Moments in Olympic History Ser.). (ENG.). 2003. Set lib. bdg. 172.35 *(978-1-4042-0933-6(6)*, 0361dc31-1865-44b6-a996-8d4495e5c6e0) Rosen Publishing Group, Inc., The.
Gustaitis, Joseph. Snowboard. 2009. (Winter Olympic Sports Ser.). (ENG., Illus.). 32p. (J). (gr. 3-6). lib. bdg. *(978-0-7787-4026-1(9))* Crabtree Publishing Co.
—Speed Skating. 2009. (Winter Olympic Sports Ser.). (ENG., Illus.). 32p. (J). (gr. 3-6). lib. bdg. *(978-0-7787-4027-8(7))* Crabtree Publishing Co.
Hellebuyck, Adam & Deimel, Laura. Olympics. 2019. (21st Century Skills Library: Global Citizens: Sports Ser.). (ENG.). 32p. (J). (gr. 4-7). pap. 14.21 *(978-1-5341-5039-3(0)*, 213463); (Illus.). lib. bdg. 32.07 *(978-1-5341-4753-9(5)*, 213462) Cherry Lake Publishing.
—Special Olympics. 2019. (21st Century Skills Library: Global Citizens: Sports Ser.). (ENG., Illus.). 32p. (J). (gr. 4-7). pap. 14.21 *(978-1-5341-5040-9(4)*, 213467); lib. bdg. 32.07 *(978-1-5341-4754-6(3)*, 213466) Cherry Lake Publishing.
Herman, Gail. What Are the Summer Olympics? 2016. (What Is... ? Ser.). lib. bdg. 16.00 *(978-0-606-38413-1(8))* Turtleback.
Herman, Gail & Who HQ. What Are the Summer Olympics? Marchesi, Stephen, illus. 2016. (What Was? Ser.). 112p. (J). (gr. 3-7). 5.99 *(978-0-448-48834-9(5)*, Penguin Workshop) Penguin Young Readers Group.
Hernandez, Laurie. I Got This: To Gold & Beyond. (ENG., Illus.). 240p. (J). (gr. 3-7). 2018. pap. 8.99 *(978-0-06-267732-7(2))* 2017. 17.99 *(978-0-06-267731-0(4)*, HarperCollins) HarperCollins Pubs.
Herzog, Brad. G Is for Gold Medal: An Olympics Alphabet. Bowles, Doug, illus. rev. ed. 2011. (Sports Alphabet Ser.). (ENG.). 32p. (J). (gr. 1-4). 15.95 *(978-1-58536-462-6(2)*, 202184) Sleeping Bear Pr.
—G Is for Gold Medal: An Olympics Alphabet. Bowles, Doug, illus. 2015. (Av2 Fiction Readalong 2016 Ser.). (ENG.). (J). (gr. 1-4). lib. bdg. 34.28 *(978-1-4896-3738-3(9)*, AV2 by Weigl) Weigl Pubs., Inc.
Hess, Debra & Olson, Tod. The Modern Olympics: Battling for Peace. 2006. (Lynx2 Social Studies). (ENG., Illus.). 32p. (J). (gr. 6-8). pap. 13.60 *(978-1-4190-2308-8(X))* Heinemann-Raintree.
Hofstetter, Adam. Olympic Basketball. 2007. 52p. pap. 26.50 *(978-1-4358-3778-2(9))* Rosen Publishing Group, Inc., The.
Hofstetter, Adam B. Olympic Basketball. 2009. (Great Moments in Olympic History Ser.). 48p. (gr. 5-6). 53.00 *(978-1-61513-157-0(4)*, Rosen Reference) Rosen Publishing Group, Inc., The.
—Olympic Gymnastics. (Great Moments in Olympic History Ser.). 48p. (gr. 5-6). 2009. 53.00 *(978-1-61513-160-0(4))* 2007. (ENG., Illus.). (J). lib. bdg. 34.47 *(978-1-4042-0968-8(9)*, 798df64e-e4dc-4583-9f17-1d448c33c199) Rosen Publishing Group, Inc., The. (Rosen Reference).
Hunter, Nick. The 2012 London Olympics: An Unofficial Guide. 2011. (Olympics Ser.). (ENG.). 32p. (J). (gr. 3-5). 33.32 *(978-1-4109-4119-0(1)*, 115049); pap. 7.99 *(978-1-4109-4125-1(6)*, 115054) Capstone. (Heinemann).
Johnson, Robin. Bobsleigh, Luge, & Skeleton. 2009. (Winter Olympic Sports Ser.). (ENG., Illus.). 32p. (J). (gr. 3-6). lib. bdg. *(978-0-7787-4024-7(2))* Crabtree Publishing Co.
—Olympic Heroes & Zeroes. 2012. (ENG., Illus.). 48p. (J). *(978-0-7787-7930-8(0))*; pap. *(978-0-7787-7939-1(4))* Crabtree Publishing Co.
Keen, Marian. Lexi & Hippocrates: Find Trouble at the Olympics. Jodie, Dias & Wendy, Watson, illus. 2014. (ENG.). 92p. pap. *(978-1-77141-026-7(4)*, Influence Publishing) Lean Marketing Pr.
Kehm, Greg. Olympic Swimming & Diving. (Great Moments in Olympic History Ser.). 48p. (gr. 5-6). 2009. 53.00 *(978-1-61513-162-4(0)*, Rosen Reference) 2007. (ENG., Illus.). (YA). lib. bdg. 34.47 *(978-1-4042-0970-1(0)*, f230c654-7ef6-4adb-bc81-9080dc33cd67) Rosen Publishing Group, Inc., The.
Kelley, K. C. Choose a Career Adventure at the Olympics. 2016. (Bright Futures Press: Choose a Career Adventure Ser.). (ENG., Illus.). 32p. (J). (gr. 4-6). 32.07 *(978-1-63471-914-8(X)*, 208977) Cherry Lake Publishing.
Kennedy, Mike. Michael Phelps, 1 vol. 2009. (People We Should Know (Second Series) Ser.). (ENG.). 48p. (J). (gr. 3-5). pap. 11.50 *(978-1-4339-2151-3(0)*, c10eb56c-5cde-4362-a61e-2c47cff7d4b5); lib. bdg. 33.67 *(978-1-4339-1950-3(8)*, 9c4d1374-f328-4c9d-9fa4-58c0d6e8c863) Stevens, Gareth Publishing LLLP. (Gareth Stevens Learning Library).
Labrecque, Ellen. Alpine Skiing. 2018. (21st Century Skills Library: Global Citizens: Olympic Sports Ser.). (ENG., Illus.). 32p. (J). (gr. 4-7). pap. 14.21 *(978-1-5341-0849-3(1)*, 210760); lib. bdg. 32.07 *(978-1-5341-0750-2(9)*, 210759) Cherry Lake Publishing.
—Curling. 2018. (21st Century Skills Library: Global Citizens: Olympic Sports Ser.). (ENG., Illus.). 32p. (J). (gr. 4-7). pap. 14.21 *(978-1-5341-0853-0(X)*, 210776); lib. bdg. 32.07 *(978-1-5341-0754-0(1)*, 210775) Cherry Lake Publishing.
—Figure Skating. 2018. (21st Century Skills Library: Global Citizens: Olympic Sports Ser.). (ENG.). 32p. (J). (gr. 4-7).

pap. 14.21 *(978-1-5341-0855-4(6)*, 210784); (Illus.). lib. bdg. 32.07 *(978-1-5341-0756-4(8)*, 210783) Cherry Lake Publishing.

—Ice Hockey. 2018. (21st Century Skills Library: Global Citizens: Olympic Sports Ser.). (ENG., Illus.). 32p. (J). (gr. 4-7). pap. 14.21 *(978-1-5341-0851-6(3)*, 210768); lib. bdg. 32.07 *(978-1-5341-0752-6(5)*, 210767) Cherry Lake Publishing.

—Nordic Skiing. 2018. (21st Century Skills Library: Global Citizens: Olympic Sports Ser.). (ENG.). 32p. (J). (gr. 4-7). pap. 14.21 *(978-1-5341-0850-9(5)*, 210764); (Illus.). lib. bdg. 32.07 *(978-1-5341-0751-9(7)*, 210763) Cherry Lake Publishing.

—Sliding. 2018. (21st Century Skills Library: Global Citizens: Olympic Sports Ser.). (ENG., Illus.). 32p. (J). (gr. 4-7). pap. 14.21 *(978-1-5341-0852-3(1)*, 210772); lib. bdg. 32.07 *(978-1-5341-0753-3(3)*, 210771) Cherry Lake Publishing.

—Snowboarding. 2018. (21st Century Skills Library: Global Citizens: Olympic Sports Ser.). (ENG.). 32p. (J). (gr. 4-7). pap. 14.21 *(978-1-5341-0848-6(3)*, 210756); (Illus.). lib. bdg. 32.07 *(978-1-5341-0749-6(5)*, 210755) Cherry Lake Publishing.

—Speed Skating. 2018. (21st Century Skills Library: Global Citizens: Olympic Sports Ser.). (ENG., Illus.). 32p. (J). (gr. 4-7). pap. 14.21 *(978-1-5341-0854-7(8)*, 210780); lib. bdg. 32.07 *(978-1-5341-0755-7(X)*, 210779) Cherry Lake Publishing.

Lacey, Minna. Story of the Olympics. 2008. (Young Reading Series 2 Gift Bks). 64p. (J). 8.99 *(978-0-7945-1934-6(2)*, Usborne) EDC Publishing.

Lanser, Amanda. The Science Behind Swimming, Diving, & Other Water Sports. 2016. (Science of the Summer Olympics Ser.). (ENG., Illus.). 32p. (J). pap. 48.70 *(978-1-4914-8169-1(2)*, 23985) Capstone.

LeBoutillier, Nate. Basketball. 2012. (J). 35.65 *(978-1-60818-208-4(8)*, Creative Education) Creative Co., The.

—Gymnastics. 2012. (J). 35.65 *(978-1-60818-210-7(X)*, Creative Education) Creative Co., The.

—Swimming. 2012. (J). 35.65 *(978-1-60818-211-4(8)*, Creative Education) Creative Co., The.

—Volleyball. 2012. (Summer Olympic Legends Ser.). (ENG., Illus.). 48p. (J). (gr. 5-8). 35.65 *(978-1-60818-213-8(4)*, 22293, Creative Education) Creative Co., The.

Levin, Ina. Journey to Athens: Grades 4-6. 2004. (U. S. Olympic Committee's Activity Book Ser.). (ENG.). 64p. (J). pap. 9.99 *(978-1-58000-121-2(1))* Griffin Publishing Group.

Levin, Ina & Siskind, Ellyn. Journey to Athens: Grades 1-3. 2004. (U. S. Olympic Committee's Activity Book Ser.). (ENG., Illus.). 32p. (J). pap. 7.99 *(978-1-58000-120-5(3))* Griffin Publishing Group.

Linde, Barbara. Olympic Wrestling. 2009. (Great Moments in Olympic History Ser.). 48p. (gr. 5-6). 53.00 *(978-1-61513-166-2(3)*, Rosen Reference) Rosen Publishing Group, Inc., The.

Linde, Barbara M. Olympic Wrestling, 1 vol. 2007. (Great Moments in Olympic History Ser.). (ENG., Illus.). 48p. (YA). (gr. 5-6). lib. bdg. 34.47 *(978-1-4042-0972-5(7)*, ee6cb8eb-6a82-4f4b-98eb-35a4a88d2322) Rosen Publishing Group, Inc., The.

Marsh, Carole. Greece: A Volcanic Land of Ancient Olympic Origins! 2009. (It's Your World Ser.). 48p. (J). (gr. 2-9). pap. 7.99 *(978-0-635-06818-7(4))* Gallopade International.

McCarthy, Meghan. The Wildest Race Ever: The Story of the 1904 Olympic Marathon. McCarthy, Meghan, illus. 2016. (ENG., Illus.). 48p. (J). (gr. -1-3). 18.99 *(978-1-4814-0639-0(6)*, Simon & Schuster/Paula Wiseman Bks.) Simon & Schuster/Paula Wiseman Bks.

McDonald, Scott. Record Breakers. 2020. (J). *(978-1-4222-4447-0(4))* Mason Crest.

Michael Phelps. rev. ed. 2009. (Amazing Athletes Ser.). (gr. 2-5). pap. 6.95 *(978-0-7613-4138-3(2)*, First Avenue Editions) Lerner Publishing Group.

Moening, Kate. Simone Biles: Olympic Gymnast. 2020. (Women Leading the Way Ser.). (ENG.). 24p. (J). (gr. k-3). lib. bdg. 26.95 *(978-1-64487-123-2(8)*, Blastoff! Readers) Bellwether Media.

Morey, Allan. Basketball. 2015. (Summer Olympic Sports Ser.). (ENG., Illus.). 32p. (J). (gr. 2-4). 19.95 *(978-1-60753-806-6(7))* Amicus Learning.

—Gymnastics. 2015. (Summer Olympic Sports Ser.). (ENG., Illus.). 32p. (J). (gr. 2-4). 19.95 *(978-1-60753-808-0(3))* Amicus Learning.

—Swimming & Diving. 2015. (Summer Olympic Sports Ser.). (ENG., Illus.). 32p. (J). (gr. 2-4). 19.95 *(978-1-60753-809-7(1))* Amicus Learning.

Nardo, Don. Massacre in Munich: How Terrorists Changed the Olympics & the World. 2016. (Captured History Sports Ser.). (ENG., Illus.). 64p. (J). (gr. 5-9). lib. bdg. 35.32 *(978-0-7565-5292-3(3)*, 130887, Compass Point Bks.) Capstone.

Nussbaum, Ben. Showdown: Olympics. 2018. (TIME(r): Informational Text Ser.). (ENG., Illus.). 48p. (J). (gr. 5-8). pap. 13.99 *(978-1-4258-4999-3(7))* Teacher Created Materials, Inc.

Osborne, M. K. El Atletismo. 2020. (Deportes Olímpicos de Verano Ser.). (SPA.). 32p. (J). (gr. 2-5). lib. bdg. *(978-1-68151-899-2(6)*, 10703) Amicus.

—El Baloncesto. 2020. (Deportes Olímpicos de Verano Ser.). (SPA.). 32p. (J). (gr. 2-5). lib. bdg. *(978-1-68151-895-4(3)*, 10705) Amicus.

—La Gimnasia. 2020. (Deportes Olímpicos de Verano Ser.). (SPA.). 32p. (J). (gr. 2-5). lib. bdg. *(978-1-68151-897-8(X)*, 10701) Amicus.

—Los Deportes de Combate. 2020. (Deportes Olímpicos de Verano Ser.). (SPA.). 32p. (J). (gr. 2-5). lib. bdg. *(978-1-68151-896-1(1)*, 10706) Amicus.

—La Natación y Los Saltos Ornamentales. 2020. (Deportes Olímpicos de Verano Ser.). (SPA.). 32p. (J). (gr. 2-5). lib. bdg. *(978-1-68151-898-5(8)*, 10702) Amicus.

—Track & Field. 2020. (Summer Olympic Sports Ser.). (ENG.). 32p. (J). (gr. 2-5). *(978-1-68151-825-1(2)*, 10699) Amicus.

—El Vóleibol. 2020. (Deportes Olímpicos de Verano Ser.). (SPA.). 32p. (J). (gr. 2-5). lib. bdg. *(978-1-68151-900-5(3)*, 10704) Amicus.

—Volleyball. 2nd ed. 2020. (Summer Olympic Sports Ser.). (ENG., Illus.). 32p. (J). (gr. 2-4). pap. 11.99 *(978-1-68152-554-9(2)*, 10753) Amicus.

Osborne, Mary Pope & Boyce, Natalie Pope. Ancient Greece & the Olympics: A Nonfiction Companion to Magic Tree House #16: Hour of the Olympics. Murdocca, Sal, illus. 2004. (Magic Tree House (R) Fact Tracker Ser.: 10). 128p. (J). (gr. 2-5). pap. 6.99 *(978-0-375-82378-7(6)*, Random Hse. Bks. for Young Readers) Random Hse. Children's Bks.

Page, Jason. Basketball, Soccer, & Other Ball Games. 2008. (Olympic Sports Ser.). (ENG., Illus.). 32p. (J). (gr. 4-7). pap. *(978-0-7787-4029-2(3))*; lib. bdg. *(978-0-7787-4012-4(9))* Crabtree Publishing Co.

—Cycling, Shooting, & Show Jumping: Archery, Weightlifting, & a Whole Lot More. 2008. (Olympic Sports Ser.). (ENG., Illus.). 32p. (J). (gr. 3-7). pap. *(978-0-7787-4030-8(7))*; (gr. 4-7). lib. bdg. *(978-0-7787-4013-1(7))* Crabtree Publishing Co.

—Decathlon, High Jump, & Other Field Events. 2008. (Olympic Sports Ser.). (ENG., Illus.). 32p. (J). (gr. 3-7). pap. *(978-0-7787-4031-5(5))*; lib. bdg. *(978-0-7787-4014-8(5))* Crabtree Publishing Co.

—Gymnastics Events. 2008. (Olympic Sports Ser.). (ENG., Illus.). 32p. (J). (gr. 3-7). pap. *(978-0-7787-4032-2(3))*; lib. bdg. *(978-0-7787-4015-5(3))* Crabtree Publishing Co.

—Martial Arts, Boxing, & Other Combat Sports: Fencing, Judo, Wrestling, Taekwondo, & a Whole Lot More, 1 vol. 2008. (Olympic Sports Ser.). (ENG., Illus.). 32p. (J). (gr. 3-7). pap. *(978-0-7787-4033-9(1))*; lib. bdg. *(978-0-7787-4016-2(1))* Crabtree Publishing Co.

—Rowing, Sailing, & Other Sports on the Water. 2008. (Olympic Sports Ser.). (ENG., Illus.). 32p. (J). (gr. 3-7). pap. *(978-0-7787-4034-6(X))*; lib. bdg. *(978-0-7787-4017-9(X))* Crabtree Publishing Co.

—Sprints, Hurdles, & Other Track Events, 1 vol. 2008. (Olympic Sports Ser.). (ENG., Illus.). 32p. (J). (gr. 3-7). pap. *(978-0-7787-4035-3(8))*; lib. bdg. *(978-0-7787-4018-6(8))* Crabtree Publishing Co.

—Swimming, Diving, & Other Water Sports. 2008. (Olympic Sports Ser.). (ENG., Illus.). 32p. (J). (gr. 3-7). pap. *(978-0-7787-4036-0(6))*; lib. bdg. *(978-0-7787-4019-3(6))* Crabtree Publishing Co.

Parry, Jim & Girginov, Vassil. The Olympic Games Explained: A Student Guide to the Evolution of the Modern Olympic Games. (Student Sport Studies). (ENG., Illus.). 2005. 288p. 64.95 *(978-0-415-34604-7(5)*, RU27968) 2004. 292p. 210.00 *(978-0-415-34603-0(7)*, RU27967) Taylor & Francis Group. (Routledge).

Patrick, Jean L. S. Long-Armed Ludy & the First Women's Olympics. Gustavson, Adam, illus. 2017. 32p. (J). (gr. 1-4). lib. bdg. 16.99 *(978-1-58089-546-0(8))* Charlesbridge Publishing, Inc.

Pemu, Dennis. The Complete Guide to Sports. 2015. (Illus.). 144p. (J). *(978-1-4351-6166-5(1))* Barnes & Noble, Inc.

Peterson, Christine. The Science Behind Swimming, Diving, & Other Water Sports. 2016. (Science of the Summer Olympics Ser.). (ENG., Illus.). 32p. (J). (gr. 3-9). lib. bdg. 28.65 *(978-1-4914-8157-8(9)*, 130636, Capstone Pr.) Capstone.

Peterson, Christine, et al. Science of the Summer Olympics. 2016. (Science of the Summer Olympics Ser.). (ENG., Illus.). 32p. (J). (gr. 3-9). 122.60 *(978-1-4914-8173-8(0)*, 23989, Capstone Pr.) Capstone.

Phelps, Michael & Abrahamson, Alan. How to Train with a T. Rex & Win 8 Gold Medals. Jenkins, Ward, illus. 2009. (ENG.). 32p. (J). (gr. -1-3). 19.99 *(978-1-4169-8669-0(3)*, Simon & Schuster Bks. For Young Readers) Simon & Schuster Bks. For Young Readers.

Powell, Jillian. Olympic Heroes: Band 05/Green (Collins Big Cat) 2012. (Collins Big Cat Ser.). (ENG., Illus.). 24p. (J). (gr. k-1). pap. 8.99 *(978-0-00-746190-5(9))* HarperCollins Pubs. Ltd. GBR. Dist: Independent Pubs. Group.

Raisman, Aly. Fierce: How Competing for Myself Changed Everything. 2018. (ENG., Illus.). 368p. (YA). (gr. 7-17). pap. 12.99 *(978-0-316-47268-5(9))* Little, Brown Bks. for Young Readers.

Raisman, Aly & Lawrence, Blythe. Fierce: How Competing for Myself Changed Everything. 2017. (Illus.). 358p. (YA). *(978-0-316-48063-5(0))* Little Brown & Co.

Rose, Simon. Canada's Olympic Torch. 2010. (Illus.). 24p. *(978-1-77071-580-6(0))*; pap. *(978-1-77071-587-5(8))* Weigl Educational Pubs. Ltd.

—Le Flambeau Olympique: Les Emblèmes Canadiens. McMann, Julie, tr. from ENG. 2011. (FRE.). 24p. (YA). (gr. 2-4). *(978-1-77071-411-3(1))* Weigl Educational Pubs. Ltd.

Roza, Greg. Olympic Math: Working with Percentages & Decimals. 2009. (PowerMath: Advanced Proficiency Plus Ser.). 32p. (gr. 5-5). 47.90 *(978-1-60851-363-5(7)*, PowerKids Pr.) Rosen Publishing Group, Inc., The.

—Olympic Math: Working with Percents & Decimals, 1 vol. 2009. (Math for the REAL World Ser.). (ENG., Illus.). 32p. (gr. 5-5). pap. 10.00 *(978-1-4042-6057-3(9)*, c15f1c62-dd2a-43b8-aed7-e9424a72102c) Rosen Publishing Group, Inc., The.

Rule, Heather. Women in the Olympics. 2017. (Women in Sports Ser.). (ENG., Illus.). 48p. (J). (gr. 4-8). lib. bdg. 34.21 *(978-1-5321-1159-4(2)*, 25894, SportsZone) ABDO Publishing Co.

Scheff, Matt. The Summer Olympics: World's Best Athletic Competition. 2020. (Big Game (Lerner (tm) Sports) Ser.). (ENG., Illus.). 32p. (J). (gr. 2-5). 30.65 *(978-1-5415-9757-0(5)*, c102949c-fedc-4ea0-bc0d-6adb1e1d2ccc, Lerner Pubns.) Lerner Publishing Group.

Schwartz, Heather E. Simone Manuel: Swimming Star. 2018. (Women Sports Stars Ser.). (ENG., Illus.). 32p. (J). (gr. 3-9). lib. bdg. 28.65 *(978-1-5157-9707-4(4)*, 136855, Capstone Pr.) Capstone.

Seed, Andy. Winter Olympics: Band 10 White/Band 12 Copper (Collins Big Cat Progress) 2014. (Collins Big Cat Progress Ser.). (ENG., Illus.). 32p. (YA). (gr. 7). pap. 9.99 *(978-0-00-751924-8(9))* HarperCollins Pubs. Ltd. GBR. Dist: Independent Pubs. Group.

Sherrow, Victoria. Wilma Rudolph. Johnson, Larry, illus. 2006. (Yo Solo Biografías Ser.). (ENG & SPA.). 48p. (J). (gr. 2-3). lib. bdg. 23.93 *(978-0-8225-6260-3(X)*, Ediciones Lerner) Lerner Publishing Group.

Simon, Francesca. Horrid Henry: Horrid Henry's Gold Medal Games: Colouring, Puzzles & Activities. 2017. (Horrid Henry Ser.). (ENG., Illus.). 24p. (J). (gr. 1-3). pap. 8.99 *(978-1-5101-0127-2(6)*, Orion Children's Bks.) Hachette Children's Group GBR. Dist: Hachette Bk. Group.

Simonds, Lucy. The Olympics. 2007. (Trackers-Math Ser.). (gr. 2-5). pap. 5.00 *(978-1-59055-911-6(8))* Pacific Learning, Inc.

Simons, Lisa M. Bolt. The First Olympics of Ancient Greece, 1 vol. 2014. (Ancient Greece Ser.). (ENG., Illus.). 24p. (J). (gr. 1-3). 27.99 *(978-1-4914-0273-3(3)*, 125818, Capstone Pr.) Capstone.

Smith-Llera, Danielle. Black Power Salute: How a Photograph Captured a Political Protest. 2017. (Captured History Sports Ser.). (ENG., Illus.). 64p. (J). (gr. 5-9). lib. bdg. 35.32 *(978-0-7565-5526-9(4)*, 134411, Compass Point Bks.) Capstone.

Smith, Nikkolas, illus. The Golden Girls of Rio. 2016. (ENG.). 32p. (J). (gr. -1-3). 16.99 *(978-1-5107-2247-7(5)*, Sky Pony Pr.) Skyhorse Publishing Co., Inc.

Sonneborn, Liz. Murder at the 1972 Olympics in Munich. 2009. (Terrorist Attacks Ser.). 64p. (gr. 5-5). 58.50 *(978-1-60853-308-4(5))* Rosen Publishing Group, Inc., The.

Stewart, Mark. The Olympics, 1 vol. 2009. (Ultimate 10: Sports Ser.). (ENG., Illus.). 48p. (gr. 3-3). (J). pap. 11.50 *(978-1-4339-2208-4(8)*, cc4e1e2a-d660-4454-b8f6-7e9569588faa); (YA). lib. bdg. 33.67 *(978-0-8368-9160-7(0)*, 09b366d3-4a5d-4694-87e8-ea2b518b17b9) Stevens, Gareth Publishing LLLP.

Sullivan, Erin Ash. Math at the Olympics & Matemáticas en las Olimpiadas: 6 English, 6 Spanish Adaptations. 2011. (ENG & SPA.). (J). 97.00 net. *(978-1-4108-5707-1(7))* Benchmark Education Co.

Torsiello, David P. Michael Phelps: Swimming for Olympic Gold, 1 vol. 2009. (Hot Celebrity Biographies Ser.). (ENG., Illus.). 48p. (gr. 5-7). pap. 11.53 *(978-0-7660-3630-7(8)*, 6e3a4df6-ddb2-4b4a-8123-96488a794dc2) Enslow Publishing, LLC.

Walters, John. Top 10 Olympic Champions. 2018. (Top 10 in Sports Ser.). (ENG.). 24p. (J). (gr. 2-5). lib. bdg. 32.79 *(978-1-5038-2727-1(5)*, 212553) Child's World, Inc, The.

Watson, Stephanie. The Science Behind Soccer, Volleyball, Cycling, & Other Popular Sports. 2016. (Science of the Summer Olympics Ser.). (ENG., Illus.). 32p. (J). (gr. 3-9). lib. bdg. 28.65 *(978-1-4914-8160-8(9)*, 130639, Capstone Pr.) Capstone.

Waxman, Laura Hamilton. Bobsled & Luge. 2017. (Winter Olympic Sports Ser.). (ENG.). 32p. (J). (gr. 2-5). 20.95 *(978-1-68151-150-4(9)*, 14691) Amicus.

—Figure Skating. 2017. (Winter Olympic Sports Ser.). (ENG.). 32p. (J). (gr. 2-5). 20.95 *(978-1-68151-148-1(7)*, 14692) Amicus.

—Skiing. 2017. (Winter Olympic Sports Ser.). (ENG.). 32p. (J). (gr. 1-4). 20.95 *(978-1-68151-151-1(7)*, Amicus High Interest) Amicus Learning.

—Speed Skating. 2017. (Winter Olympic Sports Ser.). (ENG., Illus.). 32p. (J). (gr. 2-5). 20.95 *(978-1-68151-153-5(3)*, 14696) Amicus.

—Winter Olympic Sports: Bobsled & Luge. 2017. (Winter Olympic Sports Ser.). (ENG.). 32p. (J). (gr. 2-5). pap. 9.99 *(978-1-68152-181-7(4)*, 14810) Amicus.

—Winter Olympic Sports: Figure Skating. 2017. (Winter Olympic Sports Ser.). (ENG.). 32p. (J). (gr. 2-5). pap. 9.99 *(978-1-68152-179-4(2)*, 14811) Amicus.

—Winter Olympic Sports: Ice Hockey & Curling. 2017. (Winter Olympic Sports Ser.). (ENG., Illus.). 32p. (J). (gr. 2-5). pap. 9.99 *(978-1-68152-180-0(6)*, 14812) Amicus.

—Winter Olympic Sports: Skiing. 2017. (Winter Olympic Sports Ser.). (ENG.). 32p. (J). (gr. 2-5). pap. 9.99 *(978-1-68152-182-4(2)*, 14813) Amicus.

—Winter Olympic Sports: Speed Skating. 2017. (Winter Olympic Sports Ser.). (ENG., Illus.). 32p. (J). (gr. 2-5). pap. 9.99 *(978-1-68152-184-8(9)*, 14815) Amicus.

Westcott, Jim. Olympic Greats. 2017. (Rank It! Ser.). (ENG.). 32p. (J). (gr. 4-6). pap. 9.99 *(978-1-64466-210-6(8)*, 11474); (Illus.). lib. bdg. *(978-1-68072-176-8(3)*, 10536) Black Rabbit Bks. (Bolt).

Williams, Heather. Miracle on Ice. 2018. (21st Century Skills Library: Sports Unite Us Ser.). (ENG., Illus.). 32p. (J). (gr. 3-6). lib. bdg. 32.07 *(978-1-5341-2957-3(X)*, 211872) Cherry Lake Publishing.

Yomtov, Nel. Defying Hitler: Jesse Owens' Olympic Triumph. Garcia, Eduardo, illus. 2018. (Greatest Sports Moments Ser.). (ENG.). 32p. (J). (gr. 3-9). lib. bdg. 31.32 *(978-1-5435-2865-7(1)*, 138368, Capstone Pr.) Capstone.

Zuehlke, Jeffrey. Michael Phelps. 2005. (First Step Nonfiction Ser.). (Illus.). 32p. (J). (gr. 2-5). per. 5.95 *(978-0-8225-2631-5(X))*; (gr. 3-7). lib. bdg. 23.93 *(978-0-8225-2431-1(7))* Lerner Publishing Group.

OLYMPICS—FICTION

Ahearn, Dan & Ahearn, Janet. Olympic Dreams. 2011. (Navigators Ser.). (J). pap. *(978-1-61672-964-6(3))* Benchmark Education Co.

Arena, Felice & Kettle, Phil. Olympics. Cox, David, illus. 2004. (J). pap. *(978-1-59336-374-1(5))* Mondo Publishing.

Charles, Norma. Chasing a Star. 2009. (ENG., Illus.). 182p. (YA). (gr. 5-8). pap. *(978-1-55380-077-4(X))* Ronsdale Pr.

Debnam, Mio. Animalympics, 5 BK Set. 2010. (ENG.). 140p. (J). (gr. -1-3). pap. 23.00 *(978-988-98819-0-0(X))* Haven Bks.

Dixon, Franklin W. & Keene, Carolyn. Gold Medal Murder, 4. 2010. (Nancy Drew/Hardy Boys Ser.: 4). (ENG.). 176p. (J). (gr. 3-7). pap. 7.99 *(978-1-4424-0326-0(8)*, Aladdin) Simon & Schuster Children's Publishing.

Farmer, Tom. Once upon a Daydream: The Story of Patrick & the Clumsy Camel. 2013. 44p. pap. 17.44 *(978-1-4669-6912-4(1))* Trafford Publishing.

Feinstein, John. Rush for the Gold: Mystery at the Olympics (the Sports Beat, 6) 2013. (Sports Beat Ser.: 6). 320p. (J). (gr. 5). pap. 10.99 *(978-0-375-87168-9(3)*, Yearling) Random Hse. Children's Bks.

Freitas, Donna. Gold Medal Winter. 2017. (ENG.). 336p. (J). (gr. 5-9). pap. 7.99 *(978-0-545-64378-8(3)*, Scholastic Pr.) Scholastic, Inc.

Golub, Osu. Penguins Go for the Gold. 2009. 16p. pap. 10.00 *(978-1-4490-3907-3(3))* AuthorHouse.

Goscinny, René. Asterix aux jeux Olympiques. 21.95 *(978-2-01-210012-1(0))* Hachette Groupe Livre FRA. Dist: Distribooks, Inc.

Holub, Joan & Williams, Suzanne. Artemis the Loyal. 2013. (Goddess Girls Ser.: 7). (ENG., Illus.). 288p. (J). (gr. 3-7). 16.99 *(978-1-4424-8594-5(9)*, Aladdin) Simon & Schuster Children's Publishing.

—The Girl Games. (Goddess Girls Ser.). (ENG., 320p. (J). (gr. 3-7). 2014. Illus.). 17.99 *(978-1-4424-9575-3(8))* 2012. pap. 7.99 *(978-1-4424-4933-6(0))* Simon & Schuster Children's Publishing. (Aladdin).

—The Girls' Games. 2012. (Goddess Girls Ser.). lib. bdg. 18.40 *(978-0-606-26349-8(7))* Turtleback.

Jamieson, Victoria. Olympig! 2016. lib. bdg. 19.65 *(978-0-606-38844-3(3))* Turtleback.

Kelly, David A. MVP #1: the Gold Medal Mess. Brundage, Scott, illus. 2016. (Most Valuable Players Ser.: 1). 128p. (J). (gr. 1-4). 5.99 *(978-0-553-51319-6(2)*, Random Hse. Bks. for Young Readers) Random Hse. Children's Bks.

Khalili, Davood. Developing Olympian Character, 1 vol. 2010. 32p. pap. 24.95 *(978-1-4489-5281-6(6))* PublishAmerica, Inc.

Lewis, Beverly. Girls Only! 2008. (Girls Only (Go!) Ser.: Vols. 5-8). (ENG.). (J). (gr. 4-7). 510p. pap. 20.00 *(978-0-7642-0462-3(9))*; Vols. 1-4. 512p. pap. 21.00 *(978-0-7642-0461-6(0))* Bethany Hse. Pubs.

MacGregor, Roy. Murder at the Winter Games (#18), No. 18. 2004. (Screech Owls Ser.: 18). (ENG., Illus.). 128p. (J). (gr. 3-7). mass mkt. 4.95 *(978-0-7710-5647-5(8)*, Screech Owls) McClelland & Stewart CAN. Dist: Penguin Random Hse. LLC.

Malaspina, Ann. Touch the Sky: Alice Coachman, Olympic High Jumper. Velasquez, Eric, illus. 2012. (ENG.). 32p. (J). (gr. -1-3). 16.99 *(978-0-8075-8035-6(X)*, 080758035X) Whitman, Albert & Co.

Morgan, Winter. Attack on Minecrafters Academy. 2017. (Unofficial Minecrafters Academy Ser.: 4). lib. bdg. 18.40 *(978-0-606-40309-2(4))* Turtleback.

Osborne, Mary Pope. La Hora de Los Juegos Olímpicos. Brovelli, Marcela, tr. Murdocca, Sal, illus. 2007. (Casa del Árbol Ser.: 16).Tr. of Hour of the Olympics Games. (ENG & SPA.). 68p. (J). per. 6.99 *(978-1-933032-22-1(7))* Lectorum Pubns., Inc.

—Hour of the Olympics. unabr. ed. 2004. (Magic Tree House Ser.: No. 16). 70p. (J). (gr. k-3). pap. 17.00 incl. audio *(978-0-8072-0785-7(3)*, LFTR 244 SP, Listening Library) Random Hse. Audio Publishing Group.

Panayotis. Junior & Bo's Trip to the Olympics. Theophilopoulos, Andrew, illus. 2007. 104p. per. 10.95 *(978-1-934246-26-9(3))* Peppertree Pr., The.

Peyo. The Smurf Championship Games. 2012. (Simon & Schuster Ready-To-Read Level 2 Ser.). lib. bdg. 13.55 *(978-0-606-26363-4(2))* Turtleback.

—The Smurfs Graphic Novels Boxed Set: Vol. #10-12. 2013. (Smurfs Graphic Novels Ser.). (ENG., Illus.). 168p. (J). (gr. 2-5). pap. 17.99 *(978-1-59707-386-8(5)*, 900117999, Papercutz) Mad Cave Studios.

Peyo & Delporte, Yvan. The Smurfs #11: the Smurf Olympics: The Smurf Olympics, Vol. 11. 2012. (Smurfs Graphic Novels Ser.: 11). (ENG., Illus.). 56p. (J). (gr. 2-4). 10.99 *(978-1-59707-302-8(4)*, 900080979, Papercutz) Mad Cave Studios.

Richards, Jean. The First Olympic Games: A Gruesome Greek Myth with a Happy Ending. Thacker, Kat, illus. 2004. 32p. pap. 10.95 *(978-0-7613-2443-0(7)*, Millbrook Pr.) Lerner Publishing Group.

Riley, Lehman & Austin, Megan. The Life of Babe Didrikson: "Greatness Is Never Forgotten" Wallace, Joshua, illus. 2005. 47p. (J). pap. *(978-0-9760523-2-6(6))* Matter of Africa America Time.

Rosen, Robert. My Favorite Sport. De Polonia, Nina, illus. 2017. (Play Time Ser.). (ENG.). 24p. (gr. -1-2). 28.50 *(978-1-68342-716-2(5)*, 9781683427162) Rourke Educational Media.

—My Favorite Sport. de Polonia, Nina, illus. 2017. (Play Time Ser.). (ENG.). 24p. (gr. -1-2). pap. 9.95 *(978-1-68342-768-1(8)*, 9781683427681) Rourke Educational Media.

Stilton, Gerónimo. Geronimo & the Gold Medal Mystery. 2008. (Geronimo Stilton Ser.). (Illus.). 87p. (J). (gr. 2-5). lib. bdg. 14.65 *(978-0-7569-8803-6(9))* Perfection Learning Corp.

Terrell, Brandon. Grit & Gold. Garcia, Eduardo, illus. 2016. (Time Machine Magazine Ser.). (ENG.). 128p. (J). (gr. 3-6). lib. bdg. 23.99 *(978-1-4965-2597-0(3)*, 130726) Capstone.

—Harmony & Hoops. Garcia, Eduardo, illus. 2016. (Time Machine Magazine Ser.). (ENG.). 128p. (J). (gr. 3-6). lib. bdg. 23.99 *(978-1-4965-2596-3(5)*, 130725) Capstone.

—Pluck & Perfection. Max, Iman, illus. 2016. (Time Machine Magazine Ser.). (ENG.). 128p. (J). (gr. 3-6). lib. bdg. 23.99 *(978-1-4965-2595-6(7)*, 130724, Stone Arch Bks.) Capstone.

—Valor & Victory. Max, Iman, illus. 2016. (Time Machine Magazine Ser.). (ENG.). 128p. (J). (gr. 3-6). lib. bdg. 23.99 *(978-1-4965-2594-9(9)*, 130723, Stone Arch Bks.) Capstone.

Tobey, Carole A. The Frog Olympics. 2005. (Illus.). 70p. (J). per. 12.00 *(978-0-9773648-3-1(6))* Legend eXpress Publishing.

Yardley Hastings Primary School. Tim & Holly's Olympic Adventure. 2012. 74p. pap. *(978-1-909039-52-0(7))* Legend Pr.

OMAN

Barnett, Tracy. Oman. 2003. (Modern Middle East Nations & Their Strategic Place in the World Ser.). (Illus.). 112,128p. (YA). (gr. 7-18). lib. bdg. *(978-1-59084-517-2(X))* Mason Crest.

Ejaz, Khadija. We Visit Oman. 2011. (Your Land & My Land Ser.). (Illus.). 64p. (J). (gr. 4-7). lib. bdg. 33.95 *(978-1-58415-962-9(6))* Mitchell Lane Pubs.

Issac, Michael. A Historical Atlas of Oman. (Historical Atlases of South Asia, Central Asia, & the Middle East Ser.). 64p. (gr. 6-6). 2009. 61.20 *(978-1-61513-326-0(7))* 2003. (ENG., Illus.). lib. bdg. 37.13 *(978-0-8239-4500-9(6)*, 626e6226-eccf-4ce0-9944-dcabab7d02ed) Rosen Publishing Group, Inc., The.

King, David C. Oman, 1 vol. 2009. (Cultures of the World (First Edition)(r) Ser.). (ENG., Illus.). 144p. (gr. 5-5). lib. bdg. 49.79

(978-0-7614-3120-6(9), c7a59747-fee8-4b03-ae3f-be7a084a0f87) Cavendish Square Publishing LLC.

Rinaldo, Denise. Lost City Spotted from Space! Is There a Hidden Land under the Sand? 2011. (J). pap. (978-0-545-32929-3(9)) Scholastic, Inc.

ONASSIS, JACQUELINE KENNEDY, 1929-1994

Cardillo, Margaret. Just Being Jackie. Denos, Julia, illus. 2018. (ENG.). 32p. (J). (gr. -1-3). 17.99 (978-0-06-248502-1(4), Balzer & Bray) HarperCollins Pubs.

Raatma, Lucia. Jacqueline Kennedy, 1 vol. 2010. (First Ladies Ser.). (ENG.). 24p. (J). (gr. -1-2). lib. bdg. 27.32 (978-1-4296-5009-0(5), 112958, Capstone Pr.) Capstone.

Strand, Jennifer. Jacqueline Kennedy. 2017. (First Ladies (Launch!) Ser.). (ENG., Illus.). 24p. (J). (gr. -1-2). lib. bdg. 31.36 (978-1-5321-2016-9(8), 25282, Abdo Zoom-Launch) ABDO Publishing Co.

ONE-ACT PLAYS

Sacco, Christopher & Haehnel, Alan. The Education of Janet O'Malley: One-Act Comedy Play. 2003. (YA). pap. 4.25 (978-1-932404-10-4(4), 728) Brooklyn Pubs.

O'NEILL, EUGENE, 1888-1953

Bloom, Harold, ed. Long Day's Journey into Night- Eugene O'Neill. 2nd rev. ed. 2009. (Bloom's Modern Critical Interpretations Ser.). (ENG.). 248p. (gr. 9-18). 45.00 (978-1-60413-390-5(2), P165436, Facts On File) Infobase Holdings, Inc.

Hermann, Spring. Reading & Interpreting the Works of Eugene O'Neill, 1 vol. 2016. (Lit Crit Guides). (ENG., Illus.). 176p. (gr. 6-6). 41.60 (978-0-7660-7913-7(9), 162cc17a-1461-40fa-9c77-244edb1ef2d8) Enslow Publishing, LLC.

—A Student's Guide to Eugene O'Neill, 1 vol. 2009. (Understanding Literature Ser.). (ENG., Illus.). 176p. (gr. 9-10). lib. bdg. 31.93 (978-0-7660-2886-9(0), 01e2bf4d-7662-492b-9661-ec72b936f038) Enslow Publishing, LLC.

ONTARIO

Adams, Carly. Queens of the Ice: They Were Fast, They Were Fierce, They Were Teenage Girls, 1 vol. 2011. (Lorimer Recordbooks Ser.). (ENG., Illus.). 136p. (YA). (gr. 7-12). 8.99 (978-1-55277-720-6(0), 8d1b677f-79a6-46b8-b135-cf0face61030) James Lorimer & Co. Ltd., Pubs. CAN. Dist: Lerner Publishing Group.

Brignall, Richard. Big Train: The Legendary Ironman of Sport, Lionel Conacher, 1 vol. 2009. (Lorimer Recordbooks Ser.). (ENG., Illus.). 168p. (YA). (gr. 6-12). 16.95 (978-1-55277-451-9(1), 451); 9.95 (978-1-55277-450-2(3), 450) James Lorimer & Co. Ltd., Pubs. CAN. Dist: Formac Lorimer Bks. Ltd.

Cooper, John, Jr. & Cooper, John. Season of Rage: Hugh Burnett & the Struggle for Civil Rights. 2005. (ENG., Illus.). 80p. (J). (gr. 5-12). pap. 9.95 (978-0-88776-700-5(1), Tundra Bks.) Tundra Bks. CAN. Dist: Penguin Random Hse. LLC.

Gorman, Lovenia. A Is for Algonquin: An Ontario Alphabet. Rose, Melanie, illus. rev. ed. 2005. (Discover Canada Province by Province Ser.). (ENG.). 40p. (J). (gr. 1-3). 17.95 (978-1-58536-263-9(8), 202078) Sleeping Bear Pr.

ONTARIO—FICTION

Autio, Karen. Sabotage, 1 vol. 2014. (ENG.). 293p. (J). (gr. 4-7). pap. 10.95 (978-1-55039-208-1(5)) Sono Nis Pr. CAN. Dist: Orca Bk. Pubs. USA.

Awad, Shelley. The Greenhouse Kids: Dan Delion's Secret. Zonta, Rose, illus. 2009. 127p. (J). pap. (978-0-88887-379-8(4)) Borealis Pr.

Batchelor, Rhonda. She Loves You. 2008. (ENG.). 136p. (YA). (gr. 7-8). pap. 11.99 (978-1-55002-789-1(1)) Dundurn Pr. CAN. Dist: Publishers Group West (PGW).

Bell, Aaron. Jak's Story. 2010. (ENG., Illus.). 96p. (YA). (gr. 4). pap. 10.99 (978-1-55488-710-1(0)) Dundurn Pr. CAN. Dist: Publishers Group West (PGW).

Bow, James. The Young City: The Unwritten Books. 2008. (Unwritten Bks.: 3). (ENG.). 264p. (YA). (gr. 7). pap. 12.99 (978-1-55002-846-1(4)) Dundurn Pr. CAN. Dist: Publishers Group West (PGW).

Bow, Patricia. The Prism Blade: Passage to Mythrin. 2008. (Passage to Mythrin Ser.: 2). (ENG.). 272p. (YA). (gr. 7-12). pap. 12.99 (978-1-55002-809-6(X)) Dundurn Pr. CAN. Dist: Publishers Group West (PGW).

—The Ruby Kingdom: Passage to Mythrin. 2007. (Passage to Mythrin Ser.: 1). (ENG.). 256p. (YA). (gr. 7). pap. 12.99 (978-1-55002-667-2(4)) Dundurn Pr. CAN. Dist: Publishers Group West (PGW).

Brouwer, Sigmund. Timberwolf Chase, 1 vol. Griffiths, Dean, illus. 2006. (Orca Echoes Ser.). (ENG.). 64p. (J). (gr. 1-3). per. 6.95 (978-1-55143-548-0(9)) Orca Bk. Pubs. USA.

Brummel Crook, Connie. Meyer's Creek. 2013. (ENG.). 278p. (J). pap. 12.95 (978-1-55005-211-4(X), 83b4def3-8c68-4821-9b9f-4122b20c5a43) Fitzhenry & Whiteside, Ltd. CAN. Dist: Firefly Bks., Ltd.

—No Small Victory, 1 vol. 2010. (ENG.). 232p. (J). (gr. 3-6). pap. 12.95 (978-1-55455-169-9(2), 26a8fa17-5a4d-48c4-aa55-7a9c42116658) Trifolium Bks., Inc. CAN. Dist: Firefly Bks., Ltd.

Charles, Rie. No More Dragons. 2010. (ENG., Illus.). 112p. (J). (gr. 5-7). pap. 9.95 (978-1-926607-12-2(0), Napoleon & Co.) Dundurn Pr. CAN. Dist: Publishers Group West (PGW).

Clavette, Taylor. Shapeshifter's Mark. 2012. 168p. (gr. 10-12). 22.95 (978-1-4697-9266-8(4)); pap. 12.95 (978-1-4697-9264-4(8)) iUniverse, Inc.

Cliffe, Susan. Thread of Deceit, 1 vol. 2005. (ENG., Illus.). 200p. (YA). (gr. 7-12). pap. (978-1-894549-38-7(4), Sumach Pr.) Canadian Scholars.

Crawley, Oksanna. So, You Be Keon & I'll Be Mahovlich. 2009. 28p. pap. 13.99 (978-1-4490-0243-5(9)) AuthorHouse.

Croza, Laurel. From There to Here, 1 vol. James, Matt, illus. 2014. (ENG.). 32p. (J). (gr. -1-2). 18.95 (978-1-55498-365-0(7)) Groundwood Bks. CAN. Dist: Publishers Group West (PGW).

Curtis, Christopher Paul. Elijah of Buxton (Scholastic Gold), 1 vol. (ENG.). (J). (gr. 4-7). 2009. 368p. pap. 7.99 (978-0-439-02345-0(9), Scholastic Paperbacks) 2007. 352p. 19.99 (978-0-439-02344-3(0), Scholastic Pr.) Scholastic, Inc.

Desclouds, Rick. My Year with the ESL Boys. 2009. 280p. pap. 22.92 (978-1-4269-0621-3(8)) Trafford Publishing.

Donoghue, Emma. The Lotterys Plus One. l.t. ed. 2018. (ENG.). (J). lib. bdg. 22.99 (978-1-4328-4994-8(8)) Thorndike Pr. Gale.

—The Lotterys Plus One. Hadilaksono, Caroline, illus. 2018. (ENG.). 336p. (J). (gr. 3-7). pap. 7.99 (978-0-545-92584-6(3)) Scholastic, Inc.

Doyle, Brian. Pure Spring, 1 vol. 2007. (ENG.). 160p. (J). (gr. 6-9). pap. 8.95 (978-0-88899-775-3(2)) Groundwood Bks. CAN. Dist: Publishers Group West (PGW).

Dublin, Anne. 44 Hours or Strike!, 1 vol. 2015. (ENG., Illus.). 136p. (J). (gr. 5-9). pap. 11.95 (978-1-927583-76-0(4)) Second Story Pr. CAN. Dist: Orca Bk. Pubs. USA.

Etienne, Doris. The Jewels of Sofia Tate. 2009. (ENG.). 272p. (J). (gr. 6). pap. 12.99 (978-1-55488-230-4(3)) Dundurn Pr. CAN. Dist: Publishers Group West (PGW).

Forchuk Skrypuch, Marsha. Aram's Choice, 1 vol. Wood, Muriel, illus. 2006. (New Beginnings Ser.). (ENG.). 84p. (J). (gr. 1-2). per. 8.95 (978-1-55041-354-0(6), fa8bb5f9-8781-4ebd-958c-14862dfdebd) Trifolium Bks., Inc. CAN. Dist: Firefly Bks., Ltd.

Freedman, Zelda. Rosie's Dream Cape. Bevilacqua, Silvana, illus. 2005. (ENG.). 116p. (J). pap. 6.95 (978-1-55380-025-5(7)) Ronsdale Pr. CAN. Dist: Literary Pr. Group of Canada.

Gamble, Adam & Jasper, Mark. Good Night Toronto. Stevenson, Harvey, illus. 2011. (Good Night Our World Ser.). (ENG.). 20p. (J). (gr. k — 1). bds. 9.95 (978-1-60219-048-1(8)) Good Night Bks.

Girard, M-E. Girl Mans Up. (ENG.). (YA). (gr. 9). 2018. 400p. pap. 11.99 (978-0-06-240418-3(0)) 2016. 384p. 17.99 (978-0-06-240417-6(2)) HarperCollins Pubs. (HarperCollins).

Gromosiak, Paul. Owahonton: Maid of the Mist. 2012. (ENG.). (J). pap. 12.95 (978-1-4675-4107-7(9)) Independent Pub.

Henighan, Tom. Doom Lake Holiday. 2009. (ENG.). 240p. (YA). (gr. 6). pap. 12.99 (978-1-55002-847-8(2)) Dundurn Pr. CAN. Dist: Publishers Group West (PGW).

Hill, James. Larry the Lunker. 2004. 35p. pap. 24.95 (978-1-4137-2972-6(X)) PublishAmerica, Inc.

Hopkinson, Nalo. The Chaos. 2013. (ENG., Illus.). 256p. (YA). (gr. 9). pap. 11.99 (978-1-4424-5926-7(3), McElderry, Margaret K. Bks.) McElderry, Margaret K. Bks.

Ibbitson, John. The Landing. 2008. 160p. (J). (gr. 7-9). 17.95 (978-1-55453-234-6(5)); pap. 7.95 (978-1-55453-238-4(8)) Kids Can Pr., Ltd. CAN. Dist: Hachette Bk. Group.

Jacobs, Lily. The Littlest Bunny in Ottawa: An Easter Adventure. Dunn, Robert, illus. 2015. (Littlest Bunny Ser.). (ENG.). 32p. (J). (gr. -1-3). 9.99 (978-1-4926-1174-5(3), Hometown World) Sourcebooks, Inc.

—The Littlest Bunny in Toronto: An Easter Adventure. Dunn, Robert, illus. 2015. (Littlest Bunny Ser.). (ENG.). 32p. (J). (gr. -1-3). 9.99 (978-1-4926-1213-1(8), Hometown World) Sourcebooks, Inc.

James, Eric. The Spooky Express Toronto. Piwowarski, Marcin, illus. 2017. (Spooky Express Ser.). (ENG.). 32p. (J). (gr. k-6). 9.99 (978-1-4926-5403-2(5), Hometown World) Sourcebooks, Inc.

—Tiny the Ottawa Easter Bunny. 2018. (Tiny the Easter Bunny Ser.). (ENG.). 40p. (J). (gr. k-3). 9.99 (978-1-4926-5956-3(8), Hometown World) Sourcebooks, Inc.

Jocelyn, Marthe. Mable Riley: A Reliable Record of Humdrum, Peril, & Romance. 2007. 279p. (gr. 4-7). 17.00 (978-0-7569-8183-9(2)) Perfection Learning Corp.

Johnston, Julie. A Very Fine Line. 208p. (YA). (gr. 7). 2008. pap. 10.95 (978-0-88776-829-3(6)) 2006. 18.95 (978-0-88776-746-3(X)) Tundra Bks. CAN. (Tundra Bks.). Dist: Penguin Random Hse. LLC.

Kerbel, Deborah. Lure. 2010. (ENG.). 200p. (YA). (gr. 9). pap. 12.99 (978-1-55488-754-5(2)) Dundurn Pr. CAN. Dist: Publishers Group West (PGW).

Koehler, Hanne Lore & Laraya-Coutts, Corie. A Tale of a Malipayon Warrior. 2010. 128p. 21.95 (978-1-4502-1344-8(8)); pap. 11.95 (978-1-4502-1346-2(4)) iUniverse, Inc.

Leavey, Peggy Dymond. Growing up Ivy. 2010. (ENG.). 256p. (YA). (gr. 4-8). pap. 10.99 (978-1-55488-723-1(2)) Dundurn Pr. CAN. Dist: Publishers Group West (PGW).

Leznoff, Glenda. Heartache & Other Natural Shocks. 2015. (Illus.). 384p. (YA). (gr. 9). 19.99 (978-1-77049-836-5(2), Tundra Bks.) Tundra Bks. CAN. Dist: Penguin Random Hse. LLC.

Lottridge, Celia. The Listening Tree, 1 vol. 2010. (ENG.). 154p. (J). (gr. 4-6). pap. 11.95 (978-1-55455-052-4(1), 9f0bfe2e-3d5f-41a8-a347-4a63232b6e17) Trifolium Bks., Inc. CAN. Dist: Firefly Bks., Ltd.

MacDonald, Frances. The Screaming Tunnel. 2012. (ENG.). 140p. (J). pap. 15.99 (978-1-926780-23-8(X), d7954a33-9004-486f-9283-b96ff1427a57) Key Publishing Hse., Inc., The CAN. Dist: Baker & Taylor Publisher Services (BTPS).

MacGregor, Roy. The Ghost of the Stanley Cup, 11. 2013. (Screech Owls Ser.: 11). (ENG.). 176p. (J). (gr. 4-7). pap. 8.99 (978-1-77049-416-9(2), Tundra Bks.) Tundra Bks. CAN. Dist: Penguin Random Hse. LLC.

Malik, Katherine. Giselle's Magical World, 1 vol. 2009. 150p. pap. 24.95 (978-1-4489-1902-4(9)) America Star Bks.

Martin, Mary. Grandma's Goose. Hoover, Charity, illus. 2012. 188p. (978-0-7399-2452-5(4)) Rod & Staff Pubs., Inc.

Maruno, Jennifer. Cherry Blossom Winter. 2013. 208p. pap. (978-1-4596-6307-7(1)) ReadHowYouWant.com, Ltd.

—Cherry Blossom Winter: A Cherry Blossom Book. 2012. (Cherry Blossom Book Ser.: 2). (ENG.). 176p. (J). pap. 9.99 (978-1-4597-0211-0(5)) Dundurn Pr. CAN. Dist: Publishers Group West (PGW).

—When the Cherry Blossoms Fell: A Cherry Blossom Book. 2009. (Cherry Blossom Book Ser.: 1). (ENG.). 144p. (J). (gr. 4-7). pap. 10.99 (978-1-894917-83-4(9), Napoleon & Co.) Dundurn Pr. CAN. Dist: Publishers Group West (PGW).

Matthews, Curtis. Boots Meets the Grizzly Bears. 2007. 164p. per. 13.95 (978-1-4343-3372-8(8)) AuthorHouse.

McClintock, Norah. From the Dead, 1 vol. 2014. (Seven Sequels Ser.: 2). (ENG., Illus.). 288p. (J). (gr. 4-7). pap. 10.95 (978-1-4598-0537-8(2)) Orca Bk. Pubs. USA.

McFarlane, Leslie. McGonigle Scores! 2006. (ENG.). 256p. (J). pap. 9.95 (978-1-55263-834-7(0)) Leaf Storm Pr.

McNamee, Graham. Bonechiller. 2012. (ENG.). 304p. (YA). (gr. 7). pap. 11.99 (978-0-307-97593-5(2), Ember) Random Hse. Children's Bks.

McNaughton, Janet. To Dance at the Palais Royale. 2006. (ENG.). 252p. (J). (gr. 5-8). mass mkt. 6.99 (978-0-00-639541-6(4), Harper Trophy) HarperCollins Pubs.

Montague, Gay & Wise, Erin. Peace Is a Bright Delight. 2008. 28p. pap. 13.99 (978-1-4389-2153-2(5)) AuthorHouse.

Montgomery, L. M. Jane of Lantern Hill. 2014. (ENG.). 272p. (YA). (gr. 5-12). pap. 11.99 (978-1-4022-8930-9(8)) Sourcebooks, Inc.

Norman, C. S. The Lockview Logans: Fire One. 2012. 316p. (gr. 4-6). pap. 18.95 (978-1-4697-9840-0(9)) iUniverse, Inc.

Peacock, Shane. Double You, 1 vol. 2014. (Seven Sequels Ser.: 3). (ENG., Illus.). 272p. (J). (gr. 4-7). pap. 10.95 (978-1-4598-0534-7(8)) Orca Bk. Pubs. USA.

Pearce, Jacqueline. Siege, 1 vol. 2014. (Orca Currents Ser.). (ENG.). 136p. (J). (gr. 4-7). pap. 9.95 (978-1-4598-0751-8(0)) Orca Bk. Pubs. USA.

Pearl, Beverly. Poison Ivy. 2008. (ENG.). 71p. pap. 9.99 (978-1-4357-1386-4(9)) Lulu Pr., Inc.

—Poison Ivy, the Pocket Book. 2008. 105p. pap. 14.95 (978-1-4357-2328-3(7)) Lulu Pr., Inc.

Pignat, Caroline. Wild Geese, 1 vol. 2010. (ENG., Illus.). 335p. (J). (gr. 5-9). pap. 12.95 (978-0-88995-432-8(1), 5892848d-5e36-48df-8137-257e91a4ebc2) Trifolium Bks., Inc. CAN. Dist: Firefly Bks., Ltd.

Pollock, Beth. Harley's Gift, 1 vol. 2007. (Lorimer Streetlights Ser.). (ENG.). 128p. (J). (gr. 2-5). 7.95 (978-1-55028-992-3(6), 992) James Lorimer & Co. Ltd., Pubs. CAN. Dist: Formac Lorimer Bks. Ltd.

Posesorski, Sherie. Escape Plans. Pearcey, Dawn, illus. 2005. 272p. (J). (gr. 5). 8.95 (978-1-55050-177-3(1)) Coteau Bks. CAN. Dist: Fitzhenry & Whiteside, Ltd.

Radford, Heather. The Asquinn Twins: Frontier Life. Oakley, Darlene, ed. 2012. 104p. (978-1-77097-693-1(0)); pap. (978-1-77097-694-8(9)) FriesenPress.

Ridge, Yolanda. Road Block, 1 vol. 2012. (Orca Young Readers Ser.). (ENG.). 168p. (J). (gr. 4-7). pap. 7.95 (978-1-4598-0045-8(1)) Orca Bk. Pubs. USA.

Ross, Jeff. Up North, 1 vol. 2017. (Orca Soundings Ser.). (ENG.). 144p. (YA). (gr. 8-12). pap. 9.95 (978-1-4598-1456-1(8)) Orca Bk. Pubs. USA.

Scrimger, Richard. The Wolf & Me, 1 vol. 2014. (Seven Sequels Ser.: 4). (ENG., Illus.). 256p. (J). (gr. 4-7). pap. 10.95 (978-1-4598-0531-6(3)) Orca Bk. Pubs. USA.

Shawyer, Jo. Legend of the Paymaster's Gold. 2012. (ENG., Illus.). 136p. (YA). (gr. 6). pap. 12.99 (978-1-55488-990-7(1), 9781554889907) Dundurn Pr. CAN. Dist: Publishers Group West (PGW).

Sherrard, Valerie. Watcher. 2009. (ENG.). 224p. (YA). (gr. 6-18). pap. 10.99 (978-1-55488-431-5(4)) Dundurn Pr. CAN. Dist: Publishers Group West (PGW).

Smallman, Steve. Santa Is Coming to Toronto. Dunn, Robert, illus. 2nd ed. 2019. (Santa Is Coming... Ser.). (ENG.). 40p. (J). (gr. -1-3). 12.99 (978-1-7282-0105-4(5), Hometown World) Sourcebooks, Inc.

Staunton, Ted. Coda, 1 vol. 2014. (Seven Sequels Ser.: 5). (ENG., Illus.). 224p. (J). (gr. 4-7). pap. 10.95 (978-1-4598-0549-1(6)) Orca Bk. Pubs. USA.

Stevenson, Steve. The Heist at Niagara Falls. 2013. (Agatha Girl of Mystery Ser.: 4). lib. bdg. 16.00 (978-0-606-32128-0(4)) Turtleback.

Stinson, Kathy. Highway of Heroes, 1 vol. 2010. (ENG., Illus.). 32p. (J). (gr. 4-8). 9.95 (978-1-55455-182-8(X), 5723d8f4-51c0-4d20-b125-fd8081d33f7e) Fitzhenry & Whiteside, Ltd. CAN. Dist: Firefly Bks., Ltd.

—One Year Commencing. 2006. (ENG.). 152p. pap. 11.95 (978-1-895449-65-5(0)) Thistledown Pr., Ltd. CAN. Dist: Univ. of Toronto Pr.

Sutherland, Suzanne. When We Were Good, 1 vol. 2013. (ENG.). 240p. (YA). (gr. 9-12). pap. 12.95 (978-1-927513-11-8(1), Sumach Pr.) Canadian Scholars.

Taylor, Drew Hayden. The Night Wanderer: A Native Gothic Novel. 5th ed. 2007. (ENG., Illus.). 228p. (YA). (gr. 7-12). pap. 12.95 (978-1-55451-099-3(6), 9781554510993) Annick Pr., Ltd. CAN. Dist: Publishers Group West (PGW).

Towell, Ann. Grease Town. 2010. 240p. (YA). (gr. 7-9). 17.95 (978-0-88776-983-2(7), Tundra Bks.) Tundra Bks. CAN. Dist: Penguin Random Hse. LLC.

Vandervelde, Beatrice. Home Ice, 1 vol. 2004. (Lorimer Sports Stories Ser.: 76). (ENG.). 104p. (J). (gr. 4-8). 16.95 (978-1-55028-863-6(6), 863) James Lorimer & Co. Ltd., Pubs. CAN. Dist: Formac Lorimer Bks. Ltd.

Walmsley, Tom. Kid Stuff: A Novel. 2004. (ENG.). 288p. pap. 17.95 (978-1-55152-153-4(9), 187) Arsenal Pulp Pr. CAN. Dist: Consortium Bk. Sales & Distribution.

Walters, Eric. The Falls. 2008. (ENG.). 336p. (J). (gr. 3-7). 12.00 (978-0-14-331246-8(4), Puffin Canada) PRH Canada Young Readers CAN. Dist: Penguin Random Hse. LLC.

Westley, William. Charlie & Crow. 2011. 66p. 24.99 (978-1-4628-6802-5(9)); pap. 15.99 (978-1-4628-6801-8(0)) Xlibris Corp.

Wilson, David. The Adventures of Jack Bennett Winter Rescue. 2013. 116p. pap. (978-0-9919509-0-4(9)) Wilson, David.

Young, Jennifer Hayman. Aliens, Eh! 2011. 248p. (gr. 4-6). pap. 16.95 (978-1-4620-0588-8(8)) iUniverse, Inc.

OPERA

see also Ballet

Battaglia, Stephen. Mr. Mcsymphony's It's All about Opera. 2008. (ENG.). 30p. pap. 9.99 (978-1-4196-8091-5(9)) CreateSpace Independent Publishing Platform.

Cohan, George M. & Schwaeber, Barbie. Give My Regards to Broadway. Newsom, Carol, illus. 2008. (American Favorites Ser.). (ENG.). 32p. (J). (gr. -1-3). 14.95 (978-1-59249-726-3(8)); 8.95 (978-1-59249-727-0(6)) Soundprints.

Dunn, Mary R. I Want to Be in Musicals. (Dream Jobs Ser.). 24p. (gr. 2-3). 2009. 42.50 (978-1-61512-215-8(X), PowerKids Pr.) 2008. (ENG., Illus.). (YA). lib. bdg. 26.27 (978-1-4042-4470-2(0), 4dbd29f9-d7a0-4843-b694-02ce7f7ec6f8) Rosen Publishing Group, Inc., The.

Dunn, Mary R. & Alamán, Eduardo. Quiero Trabajar en Los Musicales, 1 vol. 2009. (Trabajos de Ensueño (Dream Jobs) Ser.). (SPA.). 24p. (gr. 2-3). pap. 8.25 (978-1-4358-3435-4(6), 062b8373-0a52-42d8-be37-b45a344e896a, PowerKids Pr.); (Illus.). (J). lib. bdg. 26.27 (978-1-4042-8153-0(3), e9477ed8-5664-4202-83cd-a73a13cf47a8) Rosen Publishing Group, Inc., The.

Kushner, Tony. Brundibar. Sendak, Maurice, illus. 2003. (ENG.). 56p. (J). (gr. 5-9). 24.99 (978-0-7868-0904-2(3)) Little, Brown Bks. for Young Readers.

Lindsay, Liddy. Opera a to Z: A Beginner's Guide to Opera. 2013. (Illus.). 60p. (J). pap. 24.95 (978-0-9854248-3-1(4)) Pinwheel Bks.

Riggs, Kate. Opera Music. 2008. (World of Music Ser.). (Illus.). 24p. (J). (gr. -1). lib. bdg. 24.25 (978-1-58341-568-9(8), Creative Education) Creative Co., The.

Walker, Geof. William Shakespeare's 'the Tempest' - a playscript for younger Students. 2005. (ENG.). 28p. 19.46 (978-1-4116-7138-6(4)) Lulu Pr., Inc.

—William Shakespeare's 'Twelfth Night' - a playscript for younger Students. 2006. 52p. pap. 19.51 (978-1-4116-7137-9(6)) Lulu Pr., Inc.

OPERA—FICTION

Brian, Janeen. Cat-Astrophe at the Opera, 1 vol. rev. ed. 2013. (Literary Text Ser.). (ENG., Illus.). 28p. (J). (gr. 2-3). pap. 10.99 (978-1-4333-5597-4(3)) Teacher Created Materials, Inc.

—Cat-Astrpohe at the Opera. rev. ed. 2013. (Literary Text Ser.). (ENG., Illus.). 28p. (J). (gr. 2-3). lib. bdg. 19.96 (978-1-4807-1719-0(3)) Teacher Created Materials, Inc.

Clement, Gary. The Great Poochini. 2004. (J). (gr. 1-4). spiral bd. (978-0-616-03027-1(4)) Canadian National Institute for the Blind/Institut National Canadien pour les Aveugles.

Francis, Pauline, retold by. The Phantom of the Opera, 1 vol. 2010. (Essential Classics - Horror Ser.). (ENG., Illus.). 56p. pap. (978-0-237-54095-1(9)) Evans Brothers, Ltd.

Heidenreich, Elke. Some Folk Think the South Pole's Hot: The Three Tenors Play the Antarctic. Buchholz, Quint, illus. 2004. (ENG.). 64p. (J). 17.95 (978-1-56792-170-0(1)) Godine, David R. Pub.

Howard, A. G. RoseBlood. (ENG.). 432p. (gr. 8-17). 2018. (J). pap. 10.99 (978-1-4197-2723-8(0), 1124203, Amulet Bks.) 2017. (YA). pap. 8.95 (978-1-4197-2342-1(1)) Abrams, Inc.

—RoseBlood. 2018. (J). lib. bdg. 20.85 (978-0-606-40729-8(4)) Turtleback.

Husain, Shahrukh & Barefoot Books. Barefoot Books Stories from the Opera. Mayhew, James, illus. 2015. 96p. (J). (gr. 2-6). 16.99 (978-1-78285-253-7(0)) Barefoot Bks., Inc.

Huser, Glen. The Golden Touch, 1 vol. Béha, Philippe, illus. 2015. (ENG.). 64p. (J). (gr. 1-3). 18.00 (978-1-896580-73-9(4)) Tradewind Bks. CAN. Dist: Orca Bk. Pubs. USA.

Knighton, Kate, retold by. Phantom of the Opera. 2008. (Young Reading Series 2 Gift Bks). 64p. (J). 8.99 (978-0-7945-2082-3(0), Usborne) EDC Publishing.

Rigby Education Staff. The Night Out. (Sails Literacy Ser.). (Illus.). 16p. (gr. 2-3). 27.00 (978-0-7635-9952-2(2), 699522C99) Rigby Education.

Rosner, Gillian, tr. The Phantom of the Opera: Based on the Novel by Gaston Leroux. Druvert, Hélène, illus. 2016. (ENG.). 40p. (J). (gr. k-2). 19.95 (978-1-4197-2086-4(4), 1648901, Abrams Bks. for Young Readers) Abrams, Inc.

Svingen, Arne. The Ballad of a Broken Nose. Dickson, Kari, tr. 2016. (ENG., Illus.). 224p. (J). (gr. 5). 16.99 (978-1-4814-1542-2(5), McElderry, Margaret K. Bks.) McElderry, Margaret K. Bks.

Thomas, Novene. The Enchanted Opera: Supernaturally Enchanting & Spiritually Enlightening. 2013. 192p. pap. 13.95 (978-1-62212-986-7(5), Strategic Bk. Publishing) Strategic Book Publishing & Rights Agency (SBPRA).

Turnbull, Ann. Mary Ann & Miss Mozart. 2009. (Historical House Ser.). 166p. (YA). (gr. 5-18). pap. 5.99 (978-0-7945-2332-9(3), Usborne) EDC Publishing.

OPERA HOUSES

see Theaters

OPERAS—STORIES, PLOTS, ETC.

Balfe, Roberta Rymer, et al. A Young Person's Introduction to the Arts Featuring the Opera La Cenerentola (Cinderella) by Gioachino [sic] Rossini: Music, Drama, Language, Costumes, Games, Puzzles. 2008. (Illus.). 24p. (J). (978-0-9785364-0-4(1)) Young Patronesses of the Opera, The.

Bredin, Henrietta & McEwen, Priscilla. The Prince & the Goosegirl: A Story with Activities Based on the Opera by Humperdinck. 2006. (Illus.). 30p. (J). (gr. k-4). reprint ed. pap. 17.00 (978-1-4223-5538-1(1)) DIANE Publishing Co.

Husain, Shahrukh & Mayhew, James. The Barefoot Book of Stories from the Opera. 2007. (ENG., Illus.). 80p. (J). pap. 16.99 (978-1-84686-098-0(9)) Barefoot Bks., Inc.

Teis, Kyra. The Magic Flute, 1 vol. Teis, Kyra, illus. 2008. (ENG., Illus.). 32p. (J). (gr. k-9). 17.95 (978-1-59572-058-0(8)) Star Bright Bks., Inc.

OPIATES

see Narcotics

OPINION, PUBLIC

see Public Opinion

OPOSSUMS

Berne, Emma Carlson. Opossums, 1 vol. 2014. (Scavengers: Eating Nature's Trash Ser.). (ENG., Illus.). 24p. (J). (gr. 2-3). lib. bdg. 25.27 (978-1-4777-6602-6(2), fb3000cd-9429-412b-8330-a5950cc4ad09, PowerKids Pr.) Rosen Publishing Group, Inc., The.

Early Macken, JoAnn. Opossums, 1 vol. (Animals That Live in the Forest (First Edition) Ser.). (ENG., 24p. (gr. 1-1). 2004. Illus.). lib. bdg. 25.27 (978-0-8368-4483-2(1), 3ebb6d46-b3b5-48ce-a0f9-461bcf0c415f) 2nd rev. ed. 2009. (J). pap. 9.15 (978-1-4339-2481-1(1), 7ac94921-0397-4d5a-abae-c701443b2c96) 2nd rev. ed. 2009. (J). lib. bdg. 25.27 (978-1-4339-2405-7(6), b33a72c5-3d88-4f11-982e-08c0e0a220e8) Stevens, Gareth Publishing LLLP.

—Opossums / Zarigüeyas, 1 vol. 2nd rev. ed. 2009. (Animals That Live in the Forest / Animales Del Bosque Ser.). 24p. (J). (gr. 1-1). (SPA & ENG.). pap. 9.15 (978-1-4339-2488-0(9), 35d477ca-1c22-45de-af63-a55a32fdf0e4); (ENG & SPA.). lib. bdg. 25.27 (978-1-4339-2437-8(4), 69112cbd-0941-4642-9a9c-9f192f18fa70) Stevens, Gareth Publishing LLLP. (Weekly Reader Leveled Readers).

Green, Emily. Opossums. 2011. (Backyard Wildlife Ser.). (ENG., Illus.). 24p. (J). (gr. k-3). lib. bdg. 26.95 (978-1-60014-561-2(2), Blastoff! Readers) Bellwether Media.

M N O

—Opossums. 2011. (Backyard Wildlife Ser.). 24p. (J). (gr. k-1). lib. bdg. 22.00 *(978-0-531-20137-4(6)*, Children's Pr.) Scholastic Library Publishing.

Kissock, Heather. Opossums. 2016. (Illus.). 24p. (J). *(978-1-4896-5396-3(1))* Weigl Pubs., Inc.

Linde, Barbara M. The Life Cycle of an Opossum, 1 vol. 2011. (Nature's Life Cycles Ser.). (ENG., Illus.). 24p. (J). (gr. 2-3). pap. 9.15 *(978-1-4339-4680-6(7)*, 33cb67a2-ac20-4d34-a5ae-89972ec759f8); lib. bdg. 25.27 *(978-1-4339-4679-0(3)*, 26024a52-f9de-49f3-a3b0-360f2a047696) Stevens, Gareth Publishing LLLP. (Gareth Stevens Learning Library).

McGill, Jordan. Opossums. 2011. (J). *(978-1-61690-579-8(4))*; 27.13 *(978-1-61690-933-8(1))* Weigl Pubs., Inc.

Moore Niver, Heather. Opossums after Dark, 1 vol. 2015. (Animals of the Night Ser.). (ENG.). 32p. (gr. 3-3). pap. 11.52 *(978-0-7660-7302-9(5)*, 60a99e30-bcb9-4914-8dc5-cca29e4b1ab9); (Illus.). lib. bdg. 26.93 *(978-0-7660-7304-3(1)*, 46ba00f8-95c7-410a-b62e-76e01e622b64) Enslow Publishing, LLC.

Nichols, Catherine. Tricky Opossums. 2008. (Gross-Out Defenses Ser.). (Illus.). 24p. (J). (gr. k-3). lib. bdg. 26.99 *(978-1-59716-718-5(5))* Bearport Publishing Co., Inc.

Quinlivan, Ada. Opossums, 1 vol. 2016. (Creatures of the Forest Habitat Ser.). (ENG.). 24p. (J). (gr. 3-3). 25.27 *(978-1-4994-2928-2(2)*, 405f406f-7338-44f2-a5df-9094691b6324, PowerKids Pr.) Rosen Publishing Group, Inc., The.

Rathburn, Betsy. Opossums. 2018. (North American Animals Ser.). (ENG., Illus.). 24p. (J). (gr. k-3). lib. bdg. 26.95 *(978-1-62617-729-1(5)*, Blastoff! Readers) Bellwether Media.

Schuh, Mari. Opossums. 2016. (My First Animal Library). (Illus.). 24p. (J). (gr. k-2). lib. bdg. 25.65 *(978-1-62031-289-6(1)*, Bullfrog Bks.) Jump! Inc.

Tatlock, Ann. Backyard Jungle Safari Opossums: Opossums. 2015. (ENG., Illus.). 32p. (J). 26.50 *(978-1-62469-100-3(5))* Purple Toad Publishing, Inc.

Terhune, Charlotte. There's a Possum in the Pillows. 2005. (Illus.). 14p. (J). 12.00 *(978-0-9764893-1-3(7))* Where-I-Live / Foster Pr.

Walker, Sally M. Opossums. 2008. (Early Bird Nature Bks.). (ENG., Illus.). 48p. (J). (gr. 2-5). lib. bdg. 26.60 *(978-0-8225-3055-8(4))* Lerner Publishing Group.

Webster, Christine. Opossums. (J). 2012. *(978-1-61913-067-8(X))* 2012. *(978-1-61913-264-1(8))* 2007. (Illus.). 24p. (gr. -1-3). lib. bdg. 24.45 *(978-1-59036-677-6(8))* Weigl Pubs., Inc.

—Opossums. Hudak, Heather C., ed. 2007. (Backyard Animals Ser.). (Illus.). 24p. (J). (gr. -1-3). pap. 8.95 *(978-1-59036-678-3(6))* Weigl Pubs., Inc.

OPOSSUMS—FICTION

Ballard, John E. & Shiply, Lyn. What Is That Sound! 2011. 40p. pap. 24.95 *(978-1-4560-0988-5(5))* America Star Bks.

Bannister, Barbara. Possum's Three Fine Friends. Baron, Kathy, illus. 2006. (ENG.). 32p. (gr. 1-3). pap. 9.95 *(978-1-57874-096-3(7)*, Kaeden Bks.) Kaeden Corp.

Berkes, Marianne. Anybody Home?, 1 vol. Dickinson, Rebecca, illus. 2013. 32p. (J). (gr. -1-3). (SPA.). 17.95 *(978-1-60718-714-1(0))*; (ENG.). 17.95 *(978-1-60718-618-2(7)*, 9781607186182); (ENG.). pap. 9.95 *(978-1-60718-630-4(6))* Arbordale Publishing.

Blom, Jen K. Possum Summer. Rayyan, Omar, illus. 2011. (ENG.). 256p. (J). (gr. 3-7). 17.95 *(978-0-8234-2331-6(X))* Holiday Hse., Inc.

Burgess, Thornton W. The Adventures of Unc' Billy Possum. 2007. 140p. (gr. 4-7). per. 13.95 *(978-1-60312-337-2(7))*; 24.95 *(978-1-60312-675-5(9))* Aegypan.

—The Adventures of Unc' Billy Possum. (J). 18.95 *(978-0-8488-0382-7(5))* Amereon Ltd.

—The Adventures of Unc' Billy Possum. Cady, Harrison & Stewart, Pat Ronson, trs. Cady, Harrison & Stewart, Pat Ronson, illus. 2003. (Dover Children's Thrift Classics Ser.). (ENG.). 96p. (J). (gr. 3-8). pap. 5.00 *(978-0-486-43031-7(6)*, 430316) Dover Pubns., Inc.

—The Adventures of Unc' Billy Possum. 2011. 140p. 24.95 *(978-1-4638-9563-1(1))* Rodgers, Alan Bks.

Chaconas, Dori. The Babysitters. McCue, Lisa, illus. 2014. (Cork & Fuzz Ser.: 6). 32p. (J). (gr. 1-3). pap. 4.99 *(978-0-448-48050-3(6)*, Penguin Young Readers) Penguin Young Readers Group.

—The Collectors, 4 vols. McCue, Lisa, illus. 2010. (Cork & Fuzz Ser.: 4). 32p. (J). (gr. 1-3). mass mkt. 4.99 *(978-0-14-241714-0(9)*, Penguin Young Readers) Penguin Young Readers Group.

—Finders Keepers, 5 vols. McCue, Lisa, illus. 2011. (Cork & Fuzz Ser.: 5). 32p. (J). (gr. 1-3). mass mkt. 4.99 *(978-0-14-241869-7(2)*, Penguin Young Readers) Penguin Young Readers Group.

—Good Sports. McCue, Lisa, illus. 2010. (Cork & Fuzz Ser.: 3). 32p. (J). (gr. 1-3). mass mkt. 4.99 *(978-0-14-241713-3(0)*, Penguin Young Readers) Penguin Young Readers Group.

—Short & Tall. McCue, Lisa, illus. 2006. (Penguin Young Readers: Level 3 Ser.: 2). (ENG.). 32p. (J). (gr. 1-3). 16.19 *(978-0-670-05985-0(4)*, Viking) Penguin Publishing Group.

—Short & Tall No. 2, 2 vols. McCue, Lisa, illus. 2010. (Cork & Fuzz Ser.: 2). 32p. (J). (gr. 1-3). mass mkt. 4.99 *(978-0-14-241594-8(4)*, Penguin Young Readers) Penguin Young Readers Group.

—The Swimming Lesson. McCue, Lisa, illus. 2014. (Cork & Fuzz Ser.: 7). 32p. (J). (gr. 1-3). pap. 5.99 *(978-0-448-48051-0(4)*, Penguin Young Readers) Penguin Young Readers Group.

—Wait a Minute. McCue, Lisa, illus. 2015. (Cork & Fuzz Ser.: 9). 32p. (J). (gr. 1-3). 4.99 *(978-0-14-750856-0(8)*, Penguin Young Readers) Penguin Young Readers Group.

Collins, Nafessa. Mrs. Precious & the Possum. 2012. 56p. (gr. -1). pap. 8.95 *(978-1-4759-1273-9(0))* iUniverse, Inc.

Degroat, Diane. Ants in Your Pants, Worms in Your Plants! 2011. (Gilbert Ser.). (ENG., Illus.). 32p. (J). (gr. -1-3). 17.99 *(978-0-06-176511-7(2)*, HarperCollins) HarperCollins Pubs.

deGroat, Diane. Gilbert & the Lost Tooth. deGroat, Diane, illus. 2012. (I Can Read Level 2 Ser.). (ENG., Illus.). 32p. (J). (gr. k-3). pap. 4.99 *(978-0-06-125216-7(6)*, HarperCollins) HarperCollins Pubs.

Degroat, Diane. Gilbert & the Lost Tooth. 2012. (I Can Read Level 2 Ser.). (ENG., Illus.). 32p. (J). (gr. k-3). 16.99 *(978-0-06-125214-3(X)*, HarperCollins) HarperCollins Pubs.

deGroat, Diane. Gilbert, the Surfer Dude. deGroat, Diane, illus. 2010. (I Can Read Level 2 Ser.). (ENG., Illus.). 32p. (J). (gr. k-3). pap. 4.99 *(978-0-06-125213-6(1)*, HarperCollins) HarperCollins Pubs.

—Gilbert, the Surfer Dude. 2009. (Illus.). 31p. (J). lib. bdg. 18.89 *(978-0-06-125212-9(3))* HarperCollins Pubs.

Degroat, Diane. Last One in Is a Rotten Egg! 2011. (Gilbert Ser.). (ENG., Illus.). 32p. (J). (gr. -1-3). pap. 7.99 *(978-0-06-089296-8(X)*, HarperCollins) HarperCollins Pubs.

Desmet, Sara. Scared Silly. Desmet, Sara, illus. 2006. (Illus.). 32p. (J). (gr. -1-3). 15.95 *(978-1-60108-009-7(3))* Red Cygnet Pr.

Hinchcliffe, L. T. For the Love of Prudence Possum. 2008. 76p. pap. 15.50 *(978-1-60693-136-3(9)*, Eloquent Bks.) Strategic Book Publishing & Rights Agency (SBPRA).

Holtam, Elizabeth T. A Possum in My Pocket. 2013. 28p. pap. 21.99 *(978-1-4797-7889-8(3))* Xlibris Corp.

Jason June, Jason. Whobert Whover, Owl Detective. Pauwels, Jess, illus. 2017. (ENG.). 40p. (J). (gr. -1-1). 17.99 *(978-1-4814-6271-6(7)*, McElderry, Margaret K. Bks.) McElderry, Margaret K. Bks.

Kasza, Keiko. No Te Rias, Pepe. (Buenas Noches Ser.). (SPA.). (J). (gr. k-3). *(978-958-04-3623-2(1))* Norma S.A.

Landry, Leo. What's up, Chuck? Landry, Leo, illus. 2016. (Illus.). 48p. (J). (gr. k-3). lib. bdg. 12.95 *(978-1-58089-698-6(7))* Charlesbridge Publishing, Inc.

Lang, Valerie E. Jet's Day: A Whisker Team Story. 2011. 32p. pap. 13.00 *(978-1-61204-178-0(7)*, Strategic Bk. Publishing) Strategic Book Publishing & Rights Agency (SBPRA).

Martin, Anne E. Midnight Kitties. 2007. (Illus.). 35p. (J). per. 13.99 *(978-1-59879-245-4(8))* Lifevest Publishing, Inc.

Milliken, Lyndsay Nicole. Blossom Plays Possum: (Because She's Shy) McDonnell, Janet, illus. 2017. (ENG.). 32p. (J). 15.95 *(978-1-4338-2735-8(2)*, Magination Pr.) American Psychological Assn.

Osmond, Jimmy. Awesome Possum Family Band. 2014. (ENG., Illus.). 40p. (J). (gr. -1-3). 16.99 *(978-1-62157-211-4(0)*, Regnery Kids) Regnery Publishing.

Sanders, Cecilia. Wanted Dead or Alive. 2010. 36p. pap. 16.99 *(978-1-4520-7023-0(7))* AuthorHouse.

Sargent, Dave & Sargent, Pat. Pokey Opossum: I'm Kinda Slow, 15 vols., Vol. 18. Huff, Jeane, illus. 2nd rev. ed. 2003. (Animal Pride Ser.: 18). 42p. (J). pap. 10.95 *(978-1-56763-794-6(9))*; lib. bdg. 20.95 *(978-1-56763-793-9(0))* Ozark Publishing.

Tashlin, Frank. The Possum That Didn't. 2016. (ENG., Illus.). 64p. (gr. 5-5). pap. 3.99 *(978-0-486-80080-6(6)*, 800806) Dover Pubns., Inc.

Tingwald, July Ann. Orrie's Christmas. Powell, James, illus. 2007. 42p. 9.00 *(978-0-9706728-5-8(3))* New Millenium Pr., The.

Walker, Sally M. Opossum at Sycamore Road. Snyder, Joel, illus. 2011. (Smithsonian's Backyard Ser.). (ENG.). 32p. (J). (gr. -1-3). 8.95 *(978-1-60727-640-1(2))* Soundprints.

Weston Woods Staff, creator. Possum Magic. 2011. 38.75 *(978-0-545-14784-2(0))*; 18.95 *(978-0-545-08634-9(5))* Weston Woods Studios, Inc.

Wulfekotte, Dana. Rabbit & Possum. Wulfekotte, Dana, illus. 2018. (ENG., Illus.). 40p. (J). (gr. -1-3). 17.99 *(978-0-06-245581-9(8)*, Greenwillow Bks.) HarperCollins Pubs.

OPPENHEIMER, J. ROBERT, 1904-1967

Allman, Toney. J. Robert Oppenheimer: Theoretical Physicist, Atomic Pioneer. 2005. (Giants of Science Ser.). (ENG., Illus.). 64p. (J). (gr. 3-7). lib. bdg. 28.35 *(978-1-56711-889-6(5)*, Blackbirch Pr., Inc.) Cengage Gale.

OPPOSITES

see Polarity

OPTICAL ILLUSIONS

Cobb, Vicki. On Stage. 2008. pap. 52.95 *(978-0-8225-9450-5(1))* Lerner Publishing Group.

—On Stage. Gold, Michael, photos by. 2005. (Where's the Science Here? Ser.). (ENG., Illus.). 48p. (gr. 3-5). lib. bdg. 23.93 *(978-0-7613-2774-5(6)*, Millbrook Pr.) Lerner Publishing Group.

Einhorn, Nicholas. Stand-up Magic & Optical Illusions, 1 vol. 2010. (Inside Magic Ser.). (ENG., Illus.). 64p. (YA). (gr. 6-6). 37.13 *(978-1-4358-9452-5(9)*, 72d76f25-304f-4c37-822f-6795a1e7e82c, Rosen Reference) Rosen Publishing Group, Inc., The.

Hanson, Anders & Mann, Elissa. Cool Optical Illusions: Creative Activities That Make Math & Science Fun for Kids! 2013. (Cool Art with Math & Science Ser.). (ENG.). 32p. (J). (gr. 3-6). lib. bdg. 34.21 *(978-1-61783-822-4(5)*, 4590, Checkerboard Library) ABDO Publishing Co.

Honeycutt, Brad. Exceptional Eye Tricks. 2013. (Illus.). 128p. pap. 9.95 *(978-1-936140-73-2(X)*, Imagine Publishing) Charlesbridge Publishing, Inc.

IllusionWorks & IllusionWorks. Amazing Optical Illusions. 2004. (ENG., Illus.). 32p. (J). (gr. 1-3). 16.95 *(978-1-55297-961-7(X)*, 7636ddc1-61c2-4a8e-a0b6-7a5d1228a5d7); pap. 6.95 *(978-1-55297-962-4(8)*, 4c684226-c315-4a77-978f-5acb4c04d4af) Firefly Bks., Ltd.

Kay, Keith. A Little Giant(r) Book: Optical Illusions. 2007. (Illus.). 352p. (J). (gr. 3-7). pap. 6.95 *(978-1-4027-4971-1(6))* Sterling Publishing Co., Inc.

Loh-Hagan, Virginia. Gravity Hills. 2018. (Urban Legends: Don't Read Alone! Ser.). (ENG., Illus.). 32p. (J). (gr. 4-8). pap. 14.21 *(978-1-5341-0861-5(0)*, 210808); lib. bdg. 32.07 *(978-1-5341-0762-5(2)*, 210807) Cherry Lake Publishing. (45th Parallel Press).

Magic Eye, Inc. Staff. Harry Potter Magic Eye Book: 3D Magical Moments. 2011. (ENG.). 32p. 16.99 *(978-1-4494-0141-2(4))* Andrews McMeel Publishing.

Muir, Duncan. Optical Illusions. 2003. (Knowledge Masters Ser.). (Illus.). 32p. (YA). pap. incl. cd-rom *(978-1-903954-61-4(4)*, Pavilion Children's Books) Pavilion Bks.

National Geographic. Xtreme Illusions 2: Mind-Blowing Illusions, Wacky Brain Teasers, Awesome Puzzles. 2015. 48p. (J). (gr. 3-7). 16.99 *(978-1-4263-1974-7(6)*, National Geographic Kids) Disney Publishing Worldwide.

National Geographic Kids. What in the World? Fun-Tastic Photo Puzzles for Curious Minds. 2014. (Illus.). 48p. (J). (gr. 3-7). 16.99 *(978-1-4263-1517-6(1)*, National Geographic Kids) Disney Publishing Worldwide.

—What in the World? Look Again. 2015. (Illus.). 48p. (J). (gr. 3-7). 16.99 *(978-1-4263-2080-4(9)*, National Geographic Kids) Disney Publishing Worldwide.

Olson, Elsie. Magic Tricks with Optical Illusions. 2019. (Lightning Bolt Books (r) — Magic Tricks Ser.). (ENG., Illus.). 24p. (J). (gr. 1-3). 29.32 *(978-1-5415-3896-2(X)*, 86686e6c-6ceb-4c9d-8cca-e332a715d694, Lerner Pubns.); pap. 9.99 *(978-1-5415-4581-6(8)*, 381d3a1b-ef93-40f0-8c72-6bf3e71a45ed) Lerner Publishing Group.

Taplin, Sam. Optical Illusions Tin. 2013. (Activity Tins Ser.). 80p. (J). 14.99 *(978-0-7945-3338-0(8)*, Usborne) EDC Publishing.

—50 Optical Illusions. Seckel, Al, illus. 2010. (Activity Cards Ser.). 50p. (J). 9.99 *(978-0-7945-2664-1(0)*, Usborne) EDC Publishing.

Wick, Walter. Walter Wick's Optical Tricks (10th Anniversary Edition) 10th Anniversary Edition. Wick, Walter, photos by. 10th anniv. ed. 2008. (ENG., Illus.). 48p. (J). (gr. -1-3). 16.99 *(978-0-439-85520-4(9)*, Cartwheel Bks.) Scholastic, Inc.

OPTICAL MASERS

see Lasers

OPTICS

see also Color; Light; Perspective; Radiation; Vision

Allman, Toney. From Octopus Eyes to Powerful Lenses, 1 vol. 2006. (Imitating Nature Ser.). (ENG., Illus.). 32p. (gr. 3-6). lib. bdg. 28.88 *(978-0-7377-3631-1(3)*, 13af9fff-1269-4817-bcb6-15cb16cb2077, KidHaven Publishing) Greenhaven Publishing LLC.

Bodach, Vijaya Khisty. Reflection. 2008. (Discovering & Exploring Science Ser.). (Illus.). 16p. (J). (gr. -1-3). lib. bdg. 12.95 *(978-0-7569-8428-1(9))* Perfection Learning Corp.

Brasch, Nicolas. Why Do Shadows Lengthen?, 1 vol. 2010. (Solving Science Mysteries Ser.). (ENG., Illus.). 24p. (gr. 4-5). (J). pap. 9.25 *(978-1-61531-913-8(1)*, 1567c549-a675-4d53-b750-6824f69e7aa2, PowerKids Pr.); (YA). lib. bdg. 26.27 *(978-1-61531-891-9(7)*, 82df3909-363c-42ec-9e66-87d93386a3b0) Rosen Publishing Group, Inc., The.

—Why Do Shadows Lengthen? All about Light. 2010. (Illus.). 24p. (J). 49.50 *(978-1-61531-914-5(X)*, PowerKids Pr.) Rosen Publishing Group, Inc., The.

Davies, Monika. Helping People See (Grade 3) rev. ed. 2018. (Smithsonian: Informational Text Ser.). (ENG., Illus.). 32p. (J). (gr. 3-4). pap. 12.99 *(978-1-4938-6686-1(9))* Teacher Created Materials, Inc.

Ferrie, Chris. Optical Physics for Babies. 2017. (J). *(978-1-4926-5606-7(2))*; (Baby University Ser.: 0). (Illus.). 24p. (gr. -1-k). bds. 9.99 *(978-1-4926-5621-0(6))* Sourcebooks, Inc.

Fink, Charles. Light Show: Reflection & Absorption. 2009. (Amazing Science Ser.). 24p. (gr. 3-3). 42.50 *(978-1-61511-329-3(0)*, PowerKids Pr.) Rosen Publishing Group, Inc., The.

Hamilton, Gina L. Light. 2016. (J). *(978-1-5105-2239-8(5))* SmartBook Media, Inc.

—Light. 2008. (Science Q & A Ser.). (Illus.). 48p. (YA). (gr. 5-8). pap. 10.95 *(978-1-59036-947-0(5))*; lib. bdg. 29.05 *(978-1-59036-946-3(7))* Weigl Pubs., Inc.

—Light Q & A. 2013. (J). *(978-1-62127-415-5(2))*; pap. *(978-1-62127-421-6(7))* Weigl Pubs., Inc.

Hewitt, Sally. Amazing Light. 2007. (Amazing Science Ser.). (ENG.). 32p. (J). pap. *(978-0-7787-3626-4(1))* Crabtree Publishing Co.

Hughes, Susan. Is It Transparent or Opaque? 2012. (ENG., Illus.). 24p. (J). *(978-0-7787-2052-2(7))*; pap. *(978-0-7787-2059-1(4))* Crabtree Publishing Co.

Jennings, Terry. Light & Dark. 2009. (Science Alive Ser.). (ENG., Illus.). 32p. (J). (gr. 4-7). pap. *(978-1-897563-56-4(6))* Saunders Bk. Co.

Jennings, Terry J. Light & Dark. 2009. (J). 28.50 *(978-1-59920-270-9(0))* Black Rabbit Bks.

Kenney, Karen Latchana. The Science of Color: Investigating Light. 2015. (Science in Action Ser.). (ENG., Illus.). 32p. (J). (gr. 3-6). 32.79 *(978-1-62403-960-7(X)*, 19417, Checkerboard Library) ABDO Publishing Co.

Kittinger, Jo S. Light (a True Book: Physical Science) (Library Edition) 2019. (True Book (Relaunch) Ser.). (ENG., Illus.). 48p. (J). (gr. 3-5). lib. bdg. 31.00 *(978-0-531-13140-4(8)*, Children's Pr.) Scholastic Library Publishing.

Levy, Janey. Renaissance Paintings: Using Perspective to Represent Three-Dimensional Objects. 2005. (Math for the REAL World Ser.). 32p. 47.50 *(978-1-4042-5220-2(7)*, Rosen Classroom) Rosen Publishing Group, Inc., The.

O'Dea, Lori. Tools for Seeing. 2017. (Text Connections Guided Close Reading Ser.). (J). (gr. k). *(978-1-4900-1767-9(4))* Benchmark Education Co.

Richards, Roy. En Optica. (Coleccion 101 Trucos Cientificos). (SPA., Illus.). (J). (gr. 3-5). pap. *(978-950-724-175-8(2)*, LMA8751) Lumen ARG. Dist: Lectorum Pubns., Inc.

Romero, Libby. National Geographic Readers: Ibn AlHaytham: The Man Who Discovered How We See. 2016. (Readers Bios Ser.). (Illus.). 48p. (J). (gr. 1-3). pap. 4.99 *(978-1-4263-2500-7(2)*, National Geographic Kids) Disney Publishing Worldwide.

Rooney, Anne. Optical Engineering & the Science of Light. 2013. (ENG.). 32p. (J). *(978-0-7787-1228-2(1))*; (Illus.). pap. *(978-0-7787-1232-9(X))* Crabtree Publishing Co.

Shaffer, Jody Jensen. Vampires & Light, 6 vols. Flocco, Gervasio, illus. 2013. (Monster Science Ser.). (ENG.). 32p. (J). (gr. 3-4). pap. 48.60 *(978-1-62065-821-5(6)*, 19402); lib. bdg. 31.32 *(978-1-4296-9928-0(0)*, 120638) Capstone. (Capstone Pr.).

Spilsbury, Richard & Spilsbury, Louise. What Is Light? Exploring Science with Hands-On Activities, 1 vol. 2007. (In Touch with Basic Science Ser.). (ENG., Illus.). 32p. (gr. 3-3). lib. bdg. 26.60 *(978-0-7660-3097-8(0)*, 9482faf9-028c-468b-9d70-cacec94c16fb, Enslow Elementary) Enslow Publishing, LLC.

Strom, Laura Layton. Mirror Power. 2007. (Shockwave: Technology & Manufacturing Ser.). (ENG., Illus.). 36p. (J). (gr. 3-5). 25.00 *(978-0-531-17588-0(X)*, Children's Pr.) Scholastic Library Publishing.

Torrence, Jack. Light Show: Reflection & Absorption, 1 vol. 2008. (Real Life Readers Ser.). (ENG.). 24p. (gr. 3-3). pap. 8.25 *(978-1-4358-0096-0(6)*, a2dafbf8-b955-4129-acd3-e7c864fbcc88, Rosen Classroom) Rosen Publishing Group, Inc., The.

Walker, Sally M. Light. 2006. (Illus.). 48p. (J). pap. 8.95 *(978-0-8225-2842-5(8))* Lerner Publishing Group.

—Light. King, Andy, photos by. 2005. (Early Bird Energy Ser.). (ENG., Illus.). 48p. (gr. 2-5). lib. bdg. 26.60 *(978-0-8225-2925-5(4)*, Lerner Pubns.) Lerner Publishing Group.

Whitfield, David. Rainbows. (Sky Science (Library) Ser.). (J). 2012. (ENG., Illus.). 24p. (gr. 3-5). pap. 12.95 *(978-1-61913-546-8(9)*, 1346030, AV2 by Weigl) 2006. (Illus.). 24p. (gr. 3-7). pap. 24.45 *(978-1-59036-414-7(7))* 2006. pap. 8.95 *(978-1-59036-420-8(1))* Weigl Pubs., Inc.

Williams, Brian. The Science of a Pair of Glasses, 1 vol. 2009. (Science Of... Ser.). (ENG., Illus.). 32p. (YA). (gr. 4-5). lib. bdg. 28.67 *(978-1-4339-0044-0(0)*, 31f40d75-9525-4c30-8af8-0b5b56cd1ff5) Stevens, Gareth Publishing LLLP.

Yasuda, Anita. Explore Light & Optics! With 25 Great Projects. Stone, Bryan, illus. 2016. (Explore Your World Ser.). (ENG.). 96p. (J). (gr. 1-5). 19.95 *(978-1-61930-376-8(0)*, 249eee93-cd95-4566-a2bd-cbe9681cb26b); pap. 14.95 *(978-1-61930-380-5(9)*, 43f6238f-1c00-4c39-b7ec-01737b816ac2) Nomad Pr.

OPTICS—EXPERIMENTS

Jackson, Tom. Experiments with Light & Color, 1 vol. 2010. (Cool Science Ser.). (ENG., Illus.). 32p. (J). (gr. 4-5). pap. 11.50 *(978-1-4339-3454-4(X)*, ae1e39cc-058a-41f7-9f7b-fd2a25aa0fef); lib. bdg. 30.67 *(978-1-4339-3453-7(1)*, 371ab775-e76c-46eb-9e22-c01ad4211ac3) Stevens, Gareth Publishing LLLP. (Gareth Stevens Learning Library).

Kessler, Colleen. A Project Guide to Light & Optics. 2011. (Physical Science Projects for Kids Ser.). (Illus.). 48p. (J). (gr. 3-6). lib. bdg. 29.95 *(978-1-58415-969-8(3)*, 1327831) Mitchell Lane Pubs.

Rau, Dana Meachen. Light. 2009. (Explorer Library: Science Explorer Ser.). (ENG., Illus.). 32p. (gr. 4-8). lib. bdg. 32.07 *(978-1-60279-531-0(2)*, 200285) Cherry Lake Publishing.

OPTIONS (FINANCE)

see Stock Exchanges

OPTOMETRY

see also Eye

Harmon, Daniel E. Jump-Starting a Career in Optometry & Ophthalmology, 1 vol. 2018. (Health Care Careers in 2 Years Ser.). (ENG.). 80p. (gr. 7-7). pap. 16.30 *(978-1-5081-8504-8(2)*, 8978eba1-0332-4a90-8108-cbb25cff9e82, Rosen Young Adult) Rosen Publishing Group, Inc., The.

ORANGES

Brannon, Cecelia H. Oranges, 1 vol. 2017. (All about Food Crops Ser.). (ENG.). 24p. (gr. k-1). lib. bdg. 24.27 *(978-0-7660-8581-7(3)*, 317bfd7d-a663-4f7e-abf0-ba80adb6cba0) Enslow Publishing, LLC.

deMarin, Layne. Oranges: from Fruit to Juice, 1 vol. 2011. (Wonder Readers Fluent Level Ser.). (ENG.). 16p. (gr. -1-2). (J). pap. 6.25 *(978-1-4296-7926-8(3)*, 118258); pap. 35.94 *(978-1-4296-8135-3(7))* Capstone. (Capstone Pr.).

Hill, Christina. Lue Gim Gong: The Citrus Wizard (Florida) rev. ed. 2016. (Social Studies: Informational Text Ser.). (ENG., Illus.). 32p. (J). (gr. 4-8). pap. 11.99 *(978-1-4938-3549-2(1))* Teacher Created Materials, Inc.

Jacobson, Ryan. Orange Juice. 2016. (J). *(978-1-4896-4535-7(7))* Weigl Pubs., Inc.

Turning Oranges into Juice, 1 vol. 2014. (Step-By-Step Transformations Ser.). (ENG.). 24p. (gr. 1-1). lib. bdg. 25.93 *(978-1-62713-016-5(0)*, c8daa1ee-1e88-4675-852e-7ec102577c7f) Cavendish Square Publishing LLC.

Will Mayo, Gretchen. Orange Juice, 1 vol. 2004. (Where Does Our Food Come From? Ser.). (ENG., Illus.). 24p. (gr. 2-4). pap. 9.15 *(978-0-8368-4075-9(5)*, 65600fe6-d0db-4c78-9990-55b7bb5a6bec); lib. bdg. 23.67 *(978-0-8368-4068-1(2)*, 1dd46421-10a4-42e5-aa9b-10a4f6ceea84) Stevens, Gareth Publishing LLLP. (Weekly Reader Leveled Readers).

ORANGUTANS

Antle, Bhagavan "Doc". Suryia: An Orangutan's Story. 2018. (ENG., Illus.). 32p. (J). 14.99 *(978-1-68383-195-2(0)*, Earth Aware Editions) Insight Editions.

Borgert-Spaniol, Megan. Orangutans. 2013. (Animal Safari Ser.). (ENG., Illus.). 24p. (J). (gr. k-3). lib. bdg. 26.95 *(978-1-60014-913-9(8)*, Blastoff! Readers) Bellwether Media.

Bredeson, Carmen. Orangutans up Close, 1 vol. 2009. (Zoom in on Animals! Ser.). (ENG., Illus.). 24p. (gr. k-2). pap. 10.95 *(978-1-59845-419-2(6)*, 22d231db-6b79-4437-ba85-b0cb270d201b); lib. bdg. 25.60 *(978-0-7660-3078-7(4)*, 8da33480-096f-4238-863d-abc29793c702) Enslow Publishing, LLC. (Enslow Elementary).

Clausen-Grace, Nicki. Orangutans. 2018. (Wild Animal Kingdom (Continuation) Ser.). (ENG.). 32p. (gr. 2-7). 9.95 *(978-1-68072-736-4(2))*; (J). (gr. 4-6). pap. 9.99 *(978-1-64466-289-2(2)*, 12409); (J). (gr. 4-6). lib. bdg. *(978-1-68072-442-4(8)*, 12408) Black Rabbit Bks. (Bolt).

Davis, Patricia. Orangutans. 2009. (Illus.). 52p. (J). *(978-0-7172-8030-8(6))* Grolier, Ltd.

De la Bédoyère, Camilla. Why Why Why Are Orang-Utans So Hairy? 2008. (Why Why Why Ser.). (Illus.). 32p. (J). (gr. 4-7). pap. *(978-1-84810-003-9(5))* Miles Kelly Publishing, Ltd.

De Medeiros, Michael. Orangutans. 2008. (Amazing Animals Ser.). (Illus.). 24p. (J). (gr. 2-4). pap. 8.95 *(978-1-59036-967-8(X))*; lib. bdg. 24.45 *(978-1-59036-966-1(1))* Weigl Pubs., Inc.

Eason, Sarah. Save the Orangutan, 1 vol. Geeson, Andrew & Veldhoven, Marijke, illus. 2009. (Save The... Ser.). (ENG.). 32p. (J). (gr. 2-3). lib. bdg. 28.93 *(978-1-4358-2811-7(9)*, 492d61bc-0b16-49d1-8713-bd64cfb91440) Rosen Publishing Group, Inc., The.

The check digit for ISBN-10 appears in parentheses after the full ISBN-13

Ganeri, Anita. Survival in the Jungle. 2011. (ENG.). 24p. (J). pap. *(978-0-7787-7880-6(0))*; (gr. 3-6). *(978-0-7787-7858-5(4))* Crabtree Publishing Co.

Goldish, Meish. Orangutans. 2008. (Smart Animals! Ser.). (Illus.). 32p. (J). (gr. 2-5). lib. bdg. 28.50 *(978-1-59716-578-5(6))* Bearport Publishing Co., Inc.

Grunbaum, Mara. Orangutans (Nature's Children) (Library Edition) 2018. (Nature's Children, Fourth Ser.). (ENG., Illus.). 48p. (J). (gr. 3-5). lib. bdg. 30.00 *(978-0-531-23481-5(9))*, Children's Pr.) Scholastic Library Publishing.

Hansen, Grace. Help the Orangutans. 2018. (Little Activists: Endangered Species Ser.). (ENG., Illus.). 24p. (J). (gr. -1-2). lib. bdg. 32.79 *(978-1-5321-8202-0(3)*, 29863, Abdo Kids) ABDO Publishing Co.

Irvine, Georgeanne. Karen's Heart: The True Story of a Brave Baby Orangutan. 2018. (Illus.). (J). *(978-1-943198-04-7(7))* Southwestern Publishing Hse., Inc.

Katirgis, Jane & Harkrader, Lisa. Endangered Orangutans, 1 vol. 2015. (Wildlife at Risk Ser.). (ENG.). 48p. (gr. 6-6). pap. 12.70 *(978-0-7660-6884-1(6)*, edc7210b-3895-4160-9d08-881d8bd2dcdb); (Illus.). 29.60 *(978-0-7660-6886-5(2)*, afa22f93-22fb-4d79-baa6-cbcc0a326e2d) Enslow Publishing, LLC.

Kelley, K. C. Baby Orangutans. 2018. (Spot Baby Animals Ser.). (ENG.). 16p. (J). (gr. -1-2). pap. 7.99 *(978-1-68152-255-5(1)*, 14847) Amicus.

Knudsen, Shannon. Climbing Orangutans. 2007. (Pull Ahead Books-Animals Ser.). (ENG., Illus.). 32p. (J). (gr. k-3). lib. bdg. 22.60 *(978-0-8225-6704-2(0)*, Lerner Pubns.) Lerner Publishing Group.

Knudson, Shannon. Climbing Orangutans. 2009. pap. 40.95 *(978-0-8225-9317-1(3))* Lerner Publishing Group.

Kueffner, Sue. Orangutans. 2006. (Illus.). 45p. (J). *(978-1-59939-113-7(9)*, Reader's Digest Young Families, Inc.) Studio Fun International.

Kueffner, Susan. Orangutans, 1 vol. (Amazing Animals Ser.). (ENG.). 48p. (gr. 3-5). 2009. pap. 11.50 *(978-1-4339-2016-5(6)*, 88372046-a549-49ab-9dd8-3435ec26fec7, Gareth Stevens Learning Library) 2008. (YA). lib. bdg. 30.67 *(978-0-8368-9099-0(X)*, 7416a2a6-87e8-43d6-95f9-9e41865feed9) Stevens, Gareth Publishing LLLP.

Leaf, Christina. Baby Orangutans. 2015. (Super Cute! Ser.). (ENG., Illus.). 24p. (J). (gr. k-3). lib. bdg. 26.95 *(978-1-62617-171-8(8)*, Blastoff! Readers) Bellwether Media.

Los Orangutanes y Sus Nidos. 2017. (Animales Constructores Ser.). (Illus.). 24p. (J). (gr. 1-4). lib. bdg. 20.95 *(978-1-68151-282-2(3)*, 14723) Amicus.

Morgan, Sally. Orangutans. 2006. (QEB Animal Lives Ser.). (Illus.). 32p. (J). (gr. 4-7). lib. bdg. 19.95 *(978-1-59566-204-0(9))* QEB Publishing Inc.

Orme, Helen. Orangutans in Danger. 2006. (Wildlife Survival Ser.). (Illus.). 32p. (J). (gr. 2-5). lib. bdg. 28.50 *(978-1-59716-263-0(9))* Bearport Publishing Co., Inc.

Owen, Ruth. Orangutans, 1 vol. 2011. (World's Smartest Animals Ser.). (ENG., Illus.). 32p. (J). (gr. 2-3). pap. 12.75 *(978-1-61533-419-3(X)*, 2fc73dc8-ca50-474f-9fe0-200cd80fd703); lib. bdg. 31.27 *(978-1-61533-381-3(9)*, 5bba6d58-253f-4c58-a72b-0350b013ee80) Rosen Publishing Group, Inc., The. (Windmill Bks.).

Raum, Elizabeth. L' orang-Outan et Son Nid. Martí, Romina, illus. 2017. (Animaux Architectes Ser.). (FRE.). 24p. (J). (gr. 1-4). *(978-1-77092-383-6(7)*, 17614) Amicus.

—Orangutans Build Tree Nests. Martí, Romina, illus. 2017. (Animal Builders Ser.). (ENG.). 24p. (J). (gr. 1-4). lib. bdg. 20.95 *(978-1-68151-172-6(X)*, 14665) Amicus.

—Orangutans Build Tree Nests: Animal Builders. Martí, Romina, illus. 2018. (Animal Builders Ser.). 24p. (J). (gr. 1-4). pap. 9.99 *(978-1-68152-153-4(9)*, 14784) Amicus.

Ring, Susan. Elok. 2009. (J). *(978-1-60596-660-1(6))*; *(978-1-60596-659-5(2))* Weigl Pubs., Inc.

—Project Orangutan. Marshall, Diana & Nault, Jennifer, eds. 2003. (Zoo Life Ser.). (Illus.). 24p. (J). pap. 8.95 *(978-1-59036-058-3(3))* Weigl Pubs., Inc.

Sabatino, Michael. Being an Orangutan, 1 vol. 2013. (Can You Imagine? Ser.). (ENG., Illus.). 32p. (J). (gr. 2-3). pap. 11.50 *(978-1-4824-3283-1(8)*, 3d0dd16c-6fa2-4ce5-8af6-f8547a47df15) Rosen Publishing Group, Inc., The.

—Being an Orangutan, 1 vol. 2013. (Can You Imagine? Ser.). (ENG., Illus.). 32p. (J). (gr. 2-3). lib. bdg. 27.92 *(978-1-4824-0137-0(1)*, 92fd3c54-af41-471f-9bf5-4512c637713d) Stevens, Gareth Publishing LLLP.

Schuh, Mari. The Supersmart Orangutan. 2018. (Lightning Bolt Books (r) — Supersmart Animals Ser.). (ENG., Illus.). 24p. (J). (gr. 1-3). 29.32 *(978-1-5415-1963-1(3)*, b72911af-efcc-44ea-80ce-21cfcaf1e00f, Lerner Pubns.) Lerner Publishing Group.

Shaw, Gina. Curious about Orangutans. 2017. (Smithsonian Ser.). (Illus.). 32p. (J). (gr. 1-3). pap. 4.99 *(978-0-515-15901-1(8)*, Penguin Young Readers Licenses) Penguin Young Readers Group.

Silvey, Anita. Undaunted: The Wild Life of Biruté Mary Galdikas & Her Fearless Quest to Save Orangutans. 2019. (Illus.). 96p. (J). (gr. 3-7). 18.99 *(978-1-4263-3356-9(0))*; (ENG., lib. bdg. 28.90 *(978-1-4263-3357-6(9))* Disney Publishing Worldwide. (National Geographic Kids).

Soundprints, creator. Orang Utan's Playtime. 2011. (Let's Go to the Zoo! Ser.). (ENG., Illus.). 16p. (gr. -1). 5.95 *(978-1-60727-456-8(6))* Soundprints.

Statts, Leo. Orangutans. 2016. (Rain Forest Animals Ser.). (ENG.). 24p. (J). (gr. -1-2). 49.94 *(978-1-68079-363-5(2)*, 22984, Abdo Zoom-Launch) ABDO Publishing Co.

Storm, Marysa. Orangutans. 2020. (Awesome Animal Lives Ser.). (ENG.). 24p. (J). (gr. k-3). pap. 8.99 *(978-1-64466-101-7(2)*, 14399, Bolt Jr.) Black Rabbit Bks.

Swanson, Diane. Welcome to the World of Orangutans, 1 vol. 2003. (Welcome to the World Ser.: 0). (ENG., Illus.). 28p. (J). (gr. -1-2). pap. 7.95 *(978-1-55285-472-3(8)*, cc43305e-a6ac-4c66-8528-33fdedd49155) Whitecap Bks., Ltd. CAN. Dist: Firefly Bks., Ltd.

Taylor, Trace. Orangutan. 2017. (1-3Y Animals Ser.). (ENG.). 20p. (J). (gr. k-2). pap. 8.00 *(978-1-59301-442-1(2))* American Reading Co.

ORANGUTANS—FICTION

Doerrfeld, Cori. Wild Baby. Doerrfeld, Cori, illus. 2019. (ENG., Illus.). 32p. (J). (gr. -1-3). 17.99 *(978-0-06-269894-0(X)*, HarperCollins) HarperCollins Pubs.

—Wild Baby Board Book. Doerrfeld, Cori, illus. 2019. (ENG., Illus.). 36p. (J). (gr. -1 — 1). bds. 7.99 *(978-0-06-269893-3(1)*, HarperFestival) HarperCollins Pubs.

Law, Felicia. Olivia the Orangutan: A Tale of Helpfulness, 1 vol. Spoor, Mike, illus. 2010. (Animal Fair Values Ser.). (ENG.). 32p. (J). (gr. 2-2). pap. 11.55 *(978-1-60754-917-8(4)*, 935aef9f-83cd-4dae-94b4-dad804e02684); lib. bdg. 27.27 *(978-1-60754-906-2(9)*, 1b48ee8e-0a2e-4ed2-a7a6-7bfa68e13ddf) Rosen Publishing Group, Inc., The. (Windmill Bks.).

Lumry, Amanda & Hurwitz, Laura. Operation Orangutan. 2007. (Adventures of Riley (Unnumberd) Ser.). (Illus.). 36p. (J). (gr. -1-3). 15.95 *(978-0-9748411-4-4(5))* Eaglemont Pr.

McNaney, Jeanne. Miracle in Sumatra: The Story of Gutsy Gus. Cochard, David, illus. 2009. (ENG.). 32p. (J). (gr. -1-3). 16.95 *(978-0-9814534-6-0(5))* Ovation Bks.

Romanelli, Serena. El Pequeno Coco. Lamas, Blanca Rosa, tr. from GER. De Beer, Hans, illus. 2004.Tr. of Kleiner Dodo was Spielst du? (SPA.). 24p. (J). (gr. k-4). reprint ed. 16.00 *(978-0-7567-7707-4(0))* DIANE Publishing Co.

Schrefer, Eliot. Rescued. (Ape Quartet Ser.: 3). (ENG.). 272p. (YA). (gr. 7). 2017. pap. 12.99 *(978-1-338-19638-2(3))* 2016. 18.99 *(978-0-545-65503-3(X)*, Scholastic Pr.) Scholastic, Inc.

Wurge, B. B. The Last Notebook of Leonardo. 2010. (LeapKids Ser.). (ENG., Illus.). 154p. (J). (gr. 1-7). pap. 9.95 *(978-1-935248-14-9(6))* Leapfrog Pr.

ORATORY

see Public Speaking

ORBITING VEHICLES

see Artificial Satellites

ORCHARDS

see Fruit Culture

ORCHESTRA

see also Bands (Music); Orchestral Music

Almeida, Artie. The Ultimate Game & Activity Pack for Orchestra: Grades 3-6. 2004. act. bk. ed. 39.95 *(978-0-89328-006-2(2)*, 30/1966H) Heritage Music Pr.

Claudio, Abbado. Yo Sere Director de Orquesta. 2007. (SPA.). 48p. (J). (gr. 4-5). 23.99 *(978-84-8470-052-4(6))* Corimbo, Editorial S.L. ESP. Dist: Lectorum Pubns., Inc.

Fullman, Joe. The Ultimate Guide to Music: A Fascinating Introduction to Music & the Instruments of the Orchestra. 2016. (Y Ser.). (ENG., Illus.). 96p. (J). (gr. 3-7). 19.95 *(978-1-78312-091-8(6))* Carlton Kids GBR. Dist: Two Rivers Distribution.

Hood, Susan. Ada's Violin: The Story of the Recycled Orchestra of Paraguay. Comport, Sally Wern, illus. 2016. (ENG.). 40p. (J). (gr. -1-3). 18.99 *(978-1-4814-3095-1(5)*, Simon & Schuster Bks. For Young Readers) Simon & Schuster Bks. For Young Readers.

—El Violín de Ada (Ada's Violin) La Historia de la Orquesta de Instrumentos Reciclados Del Paraguay. McConnell, Shelley, tr. Comport, Sally Wern, illus. 2016. (SPA.). 40p. (J). (gr. -1-3). 19.99 *(978-1-4814-6657-8(7)*, Simon & Schuster Bks. For Young Readers) Simon & Schuster Bks. For Young Readers.

Rubin, Daniel. Orchestra. (ENG.). 48p. (J). pap. 9.95 *(978-0-88899-051-8(0))* Groundwood Bks. CAN. Dist: Publishers Group West (PGW).

Swalin, Benjamin. Hard Circus Road: The Odyssey of the North Carolina Symphony. McVaugh, Julia A., ed. (Illus.). 158p. (YA). 24.95 *(978-0-9618952-0-4(9))* North Carolina Symphony Society, Inc., The.

Ustinov, Peter. The Orchestra. (J). (gr. -1-18). 19.98 incl. audio Music for Little People, Inc.

ORCHESTRA—FICTION

Barnes, Peter W. Maestro Mouse: And the Mystery of the Missing Baton. Barnes, Cheryl Shaw, illus. 2013. (ENG.). 40p. (J). (gr. k-5). 16.95 *(978-1-62157-036-3(3)*, Little Patriot Pr.) Regnery Publishing.

—Maestro Mouse: And the Mystery of the Missing Baton. Barnes, Cheryl Shaw, illus. 2005. 32p. (J). 16.95 *(978-1-893622-17-3(7)*, VSP Bks.) Vacation Spot Publishing.

Brezenoff, Steve. Field Trip Mysteries: the Symphony That Was Silent. Calo, Marcos, illus. 2011. (Field Trip Mysteries Ser.). (ENG.). 88p. (J). (gr. 3-6). pap. 5.95 *(978-1-4342-3429-2(0)*, 116450, Stone Arch Bks.) Capstone.

Disney Books. Minnie: Easter Bonnet Parade: Includes Stickers. 2013. (ENG., Illus.). 24p. (J). (gr. -1-k). pap. 5.99 *(978-1-4231-6416-6(4)*, Disney Press Books) Disney Publishing Worldwide.

Gantry, Chris. The Underwater Orchestra. Burns, Theresa, illus. 2013. 38p. (J). 16.98 *(978-1-940224-19-0(5))* Taylor and Seale Publishing.

Huthmaker, Dixie. Trapped in Half Position. 2005. pap. 10.95 *(978-1-59330-317-4(3))* Aventine Pr.

King, Dedie. I See the Sun in Russia. Ossapova, Irina, tr. Inglese, Judith, illus. 2012. (I See the Sun Ser.: 4). (RUS.). 40p. (J). (gr. 1-7). 12.95 *(978-1-935874-08-9(X))* Satya Hse. Pubns.

Legrand, Claire. The Year of Shadows. Kwasny, Karl, illus. 2013. (ENG.). 416p. (J). (gr. 3-7). 16.99 *(978-1-4424-4294-8(8)*, Simon & Schuster Bks. For Young Readers) Simon & Schuster Bks. For Young Readers.

Snicket, Lemony, pseud. The Composer Is Dead. Ellis, Carson, illus. 2009. (ENG.). 40p. (J). (gr. k-5). 17.99 *(978-0-06-123627-3(6)*, HarperCollins) HarperCollins Pubs.

Taplin, Sam. Noisy Orchestra. 2013. (Noisy Bks). 10p. (J). ring bd. 19.99 *(978-0-7945-3334-2(5)*, Usborne) EDC Publishing.

Tripp, Paul. Tubby the Tuba. Cole, Henry, illus. 2006. 32p. (J). (gr. -1-3). 17.99 *(978-0-525-47717-4(9)*, Dutton Books for Young Readers) Penguin Young Readers Group.

Wallis, Quvenzhané. Shai & Emmie Star in to the Rescue! Miller, Sharee, illus. (Shai & Emmie Story Ser.). (ENG.). 128p. (J). (gr. 1-5). 2019. pap. 6.99 *(978-1-4814-5889-4(2))* 2018. 15.99 *(978-1-4814-5888-7(4))* Simon & Schuster Bks. For Young Readers. (Simon & Schuster Bks. For Young Readers).

Wilson, Budge. A Fiddle for Angus. 2004. (Illus.). (J). (gr. k-3). spiral bd. *(978-0-616-11140-6(1))* Canadian National Institute for the Blind/Institut National Canadien pour les Aveugles.

ORCHESTRAL MUSIC

Heyens, Gudrun, et al. Fun & Games with the Alto Recorder Bk. 1: Tune. 2004. (ENG.). 46p. pap. 12.99 *(978-1-902455-14-3(2)*, 49012927) Schott Music Corp.

—Fun & Games with the Alto Recorder Bk. 1: Tutor Book 1. 2004. (ENG.). 80p. pap. 17.99 *(978-1-902455-13-6(4)*, 49012926) Schott Music Corp.

—Fun & Games with the Alto Recorder Bk. 2: Tune. 2005. (ENG.). 92p. pap. 15.99 *(978-1-902455-16-7(9)*, 49012929) Schott Music Corp.

Levin, Herbert & Levin, Gail. Symphonics R Us. 2006. 70p. pap. 16.00 *(978-1-891278-41-9(X))* Barcelona Pubs.

Masters of Music, 12 bks., Set. 2004. (Masters of Music Ser.). (Illus.). 7p. (gr. 4-8). lib. bdg. 239.40 *(978-1-58415-253-8(2))* Mitchell Lane Pubs.

ORCHIDS

Wallace, Ian. The Slippers' Keeper, 1 vol. 2015. (ENG., Illus.). 36p. (J). (gr. k-3). 18.95 *(978-1-55498-414-5(9))* Groundwood Bks. CAN. Dist: Publishers Group West (PGW).

ORDNANCE

see also names of general and specific military ordnance, e.g. Atomic Weapons; also names of armies with the subdivision Ordnance and Ordnance Stores, e.g. U. S. Army—Ordnance and Ordnance Stores

Adams, Simon. Artillery. 2009. (War Machines Ser.). (YA). (gr. 5-9). 28.50 *(978-1-59920-226-6(3))* Black Rabbit Bks.

Finn, Denny Von. M109A6 Paladins. 2012. (Military Vehicles Ser.). (ENG., Illus.). 24p. (J). (gr. 3-7). lib. bdg. 26.95 *(978-1-60014-820-0(4)*, Epic Bks.) Bellwether Media.

Gilpin, Daniel. Military Vehicles, 1 vol. Pang, Alex, illus. 2011. (Machines Close-Up Ser.). (ENG.). 32p. (gr. 4-4). 31.21 *(978-1-60870-109-4(3)*, 14a3a8bb-2574-46e7-aa93-863cf03f9611) Cavendish Square Publishing LLC.

LaPierre, Yvette. How Do Robots Defuse Bombs? 2018. (How'd They Do That? Ser.). (ENG., Illus.). 32p. (J). (gr. 4-6). lib. bdg. 28.65 *(978-1-5435-4139-7(9)*, 139093, Capstone Pr.) Capstone.

Peak, Doris-Jean. Wernher Von Braun: Alabama's Rocket Scientist. 2009. (Alabama Roots Biography Ser.). (Illus.). 112p. (J). *(978-1-59421-044-0(6))* Seacoast Publishing, Inc.

OREGON

Aronin, Miriam. How Many People Traveled the Oregon Trail? And Other Questions about the Trail West. 2012. (Six Questions of American History Ser.). (ENG.). 48p. (gr. 4-6). pap. 56.72 *(978-0-7613-9237-8(8))*; (Illus.). (J). pap. 11.99 *(978-0-7613-8566-0(5)*, cb80b72c-4ecb-42fa-980f-9c951f655ece) Lerner Publishing Group.

Bratvold, Gretchen. Oregon. 2012. (J). lib. bdg. 25.26 *(978-0-7613-4552-7(3)*, Lerner Pubns.) Lerner Publishing Group.

Hart, Joyce. Oregon, 1 vol. Santoro, Christopher, illus. 2006. (It's My State! (First Edition)(r) Ser.). (ENG.). 80p. (gr. 4-4). lib. bdg. 34.07 *(978-0-7614-1908-2(X)*, fb0fdbb1-981d-4a0c-86aa-7295716f0f8a) Cavendish Square Publishing LLC.

Hart, Joyce, et al. Oregon, 1 vol. 3rd rev. ed. 2015. (It's My State! (Third Edition)(r) Ser.). (ENG., Illus.). 80p. (gr. 4-4). 35.93 *(978-1-62713-172-8(8)*, b568ceee-b8c8-4229-8f36-87807567c912) Cavendish Square Publishing LLC.

Heinrichs, Ann. Oregon. Kania, Matt, illus. 2017. (U. S. A. Travel Guides). (ENG.). 40p. (J). (gr. 2-5). lib. bdg. 38.50 *(978-1-5038-1977-1(9)*, 211613) Child's World, Inc, The.

Labella, Susan. Oregon. 2006. (Rookie Read-About Geography Ser.). (ENG., Illus.). 32p. (J). (gr. 1-2). lib. bdg. 20.50 *(978-0-516-25386-2(7))* Scholastic Library Publishing.

Lusted, Marcia Amidon. Oregon: The Beaver State, 1 vol. 2010. (Our Amazing States Ser.). (ENG.). 24p. (J). (gr. 3-3). pap. 9.25 *(978-1-4358-9786-1(2)*, 38a8ee97-0d12-47fd-a879-988e8037fb6d); lib. bdg. 26.27 *(978-1-4358-9346-7(8)*, f800497b-a416-4f29-a9d9-879f64d5a79e) Rosen Publishing Group, Inc., The. (PowerKids Pr.).

Madson, Trish. O Is for Oregon: A Beaver State ABC Primer. W. Miles, David, illus. 2017. (ENG.). 20p. (J). (gr. -1 — 1). bds. 12.99 *(978-1-944822-72-9(0)*, 552272) Familius LLC.

Marsh, Carole. Oregon Current Events Projects: 30 Cool, Activities, Crafts, Experiments & More for Kids to Do to Learn about Your State! 2003. (Oregon Experience Ser.). 32p. (gr. k-5). pap. 5.95 *(978-0-635-02056-7(4)*, Marsh, Carole Bks.) Gallopade International.

—Oregon Geography Projects: 30 Cool, Activities, Crafts, Experiments & More for Kids to Do to Learn about Your State! 2003. (Oregon Experience Ser.). 32p. (gr. k-5). pap. 5.95 *(978-0-635-01856-4(X)*, Marsh, Carole Bks.) Gallopade International.

—Oregon Government Projects: 30 Cool, Activities, Crafts, Experiments & More for Kids to Do to Learn about Your State! 2003. (Oregon Experience Ser.). 32p. (gr. k-5). pap. 5.95 *(978-0-635-01956-1(6)*, Marsh, Carole Bks.) Gallopade International.

—Oregon People Projects: 30 Cool, Activities, Crafts, Experiments & More for Kids to Do to Learn about Your State! 2003. (Oregon Experience Ser.). 32p. (gr. k-5). pap. 5.95 *(978-0-635-02006-2(8)*, Marsh, Carole Bks.) Gallopade International.

—Oregon Symbols & Facts Projects: 30 Cool, Activities, Crafts, Experiments & More for Kids to Do to Learn about Your State! 2003. (Oregon Experience Ser.). 32p. (gr. k-5). pap. 5.95 *(978-0-635-01906-6(X)*, Marsh, Carole Bks.) Gallopade International.

Murray, Julie. Oregon, 1 vol. 2006. (United States Ser.). (ENG., Illus.). 32p. (gr. 2-4). 27.07 *(978-1-59197-696-7(0)*, Buddy Bks.) ABDO Publishing Co.

Peters, S. True. How to Draw Oregon's Sights & Symbols. 2009. (Kid's Guide to Drawing America Ser.). 32p. (gr. k-k). 50.50 *(978-1-61511-090-2(9)*, PowerKids Pr.) Rosen Publishing Group, Inc., The.

Peterson del Mar, David. Oregon's Promise: An Interpretive History. 2003. (ENG., Illus.). 320p. pap. 19.95 *(978-0-87071-558-7(5))* Oregon State Univ. Pr.

Smith, Roland & Smith, Marie. B Is for Beaver: An Oregon Alphabet. Roydon, Michael, illus. 2003. (Discover America State by State Ser.). (ENG.). 40p. (J). (gr. 1-3). 18.99 *(978-1-58536-071-0(6)*, 201970) Sleeping Bear Pr.

Sonneborn, Liz. Oregon, 1 vol. 2005. (Portraits of the States Ser.). (ENG., Illus.). 32p. (gr. 3-5). pap. 11.50 *(978-0-8368-4692-8(3)*, 372b4047-49b7-4c7a-946f-3db4c07f37b4); lib. bdg. 28.67 *(978-0-8368-4673-7(7)*, 879336b8-fcf2-447f-a895-747cf61e0a4f) Stevens, Gareth Publishing LLLP. (Gareth Stevens Learning Library).

Stefoff, Rebecca. Oregon, 1 vol. 2nd rev. ed. 2006. (Celebrate the States (Second Edition) Ser.). (ENG., Illus.). 144p. (gr. 6-6). lib. bdg. 39.79 *(978-0-7614-2022-4(3)*, 1474d5c6-a350-4528-bed3-401278e60025) Cavendish Square Publishing LLC.

Way, Jennifer. Oregon, 1 vol. Brusca, Maria Cristina, tr. 2005. (Bilingual Library of the United States of America Ser.: Set 2). (ENG & SPA., Illus.). 32p. (J). (gr. 2-2). lib. bdg. 28.93 *(978-1-4042-3102-3(1)*, b36d746d-3d1e-4107-a29e-823f060a901f) Rosen Publishing Group, Inc., The.

OREGON—FICTION

Albright, Emily. Perfect Harmony. 2018. (ENG.). 304p. (YA). pap. 12.99 *(978-1-944995-82-9(X))* Amberjack Publishing Co.

Angstrom, Gwen R. Silent, Snowy Night in Sunriver, Book 2: The Eemlets & Grandma Eema Stories. 2007. 76p. per. 19.95 *(978-1-4241-9000-3(2))* America Star Bks.

Arnold, Elana K. The Question of Miracles. 2016. (ENG.). 256p. (J). (gr. 5-7). pap. 7.99 *(978-0-544-66852-2(9)*, 1625476, Clarion Bks.) HarperCollins Pubs.

Asher, Jay. What Light. 2017. (ENG.). 272p. (YA). (gr. 7). pap. 10.99 *(978-0-448-49364-0(0)*, Razorbill) Penguin Young Readers Group.

—What Light. 2017. lib. bdg. 22.10 *(978-0-606-40488-4(0))* Turtleback.

Beatty, Cherie B. Meet Lewis the Duck. 2009. 24p. pap. 12.99 *(978-1-4389-5116-4(7))* AuthorHouse.

Bernal, Estela. Can You See Me Now? 2014. (ENG.). v, 161p. (J). pap. 10.95 *(978-1-55885-783-4(4)*, Piñata Books) Arte Publico Pr.

Blackaby, Susan. The Twelve Days of Christmas in Oregon. Conahan, Carolyn Digby, illus. (Twelve Days of Christmas in America Ser.). (ENG.). (J). (-k). 2018. 22p. bds. 7.95 *(978-1-4549-2997-0(9))* 2014. 40p. 12.95 *(978-1-4549-0891-3(2))* Sterling Publishing Co., Inc.

Boat, Patty. A Disappointing Homecoming: (A Soldier's Story), 1 vol. 2009. 158p. pap. 24.95 *(978-1-61546-997-0(4))* PublishAmerica, Inc.

Buyer, Robert L. & Coute, Ursula T. Following the North Star. 2013. 52p. pap. 23.95 *(978-1-4624-0611-1(4)*, Inspiring Voices) Author Solutions, LLC.

Caletti, Deb. The Six Rules of Maybe. 2011. (ENG.). 352p. (YA). (gr. 7). pap. 12.99 *(978-1-4169-7971-5(9)*, Simon Pulse) Simon Pulse.

Carlson, Melody. Girl Power, 1 vol. 2016. (Faithgirlz / Girls of Harbor View Ser.). (ENG.). 272p. (J). pap. 9.99 *(978-0-310-75361-2(9))* Zonderkidz.

Castro, Shirley. The Pelican Family Series — Stelly & the Sticky, Gooey Taffy. Castro, Christopher, illus. 2011. 36p. (J). 15.00 *(978-0-9790307-3-4(0))* Castro, Shirley.

Christie, Ed. The Sweet Smell of Rotten Eggs: Volume Two, the Dude Ranch Rangers. 2009. 108p. pap. 10.95 *(978-1-4401-3764-8(1))* iUniverse, Inc.

Clark, Lillian. Immoral Code. 2019. 320p. (YA). (gr. 7). 17.99 *(978-0-525-58046-1(8)*, Knopf Bks. for Young Readers) Random Hse. Children's Bks.

Cleary, Beverly. Emily's Runaway Imagination. Dockray, Tracy, illus. 2008. (ENG.). 288p. (J). (gr. 3-7). pap. 7.99 *(978-0-380-70923-6(6)*, HarperCollins) HarperCollins Pubs.

—Emily's Runaway Imagination. 221p. (J). (gr. 2-4). pap. 4.95 *(978-0-8072-1416-9(7)*, Listening Library) Random Hse. Audio Publishing Group.

Davis, Susan Page. Sarah's Long Ride. 2007. (Piper Ranch Ser.). 173p. (J). (gr. 3-7). per. 8.99 *(978-1-59166-737-7(2))* BJU Pr.

Dickson, Darnell G. Small Town, Big Dreams: A Dane Jordan Sports Novel. 2008. pap. 14.99 *(978-1-59955-229-3(9))* Cedar Fort, Inc./CFI Distribution.

Elliott, Jenny. Save Me. 2015. (ENG.). 336p. (YA). (gr. 7-12). pap. 10.99 *(978-1-250-06147-8(4)*, 900141885) Feiwel & Friends.

Emshaw, Shea. The Wicked Deep. (ENG.). (YA). (gr. 9). 2019. 336p. pap. 12.99 *(978-1-4814-9735-0(9))* 2018. (Illus.). 320p. 19.99 *(978-1-4814-9734-3(0))* Simon Pulse. (Simon Pulse).

Everett, Forrest. Old MacDonald Had a Farm in Oregon. Sergeeva, Mary, illus. 2018. (Old MacDonald Had a Farm Regional Board Ser.). (ENG.). 16p. (J). (gr. k-3). bds. 12.99 *(978-1-64170-014-6(9)*, 550014) Familius LLC.

—Row, Row, Row Your Boat in Oregon. Sergeeva, Mary, illus. 2018. (Row, Row, Row Your Boat Regional Board B Ser.). (ENG.). 16p. (J). (gr. k-3). bds. 12.99 *(978-1-64170-015-3(7)*, 550015) Familius LLC.

Forman, Gayle. If I Stay. 2011. (If I Stay Ser.: BK.1). (YA). 10.36 *(978-0-7848-3573-9(X)*, Everbind) Marco Bk. Co.

—If I Stay. (ENG.). (YA). (gr. 7). 2021. 272p. pap. 5.99 *(978-0-593-40384-6(3)*, Penguin Books) 2018. 288p. mass mkt. 7.99 *(978-0-451-48064-4(3)*, Speak) 2010. 320p. 11.99 *(978-0-14-241543-6(X)*, Speak) Penguin Young Readers Group.

—If I Stay. 2010. (If I Stay Ser.: BK.1). (ENG.). 262p. (YA). (gr. 9-12). 18.45 *(978-1-60686-742-6(3))* Perfection Learning Corp.

—If I Stay. l.t. ed. 2014. (If I Stay Ser.: BK.1). (ENG.). (YA). 482p. 23.99 *(978-1-4104-7543-5(3))*; 480p. pap. 12.99 *(978-1-59413-814-0(1)*, Large Print Pr.) Thorndike Pr.

—If I Stay. 2018. lib. bdg. 18.40 *(978-0-606-41304-6(9))* 2010. (If I Stay Ser.: BK.1). (YA). lib. bdg. 22.10 *(978-0-606-14395-0(5))* Turtleback.

Grandpa & Little Guy. 2004. (J). 15.95 *(978-0-9764012-0-9(7))* Rockmill Publishing Co.

MNO

Hancock, Dennis & Uyen. The Tree House on the Bluff. Hancock, Uyen, illus. 2012. 36p. pap. 24.95 *(978-1-4626-7318-6(X))* America Star Bks.

Harrison, Lisi. Monster High. 2011. (Monster High Ser.: 1). (YA). lib. bdg. 19.65 *(978-0-606-23459-7(4))* Turtleback.

Hart, Melissa. Avenging the Owl. 2018. (ENG.). 224p. (J). (gr. 5-8). pap. 9.99 *(978-1-5107-2628-4(4)*, Sky Pony Pr.) Skyhorse Publishing Co., Inc.

Henry, April. The Night She Disappeared. 2013. (ENG.). 256p. (YA). (gr. 7-12). pap. 10.99 *(978-1-250-01674-4(6)*, 900087088) Square Fish.

Hensley, Nathaniel. The Strange Tale of Hector & Hannah Crowe. 2015. (ENG.). 222p. (J). (gr. 8-18). 13.95 *(978-1-937240-49-3(5))* Casa de Snapdragon LLC.

Hermes, Patricia. The Wild Year Bk. 3: Joshua's Oregon Trail Diary. 2003. (My America Ser.). (ENG., Illus.). 112p. (J). 12.95 *(978-0-439-37055-4(8))* Scholastic, Inc.

Herrick, Ann. Walk Softly & Watch Out for Bigfoot. 2006. (YA). pap. 9.95 *(978-0-7599-4489-3(X))* Hard Shell Word Factory.

Houck, Colleen. Tiger's Quest. 2013. (Tiger's Curse Ser.: 2). (ENG.). 512p. (J). (gr. 7). pap. 11.95 *(978-1-4549-0358-1(9))* Sterling Publishing Co., Inc.

Humphrey, Matthew J. Coastal Magic. 2007. lib. bdg. 21.95 *(978-1-59872-997-9(7))* Instant Pub.

Hutchens, Calvin. The Adventures of Otis Possum. 2007. 52p. per. 16.95 *(978-1-4241-7065-4(6))* America Star Bks.

Jacobs, Lily. The Littlest Bunny in Oregon: An Easter Adventure. Dunn, Robert, illus. 2015. (Littlest Bunny Ser.). (ENG.). 32p. (J). (gr. -1-3). 9.99 *(978-1-4926-1171-4(9)*, Hometown World) Sourcebooks, Inc.

James, Eric. Santa's Sleigh Is on Its Way to Portland: A Christmas Adventure. Dunn, Robert, illus. 2016. (Santa's Sleigh Is on Its Way Ser.). (ENG.). 32p. (J). (gr. k-2). 12.99 *(978-1-4926-4352-4(1)*, 9781492643524, Hometown World) Sourcebooks, Inc.

—The Spooky Express Oregon. Piwowarski, Marcin, illus. 2017. (Spooky Express Ser.). (ENG.). 32p. (J). (gr. k-6). 9.99 *(978-1-4926-5391-2(8)*, Hometown World) Sourcebooks, Inc.

—Tiny the Oregon Easter Bunny. 2018. (Tiny the Easter Bunny Ser.). (ENG.). 40p. (J). (gr. k-3). 9.99 *(978-1-4926-5955-6(X)*, Hometown World) Sourcebooks, Inc.

Jarvis McGraw, Eloise. Sawdust in His Shoes. 2018. (Illus.). 278p. (gr. 3-7). pap. 9.95 *(978-0-87486-826-5(2))* Plough Publishing Hse.

Jessell, Tim, illus. Mystery of the Fallen Treasure. 2013. (Boxcar Children Mysteries Ser.: 132). (ENG.). 128p. (J). (gr. 2-5). 15.99 *(978-0-8075-5508-8(8)*, 807555088); 5.99 *(978-0-8075-5506-4(1)*, 807555061) Random Hse. Children's Bks. (Random Hse. Bks. for Young Readers).

Kehret, Peg. Escaping the Giant Wave. 2004. (ENG., Illus.). 160p. (J). (gr. 3-7). pap. 7.99 *(978-0-689-85273-2(8)*, Aladdin) Simon & Schuster Children's Publishing.

Kelso, Mary Jean. One Family's Christmas. Snider, K. C., illus. 2008. 24p. pap. 10.95 *(978-1-935137-05-4(0))* Guardian Angel Publishing, Inc.

Kerley, Barbara. Portland Baby. Cleland, Josh, illus. 2017. (Local Baby Bks.). (ENG.). 22p. (J). (gr. -1 — 1). bds. 8.95 *(978-1-946064-05-9(X)*, 806405) Duo Pr. LLC.

Kimmel, Eric A. I Want a Real Bike in Oregon. Cleland, Josh, illus. 2018. (ENG.). 32p. (J). (gr. 1-3). 17.99 *(978-1-5132-6127-0(4)*, West Winds Pr.) West Margin Pr.

Kopp, J. J. Aurora, Daughter of the Dawn: A Story of New Beginnings. Will, Clark Moor, illus. 2012. (ENG.). 72p. (YA). (gr. 6-12). pap. 12.95 *(978-0-87071-671-3(9))* Oregon State Univ. Pr.

LaZebnik, Claire. The Trouble with Flirting. 2013. (ENG.). 336p. (YA). (gr. 8). pap. 9.99 *(978-0-06-192127-8(0)*, HarperTeen) HarperCollins Pubs.

Madson, Trish. 12 Little Elves Visit Oregon, Volume 4. Han, Sadie, illus. 2017. (12 Little Elves Ser.: 4). (ENG.). 32p. (J). (gr. -1-1). 16.99 *(978-1-945547-10-2(3)*, 554710) Familius LLC.

Marciano, Johnny & Chenoweth, Emily. Klawde: Evil Alien Warlord Cat: Enemies #2. Mommaerts, Robb, illus. 2019. (Klawde: Evil Alien Warlord Cat Ser.: 2). 224p. (J). (gr. 3-7). 14.99 *(978-1-5247-8722-6(1)*, Penguin Workshop) Penguin Young Readers Group.

Martha, Morales. Ariana Leaves San Francisco. Chiu, Bessie, illus. 2011. 28p. pap. 8.50 *(978-1-61170-017-6(5))* Robertson Publishing.

McCarthy, Dan. Good Night Oregon. Veno, Joe, illus. 2010. (Good Night Our World Ser.). (ENG.). 20p. (J). (gr. k — 1). bds. 9.95 *(978-1-60219-041-2(0))* Good Night Bks.

McCollum, Lynn Tragesser. The Green School Caper: The Adventures of the Five Amigos. 2008. 164p. pap. 9.95 *(978-1-4327-2564-8(5))* Outskirts Pr., Inc.

Mcdonald, Megan. Cloudy with a Chance of Boys. 2011. (Sisters Club Ser.: 3). (Illus.). 272p. (J). (gr. 3-7). 15.99 *(978-0-7636-4615-8(6))* Candlewick Pr.

McDonald, Megan. The Sisters Club. 2008. (Sisters Club Ser.: 1). (ENG., Illus.). 208p. (J). (gr. 3-7). pap. 7.99 *(978-0-7636-3251-9(1))* Candlewick Pr.

Mcdonald, Megan. The Sisters Club. 2008. (Sisters Club Ser.: 1). lib. bdg. 16.00 *(978-1-4178-1785-6(2))* Turtleback.

McDonald, Megan. The Sisters Club: Cloudy with a Chance of Boys. 2012. (Sisters Club Ser.: 3). (ENG., Illus.). 272p. (J). (gr. 3-7). pap. 6.99 *(978-0-7636-5577-8(5))* Candlewick Pr.

—The Sisters Club: Rule of Three. (Sisters Club Ser.: 2). (ENG., Illus.). 240p. (J). (gr. 3-7). 2010. pap. 7.99 *(978-0-7636-4830-5(2))* 2009. 15.99 *(978-0-7636-4153-5(7))* Candlewick Pr.

Meloy, Colin. Under Wildwood. Ellis, Carson, illus. (Wildwood Chronicles Ser.: 2). (ENG.). (J). (gr. 3). 2013. 592p. pap. 9.99 *(978-0-06-202473-2(6))* 2012. 576p. 17.99 *(978-0-06-202471-8(X))* HarperCollins Pubs. (Balzer & Bray).

—Wildwood. Ellis, Carson, illus. (Wildwood Chronicles Ser.: 1). (ENG.). (J). (gr. 3). 2012. 576p. pap. 9.99 *(978-0-06-202470-1(1))* 2011. 560p. 19.99 *(978-0-06-202468-8(X))* HarperCollins Pubs. (Balzer & Bray).

—Wildwood. Ellis, Carson, illus. 2012. (Wildwood Chronicles Ser.: 1). (J). lib. bdg. 20.85 *(978-0-606-26864-6(2))* Turtleback.

—Wildwood Imperium. Ellis, Carson, illus. 2015. (Wildwood Chronicles Ser.: 3). (ENG.). 592p. (J). (gr. 3). pap. 9.99 *(978-0-06-202476-3(0)*, Balzer & Bray) HarperCollins Pubs.

Morrow, Dj. Charlie & Joe. 2013. 28p. pap. 24.95 *(978-1-62709-833-5(X))* America Star Bks.

Nelson, Blake. The New Rules of High School. 2004. (ENG.). 240p. (YA). (gr. 7-18). reprint ed. 7.99 *(978-0-14-240242-9(7)*, Speak) Penguin Young Readers Group.

—Paranoid Park. 2008. (ENG.). 192p. (YA). (gr. 7-18). 6.99 *(978-0-14-241156-8(6)*, Puffin Books) Penguin Young Readers Group.

—Phoebe Will Destroy You. (ENG.). (YA). (gr. 9). 2019. 272p. pap. 11.99 *(978-1-4814-8817-4(1))* 2018. (Illus.). 256p. 18.99 *(978-1-4814-8816-7(3))* Simon Pulse. (Simon Pulse).

Ockler, Sarah. The Summer of Chasing Mermaids. 2015. (ENG., Illus.). 416p. (YA). (gr. 9). 17.99 *(978-1-4814-0127-2(0)*, Simon Pulse) Simon Pulse.

O'Dell, Kathryn L. From Wagon to Train. Chalk, Chris, illus. 2017. (Text Connections Guided Close Reading Ser.). (J). (gr. 2). *(978-1-4900-1854-6(9))* Benchmark Education Co.

Oneill, Elizabeth. Alfred Visits Oregon. 2008. 24p. pap. 12.00 *(978-0-9799121-8-4(0))* Funny Bone Bks.

Palmer, Connie. I Will Run Free No More, 1 vol. 2009. 49p. pap. 16.95 *(978-1-4489-7122-0(5))* America Star Bks.

Parenteau, Shirley. Dolls of War. (Friendship Dolls Ser.: 3). 320p. (J). (gr. 3-7). 2019. (ENG.). pap. 7.99 *(978-1-5362-0889-4(2))* 2017. 16.99 *(978-0-7636-9069-4(4))* Candlewick Pr.

—Ship of Dolls. 2014. (Friendship Dolls Ser.: 1). (ENG.). 272p. (J). (gr. 3-7). 16.99 *(978-0-7636-7003-0(0))* Candlewick Pr.

Parnell, Robyn. The Mighty Quinn. DeYoe, Katie & Aaron, illus. 2013. (ENG.). 272p. (J). (gr. 2-7). pap. 10.95 *(978-1-938063-10-7(4)*, Mighty Media Junior Readers) Mighty Media Pr.

Platt, Randall. Hellie Jondoe. 2009. (ENG.). 224p. (J). (gr. 7-18). pap. 16.95 *(978-0-89672-663-5(0)*, P170570) Texas Tech Univ. Pr.

—Incommunicado. (ENG.). (J). 2017. 352p. (gr. 5-8). pap. 9.99 *(978-1-5107-0991-1(6))* 2014. 336p. (gr. 4-7). 14.95 *(978-1-62914-646-1(3))* Skyhorse Publishing Co., Inc. (Sky Pony Pr.).

Rand, Johnathan. American Chillers #29 Oregon Oceanauts. 2010. 208p. (J). pap. 5.99 *(978-1-893699-24-3(2))* AudioCraft Publishing, Inc.

Reece, Colleen L. Wilderness Warriors. 2012. 114p. 18.95 *(978-1-61633-309-6(X))*; pap. 8.95 *(978-1-61633-310-2(3))* Guardian Angel Publishing, Inc.

Reed, Amy. Nowhere Girls. 2017. (ENG.). (YA). (gr. 9). pap. 12.99 *(978-1-5344-1555-3(6))* Simon & Schuster.

—The Nowhere Girls. (ENG., Illus.). (YA). (gr. 9). 2019. 432p. pap. 12.99 *(978-1-4814-8174-8(6))* 2017. 416p. 19.99 *(978-1-4814-8173-1(8))* Simon Pulse. (Simon Pulse).

Rescue Flight! 2003. 150p. (J). (gr. 4-6). per. 12.95 *(978-0-9740202-0-4(6))* Skyword Pr.

Rice, Dona Herwick & Shannon, Catherine. Narcissa Whitman & the Westward Movement, 1 vol. rev. ed. 2009. (Reader's Theater Ser.). (ENG., Illus.). 32p. (J). (gr. 3-8). pap. 11.99 *(978-1-4333-0542-9(9))* Teacher Created Materials, Inc.

Salisbury, Graham. Banjo. 2019. (ENG.). 224p. (J). (gr. 5). 16.99 *(978-0-375-84264-1(0)*, Lamb, Wendy Bks.) Random Hse. Children's Bks.

Schlick Noe, Katherine. Something to Hold. 2011. (ENG., Illus.). 256p. (J). (gr. 5-7). 17.99 *(978-0-547-55813-4(9)*, 1453477, Clarion Bks.) HarperCollins Pubs.

Schroeder, Lisa. The Day Before. 2012. (ENG.). 336p. (YA). (gr. 9). pap. 12.99 *(978-1-4424-1744-1(7)*, Simon Pulse) Simon Pulse.

—It's Raining Cupcakes. 2011. (ENG., Illus.). 208p. (J). (gr. 3-7). pap. 7.99 *(978-1-4169-9085-7(2)*, Aladdin) Simon & Schuster Children's Publishing.

Scofield, Chris. The Shark Curtain. 2015. (ENG., Illus.). 356p. (J). (gr. 6). pap. 13.95 *(978-1-61775-313-8(0)*, Black Sheep) Akashic Bks.

Sheley, Kristen. Partners in Time #5: A Change of Course. 2010. 236p. 25.95 *(978-1-4502-6658-1(4))*; pap. 15.95 *(978-1-4502-6657-4(6))* iUniverse, Inc.

Shumaker, Bonnie. High on the Saddle: An Intergenerational Adventure into the Mountains of Oregon. Beebe, Elecia, illus. 2018. (ENG.). 48p. (J). pap. 12.95 *(978-1-55571-923-4(6)*, Grid Pr.) L & R Publishing, LLC.

Smallman, Steve. Santa Is Coming to Portland. Dunn, Robert, illus. 2nd ed. 2019. (Santa Is Coming... Ser.). (ENG.). 40p. (J). (gr. -1-3). 12.99 *(978-1-7282-0096-5(2)*, Hometown World) Sourcebooks, Inc.

Stelljes, Susan. Wonder Dog: The Story of Silverton Bobbie. 2005. (Illus.). 167p. (YA). pap. 14.95 *(978-0-9761124-7-1(7))* For The Love of Dog Bks.

Sully, Katherine. Night-Night Oregon. Poole, Helen, illus. 2017. (Night-Night Ser.). (ENG.). 20p. (J). (gr. -1-1). bds. 9.99 *(978-1-4926-5484-1(1)*, Hometown World) Sourcebooks, Inc.

Walton, Rick. 10 Little Monsters Visit Oregon. Smiley, Jess Smart, illus. 2014. (ENG.). 32p. (J). (gr. -1-3). 16.95 *(978-1-939629-29-6(2)*, 552929) Familius LLC.

Watson, Renee. This Side of Home. 2015. (ENG.). 336p. (YA). (gr. 7). 18.99 *(978-1-59990-668-3(6)*, 900074806, Bloomsbury USA Childrens) Bloomsbury Publishing USA.

Watson, Renée. This Side of Home. 2017. (ENG.). 352p. (YA). pap. 10.99 *(978-1-61963-930-0(0)*, 900152550, Bloomsbury USA Childrens) Bloomsbury Publishing USA.

Waugh, Peter. Cannon Beach Mouse Caper. 2007. 128p. per. 13.95 *(978-0-944638-68-2(6))* Educare Pr.

Westover, Steve. Crater Lake: Battle for Wizard Island. 2012. pap. 14.99 *(978-1-59955-960-5(9))* Cedar Fort, Inc./CFI Distribution.

—Return of the Mystic Gray. 2013. 15.99 *(978-1-4621-1187-9(4))* Cedar Fort, Inc./CFI Distribution.

Whitney, Barbara I. Barbara's Quest to Find a Messenger: Journeys I & II. 2009. 40p. pap. 19.49 *(978-1-4415-0159-2(2))* Xlibris Corp.

Winters, Cat. The Cure for Dreaming. 2016. (ENG., Illus.). 384p. (YA). (gr. 8-17). pap. 9.95 *(978-1-4197-1941-7(6)*, 1075303, Amulet Bks.) Abrams, Inc.

Wolff, Virginia Euwer. Bat 6. 256p. (J). (gr. 4-6). pap. 4.99 *(978-0-8072-8223-6(5))*; 2004. (gr. 5-9). pap. 36.00 incl. audio *(978-0-8072-8222-9(7)*, YYA144SP) Random Hse. Audio Publishing Group. (Listening Library).

Young, Judy. A Book for Black-Eyed Susan. Ettlinger, Doris, illus. 2011. (Tales of Young Americans Ser.). (ENG.). 32p. (J). (gr. 1-4). lib. bdg. 16.95 *(978-1-58536-463-3(0)*, 202185) Sleeping Bear Pr.

OREGON—HISTORY

Aronin, Miriam. How Many People Traveled the Oregon Trail? And Other Questions about the Trail West. 2012. (Six Questions of American History Ser.). (ENG., Illus.). 48p. (J). (gr. 4-6). lib. bdg. 30.65 *(978-0-7613-5332-4(1)*, feb9aceb-5243-49a1-b0d3-f994e3938250, Lerner Pubns.) Lerner Publishing Group.

Bodden, Valerie. Oregon. 2009. (This Land Called America Ser.). 32p. (YA). (gr. 3-6). 19.95 *(978-1-58341-790-4(7))* Creative Co., The.

Boekhoff, P. M. & Kallen, Stuart A. Oregon. 2003. (Seeds of a Nation Ser.). (Illus.). 48p. (J). (gr. 3-5). 23.70 *(978-0-7377-1482-1(4)*, Kidhaven) Cengage Gale.

The Famous Oregon Events Guide ~ 2006. 2005. (YA). per. 15.95 *(978-1-881005-50-6(X))* Gail's Guides.

Friesen, Helen Lepp. Oregon: The Beaver State. 2012. (J). *(978-1-61913-393-8(8))*; pap. *(978-1-61913-394-5(6))* Weigl Pubs., Inc.

Gregory, Josh. Oregon (a True Book: My United States) (Library Edition) 2018. (True Book (Relaunch) Ser.). (ENG., Illus.). 48p. (J). (gr. 3-5). 31.00 *(978-0-531-23575-1(0)*, Children's Pr.) Scholastic Library Publishing.

Hamilton, John. Oregon, 1 vol. 2016. (United States of America Ser.). (ENG., Illus.). 48p. (J). (gr. 5-9). 34.21 *(978-1-68078-339-1(4)*, 21663, Abdo & Daughters) ABDO Publishing Co.

Harness, Cheryl. The Tragic Tale of Narcissa Whitman & a Faithful History of the Oregon Trail (Direct Mail Edition) 2006. (Cheryl Harness Histories Ser.). (Illus.). 144p. (J). (gr. 5-9). 16.95 *(978-0-7922-5920-6(3)*, National Geographic Kids) Disney Publishing Worldwide.

Hart, Joyce & Laks Gorman, Jacqueline. Oregon, 1 vol. 2nd rev. ed. 2012. (It's My State! (Second Edition)(r) Ser.). (ENG.). 80p. (gr. 4-4). 34.07 *(978-1-60870-525-2(0)*, 53b37e11-69da-490a-b8ec-3583e0962819) Cavendish Square Publishing LLC.

Jerome, Kate B. Lucky to Live in Oregon. 2017. (Arcadia Kids Ser.). (ENG., Illus.). 32p. (J). 16.99 *(978-0-7385-2791-8(2))* Arcadia Publishing.

—The Wise Animal Handbook Oregon. 2017. (Arcadia Kids Ser.). (ENG., Illus.). 32p. (J). 16.99 *(978-0-7385-2839-7(0))* Arcadia Publishing.

Kent, Deborah. America the Beautiful: Oregon (Revised Edition) 2014. (America the Beautiful, Third Ser. (Revised Edition) Ser.). (ENG., Illus.). 144p. (J). lib. bdg. 40.00 *(978-0-531-28288-5(0))* Scholastic Library Publishing.

Leedom, Karen L. A Is for Astoria. Bailey, Sally, illus. 2010. 32p. 15.00 *(978-0-9826252-0-0(0))* Rivertide Publishing.

Marsh, Carole. Exploring Oregon Through Project-Based Learning: Geography, History, Government, Economics & More. 2016. (Oregon Experience Ser.). (ENG.). (J). pap. 9.99 *(978-0-635-12361-9(4))* Gallopade International.

—I'm Reading about Oregon. 2014. (Oregon Experience Ser.). (ENG., Illus.). (J). pap., pap. 8.99 *(978-0-635-11312-2(0))* Gallopade International.

—Oregon History Projects: 30 Cool, Activities, Crafts, Experiments & More for Kids to Do to Learn about Your State! 2003. (Oregon Experience Ser.). 32p. (gr. k-5). pap. 5.95 *(978-0-635-01806-9(3)*, Marsh, Carole Bks.) Gallopade International.

Matchette, Katharine E. Discovering Oregon. Comfort, Mike & Baisley, Stephen, illus. Matchette, Dennis, photos by. (YA). (gr. 5-9). spiral bd. 13.00 *(978-0-9645045-4-7(5))* Deka Pr.

Maynard, Charles W. Fort Clatsop. 2009. (Famous Forts Throughout American History Ser.). 24p. (gr. 3-4). 42.50 *(978-1-61512-515-9(9)*, PowerKids Pr.) Rosen Publishing Group, Inc., The.

Nobleman, Marc Tyler. Thirty Minutes over Oregon: A Japanese Pilot's World War II Story. Iwai, Melissa, illus. 2018. (ENG.). 40p. (J). (gr. 1-4). 17.99 *(978-0-544-43076-1(X)*, 1595751, Clarion Bks.) HarperCollins Pubs.

Olson, Steven P. The Oregon Trail, 1 vol. 2004. (Primary Sources in American History Ser.). (ENG., Illus.). 64p. (gr. 5-8). lib. bdg. 37.13 *(978-0-8239-4512-2(X)*, 62403f74-8a1c-4b94-852b-0d437b0ca078, Rosen Reference) Rosen Publishing Group, Inc., The.

Publications International Ltd. Staff. Yesterday & Today Portland. 2009. 192p. 24.95 *(978-1-4127-7793-3(3))* Publications International, Ltd.

Roza, Greg. Oregon: Past & Present, 1 vol. 2010. (United States: Past & Present Ser.). (ENG., Illus.). 48p. (J). (gr. 5-5). pap. 12.75 *(978-1-4358-8480-9(9)*, 1bf5deda-c5a8-48d7-8548-428808ac9e88); lib. bdg. 34.47 *(978-1-4358-3515-3(8)*, 0fcec383-6a5c-4031-885e-f692e8c67f50) Rosen Publishing Group, Inc., The. (Rosen Reference).

Shannon, Terry Miller. Oregon. 2009. (From Sea to Shining Sea, Second Ser.). (ENG.). 80p. (J). pap. 7.95 *(978-0-531-21142-7(8)*, Children's Pr.) Scholastic Library Publishing.

Skewes, John. Larry Loves Portland! A Larry Gets Lost Book. Skewes, John, illus. 2014. (Larry Gets Lost Ser.). (ENG., Illus.). 20p. (J). (— 1). bds. 10.99 *(978-1-57061-935-9(2)*, Little Bigfoot) Sasquatch Bks.

Skewes, John, illus. Portland ABC: a Larry Gets Lost Book. 2014. (Larry Gets Lost Ser.). 32p. (J). (gr. -1-k). 14.99 *(978-1-57061-920-5(4)*, Little Bigfoot) Sasquatch Bks.

Skewes, John & Mullin, Michael. Larry Gets Lost in Portland. Skewes, John, illus. 2012. (Larry Gets Lost Ser.). (ENG., Illus.). 32p. (J). (gr. -1-2). 17.99 *(978-1-57061-679-2(5)*, Little Bigfoot) Sasquatch Bks.

Skogen, J. M. On the Hardwood: Portland Trail Blazers. 2013. (On the Hardwood Ser.). (ENG., Illus.). 48p. (J). (gr. 3-8). pap. 8.95 *(978-1-61570-838-3(3))* Scobre Pr. Corp.

Smith, Steven Michael. New Carissa: The Ship That Refused to Die. 2010. 52p. pap. 22.99 *(978-1-4520-6612-7(4))* AuthorHouse.

Spenser & Mom. Spenser Goes to Portland. Jacobsen, Amie, illus. 2008. (ENG.). 32p. (J). 14.95 *(978-0-9817598-0-7(7)*, cf47a802-b05d-4aa8-9dd0-abec385a8af9) Simple Fish Bk. Co., LLC.

Way, Jennifer. Oregon. 2009. (Bilingual Library of the United States of America Ser.). (ENG & SPA.). 32p. (gr. 2-2). 47.90 *(978-1-60853-381-7(6)*, Editorial Buenas Letras) Rosen Publishing Group, Inc., The.

Williams, Jack. The Modoc of California. 2009. (Library of Native Americans Ser.). 64p. (gr. 4-4). 58.50 *(978-1-60853-754-9(4)*, PowerKids Pr.) Rosen Publishing Group, Inc., The.

—The Mojave of California. 2009. (Library of Native Americans Ser.). 64p. (gr. 4-4). 58.50 *(978-1-60853-755-6(2)*, PowerKids Pr.) Rosen Publishing Group, Inc., The.

Winans, Jay D. Oregon. 2011. (Guide to American States Ser.). (Illus.). 48p. (YA). (gr. 3-6). 29.99 *(978-1-61690-809-6(2))*; (J). *(978-1-61690-485-2(2))* Weigl Pubs., Inc.

—Oregon: The Beaver State. 2016. (J). *(978-1-4896-4926-3(3))* Weigl Pubs., Inc.

Ziff, John. Northwest: Idaho, Oregon, Washington, Vol. 19. 2015. (Let's Explore the States Ser.). (Illus.). 64p. (J). (gr. 5). 23.95 *(978-1-4222-3331-3(6))* Mason Crest.

OREGON NATIONAL HISTORIC TRAIL

Aronin, Miriam. How Many People Traveled the Oregon Trail? And Other Questions about the Trail West. 2012. (Six Questions of American History Ser.). (ENG.). 48p. (gr. 4-6). pap. 56.72 *(978-0-7613-9237-8(8))*; (Illus.). (J). pap. 11.99 *(978-0-7613-8566-0(5)*, cb80b72c-4ecb-42fa-980f-9c951f655ece); (Illus.). (J). lib. bdg. 30.65 *(978-0-7613-5332-4(1)*, feb9aceb-5243-49a1-b0d3-f994e3938250, Lerner Pubns.) Lerner Publishing Group.

Dean, Arlan. The Oregon Trail: From Independence, Missouri to Oregon City, Oregon. 2009. (Famous American Trails Ser.). 24p. (gr. 3-3). 42.50 *(978-1-61512-490-9(X)*, PowerKids Pr.) Rosen Publishing Group, Inc., The.

Doeden, Matt. Oregon Trail: An Interactive History Adventure. 2013. (You Choose: History Ser.). (ENG., Illus.). 112p. (J). (gr. 3-7). 32.65 *(978-1-4765-0254-0(4)*, 122324) Capstone.

—The Oregon Trail: An Interactive History Adventure. 2013. (You Choose: History Ser.). (ENG.). 112p. (J). (gr. 3-7). pap. 6.95 *(978-1-4765-3607-1(4)*, 123611) Capstone.

Dunn, Joeming W. The Oregon Trail, 1 vol. Smith, Tim, illus. 2008. (Graphic History Ser.). (ENG.). 32p. (J). (gr. 3-8). 32.79 *(978-1-60270-183-0(0)*, 9058, Graphic Planet - Fiction) Magic Wagon.

Figley, Marthy Rhodes. Clara Morgan & the Oregon Trail Journey. Orback, Craig, illus. 2011. (History Speaks: Picture Books Plus Reader's Theater Ser.). 48p. pap. 56.72 *(978-0-7613-7631-6(3))* Lerner Publishing Group.

Figley, Marthy Rhodes & Figley, Marty Rhodes. Clara Morgan & the Oregon Trail Journey. Orback, Craig, illus. 2011. (History Speaks: Picture Books Plus Reader's Theater Ser.). (ENG.). 48p. (gr. 2-4). pap. 9.95 *(978-0-7613-7115-1(X))* Lerner Publishing Group.

Freedman, Jeri. Life As a Pioneer on the Oregon Trail, 1 vol. 2015. (Life As... Ser.). (ENG., Illus.). 32p. (gr. 3-3). pap. 11.58 *(978-1-5026-1075-1(2)*, f8b32e82-39dd-43e3-8323-f276e1cf91c9) Cavendish Square Publishing LLC.

Group/McGraw-Hill, Wright. History: The Oregon Trail, 6 vols. (Book2WebTM Ser.). (gr. 4-8). 36.50 *(978-0-322-04452-4(9))* Wright Group/McGraw-Hill.

Gunderson, Jessica. Your Life As a Pioneer on the Oregon Trail. Dougherty, Rachel, illus. 2012. (Way It Was Ser.). (ENG.). 32p. (J). (gr. 2-5). pap. 8.95 *(978-1-4048-7250-9(7)*, 118193, Picture Window Bks.) Capstone.

Harness, Cheryl. The Tragic Tale of Narcissa Whitman & a Faithful History of the Oregon Trail (Direct Mail Edition) 2006. (Cheryl Harness Histories Ser.). (Illus.). 144p. (J). (gr. 5-9). 16.95 *(978-0-7922-5920-6(3)*, National Geographic Kids) Disney Publishing Worldwide.

Hunsaker, Joyce Badgley. Seeing the Elephant: Voices from the Oregon Trail. 2003. (ENG., Illus.). 272p. 24.95 *(978-0-89672-504-1(9)*, P171779) Texas Tech Univ. Pr.

Jeffrey, Gary. The Oregon Trail, 1 vol. Poluzzi, Allesandro, illus. 2012. (Graphic History of the American West Ser.). (ENG.). 24p. (J). (gr. 3-3). pap. 9.15 *(978-1-4339-6745-0(6)*, 6cef5d54-63c3-4008-83af-ed9d14b18589, Gareth Stevens Learning Library); lib. bdg. 26.60 *(978-1-4339-6743-6(X)*, 0ad4de6b-3511-4850-a21f-171ad1720118) Stevens, Gareth Publishing LLLP.

Landau, Elaine. True Books: Oregon Trail. 2006. (True Bks.). (ENG., Illus.). 48p. (J). (gr. 3-7). pap. 6.95 *(978-0-516-27903-9(3)*, Children's Pr.) Scholastic Library Publishing.

Loh-Hagan, Virginia. Heading West: Oregon Trail & Westward Expansion. 2019. (Behind the Curtain Ser.). (ENG.). 32p. (J). (gr. 4-8). pap. 14.21 *(978-1-5341-3995-4(8)*, 212809); (Illus.). lib. bdg. 32.07 *(978-1-5341-4339-5(4)*, 212808) Cherry Lake Publishing. (45th Parallel Press).

Lynette, Rachel. The Oregon Trail, 1 vol. 2013. (Pioneer Spirit: the Westward Expansion Ser.). (ENG.). 24p. (J). (gr. 2-3). 26.27 *(978-1-4777-0786-9(7)*, 85daa1aa-68ff-435a-9f1f-19327c89708a); (Illus.). pap. 9.25 *(978-1-4777-0905-4(3)*, ab0ff1dd-2296-4d9a-9b10-8084ed8aad2a) Rosen Publishing Group, Inc., The. (PowerKids Pr.).

Marciniak, Kristin. The Oregon Trail & Westward Expansion: A History Perspectives Book. 2013. (Perspectives Library). (ENG., Illus.). 32p. (J). (gr. 4-8). 32.07 *(978-1-62431-419-3(8)*, 202796); pap. 14.21 *(978-1-62431-495-7(3)*, 202798) Cherry Lake Publishing.

Murray, Laura K. The Oregon Trail, 1 vol. 2016. (Wild West Ser.). (ENG., Illus.). 48p. (J). (gr. 4-8). lib. bdg. 35.64 *(978-1-68078-258-5(4)*, 22117) ABDO Publishing Co.

Nash, Nancy. Mama's Books: An Oregon Trail Story. Burke, Ruth Anne, illus. 2013. (J). pap. 9.95 *(978-0-9838653-6-0(1))* Doorlight Pubns.

Olson, Steven. The Oregon Trail: A Primary Source History of the Route to the American West. 2009. (Primary Sources in American History Ser.). 64p. (gr. 5-8). 58.50 *(978-1-60851-501-1(X))* Rosen Publishing Group, Inc., The.

Olson, Steven P. The Oregon Trail, 1 vol. 2004. (Primary Sources in American History Ser.). (ENG., Illus.). 64p. (gr. 5-8). lib. bdg. 37.13 *(978-0-8239-4512-2(X)*,

62403f74-8a1c-4b94-852b-0d437b0ca078, Rosen Reference) Rosen Publishing Group, Inc., The.

The Oregon Trail. 2013. (Pioneer Spirit: the Westward Expansion Ser.). 24p. (J). (gr. 3-6). pap. 49.50 (978-1-4777-0906-1(1), PowerKids Pr.) Rosen Publishing Group, Inc., The.

Proudfit, Benjamin. The Oregon Trail, 1 vol. 2016. (Road Trip: Famous Routes Ser.). (ENG., Illus.). 24p. (J). (gr. 2-3). pap. 9.15 (978-1-4824-4675-3(8), 53ed9fe6-616c-4dc6-8df4-b88b51808ee6) Stevens, Gareth Publishing LLLP.

Stefoff, Rebecca. Surviving the Oregon Trail: Stories in American History, 1 vol. 2012. (Stories in American History Ser.). (ENG., Illus.). 128p. (gr. 5-6). 35.93 (978-0-7660-3955-1(2), c1760ce8-dc06-4e25-9147-347b87cd367f); pap. 13.88 (978-1-4644-0025-4(3), c88db0fb-07e6-4a6c-9422-5bd8161ac3b2) Enslow Publishing, LLC.

Uschan, Michael V. The Oregon Trail, 1 vol. 2004. (Landmark Events in American History Ser.). (ENG., Illus.). 48p. (gr. 5-8). pap. 15.05 (978-0-8368-5414-5(4), 8ae2420a-0a80-45c2-8ba1-444c4537e421, Gareth Stevens Secondary Library) Stevens, Gareth Publishing LLLP.

OREGON NATIONAL HISTORIC TRAIL—FICTION

Bly, Stephen A. The Lost Wagon Train. 2005. (Retta Barre's Oregon Trail Ser.: Vol. 1). 110p. pap. 5.99 (978-1-58134-391-5(4), Crossway Bibles) Crossway.

Carr, Mary Jane. Children of the Covered Wagon. 2007. (Illus.). 266p. per. 9.95 (978-1-932971-50-7(5)) Christian Liberty Pr.

Kelso, Mary Jean. The Christmas Angel. Snider, K. C., illus. 2007. 32p. (J). 11.95 (978-1-933090-58-0(8)) Guardian Angel Publishing, Inc.

Lee, Stacey. Under a Painted Sky. 2016. lib. bdg. 22.10 (978-0-606-38391-2(3)) Turtleback.

Marsh, Carole. The Mystery on the Oregon Trail. 2010. (Real Kids, Real Places Ser.). (Illus.). 158p. (J). 18.99 (978-0-635-07440-9(0), Marsh, Carole Mysteries) Gallopade International.

—The Mystery on the Oregon Trail. Friedlander, Randolyn, illus. 2010. (Real Kids, Real Places Ser.). 32p. pap. 7.99 (978-0-635-07441-6(9), Marsh, Carole Mysteries) Gallopade International.

Messner, Kate. Rescue on the Oregon Trail (Ranger in Time #1) McMorris, Kelley, illus. 2015. (Ranger in Time Ser.: 1). (ENG.). 144p. (J). (gr. 2-5). pap. 5.99 (978-0-545-63914-9(X), Scholastic Pr.) Scholastic, Inc.

Pierpoint, Eric. The Last Ride of Caleb O'Toole. 2013. (ENG., Illus.). 304p. (J). (gr. 4-7). pap. 11.99 (978-1-4022-8171-6(4), 9781402281716) Sourcebooks, Inc.

Wiley, Jesse. The Oregon Trail: Danger at the Haunted Gate. 2018. (Oregon Trail Ser.: 2). (ENG., Illus.). 160p. (J). (gr. 1-5). 14.99 (978-1-328-55001-9(X), 1724255, Clarion Bks.) HarperCollins Pubs.

—The Oregon Trail: Danger at the Haunted Gate. 2018. (Oregon Trail Ser.: 2). (ENG., Illus.). 160p. (J). (gr. 1-5). pap. 7.99 (978-1-328-54997-6(6), 1724097, Clarion Bks.) HarperCollins Pubs.

—The Oregon Trail: the Race to Chimney Rock. 2018. (Oregon Trail Ser.: 1). (ENG., Illus.). 160p. (J). (gr. 1-5). pap. 7.99 (978-1-328-54996-9(8), 1724095, Clarion Bks.) HarperCollins Pubs.

—The Oregon Trail: the Search for Snake River. 2018. (Oregon Trail Ser.: 3). (ENG., Illus.). 160p. (J). (gr. 1-5). pap. 7.99 (978-1-328-54998-3(4), 1724099, Clarion Bks.) HarperCollins Pubs.

—The Oregon Trail: the Search for Snake River. 2018. (Oregon Trail Ser.: 3). (ENG., Illus.). 160p. (J). (gr. 1-5). 14.99 (978-1-328-55002-6(8), 1724257, Clarion Bks.) HarperCollins Pubs.

Wilson, Laura. How I Survived the Oregon Trail: The Journal of Jesse Adams. 2006. (Illus.). 37p. (J). (gr. 4-8). reprint ed. pap. 10.00 (978-0-7567-9925-0(2)) DIANE Publishing Co.

Young, Judy & Scillian, Devin. Westward Journeys. Farnsworth, Bill et al, illus. 2013. (American Adventures Ser.). (ENG.). 96p. (J). (gr. 3-6). pap. 6.99 (978-1-58536-860-0(1), 202367) Sleeping Bear Pr.

OREGON TRAIL

see Oregon National Historic Trail

ORGANIC CHEMISTRY

see Chemistry, Organic

ORGANIC FARMING

Barker, David M. Organic Foods. 2016. (Growing Green Ser.). (ENG., Illus.). 64p. (J). (gr. 6-8). lib. bdg. 34.65 (978-1-4677-9391-9(4), f40b3938-c42d-4f5c-a23c-06e265ed9da8); E-Book 51.99 (978-1-4677-9712-2(X)) Lerner Publishing Group. (Lerner Pubns.).

Centore, Michael. Organic Foods. 2017. 64p. (J). (978-1-4222-3740-3(0)) Mason Crest.

Flounders, Anne. Growing Good Food. 2014. (Core Content Science — Our Green Earth Ser.). (ENG., Illus.). 32p. (J). (gr. 2-4). pap. 8.99 (978-1-939656-31-5(1), b5ddbe16-670e-4d6f-aaa0-73a7f8eb09a0) Red Chair Pr.

Francis, Amy, ed. The Local Food Movement, 1 vol. 2010. (At Issue Ser.). (ENG.). 160p. (gr. 10-12). 41.03 (978-0-7377-4888-8(5), 6fe1c1fe-be46-4f19-86e6-8d736c660a46); pap. 28.80 (978-0-7377-4889-5(3), 1e81c7be-6b76-4797-9831-b4453f810fa5) Greenhaven Publishing LLC. (Greenhaven Publishing).

Hodge, Deborah. Up We Grow! A Year in the Life of a Small, Local Farm. Harris, Brian, illus. 2010. (ENG.). 32p. (J). (gr. -1-2). 16.95 (978-1-55453-561-3(1)) Kids Can Pr., Ltd. CAN. Dist: Hachette Bk. Group.

Hurt, Avery Elizabeth, ed. Corporate Farming, 1 vol. 2017. (Opposing Viewpoints Ser.). (ENG.). 208p. (gr. 10-12). pap. 34.80 (978-1-5345-0049-5(9), ec286b49-a974-457a-95b4-96ed6dd599cc) Greenhaven Publishing LLC.

Mickelson, Trina. Free-Range Farming. 2016. (Growing Green Ser.). (ENG., Illus.). 64p. (J). (gr. 6-8). lib. bdg. 34.65 (978-1-4677-9389-6(2), 342e135f-f732-4b1c-b5ef-016654f9c69f); E-Book 51.99 (978-1-4677-9710-8(3)) Lerner Publishing Group. (Lerner Pubns.).

Orr, Tamra B. Organic Farmer. 2009. (21st Century Skills Library: Cool Careers Ser.). (ENG., Illus.). 32p. (gr. 4-8). lib. bdg. 32.07 (978-1-60279-500-6(2), 200312) Cherry Lake Publishing.

Reilly, Kathleen M. Food: 25 Amazing Projects Investigate the History & Science of What We Eat. Rizvi, Farah, illus. 2010. (Build It Yourself Ser.). (ENG.). 128p. (J). (gr. 3-7). pap. 15.95 (978-1-934670-59-0(6), 10795b12-35f6-47e5-9b01-349fde845448) Nomad Pr.

—Food - 25 Amazing Projects: Investigate the History & Science of What We Eat. Rizvi, Farah, illus. 2010. (Build It Yourself Ser.). (ENG.). 128p. (J). (gr. 3-7). 21.95 (978-1-934670-60-6(X), 001bdaf8-506b-4c5f-bb04-c719caf0d3a6) Nomad Pr.

Rice, Dona Herweck. Organic Farming. rev. ed. 2018. (Smithsonian: Informational Text Ser.). (ENG., Illus.). 32p. (gr. 3-5). pap. 11.99 (978-1-4938-6692-2(3)) Teacher Created Materials, Inc.

Rissman, Rebecca. Eating Organic, 1 vol. 2015. (Food Matters Ser.). (ENG., Illus.). 48p. (J). (gr. 4-8). 35.64 (978-1-62403-862-4(X), 18094) ABDO Publishing Co.

Shackleton, Caroline. Money Tree: the Business of Organics High Intermediate Book with Online Access, 1 vol. 2014. (ENG., Illus.). 28p. (J). pap., E-Book 9.50 (978-1-107-63678-1(7)) Cambridge Univ. Pr.

ORGANIC GARDENING

Aloian, Molly. Green Gardening & Composting. 2013. (ENG.). 24p. (J). (978-0-7787-0262-7(6)); pap. (978-0-7787-0276-4(6)) Crabtree Publishing Co.

Dunn-Georgiou, Elisha. Everything You Need to Know about Organic Foods. 2009. (Need to Know Library). 64p. (gr. 5-5). 58.50 (978-1-60854-079-2(0)) Rosen Publishing Group, Inc., The.

Korrow, Chris. The Organic Bug Book, 1 vol. Korrow, Chris, illus. 2013. (Illus.). 44p. (J). pap. 11.95 (978-1-58420-145-8(2), Lindisfarne Bks.) SteinerBooks, Inc.

Loh-Hagan, Virginia. Organic Garden. 2016. (D. I. Y. Make It Happen Ser.). (ENG., Illus.). 32p. (J). (gr. 4-8). 32.07 (978-1-63471-102-9(5), 208519, 45th Parallel Press) Cherry Lake Publishing.

Scholl, Elizabeth. Organic Gardening for Kids. 2009. (Gardening for Kids Ser.). (Illus.). 48p. (YA). (gr. 1-4). lib. bdg. 29.95 (978-1-58415-815-8(8)) Mitchell Lane Pubs.

Siddals, Mary McKenna. Compost Stew: An a to Z Recipe for the Earth. Wolff, Ashley, illus. 2014. 40p. (J). (gr. -1-2). 8.99 (978-0-385-75538-2(4), Dragonfly Bks.) Random Hse. Children's Bks.

Spilsbury, Louise. How Community Gardens Work, 1 vol. 2013. (EcoWorks Ser.). 32p. (J). (gr. 3-4). (ENG.). pap. 11.50 (978-1-4339-9557-6(3), e543f05e-cb19-458a-8935-c9143516f10a); pap. 63.00 (978-1-4339-9558-3(1)); (ENG., Illus.). lib. bdg. 29.27 (978-1-4339-9556-9(5), b058ae06-34b6-45ad-9f9f-deec6a4e83ad) Stevens, Gareth Publishing LLLP.

Winckler, Suzanne. Planting the Seed: A Guide to Gardening. 2005. (Illus.). 64p. (gr. 5-12). 25.76 (978-0-8225-0081-0(7)) Lerner Publishing Group.

ORGANICULTURE

see Organic Farming; Organic Gardening

ORGANIZATION, INTERNATIONAL

see International Organization

ORGANIZATION AND MANAGEMENT

see Management

ORGANIZED CRIME

see Racketeering

ORGANIZED LABOR

see Labor Unions

ORIENTATION

Champion, Neil. Finding Your Way. 2010. (Survive Alive Ser.). (ENG.). 32p. (J). (gr. 3-7). lib. bdg. 28.50 (978-1-60753-038-1(4), 17221) Amicus.

Champion, Neil & Ganeri, Anita. Finding Food & Water. 2011. (How the World Makes Music Ser.). 32p. (gr. 4-7). lib. bdg. 31.35 (978-1-59920-478-9(9)) Black Rabbit Bks.

De Capua, Sarah. Como Nos Orientamos? 2005. (Rookie Reader Español Ser.). (SPA., Illus.). 32p. (J). (gr. k-2). lib. bdg. 19.50 (978-0-516-24442-6(6), Children's Pr.) Scholastic Library Publishing.

Grack, Rachel. Navigation from Then to Now. 2019. (Sequence Developments in Technology Ser.). (ENG.). 32p. (J). (gr. 2-5). pap. 9.99 (978-1-68152-469-6(4), 11055) Amicus.

Greve, Meg. North, South, East, & West. 2009. (Little World Geography Ser.). (ENG., Illus.). 24p. (gr. k-2). pap. 9.95 (978-1-60694-534-6(3), 9781606945346) Rourke Educational Media.

Katirgis, Jane. Up & Down, 1 vol. 2011. (All about Opposites Ser.). (ENG., Illus.). 24p. (gr. -1-1). pap. 10.35 (978-1-59845-258-7(4), 9b6ef717-bdc4-406f-af78-51a42e64ce90); lib. bdg. 25.27 (978-0-7660-3913-1(7), e6174b0e-e323-4f82-a84b-b36009fc8899) Enslow Publishing, LLC. (Enslow Publishing).

McDonnell, Rory. In or Out?, 1 vol. 2019. (All about Opposites Ser.). (ENG.). 24p. (gr. k-k). pap. 9.15 (978-1-5382-3726-7(1), aab60d62-bcf5-4582-b0cd-4f955300d036) Stevens, Gareth Publishing LLLP.

—Up or Down?, 1 vol. 2019. (All about Opposites Ser.). (ENG.). 24p. (gr. k-k). 24.27 (978-1-5382-3736-6(9), ccf7ee8d-a6d9-497b-909d-97dbc1554093) Stevens, Gareth Publishing LLLP.

Nelson, Robin. Staying Clean. 2005. (Pull Ahead Books — Health Ser.). (ENG., Illus.). 32p. (J). (gr. k-3). lib. bdg. 22.65 (978-0-8225-2638-4(7), 1f5dfddc-6e7c-4098-8a27-e43a960b4149, Lerner Pubns.) Lerner Publishing Group.

Rivera, Sheila. Above & Below. 2005. (First Step Nonfiction — Location Ser.). (ENG., Illus.). 8p. (J). (gr. k-2). pap. 5.99 (978-0-8225-5355-7(4), 80b6e614-616c-4f98-b5e8-f604125eb458) Lerner Publishing Group.

—Behind & in Front. 2005. (First Step Nonfiction — Location Ser.). (ENG., Illus.). 8p. (J). (gr. k-2). pap. 5.99 (978-0-8225-5352-6(X), 166f0b8b-882e-4b19-a112-1d67b7667fa2) Lerner Publishing Group.

—Left & Right. 2004. (First Step Nonfiction Ser.). (J). pap. 3.95 (978-0-8225-5351-9(1), Lerner Pubns.) Lerner Publishing Group.

Savage, Jeff. Carly Patterson. 2005. (Amazing Athletes Ser.). (Illus.). 32p. (J). 23.93 (978-0-8225-2639-1(5), Lerner Pubns.) Lerner Publishing Group.

Woods, Michael & Woods, Mary B. The History of Medicine. 2005. (Major Inventions Through History Ser.). (ENG., Illus.). 56p. (gr. 5-8). lib. bdg. 26.60 (978-0-8225-2636-0(0), Twenty-First Century Bks.) Lerner Publishing Group.

Zubek, Adeline. Front or Back?, 1 vol. 2019. (All about Opposites Ser.). (ENG.). 24p. (gr. k-k). 24.27 (978-1-5382-3720-5(2), 51b658b4-75d7-4fad-bf16-9ee1c130c2f9) Stevens, Gareth Publishing LLLP.

ORIGAMI

see also Paper Work

Amazing Geogami. 2007. (978-1-884270-11-6(5)); (978-1-884270-10-9(7)) Hall, Nancy Inc.

Amazing Origami. 2013. (Amazing Origami Ser.). 32p. (J). (gr. 2-5). pap. 378.00 (978-1-4339-9814-0(9)); pap. 63.00 (978-1-4339-9813-3(0)) Stevens, Gareth Publishing LLLP.

Amazing Origami: Set 2, 12 vols. 2014. (Amazing Origami Ser.). (ENG.). 32p. (J). (gr. 2-3). lib. bdg. 175.62 (978-1-4824-2198-9(4), ea5cbf18-e304-4529-9326-a3ac8ef6105f) Stevens, Gareth Publishing LLLP.

Amazing Origami: Set 4, 12 vols. 2016. (Amazing Origami Ser.). (ENG.). 00032p. (J). (gr. 2-3). lib. bdg. 175.62 (978-1-4824-5848-0(9), 9add5793-4dbc-4821-9955-92dc22613dbe) Stevens, Gareth Publishing LLLP.

Angleberger, Tom. ART2-D2's Guide to Folding & Doodling. 2013. (Illus.). 163p. (J). pap. (978-1-4197-0994-4(1), Amulet Bks.) Abrams, Inc.

—Art2-D2's Guide to Folding & Doodling (an Origami Yoda Activity Book) (Origami Yoda Ser.). (ENG., Illus.). (J). (gr. 3-7). 2016. 192p. pap. 8.99 (978-1-4197-2028-4(7), 1042403) 2013. 176p. 12.95 (978-1-4197-0534-2(2), 1042401) Abrams, Inc. (Amulet Bks.).

—Darth Paper Strikes Back (Origami Yoda #2) An Origami Yoda Book. 2015. (Origami Yoda Ser.). (ENG., Illus.). 176p. (J). (gr. 3-7). pap. 8.99 (978-1-4197-1640-9(9), 697403, Amulet Bks.) Abrams, Inc.

Animal Kingdom Origami, 12 vols. 2017. (Animal Kingdom Origami Ser.). 32p. (ENG.). (gr. 3-3). 175.62 (978-1-4994-3398-2(0), 88eaccaf-26d9-406f-bb5b-8b0949c4db1d); (gr. 8-8). pap. 70.50 (978-1-5081-5370-2(1)) Rosen Publishing Group, Inc., The. (PowerKids Pr.).

Arcturus Publishing. Incredible Origami: 95 Amazing Paper-Folding Projects, Includes Origami Paper. 2017. (ENG.). 256p. pap. 16.99 (978-1-78428-855-6(1), 8c299850-002d-498e-a27c-f17fbfe6bdff) Arcturus Publishing GBR. Dist: Baker & Taylor Publisher Services (BTPS).

Ard, Catherine. Origami Bugs, 1 vol. 2014. (Amazing Origami Ser.). (ENG., Illus.). 32p. (J). (gr. 2-3). 29.27 (978-1-4824-2199-6(2), 7829330c-1e57-4036-b637-a041139bb3e5) Stevens, Gareth Publishing LLLP.

—Origami Holidays, 1 vol. 2014. (Amazing Origami Ser.). (ENG., Illus.). 32p. (J). (gr. 2-3). 29.27 (978-1-4824-2200-9(X), 693f3cfd-b8f3-4b1d-b99f-14898ea14b01) Stevens, Gareth Publishing LLLP.

—Origami Monsters, 1 vol. 2014. (Amazing Origami Ser.). (ENG., Illus.). 32p. (J). (gr. 2-3). 29.27 (978-1-4824-2201-6(8), da7d56a7-09c5-4274-b401-3ba51266f131) Stevens, Gareth Publishing LLLP.

—Origami on the Move, 1 vol. 2014. (Amazing Origami Ser.). (ENG., Illus.). 32p. (J). (gr. 2-3). 29.27 (978-1-4824-2202-3(6), 8f2d879d-bf21-4541-b109-25ea1972a95e) Stevens, Gareth Publishing LLLP.

—Origami Planes, 1 vol. 2014. (Amazing Origami Ser.). (ENG., Illus.). 32p. (J). (gr. 2-3). 29.27 (978-1-4824-2203-0(4), 1f9a8b91-7330-49db-9105-e06fc3864e6a) Stevens, Gareth Publishing LLLP.

—Origami Space, 1 vol. 2014. (Amazing Origami Ser.). (ENG., Illus.). 32p. (J). (gr. 2-3). 29.27 (978-1-4824-2204-7(2), c36e64e8-2dac-4679-981a-50146d3ca197) Stevens, Gareth Publishing LLLP.

Arnstein, Bennett Roy. The Saturday Afternoon Public Library Origami Club Manual: Not Just Another Origami Book. 2004. (Illus.). 69p. 11.95 (978-0-9620058-2-4(7)) Arnstein, Bennett.

Azzità, Emanuele. Origami Arts & Crafts, 1 vol. 2017. (Exciting Origami Ser.). (ENG.). 48p. (gr. 3-3). pap. 12.70 (978-0-7660-8761-3(1), 5ce63074-d017-4249-93b2-e6663ef181f7); lib. bdg. 29.60 (978-0-7660-8646-3(1), d3b56eae-34f2-4182-91fe-f15375cc1e61) Enslow Publishing, LLC.

—Origami Birds, 1 vol. 2017. (Exciting Origami Ser.). (ENG.). 48p. (gr. 3-3). pap. 12.70 (978-0-7660-8759-0(X), 87513f53-e769-40da-9da6-73afed41890c); lib. bdg. 29.60 (978-0-7660-8648-7(8), 95951d72-5bdb-424a-bff4-2875b4289d9e) Enslow Publishing, LLC.

—Origami Land & Sea Animals, 1 vol. 2017. (Exciting Origami Ser.). (ENG.). 48p. (gr. 3-3). lib. bdg. 29.60 (978-0-7660-8718-7(2), ba2c5a28-2632-4875-a37b-e19c2f84e6a9) Enslow Publishing, LLC.

Bolitho, Mark. Fold Your Own Origami Air Force, 1 vol. 2013. (Origami Army Ser.). (ENG.). 32p. (J). (gr. 4-5). 30.17 (978-1-4777-1319-8(0), 7e8cecf2-ebe7-49f0-80d2-eef4f33bfa12); pap. 12.75 (978-1-4777-1469-0(3), d136c147-9f3b-4b8d-9e62-0f1bc836da42) Rosen Publishing Group, Inc., The. (PowerKids Pr.).

—Fold Your Own Origami Army, 1 vol. 2013. (Origami Army Ser.). (ENG.). 32p. (J). (gr. 4-5). 30.17 (978-1-4777-1317-4(4), 79e2de33-f8c5-4926-8d23-a97cb935d271); pap. 12.75 (978-1-4777-1465-2(0), ddcdf6cf-df53-493d-b4c4-feb11e84fd28) Rosen Publishing Group, Inc., The. (PowerKids Pr.).

—Fold Your Own Origami Navy, 1 vol. 2013. (Origami Army Ser.). (ENG.). 32p. (J). (gr. 4-5). 30.17 (978-1-4777-1318-1(2), bf7d4de7-f93a-46c8-91c4-ba2855630374); pap. 12.75 (978-1-4777-1467-6(7), 27357e93-155b-4e06-aea9-a429de38b1ea) Rosen Publishing Group, Inc., The. (PowerKids Pr.).

—Fold Your Own Origami Weapons, 1 vol. 2013. (Origami Army Ser.). (ENG.). 32p. (J). (gr. 4-5). 30.17 (978-1-4777-1320-4(4), d9bcbd15-0319-4281-aa7f-22af4b647f9d); pap. 12.75 (978-1-4777-1471-3(5), abf46ea1-7817-4701-98dd-6a5b4effc1a2) Rosen Publishing Group, Inc., The. (PowerKids Pr.).

Boursin, Didier. Easy Origami. 2005. (ENG., Illus.). 64p. (J). (gr. 2-8). pap. 9.95 (978-1-55297-939-6(3), 97291e41-fe90-4e1b-8b52-e3245633bc97) Firefly Bks., Ltd.

Braun, Eric. Let's Rock! Science Adventures with Rudie the Origami Dinosaur, 1 vol. Christoph, Jamey, illus. 2013. (Origami Science Adventures Ser.). (ENG.). 24p. (J). (gr. -1-3). pap. 6.95 (978-1-4048-8068-9(2), 121840, Picture Window Bks.) Capstone.

Buckingham, Marie. Space Bomber! Expert-Level Paper Airplanes: 4D an Augmented Reading Paper-Folding Experience. 2018. (Paper Airplanes with a Side of Science 4D Ser.). (ENG., Illus.). 32p. (J). (gr. 3-6). lib. bdg. 33.99 (978-1-5435-0794-2(8), 137530, Capstone Classroom) Capstone.

—Spinning Blimp! Beginning-Level Paper Airplanes: 4D an Augmented Reading Paper-Folding Experience. 2018. (Paper Airplanes with a Side of Science 4D Ser.). (ENG., Illus.). 32p. (J). (gr. 3-6). lib. bdg. 33.99 (978-1-5435-0797-3(2), 137533, Capstone Classroom) Capstone.

Butler, Tom. Origami Animals, 1 vol. 2016. (Mastering Origami Ser.). (ENG.). 48p. (gr. 5-6). pap. 12.70 (978-0-7660-7944-1(9), c6fc5365-cabc-4086-aa28-771e0037c2c6) Enslow Publishing, LLC.

—Origami Toys & Games, 1 vol. 2016. (Mastering Origami Ser.). (ENG.). 48p. (gr. 5-6). pap. 12.70 (978-0-7660-7948-9(1), 6d4fc437-202e-4258-ad51-40d8fc49de0f) Enslow Publishing, LLC.

—Origami Vehicles, 1 vol. 2016. (Mastering Origami Ser.). (ENG.). 48p. (gr. 5-6). pap. 12.70 (978-0-7660-7952-6(X), a1fb0880-cbdc-49f2-b937-1a64b33115ed) Enslow Publishing, LLC.

—Practical Origami, 1 vol. 2016. (Mastering Origami Ser.). (ENG.). 48p. (gr. 5-6). pap. 12.70 (978-0-7660-7955-7(4), e458fd38-928d-432f-89a8-89cc1f445f3b) Enslow Publishing, LLC.

CICO Kidz. My First Origami Book: 35 Fun Papercrafting Projects for Children Aged 7+ 2018. (ENG., Illus.). 128p. (J). pap. 14.95 (978-1-78249-671-7(8), 1782496718, Cico Kidz) Ryland Peters & Small GBR. Dist: WIPRO.

Cook, Trevor, et al. Origami: A Step-By-Step Introduction to the Art of Paper Folding. 2012. (ENG., Illus.). 96p. (J). pap. 12.95 (978-1-84858-650-5(7), 95f7aaf5-66d0-469a-961e-a58fd7406984) Arcturus Publishing GBR. Dist: Baker & Taylor Publisher Services (BTPS).

Dare, Sterling. Money Menagerie: A Collection of Wild or Strange Animals. 2004. 15.00 (978-0-9727938-3-4(6)) H & R Magic Bks.

Dewar, Andrew. Origami Bible Stories for Kids Kit: Folded Paper Figures & Stories Bring the Bible to Life! 64 Paper Models with a Full-Color Instruction Book & 4 Backdrops. Roy, Suman, illus. 2018. 64p. 14.99 (978-0-8048-4851-0(3)) Tuttle Publishing.

Diaz, James. Popigami: When Everyday Paper Pops! Diaz, Francesca, illus. 2007. (ENG.). 8p. (J). (gr. -1). 19.95 (978-1-58117-641-4(4), Intervisual/Piggy Toes) Bendon, Inc.

Everything Origami. 2015. (Everything Origami Ser.). (ENG.). 32p. (J). (gr. 3-4). pap., pap., pap. 423.00 (978-1-4777-5677-5(9), Windmill Bks.) Rosen Publishing Group, Inc., The.

Exciting Origami. 2017. (Exciting Origami Ser.). 48p. (gr. 3-3). pap. 46.80 (978-0-7660-8807-8(3)); (ENG.). lib. bdg. 118.40 (978-0-7660-8592-3(9), f8c1dc51-7808-4dec-87a3-ebc4ad0b9efe) Enslow Publishing, LLC.

Fold Your Own Origami Air Force. 2013. (Origami Army Ser.). 32p. (J). (gr. 3-6). pap. 70.50 (978-1-4777-1470-6(7), PowerKids Pr.) Rosen Publishing Group, Inc., The.

Fold Your Own Origami Army. 2013. (Origami Army Ser.). 32p. (J). (gr. 3-6). pap. 70.50 (978-1-4777-1466-9(9), PowerKids Pr.) Rosen Publishing Group, Inc., The.

Fold Your Own Origami Navy. 2013. (Origami Army Ser.). 32p. (J). (gr. 3-6). pap. 70.50 (978-1-4777-1468-3(5), PowerKids Pr.) Rosen Publishing Group, Inc., The.

Fold Your Own Origami Weapons. 2013. (Origami Army Ser.). 32p. (J). (gr. 3-6). pap. 70.50 (978-1-4777-1472-0(3), PowerKids Pr.) Rosen Publishing Group, Inc., The.

Fullman, Joe. Arctic Origami, 1 vol. 2016. (Amazing Origami Ser.). (ENG.). 32p. (J). (gr. 2-3). pap. 11.50 (978-1-4824-5920-3(5), 883f722a-e1d1-4cf6-bce8-329ce408db9e) Stevens, Gareth Publishing LLLP.

—Desert Origami, 1 vol. 2016. (Amazing Origami Ser.). (ENG.). 32p. (J). (gr. 2-3). pap. 11.50 (978-1-4824-5924-1(8), feda1413-0878-4e27-8f72-20689b4490ca) Stevens, Gareth Publishing LLLP.

—Floating Origami, 1 vol. 2015. (Amazing Origami Ser.). (ENG.). 32p. (J). (gr. 2-3). lib. bdg. 29.27 (978-1-4824-4167-3(5), a35208d9-0f21-40e1-9bbf-8b0c222d5d47) Stevens, Gareth Publishing LLLP.

—Flying Origami, 1 vol. 2015. (Amazing Origami Ser.). (ENG.). 32p. (J). (gr. 2-3). pap. 11.50 (978-1-4824-4155-0(1),

09ed6451-ad2d-4b66-b76a-698c3fdce8b5) Stevens, Gareth Publishing LLLP.

—Jungle Origami, 1 vol. 2016. (Amazing Origami Ser.). (ENG.). 32p. (J). (gr. 2-3). pap. 11.50 *(978-1-4824-5928-9(0)*, cfd76b26-d785-4e39-92e3-5e2b65a1904a) Stevens, Gareth Publishing LLLP.

—Ocean Origami, 1 vol. 2016. (Amazing Origami Ser.). (ENG.). 32p. (J). (gr. 2-3). pap. 11.50 *(978-1-4824-5932-6(9)*, b574acee-e4d0-4930-8029-56da4ba19c68) Stevens, Gareth Publishing LLLP.

—Origami Games, 1 vol. 2015. (Amazing Origami Ser.). (ENG.). 32p. (J). (gr. 2-3). pap. 11.50 *(978-1-4824-4159-8(4)*, 81bf94ef-2c49-47a1-8247-e1355a67564f) Stevens, Gareth Publishing LLLP.

—Origami Magic, 1 vol. 2015. (Amazing Origami Ser.). (ENG.). 32p. (J). (gr. 2-3). pap. 11.50 *(978-1-4824-4163-5(2)*, 0beef321-3c28-404c-83ff-09476743c73e) Stevens, Gareth Publishing LLLP.

—Plant-Eating Dinosaurs, 1 vol. 2018. (Amazing Origami Ser.). (ENG.). 32p. (J). (gr. 2-3). pap. 11.50 *(978-1-5382-3464-8(5)*, 82230854-1521-42da-8b18-0667036686d2); lib. bdg. 29.27 *(978-1-5382-3466-2(1)*, e2bd0a0a-2934-4c11-8cf8-aef130c48bc4) Stevens, Gareth Publishing LLLP.

—Safari Origami, 1 vol. 2016. (Amazing Origami Ser.). (ENG.). 32p. (J). (gr. 2-3). pap. 11.50 *(978-1-4824-5936-4(1)*, d73da820-af77-4dd0-bf75-a4621393c86c) Stevens, Gareth Publishing LLLP.

—Sea Monsters & Flying Monsters, 1 vol. 2018. (Amazing Origami Ser.). (ENG.). 32p. (J). (gr. 2-3). pap. 11.50 *(978-1-5382-3468-6(8)*, f8d7e5d3-d319-4f31-9e32-2cd4a58e6d36); lib. bdg. 29.27 *(978-1-5382-3470-9(X)*, ee9d8265-209c-4319-ad83-b76d3d7dfebe) Stevens, Gareth Publishing LLLP.

—Snapping & Speaking Origami, 1 vol. 2015. (Amazing Origami Ser.). (ENG.). 32p. (J). (gr. 2-3). pap. 11.50 *(978-1-4824-4175-8(6)*, e1ee5931-3378-44c1-9163-fc464fe81a7e) Stevens, Gareth Publishing LLLP.

—Woodland Origami, 1 vol. 2016. (Amazing Origami Ser.). (ENG.). 32p. (J). (gr. 2-3). pap. 11.50 *(978-1-4824-5940-1(X)*, a21b3fdd-c735-4f32-a729-77ac5686420c) Stevens, Gareth Publishing LLLP.

Gardiner, Matthew. Everything Origami Set. 2015. (Everything Origami Ser.). (ENG., Illus.). 32p. (J). pap., pap., pap. 70.50 *(978-1-4777-5678-2(7)*, Windmill Bks.) Rosen Publishing Group, Inc., The.

George, Anna. Origami Birds: Easy & Fun Paper-Folding Projects. 2016. (Super Simple Origami Ser.). (ENG., Illus.). 32p. (J). (gr. k-4). lib. bdg. 34.21 *(978-1-68078-446-6(3)*, 23751, Super SandCastle) ABDO Publishing Co.

—Origami Dinosaurs: Easy & Fun Paper-Folding Projects. 2016. (Super Simple Origami Ser.). (ENG., Illus.). 32p. (J). (gr. k-4). lib. bdg. 34.21 *(978-1-68078-447-3(1)*, 23753, Super SandCastle) ABDO Publishing Co.

—Origami Farm Animals: Easy & Fun Paper-Folding Projects. 2016. (Super Simple Origami Ser.). (ENG., Illus.). 32p. (J). (gr. k-4). lib. bdg. 34.21 *(978-1-68078-448-0(X)*, 23755, Super SandCastle) ABDO Publishing Co.

—Origami Insects: Easy & Fun Paper-Folding Projects. 2016. (Super Simple Origami Ser.). (ENG., Illus.). 32p. (J). (gr. k-4). lib. bdg. 34.21 *(978-1-68078-449-7(8)*, 23757, Super SandCastle) ABDO Publishing Co.

—Origami Pets: Easy & Fun Paper-Folding Projects. 2016. (Super Simple Origami Ser.). (ENG., Illus.). 32p. (J). (gr. k-4). lib. bdg. 34.21 *(978-1-68078-450-3(1)*, 23759, Super SandCastle) ABDO Publishing Co.

—Origami Zoo Animals: Easy & Fun Paper-Folding Projects. 2016. (Super Simple Origami Ser.). (ENG., Illus.). 32p. (J). (gr. k-4). lib. bdg. 34.21 *(978-1-68078-451-0(X)*, 23761, Super SandCastle) ABDO Publishing Co.

Hanson, Anders Mann & Mann, Elissa. Cool Paper Folding: Creative Activities That Make Math & Science Fun for Kids! 2013. (Cool Art with Math & Science Ser.). (ENG.). 32p. (J). (gr. 3-6). lib. bdg. 34.21 *(978-1-61783-823-1(3)*, 4592, Checkerboard Library) ABDO Publishing Co.

Harbo, Christopher. Easy Origami Decorations: An Augmented Reality Crafting Experience. 2017. (Origami Crafting 4D Ser.). (ENG., Illus.). 24p. (J). (gr. 1-3). lib. bdg. 30.65 *(978-1-5157-3585-4(0)*, 133585, Capstone Pr.) Capstone.

—Easy Origami Greeting Cards: An Augmented Reality Crafting Experience. 2017. (Origami Crafting 4D Ser.). (ENG., Illus.). 24p. (J). (gr. 1-3). lib. bdg. 30.65 *(978-1-5157-3587-8(7)*, 133587, Capstone Pr.) Capstone.

—Easy Origami Ornaments: An Augmented Reality Crafting Experience. 2017. (Origami Crafting 4D Ser.). (ENG., Illus.). 24p. (J). (gr. 1-3). lib. bdg. 30.65 *(978-1-5157-3586-1(9)*, 133586, Capstone Pr.) Capstone.

—Origami Explosion: Scorpions, Whales, Boxes, & More! 2015. (Origami Paperpalooza Ser.). (ENG., Illus.). 32p. (J). (gr. 3-9). lib. bdg. 28.65 *(978-1-4914-2023-2(5)*, 127500, Capstone Pr.) Capstone.

—Origami Folding Frenzy: Boats, Fish, Cranes, & More! 2015. (Origami Paperpalooza Ser.). (ENG., Illus.). 32p. (J). (gr. 3-9). lib. bdg. 28.65 *(978-1-4914-2021-8(9)*, 127497, Capstone Pr.) Capstone.

—Origami Palooza: Dragons, Turtles, Birds, & More! 2015. (Origami Paperpalooza Ser.). (ENG., Illus.). 32p. (J). (gr. 3-9). lib. bdg. 28.65 *(978-1-4914-2024-9(3)*, 127502, Capstone Pr.) Capstone.

—Origami Paperpalooza. 2015. (Origami Paperpalooza Ser.). (ENG.). 32p. (J). (gr. 3-9). 122.60 *(978-1-4914-2548-0(2)*, 22532, Capstone Pr.) Capstone.

—Origami Paperpalooza! 2015. (ENG., Illus.). 144p. (J). (gr. 3-9). pap., pap., pap. 14.95 *(978-1-62370-227-4(5)*, 127865, Capstone Young Readers) Capstone.

—Origami Papertainment: Samurai, Owls, Ninja Stars, & More! 2015. (Origami Paperpalooza Ser.). (ENG., Illus.). 32p. (J). (gr. 3-9). lib. bdg. 28.65 *(978-1-4914-2022-5(7)*, 127498, Capstone Pr.) Capstone.

Harbo, Christopher L. Easy Animal Origami, 1 vol. 2010. (Easy Origami Ser.). (ENG.). 24p. (J). (gr. 1-3). lib. bdg. 25.99 *(978-1-4296-5384-8(1)*, 113810, Capstone Pr.) Capstone.

—Easy Magician Origami, 1 vol. 2011. (Easy Origami Ser.). (ENG.). 24p. (J). (gr. 1-3). lib. bdg. 25.99 *(978-1-4296-6000-6(7)*, 114937, Capstone Pr.) Capstone.

—Easy Ocean Origami, 1 vol. 2010. (Easy Origami Ser.). (ENG.). 24p. (J). (gr. 1-3). lib. bdg. 25.99 *(978-1-4296-5385-5(X)*, 113811, Capstone Pr.) Capstone.

—Easy Origami, 6 vols., Set. Incl. Easy Animal Origami. 2010. lib. bdg. 25.99 *(978-1-4296-5384-8(1)*, 113810); Easy Magician Origami. 2011. lib. bdg. 25.99 *(978-1-4296-6000-6(7)*, 114937); Easy Ocean Origami. 2010. lib. bdg. 25.99 *(978-1-4296-5385-5(X)*, 113811); Easy Origami Toys. 2010. lib. bdg. 25.99 *(978-1-4296-5386-2(8)*, 113812); Easy Space Origami. 2011. lib. bdg. 25.99 *(978-1-4296-6001-3(5)*, 114938); (J). (gr. 1-3). (Easy Origami Ser.). (ENG.). 24p. 2011. 167.94 o.p. *(978-1-4296-6137-9(2)*, 15999, Capstone Pr.) Capstone.

—Easy Origami Toys, 1 vol. 2010. (Easy Origami Ser.). (ENG.). 24p. (J). (gr. 1-3). lib. bdg. 25.99 *(978-1-4296-5386-2(8)*, 113812, Capstone Pr.) Capstone.

—Easy Space Origami, 1 vol. 2011. (Easy Origami Ser.). (ENG.). 24p. (J). (gr. 1-3). lib. bdg. 25.99 *(978-1-4296-6001-3(5)*, 114938, Capstone Pr.) Capstone.

Hardyman, Roby. Origami Fun: Pets. 2017. (Origami Fun Ser.). (ENG., Illus.). 24p. (J). (gr. 3-8). lib. bdg. 26.95 *(978-1-62617-714-7(7)*, Express Bks.) Bellwether Media.

Hardyman, Robyn. Origami Fun: Aircraft. 2017. (Origami Fun Ser.). (ENG., Illus.). 24p. (J). (gr. 3-8). lib. bdg. 26.95 *(978-1-62617-707-9(4))* Bellwether Media.

—Origami Fun: Birds. 2017. (Origami Fun Ser.). (ENG., Illus.). 24p. (J). (gr. 3-8). lib. bdg. 26.95 *(978-1-62617-708-6(2)*, Express Bks.) Bellwether Media.

—Origami Fun: Dinosaurs. 2017. (Origami Fun Ser.). (ENG., Illus.). 24p. (J). (gr. 3-8). lib. bdg. 26.95 *(978-1-62617-709-3(0)*, Express Bks.) Bellwether Media.

—Origami Fun: Farm Animals. 2017. (Origami Fun Ser.). (ENG., Illus.). 24p. (J). (gr. 3-8). lib. bdg. 26.95 *(978-1-62617-710-9(4)*, Express Bks.) Bellwether Media.

—Origami Fun: Holidays. 2017. (Origami Fun Ser.). (ENG., Illus.). 24p. (J). (gr. 3-8). lib. bdg. 26.95 *(978-1-62617-711-6(2))* Bellwether Media.

—Origami Fun: Jungle Animals. 2017. (Origami Fun Ser.). (ENG., Illus.). 24p. (J). (gr. 3-8). lib. bdg. 26.95 *(978-1-62617-712-3(0)*, Express Bks.) Bellwether Media.

—Origami Fun: Ocean Animals. 2017. (Origami Fun Ser.). (ENG., Illus.). 24p. (J). (gr. 3-8). 26.95 *(978-1-62617-713-0(9)*, Express Bks.) Bellwether Media.

Holiday Origami: Set 2, 12 vols. 2014. (Holiday Origami Ser.). (ENG.). 32p. (J). (gr. 2-3). lib. bdg. 181.62 *(978-1-4777-5722-2(8)*, 2b42823e-804c-42ea-bd1f-ab4cb68f853e, PowerKids Pr.) Rosen Publishing Group, Inc., The.

Idea Network LA Inc. Origami: 15 Easy & Fun Origami Designs. 2006. (CHI & SPA.). (J). DVD 24.95 *(978-0-9773301-0-2(9))* Idea Network LA Inc.

Imamori, Mitsuhiko. Everybody Kirigami! 2014. (Illus.). 88p. pap. 18.95 *(978-1-939130-17-4(4)*, Vertical) Kodansha America, Inc.

Ives, Rob. Amazing Origami Animals. 2019. (Amazing Origami Ser.). (ENG., Illus.). 32p. (J). (gr. 3-6). 27.99 *(978-1-5415-0123-2(3)*, 0ea35943-0cac-44f5-851f-9c6204810dfa, Hungry Tomato (r)) Lerner Publishing Group.

—Amazing Origami Dinosaurs. 2019. (Amazing Origami Ser.). (ENG., Illus.). 32p. (J). (gr. 3-6). 27.99 *(978-1-5415-0126-3(8)*, 1d6ca8f5-d204-4d75-9d64-cce0e7c71196, Hungry Tomato (r)) Lerner Publishing Group.

—Amazing Origami Gifts. 2019. (Amazing Origami Ser.). (ENG., Illus.). 32p. (J). (gr. 3-6). 27.99 *(978-1-5415-0124-9(1)*, f0029e7e-fb82-4ee8-a099-6ff5561f5915, Hungry Tomato (r)) Lerner Publishing Group.

—Amazing Origami Vehicles. 2019. (Amazing Origami Ser.). (ENG., Illus.). 32p. (J). (gr. 3-6). 27.99 *(978-1-5415-0125-6(X)*, 1ea8c9f2-8daa-4666-ae38-6729383d770e, Hungry Tomato (r)) Lerner Publishing Group.

Jezewski, Mayumi. 500 Irresistible Origamis. 2018. (ENG., Illus.). 520p. pap. 9.95 *(978-0-2281-0150-5(6)*, e3ca196f-2578-4972-9d30-ada4c5999572) Firefly Bks., Ltd.

Johnson, Anne Akers. Origami. 88p. (J). 2005. (SPA., Illus.). spiral bd. 19.95 *(978-987-1078-26-4(9))* 2004. (ENG.). spiral bd. 19.95 *(978-987-1078-15-8(3))* Klutz Latino MEX. Dist: Independent Pubs. Group.

Kallevig, Christine P. Nature Fold-along Stories: Quick & Easy Origami Tales about Plants & Animals. 2009. (ENG., Illus.). 80p. (Orig.). (J). (gr. k-8). pap. 11.95 *(978-0-9628769-2-9(5))* Storytime Ink International.

Kenney, Karen Latchana. Folding Tech: Using Origami & Nature to Revolutionize Technology. 2020. (ENG., Illus.). 104p. (YA). (gr. 6-12). 37.32 *(978-1-5415-3304-2(6)*, c3c8a4a5-ccd8-4f11-bc7a-dcd4878fac09, Twenty-First Century Bks.) Lerner Publishing Group.

LaFosse, Michael. Making Origami Cards Step by Step, 1 vol. 2003. (Kid's Guide to Origami Ser.). (ENG., Illus.). 24p. (J). (gr. 3-4). lib. bdg. 28.93 *(978-0-8239-6701-8(8)*, de2e6bf4-8526-46ce-b567-7bade4fb8f44, PowerKids Pr.) Rosen Publishing Group, Inc., The.

—Making Origami Science Experiments Step by Step, 1 vol. 2003. (Kid's Guide to Origami Ser.). (ENG., Illus.). 24p. (J). (gr. 3-4). lib. bdg. 28.93 *(978-0-8239-6705-6(0)*, 3febf6e4-92a7-4741-934b-29290f9b05ea, PowerKids Pr.) Rosen Publishing Group, Inc., The.

LaFosse, Michael G. Making Origami Cards Step by Step. 2009. (Kid's Guide to Origami Ser.). 24p. (gr. 3-4). 47.90 *(978-1-61511-183-1(2)*, PowerKids Pr.) Rosen Publishing Group, Inc., The.

—Making Origami Masks Step by Step. 2009. (Kid's Guide to Origami Ser.). 24p. (gr. 3-4). 47.90 *(978-1-61511-188-6(3)*, PowerKids Pr.) Rosen Publishing Group, Inc., The.

—Making Origami Puzzles Step by Step. 2009. (Kid's Guide to Origami Ser.). 24p. (gr. 3-4). 47.90 *(978-1-61511-194-7(8)*, PowerKids Pr.) Rosen Publishing Group, Inc., The.

—Making Origami Science Experiments Step by Step. 2009. (Kid's Guide to Origami Ser.). 24p. (gr. 3-4). 47.90 *(978-1-61511-195-4(6)*, PowerKids Pr.) Rosen Publishing Group, Inc., The.

Lim, Annalees. Origami Crafts, 1 vol., 1. 2015. (10-Minute Crafts Ser.). (ENG., Illus.). 24p. (J). (gr. 2-3). pap. 11.60 *(978-1-5081-9097-4(6)*, 5eac8067-3dd2-421b-9031-d07da5bb6820, Windmill Bks.) Rosen Publishing Group, Inc., The.

Linde, Barbara M. Origami: Identifying Right Angles in Geometric Figures, 1 vol. (Math for the REAL World Ser.). 24p. (gr. 3-4). 2010. (ENG., Illus.). pap. 8.25 *(978-0-8239-8882-2(1)*, aad0e9e3-8a5d-430c-9246-c672e0800f9e) 2009. 45.00 *(978-1-60851-382-6(3))* 2003. (ENG., Illus.). (J). lib. bdg. 26.27 *(978-0-8239-8968-3(2)*, 01de8dbf-a7f7-447d-a41a-89358d04ad5f) Rosen Publishing Group, Inc., The. (PowerKids Pr.).

Maekawa, Jun & Origami. Genuine Japanese Origami: 33 Mathematical Models Based upon √2. Hatori, Koshiro, tr. 2012. (Dover Origami Papercraft Ser.). (ENG.). 160p. (gr. 7). pap. 24.95 *(978-0-486-48331-3(2)*, 483312) Dover Pubns., Inc.

Mastering Origami, 8 vols. 2016. (Mastering Origami Ser.). 48p. (ENG.). (gr. 5-6). lib. bdg. 118.40 *(978-0-7660-7943-4(0)*, bf6b76ef-5fd8-4148-8577-b2c5b8ff2185); (gr. 6-5). pap. 46.80 *(978-0-7660-7985-4(6))* Enslow Publishing, LLC.

Meinking, Mary. Easy Origami. 2008. (Origami Ser.). (ENG.). 32p. (J). (gr. 3-9). 30.65 *(978-1-4296-2020-8(X)*, 94912, Capstone Pr.) Capstone.

—Not-Quite-So-Easy Origami, 1 vol. 2008. (Origami Ser.). (ENG.). 32p. (J). (gr. 3-9). 28.65 *(978-1-4296-2021-5(8)*, 94913, Capstone Pr.) Capstone.

Meinking, Mary & Alexander, Chris. Easy Origami: A Step-By-Step Guide for Kids. 2010. (Origami Ser.). (ENG., Illus.). 112p. (J). (gr. 3-9). pap., pap., pap. 12.95 *(978-1-4296-5034-2(6)*, 113084, Capstone Pr.) Capstone.

Miles, Lisa. Origami Birds & Butterflies, 1 vol. 2013. (Amazing Origami Ser.). 32p. (J). (gr. 2-3). (ENG.). pap. 11.50 *(978-1-4339-9645-0(6)*, 217a5191-9ff1-4702-81e1-ef72b3479194); pap. 63.00 *(978-1-4339-9646-7(4))*; (ENG., Illus.). lib. bdg. 29.27 *(978-1-4339-9644-3(8)*, 0ced0108-f225-481b-b7ea-6a5d7d567efd) Stevens, Gareth Publishing LLLP.

—Origami Dinosaurs, 1 vol. 2013. (Amazing Origami Ser.). 32p. (J). (gr. 2-3). (ENG.). pap. 11.50 *(978-1-4339-9649-8(9)*, c3d99caa-088b-4159-b390-36e1d69910c7); pap. 63.00 *(978-1-4339-9650-4(2))*; (ENG., Illus.). lib. bdg. 29.27 *(978-1-4339-9648-1(0)*, b0b0bef7-b222-4830-a7b2-f087dd008595) Stevens, Gareth Publishing LLLP.

—Origami Farm Animals, 1 vol. 2013. (Amazing Origami Ser.). 32p. (J). (gr. 2-3). (ENG.). pap. 11.50 *(978-1-4339-9653-5(7)*, 6f1a15f2-5302-478c-8a11-48fd5eee1c2a); pap. 63.00 *(978-1-4339-9654-2(5))*; (ENG., Illus.). lib. bdg. 29.27 *(978-1-4339-9652-8(9)*, 795168cf-27ac-47b6-b2c4-c0b9a4d2e0a7) Stevens, Gareth Publishing LLLP.

—Origami Pets, 1 vol. 2013. (Amazing Origami Ser.). 32p. (J). (gr. 2-3). (ENG.). pap. 11.50 *(978-1-4339-9657-3(X)*, 6e6f4732-641b-4de2-acaa-eceb8d590065); pap. 63.00 *(978-1-4339-9658-0(8))*; (ENG., Illus.). lib. bdg. 29.27 *(978-1-4339-9656-6(1)*, 40adfff3-6af6-4f2f-b379-6f2ebb735abe) Stevens, Gareth Publishing LLLP.

—Origami Sea Creatures, 1 vol. 2013. (Amazing Origami Ser.). 32p. (J). (gr. 2-3). (ENG.). pap. 11.50 *(978-1-4339-9661-0(8)*, 90f44aac-29ae-44b4-93bd-e966b71226e8); pap. 63.00 *(978-1-4339-9662-7(6))*; (ENG., Illus.). lib. bdg. 29.27 *(978-1-4339-9660-3(X)*, a11891c0-4854-4ac1-bac3-b849f7c98e9f) Stevens, Gareth Publishing LLLP.

—Origami Wild Animals, 1 vol. 2013. (Amazing Origami Ser.). 32p. (J). (gr. 2-3). (ENG.). pap. 11.50 *(978-1-4339-9665-8(0)*, bdf1c2fa-7a5e-40ae-9f63-11a9e8026d73); pap. 63.00 *(978-1-4339-9666-5(9))*; (ENG., Illus.). lib. bdg. 29.27 *(978-1-4339-9664-1(2)*, 232c5825-b1aa-4209-a962-8ead8ba2170a) Stevens, Gareth Publishing LLLP.

Montevecchi, Mila Bertinetti. Origami for Kids: 20 Projects to Make Plus 100 Papers to Fold. 2019. (ENG., Illus.). 276p. (J). pap. 24.99 *(978-1-64124-028-4(8)*, 0284) Fox Chapel Publishing Co., Inc.

Montroll, John. Batman Origami: Amazing Folding Projects for the Dark Knight. Ku, Min Sung, illus. 2015. (DC Origami Ser.). (ENG.). 48p. (J). (gr. 3-7). lib. bdg. 28.65 *(978-1-4914-1786-7(2)*, 127202, Stone Arch Bks.) Capstone.

—DC Origami. Ku, Min Sung, illus. 2015. (DC Origami Ser.). (ENG.). 48p. (J). (gr. 4-5). 122.60 *(978-1-4914-1790-4(0)*, 22132, Stone Arch Bks.) Capstone.

—DC Super Heroes Origami: 21 Folding Projects for Batman, Superman, & More! 2017. (J). lib. bdg. *(978-1-5157-5930-0(X)*, Capstone Young Readers) Capstone.

—Dollar Bill Origami. 2003. (Illus.). 120p. (YA). per. 14.94 net. *(978-1-877656-17-0(8))* Antroll Publishing Co.

—Easy Origami Animals 4D: An Augmented Reading Paper Folding Experience. 2018. (Easy Origami Animals 4D Ser.). (ENG.). 32p. (J). (gr. 3-5). 135.96 *(978-1-5435-1316-5(6)*, 27947, Capstone Classroom) Capstone.

—Easy Origami Jungle Animals: 4D an Augmented Reading Paper Folding Experience. 2018. (Easy Origami Animals 4D Ser.). (ENG., Illus.). 32p. (J). (gr. 3-5). lib. bdg. 33.99 *(978-1-5435-1306-6(9)*, 137752, Capstone Pr.) Capstone.

—Easy Origami Polar Animals: 4D an Augmented Reading Paper Folding Experience. 2018. (Easy Origami Animals 4D Ser.). (ENG., Illus.). 32p. (J). (gr. 3-5). lib. bdg. 33.99 *(978-1-5435-1304-2(2)*, 137750, Capstone Pr.) Capstone.

—Easy Origami Woodland Animals: 4D an Augmented Reading Paper Folding Experience. 2018. (Easy Origami Animals 4D Ser.). (ENG., Illus.). 32p. (J). (gr. 3-5). lib. bdg. 33.99 *(978-1-5435-1305-9(0)*, 137751, Capstone Pr.) Capstone.

—Justice League Origami: Amazing Folding Projects for the JLA. Ku, Min Sung, illus. 2015. (DC Origami Ser.). (ENG.). 48p. (J). (gr. 3-7). lib. bdg. 28.65 *(978-1-4914-1789-8(7)*, 127205, Stone Arch Bks.) Capstone.

—Superman Origami: Amazing Folding Projects for the Man of Steel. Ku, Min Sung, illus. 2015. (DC Origami Ser.). (ENG.). 48p. (J). (gr. 3-7). lib. bdg. 28.65 *(978-1-4914-1787-4(0)*, 127203, Stone Arch Bks.) Capstone.

—Wonder Woman Origami: Amazing Folding Projects for the Warrior Princess. Ku, Min Sung, illus. 2015. (DC Origami Ser.). (ENG.). 48p. (J). (gr. 3-7). lib. bdg. 28.65 *(978-1-4914-1788-1(9)*, 127204, Stone Arch Bks.) Capstone.

O'Brien, Eileen & Needham, Kate. Origami Pack. 2004. (Activity Kits Ser.). 24p. (J). act. bk. ed. 14.95 *(978-0-7945-0460-1(4))* EDC Publishing.

Ono, Mari. Fun Origami for Children: Pets! 12 Amazing Animals to Fold. 2018. (ENG., Illus.). 32p. (J). pap. 12.95 *(978-1-78249-580-2(0)*, 1782495800, CICO Books) Ryland Peters & Small GBR. Dist: WIPRO.

Ono, Mari & Ono, Roshin. Fun Origami for Children: Flight! 12 Paper Planes & Other Flying Objects to Fold for Fun! 2018. (ENG., Illus.). 32p. (J). pap. 12.95 *(978-1-78249-579-6(7)*, 9124101680, CICO Books) Ryland Peters & Small GBR. Dist: WIPRO.

—Origami for Children: 35 Easy-to-Follow Step-by-Step Projects. 2008. (ENG., Illus.). 128p. *(978-1-906094-38-6(1)*, CICO Books) Ryland Peters & Small.

—Origami for Children: Book & Paper Pack with 35 Projects, Pack. 2009. (ENG., Illus.). 128p. (J). (gr. 3-11). pap. 19.95 *(978-1-906525-80-4(3)*, 1906525803, CICO Books) Ryland Peters & Small GBR. Dist: WIPRO.

Ono, Mari & Shingu, Fumiaki. Fun Origami for Children: Wild! 12 Amazing Animals to Fold. 2017. (ENG., Illus.). 32p. (J). (gr. 5-7). pap. 12.95 *(978-1-78249-467-6(7)*, 1782494677, Cico Kidz) Ryland Peters & Small GBR. Dist: WIPRO.

Ono, Mari & Takai, Hiroaki. Fun Origami for Children: Dino! 12 Daring Dinosaurs to Fold. 2017. (ENG., Illus.). 32p. (J). (gr. 5-7). pap. 12.95 *(978-1-78249-466-9(9)*, 1782494669, Cico Kidz) Ryland Peters & Small GBR. Dist: WIPRO.

Origami Army. 2013. (Origami Army Ser.). 32p. (J). (gr. 3-6). pap. 282.00 *(978-1-4777-2733-1(7))*; (gr. 3-6). pap. 47.00 *(978-1-4777-2732-4(9))*; (ENG.). (gr. 4-5). 121.08 *(978-1-4777-1548-2(7)*, 21d238b7-5479-4501-b291-31e54d52060b) Rosen Publishing Group, Inc., The. (PowerKids Pr.).

Origami Holidays, 12 vols. 2016. (Origami Holidays Ser.). 32p. (gr. 3-3). (ENG.). 175.62 *(978-1-4994-2252-8(0)*, 945c765a-6741-4f50-8bbf-fa1d75f95cd5); pap. 70.50 *(978-1-4994-2452-2(3))* Rosen Publishing Group, Inc., The. (PowerKids Pr.).

Origami Safari. 2014. (Origami Safari Ser.). 32p. (J). (gr. 3-6). 165.00 *(978-1-4777-9113-4(2))* Windmill Bks.

Owen, Ruth. Christmas & Hanukkah Origami, 1 vol. 2012. (Holiday Origami Ser.). (ENG., Illus.). 32p. (J). (gr. 2-3). 30.27 *(978-1-4488-7860-4(8)*, 5e0d435a-c157-48a9-a337-2b5721a423ef); pap. 12.75 *(978-1-4488-7919-9(1)*, cadb6e3d-2209-4b3c-8cb2-2d3ca3e172f5) Rosen Publishing Group, Inc., The. (PowerKids Pr.).

—Desert Animals, 1 vol. 2014. (Origami Safari Ser.). (ENG., Illus.). 32p. (J). (gr. 2-3). pap. 12.75 *(978-1-4777-9242-1(2)*, 01398ad7-8d19-4733-8937-5321e16a5359, Windmill Bks.) Rosen Publishing Group, Inc., The.

—Easter Origami, 1 vol. 2012. (Holiday Origami Ser.). (ENG., Illus.). 32p. (J). (gr. 2-3). 30.27 *(978-1-4488-7861-1(6)*, 4272bc66-0cb3-4322-8f2d-94283c64be72); pap. 12.75 *(978-1-4488-7920-5(5)*, d2b384c1-cfcf-4c22-92c0-50c3b0db6e2b) Rosen Publishing Group, Inc., The. (PowerKids Pr.).

—Grassland Animals, 1 vol. 2014. (Origami Safari Ser.). (ENG., Illus.). 32p. (J). (gr. 2-3). lib. bdg. 30.27 *(978-1-4777-9253-7(8)*, d8de5b15-1109-4918-bd8e-1d281155910a, Windmill Bks.) Rosen Publishing Group, Inc., The.

—Halloween Origami, 1 vol. 2012. (Holiday Origami Ser.). (ENG., Illus.). 32p. (J). (gr. 2-3). 30.27 *(978-1-4488-7862-8(4)*, 985b4bde-c1ad-42f4-b9cb-085f5de4da0a); pap. 12.75 *(978-1-4488-7921-2(3)*, d57228a0-bc8b-408e-aa8d-f240d1a8682e) Rosen Publishing Group, Inc., The. (PowerKids Pr.).

—Independence Day Origami, 1 vol. 2012. (Holiday Origami Ser.). (ENG., Illus.). 32p. (J). (gr. 2-3). 30.27 *(978-1-4488-7863-5(2)*, 1830f606-aafc-4110-9c99-e30932679ee3); pap. 12.75 *(978-1-4488-7922-9(1)*, b926e860-9223-42a7-800a-67011231f16a) Rosen Publishing Group, Inc., The. (PowerKids Pr.).

—Jungle Animals, 1 vol. 2014. (Origami Safari Ser.). (ENG., Illus.). 32p. (J). (gr. 2-3). lib. bdg. 30.27 *(978-1-4777-9238-4(4)*, 50c51553-ca9b-43d6-b0b6-37943382537c, Windmill Bks.) Rosen Publishing Group, Inc., The.

—More Christmas Origami, 1 vol. 2014. (Holiday Origami Ser.). (ENG., Illus.). 32p. (J). (gr. 2-3). 30.27 *(978-1-4777-5706-2(6)*, bf15012d-ce90-4736-990f-d05495dc67d3, PowerKids Pr.) Rosen Publishing Group, Inc., The.

—More Halloween Origami, 1 vol. 2014. (Holiday Origami Ser.). (ENG.). 32p. (J). (gr. 2-3). 30.27 *(978-1-4777-5702-4(3)*, 9a5e29ce-af44-47b7-accc-235bb4810d98, PowerKids Pr.) Rosen Publishing Group, Inc., The.

—More Hanukkah Origami, 1 vol. 2014. (Holiday Origami Ser.). (ENG., Illus.). 32p. (J). (gr. 2-3). 30.27 *(978-1-4777-5714-7(7)*, cb376c6d-ca42-4d79-9d7d-867d502c0151, PowerKids Pr.) Rosen Publishing Group, Inc., The.

—More Thanksgiving Origami, 1 vol. 2014. (Holiday Origami Ser.). (ENG., Illus.). 32p. (J). (gr. 2-3). 30.27 *(978-1-4777-5710-9(4)*, 4369907f-e861-4a42-92b4-2d70c7f0a490, PowerKids Pr.) Rosen Publishing Group, Inc., The.

—More Valentine's Day Origami, 1 vol. 2014. (Holiday Origami Ser.). (ENG., Illus.). 32p. (J). (gr. 2-3). 30.27 *(978-1-4777-5698-0(1)*, 763a2325-9a75-4449-9a32-994a9dbdfaa5, PowerKids Pr.) Rosen Publishing Group, Inc., The.

—Mountain Animals, 1 vol. 2014. (Origami Safari Ser.). (ENG., Illus.). 32p. (J). (gr. 2-3). lib. bdg. 30.27

(978-1-4777-9257-5(0), f50c8359-ff6a-4cc0-b588-52347afedb13, Windmill Bks.) Rosen Publishing Group, Inc., The.

—Ocean Animals, 1 vol. 2014. (Origami Safari Ser.). (ENG., Illus.). 32p. (J). (gr. 2-3). lib. bdg. 30.27 (978-1-4777-9249-0(X), 722f7fdc-ce3a-4688-a6f6-1310864dd48b, Windmill Bks.) Rosen Publishing Group, Inc., The.

—Polar Animals, 1 vol. 2014. (Origami Safari Ser.). (ENG., Illus.). 32p. (J). (gr. 2-3). lib. bdg. 30.27 (978-1-4777-9245-2(7), 8c95d87c-247e-4a5d-b4a0-692a1e4b06f4, Windmill Bks.) Rosen Publishing Group, Inc., The.

—St. Patrick's Day Origami, 1 vol. 2014. (Holiday Origami Ser.). (ENG., Illus.). 32p. (J). (gr. 2-3). 30.27 (978-1-4777-5718-5(X), 62f1622e-cff7-4989-ab7c-dfe7249a03be, PowerKids Pr.) Rosen Publishing Group, Inc., The.

—Thanksgiving Origami, 1 vol. 2012. (Holiday Origami Ser.). (ENG., Illus.). 32p. (J). (gr. 2-3). 30.27 (978-1-4488-7864-2(0), 03e395a0-6577-4961-abdc-1baf872dd25e); pap. 12.75 (978-1-4488-7923-6(X), 6bafb57d-e2fd-47de-95b1-031628624b51) Rosen Publishing Group, Inc., The. (PowerKids Pr.).

—Valentine's Day Origami, 1 vol. 2012. (Holiday Origami Ser.). (ENG., Illus.). 32p. (J). (gr. 2-3). 30.27 (978-1-4488-7865-9(9), 5d861dd6-ac8f-47e4-b3bd-ea0f1d195d7e); pap. 12.75 (978-1-4488-7924-3(8), 1465687d-e3ff-4c3d-9fee-ab16d11fd7fc) Rosen Publishing Group, Inc., The. (PowerKids Pr.).

Palacios, Vicente. Origami Animals. 2012. (Dover Origami Papercraft Ser.). (ENG., Illus.). 64p. (gr. 7). pap. 9.95 (978-0-486-47874-6(2)) Dover Pubns., Inc.

Ramon, Emilie & Ramon, Emilie. 500 Fun Origamis. 2018. (ENG., Illus.). 520p. pap. 9.95 (978-0-2281-0148-2(4), 370d42d2-0386-4797-85ed-4e6db54814fa) Firefly Bks., Ltd.

Rau, Dana Meachen. Folding Origami. Petelinsek, Kathleen, illus. 2013. (How-To Library). (ENG.). 32p. (J). (gr. 3-6). 32.07 (978-1-62431-145-1(8), 202900); pap. 14.21 (978-1-62431-277-9(2), 202902) Cherry Lake Publishing.

Robinson, Nick. My First Origami Book — Christmas: With 24 Sheets of Origami Paper! 2013. (Dover Origami Papercraft Ser.). (ENG.). 96p. (J). (gr. 2). pap. 12.99 (978-0-486-49182-0(X), 49182X) Dover Pubns., Inc.

Schultz, Walter-Alexandre. Origami Dinosaurs, 1 vol. 2017. (Exciting Origami Ser.). (ENG.). 48p. (gr. 3-3). lib. bdg. 29.60 (978-0-7660-8650-0(X), 4a9dbe26-33e7-4819-9034-3fbce73ae335) Enslow Publishing, LLC.

Schwartz, Heather E. Origami: Dividing Fractions. 2019. (Mathematics in the Real World Ser.). (ENG., Illus.). 32p. (gr. 5-8). pap. 11.99 (978-1-4258-5877-3(5)) Teacher Created Materials, Inc.

Shingu, Fumiaki. Easy Origami. 2007. (Illus.). 64p. (J). (978-1-60311-000-6(3)) Mud Puddle, Inc.

Song, Sok. Everyday Origami: A Foldable Fashion Guide. Song, Sok, illus. 2016. (Fashion Origami Ser.). (ENG., Illus.). 48p. (J). (gr. 4-8). lib. bdg. 32.65 (978-1-5157-1630-3(9), 132464, Capstone Pr.) Capstone.

—Origami Accessories: A Foldable Fashion Guide. Song, Sok, illus. 2016. (Fashion Origami Ser.). (ENG., Illus.). 48p. (J). (gr. 4-8). lib. bdg. 32.65 (978-1-5157-1623-5(6), 132463, Capstone Pr.) Capstone.

—Origami Chic: A Guide to Foldable Fashion. Song, Sok, illus. 2016. (ENG., Illus.). 240p. (J). (gr. 3-3). pap., pap., pap. 14.95 (978-1-62370-771-2(4), 132466, Capstone Young Readers) Capstone.

—Origami Outfits: A Foldable Fashion Guide. Song, Sok, illus. 2016. (Fashion Origami Ser.). (ENG., Illus.). 48p. (J). (gr. 4-8). lib. bdg. 32.65 (978-1-5157-1631-0(7), 132465, Capstone Pr.) Capstone.

Souleres, Caroline & Souleres, Caroline. 500 Fluorescent Origamis. 2018. (ENG., Illus.). 520p. pap. 9.95 (978-0-2281-0149-9(2), 228ca8e1-d8da-41d7-8ef3-feea9191ee8c) Firefly Bks., Ltd.

Stadler, Charlotte. Origami. 2011. (Early Connections Ser.). (J). (978-1-61672-614-0(8)) Benchmark Education Co.

Thomas, Rachael L. Origami: Classic Paper Folding. 2019. (Cool Paper Art Ser.). (ENG., Illus.). 32p. (J). (gr. 3-6). lib. bdg. 34.21 (978-1-5321-1946-0(1), 32477, Checkerboard Library) ABDO Publishing Co.

Troupe, Thomas Kingsley. Magnet Power! Science Adventures with MAG-3000 the Origami Robot, 1 vol. Christoph, Jamey, illus. 2013. (Origami Science Adventures Ser.). (ENG.). 24p. (J). (gr. -1-3). pap. 6.95 (978-1-4048-8070-2(4), 121841, Picture Window Bks.) Capstone.

Tsin, Justin. What Would You Imagine? 2008. (Illus.). 32p. (gr. k-3). per. 19.95 (978-1-60396-039-7(2)) Santillana USA Publishing Co., Inc.

Yates, Jane. Dollar Bill Origami, 1 vol. 2016. (Cool Crafts for Kids Ser.). (ENG.). 32p. (J). (gr. 3-3). pap. 12.75 (978-1-4994-8226-3(4), 5c547e7d-26e0-4eef-a8ad-3f1e9983fd2b, Windmill Bks.) Rosen Publishing Group, Inc., The.

Yee, Tammy. Easy Butterfly Origami. 2015. (Dover Origami Papercraft Ser.). (ENG.). 64p. (gr. 3). pap. 9.99 (978-0-486-78457-1(6), 784576) Dover Pubns., Inc.

ORIGIN OF HUMAN BEINGS

see Human Beings—Origin

ORIGIN OF SPECIES

see Evolution

ORNAMENT

see Decoration and Ornament

ORNAMENTAL ALPHABETS

see Lettering

ORNAMENTAL DESIGN

see Design, Decorative

ORNITHOLOGY

see Birds

ORPHANAGES

Benge, Janet & Benge, Geoff. Christian Heroes - Then & Now - Lillian Trasher: The Greatest Wonder in Egypt. 2003. (Christian Heroes Ser.). (ENG.). 189p. (YA). pap. 11.99 (978-1-57658-305-0(8)) YWAM Publishing.

Jocelyn, Marthe. A Home for Foundlings: A Lord Museum Book. 2005. (Lord Museum Ser.). (Illus.). 120p. (J). (gr. 5-12). pap. 16.95 (978-0-88776-709-8(5), Tundra Bks.) Tundra Bks. CAN. Dist: Penguin Random Hse. LLC.

Richards, Laurae. Coming Home. 2013. 28p. pap. 16.95 (978-1-4624-0769-9(2), Inspiring Voices) Author Solutions, LLC.

Skrypuch, Marsha Forchuk. Last Airlift: A Vietnamese Orphan's Rescue from War   (ENG., Illus.). 120p. (J). (gr. 3-7). 2013. pap. 12.95 (978-0-9869495-1-7(5)) 2012. 17.95 (978-0-9869495-4-8(X)) Pajama Pr. CAN. Dist: Publishers Group West (PGW).

ORPHANAGES—FICTION

Alders, Willa. Leafy Finds a Home. Burns, Sandra, illus. 2013. 24p. pap. 8.99 (978-1-938768-13-2(2)) Gypsy Pubns.

Authords, D. K. Being Alone. 2013. 120p. pap. 19.95 (978-1-63000-114-8(7)) America Star Bks.

Bartók, Mira. The Wonderling. Bartók, Mira, illus. 2017. (ENG., Illus.). 464p. (J). (gr. 5-9). 21.99 (978-0-7636-9121-9(6)) Candlewick Pr.

Bartok, Mira. The Wonderling. Bartok, Mira, illus. 2019. (ENG., Illus.). 464p. (J). (gr. 5-9). pap. 9.99 (978-1-5362-0890-0(6)) Candlewick Pr.

Bastian, Kimberlee Ann. The Orphan, the Soulcatcher, & the Black Blizzard. 2012. 258p. pap. 22.50 (978-1-105-06633-7(9)) Lulu.com GBR. Dist: Lulu Pr., Inc.

Bragg, Jane. Teddy Bears Christmas Miracle. 2009. (ENG.). 49p. pap. 18.70 (978-0-557-22087-8(4)) Lulu Pr., Inc.

Brezenoff, Steve. The Sleeper, 1 vol. Percival, Tom, illus. 2012. (Ravens Pass Ser.). (ENG.). 96p. (J). (gr. 3-6). pap. 6.15 (978-1-4342-4211-2(0), 120269); lib. bdg. 25.32 (978-1-4342-3792-7(3), 117091) Capstone. (Stone Arch Bks.).

Burch, Genny. My Name Is Bobby Claus: A fictional Christmas story for Children. 2009. 36p. pap. 15.99 (978-1-4490-4233-2(3)) AuthorHouse.

Chapmon, Rachelle. Mari. 2009. 148p. pap. 11.99 (978-1-4389-6310-5(6)) AuthorHouse.

Darke, J. A. The Screaming Bridge. Evergreen, Nelson, illus. 2015. (Spine Shivers Ser.). (ENG.). 128p. (J). (gr. 4-6). lib. bdg. 27.32 (978-1-4965-0219-3(1), 128033, Stone Arch Bks.) Capstone.

Doty, Kathryn Adams. Wild Orphan. 2006. (ENG.). 144p. (gr. 3-7). per. 14.95 (978-1-889020-20-4(6)) Edinborough Pr.

Durrant, S. E. Little Bits of Sky. Harnett, Katie, illus. 2017. (ENG.). 208p. (J). (gr. 3-7). 16.95 (978-0-8234-3839-6(2)) Holiday Hse., Inc.

Flores-Galbis, Enrique. 90 Miles to Havana. 2012. (ENG.). 304p. (J). (gr. 4-7). pap. 8.99 (978-1-250-00559-5(0), 900081145) Square Fish.

Gazdag, Adam. The Non Born Heir. 2010. (ENG.). 313p. pap. 19.27 (978-0-557-17709-7(X)) Lulu Pr., Inc.

Griser, Carol. Breona's New Life. 2009. 24p. pap. 14.00 (978-1-4389-4975-8(8)) AuthorHouse.

Grizzard, Sue H. Princess Caylee: An Incredible Birthday Wish Come True. 2009. 44p. pap. 19.95 (978-1-4490-4001-7(2)) AuthorHouse.

Hargrave, Kiran Millwood. The Island at the End of Everything. 2018. (ENG.). 256p. (J). (gr. 5). lib. bdg. 19.99 (978-0-553-53533-4(1), Knopf Bks. for Young Readers) Random Hse. Children's Bks.

Hueller, Andy. Skipping Stones at the Center of the Earth: A Middle Grade Novel. 2011. 241p. (J). pap. 8.99 (978-1-59955-488-4(7), Bonneville Bks.) Cedar Fort, Inc./CFI Distribution.

Johnson, D. C. & Rowan, Ron. The Secret of MeadowBrook Orphanage. 2012. 528p. (gr. -1). pap. 18.30 (978-1-4669-1866-5(7)) Trafford Publishing.

Khan, Rukhsana. Wanting Mor, 1 vol. 2009. (ENG.). 192p. (J). (gr. 5-9). pap. 10.99 (978-0-88899-862-0(7)) Groundwood Bks. CAN. Dist: Publishers Group West (PGW).

Laurie, Victoria. Oracles of Delphi Keep. (Oracles of Delphi Keep Ser.: 1). (J). 2010. 576p. (gr. 3-7). 8.99 (978-0-440-42258-7(2), Yearling)1. 2009. (ENG.). 560p. (gr. 6-8). lib. bdg. 22.44 (978-0-385-90561-9(0), Delacorte Pr.) Random Hse. Children's Bks.

Legrand, Claire. The Cavendish Home for Boys & Girls. Watts, Sarah, illus. (ENG.). (J). (gr. 5). 2013. 368p. pap. 8.99 (978-1-4424-4292-4(1)) 2012. 352p. 17.99 (978-1-4424-4291-7(3)) Simon & Schuster Bks. For Young Readers. (Simon & Schuster Bks. For Young Readers).

Lynn, Jenna. Metropolis Orphanage: Book 1. Cruz, Abigail Dela, illus. 2018. (Robyn Hood Ser.). (ENG.). 48p. (J). (gr. 3-7). lib. bdg. 34.21 (978-1-5321-3376-3(6), 31175, Spellbound) Magic Wagon.

Mandeville, Terry M. Just Waiting for My Family. l.t. ed. 2005. (Illus.). 52p. (J). 14.95 (978-0-9762475-0-0(X)) Mandeville, Terry M.

Nesbet, Anne. The Orphan Band of Springdale. 2018. (ENG.). 448p. (J). (gr. 5-9). 18.99 (978-0-7636-8804-2(5)) Candlewick Pr.

Panckridge, Michael & Harvey, Pam. Ghost of a Chance. 2007. (ENG.). 208p. (978-0-207-20063-2(7)) HarperCollins Pubs. Australia.

Patterson, Valerie O. Operation Oleander. 2015. (ENG.). 192p. (J). (gr. 5-7). pap. 7.99 (978-0-544-43935-1(X), 1596834, Clarion Bks.) HarperCollins Pubs.

Pinkney, Andrea Davis. Bird in a Box. 2012. (ENG., Illus.). 288p. (J). (gr. 3-7). pap. 8.99 (978-0-316-07402-5(0)) Little, Brown Bks. for Young Readers.

—Bird in a Box. Qualls, Sean, illus. 2012. (J). lib. bdg. 18.45 (978-0-606-26157-9(5)) Turtleback.

Riggs, Ransom. Hollow City. Riggs, Ransom, illus. 2015. (Miss Peregrine's Peculiar Children Ser.: 2). (Illus.). lib. bdg. 22.10 (978-0-606-36394-5(7)) Turtleback.

—Hollow City: The Second Novel of Miss Peregrine's Peculiar Children. 2015. (Miss Peregrine's Peculiar Children Ser.: 2). (Illus.). 416p. (YA). (gr. 9). pap. 14.99 (978-1-59474-735-9(0)) Quirk Bks.

—Hollow City: The Second Novel of Miss Peregrine's Peculiar Children. Riggs, Ransom, illus. 2014. (Miss Peregrine's Peculiar Children Ser.: 2). (Illus.). 352p. (YA). (gr. 9). 18.99 (978-1-59474-612-3(5)) Quirk Bks.

—Hollow City: the Graphic Novel: The Second Novel of Miss Peregrine's Peculiar Children. 2016. (Miss Peregrine's Peculiar Children: the Graphic Novel Ser.: 2). (ENG., Illus.). 272p. (YA). (gr. 8-17). 20.00 (978-0-316-30679-9(7)) Yen Pr. LLC.

—Miss Peregrine's Home for Peculiar Children. (Miss Peregrine's Peculiar Children Ser.: 1). (Illus.). (YA). (gr. 9). 2013. 384p. pap. 14.99 (978-1-59474-603-1(6)) 2011. 352p. 18.99 (978-1-59474-476-1(9)) Quirk Bks.

—Miss Peregrine's Home for Peculiar Children. l.t. ed. 2012. (ENG.). 484p. (J). (gr. 8-12). 23.99 (978-1-4104-5023-4(6)) Thorndike Pr.

—Miss Peregrine's Home for Peculiar Children. 2013. (Miss Peregrine's Peculiar Children Ser.: 1). (SWE.). lib. bdg. 22.10 (978-0-606-32081-8(4)) Turtleback.

—Miss Peregrine's Home for Peculiar Children (Movie Tie-In Edition) 2016. (Miss Peregrine's Peculiar Children Ser.: 1). (Illus.). 392p. (YA). (gr. 9). pap. 11.99 (978-1-59474-902-5(7)) Quirk Bks.

—Miss Peregrine's Peculiar Children Boxed Set, 3 vols. 2015. (Miss Peregrine's Peculiar Children Ser.). (Illus.). 1216p. (YA). (gr. 9). 44.97 (978-1-59474-890-5(X)) Quirk Bks.

Riggs, Ransom, et al. Miss Peregrine's Home for Peculiar Children. 2011. pap. (978-1-59474-574-4(9)) Quirk Bks.

Roesti, Delores. Mareena Maree Mulligan & the Flying Wheel Chair: Book 1: School Days. 2007. 81p. pap. 9.95 (978-0-7414-4048-8(2)) Infinity Publishing.

Roesti, Delores Anne. Mareena Maree Mulligan & the Flying Wheelchair Book #3: Temptation's Talking, 1 vol. 2010. 93p. pap. 16.95 (978-1-4489-6692-9(2)) PublishAmerica, Inc.

Sharp, Cathy. The Boy with the Latch Key (Halfpenny Orphans, Book 4) 2018. (Halfpenny Orphans Ser.: 4). (ENG.). 416p. 12.99 (978-0-00-827672-0(2), HarperCollins) HarperCollins Pubs.

Stewart, Trenton Lee. The Extraordinary Education of Nicholas Benedict. Sudyka, Diana, illus. (Mysterious Benedict Society Ser.). (ENG.). (J). (gr. 3-7). 2013. 496p. pap. 9.99 (978-0-316-17620-0(6)) 2012. 480p. 39.99 (978-0-316-17619-4(2)) Little, Brown Bks. for Young Readers.

—The Extraordinary Education of Nicholas Benedict. 2013. (Mysterious Benedict Society Ser.: 0). (J). lib. bdg. 19.65 (978-0-606-31743-6(0)) Turtleback.

Thompson-Swift, Joseph. The Adventures of Primrose Perfect. 2011. 248p. pap. (978-1-907652-88-2(4)) Grosvenor Hse. Publishing Ltd.

Tripp, Valerie. Nellie's Promise. England, Tamara, ed. Andreasen, Dan, illus. 2004. (American Girls Collection: Samantha Stories Ser.). (ENG.). 96p. (J). (gr. 2-4). pap. 18.69 (978-1-58485-890-4(7)) American Girl Publishing, Inc.

Williams, Karen Lynn. Lubuto Means Light. Grifalconi, Ann, illus. 2010. (ENG.). 32p. 16.95 (978-1-59078-716-8(1)) Highlights Pr., c/o Highlights for Children, Inc.

Woodell, Rejoice. Kohara, the White Veiled City. 2011. 138p. pap. 19.99 (978-1-4568-7969-3(3)) Xlibris Corp.

The Year We Sailed the Sun. 2015. (ENG., Illus.). 432p. (J). (gr. 3-7). 17.99 (978-0-689-85827-7(2), Atheneum/Richard Jackson Bks.) Simon & Schuster Children's Publishing.

ORPHANS

DePrince, Michaela & Deprince, Elaine. Ballerina Dreams: from Orphan to Dancer (Step into Reading, Step 4) Morrison, Frank, illus. 2014. (Step into Reading Ser.). (ENG.). 48p. (J). (gr. 2-4). 5.99 (978-0-385-75515-3(5), Random Hse. Bks. for Young Readers) Random Hse. Children's Bks.

Ellis, Deborah. Our Stories, Our Songs: African Children Talk about AIDS, 1 vol. 2005. (ENG., Illus.). 112p. (YA). (gr. 6-12). pap. 14.95 (978-1-55041-912-2(9), 4f99143f-bf44-4ce2-b81c-0ff5552486cf) éditeur, Annika Parance CAN. Dist: Firefly Bks., Ltd.

Gutwein, Austin & Hillard, Todd. Take Your Best Shot: Do Something Bigger Than Yourself, 1 vol. 2009. (ENG., Illus.). 240p. (YA). (gr. 7-12). pap. 14.99 (978-1-4003-1515-4(8), Tommy Nelson) Nelson, Thomas Inc.

Langston-George, Rebecca. Orphan Trains: Taking the Rails to a New Life. 2016. (Encounter: Narrative Nonfiction Stories Ser.). (ENG., Illus.). 128p. (J). (gr. 3-6). pap. 6.95 (978-1-62370-630-2(0), 131148); lib. bdg. 31.32 (978-1-4914-8551-4(5), 131147) Capstone. (Capstone Young Readers).

Littlefield, Holly. Children of the Orphan Trains. 2005. (Picture the American Past Ser.). (Illus.). 48p. (gr. 2-5). lib. bdg. 22.60 (978-1-57505-466-7(3)) Lerner Publishing Group.

Lynette, Rachel. Ana Dodson: Advocate for Peruvian Orphans, 1 vol. 2007. (Young Heroes Ser.). (ENG., Illus.). 48p. (gr. 4-8). lib. bdg. 37.33 (978-0-7377-3865-0(0), 6d90ce7f-1cc6-4e42-965d-a5e47e40dd5a, KidHaven Publishing) Greenhaven Publishing LLC.

MacKenzie, Catherine. Helen Roseveare: What's in the Parcel? rev. ed. 2012. (Little Lights Ser.). (ENG.). 24p. (J). 7.99 (978-1-84550-383-3(X), a968cdf5-b466-4c2a-886f-66cec838ae8d) Christian Focus Pubns. GBR. Dist: Baker & Taylor Publisher Services (BTPS).

Naidoo, Beverley, intro. Making It Home: Real-Life Stories from Children Forced to Flee. 2005. (ENG., Illus.). 128p. (J). (gr. 3-7). 6.99 (978-0-14-240455-3(1), Puffin Books) Penguin Young Readers Group.

Raum, Elizabeth. Orphan Trains: An Interactive History Adventure. 2010. (You Choose: History Ser.). (ENG.). 112p. (J). (gr. 3-4). pap. 41.70 (978-1-4296-6441-7(X), 16181); pap. 6.95 (978-1-4296-6273-4(5), 115419); (Illus.). 32.65 (978-1-4296-5479-1(1), 113879) Capstone. (Capstone Pr.).

Richards, Laurae. Coming Home. 2013. 28p. pap. 16.95 (978-1-4624-0769-9(2), Inspiring Voices) Author Solutions, LLC.

Robertson, David A. Scars. Henderson, Scott B., illus. 2010. (7 Generations Ser.: 2). (ENG.). 30p. (YA). (gr. 7-12). pap. (978-1-55379-228-4(9), 4ae83eb9-baca-4c13-a381-ea5771ba95b7, HighWater Pr.) Portage & Main Pr.

Ruckel, Izidor. Abandoned for Life: The Incredible Story of One Romanian Orphan, Hidden from the World. His Life. His Words. Bramsch, Joan, ed. 2003. (YA). mass mkt. 19.97 (978-0-934334-13-6(7)) JB Information Station.

Shames, Stephen. Transforming Lives: Turning Uganda's Forgotten Children into Leaders. Shames, Stephen, photos by. 2009. (Illus.). 40p. (YA). pap. 12.95 (978-1-59572-213-3(0)) Star Bright Bks., Inc.

Skrypuch, Marsha Forchuk. Last Airlift: A Vietnamese Orphan's Rescue from War   (ENG., Illus.). 120p. (J). (gr. 3-7). 2013. pap. 12.95 (978-0-9869495-1-7(5)) 2012. 17.95 (978-0-9869495-4-8(X)) Pajama Pr. CAN. Dist: Publishers Group West (PGW).

—One Step at a Time: A Vietnamese Child Finds Her Way. (ENG., Illus.). 128p. (J). (gr. 3-7). 2014. pap. 12.95 (978-1-927485-02-6(9)) 2013. 17.95 (978-1-927485-01-9(0)) Pajama Pr. CAN. Dist: Publishers Group West (PGW).

Stevens, Dylan. Wooded Sanctuary. 2004. 136p. (YA). pap. 13.95 (978-0-595-31093-7(1)) iUniverse, Inc.

Uschan, Michael V. Matt Dalio: China Care Founder, 1 vol. 2007. (Young Heroes Ser.). (ENG., Illus.). 48p. (gr. 4-8). lib. bdg. 37.33 (978-0-7377-3670-0(4), e231fb42-b839-43a5-9260-86aa8bb082c1, KidHaven Publishing) Greenhaven Publishing LLC.

Warren, Andrea. We Rode the Orphan Trains. 2004. (ENG., Illus.). 144p. (J). (gr. 5-7). reprint ed. pap. 10.99 (978-0-618-43235-6(3), 410538, Clarion Bks.) HarperCollins Pubs.

ORPHANS—FICTION

Adams, W. Royce. Jay. 2005. viii, 115p. (YA). pap. (978-1-58832-120-6(7)) Unlimited Publishing LLC.

Aguila, Priscilla. As Different As Can Be. 2006. 48p. pap. 17.96 (978-1-4116-5609-3(1)) Lulu Pr., Inc.

Aiken, Joan. Go Saddle the Sea. 2007. (ENG., Illus.). 384p. (YA). (gr. 7). pap. 6.95 (978-0-15-206064-0(2), 1198214, Clarion Bks.) HarperCollins Pubs.

Akita, Yoshinobu. Orphen, Vol. 4. 2006. (Orphen Ser.). (Illus.). 168p. (YA). pap. 9.99 (978-1-4139-0269-3(3)) ADV Manga.

Alcott, Louisa. Eight Cousins. 2005. 29.95 (978-1-4218-0976-2(1), 1st World Library - Literary Society) 1st World Publishing, Inc.

—Eight Cousins. 2013. (Works of Louisa May Alcott). 291p. reprint ed. lthr. 79.00 (978-0-7812-1633-3(8)) Reprint Services Corp.

—Eight Cousins, or, the Aunt-Hill. 2010. 250p. pap. 16.95 (978-1-60444-100-0(3)) IndoEuropeanPublishing.com.

—Little Men: Life at Plumfield with Jo's Boys. 2013. (Works of Louisa May Alcott). 292p. reprint ed. lthr. 79.00 (978-0-7812-1629-6(X)) Reprint Services Corp.

Alexander, Lloyd. The Book of Three. 2006. (Chronicles of Prydain Ser.: 1). (ENG., Illus.). 224p. (J). (gr. 3-7). pap. 7.99 (978-0-8050-8048-3(1), 900038435) Square Fish.

Alger, Horatio. Facing the World. 2006. pap. (978-1-4065-0704-1(0)) Dodo Pr.

—Fame & Fortune: Or: the Progress of Richard Hunter. 2007. (ENG.). 160p. per. 19.99 (978-1-4346-5061-0(8)) Creative Media Partners, LLC.

—Frank & Fearless or the Fortunes of Jasper Kent. 2007. 228p. 20.99 (978-1-4280-7465-1(1)); per. 14.99 (978-1-4280-7470-5(8)) IndyPublish.com.

—Frank Fowler, the Cash Boy. reprint ed. pap. 79.00 (978-1-4047-3558-3(5)) Classic Textbooks.

—Frank Fowler, the Cash Boy. 2013. (Works of Horatio Alger Jr.). 254p. reprint ed. lthr. 79.00 (978-0-7812-3558-7(8)) Reprint Services Corp.

—Joe's Luck. 2005. 28.95 (978-1-4218-1455-1(2)); 264p. pap. 13.95 (978-1-4218-1555-8(9)) 1st World Publishing, Inc. (1st World Library - Literary Society).

—Joe's Luck: Or, Always Wide Awake. 2006. (ENG.). 176p. pap. 19.99 (978-1-4264-0883-0(8)); 170p. pap. 21.99 (978-1-4264-0864-9(1)) Creative Media Partners, LLC.

—Joe's Luck: Or, Always Wide Awake. 2006. pap. (978-1-4065-0713-3(X)) Dodo Pr.

—The Young Outlaw: Or, Adrift in the Streets. 2004. (Illus.). 15.90 (978-1-4145-0294-6(X)) Pavilion Pr., Inc.

Anderson, Natalie C. City of Saints & Thieves. 2018. (ENG.). 432p. (YA). (gr. 7). pap. 11.99 (978-0-399-54759-1(2), Speak) Penguin Young Readers Group.

Anthony, Horowitz. Ark Angel. 2007. (Alex Rider Ser.: Bk. 6). 326p. (gr. 5-9). 19.00 (978-0-7569-8134-1(4)) Perfection Learning Corp.

—Ark Angel. 2007. (Alex Rider Ser.: 6). 326p. lib. bdg. 19.65 (978-1-4177-7664-1(1)) Turtleback.

—Point Blanc. 2004. (Alex Rider Ser.: Bk. 2). (SPA.). 264p. 7.95 (978-84-414-1410-5(6)) Editorial Edaf, S.L. ESP. Dist: Spanish Pubs., LLC.

—Russian Roulette. 2014. (Alex Rider Ser.: 10). lib. bdg. 19.65 (978-0-606-36189-7(8)) Turtleback.

—Scorpia Rising, 9 vols. (J). 2012. 256.75 (978-1-4561-3362-7(4)) 2012. 1.25 (978-1-4640-0577-0(X)) 2012. 90.75 (978-1-4561-3363-4(2)) 2011. 122.75 (978-1-4561-3365-8(9)) 2011. 120.75 (978-1-4561-3367-2(5)) Recorded Bks., Inc.

—Scorpia Rising. 2012. (Alex Rider Ser.: 9). lib. bdg. 19.65 (978-0-606-23638-6(4)) Turtleback.

—Stormbreaker. 2004. (Alex Rider Ser.: Bk. 1). 208p. (J). (gr. 4-7). pap. 38.00 incl. audio (978-0-8072-2277-5(1), Listening Library) Random Hse. Audio Publishing Group.

Atwood, Megan. Beat the Odds, No. 2. 2016. (Contest Ser.: 2). (ENG.). 104p. (YA). (gr. 6-12). lib. bdg. 27.99 (978-1-4677-7507-6(X), 38d912b5-2276-4d6a-aa56-773654534b56, Darby Creek) Lerner Publishing Group.

—Turn the Tables. 2016. (Contest Ser.: 5). (ENG.). 112p. (YA). (gr. 6-12). E-Book 42.65 (978-1-4677-8835-9(X), 9781467788359, Darby Creek) Lerner Publishing Group.

Auxier, Jonathan. The Night Gardener. (ENG.). 2015. 384p. (YA). (gr. 3-7). pap. 9.99 (978-1-4197-1531-0(3), 1076503) 2014. 368p. (J). (gr. 5-17). 19.99 (978-1-4197-1144-2(X), 1076501, Amulet Bks.) Abrams, Inc.

—The Night Gardener. 2015. (J). lib. bdg. 19.60 (978-0-606-36891-9(4)) Turtleback.

—Peter Nimble & His Fantastic Eyes. 2012. (ENG.). 400p. (YA). (gr. 5-17). pap. 9.95 (978-1-4197-0421-5(4), 693403, Amulet Bks.) Abrams, Inc.

—Sweep: The Story of a Girl & Her Monster. (ENG.). (J). (gr. 3-7). 2020. 384p. pap. 9.99 (978-1-4197-3702-2(3), 1191203) 2018. 368p. 18.99 (978-1-4197-3140-2(8), 1191201) Abrams, Inc. (Amulet Bks.).

Avi. Crispin: La Cruz de Plomo. 2004.Tr. of Crispin: The Cross of Lead. (SPA., Illus.). (YA). pap. 7.99 (978-84-348-9601-7(X)) SM Ediciones ESP. Dist: Lectorum Pubns., Inc.

—Crispin: the Cross of Lead (Newbery Medal Winner) 2004. (Crispin Ser.). (ENG.). 320p. (J). (gr. 3-7). reprint ed. pap.

8.99 (978-0-7868-1658-3(9)) Little, Brown Bks. for Young Readers.

—Crispin: the End of Time. 2011. (ENG.). 240p. (J). (gr. 5). pap. 7.99 (978-0-06-174083-1(7), Balzer & Bray) HarperCollins Pubs.

—Murder at Midnight. 2011. (ENG.). 256p. (J). (gr. 3-7). pap. 7.99 (978-0-545-08091-0(6), Scholastic Paperbacks) Scholastic, Inc.

Aviation Book Company Staff. Crispin: The Cross of Lead. 2004. (J). (gr. 3-6). 18.40 (978-0-613-74965-7(0)) Turtleback.

Babbitt, Natalie. The Moon over High Street. 2012. (J). (ENG.). 160p. (gr. 4-9). 17.99 (978-0-545-37636-5(X), Di Capua, Michael); 148p. pap. (978-0-545-46740-7(3)) Scholastic, Inc.

Bacigalupi, Paolo. The Drowned Cities. 2013. (ENG.). 464p. (J). (gr. 10-17). pap. 12.99 (978-0-316-05622-9(7)) 2012. 448p. (YA). 17.99 (978-0-316-20037-0(9)) Little, Brown Bks. for Young Readers.

—The Drowned Cities. 2012. 352p. (978-1-59606-506-2(0)) Subterranean Pr.

—The Drowned Cities. 2013. (J). lib. bdg. 22.10 (978-0-606-31749-8(X)) Turtleback.

Bailey, Em. Shift. 2016. (ENG.). 320p. (YA). (gr. 9). pap. 18.99 (978-1-76012-698-8(5)) Hardie Grant Children?s Publishing AUS. Dist: Independent Pubs. Group.

Bailey, Kristin. Legacy of the Clockwork Key. (Secret Order Ser.: 1). (ENG., (YA). (gr. 9). 2014. Illus.). 432p. pap. 9.99 (978-1-4424-4027-2(9)) 2013. 416p. 17.99 (978-1-4424-4026-5(0)) Simon Pulse. (Simon Pulse).

—Shadow of the War Machine. 2015. (Secret Order Ser.: 3). (ENG., Illus.). 448p. (YA). (gr. 9). 17.99 (978-1-4424-6805-4(X), Simon Pulse) Simon Pulse.

Banks, Kimberly E. Mask Man. Wroe, Dameon K., ed. 2003. 57p. (YA). pap. 9.99 (978-0-9740685-0-3(0)) Another Ep Publishing.

Baratz-Logsted, Lauren. The Education of Bet. 2011. (ENG.). 192p. (YA). (gr. 7). pap. 11.99 (978-0-547-55024-4(3), 1450234, Clarion Bks.) HarperCollins Pubs.

Bardugo, Leigh. Ruin & Rising. 2014. (Shadow & Bone Trilogy Ser.: 3). (ENG., Illus.). 432p. (YA). (gr. 7-12). 19.99 (978-0-8050-9461-9(X), 900078589, Holt, Henry & Co. Bks. For Young Readers) Holt, Henry & Co.

—Shadow & Bone. 2012. (Shadow & Bone Trilogy Ser.: 1). (ENG.). 368p. (YA). (gr. 7-12). 19.99 (978-0-8050-9459-6(8), 900078585, Holt, Henry & Co. Bks. For Young Readers) Holt, Henry & Co.

—Shadow & Bone. 2013. (Shadow & Bone Trilogy Ser.: 1). (ENG.). 416p. (YA). (gr. 7-12). pap. 10.99 (978-1-250-02743-6(8), 900098315) Square Fish.

—Shadow & Bone. 2013. (Grisha Trilogy Ser.: 1). (YA). lib. bdg. 22.10 (978-0-606-31903-4(4)) Turtleback.

—Siege & Storm. 2013. (Shadow & Bone Trilogy Ser.: 2). (ENG., Illus.). 448p. (YA). (gr. 7). 19.99 (978-0-8050-9460-2(1), 900078587, Holt, Henry & Co. Bks. For Young Readers) Holt, Henry & Co.

—Siege & Storm. 2014. (Shadow & Bone Trilogy Ser.: 2). (ENG.). 496p. (YA). (gr. 7). pap. 10.99 (978-1-250-04443-3(X), 900128342) Square Fish.

Barfield, Bryce. Eliza Meets a Kind Traveler. 2017. (ENG., Illus.). (J). pap. 9.95 (978-1-947491-81-6(4)) Yorkshire Publishing Group.

Barnhill, Kelly. The Ogress & the Orphans. (ENG.). 2023. 416p. (gr. 6-8). 28.69 **(978-1-5364-8190-7(4))** 2022. 400p. (J). (gr. 5-13). 19.95 (978-1-64375-074-3(7), 74074) Algonquin Young Readers.

—The Ogress & the Orphans. l.t. ed. 2022. (ENG.). lib. bdg. 22.99 Cengage Gale.

Bath, K. P. The Secret of Castle Cant. 2005. 1.00 (978-1-4237-3189-4(1)) Recorded Bks., Inc.

Bauer, Joan. Raising Lumie. 2020. (ENG.). 288p. (J). (gr. 5). 16.99 (978-0-593-11320-2(9), Viking Books for Young Readers) Penguin Young Readers Group.

Bayard, Louis. Lucky Strikes. 2016. (ENG., Illus.). 320p. (YA). 29.99 (978-1-62779-390-2(9), 900148815, Holt, Henry & Co. Bks. For Young Readers) Holt, Henry & Co.

—Lucky Strikes. 2017. (YA). lib. bdg. 20.85 (978-0-606-39951-7(8)) Turtleback.

Beake, Lesley. Home Now. Littlewood, Karin, illus. 2007. 32p. (J). (ENG.). (gr. -1-3). pap. 6.95 (978-1-58089-163-9(2)); (gr. k-3). 16.95 (978-1-58089-162-2(4)) Charlesbridge Publishing, Inc.

Beasley, Cassie. Circus Mirandus. 2016. (SPA.). 25.99 (978-84-246-5686-7(5)) La Galera, S.A. Editorial ESP. Dist: Lectorum Pubns., Inc.

—Circus Mirandus. 2016. (ENG., Illus.). 320p. (J). (gr. 4-7). pap. 8.99 (978-0-14-751554-4(8), Puffin Books) Penguin Young Readers Group.

—Circus Mirandus. l.t. ed. 2020. (ENG.). lib. bdg. 22.99 (978-1-4328-7834-4(4)) Thorndike Pr.

—Circus Mirandus. 2016. (ENG.). 304p. (J). (gr. 3-7). 19.65 (978-0-606-39311-9(0)) Turtleback.

Beltz, Temre. The Tragical Tale of Birdie Bloom. (ENG., Illus.). (J). (gr. 3-7). 2020. 384p. pap. 7.99 (978-0-06-283584-0(X)) 2019. 368p. 16.99 (978-0-06-283583-3(1)) HarperCollins Pubs. (HarperCollins).

Bemis, John Claude. The Nine Pound Hammer: Book 1 of the Clockwork Dark. 2010. (Clockwork Dark Ser.: 1). (ENG.). 384p. (J). (gr. 3-7). pap. 8.99 (978-0-375-85565-8(3), Yearling) Random Hse. Children's Bks.

Bennion, Jay B. From Here to There. 2013. 136p. pap. 9.99 (978-0-9826175-0-2(X)) Pearl Publishing, LLC.

Bergstrom, Sarah. Desert Dwellers Born by Fire: The First Book in the Paintbrush Saga. 2015. (ENG., Illus.). 312p. (J). (gr. -1-12). pap. 12.95 (978-1-78279-587-2(1), Lodestone Bks.) Hunt, John Publishing Ltd. GBR. Dist: National Bk. Network.

Berkeley, Jon. Between the Light. Dorman, Brandon, illus. 2008. (Julie Andrews Collection). (J). lib. bdg. 17.89 (978-0-06-075514-0(8)) HarperCollins Pubs.

—The Palace of Laughter. Dorman, Brandon, illus. 2006. (Wednesday Tales Ser.: No. 1). 427p. (J). (gr. 3-7). 16.99 (978-0-06-075507-2(5), Julie Andrews Collection) HarperCollins Pubs.

—The Tiger's Egg. Dorman, Brandon, illus. (Wednesday Tales Ser.: No. 2). (J). 2009. (ENG.). 432p. pap. 7.99 (978-0-06-075512-6(1), Harper Trophy) 2007. 416p. (gr. 3-7). 16.99 (978-0-06-075510-2(5), Julie Andrews Collection) HarperCollins Pubs.

Bermudez, Cyn. Taken Away, 1 vol. 2018. (Brothers Ser.). (ENG.). 88p. (YA). (gr. 2-3). 24.55 (978-1-5383-8230-1(X), 64d26459-86cf-46ad-a761-3c76fa06bbab); pap. 14.85 (978-1-5383-8229-5(6), c107d7b5-9fea-4acb-a690-0e18e5649a83) Enslow Publishing, LLC.

Berryman, Chelsea. Missing Pages. 2007. 77p. pap. 19.95 (978-1-60441-747-0(1)) America Star Bks.

Besser, Kenneth/R. Arnie Carver & the Plague of Demeverde. 2007. (Illus.). x, 338p. (J). (978-1-934316-02-3(4)) RTMC Organization, LLC.

Bethers, Linda, retold by. Christmas Oranges. 2004. 13p. pap. 3.95 (978-1-57734-546-6(0), 01114387) Covenant Communications, Inc.

Biedrzycki, David. Ace Lacewing, Bug Detective: the Big Swat. Biedrzycki, David, illus. 2010. (Ace Lacewing, Bug Detective Ser.). (Illus.). 44p. (J). (gr. k-4). 16.95 (978-1-57091-747-9(7)) Charlesbridge Publishing, Inc.

Billingsley, Franny. The Folk Keeper. unabr. ed. 2004. 176p. (J). (gr. 5-9). pap. 36.00 incl. audio (978-0-8072-0662-1(8), Listening Library) Random Hse. Audio Publishing Group.

Binns, B. A. Pull. 2010. 310p. (YA). (gr. 9-18). 16.95 (978-1-934813-43-0(5)) Westside Bks.

Black, Holly. The Cruel Prince. 2023. (YA). 45.00 (978-1-955876-16-2(9)) LitJoy Crate.

—The Cruel Prince. 2018. (Folk of the Air Ser.: 1). (ENG.). (YA). (gr. 9-17). 416p. pap. 12.99 (978-0-316-31031-4(X)); (Illus.). 384p. 19.99 (978-0-316-31027-7(1)) Little, Brown Bks. for Young Readers.

Blackwood, Sage. Jinx's Fire. (Jinx Ser.: 3). (ENG.). 400p. (J). (gr. 3-7). 2016. pap. 9.99 (978-0-06-212997-0(X)) 2015. 16.99 (978-0-06-212996-3(1)) HarperCollins Pubs. (Tegen, Katherine Bks).

—Jinx's Magic. 2014. (Jinx Ser.: 2). (ENG.). 400p. (J). (gr. 3-7). 16.99 (978-0-06-212993-2(7), Tegen, Katherine Bks) HarperCollins Pubs.

Blagden, Scott. Dear Life, You Suck. 2015. (ENG.). 320p. (YA). (gr. 9). pap. 9.99 (978-0-544-33621-6(6), 1584167, Clarion Bks.) HarperCollins Pubs.

Blake, Heather Lynn. Anne's Quest: The Wishing Stone. 2005. (ENG.). 153p. pap. 24.95 (978-1-4137-5749-1(9)) PublishAmerica, Inc.

Booher, Brock. The Charity Chip. 2015. pap. 16.99 (978-1-4621-1669-0(8)) Cedar Fort, Inc./CFI Distribution.

Boone, Martina. Illusion. 2016. (Heirs of Watson Island Ser.). (ENG., Illus.). 480p. (YA). (gr. 9). 17.99 (978-1-4814-1128-8(4), Simon Pulse) Simon Pulse.

Bouani, Jennifer. Tyler & His Solve-A-Matic Machine: (1st Edition) 2006. (Future Business Leaders' Ser.). (Illus.). 118p. (J). (gr. 4-7). per. 6.99 (978-0-9779265-0-3(8)) Bouje Publishing, LLC.

Boyne, John. The Boy at the Top of the Mountain. 2017. (J). lib. bdg. 18.40 (978-0-606-39937-1(2)) Turtleback.

Bradbury, Jennifer. Outside In. 2017. (ENG., Illus.). 288p. (J). (gr. 3-7). 17.99 (978-1-4424-6827-6(0), Atheneum/Caitlyn Dlouhy Books) Simon & Schuster Children's Publishing.

Braden, Stephanie. The Wishing Well. 2012. 48p. pap. 16.95 (978-1-62709-450-4(4)) America Star Bks.

Bradford, Chris. The Way of the Dragon, 3. 2012. (Young Samurai Ser.). (ENG.). 512p. (J). (gr. 6-8). 22.44 (978-1-4231-3779-5(5)) Hyperion Bks. for Children.

—The Way of the Sword. l.t. ed. 2012. (Young Samurai Ser.). (ENG.). 547p. (J). (gr. 6-9). 23.99 (978-1-4104-4404-2(X)) Thorndike Pr.

—The Way of the Warrior, 1. 2008. (Young Samurai Ser.). (ENG.). 384p. (J). (gr. 6-8). 22.44 (978-1-4231-1986-9(X)) Hyperion Bks. for Children.

—The Way of the Warrior. l.t. ed. 2011. (Young Samurai Ser.). (ENG.). 328p. (J). 23.99 (978-1-4104-4329-8(9)) Thorndike Pr.

—Young Samurai: the Way of the Sword, 2. 2011. (Young Samurai Ser.). (ENG.). 448p. (gr. 6-8). 22.44 (978-1-4231-2937-0(7)) Hyperion Bks. for Children.

—Young Samurai the Way of the Warrior: The Way of the Warrior, Bk. 1. 2008. (Young Samurai Ser.: 1). (Illus.). 352p. (J). (gr. 6-10). pap. 12.99 (978-0-14-132430-2(9)) Penguin Bks., Ltd. GBR. Dist: Independent Pubs. Group.

Bradley, Kimberly Brubaker. The War I Finally Won. (ENG.). (J). (gr. 4-7). 2018. 416p. 9.99 (978-0-14-751681-7(1), Puffin Books) 2017. 400p. 18.99 (978-0-525-42920-3(4), Dial Bks) Penguin Young Readers Group.

Breach, Jen. Clem Hetherington & the Ironwood Race. Holgate, Douglas, illus. 2018. (Clem Hetherington Ser.: 1). (ENG.). 208p. (J). (gr. 3-7). pap. 14.99 (978-0-545-81446-1(4), Graphix) Scholastic, Inc.

Bredsdorff, Bodil. The Crow-Girl: The Children of Crow Cove. Ingwersen, Faith, tr. 2006. (Children of Crow Cove Ser.: 1). (ENG., Illus.). 160p. (J). (gr. 3-7). reprint ed. pap. 16.99 (978-0-374-40003-3(2), 900038846, Farrar, Straus & Giroux (BYR)) Farrar, Straus & Giroux.

—The Crow-Girl: The Children of Crow Cove. Ingwersen, Faith, tr. from DAN. 2007. (Illus.). 155p. (gr. 3-7). 18.00 (978-0-7569-8186-0(7)) Perfection Learning Corp.

Brewer, Heather. Eighth Grade Bites #1: The Chronicles of Vladimir Tod. 2008. (Chronicles of Vladimir Tod Ser.: 1). (ENG.). 192p. (YA). (gr. 7). 10.99 (978-0-14-241187-2(6), Speak) Penguin Young Readers Group.

—Eleventh Grade Burns, 4. 4th ed. 2010. (Chronicles of Vladimir Tod Ser.: 4). (ENG.). 208p. (J). (gr. 7-12). 24.94 (978-0-525-42243-3(9)) Penguin Young Readers Group.

—Eleventh Grade Burns #4: The Chronicles of Vladimir Tod, 4 vols. 2010. (Chronicles of Vladimir Tod Ser.: 4). (ENG.). 320p. (YA). (gr. 7-18). 10.99 (978-0-14-241647-1(9), Speak) Penguin Young Readers Group.

—Ninth Grade Slays #2: The Chronicles of Vladimir Tod, 2 vols. 2009. (Chronicles of Vladimir Tod Ser.: 2). (ENG.). 288p. (YA). (gr. 7-18). 10.99 (978-0-14-241342-5(9), Speak) Penguin Young Readers Group.

—Tenth Grade Bleeds. 2010. (Chronicles of Vladimir Tod Ser.: 03). lib. bdg. 19.65 (978-0-606-10594-1(8)) Turtleback.

—Tenth Grade Bleeds #3: The Chronicles of Vladimir Tod. 2010. (Chronicles of Vladimir Tod Ser.: 3). (ENG.). 304p. (YA). (gr. 7-18). pap. 10.99 (978-0-14-241560-3(X), Speak) Penguin Young Readers Group.

Brockway, Stephanie. The Mystic Phyles: Beasts. Masiello, Ralph, illus. 2011. 144p. (J). (gr. 4-7). 15.95 (978-1-57091-718-9(3)) Charlesbridge Publishing, Inc.

Brown, Jeff. The True Joy of Christmas. 2012. 28p. pap. 16.99 (978-1-4624-0365-3(4), Inspiring Voices) Author Solutions, LLC.

Bruchac, Joseph. Whisper in the Dark. 2009. (ENG., Illus.). 192p. (J). (gr. 5). pap. 7.99 (978-0-06-058089-6(5), HarperCollins) HarperCollins Pubs.

Buck, Alicia. Out of the Ashes. 2015. 281p. (YA). pap. 17.99 (978-1-4621-1727-7(9)) Cedar Fort, Inc./CFI Distribution.

Buckey, Sarah Masters. Clue in the Castle Tower: A Samantha Mystery. Ross, Peg, ed. Giovine, Sergio, illus. 2011. (American Girl Mysteries Ser.). (ENG.). 184p. (YA). (gr. 4-6). pap. 21.19 (978-1-59369-752-5(X)) American Girl Publishing, Inc.

—The Stolen Sapphire. 2007. (American Girl Mysteries Ser.). (Illus.). 181p. (gr. 4-7). 17.45 (978-0-7569-8278-2(2)) Perfection Learning Corp.

Buckley, Michael. The Fairy-Tale Detectives. (Sisters Grimm Ser.: 1). (J). 2008. 81.45 (978-1-4361-0398-5(3)) 2007. 214.75 (978-1-4193-6197-5(X)) 2007. 1.25 (978-1-4193-6193-7(7)) 2006. 86.75 (978-1-4193-8749-4(9)) 2006. 74.75 (978-1-4193-6196-8(1)) 2006. 71.75 (978-1-4193-6198-2(8)) 2006. 89.75 (978-1-4193-8747-0(2)) Recorded Bks., Inc.

—The Fairy-Tale Detectives: And the Unusual Suspects. Ferguson, Peter, illus. 2012. 580p. (J). (978-1-4351-4487-3(2), Amulet Bks.) Abrams, Inc.

—The Fairy-Tale Detectives (the Sisters Grimm #1) 10th Anniversary Edition. 10th anniv. ed. 2017. (Sisters Grimm Ser.). (ENG., Illus.). 288p. (J). (gr. 3-7). pap. 9.99 (978-1-4197-2005-5(8), 580406) Abrams, Inc.

—A Very Grimm Guide. Ferguson, Peter, illus. 2012. (Sisters Grimm Ser.). (ENG.). 128p. (J). (gr. 3-7). 17.99 (978-1-4197-0201-3(7), 1019601, Amulet Bks.) Abrams, Inc.

Bulla, Clyde Robert. A Lion to Guard Us. Chessare, Michele, illus. 2018. (ENG.). 128p. (J). (gr. 3-7). pap. 9.99 (978-0-06-440333-7(5), HarperCollins) HarperCollins Pubs.

Bunney, Ron. No One Owns Me. 2004. (Illus.). 256p. (YA). pap. 13.50 (978-1-920731-86-1(5)) Fremantle Pr. AUS. Dist: Independent Pubs. Group.

Bunting, Eve. Train to Somewhere. Himler, Ronald, illus. 2004. 32p. (gr. -1-3). 18.00 (978-0-7569-4260-1(8)) Perfection Learning Corp.

Burgess, Melvin. Nicholas Dane. 2013. (ENG.). 432p. (YA). (gr. 8-12). 26.19 (978-0-312-55146-9(0), 900074424) Square Fish.

Burnett, Frances. Frances Hodgson Burnett's the Secret Garden. Barrager, Brigette, illus. 2017. (J). (978-1-5182-2305-1(2), Golden Bks.) Random Hse. Children's Bks.

—A Little Princess. 2008. 156p. 25.95 (978-1-60664-768-4(7)); pap. 13.95 (978-1-60664-141-5(7)) Aegypan.

—A Little Princess. 2008. 212p. (gr. 2-4). 27.99 (978-0-554-29155-0(X)) Creative Media Partners, LLC.

—A Little Princess. Aldous, Kate, illus. 2005. 62p. (J). (gr. 4-7). 8.95 (978-0-7945-1123-4(6), Usborne) EDC Publishing.

—A Little Princess. 2012. 212p. pap. 8.99 (978-1-60796-454-4(6)) Meirovich, Igal.

—A Little Princess. 188p. 2009. pap. 13.95 (978-1-4385-0876-4(X)) 2008. pap. 13.45 (978-1-4385-0194-9(3)) Standard Publications, Inc. (Bk. Jungle).

—A Little Princess. Engelbreit, Mary, illus. 2007. (Mary Engelbreit's Classic Library). (ENG.). 304p. (J). (gr. 3-7). 9.99 (978-0-06-008137-9(6), HarperFestival) HarperCollins Pubs.

—A Little Princess. 2012. (Children's Classics Ser.). (ENG.). 186p. pap. 19.99 (978-1-909438-52-1(9), Sovereign) Bollinger, Max GBR. Dist: Lightning Source UK, Ltd.

—A Little Princess: Being the whole story of Sara Crewe now told for T. 2007. 196p. per. 19.99 (978-1-4346-7028-1(7)); (ENG.). 210p. per. 22.99 (978-1-4346-7029-8(5)) Creative Media Partners, LLC.

—A Little Princess: The Story of Sara Crewe. (J). 16.95 (978-0-8488-1253-9(0)) Amereon Ltd.

—A Little Princess: The Story of Sara Crewe. Warren, Eliza, ed. Marcos, Pablo, illus. 2006. 239p. (YA). reprint ed. 10.00 (978-0-7567-9835-2(3)) DIANE Publishing Co.

—A Little Princess: The Story of Sara Crewe. 2005. 112p. per. 4.95 (978-1-4209-2529-6(6)) Digireads.com Publishing.

—A Little Princess: The Story of Sara Crewe. 2006. pap. (978-1-4065-0559-7(5)) Dodo Pr.

—A Little Princess: The Story of Sara Crewe. l.t. ed. 2005. 376p. pap. (978-1-84637-117-2(1)) Echo Library.

—A Little Princess: The Story of Sara Crewe. 2004. reprint ed. pap. 1.99 (978-1-4192-0213-1(8)); pap. 22.95 (978-1-4191-0213-4(3)) Kessinger Publishing, LLC.

—A Little Princess: The Story of Sara Crewe. 2006. 204p. (YA). 19.95 (978-1-934169-20-9(X)); pap. 7.95 (978-1-934169-21-6(8)) Norilana Bks.

—A Little Princess: The Story of Sara Crewe. 2005. (Twelve-Point Ser.). lib. bdg. 25.00 (978-1-58287-320-6(8)); lib. bdg. 26.00 (978-1-58287-814-0(5)) North Bks.

—A Little Princess: The Story of Sara Crewe. Rust, Graham, illus. (J). pap. 22.95 (978-0-590-24079-6(X)) Scholastic, Inc.

—A Little Princess: The Story of Sara Crewe. l.t. ed. 2003. 342p. pap. 10.95 (978-0-7862-6247-2(8)) Thorndike Pr.

—A Little Princess: With a Discussion of Generosity. Gribbon, Sean & Jael, trs. Gribbon, Sean & Jael, illus. 2003. (Values in Action Illustrated Classics Ser.). (J). (978-1-59203-050-7(5)) Learning Challenge, Inc.

—Petite Princess. pap. 19.95 (978-2-07-051994-1(5)) Gallimard, Editions FRA. Dist: Distribooks, Inc.

—Sara Crewe. l.t. ed. 2006. 92p. pap. (978-1-84637-263-6(1)) Echo Library.

—Sara Crewe. 2009. 68p. pap. 7.95 (978-1-60664-388-4(6)) Rodgers, Alan Bks.

—Sara Crewe or What Happened at Miss Minc. 2005. pap. 20.95 (978-0-7661-9708-4(5)) Kessinger Publishing, LLC.

—Sara Crewe or What Happened at Miss Minchin's. 2006. (ENG.). 88p. per. 8.95 (978-1-59462-359-2(7), 395, Bk. Jungle) Standard Publications, Inc.

—Sara Crewe, or What Happened at Miss Minchin's. 2007. 48p. per. (978-1-4068-4489-4(6)) Echo Library.

—The Secret Garden. 2012. (Illus.). 304p. (978-1-4351-4212-1(8)) Barnes & Noble, Inc.

—The Secret Garden. Robinson, Charles, illus. 2011. 304p. (J). (978-1-4351-3344-0(7)) Barnes & Noble, Inc.

—The Secret Garden, 1 vol. Simon, Ute, illus. 2011. (Calico Illustrated Classics Ser.: No. 3). (ENG.). 112p. (J). (gr. 2-5). 38.50 (978-1-61641-108-4(2), 4023, Calico Chapter Bks.) ABDO Publishing Co.

—The Secret Garden: A Young Reader's Edition of the Classic Story. (J). 22.95 (978-0-8488-0692-7(1)) Amereon Ltd.

—The Secret Garden: A Young Reader's Edition of the Classic Story. 2004. (Illus.). (J). (gr. 1-4). spiral bd. (978-0-616-14565-4(9)); spiral bd. (978-0-616-14566-1(7)) Canadian National Institute for the Blind/Institut National Canadien pour les Aveugles.

—The Secret Garden: A Young Reader's Edition of the Classic Story. (English As a Second Language Bk.). (Illus.). 92p. pap. 4.46 net. (978-0-582-53417-9(8)) Longman Publishing Group.

—The Secret Garden: With a Discussion of Compassion. Lauter, Richard, illus. 2003. (Values in Action Illustrated Classics Ser.). 191p. (J). (978-1-59203-037-8(8)) Learning Challenge, Inc.

—The Secret Garden Book & Charm. Tudor, Tasha, illus. deluxe ed. 2005. (Charming Classics). 368p. (J). 9.99 (978-0-06-075771-7(X), HarperFestival) HarperCollins Pubs.

Burnett, Frances Hodgson. Classic Starts(r): a Little Princess. Corvino, Lucy, illus. 2005. (Classic Starts(r) Ser.). 160p. (J). (gr. 2-4). 6.95 (978-1-4027-1275-3(8)) Sterling Publishing Co., Inc.

—A Little Princess. Rust, Graham, illus. 2019. (ENG.). 192p. (J). (gr. 4-7). reprint ed. 18.95 (978-0-87923-784-4(8)) Godine, David R. Pub.

—A Little Princess. 2012. (ENG., Illus.). 280p. (978-1-905716-04-3(4), Collector's Library, The) Pan Macmillan.

—A Little Princess. (Puffin Classics Ser.). (Illus.). (J). (gr. 5-7). 2012. 310p. 16.99 (978-0-14-134171-2(8)) 2008. (ENG., 320p. 8.99 (978-0-14-132112-7(1)) Penguin Young Readers Group. (Puffin Books).

—The Secret Garden. Moore, Inga, illus. 2010. (ENG.). 272p. (J). (gr. 1-4). pap. 19.99 (978-0-7636-4732-2(2)) Candlewick Pr.

—The Secret Garden. 2003. (Illus.). 288p. (gr. 12-18). mass mkt. 5.95 (978-0-451-52883-4(2), Signet) Penguin Publishing Group.

—The Secret Garden. 2013. (Vintage Children's Classics Ser.). (ENG.). 384p. (J). (gr. 4-7). pap. 12.99 (978-0-09-957295-4(8)) Penguin Random Hse. GBR. Dist: Independent Pubs. Group.

—The Secret Garden. 2008. (Puffin Classics Ser.). (Illus.). 368p. (J). (gr. 3-7). 8.99 (978-0-14-132106-6(7), Puffin Books) Penguin Young Readers Group.

—The Secret Garden. 2003. (Modern Library Classics Ser.). 288p. (J). (gr. 3-7). pap. 10.00 (978-0-8129-6998-6(7), Modern Library) Random House Publishing Group.

—The Secret Garden: Special Edition with Tasha Tudor Art & Bonus Materials. Tudor, Tasha, illus. 100th anniv. ed. 2010. (ENG.). 384p. (J). (gr. 4-18). reprint ed. pap. 9.99 (978-0-06-440188-3(X), HarperCollins) HarperCollins Pubs.

Burnett, Frances Hodgson & Hunt, Peter. The Secret Garden. 2011. (Oxford World's Classics Ser.). (ENG.). 288p. (gr. 7-18). pap. 8.95 (978-0-19-958822-0(8)) Oxford Univ. Pr., Inc.

Burt, Jake. Greetings from Witness Protection! 2018. (ENG.). 384p. (J). pap. 8.99 (978-1-250-17904-3(1), 900164745) Square Fish.

Bush, Suzanne & Takes, Deb. Time Will Tell. 2004. 279p. (YA). lib. bdg. 15.95 (978-0-9747426-0-1(0)) Imagining Possibilities.

Byng, Georgia. Molly Moon & the Morphing Mystery. 2011. (Molly Moon Ser.: 5). (ENG.). 416p. (J). (gr. 3-7). pap. 7.99 (978-0-06-166162-4(7), HarperCollins) HarperCollins Pubs.

—Molly Moon Detiene el Mundo. 2004. (SPA.). 358p. (gr. 5-8). 18.99 (978-84-348-9610-9(9)) SM Ediciones ESP. Dist: Lectorum Pubns., Inc.

—Molly Moon Stops the World. (Illus.). (J). 2004. 384p. 16.99 (978-0-06-051410-5(8)) 2005. (Molly Moon Ser.: 2). (ENG., 416p. (gr. 3-7). reprint ed. pap. 7.99 (978-0-06-051415-0(9), HarperCollins) HarperCollins Pubs.

—Molly Moon y el Increible Libro. 2003. (SPA.). 349p. (J). 18.99 (978-84-348-9076-3(3)) SM Ediciones ESP. Dist: Lectorum Pubns., Inc.

—Molly Moon's Incredible Book of Hypnotism. 2003. 135.92 (978-0-06-057217-4(5)) 2003. (Molly Moon Ser.: 1). (ENG., Illus.). 384p. (J). (gr. 3-7). 17.99 (978-0-06-051406-8(X), HarperCollins) 2004. (Molly Moon Ser.: 1). (ENG., Illus.). 384p. (J). (gr. 3-7). reprint ed. pap. 7.99 (978-0-06-051409-9(4), HarperCollins) HarperCollins Pubs.

—Molly Moon's Incredible Book of Hypnotism. 2004. (Molly Moon Ser.). 371p. (gr. 3-7). 18.00 (978-0-7569-3484-2(2)) Perfection Learning Corp.

Byrne, Michael. Lottery Boy. 2016. (ENG.). 304p. (YA). (gr. 7). 16.99 (978-0-7636-7996-5(8)) Candlewick Pr.

Byrne, Mike, illus. Great Expectations: A BabyLit Storybook, 1 vol. 2018. (BabyLit Ser.). 28p. (J). (gr. -1-k). 12.99 (978-1-4236-4984-7(2)) Gibbs Smith, Publisher.

Calhoun, Dia. After the River the Sun. Slater, Kate, illus. 2013. (ENG.). 368p. (J). (gr. 4-7). 16.99 (978-1-4424-3985-6(8)) Simon & Schuster Children's Publishing.

Campbell, H. David. Merribell: A Comforting Story. Thomas, Darlene Kay, illus. 2011. (ENG.). 218p. (gr. 2-2). 23.95 (978-1-4620-4477-1(8)); pap. 13.95 (978-1-4620-4476-4(X)) iUniverse, Inc.

Campbell, K. G. A Small Zombie Problem. 2019. (Zombie Problems Ser.: 1). (Illus.). 240p. (J). (gr. 3-7). 16.99 (978-0-553-53955-4(8), Knopf Bks. for Young Readers) Random Hse. Children's Bks.

Canfield, Dorothy. Understood Betsy. 2004. reprint ed. pap. 1.99 (978-1-4192-9201-9(3)); pap. 24.95 (978-1-4179-0955-1(2)) Kessinger Publishing, LLC.

Cardarelli, Mario. Bunny, an Orphan's Story. 2008. 44p. pap. 18.99 (978-1-4389-1597-5(7)) AuthorHouse.

Carey, Anna. Eve. (Eve Ser.: 1). (ENG.). (YA). (gr. 8). 2012. 352p. pap. 9.99 (978-0-06-204851-6(1)) 2011. 336p. 17.99 (978-0-06-204850-9(3)) HarperCollins Pubs. (HarperCollins).

—Eve. 2012. (SPA.). 224p. (YA). pap. 20.95 (978-84-9918-434-0(0)) Roca Editorial ESP. Dist: Spanish Pubs., LLC.

Carlon, Mick. Riding on Duke's Train. 2011. (LeapKids Ser.). (ENG.). 160p. (J). (gr. k-7). pap. 9.95 *(978-1-935248-06-4(5))* Leapfrog Pr.

Carlson-Voiles, Polly. Summer of the Wolves. 2013. (ENG.). 352p. (J). (gr. 5-7). pap. 7.99 *(978-0-544-02276-8(9),* 1528497, Clarion Bks.) HarperCollins Pubs.

Carman, Patrick. The House of Power. 2008. (Atherton Ser.: 1). (ENG., Illus.). 384p. (J). (gr. 3-7). pap. 9.99 *(978-0-316-16671-3(5))* Little, Brown Bks. for Young Readers.

—Into the Mist, 5. 2011. (Land of Elyon Ser.: Bk. 4). 304p. (J). (gr. 4-6). 18.69 *(978-0-439-89998-7(2))* Scholastic, Inc.

—Rivers of Fire. 2009. (Atherton Ser.: 2). (ENG., Illus.). 336p. (J). (gr. 3-7). pap. 17.99 *(978-0-316-16673-7(1))* Little, Brown Bks. for Young Readers.

Carmichael, Clay. Wild Things. 2012. (ENG.). 184p. (J). (gr. 4-7). pap. 9.99 *(978-1-59078-914-8(8),* Astra Young Readers) Astra Publishing Hse.

—Wild Things, 6 vols. 2010. (J). 77.75 *(978-1-4498-0632-3(5))* Recorded Bks., Inc.

Carolyn, Reeder. Shades of Gray. 2014. (ENG.). 160p. (J). (gr. 5-12). 11.24 *(978-1-63245-242-9(1))* Lectorum Pubns., Inc.

Casey, Barbara. The Cadence of Gypsies. 2011. (ENG.). 272p. (J). (gr. 7-12). 16.95 *(978-0-9820812-8-0(6),* Hungry Goat Pr.) Gauthier Pubns. Inc.

Cashore, Kristin. Jane, Unlimited. 2018. (Illus.). 480p. (YA). (gr. 9). pap. 10.99 *(978-0-14-751310-6(3),* Speak) Penguin Young Readers Group.

Cavanagh, Peter J. Fungie: The Dingle Dolphin. 2008. 48p. per. 24.95 *(978-1-4241-8356-2(1))* America Star Bks.

Chee, Traci. The Reader. (Reader Ser.: 1). 464p. (YA). (gr. 7). 2017. pap. 11.99 *(978-0-14-751805-7(9),* Speak)Bk. 1. 2016. 19.99 *(978-0-399-17677-7(2),* G.P. Putnam's Sons Books for Young Readers) Penguin Young Readers Group.

—The Reader. 2017. (Sea of Ink & Gold Ser.: 1). lib. bdg. 22.10 *(978-0-606-40001-5(X))* Turtleback.

—The Speaker. 2018. (Reader Ser.: 2). 512p. (YA). (gr. 7). pap. 10.99 *(978-0-14-751806-4(7),* Speak) Penguin Young Readers Group.

—The Storyteller. 2019. (Reader Ser.: 3). 544p. (YA). (gr. 7). pap. 10.99 *(978-0-14-751807-1(5),* Penguin Books) Penguin Young Readers Group.

Chima, Cinda Williams. The Wizard Heir. 2008. (Heir Chronicles Ser.: 2). (ENG.). 480p. (YA). (gr. 7-17). pap. 12.99 *(978-1-4231-0488-9(9))* Little, Brown Bks. for Young Readers.

Chimombo, S. The Bird Boy's Song. 2004. 96p. pap. *(978-99908-48-07-6(6))* Wasi Pubns. ZWE. Dist: Michigan State Univ. Pr.

Ching, Lorilei. He Ping: An Orphan's Destiny. 2013. 32p. pap. 13.95 *(978-1-4624-0807-8(9),* Inspiring Voices) Author Solutions, LLC.

Chriss, Granddad. The Adventures of Barazaburg. 2011. 54p. 24.99 *(978-1-4568-7988-4(X));* pap. 15.99 *(978-1-4568-7987-7(1))* Xlibris Corp.

Christopher, Matt. Dirt Bike Runaway. 2008. (New Matt Christopher Sports Library). 176p. (J). (gr. 4-6). lib. bdg. 26.60 *(978-1-59953-215-8(8))* Norwood Hse. Pr.

Chronicles of Avonlea. 2004. 142p. (YA). pap. 7.95 *(978-1-57646-893-7(3))* Quiet Vision Publishing.

Clare, Cassandra. Clockwork Angel. (Infernal Devices Ser.: 1). (ENG., Illus.). (YA). (gr. 9). 2015. 544p. pap. 14.99 *(978-1-4814-5602-9(4))* 2010. 496p. 24.99 *(978-1-4169-7586-1(1))* McElderry, Margaret K. Bks. (McElderry, Margaret K. Bks.).

—Clockwork Angel. 2013. (CHI & ENG.). 240p. (YA). (gr. 8-17). pap. *(978-986-6000-84-3(2))* Spring International Pubs.

—Clockwork Angel. 2015. (Infernal Devices Ser.: Bk. 1). 544p. (YA). lib. bdg. 25.75 *(978-0-606-37737-9(9))* 2012. (Infernal Devices Graphic Novel Ser.: 1). lib. bdg. 24.55 *(978-0-606-32257-7(4))* Turtleback.

—Clockwork Prince. (Infernal Devices Ser.: 2). (YA). 2015. (ENG., Illus.). 560p. (gr. 9). pap. 14.99 *(978-1-4814-5601-2(6))* 2011. (ENG., Illus.). 528p. (gr. 9-18). 24.99 *(978-1-4169-7588-5(8))* 2011. 502p. *(978-1-4424-5174-2(2))* McElderry, Margaret K. Bks. (McElderry, Margaret K. Bks.).

—Clockwork Prince. 2015. (Infernal Devices Ser.: Bk. 2). 560p. (YA). lib. bdg. 25.75 *(978-0-606-37895-6(2))* 2013. (Infernal Devices Graphic Novel Ser.: 2). lib. bdg. 24.55 *(978-0-606-32258-4(2))* Turtleback.

—Clockwork Princess. 2013. (YA). (Infernal Devices Ser.: 3). (ENG., Illus.). 592p. (gr. 9). 24.99 *(978-1-4169-7590-8(X));* 570p. *(978-1-4424-8541-9(8))* McElderry, Margaret K. Bks. (McElderry, Margaret K. Bks.).

—The Infernal Devices: Clockwork Angel; Clockwork Prince; Clockwork Princess. 2013. (Infernal Devices Ser.: Bks. 1-3). (ENG.). 1520p. (YA). (gr. 9). 74.99 *(978-1-4424-8372-9(5),* McElderry, Margaret K. Bks.) McElderry, Margaret K. Bks.

—The Infernal Devices: Clockwork Angel. 2012. (Infernal Devices Ser.: 1). (ENG.). 240p. (gr. 8-17). pap. 13.00 *(978-0-316-20098-1(0),* Yen Pr.) Yen Pr. LLC.

Clark, Brenda. Spiro & Zinger Rescue the Orphans: Spiro the Shooting Star - Book Three, 1 vol. 2010. 70p. pap. 19.95 *(978-1-4489-3992-3(5))* America Star Bks.

Coats, J. Anderson. The Many Reflections of Miss Jane Deming. 2017. (ENG., Illus.). 288p. (J). (gr. 5-7). 16.99 *(978-1-4814-6496-3(5),* Atheneum Bks. for Young Readers) Simon & Schuster Children's Publishing.

Coatsworth, Elizabeth Jane & Sewell, Helen. The Fair American. 2005. (ENG., Illus.). 137p. (J). (gr. 3-4). pap. 11.95 *(978-1-883937-85-0(X))* Ignatius Pr.

Collier, James Lincoln. Me & Billy. 0 vols. unabr. ed. 2013. (ENG.). 194p. (J). (gr. 5-7). pap. 9.99 *(978-1-4778-1706-3(9),* 9781477817063, Two Lions) Amazon Publishing.

Collingwood, Harry. The Log of a Privateersman. 2008. 216p. 26.95 *(978-1-60664-899-5(3));* pap. 15.95 *(978-1-60664-018-0(6))* Aegypan.

Collins, Pat Lowery. Hidden Voices: The Orphan Musicians of Venice. 2009. (ENG., Illus.). 352p. (YA). (gr. 7). 17.99 *(978-0-7636-3917-4(6))* Candlewick Pr.

Collins, Sonny. Mouse Tails. 2006. (ENG.). 52p. per. 16.95 *(978-1-4241-4589-8(9))* PublishAmerica, Inc.

Cook, Kristi. Eternal. (ENG., Illus.). (YA). (gr. 9). 2014. 432p. pap. 9.99 *(978-1-4424-8531-0(0))* 2013. 416p. 16.99 *(978-1-4424-8532-7(9))* Simon Pulse. (Simon Pulse).

—Haven. 2012. (ENG.). 448p. (YA). (gr. 9). pap. 12.99 *(978-1-4424-0761-9(1),* Simon Pulse) Simon Pulse.

—Mirage. (ENG., (YA). (gr. 9). 2013. Illus.). 416p. pap. 12.99 *(978-1-4424-4300-6(6))* 2012. 384p. 16.99 *(978-1-4424-4299-3(9))* Simon Pulse. (Simon Pulse).

Cooney, Caroline B. If the Witness Lied. 2010. (ENG.). 224p. (YA). (gr. 7). pap. 8.99 *(978-0-385-73449-3(2),* Ember) Random Hse. Children's Bks.

Cooper, Paul Fenimore. Tal, His Marvelous Adventures with Noom-Zor-Noom. Reeves, Ruth, illus. 80th ed. 2009. 305p. (J). pap. 12.95 *(978-1-930900-41-7(4))* Purple Hse. Pr.

Cormier, Robert. Heroes. 2006. (York Notes Ser.). (ENG., Illus.). 112p. pap. *(978-1-4058-3559-6(1))* Pearson Education, Ltd.

Couloumbis, Audrey. The Misadventures of Maude March. 2007. (Maude March Ser.: 1). (ENG., Illus.). 320p. (J). (gr. 3-7). 8.99 *(978-0-375-83247-5(5),* Yearling) Random Hse. Children's Bks.

—The Misadventures of Maude March: Or Trouble Rides a Fast Horse. 2007. (Illus.). 295p. (gr. 3-7). 18.00 *(978-0-7569-7770-2(3))* Perfection Learning Corp.

Cowling, Douglas. Vivaldi's Ring of Mystery. Fernandez, Laura & Jacobson, Rick, illus. 2004. (ENG.). 44p. (J). *(978-0-439-96904-8(2),* North Winds Pr) Scholastic Canada, Ltd.

Crawford, Clint. The Rag Tag Gang, 1 vol. 2009. 83p. pap. 19.95 *(978-1-4489-9697-1(X))* America Star Bks.

Creech, Sharon. The Castle Corona. Diaz, David, illus. (J). 2013. (ENG.). 352p. (gr. 3-7). pap. 7.99 *(978-0-06-206395-3(2),* HarperCollins) 2007. 336p. (gr. 4-7). lib. bdg. 19.89 *(978-0-06-084622-0(4),* Cotler, Joanna Books) HarperCollins Pubs.

—The Great Unexpected. (ENG.). (J). (gr. 3-7). 2013. 256p. pap. 7.99 *(978-0-06-189234-9(3))* 2012. (Illus.). 240p. 16.99 *(978-0-06-189232-5(7))* HarperCollins Pubs. (HarperCollins).

—Ruby Holler. 2012. (ENG.). 288p. (J). (gr. 3-7). pap. 7.99 *(978-0-06-056015-7(0),* HarperCollins) HarperCollins Pubs.

—Ruby Holler. 2004. (Joanna Cotler Bks.). 310p. (gr. 3-7). 17.00 *(978-0-7569-1940-5(1))* Perfection Learning Corp.

—Ruby Holler. 2012. (J). (gr. 3-6). 17.20 *(978-0-613-86272-1(4))* Turtleback.

—The Unfinished Angel. 2013. (ENG.). 160p. (J). (gr. 3-7). pap. 7.99 *(978-0-06-143097-8(6),* HarperCollins) HarperCollins Pubs.

Croggon, Alison. The Singing: Book Four of Pellinor. 2017. (Pellinor Ser.). (ENG.). 496p. (J). (gr. 7). pap. 9.99 *(978-0-7636-9446-3(0))* Candlewick Pr.

Cummings, Pat. Trace. 2019. (ENG., Illus.). 320p. (J). (gr. 3-7). 16.99 *(978-0-06-269884-1(2),* HarperCollins) HarperCollins Pubs.

Cummins, Maria S. The Lamplighter. 2011. 308p. pap. 16.99 *(978-1-61203-228-3(1))* Bottom of the Hill Publishing.

Cushman, Karen. Rodzina. 2020.Tr. of Rodzina. (ENG.). 240p. (J). (gr. 3-7). pap. 7.99 *(978-0-358-09751-8(7),* 1747610, Clarion Bks.) HarperCollins Pubs.

Dahl, Roald. The BFG. 2016. (CHI.). 112p. (J). (gr. 3-6). pap. *(978-986-479-012-8(9))* Commonwealth Publishing Co., Ltd.

—The BFG. 30th rev. ed. 2014. (ENG.). 208p. (J). (gr. 2-12). 11.24 *(978-1-63245-341-9(X))* Lectorum Pubns., Inc.

—The BFG. 2009. 9.00 *(978-0-7848-2054-4(6),* Everbind) Marco Bk. Co.

—The BFG. 2007. (SWE., Illus.). 17.00 *(978-0-7569-8233-1(2))* Penguin Publishing Group.

—The BFG. 2019. (ENG., Illus.). 224p. (J). (gr. 3-7). 17.99 *(978-1-9848-3715-8(X),* Puffin Books) Penguin Young Readers Group.

—The BFG. Blake, Quentin, illus. 30th anniv. ed. 2007. (ENG.). 224p. (J). (gr. 3-7). 8.99 *(978-0-14-241038-7(1),* Puffin Books) Penguin Young Readers Group.

—The BFG. 2005. (J). 1.25 *(978-1-4193-5995-8(9))* Recorded Bks., Inc.

—The BFG. 2007. (SWE.). 18.40 *(978-1-4177-8612-1(4))* Turtleback.

Dallas, Sandra. Someplace to Call Home. (ENG., Illus.). 240p. (J). (gr. 3-6). 2020. pap. 9.99 *(978-1-58536-415-2(0),* 204766) 2019. 15.95 *(978-1-58536-414-5(2),* 204752) Sleeping Bear Pr.

Dalmatian Press Staff, adapted by. Heidi. (SPA., Illus.). (YA). 11.95 *(978-84-7281-082-2(8),* AF1082) Auriga, Ediciones S.A. ESP. Dist: Continental Bk. Co., Inc.

—Heidi. (Young Collector's Illustrated Classics Ser.). (Illus.). 192p. (J). (gr. 3-7). 9.95 *(978-1-56156-455-2(9))* Kidsbooks, LLC.

—Oliver Twist. Date not set. (C). pap. *(978-0-7593-9612-8(4),* Cengage Learning) CENGAGE Learning.

La Dama de Cobre (the Copper Lady) 2006. (J). pap. 6.95 *(978-0-8225-6616-8(8),* Ediciones Lerner) Lerner Publishing Group.

Danforth, Emily M. The Miseducation of Cameron Post. 2012. (ENG.). 480p. (YA). (gr. 9). 17.99 *(978-0-06-202056-7(0),* Balzer & Bray) HarperCollins Pubs.

D'Arcy, Megan. Be Happy. Gawthrop, Shaughn, illus. 2011. 32p. (J). 14.95 *(978-1-879094-95-6(9))* Momentum Bks., LLC.

Daunis, Marcia Prosco. Miller's Ben. 2008. 159p. pap. 24.95 *(978-1-60672-759-1(1))* America Star Bks.

Davidson, Jenny. The Explosionist. 2008. 464p. (YA). (gr. 7-18). lib. bdg. 18.89 *(978-0-06-123976-2(3),* HarperTeen) HarperCollins Pubs.

Davies, Anna. Wrecked. 2013. (ENG., Illus.). 336p. (YA). (gr. 9). pap. 9.99 *(978-1-4424-3279-6(9),* Simon & Schuster Bks. For Young Readers) Simon & Schuster Bks. For Young Readers.

Davis, Susan Page. Sarah's Long Ride. 2007. (Piper Ranch Ser.). 173p. (J). (gr. 3-7). per. 8.99 *(978-1-59166-737-7(2))* BJU Pr.

De Haven, Tom. The Orphan's Tent. 2005. (Illus.). 192p. mass mkt. 5.99 *(978-0-7434-9772-5(4))* ibooks, Inc.

De Leeuw, Cateau. Fear in the Forest. Vosburgh, Leonard, illus. 2014. (ENG.). 123p. (J). pap. 14.95 *(978-1-932350-43-2(8))* Bethlehem Bks.

De Lint, Charles. The Cats of Tanglewood Forest. 2014. (J). lib. bdg. 22.10 *(978-0-606-36532-1(X))* Turtleback.

De Stefano, Lauren. A Curious Tale of the In-Between. 2016. (J). lib. bdg. 19.65 *(978-0-606-39553-3(9))* Turtleback.

DeFelice, Cynthia. The Apprenticeship of Lucas Whitaker. 2007. (ENG.). 160p. (J). (gr. 5-9). per. 16.99 *(978-0-374-40014-9(8),* 900042005) Square Fish.

del Rio, Tania. Warren the 13th & the All-Seeing Eye: A Novel. Staehle, Will, illus. 2015. (Warren The 13th Ser.: 1). 256p. (J). (gr. 5). 16.95 *(978-1-59474-803-5(9))* Quirk Bks.

Delaney, Joseph. Ghost Prison. 2014. (ENG.). 112p. (YA). (gr. 6-12). pap. 8.99 *(978-1-4926-0174-6(8))* Sourcebooks, Inc.

D'Elia, Amy & Clerman, Lisa. Dreams Come True: A story about the blessing of Adoption. 2007. *(978-0-9777744-1-8(4))* Finneran, Lisa.

Denenberg, Barry. A True Patriot: The Journal of William Thomas Emerson, a Revolutionary War Patriot. 2012. lib. bdg. 17.20 *(978-0-606-26736-6(0))* Turtleback.

Denton, Shannon Eric & Warner, Gertrude Chandler. The Boxcar Children, 1 vol. Dubisch, Michael, illus. 2009. (Boxcar Children Graphic Novels Ser.). (ENG.). 32p. (J). (gr. 3-8). lib. bdg. 32.79 *(978-1-60270-586-9(0),* 3669, Graphic Planet - Fiction) Magic Wagon.

Desio, Delores. The Legend of Ruby O'Grady: Grandma Was A Hippie. 2011. 122p. pap. 19.95 *(978-1-4560-7039-7(8))* America Star Bks.

DeStefano, Lauren. Dreaming Dangerous. 2018. (ENG.). 208p. (J). 16.99 *(978-1-68119-447-9(3),* 900172801, Bloomsbury Children's Bks.) Bloomsbury Publishing USA.

—Fever, 7 vols. 2012. (Chemical Garden Trilogy: Bk. 2). (YA). 102.75 *(978-1-4640-1914-2(2))* Recorded Bks., Inc.

—Fever. (Chemical Garden Trilogy Ser.: 2). (ENG., (YA). (gr. 9). 2013. Illus.). 368p. pap. 12.99 *(978-1-4424-0908-8(8))* 2012. 352p. 17.99 *(978-1-4424-0907-1(X))* Simon & Schuster Bks. For Young Readers. (Simon & Schuster Bks. For Young Readers).

—Fiebre. (Chemical Garden Trilogy: Bk. 2).Tr. of Fever. (SPA.). 352p. pap. 18.95 *(978-84-96886-28-5(X))* Ediciones Urano S. A. ESP. Dist: Spanish Pubs., LLC.

—Sever. 2013. (Chemical Garden Trilogy Ser.: 3). (ENG.). 400p. (YA). (gr. 9). pap. 9.99 *(978-1-4424-0910-1(X))* Simon & Schuster.

—Sever. 2013. (Chemical Garden Trilogy Ser.: 3). (ENG.). 384p. (YA). (gr. 9). 17.99 *(978-1-4424-0909-5(6),* Simon & Schuster Bks. For Young Readers) Simon & Schuster Bks. For Young Readers.

—Wither, 9 vols. (Chemical Garden Ser.: 1). (YA). 90.75 *(978-1-4561-2060-3(3));* 256.75 *(978-1-4561-2059-7(X));* 1.25 *(978-1-4561-2064-1(6));* 2011. 122.75 *(978-1-4561-2061-0(1));* 2011. 120.75 *(978-1-4561-2063-4(8))* Recorded Bks., Inc.

—Wither. 2011. (Chemical Garden Trilogy Ser.: 1). (ENG.). 384p. (YA). (gr. 9). pap. 13.99 *(978-1-4424-0906-4(1),* Simon & Schuster Bks. For Young Readers) Simon & Schuster Bks. For Young Readers.

Dicamillo, Kate. The Magician's Elephant. 2015. lib. bdg. 17.20 *(978-0-606-37891-8(X))* Turtleback.

DiCamillo, Kate. The Magician's Elephant. Tanaka, Yoko, illus. (ENG.). (J). (gr. 3-7). 2015. 224p. pap. 8.99 *(978-0-7636-8088-6(5))* 2009. 208p. 18.99 *(978-0-7636-4410-9(2))* Candlewick Pr.

Dicamillo, Kate. The Magician's Elephant. Lt. ed. 2010. (ENG.). 242p. 23.95 *(978-1-4104-2493-8(6))* Thorndike Pr.

—The Magician's Elephant. 2011. lib. bdg. 17.20 *(978-0-606-15375-1(6))* Turtleback.

Dickens, Charles. Classic Starts(r): Oliver Twist: Retold from the Charles Dickens Original. Andreasen, Dan, illus. 2006. (Classic Starts(r) Ser.). 160p. (J). (gr. 2-4). 7.99 *(978-1-4027-2665-1(1))* Sterling Publishing Co., Inc.

—David Copperfield, 1 vol. McWilliam, Howard, illus. 2010. (Calico Illustrated Classics Ser.). (ENG.). 112p. (J). (gr. 2-5). 38.50 *(978-1-60270-745-0(6),* 3991, Calico Chapter Bks.) ABDO Publishing Co.

—David Copperfield. 2008. (Bring the Classics to Life Ser.). (Illus.). 72p. (gr. 4-12). pap., act. bk. ed. 10.95 *(978-1-55576-322-0(7),* EDCTR-408B) EDCON Publishing Group.

—David Copperfield. 2009. 186p. pap. 19.99 *(978-1-4590-4328-2(6))* General Bks. LLC.

—David Copperfield. 2006. (Oberon Modern Playwrights Ser.). (ENG.). 126p. per. 14.95 *(978-1-84002-570-5(0),* 900242906) Oberon Bks., Ltd. GBR. Dist: Macmillan.

—David Copperfield, 1 vol. 2009. (Real Reads Ser.). (ENG., Illus.). 64p. (J). (gr. 5-5). pap. 14.55 *(978-1-60754-383-1(4),* c5e07a78-19a4-4f2e-8cb9-6c68f7cc7a4c, Windmill Bks.) Rosen Publishing Group, Inc., The.

—David Copperfield, 1 vol. 2009. (Foundation Classics Ser.). (ENG.). 56p. (J). (gr. 5-5). lib. bdg. 32.60 *(978-1-60754-852-2(6),* 2f99677f-33bf-48ec-ae78-c9d2ee798299, Windmill Bks.) Rosen Publishing Group, Inc., The.

—David Copperfield. 2006. (Oxford Progressive English Readers Ser.). (ENG., Illus.). 103p. (J). (gr. 4-7). per. *(978-0-19-597140-8(X))* Oxford Univ. Pr.

—Great Expectations. 2019. (ENG.). 470p. (YA). (gr. 7). pap. 19.89 *(978-1-7274-9559-1(4))* CreateSpace Independent Publishing Platform.

—Great Expectations. 2020. (ENG.). 416p. (J). (gr. 3-7). pap. *(978-1-77426-072-2(7))* East India Publishing Co.

—Great Expectations. 2019. (ENG.). 552p. (J). (gr. 3-7). pap. 21.99 *(978-1-7036-4774-7(2));* 498p. (YA). (gr. 7). pap. 32.99 *(978-1-0890-6847-1(6));* 552p. (YA). (gr. 7). pap. 30.99 *(978-1-6867-1072-8(0));* 552p. (YA). (gr. 7). pap. 34.99 *(978-1-0810-7252-0(0));* 552p. (YA). (gr. 7). pap. 30.99 *(978-1-0713-5331-8(4));* 668p. (YA). (gr. 7). pap. 24.95 *(978-1-0703-4968-8(2))* Independently Published.

—Great Expectations. Donnelly, Karen, illus. 2013. (Charles Dickens Ser.). (ENG.). 64p. pap. 7.95 *(978-1-906230-01-2(3))* Real Reads Ltd. GBR. Dist: Casemate Pubs. & Bk. Distributors, LLC.

—Great Expectations. 2013. (Differentiated Timeless Classics Ser.). (ENG.). 80p. (YA). (gr. 4-12). 14.95 *(978-1-62250-718-4(5))* Saddleback Educational Publishing, Inc.

—Great Expectations. 2018. (ENG., Illus.). 466p. (J). (gr. 4-6). 24.99 *(978-1-5154-2681-3(5))* Wilder Pubns., Corp.

—Great Expectations: Abridged Edition. 2011. (Puffin Classics Ser.). (ENG.). 432p. (J). (gr. 5-7). pap. 8.99 *(978-0-14-133013-6(9),* Puffin Books) Penguin Young Readers Group.

—Great Expectations: The Graphic Novel, 1 vol. 2010. (Classic Graphic Novel Collection). (ENG.). 160p. (gr. 7-10). 41.03 *(978-1-4205-0372-2(3),* c93617a4-5093-4c70-be39-d2ee1429dc17, Lucent Pr.) Greenhaven Publishing LLC.

—Oliver Twist, 1 vol. 2009. (Foundation Classics Ser.). (ENG., Illus.). 56p. (J). (gr. 5-5). lib. bdg. 32.60 *(978-1-60754-542-2(X),* 9899534b-2ed0-46e5-86cf-4f5e01b17974, Windmill Bks.) Rosen Publishing Group, Inc., The.

—Oliver Twist, 1 vol. McWilliam, Howard, illus. 2011. (Calico Illustrated Classics Ser.: No. 3). (ENG.). 112p. (J). (gr. 2-5). 38.50 *(978-1-61641-106-0(6),* 4019, Calico Chapter Bks.) ABDO Publishing Co.

—Oliver Twist. abr. ed. Date not set. (Nelson Readers Ser.). (J). pap. *(978-0-17-557020-1(5))* Addison-Wesley Longman, Inc.

—Oliver Twist. 2014. (Graphic Classics Ser.). (Illus.). 48p. (gr. 2-7). pap. 8.95 *(978-1-905087-97-6(7))* Book Hse. GBR. Dist: Black Rabbit Bks.

—Oliver Twist. 2013. 274p. pap. 14.99 *(978-1-4837-0319-0(3))* Bottom of the Hill Publishing.

—Oliver Twist. Belli, Alfredo, illus. 2008. (Green Apple Step Two Ser.). (ENG.). 96p. (J). (gr. 5). pap. incl. audio compact disk *(978-88-530-0580-9(7))* Cideb.

—Oliver Twist. 2008. (Bring the Classics to Life Ser.). (ENG., Illus.). 72p. (gr. 3-12). pap., act. bk. ed. 10.95 *(978-1-55576-325-1(1),* EDCTR-308B) EDCON Publishing Group.

—Oliver Twist. abr. ed. (J). 9.95 *(978-1-56156-372-2(2))* Kidsbooks, LLC.

—Oliver Twist. 2013. (Vintage Children's Classics Ser.). (Illus.). 736p. (J). (gr. 4-7). pap. 12.99 *(978-0-09-958263-2(5))* Penguin Random Hse. GBR. Dist: Independent Pubs. Group.

—Oliver Twist. Donnelly, Karen, illus. 2013. (Charles Dickens Ser.). (ENG.). 64p. pap. 7.95 *(978-1-906230-00-5(5))* Real Reads Ltd. GBR. Dist: Casemate Pubs. & Bk. Distributors, LLC.

—Oliver Twist, 1 vol. Donnelly, Karen, illus. 2009. (Real Reads Ser.). (ENG.). 64p. (YA). (gr. 5-5). pap. 14.55 *(978-1-60754-153-0(X),* 86478a93-d43b-486b-9cbe-5c249a8a89cd, Windmill Bks.) Rosen Publishing Group, Inc., The.

—Oliver Twist. Morgan, Richard & Fennell, Tracy, illus. 2008. 48p. (J). (gr. 4-7). pap. 10.00 *(978-1-4190-5075-6(3))* Steck-Vaughn.

—Oliver Twist: With a Discussion of Honesty. 2003. (Values in Action Illustrated Classics Ser.). (J). *(978-1-59203-051-4(3))* Learning Challenge, Inc.

Dickerson, Melanie. The Orphan's Wish, 1 vol. 2018. (ENG.). 352p. (YA). 16.99 *(978-0-7180-7483-8(1))* Nelson, Thomas Inc.

Dimpel, Matt. The War of the Serpent Swords. 2011. 230p. pap. 24.95 *(978-1-4626-3169-8(X))* PublishAmerica, Inc.

Dixon, John. Phoenix Island. 2014. (ENG.). 320p. pap. 17.99 *(978-1-4767-3865-9(3),* Gallery Bks.) Gallery Bks.

Doder, Joshua. Grk Smells a Rat. 2009. (J). *(978-0-385-90654-8(4),* Delacorte Pr) Random House Publishing Group.

Domínguez, José A. Mamerto: A Children's Story. 2006. (J). mass mkt. 12.50 *(978-1-59835-022-7(6))* Cambridge BrickHouse, Inc.

Domínguez, María, et al. Estrella de Fútbol: Soccer Star. 2015. (ENG & SPA., Illus.). 32p. (J). *(978-1-4806-9267-1(0))* Scholastic, Inc.

Donne, Alexa. Brightly Burning. (ENG.). (YA). (gr. 7). 2020. 416p. pap. 9.99 *(978-1-328-60438-5(1),* 1732068) 2018. 400p. 17.99 *(978-1-328-94893-9(5),* 1705605) HarperCollins Pubs. (Clarion Bks.).

Dowell, Frances O'Roark. Where I'd Like to Be. 2004. (Aladdin Fiction Ser.). 232p. (gr. 5-9). 17.00 *(978-0-7569-4357-8(4))* Perfection Learning Corp.

—Where I'd Like to Be. (ENG., (J). (gr. 5-9). 2003. Illus.). 240p. 17.99 *(978-0-689-84420-1(4))* 2004. 256p. reprint ed. pap. 7.99 *(978-0-689-87067-5(1))* Simon & Schuster Children's Publishing. (Atheneum Bks. for Young Readers).

—Where I'd Like to Be. Lt. ed. 2003. 162p. (J). 22.95 *(978-0-7862-5741-6(5))* Thorndike Pr.

Dower, Laura. Maggie's Magic Chocolate Moon. Lazuli, Lilly, illus. 2016. (Dessert Diaries). (ENG.). 160p. (J). (gr. 4-8). pap. 5.95 *(978-1-4965-4141-3(3),* 133429, Stone Arch Bks.) Capstone.

Doyle, Brian. Easy Avenue, 1 vol. 2nd ed. 2004. (ENG.). 144p. (J). (gr. 6-9). pap. 6.95 *(978-0-88899-605-3(5))* Groundwood Bks. CAN. Dist: Publishers Group West (PGW).

Doyle, Sheldon. Purple Mountain's Majesty. A Novel. 2008. (ENG.). 215p. pap. 21.95 *(978-1-4357-2017-6(2))* Lulu Pr., Inc.

Drake, Raelyn. Picking up Speed. 2018. (Superhuman Ser.). (ENG.). 104p. (YA). (gr. 6-12). pap. 7.99 *(978-1-5415-1050-0(X),* a3c8eb1b-eecb-4d50-a140-ef741d3cd510); 25.32 *(978-1-5124-9831-8(9),* 0d62eed7-3333-4987-81f2-288feafcf1dd) Lerner Publishing Group. (Darby Creek).

Du Jardin, Rosamond. Young & Fair. 2003. (YA). pap. 12.95 *(978-1-930009-79-0(8),* 800-691-7779) Image Cascade Publishing.

Duble, Kathleen Benner. Madame Tussaud's Apprentice: An Untold Story of Love in the French Revolution. 2014. (ENG.). 224p. (YA). 17.99 *(978-1-4405-8116-8(9),* Simon Pulse) Simon Pulse.

Dublin, Anne. The Baby Experiment: A Novel (Large Print 16pt) 2013. 172p. pap. *(978-1-4596-6337-4(3))* ReadHowYouWant.com, Ltd.

Dunkle, Clare B. The Hollow Kingdom: Book I — the Hollow Kingdom Trilogy. 2006. (Hollow Kingdom Trilogy Ser.: 1). (ENG.). 240p. (J). (gr. 6-9). reprint ed. pap. 16.99 *(978-0-8050-8108-4(9),* 900039576, Holt, Henry & Co. Bks. For Young Readers) Holt, Henry & Co.

—The House of Dead Maids: A Chilling Prelude to Wuthering Heights. Arrasmith, Patrick, illus. 2011. (ENG.). 176p. (YA). (gr. 7-12). pap. 16.99 *(978-0-312-55155-1(X),* 900074432) Square Fish.

Dunn, Joeming & Warner, Gertrude Chandler. The Lighthouse Mystery, 1 vol., Bk. 14. Dunn, Ben, illus. 2011. (Boxcar Children Graphic Novels Ser.). (ENG.). 32p. (J). (gr. 2-8). 32.79 *(978-1-61641-122-0(8)*, 3684, Graphic Planet - Fiction) Magic Wagon.

—The Woodshed Mystery, 1 vol., Bk. 13. Dunn, Ben, illus. 2011. (Boxcar Children Graphic Novels Ser.). (ENG.). 32p. (J). (gr. 3-8). 32.79 *(978-1-61641-121-3(X)*, 3683, Graphic Planet - Fiction) Magic Wagon.

Durrant, S. E. Little Bits of Sky. Harnett, Katie, illus. 2017. (ENG.). 208p. (J). (gr. 3-7). 16.95 *(978-0-8234-3839-6(2))* Holiday Hse., Inc.

Eagar, Lindsay. Race to the Bottom of the Sea. (ENG.). 432p. (J). (gr. 3-7). 2019. pap. 9.99 *(978-0-7636-9877-5(6))* 2017. 17.99 *(978-0-7636-7923-1(2))* Candlewick Pr.

Edge, Christopher. Twelve Minutes to Midnight. 2014. (Penelope Tredwell Mysteries Ser.: 1). (ENG.). 256p. (J). (gr. 3-7). 16.99 *(978-0-8075-8133-9(X)*, 080758133X) Whitman, Albert & Co.

Edwards, Garth. Escape from Mercy Hall. 2012. (Thorn Gate Trilogy Ser.). (Illus.). 192p. (J). (gr. 4-6). pap. 7.99 *(978-0-9567122-4-0(X))* Lerner Publishing Group.

Edwards, Judith. Invasion on the Mountain: The Adventures of Will Ryan & the Civilian Conservation Corps, 1933, Book I. 2011. (Images from the Past Ser.). (ENG., Illus.). 90p. (J). (gr. 4-7). pap. 12.50 *(978-1-884592-55-3(4))* Applewood Bks.

—Trouble on the Mountain: The Adventures of Will Ryan & the Civilian Conservation Corps, 1934-35 Book II. 2012. (Images from the Past Ser.). (ENG., Illus.). 118p. (J). (gr. 3-7). pap. 12.50 *(978-1-884592-60-7(0))* Applewood Bks.

Edwards, Julie Andrews. Mandy. 2nd ed. 2006. (ENG., Illus.). 320p. (J). (gr. 3-7). 17.99 *(978-0-06-113162-2(8))*; pap. 9.99 *(978-0-06-120707-5(1))* HarperCollins Pubs. (HarperCollins).

Edwards, S. Neil. My Dog, Digger. 2006. 122p. pap. 19.95 *(978-1-4241-0514-4(5))* America Star Bks.

Eliot, Ethel. The Little House in the Fairy Wood. 2006. 108p. per. 9.95 *(978-1-59818-097-8(5))*; 22.95 *(978-1-59818-343-6(5))* Aegypan.

Eliot, Ethel Cook. The Little House in the Fairy Wood. 2017. (ENG., Illus.). (J). 22.95 *(978-1-374-81790-6(2))* Capital Communications, Inc.

—The Little House in the Fairy Wood. 2015. (ENG., Illus.). (J). 22.95 *(978-1-297-76874-3(4))* Creative Media Partners, LLC.

Ellis, Deborah. The Heaven Shop, 1 vol. 2007. (ENG., Illus.). 186p. (YA). (gr. 6-9). per. 12.95 *(978-1-55455-086-9(6)*, eadf642d-0c21-4d47-964b-d476c82614cf) Fitzhenry & Whiteside, Ltd. CAN. Dist: Firefly Bks., Ltd.

—No Ordinary Day, 1 vol. 2011. (ENG.). (J). 144p. (gr. 3-7). 16.95 *(978-1-55498-134-2(4))*; 160p. (gr. 4-7). pap. 9.95 *(978-1-55498-108-3(5))* Groundwood Bks. CAN. Dist: Publishers Group West (PGW).

—No Ordinary Day. 2013. 164p. pap. *(978-1-4596-6451-7(5))* ReadHowYouWant.com, Ltd.

Ellis, Mary. Elephant Child. MacDonald Denton, Kady, illus. 2010. (ENG.). 128p. (gr. 2-4). pap. 7.99 *(978-0-00-712820-4(7)*, HarperCollins Children's Bks.) HarperCollins Pubs. Ltd. GBR. Dist: HarperCollins Pubs.

Ellis, Sarah. The Several Lives of Orphan Jack, 1 vol. St-Aubin, Bruno, illus. 2004. (ENG.). 88p. (J). (gr. 2-5). pap. 8.95 *(978-0-88899-618-3(7))* Groundwood Bks. CAN. Dist: Publishers Group West (PGW).

Emerson, Alice B. Ruth Fielding at Snow Camp or Lost in the Backwoods. 2005. reprint ed. pap. 24.95 *(978-1-4179-3132-3(9))* Kessinger Publishing, LLC.

—Ruth Fielding in the Red Cross or Doing. 2005. pap. 24.95 *(978-1-4179-1799-0(7))* Kessinger Publishing, LLC.

—Ruth Fielding on the St. Lawrence or the. 2005. pap. 24.95 *(978-0-7661-9911-8(8))* Kessinger Publishing, LLC.

Emery, Joanna. Brothers of the Falls. Erickson, David, illus. 2004. (Adventures in America Ser.). (gr. 4). 14.95 *(978-1-893110-37-3(0))* Silver Moon Pr.

Fagan, Deva. Circus Galacticus. 2013. (ENG.). 304p. (J). (gr. 4-6). 17.44 *(978-0-547-58136-1(X))* Harcourt Children's Bks.

Falkner, John Meade. Moonfleet: A Classic Tale of Smuggling. Marks, Alan, illus. 2007. (Young Reading Series 3 Gift Bks). 63p. (J). (gr. 4-7). 8.99 *(978-0-7945-1906-3(7)*, Usborne) EDC Publishing.

Fenn, G. Manville. Brownsmith's Boy. 2008. 260p. 29.95 *(978-1-60664-780-6(6))* Aegypan.

Ferguson, M. J. The Mirror in the Box: A Children's Story & a Parable. 2013. 66p. (gr. 4-6). pap. 9.99 *(978-1-4497-7804-0(6)*, WestBow Pr.) Author Solutions, LLC.

Ficklin, Jonene H. The Garden Gate. 2005. (YA). 14.95 *(978-0-9761188-2-4(3))* Victor's Crown Publishing.

Fiona Fox Staff, ed. The Secret Garden. 2012. (ENG., Illus.). 64p. 15.00 *(978-1-84135-837-6(1))* Award Pubns. Ltd. GBR. Dist: Parkwest Pubns., Inc.

Fisher, Dorothy Canfield. Understood Betsy. 2018. (ENG., Illus.). 108p. (J). 12.99 *(978-1-5154-3494-8(X))* Wilder Pubns., Corp.

Forman, M. L. Adventurers Wanted, Book 1: Slathbog's Gold. 2011. (Adventurers Wanted Ser.: 1). (ENG.). 416p. (J). (gr. 5). mass mkt. 9.99 *(978-1-60641-681-5(2)*, 5053131, Shadow Mountain) Shadow Mountain Publishing.

—Adventurers Wanted, Book 2: The Horn of Moran. 2011. 400p. 39.99 *(978-1-60641-255-8(8))* Deseret Bk. Co.

—Adventurers Wanted, Book 2: The Horn of Moran. 2012. (Adventurers Wanted Ser.: 2). (ENG.). 384p. (J). (gr. 5). pap. 9.99 *(978-1-60908-911-5(1)*, 5069125, Shadow Mountain) Shadow Mountain Publishing.

—Adventurers Wanted, Book 3: Albrek's Tomb. 2013. (Adventurers Wanted Ser.: 3). (ENG.). 504p. (J). (gr. 5). pap. 9.99 *(978-1-60907-339-8(8)*, 5097801, Shadow Mountain) Shadow Mountain Publishing.

—Adventurers Wanted, Book 4: Sands of Nezza. 2013. (Adventurers Wanted Ser.: 4). (ENG.). 400p. (J). (gr. 5). 19.99 *(978-1-60907-329-9(0)*, 5097486, Shadow Mountain) Shadow Mountain Publishing.

—Adventures Wanted, Book 3: Albrek's Tomb. 2012. x, 494p. (YA). 19.99 *(978-1-60908-892-7(1))* Deseret Bk. Co.

Forman, Mark. The Horn of Moran. 2011. 400p. (YA). (gr. 3-18). 18.99 *(978-1-60641-226-8(4)*, Shadow Mountain) Shadow Mountain Publishing.

—Slathbog's Gold. 2009. (Adventurers Wanted Ser.: Bk. 1). 432p. (J). 17.95 *(978-1-60641-029-5(6)*, Shadow Mountain) Shadow Mountain Publishing.

Forster, Miriam. City of a Thousand Dolls. 2013. (ENG.). 368p. (YA). (gr. 8). 17.99 *(978-0-06-212130-1(8)*, HarperTeen) HarperCollins Pubs.

Forte, Joseph. At the Window. 2013. 32p. pap. *(978-1-4602-2190-7(7))* FriesenPress.

Foster, Stewart. Bubble. 2017. (ENG., Illus.). 352p. (J). (gr. 3-5). 16.99 *(978-1-4814-8742-9(6)*, Simon & Schuster Bks. For Young Readers) Simon & Schuster Bks. For Young Readers.

Fox, Jennifer. Meet the Boxtrolls. 2014. (Passport to Reading Level 2 Ser.). (J). lib. bdg. 13.55 *(978-0-606-36529-1(X))* Turtleback.

Francis, Pauline, retold by. The Turn of the Screw, 1 vol. 2010. (Essential Classics - Horror Ser.). (ENG., Illus.). 48p. pap. *(978-0-237-54110-1(6))* Evans Brothers, Ltd.

Frazier, Neta. The Stout-Hearted Seven: Orphaned on the Oregon Trail. 2017. (Great Leaders & Events Ser.). (ENG.). (J). (gr. 4-8). lib. bdg. 35.99 *(978-1-942875-43-7(6))* Quarto Publishing Group USA.

Frederick Marryat. The Children of the New Forest. 2007. 412p. per. 17.95 *(978-1-4218-4823-5(6))*; 33.95 *(978-1-4218-4726-9(4))* 1st World Publishing, Inc. (1st World Library - Literary Society).

Freedman, Nancy Price. Isak & the Oranges: The Half-Orphans of HOA (Hebrew Orphan Asylum, NY) 2015. (ENG., Illus.). 107p. (J). pap. 10.95 *(978-1-4787-5564-7(4))* Outskirts Pr., Inc.

Freeman, Blake. Haibu Lost in New York. 2018. (Haibu Ser.). (ENG., Illus.). 144p. (J). (gr. 1-4). 18.99 *(978-1-5132-6221-5(1))*; pap. 7.99 *(978-1-5132-6220-8(3))* West Margin Pr. (Graphic Arts Bks.).

French, Vivian. The Bag of Bones: The Second Tale from the Five Kingdoms. Collins, Ross, illus. 2009. (Tales from the Five Kingdoms Ser.: 2). (ENG.). 256p. (J). (gr. 3-7). 14.99 *(978-0-7636-4255-6(X))* Candlewick Pr.

Frost, C. Amethyst. Mourning under the Bridge. 2012. 280p. pap. 9.99 *(978-0-9847236-2-1(5))* Frost, C. A.

Funaro, Gregory. Alistair Grim's Odd Aquaticum. 2016. (Alistair Grim Ser.: 2). (ENG.). 448p. (J). (gr. 3-7). pap. 7.99 *(978-1-4847-0900-9(4))* Hyperion Bks. for Children.

—Alistair Grim's Odditorium. 2015. (J). lib. bdg. 18.40 *(978-0-606-37399-9(3))* Turtleback.

Funke, Cornelia. The Thief Lord. Birmingham, Christian, illus. 2010.Tr. of Herr der Diebe. (ENG.). 368p. (J). (gr. 4-7). pap. 9.99 *(978-0-545-22770-4(4))* Scholastic, Inc.

Gaiman, Neil. The Graveyard Book. 2009. (CHI.). 304p. (J). (gr. 5-8). pap. *(978-957-33-2574-1(8))* Crown Publishing Co., Ltd.

—The Graveyard Book. McKean, Dave, illus. (J). 2018. (ENG.). 368p. (gr. 5). pap. 10.99 *(978-0-06-053094-5(4)*, HarperCollins) 2008. 552p. pap. 17.99 *(978-0-06-170912-8(3))* 2008. (ENG.). 368p. (gr. 5-7). 17.99 *(978-0-06-053092-1(8)*, HarperCollins) 2008. (ENG.). 320p. (gr. 5-7). lib. bdg. 18.89 *(978-0-06-053093-8(6)*, HarperCollins) HarperCollins Pubs.

—The Graveyard Book. 2009. 19.00 *(978-1-60686-823-2(3))* Perfection Learning Corp.

—The Graveyard Book. 2011. (Literature Kit Ser.). (ENG., Illus.). 55p. pap. 12.95 *(978-1-55319-559-7(0)*, Classroom Complete Pr.) Rainbow Horizons Publishing, Inc.

—The Graveyard Book, 7 vols. 2008. (J). 100.75 *(978-1-4361-5887-9(7))*; 256.75 *(978-1-4361-5882-4(6))* Recorded Bks., Inc.

—The Graveyard Book. l.t. ed. 2009. (ENG.). 373p. (YA). 23.95 *(978-1-4104-1441-0(8))* Thorndike Pr.

—The Graveyard Book. 2010. (J). lib. bdg. 19.65 *(978-0-606-14883-2(3))* Turtleback.

—The Graveyard Book Commemorative Edition. McKean, Dave, illus. 2014. (ENG.). 352p. (J). (gr. 5-7). pap. 9.99 *(978-0-06-234918-7(X)*, HarperCollins) HarperCollins Pubs.

—El Libro Del Cementerio. (SPA.). 2010. 256p. pap. 20.95 *(978-84-9918-146-2(5))* Vol. 1. 2009. 306p. (YA). 20.95 *(978-84-9918-030-4(2))* Roca Editorial ESP. Dist: Spanish Pubs., LLC.

Gaiman, Neil & Russell, P. Craig. The Graveyard Book Graphic Novel: Volume 1, Vol. 1. Russell, P. Craig, illus. 2014. (ENG., Illus.). 192p. (J). (gr. 3-7). 19.99 *(978-0-06-219481-7(X)*, Quill Tree Bks.) HarperCollins Pubs.

—The Graveyard Book Graphic Novel: Volume 2, Vol. 2. Russell, P. Craig, illus. 2014. (ENG., Illus.). 176p. (J). (gr. 3-7). 19.99 *(978-0-06-219483-1(6)*, Quill Tree Bks.) HarperCollins Pubs.

Galdos, Benito Perez. Tristana. Costa, Margaret Jull, tr. 2014. (NYRB Classics Ser.). 192p. pap. 14.95 *(978-1-59017-765-5(7)*, NYRB Classics) New York Review of Bks., Inc., The.

Garcia, Kami. Teen Titans: Raven. Picolo, Gabriel, illus. 2019. 192p. (YA). (gr. 7). pap. 16.99 *(978-1-4012-8623-1(2)*, DC Ink) DC Comics.

Gardner, Sally. The Red Necklace. 2009. (ENG.). 400p. (YA). (gr. 7-18). 8.99 *(978-0-14-241488-0(3)*, Speak) Penguin Young Readers Group.

—The Red Necklace: A Story of the French Revolution. 2009. (ENG.). 378p. (YA). (gr. 7). lib. bdg. 19.80 *(978-1-5311-8287-8(9))* Perfection Learning Corp.

—The Red Necklace: A Story of the French Revolution. l.t. ed. 2008. 583p. 23.95 *(978-1-4104-1016-0(1))* Thorndike Pr.

Garinger, Alan K. Alone: The Journey of the Boy Sims. 2008. (J). 15.95 *(978-0-87195-266-0(1))*; pap. 7.95 *(978-0-87195-267-7(X))* Indiana Historical Society.

Garlick, Nicholas. Storm Horse. 2017. 242p. (J). pap. *(978-0-545-90415-5(3))* Scholastic, Inc.

Gemeinhart, Dan. The Midnight Children. 2022. (ENG.). 352p. (J). 16.99 *(978-1-250-19672-9(8)*, 900194233, Holt, Henry & Co. Bks. For Young Readers) Holt, Henry & Co.

George, Jessica Day. Dragon Slippers. 2008. (Dragon Slippers Ser.). (ENG., Illus.). 352p. (YA). (gr. 5). pap. 9.99 *(978-1-59990-275-3(3)*, 900051439, Bloomsbury USA Childrens) Bloomsbury Publishing USA.

—Dragon Slippers. l.t. ed. 2008. (Thorndike Literacy Bridge Middle Reader Ser.). 391p. (J). (gr. 4-7). 22.95 *(978-1-4104-0337-7(8))* Thorndike Pr.

—The Rose Legacy. 2018. (Rose Legacy Ser.). (ENG.). 272p. (J). 17.99 *(978-1-59990-647-8(3)*, 900074530, Bloomsbury Children's Bks.) Bloomsbury Publishing USA.

Giff, Patricia Reilly. Eleven. (ENG.). (J). 2009. 176p. (gr. 3-7). 7.99 *(978-0-440-23802-7(1)*, Yearling) 2008. 164p. (gr. 4-6). lib. bdg. 21.19 *(978-0-385-90098-0(8)*, Lamb, Wendy Bks.) Random Hse. Children's Bks.

—Gingersnap. 2014. (ENG.). 160p. (J). (gr. 3-7). 6.99 *(978-0-440-42178-8(0)*, Yearling) Random Hse. Children's Bks.

—Pictures of Hollis Woods. 2014. (ENG.). 176p. (J). (gr. 3-7). 11.24 *(978-1-63245-318-1(5))* Lectorum Pubns., Inc.

—Pictures of Hollis Woods. 2004. (ENG.). 176p. (J). (gr. 3-7). 8.99 *(978-0-440-41578-7(0)*, Yearling) Random Hse. Children's Bks.

Gildea, Kathy. The Adventures of Baylee Beagle — Annabelle Beagle. Larson, Amanda, illus. 2005. 28p. (J). 7.95 *(978-0-9767096-1-9(9))* Maxim Pr.

—The Adventures of Baylee Beagle — Greenville. 2005. (Illus.). 20p. (J). 7.95 *(978-0-9767096-0-2(0))* Maxim Pr.

—The Adventures of Baylee Beagle — Hurricane Hound. Larson, Amanda, illus. 2005. 28p. (J). 7.95 *(978-0-9767096-2-6(7))* Maxim Pr.

Glasgow, Kathleen. How to Make Friends with the Dark. (ENG.). (YA). (gr. 9). 2020. 448p. pap. 12.99 *(978-1-101-93478-4(6)*, Ember) 2019. 432p. 18.99 *(978-1-101-93475-3(1)*, Delacorte Pr.) 2019. 432p. lib. bdg. 21.99 *(978-1-101-93477-7(8)*, Delacorte Pr.) Random Hse. Children's Bks.

Gleitzman, Morris. Once. 2013. (Once Ser.: 1). (ENG.). 192p. (YA). (gr. 7). pap. 10.99 *(978-0-312-65304-0(2)*, 900069444) Square Fish.

—Then. 2013. (Once Ser.: 2). (ENG.). 224p. (YA). (gr. 7). pap. 11.99 *(978-1-250-00341-6(5)*, 900079882) Square Fish.

—Then. 2013. (YA). lib. bdg. 20.85 *(978-0-606-31904-1(2))* Turtleback.

Godden, Rumer. The Story of Holly & Ivy. Cooney, Barbara, illus. 2006. (ENG.). 32p. (J). (gr. k-3). 17.99 *(978-0-670-06219-5(7)*, Viking Books for Young Readers) Penguin Young Readers Group.

Golding, Julia. Cat among the Pigeons, 2. 2006. (Cat Royal Adventure Ser.: 2). (ENG.). 400p. (J). (gr. 6-8). 22.44 *(978-0-312-60215-4(4)*, 900064230) Square Fish.

—Cat o'Nine Tails. 2018. (ENG., Illus.). 374p. (J). (gr. 5-9). pap. *(978-1-910426-18-0(0))* Frost Wolf.

—Den of Thieves. 2018. (ENG., Illus.). 406p. (J). (gr. 5-9). pap. *(978-1-910426-16-6(4))* Frost Wolf.

—The Diamond of Drury Lane, 1. 2009. (Cat Royal Adventure Ser.: 1). (ENG., Illus.). 424p. (J). (gr. 6-8). 22.44 *(978-0-312-56123-9(7)*, 900058857) Square Fish.

Gonick, Larry. Kokopelli & Company in Attack of the Smart Pies. 2005. (ENG., Illus.). 192p. (J). 15.95 *(978-0-8126-2740-4(7))* Cricket Bks.

Goudge, Elizabeth. The Little White Horse. movie tie-in ed. 2008. (ENG., Illus.). 224p. (J). (gr. 4-7). pap. *(978-0-7459-6118-7(5))* Lion Hudson PLC GBR. Dist: Independent Pubs. Group.

Graff, Lisa. A Tangle of Knots. 2013. (ENG.). 240p. (J). (gr. 3-7). 17.99 *(978-0-399-25517-5(6)*, Philomel Bks.) Penguin Young Readers Group.

Grant, Holly. The League of Beastly Dreadfuls Book 1. (League of Beastly Dreadfuls Ser.: 1). (Illus.). (J). (gr. 3-7). 2016. 336p. 8.99 *(978-0-385-37010-3(5)*, Yearling) 2015. 320p. 16.99 *(978-0-385-37007-3(5)*, Random Hse. Bks. for Young Readers) Random Hse. Children's Bks.

—The Witch's Glass. Portillo, Josie, illus. 2017. (League of Beastly Dreadfuls Ser.: Bk. 3). 305p. (J). pap. *(978-1-101-93369-5(0))* Random Hse., Inc.

Gratton, Tessa. Blood Magic. 2012. (Blood Journals). (ENG.). 416p. (YA). (gr. 8-12). lib. bdg. 26.19 *(978-0-375-96733-7(8))* Random House Publishing Group.

—Blood Magic. 2011. 408p. (YA). pap. *(978-0-375-86486-5(5))* Random Hse. Children's Bks.

Gray, Claudia. Defy the Fates. 2019. (Defy the Stars Ser.: 3). (ENG.). 480p. (YA). (gr. 9-17). 18.99 *(978-0-316-44075-2(2))* Little, Brown Bks. for Young Readers.

—Defy the Stars. 2018. (Defy the Stars Ser.: 1). (ENG.). 528p. (YA). (gr. 9-17). pap. 23.99 *(978-0-316-39404-8(1))* Little, Brown Bks. for Young Readers.

—Defy the Worlds. 2019. (Defy the Stars Ser.: 2). (ENG.). 496p. (YA). (gr. 9-17). pap. 12.99 *(978-0-316-39407-9(6))* Little, Brown Bks. for Young Readers.

Great, Alex. Balkan Tales. 2009. 134p. pap. 18.36 *(978-1-4452-4363-4(6))* Lulu Pr., Inc.

Greenburg, Dan. Secrets of Dripping Fang, Book One: The Onts. Fischer, Scott M., illus. 2005. (Secrets of Dripping Fang Ser.: Bk. 1). (ENG.). 144p. (J). (gr. 3-7). 12.99 *(978-0-15-205457-1(X)*, 1196419, Clarion Bks.) HarperCollins Pubs.

—Secrets of Dripping Fang, Book Two: Treachery & Betrayal at Jolly Days. Fischer, Scott M., illus. 2006. (Secrets of Dripping Fang Ser.: Bk. 2). (ENG.). 144p. (J). (gr. 3-7). 12.99 *(978-0-15-205463-2(4)*, 1196437, Clarion Bks.) HarperCollins Pubs.

Grew, David. The Wild Dog of Edmonton. Segner, Ellen, illus. 2011. 208p. 44.95 *(978-1-258-09902-2(0))* Literary Licensing, LLC.

Griffin, A. C. America's Child. 2008. (J). pap. 9.99 *(978-0-88092-492-4(6))* Royal Fireworks Publishing Co.

Griffith, A. J. America's Child. 2008. (J). pap. 9.99 *(978-0-88092-493-1(4))* Royal Fireworks Publishing Co.

Grogan, Joy. Into the Fold. 2003. 156p. per. 15.00 *(978-0-9740321-6-0(6))* Open Bk. Publishing.

The Guardians. 2014. (ENG., Illus.). 288p. (J). (gr. 4-8). pap. 7.99 *(978-1-4814-1834-8(3)*, Aladdin) Simon & Schuster Children's Publishing.

Gustafson, Scott. Eddie: The Lost Youth of Edgar Allan Poe. Gustafson, Scott, illus. 2012. (ENG., Illus.). 208p. (J). (gr. 3-7). pap. 6.99 *(978-1-4169-9765-8(2)*, Simon & Schuster Bks. For Young Readers) Simon & Schuster Bks. For Young Readers.

—Eddie: The Lost Youth of Edgar Allan Poe. Gustafson, Scott, illus. 2011. (ENG., Illus.). 208p. (J). (gr. 3-7). 15.99 *(978-1-4169-9764-1(4))* Simon & Schuster, Inc.

Guterson, Ben. The Secrets of Winterhouse. Bristol, Chloe, illus. 2019. (Winterhouse Ser.: 2). (ENG.). 400p. (J). pap. 9.99 *(978-1-250-23352-3(6)*, 900174324) Square Fish.

—Winterhouse. Bristol, Chloe, illus. 2018. (Winterhouse Ser.: 1). (ENG.). 400p. (J). pap. 8.99 *(978-1-250-29419-7(3)*, 900174321) Square Fish.

Guzman, Lila & Guzman, Rick. Lorenzo's Revolutionary Quest. 2003. 176p. (J). pap. 9.95 *(978-1-55885-392-8(8)*, Piñata Books) Arte Publico Pr.

—Lorenzo's Secret Mission. 2005. 153p. (gr. 4-7). 19.95 *(978-0-7569-5599-1(8))* Perfection Learning Corp.

Habel, Lia. Dearly, Departed: a Zombie Novel. 2012. (Gone with the Respiration Ser.: 1). (ENG.). 496p. (YA). (gr. 8-12). pap. 10.99 *(978-0-345-52332-7(6)*, Del Rey) Random Hse. Worlds.

Haberdasher, Violet. Knightley Academy. 2011. (ENG.). 512p. (J). (gr. 3-7). pap. 5.99 *(978-1-4169-9144-1(1)*, Aladdin) Simon & Schuster Children's Publishing.

—Knightley Academy. 2010. (ENG.). 480p. (J). (gr. 3-7). 16.99 *(978-1-4169-9143-4(3)*, Simon & Schuster/Paula Wiseman Bks.) Simon & Schuster/Paula Wiseman Bks.

—The Secret Prince: A Knightley Academy Book. (ENG.). 512p. (J). (gr. 3-7). 2012. pap. 7.99 *(978-1-4169-9146-5(8))* 2011. 16.99 *(978-1-4169-9145-8(X))* Simon & Schuster/Paula Wiseman Bks. (Simon & Schuster/Paula Wiseman Bks.).

Haddix, Margaret Peterson. Palace of Mirrors. 2010. (Palace Chronicles Ser.: 2). (ENG.). 320p. (J). (gr. 5-9). pap. 8.99 *(978-1-4424-0667-4(4)*, Simon & Schuster Bks. For Young Readers) Simon & Schuster Bks. For Young Readers.

Hagman, Harvey. Majesty from Assateague, 1 vol. 2009. (ENG., Illus.). 80p. (J). pap. 8.95 *(978-0-87033-552-5(9)*, 3670, Cornell Maritime Pr./Tidewater Pubs.) Schiffer Publishing, Ltd.

Hahn, Mary Downing. The Ghost of Crutchfield Hall. 2011. (ENG.). 160p. (J). (gr. 5-7). pap. 7.99 *(978-0-547-57715-9(X)*, 1458473, Clarion Bks.) HarperCollins Pubs.

—Promises to the Dead. 2009. (ENG.). 208p. (J). (gr. 5-7). pap. 7.99 *(978-0-547-25838-6(0)*, 1402071, Clarion Bks.) HarperCollins Pubs.

Halpern, Jake & Kujawinski, Peter. Edgeland. 2018. (ENG., Illus.). 288p. (J). (gr. 5). 8.99 *(978-0-14-751741-8(9)*, Puffin Books) Penguin Young Readers Group.

Hand, Cynthia, et al. My Plain Jane. (Lady Janies Ser.). (ENG.). (YA). (gr. 8). 2019. 480p. pap. 10.99 *(978-0-06-265278-2(8))* 2018. 464p. 17.99 *(978-0-06-265277-5(X))* HarperCollins Pubs. (HarperTeen).

Hanley, Victoria. Violet Wings. 2009. (ENG.). 368p. (J). (gr. 6-8). lib. bdg. 21.19 *(978-1-60684-039-9(8))* Farshore GBR. Dist: Children's Plus, Inc.

Hansen, Joyce. One True Friend. 2005. (ENG.). 160p. (J). (gr. 5-7). pap. 11.95 *(978-0-618-60991-8(1)*, 100443, Clarion Bks.) HarperCollins Pubs.

Hardinge, Frances. Fly Trap. 2012. 592p. (J). (gr. 5). pap. 7.99 *(978-0-06-088046-0(5))* HarperCollins Pubs.

Hardy, Janice. The Healing Wars: Book II: Blue Fire. (Healing Wars Ser.: II). (ENG.). (J). (gr. 5). 2011. 400p. pap. 7.99 *(978-0-06-174744-1(0))*Bk. 2. 2010. 384p. 16.99 *(978-0-06-174741-0(6))* HarperCollins Pubs. (Balzer & Bray).

—The Shifter. 2009. (Healing Wars Ser.). 384p. (J). (gr. 5-18). lib. bdg. 17.89 *(978-0-06-176177-5(X))* HarperCollins Pubs.

Harlow, Joan Hiatt. Midnight Rider. 2006. (ENG.). 384p. (J). (gr. 4-9). pap. 8.99 *(978-0-689-87010-1(8)*, McElderry, Margaret K. Bks.) McElderry, Margaret K. Bks.

—Thunder from the Sea. 2004. (ENG., Illus.). 208p. (J). (gr. 3-7). 17.99 *(978-0-689-86403-2(5)*, McElderry, Margaret K. Bks.) McElderry, Margaret K. Bks.

Harris, Christine. Undercover Girl #5: Twisted. 2007. (ENG.). 136p. (J). per. 10.95 *(978-1-59594-151-0(7)*, Wingspan Pr.) WingSpan Publishing.

Harris, Neil Patrick. The Magic Misfits. Martin, Lissy & Hilton, Kyle, illus. (Magic Misfits Ser.: 1). (ENG.). (J). (gr. 3-7). 2018. 288p. pap. 8.99 *(978-0-316-35557-5(7))* 2017. 272p. 16.99 *(978-0-316-39182-5(4))* 2017. 336p. 34.99 *(978-0-316-43984-8(3))* Little, Brown Bks. for Young Readers.

—The Magic Misfits: the Minor Third. 2019. (Magic Misfits Ser.: 3). (ENG.). (J). (gr. 3-7). Illus.). 336p. 16.99 *(978-0-316-39187-0(5))*; 400p. 36.99 *(978-0-316-42589-6(3))* Little, Brown Bks. for Young Readers.

—The Magic Misfits: the Second Story. Martin, Lissy & Hilton, Kyle, illus. (Magic Misfits Ser.: 2). (ENG.). (J). (gr. 3-7). 2019. 352p. pap. 8.99 *(978-0-316-39184-9(0))* 2018. 336p. 16.99 *(978-0-316-39185-6(9))* 2018. 400p. 37.99 *(978-0-316-41986-4(9))* Little, Brown Bks. for Young Readers.

Harris, Neil Patrick & Azam, Alec. The Magic Misfits: The Second Story. Martin, Lissy, illus. 2018. xii, 312p. (J). *(978-0-316-48724-5(4))*; *(978-0-316-52639-5(8))* Little Brown & Co.

Harrison, Michelle. 13 Curses. 2012. (13 Treasures Trilogy Ser.: 2). (ENG.). 512p. (J). (gr. 5-9). pap. 23.99 *(978-0-316-04149-2(1))* Little, Brown Bks. for Young Readers.

—13 Curses. 2012. (13 Treasures Ser.: 2). (J). lib. bdg. 19.65 *(978-0-606-26160-9(5))* Turtleback.

Hawes, Charles Boardman. The Dark Frigate. Chappell, Warren, illus. 2018. (ENG.). 240p. (gr. 3-7). pap. 7.99 *(978-0-486-82392-8(X)*, 82392X) Dover Pubns., Inc.

—The Dark Frigate. 2005. pap. 27.95 *(978-1-4179-3209-2(0))* Kessinger Publishing, LLC.

Hawthorne, Rachel. Dark Guardian #4: Shadow of the Moon. 2010. (Dark Guardian Ser.: 4). (ENG.). 256p. (YA). (gr. 9-18). pap. 8.99 *(978-0-06-196290-5(2)*, HarperTeen) HarperCollins Pubs.

Hayes, Sean & Icenogle, Scott. Plum. Thompson, Robin, illus. 2018. (ENG.). 48p. (J). (gr. -1-3). 17.99 *(978-1-5344-0404-5(X)*, Simon & Schuster Bks. For Young Readers) Simon & Schuster Bks. For Young Readers.

Heimerdinger, Chris. Escape from Zarahemla. 2011. 263p. (YA). pap. *(978-1-60861-539-1(1))* Covenant Communications.

Helldorfer, M. C. Anne of Green Gables. Beier, Ellen, illus. 2003. 40p. (J). (gr. -1-2). pap. 7.99 *(978-0-440-41614-2(0)*, Dragonfly Bks.) Random Hse. Children's Bks.

Hembree, G. Wil. The Willisby Orphans: In the Keys to the Bottomless Pit. 2011. 552p. (gr. -1 — 1). 44.95

(978-1-4497-2366-8(7)); pap. 34.95 *(978-1-4497-2365-1(9))* Author Solutions, LLC. (WestBow Pr.).

Hemphill, Kris. Ambush in the Wilderness. 2003. (Adventures in America Ser.). (Illus.). 90p. (gr. 4). 14.95 *(978-1-893110-34-2(6))* Silver Moon Pr.

Hendershot, Eric. At Season's End. 2012. 164p. (YA). pap. 13.99 *(978-1-59955-995-7(1))* Cedar Fort, Inc./CFI Distribution.

Henderson, Lauren. Kiss Me Kill Me. 2009. (Scarlett Wakefield Ser.). 272p. (YA). (gr. 9). pap. 10.99 *(978-0-385-73488-2(3))*, Delacorte Pr.) Random Hse. Children's Bks.

—Kisses & Lies, 2. 2009. (Scarlett Wakefield Novels Ser.). (ENG.). 320p. (J). (gr. 9-12). lib. bdg. 26.19 *(978-0-385-90486-5(X))*, Delacorte Pr.) Random Hse. Children's Bks.

Henderson, Leah. One Shadow on the Wall. (ENG.). 448p. (J). (gr. 3-7). 2018. pap. 8.99 *(978-1-4814-6296-9(2))* 2017. (Illus.). 18.99 *(978-1-4814-6295-2(4))* Simon & Schuster Children's Publishing. (Atheneum Bks. for Young Readers).

Heneghan, Judith. The Magician's Apprentice. 2008. (Illus.). 168p. (J). (gr. 3-7). 16.95 *(978-0-8234-2150-3(3))* Holiday Hse., Inc.

Herbert, Bethany Zohner. The Perfect Fool. 2015. 279p. (YA). pap. 17.99 *(978-1-4621-1620-1(5))* Cedar Fort, Inc./CFI Distribution.

Hering, Marianne. Trouble on the Orphan Train. 2016. (AIO Imagination Station Bks.: 18). (ENG.). 144p. (J). pap. 5.99 *(978-1-58997-805-8(6))*, 20_27692) Focus on the Family Publishing.

Hest, Amy. When Jessie Came Across the Sea. 2003. 17.20 *(978-0-613-69484-1(8))* Turtleback.

Hicks, Jamara. Calvin Gets a Family. 2009. 24p. pap. 12.00 *(978-1-4490-4754-2(8))* AuthorHouse.

Higgins, Simon. Moonshadow: the Nightmare Ninja. 2012. (Moonshadow Ser.: 2). (ENG.). 384p. (J). (gr. 3-7). pap. 19.99 *(978-0-316-05534-5(4))* Little, Brown Bks. for Young Readers.

Hill, Kirkpatrick. Bo at Ballard Creek. Pham, LeUyen, illus. 2014. (ENG.). 304p. (J). (gr. 3-7). pap. 13.99 *(978-1-250-04425-9(1))*, 900128317) Square Fish.

Hoban, Julia. Willow. (ENG.). (YA). (gr. 9-18). 2010. 336p. 9.99 *(978-0-14-241666-2(5))*, Speak) 2009. 224p. 26.19 *(978-0-8037-3356-5(9))* Penguin Young Readers Group.

Hobbs, Valerie. Maggie & Oliver or a Bone of One's Own. Thermes, Jennifer, illus. 2013. (ENG.). 208p. (J). (gr. 8-12). pap. 21.19 *(978-1-250-01672-0(X))*, 9781250016720) Square Fish.

Hobbs, William. Jason's Gold. unabr. ed. 2004. 240p. (J). (gr. 5-9). pap. 38.00 incl. audio *(978-0-8072-8229-8(4))*, Listening Library) Random Hse. Audio Publishing Group.

Holder, Nancy & Viguie, Debbie. Unleashed. 2012. (Wolf Spring Chronicles Ser.: 1). (ENG.). 400p. (YA). (gr. 7). pap. 9.99 *(978-0-385-74099-9(9))*, Ember) Random Hse. Children's Bks.

Holm, Jennifer L. Boston Jane: the Claim. 2010. (Boston Jane Ser.: 3). (ENG.). 224p. (J). (gr. 3-7). pap. 8.99 *(978-0-375-86206-9(4))*, Yearling) Random Hse. Children's Bks.

—Boston Jane: Wilderness Days. 2010. (Boston Jane Ser.: 2). (ENG.). 256p. (J). (gr. 3-7). pap. 8.99 *(978-0-375-86205-2(6))*, Yearling) Random Hse. Children's Bks.

—The Claim. 2010. (Boston Jane Ser.: No. 3). (ENG.). 224p. (J). (gr. 4-6). lib. bdg. 22.44 *(978-0-375-96206-6(9))* Random House Publishing Group.

—Wilderness Days. 2004. (Boston Jane Ser.: No. 2). 256p. (J). (gr. 5-18). pap. 5.99 *(978-0-06-440881-3(7))*, Harper Trophy) HarperCollins Pubs.

—Wilderness Days. 2010. (Boston Jane Ser.: No. 2). (ENG.). 256p. (J). (gr. 4-6). lib. bdg. 22.44 *(978-0-375-96205-9(0))* Random House Publishing Group.

Hooper, R. M. J. The Secret of Crescent Grey. 2009. 340p. pap. 19.99 *(978-1-4363-3206-4(0))* Xlibris Corp.

Hopkinson, Deborah. Into the Firestorm: a Novel of San Francisco 1906. 2008. (ENG.). 208p. (J). (gr. 3-7). per. 7.99 *(978-0-440-42129-0(2))*, Yearling) Random Hse. Children's Bks.

Hoppenstedt, Elbert M. President Harrison's Horse Race. 2006. (ENG.). 48p. per. 16.95 *(978-1-4241-5017-5(5))* PublishAmerica, Inc.

Horowitz, Anthony. Ark Angel. 2007. (Alex Rider Ser.: 6). (ENG.). 352p. (J). (gr. 5-18). 8.99 *(978-0-14-240738-7(0))*, Puffin Books) Penguin Young Readers Group.

—Eagle Strike. 2006. (Alex Rider Ser.: 4). (ENG.). 368p. (J). (gr. 5-18). 8.99 *(978-0-14-240613-7(9))*, Puffin Books) Penguin Young Readers Group.

—The Falcon's Malteser. 2004. (Diamond Brothers Ser.: No. 1). (ENG.). 208p. (J). (gr. 3-7). 7.99 *(978-0-14-240219-1(2))*, Puffin Books) Penguin Young Readers Group.

—Point Blank. 2006. (Alex Rider Ser.: 2). (ENG.). 320p. (J). (gr. 5-18). 9.99 *(978-0-14-240612-0(0))*, Puffin Books) Penguin Young Readers Group.

—Russian Roulette: The Story of an Assassin. 2014. (Alex Rider Ser.: 10). (ENG.). 432p. (J). (gr. 5). pap. 9.99 *(978-0-14-751231-4(X))*, Puffin Books) Penguin Young Readers Group.

—Scorpia. 2006. (Alex Rider Ser.: 5). (ENG.). 416p. (J). (gr. 5-18). pap. 8.99 *(978-0-14-240578-9(7))*, Puffin Books) Penguin Young Readers Group.

—Scorpia Rising. 2012. (Alex Rider Ser.: 9). (ENG.). 432p. (J). (gr. 5-18). 9.99 *(978-0-14-241985-4(0))*, Puffin Books) Penguin Young Readers Group.

—Skeleton Key. 2006. (Alex Rider Ser.: 3). (ENG.). 368p. (J). (gr. 5-18). 8.99 *(978-0-14-240614-4(7))*, Puffin Books) Penguin Young Readers Group.

—Skeleton Key: the Graphic Novel. Kanako & Yuzuru, illus. 2009. (Alex Rider Ser.: Bk. 3). (ENG.). 176p. (J). (gr. 5-18). pap. 16.99 *(978-0-399-25418-5(8))*, Philomel Bks.) Penguin Young Readers Group.

—Snakehead. 2008. (Alex Rider Ser.: 7). (ENG.). 432p. (J). (gr. 5-18). pap. 8.99 *(978-0-14-241212-1(0))*, Puffin Books) Penguin Young Readers Group.

—Stormbreaker. 2006. (Alex Rider Ser.: 1). (ENG.). 304p. (J). (gr. 5-18). 9.99 *(978-0-14-240611-3(2))*, Puffin Books) Penguin Young Readers Group.

—Stormbreaker: the Graphic Novel. Kanako & Yuzuru, illus. 2006. (Alex Rider Ser.). (ENG.). 144p. (J). (gr. 5-18). pap. 14.99 *(978-0-399-24633-3(9))*, Philomel Bks.) Penguin Young Readers Group.

Houck, Colleen. Tiger's Curse, Bk. 1. 2012. (Tiger's Curse Ser.: 1). (ENG.). 456p. (J). (gr. 7). pap. 12.99 *(978-1-4549-0249-2(3))* Sterling Publishing Co., Inc.

—Tiger's Curse. 2012. (Tiger's Curse Ser.: Bk. 1). lib. bdg. 20.80 *(978-0-606-23822-9(0))* Turtleback.

—Tiger's Destiny. 2015. (Tiger's Curse Ser.: 4). (ENG.). 464p. (J). (gr. 7). pap. 12.99 *(978-1-4549-0356-7(2))* Sterling Publishing Co., Inc.

—Tiger's Quest. 2013. (Tiger's Curse Ser.: 2). (ENG.). 512p. (J). (gr. 7). pap. 11.95 *(978-1-4549-0358-1(9))* Sterling Publishing Co., Inc.

—Tiger's Voyage. 2014. (Tiger's Curse Ser.: 3). (ENG.). 568p. (J). (gr. 7). pap. 12.99 *(978-1-4549-0357-4(0))* Sterling Publishing Co., Inc.

Howard, Ellen. Edith Herself. 2007. (ENG.). 144p. (J). (gr. 3-7). pap. 10.95 *(978-1-4169-6454-4(1))*, Simon & Schuster/Paula Wiseman Bks.) Simon & Schuster/Paula Wiseman Bks.

—The Gate in the Wall. 2007. (ENG.). 160p. (J). (gr. 3-7). pap. 9.95 *(978-1-4169-6796-5(6))*, Simon & Schuster/Paula Wiseman Bks.) Simon & Schuster/Paula Wiseman Bks.

Howell, Robert. Third Times the Charm. 2007. (ENG.). 224p. (gr. 4-7). per. 12.95 *(978-1-897235-20-1(8))* Thistledown Pr., Ltd. CAN. Dist: Univ. of Toronto Pr.

Huber, Morgan. Nanite. 2013. 140p. pap. 19.95 *(978-1-63004-633-0(7))* America Star Bks.

Hue, Wendy. Tópé Arrives. 2011. (Illus.). 100p. pap. 12.10 *(978-1-4567-7640-4(1))* AuthorHouse.

Hull, Norman. Robin's Big Brother. 2011. 56p. (gr. 4-6). pap. 9.99 *(978-1-4634-3691-9(2))* AuthorHouse.

Hussey, Charmian. The Valley of Secrets. Crump, Christopher, illus. 2006. (ENG.). 400p. (J). (gr. 7-12). per. 17.99 *(978-1-4169-0015-3(2))*, Simon Pulse) Simon Pulse.

Hutchinson, Shaun David. The Five Stages of Andrew Brawley. Larsen, Christine, illus. 2015. (ENG.). 304p. (YA). (gr. 7). 19.99 *(978-1-4814-0310-8(9))*, Simon Pulse) Simon Pulse.

Ibbotson, Eva. Dial-A-Ghost. Hawkes, Kevin, illus. 2003. (ENG.). 224p. (J). (gr. 3-7). pap. 6.99 *(978-0-14-250018-7(6))*, Puffin Books) Penguin Young Readers Group.

—Journey to the River Sea. Hawkes, Kevin, illus. 2003. (ENG.). 304p. (J). (gr. 3-7). pap. 8.99 *(978-0-14-250184-9(0))*, Puffin Books) Penguin Young Readers Group.

—Journey to the River Sea. Hawkes, Kevin, illus. 2003. 298p. (gr. 3-7). 18.00 *(978-0-7569-1552-0(X))* Perfection Learning Corp.

Iinuma, Yuuki. Itsuwaribito , Vol. 14. 2015. (ENG.). 192p. pap. 9.99 *(978-1-4215-6525-5(0))* Viz Media.

Imbernón, Maite & Dickens, Charles. Oliver Twist. 2003. (Timeless Classics Ser.). (SPA., Illus.). 92p. (J). pap. 10.95 *(978-84-204-5750-5(7))* Santillana USA Publishing Co., Inc.

In a World Just Right. 2015. (ENG., Illus.). 432p. (YA). (gr. 7). 18.99 *(978-1-4814-1660-3(X))* Simon & Schuster Children's Publishing.

Inman, Robert. The Christmas Bus. Baskin, Lyle, illus. 2006. 77p. 19.95 *(978-0-9760963-6-8(6))* Novello Festival Pr.

Ireland, Justina. Vengeance Bound. 2013. (ENG.). 320p. (YA). (gr. 9). 17.99 *(978-1-4424-4462-1(2))*, Simon & Schuster Bks. For Young Readers) Simon & Schuster Bks. For Young Readers.

Isbell, Tom. The Capture. 2016. (Prey Trilogy Ser.: 2). (ENG.). 448p. (YA). (gr. 8). 17.99 *(978-0-06-221605-2(8))*, HarperTeen) HarperCollins Pubs.

—The Prey. 2015. (Prey Trilogy Ser.: 1). (ENG.). 416p. (YA). (gr. 8). 17.99 *(978-0-06-221601-4(5))*, HarperTeen) HarperCollins Pubs.

Jacobson, Jennifer Richard. Paper Things. 2015. (ENG.). 384p. (J). (gr. 5). 17.99 *(978-0-7636-6323-0(9))* Candlewick Pr.

—Paper Things. 2017. (ENG.). (J). (gr. 5). lib. bdg. 19.65 *(978-0-606-39841-1(4))* Turtleback.

Jacques, Brian. Voyage of Slaves. 2007. (Castaways of the Flying Dutchman Ser.: 3). (ENG.). 320p. (gr. 12-18). 7.99 *(978-0-441-01528-3(X))*, Ace) Penguin Publishing Group.

James, Brian. The Heights. 2009. (ENG.). 272p. (YA). (gr. 7-12). 22.44 *(978-0-312-60736-4(9))* Square Fish.

James-Carde, Genice. A Father for Me. Thomas, Michael Lee, illus. 2011. 20p. pap. 24.95 *(978-1-4560-3951-6(2))* America Star Bks.

James, Helen Foster & Loh, Virginia Shin-Mui. Paper Son: Lee's Journey to America. Ong, Wilson, illus. 2013. (Tales of Young Americans Ser.). (ENG.). 32p. (J). (gr. 1-4). 17.99 *(978-1-58536-833-4(4))*, 202366) Sleeping Bear Pr.

James, Will. Cowboy in the Making. rev. ed. (Illus.). 104p. (J). (gr. 4-6). pap. 15.00 *(978-0-87842-439-9(3))*, 811) Mountain Pr. Publishing Co., Inc.

Jarvis McGraw, Eloise. Sawdust in His Shoes. 2018. (Illus.). 278p. (gr. 3-7). pap. 9.95 *(978-0-87486-826-5(2))* Plough Publishing Hse.

Jarvis, Robin. The Whitby Witches (Modern Classics) 2017. (Modern Classics Ser.). (ENG., Illus.). 336p. (J). (gr. 6). pap. 7.99 *(978-1-4052-8540-7(0))* Farshore GBR. Dist: HarperCollins Pubs.

Jennings, Patrick. Wish Riders. 2008. (ENG.). 288p. pap. 6.99 *(978-1-4231-0015-7(8))* Hyperion Pr.

Jennings, Paul. A Different Boy. 2019. (Different Ser.). (ENG., Illus.). 112p. (J). (gr. 5-9). pap. 11.99 *(978-1-76052-350-3(X))* Allen & Unwin AUS. Dist: Independent Pubs. Group.

Jennings, Sharon. Home Free, 1 vol. 2009. (Gutsy Girl Ser.: 1). (ENG., Illus.). 154p. (J). (gr. 4-7). pap. 8.95 *(978-1-897187-55-5(6))* Second Story Pr. CAN. Dist: Orca Bk. Pubs. USA.

Jessell, Tim, illus. The Boardwalk Mystery. 2013. (Boxcar Children Mysteries Ser.: 131). (ENG.). 144p. (J). (gr. 2-5). pap. 6.99 *(978-0-8075-0803-9(9))*, 807508039);131. 15.99 *(978-0-8075-0802-2(0))*, 807508020) Random Hse. Children's Bks. (Random Hse. Bks. for Young Readers).

—The Boxcar Children Deluxe Hardcover Boxed Gift Set (#1-3), Set. 2013. (Boxcar Children Mysteries Ser.). (ENG.). 538p. (J). (gr. 2-5). lib. bdg., lib. bdg., lib. bdg. 45.00 *(978-0-8075-0864-0(0))*, 807508640, Random Hse. Bks. for Young Readers) Random Hse. Children's Bks.

—The Garden Thief. 2012. (Boxcar Children Mysteries Ser.: 130). (ENG.). 128p. (J). (gr. 2-5). 5.99 *(978-0-8075-2752-8(1))*, 807527521); 15.99 *(978-0-8075-2751-1(3))*, 807527513) Random Hse. Children's Bks. (Random Hse. Bks. for Young Readers).

—Mystery of the Fallen Treasure. 2013. (Boxcar Children Mysteries Ser.: 132). (ENG.). 128p. (J). (gr. 2-5). 15.99 *(978-0-8075-5508-8(8))*, 807555088); 5.99 *(978-0-8075-5506-4(1))*, 807555061) Random Hse. Children's Bks. (Random Hse. Bks. for Young Readers).

—The Mystery of the Stolen Snowboard. 2014. (Boxcar Children Mysteries Ser.: 134). (ENG.). 128p. (J). (gr. 2-5). 15.99 *(978-0-8075-8728-7(1))*, 807587281, Random Hse. Bks. for Young Readers) Random Hse. Children's Bks.

—The Mystery of the Wild West Bandit. 2014. (Boxcar Children Mysteries Ser.: 135). (ENG.). 128p. (J). (gr. 2-5). 15.99 *(978-0-8075-8725-6(7))*, 807587257, Random Hse. Bks. for Young Readers) Random Hse. Children's Bks.

—The Return of the Graveyard Ghost. 2013. (Boxcar Children Mysteries Ser.: 133). (ENG.). 128p. (J). (gr. 2-5). 5.99 *(978-0-8075-6936-8(4))*, 807569364); 15.99 *(978-0-8075-6935-1(6))*, 807569356) Random Hse. Children's Bks. (Random Hse. Bks. for Young Readers).

Jinks, Catherine. Babylonne. 2008. (ENG., Illus.). 400p. (YA). (gr. 7). 18.99 *(978-0-7636-3650-0(9))* Candlewick Pr.

—The Last Bogler. 2017. (How to Catch a Bogle Ser.: 3). (ENG.). 336p. (J). (gr. 5-7). pap. 7.99 *(978-0-544-81309-0(X))*, 1641901, Clarion Bks.) HarperCollins Pubs.

—A Plague of Bogles. 2015. (How to Catch a Bogle Ser.: 2). (ENG.). 336p. (J). (gr. 5-7). pap. 6.99 *(978-0-544-54067-5(0))*, 1608871); (Illus.). 16.99 *(978-0-544-08747-7(X))*, 1538140) HarperCollins Pubs. (Clarion Bks.).

Johnson, Gerald J. J. Misty's Christmas Present, 1 vol. Miltenberger, Jeri & Miltenberger, Dave, illus. 2010. 32p. 24.95 *(978-1-4512-1330-0(1))* PublishAmerica, Inc.

Johnson, Mary L. Flinthills Frannie, 1 vol. 2009. 43p. pap. 24.95 *(978-1-61546-886-7(2))* America Star Bks.

Johnson, Nancy. A Sweet-Sounding Place: A Civil War Story. 2008. (ENG.). 128p. (J). (gr. 3-7). pap. 10.95 *(978-0-89272-770-4(5))* Down East Bks.

Johnson, Sarah Blake. Crossings. 2017. 309p. (YA). pap. 17.99 *(978-1-4621-1957-8(3))* Cedar Fort, Inc./CFI Distribution.

Johnston, Mike. Confessions of a Dork Lord. Altés, Marta, illus. 2020. (Confessions of a Dork Lord Ser.: 1). 352p. (J). (gr. 3-7). 13.99 *(978-1-5247-4081-8(0))*, G.P. Putnam's Sons Books for Young Readers) Penguin Young Readers Group.

Jones, Chris. Cameron Jack & the Ghosts of World War 2. 2010. 120p. pap. 12.49 *(978-1-4520-2839-2(7))* AuthorHouse.

Jones, Diana Wynne. Earwig & the Witch. Zelinsky, Paul O., illus. 2012. (ENG.). 128p. (J). (gr. 3-7). 15.99 *(978-0-06-207511-6(X))*, Greenwillow Bks.) HarperCollins Pubs.

—Enchanted Glass. 2011. (ENG.). 304p. (J). (gr. 3-7). pap. 7.99 *(978-0-06-186685-2(7))*, Greenwillow Bks.) HarperCollins Pubs.

Jones, Sandra. Sasha's Little Red Box: An Adoption Story. 2008. 27p. pap. 24.95 *(978-1-60703-187-1(6))* America Star Bks.

Jones, Sandy. Anya's Gift: A Tale of Two Christmases, 1 vol. Yourell, Pam, illus. 2009. 48p. pap. 24.95 *(978-1-61546-129-5(9))* America Star Bks.

Joyce, Kelley A. Amos the Elf & His Magical Pajamas. Beckman, Jeff & Aguirre, Diego, illus. 2012. 38p. pap. 9.95 *(978-0-9881822-0-2(3))* Elf Garb.

Joyce, William. Toothiana, Queen of the Tooth Fairy Armies. Joyce, William, illus. 2018. (Guardians Ser.: 3). (ENG., Illus.). 256p. (J). (gr. 2-6). pap. 8.99 *(978-1-4424-3053-2(2))*, Atheneum Bks. for Young Readers) Simon & Schuster Children's Publishing.

Kacer, Kathy. Stones on a Grave, 1 vol. 2015. (Secrets Ser.: 4). (ENG.). 240p. (YA). (gr. 8-12). pap. 14.95 *(978-1-4598-0659-7(X))* Orca Bk. Pubs. USA.

Kares, P. S. Hole-in-the-Wall with the Prairie Orphans. 2009. 32p. pap. 24.95 *(978-1-60813-521-9(7))* America Star Bks.

Katz, Nikki. The Midnight Dance. 2018. (ENG.). 336p. (YA). pap. 16.99 *(978-1-250-18812-0(1))*, 900192048) Square Fish.

Kehoe, Tim. Furious Jones & the Assassin's Secret. 2014. (ENG., Illus.). 336p. (J). (gr. 3-7). 16.99 *(978-1-4424-7337-9(1))*, Simon & Schuster Bks. For Young Readers) Simon & Schuster Bks. For Young Readers.

Kellogg, Elijah. Charlie Bell, the Waif of Elm Island by Rev Elijah Kellogg. 2006. 352p. per. 23.99 *(978-1-4255-3559-9(3))* Michigan Publishing.

Kennedy, Emma. The Case of the Fatal Phantom, 3 vols. Marc, Sylvain, illus. 2012. (Wilma Tenderfoot Ser.: 3). (ENG.). 351p. (J). (gr. 3-6). 17.95 *(978-0-8037-3542-2(1))* Penguin Young Readers Group.

—Wilma Tenderfoot: the Case of the Frozen Hearts. 2012. (Wilma Tenderfoot Ser.: 1). (ENG.). 368p. (J). (gr. 3-7). 7.99 *(978-0-14-242140-6(5))*, Puffin Books) Penguin Young Readers Group.

Key, Watt. Alabama Moon. (Alabama Moon Ser.: 1). (ENG.). (J). (gr. 5-9). 2008. 304p. pap. 8.99 *(978-0-312-38428-9(9))*, 900053363) 2010. 320p. pap. 8.99 *(978-0-312-64480-2(9))*, 900068607) Square Fish.

Kieffer, Jean-Francois. The Tournament, Vol. 3. Chevrier, Janet, tr. 2013. (Adventures of Loupio Ser.: 3). (ENG., Illus.). 44p. (J). (gr. 1-7). pap. 8.99 *(978-1-58617-853-6(9))* Ignatius Pr.

Kimmel, Elizabeth Cody. The Boxtrolls: a Novel. 2014. (ENG., Illus.). 256p. (J). E-Book *(978-0-316-33263-7(1))* Little Brown & Co.

Kindl, Patrice. Goose Chase. 2010. (ENG.). 240p. (J). (gr. 5-7). pap. 7.99 *(978-0-547-33164-5(9))*, 1417430, Clarion Bks.) HarperCollins Pubs.

King, Emily R. The Hundredth Queen. 2017. (Hundredth Queen Ser.: 1). (YA). (ENG.). 300p. (gr. 10-13). pap. 9.99 *(978-1-5039-4365-0(8))*, 9781503943650, Skyscape); *(978-1-5039-9865-0(7))* Amazon Publishing.

Kinra, Richa, illus. The Princess Panda Tea Party: A Cerebral Palsy Fairy Tale. 2014. 45p. (J). pap. 14.95 *(978-1-61599-219-5(7))* Loving Healing Pr., Inc.

Kipling, Rudyard. Kim. 2008. (Bring the Classics to Life Ser.). (ENG., Illus.). 72p. (gr. 5-12). pap., act. bk. ed. 10.95 *(978-0-931334-69-6(1))*, EDCTR-503B) EDCON Publishing Group.

Kirby, Jessi. In Honor. (ENG.). (YA). (gr. 9). 2013. Illus.). 256p. pap. 9.99 *(978-1-4424-1698-7(X))* 2012. 240p. 16.99 *(978-1-4424-1697-0(1))* Simon & Schuster Bks. For Young Readers. (Simon & Schuster Bks. For Young Readers).

Kirby, Susan E. A No-Fuss Christmas. 2010. (J). *(978-1-60682-059-9(1))* BJU Pr.

Kline, Christina Baker. Orphan Train Girl. (ENG.). 240p. (J). (gr. 3-7). 2018. pap. 7.99 *(978-0-06-244595-7(2))* 2017. (Illus.). 17.99 *(978-0-06-244594-0(4))* HarperCollins Pubs. (HarperCollins).

—Orphan Train Girl (Young Readers Edition) 2018. (J). lib. bdg. 18.40 *(978-0-606-41376-3(6))* Turtleback.

Koertge, Ronald. Strays. (ENG., 176p. (YA). (gr. 9). 2010. Illus.). pap. 7.99 *(978-0-7636-4377-5(7))* 2007. 16.99 *(978-0-7636-2705-8(4))* Candlewick Pr.

Koja, Kathe. Buddha Boy. 2004. (ENG.). 128p. (YA). (gr. 7-11). reprint ed. 7.99 *(978-0-14-240209-2(5))*, Speak) Penguin Young Readers Group.

—Buddha Boy. 2004. 117p. (gr. 3-7). 16.00 *(978-0-7569-3117-9(7))* Perfection Learning Corp.

Konigbagbe, Olutobi. Joy in the Morning. 2012. (Illus.). 100p. pap. 18.99 *(978-1-908064-14-1(5))* Grace Publishing Group.

Kovalkova-McKenna, Svetlana & McKenna, Konstantin. Oberon. 2009. 44p. pap. 7.26 *(978-0-557-06114-3(8))* Lulu Pr., Inc.

Laar-Yond C.T. Six Fingers & the Blue Warrior. Playcrib, illus. 2013. 36p. pap. 14.00 *(978-1-62212-177-9(5))*, Strategic Bk. Publishing) Strategic Book Publishing & Rights Agency (SBPRA).

Lackey, Mercedes & Edghill, Rosemary. Shadow Grail #1: Legacies, No. 1. 2010. (Shadow Grail Ser.: 1). (ENG.). 320p. (YA). (gr. 8-12). pap. 17.99 *(978-0-7653-1761-2(3))*, 900041772, Tor Teen) Doherty, Tom Assocs., LLC.

—Shadow Grail #2: Conspiracies: Conspiracies. 2011. (Shadow Grail Ser.: 2). (ENG.). 352p. (YA). (gr. 8-12). pap. 18.99 *(978-0-7653-1762-9(1))*, 900041774, Tor Teen) Doherty, Tom Assocs., LLC.

—Shadow Grail #3: Sacrifices. 2013. (Shadow Grail Ser.: 3). (ENG.). 304p. (YA). (gr. 8-12). pap. 17.99 *(978-0-7653-1763-6(X))*, 900041776, Tor Teen) Doherty, Tom Assocs., LLC.

LaCour, Nina. We Are Okay. (ENG.). (YA). (gr. 9). 2019. 256p. pap. 11.99 *(978-0-14-242293-9(2))*, Penguin Books) 2017. 240p. 17.99 *(978-0-525-42589-2(6))*, Dutton Books for Young Readers) Penguin Young Readers Group.

LaFaye, A. Stella Stands Alone. 2010. (ENG.). 256p. (YA). (gr. 7). pap. 7.99 *(978-1-4169-8647-8(2))*, Simon & Schuster Bks. For Young Readers) Simon & Schuster Bks. For Young Readers.

—Water Steps. 2009. (ENG., Illus.). 208p. (J). (gr. 2-7). 16.95 *(978-1-57131-687-5(6))*; pap. 6.95 *(978-1-57131-686-8(8))* Milkweed Editions.

—Worth. unabr. ed. 2006. (Live Oak Histories Ser.). (J). (gr. 3-6). pap. 28.95 incl. audio compact disk *(978-1-59519-767-2(2))* Live Oak Media.

—Worth. 2006. 144p. (J). (gr. 4-7). 13.65 *(978-0-7569-6614-0(0))* Perfection Learning Corp.

LaFevers, R. L. The Basilisk's Lair. Murphy, Kelly, illus. 2011. (Nathaniel Fludd, Beastologist Ser.: 2). (ENG.). 160p. (J). (gr. 1-4). pap. 6.99 *(978-0-547-54957-6(1))*, 1450109, Clarion Bks.) HarperCollins Pubs.

—Flight of the Phoenix Bk. 1. Murphy, Kelly, illus. 2010. (Nathaniel Fludd, Beastologist Ser.: 1). (ENG.). 144p. (J). (gr. 1-4). pap. 6.99 *(978-0-547-40845-3(5))*, 1428742, Clarion Bks.) HarperCollins Pubs.

—The Wyverns' Treasure. 2012. (Nathaniel Fludd, Beastologist Ser.: 3). lib. bdg. 16.00 *(978-0-606-24516-6(2))* Turtleback.

LaFleur, Suzanne. Eight Keys. 2012. (ENG.). 224p. (J). (gr. 4-7). 7.99 *(978-0-375-87213-6(2))*, Yearling) Random Hse. Children's Bks.

Landis, Matthew. League of American Traitors. 2017. (ENG.). 256p. (J). (gr. 8-8). 16.99 *(978-1-5107-0735-1(2))*, Sky Pony Pr.) Skyhorse Publishing Co., Inc.

Langrish, Katherine. Troll Fell. 2004. (Illus.). 272p. (J). (gr. 5-18). (ENG.). 16.99 *(978-0-06-058304-0(5))*; lib. bdg. 16.89 *(978-0-06-058305-7(3))* HarperCollins Pubs.

—Troll Mill. 2008. (ENG., Illus.). 336p. (YA). (gr. 7). pap. 7.99 *(978-0-06-058309-5(6))*, Eos) HarperCollins Pubs.

Lansdale, Joe R. All the Earth, Thrown to the Sky. 2012. (ENG.). 256p. (YA). (gr. 7). pap. 8.99 *(978-0-385-73932-0(X))*, Ember) Random Hse. Children's Bks.

Larson, Kirby. Audacity Jones to the Rescue. 2016. (Audacity Jones Ser.: 1). (ENG.). 224p. (J). (gr. 3-7). pap. 6.99 *(978-0-545-84060-6(0))*, Scholastic Pr.) Scholastic, Inc.

—Audacity Jones to the Rescue. 2016. (Audacity Jones Ser.: 1). lib. bdg. 17.20 *(978-0-606-39708-7(6))* Turtleback.

—Hattie Big Sky. (Hattie Ser.: 1). (YA). (gr. 7-7). 2008. (ENG.). 304p. 8.99 *(978-0-385-73595-7(2))*, Yearling) 2007. 336p. pap. 9.99 *(978-0-440-23941-3(9))*, Ember) Random Hse. Children's Bks.

—Hattie Big Sky. l.t. ed. 2007. (Literacy Bridge Young Adult Ser.). 381p. (YA). (gr. 7-12). 23.95 *(978-0-7862-9697-2(6))* Thorndike Pr.

—Hattie Ever After. 2014. (Hattie Ser.: 2). (ENG.). 256p. (YA). (gr. 7). pap. 8.99 *(978-0-375-85090-5(2))*, Ember) Random Hse. Children's Bks.

Lasky, Kathryn. Christmas after All. 2012. (Dear America Ser.). (ENG.). 192p. (J). (gr. 3-9). 12.99 *(978-0-545-38177-2(0))* Scholastic, Inc.

—Tangled in Time: the Portal. 2019. (ENG.). (J). (gr. 3-7). 400p. pap. 6.99 *(978-0-06-269326-6(3))*; (Illus.). 384p. 16.99 *(978-0-06-269325-9(5))* HarperCollins Pubs. (HarperCollins).

Laurie, Victoria. The Curse of Deadman's Forest. (ENG.). 432p. (J). 2011. (gr. 3-7). 8.99 *(978-0-440-42259-4(0))*, Yearling)2. 2010. (Oracles of Delphi Keep Ser.: No. 2). (gr. 6-8). lib. bdg. 22.44 *(978-0-385-90562-6(9))*, Delacorte Pr.) Random Hse. Children's Bks.

—Oracles of Delphi Keep. (Oracles of Delphi Keep Ser.: 1). (J). 2010. 576p. (gr. 3-7). 8.99 *(978-0-440-42258-7(2))*, Yearling)1. 2009. (ENG.). 560p. (gr. 6-8). lib. bdg. 22.44 *(978-0-385-90561-9(0))*, Delacorte Pr.) Random Hse. Children's Bks.

M N O

Lavender, William. Just Jane: A Daughter of England Caught in the Struggle of the American Revolution. 2005. (Great Episodes Ser.). (ENG.). 336p. (YA). (gr. 7-12). pap. 15.95 *(978-0-15-205472-4(3)*, 1196465, Clarion Bks.) HarperCollins Pubs.

Lawrence, Caroline. The Case of the Deadly Desperados, 1. 2013. (P. K. Pinkerton Novels Ser.: 1). (ENG.). 272p. (J). (gr. 4-6). 21.19 *(978-0-399-25633-2(4))* Penguin Young Readers Group.

—P. K. Pinkerton & the Case of the Deadly Desperados. 2013. (P. K. Pinkerton Ser.: 1). (ENG.). 304p. (J). (gr. 3-7). pap. 8.99 *(978-0-14-242381-3(5)*, Puffin Books) Penguin Young Readers Group.

—P. K. Pinkerton & the Pistol-Packing Widows. 2015. (P. K. Pinkerton Ser.: 3). (ENG.). 320p. (J). (gr. 3-7). 7.99 *(978-0-14-751130-0(5)*, Puffin Books) Penguin Young Readers Group.

Lawrence, Susan. The Long Ride Home. Hutcheon, Nathan, illus. 2017. 139p. (J). *(978-1-62856-445-7(8))* BJU Pr.

Le Feuvre, Amy. Harebell's Friend. 2004. (Golden Inheritance Ser.: Vol. 8). (Illus.). 140p. (J). pap. *(978-0-921100-84-3(1))* Inheritance Pubns.

Lee, Y. S. The Agency 2: the Body at the Tower. 2010. (Agency Ser.: 2). (ENG., Illus.). 352p. (YA). (gr. 7-18). 16.99 *(978-0-7636-4968-5(6))* Candlewick Pr.

—The Agency 3: the Traitor in the Tunnel. 2012. (Agency Ser.: 3). (ENG., Illus.). 384p. (YA). (gr. 7). 16.99 *(978-0-7636-5316-3(0))* Candlewick Pr.

—The Agency: a Spy in the House. 2016. (Agency Ser.: 1). (ENG.). 352p. (YA). (gr. 7). pap. 9.99 *(978-0-7636-8748-9(0))* Candlewick Pr.

—A Spy in the House, 1. 2010. (Agency Ser.: Bk. 1). (ENG., Illus.). 352p. (YA). (gr. 7-12). 22.44 *(978-0-7636-4067-5(0))* Candlewick Pr.

L'Engle, Madeleine. Meet the Austins: Book One of the Austin Family Chronicles. 2008. (Austin Family Ser.: 1). (ENG., Illus.). 240p. (J). (gr. 6-12). pap. 9.99 *(978-0-312-37931-5(5)*, 900050194) Square Fish.

—The Moon by Night: Book Two of the Austin Family Chronicles, Bk. 2. 2008. (Austin Family Ser.: 2). (ENG.). 288p. (J). (gr. 6-12). pap. 11.99 *(978-0-312-37932-2(3)*, 900050195) Square Fish.

Leppard, Lois Gladys. The Mandie Collection. (ENG.). (J). (gr. 3-8). 2011. 366p. pap. 16.00 *(978-0-7642-0932-1(9))* 2011. 382p. pap. 16.00 *(978-0-7642-0878-2(0))* 2011. 368p. pap. 16.00 *(978-0-7642-0689-4(3))* 2011. 368p. pap. 16.00 *(978-0-7642-0877-5(2))* Vol. 1. 2007. 544p. pap. 16.99 *(978-0-7642-0446-3(7))* Vol. 2. 2008. (Illus.). 576p. pap. 17.99 *(978-0-7642-0538-5(2))* Bethany Hse. Pubs.

—Mandie Collection, Vol. 3. 2008. (ENG.). 608p. (J). pap. 18.99 *(978-0-7642-0593-4(5))* Bethany Hse. Pubs.

Lethcoe, Jason, illus. You Wish. 2007. 215p. (J). *(978-1-4287-1806-7(0)*, Grosset & Dunlap) Penguin Publishing Group.

Levine, Gail Carson. Dave at Night. 2006. (ENG.). 304p. (J). (gr. 3-7). reprint ed. pap. 9.99 *(978-0-06-440747-2(0)*, HarperCollins) HarperCollins Pubs.

—Dave at Night. 2004. 281p. (gr. 3-7). 17.00 *(978-0-7569-4101-7(6))* Perfection Learning Corp.

—Dave at Night. unabr. ed. 2004. 278p. (J). (gr. 4-7). pap. 38.00 incl. audio *(978-0-8072-8379-0(7)*, YA174SP, Listening Library) Random Hse. Audio Publishing Group.

Lincoln Collier, James. The Corn Raid. 2004. 142p. (J). lib. bdg. 16.92 *(978-1-4242-0768-8(1))* Fitzgerald Bks.

Lindgren, Astrid & Crampton, Patricia. The Red Bird. Tornqvist, Marit, illus. 2005. (J). 5.99 *(978-0-439-62797-9(4)*, Levine, Arthur A. Bks.) Scholastic, Inc.

Lisle, Janet Taylor. The Crying Rocks. 2005. 281p. (YA). (gr. 7-12). 14.65 *(978-0-7569-5507-6(6))* Perfection Learning Corp.

Literature Connections English: Jane Eyre. 2004. (gr. 6-12). *(978-0-395-77557-8(4)*, 2-80126) Holt McDougal.

Llorente, Pilar Molina. Aura Gris. (SPA.). 192p. (YA). (gr. 5-8). *(978-84-216-0993-4(9)*, BU3870) Bruño, Editorial ESP. Dist: Lectorum Pubns., Inc.

Lloyd, Natalie. The Key to Extraordinary. 2017. (ENG.). 240p. (J). (gr. 3-7). pap. 8.99 *(978-0-545-55276-9(1)*, Scholastic Pr.) Scholastic, Inc.

Lo, Malinda. Ash. 10th ed. 2019. (ENG.). 304p. (YA). (gr. 8-17). pap. 10.99 *(978-0-316-53131-3(6))* Little, Brown Bks. for Young Readers.

Lockhart, E. Genuine Fraud. 2017. (YA). *(978-1-5247-7067-9(1)*, Delacorte Pr) Random House Publishing Group.

—Genuine Fraud. 2019. (ENG.). 288p. (YA). (gr. 7). pap. 11.99 *(978-0-385-74478-2(1)*, Ember) Random Hse. Children's Bks.

Lois, Lowry. Gathering Blue. unabr. ed. 2004. (Middle Grade Cassette Librariestm Ser.). 224p. (J). (gr. 5-9). pap. 38.00 incl. audio *(978-0-8072-0989-9(9)*, S YA 250 SP, Listening Library) Random Hse. Audio Publishing Group.

—Gathering Blue. 2013. (Giver Quartet Ser.: 2). lib. bdg. 20.85 *(978-0-606-31673-6(6))* Turtleback.

London, J. A. After Daybreak: A Darkness Before Dawn Novel. 2013. (Darkness Before Dawn Ser.: 3). (ENG., Illus.). 336p. (YA). (gr. 9). pap. 9.99 *(978-0-06-202067-3(6)*, HarperTeen) HarperCollins Pubs.

—Darkness Before Dawn. 2012. (Darkness Before Dawn Ser.: 1). (ENG., Illus.). 368p. (YA). (gr. 9). pap. 9.99 *(978-0-06-202065-9(X)*, HarperTeen) HarperCollins Pubs.

London, Victoria. Emily Cobbs & the Naked School Bk. 1: A Gifted Girls Series. 2005. (Gifted Girls Ser.). (J). per. 7.99 *(978-1-59748-857-0(7))* Sparklesoup LLC.

—Emily Cobbs Collection, Bks. 1 & 2. 2nd ed. 2005. (Gifted Girls Ser.). 164p. (J). pap. 10.95 *(978-1-59748-358-2(3))* Sparklesoup LLC.

—Emily Cobbs Collection Bk. 1 & Bk. 2: A Gifted Girls Series. 2005. (Gifted Girls Ser.). (J). per. 12.95 *(978-1-59748-859-4(3))* Sparklesoup LLC.

Long, Christopher E. & Warner, Gertrude Chandler. Tree House Mystery, 1 vol. Bloodworth, Mark, illus. 2010. (Boxcar Children Graphic Novels Ser.). (ENG.). 32p. (J). (gr. 3-8). 32.79 *(978-1-60270-716-0(2)*, 3677, Graphic Planet - Fiction) Magic Wagon.

Love, D. Anne. The Puppeteer's Apprentice. 2004. (ENG., Illus.). 192p. (J). (gr. 3-7). reprint ed. pap. 9.99 *(978-0-689-84425-6(5)*, McElderry, Margaret K. Bks.) McElderry, Margaret K. Bks.

—The Puppeteer's Apprentice. 2004. (Aladdin Historical Fiction Ser.). 185p. (gr. 3-7). 17.00 *(978-0-7569-4323-3(X))* Perfection Learning Corp.

Lovric, Michelle. The Undrowned Child, 1. 2012. (Undrowned Child Ser.). (ENG.). 464p. (J). (gr. 6-8). lib. bdg. 22.44 *(978-0-385-90814-6(8)*, Delacorte Pr.) Random Hse. Children's Bks.

Lowry, Lois. Gathering Blue. (Giver Quartet Ser.: 2). (ENG.). 256p. (YA). (gr. 7). 2013. pap. 11.99 *(978-0-547-90414-6(2)*, 1510989) 2012. 19.99 *(978-0-547-99568-7(7)*, 1525434) HarperCollins Pubs. (Clarion Bks.).

—The Willoughbys. 2008. (Willoughbys Ser.). (ENG., Illus.). 176p. (J). (gr. 1-4). 17.99 *(978-0-618-97974-5(3)*, 1025183, Clarion Bks.) HarperCollins Pubs.

—The Willoughbys. 2010. (ENG.). 176p. (J). (gr. 3-7). 7.99 *(978-0-385-73776-0(9)*, Yearling) Random Hse. Children's Bks.

—The Windeby Puzzle: History & Story. 2023. (ENG., Illus.). 224p. (J). (gr. 5). 19.99 *(978-0-358-67250-0(3)*, Clarion Bks.) HarperCollins Pubs.

Lunievicz, Joe. Open Wounds. 2011. 352p. (YA). (gr. 9-18). 16.95 *(978-1-934813-51-5(6))* Westside Bks.

Lupica, Mike. Fast Break. 2016. (ENG.). 288p. (J). (gr. 5). pap. 8.99 *(978-1-101-99783-3(4)*, Puffin Books) Penguin Young Readers Group.

—Fast Break. 2016. (ENG.). 288p. (J). (gr. 5). 19.65 *(978-0-606-39313-3(7))* Turtleback.

—Heat. 2007. (ENG.). 256p. (J). (gr. 5-18). 8.99 *(978-0-14-240757-8(7)*, Puffin Books) Penguin Young Readers Group.

—Heat. 2007. 220p. (gr. 5-9). 18.00 *(978-0-7569-8131-0(X))* Perfection Learning Corp.

—Heat. 2007. 18.40 *(978-1-4177-7264-3(6))* Turtleback.

Luxa, Sue. Denver Days. 2004. (Illus.). 82p. (J). pap. 8.95 *(978-1-890437-98-5(0)*, 1234247) Western Reflections Publishing Co.

Lyle, Cindy. The Creation Chronicles - the Dragon Within. 2013. 320p. *(978-1-4602-2618-6(6))* FriesenPress.

Lyons, CJ. The Color of Lies, 1 vol. 2019. (ENG.). 336p. (YA). pap. 10.99 *(978-0-310-76533-2(1))* Blink.

—The Colour of Lies, 1 vol. 2018. (ENG.). 352p. (YA). 17.99 *(978-0-310-76535-6(8))* Blink.

Maccoll, Michaela & Nichols, Rosemary. Rory's Promise. 2014. (Hidden Histories Ser.). (ENG.). 288p. (J). (gr. 4-7). 16.95 *(978-1-62091-623-0(1)*, Calkins Creek) Highlights Pr., c/o Highlights for Children, Inc.

MacDonald, Betty. Nancy & Plum. GrandPre, Mary, illus. 2011. 240p. (J). (gr. 3-7). 7.99 *(978-0-375-85986-1(1)*, Yearling) Random Hse. Children's Bks.

Machado, Ana Maria. Until the Day Arrives, 1 vol. Springer, Jane, tr. from POR. 2014. (ENG.). 152p. (J). (gr. 5-8). 16.95 *(978-1-55498-455-8(6))* Groundwood Bks. CAN. Dist: Publishers Group West (PGW).

MacLean, Betty. Jiali's Traveling Heart. Kinra, Richa, illus. 2013. 34p. (J). 17.95 *(978-1-60131-157-3(5)*, Castlebridge Bks.) Big Tent Bks.

Maguire, Gregory. Missing Sisters. 2009. 192p. (J). 16.99 *(978-0-06-123204-6(1))*; (ENG.). (gr. 3-7). pap. 6.99 *(978-0-06-123203-9(3)*, HarperCollins) HarperCollins Pubs.

—What-The-Dickens: The Story of a Rogue Tooth Fairy. 2008. (ENG., Illus.). 304p. (gr. 4-7). pap. 10.99 *(978-0-7636-4147-4(2))* Candlewick Pr.

—What-the-Dickens: The Story of a Rogue Tooth Fairy. 2007. (ENG.). 304p. (J). (gr. 4-8). 24.80 *(978-1-4287-6555-9(7)*, Follettbound) Follett School Solutions.

Malam, John, retold by. Oliver Twist. 2014. (Graphic Classics Ser.). (Illus.). 48p. (gr. 3-6). 37.10 *(978-1-908973-89-4(7))* Book Hse. GBR. Dist: Black Rabbit Bks.

Malot, Hector & Crewe-Jones, Florence. Nobody's Boy: Companion Story to Nobody's Girl. Gooch, Thelma & Gruelle, Johnny, illus. 2006. 237p. (J). pap. *(978-1-894666-75-6(5))* Inheritance Pubns.

—Nobody's Girl: Companion Story to Nobody's Boy. Gooch, Thelma, illus. 2006. 220p. (J). pap. *(978-1-894666-76-3(3))* Inheritance Pubns.

Mama Jamie. I Will Call Myself Future. 2012. 34p. pap. 15.95 *(978-1-4497-5500-3(3)*, WestBow Pr.) Author Solutions, LLC.

Manale, Shizumi & Marshall, Richard. Running with Cosmos Flowers: The Children of Hiroshima, 1 vol. 2014. (ENG., Illus.). 152p. (YA). (gr. 8-8). 16.99 *(978-1-4556-1966-5(3)*, Pelican Publishing) Arcadia Publishing.

Mantchev, Lisa. Eyes Like Stars: Theatre Illuminata, Act I. 2010. (Theatre Illuminata Ser.: 1). (ENG.). 384p. (YA). (gr. 7-12). pap. 17.99 *(978-0-312-60866-8(7)*, 900065167) Square Fish.

—Perchance to Dream: Theatre Illuminata #2, 2. 2011. (Theatre Illuminata Ser.: 2). (ENG.). 368p. (YA). (gr. 7-12). pap. 17.99 *(978-0-312-67510-3(0)*, 900072953) Square Fish.

Marciano, John Bemelmans. Madeline & the Old House in Paris. 2013. (Madeline Ser.). (ENG., Illus.). 48p. (J). (gr. -1-2). 18.99 *(978-0-670-78485-1(0)*, Viking Books for Young Readers) Penguin Young Readers Group.

—Madeline at the White House. (Madeline Ser.). (Illus.). (J). (gr. -1-2). 2020. 34p. bds. 9.99 *(978-0-593-11800-9(6)*, Viking Books for Young Readers) 2016. 48p. pap. 9.99 *(978-1-101-99780-2(X)*, Puffin Books) 2011. 48p. 19.99 *(978-0-670-01228-2(9)*, Viking Books for Young Readers) Penguin Young Readers Group.

—Madeline at the White House. 2016. (Madeline Ser.). lib. bdg. 19.65 *(978-0-606-38845-0(1))* Turtleback.

Marillier, Juliet. Raven Flight: A Shadowfell Novel. 2014. (Shadowfell Ser.). (ENG.). 416p. (YA). (gr. 7). pap. 9.99 *(978-0-375-87197-9(7)*, Ember) Random Hse. Children's Bks.

—Shadowfell. 2013. (Shadowfell Ser.). (ENG., Illus.). 416p. (YA). (gr. 7). pap. 14.99 *(978-0-375-87196-2(9)*, Ember) Random Hse. Children's Bks.

Marks, Alan, illus. The Story of Heidi. 2007. (Picture Book Classics Ser.). 24p. (J). (gr. -1-3). 9.99 *(978-0-7945-1716-8(1)*, Usborne) EDC Publishing.

Marryat. Oxford Bookworms Library: the Children of the New Forest: Level 2: 700-Word Vocabulary. 3rd ed. 2008. (ENG., Illus.). 64p. 11.00 *(978-0-19-479054-3(1))* Oxford Univ. Pr., Inc.

Marryat, Captian. The Children of the New Forest. 2008. 332p. (gr. 8-12). 29.99 *(978-0-554-29238-0(6))*; 28.99 *(978-0-554-38541-9(4))* Creative Media Partners, LLC.

—The Children of the New Forest. 2007. 312p. per. *(978-1-4065-5647-6(5))* Dodo Pr.

—The Children of the New Forest. 2006. 216p. pap. *(978-1-84637-527-9(4))*; pap. *(978-1-84702-355-1(X))* Echo Library.

—The Children of the New Forest. 2004. reprint ed. pap. 1.99 *(978-1-4192-5655-4(6))*; pap. 28.95 *(978-1-4191-5655-7(1))* Kessinger Publishing, LLC.

—The Children of the New Forest. 2008. 292p. pap. 16.95 *(978-1-60597-491-0(9)*, Bk. Jungle) Standard Publications, Inc.

Marryat, Frederick. Children of the New Forest (Yesterday's Classics) 2007. (J). pap. 12.95 *(978-1-59915-050-5(6))* Yesterday's Classics.

Marsh, Katherine. The Door by the Staircase. Murphy, Kelly, illus. 2017. (ENG.). 288p. (J). (gr. 3-7). pap. 7.99 *(978-1-4231-3785-6(X))* Hyperion Bks. for Children.

—Nowhere Boy. 2020. (ENG.). 384p. (J). pap. 8.99 *(978-1-250-21145-3(X)*, 900198061) Square Fish.

Marshall, G. Skies of Dawn. 2007. 160p. per. 12.95 *(978-0-595-42946-2(7))* iUniverse, Inc.

Martin, Ann M. Best Friends. 2008. (Illus.). 195p. (J). pap. *(978-0-545-05062-3(6))* Scholastic, Inc.

—Needle & Thread. Andreasen, Dan, illus. 2007. 205p. (J). pap. *(978-0-545-03660-3(7))* Scholastic, Inc.

Maruno, Jennifer. Totem, 0 vols. 2014. (ENG.). 168p. (YA). pap. 10.99 *(978-1-4597-1934-7(4)*, 9781459719347) Dundurn Pr. CAN. Dist: Publishers Group West (PGW).

—Warbird. 2010. (ENG., Illus.). 120p. (J). (gr. 4-7). pap. 9.95 *(978-1-926607-11-5(2)*, Napoleon & Co.) Dundurn Pr. CAN. Dist: Publishers Group West (PGW).

Mason, Conrad. The Watchmen of Port Fayt. 2015. (ENG.). 400p. (J). (gr. 3-7). 17.99 *(978-0-545-83308-0(6))* Scholastic, Inc.

Matthews, L. S. Lexi. 2008. 200p. (J). pap. *(978-0-385-73575-9(8)*, Delacorte Pr) Random House Publishing Group.

Matute, Ana María. El Polizón del Ulises. (SPA.). 96p. (J). *(978-84-264-3401-2(0)*, LM4015) Editorial Lumen ESP. Dist: Lectorum Pubns., Inc.

McClure, Wendy. Wanderville. 2014. (Wanderville Ser.: 1). (ENG.). 240p. (J). (gr. 3-7). pap. 7.99 *(978-1-59514-701-1(2)*, Razorbill) Penguin Young Readers Group.

McDougal-Littell Publishing Staff. Literature Connections Spanish. 2004. (McDougal Littell Literature Connections Ser.). (SPA.). 576p. (gr. 12-12). stu. ed. 16.90 *(978-0-395-81741-4(2)*, 2-70491) Great Source Education Group, Inc.

Mcentire, Myra. Hourglass, 1. 2012. (Hourglass Ser.). (ENG.). 400p. (YA). (gr. 9-12). 26.19 *(978-1-60684-144-0(0))* Farshore GBR. Dist: Children's Plus, Inc.

McGowan, Jennifer. Maid of Secrets. (Maids of Honor Ser.). (ENG.). (YA). (gr. 7). 2014. 432p. pap. 9.99 *(978-1-4424-4139-2(9))* 2013. 416p. 17.99 *(978-1-4424-4138-5(0))* Simon & Schuster Bks. For Young Readers. (Simon & Schuster Bks. For Young Readers).

McGowan, Maureen. Deviants, 0 vols. 2012. (Dust Chronicles Ser.: 1). (ENG.). 322p. (YA). (gr. 7-12). pap. 9.99 *(978-1-4778-1032-3(3)*, 9781477810323, Skyscape) Amazon Publishing.

McIntosh, Will. Watchdog. 2019. (ENG.). 192p. (J). (gr. 5). 8.99 *(978-1-5247-1387-4(2)*, Yearling) Random Hse. Children's Bks.

McKenzie, Sophie. Every Second Counts. 2016. 405p. (YA). pap. *(978-1-4814-3927-5(8))* Simon & Schuster Children's Publishing.

—In a Split Second. 2015. (ENG., Illus.). 368p. (YA). (gr. 7). 17.99 *(978-1-4814-1394-7(5))* Simon & Schuster Children's Publishing.

McKernan, Victoria. The Devil's Paintbox, 1. 2010. (Devil's Paintbox Ser.). (ENG.). 368p. (J). (gr. 9-12). lib. bdg. 22.44 *(978-0-375-93750-7(1))* Random House Publishing Group.

—The Devil's Paintbox. (ENG.). (YA). (gr. 9). 2013. 384p. pap. 9.99 *(978-0-449-81655-4(9)*, Ember) 2010. 368p. mass mkt. 8.99 *(978-0-440-23962-8(1)*, Laurel Leaf) Random Hse. Children's Bks.

McLelland, Brad & Sylvester, Louis. The Fang of Bonfire Crossing: Legends of the Lost Causes. 2020. (Legends of the Lost Causes Ser.: 2). (ENG.). 400p. (J). pap. 20.99 *(978-1-250-23360-8(7)*, 900174394) Square Fish.

McNichol, John. The Tripods Attack! 2008. (Young Chesterton Chronicles Ser.). 367p. (YA). (gr. 8-12). pap. 17.95 *(978-1-933184-26-5(4))* Sophia Institute Pr.

McQuestion, Karen. Life on Hold, 0 vols. unabr. ed. 2011. (ENG.). 196p. (YA). (gr. 3-6). pap. 9.95 *(978-1-935597-27-8(2)*, 9781935597278, Skyscape) Amazon Publishing.

Meade, L. T. The Children's Pilgrimage. 2017. (ENG., Illus.). (J). 25.95 *(978-1-374-91664-7(1))*; pap. 15.95 *(978-1-374-91663-0(3))* Capital Communications, Inc.

Meehan, Thomas. Annie. 2013. (Annie Book Ser.). (ENG.). 272p. (J). (gr. 5). pap. 8.99 *(978-0-14-751114-0(3)*, Puffin Books) Penguin Young Readers Group.

Meigs, Elizabeth Bleecker. The White Winter: A Story of Scarlet Hill. Chapman, Frederick T., illus. 2011. 208p. 44.95 *(978-1-258-08230-7(6))* Literary Licensing, LLC.

Meloy, Colin. Wildwood Imperium. Ellis, Carson, illus. 2015. (Wildwood Chronicles Ser.: 3). (ENG.). 592p. (J). (gr. 3). pap. 9.99 *(978-0-06-202476-3(0)*, Balzer & Bray) HarperCollins Pubs.

Messenger, Shannon. Let the Sky Fall. 2013. (Sky Fall Ser.: 1). (ENG., (YA). (gr. 7). Illus.). 432p. pap. 12.99 *(978-1-4424-5042-4(8))*; 416p. 17.99 *(978-1-4424-5041-7(X))* Simon Pulse. (Simon Pulse).

—Let the Storm Break. 2014. (Sky Fall Ser.: 2). (ENG., Illus.). 400p. (YA). (gr. 7). 17.99 *(978-1-4424-5044-8(4)*, Simon Pulse) Simon Pulse.

Messner, Kate. Spitfire. 2007. (ENG.). (J). pap. *(978-1-59531-018-7(5))* North Country Bks., Inc.

Meyer, Kai. Dark Reflections: The Water Mirror; the Stone Light; the Glass Word. Crawford, Elizabeth D., tr. 2010. (Dark Reflections Trilogy Ser.). (ENG.). 896p. (YA). (gr. 7). pap. 9.99 *(978-1-4424-0938-5(X)*, McElderry, Margaret K. Bks.) McElderry, Margaret K. Bks.

—The Glass Word. Crawford, Elizabeth D., tr. 2008. (ENG.). 288p. (YA). (gr. 7). (Dark Reflections Trilogy Ser.: 3). pap. 9.99 *(978-0-689-87792-6(7))*; (Dark Reflections Trilogy: Bk. 3). 16.99 *(978-0-689-87791-9(9))* McElderry, Margaret K. Bks. (McElderry, Margaret K. Bks.).

—The Stone Light. Crawford, Elizabeth D., tr. 2007. (Dark Reflections Trilogy Ser.: 2). (ENG.). 384p. (YA). (gr. 7-12). pap. 8.99 *(978-0-689-87790-2(0)*, McElderry, Margaret K. Bks.) McElderry, Margaret K. Bks.

Meyer, L. A. Mississippi Jack: Being an Account of the Further Waterborne Adventures of Jacky Faber, Midshipman, Fine Lady, & Lily of the West. (Bloody Jack Adventures Ser.: 5). (ENG., Illus.). 624p. (YA). (gr. 7-12). 2007. 17.00 *(978-0-15-206003-9(0)*, 1198027) 2nd ed. 2010. pap. 8.99 *(978-0-15-206632-1(2)*, 1099015) HarperCollins Pubs. (Clarion Bks.).

—Rapture of the Deep: Being an Account of the Further Adventures of Jacky Faber, Soldier, Sailor, Mermaid, Spy. 2011. (Bloody Jack Adventures Ser.: 7). (ENG.). 464p. (YA). (gr. 9). pap. 9.99 *(978-0-547-55120-3(7)*, 1450433, Clarion Bks.) HarperCollins Pubs.

—The Wake of the Lorelei Lee: Being an Account of the Further Adventures of Jacky Faber, on Her Way to Botany Bay. 2012. (Bloody Jack Adventures Ser.: 8). (ENG.). 576p. (YA). (gr. 9). pap. 12.99 *(978-0-547-72194-1(3)*, 1482451, Clarion Bks.) HarperCollins Pubs.

—The Wake of the Lorelei Lee: Being an Account of the Further Adventures of Jacky Faber, on Her Way to Botany Bay. 2010. (Bloody Jack Adventures Ser.: Bk. 8). audio compact disk 29.95 *(978-1-59316-484-3(X))* Listen & Live Audio, Inc.

Michaelis, Antonia. The Secret of the Twelfth Continent. 2013. (ENG., Illus.). 288p. (J). (gr. 2-7). 14.95 *(978-1-62087-539-1(X)*, 620539, Sky Pony Pr.) Skyhorse Publishing Co., Inc.

Michaels, Rune. Fix Me. 2011. (ENG., Illus.). 160p. (YA). (gr. 9). 16.99 *(978-1-4169-5772-0(3)*, Atheneum Bks. for Young Readers) Simon & Schuster Children's Publishing.

Miklowitz, Gloria D. Secrets in the House of Delgado. 2004. (ENG.). 192p. (J). (gr. 4-18). pap. 8.00 *(978-0-8028-5210-6(6))* Eerdmans, William B. Publishing Co.

Mobley, Jeannie. Bobby Lee Claremont & the Criminal Element. 2017. (ENG., Illus.). 246p. (J). (gr. 3-7). 16.95 *(978-0-8234-3781-8(7))* Holiday Hse., Inc.

Molesworth, Mary Louisa. The Cuckoo Clock. 2004. reprint ed. pap. 1.99 *(978-1-4192-5839-8(7))*; pap. 19.95 *(978-1-4191-5839-1(2))* Kessinger Publishing, LLC.

Monsef, Kiyash. Once There Was. 2023. (Once There Was Ser.). (ENG., Illus.). 416p. (J). (gr. 5). 18.99 *(978-1-6659-2850-2(6)*, Simon & Schuster Bks. For Young Readers) Simon & Schuster Bks. For Young Readers.

Montgomery, L. M. Akin to Anne: Tales of Other Orphans. (YA). 22.95 *(978-0-8488-2656-7(6))* Amereon Ltd.

—Ana la de Avonlea. García Díaz, José, tr. 5th ed. (Ana la de Tejas Verdes Ser.: 2).Tr. of Anne of Avonlea. (SPA., Illus.). 254p. (J). (gr. 5-8). *(978-84-7888-632-6(X)*, SAL3943) Emece Editores ESP. Dist: Lectorum Pubns., Inc.

—Ana la de Ingleside. 2nd ed. (Ana la de Tejas Verdes Ser.: 6).Tr. of Anne of Ingleside. (SPA., Illus.). 288p. (J). (gr. 5-8). *(978-84-7888-634-0(6)*, SAL3088) Emece Editores ESP. Dist: Lectorum Pubns., Inc.

—Ana la de Isla. 4th ed. (Ana la de Tejas Verdes Ser.: 3).Tr. of Anne of the Island. (SPA., Illus.). 240p. (YA). (gr. 5-8). *(978-84-7888-635-7(4)*, SAL5036) Emece Editores ESP. Dist: Lectorum Pubns., Inc.

—Ana la de Tejas Verdes. García Díaz, José, tr. 7th ed. (Ana la de Tejas Verdes Ser.: 1).Tr. of Anne of Green Gables. (SPA., Illus.). 288p. (J). (gr. 5-8). *(978-84-7888-633-3(8))* Emece Editores ESP. Dist: Lectorum Pubns., Inc.

—Anne of Avonlea. 2004. 352p. per. 15.95 *(978-1-59540-109-0(1))* 1st World Publishing, Inc.

—Anne of Avonlea. 2018. (ENG., Illus.). 250p. (J). (gr. 3-7). pap. *(978-93-5297-101-5(9))* Alpha Editions.

—Anne of Avonlea. (ENG., Illus.). (J). 2018. 400p. pap. 17.95 *(978-1-376-49928-5(2))* 2015. 27.95 *(978-1-297-91573-4(9))* Creative Media Partners, LLC.

—Anne of Avonlea. 2005. pap. *(978-1-905432-15-8(1))* Dodo Pr.

—Anne of Avonlea. 2005. (Aladdin Classics Ser.). (ENG., Illus.). 416p. (J). (gr. 4-7). pap. 5.99 *(978-1-4169-0328-4(3)*, Aladdin) Simon & Schuster Children's Publishing.

—Anne of Avonlea. 2018. (Anne of Green Gables: the Complete Collection: 2). (ENG.). 336p. (J). (gr. 6-12). 8.99 *(978-1-78226-444-6(2)*, 5ab6e735-475a-4e0f-a18b-99628df1f473) Sweet Cherry Publishing GBR. Dist: Baker & Taylor Publisher Services (BTPS).

—Anne of Avonlea. 2018. (ENG., Illus.). 276p. (YA). 24.99 *(978-1-5287-0644-5(7)*, Classic Bks. Library) The Editorium, LLC.

—Anne of Avonlea. 2019. (ENG.). 262p. (J). pap. 11.89 *(978-1-7278-8486-9(8))* CreateSpace Independent Publishing Platform.

—Anne of Avonlea. (ENG.). 2019. 268p. (J). pap. 12.99 *(978-1-7018-6034-6(1))* 2019. 386p. (J). pap. 22.99 *(978-1-0899-1022-0(3))* 2019. 386p. (J). pap. 22.99 *(978-1-0830-1790-1(X))* 2019. 546p. (J). pap. 36.99 *(978-1-0825-6163-4(0))* 2019. 386p. (J). pap. 22.99 *(978-1-0807-5704-6(X))* 2019. 546p. (J). pap. 35.99 *(978-1-0800-7977-3(7))* 2019. 818p. (J). pap. 46.99 *(978-1-0781-0625-2(8))* 2019. 544p. (J). pap. 35.99 *(978-1-0780-6471-2(7))* 2019. 546p. (J). pap. 31.99 *(978-1-0753-6837-0(5))* 2019. 386p. (YA). pap. 22.99 *(978-1-0726-8331-5(8))* 2019. 546p. (YA). pap. 30.99 *(978-1-0707-5140-5(5))* 2019. 268p. (YA). pap. 18.99 *(978-1-0705-9376-0(1))* 2019. 568p. (YA). pap. 33.99 *(978-1-0987-6527-9(3))* 2019. 364p. (YA). pap. 19.99 *(978-1-0968-7536-9(5))* 2019. 268p. (YA). pap. 16.99 *(978-1-0954-6547-9(3))* 2019. 546p. (YA). pap. 34.99 *(978-1-0916-4683-4(X))* 2019. 506p. (YA). pap. 29.99 *(978-1-7965-5870-8(2))* 2019. (Illus.). 546p. (YA). pap. 34.99 *(978-1-7929-7537-0(6))* 2018. (Illus.). 240p. (YA). pap. 15.99 *(978-1-7919-1487-5(X))* Independently Published.

—Anne of Avonlea. 2019. (ENG.). 252p. (J). pap. 27.99 (978-1-7077-7448-7(X)) Independently Published.
—Anne of Avonlea. 2012. (World Classics Ser.). (ENG.). 228p. pap. 19.99 (978-1-909438-94-1(4), Sovereign) Bollinger, Max GBR. Dist: Gardners Bks. Ltd., Lightning Source UK, Ltd.
—Anne of Avonlea. l.t. ed. 2006. (ENG.). pap. (978-1-4068-3173-3(5)) Echo Library.
—Anne of Green Gables. 400p. 2005. 33.95 (978-1-4218-0660-0(6), 1st World Library - Literary Society) 2004. per. 16.95 (978-1-59540-110-6(5)) 1st World Publishing, Inc.
—Anne of Green Gables, 1 vol. Castelao, Patricia, illus. 2011. (Calico Illustrated Classics Ser.: No. 4). (ENG.). 112p. (J). (gr. 2-5). 38.50 (978-1-61641-612-6(2), 4039, Calico Chapter Bks.) ABDO Publishing Co.
—Anne of Green Gables. 2009. 292p. 27.99 (978-1-60512-375-2(7)); pap. 14.99 (978-1-60512-475-9(3)) Akasha Publishing, LLC. (Akasha Classics).
—Anne of Green Gables. 2012. (World Classics Ser.). (ENG.). 260p. pap. 19.99 (978-1-909438-96-5(0), Sovereign) Bollinger, Max GBR. Dist: Lightning Source UK, Ltd.
—Anne of Green Gables. 2008. 316p. 29.99 (978-0-554-23545-5(5)) 2008. 316p. 28.99 (978-0-554-32848-5(8)) 2007. (ENG.). 312p. pap. 24.99 (978-1-4264-4662-7(4)) Creative Media Partners, LLC.
—Anne of Green Gables. 2008. (Anne of Green Gables Ser.). (ENG.). 366p. (J). (gr. 4-7). pap. 9.95 (978-0-9782552-6-8(7)) Davenport Pr. CAN. Dist: Independent Pubs. Group.
—Anne of Green Gables. 2007. per. 6.99 (978-1-4209-2922-5(4)) Digireads.com Publishing.
—Anne of Green Gables. 2007. 284p. per. (978-1-4065-6399-3(4)) Dodo Pr.
—Anne of Green Gables. 2007. 572p. (978-1-84702-773-3(3)) 2006. pap. (978-1-4068-2170-3(5)) 2006. pap. (978-1-4068-3174-0(3)) Echo Library.
—Anne of Green Gables. 2009. 242p. pap. 8.58 (978-0-217-43952-7(7)) General Bks. LLC.
—Anne of Green Gables. 2005. (My First Classics Ser.). 112p. (J). (gr. k-3). pap., pap. 4.99 (978-0-06-079147-6(0), HarperFestival) HarperCollins Pubs.
—Anne of Green Gables. 2005. 21.99 (978-1-4142-5125-7(4)) IndyPublish.com.
—Anne of Green Gables. 2004. reprint ed. pap. 1.99 (978-1-4192-0717-4(2)); pap. 27.95 (978-1-4191-0717-7(8)) Kessinger Publishing, LLC.
—Anne of Green Gables. l.t. ed. 2009. (World Classics Ser.). (ENG.). 384p. pap. 21.95 (978-1-59688-123-5(2)) Large Print Bk. Co., The.
—Anne of Green Gables. 2003. (ENG.). 320p. (gr. 5-7). 5.95 (978-0-451-52882-7(4), Signet) Penguin Publishing Group.
—Anne of Green Gables. 2008. (Puffin Classics Ser.). (Illus.). 464p. (J). (gr. 3-7). 8.99 (978-0-14-132159-2(8), Puffin Books) Penguin Young Readers Group.
—Anne of Green Gables. 2003. 320p. (J). (gr. 4-7). 12.60 (978-0-7569-1848-4(0)) Perfection Learning Corp.
—Anne of Green Gables. 2008. (Modern Library Classics Ser.). (ENG.). 320p. pap. 11.00 (978-0-8129-7903-9(6), Modern Library) Random House Publishing Group.
—Anne of Green Gables. 2014. (Official Anne of Green Gables Ser.: 1). 352p. (YA). (gr. 5-12). pap. 13.99 (978-1-4022-8894-4(8)) Sourcebooks, Inc.
—Anne of Green Gables. 2009. 224p. pap. 15.45 (978-1-4385-1847-3(1), Bk. Jungle) Standard Publications, Inc.
—Anne of Green Gables. 2008. 316p. pap. 16.95 (978-1-60096-101-4(0)); pap. 16.95 (978-1-60096-565-4(2)) The Editorium, LLC.
—Anne of Green Gables: Norton Critical Edition. Rubio, Mary Henley & Waterston, Elizabeth, eds. 2007. (Norton Critical Editions Ser.: 0). (ENG., Illus.). 464p. (C). (gr. 9-12). per. 16.00 net. (978-0-393-92695-8(8), 92695) Norton, W. W. & Co., Inc.
—The Anne of Green Gables Collection: Six Complete & Unabridged Novels in One Volume. 2013. 1140p. (978-1-78139-344-4(3)) Benediction Classics.
—Anne of the Island. 2018. (ENG., Illus.). 240p. (J). (gr. 2-5). pap. (978-93-5297-102-2(7)) Alpha Editions.
—Anne of the Island. 2017. (ENG., Illus.). (J). 28.99 (978-1-366-55836-7(7)) Blurb, Inc.
—Anne of the Island. 2017. (ENG., Illus.). (J). 25.95 (978-1-374-89884-4(8)); pap. 15.95 (978-1-374-89883-7(X)) Capital Communications, Inc.
—Anne of the Island. (ENG., Illus.). (J). 2017. pap. 15.90 (978-1-375-53109-2(3)) 2015. 26.95 (978-1-297-59159-4(3)) Creative Media Partners, LLC.
—Anne of the Island. 2008. (Anne of Green Gables Ser.). (ENG.). 272p. (J). (gr. 4-7). pap. 9.95 (978-0-9782552-8-2(3)) Davenport Pr. CAN. Dist: Independent Pubs. Group.
—Anne of the Island. 2006. (ENG.). pap. (978-1-4068-2171-0(3)) Echo Library.
—Anne of the Island. 2010. (Puffin Classics Ser.). (ENG.). 368p. (J). (gr. 5-7). pap. 7.99 (978-0-14-132736-5(7), Puffin Books) Penguin Young Readers Group.
—Anne of the Island. 2018. (Anne of Green Gables: the Complete Collection: 3). (ENG.). 312p. (J). (gr. 6-12). 8.99 (978-1-78226-445-3(0), 6a902ad3-6883-4c7e-8532-21673815d7a9) Sweet Cherry Publishing GBR. Dist: Baker & Taylor Publisher Services (BTPS).
—Anne of the Island. 2018. (ENG., Illus.). 258p. (YA). 24.99 (978-1-5287-0650-6(1), Classic Bks. Library) The Editorium, LLC.
—Anne of the Island. 2019. (ENG.). 250p. (J). pap. 11.89 (978-1-7278-8584-2(8)) CreateSpace Independent Publishing Platform.
—Anne of the Island. (ENG.). (J). 2019. 252p. pap. 11.99 (978-1-7018-6205-0(0)) 2019. 352p. pap. 19.99 (978-1-0899-1090-9(8)) 2019. 788p. pap. 45.99 (978-1-0828-3158-4(1)) 2019. 498p. pap. 33.99 (978-1-0825-6062-0(6)) 2019. 466p. pap. 32.99 (978-1-0799-0876-3(5)) 2019. 788p. pap. 45.99 (978-1-0804-7520-9(6)) 2019. 740p. pap. 43.99 (978-1-0776-6557-6(1)) 2019. 352p. pap. 19.99 (978-1-0726-8332-2(6)) 2019. 498p. pap. 31.99 (978-1-0753-6839-4(1)) 2019. 342p. pap. 19.99 (978-1-0968-7543-7(8)) 2019. 526p. pap. 29.99 (978-1-0985-3618-3(5)) 2019. 252p. pap. 17.99 (978-1-0705-9734-8(1)) 2019. 500p. pap. 29.99 (978-1-0707-5185-6(5)) 2019. 498p. pap. 32.99 (978-1-0916-4685-8(6)) 2019. 462p. pap. 25.99 (978-1-7965-5869-2(9)) 2019. 136p. pap. 8.60 (978-1-7953-3769-4(9)) 2018. (Illus.). 224p. pap. 14.99 (978-1-7919-1456-1(X)) Independently Published.
—Anne of the Island. 2019. (ENG.). 232p. (J). pap. 27.99 (978-1-7077-7514-9(1)) Independently Published.
—Anne of the Island. 2012. (World Classics Ser.). (ENG.). 212p. pap. 19.99 (978-1-909438-92-7(8), Sovereign) Bollinger, Max GBR. Dist: Lightning Source UK, Ltd.
—Anne of the Island. l.t. ed. 2006. (ENG.). pap. (978-1-4068-3175-7(1)) Echo Library.
—Anne of the Island. 2004. reprint ed. pap. 1.99 (978-1-4192-0718-1(0)); pap. 30.95 (978-1-4179-0885-1(8)) Kessinger Publishing, LLC.
—Anne of the Island. l.t. ed. 2004. 396p. 26.00 (978-1-58287-640-5(1)) North Bks.
—Emily Climbs. 2009. (ENG.). 376p. pap. 16.95 (978-0-7710-9382-1(9), New Can Library) McClelland & Stewart CAN. Dist: Random Hse., Inc.
—Emily Climbs: Emily of New Moon Series. 2014. (Emily Ser.: 2). (ENG.). 368p. (YA). (gr. 5-12). pap. 13.99 (978-1-4022-8915-6(4)) Sourcebooks, Inc.
—Emily of New Moon. 2019. (ENG.). (J). (gr. 5-12). 700p. pap. 39.99 (978-1-6967-9800-6(0)); 704p. pap. 27.99 (978-1-6984-6657-6(9)); 700p. pap. 39.99 (978-1-6910-9002-0(6)); 700p. pap. 39.99 (978-1-6949-7463-1(4)); 562p. pap. 35.99 (978-1-0864-2303-7(8)); 342p. pap. 19.99 (978-1-6862-9811-0(0)); 704p. pap. 34.99 (978-1-0803-9453-1(2)); 704p. pap. 45.99 (978-1-0784-0299-6(X)); 704p. pap. 25.99 (978-1-0799-5146-2(6)); 562p. pap. 30.99 (978-1-0775-9085-4(7)); 704p. pap. 39.99 (978-1-0761-2343-5(0)); 702p. pap. 39.99 (978-1-0974-8467-6(2)); 468p. pap. 26.99 (978-1-0957-2882-6(2)); 704p. pap. 44.99 (978-1-0917-4644-2(3)); 704p. pap. 44.99 (978-1-7969-7316-7(5)); 702p. pap. 30.99 (978-1-7965-6239-2(4)) Independently Published.
—Emily of New Moon. 2019. (ENG.). (J). (gr. 5-12). 330p. pap. 33.99 (978-1-7077-8544-5(9)); 342p. pap. 14.99 (978-1-7018-6548-8(3)) Independently Published.
—Emily's Quest. 2009. (ENG.). 272p. pap. 19.95 (978-0-7710-9383-8(7), New Can Library) McClelland & Stewart CAN. Dist: Random Hse., Inc.
—Emily's Quest. 2014. (Emily Ser.: 3). (ENG.). 256p. (YA). (gr. 5-12). pap. 12.99 (978-1-4022-8918-7(9)) Sourcebooks, Inc.
Montgomery, Lucy Maud. Anne of Avonlea. 2019. (ENG.). (J). (gr. 3-7). 276p. pap. 12.95 (978-0-368-78940-3(3)); 96p. pap. 12.71 (978-0-368-28129-7(9)) Blurb, Inc.
—Anne of Avonlea. (ENG.). (gr. 3-7). 2020. 170p. (YA). pap. 9.99 (978-1-6594-8477-9(4)) 2018. (Illus.). 594p. (J). pap. 34.99 (978-1-7916-6454-1(7)) Independently Published.
—Anne of Avonlea. Blake, Sheba, ed. 2020. (ENG.). 254p. (YA). (gr. 3-7). pap. 14.99 (978-1-222-29341-8(2)) Indy Pub.
—Anne of Avonlea. 2008. (ENG., Illus.). 268p. (J). (gr. 3-7). 18.99 (978-1-4341-1489-1(9), Waking Lion Press) The Editorium, LLC.
—Anne of Green Gables. 2013. (Word Cloud Classics Ser.). (ENG.). 264p. (YA). pap. 14.99 (978-1-60710-728-6(7), Canterbury Classics) Printers Row Publishing Group.
—Anne of Green Gables: Stories for Young Readers, 1 vol. Smith, David Preston, illus. 2008. (ENG.). 46p. (J). (gr. 1-3). pap. 12.95 (978-1-55109-662-9(5), 3b164d3e-d44c-49e5-9188-05373178fc3d) Nimbus Publishing, Ltd. CAN. Dist: Baker & Taylor Publisher Services (BTPS).
—Anne of the Island. 2019. (ENG.). (J). (gr. 2-5). 276p. pap. 12.95 (978-0-368-79656-2(6)); 94p. pap. 12.55 (978-0-368-28130-3(2)) Blurb, Inc.
—Anne of the Island. 2018. (ENG.). 328p. (J). (gr. 2-5). 44.95 (978-0-343-91137-9(X)); pap. 27.95 (978-0-343-91136-2(1)) Creative Media Partners, LLC.
—Anne of the Island. 2019. (ENG.). (J). (gr. 2-5). 734p. pap. 46.99 (978-1-6881-5126-0(5)); 736p. pap. 43.99 (978-1-0968-8163-6(2)); 448p. pap. 25.99 (978-1-0932-8992-3(9)) Independently Published.
—Emily of New Moon. 2018. (ENG., Illus.). 184p. (J). (gr. 4-7). pap. 6.95 (978-0-464-89423-0(9)) Blurb, Inc.
—Emily of New Moon. (ENG.). (J). 2019. 626p. (gr. 4-7). pap. 35.99 (978-1-0865-5466-3(3)) 2019. 628p. (gr. k-6). pap. 34.99 (978-1-0934-3679-2(4)) 2018. (Illus.). 628p. (gr. 4-7). pap. 35.99 (978-1-7915-2706-8(X)) Independently Published.
Montgomery, Lucy Maud & Grandma's Treasures. Anne of Avonlea. 2019. (ENG.). 252p. (YA). (gr. 3-7). (978-1-7948-2437-9(5)) Lulu Pr., Inc.
Montgomery, Lucy Maud & Montgomery, L. M. Emily of New Moon. 2019. (ENG., Illus.). 316p. (J). (gr. k-6). 19.99 (978-1-5154-3983-7(6)); pap. 9.99 (978-1-5154-3982-0(8)) Wilder Pubns., Corp.
Montgomery, Lucy Maud & Treasures, Grandma's. Anne of Avonlea. 2019. (ENG.). 252p. (YA). (gr. 3-7). pap. (978-1-7948-2462-1(6)) Lulu Pr., Inc.
Montgomery, R. A. Chinese Dragons. Semionov, Vladimir, illus. 2009. (ENG.). 144p. (J). (gr. 4-8). pap. 7.99 (978-1-933390-30-7(1)) Chooseco LLC.
Montgomery, Ross. Max & the Millions. 2018. 265p. (J). pap. (978-1-5247-1887-9(4)) Earthscan Canada.
—Max & the Millions. 2018. (ENG.). 272p. (J). (gr. 3-7). 16.99 (978-1-5247-1884-8(X), Lamb, Wendy Bks.) Random Hse. Children's Bks.
Moore, Stephanie Perry. Better Than Picture Perfect, No. 2. 2014. (Sharp Sisters Ser.: 2). (ENG.). 160p. (YA). (gr. 6-12). pap. 7.95 (978-1-4677-4486-7(7), add2aaa3-7821-4781-9f47-582ec3843188, Darby Creek) Lerner Publishing Group.
Moreton, Clara. Frank & Fanny: A Rural Story. 2017. (ENG., Illus.). (J). pap. 10.95 (978-1-374-84019-5(X)) Capital Communications, Inc.
Morgan, Clay. The Boy Who Spoke Dog. 2005. 176p. (J). (gr. 3-7). 5.99 (978-0-14-240343-3(1), Puffin Books) Penguin Young Readers Group.
Morgen, A. M. The Inventors at No. 8. (ENG., Illus.). (J). (gr. 3-7). 2019. 368p. pap. 7.99 (978-0-316-47151-0(8)) 2018. 352p. 16.99 (978-0-316-47149-7(6)) Little, Brown Bks. for Young Readers.
Morpurgo, Michael. Kaspar the Titanic Cat. Foreman, Michael, illus. 2012. (ENG.). 208p. (J). (gr. 3-7). 16.99 (978-0-06-200618-9(5), Balzer & Bray) HarperCollins Pubs.
Moser, Fiadhnait. The Flourishing of Floralie Laurel. 2018. (ENG., Illus.). 336p. (J). (gr. 4-9). 16.99 (978-1-4998-0668-7(X), Yellow Jacket) Bonnier Publishing USA.
Mosher, Richard. Zazoo. 2004. (ENG.). 272p. (YA). (gr. 7-18). reprint ed. pap. 15.95 (978-0-618-43904-1(8)) Houghton Mifflin Harcourt Publishing Co.
Motomi, Kyousuke. Dengeki Daisy, Vol. 16. Vol. 16. 2015. (Dengeki Daisy Ser.: 16). (ENG., Illus.). 192p. pap. 9.99 (978-1-4215-7771-5(2)) Viz Media.
Moulton, Mark Kimball. A Cricket's Carol. Blowers, Lisa, illus. 2004. 32p. (J). 14.95 (978-0-8249-5488-8(2), Ideals Pubns.) Worthy Publishing.
Mourlevat, Jean-Claude. Winter's End. Bell, Anthea, tr. 2009. (ENG., Illus.). 432p. (YA). (gr. 9-18). 17.99 (978-0-7636-4450-5(1)) Candlewick Pr.
Muchamore, Robert. The Dealer. (Cherub Ser.: 2). (ENG.). (YA). (gr. 7). 2011. 336p. pap. 12.99 (978-1-4424-1361-0(1)) 2010. 320p. 19.99 (978-1-4169-9941-6(8)) Simon Pulse. (Simon Pulse).
—Maximum Security. 2012. (Cherub Ser.: 3). (ENG.). 320p. (YA). (gr. 7). pap. 12.99 (978-1-4424-1362-7(X), Simon Pulse) Simon Pulse.
Munda, Rosaria. Fireborne. 2019. (Aurelian Cycle Ser.: 1). (ENG.). 448p. (YA). (gr. 7). 18.99 (978-0-525-51821-1(5), G.P. Putnam's Sons Books for Young Readers) Penguin Young Readers Group.
Murdock, Catherine Gilbert. Wisdom's Kiss. 2013. (ENG.). 320p. (YA). (gr. 7). pap. 8.99 (978-0-547-85540-0(0), 1501132, Clarion Bks.) HarperCollins Pubs.
Muschla, Gary Robert. Crusader. 2006. (YA). pap. (978-0-88092-491-7(8)) Royal Fireworks Publishing Co.
Myhre, Jennifer. A Chameleon, a Boy, & a Quest. 2015. (ENG., Illus.). 176p. (J). pap. 16.99 (978-1-942572-08-4(5)) New Growth Pr.
Myklusch, Matt. The Accidental Hero. 2011. (Jack Blank Adventure Ser.: 1). (ENG., Illus.). 496p. (J). (gr. 3-7). pap. 9.99 (978-1-4169-9562-3(5), Aladdin) Simon & Schuster Children's Publishing.
—Jack Blank & the Imagine Nation. 2010. (Jack Blank Adventure Ser.: Bk. 1). (ENG., Illus.). 480p. (J). (gr. 3-7). 19.99 (978-1-4169-9561-6(7), Aladdin) Simon & Schuster Children's Publishing.
—The Secret War. 2012. (Jack Blank Adventure Ser.: 2). (ENG., Illus.). 560p. (J). (gr. 3-7). pap. 10.99 (978-1-4169-9565-4(X), Aladdin) Simon & Schuster Children's Publishing.
—The Secret War. 2011. (Jack Blank Adventure Ser.: 2). (ENG., Illus.). 544p. (J). (gr. 3-7). lib. bdg. 16.99 (978-1-4169-9564-7(1), Simon & Schuster/Paula Wiseman Bks.) Simon & Schuster/Paula Wiseman Bks.
Nannestad, Katrina. When Mischief Came to Town. 2018. (ENG.). 192p. (J). (gr. 5-7). pap. 9.99 (978-1-328-74094-6(3), 1677139, Clarion Bks.) HarperCollins Pubs.
Naylor, Phyllis Reynolds. Emily's Fortune, 1. 2011. (Emily Ser.: 1). 160p. (J). (gr. 3-7). 6.99 (978-0-375-84492-8(9), Yearling) Random Hse. Children's Bks.
—Sang Spell. 2013. (ENG., Illus.). 224p. (YA). (gr. 7). pap. 13.99 (978-1-4814-1589-7(1), Atheneum Bks. for Young Readers) Simon & Schuster Children's Publishing.
Nelson, D. A. Darkisle. 2008. (ENG.). 272p. (J). (gr. 4-6). lib. bdg. 22.44 (978-0-385-90600-5(5)) Random House Publishing Group.
Niball, Ellen Cook. Secret of St. Nicholas. 2010. 32p. 16.95 (978-0-9818154-1-1(3)) Fairland Bks.
Nielsen, Jennifer A. The False Prince. 2012. (Ascendance Trilogy: Bk. 1). (ENG.). (J). (gr. 5-8). 64.99 (978-1-61707-596-4(5)) Findaway World, LLC.
—The False Prince. 2012. (Ascendance Trilogy: Bk. 1). (Illus.). 342p. (J). pap. (978-0-545-43347-1(9), Scholastic Pr.) Scholastic, Inc.
—The False Prince. 2013. (Ascendance Trilogy Ser.: 1). lib. bdg. 18.40 (978-0-606-31491-6(1)) Turtleback.
—The False Prince (the Ascendance Series, Book 1) (ENG.). 352p. 2013. (Ascendance Ser.: 1). (YA). (gr. 3-7). pap. 8.99 (978-0-545-28414-1(7), Scholastic Paperbacks) 2012. (Ascendance Ser.: 1). (Illus.). (YA). (gr. 3-7). 18.99 (978-0-545-28413-4(9), Scholastic Pr.) 2012. (Ascendance Trilogy: Bk. 1). E-Book 17.99 (978-0-545-39249-5(7)) Scholastic, Inc.
Novak, Ali. My Life with the Walter Boys. (ENG.). (YA). 2019. 400p. (gr. 8-12). pap. 11.99 (978-1-7282-0547-2(6)) 2014. 368p. (gr. 7-12). pap. 10.99 (978-1-4022-9786-1(6), 9781402297861) Sourcebooks, Inc.
Novel Units. The Pinballs Novel Units Student Packet. 2019. (ENG.). (J). pap. 13.99 (978-1-56137-827-2(5), Novel Units, Inc.) Classroom Library Co.
—The Pinballs Novel Units Teacher Guide. 2019. (ENG.). (J). pap. 12.99 (978-1-56137-082-5(7), Novel Units, Inc.) Classroom Library Co.
Nye, Bill & Mone, Gregory. Jack & the Geniuses: At the Bottom of the World. Iluzada, Nicholas, illus. (ENG.). (J). (gr. 3-7). 2018. 272p. pap. 8.99 (978-1-4197-3288-1(9), 1152603) 2017. 256p. 13.95 (978-1-4197-2303-2(0), 1152601, Amulet Bks.) Abrams, Inc.
—Lost in the Jungle: Jack & the Geniuses Book #3. Iluzada, Nicholas, illus. (Jack & the Geniuses Ser.). (ENG.). 288p. (J). (gr. 3-7). 2019. pap. 7.99 (978-1-4197-3485-4(7), 1158103) 2018. 13.99 (978-1-4197-2867-9(9), 1158101) Abrams, Inc. (Amulet Bks.).
Ogilvy, Ian. Measle & the Wrathmonk. 2004. 224p. (J). (gr. 4-6). 15.99 (978-0-06-058685-0(0)) HarperCollins Pubs.
Oladokun, Alexander. Acrux Manor: The Prodigal's Curse (Hardcover) 2013. (ENG.). 204p. 28.50 (978-1-300-68651-4(0)) Lulu Pr., Inc.
Olds, Barbara Anne. Haven House. Amatrula, Michele, illus. 2007. (ENG.). 148p. (J). (gr. 4-6). pap. 10.95 (978-0-9744446-0-4(X)) All About Kids Publishing.
Oliveira, Luis. The DogMan 2. 2009. (ENG.). 60p. pap. 15.50 (978-0-578-02385-4(7)) Desktop Prepress Services.
Oliver, Lauren. Delirium, 1. 2016. (Delirium Trilogy Ser.: 1). (ENG.). 480p. (YA). (gr. 9-12). pap. 15.99 (978-0-06-172683-5(4), HarperCollins) HarperCollins Pubs.
—Delirium. 2016. (Delirium Ser.: 1). (YA). lib. bdg. 20.85 (978-0-606-23575-4(2)) Turtleback.
—Delirium Stories: Hana, Annabel, Raven & Alex. (Delirium Ser.). (YA). 2016. lib. bdg. 20.85 (978-0-606-38920-4(2)) 2013. lib. bdg. 20.85 (978-0-606-31834-1(8)) Turtleback.
—Delirium Stories: Hana, Annabel, & Raven. 2013. (Delirium Trilogy Ser.). (ENG.). 224p. (YA). (gr. 9). pap. 9.99 (978-0-06-226778-8(7), HarperCollins) HarperCollins Pubs.
—Delirium Stories: Hana, Annabel, Raven, & Alex. 2016. (Delirium Story Ser.). (ENG.). 224p. (YA). (gr. 9). pap. 9.99 (978-0-06-248432-1(X), HarperCollins) HarperCollins Pubs.
—Delirium: the Special Edition. 2011. (Delirium Trilogy Ser.: 1). (ENG.). 480p. (YA). (gr. 9). 17.99 (978-0-06-211243-9(0), HarperCollins) HarperCollins Pubs.
—Liesl & Po. Acedera, Kei, illus. 2012. (ENG.). 336p. (J). (gr. 3-7). pap. 7.99 (978-0-06-201452-8(8), HarperCollins) HarperCollins Pubs.
—Liesl & Po. 2012. (J). lib. bdg. 17.20 (978-0-606-26853-0(7)) Turtleback.
Oliver, Lauren & Chester, H. C. Curiosity House: the Screaming Statue. 2017. (Curiosity House Ser.: 2). (ENG.). 384p. (J). (gr. 3-7). pap. 6.99 (978-0-06-227085-6(0), HarperCollins) HarperCollins Pubs.
—Curiosity House: the Shrunken Head. Lacombe, Benjamin, illus. 2015. (Curiosity House Ser.: 1). (ENG.). 368p. (J). (gr. 3-7). 16.99 (978-0-06-227081-8(8), HarperCollins) HarperCollins Pubs.
—The Screaming Statue. 2016. (Illus.). 361p. (J). (978-0-06-245885-8(X)) Harper & Row Ltd.
Oliver, Lin & Baker, Theo. Sound Bender. 2011. (ENG.). 272p. (J). (gr. 5-9). 16.99 (978-0-545-19692-5(2), Scholastic Pr.) Scholastic, Inc.
Olmstead, Kathleen & Porter, Eleanor H. Pollyanna. Akib, Jamel, illus. 2007. (Classic Starts Ser.). 154p. (J). (978-1-4287-4209-3(3)) Sterling Publishing Co., Inc.
Olswanger, Anna. Greenhorn. Nerlove, Miriam, illus. 2012. (ENG.). (J). 48p. 17.95 (978-1-58838-235-1(4), 8806); E-Book 9.99 (978-1-60306-159-9(2), 8807) NewSouth, Inc. (NewSouth Bks.).
Ormand, Kate. The Pack. 2017. (ENG.). 304p. (J). 16.99 (978-1-5107-1218-8(6), Sky Pony Pr.) Skyhorse Publishing Co., Inc.
Ormsbee, K. E. The Doorway & the Deep. 2016. (Water & the Wild Ser.: 2). (ENG., Illus.). 480p. (J). (gr. 3-7). 16.99 (978-1-4521-3636-3(X)) Chronicle Bks. LLC.
—The Water & the Wild. Mora, Elsa, illus. 2015. (Water & the Wild Ser.). (ENG.). 448p. (J). (gr. 3-7). 16.99 (978-1-4521-1386-9(6)) Chronicle Bks. LLC.
Osborne, Jill. Riley Mae & the Sole Fire Safari, 1 vol. 2014. (Faithgirlz / the Good News Shoes Ser.: 3). (ENG.). 256p. (J). pap. 7.99 (978-0-310-74283-8(8)) Zonderkidz.
Otis, James. Peter of New Amsterdam: A story of Old New York. 2007. 136p. per. 9.95 (978-0-9790876-2-2(7)) Living Bks. Pr.
Ott, Alexandra. Rules for Thieves. 2017. (Rules for Thieves Ser.: 1). (ENG., Illus.). 320p. (J). (gr. 3-7). 17.99 (978-1-4814-7274-6(7), Aladdin) Simon & Schuster Children's Publishing.
—Rules for Thieves. 2018. (Rules for Thieves Ser.: 1). (ENG.). 336p. (J). (gr. 3-7). pap. 8.99 (978-1-4814-7275-3(5), Simon & Schuster/Paula Wiseman Bks.) Simon & Schuster/Paula Wiseman Bks.
—The Shadow Thieves. 2018. (Rules for Thieves Ser.: 2). (ENG., Illus.). 400p. (J). (gr. 3-7). 17.99 (978-1-4814-7277-7(1), Aladdin) Simon & Schuster Children's Publishing.
Otten, Charlotte F. Home in a Wilderness Fort: Copper Harbor 1844. 2006. (Illus.). 232p. (J). (gr. 2-7). per. 14.95 (978-0-9766104-5-8(0)) Arbutus Pr.
Palmer, Pamela. Horse of the Dawn. 2005. 89p. pap. 16.95 (978-1-4137-9545-5(5)) PublishAmerica, Inc.
Papp, Robert, illus. The Amazing Mystery Show. 2010. (Boxcar Children Mysteries Ser.: 123). (ENG.). 128p. (J). (gr. 2-5). pap. 7.99 (978-0-8075-0315-7(0), 807503150);No. 123. 14.99 (978-0-8075-0314-0(2), 807503142) Random Hse. Children's Bks. (Random Hse. Bks. for Young Readers).
—The Clue in the Recycling Bin. 2011. (Boxcar Children Mysteries Ser.: 126). (ENG.). 128p. (J). (gr. 2-5). pap. 6.99 (978-0-8075-1209-8(5), 807512095); lib. bdg. 14.99 (978-0-8075-1208-1(7), 807512087) Random Hse. Children's Bks. (Random Hse. Bks. for Young Readers).
—The Ghost of the Chattering Bones. 2007. (Boxcar Children Ser.). 120p. 15.00 (978-0-7569-7611-8(1)) Perfection Learning Corp.
—The Great Turkey Heist. 2011. (Boxcar Children Mysteries Ser.: 129). (ENG.). (J). (gr. 2-5). 144p. 6.99 (978-0-8075-3051-1(4), 807530514); 128p. lib. bdg. 14.99 (978-0-8075-3050-4(6), 807530506) Random Hse. Children's Bks. (Random Hse. Bks. for Young Readers).
—Monkey Trouble. 2011. (Boxcar Children Mysteries Ser.: 127). (ENG.). 128p. (J). (gr. 2-5). pap. 7.99 (978-0-8075-5240-7(2), 807552402); lib. bdg. 14.99 (978-0-8075-5239-1(9), 807552399) Random Hse. Children's Bks. (Random Hse. Bks. for Young Readers).
—Spooktacular Special. 2013. (Boxcar Children Mysteries Ser.). (ENG.). 400p. (J). (gr. 2-5). 9.99 (978-0-8075-7605-2(0), 807576050, Random Hse. Bks. for Young Readers) Random Hse. Children's Bks.
—The Spy Game. 2009. (Boxcar Children Mysteries Ser.: 118). (ENG.). 128p. (J). (gr. 2-5). 14.99 (978-0-8075-7603-8(4), 807576034, Random Hse. Bks. for Young Readers) Random Hse. Children's Bks.
—The Spy in the Bleachers. 2010. (Boxcar Children Mysteries Ser.: 122). (ENG.). 128p. (J). (gr. 2-5). 14.99 (978-0-8075-7606-9(9), 807576069);No. 122. pap. 6.99 (978-0-8075-7607-6(7), 807576077) Random Hse. Children's Bks. (Random Hse. Bks. for Young Readers).
—The Zombie Project. 2011. (Boxcar Children Mysteries Ser.: 128). (ENG.). 128p. (J). (gr. 2-5). 6.99

MNO

(978-0-8075-9493-3(8), 807594938); lib. bdg. 14.99 *(978-0-8075-9492-6(X),* 080759492X) Random Hse. Children's Bks. (Random Hse. Bks. for Young Readers).

Parker, Richard. Voyage to Tasmani. Seward, Prudence, illus. 2011. 128p. 40.95 *(978-1-258-08572-8(0))* Literary Licensing, LLC.

Parry, Rosanne. Written in Stone. 2014. (Illus.). 208p. (J). (gr. 4-7). pap. 7.99 *(978-0-375-87135-1(7),* Yearling) Random Hse. Children's Bks.

Patterson, James. The Dangerous Days of Daniel X. 2014. lthr. 79.00 *(978-1-62715-506-9(6))* Leatherbound Bestsellers.

—The Dangerous Days of Daniel X. (Daniel X Ser.: 1). (ENG.). (J). (gr. 3-7). 2010. Illus.). 272p. pap. 8.99 *(978-0-316-11970-2(9))* 2009. 288p. mass mkt. 7.99 *(978-0-446-50913-8(2))* 2008. 304p. pap. 19.99 *(978-0-316-03025-0(2))* Little Brown & Co. (Jimmy Patterson).

—The Dangerous Days of Daniel X. 2010. (Daniel X Ser.: 1). (J). lib. bdg. 18.45 *(978-0-606-14720-0(9))* Turtleback.

—Daniel X: Armageddon. (Daniel X Ser.: 5). (ENG.). (J). (gr. 3-7). 2013. 320p. pap. 17.99 *(978-0-316-10177-6(X))* 2012. 304p. 16.99 *(978-0-316-10179-0(6))* 2012. 384p. 28.00 *(978-0-316-22421-5(9))* Little Brown & Co. (Jimmy Patterson).

—Daniel X: Demons & Druids. (Daniel X Ser.: 3). (ENG.). (J). (gr. 3-7). 2011. 304p. pap., pap. 8.99 *(978-0-316-03830-0(X))* 2010. 320p. 33.99 *(978-0-316-08731-5(9))* Little Brown & Co. (Jimmy Patterson).

—Watch the Skies. 2014. lthr. 79.00 *(978-1-62715-571-7(6))* Leatherbound Bestsellers.

—Watch the Skies. 2010. (Daniel X Ser.: 2). (J). lib. bdg. 18.45 *(978-0-606-10550-7(6))* Turtleback.

Patterson, James & Grabenstein, Chris. Armageddon. 2013. (Daniel X Ser.: 5). (J). lib. bdg. 18.45 *(978-0-606-31747-4(3))* Turtleback.

—Daniel X: Lights Out. 2015. (Daniel X Ser.: 6). (ENG.). 272p. (J). (gr. 3-7). 32.99 *(978-0-316-20745-4(4),* Jimmy Patterson) Little Brown & Co.

Patterson, James & Rust, Ned. Daniel X: Game Over. 2011. (Daniel X Ser.: 4). (ENG.). 240p. (J). (gr. 3-7). 32.99 *(978-0-316-10178-3(8),* Jimmy Patterson) Little Brown & Co.

—Daniel X: Watch the Skies. (Daniel X Ser.: 2). (ENG.). (J). (gr. 3-7). 2010. 288p. pap. 8.99 *(978-0-316-11969-6(5))* 2009. 352p. pap. 19.99 *(978-0-316-04363-2(X))* Little Brown & Co. (Jimmy Patterson).

—Game Over. 2012. (Daniel X Ser.: 4). (J). lib. bdg. 18.45 *(978-0-606-26165-4(6))* Turtleback.

Patterson, James & Sadler, Adam. Daniel X: Demons & Druids. 2010. (Daniel X Ser.: 3). (ENG.). 256p. (J). (gr. 3-7). 31.99 *(978-0-316-03698-6(6),* Jimmy Patterson) Little Brown & Co.

Paulsen, Gary. Northwind. 2022. (ENG.). 256p. (J). 18.99 *(978-0-374-31420-0(9),* 900225846, Farrar, Straus & Giroux (BYR)) Farrar, Straus & Giroux.

—Northwind. 2024. (ENG.). 256p. (gr. 6-8). 24.94 ***(978-1-5364-8333-8(8))*** Square Fish.

Pavlou, Stel. Daniel Coldstar #2: the Betrayer. 2019. (Daniel Coldstar Ser.: 2). (ENG.). 304p. (J). (gr. 3-7). 16.99 *(978-0-06-212609-2(1),* HarperCollins) HarperCollins Pubs.

Peacock, Shane. The Dark Missions of Edgar Brim: Monster. 2019. (Dark Missions of Edgar Brim Ser.: 2). 288p. (YA). (gr. 7). pap. 9.99 *(978-0-7352-6273-7(X),* Penguin Teen) PRH Canada Young Readers CAN. Dist: Penguin Random Hse. LLC.

Pearson, Ridley. Peter & the Starcatchers-Peter & the Starcatchers, Book One. rev. ed. 2006. (Peter & the Starcatchers Ser.: 1). (ENG., Illus.). 480p. (J). (gr. 5-9). reprint ed. pap. 9.99 *(978-0-7868-4907-9(X),* Disney-Hyperion) Disney Publishing Worldwide.

Peart, Hendry. Red Falcons of Tremoine. Brevannes, Maurice, illus. 2007. (ENG.). 256p. (J). (gr. 4-6). pap. 13.95 *(978-1-932350-15-9(2))* Ignatius Pr.

Peart, Jane. Orphan Train West Trilogy. 2004. (Orphan Train West Ser.). pap. 11.98 *(978-0-8007-5843-1(9))* Baker Publishing Group.

Peck, Robert Newton. Horse Thief. 2003. 277p. (YA). (gr. 7). 13.65 *(978-0-7569-1461-5(2))* Perfection Learning Corp.

Peet, Mal & Rosoff, Meg. Beck. 2019. (ENG.). 272p. (YA). (gr. 11). pap. 8.99 *(978-1-5362-0642-5(3))* Candlewick Pr.

Pennypacker, Sara. Pax, Journey Home. Klassen, Jon, illus. 2021. 246p. (J). *(978-0-06-314400-2(X)); (978-0-06-320674-8(9))* Addison Wesley.

—Pax, Journey Home. Klassen, Jon, illus. (Pax Ser.). (ENG.). (J). (gr. 3-7). 2023. 272p. pap. 9.99 *(978-0-06-293036-1(2))* 2021. 272p. E-Book *(978-0-06-293037-8(0),* 9780062930378) 2021. 256p. 17.99 *(978-0-06-293034-7(6))* HarperCollins Pubs. (Balzer & Bray).

Peters, Julie Anne. Rage: a Love Story. 2010. 304p. (YA). (gr. 9). pap. 9.99 *(978-0-375-84411-9(2),* Knopf Bks. for Young Readers) Random Hse. Children's Bks.

Petersen, Alicia. A Sparrow Alone. 2004. 154p. (YA). 8.99 *(978-1-59166-204-4(4))* BJU Pr.

Peterson Haddix, Margaret. El desafío final: The 39 Clues 10. 2013. (SPA.). 304p. (J). pap. 14.99 *(978-84-08-10876-4(X))* Noguer y Caralt Editores, S. A. ESP. Dist: Lectorum Pubns., Inc.

Petrucha, Stefan. Ripper. (ENG.). 432p. (YA). (gr. 7). 2013. pap. 9.99 *(978-0-14-242418-6(8),* Speak) 2012. 26.19 *(978-0-399-25524-3(9))* Penguin Young Readers Group.

Pfeffer, Susan Beth. Revenge of the Aztecs. 2004. 118p. (J). lib. bdg. 16.92 *(978-1-4242-0763-3(0))* Fitzgerald Bks.

Philbrick, Rodman. The Mostly True Adventures of Homer P. Figg (Scholastic Gold) 2011. (ENG.). 240p. (J). (gr. 4-7). pap. 8.99 *(978-0-439-66821-7(2),* Scholastic Paperbacks) Scholastic, Inc.

Phillips, Dixie. One Noble Journey. Sponaugle, Kim, illus. 2009. 16p. pap. 9.95 *(978-1-935137-86-3(7))* Guardian Angel Publishing, Inc.

Pickett, Lanaya A. Walking with Angels. 2011. 192p. 23.95 *(978-1-4620-2306-6(1));* pap. 13.95 *(978-1-4620-2307-3(X))* iUniverse, Inc.

Pierpoint, Eric. The Last Ride of Caleb O'Toole. 2013. (ENG., Illus.). 304p. (J). (gr. 4-7). pap. 11.99 *(978-1-4022-8171-6(4),* 9781402281716) Sourcebooks, Inc.

Pinkney, Andrea Davis. Bird in a Box. Qualls, Sean, illus. 2012. (J). lib. bdg. 18.45 *(978-0-606-26157-9(5))* Turtleback.

Platt, Randall. Hellie Jondoe. 2009. (ENG.). 224p. (J). (gr. 7-18). pap. 16.95 *(978-0-89672-663-5(0),* P170570) Texas Tech Univ. Pr.

Poblocki, Dan. The Missing (Shadow House, Book 4) 2018. (Shadow House Ser.: 4). (ENG.). 224p. (J). (gr. 3-7). 12.99 *(978-1-338-24578-3(3))* Scholastic, Inc.

—No Way Out (Shadow House, Book 3) 2017. (Shadow House Ser.: 3). (ENG., Illus.). 224p. (J). (gr. 3-7). 12.99 *(978-0-545-92552-5(5))* Scholastic, Inc.

Polacco, Patricia. The Bravest Man in the World. Polacco, Patricia, illus. 2019. (ENG., Illus.). 56p. (J). (gr. -1-3). 17.99 *(978-1-4814-9461-8(9),* Simon & Schuster Bks. For Young Readers) Simon & Schuster Bks. For Young Readers.

Porter, Eleanor. Pollyanna. 2018. (ENG., Illus.). 258p. (J). (gr. 4-7). 27.20 *(978-1-7317-0764-2(9));* pap. 15.14 *(978-1-7317-0765-9(7))* Simon & Brown.

Porter, Eleanor H. Pollyanna. (J). 21.95 *(978-0-8488-1445-8(2))* Amereon Ltd.

—Pollyanna. abr. ed. 2006. 210p. (J). (gr. 3-7). per. 8.99 *(978-1-59166-669-1(4))* BJU Pr.

—Pollyanna. Hindley, Kate, illus. 2017. (Alma Junior Classics Ser.). (ENG.). 288p. (J). pap. 12.00 *(978-1-84749-640-9(7),* 900184120, Alma Classics) Bloomsbury Publishing USA.

—Pollyanna. l.t. ed. 2007. (ENG.). 206p. pap. 22.99 *(978-1-4346-1071-3(3))* Creative Media Partners, LLC.

—Pollyanna. 2005. 104p. per. 4.95 *(978-1-4209-2555-5(5))* Digireads.com Publishing.

—Pollyanna. 2011. (Dover Children's Evergreen Classics Ser.). (ENG.). 208p. (J). (gr. 3-8). pap. 7.99 *(978-0-486-43206-9(8),* 432068) Dover Pubns., Inc.

—Pollyanna. Date not set. (J). 14.99 *(978-0-06-028226-4(6));* 32p. pap. 4.99 *(978-0-06-443536-9(9))* HarperCollins Pubs.

—Pollyanna. 2018. (ENG., Illus.). 120p. (J). (gr. 4-7). pap. 5.99 *(978-1-7268-3443-8(3))* Independently Published.

—Pollyanna. 2016. (J). pap. *(978-1-5124-2614-4(8))* Lerner Publishing Group.

—Pollyanna & Pollyanna Grows Up. 2004. pap. 11.95 *(978-1-4145-0603-6(1))* Pavilion Pr., Inc.

Porter, Pamela. I'll Be Watching. 2013. 336p. pap. *(978-1-4596-6449-4(3))* ReadHowYouWant.com, Ltd.

Poston, Ashley. Heart of Iron. 2019. (ENG.). 496p. (YA). (gr. 8). pap. 9.99 *(978-0-06-265286-7(9))* 2018. 467p. (J). *(978-0-06-284485-9(7))* HarperCollins Pubs. (Balzer & Bray).

—Soul of Stars. 2019. (ENG., Illus.). 448p. (YA). (gr. 8). 17.99 *(978-0-06-284733-1(3),* Balzer & Bray) HarperCollins Pubs.

Potter, Ellen. The Humming Room: A Novel Inspired by the Secret Garden. 2013. (ENG.). 208p. (J). (gr. 4-7). pap. 9.99 *(978-1-250-01666-9(5),* 900087030) Square Fish.

Price, Lissa. Starters. 2013. (Starters Ser.: 1). (ENG.). 384p. (YA). (gr. 7). pap. 10.99 *(978-0-385-74248-1(7),* Ember) Random Hse. Children's Bks.

Price, Roy. The Gnome Guardian: Polly's Adventure. 2012. 64p. pap. 13.66 *(978-1-4678-9701-3(9))* AuthorHouse.

Prineas, Sarah. The Magic Thief: Found. Caparo, Antonio Javier, illus. 2011. (Magic Thief Ser.: 3). (ENG.). 384p. (J). (gr. 5). pap. 7.99 *(978-0-06-137595-8(0),* HarperCollins) HarperCollins Pubs.

Pullman, Philip. The Ruby in the Smoke. 2009. 9.84 *(978-0-7848-2919-6(5),* Everbind) Marco Bk. Co.

—The Ruby in the Smoke. 2008. (Sally Lockhart Mystery Ser.: Bk. 1). (ENG.). 230p. (YA). (gr. 7-18). 22.44 *(978-0-394-98826-9(4))* Random House Publishing Group.

—The Ruby in the Smoke. 2003. (Sally Lockhart Ser.: Bk. 1). (Illus.). (YA). pap. 9.95 *(978-0-375-82545-3(2),* Knopf Bks. for Young Readers) Random Hse. Children's Bks.

—The Ruby in the Smoke: a Sally Lockhart Mystery. 2008. (Sally Lockhart Ser.: Bk. 1). (ENG.). 256p. (YA). (gr. 7). pap. 10.99 *(978-0-375-84516-1(X),* Ember) Random Hse. Children's Bks.

Qualey, Marsha. Thin Ice. 2007. 214p. (YA). *(978-0-9793444-0-4(9))* Quercus Pr.

Raasch, Sara. Frost Like Night. (Snow Like Ashes Ser.: 3). (ENG.). (YA). (gr. 9). 2017. 512p. pap. 10.99 *(978-0-06-228699-4(4))* 2016. (Illus.). 496p. 17.99 *(978-0-06-228698-7(6))* HarperCollins Pubs. (Balzer & Bray).

—Ice Like Fire. (Illus.). (YA). 2016. (Snow Like Ashes Ser.: 2). (ENG.). 512p. (gr. 9). pap. 9.99 *(978-0-06-228696-3(X),* Balzer & Bray) 2015. (Snow Like Ashes Ser.: 2). (ENG.). 496p. (gr. 9-12). 17.99 *(978-0-06-228695-6(1),* Balzer & Bray) 2015. 496p. pap. *(978-0-06-242793-9(8))* HarperCollins Pubs.

—Snow Like Ashes. (Snow Like Ashes Ser.: 1). (ENG., Illus.). (YA). (gr. 9). 2015. 448p. pap. 15.99 *(978-0-06-228693-2(5))* 2014. 432p. 17.99 *(978-0-06-228692-5(7))* HarperCollins Pubs. (Balzer & Bray).

Rand, Edward A. The Knights of the White Shield; or, up-the-Ladder Club Series, Round One Play. 2007. 120p. per. *(978-1-4068-3739-1(3))* Echo Library.

Randall, Alice. The Diary of B. B. Bright, Possible Princess. 2012. (J). *(978-1-61858-016-0(7))* Turner Publishing Co.

Randall, Alice & Randall Williams, Caroline. The Diary of B. B. Bright, Possible Princess. Strickland, Shadra, illus. 2012. (ENG.). 192p. (J). (gr. 2-6). 27.99 *(978-1-61858-015-3(9))* Turner Publishing Co.

Redding, LaTisha. Calling the Water Drum, 1 vol. Boyd, Aaron, illus. 2016. (ENG.). 32p. (J). (gr. -1-5). 17.95 *(978-1-62014-194-6(9),* 1dbccc72-9d38-4d4a-8811-50b865e16029) Lee & Low Bks., Inc.

Reh, Rusalka. Pizzicato: The Abduction of the Magic Violin, 0 vols. Wilson, David Henry, tr. 2011. (ENG.). 132p. (J). (gr. 4-6). pap. 9.95 *(978-1-61109-004-8(0),* 9781611090048, Two Lions) Amazon Publishing.

Resau, Laura. Red Glass. 2009. (ENG.). 304p. (YA). (gr. 7). pap. 9.99 *(978-0-440-24025-9(5),* Delacorte Bks. for Young Readers) Random Hse. Children's Bks.

Rewa. Molly May on the High Seas. (Illus.). 9.95 *(978-0-9726375-1-0(6))* Little Red Cat Publishing.

Reynolds Naylor, Phyllis. Sang Spell. 224p. (YA). (gr. 5-18). pap. 4.99 *(978-0-8072-8294-6(4),* Listening Library) Random Hse. Audio Publishing Group.

Richards, Laura E. Captain January. 2004. reprint ed. pap. 15.95 *(978-1-4191-1199-0(X));* pap. 1.99 *(978-1-4192-1199-7(4))* Kessinger Publishing, LLC.

Richardson, Arleta. Across the Border. 2016. (Beyond the Orphan Train Ser.: 4). (ENG.). 192p. (J). (gr. 3-6). pap. 7.99 *(978-0-7814-1358-9(3),* 136205) Cook, David C.

—Prairie Homestead. 2016. (Beyond the Orphan Train Ser.: 3). (ENG.). 192p. (J). pap. 7.99 *(978-0-7814-1357-2(5),* 136204) Cook, David C.

—Whistle Stop West. 2003. (Orphans' Journey Ser.: Vol. 2). 144p. (J). (gr. 3-7). pap., pap. 5.99 *(978-0-7814-3537-6(4),* 0781435374) Cook, David C.

Riggs, Ransom. Library of Souls. 2017. (Miss Peregrine's Peculiar Children Ser.: 3). (ENG.). (YA). (gr. 9). lib. bdg. 23.30 *(978-0-606-39808-4(2))* Turtleback.

—Library of Souls: The Third Novel of Miss Peregrine's Peculiar Children. 2015. (Miss Peregrine's Peculiar Children Ser.: 3). (Illus.). 400p. (YA). (gr. 9). 18.99 *(978-1-59474-758-8(X))* Quirk Bks.

Rigsby, Annelle & Raffa, Edwina. Race to Kitty Hawk. 2003. (Adventures in America Ser.). (Illus.). 84p. (gr. 4). 14.95 *(978-1-893110-33-5(8))* Silver Moon Pr.

Rinaldi, Ann. Juliet's Moon. 2010. (ENG., Illus.). 256p. (YA). (gr. 7). pap. 14.99 *(978-0-547-25874-4(7),* 1402328, Clarion Bks.) HarperCollins Pubs.

Riordan, Rick. Daughter of the Deep. Naidu, Lavanya, illus. 2021. xii, 336p. (J). ***(978-1-368-08084-2(7))*** Disney Pr.

—Daughter of the Deep. (ENG.). 2023. 368p. (J). (gr. 5-9). pap. 9.99 *(978-1-368-07793-4(5),* Disney-Hyperion) 2023. 368p. (gr. 6-8). 26.19 ***(978-1-5364-7874-7(1))*** 2021. (Illus.). 352p. (J). (gr. 5-9). 19.99 *(978-1-368-07792-7(7),* Disney-Hyperion) Disney Publishing Worldwide.

Roberts, Kelly Hughes. The Road to Chianti. 2012. 214p. (gr. 4-6). 33.99 *(978-1-4525-5963-6(5));* pap. 15.99 *(978-1-4525-5961-2(9))* Balboa Pr.

Robins, Eleanor. The Secret Message, 1 vol. unabr. ed. 2011. (Carter High Mysteries Ser.). (ENG.). 48p. (YA). (gr. 9-12). 9.75 *(978-1-61651-568-3(6))* Saddleback Educational Publishing, Inc.

Roesti, Delores. Mareena Maree Mulligan & the Flying Wheel Chair: Book 1: School Days. 2007. 81p. pap. 9.95 *(978-0-7414-4048-8(2))* Infinity Publishing.

Roman, Annette. 1 World Manga, Vol. 5. Ng, Leandro, illus. 2007. (1 World Manga Ser.). (ENG.). 240p. pap. 3.99 *(978-1-4215-1169-6(X))* Viz Media.

Ross, Alice & Ross, Kent. La Dama de Cobre. Bowman, Leslie, illus. 2006. (Yo Solo - Historia (on My Own - History) Ser.). (SPA.). 48p. (gr. 2-4). lib. bdg. 25.26 *(978-0-8225-6262-7(6))* Lerner Publishing Group.

Ross, Joel. The Fog Diver. 2015. (Fog Diver Ser.: 1). (ENG.). 336p. (J). (gr. 3-7). 16.99 *(978-0-06-235293-4(8),* HarperCollins) HarperCollins Pubs.

—The Lost Compass. 2016. (Fog Diver Ser.: 2). (ENG.). 352p. (J). (gr. 3-7). 16.99 *(978-0-06-235297-2(0),* HarperCollins) HarperCollins Pubs.

Rossell, Judith. Withering-By-Sea. Rossell, Judith, illus. 2017. (ENG., Illus.). 288p. (J). (gr. 3-7). pap. 8.99 *(978-1-4814-4368-5(2))* Simon & Schuster Children's Publishing.

—Wormwood Mire. Rossell, Judith, illus. 2017. (ENG., Illus.). 288p. (J). (gr. 3-7). 16.99 *(978-1-4814-4370-8(4),* Atheneum Bks. for Young Readers) Simon & Schuster Children's Publishing.

Rubright, Lynn. Mama's Window. Smith, Duane, illus. 2005. 89p. (J). 16.95 *(978-1-57480-160-6(0))* Lee & Low Bks., Inc.

Rudden, Dave. The Endless King. 2018. (J). *(978-0-553-52305-8(8))* Random Hse., Inc.

—The Forever Court (Knights of the Borrowed Dark, Book 2) 2017. (Knights of the Borrowed Dark Ser.: 2). (ENG.). 432p. (J). (gr. 5). 16.99 *(978-0-553-52301-0(5),* Random Hse. Bks. for Young Readers) Random Hse. Children's Bks.

Rue, Nancy N. Sophie Steps Up, 1 vol. 2009. (Faithgirlz! Ser.: No. 4). (ENG.). 128p. (J). pap. 6.99 *(978-0-310-71841-3(4))* Zonderkidz.

Rugg, Jim & Maruca, Brian. The Street Angel Gang. 2017. (ENG., Illus.). 40p. (YA). 19.99 *(978-1-5343-0366-9(9),* b946d656-558a-4949-8e8b-e6d491cbac95) Image Comics.

Rundell, Katherine. Cartwheeling in Thunderstorms. Castrillón, Melissa & Castrillón, Melissa, illus. 2014. (ENG.). 256p. (J). (gr. 3-7). 18.99 *(978-1-4424-9061-1(6),* Simon & Schuster Bks. For Young Readers) Simon & Schuster Bks. For Young Readers.

SaBerre, Kristen. A Noble Cause. 2018. (Suddenly Royal Ser.). (ENG.). 112p. (YA). (gr. 6-12). pap. 7.99 *(978-1-5415-2639-6(2),* 38f3af7a-8598-4396-82c0-6ccb288be95c); lib. bdg. 26.65 *(978-1-5415-2569-6(8),* eef4bf2d-fdad-48be-b43c-f1e8c406a1fb) Lerner Publishing Group. (Darby Creek).

Salerni, Dianne K. The Eighth Day. McClellan, David, illus. 2015. (Eighth Day Ser.: 1). (ENG.). 336p. (J). (gr. 3-7). pap. 6.99 *(978-0-06-227216-4(0),* HarperCollins) HarperCollins Pubs.

—The Eighth Day. 2014. (Eighth Day Ser.: 1). (ENG., Illus.). 320p. (J). (gr. 3-7). 16.99 *(978-0-06-227215-7(2),* HarperCollins) HarperCollins Pubs.

—The Inquisitor's Mark. 2015. (Eighth Day Ser.: 2). (ENG.). 352p. (J). (gr. 3-7). 16.99 *(978-0-06-227218-8(7),* HarperCollins) HarperCollins Pubs.

—The Morrigan's Curse. 2016. (Eighth Day Ser.: 3). (ENG.). 400p. (J). (gr. 3-7). 16.99 *(978-0-06-227221-8(7),* HarperCollins) HarperCollins Pubs.

Sandwall-Bergstrom, Martha. Goldie at the Farm, 25 vols. Stalsjo, Eva, illus. (ENG.). 24p. 17.95 *(978-0-86315-485-0(9))* Floris Bks. GBR. Dist: SteinerBooks, Inc.

Sandwall-Bergström, Martha. Goldie at the Orphanage, 25 vols. Stålsjö, Eva, illus. 2004. (ENG.). 24p. (J). 16.95 *(978-0-86315-443-0(3))* Floris Bks. GBR. Dist: SteinerBooks, Inc.

Saunders, Margaret Marshall. Tilda Jane. 2008. (Fiction Treasures Ser.). (ENG.). 318p. pap. 16.95 *(978-0-88780-780-0(1),* 780) Formac Publishing Co., Ltd. CAN. Dist: Formac Lorimer Bks. Ltd.

Savage, Melissa. Lemons. 2018. (ENG.). 320p. (J). (gr. 3-7). 8.99 *(978-1-5247-0015-7(0),* Yearling) Random Hse. Children's Bks.

Scarrow, Kristine. Throwaway Girl. 2014. (ENG.). 184p. (YA). pap. 12.99 *(978-1-4597-1407-6(5))* Dundurn Pr. CAN. Dist: Publishers Group West (PGW).

Schlitz, Laura Amy. Splendors & Glooms. (ENG.). 400p. (J). 2017. (gr. 5-9). pap. 10.99 *(978-0-7636-9449-4(5))* 2012. (Illus.). (gr. 4-7). 17.99 *(978-0-7636-5380-4(2))* Candlewick Pr.

—Splendors & Glooms. 2014. (ENG.). (J). (gr. 4-7). lib. bdg. 18.60 *(978-1-62765-443-2(7))* Perfection Learning Corp.

—Splendors & Glooms. 2014. lib. bdg. 18.40 *(978-0-606-35170-6(1))* Turtleback.

Schmid, Susan Maupin. Ghost of a Chance. Marlin, Lissy, illus. 2017. (100 Dresses Ser.: 2). 320p. (J). (gr. 3-7). 16.99 *(978-0-553-53373-6(8),* Random Hse. Bks. for Young Readers) Random Hse. Children's Bks.

—If the Magic Fits. 2017. (100 Dresses Ser.: 1). 320p. (J). (gr. 3-7). 7.99 *(978-0-553-53369-9(X),* Yearling) Random Hse. Children's Bks.

—The Starlight Slippers. 2018. (100 Dresses Ser.: 3). (Illus.). 336p. (J). (gr. 3-7). 16.99 *(978-0-553-53377-4(0),* Random Hse. Bks. for Young Readers) Random Hse. Children's Bks.

Schrefer, Eliot. Orphaned (Ape Quartet #4) 2018. (Ape Quartet Ser.: 4). (ENG., Illus.). 336p. (YA). (gr. 7-7). 18.99 *(978-0-545-65505-7(6),* Scholastic Pr.) Scholastic, Inc.

Scott, Elaine. Secrets of the Cirque Medrano. 2008. (Illus.). 216p. (J). (gr. 5-9). 15.95 *(978-1-57091-712-7(4))* Charlesbridge Publishing, Inc.

—The Spanish Web: An Encounter with Picasso. 2004. (Art Encounters Ser.). (J). 15.95 *(978-0-8230-0410-2(4));* pap. 6.99 *(978-0-8230-0413-3(9))* Watson-Guptill Pubns., Inc.

Scott, Lisa Ann. Back on the Map. 2017. (ENG.). 320p. (J). (gr. 2-7). 15.99 *(978-1-5107-1353-6(0),* Sky Pony Pr.) Skyhorse Publishing Co., Inc.

Seabag-Montefiore, Mary, retold by. David Copperfield. 2008. (Young Reading Series 3 Gift Books - Famous Lives Ser.). 64p. (J). 8.99 *(978-0-7945-2097-7(9),* Usborne) EDC Publishing.

Seabrooke, Brenda. Stonewolf. 2004. (ENG.). 240p. (J). (gr. 7-18). tchr. ed. 16.95 *(978-0-8234-1848-0(0))* Holiday Hse., Inc.

Sedgwick, Julian. The Black Dragon. Moffett, Patricia, illus. (Mysterium Ser.). (ENG.). 352p. (J). (gr. 4-8). 2018. pap. 9.99 *(978-1-5415-1489-8(0),* 6c0683dc-fa47-4097-b4fd-1f7a2d9c8e98) 2016. E-Book 29.32 *(978-1-4677-9555-5(0))* Lerner Publishing Group. (Carolrhoda Bks.).

—The Wheel of Life & Death, No. 3. Moffett, Patricia, illus. 2018. (Mysterium Ser.). (ENG.). 344p. (J). (gr. 4-8). 18.99 *(978-1-4677-7569-4(X),* e1dc9978-31c7-4613-afa7-14b9bae2030a, Carolrhoda Bks.) Lerner Publishing Group.

Sedgwick, Marcus. The Book of Dead Days. 2006. (Book of Dead Days Ser.: 1). (ENG.). 288p. (YA). (gr. 5-12). reprint ed. per. 7.99 *(978-0-385-74704-2(7),* Lamb, Wendy Bks.) Random Hse. Children's Bks.

Seidler, Tor. The Dulcimer Boy. Selznick, Brian, illus. 2003. 160p. (J). (gr. 3-7). lib. bdg. 16.89 *(978-0-06-623610-0(X))* HarperCollins Pubs.

—The Dulcimer Boy. Selznick, Brian, illus. 2004. 153p. (gr. 5-7). 17.00 *(978-0-7569-3520-7(2))* Perfection Learning Corp.

Seidman, Richard. The Secret of Ebbets Field. 2017. (J). mass mkt. 11.95 *(978-1-55571-859-6(0),* Paloma Bks.) L & R Publishing, LLC.

Seki, Sunny. Yuko-Chan & the Daruma Doll: The Adventures of a Blind Japanese Girl Who Saves Her Village - Bilingual English & Japanese Text. 2012. (Illus.). 32p. (J). (gr. -1-3). 15.95 *(978-4-8053-1187-5(8))* Tuttle Publishing.

Selznick, Brian. The Invention of Hugo Cabret. 2007. (CHI., Illus.). 534p. (J). *(978-957-570-894-8(6))* Eastern Publishing Co., Ltd., The.

—The Invention of Hugo Cabret. 2008. (CHI., Illus.). 465p. (J). pap. *(978-7-5448-0279-6(5))* Jieli Publishing Hse.

—The Invention of Hugo Cabret. Selznick, Brian, illus. 2007. (ENG., Illus.). 544p. (J). (gr. 4-7). 29.99 *(978-0-439-81378-5(6),* Scholastic Pr.); 534p. *(978-1-4071-0348-8(2))* Scholastic, Inc.

Seredy, Kate. Philomena. Seredy, Kate, illus. 2008. (Illus.). 93p. (J). pap. 11.95 *(978-1-932350-19-7(5))* Bethlehem Bks.

Seydou, Garba B. The One Man Army. 2012. 58p. pap. 16.95 *(978-1-4626-8958-3(2))* America Star Bks.

Shane, Rachel. Alice in Wonderland High. 2015. (ENG.). 300p. (YA). 17.99 *(978-1-4405-8466-4(4),* Simon Pulse) Simon Pulse.

Shapiro, David L. Sara's Journey. 2005. (ENG.). 224p. (gr. 7-12). per. 16.95 *(978-0-8276-0776-7(8))* Jewish Pubn. Society.

Sharenow, Robert. The Girl in the Torch. 2015. (ENG.). 304p. (J). (gr. 3-7). 16.99 *(978-0-06-222795-9(5),* Balzer & Bray) HarperCollins Pubs.

Sharp, Cathy. The Boy with the Latch Key (Halfpenny Orphans, Book 4) 2018. (Halfpenny Orphans Ser.: 4). (ENG.). 416p. 12.99 *(978-0-00-827672-0(2),* HarperCollins) HarperCollins Pubs.

Sharplin, Emory. Scrap. 2013. 352p. (J). pap. 14.95 *(978-1-938416-35-4(X))* River Grove Bks.

Shearer, Alex. Sky Run. 2014. (Cloud Hunters Ser.). (ENG.). 288p. (J). (gr. 2-7). 14.95 *(978-1-62873-593-2(7),* Sky Pony Pr.) Skyhorse Publishing Co., Inc.

Shefelman, Janice. Anna Maria's Gift. Papp, Robert, illus. 2011. (Stepping Stone Book(TM) Ser.). 112p. (J). (gr. 2-5). pap. 4.99 *(978-0-375-85882-6(2),* Random Hse. Bks. for Young Readers) Random Hse. Children's Bks.

Shefelman, Janice Jordan. Anna Maria's Gift. Papp, Robert, illus. 2010. (Stepping Stones Chapter Book: History Ser.). (ENG.). 112p. (J). (gr. 1-4). lib. bdg. 17.44 *(978-0-375-95881-6(9))* Random House Publishing Group.

Showalter, Gena. Alice in Zombieland. 2013. (White Rabbit Chronicles Ser.: 1). (ENG.). 416p. pap. 10.99 *(978-0-373-21089-3(2),* Harlequin Teen) Harlequin Enterprises ULC CAN. Dist: HarperCollins Pubs.

—Alice in Zombieland. 2013. (J). lib. bdg. 20.85 *(978-0-606-31712-2(0))* Turtleback.

—The Queen of Zombie Hearts. 2014. (White Rabbit Chronicles Ser.: 3). (ENG.). 464p. (YA). 18.99 *(978-0-373-21131-9(7),* Harlequin Teen) Harlequin Enterprises ULC CAN. Dist: HarperCollins Pubs.

—Through the Zombie Glass. 2014. (White Rabbit Chronicles Ser.: 2). (ENG.). 480p. (YA). pap. 12.99

(978-0-373-21129-6(5), Harlequin Teen) Harlequin Enterprises ULC CAN. Dist: HarperCollins Pubs.

Simmons, Andrew & Averdonz, N. R. I Was an Eighth-Grade Ninja, 1 vol., 1. Padilla, Ariel, illus. 2007. (Z Graphic Novels / Tomo Ser.). (ENG.). 160p. (J). (gr. 3-7). pap. 6.99 *(978-0-310-71300-5(5))* Zondervan.

Simon, Nadine. Flickers of True Destiny. 2010. 58p. pap. 11.95 *(978-1-60860-948-2(0)*, Eloquent Bks.) Strategic Book Publishing & Rights Agency (SBPRA).

Skelton, Matthew. The Story of Cirrus Flux. 2012. (ENG., Illus.). 304p. (J). (gr. 4-6). lib. bdg. 21.19 *(978-0-385-90398-1(7))* Random House Publishing Group.

Skot, Joelle. The Legend of the Blue Squid. 2008. (Illus.). (J). per. 16.99 *(978-1-933156-16-3(3)*, Visikid Bks.) GSVQ Publishing.

Skrypuch, Marsha Forchuk. Call Me Aram, 1 vol. Wood, Muriel, illus. 2008. (New Begininngs Ser.). (ENG.). 86p. (J). (gr. 4-6). 16.95 *(978-1-55455-000-5(9)*, 7c62f834-f311-47df-9b12-d300eb5d35c9) Fitzhenry & Whiteside, Ltd. CAN. Dist: Firefly Bks., Ltd.

—Call Me Aram, 1 vol. Wood, Muriel, illus. 2008. (New Begininngs Ser.). (ENG.). 86p. (J). (gr. 4-6). pap. 9.95 *(978-1-55455-001-2(7)*, db65e2ae-6abd-4783-9938-9a307fa1f9e3) Trifolium Bks., Inc. CAN. Dist: Firefly Bks., Ltd.

—Nobody's Child. 2003. (ENG.). 248p. (YA). (gr. 7). pap. 8.99 *(978-1-55002-442-5(6))* Dundurn Pr. CAN. Dist: Publishers Group West (PGW).

Sleiman, Dina L. Dauntless. 2015. (Valiant Hearts Ser.: 1). (ENG.). 368p. (YA). pap. 16.00 *(978-0-7642-1312-0(1))* Bethany Hse. Pubs.

Sloan, Holly Goldberg. Counting by 7s. 2015. (CHI.). 392p. (J). pap. *(978-986-6104-68-8(0))* DaskoviK, Izdatel'sko-torgovaja korporacija.

—Counting by 7s. 2014. (ENG.). (J). (gr. 5). lib. bdg. 19.60 *(978-1-62765-616-0(2))* Perfection Learning Corp.

—Counting by 7s. 2014. (gr. 5-8). lib. bdg. 19.65 *(978-0-606-36583-3(4))* Turtleback.

—Counting By 7s. (ENG.). (J). (gr. 5-9). 2014. 416p. 9.99 *(978-0-14-242286-1(X)*, Puffin Books) 2013. 384p. 18.99 *(978-0-8037-3855-3(2)*, Dial Bks) Penguin Young Readers Group.

Smith, Cynthia Leitich. Blessed. 2011. (Tantalize Ser.: 3). (ENG., Illus.). 480p. (YA). (gr. 9-18). 17.99 *(978-0-7636-4326-3(2))* Candlewick Pr.

—Tantalize. 2008. (Tantalize Ser.: 1). (ENG., Illus.). 336p. (YA). (gr. 9). pap. 9.99 *(978-0-7636-4059-0(X))* Candlewick Pr.

Smith, Sarah. The Other Side of Dark. 2010. (ENG.). 320p. (YA). (gr. 7-18). 16.99 *(978-1-4424-0280-5(6)*, Atheneum Bks. for Young Readers) Simon & Schuster Children's Publishing.

Smithem, Beth. Cocoa Bean & Squirt. 2010. 68p. pap. 10.49 *(978-1-4520-1929-1(0))* AuthorHouse.

Snedeker, Caroline Dale & Barney, Maginel Wright. Downright Dencey. 2003. (Young Adult Library). (ENG., Illus.). 274p. (J). (gr. 4-6). pap. 12.95 *(978-1-883937-79-9(5))* Ignatius Pr.

Snicket, Lemony, pseud. El Ascensor Artificioso. 2004. (Coleccion Una Serie de Catastroficas Desdichas A Series of Unfortunate Events Ser.). (SPA., Illus.). 232p. (YA). 12.95 *(978-84-8441-215-1(6))* Grijalbo Mondadori, S.A.-Montena ESP. Dist: Lectorum Pubns., Inc.

—The Austere Academy. Helquist, Brett, illus. 2008. (Series of Unfortunate Events Ser.: Bk. 5). (ENG.). 240p. (J). (gr. 5-18). pap. 6.99 *(978-0-06-114634-3(X)*, Harper Trophy) HarperCollins Pubs.

—The Bad Beginning. 2007. (Ser. of Unfortunate Events Ser.: 1). (J). lib. bdg. 17.20 *(978-1-4177-8840-8(2))* Turtleback.

—The Bad Beginning or, Orphans! 2007. (Series of Unfortunate Events Ser.: 1). (ENG., Illus.). 176p. (J). (gr. 5-9). pap. 7.99 *(978-0-06-114630-5(7)*, HarperCollins) HarperCollins Pubs.

—Una Funesta Finestra. pap. 21.95 *(978-88-7782-953-5(2))* Salani ITA. Dist: Distribooks, Inc.

—The Grim Grotto. 2004. (Series of Unfortunate Events Ser.: 11). (ENG., Illus.). 352p. (J). (gr. 5-6). 13.99 *(978-0-06-441014-4(5)*, HarperCollins) HarperCollins Pubs.

—Un Infausto Inizio. pap. 23.95 *(978-88-7782-951-1(6))* Salani ITA. Dist: Distribooks, Inc.

—The Loathsome Library, Bks. 1-6. Helquist, Brett, illus. 2005. (Series of Unfortunate Events Ser.: Bks. 1-6). (J). (gr. 5). 65.00 *(978-0-06-083353-4(X))* HarperCollins Pubs.

—The Miserable Mill, 13 vols. Helquist, Brett, illus. 2008. (Series of Unfortunate Events Ser.: Bk. 4). (ENG.). 208p. (J). (gr. 5-18). pap. 6.99 *(978-0-06-114632-9(3)*, Harper Trophy) HarperCollins Pubs.

—Piege au College. pap. 24.95 *(978-2-09-282599-0(2))* Nathan, Fernand FRA. Dist: Distribooks, Inc.

—A Series of Unfortunate Events #10: the Slippery Slope. Helquist, Brett & Kupperman, Michael, illus. 2003. (Series of Unfortunate Events Ser.: 10). (ENG.). 352p. (J). (gr. 5-6). 13.99 *(978-0-06-441013-7(7)*, HarperCollins) HarperCollins Pubs.

—A Series of Unfortunate Events #2: the Reptile Room. Helquist, Brett & Kupperman, Michael, illus. 2007. (Series of Unfortunate Events Ser.: 2). (ENG.). 192p. (J). (gr. 5-9). pap. 7.99 *(978-0-06-114631-2(5)*, HarperCollins) HarperCollins Pubs.

—A Series of Unfortunate Events Box: the Gloom Looms (Books 10-12), Bks. 10-12. Helquist, Brett, illus. 2005. (Series of Unfortunate Events Ser.: Bks. 10-12). (ENG.). (J). (gr. 5). 41.99 *(978-0-06-083909-3(0)*, HarperCollins) HarperCollins Pubs.

—The Slippery Slope. Helquist, Brett, illus. 2003. (Series of Unfortunate Events Ser.: Bk. 10). (YA). (gr. 5-18). 197.82 *(978-0-06-057743-8(6))*; 352p. (J). (gr. 3-6). lib. bdg. 15.89 *(978-0-06-029641-4(0))* HarperCollins Pubs.

—The Trouble Begins. Helquist, Brett, illus. movie tie-in ed. 2004. (Series of Unfortunate Events Ser.: Bks. 1-3). (J). 35.99 *(978-0-06-075773-1(6))* HarperCollins Pubs.

—The Wide Window or, Disappearance! 2007. (Series of Unfortunate Events Ser.: 3). (ENG., Illus.). 208p. (J). (gr. 5). pap. 7.99 *(978-0-06-114633-6(1)*, HarperCollins) HarperCollins Pubs.

Sniegoski, Thomas E. The Fallen 1: The Fallen & Leviathan, 1. 2010. (Fallen Ser.: 1). (ENG.). 544p. (YA). (gr. 11-12). pap. 14.99 *(978-1-4424-0862-3(6)*, Simon Pulse) Simon Pulse.

—The Fallen 2: Aerie & Reckoning. 2010. (Fallen Ser.: 2). (ENG.). 576p. (YA). (gr. 11-18). pap. 13.99 *(978-1-4424-0863-0(4)*, Simon Pulse) Simon Pulse.

—The Fallen 3 Vol. 3: End of Days. 2011. (Fallen Ser.: 3). (ENG.). 384p. (YA). (gr. 9). pap. 9.99 *(978-1-4424-2349-7(8)*, Simon Pulse) Simon Pulse.

Snyder, Laurel. Orphan Island. (ENG.). 288p. (J). (gr. 3-7). 2018. pap. 7.99 *(978-0-06-244342-7(9))* 2017. (Illus.). 16.99 *(978-0-06-244341-0(0))* HarperCollins Pubs. (Waldon Pond Pr.).

Soileau, Hodges, illus. The Black Widow Spider Mystery. 2004. (Boxcar Children Special Ser.). 130p. (gr. 2-7). 15.50 *(978-0-7569-3266-4(1))* Perfection Learning Corp.

—The Comic Book Mystery. 2003. (Boxcar Children Ser.). 106p. (gr. 4-7). 15.00 *(978-0-7569-1611-4(9))* Perfection Learning Corp.

—The Great Shark Mystery. 2003. (Boxcar Children Special Ser.). 130p. (gr. 4-7). 15.50 *(978-0-7569-1616-9(X))* Perfection Learning Corp.

—The Mystery at Skeleton Point. 2003. (Boxcar Children Ser.). 120p. (gr. 4-7). 15.00 *(978-0-7569-1609-1(7))* Perfection Learning Corp.

Sonneborn, Scott. The Frankenstein Journals, 1 vol. Banks, Timothy, illus. 2014. (Frankenstein Journals). (ENG.). 160p. (J). (gr. 2-4). 9.95 *(978-1-4342-9130-1(8)*, 125575, Stone Arch Bks.) Capstone.

—A Pain in the Butt. Banks, Timothy, illus. 2015. (Frankenstein Journals). (ENG.). 80p. (J). (gr. 2-4). 22.65 *(978-1-4965-0222-3(1)*, 128036, Stone Arch Bks.) Capstone.

Sowards, Ben, illus. Christmas Oranges. 2004. 32p. 17.95 *(978-1-59156-098-2(5))* Covenant Communications, Inc.

Spence, Eleanor. Jamberoo Road. 2007. (ENG.). 184p. (J). (gr. 7-9). pap. 12.95 *(978-1-932350-17-3(9))* Ignatius Pr.

—The Switherby Pilgrims: A Tale of the Australian Bush. 2006. (ENG.). 195p. (J). (gr. 4-11). pap. 12.95 *(978-1-883937-99-7(X))* Ignatius Pr.

Spies, Ben. Weirdo. Spies, Robert, illus. 2015. (ENG.). 54p. (J). pap. *(978-0-473-33563-2(8))* Spies Publishing.

Spinale, Wendy. Everland (the Everland Trilogy, Book 1) (Everland Trilogy Ser.: 1). (ENG.). (YA). (gr. 7-7). 2017. 336p. pap. 10.99 *(978-1-338-09553-1(6)*, Scholastic Paperbacks) 2016. 320p. 17.99 *(978-0-545-83694-4(8)*, Scholastic Pr.) Scholastic, Inc.

Sposito, Pipi, illus. Charles Dickens: Great Expectations. 2021. (Sweet Cherry Easy Classics Ser.: 2). (ENG.). 96p. (J). 6.95 *(978-1-78226-744-7(1)*, aae9966f-3007-42ff-b8c1-f8dedf20addc) Sweet Cherry Publishing GBR. Dist: Baker & Taylor Publisher Services (BTPS).

Spotswood, Jessica. The Last Summer of the Garrett Girls. 2018. 368p. (YA). (gr. 8-12). pap. 10.99 *(978-1-4926-2219-2(2))* Sourcebooks, Inc.

Springer, Audrey. Rusty's Gift. Richards, Kris, illus. 2012. 28p. 24.95 *(978-1-4626-6589-1(6))* America Star Bks.

Spyri, Johanna. Heidi. 2014. (ENG.). 345p. 17.50 *(978-1-78270-044-9(7))* Award Pubns. Ltd. GBR. Dist: Parkwest Pubns., Inc.

—Heidi. 2008. (Bring the Classics to Life Ser.). (Illus.). 72p. (gr. 1-12). pap., act. bk. ed. 10.95 *(978-1-55576-178-3(X)*, EDCTR-107B) EDCON Publishing Group.

—Heidi. 2003. pap. *(978-1-84637-585-9(1))* Echo Library.

—Heidi. Kirk, Maria L., illus. 2015. (First Avenue Classics (tm) Ser.). (ENG.). 192p. (YA). (gr. 3-8). E-Book 19.99 *(978-1-4677-5846-8(9)*, First Avenue Editions) Lerner Publishing Group.

—Heidi. 2013. (ENG., Illus.). 336p. (J). (gr. 2-7). 14.95 *(978-1-62087-686-2(8)*, 620686, Sky Pony Pr.) Skyhorse Publishing Co., Inc.

—Heidi: With a Discussion of Optimism. Clift, Eva, illus. 2003. (Values in Action Illustrated Classics Ser.). 190p. (J). *(978-1-59203-030-9(0))* Learning Challenge, Inc.

Spyri, Johanna & Blaisdell, Robert. Heidi: Adapted for Young Readers. Kliros, Thea, illus. 2011. (Dover Children's Thrift Classics Ser.). (ENG.). 80p. (J). (gr. 3-8). pap. 4.00 *(978-0-486-40166-9(9)*, 401669) Dover Pubns., Inc.

Spyri, Johanna & Lacey, Mike. Heidi, 1 vol. 2011. (Calico Illustrated Classics Ser.: No. 4). (ENG., Illus.). 112p. (J). (gr. 2-5). 38.50 *(978-1-61641-613-3(0)*, 4041, Calico Chapter Bks.) ABDO Publishing Co.

St. Crow, Lili. Betrayals, 10 vols. 2010. (Strange Angels Ser.: 2). (YA). 95.75 *(978-1-4407-7156-9(1))* Recorded Bks., Inc.

—Betrayals. 2009. (Strange Angels Ser.: 2). lib. bdg. 20.85 *(978-0-606-09020-9(7))* Turtleback.

—Betrayals: A Strange Angels Novel, 2. 2009. (Strange Angels Ser.: 2). (ENG., Illus.). 304p. (YA). (gr. 7-18). pap. 26.19 *(978-1-59514-252-8(5)*, Razorbill) Penguin Young Readers Group.

—Defiance, 4. 2011. (Strange Angels Ser.: 4). (ENG.). 304p. (YA). (gr. 7-18). 26.19 *(978-1-59514-392-1(0)*, Razorbill) Penguin Young Readers Group.

—Jealousy, 10 vols. 2010. (Strange Angels Ser.: 3). (J). 86.75 *(978-1-4498-2774-8(8))*; 68.75 *(978-1-4498-2773-1(X))*; 83.75 *(978-1-4498-2776-2(4))*; 1.25 *(978-1-4498-2777-9(2))*; 209.75 *(978-1-4498-2772-4(1))* Recorded Bks., Inc.

—Jealousy. 2010. (Strange Angels Ser.: 3). lib. bdg. 20.85 *(978-0-606-14566-4(4))* Turtleback.

—Jealousy: A Strange Angels Novel. 2010. (Strange Angels Ser.: 3). (ENG.). 320p. (YA). (gr. 7-18). 9.99 *(978-1-59514-290-0(8)*, Razorbill) Penguin Young Readers Group.

—Strange Angels, 9 vols. 2009. (Strange Angels Ser.: 1). (J). 181.75 *(978-1-4407-6194-2(9))*; 117.75 *(978-1-4407-6197-3(3))*; 84.75 *(978-1-4407-6195-9(7))*; 114.75 *(978-1-4407-6199-7(X))*; 87.75 *(978-1-4407-6193-5(0))* Recorded Bks., Inc.

—Strange Angels. 2009. (Strange Angels Ser.: 1). lib. bdg. 20.85 *(978-0-606-08957-9(8))* Turtleback.

St. Jean, Alan. Aidan of Oren: The Journey Begins. Friedman, Judith, illus. 2004. (ENG.). 208p. (J). (gr. 4-7). 19.95 *(978-0-9724853-5-7(X))* Keene Publishing.

St. John, Lauren. Dolphin Song. 2008. (Legend of the Animal Healer Ser.). (ENG.). 246p. (J). (gr. 4-6). 21.19 *(978-0-8037-3214-8(7))* Penguin Young Readers Group.

—The Elephant's Tale. 2011. (Legend of the Animal Healer Ser.). (ENG.). (J). 208p. (gr. 4-6). 21.19 *(978-0-8037-3291-9(0))*; 240p. (gr. 3-7). 6.99 *(978-0-14-241879-6(X)*, Puffin Books) Penguin Young Readers Group.

—The White Giraffe. 2008. (ENG., Illus.). 208p. (J). (gr. 2-5). 8.99 *(978-0-14-241152-0(3)*, Puffin Books) Penguin Young Readers Group.

Stanley, Diane. Raising Sweetness, 4 bks. Karas, G. Brian, illus. 2004. (J). pap. 39.95 incl. audio compact disk *(978-1-59112-524-2(3))* Live Oak Media.

—Raising Sweetness. 2003. (Illus.). (J). 25.95 incl. audio *(978-1-59112-266-1(X))*; 28.95 incl. audio compact disk *(978-1-59112-516-7(2))* Live Oak Media.

—Raising Sweetness, 4 bks. Stanley, Diane, illus. 2003. (Illus.). (J). pap. 37.95 incl. audio *(978-1-59112-267-8(8))* Live Oak Media.

—Sweetness Series. Karas, G. Brian, illus. 2003. pap. 34.95 incl. audio compact disk *(978-1-59112-860-1(9))*; pap. 30.95 incl. audio *(978-1-59112-847-2(1))* Live Oak Media.

Stark-Mcginnis, Sandy. Extraordinary Birds. (ENG.). (J). 2020. 240p. pap. 8.99 *(978-1-5476-0143-1(4)*, 900199962) 2019. 224p. 16.99 *(978-1-5476-0100-4(0)*, 900198461) Bloomsbury Publishing USA. (Bloomsbury Children's Bks.).

Stentiford, Tyler Michael. A Darker Secret. 2009. (ENG.). 128p. (YA). pap. 9.99 *(978-1-60138-315-0(0))* Atlantic Publishing Group, Inc.

Stevenson, James. Runaway Horse! Date not set. (J). 15.99 *(978-0-06-051978-0(9))*; 16.89 *(978-0-06-051979-7(7))* HarperCollins Pubs.

Stewart, Paul. Far-Flung Adventures: Hugo Pepper. 2012. (Far-Flung Adventures Ser.). (ENG.). 272p. (J). (gr. 3-7). 7.99 *(978-0-385-75223-7(7)*, Yearling) Random Hse. Children's Bks.

Stewart, Trenton Lee. The Extraordinary Education of Nicholas Benedict. Sudyka, Diana, illus. 2013. (Mysterious Benedict Society Ser.). (ENG.). 496p. (J). (gr. 3-7). pap. 9.99 *(978-0-316-17620-0(6))* Little, Brown Bks. for Young Readers.

—The Extraordinary Education of Nicholas Benedict. 2013. (Mysterious Benedict Society Ser.: 0). (J). lib. bdg. 19.65 *(978-0-606-31743-6(0))* Turtleback.

—The Mysterious Benedict Society. Ellis, Carson, illus. (Mysterious Benedict Society Ser.: 1). (ENG.). (J). (gr. 3-7). 2008. 512p. pap. 9.99 *(978-0-316-00395-7(6))* 2007. 496p. 19.99 *(978-0-316-05777-6(0))* Little, Brown Bks. for Young Readers.

—The Mysterious Benedict Society. 2021. (Mysterious Benedict Society Ser.). (ENG., Illus.). 496p. (J). (gr. 3-7). pap. 9.99 *(978-0-316-29760-8(7))* Little, Brown Bks. for Young Readers.

—The Mysterious Benedict Society. 2009. 17.45 *(978-1-60686-527-9(7))* Perfection Learning Corp.

—The Mysterious Benedict Society. 2010. (Mysterious Benedict Society Ser.: 3). (J). lib. bdg. 19.65 *(978-0-606-15117-7(6))* Turtleback.

—The Mysterious Benedict Society. Ellis, Carson, illus. 2008. (Mysterious Benedict Society Ser.: 1). 485p. (J). (gr. 3-7). lib. bdg. 19.65 *(978-1-4178-1817-4(4))* Turtleback.

—The Mysterious Benedict Society & the Prisoner's Dilemma. Sudyka, Diana, illus. (Mysterious Benedict Society Ser.: 3). (ENG.). 400p. (J). (gr. 3-7). 2010. pap. 9.99 *(978-0-316-04550-6(0))* 2009. 36.99 *(978-0-316-04552-0(7))* Little, Brown Bks. for Young Readers.

Stiefvater, Maggie. The Scorpio Races. (ENG.). (YA). (gr. 8-12). 2013. 448p. pap. 12.99 *(978-0-545-22491-8(8)*, Scholastic Paperbacks) 2011. 416p. 19.99 *(978-0-545-22490-1(X)*, Scholastic Pr.) Scholastic, Inc.

—The Scorpio Races. 2013. lib. bdg. 22.10 *(978-0-606-31501-2(2))* Turtleback.

—The Scorpio Races (Unabridged Edition), 1 vol. unabr. ed. 2011. (ENG.). 5p. (J). audio compact disk 79.99 *(978-0-545-35705-0(5))* Scholastic, Inc.

Stone, Marie. On Their Own: A Journey to Jamestown. 2006. (Illus.). 166p. (J). (gr. 3-7). per. 8.95 *(978-1-57249-385-8(2)*, White Mane Kids) White Mane Publishing Co., Inc.

Stork, Francisco X. The Last Summer of the Death Warriors. 2012. (ENG.). 352p. (J). (gr. 9-12). 26.19 *(978-0-545-15134-4(1)*, Levine, Arthur A. Bks.) Scholastic, Inc.

Stratton, Allan. Chanda's Wars. 2011. 10.36 *(978-0-7848-3486-2(5)*, Everbind) Marco Bk. Co.

Stratton-Porter, Gene. Freckles. (J). reprint ed. lib. bdg. 24.95 *(978-0-89190-949-1(4)*, Rivercity Pr.) Amereon Ltd.

—Freckles. 2017. (ENG., Illus.). (J). pap. 11.99 *(978-1-366-50926-0(9))* Blurb, Inc.

—Freckles. 2017. (ENG., Illus.). (J). (gr. 3-7). 24.95 *(978-1-374-90678-5(6))*; pap. 14.95 *(978-1-374-90677-8(8))* Capital Communications, Inc.

—Freckles. (ENG., 2017. Illus.). (J). (gr. 3-7). pap. 17.95 *(978-1-375-50440-9(1))* 2015. (Illus.). (J). 27.95 *(978-1-297-91217-7(9))* 2015. (Illus.). (J). 27.95 *(978-1-297-66159-4(1))* 2007. 248p. pap. 22.99 *(978-1-4264-5654-1(9))* Creative Media Partners, LLC.

—Freckles. 2006. 236p. (YA). 19.95 *(978-1-934169-32-2(3))*; pap. 8.95 *(978-1-934169-33-9(1))* Norilana Bks.

—Freckles. 2008. (ENG., Illus.). 264p. (J). (gr. 3-7). 18.99 *(978-1-4341-1607-9(7)*, Boomer Bks.) The Editorium, LLC.

Strutt, Lesley. On the Edge. 2019. (ENG.). 252p. pap. 19.95 *(978-1-77133-597-3(1))* Inanna Pubns. & Education, Inc. CAN. Dist: SPD-Small Pr. Distribution.

Surget, Alain. Escape from Veracruz. 2015. (Jolly Roger Ser.). (Illus.). 96p. (gr. 3-6). 28.50 *(978-1-909645-44-8(3))* Book Hse. GBR. Dist: Black Rabbit Bks.

—The Ghost Ship. 2015. (Jolly Roger Ser.). (Illus.). 96p. (gr. 3-6). 28.50 *(978-1-909645-41-7(9))* Book Hse. GBR. Dist: Black Rabbit Bks.

—The Plumed Serpent's Gold. 2015. (Jolly Roger Ser.). (Illus.). 96p. (gr. 3-6). 28.50 *(978-1-909645-43-1(5))* Book Hse. GBR. Dist: Black Rabbit Bks.

—Shark Island. 2015. (Jolly Roger Ser.). (Illus.). 96p. (gr. 3-6). 28.50 *(978-1-909645-42-4(7))* Book Hse. GBR. Dist: Black Rabbit Bks.

Swan, Bill. Corner Kick, 1 vol. 2004. (Lorimer Sports Stories Ser.: 66). (ENG.). 144p. (J). (gr. 4-8). 16.95 *(978-1-55028-817-9(2)*, 817) James Lorimer & Co. Ltd., Pubs. CAN. Dist: Formac Lorimer Bks. Ltd.

Taylor, Laini. Strange the Dreamer. LitJoy Crate et al, illus. 2021. (YA). 59.99 *(978-1-7350633-7-9(1))* LitJoy Crate.

—Strange the Dreamer. 2017. 536p. (YA). *(978-0-316-43120-0(6))* Little Brown & Co.

—Strange the Dreamer. (Strange the Dreamer Ser.: 1). (ENG.). (YA). (gr. 9-17). 2018. 560p. pap. 14.99 *(978-0-316-34167-7(3))* 2017. 544p. 22.99 *(978-0-316-34168-4(1))* Little, Brown Bks. for Young Readers.

—Strange the Dreamer. 2018. (J). lib. bdg. 24.50 *(978-0-606-40987-2(4))* Turtleback.

Taylor, Richard A. Ships of Children. 2nd rev. ed. 2006. (Illus.). 191p. (YA). lib. bdg. 37.95 *(978-0-9764403-7-6(7))* Klare Taylor Pubs.

Taylor, Shirley A. The Stable Boy. Hall, Wendell E., illus. 2012. (ENG.). 40p. (J). (gr. 2-17). 17.95 *(978-1-935166-79-5(4))* Parkhurst Brothers, Inc., Pubs.

Teele, Elinor. The Mechanical Mind of John Coggin. 2016. (ENG., Illus.). 352p. (J). (gr. 3-7). 16.99 *(978-0-06-234510-3(9)*, Waldon Pond Pr.) HarperCollins Pubs.

Tewee, Laqaixit. Winterbloom & the Magical Swan: Book 1 Discovery of the Moon Treasure. 2012. 68p. pap. 31.99 *(978-1-4653-9933-5(X))* Xlibris Corp.

Thompson, Michelle. Taming the Wind. 2010. 176p. pap. 12.99 *(978-1-59955-379-5(1))* Cedar Fort, Inc./CFI Distribution.

Thoms, Gigi. Noble Pocket. 2016. (YA). pap. 18.99 *(978-1-4621-1773-4(2)*, Horizon Pubs.) Cedar Fort, Inc./CFI Distribution.

Tiernan, Cate. Darkest Fear. 2014. (Birthright Ser.: 1). (ENG., Illus.). 368p. (YA). (gr. 9). pap. 9.99 *(978-1-4424-8245-6(1)*, Simon Pulse) Simon Pulse.

Tollefson, Carol & Shelton, Kim. McTavich That Rascal Squirrel. 2015. (ENG., Illus.). 20p. pap. 12.00 *(978-1-62288-101-7(X)*, P476290) Austin, Stephen F. State Univ. Pr.

Townsend, Daniel. Trumpet. 2008. 24p. pap. 24.95 *(978-1-4241-9387-5(7))* America Star Bks.

Trevayne, Emma. Spindrift & the Orchid. (ENG.). 256p. (J). (gr. 3-7). 2019. pap. 8.99 *(978-1-4814-6260-0(1))* 2018. (Illus.). 17.99 *(978-1-4814-6259-4(8))* Simon & Schuster Bks. For Young Readers. (Simon & Schuster Bks. For Young Readers).

Tsutsumi, Robert Kondo and Dice. The Dam Keeper. 2017. (Dam Keeper Ser.: 1). (ENG., Illus.). 160p. (J). 25.99 *(978-1-62672-426-6(1)*, 900156878, First Second Bks.) Roaring Brook Pr.

Tucker, David J. The Fourth Gift. 2010. 96p. 12.99 *(978-1-59955-438-9(0))* Cedar Fort, Inc./CFI Distribution.

Tyre, Lisa Lewis. Hope in the Holler. 2019. 240p. (J). (gr. 5). 8.99 *(978-0-399-54632-7(4)*, Puffin Books) Penguin Young Readers Group.

—Hope in the Holler. 2020. (Penworthy Picks YA Fiction Ser.). (ENG.). 212p. (J). (gr. 4-5). 20.96 *(978-1-64697-195-4(7))* Penworthy Co., LLC, The.

Ure, Jean. Daisy May. Donnelly, Karen, illus. 2011. (ENG.). 96p. pap. 5.99 *(978-0-00-713369-7(3)*, HarperCollins Children's Bks.) HarperCollins Pubs. Ltd. GBR. Dist: HarperCollins Pubs.

van Arsdale, Peternelle. The Beast Is an Animal. (ENG.). 352p. (YA). (gr. 9). 2018. pap. 11.99 *(978-1-4814-8842-6(2))* 2017. (Illus.). 17.99 *(978-1-4814-8841-9(4))* McElderry, Margaret K. Bks. (McElderry, Margaret K. Bks.).

Van Draanen, Wendelin. Runaway. 2012. (ENG.). 272p. (YA). (gr. 5). pap. 9.99 *(978-0-307-97597-3(5)*, Ember) Random Hse. Children's Bks.

Van Hamme, Jean. The Heir, Vol. 1. Francq, Philippe, illus. 2008. (Largo Winch Ser.: 1). 96p. pap. 19.95 *(978-1-905460-48-9(1))* CineBook GBR. Dist: National Bk. Network.

VanArsdale, Anthony, illus. The Mystery at the Calgary Stampede. 2015. 104p. (J). *(978-1-4806-9406-4(1))* Whitman, Albert & Co.

—The Shackleton Sabotage. 2017. (Boxcar Children Great Adventure Ser.: 4). (ENG.). 160p. (J). (gr. 2-5). 12.99 *(978-0-8075-0687-5(7)*, 807506877, Random Hse. Bks. for Young Readers) Random Hse. Children's Bks.

—The Sleepy Hollow Mystery. 2015. 111p. (J). *(978-1-4806-9407-1(X))* Whitman, Albert & Co.

Vander Zee, Ruth. Always with You. Himler, Ron, illus. 2008. (ENG.). 32p. (J). (gr. -1-3). 17.00 *(978-0-8028-5295-3(5)*, Eerdmans Bks For Young Readers) Eerdmans, William B. Publishing Co.

Ventrella, Kim. Bone Hollow, 1 vol. 2019. (ENG.). 240p. (J). (gr. 3-7). 17.99 *(978-1-338-04274-0(2)*, Scholastic Pr.) Scholastic, Inc.

Verrico, Susan. Privateer's Apprentice. 2018. 192p. (J). (gr. 3-7). pap. 7.95 *(978-1-68263-040-2(4))* Peachtree Publishing Co. Inc.

Verrone, Patric C. W. Sharktooth. 2009. 229p. pap. 14.76 *(978-0-557-09535-3(2))* Lulu Pr., Inc.

Vincent, Victoria. The City of Kind Words: A Story by Tory. l.t. ed. 2006. (Illus.). 56p. (J). per. 19.95 *(978-0-9788950-0-6(2))* All Over Creation.

Voisin, Mandy Madson. Star of Deliverance. 2014. pap. 17.99 *(978-1-4621-1454-2(7))* Cedar Fort, Inc./CFI Distribution.

Wait, Lea. Stopping to Home. 2003. (ENG.). 160p. (J). (gr. 3-7). pap. 8.99 *(978-0-689-83849-1(2)*, Simon & Schuster/Paula Wiseman Bks.) Simon & Schuster/Paula Wiseman Bks.

Walker, Keegan Holmes. Sebastianus: The War Begins. 2010. 304p. pap. 18.95 *(978-1-4502-5580-6(9))* iUniverse, Inc.

Wallace, Barbara Brooks. The Perils of Peppermints. 2005. (ENG., Illus.). 272p. (J). (gr. 3-7). pap. 12.99 *(978-0-689-85045-5(X)*, Simon & Schuster/Paula Wiseman Bks.) Simon & Schuster/Paula Wiseman Bks.

Walsh, Pat. The Crowfield Demon. 2013. 360p. (J). *(978-0-545-37350-0(6))* Scholastic, Inc.

Walter, Jon. Close to the Wind. 2017. (ENG.). 320p. (J). (gr. 5-7). pap. 8.99 *(978-0-545-82275-6(0))* Scholastic, Inc.

Walters, Eric. Diamonds in the Rough, 1 vol. 2014. (ENG.). 236p. (YA). (gr. 7-11). pap. 12.95 *(978-1-55455-308-2(3)*, 5d6e5cd8-91bd-4323-9bff-e86b1675c2b9) Trifolium Bks., Inc. CAN. Dist: Firefly Bks., Ltd.

Warner, Gertrude Chandler. Blue Bay Mystery, 1 vol. Dubisch, Michael, illus. 2009. (Boxcar Children Graphic Novels Ser.). (ENG.). 32p. (J). (gr. 3-8). 32.79 *(978-1-60270-591-3(7)*, 3674, Graphic Planet - Fiction) Magic Wagon.

—The Box-Car Children. Gregory, Dorothy Lake, illus. 2020. (ENG.). 64p. (J). (gr. 2-5). pap. 6.99 *(978-1-4209-6966-5(8))* Digireads.com Publishing.

—The Box-Car Children. 2019. (ENG.). 70p. (J). (gr. 2-5). pap. 5.99 *(978-1-6777-0963-2(4))* Independently Published.

—The Box-Car Children. Gregory, Dorothy Lake, illus. 2019. (ENG.). 88p. (J). (gr. 1-5). 14.99 *(978-1-5154-4203-5(9))*; pap. 6.49 *(978-1-5154-4204-2(7))* Jorge Pinto Bks. (Illustrated Bks.).

—The Box-Car Children: The Original 1924 Edition. 2020. (ENG.). 160p. (J). (gr. 2-5). 14.99 *(978-0-486-83851-9(X)*, 83851X) Dover Pubns., Inc.

—The Boxcar Children. Date not set. (Boxcar Children Ser.: No. 1). (J). (gr. 2-5). lib. bdg. 18.95 *(978-0-8488-1712-1(5))* Amereon Ltd.

—The Boxcar Children. (Boxcar Children Ser.: No. 1). 154p. (J). (gr. 2-5). pap. 3.95 *(978-0-8072-1447-3(7)*, Listening Library) Random Hse. Audio Publishing Group.

—The Boxcar Children. Deal, L. Kate, illus. 2020. (Boxcar Children Ser.). (ENG.). 160p. (J). (gr. 2-6). lib. bdg. 31.36 *(978-1-5321-4473-8(3)*, 35163, Chapter Bks.) Spotlight.

—The Boxcar Children Fully Illustrated Edition. Gilbert, Anne Yvonne & Powers, Gretchen Ellen, illus. 2017. (Boxcar Children Mysteries Ser.). (ENG.). 168p. (J). (gr. 2-5). 34.99 *(978-0-8075-0925-8(6)*, 807509256, Random Hse. Bks. for Young Readers) Random Hse. Children's Bks.

—The Haunted Cabin Mystery, 1 vol. Bloodworth, Mark, illus. 2010. (Boxcar Children Graphic Novels Ser.). (ENG.). 32p. (J). (gr. 3-8). 32.79 *(978-1-60270-717-7(0)*, 3678, Graphic Planet - Fiction) Magic Wagon.

—The Lighthouse Mystery. (Boxcar Children Ser.: No. 8). 147p. (J). (gr. 2-5). pap. 3.95 *(978-0-8072-1474-9(4)*, Listening Library) Random Hse. Audio Publishing Group.

—Mike's Mystery. (Boxcar Children Ser.: No. 5). 128p. (J). (gr. 2-5). pap. 3.95 *(978-0-8072-1462-6(0)*, Listening Library) Random Hse. Audio Publishing Group.

—Mike's Mystery, 1 vol. Dubisch, Michael, illus. 2009. (Boxcar Children Graphic Novels Ser.). (ENG.). 32p. (J). (gr. 3-8). 32.79 *(978-1-60270-590-6(9)*, 3673, Graphic Planet - Fiction) Magic Wagon.

—The Mystery of the Runaway Ghost. Soileau, Hodges, illus. 2004. (Boxcar Children Ser.). 135p. (J). 12.65 *(978-0-7569-3264-0(5))* Perfection Learning Corp.

—Mystery Ranch. (Boxcar Children Ser.: No. 4). 128p. (J). (gr. 2-5). pap. 3.95 *(978-0-8072-1450-3(7)*, Listening Library) Random Hse. Audio Publishing Group.

—Mystery Ranch, 1 vol. Dubisch, Michael, illus. 2009. (Boxcar Children Graphic Novels Ser.). (ENG.). 32p. (J). (gr. 3-8). 32.79 *(978-1-60270-589-0(5)*, 3672, Graphic Planet - Fiction) Magic Wagon.

—Snowbound Mystery, 1 vol. Dubisch, Mike, illus. 2010. (Boxcar Children Graphic Novels Ser.). (ENG.). 32p. (J). (gr. 3-8). 32.79 *(978-1-60270-715-3(4)*, 3676, Graphic Planet - Fiction) Magic Wagon.

—The Yellow House Mystery. (Boxcar Children Ser.: No. 3). 191p. (J). (gr. 2-5). pap. 3.95 *(978-0-8072-1449-7(3)*, Listening Library) Random Hse. Audio Publishing Group.

—The Yellow House Mystery, 1 vol. Dubisch, Michael, illus. 2009. (Boxcar Children Graphic Novels Ser.). (ENG.). 32p. (J). (gr. 3-8). 32.79 *(978-1-60270-588-3(7)*, 3671, Graphic Planet - Fiction) Magic Wagon.

—The Yellow House Mystery, No. 3. Dubisch, Mike, illus. 2009. (Boxcar Children Graphic Novels Ser.). (ENG.). 32p. (J). (gr. 2-5). 6.99 *(978-0-8075-2869-3(2))* Whitman, Albert & Co.

Warner, Gertrude Chandler, creator. The Boxcar Children Guide to Adventure: A How-To for Mystery Solving, Make-It-Yourself Projects, & More. 2014. (Boxcar Children Mysteries Ser.). (ENG., Illus.). 144p. (J). (gr. 2-5). 12.99 *(978-0-8075-0905-0(1)*, 807509051, Random Hse. Bks. for Young Readers) Random Hse. Children's Bks.

—The Creature in Ogopogo Lake. 2006. (Boxcar Children Mysteries Ser.: 108). (ENG., Illus.). 128p. (J). (gr. 2-5). lib. bdg. 14.99 *(978-0-8075-1336-1(9)*, 807513369); per. 6.99 *(978-0-8075-1337-8(7)*, 807513377) Random Hse. Children's Bks. (Random Hse. Bks. for Young Readers).

—The Creepy Clues Special. 2017. (Boxcar Children Mysteries Ser.). (ENG., Illus.). 336p. (J). (gr. 2-5). pap. 9.99 *(978-0-8075-2848-8(X)*, 080752848X, Random Hse. Bks. for Young Readers) Random Hse. Children's Bks.

—The Ghost at the Drive-In Movie. 2008. (Boxcar Children Mysteries Ser.: 116). (ENG., Illus.). 128p. (J). (gr. 2-5). 14.99 *(978-0-8075-5577-4(0)*, 807555770, Random Hse. Bks. for Young Readers) Random Hse. Children's Bks.

—The Ghost-Hunting Special. 2015. (Boxcar Children Mysteries Ser.). (ENG., Illus.). 352p. (J). (gr. 2-5). 9.99 *(978-0-8075-2846-4(3)*, 807528463, Random Hse. Bks. for Young Readers) Random Hse. Children's Bks.

—The Ghost of the Chattering Bones. 2005. (Boxcar Children Mysteries Ser.: 102). (ENG., Illus.). 128p. (J). (gr. 2-5). pap. 6.99 *(978-0-8075-0874-9(8)*, 807508748, Random Hse. Bks. for Young Readers) Random Hse. Children's Bks.

—The Giant Yo-Yo Mystery. 2006. (Boxcar Children Mysteries Ser.: 107). (ENG., Illus.). 144p. (J). (gr. 2-5). per. 5.99 *(978-0-8075-0879-4(9)*, 807508799, Random Hse. Bks. for Young Readers) Random Hse. Children's Bks.

—The Great Detective Race. 2008. (Boxcar Children Mysteries Ser.: 115). (ENG., Illus.). 128p. (J). (gr. 2-5). 14.99 *(978-0-8075-5573-6(8)*, 807555738); pap. 5.99 *(978-0-8075-5574-3(6)*, 807555746) Random Hse. Children's Bks. (Random Hse. Bks. for Young Readers).

—The Haunted Legends Special. 2016. (Boxcar Children Mysteries Ser.). (ENG., Illus.). 368p. (J). (gr. 2-5). 9.99 *(978-0-8075-0724-7(5)*, 807507245, Random Hse. Bks. for Young Readers) Random Hse. Children's Bks.

—The Legend of the Irish Castle. 2016. (Boxcar Children Mysteries Ser.: 142). (ENG., Illus.). 128p. (J). (gr. 2-5). 15.99 *(978-0-8075-0705-6(9)*, 807507059, Random Hse. Bks. for Young Readers) Random Hse. Children's Bks.

—The Mystery at the Calgary Stampede. 2015. (Boxcar Children Mysteries Ser.: 140). (ENG., Illus.). 128p. (J). (gr. 2-5). 15.99 *(978-0-8075-2840-2(4)*, 807528404, Random Hse. Bks. for Young Readers) Random Hse. Children's Bks.

—The Mystery of the Grinning Gargoyle. 2014. (Boxcar Children Mysteries Ser.: 137). (ENG., Illus.). 128p. (J). (gr. 2-5). pap. 5.99 *(978-0-8075-0893-0(4)*, 807508934, Random Hse. Bks. for Young Readers) Random Hse. Children's Bks.

—The Mystery of the Missing Pop Idol. 2015. (Boxcar Children Mysteries Ser.: 138). (ENG., Illus.). 128p. (J). (gr. 2-5). 15.99 *(978-0-8075-5605-4(X)*, 080755605X, Random Hse. Bks. for Young Readers) Random Hse. Children's Bks.

—The Mystery of the Soccer Snitch. 2014. (Boxcar Children Mysteries Ser.: 136). (ENG., Illus.). 128p. (J). (gr. 2-5). pap. 6.99 *(978-0-8075-0896-1(9)*, 807508969, Random Hse. Bks. for Young Readers) Random Hse. Children's Bks.

—The Mystery of the Stolen Dinosaur Bones. 2015. (Boxcar Children Mysteries Ser.: 139). (ENG., Illus.). 128p. (J). (gr. 2-5). 15.99 *(978-0-8075-5608-5(4)*, 807556084, Random Hse. Bks. for Young Readers) Random Hse. Children's Bks.

—The Rock 'n' Roll Mystery. 2006. (Boxcar Children Mysteries Ser.: 109). (ENG., Illus.). 128p. (J). (gr. 2-5). lib. bdg. 14.99 *(978-0-8075-7089-0(3)*, 807570893); per. 5.99 *(978-0-8075-7090-6(7)*, 807570907) Random Hse. Children's Bks. (Random Hse. Bks. for Young Readers).

—The Seattle Puzzle. 2007. (Boxcar Children Mysteries Ser.: 111). (ENG., Illus.). (J). (gr. 2-5). 128p. lib. bdg. 14.99 *(978-0-8075-5560-6(6)*, 807555606); 112p. per. 5.99 *(978-0-8075-5561-3(4)*, 807555614) Random Hse. Children's Bks. (Random Hse. Bks. for Young Readers).

—The Sleepy Hollow Mystery. 2015. (Boxcar Children Mysteries Ser.: 141). (ENG., Illus.). 128p. (J). (gr. 2-5). 15.99 *(978-0-8075-2843-3(9)*, 807528439, Random Hse. Bks. for Young Readers) Random Hse. Children's Bks.

—The Sword of the Silver Knight. 2005. (Boxcar Children Mysteries Ser.: 103). (ENG., Illus.). 128p. (J). (gr. 2-5). per. 6.99 *(978-0-8075-0876-3(4)*, 807508764, Random Hse. Bks. for Young Readers) Random Hse. Children's Bks.

—The Vanishing Passenger. 2006. (Boxcar Children Mysteries Ser.: 106). (ENG., Illus.). 112p. (J). (gr. 2-5). per. 7.99 *(978-0-8075-1067-4(X)*, 080751067X, Random Hse. Bks. for Young Readers) Random Hse. Children's Bks.

Wass, Eliza. The Life & Death Parade. 2019. (ENG.). 256p. (YA). (gr. 9-17). pap. 9.99 *(978-1-4847-8752-6(8))* Hyperion Bks. for Children.

Watson, Jude. Loot. 2015. (ENG.). 272p. (J). (gr. 3-7). pap. 8.99 *(978-0-545-46803-9(5)*, Scholastic Paperbacks) Scholastic, Inc.

Watson, Renee. What Momma Left Me. 2019. (ENG.). 240p. (YA). 17.99 *(978-1-5476-0173-8(6)*, 900201596); pap. 10.99 *(978-1-68119-949-8(1)*, 900194102) Bloomsbury Publishing USA. (Bloomsbury Young Adult).

Watts, Irene N. When the Bough Breaks. 2007. 152p. (YA). (gr. 7-7). pap. 9.95 *(978-0-88776-821-7(0)*, Tundra Bks.) Tundra Bks. CAN. Dist: Penguin Random Hse. LLC.

Webb, Holly. Return to the Secret Garden. (ENG.). (J). (gr. 3-7). 2019. 240p. pap. 11.99 *(978-1-4926-8424-4(4))* 2016. 224p. 16.99 *(978-1-4926-3909-1(5)*, 9781492639091) Sourcebooks, Inc.

—Rose. 2013. (Rose Ser.: 1). (ENG.). 240p. (J). (gr. 3-6). pap. 12.99 *(978-1-4022-8581-3(7)*, 9781402285813) Sourcebooks, Inc.

—Rose & the Lost Princess. 2014. (Rose Ser.: 2). (ENG.). 256p. (J). (gr. 3-6). pap. 10.99 *(978-1-4022-8584-4(1))* Sourcebooks, Inc.

—Rose & the Magician's Mask. 2014. (Rose Ser.: 3). (ENG.). 224p. (J). (gr. 3-6). pap. 10.99 *(978-1-4926-0430-3(5)*, 9781492604303) Sourcebooks, Inc.

Weber, John. Orphan. 2010. 266p. (YA). (gr. 7-18). 16.95 *(978-1-934813-38-6(9))* Westside Bks.

Webster, Jean. Daddy-Long-Legs. (J). 19.95 *(978-0-8488-0323-0(X))* Amereon Ltd.

—Daddy-Long-Legs. Webster, Jean, illus. 2018. (Alma Junior Classics Ser.). (ENG., Illus.). 224p. pap. 9.95 *(978-1-84749-651-5(2)*, 900200349, Alma Classics) Bloomsbury Publishing USA.

—Daddy-Long-Legs. 2016. (ENG., Illus.). (J). 26.95 *(978-1-358-17233-5(1))* Creative Media Partners, LLC.

—Daddy-Long-Legs. 2004. reprint ed. pap. 19.95 *(978-1-4191-1490-8(5))*; pap. 1.99 *(978-1-4192-1490-5(X))* Kessinger Publishing, LLC.

—Daddy-Long-Legs. 2016. (ENG., Illus.). (J). pap. 4.50 *(978-1-68422-026-7(2))* Martino Fine Bks.

—Daddy-Long-Legs. 2011. (Puffin Classics Ser.). (Illus.). 198p. (J). (gr. 5-7). pap. 7.99 *(978-0-14-133111-9(9)*, Puffin Books) Penguin Young Readers Group.

—Dear Enemy. (J). 21.95 *(978-0-8488-0324-7(8))* Amereon Ltd.

—Dear Enemy. 2013. (Best Sellers of 1916 Ser.). 425p. reprint ed. lthr. 69.00 *(978-0-7426-1275-4(9))* Classic Bks.

—Dear Enemy. 2004. reprint ed. pap. 31.95 *(978-1-4179-1744-0(X))* Kessinger Publishing, LLC.

Wedekind, Annie. Mercury's Flight: The Story of a Lipizzaner Stallion. 2011. (Breyer Horse Collection: 4). (ENG.). 128p. (J). (gr. 4-7). pap. 10.99 *(978-0-312-64451-2(5)*, 900068505) Feiwel & Friends.

Weekes, Patrick. Feeder. 2018. (ENG., Illus.). 304p. (YA). (gr. 9). 17.99 *(978-1-5344-0016-0(8)*, McElderry, Margaret K. Bks.) McElderry, Margaret K. Bks.

Welsh, Charles. Goody Two Shoes. 2005. reprint ed. pap. 22.95 *(978-1-4179-6775-9(7))* Kessinger Publishing, LLC.

West, Madeleine. Lily d V. A. P: Orphan Annie, Volume 1. 2020. (Lily d, V. A. P Ser.: 1). (ENG.). 112p. (J). (gr. k-2). pap. 9.99 *(978-1-76068-300-9(0))* Little Hare Bks. AUS. Dist: Independent Pubs. Group.

Westerfeld, Scott. Spill Zone Book 2: The Broken Vow. Puvilland, Alex, illus. 2019. (Spill Zone Ser.: 2). (ENG.). 240p. (YA). pap. 17.99 *(978-1-250-30942-6(5)*, 900198487, First Second Bks.) Roaring Brook Pr.

Westley, William. Charlie & Crow. 2011. 66p. 24.99 *(978-1-4628-6802-5(9))*; pap. 15.99 *(978-1-4628-6801-8(0))* Xlibris Corp.

Wexler, Django. The Forbidden Library. 2015. (Forbidden Library: 1). (ENG., Illus.). 400p. (J). (gr. 5). 8.99 *(978-0-14-242681-4(4)*, Puffin Books) Penguin Young Readers Group.

Wheeler, Kim. The Adventures of Jonny Plumb. 2013. 174p. pap. *(978-0-7552-1568-3(0)*, Bright Pen) Authors OnLine, Ltd.

Whelan, Gloria. Listening for Lions. 2006. (ENG.). 208p. (J). (gr. 5-9). pap. 9.99 *(978-0-06-058176-3(X)*, HarperCollins) HarperCollins Pubs.

—Listening for Lions. 2007. 194p. (gr. 5-9). 16.00 *(978-0-7569-7800-6(9))* Perfection Learning Corp.

White, Andrea. Windows on the World. 2011. 238p. (J). 18.95 *(978-1-60898-105-2(3))*; pap. 9.95 *(978-1-60898-106-9(1))* namelos llc.

White, Ellen Emerson. Voyage on the Great Titanic. 2010. (Dear America Ser.). (ENG., Illus.). 208p. (J). (gr. 3-9). 12.99 *(978-0-545-23834-2(X)*, Scholastic Pr.) Scholastic, Inc.

Wicke, Ed. The Muselings. Douglas, Janine, illus. 2012. 212p. pap. 9.99 *(978-0-9840718-8-3(1))* Blacknblue Pr.

Williams, Mary. Brothers in Hope: The Story of the Lost Boys of Sudan, 1 vol. Christie, R. Gregory, illus. 2013. (ENG.). 40p. (J). (gr. 2-5). 20.95 *(978-1-58430-232-2(1)*, leelowbooks) Lee & Low Bks., Inc.

Wilson, Laurie Harman. The Treasures of Destiny. 2012. 72p. pap. 7.95 *(978-0-9848050-3-7(6)*, Little Creek Bks.) Jan-Carol Publishing, INC.

Winter, Barbara. Trapped in Gallipoli. 2007. (Illus.). 48p. (YA). lib. bdg. 15.00 *(978-1-4242-1643-7(5))* Dingles & Co.

Wolk, Lauren. Beyond the Bright Sea. 2017. (ENG.). 304p. (J). (gr. 5). 18.99 *(978-1-101-99485-6(1)*, Dutton Books for Young Readers) Penguin Young Readers Group.

Wood, Francis Eusene. The Christmas Letter. Wood, Christine & Marken, Jon, eds. McDermott, Robert, illus. Wood, Christine, photos by. 2007. pap. 9.95 *(978-0-9746372-6-6(2))* Tip-Of-The-Moon Publishing Co.

Wood, Maryrose. The Hidden Gallery. Klassen, Jon, illus. 2011. (Incorrigible Children of Ashton Place Ser.: Bk. 2). (J). (gr. 3-7). 16.89 *(978-0-06-179114-7(8))* HarperCollins Pubs.

—The Incorrigible Children of Ashton Place: Book I: the Mysterious Howling. Klassen, Jon, illus. 2015. (Incorrigible Children of Ashton Place Ser.: 1). (ENG.). 288p. (J). (gr. 3-7). pap. 7.99 *(978-0-06-236693-1(9)*, Balzer & Bray) HarperCollins Pubs.

—The Incorrigible Children of Ashton Place: Book II: the Hidden Gallery. Klassen, Jon, illus. 2015. (Incorrigible Children of Ashton Place Ser.: 2). (ENG.). 336p. (J). (gr. 3-7). pap. 7.99 *(978-0-06-236694-8(7)*, Balzer & Bray) HarperCollins Pubs.

—The Incorrigible Children of Ashton Place: The Mysterious Howling Howlin G, Bk. I. Klassen, Jon, illus. 2010. (Incorrigible Children of Ashton Place Ser.: 1). (ENG.). 272p. (J). (gr. 3-7). 16.99 *(978-0-06-179105-5(9)*, Balzer & Bray) HarperCollins Pubs.

—The Incorrigible Children of Ashton Place: Book III: The Unseen Guest. Klassen, Jon, illus. 2015. (Incorrigible Children of Ashton Place Ser.: 3). (ENG.). 352p. (J). (gr. 3-7). pap. 6.99 *(978-0-06-236695-5(5)*, Balzer & Bray) HarperCollins Pubs.

—The Incorrigible Children of Ashton Place: Book IV Bk. 4: The Interrupted Tale. Wheeler, Eliza, illus. 2015. (Incorrigible Children of Ashton Place Ser.: 4). (ENG.). 400p. (J). (gr. 3-7). pap. 9.99 *(978-0-06-179123-9(7)*, Balzer & Bray) HarperCollins Pubs.

—The Incorrigible Children of Ashton Place: Book V: The Unmapped Sea. Wheeler, Eliza, illus. 2016. (Incorrigible Children of Ashton Place Ser.: 5). (ENG.). 416p. (J). (gr. 3-7). pap. 8.99 *(978-0-06-211042-8(X)*, Balzer & Bray) HarperCollins Pubs.

—The Incorrigible Children of Ashton Place: Book VI: The Long-Lost Home. Wheeler, Eliza, illus. (Incorrigible Children of Ashton Place Ser.: 6). (ENG.). 448p. (J). (gr. 3-7). 2019. pap. 7.99 *(978-0-06-211045-9(4))* 2018. 15.99 *(978-0-06-211044-2(6))* HarperCollins Pubs. (Balzer & Bray).

Wood, Maryrose & Klassen, Jon. The Hidden Gallery. 2011. (Incorrigible Children of Ashton Place Ser.: 2). (ENG., Illus.). 320p. (J). (gr. 3-7). 17.99 *(978-0-06-179112-3(1)*, Balzer & Bray) HarperCollins Pubs.

Woodruff, Elvira. Fearless. 2011. (ENG.). 240p. (YA). (gr. 4-7). pap. 6.99 *(978-0-439-67704-2(1)*, Scholastic Pr.) Scholastic, Inc.

Woodson, Jacqueline. Miracle's Boys. 2010. (ENG.). 176p. (J). (gr. 5-18). 8.99 *(978-0-14-241553-5(7)*, Puffin Books) Penguin Young Readers Group.

—Peace, Locomotion. (ENG.). (J). 2010. 176p. (gr. 5-18). 8.99 *(978-0-14-241512-2(X)*, Puffin Books) 2009. 144p. (gr. 4-6). 22.44 *(978-0-399-24655-5(X))* Penguin Young Readers Group.

Woolston, Blythe. MARTians. (ENG.). 224p. (gr. 7). 2018. (J). pap. 7.99 *(978-1-5362-0056-0(5))* 2015. (YA). 16.99 *(978-0-7636-7756-5(6))* Candlewick Pr.

Worley, Rob M. & Warner, Gertrude Chandler. Surprise Island, 1 vol. Dubisch, Michael, illus. 2009. (Boxcar Children Graphic Novels Ser.). (ENG.). 32p. (J). (gr. 3-8). 32.79 *(978-1-60270-587-6(9)*, 3670, Graphic Planet - Fiction) Magic Wagon.

Wulf, Linda Press. The Night of the Burning. 2007. 224p. pap. *(978-0-7475-9051-4(6))* Bloomsbury Publishing Plc.

Yancey, Rick. The Curse of the Wendigo. 2011. (Monstrumologist Ser.: 2). (ENG.). 464p. (YA). (gr. 9). pap. 13.99 *(978-1-4169-8451-1(8)*, Simon & Schuster Bks. For Young Readers) Simon & Schuster Bks. For Young Readers.

—The Final Descent. 2013. (Monstrumologist Ser.: 4). (ENG., Illus.). 320p. (YA). (gr. 9). 18.99 *(978-1-4424-5153-7(X)*, Simon & Schuster Bks. For Young Readers) Simon & Schuster Bks. For Young Readers.

—The Isle of Blood. (Monstrumologist Ser.: 3). (ENG.). 560p. (YA). (gr. 9). 2012. pap. 13.99 *(978-1-4169-8453-5(4))* 2011. (Illus.). 18.99 *(978-1-4169-8452-8(6))* Simon & Schuster Bks. For Young Readers. (Simon & Schuster Bks. For Young Readers).

—The Monstrumologist. 2010. (Monstrumologist Ser.: 1). (ENG.). 464p. (YA). (gr. 9). pap. 13.99 *(978-1-4169-8449-8(6)*, Simon & Schuster Bks. For Young Readers) Simon & Schuster Bks. For Young Readers.

Yates, Alexander. The Winter Place. 2015. (ENG., Illus.). 448p. (YA). (gr. 9). 17.99 *(978-1-4814-1981-9(1))* Simon & Schuster Children's Publishing.

The Year We Sailed the Sun. 2015. (ENG., Illus.). 432p. (J). (gr. 3-7). 17.99 *(978-0-689-85827-7(2)*, Atheneum/Richard Jackson Bks.) Simon & Schuster Children's Publishing.

Yep, Laurence. The Magic Paintbrush. Wang, Suling, illus. 2003. (ENG.). 96p. (J). (gr. 3-7). pap. 6.99 *(978-0-06-440852-3(3)*, HarperCollins) HarperCollins Pubs.

—The Magic Paintbrush. Wang, Suling, illus. 2003. 89p. (J). (gr. 3-7). 12.65 *(978-0-7569-1444-8(2))* Perfection Learning Corp.

—The Tiger's Apprentice. 2005. (Tiger's Apprentice Ser.: Bk. 1). 184p. (J). lib. bdg. 24.62 *(978-1-4242-0449-6(6))* Fitzgerald Bks.

—The Tiger's Apprentice. 2005. (Tiger's Apprentice (Tandem Library) Ser.). 184p. (gr. 5-9). 17.00 *(978-0-7569-5074-3(0))* Perfection Learning Corp.

Youme. Sélavi: A Haitian Story of Hope, 1 vol. Youme, illus. 2005. (ENG., Illus.). 40p. (J). (gr. 3-5). pap. 12.95 *(978-0-938317-95-1(4)*, 23353382, Cinco Puntos Press) Lee & Low Bks., Inc.

Young, Moira. Blood Red Road. (Dust Lands Ser.: 1). (ENG.). (YA). (gr. 9). 2012. 480p. pap. 12.99 *(978-1-4424-2999-4(2))* 2011. (Illus.). 464p. 17.99 *(978-1-4424-2998-7(4))* McElderry, Margaret K. Bks. (McElderry, Margaret K. Bks.).

—Blood Red Road, 9 vols. 2011. (YA). 122.75 *(978-1-4618-0629-5(1))*; 286.75 *(978-1-4618-0634-9(8))*; 1.25 *(978-1-4640-2632-4(7))*; 120.75 *(978-1-4618-0633-2(X))*; 120.75 *(978-1-4618-0630-1(5))* Recorded Bks., Inc.

—Raging Star. (Dust Lands Ser.: 3). (ENG., Illus.). 448p. (YA). (gr. 9). 2015. pap. 13.99 *(978-1-4424-3003-7(6))* 2014. 17.99 *(978-1-4424-3002-0(8))* McElderry, Margaret K. Bks. (McElderry, Margaret K. Bks.).

—Rebel Heart. 2013. (Dust Lands Ser.: 2). (ENG., Illus.). 448p. (YA). (gr. 9). pap. 13.99 *(978-1-4424-3001-3(X)*, McElderry, Margaret K. Bks.) McElderry, Margaret K. Bks.

Zafon, Carlos Ruiz. The Midnight Palace. 2012. (ENG.). 320p. (YA). (gr. 7-17). pap. 17.99 *(978-0-316-04474-5(1))* Little, Brown Bks. for Young Readers.

Zdunich, Terrance. The Molting: Issue #1 Guilty Susie. 2009. pap. 7.99 *(978-1-61623-120-0(3))* Independent Pub.

Zweig, Eric. Fever Season. 2009. (ENG.). 256p. (YA). (gr. 4-18). pap. 10.99 *(978-1-55488-432-2(2))* Dundurn Pr. CAN. Dist: Publishers Group West (PGW).

ORR, BOBBY, 1948-

Kootstra, Kara. The Boy in Number Four. Thomson, Regan, illus. 2014. (ENG.). 32p. (J). (gr. k-3). 14.99 *(978-0-670-06713-8(X)*, Puffin Canada) PRH Canada Young Readers CAN. Dist: Penguin Random Hse. LLC.

ORWELL, GEORGE, 1903-1950

Boerst, William J. Generous Anger: The Story of George Orwell. 2004. (World Writers Ser.). (Illus.). 112p. (YA). (gr. 6-12). 23.95 *(978-1-883846-74-9(9)*, First Biographies) Reynolds, Morgan Inc.

Borus, Audrey. Reading & Interpreting the Works of George Orwell, 1 vol. 2016. (Lit Crit Guides). (ENG., Illus.). 176p. (gr. 6-6). 41.60 *(978-0-7660-8354-7(3)*, 953ea8b5-6619-4c98-93ca-032608f6fca5) Enslow Publishing, LLC.

George Orwell 1984: The Political Pen. 2014. (ENG.). 180p. (J). (gr. 3-7). pap. 13.95 *(978-1-59077-354-3(3))* Evans, M. & Co., Inc.

OSCEOLA, SEMINOLE CHIEF, 1804-1838

Hunt, Santana. Osceola, 1 vol. 2015. (Native American Heroes Ser.). (ENG., Illus.). 24p. (J). (gr. 1-2). pap. 9.15 *(978-1-4824-2689-2(7)*, a0ad4dd5-1260-4402-a69d-7514e09eb68a) Stevens, Gareth Publishing LLLP.

Sanford, William R. Seminole Chief Osceola, 1 vol. 2013. (Native American Chiefs & Warriors Ser.). (ENG.). 48p. (gr. 5-7). pap. 11.53 *(978-1-4644-0263-0(9)*, 59695d5a-2126-4dac-9e71-8bf2d52c49f8); (Illus.). (J). lib. bdg. 25.27 *(978-0-7660-4117-2(4)*, 71a840ed-b1cb-4569-abd7-17f460cdc077) Enslow Publishing, LLC.

OSTEOLOGY

see Bones

OSTRICHES

Awesome Ostriches. 2013. (Great Big Animals Ser.). 24p. (J). (gr. k-2). pap. 48.90 *(978-1-4339-9418-0(6))* Stevens, Gareth Publishing LLLP.

Calhoun, Kelly. Fast & Flightless: Ostrich. 2015. (Guess What Ser.). (ENG., Illus.). 24p. (J). (gr. k-2). 30.64 *(978-1-63362-627-0(X)*, 206664) Cherry Lake Publishing.

—Velocidad Sin Vuelo (Fast & Flightless) Avestruz (Ostrich) 2016. (Adivina (Guess What) Ser.). (SPA., Illus.). 24p. (J). (gr. k-2). 30.64 *(978-1-63471-446-4(6)*, 208847) Cherry Lake Publishing.

Cunningham, Kevin. Zebras & Ostriches. 2016. (21st Century Junior Library: Better Together Ser.). (ENG., Illus.). 24p. (J). (gr. 2-5). 29.21 *(978-1-63471-082-4(7)*, 208407) Cherry Lake Publishing.

Emminizer, Theresa. Ostrich: The Largest Bird, 1 vol. 2019. (Animal Record Breakers Ser.). (ENG.). 24p. (gr. 2-3). pap. 9.25 *(978-1-7253-0874-9(6)*, 04eac43b-8564-4ce6-b0c8-47101ee5e612, PowerKids Pr.) Rosen Publishing Group, Inc., The.

Gibbs, Maddie. Ostriches, 1 vol. 2011. (Safari Animals Ser.). (ENG.). 24p. (J). (gr. 1-1). pap. 9.25 *(978-1-4488-2600-1(4)*, 9bf51e08-234c-4a55-a9c5-6ef9bca35e7e); lib. bdg. 26.27 *(978-1-4488-2509-7(1)*, a5ebbcd0-6612-4319-a851-b7884710a743) Rosen Publishing Group, Inc., The. (PowerKids Pr.).

—Ostriches: Avestruces, 1 vol. 2011. (Safari Animals / Animales de Safari Ser.). (SPA & ENG.). 24p. (J). (gr. 1-1). lib. bdg. 26.27 *(978-1-4488-3121-0(0)*, 01477276-7985-4106-8899-964e3f49da9e) Rosen Publishing Group, Inc., The.

Gish, Melissa. Ostriches. (Living Wild Ser.). (ENG., Illus.). 48p. (J). (gr. 4-7). 2017. pap. 12.00 *(978-1-62832-302-3(7)*, 20614, Creative Paperbacks) 2016. *(978-1-60818-706-5(3)*, 20616, Creative Education) Creative Co., The.

Hansen, Grace. Ostriches, 1 vol. 2016. (Super Species Ser.). (ENG., Illus.). 24p. (J). (gr. -1-2). lib. bdg. 32.79 *(978-1-68080-547-5(9)*, 21374, Abdo Kids) ABDO Publishing Co.

Harasymiw, Teppo. Ostriches, 1 vol. 2010. (Animals That Live in the Grasslands Ser.). (ENG.). 24p. (J). (gr. 1-1). pap. 9.15 *(978-1-4339-3879-5(0)*, 906b0340-adff-4ce1-8a74-2e51a3fbc85d); lib. bdg. 25.27 *(978-1-4339-3878-8(2)*, cacfc1f0-5f5f-497c-bbc1-712cc95d2c4a) Stevens, Gareth Publishing LLLP.

Herriott, Charlotte. Cheetah vs. Ostrich, 1 vol. 2015. (Bizarre Beast Battles Ser.). (ENG., Illus.). 24p. (J). (gr. 2-3). pap. 9.15 *(978-1-4824-2784-4(2)*,

ced85b28-de2a-4628-ab95-20815baf1b28) Stevens, Gareth Publishing LLLP.
Jacobs, Liza. Ostriches. 2003. (Wild Wild World Ser.). (Illus.). 24p. (J). 21.20 *(978-1-4103-0040-9(4),* Blackbirch Pr., Inc.) Cengage Gale.
Lunis, Natalie. Ostrich: The World's Biggest Bird. 2007. (SuperSized! Ser.). (Illus.). 24p. (J). (gr. k-3). lib. bdg. 21.28 *(978-1-59716-394-1(5),* 1265939) Bearport Publishing Co., Inc.
Markovics, Joyce. My Legs Are Long & Strong (Ostrich) 2014. (Zoo Clues Ser.). 24p. (J). (gr. -1-3). lib. bdg. 26.99 *(978-1-62724-108-3(6))* Bearport Publishing Co., Inc.
Markovics, Joyce L. MIS Patas Son Largas y Fuertes. 2015. (Pistas de Animales Ser.). (SPA.). 24p. (J). (gr. -1-3). lib. bdg. 26.99 *(978-1-62724-582-1(0))* Bearport Publishing Co., Inc.
Moore Niver, Heather. Ostriches Are Not Pets!, 1 vol. 2013. (When Pets Attack! Ser.). (ENG.). 32p. (J). (gr. 3-4). 29.27 *(978-1-4339-9283-4(3),* 49ae0d97-6fc9-4c70-b1cc-e71b0b57002e); pap. 11.50 *(978-1-4339-9284-1(1),* ee3d7371-2cfd-4742-b0cb-7ca9547bce11) Stevens, Gareth Publishing LLLP.
Nagelhout, Ryan. Awesome Ostriches, 1 vol. 2013. (Great Big Animals Ser.). (ENG.). 24p. (J). (gr. k-k). pap. 9.15 *(978-1-4339-9417-3(8),* 67c4d66a-6563-49b8-882d-313e7d0eca86); (Illus.). lib. bdg. 25.27 *(978-1-4339-9416-6(X),* 00f5efc2-c67b-4032-bfd8-6af970236c10) Stevens, Gareth Publishing LLLP.
—Awesome Ostriches / Avestruces Increíbles, 1 vol. 2013. (Great Big Animals / Superanimales Ser.). (SPA & ENG.). 24p. (J). (gr. k-k). 25.27 *(978-1-4339-9450-0(X),* b6002dc6-4ee3-48bf-9fa0-279a2ec21de9) Stevens, Gareth Publishing LLLP.
Ostriches Are Not Pets! 2013. (When Pets Attack! Ser.). 32p. (J). (gr. 3-6). pap. 63.00 *(978-1-4339-9285-8(X))* Stevens, Gareth Publishing LLLP.
Riggs, Kate. L' autruche. 2018. (Planète Animaux Ser.). (FRE., Illus.). 24p. (J). *(978-1-77092-394-2(2),* 19683) Creative Co., The.
—Ostriches. 2018. (Amazing Animals Ser.). (ENG., Illus.). 24p. (J). (gr. 1-3). pap. 8.99 *(978-1-62832-496-9(1),* 19628, Creative Paperbacks); *(978-1-60818-880-2(9),* 19630, Creative Education) Creative Co., The.
Schuetz, Kari. Ostriches. 2013. (Animal Safari Ser.). (ENG., Illus.). 24p. (J). (gr. k-3). lib. bdg. 26.95 *(978-1-60014-866-8(2),* Blastoff! Readers) Bellwether Media.
Silverman, Buffy. Can You Tell an Ostrich from an Emu. 2012. (Animal Look-Alikes Ser.). (Illus.). 32p. (J). (gr. k-2). lib. bdg. 25.26 *(978-0-7613-6741-3(1),* Lerner Pubns.) Lerner Publishing Group.
—Can You Tell an Ostrich from an Emu? 2012. (Animal Look-Alikes Ser.). 32p. (gr. k-2). pap. 45.32 *(978-0-7613-9258-3(0))* Lerner Publishing Group.
Stout, Frankie. Ostriches: Nature's Biggest Birds. (Things with Wings Ser.). 24p. (gr. 2-3). 2009. 42.50 *(978-1-60854-353-3(6))* 2008. (ENG., Illus.). (J). lib. bdg. 26.27 *(978-1-4042-4498-6(0),* bf58f29d-ee35-4040-b5a8-3e6ebd387c91) Rosen Publishing Group, Inc., The. (PowerKids Pr.).
Ward, Finn. Avestruces / Ostriches at the Zoo, 1 vol. 2015. (Animales Del Zoológico / Zoo Animals Ser.). (ENG & SPA.). 24p. (J). (gr. k-k). lib. bdg. 24.27 *(978-1-4824-3233-6(1),* 731d26f5-1697-4042-92b4-fcd396f0fed3) Stevens, Gareth Publishing LLLP.
—Ostriches at the Zoo, 1 vol. 2015. (Zoo Animals Ser.). (ENG., Illus.). 24p. (J). (gr. k-k). pap. 9.15 *(978-1-4824-2601-4(3),* c10efd1c-803c-4945-89ee-c9ddf9b8b6c0) Stevens, Gareth Publishing LLLP.
Waxman, Laura Hamilton. Ostriches: Fast Flightless Birds. 2016. (Comparing Animal Traits Ser.). (ENG., Illus.). 32p. (J). (gr. 2-4). 26.65 *(978-1-4677-9509-8(7),* 490a8e61-da0f-41e1-8eee-85cc4930bb77, Lerner Pubns.) Lerner Publishing Group.
Yasuda, Anita. Avestruces. 2013. (Animales en la Granja Ser.). (SPA., Illus.). 24p. (J). (gr. -1-3). lib. bdg. 27.13 *(978-1-62127-589-3(2),* AV2 by Weigl) Weigl Pubs., Inc.
—Ostriches. 2012. (J). 27.13 *(978-1-61913-277-1(X));* (ENG., Illus.). 24p. pap. 12.95 *(978-1-61913-281-8(8),* AV2 by Weigl) Weigl Pubs., Inc.

OSTRICHES—FICTION

Belonie, Shannon. Teaching an Ostrich to Fly. 2008. 16p. pap. 8.74 *(978-1-4343-5519-5(5))* AuthorHouse.
Brown, Ken. Why Can't I Fly? (ENG., Illus.). 32p. (J). pap. 9.99 *(978-1-84270-017-4(0))* Andersen Pr. GBR. Dist: Trafalgar Square Publishing.
Del Riego, Erica. The Heart of Life. 2010. 36p. pap. 17.75 *(978-1-4389-7572-6(4))* AuthorHouse.
Dominguez, Angela. How Are You? / ¿Cómo Estás? 2018. (ENG., Illus.). 32p. (J). 18.99 *(978-1-250-12686-3(X),* 900175268, Holt, Henry & Co. Bks. For Young Readers) Holt, Henry & Co.
Harrison, Casey. I'm an Ostrich. 2012. 24p. pap. 9.99 *(978-0-9853650-4-2(8))* Mindstir Media.
Henderson, Susan Sinclair. Penelope's Journey Home. 2013. 48p. pap. 9.99 *(978-1-4908-0420-0(X),* WestBow Pr.) Author Solutions, LLC.
Idle, Molly. Flora & the Ostrich: An Opposites Book by Molly Idle (Flora & Flamingo Board Books, Picture Books for Toddlers, Baby Books with Animals) 2017. (Flora & Friends Ser.). (ENG., Illus.). 20p. (J). (gr. -1 — 1). bds. 9.99 *(978-1-4521-4658-4(6))* Chronicle Bks. LLC.
Kok, Gemma. Scribble. 2008. 42p. pap. 17.94 *(978-1-4092-2060-2(5))* Lulu Pr., Inc.
—Scribble (Printed in black & White) 2008. (ENG.). 42p. pap. 7.96 *(978-1-4092-2531-7(3))* Lulu Pr., Inc.
Kulka, Joe. Undercover Ostrich. Kulka, Joe, illus. 2019. (ENG., Illus.). 32p. (J). (gr. -1-3). 17.99 *(978-1-5124-9787-8(8),* 053dc6c1-2486-4aab-be89-cd9487302742, Carolrhoda Bks.) Lerner Publishing Group.
Morrow, John. Ostrich Egg Omelets. 2017. (ENG., Illus.). (J). 19.99 *(978-0-9790832-1-1(4))* 405 Pubns.
Rea, Monique. Toulouse the Moose & the Mystery Guests. 2012. 34p. pap. 13.99 *(978-0-9788926-4-7(X))* Trails of Discovery.
Stockton, Lucille. Hallo, Mallo & Pallo: The Ostracized Ostrich Family. Sampson, April, illus. 2005. 31p. (J). 19.95 *(978-1-59408-511-6(0))* Cork Hill Pr.
Wallace, Karen. Flash Harriet & the Outrageous Ostrich Egg Mystery. (ENG., Illus.). 64p. (J). pap. *(978-0-340-61961-2(9))* Hodder & Stoughton.
Wilson, D. Arthur. Little Red Rhupert. 2006. 15.95 *(978-0-9785144-0-2(8))* Ostrageous Publishing.

OTTERS

Costain, Meredith. Otter, 1 vol. Hanna, Gary, illus. 2016. (Wild World Ser.). (ENG.). 32p. (J). (gr. 1-2). pap. 11.00 *(978-1-4994-8218-8(3),* 67fa22af-561a-4c9d-9be5-b159f4f552ed, Windmill Bks.) Rosen Publishing Group, Inc., The.
Drumlin, Sam. Sea Otters, 1 vol. 2013. (PowerKids Readers: Sea Friends Ser.). (ENG., Illus.). 24p. (J). (gr. k-k). pap. 9.25 *(978-1-4488-9744-5(0),* a4e70edb-f3c2-4b64-b5e9-3a9cdb8fc1af); lib. bdg. 26.27 *(978-1-4488-9643-1(6),* c39cb14f-0c12-4cf9-a434-1d802a3566d1) Rosen Publishing Group, Inc., The. (PowerKids Pr.).
—Sea Otters: Las Nutrias Marinas, 1 vol. Alamán, Eduardo, tr. 2013. (PowerKids Readers: Los Amigos Del Mar / Sea Friends Ser.). (SPA & ENG., Illus.). 24p. (J). (gr. k-k). lib. bdg. 26.27 *(978-1-4488-9976-0(1),* 11a25dcf-c066-47d5-a1b1-93bb74c30bb2, PowerKids Pr.) Rosen Publishing Group, Inc., The.
Emminizer, Theresa. What If Sea Otters Disappeared? 2019. (Life Without Animals Ser.). (ENG.). 24p. (gr. 1-2). 48.90 *(978-1-5382-3823-3(3))* Stevens, Gareth Publishing LLLP.
Esbaum, Jill. Explore My World Sea Otters. 2017. (Explore My World Ser.). (Illus.). 32p. (J). (gr. -1-k). pap. 4.99 *(978-1-4263-2825-1(7),* National Geographic Kids) Disney Publishing Worldwide.
Esbensen, Barbara Juster. Playful Slider: The North American River Otter. Brown, Mary Barrett, illus. 2011. (Fesler-Lampert Minnesota Heritage Ser.). (ENG.). 32p. pap. 11.95 *(978-0-8166-7765-8(4))* Univ. of Minnesota Pr.
Evans, Shira. National Geographic Readers: Peek, Otter. 2016. (Readers Ser.). 24p. (J). (gr. -1-k). pap. 4.99 *(978-1-4263-2436-9(7));* (ENG.). lib. bdg. 13.90 *(978-1-4263-2437-6(5))* Disney Publishing Worldwide. (National Geographic Kids).
Feldman, Thea. A Sea Otter to the Rescue: Ready-To-Read Level 2. Sanson, Rachel, illus. 2019. (Tails from History Ser.). (ENG.). 32p. (J). (gr. k-2). pap. 4.99 *(978-1-5344-4337-2(1),* Simon Spotlight) Simon Spotlight.
Gates, Margo. Sea Otters. 2013. (Animal Safari Ser.). (ENG., Illus.). 24p. (J). (gr. k-3). lib. bdg. 26.95 *(978-1-60014-915-3(4),* Blastoff! Readers) Bellwether Media.
Gish, Ashley. Sea Otters. 2019. (X-Books: Marine Mammals Ser.). (ENG.). 32p. (J). (gr. 3-6). *(978-1-64026-192-1(3),* 19224, Creative Education) Creative Co., The.
Goldsworthy, Kaite. Otters. 2011. (J). (gr. 2-4). pap. 12.95 *(978-1-61690-627-6(8),* AV2 by Weigl); (Illus.). 24p. 27.13 *(978-1-61690-621-4(9))* Weigl Pubs., Inc.
Green, Jen. River Otters. 2008. (Illus.). 52p. (J). *(978-0-7172-6283-0(9))* Grolier, Ltd.
—Sea Otter. 2013. (Science Slam: the Deep End-Animal Life Underwater Ser.). 24p. (J). (gr. -1-3). lib. bdg. 26.99 *(978-1-61772-922-5(1))* Bearport Publishing Co., Inc.
Johnson, Jinny. Sea Otter. 2014. (North American Mammals Ser.). (ENG., Illus.). 24p. (J). (gr. 1-4). 28.50 *(978-1-62588-037-6(5),* 17375) Black Rabbit Bks.
King, Zelda. Sea Otters. (Illus.). 24p. (J). 2012. 49.50 *(978-1-4488-5140-9(8),* PowerKids Pr.) 2011. (ENG., (gr. 2-3). pap. 9.25 *(978-1-4488-5139-3(4),* c5d3ab92-4f49-4895-b41e-fa73f07b7667, PowerKids Pr.) 2011. (ENG., (gr. 2-3). lib. bdg. 26.27 *(978-1-4488-5004-4(5),* 101bf335-8639-440f-ac4a-8228e2c0b5f1) Rosen Publishing Group, Inc., The.
Lajiness, Katie. Otters: Tool Users. 2018. (Awesome Animal Powers Ser.). (ENG., Illus.). 32p. (J). (gr. 2-5). lib. bdg. 34.21 *(978-1-5321-1502-8(4),* 28858, Big Buddy Bks.) ABDO Publishing Co.
Laughlin, Kara L. Sea Otters. 2017. (In the Deep Blue Sea Ser.). (ENG.). 24p. (J). (gr. k-3). lib. bdg. 32.79 *(978-1-5038-1689-3(3),* 211522) Child's World, Inc, The.
Lawrence, Ellen. Giant Otter. 2016. (Apex Predators of the Amazon Rain Forest Ser.). (ENG., Illus.). 24p. (J). (gr. -1-3). 26.99 *(978-1-68402-034-8(4))* Bearport Publishing Co., Inc.
—River Otter. 2016. (Swamp Things: Animal Life in a Wetland Ser.). (ENG.). 24p. (J). (gr. -1-3). 26.99 *(978-1-944102-54-8(X))* Bearport Publishing Co., Inc.
Leach, Michael. Otter, 1 vol. 2008. (Animal Neighbors Ser.). (ENG.). 32p. (gr. 3-3). (J). 28.93 *(978-1-4358-4993-8(0),* ed4b9b36-c856-434e-ae78-b7f4fc0530f1); pap. 11.60 *(978-1-4042-4570-9(7),* 25ffc450-fb42-4502-8683-9819fcafd196, Rosen Classroom) Rosen Publishing Group, Inc., The.
Leaf, Christina. Baby Sea Otters. 2014. (Super Cute! Ser.). (ENG., Illus.). 24p. (J). (gr. k-3). lib. bdg. 26.95 *(978-1-60014-976-4(6),* Blastoff! Readers) Bellwether Media.
Levine, Michelle. Let's Look at Sea Otters. 2010. pap. 45.32 *(978-0-7613-6978-3(3))* Lerner Publishing Group.
Litwin, Stephanie K. Raising Otter. 2011. 32p. pap. 14.99 *(978-1-4634-2595-1(3))* AuthorHouse.
London, Jonathan. Otters Love to Play. So, Meilo, illus. (Read & Wonder Ser.). (ENG.). 32p. (J). (gr. k-4). 2018. 7.99 *(978-1-5362-0324-0(6))* 2016. 17.99 *(978-0-7636-6913-3(X))* Candlewick Pr.
Lynch, Seth. Otters at the Zoo, 1 vol. 2019. (Zoo Animals Ser.). (ENG.). 24p. (gr. k-k). pap. 9.15 *(978-1-5382-3938-4(8),* fe6db6bb-df1e-4b34-84f5-b9e582544d23) Stevens, Gareth Publishing LLLP.
Lynette, Rachel. Giant River Otters. 2013. (Jungle Babies of the Amazon Rain Forest Ser.). 24p. (J). (gr. -1-3). lib. bdg. 21.32 *(978-1-61772-754-2(7))* Bearport Publishing Co., Inc.
Mara, Wil. Otters, 1 vol. 2008. (Animals, Animals Ser.). (ENG.). 48p. (gr. 5-5). lib. bdg. 32.64 *(978-0-7614-2527-4(6),* 74d737e2-938d-43fb-966c-2e6d5f82b4f2) Cavendish Square Publishing LLC.
Marsh, Laura. National Geographic Readers: Sea Otters. 2014. (Readers Ser.). (Illus.). 32p. (J). (gr. -1-k). pap. 4.99 *(978-1-4263-1751-4(4),* National Geographic Kids) Disney Publishing Worldwide.
Marsico, Katie & Gregory, Josh. Nature's Children: Otters. 2015. (ENG.). 48p. (J). pap. 6.95 *(978-0-531-21190-8(8),* Orchard Bks.) Scholastic Library Publishing.
Mason, Adrienne. Otters. Ogle, Nancy Gray, illus. 2003. (Kids Can Press Wildlife Ser.). (ENG.). 32p. (J). (gr. k-5). 11.99 *(978-1-55337-407-7(X))* Kids Can Pr., Ltd. CAN. Dist: Hachette Bk. Group.
McDonnell, Rory. Odd & Even with Otters, 1 vol. 2017. (Animal Math Ser.). (ENG.). 24p. (J). (gr. 1-2). pap. 9.15 *(978-1-5382-0852-6(0),* d3db3c5f-a581-4da2-937b-b2a516f99b12) Stevens, Gareth Publishing LLLP.
McLellan, Joe. Nikik & Wapus Save the People, 1 vol. Traverse, Jackie, illus. 2015. (ENG.). 32p. (J). mass mkt. 10.95 *(978-1-894717-70-0(8),* baddc49e-5bc9-4569-a55f-6ed5d2b298d0) Pemmican Pubns., Inc. CAN. Dist: Firefly Bks., Ltd.
Miles, Victoria. Sea Otter Pup, 1 vol. Gatt, Elizabeth, illus. (ENG.). (J). (gr. -1 — 1). 2017. 28p. 6.95 *(978-1-4598-1506-3(8))* 2013. 26p. bds. 10.95 *(978-1-4598-0467-8(8))* Orca Bk. Pubs. USA.
Miller, Sara Swan. Otters. (Paws & Claws Ser.). 24p. (gr. 2-3). 2009. 42.50 *(978-1-60851-151-8(0))* 2008. (ENG., Illus.). (J). lib. bdg. 26.27 *(978-1-4042-4162-6(0),* 042c1b3d-d70e-412d-9254-d679925450e1) Rosen Publishing Group, Inc., The. (PowerKids Pr.).
Newman, Patricia. Sea Otter Heroes: The Predators That Saved an Ecosystem. 2017. (ENG., Illus.). 56p. (J). (gr. 4-8). 33.32 *(978-1-5124-2631-1(8),* bdb5dec7-eab1-434b-9e98-f6d597589e5d); E-Book 47.99 *(978-1-5124-2844-5(2));* E-Book 47.99 *(978-1-5124-3885-7(5),* 9781512438857); E-Book 9.99 *(978-1-5124-3884-0(7),* 9781512438840) Lerner Publishing Group. (Millbrook Pr.).
Rathburn, Betsy. River Otters. 2018. (North American Animals Ser.). (ENG., Illus.). 24p. (J). (gr. k-3). lib. bdg. 26.95 *(978-1-62617-730-7(9),* Blastoff! Readers) Bellwether Media.
Ring, Susan. Project Otter. Kissock, Heather & Marshall, Diana, eds. 2003. (Zoo Life Ser.). (Illus.). 24p. (J). pap. 8.95 *(978-1-59036-059-0(1))* Weigl Pubs., Inc.
Schuh, Mari. Sea Otters. 2015. (Illus.). 24p. (J). lib. bdg. *(978-1-62031-191-2(7),* Bullfrog Bks.) Jump! Inc.
Slade, Suzanne. What If There Were No Sea Otters? A Book about the Ocean Ecosystem, 1 vol. Schwartz, Carol, illus. 2010. (Food Chain Reactions Ser.). (ENG.). 24p. (J). (gr. 2-4). pap. 9.95 *(978-1-4048-6397-2(4),* 114148, Picture Window Bks.) Capstone.
Sommer, Nathan. Sea Otters. 2018. (Ocean Life up Close Ser.). (ENG., Illus.). 24p. (J). (gr. k-3). lib. bdg. 26.95 *(978-1-62617-766-6(X),* Blastoff! Readers) Bellwether Media.
Steinhardt, Kim. Sabby the Sea Otter: A Pup's True Adventure & Triumph. 2020. (ENG., Illus.). 32p. (J). (gr. k-5). 17.95 *(978-1-61035-353-3(6),* Craven Street Bks.) Linden Publishing Co., Inc.
Suen, Anastasia. Sea Otters. 2020. (Spot Arctic Animals Ser.). (ENG.). 16p. (J). (gr. -1-2). lib. bdg. *(978-1-68151-799-5(X),* 10673) Amicus.
Wendorff, Anne. Sea Otters. 2008. (Oceans Alive Ser.). (ENG., Illus.). 24p. (J). (gr. k-3). lib. bdg. 26.95 *(978-1-60014-207-9(9))* Bellwether Media.
Wilsdon, Christina. Otters. 2007. (J). *(978-1-59939-138-0(4),* Reader's Digest Young Families, Inc.) Studio Fun International.
Woodward, Molly. It's Nice to Be an Otter. Leeson, Tom and Pat, photos by. 2016. (ENG., Illus.). 20p. (J). bds. 8.99 *(978-1-59714-335-6(9))* Heyday.

OTTERS—FICTION

Anderson, Dee, retold by. Otter Gets Tricked! A Cherokee Trickster Story. Lt. ed. 2004. (Illus.). 32p. (J). pap. 6.00 *(978-0-9755934-1-7(2))* Colonel Davenport Historical Foundation.
Applegate, Katherine. Odder. 2023. (SPA.). 296p. (J). (gr. 4-7). pap. 15.95 **(978-607-557-713-5(0))** Editorial Oceano de Mexico MEX. Dist: Independent Pubs. Group.
—Odder. Santoso, Charles, illus. 2022. (ENG.). 288p. (J). 16.99 *(978-1-250-14742-4(5),* 900181554) Feiwel & Friends.
Autio, Karen. Kah-Lan the Adventurous Sea Otter, 1 vol. Lott, Sheena, illus. 2016. (ENG.). 64p. (J). (gr. 1-3). 9.95 *(978-1-55039-244-9(1))* Sono Nis Pr. CAN. Dist: Orca Bk. Pubs. USA.
Bleu, Kennedy. Cotter Otter in Treasure Water. Goembel, Ponder, illus. 2014. (ENG.). 24p. (J). pap. 24.95 *(978-1-63004-814-3(3))* America Star Bks.
Bowman, Crystal. Otter & Owl's Helpful Hike, 1 vol. Zimmer, Kevin J., illus. 2008. (I Can Read! / Otter & Owl Ser.). (ENG.). 32p. (J). pap. 4.99 *(978-0-310-71706-5(X));* pap. 4.99 *(978-0-310-71704-1(3))* Zonderkidz.
Burgess, Thornton W. Little Joe Otter. (J). 18.95 *(978-0-8488-0398-8(1))* Amereon Ltd.
Casanova, Mary. Utterly Otterly Day. Hoyt, Ard, illus. 2008. (ENG.). 40p. (J). (gr. -1-3). 19.99 *(978-1-4169-0868-5(4),* Simon & Schuster Bks. For Young Readers) Simon & Schuster Bks. For Young Readers.
—Utterly Otterly Night. Hoyt, Ard, illus. 2011. (ENG.). 40p. (J). (gr. -1-1). 19.99 *(978-1-4169-7562-5(4),* Simon & Schuster Bks. For Young Readers) Simon & Schuster Bks. For Young Readers.
Chapman, Jane. With Your Paw in Mine. Chapman, Jane, illus. 2018. (ENG., Illus.). 32p. (J). (gr. -1-2). 17.99 *(978-1-68010-084-6(X))* Tiger Tales.
Collins, Yvonne & Rideout, Sandy. The Black Sheep. 2007. 348p. (J). *(978-1-4287-4665-7(X))* Hyperion Pr.
Connors, Lisa. Nico: Nutria Por un Dia - Oliver's Otter Phase: Spanish, 1 vol. Jones, Karen, illus. 2018. (SPA.). 32p. (J). (gr. k-1). pap. 11.95 *(978-1-60718-467-6(2),* 8067796d-08c0-437d-97c0-95e59745d2d6) Arbordale Publishing.
—Oliver's Otter Phase, 1 vol. Jones, Karen, illus. 2018. (ENG.). 32p. (J). (gr. k-3). 17.95 *(978-1-60718-451-5(6),* 9781607184515); pap. 11.95 *(978-1-60718-462-1(1),* 9781607184621) Arbordale Publishing.
Curtis, Jennifer Keats. Saving Squeak: The Otter Tale, 1 vol. 2010. (ENG., Illus.). 32p. (J). (gr. -1-3). 14.99 *(978-0-7643-3588-4(X),* 4018) Schiffer Publishing, Ltd.
Dana, Katherine. Never Invite an Otter to Stay the Night. 2011. 60p. 29.95 *(978-1-60844-956-9(4));* pap. 19.95 *(978-1-4575-0158-6(9))* Dog Ear Publishing, LLC.
deRubertis, Barbara. Oliver Otter's Own Office. Alley, R. W., illus. 2011. (Animal Antics A to Z Ser.). 32p. (J). pap. 45.32 *(978-0-7613-7661-3(5));* (gr. -1-3). pap. 7.95 *(978-1-57565-327-3(3),* 419a901e-b7f6-4632-9be1-6d21f81440fe, Kane Press) Astra Publishing Hse.
deRubertis, Barbara & DeRubertis, Barbara. Oliver Otter's Own Office. Alley, R. W., illus. 2012. (Animal Antics A to Z Ser.). 32p. (J). (gr. 2 — 1). cd-rom 7.95 *(978-1-57565-408-9(3))* Astra Publishing Hse.
Dodd, Emma. Together. Dodd, Emma, illus. (Emma Dodd's Love You Bks.). (ENG., Illus.). (J). (— 1). 2018. 22p. bds. 9.99 *(978-0-7636-9940-6(3))* 2016. 24p. 14.99 *(978-0-7636-8940-7(8))* Candlewick Pr.
Dohlke, Nora. The Wonderful Adventures of Ozzie Sea Otter (Spanish) Stearns, Forest, illus. 2009. (ENG.). 98p. 19.95 *(978-0-9822046-2-7(0))* Bay Publishing.
—The Wonderful Adventures of Ozzie the Sea Otter. Stearns, Forest, illus. 2009. 98p. (J). 19.95 *(978-0-9822046-0-3(4))* Bay Publishing.
—The Wonderful Adventures of Ozzie the Sea Otter (Book & CD) Stearns, Forest, illus. 2009. (ENG.). 98p. 26.95 *(978-0-9822046-1-0(2))* Bay Publishing.
Eagle, Golden. You Can Play All Day If You Know the Way: Otter Medicine. 2005. (Illus.). 18p. (J). per. 12.99 *(978-1-932338-64-5(0))* Lifevest Publishing, Inc.
Ealy, Gerald & Ealy, Gerald. I Made a Wish to Be a Fish. 2012. 32p. pap. 9.95 *(978-0-9843837-5-7(1))* G340 Publishing.
Fraser, Mary Ann. Milton & Odie & the Bigger-Than-Bigmouth Bass. Fraser, Mary Ann, illus. 2019. (Illus.). 32p. (J). (gr. -1-3). lib. bdg. 16.99 *(978-1-62354-098-2(4))* Charlesbridge Publishing, Inc.
Galvin, Laura. River Otter at Autumn Lane. Leeper, Christopher, illus. 2003. (ENG.). 32p. (J). (gr. -1-3). 9.95 *(978-1-931465-66-3(5),* PB5073) Soundprints.
Galvin, Laura Gates. River Otter at Autumn Lane. Leeper, Christopher J., illus. 2011. (Smithsonian's Backyard Ser.). (ENG.). 32p. (J). (gr. -1-3). 8.95 *(978-1-60727-642-5(9));* 19.95 *(978-1-60727-641-8(0))* Soundprints.
—River Otter at Autumn Lane. Leeper, Christopher, illus. 2005. (Smithsonian's Backyard Ser.). (ENG.). 32p. (J). (gr. -1-2). 19.95 *(978-1-931465-63-2(0),* BC5023); 15.95 *(978-1-931465-61-8(4),* B5023) Soundprints.
Garton, Sam. I Am Otter. Garton, Sam, illus. 2014. (ENG., Illus.). 32p. (J). (gr. -1-3). 16.99 *(978-0-06-224775-9(1),* Balzer & Bray) HarperCollins Pubs.
—I Am Otter Board Book. 2016. (ENG., Illus.). 34p. (J). (gr. -1 — 1). bds. 7.99 *(978-0-06-240908-9(5),* Balzer & Bray) HarperCollins Pubs.
—Otter: Hello, Sea Friends! 2016. (My First I Can Read Ser.). (ENG., Illus.). 32p. (J). (gr. -1-3). pap. 4.99 *(978-0-06-236660-3(2),* Balzer & Bray) HarperCollins Pubs.
—Otter Goes to School. Garton, Sam, illus. 2016. (ENG., Illus.). 32p. (J). (gr. -1-3). 17.99 *(978-0-06-235225-5(3),* Balzer & Bray) HarperCollins Pubs.
—Otter: I Love Books! Garton, Sam, illus. 2019. (My First I Can Read Ser.). (ENG., Illus.). 32p. (J). (gr. -1-3). 17.99 *(978-0-06-284508-5(X),* Balzer & Bray) HarperCollins Pubs.
—Otter: Let's Go Swimming! Garton, Sam, illus. 2017. (My First I Can Read Ser.). (ENG., Illus.). 32p. (J). (gr. -1-3). pap. 4.99 *(978-0-06-236663-4(7),* Balzer & Bray) HarperCollins Pubs.
—Otter Loves Easter! An Easter & Springtime Book for Kids. Garton, Sam, illus. 2017. (ENG., Illus.). 32p. (J). (gr. -1-3). pap. 9.99 *(978-0-06-236667-2(X),* Balzer & Bray) HarperCollins Pubs.
—Otter Loves Halloween! Garton, Sam, illus. 2015. (ENG., Illus.). 32p. (J). (gr. -1-3). 9.99 *(978-0-06-236666-5(1),* Balzer & Bray) HarperCollins Pubs.
—Otter: Oh No, Bath Time! Garton, Sam, illus. 2016. (My First I Can Read Ser.). (ENG., Illus.). 32p. (J). (gr. -1-3). pap. 4.99 *(978-0-06-236657-3(2),* Balzer & Bray) HarperCollins Pubs.
—Otter: the Best Job Ever! Garton, Sam, illus. 2016. (My First I Can Read Ser.). (ENG., Illus.). 32p. (J). (gr. -1-3). pap. 5.99 *(978-0-06-236654-2(8),* Balzer & Bray) HarperCollins Pubs.
Garton, Sam, illus. Otter: Hello, Sea Friends! 2016. 32p. (J). *(978-1-5182-2257-3(9),* Balzer & Bray) HarperCollins Pubs.
—Otter: Let's Go Swimming! 2017. 32p. (J). *(978-1-5182-4207-6(3),* Balzer & Bray) HarperCollins Pubs.
Grandpa & Little Guy. 2004. (J). 15.95 *(978-0-9764012-0-9(7))* Rockmill Publishing Co.
Halfmann, Janet. Good Night, Little Sea Otter: Burmese Karen/English, 1 vol. Williams, Wish, illus. 2012. (ENG.). 24p. (J). 5.95 *(978-1-59572-371-0(4))* Star Bright Bks., Inc.
—Good Night, Little Sea Otter: Burmese/English, 1 vol. Williams, Wish, illus. 2012. (ENG.). 24p. (J). pap. 5.95 *(978-1-59572-370-3(6))* Star Bright Bks., Inc.
—Good Night, Little Sea Otter: English, 1 vol. Williams, Wish, illus. (ENG.). (J). 2012. 24p. 15.95 *(978-1-59572-277-5(7))* 2010. 32p. (gr. -1-3). pap. 5.95 *(978-1-59572-254-6(8))* Star Bright Bks., Inc.
—Good Night, Little Sea Otter: Hmong/English, 1 vol. Williams, Wish, illus. 2012. (ENG.). 24p. (J). pap. 5.95 *(978-1-59572-365-9(X))* Star Bright Bks., Inc.
—Good Night, Little Sea Otter: Portugese/English, 1 vol. Williams, Wish, illus. 2012. (ENG.). 24p. (J). pap. 5.95 *(978-1-59572-359-8(5))* Star Bright Bks., Inc.
Hicks, Aniya & Hicks, Michelle. Fun Back in Ruskin Town. 2012. 24p. pap. 24.95 *(978-1-4626-8245-4(6))* America Star Bks.
Hoban, Russell. Emmet Otter's Jug-Band Christmas. Hoban, Lillian, illus. 2017. (ENG.). 48p. (J). (gr. -1-2). 16.99 *(978-1-5247-1457-4(7),* Doubleday Bks. for Young Readers) Random Hse. Children's Bks.
Howe, James. Otter & Odder: A Love Story. Raschka, Chris, illus. 2012. (ENG.). 40p. (J). (gr. 1-4). 14.00 *(978-0-7636-4174-0(X))* Candlewick Pr.
Humphreys, Neil. Telling the Otters to Leave Home Was a Really Big Mistake: Abbie Rose & the Magic Suitcase. Koon, Cheng Puay, illus. 2019. (ENG.). 32p. (J). (gr. -1 — 1). pap. 13.99 *(978-981-4828-76-5(9))* Marshall Cavendish International (Asia) Private Ltd. SGP. Dist: Independent Pubs. Group.

MNO

Jacques, Brian. Taggerung. 2003. (Redwall Ser.). 1.00 *(978-1-4175-5326-6(X))* Recorded Bks., Inc.

—Taggerung: A Tale from Redwall. Chalk, Gary, illus. 2003. (Redwall Ser.: 14). (ENG.). 448p. (J). (gr. 5-18). pap. 9.99 *(978-0-14-250154-2(9)*, Firebird) Penguin Young Readers Group.

Keiser, Frances R. Annie the River Otter: The Adventures of Pelican Pete. Keiser, Hugh M., illus. l.t. ed. 2006. (ENG.). 34p. (J). 19.99 *(978-0-9668845-4-8(X))* Sagaponack Bks.

Keller, Laurie. Do unto Otters: A Book about Manners. Keller, Laurie, illus. 2007. (ENG., Illus.). 40p. (J). (gr. k-3). 21.99 *(978-0-8050-7996-8(3)*, 900034600, Holt, Henry & Co. Bks. For Young Readers) Holt, Henry & Co.

—Do unto Otters: A Book about Manners. Keller, Laurie, illus. 2009. (ENG., Illus.). 40p. (J). (gr. k-3). pap. 9.99 *(978-0-312-58140-4(8)*, 900061994) Square Fish.

LeapFrog Staff. Ozzie & Mack. 2008. (J). pap. 49.99 *(978-1-59319-924-1(4))*; pap. 39.99 *(978-1-59319-976-0(7))* LeapFrog Enterprises, Inc.

Leavy, Diana C. Backstroke the Sea Otter & the Perfect Day. 2003. 32p. (J). per. *(978-1-59196-258-8(7))* Instant Pub.

McSorley, Paul J. & Bearss, Patricia. The Adventures of Forealdo: Finding Millie. 2012. 34p. 24.95 *(978-1-4626-6721-5(X))* America Star Bks.

Meadows, Daisy. Chloe Slipperslide's Secret. 2016. (Magic Animal Friends Ser.: 11). lib. bdg. 14.75 *(978-0-606-38801-6(X))* Turtleback.

Morrow, Dj. Charlie & Joe. 2013. 28p. pap. 24.95 *(978-1-62709-833-5(X))* America Star Bks.

Otter, Otter. (J). 26.20 *(978-0-8136-8416-1(1))*; (gr. -1-3). 59.50 *(978-0-8136-7954-9(0))* Modern Curriculum Pr.

Paul J McSorley; Illustrated By Patricia. The Adventures of Forealdo. Bearss, Patricia, illus. 2011. 36p. pap. 24.95 *(978-1-4560-8429-5(1))* America Star Bks.

Reidy, Jean. Pup 681: A Sea Otter Rescue Story. Crowley, Ashley, illus. 2019. (ENG.). 40p. (J). 17.99 *(978-1-250-11450-1(0)*, 900171459, Holt, Henry & Co. Bks. For Young Readers) Holt, Henry & Co.

Reminick, Gerald. Ollie Otter's Special Gift: A Story from Quiet Pond. Quintero, Michelle, illus. 2013. 32p. (J). 10.00 *(978-1-889901-60-2(1)*, Palo Alto Bks.) Glencannon Pr.

Rylant, Cynthia. The Otter. McDaniels, Preston, illus. 2016. (Lighthouse Family Ser.: 6). (ENG.). 48p. (J). (gr. 1-5). 17.99 *(978-1-4814-6045-3(5)*, Beach Lane Bks.) Beach Lane Bks.

Soundprints Staff. Smithsonian Oceanic Collection Micro 4 Book Set. 2007. (ENG.). 32p. 14.95 *(978-1-59249-749-2(7))*; 14.95 *(978-1-59249-748-5(9))* Soundprints.

Swenson, Lynn. Rollie & Mollie: Disappearing Act. Baker, David, illus. 2012. 26p. 24.95 *(978-1-4626-5277-8(8))* America Star Bks.

Tomlinson, Jill. The Otter Who Wanted to Know. Howard, Paul, illus. 2014. (ENG.). 96p. (J). (gr. -1-2). pap. 5.99 *(978-1-4052-7194-3(9))* Farshore GBR. Dist: HarperCollins Pubs.

Voake, Steve. Daisy Dawson & the Secret Pond. Meserve, Jessica, illus. 2010. (Daisy Dawson Ser.: 2). (ENG.). 96p. (J). (gr. 1-4). pap. 6.99 *(978-0-7636-4730-8(6))* Candlewick Pr.

Wargin, Kathy-jo. Otter Out of Water. Bendall-Brunello, John, illus. 2014. (ENG.). 32p. (J). (gr. k-3). 15.95 *(978-1-58536-431-2(2)*, 203005) Sleeping Bear Pr.

Watt, Fiona. That's Not My Otter. 2018. (Touchy-Feely Board Bks.). (ENG.). 10p. (J). 9.99 *(978-0-7945-4105-7(4)*, Usborne) EDC Publishing.

Webster, Christine. Otter Everywhere: Brand New Readers. Nihoff, Tim, illus. 2007. (Brand New Readers Ser.). (ENG.). 48p. (J). (gr. -1-3). pap. 6.99 *(978-0-7636-2922-9(7))* Candlewick Pr.

OUTBOARD MOTORS

see Motorboats

OUTDOOR COOKERY

see Outdoor Cooking

OUTDOOR COOKING

Conners, Christine & Conners, Tim. Scout's Deck of Outdoor Recipe Cards. 2015. (Illus.). 64p. 14.95 *(978-1-4930-0811-7(0)*, Falcon Guides) Globe Pequot Pr., The.

Jorgensen, Katrina. Food, Football, & Fun! Sports Illustrated Kids' Football Recipes. 2015. (Sports Illustrated Kids Ser.). (ENG., Illus.). 144p. (J). (gr. 3-9). pap., pap., pap. 15.95 *(978-1-62370-230-4(5)*, 127868, Capstone Young Readers) Capstone.

—Football Tailgating Recipes: Tasty Treats for the Stadium Crowd. 2015. (Football Cookbooks Ser.). (ENG.). 48p. (J). (gr. 3-9). lib. bdg. 31.99 *(978-1-4914-2137-6(1)*, 127620) Capstone.

Labat, Yancey C., illus. Let's Have a Cookout! 2007. 56p. (J). *(978-0-439-83228-1(4))* Scholastic, Inc.

Omoth, Tyler. Grill Master: Finger-Licking Grilled Recipes. 2017. (Kids Can Cook! Ser.). (ENG., Illus.). 32p. (J). (gr. 3-9). lib. bdg. 28.65 *(978-1-5157-3815-2(9)*, 133718, Capstone Pr.) Capstone.

Proudfit, Benjamin. Let's Go to a Cookout!, 1 vol. 2019. (Time to Celebrate! Ser.). (ENG.). 24p. (gr. k-k). pap. 9.15 *(978-1-5382-3890-5(X)*, 798be2d0-1d13-4ae3-880f-d1900279f3ac) Stevens, Gareth Publishing LLLP.

OUTDOOR LIFE

see also Camping; Country Life; Hiking; Mountaineering; Nature Study; Sports; Wilderness Survival

Abdo, Kenny. How to Survive a Blizzard. 2018. (How to Survive Ser.). (ENG., Illus.). 24p. (J). (gr. 2-8). lib. bdg. 31.36 *(978-1-5321-2323-8(X)*, 28413, Abdo Zoom-Fly) ABDO Publishing Co.

Aloian, Molly. The Yangtze: China's Majestic River, 1 vol. 2010. (Rivers Around the World Ser.). (ENG., Illus.). 32p. (J). (gr. 5-8). pap. *(978-0-7787-7472-3(4))*; lib. bdg. *(978-0-7787-7449-5(X))* Crabtree Publishing Co.

Beard, Lina & Beard, Adelia B. The American Girl's Handy Book: Making the Most of Outdoor Fun. 2018. (Illus.). 488p. (J). (gr. 4-7). 19.95 *(978-1-4930-3679-0(3)*, Lyons Pr.) Globe Pequot Pr., The.

Brennan, Stephen & Brennan, Finn. The Adventurous Boy's Handbook: For Ages 9 To 99. 2nd ed. 2011. (ENG., Illus.). 224p. (J). (gr. 2-5). pap. 12.95 *(978-1-61608-163-8(5)*, 608163) Skyhorse Publishing Co., Inc.

Brennan, Stephen & Brennan, Finn, eds. The Adventurous Boy's Handbook. 2014. (ENG., Illus.). 320p. 17.95 *(978-1-62873-707-3(7))* Skyhorse Publishing Co., Inc.

Brennan, Stephen & Brennan, Lara, eds. The Adventurous Girl's Handbook. 2014. (ENG., Illus.). 320p. 17.95 *(978-1-62873-708-0(5))* Skyhorse Publishing Co., Inc.

Butterfield, Moira. Survive & Thrive: A Pocket Guide to Wilderness Safety Skills, Plus 16 Quick-Check Skill Cards. 2016. (ENG., Illus.). 112p. (J). (gr. 3-7). pap. 11.99 *(978-1-4380-0842-4(2))* Sourcebooks, Inc.

Cain, Marie Mowery. Beyond the Backyard. 2013. (Big Books, Blue Ser.). (ENG & SPA., Illus.). 16p. pap. 33.00 *(978-1-59246-022-9(4))* Big Books, by George!

—Let's Move. 2013. (Big Books, Blue Ser.). (ENG & SPA., Illus.). 16p. pap. 33.00 *(978-1-59246-012-0(7))* Big Books, by George!

Cassany, Mia. Wilderness: Earth's Amazing Habitats. Navarro, Marcos, illus. 2019. (ENG.). 48p. (J). (gr. 1-4). 19.95 *(978-3-7913-7372-0(2))* Prestel Verlag GmbH & Co KG. DEU. Dist: Penguin Random Hse. LLC.

Challoner, Jack. Maker Lab Outdoors: 25 Super Cool Projects: Build, Invent, Create, Discover. 2018. (Illus.). 160p. (J). *(978-1-4654-7392-9(0))* Dorling Kindersley Publishing, Inc.

Dalton, Kippy. Outdoor Fun. 2016. (Spring Forward Ser.). (J). (gr. 1). *(978-1-4900-3712-7(8))* Benchmark Education Co.

Devera, Czeena. In My Backyard. 2019. (I Can See Ser.). (ENG.). 16p. (J). (gr. -1-2). pap. 11.36 *(978-1-5341-3917-6(6)*, 212501, Cherry Blossom Press) Cherry Lake Publishing.

Eggerling, Kristin J. Breath of Wilderness: The Life of Sigurd Olson. 2014. (ENG., Illus.). 112p. (J). (gr. 4-7). pap. 12.95 *(978-1-938486-10-4(2))* Fulcrum Publishing.

Encyclopaedia Britannica, Inc. Staff, compiled by. Discover English with Ben & Bella: Series 1: Outdoors. 2010. 180.00 *(978-1-61535-348-4(8))* Encyclopaedia Britannica, Inc.

Ferguson, Ollie & Ferguson, Harry. Ollie & Harry's Marvelous Adventures. 2019. (ENG., Illus.). 160p. (J). (gr. 3-10). 19.95 *(978-1-324-00395-3(2)*, 340395, Norton Young Readers) Norton, W. W. & Co., Inc.

Field & Stream's Guide to the Outdoors, 8 vols. 2014. (Field & Stream's Guide to the Outdoors Ser.). (ENG.). 96p. (J). (gr. 6-8). lib. bdg. 150.40 *(978-1-4824-2306-8(5)*, 9d467ccd-7617-4e49-88c2-336ee5d2046a) Stevens, Gareth Publishing LLLP.

Field & Stream's Guide to the Outdoors: Set 2, 6 vols. 2015. (Field & Stream's Guide to the Outdoors Ser.). (ENG.). 96p. (J). (gr. 6-8). lib. bdg. 112.80 *(978-1-4824-2563-5(7)*, 4a36a531-20c5-4f22-9659-6fcaff4696cb) Stevens, Gareth Publishing LLLP.

Gamble, Adam & Jasper, Mark. Good Night Mountains. 2013. (Good Night Our World Ser.). (ENG., Illus.). 24p. (J). (— 1). bds. 9.95 *(978-1-60219-090-0(9))* Good Night Bks.

Garrison, Hal. Cave Diving, 1 vol. 2017. (Daredevil Sports Ser.). (ENG.). 32p. (J). (gr. 1-2). pap. 11.50 *(978-1-5382-1113-7(0)*, d8fcf5ef-d4c0-4247-b515-baf44457828e) Stevens, Gareth Publishing LLLP.

Get Outdoors, 8 vols., Set 1. Incl. Canoeing & Kayaking. Rock, Lois. (J). lib. bdg. 28.93 *(978-1-4358-3041-7(5)*, 696db044-ecf8-4a6b-8c3a-12c881e70baf, PowerKids Pr.); Fishing. Ross, Nick. (YA). lib. bdg. 28.93 *(978-1-4358-3042-4(3)*, cc938c0d-7b64-4c42-a7c1-03ec00dd9d46); Orienteering. Champion, Neil. (YA). lib. bdg. 28.93 *(978-1-4358-3044-8(X)*, ea7e2e27-062f-4bd6-b3f0-35dab72c488f); Rock Climbing. Champion, Neil. (YA). lib. bdg. 28.93 *(978-1-4358-3043-1(1)*, e8705b55-1322-4389-8dc6-a91906d7217a); (gr. 4-4). 2009. (Get Outdoors Ser.). (ENG., Illus.). 32p. 2009. Set lib. bdg. 115.72 *(978-1-4358-3231-2(0)*, f5aa904c-7f13-4530-bbf1-9e6c19864afc, PowerKids Pr.) Rosen Publishing Group, Inc., The.

Heidtke, John. Family Outdoor Journal. 2008. (YA). pap. *(978-0-9792739-4-0(3))* Ajoyin Publishing, Inc.

Hinman, Bonnie. Get Outside in Summer. 2019. (Get Outside Ser.). (ENG., Illus.). 32p. (J). (gr. 2-3). 31.35 *(978-1-64185-333-0(6)*, 1641853336, Focus Readers) North Star Editions.

Hoenecke, Karen. At the Park. Biddle, Bruce, illus. 2003. (Bridging School to Home Series B). (ENG.). 8p. (gr. k-1). pap. 7.95 *(978-1-879835-37-5(1)*, Kaeden Bks.) Kaeden Corp.

Holden, Pam. Look Outside, 1 vol. 2017. (ENG., Illus.). 23p. (J). pap. *(978-1-77654-222-2(3)*, Red Rocket Readers) Flying Start Bks.

Honovich, Nancy & Beer, Julie. National Geographic Kids Get Outside Guide: All Things Adventure, Exploration, & Fun! 2014. (Illus.). 160p. (J). (gr. 3-7). pap. 14.99 *(978-1-4263-1502-2(3)*, National Geographic Kids) Disney Publishing Worldwide.

Johnson, Rich & James, Robert F. Outdoor Life's Disaster Survival Guide, 1 vol. 2015. (Field & Stream's Guide to the Outdoors Ser.). (ENG., Illus.). 96p. (J). (gr. 6-8). lib. bdg. 37.60 *(978-1-4824-3189-6(0)*, 16315027-2bda-4d91-826c-b13451c9e557) Stevens, Gareth Publishing LLLP.

Kallen, Stuart A. Careers If You Like the Outdoors. 2017. (ENG.). 80p. (YA). (gr. 5-12). 39.93 *(978-1-68282-140-4(4))* ReferencePoint Pr., Inc.

Let's Go Outdoors! 2015. (Let's Go Outdoors! Ser.). (ENG.). 24p. (J). (gr. k-k). pap., pap., pap. 293.40 *(978-1-4824-3483-5(0))*; pap., pap., pap. 48.90 *(978-1-4824-3484-2(9))*; lib. bdg. 145.62 *(978-1-4824-2540-6(8)*, f0d8c61a-42e3-4f96-b531-09d1e119be57) Stevens, Gareth Publishing LLLP.

Lowrie, Paul. Hooray for Minnesota Lakes. 2008. 19.95 *(978-0-9755801-8-9(3))* Questmarc Publishing.

—Hooray for Minnesota Winters. 2008. 19.95 *(978-0-9755801-9-6(1))* Questmarc Publishing.

Navarre, Gabrielle. Cool Careers Without College for People Who Love Nature, 1 vol. 2013. (Cool Careers Without College Ser.). (ENG., Illus.). 144p. (J). (gr. 7-7). 41.12 *(978-1-4777-1821-6(4)*, c656b8de-9347-4f99-baa5-1186c07395a6) Rosen Publishing Group, Inc., The.

Nickens, T. Edward. Field & Stream's Guide to Outdoor Survival, 1 vol. of, The Editors of Field and Stream, ed. 2014. (Field & Stream's Guide to the Outdoors Ser.). (ENG., Illus.). 96p. (J). (gr. 6-8). 37.60 *(978-1-4824-2304-4(9)*, aa112e67-b232-467b-94e1-32bb8d2d3b94) Stevens, Gareth Publishing LLLP.

Outdoor Adventure, 12 vols. 2014. (Outdoor Adventure Ser.). (ENG.). 32p. (J). (gr. 1-1). 161.58 *(978-1-4824-1175-1(X)*, 25b0a2ac-801d-4fb7-b1bf-f40b9e9daa27) Stevens, Gareth Publishing LLLP.

Outdoor Book IR. 2017. (Outdoor Book Ser.). (ENG.). (J). 9.99 *(978-0-7945-3968-9(8)*, Usborne) EDC Publishing.

Paulsen, Gary. Puppies, Dogs, & Blue Northers: Reflections on Being Raised by a Pack of Sled Dogs. 2007. (ENG., Illus.). 80p. (J). (gr. 5-7). pap. 7.99 *(978-0-15-206103-6(7)*, 1198332, Clarion Bks.) HarperCollins Pubs.

—Woodsong. 2007. (ENG., Illus.). 144p. (J). (gr. 5-9). pap. 7.99 *(978-1-4169-3939-9(3)*, Simon & Schuster Bks. For Young Readers) Simon & Schuster Bks. For Young Readers.

Percival, Tom, illus. 50 Things to Do Before You're 11 3/4: an Outdoor Adventure Handbook. 2018. (ENG.). 96p. (J). (gr. 3-7). pap. 9.99 *(978-0-7636-9337-4(5))* Candlewick Pr.

Pipe, Jim. How to Survive on a Desert Island, 1 vol. 2012. (Tough Guides). (ENG., Illus.). 32p. (J). (gr. 4-5). pap. 11.00 *(978-1-4488-7935-9(3)*, 2573f758-7322-46f5-be26-8dba06231ae9); lib. bdg. 28.93 *(978-1-4488-7870-3(5)*, f49d186b-1246-41da-9335-5179a4319e3e) Rosen Publishing Group, Inc., The. (PowerKids Pr.).

Rice, William B. Survival! Desert, 1 vol. 2nd rev. ed. 2012. (TIME for KIDS(r): Informational Text Ser.). (ENG., Illus.). 48p. (gr. 4-5). pap. 13.99 *(978-1-4333-4818-1(7))* Teacher Created Materials, Inc.

—Survival! Jungle, 1 vol. 2nd rev. ed. 2012. (TIME for KIDS(r): Informational Text Ser.). (ENG., Illus.). 48p. (gr. 4-5). pap. 13.99 *(978-1-4333-4820-4(9))* Teacher Created Materials, Inc.

Rinella, Steven. Catch a Crayfish, Count the Stars: Fun Projects, Skills, & Adventures for Outdoor Kids. Temescu, Max, illus. 2023. 368p. (gr. 3-7). 26.99 ***(978-0-593-44897-7(9)**, Random House)* Random House Publishing Group.

Royston, Angela. How to Survive in the Desert, 1 vol. 2012. (Tough Guides). (ENG., Illus.). 32p. (J). (gr. 4-5). pap. 11.00 *(978-1-4488-7932-8(9)*, 1299e474-93fe-46fb-82d0-ec90713099fe); lib. bdg. 28.93 *(978-1-4488-7867-3(5)*, e3b27a32-dfac-49b8-8446-3439722de5c2) Rosen Publishing Group, Inc., The. (PowerKids Pr.).

—How to Survive in the Rain Forest, 1 vol. 2012. (Tough Guides). (ENG., Illus.). 32p. (J). (gr. 4-5). pap. 11.00 *(978-1-4488-7934-2(5)*, 7fd52be1-8723-411a-aec2-1f3e01353445); lib. bdg. 28.93 *(978-1-4488-7869-7(1)*, bdb8234b-5919-467c-9a7b-63a3de14f110) Rosen Publishing Group, Inc., The. (PowerKids Pr.).

SANCHEZ, Anita. Wait till It Gets Dark. 2017. (Illus.). 64p. (J). (gr. 3-7). 14.95 *(978-1-63076-318-3(7))* Muddy Boots Pr.

Slade, Suzanne. Adventures Outdoors, 10 vols., Set. Incl. Let's Go Camping. lib. bdg. 28.93 *(978-1-4042-3650-9(3)*, f039084b-bdbf-4b66-a8b2-6c0d154eb825); Let's Go Canoeing & Kayaking. lib. bdg. 28.93 *(978-1-4042-3649-3(X)*, f4f4d625-f944-4bfb-921d-b572c4a206c6); Let's Go Fishing. lib. bdg. 28.93 *(978-1-4042-3647-9(3)*, d36f87e4-227c-43e3-a423-fd082bb16fa2); Let's Go Hiking. lib. bdg. 28.93 *(978-1-4042-3651-6(1)*, 49dc087a-9657-453e-a445-40a3b422839d); Let's Go Hunting. lib. bdg. 28.93 *(978-1-4042-3646-2(5)*, 077884c0-c5a6-40d6-8e50-611ae72ed682); Let's Go Snowboarding. lib. bdg. 28.93 *(978-1-4042-3648-6(1)*, c8062675-0524-4653-bf8b-76323721e916); (Illus.). 32p. (J). (gr. 4-5). (Adventures Outdoors Ser.). (ENG.). 2006. Set lib. bdg. 144.65 *(978-1-4042-3603-5(1)*, ab121502-86ce-4a7c-b2b7-d3ece27d882e, PowerKids Pr.) Rosen Publishing Group, Inc., The.

Sole Survivor, 12 vols. 2016. (Sole Survivor Ser.). 48p. (ENG.). (gr. 4-5). lib. bdg. 201.60 *(978-1-4824-4974-7(9)*, ce6ab41e-c5f1-4ed8-9b1d-b025dab080fc); (gr. 5-4). pap. 84.30 *(978-1-4824-5302-7(9))* Stevens, Gareth Publishing LLLP.

Spilsbury, Louise. Surviving the Ice, 1 vol. 2016. (Sole Survivor Ser.). (ENG.). 48p. (gr. 4-5). pap. 15.05 *(978-1-4824-5087-3(9)*, 1096ebbb-2ef9-477f-92e3-2a9813e0bdbc) Stevens, Gareth Publishing LLLP.

—Surviving the Mountain, 1 vol. 2016. (Sole Survivor Ser.). (ENG.). 48p. (gr. 4-5). pap. 15.05 *(978-1-4824-5083-5(6)*, 1fbe87ef-f74b-45a5-9f8c-8af86b8de947) Stevens, Gareth Publishing LLLP.

Taylor, Charlotte. Ways to Make Money Working Outside, 1 vol. 2019. (Cash in on Your Skills Ser.). (ENG.). 80p. (gr. 7-7). pap. 18.60 *(978-1-9785-1548-2(0)*, 6c65ffdb-9e47-4ee8-820a-5c8c71c2a457) Enslow Publishing, LLC.

Wild Outdoors. 2011. (Wild Outdoors Ser.). (ENG.). 32p. (gr. 1-2). lib. bdg. 136.60 *(978-1-4296-6514-8(9)*, Capstone Pr.) Capstone.

OUTDOOR LIFE—FICTION

Aimard, Gustave. The Indian Scout: a Story of the Aster City. 2006. (ENG.). 464p. per. 37.95 *(978-1-4286-1776-6(0))* Kessinger Publishing, LLC.

Allen, Quinc. The Outdoor Chums. 2006. pap. *(978-1-4065-0782-9(2))* Dodo Pr.

—The Outdoor Chums after Big Game (illust. 2006. pap. *(978-1-4065-0780-5(6))* Dodo Pr.

—The Outdoor Chums on the Gulf. 2006. pap. *(978-1-4065-0781-2(4))* Dodo Pr.

Ballantyne, R. M. Red Rooney: Or, the Last of the Crew. 2007. (R. M. Ballantyne Collection). (Illus.). 408p. 22.00 *(978-1-934554-08-1(1))* Vision Forum, Inc., The.

Byrne, Marlene. Kick the Can. Graber, Jesse, illus. 2009. 61p. pap. 9.99 *(978-0-9777135-3-0(9))* Good Stories Publishing.

Clark, Henry Scott. The Legionaires: A Story of the Great Raid. 2005. reprint ed. pap. 34.95 *(978-1-4191-3923-9(1))* Kessinger Publishing, LLC.

Cole, Henry. On the Way to the Beach. Cole, Henry, illus. 2003. (ENG., Illus.). 32p. (J). (gr. -1-3). 16.99 *(978-0-688-17515-3(5)*, Greenwillow Bks.) HarperCollins Pubs.

Covell, David. Run Wild. 2018. (Illus.). 40p. (J). (-k). 18.99 *(978-0-670-01411-8(7)*, Viking Books for Young Readers) Penguin Young Readers Group.

Dilz, Ric. My Grandma Could Do Anything in the Great Outdoors! 2008. (Illus.). 32p. (J). 14.95 *(978-0-9758704-6-4(7))* Ric Design LLC.

Grant, Robert. Jack in the Bush or A Summer on a Salmon River. 2005. pap. 33.95 *(978-1-4179-5573-2(2))* Kessinger Publishing, LLC.

Henkes, Kevin. In the Middle of Fall Board Book. Dronzek, Laura, illus. 2018. (ENG.). 36p. (J). (gr. -1 — 1). bds. 8.99 *(978-0-06-274726-6(6)*, Greenwillow Bks.) HarperCollins Pubs.

Keough, Rob. Wolf Summer. 2009. (Gem Lakes Ser.: 2). (ENG., Illus.). 192p. (YA). pap. 11.95 *(978-1-894283-87-8(2)*, Great Plains Teen Fiction) Great Plains Pubns. CAN. Dist: Independent Pubs. Group.

London, Jonathan. Grizzly Peak. London, Sean, illus. 2017. (Aaron's Wilderness Ser.). (ENG.). 174p. (YA). (gr. 3-7). pap. 12.99 *(978-1-943328-77-2(3)*, West Winds Pr.) West Margin Pr.

Manning, Mick. Adventures with Max & Kate, 1 vol. 2018. (Let's Read with Max & Kate Ser.). (ENG.). 24p. (J). (gr. 1-2). 25.27 *(978-1-5383-4037-0(2)*, 47df20a5-2af7-47ed-944a-5e3b17719663); pap. 9.25 *(978-1-5383-4038-7(0)*, 9b3da1ed-7ea9-427f-a58a-93034e28e34e) Rosen Publishing Group, Inc., The. (PowerKids Pr.).

—Outdoors with Max & Kate, 1 vol. 2018. (Let's Read with Max & Kate Ser.). (ENG.). 24p. (J). (gr. 1-2). 25.27 *(978-1-5383-4069-1(0)*, db38b6f7-519b-491e-bb71-6422d7ae1e04); pap. 9.25 *(978-1-5383-4070-7(4)*, 6f9144f8-b5a0-4f78-ad87-36d5aefec6d1) Rosen Publishing Group, Inc., The. (PowerKids Pr.).

Mullendore, Bryan L. Scott's Many Adventures. 2010. 54p. pap. 22.95 *(978-0-557-63648-8(5))* Lulu Pr., Inc.

Peep for Keeps. 2005. 43p. (J). 3.99 *(978-0-9763213-4-7(3))* OHC Group LLC.

Pringle, Cindy & Pringle, Kirby. Happy Tails: The Call of Nature. 2008. (ENG., Illus.). 32p. (J). (gr. 2-7). *(978-0-9777126-1-8(3))* Dogtown Artworks.

Santillo, LuAnn. Mike. Santillo, LuAnn, ed. 2003. (Half-Pint Kids Readers Ser.). (Illus.). 7p. (J). (gr. -1-1). pap. 1.00 *(978-1-59256-100-1(4))* Half-Pint Kids, Inc.

Sedita, Francesco. Miss Popularity Goes Camping. 2009. (ENG.). 142p. (J). lib. bdg. 15.38 *(978-1-4242-4383-9(1))* Fitzgerald Bks.

Seton, Ernest Thompson. Two Little Savages. 2011. (Dover Children's Classics Ser.). (ENG., Illus.). 320p. (J). (gr. 3-8). pap. 14.95 *(978-0-486-20985-2(7)*, 209857) Dover Pubns., Inc.

—Two Little "Savages" The Adventures of Two Boys Who Lived As American Indians. Seton, Ernest Thompson, illus. 2010. (ENG., Illus.). 313p. (J). (gr. 4-7). pap. 18.00 *(978-1-60419-033-5(7))* Axios Pr.

Thomes, William Henry. The Bushrangers a Yankee's Adventures During His Second Visit to Australia by William H Thomes. 2006. 420p. per. 26.99 *(978-1-4255-4567-3(X))* Michigan Publishing.

Walker, Lane. The Boss on Redemption Road. 2014. 176p. pap. 9.99 *(978-1-58169-563-2(2)*, Evergreen Pr.) Genesis Communications, Inc.

Wang, Adria. My World: My Outdoors. Nicholls, Paul, illus. 2005. (My World Bks.). 10p. (J). 4.95 *(978-1-58117-249-2(4)*, Intervisual/Piggy Toes) Bendon, Inc.

Wright, Caleb E. Marcus Blair A Story of Provincial Times. 2006. pap. 22.95 *(978-1-4286-6303-9(7))* Kessinger Publishing, LLC.

OUTDOOR SURVIVAL

see Wilderness Survival

OUTER BANKS (N.C.)—HISTORY

Gamble, Adam & Jasper, Mark. Good Night Outer Banks. Veno, Joe, illus. 2018. (Good Night Our World Ser.). 20p. (J). (— 1). bds. 9.95 *(978-1-60219-604-9(4))* Good Night Bks.

OUTER SPACE

Abbott, Simon, illus. 100 Questions about Outer Space: And All the Answers, Too! 2018. (100 Questions Ser.). (ENG.). 48p. (J). 7.99 *(978-1-4413-2617-1(0)*, dacc02d3-1a11-49e1-bbdd-d08555de9f53) Peter Pauper Pr. Inc.

Aldrin, Buzz. Look to the Stars. Minor, Wendell, illus. 2009. (ENG.). 40p. (J). (gr. 1-3). 18.99 *(978-0-399-24721-7(1)*, G.P. Putnam's Sons Books for Young Readers) Penguin Young Readers Group.

Allen, Kathy. Let's Draw Aliens & Spaceships with Crayola (r) ! Clark, Neil, illus. 2019. (Let's Draw with Crayola (r) ! Ser.). (ENG.). 32p. (J). (gr. -1-3). 29.32 *(978-1-5415-1103-3(4)*, 00325c19-485a-4586-867d-a18e89c13ed2); pap. 6.99 *(978-1-5415-4606-6(7)*, 28081bbf-d4af-4d9d-a604-b677f1677cc8) Lerner Publishing Group. (Lerner Pubns.).

Amson-Bradshaw, Georgia. Earth & Space, 1 vol. 2017. (Science in a Flash Ser.). (ENG.). 32p. (J). (gr. 5-5). pap. 11.50 *(978-1-5382-1487-9(3)*, 64480c70-b6f7-4502-a49c-badcffb49c16); lib. bdg. 28.27 *(978-1-5382-1392-6(3)*, 8edf34c0-8b65-4f79-880c-a576c6bba306) Stevens, Gareth Publishing LLLP.

Arlon, Penelope & Gordon-Harris, Tory. Planets. 2012. (J). lib. bdg. *(978-0-531-22957-6(2))* Scholastic, Inc.

AZ Books Staff. Amazing Space. Ivinskaya, Snezhana, ed. 2012. (Encyclopedia with Flaps Ser.). (ENG.). 22p. (J). (gr. 1-3). bds. 13.95 *(978-1-61889-150-1(2))* AZ Bks. LLC.

Becker, Helaine. National Geographic Kids Everything Space: Blast off for a Universe of Photos, Facts, & Fun! 2015. (National Geographic Kids Everything Ser.). (Illus.). 64p. (J). (gr. 3-7). pap. 12.99 *(978-1-4263-2074-3(4)*, National Geographic Kids) Disney Publishing Worldwide.

Becklake, Sue & Kelly, Miles. Space. Kelly, Richard, ed. 2017. (ENG., Illus.). 48p. (J). pap. 9.95 *(978-1-84810-911-7(3))* Miles Kelly Publishing, Ltd. GBR. Dist: Parkwest Pubns., Inc.

Berkowitz, Jacob. Out of This World: The Amazing Search for an Alien Earth. 2009. (Illus.). 40p. (J). (gr. 3-7). 16.95

(978-1-55453-197-4(7)) Kids Can Pr., Ltd. CAN. Dist: Hachette Bk. Group.

Beth, Georgia & Fielder, Heidi. Growing Plants in Space. rev. ed. 2019. (Smithsonian: Informational Text Ser.). (ENG., Illus.). 32p. (J). (gr. 2-3). pap. 10.99 *(978-1-4938-6670-0(2))* Teacher Created Materials, Inc.

Bow, James. Deep Space Extremes, 1 vol. 2008. (Extreme Nature Ser.). (ENG., Illus.). 32p. (J). (gr. 2-3). pap. *(978-0-7787-4522-8(8))* Crabtree Publishing Co.

Bowman, Donna H. What Is the Moon Made Of? And Other Questions Kids Have about Space, 1 vol. Lubach, Peter, illus. 2010. (Kids' Questions Ser.). (ENG.). 24p. (J). (gr. k-2). pap. 7.49 *(978-1-4048-6726-0(0)*, 115554, Picture Window Bks.) Capstone.

Britannica, Learning Library. Exploring Space. 2003. (Illus.). 64p. 14.95 *(978-1-59339-031-0(9))* Encyclopaedia Britannica, Inc.

Cain, Marie Mowery. Wide Open Space. 2013. (Big Books, Blue Ser.). (ENG & SPA., Illus.). 16p. pap. 33.00 *(978-1-59246-002-1(X))* Big Books, by George!

Canavan, Thomas. Why Are Black Holes Black? Questions & Answers about Space. 2013. (Science F. A. Q. Ser.). 32p. (gr. 3-6). 31.35 *(978-1-78212-395-8(4))* Arcturus Publishing GBR. Dist: Black Rabbit Bks.

Carson, Mary Kay. Exploring the Solar System: A History with 22 Activities. rev. ed. 2008. (For Kids Ser.: 25). (ENG., Illus.). 176p. (J). (gr. 4-7). pap. 19.99 *(978-1-55652-715-9(2))* Chicago Review Pr., Inc.

Coupper, Heather. Atlas Visual del Espacio. (Colección Atlas Visual). (SPA., Illus.). 64p. (YA). (gr. 5-8). *(978-84-216-1816-5(4)*, BU5067) Bruño, Editorial ESP. Dist: Lectorum Pubns., Inc.

Dakota, Heather. Space. Myers, Lawrence E., illus. 2008. 64p. (J). pap. *(978-0-545-08503-8(9))* Scholastic, Inc.

Daynes, Katie. Living in Space. Fox, Christyan & Pang, Alex, illus. 2003. (Usborne Beginners Ser.). 32p. (J). (gr. 1). lib. bdg. 12.99 *(978-1-58086-930-0(0)*, Usborne) EDC Publishing.

—See Inside Space. Allen, Peter, illus. 2009. (See Inside Board Bks). 16p. (J). (gr. 2). bds. 12.99 *(978-0-7945-2088-5(X)*, Usborne) EDC Publishing.

Daynes, Katie & Wray, Zoe. Life in Space. Fox, Christyan & Pang, Alex, illus. 2008. (Usborne Beginners Ser.). 32p. (J). *(978-0-545-06963-2(7))* Scholastic, Inc.

De la Bédoyère, Camilla & Kelly, Miles. Spot 50 Space. Kelly, Richard, ed. 2013. (Illus.). 56p. (J). pap. 9.95 *(978-1-84810-905-6(9))* Miles Kelly Publishing, Ltd. GBR. Dist: Parkwest Pubns., Inc.

DeSantis, Andrea, illus. Space Kids: An Introduction for Young Explorers. 2018. (ENG.). 40p. (J). (gr. 2). 24.95 *(978-3-89955-795-4(6))* Die Gestalten Verlag DEU. Dist: Ingram Publisher Services.

DiSiena, Laura Lyn & Eliot, Hannah. Saturn Could Sail: And Other Fun Facts. Oswald, Pete & Spurgeon, Aaron, illus. 2014. (Did You Know? Ser.). (ENG.). 32p. (J). (gr. -1-3). 17.99 *(978-1-4814-1429-6(1))*; pap. 7.99 *(978-1-4814-1428-9(3))* Little Simon. (Little Simon).

DK. Pop-Up Peekaboo! Space. 2019. (Pop-Up Peekaboo! Ser.). (ENG., Illus.). 12p. (J). (— 1). bds. 12.99 *(978-1-4654-7933-4(3)*, DK Children) Dorling Kindersley Publishing, Inc.

—Ultimate Sticker Book: Space: More Than 250 Reusable Stickers. 2016. (Ultimate Sticker Book Ser.). (ENG.). 32p. (J). (gr. k-3). pap. 6.99 *(978-1-4654-4881-1(0)*, DK Children) Dorling Kindersley Publishing, Inc.

Dorling Kindersley Publishing Staff. Sticker Encyclopedia Space. 2009. (Sticker Encyclopedias Ser.). (ENG.). 96p. (J). (gr. k-2). pap. 12.99 *(978-0-7566-5839-7(X)*, DK Children) Dorling Kindersley Publishing, Inc.

Dowswell, Paul. Mi Primera Enciclopedia del Espacio. 2004. (Titles in Spanish Ser.) Tr. of First Encyclopedia of Space. (SPA.). (J). pap. 9.95 *(978-0-7460-5075-0(5))* EDC Publishing.

—The Usborne Little Encyclopedia of Space. Bines, Gary & Hancock, David, illus. 2005. 64p. (J). (gr. -1-3). 6.95 *(978-0-7945-1091-6(4)*, Usborne) EDC Publishing.

Doyle, Bill. The Space Explorer's Guide to the Universe. Labat, Yancey C., illus. 2003. (Space University Ser.). 48p. (J). *(978-0-439-55739-9(9))* Scholastic, Inc.

Duhamel, Megan. Space. 2010. (Illus.). 16p. (J). *(978-0-545-13723-2(3))* Scholastic, Inc.

Dyer, Alan. Space. 2007. (Insiders Ser.). (ENG., Illus.). 64p. (J). (gr. 3-7). 19.99 *(978-1-4169-3860-6(5)*, Simon & Schuster Bks. For Young Readers) Simon & Schuster Bks. For Young Readers.

Earth & Space. (Illus.). (J). Date not set. 48p. 5.98 *(978-1-4054-0206-4(7))* 2003. 256p. 12.98 *(978-1-4054-1543-9(6))* Parragon, Inc.

Earth & Space, 10 vols. 2007. (Earth & Space Ser.). (ENG.). (J). (gr. 6-6). lib. bdg. 172.35 *(978-1-4042-1103-2(9)*, 454ff4c9-f56b-4996-ab5c-0538cecfeae3, Rosen Reference) Rosen Publishing Group, Inc., The.

Eboch, M. M., ed. Commercial Space Exploration, 1 vol. 2018. (Introducing Issues with Opposing Viewpoints Ser.). (ENG.). 120p. (gr. 7-10). 43.63 *(978-1-5345-0359-5(5)*, baebd8da-b43f-4728-bb2e-a205d425e90a) Greenhaven Publishing LLC.

Explore Outer Space: Set 2. 2013. (Explore Outer Space Ser.). 32p. (J). (gr. 3-6). 277.75 *(978-1-4777-1541-3(X))* Windmill Bks.

Ferrie, Chris. There Was a Black Hole That Swallowed the Universe. Batori, Susan, illus. 2019. 40p. (J). (gr. -1-3). 17.99 *(978-1-4926-8077-2(X))* Sourcebooks, Inc.

Flynn, Mike. Outer Space Explained, 1 vol. 2014. (Guide for Curious Minds Ser.). (ENG.). 151p. (J). (gr. 8-8). 42.41 *(978-1-4777-8128-9(5)*, e199e5c5-9611-4012-9033-e7dd10a6e31a, Rosen Young Adult) Rosen Publishing Group, Inc., The.

Ford, Harry & Barnham, Kay. Outer Space. 2003. (Knowledge Masters Ser.). (Illus.). 32p. (YA). pap. incl. cd-rom *(978-1-903954-09-6(6)*, Pavilion Children's Books) Pavilion Bks.

Fun Fact File: Space!, 12 vols. 2014. (Fun Fact File: Space! Ser.). (ENG.). 32p. (J). (gr. 2-3). 167.58 *(978-1-4824-0995-6(X)*, ad278efb-88cb-4b5d-a410-3ad33de5d910) Stevens, Gareth Publishing LLLP.

Gallagher, Belinda & Camilla, De La Bedoyere. Space: Identify & Record Your Sightings. Kelly, Richard, ed. 2017. (Illus.). 96p. (J). pap., instr.'s hndbk. ed. 9.95 *(978-1-78209-166-0(1))* Miles Kelly Publishing, Ltd. GBR. Dist: Parkwest Pubns., Inc.

Ganeri, Anita, et al. Earth & Space: Questions & Answers. 2012. (Illus.). 256p. (J). *(978-1-4351-4349-4(3))* Barnes & Noble, Inc.

The Geek's Guide to Space, 10 vols. 2017. (Geek's Guide to Space Ser.). (ENG.). 192p. (gr. 9-9). 231.35 *(978-1-4994-6664-5(1)*, f2d85375-6e2c-4fc4-ba4c-1ac30436e3af, Rosen Young Adult) Rosen Publishing Group, Inc., The.

Gitlin, Martin. Personal Space Travel. 2017. (21st Century Skills Innovation Library: Emerging Tech Ser.). (ENG., Illus.). 32p. (J). (gr. 4-8). lib. bdg. 32.07 *(978-1-63472-703-7(7)*, 210138) Cherry Lake Publishing.

Goldberg, Marc. If You Had to Draw a Universe for Me ... 50 Questions About the Universe, Matter & Scientists. 2018. (ENG., Illus.). ix, 112p. (J). pap. *(978-981-327-721-2(1))* World Scientific Publishing Co. Pte Ltd.

Goldstein, Margaret J. Garbage in Space: A Space Discovery Guide. 2017. (Space Discovery Guides). (ENG., Illus.). 48p. (J). (gr. 4-6). 31.99 *(978-1-5124-2590-1(7)*, de8456a6-c6ec-4c0f-9995-6893b50a2be5, Lerner Pubns.) Lerner Publishing Group.

Grego, Peter. My Little Book of Space. 2014. (Illus.). 64p. (J). *(978-1-4351-5530-5(0))* Barnes & Noble, Inc.

Gregoire, Maryellen. Things in Space. 2011. (Wonder Readers Emergent Level Ser.). (ENG.). 8p. (gr. -1-1). pap. 35.94 *(978-1-4296-8235-0(3)*, Capstone Pr.) Capstone.

Hantula, Richard & Asimov, Isaac. Asteroides (Asteroids), 1 vol. 2003. (Isaac Asimov's Biblioteca Del Universo Del Siglo XXI (Isaac Asimov's 21st Century Library of the Universe) Ser.) Tr. of Asteroids. (SPA., Illus.). 32p. (gr. 3-5). lib. bdg. 28.67 *(978-0-8368-3853-4(X)*, e7081b8a-3755-4cd1-a05e-618a7dc0d3be, Gareth Stevens Learning Library) Stevens, Gareth Publishing LLLP.

Harrison, Paul. Space. (Up Close Ser.). 24p. (gr. 3-3). 2009. 47.90 *(978-1-60854-704-3(3)*, PowerKids Pr.) 2007. (ENG., Illus.). (J). lib. bdg. 28.93 *(978-1-4042-4221-0(X)*, bb169a83-a8ed-4f24-99a9-b55990fbeb48) Rosen Publishing Group, Inc., The.

Hartson, Tamara. Night Skies of Canada, 1 vol. 2018. (Super Explorers Ser.). (ENG., Illus.). 64p. (J). pap. 6.99 *(978-1-926700-86-1(4)*, 32209b59-500b-4d48-9fde-52b3e05be1b4) Blue Bike Bks. CAN. Dist: Lone Pine Publishing USA.

—Planets, 1 vol. 2018. (Mega Machines Ser.). (ENG., Illus.). 64p. (J). pap. 6.99 *(978-1-926700-88-5(0)*, 9d23404f-6062-4abf-bf4b-368c290af7e8) Blue Bike Bks. CAN. Dist: Lone Pine Publishing USA.

—Space, 1 vol. 2017. (Super Explorers Ser.). (ENG., Illus.). 64p. (J). pap. 6.99 *(978-1-926700-72-4(4)*, ad288c7a-bacc-497a-b692-6a7421af7fd0) Blue Bike Bks. CAN. Dist: Lone Pine Publishing USA.

Haslam, Andrew, et al. Space. (Make It Work! Ser.). (Illus.). 48p. (J). pap. 7.99 *(978-0-590-24690-3(9))* Scholastic, Inc.

Hersey, John, illus. Amazing Space: Go on a Journey to the Edge of the Universe. 2019. (ENG.). 48p. (J). (gr. 2-7). 19.99 *(978-1-78312-393-3(1))* Carlton Bks., Ltd. GBR. Dist: Two Rivers Distribution.

Hirschmann, Kris. Space & the Planets. Bollinger, Peter, illus. 2003. (Magic School Bus Science Fact Finder Ser.). (ENG.). 96p. (J). (gr. 3-6). 16.19 *(978-0-439-38175-8(4))* Scholastic, Inc.

Hofer, Charles. Spacecraft, 1 vol. 2007. (World's Fastest Machines Ser.). (ENG., Illus.). 24p. (gr. 2-3). lib. bdg. 26.27 *(978-1-4042-4178-7(7)*, dd6386e5-aacf-44eb-9c62-fef0e351ba99, PowerKids Pr.) Rosen Publishing Group, Inc., The.

Howell, Laura & Rogers, Kirsteen. Earth & Space. 2004. (Library of Science Ser.). 64p. (J). lib. bdg. 17.95 *(978-1-58086-373-5(6))* EDC Publishing.

Hubbard, Ben & Langley, Andrew. Adventures in Space. 2015. (Adventures in Space Ser.). (ENG.). 48p. (J). (gr. 4-6). 143.96 *(978-1-4846-2518-7(8)*, 23580, Heinemann) Capstone.

Jackson, Tom. What's Inside a Black Hole? Theories about Space Phenomena, 1 vol. 2018. (Beyond the Theory: Science of the Future Ser.). (ENG.). 48p. (gr. 5-6). lib. bdg. 33.60 *(978-1-5382-2667-4(7)*, 84ded446-50dd-45d5-bba7-f372fce9496a) Stevens, Gareth Publishing LLLP.

Jefferis, David. Space Colonists. 2017. (Our Future in Space Ser.). (Illus.). 32p. (J). (gr. 5-5). *(978-0-7787-3534-2(6))*; pap. *(978-0-7787-3538-0(9))* Crabtree Publishing Co.

—Space Tourists. 2017. (Our Future in Space Ser.). (Illus.). 32p. (J). (gr. 5-5). *(978-0-7787-3536-6(2))*; pap. *(978-0-7787-3548-9(6))* Crabtree Publishing Co.

—Space Workers. 2017. (Our Future in Space Ser.). (Illus.). 32p. (J). (gr. 5-5). *(978-0-7787-3537-3(0))*; pap. *(978-0-7787-3549-6(4))* Crabtree Publishing Co.

—Star Spotters: Telescopes & Observatories. 2008. (Exploring Our Solar System Ser.). (ENG., Illus.). 32p. (J). (gr. 4-9). pap. *(978-0-7787-3742-1(X))* Crabtree Publishing Co.

Jones, Rob Lloyd. Look Inside Space. 2012. (Look Inside Board Bks). 14p. (J). bds. 14.99 *(978-0-7945-3282-6(9)*, Usborne) EDC Publishing.

Kelley, K. C. Space. 2018. (Spot Awesome Nature Ser.). (ENG.). 16p. (J). (gr. -1-2). pap. 7.99 *(978-1-68152-249-4(7)*, 14825) Amicus.

Keppeler, Jill. 20 Fun Facts about Astronomy, 1 vol. 2017. (Fun Fact File: Earth Science Ser.). (ENG.). 32p. (J). (gr. 2-3). pap. 11.50 *(978-1-5382-1173-1(4)*, 78e1f8bc-ab36-4dea-a9ff-0d82b32c2ff2) Stevens, Gareth Publishing LLLP.

Kopp, Megan. Unlocking the Secrets of the Solar System. 2019. (Mission: Space Science Ser.). (Illus.). 48p. (J). (gr. 5-5). *(978-0-7787-5396-4(4))*; pap. *(978-0-7787-5407-7(3))* Crabtree Publishing Co.

Kurtz, Kevin. Cutting-Edge Space Tourism. 2019. (Searchlight Books (tm) — New Frontiers of Space Ser.). (ENG., Illus.). 32p. (J). (gr. 3-5). pap. 9.99 *(978-1-5415-7486-1(9)*, c0323055-a890-4581-8d18-e493505a8663); lib. bdg. 30.65 *(978-1-5415-5744-4(1)*, 41826025-3a04-4f45-ac6e-e861b4f83121) Lerner Publishing Group. (Lerner Pubns.).

LaBaff, Stephanie. Draw Aliens & Space Objects in 4 Easy Steps: Then Write a Story, 1 vol. 2012. (Drawing in 4 Easy Steps Ser.). (ENG., Illus.). 48p. (gr. 3-3). lib. bdg. 27.93 *(978-0-7660-3841-7(6)*, fb4abb06-e1ce-4ca3-bab3-1a88c990b59b) Enslow Publishing, LLC.

Launch into Space!, 12 vols. 2015. (Launch into Space! Ser.). (ENG.). 32p. (J). (gr. 3-4). lib. bdg. 161.58 *(978-0-7660-6682-3(7)*, f43e1365-3dea-4305-8ed7-716f8c102688) Enslow Publishing, LLC.

Let's Find Out! Space, 24 vols. 2014. (Let's Find Out! Space Science Ser.). (ENG.). 32p. (J). (gr. 2-3). 312.72 *(978-1-62275-757-2(2)*, 9d15a01e-bb30-477a-b520-13402a3782fe) Rosen Publishing Group, Inc., The.

Little & Large Sticker Activity - Space. 2006. (J). 3.99 *(978-1-933581-36-1(0))* Byeway Bks.

Loh-Hagan, Virginia. Lost in Space Hacks. 2019. (Could You Survive? Ser.). (ENG.). 32p. (J). (gr. 4-8). pap. 14.21 *(978-1-5341-5069-0(2)*, 213583); (Illus.). lib. bdg. 32.07 *(978-1-5341-4783-6(7)*, 213582) Cherry Lake Publishing. (45th Parallel Press).

Looking at Space. (Jump Ser.). 36p. (J). (gr. 2-7). pap. *(978-1-882210-20-6(4))* Action Publishing, Inc.

Martin, Ruth. Little Explorers: Outer Space. Sanders, Allan, illus. 2016. (Little Explorers Ser.). (ENG.). 18p. (J). (gr. -1-3). 10.99 *(978-1-4998-0250-4(1))* Little Bee Books Inc.

McGill, Jordan, ed. Space. 2011. (gr. 3-5). (J). pap. 13.95 *(978-1-61690-865-2(3)*, AV2 by Weigl); (Illus.). 32p. (YA). 28.55 *(978-1-61690-859-1(9))* Weigl Pubs., Inc.

Media, Cont. Sun Moon Stars. 2008. (ENG., Illus.). 48p. (YA). 12.99 *(978-1-931703-09-3(4))* Creative Publishing Consultants.

Miles, Lisa. Astronomy & Space. 2010. (Complete Bks). 96p. (J). pap. 14.99 *(978-0-7945-2626-9(8)*, Usborne) EDC Publishing.

Miller, Ron. Space Exploration. 2007. (Space Innovations Ser.). (ENG., Illus.). 112p. (gr. 6-8). lib. bdg. 31.93 *(978-0-8225-7155-1(2))* Lerner Publishing Group.

Minter, Laura & Williams, Tia. The Space Craft Book: 15 Things a Space Fan Can't Do Without! 2018. (ENG., Illus.). 64p. pap. 9.95 *(978-1-78494-365-3(7)*, GM0309) GMC Distribution GBR. Dist: Ingram Publisher Services.

Morris, Ting & Morris, Neil. Space. Turvey, Raymond, illus. 2006. (Sticky Fingers Ser.). 32p. (J). lib. bdg. 27.10 *(978-1-59771-032-9(6))* Sea-To-Sea Pubns.

Murtagh, Ciaran. Collins Big Cat Phonics for Letters & Sounds - Space Science: Band 07/Turquoise, Bd. 7. 2018. (Collins Big Cat Phonics Ser.). (ENG., Illus.). 24p. (J). (gr. 1-2). pap. 6.99 *(978-0-00-825181-9(9))* HarperCollins Pubs. Ltd. GBR. Dist: Independent Pubs. Group.

Musgrave, Ruth A. National Geographic Kids Little Kids First Board Book: Space. 2019. (First Board Bks.). (Illus.). 26p. (J). (gr. -1 — 1). bds. 7.99 *(978-1-4263-3314-9(5)*, National Geographic Kids) Disney Publishing Worldwide.

Nardo, Don. Destined for Space: Our Story of Exploration, 1 vol. 2012. (Smithsonian Ser.). (ENG.). 64p. (J). (gr. 2-6). pap. 8.95 *(978-1-4296-8024-0(5)*, 118356, Capstone Pr.) Capstone.

National Geographic Learning. Reading Expeditions (Science: Earth Science): Exploring Space. 2006. (Nonfiction Reading & Writing Workshops Ser.). (ENG., Illus.). 32p. (J). pap. 18.95 *(978-0-7922-8870-1(X))* CENGAGE Learning.

Nicolson, Cynthia Pratt & Bourgeois, Paulette. The Jumbo Book of Space. Nicolson, Cynthia Pratt & Slavin, Bill, illus. 2007. (Jumbo Bks.). 208p. (J). 17.95 *(978-1-55453-020-5(2))* Kids Can Pr., Ltd. CAN. Dist: Hachette Bk. Group.

O'Hearn, Michael. Awesome Space Robots. 2013. (Robots Ser.). (ENG.). 32p. (J). (gr. 3-4). pap. 50.74 *(978-1-62065-779-9(1)*, 19361, Capstone Pr.) Capstone.

O'Brien, Eileen. Space. 2008. (Discovery Nature Ser.). 48p. (YA). (gr. 3-18). 8.99 *(978-0-7945-2242-1(4)*, Usborne) EDC Publishing.

Ortler, Brett. Outer Space Activity Book. Juliano, Phil, illus. 2017. (Color & Learn Ser.). (ENG.). 64p. (J). (gr. k-5). pap. 6.95 *(978-1-59193-708-1(6)*, Adventure Pubns.) AdventureKEEN.

Outer Space. Date not set. (Illus.). 12p. (J). 3.98 *(978-1-4054-0498-3(1))* Parragon, Inc.

Outer Space. 2014. (Ken Jennings' Junior Genius Guides). (ENG., Illus.). 160p. (J). (gr. 3-5). pap. 9.99 *(978-1-4814-0170-8(X)*, Little Simon) Little Simon.

Oxlade, Chris. Why Why Why... Do Astronauts Float in Space? 2010. (Why Why Why Ser.). 32p. (J). (gr. 1-3). lib. bdg. 18.95 *(978-1-4222-1578-4(4))* Mason Crest.

Parisi, Anthony. First Look at Space. Pindroh, Paula, illus. 2011. (ENG.). 16p. (J). *(978-1-60727-225-0(3)*, Blackbirch Pr., Inc.) Soundprints.

Parker. Space Mysteries - Space Busters. 2004. (YA). pap. 48.30 *(978-1-4109-0293-1(5))* Harcourt Schl. Pubs.

Penguin Books Staff, ed. Space. (Learners Ser.). (Illus.). 48p. (J). 3.50 *(978-0-7214-1702-8(7)*, Dutton Juvenile) Penguin Publishing Group.

Ponto, Joanna & Boekhoff, P. M. Kids Love Space Crafts, 1 vol. 2018. (Kids Love Crafts Ser.). (ENG.). 32p. (J). (gr. 3-3). 26.93 *(978-1-9785-0200-0(1)*, 4658cdb5-9c3c-46a2-9881-feeffaefe474) Enslow Publishing, LLC.

Pulliam, Christine & Daniels, Patricia. Space Encyclopedia: A Tour of Our Solar System & Beyond. Aguilar, David A., illus. 2013. 191p. (J). *(978-1-4263-1629-6(1))* National Geographic Society.

¿Que Hay en el Espacio? (Coleccion Primeros Pasos en la Ciencia). (SPA., Illus.). (J). (gr. 1-3). pap. *(978-950-724-099-7(3)*, LMA8217) Lumen ARG. Dist: Lectorum Pubns., Inc.

Red Bird Press Staff. Space. 2004. (Mission Xtreme 3D Ser.). 18p. (J). pap. 5.95 *(978-1-902626-62-8(1))* Red Bird Publishing GBR. Dist: Weatherhill, Inc.

Redfern, Nick. True Stories of Space Exploration Conspiracies, 1 vol. 2014. (Off the Record! Ser.). (ENG.). 248p. (YA). (gr. 7-7). 41.47 *(978-1-4777-7833-3(0)*, 51f7c5d4-2961-4920-9bc1-f1e3cdf2c294) Rosen Publishing Group, Inc., The.

Ripley's Entertainment Inc. Zoom! Graziano, John, illus. 2012. (Ripley's Shout Outs Ser.: 2). (ENG.). 96p. (J). (gr. 2-5). pap. 4.99 *(978-0-545-38076-8(6))* Scholastic, Inc.

Romaine, Garret. Solar System, Space Rocks, & Beyond: Exploring the Wonders of Space Particles & Meteorites. 2018. (Geology Lab for Kids Ser.). (ENG., Illus.). 32p. (J). (gr. 3-6). lib. bdg. 27.99 *(978-1-63159-457-1(5)*, 56468e7a-d008-44da-aa7c-7ad266addf08, Quarry Bks.) Quarto Publishing Group USA.

Rooney, Anne. A Math Journey Through Space. 2014. (Go Figure! Ser.). (ENG., Illus.). 32p. (J). (gr. 4-4). *(978-0-7787-0730-1(X))* Crabtree Publishing Co.

Royston, Angela. Space. 2015. (Research on the Edge Ser.). (ENG., Illus.). 32p. (J). (gr. 3-8). 31.35 *(978-1-62588-158-8(4)*, 19356, Smart Apple Media) Black Rabbit Bks.

Roytman, Arkady & Coloring Books Staff. Outer Space. 2011. (Dover Space Coloring Bks.). (ENG., Illus.). 32p. (J). (gr. 3-5). pap. 6.99 *(978-0-486-48392-4(4)*, 483924) Dover Pubns., Inc.

Roza, Greg. Space Math. 2009. (Reading Room Collection 2 Ser.). 24p. (gr. 3-4). 42.50 *(978-1-60851-989-7(9)*, PowerKids Pr.) Rosen Publishing Group, Inc., The.

Rustad, Martha E. H. Exploring Space. 2012. (Exploring Space Ser.). (ENG.). 24p. (gr. k-1). pap. 250.20 *(978-1-4296-8333-3(3)*, Capstone Pr.) Capstone.

Samuel, Nigel. The 10 Coolest Wonders of the Universe. 2008. (Illus.). (J). 14.99 *(978-1-55448-490-4(1))* Scholastic Library Publishing.

Science Readers Staff & Jankowski, Connie. From Hubble to Hubble: Astromers & Outer Space, 1 vol. rev. ed. 2007. (Science: Informational Text Ser.). (ENG., Illus.). 32p. (gr. 4-6). pap. 12.99 *(978-0-7439-0564-0(4))* Teacher Created Materials, Inc.

—The Wonder of Outer Space, 1 vol. rev. ed. 2007. (Science: Informational Text Ser.). (ENG., Illus.). 32p. (gr. 4-6). pap. 12.99 *(978-0-7439-0563-3(6))* Teacher Created Materials, Inc.

Secrets of Space, 3 vols. lib. bdg. 50.94 *(978-0-8050-5022-6(1)*, Twenty-First Century Bks.) Lerner Publishing Group.

Smith, A. Book of Astronomy & Space. 2004. (Complete Bks.). (SPA., Illus.). 96p. (J). lib. bdg. 22.95 *(978-1-58086-385-8(X))* EDC Publishing.

Spilsbury, Louise. Projects with Space, 1 vol. 2014. (Make & Learn Ser.). (ENG., Illus.). 32p. (J). (gr. 4-4). lib. bdg. 29.27 *(978-1-4777-7177-8(8)*, 231dccaa-d3a6-4680-b796-a5a23f048391, PowerKids Pr.) Rosen Publishing Group, Inc., The.

Spilsbury, Richard & Spilsbury, Louise. In Space, 1 vol. 2016. (Science on Patrol Ser.). (ENG.). 48p. (J). (gr. 4-5). pap. 15.05 *(978-1-4824-5972-2(8)*, ef854f9b-11a3-4155-8d98-1d265f20cd4a) Stevens, Gareth Publishing LLLP.

Stott, Carole. Eye Wonder: Space: Open Your Eyes to a World of Discovery. 2016. (Eye Wonder Ser.). (ENG., Illus.). 56p. (J). (gr. k-4). 10.99 *(978-1-4654-1856-2(3)*, DK Children) Dorling Kindersley Publishing, Inc.

—Mission: Space: Explore the Galaxy. 2016. (Illus.). 128p. (J). *(978-1-4654-5376-1(8))* Dorling Kindersley Publishing, Inc.

The Sun. (Eyes on Adventure Ser.). (J). 32p. (gr. 1). pap. *(978-1-882210-62-6(X))*; 42p. (gr. 4-8). pap. *(978-1-882210-49-7(2))* Action Publishing, Inc.

The Sun. 2009. (FACT ATLAS Ser.). 72p. (J). (gr. 3-7). pap. 13.99 *(978-0-8437-1896-6(X))* Hammond World Atlas Corp.

Swanson, Jennifer. Astronaut-Aquanaut: How Space Science & Sea Science Interact. 2018. (Illus.). 96p. (J). (gr. 3-7). 18.99 *(978-1-4263-2867-1(2)*, National Geographic Kids) Disney Publishing Worldwide.

Swaiting, Todd. What Is Space Junk?, 1 vol. 2018. (Space Mysteries Ser.). (ENG.). 32p. (gr. 2-3). 29.27 *(978-1-5382-1967-6(0)*, 62837891-850b-442a-9b72-e24a846c4067) Stevens, Gareth Publishing LLLP.

Tejido, Jomike. Jumbo Stickers for Little Hands: Outer Space: Includes 75 Stickers. 2018. (Jumbo Stickers for Little Hands Ser.). (ENG., Illus.). 24p. (J). (gr. -1-k). pap. 7.95 *(978-1-63322-547-3(X)*, 302045, Moondance) Quarto Publishing Group USA.

Time for Kids Editors. Space. 2014. (Time for Kids X-Why-Z Ser.). (ENG., Illus.). 96p. (J). (gr. -1-1). 14.95 *(978-1-61893-126-9(1)*, Time For Kids) Time Inc. Bks.

—Stellar Space. 2014. (Time for Kids Book of Why Ser.). (ENG., Illus.). 48p. (J). (gr. 3-17). pap. 4.99 *(978-1-60320-985-4(9)*, Time For Kids) Time Inc. Bks.

Wadsworth, Pamela. Amser a Gofod. 2005. (WEL., Illus.). 24p. pap. *(978-1-85596-241-5(1))* Dref Wen.

—Rhagor Am Amser a Gofod. 2005. (WEL., Illus.). 24p. pap. *(978-1-85596-242-2(X))* Dref Wen.

Walsh, Kenneth. Outer Space, 1 vol. 2nd rev. ed. 2011. (TIME for KIDS(r): Informational Text Ser.). (ENG.). 28p. (gr. 2-3). pap. 10.99 *(978-1-4333-3632-4(4))* Teacher Created Materials, Inc.

Walsh, Kieran. Space Math. 2005. (Math & My World Ser.). (Illus.). 48p. (J). (gr. 4-6). lib. bdg. 20.95 *(978-1-59515-494-1(9))* Rourke Educational Media.

Willett, Edward. Space Q&a. 2014. (Science Discovery Ser.). (ENG., Illus.). 48p. (J). (gr. 4-7). lib. bdg. 28.55 *(978-1-4896-0692-1(0)*, AV2 by Weigl) Weigl Pubs., Inc.

Williams, Dave. Destination: Space. 2019. (Dr. Dave Astronaut Ser.). (ENG.). 52p. (J). (gr. 4-6). 22.96 *(978-1-64310-805-6(0))* Penworthy Co., LLC, The.

Williams, Dave & Cunti, Loredana. Destination: Space. 2018. (Dr. Dave - Astronaut Ser.). (Illus.). 52p. (J). (gr. 4-7). pap. 12.95 *(978-1-77321-057-5(2))* Annick Pr., Ltd. CAN. Dist: Publishers Group West (PGW).

Wolny, Philip. Weapons Satellites. 2009. (Library of Satellites Ser.). 64p. (gr. 5-8). 58.50 *(978-1-60853-834-8(6)*, Rosen Reference) Rosen Publishing Group, Inc., The.

World Book, Inc. Staff, contrib. by. Human Space Exploration. 2010. (J). *(978-0-7166-9543-1(X))* World Bk., Inc.

—Zac Newton Investigates Spectacular Space. 2018. (J). *(978-0-7166-4061-5(9))* World Bk., Inc.

Wynne, Patricia J. & Silver, Donald M. My First Book about Outer Space. 2015. (Dover Science for Kids Coloring Bks.).

M N O

(ENG.). 48p. (J). (gr. 3-8). pap. 5.99 *(978-0-486-78329-1(4)*, 783294) Dover Pubns., Inc.

OUTER SPACE—COMMUNICATION

see Interstellar Communication

OUTER SPACE—EXPLORATION

Alexander, Florence & Alexander, Stanley. Space Exploration. l.t. ed. 2003. (Come with Me & See Ser.). (ENG & SPA., Illus.). 32p. (J). 7.99 *(978-0-915960-75-0(3))* Ebon Research Systems Publishing, LLC.

Allan, John. Journey to Mars. 2019. (Math Adventures (Step 1) Ser.). (ENG., Illus.). 32p. (J). (gr. 1-3). lib. bdg. 29.32 *(978-1-912108-23-7(2)*, ff5cfee6-9b6a-4353-b54c-fa4a04ca2719, Hungry Tomato (r)) Lerner Publishing Group.

Anderson, AnnMarie. Satellite Space Mission (the Magic School Bus Rides Again) Artful Doodlers Ltd., illus. 2018. (Magic School Bus Rides Again Ser.: 4). (ENG.). 96p. (J). (gr. 1-3). pap. 5.99 *(978-1-338-26251-3(3))* Scholastic, Inc.

Anderson, Clayton. A Is for Astronaut: Blasting Through the Alphabet. Brundage, Scott, illus. 2018. (ENG.). 32p. (J). (gr. 1-4). 16.99 *(978-1-58536-396-4(0)*, 204409) Sleeping Bear Pr.

Arnold, Tedd. Fly Guy Presents: Space. 2013. (Fly Guy Presents Ser.). lib. bdg. 13.55 *(978-0-606-32353-6(8))* Turtleback.

Bailey, Diane. The Future of Space Exploration. 2012. (What's Next? Ser.). (Illus.). 48p. (J). (gr. 5-12). 23.95 *(978-1-60818-223-7(1)*, Creative Education) Creative Co., The.

Bailey, Gerry. Space Challenge, 1 vol. 2011. (Planet SOS Ser.). (ENG., Illus.). 48p. (J). (gr. 4-5). pap. 15.05 *(978-1-4339-4983-8(0)*, d67e6b5c-246b-4c2d-80a1-4c7443aeedd9, Gareth Stevens Learning Library) Stevens, Gareth Publishing LLLP.

Baker, David. Satellites. 2008. (Exploring Space Ser.). (Illus.). 32p. (J). (gr. 4-6). lib. bdg. 26.00 *(978-1-59036-777-3(4))* Weigl Pubs., Inc.

—The Shuttle. 2008. (Exploring Space Ser.). (Illus.). 32p. (J). (gr. 4-6). lib. bdg. 26.00 *(978-1-59036-767-4(7))* Weigl Pubs., Inc.

Baker, David & Kissock, Heather. The International Space Station. 2016. (Illus.). 32p. (J). *(978-1-4896-5824-1(6)*, AV2 by Weigl) Weigl Pubs., Inc.

—Rockets. 2016. (Illus.). 32p. (J). *(978-1-4896-5821-0(1)*, AV2 by Weigl) Weigl Pubs., Inc.

—Satellites. 2008. (Exploring Space Ser.). (Illus.). 32p. (J). (gr. 4-6). pap. 9.95 *(978-1-59036-778-0(2))* Weigl Pubs., Inc.

—The Shuttle. 2008. (Exploring Space Ser.). (Illus.). 32p. (J). (gr. 4-6). pap. 9.95 *(978-1-59036-768-1(5))* Weigl Pubs., Inc.

Banquieri, Eduardo. Space. 2005. (Our Planet Ser.). (Illus.). 32p. (gr. 4-6). lib. bdg. 28.00 *(978-0-7910-9009-1(4)*, Chelsea Clubhse.) Infobase Holdings, Inc.

Barchers, Suzanne I. Revolution in Space, 1 vol. 2010. (It Works! Ser.). (ENG.). 32p. (gr. 3-3). 31.21 *(978-0-7614-4377-3(0)*, ba8ed6a1-c3a6-424a-b08c-e9a4b66a6d69) Cavendish Square Publishing LLC.

Basher, Simon. Basher Basics: Space Exploration. Basher, Simon, illus. 2019. (Basher Basics Ser.). (ENG., Illus.). 64p. (J). 12.99 *(978-0-7534-7507-2(3)*, 900201812); pap. 8.99 *(978-0-7534-7506-5(5)*, 900201771) Roaring Brook Pr. (Kingfisher).

Bellisario, Gina. To the Stars! Moran, Mike, illus. 2017. (Cloverleaf Books (tm) — Space Adventures Ser.). (ENG.). 24p. (J). (gr. k-2). 25.32 *(978-1-5124-2537-6(0)*, 4b03fa2e-d854-4efa-8c3f-68749cf82c18); E-Book 38.65 *(978-1-5124-3896-3(0)*, 9781512438963); E-Book 38.65 *(978-1-5124-2834-6(5))* Lerner Publishing Group. (Millbrook Pr.).

Block, Dakota. Exploring the Solar System, 1 vol. 2012. (Exploring Earth & Space Ser.). (ENG., Illus.). 24p. (J). (gr. 1-2). 26.27 *(978-1-4488-8572-5(8)*, 0fa49534-491c-44f5-b5df-f9eca902d269, PowerKids Pr.) Rosen Publishing Group, Inc., The.

Bortz, Fred. Envisioning Outer Space: Where Science & Fiction Meet. 2015. (J). *(978-1-4677-6305-9(5))*; lib. bdg. *(978-1-4677-3740-1(2))* Twenty First Century Bks.

Bow, James. Deep Space Extremes. 2008. (Extreme Nature Ser.). (ENG., Illus.). 32p. (J). (gr. 2-4). lib. bdg. *(978-0-7787-4505-1(8))* Crabtree Publishing Co.

—Space Entrepreneurs. 2018. (Science & Technology Start-Up Stars Ser.). (ENG., Illus.). 32p. (J). (gr. 5-5). *(978-0-7787-4423-8(X))* Crabtree Publishing Co.

Braun, Eric. Awesome, Disgusting, Unusual Facts about Space. 2018. (Our Gross, Awesome World Ser.). (ENG.). 24p. (J). (gr. 4-6). pap. 8.99 *(978-1-64466-308-0(2)*, 12527); (Illus.). lib. bdg. 28.50 *(978-1-68072-613-8(7)*, 12526) Black Rabbit Bks. (Hi Jinx).

—Beurk! le Livre Différent et Fascinant Sur L'espace. 2018. (Notre Monde: dégoûtant Mais Génial! Ser.). (FRE.). 24p. (J). (gr. 4-6). *(978-1-77092-451-2(5)*, 12586, Hi Jinx) Black Rabbit Bks.

Bredeson, Carmen & Dyson, Marianne. Astronauts Explore the Galaxy, 1 vol. 2015. (Launch into Space! Ser.). (ENG.). 32p. (gr. 3-4). pap. 11.52 *(978-0-7660-6813-1(7)*, 00d8f81b-f083-40b8-973d-f9b231a12e9f); (Illus.). 26.93 *(978-0-7660-6815-5(3)*, f403da6b-59be-4669-b4df-051d43179460) Enslow Publishing, LLC.

—Exploring the Solar System, 1 vol. 2015. (Launch into Space! Ser.). (ENG.). 32p. (gr. 3-4). pap. 11.52 *(978-0-7660-6825-4(0)*, 4b64b9fb-0a7e-440c-b8c2-341749f50b25); (Illus.). 26.93 *(978-0-7660-6827-8(7)*, ed937177-22ca-436f-8a1b-517879459bec) Enslow Publishing, LLC.

Bright, Michael. Journey into Space, 1 vol. 2017. (Planet Earth Ser.). (ENG.). 32p. (gr. 5-5). 27.93 *(978-1-5081-5393-1(0)*, 9957189a-809e-433e-9c58-a44b80a877cd, PowerKids Pr.) Rosen Publishing Group, Inc., The.

Brownell, Richard. Space Exploration, 1 vol. 2012. (World History Ser.). (ENG., illus.). 96p. (gr. 7-7). lib. bdg. 41.53 *(978-1-4205-0875-8(X)*, b8f4ade5-2bdd-4146-9ae3-68d833d9011f, Lucent Pr.) Greenhaven Publishing LLC.

Buckley, James, Jr. Space Exploration, Vol. 7. 2016. (Solar System Ser.: Vol. 7). (ENG., Illus.). 48p. (J). (gr. 5-8). 20.95 *(978-1-4222-3644-4(7))* Mason Crest.

Carlson-Berne, Emma. Totally Wacky Facts about Exploring Space. 2015. (Mind Benders Ser.). (ENG., Illus.). 112p. (J). (gr. 3-6). lib. bdg. 23.99 *(978-1-4914-6524-0(7)*, 129023, Capstone Pr.) Capstone.

Carroll, Jillian. Hot Spot. 2003. (J). pap. *(978-1-58417-235-2(5))*; lib. bdg. *(978-1-58417-234-5(7))* Lake Street Pubs.

—Zoom Around a Moon. 2003. (J). pap. *(978-1-58417-241-3(X))*; lib. bdg. *(978-1-58417-240-6(1))* Lake Street Pubs.

Carson, Mary Kay. Mission to Pluto: The First Visit to an Ice Dwarf & the Kuiper Belt. 2017. (Scientists in the Field Ser.). (ENG., Illus.). 80p. (J). (gr. 5-7). 18.99 *(978-0-544-41671-0(6)*, 1594758, Clarion Bks.) HarperCollins Pubs.

Cerullo, Mary M. & Nardo, Don. Smithsonian. 2012. (Smithsonian Ser.). (ENG.). (gr. 2-6). pap. 107.40 *(978-1-4296-8526-9(3))* Capstone.

Clarke, Penny. The Story of the Exploration of Space. Antram, David et al, illus. 2013. 64p. (J). *(978-1-4351-5030-0(9))* Barnes & Noble, Inc.

Clay, Kathryn. Astronaut in Training. 2017. (Little Astronauts Ser.). (ENG., Illus.). 32p. (J). (gr. -1-2). lib. bdg. 28.65 *(978-1-5157-3660-8(1)*, 133645, Capstone Pr.) Capstone.

—Living in Space. 2017. (Little Astronauts Ser.). (ENG., Illus.). 32p. (J). (gr. -1-2). lib. bdg. 28.65 *(978-1-5157-3657-8(1)*, 133642, Capstone Pr.) Capstone.

—Space Flights. 2017. (Little Astronauts Ser.). (ENG., Illus.). 32p. (J). (gr. -1-2). lib. bdg. 28.65 *(978-1-5157-3659-2(8)*, 133644, Capstone Pr.) Capstone.

—Spacewalks. 2017. (Little Astronauts Ser.). (ENG., Illus.). 32p. (J). (gr. -1-2). lib. bdg. 28.65 *(978-1-5157-3658-5(X)*, 133643, Capstone Pr.) Capstone.

Cole, Joanna. Lost in the Solar System. Degen, Bruce, illus. 2010. (Magic School Bus Ser.). (ENG.). (J). (gr. 2-5). audio compact disk 18.99 *(978-0-545-22337-9(7))* Scholastic, Inc.

Collins, Ailynn. Probe Power: How Space Probes Do What Humans Can't. 2019. (Future Space Ser.). (ENG., Illus.). 32p. (J). (gr. 3-9). pap. 7.95 *(978-1-5435-7518-7(8)*, 141049); lib. bdg. 28.65 *(978-1-5435-7269-8(3)*, 140600) Capstone.

Countdown to Space, 40 bks. , Set. (Illus.). (YA). (gr. 4-10). lib. bdg. 758.00 *(978-0-89490-562-9(7))* Enslow Publishing, LLC.

(Del) Space Mysteries: Set 2. 2013. (Space Mysteries Ser.). 32p. (J). (gr. 2-5). 279.80 *(978-1-4824-0003-8(0))* Stevens, Gareth Publishing LLLP.

Dickmann, Nancy. Exploring Beyond the Solar System, 1 vol. 2015. (Spectacular Space Science Ser.). (ENG., Illus.). 48p. (J). (gr. 5-6). 33.47 *(978-1-4994-3641-9(6)*, c661c4b7-cd32-45d1-9413-c0fe5359a666, Rosen Central) Rosen Publishing Group, Inc., The.

—Exploring Comets, Asteroids, & Other Objects in Space, 1 vol. 2015. (Spectacular Space Science Ser.). (ENG., Illus.). 48p. (J). (gr. 5-6). 33.47 *(978-1-4994-3637-2(8)*, 670562d8-c46b-4c18-a44e-6c803f2766d7, Rosen Central) Rosen Publishing Group, Inc., The.

—Exploring Space, 1 vol. 2018. (Space Facts & Figures Ser.). (ENG., Illus.). 32p. (J). (gr. 2-3). 28.93 *(978-1-5081-9510-8(2)*, 90f7e2bf-0b9a-48c5-9abd-76506497396b, Windmill Bks.) Rosen Publishing Group, Inc., The.

—Exploring the Inner Planets, 1 vol. 2015. (Spectacular Space Science Ser.). (ENG., Illus.). 48p. (J). (gr. 5-6). 33.47 *(978-1-4994-3629-7(7)*, ab513eb5-c984-4eb0-b82d-98012308a5f4, Rosen Central) Rosen Publishing Group, Inc., The.

—Exploring the Outer Planets, 1 vol. 2015. (Spectacular Space Science Ser.). (ENG., Illus.). 48p. (J). (gr. 5-6). 33.47 *(978-1-4994-3633-4(5)*, ef7913ac-eba6-4b92-979c-fa099a799c59, Rosen Central) Rosen Publishing Group, Inc., The.

Dinmont, Kerry. Tom's Telescope: A Book about the Moon & the Sun. 2017. (My Day Readers Ser.). (ENG.). 24p. (J). (gr. -1-2). lib. bdg. 32.79 *(978-1-5038-2017-3(3)*, 211868) Child's World, Inc, The.

DK. DKfindout! Space Travel. 2019. (DK Findout! Ser.). (ENG., Illus.). 64p. (J). (gr. 1-4). 16.99 *(978-1-4654-7932-7(5))*; pap. 10.99 *(978-1-4654-7931-0(7))* Dorling Kindersley Publishing, Inc. (DK Children).

—Super Space Encyclopedia: The Furthest, Largest, Most Spectacular Features of Our Universe. 2019. (DK Super Nature Encyclopedias Ser.). (ENG., Illus.). 208p. (J). (gr. 4-7). 24.99 *(978-1-4654-8171-9(0)*, DK Children) Dorling Kindersley Publishing, Inc.

Dorling Kindersley Publishing Staff. Moon Landings: Level 3. 2019. (ENG., Illus.). 64p. (J). *(978-0-241-35853-5(1))* Dorling Kindersley Publishing, Inc.

—Space Travel. 2019. (ENG., Illus.). 64p. (J). pap. *(978-0-241-35839-9(6))* Dorling Kindersley Publishing, Inc.

Doudna, Kelly. Space Exploration. 2016. (Exploring Our Universe Ser.). (ENG., Illus.). 32p. (J). (gr. 3-6). lib. bdg. 32.79 *(978-1-68078-407-7(2)*, 23673, Checkerboard Library) ABDO Publishing Co.

Dugan, Christine. Space Exploration, 1 vol. 2nd rev. ed. (TIME for KIDS(r): Informational Text Ser.). (ENG., 32p. (gr. 3-5). 2014. Illus.). (J). lib. bdg. 25.96 *(978-1-4807-1083-2(0))* 2012. pap. 12.99 *(978-1-4333-3674-4(X))* Teacher Created Materials, Inc.

Elish, Dan. NASA, 1 vol. 2007. (Kaleidoscope: Space Ser.). (ENG., Illus.). 48p. (gr. 4-4). lib. bdg. 32.64 *(978-0-7614-2046-0(0)*, 7d2c4392-852c-4109-8304-40daa8b73ba5) Cavendish Square Publishing LLC.

Encyclopaedia Britannica, Inc. Staff, compiled by. Britannica Illustrated Science Library: Space Exploration, 16 vols. 2008. (Illus.). (J). 29.95 *(978-1-59339-397-7(0))* Encyclopaedia Britannica, Inc.

—Exploring Space. 2003. (Britannica Learning Library). (gr. 2-5). 14.95 *(978-1-59339-000-6(9)*, 049901-EN-REF) Encyclopaedia Britannica, Inc.

—Space Exploration. 2008. 49.95 *(978-1-59339-689-3(9))* Encyclopaedia Britannica, Inc.

Engel, Christiane, illus. Astronauts. 2018. (First Explorers Ser.). (ENG.). 10p. (J). (— 1). bds. 9.95 *(978-1-4549-2940-6(5))* Sterling Publishing Co., Inc.

Explore Outer Space: Sets 1 - 2. 2013. (Explore Outer Space Ser.). 32p. (J). (gr. 3-6). 429.25 *(978-1-61533-869-6(1))*; pap. 170.00 *(978-1-61533-882-5(9))*; pap. 1020.00 *(978-1-61533-883-2(7))* Windmill Bks.

Explore Space. (Color & Learn Ser.). 36p. (J). (gr. 1-5). pap. *(978-1-882210-13-8(1))* Action Publishing, Inc.

Exploring Space. 2004. (J). cd-rom *(978-0-9764218-3-2(6))* Dawasoft.

Exploring Space. (Eyes on Adventure Ser.). (Illus.). 32p. (J). (gr. 1-18). 7.95 *(978-1-56156-488-0(5))* Kidsbooks, LLC.

Exploring Space, 6 vols. (Sunshinetm Science Ser.). 24p. (gr. 1-2). 31.50 *(978-0-7802-0294-8(5))* Wright Group/McGraw-Hill.

Fabiny, Sarah & Who HQ. What Is NASA? Hammond, Ted, illus. 2019. (What Was? Ser.). 112p. (J). (gr. 3-7). 5.99 *(978-1-5247-8603-8(9))*; 15.99 *(978-1-5247-8605-2(5))* Penguin Young Readers Group. (Penguin Workshop).

Faust, Daniel R. After Earth: Living on a Different Planet. 2008. (Jr. Graphic Environmental Dangers Ser.). (ENG.). 24p. (J). 47.90 *(978-1-61532-099-8(7)*, PowerKids Pr.) Rosen Publishing Group, Inc., The.

—Más Allá de la Tierra: Vivir en Otro Planeta, 1 vol. 2009. (Historietas Juveniles: Peligros Del Medioambiente (Jr. Graphic Environmental Dangers) Ser.). (SPA., Illus.). 24p. (gr. 4-4). pap. 10.60 *(978-1-4358-8472-4(8)*, 7b74d532-cf15-43b9-bf13-828cca7b1dea); (YA). lib. bdg. 28.93 *(978-1-4358-8471-7(X)*, 564ad328-dade-409e-b98f-5396878a160c) Rosen Publishing Group, Inc., The.

Felix, Rebecca. 12 Things to Know about Space Exploration. 2015. (Today's News Ser.). (ENG., Illus.). 32p. (J). (gr. 3-6). 32.80 *(978-1-63235-032-9(7)*, 11610, 12-Story Library) Bookstaves, LLC.

From Earth to the Stars. 2017. (From Earth to the Stars Ser.). 48p. (gr. 10-12). pap. 56.20 *(978-1-5081-0529-9(4))*; (ENG.). (gr. 6-7). 113.64 *(978-1-5081-0527-5(8)*, 85bb2ff4-2339-451d-b368-04a3447c1c16) Rosen Publishing Group, Inc., The. (Britannica Educational Publishing).

Furgang, Adam. Human Spaceflight, 1 vol. 2017. (From Earth to the Stars Ser.). (ENG.). 48p. (gr. 6-7). pap. 15.05 *(978-1-68048-669-8(1)*, 0dee7fa1-36a8-4491-ace1-54cb3d373420, Britannica Educational Publishing) Rosen Publishing Group, Inc., The.

Furgang, Kathy. Rocket Science & Spacecraft Fundamentals, 1 vol. 2017. (From Earth to the Stars Ser.). (ENG., Illus.). 48p. (J). (gr. 6-7). pap. 15.05 *(978-1-68048-673-5(X)*, 20385597-10e1-429a-85e0-3ffdb1c250b7, Britannica Educational Publishing) Rosen Publishing Group, Inc., The.

Furstinger, Nancy. Robots in Space. 2014. (Lightning Bolt Books (r) — Robots Everywhere! Ser.). (ENG., Illus.). 32p. (J). (gr. 1-3). pap. 9.99 *(978-1-4677-4510-9(3)*, 865977fb-31b3-4865-a160-1ef1d1c30c35); lib. bdg. 29.32 *(978-1-4677-4055-5(1)*, ea912cc8-ca06-4b2d-a579-a1c46f9dc90f, Lerner Pubns.) Lerner Publishing Group.

Galat, Joan Marie. Absolute Expert - Space: All the Latest Facts from the Field. 2020. (Absolute Expert Ser.). (Illus.). 112p. (J). (gr. 3-7). 14.99 *(978-1-4263-3669-0(1)*, National Geographic Kids) Disney Publishing Worldwide.

—Absolute Expert: Space: All the Latest Facts from the Field. 2020. (Absolute Expert Ser.). (ENG., Illus.). 112p. (J). (gr. 3-7). lib. bdg. 24.90 *(978-1-4263-3670-6(5)*, National Geographic Kids) Disney Publishing Worldwide.

Gifford, Clive. Astronomy, Astronauts, & Space Exploration. 2015. (Watch This Space! Ser.). (ENG., Illus.). 32p. (J). (gr. 4-5). lib. bdg. *(978-0-7787-2021-8(7))* Crabtree Publishing Co.

Gitlin, Martin. Careers in Personal Space Travel. 2018. (Bright Futures Press: Emerging Tech Careers Ser.). (ENG., Illus.). 32p. (J). (gr. 4-7). lib. bdg. 32.07 *(978-1-5341-2976-4(6)*, 211948) Cherry Lake Publishing.

Goldsmith, Mike. Listopia: Space. 2016. (ENG., Illus.). 208p. (J). (gr. 2-5). pap. 9.99 *(978-1-4998-0280-1(3))* Little Bee Books Inc.

Goldsworthy, Steve. Famous Explorers. 2011. (J). (gr. 4-6). pap. 13.95 *(978-1-61690-636-8(7)*, AV2 by Weigl); (Illus.). 32p. (YA). (gr. 2-5). 28.55 *(978-1-61690-632-0(4))* Weigl Pubs., Inc.

—Space Explorers. 2017. (Illus.). 32p. (J). *(978-1-4896-5815-9(7)*, AV2 by Weigl) Weigl Pubs., Inc.

Grack, Rachel. Space Travel from Then to Now. 2019. (Sequence Developments in Technology Ser.). (ENG.). 32p. (J). (gr. 2-5). pap. 9.99 *(978-1-68152-473-3(2)*, 11057); lib. bdg. *(978-1-68151-687-5(X)*, 10817) Amicus.

Green, Jen. The Story of the Race to the Moon. Mark Bergin, illus. 2017. (Explorers Ser.). 32p. (gr. 3-6). 31.35 *(978-1-910706-92-3(2))* Book Hse. GBR. Dist: Black Rabbit Bks.

Greve, Tom. Thanks, Nasa! 2012. (Let's Explore Science Ser.). (ENG.). 48p. (gr. 4-6). pap. 10.95 *(978-1-61810-253-9(2)*, 9781618102539) Rourke Educational Media.

Gross, Miriam. All about Space Missions. 2009. (Blast Off! Ser.). 24p. (gr. 2-3). 42.50 *(978-1-61511-623-2(0)*, PowerKids Pr.) Rosen Publishing Group, Inc., The.

Gross, Miriam J. All about Space Missions, 1 vol. 2009. (Blast Off! Ser.). (ENG.). 24p. (J). (gr. 2-3). pap. 9.25 *(978-1-4358-3138-4(1)*, 2c9aa5cb-9bae-4a8e-b34e-87d3674163db); lib. bdg. 26.27 *(978-1-4358-2740-0(6)*, 255befb5-8e9f-4767-9624-23cb3c6fd2c9) Rosen Publishing Group, Inc., The. (PowerKids Pr.).

Group/McGraw-Hill, Wright. History: Space Exploration, 6 vols. (Book2WebTM Ser.). (gr. 4-8). 36.50 *(978-0-322-04456-2(1))* Wright Group/McGraw-Hill.

Hamilton, John. Cassini: Unlocking the Secrets of Saturn. 2017. (Xtreme Spacecraft Ser.). (ENG., Illus.). 32p. (J). (gr. 3-9). lib. bdg. 32.79 *(978-1-5321-1011-5(1)*, 25598, Abdo & Daughters) ABDO Publishing Co.

—Curiosity Rover: Searching for Life on Mars. 2017. (Xtreme Spacecraft Ser.). (ENG., Illus.). 32p. (J). (gr. 3-9). lib. bdg. 32.79 *(978-1-5321-1009-2(X)*, 25594, Abdo & Daughters) ABDO Publishing Co.

—Hubble Space Telescope: Photographing the Universe. 2017. (Xtreme Spacecraft Ser.). (ENG., Illus.). 32p. (J). (gr. 3-9). lib. bdg. 32.79 *(978-1-5321-1012-2(X)*, 25600, Abdo & Daughters) ABDO Publishing Co.

—Humans to Mars. 2018. (Mission to Mars Ser.). (ENG., Illus.). 48p. (J). (gr. 5-9). lib. bdg. 34.21 *(978-1-5321-1592-9(X)*, 28760, Abdo & Daughters) ABDO Publishing Co.

—New Horizons: Exploring Jupiter, Pluto, & Beyond. 2017. (Xtreme Spacecraft Ser.). (ENG., Illus.). 32p. (J). (gr. 3-9). lib. bdg. 32.79 *(978-1-5321-1010-8(3)*, 25596, Abdo & Daughters) ABDO Publishing Co.

—Rosetta: Voyage to a Comet. 2017. (Xtreme Spacecraft Ser.). (ENG., Illus.). 32p. (J). (gr. 3-9). lib. bdg. 32.79 *(978-1-5321-1013-9(8)*, 25602, Abdo & Daughters) ABDO Publishing Co.

Hamilton, Tracy Brown. All about Spacecraft, 1 vol. 2016. (Let's Find Out! Transportation Ser.). (ENG., Illus.). 32p. (J). (gr. 2-3). lib. bdg. 26.06 *(978-1-68048-445-8(1)*, 5bc59e5b-21fc-43ba-9dd5-62c742978fcd) Rosen Publishing Group, Inc., The.

Hand, Carol. Colonizing Planets, 1 vol. 2018. (Sci-Fi or STEM? Ser.). (ENG., Illus.). 64p. (J). (gr. 7-7). lib. bdg. 36.13 *(978-1-5081-8029-6(6)*, 5918b82a-8673-44b5-96f9-81fdd831e671) Rosen Publishing Group, Inc., The.

Hantula, Richard & Asimov, Isaac. Global Space Programs, 1 vol. 2005. (Isaac Asimov's 21st Century Library of the Universe: Past & Present Ser.). (ENG., Illus.). 32p. (gr. 3-5). lib. bdg. 28.67 *(978-0-8368-3982-1(X)*, c7836922-1a80-4909-93cd-08c7133b3aa2) Stevens, Gareth Publishing LLLP.

Harmon, Daniel E. The Early Days of Space Exploration, 1 vol. 2017. (From Earth to the Stars Ser.). (ENG., Illus.). 7.2p. (J). (gr. 6-7). pap. 15.05 *(978-1-68048-665-0(9)*, 1a1ea672-46cc-4314-96dc-37b124d52795, Britannica Educational Publishing) Rosen Publishing Group, Inc., The.

Harris, Joseph. Space Exploration: The Impact of Science & Technology, 1 vol. 2009. (Pros & Cons Ser.). (ENG.). 64p. (YA). (gr. 5-8). lib. bdg. 37.67 *(978-1-4339-1989-3(3)*, ab953dc5-378f-4f08-a3f3-bc401f1ab08b) Stevens, Gareth Publishing LLLP.

Hartson, Tamara. Space, 1 vol. 2017. (Super Explorers Ser.). (ENG., Illus.). 64p. (J). pap. 6.99 *(978-1-926700-72-4(4)*, ad288c7a-bacc-497a-b692-6a7421af7fd0) Blue Bike Bks. CAN. Dist: Lone Pine Publishing USA.

Haugen, David M., ed. Space Exploration, 1 vol. 2011. (At Issue Ser.). (ENG.). 120p. (gr. 10-12). 41.03 *(978-0-7377-5596-1(2)*, 6f8d2418-da49-4bd8-bf2a-d78559fddb4a); pap. 28.80 *(978-0-7377-5597-8(0)*, 082a0206-d26a-480a-b96a-5bcfb1bd0c62) Greenhaven Publishing LLC. (Greenhaven Publishing).

Head, Honor. Top Secret Science in Space. 2019. (Top Secret Science Ser.). (Illus.). 48p. (J). (gr. 5-5). *(978-0-7787-5996-6(2))*; pap. *(978-0-7787-6034-4(0))* Crabtree Publishing Co.

Hermsen, Sarah. Space Exploration Library Cumulative Index. 2004. (Space Exploration Reference Library). (ENG.). 42p. (J). lib. bdg. 5.00 *(978-0-7876-9214-8(X)*, UXL) Cengage Gale.

Hirsch, Rebecca E. Space Vehicles in Action (an Augmented Reality Experience) 2020. (Space in Action: Augmented Reality (Alternator Books (r)) Ser.). (ENG., Illus.). 32p. (J). (gr. 3-6). lib. bdg. 31.99 *(978-1-5415-7882-1(1)*, 7771913d-8045-4c13-8e35-f0c00ee7aa90, Lerner Pubns.) Lerner Publishing Group.

The History of Space Exploration, 8 vols. 2004. (History of Space Exploration Ser.). (ENG.). 48p. (gr. 5-8). lib. bdg. 202.02 *(978-0-8368-5704-7(6)*, 3b3908c3-5106-4098-a687-08b6b7f06ea2) Stevens, Gareth Publishing LLLP.

Hofer, Charles. Spacecraft. 2009. (World's Fastest Machines Ser.). 24p. (gr. 2-3). 42.50 *(978-1-60854-855-2(4)*, PowerKids Pr.) Rosen Publishing Group, Inc., The.

Holcroft, John & Candlewick Press Staff. Space Exploration: Panorama Pops. Holcroft, John, illus. 2015. (Panorama Pops Ser.). (ENG., Illus.). 30p. (J). (gr. k-4). 8.99 *(978-0-7636-7699-5(3))* Candlewick Pr.

Hopping, Lorraine Jean. Space Rocks: The Story of Planetary Geologist Adriana Ocampo. 2006. (ENG., Illus.). 128p. (gr. 7-9). per. 19.95 *(978-0-309-09555-6(7)*, Joseph Henry Pr.) National Academies Pr.

Huddleston, Emma. Exploring Kennedy Space Center. 2019. (Travel America's Landmarks Ser.). (ENG., Illus.). 32p. (J). (gr. 2-3). pap. 9.95 *(978-1-64185-854-0(0)*, 1641858540); lib. bdg. 31.35 *(978-1-64185-785-7(4)*, 1641857854) North Star Editions. (Focus Readers).

Hurt, Avery Elizabeth, ed. The Future of Space Exploration, 1 vol. 2019. (Opposing Viewpoints Ser.). (ENG.). 176p. (gr. 10-12). pap. 34.80 *(978-1-5345-0503-2(2)*, 91f0b196-3ec4-4300-863a-81424563190c) Greenhaven Publishing LLC.

Hutmacher, Kimberly M. The Universe Began with a Bang & Other Cool Space Facts. 2019. (Mind-Blowing Science Facts Ser.). (ENG., Illus.). 32p. (J). (gr. 4-6). lib. bdg. 28.65 *(978-1-5435-5769-5(4)*, 139725) Capstone.

Hwang, William Liang & Mian, Matthew K., eds. InnoWorks: Explorations, Student Edition. 2006. (YA). spiral bd. *(978-0-9771380-4-3(6))* United InnoWorks Academy.

Ingebretsen, Karen, et al. Human Space Exploration. 2006. (World Book's Solar System & Space Exploration Library). (Illus.). 63p. (J). *(978-0-7166-9509-7(X))* World Bk., Inc.

Jackson, Tom. The Universe: An Illustrated History of Astronomy. 2012. (Illus.). 144p. (J). *(978-0-9853230-2-8(7))* Shelter Harbor Pr.

Jefferis, David. Space Explorers. 2017. (Our Future in Space Ser.). (Illus.). 32p. (J). (gr. 5-5). *(978-0-7787-3535-9(4))*; pap. *(978-0-7787-3540-3(0))* Crabtree Publishing Co.

Jemison, Mae & Rau, Dana Meachen. Journey Through Our Solar System. 2013. (True Book™—Dr. Mae Jemison & 100 Year Starship™ Ser.). (ENG., Illus.). 48p. (J). lib. bdg. 29.00 *(978-0-531-25501-8(8))* Scholastic Library Publishing.

Jenkins, Martin. Exploring Space: from Galileo to the Mars Rover & Beyond. Biesty, Stephen, illus. 2017. (ENG.). 64p. (J). (gr. 3-7). 17.99 *(978-0-7636-8931-5(9))* Candlewick Pr.

Jones, Tom. Ask the Astronaut: A Galaxy of Astonishing Answers to Your Questions on Spaceflight. 2016. (Illus.). 224p. (gr. 5-12). pap. 12.95 *(978-1-58834-537-0(8)*, Smithsonian Bks.) Smithsonian Institution Scholarly Pr.

Kain, Kathleen. Telescopes & Space Probes. 2006. (World Book's Solar System & Space Exploration Library). (Illus.). 63p. (J). *(978-0-7166-9510-3(3))* World Bk., Inc.

Keiser, Cody. Exploring Uranus. 2017. (Journey Through Our Solar System Ser.). 24p. (gr. 1-2). 49.50 *(978-1-5345-2253-4(0)*, KidHaven Publishing); (ENG.). pap. 9.25 *(978-1-5345-2289-3(1)*, 1f4b99e1-69c6-4e0a-be0b-444667c46c2c); (ENG.). lib. bdg. 26.23 *(978-1-5345-2281-7(6)*, 3953ed88-aac1-416d-a509-2b8a28a8c7e5) Greenhaven Publishing LLC.

Kelley, K. C. Astronauts!, Vol. 10. 2015. (Scientists in Action Ser.). (Illus.). 48p. (J). (gr. 5). 20.95 *(978-1-4222-3418-1(5))* Mason Crest.

—Blast off to Space. 2018. (Amazing Adventures Ser.). (ENG.). 16p. (J). (gr. k-2). lib. bdg. *(978-1-68151-315-7(3)*, 14881); (Illus.). pap. 7.99 *(978-1-68152-271-5(3)*, 14887) Amicus.

Kelly, Erin. The Space Book (Side by Side) (Library Edition) 2019. (Side by Side Ser.). (ENG., Illus.). 24p. (J). (gr. k-k). lib. bdg. 26.00 *(978-0-531-23842-4(3)*, Children's Pr.) Scholastic Library Publishing.

Kelly, Tracey. Communication Technology: From Smoke Signals to Smartphones. 2019. (History of Inventions Ser.). (ENG.). 24p. (J). (gr. 2-4). lib. bdg. *(978-1-78121-456-5(5)*, 16733) Brown Bear Bks.

Kenney, Karen Latchana. Breakthroughs in Planet & Comet Research. 2019. (Space Exploration (Alternator Books (r)) Ser.). (ENG., Illus.). 32p. (J). (gr. 3-6). 29.32 *(978-1-5415-3870-2(6)*, fee970a7-9c67-48b0-a7b4-dc837a3ff879, Lerner Pubns.) Lerner Publishing Group.

—Breakthroughs in the Search for Extraterrestrial Life. 2019. (Space Exploration (Alternator Books (r)) Ser.). (ENG., Illus.). 32p. (J). (gr. 3-6). 29.32 *(978-1-5415-3872-6(2)*, be10ae37-ef0f-4396-8317-c713fbd7bc41, Lerner Pubns.) Lerner Publishing Group.

Keppeler, Eric. More Freaky Space Stories, 1 vol. 2019. (Freaky True Science Ser.). (ENG.). 32p. (gr. 4-5). pap. 11.50 *(978-1-5382-4062-5(9)*, 242e9922-9f68-4957-a807-c0a26d7fdb35) Stevens, Gareth Publishing LLLP.

Kerrod, Robin. Space. 2003. 48p. (J). lib. bdg. 27.10 *(978-1-58340-351-8(5))* Black Rabbit Bks.

Khan, Hena. The Space Explorer's Guide to Earth's Neighborhood. 2003. (Space University Ser.). (Illus.). 48p. (J). *(978-0-439-55741-2(0))* Scholastic, Inc.

Khan, Hena & Dyson, Marianne J. The Space Explorer's Guide to Out-Of-This-World Science. 2004. (Space University Ser.). (Illus.). 48p. (J). *(978-0-439-55747-4(X))* Scholastic, Inc.

Klepeis, Alicia Z. Moon Base & Beyond: The Lunar Gateway to Deep Space. 2019. (Future Space Ser.). (ENG., Illus.). 32p. (J). (gr. 3-9). pap. 7.95 *(978-1-5435-7515-6(3)*, 141046); lib. bdg. 28.65 *(978-1-5435-7267-4(7)*, 140598) Capstone.

Kluger, Jeffrey. Disaster Strikes! The Most Dangerous Space Missions of All Time. 2019. (ENG., Illus.). 224p. (J). (gr. 3-7). 18.99 *(978-1-9848-1275-9(0)*, Philomel Bks.) Penguin Young Readers Group.

Kopp, Megan. Journeys to Outer Space. 2019. (Mission: Space Science Ser.). (Illus.). 48p. (J). (gr. 5-5). *(978-0-7787-5393-3(X))*; pap. *(978-0-7787-5404-6(9))* Crabtree Publishing Co.

Kortemeier, Todd. Searching for Alien Life. 2017. (Science Frontiers Ser.). (ENG., Illus.). 32p. (J). (gr. 3-6). 32.80 *(978-1-63235-380-1(6)*, 11874, 12-Story Library) Bookstaves, LLC.

Kortenkamp, Steve. Show Me Space: My First Picture Encyclopedia, 1 vol. 2013. (My First Picture Encyclopedias Ser.). (ENG.). 32p. (J). (gr. -1-2). pap. 8.10 *(978-1-4765-3790-0(9)*, 123750, Capstone Pr.) Capstone.

Kranz, Rachel. La exploración del Espacio. 2011. (SPA.). 32p. (J). pap. 49.00 net. *(978-1-4108-2344-1(X)*, A2344X) Benchmark Education Co.

Krieger, Emily. National Geographic Kids Funny Fill-in: My Space Adventure. 2013. (Illus.). 48p. (J). (gr. 3-7). pap. 4.99 *(978-1-4263-1354-7(3)*, National Geographic Kids) Disney Publishing Worldwide.

Kruesi, Liz. Discover Space Exploration. 2016. (Searchlight Books (tm) — What's Cool about Science? Ser.). (ENG., Illus.). 40p. (J). (gr. 3-5). 30.65 *(978-1-5124-0811-9(5)*, 1fb5a99a-38ad-49de-bf70-ed8d315026f8, Lerner Pubns.) Lerner Publishing Group.

—Finding Earthlike Planets. 2018. (Destination Space Ser.). (ENG., Illus.). 48p. (J). (gr. 5-6). pap. 11.95 *(978-1-63517-567-7(4)*, 1635175674); lib. bdg. 34.21 *(978-1-63517-495-3(3)*, 1635174953) North Star Editions. (Focus Readers).

—Voyage to Pluto. 2018. (Destination Space Ser.). (ENG., Illus.). 48p. (J). (gr. 5-6). pap. 11.95 *(978-1-63517-572-1(0)*, 1635175720); lib. bdg. 34.21 *(978-1-63517-500-4(3)*, 1635175003) North Star Editions. (Focus Readers).

—Voyage to Pluto. 2018. (Illus.). 48p. (J). pap. *(978-1-4896-9801-8(9)*, AV2 by Weigl) Weigl Pubs., Inc.

Labrecque, Ellen. Yvonne Brill & Satellite Propulsion. 2017. (21st Century Junior Library: Women Innovators Ser.). (ENG., Illus.). 24p. (J). (gr. 2-5). lib. bdg. 29.21 *(978-1-63472-184-4(5)*, 209308) Cherry Lake Publishing.

Lakin, Patricia. The Stellar Story of Space Travel: Ready-To-Read Level 3. Burroughs, Scott, illus. 2016. (History of Fun Stuff Ser.). (ENG.). 48p. (J). (gr. 1-3). pap. 4.99 *(978-1-4814-5623-4(7)*, Simon Spotlight) Simon Spotlight.

Langley, Andrew. Chris Hadfield & the International Space Station. 2015. (Adventures in Space Ser.). (ENG., Illus.). 48p. (J). (gr. 4-6). 35.99 *(978-1-4846-2517-0(X)*, 130014, Heinemann) Capstone.

—Planet Hunting: Racking up Data & Looking for Life. 2019. (Future Space Ser.). (ENG., Illus.). 32p. (J). (gr. 3-9). pap. 7.95 *(978-1-5435-7516-3(1)*, 141047); lib. bdg. 28.65 *(978-1-5435-7270-4(7)*, 140601) Capstone.

—Sally Ride & the Shuttle Missions. 2015. (Adventures in Space Ser.). (ENG., Illus.). 48p. (J). (gr. 4-6). 35.99 *(978-1-4846-2516-3(1)*, 130013, Heinemann) Capstone.

—Space Telescopes: Instagram of the Stars. 2019. (Future Space Ser.). (ENG., Illus.). 32p. (J). (gr. 3-9). pap. 7.95 *(978-1-5435-7519-4(6)*, 141050); lib. bdg. 28.65 *(978-1-5435-7271-1(5)*, 140602) Capstone.

Larson, Kirsten W. Space Robots. (Robotics in Our World Ser.). (ENG., Illus.). 32p. (J). (gr. 2-5). 2018. pap. 9.99 *(978-1-68152-178-7(4)*, 14809) 2017. 20.95 *(978-1-68151-147-4(9)*, 14690) Amicus.

Lassieur, Allison. International Space Station: An Interactive Space Exploration Adventure. 2016. (You Choose: Space Ser.). (ENG., Illus.). 112p. (J). (gr. 3-7). lib. bdg. 32.65 *(978-1-4914-8104-2(8)*, 130588, Capstone Pr.) Capstone.

Launch into Space! 2015. (Launch into Space! Ser.). (ENG.). 32p. (J). (gr. 3-4). pap., pap., pap. 378.72 *(978-0-7660-6683-0(5))* Enslow Publishing, LLC.

Law, Felicia & Bailey, Gerry. Trouble in Space. Noyes, Leighton, illus. 2015. (Science to the Rescue Ser.). (ENG.). 32p. (J). (gr. 4-4). *(978-0-7787-1676-1(7))* Crabtree Publishing Co.

Lombardo, Jennifer. Space Exploration Throughout History: From Telescopes to Tourism, 1 vol. 2019. (World History Ser.). (ENG.). 104p. (gr. 7-7). 41.53 *(978-1-5345-6712-2(7)*, 47fb66b6-eab7-446c-ae36-dc30db49b477, Lucent Pr.) Greenhaven Publishing LLC.

The Magic School Bus: Lost in the Solar System. 2011. (J). audio compact disk 9.99 *(978-0-545-22880-0(8))* Scholastic, Inc.

Mallick, Nita. Space Exploration, 1 vol. 2016. (Study of Science Ser.). (ENG., Illus.). 124p. (J). (gr. 8-8). lib. bdg. 37.82 *(978-1-5081-0427-8(1)*, c0f0da99-b423-4e52-b0f5-89e423be5633) Rosen Publishing Group, Inc., The.

Mason Crest Publishers Staff, contrib. by. Space Exploration, Vol. 6. 2019. (Science & Technology Ser.). 48p. (J). (gr. 8). 27.93 *(978-1-4222-4208-7(0))* Mason Crest.

Mason, Jenny. Space Exploration: From Galileo Galilei to Neil Degrasse Tyson. 2018. (STEM Stories Ser.). (ENG., Illus.). 32p. (J). (gr. 3-6). lib. bdg. 32.79 *(978-1-5321-1549-3(0)*, 28952, Checkerboard Library) ABDO Publishing Co.

McMahon, Michael. Why Do Stars Twinkle?, 1 vol. 2010. (Solving Science Mysteries Ser.). (ENG., Illus.). 24p. (gr. 4-5). (J). pap. 9.25 *(978-1-61531-921-3(2)*, ee0bbc47-47cf-4000-9754-0d04979b329a, PowerKids Pr.); (YA). lib. bdg. 26.27 *(978-1-61531-895-7(X)*, 5cb41215-5515-48d4-961e-8de23820e0e3) Rosen Publishing Group, Inc., The.

McMahon, Peter. The Space Adventurer's Guide: Your Passport to the Coolest Things to See & Do in the Universe. Holinaty, Josh, illus. 2018. (ENG.). 100p. (J). (gr. 3-7). pap. 17.99 *(978-1-77138-032-4(2))* Kids Can Pr., Ltd. CAN. Dist: Hachette Bk. Group.

Meet NASA Inventor Robert Hoyt & His Team's Web-Spinning Space Spiders. 2017. (J). *(978-0-7166-6157-3(8))* World Bk., Inc.

Mikoley, Kate. The Hubble Telescope Launch, 1 vol. 2018. (History Just Before You Were Born Ser.). (ENG.). 32p. (gr. 4-5). 28.27 *(978-1-5382-3027-5(5)*, 61df2c1e-7557-4122-8243-298a0400d806) Stevens, Gareth Publishing LLLP.

Miller, Derek. Investigating Space Through Modeling, 1 vol. 2019. (Science Investigators Ser.). (ENG.). 48p. (gr. 5-5). pap. 13.93 *(978-1-5026-5252-2(8)*, 9340a597-bebf-49fd-a1ea-f28470fde29f) Cavendish Square Publishing LLC.

Miller, Gary. The Outer Limits: The Future of Space Exploration. 2009. (Current Science Ser.). (ENG.). 48p. (J). (gr. 4-6). pap. 8.95 *(978-1-4339-2246-6(0)*, Gareth Stevens Learning Library) Stevens, Gareth Publishing LLLP.

—The Outer Limits: the Future of Space Exploration, 1 vol. 2009. (Current Science Ser.). (ENG.). 48p. (YA). (gr. 4-6). lib. bdg. 33.67 *(978-1-4339-2242-8(8)*, 0a3856e3-925d-4df0-a4d0-35b9136b6483) Stevens, Gareth Publishing LLLP.

Mills, Nathan & Block, Dakota. Exploring the Solar System, 1 vol. 2012. (Rosen Readers Ser.). (ENG., Illus.). 24p. (J). (gr. 1-2). pap. 8.25 *(978-1-4488-8857-3(3)*, 299c01d7-d01b-4f63-af8e-f4cbbba42b72, Rosen Classroom) Rosen Publishing Group, Inc., The.

Mills, Nathan & Stiegler, Lorraine. Space Probes, 1 vol. 2012. (Rosen Readers Ser.). (ENG., Illus.). 24p. (J). (gr. 1-2). pap. 8.25 *(978-1-4488-8869-6(7)*, 01e87361-02cb-470b-82d9-7854c8f69298, Rosen Classroom) Rosen Publishing Group, Inc., The.

Mitton, Tony & Parker, Ant. Roaring Rockets. 2017. (Amazing Machines Ser.). (ENG.). 20p. (J). bds. 6.99 *(978-0-7534-7371-9(2)*, 900178401, Kingfisher) Roaring Brook Pr.

Moore, Phillip. When Did American Astronauts Explore? 2012. (Level C Ser.). (ENG., Illus.). 16p. (J). (gr. k-2). pap. 7.95 *(978-1-927136-26-3(1)*, 19430) RiverStream Publishing.

Morey, Allan. The Hubble Space Telescope. 2017. (Space Tech Ser.). (ENG., Illus.). 24p. (J). (gr. 3-7). lib. bdg. 26.95 *(978-1-62617-700-0(7)*, Epic Bks.) Bellwether Media.

—Mars Rovers. 2017. (Space Tech Ser.). (ENG., Illus.). 24p. (J). (gr. 3-7). lib. bdg. 26.95 *(978-1-62617-703-1(1)*, Epic Bks.) Bellwether Media.

—Robonauts. 2017. (Space Tech Ser.). (ENG., Illus.). 24p. (J). (gr. 3-7). lib. bdg. 26.95 *(978-1-62617-704-8(X)*, Epic Bks.) Bellwether Media.

—Rockets. 2017. (Space Tech Ser.). (ENG., Illus.). 24p. (J). (gr. 3-7). lib. bdg. 26.95 *(978-1-62617-705-5(8)*, Epic Bks.) Bellwether Media.

Moskal, Greg. The History of Space Exploration: Sequencing Events Chronologically on a Timeline, 1 vol. (Math for the REAL World Ser.). (ENG., Illus.). 24p. (gr. 3-4). 2010. pap. 8.25 *(978-0-8239-8850-1(3)*, f4967c3d-3497-45f7-a928-6133c53c74b3) 2003. (J). lib. bdg. 26.27 *(978-0-8239-8962-1(3)*, e85142dc-e3fb-4583-9ec4-3f8b97b40e52) Rosen Publishing Group, Inc., The. (PowerKids Pr.).

Nagel, Rob. Space Exploration - Almanac, 2 vols. 2004. (Space Exploration Reference Library). (ENG., Illus.). 400p. lib. bdg. 191.00 *(978-0-7876-9209-4(3)*, UXL) Cengage Gale.

Nagelhout, Ryan. Astronauts, 1 vol., 1. 2015. (Out of the Lab: Extreme Jobs in Science Ser.). (ENG., Illus.). 32p. (J). (gr. 4-5). pap. 11.00 *(978-1-5081-4509-7(1)*, dc55125e-6388-467f-9dc7-d26038656618, PowerKids Pr.) Rosen Publishing Group, Inc., The.

—Space Robots, 1 vol. 2016. (Robots & Robotics Ser.). (ENG.). 32p. (J). (gr. 5-5). 27.93 *(978-1-4994-2183-5(4)*, 7f71bf35-5c46-4d47-9800-548862342e18, PowerKids Pr.) Rosen Publishing Group, Inc., The.

Nardo, Don. Destined for Space: Our Story of Exploration. 2012. (Smithsonian Ser.). (ENG.). 64p. (gr. 4-5). pap. 53.70 *(978-1-4296-8524-5(7))* Capstone.

—Hubble Deep Field: How a Photo Revolutionized Our Understanding of the Universe. 2017. (Captured Science History Ser.). (ENG., Illus.). 64p. (J). (gr. 5-9). lib. bdg. 35.32 *(978-0-7565-5643-3(0)*, 136083, Compass Point Bks.) Capstone.

National Geographic Learning. Language, Literacy & Vocabulary - Reading Expeditions (Earth Science): Stars. 2007. (ENG., Illus.). 36p. (J). pap. 20.95 *(978-0-7922-5433-1(3))* CENGAGE Learning.

—Reading Expeditions (Social Studies: World Explorers): Missions in Space 1955-Present. 2007. (ENG., Illus.). 32p. (J). pap. 18.95 *(978-0-7922-4546-9(6))* CENGAGE Learning.

Newland, Sonya. Space Exploration: Triumphs & Tragedies, 1 vol. 2016. (Crabtree Chrome Ser.). (ENG., Illus.). 48p. (J). (gr. 6-9). pap. *(978-0-7787-2231-1(7))* Crabtree Publishing Co.

Nicolson, Cynthia. Discover Space. Slavin, Bill, illus. 2005. 32p. (J). lib. bdg. 15.38 *(978-1-4242-1193-7(X))* Fitzgerald Bks.

Nicolson, Cynthia Pratt. Discover Space. Slavin, Bill, illus. 2005. (Kids Can Read! Ser.). 32p. (J). (gr. 1-3). 3.95 *(978-1-55337-824-2(5))* Kids Can Pr., Ltd. CAN. Dist: Hachette Bk. Group.

O'Brien, Cynthia. Searching for Extraterrestrials. 2019. (Mission: Space Science Ser.). (Illus.). 48p. (J). (gr. 5-5). *(978-0-7787-5394-0(8))*; pap. *(978-0-7787-5405-3(7))* Crabtree Publishing Co.

O'Brien, Eileen & Denne, Ben. Space. 2004. (Discovery Program Ser.). (SPA., Illus.). 48p. (J). pap. 8.95 *(978-0-7945-0126-6(5)*, Usborne); lib. bdg. 16.95 *(978-1-58086-388-9(4))* EDC Publishing.

O'Hearn, Michael. Awesome Space Robots, 1 vol. 2013. (Robots Ser.). (ENG.). 32p. (J). (gr. 3-9). lib. bdg. 28.65 *(978-1-4296-9918-1(3)*, 120630); (Illus.). pap. 8.29 *(978-1-62065-778-2(3)*, 121743) Capstone.

Orr, Tamra B. Space Discoveries. 2018. (Marvelous Discoveries Ser.). (ENG., Illus.). 32p. (J). (gr. 2-5). lib. bdg. 28.65 *(978-1-5435-2616-5(0)*, 138087, Capstone Pr.) Capstone.

—Space, Incorporated: The Future of Commercial Space Travel. 2019. (Future Space Ser.). (ENG., Illus.). 32p. (J). (gr. 3-9). pap. 7.95 *(978-1-5435-7520-0(X)*, 141051); lib. bdg. 28.65 *(978-1-5435-7266-7(9)*, 140597) Capstone.

Owen, David. Final Frontier: Voyages into Outer Space. 2004. (ENG., Illus.). 128p. (J). (gr. 6-9). pap. 9.95 *(978-1-55297-775-0(7)*, 86940327-48ff-48fc-8111-cf7089f42efb) Firefly Bks., Ltd.

Paris, Stephanie. 20th Century: Race to the Moon, 1 vol. 2nd rev. ed. 2013. (TIME for KIDS(r): Informational Text Ser.). (ENG., Illus.). 64p. (J). (gr. 4-8). pap. 14.99 *(978-1-4333-4899-0(3))* Teacher Created Materials, Inc.

—21st Century: Mysteries of Deep Space, 1 vol. 2nd rev. ed. 2013. (TIME for KIDS(r): Informational Text Ser.). (ENG., Illus.). 64p. (J). (gr. 4-8). pap. 14.99 *(978-1-4333-4900-3(0))* Teacher Created Materials, Inc.

Paris, Stephanie & Kuligowski, Stephanie. 22nd Century - Future of Space, 1 vol. 2nd rev. ed. 2013. (TIME for KIDS(r): Informational Text Ser.). (ENG., Illus.). 64p. (J). (gr. 4-8). pap. 14.99 *(978-1-4333-4901-0(9))* Teacher Created Materials, Inc.

Parker, Steve. In Space. 2010. (J). 28.50 *(978-1-59920-285-3(9))* Black Rabbit Bks.

—Looking Beyond. West, David, illus. 2015. (Story of Space Ser.). (ENG.). 32p. (J). (gr. 3-6). 31.35 *(978-1-62588-076-5(6)*, 1389436) Black Rabbit Bks.

—Space Exploration. 2010. (How It Works Ser.). 40p. (J). (gr. 3-18). lib. bdg. 19.95 *(978-1-4222-1799-3(X))* Mason Crest.

—Space Stations. West, David, illus. 2015. (Story of Space Ser.). (ENG.). 32p. (J). (gr. 3-6). 31.35 *(978-1-62588-081-9(2))* Black Rabbit Bks.

Parker, Steve & Snedding, Robert. A Brief Illustrated History of Space Exploration. 2017. (Brief Illustrated History Ser.). (ENG., Illus.). 32p. (J). (gr. 3-6). lib. bdg. 27.99 *(978-1-5157-2519-0(7)*, Capstone Pr.) Capstone.

Parker, Steve & Twist, Clint. Exploring Space. 2013. (Illus.). 48p. (J). *(978-1-4351-5088-1(0))* Barnes & Noble, Inc.

Parker, Steve & West, David. In Space, 1 vol. West, David, illus. 2012. (Future Transport Ser.). (ENG., Illus.). 32p. (gr. 5-5). 31.21 *(978-1-60870-778-2(4)*, 7d0ec3ee-2ca3-4295-9570-95db2ba69517) Cavendish Square Publishing LLC.

Parks, Peggy J. Space Research. 2010. (Inside Science Ser.). (Illus.). 96p. (J). (gr. 7-12). 41.27 *(978-1-60152-111-8(1)*, 1316146) ReferencePoint Pr., Inc.

Peters, Elisa. Outer Space, 1 vol. 2012. (PowerKids Readers: the Universe Ser.). (ENG., Illus.). 24p. (J). (gr. k-k). 26.27 *(978-1-4488-7390-6(8)*, bba0a76e-6aae-49fb-9158-a8be4335e7a1); pap. 9.25 *(978-1-4488-7469-9(6)*, a9b9c8c6-038e-4253-8c2d-0a211d9258d5) Rosen Publishing Group, Inc., The. (PowerKids Pr.).

—Outer Space: El Espacio Exterior, 1 vol. 2012. (PowerKids Readers: el Universo / the Universe Ser.). (SPA & ENG., Illus.). 24p. (J). (gr. k-k). lib. bdg. 26.27 *(978-1-4488-7826-0(8)*, ee62d2ea-4c9c-4a9b-9758-d58195a510b1, PowerKids Pr.) Rosen Publishing Group, Inc., The.

Peterson, Christy. Cutting-Edge Hubble Telescope Data. 2019. (Searchlight Books (tm) — New Frontiers of Space Ser.). (ENG., Illus.). 32p. (J). (gr. 3-5). pap. 9.99 *(978-1-5415-7484-7(2)*, 693e0d9b-052e-4873-9c6a-b5ed1addd6f4); lib. bdg. 30.65 *(978-1-5415-5581-5(3)*, a753add7-1035-45de-a9bf-367b895f49d6) Lerner Publishing Group. (Lerner Pubns.).

Peterson, Judy Monroe. Exploring Space: Astronauts & Astronomers. (Extreme Scientists Ser.). 24p. (gr. 2-3). 2009. 42.50 *(978-1-61512-451-0(9)*, PowerKids Pr.) 2008. (ENG., Illus.). (YA). lib. bdg. 26.27 *(978-1-4042-4528-0(6)*, 37f0a133-74a4-413d-9e09-42dd5e033e65) Rosen Publishing Group, Inc., The.

Peterson, Megan Cooley & Rustad, Martha E. H. The First Space Missions, 1 vol. 2014. (Famous Firsts Ser.). (ENG., Illus.). 24p. (J). (gr. -1-2). 27.32 *(978-1-4914-0576-5(7)*, 125914, Capstone Pr.) Capstone.

Petrikowski, Nicki Peter. Critical Perspectives on the Viability of Human Life on Other Planets, 1 vol. 2016. (Analyzing the Issues Ser.). (ENG.). 208p. (gr. 8-8). 50.93 *(978-0-7660-7674-7(1)*, 963ad279-23df-4f9d-b8fa-584403eefd5b) Enslow Publishing, LLC.

Polinsky, Paige. Sara Seager: Planetary Scientist. 2019. (Women Leading the Way Ser.). (ENG., Illus.). 24p. (J). (gr. k-3). pap. 7.99 *(978-1-61891-505-4(3)*, 12155, Blastoff! Readers) Bellwether Media.

Polinsky, Paige V. Sara Seager: Planetary Scientist. 2019. (Women Leading the Way Ser.). (ENG., Illus.). 24p. (J). (gr. k-3). lib. bdg. 26.95 *(978-1-62617-944-8(1)*, Blastoff! Readers) Bellwether Media.

Porterfield, Jason. The Benefits of Spaceflight & Space Exploration, 1 vol. 2017. (From Earth to the Stars Ser.). (ENG., Illus.). 48p. (J). (gr. 6-7). pap. 15.05 *(978-1-68048-661-2(6)*, 07a1fc2e-e593-4f4c-8cc2-4edd2b8b4411, Britannica Educational Publishing) Rosen Publishing Group, Inc., The.

Priddy, Roger. Smart Kids Space: With More Than 30 Stickers. 2018. (Smart Kids Ser.). (ENG., Illus.). 24p. (J). pap. 5.99 *(978-0-312-52289-6(4)*, 900175811) St. Martin's Pr.

Rauf, Don. Choose a Career Adventure at NASA. 2016. (Bright Futures Press: Choose a Career Adventure Ser.). (ENG., Illus.). 32p. (J). (gr. 4-6). 32.07 *(978-1-63471-913-1(1)*, 208973) Cherry Lake Publishing.

Rich, Mari. Space, Vol. 10. Gilmore, Malinda & Pouson, Mel, eds. 2016. (Black Achievement in Science Ser.). (Illus.). 64p. (J). (gr. 7). 23.95 *(978-1-4222-3563-8(7))* Mason Crest.

Ringstad, Arnold. How Do Engineers Reuse Rockets? 2018. (How'd They Do That? Ser.). (ENG., Illus.). 32p. (J). (gr. 4-6). lib. bdg. 28.65 *(978-1-5435-4135-9(6)*, 139089, Capstone Pr.) Capstone.

—NASA Takes Photography into Space. 2017. (Defining Images Ser.). (ENG., Illus.). 112p. (J). (gr. 6-12). lib. bdg. 41.36 *(978-1-5321-1017-7(0)*, 25610, Essential Library) ABDO Publishing Co.

Robots Exploring Space, 12 vols. 2016. (Robots Exploring Space Ser.). 32p. (gr. 5-5). (ENG.). 167.58 *(978-1-4994-2253-5(9)*, 554a68ee-24df-4527-af57-59d0039be47b); pap. 60.00 *(978-1-5081-5254-5(3))* Rosen Publishing Group, Inc., The. (PowerKids Pr.).

Ross, Jerry L. & Gunderson, Susan G. Becoming a Spacewalker: My Journey to the Stars. 2014. (ENG., Illus.). 40p. (J). 16.95 *(978-1-55753-693-8(7)*, P232663) Purdue Univ. Pr.

Rowland, Andrew, illus. Space. 2015. 17p. (J). *(978-1-4351-5936-5(5))* Barnes & Noble, Inc.

Royston, Angela. Space Blog. 2010. (ENG., Illus.). 32p. (J). *(978-0-7787-9910-8(7))*; pap. *(978-0-7787-9931-3(X))* Crabtree Publishing Co.

Roza, Greg. The Hubble Space Telescope: Understanding & Representing Numbers in the Billions. (PowerMath: Proficiency Plus Ser.). 32p. 2009. (gr. 4-5). 47.90 *(978-1-60851-422-9(6))* 2004. (ENG., Illus.). (J). (gr. 5-6). lib. bdg. 28.93 *(978-1-4042-2931-0(0)*, 7af2f6d7-2234-4b48-ae6e-bc071138672d) Rosen Publishing Group, Inc., The. (PowerKids Pr.).

—The Hubble Space Telescope: Understanding & Representing Numbers up to 1 Billion, 1 vol. 2010. (Math for the REAL World Ser.). (ENG., Illus.). 32p. (gr. 5-6). pap. 10.00 *(978-1-4042-5129-8(4)*, 881be7c6-f2f5-4e5e-bf41-3aab27d0b7a2) Rosen Publishing Group, Inc., The.

Rustad, Martha E. H. Life in Space. 2018. (Astronaut's Life Ser.). (ENG., Illus.). 24p. (J). (gr. -1-2). lib. bdg. 27.32 *(978-1-5157-9817-0(8)*, 136883, Capstone Pr.) Capstone.

—NASA. 2012. (Exploring Space Ser.). (ENG.). 24p. (gr. k-1). pap. 41.70 *(978-1-4296-8329-6(5)*, Capstone Pr.) Capstone.

—NASA, 1 vol. 2012. (Exploring Space Ser.). (ENG.). 24p. (J). (gr. -1-2). lib. bdg. 27.32 *(978-1-4296-7581-9(0)*, 117178, Capstone Pr.) Capstone.

—Working in Space. 2018. (Astronaut's Life Ser.). (ENG., Illus.). 24p. (J). (gr. -1-2). lib. bdg. 27.32 *(978-1-5157-9820-0(8)*, 136888, Capstone Pr.) Capstone.

Sabol, Stephanie. Where Is Our Solar System? 2019. (Who HQ Ser.). (ENG.). 112p. (J). (gr. 2-4). 16.36 *(978-1-64310-813-1(1))* Penworthy Co., LLC, The.

Sabol, Stephanie & Who HQ. Where Is Our Solar System? Hammond, Ted, illus. 2018. (Where Is? Ser.). 112p. (J). (gr. 3-7). 5.99 *(978-0-515-15818-2(6)*, Penguin Workshop) Penguin Young Readers Group.

Salzano, Tammi J. Destination, Space. 2006. (Illus.). 30p. (J). *(978-0-439-88736-6(4))* Scholastic, Inc.

Saunders-Smith, Gail. Robots in Space, 1 vol. 2014. (Cool Robots Ser.). (ENG., Illus.). 24p. (J). (gr. -1-2). 27.32 *(978-1-4914-0585-7(6)*, 125923, Capstone Pr.) Capstone.

Schmermund, Elizabeth. Telescopes, Probes, Spacecraft, & the Future of Space Exploration, 1 vol. 2016. (Space Systems Ser.). (ENG., Illus.). 112p. (J). (gr. 8-8). lib. bdg. 44.50 *(978-1-5026-2293-8(9)*, 52e40515-3c6c-4de4-ac0e-ba5bb8c321c9) Cavendish Square Publishing LLC.

The Science of Space. 2016. (Illus.). 48p. (J). *(978-1-4222-3515-7(7))* Mason Crest.

Science Readers Staff & Jankowski, Connie. From Hubble to Hubble: Astromers & Outer Space, 1 vol. rev. ed. 2007. (Science: Informational Text Ser.). (ENG., Illus.). 32p. (gr. 4-6). pap. 12.99 *(978-0-7439-0564-0(4))* Teacher Created Materials, Inc.

Shackleton, Caroline. Lift off: Exploring the Universe High Intermediate Book with Online Access, 1 vol. 2014. (ENG., Illus.). 28p. (J). pap., E-Book 9.50 *(978-1-107-69249-7(0))* Cambridge Univ. Pr.

M N O

Sipe, Nicole. Living & Working in Space. rev. ed. 2018. (Smithsonian: Informational Text Ser.). (ENG., Illus.). 32p. (J). (gr. 4-8). pap. 11.99 *(978-1-4938-6712-7(1))* Teacher Created Materials, Inc.

Smibert, Angie. Space Myths, Busted! 2017. (Science Myths, Busted! Ser.). (ENG., Illus.). 32p. (J). (gr. 3-6). 32.80 *(978-1-63235-305-4(9)*, 11810, 12-Story Library) Bookstaves, LLC.

Space Exploration. 2011. (ENG., Illus.). 128p. (gr. 4-9). 24.95 *(978-0-8160-8054-0(2)*, P189800, Ferguson Publishing Company) Infobase Holdings, Inc.

Space Exploration: Science, Technology, Engineering (Calling All Innovators: a Career for You) (Library Edition) 2014. (Calling All Innovators: a Career for You Ser.). (ENG.). 64p. (J). (gr. 5-8). lib. bdg. 32.00 *(978-0-531-20615-7(7)*, Children's Pr.) Scholastic Library Publishing.

Space Explorers, 12 vols. 2017. (Space Explorers Ser.). (ENG.). (J). (gr. 2-2). lib. bdg. 161.58 *(978-0-7660-9269-3(0)*, f55d26b1-1ce0-4562-8ac8-4bbf3d89d258) Enslow Publishing, LLC.

Space Mysteries: Set 3, 12 vols. 2018. (Space Mysteries Ser.). (ENG.). 32p. (gr. 2-3). lib. bdg. 175.62 *(978-1-5382-2190-7(X)*, f35bf2eb-2bbc-48dd-a995-4c4f0219c238) Stevens, Gareth Publishing LLLP.

Sparrow, Giles. Exploring the Universe, 1 vol. 2006. (Secrets of the Universe Ser.). (ENG., Illus.). 48p. (gr. 6-8). lib. bdg. 33.67 *(978-0-8368-7276-7(2)*, b9c1e309-ac1e-4409-923b-d6b8b6a1a3cd, Gareth Stevens Secondary Library) Stevens, Gareth Publishing LLLP.

—Probing Deep Space, 1 vol. 2006. (Secrets of the Universe Ser.). (ENG., Illus.). 48p. (gr. 6-8). lib. bdg. 33.67 *(978-0-8368-7279-8(7)*, 1fc28e8c-561b-4afa-a044-60d80f56400a, Gareth Stevens Secondary Library) Stevens, Gareth Publishing LLLP.

—Space Exploration. 2011. (Exploring Space: Space Travel Guides). 32p. (gr. 3-6). lib. bdg. 31.35 *(978-1-59920-665-3(X))* Black Rabbit Bks.

Sparrow, Giles, et al. Exploring Space, 1 vol. 2015. (Discoveries in Space Science Ser.). (ENG., Illus.). 80p. (YA). (gr. 9-9). lib. bdg. 37.36 *(978-1-5026-1012-6(4)*, a6a63c3c-9a0a-4ab9-807c-85d4044a4a6e) Cavendish Square Publishing LLC.

—Shuttles & Space Missions, 1 vol. 2015. (Discoveries in Space Science Ser.). (ENG., Illus.). 80p. (YA). (gr. 9-9). lib. bdg. 37.36 *(978-1-5026-1016-4(7)*, 69c4d247-85f3-419b-99f3-58f67e00afea) Cavendish Square Publishing LLC.

Squishy, Fishy Robot Explorers: Meet NASA Inventor Mason Peck & His Team's. 2017. (J). *(978-0-7166-6156-6(X))* World Bk., Inc.

Staff, Gareth Editorial Staff. Space Exploration, 1 vol. 2003. (Discovery Channel School Science: Universes Large & Small Ser.). (ENG., Illus.). 32p. (gr. 5-7). lib. bdg. 28.67 *(978-0-8368-3373-7(2)*, 09ab0b4a-e97d-4772-a1d3-72ec7d345831, Gareth Stevens Learning Library) Stevens, Gareth Publishing LLLP.

Stiegler, Lorraine. Space Probes, 1 vol. 2012. (Exploring Earth & Space Ser.). (ENG., Illus.). 24p. (J). (gr. 1-2). 26.27 *(978-1-4488-8580-0(9)*, eca19de1-0ae6-4e72-9bee-c32de37e94dd, PowerKids Pr.) Rosen Publishing Group, Inc., The.

Stone, Tanya Lee. Mercury, 1 vol. 2003. (Blastoff! Ser.). (ENG., Illus.). 64p. (gr. 5-5). 34.07 *(978-0-7614-1403-2(7)*, 55b133bf-ce16-476e-8948-6f371fb14a47) Cavendish Square Publishing LLC.

—Venus, 1 vol. 2003. (Blastoff! Ser.). (ENG., Illus.). 64p. (gr. 5-5). 34.07 *(978-0-7614-1405-6(3)*, b640cfb3-0bfa-4da9-873d-384df522d210) Cavendish Square Publishing LLC.

Swatling, Todd. What Happens to Space Probes?, 1 vol. 2018. (Space Mysteries Ser.). (ENG.). 32p. (gr. 2-3). 29.27 *(978-1-5382-1959-1(X)*, 41b9eae3-a043-4dcc-95fc-2b04d56f53fc) Stevens, Gareth Publishing LLLP.

Teitelbaum, Michael. Mars & Venus Space Exploration: Set Of 6. 2011. (Navigators Ser.). (J). pap. 50.00 net. *(978-1-4108-6243-3(7))* Benchmark Education Co.

—Mars & Venus: Space Exploration: Text Pairs. 2008. (Bridges/Navigators Ser.). (J). (gr. 6). 94.00 *(978-1-4108-8445-9(7))* Benchmark Education Co.

Thomas, Rachael L. Revolutionary Robots in Space. 2019. (Cosmos Chronicles (Alternator Books (r)) Ser.). (ENG., Illus.). 32p. (J). (gr. 3-6). pap. 10.99 *(978-1-5415-7370-3(6)*, ac8379ce-a411-4aca-bf09-d9827e7dc129, Lerner Pubns.) Lerner Publishing Group.

—Trailblazing Space Scientists. 2019. (Cosmos Chronicles (Alternator Books (r)) Ser.). (ENG., Illus.). 32p. (J). (gr. 3-6). pap. 10.99 *(978-1-5415-7372-7(2)*, 4500078f-d14f-4d62-9efd-560dc7b43f49); lib. bdg. 29.32 *(978-1-5415-5595-2(3)*, e78b7377-6bca-4a08-942b-2f6650836968) Lerner Publishing Group. (Lerner Pubns.).

Thompson, Ben & Slader, Erik. The Race to Space: Countdown to Liftoff (Epic Fails #2) Foley, Tim, illus. 2018. (Epic Fails Ser.: 2). (ENG.). 160p. (J). pap. 8.99 *(978-1-250-15062-2(0)*, 900182551) Roaring Brook Pr.

Trotman, Felicity. Exploration of Space. 2010. (History of Exploration Ser.). 48p. 32.80 *(978-1-84898-302-1(6))* Black Rabbit Bks.

Vogt, Gregory L. Missions to Mars. 2018. (Destination Space Ser.). (ENG., Illus.). 48p. (J). (gr. 5-6). pap. 11.95 *(978-1-63517-568-4(2)*, 1635175682); lib. bdg. 34.21 *(978-1-63517-496-0(1)*, 1635174961) North Star Editions. (Focus Readers).

Walliman, Dominic. Professor Astro Cat's Frontiers of Space. Newman, Ben, illus. 2nd ed. 2013. (Professor Astro Cat Ser.). (ENG.). 64p. (J). (gr. 2-5). 19.95 *(978-1-909263-07-9(9))* Flying Eye Bks. GBR. Dist: Penguin Random Hse. LLC.

Waxman, Laura Hamilton. Exploring Black Holes. 2011. (Searchlight Books (tm) — What's Amazing about Space? Ser.). (ENG., Illus.). 40p. (J). (gr. 3-5). pap. 9.99 *(978-0-7613-7877-8(4)*, 3956c271-e45e-4bbb-8ee4-7c6baac29400) Lerner Publishing Group.

Way, Steve & Bailey, Gerry. Space, 1 vol. 2008. (Simply Science Ser.). (ENG., Illus.). 32p. (YA). (gr. 3-5). lib. bdg. 28.67 *(978-0-8368-9232-1(1)*, 17882e13-4ca7-4806-ac29-b0cecdacda37) Stevens, Gareth Publishing LLLP.

Wimmer, Teresa. National Aeronautics & Space Administration. (Agents of Government Ser.). (ENG.). 48p. (J). (gr. 4-7). 2016. pap. 12.00 *(978-1-62832-148-7(2)*, 20844, Creative Paperbacks) 2015. (Illus.). *(978-1-60818-547-4(8)*, 20843, Creative Education) Creative Co., The.

Windsor, Susan, illus. Space: God's Majestic Handiwork. 2017. 111p. (J). pap. *(978-1-946246-03-5(4))* Institute for Creation Research.

Woolf, Alex. The Science of Spacecraft: the Cosmic Truth about Rockets, Satellites, & Probes (the Science of Engineering) (Library Edition) Myer, Ed & Beach, Bryan, illus. 2019. (Science Of... Ser.). (ENG.). 32p. (J). (gr. 3-3). lib. bdg. 29.00 *(978-0-531-13197-8(1)*, Watts, Franklin) Scholastic Library Publishing.

World Book, Inc. Staff, contrib. by. Encyclopedia of Space. 2013. (J). *(978-0-7166-7523-5(4))* World Bk., Inc.

—Human Space Exploration. 2nd ed. 2006. (World Book's Solar System & Space Exploration Library). (Illus.). 64p. (J). *(978-0-7166-9514-1(6))* World Bk., Inc.

—Space Exploration. 2011. (J). *(978-0-7166-1792-1(7))* World Bk., Inc.

—Stargazing to Space Travel: A Timeline of Space Exploration. 2016. (Illus.). 40p. (J). *(978-0-7166-3545-1(3))* World Bk.-Childcraft International.

—Telescopes & Space Probes. 2nd ed. 2006. (Illus.). 64p. (J). *(978-0-7166-9520-2(0))* World Bk., Inc.

Zobel, Derek. NASA. 2010. (Exploring Space Ser.). (ENG., Illus.). 24p. (J). (gr. k-3). lib. bdg. 26.95 *(978-1-60014-293-2(1)*, Blastoff! Readers) Bellwether Media.

OUTER SPACE—FICTION

Act-Two Staff. Space Mission. 2004. (Illus.). (J). pap. 8.99 incl. cd-rom *(978-0-7868-3418-1(8))* Hyperion Bks. for Children.

Adventures Beyond the Solar System: Planetron & Me. 2005. (J). audio, cd-rom 24.95 *(978-0-9771381-5-9(1))* Williams, Geoffrey T.

Adventures in the Solar System: Planetron & Me. 2005. (J). audio, cd-rom 24.95 *(978-0-9771381-4-2(3))* Williams, Geoffrey T.

Auerbach, Annie. My Race into Space! A Water Wonder Book. Garofoli, Viviana, illus. 2005. 18p. (J). 9.95 *(978-1-58117-351-2(2)*, Intervisual/Piggy Toes) Bendon, Inc.

Bartol, Amy A. Sea of Stars, 0 vols. 2015. (Kricket Ser.: 2). (ENG.). 320p. pap. 14.95 *(978-1-4778-2823-6(0)*, 9781477828236, 47North) Amazon Publishing.

Bean, Raymond. First Family in Space. Vimislik, Matthew, illus. 2016. (Out of This World Ser.). (ENG.). 112p. (J). (gr. 2-5). lib. bdg. 32.65 *(978-1-4965-3617-4(7)*, 132833, Stone Arch Bks.) Capstone.

—Trouble on Venus. Vimislik, Matthew, illus. 2016. (Out of This World Ser.). (ENG.). 112p. (J). (gr. 2-5). lib. bdg. 32.65 *(978-1-4965-3614-3(2)*, 132830, Stone Arch Bks.) Capstone.

Beecroft, Simon. Stand Aside-Bounty Hunters! 2009. (Star Wars: the Clone Wars DK Readers Ser.). lib. bdg. 13.55 *(978-0-606-07065-2(6))* Turtleback.

Bloomsbury USA. Lift & Look: in Space. 2016. (ENG., Illus.). 12p. (J). (— 1). bds. 8.99 *(978-1-61963-826-6(6)*, 9781619638266, Bloomsbury Activity Bks.) Bloomsbury Publishing USA.

Brezenoff, Steve. The Final Mission. Calle Velez, Juan, illus. 2019. (Michael Dahl Presents: Screams in Space 4D Ser.). (ENG.). 112p. (J). (gr. 3-5). lib. bdg. 27.32 *(978-1-4965-7902-7(X)*, 139612, Stone Arch Bks.) Capstone.

Brockington, Drew. CatStronauts: Robot Rescue. 2018. (CatStronauts Ser.: 4). (J). lib. bdg. 19.65 *(978-0-606-40982-7(3))* Turtleback.

—CatStronauts: Robot Rescue. 2018. (CatStronauts Ser.: 4). (ENG., Illus.). 184p. (J). (gr. 1-5). pap. 9.99 *(978-0-316-30756-7(4))* Little, Brown Bks. for Young Readers.

—CatStronauts: Space Station Situation. 2017. (CatStronauts Ser.: 3). (ENG., Illus.). 168p. (J). (gr. 1-5). pap. 9.99 *(978-0-316-30753-6(X))* Little, Brown Bks. for Young Readers.

Brophy, Ann. Novus 3 & Me: Six Short Stories about Friendship. 2010. 44p. pap. 18.49 *(978-1-4490-7132-5(5))* AuthorHouse.

Caine, Rachel, pseud & Aguirre, Ann. Honor Bound. (Honors Ser.: 2). (ENG.). (YA). (gr. 8). 2020. 496p. pap. 12.99 *(978-0-06-257103-8(6))* 2019. (Illus.). 480p. 17.99 *(978-0-06-257102-1(8))* HarperCollins Pubs. (Tegen, Katherine Bks).

Calandrelli, Emily. Ada Lace, Take Me to Your Leader. 2018. (Ada Lace Adventure Ser.: 3). lib. bdg. 17.20 *(978-0-606-41405-0(3))* Turtleback.

Camper, Cathy. Lowriders in Space, 1 vol. the Third, Raul, illus. 2014. (Lowriders Ser.). (ENG.). 112p. (J). (gr. 3-7). pap. 9.99 *(978-1-4521-2869-6(3)*, da9edee5-f1ff-4bfb-91f6-5ca5cf0178dd) Chronicle Bks. LLC.

Carson, Penny & Hess, Amy. Simon Goes Camping. 2008. 19p. 10.95 *(978-1-4357-1560-8(8))* Lulu Pr., Inc.

Castellan, Andrea. Mickey Mouse & the Orbiting Nightmare. 2011. (ENG., Illus.). 128p. (J). pap. *(978-1-60886-630-4(0))* BOOM! Studios.

Chang, Ifay, as told by. Outopians. 2007. (Illus.). 27p. (YA). pap. *(978-0-9771594-1-3(8))* TLC Information Services.

Chiaramonti, Gregory. Probie the Space Probe, Mission One: the Ocean of Europa. 2007. 32p. (J). 16.72 *(978-0-615-13848-0(9))* Chiaramonti, Gregory.

Connely, Chris L. & Vaughan, Mark. An Alien from Earth. 2003. 175p. per. 9.95 *(978-0-9745544-0-2(5))* Lewis Lynn Bks.

Cook, Julia. Personal Space Camp. Hartman, Carrie, illus. 2007. (ENG.). 32p. (J). (gr. k-3). pap. 10.95 *(978-1-931636-87-2(7)*, A134) National Ctr. For Youth Issues.

Cottrell Boyce, Frank. Cosmic. 2011. (ENG.). 336p. (J). (gr. 3-7). pap. 9.99 *(978-0-06-183688-6(5)*, Waldon Pond Pr.) HarperCollins Pubs.

Dahl, Roald. Charlie & the Great Glass Elevator. Blake, Quentin, illus. (ENG.). (J). (gr. 3-7). 2007. 192p. 8.99 *(978-0-14-241032-5(2))* 2005. 176p. pap. 7.99 *(978-0-14-240412-6(8))* Penguin Young Readers Group. (Puffin Books).

—Charlie & the Great Glass Elevator. 2007. 18.40 *(978-1-4177-8610-7(8))* Turtleback.

Dinardo, Jeff. Field Trip to Mars (Book 1) Clegg, Dave, illus. 2018. (Funny Bone Books (tm) First Chapters — the Jupiter Twins Ser.). (ENG.). 32p. (J). (gr. k-2). pap. 4.99 *(978-1-63440-253-8(7)*, a36c3066-7240-49c6-8199-6603c4e655a8); lib. bdg. 19.99 *(978-1-63440-249-1(9)*, 6e39dd05-728c-4f2b-a77c-a147a05d70b4) Red Chair Pr.

—Lost on Earth (Book 2) Clegg, Dave, illus. 2018. (Funny Bone Books (tm) First Chapters — the Jupiter Twins Ser.: Vol. 2). (ENG.). 32p. (J). (gr. k-2). lib. bdg. 19.99 *(978-1-63440-250-7(2)*, 2095c0c4-de74-4dce-8ea1-005fdbc5304d) Red Chair Pr.

—Party on Pluto (Book 4) Clegg, Dave, illus. 2018. (Funny Bone Books (tm) First Chapters — the Jupiter Twins Ser.). (ENG.). 32p. (J). (gr. k-2). pap. 4.99 *(978-1-63440-256-9(1)*, 87d1a80e-6152-46fc-9771-54bebed1096c); lib. bdg. 19.99 *(978-1-63440-252-1(9)*, 089f8f27-9295-4aac-8f56-a859d89d15a0) Red Chair Pr.

—Scout Trip to Saturn (Book 3) Clegg, Dave, illus. 2018. (Funny Bone Books (tm) First Chapters — the Jupiter Twins Ser.). (ENG.). 32p. (J). (gr. k-2). pap. 4.99 *(978-1-63440-255-2(3)*, bac7dde8-6758-450f-824b-41607ade5c01); lib. bdg. 19.99 *(978-1-63440-251-4(0)*, 2209adee-6f57-4c9f-9075-4e7d59fa6385) Red Chair Pr.

Disney Press Editors. Ewoks Join the Fight. 2015. (Star Wars: World of Reading Ser.). (J). lib. bdg. 13.55 *(978-0-606-36912-1(0))* Turtleback.

Doeden, Matt. Hansel & Gretel: An Interactive Fairy Tale Adventure. Miramon, Sabrina, illus. 2017. (You Choose: Fractured Fairy Tales Ser.). (ENG.). 112p. (J). (gr. 3-7). pap. 6.95 *(978-1-5157-6952-1(6)*, 135424); lib. bdg. 32.65 *(978-1-5157-6944-6(5)*, 135418) Capstone. (Capstone Pr.).

Edick, Grant. Space Station. 2004. (Two Boys Adventure Story Ser.). 98p. (J). (gr. 3-6). 15.95 *(978-0-9677839-9-4(2))* Wysteria Publishing.

Emerson, Kevin. The Shores Beyond Time. (Chronicle of the Dark Star Ser.: 3). (ENG.). 512p. (J). (gr. 3-7). 2020. pap. 8.99 *(978-0-06-230678-4(2))* 2019. 16.99 *(978-0-06-230677-7(4))* HarperCollins Pubs. (Waldon Pond Pr.).

Evans, D. L. & Sinclair, Valerie. How Rolly Robot Saved the Starbabies, 1 vol. 2012. (ENG., Illus.). 32p. (J). *(978-1-55455-201-6(X))* Fitzhenry & Whiteside, Ltd.

Farber, Erica, et al. The Alien from Outer Space, 2. 2006. (Mercer Mayer's Critter Kids Adventures Ser.). (ENG., Illus.). 32p. (J). (gr. k-3). 17.44 *(978-0-7696-4763-0(4))* School Specialty, Incorporated.

Finn, Caitlin. Harold the Misfit. 2012. 24p. pap. 14.93 *(978-1-4669-5131-0(1))* Trafford Publishing.

Freestone, Annie. The Little Mars Rovers. 2008. 36p. pap. 13.95 *(978-1-59858-459-2(6))* Dog Ear Publishing, LLC.

Gioseffi, Anthony P. Mainframe. 2007. 144p. per. 11.95 *(978-0-595-44953-8(0))* iUniverse, Inc.

Girard, Philippe. Gustave et le Capitaine Planète. Girard, Philippe, illus. 2004. (Mon Roman Ser.). (FRE., Illus.). 96p. (J). (gr. 2). pap. *(978-2-89021-649-5(7))* Diffusion du livre Mirabel (DLM).

Goguen, Martha M. Andromed: Dream Believe Achieve Series. Walker, Patricia M., illus. 2011. 36p. pap. *(978-1-897435-35-9(5))* Agio Publishing Hse.

Golden Books. Sponge in Space! (SpongeBob SquarePants) Martinez, Heather, illus. 2012. (Little Golden Book Ser.). (ENG.). 24p. (J). (gr. k-k). 4.99 *(978-0-307-92990-7(6)*, Golden Bks.) Random Hse. Children's Bks.

Granny J. Pinky Visits Outer Space: Pinky Frink's Adventures. 2012. (ENG.). 36p. pap. 17.99 *(978-1-300-06064-2(6))* Lulu Pr., Inc.

Guibert, Emmanuel. Sardine in Outer Space. Sfar, Joann, illus. deluxe ed. 2006. (Sardine in Outer Space Ser.: 1). (ENG.). 128p. (J). (gr. 1-5). pap. 17.99 *(978-1-59643-126-3(1)*, 900032000, First Second Bks.) Roaring Brook Pr.

Harber, Chris. Simon the Policeman on the Number Planet. Harber, Hulya, illus. 2013. 28p. pap. *(978-0-7552-1560-7(5)*, Bright Pen) Authors OnLine, Ltd.

Harrison, Zac. Robot Warriors, 1 vol. 2013. (Hyperspace High Ser.). (ENG., Illus.). 288p. (J). (gr. 4-8). pap. 8.95 *(978-1-4342-6312-4(6)*, 123758, Stone Arch Bks.) Capstone.

Hawking, Lucy & Hawking, Stephen. George's Cosmic Treasure Hunt. Parsons, Garry, illus. 2009. (George's Secret Key Ser.). (ENG.). 320p. (J). (gr. 3-7). 19.99 *(978-1-4169-8671-3(5)*, Simon & Schuster Bks. For Young Readers) Simon & Schuster Bks. For Young Readers.

—George's Cosmic Treasure Hunt. Parsons, Garry, illus. 2011. (George's Secret Key Ser.). (ENG.). 352p. (J). (gr. 3-7). pap. 12.99 *(978-1-4424-2175-2(4)*, Simon & Schuster Bks. For Young Readers) Simon & Schuster Bks. For Young Readers.

Hawking, Stephen & Hawking, Lucy. George's Secret Key to the Universe. Parsons, Garry, illus. l.t. ed. 2008. (Literacy Bridge Middle Reader Ser.). 359p. (J). (gr. 3-7). 24.95 *(978-1-4104-0638-5(5))* Thorndike Pr.

Hinote Lanier, Wendy. Rockets. 2019. (Let's Fly Ser.). (ENG., Illus.). 32p. (J). (gr. 2-3). 31.35 *(978-1-64185-341-5(7)*, 1641853417, Focus Readers) North Star Editions.

Hoena, Blake A. Ooze Slingers from Outer Space. Harpster, Steve, illus. 2007. (Graphic Sparks Ser.). (ENG.). 40p. (J). (gr. 2-5). per. 5.95 *(978-1-59889-410-3(2)*, 93557, Stone Arch Bks.) Capstone.

Hole, Stian. Garmann's Secret. 2011. (ENG., Illus.). 56p. (J). 17.00 *(978-0-8028-5400-1(1)*, Eerdmans Bks For Young Readers) Eerdmans, William B. Publishing Co.

Klein, Joel & Klein, Abby. The Night I Saved the Universe: From the Files of the Galactic Police Department. 2009. 126p. (J). *(978-0-545-12933-6(8))* Scholastic, Inc.

Knife & Packer. Spash Mash. Knife & Packer, illus. 2016. (Illus.). 93p. (J). pap. 6.99 *(978-1-61067-397-6(2))* Kane Miller.

Korté, Steve. Superman & the Showdown at Saturn: A Solar System Adventure. Schigiel, Gregg, illus. 2018. (Superman Solar System Adventures Ser.). (ENG.). 32p. (J). (gr. 4-8). lib. bdg. 27.99 *(978-1-5435-1572-5(X)*, 137927, Capstone Pr.) Capstone.

Lehman, Seth. The Color Pets. 2006. (Illus.). 52p. (J). 7.00 net. *(978-0-9787986-0-4(0))* 4All Ages LLC.

Lem, Stanislaw. The Seventh Voyage: a Graphic Novel. Kandel, Michael, tr. Muth, Jon J., illus. 2019.Tr. of Star Diaries. (ENG.). 80p. (YA). (gr. 3-7). 19.99 *(978-0-545-00462-6(4)*, Graphix) Scholastic, Inc.

Long, Ethan. Clara & Clem in Outer Space. 2013. (Penguin Young Readers, Level 1 Ser.). (ENG.). 32p. (J). (gr. k-1). pap. 5.99 *(978-0-448-46721-4(6)*, Penguin Young Readers) Penguin Young Readers Group.

McBride, Earvin, Jr. Space - M. D. 3001. McBride, Earvin, Jr., illus. 2nd unabr. ed. 2003. (Earvin MacBride's Amazing Sci-Fi & Adventure Heroes Ser.). (Illus.). 329p. (J). (gr. 7-12). pap. 4.95 *(978-1-892511-09-6(6))* MacBride, E. J. Pubn., Inc.

McNamara, Margaret. The Three Little Aliens & the Big Bad Robot. Fearing, Mark, illus. 2011. (ENG.). 40p. (J). (gr. -1-3). 18.99 *(978-0-375-86689-0(2))* Random Hse. Children's Bks.

McNamee, Kevin. Just for Today. Movshina, Marina, illus. 2012. 16p. pap. 9.95 *(978-1-61633-314-0(6))* Guardian Angel Publishing, Inc.

Meister, Cari. Buzz Beaker & the Outer Space Trip. McGuire, Bill, illus. 2010. (Buzz Beaker Bks.). (ENG.). 32p. (J). (gr. 2-3). pap. 6.25 *(978-1-4342-2800-0(2)*, 114067, Stone Arch Bks.) Capstone.

Metz, Melinda. S. M. A. R. T. S. & the Mars Mission Mayhem. McKenzie, Heath, illus. 2016. (S. M. A. R. T. S. Ser.). (ENG.). 128p. (J). (gr. 3-6). pap. 9.95 *(978-1-4965-3018-9(7)*, 131905, Stone Arch Bks.) Capstone.

Meyers, Haily & Meyers, Kevin. 3-2-1 Blast Off! A Journey to Our Solar System, 1 vol. 2018. (Lucy Darling Ser.). (Illus.). 20p. (J). (-k). bds. 14.99 *(978-1-4236-5033-1(6))* Gibbs Smith, Publisher.

Miller, Jeff. The Nerdy Dozen #2: Close Encounters of the Nerd Kind. 2015. (Nerdy Dozen Ser.: 2). (ENG.). 272p. (J). (gr. 3-7). 16.99 *(978-0-06-227265-2(9)*, HarperCollins) HarperCollins Pubs.

Molloy, Tom. Everything but the Beach: A Slice of Manchester Life. 2012. (ENG., Illus.). 192p. (J). pap. 9.60 *(978-1-291-15817-5(0))* Lulu Pr., Inc.

Montgomery, R. A. Trouble on Planet Earth. 2007. 144p. (J). pap. *(978-1-86504-933-5(6))* Chooseco LLC.

—Trouble on Planet Earth. Trod, Mariano et al, illus. 2006. (ENG.). 144p. (J). (gr. 4-8). per. 6.99 *(978-1-933390-11-6(5)*, CHCL11) Chooseco LLC.

—Trouble on Planet Earth. 2005. (Illus.). 113p. (J). pap. *(978-0-7608-9699-0(2))* Sundance/Newbridge Educational Publishing.

Moodey, Mary. Christopher Counts the Constellation, bks. 500, bk. 500. Shingle, Jude, illus. 500th l.t. ed. 2012. (ENG.). 37p. 16.99 *(978-0-9853579-0-0(8))* MarMooWorks,LLC.

Moore, Brenna L. Out of Place in Outer Space. 2013. 28p. pap. 11.95 *(978-1-4787-0706-6(2))* Outskirts Pr., Inc.

Oppel, Kenneth. Starclimber. (ENG.). 400p. (YA). (gr. 8-8). 2010. pap. 11.99 *(978-0-06-085059-3(0))* 2009. (Illus.). 17.99 *(978-0-06-085057-9(4))* HarperCollins Pubs. (HarperCollins).

O'Ryan, Ray. The Annoying Crush. Kraft, Jason, illus. 2014. (Galaxy Zack Ser.: 9). (ENG.). 128p. (J). (gr. k-4). 17.99 *(978-1-4424-9364-3(X))*; pap. 5.99 *(978-1-4424-9363-6(1))* Little Simon. (Little Simon).

—The Annoying Crush. 2014. (Galaxy Zack Ser.: 9). lib. bdg. 16.00 *(978-0-606-36093-7(X))* Turtleback.

—Drake Makes a Splash! Jack, Colin, illus. 2014. (Galaxy Zack Ser.: 8). (ENG.). 128p. (J). (gr. k-4). pap. 6.99 *(978-1-4424-9360-5(7)*, Little Simon) Little Simon.

—A Galactic Easter! Jack, Colin, illus. 2014. (Galaxy Zack Ser.: 7). (ENG.). 128p. (J). (gr. k-4). pap. 6.99 *(978-1-4424-9357-5(7)*, Little Simon) Little Simon.

—A Galactic Easter! 2014. (Galaxy Zack Ser.: 7). lib. bdg. 16.00 *(978-0-606-35428-8(X))* Turtleback.

—A Green Christmas! Jack, Colin, illus. 2013. (Galaxy Zack Ser.: 6). (ENG.). 128p. (J). (gr. k-2). 17.99 *(978-1-4424-8225-8(7))*; pap. 6.99 *(978-1-4424-8224-1(9))*; pap. 6.99 *(978-1-4424-8224-1(9))* Little Simon. (Little Simon).

—A Green Christmas! 2013. (Galaxy Zack Ser.: 6). lib. bdg. 14.75 *(978-0-606-35185-0(X))* Turtleback.

Packer. Space Mash. Knife, illus. 2016. 93p. (J). *(978-1-61067-477-5(4))* Kane Miller.

Pilkey, Dav. Ricky Ricotta's Mighty Robot vs. the Naughty Nightcrawlers from Neptune (Ricky Ricotta's Mighty Robot #8) Santat, Dan, illus. 2016. (Ricky Ricotta's Mighty Robot Ser.: 8). (ENG.). 128p. (J). (gr. -1-3). pap. 5.99 *(978-0-439-37709-6(9))* Scholastic, Inc.

Rand, Johnathan. Freddie Fernortner #9: Attack of the Dust Bunnies from Outer Space. 2008. 96p. (J). pap. 4.99 *(978-1-893699-95-3(1))* AudioCraft Publishing, Inc.

Regan, Dian Curtis. Space Boy & His Dog. Neubecker, Robert, illus. 2015. (Space Boy Ser.). (ENG.). 32p. (J). (gr. -1-2). 16.95 *(978-1-59078-955-1(5)*, Astra Young Readers) Astra Publishing Hse.

—Space Boy & the Snow Monster. Neubecker, Robert, illus. 2017. (Space Boy Ser.). (ENG.). 32p. (J). (gr. -1-2). 17.95 *(978-1-59078-957-5(1)*, Astra Young Readers) Astra Publishing Hse.

—Space Boy & the Space Pirate. Neubecker, Robert, illus. 2016. (Space Boy Ser.). (ENG.). 40p. (J). (gr. -1-2). 16.95 *(978-1-59078-956-8(3)*, Astra Young Readers) Astra Publishing Hse.

Rockwell, Carey. The Revolt on Venus. 2007. 120p. per. *(978-1-4068-3961-6(2))* Echo Library.

—The Space Pioneers. 2007. 120p. per. *(978-1-4068-3962-3(0))* Echo Library.

—Treachery in Outer Space. 2017. (ENG., Illus.). (J). 23.95 *(978-1-374-97145-5(6))*; pap. 13.95 *(978-1-374-97144-8(8))* Capital Communications, Inc.

Rosenthal, Adam. Adventures of Snizznsnozz. 2011. 24p. pap. 11.32 *(978-1-4634-0736-0(X))* AuthorHouse.

Roth, Jonathan. Party Crashers, 2. 2019. (Beep & Bob Ser.). (ENG.). 128p. (J). (gr. 2-4). 15.59 *(978-1-64310-827-8(1))* Penworthy Co., LLC, The.

—Party Crashers. Roth, Jonathan, illus. 2018. (Beep & Bob Ser.: 2). (ENG., Illus.). 128p. (J). (gr. 1-4). 16.99 *(978-1-4814-8856-3(2))*; pap. 6.99 *(978-1-4814-8855-6(4))* Simon & Schuster Children's Publishing. (Aladdin).

—Take Us to Your Sugar, 3. 2019. (Beep & Bob Ser.). (ENG.). 128p. (J). (gr. 2-4). 15.59 (978-1-64310-828-5(X)) Penworthy Co., LLC, The.

—Take Us to Your Sugar. Roth, Jonathan, illus. 2018. (Beep & Bob Ser.: 3). (ENG., Illus.). 128p. (J). (gr. 1-4). 16.99 (978-1-4814-8859-4(7)); pap. 5.99 (978-1-4814-8858-7(9)) Simon & Schuster Children's Publishing. (Aladdin).

—Too Much Space!, 1. 2019. (Beep & Bob Ser.). (ENG.). 128p. (J). (gr. 2-4). 15.59 (978-1-64310-829-2(8)) Penworthy Co., LLC, The.

—Too Much Space! Roth, Jonathan, illus. 2018. (Beep & Bob Ser.: 1). (ENG., Illus.). 128p. (J). (gr. 1-4). 17.99 (978-1-4814-8853-2(8)); pap. 5.99 (978-1-4814-8852-5(X)) Simon & Schuster Children's Publishing. (Aladdin).

Rouss, Sylvia A. Reach for the Stars. 2005. (Illus.). 40p. (J). (gr. 3-7). 16.95 (978-1-930143-82-1(6)); pap. 9.95 (978-1-930143-83-8(4)) Simcha Media Group. (Devora Publishing).

Santillo, LuAnn. The Big Job. Santillo, LuAnn, ed. 2003. (Half-Pint Kids Readers Ser.). (Illus.). 7p. (J). (gr. -1-1). pap. (978-1-59256-044-8(X)) Half-Pint Kids, Inc.

—Outerspace, 6 vols. Santillo, LuAnn, ed. 2003. (Half-Pint Kids Readers Ser.). (Illus.). 42p. (J). (gr. -1-1). pap. 6.95 (978-1-59256-042-4(3)) Half-Pint Kids, Inc.

Schooley, Bob & McCorkle, Mark. Liar of Kudzu. 2008. (ENG.). 192p. (J). (gr. 5-9). pap. 9.99 (978-1-4169-1489-1(7), Simon & Schuster Bks. For Young Readers) Simon & Schuster Bks. For Young Readers.

—Liar of Kudzu. 2007. (ENG.). 183p. (J). (gr. 6-8). 18.69 (978-1-4169-1488-4(9)) Simon & Schuster, Inc.

Scott, Janine. Café Cosmos, 1 vol. Wood, Hannah, illus. 2009. (Treasure Chest Readers Ser.). (ENG.). 24p. (J). (gr. 1-1). pap. 9.15 (978-1-60754-674-0(4), 1dece89f-fea7-4a4b-b784-8d6413382311); lib. bdg. 27.27 (978-1-60754-673-3(6), 16ffcaf2-b162-4e05-83e0-eb19ec85efb5) Rosen Publishing Group, Inc., The. (Windmill Bks.).

—Mars Mouse, 1 vol. Wood, Hannah, illus. 2009. (Treasure Chest Readers Ser.). (ENG.). 24p. (J). (gr. 1-1). pap. 9.15 (978-1-60754-677-1(9), 91ae73ab-a879-4fb8-9c38-fd87648aaf30); lib. bdg. 27.27 (978-1-60754-676-4(0), c87bb159-35dd-4473-a072-85a046b4d8b0) Rosen Publishing Group, Inc., The. (Windmill Bks.).

Shannon, Ronnie Jay. Samurai Force: the Final Hope: The Junior Novel. 2007. (ENG.). 76p. per. 19.95 (978-1-4241-6528-5(8)) America Star Bks.

Shirai, Shiro, illus. Disney Manga: Pixar's Wall-E. 2018. (Disney Manga: Pixar's WALL E Ser.). 144p. (J). (gr. 1-1). pap. 10.99 (978-1-4278-5771-2(7), 2acaa296-e525-4288-8c30-11a544decd87, TOKYOPOP Manga) TOKYOPOP, Inc.

Smiley, Mark. A Journey Far Away. 2006. 164p. pap. 13.95 (978-1-59526-494-7(9)) Aeon Publishing Inc.

Snyder, Maria V. Navigating the Stars. 2018. (ENG.). 444p. (YA). (gr. 18-18). pap. 17.95 (978-1-946381-01-9(2)) Snyder, Maria V.

Spoonmore, Scott. Seymour the Semi- Space Truckin' Sponaugle, Kim, illus. 2012. 24p. 19.95 (978-1-61633-282-2(4)); pap. 11.95 (978-1-61633-283-9(2)) Guardian Angel Publishing, Inc.

Stilton, Gerónimo. Rescue Rebellion. 2015. (Geronimo Stilton Spacemice Ser.: 5). lib. bdg. 17.20 (978-0-606-37775-1(1)) Turtleback.

Strub, Scott Richard. Otto the Outerspace Octopus. 2007. (J). per. 10.00 (978-1-59872-782-1(6)) Instant Pub.

Thompson, Craig. Space Dumplins: a Graphic Novel. Thompson, Craig, illus. 2015. (ENG., Illus.). 320p. (J). (gr. 3-7). pap. 18.99 (978-0-545-56543-1(X), Graphix) Scholastic, Inc.

Todd, Ruthven. Space Cat & the Kittens. Galdone, Paul, illus. 2018. (ENG.). 96p. (gr. 1-5). 16.95 (978-0-486-82275-4(3), 822753) Dover Pubns., Inc.

Trine, Greg. Willy Maykit in Space. Burks, James, illus. (ENG.). 208p. (J). (gr. 3-7). 2016. pap. 7.99 (978-0-544-66848-5(0), 1625468) 2015. 14.99 (978-0-544-31351-4(8), 1581676) HarperCollins Pubs. (Clarion Bks.).

Tucker, Susan K. Ridiculously Ridiculous. Foster, Jack, illus. 2012. 16p. pap. 9.95 (978-1-61633-346-1(4)) Guardian Angel Publishing, Inc.

Underwood, Deborah. Interstellar Cinderella: (Princess Books for Kids, Books about Science) Hunt, Meg, illus. 2015. (Future Fairy Tales Ser.). (ENG.). 40p. (J). (gr. -1-k). 17.99 (978-1-4521-2532-9(5)) Chronicle Bks. LLC.

Winn, L. B. Butterpod Jerome & the Planet of Gabool. Winn, L. B., illus. 2007. (Illus.). (J). pap. 18.95 (978-0-9791884-0-4(7)) Winn, Lynnette.

Wong, Clarissa. Guardians of the Galaxy: These Are the Guardians, 1 vol. Lim, Ron & Pinto, Marcelo, illus. 2015. (World of Reading Level 1 Ser.). (ENG.). 32p. (J). (gr. -1-3). 31.36 (978-1-61479-360-1(3), 18195) Spotlight.

Wyneken, Cherise. Spaceship Lands in Africa, 1 vol. 2010. 50p. pap. 16.95 (978-1-4489-5417-9(7)) America Star Bks.

Yaccarino, Dan. Zorgoochi Intergalactic Pizza: Delivery of Doom. Yaccarino, Dan, illus. 2014. (ENG., Illus.). 336p. (J). (gr. 3-7). 16.99 (978-1-250-00844-2(1), 900083572) Feiwel & Friends.

Yamamoto, Lun Lun. Swans in Space. (ENG., Illus.). (J). Vol. 2. 2010. 160p. pap. 8.99 (978-1-897376-94-2(4), 34f039d5-dc1a-4512-a30c-e1271c99bef9) Vol. 3. 2011. 128p. pap. 8.99 (978-1-897376-95-9(2), c3e02c59-9b09-431b-b309-d84af4538c18) URON Entertainment Corp. CAN. Dist: Diamond Comic Distributors, Inc.

Young, Craig. Arrr Marks the Spot. 2011. 32p. pap. (978-1-926959-06-1(X)) 1889 Labs Ltd.

Young, Timothy. I'm Going to Outer Space!, 1 vol. 2017. (ENG., Illus.). 32p. (J). (gr. -1-3). 16.99 (978-0-7643-5385-7(3), 8936) Schiffer Publishing, Ltd.

OUTLAWS

see Robbers and Outlaws

OVERLAND JOURNEYS TO THE PACIFIC

Améz, Lynda. My Wagon Train Adventure, 1 vol. 2015. (My Place in History Ser.). (ENG., Illus.). 24p. (J). (gr. 2-3). pap. 9.15 (978-1-4824-4002-7(4), 123566d3-91e8-4ad7-bc2b-ead566925690) Stevens, Gareth Publishing LLLP.

Aronin, Miriam. How Many People Traveled the Oregon Trail? And Other Questions about the Trail West. 2012. (Six Questions of American History Ser.). (ENG.). 48p. (gr. 4-6). pap. 56.72 (978-0-7613-9237-8(8)); (Illus.). (J). pap. 11.99 (978-0-7613-8566-0(5), cb80b72c-4ecb-42fa-980f-9c951f655ece); (Illus.). (J). lib. bdg. 30.65 (978-0-7613-5332-4(1), feb9aceb-5243-49a1-b0d3-f994e3938250, Lerner Pubns.) Lerner Publishing Group.

Braidich, Victoria. Making History: A Covered Wagon, 1 vol. 2005. (Content-Area Literacy Collections). (ENG.). 24p. (gr. 3-4). pap. 8.85 (978-1-4042-5589-0(3), 42736b4c-1aa8-4a79-a315-ec5a5e77ef3f) Rosen Publishing Group, Inc., The.

Bryant, Jill. Wagon Train. 2003. (Real Life Stories Ser.). (Illus.). 24p. (J). lib. bdg. 24.45 (978-1-59036-082-8(6)) Weigl Pubs., Inc.

Bush Gibson, Karen. The Oregon Trail: The Journey Across the Country from Lewis & Clark to the Transcontinental Railroad with 25 Projects. Casteel, Tom, illus. 2017. (Build It Yourself Ser.). (ENG.). 128p. (J). (gr. 4-6). 22.95 (978-1-61930-572-4(0), 77e126b1-8fea-4a6d-9002-3d16341b9cf2); pap. 17.95 (978-1-61930-576-2(3), 5f3f185d-9f42-4cab-8d89-e2a51abc3da8) Nomad Pr.

Dean, Arlan. The Old Spanish Trail: From Santa Fe, New Mexico to Los Angeles, California. 2009. (Famous American Trails Ser.). 24p. (gr. 3-3). 42.50 (978-1-61512-489-3(6), PowerKids Pr.) Rosen Publishing Group, Inc., The.

—The Oregon Trail: From Independence, Missouri to Oregon City, Oregon. 2009. (Famous American Trails Ser.). 24p. (gr. 3-3). 42.50 (978-1-61512-490-9(X), PowerKids Pr.) Rosen Publishing Group, Inc., The.

—The Overland Trail: From Atchison, Kansas to Ft. Bridger, Wyoming. 2009. (Famous American Trails Ser.). 24p. (gr. 3-3). 42.50 (978-1-61512-491-6(8), PowerKids Pr.) Rosen Publishing Group, Inc., The.

Doeden, Matt. Oregon Trail: An Interactive History Adventure. 2013. (You Choose: History Ser.). (ENG., Illus.). 112p. (J). (gr. 3-7). 32.65 (978-1-4765-0254-0(4), 122324) Capstone.

—The Oregon Trail: An Interactive History Adventure. 2013. (You Choose: History Ser.). (ENG.). 112p. (J). (gr. 3-7). pap. 6.95 (978-1-4765-3607-1(4), 123611) Capstone.

Domnauer, Teresa. True Books: Westward Expansion. 2010. (True Book Ser.). (ENG., Illus.). 48p. (J). (gr. 2-5). 29.00 (978-0-531-20586-0(X)) Scholastic Library Publishing.

Dunn, Joeming W. The Oregon Trail, 1 vol. Smith, Tim, illus. 2008. (Graphic History Ser.). (ENG.). 32p. (J). (gr. 3-8). 32.79 (978-1-60270-183-0(0), 9058, Graphic Planet - Fiction) Magic Wagon.

Figley, Marthy Rhodes. Clara Morgan & the Oregon Trail Journey. Orback, Craig, illus. 2011. (History Speaks: Picture Books Plus Reader's Theater Ser.). 48p. pap. 56.72 (978-0-7613-7631-6(3)) Lerner Publishing Group.

Figley, Marthy Rhodes & Figley, Marty Rhodes. Clara Morgan & the Oregon Trail Journey. Orback, Craig, illus. 2011. (History Speaks: Picture Books Plus Reader's Theater Ser.). (ENG.). 48p. (gr. 2-4). pap. 9.95 (978-0-7613-7115-1(X)) Lerner Publishing Group.

Francis, Dorothy Brenner. Courage on the Oregon Trail. 2003. (Reading Essentials in Social Studies). (Illus.). 40p. pap. 8.00 (978-0-7891-5872-7(8)) Perfection Learning Corp.

Freedman, Jeri. Life As a Pioneer on the Oregon Trail, 1 vol. 2015. (Life As... Ser.). (ENG., Illus.). 32p. (gr. 3-3). pap. 11.58 (978-1-5026-1075-1(2), f8b32e82-39dd-43e3-8323-f276e1cf91c9) Cavendish Square Publishing LLC.

Friedman, Mel. True Books: the Oregon Trail. 2010. (True Book Ser.). (ENG., Illus.). 48p. (J). (gr. 2-5). 29.00 (978-0-531-20584-6(3)) Scholastic Library Publishing.

Gingrich, Callista. From Sea to Shining Sea. Arciero, Susan, illus. 2014. (Ellis the Elephant Ser.: 4). (ENG.). 40p. (J). (gr. -1-3). 14.99 (978-1-62157-253-4(6), Regnery Kids) Regnery Publishing.

Greathouse, Lisa. Crossing a Continent (California) rev. ed. 2017. (Social Studies: Informational Text Ser.). (ENG., Illus.). 32p. (J). (gr. 3-5). pap. 11.99 (978-1-4258-3241-4(5)) Teacher Created Materials, Inc.

Gunderson, Jessica. Your Life As a Pioneer on the Oregon Trail. Dougherty, Rachel, illus. 2012. (Way It Was Ser.). (ENG.). 32p. (J). (gr. 2-5). pap. 8.95 (978-1-4048-7250-9(7), 118193, Picture Window Bks.) Capstone.

Hale, Nathan. Donner Dinner Party (Nathan Hale's Hazardous Tales #3) A Pioneer Tale. 2013. (Nathan Hale's Hazardous Tales Ser.). (ENG., Illus.). 128p. (J). (gr. 3-7). 14.99 (978-1-4197-0856-5(2), 1048001) Abrams, Inc.

Harberts, Bernie. Woody & Maggie Walk Across America. 2006. (Illus.). 40p. (J). 16.96 (978-0-9787722-9-1(6)) RiverEarth.

Harkins, Susan Sales & Harkins, William H. The Donner Party. 2008. (What's So Great About... ? Ser.). (Illus.). 32p. (J). (gr. 2-4). lib. bdg. 25.70 (978-1-58415-669-7(4)) Mitchell Lane Pubs.

Harness, Cheryl. The Tragic Tale of Narcissa Whitman & a Faithful History of the Oregon Trail (Direct Mail Edition) 2006. (Cheryl Harness Histories Ser.). (Illus.). 144p. (J). (gr. 5-9). 16.95 (978-0-7922-5920-6(3), National Geographic Kids) Disney Publishing Worldwide.

Hill, William E. The California Trail: Yesterday & Today. 2017. (Illus.). xviii, 343p. (978-0-87004-604-9(7)) Caxton Pr.

Hunsaker, Joyce Badgley. Seeing the Elephant: Voices from the Oregon Trail. 2003. (ENG., Illus.). 272p. 24.95 (978-0-89672-504-1(9), P171779) Texas Tech Univ. Pr.

Jeffrey, Gary. The Gold Rush, 1 vol. Boccanfuso, Emanuele, illus. 2012. (Graphic History of the American West Ser.). (ENG.). 24p. (J). (gr. 3-3). pap. 9.15 (978-1-4339-6741-2(3), d8c17dfc-f3a5-4164-8524-fb24d040f192, Gareth Stevens Learning Library) Stevens, Gareth Publishing LLLP.

—The Oregon Trail, 1 vol. Poluzzi, Allesandro, illus. 2012. (Graphic History of the American West Ser.). (ENG.). 24p. (J). (gr. 3-3). pap. 9.15 (978-1-4339-6745-0(6), 6cef5d54-63c3-4008-83af-ed9d14b18589, Gareth Stevens Learning Library); lib. bdg. 26.60 (978-1-4339-6743-6(X), 0ad4de6b-3511-4850-a21f-171ad1720118) Stevens, Gareth Publishing LLLP.

LaClair, Teresa. Americans Move West (1846-1860) 2013. (Illus.). 48p. (J). pap. (978-1-4222-2417-5(1)) Mason Crest.

—Americans Move West (1846-1860) Rakove, Jack N., ed. 2012. (How America Became America Ser.). (Illus.). 48p. (J). (gr. 3-4). 19.95 (978-1-4222-2403-8(1)) Mason Crest.

—Americans Move West, 1846-1860. 2019. (978-1-5105-3600-5(0)) SmartBook Media, Inc.

Landau, Elaine. True Books: Oregon Trail. 2006. (True Bks.). (ENG., Illus.). 48p. (J). (gr. 3-7). pap. 6.95 (978-0-516-27903-9(3), Children's Pr.) Scholastic Library Publishing.

Levy, Janey. Life on a Wagon Train. 2003. (Rosen Real Readers Big Bookstm Ser.). (ENG.). 16p. (gr. 2-3). 37.95 (978-1-4042-6224-9(5)) Rosen Publishing Group, Inc., The.

Loh-Hagan, Virginia. Heading West: Oregon Trail & Westward Expansion. 2019. (Behind the Curtain Ser.). (ENG.). 32p. (J). (gr. 4-8). pap. 14.21 (978-1-5341-3995-4(8), 212809); (Illus.). lib. bdg. 32.07 (978-1-5341-4339-5(4), 212808) Cherry Lake Publishing. (45th Parallel Press).

Lynette, Rachel. The Oregon Trail, 1 vol. 2013. (Pioneer Spirit: the Westward Expansion Ser.). (ENG.). 24p. (J). (gr. 2-3). 26.27 (978-1-4777-0786-9(7), 85daa1aa-68ff-435a-9f1f-19327c89708a); (Illus.). pap. 9.25 (978-1-4777-0905-4(3), ab0ff1dd-2296-4d9a-9b10-8084ed8aad2a) Rosen Publishing Group, Inc., The. (PowerKids Pr.).

Marciniak, Kristin. The Oregon Trail & Westward Expansion: A History Perspectives Book. 2013. (Perspectives Library). (ENG., Illus.). 32p. (J). (gr. 4-8). 32.07 (978-1-62431-419-3(8), 202796); pap. 14.21 (978-1-62431-495-7(3), 202798) Cherry Lake Publishing.

Marsh, Sarah Glenn. Alice Across America: The Story of the First Women's Cross-Country Road Trip. Ford, Gilbert, illus. 2020. (ENG.). 48p. (J). 18.99 (978-1-250-29702-0(8), 900195861, Holt, Henry & Co. Bks. For Young Readers) Holt, Henry & Co.

McNeese, Tim. The Oregon Trail. 2009. (ENG., Illus.). 152p. (gr. 6-12). 35.00 (978-1-60413-027-0(X), P161434, Facts On File) Infobase Holdings, Inc.

Morley, Jacqueline. You Wouldn't Want to... Be an American Pioneer! Antram, David, illus. rev. ed. 2012. (ENG.). 32p. (J). lib. bdg. 29.00 (978-0-531-27500-9(0)) Scholastic Library Publishing.

Nolan, Frederick. Trailblazing the Way West. 2015. (Wild West Ser.). (Illus.). 64p. (J). (gr. 9-12). 39.95 (978-1-78404-081-9(9)) Arcturus Publishing GBR. Dist: Black Rabbit Bks.

Olson, Steven. The Oregon Trail: A Primary Source History of the Route to the American West. 2009. (Primary Sources in American History Ser.). 64p. (gr. 5-8). 58.50 (978-1-60851-501-1(X)) Rosen Publishing Group, Inc., The.

Olson, Steven P. The Oregon Trail, 1 vol. 2004. (Primary Sources in American History Ser.). (ENG., Illus.). 64p. (gr. 5-8). lib. bdg. 37.13 (978-0-8239-4512-2(X), 62403f74-8a1c-4b94-852b-0d437b0ca078, Rosen Reference) Rosen Publishing Group, Inc., The.

The Oregon Trail. 2013. (Pioneer Spirit: the Westward Expansion Ser.). 24p. (J). (gr. 3-6). pap. 49.50 (978-1-4777-0906-1(1), PowerKids Pr.) Rosen Publishing Group, Inc., The.

Quasha, Jennifer. Covered Wagons: Hands-on Projects about America's Westward Expansion. 2009. (Great Social Studies Projects Ser.). 24p. (gr. 3-3). 42.50 (978-1-61513-208-9(2), PowerKids Pr.) Rosen Publishing Group, Inc., The.

Rajczak Nelson, Kristen. The Donner Party, 1 vol. 2015. (Doomed! Ser.). (ENG., Illus.). 32p. (J). (gr. 4-5). pap. 11.50 (978-1-4824-2928-2(4), b65c6e2c-00a0-43be-b0b6-56abfacb7c74) Stevens, Gareth Publishing LLLP.

—Life on a Wagon Train, 1 vol. 2013. (What You Didn't Know about History Ser.). (ENG., Illus.). 24p. (J). (gr. 2-3). pap. 9.15 (978-1-4339-8445-7(8), 9b458fc3-3d4c-4a1d-a23f-1647e3661dab); lib. bdg. 25.27 (978-1-4339-8444-0(X), cd79e9b1-b73f-4f37-9a43-5ef18bc1fd78) Stevens, Gareth Publishing LLLP.

Sechrist, Darren. Westward, Ho!, 1 vol. 2008. (ENG., Illus.). 32p. (J). pap. (978-0-7787-4217-3(2)) Crabtree Publishing Co.

Smith-Llera, Danielle. Stranded in the Sierra Nevada: The Story of the Donner Party. 2015. (Adventures on the American Frontier Ser.). (ENG., Illus.). 32p. (J). (gr. 3-6). pap. 7.95 (978-1-4914-4912-7(8), 128747, Capstone Pr.) Capstone.

Steele, Christy. Famous Wagon Trails, 1 vol. 2004. (America's Westward Expansion Ser.). (ENG., Illus.). 48p. (gr. 5-8). pap. 15.05 (978-0-8368-5795-5(X), 960f15d9-0f17-470d-96a8-1bb79b286c9a); lib. bdg. 33.67 (978-0-8368-5788-7(7), cdb80fe3-5c8f-4fd5-b8ec-0282bee0fc85) Stevens, Gareth Publishing LLLP. (Gareth Stevens Secondary Library).

Stefoff, Rebecca. Surviving the Oregon Trail: Stories in American History, 1 vol. 2012. (Stories in American History Ser.). (ENG., Illus.). 128p. (gr. 5-6). 35.93 (978-0-7660-3955-1(2), c1760ce8-dc06-4e25-9147-347b87cd367f); pap. 13.88 (978-1-4644-0025-4(3), c88db0fb-07e6-4a6c-9422-5bd8161ac3b2) Enslow Publishing, LLC.

Stoltman, Joan. 20 Fun Facts about Westward Expansion, 1 vol. 2018. (Fun Fact File: U. S. History! Ser.). (ENG.). 32p. (gr. 2-3). pap. 11.50 (978-1-5382-1919-5(0), 5a247029-dcc4-48e0-b42c-9d50f95dca60); lib. bdg. 27.93 (978-1-5382-1921-8(2), 6fc1b9f0-d70b-4b5a-91f9-771df24f3eb9) Stevens, Gareth Publishing LLLP.

Stuckey, Rachel. Wagon Trains Heading West, 1 vol. 2015. (True History of the Wild West Ser.). (ENG., Illus.). 32p. (J). (gr. 5-5). pap. 11.00 (978-1-4994-1179-9(0), 4af2b5b8-0212-4d7a-bc56-2f78656030dc, PowerKids Pr.) Rosen Publishing Group, Inc., The.

Wadsworth, Ginger. Survival in the Snow. Orback, Craig, illus. 2011. 48p. (J). pap. 6.95 (978-0-7613-3941-0(8), First Avenue Editions) Lerner Publishing Group.

OVERLAND JOURNEYS TO THE PACIFIC—FICTION

Bly, Stephen A. The Lost Wagon Train. 2005. (Retta Barre's Oregon Trail Ser.: Vol. 1). 110p. pap. 5.99 (978-1-58134-391-5(4), Crossway Bibles) Crossway.

Buffalo Storm. 2014. (ENG., Illus.). 32p. (J). (gr. -1-3). pap. 7.99 (978-0-544-33921-7(5), 1584492, Clarion Bks.) HarperCollins Pubs.

Carson, Rae. Walk on Earth a Stranger. 2015. (Gold Seer Trilogy Ser.: 1). (ENG.). 448p. (YA). (gr. 8). 17.99 (978-0-06-224291-4(1), Greenwillow Bks.) HarperCollins Pubs.

Coerr, Eleanor. The Josefina Story Quilt. Degen, Bruce, illus. 2003. (I Can Read! Level 3 Ser.). 64p. (J). (gr. 2-4). lib. bdg. 13.55 (978-0-8335-2723-3(1)) Turtleback.

Crawford, Neil. The Journeyers. 2006. (ENG.). 248p. (J). per. (978-0-9778205-4-2(8)) Helm Publishing.

Fitzgerald, John D. Brave Buffalo Fighter. 2003. (Young Adult Bookshelf Ser.). (ENG.). 192p. pap. 11.95 (978-1-883937-59-1(0)) Ignatius Pr.

Frazier, Neta. The Stout-Hearted Seven: Orphaned on the Oregon Trail. 2017. (Great Leaders & Events Ser.). (ENG.). (J). (gr. 4-8). lib. bdg. 35.99 (978-1-942875-43-7(6)) Quarto Publishing Group USA.

Hopkinson, Deborah. Apples to Oregon. 2014. 17.00 (978-1-63419-642-0(2)) Perfection Learning Corp.

—Apples to Oregon: Being the (Slightly) True Narrative of How a Brave Pioneer Father Brought Apples, Peaches, Pears, Plums, Grapes, & Cherries (and Children) Across the Plains. Carpenter, Nancy, illus. 2008. (ENG.). 40p. (J). (gr. -1-3). 8.99 (978-1-4169-6746-0(X), Aladdin) Simon & Schuster Children's Publishing.

—Apples to Oregon: Being the (Slightly) True Narrative of How a Brave Pioneer Father Brought Apples, Peaches, Pears, Plums, Grapes, & Cherries (and Children) Across the Plains. Carpenter, Nancy, illus. 2004. (ENG.). 40p. (J). (gr. -1-3). 19.99 (978-0-689-84769-1(6)) Simon & Schuster, Inc.

Kimmel, E. Cody. West on the Wagon Train. Snow, Scott, illus. 2003. (Adventures of Young Buffalo Bill Ser.). (ENG.). 160p. (J). 15.99 (978-0-06-029113-6(3)) HarperCollins Pubs.

Lawlor, Laurie. He Will Go Fearless. (ENG.). 224p. (J). (gr. 5-9). 2012. pap. 10.99 (978-0-689-86580-0(5)) 2006. 15.95 (978-0-689-86579-4(1)) Simon & Schuster Bks. For Young Readers. (Simon & Schuster Bks. For Young Readers).

McKernan, Victoria. The Devil's Paintbox, 1. 2010. (Devil's Paintbox Ser.). (ENG.). 368p. (J). (gr. 9-12). lib. bdg. 22.44 (978-0-375-93750-7(1)) Random House Publishing Group.

—The Devil's Paintbox. (ENG.). (YA). (gr. 9). 2013. 384p. pap. 9.99 (978-0-449-81655-4(9), Ember) 2010. 368p. mass mkt. 8.99 (978-0-440-23962-8(1), Laurel Leaf) Random Hse. Children's Bks.

Napoli, Donna Jo. The Crossing. Madsen, Jim, illus. 2011. (ENG.). 40p. (J). (gr. -1-3). 19.99 (978-1-4169-9474-9(2), Atheneum Bks. for Young Readers) Simon & Schuster Children's Publishing.

Thompson, Gare. Our Journey West: An Adventure on the Oregon Trail. 2003. 40p. (J). pap. 6.99 (978-0-7922-5199-6(7)) CENGAGE Learning.

Wilson, Laura. How I Survived the Oregon Trail: The Journal of Jesse Adams. 2006. (Illus.). 37p. (J). (gr. 4-8). reprint ed. pap. 10.00 (978-0-7567-9925-0(2)) DIANE Publishing Co.

Wolf, Allan. New Found Land: Lewis & Clark's Voyage of Discovery. 2007. (ENG., Illus.). 512p. (YA). (gr. 7-9). per. 19.99 (978-0-7636-3288-5(0)) Candlewick Pr.

OVERWEIGHT

see Weight Control

OWENS, JESSE, 1913-1980

Adler, David A. A Picture Book of Jesse Owens. Casilla, Robert, illus. 2019. (Picture Book Biography Ser.). 32p. (J). (gr. -1-3). pap. 7.99 (978-0-8234-4270-6(5)) Holiday Hse., Inc.

Buckley, James, Jr. & Who HQ. Who Was Jesse Owens? Copeland, Gregory, illus. 2015. (Who Was? Ser.). 112p. (J). (gr. 3-7). 6.99 (978-0-448-48307-8(6), Penguin Workshop) Penguin Young Readers Group.

Buckley, James. Who Was Jesse Owens? Copeland, Gregory, illus. 2015. 106p. (J). (978-1-4806-9215-2(8), Grosset & Dunlap) Penguin Publishing Group.

—Who Was Jesse Owens? 2015. (Who Was... ? Ser.). (Illus.). 106p. (J). lib. bdg. 16.00 (978-0-606-36754-7(3)) Turtleback.

Burgan, Michael. Olympic Gold 1936: How the Image of Jesse Owens Crushed Hitler's Evil Myth. 2017. (Captured History Sports Ser.). (ENG., Illus.). 64p. (J). (gr. 5-9). lib. bdg. 35.32 (978-0-7565-5528-3(0), 134413, Compass Point Bks.) Capstone.

Burlingame, Jeff. Jesse Owens: I Always Loved Running, 1 vol. 2008. (African-American Biography Library). (ENG., Illus.). 128p. (gr. 6-7). lib. bdg. 35.93 (978-0-7660-3497-6(6), c6efb6b4-5e32-43da-8578-9363fa4e2314) Enslow Publishing, LLC.

Eboch, M. M. Jesse Owens: Young Record Breaker. Henderson, Meryl, illus. 2008. (Childhood of Famous Americans Ser.). (ENG.). 208p. (J). (gr. 3-7). pap. 7.99 (978-1-4169-3922-1(9), Aladdin) Simon & Schuster Children's Publishing.

Hind, Devon & Bergstresser, Kate, trs. Jesse Owens: World's Fastest Human. 2003. (Alabama Roots Biography Ser.). (Illus.). 120p. (J). (978-1-878561-38-1(3)) Seacoast Publishing, Inc.

Hoena, Blake. Jesse Owens: Athletes Who Made a Difference. Shephard, David, illus. 2020. (Athletes Who Made a Difference Ser.). (ENG.). 32p. (J). (gr. 3-6). 27.99 (978-1-5415-7815-9(5), 6f1177d5-000e-4572-8f43-0fa3db9ff35d); pap. 8.99 (978-1-7284-0295-6(6), 40623995-5723-437b-9ae3-f10d764102c0) Lerner Publishing Group. (Graphic Universe™).

Jesse Owens. 2004. (Illus.). 112p. pap. 9.95 (978-0-8225-5318-2(X)) Lerner Publishing Group.

Mckissack, Patricia & Mckissack, Fredrick. Jesse Owens: Legendary Track Star, 1 vol. 2013. (Famous African Americans Ser.). (ENG.). 24p. (gr. k-2). pap. 10.35 (978-1-4644-0199-2(3), 4261b8b0-7a97-4f86-92d0-a7b892e91f1e, Enslow Elementary); (Illus.). 25.27 (978-0-7660-4104-2(2), 99a92186-6ddf-45a7-a2b6-3866e32768d3) Enslow Publishing, LLC.

Shafer, Susan. Jesse Owens: Fastest Human. 2005. (J). pap. (978-1-4108-4207-7(X)) Benchmark Education Co.

Stanmyre, Jackie F. Jesse Owens: Facing down Hitler, 1 vol. 2015. (Game-Changing Athletes Ser.). (ENG., Illus.). 112p. (YA). (gr. 9-9). lib. bdg. 44.50 (978-1-5026-1049-2(3),

MNO

a30ea382-851d-40c9-88f1-43a857e01970) Cavendish Square Publishing LLC.

Streissguth, Tom. Jesse Owens. (Sports Heroes & Legends Ser.). (ENG., Illus.). 112p. (gr. 5-12). 2005. lib. bdg. 30.60 *(978-0-8225-3070-1(8))* 2004. lib. bdg. 27.93 *(978-0-8225-2256-0(X))* Lerner Publishing Group.

Sutcliffe, Jane. Jesse Owens. Porter, Janice Lee, illus. 2006. (On My Own Biographies Ser.). 48p. 17.00 *(978-0-7569-6702-4(3))* Perfection Learning Corp.

Williams, Heather. Jesse Owens. 2018. (21st Century Skills Library: Sports Unite Us Ser.). (ENG., Illus.). 32p. (J). (gr. 3-6). lib. bdg. 32.07 *(978-1-5341-2959-7(6)*, 211880) Cherry Lake Publishing.

Yomtov, Nel. Defying Hitler: Jesse Owens' Olympic Triumph. Garcia, Eduardo, illus. 2018. (Greatest Sports Moments Ser.). (ENG.). 32p. (J). (gr. 3-9). lib. bdg. 31.32 *(978-1-5435-2865-7(1)*, 138368, Capstone Pr.) Capstone.

OWLS

Albertson, Al. Great Gray Owls. 2020. (Animals of the Forest Ser.). (ENG.). 24p. (J). (gr. k-3). lib. bdg. 26.95 *(978-1-64487-127-0(0)*, Blastoff! Readers) Bellwether Media.

Alinsky, Shelby. Hoot, Owl! (1 Hardcover/1 CD) 2017. (National Geographic Kids Ser.). (ENG.). (J). 29.95 *(978-1-4301-2653-9(1))* Live Oak Media.

—Hoot, Owl! (1 Paperback/1 CD) 2017. (National Geographic Kids Ser.). (ENG.). (J). pap. 19.95 *(978-1-4301-2652-2(3))* Live Oak Media.

—Hoot, Owl! (4 Paperbacks/1 CD), 4 vols. 2017. (National Geographic Kids Ser.). (ENG.). (J). pap. 31.95 *(978-1-4301-2654-6(X))* Live Oak Media.

—National Geographic Readers: Hoot, Owl! 2015. (Readers Ser.). (Illus.). 24p. (J). (gr. -1-k). pap. 4.99 *(978-1-4263-2125-2(2)*, National Geographic Kids) Disney Publishing Worldwide.

Arjas, Pirkko & Butcher, Sally K., illus. Friend Owl: A Children's Book. 1000th ed. 2005. 48p. (J). 18.00 *(978-0-9762132-0-8(6))* Old Bess Publishing Co.

Arnold, Quinn M. Barn Owls. 2019. (Creatures of the Night Ser.). (ENG.). 24p. (J). (gr. 1-4). *(978-1-64026-117-4(6)*, 18937, Creative Education); pap. 8.99 *(978-1-62832-680-2(8)*, 18938, Creative Paperbacks) Creative Co., The.

Bergeron, Alain M. & Quintin, Michel. Do You Know Owls?, 1 vol. Doll, Pamela, tr. Sampar, illus. 2019. (Do You Know? Ser.). (ENG.). 64p. (J). (gr. 2-4). 9.95 *(978-1-55455-352-5(0)*, 9a06904f-5aee-4afd-ab26-c220b289bf08) Fitzhenry & Whiteside, Ltd. CAN. Dist: Firefly Bks., Ltd.

Bodden, Valerie. Owls. 2013. (Illus.). 24p. (J). 25.65 *(978-1-60818-088-2(3)*, Creative Education) Creative Co., The.

Bone, Emily. Owls. Cooper, Jenny & Watson, Richard, illus. 2013. (Usborne Beginners Ser.). (ENG.). 32p. (J). 9.99 *(978-0-7945-3401-1(5)*, Usborne) EDC Publishing.

Burke, Zoe. Owls & Loons. Inuit artists and printmakers of Kinngait Studios, illus. 2016. 24p. (J). bds. 10.95 *(978-0-7649-7542-4(0)*, POMEGRANATE KIDS) Pomegranate Communications, Inc.

Camisa, Kathryn. Barn Owl. 2016. (Weird but Cute Ser.). (ENG., Illus.). 24p. (J). (gr. -1-3). 26.99 *(978-1-943553-27-3(0))* Bearport Publishing Co., Inc.

Carr, Aaron. Owls. 2014. (Illus.). 24p. (J). *(978-1-62127-213-7(3))* Weigl Pubs., Inc.

Caswell, Deanna. Baby Owls. 2018. (Adorable Animals Ser.). (ENG.). 32p. (J). (gr. 4-6). pap. 9.99 *(978-1-64466-245-8(0)*, 12235); lib. bdg. *(978-1-68072-398-4(7)*, 12234) Black Rabbit Bks. (Bolt).

Clausen-Grace, Nicki. Owls. 2018. (Wild Animal Kingdom (Continuation) Ser.). (ENG.). 32p. (gr. 2-7). 9.95 *(978-1-68072-737-1(0))*; (J). (gr. 4-6). pap. 9.99 *(978-1-64466-290-8(6)*, 12413); (J). (gr. 4-6). lib. bdg. *(978-1-68072-443-1(6)*, 12412) Black Rabbit Bks. (Bolt).

Courtauld, Sarah. Owls: Internet-Referenced. Hussey, Lorna, illus. 2009. (First Reading Level 3 Ser.). 48p. (J). (gr. 2). 6.99 *(978-0-7945-2502-6(4)*, Usborne) EDC Publishing.

Dahlen, Noelle. Spark - Owls Coloring Book. 2015. (Dover Animal Coloring Bks.). (ENG., Illus.). 64p. (J). (gr. 1-4). pap. 5.99 *(978-0-486-80211-4(6)*, 802116) Dover Pubns., Inc.

Danielson, Ethan. Owls, 1 vol., 1. 2015. (Raptors! Ser.). (ENG., Illus.). 24p. (J). (gr. 3-4). 25.27 *(978-1-5081-4252-2(1)*, f7cd647b-17a0-433a-91a2-bcb79793e666, PowerKids Pr.) Rosen Publishing Group, Inc., The.

Dibble, Traci. Where Can Owls Nest? 2015. (1-3Y Birds Ser.). (ENG., Illus.). 28p. (J). pap. 9.60 *(978-1-63437-668-6(4))* American Reading Co.

Dieker, Wendy Strobel. El Búho (Owls) 2017. (Spot Backyard Animals Ser.). (ENG & SPA., Illus.). 16p. (J). (gr. k-3). 17.95 *(978-1-68151-274-7(2)*, Amicus Readers) Amicus Learning.

—Owls. 2018. (Spot Backyard Animals Ser.). (ENG., Illus.). 16p. (J). (gr. -1-2). pap. 7.99 *(978-1-68152-219-7(5)*, 14750) Amicus.

Dinmont, Kerry. It's a Snowy Owl! 2018. (Bumba Books (r) — Polar Animals Ser.). (ENG., Illus.). 24p. (J). (gr. -1-1). pap. 8.99 *(978-1-5415-2697-6(X)*, 12d23341-f85c-464f-99bc-61b5bc5608a0) Lerner Publishing Group.

Dunn, Mary R. Owls, 1 vol. 2011. (Nocturnal Animals Ser.). (ENG.). 24p. (J). (gr. -1-2). pap. 7.29 *(978-1-4296-7119-4(X)*, 116771); (gr. -1-2). lib. bdg. 27.32 *(978-1-4296-5997-0(1)*, 114928); (gr. k-1). pap. 43.74 *(978-1-4296-7122-4(X)*, 16701) Capstone. (Capstone Pr.).

Dyan, Penelope. The Comeback Kids, Book 8, the Antioch Burrowing Owl. Weigand, John D., photos by. 2009. (Illus.). 60p. pap. 22.00 *(978-1-935118-86-2(2))* Bellissima Publishing, LLC.

Early Macken, JoAnn. Owls, 1 vol. (Animals That Live in the Forest (First Edition) Ser.). (ENG., 24p. (gr. 1-1). 2004. Illus.). lib. bdg. 25.27 *(978-0-8368-4484-9(X)*, 28d3cbb6-7dd1-45c7-b9ce-0464c2ef3025) 2nd rev. ed. 2009. (J). pap. 9.15 *(978-1-4339-2482-8(X)*, ae38185a-01be-49b6-9c27-c0214f3a2622) 2nd rev. ed. 2009. (J). lib. bdg. 25.27 *(978-1-4339-2406-4(4)*, 1d66d5da-e422-492a-978a-f6cd8370454b) Stevens, Gareth Publishing LLLP.

—Owls / Búhos y Lechuzas, 1 vol. 2nd rev. ed. 2009. (Animals That Live in the Forest / Animales Del Bosque Ser.). (SPA & ENG.). 24p. (J). (gr. 1-1). pap. 9.15 *(978-1-4339-2489-7(7)*, b952139e-c1d0-4577-a422-ec51f76537d0); lib. bdg. 25.27 *(978-1-4339-2438-5(2)*, d985d615-1ad6-4f09-a1bb-7807a1a9615c) Stevens, Gareth Publishing LLLP. (Weekly Reader Leveled Readers).

Ford, Ansley Watson & Holt, Denver W. Snowy Owls: Whoo Are They?, 1 vol. Bohman, Jennifer White, illus. 2008. (ENG.). 64p. (J). (gr. 3-7). pap. 12.00 *(978-0-87842-543-3(8))* Mountain Pr. Publishing Co., Inc.

Franks, Katie. Owls up Close. (Nature up Close Ser.). 24p. 2009. (gr. k-1). 42.50 *(978-1-61514-827-1(2))* 2007. (ENG., Illus.). (J). (gr. 1-1). lib. bdg. 26.27 *(978-1-4042-4140-4(X)*, e73e43fa-70e5-47b3-ac72-004c6ac87924) Rosen Publishing Group, Inc., The. (PowerKids Pr.).

—Owls up Close / Los Buhos. 2009. (Nature up Close / la naturaleza de cerca Ser.). (ENG & SPA.). 24p. (gr. k-1). 42.50 *(978-1-61514-833-2(7)*, Editorial Buenas Letras) Rosen Publishing Group, Inc., The.

—Owls up Close/Los Buhos, 1 vol. Sanz, Pilar, tr. 2007. (Nature up Close / la Naturaleza de Cerca Ser.). (ENG & SPA., Illus.). 24p. (J). (gr. 1-1). lib. bdg. 26.27 *(978-1-4042-7678-9(5)*, 20f24430-163b-4691-9144-e2460e1b9794, Editorial Buenas Letras) Rosen Publishing Group, Inc., The.

Frick, Ivi. Hunting with Great Horned Owls, 1 vol. 2012. (Animal Attack! Ser.). (ENG., Illus.). 24p. (J). (gr. 2-3). pap. 9.15 *(978-1-4339-7072-6(4)*, 7bf148be-e4c6-48fc-a24f-24be0f6a46a4); lib. bdg. 25.27 *(978-1-4339-7071-9(6)*, 2f2ec034-485f-4c4f-96a2-ea153fa94209) Stevens, Gareth Publishing LLLP.

Frost, Helen. Snowy Owls [Scholastic]. 2009. (Polar Animals Ser.). 24p. (gr. k-1). pap. 0.34 *(978-1-4296-4228-6(9)*, Pebble) Capstone.

George, Jean Craighead. Winter Moon. 2003. (J). (gr. 3-7). 20.75 *(978-0-8446-7244-1(0))* Smith, Peter Pub., Inc.

Gibbons, Gail. Owls. 2006. (ENG., Illus.). 32p. (J). (gr. -1-3). 7.99 *(978-0-8234-2014-8(0))* Holiday Hse., Inc.

Gilbert, Betty. Buffy the Burrowing Owl. 2008. (Illus.). 40p. (J). 13.95 *(978-0-942407-88-4(1))* Father & Son Publishing.

Gilkerson, Patricia. My Adventure with Owls. 2009. (ENG.). 44p. (J). 8.99 *(978-1-59092-460-0(6))* Blue Forge Pr.

Gish, Melissa. Owls. 2011. (Living Wild Ser.). (ENG., Illus.). 48p. (J). (gr. 5-8). 35.65 *(978-1-60818-081-3(6)*, 23894, Creative Education) Creative Co., The.

Gonzales, Doreen. Owls in the Dark, 1 vol. 2009. (Creatures of the Night Ser.). (ENG., Illus.). 24p. (J). (gr. 2-3). 26.27 *(978-1-4042-8097-7(9)*, f1eaffc7-40ee-424e-a58d-afa5cd9d9833); pap. 9.25 *(978-1-4358-3251-0(5)*, 13f3fb0b-a621-441a-bfd8-7889db555344, PowerKids Pr.) Rosen Publishing Group, Inc., The.

Gove-Berg, Christie. Greta the Great-Horned Owl: A True Story of Rescue & Rehabilitation. 2019. (Wildlife Rescue Stories Ser.). (ENG., Illus.). 32p. (J). (gr. -1-3). 14.95 *(978-1-59193-815-6(5)*, Adventure Pubns.) AdventureKEEN.

Gregory, Josh. Owls. 2013. (Nature's Children Ser.). (ENG.). 48p. (J). pap. 6.95 *(978-0-531-24305-3(2)*, Children's Pr.) Scholastic Library Publishing.

Gregson, Agatha. I See an Owl, 1 vol. 2018. (In My Backyard Ser.). (ENG.). 24p. (gr. k-k). 25.27 *(978-1-5382-2878-4(5)*, 9e64a706-cacc-4c38-808d-72b2b2861e00) Stevens, Gareth Publishing LLLP.

Hill, Melissa. Barn Owls. 2015. (Owls Ser.). (ENG., Illus.). 24p. (J). (gr. -1-2). pap. 6.95 *(978-1-4914-6051-1(2)*, 128965, Capstone Pr.) Capstone.

—Burrowing Owls. 2015. (Owls Ser.). (ENG., Illus.). 24p. (J). (gr. -1-2). pap. 6.95 *(978-1-4914-6052-8(0)*, 128966, Capstone Pr.) Capstone.

—Great Horned Owls. 2015. (Owls Ser.). (ENG., Illus.). 24p. (J). (gr. -1-2). pap. 6.95 *(978-1-4914-6053-5(9)*, 128967, Capstone Pr.) Capstone.

—Owls. 2015. (Owls Ser.). (ENG.). 24p. (J). (gr. k-1). 117.28 *(978-1-4914-6942-2(0)*, 22982, Capstone Pr.) Capstone.

—Snowy Owls. 2015. (Owls Ser.). (ENG., Illus.). 24p. (J). (gr. -1-2). pap. 6.95 *(978-1-4914-6054-2(7)*, 128969, Capstone Pr.) Capstone.

Hirsch, Rebecca E. Snowy Owls: Stealthy Hunting Birds. 2016. (Comparing Animal Traits Ser.). (ENG., Illus.). 32p. (J). (gr. 2-4). E-Book 39.99 *(978-1-4677-9628-6(X)*, Lerner Pubns.) Lerner Publishing Group.

Hiscock, Bruce. Ookpik: The Travels of a Snowy Owl. 2008. (ENG., Illus.). 32p. (J). (gr. 2-k). 16.95 *(978-1-59078-461-7(8)*, Astra Young Readers) Astra Publishing Hse.

Holland, Mary. Otis, el Búho. 2017. (SPA., Illus.). 32p. (J). (gr. 2-3). pap. 11.95 *(978-1-62855-941-5(1)*, 18eb0bb0-55cd-497e-9e83-9604e1995b13) Arbordale Publishing.

—Otis the Owl. 2017. (SPA & ENG., Illus.). 32p. (J). (gr. k-3). 17.95 *(978-1-62855-939-2(X))* Arbordale Publishing.

Houghton, Gillian. Buhos: Por Dentro y Por Fuera, 1 vol. Gonzalez, Tomas, tr. Studio Stalio, illus. 2003. (Explora la Naturaleza (Getting into Nature) Ser.). (SPA.). 32p. (YA). (gr. 3-4). lib. bdg. 28.93 *(978-1-4042-2866-5(7)*, df796752-5f20-42e0-9373-c15cde7c3bad) Rosen Publishing Group, Inc., The.

—Buhos: Por dentro y por fuera (Owls: Inside & Out) 2009. (Explora la Naturaleza (Getting into Nature) Ser.). (SPA.). 32p. (gr. 3-4). 47.90 *(978-1-61512-335-3(0)*, Editorial Buenas Letras) Rosen Publishing Group, Inc., The.

—Owl, 1 vol. 2004. (Getting into Nature Ser.). (ENG., Illus.). 32p. (J). (gr. 3-4). lib. bdg. 28.93 *(978-0-8239-4208-4(2)*, 6f853168-af2f-43f7-b7e2-38d0885aa389) Rosen Publishing Group, Inc., The.

—Owls: Inside & Out. 2009. (Getting into Nature Ser.). 32p. (gr. 3-4). 47.90 *(978-1-61512-724-5(0)*, PowerKids Pr.) Rosen Publishing Group, Inc., The.

Houts, Michelle. Silent Swoop: An Owl, an Egg, & a Warm Shirt Pocket. Hoeffner, Deb, illus. 2019. 32p. (J). (gr. -1-3). 16.95 *(978-1-58469-646-9(X)*, Dawn Pubns.) Sourcebooks, Inc.

Jacobs, Liza. Owls. 2003. (Wild Wild World Ser.). (Illus.). 24p. (J). 23.70 *(978-1-4103-0050-8(1)*, Blackbirch Pr., Inc.) Cengage Gale.

Jaycox, Jaclyn. Snowy Owls Are Awesome. 2019. (Polar Animals Ser.). (ENG., Illus.). 32p. (J). (gr. -1-2). pap. 7.95 *(978-1-9771-1001-5(0)*, 140944, Pebble) Capstone.

Landau, Elaine. Snowy Owls: Hunters of the Snow & Ice, 1 vol. 2010. (Animals of the Snow & Ice Ser.). (ENG., Illus.). 32p. (gr. 3-3). 26.60 *(978-0-7660-3464-8(X)*, 0df7a6e0-02a0-410b-ba3a-51c5b761a8de) Enslow Publishing, LLC.

Lang, Aubrey. Baby Owl, 1 vol. Lynch, Wayne, photos by. 2004. (Nature Babies Ser.). (ENG., Illus.). 36p. (J). (gr. k-3). 16.95 *(978-1-55041-796-8(7)*, 51cd5abe-0798-434c-97e9-1a8525e97416); pap. 8.95 *(978-1-55041-798-2(3)*, 88cc6346-d100-43f4-a391-7f07cbef3653) Trifolium Bks., Inc. CAN. Dist: Firefly Bks., Ltd.

Lawrence, Riley. Snowy Owls of the Tundra. 2017. (Animals of the Tundra Ser.). 24p. (gr. 1-2). 49.50 *(978-1-5345-2216-9(6)*, KidHaven Publishing) Greenhaven Publishing LLC.

Leaf, Christina. Baby Owls. 2015. (Super Cute! Ser.). (ENG., Illus.). 24p. (J). (gr. k-3). lib. bdg. 26.95 *(978-1-62617-172-5(6)*, Blastoff! Readers) Bellwether Media.

—Great-Horned Owls. 2015. (North American Animals Ser.). (ENG., Illus.). 24p. (J). (gr. k-3). lib. bdg. 26.95 *(978-1-62617-189-3(0)*, Blastoff! Readers) Bellwether Media.

Loughrey, Anita. Owl's Winter Rescue. Howarth, Daniel, illus. 2016. (J). *(978-1-4351-6415-4(6))* Barnes & Noble, Inc.

Lundgren, Julie. Owls. 2009. (Illus.). 24p. (J). pap. 7.95 *(978-1-60694-773-9(7))* Rourke Educational Media.

Lundgren, Julie & Lundgren. Julie. Owls. 2009. (Illus.). 24p. (J). (gr. 2-5). lib. bdg. 22.79 *(978-1-60694-395-3(2))* Rourke Educational Media.

Lynch, Annabelle. Owls & Owlets. 2017. (Animals & Their Babies Ser.). (Illus.). 24p. (J). (gr. k-3). 28.50 *(978-1-62588-418-3(4)*, Smart Apple Media) Black Rabbit Bks.

Mara, Wil. Owls, 1 vol. 2014. (Backyard Safari Ser.). (ENG.). 32p. (gr. 3-3). 31.21 *(978-1-62712-298-6(2)*, 4e8361ae-f633-44c7-9494-f859a0df1f38) Cavendish Square Publishing LLC.

Markle, Sandra. Owls. (Animal Predators Ser.). (ENG., Illus.). 40p. (gr. 3-6). 2005. (J). pap. 8.99 *(978-1-57505-745-3(X)*, f2d46737-d846-49ab-97b0-bc68c2724ae2, First Avenue Editions) 2004. lib. bdg. 26.60 *(978-1-57505-729-3(8))* Lerner Publishing Group.

Marsh, Laura. National Geographic Readers: Owls. 2014. (Readers Ser.). (Illus.). 32p. (J). (gr. -1-k). pap. 5.99 *(978-1-4263-1743-9(3)*, National Geographic Kids) Disney Publishing Worldwide.

Mattern, Joanne. Owls Are Night Animals, 1 vol. 2007. (Night Animals Ser.). (ENG., Illus.). 24p. (gr. 1-3). pap. 9.15 *(978-0-8368-7855-4(8)*, d0c35c77-d4ef-4576-8de7-438574c159ce); lib. bdg. 24.67 *(978-0-8368-7848-6(5)*, fa5df795-8cf6-4f7c-bdd1-0b6f0dd7963a) Stevens, Gareth Publishing LLLP. (Weekly Reader Leveled Readers).

—Owls Are Night Animals / Los Búhos Son Animales Nocturnos, 1 vol. 2007. (Night Animals / Animales Nocturnos Ser.). (SPA & ENG., Illus.). 24p. (gr. 1-3). pap. 9.15 *(978-0-8368-8052-6(8)*, 3f85e3f7-d3a7-4cad-8874-37fcd854e47f); lib. bdg. 24.67 *(978-0-8368-8045-8(5)*, 4c36d61f-6d51-4d8c-a0b8-4c9778a09a9d) Stevens, Gareth Publishing LLLP. (Weekly Reader Leveled Readers).

Meister, Cari. Do You Really Want to Meet an Owl? Fabbri, Daniele, illus. 2016. (Do You Really Want to Meet ... ? Ser.). (ENG.). 24p. (J). (gr. 1-4). pap. 8.99 *(978-1-68152-119-0(9)*, 15600); lib. bdg. 20.95 *(978-1-60753-948-3(9)*, 15594) Amicus.

Miller, Sara Swan. Owls. (Paws & Claws Ser.). 24p. (gr. 2-3). 2009. 42.50 *(978-1-60851-152-5(9))* 2008. (ENG., Illus.). (J). lib. bdg. 26.27 *(978-1-4042-4165-7(5)*, 5f20c20f-123e-4716-a561-c388700d384e) Rosen Publishing Group, Inc., The. (PowerKids Pr.).

Minsky, Howie. Look at the Owl. 2019. (Hello, Everglades! Ser.). (ENG., Illus.). 16p. (J). (gr. -1-2). pap. 11.36 *(978-1-5341-5732-3(8)*, 214171, Cherry Blossom Press) Cherry Lake Publishing.

—Owl Looks Around. 2019. (Hello, Everglades! Ser.). (ENG.). 16p. (J). (gr. -1-2). pap. 11.36 *(978-1-5341-5731-6(X)*, 214168, Cherry Blossom Press) Cherry Lake Publishing.

Mudd-Ruth, Maria. Owls, 1 vol. 2006. (Animals, Animals Ser.). (ENG., Illus.). 48p. (gr. 5-5). 32.64 *(978-0-7614-1752-1(4)*, 79ee8b3c-9f85-413c-8b49-3ff11a2c3217) Cavendish Square Publishing LLC.

Murray, Julie. Búhos. 2017. (¡Me Gustan Los Animales! (I Like Animals! Set 2) Ser.).Tr. of Owls. (SPA.). 24p. (J). (gr. -1-2). lib. bdg. 31.36 *(978-1-5321-0182-3(1)*, 25190, Abdo Kids) ABDO Publishing Co.

—Owls. (Animal Kingdom Ser.). (ENG., Illus.). (J). 2019. 32p. (gr. 2-5). lib. bdg. 34.21 *(978-1-5321-1646-9(2)*, 32403, Big Buddy Bks.) 2016. 24p. (gr. -1-2). lib. bdg. 31.36 *(978-1-68080-906-0(7)*, 23287, Abdo Kids) ABDO Publishing Co.

Oddey the Owl. 2005. (J). 9.95 *(978-0-9765502-0-4(2))* ONTRAK.

O'Shaughnessy, Ruth. Owls after Dark, 1 vol. 2015. (Animals of the Night Ser.). (ENG.). 32p. (gr. 3-4). pap. 11.52 *(978-0-7660-6758-5(0)*, 54c41c4b-7e2b-4320-b119-ff397b94ddca); (Illus.). 26.93 *(978-0-7660-6760-8(2)*, 8ea0d16a-1fe6-48f5-923e-89d2ccb7d34d) Enslow Publishing, LLC.

Owen, Ruth. Snowy Owls, 1 vol. 2013. (Polar Animals: Life in the Freezer Ser.). (ENG., Illus.). 32p. (gr. 2-3). 29.93 *(978-1-4777-0223-9(7)*, b02ea7b3-5316-4fca-a6eb-4167924bdfca); pap. 11.00 *(978-1-4777-0233-8(4)*, 7ec18780-1441-48df-b93f-53cf193f1189) Rosen Publishing Group, Inc., The. (Windmill Bks.).

Owls, 6 bks. 2005. (Animal Predators Ser.). (Illus.). 40p. (J). (gr. 3-6). pap. 46.95 *(978-0-8225-5490-5(9))* Lerner Publishing Group.

Owls: Individual Title Six-Packs. (Story Steps Ser.). (gr. k-2). 32.00 *(978-0-7635-9800-6(3))* Rigby Education.

Parker, Steve. Owls, 1 vol. Morandi, Andrea, illus. 2010. (I Love Animals Ser.). (ENG.). 24p. (J). (gr. 2-2). lib. bdg. 27.27 *(978-1-61533-229-8(4)*, 2e44d7e7-63be-4cfd-8f11-9975e9f0b6de, Windmill Bks.) Rosen Publishing Group, Inc., The.

Patrick, Roman. Snowy Owls, 1 vol. 2010. (Animals That Live in the Tundra Ser.). (ENG., Illus.). 24p. (J). (gr. 1-1). pap. 9.15 *(978-1-4339-3909-9(6)*, ac142144-1516-4a20-9b17-64a8066fd2db); lib. bdg. 25.27 *(978-1-4339-3908-2(8)*, 34ff0d59-a960-4d82-8c69-6749c0e002fb) Stevens, Gareth Publishing LLLP.

Phillips, Dee. Burrowing Owl's Hideaway. 2015. (Illus.). 24p. (J). lib. bdg. 26.99 *(978-1-62724-307-0(0))* Bearport Publishing Co., Inc.

—Spotted Owl. 2013. (Science Slam: Treed-Animal Life in the Trees Ser.). 24p. (J). (gr. -1-3). lib. bdg. 26.99 *(978-1-61772-910-2(8))* Bearport Publishing Co., Inc.

Pringle, Laurence. Owls! Strange & Wonderful. Henderson, Meryl Learnihan, illus. 2016. (Strange & Wonderful Ser.). (ENG.). 32p. (J). (gr. 2-5). 16.95 *(978-1-62091-651-3(7)*, Astra Young Readers) Astra Publishing Hse.

Quality Productions Staff. Lechuzas. Rountree, Monica, tr. 2003. (Zoobooks Ser.). Orig. Title: Owls. (SPA., Illus.). 24p. (J). (gr. 1-7). lib. bdg. 15.95 *(978-1-888153-81-1(4))* National Wildlife Federation.

—Owls. rev. ed. 2003. (Illus.). 24p. (J). (gr. 1-7). 10.95 *(978-1-888153-93-4(8)*, Zoo Bks.) National Wildlife Federation.

Read, Tracy C. Exploring the World of Owls. 2011. (Exploring the World Of Ser.). (ENG., Illus.). 24p. (J). (gr. 3-7). 16.95 *(978-1-55407-883-7(0)*, 389d46e4-c102-4530-b7df-956e2fdbb1b0); pap. 6.95 *(978-1-55407-957-5(8)*, 3aa803db-0fd0-4f36-9b68-2be22102d442) Firefly Bks., Ltd.

Reher, Matt. Farmers Like Barn Owls. 2017. (1G Predator Animals Ser.). (ENG., Illus.). 28p. (J). pap. 9.60 *(978-1-63437-675-4(7))* American Reading Co.

Ricciuti, Edward R. Adivina Quién Baja en Picada / Guess Who Swoops, 1 vol. 2008. (Adivina Quién / Guess Who? Ser.). (ENG & SPA., Illus.). 32p. (gr. k-2). lib. bdg. 25.50 *(978-0-7614-2468-0(7)*, 47fe6237-6707-4e32-83ed-087e5fd375c1) Cavendish Square Publishing LLC.

—Adivina Quién Baja en Picada (Guess Who Swoops), 1 vol. 2008. (Adivina Quién (Guess Who?) Ser.). (SPA., Illus.). 32p. (gr. k-2). lib. bdg. 25.50 *(978-0-7614-2387-4(7)*, dd914657-2c3d-47f8-8d67-e08d2b86b048) Cavendish Square Publishing LLC.

—Guess Who Swoops, 1 vol. (Guess Who? Ser.). (ENG., Illus.). 32p. (gr. k-1). 2008. pap. 9.23 *(978-0-7614-3323-1(6)*, 49c923bc-183f-4281-b218-daf8f0bb924d) 2005. lib. bdg. 25.50 *(978-0-7614-1553-4(X)*, 605597a5-4dd8-49ba-98f2-646414fac740) Cavendish Square Publishing LLC.

Riley, Joelle. Quiet Owls. 2004. (Pull Ahead Bks.). (Illus.). 32p. (J). 22.60 *(978-0-8225-3771-7(0)*, Carolrhoda Bks.) Lerner Publishing Group.

Rustad, Martha E. H. Owls. 2013. (ENG., Illus.). 24p. (J). lib. bdg. 25.65 *(978-1-62031-071-7(6))* Jump! Inc.

Sandoval, Gustavo. Owls & Owlets, 1 vol. 2017. (Animal Family Ser.). (ENG.). 24p. (gr. k-k). pap. 9.15 *(978-1-4824-6385-9(7)*, ddf8cbff-dff8-4b59-9eb3-74901f445710) Stevens, Gareth Publishing LLLP.

Schuetz, Kari. Owls. 2011. (Backyard Wildlife Ser.). (ENG., Illus.). 24p. (J). (gr. k-3). lib. bdg. 26.95 *(978-1-60014-598-8(1))* Bellwether Media.

Smalley, Carol Parenzan. Threat to the Spotted Owl. 2008. (On the Verge of Extinction Ser.). (Illus.). 32p. (YA). (gr. 2-5). lib. bdg. 25.70 *(978-1-58415-687-1(2))* Mitchell Lane Pubs.

Sollinger, Emily. Owls: Birds of the Night. Rallis, Chris, illus. 2014. (Penguin Young Readers, Level 3 Ser.). 48p. (J). (gr. 1-3). pap. 4.99 *(978-0-448-48135-7(9)*, Penguin Young Readers) Penguin Young Readers Group.

Sommer, Nathan. Owls. 2018. (Birds of Prey Ser.). (ENG., Illus.). 24p. (J). (gr. 3-7). lib. bdg. 26.95 *(978-1-62617-881-6(X)*, Epic Bks.) Bellwether Media.

Storm, Marysa. Owls. 2020. (Awesome Animal Lives Ser.). (ENG.). 24p. (J). (gr. k-3). pap. 8.99 *(978-1-64466-102-4(0)*, 14403, Bolt Jr.) Black Rabbit Bks.

Suen, Anastasia. Snowy Owls. 2020. (Spot Arctic Animals Ser.). (ENG.). 16p. (J). (gr. -1-2). lib. bdg. *(978-1-68151-800-8(7)*, 10674) Amicus.

Taylor, Trace & Cline, Gina. Owls. Taylor, Trace, illus. 2017. (2G Predator Animals Ser.). (ENG., Illus.). 32p. (J). pap. 8.00 *(978-1-61406-133-5(5))* American Reading Co.

Tekiela, Stan. Our Love of Owls. 2018. (Our Love of Wildlife Ser.). (ENG., Illus.). 48p. 9.95 *(978-1-59193-813-2(9)*, Adventure Pubns.) AdventureKEEN.

Thomson, Ruth. The Life Cycle of an Owl, 1 vol. 2009. (Learning about Life Cycles Ser.). (ENG.). 24p. (J). (gr. 2-2). lib. bdg. 26.27 *(978-1-4358-2833-9(X)*, 3baffc10-133f-43d4-b5db-ae16d480f699) Rosen Publishing Group, Inc., The.

Warhol, Tom. Owls, 1 vol. 2008. (Animal Ways Ser.). (ENG., Illus.). 112p. (gr. 6-6). lib. bdg. 38.36 *(978-0-7614-2537-3(3)*, ff185028-7fdb-4ddb-b2cd-8b1314fd2f32) Cavendish Square Publishing LLC.

Wechsler, Doug. Great Horned Owls. 2009. (Really Wild Life of Animals Ser.). 24p. (gr. 3-4). 42.50 *(978-1-60854-194-2(0)*, PowerKids Pr.) Rosen Publishing Group, Inc., The.

Wilson, Mark. Owling: Enter the World of the Mysterious Birds of the Night. 2019. (ENG., Illus.). 120p. (J). (gr. 3-7). 18.95 *(978-1-61212-962-4(5)*, 622962) Storey Publishing, LLC.

Winnick, Nick. Owls. 2010. (Backyard Animals Ser.). (Illus.). 24p. (J). (gr. 2-4). pap. 11.95 *(978-1-60596-953-4(2))*; lib. bdg. 25.70 *(978-1-60596-952-7(4))* Weigl Pubs., Inc.

Wyatt, Laura. Those Outrageous Owls. Weaver, Steve, illus. Moore, H. G., photos by. 2006. (Those Amazing Animals Ser.). (ENG.). (J). (gr. -1-12). 55p. 14.95 *(978-1-56164-365-3(3))*; 58p. per. 9.95 *(978-1-56164-366-0(1))* Pineapple Pr., Inc.

OWLS—FICTION

Alexander, Heather. Wallace & Grace & the Cupcake Caper. Zarrin, Laura, illus. (Wallace & Grace Ser.). (ENG.). 80p. (J). 2018. pap. 7.99 *(978-1-68119-011-2(7)*, 900154812, Bloomsbury Children's Bks.) 2017. 9.99 *(978-1-68119-010-5(9)*, 900154813, Bloomsbury USA Childrens) Bloomsbury Publishing USA.

—Wallace & Grace & the Lost Puppy. Zarrin, Laura, illus. 2017. (Wallace & Grace Ser.). (ENG.). 80p. (J). 9.99

(978-1-68119-012-9(5), 900154800, Bloomsbury USA Childrens) Bloomsbury Publishing USA.
Allen, Jonathan. I'm Not Sleepy! 2012. (Baby Owl Ser.). (ENG., Illus.). 26p. (J). (gr. k — 1). bds. 6.95 *(978-1-907967-37-5(0))* Boxer Bks., Ltd. GBR. Dist: Sterling Publishing Co., Inc.
Anastasio, Dina. How Raven Became Black & Owl Got Its Spots & Por qué el cuervo es negro y el búho tiene Manchitas: 6 English, 6 Spanish Adaptations. 2011. (ENG & SPA.). (J). 75.00 net. *(978-1-4108-5626-5(7))* Benchmark Education Co.
Anastasio, Dina, retold by. How Raven Became Black & Owl Got Its Spots: Set Of 6. 2010. (Early Connections Ser.). (J). pap. 37.00 net. *(978-1-4108-1093-9(3))* Benchmark Education Co.
Anaya, Rudolfo. Owl in a Straw Hat: El Tecolote Del Sombrero de Paja. Lamadrid, Enrique R., tr. El Moisés, El, illus. 2017. (ENG.). 44p. (J). 16.95 *(978-0-89013-630-0(0))* Museum of New Mexico Pr.
Avi. Poppy. Floca, Brian, illus. 2020. (Poppy Ser.: 3). (ENG.). 192p. (J). (gr. 3-7). pap. 9.99 *(978-0-380-72769-8(2)*, HarperCollins) HarperCollins Pubs.
—Poppy. 2006. (Poppy Stories Ser.: 2). (J). (gr. 3-6). lib. bdg. 17.20 *(978-0-613-03338-1(8))* Turtleback.
Bailey, Arthur Scott. The Tale of Solomon Owl. 2018. (ENG., Illus.). 62p. (YA). (gr. 7-12). pap. *(978-93-5297-579-2(0))* Alpha Editions.
—The Tale of Solomon Owl. (ENG., Illus.). (J). 2017. pap. 12.95 *(978-1-375-45157-4(X))* 2015. 124p. 22.95 *(978-1-340-20436-5(3))* Creative Media Partners, LLC.
—The Tale of Solomon Owl. 2017. (ENG., Illus.). (J). pap. *(978-0-649-51571-4(4))* Trieste Publishing Pty Ltd.
—Tuck-Me-In Tales: The Tale of Solomon Ow. 2006. (Illus.). pap. *(978-1-4065-0452-1(1))* Dodo Pr.
Balboni, Mary. The Birds of Winslow. 2010. 20p. 10.49 *(978-1-4490-2712-4(1))* AuthorHouse.
Batsel, Hannah. A Is for Another Rabbit. Batsel, Hannah, illus. 2020. (ENG., Illus.). 32p. (J). (gr. -1-2). 17.99 *(978-1-5415-2950-2(2)*, 560c7d12-c42e-4a7b-8ba7-b224ff9b6a7f, Carolrhoda Bks.) Lerner Publishing Group.
Beatty, Connie. Why Owls Say Who. Beatty, Connie & Phillippi, Faith, illus. 2008. 20p. per. 24.95 *(978-1-4137-6715-5(X))* America Star Bks.
Bernstein, Ariel. I Have a Balloon. Magoon, Scott, illus. 2017. (ENG.). 40p. (J). (gr. -1-3). 19.99 *(978-1-4814-7250-0(X)*, Simon & Schuster/Paula Wiseman Bks.) Simon & Schuster/Paula Wiseman Bks.
—Where Is My Balloon? Magoon, Scott, illus. 2019. (ENG.). 40p. (J). (gr. -1-3). 17.99 *(978-1-5344-1451-8(7)*, Simon & Schuster Bks. For Young Readers) Simon & Schuster Bks. For Young Readers.
Billows, Denis. Down in Bluebell Wood. 2010. 164p. pap. 11.99 *(978-1-4490-8822-4(8))* AuthorHouse.
Bingamon-Haller, Mary. The Great Horned Owl. Burns, Sandra, illus. 2013. 28p. pap. 8.99 *(978-1-938768-12-5(4))* Gypsy Pubns.
Black, Cary & Schott, Gretchen Victoria. French Quarter Tori & the Red Owl. Travis, Caroline, illus. 2012. 38p. pap. 14.95 *(978-0-9754279-7-2(0))*; pap. 12.95 *(978-0-9754279-8-9(9))* Red Owl Pubns.
Bodoh, Tony. Hannah's Animal Farm. 2008. 28p. pap. 14.95 *(978-1-4327-2046-9(5))* Outskirts Pr., Inc.
A Book of Sleep. 2011. (ENG.). 24p. (J). (gr. k — 1). bds. 6.99 *(978-0-375-86618-0(3)*, Knopf Bks. for Young Readers) Random Hse. Children's Bks.
Boto, Julie & Boto, Thomas. Nora & the Powerful Light: An Owlegories Tale. 2018. (Owlegories Ser.). (ENG., Illus.). 32p. (J). 12.99 *(978-1-5064-3312-7(X)*, Sparkhouse Family) 1517 Media.
Boto, Thomas & Boto, Julie. Gus & the Caterpillar Caper: An Owlegories Tale. 2018. (Owlegories Ser.). (ENG.). 32p. (J). 12.99 *(978-1-5064-3311-0(1)*, Sparkhouse Family) 1517 Media.
Bowman, Crystal. Otter & Owl's Helpful Hike, 1 vol. Zimmer, Kevin J., illus. 2008. (I Can Read! / Otter & Owl Ser.). (ENG.). 32p. (J). pap. 4.99 *(978-0-310-71706-5(X))*; pap. 4.99 *(978-0-310-71704-1(3))* Zonderkidz.
Branford, Anna. The Midnight Owl. Coutts, Lisa, illus. 2016. (Lily the Elf Ser.). (ENG.). 47p. (J). *(978-1-61067-625-0(4))* Kane Miller.
—The Midnight Owl: Lily the Elf. Coutts, Lisa, illus. 2017. 47p. (J). pap. 4.99 *(978-1-61067-529-1(0))* Kane Miller.
Brodien-Jones, Christine. The Owl Keeper. Kneen, Maggie, illus. 2011. (ENG.). 320p. (J). (gr. 3-7). 8.99 *(978-0-385-73815-6(3)*, Yearling) Random Hse. Children's Bks.
Brown, Ruby. Cuddles for Mommy. Macnaughton, Tina, illus. 2016. (ENG.). 32p. (J). (gr. -1-3). 16.99 *(978-1-4998-0203-0(X))* Little Bee Books Inc.
Bruchac, Joseph. Wabi: A Hero's Tale. 2007. 208p. (YA). (gr. 7-18). pap. 9.99 *(978-0-14-240947-3(2)*, Speak) Penguin Young Readers Group.
Bunting, Sarah Clare. Why Are You So Lazy Owl? 2011. (ENG.). 16p. 12.50 *(978-1-4709-4837-5(0))* Lulu Pr., Inc.
Burke, Maria. The Ark of Dun Ruah. 2013. (Ark of Dun Ruah Ser.: 01). (ENG., Illus.). 256p. (J). pap. 26.00 *(978-1-85607-794-1(2))* Currach Pr. IRL. Dist: Dufour Editions, Inc.
Callahan, Susan. A New Way. 2012. 20p. pap. 17.99 *(978-1-4772-4507-1(3))* AuthorHouse.
Cefalo, Maria Raffaella. If Dreams Could Talk. 2012. (ENG.). 25p. (J). pap. 27.95 *(978-1-4327-9708-9(5))*; pap. 17.95 *(978-1-4327-9623-5(2))* Outskirts Pr., Inc.
Chambers, Melinda. We Are Whoooo We Are. Spiker, Sue Ann, illus. 2006. 32p. (J). 16.95 *(978-0-929915-46-3(1))* Headline Bks., Inc.
Chandler, Tony. The Journey. 2013. 242p. pap. *(978-1-77115-091-0(2))* Double Dragon ebooks.
Charman, Katrina. The Cloud Kingdom: a Branches Book (the Last Firehawk #7) Tondora, Judit, illus. 2019. (Last Firehawk Ser.: 7). (ENG.). 96p. (J). (gr. 1-3). pap. 5.99 *(978-1-338-30717-7(7))* Scholastic, Inc.
—The Cloud Kingdom: a Branches Book (the Last Firehawk #7) (Library Edition), Vol. 7. Tondora, Judit, illus. 2019. (Last Firehawk Ser.: 7). (ENG.). 96p. (J). (gr. 1-3). 24.99 *(978-1-338-30718-4(5))* Scholastic, Inc.
—The Crystal Caverns: a Branches Book (the Last Firehawk #2) (Library Edition) Norton, Jeremy, illus. 2017. (Last Firehawk Ser.: 2). (ENG.). 96p. (J). (gr. 1-3). 15.99 *(978-1-338-12252-7(5))* Scholastic, Inc.
—The Ember Stone: a Branches Book (the Last Firehawk #1) Norton, Jeremy, illus. 2017. (Last Firehawk Ser.: 1). (ENG.). 96p. (J). (gr. 1-3). pap. 5.99 *(978-1-338-12213-8(4))* Scholastic, Inc.
—Lullaby Lake: a Branches Book (the Last Firehawk #4) Norton, Jeremy, illus. 2018. (Last Firehawk Ser.: 4). (ENG.). 96p. (J). (gr. 1-3). pap. 5.99 *(978-1-338-12267-1(3))* Scholastic, Inc.
—Lullaby Lake: a Branches Book (the Last Firehawk #4) (Library Edition), Vol. 4. Norton, Jeremy, illus. 2018. (Last Firehawk Ser.: 4). (ENG.). 96p. (J). (gr. 1-3). lib. bdg. 24.99 *(978-1-338-12271-8(1))* Scholastic, Inc.
—The Shadowlands: a Branches Book (the Last Firehawk #5) Norton, Jeremy, illus. 2019. (Last Firehawk Ser.: 5). (ENG.). 96p. (J). (gr. 1-3). pap. 5.99 *(978-1-338-30711-5(8))* Scholastic, Inc.
—The Whispering Oak: a Branches Book (the Last Firehawk #3), 1 vol., Vol. 3. Norton, Jeremy, illus. 2018. (Last Firehawk Ser.: 3). (ENG.). 96p. (J). (gr. 1-3). pap. 5.99 *(978-1-338-12255-8(X))* Scholastic, Inc.
Chase, Kit. Oliver's Tree. Chase, Kit, illus. 2014. (ENG., Illus.). 32p. (J). (gr. -1-k). 17.99 *(978-0-399-25700-1(4)*, G.P. Putnam's Sons Books for Young Readers) Penguin Young Readers Group.
Chronicle Books & ImageBooks. Little Owl: Finger Puppet Book: (Finger Puppet Book for Toddlers & Babies, Baby Books for First Year, Animal Finger Puppets) 2011. (Little Finger Puppet Board Bks.). (ENG.). 12p. (J). (gr. -1 — 1). 7.99 *(978-1-4521-0221-4(X))* Chronicle Bks. LLC.
Cochran, Randy. Critter Golf Ii: Chaos at Owl's Nest. 2013. 148p. pap. 10.95 *(978-1-4787-0302-0(4))* Outskirts Pr., Inc.
Coe, Catherine. A Magical Beginning. 2016. (Illus.). 83p. (J). *(978-0-545-92890-8(7))* Scholastic, Inc.
Councilman, Janet H. Rocky & His Responsible Band of Cowboys, 1 vol. 2009. pap. 24.95 *(978-1-60749-384-6(5))* America Star Bks.
Davies, Gill. Brave Little Owl. Twinney, Dick, illus. 2006. (ENG.). 24p. (J). *(978-1-55168-279-2(6))* Fenn, H. B. & Co., Ltd.
Davies, Nicola. White Owl, Barn Owl: Read & Wonder. Foreman, Michael, illus. 2009. (Read & Wonder Ser.). (ENG.). 32p. (J). (gr. -1-3). pap. 8.99 *(978-0-7636-4143-6(X))* Candlewick Pr.
—White Owl, Barn Owl with Audio, Peggable: Read, Listen, & Wonder. Foreman, Michael, illus. 2009. (Read, Listen, & Wonder Ser.). (ENG.). 32p. (J). (gr. -1-3). pap. 9.99 *(978-0-7636-4194-8(4))* Candlewick Pr.
Debowski, Sharon. The Snowman, the Owl, & the Groundhog. 2007. (J). lib. bdg. 15.95 *(978-1-60227-468-6(1))*; (Illus.). 32p. (gr. -1-4). 14.95 *(978-1-60227-470-9(3))* Above the Clouds Publishing.
Del Riego, Erica. The Heart of Life. 2010. 36p. pap. 17.75 *(978-1-4389-7572-6(4))* AuthorHouse.
Denise, Christopher. Knight Owl (Caldecott Honor Book) 2022. (ENG., Illus.). 48p. (J). (gr. -1-3). 17.99 *(978-0-316-31062-8(X))* Little, Brown Bks. for Young Readers.
Dodd, Emma. Happy. Dodd, Emma, illus. (Emma Dodd's Love You Bks.). (ENG., Illus.). (J). (— 1). 2017. 22p. bds. 10.99 *(978-0-7636-9642-9(0))* 2015. 24p. 12.99 *(978-0-7636-8008-4(7))* Candlewick Pr.
Donald, George Mac. Cross Purposes. 2012. 104p. pap. 25.95 *(978-1-4474-5057-3(4))* Borah Pr.
Donaldson, Julia. The Further Adventures of the Owl & the Pussy-Cat. Voake, Charlotte, illus. 2017. (ENG.). 32p. (J). (gr. -1-2). 16.99 *(978-0-7636-9081-6(3))* Candlewick Pr.
Dyas, Amy. The Robins of St Lawrence Church. 2009. 128p. pap. 29.96 *(978-0-9786567-8-2(4))* Parson Place Pr., LLC.
Eagle, Golden. The Owl Who Lives in My House. l.t. ed. 2003. (Illus.). 24p. (J). per. 12.99 *(978-1-932338-34-8(9))* Lifevest Publishing, Inc.
Eisan, Daniel. The Lonely Peach. 2011. (Illus.). 48p. pap. 15.99 *(978-1-4628-5634-3(9))* Xlibris Corp.
Eisele, Barbara. Miss Thistle & Friends. 2009. 48p. pap. 12.99 *(978-1-4490-2007-1(0))* AuthorHouse.
Elliott, Rebecca. Baxter Is Missing: a Branches Book (Owl Diaries #6) Elliott, Rebecca, illus. 2017. (Owl Diaries: 6). (ENG., Illus.). 80p. (J). (gr. k-2). pap. 6.99 *(978-1-338-04284-9(X))* Scholastic, Inc.
—Eva & Baby Mo, 10. 2019. (Branches Early Ch Bks). (ENG.). 71p. (J). (gr. 2-3). 15.36 *(978-0-87617-985-7(5))* Penworthy Co., LLC, The.
—Eva & Baby Mo: a Branches Book (Owl Diaries #10) Elliott, Rebecca, illus. 2019. (Owl Diaries: 10). (ENG., Illus.). 80p. (J). (gr. k-2). pap. 4.99 *(978-1-338-29857-4(7))* Scholastic, Inc.
—Eva & Baby Mo: a Branches Book (Owl Diaries #10) (Library Edition), Vol. 10. Elliott, Rebecca, illus. 2019. (Owl Diaries: 10). (ENG., Illus.). 80p. (J). (gr. k-2). lib. bdg. 24.99 *(978-1-338-29858-1(5))* Scholastic, Inc.
—Eva & the Lost Pony, 8. 2019. (Branches Early Ch Bks). (ENG.). 72p. (J). (gr. 2-3). 15.36 *(978-0-87617-986-4(3))* Penworthy Co., LLC, The.
—Eva & the Lost Pony. 2018. (Owl Diaries — Branches Ser.: 8). lib. bdg. 14.75 *(978-0-606-41142-4(9))* Turtleback.
—Eva & the Lost Pony: a Branches Book (Owl Diaries #8) Elliott, Rebecca, illus. 2018. (Owl Diaries: 8). (ENG., Illus.). 80p. (J). (gr. k-2). pap. 4.99 *(978-1-338-16303-2(5))* Scholastic, Inc.
—Eva & the Lost Pony: a Branches Book (Owl Diaries #8) (Library Edition), Vol. 8. Elliott, Rebecca, illus. 2018. (Owl Diaries: 8). (ENG., Illus.). 80p. (J). (gr. k-2). lib. bdg. 24.99 *(978-1-338-16304-9(3))* Scholastic, Inc.
—Eva & the New Owl: a Branches Book (Owl Diaries #4) Elliott, Rebecca, illus. 2016. (Owl Diaries: 4). (ENG., Illus.). 80p. (J). (gr. k-2). pap. 5.99 *(978-0-545-82559-7(8))* Scholastic, Inc.
—Eva at the Beach: a Branches Book (Owl Diaries #14) Elliott, Rebecca, illus. 2021. (Owl Diaries: 14). (ENG., Illus.). 80p. (J). (gr. k-2). pap. 5.99 *(978-1-338-29879-6(8))* Scholastic, Inc.
—Eva at the Beach: a Branches Book (Owl Diaries #14) (Library Edition) Elliott, Rebecca, illus. 2021. (Owl Diaries: 14). (ENG., Illus.). 80p. (J). (gr. k-2). lib. bdg. 24.99 *(978-1-338-29881-9(X))* Scholastic, Inc.
—Eva in the Band: a Branches Book (Owl Diaries #17) Elliott, Rebecca, illus. 2022. (Owl Diaries). (ENG.). 80p. (J). (gr. k-2). 24.99 *(978-1-338-74544-3(1))*; pap. 5.99 *(978-1-338-74543-6(3))* Scholastic, Inc.
—Eva in the Spotlight: a Branches Book (Owl Diaries #13) Elliott, Rebecca, illus. 2020. (Owl Diaries: 13). (ENG., Illus.). 80p. (J). (gr. k-2). pap. 4.99 *(978-1-338-29875-8(5))* Scholastic, Inc.
—Eva in the Spotlight: a Branches Book (Owl Diaries #13) (Library Edition) Elliott, Rebecca, illus. 2020. (Owl Diaries: 13). (ENG., Illus.). 80p. (J). (gr. k-2). lib. bdg. 24.99 *(978-1-338-29876-5(3))* Scholastic, Inc.
—Eva Sees a Ghost. 2015. (Owl Diaries: 2). lib. bdg. 14.75 *(978-0-606-37038-7(2))* Turtleback.
—Eva Sees a Ghost: a Branches Book (Owl Diaries #2) Elliott, Rebecca, illus. 2015. (Owl Diaries: 2). (ENG., Illus.). 80p. (J). (gr. k-2). pap. 5.99 *(978-0-545-78783-3(1))* Scholastic, Inc.
—Eva Sees a Ghost: a Branches Book (Owl Diaries #2) (Library Edition) Elliott, Rebecca, illus. 2015. (Owl Diaries: 2). (ENG., Illus.). 80p. (J). (gr. k-2). 24.99 *(978-0-545-78784-0(X))* Scholastic, Inc.
—Eva's Big Sleepover, 9. 2019. (Branches Early Ch Bks). (ENG.). 72p. (J). (gr. 2-3). 15.36 *(978-0-87617-987-1(1))* Penworthy Co., LLC, The.
—Eva's Big Sleepover. 2018. (Owl Diaries — Branches Ser.: 9). lib. bdg. 14.75 *(978-0-606-41508-8(4))* Turtleback.
—Eva's Big Sleepover: a Branches Book (Owl Diaries #9) Elliott, Rebecca, illus. 2018. (Owl Diaries: 9). (ENG., Illus.). 80p. (J). (gr. k-2). pap. 4.99 *(978-1-338-16306-3(X))* Scholastic, Inc.
—Eva's Big Sleepover: a Branches Book (Owl Diaries #9) (Library Edition), Vol. 9. Elliott, Rebecca, illus. 2018. (Owl Diaries: 9). (ENG., Illus.). 80p. (J). (gr. k-2). lib. bdg. 24.99 *(978-1-338-16307-0(8))* Scholastic, Inc.
—Eva's Campfire Adventure, 12. 2020. (Branches Early Ch Bks). (ENG.). 72p. (J). (gr. 2-3). 15.36 *(978-1-64697-303-3(8))* Penworthy Co., LLC, The.
—Eva's Campfire Adventure: a Branches Book (Owl Diaries #12) Elliott, Rebecca, illus. 2019. (Owl Diaries: 12). (ENG., Illus.). 80p. (J). (gr. k-2). pap. 4.99 *(978-1-338-29869-7(0))* Scholastic, Inc.
—Eva's Campfire Adventure: a Branches Book (Owl Diaries #12) (Library Edition), Vol. 12. Elliott, Rebecca, illus. 2019. (Owl Diaries: 12). (ENG., Illus.). 80p. (J). (gr. k-2). lib. bdg. 24.99 *(978-1-338-29871-0(2))* Scholastic, Inc.
—Eva's New Pet: a Branches Book (Owl Diaries #15) Elliott, Rebecca, illus. 2021. (Owl Diaries: 15). (ENG., Illus.). 80p. (J). (gr. k-2). pap. 5.99 *(978-1-338-74537-5(9))* Scholastic, Inc.
—Eva's New Pet: a Branches Book (Owl Diaries #15) (Library Edition) Elliott, Rebecca, illus. 2021. (Owl Diaries: 15). (ENG., Illus.). 80p. (J). (gr. k-2). lib. bdg. 24.99 *(978-1-338-74538-2(7))* Scholastic, Inc.
—Eva's Treetop Festival. 2015. (Owl Diaries: 1). lib. bdg. 14.75 *(978-0-606-36337-2(8))* Turtleback.
—Eva's Treetop Festival: a Branches Book (Owl Diaries #1), 1 vol., Bk. 1. Elliott, Rebecca, illus. 2015. (Owl Diaries: 1). (ENG., Illus.). 80p. (J). (gr. k-2). pap. 5.99 *(978-0-545-68362-3(9)*, b705f388-0996-4860-8f27-1a68fd6e0f94) Scholastic, Inc.
—Get Well, Eva: a Branches Book (Owl Diaries #16) Elliott, Rebecca, illus. 2022. (Owl Diaries). (ENG.). 80p. (J). (gr. k-2). 24.99 *(978-1-338-74541-2(7))*; pap. 5.99 *(978-1-338-74540-5(9))* Scholastic, Inc.
—Trip to the Pumpkin Farm, 11. 2020. (Branches Early Ch Bks). (ENG.). 72p. (J). (gr. 2-3). 15.36 *(978-1-64697-304-0(6))* Penworthy Co., LLC, The.
—Trip to the Pumpkin Farm: a Branches Book (Owl Diaries #11) Elliott, Rebecca, illus. 2019. (Owl Diaries: 11). (ENG., Illus.). 80p. (J). (gr. k-2). pap. 6.99 *(978-1-338-29864-2(X))* Scholastic, Inc.
—Trip to the Pumpkin Farm: a Branches Book (Owl Diaries #11) (Library Edition) Elliott, Rebecca, illus. 2019. (Owl Diaries: 11). (ENG., Illus.). 80p. (J). (gr. k-2). lib. bdg. 24.99 *(978-1-338-29865-9(8))* Scholastic, Inc.
—Warm Hearts Day: a Branches Book (Owl Diaries #5) Elliott, Rebecca, illus. 2016. (Owl Diaries: 5). (ENG., Illus.). 80p. (J). (gr. k-2). pap. 5.99 *(978-1-338-04280-1(7))* Scholastic, Inc.
—The Wildwood Bakery, 7. 2019. (Branches Early Ch Bks). (ENG.). 72p. (J). (gr. 2-3). 15.36 *(978-0-87617-988-8(X))* Penworthy Co., LLC, The.
—The Wildwood Bakery. 2017. (Owl Diaries — Branches Ser.: 7). lib. bdg. 14.75 *(978-0-606-40660-4(3))* Turtleback.
—The Wildwood Bakery: a Branches Book (Owl Diaries #7) Elliott, Rebecca, illus. 2017. (Owl Diaries: 7). (ENG., Illus.). 80p. (J). (gr. k-2). pap. 4.99 *(978-1-338-16300-1(0))* Scholastic, Inc.
—The Wildwood Bakery: a Branches Book (Owl Diaries #7) (Library Edition) Elliott, Rebecca, illus. 2017. (Owl Diaries: 7). (ENG., Illus.). 80p. (J). (gr. k-2). lib. bdg. 15.99 *(978-1-338-16301-8(9))* Scholastic, Inc.
—A Woodland Wedding. 2016. (Owl Diaries: 3). (ENG.). 80p. (J). (gr. k-2). lib. bdg. 14.75 *(978-0-606-38068-3(X))* Turtleback.
—A Woodland Wedding: a Branches Book (Owl Diaries #3) (Library Edition), Vol. 3. Elliott, Rebecca, illus. 2016. (Owl Diaries: 3). (ENG., Illus.). 80p. (J). (gr. k-2). 24.99 *(978-0-545-82558-0(X))* Scholastic, Inc.
Emerson, Joan. Meet the Beanie Boos (Beanie Boos) 2018. (Beanie Boos Ser.). (ENG.). 24p. (J). (gr. -1-3). pap. 4.99 *(978-1-338-25621-5(1))* Scholastic, Inc.
Fabrizio, Anthony. The Last Forest, 1 vol. 2009. 64p. pap. 19.95 *(978-1-61546-861-4(7))* America Star Bks.
Filoche, Eric. Hey ! We're Talking about Ourselves ! 2013. 68p. pap. *(978-2-9538737-4-0(0))* Koshkindom.
Fitzpatrick, Marie-Louise. Owl Bat Bat Owl. Fitzpatrick, Marie-Louise, illus. 2017. (ENG., Illus.). 32p. (J). (gr. -1-2). 15.99 *(978-0-7636-9161-5(5))* Candlewick Pr.
Frank, Rochelle. So What, Saw-Whet? Gast, Linda, photos by. 2004. (Illus.). (J). per. 9.95 *(978-0-9746792-0-4(8))* Hummingbird Mountain Pr.
Freedman, Claire. The Monster of the Woods! Julian, Russell, illus. 2013. (ENG.). 32p. (J). pap. *(978-0-545-51571-9(8)*, Cartwheel Bks.) Scholastic, Inc.
French, Jennifer Pratt. Hoot Owl Shares the Dawn 2004. 128p. (YA). per. 9.95 *(978-0-9709104-4-8(4))* Hickory Tales Publishing.
Friester, Paul. Owl Howl. Goossens, Philippe, illus. 2014. (ENG.). 32p. (J). (gr. -1-2). 15.95 *(978-0-7358-4188-8(8))* North-South Bks., Inc.
—Owl Howl & the BLU-BLU. Goossens, Philippe, illus. 2016. (ENG.). 32p. (J). (gr. -1-1). 15.95 *(978-0-7358-4246-5(9))* North-South Bks., Inc.
—Owl Howl Board Book. Goossens, Philippe, illus. 2nd rev. ed. 2016. (ENG.). 26p. (J). (gr. -1-1). bds. 8.95 *(978-0-7358-4234-2(5))* North-South Bks., Inc.
—Owl Howls Again! Goossens, Philippe, illus. 2015. (ENG.). 32p. (J). (gr. -1-1). 15.95 *(978-0-7358-4129-1(2))* North-South Bks., Inc.
Furuya, Michael, illus. Keoni's Special Gift. 2009. (J). *(978-1-56647-915-8(0))* Mutual Publishing LLC.
Gadsby, Maggie. Owl Be Home for Christmas. 2012. (J). 14.95 *(978-1-62086-064-9(3))* Amplify Publishing Group.
Galante, Cecilia. Little Wings #4: the One & Only Willa Bean. Valiant, Kristi, illus. 2012. (Little Wings Ser.: 4). 112p. (J). (gr. 1-4). pap. 4.99 *(978-0-375-86950-1(6)*, Random Hse. Bks. for Young Readers) Random Hse. Children's Bks.
—The One & Only Willa Bean, 4. Valiant, Kristi, illus. 2013. (Little Wings Ser.: No. 4). (ENG.). 112p. (J). (gr. 1-3). lib. bdg. 17.44 *(978-0-375-96950-8(0))* Random House Publishing Group.
Gardner Johnson, Jaime. The Ghost of Donley Farm, 1 vol. Allen Klein, Laurie, illus. 2015.Tr. of [the Ghost of Donley Farm] [Spanish Edition]. (ENG.). 32p. (J). (gr. k-3). 17.95 *(978-1-62855-451-9(7))*; pap. 9.95 *(978-1-62855-459-5(2))* Arbordale Publishing.
Garza, Xavier & Gabriela, Baeza Ventura. Vincent Ventura & the Mystery of the Witch Owl / Vincent Ventura y el Misterio de la Bruja Lechuza: A Monster Fighter Mystery / Serie Exterminador de Monstruos. 2019. (SPA & ENG., Illus.). 122p. (J). (gr. 4-7). pap. 9.95 *(978-1-55885-890-9(3)*, Piñata Books) Arte Publico Pr.
George, Jean Craighead. There's an Owl in the Shower. Merrill, Christine Herman, illus. 2019. (ENG.). 144p. (J). (gr. 3-7). pap. 9.99 *(978-0-06-440682-6(2)*, HarperCollins) HarperCollins Pubs.
Gianferrari, Maria. Whoo-Ku Haiku: a Great Horned Owl Story. Voss, Jonathan, illus. 2020. (ENG.). 32p. (J). (gr. -1-3). 18.99 *(978-0-399-54842-0(4)*, G.P. Putnam's Sons Books for Young Readers) Penguin Young Readers Group.
Giraldo, Maria Loretta & Hagen, Katie ten. Abracadabra! The Magic of Trying. Bertelle, Nicoletta, illus. 2018. 32p. (J). *(978-1-4338-2874-4(X)*, Magination Pr.) American Psychological Assn.
Glass, Shelby. Something Is Everything. 2012. 36p. pap. 19.99 *(978-1-4772-6581-9(3))* AuthorHouse.
Gliori, Debi. Little Owl's Egg. Brown, Alison, illus. (ENG.). 32p. (J). 2018. bds. 7.99 *(978-1-68119-893-4(2)*, 900191670, Bloomsbury Children's Bks.) 2017. 16.99 *(978-1-68119-324-3(8)*, 900170041, Bloomsbury USA Childrens) Bloomsbury Publishing USA.
Gordon, Pauline C. Animals in My Backyard! Joey, the Flying Squirrel. 2012. 28p. pap. 15.99 *(978-1-4771-1961-7(2))* Xlibris Corp.
Gram, Golden. Gail the Snail: Night Owl. 2008. 20p. pap. 11.95 *(978-1-59858-859-0(1))* Dog Ear Publishing, LLC.
Grandpa Dennis, as told by. George Washington's Smallest Army: The Miracle Before Trenton. 2009. 216p. (J). pap. 17.49 *(978-1-4389-3147-0(6))* AuthorHouse.
Grant, V. F. Stories from Grimley Forest. 2011. 48p. (gr. 1-2). pap. 19.50 *(978-1-4567-4709-1(6))* AuthorHouse.
Green, Joanne. Hootah's Baby. 2012. 46p. pap. *(978-1-897512-53-1(8))* Saga Bks.
Groce, Michelle. Jasper. Duis, Laura, illus. 2003. 174p. (J). 17.95 *(978-0-9708972-6-8(X))* Novello Festival Pr.
Gwyer, Gillian K. Podnockery Forest - Owl & the Trickster. 2013. 40p. pap. *(978-1-4602-3974-2(1))* FriesenPress.
Hanson, Anders. Night Owl. Haberstroh, Anne, illus. 2006. (Fact & Fiction Ser.). 24p. (J). pap. 48.42 *(978-1-59679-954-7(4))* ABDO Publishing Co.
Harary, Keith. The Owls of the Enchanted Forest. Gonina, Luba, illus. 2008. 52p. (J). pap. 15.88 *(978-0-9799196-8-8(1))* Owl Pals.
—The Owls of the Enchanted Forest - 2007 Special Collector's Edition. Gonina, Luba, illus. 2007. 50p. (J). 50.00 incl. DVD *(978-0-9799196-3-3(0))* Owl Pals.
Haughton, Chris. Little Owl Lost. Haughton, Chris, illus. (ENG., Illus.). (J). 2013. 30p. (-k). bds. 10.99 *(978-0-7636-6750-4(1))* 2010. 32p. (gr. -1-k). 17.99 *(978-0-7636-5022-3(6))* Candlewick Pr.
Hawkins, Linda J. Who Gives a Hoot? Hunter Hoot,the Great Horned Owl. 2012. (ENG., Illus.). 40p. (J). pap. 9.99 *(978-1-937008-06-2(1))* Heart to Heart Publishing, Inc.
Hecht, Tracey. The Ominous Eye: The Nocturnals Book 2. Liebman, Kate, illus. 2016. (Nocturnals Ser.: 2). (ENG.). 208p. (J). (gr. 3-5). 15.99 *(978-1-944020-03-3(9)*, Fabled Films Pr. LLC) Fabled Films LLC.
Hemmings, Lisa & O'Keefe, Allan. Imagine Me with the Three Owls: Feeling Great. 2012. 32p. pap. 13.95 *(978-1-4525-0551-0(9))* Balboa Pr.
Heroux, Matthew & Kirwan, Wednesday. Owl Love You. 2018. (ENG., Illus.). 32p. (J). (gr. -1-3). 16.95 *(978-1-944903-35-0(6)*, 1320501, Cameron Kids) Cameron + Co.
Hiaasen, Carl. Hoot. 2004. (ENG.). 320p. (YA). (gr. 5). reprint ed. pap. 9.99 *(978-0-375-82916-1(4)*, Ember) Random Hse. Children's Bks.
Hiaasen, Carl. Hoot. 2014. 17.00 *(978-1-63419-707-6(0))* Perfection Learning Corp.
Hills, Tad. Rocket Writes a Story. Hills, Tad, illus. 2012. (Rocket Ser.). (ENG., Illus.). 40p. (J). (gr. -1-3). 17.99 *(978-0-375-87086-6(5)*, Schwartz & Wade Bks.) Random Hse. Children's Bks.
Huggins, Peter. Trosclair & the Alligator, 1 vol. Gardiner, Lindsey, illus. 2005. (ENG.). 32p. (J). (gr. -1-3). 15.95 *(978-1-932065-98-5(9))* Star Bright Bks., Inc.
Hutchins, Pat. Good-Night, Owl! Hutchins, Pat, illus. 2015. (Classic Board Bks.). (ENG., Illus.). 34p. (J). (gr. -1 — 1). bds. 8.99 *(978-1-4814-4424-8(7)*, Little Simon) Little Simon.
I Am A Dog. 2008. (Illus.). 26p. 24.95 *(978-0-9801054-0-7(4))* Teahouse of Danger.

MNO

Irvin-Marston, Hope. My Little Book of Burrowing Owls. Magdalena-Brown, Maria, illus. 2nd ed. 2004. (ENG.). 32p. (J). pap. 7.95 *(978-0-89317-054-7(2)*, WW-0542, Windward Publishing) Finney Co., Inc.

Jacquemain, Patti. Journey of the Great Bear: Through California's Golden Past. Jacquemain, Patti, illus. 2006. (Illus.). (J). *(978-0-929702-10-0(7))* Mission Creek Studios.

Jason June, Jason. Whobert Whover, Owl Detective. Pauwels, Jess, illus. 2017. (ENG.). 40p. (J). (gr. -1-1). 17.99 *(978-1-4814-6271-6(7)*, McElderry, Margaret K. Bks.) McElderry, Margaret K. Bks.

Johnson, Katharine. The Mukluk Ball. Schwab, Alicia, illus. 2018. (ENG.). 32p. (J). 16.95 *(978-1-68134-116-3(6))* Minnesota Historical Society Pr.

Judge, Lita. Hoot & Peep. 2016. (Hoot & Peep Ser.). (ENG., Illus.). 40p. (J). (-k). 17.99 *(978-0-525-42837-4(2)*, Dial Bks) Penguin Young Readers Group.

Kail, Leanna. The Owl Who Couldn't Whoo. Rottinger, Amy, illus. 2013. 24p. pap. 11.95 *(978-1-61244-129-0(7))* Halo Publishing International.

Keats Curtis, Jennifer. Baby Owl's Rescue, 1 vol. Jacques, Laura, illus. 2009. (ENG.). 32p. (J). (gr. -1-3). 16.95 *(978-1-934359-95-2(5)*, 9781934359952) Arbordale Publishing.

Kelly, Jacqueline. Who Gives a Hoot?: Calpurnia Tate, Girl Vet. Meyer, Jennifer L., illus. 2018. (Calpurnia Tate, Girl Vet Ser.: 3). (ENG.). 128p. (J). pap. 6.99 *(978-1-250-14339-6(X)*, 900161290) Square Fish.

Kim, Melissa & Fitch, Jada. A Snowy Owl Story, 1 vol. 2015. (ENG.). 24p. (J). bds. 12.95 *(978-1-939017-48-2(3)*, ed96c2d3-7f04-4596-8e45-195bf11576e9) Islandport Pr., Inc.

Kindl, Patrice. Owl in Love. 2004. (ENG.). 224p. (YA). (gr. 7-18). pap. 14.95 *(978-0-618-43910-2(2))* Houghton Mifflin Harcourt Publishing Co.

Lambert, Jonny. The Great Aaa-Ooo! 2016. (ENG., Illus.). 32p. (J). pap. *(978-1-84869-276-3(5))* Tiger Tales.

Lamm, C. Drew. Screech Owl at Midnight Hollow. Snyder, Joel, illus. 2011. (Smithsonian's Backyard Ser.). (ENG.). 32p. (J). (gr. -1-3). 19.95 *(978-1-60727-643-2(7))* Soundprints.

Lansdowne, Marcella. The Adventures of Patty & Annabel: The Javelinas & Releasing the Cords. 2009. 28p. pap. 15.95 *(978-1-4389-1645-3(0))* AuthorHouse.

Lasky, Kathryn. The Capture. l.t. ed. 2007. (Guardians of Ga'Hoole Ser.: Bk. 1). 228p. (YA). 22.95 *(978-0-7862-9865-5(0))* Thorndike Pr.

—The Capture. 2003. (Guardians of Ga'Hoole Ser.: 1). (gr. 3-6). lib. bdg. 17.20 *(978-0-613-67484-3(7))* Turtleback.

—The Capture (Guardians of Ga'Hoole #1) 2003. (Guardians of Ga'hoole Ser.: 1). (ENG.). 240p. (gr. 4-7). mass mkt. 7.99 *(978-0-439-40557-7(2)*, Scholastic Paperbacks) Scholastic, Inc.

—The Golden Tree. 2007. (Guardians of Ga'Hoole Ser.: 12). (Illus.). 192p. lib. bdg. 17.20 *(978-1-4177-8260-4(9))* Turtleback.

—The Journey. l.t. ed. 2007. (Guardians of Ga'Hoole Ser.: Bk. 2). (Illus.). 271p. (J). (gr. 3-7). 22.95 *(978-1-4104-0293-6(2))* Thorndike Pr.

—The Rescue (Guardians of Ga'Hoole #3). 3. 2004. (Guardians of Ga'hoole Ser.: 3). (ENG., Illus.). 208p. (gr. 4-7). pap. 7.99 *(978-0-439-40559-1(9))* Scholastic, Inc.

—The River of Wind. 2007. (Guardians of Ga'Hoole Ser.: 13). lib. bdg. 17.20 *(978-1-4177-8261-1(7))* Turtleback.

Laurie, Peter. Mauby & the Hurricane. 2007. (Illus.). 56p. pap. 16.00 *(978-1-4050-7718-7(2))* Macmillan Caribbean GBR. Dist: Interlink Publishing Group, Inc.

Leadbetter, Lesley. Harold the Owl Who Couldn't Sleep. Leszek, Cedryll, illus. 2012. 30p. (J). pap. *(978-1-921869-89-1(5)*, Digital Publishing Centre) Interactive Pubns. Pty. Ltd.

Lear, Edward. Buho y la Gatita.Tr. of Owl & the Cat. (SPA., Illus.). 32p. (J). 14.95 *(978-84-261-3023-5(2))* Juventud, Editorial ESP. Dist: AIMS International Bks., Inc.

Leist, Christina. Jack the Bear. 2009. (ENG., Illus.). 40p. (J). (gr. -1-3). 16.95 *(978-1-894965-97-2(3))* Simply Read Bks. CAN. Dist: Ingram Publisher Services.

Litton, Jonathan. Hoot: A Hide-And-Seek Book of Counting! Galloway, Fhiona, illus. 2014. (My Little World Ser.). (ENG.). 16p. (J). (gr. -1-k). bds. 7.99 *(978-1-58925-595-1(X))* Tiger Tales.

London, Lewis. Wesley Owl. 2010. (Illus.). 36p. (J). pap. 16.99 *(978-1-4490-6122-7(2))* AuthorHouse.

Loyie, Larry & Brissenden, Constance. As Long As the Rivers Flow, 1 vol. Holmlund, Heather D., illus. 2005. (ENG.). 48p. (J). (gr. 4-3). pap. 9.99 *(978-0-88899-696-1(9))* Groundwood Bks. CAN. Dist: Publishers Group West (PGW).

Lucas, Ronne Kay. How the Cactus Got Its Thorns. 2013. 20p. pap. 24.95 *(978-1-4626-8915-6(9))* America Star Bks.

MacGregor, Roy. Trouble at the Top of the World. 2009. (Screech Owls Ser.: 22). (ENG.). 136p. (J). (gr. 3-7). mass mkt. 5.95 *(978-0-7710-5609-3(5)*, Screech Owls) McClelland & Stewart CAN. Dist: Penguin Random Hse. LLC.

MacGregor, Roy & MacGregor, Roy. The Complete Screech Owls, Volume 5, Vol. 5. 2007. (Complete Screech Owls Ser.: 5). (ENG.). 488p. (J). (gr. 3-7). per. 15.95 *(978-0-7710-5497-6(1)*, Screech Owls) McClelland & Stewart CAN. Dist: Penguin Random Hse. LLC.

Magsamen, Sandra. Owl Always Love You! Magsamen, Sandra, illus. 2018. (ENG.). 10p. (J). (gr. -1 — 1). bds. 7.99 *(978-0-545-92800-7(1)*, Cartwheel Bks.) Scholastic, Inc.

Maresca, Beth Anne, illus. Megan Owlet. 2015. (ENG.). 32p. (J). (gr. -1-k). 16.99 *(978-1-63220-404-2(5)*, Sky Pony Pr.) Skyhorse Publishing Co., Inc.

Marino, Gianna. Too Tall Houses. 2012. 40p. (J). (gr. -1-k). 18.99 *(978-0-670-01314-2(5)*, Viking Books for Young Readers) Penguin Young Readers Group.

Markowitz, Susan Meredith. The Great Green Forest & el gran bosque Verde: 6 English, 6 Spanish Adaptations. 2011. (ENG & SPA.). (J). 75.00 net. *(978-1-4108-5653-1(4))* Benchmark Education Co.

Mcallister, Herb West. Doo West to Toadstool. 2011. 44p. pap. 21.99 *(978-1-4628-5530-8(X))* Xlibris Corp.

McCall, Angie. Orlando the Oak. McCall, Tony, illus. 2007. (ENG.). 26p. per. 15.99 *(978-1-4257-7952-8(2))* Xlibris Corp.

McLean, Danielle. Good Night, I Love You. Macnaughton, Tina, illus. 2018. (ENG.). 16p. (J). (gr. -1-k). bds. 9.99 *(978-1-68010-540-7(X))* Tiger Tales.

McMilin, Jack. Dodger the Dragon, 1 vol. Nevarez, Lisa, illus. 2009. pap. 24.95 *(978-1-60703-930-3(3))* PublishAmerica, Inc.

Mercer, M. J. O'No It's Henry. 2010. 24p. 12.99 *(978-1-4520-2125-6(2))* AuthorHouse.

Montgomery, R. A. Owl Tree. Utomo, Gabhor, illus. 2009. (ENG.). 80p. (Orig.). (J). (gr. 3-3). pap. 7.99 *(978-1-933390-80-2(8))* Chooseco LLC.

Moroney, Trace, creator. The Owl & the Pussy Cat. 2008. (Illus.). 10p. (gr. -1-1). bds. 4.99 *(978-1-74178-515-9(4))* Gardner Pubns.

Naughton, Geraldine. Owl's Birthday. 2010. 20p. 12.68 *(978-1-4269-4481-9(0))* Trafford Publishing.

Niddrie, June. Great Scott & Otis. 2010. 56p. pap. 23.30 *(978-0-557-31863-6(7))* Lulu Pr., Inc.

Novel Units. I Heard the Owl Call My Name Novel Units Teacher Guide. 2019. (ENG.). (YA). pap. 12.99 *(978-1-56137-142-6(4)*, Novel Units, Inc.) Classroom Library Co.

—Owls in the Family Novel Units Teacher Guide. 2019. (ENG.). (J). pap. 12.99 *(978-1-56137-199-0(8)*, Novel Units, Inc.) Classroom Library Co.

Orobosa-Ogbeide, Kathryn. The Owl That Couldn't Fly. 2012. 12p. pap. 12.68 *(978-1-4669-1892-4(6))* Trafford Publishing.

Otis, Chad. Oliver the Curious Owl. 2020. (ENG., Illus.). 40p. (J). (gr. -1-3). 17.99 *(978-0-316-52987-7(7))* Little, Brown Bks. for Young Readers.

Paquet, Claudine, et al. Antonio, Plumero y Manchitas. 2006. (SPA., Illus.). 110p. (J). pap. *(978-958-30-2016-2(8))* Panamericana Editorial.

Parrish, Emma. Little Owl Says Goodnight: A Slide-And-Seek Book. 2016. (Slide-And-Seek Ser.). (ENG., Illus.). 10p. (J). (gr. -1-k). bds. 9.99 *(978-1-4998-0406-5(7))* Little Bee Books Inc.

Pauline Wall & Shelley Smith. What the Owl Saw: (a Christmas Story) 2012. 20p. pap. 15.19 *(978-1-4669-2813-8(1))* Trafford Publishing.

Pendergrass, Daphne. Owlette & the Giving Owl: Ready-To-Read Level 1. Style Guide, illus. 2017. (PJ Masks Ser.). (ENG.). 32p. (J). (gr. -1-1). 16.99 *(978-1-5344-0376-5(0))*; pap. 4.99 *(978-1-5344-0375-8(2))* Simon Spotlight. (Simon Spotlight).

Perales, Alonso M. Brujas, Lechuzas y Espantos/Witches, Owls & Spooks. Pluecker, John, tr. from SPA. 2008. (ENG & SPA., Illus.). 96p. (J). (gr. 3-7). pap. 9.95 *(978-1-55885-512-0(2)*, Piñata Books) Arte Publico Pr.

Peters, Lou. The Owl & the Turtle. 2010. 32p. pap. 15.95 *(978-0-557-51727-5(3))* Lulu Pr., Inc.

Pevear, Ted F. & Pevear, Linda W. The Date in the Junk Yard. 2012. 28p. 24.95 *(978-1-62709-781-9(3))*; pap. 24.95 *(978-1-4626-8994-1(9))* America Star Bks.

—Finding Little Feathers a Hub-A-Son. 2012. 24p. 24.95 *(978-1-4626-5874-9(1))* America Star Bks.

Potter, Alan Mitchell & Williams, Virginia. Hoo-Hoo Hooty-Hoo-Who. 2005. 9.00 *(978-0-8059-9807-8(1))* Dorrance Publishing Co., Inc.

Priddy, Roger. Little Friends: Home Sweet Home: A Lift-The-Flap Book. 2014. (Little Friends Ser.). (ENG.). 10p. (J). (gr. -1 — 1). bds. 6.99 *(978-0-312-51679-6(7)*, 900126035) St. Martin's Pr.

Rixon, Denise. The Owl That Barked: Tammy, 1 vol. 2009. 203p. pap. 24.95 *(978-1-4489-8472-5(6))* America Star Bks.

Rose, A. First Flight. 2011. 24p. pap. 15.99 *(978-1-4628-7747-8(8))* Xlibris Corp.

Rouncville, Bibi. Gimbels & Gooseberries. 2010. (ENG.). 52p. pap. 9.50 *(978-0-557-21585-0(4))* Lulu Pr., Inc.

Runton, Andy. Owly & Wormy, Bright Lights & Starry Nights. Runton, Andy, illus. 2012. (ENG., Illus.). 40p. (J). (gr. -1-3). 19.99 *(978-1-4169-5775-1(8)*, Atheneum Bks. for Young Readers) Simon & Schuster Children's Publishing.

—Owly & Wormy, Friends All Aflutter! Runton, Andy, illus. 2011. (ENG., Illus.). 40p. (J). (gr. -1-2). 17.99 *(978-1-4169-5774-4(X)*, Atheneum Bks. for Young Readers) Simon & Schuster Children's Publishing.

Russell, D. Z. The Amazing Adventures of Andy Owl: A Children's Guide to Understanding Music. Stone, John, illus. 2003. 34p. (J). per. 7.95 *(978-0-9725398-0-7(8))* World Famous Children's Bks.

Sargent, Dave & Sargent, David, Jr. Hoot Owl: Mind Your Mamma, 19 vols., Vol. 9. Lenoir, Jane, illus. 2003. (Feather Tales Ser.: 9). 42p. (J). pap. 10.95 *(978-1-56763-736-6(1))* Ozark Publishing.

Sargent, Dave & Sargent, David M., Jr. Hoot Owl: Mind Your Mamma, 20 vols., Vol. 9. Lenoir, Jane, illus. 2nd ed. 2003. (Feather Tales Ser.: 9). 42p. (J). lib. bdg. *(978-1-56763-735-9(3))* Ozark Publishing.

Sassi, Laura. Love Is Kind, 1 vol. Chaperon, Lison, illus. 2019. (ENG.). 28p. (J). bds. 9.99 *(978-0-310-75484-8(4))* Zonderkidz.

Schmidt-Kyanka, Anita. Sapsucker Blues: The Story of an Endearing Family of Great Blue Herons. 2013. 48p. pap. 20.99 *(978-1-4808-0250-6(6))* Archway Publishing.

Scull, Paul E. Los Animales Cuentan Su Histori. 2011. 20p. pap. *(978-1-4269-7319-2(5))* Trafford Publishing (UK) Ltd.

The Secret Song & Other Stories: Individual Title Six-Pack. (Story Steps Ser.). (gr. k-2). 48.00 *(978-0-7635-9808-2(9))* Rigby Education.

Seymour, Mary Sue. Friends in a Storm. Flynn, Samantha, illus. 2013. 20p. pap. 9.95 *(978-1-61633-376-8(6))* Guardian Angel Publishing, Inc.

Shannon, Star Erian. Erian's Friend Jeremiah the Owl. 2003. (J). pap. 9.00 *(978-0-8059-6068-6(6))* Dorrance Publishing Co., Inc.

Sharmat, Marjorie Weinman. Nate the Great on the Owl Express. Sharmat, Mitchell & Weston, Martha, illus. 2004. (Nate the Great Ser.). (ENG.). 80p. (J). (gr. 1-4). 5.99 *(978-0-440-41927-3(1)*, Yearling) Random Hse. Children's Bks.

Silvey, Diane. Time of the Thunderbird. Mantha, John, illus. 2008. (ENG.). 88p. (J). (gr. 6-5). pap. 11.99 *(978-1-55002-792-1(1))* Dundurn Pr. CAN. Dist: Publishers Group West (PGW).

Smith, Jeffrey B. Stubby. 2006. 15p. 8.28 *(978-1-4116-8215-3(7))* Lulu Pr., Inc.

Squires, R. L. Peaches & Cream, 1 vol. Collier, Kevin Scott, illus. 2009. 31p. pap. 24.95 *(978-1-60749-164-4(8))* America Star Bks.

Squires, Ricky. Lily & Ike, 1 vol. 2010. 32p. 24.95 *(978-1-4512-9308-1(9))* PublishAmerica, Inc.

Srinivasan, Divya. Little Owl's 1-2-3. Srinivasan, Divya, illus. 2015. (Little Owl Ser.). (Illus.). 18p. (J). (— 1). bds. 6.99 *(978-0-451-47454-4(6)*, Viking Books for Young Readers) Penguin Young Readers Group.

—Little Owl's Colors. Srinivasan, Divya, illus. 2015. (Little Owl Ser.). (Illus.). 18p. (J). (— 1). bds. 7.99 *(978-0-451-47456-8(2)*, Viking Books for Young Readers) Penguin Young Readers Group.

—Little Owl's Day. Srinivasan, Divya, illus. 2014. (Little Owl Ser.). (Illus.). 40p. (J). (gr. -1-k). 17.99 *(978-0-670-01650-1(0)*, Viking Books for Young Readers) Penguin Young Readers Group.

—Little Owl's Night. (Little Owl Ser.). (Illus.). (J). 2013. 34p. (— 1). bds. 6.99 *(978-0-670-01579-5(2))* 2011. 40p. (gr. -1-k). 18.99 *(978-0-670-01295-4(5))* Penguin Young Readers Group. (Viking Books for Young Readers).

—Little Owl's Snow. 2018. (Little Owl Ser.). (Illus.). 40p. (J). (-k). 18.99 *(978-0-670-01651-8(9)*, Viking Books for Young Readers) Penguin Young Readers Group.

Staheli, Bee, ed. The Owl Who Couldn't Say Whoo. Clish, Lori, illus. l.t. ed. (J). (gr. k-5). pap. 7.95 *(978-1-928632-50-4(5))* Writers Marketplace:Consulting, Critiquing & Publishing.

Stein, Renea. The Wise Old Owl & Those Tricky Times Tables. 2008. 36p. pap. 24.95 *(978-1-60474-228-2(3))* America Star Bks.

Sterer, Gideon & Kalish, Ellen. The Christmas Owl: Based on the True Story of a Little Owl Named Rockefeller. Kaulitzki, Ramona, illus. 2021. (ENG.). 40p. (J). (gr. -1-3). 18.99 *(978-0-316-29912-1(X))* Little, Brown Bks. for Young Readers.

Stewart, Bob. Baily Bumble Bee. Gorum, Jerry, illus. 2009. (ENG.). 32p. pap. 14.49 *(978-1-4389-7254-1(7))* AuthorHouse.

Stone, Kate & Accord Publishing, Accord. One Spooky Night: A Halloween Adventure. 2011. (ENG.). 36p. (J). pap. 11.99 *(978-1-4494-0330-0(1))* Andrews McMeel Publishing.

There's an Owl in the Closet. 2013. (ENG., Illus.). 32p. (J). pap. 9.99 *(978-1-4908-0932-8(5)*, 66d9b4b7-82f7-45ae-ba40-bce8b78ef692, WestBow Pr.) Author Solutions, LLC.

Thomas, Christie. Quinn's Promise Rock: No Matter Where, God Is Always There. 2019. (ENG., Illus.). 32p. (J). (gr. -1-2). 17.99 *(978-0-7369-7432-5(6)*, 6974325) Harvest Hse. Pubs.

Timms, E. H. Ring of Nine. 2010. 156p. pap. 16.95 *(978-1-4452-4512-6(4))* Lulu Pr., Inc.

Tomlinson, Jill. The Owl Who Was Afraid of the Dark. Howard, Paul, illus. 2014. (ENG.). 112p. (gr. -1-2). pap. 5.99 *(978-1-4052-7197-4(3))* Farshore GBR. Dist: HarperCollins Pubs.

—Owl Who Was Afraid of the Dark. (ENG., Illus.). 95p. (J). pap. 6.99 *(978-0-7497-0795-8(X))* Farshore GBR. Dist: Trafalgar Square Publishing.

—The Owl Who Was Afraid of the Dark. Howard, Paul, illus. 2022. (ENG.). 32p. (J). (gr. k-2). pap. 7.99 *(978-1-4052-0177-3(0))* Farshore GBR. Dist: HarperCollins Pubs.

Turner, Mary. The Quiet & Still Owl. 2012. 40p. pap. 21.99 *(978-1-4691-2795-8(4))* Xlibris Corp.

Uihlein, Mary. Hello Little Owl. Uihlein, Mary, illus. 2012. (Illus.). 24p. 22.95 *(978-1-61493-140-9(2))*; pap. 12.95 *(978-1-61493-139-3(9))* Peppertree Pr., The.

—Hello Little Owl, I Am Hermit Crab! Uihlein, Mary, illus. 2013. (Illus.). 28p. 24.95 *(978-1-61493-159-1(3))*; pap. 12.95 *(978-1-61493-158-4(5))* Peppertree Pr., The.

Ulbrich, Jasper. The Little Owl. 2009. (Illus.). 32p. pap. 16.50 *(978-1-60860-047-2(5)*, Eloquent Bks.) Strategic Book Publishing & Rights Agency (SBPRA).

Waddell, Martin. Owl Babies. Benson, Patrick, illus. (ENG.). (J). 2017. 32p. (gr. -1-2). 17.99 *(978-0-7636-9519-4(X))* 2015. 22p. (— 1). bds. 7.99 *(978-0-7636-7961-3(5))* Candlewick Pr.

—Owl Babies. (Illus.). 25p. (J). (CHI, ENG, URD, TUR & VIE.). *(978-1-85430-343-1(0)*, 93441); (ENG, VIE, URD, TUR & CHI., *(978-1-85430-348-6(1)*, 93442) Little Tiger Pr. Group.

—Owl Babies: Padded Board Book. Benson, Patrick, illus. 2019. (ENG.). 24p. (J). (— 1). bds. 9.99 *(978-1-5362-0963-1(5))* Candlewick Pr.

—Owl Babies Book & Toy Gift Set. Benson, Patrick, illus. 2016. (ENG.). 22p. (J). (-k). bds. 15.99 *(978-0-7636-8898-1(3))* Candlewick Pr.

—Owl Babies Lap-Size Board Book. Benson, Patrick, illus. 2018. (ENG.). 22p. (J). (— 1). bds. 12.99 *(978-0-7636-9520-0(3))* Candlewick Pr.

Walden, Libby. Noisy Touch & Feel: Owl Says Hoot. Enright, Amanda, illus. 2016. (Noisy Touch & Feel Ser.). (ENG.). 12p. (J). bds. 14.99 *(978-1-62686-576-1(0)*, Silver Dolphin Bks.) Readerlink Distribution Services, LLC.

Walker, Mary. The Flower Tree. 2010. (Illus.). 50p. pap. 12.95 *(978-1-4327-3588-3(8))* Outskirts Pr., Inc.

Wentz, Andrea, illus. Nora & the Growing Tree: An Owlegories Tale. 2018. (Owlegories Ser.). 32p. (J). (gr. -1-3). 12.99 *(978-1-5064-3309-7(X)*, Sparkhouse Family) 1517 Media.

—Twitch & the Invisible Wind: An Owlegories Tale. 2017. (Owlegories Ser.). 32p. (J). 12.99 *(978-1-5064-3305-9(7)*, Sparkhouse Family) 1517 Media.

West, Judy & Westerink, Gerda. The Christmas Owls, 50 vols. 2004. (ENG., Illus.). 32p. (J). 16.95 *(978-0-86315-421-8(2))* Floris Bks. GBR. Dist: SteinerBooks, Inc.

Westerman, Robert. Alohalani Kalikimaka Auntie: Sheet Music & Lyrics. Westerman, Robert, . 2006. (Illus.). 12p. (J). 6.95 *(978-0-9761992-1-2(1))* Gold Boy Music & Pubn.

Wildsmith, Brian. The Owl & the Woodpecker, 1 vol. Wildsmith, Brian, illus. 2006. (ENG., Illus.). 32p. (J). (gr. -1-3). 16.95 *(978-1-59572-043-6(X))*; pap. 7.99 *(978-1-59572-050-4(2))* Star Bright Bks., Inc.

Willard, Gerald. Amy Firefly. 2009. 40p. pap. 18.50 *(978-1-60693-448-7(1)*, Eloquent Bks.) Strategic Book Publishing & Rights Agency (SBPRA).

Williams, Raymond. Tales from the Willow Tree. 2012. (Illus.). 28p. pap. 8.50 *(978-1-78035-343-2(X)*, Fastprint Publishing) Upfront Publishing Ltd. GBR. Dist: Printondemand-worldwide.com.

Willis, Jeanne. Fly, Chick, Fly! Ross, Tony, illus. 2012. (Andersen Press Picture Bks). (ENG.). 32p. (J). (gr. -1-3). 16.95 *(978-1-4677-0314-7(1))* Lerner Publishing Group.

Wilson, Karma. Bear's New Friend. Chapman, Jane, illus. 2009. (Bear Bks.). (ENG.). 34p. (J). (gr. -1-2). bds. 7.99 *(978-1-4169-5438-5(4)*, Little Simon) Little Simon.

—Bear's New Friend. Chapman, Jane, illus. 2006. (Bear Bks.). (ENG.). 40p. (J). (gr. -1-3). 18.99 *(978-0-689-85984-7(8)*, McElderry, Margaret K. Bks.) McElderry, Margaret K. Bks.

Wilson, Robert. Pippy: The Miracle of A Dream. 2011. 136p. 21.95 *(978-1-4620-6634-6(8))*; pap. 11.95 *(978-1-4620-6633-9(X))* iUniverse, Inc.

Winbolt-Lewis, Martin. Owliviah. Cressey, Roger, illus. 2013. 56p. (J). pap. *(978-1-78222-075-6(5))* Paragon Publishing, Rothersthorpe.

Wolff, Susan. Quackers Wants to Fly. Currie, Justin, illus. 2013. 32p. pap. 8.95 *(978-1-60653-074-0(7))* High Hill Pr.

Wolverton, Barry. Neversink. Nielson, Sam, illus. 2012. xiii, 287p. (J). *(978-0-06-202792-4(1))* Longman Publishing.

Woman, Magpie Sleeping. Big Eyes: The Keeper of the Night. 2013. 24p. pap. 24.95 *(978-1-4626-9569-0(8))* America Star Bks.

Won, Brian. Hooray for Today! 2016. (ENG., Illus.). 40p. (J). (gr. -1-3). 16.99 *(978-0-544-74803-3(4)*, 1633259, Clarion Bks.) HarperCollins Pubs.

Wood, A. J. The Christmas Hat. Kneen, Maggie, illus. 2004. (ENG.). 24p. (J). *(978-1-55168-267-9(2))* Fenn, H. B. & Co., Ltd.

Yolen, Jane. Owl Moon. 2013. lib. bdg. 18.40 *(978-0-606-36222-1(3))* Turtleback.

Young, Lynn. Adventures with Looka, 1 vol. 2009. 48p. pap. 16.95 *(978-1-60813-959-0(X))* America Star Bks.

Zaglada, Vladimir. Gymmy the Owl & His Friends. 2012. 52p. pap. 24.99 *(978-1-4772-0226-5(9))* AuthorHouse.

—Gymmy the Owl & His Friends: Tales in Rhyme about the Animal Kingdom's Natural Gymnasts. 2012. 52p. pap. 24.99 *(978-1-4685-6011-4(5))* AuthorHouse.

OXYACETYLENE WELDING

see Welding

OZ (IMAGINARY PLACE)—FICTION

Anfuso, Dennis & Lindsay, Alan. Oz House. 2012. (ENG.). 321p. pap. 19.95 *(978-1-57433-041-0(1))* Interset Pr.

Baum, L. Frank. Adventures in Oz: Dorothy & the Wizard in Oz, the Road to Oz, the Emerald City of Oz. 2007. 296p. 24.95 *(978-1-60459-017-3(3))*; per. 12.95 *(978-1-60459-016-6(5))* Wilder Pubns., Corp.

—Adventures in Oz: The Patchwork Girl of Oz, Little Wizard Stories of Oz, Tik-Tok of Oz. 2007. 268p. 24.95 *(978-1-60459-019-7(X))*; per. 12.99 *(978-1-60459-018-0(1))* Wilder Pubns., Corp.

—Adventures in Oz: The Tin Woodman of Oz, the Magic of Oz, Glinda of Oz. 2007. 284p. 24.95 *(978-1-60459-023-4(8))*; per. 12.99 *(978-1-60459-022-7(X))* Wilder Pubns., Corp.

—Adventures in Oz: The Wonderful Wizard of Oz, the Marvelous Land of Oz, Ozma of Oz. 2007. 264p. per. 12.99 *(978-1-60459-014-2(9))*; per. 24.95 *(978-1-60459-015-9(7))* Wilder Pubns., Corp.

—Collected Short Stories of L. Frank Baum. 2006. (J). 29.95 *(978-1-930764-14-9(6))* International Wizard of Oz Club, The.

—Complete Book of Oz: The Wonderful Wizard of Oz, the Marvelous Land of Oz, & Ozma of Oz, Vol. 1. 2009. 268p. (J). 24.95 *(978-1-60459-711-0(9))* Wilder Pubns., Corp.

—Dorothy & the Wizard in Oz. 2019. (ENG.). (J). 142p. pap. 6.99 *(978-0-368-73134-1(0))*; 98p. pap. 10.71 *(978-0-368-25974-6(9))* Blurb, Inc.

—Dorothy & the Wizard in Oz. (ENG.). (J). 2019. 244p. pap. 9.99 *(978-1-7121-7489-0(4))* 2019. 244p. pap. 11.99 *(978-1-7016-1879-4(6))* 2019. 332p. pap. 14.99 *(978-1-6996-1197-5(1))* 2019. 334p. pap. 19.99 *(978-1-6949-5664-4(4))* 2019. 334p. pap. 19.99 *(978-1-6907-1041-7(1))* 2019. 276p. pap. 19.99 *(978-1-6935-2914-6(9))* 2019. 482p. pap. 30.99 *(978-1-6865-0513-3(2))* 2019. 334p. pap. 21.99 *(978-1-0804-6450-0(6))* 2019. 296p. pap. 19.99 *(978-1-0828-0289-8(1))* 2019. 244p. pap. 15.99 *(978-1-0861-6605-7(1))* 2019. 260p. pap. 18.99 *(978-1-0723-4222-9(7))* 2019. 488p. pap. 26.99 *(978-1-0756-3610-3(8))* 2019. 402p. pap. 24.99 *(978-1-0968-8175-9(6))* 2019. 190p. pap. 10.99 *(978-1-0979-8618-7(7))* 2019. 246p. pap. 15.99 *(978-1-0989-5773-5(3))* 2019. 336p. pap. 19.99 *(978-1-0704-5458-0(3))* 2019. 402p. pap. 24.99 *(978-1-0994-9744-5(2))* 2019. 246p. pap. 15.99 *(978-1-0931-9183-7(X))* 2019. 334p. pap. 21.99 *(978-1-0936-9118-4(2))* 2019. 282p. pap. 18.99 *(978-1-0917-8010-1(2))* 2019. 282p. pap. 16.99 *(978-1-7965-5884-5(2))* 2019. (Illus.). 184p. pap. 14.00 *(978-1-7938-3201-6(3))* 2018. (Illus.). 470p. pap. 30.99 *(978-1-7915-2681-8(0))* Independently Published.

—Dorothy & the Wizard in Oz. 2004. reprint ed. pap. 20.95 *(978-1-4191-1655-1(X))*; pap. 1.99 *(978-1-4192-1655-8(4))* Kessinger Publishing, LLC.

—Dorothy & the Wizard in Oz, 1 vol. 2nd ed. 2016. (Wizard of Oz Collection). (ENG., Illus.). 172p. (J). (gr. 4-8). 7.99 *(978-1-78226-308-1(X)*, 29ba1016-650a-4197-a7b9-28139a06af9f) Sweet Cherry Publishing GBR. Dist: Baker & Taylor Publisher Services (BTPS).

—Dorothy & the Wizard in Oz. 2017. (ENG., Illus.). (J). pap. *(978-0-649-07630-7(3))* Trieste Publishing Pty Ltd.

—Dorothy & the Wizard of Oz. 2005. pap. *(978-1-4065-0075-2(5))* Dodo Pr.

—Dorothy & the Wizard of Oz. l.t. ed. 2004. (Large Print Ser.). lib. bdg. 25.00 *(978-1-58287-769-3(6))* North Bks.

—The Emerald City of Oz. 2007. 144p. per. 11.95 *(978-1-60312-256-6(7))* Aegypan.

—The Emerald City of Oz. (Oz Ser.). (YA). (gr. 5-8). 21.95 *(978-0-8488-0733-7(2))* Amereon Ltd.

—The Emerald City of Oz. 2003. (Twelve-Point Ser.). lib. bdg. 24.00 *(978-1-58287-254-4(6))* North Bks.

—Glinda of Oz. rev. ed. 2006. 184p. 26.95 *(978-1-4218-1786-6(1))*; pap. 11.95 *(978-1-4218-1886-3(8))* 1st World Publishing, Inc. (1st World Library - Literary Society).

—Glinda of Oz. 2007. 108p. 22.95 *(978-1-60312-591-8(4))* Aegypan.

—Glinda of Oz. (Oz Ser.). (YA). (gr. 5-8). 21.95 *(978-0-8488-0784-9(7))* Amereon Ltd.

—Glinda of Oz. (Twelve-Point Ser.). 2003. lib. bdg. 24.00 (978-1-58287-256-8(2)) 2004. 210p. 25.00 (978-1-58287-740-2(8)) North Bks.
—Glinda of Oz. John R Neill, illus. 2010. 144p. pap. 5.88 (978-1-60386-310-0(9), Merchant Bks.) Rough Draft Printing.
—Large Hardback 1: L. Frank Baum's Original Oz Series. Wonderful Wizard of Oz, Marvelous Land of Oz, Ozma of Oz, Dorothy & the Wizard I. 2011. 1194p. (978-1-905921-22-5(5)) Shoes & Ships & Sealing Wax Ltd.
—Little Wizard Stories of Oz. Neill, John R., illus. 2011. (Dover Children's Classics Ser.). (ENG.). 160p. (J). (gr. 3-5). pap. 14.99 (978-0-486-47644-5(8)) Dover Pubns., Inc.
—The Lost Princess of Oz. (Oz Ser.). (YA). (gr. 5-8). 22.95 (978-0-8488-0786-3(3)) Amereon Ltd.
—The Lost Princess of Oz. (Twelve-Point Ser.). 2003. lib. bdg. 24.00 (978-1-58287-255-1(4)) 2004. 241p. 25.00 (978-1-58287-739-6(4)) North Bks.
—The Magic of Oz. 2007. 108p. (gr. 4-7). per. 9.95 (978-1-60312-334-1(2)); 22.95 (978-1-60312-671-7(6)) Aegypan.
—The Magic of Oz. 2004. (Twelve-Point Ser.). lib. bdg. 24.00 (978-1-58287-279-7(1)); lib. bdg. 25.00 (978-1-58287-775-4(0)) North Bks.
—El Maravilloso Mago de Oz. (Oz Ser.).Tr. of Wonderful Wizard of Oz. (SPA., Illus.). 160p. (YA). (gr. 5-8). 14.95 (978-84-7281-184-3(0), AF1184) Auriga, Ediciones S.A. ESP. Dist: Continental Bk. Co., Inc.
—The Marvelous Land of Oz. 2007. 120p. per. 10.95 (978-1-60312-149-1(8)) Aegypan.
—The Marvelous Land of Oz. 2004. (Twelve-Point Ser.). lib. bdg. 24.00 (978-1-58287-272-8(4)); lib. bdg. 25.00 (978-1-58287-768-6(8)) North Bks.
—Mini Classic - the Wonderful Wizard of Oz. 2017. (ENG.). 320p. (J). pap. 12.95 (978-1-78209-846-1(1)) Parkwest Pubns., Inc.
—Oz, the Complete Collection, Volume 1: The Wonderful Wizard of Oz; the Marvelous Land of Oz; Ozma of Oz. 2013. (Oz, the Complete Collection: 1). (ENG., Illus.). 592p. (J). (gr. 3-7). 19.99 (978-1-4424-8889-2(1)); pap. 12.99 (978-1-4424-8547-1(7)) Simon & Schuster Children's Publishing. (Aladdin).
—Oz, the Complete Collection, Volume 2: Dorothy & the Wizard in Oz; the Road to Oz; the Emerald City of Oz, Vol. 2. 2013. (Oz, the Complete Collection: 2). (ENG.). 656p. (J). (gr. 3-7). pap. 12.99 (978-1-4424-8548-8(5), Aladdin) Simon & Schuster Children's Publishing.
—Oz, the Complete Collection, Volume 2: Dorothy & the Wizard in Oz; the Road to Oz; the Emerald City of Oz. 2013. (Oz, the Complete Collection: 2). (ENG.). 656p. (J). (gr. 3-7). 19.99 (978-1-4424-8890-8(5), Simon & Schuster/Paula Wiseman Bks.) Simon & Schuster/Paula Wiseman Bks.
—Oz, the Complete Collection, Volume 3: The Patchwork Girl of Oz; Tik-Tok of Oz; the Scarecrow of Oz. 2013. (Oz, the Complete Collection: 3). (ENG.). 720p. (J). (gr. 3-7). 19.99 (978-1-4424-8892-2(1)); Vol. 3. pap. 12.99 (978-1-4424-8549-5(3)) Simon & Schuster Children's Publishing. (Aladdin).
—Oz, the Complete Collection, Volume 4: Rinkitink in Oz; the Lost Princess of Oz; the Tin Woodman of Oz. 2013. (Oz, the Complete Collection: 4). (ENG.). 656p. (J). (gr. 3-7). 19.99 (978-1-4424-8893-9(X)); Vol. 4. pap. 12.99 (978-1-4424-8550-1(7)) Simon & Schuster Children's Publishing. (Aladdin).
—Oz, the Complete Hardcover Collection (Boxed Set) Oz, the Complete Collection, Volume 1; Oz, the Complete Collection, Volume 2; Oz, the Complete Collection, Volume 3; Oz, the Complete Collection, Volume 4; Oz, the Complete Collection, Volume 5. 2013. (Oz, the Complete Collection). (ENG.). 3200p. (J). (gr. 3-7). 99.99 (978-1-4424-8903-5(0), Aladdin) Simon & Schuster Children's Publishing.
—Oz, the Complete Paperback Collection (Boxed Set) Oz, the Complete Collection, Volume 1; Oz, the Complete Collection, Volume 2; Oz, the Complete Collection, Volume 3; Oz, the Complete Collection, Volume 4; Oz, the Complete Collection, Volume 5. 2013. (Oz, the Complete Collection). (ENG.). 3200p. (J). (gr. 3-7). pap. 64.99 (978-1-4424-8902-8(2), Aladdin) Simon & Schuster Children's Publishing.
—Ozma of Oz. 2007. 108p. (gr. 4-7). per. 9.95 (978-1-60312-150-7(1)) Aegypan.
—Ozma of Oz. (Twelve-Point Ser.). 2003. lib. bdg. 24.00 (978-1-58287-252-0(X)) 2004. 210p. 25.00 (978-1-58287-736-5(X)) North Bks.
—The Patchwork Girl of Oz. 2007. 152p. (gr. -1-7). 24.95 (978-1-60312-632-8(5)); per. 12.95 (978-1-60312-374-7(1)) Aegypan.
—The Patchwork Girl of Oz. (Oz Ser.). (YA). (gr. 5-8). 25.95 (978-0-8488-0705-4(7)) Amereon Ltd.
—The Patchwork Girl of OZ. l.t. ed. 2004. (Large Print Ser.). lib. bdg. 25.00 (978-1-58287-771-6(8)) North Bks.
—Rinkitink in Oz. rev. ed. 2006. 216p. 27.95 (978-1-4218-1791-0(8)); pap. 12.95 (978-1-4218-1891-7(4)) 1st World Publishing, Inc. (1st World Library - Literary Society).
—Rinkitink in Oz. (Oz Ser.). (YA). (gr. 5-8). 22.95 (978-0-8488-0735-1(9)) Amereon Ltd.
—Rinkitink in Oz. 2019. (ENG.). 102p. (J). pap. 10.90 (978-0-368-26362-0(2)) Blurb, Inc.
—Rinkitink in Oz. 2019. (ENG.). (J). 176p. pap. 21.99 (978-1-7072-3787-6(5)); 410p. pap. 42.99 (978-1-7068-6636-7(4)); 408p. pap. 16.99 (978-1-7018-0886-7(2)); 408p. pap. 16.99 (978-1-6996-1486-0(5)); 408p. pap. 24.99 (978-1-6967-8987-5(7)); 408p. pap. 24.99 (978-1-6949-5804-4(3)); 310p. pap. 19.99 (978-1-6935-8173-1(6)); 284p. pap. 16.99 (978-1-6933-6693-2(2)); 284p. pap. 16.99 (978-1-6899-7536-0(9)); 148p. pap. 10.99 (978-1-0895-3888-2(X)); 316p. pap. 21.99 (978-1-0871-4687-4(9)); 316p. pap. 17.99 (978-1-0774-0326-0(7)); 590p. pap. 33.99 (978-1-0756-3631-8(0)); 316p. pap. 21.99 (978-1-0723-6178-7(7)); 412p. pap. 24.99 (978-1-0704-5958-5(5)); 412p. pap. 24.99 (978-1-0973-3312-7(4)); 302p. pap. 17.99 (978-1-0958-4123-5(8)) Independently Published.
—Rinkitink in Oz. 2004. reprint ed. pap. 20.95 (978-1-4191-6718-8(9)); pap. 1.99 (978-1-4192-6718-5(3)) Kessinger Publishing, LLC.
—Rinkitink in Oz. 2004. (Twelve-Point Ser.). lib. bdg. 24.00 (978-1-58287-278-0(3)); lib. bdg. 25.00 (978-1-58287-774-7(2)) North Bks.
—The Road to Oz. (Oz Ser.). (YA). (gr. 5-8). 20.95 (978-0-8488-0788-7(X)) Amereon Ltd.
—The Road to Oz. 2004. (Twelve-Point Ser.). lib. bdg. 24.00 (978-1-58287-274-2(0)); lib. bdg. 25.00 (978-1-58287-770-9(X)) North Bks.
—The Scarecrow of Oz. (Oz Ser.). (YA). (gr. 5-8). 20.95 (978-0-8488-0707-8(3)) Amereon Ltd.
—The Scarecrow of Oz. 2004. (Twelve-Point Ser.). lib. bdg. 24.00 (978-1-58287-277-3(5)); lib. bdg. 25.00 (978-1-58287-773-0(4)) North Bks.
—Tik-Tok of Oz. 2007. 128p. (gr. -1-7). per. 10.95 (978-1-60312-333-4(4)); 23.95 (978-1-60312-670-0(8)) Aegypan.
—Tik-Tok of Oz. 2004. (Twelve-Point Ser.). lib. bdg. 24.00 (978-1-58287-276-6(7)); lib. bdg. 25.00 (978-1-58287-772-3(6)) North Bks.
—The Tin Woodman of Oz. rev. ed. 2006. 204p. 27.95 (978-1-4218-1789-7(6)); pap. 12.95 (978-1-4218-1889-4(2)) 1st World Publishing, Inc. (1st World Library - Literary Society).
—The Tin Woodman of Oz. 2008. 116p. (gr. 4-7). 22.95 (978-1-60664-947-3(7)); per. 9.95 (978-1-60312-497-3(7)) Aegypan.
—The Tin Woodman of Oz. 2009. 174p. (gr. 4-7). 25.99 (978-1-60512-317-2(X)); pap. 12.99 (978-1-60512-417-9(6)) Akasha Publishing, LLC. (Akasha Classics).
—The Tin Woodman of Oz. (J). 20.95 (978-0-8488-0709-2(X)) Amereon Ltd.
—The Tin Woodman of Oz. (ENG.). (J). 2019. 98p. pap. 10.71 (978-0-368-26372-9(X)) 2018. (Illus.). 168p. 29.99 (978-1-388-99712-0(6)) Blurb, Inc.
—The Tin Woodman of Oz. 2005. pap. (978-1-4065-0079-0(8)) Dodo Pr.
—The Tin Woodman of Oz. l.t. ed. 2005. 256p. pap. (978-1-84637-112-7(0)) Echo Library.
—The Tin Woodman of Oz. (ENG.). (J). 2019. 350p. pap. 14.99 (978-1-7018-3895-6(8)) 2019. 352p. pap. 36.99 (978-1-7077-9143-9(0)) 2019. 354p. pap. 19.99 (978-1-6967-0449-6(9)) 2019. 350p. pap. 14.99 (978-1-6996-4268-9(0)) 2019. 142p. pap. 6.99 (978-1-7026-1743-7(2)) 2019. 136p. pap. 11.99 (978-1-0886-8304-0(5)) 2019. 352p. pap. 19.99 (978-1-6949-7276-7(3)) 2019. 258p. pap. 15.99 (978-1-6940-6689-3(4)) 2019. 324p. pap. 21.99 (978-1-6935-8484-8(0)) 2019. 258p. pap. 15.99 (978-1-6894-0758-8(1)) 2019. 354p. pap. 19.99 (978-1-0783-9569-4(1)) 2019. 354p. pap. 24.99 (978-1-0799-5145-5(8)) 2019. 302p. pap. 21.99 (978-1-0827-4913-1(3)) 2019. 356p. pap. 19.99 (978-1-0706-6318-0(2)) 2019. 258p. pap. 16.99 (978-1-0707-8126-6(6)) 2019. 426p. pap. 24.99 (978-1-0734-9978-6(2)) 2019. 356p. pap. 19.99 (978-1-0974-6096-0(7)) 2019. 354p. pap. 19.99 (978-1-0995-7277-7(0)) 2019. 354p. pap. 22.99 (978-1-0917-4633-6(8)) 2019. 354p. pap. 21.99 (978-1-7969-2399-5(0)) 2019. (Illus.). 358p. pap. 24.99 (978-1-7930-0584-7(2)) 2018. (Illus.). 138p. pap. 12.99 (978-1-7920-0107-9(X)) Independently Published.
—The Tin Woodman of Oz. (Twelve-Point Ser.). 2003. lib. bdg. 24.00 (978-1-58287-257-5(0)) 2004. 230p. 25.00 (978-1-58287-741-9(6)) North Bks.
—The Tin Woodman of Oz. 2009. 136p. pap. 10.95 (978-1-4385-2196-1(0), Bk. Jungle) Standard Publications, Inc.
—The Tin Woodman of Oz, 1 vol. 2nd ed. 2016. (Wizard of Oz Collection: 12). (ENG., Illus.). 180p. (J). (gr. 4-8). 7.99 (978-1-78226-316-6(0), 53a82a0c-e884-4db9-856b-3a73fd415735) Sweet Cherry Publishing GBR. Dist: Baker & Taylor Publisher Services (BTPS).
—The Tin Woodman of Oz. 2008. 308p. (gr. 4-7). 32.95 (978-1-4344-7192-5(6)); pap. 19.95 (978-1-4344-7191-8(8)) Wildside Pr., LLC.
—The Treasury of Oz. 2007. 784p. 49.99 (978-1-60459-028-9(9)) Wilder Pubns., Corp.
—The Tresury of Oz: The Wonderful Wizard of Oz, the Marvelous Land of Oz, Ozma of Oz, Dorothy & the Wizard in Oz, the Road to Oz, the Emerald City Of. 2007. 548p. per. 19.49 (978-1-60459-029-6(7)) Wilder Pubns., Corp.
—The Wizard of Oz. Evangelista, Mauro, illus. 2007. (Usborne Young Reading: Series Two Ser.). 64p. (J). (gr. 3-7). 8.99 (978-0-7945-1457-0(X), Usborne) EDC Publishing.
—The Wizard of Oz. 2013. (ENG., Illus.). 176p. (978-1-907360-90-9(5), Collector's Library, The) Pan Macmillan.
—The Wizard of Oz. 2012. (Puffin Classics Ser.). (Illus.). 224p. (J). (gr. 5). 16.99 (978-0-14-134173-6(4), Puffin Books) Penguin Young Readers Group.
—The Wizard of Oz. (SPA.). 256p. (J). 9.95 (978-84-204-3509-1(0)) Santillana USA Publishing Co., Inc.
—The Wizard of Oz. 2012. (ENG., Illus.). (J). (gr. 4-7). 14.99 (978-1-61382-935-6(3)) Simon & Brown.
—The Wizard of Oz, 1 vol. 2009. (Foundation Classics Ser.). (ENG., Illus.). 56p. (J). (gr. 5-5). lib. bdg. 32.60 (978-1-60754-544-6(6), 7bc18ae4-87d9-434a-bc82-af93c953dd7f, Windmill Bks.) Rosen Publishing Group, Inc., The.
—The Wizard of Oz. Zwerger, Lisbeth, illus. 2004. 103p. (J). (gr. 4-8). reprint ed. 20.00 (978-0-7567-7708-1(9)) DIANE Publishing Co.
—The Wizard of Oz. 2004. reprint ed. pap. 19.95 (978-1-4191-8832-9(1)) Kessinger Publishing, LLC.
—The Wizard of Oz: And Other Wonderful Books of Oz: the Emerald City of Oz & Glinda of Oz (Penguin Classics Deluxe Edition) Sumpter, Rachell, illus. deluxe ed. 2012. (Penguin Classics Deluxe Edition Ser.). 432p. (gr. 5). pap. 17.00 (978-0-14-310663-0(5), Penguin Classics) Penguin Publishing Group.
—The Wizard of Oz Book & Charm. deluxe ed. 2005. (Charming Classics). 208p. (J). 9.99 (978-0-06-075772-4(8), HarperFestival) HarperCollins Pubs.
—A Wonderful Welcome to Oz: The Marvelous Land of Oz, Ozma of Oz, & the Emerald City of Oz. Maguire, Gregory, ed. Neill, John R., illus. 2006. (Modern Library Classics Ser.). 624p. per. 17.00 (978-0-8129-7494-2(8), Modern Library) Random House Publishing Group.
—The Wonderful Wizard of Oz. 180p. 2005. 26.95 (978-1-4218-0652-5(5)) 2004. pap. 11.95 (978-1-59540-102-1(4)) 1st World Publishing, Inc. (1st World Library - Literary Society).
—The Wonderful Wizard of Oz. (Oz Ser.). (YA). (gr. 5-8). 20.95 (978-0-88411-772-8(3)) Amereon Ltd.
—The Wonderful Wizard of Oz. 2014. (ENG., Illus.). 167p. 17.50 (978-1-78270-042-5(0)) Award Pubns. Ltd. GBR. Dist: Parkwest Pubns., Inc.
—The Wonderful Wizard of Oz. 2017. (ENG., Illus.). (J). pap. 12.95 (978-1-374-89899-8(6)) Capital Communications, Inc.
—The Wonderful Wizard of Oz. 2007. (ENG.). 134p. pap. 19.99 (978-1-4264-4884-3(8)); 374p. pap. 18.99 (978-1-4264-4841-6(4)) Creative Media Partners, LLC.
—The Wonderful Wizard of Oz. Denslow, W. W., illus. 2015. (Dover Children's Classics Ser.). (ENG.). 308p. (J). (gr. 3-6). reprint ed. pap. 16.99 (978-0-486-20691-2(2), 206912) Dover Pubns., Inc.
—The Wonderful Wizard of Oz. 2017. (ENG., Illus.). (J). pap. 14.25 (978-1-387-05021-5(4)) Lulu Pr., Inc.
—The Wonderful Wizard of Oz. 2003. (Modern Library Classics Ser.). (Illus.). 224p. pap. 15.00 (978-0-8129-7011-1(X), Modern Library) Random House Publishing Group.
—The Wonderful Wizard of Oz. (ENG., Illus.). (J). 2012. 138p. (gr. 3). pap. 8.00 (978-1-61382-347-7(9)) 2012. (gr. 1-7). 14.99 (978-1-61382-939-4(6)) 2011. (gr. 1-7). 14.99 (978-1-61382-942-4(6)) Simon & Brown.
—The Wonderful Wizard of Oz, 1 vol. 2nd ed. 2016. (Wizard of Oz Collection: 1). (ENG.). 160p. (J). (gr. 4-8). 7.99 (978-1-78226-305-0(5), c29df6fd-bb3b-44d9-a9ac-04b48ca1bb83) Sweet Cherry Publishing GBR. Dist: Baker & Taylor Publisher Services (BTPS).
—The Wonderful Wizard of Oz. 2011. (ENG., Illus.). 322p. (J). (gr. 1-7). 37.95 (978-1-59687-487-9(2), ipicturebooks) ibooks, Inc.
—The Wonderful Wizard of Oz: A Classic Story about Cooperation. 2003. (Illus.). 32p. per. 3.95 (978-0-9747133-5-9(X), Values to Live By Classic Stories) Thomas, Frederic Inc.
—7 Books In: L. Frank Baum's Original Oz Series, Volume 1 of 2. the Wonderful Wizard of Oz, the Marvelous Land of Oz, Ozma of Oz, Dorothy & the W. 2008. 820p. (978-1-905921-02-7(0)) Shoes & Ships & Sealing Wax Ltd.
—7 Books In: L. Frank Baum's Oz Series, volume 1 of 2. the Wonderful Wizard of Oz, the Marvelous Land of Oz, Ozma of Oz, Dorothy & the Wizard In. 2008. 824p. pap. (978-1-905921-01-0(2)) Shoes & Ships & Sealing Wax Ltd.
—8 Books In: L. Frank Baum's Original Oz Series, volume 2 of 2. Little Wizard Stories of Oz, Tik-Tok of Oz, the Scarecrow of Oz, Rinkitink in Oz, T. 2008. 764p. (978-1-905921-03-4(9)) Shoes & Ships & Sealing Wax Ltd.
Baum, L. Frank, creator. Rinkitink in Oz. 2015. (ENG., Illus.). 320p. (J). (gr. 4-7). 26.95 (978-1-296-81473-1(4)) Creative Media Partners, LLC.
Baum, L. Frank, told to. The Emerald City of Oz. l.t. ed. 2004. (Large Print Ser.). 285p. 25.00 (978-1-58287-738-9(6)) North Bks.
Baum, L. Frank & Denslow, W. W. The Wonderful Wizard of Oz. 2012. (Illus.). 232p. (978-1-4351-3973-2(9)) Barnes & Noble, Inc.
Baum, L. Frank & Neill, John R., illus. The Emerald City of Oz: Novels 6 Through 10 of the Oz Series. 2014. viii, 791p. (J). (978-1-4351-5615-9(3)) Barnes & Noble, Inc.
Baum, L. Frank & Neill, John R. III. Dorothy & the Wizard in Oz. 2018. (ENG., Illus.). 228p. (J). pap. 14.95 (978-1-378-96327-2(X)) Creative Media Partners, LLC.
Baum, L. Frank & Thompson, Ruth Plumly. Oz, the Complete Collection, Volume 5: The Magic of Oz; Glinda of Oz; the Royal Book of Oz. 2013. (Oz, the Complete Collection: 5). (ENG.). 576p. (J). (gr. 3-7). pap. 12.99 (978-1-4424-8551-8(5), Aladdin) Simon & Schuster Children's Publishing.
—Oz, the Complete Collection, Volume 5 Vol. 5: The Magic of Oz; Glinda of Oz; the Royal Book of Oz. 2013. (Oz, the Complete Collection: 5). (ENG.). 576p. (J). (gr. 3-7). 19.99 (978-1-4424-8894-6(8), Aladdin) Simon & Schuster Children's Publishing.
Baum, Roger S. The Lion of Oz & the Badge of Courage. Coons, Dean, illus. 2nd ed. 2003. 247p. (J). 24.95 (978-1-57072-255-4(2)) Overmountain Pr.
—The Oz Odyssey. Seitzinger, Victoria, illus. 2006. 176p. (J). 19.95 (978-1-57072-299-8(4)) Overmountain Pr.
—Toto of Oz & the Surprise Party. Seitzinger, Victoria, illus. 2004. (ENG.). 32p. (J). 13.95 (978-1-57072-284-4(6), 1233723) Overmountain Pr.
Bracken, Beth. The Wizard of Oz, 1 vol. 2013. (Wizard of Oz Ser.). (ENG., Illus.). 32p. (J). (gr. -1-3). 14.95 (978-1-62370-026-3(4), 123810, Capstone Young Readers) Capstone.
Burns, Laura J. Bewitched in Oz, 1 vol. 2014. (Bewitched in Oz Ser.). (ENG., Illus.). 256p. (J). (gr. 4-8). 12.95 (978-1-62370-129-1(5), 125714, Capstone Young Readers); lib. bdg. 30.65 (978-1-4342-9207-0(X), 125712, Stone Arch Bks.) Capstone.
—Magic Below. 2016. (Bewitched in Oz Ser.). (ENG.). 240p. (J). (gr. 4-8). lib. bdg. 30.65 (978-1-4965-2603-8(1), 130909, Stone Arch Bks.) Capstone.
Conlon, Mara, adapted by. Scratch & Sketch Wizard of Oz: An Art Activity Story Book for Artists on Both Sides of the Rainbow. 2005. (Activity Book Ser.). (Illus.). 64p. (J). 14.99 (978-1-59359-906-5(4)) Peter Pauper Pr. Inc.
Einhorn, Edward. The Living House of Oz. Shanower, Eric, illus. 2005. 239p. (J). 27.95 (978-1-929527-08-3(X)) Hungry Tiger Pr.
Evans, Robert J. Dorothy's Mystical Adventures in Oz. 2004. reprint ed. pap. 1.99 (978-1-4192-1658-9(9)) Kessinger Publishing, LLC.
Florence, Debbi Michiko. Dorothy & Toto. Roe, Monika, illus. 2016. (Dorothy & Toto Ser.). (ENG.). 40p. (J). (gr. k-2). 90.60 (978-1-4795-8714-8(1), 24142) Capstone.
Gardner, Martin & Nye, Russel B. The Wizard of Oz & Who He Was. 2011. 220p. 44.95 (978-1-258-00799-7(1)) Literary Licensing, LLC.
Kirshenblatt, Shane. Dorothy Gale - Journey to Oz. 2005. 64p. Vol. 2. 7.99 (978-1-894998-89-5(8)) Vol. 3. 7.99 (978-1-894998-90-1(1)) Lake, Jack Productions, Inc. CAN. Dist: Hushion Hse. Publishing, Ltd.
Ladybird. The Wizard of Oz. 2016. (First Favourite Tales Ser.). (Illus.). 32p. (J). (gr. -1-k). 8.99 (978-0-7232-9219-7(1)) Penguin Bks., Ltd. GBR. Dist: Independent Pubs. Group.
Landes, William-Alan & Standish, Marilyn. The Wizard of Oz. rev. ed. 2003. (Wondrawhopper Ser.). 40p. (J). (gr. 3-12). pap. 6.00 (978-0-88734-105-2(5)) Players Pr., Inc.
Martin, Dick. The Ozmapolitan of Oz. 2006. (J). 24.95 (978-1-930764-11-8(1)) International Wizard of Oz Club, The.
McGraw, Eloise Jarvis & McGraw, Lauren Lynn. The Forbidden Fountain of Oz. 2006. (J). 24.95 (978-1-930764-12-5(X)) International Wizard of Oz Club, The.
Mula, Tom. The Hackers of Oz. 2012. 272p. (-18). 21.95 (978-1-4575-1562-0(8)); pap. 14.99 (978-1-4575-1564-4(4)) Dog Ear Publishing, LLC.
Paige, Danielle. Dorothy Must Die. (Dorothy Must Die Ser.: 1). (ENG.). (YA). (gr. 9-12). 2014. 464p. 17.99 (978-0-06-228067-1(8)) 9th ed. 2015. 480p. pap. 12.99 (978-0-06-228068-8(6)) HarperCollins Pubs. (HarperCollins).
—Dorothy Must Die. 2015. (Dorothy Must Die Ser.: 1). (YA). lib. bdg. 20.85 (978-0-606-36510-9(9)) Turtleback.
—Dorothy Must Die 2-Book Box Set: Dorothy Must Die, the Wicked Will Rise. 2016. (Dorothy Must Die Ser.). (ENG.). 800p. (YA). (gr. 9). pap. 19.98 (978-0-06-256982-0(1), HarperCollins) HarperCollins Pubs.
—Dorothy Must Die Stories: No Place Like Oz, the Witch Must Burn, the Wizard Returns. 2015. (Dorothy Must Die Novella Ser.). (ENG., Illus.). 416p. (YA). (gr. 9). pap. 10.99 (978-0-06-228079-4(1), HarperCollins) HarperCollins Pubs.
—Dorothy Must Die Stories: No Place Like Oz, the Witch Must Burn, the Wizard Returns. 2015. (Dorothy Must Die Ser.). (YA). lib. bdg. 20.85 (978-0-606-37248-0(2)) Turtleback.
—Dorothy Must Die Stories Volume 2: Heart of Tin, the Straw King, Ruler of Beasts. 2016. (Dorothy Must Die Novella Ser.). (ENG.). 336p. (YA). (gr. 9). pap. 10.99 (978-0-06-240397-1(4), HarperCollins) HarperCollins Pubs.
—The End of Oz. 2017. 304p. (YA). (978-0-06-266023-7(3)) Harper & Row Ltd.
—The End of Oz. (Dorothy Must Die Ser.: 4). (ENG.). 304p. (YA). (gr. 9). 2018. pap. 10.99 (978-0-06-242378-8(9)) 2017. 18.99 (978-0-06-242377-1(0)) HarperCollins Pubs. (HarperCollins).
—The Wicked Will Rise. (Dorothy Must Die Ser.: 2). (ENG.). (YA). (gr. 9). 2016. 320p. pap. 12.99 (978-0-06-228071-8(6)) 2015. 304p. 17.99 (978-0-06-228070-1(8)) HarperCollins Pubs. (HarperCollins).
—The Wicked Will Rise. 2016. (Dorothy Must Die Ser.: 2). (YA). lib. bdg. 20.85 (978-0-606-38170-3(8)) Turtleback.
—Yellow Brick War. 2016. (978-0-06-245860-5(4)); (Dorothy Must Die Ser.: 3). (ENG.). 288p. (YA). (gr. 9-12). 18.99 (978-0-06-228073-2(2), HarperCollins) HarperCollins Pubs.
Pearse, Asha, illus. Wizard of Oz. 2017. (10 Minute Classics Ser.). (ENG.). 32p. (J). (gr. 1-4). 16.99 (978-1-4867-1221-2(5), 341fccfd-893b-4e64-bc14-77b725bee85d) Flowerpot Pr.
—Wizard of Oz. 2017. (ENG.). 32p. (J). (gr. 1-5). (978-1-4867-1269-4(X)) Flowerpot Children's Pr. Inc.
—Wizard of Oz. 2014. (ENG.). 16p. (J). (gr. -1-4). 7.99 (978-1-4867-0009-7(8)) Flowerpot Children's Pr. Inc. CAN. Dist: Cardinal Pubs. Group.
Price, Nick, illus. The Wonderful Wizard of Oz. 2009. (ENG.). 12p. (J). 8.95 (978-1-58117-856-2(5), Intervisual/Piggy Toes) Bendon, Inc.
Rand McNally Staff, creator. Rand Mcnally fabMAP Chicago: Lincoln Park/Lakeview. 2008. (Rand Mcnally Fab Map Chicago Ser.). (Illus.). (J). (gr. 2-18). reprint ed. 5.95 (978-0-528-87187-0(0)) Macmillan Publishing Co., Inc.
Rayburn, Tricia. Ruby's Slippers. 2010. (ENG.). 352p. (J). (gr. 4-8). pap. 7.99 (978-1-4169-8701-7(0)) Simon & Schuster, Inc.
Ridley, R. W. Banshee Worm King. 2012. 242p. pap. 9.99 (978-0-9792067-5-7(8)) Middlebury Hse. Publishing.
Robinson, Robin, illus. L. Frank Baum's the Wonderful Wizard of Oz. 2013. (Penguin Young Readers, Level 4 Ser.). 48p. (J). (gr. 3-4). mass mkt. 5.99 (978-0-448-45588-4(9), Penguin Young Readers) Penguin Young Readers Group.
Santore, Charles. Wizard of Oz Coloring Book: The Classic Edition. 2017. (Classic Edition Ser.). (ENG., Illus.). 52p. (J). (gr. 1). pap. 10.99 (978-1-60433-706-8(0), Applesauce Pr.) Cider Mill Pr. Bk. Pubs., LLC.
Shanower, Eric. Adventures in Oz. Shanower, Eric, illus. 2007. (Illus.). 256p. (J). (gr. 5-7). 75.00 (978-1-60010-071-0(6)) Idea & Design Works, LLC.
—The Salt Sorcerer of Oz & Other Stories. Shanower, Eric, illus. 2003. (Oz Ser.). (Illus.). 288p. (J). 24.95 (978-1-929527-06-9(3)) Hungry Tiger Pr.
Smith, Jeff & Robertson, Barny. Pirates of the 'I Don't Care'-Ibbean: A Kids' Musical about Storing up Treasures in Heaven. 2007. (ENG.). 104p. pap. 7.99 (978-0-8341-7595-2(9), 0834175959) Lillenas Publishing Co.
Smith, Sherwood. The Emerald Wand of Oz. Stout, William, illus. 2007. 262p. (J). 17.00 (978-1-4223-6710-0(X)) DIANE Publishing Co.
—The Emerald Wand of Oz. Stout, William, illus. 2005. (ENG.). 272p. (J). (gr. -1-17). 16.99 (978-0-06-029607-0(0)) HarperCollins Pubs.
Stine, R. L. Lizard of Oz. 2016. (Goosebumps Most Wanted Ser.: 10). (ENG.). 160p. (J). (gr. 3-7). 17.20 (978-0-606-39142-9(8)) Turtleback.
Sundstrom, Dainel H. The Return of Oz. 2007. pap. 10.00 (978-0-8059-8944-1(7)) Dorrance Publishing Co., Inc.
Thompson, Ruth Plumly. The Enchanted Island of Oz. 2006. (J). 24.95 (978-1-930764-10-1(3)) International Wizard of Oz Club, The.
—The Royal Book of Oz. 2004. reprint ed. pap. 1.99 (978-1-4192-8123-5(2)); pap. 20.95 (978-1-4191-8123-8(8)) Kessinger Publishing, LLC.

—The Wonder Book. 2006. (J). 24.95 *(978-1-930764-15-6(4))* International Wizard of Oz Club, The.
—Yankee in Oz. 2006. (J). 24.95 *(978-1-930764-13-2(8))* International Wizard of Oz Club, The.
Thompson, Ruth Plumly & Baum, L. Frank. The Silver Princess in Oz. Neill, John R., illus. 2011. 248p. 46.95 *(978-1-258-01166-6(2))* Literary Licensing, LLC.

OZARK MOUNTAINS REGION

Arnold, Jude. The Lipizzan Reunion: A True Story. 2009. 48p. pap. 19.49 *(978-1-4389-7060-8(9))* AuthorHouse.

OZARK MOUNTAINS REGION—FICTION

Ellis, Edward Sylvester & Coghlan, John. The Camp in the Mountains. 2004. (Illus.). 200p. (J). pap. 19.95 *(978-0-9713470-8-3(5))* Phoenix International, Inc.
The Hunters of the Ozark. 2004. (Illus.). 224p. (J). pap. 19.95 *(978-0-9713470-2-1(6))* Phoenix International, Inc.
Jones, Don. When the Firewood Comes. 2009. 86p. pap. 19.95 *(978-1-4489-9667-4(8))* America Star Bks.
McDougal-Littell Publishing Staff. Literature Connections English: Where the Red Fern Grows. 2004. (McDougal Littell Literature Connections Ser.). (ENG.). 328p. (gr. 7-7). 16.90 *(978-0-395-77528-8(0), 2-80097)* Great Source Education Group, Inc.
Rawls, Wilson. Where the Red Fern Grows. 249p. (YA). (gr. 5-18). pap. 5.99 *(978-0-8072-1467-1(1))*; pap. 5.99 *(978-0-8072-1358-2(6))* Random Hse. Audio Publishing Group. (Listening Library).
—Where the Red Fern Grows. Lt. ed. 2005. 376p. pap. 10.95 *(978-0-7862-7312-6(7),* Large Print Pr.) Thorndike Pr.

P

PACIFIC ISLANDS

see Islands of the Pacific

PACIFIC NORTHWEST

see Northwest, Pacific

PACIFIC OCEAN

Cerullo, Mary M. Journey to Shark Island: A Shark Photographer's Close Encounters, 1 vol. Rotman, Jeffrey L., illus. Rotman, Jeffrey L., photos by. 2014. (Shark Expedition Ser.). (ENG.). 40p. (J). (gr. 5-9). lib. bdg. 32.65 *(978-0-7565-4887-2(X),* 124954, Compass Point Bks.) Capstone.
Cerullo, Mary M. & Simmons, Beth E. Sea Secrets: Tiny Clues to a Big Mystery. Carlson, Kirsten., illus. 2015. (Long Term Ecological Research Ser.). 32p. (J). (gr. 1-5). pap. 9.95 *(978-1-63076-075-5(7))* Taylor Trade Publishing.
Cooke, Tim. The Exploration of Australasia & the Pacific, 1 vol. 2013. (Explorers Discovering the World Ser.). (ENG., Illus.). 48p. (J). (gr. 4-5). 34.60 *(978-1-4339-8619-2(1),* ec0edf2d-ed07-4e92-ba70-296e42d30db9); pap. 15.05 *(978-1-4339-8620-8(5),* 853f1283-6353-4497-bd33-0f55f696e02d) Stevens, Gareth Publishing LLLP. (Gareth Stevens Learning Library).
Davies, Monika. How Deep in the Ocean? Ocean Animal Habitats. Marti, Romina, illus. 2018. (Animals Measure Up Ser.). (ENG.). 24p. (J). (gr. 1-4). pap. 9.99 *(978-1-68152-304-0(3),* 15018); lib. bdg. *(978-1-68151-384-3(6),* 15012) Amicus.
Freed, Kira. The Terrific Pacific. 2017. (Text Connections Guided Close Reading Ser.). (J). (gr. 1). *(978-1-4900-1807-2(7))* Benchmark Education Co.
Gonzales, Doreen. The Huge Pacific Ocean, 1 vol. 2013. (Our Earth's Oceans Ser.). (ENG.). 48p. (gr. 3-3). 27.93 *(978-0-7660-4090-8(9),* f7a3a0f0-985f-4e03-a542-5c3c90e5e302); pap. 11.53 *(978-1-4644-0151-0(9),* 12ba4814-8b07-4cb5-b4c3-228cc2f659a3, Enslow Elementary) Enslow Publishing, LLC.
Green, Jen. Pacific Ocean, 1 vol. 2005. (Oceans & Seas Ser.). (ENG., Illus.). 48p. (gr. 5-8). pap. 15.05 *(978-0-8368-6283-6(X),* 65b54abb-14ad-4e72-baf5-9032daf6cf61); lib. bdg. 33.67 *(978-0-8368-6275-1(9),* d667bf2a-6004-4a22-944c-2cd4ef77580a) Stevens, Gareth Publishing LLLP. (Gareth Stevens Secondary Library).
Jeffrey, Gary. War in the Pacific. 2012. (ENG., Illus.). 48p. (J). *(978-0-7787-4197-8(4))*; pap. *(978-0-7787-4204-3(0))* Crabtree Publishing Co.
Kopp, Megan. Pacific Ocean. 2016. (Illus.). 32p. (J). *(978-1-4896-4739-9(2))* Weigl Pubs., Inc.
Mara, Wil. The Four Oceans. 2005. (Rookie Read-About Geography Ser.). (ENG., Illus.). 32p. (J). (gr. 1-2). per. 5.95 *(978-0-516-25817-1(6),* Children's Pr.) Scholastic Library Publishing.
Nagelhout, Ryan. Vasco Núñez de Balboa, 1 vol. 2016. (Spotlight on Explorers & Colonization Ser.). (ENG., Illus.). 48p. (J). (gr. 6-6). pap. 12.75 *(978-1-4777-8828-8(X),* 4c61e68-f789-41e8-9338-29be4c5b7bdc) Rosen Publishing Group, Inc., The.
Oachs, Emily Rose. Pacific Ocean. 2016. (Discover the Oceans Ser.). (ENG., Illus.). 24p. (J). (gr. k-3). lib. bdg. 26.95 *(978-1-62617-333-0(8),* Blastoff! Readers) Bellwether Media.
Olson, Tod. Lost in the Pacific, 1942: Not a Drop to Drink (Lost #1) 2016. (Lost Ser.: 1). (ENG., Illus.). 176p. (J). (gr. 5-9). 14.99 *(978-0-545-92811-3(7),* Scholastic Nonfiction) Scholastic, Inc.
Otfinoski, Steven. Vasco Nunez de Balboa: Explorer of the Pacific, 1 vol. 2006. (Great Explorations Ser.). (ENG., Illus.). 80p. (gr. 6-6). 36.93 *(978-0-7614-1609-8(9),* a881b4cb-52a0-4091-bbf7-8a7718d7fcd7) Cavendish Square Publishing LLC.
Ray, Deborah Kogan. The Impossible Voyage of Kon-Tiki. Ray, Deborah Kogan, illus. 2015. (Illus.). 40p. (J). (gr. 2-5). lib. bdg. 16.95 *(978-1-58089-620-7(0))* Charlesbridge Publishing, Inc.
Rogers, Juniata. The Pacific Ocean. 2018. (Oceans of the World Ser.). (ENG.). 24p. (J). (gr. -1-2). lib. bdg. 32.79 *(978-1-5038-2504-8(3),* 212365) Child's World, Inc, The.
Sandler, Michael. Oceans: Surviving in the Deep Sea. 2005. (X-treme Places Ser.). (Illus.). 32p. (J). (gr. 2-5). lib. bdg. 25.27 *(978-1-59716-087-2(3))* Bearport Publishing Co., Inc.
Tarbox, A. D. An Ocean Food Chain: Nature's Bounty. 2015. (Odysseys in Nature Ser.). (ENG., Illus.). 80p. (J). (gr. 7-10). *(978-1-60818-541-2(9),* 20971, Creative Education) Creative Co., The.
Webb, Sophie. Far from Shore: Chronicles of an Open Ocean Voyage. 2011. (ENG., Illus.). 80p. (J). (gr. 5-7). 18.99 *(978-0-618-59729-1(8),* 567897, Clarion Bks.) HarperCollins Pubs.
Weintraub, Aileen. The Pacific Ocean: The Largest Ocean. 2009. (Great Record Breakers in Nature Ser.). 24p. (gr. 3-4). 42.50 *(978-1-61513-185-3(X),* PowerKids Pr.) Rosen Publishing Group, Inc., The.

PACIFIC RAILROADS

Caswell, Max. My Life As a Chinese Immigrant, 1 vol. 2017. (My Place in History Ser.). (ENG.). 24p. (J). (gr. 2-3). pap. 9.15 *(978-1-5382-0293-7(X),* b9a1b810-4d98-4291-8560-1023b40012c0) Stevens, Gareth Publishing LLLP.
Dolan, Edward F., Jr. & Dolan, Edward F. The Transcontinental Railroad, 1 vol. 2003. (Kaleidoscope: American History Ser.). (ENG., Illus.). 48p. (gr. 4-4). 32.64 *(978-0-7614-1455-1(X),* d8770898-99bc-4987-8e78-a36217f24914) Cavendish Square Publishing LLC.
Fine, Jil. High Interest Books: Trail Blazers of the West: the Transcontinental Railroad. 2005. (High Interest Bks.). (ENG., Illus.). 48p. (J). (gr. 4-7). per. 6.95 *(978-0-516-25098-4(1),* Children's Pr.) Scholastic Library Publishing.
Greathouse, Lisa. Crossing a Continent (California) rev. ed. 2017. (Social Studies: Informational Text Ser.). (ENG., Illus.). 32p. (J). (gr. 3-5). pap. 11.99 *(978-1-4258-3241-4(5))* Teacher Created Materials, Inc.
Halpern, Monica. Railroad Fever (Direct Mail Edition) Building the Transcontinental Railroad 1830-1870. 2004. (Crossroads America Ser.). (ENG., Illus.). 40p. (J). (gr. 5-9). 12.95 *(978-0-7922-6767-6(2))* National Geographic Society.
Kraft, Eric. The Transcontinental Railroad & el ferrocarril Transcontinental: 6 English, 6 Spanish Adaptations. 2011. (ENG & SPA.). (J). 97.00 net. *(978-1-4108-5709-5(3))* Benchmark Education Co.
Lynette, Rachel. The Transcontinental Railroad, 1 vol. 2013. (Pioneer Spirit: the Westward Expansion Ser.). (ENG.). 24p. (J). (gr. 2-3). 26.27 *(978-1-4777-0785-2(9),* 56fc3c90-8a3f-4d6c-8b10-da957491801a); (Illus.). pap. 9.25 *(978-1-4777-0903-0(7),* 9e793ea2-5a60-4efb-8f00-26c84803618c) Rosen Publishing Group, Inc., The. (PowerKids Pr.).
Nardo, Don. The Golden Spike: How a Photograph Celebrated the Transcontinental Railroad. 2015. (Captured History Ser.). (ENG., Illus.). 64p. (J). (gr. 5-9). lib. bdg. 35.32 *(978-0-7565-4991-6(4),* 127634, Compass Point Bks.) Capstone.
National Geographic Learning. Reading Expeditions (Social Studies: Seeds of Change in American History): Building the Transcontinental Railroad. 2007. (ENG., Illus.). 40p. (J). pap. 21.95 *(978-0-7922-8690-5(1))* CENGAGE Learning.
Perritano, John. True Books: the Transcontinental Railroad. 2010. (True Book Ser.). (ENG.). 48p. (J). (gr. 2-5). 29.00 *(978-0-531-20585-3(1))* Scholastic Library Publishing.
Rajczak, Michael. The Transcontinental Railroad, 1 vol., Vol. 1. 2013. (What You Didn't Know about History Ser.). (ENG., Illus.). 24p. (J). (gr. 2-3). 25.27 *(978-1-4824-0600-9(4),* 7acf73a1-4ad9-461e-a523-2d300a808728) Stevens, Gareth Publishing LLLP.
Redmond, Shirley Raye. Blind Tom: The Horse Who Helped Build the Great Railroad. Bradley, Lois, illus. 2009. (J). pap. 10.00 *(978-0-87842-558-7(6))* Mountain Pr. Publishing Co., Inc.
Roberts, Russell. The Railroad Fuels Westward Expansion (1870s) 2012. (Illus.). 47p. (J). lib. bdg. 29.95 *(978-1-61228-290-9(3))* Mitchell Lane Pubs.
Shea, Therese. The Transcontinental Railroad: Using Algebra to Represent Situations & Solve Problems. 2006. (Math Big Bookstm Ser.). (ENG.). 32p. (gr. 6-7). 47.50 *(978-1-4042-6365-9(9))* Rosen Publishing Group, Inc., The.
Stein, R. Conrad. The Incredible Transcontinental Railroad: Stories in American History, 1 vol. 2012. (Stories in American History Ser.). (ENG., Illus.). 128p. (gr. 5-6). lib. bdg. 35.93 *(978-0-7660-3956-8(0),* f5371024-bccd-4f8f-993e-33924ec3c638) Enslow Publishing, LLC.
The Transcontinental Railroad. 2013. (Pioneer Spirit: the Westward Expansion Ser.). 24p. (J). (gr. 3-6). pap. 49.50 *(978-1-4777-0904-7(5),* PowerKids Pr.) Rosen Publishing Group, Inc., The.
Uschan, Michael V. The Transcontinental Railroad, 1 vol. 2009. (American History Ser.). (ENG.). 104p. (gr. 7-7). 41.03 *(978-1-4205-0105-6(4),* e3813323-b9e7-4454-97f9-ca01eaaab6e2); pap. 29.30 *(978-1-4205-0303-6(0),* 9b01852c-22f5-439f-a3d4-0f929415639d) Greenhaven Publishing LLC. (Lucent Pr.).
—The Transcontinental Railroad, 1 vol. 2003. (Landmark Events in American History Ser.). (ENG., Illus.). 48p. (J). (gr. 5-8). pap. 15.05 *(978-0-8368-5410-7(1),* 1e383fb5-2ffb-4d1c-a683-741a73060a32); lib. bdg. 33.67 *(978-0-8368-5382-7(2),* d0f576fb-46eb-4602-be10-44e089049cf0) Stevens, Gareth Publishing LLLP. (Gareth Stevens Secondary Library).

PACIFIC STATES

Here are entered works discussing collectively the states of California, Oregon, and Washington.

Bartley, Niccole. The West Coast. 2014. (Land That I Love: Regions of the United States Ser.). (Illus.). 32p. (J). (gr. 3-6). pap. 60.00 *(978-1-4777-6633-0(2),* PowerKids Pr.) Rosen Publishing Group, Inc., The.
Connors, Kathleen. Let's Explore the Pacific Northwest, 1 vol. 2013. (Road Trip: Exploring America's Regions Ser.). (ENG.). 24p. (J). (gr. 2-3). pap. 9.15 *(978-1-4339-9140-0(3),* 458789ee-ba1e-44b2-9b44-a385af9569ab); (Illus.). lib. bdg. 25.27 *(978-1-4339-9139-4(X),* 3d88b390-0fd2-406c-b68c-890574537329) Stevens, Gareth Publishing LLLP.
Let's Explore the Pacific Northwest. 2013. (Road Trip: Exploring America's Regions Ser.). 24p. (J). (gr. 2-5). pap. 48.90 *(978-1-4339-9141-7(1))* Stevens, Gareth Publishing LLLP.

PACKAGING

Blaxland, Wendy. Cans, 1 vol. 2010. (How Are They Made? Ser.). (ENG.). 32p. (gr. 4-4). lib. bdg. 21.27 *(978-0-7614-4753-5(9),* 541233ca-e120-47b2-8432-f56f4a2efade) Cavendish Square Publishing LLC.
Chapman, Gillian & Robson, Pam. Making Art with Packaging, 1 vol. 2007. (Everyday Art Ser.). (ENG., Illus.). 32p. (YA). (gr. 4-5). lib. bdg. 30.27 *(978-1-4042-3724-7(0),* c5617d61-ea66-406a-8526-604a929e9e5c) Rosen Publishing Group, Inc., The.
Walker, Kate. Metal Cans, 1 vol. Vanzet, Gaston, illus. 2011. (Recycling Ser.). (ENG.). 32p. (J). (gr. 1-1). 31.21 *(978-1-60870-131-5(X),* 34802586-f8a0-48da-9aae-5eaaed2ca814) Cavendish Square Publishing LLC.

PACKAGING—FICTION

Rice, Franny L. Zip-Lock Zack. 2011. 28p. (gr. 1-2). 12.03 *(978-1-4567-1607-3(7))* AuthorHouse.
Santillo, LuAnn. Packing. Santillo, LuAnn, ed. 2003. (Half-Pint Kids Readers Ser.). (Illus.). 7p. (J). (gr. -1-1). pap. 1.00 *(978-1-59256-072-1(5))* Half-Pint Kids, Inc.

PACKING INDUSTRY

see Meat Industry and Trade

PADDINGTON BEAR (FICTITIOUS CHARACTER)—FICTION

Bond, Michael. Love from Paddington. Fortnum, Peggy & Alley, R. W., illus. (Paddington Ser.). (ENG.). 144p. (J). (gr. 3-7). 2016. pap. 5.99 *(978-0-06-242526-3(9))* 2014. 9.99 *(978-0-06-236816-4(8))* HarperCollins Pubs. (HarperCollins).
—More about Paddington. Fortnum, Peggy, illus. 2015. (Paddington Ser.). (ENG.). 176p. (J). (gr. 3-7). 9.99 *(978-0-06-231220-4(0),* HarperCollins) HarperCollins Pubs.
—Paddington. Alley, R. W., illus. 2007. (Paddington Ser.). (ENG.). 32p. (J). (gr. -1-3). 19.99 *(978-0-06-117074-4(7),* HarperCollins) HarperCollins Pubs.
—Paddington & the Christmas Surprise. Alley, R. W., illus. 2008. (Paddington Ser.). (ENG.). 32p. (J). (gr. -1-3). 16.99 *(978-0-06-168740-2(5),* HarperCollins) HarperCollins Pubs.
—Paddington & the Christmas Surprise: A Christmas Holiday Book for Kids. Alley, R. W., illus. 2015. (Paddington Ser.). (ENG.). 32p. (J). (gr. -1-3). 17.99 *(978-0-06-231842-8(X),* HarperCollins) HarperCollins Pubs.
—Paddington at Large. Fortnum, Peggy, illus. 2016. (Paddington Ser.). (ENG.). 176p. (J). (gr. 3-7). 9.99 *(978-0-06-231224-2(3),* HarperCollins) HarperCollins Pubs.
—Paddington at St. Paul's. Alley, R. W., illus. 2019. (Paddington Ser.). (ENG.). 32p. (J). (gr. -1-3). 17.99 *(978-0-06-288785-6(8),* HarperCollins) HarperCollins Pubs.
—Paddington at the Barber Shop. Alley, R. W., illus. 2017. (I Can Read Level 1 Ser.). (ENG.). 32p. (J). (gr. -1-3). 16.99 *(978-0-06-243080-9(7))*; pap. 4.99 *(978-0-06-243079-3(3))* HarperCollins Pubs. (HarperCollins).
—Paddington at the Circus. Alley, R. W., illus. 2016. (Paddington Ser.). (ENG.). 32p. (J). (gr. -1-3). 17.99 *(978-0-06-231843-5(8),* HarperCollins) HarperCollins Pubs.
—Paddington at Work. Fortnum, Peggy, illus. (Paddington Ser.). (ENG.). 176p. (J). (gr. 3-7). 2018. pap. 6.99 *(978-0-06-243312-1(1))* 2017. 9.99 *(978-0-06-231226-6(X))* HarperCollins Pubs. (HarperCollins).
—Paddington Bear All Day. braille ed. 2004. (Illus.). (J). (gr. 1). spiral bd., bds. *(978-0-616-01860-6(6))* Canadian National Institute for the Blind/Institut National Canadien pour les Aveugles.
—Paddington Bear All Day. Alley, R. W., illus. 2004. 12p. (J). *(978-1-85269-444-9(0))*; *(978-1-85269-445-6(9))*; *(978-1-85269-456-2(4))*; *(978-1-85269-443-2(2))*; *(978-1-85269-442-5(4))* Mantra Lingua.
—Paddington Bear Goes to Market. Alley, R. W., illus. 2004. 12p. (J). *(978-1-85269-455-5(6))*; *(978-1-85269-451-7(3))* Mantra Lingua.
—Paddington Collector's Quintet: 5 Fun-Filled Stories in 1 Box! Alley, R. W., illus. 2018. (I Can Read Level 1 Ser.). (ENG.). 160p. (J). (gr. -1-3). pap. 19.99 *(978-0-06-267138-7(3),* HarperCollins) HarperCollins Pubs.
—Paddington Goes to Town. Fortnum, Peggy, illus. (Paddington Ser.). (ENG.). 176p. (J). (gr. 3-7). 2018. pap. 6.99 *(978-0-06-243313-8(X))* 2017. 9.99 *(978-0-06-231228-0(6))* HarperCollins Pubs. (HarperCollins).
—Paddington Goes to Town. Fortnum, Peggy, illus. 2003. (Paddington Bear Adventures Ser.). 136p. (J). (gr. 3-7). 12.60 *(978-0-8124-2266-5(X))* Perfection Learning Corp.
—Paddington Helps Out. Fortnum, Peggy, illus. 2015. (Paddington Ser.). (ENG.). 160p. (J). (gr. 3-7). 9.99 *(978-0-06-231230-3(8),* HarperCollins) HarperCollins Pubs.
—Paddington Here & Now. Alley, R. W., illus. 176p. (J). 2009. pap. 5.99 *(978-0-06-147366-1(9))* 2008. (ENG.). (gr. 3-7). 15.99 *(978-0-06-147364-7(2))* HarperCollins Pubs.
—Paddington Here & Now. Alley, R. W., illus. 2018. (Paddington Ser.). (ENG.). 192p. (J). (gr. 3-7). 9.99 *(978-0-06-231723-0(7),* HarperCollins) HarperCollins Pubs.
—Paddington Marches On. Fortnum, Peggy, illus. 2016. (Paddington Ser.). (ENG.). 176p. (J). (gr. 3-7). 9.99 *(978-0-06-231232-7(4),* HarperCollins) HarperCollins Pubs.
—Paddington on Top. Fortnum, Peggy, illus. 2018. (Paddington Ser.). (ENG.). 176p. (J). (gr. 3-7). pap. 6.99 *(978-0-06-243314-5(8))*; 9.99 *(978-0-06-231234-1(0))* HarperCollins Pubs. (HarperCollins).
—Paddington Races Ahead. Fortnum, Peggy & Alley, R. W., illus. 2019. (Paddington Ser.). (ENG.). 192p. (J). (gr. 3-7). pap. 6.99 *(978-0-06-243316-9(4),* HarperCollins) HarperCollins Pubs.
—Paddington Takes the Air. Fortnum, Peggy, illus. 2018. (Paddington Ser.). (ENG.). 176p. (J). (gr. 3-7). 9.99 *(978-0-06-231238-9(3),* HarperCollins) HarperCollins Pubs.
—Paddington Takes the Air. Fortnum, Peggy, illus. 2019. (Paddington Ser.). (ENG.). 176p. (J). (gr. 3-7). pap. 6.99 *(978-0-06-243315-2(6),* HarperCollins) HarperCollins Pubs.
—Paddington Takes the Test. Fortnum, Peggy, illus. 2016. (Paddington Ser.). (ENG.). 176p. (J). (gr. 3-7). 9.99 *(978-0-06-231240-2(5),* HarperCollins) HarperCollins Pubs.
—The Paddington Treasury: Six Classic Bedtime Stories. Alley, R. W., illus. 2014. (Paddington Ser.). (ENG.). 160p. (J). (gr. -1-3). 21.99 *(978-0-06-231242-6(1),* HarperCollins) HarperCollins Pubs.
—Paddington's Day Off. Alley, R. W., illus. 2017. (I Can Read Level 1 Ser.). (ENG.). 32p. (J). (gr. -1-3). pap. 4.99 *(978-0-06-243073-1(4),* HarperCollins) HarperCollins Pubs.
—Paddington's Finest Hour. Fortnum, Peggy & Alley, R. W., illus. 2017. (Paddington Ser.). (ENG.). 144p. (J). (gr. 3-7). 9.99 *(978-0-06-266972-8(9),* HarperCollins) HarperCollins Pubs.
—Paddington's Finest Hour. Alley, R. W., illus. 2017. (ENG.). 128p. (J). *(978-0-00-822619-0(9))* HarperCollins Pubs.
—Paddington's Prize Picture. Alley, R. W., illus. 2017. (I Can Read Level 1 Ser.). (ENG.). 32p. (J). (gr. -1-3). pap. 4.99 *(978-0-06-243076-2(9),* HarperCollins) HarperCollins Pubs.
—Paddington's Prize Picture. Alley, R. W., illus. 2017. 29p. (J). *(978-1-5182-4206-9(5))* Harper & Row Ltd.
Bond, Michael & Webster, Christy. Paddington Plays On. Alley, R. W., illus. 2016. 32p. (J). *(978-1-5182-3398-2(8))* Harper & Row Ltd.
Collins, Harper & Harper Collins / LeapFrog. Paddington Bear. 2008. (J). 11.99 *(978-1-59319-989-0(9))* LeapFrog Enterprises, Inc.
Macri, Thomas. Paddington 2: Paddington's Family & Friends. 2017. (I Can Read Level 1 Ser.). (ENG., Illus.). 32p. (J). (gr. -1-3). pap. 4.99 *(978-0-06-282441-7(4),* HarperCollins) HarperCollins Pubs.

PADEREWSKI, IGNACE JAN, 1860-1941

Roberto, Brother. Music for Millions: A Story of Ignace Paderewski. Jagodits, Carolyn Lee, illus. 2011. 94p. 38.95 *(978-1-258-09336-5(7))* Literary Licensing, LLC.

PAGANINI, NICOLO, 1782-1840

Frisch, Aaron. Dark Fiddler. Kelley, Gary, illus. 2008. (ENG.). 32p. (J). (gr. 1-3). 17.95 *(978-1-56846-200-4(X),* 22043, Creative Editions) Creative Co., The.

PAIGE, SATCHEL, 1906-1982

Cline-Ransome, Lesa. Satchel Paige. Ransome, James E., illus. 2004. 31p. (J). (gr. k-4). reprint ed. pap. 7.00 *(978-0-7567-7799-9(2))* DIANE Publishing Co.
—Satchel Paige. Ransome, James E., illus. 2003. (ENG.). 40p. (J). (gr. 1-5). 8.99 *(978-0-689-85681-5(4),* Simon & Schuster/Paula Wiseman Bks.) Simon & Schuster/Paula Wiseman Bks.
Frystak, Timothy D. Jackie Robinson: With Profiles of Satchel Paige & & Branch Rickey. 2006. (Biographical Connections Ser.). (Illus.). 112p. (J). *(978-0-7166-1828-7(1))* World Bk., Inc.

PAINE, THOMAS, 1737-1809

Aldritt, Jeremy. Thomas Paine & the Power of Common Sense, 1 vol. 2015. (Spotlight on American History Ser.). (ENG., Illus.). 24p. (J). (gr. 4-6). pap. 11.00 *(978-1-4994-1765-4(9),* 6d93e3a5-db18-41c4-af43-5de9b1569455, PowerKids Pr.) Rosen Publishing Group, Inc., The.
Crompton, Samuel Willard. Thomas Paine: Fighting for American Independence, 1 vol. 2017. (Rebels with a Cause Ser.). (ENG.). 128p. (gr. 8-8). lib. bdg. 38.93 *(978-0-7660-8515-2(5),* 9bbb932c-af6f-4b5e-9b36-0aa7fa6f6bff) Enslow Publishing, LLC.
Hurt, Avery Elizabeth. Thomas Paine's Common Sense, 1 vol. 2018. (America's Most Important Documents: Inquiry into Historical Sources Ser.). (ENG.). 64p. (gr. 6-6). lib. bdg. 37.36 *(978-1-5026-3601-0(8),* c05511b4-ee61-48f5-bf4c-393681f4ec9d) Cavendish Square Publishing LLC.
Jeffrey, Gary. Thomas Paine Writes Common Sense, 1 vol. 2011. (Graphic Heroes of the American Revolution Ser.). (ENG.). 24p. (gr. 3-3). (J). pap. 9.15 *(978-1-4339-6029-1(X),* 0b304be1-d0ef-44f8-8344-e85077307d9a, Gareth Stevens Learning Library); (YA). lib. bdg. 26.60 *(978-1-4339-6028-4(1),* 68e1aab1-5954-40b5-8644-751c4fa60a0d) Stevens, Gareth Publishing LLLP.
Marsh, Carole. Thomas Paine. 2004. 12p. (gr. k-4). 2.95 *(978-0-635-02369-8(5))* Gallopade International.
McCartin, Brian. Thomas Paine: Common Sense, & Revolutionary Pamphleteering. 2009. (Library of American Lives & Times Ser.). 112p. (gr. 5-5). 69.20 *(978-1-60853-509-5(6))* Rosen Publishing Group, Inc., The.
Nagelhout, Ryan. Thomas Paine's Common Sense, 1 vol. 2013. (Documents That Shaped America Ser.). (ENG.). 32p. (J). (gr. 4-5). 29.27 *(978-1-4339-9013-7(X),* 6422b8d2-5c0a-49a8-abeb-412a02746314); pap. 11.50 *(978-1-4339-9014-4(8),* cbade4d6-c6c0-4be1-8220-bf76bf726e50) Stevens, Gareth Publishing LLLP.
Rauf, Don. Thomas Paine: Author of Common Sense, 1 vol. 2017. (Spotlight on Civic Courage: Heroes of Conscience Ser.). (ENG., Illus.). 48p. (J). (gr. 6-6). 33.47 *(978-1-5383-8100-7(1),* 82c374e6-6b8f-4c4a-a82d-9d449ee2c3ad); pap. 12.75 *(978-1-5383-8097-0(8),* 870356b7-d649-44d9-a836-aaf70ed6a868) Rosen Publishing Group, Inc., The.
Thomas Paine's Common Sense. 2013. (Documents That Shaped America Ser.). 32p. (J). (gr. 4-6). pap. 63.00 *(978-1-4339-9015-1(6))* Stevens, Gareth Publishing LLLP.
Waxman, Laura Hamilton. An Uncommon Revolutionary: A Story about Thomas Paine. Orback, Craig, illus. 2003. (Creative Minds Biography Ser.). (J). pap. 5.95 *(978-1-57505-608-1(9),* Carolrhoda Bks.) Lerner Publishing Group.

PAINTED GLASS

see Glass Painting and Staining

PAINTERS

see also Artists

also names of individual painters

Alvarez, Mateo. Diego Rivera: Famous Mexican Painter, 1 vol. 2015. (Exceptional Latinos Ser.). (ENG., Illus.). 24p. (J). (gr. 3-4). pap. 10.35 *(978-0-7660-6702-8(5),* 3596e525-8f1c-40ac-8bd9-b2d6f4e062e4) Enslow Publishing, LLC.
Bacon, Dolores. Pictures Every Child Should Know (Illust. 2006. pap. *(978-1-4065-0424-8(6))* Dodo Pr.

Bankston, John. Diego Rivera. 2003. (Latinos in American History Ser.). (Illus.). 56p. (J). (gr. 4-8). lib. bdg. 29.95 *(978-1-58415-208-8(7))* Mitchell Lane Pubs.

Berenger, Al. Pocket Bios: Frida Kahlo. Berenger, Al, illus. 2018. (Pocket Bios Ser.). (ENG., Illus.). 32p. (J). 14.99 *(978-1-250-16875-7(9)*, 900187746) Roaring Brook Pr.

Bernier-Grand, Carmen T. Diego: Bigger Than Life, 0 vols. Diaz, David, illus. 2012. (ENG.). 64p. (YA). (gr. 9-12). 18.99 *(978-0-7614-5383-3(0)*, 9780761453833, Two Lions) Amazon Publishing.

Bodden, Valerie. Vincent Van Gogh. 2016. (Odysseys in Artistry Ser.). (ENG., Illus.). 80p. (J). (gr. 7-10). *(978-1-60818-721-8(7)*, 20665, Creative Education) Creative Co., The.

Bogart, Jo Ellen. Capturing Joy: The Story of Maud Lewis. Lang, Mark, illus. 2011. 32p. (J). (gr. 3-7). pap. 8.95 *(978-1-77049-262-2(3)*, Tundra Bks.) Tundra Bks. CAN. Dist: Penguin Random Hse. LLC.

—Emily Carr: At the Edge of the World. Newhouse, Maxwell, illus. 2003. 40p. (J). (gr. 5-18). 22.95 *(978-0-88776-640-4(4)*, Tundra Bks.) Tundra Bks. CAN. Dist: Penguin Random Hse. LLC.

Bowen, Richard. Vincent Van Gogh: Modern Artist. 2013. (People of Importance Ser.: 21). (Illus.). 32p. (J). (gr. 4-18). 19.95 *(978-1-4222-2858-6(4))* Mason Crest.

Brown, Isobel. Klimt, Vol. 7. 2015. (Great Artists Collection). (Illus.). 64p. (J). (gr. 7). lib. bdg. 23.95 *(978-1-4222-3260-6(3))* Mason Crest.

Brown, Monica. Frida Kahlo & Her Animalitos. Parra, John, illus. 2017. (ENG.). 40p. (J). (gr. -1-3). 18.95 *(978-0-7358-4269-4(8))* North-South Bks., Inc.

Collard, Sneed B., III. Jacob Lawrence, 1 vol. 2010. (American Heroes Ser.). (ENG.). 48p. (gr. 3-3). 32.64 *(978-0-7614-4058-1(5)*, 19d54f3f-2d13-43c3-a7af-77244e0ba9a9) Cavendish Square Publishing LLC.

Collier Hillstrom, Laurie. Frida Kahlo: Painter, 1 vol. 2008. (Twentieth Century's Most Influential Hispanics Ser.). (ENG., Illus.). 104p. (gr. 7-10). 41.03 *(978-1-4205-0019-6(8)*, a30b590c-d8db-4a58-ac9e-a9a77f8fe4a0, Lucent Pr.) Greenhaven Publishing LLC.

Connolly, Sean. Botticelli, 1 vol. 2004. (Lives of the Artists Ser.). (ENG., Illus.). 48p. (gr. 5-8). pap. 15.05 *(978-0-8368-5653-8(8)*, cbd8f260-ac85-455d-9253-44aa25bdc952); lib. bdg. 33.67 *(978-0-8368-5648-4(1)*, f4b213e1-9465-4777-beef-1b7895989864) Stevens, Gareth Publishing LLLP. (Gareth Stevens Secondary Library).

Crabtree, Marc. Meet My Neighbor, the Artist. 2009. (Meet my Neighbor Ser.). (ENG., Illus.). 24p. (J). (gr. k-2). pap. *(978-0-7787-4579-2(1))*; lib. bdg. *(978-0-7787-4569-3(4))* Crabtree Publishing Co.

Crispino, Enrica. Van Gogh. 2008. (Art Masters Ser.). 64p. (YA). (gr. 6-18). lib. bdg. 24.95 net. *(978-1-934545-05-8(8))* Oliver Pr., Inc.

Debon, Nicolas. Four Pictures by Emily Carr, 1 vol. 2007. (ENG., Illus.). 40p. (J). (gr. 2-7). pap. 6.95 *(978-0-88899-814-9(7))* Groundwood Bks. CAN. Dist: Publishers Group West (PGW).

Devera, Czeena. Frida Kahlo. Bane, Jeff, illus. 2017. (My Early Library: My Itty-Bitty Bio Ser.). (ENG.). 24p. (J). (gr. k-1). 30.64 *(978-1-63472-815-7(7)*, 209686) Cherry Lake Publishing.

Dickens, Rosie. Impressionists. Blackwood, Freyda, illus. 2009. (Young Reading Ser.). 64p. (J). 6.99 *(978-0-7945-2154-7(1)*, Usborne) EDC Publishing.

Etinde-Crompton, Charlotte & Crompton, Samuel Willard. Alma Woodsey Thomas: Painter & Educator, 1 vol. 2019. (Celebrating Black Artists Ser.). (ENG.). 104p. (gr. 7-7). 38.93 *(978-1-9785-1468-3(9)*, e209b4fd-1309-4def-935a-f3066ac49b20) Enslow Publishing, LLC.

—Robert S. Duncanson: Landscape Painter, 1 vol. 2019. (Celebrating Black Artists Ser.). (ENG.). 104p. (gr. 7-7). 38.93 *(978-1-9785-1477-5(8)*, 235c7188-7394-4cf8-ae19-ef3ec8a25549) Enslow Publishing, LLC.

Ewasiuk, Sandee. Painting Skills Lab. 2018. (Art Skills Lab Ser.). (Illus.). 32p. (J). (gr. 4-4). *(978-0-7787-5223-3(2))* Crabtree Publishing Co.

Fabiny, Sarah. Who Was Frida Kahlo? 2013. (Who Was... ? Ser.). lib. bdg. 16.00 *(978-0-606-34164-6(1))* Turtleback.

Fabiny, Sarah & Who HQ. Who Was Frida Kahlo? Hoare, Jerry, illus. 2013. (Who Was? Ser.). 112p. (J). (gr. 3-7). 6.99 *(978-0-448-47938-5(9)*, Penguin Workshop) Penguin Young Readers Group.

Feldman, Thea. A Parrot in the Painting: The Story of Frida Kahlo & Bonito (Ready-To-Read Level 2) Sanson, Rachel, illus. 2018. (Tails from History Ser.). (ENG.). 32p. (J). (gr. k-2). 17.99 *(978-1-5344-2230-8(7))*; pap. 4.99 *(978-1-5344-2229-2(3))* Simon Spotlight. (Simon Spotlight).

Flor Ada, Alma & Campoy, F. Isabel, contrib. by. Pasos. (Literature Collection of Puertas Al Sol Ser.).Tr. of Steps. (SPA.). 32p. (J). (gr. k-6). pap. 13.95 *(978-1-59437-704-4(9))* Santillana USA Publishing Co., Inc.

—Paths. (Literature Collection of Gateways to the Sun Ser.). 48p. (J). (gr. k-6). pap. 16.95 *(978-1-59437-722-8(7))* Santillana USA Publishing Co., Inc.

—Voces. (Literature Collection of Puertas Al Sol Ser.).Tr. of Voices. (SPA.). 32p. (J). (gr. k-6). pap. 13.95 *(978-1-59437-707-5(3))* Santillana USA Publishing Co., Inc.

Heine, Florian. 13 Painters Children Should Know. 2012. (13 Children Should Know Ser.). (ENG., Illus.). 48p. (J). (gr. 3-7). 14.95 *(978-3-7913-7086-6(3))* Prestel Verlag GmbH & Co KG. DEU. Dist: Penguin Random Hse. LLC.

Hersey, Bob, illus. Norman Rockwell: A Pop-Up Art Experience. 2004. 6p. (J). (gr. k-4). reprint ed. 19.00 *(978-0-7567-7642-8(2))* DIANE Publishing Co.

Holzhey, Magdalena. Frida Kahlo: The Artist in the Blue House. 2015. (ENG., Illus.). 32p. (J). (gr. 3-7). pap. 9.95 *(978-3-7913-7229-7(7))* Prestel Verlag GmbH & Co KG. DEU. Dist: Penguin Random Hse. LLC.

January, Brendan. Leonardo Da Vinci: Renaissance Painter. 2013. (People of Importance Ser.: 21). (Illus.). 32p. (J). (gr. 4-18). 19.95 *(978-1-4222-2848-7(7))* Mason Crest.

Ketchum, William C. Grandma Moses: An American Original, Vol. 8. 2018. (American Artists Ser.). 80p. (J). (gr. 7). 33.27 *(978-1-4222-4160-8(2))* Mason Crest.

Koja, Stephan. Gustav Klimt: A Painted Fairy Tale. 2007. (Adventures in Art Ser.). (Illus.). 28p. (J). (gr. 6-8). 14.95 *(978-3-7913-3704-3(1))* Prestel Publishing.

Kuiper, Kathleen, ed. The 100 Most Influential Painters & Sculptors of the Renaissance, 1 vol. 2010. (Britannica Guide to the World's Most Influential People Ser.). (ENG., Illus.). 376p. (YA). (gr. 10-10). lib. bdg. 56.59 *(978-1-61530-004-4(X)*, deb5d486-8e60-40ab-9222-0c87fd73c880) Rosen Publishing Group, Inc., The.

Kuligowski, Stephanie. Leonardo Da Vinci: Renaissance Artist & Inventor, 1 vol. rev. ed. 2012. (Social Studies: Informational Text Ser.). (ENG.). 32p. (gr. 4-8). pap. 11.99 *(978-1-4333-5008-5(4))* Teacher Created Materials, Inc.

La Bella, Laura. Careers in Painting & Wall Covering, 1 vol., 1. 2015. (Essential Careers Ser.). (ENG.). 80p. (J). (gr. 6-6). 37.47 *(978-1-4994-6219-7(0)*, eba87457-acad-49af-908e-aa2ef3d0153b, Rosen Young Adult) Rosen Publishing Group, Inc., The.

Landau, Jennifer. Vincent Van Gogh: Master of Post-Impressionist Painting, 1 vol. 2015. (Britannica Beginner Bios Ser.). (ENG., Illus.). 32p. (J). (gr. 2-3). 26.06 *(978-1-62275-946-0(X)*, 061286c9-3523-4bc2-88dd-fa4ae70dd02d, Britannica Educational Publishing) Rosen Publishing Group, Inc., The.

Larsen, Wayne. A. Y. Jackson: A Love for the Land. 2003. (ENG., Illus.). 192p. pap. 15.95 *(978-1-894852-06-7(0))* Dundurn Pr. CAN. Dist: Publishers Group West (PGW).

Larsson, Carl. A Family: Paintings from a Bygone Age, 24 vols. 2007. (ENG., Illus.). 30p. (J). (gr. 1). *(978-0-86315-583-3(9))* Floris Bks.

Lossani, Chiara. Vincent Van Gogh & the Colors of the Wind. Monaco, Octavia, illus. 2011. (ENG.). 40p. (YA). (gr. 2). 19.00 *(978-0-8028-5390-5(0)*, Eerdmans Bks For Young Readers) Eerdmans, William B. Publishing Co.

Marín, Guadalupe Rivera. My Papá Diego & Me (Mi Papa Diego y Yo) Memories of My Father & His Art (Recuerdos de Mi Padre y Su Arte) Rivera, Diego, illus. 2013. (SPA & ENG.). 32p. (J). (gr. k-5). 18.95 *(978-0-89239-228-5(2))* Lee & Low Bks., Inc.

Marsh, Carole. Diego Rivera: Acclaimed Mural Painter: Acclaimed Mural Painter. 2003. 12p. (gr. k-4). 2.95 *(978-0-635-02137-3(4))* Gallopade International.

Mecum, Shelly & Chun, Peggy. Watercolor Cat. 2007. 48p. 14.95 *(978-1-56647-838-0(3))* Mutual Publishing LLC.

Medina, Mariana & Mcintosh Wooten, Sara. Frida Kahlo: Self-Portrait Artist, 1 vol. 2015. (Influential Latinos Ser.). (ENG., Illus.). 128p. (gr. 7-7). 38.93 *(978-0-7660-6997-8(4)*, 07bd4b04-4536-45a2-b6f1-5574150be40a) Enslow Publishing, LLC.

Mis, Melody S. Vermeer. 2009. (Meet the Artist Ser.). 24p. (gr. 2-3). 42.50 *(978-1-61514-633-8(4)*, PowerKids Pr.) Rosen Publishing Group, Inc., The.

Mofford, Juliet. Raphael. 2009. (Art Profiles for Kids Ser.). (Illus.). 48p. (YA). (gr. 4-7). lib. bdg. 29.95 *(978-1-58415-745-8(3))* Mitchell Lane Pubs.

Morales, Yuyi. Viva Frida. Morales, Yuyi & O'Meara, Tim, illus. 2014. (ENG.). 40p. (J). (gr. -1-3). 19.99 *(978-1-59643-603-9(4)*, 900065746) Roaring Brook Pr.

Murray, Stuart A. P. John Trumbull: Painter of the Revolutionary War: Painter of the Revolutionary War. 2008. (ENG., Illus.). 83p. (C). (gr. 6-18). lib. bdg. 180.00 *(978-0-7656-8150-8(1)*, Y182501) Routledge.

Nardo, Don. Frida Kahlo, 1 vol. 2012. (Eye on Art Ser.). (ENG., Illus.). 104p. (gr. 7-7). lib. bdg. 41.03 *(978-1-4205-0850-5(4)*, 0d29b11b-0d31-429f-894d-3e5dbb106df0, Lucent Pr.) Greenhaven Publishing LLC.

Nelson, Andy. The Renaissance Painters Coloring Book: Donatello, Raphael, Leonardo & Michelangelo. 2nd ed. 2004. (Illus.). 96p. (J). (gr. 1-6). pap. 8.95 *(978-0-929636-27-6(9))* Syren Bk. Co.

Newbold, Amy. If Da Vinci Painted a Dinosaur, 1 vol. Newbold, Greg, illus. 2018. (Reimagined Masterpiece Ser.: 0). (ENG.). 40p. (J). (gr. 1-5). 17.95 *(978-0-88448-667-1(2)*, 884667) Tilbury Hse. Pubs.

Nichols, Catherine. Vincent Van Gogh, 1 vol. 2005. (Primary Source Library of Famous Artists Ser.). (ENG., Illus.). 32p. (J). (gr. 3-4). lib. bdg. 27.60 *(978-1-4042-2766-8(0)*, 3e3645d4-164e-485e-9aca-4e16e3764974, PowerKids Pr.) Rosen Publishing Group, Inc., The.

—Vincent van Gogh. 2009. (Primary Source Library of Famous Artists Ser.). 32p. (gr. 3-4). 42.50 *(978-1-60854-105-8(3)*, PowerKids Pr.) Rosen Publishing Group, Inc., The.

Olson, Greg. George Caleb Bingham: Frontier Artist, Missouri Politician. 2017. (ENG., Illus.). 48p. (J). lib. bdg. 27.00 *(978-1-61248-206-4(6))* Truman State Univ. Pr.

Pezzi, Bryan. Emily Carr. 2010. (Illus.). 24p. *(978-1-77071-599-8(1))*; pap. *(978-1-77071-605-6(X))* Weigl Educational Pubs. Ltd.

Raynham, Alex. Leonardo Da Vinci. 3rd ed. 2013. (Illus.). 64p. pap. 11.00 *(978-0-19-423670-6(6))* Oxford Univ. Pr., Inc.

Reef, Catherine. Frida & Diego: Art, Love, Life. 2014. (ENG., Illus.). 176p. (YA). (gr. 7-12). 18.99 *(978-0-547-82184-9(0)*, 1497178, Clarion Bks.) HarperCollins Pubs.

Restrepo, Felipe. Francis Bacon -Retrato de una Pesadilla. 2006. (SPA.). 136p. (YA). *(978-958-30-1693-6(4))* Panamericana Editorial.

Rockett, Paul. Pieter Bruegel, 1 vol., 1. 2015. (Inspiring Artists Ser.). (ENG.). 48p. (J). (gr. 7-7). 33.47 *(978-1-5081-7060-0(6)*, 4ef62c9a-0255-413d-a7c6-b8021fd6b868, Rosen Young Adult) Rosen Publishing Group, Inc., The.

Romeo, Francesca. Leonardo Da Vinci. 2008. (Art Masters Ser.). 64p. (YA). (gr. 6-18). lib. bdg. 24.95 net. *(978-1-934545-00-3(7))* Oliver Pr., Inc.

Rubin, Susan Goldman. Degas & the Dance: The Painter & the Petits Rats, Perfecting Their Art. 2005. (Illus.). 31p. (J). (gr. 4-8). reprint ed. 18.00 *(978-0-7567-9291-6(6))* DIANE Publishing Co.

—Diego Rivera: An Artist for the People. 2013. (ENG., Illus.). 56p. (J). (gr. 3-7). 22.95 *(978-0-8109-8411-0(3)*, 666701, Abrams Bks. for Young Readers) Abrams, Inc.

Salvi, Francesco. The Impressionists. 2008. (Art Masters Ser.). 64p. (YA). (gr. 6-18). lib. bdg. 24.95 net. *(978-1-934545-03-4(1))* Oliver Pr., Inc.

Sanchez Vegara, Maria Isabel & Fan, Eng Gee. Frida Kahlo (Little People Big Dreams) 2016. (Little People, Big Dreams Ser.). (ENG., Illus.). 32p. (J). 14.99 *(978-1-84780-770-0(4)*, Frances Lincoln Children's Bks.) Quarto Publishing Group UK GBR. Dist: Littlehampton Bk Services, Ltd.

Sherman, Patrice. John James Audubon. 2011. (ENG., Illus.). 152p. (gr. 6-12). 35.00 *(978-1-60413-953-2(6)*, P189964, Facts On File) Infobase Holdings, Inc.

Soni, Jaymee & Schubert, Charles. A Kid at Art - Wassily Kandinsky. 2003. (J). pap. 14.99 *(978-0-9743760-2-8(7))* Little Noggin LLC.

Taylor, Charlotte. Get to Know Georgia O'Keeffe, 1 vol. 2015. (Famous Artists Ser.). (ENG.). 48p. (gr. 3-4). pap. 12.70 *(978-0-7660-7224-4(X)*, e83360bf-51ab-4915-ad5c-6d231c79232e) Enslow Publishing, LLC.

—Get to Know John Singer Sargent, 1 vol. 2015. (Famous Artists Ser.). (ENG., Illus.). 48p. (gr. 3-4). 29.60 *(978-0-7660-7230-5(4)*, 923283b7-e81a-41dc-8aa9-f3b330aef688) Enslow Publishing, LLC.

—Get to Know Mary Cassatt, 1 vol. 2015. (Famous Artists Ser.). (ENG., Illus.). 48p. (J). (gr. 3-4). 29.60 *(978-0-7660-7234-3(7)*, 5f719eec-b4d7-410b-b785-8562b7f44c28) Enslow Publishing, LLC.

—Get to Know Norman Rockwell, 1 vol. 2015. (Famous Artists Ser.). (ENG., Illus.). 48p. (gr. 3-4). 29.60 *(978-0-7660-7238-1(X)*, 3d18bb4b-e96e-4c96-989c-1c3116006244) Enslow Publishing, LLC.

Thomson, Ruth. Vincent Van Gogh, 1 vol., 1. 2015. (Inspiring Artists Ser.). (ENG.). 48p. (J). (gr. 7-7). 33.47 *(978-1-5081-7056-3(8)*, 16e5c66d-9659-44f1-91ff-52e7b68922cb, Rosen Young Adult) Rosen Publishing Group, Inc., The.

Tonatiuh, Duncan. Diego Rivera: His World & Ours. 2011. (ENG., Illus.). 40p. (J). (gr. 1-4). 18.99 *(978-0-8109-9731-8(2)*, 692401) Abrams, Inc.

van Gogh, Vincent. Make a Masterpiece — Van Gogh's Starry Night. 2014. (Dover Little Activity Bks.). (ENG.). 4p. (J). (gr. k-3). pap. 2.50 *(978-0-486-78950-7(0)*, 789500) Dover Pubns., Inc.

—Vincent's Colors. 2005. (Illustrated Biographies by Chronicle Bks.). (ENG., Illus.). 48p. (J). (gr. -1-17). 16.99 *(978-0-8118-5099-5(4))* Chronicle Bks. LLC.

van Gogh, Vincent & Lach, William. Vincent's Colors: Words & Pictures by Van Gogh. 2005. (Illus.). 48p. (J). 14.95 *(978-1-58839-155-1(8))* Metropolitan Museum of Art, The.

Venezia, Mike. Diego Velázquez. Venezia, Mike, illus. 2004. (Getting to Know the World's Greatest Artists Ser.). (ENG., Illus.). 32p. (J). (gr. 3-4). pap. 6.95 *(978-0-516-26980-1(1)*, Children's Pr.) Scholastic Library Publishing.

—Georgia o'Keeffe (Revised Edition) (Getting to Know the World's Greatest Artists) Venezia, Mike, illus. 2015. (Getting to Know the World's Greatest Artists Ser.). (ENG., Illus.). 40p. (J). (gr. 3-4). pap. 7.95 *(978-0-531-21291-2(2)*, Children's Pr.) Scholastic Library Publishing.

—Horace Pippin. Venezia, Mike, illus. 2007. (Getting to Know the World's Greatest Artists Ser.). (ENG., Illus.). 32p. (J). (gr. 3-4). 28.00 *(978-0-531-18527-8(3)*, Children's Pr.) Scholastic Library Publishing.

Venezia, Mike & Magritte, Rene. René Magritte. Venezia, Mike, illus. 2003. (Getting to Know the World's Greatest Artists Ser.). (ENG., Illus.). 32p. (J). (gr. 3-4). pap. 6.95 *(978-0-516-27814-8(2)*, Children's Pr.) Scholastic Library Publishing.

Wenzel, Angela. 13 Artists Children Should Know. 2009. (13 Children Should Know Ser.). (ENG., Illus.). 48p. (J). (gr. 3-7). 14.95 *(978-3-7913-4173-6(1))* Prestel Verlag GmbH & Co KG. DEU. Dist: Penguin Random Hse. LLC.

Whiting, Jim. Claude Monet. 2007. (Art Profiles for Kids Ser.). (Illus.). 48p. (YA). (gr. 4-7). lib. bdg. 29.95 *(978-1-58415-563-8(9))* Mitchell Lane Pubs.

—Vincent Van Gogh. 2007. (Art Profiles for Kids Ser.). (Illus.). 48p. (YA). (gr. 4-7). lib. bdg. 29.95 *(978-1-58415-564-5(7))* Mitchell Lane Pubs.

Wood, Alix. Johannes Vermeer, 1 vol. 2013. (Artists Through the Ages Ser.). (ENG., Illus.). 32p. (J). (gr. 2-3). pap. 11.00 *(978-1-61533-633-3(8)*, 0b49d21b-ed88-4285-babf-044a5a73f5b9); lib. bdg. 29.93 *(978-1-61533-623-4(0)*, fcf77482-fd27-4f4c-8bba-2c5d8413185d) Rosen Publishing Group, Inc., The. (Windmill Bks.).

—Vincent Van Gogh, 1 vol. 2013. (Artists Through the Ages Ser.). (ENG., Illus.). 32p. (gr. 2-3). 29.93 *(978-1-61533-622-7(2)*, cb601fd8-ed7e-42e5-b696-68547669498e); pap. 11.00 *(978-1-61533-631-9(1)*, 122108d6-6d93-42d7-a5d9-7afc23e6b28c) Rosen Publishing Group, Inc., The. (Windmill Bks.).

Zaczek, Iain. Édouard Manet, 1 vol. 2014. (Great Artists Ser.). (ENG., Illus.). 32p. (J). (gr. 4-4). pap. 11.50 *(978-1-4824-1217-8(9)*, 6dcfd654-b353-41b8-adeb-81dfa8799daa) Stevens, Gareth Publishing LLLP.

—Vincent Van Gogh. 2014. (Great Artists Ser.). 32p. (J). (gr. 3-6). pap. 63.00 *(978-1-4824-1249-9(7))* Stevens, Gareth Publishing LLLP.

PAINTERS—FICTION

Baillie, James. The Steam Genie. 2005. 53p. (YA). 11.84 *(978-1-4116-3998-0(7))* Lulu Pr., Inc.

Blain, Christophe. Los Hielos, Vol. 2. 2005. (Isaac el Pirata Ser.). (SPA., Illus.). 48p. (YA). (gr. 8-17). 19.95 *(978-1-59497-114-3(5))* Public Square Bks.

Clancy, Kaycee. Sky Painters. 2007. 41p. per. 11.95 *(978-0-9776777-8-8(8))* Legacy Publishing Services, Inc.

Cullen, Lyn. I Am Rembrandt's Daughter. 2011. 8.88 *(978-0-7848-3491-6(1)*, Everbind) Marco Bk. Co.

Greene, Sefton. Space Painters. 2003. 18p. bds. *(978-1-904502-30-2(X))* MediaWorld/BestBooks.

Hawes, Louise. The Vanishing Point. 2007. (ENG.). 240p. (J). (gr. 5-7). pap. 15.95 *(978-0-618-74788-7(5)*, 487465, Clarion Bks.) HarperCollins Pubs.

James, Wayan. My Friend the Painter, 1 vol. 2016. (Rosen REAL Readers: STEM & STEAM Collection). (ENG.). 12p. (gr. 1-2). pap. 6.33 *(978-1-5081-2661-4(5)*, aa92d171-514d-4a9c-a632-9b3f8e2fbe0a, Rosen Classroom) Rosen Publishing Group, Inc., The.

Joyce, Mere. Getting the Brush Off, 1 vol. 2017. (Orca Limelights Ser.). (ENG.). 120p. (J). (gr. 4-7). pap. 9.95 *(978-1-4598-1358-8(8))* Orca Bk. Pubs. USA.

Juliette, the Modern Art Monkey: Individual Title Six-Packs. (Bookweb Ser.). 32p. (gr. 5-18). 34.00 *(978-0-7635-3776-0(4))* Rigby Education.

Lamballe, Jérôme. The Curious Story of Pablo Picasslug. 2010. 28p. 16.95 *(978-1-4452-8949-6(0))* Lulu Pr., Inc.

The Magnificent Mural, 6 vols., Pack. (Bookweb Ser.). 32p. (gr. 6-18). 34.00 *(978-0-7578-0889-0(1))* Rigby Education.

McDougal-Littell Publishing Staff. Literature Connections Spanish: Yo, Juan de Pareja (I, Juan de Pareja) 2004. (McDougal Littell Literature Connections Ser.). (SPA.). 256p. (gr. 7-7). 16.90 *(978-0-395-84375-8(8)*, 2-70788) Great Source Education Group, Inc.

Moss, Marissa. Caravaggio: Painter on the Run. 2016. (ENG., Illus.). 345p. (YA). (gr. 7-12). 16.95 *(978-1-939547-29-3(6)*, 1539c575-a382-4f0e-b72d-18c9c2260ca3) Creston Bks.

Osborne, Mary A. Nonna's Book of Mysteries. 2010. (ENG., Illus.). 352p. (gr. 8-17). pap. 16.95 *(978-1-936181-16-2(9))* Lake Street Pr.

Perkins, Mitali. Rickshaw Girl. Hogan, Jamie, illus. 2008. (ENG.). 96p. (J). (gr. 2-5). pap. 7.99 *(978-1-58089-309-1(0))* Charlesbridge Publishing, Inc.

Rogerson, Margaret. An Enchantment of Ravens. (ENG., Illus.). (YA). (gr. 9). 2018. 320p. pap. 12.99 *(978-1-4814-9759-6(6))* 2017. 304p. 19.99 *(978-1-4814-9758-9(8))* McElderry, Margaret K. Bks. (McElderry, Margaret K. Bks.).

Russo, Richard. Bridge of Sighs: A Novel. 2007. (ENG.). pap. *(978-0-7393-2751-7(8))* Random Hse. Large Print.

Verplancke, Klaas. Magritte's Apple. 2016. (ENG., Illus.). 40p. (J). (gr. -1-2). 19.95 *(978-1-63345-016-5(3)*, 1643301) Museum of Modern Art.

Wynne-Jones, Tim. On Tumbledown Hill, 1 vol. Petricic, Dusan, illus. 2008. (ENG.). 32p. (J). (gr. k-3). pap. 5.95 *(978-0-88995-409-0(7)*, b535b8c2-8843-44c4-a062-fb6fcb6cb8f6) Red Deer Pr. CAN. Dist: Firefly Bks., Ltd.

PAINTERS—FRANCE

Björk, Christina. Linnea in Monet's Garden. Sandin, Joan, tr. Anderson, Lena, illus. 2012. 48p. (J). (gr. k-3). 16.99 *(978-1-4022-7729-0(6))* Sourcebooks, Inc.

Bober, Suzanne & Merberg, Julie. A Picnic with Monet. 2003. (Mini Masters Ser.: 3). (ENG., Illus.). 22p. (J). (gr. -1-7). bds. 7.99 *(978-0-8118-4046-0(8))* Chronicle Bks. LLC.

Brooks, Susie. Claude Monet, 1 vol., 1. 2015. (Inspiring Artists Ser.). (ENG.). 48p. (J). (gr. 7-7). 33.47 *(978-1-5081-7063-1(0)*, eeb7bed4-d14e-4869-976c-339b7e2f3918, Rosen Young Adult) Rosen Publishing Group, Inc., The.

Connolly, Sean. Claude Monet, 1 vol. 2004. (Lives of the Artists Ser.). (ENG., Illus.). 48p. (gr. 5-8). pap. 15.05 *(978-0-8368-5655-2(4)*, 4a0a3de8-c2f3-4847-ad47-7b72fc925ec7, Gareth Stevens Secondary Library) Stevens, Gareth Publishing LLLP.

Dickins, Rosie & Ball, Karen. Leonardo Da Vinci. Unzner, Christa, illus. 2007. (Famous Lives Gift Bks). 63p. (J). (gr. 4-7). 8.99 *(978-0-7945-1594-2(0)*, Usborne) EDC Publishing.

Harris, Nathaniel. Paul Cézanne. 2003. (Artists in Their Time Ser.). (ENG., Illus.). 48p. (J). 24.00 *(978-0-531-12242-6(5)*, Watts, Franklin) Scholastic Library Publishing.

Kallen, Stuart A. Claude Monet, 1 vol. 2008. (Eye on Art Ser.). (ENG., Illus.). 112p. (gr. 7-7). lib. bdg. 41.03 *(978-1-4205-0074-5(0)*, 903ee674-0b0f-4a3d-b42d-5b994a5d0a9a, Lucent Pr.) Greenhaven Publishing LLC.

Kelley, True. Smart about Art: Pierre-Auguste Renoir: Paintings That Smile. 2005. (Smart about Art Ser.). (Illus.). 32p. (J). (gr. k-4). mass mkt. 7.99 *(978-0-448-43371-4(0)*, Grosset & Dunlap) Penguin Young Readers Group.

Lomberg, Michelle. Claude Monet. 2016. (Illus.). 32p. (J). *(978-1-4896-4619-4(1))* Weigl Pubs., Inc.

Macdonald, Maryann. Rosa's Animals: The Story of Rosa Bonheur & Her Painting Menagerie. 2018. (ENG., Illus.). 64p. (J). (gr. 3-7). 21.99 *(978-1-4197-2850-1(4)*, 1162601, Abrams Bks. for Young Readers) Abrams, Inc.

Markel, Michelle. The Fantastic Jungles of Henri Rousseau. Hall, Amanda, illus. 40p. (J). 2019. (ENG.). *(978-0-8028-5523-7(7))* 2012. 17.00 *(978-0-8028-5364-6(1))* Eerdmans, William B. Publishing Co. (Eerdmans Bks For Young Readers).

Mis, Melody S. Edgar Degas. (Meet the Artist Ser.). 24p. (gr. 2-3). 2009. 42.50 *(978-1-61514-628-4(8)*, PowerKids Pr.) 2007. (ENG., Illus.). (YA). lib. bdg. 26.27 *(978-1-4042-3839-8(5)*, 58717505-4caa-4597-bf6f-c42d534b0936) Rosen Publishing Group, Inc., The.

—Edouard Manet. (Meet the Artist Ser.). 24p. (gr. 2-3). 2009. 42.50 *(978-1-61514-629-1(6)*, PowerKids Pr.) 2007. (ENG., Illus.). (J). lib. bdg. 26.27 *(978-1-4042-3841-1(7)*, 41a9fc1c-05de-4cd4-bd9a-614ed331338d) Rosen Publishing Group, Inc., The.

—Paul Cezanne. (Meet the Artist Ser.). 24p. (gr. 2-3). 2009. 42.50 *(978-1-61514-631-4(8)*, PowerKids Pr.) 2007. (ENG., Illus.). (YA). lib. bdg. 26.27 *(978-1-4042-3842-8(5)*, ac667c47-185a-47c0-bbd2-a9f7d1011051) Rosen Publishing Group, Inc., The.

Nichols, Catherine. Claude Monet. (Primary Source Library of Famous Artists Ser.). 32p. (gr. 3-4). 2009. 42.50 *(978-1-60854-100-3(2))* 2005. (ENG., Illus.). (J). lib. bdg. 27.60 *(978-1-4042-2761-3(X)*, d98df970-1792-480c-87b1-27f64d46cc85) Rosen Publishing Group, Inc., The. (PowerKids Pr.).

—Pierre-Auguste Renoir. (Primary Source Library of Famous Artists Ser.). 32p. (gr. 3-4). 2009. 42.50 *(978-1-60854-104-1(5))* 2005. (ENG., Illus.). (J). lib. bdg. 27.60 *(978-1-4042-2765-1(2)*, cc309da8-8b19-4fb3-b670-da92beba1bb0) Rosen Publishing Group, Inc., The. (PowerKids Pr.).

Rubin, Susan Goldman. Matisse Dance with Joy. 2008. (Mini Masters Modern Ser.). (ENG., Illus.). 26p. (J). (gr. -1 — 1). bds. 6.99 (978-0-8118-6288-2(7)) Chronicle Bks. LLC.

Sánchez, Consuelo. Claudet Monet. 2005. (SPA.). 132p. (YA). (978-958-30-1869-5(4)) Panamericana Editorial.

Somervill, Barbara A. Pierre-Auguste Renoir. 2007. (Art Profiles for Kids Ser.). (Illus.). 48p. (YA). (gr. 4-7). lib. bdg. 29.95 (978-1-58415-566-9(3)) Mitchell Lane Pubs.

Spence, David. Gauguin. 2010. (Great Artists & Their World Ser.). (Illus.). 48p. (YA). 32.80 (978-1-84898-316-8(6)) Black Rabbit Bks.

—Gauguin: Huida al Eden. (Coleccion Grandes Artistas).Tr. of Gauguin: Escape to Eden. (SPA.). 266p. (YA). (gr. 5-8). 12.76 (978-84-8211-138-4(8)) Celeste Ediciones, S.A. ESP. Dist: Lectorum Pubns., Inc.

—Monet. 2013. (Ticktock Essential Artists Ser.). (ENG.). 32p. (J). (gr. 4-7). 21.19 (978-1-84696-973-7(5), TickTock Books) Octopus Publishing Group GBR. Dist: Children's Plus, Inc.

—Monet: Impresionismo. (Coleccion Grandes Artistas). (SPA.). 220p. (YA). (gr. 5-8). 12.76 (978-84-8211-133-9(7)) Celeste Ediciones, S.A. ESP. Dist: Lectorum Pubns., Inc.

—Renoir. 2010. (Great Artists & Their World Ser.). 48p. 32.80 (978-1-84898-317-5(4)) Black Rabbit Bks.

—Renoir. 2013. (Ticktock Essential Artists Ser.). (ENG.). 32p. (J). (gr. 4-7). 21.19 (978-1-84696-972-0(7), TickTock Books) Octopus Publishing Group GBR. Dist: Children's Plus, Inc.

Stamford, Tasha. Monet, Vol. 7. 2015. (Great Artists Collection). (Illus.). 64p. (J). (gr. 7). lib. bdg. 23.95 (978-1-4222-3261-3(1)) Mason Crest.

Swigelson, Kayce M. The Grand Adventures of Petit Louis. Swigelson, Kayce M., illus. 2013. (Illus.). 54p. 24.95 (978-0-9889643-1-0(7)) MathisJones Communications, LLC.

Tracy, Kathleen. Edouard Manet. 2009. (Art Profiles for Kids Ser.). (Illus.). 48p. (YA). (gr. 4-7). lib. bdg. 29.95 (978-1-58415-746-5(1)) Mitchell Lane Pubs.

—Paul Cezanne. 2007. (Art Profiles for Kids Ser.). (Illus.). 48p. (YA). (gr. 4-7). lib. bdg. 29.95 (978-1-58415-565-2(5)) Mitchell Lane Pubs.

Venezia, Mike. Camille Pissarro. Venezia, Mike, illus. 2004. (Getting. . Know Artists Ser.). (ENG., Illus.). 32p. (J). (gr. 3-4). pap. 6.95 (978-0-516-26977-1(1), Children's Pr.) Scholastic Library Publishing.

—Camille Pissarro. 2003. (Getting to Know World Artists Ser.). (ENG., Illus.). 32p. (J). 28.00 (978-0-516-22577-7(4), Children's Pr.) Scholastic Library Publishing.

—Eugene Delacroix. Venezia, Mike, illus. 2003. (Getting to Know World Artists Ser.). (ENG., Illus.). 32p. (J). 28.00 (978-0-516-22576-0(6), Children's Pr.) Scholastic Library Publishing.

Waldron, Ann. Who Was Claude Monet? 2009. (Who Was... ? Ser.). lib. bdg. 16.00 (978-0-606-04028-0(5)) Turtleback.

Waldron, Ann & Who HQ. Who Was Claude Monet? Marchesi, Stephen, illus. 2009. (Who Was? Ser.). 112p. (J). (gr. 3-7). pap. 5.99 (978-0-448-44985-2(4), Penguin Workshop) Penguin Young Readers Group.

Winter, Jeanette. Henri's Scissors. Winter, Jeanette, illus. 2013. (ENG., Illus.). 40p. (J). (gr. k-3). 18.99 (978-1-4424-6484-1(4), Beach Lane Bks.) Beach Lane Bks.

Wood, Alix. Claude Monet, 1 vol. 2013. (Artists Through the Ages Ser.). (ENG., Illus.). 32p. (J). (gr. 2-3). pap. 11.00 (978-1-61533-627-2(3), c668e58e-49ae-4910-8c6d-9f3d705b571d); lib. bdg. 29.93 (978-1-61533-620-3(6), 0181c944-67ee-4fed-be4a-4e6e2f2a3d75) Rosen Publishing Group, Inc., The. (Windmill Bks.).

—Paul Cézanne, 1 vol. 2013. (Artists Through the Ages Ser.). (ENG., Illus.). 32p. (J). (gr. 2-3). pap. 11.00 (978-1-61533-625-8(7), cc4e1b40-5755-457a-aa22-ff0574837e48); lib. bdg. 29.93 (978-1-61533-619-7(2), d37efbe6-97fb-4d88-856f-e1aadb3d3fc4) Rosen Publishing Group, Inc., The. (Windmill Bks.).

Zaczek, Iain. Georges Seurat. 2014. (Great Artists Ser.). 32p. (J). (gr. 3-6). pap. 63.00 (978-1-4824-1248-2(9)) Stevens, Gareth Publishing LLLP.

—Paul Cézanne, 1 vol. 2014. (Great Artists Ser.). (ENG.). 32p. (J). (gr. 4-4). pap. 11.50 (978-1-4824-1216-1(0), 98f5a997-cd9f-417a-88e1-4816979fae96) Stevens, Gareth Publishing LLLP.

PAINTERS—SPAIN

Mis, Melody S. El Greco. (Meet the Artist Ser.). 24p. (gr. 2-3). 2009. 42.50 (978-1-61514-630-7(X), PowerKids Pr.) 2007. (ENG., Illus.). (YA). lib. bdg. 26.27 (978-1-4042-3844-2(1), d1312f51-46b5-42b5-8f69-f2e209e31d6e) Rosen Publishing Group, Inc., The.

Toyne, Jessica. Dali, Vol. 7. 2015. (Great Artists Collection). (Illus.). 64p. (J). (gr. 7). lib. bdg. 23.95 (978-1-4222-3258-3(1)) Mason Crest.

Venezia, Mike. Francisco Goya (Revised Edition) (Getting to Know the World's Greatest Artists) (Library Edition) Venezia, Mike, illus. 2016. (Getting to Know the World's Greatest Artists Ser.). (ENG.). 40p. (J). (gr. 3-4). lib. bdg. 29.00 (978-0-531-21667-5(5), Children's Pr.) Scholastic Library Publishing.

PAINTERS—UNITED STATES

Abrams, Dennis. Georgia O'Keeffe: Artist. 2nd rev. ed. 2009. (ENG., Illus.). 144p. (gr. 6-12). 35.00 (978-1-60413-336-3(8), P165458, Facts On File) Infobase Holdings, Inc.

Berne, Emma Carlson. Frida Kahlo: Groundbreaking Artist, 1 vol. 2009. (Essential Lives Set 4 Ser.). (ENG., Illus.). 112p. (YA). (gr. 6-12). lib. bdg. 41.36 (978-1-60453-701-7(9), 6693, Essential Library) ABDO Publishing Co.

Brown, Elizabeth. Dancing Through Fields of Color: The Story of Helen Frankenthaler. Sicuro, Aimée, illus. 2019. (ENG.). 40p. (J). (gr. -1-3). 19.99 (978-1-4197-3410-6(5), 1190801, Abrams Bks. for Young Readers) Abrams, Inc.

Bryant, Jen. A Splash of Red: the Life & Art of Horace Pippin. Sweet, Melissa, illus. 2013. 40p. (J). (gr. k-3). 18.99 (978-0-375-86712-5(0), Knopf Bks. for Young Readers) Random Hse. Children's Bks.

Burleigh, Robert. George Bellows: Painter with a Punch! 2012. (ENG., Illus.). 40p. (J). (gr. 3-7). 19.95 (978-1-4197-0166-5(5), 649401, Abrams Bks. for Young Readers) Abrams, Inc.

Davies, Jacqueline. The Boy Who Drew Birds: A Story of John James Audubon. Sweet, Melissa, illus. 2004. (ENG.). 32p. (J). (gr. -1-3). tchr. ed. 17.99 (978-0-618-24343-3(7), 584353, Clarion Bks.) HarperCollins Pubs.

Dickinson, Stephanie E. Jacob Lawrence: Painter, 1 vol. 2016. (Artists of the Harlem Renaissance Ser.). (ENG.). 128p. (YA). (gr. 9-9). 47.36 (978-1-5026-1070-6(1), 0395c066-77ae-4d79-b463-433e205eaf7e) Cavendish Square Publishing LLC.

Etinde-Crompton, Charlotte & Crompton, Samuel Willard. Henry Ossawa Tanner: Landscape Painter & Expatriate, 1 vol. 2019. (Celebrating Black Artists Ser.). (ENG.). 104p. (gr. 7-7). 38.93 (978-1-9785-0362-5(8), 4e0bcabe-039c-471f-8dcc-16bc7a958958) Enslow Publishing, LLC.

Fabiny, Sarah & Who HQ. Who Was Norman Rockwell? Copeland, Gregory, illus. 2019. (Who Was? Ser.). 112p. (J). (gr. 3-7). 5.99 (978-0-448-48864-6(7), Penguin Workshop) Penguin Young Readers Group.

Greenberg, Jan & Jordan, Sandra. Action Jackson. Parker, Robert Andrew, illus. 2007. (ENG.). 32p. (J). (gr. 1-5). pap. 8.99 (978-0-312-36751-0(1), 900042355) Square Fish.

Igus, Toyomi. Going Back Home: An Artist Returns to the South, 1 vol. Wood, Michele, illus. 2013. (ENG.). 32p. (J). (gr. 3-5). pap. 11.95 (978-0-89239-197-4(9), leelowcbp, Children's Book Press) Lee & Low Bks., Inc.

Jordan, Sandra & Greenberg, Jan. Action Jackson. Parker, Robert Andrew, illus. pap. incl. audio compact disk (978-1-59112-965-3(6)); pap. incl. audio (978-1-59112-961-5(3)) Live Oak Media.

Koerner, Henry. The Early Works of Henry Koerner 1945-1957. 2004. (Illus.). 96p. (YA). (gr. 13-18). pap. 35.00 (978-0-9703425-5-3(1)) Frick Art & Historical Ctr.,The.

Kopp, Megan. Grandma Moses. 2016. (Illus.). 32p. (J). (978-1-4896-4621-7(3)) Weigl Pubs., Inc.

Maurer, Tracy Nelson. Samuel Morse, That's Who! The Story of the Telegraph & Morse Code. Ramón, El Primo, illus. 2019. (ENG.). 40p. (J). 19.99 (978-1-62779-130-4(2), 900136046, Holt, Henry & Co. Bks. For Young Readers) Holt, Henry & Co.

McLellan, Richard A. The Land of Truth & Phantasy: Life & Painting at Ring Farm USA. Wyeth, Andrew N. & Kuerner, Karl J., illus. gif. ed. 2005. (ENG.). 187p. 24.00 (978-0-9747536-0-7(2)) McLellan Bks.

O'Connor, Jane. Mary Cassatt: Family Pictures. Kalis, Jennifer, illus. 2003. (Smart about Art Ser.). (ENG.). 32p. (J). (gr. k-4). mass mkt. 7.99 (978-0-448-43152-9(1), Grosset & Dunlap) Penguin Young Readers Group.

Reich, Susanna. Painting the Wild Frontier: The Art & Adventures of George Catlin. 2008. (ENG., Illus.). 176p. (J). (gr. 5-7). 22.00 (978-0-618-71470-4(7), 100506, Clarion Bks.) HarperCollins Pubs.

Rodriguez, Rachel Victoria. Through Georgia's Eyes. Paschkis, Julie, illus. rev. ed. 2006. (ENG.). 32p. (J). (gr. k-3). 19.99 (978-0-8050-7740-7(5), 900031594, Holt, Henry & Co. Bks. For Young Readers) Holt, Henry & Co.

Show Me America, 5 vols., Set. Incl. Dorothea Lange: Photographer of the People: Photographer of the People. King, David C. 88p. (C). 2009. lib. bdg. 180.00 (978-0-7656-8154-6(4), Y181941); George Catlin: Painter of Indian Life: Painter of Indian Life. Worth, Richard. 80p. (C). 2009. lib. bdg. 180.00 (978-0-7656-8152-2(8), Y182314); John Trumbull: Painter of the Revolutionary War: Painter of the Revolutionary War. Murray, Stuart A. P. 83p. (C). 2008. lib. bdg. 180.00 (978-0-7656-8150-8(1), Y182501); Lewis Hine: Photographer of Americans at Work: Photographer of Americans at Work. Worth, Richard. 80p. (C). 2009. lib. bdg. 180.00 (978-0-7656-8153-9(6), Y182862); Mathew Brady: Photographer of Our Nation: Photographer of Our Nation. Murray, Stuart A. P. 83p. 2009. lib. bdg. 180.00 (978-0-7656-8151-5(X), Y182957); (Illus.). (gr. 6-18). (ENG.). 2009. Set lib. bdg. 165.00 (978-0-7656-8149-2(8), Y183560) Routledge.

Sonder, Ben. The Legacy of Norman Rockwell, Vol. 8. 2018. (American Artists Ser.). 144p. (J). (gr. 7). 35.93 (978-1-4222-4161-5(0)) Mason Crest.

Stephens, Pamela Geiger. Dropping in on Romare Bearden. McNeill, Jim, illus. 2007. (ENG.). 32p. (J). 15.95 (978-1-56290-539-2(2)) Crystal Productions.

Tate, Don. It Jes' Happened: When Bill Traylor Started to Draw, 1 vol. Christie, R. Gregory, illus. (ENG.). (J). 2019. 32p. (gr. 1-6). pap. 11.95 (978-1-64379-055-8(2), leelowbooks) 2012. 1p. 17.95 (978-1-60060-260-3(6)) Lee & Low Bks., Inc.

Taylor, Charlotte. Get to Know Georgia O'Keeffe, 1 vol. 2015. (Famous Artists Ser.). (ENG., Illus.). 48p. (gr. 3-4). 29.60 (978-0-7660-7226-8(6), f6a161e3-09a3-4788-a42f-f788f7263b40) Enslow Publishing, LLC.

Venezia, Mike. Winslow Homer. Venezia, Mike, illus. 2004. (Getting. . Know Artists Ser.). (ENG., Illus.). 32p. (J). (gr. 3-4). pap. 6.95 (978-0-516-26979-5(8), Children's Pr.) Scholastic Library Publishing.

Wallace, Sandra Neil. Between the Lines: How Ernie Barnes Went from the Football Field to the Art Gallery. Collier, Bryan, illus. 2018. (ENG.). 48p. (J). (gr. -1-3). 18.99 (978-1-4814-4387-6(9), Simon & Schuster Bks. For Young Readers) Simon & Schuster Bks. For Young Readers.

Worth, Richard. George Catlin: Painter of Indian Life: Painter of Indian Life. 2009. (ENG., Illus.). 80p. (C). (gr. 6-18). lib. bdg. 180.00 (978-0-7656-8152-2(8), Y182314) Routledge.

PAINTING

see also Animal Painting and Illustration; Color; Composition (Art); Finger Painting; Flower Painting and Illustration; Impressionism (Art); Landscape Painting; Marine Painting; Perspective; Post-Impressionism (Art); Stencil Work; Textile Painting; Watercolor Painting

Aigner-Clark, Julie. Master Pieces. Zaidi, Nadeem, illus. 2004. (SPA.). 10p. (J). 9.95 (978-970-718-211-0(3), Silver Dolphin Bks.) Readerlink Distribution Services, LLC.

Alexander, Heather. A Child's Introduction to Art: The World's Greatest Paintings & Sculptures. Hamilton, Meredith, illus. 2014. (Child's Introduction Ser.). (ENG.). 96p. (J). (gr. -1-17). 19.99 (978-1-57912-956-9(0), 81956, Black Dog & Leventhal Pubs. Inc.) Running Pr.

Ancona, George. Murals: Walls That Sing, 1 vol. 2003. (ENG., Illus.). 32p. (YA). 17.95 (978-0-7614-5131-0(5)) Marshall Cavendish Corp.

Anderson, Robert. Artists in Their Time: Paul Gauguin. 2003. (Artists in Their Time Ser.). (ENG., Illus.). 48p. (J). (gr. 5-7). pap. 6.95 (978-0-531-16647-5(3), Watts, Franklin) Scholastic Library Publishing.

Anholt, Laurence. Anholt's Artists Activity Book. 2012. (ENG.). 48p. (J). (gr. k-3). pap. 11.99 (978-1-4380-0114-2(2)) Sourcebooks, Inc.

Armstrong, Carole. My Sticker Art Gallery: Monet. (ENG., Illus.). 12p. (J). (gr. 2-18). pap. (978-0-7112-0962-6(6)) ReiseArt Buchhandlung GmbH.

The Art of Glass Painting. 2004. (Classic Craft Cases Ser.). (Illus.). 64p. (978-1-84229-801-5(1)) Top That! Publishing PLC.

Bac, F. Sehnaz. Stone Painting for Kids: Designs to Spark Your Creativity. 2018. (ENG., Illus.). 96p. pap. 19.95 (978-0-486-81903-7(5), 819035) Dover Pubns., Inc.

Bacon, Dolores. Pictures Every Child Should Know (Illust. 2006. pap. (978-1-4065-0424-8(6)) Dodo Pr.

Barlowe, Dot. Flower Gardens to Paint or Color. 2007. (Dover Flower Coloring Bks.). (ENG., Illus.). 48p. (gr. 3-5). 5.99 (978-0-486-46204-2(8), 462048) Dover Pubns., Inc.

Binam, Sharyn. The Sidload: Garden. 2004. 64p. pap. 11.95 (978-1-57377-186-3(4), 0-1988-4-02500-9) Eas'l Pubns.

Bodden, Valerie. History Paintings. 2013. (Brushes with Greatness Ser.). (ENG.). 48p. (J). (gr. 5-9). pap. 12.00 (978-0-89812-763-8(7), 21944, Creative Paperbacks) Creative Co., The.

Booth, Elaine. This Painting Has Action! 2017. (Text Connections Guided Close Reading Ser.). (J). (gr. k). (978-1-4900-1764-8(X)) Benchmark Education Co.

Conway, Agnes Ethel & Conway, Martin. The Book of Art for Young People. 2007. (ENG., Illus.). 136p. per. (978-1-4065-1514-5(0)) Dodo Pr.

Courtauld, Sarah. Story of Art Sticker Book. 2012. (Art Ser.). 42p. (J). pap. 9.99 (978-0-7945-3295-6(0), Usborne) EDC Publishing.

Crabtree, Marc. Meet My Neighbor, the Artist. 2009. (Meet my Neighbor Ser.). (ENG., Illus.). 24p. (J). (gr. k-2). pap. (978-0-7787-4579-2(1)); lib. bdg. (978-0-7787-4569-3(4)) Crabtree Publishing Co.

Crismon, Joy. Chinese Brush Painting. 84p. (J). (gr. 1-7). pap. (978-1-56861-049-8(1)) Swift Learning Resources.

Davies, Carolyn. Pont Library: Josef Herman in Wales. 2004. (ENG., Illus.). 32p. pap. 15.95 (978-1-85902-999-2(X)) Beekman Bks., Inc.

Delafosse, Claude. Paintings. Ross, Tony, illus. 2nd ed. 2018. (My First Discoveries Ser.).Tr. of Tableaux. (ENG.). 34p. (J). (gr. k-2). spiral bd. 19.99 (978-1-85103-464-2(1), 1851034641) Moonlight Publishing, Ltd. GBR. Dist: Independent Pubs. Group.

D'Elia, Una. Painting in the Renaissance, 1 vol. 2009. (Renaissance World Ser.). (ENG., Illus.). 32p. (J). (gr. 5-8). pap. (978-0-7787-4612-6(7)); lib. bdg. (978-0-7787-4592-1(9)) Crabtree Publishing Co.

Dickens, Rosie. Famous Paintings: Internet-Linked. 2009. (Famous Paintings Ser.). 96p. (YA). (gr. 4-18). 16.99 (978-0-7945-2542-2(3), Usborne) EDC Publishing.

Dinmont, Kerry. Lee Paints a Picture: A Book about Colors. 2017. (My Day Readers Ser.). (ENG.). 24p. (J). (gr. -1-2). lib. bdg. 32.79 (978-1-5038-2013-5(0), 211864) Child's World, Inc, The.

Disney Princess Paint n' Play with Sticker Rolls. 2005. (J). spiral bd. (978-1-59487-148-1(5)) Artist Studios, Ltd.

Dorling Kindersley Publishing Staff. My Art Book. 2011. (ENG., Illus.). 80p. (J). (gr. 2-5). 15.99 (978-0-7566-7582-0(0), DK Children) Dorling Kindersley Publishing, Inc.

Dubowski, Mark. Discovery in the Cave. Barnard, Bryn, illus. 2010. (Step into Reading Ser.). 48p. (J). (gr. 2-4). pap. 5.99 (978-0-375-85893-2(8), Random Hse. Bks. for Young Readers) Random Hse. Children's Bks.

Felix, Rebecca. Cool Crayons, Chalks, & Paints: Crafting Creative Toys & Amazing Games. 2015. (Cool Toys & Games Ser.). (ENG., Illus.). 32p. (J). (gr. 3-6). lib. bdg. 34.21 (978-1-68078-048-2(4), 19101, Checkerboard Library) ABDO Publishing Co.

Fisher, Diana. Rockin' Crafts: Everything You Need to Become a Rock-Painting Craft Star! 2012. (Craft Star Ser.). (Illus.). 64p. (J). (gr. 2-4). 32.80 (978-1-936309-40-5(8)) Quarto Publishing Group USA.

Fitzrandolph, Joyce. Learn to Paint with the Alexander Brush Club. (Illus.). 24p. (J). (gr. 4-6). pap. (978-1-883576-32-5(6), KT-220B) Alexander Art L.P.

Flor Ada, Alma & Campoy, F. Isabel, contrib. by. Blue & Green. (Literature Collection of Gateways to the Sun Ser.). 32p. (J). (gr. k-6). pap. 13.95 (978-1-59437-714-3(6)) Santillana USA Publishing Co., Inc.

Foa, Emma. Edward Hopper. 2003. (Artists in Their Time Ser.). (ENG., Illus.). 48p. (J). 24.00 (978-0-531-12240-2(9)); (gr. 5-7). pap. 6.95 (978-0-531-16641-3(4)) Scholastic Library Publishing. (Watts, Franklin).

Foldvary-Anderson, Carol. 3-D Coloring Book — Hearts. 2012. (Dover Romance Coloring Bks.). (ENG., Illus.). 32p. (J). (gr. 2-6). pap. 5.99 (978-0-486-49013-7(0), 490130) Dover Pubns., Inc.

Fretland VanVoorst, Jenny. Painting. 2016. (Artist's Studio Ser.). (Illus.). 24p. (J). (gr. k-2). lib. bdg. 25.65 (978-1-62031-282-7(4), Bullfrog Bks.) Jump! Inc.

Frida Kahlo. 2018. (J). (978-0-7166-2282-6(3)) World Bk., Inc.

Frisch-Schmoll, Joy. Still Lifes. 2013. (Brushes with Greatness Ser.). (ENG.). 48p. (J). (gr. 5-9). pap. 12.00 (978-0-89812-766-9(1), 21947, Creative Paperbacks) Creative Co., The.

Gibson, Ray. What Shall I Paint? Everett, Felicity, ed. Kennard, Michaela, illus. 2006. (What Shall I Do Today? Ser.). 32p. (J). (gr. 2). lib. bdg. 15.95 (978-1-58086-549-4(6)) EDC Publishing.

Gluck, Larry. The Basic Painting Course. 2004. (YA). spiral bd. (978-1-929473-05-2(2)) Renaissance Pubns.

Gray, Savannah. We Can Feel Art! 2017. (Text Connections Guided Close Reading Ser.). (J). (gr. 1). (978-1-4900-1808-9(5)) Benchmark Education Co.

Handler, Daniel. Girls Standing on the Lawn. Kalman, Maira, illus. 2014. (ENG.). 64p. (gr. 5-17). 14.95 (978-0-87070-908-1(9)) Museum of Modern Art.

Hansen, Grace. American Paint Horses. 2016. (Horses (Abdo Kids Jumbo) Ser.). (ENG., Illus.). 24p. (J). (gr. -1-2). lib. bdg. 32.79 (978-1-68080-925-1(3), 23325, Abdo Kids) ABDO Publishing Co.

Harron, Nancy. Harron's Nest Floor Decor & More. 2004. 68p. pap. 16.95 (978-1-57377-202-0(X), 0-1988-4-2524) Eas'l Pubns.

Henry, Sally. Drawing, 12 vols., Set 1. Incl. Card Making. lib. bdg. 30.27 (978-1-4358-2506-2(3), e98332e3-5734-417a-8826-e23c60aa3200); Clay Modeling. lib. bdg. 30.27 (978-1-4358-2508-6(X), 89020edc-cf7d-44e6-b170-245ed1de5a49); Collage. lib. bdg. 30.27 (978-1-4358-2509-3(8), 20c79d9c-abd9-4986-9397-8a8a9d4eb5c8); lib. bdg. 30.27 (978-1-4358-2510-9(1), f7777292-91bc-44d7-80b5-fb82d73b69b1); Painting. lib. bdg. 30.27 (978-1-4358-2511-6(X), 7296eaa9-fbdb-41c1-bcde-f7eaeeee7b12); Paper Folding. lib. bdg. 30.27 (978-1-4358-2507-9(1), 09a8d395-82f9-4f76-94aa-1532ef08ccf5); (J). (gr. 3-4). (Make Your Own Art Ser.). (ENG., Illus.). 32p. 2008. Set lib. bdg. 181.62 (978-1-4358-2549-9(7), 3fce187b-c18a-47c1-b974-447e2b54b804, PowerKids Pr.) Rosen Publishing Group, Inc., The.

—Painting, 1 vol. 2008. (Make Your Own Art Ser.). (ENG., Illus.). 32p. (gr. 3-4). pap. 12.75 (978-1-4358-2644-1(2), 0c88a250-e146-465f-81e7-77c22884ad32, PowerKids Pr.) Rosen Publishing Group, Inc., The.

Henry, Sally & Cook, Trevor. Make Your Own Art: Set 2, 10 vols. Incl. Eco Crafts. lib. bdg. 30.27 (978-1-4488-1582-1(7), 9954893c-0fed-4f20-854d-2d05e915234b); Making Masks. 30.27 (978-1-4488-1583-8(5), fcf75343-3ae6-4fcf-9ad0-59c260787f14); Making Mosaics. 30.27 (978-1-4488-1585-2(1), b486d950-5a61-4480-bf95-a93f3b05f98a); Making Puppets. 30.27 (978-1-4488-1584-5(3), 91ded940-cb87-486c-916d-7905a13bfef3); Papier-Mâché. 30.27 (978-1-4488-1587-6(8), 140b6f37-b163-4556-bfa4-cb69696f6108); (J). (gr. 3-4). (Make Your Own Art Ser.). (ENG., Illus.). 32p. 2010. Set lib. bdg. 151.35 (978-1-4488-1625-5(4), ab4eeb4f-5340-4fa7-af2c-a6391e8949de, PowerKids Pr.) Rosen Publishing Group, Inc., The.

Hill, Z. B. Painting. 2014. (Art Today! Ser.: 10). 64p. (J). (gr. 7-18). 23.95 (978-1-4222-3173-9(9)) Mason Crest.

Holden, Pam. I Like to Paint, 1 vol., Set. 2009. (Red Rocket Readers Ser.). (ENG., Illus.). 16p. (gr. -1-1). pap. (978-1-877435-97-3(X)) Flying Start Bks.

Hyde, Margaret, ed. Van Gogh for Kids, 1 vol. 2nd ed. 2005. (Great Art for Kids Ser.). (ENG., Illus.). 12p. (J). (gr. -1 — 1). bds. 8.95 (978-1-58980-279-7(9), Pelican Publishing) Arcadia Publishing.

Hyde, Margaret E., ed. Picasso for Kids, 1 vol. 2004. (Great Art for Kids Ser.). (ENG., Illus.). 12p. (J). 8.95 (978-1-58980-205-6(5), Pelican Publishing) Arcadia Publishing.

Jakopovich, Kathy. Paint on a Happy Face, Vol. 2. 2004. 68p. pap. 11.95 (978-1-57377-198-6(8), 0-1988-4-02516-0) Eas'l Pubns.

Jo Tuttle, Mary. Tuttles Touches. 2004. 60p. pap. 11.95 (978-1-57377-203-7(8), 0-1988-4-2526-9) Eas'l Pubns.

Klein, Carol Swartout. Painting for Peace in Ferguson. 2nd ed. 2015. (ENG.). 54p. (J). (gr. 2-3). 25.95 (978-0-9963901-0-1(3)); pap. 15.95 (978-0-9892079-9-7(4)) TreeHse. Publishing Group.

KRANZ, Linda. Let's Rock! 2017. (Illus.). 64p. (J). (gr. -1-12). pap. 12.95 (978-1-63076-294-0(6)) Muddy Boots Pr.

Kuiper, Kathleen, ed. The 100 Most Influential Painters & Sculptors of the Renaissance, 1 vol. 2010. (Britannica Guide to the World's Most Influential People Ser.). (ENG., Illus.). 376p. (YA). (gr. 10-10). lib. bdg. 56.59 (978-1-61530-004-4(X), deb5d486-8e60-40ab-9222-0c87fd73c880) Rosen Publishing Group, Inc., The.

Kutschbach, Doris. The Art Treasure Hunt: I Spy with My Little Eye. 2012. (ENG., Illus.). 48p. (J). (gr. -1-3). 14.95 (978-3-7913-7097-2(9)) Prestel Verlag GmbH & Co KG. DEU. Dist: Penguin Random Hse. LLC.

La Valette, Desiree, et al. Keith Haring: I Wish I Didn't Have to Sleep. 2014. (ENG., Illus.). 32p. (J). (gr. 3-7). pap. 10.99 (978-3-7913-7219-8(X)) Prestel Verlag GmbH & Co KG. DEU. Dist: Penguin Random Hse. LLC.

Lang, Annie J. Who Let the Kids Out. 2003. 48p. pap. 10.95 (978-1-57377-168-9(6)) Eas'l Pubns.

Lappe, S. M. Street Painting: A Guide for Young Artists. 2011. 36p. pap. 13.95 (978-1-60976-963-5(5), Strategic Bk. Publishing) Strategic Book Publishing & Rights Agency (SBPRA).

Las pinturas de Pepe: Individual Title-Six Packs. (Chiquilibros Ser.). (SPA.). (gr. k-1). 23.00 (978-0-7635-8608-9(0)) Rigby Education.

Let's Paint! (Early Intervention Levels Ser.). 23.10 (978-0-7362-0012-7(6)) CENGAGE Learning.

Levy, Janey. Renaissance Paintings: Using Perspective to Represent Three-Dimensional Objects, 1 vol. (Math for the REAL World Ser.). 32p. 2009. (ENG., Illus.). (gr. 5-6). pap. 10.00 (978-1-4042-5115-1(4), 4edb657e-f25d-4c96-94d1-fcb8fd7410a1) 2009. (gr. 4-5). 47.90 (978-1-60851-416-8(1), PowerKids Pr.) 2005. 47.50 (978-1-4042-5220-2(7), Rosen Classroom) 2004. (ENG., Illus.). (J). (gr. 5-6). lib. bdg. 28.93 (978-1-4042-2926-6(4), d74fba5b-a79f-4ac2-b2b6-0fe322b4823d, PowerKids Pr.) Rosen Publishing Group, Inc., The.

Make Your Own Art: Sets 1-2, 22 vols. Incl. Make Your Own Art: Set 2. 2010. lib. bdg. 151.35 (978-1-4488-1625-5(4), ab4eeb4f-5340-4fa7-af2c-a6391e8949de); Set 1. Drawing. 2008. lib. bdg. 181.62 (978-1-4358-2549-9(7), 3fce187b-c18a-47c1-b974-447e2b54b804); (J). (gr. 3-4). (Make Your Own Art Ser.). (ENG., Illus.). 32p. 2010. Set lib. bdg. 332.97 (978-1-4488-1626-2(2), a3f3628d-9f30-4b44-93b7-bf632de74ed6, PowerKids Pr.) Rosen Publishing Group, Inc., The.

McLean, Sandra. Monkey Business. 2004. (Illus.). 68p. pap. 10.95 (978-1-57377-187-0(2), 0-1988-4-02502-3) Eas'l Pubns.

McLewn, Sandra. Cuisine D'art. 2004. 60p. pap. 11.95 (978-1-57377-199-3(6), 0-1988-4-02518-4) Eas'l Pubns.

Medina, Sarah. Having Fun with Paint, 1 vol. 2007. (Fun Art Projects Ser.). (ENG., Illus.). 24p. (J). (gr. 2-2). lib. bdg. 28.93

(978-1-4042-3718-6(6), 40593bc8-e3d7-4339-8f5f-783b88f46c45, PowerKids Pr.) Rosen Publishing Group, Inc., The.

Meet the Artists, 6 vols., Pack. (Bookweb Ser.). 32p. (gr. 6-18). 34.00 *(978-0-7578-0905-7(7))* Rigby Education.

Micklethwait, Lucy. I Spy Colors in Art. 2007. (ENG., Illus.). 40p. (J). (gr. -1-3). 19.99 *(978-0-06-134837-2(6),* Greenwillow Bks.) HarperCollins Pubs.

Munro, Roxie. Masterpiece Mix. 32p. (J). (gr. -1-3). 2019. pap. 8.99 *(978-0-8234-4435-9(X))* 2017. (ENG., Illus.). 16.95 *(978-0-8234-3699-6(3))* Holiday Hse., Inc.

My Little Pony Paint n' Play. 2005. (J). spiral bd. *(978-1-59487-072-9(1))* Artist Studios, Ltd.

My Little Pony Paint n' Play with Sticker Rolls. 2005. (J). spiral bd. *(978-1-59487-143-6(4))* Artist Studios, Ltd.

Nardo, Don & Parks, Peggy J. Painting, 1 vol. 2012. (Eye on Art Ser.). (ENG., Illus.). 112p. (gr. 7-7). lib. bdg. 41.03 *(978-1-4205-0549-8(1),* 8729a141-a023-4396-bfa2-b6fe905a7aba, Lucent Pr.) Greenhaven Publishing LLC.

Newbold, Amy. If Da Vinci Painted a Dinosaur, 1 vol. Newbold, Greg, illus. 2018. (Reimagined Masterpiece Ser.: 0). (ENG.). 40p. (J). (gr. 1-5). 17.95 *(978-0-88448-667-1(2),* 884667) Tilbury Hse. Pubs.

Newlands, Anne. The Group of Seven & Tom Thomson: An Introduction. 2008. (ENG., Illus.). 64p. (gr. 5-18). pap. 14.95 *(978-1-895565-54-6(5),* abf3a372-a1bd-49ae-aaa3-774c8583e767) Firefly Bks., Ltd.

Noble, Marty. Color Your Own Great Paintings by Women Artists. 2006. (Dover Art Masterpieces to Color Ser.). (ENG., Illus.). 32p. (gr. 3-8). pap. 4.99 *(978-0-486-45108-4(9),* 451089) Dover Pubns., Inc.

Nudelman, Edward, ed. A Halloween Reader. 2004. (Illus.). 12p. 8.95 *(978-1-58980-260-5(8),* Pelican Publishing) Arcadia Publishing.

O'Dea, Rory & Benchmark Education Co. Staff. Opinions about Art - a Study of Paintings from the Romantic Era. 2014. (Text Connections Ser.). (J). (gr. 5). *(978-1-4900-1384-8(9))* Benchmark Education Co.

Paint (Jump Ser.). (Illus.). 36p. (J). (gr. 2-6). pap. *(978-1-882210-32-9(8))* Action Publishing, Inc.

Painting the Car: KinderConcepts Individual Title Six-Packs. (Kinderstarters Ser.). 8p. (gr. -1-1). 21.00 *(978-0-7635-8732-1(X))* Rigby Education.

Palomaki, Kurt. Floating Men & Pale Faces: The Paintings of Kurt Palomaki. 2003. (Illus.). 48p. (YA). per. 19.99 *(978-0-9645655-5-5(2))* BurnhillWolf.

Papel, Dibujos y Pinturas. (One Hundred One Things to Do Ser.).Tr. of Paper, Drawing & Painting. (SPA.). (J). (gr. 3-5). pap. 4.76 *(978-950-724-204-5(X))* Lumen ARG. Dist: Lectorum Pubns., Inc.

Pete Paints a Picture, 6 Packs. (Story Steps Ser.). (gr. k-2). 20.00 *(978-0-7635-9602-6(7))* Rigby Education.

Peters, Scott. Painting Shapes. 2011. (Early Connections Ser.). (J). *(978-1-61672-332-3(7))* Benchmark Education Co.

Powell, William F. Color Mixing Recipes for Portraits: More Than 500 Color Combinations for Skin, Eyes, Lips & Hair. 2006. (Color Mixing Recipes Ser.). (ENG., Illus.). 48p. 9.95 *(978-1-56010-990-7(4),* 1560109904, Walter Foster) Quarto Publishing Group USA.

Price, Jamie Mills. Christmastime: Between the Vines, Vol. 3. 2004. 84p. pap. 12.95 *(978-1-57377-195-5(3),* 0-1988-4-02510-8) Eas'l Pubns.

QEB Learn Art National Book Stores Edition: Painting. 2006. (J). per. *(978-1-59566-281-1(2))* QEB Publishing Inc.

QEB Let's Start! Art National Book Stores Edition: Painting. 2006. (J). per. *(978-1-59566-303-0(7))* QEB Publishing Inc.

Raczka, Bob. Artful Reading. 2007. (Bob Raczka's Art Adventures Ser.). (ENG., Illus.). 32p. (gr. -1-3). lib. bdg. 25.26 *(978-0-8225-6754-7(7),* Millbrook Pr.) Lerner Publishing Group.

Raczka, Robert. More Than Meets the Eye: Seeing Art with All Five Senses. 2003. (Bob Raczka's Art Adventures Ser.). (ENG., Illus.). 32p. (J). (gr. k-12). lib. bdg. 25.32 *(978-0-7613-2797-4(5),* 34aaf006-7026-4540-aaf4-c1ca727ff5c2, Millbrook Pr.) Lerner Publishing Group.

Rau, Dana Meachen. Painting Rocks. 2012. (How-To Library). (ENG.). 32p. (gr. 3-6). pap. 14.21 *(978-1-61080-653-4(0),* 202263); (Illus.). 32.07 *(978-1-61080-479-0(1),* 202089) Cherry Lake Publishing.

Rendall, Richard. Hand-Painted Porcelain Plates: Nineteenth Century to the Present, 1 vol. 2003. (ENG., Illus.). 240p. (gr. 10-13). 59.99 *(978-0-7643-1692-0(3),* 1814) Schiffer Publishing, Ltd.

Riggs, Kate. What Is Realism? 2016. (Art World Ser.). (ENG., Illus.). 24p. (J). (gr. 1-4). *(978-1-60818-628-0(8),* 20462, Creative Education) Creative Co., The.

—What Is Romanticism? 2016. (Art World Ser.). (ENG., Illus.). 24p. (J). (gr. 1-4). *(978-1-60818-629-7(6),* 20465, Creative Education) Creative Co., The.

Schwake, Susan. Art Lab for Kids: Express Yourself: 52 Creative Adventures to Find Your Voice Through Drawing, Painting, Mixed Media, & Sculpture, Volume 19. 2018. (Lab for Kids Ser.: 19). (ENG., Illus.). 144p. (J). (gr. -1-5). pap. 24.99 *(978-1-63159-592-9(X),* 305221, Quarry Bks.) Quarto Publishing Group USA.

Shirodkar, Suhag. Captured in Miniature. 2010. (ENG., Illus.). 56p. 16.95 *(978-0-944142-61-5(3))* Mapin Publishing Pvt. Ltd IND. Dist: National Bk. Network.

Singer, Agathe. Anywhere, Anytime Art: Gouache: An Artist's Guide to Painting with Gouache on the Go! 2018. (Anywhere, Anytime Art Ser.). (ENG., Illus.). 128p. pap. 16.95 *(978-1-63322-496-4(1),* 301343, Walter Foster Jr) Quarto Publishing Group USA.

Smith, Lucy. How to Draw Horses. Chapman, Chris et al, illus. rev. ed. 2006. (Kid Kits Ser.). 32p. (J). (gr. 4). pap. 13.99 *(978-1-58086-969-0(6))* EDC Publishing.

Smith, Thomasina. Fantastic Faces to Paint Yourself! Become a Pirate, a Ghoul, a Spotty Dog & More. 2016. (Illus.). 64p. (J). (gr. -1-12). 9.99 *(978-1-86147-470-4(9),* Armadillo) Anness Publishing GBR. Dist: National Bk. Network.

Spence, David. The Impressionists: Monet, Cezanne, Renoir, Degas. 2010. (ENG.). 128p. (J). (gr. 4-7). pap. 12.95 *(978-1-84696-217-2(X),* TickTock Books) Octopus Publishing Group GBR. Dist: Independent Pubs. Group.

—Monet. 2013. (Ticktock Essential Artists Ser.). (ENG.). 32p. (J). (gr. 4-7). 21.19 *(978-1-84696-973-7(5),* TickTock Books) Octopus Publishing Group GBR. Dist: Children's Plus, Inc.

—Rembrandt. 2013. (Ticktock Essential Artists Ser.). (ENG.). 32p. (J). (gr. 4-7). 21.19 *(978-1-84696-977-5(8),* TickTock Books) Octopus Publishing Group GBR. Dist: Children's Plus, Inc.

—Renoir. 2013. (Ticktock Essential Artists Ser.). (ENG.). 32p. (J). (gr. 4-7). 21.19 *(978-1-84696-972-0(7),* TickTock Books) Octopus Publishing Group GBR. Dist: Children's Plus, Inc.

Spence, David & Ticktock Media, Ltd. Staff. Michelangelo. 2013. (Ticktock Essential Artists Ser.). (ENG.). 32p. (J). (gr. 4-7). 21.19 *(978-1-84696-979-9(4),* TickTock Books) Octopus Publishing Group GBR. Dist: Children's Plus, Inc.

Strawberry Shortcake Paint n' Play with Sticker Rolls. 2005. (J). spiral bd. *(978-1-59487-146-7(9))* Artist Studios, Ltd.

Taylor, Diane C. The Renaissance Artists: With History Projects for Kids. 2018. (the Renaissance for Kids Ser.). (ENG., Illus.). 112p. (J). (gr. 5-10). 22.95 *(978-1-61930-686-8(7),* de1b17a4-a94f-4e47-9707-10401e3e77e3) Nomad Pr.

Teenage Mutant Ninja Turtles Paint Master Activity Books. 2004. (J). act. bk. ed. 2.99 *(978-0-7666-1302-7(X),* 15330); act. bk. ed. 2.99 *(978-0-7666-1301-0(1),* 15330) Modern Publishing.

Thomas, Danita & Thomas, John E. The Ultimate Book of Holiday Kid Concoctions: More Than 50 Wacky, Wild, & Crazy Concoctions for All Occasions. 2006. (Ultimate Book of Kid Concoctions Ser.). (Illus.). 80p. (J). (gr. 4-7). per. 14.99 *(978-0-8054-4445-2(9))* B&H Publishing Group.

—The Ultimate Book of Kid Concoctions. 2006. (Illus.). 80p. (J). (gr. 4-7). per. 14.99 *(978-0-8054-4443-8(2))* B&H Publishing Group.

Thomas, John E. & Thomas, Danita. The Ultimate Book of Kid Concoctions 2. 2006. (Illus.). 80p. (J). (gr. 4-7). per. 14.99 *(978-0-8054-4444-5(0))* B&H Publishing Group.

Top That Publishing Staff, ed. Drawing with Pastels. 2006. 64p. *(978-1-84510-615-7(6))* Top That! Publishing PLC.

—Glass Painting. 2004. (Creative Studios Ser.). (ENG., Illus.). 48p. (J). *(978-1-84510-248-7(7))* Top That! Publishing PLC.

Torres, Laura. Rocas Pintadas. 2004. (SPA & ENG.). 64p. (J). spiral bd. 17.95 *(978-968-5528-07-8(1))* Klutz Latino MEX. Dist: Independent Pubs. Group.

Toyne, Jessica. Dali, Vol. 7. 2015. (Great Artists Collection). (Illus.). 64p. (J). (gr. 7). lib. bdg. 23.95 *(978-1-4222-3258-3(1))* Mason Crest.

VanVoorst, Jenny Fretland. La Pintura. 2016. (El Estudio del Artista (Artist's Studio)).Tr. of Painting. (SPA., Illus.). 24p. (J). (gr. k-2). lib. bdg. 25.65 *(978-1-62031-325-1(1),* Bullfrog Bks.) Jump! Inc.

Watt, Fiona. 50 Things to Draw & Paint. (50 Things to Make & Do Ser.). (J). 2009. 104p. spiral bd. 9.99 *(978-0-7945-2463-0(X))* 2006. (Illus.). 50p. (gr. 1-4). 9.99 *(978-0-7945-1215-6(1))* EDC Publishing. (Usborne).

Wenzel, Angela. 13 Art Mysteries Children Should Know. 2011. (13 Children Should Know Ser.). (ENG., Illus.). 48p. (J). (gr. 3-7). 14.95 *(978-3-7913-7044-6(8))* Prestel Verlag GmbH & Co KG. DEU. Dist: Penguin Random Hse. LLC.

—13 Artists Children Should Know. 2009. (13 Children Should Know Ser.). (ENG., Illus.). 48p. (J). (gr. 3-7). 14.95 *(978-3-7913-4173-6(1))* Prestel Verlag GmbH & Co KG. DEU. Dist: Penguin Random Hse. LLC.

—13 Paintings Children Should Know. 2009. (13 Children Should Know Ser.). (ENG., Illus.). 48p. (J). (gr. 3-7). 14.95 *(978-3-7913-4323-5(8))* Prestel Verlag GmbH & Co KG. DEU. Dist: Penguin Random Hse. LLC.

Wilmes, Liz & Wilmes, Dick. Easel Art. Koeller, Carol, illus. 2004. 128p. (J). pap. 12.95 *(978-0-943452-25-8(2))* Building Blocks, LLC.

Wisner, Karen. Country Seasons, Vol. 3. 2004. 60p. pap. 11.95 *(978-1-57377-201-3(1),* 0-1988-4-2522-1) Eas'l Pubns.

Wood, Alix. Acrylics, 1 vol. 2018. (Make a Masterpiece Ser.). (ENG.). 32p. (J). (gr. 3-4). pap. 11.50 *(978-1-5382-3576-8(5),* f5390739-2ad7-462c-978b-4ff690fbddef); lib. bdg. 28.27 *(978-1-5382-3578-2(1),* 8aaf3319-ceff-4a76-9749-a176960d7f3f) Stevens, Gareth Publishing LLLP.

Zhang, Gui Jie. The Bamboo Forest: I Truly Love You, & God Loves You Too, 1 vol. 2009. 47p. pap. 24.95 *(978-1-60836-292-9(2))* America Star Bks.

PAINTING, ABSTRACT

see Art, Abstract

PAINTING—COLOR REPRODUCTION

see Prints

PAINTING, DUTCH

Nichols, Catherine. Vincent Van Gogh, 1 vol. 2005. (Primary Source Library of Famous Artists Ser.). (ENG., Illus.). 32p. (J). (gr. 3-4). lib. bdg. 27.60 *(978-1-4042-2766-8(0),* 3e3645d4-164e-485e-9aca-4e16e3764974, PowerKids Pr.) Rosen Publishing Group, Inc., The.

—Vincent van Gogh. 2009. (Primary Source Library of Famous Artists Ser.). 32p. (gr. 3-4). 42.50 *(978-1-60854-105-8(3),* PowerKids Pr.) Rosen Publishing Group, Inc., The.

Spence, David. Rembrandt. 2013. (Ticktock Essential Artists Ser.). (ENG.). 32p. (J). (gr. 4-7). 21.19 *(978-1-84696-977-5(8),* TickTock Books) Octopus Publishing Group GBR. Dist: Children's Plus, Inc.

Wood, Alix. Vincent Van Gogh, 1 vol. 2013. (Artists Through the Ages Ser.). (ENG., Illus.). 32p. (gr. 2-3). 29.93 *(978-1-61533-622-7(2),* cb601fd8-ed7e-42e5-b696-68547669498e); pap. 11.00 *(978-1-61533-631-9(1),* 122108d6-6d93-42d7-a5d9-7afc23e6b28c) Rosen Publishing Group, Inc., The. (Windmill Bks.).

PAINTING—FICTION

Aboff, Marcie. The Mystery of the Disappearing Painting. 2016. (Spring Forward Ser.). (J). (gr. 2). *(978-1-4900-9453-3(9))* Benchmark Education Co.

Adams, Jesse. Farmer Dillo Paints His Barn. Speer, Julie & Davis, Christopher Owen, illus. 2007. (J). (gr. -1-3). pap. 12.95 *(978-1-59166-808-4(5))* BJU Pr.

Agee, Jon. The Incredible Painting of Felix Clousseau. 2015. 32p. pap. 8.00 *(978-1-61003-620-7(4))* Center for the Collaborative Classroom.

Alphin, Elaine Marie. Simon Says. 2005. (ENG.). 264p. (YA). (gr. 9-12). pap. 14.95 *(978-0-15-204678-1(X),* 1194100, Clarion Bks.) HarperCollins Pubs.

Ardwin, Juanita. Remember When, 1 vol. 2009. 40p. pap. 19.95 *(978-1-4489-2008-2(6))* PublishAmerica, Inc.

Asch, Frank. Bread & Honey. 2015. lib. bdg. 18.40 *(978-0-606-36290-0(8))* Turtleback.

Austin, Rikey. Sandy Paints a Picture: Alice's Bear Shop. 2012. 28p. pap. *(978-1-78092-155-6(1))* MX Publishing, Ltd.

Bang, Molly. When Sophie's Feelings Are Really, Really Hurt. Bang, Molly, illus. 2015. (ENG., Illus.). 40p. (J). (gr. -1-3). 18.99 *(978-0-545-78831-1(5),* Blue Sky Pr., The) Scholastic, Inc.

Barnett, Mac. Oh No! Not Again! (or How I Built a Time Machine to Save History) (or at Least My History Grade) Santat, Dan, illus. 2012. (Oh No! Picture Book Ser.). (ENG.). 40p. (J). (gr. -1-3). 17.99 *(978-1-4231-4912-5(2))* Little, Brown Bks. for Young Readers.

Beaumont, Karen. I Ain't Gonna Paint No More! Catrow, David, illus. 2005. (ENG.). 32p. (J). (gr. -1-3). 17.99 *(978-0-15-202488-8(3),* 1192948, Clarion Bks.) HarperCollins Pubs.

—I Ain't Gonna Paint No More! Lap Board Book. Catrow, David, illus. 2012. (ENG.). 30p. (J). (gr. -1 — 1). bds. 12.99 *(978-0-547-87035-9(3),* 1504857, Clarion Bks.) HarperCollins Pubs.

Bell, Kristen & Hart, Benjamin. The World Needs More Purple Schools. Wiseman, Daniel, illus. 2022. (My Purple World Ser.). 40p. (J). (gr. -1-2). 18.99 *(978-0-593-43490-1(0));* (ENG.). lib. bdg. 21.99 *(978-0-593-43491-8(9))* Random Hse. Children's Bks. (Random Hse. Bks. for Young Readers).

Bledsoe, Michele & Bledsoe, Richard. The Secret Kingdom. 2013. 36p. 20.95 *(978-1-4787-0362-4(8))* Outskirts Pr., Inc.

Bond, Michael. Paddington's Prize Picture. Alley, R. W., illus. 2017. 29p. (J). *(978-1-5182-4206-9(5))* Harper & Row Ltd.

Brennan-Nelson, Denise & Brennan, Rosemarie. Willow. Moore, Cyd, illus. 2008. (ENG.). 32p. (J). (gr. 1-4). 16.95 *(978-1-58536-342-1(1),* 202132) Sleeping Bear Pr.

Bridges, Shirin Yim. The Umbrella Queen. 2008. (ENG., Illus.). 40p. (J). (gr. k-3). 17.99 *(978-0-06-075040-4(5),* Greenwillow Bks.) HarperCollins Pubs.

Bryant, Megan E. Glow. 2018. (ENG.). 272p. (YA). (gr. 8-12). pap. 9.99 *(978-0-8075-2965-2(6),* 807529656) Whitman, Albert & Co.

Buchholz, Quint. El Coleccionista de Momentos. 2nd ed. 2003. (Rosa y Manzana Ser.). (SPA., Illus.). 48p. (J). *(978-84-89804-16-6(8))* Lóguez Ediciones ESP. Dist: Lectorum Pubns., Inc.

Campoy, F. Isabel & Howell, Theresa. Maybe Something Beautiful: How Art Transformed a Neighborhood. López, Rafael, illus. 2016. (ENG.). 40p. (J). (gr. -1-3). 19.99 *(978-0-544-35769-3(8),* 1587128, Clarion Bks.) HarperCollins Pubs.

Capatti, Bérénice. Klimt & His Cat. Monaco, Octavia, illus. 2004. (ENG.). 40p. (J). 20.00 *(978-0-8028-5282-3(3))* Eerdmans, William B. Publishing Co.

Cardwell, Michelle. Seeing the World Through Different Eyes. 2009. 32p. pap. 12.99 *(978-1-4389-9776-6(0))* AuthorHouse.

Carle, Eric. The Artist Who Painted a Blue Horse. 2012. (CHI.). 24p. (J). (gr. -1-k). *(978-957-762-524-3(X))* Hsin Yi Pubns.

—The Artist Who Painted a Blue Horse. 2014. (JPN.). 25p. (J). *(978-4-03-348280-4(6))* Kaisei-Sha.

—The Artist Who Painted a Blue Horse. Carle, Eric, illus. (ENG., Illus.). (J). (gr. -1 — 1). 2013. 22p. bds. 8.99 *(978-0-399-16402-6(2))* 2011. 32p. 18.99 *(978-0-399-25713-1(6))* Penguin Young Readers Group.

Cohn, Diana. Mr Goethes Garden, 1 vol. Mirocha, Paul, illus. 2003. 32p. (J). 17.95 *(978-0-88010-521-7(6))* SteinerBooks, Inc.

Cotter, Charis. The Painting. 2017. (Illus.). 288p. (J). (gr. 4-7). 16.99 *(978-1-101-91887-6(X),* Tundra Bks.) Tundra Bks. CAN. Dist: Penguin Random Hse. LLC.

Coulton, Mia. Danny Paints a Picture. Coulton, Mia, photos by. 2004. (ENG., Illus.). pap. 5.35 *(978-0-9746475-5-5(1))* Maryruth Bks., Inc.

Crain, Kira. SEK Statton. 2009. (GER.). 136p. 29.95 *(978-1-4092-6127-8(1))* Lulu Pr., Inc.

Crow, Melinda Melton. Let's Paint the Garage!, 1 vol. Thompson, Chad, illus. 2012. (Wonder Wheels Ser.). (ENG.). 32p. (J). (gr. -1-1). pap. 6.25 *(978-1-4342-4238-9(2),* 120296); lib. bdg. 22.65 *(978-1-4342-4016-3(9),* 118397) Capstone. (Stone Arch Bks.).

Davis, Chasta. The Easter Bunny & His Famous Painted Eggs. 2011. 28p. pap. 24.95 *(978-1-4512-1649-3(1))* America Star Bks.

Dean, James & Dean, Kimberly. Pete the Cat: a Pet for Pete. Dean, James, illus. 2014. (My First I Can Read Ser.). (ENG., Illus.). 32p. (J). (gr. -1-3). pap. 5.99 *(978-0-06-230379-0(1),* HarperCollins) HarperCollins Pubs.

deRubertis, Barbara. Polly Porcupine's Painting Prize. Alley, R. W., illus. 2011. (Animal Antics A to Z Ser.). 32p. (J). pap. 45.32 *(978-0-7613-7662-0(3));* lib. bdg. 22.60 *(978-1-57565-337-2(0))* Astra Publishing Hse.

deRubertis, Barbara & DeRubertis, Barbara. Polly Porcupine's Painting Prizes. Alley, R. W., illus. 2012. (Animal Antics A to Z Ser.). 32p. (J). (gr. 2 — 1). cd-rom 7.95 *(978-1-57565-409-6(1))* Astra Publishing Hse.

DiLorenzo, Barbara. Quincy: The Chameleon Who Couldn't Blend In. 2018. (ENG., Illus.). 40p. (J). (gr. -1-3). 17.99 *(978-1-4998-0542-0(X))* Little Bee Books Inc.

Dolson, Carol Bland. Hattie & the Higgledy-Piggledy Hedge. Rabon, Elaine Hearn, illus. 2012. (ENG.). 32p. (J). 18.95 *(978-0-9827614-4-1(9),* 9780982761441) Miglior Pr.

Donaldson, Julia. The Magic Paintbrush. Stewart, Joel, illus. 2017. (ENG.). 32p. (J). (gr. -1-1). pap. 14.99 *(978-1-5098-3046-6(4),* 900326053, Macmillan Children's Bks.) Pan Macmillan GBR. Dist: Macmillan.

Falwell, Cathryn. Butterflies for Kiri. 2003. (ENG., Illus.). 32p. (J). *(978-1-58430-100-4(7))* Lee & Low Bks., Inc.

Faruqi, Saadia. Yasmin the Painter. Aly, Hatem, illus. 2018. (Yasmin Ser.). (ENG.). 32p. (J). (gr. k-2). 22.65 *(978-1-5158-2728-3(3),* 137932, Picture Window Bks.) Capstone.

Flavin, Teresa. The Crimson Shard. (ENG.). (J). (gr. 4-7). 2015. 288p. pap. 6.99 *(978-0-7636-7172-3(X))* 2012. (Illus.). 256p. 15.99 *(978-0-7636-6093-2(0))* Candlewick Pr. (Templar).

Flores, Carolyn Dee. Amazing Watercolor Fish, the / el Asombroso Pez Acuarela. Flores, Carolyn Dee, illus. 2018. (ENG & SPA., Illus.). 32p. (J). (gr. -1-2). 17.95 *(978-1-55885-873-2(3),* Piñata Books) Arte Publico Pr.

Fortune, Tracy. Kaila's Garden. 2009. 32p. pap. 14.98 *(978-0-557-02254-0(1))* Lulu Pr., Inc.

Frueh, Stacy. Jonah's Weird, but Totally Cool Field Tr. 2005. 50p. pap. 16.95 *(978-1-4137-9818-0(7))* PublishAmerica, Inc.

Fulton-Vengco, Aletha. Felicidad's Sidewalk Art. 2009. 36p. 14.80 *(978-0-578-00890-5(4))* Vengco, Aletha Fulton.

Gerstein, Mordicai. The First Drawing. 2013. (ENG., Illus.). 40p. (J). (gr. -1-3). 18.99 *(978-0-316-20478-1(1))* Little, Brown Bks. for Young Readers.

Golden Books. Snow Wonder! (Frosty the Snowman) Golden Books, illus. 2013. (ENG., Illus.). 128p. (J). (gr. -1-2). pap. 7.99 *(978-0-385-37179-7(9),* Golden Bks.) Random Hse. Children's Bks.

Graves, Sue. Oh, George! Collins, Ross, illus. 2005. (Reading Corner Ser.). 24p. (J). (gr. k-3). lib. bdg. 22.80 *(978-1-59771-000-8(8))* Sea-To-Sea Pubns.

Gutiérrez, Elisa. Picturescape. rev. ed. 2007. (ENG., Illus.). 40p. (J). (gr. -1-3). pap. 9.95 *(978-1-894965-65-1(5))* Simply Read Bks. CAN. Dist: Ingram Publisher Services.

Hahn, Blair. My Purple Toes. Nation, Tate, illus. 2010. 24p. (J). 10.99 *(978-0-9844556-4-5(7))* My Purple Toes, LLC.

Hardy, Sarah Frances. Paint Me! Hardy, Sarah Frances, illus. 2014. (ENG., Illus.). 32p. (J). (-k). 14.95 *(978-1-62873-813-1(8),* Sky Pony Pr.) Skyhorse Publishing Co., Inc.

Harris, Patricia. The Car of Many Colors, 1 vol. 2017. (Colorful Cars Ser.). (ENG.). 24p. (gr. 1-1). pap. 9.25 *(978-1-5383-2087-7(8),* 47d4dd1a-6377-4001-9c8f-f9af1c137d72, PowerKids Pr.) Rosen Publishing Group, Inc., The.

Harrison, Penny & Harrison, Penny. The Art Garden: Sowing the Seeds of Creativity. Pratley, Penelope, illus. 2018. (ENG.). 32p. (J). (gr. k-2). 17.99 *(978-1-925335-59-0(3),* 317691, EK Bks.) Exisle Publishing Pty Ltd. AUS. Dist: Hachette UK Distribution.

Hewitt, Christine. A Mystical Journey. 2009. 80p. pap. 12.45 *(978-0-557-06314-7(0))* Lulu Pr., Inc.

Hicer, Nancy. Rosa's Painting, 1 vol. 2015. (Rosen REAL Readers: STEM & STEAM Collection). (ENG.). 8p. (gr. k-1). pap. 5.46 *(978-1-4994-9608-6(7),* f8cfed05-442c-4c6c-b4f1-715f15887d30, Rosen Classroom) Rosen Publishing Group, Inc., The.

Hieber, Leanna Renee. Darker Still. 2011. (Magic Most Foul Ser.: 1). (ENG.). 336p. (YA). (gr. 7-12). pap. 8.99 *(978-1-4022-6052-0(0))* Sourcebooks, Inc.

Hoffman, Peter. A Ferret in a Garret. Olson, Cindy, illus. 2008. 36p. (J). 24.99 *(978-0-9790247-6-4(5))* Artpacks.

Holden, Pam. Animal Art, 1 vol. Storey, Jim, illus. 2009. (Red Rocket Readers Ser.). (ENG.). 16p. (gr. 1-1). pap. *(978-1-877419-73-7(7),* Red Rocket Readers) Flying Start Bks.

I Love to Paint. 2003. (Illus.). (J). per. *(978-1-57657-961-9(1))* Paradise Pr., Inc.

Johnson, Angela. Daddy Calls Me Man. Mitchell, Rhonda, illus. 2014. 32p. pap. 7.00 *(978-1-61003-309-1(4))* Center for the Collaborative Classroom.

Johnson, D. B. Magritte's Marvelous Hat. Johnson, D. B., illus. 2012. (ENG., Illus.). 32p. (J). (gr. -1-3). 17.99 *(978-0-547-55864-6(3),* 1453619, Clarion Bks.) HarperCollins Pubs.

Kalar, Bonnie. Ann Paints & Plays. Spreen, Kathe, illus. Date not set. 12p. (J). (gr. -1-2). pap. *(978-1-891619-40-3(3))* Corona Pr.

King, Kirsty. My New Friends. 2005. 52p. pap. *(978-1-84401-576-4(9))* Athena Pr.

Kravetz, Nathan. A Horse of Another Color. 2011. 68p. (gr. 4-6). pap. 10.95 *(978-1-4620-0591-8(8))* iUniverse, Inc.

Kuenzler, Lou. Not yet Zebra. Woolf, Julia, illus. 2018. (ENG.). 32p. (J). (gr. -1-1). 16.95 *(978-0-571-34288-4(4),* Faber & Faber Children's Bks.) Faber & Faber, Inc.

Kyle, Tracey. A Paintbrush for Paco. Heinsz, Joshua, illus. 2018. (ENG.). 40p. (J). (gr. -1-3). 17.99 *(978-1-4998-0544-4(6))* Little Bee Books Inc.

Ladybird. The Magic Paintbrush Activity Book - Ladybird Readers Level 2. 2019. (Ladybird Readers Ser.). (ENG., Illus.). 16p. (J). (gr. k-2). pap. 5.99 *(978-0-241-35823-8(X))* Penguin Random Hse. AUS. Dist: Independent Pubs. Group.

Lawson, JonArno. Uncle Holland, 1 vol. Nelson, Natalie, illus. 2017. (ENG.). 32p. (J). (gr. k-2). 17.95 *(978-1-55498-929-4(9))* Groundwood Bks. CAN. Dist: Publishers Group West (PGW).

Lodding, Linda Ravin. Painting Pepette. Fletcher, Claire, illus. 2016. (ENG.). 40p. (J). (gr. -1-3). 17.99 *(978-1-4998-0136-1(X))* Little Bee Books Inc.

Look, Lenore. Brush of the Gods. So, Meilo, illus. 2013. 40p. (J). (gr. -1-3). 17.99 *(978-0-375-87001-9(6),* Schwartz & Wade Bks.) Random Hse. Children's Bks.

Lukacs, Krisztian. Bud & Barnie: Let's Paint! 2011. 50p. pap. 19.99 *(978-1-4475-7901-4(1))* Lulu Pr., Inc.

Markun, Patricia M. The Little Painter of Sabana Grande. Casilla, Robert, illus. 2014. (ENG.). 32p. (J). (gr. -1-3). 13.99 *(978-1-4814-4458-3(1),* Simon & Schuster Bks. For Young Readers) Simon & Schuster Bks. For Young Readers.

Mayhew, James & McQuillan, Mary. Katie & the British Artists. 2015. (Katie Ser.). (ENG., Illus.). 32p. (J). (gr. -1-k). 9.99 *(978-1-4083-3190-3(X))* Hodder & Stoughton GBR. Dist: Hachette Bk. Group.

—Katie & the Waterlily Pond. 2015. (Katie Ser.). (ENG., Illus.). 32p. (J). (gr. -1-k). pap. 10.99 *(978-1-4083-3245-0(0))* Hodder & Stoughton GBR. Dist: Hachette Bk. Group.

McPhail, David. Big Brown Bear/el Gran Oso Pardo: Bilingual English-Spanish. McPhail, David, illus. 2007. (Big Brown Bear Ser.). (ENG., Illus.). 28p. (J). (gr. -1-3). pap. 5.99 *(978-0-15-205970-5(9),* 1197929, Clarion Bks.) HarperCollins Pubs.

Meadows, Daisy. Violet the Painting Fairy. 2015. (Illus.). 65p. (J). *(978-0-545-72413-5(9))* Scholastic, Inc.

Merberg, Julie & Bober, Suzanne. Dreaming with Rousseau. 2007. (Mini Masters Ser.: 10). (ENG., Illus.). 22p. (J). (gr. -1 — 1). bds. 6.99 *(978-0-8118-5712-3(3))* Chronicle Bks. LLC.
—Painting with Picasso. 2006. (Mini Masters Ser.: 6). (ENG., Illus.). 22p. (J). (gr. -1 — 1). bds. 7.99 *(978-0-8118-5505-1(8))* Chronicle Bks. LLC.
Montserrat, Gisbert. Dali, pintame un sueño. 2004. (SPA., Illus.). (J). 19.99 *(978-84-8488-127-8(X))* Serres, Ediciones, S. L. ESP. Dist: Lectorum Pubns., Inc.
Mullarkey, Lisa. Freckles the Pig. Franco, Paula, illus. 2017. (Farmyard Friends Ser.). (ENG.). 32p. (J). (gr. -1-3). lib. bdg. 32.79 *(978-1-5321-4044-0(4),* 25516, Calico Chapter Bks) Magic Wagon.
Nez, John, illus. The Dragon Painter. 2006. (First Reading Level 4 Ser.). 48p. (J). (gr. 1-4). 8.99 *(978-0-7945-1275-0(5),* Usborne) EDC Publishing.
Ortiz, Raquel M. & Ventura, Gabriela Baeza. Sofi & the Magic, Musical Mural. Dominguez, Maria, illus. 2015. (SPA & ENG.). (J). 17.95 *(978-1-55885-803-9(2),* Piñata Books) Arte Publico Pr.
Perkins, Mitali. Rickshaw Girl. Hogan, Jamie, illus. 2007. 96p. (J). (gr. 2-5). 14.95 *(978-1-58089-308-4(2))* Charlesbridge Publishing, Inc.
Peschke, Marci. Art Queen. Mourning, Tuesday, illus. 2018. (Kylie Jean Ser.). (ENG.). 112p. (J). (gr. 1-3). lib. bdg. 22.65 *(978-1-5158-2927-0(8),* 138470, Picture Window Bks.) Capstone.
Pinkwater, Daniel M. Bear's Picture. Johnson, D. B., illus. 2008. (ENG.). 32p. (J). (gr. -1-3). 16.00 *(978-0-618-75923-1(9),* 543218, Clarion Bks.) HarperCollins Pubs.
Plummer, David & Archambault, John. I Paint a Rainbow. Hollander, Sarah, illus. 2007. (J). *(978-1-58669-228-5(3)); (978-1-58669-227-8(5))* Childcraft Education Corp.
Poulsen, David A. The Prisoners & the Paintings. 5th ed. 2008. (Salt & Pepper Chronicles: No. 5). (ENG.). 176p. (J). (gr. 2-7). *(978-1-55470-015-8(9))* Me to We.
Publications International Ltd. Staff. Play A Sound Video Fifi's Painting Party. 2008. 24p. 19.98 *(978-1-4127-9435-0(8),* PIL Kids) Publications International, Ltd.
Randolph, Joanne. A Rock for Mom, 1 vol. 2015. (Rosen REAL Readers: STEM & STEAM Collection). (ENG.). 8p. (gr. k-1). pap. 5.46 *(978-1-4994-9533-1(1),* facb81a8-0a35-4b15-b4a4-42ba62ab3a15, Rosen Classroom) Rosen Publishing Group, Inc., The.
Rey, H. A. Curious George: Time for School Lift-The-Flaps (CGTV) 2011. (Curious George Ser.). (ENG., Illus.). 16p. (J). (gr. -1-3). 6.99 *(978-0-547-42230-5(X),* 1431226, Clarion Bks.) HarperCollins Pubs.
Reynolds, Peter H. Sky Color. Reynolds, Peter H., illus. 2012. (Creatrilogy Ser.). (ENG., Illus.). 32p. (J). (gr. k-4). 15.00 *(978-0-7636-2345-6(8))* Candlewick Pr.
Rigby Education Staff. Tom Sawyer: Jumbled Tumble. (gr. k-2). 26.00 *(978-0-7635-2424-1(7))* Rigby Education.
Robins, Eleanor. Art Show Mystery, 1 vol. unabr. ed. 2011. (Carter High Mysteries Ser.). (ENG.). 48p. (YA). (gr. 9-12). 9.75 *(978-1-61651-560-7(0))* Saddleback Educational Publishing, Inc.
Rørvik, Bjø F. The Little Paintbrush. Hansen, Thore, illus. 2014. (ENG.). 32p. (J). (gr. -1-k). 12.95 *(978-1-62087-996-2(4),* 620996, Sky Pony Pr.) Skyhorse Publishing Co., Inc.
Ross, Donald. The Scribble Squad in the Weird Weird West. 2016. (ENG., Illus.). 256p. (J). 13.99 *(978-1-4494-6921-4(3))* Andrews McMeel Publishing.
Ross, Jill. What's the Matter, Mr. Ticklebritches? Pruitt, Gwendolyn, illus. 2010. (ENG.). 70p. (J). (gr. 3-7). pap. 9.95 *(978-1-59825-948-3(2))* Shenanigans Series.
Rouillard, Wendy W. Barnaby's Tree House. 2005. (Illus.). 30p. (J). *(978-0-9651070-4-4(3))* Barnaby & Co.
Rudolph, Tammy. Lucy's Mysterious Paint Brush. 2005. 17.00 *(978-0-8059-9765-1(2))* Dorrance Publishing Co., Inc.
Salter-Mathieson, Nigel C. S. Little Chief Mischief: From Tales of the Menehune. Gruen, Chuck, illus. 2011. 44p. pap. 35.95 *(978-1-258-10135-0(1))* Literary Licensing, LLC.
Schwartz, Amy. Begin at the Beginning: A Little Artist Learns about Life. Schwartz, Amy, illus. 2005. (Illus.). 40p. (J). (gr. -1-2). lib. bdg. 16.89 *(978-0-06-000112-4(7))* HarperCollins Pubs.
Siminovich, Lorena. Alex & Lulu: Two of a Kind. Siminovich, Lorena, illus. 2009. (ENG., Illus.). 32p. (J). (gr. -1-3). 14.99 *(978-0-7636-4423-9(4),* Templar) Candlewick Pr.
Simko, Joe. The Sweet Rot, Book 2: Raiders of the Lost Art, 1 vol. 2011. (ENG., Illus.). 80p. (YA). (gr. 8-12). 19.99 *(978-0-7643-3828-1(5),* 4192, Schiffer Publishing Ltd) Schiffer Publishing, Ltd.
Spencer, Hannah. With All Best Wishes, Mrs Butterbean. 2008. 28p. pap. 13.50 *(978-1-60693-138-7(5),* Eloquent Bks.) Strategic Book Publishing & Rights Agency (SBPRA).
St. Aubin, Anne. Drafus the Daring Dragon. 2008. 24p. pap. 16.49 *(978-1-4343-8875-9(1))* AuthorHouse.
Strauss, Victoria. Color Song, 0 vols. 2014. (Passion Blue Novel Ser.: 2). (ENG.). 344p. (YA). (gr. 7-9). pap. 9.99 *(978-1-4778-2504-4(5),* 9781477825044, Skyscape) Amazon Publishing.
Sweet, Melissa. Carmine: A Little More Red. 2008. (ENG., Illus.). 40p. (J). (gr. -1-3). pap. 6.95 *(978-0-618-99717-6(2),* 1028081, Clarion Bks.) HarperCollins Pubs.
Tim's Paintings: Individual Title-Six Packs. (Chiquilibros Ser.). (gr. k-1). 23.00 *(978-0-7635-0430-4(0))* Rigby Education.
Tom Sawyer: 6 Small Books. (gr. k-2). 23.00 *(978-0-7635-8507-5(6))* Rigby Education.
Town, Vicky. Mayhem in the Museum. 2013. 74p. pap. 9.99 *(978-1-61720-974-1(0))* Wilder Pubns., Corp.
Twohy, Mike. Mouse & Hippo. Twohy, Mike, illus. 2017. (ENG., Illus.). 32p. (J). (gr. -1-3). 17.99 *(978-1-4814-5124-6(3),* Simon & Schuster/Paula Wiseman Bks.) Simon & Schuster/Paula Wiseman Bks.
Wells, Rosemary. Ruby's Rainbow. 2012. (Max & Ruby Ser.). lib. bdg. 13.55 *(978-0-606-26091-6(9))* Turtleback.
West, Jacqueline. The Shadows. l.t. ed. 2010. (Books of Elsewhere Ser.: Vol. 1). (ENG.). 268p. 23.99 *(978-1-4104-3139-4(8))* Thorndike Pr.
—The Shadows. 2011. (Books of Elsewhere Ser.: 1). lib. bdg. 17.20 *(978-0-606-23070-4(X))* Turtleback.
—The Shadows: The Books of Elsewhere: Volume 1. 2011. (Books of Elsewhere Ser.: 1). (ENG.). 272p. (J). (gr. 5-7). 8.99 *(978-0-14-241872-7(2),* Puffin Books) Penguin Young Readers Group.
Whipp, Jo. Otis & Baby Jean. Whipp, Katie, illus. 2012. 26p. 24.95 *(978-1-4626-5049-1(X))* America Star Bks.
Wiesner, David. Art & Max. 2011. (JPN.). 40p. (J). (gr. k-3). *(978-4-7764-0448-4(6))* BL Publishing Co., Ltd.
—Art & Max. 2011. (CHI.). 40p. (J). (gr. k-3). *(978-986-189-233-7(8))* Grimm Cultural Ent., Co., Ltd.
—Art & Max. 2010. (ENG., Illus.). 40p. (J). (gr. -1-3). 17.99 *(978-0-618-75663-6(9),* 100534, Clarion Bks.) HarperCollins Pubs.
—Art & Max. 2012. (CHI.). 37p. (J). *(978-7-5434-9586-9(4))* Hebei Jiaoyu Chubanshe.
Williams, John Joseph. The Frightened Garden. 2013. 98p. (J). pap. *(978-1-78299-167-0(0))* FeedARead.com.
Wilson, Martha. Latin Primer II - Student. 3rd ed. 2003. (ENG & LAT.). 138p. (gr. 3-6). spiral bd. 17.00 *(978-1-885767-52-3(8))* Canon Pr.
Zibart, Rosemary. I Have a Grandma Who ... Herzlich, Valori, illus. 2014. (J). *(978-1-929115-25-9(3))* Azro Pr., Inc.

PAINTING, FINGER

see Finger Painting

PAINTING—HISTORY

Fandel, Jennifer. Pablo Picasso. 2005. (Xtraordinary Artists Ser.). (Illus.). 48p. (J). (gr. 5-9). lib. bdg. 21.95 *(978-1-58341-331-9(6),* Creative Education) Creative Co., The.
Forte, Virginia. The History of Western Painting, 1 vol. 2015. (Britannica Guide to the Visual & Performing Arts Ser.). (ENG., Illus.). 280p. (J). (gr. 9-10). 47.59 *(978-1-68048-070-2(7),* 8cd1db3a-eb28-4093-9fb9-d10971e6d6b6, Britannica Educational Publishing) Rosen Publishing Group, Inc., The.
Harris, Nathaniel. Paul Cézanne. 2003. (Artists in Their Time Ser.). (ENG., Illus.). 48p. (J). 24.00 *(978-0-531-12242-6(5),* Watts, Franklin) Scholastic Library Publishing.
Heine, Florian. 13 Painters Children Should Know. 2012. (13 Children Should Know Ser.). (ENG., Illus.). 48p. (J). (gr. 3-7). 14.95 *(978-3-7913-7086-6(3))* Prestel Verlag GmbH & Co KG. DEU. Dist: Penguin Random Hse. LLC.
Lyons, Deborah. Edward Hopper: Summer at the Seaside. 2003. (Adventures in Art Ser.). (Illus.). 30p. (gr. 5-18). 14.95 *(978-3-7913-2737-2(2))* Prestel Publishing.
Manning, Mick. The Story of Paintings: A History of Art for Children. Granström, Brita, illus. 2017. (ENG.). 88p. (J). (gr. 3-9). 17.99 *(978-1-4549-2702-0(X))* Sterling Publishing Co., Inc.
Nichols, Catherine. Claude Monet, 1 vol. 2005. (Primary Source Library of Famous Artists Ser.). (ENG., Illus.). 32p. (J). (gr. 3-4). lib. bdg. 27.60 *(978-1-4042-2761-3(X),* d98df970-1792-480c-87b1-27f64d46cc85, PowerKids Pr.) Rosen Publishing Group, Inc., The.
—Pierre-Auguste Renoir, 1 vol. 2005. (Primary Source Library of Famous Artists Ser.). (ENG., Illus.). 32p. (J). (gr. 3-4). lib. bdg. 27.60 *(978-1-4042-2765-1(2),* cc309da8-8b19-4fb3-b670-da92beba1bb0, PowerKids Pr.) Rosen Publishing Group, Inc., The.
Sherrow, Victoria & Buonarroti, Michelangelo. Claude Monet, 1 vol. 2005. (Great Artists Ser.). (ENG., Illus.). 40p. (gr. 4-6). 28.36 *(978-1-59270-009-7(8),* 55f6e21e-a7fe-4df8-8e36-df4da5d8aecc) Cavendish Square Publishing LLC.
Thurlby, Paul. The Great Art Activity Book. 2019. (National Gallery Paul Thurlby Ser.). (ENG., Illus.). 64p. (J). (gr. 1-3). pap. 15.99 *(978-1-4449-3427-4(9))* Hachette Children's Group GBR. Dist: Hachette Bk. Group.
Weller, Alan & Dover Publications Inc. Staff. Spot the Differences: Art Masterpieces, Bk. 2. 2010. (Dover Kids Activity Bks.: Bk. 2). (ENG., Illus.). 64p. (J). (gr. 3-5). 10.99 *(978-0-486-47300-0(7),* 473007) Dover Pubns., Inc.
Wheatley, Abigail. The Story of Painting. Riley, Janis, ed. Mayer, Uwe & McNee, Ian, illus. 2007. (Story of Painting Ser.). 96p. (J). (gr. 4-7). pap. 10.99 *(978-0-7945-1678-9(5),* Usborne) EDC Publishing.

PAINTING, ITALIAN

Spence, David & Ticktock Media, Ltd. Staff. Michelangelo. 2013. (Ticktock Essential Artists Ser.). (ENG.). 32p. (J). (gr. 4-7). 21.19 *(978-1-84696-979-9(4),* TickTock Books) Octopus Publishing Group GBR. Dist: Children's Plus, Inc.
Venezia, Mike. Getting to Know the World's Greatest Artists - Titian. Venezia, Mike, illus. 2003. (Getting to Know the World's Greatest Artists Ser.). (ENG., Illus.). 32p. (J). (gr. 3-4). pap. 6.95 *(978-0-516-26975-7(5),* Children's Pr.) Scholastic Library Publishing.
—Titian. Venezia, Mike, illus. 2003. (Getting to Know World Artists Ser.). (ENG., Illus.). 32p. (J). 28.00 *(978-0-516-22575-3(8),* Children's Pr.) Scholastic Library Publishing.

PAINTING, RELIGIOUS

see Christian Art and Symbolism

PAINTING—TECHNIQUE

Boase, Petra. Show Me How I Can Paint: Arty Activities for Kids Shown Step by Step. 2016. (Illus.). 48p. (J). (gr. -1-12). 7.99 *(978-1-86147-463-6(6),* Armadillo) Anness Publishing GBR. Dist: National Bk. Network.
Bolte, Mari. Acrylics, 1 vol. Ice, Dawn, illus. 2013. (Paint It Ser.). (ENG.). 32p. (J). (gr. 3-9). 28.65 *(978-1-4765-3109-0(9),* 123091) Capstone.
—Paint It: The Art of Acrylics, Oils, Pastels, & Watercolors, 1 vol. Ice, Dawn, illus. 2013. (Craft It Yourself Ser.). (ENG.). 144p. (J). (gr. 3-9). pap., pap., pap. 14.95 *(978-1-62370-009-6(4),* 123602, Capstone Young Readers) Capstone.
—Watercolors, 1 vol. Ice, Dawn, illus. 2013. (Paint It Ser.). (ENG.). 32p. (J). (gr. 3-9). 28.65 *(978-1-4765-3108-3(0),* 123090, Capstone Pr.) Capstone.
Calver, Paul. Painting, 1 vol. 2014. (Mini Artist Ser.). (ENG., Illus.). 24p. (J). (gr. 1-2). lib. bdg. 26.27 *(978-1-4777-9119-6(1),* 2d3af529-d34f-48a1-974c-1ba0552b3a71, Windmill Bks.) Rosen Publishing Group, Inc., The.
Davidson, Susanna. The Snow Queen Magic Painting. 2017. (Magic Painting Bks.). (ENG.). 16p. pap. 9.99 *(978-0-7945-4139-2(9),* Usborne) EDC Publishing.
Editors of Klutz. Glitter Face Painting. 2016. (ENG.). 54p. (J). (gr. 3-7). 26.99 *(978-1-338-03751-7(X))* Klutz.
Ewasiuk, Sandee. Painting Skills Lab. 2018. (Art Skills Lab Ser.). (Illus.). 32p. (J). (gr. 4-4). *(978-0-7787-5223-3(2))* Crabtree Publishing Co.
Franco, Nick. Are You Ready to Paint? 2010. 17p. 19.25 *(978-0-615-24474-7(2))* Franco, Nick Art.
Hanson, Anders. Cool Painting: The Art of Creativity for Kids, 1 vol. 2008. (Cool Art Ser.). (ENG.). 32p. (J). (gr. 3-6). 34.21 *(978-1-60453-143-5(6),* 4576, Checkerboard Library) ABDO Publishing Co.
Hardy, Emma. My First Rock Painting Book: 35 Fun Craft Projects for Children Aged 7+ 2018. (ENG., Illus.). 112p. (J). pap. 14.95 *(978-1-78249-609-0(2),* 1782496092, Cico Kidz) Ryland Peters & Small GBR. Dist: WIPRO.
Hendler, Muncie. Dover Masterworks: Color Your Own Modern Art Paintings. 2013. (Adult Coloring Books: Art & Design Ser.). (ENG.). 64p. (gr. 3). pap. 6.99 *(978-0-486-78024-5(4),* 780244) Dover Pubns., Inc.
Henry, Sally. Painting, 1 vol. 2008. (Make Your Own Art Ser.). (ENG., Illus.). 32p. (J). (gr. 3-4). lib. bdg. 30.27 *(978-1-4358-2511-6(X),* 7296eaa9-fbdb-41c1-bcde-f7eaeeee7b12, PowerKids Pr.) Rosen Publishing Group, Inc., The.
Hewett, Angela, illus. Bumper Junior Art: Colour by Numbers. 2013. (ENG.). 64p. (J). (gr. -1-3). pap. 8.50 *(978-1-84135-998-4(X))* Parkwest Pubns., Inc.
Hicks, Angie, illus. Alien. 2012. (ENG.). 24p. (J). 4.95 *(978-1-84135-585-6(2))* Award Pubns. Ltd. GBR. Dist: Parkwest Pubns., Inc.
—Butterfly. 2012. (ENG.). 24p. (J). 4.95 *(978-1-84135-582-5(8))* Award Pubns. Ltd. GBR. Dist: Parkwest Pubns., Inc.
—Fish. 2012. (ENG.). 24p. (J). 4.95 *(978-1-84135-584-9(4))* Award Pubns. Ltd. GBR. Dist: Parkwest Pubns., Inc.
—Junior Art Colour By Numbers: Lion. 2012. (ENG.). 16p. (J). 3.25 *(978-1-84135-857-4(6))* Award Pubns. Ltd. GBR. Dist: Parkwest Pubns., Inc.
—Pirate. 2012. (ENG.). 24p. (J). 4.95 *(978-1-84135-583-2(6))* Award Pubns. Ltd. GBR. Dist: Parkwest Pubns., Inc.
Iossa, Federica, illus. Dinosaurs Magic Painting Book. 2018. (Magic Painting Bks.). (ENG.). 16p. pap. 9.99 *(978-0-7945-4126-2(7),* Usborne) EDC Publishing.
Learn to Paint & Draw. 2009. (Reference Ser.). 128p. *(978-1-4075-2106-0(3))* Parragon, Inc.
Lundie, Isobel. Pirates. 2013. (Start with Art Ser.). (ENG., Illus.). 32p. (J). *(978-1-911242-67-3(9))* Book Hse.
McGuinness, Denis E., ed. Painting: Materials, Technique, Styles, & Practice, 1 vol. 2016. (Britannica's Practical Guide to the Arts Ser.). (ENG., Illus.). 128p. (J). (gr. 10-10). lib. bdg. 37.82 *(978-1-68048-373-4(0),* 9900450f-041a-4bc4-ae8e-fbfcc4e793a8) Rosen Publishing Group, Inc., The.
Mehtani, Henu. Handprint Animals. 2017. (Handprint Art Ser.). (Illus.). 32p. (J). (gr. 1-2). *(978-0-7787-3108-5(1))* Crabtree Publishing Co.
—Handprint Garden. 2017. (Handprint Art Ser.). (Illus.). 32p. (J). (gr. 1-2). *(978-0-7787-3110-8(3))* Crabtree Publishing Co.
—Handprint People. 2017. (Handprint Art Ser.). (Illus.). 32p. (J). (gr. 1-2). *(978-0-7787-3111-5(1))* Crabtree Publishing Co.
—Handprint Transportation. 2017. (Handprint Art Ser.). (Illus.). 32p. (J). (gr. 1-2). *(978-0-7787-3109-2(X))* Crabtree Publishing Co.
Muller, Brunhild. Painting with Children: Colour & Child Development, 30 vols. Maclean, Donald, tr. 5th rev. ed. 2008. (Illus.). 48p. pap. 15.95 *(978-0-86315-366-2(6))* Floris Bks. GBR. Dist: Consortium Bk. Sales & Distribution.
Nelson, Robin. De la cera a la crayon (from Wax to Crayon) 2006. (De Principio a Fin (Start to Finish) Ser.). (Illus.). 24p. (J). (gr. 4-7). per. 5.95 *(978-0-8225-6635-9(4),* Ediciones Lerner) Lerner Publishing Group.
—De la Cera Al Crayon. Translations.com Staff, tr. from ENG. 2006. (De Principio a Fin (Start to Finish) Ser.).Tr. of From Wax to Crayon. (SPA., Illus.). 24p. (gr. 3-5). lib. bdg. 19.93 *(978-0-8225-6493-5(9),* Ediciones Lerner) Lerner Publishing Group.
Noble, Marty. Dover Masterworks: Color Your Own Famous American Paintings. 2013. (Adult Coloring Books: Art & Design Ser.). (ENG.). 64p. (gr. 3). pap. 6.99 *(978-0-486-77942-3(4),* 779424) Dover Pubns., Inc.
—Dover Masterworks: Color Your Own Impressionist Paintings. 2013. (Adult Coloring Ser.). (ENG.). 64p. (gr. 3). pap. 5.99 *(978-0-486-78025-2(2))* Dover Pubns., Inc.
—Dover Masterworks: Color Your Own Monet Paintings. 2013. (Adult Coloring Books: Art & Design Ser.). (ENG.). 64p. (gr. 3). pap. 6.99 *(978-0-486-77945-4(9),* 779459) Dover Pubns., Inc.
—Dover Masterworks: Color Your Own Renoir Paintings. 2013. (Adult Coloring Ser.). (ENG.). 64p. (gr. 3). pap. 5.99 *(978-0-486-77946-1(7))* Dover Pubns., Inc.
—Dover Masterworks: Color Your Own Van Gogh Paintings. 2013. (Adult Coloring Books: Art & Design Ser.). (ENG.). 64p. (gr. 3). pap. 6.99 *(978-0-486-77950-8(5),* 779505) Dover Pubns., Inc.
O'Brien, Gregory. Back & Beyond: New Zealand in Painting for the Young & Curious. 2008. (ENG., Illus.). 104p. 24.95 *(978-1-86940-404-8(1))* Auckland Univ. Pr. NZL. Dist: Independent Pubs. Group.
Robins, Deri. Painting: Amazing Ideas & Techniques to Help You Create Fabulous Art. 2006. (Art Smart Ser.). (ENG., Illus.). 32p. (J). (gr. 4-6). pap. 9.95 *(978-1-58728-534-9(7),* 1253682) Cooper Square Publishing Llc.
Scrace, Carolyn. Learn, Press-Out & Play Safari Animals. 2018. (Learn, Press-Out & Play Ser.). (ENG., Illus.). 48p. (J). (gr. k). pap. 8.95 *(978-1-912233-29-8(0),* Scribblers) Book Hse. GBR. Dist: Sterling Publishing Co., Inc.
—Princesses & Ballerinas. 2013. (Start with Art Ser.). (ENG., Illus.). 32p. (J). *(978-1-911242-68-0(7))* Book Hse.
—Safari Animals. 2013. (Start with Art Ser.). (ENG., Illus.). 32p. (J). (gr. k). *(978-1-911242-69-7(5))* Book Hse.
Watt, Fiona. Complete Book of Art Ideas. rev. ed. 2011. (Art Ser.). 288p. (J). pap. 19.99 *(978-0-7945-2642-9(X),* Usborne) EDC Publishing.
—365 Things to Draw & Paint. 2011. (Activity Books Ser.). 128p. (J). pap. 24.99 *(978-0-7945-2707-5(8),* Usborne) EDC Publishing.

PAINTINGS

see Painting

PAIR SYSTEM

see Binary System (Mathematics)

PAKISTAN

Aykroyd, Clarissa. Pakistan. (Major Muslim Nations Ser.). (YA). 2010. 128p. (gr. 7-18). 25.95 *(978-1-4222-1408-4(7))* 2008. pap. 14.95 *(978-1-4222-1438-1(9))* Mason Crest.
Barker, Geoff. Discover Pakistan, 1 vol. 2011. (Discover Countries Ser.). (ENG.). 32p. (YA). (gr. 4-4). lib. bdg. 30.27 *(978-1-4488-5271-0(4),* 44b29397-493b-469c-91ec-7be54b0d29ca) Rosen Publishing Group, Inc., The.
Brown, Dinah. Who Is Malala Yousafzai? Thomson, Andrew, illus. 2015. (Who Was-? Chapters Ser.). (ENG.). 112p. (J). (gr. 3-6). 18.69 *(978-1-4844-6131-0(2),* Penguin Workshop) Penguin Young Readers Group.
—Who Is Malala Yousafzai? 2015. (Who Is... ? Ser.). lib. bdg. 16.00 *(978-0-606-37551-1(1))* Turtleback.
Donaldson, Madeline. Pakistan. 2009. pap. 52.95 *(978-0-7613-4730-9(5))* Lerner Publishing Group.
Fazzi, Cindy. How to Draw Pakistan's Sights & Symbols. (Kid's Guide to Drawing the Countries of the World Ser.). 48p. (gr. 4-4). 2009. 53.00 *(978-1-61511-120-6(4))* 2004. (ENG.). (J). 32.93 *(978-1-4042-2739-2(3),* 4a0daa99-0db4-4160-9590-12493ee2cd64) Rosen Publishing Group, Inc., The. (PowerKids Pr.).
Graham, Ian. Pakistan. 2003. (Country Files Ser.). 32p. (J). lib. bdg. 24.25 *(978-1-58340-239-9(X))* Black Rabbit Bks.
Hansen, Grace. Malala Yousafzai: Education Activist, 1 vol. 2015. (History Maker Biographies (Abdo Kids Jumbo) Ser.). (ENG.). 24p. (J). (gr. -1-2). lib. bdg. 32.79 *(978-1-62970-703-7(1),* 17013, Abdo Kids) ABDO Publishing Co.
—Malala Yousafzai: Education Activist. 2017. (History Maker Biographies Ser.). (ENG.). 24p. (J). (gr. -1-2). pap. 7.95 *(978-1-4966-1226-7(4),* 134990, Capstone Classroom) Capstone.
Harmon, Daniel E. Pervez Musharraf: President of Pakistan, 1 vol. 2007. (Newsmakers Ser.). (ENG., Illus.). 112p. (YA). (gr. 9-10). lib. bdg. 39.80 *(978-1-4042-1905-2(6),* 2b59f01f-5a05-4609-971b-4dbb22d8f3e5) Rosen Publishing Group, Inc., The.
Kiesbye, Stefan, ed. How Should the U. S. Proceed in Afghanistan?, 1 vol. 2009. (At Issue Ser.). (ENG., Illus.). 96p. (gr. 10-12). 41.03 *(978-0-7377-4424-8(3),* 9d8c3c8f-a329-410a-862c-64df381ca90e); pap. 28.80 *(978-0-7377-4425-5(1),* 4138f1b8-6246-4f23-b7b8-666ae7482a98) Greenhaven Publishing LLC. (Greenhaven Publishing).
Kumar, Monica & Kumar, Asha. The Great Desert Adventure. 2008. (HIN & ENG., Illus.). 32p. (J). *(978-0-9797191-1-0(9))* MeeraMasi, Inc.
Labrecque, Ellen. It's Cool to Learn about Countries: Pakistan. 2010. (Explorer Library: Social Studies Explorer Ser.). (ENG., Illus.). 48p. (gr. 4-8). lib. bdg. 34.93 *(978-1-60279-828-1(1),* 200522) Cherry Lake Publishing.
Langston-George, Rebecca. For the Right to Learn: Malala Yousafzai's Story. Bock, Janna Rose, illus. 2016. (Encounter: Narrative Nonfiction Picture Bks.). (ENG.). 40p. (J). (gr. 3-6). pap. 7.95 *(978-1-4914-6556-1(5),* 129041, Capstone Pr.) Capstone.
—For the Right to Learn: Malala Yousafzai's Story. Bock, Janna, illus. 2015. (Encounter: Narrative Nonfiction Picture Bks.). (ENG.). 40p. (J). (gr. 3-6). lib. bdg. 29.32 *(978-1-4914-6071-9(7),* 128971, Capstone Pr.) Capstone.
Leggett Abouraya, Karen & Roth, Susan L. Malala Yousafzai: Warrior with Words, 1 vol. 2019. (ENG., Illus.). 40p. (J). (gr. k-3). pap. 11.95 *(978-1-62014-799-3(8),* leelowbooks) Lee & Low Bks., Inc.
Morgan, Sally. Focus on Pakistan, 1 vol. 2007. (World in Focus Ser.). (ENG.). 64p. (gr. 5-8). pap. 15.05 *(978-0-8368-6759-6(9),* 0f3b8e6c-85f0-4021-8535-12dc80c27095); (Illus.). lib. bdg. 36.67 *(978-0-8368-6752-7(1),* 187d7f51-675a-44b0-be6b-85ae040b3d44) Stevens, Gareth Publishing LLLP. (Gareth Stevens Secondary Library).
Mortenson, Greg. Listen to the Wind: The Story of Dr. Greg & Three Cups of Tea. Roth, Susan L., illus. 2009. 32p. (J). (gr. 1-3). 18.99 *(978-0-8037-3058-8(6),* Dial Bks) Penguin Young Readers Group.
—Stones into Schools: Promoting Peace, One School at a Time. 2011. (ENG.). 240p. (J). (gr. 3-18). 16.99 *(978-0-8037-3687-0(8),* Dial) Penguin Publishing Group.
Mortenson, Greg & Relin, David Oliver. Three Cups of Tea: Young Readers Edition: One Man's Journey to Change the World... One Child at a Time. 2009. (ENG., Illus.). 240p. (J). (gr. 3-7). 9.99 *(978-0-14-241412-5(3),* Puffin Books) Penguin Young Readers Group.
Murray, Julie. Pakistan, 1 vol. 2014. (Explore the Countries Ser.). (ENG.). 40p. (J). (gr. 2-5). 35.64 *(978-1-62403-346-9(6),* 1368, Big Buddy Bks.) ABDO Publishing Co.
O'Donnell, Kerri. A Primary Source Guide to Pakistan. 2009. (Countries of the World). 24p. (gr. 2-3). 42.50 *(978-1-61512-042-0(4),* PowerKids Pr.) Rosen Publishing Group, Inc., The.
Rengel, Marian. Pakistan: A Primary Source Cultural Guide, 1 vol. 2003. (Primary Sources of World Cultures Ser.). (ENG., Illus.). 128p. (gr. 4-5). lib. bdg. 43.60 *(978-0-8239-4001-1(2),* 696d2423-f6af-4ca0-bfa8-e880f8a3598c) Rosen Publishing Group, Inc., The.
Roraback, Amanda. Pakistan in a Nutshell. 2nd ed. 2004. (Nutshell Notes Ser.). (Illus.). 64p. pap. 7.95 *(978-0-9702908-9-2(6))* Enisen Publishing.
Schumacher, Cassandra. True Teen Stories from Afghanistan & Pakistan: Surviving the Taliban, 1 vol. 2018. (Surviving Terror: True Teen Stories from Around the World Ser.). (ENG.). 112p. (J). (gr. 8-8). 45.93 *(978-1-5026-3550-1(X),* dbc4abf8-86f7-438c-ab95-d6449c760225) Cavendish Square Publishing LLC.
Sheehan, Sean & Samiuddin, Shahrezad. Pakistan, 1 vol. 2nd rev. ed. 2006. (Cultures of the World (Second Edition)(r) Ser.). (ENG., Illus.). 144p. (gr. 5-5). 49.79 *(978-0-7614-1787-3(7),* 8bfaf7ce-006d-4823-b82a-40c45b9e84fa) Cavendish Square Publishing LLC.

Sheehan, Sean, et al. Pakistan, 1 vol. 3rd rev. ed. 2014. (Cultures of the World (Third Edition)(r) Ser.). (ENG., Illus.). 144p. (gr. 5-5). 48.79 (978-1-5026-0082-0(X), 30ddb4e8-8710-44f5-9931-d58056f64978) Cavendish Square Publishing LLC.

Sheen, Barbara. Foods of Pakistan, 1 vol. 2011. (Taste of Culture Ser.). (ENG., Illus.). 64p. (gr. 3-6). 36.83 (978-0-7377-5883-2(X), 981ce68a-9ec6-489a-8fbd-6ecdf04396ec, KidHaven Publishing) Greenhaven Publishing LLC.

Simmons, Walter. Pakistan. 2011. (Illus.). 32p. (J). lib. bdg. (978-0-531-20958-5(X)); (ENG., (gr. 3-7). lib. bdg. 27.95 (978-1-60014-593-3(0), Blastoff! Readers) Bellwether Media.

Sonneborn, Liz. Enchantment of the World: Pakistan. 2012. (Enchantment of the World, Second Ser.). (ENG., Illus.). 144p. (J). (gr. 5-8). lib. bdg. 40.00 (978-0-531-27544-3(2), Children's Pr.) Scholastic Library Publishing.

Strand, Jennifer. Malala Yousafzai. 2016. (Great Women Ser.). (ENG.). 24p. (J). (gr. -1-2). 49.94 (978-1-68079-390-1(X), 23011, Abdo Zoom-Launch) ABDO Publishing Co.

Taus-Bolstad, Stacy. Pakistan in Pictures. 2003. (Visual Geography Ser.). (Illus.). 80p. (J). (gr. 5-12). 27.93 (978-0-8225-4682-5(5)) Lerner Publishing Group.

Thomson, Sarah & Relin, David Oliver. Three Cups of Tea. adapted ed. 2009. 10.36 (978-0-7848-3360-5(5), Everbind) Marco Bk. Co.

—Three Cups of Tea. ed. 2009. lib. bdg. 19.65 (978-0-606-07164-2(4)) Turtleback.

Wang, Andrea. Malala Yousafzai: Nobel Peace Prize Winner & Education Activist, 1 vol. 2015. (Newsmakers Ser.). (ENG.). 48p. (J). (gr. 4-8). lib. bdg. 35.64 (978-1-62403-646-0(5), 17191) ABDO Publishing Co.

Worth, Richard. Pervez Musharraf. 2nd rev. ed. 2007. (Modern World Leaders Ser.). (ENG., Illus.). 104p. (gr. 7-12). lib. bdg. 30.00 (978-0-7910-9264-4(X), P124699, Facts On File) Infobase Holdings, Inc.

PAKISTAN—FICTION

Antieau, Kim. Broken Moon. 2007. (ENG.). 192p. (YA). (gr. 9-12). 16.99 (978-1-4169-1767-0(5), McElderry, Margaret K. Bks.) McElderry, Margaret K. Bks.

Ellis, Deborah. Mud City, 1 vol. 2015. (Breadwinner Ser.: 3). (ENG., Illus.). 168p. (J). (gr. 5-9). pap. 10.99 (978-1-55498-773-3(3)) Groundwood Bks. CAN. Dist: Publishers Group West (PGW).

—Mud City. 2013. 156p. pap. (978-1-4596-6445-6(0)) ReadHowYouWant.com, Ltd.

Francesco, D'Adamo. Iqbal. 2014. (ENG.). 128p. (J). (gr. 3-7). 11.24 (978-1-63245-261-0(8)) Lectorum Pubns., Inc.

Hawke, Rosanne. Spirit of a Mountain Wolf, 1 vol. 2014. (Scarlet Voyage Ser.). (ENG.). (gr. 9-10). 208p. 39.93 (978-1-62324-033-2(6), 32098452-56b1-449a-a4cc-287fb22f83f9); (Illus.). 216p. (YA). pap. 13.88 (978-1-62324-034-9(4), 751f42df-3bc6-4b75-8ba8-9edc9b34e0b9) Enslow Publishing, LLC.

Khan, Rukhsana. King for a Day, 1 vol. Krömer, Christiane, illus. (ENG.). 32p. (J). 2019. (gr. 1-5). pap. 10.95 (978-1-64379-056-5(0), leelowbooks) 2014. 17.95 (978-1-60060-659-5(8)) Lee & Low Bks., Inc.

Laidlaw, S. J. An Infidel in Paradise. 2013. (Illus.). 272p. (YA). (gr. 7). 19.95 (978-1-77049-304-9(2), Tundra Bks.) Tundra Bks. CAN. Dist: Penguin Random Hse. LLC.

Mortenson, Greg & Husain, Farzana. Listen to the Children: The Story of Dr. Greg & Stones into Schools. Roth, Susan L., illus. 2011. (ENG.). 32p. (J). (gr. 1-3). 17.99 (978-0-8037-3593-4(6), Dial) Penguin Publishing Group.

Qamar, Amjed. Beneath My Mother's Feet. (ENG.). 208p. (YA). (gr. 7). 2011. pap. 12.99 (978-1-4424-1451-8(0)) 2008. 16.99 (978-1-4169-4728-8(0)) Simon & Schuster Children's Publishing. (Atheneum Bks. for Young Readers).

Saeed, Aisha. Amal Unbound. (ENG.). 240p. (J). (gr. 5-9). 2020. 8.99 (978-0-399-54469-9(0), Puffin Books) 2018. 17.99 (978-0-399-54468-2(2), Nancy Paulsen Books) Penguin Young Readers Group.

Shea, Pegi Deitz & Deitz Shea, Pegi. The Carpet Boy's Gift, 1 vol. Morin, Leane, illus. 2005. (ENG.). 40p. (J). (gr. 3-6). 16.95 (978-0-88448-248-2(0)) Tilbury Hse. Pubs.

Smith, Roland. The Edge. 2016. (Peak Marcello Adventure Ser.: 2). (ENG.). 240p. (YA). (gr. 7). pap. 7.99 (978-0-544-81354-0(5), 1641953, Clarion Bks.) HarperCollins Pubs.

Staples, Suzanne Fisher. Haveli. 2012. (Shabanu Ser.). 336p. (YA). (gr. 7). pap. 9.99 (978-0-307-97789-2(7), Ember) Random Hse. Children's Bks.

—Haveli. 2006. 21.50 (978-0-8446-7291-5(2)) Smith, Peter Pub., Inc.

—The House of Djinn. 2012. (Shabanu Ser.). (ENG.). 224p. (YA). (gr. 7). pap. 8.99 (978-0-307-97642-0(4), Ember) Random Hse. Children's Bks.

—Shabanu: Daughter of the Wind. 3rd ed. (J). pap. 3.99 (978-0-13-800053-0(0)) Prentice Hall (Schl. Div.).

—Shabanu: Daughter of the Wind. 2012. (Shabanu Ser.). (Illus.). 288p. (YA). (gr. 7). pap. 10.99 (978-0-307-97788-5(9), Ember) Random Hse. Children's Bks.

—Under the Persimmon Tree. 2008. (Illus.). 281p. (gr. 7-12). 20.00 (978-0-7569-9004-6(1)) Perfection Learning Corp.

—Under the Persimmon Tree. 2008. (ENG., Illus.). 304p. (YA). (gr. 7-12). pap. 13.99 (978-0-312-37776-2(2), 900049283) Square Fish.

PAKISTAN—HISTORY

Aretha, David. Malala Yousafzai & the Girls of Pakistan. 2014. (ENG.). (J). 27.45 (978-1-59935-454-5(3)) Reynolds, Morgan Inc.

Aykroyd, Clarissa. Pakistan, Vol. 13. 2015. (Major Nations of the Modern Middle East Ser.). (Illus.). 128p. (J). (gr. 7). lib. bdg. 25.95 (978-1-4222-3445-7(2)) Mason Crest.

Berlatsky, Noah, ed. East Pakistan, 1 vol. 2012. (Genocide & Persecution Ser.). (ENG.). 216p. (gr. 10-12). lib. bdg. 43.63 (978-0-7377-6256-3(X), 7590fdc9-e67c-4f36-868d-6c8c316088ad, Greenhaven Publishing) Greenhaven Publishing LLC.

Cantor, Rachel Anne. Pakistan. 2016. (Countries We Come From Ser.). (ENG., Illus.). 32p. (J). (gr. -1-3). 28.50 (978-1-68402-060-7(3)) Bearport Publishing Co., Inc.

Clements, Gillian. Indus Valley City. 2009. (Building History Ser.). (Illus.). 32p. (J). (gr. 3-5). lib. bdg. 27.10 (978-1-59771-144-9(6)) Sea-To-Sea Pubns.

Corey, Shana. Malala: a Hero for All. Sayles, Elizabeth, illus. 2016. (Step into Reading Ser.). 48p. (J). (gr. 2-4). pap. 4.99 (978-0-553-53761-1(X), Random Hse. Bks. for Young Readers) Random Hse. Children's Bks.

Donaldson, Madeline. Pakistan. 2009. (Country Explorers Ser.). (ENG., Illus.). 48p. (J). (gr. 2-4). 29.32 (978-1-58013-599-3(4), a4d4f776-a5fc-4d76-be01-5f8f28d9860a, Lerner Pubns.) Lerner Publishing Group.

Greenberger, Robert. A Historical Atlas of Pakistan. 2009. (Historical Atlases of South Asia, Central Asia, & the Middle East Ser.). 64p. (gr. 6-6). 61.20 (978-1-61513-327-7(5)) Rosen Publishing Group, Inc., The.

HARMON, Daniel E. Pervez Musharraf: President of Pakistan. 2009. (Newsmakers Ser.). 112p. (gr. 9-10). 63.90 (978-1-60851-135-8(9)) Rosen Publishing Group, Inc., The.

Hinman, Bonnie. We Visit Pakistan. 2011. (Your Land & My Land Ser.). (Illus.). 64p. (J). (gr. 4-7). lib. bdg. 33.95 (978-1-58415-960-5(X)) Mitchell Lane Pubs.

Kaminski, Leah. Assalam-O-Alaikum, Pakistan. 2019. (Countries of the World Ser.). (ENG.). 48p. (J). (gr. 4-8). pap. 17.07 (978-1-5341-5096-6(X), 213691); (Illus.). lib. bdg. 39.21 (978-1-5341-4810-9(8), 213690) Cherry Lake Publishing.

Klepeis, Alicia Z. Pakistan. 2019. (Country Profiles Ser.). (ENG., Illus.). 32p. (J). (gr. 3-8). lib. bdg. 27.95 (978-1-64487-052-5(5), Blastoff! Discovery) Bellwether Media.

Kwek, Karen & Haque, Jameel. Welcome to Pakistan, 1 vol. 2011. (Welcome to My Country Ser.). (ENG.). 48p. (gr. 3-3). 31.21 (978-1-60870-158-2(1), 1a21d2ce-0fb9-434b-aa7f-5b491057f7e1) Cavendish Square Publishing LLC.

Langley, Andrew. Pakistan in Our World. 2011. (Countries in Our World Ser.). 32p. (YA). (gr. 4-7). lib. bdg. 28.50 (978-1-59920-392-8(8)) Black Rabbit Bks.

Malala, a Brave Girl from Pakistan/Iqbal, a Brave Boy from Pakistan: Two Stories of Bravery. 2014. (ENG., Illus.). 40p. (J). (gr. 1-5). 17.99 (978-1-4814-2294-9(4), Beach Lane Bks.) Beach Lane Bks.

Mohiuddin, Yasmeen Niaz. Pakistan: A Global Studies Handbook, 1 vol. 2006. (Global Studies - Asia Ser.). (ENG., Illus.). 408p. (C). 67.00 (978-1-85109-801-9(1), 900322362) ABC-CLIO, LLC.

Naden, Corinne. Benazir Bhutto, 1 vol. 2011. (Leading Women Ser.). (ENG., Illus.). 96p. (J). (gr. 7-7). 42.64 (978-0-7614-4952-2(3), 4cb4dc26-f281-494e-b9ea-ec4657c25e37) Cavendish Square Publishing LLC.

Niver, Heather Moore. Malala Yousafzai, 1 vol., 1. 2015. (Britannica Beginner Bios Ser.). (ENG., Illus.). 32p. (J). (gr. 2-3). lib. bdg. 26.06 (978-1-68048-253-9(X), 6e887405-0ba1-49a1-944d-603e52a8a725, Britannica Educational Publishing) Rosen Publishing Group, Inc., The.

Peters, Elisa. Malala Yousafzai: Pakistani Activist for Female Education, 1 vol. 2017. (Spotlight on Civic Courage: Heroes of Conscience Ser.). (ENG., Illus.). 48p. (J). (gr. 6-6). 33.47 (978-1-5081-7749-4(X), 92731d4f-26f7-4da6-ae6b-19013b03ff01) Rosen Publishing Group, Inc., The.

Rengel, Marian. Pakistan: A Primary Source Cultural Guide. 2009. (Primary Sources of World Cultures Ser.). 128p. (gr. 4-5). 79.90 (978-1-60851-928-6(7)) Rosen Publishing Group, Inc., The.

Shoup, Kate. Pakistan, 1 vol. 2018. (Exploring World Cultures (First Edition) Ser.). (ENG.). 32p. (gr. 3-3). 31.64 (978-1-5026-3806-9(1), 37404efb-415f-4730-ba2c-70f144da0624) Cavendish Square Publishing LLC.

Simmons, Walter. Pakistan. 2011. (Illus.). 32p. (J). lib. bdg. (978-0-531-20958-5(X)) Bellwether Media.

Stoltman, Joan. Malala Yousafzai, 1 vol. 2018. (Little Biographies of Big People Ser.). (ENG.). 24p. (gr. 1-2). 24.27 (978-1-5382-2894-4(7), e07fe2cf-0feb-42cd-b6b7-4a6037f33745) Stevens, Gareth Publishing LLLP.

World Book, Inc. Staff, contrib. by. Independence of India & Pakistan. 2010. (J). (978-0-7166-1506-4(1)) World Bk., Inc.

Yousafzai, Malala. I Am Malala: How One Girl Stood up for Education & Changed the World (Young Readers Edition) (ENG., (J). (gr. 5-17). 2016. Illus.). 256p. pap. 10.99 (978-0-316-32791-6(3)) 2014. (Illus.). 240p. 18.99 (978-0-316-32793-0(X)) 2015. 240p. 17.00 (978-0-316-31119-9(7)) Little, Brown Bks. for Young Readers.

—I Am Malala: The Girl Who Stood up for Education & Was Shot by the Taliban. 2016. (J). lib. bdg. 22.10 (978-0-606-37164-3(8)) Turtleback.

—I Am Malala 9c Solid Floor Display: How One Girl Stood up for Education & Changed the World (Young Readers Edition) 2014. (ENG.). 256p. (J). (gr. 5-17). 153.00 (978-0-316-33917-9(2)) Little, Brown Bks. for Young Readers.

—I Am Malala PB 9c Solid Floor Display: How One Girl Stood up for Education & Changed the World (Young Readers Edition) 2016. (ENG.). 256p. (J). (gr. 5-17). 98.91 (978-0-316-30398-9(4)) Little, Brown Bks. for Young Readers.

Yousafzai, Malala & McCormick, Patricia. I Am Malala: The Girl Who Stood up for Education & Was Shot by the Taliban. l.t. ed. 2017. (ENG., Illus.). 302p. 22.99 (978-1-4104-9916-5(2)) Cengage Gale.

PALACES

Ball, Jacqueline A. Windsor Castle: England's Royal Fortress. 2005. (Castles, Palaces, & Tombs Ser.). (Illus.). 32p. (J). lib. bdg. 28.50 (978-1-59716-005-6(9)) Bearport Publishing Co., Inc.

Cullis, Megan. See Inside Famous Palaces. 2015. (See Inside Board Bks.). (ENG.). 16p. (J). (gr. k-5). 14.99 (978-0-7945-3477-6(5), Usborne) EDC Publishing.

Dyan, Penelope. A Royal Residence — A Kid's Guide to Windsor Castle. Weigand, John D., photos by. 2011. (Illus.). 40p. pap. 12.95 (978-1-935630-65-4(2)) Bellissima Publishing, LLC.

Hodge, Susie. The Forbidden City, 1 vol. 2004. (Places in History Ser.). (ENG., Illus.). 48p. (gr. 5-8). pap. 15.05 (978-0-8368-5817-4(4), 9fce9bee-9dae-4830-8d54-c92cf43c7a3a, World Almanac Library) Stevens, Gareth Publishing LLLP.

Lee, Sally. Castles & Palaces, 1 vol. 2013. (Royalty Ser.). (ENG.). 24p. (J). (gr. -1-2). lib. bdg. 27.32 (978-1-62065-121-6(1), 120814, Capstone Pr.) Capstone.

Mason, Anthony. Versailles, 1 vol. 2004. (Places in History Ser.). (ENG., Illus.). 48p. (gr. 5-8). lib. bdg. 33.67 (978-0-8368-5815-0(8), a9cb173a-1363-442e-b942-0f91eb84c1a1, World Almanac Library) Stevens, Gareth Publishing LLLP.

Tagliaferro, Linda. Palace of Versailles. 2018. (Castles, Palaces Tombs Ser.). (ENG.). 32p. (J). (gr. 2-7). 7.99 (978-1-64280-065-4(1)) Bearport Publishing Co., Inc.

PALACES—FICTION

Al-Zeheri, Ali. The Princess & the Gold. 2009. 32p. pap. 12.99 (978-1-4490-2091-0(7)) AuthorHouse.

Dadey, Debbie. The Crook & the Crown. Avakyan, Tatevik, illus. 2015. (Mermaid Tales Ser.: 13). (ENG.). 128p. (J). (gr. 1-4). pap. 6.99 (978-1-4814-4075-2(6), Aladdin) Simon & Schuster Children's Publishing.

East, Jacqueline, illus. Princess Palace: A Three-Demensional Playset. 2006. 8p. (J). (gr. -1-3). 22.95 (978-1-58117-492-2(6), Intervisual/Piggy Toes) Bendon, Inc.

Fairy Palaces Magic Painting Book. 2017. (Magic Painting Bks.). (ENG.). (J). pap. 9.99 (978-0-7945-3876-7(2), Usborne) EDC Publishing.

Gil, Carmen. Que Fastidio Ser Princesa! (It's a Pain to Be a Princess) (It's a Pain to Be a Princess) Montero Galan, Daniel, illus. 2012. (SPA.). 28p. (J). (gr. k-3). 14.95 (978-84-15241-14-0(3)) Cuento de Luz SL ESP. Dist: Publishers Group West (PGW).

Marsh, Carole. The Mystery at Mount Fuji: Tokyo, Japan, 7. 2007. (Carole Marsh Mysteries: Around the World in 80 Mysteries Ser.). (ENG., Illus.). 131p. (J). (gr. 4-6). 22.44 (978-0-635-06207-9(0)) Gallopade International.

—The Mystery at Mt. Fuji: Tokyo, Japan. 2007. (Around the World in 80 Mysteries Ser.). (Illus.). 131p. (J). (gr. 3-5). 14.95 (978-0-635-06211-6(9)) Gallopade International.

Muthu, Antony M. Athim. 2008. 48p. pap. 19.49 (978-1-4389-3074-9(7)) AuthorHouse.

Nicola Baxter Staff. Fairy Palace Pop up. 2009. (978-1-84322-574-4(3)) Bookmart Ltd.

Norman, Cook. Sam & the Glass Palace. 2005. (Illus.). 108p. pap. 8.00 (978-1-903087-42-8(2)) DayOne Pubns. GBR. Dist: Send The Light Distribution LLC.

Parker, Danny & Shield, Guy. Plastic Palace, Volume 4. 2017. (Lola's Toy Box Ser.: 4). (ENG., Illus.). 96p. (J). (gr. k-2). pap. 6.99 (978-1-76012-439-7(7)) Hardie Grant Children?s Publishing AUS. Dist: Independent Pubs. Group.

Princess Protection Program Staff. The Palace of Mystery, No. 4. 2010. (Princess Protection Program Ser.). 144p. pap. 4.99 (978-1-4231-2727-7(7)) Disney Pr.

Wethington. Constance. The Butterfly's Ball. 2013. 20p. pap. 24.95 (978-1-4626-8640-7(0)) America Star Bks.

PALEOBOTANY

see Plants, Fossil

PALEOLITHIC PERIOD

see Stone Age

PALEONTOLOGISTS

Barnham, Kay. History VIPs: Mary Anning. 2017. (History VIPs Ser.). (ENG., Illus.). 32p. (J). (gr. 4-6). pap. 11.99 (978-0-7502-9914-5(2), Wayland) Hachette Children's Group GBR. Dist: Hachette Bk. Group.

Bennett, Leonie. Dinosaur Fossils. 2007. (I Love Reading Ser.). (Illus.). 24p. (J). (gr. -1-2). lib. bdg. 19.96 (978-1-59716-555-6(7)) Bearport Publishing Co., Inc.

—Dinosaur Hunting. 2007. (I Love Reading Ser.). (Illus.). 24p. (J). (gr. -1-2). lib. bdg. 25.65 (978-1-59716-554-9(9)) Bearport Publishing Co., Inc.

Butz, Steve. The Bone Race: A Quest for Dinosaur Fossils. 2007. (ENG.). 248p. (YA). (gr. 7). pap. (978-1-933255-30-9(7)) DNA Pr.

Buzzeo, Toni. When Sue Found Sue: Sue Hendrickson Discovers Her T. Rex. Sudyka, Diana, illus. 2019. (ENG.). 32p. (J). (gr. 1-4). 18.99 (978-1-4197-3163-1(7), 1143101, Abrams Bks. for Young Readers) Abrams, Inc.

Chrisp, Peter. Dinosaur Detectives. 2009. (DK Readers Level 4 Ser.). (ENG.). 48p. (J). (gr. 2-4). 16.19 (978-0-7566-5598-3(6)) Dorling Kindersley Publishing, Inc.

Claybourne, Anna. Mary Anning Fossil Hunter: Band 17/Diamond, Bd. 17. 2017. (Collins Big Cat Ser.). (ENG., Illus.). 56p. (J). pap. 12.99 (978-0-00-820893-6(X)) HarperCollins Pubs. Ltd. GBR. Dist: Independent Pubs. Group.

Close, Edward. Dinosaur Hunters. 2013. (Discovery Education: Discoveries & Inventions Ser.). 32p. (J). (gr. 3-6). pap. 60.00 (978-1-4777-1499-7(5), PowerKids Pr.) Rosen Publishing Group, Inc., The.

Cohen, Roger. Danger in the Desert: True Adventures of a Dinosaur Hunter. 2008. (Sterling Point Bks.). (ENG., Illus.). 189p. (J). (gr. 5-8). 21.19 (978-1-4027-5706-8(9)) Sterling Publishing Co., Inc.

Coupe, Robert. Dinosaur Hunters, 1 vol. 2013. (Discovery Education: Discoveries & Inventions Ser.). (ENG., Illus.). 32p. (J). (gr. 4-5). pap. 11.00 (978-1-4777-1498-0(7), f837c010-ff5a-4403-a282-6c1d04131458); lib. bdg. 28.93 (978-1-4777-1328-0(X), 3dbc2cb1-4214-461f-a4cf-5a85fe120db5) Rosen Publishing Group, Inc., The. (PowerKids Pr.).

Dowell, Lori. Be a Paleontologist, 1 vol. 2014. (Be a Scientist! Ser.). 32p. (J). (gr. 3-4). (ENG.). pap. 11.50 (978-1-4824-1209-3(8), 08e83023-2625-4f54-b7c2-034dd414e89d); pap. 63.00 (978-1-4824-1200-0(4)) Stevens, Gareth Publishing LLLP.

Duffield, Katy. I Dig Dinosaurs! 2018. (Let's Find Out Ser.). (ENG., Illus.). 16p. (gr. -1-2). lib. bdg. 28.50 (978-1-64156-192-1(0), 9781641561921) Rourke Educational Media.

Enik, Ted. Sticks 'n' Stones 'n' Dinosaur Bones: Being a Whimsical Take on a (pre)Historical Event, 1 vol. Newland, G. F., illus. 2017. (Unhinged History Ser.: 1). (ENG.). 48p. (J). (gr. -1-3). 16.99 (978-0-7643-5394-9(2), 7730) Schiffer Publishing, Ltd.

Fern, Tracey. Barnum's Bones: How Barnum Brown Discovered the Most Famous Dinosaur in the World, 1 vol. Kulikov, Boris, illus. 2012. (ENG.). 40p. (J). (gr. k-4). 18.99 (978-0-374-30516-1(1), 900065867, Farrar, Straus & Giroux (BYR)) Farrar, Straus & Giroux.

Goldish, Meish. The Fossil Feud: Marsh & Cope's Bone Wars. 2006. (Fossil Hunters Ser.). (Illus.). 32p. (YA). (gr. 2-5). lib. bdg. 28.50 (978-1-59716-256-2(6)) Bearport Publishing Co., Inc.

Hill, David. Dinosaur Hunter: Joan Wiffen's Awesome Fossil Discoveries. Phoebe Morris & Hill, David Spence, illus. 2019. (David Hill Kiwi Legends Ser.). 32p. (J). (gr. -1-k). 19.99 (978-0-14-377322-1(4)) Penguin Group New Zealand, Ltd. NZL. Dist: Independent Pubs. Group.

Holmes, Thom. Dinosaur Scientist: Careers Digging up the Past, 1 vol. 2010. (Wild Science Careers Ser.). (ENG., Illus.). 128p. (gr. 5-6). lib. bdg. 35.93 (978-0-7660-3053-4(9), 5470a859-3d09-4f3e-a250-dc58316c6710) Enslow Publishing, LLC.

—Paleontologists: Searching for Dinosaur Bones, 1 vol. 2015. (Extreme Science Careers Ser.). (ENG., Illus.). 128p. (gr. 7-7). 38.93 (978-0-7660-6964-0(8), 490e0a5e-4a21-425f-bb6a-eb95417ab7cd) Enslow Publishing, LLC.

Kurtz, Jane. Mister Bones: Dinosaur Hunter (Ready-To-Read Level 1) Haverfield, Mary, illus. 2004. (Ready-To-Read Ser.). (ENG.). 32p. (J). (gr. -1-1). pap. 4.99 (978-0-689-85960-1(0), Simon Spotlight) Simon Spotlight.

Lendler, Ian. The First Dinosaur: How Science Solved the Greatest Mystery on Earth. Butzer, C. M., illus. 2019. (ENG.). 224p. (J). (gr. 5). 24.99 (978-1-5344-2700-6(7), McElderry, Margaret K. Bks.) McElderry, Margaret K. Bks.

—The First Dinosaur: How Science Solved the Greatest Mystery on Earth. Butzer, C. M., illus. 2019. 220p. (J). (978-1-5344-2701-3(5)) Simon & Schuster, Inc.

Lucas Donald, Rhonda. Dino Treasures, 1 vol. Morrison, Cathy, illus. 2015. (ENG.). 32p. (J). (gr. 1-4). 17.95 (978-1-62855-450-2(9)) Arbordale Publishing.

McGowan, Chris. Dinosaur Discovery: Everything You Need to Be a Paleontologist. Schmidt, Erica Lyn, illus. 2011. (ENG.). 48p. (J). (gr. 2-6). 19.99 (978-1-4169-4764-6(7), Simon & Schuster Bks. For Young Readers) Simon & Schuster Bks. For Young Readers.

Miller, Connie Colwell. I'll Be a Paleontologist. Baroncelli, Silvia, illus. 2016. (When I Grow Up Ser.). (ENG.). 24p. (J). (gr. k-3). 20.95 (978-1-60753-763-2(X)) Amicus Learning.

—Paléontologue. Baroncelli, Silvia, illus. 2016. (Plus Tard, Je Serai... Ser.). (FRE.). 24p. (J). (gr. 1-4). (978-1-77092-357-7(8), 17620) Amicus.

National Park Service Staff, ed. Junior Paleontologist Activity Book: Ages 5 to 12: Explore, Learn, Protect. Wood, Ethan, illus. rev. ed. 2012. (ENG.). 22p. (gr. k-6). 6.00 (978-0-16-090846-0(9)) National Park Service Div. of Pubns.

Owen, Ruth. Paleontologists & Archaeologists. 2013. (Out of the Lab: Extreme Jobs in Science Ser.). 32p. (J). (gr. 3-6). pap. 60.00 (978-1-4777-1387-7(5)); (ENG.). (gr. 4-5). pap. 11.00 (978-1-4777-1380-8(8), 8b4650ad-1ba3-4d8e-ad22-1e4d3eb5df2b); (ENG., Illus.). (gr. 4-5). 28.93 (978-1-4777-1290-0(9), 94a63289-9f55-4841-abf4-5202f333f2ab) Rosen Publishing Group, Inc., The. (PowerKids Pr.).

Peterson, Judy Monroe. Fossil Finders: Paleontologists. 2009. (Extreme Scientists Ser.). 24p. (gr. 2-3). 42.50 (978-1-61512-452-7(7), PowerKids Pr.) Rosen Publishing Group, Inc., The.

Walker, Sally M. Mary Anning: Fossil Hunter. Saroff, Phyllis V., illus. 2007. (On My Own Biographies Ser.). 48p. (J). (gr. 2-5). per. 6.95 (978-1-57505-457-5(4), First Avenue Editions) Lerner Publishing Group.

PALEONTOLOGY

see Fossils

PALESTINE

Carew-Miller, Anna. The Palestinians. 2010. (Major Muslim Nations Ser.). 135p. (YA). (gr. 5-18). lib. bdg. 25.95 (978-1-4222-1389-6(7)) Mason Crest.

Katz, Samuel M. Jerusalem or Death: Palestinian Terrorism. 72p. (YA). (gr. 9-18). 19.95 (978-1-58013-208-4(1), Kar-Ben Publishing); 2003. (Illus.). (J). (gr. 6-12). 26.60 (978-0-8225-4033-5(9)) Lerner Publishing Group.

Lusted, Marcia. Understanding Palestine Today. 2014. (Illus.). 63p. (J). (gr. 3-6). 33.95 (978-1-61228-655-6(0)) Mitchell Lane Pubs.

PALESTINE—FICTION

Booth, Bradley. Escape from Egypt. 2009. (J). pap. 11.99 (978-0-8163-2305-0(4)) Pacific Pr. Publishing Assn.

Ellis, Deborah. The Cat at the Wall, 1 vol. 2014. (ENG., Illus.). 144p. (J). (gr. 4-7). 16.95 (978-1-55498-491-6(2)); pap. 9.95 (978-1-55498-707-8(5)) Groundwood Bks. CAN. Dist: Publishers Group West (PGW).

Evans, Loralee. The King's Heir. 2006. 287p. (YA). (gr. 8-12). per. 18.99 (978-1-55517-865-9(0), Bonneville Bks.) Cedar Fort, Inc./CFI Distribution.

Heimerdinger, Chris. Kingdoms & Conquerors: A Novel. 2005. 434p. (YA). (978-1-59156-740-0(8)) Covenant Communications.

Laurel Carter, Anne. The Shepherd's Granddaughter. 2013. 236p. pap. (978-1-4596-6490-6(6)) ReadHowYouWant.com, Ltd.

Martin, Gary & Zondervan Bibles Staff. The Sword of Revenge, 1 vol., 7. Cariello, Sergio, illus. 2009. (Z Graphic Novels / Son of Samson Ser.). (ENG.). 160p. (J). pap. 6.99 (978-0-310-71285-5(8)) Zondervan.

Muñiz-Huberman, Angelina & Menton, Seymour. Dreaming of Safed. 2014. 126p. (YA). pap. (978-1-935604-61-7(9)) Gaon Bks.

Novel Units. The Bronze Bow Novel Units Teacher Guide. 2019. (ENG.). (J). pap. 12.99 (978-1-56137-726-8(0), Novel Units, Inc.) Classroom Library Co.

Phillips, Dixie & Sharon, et al. Bethlehem's King Size Bed. 2013. 24p. pap. 7.95 (978-1-61633-423-9(1)) Guardian Angel Publishing, Inc.

Rucinski, Sandra. The Story of Jesus According to Tobin. 2009. 32p. pap. 14.50 (978-1-60860-372-5(5), Eloquent Bks.) Strategic Book Publishing & Rights Agency (SBPRA).

Silverberg, Selma Kritzer. Naomi's Song. 2009. (ENG.). 142p. (gr. 7-18). pap. 19.95 (978-0-8276-0886-3(1)) Jewish Pubn. Society.

Studer, Diana. The Tabby's Gift. 2009. 24p. pap. 12.55 (978-1-4389-5582-7(0)) AuthorHouse.

Travis, Lucille. Tirzah. Garber, S. David, ed. 2004. (ENG.). 160p. (YA). (gr. 4-7). pap. 9.99 (978-0-8361-3546-6(6)) Herald Pr.

PALESTINE—HISTORY

Carew-Miller, Anna. The Palestinians, Vol. 13. 2015. (Major Nations of the Modern Middle East Ser.). (Illus.). 136p. (J). (gr. 7). lib. bdg. 25.95 (978-1-4222-3448-8(7)) Mason Crest.

Hayhurst, Chris. Israel's War of Independence. 2009. (War & Conflict in the Middle East Ser.). 64p. (gr. 5-5). 58.50 (978-1-60854-736-4(1)) Rosen Publishing Group, Inc., The.

—Israel's War of Independence: Al-Nakba, 1 vol. 2003. (War & Conflict in the Middle East Ser.). (ENG., Illus.). 64p. (gr. 5-5). lib. bdg. 37.13 (978-0-8239-4548-1(0), 39fee87d-eaa3-46f8-8aad-505b4eeb67b5) Rosen Publishing Group, Inc., The.

Immell, Myra, ed. The Creation of the State of Israel, 1 vol. 2009. (Perspectives on Modern World History Ser.). (ENG., Illus.). 224p. (gr. 10-12). 49.43 (978-0-7377-4556-6(8), 2d04d54d-7c12-4cc2-a77c-863ec3ac2d0c, Greenhaven Publishing) Greenhaven Publishing LLC.

Jones, Graham. How They Lived in Bible Times. Deverell, Richard, illus. 2003. 48p. 6.49 (978-1-85999-435-1(0)) Scripture Union GBR. Dist: Gabriel Resources.

Lusted, Marcia Amidon. The Israeli-Palestinian Conflict. 2017. (Special Reports Set 3 Ser.). (ENG., Illus.). 112p. (J). (gr. 6-12). lib. bdg. 41.36 (978-1-5321-1333-8(1), 27541, Essential Library) ABDO Publishing Co.

Marabini, Sergio. Arafat. 2004. (Protagonistas Ser.). (SPA.). 96p. (YA). (978-987-1129-64-5(5)) Grupo Visor E.A.S.A.

Mason, Paul. Israel & Palestine, 1 vol. 2009. (Global Hotspots Ser.). (ENG.). 32p. (gr. 5-5). lib. bdg. 21.27 (978-0-7614-3181-7(0), 934277a6-9922-4bda-bb3e-f52728915c35) Cavendish Square Publishing LLC.

Wingate, Katherine. The Intifadas. (War & Conflict in the Middle East Ser.). 64p. (gr. 5-5). 2009. 58.50 (978-1-60854-738-8(8)) 2003. (ENG., Illus.). lib. bdg. 37.13 (978-0-8239-4546-7(4), 2a6fb851-288c-4e25-a051-e940593c5539) Rosen Publishing Group, Inc., The.

PALMER, NATHANIEL BROWN, 1799-1877

Sanford, Candace. Captain Nathaniel Brown Palmer. Scala, Susan, illus. 2007. 96p. (YA). pap. 14.95 (978-0-9773725-9-1(6)) Flat Hammock Pr.

PALSY, CEREBRAL

see Cerebral Palsy

PANAMA

Adamson, Heather. Panama. 2016. (Exploring Countries Ser.). (ENG., Illus.). 32p. (J). (gr. 3-7). lib. bdg. 27.95 (978-1-62617-345-3(1), Blastoff! Readers) Bellwether Media.

Augustin, Byron. Panama. 2005. (Enchantment of the World Ser.). (ENG., Illus.). 144p. (YA). (gr. 5-9). 39.00 (978-0-516-23676-6(8)) Scholastic Library Publishing.

Freire, Carolina. Panama, 1 vol. 2004. (Countries of the World Ser.). (ENG., Illus.). 96p. (gr. 6-8). lib. bdg. 33.67 (978-0-8368-3117-7(9), 9cb6c953-507b-434a-a5d6-2293a51b3446) Stevens, Gareth Publishing LLLP.

Hinman, Bonnie. We Visit Panama. 2010. (Your Land & My Land Ser.). (Illus.). 64p. (J). (gr. 3-6). lib. bdg. 33.95 (978-1-58415-893-6(X)) Mitchell Lane Pubs.

Matrishon, Maible. Island Experiences - Adventures in Bocas Del Toro, on the Caribbean Coast of Panama. 2013. 40p. pap. (978-0-9808653-9-4(5), Matrishon Media) Wider Vision Publishing.

Nevins, Debbie, et al. Panama, 1 vol. 3rd enl. rev. ed. 2016. (Cultures of the World (Third Edition)(r) Ser.). (ENG., Illus.). 144p. (J). (gr. 5-5). 48.79 (978-1-5026-2215-0(7), d54ecd66-1249-40d2-a7d9-3b41fae80eac) Cavendish Square Publishing LLC.

Perritano, John. Panama. 2018. (Illus.). 32p. (J). (978-1-4896-7514-9(0), AV2 by Weigl) Weigl Pubs., Inc.

Shields, Charles J. Panama. 2010. (Central America Today Ser.). 63p. (YA). (gr. 7-18). pap. 9.95 (978-1-4222-0718-5(8)); (Illus.). (gr. 9-12). 21.95 (978-1-4222-0651-5(3)) Mason Crest.

—Panama, Vol. 8. Henderson, James D., ed. 2015. (Discovering Central America: History, Politics, & Culture Ser.). (Illus.). 64p. (J). (gr. 7). lib. bdg. 22.95 (978-1-4222-3292-7(1)) Mason Crest.

Streissguth, Tom. Panama in Pictures. 2nd ed. 2005. (Visual Geography Series, Second Ser.). (ENG., Illus.). 80p. (gr. 5-12). 31.93 (978-0-8225-2395-6(7)) Lerner Publishing Group.

PANAMA—FICTION

Andrews, Carol. The Giggle Wind. 2003. (Illus.). 40p. 17.95 (978-0-9725609-2-4(0)) Diakonia Publishing.

Appleton, Victor. The Moving Picture Boys at Panama. 2005. 27.95 (978-1-4218-1499-5(4)); 208p. pap. 12.95 (978-1-4218-1599-2(0)) 1st World Publishing, Inc. (1st World Library - Literary Society).

—The Moving Picture Boys at Panama. 2004. reprint ed. pap. 1.99 (978-1-4192-7472-5(4)); pap. 20.95 (978-1-4191-7472-8(X)) Kessinger Publishing, LLC.

Giménez Llort, Lydia. The man who wore a Panama Hat. 2009. 36p. pap. 20.50 (978-1-4092-7060-7(2)) Lulu Pr., Inc.

Markun, Patricia M. The Little Painter of Sabana Grande. Casilla, Robert, illus. 2014. (ENG.). 32p. (J). (gr. -1-3). 13.99 (978-1-4814-4458-3(1), Simon & Schuster Bks. For Young Readers) Simon & Schuster Bks. For Young Readers.

Oertel, Andreas. Panama Pursuit. 2016. (Shenanigans Ser.). (ENG.). 192p. (J). (gr. 4-7). pap. 9.95 (978-1-77203-097-6(X), Wandering Fox) Heritage Hse. CAN. Dist: Orca Bk. Pubs. USA.

Payson, Howard. The Boy Scouts at the Panama Canal. 2007. 332p. per. 19.95 (978-1-60466-006-7(6)) Capricorn Hse. Publishing.

—The Boy Scouts at the Panama Canal. 2005. reprint ed. pap. 30.95 (978-1-4179-2457-8(8)) Kessinger Publishing, LLC.

—The Boy Scouts at the Panama Canal. 2005. pap. 30.95 (978-1-885529-44-2(9)) Stevens Publishing.

Popcorn, Socks, & Salvation. 2008. 32p. pap. 4.99 (978-0-8341-2350-2(9), 083-412-3509) Beacon Hill Pr. of Kansas City.

Ross, Jeff. Dawn Patrol, 1 vol. 2012. (Orca Sports Ser.). (ENG.). 160p. (J). (gr. 4-7). pap. 9.95 (978-1-4598-0062-5(1)) Orca Bk. Pubs. USA.

Roy, Lillian Elizabeth. Polly's Southern Cruise: The Polly Brewster Series. Barbour, H. S., illus. 2011. 294p. 48.95 (978-1-258-10514-3(4)) Literary Licensing, LLC.

Wells, Helen. Cherry Ames, Army Nurse. 2005. (Cherry Ames Nurse Stories Ser.: Bk. 3). 224p. (J). (gr. 4-7). 14.95 (978-0-9771597-2-7(8)) Springer Publishing Co., Inc.

PANAMA CANAL (PANAMA)

Anderson, Dale. Building the Panama Canal, 1 vol. 2004. (Landmark Events in American History Ser.). (ENG., Illus.). 48p. (gr. 5-8). (J). pap. 15.05 (978-0-8368-5422-0(5), e4a10785-512d-46cb-8ef2-4f51aa259f48); lib. bdg. 33.67 (978-0-8368-5394-0(6), 14616fbd-3327-4ce7-a368-8ea60899d0e6) Stevens, Gareth Publishing LLLP. (Gareth Stevens Secondary Library).

Anderson, Dale & Crewe, Sabrina. Building the Panama Canal, 1 vol. 2004. (Events That Shaped America Ser.). (ENG., Illus.). 32p. (gr. 3-5). lib. bdg. 28.67 (978-0-8368-3413-0(5), 63ede30e-7074-42ee-af41-f0a4beba7e62, Gareth Stevens Learning Library) Stevens, Gareth Publishing LLLP.

Benoit, Peter. The Panama Canal. 2013. (ENG.). 64p. (J). pap. 8.95 (978-0-531-27670-9(8)) Scholastic Library Publishing.

Currie, Stephen. The Panama Canal. 2014. (History's Great Structures). (ENG., Illus.). 96p. (J). lib. bdg. (978-1-60152-710-3(1)) ReferencePoint Pr., Inc.

DuTemple, Lesley A. The Panama Canal: Great Building Feats Series. 2003. (Great Building Feats Ser.). (Illus.). 96p. (J). (gr. 5-9). 27.93 (978-0-8225-0079-7(5)) Lerner Publishing Group.

Hoffman, Mary Ann. The Panama Canal: Global Gateway, 1 vol. 2008. (Real Life Readers Ser.). (ENG.). 32p. (gr. 5-6). pap. 10.00 (978-1-4358-0207-0(1), fd4d9505-ac5e-4bb8-8c65-6616863a3ada, Rosen Classroom) Rosen Publishing Group, Inc., The.

LaPierre, Yvette. Engineering the Panama Canal. 2017. (Building by Design Set 2 Ser.). (ENG., Illus.). 48p. (J). (gr. 4-8). lib. bdg. 35.64 (978-1-5321-1375-8(7), 27673) ABDO Publishing Co.

Mann, Elizabeth. The Panama Canal: The Story of How a Jungle Was Conquered & the World Made Smaller. Rangel, Fernando, illus. 2006. (Wonders of the World Book Ser.). (ENG.). 48p. (J). (gr. 4-8). pap. 12.95 (978-1-931414-14-2(9), 30630de7-6f19-49f3-b7bf-dc8362d2fc99) Mikaya Pr.

Miller, Heather. The Panama Canal. 2014. (Great Idea Ser.). (ENG., Illus.). 48p. (J). (gr. 4-6). lib. bdg. 26.60 (978-1-59953-594-4(7)) Norwood Hse. Pr.

Pascal, Janet. What Is the Panama Canal? 2014. (What Is... ? Ser.). lib. bdg. 16.00 (978-0-606-35688-6(6)) Turtleback.

Pascal, Janet B. & Who HQ. What Is the Panama Canal? Foley, Tim, illus. 2014. (What Was? Ser.). 112p. (J). (gr. 3-7). 5.99 (978-0-448-47899-9(4), Penguin Workshop) Penguin Young Readers Group.

Roberts, Russell. Building the Panama Canal. 2008. (Monumental Milestones Ser.). (Illus.). 48p. (YA). (gr. 4-7). lib. bdg. 29.95 (978-1-58415-692-5(9)) Mitchell Lane Pubs.

Ryckman, Tatiana. The Panama Canal, 1 vol. 2017. (Routes of Cross-Cultural Exchange Ser.). (ENG., Illus.). 96p. (YA). (gr. 8-8). 44.50 (978-1-5026-2692-9(6), e2a921f1-45a7-4e88-bbf0-698bae2622ee) Cavendish Square Publishing LLC.

Stefoff, Rebecca. Panama Canal. 2016. (Engineering Wonders Ser.). (ENG., Illus.). 32p. (J). (gr. 3-6). lib. bdg. 27.99 (978-1-4914-8198-1(6), 130671, Capstone Pr.) Capstone.

PANDAS

Austen, Mary. Panda Bears, 1 vol. 2016. (Bears of the World Ser.). (ENG.). 24p. (J). (gr. 3-3). 25.27 (978-1-4994-2040-1(4), b496c59a-7705-424a-b16c-58f041516565, PowerKids Pr.) Rosen Publishing Group, Inc., The.

Bell, Samantha S. Giant Pandas Are Awesome. 2018. (Animals Are Awesome Ser.). (ENG., Illus.). 32p. (J). (gr. 3-6). 32.80 (978-1-63235-435-8(7), 13813, 12-Story Library) Bookstaves, LLC.

Besel, Jen. Panda Cubs. 2020. (Baby Animals Ser.). (ENG.). 24p. (J). (gr. k-3). lib. bdg. (978-1-62310-141-1(7), 14382, Bolt Jr.) Black Rabbit Bks.

Bodden, Valerie. Pandas. 2013. (Amazing Animals Ser.). (ENG., Illus.). 24p. (J). (gr. 1-4). 25.65 (978-1-60818-089-9(1), 23055, Creative Education) Creative Co., The.

Bodkin, Odds. Belly Button. 2003. (Illus.). 12p. (J). bds. (978-0-9657170-5-2(4)) Perkins Schl. for the Blind.

Borgert-Spaniol, Megan. Red Pandas. 2015. (Animal Safari Ser.). (ENG., Illus.). 24p. (J). (gr. k-3). lib. bdg. 26.95 (978-1-62617-213-5(7), Blastoff! Readers) Bellwether Media.

Bortolotti, Dan. Panda Rescue: Changing the Future for Endangered Wildlife. 2003. (Firefly Animal Rescue Ser.). (ENG., Illus.). 64p. (J). (gr. 5-18). 19.95 (978-1-55297-598-5(3), 50fed52f-f28f-4567-a3b3-b15f005efc37); pap. 9.95 (978-1-55297-557-2(6), 785b8409-3d57-4ab9-8120-d0c29c37561d) Firefly Bks., Ltd.

Boyer, Crispin. So Cute! Pandas. 2019. (Cool/Cute Ser.). (Illus.). 32p. (J). (gr. -1-k). 6.99 (978-1-4263-3363-7(3), National Geographic Kids) Disney Publishing Worldwide.

Bright, Michael. Exploring Nature - Bears & Pandas: An Intriguing Insight into the Lives of Brown Bears, Polar Bears, Black Bears, Pandas & Others, with 190 Exciting Images: Bears & Pandas: Bears & Pandas. 2015. (ENG., Illus.). 64p. (J). (gr. -1-2). 12.99 (978-1-86147-389-9(3), Armadillo) Anness Publishing GBR. Dist: National Bk. Network.

Butterfield, Moira. Panda. (Who Am I? Ser.). (Illus.). 32p. lib. bdg. 24.25 (978-1-930643-91-8(8)) Chrysalis Education.

Cain, Marie Mowery. Look at That Face. 2013. (Big Books, Blue Ser.). (ENG & SPA., Illus.). 16p. pap. 33.00 (978-1-59246-004-5(6)) Big Books, by George!

Candy Cane Press, creator. Baby Panda Book & Toy Gift Set, Set. 2006. (Illus.). 26p. (J). bds. 16.95 (978-0-8249-6675-1(9), Ideals Pubns.) Worthy Publishing.

Caravan, Jill. Pandas, Vol. 12. 2018. (Animals in the Wild Ser.). (Illus.). 72p. (J). (gr. 7). 33.27 (978-1-4222-4173-8(4)) Mason Crest.

—Pandas: A Portrait of the Animal World. (Portrait of the Animal World Ser.). (Illus.). 72p. 2013. pap. 9.95 (978-1-59764-317-7(3)) 2nd rev. ed. 2012. 12.95 (978-1-59764-230-9(4)) New Line Bks.

Caswell, Deanna. Baby Pandas. 2018. (Adorable Animals Ser.). (ENG.). 32p. (J). (gr. 4-6). pap. 9.99 (978-1-64466-246-5(9), 12239); lib. bdg. (978-1-68072-399-1(5), 12238) Black Rabbit Bks. (Bolt).

Clark, Willow. Pandas, 1 vol. 2012. (Animals of Asia Ser.). (ENG., Illus.). 24p. (J). (gr. 2-3). pap. 9.25 (978-1-4488-7487-3(4), 2b262f18-53c4-4817-913f-17290aa808a3); lib. bdg. 26.27 (978-1-4488-7414-9(9), 6dfc5eea-8b59-428e-bca3-f8cb03b7d804) Rosen Publishing Group, Inc., The. (PowerKids Pr.).

Costain, Meredith. Panda, 1 vol. Jackson-Carter, Stuart, illus. 2016. (Wild World Ser.). (ENG.). 32p. (J). (gr. 1-2). 28.93 (978-1-4994-8221-8(3), 4d9824b9-a333-44a8-96b8-4f8edb5d8dba, Windmill Bks.) Rosen Publishing Group, Inc., The.

Crossingham, John & Kalman, Bobbie. Endangered Pandas, 1 vol. 2005. (Earth's Endangered Animals Ser.). (ENG., Illus.). 32p. (J). (gr. 3-5). pap. (978-0-7787-1904-5(9)) Crabtree Publishing Co.

Cruickshank, Don. Giant Pandas. 2006. (Amazing Animals Ser.). (Illus.). 24p. (J). (gr. 3-7). pap. 8.95 (978-1-59036-395-9(7)); lib. bdg. 24.45 (978-1-59036-389-8(2)) Weigl Pubs., Inc.

Daly, Ruth. Bringing Back the Giant Panda. 2018. (Animals Back from the Brink Ser.). (Illus.). 32p. (J). (gr. 4-4). (978-0-7787-4902-8(9)) Crabtree Publishing Co.

Dudley, Karen. Giant Pandas with Code. 2012. (Animals on the Brink Ser.). (ENG., Illus.). 48p. (J). (gr. 4-7). pap. 14.95 (978-1-61913-434-8(9)); lib. bdg. 29.99 (978-1-61913-433-1(0)) Weigl Pubs., Inc. (AV2 by Weigl).

Eason, Sarah. Save the Panda, 1 vol. Geeson, Andrew & Veldhoven, Marijke, illus. 2009. (Save The... Ser.). (ENG.). 32p. (J). (gr. 2-3). lib. bdg. 28.93 (978-1-4358-2812-4(7), 23d90f59-f8f6-440f-ad8e-3c2b59d0112f) Rosen Publishing Group, Inc., The.

Eszterhas, Suzi. Panda Opposites. 2019. (ENG., Illus.). 24p. (J). (gr. -1-1). bds. 9.95 (978-1-77147-330-9(4)) Owlkids Bks. Inc. CAN. Dist: Publishers Group West (PGW).

Faundez, Anne. Animals in Danger. 2004. (QEB Start Reading Ser.). (Illus.). 24p. (J). lib. bdg. 15.95 (978-1-59566-009-1(7)) QEB Publishing Inc.

Firestone, Mary. Top 50 Reasons to Care about Giant Pandas: Animals in Peril, 1 vol. 2010. (Top 50 Reasons to Care about Endangered Animals Ser.). (ENG., Illus.). 104p. (gr. 5-6). 35.93 (978-0-7660-3451-8(8), c5bfbc54-6017-401a-a33a-46c06223b44d) Enslow Publishing, LLC.

Franks, Katie. Pandas. 2014. (Zoo's Who's Who Ser.). (Illus.). 24p. (J). (gr. k-2). pap. 49.50 (978-1-4777-6582-1(4), PowerKids Pr.) Rosen Publishing Group, Inc., The.

Gallagher, Debbie. Pandas, 1 vol. 2010. (Zoo Animals Ser.). (ENG.). 32p. (gr. 2-2). lib. bdg. 21.27 (978-0-7614-4745-0(8), 21c449c2-ee6a-4ed1-b4fb-246741d551dd) Cavendish Square Publishing LLC.

Gardner, Robert. How Heavy Is Heavy? Science Projects with Weight, 1 vol. 2014. (Hot Science Experiments Ser.). (ENG.). 48p. (gr. 3-4). pap. 11.53 (978-0-7660-6601-4(0), 00044fdd-2a98-406e-bafa-21046483ad3f, Enslow Elementary) Enslow Publishing, LLC.

Gervasio, Christine. Pandas Live to Eat. 2014. (1B Animal Behaviors Ser.). (ENG., Illus.). 32p. (J). pap. 8.00 (978-1-63437-015-8(5)) American Reading Co.

Gibbons, Gail. Giant Pandas. 2004. (ENG., Illus.). 32p. (J). (gr. -1-3). pap. 7.99 (978-0-8234-1828-2(6)) Holiday Hse., Inc.

Gish, Melissa. Living Wild: Pandas. 2012. (Living Wild Ser.). (ENG.). 48p. (J). (gr. 4-7). pap. 12.00 (978-0-89812-674-7(6), 22679, Creative Paperbacks) Creative Co., The.

—Panda. 2019. (Spotlight on Nature Ser.). (ENG.). 32p. (J). (gr. 4-7). pap. 9.99 (978-1-62832-746-5(4), 19185, Creative Paperbacks) Creative Co., The.

—Pandas. 2011. (Illus.). 48p. (J). 35.65 (978-1-60818-082-0(4), Creative Education) Creative Co., The.

—Red Pandas. 2018. (ENG.). 48p. (J). (gr. 5-8). pap. 13.99 (978-1-62832-565-2(8), 19778, Creative Paperbacks); (gr. 4-7). (978-1-60818-960-1(0), 19770, Creative Education) Creative Co., The.

Green, Carl R. & Katirgis, Jane. Endangered Giant Pandas, 1 vol. 2015. (Wildlife at Risk Ser.). (ENG.). 48p. (gr. 6-6). pap. 12.70 (978-0-7660-6892-6(7), e550618c-4567-436c-b07e-aeb1e1039fab); (Illus.). 29.60 (978-0-7660-6894-0(3), f9608cb5-2126-43f1-a43d-a1bfbc2fb8bc) Enslow Publishing, LLC.

Gregory, Josh. Red Pandas. 2016. (Nature's Children Ser.). (ENG., Illus.). 48p. (J). pap. 6.95 (978-0-531-21936-2(4), Children's Pr.) Scholastic Library Publishing.

Herrington, Lisa M. Giant Pandas (Nature's Children) (Library Edition) 2019. (Nature's Children, Fourth Ser.). (ENG., Illus.). 48p. (J). (gr. 3-5). lib. bdg. 30.00 (978-0-531-12716-2(8), Children's Pr.) Scholastic Library Publishing.

Idzikowski, Lisa. How Pandas Grow Up, 1 vol. 2018. (Animals Growing Up Ser.). (ENG.). 24p. (gr. 1-2). 24.27 (978-0-7660-9655-4(6), bb05dac6-994e-49ce-9089-e19001c59cb5) Enslow Publishing, LLC.

Jazynka, Kitson. National Geographic Kids Mission: Panda Rescue: All about Pandas & How to Save Them. 2016. (NG Kids Mission: Animal Rescue Ser.). (Illus.). 112p. (J). (gr. 5-9). pap. 12.99 (978-1-4263-2088-0(4), National Geographic Kids) Disney Publishing Worldwide.

Keller, Susanna. Meet the Panda, 1 vol. 2010. (At the Zoo Ser.). (ENG.). 24p. (J). (gr. 1-1). pap. 9.25 (978-1-4358-9726-7(9), 3268e4ef-6ccd-4416-944a-f29fcdf4ae7b); (Illus.). lib. bdg. 26.27 (978-1-4358-9307-8(7), 8226a0fc-dc2f-4441-ad4d-c27c1d014b27) Rosen Publishing Group, Inc., The. (PowerKids Pr.).

Kennedy Shea, Bobby. Patterns with Pandas, 1 vol. 2013. (Animal Math Ser.). (ENG.). 24p. (J). (gr. 1-2). pap. 9.15 (978-1-4339-9319-0(8), c05f70c0-c50a-4c4f-bcb1-6a5ab18aee27); (Illus.). lib. bdg. 25.27 (978-1-4339-9318-3(X), ff6b0c97-0f78-40e9-a979-00b688142e6e) Stevens, Gareth Publishing LLLP.

Kueffner, Susan. Pandas, 1 vol. (Amazing Animals Ser.). (ENG.). 48p. (gr. 3-5). 2009. pap. 11.50 (978-1-4339-2017-2(4), 387ad7d0-87f0-4680-a820-d4b77e3c112a, Gareth Stevens Learning Library) 2008. (YA). lib. bdg. 30.67 (978-0-8368-9100-3(7), 55235756-991d-49fb-abe5-c5592306bae2) Stevens, Gareth Publishing LLLP.

—Pandas. 2007. (J). (978-1-59939-126-7(0), Reader's Digest Young Families, Inc.) Studio Fun International.

Letkeman, Candice. All about Pandas. 2018. (Illus.). 24p. (978-1-4896-5674-2(X), AV2 by Weigl) Weigl Pubs., Inc.

Levine, Michelle. Giant Pandas. 2006. (Pull Ahead Books-Animals Ser.). (ENG., Illus.). 32p. (J). (gr. k-3). lib. bdg. 22.60 (978-0-8225-3482-2(7), Lerner Pubns.) Lerner Publishing Group.

Macheske, Felicia. Round & Rare: Giant Panda. 2017. (Guess What Ser.). (ENG., Illus.). 24p. (J). (gr. k-2). lib. bdg. 30.64 (978-1-63472-170-7(5), 209252) Cherry Lake Publishing.

Macleod, Steve. Panda Gigante. 2012. (SPA.). (J). 27.13 (978-1-61913-175-0(7)) Weigl Pubs., Inc.

Markle, Sandra. How Many Baby Pandas? / Scholastic Book Fair Edition. 2009. (Illus.). 32p. (J). pap. 4.99 (978-0-8027-2070-2(6)) Walker & Co.

Marsh, Laura. National Geographic Readers: Red Pandas. 2015. (Readers Ser.). (Illus.). 32p. (J). (gr. -1-k). pap. 4.99 (978-1-4263-2121-4(X), National Geographic Kids) Disney Publishing Worldwide.

Miller, Sara Swan. Red Pandas. (Paws & Claws Ser.). 24p. (gr. 2-3). 2009. 42.50 (978-1-60851-153-2(7)) 2008. (ENG., Illus.). (J). lib. bdg. 26.27 (978-1-4042-4164-0(7), 4f180ce1-f044-411f-a81d-543f9dc2f512) Rosen Publishing Group, Inc., The. (PowerKids Pr.).

Min, Fang. The Giant Panda. Daggers, Ben, tr. 2011. (Discovering China Ser.). (ENG., Illus.). 112p. 16.95 (978-1-60220-130-9(7)) Shanghai Pr.

Moldovo, Eustacia. Baby Pandas at the Zoo, 1 vol. 2015. (All about Baby Zoo Animals Ser.). (ENG., Illus.). 24p. (gr. -1-1). 24.27 (978-0-7660-7079-0(4), 780286b2-899a-4146-a601-b98b84fa95fd); pap. 10.35 (978-0-7660-7077-6(8), 5063e83a-2870-452f-a74f-ad2c3b725759) Enslow Publishing, LLC.

Murray, Julie. Panda Cubs. 2018. (Baby Animals (Abdo Kids Junior) Ser.). (ENG., Illus.). 24p. (J). (gr. -1-2). lib. bdg. 31.36 (978-1-5321-8166-5(3), 29889, Abdo Kids) ABDO Publishing Co.

—Pandas. 2019. (Animal Kingdom Ser.). (ENG., Illus.). 32p. (J). (gr. 2-5). lib. bdg. 34.21 (978-1-5321-1647-6(0), 32405, Big Buddy Bks.) ABDO Publishing Co.

National Geographic. National Geographic Readers: Favorite Animals Collection. 2013. (Readers Ser.). (Illus.). 128p. (J). (gr. -1-k). pap. 7.99 (978-1-4263-1333-2(0), National Geographic Kids) Disney Publishing Worldwide.

Olson, Bethany. Baby Pandas. 2013. (Super Cute! Ser.). (ENG., Illus.). 24p. (J). (gr. k-3). lib. bdg. 26.95 (978-1-60014-930-6(8), Blastoff! Readers) Bellwether Media.

Osborne, Mary Pope & Boyce, Natalie Pope. Pandas & Other Endangered Species: A Nonfiction Companion to Magic Tree House Merlin Mission #20: a Perfect Time for Pandas. Murdocca, Sal, illus. 2012. (Magic Tree House (R) Fact Tracker Ser.: 26). 128p. (J). (gr. 2-5). 6.99 (978-0-375-87025-5(3), Random Hse. Bks. for Young Readers) Random Hse. Children's Bks.

—Pandas & Other Endangered Species: A Perfect Time for Pandas. 2012. (Magic Tree House Fact Tracker Ser.: 26). lib. bdg. 16.00 (978-0-606-26400-6(0)) Turtleback.

Peterson, Megan Cooley & Rustad, Martha E. H. Giant Pandas Are Awesome! 2015. (Awesome Asian Animals Ser.). (ENG., Illus.). 32p. (J). (gr. -1-2). lib. bdg. 27.99 (978-1-4914-3905-0(X), 128622, Capstone Pr.) Capstone.

Pohl, Kathleen. Pandas, 1 vol. 2007. (Animals I See at the Zoo Ser.). (ENG.). 24p. (gr. k-2). pap. 9.15 (978-0-8368-8227-8(X), d77ba2ef-b549-4d0d-bff2-2e5a20d543ba); (Illus.). lib. bdg. 24.67 (978-0-8368-8220-9(2), f85a94ea-627f-438d-89d0-4ddc862a7bd4) Stevens, Gareth Publishing LLLP. (Weekly Reader Leveled Readers).

Portman, Michael. Pandas in Danger, 1 vol. 2011. (Animals at Risk Ser.). (ENG., Illus.). 24p. (J). (gr. 2-3). pap. 9.15 (978-1-4339-5800-7(7), c80e0d1c-b0c9-432e-9723-da7669bccc9e); lib. bdg. 25.27 (978-1-4339-5798-7(1), fd6894e4-5240-43c3-93ff-640e9e2605a9) Stevens, Gareth Publishing LLLP. (Gareth Stevens Learning Library).

Quinton, Sasha. Root-A-Toot: A Phonics Reader. 2009. (Illus.). pap. (978-1-936199-01-3(7)) Book Shop, Ltd., The.

Rebman, Nick. Pandas. 2018. (Animals Ser.). (ENG., Illus.). 16p. (J). (gr. k-1). pap. 7.95 (978-1-63517-954-5(8), 1635179548); lib. bdg. 25.64 (978-1-63517-853-1(3), 1635178533) North Star Editions. (Focus Readers).

Riggs, Kate. Pandas. 2015. (Seedlings Ser.). (ENG.). 24p. (J). (gr. -1-k). (978-1-60818-514-6(1), 21241, Creative Education) Creative Co., The.

—Seedlings: Pandas. 2015. (Seedlings Ser.). (ENG.). 24p. (J). (gr. -1-1). pap. 9.99 (978-1-62832-114-2(8), 21242, Creative Paperbacks) Creative Co., The.

Royston, Angela. Save the Giant Panda, 1 vol., 1. 2013. (Animal SOS! Ser.). (ENG.). 32p. (J). (gr. 2-3). pap. 11.00 (978-1-4777-6035-2(0), 0183aae7-8f14-4cf6-8944-7964556b37e6, Windmill Bks.) Rosen Publishing Group, Inc., The.

Rudolph, Jessica. MIS Bigotes Son Largos y Blancos (Red Panda) 2016. (Pistas de Animales 2/Zoo Clues 2 Ser.). (SPA.). 24p. (J). (gr. -1-3). 26.99 (978-1-944102-79-1(5)) Bearport Publishing Co., Inc.

—My Whiskers Are Long & White (Red Panda) 2016. (Zoo Clues 2 Ser.). (ENG., Illus.). 24p. (J). (gr. -1-3). 26.99 (978-1-944102-61-6(2)) Bearport Publishing Co., Inc.

Ryder, Joanne. Little Panda: The World Welcomes Hua Mei at the San Diego Zoo. 2004. (ENG., Illus.). 32p. (J). (gr. k-3). 8.99 (978-0-689-86616-6(X), Simon & Schuster Bks. For

Young Readers) Simon & Schuster Bks. For Young Readers.

—Panda Kindergarten. Feng, Katherine, photos by. 2014. (Illus.). 32p. pap. 8.00 *(978-1-61003-332-9(9))* Center for the Collaborative Classroom.

—Panda Kindergarten. 2015. (ENG., Illus.). 32p. (J). (gr. -1-3). pap. 7.99 *(978-0-06-057852-7(1)*, HarperCollins) HarperCollins Pubs.

—Panda Kindergarten. Feng, Katherine, illus. 2009. (ENG.). 32p. (J). (gr. -1-3). 17.99 *(978-0-06-057850-3(5)*, HarperCollins) HarperCollins Pubs.

Salomon, David. Baby Panda Goes Wild! 2019. (Step into Reading Ser.). (Illus.). 48p. (J). (gr. k-3). pap. 4.99 *(978-0-525-57916-8(8)*, Random Hse. Bks. for Young Readers) Random Hse. Children's Bks.

Schreiber, Anne. National Geographic Readers: Pandas. 2010. (Readers Ser.). (Illus.). 32p. (J). (gr. 1-3). (ENG.). 14.90 *(978-1-4263-0611-2(3))*; pap. 4.99 *(978-1-4263-0610-5(5))* Disney Publishing Worldwide. (National Geographic Kids).

—Pandas (1 Hardcover/1 CD) 2017. (National Geographic Kids Ser.). (ENG.). (J). 29.95 *(978-1-4301-2661-4(2))* Live Oak Media.

—Pandas (1 Paperback/1 CD) 2017. (National Geographic Kids Ser.). (ENG.). (J). pap. 19.95 *(978-1-4301-2660-7(4))* Live Oak Media.

—Pandas (4 Paperbacks/1 CD), 4 vols. 2017. (National Geographic Kids Ser.). (ENG.). (J). pap. 31.95 *(978-1-4301-2662-1(0))* Live Oak Media.

Schuetz, Kari. Giant Pandas. 2011. (Animal Safari Ser.). (ENG., Illus.). 24p. (J). (gr. k-3). lib. bdg. 26.95 *(978-1-60014-603-9(1)*, Blastoff! Readers) Bellwether Media.

Schuh, Mari. Giant Pandas. 2017. (Black & White Animals Ser.). (ENG., Illus.). 24p. (J). (gr. -1-2). lib. bdg. 22.65 *(978-1-5157-3372-0(6)*, 133368, Pebble) Capstone.

Shea, Bobby Kennedy. Patterns with Pandas. 2013. (Animal Math Ser.). 24p. (J). (gr. 1-3). pap. 48.90 *(978-1-4339-9320-6(1))* Stevens, Gareth Publishing LLLP.

Shea, Mary Molly. Deadly Pandas, 1 vol. 2017. (Cutest Animals... That Could Kill You! Ser.). (ENG.). 24p. (J). (gr. 2-3). pap. 9.15 *(978-1-5382-1080-2(0)*, b0163cb7-089b-47d7-8161-fff07492cb3d) Stevens, Gareth Publishing LLLP.

Simon, Mary Manz. Panda Is Polite. 2006. (First Virtuestm for Toddlers Ser.). (Illus.). 20p. (J). 5.99 *(978-0-7847-1577-2(7)*, 04071) Standard Publishing.

Soundprints, creator. Panda's Busy Day. 2011. (Let's Go to the Zoo! Ser.). (ENG., Illus.). 16p. (gr. -1). 5.95 *(978-1-60727-455-1(8))* Soundprints.

Staff, Gareth Editorial Staff. Pandas, 1 vol. 2004. (All about Wild Animals Ser.). (ENG., Illus.). 32p. (J). (gr. 2-4). lib. bdg. 28.67 *(978-0-8368-4121-3(2)*, 6461d8a5-bc68-4370-bb4e-0fb8f4467dd9, Gareth Stevens Learning Library) Stevens, Gareth Publishing LLLP.

Star, Fleur, et al. Panda. 2008. (DK Watch Me Grow Ser.). (ENG., Illus.). 24p. (J). (gr. -1-3). 22.44 *(978-0-7566-3432-2(6))* Dorling Kindersley Publishing, Inc.

Stone, Lynn M. Giant Pandas. Su, Keren, photos by. 2003. (Nature Watch Ser.). (ENG., Illus.). 48p. (J). (gr. 4-8). 27.93 *(978-1-57505-343-1(8)*, Carolrhoda Bks.) Lerner Publishing Group.

Strother, Ruth. Absolute Expert - Pandas: All the Latest Facts from the Field with National Geographic Explorer Mark Brody. 2019. (Absolute Expert Ser.). (Illus.). 112p. (J). (gr. 3-7). 14.99 *(978-1-4263-3431-3(1)*, National Geographic Kids) Disney Publishing Worldwide.

—Absolute Expert: Pandas: All the Latest Facts from the Field with National Geographic Explorer Mark Brody. 2019. (Absolute Expert Ser.). (ENG., Illus.). 112p. (J). (gr. 3-7). lib. bdg. 24.90 *(978-1-4263-3432-0(X)*, National Geographic Kids) Disney Publishing Worldwide.

Thimmesh, Catherine. Camp Panda: Helping Cubs Return to the Wild. 2018. (ENG., Illus.). 64p. (J). (gr. 5-7). 17.99 *(978-0-544-81891-0(1)*, 1642679, Clarion Bks.) HarperCollins Pubs.

Torres, John. Threat to the Giant Panda. 2008. (On the Verge of Extinction Ser.). (Illus.). 32p. (J). (gr. 2-5). lib. bdg. 25.70 *(978-1-58415-689-5(9))* Mitchell Lane Pubs.

Trueit, Trudi Strain. Giant Pandas. 2015. (Wild Bears Ser.). (ENG., Illus.). 24p. (J). (gr. 1-4). lib. bdg. 19.95 *(978-1-60753-774-8(5)*, 15290) Amicus.

Turnbull, Stephanie. Panda. 2015. (ENG., Illus.). 24p. (J). pap. 8.95 *(978-1-77092-217-4(2))* RiverStream Publishing.

Volke, Gordon, et al, illus. Panda Patrol Sticker, Story & Activitity Book, Vol. 2. 2004. 16p. pap., act. bk. ed. 6.00 *(978-1-84161-112-9(3))* Ravette Publishing, Ltd. GBR. Dist: Parkwest Pubns., Inc.

—Panda Patrol Sticker, Story & Activity Book. 2004. 16p. pap., act. bk. ed. 6.00 *(978-1-84161-072-6(0))* Ravette Publishing, Ltd. GBR. Dist: Parkwest Pubns., Inc.

—Panda Patrol Travel Games with Stickers. 2004. 16p. pap., act. bk. ed. 6.00 *(978-1-84161-110-5(7))* Ravette Publishing, Ltd. GBR. Dist: Parkwest Pubns., Inc.

Zeiger, Jennifer. Pandas. 2012. (Nature's Children Ser.). (ENG.). 48p. (J). (gr. 3-5). lib. bdg. 28.00 *(978-0-531-20905-9(9)*, Children's Pr.) Scholastic Library Publishing.

PANDAS—FICTION

Alderfer, Lauren. Mindful Monkey, Happy Panda. MacLean, Kerry Lee, illus. 2011. (ENG.). 32p. (J). (gr. -1-3). 18.95 *(978-0-86171-683-8(3))* Wisdom Pubns.

Alfred Sole. Pandi's Adventures in Afric. Patradol Kitcharoen, illus. 2012. 86p. pap. 23.97 *(978-1-61897-493-8(9)*, Strategic Bk. Publishing) Strategic Book Publishing & Rights Agency (SBPRA).

Amara, Phil & Chin, Oliver. The Discovery of Fireworks & Gunpowder: The Asian Hall of Fame. Calle, Juan, illus. 2018. (Asian Hall of Fame Ser.). (ENG.). 40p. (J). (gr. -1-3). 16.95 *(978-1-59702-142-5(3))* Immedium.

—The Discovery of Ramen: The Asian Hall of Fame. 2017. (Asian Hall of Fame Ser.). (ENG., Illus.). 40p. (J). (gr. -1-3). 16.95 *(978-1-59702-134-0(2))* Immedium.

Antony, Steve. Please, Mr. Panda. Antony, Steve, illus. 2014. (ENG., Illus.). 32p. (J). (gr. -1-k). 16.99 *(978-0-545-78892-2(7)*, Scholastic Pr.) Scholastic, Inc.

—Thank You, Mr. Panda. 2017. (ENG., Illus.). 32p. (J). (gr. -1-k). 16.99 *(978-1-338-15836-6(8)*, Scholastic Pr.) Scholastic, Inc.

Austin, Rikey. Ting Finds a Bell: Alice's Bear Shop. 2012. 28p. pap. *(978-1-78092-158-7(6))* MX Publishing, Ltd.

Bamboo Zoo Set: Meet Lester Panda & his Friends. 2006. (J). 17.95 *(978-0-9774493-1-6(9))* Bamboo Zoo, LLC.

Bedford, David. Birdy & Bou. Stanley, Mandy, illus. 2018. (J). *(978-1-4351-6727-8(9))* Barnes & Noble, Inc.

Bell, Frank. Feng Suey's Special Garden. Seaman, Paul, illus. 2004. 24p. pap. 7.00 *(978-1-84161-071-9(2))* Ravette Publishing, Ltd. GBR. Dist: Parkwest Pubns., Inc.

—How Slip Slap Slop Got His Name. Seaman, Paul, illus. 2004. 24p. pap. 7.00 *(978-1-84161-069-6(0))* Ravette Publishing, Ltd. GBR. Dist: Parkwest Pubns., Inc.

—Ma Jong & the Magic Carpet. Seaman, Paul, illus. 2004. 24p. pap. 7.00 *(978-1-84161-070-2(4))* Ravette Publishing, Ltd. GBR. Dist: Parkwest Pubns., Inc.

Bernal, Sandra Marie. I Want a Pand. 2011. 32p. pap. 24.95 *(978-1-4626-2897-1(4))* America Star Bks.

Book Buddy: Panda with Story Book. Orig. Title: Child's Play. (Illus.). 10p. (J). (gr. -1-3). reprint ed. *(978-1-881469-44-5(1))* Safari, Ltd.

Bowen, Sherry. Little Panda. Wallace, Chad, illus. 2003. (Books for Young Learners). (ENG.). 12p. (J). 5.75 net. *(978-1-57274-673-2(4)*, 2459, Bks. for Young Learners) Owen, Richard C. Pubs., Inc.

Brennan, Sarah. The Tale of Pin Yin Panda. Harrison, Harry, illus. 2012. (ENG.). 32p. (J). 24.95 *(978-1-937160-15-9(7))* Eliassen Creative.

Briant, Ed. A Day at the Beach, No. 1. Briant, Ed, illus. 2006. (Illus.). 32p. (J). (gr. -1). 17.89 *(978-0-06-079982-3(X))* HarperCollins Pubs.

Brighter Minds, creator. Fact Book. 2008. (DreamWorks Kung Fu Panda Ser.). (Illus.). 10p. (J). (gr. -1-3). 9.95 *(978-1-57791-420-4(1))* Brighter Minds Children's Publishing.

—Kung Fu Panda: Create-A-Story. 2008. (Illus.). 8p. (J). (gr. k-2). 9.95 *(978-1-57791-419-8(8))* Brighter Minds Children's Publishing.

—Kung Fu Panda Magnetic Storybook. 2008. (DreamWorks Kung Fu Panda Ser.). (Illus.). 10p. (J). (gr. 1-3). bds. 12.95 *(978-1-57791-421-1(X))* Brighter Minds Children's Publishing.

Buffomante, Maya. How Pandas Became Black & White. 2012. 24p. pap. *(978-1-4602-0613-3(4))* FriesenPress.

Capucilli, Alyssa Satin. Panda Kisses. Widdowson, Kay, illus. 2008. (Step into Reading: Step 1 Ser.). (ENG.). 32p. (J). (gr. -1-1). lib. bdg. 16.19 *(978-0-375-94562-5(8))* Random House Publishing Group.

—Panda Kisses. Widdowson, Kay, illus. 2008. (Step into Reading Ser.). 32p. (J). (gr. -1-1). pap. 5.99 *(978-0-375-84562-8(3)*, Random Hse. Bks. for Young Readers) Random Hse. Children's Bks.

Chihak, Sheena. Kung Fu Panda 3-D Puzzle Book. Salesse, Alain, illus. 2008. 10p. (J). 9.99 *(978-0-696-23485-9(8))* Meredith Bks.

—Kung Fu Panda: Paws of Power Activity Kit. 2008. (Illus.). 32p. (J). 14.99 *(978-0-696-23483-5(1))* Meredith Bks.

Chihak, Sheena & Loki. Kung Fu Panda. Mada Design Inc, illus. 2008. (I Can Find It Ser.). 22p. (J). 7.99 *(978-0-696-23484-2(X))* Meredith Bks.

Child, Lauren. I Am Going to Save a Panda! 2010. (Charlie & Lola Ser.). lib. bdg. 13.55 *(978-0-606-10628-3(6))* Turtleback.

Chronicle Books, Chronicle & ImageBooks. Little Panda: Finger Puppet Book: (Finger Puppet Book for Toddlers & Babies, Baby Books for First Year, Animal Finger Puppets) 2009. (Little Finger Puppet Board Bks.: FING). (ENG., Illus.). 12p. (J). (gr. -1 — 1). bds. 6.99 *(978-0-8118-6999-7(7))* Chronicle Bks. LLC.

Cook, Sherry & Johnson, Terri. Pressure Pete, 26 vols. Kuhn, Jesse, illus. l.t. ed. 2006. (Quirkles — Exploring Phonics through Science Ser.: 16). 32p. (J). 7.99 *(978-1-933815-15-2(9)*, Quirkles, The) Creative 3, LLC.

Cornish, Linda Sowa Young. Pong's Birthday Journey. 2006. (J). pap. 15.00 *(978-0-8059-6993-1(4))* Dorrance Publishing Co., Inc.

Crowley, Ashley. Officer Panda: Fingerprint Detective. Crowley, Ashley, illus. 2015. (Officer Panda Ser.: 1). (ENG., Illus.). 32p. (J). (gr. -1-3). 17.99 *(978-0-06-236626-9(2)*, HarperCollins) HarperCollins Pubs.

Dahl, Michael. Playdate for Panda. Vidal, Oriol, illus. 2016. (Hello Genius Ser.). (ENG.). 20p. (J). (gr. -1 — 1). bds. 7.99 *(978-1-4795-8741-4(9)*, 131130, Picture Window Bks.) Capstone.

David, Erica. Po's Two Dads. 2015. (Kung Fu Panda Ready-To-Read Ser.). lib. bdg. 13.55 *(978-0-606-38241-0(0))* Turtleback.

Davies, Jacqueline. Panda Pants. Hanson, Sydney, illus. 2016. 32p. (J). (gr. -1-2). 17.99 *(978-0-553-53576-1(5)*, Knopf Bks. for Young Readers) Random Hse. Children's Bks.

Dillard, Sarah. First Day at Zoo School. Dillard, Sarah, illus. 2014. (ENG., Illus.). 40p. (J). (gr. k-2). 14.99 *(978-1-58536-890-7(3)*, 203670) Sleeping Bear Pr.

Disney Publishing Staff & Studiomouse Staff. Panda Cub Explores. 2011. (ENG., Illus.). 20p. (J). *(978-1-59069-944-7(0))* Studio Mouse LLC.

DreamWorks. Kung Fu Panda: Po's Tasty Training. 2008. (J). 13.99 *(978-1-59319-981-4(3))* LeapFrog Enterprises, Inc.

DreamWorks & DreamWorks / LeapFrog. Kung Fu Panda: L'Entrainement Gourmand. 2008. (J). 20.79 *(978-1-59319-946-3(5))* LeapFrog Enterprises, Inc.

Duncan, Randy. Miranda & Her Pand. 2009. 28p. pap. 12.49 *(978-1-4389-6132-3(4))* AuthorHouse.

Evans, Ruth Todd. The Panda Who Would Not Eat. Evans, Ruth Todd, illus. 2007. (Illus.). 32p. (J). (gr. -1-3). per. 9.95 *(978-0-932653-84-0(7))* Sunbelt Pubns., Inc.

Forsythe, Amanda J. The Contabulous Adventures of M E. 2012. 28p. 24.95 *(978-1-4626-6531-0(4))* America Star Bks.

Franklin, Deborah. Annette's Christmas Gift. 2008. (Illus.). 24p. (YA). 7.00 *(978-0-8059-7482-9(2))* Dorrance Publishing Co., Inc.

Gaiman, Neil. Chu's Day. Rex, Adam, illus. (ENG.). (J). (gr. -1-3). 2014. 40p. pap. 6.99 *(978-0-06-201783-3(7))* 2013. 32p. 17.99 *(978-0-06-201781-9(0)*, HarperCollins) HarperCollins Pubs.

—Chu's Day at the Beach. Rex, Adam, illus. 2015. (ENG.). 32p. (J). (gr. -1-3). 17.99 *(978-0-06-222399-9(2)*, HarperCollins) HarperCollins Pubs.

—Chu's Day Board Book. Rex, Adam, illus. 2014. (ENG.). 36p. (J). (gr. -1 — 1). bds. 7.99 *(978-0-06-234746-6(2)*, HarperFestival) HarperCollins Pubs.

—Chu's First Day of School. Rex, Adam, illus. 2014. (ENG.). 32p. (J). (gr. -1-3). 18.99 *(978-0-06-222397-5(6)*, HarperCollins) HarperCollins Pubs.

—Chu's First Day of School Board Book. Rex, Adam, illus. 2015. (ENG.). 36p. (J). (gr. -1 — 1). bds. 8.99 *(978-0-06-237149-2(5)*, HarperFestival) HarperCollins Pubs.

Gallo, Tina. Like Father, Like Po. 2015. (Kung Fu Panda 8x8 Ser.). lib. bdg. 13.55 *(978-0-606-38257-1(7))* Turtleback.

—Po's Awesomely Perfect Present. 2015. (Kung Fu Panda 8x8 Ser.). lib. bdg. 13.55 *(978-0-606-37870-3(7))* Turtleback.

Gibbs, Lynne. Time to Share: A Story of Sharing, 1 vol. Mitchell, Missy, illus. 2009. (Let's Grow Together Ser.). (ENG.). 32p. (J). (gr. k-1). lib. bdg. 27.27 *(978-1-60754-757-0(0)*, a262b884-7f2d-4103-aad4-a1ff78ae63e4, Windmill Bks.) Rosen Publishing Group, Inc., The.

Gibbs, Stuart. Panda-Monium. (FunJungle Ser.). (ENG.). (J). (gr. 3-7). 2018. 384p. pap. 8.99 *(978-1-4814-4568-9(5))* 2017. (Illus.). 352p. 18.99 *(978-1-4814-4567-2(7))* Simon & Schuster Bks. For Young Readers. (Simon & Schuster Bks. For Young Readers).

—Panda-Monium. 2018. (Funjungle (Teddy Fitzroy) Ser.: 4). lib. bdg. 18.40 *(978-0-606-40849-3(5))* Turtleback.

Glass, Shelby. Something Is Everything. 2012. 36p. pap. 19.99 *(978-1-4772-6581-9(3))* AuthorHouse.

Green, John Patrick. Hippopotamister. 2016. (ENG., Illus.). 96p. (J). 18.99 *(978-1-62672-200-2(5)*, 900144759, First Second Bks.) Roaring Brook Pr.

Hay DeSimone, Corkey. Panda Promise Activity & Coloring Book. Hay DeSimone, Corkey, illus. 2006. (Illus.). (J). 4.95 *(978-0-9747921-9-4(5))* Gentle Giraffe Pr.

Heston, L. L. The Story of Pan Doo: A Panda's Progress. 2012. 24p. pap. 15.99 *(978-1-4771-2392-8(X))* Xlibris Corp.

Hunt, Elizabeth Singer. Secret Agent Jack Stalwart: Book 7: the Puzzle of the Missing Panda: China, Bk. 7. 2008. (Secret Agent Jack Stalwart Ser.: 7). (ENG., Illus.). 128p. (J). (gr. 1-4). pap. 5.99 *(978-1-60286-020-9(3))* Hachette Bk. Group.

Kuo, Fifi. The Perfect Sofa. 2019. (ENG.). 32p. (J). (gr. -1-3). 17.99 *(978-1-4998-0742-4(2))* Little Bee Books Inc.

Lin, Chris. Mandy & Pandy Play Sports. Villalta, Ingrid, illus. 2008. 20p. (J). (gr. -1-3). bds. 9.99 *(978-0-9800156-7-6(7))* Mandy & Pandy Bks., LLC.

—Mandy & Pandy Visit China. Villalta, Ingrid, illus. 2008. 20p. (J). (gr. -1-3). bds. 9.99 *(978-0-9800156-6-9(9))* Mandy & Pandy Bks., LLC.

Lumry, Amanda & Hurwitz, Laura. Project Panda. 2008. (J). *(978-1-60040-008-7(6))*; *(978-1-60040-009-4(4))* Eaglemont Pr.

Lynn, Jeffrey. The Adventures of Pablo. . the Ecuadorian Panda. 2004. (YA). per. *(978-0-9763025-0-6(0))* Penner/Lynn Publishing.

Manushkin, Fran. Bamboo for Me, Bamboo for You! Hernandez, Purificacion, illus. 2017. (ENG.). 32p. (J). (gr. -1-3). 17.99 *(978-1-4814-5063-8(8)*, Aladdin) Simon & Schuster Children's Publishing.

Martin, Bill, Jr. Panda Bear, Panda Bear, What Do You See? Carle, Eric, illus. rev. ed. 2003. (Brown Bear & Friends Ser.). (ENG.). 32p. (J). (gr. -1-k). 18.99 *(978-0-8050-1758-8(5)*, 900019009, Holt, Henry & Co. Bks. For Young Readers) Holt, Henry & Co.

McDonald, Jill, illus. Ghoulish Gang. 2008. (ENG.). 12p. (J). 9.95 *(978-1-58117-782-4(8)*, Intervisual/Piggy Toes) Bendon, Inc.

Meadows, Daisy. Mae the Panda Fairy. 2015. (Rainbow Magic — Baby Animal Rescue Fairies Ser.: 1). lib. bdg. 14.75 *(978-0-606-37049-3(8))* Turtleback.

Meldrum, Margaret. Peter Panda & His Friends. 2009. (Illus.). 24p. pap. 11.49 *(978-1-4343-7826-2(8))* AuthorHouse.

Meredith Books Staff, creator. Kung Fu Panda. 2008. (Illus.). 22p. (J). 15.95 *(978-0-696-23482-8(3))* Meredith Bks.

Milbourne, A. & Wells, R. Panda in the Park. 2004. (Look-Through Board Bks.). (Illus.). 10p. (J). (gr. -1-18). 4.95 *(978-0-7945-0158-7(3)*, Usborne) EDC Publishing.

Moody-Luther, Jacqueline. Panda Bear Cub. Nelson, Will, illus. 2006. (ENG.). 32p. (J). pap. 3.95 *(978-1-59249-585-6(0))* Soundprints.

Mucklow, Hope. Rojo the Baby Red Panda at the Zoo: An Allegory about Self-Worth Through a Red Panda & Giant Panda Comparison. 2014. (ENG., Illus.). 32p. (J). (gr. -1-3). 14.95 *(978-1-62086-593-4(9))* Amplify Publishing Group.

Muth, Jon J. Addy's Cup of Sugar: Based on a Buddhist Story of Healing (a Stillwater & Friends Book) Muth, Jon J., illus. 2020. (ENG., Illus.). 32p. (J). (gr. -1-3). 17.99 *(978-0-439-63428-1(8)*, Scholastic Pr.) Scholastic, Inc.

—Zen Ghosts (a Stillwater & Friends Book) Muth, Jon J., illus. 2010. (ENG., Illus.). 40p. (J). (gr. -1-3). 18.99 *(978-0-439-63430-4(X)*, Scholastic Pr.) Scholastic, Inc.

—Zen Shorts, 1 vol. Muth, Jon J., illus. 2010. (ENG.). (J). (gr. -1-3). audio compact disk 18.99 *(978-0-545-22760-5(7))* Scholastic, Inc.

—Zen Socks (a Stillwater & Friends Book) Muth, Jon J., illus. 2015. (ENG., Illus.). 40p. (J). (gr. -1-3). 17.99 *(978-0-545-16669-0(1)*, Scholastic Pr.) Scholastic, Inc.

—Zen Ties (a Stillwater & Friends Book) Muth, Jon J., illus. 2008. (ENG., Illus.). 40p. (J). (gr. -1-3). 18.99 *(978-0-439-63425-0(3)*, Scholastic Pr.) Scholastic, Inc.

Nagda, Ann Whitehead. A Home for Panda. Effler, Jim, illus. (Amazing Animal Adventures Ser.). (ENG.). 36p. (J). 2005. (gr. -1-2). 15.95 *(978-1-59249-045-5(X)*, B7102) 2005. (gr. -1-2). pap. 6.95 *(978-1-59249-046-2(8)*, S7102) 2005. (gr. 2-2). 8.95 *(978-1-59249-393-7(9)*, SC7102) 2005. (gr. 2-2). 19.95 *(978-1-59249-392-0(0)*, BC7102) 2003. (gr. -1-3). 2.95 *(978-1-59249-047-9(6)*, S7152) Soundprints.

—A Home for Panda. Effler, Jim, illus. 2003. (ENG.). 36p. (J). (gr. -1-3). 9.95 *(978-1-59249-058-5(1)*, PS7152) Soundprints.

—Time to Eat, Panda! 2005. (Soundprints' Read-and-Discover Ser.). (ENG., Illus.). 32p. (J). (gr. -1-1). 12.95 *(978-1-59249-148-3(0)*, PS2011) Soundprints.

Nagda, Ann Whitehead, text. Time to Eat, Panda! 2005. (Soundprints' Read-and-Discover Ser.). (ENG., Illus.). 32p. (J). (gr. -1-1). pap. 3.95 *(978-1-59249-147-6(2)*, S2011) Soundprints.

Nona Theresa Perez - Bayanin. The Birth of Nadia Mei. 2012. 24p. pap. 15.99 *(978-1-4771-0387-6(2))* Xlibris Corp.

Osborne, Mary Pope. A Perfect Time for Pandas, Bk. 20. Murdocca, Sal, illus. 2014. (Magic Tree House (R) Merlin Mission Ser.: 20). (ENG.). 144p. (J). (gr. 2-5). pap. 6.99 *(978-0-375-86798-9(8)*, Random Hse. Bks. for Young Readers) Random Hse. Children's Bks.

—A Perfect Time for Pandas. 2014. (Magic Tree House Merlin Missions Ser.: 20). lib. bdg. 16.00 *(978-0-606-35564-3(2))* Turtleback.

Panda, Jake G. The Case of the Cursed Dodo. 2014. (Illus.). 173p. (J). pap. 8.99 *(978-0-9909391-1-5(1))* Woolley Family Studios.

Pandas Are Coming! Fourth Grade Guided Comprehension Level O. (On Our Way to English Ser.). (gr. 4-18). 34.50 *(978-0-7578-7167-2(4))* Rigby Education.

Park, Linda Sue. Xander's Panda Party. Phelan, Matt, illus. (ENG.). 40p. (J). (gr. -1-3). 2017. pap. 8.99 *(978-1-328-74058-8(7)*, 1677033) 2013. 16.99 *(978-0-547-55865-3(1)*, 1453620) HarperCollins Pubs. (Clarion Bks.).

Paul, Ruth. Red Panda's Candy Apples. Paul, Ruth, illus. 2014. (ENG., Illus.). 32p. (J). (gr. -1-2). 14.99 *(978-0-7636-6758-0(7))* Candlewick Pr.

Pauley, Christa. Manda Panda & the Loons. 2013. 32p. pap. 19.99 *(978-1-62697-016-8(5))* Salem Author Services.

Pendergrass, Daphne. Secrets of the Secret Panda Village. 2015. (Kung Fu Panda 8x8 Ser.). lib. bdg. 16.00 *(978-0-606-38259-5(3))* Turtleback.

Penelope Panda's Shooting Star. 2008. (Illus.). 32p. (J). (gr. k-3). pap. 14.99 *(978-0-9717290-3-2(4))* Adrema Pr.

Pickard, Chante. The Adventures of Louie the Panda. 2006. (ENG.). 32p. per. 19.99 *(978-1-4259-0490-6(4))* AuthorHouse.

Platt, Cynthia. Panda-Monium! Vasylenko, Veronica, illus. 2011. (ENG.). 32p. (J). (gr. -1-2). 15.95 *(978-1-58925-093-2(1))*; pap. 7.95 *(978-1-58925-425-1(2))* Tiger Tales.

Powell, Richard. Peter Panda. Rhodes, Katie, illus. 2004. (Fuzzy Friends Ser.). 10p. (J). 7.95 *(978-1-58925-721-4(9))* Tiger Tales.

Prendergast, Gabrielle. Pandas on the Eastside, 1 vol. 2016. (ENG., Illus.). 192p. (J). (gr. 4-7). pap. 9.95 *(978-1-4598-1143-0(7))* Orca Bk. Pubs. USA.

Ransom, Candice. Amanda Panda & the Bigger, Better Birthday. Grove, Christine, illus. 2018. 32p. (J). (gr. -1-2). 17.99 *(978-1-5247-6819-5(7)*, Doubleday Bks. for Young Readers) Random Hse. Children's Bks.

Rim, Sujean. Chee-Kee: a Panda in Bearland. 2017. (ENG., Illus.). 40p. (J). (gr. -1-3). 17.99 *(978-0-316-40744-1(5))* Little, Brown Bks. for Young Readers.

Rix, James. Panda Panic. 2013. (Awesome Animals Ser.). (ENG., Illus.). 192p. (J). (gr. 2-4). 21.19 *(978-1-4380-0304-7(8)*, B.E.S. Publishing) Peterson's.

Sang, Franchesca Ho, compiled by. Wisdom of Pandas. 2006. (Wisdom of Animals Ser.). (Illus.). 128p. (J). (gr. k). *(978-1-59258-253-2(2))* Hylas Publishing.

Schindel, John. Busy Pandas. Husar, Lisa & Husar, Mike, photos by. 2008. (Busy Book Ser.). (Illus.). 20p. (J). (gr. -1 — 1). 6.99 *(978-1-58246-259-2(3)*, Knopf Bks. for Young Readers) Random Hse. Children's Bks.

Shealeya, Mildred. Pookie Lookie: The Pink Spotted Panda Bear. Gang, Jobie, illus. 2007. 32p. (J). per. 12.95 *(978-0-9669595-7-4(4))* SMS Cos., Inc.

Soundprints. Panda Cub in the Bamboo Forest: Wilderness Adventures. 2012. (ENG.). 32p. (J). pap. 3.95 *(978-1-60727-872-6(3))* Soundprints.

Temple, Kate & Temple, Jol. Are You My Bottom? Ghosh, Ronojoy, illus. 2019. (ENG.). 32p. (J). (gr. -1-k). 16.99 *(978-1-76063-164-2(7))* Allen & Unwin AUS. Dist: Independent Pubs. Group.

Testa, Maggie. The Power of Po. 2015. (Kung Fu Panda 8x8 Ser.). lib. bdg. 13.55 *(978-0-606-38258-8(5))* Turtleback.

Tipper, Sarah. Eviscerated Panda: Back in Bamboo. 2013. (ENG.). 346p. pap. 15.75 *(978-1-78035-624-2(2)*, Fastprint Publishing) Upfront Publishing Ltd. GBR. Dist: Printondemand-worldwide.com.

Venable, Colleen AF. Amy the Red Panda Is Writing the Best Story in the World. Chan, Ruth, illus. 2017. (ENG.). 40p. (J). (gr. -1-3). 17.99 *(978-0-06-233848-8(X)*, Greenwillow Bks.) HarperCollins Pubs.

Wacker, Eileen. Rainbow Panda & the Firecracker Fiasco. 2013. (ENG.). 40p. (J). 10.99 *(978-1-4675-1749-2(6)*, ee7a13f8-4710-4a26-a389-bc5f01119044) Oncekids.

Waldron, Kevin. Panda-Monium at Peek Zoo. Waldron, Kevin, illus. 2014. (ENG., Illus.). 40p. (J). (gr. -1-2). 16.99 *(978-0-7636-6658-3(0)*, Templar) Candlewick Pr.

Wang, Kateri. Wang Ming: The Greatest of the Great Pandas. 2012. 32p. pap. 19.99 *(978-1-4772-9042-2(7))* AuthorHouse.

Watt, Fiona. That's Not My Panda. 2013. (Touchy-Feely Board Bks). 10p. (J). ring bd. 9.99 *(978-0-7945-3332-8(9)*, Usborne) EDC Publishing.

Weatherstone, Hollie. When the Pandas Came to Scotland. Cochrane, Claire, illus. 2012. (ENG.). 24p. pap. 19.82 *(978-1-4772-3528-7(0))* AuthorHouse.

West, Tracey. Kung Fu Panda 3 Movie Novelization. 2015. lib. bdg. 17.20 *(978-0-606-38260-1(7))* Turtleback.

Xuan, Xuan Loc. Giant: A Panda of the Enchanted Forest. 2018. (ENG., Illus.). 38p. (J). 14.99 *(978-1-64124-014-7(8)*, 0147) Fox Chapel Publishing Co., Inc.

Yim, Natasha. Goldy Luck & the Three Pandas. Zong, Grace, illus. 32p. (J). (gr. -1-3). 2015. (ENG.). pap. 7.95 *(978-1-58089-653-5(7))* 2014. lib. bdg. 17.99 *(978-1-58089-652-8(9))* Charlesbridge Publishing, Inc.

Yip, Mingmei. Grandma Panda's China Storybook: Legends, Traditions & Fun. 2017. (ENG., Illus.). 32p. (J). (gr. -1-3). 9.99 *(978-0-8048-4974-6(9))* Tuttle Publishing.

Zhang, Crystal. Lil' P & His Big Problem, 1 vol. 2010. 32p. pap. 24.95 *(978-1-4489-8319-3(3))* PublishAmerica, Inc.

PANKHURST, EMMELINE, 1858-1928

Barnham, Kay. History VIPs: Emmeline Pankhurst. 2017. (History VIPs Ser.). (ENG., Illus.). 32p. (J). (gr. 4-6). 17.99 *(978-0-7502-8850-7(7)*, Wayland) Hachette Children's Group GBR. Dist: Hachette Bk. Group.

Kaiser, Lisbeth. Emmeline Pankhurst, Volume 8. Sanfelippo, Ana, illus. 2017. (Little People, BIG DREAMS Ser.: 8). (ENG.). 32p. (J). (gr. k-3). 15.99 *(978-1-78603-020-7(9)*, Frances Lincoln Children's Bks.) Quarto Publishing Group UK GBR. Dist: Hachette Bk. Group.

PANTHERS

Cain, Marie Mowery. Big Bad Cats. 2013. (Big Books, Red Ser.). (ENG & SPA., Illus.). 16p. pap. 33.00 *(978-1-59246-209-4(X))* Big Books, by George!

Caper, William. Florida Panthers: Struggle for Survival. 2007. (America's Animal Comebacks Ser.). (Illus.). 32p. (YA). (gr. 2-5). lib. bdg. 25.27 *(978-1-59716-532-7(8))* Bearport Publishing Co., Inc.

Group/McGraw-Hill, Wright. Panther Level: Adventure Journal Set. (Wildcats Ser.). (gr. 2-8). 31.95 *(978-0-322-05793-7(0))* Wright Group/McGraw-Hill.

—Panther Level: Wildcats Panther Complete Kit. (Wildcats Ser.). (gr. 2-8). 599.95 *(978-0-322-06490-4(2))* Wright Group/McGraw-Hill.

Somervill, Barbara A. Florida Panther. 2009. (21st Century Skills Library: Road to Recovery Ser.). (ENG., Illus.). 32p. (gr. 4-8). lib. bdg. 32.07 *(978-1-60279-316-3(6)*, 200212) Cherry Lake Publishing.

Wexo, John Bonnett. Panteras. Rountree, Monica, tr. 2003. (Zoobooks Ser.). Orig. Title: Bit Cats. (SPA., Illus.). 24p. (J). (gr. k-6). lib. bdg. 15.95 *(978-1-888153-80-4(6))* National Wildlife Federation.

PANTHERS—FICTION

Aryal, Aimee. Let's Go Bengals! 2008. (J). 14.95 *(978-1-932888-23-2(3))* Amplify Publishing Group.

Costello, Emily. Realm of the Panther: A Story of South Florida's Forest. 2005. (Soundprints' Wild Habitats Ser.). (ENG., Illus.). 32p. (J). (gr. 1-4). 8.95 *(978-1-59249-104-9(9))* Soundprints.

Graydon, William Murray. The Jungle Boy; or, Sexton Blake's Adventures in India. 2007. 120p. per. 14.99 *(978-1-4344-0189-2(8))* Wildside Pr., LLC.

Henderson, Milagros. Lulu the Bouncing Kangaroo. 2012. 36p. (-18). pap. 20.99 *(978-1-4772-8899-3(6))* AuthorHouse.

JohnsonMargaret. Running Wild Level 3 Lower-Intermediate. 2009. (Cambridge Experience Readers Ser.). (ENG.). 80p. pap. 14.75 *(978-84-8323-501-0(3))* Cambridge Univ. Pr.

Orr, Wendy. The Princess & Her Panther. Stringer, Lauren, illus. 2010. (ENG.). 40p. (J). (gr. -1-3). 16.99 *(978-1-4169-9780-1(6)*, Beach Lane Bks.) Beach Lane Bks.

Puerto, Carlos & Puerto, Carlos. Las Alas de la Pantera. (Barco de Vapor). (SPA.). 128p. (YA). (gr. 5-8). *(978-84-348-4667-8(5))* SM Ediciones.

Sargent, Pat. The Black Panther, 8 vols., Vol. 2. Lenoir, Jane, illus. 2003. (Barney the Bear Killer Ser.: Vol. 2). 137p. (J). lib. bdg. 26.25 *(978-1-56763-965-0(8))* Ozark Publishing.

Wallace, Bill. Danger on Panther Peak. 2008. (ENG., Illus.). 176p. (J). (gr. 3-7). pap. 6.99 *(978-1-4169-4110-1(X)*, Simon & Schuster/Paula Wiseman Bks.) Simon & Schuster/Paula Wiseman Bks.

PAPACY—HISTORY

Marchione, Margherita. Pope Pius XII: Bilingual Coloring Book. Elliott, John, illus. 2004. (SPA & ENG.). 32p. 1.00 *(978-0-8091-6721-0(2)*, 6721-2) Paulist Pr.

Stine, Megan & Who HQ. Where Is the Vatican? Conley, Laurie A., illus. 2019. (Where Is? Ser.). 112p. (J). (gr. 3-7). 5.99 *(978-1-5247-9259-6(4))*; 15.99 *(978-1-5247-9260-2(8))* Penguin Young Readers Group. (Penguin Workshop).

Worth, Richard. Pope Francis: The People's Pope, 1 vol. 2015. (Influential Latinos Ser.). (ENG., Illus.). 128p. (gr. 7-8). 38.93 *(978-0-7660-7328-9(9)*, 8c3478f2-aa7a-4674-9515-7755363d7641) Enslow Publishing, LLC.

PAPER

Cardenas, Ernesto A. Wood or Paper? 2009. 23.95 *(978-1-60698-059-0(9))*; pap. 4.95 *(978-1-60698-057-6(2))* Milo Educational Bks. & Resources.

Costain, Meredith. The Life Cycle of Paper, 1 vol. 2012. (Discovery Education: the Environment Ser.). (ENG., Illus.). 32p. (J). (gr. 4-5). pap. 11.00 *(978-1-4488-7979-3(5)*, 144caa63-7893-47a6-b446-14340c74f8cf); lib. bdg. 28.93 *(978-1-4488-7891-8(8)*, 16e4a7c6-e5bc-4716-b3e8-cafd870c29c8) Rosen Publishing Group, Inc., The. (PowerKids Pr.).

De La Bédoyère, Camilla. The Science of a Piece of Paper, 1 vol. 2009. (Science Of... Ser.). (ENG.). 32p. (YA). (gr. 4-5). lib. bdg. 28.67 *(978-1-4339-0045-7(9)*, 2c7729a0-0344-4cd2-b1ab-a6ffe146ada0) Stevens, Gareth Publishing LLLP.

Doney, Meryl. Paper Crafts, 1 vol. 2004. (Crafts from Many Cultures Ser.). (ENG., Illus.). 32p. (J). (gr. 3-5). lib. bdg. 28.67 *(978-0-8368-4046-9(1)*, 1c57fe83-5146-4e78-8265-32dbf4018d57, Gareth Stevens Learning Library) Stevens, Gareth Publishing LLLP.

From Tree to Paper. 2013. (Start to Finish, Second Ser.). (ENG., Illus.). 24p. (J). (gr. k-3). pap. 7.99 *(978-1-4677-0797-8(X)*, 4bedef84-0f12-49d7-9982-f548760c1cfb) Lerner Publishing Group.

Grack, Rachel. Tree to Paper. 2020. (Beginning to End Ser.). (ENG.). 24p. (J). (gr. k-3). lib. bdg. 26.95 *(978-1-64487-142-3(4)*, Blastoff! Readers) Bellwether Media.

Grier, Paul. Recycling Paper. 2013. (InfoMax Readers Ser.). (ENG.). 24p. (J). (gr. 2-3). pap. 49.50 *(978-1-4777-2275-6(0))*; (Illus.). pap. 8.25 *(978-1-4777-2274-9(2)*, c838cc42-3f62-4c33-8921-91f4bd7a7471) Rosen Publishing Group, Inc., The. (Rosen Classroom).

Herrington, Lisa M. Trees to Paper. 2013. (Rookie Read-About(r) Science Ser.). (ENG.). 32p. (J). lib. bdg. 23.00 *(978-0-531-24744-0(9))* Scholastic Library Publishing.

Jackson, Demi. How Is Paper Made?, 1 vol. 2015. (Everyday Mysteries Ser.). (ENG.). 24p. (J). (gr. 1-2). pap. 9.15 *(978-1-4824-3821-5(6)*, f81e73c3-ceaa-4fb0-b42a-27000d77284d) Stevens, Gareth Publishing LLLP.

James, Dawn L. Turning Trees into Paper, 1 vol. 2014. (Step-By-Step Transformations Ser.). (ENG.). 24p. (gr. 1-1). lib. bdg. 25.93 *(978-1-62713-007-3(1)*, a145068b-8204-4a03-a87a-171f9bf3f087) Cavendish Square Publishing LLC.

Langley, Andrew. Paper Products. 2008. (Everyday Materials Ser.). (ENG., Illus.). 24p. (J). (gr. k-3). pap. *(978-0-7787-4135-0(4))* Crabtree Publishing Co.

Levete, Sarah. Paper. 2006. (Material Matters Ser.). *(978-1-59389-271-5(3))* Chrysalis Education.

Lynette, Rachel. Toilet Paper. 2016. (J). *(978-1-4896-4545-6(4))* Weigl Pubs., Inc.

Moore, Phillip. Where Does Used Paper Go? 2012. (Level E Ser.). (ENG., Illus.). 16p. (J). (gr. k-2). pap. 7.95 *(978-1-927136-54-6(7)*, 19446) RiverStream Publishing.

Morris, Neil. Paper. 2010. (Materials That Matter Ser.). (ENG.). 32p. (J). (gr. 4-6). lib. bdg. 28.50 *(978-1-60753-067-1(8)*, 14866) Amicus.

Paper. (Jump Ser.). (Illus.). 36p. (J). (gr. 2-6). pap. *(978-1-882210-33-6(6))* Action Publishing, Inc.

Petelinsek, Kathleen. Crafting with Tissue Paper. Petelinsek, Kathleen, illus. 2014. (How-To Library). (ENG., Illus.). 32p. (J). (gr. 3-6). 32.07 *(978-1-63137-779-2(5)*, 205359) Cherry Lake Publishing.

Richards, Roy. En Papel. (Coleccion 101 Trucos Cientificos). (SPA., Illus.). (J). (gr. 3-5). pap. *(978-950-724-178-9(7)*, LMA8752) Lumen ARG. Dist: Lectorum Pubns., Inc.

Rivera, Andrea. Paper. 2017. (Materials Ser.). (ENG., Illus.). 24p. (J). (gr. -1-2). lib. bdg. 31.36 *(978-1-5321-2032-9(X)*, 25300, Abdo Zoom-Launch) ABDO Publishing Co.

Smith, A. G. Cut & Assemble World War II Paper Soldiers. 2017. (ENG., Illus.). 32p. (J). pap. 12.95 *(978-0-486-40581-0(8)*, 405818) Dover Pubns., Inc.

Smith, Terri Peterson. Paper. 2003. (Matter & Materials Ser.). (J). pap. *(978-1-58417-165-2(0))*; lib. bdg. *(978-1-58417-159-1(6))* Lake Street Pubs.

PAPER CRAFT

see Paper Work

PAPER FOLDING (HANDICRAFT)

see Paper Work

PAPER MAKING AND TRADE

see also Book Industries and Trade

Blaxland, Wendy. Paper, 1 vol. 2009. (How Are They Made? Ser.). (ENG.). 32p. (gr. 4-4). lib. bdg. 21.27 *(978-0-7614-3806-9(8)*, 81fcc268-4d2b-47c1-825a-c7bbdc65e4e5) Cavendish Square Publishing LLC.

Costain, Meredith. The Life Cycle of Paper, 1 vol. 2012. (Discovery Education: the Environment Ser.). (ENG., Illus.). 32p. (J). (gr. 4-5). pap. 11.00 *(978-1-4488-7979-3(5)*, 144caa63-7893-47a6-b446-14340c74f8cf); lib. bdg. 28.93 *(978-1-4488-7891-8(8)*, 16e4a7c6-e5bc-4716-b3e8-cafd870c29c8) Rosen Publishing Group, Inc., The. (PowerKids Pr.).

De La Bédoyère, Camilla. The Science of a Piece of Paper, 1 vol. 2009. (Science Of... Ser.). (ENG.). 32p. (YA). (gr. 4-5). lib. bdg. 28.67 *(978-1-4339-0045-7(9)*, 2c7729a0-0344-4cd2-b1ab-a6ffe146ada0) Stevens, Gareth Publishing LLLP.

Draper, Allison Stark. Choosing a Career in the Pulp & Paper Industry. 2009. (World of Work Ser.). 64p. (gr. 5-5). 58.50 *(978-1-60854-340-3(4))* Rosen Publishing Group, Inc., The.

From Tree to Paper. 2013. (Start to Finish, Second Ser.). (ENG., Illus.). 24p. (J). (gr. k-3). pap. 7.99 *(978-1-4677-0797-8(X)*, 4bedef84-0f12-49d7-9982-f548760c1cfb) Lerner Publishing Group.

Hinkler Studios Staff., ed. The Big Bumper Book of Paper Models. 2011. 72p. pap. 9.99 *(978-1-74184-931-8(4))* Hinkler Bks. Pty, Ltd. AUS. Dist: Ideals Pubns.

Jackson, Demi. How Is Paper Made?, 1 vol. 2015. (Everyday Mysteries Ser.). (ENG.). 24p. (J). (gr. 1-2). pap. 9.15 *(978-1-4824-3821-5(6)*, f81e73c3-ceaa-4fb0-b42a-27000d77284d) Stevens, Gareth Publishing LLLP.

Jackson, Steve. How Is Paper Recycled?, 1 vol. 2013. (Rosen Readers Ser.). (ENG.). 24p. (J). (gr. 2-2). pap. 8.25 *(978-1-4777-2254-1(8)*, 13cb4f51-30c1-4b62-8946-c40ac39ad017); pap. 49.50 *(978-1-4777-2255-8(6))* Rosen Publishing Group, Inc., The. (Rosen Classroom).

Langley, Andrew. Paper Products. 2008. (Everyday Materials Ser.). (ENG., Illus.). 24p. (J). (gr. k-3). pap. *(978-0-7787-4135-0(4))* Crabtree Publishing Co.

Llewellyn, Claire. Paper. 2005. (I Know That! Ser.). (Illus.). 24p. (J). (gr. 1-3). lib. bdg. 22.80 *(978-1-932889-54-3(X))* Sea-To-Sea Pubns.

Meachen Rau, Dana. Paper, 1 vol. 2012. (Use It! Reuse It! Ser.). (ENG.). 24p. (gr. 3-3). 25.50 *(978-1-60870-517-7(X)*, f690ec54-5905-4826-aeb0-27cbfd6141e3) Cavendish Square Publishing LLC.

Meister, Cari. From Trees to Paper. Pinilla, Albert, illus. 2019. (Who Made My Stuff? Ser.). (ENG.). 24p. (J). (gr. 1-4). lib. bdg. *(978-1-68151-697-4(7)*, 10849) Amicus.

Radford, Tracey. Make Your Own Zoo: 35 Projects for Kids Using Everyday Cardboard Packaging. Turn Your Recycling into a Zoo! 2015. (ENG., Illus.). 128p. (J). (gr. 3-11). pap. 19.95 *(978-1-78249-256-6(9)*, 1782492569, CICO Books) Ryland Peters & Small GBR. Dist: WIPRO.

Ridley, Sarah. A Paper Bag, 1 vol. 2006. (How It's Made Ser.). (ENG., Illus.). 32p. (gr. 2-4). lib. bdg. 28.67 *(978-0-8368-6703-9(3)*, 981dbc51-31cb-4d8d-b083-1ed89065e1ff, Gareth Stevens Learning Library) Stevens, Gareth Publishing LLLP.

Snyder, Inez. Trees to Paper. 2003. (How Things Are Made Ser.). (ENG., Illus.). 24p. (J). 19.00 *(978-0-516-24264-4(4)*, Children's Pr.) Scholastic Library Publishing.

PAPER MONEY

Forest, Christopher. The Dollar Bill in Translation: What It Really Means. rev. ed. 2016. (Kids' Translations Ser.). (ENG.). 32p. (J). (gr. 3-6). pap. 8.10 *(978-1-5157-6249-2(1)*, 135064, Capstone Pr.) Capstone.

Hamilton, Robert M. Dolares - Dollar Bills, 1 vol. 2015. (Monedas y Billetes / Coins & Money Ser.). (ENG & SPA.). 24p. (J). (gr. 1-1). 25.27 *(978-1-4994-0691-7(6)*, 5783a2e6-af19-4687-b062-e6f03a4c6d66, PowerKids Pr.) Rosen Publishing Group, Inc., The.

—Dollar Bills!, 1 vol. 2015. (Coins & Money Ser.). (ENG., Illus.). 24p. (J). (gr. 1-1). 25.27 *(978-1-4994-0499-9(9)*, 2d50b77f-2b92-40b8-9a6c-ec1fa8215ae6, PowerKids Pr.) Rosen Publishing Group, Inc., The.

Jozefowicz, Chris. 10 Fascinating Facts about Dollar Bills. 2016. (Rookie Star — Fact Finder Ser.). (ENG.). 32p. (J). lib. bdg. 25.00 *(978-0-531-22815-9(0)*, Children's Pr.) Scholastic Library Publishing.

Kompelein, Tracy. We Have the Skills to Know U. S. Bills!, 1 vol. 2007. (Math Made Fun Ser.). (Illus.). 24p. (J). (gr. k-3). lib. bdg. 24.21 *(978-1-59928-549-8(5)*, SandCastle) ABDO Publishing Co.

Meachen Rau, Dana. Los Billetes (Paper Money), 1 vol. 2010. (Dinero y Los Bancos (Money & Banks) Ser.). (SPA., Illus.). 24p. (gr. 2-4). pap. 9.15 *(978-1-4339-3718-7(2)*, c35a6c8e-95a6-43d3-9ee2-1349d9fc5949); (J). lib. bdg. 24.67 *(978-1-4339-3717-0(4)*, 3225b9d5-d56a-4b54-8282-95ec60ae1a88) Stevens, Gareth Publishing LLLP.

—Paper Money, 1 vol. (Money & Banks (New Edition) Ser.). (ENG., Illus.). 24p. (gr. 2-4). 2010. pap. 9.15 *(978-1-4339-3384-4(5)*, 20eef6be-86d9-4741-a2d4-82b6fb8f9baa) 2010. (J). lib. bdg. 24.67 *(978-1-4339-3383-7(7)*, a65344eb-3f38-4cdd-8951-c67b5d3a72d0) 2005. pap. 9.15 *(978-0-8368-4877-9(2)*, c2a7c902-5a7b-483d-a2a9-f2a58787566e, Weekly Reader Leveled Readers) Stevens, Gareth Publishing LLLP.

Wingard-Nelson, Rebecca. I Can Name Bills & Coins, 1 vol. 2010. (I Like Money Math! Ser.). (ENG., Illus.). 24p. (gr. k-2). pap. 10.35 *(978-0-7660-3660-4(X)*, d1652fd0-b429-47a3-948e-af3e51391448, Enslow Elementary); lib. bdg. 25.27 *(978-0-7660-3140-1(3)*, d327bac2-6207-4c5e-93e4-3b5209d3fa48) Enslow Publishing, LLC.

PAPER SCULPTURE

see Paper Work

PAPER WORK

see also names of paper crafts, e.g. Origami.

Accord Publishing, Accord. Go Fun! Paper Airplanes. 2014. (ENG.). 108p. (J). pap. 10.99 *(978-1-4494-3175-4(5))* Andrews McMeel Publishing.

Alexander, Chris. Sort-of-Difficult. 2008. (Origami Ser.). (ENG.). 32p. (J). (gr. 3-9). 28.65 *(978-1-4296-2023-9(4)*, 94915, Capstone Pr.) Capstone.

Angleberger, Tom. ART2-D2's Guide to Folding & Doodling. 2013. (Illus.). 163p. (J). pap. *(978-1-4197-0994-4(1)*, Amulet Bks.) Abrams, Inc.

Arcturus Publishing. Incredible Origami: 95 Amazing Paper-Folding Projects, Includes Origami Paper. 2017. (ENG.). 256p. pap. 16.99 *(978-1-78428-855-6(1)*, 8c299850-002d-498e-a27c-f17fbfe6bdff) Arcturus Publishing GBR. Dist: Baker & Taylor Publisher Services (BTPS).

Avery, Logan. Aviones de Papel: Componer Numeros Del 1 Al 10. rev. ed. 2019. (Mathematics in the Real World Ser.). (SPA., Illus.). 20p. (J). (gr. k-1). 8.99 *(978-1-4258-2830-1(2))* Teacher Created Materials, Inc.

—STEM. 2018. (Mathematics in the Real World Ser.). (ENG., Illus.). 20p. (J). (gr. k-1). 8.99 *(978-1-4258-5623-6(3))* Teacher Created Materials, Inc.

Baer, Sam. 100 Paper Dragons to Fold & Fly. 2015. (Tear-Off Papercraft Pads Ser.). (ENG.). 200p. (J). (gr. k-5). pap. 7.99 *(978-0-7945-3593-3(3)*, Usborne) EDC Publishing.

Barker, Cicely Mary. Flower Fairies Paper Dolls. 2005. (Flower Fairies Ser.). (ENG.). 13p. (J). (gr. -1-2). 6.99 *(978-0-7232-5432-4(X)*, Warne) Penguin Young Readers Group.

Bawden, Juliet & Moxley, Susan. Papier Mache. 2004. (Crafty Ideas Ser.). (SPA., Illus.). 32p. (J). (gr. 2-5). pap. 5.95 *(978-1-58728-127-3(9)*, Two-Can Publishing) T&N Children's Publishing.

Bell-Myers, Darcy. Pretty Ponies Paper Dolls. 2015. (ENG.). 32p. (J). (gr. -1-2). pap. 7.99 *(978-0-486-79100-5(9))* Dover Pubns., Inc.

Bianchi, Ms. The Swimmers: Paper Cut-Outs with Matisse. 2019. (ENG., Illus.). 32p. (J). (gr. 1-5). 15.95 *(978-1-58423-716-7(3))* Gingko Pr., Inc.

Bolte, Mari. Paper Presents You Can Make & Share. 2015. (Sleepover Girls Crafts Ser.). (ENG., Illus.). 32p. (J). (gr. 2-5). lib. bdg. 28.65 *(978-1-4765-7747-0(1)*, 125241, Capstone Young Readers) Capstone.

Borgert-Spaniol, Megan. Accordion Folding: Simple Paper Folding. 2019. (Cool Paper Art Ser.). (ENG., Illus.). 32p. (J). (gr. 3-6). lib. bdg. 34.21 *(978-1-5321-1943-9(7)*, 32471, Checkerboard Library) ABDO Publishing Co.

—Papermaking: Handmade Paper & Paper Products. 2019. (Cool Paper Art Ser.). (ENG., Illus.). 32p. (J). (gr. 3-6). lib. bdg. 34.21 *(978-1-5321-1947-7(X)*, 32479, Checkerboard Library) ABDO Publishing Co.

Boursin, Didier. Folding for Fun: Origami for Ages 4 & Up. 2007. (ENG., Illus.). 64p. (J). (gr. -1-12). pap. 9.95 *(978-1-55407-252-1(2)*, 8b792f40-9cbe-4efd-9c32-4933a6982227) Firefly Bks., Ltd.

Brooks, Susie. Scrap Paper Art, 1 vol. 2017. (Let's Make Art Ser.). (ENG.). 32p. (J). (gr. 2-3). 29.27 *(978-1-5383-2225-3(0)*, 2f1f5bf2-e01e-4a66-8813-68db17b2f056); pap. 12.75 *(978-1-5383-2320-5(6)*, 7ddd39eb-187d-4151-86d5-4aafbd3513b2) Rosen Publishing Group, Inc., The. (PowerKids Pr.).

Buckingham, Marie. Air Shark! Novice-Level Paper Airplanes: 4D an Augmented Reading Paper-Folding Experience. 2018. (Paper Airplanes with a Side of Science 4D Ser.). (ENG., Illus.). 32p. (J). (gr. 3-5). lib. bdg. 33.99 *(978-1-5435-0796-6(4)*, 137534, Capstone Classroom) Capstone.

—Needle Nose! Advanced-Level Paper Airplanes: 4D an Augmented Reading Paper-Folding Experience. 2018. (Paper Airplanes with a Side of Science 4D Ser.). (ENG., Illus.). 32p. (J). (gr. 3-6). lib. bdg. 33.99 *(978-1-5435-0795-9(6)*, 137532, Capstone Classroom) Capstone.

—Paper Airplanes with a Side of Science 4D, 4 vols. 2018. (Paper Airplanes with a Side of Science 4D Ser.). (ENG.). 32p. (J). (gr. 3-6). 135.96 *(978-1-5435-0809-3(X)*, 27726, Capstone Classroom) Capstone.

Carola, Leslie Conron & Grossman, Andrea. Mrs. Grossman's Sticker Magic. 2006. (Illus.). 132p. *(978-0-88363-707-4(3))* Rizzoli International Pubns., Inc.

Carson-Dellosa Publishing Staff. I Can Trace. 2009. (Big Skills for Little Hands(r) Ser.). (ENG.). 80p. (gr. -1 — 1). pap. 6.95 *(978-0-7696-6018-9(5)*, 0769660185, Brighter Child) Carson-Dellosa Publishing, LLC.

Castleforte, Brian. Papertoy Glowbots: 46 Glowing Robots You Can Make Yourself! 2016. (ENG., Illus.). 196p. (J). (gr. 5-12). pap. 22.95 *(978-0-7611-7762-3(0)*, 17762) Workman Publishing Co., Inc.

—Papertoy Monsters: Make Your Very Own Amazing Papertoys! 2010. (ENG., Illus.). 124p. (J). pap. 22.95 *(978-0-7611-5882-0(0)*, 15882) Workman Publishing Co., Inc.

Chapman, Gillian & Robson, Pam. Making Art with Packaging, 1 vol. 2007. (Everyday Art Ser.). (ENG., Illus.). 32p. (YA). (gr. 4-5). lib. bdg. 30.27 *(978-1-4042-3724-7(0)*, c5617d61-ea66-406a-8526-604a929e9e5c) Rosen Publishing Group, Inc., The.

—Making Art with Paper, 1 vol. 2007. (Everyday Art Ser.). (ENG., Illus.). 32p. (YA). (gr. 4-5). lib. bdg. 30.27 *(978-1-4042-3725-4(9)*, b7a4650a-b91c-41a3-9737-68cc2f9d3dd4) Rosen Publishing Group, Inc., The.

Chenevert, Pam. Make It Yourself! Paper Pop-Up Art. 2017. (Cool Makerspace Ser.). (ENG., Illus.). 32p. (J). (gr. 3-6). lib. bdg. 34.21 *(978-1-5321-1071-9(5)*, 25718, Checkerboard Library) ABDO Publishing Co.

Chorba, April & Editors of Klutz. Dot Jewelry: Make Pretty Paper Bracelets & Necklaces. 2013. (ENG.). 56p. (J). (gr. 3). 19.99 *(978-0-545-49278-2(5))* Klutz.

Chronicle Books. Port-A-Plant. 2013. (ENG.). 9p. 14.95 *(978-1-4521-1078-3(6))* Chronicle Bks. LLC.

CICO Kidz, compiled by. Let's Get Crafty with Paper & Glue: 25 Creative & Fun Projects for Kids Aged 2 & Up. 2016. (ENG., Illus.). 80p. (J). (gr. 2-7). pap. 12.95 *(978-1-78249-335-8(2)*, 1782493352, CICO Books) Ryland Peters & Small GBR. Dist: WIPRO.

COCHAE. Paper Sumo. 2015. (ENG., Illus.). 20p. (J). (gr. 1-17). 14.95 *(978-1-4521-4485-6(0))* Chronicle Bks. LLC.

Collins, Francis. The Second Boys' Book of Model Aeroplanes. 2004. (Illus.). 262p. per. 16.95 *(978-0-9758914-4-5(8))* Gustav's Library.

Collins, John M. The New World Champion Paper Airplane Book: Featuring the World Record-Breaking Design, with Tear-Out Planes to Fold & Fly. 2013. (ENG., Illus.). 160p. pap. 19.99 *(978-1-60774-388-0(4)*, Ten Speed Pr.) Potter/Ten Speed/Harmony/Rodale.

Cool Things Press. 75 Cool Things to Cut Out. 2008. 152p. pap. 15.95 *(978-0-615-20796-4(0))* Cool Things Pr.

Cut, Paste, & Create, 6 vols. 2007. (Cut, Paste, & Create Ser.). (ENG.). 32p. (gr. 1-3). lib. bdg. 86.01 *(978-0-8368-7718-2(7)*, 6a1315c9-7978-4d43-8d12-76fe3ca84cbf, Gareth Stevens Learning Library) Stevens, Gareth Publishing LLLP.

Dewar, Andrew. Ultimate Paper Airplanes for Kids: The Best Guide to Paper Airplanes!: Includes Instruction Book with 12 Innovative Designs & 48 Tear-Out Paper Planes. Vints, Kostya, illus. 2015. 160p. pap. 14.95 *(978-4-8053-1363-3(3))* Tuttle Publishing.

DK. Paper Craft: 50 Projects Including Card Making, Gift Wrapping, Scrapbooking, & Beautiful Pa. 2015. (ENG.). 224p. 22.99 *(978-1-4654-3943-7(9)*, DK) Dorling Kindersley Publishing, Inc.

Doney, Meryl. Paper Crafts, 1 vol. 2004. (Crafts from Many Cultures Ser.). (ENG., Illus.). 32p. (J). (gr. 3-5). lib. bdg. 28.67 *(978-0-8368-4046-9(1)*, 1c57fe83-5146-4e78-8265-32dbf4018d57, Gareth Stevens Learning Library) Stevens, Gareth Publishing LLLP.

Editors of Klutz. The Cootie Catcher Book. Editors of Klutz, ed. 2009. (ENG.). 70p. (J). (gr. 1). 14.95 *(978-1-59174-680-5(9))* Klutz.

—Dress up Your Own Paper Pups. 2015. (ENG., Illus.). 48p. (J). (gr. 1). 16.99 *(978-0-545-79864-8(7))* Klutz.

—Make Paper Lantern Animals. 2016. (ENG.). 32p. (J). (gr. 2-5). 19.99 *(978-1-338-03755-5(2))* Klutz.

—Paper Fashions. Editors of Klutz, ed. 2nd rev. ed. 2012. (ENG.). 60p. (J). (gr. 3-7). 21.99 *(978-0-545-44944-1(8))* Klutz.

—Smash Bot Battle. 2016. (ENG.). 46p. (J). (gr. 3-7). 19.99 *(978-0-545-90648-7(2))* Klutz.

—Straw-Shooter Jets. 2014. (ENG.). 60p. (J). (gr. 3). 16.99 *(978-0-545-64779-3(7))* Klutz.

—Tissue Paper Crafts. 2014. (ENG.). 64p. (J). (gr. 3). 19.99 *(978-0-545-64777-9(0))* Klutz.

—Twirled Paper. 2nd ed. 2012. (ENG.). 56p. (J). (gr. 3-7). 19.99 *(978-0-545-45991-4(5))* Klutz.

Editors of Klutz & Murphy, Pat. Paper Flying Dragons. 2012. (ENG.). 48p. (J). (gr. 3). pap. 16.99 *(978-0-545-44936-6(7))* Klutz.

Editors of Klutz & Stillinger, Doug. The Klutz Book of Paper Airplanes. 2004. (ENG., Illus.). 56p. (J). (gr. 2-5). 16.95 *(978-1-57054-830-7(7))* Klutz.

Elliot, Marion. Crafty Fun with Paper! 50 Fabulous Papercraft Projects to Make Yourself. 2014. (Illus.). 96p. (J). (gr. -1-7). 13.99 *(978-1-86147-369-1(9)*, Armadillo) Anness Publishing GBR. Dist: National Bk. Network.

Fisher, Phyllis Mae Richardson, illus. Amber: An International Friends Paper Doll from AFRICA. 2004. (ENG.). (J). 10.00 *(978-0-9745615-9-2(2))* PJs Corner Gift Shoppe.

—Chrissy: #1 in the 1989 Family Friends Paper Doll Set. l.t. ed. 2004. (ENG.). 24p. (J). 10.00 *(978-0-9745615-5-4(X))* PJs Corner Gift Shoppe.

—Janae: #3 in the 1989 Family Friends Paper Doll Set, 3 nos., no. 3. l.t. ed. 2003. (ENG.). 24p. (J). 10.00 *(978-0-9745615-7-8(6))* PJs Corner Gift Shoppe.

—Natasha: An International Friends Paper Doll from RUSSIA. 2004. (ENG.). 15p. (J). 10.00 *(978-0-9745615-8-5(4))* PJs Corner Gift Shoppe.

Flying Frog Publishing, ed. Gigantic Paper Planes. 2012. 48p. (J). 14.99 *(978-1-934967-81-2(5))* Flying Frog Publishing, Inc.

—Gigantic Sky Cruising Paper Planes. 2012. 48p. (J). 14.99 *(978-1-60745-073-3(9))* Flying Frog Publishing, Inc.

Foley, Tim. Literary Greats Paper Dolls. 2011. (Dover Paper Dolls Ser.). (ENG.). 128p. (J). (gr. 6-8). pap. 12.99 *(978-0-486-48117-3(4)*, 481174) Dover Pubns., Inc.

Forte, Imogene. Holidays & Special Days. 2004. (Fun Things to Make & Do Ser.). (Illus.). 80p. (J). per. 9.95 *(978-0-86530-616-5(8))* Incentive Pubns., Inc.

—Paper Capers. 2004. (Fun Things to Make & Do Ser.). (Illus.). 80p. (J). per. 9.95 *(978-0-86530-615-8(X))* Incentive Pubns., Inc.

French, Cathy. Make a Paper Airplane & Haz un avión de Papel: 6 English, 6 Spanish Adaptations. 2011. (ENG & SPA.). (J). 75.00 net. *(978-1-4108-5631-9(3))* Benchmark Education Co.

Garza, Carmen Lomas. Making Magic Windows, 1 vol. 2014. (Magic Windows Ser.). (ENG., Illus.). 64p. (J). (gr. 3-8). pap. 14.95 *(978-0-89239-159-2(6)*, leelowcbp) Lee & Low Bks., Inc.

Gaylord, Susan Kapuscinski & Jabbour, Joyce. Make, Draw, & Design Your Own Book. Labat, Yancey C., illus. 2006. 48p. (J). *(978-0-439-81339-6(5))* Scholastic, Inc.

Gilpin, Rebecca. Fairy Things to Make & Do. 2004. (Usborne Activities Ser.). (Illus.). 31p. (J). *(978-0-439-67250-4(3))* Scholastic, Inc.

Giulieri, Anne. Make Two Crocodiles. 2012. (Engage Literacy Blue Ser.). (ENG.). 16p. (J). (gr. k-2). pap. 36.94 *(978-1-4296-8987-8(0)*, 18390); (Illus.). pap. 6.99 *(978-1-4296-8986-1(2)*, 119999) Capstone. (Capstone Pr.).

Grack, Rachel. Tree to Paper. 2020. (Beginning to End Ser.). (ENG.). 24p. (J). (gr. k-3). lib. bdg. 26.95 *(978-1-64487-142-3(4)*, Blastoff! Readers) Bellwether Media.

Green, Gail D. Pretty Presents: Paper Creations to Share, 1 vol. 2013. (Paper Creations Ser.). (ENG.). 32p. (J). (gr. 3-9). lib. bdg. 28.65 *(978-1-62065-041-7(X)*, 120720) Capstone.

Grumpy Cat, Grumpy. Grumpy Cat Paper Dolls. 2014. (ENG.). 32p. (J). (gr. 6-12). pap. 9.99 *(978-0-486-79162-3(9)*, 791629) Dover Pubns., Inc.

—Grumpy Cat Sticker Paper Dolls. 2015. (ENG.). 4p. (J). (gr. 2-5). pap. 1.99 *(978-0-486-80320-3(1)*, 803201) Dover Pubns., Inc.

Grumpy Cat, Grumpy & Bonogofsky-Gronseth, Jimi. Grumpy Cat's Miserable Papercraft Book. 2015. (Dover Kids Activity Bks.). (ENG.). 112p. (J). (gr. 3-7). 14.95 *(978-0-486-80321-0(X)*, 80321X) Dover Pubns., Inc.

Gulliver, Amanda & Turnbull, Stephanie. Things to Make & Do with Paper. Sage, Molly, illus. 2004. (Activity Books). 32p. (J). pap. 6.95 *(978-0-7945-0674-2(7)*, Usborne) EDC Publishing.

Hankin, Rosie. Cut & Paste Farm Animals, 1 vol. 2007. (Cut, Paste, & Create Ser.). (ENG., Illus.). 32p. (J). (gr. 1-3). lib. bdg. 28.67 *(978-0-8368-7719-9(5)*, c55bd7c7-f4cf-4167-adcb-7794e23020ab, Gareth Stevens Learning Library) Stevens, Gareth Publishing LLLP.

—Cut & Paste Sea Creatures, 1 vol. 2007. (Cut, Paste, & Create Ser.). (ENG., Illus.). 32p. (gr. 1-3). lib. bdg. 28.67 *(978-0-8368-7720-5(9)*, a16eee98-21fc-4857-a182-77822f2b7240, Gareth Stevens Learning Library) Stevens, Gareth Publishing LLLP.

Hanson, Anders & Mann, Elissa. Cool Flexagon Art: Creative Activities That Make Math & Science Fun for Kids! 2013. (Cool Art with Math & Science Ser.). (ENG.). 32p. (J). (gr. 3-6). lib. bdg. 34.21 *(978-1-61783-821-7(7)*, 4588, Checkerboard Library) ABDO Publishing Co.

Hanson, Anders Mann & Mann, Elissa. Cool Paper Folding: Creative Activities That Make Math & Science Fun for Kids! 2013. (Cool Art with Math & Science Ser.). (ENG.). 32p. (J). (gr. 3-6). lib. bdg. 34.21 *(978-1-61783-823-1(3)*, 4592, Checkerboard Library) ABDO Publishing Co.

Harbo, Christopher. My First Guide to Paper Airplanes. 2015. (My First Guides). (ENG., Illus.). 24p. (J). (gr. 1-3). lib. bdg. 27.99 *(978-1-4914-2047-8(2)*, 127526, Capstone Pr.) Capstone.

—Origami Paperpalooza! 2015. (ENG., Illus.). 144p. (J). (gr. 3-9). pap., pap., pap. 14.95 *(978-1-62370-227-4(5)*, 127865, Capstone Young Readers) Capstone.

Harbo, Christopher L. Easy Origami Toys, 1 vol. 2010. (Easy Origami Ser.). (ENG.). 24p. (J). (gr. 1-3). lib. bdg. 25.99 *(978-1-4296-5386-2(8)*, 113812, Capstone Pr.) Capstone.

—Paper Airplanes, Captain Level 4, 1 vol. 2010. (Paper Airplanes Ser.). (ENG.). 32p. (J). (gr. 3-9). lib. bdg. 28.65 *(978-1-4296-4744-1(2)*, 103284, Capstone Pr.) Capstone.

—Paper Airplanes, Flight School Level 1. 2010. (Paper Airplanes Ser.). (ENG.). 32p. (J). (gr. 3-9). lib. bdg. 28.65 *(978-1-4296-4741-0(8)*, 103281, Capstone Pr.) Capstone.

—Paper Airplanes, Pilot Level 3. 2010. (Paper Airplanes Ser.). (ENG.). 32p. (J). (gr. 3-9). lib. bdg. 28.65 *(978-1-4296-4743-4(4)*, 103283, Capstone Pr.) Capstone.

Hardyman, Robyn. Origami Fun: Aircraft. 2017. (Origami Fun Ser.). (ENG., Illus.). 24p. (J). (gr. 3-8). lib. bdg. 26.95 *(978-1-62617-707-9(4))* Bellwether Media.

Hawcock, David. Make Your Own Press-Out Bulldozers. 2018. (ENG.). 22p. (gr. 2-7). pap. 12.99 *(978-0-486-82734-6(8)*, 827348) Dover Pubns., Inc.

—Make Your Own Press-Out Spaceships. 2018. (ENG.). 22p. (gr. 1-5). pap. 12.99 *(978-0-486-82503-8(5)*, 825035) Dover Pubns., Inc.

He, Xu. Happy Flight. 2007. 72p. per. 10.95 *(978-1-4303-2326-6(4))* Lulu Pr., Inc.

Henry, Sally. Drawing, 12 vols., Set 1. Incl. Card Making. lib. bdg. 30.27 *(978-1-4358-2506-2(3)*, e98332e3-5734-417a-8826-e23c60aa3200); Clay Modeling. lib. bdg. 30.27 *(978-1-4358-2508-6(X)*, 89020edc-cf7d-44e6-b170-245ed1de5a49); Collage. lib. bdg. 30.27 *(978-1-4358-2509-3(8)*, 20c79d9c-abd9-4986-9397-8a8a9d4eb5c8); lib. bdg. 30.27 *(978-1-4358-2510-9(1)*, f7777292-91bc-44d7-80b5-fb82d73b69b1); Painting. lib. bdg. 30.27 *(978-1-4358-2511-6(X)*, 7296eaa9-fbdb-41c1-bcde-f7eaeeee7b12); Paper Folding. lib. bdg. 30.27 *(978-1-4358-2507-9(1)*, 09a8d395-82f9-4f76-94aa-1532ef08ccf5); (J). (gr. 3-4). (Make Your Own Art Ser.). (ENG., Illus.). 32p. 2008. Set lib. bdg. 181.62 *(978-1-4358-2549-9(7)*, 3fce187b-c18a-47c1-b974-447e2b54b804, PowerKids Pr.) Rosen Publishing Group, Inc., The.

—Paper Folding, 1 vol. 2008. (Make Your Own Art Ser.). (ENG., Illus.). 32p. (J). (gr. 3-4). lib. bdg. 30.27 *(978-1-4358-2507-9(1)*, 09a8d395-82f9-4f76-94aa-1532ef08ccf5, PowerKids Pr.) Rosen Publishing Group, Inc., The.

Henry, Sally & Cook, Trevor. Make Your Own Art: Set 2, 10 vols. Incl. Eco Crafts. lib. bdg. 30.27 *(978-1-4488-1582-1(7)*, 9954893c-0fed-4f20-854d-2d05e915234b); Making Masks. 30.27 *(978-1-4488-1583-8(5)*, fcf75343-3ae6-4fcf-9ad0-59c260787f14); Making Mosaics. 30.27 *(978-1-4488-1585-2(1)*, b486d950-5a61-4480-bf95-a93f3b05f98a); Making Puppets. 30.27 *(978-1-4488-1584-5(3)*, 91ded940-cb87-486c-916d-7905a13bfef3); Papier-Mâché. 30.27 *(978-1-4488-1587-6(8)*, 140b6f37-b163-4556-bfa4-cb69696f6108); (J). (gr. 3-4). (Make Your Own Art Ser.). (ENG., Illus.). 32p. 2010. Set lib. bdg. 151.35 *(978-1-4488-1625-5(4)*, ab4eeb4f-5340-4fa7-af2c-a6391e8949de, PowerKids Pr.) Rosen Publishing Group, Inc., The.

—Making Mosaics, 1 vol. 2010. (Make Your Own Art Ser.). (ENG., Illus.). 32p. (J). (gr. 3-4). 30.27 *(978-1-4488-1585-2(1)*, b486d950-5a61-4480-bf95-a93f3b05f98a); pap. 12.75 *(978-1-4488-1617-0(3)*, 25c5cda6-397a-4e44-8024-552d7f3dbf66) Rosen Publishing Group, Inc., The. (PowerKids Pr.).

—Papier-Mâché, 1 vol. 2010. (Make Your Own Art Ser.). (ENG., Illus.). 32p. (J). (gr. 3-4). 30.27 *(978-1-4488-1587-6(8)*, 140b6f37-b163-4556-bfa4-cb69696f6108); pap. 12.75 *(978-1-4488-1621-7(1)*, 213bad7e-7ffe-4e7f-8942-92fad8698c8a) Rosen Publishing Group, Inc., The. (PowerKids Pr.).

Higham, Cindy. Snowflakes for All Seasons: 72 Fold & Cut Paper Snowflakes, 1 vol. 2004. Orig. Title: Snowflakes Made Easy & Fun. (ENG., Illus.). 80p. pap. 9.99 *(978-1-58685-528-4(X))* Gibbs Smith, Publisher.

Hinkler Books, ed. Littlest Pet Shop Cat & Mouse. 2012. (Paper Models Ser.). 24p. (J). 3.99 *(978-1-74185-743-6(0))* Hinkler Bks. Pty, Ltd. AUS. Dist: Ideals Pubns.

—Littlest Pet Shop Hamster & Dalmation. 2012. (Paper Models Ser.). 24p. (J). 3.99 *(978-1-74185-744-3(9))* Hinkler Bks. Pty, Ltd. AUS. Dist: Ideals Pubns.

—Littlest Pet Shop Spaniel & Monkey. 2012. (Paper Models Ser.). 24p. (J). 3.99 *(978-1-74185-745-0(7))* Hinkler Bks. Pty, Ltd. AUS. Dist: Ideals Pubns.

Hoffman, Joan. Preschool Practice. 2019. (ENG.). 30p. (J). (gr. -1-k). pap. 4.49 *(978-1-60159-116-6(0)*, f7002a79-da67-4b8e-b45a-0dd46e69721b) School Zone Publishing Co.

Holden, Pam. Paper Chains, 1 vol. 2009. (Red Rocket Readers Ser.). (ENG., Illus.). 21p. (gr. 2-2). pap. *(978-1-877435-43-0(0))* Flying Start Bks.

Holland, Gini. Paper Crafts, 1 vol. 2013. (From Trash to Treasure Ser.). (ENG.). 32p. (J). (gr. 4-5). 30.17 *(978-1-4777-1282-5(8)*, 29b9f470-98b5-4a2c-bc86-95a3ac3fdd24); pap. 12.75 *(978-1-4777-1358-7(1)*, a17f7cd2-6e67-4c37-a154-0ec8171f7bea) Rosen Publishing Group, Inc., The. (PowerKids Pr.).

Humphrey, Paul. How to Make a Mask. Fairclough, Chris, photos by. 2007. (Crafty Kids Ser.). (Illus.). 24p. (J). (gr. -1-3). lib. bdg. 24.25 *(978-1-59771-101-2(2))* Sea-To-Sea Pubns.

Indian Princess Paper Dolls. Date not set. (J). pap. 2.95 *(978-1-57122-080-6(1))* Nickel Pr.

Irvine, Joan. How to Make Super Pop-Ups. Hendry, Linda, illus. 2008. (Dover Origami Papercraft Ser.). (ENG.). 96p. (gr. 3-7). per. 9.95 *(978-0-486-46589-0(6)*, 465896) Dover Pubns., Inc.

Jackson, Paul. Best Ever Paper Planes That Really Fly! (Illus.). 36p. pap. 8.95 *(978-1-85479-334-8(9))* O'Mara, Michael Bks., Ltd. GBR. Dist: Independent Pubs. Group.

Johnson, Anne Akers. Twirly Q's: Make Irresistible Cardboard Creations. 2012. 60p. (J). (gr. 5-9). 19.99 *(978-0-545-39624-0(7))* Klutz.

Jones, Jen. Cool Crafts with Cardboard & Wrapping Paper: Green Projects for Resourceful Kids, 1 vol. 2010. (Green Crafts Ser.). (ENG.). 32p. (J). (gr. 3-9). lib. bdg. 28.65 *(978-1-4296-4765-6(5)*, 103296) Capstone.

—Cool Crafts with Newspapers, Magazines, & Junk Mail: Green Projects for Resourceful Kids, 1 vol. 2010. (Green Crafts Ser.). (ENG.). 32p. (J). (gr. 3-9). lib. bdg. 28.65 *(978-1-4296-4764-9(7)*, 103295) Capstone.

Kelly, Emery J. Paper Airplanes: Models to Build & Fly. 2003. (Activities & Crafts Ser.). (Illus.). 64p. (J). (gr. 4-7). pap. 8.95 *(978-0-8225-9903-6(1))* Lerner Publishing Group.

Klutz Editors, contrib. by. Paper Fashions Fancy. 2008. (ENG., Illus.). 58p. (J). (gr. 3-18). 21.95 *(978-1-59174-519-8(5))* Klutz.

Krcmár, Karol. Kirigami Greeting Cards: The Art of Paper Cutting & Folding. Simekova, Jela, ed. Chorvathova, Michaela, tr. Holoska, Jiri, photos by. 2005. (Kirigami Craft Books Ser.). (Illus.). 80p. (J). pap. 14.95 *(978-0-9715411-7-7(5))* Kotzig Publishing, Inc.

—Kirigami Paper Kingdom: The Art of Paper Cutting & Folding. Simekova, Jela, ed. Kovac, Stefan Patrik, tr. Holoska, Jiri, photos by. 2005. (Kirigami Craft Books Ser.). (Illus.). 112p. (J). pap. 14.95 *(978-0-9715411-6-0(7))* Kotzig Publishing, Inc.

Kumon. Let's Cut Paper, 4 vols. 2005. (Kumon First Steps Workbooks Ser.). (ENG., Illus.). 40p. (J). (gr. -1). pap. 5.95 *(978-1-933241-14-2(4))* Kumon Publishing North America, Inc.

Kumon Publishing, creator. Animals Lion & Mouse, 2 vols. 2005. (Kumon 3-D Paper Crafts Ser.). (ENG., Illus.). 16p. (J). (gr. 4-7). per. 5.95 *(978-1-933241-17-3(9))* Kumon Publishing North America, Inc.

—My Book of Amazing Crafts: Ages 5-6-7. 2006. (Kumon Workbooks Ser.). (Illus.). 34p. (J). (gr. k-2). per. 7.95 *(978-1-933241-30-2(6))* Kumon Publishing North America, Inc.

Kumon Publishing, ed. Paper Playtime Vehicles. 2012. (ENG., Illus.). 64p. (J). pap. 7.95 *(978-4-7743-0006-1(3))* Kumon Publishing North America, Inc.

Kumon Staff. Animals: Dog & Cat, 4 vols. Sarris, Eno, ed. 2006. (Kumon 3-D Paper Crafts Ser.). (ENG., Illus.). 16p. (J). (gr. -1-3). per. 5.95 *(978-1-933241-18-0(7))* Kumon Publishing North America, Inc.

Kurtz, John. Santa Claus Christmas Paper Dolls. 2013. (Dover Paper Dolls Ser.). (ENG.). 32p. (J). (gr. 1-5). 9.99 *(978-0-486-49424-1(1)*, 494241) Dover Pubns., Inc.

LaFosse, Michael. Making Origami Cards Step by Step, 1 vol. 2003. (Kid's Guide to Origami Ser.). (ENG., Illus.). 24p. (J). (gr. 3-4). lib. bdg. 28.93 *(978-0-8239-6701-8(8)*, de2e6bf4-8526-46ce-b567-7bade4fb8f44, PowerKids Pr.) Rosen Publishing Group, Inc., The.

—Making Origami Science Experiments Step by Step, 1 vol. 2003. (Kid's Guide to Origami Ser.). (ENG., Illus.). 24p. (J). (gr. 3-4). lib. bdg. 28.93 *(978-0-8239-6705-6(0)*, 3febf6e4-92a7-4741-934b-29290f9b05ea, PowerKids Pr.) Rosen Publishing Group, Inc., The.

LaFosse, Michael G. Making Origami Cards Step by Step. 2009. (Kid's Guide to Origami Ser.). 24p. (gr. 3-4). 47.90 *(978-1-61511-183-1(2)*, PowerKids Pr.) Rosen Publishing Group, Inc., The.

—Making Origami Masks Step by Step. 2009. (Kid's Guide to Origami Ser.). 24p. (gr. 3-4). 47.90 *(978-1-61511-188-6(3)*, PowerKids Pr.) Rosen Publishing Group, Inc., The.

—Making Origami Puzzles Step by Step. 2009. (Kid's Guide to Origami Ser.). 24p. (gr. 3-4). 47.90 *(978-1-61511-194-7(8)*, PowerKids Pr.) Rosen Publishing Group, Inc., The.

—Making Origami Science Experiments Step by Step. 2009. (Kid's Guide to Origami Ser.). 24p. (gr. 3-4). 47.90 *(978-1-61511-195-4(6)*, PowerKids Pr.) Rosen Publishing Group, Inc., The.

Laughlin, Kara L. Fun Things to Do with Paper Cups & Plates, 1 vol. 2014. (10 Things to Do Ser.). (ENG.). 32p. (J). (gr. -1-2). 27.99 *(978-1-4765-9897-0(5)*, 125740, Capstone Pr.) Capstone.

—Marvelous Memories: Paper Keepsake Creations, 1 vol. 2013. (Paper Creations Ser.). (ENG.). 32p. (J). (gr. 3-9). lib. bdg. 28.65 *(978-1-62065-044-8(4)*, 120723) Capstone.

Laughlin, Kara L., et al. Paper Artist: Creations Kids Can Fold, Tear, Wear, or Share. 2013. (Craft It Yourself Ser.). (ENG., Illus.). 112p. (J). (gr. 3-9). pap., pap., pap. 12.95 *(978-1-62370-004-1(3)*, 122311, Capstone Young Readers) Capstone.

—Paper Creations. 2013. (Paper Creations Ser.). (ENG.). 32p. (J). (gr. 3-9). 122.60 *(978-1-62065-045-5(2)*, 18863) Capstone.

Lee, Kyong Hwa. Amazing Paper Airplanes: The Craft & Science of Flight. 2016. (ENG., Illus.). 184p. (J). pap. 19.95 *(978-0-8263-5664-2(8)*, P496835) Univ. of New Mexico Pr.

Lim, Annalees. Fun with Paper, 1 vol. 2013. (Clever Crafts Ser.). (ENG., Illus.). 24p. (J). (gr. 2-3). 29.93 *(978-1-4777-0183-6(4)*, d05f8e6d-f808-4015-a838-135eaf27863a); pap. 11.60 *(978-1-4777-0194-2(X)*, 55ccfee2-50d6-4ea7-8bb4-b3f6da591391) Rosen Publishing Group, Inc., The. (Windmill Bks.).

—Paper Crafts, 1 vol., Vol. 1. 2013. (Craft Attack! Ser.). (ENG.). 32p. (J). (gr. 3-3). 29.27 *(978-1-4824-0211-7(4)*, 8b355986-7271-40bb-a4bf-deb1ffbc91db); pap. 11.50 *(978-1-4824-0213-1(0)*, dc67bdce-3e20-42aa-a863-5011ed84477a) Stevens, Gareth Publishing LLLP.

Littlefield, Cindy A. Pop-Out & Paint Horse Breeds: Create Paper Models of 10 Different Breeds. 2011. (ENG., Illus.). 48p. (J). (gr. 3-7). pap. 12.95 *(978-1-60342-963-4(8)*, 62963) Storey Publishing, LLC.

Llimós, Anna. Earth-Friendly Papier-Mâché Crafts in 5 Easy Steps, 1 vol. 2013. (Earth-Friendly Crafts in 5 Easy Steps Ser.). (ENG., Illus.). 32p. (gr. 3-3). lib. bdg. 26.61 *(978-0-7660-4192-9(1)*, 530a344e-3cb0-4111-a092-7d23ff98406b) Enslow Publishing, LLC.

Llimós, Anna & Llimós, Anna. Easy Paper Crafts in 5 Steps, 1 vol. 2008. (Easy Crafts in 5 Steps Ser.). (ENG., Illus.). 32p. (gr. 3-3). lib. bdg. 26.60 *(978-0-7660-3087-9(3)*, 66a7a951-4423-4347-bdb3-dd242dddedc1, Enslow Elementary) Enslow Publishing, LLC.

—Easy Paper Crafts in 5 Steps, 1 vol. 2008. (Easy Crafts in 5 Steps Ser.). (ENG., Illus.). 32p. (gr. 3-3). pap. 10.35 *(978-0-7660-3762-5(2)*, 9fcf0260-c161-4a7d-a193-4145bf4c64c8, Enslow Elementary) Enslow Publishing, LLC.

Lo Monaco, Gérard. The Small World of Paper Toys. 2015. (ENG., Illus.). 24p. (J). (gr. -1-2). 24.95 *(978-3-89955-746-6(8))* Die Gestalten Verlag DEU. Dist: Ingram Publisher Services.

Lockyer, John. Paper Making, 1 vol. 2018. (ENG., Illus.). 21p. (J). pap. *(978-1-77654-255-0(X)*, Red Rocket Readers) Flying Start Bks.

Lonergan, Lei-Seu. The Great Paper Toy Book. 2004. (YA). spiral bd. *(978-0-9759014-0-3(0))* Stonechester, Inc.

Lovett, Amber. Making Paper Airplanes. 2017. (21st Century Skills Innovation Library: Makers As Innovators Junior Ser.). (ENG., Illus.). 24p. (J). (gr. 2-5). lib. bdg. 30.64 *(978-1-63472-696-2(0)*, 210082) Cherry Lake Publishing.

Loya, Allyssa & Lincoln, Joshua A. Cardboard Maker Magic. 2020. (J). *(978-1-5415-8987-2(4))* Lerner Publishing Group.

—Paperclip Maker Magic. 2020. (J). *(978-1-5415-8989-6(0))* Lerner Publishing Group.

Loya, Allyssa, et al. Paper Maker Magic. 2020. (J). *(978-1-5415-8990-2(4))* Lerner Publishing Group.

Lum, Kwei-lin. Twisted Fairy Tales Paper Dolls. 2012. (Dover Paper Dolls Ser.). (ENG., Illus.). 32p. (gr. 6-8). pap. 9.99 *(978-0-486-48441-9(6)*, 484416) Dover Pubns., Inc.

—Voodoo Paper Dolls. 2011. (Dover Paper Dolls Ser.). (ENG., Illus.). 32p. (J). (gr. 3-5). pap. 9.99 *(978-0-486-47785-5(1))* Dover Pubns., Inc.

Lum, Kwei-lin & Paper Dolls for Grownups Staff. Speakeasy Paper Dolls: Fabulous Flappers & More from the Roaring Twenties. 2012. (Dover Paper Dolls Ser.). (ENG., Illus.). 32p. (gr. 6-8). pap. 9.99 *(978-0-486-48639-0(7)*, 486397) Dover Pubns., Inc.

Lunney, Lizz. Build Your Own Theme Park: A Paper Cut-Out Book. 2019. (ENG., Illus.). 80p. (J). pap. 18.99 *(978-1-4494-9632-6(6))* Andrews McMeel Publishing.

MacDonald, Margaret. How Can You Re-Use an Egg Carton? 2012. (Level D Ser.). (ENG., Illus.). 16p. (J). (gr. k-2). pap. 7.95 *(978-1-927136-34-8(2)*, 19411) RiverStream Publishing.

Mackey, Dean. Paper Planes That Really Fly. 2012. 128p. (J). pap. 10.99 *(978-1-74308-787-9(X))* Hinkler Bks. Pty, Ltd. AUS. Dist: Ideals Pubns.

Make Your Own Art: Sets 1-2, 22 vols. Incl. Make Your Own Art: Set 2. 2010. lib. bdg. 151.35 *(978-1-4488-1625-5(4)*, ab4eeb4f-5340-4fa7-af2c-a6391e8949de); Set 1. Drawing. 2008. lib. bdg. 181.62 *(978-1-4358-2549-9(7)*, 3fce187b-c18a-47c1-b974-447e2b54b804); (J). (gr. 3-4). (Make Your Own Art Ser.). (ENG., Illus.). 32p. 2010. Set lib. bdg. 332.97 *(978-1-4488-1626-2(2)*, a3f3628d-9f30-4b44-93b7-bf632de74ed6, PowerKids Pr.) Rosen Publishing Group, Inc., The.

Maurer, Tracy Nelson. Paper Crafts with Pizzazz. 2009. (Illus.). 32p. (J). pap. 8.95 *(978-1-60694-504-9(1))* Rourke Educational Media.

McGee, Randel. Celebrate Chinese New Year with Paper Crafts, 1 vol. 2014. (Celebrate Holidays with Paper Crafts Ser.). (ENG.). 48p. (gr. 3-4). 26.93 *(978-0-7660-6350-1(X)*, f7b1992c-23e1-4c92-a9f7-53ef7ac0ddc0) Enslow Publishing, LLC.

—Celebrate Christmas with Paper Crafts, 1 vol. 2014. (Celebrate Holidays with Paper Crafts Ser.). (ENG.). 48p. (gr. 3-4). 26.93 *(978-0-7660-6355-6(0)*, 829b3358-286f-41aa-811f-e0169c079c96) Enslow Publishing, LLC.

—Celebrate Day of the Dead with Paper Crafts, 1 vol. 2014. (Celebrate Holidays with Paper Crafts Ser.). (ENG.). 48p. (gr. 3-4). 26.93 *(978-0-7660-6360-0(7)*, b1b95642-c852-4743-a08b-27936d2a3c39) Enslow Publishing, LLC.

—Celebrate Halloween with Paper Crafts, 1 vol. 2014. (Celebrate Holidays with Paper Crafts Ser.). (ENG.). 48p. (gr. 3-4). 26.93 *(978-0-7660-6365-5(8)*, edc777a4-f749-4e8f-9e2c-905a3b7756f9) Enslow Publishing, LLC.

—Celebrate Kwanzaa with Paper Crafts, 1 vol. 2014. (Celebrate Holidays with Paper Crafts Ser.). (ENG.). 48p. (gr. 3-4). 26.93 *(978-0-7660-6370-9(4)*, 3b6a483c-ce4f-4ca8-9cce-ee55fccdf2b8) Enslow Publishing, LLC.

—Celebrate Valentine's Day with Paper Crafts, 1 vol. 2014. (Celebrate Holidays with Paper Crafts Ser.). (ENG.). 48p. (gr. 3-4). 26.93 *(978-0-7660-6375-4(5)*, ed5a99e0-73cd-46bf-9de6-978bc803cab7) Enslow Publishing, LLC.

—Paper Crafts for Chinese New Year, 1 vol. 2008. (Paper Craft Fun for Holidays Ser.). (ENG., Illus.). 48p. (gr. 3-3). pap. 11.53 *(978-1-4644-0319-4(8)*, 03c1a82f-8f81-4b13-a362-dc294ce2dbfe, Enslow Elementary) Enslow Publishing, LLC.

—Paper Crafts for Christmas, 1 vol. (Paper Craft Fun for Holidays Ser.). (ENG., Illus.). 48p. (gr. 3-5). 2009. lib. bdg. 26.93 *(978-0-7660-2952-1(2)*, 37fefbc9-8aac-4432-b3db-df33fa285ecd) 2008. pap. 11.53 *(978-1-4644-0321-7(X)*, dc1f46fd-3304-41a5-834e-8faee5bc8ace) Enslow Publishing, LLC. (Enslow Elementary).

—Paper Crafts for Day of the Dead, 1 vol. 2008. (Paper Craft Fun for Holidays Ser.). (ENG., Illus.). 48p. (gr. 3-3). pap. 11.53 *(978-1-4644-0323-1(6)*, 0b026f40-4730-47e1-b039-433135a84cf0, Enslow Elementary) Enslow Publishing, LLC.

—Paper Crafts for Easter, 1 vol. 2012. (Paper Craft Fun for Holidays Ser.). (ENG., Illus.). 48p. (gr. 3-3). pap. 11.53 *(978-1-59845-335-5(1)*, a856626e-72fc-4e49-9d6c-efa50aa823db, Enslow Elementary); lib. bdg. 27.93 *(978-0-7660-3723-6(1)*, f3d7a453-f75e-4312-be4e-1e1b8c0e307a) Enslow Publishing, LLC.

—Paper Crafts for Halloween, 1 vol. 2008. (Paper Craft Fun for Holidays Ser.). (ENG., Illus.). 48p. (gr. 3-3). pap. 11.53 *(978-1-4644-0325-5(2)*, 16b38867-65de-4433-9376-a47c3c458e6c); lib. bdg. 27.93 *(978-0-7660-2947-7(6)*, 610dfe58-179d-4626-838f-131834ab68c0) Enslow Publishing, LLC. (Enslow Elementary).

—Paper Crafts for Kwanzaa, 1 vol. 2008. (Paper Craft Fun for Holidays Ser.). (ENG., Illus.). 48p. (gr. 3-3). pap. 11.53 *(978-1-4644-0327-9(9)*, 108c01b4-c48c-4cbd-986f-c906d52dc354); lib. bdg. 27.93 *(978-0-7660-2949-1(2)*, 07ba43cf-802d-4ae2-9f3a-6b91f4d277b2) Enslow Publishing, LLC. (Enslow Elementary).

—Paper Crafts for Mardi Gras, 1 vol. 2012. (Paper Craft Fun for Holidays Ser.). (ENG., Illus.). 48p. (gr. 3-3). pap. 11.53 *(978-1-59845-334-8(3)*, 5fe996d3-ac5d-43f9-a146-3501ac646298, Enslow Elementary); lib. bdg. 27.93 *(978-0-7660-3724-3(X)*, 30ab99c7-5c11-4645-9399-96e3f6459c85) Enslow Publishing, LLC.

—Paper Crafts for Presidents' Day, 1 vol. 2012. (Paper Craft Fun for Holidays Ser.). (ENG., Illus.). 48p. (gr. 3-3). pap. 11.53 *(978-1-59845-333-1(5)*, b0bfcb15-5fd7-4773-a841-b400600588dd, Enslow Elementary); lib. bdg. 27.93 *(978-0-7660-3726-7(6)*, bac591b1-2fa7-435c-b615-7b87c4b7e8bf) Enslow Publishing, LLC.

—Paper Crafts for St. Patrick's Day, 1 vol. 2012. (Paper Craft Fun for Holidays Ser.). (ENG., Illus.). 48p. (gr. 3-3). pap. 11.53 *(978-1-59845-337-9(8)*, 4006e828-f509-4acf-a93e-521a20adac48, Enslow Elementary); lib. bdg. 27.93 *(978-0-7660-3725-0(8)*, 9a67da7a-0fad-494d-ad9c-9d553ced7d34) Enslow Publishing, LLC.

—Paper Crafts for Thanksgiving, 1 vol. 2012. (Paper Craft Fun for Holidays Ser.). (ENG., Illus.). 48p. (gr. 3-3). pap. 11.53 *(978-1-59845-336-2(X)*, 11211fe1-2dc7-4ff6-a816-9f295964b23b, Enslow Elementary); lib. bdg. 27.93 *(978-0-7660-3722-9(3)*, 96c2149d-5087-4dab-b253-976b82a1bf80) Enslow Publishing, LLC.

—Paper Crafts for the 4th of July, 1 vol. 2012. (Paper Craft Fun for Holidays Ser.). (ENG., Illus.). 48p. (gr. 3-3). pap. 11.53 *(978-1-59845-332-4(7)*, 325e5139-a38d-4eb1-a4fd-00083e05a6a5, Enslow Elementary); lib. bdg. 27.93 *(978-0-7660-3727-4(4)*, e1375e60-8cde-4742-aafb-699afc0ae36e) Enslow Publishing, LLC.

—Paper Crafts for Valentine's Day, 1 vol. 2008. (Paper Craft Fun for Holidays Ser.). (ENG., Illus.). 48p. (gr. 3-3). pap. 11.53 *(978-1-4644-0329-3(5)*, 288c7207-b89c-4bb7-9ed7-df3465df3346, Enslow Elementary) Enslow Publishing, LLC.

Medina, Sarah. Having Fun with Paper, 1 vol. 2007. (Fun Art Projects Ser.). (ENG., Illus.). 24p. (J). (gr. 2-2). lib. bdg. 28.93 *(978-1-4042-3716-2(X)*,

P
Q
R

d196f34c-345f-4583-a0b4-f267d8104d87, PowerKids Pr.) Rosen Publishing Group, Inc., The.

Menten, Ted. Evil Queens & Wicked Witches Paper Dolls. 2014. (ENG.). 32p. (J). (gr. 3-8). pap. 9.99 *(978-0-486-49497-5(7),* 494977) Dover Pubns., Inc.

—Little Goth Girl Sticker Paper Doll. 2011. (Dover Little Activity Books Paper Dolls Ser.). (ENG.). 4p. (J). (gr. 2-5). 1.99 *(978-0-486-48172-2(7),* 481727) Dover Pubns., Inc.

—Wizard of Oz Paper Dolls. 2008. (Dover Paper Dolls Ser.). (ENG., Illus.). 32p. (J). (gr. 1-5). pap. 6.99 *(978-0-486-46765-8(1),* 467651) Dover Pubns., Inc.

Mihaltchev, Atanas. Kid-Agami — Dinosaurs: Kiragami for Kids: Easy-To-Make Paper Toys. 2013. (Dover Children's Activity Bks.). (ENG.). 24p. (J). (gr. 1-5). pap. 9.99 *(978-0-486-49743-3(7))* Dover Pubns., Inc.

—Kid-Agami — Sea Life: Kiragami for Kids: Easy-To-Make Paper Toys. 2013. (Dover Kids Activity Bks.). (ENG.). 24p. (J). (gr. 1-5). pap. 9.99 *(978-0-486-49744-0(5),* 497445) Dover Pubns., Inc.

Miller, Eileen Rudisill. Harry & Meghan Sticker Paper Dolls. 2019. (Dover Little Activity Books Paper Dolls Ser.). (ENG., Illus.). 8p. (J). (gr. 1-5). 1.99 *(978-0-486-83403-0(4),* 834034) Dover Pubns., Inc.

—Nutcracker Ballet Paper Dolls with Glitter! 2011. (Dover Paper Dolls Ser.). (ENG.). 32p. (J). (gr. 1-4). pap. 12.99 *(978-0-486-48390-0(8))* Dover Pubns., Inc.

—William & Kate Sticker Paper Dolls. 2019. (Dover Little Activity Books Paper Dolls Ser.). (ENG., Illus.). 8p. (J). (gr. 1-5). 1.99 *(978-0-486-83404-7(2),* 834042) Dover Pubns., Inc.

Mitchell, David. The Magic of Flexagons: Paper Curiosities to Cut Out & Make. 2008. (ENG., Illus.). 36p. pap. 10.99 *(978-1-899618-28-6(7))* Tarquin Pubns. GBR. Dist: Independent Pubs. Group.

Moerbeek, Kees, illus. Make 24 Paper Planes: Includes Awesome Launcher Kit! 2015. (ENG.). 24p. (J). (gr. 2-6). pap. 11.99 *(978-1-4380-0640-6(3))* Sourcebooks, Inc.

Morris, Ting & Morris, Neil. Dinosaurs. Levy, Ruth & Cowne, Joanne, illus. 2006. (Sticky Fingers Ser.). 32p. (J). lib. bdg. 28.50 *(978-1-59771-029-9(6))* Sea-To-Sea Pubns.

Naylor, Amy. Whoosh! Easy Paper Airplanes for Kids: Color, Fold & Fly! 2013. (Dover Kids Activity Bks.). (ENG.). 48p. (J). (gr. -1-3). pap. 6.99 *(978-0-486-49231-5(1),* 492311) Dover Pubns., Inc.

Nemec, Nina. Play with Scissors & Little Miss Scribble. 2012. 20p. pap. 19.82 *(978-1-4772-4575-0(8))* AuthorHouse.

Newell, Keith. Models. 2005. (Art & Craft Skills (Sea-to-Sea) Ser.). (Illus.). 32p. (J). (gr. 3-6). lib. bdg. 27.10 *(978-1-932889-85-7(X),* 1247657) Sea-To-Sea Pubns.

Niark. Paper Toys: Monsters: 11 Paper Monsters to Build. 2019. (Paper Toys Ser.). (ENG., Illus.). 24p. (J). (gr. k-5). pap. 12.95 *(978-1-58423-723-5(6))* Gingko Pr., Inc.

Owen, Ruth. Paper Crafts. 2013. (From Trash to Treasure Ser.). 32p. (J). (gr. 3-6). pap. 70.50 *(978-1-4777-1359-4(X),* PowerKids Pr.) Rosen Publishing Group, Inc., The.

Paper Animals. 2004. (Art Rom Create Your Own... Ser.). (Illus.). 24p. (J). pap. incl. audio compact disk *(978-1-84229-771-1(6))* Top That! Publishing PLC.

Paper Dinosaurs. 2004. (Art Rom Create Your Own... Ser.). (Illus.). 24p. (J). pap. incl. audio compact disk *(978-1-84229-770-4(8))* Top That! Publishing PLC.

Paper Fliers. 2004. (Art Rom Create Your Own... Ser.). (Illus.). 24p. (J). pap. incl. audio compact disk *(978-1-84229-772-8(4))* Top That! Publishing PLC.

Paper Planes Boxed Kit. (J). 7.90 *(978-1-57755-401-1(9))* Flying Frog Publishing, Inc.

Papier Mache. (Jump Ser.). (Illus.). 36p. (J). (gr. 2-6). pap. *(978-1-882210-35-0(2))* Action Publishing, Inc.

Parigo, Bishop. Paper Toys: Animals: 11 Paper Animals to Build. 2016. (Paper Toys Ser.). (ENG., Illus.). 24p. (J). (gr. k-4). pap. 12.95 *(978-1-58423-648-1(5),* a4d96095-dbee-4bf3-b43b-096001817f4c) Gingko Pr., Inc.

Paschal, Janey Loree Fisher, ed. Melly: #2 in the 1989 Family Friends Paper Doll Set, 3 nos., no. 2. Fisher, Phyllis Mae Richardson, illus. l.t. ed. 2004. (ENG.). 24p. (J). act. bk. ed. 10.00 *(978-0-9745615-6-1(8))* PJs Corner Gift Shoppe.

Pasques, Patrick. Savanna Animals. 2013. (3D Paper Craft Ser.). (ENG., Illus.). 48p. (J). (gr. k). 14.95 *(978-84-92810-75-8(0))* Promotora de prensa internacional S.A ESP. Dist: Consortium Bk. Sales & Distribution.

Pereira, Diego Jourdan. Glow-in-the-Dark Zombie Sticker Paper Doll. 2014. (ENG.). 4p. (J). (gr. 1-4). 1.50 *(978-0-486-78122-8(4),* 781224) Dover Pubns., Inc.

Pérez-Reverte, Arturo. The Queen of the South. 2004. (Illus.). 384p. (J). (gr. 2-5). pap. *(978-0-9655018-2-8(5))* Knot Garden Pr.

Petelinsek, Kathleen. Crafting with Tissue Paper. Petelinsek, Kathleen, illus. 2014. (How-To Library). (ENG., Illus.). 32p. (J). (gr. 3-6). 32.07 *(978-1-63137-779-2(5),* 205359) Cherry Lake Publishing.

Phillips, Jennifer. Adorable Accessories: Paper Creations to Wear, 1 vol. 2013. (Paper Creations Ser.). (ENG.). 32p. (J). (gr. 3-9). lib. bdg. 28.65 *(978-1-62065-043-1(6),* 120722) Capstone.

—Snappy Style: Paper Decoration Creations, 1 vol. 2013. (Paper Creations Ser.). (ENG.). 32p. (J). (gr. 3-9). lib. bdg. 28.65 *(978-1-62065-042-4(8),* 120721) Capstone.

Project Runway. Project Runway Fashion Paper Doll Kit - African American Girl. 2008. (J). mass mkt. *(978-0-9819053-2-7(3))* Westrim Crafts.

—Project Runway Fashion Paper Doll Kit - Asian Girl. 2008. (J). mass mkt. 12.99 *(978-0-9819053-3-4(1))* Westrim Crafts.

—Project Runway Fashion Paper Doll Kit - Blonde Girl. 2008. (J). mass mkt. 12.99 *(978-0-9819053-6-5(6))* Westrim Crafts.

—Project Runway Fashion Paper Doll Kit - Brunette Girl. 2008. (J). mass mkt. 12.99 *(978-0-9819053-4-1(X))* Westrim Crafts.

—Project Runway Fashion Paper Doll Kit - Caucasian Girl. 2008. (J). mass mkt. 12.99 *(978-0-9819053-0-3(7))* Westrim Crafts.

—Project Runway Fashion Paper Doll Kit - Latina Girl. 2008. (J). mass mkt. 12.99 *(978-0-9819053-1-0(5))* Westrim Crafts.

Rau, Dana Meachen. Making a Paper Airplane & Other Paper Toys. 2012. (How-To Library). (ENG.). 32p. (gr. 3-6). pap. 14.21 *(978-1-61080-647-3(6),* 202257); (Illus.). 32.07 *(978-1-61080-473-8(2),* 202083) Cherry Lake Publishing.

Reynolds, Toby. Paper Sculpture, 1 vol. 2017. (Mini Artist Ser.). (ENG.). 24p. (J). (gr. 1-2). 26.27 *(978-1-5081-9408-8(4),* 21c00536-7f44-497a-8f10-09e42066a83b); pap. 11.60 *(978-1-5081-9439-2(4),* b8b81c40-8fa1-47c4-9e9f-b1a46e133af8) Rosen Publishing Group, Inc., The. (Windmill Bks.).

—Papercraft, 1 vol. 2014. (Mini Artist Ser.). (ENG.). 24p. (J). (gr. 1-2). lib. bdg. 26.27 *(978-1-4777-9123-3(X),* 96e5f214-99e4-44dd-9933-42e65b5317c8, Windmill Bks.) Rosen Publishing Group, Inc., The.

Rice, Dona Herweck. Folding Paper. rev. ed. 2019. (Smithsonian: Informational Text Ser.). (ENG., Illus.). 20p. (J). (gr. k-1). 7.99 *(978-1-4938-6639-7(7))* Teacher Created Materials, Inc.

Robinson, Nick. Fantastic Flexagons: Hexaflexagons & Other Flexible Folds to Twist & Turn. 2017. (ENG.). 96p. (J). (gr. 4-9). pap. 9.99 *(978-1-944686-10-9(X),* Racehorse Publishing) Skyhorse Publishing Co., Inc.

—My First Origami Book — Christmas: With 24 Sheets of Origami Paper! 2013. (Dover Origami Papercraft Ser.). (ENG.). 96p. (J). (gr. 2). pap. 12.99 *(978-0-486-49182-0(X),* 49182X) Dover Pubns., Inc.

Robinson, Nick & Origami. My First Origami Book-Animals. 2012. (Dover Origami Papercraft Ser.). (ENG., Illus.). 96p. (J). (gr. 2). pap. 12.99 *(978-0-486-48706-9(7),* 487067) Dover Pubns., Inc.

—My First Origami Book-Things That Go. 2012. (Dover Origami Papercraft Ser.). (ENG., Illus.). 96p. (J). (gr. 2). pap. 12.99 *(978-0-486-48707-6(5),* 487075) Dover Pubns., Inc.

Rocky Mountain Snowflakes: New Edition. 2006. 8.95 *(978-0-9661572-3-9(0))* Dream Bee Pubns.

Roi, Arnaud. Paper Toys: Robots: 12 Paper Robots to Build. 2016. (Paper Toys Ser.). (ENG., Illus.). 24p. (J). (gr. k-4). pap. 12.95 *(978-1-58423-649-8(3),* eaed9384-c8c8-40bf-a9b0-c26da39eb253) Gingko Pr., Inc.

Ross, Kathy. The Scrapbooker's Idea Book. Bosch, Nicole in den, illus. 2006. (Girl Crafts Ser.). 48p. (J). (gr. 3-7). per. 7.95 *(978-0-8225-6511-6(0),* First Avenue Editions) Lerner Publishing Group.

Rueben & Rachel's Paper Doll Book. 2003. (J). 10.00 *(978-0-9745615-3-0(3))* PJs Corner Gift Shoppe.

Ryall, Jeanette. Paper Art, 1 vol. 2012. (Awesome Art Ser.). (ENG., Illus.). 32p. (J). (gr. 3-3). 31.27 *(978-1-4488-8089-8(0),* 860340e2-de22-4511-9a23-fa258a3e9ce6); pap. 12.75 *(978-1-4488-8142-0(0),* 0779a656-72b8-4dec-91fe-e2fb517923a8) Rosen Publishing Group, Inc., The. (Windmill Bks.).

Saltzberg, Barney. Andrew Drew & Drew. 2012. (ENG., Illus.). 40p. (J). (gr. -1-1). 18.99 *(978-1-4197-0377-5(3),* 1014701, Abrams Appleseed) Abrams, Inc.

Sarris, Eno, ed. Dinosaurs: Triceratops & Pteranodon, 4 vols. 2006. (Kumon 3-D Paper Crafts Ser.). (Illus.). 16p. (J). (gr. 4-7). per. 5.95 *(978-1-933241-19-7(5))* Kumon Publishing North America, Inc.

Scraper, Katherine, et al. Boredom Busters! Try This! Free & Inexpensive Things to Make & Do. 2011. (J). pap. *(978-1-4509-5325-2(5))* Benchmark Education Co.

Shanahan, Sue. Cut & Color Paper Dolls: Maria & Megan. 2005. (Dover Paper Dolls Ser.). (ENG., Illus.). 32p. (J). (gr. -1-5). 3.95 *(978-0-486-44122-1(9))* Dover Pubns., Inc.

Sjonger, Rebecca. Maker Projects for Kids Who Love Paper Engineering. 2016. (Be a Maker! Ser.). (ENG., Illus.). 32p. (J). (gr. 5-9). *(978-0-7787-2577-0(4))* Crabtree Publishing Co.

Smith, A. Papercraft. 2004. 96p. (J). pap. 14.95 *(978-0-7945-0140-2(0))* EDC Publishing.

Song, Sok. Everyday Origami: A Foldable Fashion Guide. Song, Sok, illus. 2016. (Fashion Origami Ser.). (ENG., Illus.). 48p. (J). (gr. 4-8). lib. bdg. 32.65 *(978-1-5157-1630-3(9),* 132464, Capstone Pr.) Capstone.

—Origami Accessories: A Foldable Fashion Guide. Song, Sok, illus. 2016. (Fashion Origami Ser.). (ENG., Illus.). 48p. (J). (gr. 4-8). lib. bdg. 32.65 *(978-1-5157-1623-5(6),* 132463, Capstone Pr.) Capstone.

—Origami Outfits: A Foldable Fashion Guide. Song, Sok, illus. 2016. (Fashion Origami Ser.). (ENG., Illus.). 48p. (J). (gr. 4-8). lib. bdg. 32.65 *(978-1-5157-1631-0(7),* 132465, Capstone Pr.) Capstone.

Staff, Gareth Editorial Staff. Paper, 1 vol. 2003. (Let's Create! Ser.). (ENG., Illus.). 32p. (gr. 2-4). lib. bdg. 28.67 *(978-0-8368-3747-6(9),* 8c1913c0-c3ea-4e20-8051-5a74d17e7beb, Gareth Stevens Learning Library) Stevens, Gareth Publishing LLLP.

—Papier-Mâché, 1 vol. 2004. (Let's Create! Ser.). (ENG., Illus.). 32p. (gr. 2-4). lib. bdg. 28.67 *(978-0-8368-4017-9(8),* 90e10b76-1cc9-429f-ba2b-4b50d5347cfe, Gareth Stevens Learning Library) Stevens, Gareth Publishing LLLP.

Steadman, Barbara. Christmas Princess Sticker Paper Doll. 2005. (Dover Little Activity Books Paper Dolls Ser.). (ENG., Illus.). 4p. (J). (gr. -1-5). 1.50 *(978-0-486-44105-4(9))* Dover Pubns., Inc.

—Storybook Princess. 2004. (Dover Little Activity Books Paper Dolls Ser.). (ENG., Illus.). 4p. (J). (gr. k-3). pap. 2.50 *(978-0-486-43726-2(4),* 437264) Dover Pubns., Inc.

—Sweet Valentine. 2004. (Dover Little Activity Books Paper Dolls Ser.). (ENG., Illus.). 4p. (J). (gr. -1-5). pap. 1.50 *(978-0-486-43751-4(5))* Dover Pubns., Inc.

Steadman, Barbara, creator. Glitter Ballerina Sticker Paper Doll. 2005. (Dover Little Activity Books Paper Dolls Ser.). (ENG., Illus.). 2p. (J). (gr. 1-4). pap. 2.99 *(978-0-486-44479-6(1),* 444791) Dover Pubns., Inc.

Stillerman, Robbie. Ballerina Friends Sticker Paper Dolls. 2008. (Dover Little Activity Books Paper Dolls Ser.). (ENG., Illus.). 4p. (J). (gr. k-3). 2.50 *(978-0-486-46574-6(8),* 465748) Dover Pubns., Inc.

—Ghoulish Girls Paper Dolls. 2014. (ENG.). 32p. (J). (gr. 4-11). pap. 7.99 *(978-0-486-49489-0(6),* 494896) Dover Pubns., Inc.

—Kati & Kayla. 2005. (Dover Paper Dolls Ser.). (ENG., Illus.). 32p. (J). (gr. -1-5). pap. 3.95 *(978-0-486-44146-7(6),* 441466) Dover Pubns., Inc.

Stohs, Anita Reith. Praise God with Paper Bags. 2004. (Illus.). 64p. (J). (gr. 2-5). 10.99 *(978-0-7586-0643-3(5))* Concordia Publishing Hse.

Storey, Rita. Make Your Own Creative Cards (Do It Yourself Projects!) 2010. 24p. pap. 9.40 *(978-1-61532-593-1(X))* Rosen Publishing Group, Inc., The.

—Make Your Own Toys (Do It Yourself Projects!) 2010. 24p. pap. 9.40 *(978-1-61532-594-8(8))* Rosen Publishing Group, Inc., The.

Stunt Planes. 2004. (Fantastic Fliers Ser.). (Illus.). 48p. (J). pap. *(978-1-84229-726-1(0))* Top That! Publishing PLC.

Suen, Anastasia. How to Make a Piñata. 2018. (Step-By-Step Projects Ser.). (ENG., Illus.). 24p. (gr. k-2). lib. bdg. 28.50 *(978-1-64156-430-4(X),* 9781641564304) Rourke Educational Media.

Sun, Ming-Ju. Godey's Fashions Paper Dolls 1860-1879. 2004. (Dover Victorian Paper Dolls Ser.). (ENG.). 32p. (J). (gr. 6-8). pap. 9.99 *(978-0-486-43424-7(9),* 434249) Dover Pubns., Inc.

Supercool Fliers. 2004. (Fantastic Fliers Ser.). (Illus.). 48p. (J). pap. *(978-1-84229-729-2(5))* Top That! Publishing PLC.

Sutcliffe, Kristen. Fabric Paper Thread: 26 Projects to Stitch with Friends. 2013. (ENG., Illus.). 144p. (J). (gr. 3-8). pap. 21.95 *(978-1-60705-715-4(8))* C & T Publishing.

Thomas, Rachael L. Kirigami: Paper Cutting & Folding. 2019. (Cool Paper Art Ser.). (ENG., Illus.). 32p. (J). (gr. 3-6). lib. bdg. 34.21 *(978-1-5321-1945-3(3),* 32475, Checkerboard Library) ABDO Publishing Co.

Tierney, Tom. Art Deco Fashions Paper Dolls. 2005. (Dover Paper Dolls Ser.). (ENG., Illus.). 32p. (J). (gr. 3-8). 6.95 *(978-0-486-44158-0(X))* Dover Pubns., Inc.

—Brides from Around the World Paper Dolls. 2005. (Dover Paper Dolls Ser.). (ENG., Illus.). 32p. (J). (gr. 3-5). 9.95 *(978-0-486-44439-0(2))* Dover Pubns., Inc.

—The Dalai Lama Paper Doll. 2006. (Dover Paper Dolls Ser.). (ENG., Illus.). 32p. (J). (gr. 7-8). pap. 6.95 *(978-0-486-45181-7(X),* 45181X) Dover Pubns., Inc.

—Famous Torch Singers Paper Dolls. 2006. (Dover Celebrity Paper Dolls Ser.). (ENG., Illus.). 32p. (J). (gr. 6-8). pap. 6.95 *(978-0-486-44744-5(8))* Dover Pubns., Inc.

—Fashions of the First Ladies Paper Dolls. 2006. (Dover President Paper Dolls Ser.). (ENG., Illus.). 32p. (J). (gr. 3-8). pap. 11.99 *(978-0-486-44879-4(7),* 448797) Dover Pubns., Inc.

—French Film Stars Paper Dolls. 2005. (Dover Celebrity Paper Dolls Ser.). (ENG., Illus.). 32p. (J). (gr. 6-8). pap. 6.95 *(978-0-486-44132-0(6),* 441326) Dover Pubns., Inc.

—Glamorous Television Stars Paper Dolls. 2005. (Dover Celebrity Paper Dolls Ser.). (ENG., Illus.). 32p. (J). (gr. 7-5). pap. 6.95 *(978-0-486-44462-8(7))* Dover Pubns., Inc.

—Movie Mobsters Paper Dolls. 2011. (Dover Celebrity Paper Dolls Ser.). (ENG.). 32p. (J). (gr. 7-8). pap. 9.99 *(978-0-486-48049-7(6),* 480496) Dover Pubns., Inc.

—Newport Fashions of the Gilded Age Paper Dolls. 2005. (Dover Victorian Paper Dolls Ser.). (ENG., Illus.). 32p. (J). (gr. 6-5). pap. 8.95 *(978-0-486-44449-9(X))* Dover Pubns., Inc.

—Ziegfeld Girls Paper Dolls. 2004. (Dover Paper Dolls Ser.). (ENG., Illus.). 32p. (J). (gr. 6). pap. 5.95 *(978-0-486-43679-1(9))* Dover Pubns., Inc.

Top That! Team Staff, contrib. by. Design & Fly Paper Airplanes. 2003. (Illus.). 48p. (J). *(978-0-439-57192-0(8))* Scholastic, Inc.

Torres, Laura. Rock Your Party. 2012. (ENG., Illus.). 32p. (gr. 3-5). pap. 8.95 *(978-1-926853-86-4(5))* Saunders Bk. Co. CAN. Dist: RiverStream Publishing.

Touache, Sebastian, illus. Paper Toys: Super Heroes: 11 Paper Super Heroes to Build. 2017. (Paper Toys Ser.). (ENG.). 24p. (J). (gr. k-4). pap. 12.95 *(978-1-58423-668-9(X),* c5a14cb4-d0e6-4ac3-9fde-c9906c160d4e) Gingko Pr., Inc.

Tougui. Paper Toys: Fantasy Creatures: 11 Paper Fantasy Creatures to Build. 2017. (Paper Toys Ser.). (ENG., Illus.). 24p. (J). (gr. k-4). pap. 12.95 *(978-1-58423-650-4(7),* e6326261-2cf8-4b08-8fda-e93bb8be843f) Gingko Pr., Inc.

Tremaine, Jon. Paper Tricks. 2012. (ENG., Illus.). 32p. (gr. 3-5). pap. 8.95 *(978-1-926853-84-0(9))* Saunders Bk. Co. CAN. Dist: RiverStream Publishing.

Tucker, Mary. Cut & Create! Ocean Life. Mitchell, Judy & Lindeen, Mary, eds. Rankin, Kim, illus. 2007. 80p. (J). pap. 9.95 *(978-1-57310-526-2(0))* Teaching & Learning Co.

—Cut & Create! Spring & Summer. Mitchell, Judy & Lindeen, Mary, eds. Rankin, Kim, illus. 2007. 80p. (J). pap. 9.95 *(978-1-57310-535-4(X))* Teaching & Learning Co.

Tudor, Andy, illus. 200 Paper Planes. 2013. (200 Paper Planes Ser.). 402p. (J). pap. 13.99 *(978-0-7945-3371-7(X),* Usborne) EDC Publishing.

Tummie, Loulou &. Paper Toys: Aliens: 11 Paper Aliens to Build. 2019. (Paper Toys Ser.). (ENG., Illus.). 24p. 12.95 *(978-1-58423-722-8(8))* Gingko Pr., Inc.

Turnbull, Stephanie. Cool Stuff to Make with Paper. 2015. (ENG., Illus.). 32p. (J). pap. 9.95 *(978-1-77092-223-5(7))* RiverStream Publishing.

—Paper Crafts. 2015. (Try This! Ser.). (ENG., Illus.). 24p. (J). (gr. 3-6). 27.10 *(978-1-62588-373-5(0),* 17447) Black Rabbit Bks.

Turnbull, Stephaniel & Turnbull, Stephanie. Cool Stuff to Make with Paper. 2014. (Cool Stuff Ser.). 32p. (gr. 2-5). 31.35 *(978-1-62588-189-2(4))* Black Rabbit Bks.

Veitch, Catherine. Collins Big Cat Phonics for Letters & Sounds - Stunt Jets: Band 03/Yellow, Bd. 3. 2018. (Collins Big Cat Phonics Ser.). (ENG., Illus.). 16p. (J). (gr. k-1). pap. 6.99 *(978-0-00-825159-8(2))* HarperCollins Pubs. Ltd. GBR. Dist: Independent Pubs. Group.

Ventura, Marne. Awesome Paper Projects You Can Create. 2015. (Imagine It, Build It Ser.). (ENG., Illus.). 32p. (J). (gr. 3-9). lib. bdg. 28.65 *(978-1-4914-4293-7(X),* 128687, Capstone Pr.) Capstone.

—Cool Cardboard Projects You Can Create. 2015. (Imagine It, Build It Ser.). (ENG., Illus.). 32p. (J). (gr. 3-9). lib. bdg. 28.65 *(978-1-4914-4291-3(3),* 128684, Capstone Pr.) Capstone.

Victorian Paper Dolls. Date not set. (J). pap. 2.95 *(978-1-57122-079-0(8))* Nickel Pr.

Wallace, Holly. Paper. 2007. (How We Use Materials/Watts Ser.). (Illus.). 30p. (J). (gr. 4-7). lib. bdg. 28.50 *(978-1-59920-004-0(X))* Black Rabbit Bks.

Watt, Fiona. Cut-Out Paper Dolls. 2018. (ENG.). 100p. pap. 12.99 *(978-0-7945-4214-6(X),* Usborne) EDC Publishing.

Whatley, Charlotte. Peter Pan Paper Dolls. 2011. (Dover Paper Dolls Ser.). (ENG., Illus.). 32p. (J). (gr. 3-5). pap. 9.99 *(978-0-486-48231-6(6),* 482316) Dover Pubns., Inc.

Woodroffe, David. Making Paper Airplanes: Make Your Own Aircraft & Watch Them Fly! 2012. (ENG., Illus.). 192p. (J). (gr. 4-7). pap. 12.95 *(978-1-62087-168-3(8),* 620168, Sky Pony Pr.) Skyhorse Publishing Co., Inc.

Yates, Jane. Paper-Mache Masks, 1 vol. 2016. (Cool Crafts for Kids Ser.). (ENG.). 32p. (J). (gr. 3-3). pap. 12.75 *(978-1-4994-8234-8(5),* 2eee5d46-4a78-4831-ace0-530457fc0557, Windmill Bks.) Rosen Publishing Group, Inc., The.

—Tissue Paper Creations, 1 vol. 2016. (Cool Crafts for Kids Ser.). (ENG.). 32p. (J). (gr. 3-3). pap. 12.75 *(978-1-4994-8240-9(X),* 3083dfde-ca01-425e-a218-4db3f7bd3da8, Windmill Bks.) Rosen Publishing Group, Inc., The.

100 Birds to Fold & Fly. 2017. (Tear-Off Papercraft Pads Ser.). (ENG.). (J). pap. 7.99 *(978-0-7945-3943-6(2),* Usborne) EDC Publishing.

PAPERCRAFT

see Paper Work

PAPIER-MACHE

see Paper Work

PAPUA NEW GUINEA

Gascoigne, Ingrid. Papua New Guinea, 1 vol. 2nd rev. ed. 2009. (Cultures of the World (Second Edition)(r) Ser.). (ENG.). 144p. (gr. 5-5). lib. bdg. 49.79 *(978-0-7614-3416-0(X),* a2a863b2-0b20-4251-8c29-e45bc177c7ab) Cavendish Square Publishing LLC.

Gascoigne, Ingrid & Schumacher, Cassandra. Papua New Guinea, 1 vol. 2018. (Cultures of the World (Third Edition)(r) Ser.). (ENG.). 144p. (gr. 5-5). 48.79 *(978-1-5026-3630-0(1),* e0592e7d-464d-40d0-a242-63baa95c4594) Cavendish Square Publishing LLC.

PAPUA NEW GUINEA—FICTION

Carlson, Melody. Notes from a Spinning Planet — Papua New Guinea. 2007. (Notes from a Spinning Planet Ser.: 2). 240p. (YA). (gr. 7-12). per. 14.99 *(978-1-4000-7145-6(3),* WaterBrook Pr.) Crown Publishing Group, The.

Jones, Lloyd. Mister Pip. 2010. 256p. 21.85 *(978-0-7569-9114-2(5))* Perfection Learning Corp.

Kuelinad, Marlon. Little People's Little Happenings. 2013. 22p. pap. *(978-9980-87-916-5(5))* Univ. of Papua New Guinea Pr.

Tago, Anita. Traditional Stories from Binandere in Oro Province, Papua New Guinea. 2012. 44p. pap. *(978-9980-945-71-6(0))* Univ. of Papua New Guinea Pr.

PARABLES

see also Allegories; Fables; Jesus Christ—Parables

Adeyemi, Sam. The Parable of Dollars: Proven Strategies for Your Financial Success. 2nd ed. 2004. Orig. Title: Parable of Dollars. 208p. per. 14.95 *(978-0-9746735-1-6(X))* Summit Hse. Pubs.

Ball, Liz, illus. Miracles & Parables of Jesus: Find-the-Picture Puzzles. 2004. (Find-the-Picture Puzzle Ser.: 2). 24p. (J). pap. 2.95 *(978-0-8198-4830-7(1),* 332-221) Pauline Bks. & Media.

Black, Peter A. Parables from the Pond. 2008. 232p. per. *(978-1-897373-21-7(X))* Word Alive Pr.

Bynum, Juanita, ed. A Parable about the King. 2004.Tr. of Una Parabola Sobre el Rey. (SPA.). 32p. 8.99 *(978-0-88419-998-4(3),* Casa Creacion) Charisma Media.

Carlson, Melody. Farmer Brown's Field Trip. Björkman, Steve, illus. 2004. 40p. (gr. -1-3). 9.99 *(978-1-58134-142-3(3))* Crossway.

Clydesdale, David T., contrib. by. Acorns to Oaks: Planted, Rooted & Growing in Christ. 2007. (Illus.). 109p. pap. 6.95 *(978-5-557-71497-6(9),* Word Music) Word Entertainment.

Eder, Enelle. Create & Take Bible Crafts: Parables & Miracles. 2004. (Create & Take Bible Crafts). (Illus.). 96p. (J). pap. 11.95 *(978-1-58411-007-1(4))* Rainbow Pubs. & Legacy Pr.

Ferguson, M. J. The Mirror in the Box: A Children's Story & a Parable. 2013. 66p. (gr. 4-6). pap. 9.99 *(978-1-4497-7804-0(6),* WestBow Pr.) Author Solutions, LLC.

Gatty, Alfred. Parables from Nature (Yesterday's Classics) 2006. (Illus.). 456p. (J). per. 14.95 *(978-1-59915-005-5(0))* Yesterday's Classics.

Groenboom, Roger, et al. Sharable Parables. (Walk with Me Ser.). (gr. k-8). 24.95 *(978-1-59255-176-7(9),* 017210) Faith Alive Christian Resources.

Higgs, Liz Curtis. The Pumpkin Patch Parable, 1 vol. 2006. (Parable Ser.). (ENG., Illus.). 36p. (J). (gr. -1-2). 7.99 *(978-1-4003-0846-0(1),* Tommy Nelson) Nelson, Thomas Inc.

Holmes, Wayne & Pelletier, Christine. Lost & Found Teaching Unit. Kalvoda, LeAnn, illus. rev. ed. 2003. 96p. (J). ring bd. 35.00 *(978-1-58302-232-0(5))* Creative Ministry Solutions.

Koo, Rob, illus. More Great Buddhist Stories. 2012. (J). pap. *(978-1-935523-48-2(1))* World Tribune Pr.

Larcombe, Jennifer Rees. Danger on the Lonely Road. Björkman, Steve, illus. 2004. (Best Bible Stories Ser.). 24p. (gr. -1-3). pap. 2.99 *(978-1-58134-149-2(0))* Crossway.

Larsen, Sharon G. The Parable of the Chocolate Chips. 2008. (J). *(978-1-59038-912-6(3))* Deseret Bk. Co.

Levine, Amy-Jill & Sasso, Sandy Eisenberg. Who Is My Neighbor? Turu, Denise, illus. 2019. (ENG.). 32p. (J). (gr. -1-2). 17.00 *(978-1-947888-07-4(2),* 1947888072, Flyaway Bks.) Westminster John Knox Pr.

Littleton, Mark. Stories Jesus Told. Moroney, Trace, illus. 2004. 20p. (J). bds. 10.99 *(978-0-8254-5519-3(7))* Kregel Pubns.

Miller, Claire. The Parable of the Lost Sheep. van der Sterre, Johanna, illus. 2008. (Arch Bks.). 16p. (J). (gr. k-4). pap. 1.99 *(978-0-7586-1455-1(1))* Concordia Publishing Hse.

Phillips, Deborah. The Parable of the Princesses. 2008. (Illus.). 48p. (J). 19.99 *(978-1-59038-873-0(9))* Deseret Bk. Co.

Saunders, George. The Very Persistent Gappers of Frip. 2008. (ENG.). 88p. pap. 8.50 *(978-1-58342-557-2(8))* Dramatic Publishing Co.

—The Very Persistent Gappers of Frip. Smith, Lane, illus. 2015. (ENG.). 96p. 22.00 *(978-0-8129-8963-2(5),* Random House) Random House Publishing Group.

Smith, Cyncie. The Joyful Shepherd. 2004. (Illus.). 32p. (J). 9.99 *(978-1-56309-484-2(3),* New Hope Pubs.) Iron Stream Media.

Sproul, R. C. The Priest with Dirty Clothes. Gerard, Justin, illus. 2nd ed. 2011. (ENG.). 45p. (J). (gr. 3-7). 19.00 *(978-1-56769-210-5(9))* Ligonier Ministries.

—The Prince's Poison Cup. Gerard, Justin, illus. 2008. (ENG.). 35p. (J). (gr. 3-7). 19.00 *(978-1-56769-104-7(8))* Ligonier Ministries.
Walker, John. Pioneer Parables. 2005. (Illus.). (YA). per. 11.99 *(978-0-9677379-1-1(5))* North Gap Publishing.
White, Angel. The Seed in My Pocket. 2009. 32p. pap. *(978-1-55452-391-7(5)*, Guardian Bks.) Essence Publishing.
Young, Jeanna Stolle & Johnson, Jacqueline. Princess Hope & the Hidden Treasure, 1 vol. Aranda, Omar, illus. 2012. (Princess Parables Ser.). (ENG.). 32p. (J). 14.99 *(978-0-310-72699-9(9))* Zonderkidz.
Zondervan Staff. The Good Samaritan, 1 vol. Miles, David, illus. 2015. (I Can Read! / Adventure Bible Ser.). (ENG.). 32p. (J). pap. 4.99 *(978-0-310-74662-1(0))* Zonderkidz.

PARACHUTE TROOPS

Harasymiw, Mark J. Pararescuemen, 1 vol. 2012. (U. S. Special Forces Ser.). (ENG., Illus.). 32p. (J). (gr. 3-4). pap. 11.50 *(978-1-4339-6571-5(2)*, e1caeac4-d4b7-4ac0-b69e-ac86616c0ec9); lib. bdg. 29.27 *(978-1-4339-6569-2(0)*, 09b57886-b9e9-4d81-b6b8-a87747d34428) Stevens, Gareth Publishing LLLP. (Gareth Stevens Learning Library).
Sandler, Michael. Pararescuemen in Action. 2008. (Special Ops Ser.). (Illus.). 32p. (J). (gr. 3-6). lib. bdg. 28.50 *(978-1-59716-633-1(2))* Bearport Publishing Co., Inc.

PARACHUTES

see also Parachute Troops
Klutz Editors, contrib. by. SlingChute. (ENG.). (J). 14.95 *(978-1-57054-581-8(2))* Klutz.

PARACHUTING

see Skydiving

PARADES

Corcorane, Ann. Counting at the Parade, 1 vol. 2011. (Wonder Readers Emergent Level Ser.). (ENG.). (gr. -1-1). 8p. (J). pap. 6.25 *(978-1-4296-7864-3(X)*, 118188); 16p. pap. 35.94 *(978-1-4296-8080-6(6)*, Capstone Pr.) Capstone.
Lyons, Shelly. If You Were an Exclamation Point [LTD Commodities]. Gray, Sara, illus. 2010. (Word Fun Ser.). 24p. pap. 3.50 *(978-1-4048-6254-8(4)*, Picture Window Bks.) Capstone.
—If You Were an Exclamation Point [Readers World]. Gray, Sara, illus. 2010. (Word Fun Ser.). 24p. pap. 2.72 *(978-1-4048-6707-9(4)*, Picture Window Bks.) Capstone.
McGahey, Suzanne. Winter Guard, 1 vol. 2006. (Team Spirit! Ser.). (ENG., Illus.). 64p. (J). (gr. 6-6). lib. bdg. 37.13 *(978-1-4042-0732-5(5)*, 927981d6-70a5-4270-a983-436dd0a3255e) Rosen Publishing Group, Inc., The.
National Geographic Learning. World Windows 3 (Social Studies): New Year Celebrations: Content Literacy, Nonfiction Reading, Language & Literacy. 2011. (World Windows Ser.). (ENG., Illus.). 16p. (J). stu. ed. 10.95 *(978-1-133-49269-6(X))* Cengage Heinle.
Sweet, Melissa. Balloons over Broadway: The True Story of the Puppeteer of Macy's Parade. Sweet, Melissa, illus. 2011. (ENG., Illus.). 40p. (J). (gr. -1-3). 17.99 *(978-0-547-19945-0(7)*, 1058458, Clarion Bks.) HarperCollins Pubs.

PARADES—FICTION

Abramson, Jill & O'Connor, Jane. Puppy Parade. Melmon, Deborah, illus. 2013. (Penguin Young Readers, Level 2 Ser.). 32p. (J). (gr. 1-2). pap. 4.99 *(978-0-448-45676-8(1)*, Penguin Young Readers) Penguin Young Readers Group.
—Puppy Parade. 2013. (Penguin Young Readers Level 2 Ser.). lib. bdg. 13.55 *(978-0-606-31707-8(4))* Turtleback.
Anastos, Ernie. Ernie & the Big Newz. 2007. 32p. pap. 15.95 *(978-0-9705100-5-1(5))* NK Pubns.
Awdry, Wilbert V. & Random House Editors. Thomas & Percy & the Dragon. 2003. (Thomas & Friends Step into Reading Ser.). (gr. -1-2). lib. bdg. 13.55 *(978-0-613-89791-4(9))* Turtleback.
Balaban, Mariah. Scooby-Doo & the Thanksgiving Terror, 1 vol. Duendes Del Sur Staff, illus. 2011. (Scooby-Doo! Ser.: No. 2). (ENG.). 24p. (J). (gr. k-4). lib. bdg. 31.36 *(978-1-59961-870-8(2)*, 13248, Picture Bk.) Spotlight.
Barchers, Suzanne I. Main Street Parade, 1 vol. rev. ed. 2011. (Phonics Ser.). (ENG.). 16p. (gr. k-2). 6.99 *(978-1-4333-2921-0(2))* Teacher Created Materials, Inc.
Berenstain, Mike. The Berenstain Bears' Easter Parade: An Easter & Springtime Book for Kids. Berenstain, Mike, illus. 2014. (Berenstain Bears Ser.). (ENG., Illus.). 24p. (J). (gr. -1-3). pap. 3.99 *(978-0-06-207554-3(3)*, HarperFestival) HarperCollins Pubs.
Berenstain, Mike & Berenstain, Stan. The Berenstain Bears God Bless Our Country, 1 vol. 2015. (Berenstain Bears/Living Lights: a Faith Story Ser.). (ENG.). 24p. (J). pap. 4.99 *(978-0-310-73485-7(1))* Zonderkidz.
Black, Michael Ian. A Pig Parade Is a Terrible Idea. Hawkes, Kevin, illus. 2010. (ENG.). 40p. (J). (gr. -1-3). 19.99 *(978-1-4169-7922-7(0)*, Simon & Schuster Bks. For Young Readers) Simon & Schuster Bks. For Young Readers.
Boswell, Addie. The Rain Stomper, 0 vols. Velasquez, Eric, illus. 2012. (ENG.). 32p. (J). (gr. -1-3). 16.99 *(978-0-7614-5393-2(8)*, 9780761453932, Two Lions) Amazon Publishing.
Buzzeo, Toni. Fire up with Reading! Yoshikawa, Sachiko, illus. 2007. (Mrs. Skorupski Story Ser.). 32p. (J). (gr. -1-3). 17.95 *(978-1-932146-91-2(1)*, Upstart Bks.) Highsmith Inc.
Clark, Katie. Grandma Drove the Garbage Truck. Huntington, Amy, illus. 2006. (ENG.). 32p. (J). (gr. -1-17). 15.95 *(978-0-89272-698-1(9))* Down East Bks.
Corey, Shana. Milly & the Macy's Parade. Helquist, Brett, illus. 2006. 38p. (J). (gr. 4-8). reprint ed. 17.00 *(978-1-4223-5174-1(2))* DIANE Publishing Co.
Crow, Melinda Melton. Truck Parade, 1 vol. Thompson, Chad, illus. 2012. (Wonder Wheels Ser.). (ENG.). 32p. (J). (gr. -1-1). pap. 6.25 *(978-1-4342-4240-2(4)*, 120298); lib. bdg. 22.65 *(978-1-4342-4017-0(7)*, 118398) Capstone. (Stone Arch Bks.).
Daddis, Susan. El Día Del Desfile: Longitud. rev. ed. 2019. (Mathematics in the Real World Ser.). (SPA., Illus.). 24p. (J). (gr. 1-2). pap. 9.99 *(978-1-4258-2851-6(5))* Teacher Created Materials, Inc.
—Fun & Games: Day at the Parade: Length (Grade 1) rev. ed. 2018. (Mathematics in the Real World Ser.). (ENG., Illus.). 24p. (J). (gr. 1-2). pap. 9.99 *(978-1-4258-5689-2(6))* Teacher Created Materials, Inc.
Dartez, Cecilia. Jenny Giraffe's Mardi Gras Ride, 1 vol. Dartez, Cecilia & Green, Andy, illus. 2018. (Jenny Giraffe Ser.). (ENG.). 32p. (gr. -1-3). 8.99 *(978-1-4556-2387-7(3)*, Pelican Publishing) Arcadia Publishing.
DiPucchio, Kelly. Dress-Up Mess-up. Ross, Heather, illus. 2013. (Crafty Chloe Ser.). (ENG.). 40p. (J). (gr. -1-3). 16.99 *(978-1-4424-2124-0(X))* Simon & Schuster Children's Publishing.
Dungy, Tony & Dungy, Lauren. Here Comes the Parade! Ready-To-Read Level 2. Brantley-Newton, Vanessa, illus. 2014. (Tony & Lauren Dungy Ready-To-Reads Ser.). (ENG.). 32p. (J). (gr. k-2). pap. 4.99 *(978-1-4424-5469-9(5)*, Simon Spotlight) Simon Spotlight.
Earhart, Kristin. Roscoe & the Pony Parade. Gurney, John, illus. 2008. (Little Apple Ser.). 88p. (J). *(978-0-545-08094-1(0))* Scholastic, Inc.
Engelbreit, Mary. Queen of Easter: An Easter & Springtime Book for Kids. Engelbreit, Mary, illus. 2009. (ENG., Illus.). 32p. (J). (gr. -1-3). pap. 7.99 *(978-0-06-008186-7(4)*, HarperCollins) HarperCollins Pubs.
Estes, Don. Willy: The Little Jeep Who Wanted to Be a Fire Truck. Garrison, Sue, illus. 2003. 46p. (J). lib. bdg. 14.95 *(978-1-883551-47-6(1)*, ASP-471, Attic Studio Pr.) Attic Studio Publishing Hse.
—Willy & Friends traveling through the Seasons: The continuing story of Willy the little fire Jeep. Glass, Eric, illus. 2006. (J). *(978-1-883551-75-9(7)*, Maple Corners Press) Attic Studio Publishing Hse.
French, Vivian. Princess Katie & the Silver Pony. Gibb, Sarah, illus. 2007. (Tiara Club Ser.: No.2). 80p. (J). (gr. 1-4). 15.99 *(978-0-06-112432-7(X)*, Tegen, Katherine Bks) HarperCollins Pubs.
Genhart, Michael. Rainbow: A First Book of Pride. Passchier, Anne, illus. 2019. 24p. (J). *(978-1-4338-3087-7(6)*, Magination Pr.) American Psychological Assn.
Ginsberg, Mort. Ukey & His Magical Ukulele. 2008. 75p. pap. 19.95 *(978-1-60610-395-1(4))* America Star Bks.
Gohmann, Johanna. Pleased to Eat You: Book 3. Zolotić, Aleksandar, illus. 2018. (Electric Zombie Ser.). (ENG.). 112p. (J). (gr. 2-5). lib. bdg. 38.50 *(978-1-5321-3363-3(4)*, 31149, Calico Chapter Bks.) ABDO Publishing Co.
Harimann, Sierra. Puppies on Parade. 2014. (Illus.). 30p. (J). pap. *(978-0-545-59211-6(9))* Scholastic, Inc.
Holub, Joan. Good Luck! A St. Patrick's Day Story. Terry, Will, illus. 2007. (Ant Hill Ser.). (ENG.). 24p. (J). (gr. -1-k). lib. bdg. 11.89 *(978-1-4169-2560-6(0)*, Aladdin Library) Simon & Schuster Children's Publishing.
—Good Luck! A St. Patrick's Day Story (Ready-To-Read Pre-Level 1) Terry, Will, illus. 2007. (Ant Hill Ser.). (ENG.). 24p. (J). (gr. -1-k). pap. 4.99 *(978-1-4169-0955-2(9)*, Simon Spotlight) Simon Spotlight.
Jacobson, Jennifer Richard. Andy Shane, Hero at Last. Carter, Abby, illus. 2011. (Andy Shane Ser.: 6). (ENG.). 64p. (J). (gr. k-3). pap. 5.99 *(978-0-7636-5293-7(8))* Candlewick Pr.
—Hero at Last. Carter, Abby, illus. 2010. (Andy Shane Ser.: 6). (ENG.). 64p. (J). (gr. k-3). 14.99 *(978-0-7636-3600-5(2))* Candlewick Pr.
Janvier Gibeau, Claire. Here Comes Grandpa Now. 2009. 16p. pap. 8.49 *(978-1-4490-3829-8(8))* AuthorHouse.
Johnson, Angela. The Day Ray Got Away. LaMarca, Luke, illus. 2010. (ENG.). 40p. (J). (gr. k-3). 16.99 *(978-0-689-87375-1(1)*, Simon & Schuster Bks. For Young Readers) Simon & Schuster Bks. For Young Readers.
Jonell, Lynne. Grasshopper Magic. Dorman, Brandon, illus. 2014. (Magical Mix-Ups Ser.: 3). (ENG.). 112p. (J). (gr. 1-4). pap. 4.99 *(978-0-307-93123-8(4)*, Random Hse. Bks. for Young Readers) Random Hse. Children's Bks.
Karr, Lily. Easter Parade! Richards, Kirsten, illus. 2013. (J). *(978-0-545-56401-4(8)*, Cartwheel Bks.) Scholastic, Inc.
—Easter Parade! 2013. lib. bdg. 14.75 *(978-0-606-31494-7(6))* Turtleback.
Krulik, Nancy. Don't Be Such a Turkey! John and Wendy, illus. 2010. (Katie Kazoo, Switcheroo Ser.). 160p. (J). (gr. 2-4). pap. 6.99 *(978-0-448-45448-1(3)*, Grosset & Dunlap) Penguin Young Readers Group.
Kuphal, Shirley M. Flavor's Wild Wish. 2008. 36p. pap. 21.99 *(978-1-4363-0656-0(6))* Xlibris Corp.
Leonard, Marcia. El Hombre de Hojalata. Handelman, Dorothy, photos by. 2005. (ENG & SPA., Illus.). 32p. (J). (gr. -1-1). pap. 4.99 *(978-0-8225-3310-8(3))* Lerner Publishing Group.
London, Jonathan. Froggy Plays in the Band. Remkiewicz, Frank, illus. 2004. (Froggy Ser.). 32p. (J). (gr. -1-k). 7.99 *(978-0-14-240051-7(3)*, Puffin Books) Penguin Young Readers Group.
—Froggy Plays in the Band. Remkiewicz, Frank, illus. 2004. (Froggy Ser.). (J). (gr. -1-3). 13.65 *(978-0-7569-2955-8(5))* Perfection Learning Corp.
McCune, Susan. The Big Parade, 1 vol., 1. 2015. (Rosen REAL Readers: Social Studies Nonfiction / Fiction: Myself, My Community, My World Ser.). (ENG.). 12p. (J). (gr. k-1). pap. 6.33 *(978-1-5081-1967-8(8)*, eb043873-97dd-432e-a09b-8d91f433bfdc, Rosen Classroom) Rosen Publishing Group, Inc., The.
McGrath, Barbara Barbieri. The M & M's(r) Brand All-American Parade Book. Tagel, Peggy, illus. 2004. 12p. (J). (gr. -1-k). bds. 6.95 *(978-1-57091-430-0(3))* Charlesbridge Publishing, Inc.
—Parade Colors. Tagel, Peggy, illus. 2017. (First Celebrations Ser.: 6). 12p. (J). (— 1). bds. 6.99 *(978-1-58089-536-1(0))* Charlesbridge Publishing, Inc.
Middleton Elya, Susan. Our Celebración!, 1 vol. Aranda, Ana., illus. 2018. (ENG.). 32p. (J). (gr. 3). 18.95 *(978-1-62014-271-4(6)*, leelowbooks) Lee & Low Bks., Inc.
Miller, Pat Zietlow. The Quickest Kid in Clarksville. Morrison, Frank, illus. 2016. (ENG.). 40p. (J). (gr. k-3). 16.99 *(978-1-4521-2936-5(3))* Chronicle Bks. LLC.
Mishica, Clare. Here Comes the Parade. Richard, Ilene, illus. 2005. (Rookie Readers Ser.). (ENG.). 24p. (J). (gr. k-2). lib. bdg. 19.50 *(978-0-516-24857-8(X)*, Children's Pr.) Scholastic Library Publishing.
—Vamos al Desfile. 2006. (Rookie Reader Español Ser.). (ENG & SPA., Illus.). 32p. (J). (gr. k-2). lib. bdg. 19.50 *(978-0-516-25309-1(3))* Scholastic Library Publishing.
Moncure, Jane Belk. My Sound Parade. Thornburgh, Rebecca, illus. 2018. (Jane Belk Moncure's Sound Box Bks.). (ENG.). 32p. (J). (gr. -1-2). 35.64 *(978-1-5038-2303-7(2)*, 212158) Child's World, Inc, The.
Nolan, Allia Zobel. Animal Parade: A Lift-The-Flap Hear-the-Sound Book. Maddocks, Maria, illus. 2011. (ENG.). 10p. (J). (gr. -1 — 1). pap. 12.99 *(978-0-547-55867-7(8)*, 1453623, Clarion Bks.) HarperCollins Pubs.
Owen, Rob. Spy Boy, Cheyenne, & Ninety-Six Crayons: A "Mardi Gras" Indian's Story, 1 vol. Owen, Rob, illus. 2013. (ENG., Illus.). 32p. (J). (gr. k-3). 16.99 *(978-1-4556-1799-9(7)*, Pelican Publishing) Arcadia Publishing.
Pardo, Juan. When the Morning Comes: A Mardi Gras Indian Story, 1 vol. Smith, Vernon, illus. 2019. (ENG.). 32p. (gr. -1-3). 19.99 *(978-1-4556-2439-3(X)*, Pelican Publishing) Arcadia Publishing.
Pearson, Luke, illus. Hilda & the Bird Parade: Hilda Book 3. 2013. (Hildafolk Ser.: 3). (ENG.). 44p. (J). (gr. 3-7). 19.95 *(978-1-909263-06-2(0))* Flying Eye Bks. GBR. Dist: Penguin Random Hse. LLC.
Pitman, Gayle E. This Day in June. Litten, Kristyna, illus. 2013. 32p. (J). *(978-1-4338-1658-1(X))*; pap. *(978-1-4338-1659-8(8))* American Psychological Assn. (Magination Pr.).
Raines Day, Nancy. Hoorade Day!, 1 vol. Van Wright, Cornelius, illus. 2018. (ENG.). 32p. (J). *(978-1-59572-807-4(4))* Star Bright Bks., Inc.
Resnicoff, Stan. The BIG Parade: Los Angeles. 2012. (ENG.). (J). pap. *(978-1-4675-1540-5(X))* Independent Pub.
—The BIG Parade: New York. 2012. (ENG.). (J). pap. *(978-1-4675-1538-2(8))* Independent Pub.
—The BIG Parade: San Francisco. 2012. (ENG.). (J). pap. *(978-1-4675-1539-9(6))* Independent Pub.
Rey, H. A. Curious George Parade Day Tabbed Board Book. 2011. (Curious George Ser.). (ENG., Illus.). 14p. (J). (gr. -1 — 1). bds. 8.99 *(978-0-547-47282-9(X)*, 1438167, Clarion Bks.) HarperCollins Pubs.
Ricci, Christine. The Great Big Parade. Aikins, Dave, illus. 2007. (J). pap. *(978-1-4127-8923-3(0))* Publications International, Ltd.
Richards, Kirsten & Karr, Lily. Easter Parade!, 1 vol. Richards, Kirsten, illus. 2013. (ENG., Illus.). 24p. (J). (gr. -1-k). pap. 4.99 *(978-0-545-45824-5(2)*, Cartwheel Bks.) Scholastic, Inc.
Rowley, Julie P. The Little Purple Mardi Gras Bead, 1 vol. Paquette, John R., illus. 2016. (ENG.). 32p. pap. 9.99 *(978-1-4556-2344-0(X)*, Pelican Publishing) Arcadia Publishing.
Ryan, Pam Muñoz. Yo Ho Ho, Halloween! Fotheringham, Ed, illus. 2015. 39p. (J). pap. *(978-0-545-91590-8(2))* Scholastic, Inc.
Schories, Pat, illus. Biscuit & the Big Parade! 2018. 29p. (J). *(978-1-5444-0450-9(6))* Harper & Row Ltd.
Spiro, Ruth. Made by Maxine. Hatam, Holly, illus. 2018. 32p. (J). (gr. -1-3). 17.99 *(978-0-399-18629-5(8)*, Dial Bks) Penguin Young Readers Group.
Steers, Billy. Tractor Mac Parade's Best. 2015. (Tractor Mac Ser.). (ENG., Illus.). 32p. (J). (gr. -1-k). 9.99 *(978-0-374-30106-4(9)*, 900138384, Farrar, Straus & Giroux (BYR)) Farrar, Straus & Giroux.
Sulgit, Nicole. Caillou Leads the Parade. Poupart, Jean-Sébastien, illus. 2004. (J). *(978-0-7853-9949-0(6))* Publications International, Ltd.
Thacker, Becky. The Chorus Kids' Memorial Day Parade. Thacker, Becky, illus. 2006. (Illus.). (J). 10.95 *(978-0-9786276-1-4(X))* Mentzer Printing Ink.
Thaler, Mike. St. Patrick's Day from the Black Lagoon. Lee, Jared, illus. 2011. 61p. (J). *(978-0-545-27328-2(5))* Scholastic, Inc.
—The Thanksgiving Day from the Black Lagoon. Lee, Jared, illus. 2009. 64p. (J). *(978-0-545-16812-0(0))* Scholastic, Inc.
Wells, Rosemary. Max & the Fall Parade. 2014. (Max Ruby Ser.). lib. bdg. 13.55 *(978-0-606-36192-7(8))* Turtleback.
Zobel-Nolan, Allia. Animal Parade. Maddocks, Maria, illus. 2008. 10p. (J). (gr. -1). 12.95 *(978-1-932915-63-1(X))* Sandvik Innovations, LLC.

PARAGUAY

Augustin, Byron. Paraguay. 2005. (Enchantment of the World Ser.). (ENG., Illus.). 144p. (YA). (gr. 5-9). 39.00 *(978-0-516-23675-9(X))* Scholastic Library Publishing.
Behnke, Alison. Paraguay in Pictures. 2009. (Visual Geography Series, Second Ser.). (ENG.). 80p. (gr. 5-12). 31.93 *(978-1-57505-962-4(2))* Lerner Publishing Group.
Hernández, Roger E. Paraguay. (South America Today Ser.). 64p. 2009. (J). (gr. 4-7). 21.95 *(978-1-4222-0638-6(6))* 2007. (YA). (gr. 7-18). pap. 9.95 *(978-1-4222-0705-5(6))* Mason Crest.
Hernandez, Roger E. Paraguay, Vol. 13. Henderson, James D., ed. 2015. (Discovering South America: History, Politics, & Culture Ser.). (Illus.). 64p. (J). (gr. 7). lib. bdg. 22.95 *(978-1-4222-3301-6(4))* Mason Crest.
Jermyn, Leslie & Lin, Yong Jui. Paraguay, 1 vol. 2nd rev. ed. 2010. (Cultures of the World (Second Edition)(r) Ser.). (ENG.). 144p. (gr. 5-5). 49.79 *(978-0-7614-4858-7(6)*, 5506d8b0-d075-4fb3-943e-69fed33d651b) Cavendish Square Publishing LLC.
Jones, Naomi E., et al. Paraguay, 1 vol. 2019. (Cultures of the World (Third Edition)(r) Ser.). (ENG.). 144p. (gr. 5-5). lib. bdg. 48.79 *(978-1-5026-4738-2(9)*, 4ff217ae-fa21-47ce-87d3-a5663efe7c4a) Cavendish Square Publishing LLC.

PARAPSYCHOLOGY

see also Apparitions; Clairvoyance; Extrasensory Perception; Ghosts; Hypnotism; Mind and Body; Thought Transference
Bodden, Valerie. Cemeteries. 2017. (Creep Out Ser.). (ENG., Illus.). 24p. (J). (gr. 1-4). *(978-1-60818-806-2(X)*, 20182, Creative Education) Creative Co., The.
—Ghost Towns. 2017. (Creep Out Ser.). (ENG., Illus.). 24p. (J). (gr. 1-4). *(978-1-60818-807-9(8)*, 20184, Creative Education) Creative Co., The.
—Old Jails. 2017. (Creep Out Ser.). (ENG., Illus.). 24p. (J). (gr. 1-4). *(978-1-60818-809-3(4)*, 20188, Creative Education) Creative Co., The.
—Tombs. 2017. (Creep Out Ser.). (ENG., Illus.). 24p. (J). (gr. 1-4). *(978-1-60818-810-9(8)*, 20190, Creative Education) Creative Co., The.
Breman, Billy & Watkins, Graham. Searching for Ghosts & Poltergeists. 2011. (J). 77.70 *(978-1-4488-4778-5(8))*; (ENG.). 64p. (gr. 5-5). pap. 13.95 *(978-1-4488-4770-9(2)*, 468ab2ec-5e37-4840-9a5f-4edc175cdfcb); (ENG.). 64p. (gr. 5-5). lib. bdg. 37.13 *(978-1-4488-4762-4(1)*, b7cee3b4-74c0-4af6-bd72-10e31cf9fa61) Rosen Publishing Group, Inc., The.
Centore, Michael. Psychic Abilities. 2017. (Freaky Phenomena Ser.: Vol. 8). (ENG., Illus.). 48p. (J). (gr. 5-8). 20.95 *(978-1-4222-3779-3(6))* Mason Crest.
Cooley Peterson, Megan. Haunted Objects from Around the World. 2017. (It's Haunted! Ser.). (ENG., Illus.). 32p. (J). (gr. 3-9). lib. bdg. 28.65 *(978-1-5157-3859-6(0)*, 133759, Capstone Pr.) Capstone.
Dicker, Katie. Mysterious Messages. 2015. (Mystery! Ser.). (ENG.). 24p. (J). (gr. 2-5). 28.50 *(978-1-62588-203-5(3)*, 17360) Black Rabbit Bks.
Diker, Katie. Missing! 2015. (ENG., Illus.). 24p. (J). pap. 8.95 *(978-1-77092-232-7(6))* RiverStream Publishing.
—Mysterious Messages. 2015. (ENG., Illus.). 24p. (J). pap. 8.95 *(978-1-77092-234-1(2))* RiverStream Publishing.
—Mysterious Places. 2015. (ENG., Illus.). 24p. (J). pap. 8.95 *(978-1-77092-235-8(0))* RiverStream Publishing.
Duffield, Katy S. The Bermuda Triangle, 1 vol. 2008. (Mysterious Encounters Ser.). (ENG., Illus.). 48p. (gr. 4-8). lib. bdg. 30.63 *(978-0-7377-4046-2(9)*, ccf3731e-3eba-4f49-a71f-03b1db5300fd, KidHaven Publishing) Greenhaven Publishing LLC.
Ganeri, Anita & West, David. Lost in the Bermuda Triangle & Other Mysteries, 1 vol. 2011. (Incredible True Adventures Ser.). (ENG.). 48p. (YA). (gr. 5-5). pap. 12.75 *(978-1-4488-6662-5(6)*, bdbde0e9-a8b6-40d5-b715-6efe115f09f0); lib. bdg. 34.47 *(978-1-4488-6658-8(8)*, 05acbde8-7105-45f9-af6c-7d2cc3c643ee) Rosen Publishing Group, Inc., The. (Rosen Reference).
Green, Carl R. & Sanford, William R. Amazing Out-Of-Body Experiences, 1 vol. 2011. (Investigating the Unknown Ser.). (ENG., Illus.). 48p. (gr. 5-7). (J). lib. bdg. 27.93 *(978-0-7660-3822-6(X)*, 6c51918b-a035-477d-ae6c-61f639dd21aa); pap. 11.53 *(978-1-59845-307-2(6)*, 3440c25b-e162-4086-8557-80e337b4de19) Enslow Publishing, LLC.
Guiley, Rosemary ellen. Spirit Communications. 2009. (Mysteries, Legends, & Unexplained Phenomena Ser.). (ENG., Illus.). 128p. (gr. 7-12). 29.95 *(978-0-7910-9391-7(3)*, P171279, Facts On File) Infobase Holdings, Inc.
Harmon, Daniel E. Haunted Places & Ghostly Encounters. 2015. (J). *(978-1-61900-066-7(0))* Eldorado Ink.
Henneberg, Susan. Investigating Ghosts & the Spirit World, 1 vol. 2014. (Understanding the Paranormal Ser.). (ENG.). 48p. (YA). (gr. 5-5). 28.41 *(978-1-62275-863-0(3)*, 848def2b-790b-4288-9cb5-3b6652ae4545, Britannica Educational Publishing) Rosen Publishing Group, Inc., The.
Herbst, Judith. Vanished. 2004. (Unexplained Ser.). (Illus.). 48p. (J). pap. 8.95 *(978-0-8225-2404-5(X)*, Lerner Pubns.); (ENG., (gr. 5-12). lib. bdg. 26.60 *(978-0-8225-1631-6(4))* Lerner Publishing Group.
Kallen, Stuart A. Time Travel, 1 vol. 2009. (Mysterious Encounters Ser.). (ENG.). 48p. (gr. 4-8). 30.63 *(978-0-7377-4573-3(8)*, a9c34d8b-80a1-4df2-bbef-5701246a86ac, KidHaven Publishing) Greenhaven Publishing LLC.
Kaplan, Debbie. When I Was Big. Osadchuk, Keit, illus. 2010. (J). pap. *(978-1-57043-318-4(6))* Eckankar.
Kelly, Dave & Coddington, Andrew. The Bermuda Triangle, Stonehenge, & Unexplained Places, 1 vol. 2017. (Paranormal Investigations Ser.). (ENG.). 64p. (gr. 6-6). 35.93 *(978-1-5026-2843-5(0)*, 6259e3f1-c705-4959-a995-7fe257b4b4f7) Cavendish Square Publishing LLC.
Keppeler, Jill. More Freaky Stories about the Paranormal, 1 vol. 2019. (Freaky True Science Ser.). (ENG.). 32p. (gr. 4-5). 28.27 *(978-1-5382-4072-4(6)*, f0b17d48-5968-41af-9402-3259890863af) Stevens, Gareth Publishing LLLP.
Loh-Hagan, Virginia. Mysterious Vanishings. 2018. (Stranger Than Fiction Ser.). (ENG., Illus.). 32p. (J). (gr. 4-8). pap. 14.21 *(978-1-5341-0857-8(2)*, 210792); lib. bdg. 32.07 *(978-1-5341-0758-8(4)*, 210791) Cherry Lake Publishing. (45th Parallel Press).
Marcovitz, Hal. Teens & the Supernatural & Paranormal. Developed in Association with the Gallup Organization Staff, ed. 2013. (Gallup Youth Survey: Major Issues & Trends Ser.: 14). (Illus.). 112p. (J). (gr. 7-18). 24.95 *(978-1-4222-2959-0(9))* Mason Crest.
—Teens & the Supernatural & Paranormal. 2008. (Gallup Youth Survey, Major Issues & Trends Ser.). (Illus.). 112,128p. (J). (gr. 7-9). lib. bdg. 22.95 *(978-1-59084-876-0(4))* Mason Crest.
Marvel, Robin. Awakening Consciousness: A Boy's Guide! 2009. (J). pap. 17.95 *(978-1-932690-91-0(3))* Loving Healing Pr., Inc.
—Awakening Consciousness: A Girl's Guide. 2009. (J). pap. 16.95 *(978-1-932690-80-4(8))* Loving Healing Pr., Inc.
Merwin, E. Subterráneos Oscuros. 2018. (De Puntillas en Lugares Escalofriantes/Tiptoe into Scary Places Ser.). (SPA.). 24p. (J). (gr. k-3). 18.95 *(978-1-68402-616-6(4))* Bearport Publishing Co., Inc.
Mooney, Carla. Becoming Invisible: From Camouflage to Cloaks. 2010. (Great Idea Ser.). 48p. (J). (gr. 4-6). lib. bdg. 26.60 *(978-1-59953-378-0(2))* Norwood Hse. Pr.
Oachs, Emily Rose. Ghosts. 2018. (Investigating the Unexplained Ser.). (ENG., Illus.). 32p. (J). (gr. 3-8). lib. bdg. 27.95 *(978-1-62617-853-3(4)*, Blastoff! Discovery) Bellwether Media.
Olson, Elsie. Are You Psychic? Facts, Trivia, & Quizzes. 2017. (Mind Games Ser.). (ENG., Illus.). 32p. (J). (gr. 2-5). lib. bdg. 27.99 *(978-1-5124-3416-3(7)*, 93d7aeaa-7275-4603-815b-daf3f519273f, Lerner Pubns.) Lerner Publishing Group.
Pearce, Q. L. Mysterious Disappearances, 1 vol. 2011. (Mysterious Encounters Ser.). (ENG., Illus.). 48p. (gr. 4-8). lib. bdg. 35.23 *(978-0-7377-5840-5(6)*, f7c19a8d-93a5-4dac-987b-1530a244db80, KidHaven Publishing) Greenhaven Publishing LLC.
Peterson, Megan Cooley. Super Scary Stories. 2016. (Super Scary Stuff Ser.). (ENG., Illus.). 24p. (J). (gr. 3-5). lib. bdg.

27.99 (978-1-5157-0279-5(0), 131924, Capstone Pr.) Capstone.

Place, Robert Michael. Astrology & Divination. 2008. (ENG., Illus.). 136p. (gr. 7-12). lib. bdg. 29.95 (978-0-7910-9385-6(9), P145801, Facts On File) Infobase Holdings, Inc.

Rauf, Don. Healing. 2017. (Freaky Phenomena Ser.: Vol. 8). (ENG., Illus.). 48p. (J). (gr. 5-8). 20.95 (978-1-4222-3775-5(3)) Mason Crest.

—Personality. 2017. (Freaky Phenomena Ser.: Vol. 8). (ENG., Illus.). 48p. (J). (gr. 5-8). 20.95 (978-1-4222-3778-6(8)) Mason Crest.

—The Senses. 2017. (Freaky Phenomena Ser.: Vol. 8). (ENG., Illus.). 48p. (YA). (gr. 5-8). 20.95 (978-1-4222-3780-9(X)) Mason Crest.

Rooney, Anne. Messages from Beyond. 2009. (Amazing Mysteries Ser.). (ENG.). 32p. (J). (gr. 3-6). 28.50 (978-1-59920-363-8(4), 19254, Smart Apple Media) Black Rabbit Bks.

Schulte, Mary. The Dover Demon, 1 vol. 2009. (Mysterious Encounters Ser.). (ENG., Illus.). 48p. (gr. 4-8). 35.23 (978-0-7377-4570-2(3), 662c62b6-291d-489d-861b-7a8c091f651f, KidHaven Publishing) Greenhaven Publishing LLC.

Seeley, M. H. Freaky Stories about the Paranormal, 1 vol. 2016. (Freaky True Science Ser.). (ENG., Illus.). 32p. (J). (gr. 4-5). pap. 11.50 (978-1-4824-4846-7(7), f602e7d2-ec12-45ba-b3bb-8fe1986afffc) Stevens, Gareth Publishing LLLP.

Storm, Marysa. The Bermuda Triangle. 2020. (Little Bit Spooky Ser.). (ENG.). 24p. (J). (gr. k-3). (978-1-62310-178-7(6), 14458, Bolt Jr.) Black Rabbit Bks.

Terrell, Brandon. 12 Unsolved Mysteries. 2017. (Scary & Spooky Ser.). (ENG.). 32p. (J). (gr. 3-6). 32.80 (978-1-63235-298-9(2), 11782, 12-Story Library) Bookstaves, LLC.

Townsend, John. Gone Missing. 2009. (Amazing Mysteries Ser.). (ENG.). 32p. (J). (gr. 3-6). 28.50 (978-1-59920-364-5(2), 19253); (Illus.). pap. (978-1-897563-96-0(5), 23876) Black Rabbit Bks. (Smart Apple Media).

Vale, Jenna. Tracking Ghosts & Hauntings, 1 vol. 2018. (Paranormal Seekers Ser.). (ENG.). 64p. (J). (gr. 5-8). pap. 13.95 (978-1-5081-8567-3(0), 873f648b-e4b4-4887-b879-40653ffe8137) Rosen Publishing Group, Inc., The.

Walker, Kathryn. Mysterious Healing. 2009. (Unsolved! Ser.). (ENG., Illus.). 32p. (J). (gr. 3-5). pap. (978-0-7787-4163-3(X)); (gr. 4-6). lib. bdg. (978-0-7787-4150-3(8)) Crabtree Publishing Co.

PARAPSYCHOLOGY—FICTION

Alderson, Sarah. Losing Lila. 2013. (ENG.). 352p. (J). pap. 10.00 (978-0-85707-197-2(1), Simon & Schuster Children's) Simon & Schuster, Ltd. GBR. Dist: Simon & Schuster, Inc.

Black, Michael Ian. The Purple Kangaroo. Brown, Peter, illus. 2009. (ENG.). 32p. (J). (gr. -1-3). 19.99 (978-1-4169-5771-3(5), Simon & Schuster Bks. For Young Readers) Simon & Schuster Bks. For Young Readers.

Blythe, Daniel. Shadow Breakers. 2013. (J). (978-0-545-47980-6(0), Chicken Hse., The) Scholastic, Inc.

Bracken, Alexandra. The Darkest Legacy-The Darkest Minds, Book 4. 2018. (Darkest Minds Novel Ser.: 4). (ENG.). 576p. (YA). (gr. 7-12). 18.99 (978-1-368-02324-5(X), Disney-Hyperion) Disney Publishing Worldwide.

—The Darkest Minds. 2013. (Darkest Minds Ser.: 1). (YA). lib. bdg. 20.85 (978-0-606-36533-8(8)) Turtleback.

—The Darkest Minds Series Boxed Set [4-Book Paperback Boxed Set]-The Darkest Minds. 2018. (Darkest Minds Novel Ser.). (ENG.). 2096p. (YA). (gr. 7-12). 39.99 (978-1-368-02337-5(1), Disney-Hyperion) Disney Publishing Worldwide.

—Darkest Minds, the-A Darkest Minds Novel, Book 1. 2012. (Darkest Minds Novel Ser.: 1). (ENG.). 496p. (J). (gr. 5-9). 17.99 (978-1-4231-5737-3(0), Disney-Hyperion) Disney Publishing Worldwide.

—Darkest Minds, the (Bonus Content) 2018. (Darkest Minds Novel Ser.: 1). (ENG.). 576p. (YA). (gr. 7-12). pap. 11.99 (978-1-368-02245-3(6), Disney-Hyperion) Disney Publishing Worldwide.

—In the Afterlight. 2015. (Darkest Minds Ser.: 3). (YA). lib. bdg. 20.85 (978-0-606-37505-4(8)) Turtleback.

—In the Afterlight (Bonus Content)-A Darkest Minds Novel, Book 3. 2018. (Darkest Minds Novel Ser.: 3). (ENG.). 624p. (YA). (gr. 7-12). pap. 10.99 (978-1-368-02247-7(2), Disney-Hyperion) Disney Publishing Worldwide.

—Never Fade. 2014. (Darkest Minds Ser.: 2). (YA). lib. bdg. 20.85 (978-0-606-36534-5(6)) Turtleback.

—Never Fade (Bonus Content)-The Darkest Minds, Book 2. 2018. (Darkest Minds Novel Ser.: 2). (ENG.). 576p. (YA). (gr. 7-12). pap. 10.99 (978-1-368-02246-0(4), Disney-Hyperion) Disney Publishing Worldwide.

—Through the Dark (Bonus Content)-A Darkest Minds Collection. 2018. (Darkest Minds Novel Ser.). (ENG.). 448p. (YA). (gr. 7-12). 10.99 (978-1-368-02248-4(0), Disney-Hyperion) Disney Publishing Worldwide.

Bray, Libba. The Diviners. 2012. 578p. (YA). 9.99 (978-0-316-23242-5(4)) Little Brown & Co.

—The Diviners. (Diviners Ser.: 1). (ENG.). (YA). (gr. 10-17). 2013. 496p. pap. 16.99 (978-0-316-12610-6(1)) 2012. 800p. 52.99 (978-0-316-22426-0(X)) Little, Brown Bks. for Young Readers.

—The Diviners. 2013. (Diviners Ser.: 1). 468p. (YA). lib. bdg. 24.50 (978-0-606-32284-3(1)) Turtleback.

Brignull, Irena. The Hawkweed Legacy. 2018. (Hawkweed Ser.: 2). (ENG.). 384p. (YA). (gr. 7-17). pap. 9.99 (978-1-60286-337-8(7), Hachette Bks.) Hachette Bks.

Caine, Rachel, pseud. Ash & Quill. 2018. (Great Library: 3). (ENG.). 368p. (YA). (gr. 9). pap. 9.99 (978-0-451-47315-8(9), Berkley) Penguin Publishing Group.

Caletti, Deb. The Last Forever. 2016. (ENG., Illus.). 352p. (YA). (gr. 7-7). pap. 11.99 (978-1-4424-5002-8(9), Simon & Schuster Bks. For Young Readers) Simon & Schuster Bks. For Young Readers.

Canasi, Brittany. The Creepy Cathedral. Wood, Katie, illus. 2017. (G. H. O. S. T. Squad Ser.). (ENG.). 48p. (gr. 3-5). pap. 8.95 (978-1-68342-438-3(7), 9781683424383) Rourke Educational Media.

Card, Orson Scott. Pathfinder. (Pathfinder Trilogy Ser.). (ENG.). 672p. (YA). (gr. 7). 2011. pap. 13.99 (978-1-4169-9179-3(4)) 2010. 21.99 (978-1-4169-9176-2(X)) Simon Pulse. (Simon Pulse).

—Pathfinder. l.t. ed. 2011. (Pathfinder Ser.). (ENG.). 802p. 23.99 (978-1-4104-3681-8(0)) Thorndike Pr.

Chand, Emlyn. Farsighted. 2012. 260p. pap. 12.95 (978-0-9839308-3-9(X)) Blue Crown Pr.

Chen, Justina. Return to Me. 2013. (ENG.). 352p. (YA). (gr. 7-17). 17.99 (978-0-316-10255-1(5)) Little, Brown Bks. for Young Readers.

Cook, Hope. House of Ash. 2017. (ENG., Illus.). 320p. (gr. 8-17). 17.99 (978-1-4197-2369-8(3), 1165101, Amulet Bks.) Abrams, Inc.

Everblaze. 2014. (Keeper of the Lost Cities Ser.: 3). (ENG., Illus.). 624p. (J). (gr. 3-7). 21.99 (978-1-4424-4599-4(8), Aladdin) Simon & Schuster Children's Publishing.

French, Gillian. The Door to January, 1 vol. 2nd ed. 2019. (ENG.). 212p. (YA). pap. 14.95 (978-1-944762-61-2(2), bfd61ab4-190b-41be-a973-f62e0568c1f7) Islandport Pr., Inc.

García, Kami & Stohl, Margaret. Beautiful Darkness. 2010. (Beautiful Creatures Ser.: Bk. 2). (YA). 59.99 (978-1-60941-036-0(X)) Findaway World, LLC.

—Beautiful Darkness. 2010. (Beautiful Creatures Ser.: Bk. 2). 512p. pap. 17.99 (978-0-316-09861-8(2)) Little, Brown Bks. for Young Readers.

Garcia, Kami & Stohl, Margaret. Beautiful Darkness. 2011. (Beautiful Creatures Ser.: 2). (ENG.). 528p. (YA). (gr. 7-17). pap. 15.99 (978-0-316-07704-0(6)) Little, Brown Bks. for Young Readers.

García, Kami & Stohl, Margaret. Beautiful Darkness. 2011. (Beautiful Creatures Ser.: 2). (YA). lib. bdg. 24.50 (978-0-606-26700-7(X)) Turtleback.

Garcia, Richard. Los Espiritus de Mi Tia Otilia. 2004. (ENG & SPA., Illus.). (J). (gr. k-3). spiral bd. (978-0-616-14606-4(X)) Canadian National Institute for the Blind/Institut National Canadien pour les Aveugles.

Harris, Neil Patrick. The Magic Misfits: the Second Story. Marlin, Lissy & Hilton, Kyle, illus. (Magic Misfits Ser.: 2). (ENG.). (J). (gr. 3-7). 2019. 352p. pap. 8.99 (978-0-316-39184-9(0)) 2018. 336p. 16.99 (978-0-316-39185-6(9)) 2018. 400p. 37.99 (978-0-316-41986-4(9)) Little, Brown Bks. for Young Readers.

Harris, Neil Patrick & Azam, Alec. The Magic Misfits: The Second Story. Marlin, Lissy, illus. 2018. xii, 312p. (J). (978-0-316-48724-5(4)); (978-0-316-52639-5(8)) Little Brown & Co.

Harvey-Fitzhenry, Alyxandra. Broken, 1 vol. 2010. (ENG., Illus.). 162p. (YA). (gr. 8-12). pap. 12.95 (978-1-896580-41-8(6)) Tradewind Bks. CAN. Dist: Orca Bk. Pubs. USA.

Hendry, Frances. The Seer's Stone. l.t. ed. 2007. 160p. per. (978-1-905665-18-1(0)) Pollinger In Print.

Howard, A. G. Stain. (ENG.). (YA). (gr. 7-17). 2020. 560p. pap. 11.99 (978-1-4197-3707-7(4), 1199303, Amulet Bks.) 2019. (Illus.). 528p. 19.99 (978-1-4197-3141-9(6), 1199301) Abrams, Inc.

The Iris House. 2006. (YA). per. 12.95 (978-0-9677047-7-7(4)) Marble Hse. Editions.

Kenny, Christopher D. Another World. 2017. (ENG.). 269p. pap. 13.95 (978-1-78629-627-6(6), 0502550f-eff6-4510-bc99-941dda446b06) Austin Macauley Pubs. Ltd. GBR. Dist: Baker & Taylor Publisher Services (BTPS).

Kessler, Liz. Haunt Me. 2017. (ENG.). 384p. (YA). (gr. 7). 17.99 (978-0-7636-9162-2(3)) Candlewick Pr.

Mabry, Samantha. A Fierce & Subtle Poison. 2017. (ENG.). 288p. (YA). (gr. 8-13). pap. 13.99 (978-1-61620-698-7(5), 73698) Algonquin Young Readers.

Marr, Melissa & Pratt, Tim, eds. Rags & Bones: New Twists on Timeless Tales. 2015. (ENG.). 368p. (YA). (gr. 10-17). pap. 17.99 (978-0-316-21293-9(8)) Little, Brown Bks. for Young Readers.

McCune, D. J. Fault Lines. 2016. (Death & Co Ser.: 3). (ENG.). 352p. (YA). (gr. 8). pap. 11.99 (978-1-4714-0271-5(1)) Bonnier Publishing GBR. Dist: Independent Pubs. Group.

McDonald, Joyce. Shades of Simon Gray. 2003. (Readers Circle Ser.). 245p. (YA). 14.15 (978-0-7569-1880-4(4)) Perfection Learning Corp.

Mead, Richelle. Bloodlines: the Ruby Circle (book 6) 2015. (ENG.). 368p. (J). pap. (978-0-14-136131-4(X), Razorbill) Penguin Young Readers Group.

Messenger, Shannon. Exile. (Keeper of the Lost Cities Ser.: 2). (ENG., Illus.). (J). (gr. 3-7). 2014. 592p. pap. 9.99 (978-1-4424-4597-0(1)) 2013. 576p. 21.99 (978-1-4424-4596-3(3)) Simon & Schuster Children's Publishing. (Aladdin).

—Keeper of the Lost Cities. (Keeper of the Lost Cities Ser.: 1). (ENG., Illus.). (J). (gr. 3-7). 2013. 512p. pap. 9.99 (978-1-4424-4594-9(7)) 2012. 496p. 21.99 (978-1-4424-4593-2(9)) Simon & Schuster Children's Publishing. (Aladdin).

—Lodestar. (Keeper of the Lost Cities Ser.: 5). (ENG.). (J). (gr. 3-7). 2017. 704p. pap. 9.99 (978-1-4814-7496-2(0)) 2016. (Illus.). 688p. 21.99 (978-1-4814-7495-5(2)) Simon & Schuster Children's Publishing. (Aladdin).

—Neverseen. (Keeper of the Lost Cities Ser.: 4). (ENG., Illus.). 688p. (J). (gr. 3-7). 2016. pap. 9.99 (978-1-4814-3230-6(3)) 2015. 21.99 (978-1-4814-3229-0(X)) Simon & Schuster Children's Publishing. (Aladdin).

Nelson, Marilyn. Pemba's Song. 2008. (ENG.). 112p. (J). (gr. 7-7). 16.99 (978-0-545-02076-3(X), Scholastic Pr.) Scholastic, Inc.

Patten, E. J. The Legend Thief. Rocco, John, illus. 2014. (Hunter Chronicles Ser.: 2). (ENG.). 384p. (J). (gr. 3-7). pap. 9.99 (978-1-4424-2036-6(7), Simon & Schuster Bks. For Young Readers) Simon & Schuster Bks. For Young Readers.

Rayne, C. M. Dark Oracle. Scythe, Adam, illus. 2016. (ENG.). (J). pap. (978-615-80463-0-5(2)) GiziMap.

Rivers, Phoebe. Giving up the Ghost, 6. 2013. (Saranormal Ser.: 6). (ENG.). 160p. (J). (gr. 3-7). 15.99 (978-1-4424-6616-6(2), Simon Spotlight) Simon & Schuster Children's Publishing.

—Giving up the Ghost. 2013. (Saranormal Ser.: 6). (ENG.). 160p. (J). (gr. 3-7). pap. 5.99 (978-1-4424-6617-3(0), Simon Spotlight) Simon Spotlight.

—Kindred Spirits. 2013. (Saranormal Ser.: 8). (ENG.). 160p. (J). (gr. 3-7). 15.99 (978-1-4424-6853-5(X)); (Illus.). pap. 5.99 (978-1-4424-6852-8(1)) Simon Spotlight. (Simon Spotlight).

Rose, R. M. & Leuzinger, Shannon. Guardians or Demons. 2017. (ENG.). 419p. (YA). pap. 15.95 (978-1-78612-746-4(6), 1250bce7-2cc5-4844-8e09-9c8a726c6786) Austin Macauley Pubs. Ltd. GBR. Dist: Baker & Taylor Publisher Services (BTPS).

Schwab, Victoria & Schwab, V. E. City of Ghosts. (City of Ghosts Ser.: 1). (ENG.). (J). (gr. 4-7). 2019. 320p. pap. 8.99 (978-1-338-11102-6(7)) 2018. (Illus.). 304p. 17.99 (978-1-338-11100-2(0), Scholastic Pr.) Scholastic, Inc.

Smith, L. J. Dark Visions: The Strange Power; the Possessed; the Passion. 2009. (Dark Visions Ser.: Bks 1-3). (ENG.). 752p. (YA). (gr. 7). pap. 15.99 (978-1-4169-8956-1(0), Simon Pulse) Simon Pulse.

St. Crow, Lili. Betrayals, 10 vols. 2010. (Strange Angels Ser.: 2). (YA). 95.75 (978-1-4407-7156-9(1)) Recorded Bks., Inc.

—Betrayals. 2009. (Strange Angels Ser.: 2). lib. bdg. 20.85 (978-0-606-09020-9(7)) Turtleback.

—Betrayals: A Strange Angels Novel, 2. 2009. (Strange Angels Ser.: 2). (ENG., Illus.). 304p. (YA). (gr. 7-18). pap. 26.19 (978-1-59514-252-8(5), Razorbill) Penguin Young Readers Group.

—Strange Angels, 9 vols. 2009. (Strange Angels Ser.: 1). (J). 114.75 (978-1-4407-6199-7(X)); 84.75 (978-1-4407-6195-9(7)); 87.75 (978-1-4407-6193-5(0)); 117.75 (978-1-4407-6197-3(3)); 181.75 (978-1-4407-6194-2(9)) Recorded Bks., Inc.

—Strange Angels. 2009. (Strange Angels Ser.: 1). lib. bdg. 20.85 (978-0-606-08957-9(8)) Turtleback.

St. John, Wylly Folk. The Ghost Next Door. Hyman, Trina Schart, illus. 2019. 184p. (J). pap. (978-1-948959-08-7(9)) Purple Hse. Pr.

Stiefvater, Maggie. Blue Lily, Lily Blue (the Raven Cycle, Book 3) (Unabridged Edition), 1 vol. unabr. ed. 2014. (Raven Cycle Ser.: 3). (ENG.). 2p. (YA). (gr. 7). audio compact disk 39.99 (978-0-545-64907-0(2)) Scholastic, Inc.

Stine, R. L. Help! We Have Strange Powers! 2009. (Goosebumps HorrorLand Ser.: 10). lib. bdg. 17.20 (978-0-606-05347-1(6)) Turtleback.

Valdes-Rodriguez, Alisa. Haters, 8 vols. (YA). 2008. 198.75 (978-1-4281-2205-5(2)) 2007. 105.75 (978-1-4281-2204-8(4)) 2007. 79.75 (978-1-4281-2200-0(1)) 2006. 76.75 (978-1-4281-2202-4(8)) 2006. 102.75 (978-1-4281-2206-2(0)) 2006. 172.75 (978-1-4281-2201-7(X)) 2006. 1.25 (978-1-4281-2197-3(8)) Recorded Bks., Inc.

Weisenberg, Marit. Select Few. 2018. (Select Ser.: 2). 384p. (YA). (gr. 9). 17.99 (978-1-58089-829-4(7), Charlesbridge Teen) Charlesbridge Publishing, Inc.

White, Kiersten. Mind Games. 2013. (Mind Games Ser.: 1). (ENG.). 304p. (YA). (gr. 8). pap. 9.99 (978-0-06-213532-2(5), HarperTeen) HarperCollins Pubs.

—Paranormalcy. 2011. (Paranormalcy Ser.: 1). (ENG.). 368p. (YA). (gr. 8). pap. 9.99 (978-0-06-198585-0(6), HarperTeen) HarperCollins Pubs.

Wilson, Dianne J. Affinity. 2018. (Spirit Walker Ser.). (ENG.). 324p. (YA). (gr. 7). pap. 15.99 (978-1-5223-0023-6(6)) Pelican Ventures, LLC.

Winters, Cat. The Cure for Dreaming. 2016. (ENG., Illus.). 384p. (YA). (gr. 8-17). pap. 9.95 (978-1-4197-1941-7(6), 1075303, Amulet Bks.) Abrams, Inc.

—Odd & True. 2019. (ENG.). 368p. (gr. 7-17). pap. 9.99 (978-1-4197-3508-0(X), 1153003) Abrams, Inc.

Yee, F. C. The Epic Crush of Genie Lo. (Genie lo Novel Ser.). (ENG.). 336p. 2019. (YA). (gr. 7-17). pap. 9.99 (978-1-4197-3209-6(9), 1180403) 2017. (J). (gr. 8-17). 18.99 (978-1-4197-2548-7(3), 1180401) Abrams, Inc. (Amulet Bks.).

Young, Suzanne. Hotel for the Lost. 2016. (ENG., Illus.). 304p. (YA). (gr. 9). pap. 10.99 (978-1-4814-2301-4(0), Simon Pulse) Simon Pulse.

PARASITES

see also Bacteriology; Insect Pests

Alessi, Jolene. Zombie Grasshoppers, 1 vol. 2015. (Zombie Animals: Parasites Take Control! Ser.). (ENG.). 24p. (J). (gr. 2-3). 24.27 (978-1-4824-2846-9(6), 53944d23-4348-4010-bdb8-9cf1de940b47) Stevens, Gareth Publishing LLLP.

—Zombie Snails, 1 vol. 2015. (Zombie Animals: Parasites Take Control! Ser.). (ENG., Illus.). 24p. (J). (gr. 2-3). pap. 9.15 (978-1-4824-2848-3(2), 53ae166c-5875-4ef5-b90a-110e1ddf5263) Stevens, Gareth Publishing LLLP.

Artell, Mike. Backyard Bloodsuckers: Questions, Facts & Tongue Twisters about Creepy Crawlers. 2004. (Illus.). 80p. pap. 14.95 (978-0-673-59248-4(0)) Good Year Bks.

—Backyard Bloodsuckers: Questions, Facts & Tongue Twisters about Creepy, Crawly Creatures. 2008. (Illus.). 80p. (J). (gr. 4). pap. 14.95 (978-1-59647-271-6(5)) Good Year Bks.

Axelrod-Contrada, Joan. Body Snatchers: Flies, Wasps, & Other Creepy Crawly Zombie Makers. 2016. (Real-Life Zombies Ser.). (ENG., Illus.). 32p. (J). (gr. 3-9). lib. bdg. 28.65 (978-1-5157-2480-3(8), 132852, Capstone Pr.) Capstone.

—Mini Mind Controllers: Fungi, Bacteria, & Other Tiny Zombie Makers. 2016. (Real-Life Zombies Ser.). (ENG., Illus.). 32p. (J). (gr. 3-9). lib. bdg. 28.65 (978-1-5157-2478-0(6), 132850, Capstone Pr.) Capstone.

Bensinger, Lou. Tiny Invaders in Your Body. 2010. (Illus.). 24p. (J). 49.50 (978-1-4358-9851-6(6), 1307242); (ENG., (gr. 2-3). pap. 9.25 (978-1-4358-9850-9(8), 70e70ea5-f8e5-4a68-a6bc-3476f0959d1e); (ENG., (gr. 2-3). lib. bdg. 26.27 (978-1-4358-9379-5(4), 41640dcd-d7c1-4a93-a5f8-ae1bdb6a5218) Rosen Publishing Group, Inc., The. (PowerKids Pr.).

Christiansen, Per. Pests & Parasites, 1 vol. 2008. (Nature's Monsters: Insects & Spiders Ser.). (ENG., Illus.). 32p. (YA). (gr. 3-5). lib. bdg. 28.67 (978-0-8368-9218-5(6), 4fec2b5e-02d0-4971-9690-32f4588aaac7) Stevens, Gareth Publishing LLLP.

Ciletti, Barbara. Malaria Parasites. 2016. (Awful, Disgusting Parasites Ser.). (ENG.). 32p. (J). (gr. 4-6). 31.35 (978-1-68072-008-2(2), 10253); pap. 9.99 (978-1-64466-138-3(1), 10254) Black Rabbit Bks. (Bolt).

—Tapeworms. 2016. (Awful, Disgusting Parasites Ser.). (ENG.). 32p. (J). (gr. 4-6). pap. 9.99 (978-1-64466-140-6(3), 10262); (Illus.). 31.35 (978-1-68072-010-5(4), 10261) Black Rabbit Bks. (Bolt).

Clark, Lisa. The 10 Most Revolting Parasites. 2008. (J). 14.99 (978-1-55448-521-5(5)) Scholastic Library Publishing.

Cohn, Jessica. Parasite Collector, 1 vol. 2011. (Dirty & Dangerous Jobs Ser.). (ENG.). 32p. (gr. 3-3). 31.21 (978-1-60870-175-9(1), 7dc95fac-bfb6-4cfc-93b1-088f460bb909) Cavendish Square Publishing LLC.

Davies, Nicola. What's Eating You? Parasites — the Inside Story. Layton, Neal, illus. 2009. (Animal Science Ser.). (ENG.). 64p. (J). (gr. 3-7). pap. 7.99 (978-0-7636-4521-2(4)) Candlewick Pr.

Fleisher, Paul. Parasites: Latching on to a Free Lunch. 2006. (Discovery! Ser.). (ENG., Illus.). 112p. (J). (gr. 6-12). lib. bdg. 31.93 (978-0-8225-3415-0(0)) Lerner Publishing Group.

Graham, Ian. Microscopic Scary Creatures. 2009. (Scary Creatures Ser.). (ENG., Illus.). 32p. (J). (gr. 3-5). 27.00 (978-0-531-21673-6(X), Children's Pr.) Scholastic Library Publishing.

Harrison, Paul. Micro Bugs. (Up Close Ser.). 24p. (gr. 3-3). 2009. 47.90 (978-1-60854-696-1(9)) 2006. (ENG., Illus.). (J). lib. bdg. 28.93 (978-1-4042-3760-5(7), 64d83584-7064-42ec-8555-8bf189856047) Rosen Publishing Group, Inc., The. (PowerKids Pr.).

Jackson, Cari. Alien Invasion: Invasive Species Become Major Menaces. 2009. (Current Science Ser.). (ENG.). 48p. (J). (gr. 4-6). pap. 8.95 (978-1-4339-2128-5(6), Gareth Stevens Learning Library) Stevens, Gareth Publishing LLLP.

—Alien Invasion: Invasive Species Become Major Menaces, 1 vol. 2009. (Current Science Ser.). (ENG.). 48p. (C). (gr. 4-6). lib. bdg. 33.67 (978-1-4339-2057-8(3), 2b0ddd7e-122f-45ba-9cda-c11f2e8ea6b7) Stevens, Gareth Publishing LLLP.

Johnson, Rebecca L. Zombie Makers: True Stories of Nature's Undead. (ENG., Illus.). 48p. (J). (gr. 4-8). 2012. lib. bdg. 30.65 (978-0-7613-8633-9(5), 4eb37692-7709-421b-89bf-e9674d63b168, Millbrook Pr.) 2015. E-Book 53.32 (978-1-4677-5992-2(9), 9781467759922, Lerner Digital) Lerner Publishing Group.

Klepeis, Alicia Z. Brain Eaters: Creatures with Zombelike Diets. 2016. (Real-Life Zombies Ser.). (ENG., Illus.). 32p. (J). (gr. 3-9). lib. bdg. 28.65 (978-1-5157-2479-7(4), 132851, Capstone Pr.) Capstone.

Kopp, Megan. Parasites. 2016. (Illus.). 24p. (J). (978-1-4896-5782-4(7)) 2011. (J). (gr. 4-6). pap. 12.95 (978-1-61690-717-4(7), AV2 by Weigl) 2011. (Illus.). 24p. (YA). (gr. 2-5). 27.13 (978-1-61690-711-2(8)) Weigl Pubs., Inc.

Larson, Kirsten W. Zombies in Nature. 2015. (Freaky Nature Ser.). (ENG., Illus.). 32p. (J). (gr. 2-5). lib. bdg. 19.95 (978-1-60753-783-0(4), 15299) Amicus.

Mincks, Margaret. Head Lice. 2016. (Awful, Disgusting Parasites Ser.). (ENG.). 32p. (J). (gr. 4-6). pap. 9.99 (978-1-64466-137-6(3), 10250); (Illus.). 31.35 (978-1-68072-007-5(4), 10249) Black Rabbit Bks. (Bolt).

—Ticks. 2016. (Awful, Disgusting Parasites Ser.). (ENG.). 32p. (J). (gr. 4-6). pap. 9.99 (978-1-64466-141-3(1), 10266); (Illus.). 31.35 (978-1-68072-011-2(2), 10265) Black Rabbit Bks. (Bolt).

Nagle, Frances. Zombie Ants, 1 vol. 2015. (Zombie Animals: Parasites Take Control! Ser.). (ENG.). 24p. (J). (gr. 2-3). pap. 9.15 (978-1-4824-2828-5(8), 35235b0b-ec72-40bd-8fef-5ea72eaba6df) Stevens, Gareth Publishing LLLP.

Newman, Mark. Sooper Yooper: Environmental Defender. Heckman, Mark, illus. 2010. 48p. (J). 17.95 (978-1-933272-26-9(0)) Thunder Bay Pr.

Olexa, Keith. The Gross Science of Lice & Other Parasites, 1 vol. 2018. (Way Gross Science Ser.). (ENG.). 48p. (gr. 5-5). 33.47 (978-1-5081-8171-2(3), fd0fa5b9-8dc2-4e0d-9da6-cf97922f8377, Rosen Reference) Rosen Publishing Group, Inc., The.

Owen, Ruth. Disgusting Food Invaders. (Up Close & Gross: Microscopic Creatures Ser.). 24p. 2016. (ENG., Illus.). (J). (gr. 1-6). pap. 7.99 (978-1-944998-70-7(5)) 2011. (YA). (gr. 2-5). lib. bdg. 26.99 (978-1-61772-127-4(1)) Bearport Publishing Co., Inc.

—Gross Body Invaders. 2011. (Up Close & Gross Ser.). 24p. (YA). (gr. 2-5). lib. bdg. 26.99 (978-1-61772-126-7(3)) Bearport Publishing Co., Inc.

Parker, Barbara Keevil. Ticks. 2007. (Early Bird Nature Books). (Illus.). 48p. (J). (gr. 3-7). lib. bdg. 25.26 (978-0-8225-6464-5(5), Lerner Pubns.) Lerner Publishing Group.

Perritano, John. Bugs That Live on Us, 1 vol. 2009. (Bug Alert! Ser.). (ENG.). 32p. (gr. 3-3). lib. bdg. 31.21 (978-0-7614-3187-9(X), 72796cfb-0eb8-4f90-9ccc-6103db4876eb) Cavendish Square Publishing LLC.

Rake, Matthew. Creepy, Crawly Creatures. Mendez, Simon, illus. 2015. (Real-Life Monsters Ser.). (ENG.). 32p. (J). (gr. 3-6). lib. bdg. 27.99 (978-1-4677-6362-2(4), 5f295af2-aeaf-4fbf-830d-aaef833e4c0b, Hungry Tomato (r)) Lerner Publishing Group.

Rodger, Marguerite. Termites & Other Home Wreckers. 2010. (Creepy Crawlies Ser.). (ENG.). 32p. (J). (gr. 3-6). (978-0-7787-2503-9(0)); pap. (978-0-7787-2510-7(3)) Crabtree Publishing Co.

Spilsbury, Richard. Zoom in on Body Invaders, 1 vol. 2013. (Zoom in On... Ser.). (ENG.). 32p. (gr. 4-6). 25.60 (978-0-7660-4310-7(X), 8d2d951f-3906-41c2-91ee-7400c92745cd); pap. 10.95 (978-1-4644-0565-5(4), 3c3d7149-f896-4a85-9006-0193db2609b8) Enslow Publishing, LLC.

—Zoom in on House of Horrors, 1 vol. 2013. (Zoom in On... Ser.). (ENG.). 32p. (gr. 4-6). pap. 10.95 (978-1-4644-0569-3(7), 62e4fa37-d08f-444b-841d-2a5801e64088) Enslow Publishing, LLC.

Tilden, Thomasine E. Lewis. Worms! Parasites Plague a Village. 2011. (J). pap. *(978-0-545-32804-3(7))* Scholastic, Inc.

Torres, John A. Real-Life Zombies, 1 vol. 2019. (Creepy, Kooky Science Ser.). (ENG.). 48p. (gr. 5-5). pap. 12.70 *(978-1-9785-1389-1(5),* 06f4040d-2ff9-4fe9-b415-0c9ccf3b2476) Enslow Publishing, LLC.

Troup, Roxanne. Nasty Parasites, 1 vol. 2019. (Creepy, Kooky Science Ser.). (ENG.). 48p. (gr. 5-5). pap. 12.70 *(978-1-9785-1380-8(1),* 0ff34d1d-dc59-4cfa-8e2f-c552f966f470) Enslow Publishing, LLC.

Viegas, Jennifer. Parasites. (Germs: the Library of Disease-Causing Organisms Ser.). 48p. (gr. 5-5). 2009. 53.00 *(978-1-61512-717-7(8))* 2003. (ENG., Illus.). lib. bdg. 34.47 *(978-0-8239-4494-1(8),* 6cd12ed2-bd1e-428e-b70c-0f915d753bb3) Rosen Publishing Group, Inc., The.

Viegas, Jennifer & Baum, Margaux. Parasites, 1 vol. 2016. (Germs: Disease-Causing Organisms Ser.). (ENG., Illus.). 48p. (J). (gr. 5-5). pap. 12.75 *(978-1-4777-8847-9(6),* 16d4c2e2-f6c0-4fcb-8188-3f0b597d5e9b, Rosen Reference) Rosen Publishing Group, Inc., The.

Weir, Kirsten. Bugs That Live on Animals, 1 vol. 2009. (Bug Alert! Ser.). (ENG.). 32p. (gr. 3-3). lib. bdg. 31.21 *(978-0-7614-3189-3(6),* e9dfac96-8ca3-4b9c-9036-f436886cbeb1) Cavendish Square Publishing LLC.

Woodward, John. What Lives on Other Animals?, 1 vol. 2007. (What Lives In... ? Ser.). (ENG., Illus.). 48p. (gr. 3-5). lib. bdg. 29.67 *(978-0-8368-7860-8(4),* b89e60a5-fe55-4bea-8afa-7916c0a66c56, Gareth Stevens Learning Library) Stevens, Gareth Publishing LLLP.

World Book, Inc. Staff, contrib. by. Animals Living Alongside People. 2018. (Illus.). 48p. (J). *(978-0-7166-2732-6(9))* World Bk., Inc.

Zombie Animals: Parasites Take Control! 2015. (Zombie Animals: Parasites Take Control! Ser.). (ENG.). 24p. (J). (gr. 2-3). pap., pap., pap. 293.40 *(978-1-4824-3500-9(4))* Stevens, Gareth Publishing LLLP.

PARATROOPS

see Parachute Troops

PARCEL POST

see Postal Service

PAREJA, JUAN DE, 1606-1670—FICTION

de Trevino, Elizabeth Borton. I, Juan de Pareja. 3rd ed. pap. 3.95 *(978-0-13-800129-2(4))* Prentice Hall (Schl. Div.).

—I, Juan de Pareja. l.t. ed. 2005. 244p. 20.95 *(978-0-7862-7666-0(5))* Thorndike Pr.

De Trevino, Elizabeth Borton. I, Juan de Pareja: The Story of a Great Painter & the Slave He Helped Become a Great Artist. 2008. (ENG.). 192p. (YA). (gr. 7-12). pap. 9.99 *(978-0-312-38005-2(4),* 900050528) Square Fish.

I, Juan de Pareja. 3rd ed. (J). pap., stu. ed. *(978-0-13-667452-8(6))* Prentice Hall (Schl. Div.).

PARENT AND CHILD

see also Child Rearing; Father and Child; Mother and Child

Arquette, Kerry. Daddy Promises. McCain, Kevin, illus. 2005. 32p. (J). pap. 7.49 *(978-0-7586-0905-2(1))* Concordia Publishing Hse.

Astacio, Mrinali Alvarez, illus. Pon, Pon: A Jugar con el Bebé! 2007. (SPA.). 28p. 14.95 *(978-0-8477-1575-6(2))* Univ. of Puerto Rico Pr.

Auld, Mary. My Mom, 1 vol. 2004. (Meet the Family Ser.). (ENG., Illus.). 24p. (gr. k-2). lib. bdg. 24.67 *(978-0-8368-3927-2(7),* a2e78d11-e383-4d61-a7f9-e07ebf756630, Gareth Stevens Learning Library) Stevens, Gareth Publishing LLLP.

Beisswenger, Iffer & Eldred, Margaret. The Way We See Things: Middle Schoolers Look at Themselves & Issues They Face Everyday. Krusi, Carolynne, ed. 2004. 96p. pap. 14.95 *(978-0-9759264-0-6(3))* Anemone Publishing.

Bergren, Lisa Tawn. Mama Kisses, Papa Hugs. Zolotic, Aleksander, illus. 2020. (ENG.). 40p. (J). (gr. -1-2). 11.99 *(978-0-525-65409-4(7),* WaterBrook Pr.) Crown Publishing Group, The.

Berry, Joy. I Love Mommies & Daddies. Regan, Dana, illus. 2010. (Teach Me About Ser.). (ENG.). 20p. (J). (gr. k — 1). pap. 5.99 *(978-1-60577-001-7(9))* Berry, Joy Enterprises.

—Illness. 2009. (ENG.). 40p. (J). (gr. k — 1). bds. 7.95 *(978-1-60577-012-3(4))* Berry, Joy Enterprises.

Brown, Tracy. Frequently Asked Questions about Same-Sex Marriage & When a Parent Is Gay, 1 vol. 2012. (FAQ: Teen Life Ser.). (ENG., Illus.). 64p. (J). (gr. 5-6). lib. bdg. 37.13 *(978-1-4488-8330-1(X),* 7736c889-cf0c-4b68-b022-ac7bf27b69be) Rosen Publishing Group, Inc., The.

Burgen, Jim. What's the Big Deal about My Parents? Reeves, Dale, ed. 2006. (What's the Big Deal Ser.). 160p. (gr. 7-18). pap. 10.99 *(978-0-7847-1252-8(2),* 23335) Standard Publishing.

Carlton, Heather. Bobby's Lesson on Blessings. 2009. (ENG.). 36p. pap. 14.44 *(978-0-557-12601-9(0))* Lulu Pr., Inc.

Conversations with kids ages 7 To 10: A lovey bedtiem Book. 2007. (J). 9.95 *(978-0-9747375-1-5(8))* Joanne Faye Pr.

Corey, Dorothy. You Go Away. Fox, Lisa, illus. 2010. (ENG.). 16p. (J). (gr. -1 — 1). bds. 8.99 *(978-0-8075-9440-7(7),* 807594407) Whitman, Albert & Co.

Dalton, Sommer. While You Sleep. Baker, David, illus. 2011. 28p. pap. 24.95 *(978-1-4560-2360-7(8))* America Star Bks.

Donahue, Mary R. & Thornburgh, Gail. What's My Job? Helping Children Navigate the Rough Waters of Separation & Divorce. 2010. 32p. pap. 12.99 *(978-1-4490-4669-9(X))* AuthorHouse.

Duffy, Betsy Smeltzer. I Am Beautiful Because... I Am Creative. 2013. 24p. pap. 17.99 *(978-1-4817-0618-6(7))* AuthorHouse.

Ellis, Deborah. Our Stories, Our Songs: African Children Talk about AIDS, 1 vol. 2005. (ENG., Illus.). 112p. (J). (gr. 4-7). *(978-1-55041-913-9(7))* Fitzhenry & Whiteside, Ltd.

Feldman, Rachel S. The Little Tree. 2010. 32p. pap. 14.99 *(978-1-4520-0033-6(6))* AuthorHouse.

Fields, Julianna. Foster Families. 2010. (Changing Face of Modern Families Ser.). (Illus.). 64p. (YA). (gr. 5-18). lib. bdg. 22.95 *(978-1-4222-1497-8(4))* Mason Crest.

Fink, Thad. I Want You to Know, Son. Robert, J. Martin, illus. 2007. 26p. (J). (gr. -1-3). per. 11.99 *(978-1-59879-260-7(1))* Lifevest Publishing, Inc.

Flack, Judy. We're Having a Baby: A Story for Jack. 2010. 32p. pap. 12.99 *(978-1-4490-6873-8(1))* AuthorHouse.

Flaherty, Patrick F. & Harper, Steven. Life's Lessons from Dad: Quotes for Life Book Series. McLaughlin, Patrick, ed. 2004. per. 12.95 *(978-0-9724178-5-3(0))* Teckni-Corp, Ltd.

Ford, Vikke. Angel Anya's Adventures: Anya's Magic Heart. 2009. 28p. pap. 15.95 *(978-1-4490-0698-3(1))* AuthorHouse.

Fox-Lee, Kyme & Fox-Lee, Susan. What Are Parents? Jennings, Randy, illus. 2007. 32p. (J). 15.95 *(978-0-9753699-1-3(1))* StoryTyme Publishing.

Fox, Phoebe. Babies Nurse: Así Se Alimentan los Bebés. Geating, Karen Rivera, tr. Fox, Jim, illus. 2018. (ENG.). 32p. (J). (gr. -1-2). 14.95 *(978-1-930775-73-2(3))* Platypus Media, L.L.C.

—Babies Nurse / Así Se Alimentan Los Bebés. Geating, Karen Rivera, tr. Fox, Jim, illus. 2018. (ENG.). 32p. (J). (gr. -1-2). pap. 9.95 *(978-1-930775-72-5(5))* Platypus Media, L.L.C.

Garcia, Justine Marie. While You Were Gone Year Two. Robin, Gulack, illus. 2012. 26p. pap. 12.95 *(978-0-9836913-5-8(5))* Rose Bud Publishing Co. LLC.

Ginsburg, Sara. Look What My Parents Give Me. 2014. (ENG., Illus.). 29p. (J). *(978-1-4226-1489-1(1))* Mesorah Pubns., Ltd.

Goozh, Judi & Jeweler, Sue. Tell Me about When Moms & Dads Come Home from Jail. 2018. (Tell Me about Jail Ser.). (Illus.). 40p. (J). pap. 15.95 *(978-1-78592-806-2(6),* 696739) Kingsley, Jessica Pubs. GBR. Dist: Hachette UK Distribution.

Gorbett, Danea. Adopted Teens Only: A Survival Guide to Adolescence. 2007. 120p. per. 9.95 *(978-1-58348-481-4(7),* iUniverse Star) iUniverse, Inc.

Grollman, Earl A. Talking about Divorce & Separation: A Dialogue Between Parent & Child. Pitzer, Suzanne, illus. 2005. (J). *(978-1-56123-155-3(X))* Centering Corp.

Hahn, Donna M. Staying Safe When I Go Out. 2009. 24p. pap. 12.00 *(978-1-4389-6498-0(6))* AuthorHouse.

Hewitt, Sally. My Stepfamily. 2009. (J). 28.50 *(978-1-59920-229-7(8))* Black Rabbit Bks.

—Our New Baby. 2009. (Illus.). 32p. (J). 28.50 *(978-1-59920-232-7(8))* Black Rabbit Bks.

Hilton, Marilyn Copley. The Christian Girl's Guide to Your Mom. 2004. (Illus.). 176p. (J). pap. 9.99 *(978-1-58411-045-3(7),* Legacy Pr.) Rainbow Pubs. & Legacy Pr.

Hinds, Sandra A. I Love You Every. 2012. 32p. pap. 19.99 *(978-1-4567-2418-4(5))* AuthorHouse.

Jareaux, Marlena. 26 Things to Teach Your Parents. 2007. (Illus.). 76p. (YA). per. 10.95 *(978-0-9790415-1-8(1))* Inspired by the Beach Co.

Johnson, Alberta & Johnson, Errick C. Twelve Roses for Ann. 2008. 40p. pap. 16.99 *(978-1-4389-2988-0(9))* AuthorHouse.

Jones, Marla F. Ponder Learns to Be Thankful. 2010. 28p. pap. 13.99 *(978-1-4490-8570-4(9))* AuthorHouse.

Kerley, Barbara. You & Me Together: Moms, Dads, & Kids Around the World. 2010. (Barbara Kerley Photo Inspirations Ser.). (Illus.). 32p. (J). (gr. -1-k). pap. 7.95 *(978-1-4263-0623-5(7),* National Geographic Kids) Disney Publishing Worldwide.

Kiers, Erin L. I Have Chakras Just Like You. 2012. 24p. pap. *(978-1-4602-0343-9(7))* FriesenPress.

Kiesbye, Stefan, ed. Is Parenthood a Right or a Privilege?, 1 vol. 2009. (At Issue Ser.). (ENG., Illus.). 104p. (gr. 10-12). 41.03 *(978-0-7377-4430-9(8),* 275d9712-6d26-4ff1-baa3-dd85ec835ecc, Greenhaven Publishing) Greenhaven Publishing LLC.

Kitch, Anne E. Como Participar en la Liturgia: Un Libro de Actividades para Los Ninos Anglicanos-Episcopales. Martell, Oswald Perez, tr. Perez, Dorothy Thompson, illus. 2008. (SPA.). 48p. (J). pap. 11.95 *(978-0-8192-2331-9(X),* edefa50a-b589-4222-b291-f96aa5d45d3d) Church Publishing, Inc.

LaRamee-Jones, Shanda & McDougall, Carol. Let's Point!, 1 vol. 2017. (Baby Steps Ser.). (ENG., Illus.). 18p. (J). (gr. -1 — 1). bds. 12.95 *(978-1-77108-519-9(3),* 6774d4a4-de53-4492-a690-2d1c7c0bf306) Nimbus Publishing, Ltd. CAN. Dist: Baker & Taylor Publisher Services (BTPS).

Lovegrove, Emily. Help! I'm Being Bullied. 2007. (Illus.). 167p. per. *(978-1-905170-34-0(3))* Accent Pr. Ltd.

MacAdam, Lea. You & Rules in Your Family. 2009. (Family Matters Ser.). 48p. (gr. 5-8). 53.00 *(978-1-61512-483-1(7),* Rosen Reference) Rosen Publishing Group, Inc., The.

Marks, Jennifer L. Parents: Revised Edition. rev. ed. 2009. (People Ser.). (ENG.). 24p. (J). (gr. -1-2). lib. bdg. 24.65 *(978-1-4296-2240-0(7),* 94954) Capstone.

Martin-Finks, Nancy. Custody Battle: A Workbook for Children. Barber, David L., illus. 2005. (ENG.). 68p. (gr. 3-6). per. 19.95 *(978-1-931636-42-1(7))* National Ctr. For Youth Issues.

Martinez, Victor. Parrot in the Oven: Mi Vida. Scott, Steve, illus. rev. ed. 2004. (ENG.). 240p. (YA). (gr. 8-18). pap. 10.99 *(978-0-06-447186-2(1))* HarperCollins Español.

Maxwell, Shannon. Our Daddy Is Invincible! Biggers, Liza, illus. 40p. (J). 2011. 15.95 *(978-1-61751-003-8(3))* 2010. pap. 9.95 *(978-1-61751-002-1(5))* Kurdyla, E L Publishing LLC. (4th Division Pr.).

McCloud, Carol. BABY's BUCKET Book. Zimmer, Glenn, illus. 2014. 16p. (J). (gr. -1 — 1). bds. 7.95 *(978-0-9960999-2-9(1),* Bucket Fillosophy) Cardinal Rule Pr.

Naish, Sarah & Jefferies, Rosie. Katie Careful & the Very Sad Smile: A Story about Anxious & Clingy Behaviour. Evans, Megan, illus. 2017. (Therapeutic Parenting Bks.). (ENG.). 32p. (C). pap. 17.95 *(978-1-78592-304-3(8),* 696532) Kingsley, Jessica Pubs. GBR. Dist: Hachette UK Distribution.

National Geographic Learning. Windows on Literacy Step up (Social Studies: Me & My Family): I Help My Dad. 2007. (ENG., Illus.). 12p. pap. 11.95 *(978-0-7922-8464-2(X))* National Geographic School Publishing, Inc.

Okoronkwo, Stella. Communication with Children & Youth: A Guide for Parents, Social & Youth Workers. 2nd ed. 2012. (Illus.). 152p. (gr. 4-6). 23.99 *(978-1-4678-8176-0(7))*; pap. 14.95 *(978-1-4678-8175-3(9))* AuthorHouse.

Orgullo, Marisa. What Happens When My Parents Get Divorced?, 1 vol. 2018. (Help Me Understand Ser.). (ENG.). 24p. (gr. 3-3). 25.27 *(978-1-5081-6710-5(9),* e39d81fa-1199-43c6-b7f1-faba0e400be1, PowerKids Pr.) Rosen Publishing Group, Inc., The.

Peltier, Sylvia M. Nanny & I. Peltier, Sylvia M., illus. 2003. (Illus.). 32p. (YA). (gr. -1-18). 16.95 *(978-0-9724394-0-4(4))* Sylables.

Phelan, Thomas & Lee, Tracy. 1-2-3 Magic for Kids: Helping Your Kids Understand the New Rules. 2nd ed. 2017. (Illus.). 128p. pap. 11.99 *(978-1-4926-4786-7(1),* 9781492647867) Sourcebooks, Inc.

Pinto, Marie Parks. Does It Still Hurt. Mazzei, Miriam, illus. 2012. 30p. pap. 16.95 *(978-1-938812-02-6(6))* Full Court Pr.

—I Am Not Broken. Mazzei, Miriam, illus. 2012. (ENG.). 30p. pap. 16.95 *(978-1-938812-00-2(X))* Full Court Pr.

—Where Is Daddy? Mazzei, Miriam, illus. 2012. 30p. pap. 16.95 *(978-1-938812-06-4(9))* Full Court Pr.

Publishing, Sterling. Daddy & Me. 2008. (Illus.). 12p. (J). bds. *(978-1-934618-44-8(6))* Begin Smart LLC.

Ramnath, Vianna. Daddy Loves You! 2006. 22p. 11.99 *(978-1-4116-8867-4(8))* Lulu Pr., Inc.

Rescek, Sanja, illus. Bounce & Jiggle. 2007. (Baby Gym Ser.). 12p. (J). (gr. -1). spiral bd. *(978-1-84643-131-9(X))* Child's Play International Ltd.

—Calm & Soothe. 2007. (Baby Gym Ser.). 12p. (J). (gr. -1). spiral bd. *(978-1-84643-133-3(6))* Child's Play International Ltd.

—Touch & Tickle. 2007. (Baby Gym Ser.). 12p. (J). (gr. -1). bds. *(978-1-84643-130-2(1))* Child's Play International Ltd.

—Wiggle & Move. 2007. (Baby Gym Ser.). 12p. (J). (gr. -1). spiral bd. *(978-1-84643-132-6(8))* Child's Play International Ltd.

Rigby Education Staff. Visiting My Mom's Office. (Illus.). 8p. (J). bds. 3.95 *(978-0-7635-6452-0(4),* 764524C99) Rigby Education.

Ritchie, Jon. Babies Are Boring. Ritchie, Alex, illus. 2008. 40p. (J). *(978-0-9809970-0-2(3))* Purple Possum Publishing Inc.

Rosenfeld, Dina. It's Called Kibud Av Va'Eim: A Story about Honoring Parents. Ebert, Len, illus. 2014. (ENG.). 20p. (J). 11.99 *(978-1-929628-78-0(1))* Hachai Publishing.

Ross, Allison J. Coping When a Parent Is Mentally Ill. 2009. (Coping Ser.). 192p. (gr. 7-12). 63.90 *(978-1-61511-987-5(6))* Rosen Publishing Group, Inc., The.

Rowe, Amanda. If There Never Was a You. Skomorokhova, Olga, illus. 2019. (ENG.). 20p. (J). (gr. -1 — 1). bds. 12.99 *(978-1-64170-111-2(0),* 550111) Familius LLC.

Searching for the Words. 2nd ed. 2003. (J). spiral bd. *(978-0-9718626-2-3(1))* Holofcener, Mark.

Sermons, Faye. My Granma Lives at the Airport. 2012. 20p. pap. 12.00 *(978-1-4490-1893-1(9))* AuthorHouse.

Sheldon, Annette. Big Brother Now: A Story about Me & Our New Baby. Maizel, Karen, illus. 2008. 32p. (J). (gr. -1-1). (ENG.). 14.95 *(978-1-4338-0381-9(X))*; pap. 9.95 *(978-1-4338-0382-6(8))* American Psychological Assn. (Magination Pr.).

—Big Sister Now: A Story about Me & Our New Baby. Maizel, Karen, illus. 2005. 32p. (J). (gr. -1-1). per. 9.95 *(978-1-59147-244-5(X),* Magination Pr.) American Psychological Assn.

Sheldon, Annette & Maizel, Karen. Big Sister Now: A Story about Me & Our New Baby. Maizel, Karen, illus. 2005. (ENG., Illus.). 32p. (J). (gr. -1-3). 14.95 *(978-1-59147-243-8(1),* Magination Pr.) American Psychological Assn.

Sherman, Aliza. Everything You Need to Know about Placing Your Baby for Adoption. 2009. (Need to Know Library). 64p. (gr. 5-5). 58.50 *(978-1-60854-082-2(0))* Rosen Publishing Group, Inc., The.

Sidman, Joyce & Swan, Susan. Just Us Two: Poems about Dads. 2003. (Single Titles Ser.: Vol. 3). 32p. pap. 7.95 *(978-0-7613-1833-0(X),* Millbrook Pr.) Lerner Publishing Group.

Smith, Andrea Joy. Gladys Blackmon-Morrow: Let the Words from My Mouth... Be Acceptable in Thy Sight, O Lord... Psalms 19:14: the Woman, the Wife, the Mother. 2005. (YA). per. 14.95 *(978-0-9764396-1-5(1))* Smith, Andrea Joy.

Snow, Judith E. How It Feels to Have a Gay or Lesbian Parent: A Book by Kids for Kids of All Ages. 2004. (ENG., Illus.). (C). 136p. 165.00 *(978-1-56023-419-7(9),* HW14434); 132p. pap. 38.95 *(978-1-56023-420-3(2),* HW14375) Routledge.

Solomon, Andrew. Far from the Tree: Young Adult Edition — How Children & Their Parents Learn to Accept One Another ... Our Differences Unite Us. (ENG., Illus.). (YA). (gr. 9). 2018. 480p. pap. 13.99 *(978-1-4814-4091-2(8))* 2017. 464p. 18.99 *(978-1-4814-4090-5(X))* Simon & Schuster Bks. For Young Readers. (Simon & Schuster Bks. For Young Readers).

Sportelli-Rehak, Angela. Uncle Sam's Kids: When Duty Calls. Hinlicky, Gregg, illus. 2004. (Uncle Sam's Kids Ser.: Bk. 1). 40p. (gr. k-6). 15.95 *(978-0-9714515-1-3(6))* Abidenme Bks.

Stanton, Brandon. Little Humans. Stanton, Brandon, photos by. 2014. (ENG., Illus.). 40p. (J). (gr. -1-1). 19.99 *(978-0-374-37456-3(2),* 900123448, Farrar, Straus & Giroux (BYR)) Farrar, Straus & Giroux.

Steverson, Sylvia. I LOVE YOU Means... 2010. 32p. pap. 16.99 *(978-0-557-36954-6(1))* Lulu Pr., Inc.

Stewart, Rachel M. The Angel Inside Me. 2012. 46p. pap. 17.45 *(978-1-4525-5047-3(6))* Balboa Pr.

Sullivan, James Kevin, illus. What Went Right Today? Journal: WWRT Journal. 2007. 72p. (J). spiral bd. 12.95 *(978-0-9766990-1-9(X))* Buz-Land Presentations, Inc.

Thomas, Natasha. Mommy & Daddy Is There Really Greatness in Me? 2013. (ENG.). 24p. (J). pap. 34.95 *(978-1-4327-8767-7(5))* Outskirts Pr., Inc.

Thumann, Robin K. Peaceful Thoughts: An Interactive Journey in Positive Thinking for Children & Their Parents. Thumann, Robin K., illus. 2003. (Illus.). 44p. (J). (gr. -1-4). 19.95 *(978-0-9725118-0-3(6))* Peaceful Thoughts Pr.

Tomories, K. G. Someone Special for You to Know. 2010. 28p. pap. 13.99 *(978-1-4389-9651-6(9))* AuthorHouse.

Towne, Isobel & MacAdam, Lea. Dealing with Family Rules, 1 vol., 1. 2015. (Family Issues & You Ser.). (ENG.). 48p. (J). (gr. 5-5). pap. 12.75 *(978-1-4994-3697-6(1),* 3cb487d7-0531-4b7c-ba0b-ef7eaed9a686, Rosen Central) Rosen Publishing Group, Inc., The.

Tsioumanis, Marina. Mum & Dad Are Separating: A Practical Resource for Separating Families & Family Therapy Professionals, 2 vols. 2017. (ENG., Illus.). 176p. (C). pap. 51.95 *(978-0-86388-669-0(8),* Y329910) Routledge.

Verdick, Elizabeth. Sharing Time. Heinlen, Marieka, illus. 2009. (Toddler Tools(r) Ser.). (ENG.). 26p. (J). (gr. -1). bds. 9.99 *(978-1-57542-314-2(6),* 23142) Free Spirit Publishing Inc.

—Sharing Time / Tiempo para Compartir. Heinlen, Marieka, illus. 2016. (Toddler Tools(r) Ser.). (ENG.). 26p. (J). (— 1). bds. 9.99 *(978-1-63198-096-1(3))* Free Spirit Publishing Inc.

Young, Diana S. Daddy Doesn't Live with Me Anymore. 2010. 20p. pap. 10.83 *(978-1-4490-7550-7(9))* AuthorHouse.

PARENT AND CHILD—FICTION

Abbott, Victoria. The Perfect Jack-O'-Lantern. Piworski, Marcin, illus. 2017. (My Adventures Ser.). (ENG.). 24p. (gr. -1-2). pap. 9.95 *(978-1-68342-795-7(5),* 9781683427957) Rourke Educational Media.

Abegg, Rainbow G. Peaches & Prayers. 2004. (Illus.). 17.95 *(978-1-59156-049-4(7))* Covenant Communications, Inc.

Adelman, Hallee. My Quiet Ship: When They Argue. Sánchez, Sonia, illus. 2018. (ENG.). 32p. (J). (gr. -1-3). 16.99 *(978-0-8075-6713-5(2),* 807567132) Whitman, Albert & Co.

Adler, Denise. Thank You for Looking for Me. 2010. 20p. 12.99 *(978-1-4520-2438-7(3))* AuthorHouse.

Adler, Victoria. All of Baby, Nose to Toes. Nakata, Hiroe, illus. 2011. 30p. (J). (gr. k — 1). bds. 7.99 *(978-0-8037-3531-6(6),* Dial Bks) Penguin Young Readers Group.

Ahlberg, Janet & Ahlberg, Allan. Adiós Pequeño! Ahlberg, Janet & Ahlberg, Allan, illus. (Historias Para Dormir Ser.). Tr. of Bye Bye Baby. (SPA., Illus.). 28p. (J). (gr. k-3). 9.95 *(978-968-19-1039-6(7))* Aguilar Editorial MEX. Dist: Santillana USA Publishing Co., Inc.

Ahmed, Roda. Mae among the Stars. Burrington, Stasia, illus. 2018. (ENG.). 40p. (J). (gr. -1-3). 19.99 *(978-0-06-265173-0(0),* HarperCollins) HarperCollins Pubs.

Akchurin, Sergo. Canadian Story. 2011. 16p. 12.99 *(978-1-4269-5215-9(5))* Trafford Publishing.

Al-Araimi, Saif & Al-Rawahi, Thuria. Smart Parents Meet Mr Motivation (V2) 2010. (ENG.). 85p. pap. 16.40 *(978-0-557-20544-8(1))* Lulu Pr., Inc.

Alborough, Jez. Hug. Alborough, Jez, illus. 2009. (ENG., Illus.). 32p. (J). (gr. -1-k). pap. 5.99 *(978-0-7636-4510-6(9))* Candlewick Pr.

—Hug Lap-Size Board Book. Alborough, Jez, illus. 2005. (ENG., Illus.). 32p. (J). (— 1). bds. 12.99 *(978-0-7636-2893-2(X))* Candlewick Pr.

Aldis, Dorothy & Collins, Heather. Hiding. (FRE.). (J). pap. 7.99 *(978-0-590-24195-3(8))* Scholastic, Inc.

Ambrosio, Michael. It Takes a Lot of Love. Awes, Jennifer, illus. 2007. 32p. (J). 14.95 *(978-0-9716085-4-2(7))* LionX Publishing.

Amollo, Regina. When Mother Leaves Home. 2004. (Illus.). 35p. pap. *(978-9970-02-435-3(3))* Fountain Pubs. Ltd. UGA. Dist: Michigan State Univ. Pr.

Anastas, Margaret. A Hug for You. Winter, Susan, photos by. 2005. (ENG., Illus.). 32p. (J). (gr. -1-1). 15.99 *(978-0-06-623613-1(4))* HarperCollins Pubs.

—Mommy's Best Kisses. 2003. (ENG., Illus.). 32p. (J). (gr. -1-1). 17.99 *(978-0-06-623601-8(0),* HarperCollins) HarperCollins Pubs.

Anderson, Constance. Smelling Sunshine, 1 vol. Anderson, Constance, illus. 2013. (ENG., Illus.). 32p. (J). 16.99 *(978-1-59572-635-3(7))*; pap. 6.99 *(978-1-59572-636-0(5))* Star Bright Bks., Inc.

Anderson, Laurie Halse. Catalyst. 2003. (ENG.). 272p. (YA). (gr. 7-18). pap. 10.99 *(978-0-14-240001-2(7),* Speak) Penguin Young Readers Group.

Anderson, Peggy Perry. I Can Help! 2015. (Green Light Readers Ser.). (ENG., Illus.). 32p. (J). (gr. 1-4). pap. 4.99 *(978-0-544-52801-7(8),* 1607367, Clarion Bks.) HarperCollins Pubs.

Andreae, Giles. Keep Love in Your Heart, Little One. Vulliamy, Clara, illus. 2007. 32p. (J). (gr. -1-3). 15.95 *(978-1-58925-066-6(4))* Tiger Tales.

Apel, Kathryn. Bully on the Bus. 2018. (Illus.). 136p. (J). *(978-1-61067-871-1(0))* Kane Miller.

Ashman, Linda. All We Know. Dyer, Jane, illus. 2016. (ENG.). 40p. (J). (gr. -1-3). 17.99 *(978-0-06-168958-1(0),* HarperCollins) HarperCollins Pubs.

Atteberry, Kevan. I Love You More Than the Smell of Swamp Gas. Atteberry, Kevan, illus. 2017. (ENG., Illus.). 40p. (J). (gr. -1-3). 17.99 *(978-0-06-240871-6(2),* HarperCollins) HarperCollins Pubs.

Augustine, Kristen. Can I Tell You? 2005. 9.00 *(978-0-8059-8071-4(7))* Dorrance Publishing Co., Inc.

Ault, Kelly. Let's Sign, Baby! A Fun & Easy Way to Talk with Baby. Landry, Leo, illus. abr. ed. 2010. (ENG.). 40p. (J). (gr. k — 1). bds. 9.99 *(978-0-547-31596-6(1),* 1415353, Clarion Bks.) HarperCollins Pubs.

Babcock, Nabila. My Child, My Love. 2012. 24p. 24.95 *(978-1-4626-5214-3(X))* PublishAmerica, Inc.

Bacchus, Tamika D. Plain Jane Learns to Pray. 2011. 48p. pap. 19.99 *(978-1-61379-455-5(X))* Salem Author Services.

Bachelet, Gilles. A Story That Grows. 2019. (ENG., Illus.). 32p. (J). *(978-0-8028-5512-1(1),* Eerdmans Bks For Young Readers) Eerdmans, William B. Publishing Co.

Baer, Julie. Love Me Later. 2005. (Illus.). 28p. (J). (gr. -1-3). 16.99 *(978-1-932188-03-5(7))* Bollix Bks.

Bailey, Tressie. The Little Box Kittens. 2009. 37p. pap. 20.50 *(978-0-557-02639-5(3))* Lulu Pr., Inc.

Baker, Liza, et al. I Love You: a Keepsake Storybook Collection, 1 vol. BRYAN, Beth, ed. McPhail, David et al, illus. 2006. (ENG.). 144p. (J). (gr. -1-k). pap., pap. 10.99 *(978-0-439-84799-5(0),* Cartwheel Bks.) Scholastic, Inc.

Balcarcel, Rebecca. The Other Half of Happy: (Middle Grade Novel for Ages 9-12, Bilingual Tween Book) 2019. (ENG., Illus.). 332p. (J). (gr. 5-9). 16.99 *(978-1-4521-6998-9(5))* Chronicle Bks. LLC.

Ballengee, Fran. Sara Elizabeth, an Adoption Story. 2008. 22p. pap. 24.95 *(978-1-60610-557-3(4))* PublishAmerica, Inc.

Banting, Celia. I Only Said I Didn't Want You Because I Was Terrified. 2006. (I Only Said Ser.: 4). 240p. (YA). pap. 14.99 *(978-0-9786648-3-1(3))* Wighita Pr.

Barbara E. Barber. Saturday at the New You, 1 vol. 2013. (ENG., Illus.). 32p. (J). (gr. 1-4). reprint ed. pap. 11.95 *(978-1-880000-43-4(1),* leelowbooks) Lee & Low Bks., Inc.

Barkow, Henriette. That's My Mum. Brazell, Derek, illus. 2004. 28p. (J). (ALB & ENG.). pap. *(978-1-85269-595-8(1))*; (ENG & YOR.). pap. *(978-1-84444-381-9(7))* Mantra Lingua.

Bateman, Teresa. Hunting the Daddyosaurus. Huang, Benrei, illus. 2004. 29p. (J). (gr. k-4). reprint ed. 16.00 *(978-0-7567-7796-8(8))* DIANE Publishing Co.

Beaton, Kate. King Baby. Beaton, Kate, illus. 2016. (ENG., Illus.). 40p. (J). (gr. -1-3). 18.99 *(978-0-545-63754-1(6))* Scholastic, Inc.

Beaudette, Cathy. The Boss of Me. Beaudette, Michelle, illus. 2011. 32p. pap. *(978-1-77067-350-2(4))* FriesenPress.

Bechard, Margaret. Hanging on to Max. 2003. (ENG., Illus.). 208p. (YA). (gr. 7). pap. 11.99 *(978-0-689-86268-7(7)*, Simon Pulse) Simon Pulse.

Becker, Christie. You Will Be My Baby Even When. Brayton, Julie, illus. 2003. 32p. (J). (gr. -1-1). 14.95 *(978-0-9728116-0-6(5))* Becker, Christie.

Beckerman, Menucha. A Surprise for Mommy. 2003. (My Middos World Ser.: Vol. 4). (Illus.). 34p. (J). (gr. k-5). 5.95 *(978-1-931681-10-0(4))* Israel Bookshop Pubns.

Beckford, Avril. I Love You 65 Bulldozers. 2009. 36p. pap. 15.49 *(978-1-4389-4048-9(3))* AuthorHouse.

Benson, Nicky. I Love You More & More. Lambert, Jonny, illus. 2016. (ENG.). 24p. (J). (gr. -1-1). bds. 9.99 *(978-1-58925-227-1(6))* Tiger Tales.

Bently, Peter. Meet the Parents. Ogilvie, Sara, illus. 2014. (ENG.). 32p. (J). (gr. -1-3). 17.99 *(978-1-4814-1483-8(6)*, Simon & Schuster/Paula Wiseman Bks.) Simon & Schuster/Paula Wiseman Bks.

Benton, Jim. The Handbook. Benton, Jim, illus. 2017. (ENG., Illus.). 240p. (J). (gr. 3-7). 12.99 *(978-0-545-94240-9(3)*, Scholastic Pr.) Scholastic, Inc.

Berenstain, Stan & Berenstain, Jan. The Berenstain Bears Meet Santa Bear (Deluxe Edition) 2016. (First Time Books(R) Ser.). (Illus.). 32p. (J). (gr. -1-2). pap. 6.99 *(978-0-399-55767-5(9)*, Random Hse. Bks. for Young Readers) Random Hse. Children's Bks.

Bess, Stacey. Planting More Than Pansies: A Fable about Love. Ricks, Melissa, illus. 2003. (J). 14.95 *(978-1-57008-893-3(4)*, Shadow Mountain) Shadow Mountain Publishing.

Beverly, Cleary. Dear Mr. Henshaw. 2014. (Cleary Reissue Ser.). (ENG.). 160p. (J). (gr. 7-12). 10.24 *(978-1-63245-195-8(6))* Lectorum Pubns., Inc.

Bigler, Ashley Hansen. Once upon a Time: An Adoption Story. Hintz, Amy, illus. 2010. (J). pap. 12.99 *(978-1-59955-310-8(4))* Cedar Fort, Inc./CFI Distribution.

Binch, Caroline. The Princess & the Castle. Binch, Caroline, illus. 2005. (ENG., Illus.). 32p. (J). (gr. k-2). 8.99 *(978-0-09-943236-4(6)*, Red Fox) Random House Children's Books GBR. Dist: Independent Pubs. Group.

Blair, Candice. Rosie's Pink House, 1 vol. Cato, Andrea, illus. 2010. 18p. 24.95 *(978-1-4489-4619-8(0))* America Star Bks.

Blanda, Amanda. My Days with Nonna. 2008. (ENG.). 24p. pap. 11.49 *(978-1-4343-1889-3(3))* AuthorHouse.

Blanks, Morgan Georgia. The Desert Island. 2008. 52p. pap. 20.49 *(978-1-4343-9006-6(3))* AuthorHouse.

Blocker, Adam P. Joshua & the Spider. Taylor, Josh, illus. 2013. (ENG.). 72p. 17.99 *(978-1-939418-08-1(9))* Writer of the Round Table Pr.

Bloom, Deb-b. The Bird Who Could Fly. 2008. 24p. pap. 24.95 *(978-1-60441-383-0(2))* America Star Bks.

Boehler, Ren'Ae L. The Unicorn Fish Are Having a Party. 2008. (ENG.). 26p. per. 15.99 *(978-1-4257-9945-8(0))* Xlibris Corp.

Bonasia, Steve. Dominic & the Secret Ingredient. Van Norstrand, Kain, illus. 2012. (ENG.). 39p. (J). pap. 24.95 *(978-1-4327-9805-5(7))* Outskirts Pr., Inc.

Bondoux, Anne-Laure. The Princetta. 2008. (ENG.). 448p. (YA). (gr. 6-12). pap. 10.99 *(978-1-59990-098-8(X)*, 9781599900988, Bloomsbury USA Childrens) Bloomsbury Publishing USA.

Bonnell, Kris. A Walk with Dad. 2006. (J). pap. 5.95 *(978-1-933727-43-1(8))* Reading Reading Bks., LLC.

Borden, Louise. The Little Ships: The Heroic Rescue at Dunkirk in World War II. Foreman, Michael, illus. 2003. (ENG.). 32p. (J). (gr. 4-7). 8.99 *(978-0-689-85396-8(3)*, McElderry, Margaret K. Bks.) McElderry, Margaret K. Bks.

Borntrager, Mary Christner. Polly. 2015. (ENG.). 176p. (YA). (gr. 4-7). pap. 9.99 *(978-0-8361-3670-8(5))* Herald Pr.

Boyd, David. Closer to Hamlet. 2003. 120p. (YA). (gr. 6-9). pap. *(978-0-921156-93-2(6))* Plumleaf Press.

Bracken, Beth. Henry Helps Plant a Garden, 1 vol. Busby, Allie, illus. 2012. (Henry Helps Ser.). (ENG.). 24p. (J). (gr. -1 — 1). pap. 5.95 *(978-1-4048-7670-5(7)*, 120332, Picture Window Bks.) Capstone.

Brandeis, Madeline. Mitz & Fritz of Germany. 2011. 164p. 41.95 *(978-1-258-10138-1(6))* Literary Licensing, LLC.

Brennan-Nelson, Denise. Teach Me to Love. 2014. (ENG., Illus.). 24p. (J). (gr. -1-1). 12.99 *(978-1-58536-858-7(X)*, 203671) Sleeping Bear Pr.

Brink Hull, Amanda. Maslyn: A Different Kind of Name for a Delightful Little Girl. 2009. (Illus.). 36p. pap. 16.99 *(978-1-4389-9338-6(2))* AuthorHouse.

Brooks, Bertha. The Big Fishing Trip. 2004. (Illus.). 32p. (J). 12.00 *(978-1-58374-086-6(4))* Chicago Spectrum Pr.

Brooks, Robert. Sonrieta. Urban, Helle, illus. 2008. 40p. (YA). 17.95 *(978-0-9792294-0-4(5))* Mystic Jaguar Publishing.

Brown, Jo. Where's My Mommy? 2004. (Illus.). 32p. (J). tchr. ed. 14.95 *(978-1-58925-019-2(2))* Tiger Tales.

Brown, Margaret Wise. The Runaway Bunny Board Book: An Easter & Springtime Book for Kids. Hurd, Clement, illus. 2017. (ENG.). 34p. (J). (gr. -1 — 1). bds. 8.99 *(978-0-06-107429-5(2)*, HarperFestival) HarperCollins Pubs.

—The Runaway Bunny Lap Edition: An Easter & Springtime Book for Kids. Hurd, Clement, illus. 2017. (ENG.). 36p. (J). (gr. -1 — 1). bds. 12.99 *(978-0-694-01671-6(3)*, HarperFestival) HarperCollins Pubs.

Brown, Petra. When the Wind Blew. Brown, Petra, illus. 2017. (ENG., Illus.). 32p. (J). (gr. k-3). 16.99 *(978-1-58536-969-0(1)*, 204234) Sleeping Bear Pr.

Bunting, Eve. Flower Garden. Hewitt, Kathryn, illus. 2004. 28p. (gr. -1-2). 17.00 *(978-0-7569-4113-0(X))* Perfection Learning Corp.

—My Mom's Wedding. Papp, Lisa, illus. 2006. (ENG.). 32p. (J). (gr. 1-4). 16.95 *(978-1-58536-288-2(3)*, 202099) Sleeping Bear Pr.

Burnett, Frances. Editha's Burglar. Sandham, Henry, illus. 2005. reprint ed. pap. 15.95 *(978-1-4179-0135-7(7))* Kessinger Publishing, LLC.

Burns, Joanne. No Says the Baby When You Say Yes, a book about the terrible Twos. 2005. 1p. 5.68 *(978-1-4116-3386-5(5))* Lulu Pr., Inc.

Burton, Jeffrey. My Sweet Little Megabyte. Roode, Laura, illus. 2016. (ENG.). 16p. (J). (gr. -1 — 1). bds. 5.99 *(978-1-4814-6809-1(X)*, Little Simon) Little Simon.

Byrne, Barbara. Megan's Moon. 2004. 18p. 14.87 *(978-1-4116-1008-8(3))* Lulu Pr., Inc.

C., Brandi & Flanagan, Logan. City Morn Country Dad. 2009. pap. *(978-1-61584-398-5(1))* Independent Pub.

C. Larene Hall. Martha's Freedom Train. 2009. 100p. pap. 10.49 *(978-1-4389-7977-9(0))* AuthorHouse.

Cabrol, Marta, illus. When Do I Love You?, 1 vol. 2018. (ENG.). 20p. (J). bds. 8.99 *(978-1-4002-0990-3(0)*, Tommy Nelson) Nelson, Thomas Inc.

A Cake for Mom: Individual Title Six-Packs. (gr. -1-2). 23.00 *(978-0-7635-8997-4(7))* Rigby Education.

Calabrese, Diane Marie. My Dad's off to War. Swope, Brenda, illus. 2011. 28p. pap. 24.95 *(978-1-4560-0942-7(7))* America Star Bks.

Calabrese, Dianne. The Inspirational Guide, 1 vol. 2010. 24p. 24.95 *(978-1-4489-4844-4(4))* PublishAmerica, Inc.

Calvert, Patricia. Bigger. 2003. (ENG., Illus.). 144p. (J). (gr. 3-7). pap. 8.95 *(978-0-689-86003-4(X)*, Simon & Schuster/Paula Wiseman Bks.) Simon & Schuster/Paula Wiseman Bks.

Campbell, H. David. Merribell: A Comforting Story. Thomas, Darlene Kay, illus. 2011. (ENG.). 218p. (gr. 2-2). 23.95 *(978-1-4620-4477-1(8))*; pap. 13.95 *(978-1-4620-4476-4(X))* iUniverse, Inc.

Capdevila (Max), Francesc, illus. Thumbelina/Pulgarcita. 2004. (Bilingual Fairy Tales Ser.: BILI). (ENG.). 32p. (J). (gr. -1-7). pap. 6.99 *(978-0-8118-3928-0(1))* Chronicle Bks. LLC.

Capucilli, Alyssa Satin. Panda Kisses. Widdowson, Kay, illus. 2008. (Step into Reading: Step 1 Ser.). (ENG.). 32p. (J). (gr. -1-1). lib. bdg. 16.19 *(978-0-375-94562-5(8))* Random House Publishing Group.

—Panda Kisses. Widdowson, Kay, illus. 2008. (Step into Reading Ser.). 32p. (J). (gr. -1-1). pap. 5.99 *(978-0-375-84562-8(3)*, Random Hse. Bks. for Young Readers) Random Hse. Children's Bks.

Caraballo, Samuel. Mis Papitos: Héroes de la Cosecha. Gomez, Obed, illus. 2005. (ENG & SPA.). 32p. (J). (gr. -1-3). 16.95 *(978-1-55885-450-5(9)*, Piñata Books) Arte Publico Pr.

Carey Nevin, Judy. What Daddies Like. Six, Stephanie, illus. 2017. (ENG.). 32p. (J). (gr. -1-3). 16.99 *(978-1-4998-0197-2(1))* Little Bee Books Inc.

—What Mommies Like. Six, Stephanie, illus. 2018. (ENG.). 32p. (J). (gr. -1-3). 16.99 *(978-1-4998-0528-4(4))* Little Bee Books Inc.

Carle, Eric. Mister Seahorse. Carle, Eric, illus. 2004. (ENG., Illus.). 32p. (J). (gr. -1-k). 18.99 *(978-0-399-24269-4(4))* Penguin Young Readers Group.

Carlson, Lavelle. Eek! I Hear a Squeak & the Scurrying of Little Feet. Loehr, Jenny, illus. 2006. (ENG.). 28p. (J). (gr. -1-3). 19.95 incl. audio compact disk *(978-0-9725803-8-0(7))* Children's Publishing.

Carlstrom, Nancy White. Before You Were Born. Saport, Linda, illus. 2004. (ENG.). 32p. (J). (gr. -1-k). 17.00 *(978-0-8028-5185-7(1))* Eerdmans, William B. Publishing Co.

Carolan, Jill. Sadie's Bargain. 2008. 148p. pap. 10.94 *(978-0-615-26231-4(7))* Never Quit Productions, Inc.

Carr, Dorothy. Snow Goes Home. 2011. 24p. pap. 15.99 *(978-1-4628-6701-1(4))* Xlibris Corp.

Carr, Karen. The Christmas Wishing Quilt. 2008. 24p. pap. 12.99 *(978-1-4389-1353-7(2))* AuthorHouse.

Casciano, Christie & Moziak, Rose Mary Casciano, illus. Haunted Hockey in Lake Placid. 2012. (ENG.). 72p. (J). pap. *(978-1-59531-040-8(1))* North Country Bks., Inc.

Cassidy, Colette. DIVCO, the Little Milk Truck. 2007. (Illus.). 28p. (J). pap. 7.99 *(978-0-615-17346-7(2))* Redcay Publishing.

Catalanotto, Peter. The Newbies. Catalanotto, Peter, illus. 2015. (ENG., Illus.). 40p. (J). (gr. -1-3). 17.99 *(978-1-4814-1892-8(0))* Simon & Schuster Children's Publishing.

Centeio, Tara Jaye. Mommy Loves Her Baby. Date not set. 32p. (J). (gr. -1-1). pap. 5.99 *(978-0-06-443715-8(9))* HarperCollins Pubs.

Cerrito, Dana. On the Day Love Was Born. Gallegos, Lauren, illus. 2011. 24p. (J). pap. 10.95 *(978-0-9835048-0-1(6))* Little Hill Pubs.

Chamberlain, Karen, et al. A Feather for the Queen. 2009. 28p. pap. 13.95 *(978-1-4490-3903-5(0))* AuthorHouse.

Chandler, Richy K. You Make Your Parents Super Happy! A Book about Parents Separating. Chandler, Richy K., illus. 2017. (Illus.). 40p. (J). 15.95 *(978-1-78592-414-9(1)*, 696704) Kingsley, Jessica Pubs. GBR. Dist: Hachette UK Distribution.

Chapman, Jane. With Your Paw in Mine. Chapman, Jane, illus. 2018. (ENG., Illus.). 32p. (J). (gr. -1-2). 17.99 *(978-1-68010-084-6(X))* Tiger Tales.

Charlip, Remy. A Perfect Day. 2007. (Illus.). 40p. (J). (gr. -1). lib. bdg. 17.89 *(978-0-06-051973-5(8))* HarperCollins Pubs.

Chayce, Jorden. How High Is Up? 2011. 36p. pap. 24.95 *(978-1-4560-6999-5(3))* America Star Bks.

Childs Howard, Betsy. Arlo & the Great Big Cover-Up. Hardy, Samara, illus. 2020. (TGC Kids Ser.). (ENG.). 40p. 14.99 *(978-1-4335-6852-7(7))* Crossway.

Christy, Lucy. A Letter to My Child. 2008. (ENG.). 28p. per. 13.99 *(978-1-4363-0055-1(X))* Xlibris Corp.

Church, Caroline Jayne. Giggle!, 1 vol. Church, Caroline Jayne, illus. 2013. (ENG., Illus.). 10p. (J). (— 1). bds. 7.99 *(978-0-545-35082-2(4)*, Cartwheel Bks.) Scholastic, Inc.

—I Love You. Church, Caroline Jayne, illus. 2012. (ENG., Illus.). 6p. (J). (— 1). 12.99 *(978-0-545-46140-5(5)*, Cartwheel Bks.) Scholastic, Inc.

A City Garden, 6 Packs. (gr. -1-2). 27.00 *(978-0-7635-9441-1(5))* Rigby Education.

Clara Mulholland. Naughty Miss Bunny. 2007. 128p. per. 10.95 *(978-1-4218-3938-7(5)*, 1st World Library - Literary Society) 1st World Publishing, Inc.

Clarke, Judith. Al Capsella & Watchdogs. 164p. pap. *(978-0-7022-2294-8(1))* Univ. of Queensland Pr.

Cleary, Beverly. Ramona & Her Mother. (Ramona Quimby Ser.). 208p. (J). (gr. 3-5). pap. 4.99 *(978-0-8072-1435-0(3)*, Listening Library) Random Hse. Audio Publishing Group.

—Ramona & Her Mother: A National Book Award Winner. Rogers, Jacqueline, illus. 2020. (Ramona Ser.: 5). (ENG.). 224p. (J). (gr. 3-7). 16.99 *(978-0-688-22195-9(5))*; reprint ed. pap. 7.99 *(978-0-380-70952-6(X))* HarperCollins Pubs. (HarperCollins).

Clements, Andrew. The Last Holiday Concert. 2004. (ENG., Illus.). 176p. (J). (gr. 3-7). 19.99 *(978-0-689-84516-1(2)*, Atheneum Bks. for Young Readers) Simon & Schuster Children's Publishing.

Cochran, Bill. My Parents Are Divorced My Elbows Have Nicknames & Other Fact. Björkman, Steve, illus. 2009. (ENG.). 32p. (J). (gr. -1-3). 17.99 *(978-0-06-053942-9(9))* HarperCollins Pubs.

Coffey, M. Carol. Zoe Lucky: And the Green Gables' Mystery. 2008. 156p. pap. 12.95 *(978-1-4327-3190-8(4))* Outskirts Pr., Inc.

Collins, Yvonne & Rideout, Sandy. The Black Sheep. 2007. 348p. (J). *(978-1-4287-4665-7(X))* Hyperion Pr.

Conlon-McKenna, Marita. Under the Hawthorn Tree. Teskey, Donald, illus. 2003. (ENG.). 160p. pap. 5.95 *(978-0-86278-206-1(6))* O'Brien Pr., Ltd., The IRL. Dist: Independent Pubs. Group.

Conradt, Christine. Missing At 17. 2018. (At 17 Ser.: 1). (ENG.). 304p. (YA). (gr. 9). pap. 9.99 *(978-0-06-265164-8(1)*, HarperTeen) HarperCollins Pubs.

Cook, Julia. Scoop. Venting, Elisabeth, illus. 2007. 32p. (J). 15.95 *(978-1-934073-07-0(5))* National Ctr. For Youth Issues.

Cooney, Caroline B. The Face on the Milk Carton. 2009. 9.14 *(978-0-7848-0397-4(8)*, Everbind) Marco Bk. Co.

—The Face on the Milk Carton. 2012. (Face on the Milk Carton Ser.). (ENG.). 208p. (YA). (gr. 7). pap. 10.99 *(978-0-385-74238-2(X)*, Ember) Random Hse. Children's Bks.

—The Face on the Milk Carton. 2012. (Janie Bks.: 1). lib. bdg. 20.85 *(978-0-606-26368-9(3))* Turtleback.

—The Voice on the Radio. 2012. (Face on the Milk Carton Ser.). 208p. (YA). (gr. 7). pap. 10.99 *(978-0-385-74240-5(1)*, Ember) Random Hse. Children's Bks.

—The Voice on the Radio. 2012. (Janie Bks.: 3). lib. bdg. 20.85 *(978-0-606-26369-6(1))* Turtleback.

—What Janie Found. 2012. (Face on the Milk Carton Ser.). 208p. (YA). (gr. 7). pap. 10.99 *(978-0-385-74241-2(X)*, Ember) Random Hse. Children's Bks.

—What Janie Found. 2012. (Janie Bks.: 4). lib. bdg. 20.85 *(978-0-606-26370-2(5))* Turtleback.

—Whatever Happened to Janie? 2012. (Face on the Milk Carton Ser.). 224p. (YA). (gr. 7). pap. 10.99 *(978-0-385-74239-9(8)*, Ember) Random Hse. Children's Bks.

Cooper, Judith. Many Moons. 2008. 28p. per. 24.95 *(978-1-4241-9284-7(6))* America Star Bks.

Corentin, Philippe. Papa! (SPA.). 32p. *(978-84-95150-38-7(7))* Corimbo, Editorial S.L.

—Papa. 2003. (SPA.). (J). (gr. -1-k). 19.99 *(978-84-8470-094-4(1))* Corimbo, Editorial S.L. ESP. Dist: Lectorum Pubns., Inc.

Cowell, Cressida & Mayhew, James. Emily Brown: Emily Brown & the Elephant Emergency. 2015. (Emily Brown Ser.). (ENG., Illus.). 32p. (J). (gr. -1-k). pap. 10.99 *(978-1-4449-2343-8(9))* Hachette Children's Group GBR. Dist: Hachette Bk. Group.

Coy, John. On Your Way. Shipman, Talitha, illus. 2019. 32p. (J). (gr. -1-k). 17.99 *(978-1-5064-5258-6(2)*, Beaming Books) 1517 Media.

Coyle, Carmela LaVigna. Do Princesses Really Kiss Frogs? Gordon, Mike & Gordon, Carl, illus. 2005. (Do Princesses Ser.). (ENG.). 32p. (J). (gr. -1-2). 15.95 *(978-0-87358-880-5(0))* Cooper Square Publishing Llc.

Craft, Jerry. New Kid: A Newbery Award Winner. Craft, Jerry, illus. 2019. (ENG., Illus.). 256p. (J). (gr. 3-7). 22.99 *(978-0-06-269120-0(1))*; pap. 12.99 *(978-0-06-269119-4(8))* HarperCollins Pubs. (Quill Tree Bks.).

Craik, Dinah. The Little Lame Prince & His Traveling Cloak. 2005. reprint ed. pap. 20.95 *(978-1-4179-1940-6(X))* Kessinger Publishing, LLC.

Creech, Sharon. Absolutely Normal Chaos. 2012. (Walk Two Moons Ser.: 2). (ENG.). 256p. (J). (gr. 4-18). pap. 7.99 *(978-0-06-440632-1(6)*, HarperCollins) HarperCollins Pubs.

—Fishing in the Air. Raschka, Chris, illus. 2003. (ENG.). 32p. (J). (gr. -1-3). pap. 7.99 *(978-0-06-051606-2(2)*, HarperCollins) HarperCollins Pubs.

—Fishing in the Air, 4 bks. Raschka, Chris, illus. 2003. (J). pap. 37.95 incl. audio *(978-1-59112-226-5(0))* Live Oak Media.

—Fishing in the Air. 2003. (J). (gr. k-3). 17.20 *(978-0-613-66967-2(3))* Turtleback.

Crist-Evans, Craig. Moon over Tennessee: A Boy's Civil War Journal. Christensen, Bonnie, illus. 2003. (ENG.). 64p. (J). (gr. 5-7). pap. 8.95 *(978-0-618-31107-1(6)*, 460020, Clarion Bks.) HarperCollins Pubs.

Crosson, Denise D. Mommy's Gone to Treatment. Motz, Mike, illus. 2008. (ENG.). 44p. (J). (gr. k-3). pap. 14.95 *(978-0-9799869-1-8(5))* Central Recovery Pr.

Crowe, Chris. The Mississippi Trial 1955. 2003. (gr. 7-12). lib. bdg. 16.00 *(978-0-613-86522-7(7))* Turtleback.

Crutcher, Chris. Ironman. 2004. (ENG.). 288p. (YA). (gr. 8). pap. 10.99 *(978-0-06-059840-2(9)*, Greenwillow Bks.) HarperCollins Pubs.

Cummings, Suzy Lynch. Oh Goodness, Oh Gracious! What Have I Done to my Family? 2009. 28p. pap. 13.99 *(978-1-4490-2408-6(4))* AuthorHouse.

Currinder, Michael. Running Full Tilt. 336p. (YA). (gr. 7). 2018. pap. 10.99 *(978-1-58089-896-6(3))* 2017. lib. bdg. 17.99 *(978-1-58089-802-7(5))* Charlesbridge Publishing, Inc. (Charlesbridge Teen).

Cushenberry, Lisa. No Tears for Teary. 2009. 84p. pap. 9.99 *(978-1-60860-556-9(6)*, Strategic Bk. Publishing) Strategic Book Publishing & Rights Agency (SBPRA).

Cusimano Love, Maryann. You Are My I Love You. Ichikawa, Satomi, illus. 2012. 30p. (J). (gr. -1 — 1). bds. 7.99 *(978-0-399-24396-7(8)*, Philomel Bks.) Penguin Young Readers Group.

—You Are My I Love You: Board Book. Ichikawa, Satomi, illus. 2010. 30p. (J). (gr. -1 — 1). bds. 6.99 *(978-0-399-24395-0(X)*, Philomel Bks.) Penguin Young Readers Group.

Daddy I Wanna Be A Lawyer: And Make Lots of Money. 2004. lib. bdg. 12.95 *(978-1-932762-08-2(6))* Elderberry Press, Inc.

Dannenbring, McKinsey. A Lemon Without the Sour. 2009. 32p. pap. 14.49 *(978-1-4389-2367-3(8))* AuthorHouse.

Danziger, Paula. Amber Brown Is Feeling Blue. 2010. (Amber Brown Ser.: 7). (ENG.). 160p. (J). (gr. 2-5). 6.99 *(978-0-14-241686-0(X)*, Puffin Books) Penguin Young Readers Group.

—Amber Brown Is Feeling Blue. 2004. (Amber Brown Ser.: No. 7). 131p. (J). (gr. 2-4). pap. 17.00 incl. audio *(978-0-8072-2063-4(9)*, Listening Library) Random Hse. Audio Publishing Group.

—Amber Brown Is Feeling Blue. 2010. (Amber Brown Ser.: 7). (gr. 3-6). lib. bdg. 16.00 *(978-0-613-20096-7(9))* Turtleback.

—The Divorce Express. 2007. (ENG.). 208p. (J). (gr. 5-18). 8.99 *(978-0-14-240712-7(7)*, Puffin Books) Penguin Young Readers Group.

—Es Dia de Feria, Ambar Dorado. Ross, Tony, illus. 2007. (de Ambar / a Is for Amber Easy-To-Read Ser.).Tr. of It's a Fair Day, Amber Brown. (SPA.). 48p. (gr. k-3). pap. 8.95 *(978-1-59820-596-1(X))* Santillana USA Publishing Co., Inc.

—I, Amber Brown. Ross, Tony, illus. 2011. (Amber Brown Ser.: 8). (ENG.). 160p. (J). (gr. 2-5). 6.99 *(978-0-14-241965-6(6)*, Puffin Books) Penguin Young Readers Group.

—I, Amber Brown. 2004. (Amber Brown Ser.: No. 8). 144p. (J). (gr. 2-4). pap. 17.00 incl. audio *(978-0-8072-2064-1(7)*, Listening Library) Random Hse. Audio Publishing Group.

—It's a Fair Day, Amber Brown. Ross, Tony, illus. 2003. pap. 31.95 incl. audio compact disk *(978-1-59112-564-8(2))*; (J). (gr. -1-2). audio compact disk 28.95 *(978-1-59112-565-5(0))* Live Oak Media.

—It's a Fair Day, Amber Brown. Ross, Tony, illus. 2003. (Is for Amber Ser.: 3). (ENG.). 48p. (J). (gr. -1-3). pap. 4.99 *(978-0-698-11982-6(7)*, Penguin Young Readers) Penguin Young Readers Group.

—It's a Fair Day, Amber Brown. 2003. (Young Amber Brown Easy-To-Read Ser.: 4). (gr. k-3). lib. bdg. 13.55 *(978-0-613-61635-5(9))* Turtleback.

David, Stuart. My Brilliant Idea (and How It Caused My Downfall) 2017. (ENG.). 240p. (YA). (gr. 7). pap. 9.99 *(978-0-544-93886-1(0)*, 1658465, Clarion Bks.) HarperCollins Pubs.

Davidson, Barbara. Billys Most Difficult Choice. 2007. 49p. 16.95 *(978-1-4241-6153-9(3))* America Star Bks.

Davies, Nicola. The Pond. Fisher, Cathy, illus. 2017. 32p. (J). (gr. k-2). 16.99 *(978-1-912050-70-3(6))* Graffeg Limited GBR. Dist: Independent Pubs. Group.

Davis, Helen J. Good Times with Gregory: Birds: Rescuing a Baby Bird. Davis, Robyn L., illus. 2008. (Good Times with Gregory Ser.). 54p. (J). (gr. -1-4). 12.95 *(978-1-931522-10-4(X))* K&B Products.

Davis, Melissa. Denny the Duck. 2008. 25p. pap. 24.95 *(978-1-60672-712-6(5))* America Star Bks.

Davol, Marguerite W. Black, White, Just Right! Trivas, Irene, illus. 2019. (ENG.). 32p. (J). (gr. -1-3). pap. 7.99 *(978-0-8075-0788-9(1)*, 807507881) Whitman, Albert & Co.

Day, Kathleen. The Sweet Song of Rainbow Bird. 2012. 32p. pap. 14.75 *(978-1-4669-3555-6(3))* Trafford Publishing.

de Balzac, Honore. Le Pere Goriot. (FRE.). (YA). (gr. 7-12). 9.95 *(978-0-88436-043-8(1)*, 40280) EMC/Paradigm Publishing.

de Silva, Eugenie. The Adventures of Princess Eugenie. 2008. 35p. pap. 24.65 *(978-0-557-01213-8(9))* Lulu Pr., Inc.

De Smet, Marian. Anna's Tight Squeeze. Meijer, Marja, illus. 2003. Orig. Title: Op Slot. 32p. (J). pap. 5.95 *(978-1-58925-378-0(7))* Tiger Tales.

DeKeyser, Stacy. Jump the Cracks. 2008. (ENG.). 216p. (YA). (gr. 9-12). per. 9.95 *(978-0-7387-1274-1(4)*, 0738712744, Flux) North Star Editions.

DeMeo, Kimberly F. One Little Egg. 2013. (ENG.). 25p. (J). pap. 20.95 *(978-1-4787-1084-4(5))* Outskirts Pr., Inc.

Dessen, Sarah. This Lullaby. 2004. (ENG.). 368p. (YA). (gr. 7-18). reprint ed. pap. 11.99 *(978-0-14-250155-9(7)*, Speak) Penguin Young Readers Group.

Diggle, David Mark. Paco: The High-Performance Penguin. Preuss, Sarah Louise, illus. 2011. 24p. (J). pap. *(978-0-9871658-1-7(X))* Diggle de Doo Productions Pty, Ltd.

Dilz, Ric. My Grandma Could Do Anything! 2008. (J). 14.95 *(978-0-9758704-3-3(2))* Ric Design LLC.

—My Grandma Could Do Anything in the Great Outdoors! 2008. (Illus.). 32p. (J). 14.95 *(978-0-9758704-6-4(7))* Ric Design LLC.

Disney Books. Descendants: Mal's Diary. 2015. (ENG., Illus.). 192p. (J). (gr. 3-7). 9.99 *(978-1-4847-2685-3(5)*, Disney Press Books) Disney Publishing Worldwide.

—Descendants: Mal's Spell Book. 2015. (ENG., Illus.). 192p. (J). (gr. 3-7). 11.99 *(978-1-4847-2638-9(3)*, Disney Press Books) Disney Publishing Worldwide.

—Fairest of All-Villains, Book 1. 2009. (Villains Ser.: 1). (ENG., Illus.). 256p. (YA). (gr. 7-12). 17.99 *(978-1-4231-0629-6(6)*, Disney Press Books) Disney Publishing Worldwide.

DiTerlizzi, Angela. Baby Love. Boynton-Hughes, Brooke, illus. 2015. (ENG.). 32p. (J). (gr. -1-3). 17.99 *(978-1-4424-3392-2(2)*, Beach Lane Bks.) Beach Lane Bks.

—Baby Love. Boynton-Hughes, Brooke, illus. 2018. (Classic Board Bks.). (ENG.). 36p. (J). (gr. -1 — 1). bds. 7.99 *(978-1-5344-2035-9(5)*, Little Simon) Little Simon.

—Say What? Chou, Joey, illus. 2011. (ENG.). 32p. (J). (gr. -1-k). 19.99 *(978-1-4169-8694-2(4)*, Beach Lane Bks.) Beach Lane Bks.

Doctor McGougain. Stevie's Dreams: Doctor Mcgougain. 2012. 16p. pap. 15.99 *(978-1-4685-5345-1(3))* AuthorHouse.

Dodd, Emma. Forever. Dodd, Emma, illus. 2019. (Emma Dodd's Love You Bks.). (ENG., Illus.). 22p. (J). (— 1). bds. 10.99 *(978-1-5362-0812-2(4)*, Templar) Candlewick Pr.

—More & More. Dodd, Emma, illus. 2014. (Emma Dodd's Love You Bks.). (ENG., Illus.). 24p. (J). (-k). 12.99 *(978-0-7636-7543-1(1)*, Templar) Candlewick Pr.

Doller, Trish. Where the Stars Still Shine. 2013. (ENG.). 216p. (YA). (gr. 9). E-Book 7.99 *(978-1-61963-145-8(8)*, Bloomsbury USA Childrens) Bloomsbury Publishing USA.

Dotlich, Rebecca Kai. Mama Loves. Brown, Kathryn, illus. 2004. 32p. (J). (gr. -1-2). lib. bdg. 15.89 *(978-0-06-029408-3(6))* HarperCollins Pubs.

Dower, Laura. For Emme, Baked with Love. Lazuli, Lilly, illus. 2016. (Dessert Diaries). (ENG.). 160p. (J). (gr. 4-8). pap. 5.95 *(978-1-4965-4142-0(1),* 133430); lib. bdg. 26.65 *(978-1-4965-3122-3(1),* 132193) Capstone. (Stone Arch Bks.).

Doyle, Patrick H. T. Edgar Font's Hunt for a House to Haunt: Adventure Three: the Flint Island Treehouse. 2008. (Illus.). 300p. (J). per. 7.99 *(978-0-9786132-2-8(8))* Armadillo Bks.

Doyle, Teresa J. The Dream Box: Big Dreams for Little Sleepers. 2008. 84p. pap. 26.95 *(978-1-4343-9086-8(1))* AuthorHouse.

Duble, Kathleen Benner. Pilot Mom. Marks, Alan, illus. 2004. 32p. (J). (gr. k-3). 15.95 *(978-1-57091-555-0(5))* Charlesbridge Publishing, Inc.

Duksta, Laura. I Love You More. Keesler, Karen, illus. 2007. 34p. (J). (gr. k-2). 17.99 *(978-1-4022-1126-3(0),* Sourcebooks Jabberwocky) Sourcebooks, Inc.

Dumble, Carol. R U My Friend? 2011. 20p. pap. 11.99 *(978-1-4567-1825-1(8))* AuthorHouse.

Dungy, Tony & Dungy, Lauren. A Team Stays Together! Ready-To-Read Level 2. Brantley-Newton, Vanessa, illus. 2011. (Tony & Lauren Dungy Ready-To-Reads Ser.). (ENG.). 32p. (J). (gr. k-2). pap. 4.99 *(978-1-4424-3539-1(9),* Simon Spotlight) Simon Spotlight.

Durrant, George D. Shakespeare's Best Work: A Novel of Unexpected Family Ties & Uncommon Faith. 2003. 130p. pap. 10.95 *(978-1-55517-709-6(3),* 77093) Cedar Fort, Inc./CFI Distribution.

Earhardt, Ainsley. I'm So Glad You Were Born: Celebrating Who You Are. Barnes, Kim, illus. 2022. (ENG.). 32p. (J). 18.99 *(978-0-310-77702-1(X))* Zonderkidz.

Eaton, Kelly Toole. Kitten Trouble. 2011. 36p. pap. 21.99 *(978-1-4568-8937-1(0))* Xlibris Corp.

Edgeworth, Maria. The Parent's Assistant; or, Stories for Children. 2007. 468p. (gr. 4-7). per. *(978-1-4065-1649-4(X))* Dodo Pr.

Edgeworth, Maria & Anderson, Alexander. The Parent's Assistant; or, Stories for Children. 2016. (ENG., Illus.). (J). 25.95 *(978-1-358-39155-2(6))* Creative Media Partners, LLC.

Edwards, Nicola. You're My Little Cuddle Bug. Marshall, Natalie, illus. 2018. (You're My Little Ser.). (ENG.). 18p. (J). (gr. -1 — 1). bds. 8.99 *(978-1-68412-258-5(9),* Silver Dolphin Bks.) Printers Row Publishing Group.

Ehlert, Lois. Hands: Growing up to Be an Artist. Ehlert, Lois, illus. 2004. (ENG., Illus.). 48p. (J). (gr. -1-3). 16.99 *(978-0-15-205107-5(4),* 1195421, Clarion Bks.) HarperCollins Pubs.

—Pie in the Sky. Ehlert, Lois, illus. 2004. (ENG., Illus.). 40p. (J). (gr. -1-3). 17.99 *(978-0-15-216584-0(3),* 1201415, Clarion Bks.) HarperCollins Pubs.

Elgert, C. J. The Elder Brothers & the Padstow Crystals. 2013. 208p. *(978-1-4602-1788-7(8));* pap. *(978-1-4602-1789-4(6))* FriesenPress.

Ellis, Ann Dee. You May Already Be a Winner. 2017. 352p. (J). (gr. 5-9). 16.99 *(978-1-101-99385-9(5),* Dial Bks) Penguin Young Readers Group.

Elmquist, Laurie. Where's Burgess?, 1 vol. Parkins, David, illus. 2018. (Orca Echoes Ser.). (ENG.). 96p. (J). (gr. 1-3). pap. 6.95 *(978-1-4598-1478-3(9))* Orca Bk. Pubs. USA.

Ennis, Nancy. When Mommy & Daddy Say No, They Still Love You. Meadows, Cynthia, illus. 2014. (ENG.). 24p. (J). 14.95 net. *(978-1-61254-198-3(4))* Brown Books Publishing Group.

Ethier, Vicki. Papa & the Hen. Ethier, Vicki, illus. 2004. (Illus.). 36p. (J). 7.00 *(978-1-928972-12-9(8))* Critter Pubns.

Eubank, Patti Reeder. Count Your Blessings! 2004. (ENG., Illus.). 14p. (J). bds. 9.95 *(978-0-8249-6544-0(2),* Ideals Pubns.) Worthy Publishing.

Evyindson, Peter. Kyle's Bath, 1 vol. Wolsak, Wendy, illus. 2016. (ENG.). 32p. (J). (gr. -1-2). mass mkt. 10.95 *(978-0-919143-05-0(9),* 4c1e709c-2ae1-4447-a8bb-127d24501731) Pemmican Pubns., Inc. CAN. Dist: Firefly Bks., Ltd.

Falk, Jennifer & Morgan. A Heart Daddy for Chrissie. 2005. 43p. (J). pap. 16.00 *(978-1-4116-3585-2(X))* Lulu Pr., Inc.

Fass, Tara. Turtlebird's Double Dip Shuffle. Conn, Alexandra, illus. 2013. 18p. pap. 10.00 *(978-0-9838120-4-3(7))* Huqua Pr.

Fehr, Signe. Mama Always Comes Back. 2008. 32p. pap. 14.99 *(978-1-4389-0036-0(8))* AuthorHouse.

Feldkamp, Jim And Cate. The Adventures of Tommy & Clara on Mount Catherine. 2008. 32p. pap. 14.49 *(978-1-4389-1366-7(4))* AuthorHouse.

Felker, Linda, et al. What If? 2013. 42p. pap. 13.95 *(978-1-938101-51-9(0))* Indigo Sea Pr., LLC.

Ferreri, Della Ross. Precious Baby. Dong, Monique, illus. 2019. 20p. (J). (gr. -1 — 1). 7.99 *(978-1-5064-4773-5(2),* Beaming Books) 1517 Media.

Findlay, Chris. Ae Sma Voice. 2008. 152p. pap. *(978-1-84923-144-2(3))* YouWriteOn.

Fleischman, Paul. Seek. braille ed. 2003. (J). (gr. 2). spiral bd. *(978-0-616-15870-8(X))* Canadian National Institute for the Blind/Institut National Canadien pour les Aveugles.

—Seek. 2004. 176p. (J). (gr. 7-18). pap. 29.00 incl. audio *(978-0-8072-2285-0(2),* Listening Library) Random Hse. Audio Publishing Group.

Fleming, Meg. I Heart You. Wright, Sarah Jane, illus. 2016. (ENG.). 40p. (J). (gr. -1-3). 17.99 *(978-1-4424-8895-3(6),* Beach Lane Bks.) Beach Lane Bks.

—I Heart You. Wright, Sarah Jane, illus. 2019. (Classic Board Bks.). (ENG.). 36p. (J). (gr. -1-3). bds. 8.99 *(978-1-5344-5130-8(7),* Little Simon) Little Simon.

Flesher, Brandon. Shattered Dreams in Light. (J). 2017. (ENG., Illus.). (gr. 3-6). pap. 11.95 *(978-1-938237-25-6(0),* Flat Sole Studio) 2014. *(978-1-938237-10-2(2))* Skywater Publishing Co.

Flinn, Alex. Breathing Underwater. 2nd ed. 2019. (ENG., Illus.). 304p. (YA). (gr. 9). pap. 11.99 *(978-0-06-447257-9(4),* HarperTeen) HarperCollins Pubs.

—Breathing Underwater. unabr. ed. 2004. (Young Adult Cassette Librariestm Ser.). 272p. (J). (gr. 7-18). pap. 36.00 incl. audio *(978-0-8072-0992-9(9),* S YA 346 SP, Listening Library) Random Hse. Audio Publishing Group.

Flint, Shamini. Life of the Party! the Susie K Files 1. Heinrich, Sally, illus. 2018. (Susie K Files Ser.: 1). (ENG.). 96p. (J). (gr. 2-6). pap. 8.99 *(978-1-76029-668-1(6))* Allen & Unwin AUS. Dist: Independent Pubs. Group.

Fogliano, Julie. If I Was the Sunshine. Long, Loren, illus. 2019. (ENG.). 48p. (J). (gr. -1-3). 17.99 *(978-1-4814-7243-2(7),* Atheneum Bks. for Young Readers) Simon & Schuster Children's Publishing.

Ford, Jayme. The Adventures of Glop-A-Lopikins & the Pink Castle. 2013. 28p. pap. 24.95 *(978-1-62709-206-7(4))* America Star Bks.

Fox, Mem. Harriet, You'll Drive Me Wild! frazee, Marla, illus. 2003. (ENG.). 32p. (J). (gr. -1-3). pap. 7.99 *(978-0-15-204598-2(8),* 1193846, Clarion Bks.) HarperCollins Pubs.

—Harriet, You'll Drive Me Wild! 2003. (gr. k-3). 17.20 *(978-0-613-59897-2(0))* Turtleback.

Frederick, Heather Vogel. The Voyage of Patience Goodspeed. 2004. (ENG., Illus.). 224p. (J). (gr. 3-7). pap. 8.99 *(978-0-689-84869-8(2),* Simon & Schuster Bks. For Young Readers) Simon & Schuster Bks. For Young Readers.

Freedman, Claire. I Love You, Baby! Abbot, Judi, illus. 2017. (ENG.). 32p. (J). (gr. -1-3). 17.99 *(978-1-4814-9904-0(1),* Simon & Schuster/Paula Wiseman Bks.) Simon & Schuster/Paula Wiseman Bks.

Freeman, Suzanne. The Cuckoo's Child. 249p. (YA). (gr. 5-8). pap. 5.95 *(978-0-8072-1510-4(4),* Listening Library) Random Hse. Audio Publishing Group.

Friedman, Becky. Daniel Goes to School. 2014. (Daniel Tiger's Neighborhood 8X8 Ser.). lib. bdg. 13.55 *(978-0-606-35756-2(4))* Turtleback.

—Daniel Tries a New Food. 2015. (Daniel Tiger's Neighborhood 8X8 Ser.). lib. bdg. 13.55 *(978-0-606-37874-1(X))* Turtleback.

—Munch Your Lunch! 2018. (Daniel Tiger's Neighborhood 8X8 Ser.). (Illus.). (J). lib. bdg. 16.00 *(978-0-606-41413-5(4))* Turtleback.

Friend, Natasha. Perfect. 2004. (ENG.). 232p. (J). pap. 10.00 *(978-1-57131-651-6(5))* Milkweed Editions.

Fruchter, Jason, illus. Daniel Feels Left Out: Ready-To-Read Pre-Level 1. 2015. (Daniel Tiger's Neighborhood Ser.). (ENG.). 32p. (J). (gr. -1-k). 17.99 *(978-1-4814-3836-0(0),* Simon Spotlight) Simon Spotlight.

—Daniel Goes to School. 2014. (Daniel Tiger's Neighborhood Ser.). (ENG.). 24p. (J). (gr. -1-2). pap. 4.99 *(978-1-4814-0318-4(4),* Simon Spotlight) Simon Spotlight.

—Daniel Tries a New Food. 2015. (Daniel Tiger's Neighborhood Ser.). (ENG.). 24p. (J). (gr. -1-2). pap. 4.99 *(978-1-4814-4170-4(1),* Simon Spotlight) Simon Spotlight.

—Munch Your Lunch! 2018. (Daniel Tiger's Neighborhood Ser.). (ENG.). 16p. (J). (gr. -1-2). pap. 5.99 *(978-1-5344-1778-6(8),* Simon Spotlight) Simon Spotlight.

Frye, Timea Csonka. Wishing Star: Lost in the Woods. 2013. 32p. pap. 24.95 *(978-1-63000-931-1(8))* America Star Bks.

Gaffney, Linda. My Daddy Does GOOD Things, Too! Dabney, Undra & Goettling, Nickalas, illus. 2006. 55p. per. 10.99 *(978-0-9787501-0-7(1))* Gaffney, Linda.

Galassi, Isabel. I Want, 1 vol. 2009. 12p. pap. 24.95 *(978-1-61546-535-4(9))* America Star Bks.

Garisch, Dawn. Babyshoes. 2004. (ENG.). 288p. (J). pap. 9.99 *(978-0-689-83778-4(X))* Simon & Schuster, Ltd. GBR. Dist: Simon & Schuster, Inc.

Garner, Jazzy. The Cotton Tales of Pippa the Bunny. 2010. 20p. 12.49 *(978-1-4490-8699-2(3))* AuthorHouse.

Gasparro, Marie & Falletta, Bernadette. The Magnificent Hole. 2005. 13p. (J). 12.95 *(978-1-4116-5924-7(4))* Lulu Pr., Inc.

Gates, Josephine Scribner. The Story of Live Dolls: Being an Account of How, on a Certain June Morning. unabr. ed. 2012. (Illus.). 104p. 39.99 *(978-1-4622-8158-9(3))* Repressed Publishing LLC.

Gay, Michel. El Cochecito. 2003. (SPA.). 68p. *(978-84-8470-084-5(4))* Corimbo, Editorial S.L.

Gaylord, Laurel Porter. I Love My Mommy Because... Wolff, Ashley, illus. 2004. 22p. (J). (gr. -1 — 1). bds. 7.99 *(978-0-525-47247-6(9),* Dutton Books for Young Readers) Penguin Young Readers Group.

Geeslin, Campbell. Elena's Serenade. Juan, Ana, illus. 2004. (ENG.). 40p. (J). (gr. -1-2). 19.99 *(978-0-689-84908-4(7),* Atheneum Bks. for Young Readers) Simon & Schuster Children's Publishing.

Geise, Brenda & Merkle, Blair Geise. Love Spot. 2008. 28p. pap. 12.99 *(978-1-4389-1102-1(5))* AuthorHouse.

Geist, Christina. Sorry, Grown-Ups, You Can't Go to School! Bowers, Tim, illus. 2019. (Growing with Buddy Ser.: 2). 40p. (J). (gr. -1-2). 17.99 *(978-1-5247-7084-6(1));* (ENG.). lib. bdg. 20.99 *(978-1-5247-7085-3(X))* Random Hse. Children's Bks. (Random Hse. Bks. for Young Readers).

Gerber, Alyson. Focused. 2019. (ENG.). 304p. (J). (gr. 3-7). 16.99 *(978-1-338-18597-3(7),* Scholastic Pr.) Scholastic, Inc.

Gershman, Jenifer. Where Did Mommy's Superpowers Go? Helping Kids Understand a Parent's Serious Illness. 2011. (ENG., Illus.). 36p. (J). pap. 16.95 *(978-0-9824461-9-5(5))* SDP Publishing.

Gibbons, Alan. The Dying Photo. 2012. (Stoke Books Titles Ser.). 64p. (J). (gr. 5-8). pap. 45.32 *(978-0-7613-9217-0(3))* Stoke Bks.

Gibbs, Dreene. Am I Pretty, Momma? 2nd l.t. ed. 2004. (Illus.). 32p. (J). bds. 12.95 *(978-0-9741406-1-2(9),* 0138) Cranberry Quill Publishing Co.

Gibson, Donovan. The Ticker That Needed a Fixer. Rottinger, Amy, illus. 2011. 28p. pap. 12.95 *(978-1-935268-46-8(5))* Halo Publishing International.

Gilbert, George. George, Candy, & the Raccoon. Perez-Torres, Juliana, illus. 2008. (ENG.). 38p. pap. 16.99 *(978-1-4389-2848-7(3))* AuthorHouse.

Gilles, Almira Astudillo. Willie Wins, 1 vol. Angel, Carl, illus. 2013. (ENG.). 32p. (J). (gr. -1-3). 16.95 *(978-1-58430-023-5(X))* Lee & Low Bks., Inc.

Gillespie, Hollis. Unaccompanied Minor. 2014. (ENG.). 256p. (YA). 17.99 *(978-1-4405-6773-5(5))* Adams Media Corp.

Gliori, Debi. No Matter What Board Book. Gliori, Debi, illus. 2008. (ENG., Illus.). 24p. (J). (gr. -1 — 1). bds. 8.99 *(978-0-15-206343-6(9),* 1198999, Clarion Bks.) HarperCollins Pubs.

—No Matter What Lap Board Book. Gliori, Debi, illus. 2012. (ENG., Illus.). 24p. (J). (gr. -1 — 1). bds. 12.99 *(978-0-547-71905-4(1),* 1481812, Clarion Bks.) HarperCollins Pubs.

Gormally, Eleanor. The Little One Asks. 2013. (ENG.). 32p. (J). pap. 12.95 *(978-1-84730-407-0(9))* Veritas Pubns. IRL. Dist: Casemate Pubs. & Bk. Distributors, LLC.

Gownley, Jimmy. What Makes You Happy. Gownley, Jimmy, illus. 2009. (Amelia Rules! Ser.). (ENG., Illus.). 176p. (J). (gr. 2-7). pap. 12.99 *(978-1-4169-8605-8(7),* Atheneum Bks. for Young Readers) Simon & Schuster Children's Publishing.

Graff, Lisa. It Is Not Time for Sleeping. Castillo, Lauren, illus. 2016. (ENG.). 40p. (J). (gr. -1-3). 16.99 *(978-0-544-31930-1(3),* 1582434, Clarion Bks.) HarperCollins Pubs.

Graham, Bob. Home in the Rain. Graham, Bob, illus. 2017. (ENG., Illus.). 32p. (J). (gr. -1-2). 16.99 *(978-0-7636-9269-8(7))* Candlewick Pr.

Grandfeather Press. Roly Poly Napoleon Discovers Colors. 2011. (ENG., Illus.). 36p. (J). pap. 6.99 *(978-0-9832355-0-7(3))* Grandfeather Pr.

Graves, Jennifer. Ava's Awful Fright! 2009. 28p. pap. 15.99 *(978-1-4415-0482-1(6))* Xlibris Corp.

Greban, Quentin. Mommy, I Love You. Greban, Quentin, illus. 2005. (Illus.). 32p. *(978-0-689-03922-5(0),* Milk & Cookies) ibooks, Inc.

Greene, Marjorie. Cassie's Big Day. 2003. (Illus.). (J). 16.95 *(978-0-9741764-0-6(0))* Greene, Marjorie A.

Greenspan, Deborah. Kids' Day. 2004. (J). pap. 10.95 *(978-1-59526-197-7(4))* Aeon Publishing Inc.

Gregory, Dee. The Accidental Daughter: A Children's Story about Hope. 2008. 96p. pap. 10.49 *(978-1-4389-3338-2(X))* AuthorHouse.

Griffin, Donna. Dani & the Beans. 2008. 28p. pap. 13.50 *(978-1-4389-1175-5(0))* AuthorHouse.

Griffin, Michele. Picky, Picky Pete. 2010. (ENG.). 48p. (J). (gr. -1-3). pap. 12.95 *(978-1-935567-21-9(7),* P183708) Future Horizons, Inc.

Gutman, Anne & Hallensleben, Georg. Daddy Cuddles. 2005. (Daddy, Mommy Ser.). (ENG., Illus.). 14p. (J). (gr. -1 — 1). bds. 5.99 *(978-0-8118-4674-5(1))* Chronicle Bks. LLC.

Haddix, Margaret Peterson. Children of Exile. 2016. (Children of Exile Ser.: 1). (ENG., Illus.). 304p. (J). (gr. 5). 18.99 *(978-1-4424-5003-5(7),* Simon & Schuster Bks. For Young Readers) Simon & Schuster Bks. For Young Readers.

—Say What? Bernardin, James, illus. 2005. 91p. (J). 11.65 *(978-0-7569-5465-9(7))* Perfection Learning Corp.

Haislip, Phyllis Hall. Lottie's Courage: A Contraband Slave's Story. 2003. (Illus.). 120p. (J). pap. 7.95 *(978-1-57249-311-7(9),* White Mane Kids) White Mane Publishing Co., Inc.

Hall, John. What If I Pulled This Thread. Gilpin, Stephen, illus. 2006. 48p. 12.99 *(978-1-59379-067-7(8))* White Stone Bks.

Hall, Marjory. The Gold-Lined Box. 2003. 224p. 11.95 *(978-0-9714612-6-0(0))* Green Mansion Pr. LLC.

Hallinan, P. K. How Do I Love You? 2018. (ENG., Illus.). 22p. (J). (gr. -1-k). bds. 7.99 *(978-0-8249-1682-4(4))* Worthy Publishing.

—We're Very Good Friends, My Mother & I. 24p. (J). 7.95 *(978-0-8249-5373-7(8));* 5.95 *(978-0-8249-5374-4(6))* Worthy Publishing. (Ideals Pubns.).

Hank. 2003. (ENG.). 192p. (J). 19.95 *(978-1-890862-22-0(3),* 827a2b88-c50e-44f2-ad1d-6733447b1879) Bancroft Pr.

Hao, K. T. Who Did This? Bernatene, Poly, illus. 2008. (ENG.). 32p. (J). (gr. -1). lib. bdg. 16.50 *(978-1-933327-33-4(2))* Purple Bear Bks., Inc.

—Who Did This? Bernatene, Poly, illus. 2008. (ENG.). 32p. (J). (gr. -1). 15.95 *(978-1-933327-32-7(4))* Purple Bear Bks., Inc.

Harrington, Claudia. My Military Mom, 1 vol. Persico, Zoe, illus. 2015. (My Family Ser.). (ENG.). 32p. (J). (gr. -1-3). 32.79 *(978-1-62402-106-0(9),* 18154, Looking Glass Library) Magic Wagon.

—My Two Homes, 1 vol. Persico, Zoe, illus. 2015. (My Family Ser.). (ENG.). 32p. (J). (gr. -1-3). 32.79 *(978-1-62402-109-1(3),* 18160, Looking Glass Library) Magic Wagon.

Harris, Teresa. Summer Jackson: Grown Up. Ford, A. G., illus. 2011. (ENG.). 32p. (J). (gr. -1-2). 17.99 *(978-0-06-185757-7(2),* Tegen, Katherine Bks) HarperCollins Pubs.

Hart, Melissa. Avenging the Owl. (ENG.). 224p. (J). (gr. 5-8). 2018. pap. 9.99 *(978-1-5107-2628-4(4))* 2016. 15.99 *(978-1-63450-147-7(0))* Skyhorse Publishing Co., Inc. (Sky Pony Pr.).

Haughton, Emma. Rainy Day. Rinaldi, Angelo, illus. (Carolrhoda Picture Books Ser.). 32p. (J). 2004. pap. 6.95 *(978-1-57505-668-5(2))* 2003. (gr. -1-3). 6.95 *(978-1-57505-452-0(3),* Carolrhoda Bks.) Lerner Publishing Group.

Haven, Gayle Jeanine. Love from Both Houses, My Parents Love. 2012. 28p. pap. 19.99 *(978-1-4685-9810-0(4))* AuthorHouse.

Haworth, Margaret. When Daddy Goes Away: Rusty Books. Edwards, Paul, illus. l.t. ed. 2003. (Books That Help Ser.: Vol. 2). 34p. (J). (gr. -1-5). pap. 9.95 *(978-0-9740313-1-6(3))* Haworth, Margaret.

Hayes, Geoffrey. A Night-Light for Bunny. Date not set. 32p. (J). (gr. -1-3). pap. 5.99 *(978-0-06-443728-8(0))* HarperCollins Pubs.

—A Night-Light for Bunny. Hayes, Geoffrey, illus. 2004. (Illus.). 32p. (J). (gr. -1-3). 14.99 *(978-0-06-029163-1(X))* HarperCollins Pubs.

Helakoski, Leslie. Woolbur. Harper, Lee, illus. 2008. (ENG.). 32p. (J). (gr. -1-3). 17.99 *(978-0-06-084726-5(3),* HarperCollins) HarperCollins Pubs.

—Woolbur. 2008. (J). (gr. -1-2). 29.95 incl. audio *(978-0-8045-6971-2(1))* Spoken Arts, Inc.

Hemingway, Edith M. Road to Tater Hill. 2011. 224p. (J). (gr. 3-7). 8.99 *(978-0-375-84544-4(5),* Yearling) Random Hse. Children's Bks.

Henkes, Kevin. Owen. 2017. (SPA., Illus.). 24p. (J). pap. 9.99 *(978-1-63245-665-6(6))* Lectorum Pubns., Inc.

Henry, Nancy. Where's Papa? 2008. 24p. per. 24.95 *(978-1-60474-000-4(0))* America Star Bks.

Hepworth, Amelia. I Love You to the Moon & Back. Warnes, Tim, illus. 2017. (ENG.). 24p. (J). (gr. -1-k). bds. 9.99 *(978-1-68010-522-3(1))* Tiger Tales.

Hest, Amy. Remembering Mrs. Rossi. Maione, Heather, illus. 2007. (ENG.). 192p. (J). (gr. 3-7). 14.99 *(978-0-7636-2163-6(3))* Candlewick Pr.

—Remembering Mrs. Rossi. Maione, Heather, illus. 2010. (ENG.). 192p. (J). (gr. 3-7). 6.99 *(978-0-7636-4089-7(1))* Candlewick Pr.

Hetzer, Michael. No More Handprints: Your Child's Handprint Completes the Story. Clayton, Kim, illus. 2nd ed. 2005. 32p. (J). 18.95 *(978-0-9728222-0-6(8))* Webster Henrietta Publishing.

Higgins, M. G. Family Fix-It Plan. Taylor, Jo, illus. 2016. (Sibling Split Ser.). (ENG.). 112p. (J). (gr. 3-6). lib. bdg. 25.32 *(978-1-4965-2590-1(6),* 130719, Stone Arch Bks.) Capstone.

—The Impossible Wish. Taylor, Jo, illus. 2016. (Sibling Split Ser.). (ENG.). 112p. (J). (gr. 3-6). lib. bdg. 25.32 *(978-1-4965-2593-2(0),* 130722, Stone Arch Bks.) Capstone.

—Party of Nine. Taylor, Jo, illus. 2016. (Sibling Split Ser.). (ENG.). 112p. (J). (gr. 3-6). lib. bdg. 25.32 *(978-1-4965-2592-5(2),* 130721, Stone Arch Bks.) Capstone.

—Trouble in the City. Taylor, Jo, illus. 2016. (Sibling Split Ser.). (ENG.). 112p. (J). (gr. 3-6). lib. bdg. 25.32 *(978-1-4965-2591-8(4),* 130720, Stone Arch Bks.) Capstone.

Hightman, Jason. The Saint of Dragons. 2004. (ENG.). 304p. (J). (gr. 7-18). 16.99 *(978-0-06-054011-7(7))* HarperCollins Pubs.

Hinbest, Wendy. Frizzy Tizzy Gets New Shoes. 2011. 24p. pap. 11.95 *(978-1-4583-5827-1(5))* Lulu Pr., Inc.

—Frizzy Tizzy Goes to the Park. 2011. (ENG.). 20p. 11.95 *(978-1-4583-4346-8(4))* Lulu Pr., Inc.

Hines, Anna Grossnickle, illus. Whistling. 2003. 40p. (J). 16.89 *(978-0-06-050236-2(3))* HarperCollins Pubs.

Hodges, Lynn & Buchanan, Sue. I Love You This Much, 1 vol. Bendall-Brunello, John, illus. (ENG.). (J). 2010. 36p. pap. 6.99 *(978-0-310-72265-6(9))* 2005. 16p. (gr. -1). bds. 8.99 *(978-0-310-70961-9(X))* Zonderkidz.

Hodgkins, Fran. If You Were My Baby: A Wildlife Lullaby. Bryant, Laura J., illus. 2005. 32p. (J). (gr. -1-3). pap. 8.95 *(978-1-58469-075-7(5),* Dawn Pubns.) Sourcebooks, Inc.

Hofmeister, Nick. Adventures of Eli Deuce - SPECIAL EDITION - Fourth & Final Part Added. 2009. 360p. pap. 23.50 *(978-0-557-12192-2(2))* Lulu Pr., Inc.

Hofstad, Maryanne. Hi, Mommy & Daddy! I'm Here! 2009. 12p. pap. 9.99 *(978-1-4389-4887-4(5))* AuthorHouse.

Hogan, Janice M. As Big as the Sky. 2008. 32p. per. 24.95 *(978-1-4241-9181-9(5))* America Star Bks.

Holt, Kimberly Willis. My Louisiana Sky. 208p. (YA). (gr. 5-18). 4.99 *(978-0-8072-8291-5(X),* Listening Library) Random Hse. Audio Publishing Group.

—My Louisiana Sky. 2011. (ENG.). 224p. (J). (gr. 4-7). pap. 8.99 *(978-0-312-66095-6(2),* 900070608) Square Fish.

Hong, Denise & Hong, Andrew. Why I Love My Mom: The Ultimate Gift of the Heart. Lopez, Paul & Hong, Denise, illus. 2004. 32p. (J). lib. bdg. 17.95 *(978-0-9746503-4-0(X))* Platinum Bks.

Horowitz, Stacey & Brenner, Jordyn. My Privates Are Private. 2009. 24p. pap. 12.95 *(978-1-60844-281-2(0))* Dog Ear Publishing, LLC.

Hood, Tyline M. I Love You So Much, Goodnight. 2012. 26p. pap. 17.99 *(978-1-4685-6444-0(7))* AuthorHouse.

Hopkins, Ellen. The You I've Never Known. (ENG.). (YA). (gr. 9). 2018. 624p. pap. 14.99 *(978-1-4814-4291-6(0))* 2017. (Illus.). 608p. 18.99 *(978-1-4814-4290-9(2))* McElderry, Margaret K. Bks. (McElderry, Margaret K. Bks.).

Horn, Lorri. Dewey Fairchild, Parent Problem Solver. 2018. (Dewey Fairchild Ser.: 1). (ENG., Illus.). 252p. (J). (gr. 4-7). pap. 7.99 *(978-1-948705-12-7(5))* Amberjack Publishing Co.

—Dewey Fairchild, Parent Problem Solver: Parent Problem Solver. 2017. (Dewey Fairchild Ser.: 1). (ENG., Illus.). 252p. (J). (gr. 4-7). 13.99 *(978-1-944995-16-4(1))* Amberjack Publishing Co.

Horvath, Polly. Everything on a Waffle, 1 vol. (ENG., Illus.). 160p. (J). pap. 8.95 *(978-0-88899-442-4(7))* Groundwood Bks. CAN. Dist: Publishers Group West (PGW).

—Everything on a Waffle. 2008. (Illus.). 154p. (gr. 5-9). 18.00 *(978-0-7569-8776-3(8))* Perfection Learning Corp.

—Everything on a Waffle. 2008. (ENG., Illus.). 176p. (J). (gr. 5-9). pap. 8.99 *(978-0-312-38004-5(6),* 900050527) Square Fish.

Hostetter, Joyce Moyer. Aim. (Bakers Mountain Stories Ser.). 288p. (J). (gr. 4-7). 2019. pap. 9.95 *(978-1-68437-276-8(3))* 2016. (ENG.). 17.95 *(978-1-62979-673-4(5))* Highlights Pr., c/o Highlights for Children, Inc. (Calkins Creek).

Houk, Amanda. Mommy's New Heart, 1 vol. 2010. 22p. 24.95 *(978-1-4512-9377-7(1))* PublishAmerica, Inc.

Houran, Lori Haskins. Warts & All: A Book of Unconditional Love. Hanson, Sydney, illus. 2017. (ENG.). 32p. (J). (gr. -1-3). 15.99 *(978-0-8075-8658-7(7),* 807586587) Whitman, Albert & Co.

Hugger, M. A. Danny Malloy & His Mississippi River Samurai. 2008. 132p. 21.95 *(978-0-595-49382-1(3));* pap. 11.95 *(978-0-595-48462-1(X))* iUniverse, Inc.

Hulslander, Dyan. God's Precious Gift. 2009. 24p. pap. 14.99 *(978-1-4389-6903-9(1))* AuthorHouse.

Humphrey, Lisa. A Mother's Promise. Danioth, David, illus. 2004. 32p. (J). per. 15.95 *(978-0-9701907-9-6(4))* Illumination Arts Publishing Co., Inc.

Ibeh, Chinwe. The Moment That Sandra Won. 2011. 28p. pap. 24.95 *(978-1-4626-2938-1(5))* PublishAmerica, Inc.

Inacio, Maria St. Katie's Big Move! 2013. 20p. pap. 17.99 *(978-1-4772-8703-3(5))* AuthorHouse.

Ingold, Jeanette. Mountain Solo. 2005. (ENG.). 320p. (YA). (gr. 7-12). pap. 15.95 *(978-0-15-205358-1(1),* 1062824, Clarion Bks.) HarperCollins Pubs.

Irvin, David. Rusty, the Rainbow Trout: Moving Day. Irvin, Sioux, illus. 2007. 24p. per. 24.95 *(978-1-4241-8455-2(X))* America Star Bks.

Isol. The Menino: A Story Based on Real Events, 1 vol. Amado, Elisa, tr. 2015. (ENG., Illus.). 64p. (J). (— 1). 19.95 *(978-1-55498-778-8(4))* Groundwood Bks. CAN. Dist: Publishers Group West (PGW).

Jacoby, Sarah. Forever or a Day: (Children's Picture Book for Babies & Toddlers, Preschool Book) 2018. (ENG., Illus.).

40p. (J). (gr. -1-k). 17.99 *(978-1-4521-6463-2(0))* Chronicle Bks. LLC.
Jadoul, Émile. Good Night, Chickie. 2010. (ENG.). 26p. (J). (gr. -1-k). 14.00 *(978-0-8028-5378-3(1)*, Eerdmans Bks For Young Readers) Eerdmans, William B. Publishing Co.
Jameson, Catherine. Zoe & the Fawn. Flett, Julie, illus. 2006. (ENG.). 32p. (J). (gr. -1-k). pap. 12.95 *(978-1-894778-43-5(X))* Theytus Bks., Ltd. CAN. Dist: Orca Bk. Pubs. USA.
Jiries, Nariman. Grace-A-Lena Learns the Meaning of Self-Esteem. 2012. 36p. pap. 21.99 *(978-1-4771-0476-7(3))* Xlibris Corp.
Jobling, Curtis. My Daddy. Jobling, Curtis, illus. 2007. (ENG., Illus.). 32p. (J). (gr. -1-k). 9.99 *(978-0-00-722164-6(9)*, HarperCollins Children's Bks.) HarperCollins Pubs. Ltd. GBR. Dist: Independent Pubs. Group.
—My Daddy: Mini Edition. 2004. (Illus.). 32p. (J). 19.99 *(978-0-00-712254-7(3)*, HarperSport) HarperCollins Pubs. Ltd. GBR. Dist: Trafalgar Square Publishing.
Jocham, Tammy. Smiley Meets Twinkle. 2008. 16p. pap. 8.49 *(978-1-4389-2615-5(4))* AuthorHouse.
Joel, Billy. Goodnight, My Angel: A Lullabye. Gilbert, Yvonne, illus. 2004. (J). pap. *(978-0-439-55378-0(4))* Scholastic, Inc.
Johnson, Angela. Heaven, 3 vols. 2006. (J). 44.75 *(978-1-4281-0237-8(X))* Recorded Bks., Inc.
—Heaven. 2010. (ENG.). 160p. (YA). (gr. 7). pap. 10.99 *(978-1-4424-0342-0(X)*, Simon & Schuster Bks. For Young Readers) Simon & Schuster Bks. For Young Readers.
Johnson, Antonia. Bianca's Light. 2009. 28p. pap. 14.99 *(978-1-4389-8951-8(2))* AuthorHouse.
Johnson, Pete. How to Train Your Parents. 2003. (Illus.). 208p. pap. *(978-0-440-86439-4(9)*, Yearling) Random Hse. Children's Bks.
Johnston, Tony. Loving Hands. Bates, Amy June, illus. 2018. (ENG.). 32p. (J). (gr. -1-1). 16.99 *(978-0-7636-7993-4(3))* Candlewick Pr.
Jones, Abigail. Still a Family. 2011. 24p. pap. 15.99 *(978-1-4568-7941-9(3))* Xlibris Corp.
Jones, Debbie Knatt. Maurice ... As Read to the Students in Room D183 & D184. 2013. 150p. pap. 13.95 *(978-1-62516-536-7(6)*, Strategic Bk. Publishing) Strategic Book Publishing & Rights Agency (SBPRA).
Joosse, Barbara M. Papa, Do You Love Me? Lavallee, Barbara, illus. 2005. (Mama & Papa, Do You Love Me? Ser.: MAMA). (ENG.). 36p. (J). (gr. -1-7). 15.99 *(978-0-8118-4265-5(7))* Chronicle Bks. LLC.
Judge, Chris. The Baby Beast. Judge, Chris, illus. 2019. (ENG., Illus.). 32p. (J). (gr. -1-3). 17.99 *(978-1-5415-5512-9(0)*, 21e15890-2df1-45cc-b677-bb69be6c2532) Lerner Publishing Group.
Kabat, Vicki Marsh. Will You Still Love Me? 2012. 28p. pap. 13.99 *(978-1-4624-0346-2(8)*, Inspiring Voices) Author Solutions, LLC.
Kalechofsky, Roberta. A Boy, a Chicken & the Lion of Judah: How Ari Became a Vegetarian. 2012. (ENG., Illus.). 50p. (J). pap. 12.00 *(978-0-916288-58-7(7))* Micah Pubns.
Kane, Sharon. Little Mommy. Kane, Sharon, illus. 2008. (Little Golden Book Ser.). (Illus.). 24p. (J). (gr. -1-2). 5.99 *(978-0-375-84820-9(7)*, Golden Bks.) Random Hse. Children's Bks.
Kathleen, Judith. Attila's Wobbly Birthday Box, 1 vol. 2010. 20p. pap. 24.95 *(978-1-4489-2451-6(0))* PublishAmerica, Inc.
Kaufman Orloff, Karen. I Wanna Iguana. Catrow, David, illus. 2004. 32p. (J). (gr. -1-3). 18.99 *(978-0-399-23717-1(8)*, G.P. Putnam's Sons Books for Young Readers) Penguin Young Readers Group.
Kavanagh, Peter. I Love My Mama. Chapman, Jane, tr. Chapman, Jane, illus. 2003. 32p. (J). 12.95 *(978-1-85430-806-1(8)*, Simon & Schuster Bks. For Young Readers) Simon & Schuster Bks. For Young Readers.
Kaye, Marilyn. Better Late Than Never. 2. 2009. (Gifted Ser.). (ENG.). 224p. (YA). (gr. 6-8). pap. 22.44 *(978-0-7534-6300-0(8)*, 9780753463000) Kingfisher Publications, plc GBR. Dist: Children's Plus, Inc.
Keith, Donna. I Love You All the Same, 1 vol. 2014. (ENG., Illus.). 20p. (J). bds. 9.99 *(978-0-529-10204-1(8)*, Tommy Nelson) Nelson, Thomas Inc.
Kellerhals-Stewart, Heather. Brave Highland Heart. 2004. (Illus.). (J). (gr. k-3). spiral bd. *(978-0-616-01688-6(3))* Canadian National Institute for the Blind/Institut National Canadien pour les Aveugles.
Kelty, Colleen A. Spencer the Spectacular. 2011. 28p. pap. 24.95 *(978-1-4560-1033-1(6))* America Star Bks.
Kemp, Anna. Rhinos Don't Eat Pancakes. Ogilvie, Sara, illus. 2015. (ENG.). 32p. (J). (gr. -1-3). 17.99 *(978-1-4814-3845-2(X)*, Simon & Schuster/Paula Wiseman Bks.) Simon & Schuster/Paula Wiseman Bks.
Kerr, M. E., pseud. I'll Love You When You're More Like Me. 2014. (ENG.). 200p. (gr. 6). pap. 12.95 *(978-1-939601-06-3(1))* Ig Publishing, Inc.
Kevin, Henkes. Owen. 2006. (Coleccion Rascacielos Ser.). (SPA., Illus.). 32p. (gr. k-1). pap. 9.99 *(978-84-241-1519-7(8))* Everest Editora ESP. Dist: Lectorum Pubns., Inc.
Key, Janet Rhyme. Rosa in Bloom. 2013. 86p. (J). pap. 13.95 *(978-1-4817-1956-8(4))* AuthorHouse.
Kim, Cecil. Mommy & Daddy Love You. Ladecka, Anna, illus. 2014. (MySELF Bookshelf Ser.). (ENG.). 32p. (J). (gr. k-2). pap. 11.94 *(978-1-60357-691-8(6))*; lib. bdg. 25.27 *(978-1-59953-656-9(0))* Norwood Hse. Pr.
Kimmel, Haven. Kaline Klattermaster's Tree House. Brown, Peter, illus. 2010. (ENG.). 160p. (J). (gr. 2-7). pap. 7.99 *(978-0-689-87403-1(0)*, Atheneum Bks. for Young Readers) Simon & Schuster Children's Publishing.
Kimmelman, Leslie. You're the Cheese in My Blintz. Kaulitzki, Ramona, illus. 2020. (ENG.). 12p. (J). (gr. -1 — 1). bds. 6.99 *(978-1-5415-3467-4(0)*, 3d66852f-012f-48cc-ab8b-c39cc70b188a, Kar-Ben Publishing) Lerner Publishing Group.
King, Amy Sarig. The Year We Fell from Space (Scholastic Gold) 2021. (ENG.). 288p. (J). (gr. 3-7). pap. 7.99 *(978-1-338-23645-3(8))* Scholastic, Inc.
King-Smith, Dick. Dinosaur Trouble: A Picture Book. Bruel, Nick, illus. 2012. (ENG.). 128p. (J). (gr. 2-5). pap. 16.99 *(978-1-59643-935-1(1)*, 900122930) Roaring Brook Pr.
Kirkman, Rick & Scott, Jerry. Binge Parenting: A Baby Blues Collection. 2017. (Baby Blues Ser.). (ENG., Illus.). 208p. pap. 18.99 *(978-1-4494-8511-5(1))* Andrews McMeel Publishing.
—Gross! A Baby Blues Collection. 2016. (Baby Blues Ser.: 40). (ENG., Illus.). 208p. pap. 18.99 *(978-1-4494-7781-3(X))* Andrews McMeel Publishing.
Kissell, Casey. Awaiting Your Arrival. 2013. 20p. pap. 24.95 *(978-1-62709-188-6(2))* America Star Bks.
Klingensmith, Ryan Lee & Klingensmith, Sherri Ann. Starlight Blue: A New Baby. Rollinger, Marsha, illus. 2012. 32p. pap. 24.95 *(978-1-4626-8219-5(7))* America Star Bks.
Knesek, Marian. Zane & the Armadillo. Leipsic, Regina, illus. 2012. 26p. 24.95 *(978-1-4626-6685-0(X))* America Star Bks.
Kormos, Lawrence A. There Is A Place I Go. 2007. (Illus.). (J). *(978-1-55452-245-3(5))* Essence Publishing.
—What Is Love Mama? 2007. (Illus.). (J). *(978-1-55452-190-6(4))* Essence Publishing.
Krossing, Karen. Pure, 1 vol. 2005. (ENG.). 248p. (YA). (gr. 7-9). per. 10.95 *(978-1-896764-96-2(7))* Second Story Pr. CAN. Dist: Orca Bk. Pubs. USA.
Krug, Ken. No, Silly! Krug, Ken, illus. 2015. (ENG., Illus.). 40p. (J). (gr. -1-3). 17.99 *(978-1-4814-0066-4(5)*, Beach Lane Bks.) Beach Lane Bks.
Kupchella, Rick. Tell Me What We Did Today. Hanson, Warren, illus. (ENG.). 32p. (J). 15.95 *(978-0-9726504-0-3(7))* TRISTAN Publishing, Inc.
Kvasnosky, Laura McGee. Little Wolf's First Howling. Kvasnosky, Laura McGee & McGee, Kate Harvey, illus. 2017. (ENG.). 32p. (J). (gr. -1-2). 17.99 *(978-0-7636-8971-1(8))* Candlewick Pr.
Laditan, Bunmi. The Big Bed. Knight, Tom, illus. 2018. (ENG.). 32p. (J). 18.99 *(978-0-374-30123-1(9)*, 900138493, Farrar, Straus & Giroux (BYR)) Farrar, Straus & Giroux.
Lakin, Patricia. Dad & Me in the Morning. Steele, Robert G., illus. 2019. (ENG.). 32p. (J). (gr. -1-3). pap. 7.99 *(978-0-8075-1420-7(9)*, 807514209) Whitman, Albert & Co.
Lambert, Teres. Mommy, Do You Love Me? 2008. 20p. pap. 24.95 *(978-1-60441-911-5(3))* America Star Bks.
Lane, Sandra M. & Miles, Brenda S. The Moment You Were Born: A Story for You & Your Premature Baby. Hehenberger, Shelly, illus. 2015. 32p. (J). *(978-1-4338-1964-3(3)*, Magination Pr.) American Psychological Assn.
Lapid, Koty. The Wild Virtual Enchanted Garden. 2005. 41p. (J). per. 16.18 *(978-1-4116-2068-1(2))* Lulu Pr., Inc.
Larkin, Susan. All the Ways I Love You. East, Jacqueline, illus. 2014. (J). *(978-1-4351-5821-4(0))* Barnes & Noble, Inc.
LaRochelle, David. How Martha Saved Her Parents from Green Beans. Fearing, Mark, illus. 2013. (ENG.). 32p. (J). (gr. k-3). 17.99 *(978-0-8037-3766-2(1)*, Dial Bks) Penguin Young Readers Group.
Larsen, Mylisa. How to Put Your Parents to Bed. Cole, Babette, illus. 2016. (ENG.). 32p. (J). (gr. -1-3). 17.99 *(978-0-06-232064-3(5)*, HarperCollins) HarperCollins Pubs.
Larson, Susan. Sam (a Pastoral) 2012. (ENG.). 220p. (YA). pap. 12.95 *(978-0-9826069-9-5(0))* Savvy Pr.
Lasky, Kathryn. Before I Was Your Mother. Pham, LeUyen, illus. 2007. (ENG.). 40p. (J). (gr. k-2). 18.69 *(978-0-15-201464-3(0))* Houghton Mifflin Harcourt Publishing Co.
Lawler, Janet. If Kisses Were Colors Board Book. Jay, Alison, illus. 2010. (ENG.). 22p. (J). (gr. -1 — 1). bds. 7.99 *(978-0-8037-3530-9(8)*, Dial Bks) Penguin Young Readers Group.
Layne, Steven L. Over Land & Sea: The Story of International Adoption, 1 vol. Bower, Jan, illus. 2005. (ENG.). 32p. (J). (gr. k-3). 16.99 *(978-1-58980-182-0(2)*, Pelican Publishing) Arcadia Publishing.
Lê, Minh. The Perfect Seat. 2019. (ENG., Illus.). 32p. (J). (gr. -1-3). 16.99 *(978-1-368-02004-6(6))* Hyperion Bks. for Children.
Leach, Sara. Count Me In, 1 vol. 2011. (ENG.). 176p. (J). (gr. 4-7). pap. 9.95 *(978-1-55469-404-4(3))* Orca Bk. Pubs. USA.
Leavey, Peggy Dymond. Growing up Ivy. 2010. (ENG.). 256p. (YA). (gr. 4-8). pap. 10.99 *(978-1-55488-723-1(2))* Dundurn Pr. CAN. Dist: Publishers Group West (PGW).
Ledwidge, Maria. My Salvation Birthday. 2011. 24p. (gr. 2-4). pap. 12.95 *(978-1-4497-1771-1(3)*, WestBow Pr.) Author Solutions, LLC.
Lee, Darrien. Denim Diaries 1: 16 Going On 21. 2008. (Denim Diaries: 1). (ENG., Illus.). 181p. (YA). (gr. 9). 17.00 *(978-1-933967-71-4(4)*, Urban Renaissance) Kensington Publishing Corp.
LeFalle, Deborah. Bitty Brown Babe. Morris, Keisha, illus. 2019. 24p. (J). (gr. -1 — 1). 7.99 *(978-1-5064-4853-4(4)*, Beaming Books) 1517 Media.
L'Engle, Madeleine. Camilla. 2009. (ENG.). 272p. (YA). (gr. 7-12). pap. 18.99 *(978-0-312-56132-1(6)*, 900058867) Square Fish.
Lester, Julius. Pharaoh's Daughter: A Novel of Ancient Egypt. 2009. (ENG., Illus.). 192p. (YA). (gr. 7). pap. 7.99 *(978-0-15-206662-8(4)*, 1099001, Clarion Bks.) HarperCollins Pubs.
—When Dad Killed Mom. 2003. (YA). (gr. 7-12). mass mkt. 6.95 *(978-0-15-524698-0(4)*, Silver Whistle) Harcourt Trade Pubs.
—When Dad Killed Mom. 2003. (ENG.). 216p. (YA). (gr. 7-12). pap. 13.95 *(978-0-15-204698-9(4)*, 1194150, Clarion Bks.) HarperCollins Pubs.
Levine, Arthur A. Monday Is One Day. Hector, Julian, illus. 2015. (ENG.). 32p. (J). (gr. -1-k). 6.99 *(978-0-439-78925-7(7))* Scholastic, Inc.
Lewis, Anne Margaret. Sleeping Bear: Journey of the Cub Book 1. 2012. (ENG.). (J). pap. 8.00 *(978-1-4675-5260-8(7))* Independent Pub.
Lewis-Long, Carla. Why I'm So Special: A Book about Surrogacy. 2010. 44p. pap. 19.95 *(978-1-4389-9656-1(X))* AuthorHouse.
Lewis, Paeony. I'll Always Love You. Ives, Penny, illus. 2004. 32p. (J). pap. 5.95 *(978-1-58925-360-5(4))* Tiger Tales.
Lichtenheld, Tom. What Mess? 2012. (J). lib. bdg. 17.20 *(978-0-606-26686-4(0))* Turtleback.
Lilly, T. S. The Upgrade. 2008. 60p. pap. 16.95 *(978-1-60441-536-0(3))* America Star Bks.
Lindaman, Jane. Zip It! Carlson, Nancy, illus. 2012. (ENG.). 32p. (J). (gr. k-4). lib. bdg. 16.95 *(978-0-7613-5592-2(8)*, 5108e83a-9d94-42c9-95b4-8beb17e21d7d, Carolrhoda Bks.) Lerner Publishing Group.
Linden, Dianne. Peacekeepers. 82p. (J). stu. ed. 9.95 *(978-1-55050-297-8(2))* Coteau Bks. CAN. Dist: Fitzhenry & Whiteside, Ltd.
Lindgren, Astrid. Mio, My Son. Wikland, Ilon, illus. 2003. Tr. of Mio, Min Mio. 179p. (J). 17.95 *(978-1-930900-23-3(6))* Purple Hse. Pr.
Lindsay, Andrew. My Mum & Dad. 2018. (ENG., Illus.). 32p. (J). *(978-1-5289-2408-5(8))*; pap. *(978-1-5289-2406-1(1))* Austin Macauley Pubs. Ltd.
Line, Deirdre. All in the Dark. 2010. 24p. pap. 10.96 *(978-1-4251-4231-5(1))* Trafford Publishing.
Lippman, Laura. Liza Jane & the Dragon. Samworth, Kate, illus. 2018. (ENG.). 32p. (J). 16.95 *(978-1-61775-661-0(X)*, Black Sheep) Akashic Bks.
Living the Life Prequel - Kurtis. 2003. (Living the Life Ser.: Vol. 2). 160p. (YA). pap. 14.00 *(978-0-9710398-3-4(6))* Michael-Christopher Bks.
Livingston, Juwuan. One Word for Good. 2011. 28p. pap. 15.99 *(978-1-4568-4341-0(9))* Xlibris Corp.
Livsey, John. '38: The Great Hurricane in Quonochontaug, Rhode Island. 2004. 288p. (YA). per. 15.49 *(978-0-9754979-2-0(8))* Big Wave Bks.
Lodding, Linda Ravin. The Busy Life of Ernestine Buckmeister. Beaky, Suzanne, illus. 2011. (ENG.). 32p. (J). (gr. -1-1). 16.95 *(978-0-9799746-9-4(0))* Flashlight Pr.
Lopez, Christopher P. The Absolute Truth about Lying. Racine, Victoria, illus. 2011. 36p. pap. 24.95 *(978-1-4626-3245-9(9))* America Star Bks.
Love, Maryann Cusimano. You Are My Miracle. Ichikawa, Satomi, illus. 2012. 30p. (J). (gr. -1 — 1). bds. 7.99 *(978-0-399-25791-9(8)*, Philomel Bks.) Penguin Young Readers Group.
Lovins, Jennifer O. Opihi Baby. 2008. 32p. pap. 14.95 *(978-1-57306-285-5(5))* Bess Pr., Inc.
Lowe, Nakesha. Just Leave Me Alone. 2011. 16p. 10.70 *(978-1-4567-2641-6(2))* AuthorHouse.
Lowry, Brigid. Guitar Highway Rose: A Novel. 2006. (ENG.). 208p. (YA). (gr. 8-12). reprint ed. pap. 18.99 *(978-0-312-34296-8(9)*, 900030465, St. Martin's Griffin) St. Martin's Pr.
Lubbe, Angela C. Don't Forget about Us. 2012. 16p. pap. 15.99 *(978-1-4685-9538-3(5))* AuthorHouse.
Lucado, Max. Just in Case You Ever Wonder, 1 vol. Tharlet, Eve, illus. 2019. (Just in Case Ser.). (ENG.). (J). 30p. bds. 8.99 *(978-0-7180-7539-2(0))*; 32p. 19.99 *(978-0-7180-7538-5(2))* Nelson, Thomas Inc. (Tommy Nelson).
—Just in Case You Ever Wonder, 1 vol. (Just in Case Ser.). 32p. 2011. (ENG.). (J). 16.99 *(978-1-4003-1958-9(7)*, Tommy Nelson) 2009. (ENG.). (J). bds. 12.99 *(978-1-4003-8531-7(8))* 2005. 9.99 *(978-1-4003-0740-1(6))* Nelson, Thomas Inc.
Lukoff, Kyle. When Aidan Became a Brother, 1 vol. Juanita, Kaylani, illus. 2019. (ENG.). 32p. (J). (gr. -1-3). 19.95 *(978-1-62014-837-2(4)*, leelowbooks) Lee & Low Bks., Inc.
Lupica, Mike. Batting Order. (ENG.). (J). (gr. 3-7). 2020. 320p. pap. 8.99 *(978-1-5344-2156-1(4))* 2019. (Illus.). 304p. 19.99 *(978-1-5344-2155-4(6))* Simon & Schuster Bks. For Young Readers. (Simon & Schuster Bks. For Young Readers).
—Safe at Home. 2009. (Comeback Kids Ser.: 2). (ENG.). 192p. (J). (gr. 3-7). 7.99 *(978-0-14-241460-6(3)*, Puffin Books) Penguin Young Readers Group.
Lutz, Lisa. How to Negotiate Everything. Temairik, Jaime, illus. 2013. (ENG.). 32p. (J). (gr. -1-3). 16.99 *(978-1-4424-5119-3(X)*, Simon & Schuster Bks. For Young Readers) Simon & Schuster Bks. For Young Readers.
Lynch, Chris. Iceman. 2013. (ENG.). 176p. (YA). (gr. 7). pap. 10.99 *(978-1-4424-6001-0(6)*, Simon & Schuster Bks. For Young Readers) Simon & Schuster Bks. For Young Readers.
—Iceman. 2013. (ENG.). 160p. (YA). (gr. 7-12). 16.99 *(978-1-4424-6002-7(4))* Simon & Schuster, Inc.
Macaulay, David. Black & White: A Caldecott Award Winner. 2005. (ENG., Illus.). 32p. (J). (gr. -1-3). 8.99 *(978-0-618-63687-7(0)*, 490567, Clarion Bks.) HarperCollins Pubs.
MacDonald, Annie. Bubbles for Poppo. 2011. 32p. pap. 19.95 *(978-1-4520-1720-4(4))* AuthorHouse.
MacDonald, Margaret Read. Tunjur! Tunjur! Tunjur! A Palestinian Folktale, 0 vols. Arzoumanian, Alik, illus. 2012. (ENG.). 32p. (J). (gr. -1-2). pap. 9.99 *(978-0-7614-6312-2(7)*, 9780761463122, Two Lions) Amazon Publishing.
Mace, Aubrey. My Fairy Grandmother. 2009. 270p. pap. 16.99 *(978-1-59955-217-0(5))* Cedar Fort, Inc./CFI Distribution.
Mack, Paulette. Cookout at Grandma's House: The Adventures of Mielle & Cheeky. 2006. (ENG., Illus.). 24p. per. 10.95 *(978-1-59800-998-9(2))* Outskirts Pr., Inc.
MacLachlan, Patricia. The Truth of Me. (ENG.). (J). (gr. 1-5). 2015. 144p. pap. 7.99 *(978-0-06-199861-4(3))* 2013. 128p. 16.99 *(978-0-06-199859-1(1))* HarperCollins Pubs. (Tegen, Katherine Bks).
MacPherson, Lorry. Lynne Woke Up! Alexander, Yvonne Rabdau, illus. 2007. 20p. per. 24.95 *(978-1-4137-2536-0(8))* America Star Bks.
Maddox, Jake. Climbing Strong. 2019. (Jake Maddox JV Ser.). (ENG.). 96p. (J). (gr. 4-6). lib. bdg. 25.99 *(978-1-4965-7524-1(5)*, 139146, Stone Arch Bks.) Capstone.
—Striker's Sister. Wood, Katie, illus. 2018. (Jake Maddox Girl Sports Stories Ser.). (ENG.). 72p. (J). (gr. 3-6). lib. bdg. 25.32 *(978-1-4965-6355-2(7)*, 138071, Stone Arch Bks.) Capstone.
Magnus, Kellie. Little Lion Goes to School. Robinson, Michael, illus. l.t. ed. 2003. 16p. (J). 9.99 *(978-0-9744211-0-0(3))* Media Magic New York.
Magsamen, Sandra. Good Night, My Love. Magsamen, Sandra, illus. 2018. (ENG., Illus.). 10p. (J). (gr. -1 — 1). bds. 8.99 *(978-1-338-11093-7(4)*, Cartwheel Bks.) Scholastic, Inc.
—I Love You, Honey Bunny (Made with Love) Magsamen, Sandra, illus. 2016. (Made with Love Ser.). (ENG., Illus.). 14p. (J). (— 1). bds. 7.99 *(978-1-338-11084-5(5)*, Cartwheel Bks.) Scholastic, Inc.
—Welcome Little One. 2015. (Welcome Little One Baby Gift Collection). (ENG., Illus.). 24p. (J). (-1). bds. 7.99 *(978-1-4926-3264-1(3)*, 9781492632641) Sourcebooks, Inc.
Maier, Inger. When Fuzzy Was Afraid of Losing His Mother. Candon, Jennifer, illus. 2004. 32p. (J). 14.95 *(978-1-59147-168-4(0)*, Magination Pr.) American Psychological Assn.
Maier, Inger M. When Fuzzy Was Afraid: Of Losing His Mother. Candon, Jennifer, illus. 2004. 32p. (J). pap. 9.95 *(978-1-59147-169-1(9)*, Magination Pr.) American Psychological Assn.
Malone, Jen. Changes in Latitudes. 2017. (ENG.). 384p. (YA). (gr. 8). pap. 9.99 *(978-0-06-238017-3(6)*, HarperTeen) HarperCollins Pubs.
Mansfield, Creina. My Nutty Neighbours. 2006. (ENG., Illus.). 192p. (J). pap. 12.95 *(978-0-86278-788-2(2))* O'Brien Pr., Ltd., The IRL. Dist: Dufour Editions, Inc.
Markham, Dorothy & O'Donnell, Aileen. All about Ben: Helping Children with Attachment Issues to Understand Their Feelings. O'Donnell, Aileen, illus. 2018. (Illus.). 40p. (C). pap. 14.95 *(978-1-78592-499-6(0)*, 696838) Kingsley, Jessica Pubs. GBR. Dist: Hachette UK Distribution.
Martella, Liz. Izabella & her Wardrobe. 2007. 18p. 12.95 *(978-0-615-14941-7(3))* Martella, Liz.
Martin, Emily Winfield. The Wonderful Things You Will Be. 2015. (ENG., Illus.). 36p. (J). (gr. -1-2). 17.99 *(978-0-385-37671-6(5))*; lib. bdg. 20.99 *(978-0-375-97327-7(3))* Random Hse. Children's Bks. (Random Hse. Bks. for Young Readers).
Martinez Jover, Carmen. The Twin Kangaroo Treasure Hunt, a Gay Parenting Story. Martinez, Rosemary, illus. 2013. 32p. pap. *(978-607-00-6545-3(X))* Martinez Jover, María del Carmen Dorotea.
Marzollo, Jean. Mama Mama/Papa Papa Flip Board Book. Regan, Laura, illus. 2003. (ENG.). 32p. (J). (gr. -1 — 1). bds. 7.99 *(978-0-06-051915-5(0)*, HarperFestival) HarperCollins Pubs.
Massie, Elizabeth. Ameri-Scares: Virginia. 2013. 150p. (J). pap. 12.99 *(978-1-937530-52-5(3)*, Wonderstruck Bks.) Crossroad Pr.
Masurel, Claire. Two Homes. Denton, Kady MacDonald, illus. 2003. (ENG.). 40p. (J). (gr. -1-2). 7.99 *(978-0-7636-1984-8(1))* Candlewick Pr.
—Two Homes. 2003. 17.20 *(978-0-613-69470-4(8))* Turtleback.
Max, Max, illus. Thumbelina/Pulgarcita. 2004. (Bilingual Fairy Tales Ser.: BILI). (ENG.). 32p. (J). (gr. -1-7). 14.99 *(978-0-8118-3927-3(3))* Chronicle Bks. LLC.
Mayes, Joanne. I'm Isaac; My Brain is Green. 2008. 27p. pap. 24.95 *(978-1-60563-984-0(2))* America Star Bks.
Mazer, Norma Fox. What I Believe. 2007. (ENG., Illus.). 176p. (J). (gr. 5-9). pap. 12.95 *(978-0-15-206283-5(1))* Houghton Mifflin Harcourt Publishing Co.
—When We First Met. 2015. (ENG., Illus.). 208p. (YA). (gr. 7). pap. 14.99 *(978-1-4814-5103-1(0)*, Atheneum Bks. for Young Readers) Simon & Schuster Children's Publishing.
McBratney, Sam. Guess How Much I Love You: Baby Book. Jeram, Anita, illus. 2014. (Guess How Much I Love You Ser.). (ENG.). 64p. (J). (gr. -1 — 1). 16.99 *(978-0-7636-7023-8(5))* Candlewick Pr.
—A Surprise for the Nutbrown Hares. Jeram, Anita, illus. 2009. (J). *(978-0-7636-4903-6(1))* Candlewick Pr.
—There, There. Bates, Ivan, illus. 2015. (ENG.). 32p. (J). (-k). bds. 7.99 *(978-0-7636-7565-3(2)*, Templar) Candlewick Pr.
—You're All My Favorites. Jeram, Anita, illus. 2008. (ENG.). 32p. (J). (gr. k-k). bds. 7.99 *(978-0-7636-4297-6(5))* Candlewick Pr.
McCaughrean, Geraldine. Casting the Gods Adrift: A Tale of Ancient Egypt. Ludlow, Patricia D., illus. 2003. (ENG.). 112p. (J). (gr. 4-7). 15.95 *(978-0-8126-2684-1(2))* Cricket Bks.
Mccauley, Plum. It All Started with A Bicycle. 2011. (ENG.). 220p. pap. 11.95 *(978-1-4327-7412-7(3))* Outskirts Pr., Inc.
McCourt, Lisa. I Love You, Stinky Face. Moore, Cyd, illus. (ENG.). 32p. (J). (gr. -1 — 1). 2004. bds. 6.99 *(978-0-439-63572-1(1))* 2003. pap. 6.99 *(978-0-439-63469-4(5))* Scholastic, Inc.
McGhee, Alison. So Many Days. Yoo, Taeeun, illus. 2010. (ENG.). 40p. (J). (gr. k-2). 15.99 *(978-1-4169-5857-4(6)*, Atheneum Bks. for Young Readers) Simon & Schuster Children's Publishing.
McGriff, Shawna A. Princess Pink: Princess Pink Helps Zion, Melinda, & Jasmine Learn to Communicate about Their Parents' Divorces. 2010. 56p. pap. 24.00 *(978-1-4520-3941-1(0))* AuthorHouse.
McKay, Lise Y. The Mysterious Well. 2012. 130p. pap. 14.95 *(978-1-59663-865-5(6)*, Mount Helicon Pr.) Rock, James A. & Co. Pubs.
McKee, David. El Principe Pedro y el oso de Peluche. (SPA.). (J). 7.95 *(978-958-04-6258-3(5))* Norma S.A. COL. Dist: Distribuidora Norma, Inc.
McKellop, Holly R. To the Moon. 2012. 32p. pap. 24.95 *(978-1-4626-8034-4(8))* America Star Bks.
McNaney, Jeanne. Miracle in Sumatra: The Story of Gutsy Gus. Cochard, David, illus. 2009. (ENG.). 32p. (J). (gr. -1-3). 16.95 *(978-0-9814534-6-0(5))* Ovation Bks.
McNeal, Laura & McNeal, Tom. Crooked. 2007. (ENG.). 368p. (YA). (gr. 7-11). pap. 9.99 *(978-0-375-84191-0(1)*, Ember) Random Hse. Children's Bks.
McOmber, Rachel B., ed. McOmber Phonics Storybooks: Mom & Dad Hop-Jig. rev. ed. (Illus.). (J). *(978-0-944991-16-9(5))* Swift Learning Resources.
McTrustry, Chris. Red Goes Green, 1 vol. rev. ed. 2013. (Literary Text Ser.). (ENG., Illus.). 32p. (J). (gr. 3-4). pap. 11.99 *(978-1-4333-5641-4(4))* Teacher Created Materials, Inc.
McVicar, William E. Turtle Tries. 2008. 16p. pap. 24.95 *(978-1-60563-180-6(9))* America Star Bks.
Meagher, Ed. D. Zach & His Dog: A Story of Bonding, Love, & Loss for Children & Adults to Share Together. 2009. 56p. pap. 23.99 *(978-1-4389-4228-5(1))* AuthorHouse.
Mean Margaret. 2014. (ENG., Illus.). 176p. (J). (gr. 2-7). 16.99 *(978-1-4814-1014-4(8)*, Atheneum Bks. for Young Readers) Simon & Schuster Children's Publishing.
Meron, Renato Mas. Why Corn Kernels Pop Up. 2012. 24p. pap. 24.95 *(978-1-62709-859-5(3))* America Star Bks.
Metzger, Steve. I Love You All Year Long. Keay, Claire, illus. 2009. 20p. (J). (gr. -1-k). 8.95 *(978-1-58925-847-1(9))* Tiger Tales.
Michaels, Kat. Gentle Is the Night. 2008. (J). 15.95 *(978-0-9745052-7-5(7))* Tree Of Life Publishing.
Middlestadt, Donna. Little Miss No Name. 2004. (ENG.). 218p. pap. 24.95 *(978-1-4137-0894-3(3))* America Star Bks.

Mike. New Pet. Mike, illus. l.t. ed. 2005. (ENG., Illus.). 32p. (J). lib. bdg. 14.95 (978-0-9658365-8-6(4)) Beetle Bug Bks.

Millmann, Anita Sutherland. Zitta & Nelli. 2011. 24p. pap. 15.14 (978-1-4634-0036-1(5)) AuthorHouse.

Mlawer, Teresa, tr. Fix It!/¡a Reparar! Birkett, Georgie, illus. 2009. (Helping Hands English/Spanish Edition Ser.). (ENG.). 24p. (J). (gr. -1-k). pap. (978-1-84643-571-3(4)) Child's Play International Ltd.

—Grow It!/¡a Sembrar! Birkett, Georgie, illus. 2009. (Helping Hands English/Spanish Edition Ser.). (ENG.). 24p. (J). (gr. -1-k). pap. (978-1-84643-570-6(6)) Child's Play International Ltd.

Mohler, Marie. Little Bird's Earth Nest. 2008. 32p. 18.95 (978-1-4357-1711-4(2)) Lulu Pr., Inc.

Monte, Diane E. Coming Home: Welcome Home at Last. 2012. 24p. pap. 17.99 (978-1-4772-5713-5(6)) AuthorHouse.

Moore, Katherine Roberts. Is God Behind the Big Blue Sky? Moore, Kristen L., illus. 2010. 34p. pap. 13.95 (978-1-60911-705-4(0), Eloquent Bks.) Strategic Book Publishing & Rights Agency (SBPRA).

Moran, Alex & Sullivan, Paula. Todd's Box. 2004. (Green Light Readers Level 1 Ser.). (gr. -1-2). 13.50 (978-0-613-81968-8(3)) Turtleback.

Moreillon, Judi. Read to Me. Teis, Kyra, illus. 2003. 24p. (J). 6.95 (978-1-932065-49-7(0), 1-718-784-9112) Star Bright Bks., Inc.

—Read to Me: English, 1 vol. Teis, Kyra, illus. 2004. (ENG.). 32p. (J). (gr. -1). bds. 6.95 (978-1-59572-014-6(6)) Star Bright Bks., Inc.

Moreira, Carol. Charged, 1 vol. 2008. (Lorimer SideStreets Ser.). (ENG.). 128p. (YA). (gr. 9-12). 8.99 (978-1-55277-006-1(0), a88d78ef-84e3-4b69-9b8a-16564cc191e0); 16.95 (978-1-55277-008-5(7), 008) James Lorimer & Co. Ltd., Pubs. CAN. Dist: Lerner Publishing Group, Formac Lorimer Bks. Ltd.

Morgan, Melissa J. Grace's Twist #3. 2005. (Camp Confidential Ser.: 3). (ENG.). 160p. (J). (gr. 3-7). mass mkt. 4.99 (978-0-448-43875-7(5), Grosset & Dunlap) Penguin Young Readers Group.

Moriarty, Jaclyn. The Extremely Inconvenient Adventures of Bronte Mettlestone. 2018. (ENG., Illus.). 384p. (J). (gr. 3-7). 17.99 (978-1-338-25584-3(3), Levine, Arthur A. Bks.) Scholastic, Inc.

Morrow, Tara Jaye. Just Mommy & Me. Bratun, Katy, illus. 2004. 32p. (J). 13.89 (978-0-06-000725-6(7)) HarperCollins Pubs.

Mossiano, Lilly. My New Mommy. Mossiano, Sage, illus. 2012. 28p. pap. 24.95 (978-1-4626-8898-2(5)) PublishAmerica, Inc.

Mulholland, Clara. Naughty Miss Bunny. 2007. 128p. 25.95 (978-1-4218-3838-0(9), 1st World Library - Literary Society) 1st World Publishing, Inc.

Munsch, Robert. Love You Forever. 2014. (ENG.). 32p. (J). (gr. 3-7). 10.20 (978-1-63245-248-1(0)) Lectorum Pubns., Inc.

Murphy, Mary. I Like It When ... Board Book. Murphy, Mary, illus. 2005. (ENG., Illus.). 22p. (J). (gr. k — 1). bds. 7.99 (978-0-15-205649-0(1), 1196986, Clarion Bks.) HarperCollins Pubs.

—I Like It When ... /Me Gusta Cuando ... Bilingual English-Spanish. Murphy, Mary, illus. 2008. (ENG., Illus.). 22p. (J). (gr. -1-k). bds. 7.99 (978-0-15-206045-9(6), 1198156, Clarion Bks.) HarperCollins Pubs.

—Utterly Lovely One. 2012. (ENG., Illus.). 32p. (J). (gr. -1-k). 16.99 (978-0-7636-5267-8(9)) Candlewick Pr.

Murphy, Stuart J. Happy, Healthy Ajay! 2012. (I See I Learn Ser.: 12). (ENG., Illus.). 32p. (J). (-k). pap. 7.99 (978-1-58089-471-5(2)) Charlesbridge Publishing, Inc.

My Father the Mad Professor: Individual Title Six-Packs. (Action Packs Ser.). 120p. (gr. 3-5). 44.00 (978-0-7635-8424-5(X)) Rigby Education.

My Name Is Really Lucy! 2003. (J). pap. (978-0-9745591-1-7(3)) Roehm, Nancy Jean.

Myers, Anna. Tulsa Burning. 2004. (Illus.). 184p. (J). (gr. 3-7). 16.95 (978-0-8027-8829-0(7)) Walker & Co.

Myers, Walter Dean. The Dream Bearer. 2003. (ENG.). 192p. (J). (gr. 5-18). 15.99 (978-0-06-029521-9(X), Amistad) HarperCollins Pubs.

Nelson, Annabelle. Angelica's Hope: A Story for Young People & Their Parents about the Need to Talk about Things That No One Talks About. Palomares, Franz, illus. 2003. (SPA.). (978-0-9656732-9-7(4)) WHEEL Council, Inc., The.

Nelson, Theresa. Ruby Electric. 2004. (ENG.). 272p. (J). (gr. 5-7). reprint ed. pap. 12.99 (978-0-689-87146-7(5), Atheneum Bks. for Young Readers) Simon & Schuster Children's Publishing.

Neufeld, John. Edgar Allan. 2007. 136p. (gr. 5-9). per. 11.95 (978-0-595-45039-8(3), Backinprint.com) iUniverse, Inc.

Neville, Emily Cheney. It's Like This, Cat: A Newbery Award Winner. Weiss, Emil, illus. 2019. (ENG.). 176p. (J). (gr. 5-9). pap. 7.99 (978-0-06-440073-2(5), HarperCollins) HarperCollins Pubs.

Newman, Leslea. The Boy Who Cried Fabulous. Ferguson, Peter, illus. 2007. 32p. (J). (gr. -1-2). pap. 7.99 (978-1-58246-224-0(0), Tricycle Pr.) Random Hse. Children's Bks.

Newswanger, Rebecca. God Gave Us Fathers & Mothers. Steiner, Maria, illus. 2009. (Little Jewel Book Ser.). 24p. (J). (gr. 2). pap. 2.70 (978-0-7399-2408-2(7)) Rod & Staff Pubs., Inc.

The Night Before Kindergarten. 2014. (Night Before Ser.). (ENG.). 32p. (J). (gr. 7-12). 8.24 (978-1-63245-263-4(4)) Lectorum Pubns., Inc.

Nixon, Joan Lowery. John's Story, 1775. 2004. (J). (978-0-87935-228-8(0)) Colonial Williamsburg Foundation.

—Will's Story, 1771. 2004. (J). (978-0-87935-226-4(4)) Colonial Williamsburg Foundation.

Nkemayang, Chelsea. Split Ville. 2012. (Illus.). 36p. pap. 22.88 (978-1-4772-4177-6(9)) AuthorHouse.

Nolan, Han. Born Blue. 2003. (ENG.). 308p. (YA). (gr. 9-12). pap. 9.99 (978-0-15-204697-2(6), 1194147, Clarion Bks.) HarperCollins Pubs.

Nolen, Jerdine. Hewitt Anderson's Great Big Life. Nelson, Kadir, illus. (ENG.). 40p. (J). (gr. k-3). 2013. 8.99 (978-1-4424-6035-5(0)) 2005. 19.99 (978-0-689-86866-5(9)) Simon & Schuster/Paula Wiseman Bks. (Simon & Schuster/Paula Wiseman Bks.).

Novel Units. It's Like This, Cat Novel Units Teacher Guide. 2019. (ENG.). (J). pap. 12.99 (978-1-56137-101-3(7), Novel Units, Inc.) Classroom Library Co.

Novick, Rona Milch. Mommy, Can You Stop the Rain? Kubaszewska, Anna, illus. 2020. (ENG.). 32p. (J). 17.95 (978-1-68115-555-5(9), 0af463f0-a462-4701-8221-bd14af153516, Apples & Honey Pr.) Behrman Hse., Inc.

Oates, Joyce Carol. Freaky Green Eyes. 2003. 352p. (J). 16.99 (978-0-06-623759-6(9)) 2005. (ENG.). 368p. (YA). (gr. 8). reprint ed. pap. 10.99 (978-0-06-447348-4(1)) HarperCollins Pubs. (HarperTeen).

Ockun, Lisa C. Sammy the Tin Man. 2012. 32p. pap. 19.99 (978-1-4685-4328-5(8)) AuthorHouse.

O'Connell, Rebecca. The Baby Goes Beep. Wilson-Max, Ken, illus. 2010. (ENG.). 16p. (J). (gr. -1 — 1). bds. 7.99 (978-0-8075-0508-3(0), 807505080) Whitman, Albert & Co.

—Baby Parade. Poole, Susie, illus. 2017. (ENG.). 24p. (J). (gr. -1 — 1). bds. 7.99 (978-0-8075-0515-1(3), 807505153) Whitman, Albert & Co.

O'Dare, Helen. Love. O'Byrne, Nicola, illus. 2016. (ENG.). 26p. (J). (gr. -1 — 1). bds. 6.99 (978-1-62686-677-5(5), Silver Dolphin Bks.) Printers Row Publishing Group.

Odom, Leslie, Jr. & Robinson, Nicolette. I Love You More Than You'll Ever Know. Ruiz, Joy Hwang, illus. 2023. (ENG.). 32p. (J). 17.99 (978-1-250-26564-7(9), 900222067) Feiwel & Friends.

On the Job: Individual Title Six-Packs. (gr. -1-2). 27.00 (978-0-7635-9468-8(7)) Rigby Education.

Orgill, Rosanne Buhler. Mama Knows about Fences. 2008. 36p. 18.99 (978-1-4343-2689-8(6)) AuthorHouse.

Orr, Fran E. When Mommy Was a Soldier, 1 vol. 2008. (ENG.). 26p. 24.95 (978-1-4241-9576-3(4)) America Star Bks.

Pallone, Robert. The Adventures of Main Man: A Child's View of the World. 2010. 28p. pap. 12.95 (978-1-4490-5598-1(2)) AuthorHouse.

Palmer, Catherine. Fatal Harvest. l.t. ed. 2004. (Matthew 25 Ser.). 496p. (YA). 28.95 (978-0-7862-6259-5(1)) Thorndike Pr.

Parish, Herman. Amelia Bedelia Chapter Book #2: Amelia Bedelia Unleashed (Special Edition) 2013. (ENG., Illus.). 160p. (J). (978-0-06-227056-6(7), Harper Design) HarperCollins Pubs.

Park, Linda Sue. Gondra's Treasure. Reinhardt, Jennifer Black, illus. 2019. (ENG.). 40p. (J). (gr. -1-3). 17.99 (978-0-544-54669-1(5), 1609531, Clarion Bks.) HarperCollins Pubs.

Parker, Marjorie Blain. I Love You near & Far. Henry, Jed, illus. 2015. 24p. (J). (gr. -1-1). 9.95 (978-1-4549-0507-3(7)) Sterling Publishing Co., Inc.

Parker, Vicki Sue. The Get Well Soon... Balloon. Beebe, Susan, illus. 2005. 16p. (J). 15.00 (978-1-931117-35-7(7), BALL) Lash & Assocs. Publishing/Training, Inc.

Parkinson, Betsy. The Picky Eater. Clester, Shane, illus. 2018. (Little Boost Ser.). (ENG.). 32p. (J). (gr. -1-2). 14.95 (978-1-5158-2943-0(X), 138476); lib. bdg. 23.99 (978-1-5158-2942-3(1), 138475) Capstone. (Picture Window Bks.).

Paterson, Katherine. El Signo del Crisantemo. 2003.Tr. of Sign of the Chrysanthemum. (SPA., Illus.). 142p. (YA). (gr. 5-8). (978-84-348-6699-7(4), SM30544) SM Ediciones ESP. Dist: Lectorum Pubns., Inc.

Pau Pau. Bird Bandit, 1 vol. 2010. 56p. pap. 16.95 (978-1-4489-3991-6(7)) America Star Bks.

Paul, Ann Whitford. If Animals Celebrated Christmas. Walker, David, illus. (If Animals Kissed Good Night Ser.). (ENG.). (J). 2019. 24p. bds. 7.99 (978-0-374-31308-1(3), 900209754) 2018. 32p. 16.99 (978-0-374-30901-5(9), 900188209) Farrar, Straus & Giroux. (Farrar, Straus & Giroux (BYR)).

—If Animals Kissed Good Night. Walker, David, illus. 2014. (If Animals Kissed Good Night Ser.). (ENG.). 34p. (J). (gr. -1-1). bds. 7.99 (978-0-374-30021-0(6), 900129088, Farrar, Straus & Giroux (BYR)) Farrar, Straus & Giroux.

Peck, J. L. Mr Crabby Pants & the Zoo. 2012. 24p. pap. 17.99 (978-1-4685-7953-6(3)) AuthorHouse.

Pentz, Jane A. Horatio's Magical Journeys - Horatio's New Book. 2007. 108p. pap. 10.00 (978-1-892426-10-9(2)) LMA Publishing.

Perryman, Kawanis. Gabrielle's Prayer: Gabrielle's Wish. 2011. 28p. pap. 13.59 (978-1-4567-2731-4(1)) AuthorHouse.

Peters, Julie Anne. Define "Normal" 2003. (ENG., Illus.). 208p. (J). (gr. 7-17). pap. 10.99 (978-0-316-73489-9(6)) Little, Brown Bks. for Young Readers.

Picou, Lin. Do I Have To ... Reese, Bob, illus. 2011. (Little Birdie Readers Ser.). (ENG.). 24p. (gr. 1-2). 28.50 (978-1-61741-816-7(1), 9781617418167) Rourke Educational Media.

Pierre, Eileen. It's Not Easy Being Mean. 2010. 56p. pap. 10.00 (978-1-60860-929-1(4), Eloquent Bks.) Strategic Book Publishing & Rights Agency (SBPRA).

Pinkham, Mark Amaru. Love Me Later. 2005. 202p. 14.95 (978-1-932188-02-8(9)) Adventures Unlimited Pr.

Pinkwater, Daniel M. Mrs. Noodlekugel. Stower, Adam, illus. 2013. (Mrs. Noodlekugel Ser.: 1). (ENG.). 80p. (J). (gr. k-4). pap. 7.99 (978-0-7636-6452-7(9)) Candlewick Pr.

Pinocchio: 6 Small Books. (gr. k-2). 23.00 (978-0-7635-8513-6(0)) Rigby Education.

Pitman, Gayle E. My Maddy. Tobacco, Violet, illus. 2020. 32p. (J). (978-1-4338-3044-0(2), Magination Pr.) American Psychological Assn.

Pixton, Kaaren. Indestructibles: Mama & Baby! Chew Proof · Rip Proof · Nontoxic · 100% Washable (Book for Babies, Newborn Books, Safe to Chew) 2010. (Indestructibles Ser.). (ENG., Illus.). 12p. (J). (gr. -1 — 1). pap. 5.99 (978-0-7611-5859-2(6), 15859) Workman Publishing Co., Inc.

Powers, Elizabeth. Where Are You Taking Me? 2008. 28p. pap. 24.95 (978-1-60563-033-5(0)) America Star Bks.

Powers, John. Seymour & the Big Red Rhino. Colavecchio, Alan, illus. 2005. 32p. (J). (gr. -1-3). 14.95 (978-1-929039-21-0(2)) Ambassador Bks., Inc.

Preble, Joy. The Sweet Dead Life. 2014. (Sweet Dead Life Novel Ser.). (Illus.). 244p. (YA). (gr. 9). pap. 10.99 (978-1-61695-368-3(3), Soho Teen) Soho Pr., Inc.

Preiss, Thomas. The Boat under the Boat: A Story about the Golden Rule. 2nd rev. ed. 2004. (ENG., Illus.). 32p. (J). per. 14.95 (978-0-9798620-1-4(9)) Peralta Publishing, LLC.

Prince, Mark E. I'm Happy When. 2009. 20p. pap. 12.99 (978-1-4389-5523-0(5)) AuthorHouse.

Prins, Piet. Stefan Derksen's Polar Adventure. 2004. (Illus.). 237p. (J). pap. (978-1-894666-67-1(4)) Inheritance Pubns.

Propp, Vera W. When the Soldiers Were Gone: A Novel. 2006. 101p. (J). (gr. 4-8). reprint ed. 15.00 (978-1-4223-5310-3(9)) DIANE Publishing Co.

Quillen, Donna Mc. I Can't Wait. 2011. 50p. 24.99 (978-1-4628-8475-9(X)); pap. 15.99 (978-1-4628-8474-2(1)) Xlibris Corp.

Quinn, David. Go to Sleep, Little Creep. Spires, Ashley, illus. 2018. 32p. (J). (-k). 17.99 (978-1-101-93944-4(3), Crown Books For Young Readers) Random Hse. Children's Bks.

Quivers, Anthony S. Lil' Johnny's First Day of School. 2010. 24p. 13.99 (978-1-4520-4149-0(0)) AuthorHouse.

Rabe, Tish. Love You, Hug You, Read to You! Endersby, Frank, illus. 2015. (ENG.). 32p. (J). (gr. -1 — 1). bds. 8.99 (978-1-101-93655-9(X), Random Hse. Bks. for Young Readers) Random Hse. Children's Bks.

—¡Te Amo, Te Abrazo, Leo Contigo!/Love You, Hug You, Read to You! Endersby, Frank, illus. 2015. 32p. (J). (gr. -1 — 1). bds. 7.99 (978-1-101-93657-3(6), Random Hse. Bks. for Young Readers) Random Hse. Children's Bks.

Rainwater, Crystal. Song the Slug; Book 1, 1 vol. 2010. 24p. pap. 24.95 (978-1-4489-4215-2(2)) PublishAmerica, Inc.

Raisinghani, Jaya. Sweet Child of Mine. 2014. 16p. pap. 15.00 (978-1-4828-9218-5(9)) Partridge Pub.

—Sweet Child of Mine. 2012. 16p. pap. 15.00 (978-1-4669-3099-5(3)) Trafford Publishing.

Ramos, Jorge. I'm Just Like My Mom; I'm Just Like My Dad/Me Parezco Tanto a Mi Mama; Me Parez: Bilingual Spanish-English. Gutierrez, Akemi, illus. 2008.Tr. of Me Parezco Tanto a mi Papá. (ENG.). 40p. (J). (gr. -1-3). 16.99 (978-0-06-123968-7(2)) HarperCollins Español.

Rawlings, Marjorie Kinnan. The Yearling. Wyeth, N. C., illus. 2013. (Scribner Classics Ser.). (ENG.). 416p. (J). (gr. 5-9). 29.99 (978-1-4424-8209-8(5), Atheneum Bks. for Young Readers) Simon & Schuster Children's Publishing.

Rayner, Robert. Libby on Strike, 1 vol. 2008. (Lorimer Streetlights Ser.). (ENG.). 120p. (J). (gr. 2-4). 8.95 (978-1-55277-034-4(6), 034) James Lorimer & Co. Ltd., Pubs. CAN. Dist: Formac Lorimer Bks. Ltd.

Reedy, Trent. Gamer Army. 2018. (ENG.). 336p. (J). (gr. 3-7). 17.99 (978-1-338-04529-1(6), Levine, Arthur A. Bks.) Scholastic, Inc.

Reichert, Amy. While Mama Had a Quick Little Chat. Boiger, Alexandra, illus. 2005. (ENG.). 40p. (J). (gr. -1-2). 19.99 (978-0-689-85170-4(7), Atheneum/Richard Jackson Bks.) Simon & Schuster Children's Publishing.

Reiser, Lynn. You & Me, Baby. Gentieu, Penny, photos by. 2008. (ENG., Illus.). 32p. (J). (— 1). bds. 6.99 (978-0-375-84420-1(1), Knopf Bks. for Young Readers) Random Hse. Children's Bks.

Renninson, Lou. Frontalknutschen. pap. 17.95 (978-3-570-30008-4(0)) Bertelsman, Verlagsgruppe C. GmbH DEU. Dist: Distribooks, Inc.

Reynolds, Peter H. Love You by Heart. Reynolds, Peter H., illus. 2022. (ENG., Illus.). 32p. (J). (gr. -1-k). 9.99 (978-1-338-78363-6(7), Orchard Bks.) Scholastic, Inc.

RH Disney Staff & Disney Enterprises Inc. Staff. Best Dad in the Sea. 2003. (Step into Reading - Level 1 Ser.). (gr. k-3). lib. bdg. 13.55 (978-0-613-73685-5(0)) Turtleback.

Richmond, Lori. Bunny's Staycation (Mama's Business Trip) 2018. (ENG., Illus.). 32p. (J). (gr. -1-k). 17.99 (978-0-545-92589-1(4), Scholastic Pr.) Scholastic, Inc.

Richmond, Marianne. I Love You So... (Marianne Richmond Ser.: 0). (J). 2018. 26p. (gr. -1-k). bds. 8.99 (978-1-4926-7511-2(3)) 2015. 24p. bds. 8.99 (978-1-4926-3381-5(X)) Sourcebooks, Inc. (Sourcebooks Jabberwocky).

—If I Could Keep You Little..., (J). 2018. (Marianne Richmond Ser.: 0). (Illus.). 26p. (gr. -1-k). bds. 8.99 (978-1-4926-7510-5(5)) 2012. 24p. (gr. -1-k). bds. 8.99 (978-1-4022-7237-0(5)) 2010. (Marianne Richmond Ser.: 0). 32p. 9.95 (978-1-934082-92-8(9)) Sourcebooks, Inc. (Sourcebooks Jabberwocky).

Rideau, Nicole. What Is a Pookalaka? 2009. 28p. pap. 13.99 (978-1-4389-2275-1(2)) AuthorHouse.

Rigby Education Staff. Cinderella: Jumbled Tumble. (gr. k-2). 26.00 (978-0-7635-2420-3(4)) Rigby Education.

—Pinocchio: Jumbled Tumble. (gr. k-2). 26.00 (978-0-7635-2419-7(0)) Rigby Education.

—William Tell. (gr. k-2). 21.00 (978-0-7635-2426-5(3)) Rigby Education.

Rigby, Jill. I Put It Right There! I Swear! The story of one boy's master plan to overcome executive functioning Difficulties! 2011. 28p. pap. 12.77 (978-1-4634-3710-7(2)) AuthorHouse.

Riley-Collins, Jennifer. Daddy God. 2007. (J). pap. (978-0-9791374-1-9(1)) Favored Publishing, Inc.

Rinaldi, Ann. The Secret of Sarah Revere. 2003. (Great Episodes Ser.). (ENG.). 336p. (J). (gr. 5-7). pap. 9.99 (978-0-15-204684-2(4), 1194115, Clarion Bks.) HarperCollins Pubs.

Rinker, Sherri Duskey. How to Put an Octopus to Bed: (Going to Bed Book, Read-Aloud Bedtime Book for Kids) Schwarz, Viviane, illus. 2020. (ENG.). 40p. (J). (gr. -1-k). 17.99 (978-1-4521-4010-0(3)) Chronicle Bks. LLC.

Roberts, Mary. Once upon A Monday. Lipe, Barbara, illus. 2004. 48p. (J). per. 19.95 (978-0-9744412-0-7(1)) DinRo.

Roberts, Patricia Gaskins. My Friend Tommy Has a Daddy & a Mommy. Adams, Stephen, illus. 2012. (ENG.). 24p. pap. 17.99 (978-1-4772-3273-6(7)) AuthorHouse.

Robinson, David. My Little Man. 2013. 20p. pap. 24.95 (978-1-63004-427-5(X)) America Star Bks.

Rock, Brian. With All My Heart. Banta, Susan, illus. 2012. (ENG.). 24p. (J). (978-1-58925-648-4(4)) Tiger Tales.

Rodgers, Mary. Freaky Friday. 2009. (ENG.). 192p. (J). (gr. 5-18). reprint ed. pap. 9.99 (978-0-06-440046-6(8), HarperCollins) HarperCollins Pubs.

Rodriguez, Michelle. Never Far Away. 2013. 26p. pap. 9.99 (978-0-9900061-0-7(7)) Rodriguez, Michelle.

Rokhsar, Lillian. Babytionary. Bell, Liesl, illus. 2012. (ENG.). 40p. 17.99 (978-0-9884922-0-2(2)) Begoo Bks., LLC.

Rooney, Jodie C. Feather in Your Cap, 1 vol. 2008. (ENG.). 19p. 24.95 (978-1-60474-390-6(5)) America Star Bks.

Rosanbalm, Sunny, illus. A Gift for Baby. 2009. (SPA & ENG.). (978-0-9685754-7-5(1)) Natural Child Project Society, The.

Rosen, Marvin. Becca in Cyberland, 1 vol. 2010. 48p. pap. 16.95 (978-1-4489-9831-9(X)) America Star Bks.

Rossetti-Shustak, Bernadette. I Love You Through & Through. Church, Caroline Jayne, illus. 2005. (ENG.). 24p. (J). (gr. -1 — 1). bds. 8.95 (978-0-439-67363-1(1), Cartwheel Bks.) Scholastic, Inc.

—I Love You Through & Through / Te Quiero, Yo Te Quiero (Bilingual) (Bilingual Edition) Church, Caroline Jayne, illus. 2013. (SPA.). 24p. (J). (gr. -1 — 1). bds. 8.95 (978-0-545-58416-6(7)) Scholastic, Inc.

Rowland, Jeanna. Always Mom, Forever Dad, 1 vol. Weber, Penny, illus. 2014. (ENG.). 32p. (J). (gr. -1-3). 16.95 (978-0-88448-367-0(3), 884367) Tilbury Hse. Pubs.

Rusackas, Francesca. I Love You All Day Long. Burris, Priscilla, illus. 2004. (ENG.). 32p. (J). (gr. -1-k). reprint ed. pap. 7.99 (978-0-06-050278-2(9), HarperCollins) HarperCollins Pubs.

Salomon, Bob & Young, Rick. Beyond the Laces. 2015. (ENG., Illus.). (J). pap. 12.95 (978-1-4951-5694-6(X)) Independent Pub.

Sammy's Sneeze: Individual Title Six-Packs. (gr. -1-2). 23.00 (978-0-7635-9013-0(4)) Rigby Education.

Sanchez, Pete. A Friend for Petro. 2008. 73p. pap. 19.95 (978-1-60474-902-1(4)) America Star Bks.

Santiago, Roberto. El Ultimo Sordo. 2003. (SPA., Illus.). 95p. (978-84-236-3428-6(0), ED7340) Edebé ESP. Dist: Lectorum Pubns., Inc.

Santucci, Barbara. Loon Summer. Shine, Andrea, illus. 2004. 32p. (J). (gr. k-3). 16.00 (978-0-8028-5182-6(7)) Eerdmans, William B. Publishing Co.

Sarn, Amélie & Trouillot, Virgile. A Day of Surprises, 1 vol. 2009. (Groove High Ser.). (ENG., Illus.). 112p. (YA). (gr. 5-5). 16.93 (978-1-60754-209-4(9), 313b30a5-40a0-48ad-a8a4-eb0a2abd6b71); pap. 8.95 (978-1-60754-210-0(2), ade20f5d-a929-4448-aa6f-5adbbc16543f) Rosen Publishing Group, Inc., The. (Windmill Bks.).

Sawyer, Louise. Mother's Storybook Signs, Vol. 2. 2004. (YA). spiral bd. 19.95 (978-0-9719842-8-8(X)) Martin & Brothers.

Schaumberg, Rose Mary & Schaumberg, Emily Rose. I'll Miss My Grandma, Wouldn't You? 2008. (Illus.). 40p. pap. 16.99 (978-1-4389-1335-3(4)) AuthorHouse.

Scheuer, Benjamin. Hibernate with Me. Williams, Jemima, illus. 2019. (ENG.). 40p. (J). (gr. -1-3). 17.99 (978-1-5344-3217-8(5), Simon & Schuster Bks. For Young Readers) Simon & Schuster Bks. For Young Readers.

Schmid, Paul. A Pet for Petunia. 2011. (J). lib. bdg. 14.89 (978-0-06-196332-2(1)) HarperCollins Pubs.

—A Pet for Petunia. Schmid, Paul, illus. 2011. (ENG., Illus.). 40p. (J). (gr. -1-2). 12.99 (978-0-06-196331-5(3), HarperCollins) HarperCollins Pubs.

Schwartz, Kristi. Divorced Together: For teh Sake of the Children. 2009. (ENG.). 32p. pap. 11.95 (978-1-933916-47-7(8), Ferne Pr.) Nelson Publishing & Marketing.

Scotton, Rob. The Perfect Present for Mom & Dad. 2012. (Splat the Cat 8X8 Ser.). (J). lib. bdg. 14.75 (978-0-606-23579-2(5)) Turtleback.

—Splat the Cat: the Perfect Present for Mom & Dad: A Father's Day Gift Book from Kids. Scotton, Rob, illus. 2012. (Splat the Cat Ser.). (ENG., Illus.). 24p. (J). (gr. k-3). bds. 4.99 (978-0-06-210009-2(2), HarperFestival) HarperCollins Pubs.

Sederman, Marty & Epstein, Seymour. The Magic Box: When Parents Can't Be There to Tuck You In. Brooks, Karen Stormer, illus. 2003. 32p. (J). (gr. -1-3). 14.95 (978-1-55798-807-2(2), Magination Pr.) American Psychological Assn.

Seevers, Tim. Love, Grandp. 2009. 28p. pap. 14.99 (978-1-4389-3507-2(2)) AuthorHouse.

Segal, Howard. My Daddy the Lawyer: Mommy-Daddy Books. 2009. 16p. pap. 9.49 (978-1-4343-0883-2(9)) AuthorHouse.

Self, Jeffery. A Very, Very Bad Thing. 2017. (ENG.). 240p. (YA). (gr. 9). 17.99 (978-1-338-11840-7(4), PUSH) Scholastic, Inc.

Shannon, David. Too Many Toys. Shannon, David, illus. 2008. (ENG., Illus.). 32p. (J). (gr. -1-3). 18.99 (978-0-439-49029-0(4), Blue Sky Pr., The) Scholastic, Inc.

Shaw, Mary. Brady Brady & the Singing Tree, 11 vols. Temple, Chuck, illus. l.t. ed. 2004. 32p. (J). per. (978-0-9735557-3-8(4)) Brady Brady, Inc.

Sheets, Katherine. Captured by Henrey, 1 vol. 2010. 48p. pap. 16.95 (978-1-4489-4538-2(0)) America Star Bks.

Sheinmel, Alyssa. Faceless. 2015. (ENG.). 352p. (YA). (gr. 7). 18.99 (978-0-545-67601-4(0), Scholastic Pr.) Scholastic, Inc.

Shemtov, Yael. Sadie's Funny Feeling. 2009. 24p. pap. 16.99 (978-1-4389-6023-4(9)) AuthorHouse.

Silves, Kate. Jamie the Giraffe Learns to Dance. 2013. 20p. pap. 13.77 (978-1-4669-7305-3(6)) Trafford Publishing.

Simmons, Michael. Pool Boy. 2005. (ENG.). 192p. (YA). (gr. 7). reprint ed. pap. 7.99 (978-0-385-73196-6(5), Delacorte Bks. for Young Readers) Random Hse. Children's Bks.

Simon, Coco. Mia's Baker's Dozen, 6. 2012. (Cupcake Diaries: 6). (ENG.). 160p. (J). (gr. 3-7). pap. 6.99 (978-1-4424-4613-7(7), Simon Spotlight) Simon & Schuster Children's Publishing.

Simonds, William. Marcus; or, the Boy-Tamer by Walter Aimwell [Pseud.]. 2006. 336p. per. 23.99 (978-1-4255-3348-9(5)) Michigan Publishing.

Simoneau, D. K. We're Having a Tuesday. Cornelius, Brad, illus. 2006. (ENG.). 32p. (J). 16.95 (978-1-933302-13-3(5)) AC Pubns. Group LLC.

Singh, Sonita. Butterfly Kisses. 2018. (ENG., Illus.). 36p. (J). (gr. -1-3). (978-1-5289-2371-2(5)); pap. (978-1-5289-2372-9(3)) Austin Macauley Pubs. Ltd.

Skirvan, Pamela. The Bad Day. Skirvan, Ted, 3rd, illus. 2003. 12p. (J). (gr. k-6). pap. 4.95 (978-0-9742943-0-8(6)) Skirvan, Pamela.

Skye, Obert. Wizard for Hire. 2018. (Wizard for Hire Ser.: 1). (ENG.). 416p. (J). (gr. 5-9). 17.99 (978-1-62972-412-6(2), 5194480, Shadow Mountain) Shadow Mountain Publishing.

Slonim, David. I Loathe You. Slonim, David, illus. (ENG., Illus.). 24p. (J). (gr. -1-3). 2018. 7.99 (978-1-5344-3311-3(2)) 2012.

15.99 *(978-1-4424-2244-5(0))* Simon & Schuster Children's Publishing. (Aladdin).

Small, David. Eulalie & the Hopping Head. 2003. (Illus.). (J). 25.95 incl. audio *(978-1-59112-217-3(1))* Live Oak Media.

—Eulalie & the Hopping Head. Small, David, illus. 2003. (Illus.). (J). pap. 33.95 incl. audio *(978-1-59112-218-0(X))* Live Oak Media.

Smith, D. K. Sock 'n Boots - Share. 2010. 32p. pap. 13.60 *(978-0-557-52614-7(0))* Lulu Pr., Inc.

Smith, Jason. We Share When We Sleep. 2012. 28p. pap. 19.99 *(978-1-4772-5446-2(3))* AuthorHouse.

Smucker, Anna Egan. To Keep the South Manitou Light. 2004. (Great Lakes Books Ser.). (ENG., Illus.). 140p. 23.95 *(978-0-8143-3235-1(8),* P029609) Wayne State Univ. Pr.

Snowe, Olivia. Beauty & the Basement, 1 vol. Lamoreaux, Michelle, illus. 2014. (Twicetold Tales Ser.). (ENG.). 128p. (J). (gr. 3-6). 8.95 *(978-1-4342-9830-0(2),* 127286, Stone Arch Bks.) Capstone.

Sommer, Carl. The Donkey, Fox, & the Lion. Noé, Ignacio, illus. 2016. (ENG.). 32p. (J). (gr. k-4). lib. bdg. 16.95 *(978-1-57537-926-5(0),* Another Sommer-Time Story) Advance Publishing, Inc.

—I Am a Lion! Budwine, Greg, illus. 2014. (J). *(978-1-57537-403-1(X))* Advance Publishing, Inc.

—I Am a Lion!(Yo Soy un León!) Budwine, Greg, illus. 2009. (Another Sommer-Time Story Bilingual Ser.). (SPA & ENG.). 48p. (J). lib. bdg. 16.95 *(978-1-57537-153-5(7))* Advance Publishing, Inc.

Staehli, Melissa. I Love You to the Moon. 2013. 28p. 15.95 *(978-1-61244-205-1(6))* Halo Publishing International.

Stamps, Paula. Learning Makes Friends Fun, 1 vol. 2010. 22p. 24.95 *(978-1-4512-8765-3(8))* PublishAmerica, Inc.

Standish, Burt L. Frank Merriwell's Son. Rudman, Jack, ed. 2003. (Frank Merriwell Ser.). pap. 9.95 *(978-0-8373-9137-3(7))* Merriwell, Frank Inc.

Star, L. J. Lydia's First Christmas, 1 vol. 2010. 24p. 24.95 *(978-1-61546-593-4(6))* PublishAmerica, Inc.

Steig, William. Pedro Es una Pizza. (Buenas Noches Ser.). (SPA., Illus.). (J). (gr. -1-5). 7.95 *(978-958-04-6034-3(5))* Norma S.A. COL. Dist: Lectorum Pubns., Inc., Distribuidora Norma, Inc.

—Pete's a Pizza. 2004. (Illus.). 32p. (J). (gr. -1-2). 28.95 incl. audio compact disk *(978-1-59112-740-6(8))* Live Oak Media.

Stevens, Liza. Not Today, Celeste! A Dog's Tale about Her Human's Depression. 2016. (Illus.). 36p. (J). 17.95 *(978-1-78592-008-0(1),* 693958) Kingsley, Jessica Pubs. GBR. Dist: Hachette UK Distribution.

Stever, Susan. When Fairies Die. 2010. 28p. pap. 13.99 *(978-1-4520-0912-4(0))* AuthorHouse.

Stewart, Kymberly M. Play It Again, Rachel. 2003. 74p. (J). pap. 10.95 *(978-0-9740653-0-4(7))* Neema's Children Literature Assn., Inc.

Stinson, June. Milton Hears a Train. 2012. 32p. pap. 24.95 *(978-1-4626-8192-1(1))* America Star Bks.

Stoehr, Shelley. Crosses. 2003. 161p. (YA). pap. 13.95 *(978-0-595-26952-5(4),* Writers Club Pr.) iUniverse, Inc.

Sullivan, Paula. Todd's Box. Westcott, Nadine Bernard, illus. 2004. (Green Light Readers Level 1 Ser.). (ENG.). 24p. (J). (gr. -1-3). pap. 6.99 *(978-0-15-205094-8(9),* 1195382, Clarion Bks.) HarperCollins Pubs.

Sullivan, Therese M. & Bitner, Pamela. A Gift from Valentine. 2007. 24p. (J). per. 12.95 *(978-1-58939-981-5(1))* Virtualbookworm.com Publishing, Inc.

Sundberg, Angela M., et al. The Pottamus Family & the Unhappy Pottamus. Sundberg, Angela M. et al, illus. 2007. (J). pap. 16.00 *(978-0-8059-7478-2(4))* Dorrance Publishing Co., Inc.

Sussman, Michael. Duckworth, the Difficult Child. Sardà, Júlia, illus. 2019. (ENG.). 40p. (J). (gr. -1-3). 17.99 *(978-1-5344-0512-7(7))* Simon & Schuster Children's Publishing.

Swanson, Julie A. Going for the Record. 2004. 223p. (YA). pap. 8.00 *(978-0-8028-5273-1(4))* Eerdmans, William B. Publishing Co.

Swayne Tidwell, Deborah. Magic Eraser & Camp Real. 2009. 16p. pap. 8.50 *(978-1-4343-8916-9(2))* AuthorHouse.

Tada, Joni Eareckson. I'll Be with You Always. Nelson, Craig, illus. 2004. 32p. (gr. 8-12). 14.99 *(978-1-58134-000-6(1))* Crossway.

Tada, Joni Eareckson & Jensen, Steve. Tell Me the Promises. DiCianni, Ron, illus. 2004. 48p. (gr. 5-7). 17.99 *(978-0-89107-904-0(1))* Crossway.

Tamburri, Pasqualino. Alex & the Trampoline. 2008. 32p. (J). (gr. -1-2). 14.95 *(978-1-60227-473-0(8))* Above the Clouds Publishing.

Tansil-Mitchell, Angela. Kimmie C Sunshine: When Mommy & Daddy Loses Their Jobs. 2011. 24p. pap. 13.79 *(978-1-4567-5666-6(4))* AuthorHouse.

Tashlikowich, Natasha. The Secret of the Seven Stones. 2009. 117p. pap. 18.97 *(978-0-557-03747-6(6))* Lulu Pr., Inc.

Thiel, Annie. Cosmos' Mom & Dad Are Moving Apart. Edwards, William M. & Marjoribanks, Karen, illus. 2006. (Playdate Kids Ser.). 32p. (J). (gr. -1-3). 14.95 *(978-1-933721-04-0(9))* Playdate Kids Publishing.

Thiel Annie. The Playdate Kids Cosmos' Mom & Dad are Moving Apart 2ED 2007. 2007. 32p. 12.95 *(978-1-933721-31-6(6));* pap. 6.95 *(978-1-933721-27-9(8))* Playdate Kids Publishing.

Thomas, Dalandra. Noonimals. 2006. (J). pap. 16.95 *(978-90-78473-02-2(9))* Nooni Publishing.

Thompson, Gwendolyn. Hayride to Heaven. 2009. 40p. pap. 16.99 *(978-1-4389-6741-7(1))* AuthorHouse.

Thompson, Lauren. A Christmas Gift for Mama. Burke, Jim, illus. 2003. (J). pap. 16.95 *(978-0-590-30726-0(6))* Scholastic, Inc.

Thompson, Vivian L. Neat! Said Jeremy. 2003. 33p. (J). pap. 8.95 *(978-0-7414-1579-0(8))* Infinity Publishing.

Tiller, Amy. My Sister Is Like a Baby Bird. Tiller, Amy, illus. 2009. (ENG., Illus.). 26p. (J). 12.95 *(978-1-935130-02-4(1))* Grateful Steps.

Tillman, Nancy. Wherever You Are: My Love Will Find You. Tillman, Nancy, illus. (ENG., Illus.). 32p. (J). (gr. -1-3). 2012. bds. 8.99 *(978-1-250-01797-0(1),* 900087504) 2010. 18.99 *(978-0-312-54966-4(0),* 900055823) Feiwel & Friends.

Time Slime. 2003. 156p. (YA). (gr. 5-12). pap. 7.95 *(978-0-9702176-3-9(3),* 0004) Night Howl Productions.

Toothman, Sherry. I'm Okay, Mommy. Toothman, Lindsey, illus. 2007. 20p. per. 24.95 *(978-1-4241-8733-1(8))* America Star Bks.

Townsend, Peter. Shelly & Muffin's Big Lesson Learned. 2008. 11p. pap. 24.95 *(978-1-60672-379-1(0))* America Star Bks.

Towson, Robert. The Wrong Bus, 1 vol. 2010. 34p. 24.95 *(978-1-4489-4345-6(0))* PublishAmerica, Inc.

Treiber, Jutta & Antoni, Birgit. Porque Siempre Va a Ser Asi. 2004. (SPA., Illus.). 28p. (J). 18.99 *(978-84-89804-54-8(0))* Lóguez Ediciones ESP. Dist: Lectorum Pubns., Inc.

Trent, Shanda. Farmers' Market Day. Dippold, Jane, illus. 2013. (ENG.). 32p. (J). (gr. -1-1). 12.95 *(978-1-58925-115-1(6))* Tiger Tales.

Trice, Linda. Kenya's Song. Johnson, Pamela, illus. 2013. 32p. (J). (gr. -1-3). pap. 7.95 *(978-1-57091-847-6(3));* lib. bdg. 17.95 *(978-1-57091-846-9(5))* Charlesbridge Publishing, Inc.

Tyle, Shirley. Where Is Time, 1 vol. 2010. 30p. 24.95 *(978-1-4489-5976-1(4))* PublishAmerica, Inc.

Urda, Gary. Love You More. Bell, Jennifer A., illus. 2018. (ENG.). 40p. (J). (gr. -1-3). 17.99 *(978-1-4998-0652-6(3))* Little Bee Books Inc.

Ure, Daylene Mary. Today I'm Going to be a Hedgehog. 2008. 36p. 16.50 *(978-0-615-25326-8(1))* Ure, Daylene.

Van Buren, David. I Love You As Big As the World. Warnes, Tim, illus. 2013. (ENG.). 22p. (J). (-k). bds. 8.95 *(978-1-58925-603-3(4))* Tiger Tales.

van Genechten, Guido. Because I Love You So Much. 2004. (Illus.). 32p. (J). tchr. ed. 15.95 *(978-1-58925-039-0(7))* Tiger Tales.

Van Steenwyk, Elizabeth. Prairie Christmas. Himler, Ronald, illus. 2006. 32p. (J). (gr. k). 17.00 *(978-0-8028-5280-9(7),* Eerdmans Bks For Young Readers) Eerdmans, William B. Publishing Co.

Van Wyk, Tasja. Twins: Meet the Doctor. 2011. (Illus.). 28p. pap. 13.78 *(978-1-4567-7813-2(7))* AuthorHouse.

Vandepeer, Helen. Gifts. 2008. 76p. pap. 35.80 *(978-0-557-03191-7(5))* Lulu Pr., Inc.

Vander Zee, Ruth. Erika's Story. Innocenti, Roberto, illus. 2013. (ENG.). 24p. (J). (gr. 2-5). pap. 10.99 *(978-0-89812-891-8(9),* 22045, Creative Paperbacks) Creative Co., The.

—Mississippi Morning. Cooper, Floyd, illus. 2004. 32p. (J). 16.00 *(978-0-8028-5211-3(4))* Eerdmans, William B. Publishing Co.

Vigna, Judith. When Eric's Mom Fought Cancer. 2004. (J). (gr. 1-5). spiral bd. *(978-0-616-03063-9(0))* Canadian National Institute for the Blind/Institut National Canadien pour les Aveugles.

Villanueva, Gail D. My Fate According to the Butterfly. 2019. (ENG.). 240p. (J). (gr. 3-7). 17.99 *(978-1-338-31050-4(X),* Scholastic Pr.) Scholastic, Inc.

Voyager, Beatrice Nambouy. Mama Minko: A Survival Quest. 2010. (Illus.). 28p. pap. 15.49 *(978-1-4490-5797-8(7))* AuthorHouse.

W. Parents Are Lucky: They Don't Have to Do Chores. 2010. 24p. pap. 12.49 *(978-1-4520-7671-3(5))* AuthorHouse.

Waber, Bernard. Ask Me. Lee, Suzy., illus. 2015. (ENG.). 40p. (J). (gr. -1-3). 16.99 *(978-0-547-73394-4(1),* 1484489, Clarion Bks.) HarperCollins Pubs.

Waddell, Martin. Owl Babies. (Illus.). 25p. (J). (ENG, VIE, URD, TUR & CHI.). *(978-1-85430-348-6(1),* 93442); (CHI, ENG, URD, TUR & VIE., *(978-1-85430-343-1(0),* 93441) Little Tiger Pr. Group.

Wadham, Tim. The Queen of France. Denton, Kady MacDonald, illus. 2011. (ENG.). 32p. (J). (gr. -1-3). 16.99 *(978-0-7636-4102-3(2))* Candlewick Pr.

Walker, G. L. Good Morning Baby. 2008. 24p. pap. 10.95 *(978-1-4327-0536-7(9))* Outskirts Pr., Inc.

Wallace, Bill. Skinny-Dipping at Monster Lake. 2004. (ENG., Illus.). 224p. (J). (gr. 3-7). pap. 6.99 *(978-0-689-85151-3(0),* Simon & Schuster/Paula Wiseman Bks.) Simon & Schuster/Paula Wiseman Bks.

Walsh, Melanie. Living with Mom & Living with Dad. Walsh, Melanie, illus. 2012. (ENG., Illus.). 40p. (J). (gr. -1-2). 17.99 *(978-0-7636-5869-4(3))* Candlewick Pr.

Walter, Lee. The Gifts That Are Forgotten. 2006. 60p. pap. 16.95 *(978-1-4137-9070-2(4))* PublishAmerica, Inc.

Walvoord, Linda. Razzamadaddy, 1 vol. Yoshikawa, Sachiko, tr. Yoshikawa, Sachiko, illus. 2004. (ENG.). 32p. (J). 14.95 *(978-0-7614-5158-7(7))* Marshall Cavendish Corp.

Wan, Joyce. We Belong Together. Wan, Joyce, illus. 2011. (ENG., Illus.). 14p. (J). (gr. k — 1). bds. 6.99 *(978-0-545-30740-6(6),* Cartwheel Bks.) Scholastic, Inc.

—You Are My Magical Unicorn. Wan, Joyce, illus. 2018. (ENG., Illus.). 14p. (J). (gr. -1-k). bds. 6.99 *(978-1-338-33410-4(7),* Cartwheel Bks.) Scholastic, Inc.

Ward, Jennifer. Because You Are My Baby. Long, Sylvia, illus. 2007. (ENG.). 32p. (J). (gr. -1-1). 15.95 *(978-0-87358-911-6(4))* Cooper Square Publishing Llc.

Ward, Ruth. The Adventures of Blroor Bone. 2005. (J). lib. bdg. 18.00 *(978-1-59094-105-8(5))* Jawbone Publishing Corp.

Warwillow, Lucas D. Marick's Cross, 1 vol. 2010. 48p. pap. 16.95 *(978-1-61546-563-7(4))* America Star Bks.

Watkins, Rowboat. Big Bunny: (Funny Bedtime Read Aloud Book for Kids, Bunny Book) 2018. (ENG., Illus.). 40p. (J). (gr. -1-k). 16.99 *(978-1-4521-6390-1(1))* Chronicle Bks. LLC.

Watkins, Steve. On Blood Road (a Vietnam War Novel) 2018. (ENG.). 288p. (YA). (gr. 7-7). 18.99 *(978-1-338-19701-3(0),* Scholastic Pr.) Scholastic, Inc.

Watt, Cliff. Jenny Brown & the Search for Eusebio's Star. 2008. 77p. pap. 19.95 *(978-1-60672-169-8(0))* America Star Bks.

Watts, David, et al. Disney Pixar Read-Along Storybook & CD Box Set. 2017. (Illus.). (J). *(978-1-368-01620-9(0))* Disney Publishing Worldwide.

Watts, Irene N. When the Bough Breaks. 2007. 152p. (YA). (gr. 7-7). pap. 9.95 *(978-0-88776-821-7(0),* Tundra Bks.) Tundra Bks. CAN. Dist: Penguin Random Hse. LLC.

Weber, Lori. Yellow Mini, 1 vol. 2011. (ENG.). 243p. (YA). (gr. 7-9). pap. 9.95 *(978-1-55455-199-6(4),* 41752833-3e0a-484f-9722-80b0cdf3f540) Fitzhenry & Whiteside, Ltd. CAN. Dist: Firefly Bks., Ltd.

Weeks, Sarah. Without You. Duranceau, Suzanne, illus. 40p. (J). (gr. -1-2). 2007. (ENG.). pap. 7.99 *(978-0-06-113998-7(X),* HarperCollins) 2003. 16.99 *(978-0-06-027816-8(1),* Geringer, Laura Book) HarperCollins Pubs.

Weiss, Ellen. Whatever You Do, I Love You. Williams, Sam, illus. 2010. (ENG.). 16p. (J). (gr. -1 — 1). bds. 7.99 *(978-1-4424-0809-8(X),* Little Simon) Little Simon.

Wells, Charity. The Trouble with the Supernatural, 1 vol. 2010. 84p. pap. 19.95 *(978-1-4489-2117-1(1))* America Star Bks.

Wells, Rosemary. Hand in Hand. Wells, Rosemary, illus. 2016. (ENG., Illus.). 32p. (J). 17.99 *(978-1-62779-334-3(4),* 900150563, Holt, Henry & Co. Bks. For Young Readers) Holt, Henry & Co.

—Love Waves. Wells, Rosemary, illus. 2011. (ENG., Illus.). 32p. (J). (gr. -1-2). 15.99 *(978-0-7636-4989-0(9))* Candlewick Pr.

—Love Waves: Midi Edition. Wells, Rosemary, illus. 2012. (ENG., Illus.). 32p. (J). (gr. k — 1). 8.99 *(978-0-7636-6224-0(0))* Candlewick Pr.

Weston Woods Staff, creator. Owen. 2011. (SPA.). 38.75 *(978-0-439-02178-4(2));* 29.95 *(978-0-439-02310-8(6));* 18.95 *(978-0-439-02177-7(4))* Weston Woods Studios, Inc.

—Pete's a Pizza. 2011. 29.95 *(978-0-439-74519-2(5))* Weston Woods Studios, Inc.

—Too Many Toys! 2011. 29.95 *(978-0-545-37421-7(9))* Weston Woods Studios, Inc.

Whelan, Gloria. A Time to Keep Silent. 2004. 144p. (J). pap. 8.00 *(978-0-8028-5255-7(6))* Eerdmans, William B. Publishing Co.

Whelen-Banks, Jane. Liam Goes Poo in the Toilet: A Story about Trouble with Toilet Training. 2008. (Illus.). 32p. 13.95 *(978-1-84310-900-6(X),* 695773) Kingsley, Jessica Pubs. GBR. Dist: Hachette UK Distribution.

White, James C. David Goes Fishing. Chapin, Patrick, illus. 2003. 32p. (J). 6.95 *(978-0-9747752-0-3(7))* White, James C.

Whitney, Adeline Dutton Train. The Other Girls. 2016. (ENG., Illus.). (J). 29.95 *(978-1-358-75955-0(3))* Creative Media Partners, LLC.

Whybrow, Ian. Malicia para Principiantes: Una Aventura de Lobito y Apestosito. Quintana, Joela, tr. Ross, Tony, illus. 2005. (Libros Ilustrados (Picture Bks.)). (SPA.). 32p. (J). (gr. k-2). 16.95 *(978-0-8225-3211-8(5),* Ediciones Lerner) Lerner Publishing Group.

Whybrow, Ian & Ross, Tony. Badness for Beginners: A Little Wolf & Smellybreff Adventure. 2005. (Illus.). 32p. (J). (gr. -1-3). 16.95 *(978-1-57505-861-0(8),* Carolrhoda Bks.) Lerner Publishing Group.

Wicke, Ed. Nicklus. 2011. 184p. (J). per. 9.99 *(978-0-9677652-4-2(2),* BlacknBlue Pr. UK) Blacknblue Pr.

Wild, Margaret. Kiss Kiss! Strevens-Marzo, Bridget, illus. 2004. 26p. pap. *(978-1-877003-51-6(4))* Little Hare Bks. AUS. Dist: HarperCollins Pubs. Australia.

Wilkins, Rose. So Super-Starry. 2004. (ENG.). 256p. (J). pap. *(978-0-330-42086-0(0),* Macmillan Children's Bks.) Pan Macmillan.

Willems, Mo. Welcome: a Mo Willems Guide for New Arrivals. 2017. (ENG., Illus.). 32p. (J). (gr. -1 — 1). 15.99 *(978-1-4847-6746-7(2),* Hyperion Books for Children) Disney Publishing Worldwide.

William Tell: 6 Small Books. (gr. k-2). 23.00 *(978-0-7635-8506-8(8))* Rigby Education.

Williams-Garcia, Rita. P. S. Be Eleven. 2015. (ENG.). 304p. (J). (gr. 3-7). pap. 8.99 *(978-0-06-193864-1(5),* Quill Tree Bks.) HarperCollins Pubs.

Williams, Randy. A Hero Named Herman. 2007. 21p. pap. 24.95 *(978-1-4241-8648-8(X))* PublishAmerica, Inc.

Williams, T. H. Jo's Bright New Day. 2008. 20p. pap. 24.95 *(978-1-60474-949-6(0))* America Star Bks.

Wilson, Karma. Baby, I Love You. Williams, Sam, illus. 2009. (ENG.). 30p. (J). (gr. -1 — 1). bds. 8.99 *(978-1-4169-1910-0(4),* Little Simon) Little Simon.

—Mama Always Comes Home. Dyer, Brooke, illus. 2005. 32p. (J). (gr. -1-1). 15.99 *(978-0-06-057505-2(0))* HarperCollins Pubs.

Wilson, Leonard W. Realms of Flimenia Jeremyæs Journey. 2008. 136p. pap. 11.95 *(978-0-595-51523-3(1))* iUniverse, Inc.

Winegar, Tracy. Keeping Keller. 2008. 207p. pap. 14.99 *(978-1-59955-115-9(2))* Cedar Fort, Inc./CFI Distribution.

Wolfe, Susan Markle. The Deer from Ponchatoula, 1 vol. Welch, Gracie, illus. 2009. 24p. pap. 24.95 *(978-1-60813-519-6(5))* America Star Bks.

Woodson, Jacqueline. Coming on Home Soon. Lewis, E. B., illus. 2004. (ENG.). 32p. (J). (gr. k-3). 18.99 *(978-0-399-23748-5(8),* G.P. Putnam's Sons Books for Young Readers) Penguin Young Readers Group.

Wright, Claire. A Kiss Goodnight. Vasylenko, Veronica, illus. 2017. (Padded Board Books for Babies Ser.). (ENG.). 20p. (J). (gr. -1 — 1). bds. 6.99 *(978-1-68412-041-3(1),* Silver Dolphin Bks.) Printers Row Publishing Group.

Wright, Gail R. The Adventures of Alfred in the Greatest Fruit of All: Conflicts & Resolutions. 2011. 112p. (gr. 1-2). 28.95 *(978-1-4497-1586-1(9));* pap. 11.95 *(978-1-4497-1585-4(0))* Author Solutions, LLC. (WestBow Pr.).

Wright, Michael. Jake Starts School. Wright, Michael, illus. 2010. (ENG., Illus.). 48p. (J). (gr. -1-1). 21.19 *(978-0-312-60884-2(7),* 900065180) Square Fish.

Yang, Gene Luen & Pham, Thien. Level Up. 2016. (YA). lib. bdg. 20.85 *(978-0-606-38563-3(0))* Turtleback.

Yoo, Paula. Good Enough. 2012. (ENG.). 336p. (YA). (gr. 8). pap. 7.99 *(978-0-06-079090-5(3),* HarperTeen) HarperCollins Pubs.

You're One! 2014. (Year-By-Year Bks.). (ENG., Illus.). 16p. (J). (— 1). bds. 7.95 *(978-1-934649-46-6(5))* Bailiwick Pr.

Yvette, Sylvia. My Silly Imagination. 2012. 24p. (-18). pap. 15.99 *(978-1-4797-2966-1(3))* Xlibris Corp.

Zachariah, Abdul-Razak. The Night Is Yours. Bobo, Keturah A., illus. 2019. 32p. (J). (gr. -1-2). 17.99 *(978-0-525-55271-0(5),* Dial Bks) Penguin Young Readers Group.

Zimmerman, Mary. The Secret in the Wings: A Play. 2014. (ENG., Illus.). 128p. pap. 16.00 *(978-0-8101-2987-0(6))* Northwestern Univ. Pr.

Zschock, Martha. Hello, Philadelphia! 2011. (Hello Ser.). (ENG., Illus.). 16p. (J). (gr. -1-k). bds. 9.99 *(978-1-933212-64-7(0),* Commonwealth Editions) Applewood Bks.

—Hello, Rhode Island! 2011. (Hello Ser.). (ENG., Illus.). 16p. (J). (gr. -1-k). bds. 9.99 *(978-1-933212-62-3(4),* Commonwealth Editions) Applewood Bks.

—Hello, San Francisco! 2012. (Hello Ser.). (ENG., Illus.). 16p. (J). (gr. -1-k). bds. 9.99 *(978-1-933212-65-4(9),* Commonwealth Editions) Applewood Bks.

Zuckerman, Linda. I Will Hold You 'Til You Sleep. Muth, Jon J., illus. 2006. (J). *(978-0-439-43421-8(1),* Levine, Arthur A. Bks.) Scholastic, Inc.

PARENTS AND TEACHERS

see Home and School

PARIS (FRANCE)

Adams, Jennifer. My Little Cities: Paris: (Board Books for Toddlers, Travel Books for Kids, City Children's Books) Pizzoli, Greg, illus. 2017. (My Little Cities Ser.). (ENG.). 22p. (J). (gr. -1 — 1). bds. 9.99 *(978-1-4521-5390-2(6))* Chronicle Bks. LLC.

Anastasio, Dina. Where Is the Eiffel Tower? 2017. (Where Is... ? Ser.). lib. bdg. 16.00 *(978-0-606-40102-9(4))* Turtleback.

BeaverSimon. PARIS: CITY OF LIGHT BEGINNING BOOK WITH ONLINE ACCESS, 1 vol. 2014. (ENG., Illus.). 24p. (J). pap., E-Book, E-Book 9.50 *(978-1-107-64577-6(8))* Cambridge Univ. Pr.

Burleigh, Robert. Sylvia's Bookshop: The Story of Paris's Beloved Bookstore & Its Founder (As Told by the Bookstore Itself!) Wu, Katy, illus. 2018. (ENG.). 32p. (J). (gr. -1-3). 17.99 *(978-1-4814-7245-6(3),* Simon & Schuster/Paula Wiseman Bks.) Simon & Schuster/Paula Wiseman Bks.

Cooper, Sharon Katz. Gustave Eiffel's Spectacular Idea: The Eiffel Tower. Bock, Janna, illus. 2015. (Story Behind the Name Ser.). (ENG.). 32p. (J). (gr. 2-4). lib. bdg. 29.32 *(978-1-4795-7136-9(9),* 128896, Picture Window Bks.) Capstone.

Evans, June P. Michael in Paris. 2007. 10.00 *(978-0-8059-8933-5(1))* Dorrance Publishing Co., Inc.

Evanson, Ashley. Paris: A Book of Shapes. Evanson, Ashley, illus. 2015. (Hello, World Ser.). (Illus.). 16p. (J). (— 1). bds. 7.99 *(978-0-448-48915-5(5),* Penguin Workshop) Penguin Young Readers Group.

Fowler, Gloria. Come with Me to Paris. 2014. (ENG., Illus.). 56p. (J). 16.95 *(978-1-62326-047-7(7))* AMMO Bks., LLC.

Friedman, Samantha. What Degas Saw. 2016. (ENG., Illus.). 40p. (J). (gr. k-2). 19.95 *(978-1-63345-004-2(X),* 1648701) Museum of Modern Art.

Gardner, Alison. Passport to Paris. 2010. (Crabtree Connections Ser.). (ENG.). 24p. (J). (gr. 3-6). *(978-0-7787-9955-9(7));* pap. *(978-0-7787-9977-1(8))* Crabtree Publishing Co.

Howse, Jennifer. The Louvre. 2014. (J). *(978-1-4896-1190-1(8))* Weigl Pubs., Inc.

Jonnes, Jill. Eiffel's Tower for Young People. 2019. (For Young People Ser.). (Illus.). (YA). (gr. 7). 360p. 40.00 *(978-1-60980-905-8(X));* 368p. pap. 17.95 *(978-1-60980-917-1(3))* Seven Stories Pr. (Triangle Square).

Kissock, Heather. Eiffel Tower. 2018. (Structural Wonders of the World Ser.). (ENG.). 24p. (J). (gr. 2-5). lib. bdg. 28.55 *(978-1-4896-8181-2(7),* AV2 by Weigl) Weigl Pubs., Inc.

Kissock, Heather, ed. Eiffel Tower. 2011. (Virtual Field Trip Ser.). (Illus.). 24p. (J). (gr. 2-5). 27.13 *(978-1-61690-766-2(5));* (gr. 4-6). pap. 12.95 *(978-1-61690-770-9(3),* AV2 by Weigl) Weigl Pubs., Inc.

Leboutillier, Nate. Eiffel Tower. 2006. (Modern Wonders of the World Ser.). (Illus.). 32p. (J). (gr. 4-7). 18.95 *(978-1-58341-438-5(X),* 1262895, Creative Education) Creative Co., The.

Mansfield, Andy. Lonely Planet Kids Pop-Up Paris 1. Mansfield, Andy, illus. 2016. (Lonely Planet Kids Ser.). (ENG., Illus.). 8p. (J). (gr. -1-k). 9.99 *(978-1-76034-335-4(8),* 5335) Lonely Planet Global Ltd. IRL. Dist: Hachette Bk. Group.

Mason Crest. Paris, Vol. 8. 2016. (Major World Cities Ser.: Vol. 8). (ENG., Illus.). 48p. (J). (gr. 5-8). 20.95 *(978-1-4222-3544-7(0))* Mason Crest.

Mattern, Joanne. Paris, 1 vol. 2007. (Cities Set 2 Ser.). (Illus.). 32p. (gr. -1-3). 27.07 *(978-1-59679-720-8(7),* Checkerboard Library) ABDO Publishing Co.

Meyers, Haily & Meyers, Kevin. All Aboard! Paris: A French Primer, 1 vol. 2015. (Lucy Darling Ser.). (Illus.). 22p. (J). (— 1). bds. 11.99 *(978-1-4236-4077-6(2),* 1394332) Gibbs Smith, Publisher.

Nanji, Shenaaz. Notre Dame. 2014. (J). *(978-1-4896-1146-8(0))* Weigl Pubs., Inc.

Pezzi, Bryan. Eiffel Tower. 2007. (Structural Wonders Ser.). (Illus.). 32p. (J). (gr. 4-7). lib. bdg. 26.00 *(978-1-59036-719-3(7));* per. 9.95 *(978-1-59036-720-9(0))* Weigl Pubs., Inc.

Rice, Dona Herweck. Engineering Marvels: The Eiffel Tower: Measurement (Grade 4) 2017. (Mathematics in the Real World Ser.). (ENG., Illus.). 32p. (gr. 4-5). pap. 11.99 *(978-1-4258-5559-8(8))* Teacher Created Materials, Inc.

Riggs, Kate. Eiffel Tower. 2009. (Now That's Big Ser.). 24p. (J). (gr. 1-5). lib. bdg. 24.25 *(978-1-58341-702-7(8),* Creative Education) Creative Co., The.

Rossi, Renzo. In the Sun King's Paris with Molière, 1 vol. 2009. (Come See My City Ser.). (ENG., Illus.). 48p. (gr. 4-4). lib. bdg. 31.21 *(978-0-7614-4332-2(0),* e70ca7d2-2035-48ae-8f7f-8e5a1e648d94) Cavendish Square Publishing LLC.

Rudolph, Jessica. Paris. 2017. (Citified! Ser.). (ENG., Illus.). 24p. (J). (gr. k-3). 17.95 *(978-1-68402-233-5(9))* Bearport Publishing Co., Inc.

Sasek, M. This Is Paris. 2004. (This Is ... Ser.). (ENG., Illus.). 64p. (J). (gr. 2-12). 17.95 *(978-0-7893-1063-7(5))* Universe Publishing.

Slingerland, Janet. Engineering the Eiffel Tower. 2017. (Building by Design Ser.). (ENG., Illus.). 48p. (J). (gr. 4-8). 55.65 *(978-1-68078-950-8(3),* 26351) ABDO Publishing Co.

Stacey, Gill. Paris, 1 vol. 2004. (Great Cities of the World Ser.). (ENG., Illus.). 48p. (gr. 5-8). lib. bdg. 33.67 *(978-0-8368-5030-7(0),* 7c0b54f2-89bd-4bfd-90fc-53207c673d05, Gareth Stevens Secondary Library) Stevens, Gareth Publishing LLLP.

Thurlby, Paul. P Is for Paris. 2018. (Paul Thurlby ABC City Bks.: 0). (ENG.). 64p. (J). (gr. -1-k). 19.99 *(978-1-4926-6815-2(X))* Sourcebooks, Inc.

PARIS (FRANCE)—FICTION

Abbott, Jacob. Rollo in Paris. 2008. 116p. 22.95 *(978-1-60664-943-5(4));* pap. 9.95 *(978-1-60312-493-5(4))* Aegypan.

Abrahamson, Ruth Ann. Paris & the Purple Purse: Continuing Adventures of Magic Cookie Bean. 2011. 40p. (gr. 1-2). pap. 13.95 *(978-1-4497-1665-3(2),* WestBow Pr.) Author Solutions, LLC.
Adam D. Levine. Knights: Reign of Hellfire. 2010. (ENG.). 184p. 23.95 *(978-1-4401-7614-2(0));* pap. 13.95 *(978-1-4401-7618-0(3))* iUniverse, Inc.
Ahern, Carolyn L. Tino Turtle Travels to Paris, France. Burt Sullivan, Neallia, illus. 2007. 36p. (J). (gr. -1-4). 17.95 incl. audio compact disk *(978-0-9793158-1-7(6))* Tino Turtle Travels, LLC.
Altsheler, Joseph A. The Forest of Swords: A Story of Paris & the Marne. 2006. (World War I Ser.: Vol. 3). 284p. (J). reprint ed. 28.95 *(978-1-4218-1772-9(1));* pap. 13.95 *(978-1-4218-1872-6(8))* 1st World Publishing, Inc. (1st World Library - Literary Society).
—The Forest of Swords: A Story of Paris & the Marne. 2006. (World War I Ser.: Vol. 3). (J). reprint ed. pap. *(978-1-4068-0742-4(7))* Echo Library.
—The Forest of Swords: A Story of Paris & the Marne. 2010. (World War I Ser.: Vol. 3). 216p. (J). reprint ed. pap. *(978-1-4076-1521-9(1))* HardPr.
Angel, Ido. Vipo in Paris: The Kings of Croissants & Baguettes. 2015. (AV2 Animated Storytime Ser.). (ENG.). (J). lib. bdg. 29.99 *(978-1-4896-3902-8(0),* AV2 by Weigl) Weigl Pubs., Inc.
Axelsson, Carina. Paris. 2014. (Model Undercover Ser.: 1). (ENG.). 368p. (J). (gr. 4-7). pap. 10.99 *(978-1-4022-8587-5(6))* Sourcebooks, Inc.
Baccellia, Kim. Goddesses Can Wait. 2015. 196p. (YA). *(978-1-61271-297-0(5))* Zumaya Pubns. LLC.
Bateson, Catherine. Lisette's Paris Notebook. 2018. (ENG., Illus.). 304p. (YA). (gr. 8-12). pap. 15.99 *(978-1-76029-363-5(6))* Allen & Unwin AUS. Dist: Independent Pubs. Group.
Beck, Andrea. Pierre in the Air!, 1 vol. 2011. (Pierre le Poof Ser.: 3). (ENG., Illus.). 32p. (J). (gr. -1-k). 19.95 *(978-1-55469-032-9(3))* Orca Bk. Pubs. USA.
Bemelmans, Ludwig. Madeline. l.t. ed. 2018. (ENG., Illus.). 54p. (J). (gr. k-6). pap. *(978-4-87187-929-3(1))* Ishi Pr., Inc., The.
—Madeline. 2012. (Madeline Ser.). 36p. (J). (gr. -1-k). bds. 9.99 *(978-0-670-01407-1(9),* Viking Books for Young Readers) Penguin Young Readers Group.
—Madeline: Activity Book with Stickers. 2012. (Madeline Ser.). 32p. (J). (gr. k-3). act. bk. ed. 8.99 *(978-0-448-45903-5(5),* Grosset & Dunlap) Penguin Young Readers Group.
—Madeline's Rescue. 2004. (J). (gr. -1-2). spiral bd. *(978-0-616-11864-1(3))* Canadian National Institute for the Blind/Institut National Canadien pour les Aveugles.
Bowen, Carl. The Murders in the Rue Morgue, 1 vol. Dimaya, Emerson, illus. 2013. (Edgar Allan Poe Graphic Novels Ser.). (ENG.). 72p. (J). (gr. 5-9). 28.65 *(978-1-4342-3033-1(3),* 114578); pap. 6.10 *(978-1-4342-4259-4(5),* 120321) Capstone. (Stone Arch Bks.).
Bradley, F. T. Double Vision. 2013. (Double Vision Ser.: 1). (ENG.). 272p. (J). (gr. 3-7). pap. 6.99 *(978-0-06-210438-0(1),* HarperCollins) HarperCollins Pubs.
Brannen, Sarah S. Madame Martine. Brannen, Sarah S., illus. 2014. (ENG., Illus.). 32p. (J). (gr. -1-3). 16.99 *(978-0-8075-4905-6(3),* 807549053) Whitman, Albert & Co.
Brannen, Sarah S., illus. Madame Martine. 2015. 32p. (J). *(978-1-4896-3864-9(4))* Weigl Pubs., Inc.
Brian, Janeen. Cat-Astrophe at the Opera, 1 vol. rev. ed. 2013. (Literary Text Ser.). (ENG., Illus.). 28p. (J). (gr. 2-3). pap. 10.99 *(978-1-4333-5597-4(3))* Teacher Created Materials, Inc.
—Cat-Astrpohe at the Opera. rev. ed. 2013. (Literary Text Ser.). (ENG., Illus.). 28p. (J). (gr. 2-3). lib. bdg. 19.96 *(978-1-4807-1719-0(3))* Teacher Created Materials, Inc.
Brown, Jeff. Flat Stanley's Worldwide Adventures #11: Framed in France. Pamintuan, Macky, illus. 2014. (Flat Stanley's Worldwide Adventures Ser.: 11). (ENG.). 128p. (J). (gr. 1-5). 15.99 *(978-0-06-218985-1(9));* pap. 4.99 *(978-0-06-218984-4(0))* HarperCollins Pubs. (HarperCollins).
—Framed in France. 2014. (Flat Stanley's Worldwide Adventures Ser.: 11). (J). lib. bdg. 14.75 *(978-0-606-35480-6(8))* Turtleback.
Burt, Marissa. The 12 Dares of Christa. 2017. (ENG.). 304p. (J). (gr. 3-7). 16.99 *(978-0-06-241618-6(9),* Tegen, Katherine Bks) HarperCollins Pubs.
Cameron, Sharon. Rook. (ENG.). 464p. (YA). (gr. 7). 2016. pap. 9.99 *(978-1-338-03246-8(1))* 2015. 17.99 *(978-0-545-67599-4(5))* Scholastic, Inc. (Scholastic Pr.).
Christiansen, Rebecca. Maybe in Paris. 2017. (ENG.). 224p. (YA). (gr. 6-6). 16.99 *(978-1-5107-0880-8(4),* Sky Pony Pr.) Skyhorse Publishing Co., Inc.
Cyr, Joe. Magical Trees & Crayons: Great Stories. 2006. (Illus.). pap. 9.95 *(978-0-9778525-6-7(3))* Peppertree Pr., The.
de Brunhoff, Laurent. Babar's Guide to Paris. 2017. (ENG., Illus.). 48p. (J). (gr. k-2). 19.95 *(978-1-4197-2289-9(1),* 1153501, Abrams Bks. for Young Readers) Abrams, Inc.
De Fombelle, Timothée. The Book of Pearl. 2018. (ENG.). 368p. (J). (gr. 7). 17.99 *(978-0-7636-9126-4(7))* Candlewick Pr.
Derrick, Patricia & O'Neil, Shirley. Rathbone the Rat. Martinez, J-P Loppo, illus. 2007. 32p. (J). (gr. -1-3). 18.95 incl. audio compact disk *(978-1-933818-17-7(4))* Animalations.
Dixon, Franklin. A con Artist in Paris. 2017. 122p. (J). *(978-1-5379-7447-7(5),* Simon & Schuster/Paula Wiseman Bks.) Simon & Schuster/Paula Wiseman Bks.
—Passport to Danger. 2005. (Hardy Boys I Ser.: No. 179). 147p. (J). lib. bdg. 15.00 *(978-1-59054-847-9(7))* Fitzgerald Bks.
Doder, Joshua. Grk Takes Revenge. 2010. (J). *(978-0-385-90655-5(2)); (978-0-385-73723-4(8))* Random House Publishing Group. (Delacorte Pr).
Druvert, Hélène & Druvert, Hélène. Paris up, up & Away. 2016. (ENG., Illus.). 36p. (J). (gr. -1-1). 24.95 *(978-0-500-65059-2(4),* 565059) Thames & Hudson.
Eaton, Gordon J. Piebald & the Parade of Small Animals. 2009. 184p. pap. 14.99 *(978-1-60791-991-9(5))* Salem Author Services.
Egan, Tim. Dodsworth in Paris. Egan, Tim, illus. 2011. (Dodsworth Ser.). (ENG., Illus.). 48p. (J). (gr. 1-3). 16.19 *(978-0-618-98062-8(8))* Houghton Mifflin Harcourt Publishing Co.
—Dodsworth in Paris (Reader) Egan, Tim, illus. 2010. (Dodsworth Book Ser.). (ENG., Illus.). 48p. (J). (gr. 1-4). pap. 4.99 *(978-0-547-33192-8(4),* 1417441, Clarion Bks.) HarperCollins Pubs.
Eschberger, Beverly. The Elephants in the City of Light: An Elephant Family Adventure. Gower, Jim, illus. 2010. (J). per. 3.99 *(978-1-932926-28-6(3),* Kinkajou Pr.) Artemesia Publishing, LLC.
Francis, Pauline, retold by. The Phantom of the Opera, 1 vol. 2010. (Essential Classics - Horror Ser.). (ENG., Illus.). 56p. pap. *(978-0-237-54095-1(9))* Evans Brothers, Ltd.
Frederick, Heather Vogel. Wish You Were Eyre. (Mother-Daughter Book Club Ser.). (ENG.). (J). (gr. 4-9). 2013. 480p. pap. 8.99 *(978-1-4424-3065-5(6))* 2012. 464p. 16.99 *(978-1-4424-3064-8(8))* Simon & Schuster Bks. For Young Readers. (Simon & Schuster Bks. For Young Readers).
Froman, Annabelle. Beezeur. 2013. 34p. pap. 9.95 *(978-0-9842053-1-8(4))* Breathless Vintage Enterprises.
Fromental, Jean-Luc. Oops! Jolivet, Joëlle, illus. 2010. (ENG.). 42p. (J). (gr. -1-3). 17.95 *(978-0-8109-8749-4(X),* 681701) Abrams, Inc.
Ghislain, Gary. How I Stole Johnny Depp's Alien Girlfriend. 2011. (ENG., Illus.). 208p. (YA). (gr. 7-17). 16.99 *(978-0-8118-7460-1(5))* Chronicle Bks. LLC.
Gibbs, Stuart. The Last Musketeer #2: The Traitor's Chase. 2nd ed. 2012. (Last Musketeer Ser.: 2). (ENG.). 256p. (J). (gr. 3-7). 16.99 *(978-0-06-204841-7(4),* HarperCollins) HarperCollins Pubs.
—The Last Musketeer #2: Traitor's Chase. 2019. (ENG.). 272p. (J). (gr. 3-7). pap. 7.99 *(978-0-06-204842-4(2),* HarperCollins) HarperCollins Pubs.
—The Last Musketeer #3: Double Cross. 2019. (ENG.). 256p. (J). (gr. 3-7). pap. 7.99 *(978-0-06-204845-5(7),* HarperCollins) HarperCollins Pubs.
Greene, Bette. Morning Is a Long Time Coming. l.t. ed. 2004. (Beeler Mystery Ser.). 35.95 *(978-1-58118-122-7(1))* LRS.
Grimes, Nikki. On the Road to Paris. (Illus.). 224p. (J). 16.99 *(978-0-8037-2817-2(4),* Dial) Penguin Publishing Group.
Grover Swank, Denise. One Paris Summer, 1 vol. 2016. (ENG.). 352p. (YA). pap. 14.99 *(978-0-310-75516-6(6))* Blink.
Gruener, Nina. Kiki & Coco in Paris. 2011. (ENG., Illus.). 32p. (J). (gr. -1-3). 18.95 *(978-0-918684-50-9(1),* 1331701) Abrams, Inc.
Harris, L. Little Girl in Paris. 2004. (Madame Juliette & the Inchanded Crate Ser.: Vol. 1). (Illus.). 330p. (J). pap. 19.95 *(978-0-9749950-2-1(9))* Granny's Pub Co.
Harvey, Jacqueline. Clementine Rose & the Paris Puzzle. 2016. (Clementine Rose Ser.: 12). 160p. (J). (gr. 1-3). pap. 8.99 *(978-0-85798-788-4(7))* Random Hse. Australia AUS. Dist: Independent Pubs. Group.
Henty, George. At Agincourt: A Story of the White Hoods of Paris. 2007. (ENG.). 296p. pap. 21.99 *(978-1-4264-2133-4(8));* 284p. pap. 23.99 *(978-1-4264-2201-0(6))* Creative Media Partners, LLC.
Hess, Megan. Claris Vol. 2: The Chicest Mouse in Paris, Volume 1. 2018. (Claris Ser.: Bk. 1). (ENG., Illus.). 48p. (J). (gr. -1-3). 17.99 *(978-1-76050-259-1(6))* Hardie Grant Bks. AUS. Dist: Hachette Bk. Group.
Howard, A. G. RoseBlood. (ENG.). 432p. (gr. 8-17). 2018. (J). pap. 10.99 *(978-1-4197-2723-8(0),* 1124203, Amulet Bks.) 2017. (YA). pap. 8.95 *(978-1-4197-2342-1(1))* Abrams, Inc.
—RoseBlood. 2018. (J). lib. bdg. 20.85 *(978-0-606-40729-8(4))* Turtleback.
Hugo, Victor. The Hunchback of Notre Dame. 2008. (Bring the Classics to Life Ser.). (Illus.). 72p. (gr. 2-12). pap., act. bk. ed. 10.95 *(978-1-55576-324-4(3),* EDCTR-208B) EDCON Publishing Group.
—The Hunchback of Notre Dame: Illustrated Edition, 1 vol. 2011. (Calico Illustrated Classics Ser.: No. 4). (ENG., Illus.). 112p. (J). (gr. 2-5). 38.50 *(978-1-61641-614-0(9),* 4043, Calico Chapter Bks.) ABDO Publishing Co.
—The Hunchback of Notre Dame: With a Discussion of Compassion. Butterfield, Ned, tr. Butterfield, Ned, illus. 2003. (Values in Action Illustrated Classics Ser.). (J). *(978-1-59203-049-1(1))* Learning Challenge, Inc.
The Hunchback of Notre Dame. (Read-Along Ser.). (J). 7.99 incl. audio *(978-1-55723-992-1(4))* Walt Disney Records.
Hunt, Elizabeth Singer. Secret Agent Jack Stalwart: Book 3: the Mystery of the Mona Lisa: France, Bk. 3. 2007. (Secret Agent Jack Stalwart Ser.: 3). (ENG., Illus.). 128p. (J). (gr. 1-4). per. 5.99 *(978-1-60286-001-8(7),* Running Pr. Kids) Running Pr.
Jeanne-Marie in Gay Paris. 2003. (Illus.). 32p. (J). mass mkt. 9.99 *(978-0-9740599-1-4(9),* 2) Omnibus Publishing.
Kaldor, Connie. A Poodle in Paris. Fil & Julie, Connie, illus. 2006. (ENG.). 36p. (J). (gr. -1-2). 16.95 *(978-2-923163-12-3(5))* La Montagne Secrete CAN. Dist: Independent Pubs. Group.
Kalman, Maira. Ooh-La-la (Max in Love) 2018. (Illus.). 48p. (J). (gr. k-3). 18.95 *(978-1-68137-245-7(2),* NYR Children's Collection) New York Review of Bks., Inc., The.
Kelly, Erin. The Mystery at the Eiffel Tower: Paris, France. 2005. (Carole Marsh Mysteries Ser.). (Illus.). 144p. (J). (gr. 3-5). pap. 7.99 *(978-0-635-03468-7(9))* Gallopade International.
Knighton, Kate, retold by. Phantom of the Opera. 2008. (Young Reading Series 2 Gift Bks). 64p. (J). 8.99 *(978-0-7945-2082-3(0),* Usborne) EDC Publishing.
Layman, John. Eleanor & the Egret Volume 1. Marts, Mike, ed. 2018. (ENG., Illus.). 120p. (J). pap. 14.99 *(978-1-935002-76-5(7),* 0e6aa812-51a9-4acb-8441-2416fb2b9919) AfterShock Comics.
Lodding, Linda Ravin. Painting Pepette. Fletcher, Claire, illus. 2016. (ENG.). 40p. (J). (gr. -1-3). 17.99 *(978-1-4998-0136-1(X))* Little Bee Books Inc.
Mancuso, Jackie Clark. Paris-Chien: Adventures of an Expat Dog. 2013. (Paris-Chien Adventure Ser.: 1). (ENG., Illus.). 32p. (J). (gr. k-2). 17.95 *(978-0-615-54542-4(4))* La Librairie Parisienne.
Marsh, Carole. The Mystery at the Eiffel Tower. 2009. (Around the World in 80 Mysteries Ser.). (Illus.). 132p. (J). 18.99 *(978-0-635-07004-3(9),* Marsh, Carole Mysteries) Gallopade International.
Mary John Lewis. Pookie in Paris. 2009. 24p. pap. 12.49 *(978-1-4389-6514-7(1))* AuthorHouse.
McClintock, Barbara. The Fantastic Drawings of Danielle. 2004. (ENG., Illus.). 32p. (J). (gr. -1-3). pap. 5.95 *(978-0-618-43230-1(2),* 491158, Clarion Bks.) HarperCollins Pubs.
Meade, L. T. The Children's Pilgrimage. 2004. reprint ed. pap. 24.95 *(978-1-4191-5659-5(4));* pap. 1.99 *(978-1-4192-5659-2(9))* Kessinger Publishing, LLC.
Minou: Evaluation Guide. 2006. (J). *(978-1-55942-416-5(8))* Witcher Productions.
Modiano, Patrick. Catherine Certitude. (FRE.). pap. 17.95 *(978-2-07-051608-7(3))* Gallimard, Editions FRA. Dist: Distribooks, Inc.
Montgomery, R. A. Space Pup. Newton, Keith, illus. 2014. (ENG.). 80p. (J). (gr. 2-2). pap. 8.99 *(978-1-937133-43-6(5))* Chooseco LLC.
Nesbet, Anne. The Cabinet of Earths, 1. 2013. (ENG.). 288p. (J). (gr. 3-7). pap. 6.99 *(978-0-06-196319-3(4),* HarperCollins) HarperCollins Pubs.
Nesbit, Sara E. Mary Wants to Be an Artist. 2009. 28p. pap. 12.49 *(978-1-4490-2609-7(5))* AuthorHouse.
Nesbo, Jo. Bubble in the Bathtub. Chace, Tara F., tr. Lowery, Mike, illus. 2011. (Doctor Proctor's Fart Powder Ser.). (ENG.). (J). (gr. 3-7). 448p. pap. 8.99 *(978-1-4169-7975-3(1));* 432p. 17.99 *(978-1-4169-7974-6(3))* Simon & Schuster Children's Publishing. (Aladdin).
O'Neill, S. Rocket Robinson & the Secret of the Saint. 2018. (Illus.). 248p. (J). (gr. 5-9). pap. 14.99 *(978-1-5067-0679-5(7),* Dark Horse Books) Dark Horse Comics.
Orczy, Emmuska. Castles in the Air. 2008. 160p. 25.95 *(978-1-60664-927-5(2));* pap. 14.95 *(978-1-60664-047-0(X))* Aegypan.
Osborne, Mary Pope. Night of the New Magicians. Murdocca, Sal, illus. 2007. (Magic Tree House (R) Merlin Mission Ser.: 7). 144p. (J). (gr. 2-5). 6.99 *(978-0-375-83036-5(7),* Random Hse. Bks. for Young Readers) Random Hse. Children's Bks.
Palmer, Larry Schwarz,Iva-Marie. Romeo, Juliet & Jim: Book 1, Bk. 1. 2017. (ENG., Illus.). 288p. (YA). 34.99 *(978-1-62779-250-9(3),* 900143896, Holt, Henry & Co. Bks. For Young Readers) Holt, Henry & Co.
Paris, Harper. The Mystery of the Stolen Painting. Calo, Marcos, illus. 2014. (Greetings from Somewhere Ser.: 3). (ENG.). 128p. (J). (gr. k-4). pap. 6.99 *(978-1-4814-0296-5(X),* Little Simon) Little Simon.
Parry, Rosanne. Second Fiddle. 2012. 240p. (J). (gr. 3-7). 6.99 *(978-0-375-86166-6(1),* Yearling) Random Hse. Children's Bks.
Patterson, James & Paetro, Maxine. Confessions: the Paris Mysteries. 2014. (Confessions Ser.: 3). (ENG.). (YA). (gr. 7-17). 320p. 33.99 *(978-0-316-37084-4(3));* 352p. 35.99 *(978-0-316-40963-6(4))* Little Brown & Co. (Jimmy Patterson).
—The Paris Mysteries. 2015. (Confessions Ser.: 3). (YA). lib. bdg. 20.85 *(978-0-606-37526-9(0))* Turtleback.
Perkins, Stephanie. Anna & the French Kiss. 2010. 384p. (YA). (gr. 7-18). 18.99 *(978-0-525-42327-0(3),* Dutton Books for Young Readers) Penguin Young Readers Group.
—Isla & the Happily Ever After. 2015. (ENG.). 368p. (YA). (gr. 9-12). pap. 10.99 *(978-0-14-242627-2(X),* Speak) Penguin Young Readers Group.
Plum, Amy. Die for Me. (Die for Me Ser.: 1). (ENG.). (YA). (gr. 9). 2012. 368p. pap. 8.99 *(978-0-06-200402-4(6))* 2011. 352p. 17.99 *(978-0-06-200401-7(8))* HarperCollins Pubs. (HarperTeen).
Ponnay, Brenda. Secret Agent Josephine in Paris. Ponnay, Brenda, illus. 2013. (ENG., Illus.). 32p. (J). (gr. -1-2). pap. 19.99 *(978-1-62395-524-3(6))* Xist Publishing.
Ponnay, Brenda & Ponnay, Brenda. Secret Agent Josephine in Paris. 2013. 32p. pap. 9.99 *(978-1-62395-552-6(1))* Xist Publishing.
Presley, Daniel & Polders, Claire. A Whale in Paris. McGuire, Erin, illus. (ENG.). 256p. (J). (gr. 5). 2019. pap. 7.99 *(978-1-5344-1916-2(0))* 2018. 17.99 *(978-1-5344-1915-5(2))* Simon & Schuster Children's Publishing. (Atheneum Bks. for Young Readers).
Princess, Pula. 2005. (ENG.). 54p. pap. 20.99 *(978-1-4134-8923-1(0))* Xlibris Corp.
Punter, Russell. Kitty Kat, Kitty Kat Where Have You Been - Paris. 2018. (Picture Bks.). (ENG.). 24p. (J). 9.99 *(978-0-7945-3976-4(9),* Usborne) EDC Publishing.
Rider, Catherine. Kiss Me in Paris. 2018. (ENG.). 216p. (YA). (gr. 9-12). 16.99 *(978-1-77138-867-2(6));* pap. 10.99 *(978-1-5253-0142-1(X))* Kids Can Pr., Ltd. CAN. Dist: Hachette Bk. Group.
Rohan, Margaret de. Celia & Granny Meg go to Paris: A survival Guide. 2011. (ENG., Illus.). 184p. pap. *(978-1-84876-650-1(5))* Troubador Publishing Ltd.
—Celia & Granny Meg Return to Paris: The man with no Face. 2012. (ENG., Illus.). 176p. pap. *(978-1-78088-243-7(2))* Troubador Publishing Ltd.
Rooftoppers. 2014. (ENG., Illus.). 304p. (J). (gr. 3-7). pap. 8.99 *(978-1-4424-9059-8(4),* Simon & Schuster Bks. For Young Readers) Simon & Schuster Bks. For Young Readers.
Rosner, Gillian, tr. The Phantom of the Opera: Based on the Novel by Gaston Leroux. Druvert, Hélène, illus. 2016. (ENG.). 40p. (J). (gr. k-2). 19.95 *(978-1-4197-2086-4(4),* 1648901, Abrams Bks. for Young Readers) Abrams, Inc.
Rundell, Katherine. Rooftoppers. Fan, Terry, illus. 2013. (ENG.). 288p. (J). (gr. 3-7). 19.99 *(978-1-4424-9058-1(6),* Simon & Schuster Bks. For Young Readers) Simon & Schuster Bks. For Young Readers.
Schroeder, Lisa. My Secret Guide to Paris: a Wish Novel. (Wish Ser.). (ENG.). 224p. (J). (gr. 3-7). 2016. pap. 6.99 *(978-0-545-70810-4(9))* 2015. 16.99 *(978-0-545-70808-1(7),* Scholastic Pr.) Scholastic, Inc.
Schwab, Victoria & Schwab, V. E. Tunnel of Bones (City of Ghosts #2) 2019. (City of Ghosts Ser.: 2). (ENG., Illus.). 304p. (J). (gr. 4-7). 17.99 *(978-1-338-11104-0(3),* Scholastic Pr.) Scholastic, Inc.
Scott, Michael. The Magician. 2009. (Secrets of the Immortal Nicholas Flamel Ser.: 2). (ENG.). 496p. (YA). (gr. 7). pap. 11.99 *(978-0-385-73728-9(9),* Ember) Random Hse. Children's Bks.
Seduction. 2014. (Legacy Ser.). (ENG., Illus.). 416p. (YA). (gr. 9). 17.99 *(978-1-4814-0023-7(1)),* Simon & Schuster/Paula Wiseman Bks.) Simon & Schuster/Paula Wiseman Bks.
Shepherd, Megan. Grim Lovelies. (Grim Lovelies Ser.). (ENG.). (YA). (gr. 9). 2019. 448p. pap. 9.99 *(978-0-358-10823-8(3),* 1748887) 2018. 384p. 17.99 *(978-1-328-80918-6(8),* 1688543) HarperCollins Pubs. (Clarion Bks.).
—Midnight Beauties. 2019. (Grim Lovelies Ser.). (ENG.). 448p. (YA). (gr. 9). 17.99 *(978-1-328-81190-5(5),* 1688554, Clarion Bks.) HarperCollins Pubs.
Smadja, Brigitte. Tarte aux Escargots. pap. 17.95 *(978-2-211-03633-7(3))* Archimede Editions FRA. Dist: Distribooks, Inc.
Snyder, Karen. Mona Lisa's Makeover. LaGrange, Tiffany, illus. 2010. 24p. pap. 12.95 *(978-1-936343-15-7(0))* Peppertree Pr., The.
Soriano, Osvaldo. El Negro de Paris. (Torre de Papel Ser.). (SPA.). (J). (gr. 4-18). 8.95 *(978-958-04-3450-4(6))* Norma S.A. COL. Dist: Distribuidora Norma, Inc.
Stevenson, Steve. The Eiffel Tower Incident. 2014. (Agatha Girl of Mystery Ser.: 5). lib. bdg. 16.00 *(978-0-606-34153-0(6))* Turtleback.
Stilton, Thea. Thea Stilton & the Mystery on the Orient Express (Thea Stilton #13) A Geronimo Stilton Adventure. 2012. (Thea Stilton Ser.: 13). (ENG., Illus.). 176p. (J). (gr. 2-5). pap. 8.99 *(978-0-545-34105-9(1),* Scholastic Paperbacks) Scholastic, Inc.
Stone, Phoebe. Paris for Two. 2016. (J). (ENG.). 272p. (gr. 3-7). 16.99 *(978-0-545-44362-3(8));* 257p. *(978-1-338-04510-9(5))* Scholastic, Inc. (Levine, Arthur A. Bks.).
Surget, Alain. The Ghost Ship. 2015. (Jolly Roger Ser.). (Illus.). 96p. (gr. 3-6). 28.50 *(978-1-909645-41-7(9))* Book Hse. GBR. Dist: Black Rabbit Bks.
—The Plumed Serpent's Gold. 2015. (Jolly Roger Ser.). (Illus.). 96p. (gr. 3-6). 28.50 *(978-1-909645-43-1(5))* Book Hse. GBR. Dist: Black Rabbit Bks.
—Shark Island. 2015. (Jolly Roger Ser.). (Illus.). 96p. (gr. 3-6). 28.50 *(978-1-909645-42-4(7))* Book Hse. GBR. Dist: Black Rabbit Bks.
A Tale of Two Cities. abr. ed. (ARA., Illus.). 48p. (J). 12.00 *(978-0-86685-627-0(7))* International Bk. Ctr., Inc.
Urbain, Christophe, photos by. Emma in Paris. 2013. (ENG., Illus.). 56p. (J). (gr. k). 17.95 *(978-1-59270-139-1(6))* Enchanted Lion Bks., LLC.
Ward, Christopher. Mac in the City of Light. 2013. 220p. pap. *(978-1-4596-6323-7(3))* ReadHowYouWant.com, Ltd.
Warner, Susan & Wetherell, Elizabeth. Queechy. 2008. 328p. per. 16.95 *(978-1-60312-446-1(2))* Aegypan.
Webb, Sarah. Bridesmaid Blitz. 2012. (Ask Amy Green Ser.: 3). (ENG., Illus.). 320p. (YA). (gr. 7). pap. 6.99 *(978-0-7636-5157-2(5))* Candlewick Pr.
Wells, Carolyn. Patty in Paris. 2004. reprint ed. pap. 21.95 *(978-1-4191-4034-1(5));* pap. 1.99 *(978-1-4192-4034-8(X))* Kessinger Publishing, LLC.
—Patty in Paris. 2011. 148p. 24.95 *(978-1-4638-9969-1(6));* pap. 12.95 *(978-1-4638-0166-3(1))* Rodgers, Alan Bks.
Weston Woods Staff, creator. Madeline's Rescue. 2011. 38.75 *(978-0-439-72772-3(3));* 29.95 *(978-0-439-73488-2(6));* 18.95 *(978-0-439-72770-9(7))* Weston Woods Studios, Inc.
Whitby, Adele. Camille's Story 1910. 2015. (Secrets of the Manor Ser.: 7). (ENG., Illus.). 160p. (J). (gr. 3-7). pap. 6.99 *(978-1-4814-3988-6(X),* Simon Spotlight) Simon Spotlight.
Willems, Mo. The Story of Diva & Flea. DiTerlizzi, Tony, illus. 2015. (ENG.). 80p. (J). (gr. 1-3). 14.99 *(978-1-4847-2284-8(1),* Disney-Hyperion) Disney Publishing Worldwide.
Wright, David & Bouchard, Luc. Away Running, 1 vol. 2016. (ENG.). 312p. (YA). (gr. 8-12). pap. 14.95 *(978-1-4598-1046-4(5))* Orca Bk. Pubs. USA.
Wurge, B. B. Squiggle. 2009. (LeapKids Ser.). (ENG., Illus.). 152p. (J). (gr. 2-7). pap. 9.95 *(978-0-9815148-9-5(8))* Leapfrog Pr.

PARIS (FRANCE)—HISTORY—FICTION

Chokshi, Roshani. The Gilded Wolves: A Novel. (Gilded Wolves Ser.: 1). (ENG., Illus.). (YA). 2020. 416p. pap. 11.99 *(978-1-250-14455-3(8),* 900186061) 2019. 400p. 19.99 *(978-1-250-14454-6(X),* 900180660) St. Martin's Pr. (Wednesday Bks.).
Dickens, Charles. A Tale of Two Cities: A Classic Retelling. 2006. (Classic Retelling Ser.). (Illus.). 240p. (YA). (gr. 8-12). *(978-0-618-03150-4(2),* 2-00144) Holt McDougal.
Dickens, Charles & Hawksley, L. Dickens. A Tale of Two Cities. 2004. (Paperback Classics Ser.). 144p. (J). pap. 4.95 *(978-0-7945-0390-1(X));* lib. bdg. 12.95 *(978-1-58086-515-9(1))* EDC Publishing.
Donnelly, Jennifer. Revolution. 2011. (ENG.). 512p. (YA). (gr. 9). pap. 10.99 *(978-0-385-73764-7(5),* Ember) Random Hse. Children's Bks.
Duble, Kathleen Benner. Madame Tussaud's Apprentice: An Untold Story of Love in the French Revolution. 2014. (ENG.). 224p. (YA). 17.99 *(978-1-4405-8116-8(9),* Simon Pulse) Simon Pulse.
Fontes, Justine & Fontes, Ron. The Fifth Musketeer. Meconis, Dylan, illus. 2012. (Twisted Journeys Ser.: 19). (ENG.). 112p. (J). (gr. 4-7). pap. 45.32 *(978-0-7613-9289-7(0));* lib. bdg. 27.93 *(978-0-7613-4594-7(9))* Lerner Publishing Group. (Graphic Universe™).
Gardner, Sally. The Red Necklace. 2008. (ENG.). 384p. (J). (gr. 9-12). 24.94 *(978-0-8037-3100-4(0),* Dial) Penguin Publishing Group.
Gibbs, Stuart. The Last Musketeer #3: Double Cross. 2013. (Last Musketeer Ser.: 3). (ENG.). 256p. (J). (gr. 3-7). 16.99 *(978-0-06-204844-8(9),* HarperCollins) HarperCollins Pubs.
Henty, George. At Agincourt: A Tale of the White Hoods of Paris. 2011. 332p. pap. 19.95 *(978-1-61179-111-2(1))* Fireship Pr.
The Hunchback of Notre Dame. (Read-Along Ser.). (J). 7.99 incl. audio *(978-1-55723-992-1(4))* Walt Disney Records.
Kesterson, Casie. The Goldfish in the Chandelier. Hovland, Gary, illus. 2012. (ENG.). 32p. (gr. 2-5). 17.95 *(978-1-60606-094-0(5),* J. Paul Getty Museum) Getty Pubns.

McAlpine, Gordon. Mystery Box: A Novel about the Creators of Nancy Drew & the Hardy Boys. 2003. (ENG.). 190p. (YA). 16.95 *(978-0-8126-2680-3(X))* Cricket Bks.

Osborne, Mary Pope. Night of the New Magicians. 2007. (Magic Tree House Merlin Missions Ser.: 7). lib. bdg. 16.00 *(978-1-4177-9108-8(X))* Turtleback.

Ross, Elizabeth. Belle Epoque. 2014. (ENG.). 352p. (YA). (gr. 7). pap. 13.99 *(978-0-385-74147-7(2),* Ember) Random Hse. Children's Bks.

Scott, Elaine. Secrets of the Cirque Medrano. 2008. (Illus.). 216p. (J). (gr. 5-9). 15.95 *(978-1-57091-712-7(4))* Charlesbridge Publishing, Inc.

—The Spanish Web: An Encounter with Picasso. 2004. (Art Encounters Ser.). (J). 15.95 *(978-0-8230-0410-2(4));* pap. 6.99 *(978-0-8230-0413-3(9))* Watson-Guptill Pubns., Inc.

Selznick, Brian. The Invention of Hugo Cabret. 2007. (CHI., Illus.). 534p. (J). *(978-957-570-894-8(6))* Eastern Publishing Co., Ltd., The.

—The Invention of Hugo Cabret. 2008. (CHI., Illus.). 465p. (J). pap. *(978-7-5448-0279-6(5))* Jieli Publishing Hse.

—The Invention of Hugo Cabret. Selznick, Brian, illus. 2007. (ENG., Illus.). 544p. (J). (gr. 4-7). 29.99 *(978-0-439-81378-5(6),* Scholastic Pr.); 534p. *(978-1-4071-0348-8(2))* Scholastic, Inc.

PARKER, QUANAH, 1845?-1911

Sanford, William R. Comanche Chief Quanah Parker, 1 vol. 2013. (Native American Chiefs & Warriors Ser.). (ENG.). 48p. (gr. 5-7). pap. 11.53 *(978-1-4644-0255-5(8),* 949cfd6b-f15a-49a3-b35b-9a89a7944797); (Illus.). (J). lib. bdg. 25.27 *(978-0-7660-4095-3(X),* 3f01192a-b7dc-48bc-a9dc-9afb1ced69d5) Enslow Publishing, LLC.

PARKS, GORDON, 1912-2006

Parr, Ann. Gordon Parks: No Excuses, 1 vol. Breidenthal, Kathryn, illus. Parks, Gordon, Jr., photos by. 2006. (ENG.). 32p. (J). (gr. k-3). 16.99 *(978-1-58980-411-1(2),* Pelican Publishing) Arcadia Publishing.

PARKS, ROSA, 1913-2005

Adler, David A. A Picture Book of Rosa Parks. Casilla, Robert, illus. 2015. 32p. pap. 8.00 *(978-1-61003-405-0(8))* Center for the Collaborative Classroom.

—A Picture Book of Rosa Parks. Casilla, Robert, illus. 2004. (J). (gr. -1-2). 28.95 incl. audio compact disk *(978-1-59112-762-8(9))* Live Oak Media.

Aretha, David. The Story of Rosa Parks & the Montgomery Bus Boycott in Photographs, 1 vol. 2014. (Story of the Civil Rights Movement in Photographs Ser.). (ENG.). 48p. (gr. 5-6). 27.93 *(978-0-7660-4234-6(0),* e21f5d8c-f41e-4022-be0d-e634268e951a); pap. 11.53 *(978-1-4644-0411-5(9),* f7985370-9f23-4bf8-8b18-1ea3f16d5ddd) Enslow Publishing, LLC.

Banting, Erinn. Rosa Parks. 2005. (Great African American Women for Kids Ser.). (Illus.). 24p. (J). (gr. 2-3). lib. bdg. 26.00 *(978-1-59036-336-2(1));* (gr. 3-7). per. 8.95 *(978-1-59036-342-3(6))* Weigl Pubs., Inc.

Bednar, Chuck. Rosa Parks. 2010. (Transcending Race in America Ser.). (Illus.). 64p. (YA). (gr. 5-18). lib. bdg. 22.95 *(978-1-4222-1615-6(2))* Mason Crest.

Bjornlund, Lydia D. Rosa Parks & the Montgomery Bus Boycott, 1 vol. 2007. (Lucent Library of Black History Ser.). (ENG., Illus.). 104p. (gr. 7-7). lib. bdg. 41.03 *(978-1-4205-0010-3(4),* 6776b446-a900-4bd3-a78f-f2f693a22225, Lucent Pr.) Greenhaven Publishing LLC.

Brandt, Keith & Mattern, Joanne. Rosa Parks: Freedom Rider. Griffith, Gershom, illus. 2006. 54p. (J). pap. *(978-0-439-66045-7(9))* Scholastic, Inc.

Brown, Jonatha A. Rosa Parks, 1 vol. (People We Should Know Ser.). (Illus.). 24p. (gr. 2-4). 2006. (ENG.). lib. bdg. 24.67 *(978-0-8368-4748-2(2),* 3fd2247d-ef71-4f76-8f9d-fe2565b41a2e, Weekly Reader Leveled Readers) 2005. (SPA., pap. 9.15 *(978-0-8368-4769-7(5),* dc6d6549-aadd-4a94-970a-bd4b21cb8052, Weekly Reader Leveled Readers) 2005. (ENG., pap. 9.15 *(978-0-8368-4755-0(5),* 04e24c04-67e0-444b-8563-13ff52afad09, Weekly Reader Leveled Readers) 2005. (SPA., lib. bdg. 24.67 *(978-0-8368-4762-8(8),* 8ef1c1f4-f871-42b6-b2cd-befae7e48778) Stevens, Gareth Publishing LLLP.

Collard, Sneed B., III. Rosa Parks: The Courage to Make a Difference, 1 vol. 2007. (American Heroes Ser.). (ENG., Illus.). 48p. (gr. 3-3). lib. bdg. 32.64 *(978-0-7614-2163-4(7),* 3c36a99d-4199-4687-a280-30439851ae4b) Cavendish Square Publishing LLC.

Collins, James. Rosa Parks: Not Giving In with Buffalo Bill & Farley's Raiders. Cox, Brian T., illus. 2006. (Time Traveler's Adventure Ser.). 56p. (J). 13.50 incl. audio compact disk *(978-1-932332-17-9(0))* Toy Box Productions.

Connors, Kathleen. The Life of Rosa Parks, 1 vol., Vol. 1. 2013. (Famous Lives Ser.). (ENG.). 24p. (J). (gr. 1-2). 25.27 *(978-1-4824-0419-7(2),* b2f69321-8d88-4e1e-a43f-20dde8903ca5) Stevens, Gareth Publishing LLLP.

Daly, Ruth. Rosa Parks. 2014. (Illus.). 24p. (J). *(978-1-4896-2452-9(X))* Weigl Pubs., Inc.

Dubowski, Cathy East. Rosa Parks: Don't Give In! 2005. (Defining Moments Ser.). (Illus.). 32p. (J). (gr. 2-5). lib. bdg. 28.50 *(978-1-59716-078-0(4))* Bearport Publishing Co., Inc.

Edison, Erin. Rosa Parks, 1 vol. 2013. (Great Women in History Ser.). (ENG.). 24p. (J). (gr. -1-2) pap. 6.29 *(978-1-62065-863-5(1),* 121794); (gr. k-1). pap. 38.74 *(978-1-62065-864-2(X),* 19429); (Illus.). (gr. -1-2). lib. bdg. 24.65 *(978-1-62065-071-4(1),* 120774) Capstone. (Pebble).

Edwards, Pamela Duncan. The Bus Ride That Changed History. Shanahan, Danny, illus. 2009. (ENG.). 32p. (J). (gr. -1-3). pap. 7.99 *(978-0-547-07674-4(6),* 1042031, Clarion Bks.) HarperCollins Pubs.

Giovanni, Nikki. Rosa. Collier, Bryan, illus. rev. ed. 2005. (ENG.). 40p. (J). (gr. -1-3). 19.99 *(978-0-8050-7106-1(7),* 900029805, Holt, Henry & Co. Bks. For Young Readers) Holt, Henry & Co.

—Rosa. Collier, Bryan, illus. 2007. (ENG.). 40p. (J). (gr. -1-3). per. 8.99 *(978-0-312-37602-4(2),* 900048322) Square Fish.

—Rosa. Collier, Bryan, illus. 2011. (J). (gr. 2-5). 29.95 *(978-0-545-04261-1(5))* Weston Woods Studios, Inc.

Haldy, Emma E. Rosa Parks. Bane, Jeff, illus. 2016. (My Early Library: My Itty-Bitty Bio Ser.). (ENG.). 24p. (J). (gr. k-1). 30.64 *(978-1-63470-481-6(9),* 207655) Cherry Lake Publishing.

—Rosa Parks SP. Bane, Jeff, illus. 2018. (My Early Library: Mi Mini Biografía (My Itty-Bitty Bio) Ser.). (SPA.). 24p. (J). (gr. k-1). lib. bdg. 30.64 *(978-1-5341-2999-3(5),* 212044) Cherry Lake Publishing.

Harbison, Melissa. Rosa Parks, Vol. 9. 2018. (Civil Rights Leaders Ser.). 144p. (J). (gr. 7). lib. bdg. 35.93 *(978-1-4222-4012-0(6))* Mason Crest.

Hoe, Susan C. Rosa Parks. 2009. (Sharing the American Dream Ser.). 64p. (YA). (gr. 7-12). 22.95 *(978-1-4222-0597-6(5))* Mason Crest.

Hull, Mary, et al. Rosa Parks. 2nd rev. ed. 2008. (ENG.). 128p. (gr. 6-12). pap. 11.95 *(978-1-60413-325-7(2),* P158536, Checkmark Bks.) Infobase Holdings, Inc.

Hurt, Avery Elizabeth. Rosa Parks: Civil Rights Activist, 1 vol. 2017. (Spotlight on Civic Courage: Heroes of Conscience Ser.). (ENG., Illus.). 48p. (J). (gr. 6-6). 33.47 *(978-1-5383-8105-2(2),* 3ea91743-5014-4485-998a-c4da0612e0d4); pap. 12.75 *(978-1-5383-8102-1(8),* f1401158-4208-4b3d-88a1-f1495007bf21) Rosen Publishing Group, Inc., The.

Jazynka, Kitson. National Geographic Readers: AfricanAmerican History Makers. 2018. (Readers Bios Ser.). (Illus.). 144p. (J). (gr. 1-3). pap. 7.99 *(978-1-4263-3201-2(7),* National Geographic Kids) Disney Publishing Worldwide.

—National Geographic Readers: Rosa Parks. 2015. (Readers Bios Ser.). (Illus.). 32p. (J). (gr. 1-3). pap. 4.99 *(978-1-4263-2141-2(4),* National Geographic Kids) Disney Publishing Worldwide.

Jd, Duchess Harris & Hudak, Heather C. Rosa Parks Stays Seated. 2018. (Perspectives on American Progress Ser.). (ENG., Illus.). 48p. (J). (gr. 4-8). lib. bdg. 35.64 *(978-1-5321-1494-6(X),* 29120) ABDO Publishing Co.

Jeffrey, Gary. Rosa Parks & the Montgomery Bus Boycott, 1 vol. 2012. (Graphic History of the Civil Rights Movement Ser.). (ENG., Illus.). 24p. (J). (gr. 3-3). pap. 9.15 *(978-1-4339-7500-4(9),* 22d1d608-8b38-4dfe-bff0-ce7560a74e4c); lib. bdg. 26.60 *(978-1-4339-7499-1(1),* 184f7806-e906-404a-b9c8-b12a88f7caa0) Stevens, Gareth Publishing LLLP.

Kaiser, Lisbeth. Rosa Parks, Volume 9. Antelo, Marta, illus. 2017. (Little People, BIG DREAMS Ser.: 9). (ENG.). 32p. (J). (gr. k-3). 15.99 *(978-1-78603-018-4(7),* Frances Lincoln Children's Bks.) Quarto Publishing Group UK GBR. Dist: Hachette Bk. Group.

Kemp, Kristin. Amazing Americans: Rosa Parks, 1 vol. rev. ed. 2014. (Social Studies: Informational Text Ser.). (ENG., Illus.). 32p. (gr. 3-4). pap. 11.99 *(978-1-4333-7375-6(0))* Teacher Created Materials, Inc.

Kishel, Ann-Marie. Rosa Parks: A Life of Courage. 2006. (Pull Ahead Books — Biographies Ser.). (ENG., Illus.). 32p. (gr. k-3). (J). pap. 7.99 *(978-0-8225-5698-5(7),* 96b861c5-9d8c-48e0-b817-d743bc5612a6); lib. bdg. 22.60 *(978-0-8225-3478-5(9),* Lerner Pubns.) Lerner Publishing Group.

—Rosa Parks: Una Vida de Valentía. Translations.com Staff, tr. 2006. (Libros para Avanzar-Biografías (Pull Ahead Books-Biographies) Ser.). (ENG & SPA., Illus.). 32p. (gr. k-3). lib. bdg. 22.60 *(978-0-8225-6239-9(1))* Lerner Publishing Group.

—Rosa Parks: Una vida de valentía (A Life of Courage) 2006. (Libros para Avanzar-Biografías (Pull Ahead Books-Biographies Ser.). (Illus.). 32p. (J). (gr. 3-7). per. 6.95 *(978-0-8225-6557-4(9),* Ediciones Lerner) Lerner Publishing Group.

Kittinger, Jo S. Rosa's Bus: The Ride to Civil Rights. Walker, Steven, illus. 2010. (ENG.). 40p. (J). (gr. 2-5). 17.99 *(978-1-59078-722-9(6),* Calkins Creek) Highlights Pr., c/o Highlights for Children, Inc.

Linde, Barbara M. Rosa Parks, 1 vol. 2011. (Civil Rights Crusaders Ser.). (ENG., Illus.). 24p. (gr. 2-3). (J). pap. 9.15 *(978-1-4339-5696-6(9),* 71cefba7-22f3-4354-98bd-7e94eafa0085, Gareth Stevens Learning Library); (YA). lib. bdg. 25.27 *(978-1-4339-5694-2(2),* 044c3bb3-585b-4515-90cb-1919fa7f338a) Stevens, Gareth Publishing LLLP.

Manolis, Kay & Leslie, Tonya. Rosa Parks: A Life of Courage. 2007. (People of Character Ser.). (ENG., Illus.). 24p. (J). (gr. 2-5). lib. bdg. 26.95 *(978-1-60014-088-4(2))* Bellwether Media.

Mara, Wil. Rosa Parks. (Rookie Biographies Ser.). (ENG., Illus.). 32p. (J). (gr. 1-2). 2004. pap. 4.95 *(978-0-516-27916-9(5))* 2007. pap. 4.95 *(978-0-531-12592-2(0))* Scholastic Library Publishing. (Children's Pr.).

—Rosa Parks: Mother of the Civil Rights Movement. 2014. (Rookie Biographies(tm) Ser.). (ENG.). 32p. (J). lib. bdg. 25.00 *(978-0-531-20561-7(4))* Scholastic Library Publishing.

McCormick, Anita Louise. Rosa Parks & the Montgomery Bus Boycott. 2017. (Spotlight on the Civil Rights Movement Ser.). 48p. (J). (gr. 10-15). 70.50 *(978-1-5383-8061-1(7));* (ENG.). (gr. 6-6). pap. 12.75 *(978-1-5383-8062-8(5),* 612d67c2-9db3-411f-8126-c16ed9e6ffb3) Rosen Publishing Group, Inc., The.

McDonough, Yona Zeldis & Who HQ. Who Was Rosa Parks? Marchesi, Stephen, illus. 2010. (Who Was? Ser.). 112p. (J). (gr. 3-7). pap. 5.99 *(978-0-448-45442-9(4),* Penguin Workshop) Penguin Young Readers Group.

Meltzer, Brad. I Am Rosa Parks. Eliopoulos, Christopher, illus. 2014. (Ordinary People Change the World Ser.). 40p. (J). (gr. k-4). 15.99 *(978-0-8037-4085-3(9),* Dial Bks) Penguin Young Readers Group.

Miller, Connie Colwell. Rosa Parks & the Montgomery Bus Boycott, 1 vol. Kalal, Dan, illus. 2006. (Graphic History Ser.). (ENG.). 32p. (J). (gr. 3-9). per. 8.10 *(978-0-7368-9658-0(9),* 93445) Capstone.

Mis, Melody S. Meet Rosa Parks. (Civil Rights Leaders Ser.). 24p. (gr. 2-3). 2009. 42.50 *(978-1-61511-855-7(1),* PowerKids Pr.) 2007. (ENG., Illus.). (YA). lib. bdg. 26.27 *(978-1-4042-4210-4(4),* 4b44a5af-168d-44aa-9566-8c251e274076) Rosen Publishing Group, Inc., The.

Morretta, Alison. Rosa Parks & Civil Disobedience, 1 vol. 2016. (Primary Sources of the Civil Rights Movement Ser.). (ENG., Illus.). 64p. (gr. 6-6). 35.93 *(978-1-5026-1870-2(2),* aab07914-02e2-4aa5-9164-fec426698f87) Cavendish Square Publishing LLC.

Morris, Roz. Rosa Parks: Mother of the Civil Rights Movement. 2003. (Alabama Roots Biography Ser.). (ENG., Illus.). 109p. (J). *(978-1-878561-57-2(X))* Seacoast Publishing, Inc.

Reed, Gregory J. Dear Mrs. Parks: a Dialogue with Today's Youth, 1 vol. 2013. (ENG., Illus.). 111p. (J). (gr. 1-5). reprint ed. per. 16.95 *(978-1-880000-61-8(X),* leelowbooks) Lee & Low Bks., Inc.

Rinaldo, Denise. Rosa Parks: With a Discussion of Courage. 2003. (Values in Action Ser.). (J). *(978-1-59203-061-3(0))* Learning Challenge, Inc.

Ringgold, Faith. If a Bus Could Talk: The Story of Rosa Parks. Ringgold, Faith, illus. 2003. (ENG., Illus.). 32p. (J). (gr. k-4). pap. 8.99 *(978-0-689-85676-1(8),* Aladdin) Simon & Schuster Children's Publishing.

Roop, Peter. Take a Stand, Rosa Parks. 2005. (Illus.). 59p. (J). *(978-0-439-67625-0(8))* Scholastic, Inc.

Ruiz, Rachel. When Rosa Parks Went Fishing. Fedele, Chiara, illus. 2017. (Leaders Doing Headstands Ser.). (ENG.). 32p. (J). (gr. 1-4). lib. bdg. 28.65 *(978-1-5158-1574-7(9),* 136244, Picture Window Bks.) Capstone.

Shea, Therese. Rosa Parks, 1 vol. 2014. (Britannica Beginner Bios Ser.). (ENG., Illus.). 32p. (J). (gr. 2-3). 26.06 *(978-1-62275-697-1(5),* 620224ac-0b2f-49de-a43f-50329a4ef347, Britannica Educational Publishing) Rosen Publishing Group, Inc., The.

Shone, Rob. Rosa Parks: The Life of a Civil Rights Heroine. 2009. (Graphic Nonfiction Biographies Ser.). (ENG.). 48p. (YA). (gr. 4-5). 58.50 *(978-1-61513-026-9(8),* Rosen Reference) Rosen Publishing Group, Inc., The.

—Rosa Parks: The Life of a Civil Rights Heroine, 1 vol. Spender, Nick, illus. 2006. (Graphic Nonfiction Biographies Ser.). (ENG.). 48p. (J). (gr. 4-5). lib. bdg. 37.13 *(978-1-4042-0864-3(X),* 6428da22-86f3-4701-b64a-9c47ea50d2f3) Rosen Publishing Group, Inc., The.

—Rosa Parks: The Life of a Civil Rights Heroine, 1 vol. Spender, Nik, illus. 2006. (Graphic Nonfiction Biographies Ser.). (ENG.). 48p. (gr. 4-5). pap. 14.05 *(978-1-4042-0927-5(1),* c2923d67-40d0-41b6-a57f-742175328325) Rosen Publishing Group, Inc., The.

Stoltman, Joan. Rosa Parks, 1 vol. 2017. (Little Biographies of Big People Ser.). (ENG.). 24p. (J). (gr. 1-2). pap. 9.15 *(978-1-5382-0933-2(0),* aa3f53b1-426c-4f61-bf33-eb191f45a383) Stevens, Gareth Publishing LLLP.

—Rosa Parks, 1 vol. Garcia, Ana Maria, tr. 2017. (Pequeñas Biografías de Grandes Personajes (Little Biographies of Big People) Ser.). (SPA.). 24p. (J). (gr. 1-2). pap. 9.15 *(978-1-5382-1556-2(X),* 9be11b2b-c922-4bbc-b399-13cd29d27216); lib. bdg. 24.27 *(978-1-5382-1529-6(2),* 772b3554-c74d-4548-88b9-6c1c0c336571) Stevens, Gareth Publishing LLLP.

Strand, Jennifer. Rosa Parks. 2016. (Great Women Ser.). (ENG.). 24p. (J). (gr. -1-2). 49.94 *(978-1-68079-393-2(4),* 23014, Abdo Zoom-Launch) ABDO Publishing Co.

Susienka, Kristen. Rosa Parks, 1 vol. 2019. (African American Leaders of Courage Ser.). (ENG.). 24p. (gr. 1-2). pap. 9.25 *(978-1-7253-0854-1(1),* d8595867-a6b9-4366-8719-fdaf74e3a445, PowerKids Pr.) Rosen Publishing Group, Inc., The.

Time for Kids Editors. Rosa Parks: Civil Rights Pioneer. 2007. (Time for Kids Biographies Ser.). (Illus.). 44p. (gr. 2-4). 14.00 *(978-0-7569-8110-5(7))* Perfection Learning Corp.

Tracy, Kathleen. The Life & Times of Rosa Parks. 2008. (Illus.). 48p. (J). (gr. 4-8). lib. bdg. 29.95 *(978-1-58415-666-6(X))* Mitchell Lane Pubs.

Weidt, Maryann N. Rosa Parks. (History Maker Bios Ser.). (Illus.). (J). 2004. 48p. pap. 8.95 *(978-0-8225-4805-8(4))* 2003. 47p. 26.60 *(978-0-8225-4673-3(6))* Lerner Publishing Group. (Lerner Pubns.).

Weston Woods Staff, creator. Rosa. 2011. 18.95 *(978-0-545-14962-4(2));* 38.75 *(978-0-545-14963-1(0))* Weston Woods Studios, Inc.

Wheeler, Jill C. Rosa Parks, Set II. 2003. (Breaking Barriers Ser.). 64p. (gr. 3-8). lib. bdg. 27.07 *(978-1-57765-640-1(7),* Abdo & Daughters) ABDO Publishing Co.

Whiting, Jim. Rosa Parks. 2007. (What's So Great About...? Ser.). (Illus.). 32p. (YA). (gr. 2-4). lib. bdg. 25.70 *(978-1-58415-573-7(6))* Mitchell Lane Pubs.

PARKS

Beck, Isabel L., et al. Trophies Kindergarten: The Park. 2003. (Trophies Ser.). (gr. k-6). 13.80 *(978-0-15-329533-1(3))* Harcourt Schl. Pubs.

Beylon, Cathy. At the Amusement Park. 2004. (Dover Coloring Bks.). (ENG., Illus.). 32p. (J). (gr. -1-2). pap. 2.95 *(978-0-486-43322-6(6))* Dover Pubns., Inc.

Brinker, Spencer. At the Park. 2019. (I Spy Ser.). (ENG., Illus.). 16p. (J). (gr. -1-1). 6.99 *(978-1-64280-394-5(4))* Bearport Publishing Co., Inc.

Cantor, Rachel Anne. Haunted Amusement Parks. 2016. (Tiptoe into Scary Places Ser.). (ENG., Illus.). 24p. (J). (gr. k-3). 26.99 *(978-1-68402-050-8(6))* Bearport Publishing Co., Inc.

Clark Sawyer, J. Patterns in the Park. 2015. (J). lib. bdg. 28.50 *(978-1-62724-339-1(9))* Bearport Publishing Co., Inc.

Dale, Jay. The Environment Park. 2012. (Engage Literacy Green Ser.). (ENG.). 16p. (J). (gr. k-2). pap. 36.94 *(978-1-4296-8998-4(6),* 18395); (Illus.). pap. 6.99 *(978-1-4296-8997-7(8),* 120005) Capstone. (Capstone Pr.).

—I Am in the Park. Dybing, Michelle, illus. 2012. (Wonder Words Ser.). (ENG.). 16p. (J). (gr. k-2). pap. 36.94 *(978-1-4296-8891-8(2),* 18341, Capstone Pr.) Capstone.

Dale, Jay & Scott, Kay. I Am in the Park. Dybing, Michelle, illus. 2012. (Wonder Words Ser.). (ENG.). 16p. (J). (gr. k-2). pap. 6.99 *(978-1-4296-8890-1(4),* 119948, Capstone Pr.) Capstone.

Devera, Czeena. At the Park. 2019. (I Can See Ser.). (ENG.). 16p. (J). (gr. -1-2). pap. 11.36 *(978-1-5341-3916-9(8),* 212498, Cherry Blossom Press) Cherry Lake Publishing.

Disneyland Resort Then, Now & Forever: Remember the Moments - A Magical Souvenir. 2006. 192p. 24.95 *(978-1-4231-0256-4(8),* Disney Editions) Disney Pr.

Dunlap, Julie & Olmsted, Frederick Law. Parks for the People: The Life of Frederick Law Olmsted. 2011. (ENG., Illus.). 112p. (J). (gr. 4-7). pap. 12.95 *(978-1-55591-470-7(5))* Fulcrum Publishing.

Editorial Staff, Gareth. Things at the Park, 1 vol. 2006. (Things in My World Ser.). (ENG., Illus.). 16p. (gr. k-1). pap. 6.30 *(978-0-8368-6816-6(1),* c39592ac-5429-40dd-b892-06768d2098f4, Weekly Reader Leveled Readers) Stevens, Gareth Publishing LLLP.

—Things at the Park / Las Cosas Del Parque, 1 vol. 2006. (Things in My World / Las Cosas de Mi Mundo Ser.). (ENG & SPA., Illus.). 16p. (gr. k-1). pap. 6.30 *(978-0-8368-7228-6(2),* e8e86d10-fdc4-4678-8d5f-f5fe7200cdaf, Weekly Reader Leveled Readers) Stevens, Gareth Publishing LLLP.

Finn, Peter. Go to the Park!, 1 vol. 2019. (Go Outside! Ser.). (ENG.). 24p. (gr. k-k). pap. 9.15 *(978-1-5382-4493-7(4),* 2844463c-6662-4965-ada2-fde5ca130d52) Stevens, Gareth Publishing LLLP.

Grandma Fudgie. A Walk to the Park. 2011. 24p. pap. 12.99 *(978-1-4634-2695-8(X))* AuthorHouse.

Greathouse, Lisa. Cómo Funcionan los Parques de Diversiones. rev. ed. 2010. (Science: Informational Text Ser.). Orig. Title: How Amusement Parks Work. (SPA., Illus.). 32p. (gr. 3-5). pap. 11.99 *(978-1-4333-2149-8(1))* Teacher Created Materials, Inc.

Gregory, Helen. The Park, 1 vol. 2011. (Wonder Readers Early Level Ser.). (ENG.). 16p. (gr. -1-1). (J). pap. 6.25 *(978-1-4296-7807-0(0),* 117979); pap. 35.94 *(978-1-4296-8170-4(5))* Capstone. (Capstone Pr.).

Hill, Mary. Let's Go to a Park. 2004. (Welcome Bks.). (ENG.). 24p. (J). (gr. -1-2). pap. 4.95 *(978-0-516-25918-5(0),* Children's Pr.) Scholastic Library Publishing.

—Signs at the Park. 2003. (Welcome Bks.). (ENG., Illus.). 24p. (J). (gr. -1-2). pap. 4.95 *(978-0-516-24365-8(9),* Children's Pr.) Scholastic Library Publishing.

Hocking, Justin. Skate Parks. 2009. (Power Skateboarding Ser.). 24p. (gr. 3-4). 42.50 *(978-1-60851-338-3(6),* PowerKids Pr.) Rosen Publishing Group, Inc., The.

—Taking Action: How to Get Your City to Build a Public Skate Park. 2009. (Skateboarder's Guide to Skate Parks, Half-Pipes, Bowls, & Obstacles Ser.). 48p. (gr. 5-8). 53.00 *(978-1-60854-234-5(3),* Rosen Reference) Rosen Publishing Group, Inc., The.

—The World's Greatest Skate Parks, 1 vol. 2009. (Super Skateboarding Ser.). (ENG.). 48p. (gr. 5-8). (YA). lib. bdg. 34.47 *(978-1-4358-5046-0(7),* e754452a-d965-41ee-a1ec-f6624f9ce277); (Illus.). (J). pap. 12.75 *(978-1-4358-5390-4(3),* d49f373b-bec7-4300-a2fd-0951b8040140) Rosen Publishing Group, Inc., The.

—World's Greatest Skate Parks. 2009. (Super Skateboarding Ser.). 48p. (gr. 5-8). 53.00 *(978-1-60853-222-3(4),* Rosen Reference) Rosen Publishing Group, Inc., The.

Holub, Joan & Who HQ. Where Is Walt Disney World? Copeland, Gregory, illus. 2018. (Where Is? Ser.). 112p. (J). (gr. 3-7). 5.99 *(978-0-515-15843-4(7),* Penguin Workshop) Penguin Young Readers Group.

Hutchings, Amy. What Happens at an Amusement Park?, 1 vol. 2009. (Where People Work Ser.). (ENG.). 24p. (J). (gr. 1-1). lib. bdg. 24.67 *(978-1-4339-0073-0(4),* 7f59c7ff-7990-4bbc-9b3a-09a0a4bcef9d, Weekly Reader Leveled Readers) Stevens, Gareth Publishing LLLP.

—What Happens at an Amusement Park? / ¿Qué Pasa en un Parque de Diversiones?, 1 vol. 2009. (Where People Work / ¿dónde Trabaja la Gente? Ser.). (SPA & ENG.). 24p. (J). (gr. 1-1). pap. 9.15 *(978-1-4339-0145-4(5),* 8f9d5b62-17c1-4c7b-a568-b6017869cacf); lib. bdg. 24.67 *(978-1-4339-0081-5(5),* f8d6416e-d0ef-45ca-8e0d-99dd8c13f6b2) Stevens, Gareth Publishing LLLP. (Weekly Reader Leveled Readers).

Leigh, Johanna. Spanish Words at the Park, 1 vol., Vol. 1. 2013. (Learn My Language! Spanish Ser.). (ENG.). 24p. (J). (gr. 1-2). 25.27 *(978-1-4824-0346-6(3),* 576ce367-3d68-4c54-8a91-801c317592b8); pap. 9.15 *(978-1-4824-0345-9(5),* 365f1974-969b-4503-bad9-f33df113f046) Stevens, Gareth Publishing LLLP.

Loh-Hagan, Virginia. Roller Coasters. 2017. (21st Century Junior Library: Extraordinary Engineering Ser.). (ENG., Illus.). 24p. (J). (gr. 2-5). lib. bdg. 29.21 *(978-1-63472-164-6(0),* 209228) Cherry Lake Publishing.

Lucas, Diane & Searle, Ken. Walking with the Seasons in Kakadu. 2005. (ENG., Illus.). 32p. (J). (gr. 2-4). pap. 12.95 *(978-1-74114-471-0(X))* Allen & Unwin AUS. Dist: Independent Pubs. Group.

Lukeman, Noah. A Trip to the Amusement Park. 2015. (ENG., Illus.). 20p. (J). pap. 5.99 *(978-1-63291-487-3(5))* Morgan Rice Bks.

Marsico, Katie. Working at a Park. 2008. (21st Century Junior Library: Careers Ser.). (ENG., Illus.). 24p. (gr. 2-5). lib. bdg. 29.21 *(978-1-60279-267-8(4),* 200172) Cherry Lake Publishing.

Mattern, Joanne. Cuyahoga Valley National Park (Rookie National Parks) (Library Edition) 2018. (Rookie National Parks Ser.). (ENG., Illus.). 32p. (J). (gr. 1-2). lib. bdg. 25.00 *(978-0-531-12652-3(8),* Children's Pr.) Scholastic Library Publishing.

Mayfield, Marilee Joy. My First Book of United States Monuments & Parks. 2017. (Illus.). 51p. (J). *(978-1-4351-6637-0(X))* Barnes & Noble, Inc.

McCune, Susan. All about Our Park, 1 vol., 1. 2015. (Rosen REAL Readers: Social Studies Nonfiction / Fiction: Myself, My Community, My World Ser.). (ENG.). 8p. (J). (gr. k-1). pap. 5.46 *(978-1-5081-1722-3(5),* d96904cc-4d1f-4366-970f-12ec0c76bc7a, Rosen Classroom) Rosen Publishing Group, Inc., The.

National Geographic Learning. Windows on Literacy Step up (Science: Plants Around Us): Plants in the Park. 2007. (ENG., Illus.). 8p. (J). pap. 9.95 *(978-0-7922-8463-5(1))* CENGAGE Learning.

Nelson, Robin. How We Clean up a Park. 2014. (First Step Nonfiction — Responsibility in Action Ser.). (ENG., Illus.). 24p. (J). (gr. k-2). pap. 6.99 *(978-1-4677-3646-6(5),* e6d64a4b-6f94-484f-bb8c-c2d0ebf9cd73) Lerner Publishing Group.

On a Roll: How Communities Build State Parks. 2005. (Book Treks Ser.). (J). 37.95 *(978-0-7652-3254-0(5))* Celebration Pr.

A Park Ecosystem. 2012. (Nature Trail Ser.). (ENG., Illus.). 32p. (J). (gr. k-5). 23.95 *(978-1-4488-6626-7(X),* PowerKids Pr.) Rosen Publishing Group, Inc., The.

Parks Matter! 2004. (YA). *(978-0-88441-673-9(9))* Girl Scouts of the USA.

Randall, Jory. My Day at the Park, 1 vol. 2009. (Kid's Life! Ser.). (ENG.). 24p. (J). (gr. 1-1). pap. 9.25 *(978-1-4358-2465-2(2),* 9a1f2cab-b7a8-4e81-ab64-057074aa172f); (Illus.). lib. bdg. 26.27 *(978-1-4042-8073-1(1),* e2d8985c-548e-46f4-9c85-0c65ec5985a6) Rosen Publishing Group, Inc., The. (PowerKids Pr.).

Reasoner, Charles. First Words at the Park. Pitt, Sarah, illus. 2009. (3D Board Bks.). 12p. (J). (gr. -1-k). bds. 9.99 *(978-1-934650-39-4(0))* Just For Kids Pr., LLC.

Rissman, Rebecca. Counting at the Park, 1 vol. 2012. (I Can Count! Ser.). (ENG.). 24p. (gr. -1-k). pap. 9.95 *(978-1-4329-6700-0(2),* Heinemann) Capstone.

Ruffin, Frances E. Creating a City Park: Dividing Three-Digit Numbers by One-Digit Numbers Without Remainders, 1 vol. (Math for the REAL World Ser.). (ENG., Illus.). 24p. (gr. 3-4). 2010. pap. 8.25 *(978-0-8239-8926-3(7),* f61a8142-e5e0-4c07-8230-f8afd68bf7c1, PowerKids Pr.) 2003. (J). lib. bdg. 26.27 *(978-0-8239-8978-2(X),* 5324d1f2-d5b9-4ced-84ec-eb50ec765e3a) Rosen Publishing Group, Inc., The.

—Creating a City Park: Dividing Three-digit Numbers by One-digit Numbers Without Remainders. 2009. (PowerMath: Intermediate Ser.). 24p. (gr. 3-4). 45.00 *(978-1-60851-380-2(7),* PowerKids Pr.) Rosen Publishing Group, Inc., The.

Staff, Gareth Editorial Staff. Things at the Park, 1 vol. 2006. (Things in My World Ser.). (ENG., Illus.). 16p. (gr. k-1). lib. bdg. 21.67 *(978-0-8368-6809-8(9),* 99d3a442-747e-409f-b906-be1797eae969, Weekly Reader Leveled Readers) Stevens, Gareth Publishing LLLP.

—Things at the Park / Las Cosas Del Parque, 1 vol. 2006. (Things in My World / Las Cosas de Mi Mundo Ser.). (ENG & SPA., Illus.). 16p. (gr. k-1). lib. bdg. 21.67 *(978-0-8368-7221-7(5),* 75ebe2b3-9403-460e-a47a-692f4ba1fd9d, Weekly Reader Leveled Readers) Stevens, Gareth Publishing LLLP.

Taylor, Trace & Sanchez, Lucia M. En el Parque: At the Park. 2011. (1-3Y ARC Press Comics Ser.). (SPA & ENG.). 16p. (J). pap. 9.60 *(978-1-61541-454-3(1))* American Reading Co.

—En el parque (at the Park) 2011. (Lugares adonde voy Ser.). (SPA.). 12p. pap. 39.62 *(978-1-61541-455-0(X))* American Reading Co.

What Is a Park?, 6 Packs. (Discovery World Ser.). 16p. (gr. 1-2). 28.00 *(978-0-7635-8453-5(3))* Rigby Education.

Williams, Colleen Madonna Flood. My Adventure at the Amusement Park. 2007. 44p. (J). 8.99 *(978-1-59092-410-5(X))* Blue Forge Pr.

Wishinsky, Frieda. The Man Who Made Parks: The Story of Parkbuilder Frederick Law Olmsted. Zhang, Song Nan, illus. 2009. 32p. (J). (gr. k-4). pap. 10.95 *(978-0-88776-902-3(0),* Tundra Bks.) Tundra Bks. CAN. Dist: Penguin Random Hse. LLC.

Yazdani, Ashley Benham. A Green Place to Be: the Creation of Central Park. Yazdani, Ashley Benham, illus. 2019. (ENG., Illus.). 40p. (J). (gr. 2-5). 18.99 *(978-0-7636-9695-5(1))* Candlewick Pr.

PARKS—FICTION

Anderson, Mark A. Ma Ma, I'm Home, 1 vol. 2009. 48p. pap. 16.95 *(978-1-4489-9077-1(7))* America Star Bks.

Baker, Keith. At the Park. 2016. (Mr. & Mrs. Green Ser.). (ENG., Illus.). 32p. (J). (gr. 1-4). pap. 4.99 *(978-0-544-55556-3(2),* 1610462, Clarion Bks.) HarperCollins Pubs.

Barkley, Callie. Amy on Park Patrol. Bishop, Tracy, illus. 2017. (Critter Club Ser.: 17). (ENG.). 128p. (J). (gr. k-3). pap. 6.99 *(978-1-4814-9432-8(5),* Little Simon) Little Simon.

—Amy on Park Patrol. 2017. (Critter Club Ser.: 17). lib. bdg. 16.00 *(978-0-606-40208-8(X))* Turtleback.

Bauer, Marion Dane. Little Dog, Lost. Bell, Jennifer A., illus. 2013. (ENG.). 208p. (J). (gr. 3-7). pap. 7.99 *(978-1-4424-3424-0(4),* Atheneum Bks. for Young Readers) Simon & Schuster Children's Publishing.

Baumgarten, Josephine & Baumgarten, Michael. My Baby Monsters & I went to the Park. 2005. 32p. pap. 14.99 *(978-1-4116-6348-0(9))* Lulu Pr., Inc.

Beaty, Andrea. Sofia Valdez, Future Prez. 2019. (Questioneers Ser.). (ENG., Illus.). 40p. (J). (gr. k-2). 18.99 *(978-1-4197-3704-6(X),* 1217401) Abrams, Inc.

Benenfeld, Rikki. Let's Go to the Park. 2015. (ENG., Illus.). 36p. (J). 11.99 *(978-1-929628-82-7(X))* Hachai Publishing.

Benson, Glenda. The Adventures of Pepe & Gracie: Trouble in the Park. 2012. 20p. pap. 13.77 *(978-1-4669-0840-6(8))* Trafford Publishing.

Bloomsbury USA. Lift & Look: at the Park. 2016. (ENG., Illus.). 12p. (J). (— 1). bds. 8.99 *(978-1-61963-940-9(8),* 9781619639409, Bloomsbury Activity Bks.) Bloomsbury Publishing USA.

Booking, Walt. Teddy's Tale, 1 vol. 2006. (Neighborhood Readers Ser.). (ENG.). 12p. (gr. 1-2). pap. 5.90 *(978-1-4042-7054-1(X),* b9bd6f15-8022-48bd-ae11-5544e85a5587, Rosen Classroom) Rosen Publishing Group, Inc., The.

Bradford James Nolan. The Mouse Who Lived in Fenway Park. Jim Connelly, illus. 2009. 36p. pap. 19.99 *(978-1-4389-4491-3(8))* AuthorHouse.

Bradley, A. M. Finnegan's Magic Sunglasses. 2013. 24p. pap. 24.95 *(978-1-62709-814-4(3))* America Star Bks.

Bunting, Eve. Little Yellow Truck. Zimmer, Kevin, illus. 2019. (ENG.). 32p. (J). (gr. k-3). 16.99 *(978-1-58536-407-7(X),* 204649) Sleeping Bear Pr.

Butterworth, Nick. A Classic Treasury. Butterworth, Nick, illus. 2022. (Percy the Park Keeper Ser.). (ENG., Illus.). 240p. (J). (gr. k-2). 34.99 *(978-0-00-721137-1(6),* HarperCollins Children's Bks.) HarperCollins Pubs. Ltd. GBR. Dist: HarperCollins Pubs.

—One Snowy Night. Butterworth, Nick, illus. 2007. (ENG., Illus.). 32p. (J). 24.00 *(978-0-00-725942-7(5))* HarperCollins Pubs. Ltd. GBR. Dist: Independent Pubs. Group.

Campbell, Rod. Buster's Park. 2003. (ENG., Illus.). 14p. (J). bds. 6.99 *(978-0-333-76645-3(8))* Macmillan Pubs., Ltd. GBR. Dist: Trafalgar Square Publishing.

Carlson, Melody. Take Charge, 1 vol. 2016. (Faithgirlz / Girls of Harbor View Ser.). (ENG.). 272p. (J). (gr. 3-7). pap. 9.99 *(978-0-310-75373-5(2))* Zonderkidz.

Carmen & Thane Johnson. Dogs Don't Wear Underwear. Bianca & Annie West, illus. 2009. 20p. pap. 12.99 *(978-1-4389-4128-8(5))* AuthorHouse.

Carter, Larry. The Red Wallet. 2013. 28p. pap. 24.95 *(978-1-4626-9667-3(8))* America Star Bks.

Cleveland, Marie. Jason's Giant Dilemma: A Storybook Land Adventure. 2007. 76p. per. 19.95 *(978-1-4241-7811-7(8))* America Star Bks.

Coven, Wanda. Heidi Heckelbeck Lends a Helping Hand. Burris, Priscilla, illus. 2019. (Heidi Heckelbeck Ser.: 26). (ENG.). 128p. (J). (gr. k-4). pap. 5.99 *(978-1-5344-4529-1(3),* Little Simon) Little Simon.

Cox, Phil Roxbee. Shark in the Park. Tyler, Jenny, ed. Cartwright, Stephen, illus. rev. ed. 2006. (Phonics Readers Ser.). 16p. (J). (gr. -1-k). pap. 6.99 *(978-0-7945-1509-6(6),* Usborne) EDC Publishing.

Cox, Phil Roxbee & Cartwright, Stephen. Shark in the Park. 2004. (Easy Words to Read Ser.). (Illus.). 16p. (J). (gr. 1-18). pap. 6.95 *(978-0-7945-0171-6(0),* Usborne) EDC Publishing.

Crow, Melinda Melton. Rocky & Daisy at the Park, 1 vol. Brownlow, Mike, illus. 2013. (My Two Dogs Ser.). (ENG.). 32p. (J). (gr. 2-3). pap. 5.95 *(978-1-4342-6118-2(2),* 123268); lib. bdg. 22.65 *(978-1-4342-4163-4(7),* 119911) Capstone. (Stone Arch Bks.).

Crowne, Alyssa. Green Princess Saves the Day. Alder, Charlotte, illus. 2010. (J). (Perfectly Princess Ser.: 3). (ENG.). 80p. (gr. 1-4). 4.99 *(978-0-545-20848-2(3),* Scholastic Paperbacks); 71p. *(978-0-545-23414-6(X))* Scholastic, Inc.

Curious George at the Park Touch-And-Feel (Cgtv Board Book) 2010. (Curious George Ser.). (ENG., Illus.). 10p. (J). (gr. -1 — 1). bds. 6.99 *(978-0-547-24300-9(6),* 1099424, Clarion Bks.) HarperCollins Pubs.

Czubinski, Robert. The Many Adventures of Pig Batter: A Day at the Park, 1 vol. Czubinski, Amber, illus. 2009. 20p. pap. 24.95 *(978-1-61546-495-1(6))* America Star Bks.

Dean, Sara. The Puppy Who Found a Boy, 1 vol. Hacker, Randy, illus. 2009. 13p. pap. 24.95 *(978-1-61546-278-0(3))* America Star Bks.

DeMonte, Joe. Lucy & the Magic Factory. 2008. 79p. pap. 19.95 *(978-1-60813-119-8(X))* America Star Bks.

Denice, Sonia. Chow-E-Chowz: Saved by a Whistle. 2011. 44p. pap. 18.46 *(978-1-4567-1020-6(6))* AuthorHouse.

Dixon, Franklin W. Forever Lost: Book Three in the Lost Mystery Trilogy. 2011. (Hardy Boys (All New) Undercover Brothers Ser.: 36). (ENG.). 160p. (J). (gr. 3-7). pap. 6.99 *(978-1-4424-0264-5(4),* Aladdin) Simon & Schuster Children's Publishing.

Doherty, Kathleen. Don't Feed the Bear. Wass, Chip, illus. 2018. 32p. (J). (gr. -1). 18.99 *(978-1-4549-1979-7(5))* Sterling Publishing Co., Inc.

Dufresne, Michèle. The Water Park. 2005. (Georgie Giraffe Set 1 Ser.). (ENG.). (J). pap. 7.33 *(978-1-932570-38-0(1))* Pioneer Valley Bks.

Dugan, Jennifer. Hot Dog Girl. 2019. 320p. (J). (gr. 7). 17.99 *(978-0-525-51625-5(5),* G.P. Putnam's Sons Books for Young Readers) Penguin Young Readers Group.

Edwards, Nancy. Mom for Mayor. Chesworth, Michael, illus. 2006. (ENG.). 96p. (J). (gr. 1-5). 16.95 *(978-0-8126-2743-5(1))* Cricket Bks.

Eggers, Dave. The Eyes & the Impossible. Harris, Shawn, illus. 2023. (ENG.). 256p. (J). (gr. 3-7). 18.99 *(978-1-5247-6420-3(5));* lib. bdg. 21.99 *(978-1-5247-6421-0(3))* Random Hse. Children's Bks. (Knopf Bks. for Young Readers).

Fagan, Cary. The Hollow under the Tree, 1 vol. 2018. (ENG.). 128p. (J). (gr. 3-6). 14.95 *(978-1-55498-999-7(X))* Groundwood Bks. CAN. Dist: Publishers Group West (PGW).

Feldman, Thea. Adventure in the Park. Ward, April, illus. 2006. 20p. (J). *(978-0-696-23234-3(0))* Meredith Bks.

Galbraith, Kathryn O. Spring Babies. Pons, Adela, illus. 2019. (Babies in the Park Ser.). 20p. (J). (gr. -1 — 1). bds. 7.99 *(978-1-68263-068-6(4))* Peachtree Publishing Co. Inc.

—Winter Babies. Pons, Adela, illus. 2018. (Babies in the Park Ser.). 20p. (J). (gr. -1 — 1). bds. 6.99 *(978-1-68263-067-9(6))* Peachtree Publishing Co. Inc.

Geraldi, Michele J. Pennies at Piper Park. 2009. 24p. pap. 12.99 *(978-1-4389-2829-6(7))* AuthorHouse.

Gilmore, Cathy. Fun at the Park with Ransom & Ripley. 2011. 20p. pap. 24.95 *(978-1-4560-6643-7(9))* America Star Bks.

Going to the Park: Individual Title Six-Packs. (gr. -1-2). 23.00 *(978-0-7635-9012-3(6))* Rigby Education.

Harger, Teresa. Nicky & the Princess. 2010. 20p. pap. 12.79 *(978-1-4520-6035-4(5))* AuthorHouse.

Haugaard, Kay. No Place. 2nd ed. 2007. (ENG., Illus.). 140p. (J). (gr. 2-8). per. 6.95 *(978-1-57131-675-2(2))* Milkweed Editions.

Hensley, Sarah M. At the Park. Crowell, Knox, illus. I.t. ed. 2006. 10p. (J). (gr. -1-k). pap. 10.95 *(978-1-57332-354-3(3),* HighReach Learning, Incorporated) Carson-Dellosa Publishing, LLC.

Hill, Eric. Spot Goes to the Park. Hill, Eric, illus. 2005. (Spot Ser.). (ENG., Illus.). 24p. (J). (gr. -1 — 1). bds. 9.99 *(978-0-399-24363-9(1),* Warne) Penguin Young Readers Group.

Hinbest, Wendy. Frizzy Tizzy Goes to the Park. 2011. (ENG.). 20p. 11.95 *(978-1-4583-4346-8(4))* Lulu Pr., Inc.

Holub, Joan. Picnic! A Day in the Park (Ready-To-Read Pre-Level 1) Terry, Will, illus. 2008. (Ant Hill Ser.). (ENG.). 24p. (J). (gr. -1-k). pap. 4.99 *(978-1-4169-5133-9(4),* Simon Spotlight) Simon Spotlight.

Houran, Lori Haskins. Parks & Wrecks (Book 10) Warrick, Jessica, illus. 2018. (How to Be an Earthling Ser.). 64p. (J). (gr. 1-4). pap. 6.99 *(978-1-63592-021-5(3),* 7d90ddd2-a724-4d48-a707-23a7f6533ea1, Kane Press) Astra Publishing Hse.

Hughes, John P. A Wish for Little Tommy Turtle. White, Tara B., illus. 2011. 48p. pap. 24.95 *(978-1-4626-0011-3(5))* America Star Bks.

Hupf, Zetta & Hupf, Mitchell. Henry Goes to the Park, 1 vol. Hupf, Zetta, illus. 2009. (Illus.). 33p. pap. 24.95 *(978-1-61546-279-7(1))* America Star Bks.

Ibeh, Chinwe. The Moment That Sandra Won. 2011. 28p. pap. 24.95 *(978-1-4626-2938-1(5))* PublishAmerica, Inc.

Isaacs, Latricia. Mason & Baylee Learn to Count. 2011. 16p. (gr. -1). pap. 8.32 *(978-1-4634-0442-0(5))* AuthorHouse.

Jeffs, Dixie. The Old Man. 2013. 20p. pap. 24.95 *(978-1-62709-344-6(3))* America Star Bks.

Jenkins, Emily. Water in the Park: A Book about Water & the Times of the Day. Graegin, Stephanie, illus. 2013. 40p. (J). (gr. -1-2). 16.99 *(978-0-375-87002-6(4),* Schwartz & Wade Bks.) Random Hse. Children's Bks.

Johnson, Angela. Lottie Paris Lives Here. Fischer, Scott M., illus. 2011. (ENG.). 32p. (J). (gr. k-4). 19.99 *(978-0-689-87377-5(8),* Simon & Schuster Bks. For Young Readers) Simon & Schuster Bks. For Young Readers.

Jones, Lisa & Underwood, Edward, illus. Baby's First Cloth Book: Park. 2018. (ENG.). 8p. (J). (— 1). 18.00 *(978-0-7636-9910-9(1))* Candlewick Pr.

Joyner, Andrew. Boris on the Move. 2013. (Boris Ser.: 1). lib. bdg. 14.75 *(978-0-606-31974-4(3))* Turtleback.

—Boris on the Move: a Branches Book (Boris #1), Bk. 1. Joyner, Andrew, illus. 2013. (Boris Ser.: 1). (ENG.). 80p. (J). (gr. k-2). pap. 5.99 *(978-0-545-48443-5(X))* Scholastic, Inc.

Kean, Edward. Howdy Doody in Funland. Seiden, Art, illus. 2011. 30p. 35.95 *(978-1-258-02315-7(6))* Literary Licensing, LLC.

Kent, Lorna, illus. In the Park. 2004. 8p. (J). bds. 3.99 *(978-1-85854-097-9(6))* Brimax Books Ltd. GBR. Dist: Byeway Bks.

Kirwan-Mason, Sandra. My Doll, Dollie. 2005. (ENG.). 28p. per. 18.00 *(978-1-4208-3481-9(9))* AuthorHouse.

Knudsen, Michelle. Carl the Complainer. Cocca-Leffler, Maryann, illus. 2005. (Social Studies Connects Ser.). 32p. (J). (gr. 1-3). pap. 5.95 *(978-1-57565-157-6(2),* a9ef351d-3ed2-4993-b130-8cf5a17492d1, Kane Press) Astra Publishing Hse.

Lane, Andy. Glendale: Nashville's Magical Park. Sloan, Michael, illus. 2009. 88p. (J). 22.95 *(978-1-57736-408-5(2))* Providence Hse Pubs.

Little, Celeste. At the Park with Tommy & Scales. Motz, Mike, illus. 2012. 26p. (J). (-18). 12.95 *(978-1-60131-139-9(7),* Castlebridge Bks.) Big Tent Bks.

Lottie Paris Lives Here. 2014. (Classic Board Bks.). (ENG., Illus.). 34p. (J). (gr. -1-k). bds. 8.99 *(978-1-4814-0966-7(2),* Little Simon) Little Simon.

Lotto, Lisa Marie. Oh How We Feel When We Are Sick with the Flu: Oh the Things We See When We Go to the Park. 2008. 28p. pap. 13.99 *(978-1-4343-6009-0(1))* AuthorHouse.

Lund, Wendy E. The Fly Away Balloon. 2010. 50p. pap. 16.50 *(978-1-60911-660-6(7),* Eloquent Bks.) Strategic Book Publishing & Rights Agency (SBPRA).

Lyle-Soffe, Shari. Shoo Cat. Foster, Jack, illus. 2010. 16p. pap. 9.95 *(978-1-61633-033-0(3))* Guardian Angel Publishing, Inc.

Lynn, Cheryl. Kayla's Day at the Park. 2008. 16p. pap. 24.95 *(978-1-60813-169-3(6))* America Star Bks.

M. Ward. The Evergreens Go to the Park. 2009. (Illus.). 20p. pap. 11.49 *(978-1-4343-9761-4(0))* AuthorHouse.

MacHale, D. J. Oracle of Doom (the Library Book 3) 2018. (Library: 3). 304p. (J). (gr. 3-7). 16.99 *(978-1-101-93261-2(9),* Random Hse. Bks. for Young Readers) Random Hse. Children's Bks.

Marie, Tamara. The Adventures of Madison. 2010. 32p. pap. 17.99 *(978-1-60957-972-2(0))* Salem Author Services.

Mattiangeli, Susanna. The Hideout. Sala, Felicita, illus. 2019. (ENG.). 40p. (J). (gr. -1-3). 16.99 *(978-1-4197-3416-8(4),* 1213501, Abrams Bks. for Young Readers) Abrams, Inc.

Mayer, Mercer. Going to the Sea Park. 2009. (Little Critter: I Can Read! Ser.). (J). lib. bdg. 13.55 *(978-0-606-06964-9(X))* Turtleback.

—Little Critter: Just Critters Who Care. Mayer, Mercer, illus. 2010. (My First I Can Read Ser.). (ENG., Illus.). 32p. (J). (gr. -1-3). 16.99 *(978-0-06-083560-6(5));* pap. 4.99 *(978-0-06-083559-0(1))* HarperCollins Pubs. (HarperCollins).

Mcleod-Stecy, Tracey. The Stone Guardian. 2011. 144p. (gr. 4-6). pap. 11.95 *(978-1-4620-3954-8(5))* iUniverse, Inc.

Meachen Rau, Dana. At the Park, 1 vol. 2008. (Fun Time Ser.). (ENG., Illus.). 24p. (gr. k-1). lib. bdg. 25.50 *(978-0-7614-2613-4(2),* 675f31ba-705a-4a4a-b602-5f25431fc363) Cavendish Square Publishing LLC.

—En el Parque (at the Park), 1 vol. 2009. (Tiempo de la Diversión (Fun Time) Ser.). (SPA., Illus.). 24p. (gr. k-1). lib. bdg. 25.50 *(978-0-7614-2775-9(9),* 0189c902-e46f-48d6-856a-7c204806d681) Cavendish Square Publishing LLC.

Meisel, Paul. See Me Run. (I Like to Read Ser.). (Illus.). (J). (gr. -1-3). 2018. 32p. pap. 4.99 *(978-0-8234-4043-6(5))* 2012. (ENG., 24p. pap. 7.99 *(978-0-8234-2638-6(6))* Holiday Hse., Inc.

Messer, Celeste M. When Eagles Fly. Hoeffner, Deb, illus. 2004. 82-92p. (J). 4.95 *(978-0-9702171-8-9(8))* AshleyAlan Enterprises.

Mumford, Carole. The Magnificent: Their Yellowstone Adventure, 1 vol. 2009. 73p. pap. 19.95 *(978-1-60813-595-0(0))* America Star Bks.

Muse, Ludi. My Day at the Park. 2007. 32p. per. 13.95 *(978-1-4259-6563-1(6))* AuthorHouse.

Nan, Carol. Nana the Baby Pine Tree. 2012. 24p. pap. 24.95 *(978-1-4626-8944-6(2))* America Star Bks.

Neil, Deanna. Lost in Yellowstone: The Land of Curiosities, 1872-1873, vol. 2. 2nd rev. ed. 2015. (J). reprint ed. 19.99 *(978-0-9798800-9-4(2))* EcoSeekers, The.

O'Donnel, Liam. Scout Hits the Trail. Huerta, Catherine, illus. (Pet Tales Ser.). (ENG.). 32p. (J). (gr. -1-3). 2008. 4.95 *(978-1-59249-740-9(3))* 2007. 9.95 *(978-1-59249-742-3(X))* Soundprints.

O'Donnell, Liam. Scout Hits the Trail. Huerta, Catherine, illus. 2007. (ENG.). 32p. (J). 2.95 *(978-1-59249-741-6(1))* Soundprints.

Oliver, Veronica A. The Rainbow Colors: Learning Primary & Secondary Colors. 2011. 20p. 11.59 *(978-1-4269-4805-3(0))* Trafford Publishing.

Pace, Anne Marie. Busy-Eyed Day. Preston-Gannon, Frann, illus. 2018. (ENG.). 32p. (J). (-3). 18.99 *(978-1-4814-5903-7(1),* Beach Lane Bks.) Beach Lane Bks.

Parish, Herman. Amelia Bedelia Chapter Book #6: Amelia Bedelia Cleans Up. Avril, Lynne, illus. 2015. (Amelia Bedelia Ser.). (ENG.). 160p. (J). (gr. 1-5). pap. 6.99 *(978-0-06-233400-8(X),* Greenwillow Bks.) HarperCollins Pubs.

—Amelia Bedelia Chapter Book #6: Amelia Bedelia Cleans Up (POB) Avril, Lynne, illus. 2015. (Amelia Bedelia Ser.). (ENG.). 160p. (J). (gr. 1-5). 9.99 *(978-0-06-233403-9(4),* Greenwillow Bks.) HarperCollins Pubs.

Patricelli, Leslie. Faster! Faster! Patricelli, Leslie, illus. 2013. (Leslie Patricelli Board Bks.). (ENG., Illus.). 30p. (J). (-k). bds. 7.99 *(978-0-7636-6222-6(4))* Candlewick Pr.

—Faster! Faster!/Mas Rapido! Mas Rapido! Patricelli, Leslie, illus. 2013. (Leslie Patricelli Board Bks.). (Illus.). 30p. (J). (-k). bds. 8.99 *(978-0-7636-6611-8(4))* Candlewick Pr.

Peto, Judith E. & Talwar, Robert B. Jenny & Benny: Friends 2005. (Illus.). 28p. (J). (gr. -1-3). 16.95 *(978-0-9767511-0-6(0))* Lasting Bks. Publishing Co.

Reilly, Carmel. The Boy at the Park. Reynolds, Pat, illus. 2009. 24p. pap. 10.67 *(978-1-4190-5517-1(8))* Rigby Education.

Renek, Nava. Venice Is for Cats. 2013. (Illus.). pap. 20.00 *(978-0-923389-53-6(9))* Spuyten Duyvil Publishing.

Reynolds, Peter H. I'm Here. Reynolds, Peter H., illus. 2011. (ENG., Illus.). 32p. (J). (gr. -1-3). 18.99 *(978-1-4169-9649-1(4),* Atheneum Bks. for Young Readers) Simon & Schuster Children's Publishing.

Ricci, Christine. Dora's Picnic. Hall, Susan, illus. 2003. (Ready-to-Read Ser.: Vol. 1). (ENG.). 24p. (J). pap. 3.99 *(978-0-689-85238-1(X),* Simon Spotlight/Nickelodeon) Simon Spotlight/Nickelodeon.

Richter, Bernd & Richter, Susan. Grandma & Grandpa Visit Denali. Drashner, Diane, illus. 2008. 48p. (J). pap. 9.95 *(978-1-931353-33-5(6))* Saddle Pal Creations, Inc.

Rigby Education Staff. Headline News. (Sails Literacy Ser.). (Illus.). 16p. (gr. 1-2). 27.00 *(978-0-7635-9930-0(1),* 699301C99) Rigby Education.

Rowe, Jeannette. YoYo Goes to the Park. Rowe, Jeannette, illus. 2003. (Illus.). 12p. (J). pap. 5.95 *(978-1-58925-369-8(8))* Tiger Tales.

Roy, Ron. A Thief at the National Zoo. Bush, Timothy, illus. 2008. (Capital Mysteries Ser.: No. 9). 87p. (gr. k-3). 15.00 *(978-0-7569-8329-1(0))* Perfection Learning Corp.

Ruelle, Karen Gray. Bark Park, 1 vol. 2014. (Illus.). 32p. (J). (gr. -1-k). pap. 7.99 *(978-1-56145-773-1(6))* Peachtree Publishing Co. Inc.

Schaefer, Carole Lexa. Ciao, Baby! in the Park. Tobia, Lauren, illus. 2018. (ENG.). 28p. (J). (— 1). bds. 7.99 *(978-0-7636-8398-6(1))* Candlewick Pr.

—Ciao, Baby! Ready for a Ride. Tobia, Lauren, illus. 2018. (ENG.). 28p. (J). (— 1). bds. 7.99 *(978-0-7636-8397-9(3))* Candlewick Pr.

Schofield-Morrison, Connie. I Got the Rhythm. Morrison, Frank, illus. 2014. (ENG.). 32p. (J). (gr. -1-1). 17.99 *(978-1-61963-178-6(4),* 900123805, Bloomsbury USA Childrens) Bloomsbury Publishing USA.

Scripture Teachers: Solomon & Friends Learn about Forgiveness. 2003. pap. *(978-0-9712894-1-3(7))* Lighthouse Christian Products Co.

Singleton, Linda Joy. Cash Kat, 1 vol. Wald, Christina, illus. 2016. 39p. (J). (gr. k-1). (SPA.). pap. 11.95 *(978-1-62855-742-8(7),* 6feabda1-c792-415b-93f3-672f5c32d488); (ENG.). 17.95 *(978-1-62855-728-2(1))* Arbordale Publishing.

Sivier, Janet. Charlotte & Jackson: The Butterfly. 2012. 28p. pap. 16.09 *(978-1-4669-4555-5(9))* Trafford Publishing.

Skidmore, Marlene. In Trouble Again! 2010. 24p. pap. 9.99 *(978-0-9845208-9-3(9))* Faithful Life Pubs.

Snyder, Marilyn. A Second Chance for Tina. Shiffman, Lena, illus. 2003. (Hello Reader! Ser.). (J). *(978-0-439-44154-4(4))* Scholastic, Inc.

Stefanescu, Estera. Megan's Great Day. 2009. 20p. pap. 15.99 *(978-1-4389-6318-1(1))* AuthorHouse.

Stine, R. L. Who's Your Mummy? (Goosebumps HorrorLand #6) 2009. (Goosebumps Horrorland Ser.: 6). (ENG., Illus.). 160p. (J). (gr. 3-7). 7.99 *(978-0-439-91874-9(X),* Scholastic Paperbacks) Scholastic, Inc.

Stokely, Ted. Yaya & Uncle Ted Go Walk! 2010. 20p. 11.99 *(978-1-4520-9198-3(6))* AuthorHouse.

Stutson, Caroline. My Family Four Floors Up. Krampien, Celia, illus. 2018. (ENG.). 32p. (J). (gr. -1-2). 16.99 *(978-1-58536-991-1(8),* 204406) Sleeping Bear Pr.

Svoboda, Linda Sue. The Little Brown Bird That Could. 2012. 20p. pap. 24.95 *(978-1-4626-8043-6(7))* America Star Bks.

Tesler, Ellen. Zeke in Central Park. 2010. 32p. pap. 12.99 *(978-1-4490-7211-7(9))* AuthorHouse.

The Book Company, ed. Park. (Sparkle Bks.). 10p. (J). bds. 4.99 *(978-1-74047-332-3(9))* Book Co. Publishing Pty, Ltd., The AUS. Dist: Penton Overseas, Inc.

Thurmond, Joey. Nojoe Makes New Friends. 2009. 16p. pap. 10.99 *(978-1-4490-4156-4(6))* AuthorHouse.

Turley, Gerry, illus. Lois Looks for Bob at the Park. 2018. (Lois Looks for Bob Ser.). (ENG.). 12p. (J). (— 1). bds. 8.99 *(978-1-5362-0255-7(X))* Candlewick Pr.

Tzingoker, Lilach. Sonny's Adventure in Mystery Park. 2010. 44p. pap. 19.95 *(978-1-60911-927-0(4),* Eloquent Bks.) Strategic Book Publishing & Rights Agency (SBPRA).

A Walk in the Park. 2003. (J). per. *(978-1-57657-814-8(3))* Paradise Pr., Inc.

Ward, Kris A. Tony's Day in the Park. 2008. 42p. pap. 24.95 *(978-1-60813-351-2(6))* America Star Bks.

Weiss, Ellen. Twins in the Park: Ready-To-Read Pre-Level 1. Williams, Sam, illus. 2003. (Ready-To-Read Ser.). (ENG.). 24p. (J). (gr. -1-k). pap. 4.99 *(978-0-689-85742-3(X),* Simon Spotlight) Simon Spotlight.

West, C. The Adventures of Ice Cream & Honey Buns: A Day in the Park. 2012. 28p. pap. 16.09 *(978-1-4669-4700-9(4))* Trafford Publishing.

P Q R

Winans, Carvin. Conrad Saves Pinger Park. Harrington, Leslie, illus. 2010. 32p. (J). (gr. -1-3). 8.95 *(978-1-60349-024-5(8),* Marimba Bks.) Just Us Bks., Inc.

Written By Kimberly M Sosnowski; Illustr. Ace's Wish for a Forever Home. Sosnowski, Tiffany, illus. 2011. 28p. pap. 24.95 *(978-1-4626-3031-8(6))* America Star Bks.

Zschock, Martha. Hello, Philadelphia! 2011. (Hello Ser.). (ENG., Illus.). 16p. (J). (gr. -1-k). bds. 9.99 *(978-1-933212-64-7(0),* Commonwealth Editions) Applewood Bks.

PARKS—VOCATIONAL GUIDANCE

Hand, Carol. Working in Parks & Recreation in Your Community, 1 vol. 2018. (Careers in Your Community Ser.). (ENG.). 80p. (gr. 7-7). 37.47 *(978-1-4994-6731-4(1),* e643faf9-dc46-4b41-b931-5f16e657fcca, Rosen Young Adult) Rosen Publishing Group, Inc., The.

PARLIAMENTARY PRACTICE

Latchana Kenney, Karen. What Is a Parliamentary Government?, 1 vol., Vol. 1. 2013. (Understanding Political Systems Ser.). (ENG.). 48p. (YA). (gr. 6-8). 34.61 *(978-1-4824-0317-6(X),* 836ebace-8130-49f8-ae7e-ef854ecb0b48) Stevens, Gareth Publishing LLLP.

PARODIES

Ferrie, Chris. Goodnight Lab: A Scientific Parody. 2017. (Illus.). 32p. (J). (gr. -1-3). 17.99 *(978-1-4926-5617-3(8))* Sourcebooks, Inc.

Hysom, Dennis Joe & Walker, Christine. Wocleycat's Musical Theater. Walker, Christine, illus. 2003. (ENG., Illus.). 32p. (J). (gr. -1-3). 11.95 *(978-1-889910-26-0(0));* 18.95 *(978-1-889910-25-3(2))* Tortuga Pr.

Vande Velde, Vivian. Tales from the Brothers Grimm & the Sisters Weird. Weinman, Brad, illus. 2005. (ENG.). 144p. (J). (gr. 5-7). reprint ed. pap. 9.99 *(978-0-15-205572-1(X),* 1196759, Clarion Bks.) HarperCollins Pubs.

PARROTS

About Parrots: A Guide for Children, 1 vol. 2014. (About... Ser.: 16). (Illus.). 48p. (J). (gr. -1-2). 16.95 *(978-1-56145-795-3(7))* Peachtree Publishing Co. Inc.

Atlantic, Leonard. 95-Year-Old Parrots!, 1 vol. 2016. (World's Longest-Living Animals Ser.). (ENG., Illus.). 24p. (J). (gr. 1-2). pap. 9.15 *(978-1-4824-5616-5(8),* 79de0bd5-4bd9-4220-b7dc-75f35f908ada) Stevens, Gareth Publishing LLLP.

Barnes, J. Lou. Pet Parakeets, 1 vol. 2006. (Pet Pals Ser.). (ENG., Illus.). 32p. (gr. 3-5). lib. bdg. 28.67 *(978-0-8368-6780-0(7),* b5a6f970-9b12-4755-8ae0-f4f116e6a723, Gareth Stevens Learning Library) Stevens, Gareth Publishing LLLP.

Bjorklund, Ruth. Parrots. 2012. (Nature's Children Ser.). (ENG.). 48p. (J). pap. 6.95 *(978-0-531-25481-3(X));* lib. bdg. 28.00 *(978-0-531-26836-0(5))* Scholastic Library Publishing.

Bodden, Valerie. Parrots. 2010. (Amazing Animals Ser.). 24p. (J). (gr. -1-3). 16.95 *(978-1-58341-809-3(1),* Creative Education) Creative Co., The.

Bowman, Chris. Parrots. 2015. (Animal Safari Ser.). (ENG., Illus.). 24p. (J). (gr. k-3). lib. bdg. 26.95 *(978-1-62617-165-7(3),* Blastoff! Readers) Bellwether Media.

Bozzo, Linda. When Parrots Speak, 1 vol. 2017. (Animal Emotions Ser.). (ENG.). 32p. (gr. 3-3). pap. 11.52 *(978-0-7660-8864-1(2),* 2dc509a0-0ac6-4bd3-a9be-8a09c35a7229); lib. bdg. 26.93 *(978-0-7660-8621-0(6),* 8bdc8122-e230-4640-95cc-eaeeaed86bd4) Enslow Publishing, LLC.

Calhoun, Kelly. Flashy Feathers: Macaw. 2015. (Guess What Ser.). (ENG., Illus.). 24p. (J). (gr. k-2). 30.64 *(978-1-63362-626-3(1),* 206676) Cherry Lake Publishing.

Conure, Lunatico. Tico's Book. Durr, Carol Atkinson, illus. 2008. 36p. (J). 15.00 *(978-0-9717047-8-7(3))* Bay Media, Inc.

Dibble, Traci. Parrot Colors. 2015. (1-3Y Birds Ser.). (ENG., Illus.). 16p. (J). pap. 9.60 *(978-1-63437-669-3(2))* American Reading Co.

—The Parrot Family. 2012. (1-3Y Birds Ser.). (ENG.). 12p. (J). pap. 8.00 *(978-1-63437-843-7(1))* American Reading Co.

Donohue, Moira Rose. National Geographic Kids Chapters: Parrot Genius! And More True Stories of Amazing Animal Talents. 2014. (NGK Chapters Ser.). 112p. (J). (gr. 3-7). pap. 5.99 *(978-1-4263-1770-5(0),* National Geographic Kids) Disney Publishing Worldwide.

Dubke, Karon. Pet Parrots up Close. (Pets up Close Ser.). (ENG., 24p. (J). (gr. -1-2). 2015. Illus.). pap. 6.95 *(978-1-4914-7763-2(6),* 130166) 2014. 27.32 *(978-1-4914-0581-9(3),* 125918) Capstone. (Capstone Pr.).

Early Macken, JoAnn. Parakeets, 1 vol. 2003. (Let's Read about Pets Ser.). (ENG., Illus.). 24p. (gr. k-2). pap. 9.15 *(978-0-8368-3847-3(5),* 765c0ccd-fb94-4107-bf92-df31f2b3c5cb, Weekly Reader Leveled Readers) Stevens, Gareth Publishing LLLP.

Felipe, Juaristi. El loro de Haydn. 2004. (SPA.). 112p. (YA). 11.99 *(978-84-241-8667-8(2))* Everest Editora ESP. Dist: Lectorum Pubns., Inc.

Fetty, Margaret. Parrots. 2006. (Smart Animals! Ser.). (Illus.). 32p. (J). (gr. 2-5). lib. bdg. 28.50 *(978-1-59716-163-3(2))* Bearport Publishing Co., Inc.

Frost, Helen. Parrots [Scholastic]. 2011. (Rain Forest Animals Ser.). 24p. pap. 0.50 *(978-1-4296-6313-7(8),* Pebble) Capstone.

Gallagher, Debbie. Parrots, 1 vol. 2010. (Zoo Animals Ser.). (ENG.). 32p. (gr. 2-2). lib. bdg. 21.27 *(978-0-7614-4746-7(6),* 05a3f80c-8715-4176-bfbd-b163b8583e2c) Cavendish Square Publishing LLC.

Hanel, Rachael. Parrots. 2008. (Living Wild Ser.). (Illus.). 46p. (YA). (gr. 5-18). 22.95 *(978-1-58341-657-0(9),* Creative Education) Creative Co., The.

Haney, Johannah. Parrots, 1 vol. 2009. (Great Pets Ser.). (ENG.). 48p. (gr. 3-3). lib. bdg. 32.64 *(978-0-7614-2998-2(0),* c575f812-b500-4651-af4c-2749b9e3738e) Cavendish Square Publishing LLC.

Ho, Cammie. Parrot Parrot. 2016. (Life Cycle Bks.). (ENG., Illus.). 31p. (J). (gr. k-2). pap. 7.99 *(978-1-943241-04-0(X))* Phonic Monic.

Houston, Alecia. The Stories True of Gabby Cockatoo. Luna, Lauren, illus. 2010. 24p. pap. 11.25 *(978-1-60911-446-6(9),* Strategic Bk. Publishing) Strategic Book Publishing & Rights Agency (SBPRA).

Howard, Fran. Parrots, 1 vol. 2012. (Birds Ser.). (ENG.). 24p. (J). (gr. 1-3). lib. bdg. 25.99 *(978-1-4296-8685-3(5),* 119160, Capstone Pr.) Capstone.

Johnson, Jinny. Parrot. Woods, Michael, illus. 2007. (Zoo Animals in the Wild Ser.). 32p. (J). (gr. -1-3). lib. bdg. 28.50 *(978-1-58340-904-6(1))* Black Rabbit Bks.

Kalz, Jill. Parrots. 2006. (Wild World of Animals Ser.). (Illus.). 30p. (J). (gr. 3-5). 18.95 *(978-1-58341-434-7(7),* Creative Education) Creative Co., The.

Kawa, Katie. Playful Parakeets, 1 vol. 2011. (Pet Corner Ser.). (Illus.). 24p. (gr. k-k). (ENG.). (J). pap. 9.15 *(978-1-4339-5611-9(X),* ffce9f08-13ae-4296-8861-e9c5c5920db2); (ENG., (J). lib. bdg. 25.27 *(978-1-4339-5609-6(8),* af9ece13-c486-4333-aeaa-cc5581ff268e); 69.20 *(978-1-4339-6884-6(3))* Stevens, Gareth Publishing LLLP.

—Playful Parakeets / Pericos Juguetones, 1 vol. 2011. (Pet Corner / Rincón de Las Mascotas Ser.). (SPA & ENG., Illus.). 24p. (J). (gr. k-k). lib. bdg. 25.27 *(978-1-4339-5613-3(6),* fe3a73ba-cfeb-46c1-bbd5-29a4a6ad4ef8) Stevens, Gareth Publishing LLLP.

Klobuchar, Lisa. Cockatiels & Other Parrots. 2007. (World Book's Animals of the World Ser.). (Illus.). 64p. (J). *(978-0-7166-1327-5(1))* World Bk., Inc.

LaRoche, Amelia. Care for a Pet Parrot. 2009. (How to Convince Your Parents You Can ... Ser.). (Illus.). 32p. (J). (gr. 1-4). lib. bdg. 25.70 *(978-1-58415-795-3(X))* Mitchell Lane Pubs.

Leon, Vicki. A Rainbow of Parrots. 2nd ed. 2006. (Jean-Michel Cousteau Presents Ser.). (ENG., Illus.). 48p. (J). (gr. 4). pap. 7.95 *(978-0-9766134-2-8(5))* London Town Pr.

Lya, Maria. The Wise Parrot & a Plan to Save the Forest: A Plan to Save the Forest. 2011. (Illus.). 28p. (gr. -1). pap. 20.16 *(978-1-4567-8106-4(5))* AuthorHouse.

Macheske, Felicia. Cheerful Chirpers: Parakeet. 2017. (Guess What Ser.). (ENG., Illus.). 24p. (J). (gr. k-2). lib. bdg. 30.64 *(978-1-63472-856-0(4),* 209850) Cherry Lake Publishing.

Montgomery, Sy. Kakapo Rescue: Saving the World's Strangest Parrot. Bishop, Nic, illus. 2010. (Scientists in the Field Ser.). (ENG.). 80p. (J). (gr. 5-7). 18.00 *(978-0-618-49417-0(0),* 591725, Clarion Bks.) HarperCollins Pubs.

Murray, Julie. Parrots. 2019. (Animal Kingdom Ser.). (ENG., Illus.). 32p. (J). (gr. 2-5). lib. bdg. 34.21 *(978-1-5321-1648-3(9),* 32407, Big Buddy Bks.) ABDO Publishing Co.

Nugent, Samantha. Parrot. 2015. (Illus.). 24p. (J). *(978-1-4896-4117-5(3))* Weigl Pubs., Inc.

Owen, Ruth. Parrots, 1 vol. 2011. (World's Smartest Animals Ser.). (ENG., Illus.). 32p. (J). (gr. 2-3). pap. 12.75 *(978-1-61533-413-1(0),* f5da60f2-cb3d-4ebf-8213-9e5b21b0b5ef); lib. bdg. 31.27 *(978-1-61533-375-2(4),* 7b6ff1b3-9e09-41a6-8cd3-0dd1bf3f9ecb) Rosen Publishing Group, Inc., The. (Windmill Bks.).

Parrots. 2006. (Zooties Ser.). (J). 4.95 *(978-1-932396-20-1(9))* National Wildlife Federation.

Parrots: Early Level Satellite, 6 Packs. (Sails Literacy Ser.). 16p. (gr. 1-2). 27.00 *(978-0-7578-3160-7(5))* Rigby Education.

Rockwood, Leigh. Parrots Are Smart!, 1 vol. 2010. (Super Smart Animals Ser.). (ENG., Illus.). 24p. (J). (gr. 2-3). pap. 9.25 *(978-1-4358-9844-8(3),* dcd6711d-84b2-454d-b6db-d3f4524800ab, PowerKids Pr.); lib. bdg. 26.27 *(978-1-4358-9376-4(X),* a8dc57ca-3f97-4f01-a1c7-b15123e73d76) Rosen Publishing Group, Inc., The.

Ryndak, Rob. Parrots, 1 vol. 2014. (Jungle Animals Ser.). (ENG., Illus.). 24p. (J). (gr. k-k). 24.27 *(978-1-4824-1756-2(1),* 8da34f1e-6715-4990-9aa1-5e9e720f0a77) Stevens, Gareth Publishing LLLP.

Sexton, Colleen. Caring for Your Parakeet. 2010. (Pet Care Library). (ENG., Illus.). 24p. (J). (gr. 2-5). lib. bdg. 26.95 *(978-1-60014-470-7(5),* Blastoff! Readers) Bellwether Media.

Smith, Catherine. Parakeet, Vol. 12. 2016. (Understanding & Caring for Your Pet Ser.: Vol. 12). (ENG., Illus.). 128p. (J). (gr. 5-8). 25.95 *(978-1-4222-3701-4(X))* Mason Crest.

Sonder, Ben. Parrots. 2019. (Pet Library). (Illus.). 72p. (J). (gr. 12). lib. bdg. 34.60 *(978-1-4222-4317-6(6))* Mason Crest.

—Parrots: A Portrait of the Animal World. 2012. (Portrait of the Animal World Ser.). (Illus.). 72p. 12.95 *(978-1-59764-270-5(3))* New Line Bks.

—Parrots - Pb: A Portrait of the Animal World. 2013. (Portrait of the Animal World Ser.). (Illus.). 72p. pap. 9.95 *(978-1-59764-330-6(0))* New Line Bks.

Staff, Gareth Editorial Staff. Parrots, 1 vol. 2004. (All about Wild Animals Ser.). (ENG., Illus.). 32p. (gr. 2-4). lib. bdg. 28.67 *(978-0-8368-4122-0(0),* d5d4253d-68f7-43b0-b7ae-0f3bff54c0e0, Gareth Stevens Learning Library) Stevens, Gareth Publishing LLLP.

Statts, Leo. Parrots. 2017. (Awesome Birds Ser.). (ENG., Illus.). 24p. (J). (gr. -1-2). lib. bdg. 31.36 *(978-1-5321-2060-2(5),* 26743, Abdo Zoom-Launch) ABDO Publishing Co.

Zappa, Marcia. Kakapos, 1 vol. 2015. (World's Weirdest Animals Ser.). (ENG., Illus.). 32p. (J). (gr. 2-5). 34.21 *(978-1-62403-776-4(3),* 17854, Big Buddy Bks.) ABDO Publishing Co.

PARROTS—FICTION

The adventures of officer Byrd. 2007. (J). 16.99 *(978-0-9787322-0-2(0))* Officer Byrd Publishing Co.

Bhandari, D. Growing Wings: Parrot's Day Out. 2010. 28p. 17.99 *(978-1-4520-1102-8(8))* AuthorHouse.

Blacklidge, Barbara. Lucky: My Story. 2010. 24p. (J). pap. 12.95 *(978-1-934449-64-6(4))* Legacy Publishing Services, Inc.

Borsky, Mary. Benny Bensky & the Parrot-Napper. Hendry, Linda, illus. 2008. 128p. (J). (gr. 4-7). pap. 9.95 *(978-0-88776-840-8(7),* Tundra Bks.) Tundra Bks. CAN. Dist: Penguin Random Hse. LLC.

Boutros, Gladys. Bubba & the Sweet Pea. Balogh, Andras, illus. 2013. 86p. (J). pap. *(978-0-9873334-7-6(X))* Enlife Pty. Limited.

Brightwood, Laura. Knot for Singing Parrot. Pifer, Kimberly, ed. Brightwood, Laura, illus. 2012. (Illus.). (J). *(978-1-934409-23-7(5))* 3-C Institute for Social Development.

—Parrot's Winter Blues. Pifer, Kimberly, ed. Brightwood, Laura, illus. 2012. (Illus.). (J). *(978-1-934409-21-3(9))* 3-C Institute for Social Development.

Clawson, Kimberly. Fun O' Licious. Bellomy, Gail, illus. 2007. (ENG.). 56p. per. 16.95 *(978-1-4241-5556-9(8))* America Star Bks.

Coffey, M. Carol. Zoe Lucky: And the Green Gables' Mystery. 2008. 156p. pap. 12.95 *(978-1-4327-3190-8(4))* Outskirts Pr., Inc.

Coldon, Christine. Emmalynn: Home Tweet Home. 2011. 36p. (gr. -1). pap. 16.86 *(978-1-4567-3913-3(1))* AuthorHouse.

Colhoun, Sheelah. Elric's Florida Holiday. Cotton, Sue Lynn, illus. 2012. 20p. pap. 13.95 *(978-1-61493-110-2(0))* Peppertree Pr., The.

Connellan, Sue. Special Treasure. 2009. 40p. pap. 18.49 *(978-1-4343-7644-2(3))* AuthorHouse.

Cowley, Joy. Dan & the Parrot. 2009. pap. 8.25 *(978-1-60559-217-6(X))* Hameray Publishing Group, Inc.

Davey, Keith Peter. Squeaks Narrow Squeaks. Frost, Justine, illus. 2009. 32p. pap. 14.62 *(978-1-4120-4402-8(2))* Trafford Publishing.

Demas, Corinne & Roehrig, Artemis. The Grumpy Pirate. Anstee, Ashlyn, illus. 2020. (ENG.). 40p. (J). (gr. -1-k). 17.99 *(978-1-338-22297-5(X),* Orchard Bks.) Scholastic, Inc.

DePalma, Mary Newell. The Perfect Gift. 2010. (J). pap. *(978-0-545-15403-1(0),* Levine, Arthur A. Bks.) Scholastic, Inc.

Dicmas, Courtney. Harold Finds a Voice. Dicmas, Courtney, illus. 2013. (Child's Play Library). (Illus.). 32p. (J). *(978-1-84643-550-8(1))* Child's Play International Ltd.

Douglas, Babette. Noreen: The Real King of the Jungle. Johnson, John, illus. 2006. (Kiss a Me Teacher Creature Stories Ser.). 20p. (J). (gr. -1-3). 9.99 *(978-1-890343-25-5(0))* Kiss A Me Productions, Inc.

Dubyn, Bj. The Thrilling & Dynamic Adventures of Barbara Ann, Her Kid Brother, Billy, Jr., & Manfred the Magnificent, Their Parrot. 2008. 104p. pap. 15.99 *(978-1-4363-2652-0(4))* Xlibris Corp.

Duckers, John. The Amazing Adventures of the Silly Six. 2013. (Illus.). 188p. pap. *(978-1-78148-626-9(3))* Grosvenor Hse. Publishing Ltd.

Dugan, Karen. Always Blue for Chicu. 2010. (ENG., Illus.). 32p. (J). (gr. k-2). 16.95 *(978-0-940719-09-5(6))* Gryphon Pr., The.

Erickson, John. The Case of the Mysterious Voice. Holmes, Gerald L., illus. 2012. (Hank the Cowdog (Quality) Ser.: Vol. 58). (ENG.). 123p. (J). (gr. 3-6). pap. 5.99 *(978-1-59188-158-2(7))* Maverick Bks., Inc.

Feathers at Las Flores - Evaluation Guide: Evaluation Guide. 2006. (J). *(978-1-55942-405-9(2))* Witcher Productions.

Flambaum, Victor & Flambaum, Andrew. How to Make a Big Bang: A Cosmic Journey. 2012. (ENG.). 226p. (J). (gr. 7-10). pap. 14.95 *(978-1-936782-72-7(3))* Salem Author Services.

Flor Ada, Alma. Quiero Ayudar! Dominguez, Angela, illus. 2010.Tr. of Let Me Help! (ENG & SPA.). 32p. (J). (gr. -1-3). 16.95 *(978-0-89239-232-2(0))* Lee & Low Bks., Inc.

Fontanez, Edwin. En esta hermosa Isla. Fontanez, Edwin, illus. 2nd rev. ed. 2005. (SPA., Illus.). 32p. (J). 16.95 *(978-0-9640868-7-6(5))* Exit Studio.

Foreman, Michael. El Lorito Pelon. Diego, Rapi & Flores, Martha, illus. 2008. (SPA.). 30p. (J). (gr. 1-3). 15.99 *(978-1-930332-56-0(4))* Lectorum Pubns., Inc.

Friedman, Laurie. Love, Ruby Valentine. Avril, Lynne, illus. 2006. (Ruby Valentine Ser.). (ENG.). 32p. (J). (gr. k-3). lib. bdg. 16.95 *(978-1-57505-899-3(5),* 76ef85c3-9ebb-43e3-afc4-3afa1ae7878d, Carolrhoda Bks.) Lerner Publishing Group.

—Ruby Valentine & the Sweet Surprise. Avril, Lynne, illus. 2014. (Ruby Valentine Ser.). (ENG.). 32p. (J). (gr. k-3). 16.95 *(978-0-7613-8873-9(7),* 7491b02d-c3ff-421c-a33c-6400cf28d745, Carolrhoda Bks.) Lerner Publishing Group.

Futrell, Edgar Vernell. Twiddle de, the Talking Parrot. 2008. 28p. pap. 21.99 *(978-1-4363-0345-3(1))* Xlibris Corp.

Garson, Sarah. One, Two, Cockatoo! Garson, Sarah, illus. 2012. (ENG., Illus.). 32p. (J). (gr. k — 1). pap. 10.99 *(978-1-84270-944-3(5))* Andersen Pr. GBR. Dist: Independent Pubs. Group.

Gilley, Jane. The Adventures of Solly Polly & Georgie Porgy. 2008. 24p. pap. *(978-1-906210-70-0(5))* Grosvenor Hse. Publishing Ltd.

Gohmann, Johanna. The Very Quiet Parrot. Innerebner, Jessika von, illus. 2017. (Pirate Kids Ser.). (ENG.). 32p. (J). (gr. -1-3). lib. bdg. 32.79 *(978-1-5321-3041-0(4),* 27043, Calico Chapter Bks) Magic Wagon.

Grace, Jaylen. Porridge the Two Faced Parrot. 2013. (Illus.). 72p. pap. *(978-1-78148-227-8(6))* Grosvenor Hse. Publishing Ltd.

Graham-Morgan, Ivet. Peter the Parrot Misses Home: Misses Home. 2011. 16p. 9.98 *(978-1-4343-9791-1(2))* AuthorHouse.

Hannaford, Linda S. Petie the Parrot's Amazing Adventures: P. D. Q., 1 vol. Lee, George T., illus. 2010. 16p. pap. 24.95 *(978-1-61582-767-1(6))* PublishAmerica, Inc.

Hapka, Catherine, pseud. Blu & Friends. 2011. (I Can Read Level 2 Ser.). (ENG.). 32p. (J). (gr. k-3). pap. 3.99 *(978-0-06-201487-0(7),* HarperFestival) HarperCollins Pubs.

—Rio - Learning to Fly. 2011. (I Can Read Level 2 Ser.). (ENG.). 32p. (J). (gr. k-3). pap. 3.99 *(978-0-06-201488-7(9),* HarperFestival) HarperCollins Pubs.

Harman, Michael. The Parrot & the Fig Tree: A Story about Friendship & Respect for Nature. 2nd ed. 2009. (Jataka Tales Ser.). (Illus.). 32p. (J). (gr. -1-5). pap. 8.95 *(978-0-89800-430-4(6))* Dharma Publishing.

Harmon, Victoria Marie. Say Hello to My Little Green Friend Tiki. 2013. 20p. pap. 24.95 *(978-1-63004-192-2(0))* America Star Bks.

Harper, Benjamin. Greetings from Rio! 2011. (Rio Ser.). (ENG.). 24p. (J). (gr. -1-2). pap. 3.99 *(978-0-06-202266-0(0),* HarperFestival) HarperCollins Pubs.

Harrington, Claudia. Book 6: Pete the Very Chatty Parrot. Syed, Anoosha, illus. 2018. (Hank the Pet Sitter Ser.). (ENG.). 32p. (J). (gr. -1-3). lib. bdg. 32.79 *(978-1-5321-3174-5(7),* 28443, Calico Chapter Bks) Magic Wagon.

Harris, Patricia. Rowdy Racket in the Jungle, 1 vol. 2017. (Jungle Fun Ser.). (ENG.). 24p. (gr. 1-1). pap. 9.25 *(978-1-5383-2128-7(9),* ec7ce9a0-b552-4d8f-804f-0a305600ae07, PowerKids Pr.) Rosen Publishing Group, Inc., The.

Hay, Sam. Flight of the Pummeled Parakeet. 2015. (Undead Pets Ser.: 6). lib. bdg. 16.00 *(978-0-606-38405-6(7))* Turtleback.

—Flight of the Pummeled Parakeet #6. Cooper, Simon, illus. 2015. (Undead Pets Ser.: 6). (ENG.). 120p. (J). (gr. 1-3). 5.99 *(978-0-448-47800-5(5),* Grosset & Dunlap) Penguin Young Readers Group.

Hoffman, Mary Ann. A Parrot for Pam, 1 vol. 2006. (Neighborhood Readers Ser.). (ENG.). 8p. (gr. k-1). pap. 5.15 *(978-1-4042-5690-3(3),* 75199843-5e0f-402b-b6b1-1a68bd5ea1bf, Rosen Classroom) Rosen Publishing Group, Inc., The.

Holden, Pam. Stickybeak the Parrot, 1 vol. East, Jacqueline, illus. 2009. (Red Rocket Readers Ser.). (ENG.). 16p. (gr. -1-1). pap. *(978-1-877363-28-3(6),* Red Rocket Readers) Flying Start Bks.

Homfray, Jenny. The Adventures of Parker the Parrot. 2008. 36p. pap. 15.49 *(978-1-4389-1229-5(3))* AuthorHouse.

Huelin, Jodi. The Movie Storybook. 2011. (Rio Ser.). (ENG.). 48p. (J). (gr. -1-2). pap. 8.99 *(978-0-06-202270-7(9),* HarperFestival) HarperCollins Pubs.

I Can: Individual Title Six-Packs. (Sails Literacy Ser.). 16p. (gr. k-18). 27.00 *(978-0-7635-4396-9(9))* Rigby Education.

Jeune, Marie Carole. Rita & the Parrot. Saincilus, Larimer, illus. 2010. (HAT.). 32p. (J). pap. 16.95 *(978-1-60195-317-9(8))* International Step by Step Assn.

Judge, Lita. Good Morning to Me! Judge, Lita, illus. 2015. (ENG., Illus.). 40p. (J). (gr. -1-3). 17.99 *(978-1-4814-0369-6(9))* Simon & Schuster Children's Publishing.

Kargbo, Mariatu. Mr Byrd's Bird. 2011. 28p. pap. 24.95 *(978-1-4560-5435-9(X))* America Star Bks.

Kasten, Nancy, illus. First Feather 2003. 70p. (J). pap. 9.99 *(978-0-9744863-0-7(2))* Paulus Publishing.

Kauffman, Tracy. Gwendolyn's Wish. 2012. (-18). 24p. 24.95 *(978-1-62709-555-6(1));* 20p. pap. 24.95 *(978-1-4626-7207-3(8))* America Star Bks.

Korman, Susan. Birds of a Feather. 2011. (Rio Ser.). (ENG.). 24p. (J). (gr. -1-2). pap. 3.99 *(978-0-06-202267-7(9),* HarperFestival) HarperCollins Pubs.

Korten, Gerri. The Parakeets & the Ginkgo Tree at Hide Park. l.t. ed. 2006. (Illus.). 36p. (J). 18.85 *(978-0-9785609-7-3(3))* New Global Publishing.

La Rue, Coco. A New Pig in Town. May, Kyla, illus. 2013. 127p. (J). pap. *(978-0-545-46607-3(5))* Scholastic, Inc.

Leonardo, Cory. The Simple Art of Flying. 2019. (ENG., Illus.). 384p. (J). (gr. 3-7). 17.99 *(978-1-5344-2099-1(1),* Aladdin) Simon & Schuster Children's Publishing.

Lerasle, Magdeleine. Songs from a Journey with a Parrot: Lullabies & Nursery Rhymes from Portugal & Brazil. Fronty, Aurélia, illus. 2013. (POR & ENG.). 52p. (J). (gr. -1-k). 16.95 *(978-2-923163-99-4(0))* La Montagne Secrete CAN. Dist: Independent Pubs. Group.

Logue, Stephanie. Mango's Revenge. Murphy, Chris, illus. 2006. (J). pap. *(978-1-59336-769-5(4))* Mondo Publishing.

Lost: Individual Title, 6 Packs. (Story Steps Ser.). (gr. k-2). 23.00 *(978-0-7635-9817-4(8))* Rigby Education.

Manceau, Édouard. The Parrot Song. 2017. (ENG., Illus.). 32p. (J). (gr. -1-17). 12.95 *(978-1-84976-497-1(2),* 1653301) Tate Publishing, Ltd. GBR. Dist: Abrams, Inc.

Martinez, Victor. Parrot in the Oven: Mi Vida. Scott, Steve, illus. rev. ed. 2004. (ENG.). 240p. (YA). (gr. 8-18). pap. 10.99 *(978-0-06-447186-2(1))* HarperCollins Español.

Massenot, Véronique. The Mermaid & the Parakeet: A Children's Book Inspired by Henri Matisse. Hié, Vanessa, illus. 2016. (Children's Books Inspired by Famous Artworks Ser.). (ENG.). 32p. (J). (gr. -1-3). 14.95 *(978-3-7913-7265-5(3))* Prestel Verlag GmbH & Co KG. DEU. Dist: Penguin Random Hse. LLC.

Meissner, David. The Missing Parrot: Set Of 6. 2010. (Early Connections Ser.). (J). pap. 39.00 net. *(978-1-4108-1552-1(8))* Benchmark Education Co.

Molesworth, Mary Louisa S. Peterkin. 2009. 128p. 23.95 *(978-1-60664-659-5(1));* pap. 10.95 *(978-1-60664-287-0(1))* Rodgers, Alan Bks.

Moore, S. D. The Adventures of Pj & Split Pea. Switzer, Bobbi, illus. 2008. 36p. per. 12.95 *(978-1-4327-1288-4(8))* Outskirts Pr., Inc.

—The Adventures of PJ & Split Pea Vol. II: Nothing but the Tooth. 2010. 37p. (J). pap. 12.95 *(978-1-4327-1289-1(6))* Outskirts Pr., Inc.

Mure, Nancy S. & Torre, Tom. The Pizza Man & the Parrots. 2014. (ENG., Illus.). 40p. (J). pap. 9.98 *(978-0-7443-2136-4(0))* CamCat Publishing.

Murguia, Bethanie Deeney. Cockatoo, Too. 2018. (ENG., Illus.). 32p. (J). (gr. -1-1). bds. 7.99 *(978-1-4998-0579-6(9))* Little Bee Books Inc.

My Hat: Individual Title Six-Packs. (Sails Literacy Ser.). 16p. (gr. k-18). 27.00 *(978-0-7635-4436-2(1))* Rigby Education.

Nahal, Denise Abda. Hello Birdie! Tale of a Classroom Pet Based on a True Story. 2012. 16p. pap. 10.67 *(978-1-4669-6822-6(2))* Trafford Publishing.

Parakeet. 2004. (J). per. *(978-1-57657-398-3(2))* Paradise Pr., Inc.

Parish, John Lee. Cry Aloud: From Protest to Praise. 2007. (Illus.). 120p. per. 18.95 *(978-0-9758870-4-2(1))* Beverly Hills Publishing.

Parker, Emma & Renaud, Marguerite. Chatterbox Caz. 2010. (Illus.). 16p. pap. *(978-1-877561-77-1(0))* First Edition Ltd.

Parton, Paula. Room 17 'Where History Comes Alive!' Book Ii, Explorers. 2008. 120p. pap. 8.95 *(978-0-9794815-3-6(8))* Bellissima Publishing, LLC.

Perry, Roseann. When Mama Says No. 2009. 36p. pap. 16.99 *(978-1-4389-1938-6(7))* AuthorHouse.

Pippin, Sheila C. Katrina: Through Mango's Eyes. Pippin, Kristin A. & Pippin, Sheila C., illus. 2007. (J). (gr. -1-5). pap. 12.95 *(978-1-56167-956-0(9))* American Literary Pr.

Polly Parrot. 2006. (J). lib. bdg. 14.95 *(978-0-9774937-0-8(9))* Wood, Ella Sue.

Publications International Ltd. Staff. Look & Find Rio. 2011. 24p. (J). 7.98 (978-1-4508-1382-2(8)) Publications International, Ltd.

—Rio Large Play As Ound. 2011. 24p. (J). 17.98 (978-1-4508-0735-7(6)) Phoenix International Publications, Inc.

Punter, R. Stories of Pirates. 2004. (Young Reading Ser.: Vol. 1). 48p. (J). (gr. 2-18). pap. 5.99 (978-0-7945-0583-7(X)) EDC Publishing.

Rawson, Katherine. If You Were a Parrot, 1 vol. Rogers, Sherry, illus. 2006. (ENG.). 32p. (J). (gr. -1-3). 15.95 (978-0-9764943-9-3(6)) Arbordale Publishing.

Rey, H. A. & Rey, Margret. Curious George Feeds the Animals Book & Cd, 1 vol. 2005. (Curious George Ser.). (ENG., Illus.). 24p. (J). (gr. -1-3). audio compact disk 10.99 (978-0-618-60387-9(5), 495928, Clarion Bks.) HarperCollins Pubs.

Reza, Connie. Leah Ann Adopta un Perico. 2006. (SPA., Illus.). 32p. (J). 19.99 incl. audio compact disk (978-0-9714533-2-6(2)) Yo Puedo Publishing.

Roddie, Shen. The Gossipy Parrot. Terry, Michael, tr. Terry, Michael, illus. 2004. 32p. (J). (gr. k-2). 20.00 (978-0-7475-6079-1(X)) Bloomsbury Publishing Plc GBR. Dist: Independent Pubs. Group.

—Gossipy Parrot. Terry, Michael, illus. 2003. (J). pap. 9.99 (978-0-7475-6489-8(2)) Bloomsbury Publishing Plc GBR. Dist: Independent Pubs. Group.

Rogers, Jewels. The Princess & the Parakeet. 2011. 28p. pap. 12.50 (978-1-4567-5170-8(0)) AuthorHouse.

Rushby, Pamela. Rosie & the Audition. Konye, Paul, illus. 2009. 24p. pap. 10.67 (978-1-4190-5524-9(0)) Rigby Education.

—Rosie Goes Home. Konye, Paul, illus. 2009. (Rigby PM Stars Bridge Bks.). (ENG.). 24p. (gr. 2-3). pap. 8.25 (978-1-4190-5529-4(1)) Rigby Education.

Sanchez, Juanita L. Pancho the Green Parrot Lays an Egg, 1 vol. Ramirez, Samuel, illus. 2009. 24p. pap. 24.95 (978-1-61546-150-9(7)) America Star Bks.

Sandilands, Joyce. 3 on a Moonbeam. Padur, Simone, illus. 2004. 64p. (978-0-9734383-1-4(2)) Whitlands Publishing, Ltd.

Scillian, Devin. Memoirs of a Parrot. Bowers, Tim, illus. 2016. (ENG.). 32p. (J). (gr. k-3). 16.99 (978-1-58536-962-1(4), 204036) Sleeping Bear Pr.

Scott, Janine. The Noisy Parrot, 1 vol. Rigby, Deborah, illus. 2009. (Treasure Chest Readers Ser.). (ENG.). 24p. (J). (gr. 1-1). pap. 9.15 (978-1-60754-680-1(9), 2b2fd5e7-4c9c-454a-a346-2dda2788afe8); lib. bdg. 27.27 (978-1-60754-679-5(5), 8f7f1316-f8f0-4a48-be78-b1a3b98e3bb0) Rosen Publishing Group, Inc., The. (Windmill Bks.).

Small, Tanya. What You Say Is What You Are. 2007. pap. 7.50 (978-0-9705090-1-7(4)) MorningGlory Publishing.

Stine, R. L. Rotten School #15: Calling All Birdbrains. Park, Trip, illus. 4.99 (978-0-06-123277-0(7)) HarperCollins Pubs.

Thatcher, Stephanie. Polly Does NOT Want a Cracker. 2020. (Illus.). 32p. (J). (gr. k-2). 9.99 (978-1-988516-59-2(5)) Upstart Pr. NZL. Dist: Independent Pubs. Group.

Thompson, Chad J. Rhymes with Doug. Thompson, Chad J., illus. 2016. (ENG., Illus.). 40p. (J). (gr. -1-3). 16.99 (978-1-4814-7095-7(7), Aladdin) Simon & Schuster Children's Publishing.

True, J. J. Billy Brite: Africa & Beyond. 2011. (Illus.). 112p. pap. 14.03 (978-1-4567-7281-9(3)) AuthorHouse.

Tweti, Mira. Here, There, & Everywhere: The Story of Sreeeeeeeet the Lorikeett. Brady, Lisa, illus. 2008. 47p. (J). (gr. 4-7). (978-0-615-17122-7(2)) Parrot Pr.

Vaughn, J. D. Paula & the Parrot. Brislane, Niche, illus. 2009. 16p. pap. 8.49 (978-1-4389-8634-0(3)) AuthorHouse.

Webb, Dirk. A Warm Summer's Day. 2010. 37p. 17.00 (978-0-578-01867-6(5)) Webb, Dirk E.

What's New Cockatoo. 2005. (J). (978-0-9767179-3-5(X)) ABC Development, Inc.

Williams, Brenda May. The Unusual Pet Shop. Williams, Raymond, illus. 2012. 24p. pap. 11.50 (978-1-61897-798-4(9), Strategic Bk. Publishing) Strategic Book Publishing & Rights Agency (SBPRA).

Williams, Fawn. The Adventures of Jj the Amazon Parrot. 2011. 32p. pap. 24.95 (978-1-4626-4251-9(9)) America Star Bks.

Willis, Jeanne. Be Quiet, Parrot! Birchall, Mark, illus. 2005. (Picture Bks.). 32p. (J). (gr. k-2). 7.25 (978-1-57505-492-6(2)) Lerner Publishing Group.

Witte, Anna. El Loro Tico Tango. Witte, Anna, illus. (SPA., Illus.). 24p. (J). 2011. (gr. -1-1). 9.99 (978-1-84686-670-8(7)) 2005. pap. 6.99 (978-1-84148-971-1(9)) Barefoot Bks., Inc.

—The Parrot Tico Tango. 2005. (ENG., Illus.). 24p. (J). (gr. -1-3). pap. 6.99 (978-1-905236-11-4(5)) Barefoot Bks., Inc.

—The Parrot Tico Tango. Witte, Anna, illus. 2005. (ENG., Illus.). 24p. (J). (gr. k-3). 15.99 (978-1-84148-243-9(9)) Barefoot Bks., Inc.

Witte, Anna & Amador, Brian. The Parrot Tico Tango. Witte, Anna, illus. 2011. (Illus.). 24p. (J). (gr. -1-2). 9.99 (978-1-84686-669-2(3)) Barefoot Bks., Inc.

PARTICLES (NUCLEAR PHYSICS)

Bortz, Alfred B. The Neutron, 1 vol. 2003. (Library of Subatomic Particles Ser.). (ENG., Illus.). 64p. (gr. 6-6). lib. bdg. 37.13 (978-0-8239-4530-6(8), 7734cee7-63e6-4172-a5dc-7072ed84b9b4) Rosen Publishing Group, Inc., The.

—The Proton, 1 vol. 2003. (Library of Subatomic Particles Ser.). (ENG., Illus.). 64p. (gr. 6-6). lib. bdg. 37.13 (978-0-8239-4532-0(4), c611f070-127d-4e4f-a0b7-9e6dbc3ea107) Rosen Publishing Group, Inc., The.

Bortz, Fred. The Neutrino. 2009. (Library of Subatomic Particles Ser.). 64p. (gr. 6-6). 58.50 (978-1-60853-879-9(6)) Rosen Publishing Group, Inc., The.

—The Neutron. 2009. (Library of Subatomic Particles Ser.). 64p. (gr. 6-6). 58.50 (978-1-60853-880-5(X)) Rosen Publishing Group, Inc., The.

—The Proton. 2009. (Library of Subatomic Particles Ser.). 64p. (gr. 6-6). 58.50 (978-1-60853-886-7(9)) Rosen Publishing Group, Inc., The.

—The Quark. (Library of Subatomic Particles Ser.). 64p. (gr. 6-6). 2009. 58.50 (978-1-60853-889-8(3)) 2003. (ENG., Illus.). lib. bdg. 37.13 (978-0-8239-4533-7(2), 4e0f15ea-27b8-45c5-8469-8c5b36fa7f71) Rosen Publishing Group, Inc., The.

—Understanding Higgs Bosons, 1 vol. 2015. (Exploring the Subatomic World Ser.). (ENG., Illus.). 64p. (YA). (gr. 8-8). lib. bdg. 35.93 (978-1-5026-0550-4(3), bfcaa08f-6329-424b-910b-826f7d38dfbe) Cavendish Square Publishing LLC.

Fields, B. H. & Bortz, Fred. Understanding Neutrons, 1 vol. 2015. (Exploring the Subatomic World Ser.). (ENG., Illus.). 64p. (YA). (gr. 8-8). 35.93 (978-1-5026-0542-9(2), 589c6de3-bdba-4e1c-944a-3e94b859cb85) Cavendish Square Publishing LLC.

—Understanding Quarks, 1 vol. 2015. (Exploring the Subatomic World Ser.). (ENG., Illus.). 64p. (YA). (gr. 8-8). lib. bdg. 35.93 (978-1-5026-0548-1(1), 970b392f-2108-47c5-b194-3fb708bbc150) Cavendish Square Publishing LLC.

Latta, Sara. Smash! Exploring the Mysteries of the Universe with the Large Hadron Collider. Weigel, Jeff, illus. 2017. (ENG.). 72p. (YA). (gr. 8-12). 33.32 (978-1-4677-8551-8(2), 0035b296-315f-4339-99c8-7a59bf3fbe75); E-Book 50.65 (978-1-5124-2701-1(2), 9781512427011); E-Book 9.99 (978-1-5124-3594-8(5), 9781512435948); E-Book 50.65 (978-1-5124-3593-1(7), 9781512435931) Lerner Publishing Group. (Graphic Universe™).

The Library of Subatomic Particles, 10 vols. 2003. (Library of Subatomic Particles Ser.). (ENG., Illus.). 64p. (gr. 6-6). lib. bdg. 185.65 (978-1-4042-0145-3(9), 2975ec4e-25c8-4c49-b06b-4a54f02e3ce0) Rosen Publishing Group, Inc., The.

Scientific American Staff. Beyond Extreme Physics. 2009. (Scientific American Cutting-Edge Science Ser.). 160p. (gr. 9-9). 63.90 (978-1-60853-073-1(6)) Rosen Publishing Group, Inc., The.

Shoup, Kate. Particle Physics, 1 vol. 2018. (Great Discoveries in Science Ser.). (ENG.). 128p. (J). (gr. 9-9). 47.36 (978-1-5026-4381-0(2), 0e24178a-974e-46b7-85a7-06e983aa12fb) Cavendish Square Publishing LLC.

Ulbricht, Jaryd. The Higgs Mechanism Explained, 1 vol. 2018. (Mysteries of Space Ser.). (ENG.). 80p. (gr. 7-7). 38.93 (978-0-7660-9959-3(8), 978db4c6-2d49-4b8c-9c15-932503e8edd8) Enslow Publishing, LLC.

Wells, Robert E. What's Smaller Than a Pygmy Shrew? 2012. (J). (978-1-61913-158-3(7)) Weigl Pubs., Inc.

PARTIES

see also Entertaining

Adamson, Heather. Birthday Parties. 2010. (Special Days Ser.). (ENG.). 24p. (J). (gr. k-2). lib. bdg. 25.65 (978-1-60753-028-2(7), 17188) Amicus.

Barsocchini, Peter, creator. High School Musical 2 Party Planner. 2010. (Illus.). (J). pap. 4.99 (978-0-7666-2846-5(9)) Modern Publishing.

Beery, Barbara. Barbara Beery's Pink Princess Party Cookbook. Williams, Zac, photos by. 2011. (ENG., Illus.). 64p. (J). (gr. 2-7). spiral bd. 15.99 (978-1-4424-1231-6(3), Simon & Schuster Bks. For Young Readers) Simon & Schuster Bks. For Young Readers.

Beker, Jeanne. The Big Night Out. Dion, Nathalie, illus. 2005. 80p. (J). (gr. 4-7). pap. 15.95 (978-0-88776-719-7(2), Tundra Bks.) Tundra Bks. CAN. Dist: Penguin Random Hse. LLC.

Bokram, Karen & Faithgirlz! and Girls' Life Magazine Editors. Best Party Book Ever! From Invites to Overnights & Everything in Between, 1 vol. 2014. (Faithgirlz Ser.). (ENG., Illus.). 160p. (J). pap. 14.99 (978-0-310-74600-3(0)) Zonderkidz.

Brown, Jennifer. It's Time for a Sleepover, 1 vol. 2017. (It's Time Ser.). (ENG.). 24p. (J). (gr. 1-1). 25.27 (978-1-5081-6365-7(0), ce2a4ba3-8dda-4dda-bfbd-11821fb4dc3b, PowerKids Pr.) Rosen Publishing Group, Inc., The.

Canetti, Yanitzia. Party Colors/Colores Festivos: A World of Color. 2010. (ENG & SPA.). 24p. (J). pap. 6.99 (978-1-59835-274-0(1), BrickHouse Education) Cambridge BrickHouse, Inc.

Co-Ed Howling Noises Mystery Party Kit for 10 Players: Filled with Fun, Games & Laughter. 2004. (YA). 30.00 (978-1-932839-38-8(0)) SimpliFun Studios.

Coan, Sharon. Mi Fiesta de Cumpleaños. 2nd rev. ed. 2016. (TIME for KIDS(r): Informational Text Ser.). (SPA., Illus.). 12p. (gr. -1-k). 7.99 (978-1-4938-2972-9(6)) Teacher Created Materials, Inc.

—My Birthday Party. 2nd rev. ed. 2015. (TIME for KIDS(r): Informational Text Ser.). (ENG., Illus.). 12p. (gr. -1-k). 7.99 (978-1-4938-2063-4(X)) Teacher Created Materials, Inc.

Devore, Janna. Ballerina Cookbook. 2013. 94p. pap. (978-1-4596-5916-2(3)) ReadHowYouWant.com, Ltd.

Earle, Erin. Surprise Party!, 1 vol. 2013. (Core Math Skills: Measurement & Geometry Ser.). (ENG.). 24p. (J). (gr. 1-1). 26.27 (978-1-4777-2230-5(0), 197d47e7-4295-4b0f-9749-a6984070f523); pap. 8.25 (978-1-4777-2103-2(7), a7525908-95f3-4f8f-9414-17bdf4f66b68) Rosen Publishing Group, Inc., The. (Rosen Classroom).

—Surprise Party! Shapes & Their Attributes. 2013. (Rosen Math Readers Ser.). (ENG.). 24p. (J). (gr. 1-2). pap. 49.50 (978-1-4777-2104-9(5), Rosen Classroom) Rosen Publishing Group, Inc., The.

Encarnacion, Elizabeth. The Girls' Guide to Campfire Activities. 2008. (ENG., Illus.). 124p. (J). (gr. 5-18). pap. 12.95 (978-1-60433-003-8(1), Applesauce Pr.) Cider Mill Pr. Bk. Pubs., LLC.

Freese, Joan. Vamos a Planear una Fiesta con MATEMÁTICAS (USING MATH to Make Party Plans), 1 vol. 2008. (Las Matemáticas en Nuestro Mundo - Nivel 2 (Math in Our World - Level 2) Ser.). (SPA.). 24p. (gr. 2-2). pap. 9.15 (978-0-8368-9030-3(2), dd73ff4f-81dd-4cc9-a59b-4f46e288d9b9); (Illus.). lib. bdg. 24.67 (978-0-8368-9021-1(3), 1fef69da-0867-404f-bca6-a21aa76a8d20) Stevens, Gareth Publishing LLLP. (Weekly Reader Leveled Readers).

Gamblin, Rose Tooley. The Birthday Party. 2007. (J). (978-0-8127-0464-8(9)) Autumn Hse. Publishing Co.

Greenwald, Todd J., contrib. by. Wizards of Waverly Place Party Planner. 2009. (Wizards of Waverly Place Ser.). (Illus.). (J). pap. 4.99 (978-0-7666-3302-5(0)) Modern Publishing.

Guidone, Lisa M. What Happens at a Museum? / ¿Qué Pasa en un Museo?, 1 vol. 2008. (Where People Work / ¿dónde Trabaja la Gente? Ser.). 24p. (gr. k-2). (ENG & SPA.). (J). lib. bdg. 24.67 (978-0-8368-9282-6(8), bded1185-5170-45b7-8704-ac0765751de3); (SPA & ENG.). pap. 9.15 (978-0-8368-9381-6(6), 02d36a20-016c-4a73-a6b3-41d699d785cd) Stevens, Gareth Publishing LLLP. (Weekly Reader Leveled Readers).

Hogenkamp, S. My Birthday: Learning the IR Sound. 2009. (PowerPhonics Ser.). 24p. (gr. 1-1). 39.90 (978-1-60851-460-1(9), PowerKids Pr.) Rosen Publishing Group, Inc., The.

Holden, Pam. Happy Birthday, 1 vol. Hawley, Kelvin, illus. 2009. (Red Rocket Readers Ser.). (ENG.). 16p. (gr. -1-1). pap. (978-1-877363-03-0(0), Red Rocket Readers) Flying Start Bks.

Hurley, Jo. Slumber-lfic! Great Sleepover Ideas for You & Your Friends. Morley, Taia, illus. 2007. 63p. (J). (978-0-439-02015-2(8)) Scholastic, Inc.

Hutchings, Amy. What Happens at a Party Store?, 1 vol. 2008. (Where People Work Ser.). (ENG.). 24p. (gr. k-2). (J). lib. bdg. 24.67 (978-0-8368-9277-2(1), 18f5b77d-2d90-4cd0-be5e-7fde9286e7d4); pap. 9.15 (978-0-8368-9376-2(X), 78ed00b5-ac6f-4d1c-9983-8b2b1e554031) Stevens, Gareth Publishing LLLP. (Weekly Reader Leveled Readers).

—What Happens at a Party Store? / ¿Qué Pasa en una Tienda de Cosas para Fiestas?, 1 vol. 2008. (Where People Work / ¿dónde Trabaja la Gente? Ser.). 24p. (gr. k-2). (ENG & SPA.). (J). lib. bdg. 24.67 (978-0-8368-9283-3(6), ca84f34a-537e-4ab8-9b58-41e0b73f727c); (SPA & ENG.). pap. 9.15 (978-0-8368-9382-3(4), 9640eb2a-e999-4c8c-a18d-e1f6888a9fa2) Stevens, Gareth Publishing LLLP. (Weekly Reader Leveled Readers).

Jeffries, Joyce. Dinosaur Birthday Party, 1 vol. 2014. (Dinosaur School Ser.). (ENG.). 24p. (J). (gr. k-k). 25.27 (978-1-4824-0741-9(8), 3761c8a7-d7ae-45be-8920-0e694adfb3b8) Stevens, Gareth Publishing LLLP.

Jones, Jen. Accessory Parties: Planning a Party That Makes Your Friends Say Cool!, 1 vol. 2014. (Perfect Parties Ser.). (ENG.). 32p. (J). (gr. 3-9). lib. bdg. 28.65 (978-1-4765-4009-2(8), 124117) Capstone.

—Costume Parties: Planning a Party That Makes Your Friends Say Wow!, 1 vol. 2014. (Perfect Parties Ser.). (ENG.). 32p. (J). (gr. 3-9). lib. bdg. 28.65 (978-1-4765-4007-8(1), 124115) Capstone.

—Game Night Parties: Planning a Bash That Makes Your Friends Say Yeah!, 1 vol. 2014. (Perfect Parties Ser.). (ENG.). 32p. (J). (gr. 3-9). lib. bdg. 28.65 (978-1-4765-4006-1(3), 124114) Capstone.

—Pampering Parties: Planning a Party That Makes Your Friends Say Ahhh, 1 vol. 2014. (Perfect Parties Ser.). (ENG.). 32p. (J). (gr. 3-9). lib. bdg. 28.65 (978-1-4765-4008-5(X), 124116) Capstone.

—Planning Perfect Parties: The Girls' Guide to Fun, Fresh, Unforgettable Events. 2014. (Craft It Yourself Ser.). (ENG.). 128p. (J). (gr. 3-9). pap., pap., pap. 14.95 (978-1-62370-063-8(9), 124573, Capstone Young Readers) Capstone.

Jorgensen, Katrina. Food, Football, & Fun! Sports Illustrated Kids' Football Recipes. 2015. (Sports Illustrated Kids Ser.). (ENG., Illus.). 144p. (J). (gr. 3-9). pap., pap., pap. 15.95 (978-1-62370-230-4(5), 127868, Capstone Young Readers) Capstone.

—Football Party Recipes: Delicious Ideas for the Big Event. 2015. (Football Cookbooks Ser.). (ENG.). 48p. (J). (gr. 3-9). lib. bdg. 31.99 (978-1-4914-2136-9(3), 127619) Capstone.

—Football Tailgating Recipes: Tasty Treats for the Stadium Crowd. 2015. (Football Cookbooks Ser.). (ENG.). 48p. (J). (gr. 3-9). lib. bdg. 31.99 (978-1-4914-2137-6(1), 127620) Capstone.

Kalman, Bobbie. It Is My Birthday. 2010. (ENG., Illus.). 16p. (J). (gr. k-2). (978-0-7787-9418-9(0)); pap. (978-0-7787-9462-2(8)) Crabtree Publishing Co.

Kennedy, Thomas. It's Time for a Birthday Party, 1 vol. 2017. (It's Time Ser.). (ENG., Illus.). 24p. (J). (gr. 1-1). 25.27 (978-1-5081-6364-0(2), d9a84b51-f732-4381-bfd3-e5af6fe02968, PowerKids Pr.) Rosen Publishing Group, Inc., The.

Krulik, Nancy. Prom! The Complete Guide to a Truly Spectacular Night. Johnson, Kim, illus. 2003. 96p. (YA). 8.00 (978-0-7567-9038-7(7)) DIANE Publishing Co.

Kruse, Nancy. Treasure Hunt: A Book of Clues for Parties. 2008. 116p. pap. 12.95 (978-1-60145-565-9(8)) Booklocker.com, Inc.

Labat, Yancey C., illus. It's Party Time! 2006. 56p. (J). (978-0-439-83227-4(6)) Scholastic, Inc.

Loh-Hagan, Virginia. Surprise Party. 2017. (D. I. Y. Make It Happen Ser.). (ENG., Illus.). 32p. (J). (gr. 4-8). lib. bdg. 32.07 (978-1-63472-144-8(6), 209148, 45th Parallel Press) Cherry Lake Publishing.

Lynette, Rachel. Let's Throw a Hanukkah Party!, 1 vol. 2011. (Holiday Parties Ser.). (J). (ENG.). 24p. (gr. 2-3). 26.27 (978-1-4488-2572-1(5), 30f427ce-b4da-4174-b7fa-2655ecfcee38); (ENG.). 24p. (gr. 2-3). pap. 9.25 (978-1-4488-2733-6(7), aeb2a3ec-7106-4e9a-a6f0-702445429064); 49.50 (978-1-4488-2734-3(5)) Rosen Publishing Group, Inc., The. (PowerKids Pr.).

Lyons, Shelly. If You Were a Question Mark [LTD Commodities]. Gray, Sara, illus. 2010. (Word Fun Ser.). 24p. pap. 3.50 (978-1-4048-6253-1(6), Picture Window Bks.) Capstone.

Maile, Ruby. Why Are You Having a Party? 2012. (Level B Ser.). (ENG., Illus.). 16p. (J). (gr. k-2). pap. 7.95 (978-1-927136-10-2(5), 19459) RiverStream Publishing.

Martin, Claudia. Party Food, 1 vol. 2018. (Cooking Skills Ser.). (ENG.). 48p. (gr. 5-5). pap. 12.70 (978-1-9785-0666-4(X), 0a7f9f78-53c7-4fb7-9e6f-dea043ee9ef2); lib. bdg. 29.60 (978-1-9785-0639-8(2), ada3a236-e547-49ad-b330-ab075ef33132) Enslow Publishing, LLC.

McKissick, Katherine. Fun & Games: Planning a Perfect Party: Division (Grade 3) rev. ed. 2017. (Mathematics in the Real World Ser.). (ENG., Illus.). 32p. (J). (gr. 3-4). pap. 11.99 (978-1-4807-5799-8(3)) Teacher Created Materials, Inc.

National Geographic Learning. Windows on Literacy Step up (Social Studies: Me & My Family): Getting Ready. 2007. (ENG., Illus.). 12p. pap. 11.95 (978-0-7922-8456-7(9)) National Geographic School Publishing, Inc.

Rober, Harold. Having a Sleepover. 2017. (Bumba Books (r) — Fun Firsts Ser.). (ENG., Illus.). 24p. (J). (gr. -1-1). 26.65 (978-1-5124-2555-0(9), 567fec16-66dd-465c-9b63-27d7ade18843); E-Book 39.99 (978-1-5124-3683-9(6), 9781512436839); E-Book 39.99 (978-1-5124-2751-6(9)); E-Book 4.99 (978-1-5124-3684-6(4), 9781512436846) Lerner Publishing Group. (Lerner Pubns.).

Rosenberg, Carol & Rosenberg, Gary. Jon & Jayne's Guide to Throwing, Going To, & Surviving Parties: Advice & More from Your Average but Xtraordinary Friends. 2008. (Jon & Jayne Doe Ser.). (ENG., Illus.). 128p. (YA). (gr. 7-11). pap. 9.95 (978-0-7573-0726-3(4)) Health Communications, Inc.

Salas, Laura Purdie. C Is for Cake! A Birthday Alphabet. 2010. (Alphabet Fun Ser.). (ENG.). 32p. (gr. 1-2). pap. 47.70 (978-1-4296-5086-1(9), Capstone Pr.) Capstone.

Segarra, Mercedes. Fun Party Food: Little Chef Recipes, 1 vol. 2013. (Little Chef Ser.). (ENG.). 36p. (gr. k-2). pap. 10.35 (978-1-4644-0467-2(4), 73a01522-34e1-4cc0-92db-1671d9a63947); lib. bdg. 26.61 (978-0-7660-4262-9(6), bf35299d-c471-442e-be15-253e23752dc0) Enslow Publishing, LLC. (Enslow Elementary).

Smith, Thomasina. I Can Have a Party: Easy Decorations, Food & Games, Shown Step by Step. 2016. (Illus.). 48p. (J). (gr. -1-12). 7.99 (978-1-86147-495-7(4), Armadillo) Anness Publishing GBR. Dist: National Bk. Network.

Speechley, Greta. Birthday Crafts, 1 vol. 2010. (Creative Crafts for Kids Ser.). (ENG.). 32p. (J). (gr. 3-4). lib. bdg. 30.67 (978-1-4339-3552-7(X), b773224e-76d4-430d-a047-e555b4fdaadf); (Illus.). pap. 11.50 (978-1-4339-3553-4(8), cb8774ba-3d73-42a5-baee-c1ed6bcabcee) Stevens, Gareth Publishing LLLP. (Gareth Stevens Learning Library).

Speregen, Debra Newberger. Party Girl: How to Throw a Fab Fest. Tallardy, Laura, illus. 2008. 48p. pap. (978-0-545-04093-8(0)) Scholastic, Inc.

Thompson, Kim Mitzo. Birthday Party. 2011. (J). (gr. k-1). audio compact disk 4.99 (978-1-59922-877-8(7)) Twin Sisters IP, LLC.

Torres, Laura. Rock Your Party. 2012. (ENG., Illus.). 32p. (gr. 3-5). pap. 8.95 (978-1-926853-86-4(5)) Saunders Bk. Co. CAN. Dist: RiverStream Publishing.

Turnbull, Stephanie. Fun with Friends: Style Secrets for Girls. 2013. (Girl Talk Ser.). 32p. (gr. 4-7). 31.35 (978-1-59920-946-3(2)) Black Rabbit Bks.

Ventura, Marne & Peschke, Marci. Kylie Jean Party Craft Queen, 1 vol. Mourning, Tuesday, illus. 2014. (Kylie Jean Craft Queen Ser.). (ENG.). 32p. (J). (gr. 1-3). lib. bdg. 27.32 (978-1-4795-2191-3(4), 124029, Picture Window Bks.) Capstone.

PARTIES—FICTION

Adler, David A. Young Cam Jansen & the 100th Day of School Mystery, 15 vols. Natti, Susanna, illus. 2010. (Young Cam Jansen Ser.: 15). (ENG.). 32p. (J). (gr. 1-3). mass mkt. 4.99 (978-0-14-241685-3(1), Penguin Young Readers) Penguin Young Readers Group.

Aikins, Dave, illus. The Birthday Dance Party: Daisy's Fiesta de Quinceañera. 2006. (Dora the Explorer Ser.: 19). (ENG.). 24p. (J). (gr. -1-3). pap. 3.99 (978-1-4169-1303-0(3), Simon Spotlight/Nickelodeon) Simon Spotlight/Nickelodeon.

Alegria, Malin. Border Town #2: Quince Clash. 2012. (Border Town Ser.). (ENG.). 192p. (J). (gr. 7). pap. 5.99 (978-0-545-40241-5(7), Scholastic Paperbacks) Scholastic, Inc.

—Guerra de Quinceaneras (Quince Clash) 2013. (Border Town (Spanish) Ser.: 2). (SPA.). lib. bdg. 16.00 (978-0-606-32401-4(1)) Turtleback.

Alemagna, Beatrice. Harold Snipperpot's Best Disaster Ever. Alemagna, Beatrice, illus. 2019. (ENG., Illus.). 48p. (J). (gr. -1-3). 18.99 (978-0-06-249882-3(7), HarperCollins) HarperCollins Pubs.

Alexander, Jed. Red. 2018. (ENG., Illus.). 32p. (J). (gr. -1-3). 15.95 (978-1-944903-11-4(9), 1313501, Cameron Kids) Cameron + Co.

Allen, Francesca & Brooks, Felicity. Busy Truck. Crisp, Dan, illus. 2007. (Usborne Play Bks.). 10p. (J). (gr. -1-k). bds. 10.99 (978-0-7945-1453-2(7), Usborne) EDC Publishing.

Alpine, Rachele, et al. Best. Night. Ever: A Story Told from Seven Points of View. (Mix Ser.). (ENG., Illus.). 352p. (J). (gr. 4-8). 2018. pap. 8.99 (978-1-4814-8661-3(6)) 2017. 18.99 (978-1-4814-8660-6(8)) Simon & Schuster Children's Publishing. (Aladdin).

Anfousse, Ginette. Polo et L'anniversaire. Sarrazin, Marisol, tr. 2003. (Polo Baby Board Bks.). (FRE., Illus.). 16p. (J). (— 1). bds. (978-2-89021-656-3(X)) Diffusion du livre Mirabel (DLM).

Anna. The Magic Money Tree. 2009. (Illus.). 20p. pap. 15.49 (978-1-4389-0472-6(X)) AuthorHouse.

Arévalo, Josefina. Lo Que Paulito Olvidó. 2006. (SPA.). (J). (978-1-59835-006-7(4)) Cambridge BrickHouse, Inc.

Arnold, Tedd. Fly Guy's Big Family (Fly Guy #17) Arnold, Tedd, illus. 2017. (Fly Guy Ser.: 17). (ENG., Illus.). 32p. (J). (gr. -1-2). 6.99 (978-0-545-66316-8(4), Cartwheel Bks.) Scholastic, Inc.

Ashley, Sharon. I Wish I Could See. 2013. 24p. pap. 24.95 (978-1-4626-9700-7(3)) America Star Bks.

Averill, Esther. Jenny's Birthday Book. Averill, Esther, illus. 2005. (Jenny's Cat Club Ser.). (Illus.). 44p. (J). (gr. -1-2). reprint ed. 16.95 (978-1-59017-154-7(3), NYR Children's Collection) New York Review of Bks., Inc., The.

Avraham, Kate Aver. What Will You Be, Sara Mee? O'Brien, Anne Sibley, illus. 2010. 32p. (J). (gr. -1-3). pap. 7.95 (978-1-58089-211-7(6)) Charlesbridge Publishing, Inc.

Baena, Gloria. Invitacion a la Fiesta del Gran Gorila. Osorno, Laura, illus. 2003. (SPA.). 32p. (J). 8.95 (978-958-04-7072-4(3)) Norma S.A. COL. Dist: Distribuidora Norma, Inc.

Bailey, Linda. Stanley's Party. Slavin, Bill, illus. 2004. (ENG.). 32p. (J). (gr. -1-2). pap. 8.99 (978-1-55337-768-9(0)) Kids Can Pr., Ltd. CAN. Dist: Hachette Bk. Group.

Barchers, Suzanne I. Main Street Block Party, 1 vol. rev. ed. 2011. (Phonics Ser.). (ENG.). 16p. (gr. k-2). 6.99 *(978-1-4333-2923-4(9))* Teacher Created Materials, Inc.

Barn Party: Level M, 6 vols. 128p. (gr. 2-3). 49.95 *(978-0-7699-0983-7(3))* Shortland Pubns. (U. S. A.) Inc.

Basha, Irena Canaj. The Birthday Party, It Was Saturday... 2013. 16p. pap. 24.95 *(978-1-62709-182-4(3))* America Star Bks.

Bates, Angie. Hey Baby! 2010. (Sleepover Club Ser.). (ENG., Illus.). 144p. (J). (gr. 2-6). pap. 6.99 *(978-0-00-727704-9(0))* HarperCollins Pubs. Ltd. GBR. Dist: Independent Pubs. Group.

Bauer, Linda. Fruits & Flowers & Footprints OH MY!!! 2007. (Illus.). 29p. (J). 13.99 *(978-0-9798146-0-0(X))* Bauer, Linda.

Beck, Scott. Monster Sleepover! 2009. (ENG., Illus.). 32p. (J). (gr. k-2). 15.95 *(978-0-8109-4059-8(0)*, 601001, Abrams Bks. for Young Readers) Abrams, Inc.

Believe It Or Not!, Ripleys, compiled by. Bremner & the Party. 2018. (Story Book Ser.: 2). (ENG., Illus.). 40p. (J). 16.99 *(978-1-60991-209-3(8))* Ripley Entertainment, Inc.

Benchmark Education Company, LLC Staff, compiled by. Celebrations. 2006. (J). 148.00 *(978-1-4108-7039-1(1))* Benchmark Education Co.

Benton, Lynne. Pirate Pete. Chapman, Neil, illus. 2008. (Tadpoles Ser.). (ENG.). 24p. (J). (gr. -1-3). pap. *(978-0-7787-3892-3(2))* Crabtree Publishing Co.

Berenstain, Jan & Berenstain, Mike. Berenstain Bears & the Forgiving Tree, 1 vol. 2011. (Berenstain Bears/Living Lights: a Faith Story Ser.). (ENG., Illus.). 32p. (J). pap. 4.99 *(978-0-310-72084-3(2))* Zonderkidz.

Berenstain, Stan & Berenstain, Jan. The Berenstain Bears' Family Reunion. 2009. (Berenstain Bears — I Can Read Ser.). (J). lib. bdg. 13.55 *(978-0-606-04776-0(X))* Turtleback.

Bertrand, Diane Gonzales & Ventura, Gabriela Baeza. A Bean & Cheese Taco Birthday / un Cumpleaños con Tacos de Frijoles con Queso. Trujillo, Robert, illus. 2015. (SPA & ENG.). 32p. (J). (gr. k-3). 17.95 *(978-1-55885-812-1(1))* Arte Publico Pr.

—The Party for Papá Luis/La Fiesta para Papá Luis. Galindo, Alejandro, illus. 2010. (ENG.). 32p. (J). (gr. -1-3). 16.95 *(978-1-55885-532-8(7))* Arte Publico Pr.

Bickel, Karla. Surprise Christmas Birthday Party. Bickel, Karla, illus. l.t. ed. 2004. (Illus.). 16p. (J). (gr. -1-6). pap. 5.00 *(978-1-891452-12-3(6)*, 3) Heart Arbor Bks.

Birchall, Mark. Rabbit's Birthday Surprise. Birchall, Mark, illus. 2003. (Illus.). 32p. (J). (gr. -1-3). 15.95 *(978-0-87614-910-2(7)*, Carolrhoda Bks.) Lerner Publishing Group.

Bird, Helen & Lancett, Peter. Party Time, 3 Vols, Set. 2008. (Siti's Sisters Ser.). (ENG.). 36p. *(978-1-84167-726-2(4))* Ransom Publishing Ltd.

Birney, Betty G. Humphrey's Big Birthday Bash. Burris, Priscilla, illus. 2018. (Humphrey's Tiny Tales Ser.: 8). (ENG.). 96p. (J). (gr. k-3). 5.99 *(978-1-5247-3721-4(6)*, Puffin Books) Penguin Young Readers Group.

The Birthday Party. (Early Intervention Levels Ser.). 23.10 *(978-0-7362-0002-8(9))* CENGAGE Learning.

Black, Allyson. Crushed, Bk. 5. Spaziante, Patrick & Riley, Kellee, illus. 2011. (Scarlett & Crimson Ser.). (ENG.). 112p. (J). pap. 6.99 *(978-1-4169-9648-4(6)*, Simon Spotlight) Simon Spotlight.

Blackburn, Sheila M. Stewie Scraps & the Giant Joggers. 2008. 76p. pap. *(978-1-903853-86-3(9))* Brilliant Pubns.

—Stewie Scraps & the Trolley Cart. 2008. 72p. pap. *(978-1-903853-88-7(5))* Brilliant Pubns.

Blackstone, Stella. Bear's Birthday. Harter, Debbie, illus. 2011.Tr. of El Cumpleanos de Oso. 24p. (J). (gr. -1-1). pap. 6.99 *(978-1-84686-515-2(8))* Barefoot Bks., Inc.

Blackwell-Burke, Melissa & Kunkel, Kristen. Rhyme Time Party. 2003. (J). spiral bd. 14.95 *(978-1-58605-955-2(6)*, LeapFrog Schl. Hse.) LeapFrog Enterprises, Inc.

Blanck, Cathy. A Party for Arty. 2004. (Illus.). 32p. (J). pap. *(978-0-9753059-0-4(5))* Red Barn Reading Inc.

Blankenship, Paula. We Both Read-Lulu's Wild Party. Reinhart, Larry, illus. 2009. (We Both Read Ser.). 44p. (J). 9.95 *(978-1-60115-231-2(0))*; pap. 5.99 *(978-1-60115-232-9(9))* Treasure Bay, Inc.

Blevins, Wiley. Count on It. Kreloff, Elliot, illus. 2018. (Basic Concepts Ser.). (ENG.). 24p. (J). (gr. -1-1). pap. 6.99 *(978-1-63440-416-7(5)*, 1de9eba3-6fba-4c8b-824f-114ee278c1b1, Rocking Chair Kids) Red Chair Pr.

Bliss, Emily. Unicorn Princesses 3: Bloom's Ball. Hanson, Sydney, illus. 2017. (Unicorn Princesses Ser.: 3). (ENG.). 128p. (J). pap. 5.99 *(978-1-68119-334-2(5)*, 900170042, Bloomsbury USA Childrens) Bloomsbury Publishing USA.

—Unicorn Princesses 6: Moon's Dance. Hanson, Sydney, illus. 2018. (Unicorn Princesses Ser.: 6). (ENG.). 128p. (J). pap. 6.99 *(978-1-68119-652-7(2)*, 900179844, Bloomsbury USA Childrens) Bloomsbury Publishing USA.

Bonwill, Ann. I Don't Want to Be a Pea! Rickerty, Simon, illus. 2012. (ENG.). 32p. (J). (gr. -1-1). 14.99 *(978-1-4424-3614-5(X)*, Atheneum Bks. for Young Readers) Simon & Schuster Children's Publishing.

Border, Terry. Happy Birthday, Cupcake! Border, Terry, illus. 2015. (Illus.). 32p. (J). (gr. k-3). bds. 17.99 *(978-0-399-17160-4(6)*, Philomel Bks.) Penguin Young Readers Group.

Bowe, Julie. Birthday Glamour! 2015. (Victoria Torres, Unfortunately Average Ser.). (ENG., Illus.). 160p. (J). (gr. 4-8). lib. bdg. 27.99 *(978-1-4965-0533-0(6)*, 128605, Stone Arch Bks.) Capstone.

—Dance Fever. 2017. (Victoria Torres, Unfortunately Average Ser.). (ENG.). 160p. (J). (gr. 4-8). lib. bdg. 27.99 *(978-1-4965-3819-2(6)*, 133118, Stone Arch Bks.) Capstone.

Bowen, L. A. One Too Many Lies, 1 vol. 2018. (YA Verse Ser.). (ENG.). 200p. (YA). (gr. 3-4). 25.80 *(978-1-5383-8250-9(4)*, b5978d52-c5e7-4ca0-902e-3af9c871b80c); pap. 16.35 *(978-1-5383-8249-3(0)*, 602014c4-3603-4eb4-a045-851fb6bfd803) Enslow Publishing, LLC.

Bower, Gary. There's a Party in Heaven! A Joyful Peek at the Land of Surprises. Bower, Jan, illus. 2007. (ENG.). 32p. (J). 11.99 *(978-0-9704621-8-3(2))* Storybook Meadow Publishing.

Boynton, Sandra. Happy Birthday, Little Pookie. Boynton, Sandra, illus. 2017. (Little Pookie Ser.). (ENG., Illus.). 18p. (J). (gr. -1-k). bds. 6.99 *(978-1-4814-9770-1(7))* Simon & Schuster, Inc.

Branning, Debe. The Adventures of Chickolet Pigolet: The Bribe of Frankenbeans. Knold, Nijlon, illus. 2008. 48p. pap. 7.95 *(978-1-935137-40-5(9))* Guardian Angel Publishing, Inc.

Brian, Kate, pseud. Sweet 16. 2007. (ENG.). 288p. (YA). (gr. 7-12). pap. 9.99 *(978-1-4169-0033-7(0)*, Simon & Schuster Bks. For Young Readers) Simon & Schuster Bks. For Young Readers.

—Vengeance. 2011. (Private Ser.). (ENG.). 240p. (YA). (gr. 9). pap. 9.99 *(978-1-4169-8473-3(9)*, Simon & Schuster Bks. For Young Readers) Simon & Schuster Bks. For Young Readers.

Bridwell, Norman. Clifford's Birthday Party (Classic Storybook), 1 vol. Bridwell, Norman, illus. 50th anniv. ed. 2013. (ENG., Illus.). 32p. (J). (gr. -1-3). pap. 5.99 *(978-0-545-47956-1(8))* Scholastic, Inc.

Brown, Monica. Marisol McDonald & the Clash Bash-Marisol Mcdonald y la Fiesta Sin Igual, 1 vol. Palacios, Sara, illus. 2013. (Marisol Mcdonald Ser.). (ENG.). 40p. (J). (gr. k-3). 19.95 *(978-0-89239-273-5(8)*, leelowcbp) Lee & Low Bks., Inc.

Brown, Tameka Fryer. Around Our Way on Neighbors' Day. Riley-Webb, Charlotte, illus. 2010. (ENG.). 32p. (J). (gr. k-2). 17.95 *(978-0-8109-8971-9(9)*, 678101) Abrams, Inc.

Brownlee, Sophia Grace & McClelland, Rosie. Tea Time with Sophia Grace & Rosie. McNicholas, Shelagh, illus. 2013. (J). pap. *(978-0-545-58534-7(1)*, Orchard Bks.) Scholastic, Inc.

Bryson, Theresa. Costume Party. 2011. (Early Connections Ser.). (J). *(978-1-61672-346-0(7))* Benchmark Education Co.

Buehner, Caralyn. Snowmen at Christmas. Buehner, Mark, illus. (J). (gr. -1 — 1). 2010. 28p. bds. 7.99 *(978-0-8037-3551-4(0))* 2005. 32p. 17.99 *(978-0-8037-2995-7(2))* Penguin Young Readers Group. (Dial Bks).

Bunting, Eve. Party at the Pond. Masse, Josée, illus. 2011. (I AM a READER!: Frog & Friends Ser.). (ENG.). 40p. (J). (gr. 1-2). lib. bdg. 9.95 *(978-1-58536-549-4(1)*, 202222) Sleeping Bear Pr.

Burkhart, Jessica. Masquerade. 2012. (Canterwood Crest Ser.: 16). lib. bdg. 18.40 *(978-0-606-26887-5(1))* Turtleback.

Butler, Kristi T. A Big Surprise. Paparone, Pam, illus. 2005. (Green Light Readers Level 1 Ser.). (ENG.). 24p. (J). (gr. -1-3). pap. 5.99 *(978-0-15-205141-9(4)*, 1195515, Clarion Bks.) HarperCollins Pubs.

Byrd, Cari Grigsby. Where Did Pop Pop Go? 2013. 24p. pap. 24.95 *(978-1-62709-967-7(0))* America Star Bks.

Byrne, Marlene F. Ghost in the Graveyard. Graber, Jesse, illus. 2010. 57p. (J). pap. 9.99 *(978-0-9777135-4-7(7))* Good Stories Publishing.

Cabot, Meg. Party Princess. 2006. (Princess Diaries: Vol. 7). (ENG., Illus.). 304p. (YA). (gr. 7-12). 16.99 *(978-0-06-072453-5(6))* HarperCollins Pubs.

—The Princess Diaries, Volume VII: Party Princess, Vol. VII. 2008. (Princess Diaries: 7). (ENG.). 320p. (YA). (gr. 8). pap. 9.99 *(978-0-06-154374-6(8)*, HarperTeen) HarperCollins Pubs.

Calford, Farley. The Complete Disaster, Rhonda's Birthday Party. 2009. 86p. pap. 9.95 *(978-1-60860-210-0(9)*, Eloquent Bks.) Strategic Book Publishing & Rights Agency (SBPRA).

Callies, Debi. Frog Mill. 2008. 20p. pap. 24.95 *(978-1-60703-091-1(8))* America Star Bks.

Calonita, Jen. Winter White. 2013. (Belles Ser.: 2). (ENG.). 384p. (YA). (gr. 7-17). pap. 19.99 *(978-0-316-09118-3(9)*, Poppy) Little, Brown Bks. for Young Readers.

Cammuso, Frank. The Misadventures of Salem Hyde: Book Two: Big Birthday Bash. 2014. (Misadventures of Salem Hyde Ser.). (ENG., Illus.). 96p. (J). (gr. 1-4). 14.95 *(978-1-4197-1025-4(7)*, 1044801, Amulet Bks.) Abrams, Inc.

Cantini, Barbara. Ghoulia & the Mysterious Visitor (Book #2) 2019. (Ghoulia Ser.). (ENG., Illus.). 64p. (YA). (gr. 1-3). 9.99 *(978-1-4197-3690-2(6)*, 1254601) Abrams, Inc.

Carbone, Courtney. Princess Peppa & the Royal Ball (Peppa Pig: Scholastic Reader, Level 1), 1 vol. (Scholastic Reader, Level 1 Ser.). (ENG., 32p. (J). 2017. Illus.). (gr. -1-k). pap. 4.99 *(978-1-338-18258-3(7))* 2005. (gr. 2-5). E-Book 7.99 *(978-1-338-19011-3(3))* Scholastic, Inc.

—Sunny's Royal Ball (Sunny Day) Priori, Giulia & Legramandi, Francesco, illus. 2018. (Little Golden Book Ser.). (ENG.). 24p. (J). (-k). 4.99 *(978-1-5247-6855-3(3)*, Golden Bks.) Random Hse. Children's Bks.

Carr, Lynn. Marty Likes to Party! 2011. 20p. pap. 11.99 *(978-1-4634-4418-1(4))* AuthorHouse.

Cecil, Lauren. Lalaloopsy: Cinder Slippers & the Grand Ball. Hill, Prescott, illus. 2013. (Lalaloopsy Ser.). (ENG.). 24p. (J). (gr. -1-3). pap. 3.99 *(978-0-545-47769-7(7))* Scholastic, Inc.

—Pooh's Cleanup. Grey, Andrew, illus. 2011. (Disney Classic Pooh Ser.). (ENG.). 24p. (J). (gr. -1-3). 16.19 *(978-0-448-45558-7(7)*, Grosset & Dunlap) Penguin Publishing Group.

Chanda, J-P. Happy Birthday, SpongeBob! Martinez, Heather, illus. 2005. (SpongeBob SquarePants Ser.). (ENG.). 24p. (J). pap. 3.99 *(978-0-689-87674-5(2)*, Simon Spotlight/Nickelodeon) Simon Spotlight/Nickelodeon.

Charles, Tami. Daphne Definitely Doesn't Do Dances. Calo, Marcos, illus. 2018. (Daphne, Secret Vlogger Ser.). (ENG.). 96p. (J). (gr. 4-7). pap. 4.95 *(978-1-4965-6301-9(8)*, 138030); lib. bdg. 24.65 *(978-1-4965-6297-5(6)*, 138024) Capstone. (Stone Arch Bks.).

Charlip, Remy, creator. Dress up & Let's Have a Party. 2018. (ENG., Illus.). 32p. (J). 14.95 *(978-1-59270-234-3(1))* Enchanted Lion Bks., LLC.

Chef Jeff. Do Cows Eat Cake? 2008. 28p. pap. 13.99 *(978-1-4389-0494-8(0))* AuthorHouse.

Chloe Cow & the Party. 2004. (Play Pals Ser.). (Illus.). 12p. (J). bds. *(978-1-84229-644-8(2))* Top That! Publishing PLC.

Christopher, Matt. The Extreme Team: on Thin Ice. 4th ed. 2004. (Extreme Team Ser.: 4). (ENG., Illus.). 64p. (J). (gr. 1-4). pap. 8.99 *(978-0-316-73739-5(9))* Little, Brown Bks. for Young Readers.

Civardi, Anne. Going to a Party. Watt, Fiona, ed. Cartwright, Stephen, illus. 2007. (Usborne First Experiences Ser.). 16p. (J). (gr. -1-3). pap. 4.99 *(978-0-7945-1011-4(6)*, Usborne) EDC Publishing.

Clark, Eleanor. Mary Elizabeth: Welcome to America. 2007. (Eleanor Ser.: Bk. 1). (Illus.). 187p. (J). (gr. 4-7). 14.99 *(978-0-9753036-7-2(8))* HonorNet.

Claus, Nancy. Santa's Prize. Ferchaud, Steve, illus. 2006. (J). *(978-0-9746747-5-9(3))* Cypress Bay Publishing.

Cohen, Jerianne. Max A. Million's Birthday Party. 2008. 193p. pap. 24.95 *(978-1-60672-844-4(X))* America Star Bks.

Cohn, Rachel & Levithan, David. Sam & Ilsa's Last Hurrah. 2018. (ENG.). 224p. (YA). (gr. 7). 17.99 *(978-0-399-55384-4(3)*, Knopf Bks. for Young Readers) Random Hse. Children's Bks.

Colfer, Chris. Trollbella Throws a Party: A Tale from the Land of Stories. Dorman, Brandon, illus. 2017. (Land of Stories Ser.). (ENG.). 32p. (J). (gr. -1-3). 17.99 *(978-0-316-38340-0(6))* Little, Brown Bks. for Young Readers.

Colleen, Marcie. Going Nuts: Super Happy Party Bears 4. James, Steve, illus. 2017. (Super Happy Party Bears Ser.: 4). (ENG.). 144p. (J). pap. 5.99 *(978-1-250-10049-8(6)*, 900162461) Imprint IND. Dist: Macmillan.

—Staying a Hive, 3. James, Steve, illus. 2017. (Super Happy Party Bears Ser.). (ENG.). 144p. (J). (gr. 1-3). 18.69 *(978-1-5364-0566-8(3))* Macmillan.

—Staying a Hive: Super Happy Party Bears 3. James, Steve, illus. 2017. (Super Happy Party Bears Ser.: 3). (ENG.). 144p. (J). pap. 5.99 *(978-1-250-10047-4(X)*, 900162459) Imprint IND. Dist: Macmillan.

Cook, Tina H. Lindsey & the Yellow Masterpiece. 2011. 36p. pap. 15.99 *(978-1-4634-0306-5(2))* AuthorHouse.

Coombs, Kate. Goodnight Mr. Darcy: A BabyLit(TM) Parody Picture Book, 1 vol. 2014. (ENG., Illus.). 32p. (J). 16.99 *(978-1-4236-3670-0(8))* Gibbs Smith, Publisher.

Corderoy, Tracey. More! Warnes, Tim, illus. 2015. (ENG.). 32p. (J). (gr. -1-2). 16.99 *(978-1-58925-193-9(8))* Tiger Tales.

Coulton, Mia. Danny's Party. Coulton, Mia, photos by. 2004. (ENG., Illus.). (J). pap. 5.35 *(978-0-9746475-1-7(9))* Maryruth Bks., Inc.

Cousins, C. J. Bailey & Friends Have a Party. 2012. (ENG.). 24p. pap. 15.99 *(978-1-4772-7346-3(8))* AuthorHouse.

Cox, Judy. Happy Birthday, Mrs. Millie!, 0 vols. Mathieu, Joe, illus. 2012. (ENG.). 32p. (J). (gr. -1-2). 16.99 *(978-0-7614-6126-5(4)*, 9780761461265, Two Lions) Amazon Publishing.

Crawford, Shannon Joseph. Halloween War. 2011. 88p. pap. 19.95 *(978-1-61546-348-0(8))* America Star Bks.

Cronin, Doreen. Click, Clack, Moo I Love You! Lewin, Betsy, illus. 2017. (Click Clack Book Ser.). (ENG.). 40p. (J). (gr. -1-3). 17.99 *(978-1-4814-4496-5(4)*, Atheneum/Caitlyn Dlouhy Books) Simon & Schuster Children's Publishing.

—Click, Clack, Moo I Love You! Lewin, Betsy, illus. 2020. (Doreen Cronin: Click, Clack & More Ser.). (ENG.). 36p. (J). (gr. -1-3). 31.36 *(978-1-5321-4465-3(2)*, 35155, Picture Bk.) Spotlight.

Crow, Melinda Melton. Little Lizard's Big Party. Rowland, Andrew & Rowland, Andrew, illus. 2010. (Little Lizards Ser.). (ENG.). 32p. (J). (gr. -1-1). pap. 6.25 *(978-1-4342-2791-1(X)*, 114058, Stone Arch Bks.) Capstone.

—Rocky & Daisy & the Birthday Party. 2013. (My Two Dogs Ser.). (ENG., Illus.). 32p. (J). (gr. 1-3). pap. 35.70 *(978-1-4342-6296-7(0)*, 20268, Stone Arch Bks.) Capstone.

—Rocky & Daisy & the Birthday Party, 1 vol. Sassin, Eva, illus. 2013. (My Two Dogs Ser.). (ENG.). 32p. (J). (gr. 2-3). pap. 5.95 *(978-1-4342-6205-9(7)*, 123499); lib. bdg. 22.65 *(978-1-4342-6011-6(9)*, 123061) Capstone. (Stone Arch Bks.).

Crowne, Alyssa. Pink Princess Rules the School. Alder, Charlotte, illus. 2009. 80p. (J). pap. *(978-0-545-16077-3(4))* Scholastic, Inc.

Curious George & the Pizza Party with Downloadable Audio. 2013. (Curious George Ser.). (ENG., Illus.). 24p. (J). (gr. -1-3). pap. 4.99 *(978-0-544-10988-9(0)*, 1541242, Clarion Bks.) HarperCollins Pubs.

Curious George Pinata Party (Reader Level 1) 2009. (Curious George TV Ser.). (ENG., Illus.). 24p. (J). (gr. -1-3). pap. 4.99 *(978-0-547-11962-5(3)*, 1047234, Clarion Bks.) HarperCollins Pubs.

Czajak, Paul. Monster Needs a Party. Grieb, Wendy, illus. 2015. (Monster & Me Ser.). (ENG.). 32p. (J). (-k). 16.95 *(978-1-938063-55-8(4)*, Mighty Media Kids) Mighty Media Pr.

Darsana, Nam Aste. Guppie: God's Unified Perfect Plan Inspiring Everyone. 2011. 40p. pap. 21.99 *(978-1-4628-4535-4(5))* Xlibris Corp.

Day, Alexandra. Carl's Snowy Afternoon. Day, Alexandra, illus. 2009. (Carl Ser.). (ENG., Illus.). 32p. (J). (gr. -1-1). 13.99 *(978-0-374-31086-8(6)*, 900042212, Farrar, Straus & Giroux (BYR)) Farrar, Straus & Giroux.

de la Cruz, Melissa. Birthday Vicious. 2014. (Ashley Project Ser.: 3). (ENG., Illus.). 304p. (J). (gr. 4-8). pap. 7.99 *(978-1-4424-9038-3(1)*, Aladdin) Simon & Schuster Children's Publishing.

Dean, Karen. Kitty Kate's Tea Party. Dean, Karen, illus. 2009. (ENG., Illus.). 48p. (J). *(978-1-934363-30-0(8))* Zoe Life Christian Communications.

deGroat, Diane. Happy Birthday to You, You Belong in a Zoo. deGroat, Diane, illus. 2007. (ENG., Illus.). 32p. (J). (gr. -1-3). pap. 7.99 *(978-0-06-001029-4(8))*, HarperCollins) HarperCollins Pubs.

—Happy Birthday to You, You Belong in a Zoo. deGroat, Diane, illus. 2007. (Gilbert & Friends Ser.). (Illus.). (gr. -1-3). 17.00 *(978-0-7569-8108-2(5))* Perfection Learning Corp.

Deich, Cheri Bivin. The Messy Monkey Tea Party. Genth, Christina, illus. 2007. 32p. (J). (gr. -1-3). 15.95 *(978-1-60108-006-6(9))* Red Cygnet Pr.

Delle Donne, Elena. Elle of the Ball. 2018. (Hoops Ser.: 1). (ENG., Illus.). 160p. (J). (gr. 3-7). 17.99 *(978-1-5344-1231-6(X)*, Simon & Schuster Bks. For Young Readers) Simon & Schuster Bks. For Young Readers.

Denton, P. J. Pony Party! Denos, Julia, illus. 5th ed. 2008. (Sleepover Squad Ser.: 5). (ENG.). 96p. (J). (gr. 1-4). pap. 5.99 *(978-1-4169-5931-1(9)*, Aladdin) Simon & Schuster Children's Publishing.

dePaola, Tomie. Four Friends in Autumn. dePaola, Tomie, illus. 2004. (ENG., Illus.). 32p. (J). (gr. -1-3). 18.99 *(978-0-689-85980-9(5)*, Simon & Schuster Bks. For Young Readers) Simon & Schuster Bks. For Young Readers.

Depken, Kristen L. Happy Birthday to You! Aikins, Dave, illus. 2018. 24p. (J). *(978-1-5444-0156-0(6))* Random Hse., Inc.

—Happy Birthday to You! (Shimmer & Shine) Aikins, Dave, illus. 2018. (Step into Reading Ser.). (ENG.). 24p. (J). (gr. -1-1). pap. 5.99 *(978-1-5247-6799-0(9)*, Random Hse. Bks. for Young Readers) Random Hse. Children's Bks.

Desbordes, Astrid. Edmond, the Moonlit Party. Boutavant, Marc, illus. 2015. (ENG.). 32p. (J). (gr. -1-3). 17.95 *(978-1-59270-174-2(4))* Enchanted Lion Bks., LLC.

Dewdney, Anna. Llama Llama Birthday Party! Dewdney, Anna, illus. 2013. (Llama Llama Ser.). (Illus.). 16p. (J). (gr. -1-k). 7.99 *(978-0-448-45880-9(2)*, Grosset & Dunlap) Penguin Young Readers Group.

Dieudonné, Cléa. Party Animals! A Tall Tale of Balancing Beasts. 2017. (Illus.). 28p. (J). (gr. k-5). 19.95 *(978-0-500-65139-1(6)*, 565139) Thames & Hudson.

Disney Books. Haunted Clubhouse. 2010. (ENG., Illus.). 12p. (J). (gr. -1-k). bds. 6.99 *(978-1-4231-2832-8(X)*, Disney Press Books) Disney Publishing Worldwide.

—Minnie: Be My Sparkly Valentine. 2014. (ENG., Illus.). 24p. (J). (gr. -1-k). pap. 5.99 *(978-1-4231-6414-2(8)*, Disney Press Books) Disney Publishing Worldwide.

Donaldson, Babette. Emma Lea's First Tea Party. Van Dijk, Jerianne, illus. 2007. (ENG.). 32p. (J). 16.95 *(978-0-9792612-0-6(1))* Blue Gate Bks.

Doodler, Todd H. One Potato, Two Potato. Doodler, Todd H., illus. 2013. (ENG., Illus.). 32p. (J). (gr. -1-k). 14.99 *(978-1-4424-8517-4(5)*, Little Simon) Little Simon.

Dooley, Norah. Everybody Brings Noodles. Thornton, Peter J., illus. 40p. (J). 2005. (ENG.). (gr. k-3). pap. 7.99 *(978-1-57505-916-7(9)*, 67d3f290-0d43-43e1-922d-5168d9080e37, First Avenue Editions) 2003. (gr. -1-3). 15.95 *(978-0-87614-455-8(5)*, Carolrhoda Bks.) Lerner Publishing Group.

Dorman, Brandon & Murray, Marjorie Dennis. Halloween Night. 2013. (ENG., Illus.). 40p. (J). (gr. k-4). pap. 7.99 *(978-0-06-185773-7(4)*, Greenwillow Bks.) HarperCollins Pubs.

Dougherty, Brandi. The Valentine's Day Disaster. 2008. 204p. (J). pap. *(978-0-545-03168-4(0))* Scholastic, Inc.

Down, Reg. The Magic Knot: And other Tangles. 2007. (Illus.). 100p. (J). per. 14.95 *(978-0-9794452-0-0(5))* Lightly Pr.

Dufresne, Michèle. Surprise Party: Bella & Rosie Green Set. 2004. (Bella & Rosie Set 2 Ser.). (J). pap. 7.67 *(978-1-932570-21-2(7))* Pioneer Valley Bks.

Dunn, Janeen. I'm Afraid Your Teddy Is in Trouble Today. Nash, Scott, illus. 2017. (ENG.). 40p. (J). (gr. -1-2). 15.99 *(978-0-7636-7537-0(7))* Candlewick Pr.

Dyckman, Ame. Tea Party Rules. Campbell, K. G., illus. 2013. 36p. (J). (gr. -1-k). 18.99 *(978-0-670-78501-8(6)*, Viking Books for Young Readers) Penguin Young Readers Group.

Easley, Terriana. Bubbles & Elle: A Party for Elle. 2011. 28p. pap. 24.95 *(978-1-4626-3635-8(7))* America Star Bks.

Eastman, P. D. Go, Dog. Go! 2015. (Big Bright & Early Board Book Ser.). (ENG., Illus.). 24p. (J). (gr. -1-2). bds. 7.99 *(978-0-553-52109-2(8)*, Random Hse. Bks. for Young Readers) Random Hse. Children's Bks.

Eggleton, Jill. Clown's Party. Smith, Craig, illus. 2003. (Rigby Sails Early Ser.). (ENG.). 16p. (gr. 1-2). pap. 6.95 *(978-0-7578-8669-0(8))* Houghton Mifflin Harcourt Publishing Co.

Ehlert, Lois. Boo to You! Ehlert, Lois, illus. 2009. (ENG., Illus.). 42p. (J). (gr. -1-2). 19.99 *(978-1-4169-8625-6(1)*, Beach Lane Bks.) Beach Lane Bks.

Elizabeth's Story 1848. 2014. (Secrets of the Manor Ser.: 3). (ENG., Illus.). 160p. (J). (gr. 3-7). pap. 7.99 *(978-1-4814-1840-9(8)*, Simon Spotlight) Simon Spotlight.

Elliott, Rebecca. Eva's Big Sleepover, 9. 2019. (Branches Early Ch Bks). (ENG.). 72p. (J). (gr. 2-3). 15.36 *(978-0-87617-987-1(1))* Penworthy Co., LLC, The.

—Eva's Big Sleepover. 2018. (Owl Diaries — Branches Ser.: 9). lib. bdg. 14.75 *(978-0-606-41508-8(4))* Turtleback.

—Eva's Big Sleepover: a Branches Book (Owl Diaries #9) Elliott, Rebecca, illus. 2018. (Owl Diaries: 9). (ENG., illus.). 80p. (J). (gr. k-2). pap. 4.99 *(978-1-338-16306-3(X))* Scholastic, Inc.

—Eva's Big Sleepover: a Branches Book (Owl Diaries #9) (Library Edition), Vol. 9. Elliott, Rebecca, illus. 2018. (Owl Diaries: 9). (ENG., Illus.). 80p. (J). (gr. k-2). lib. bdg. 24.99 *(978-1-338-16307-0(8))* Scholastic, Inc.

Ellis, Kim. Bernard & His Dad. 2005. 49p. pap. 16.95 *(978-1-4137-7058-2(4))* America Star Bks.

Elrod, Julie. Splitting Hares. 2008. 36p. pap. 16.50 *(978-1-60693-484-5(8)*, Eloquent Bks.) Strategic Book Publishing & Rights Agency (SBPRA).

Emanuel, Effie Ann. The Penguin Party, 1 vol. 2009. 32p. pap. 24.95 *(978-1-60813-544-8(6))* America Star Bks.

English, Karen. Nikki & Deja: Nikki & Deja, Book One. Freeman, Laura, illus. 2009. (Nikki & Deja Ser.: 1). (ENG.). 80p. (J). (gr. -1-3). pap. 9.99 *(978-0-547-13362-1(6)*, 1048763, Clarion Bks.) HarperCollins Pubs.

—Nikki & Deja: Birthday Blues: Nikki & Deja, Book Two, Bk. 2. Freeman, Laura, illus. 2010. (Nikki & Deja Ser.: 2). (ENG.). 96p. (J). (gr. 1-4). pap. 9.99 *(978-0-547-24893-6(8)*, 1100905, Clarion Bks.) HarperCollins Pubs.

Epstein, Robin. First Pajama Party: Slumberrific Six. 2005. (Groovy Girls Ser.). (ENG., Illus.). 80p. (J). (gr. 2-5). 3.99 *(978-0-439-81431-7(6))* Scholastic, Inc.

Esbaum, Jill. If a T. Rex Crashes Your Birthday Party. Tolstikova, Dasha, illus. 2016. (ENG.). 40p. (J). (gr. -1-2). 16.95 *(978-1-4549-1550-8(1))* Sterling Publishing Co., Inc.

Eubank, Patricia Reeder. Halloween 123. 2012. (ENG., Illus.). 22p. (J). (gr. -1 — 1). bds. 6.99 *(978-0-8249-1868-2(1)*, Ideals Pubns.) Worthy Publishing.

Evans, Cordelia. Olivia & the Fancy Party. 2014. (Olivia 8x8 Ser.). lib. bdg. 13.55 *(978-0-606-35762-3(9))* Turtleback.

Evans, Rosemary R. The Little Princesses Magial Party. Taylor, Erin, illus. 2012. 40p. (J). 16.95 *(978-1-60743-759-8(7))* Wink Publishing.

Evans, Yvette Kemp. If I Take a Shower. 2008. 32p. pap. 24.95 *(978-1-4241-9953-2(0))* America Star Bks.

Facey, La-Toya S. Brielle-Elaine Tries to Fit In! Yamyamin, Floyd, illus. 2011. (ENG.). 24p. pap. 14.99 *(978-1-4634-2353-7(5))* AuthorHouse.

Faris, Stephanie. Piper Morgan Plans a Party. Fleming, Lucy, illus. 2017. (Piper Morgan Ser.: 5). (ENG.). 96p. (J). (gr. 1-4). 16.99 *(978-1-5344-0386-4(8))*; pap. 5.99 *(978-1-5344-0385-7(X))*; 5. 18.69 *(978-1-5364-2740-0(3))* Simon & Schuster Children's Publishing. (Aladdin).

Farrell, Connie. Sam's Harvest Party, 1 vol. Ellingsworth, Colleen, illus. 2009. 29p. pap. 24.95 (978-1-60813-937-8(9)) America Star Bks.

Faruqi, Saadia. Yasmin la Chef. Aparicio Publishing LLC, Aparicio Publishing, tr. from ENG. Aly, Hatem, illus. 2020. (Yasmin en Español Ser.).Tr. of Yasmin the Chef. (SPA.). 32p. (J). (gr. k-2). pap. 5.95 (978-1-5158-5734-1(4), 142098); lib. bdg. 20.65 (978-1-5158-5730-3(1), 142095) Capstone. (Picture Window Bks.).

—Yasmin the Chef. Aly, Hatem, illus. 2019. (Yasmin Ser.). (ENG.). 32p. (J). (gr. k-2). pap. 5.95 (978-1-5158-4578-2(8), 141178); lib. bdg. 22.65 (978-1-5158-3784-8(X), 139366) Capstone. (Picture Window Bks.).

Fazio, Maria R. Block Party! 2013. 28p. pap. 24.95 (978-1-4241-2603-3(7)) America Star Bks.

Feldman, Thea. Princess Party. 2006. 3p. 5.99 (978-1-932915-33-4(8)) Sandvik Publishing.

Fernandez, Joyce & Marsh, Laura. Eins und Zwei are One & Two. 2009. 22p. 15.95 (978-0-578-00208-8(6)) My Second Language Publishing, USA.

—Un et Deux are One & Two. 2009. 22p. 15.95 (978-0-615-26239-0(2)) My Second Language Publishing, USA.

—Un Is One. 2009. 21p. 15.95 (978-0-615-26238-3(4)) My Second Language Publishing, USA.

—Uno Is One. 2009. 22p. 15.95 (978-0-615-24460-0(2)) My Second Language Publishing, USA.

—Uno y Dos are One & Two. 2008. 22p. pap. 15.95 (978-0-615-26150-8(7)) My Second Language Publishing, USA.

Figueroa, Juanita Kimberly. Kendra Gives a Birthday Party. 2012. 24p. pap. 24.95 (978-1-4626-6009-4(6)) PublishAmerica, Inc.

Finzi, Ama. At Baba's House. 2011. 36p. pap. 16.46 (978-1-4269-7095-5(1)) Trafford Publishing.

Fisch, Sholly & Wolfram, Amy. Party, Party! 2015. (Teen Titans Go! Graphic Novels Ser.: 1). lib. bdg. 24.50 (978-0-606-37251-0(2)) Turtleback.

Fischer, Kelly. The Moon Throws a Birthday Party. Duckworth, Michelle, illus. 2011. 32p. (J). 19.50 (978-1-58385-237-8(9)) ktf-writers-studio.

Fitzgerald, Caroline. Animal Kingdom Goes to New York. 2011. 48p. pap. 18.46 (978-1-4520-9966-8(9)) AuthorHouse.

Fitzgerald, Joanne. This Is Me & Where I Am, 1 vol. 2006. (ENG., Illus.). 32p. (J). (gr. -1-k). bds. 9.95 (978-1-55041-786-9(X), 65890fbd-9060-4bdc-be85-bfe4aa3b3d49) Fitzhenry & Whiteside, Ltd. CAN. Dist: Firefly Bks., Ltd.

Fleischman, Sid. The Giant Rat of Sumatra. Hendrix, John, illus. 2005. 208p. (J). (gr. 5-18). 15.99 (978-0-06-074238-6(0)) HarperCollins Pubs.

Flint, Shamini. Life of the Party! the Susie K Files 1. Heinrich, Sally, illus. 2018. (Susie K Files Ser.: 1). (ENG.). 96p. (J). (gr. 2-6). pap. 8.99 (978-1-76029-668-1(6)) Allen & Unwin AUS. Dist: Independent Pubs. Group.

Flor Ada, Alma. Dear Peter Rabbit. Tryon, Leslie, illus. 2006. (Stories to Go! Ser.). (J). (gr. k-3). 12.65 (978-0-7569-7322-3(8)) Perfection Learning Corp.

Flowerpot Press, contrib. by. Sockheadz: Party. 2013. (ENG., Illus.). 20p. (J). (gr. -1-k). 8.99 (978-1-77093-617-1(3)) Flowerpot Children's Pr. Inc. CAN. Dist: Cardinal Pubs. Group.

Freedman, Claire. Dragon Jelly. Hendra, Sue, illus. 2015. (ENG.). 32p. (J). (gr. k-3). 14.99 (978-1-61963-682-8(4), 900145471, Bloomsbury USA Childrens) Bloomsbury Publishing USA.

—Scary Hairy Party. Hendra, Sue, illus. 2017. (ENG.). 32p. (J). pap. (978-1-4088-6717-4(6), 281266, Bloomsbury Children's Bks.) Bloomsbury Publishing Plc.

Friedman, Laurie. Mallory's Super Sleepover. Kalis, Jennifer, illus. (Mallory Ser.: 16). (ENG.). 160p. (J). (gr. 2-5). 2012. pap. 7.99 (978-1-4677-0209-6(9), 869ca9fe-ce75-45b6-9716-311e54cd8c12)No. 16. 2011. 15.95 (978-0-8225-8887-0(0)) Lerner Publishing Group. (Darby Creek).

—Ruby Valentine Saves the Day. Avril, Lynne, illus. 2010. (Ruby Valentine Ser.). (ENG.). 32p. (J). (gr. k-3). lib. bdg. 16.95 (978-0-7613-4213-7(3), 5712cf7b-cdd0-4bc4-bb02-98aa513f9e9a, Carolrhoda Bks.) Lerner Publishing Group.

Fronis, Aly. This Little Bunny. Rescek, Sanja, illus. 2016. (ENG.). 16p. (J). (gr. -1-k). bds. 5.99 (978-1-4998-0105-7(X)) Little Bee Books Inc.

Furgang, Kathy. A Rainbow Party: Set Of 6. 2011. (Early Connections Ser.). (J). pap. 37.00 net. (978-1-4108-1363-3(0)) Benchmark Education Co.

Gajewski, Lois. Benny, the Stubborn Bubble. 2011. 28p. (gr. 1-2). pap. 12.03 (978-1-4567-4703-9(7)) AuthorHouse.

Gallagher, Diana G. Party! The Complicated Life of Claudia Cristina Cortez, 1 vol. Garvey, Brann, illus. 2008. (Claudia Cristina Cortez Ser.). (ENG.). 88p. (J). (gr. 4-8). pap. 6.10 (978-1-4342-0867-5(2), 95228); lib. bdg. 27.32 (978-1-4342-0771-5(4), 95176) Capstone. (Stone Arch Bks.).

Gallo, Tina. Olivia Wishes on a Star. 2014. (Olivia 8x8 Ser.). lib. bdg. 13.55 (978-0-606-36118-7(9)) Turtleback.

Garratt, Irene Joyce. Happy Birthday: Two in One Stories. 2009. (Illus.). 12p. pap. 8.49 (978-1-4389-4304-6(0)) AuthorHouse.

Gaston, Sharon D. Clean Your Own House & Misery Loves Company. 2009. 40p. pap. 18.50 (978-1-4389-7831-4(6)) AuthorHouse.

Gates, Josephine Scribner. The live dolls' house Party. Keep, Virginia, illus. 2007. 104p. (J). lib. bdg. 59.00 (978-1-60304-005-1(6)) Dollworks.

Gibbs, Lynne. Molly Mouse Is Shy: A Story of Shyness, 1 vol. Mitchell, Missy, illus. 2009. (Let's Grow Together Ser.). (ENG.). 32p. (J). (gr. k-1). pap. 11.55 (978-1-60754-761-7(9), 6aac5f9c-dab3-409a-95c2-a45eaeb14dcd); lib. bdg. 27.27 (978-1-60754-756-3(2), 2e202d76-3c52-42a4-b9bb-002ce24a3c6d) Rosen Publishing Group, Inc., The. (Windmill Bks.).

Gilson. Melusine Vol. 3: The Vampires' Ball. 2008. (Melusine Ser.: 3). (Illus.). 48p. (J). (gr. 4-7). pap. 11.95 (978-1-905460-69-4(4)) CineBook GBR. Dist: National Bk. Network.

Glover, Dennis W. The Talking Flower. 2010. 32p. pap. 12.99 (978-1-4490-5599-8(0)) AuthorHouse.

Godin, Thelma Lynne. Hula-Hoopin' Queen. Brantley Newton, Vanessa, illus. 2014. (ENG.). 40p. (J). 18.95 (978-1-60060-846-9(9)) Lee & Low Bks., Inc.

—The Hula-Hoopin' Queen, 1 vol. Brantley-Newton, Vanessa, illus. 2017. (ENG.). 40p. (J). (gr. 1-5). 12.95 (978-1-62014-579-1(0), leelowbooks) Lee & Low Bks., Inc.

Godwin, Jane & Bell, Davina. Baby Day. Blackwood, Freya, illus. 2019. (ENG.). 40p. (J). (gr. -1-3). 17.99 (978-1-4814-7034-6(5)) Simon & Schuster Children's Publishing.

—Hattie Helps Out. Blackwood, Freya, illus. 2016. (ENG.). 32p. (J). (gr. -1-k). 19.99 (978-1-74343-543-4(6)) Allen & Unwin AUS. Dist: Independent Pubs. Group.

Gold, Maya. Change of a Dress, 1. 2010. (Cinderella Cleaners Ser.: 1). (ENG.). 224p. (J). (gr. 6-8). 18.69 (978-0-545-12959-6(1)) Scholastic, Inc.

Golden Books. Adventures with Grandpa! (PAW Patrol) Petrossi, Fabrizio, illus. 2018. (Little Golden Book Ser.). (ENG.). 24p. (J). (-k). 4.99 (978-1-5247-6874-4(X), Golden Bks.) Random Hse. Children's Bks.

—Puppy Birthday to You! (Paw Patrol) Petrossi, Fabrizio, illus. 2015. (Little Golden Book Ser.). (ENG.). 24p. (J). (-k). 4.99 (978-0-553-52277-8(9), Golden Bks.) Random Hse. Children's Bks.

Gonzalez Bertrand, Diane. The Ruiz Street Kids (Los Muchachos de la Calle Ruiz) Ventura, Gabriela Baeza, tr. 2006. (ENG & SPA., Illus.). (J). pap. 9.95 (978-1-55885-321-8(9), Piñata Books) Arte Publico Pr.

Goodhart, Pippa. Hoppy Birthday, Jo-Jo! Birkett, Georgie, illus. 2005. (Green Bananas Ser.). (ENG.). 48p. (J). lib. bdg. (978-0-7787-1025-7(4)) Crabtree Publishing Co.

Gownley, Jimmy. Amelia in Loosely in Disguise & Frightened: #3, 1 vol. Gownley, Jimmy, illus. 2010. (Amelia Rules! Ser.). (ENG., Illus.). 36p. (J). (gr. 2-6). 31.36 (978-1-59961-789-3(7), 2382, Graphic Novels) Spotlight.

Graves, Emma T. Total FREAK-Out. Boo, Binny, illus. 2018. (My Undead Life Ser.). (ENG.). 112p. (J). (gr. 3-6). pap. 7.95 (978-1-4965-6450-4(2), 138362, Stone Arch Bks.) Capstone.

Gritton, Steve. The Kandy Witch. 2007. (Illus.). (J). 18.95 (978-0-9795361-0-6(3)) Bad Frog Art/SMG Bks.

Grosset & Dunlap. Ruby's Tea Party. 2016. (Penguin Young Readers Level 2 Ser.). lib. bdg. 13.55 (978-0-606-38426-1(X)) Turtleback.

Guest, Elissa Haden. Iris & Walter. Davenier, Christine, illus. 2006. (Iris & Walter Ser.). 43p. (gr. 1-4). 15.95 (978-0-7569-7008-6(3)) Perfection Learning Corp.

—Iris & Walter & the Birthday Party. Davenier, Christine, illus. 2013. (Iris & Walter Ser.). (ENG.). 44p. (J). (gr. 1-4). pap. 4.99 (978-0-544-10498-3(6), 1540803, Clarion Bks.) HarperCollins Pubs.

Gunderson, Jessica. Sleeping Beauty: An Interactive Fairy Tale Adventure. Epelbaum, Mariano, illus. 2018. (You Choose: Fractured Fairy Tales Ser.). (ENG.). 112p. (J). (gr. 3-7). lib. bdg. 32.65 (978-1-5435-3006-3(0), 138603, Capstone Pr.) Capstone.

Gunnufson, Charlotte. Halloween Hustle, 0 vols. Atteberry, Kevan, illus. 2013. (ENG.). 32p. (J). (gr. -1-2). 16.99 (978-1-4778-1723-0(9), 9781477817230, Two Lions) Amazon Publishing.

Gutenberg, S. R. Abby Longbotham & the Quilt. 2008. 28p. pap. 24.95 (978-1-4241-9428-5(8)) America Star Bks.

Guy, Ginger Foglesong. Fiesta! Bilingual English-Spanish. Moreno, Rene King, illus. 2007. (ENG.). 32p. (J). (gr. -1-3). 6.99 (978-0-06-088226-6(3), Greenwillow Bks.) HarperCollins Pubs.

Hacker, Erin. The Baker of Sweet City, 1 vol. 2010. 36p. pap. 24.95 (978-1-4489-2550-6(9)) PublishAmerica, Inc.

Haesche, Richard, Sr. The Big Race. 2007. (ENG.). 222p. (J). per. 10.49 (978-0-9798536-1-6(3)) Kreative X-Pressions Pubns.

Hale, Shannon & Hale, Dean. The Princess in Black & the Perfect Princess Party. Pham, LeUyen, illus. (J). (gr. k-3). 2016. (Princess in Black Ser.: 2). (ENG.). 96p. pap. 6.99 (978-0-7636-8758-8(8)) 2015. (Princess in Black Ser.: 2). (ENG.). 96p. 15.99 (978-0-7636-6511-1(8)) 2015. 87p. (978-1-338-11281-8(3)) Candlewick Pr.

—The Princess in Black & the Perfect Princess Party, 2. 2016. (Princess in Black Ser.). (ENG.). 96p. (gr. k-3). 21.19 (978-1-4844-7927-8(0)) Candlewick Pr.

—The Princess in Black & the Perfect Princess Party. Pham, LeUyen, illus. 2018. (Princess in Black Ser.). (ENG.). 96p. (J). (gr. k-3). lib. bdg. 31.36 (978-1-5321-4220-8(X), 28557, Chapter Bks.) Spotlight.

—The Princess in Black & the Perfect Princess Party. 2016. (Princess in Black Ser.: 2). (Illus.). 87p. (J). lib. bdg. 17.20 (978-0-606-37945-8(2)) Turtleback.

Hall, Caroline V. Rhett & Abby: Abby's New Home. 2011. 40p. pap. 15.95 (978-1-4497-1887-9(6), WestBow Pr.) Author Solutions, LLC.

Hall, Kirsten. Birthday Beastie: All about Counting. Luedecke, Bev, illus. 2003. (Beastieville Ser.). 32p. (J). 19.50 (978-0-516-22891-4(9), Children's Pr.) Scholastic Library Publishing.

Hallinan, P. K. Happy Birthday! 2003. (J). (978-0-8249-6507-5(8), Ideals Pubns.) Worthy Publishing.

Hansen, Jeanne. Wow! an Upside down Cake Birthday Party! 2011. 24p. pap. 15.99 (978-1-4653-6016-8(6)) Xlibris Corp.

Hanson, Warren. Bugtown Boogie. Johnson, Steve & Fancher, Lou, illus. 2008. 32p. (J). (gr. -1-3). 17.89 (978-0-06-059938-6(3), Geringer, Laura Book) HarperCollins Pubs.

Hapka, Catherine, pseud. Friends 4 Ever? 2008. (High School Musical Stories from East High Ser.). 124p. (J). (gr. 3-7). 12.65 (978-0-7569-8820-3(9)) Perfection Learning Corp.

—Pony Scouts: Pony Party. Kennedy, Anne, illus. 2013. (I Can Read Level 2 Ser.). (ENG.). 32p. (J). (gr. -1-3). pap. 4.99 (978-0-06-208679-2(0), HarperCollins) HarperCollins Pubs.

Happy Valentine's Day Curious George. 2011. (Curious George Ser.). (ENG., Illus.). 14p. (J). (gr. -1-3). 8.99 (978-0-547-13107-8(0), 1048361, Clarion Bks.) HarperCollins Pubs.

Hargreaves, Roger. Mr. Birthday. 2007. (Mr. Men & Little Miss Ser.). (ENG., Illus.). 32p. (J). (gr. -1-2). mass mkt. 4.99 (978-0-8431-2130-8(0), Grosset & Dunlap) Penguin Young Readers Group.

Harley, Bill. Bear's All-Night Party. Ferreira, Melissa, illus. 2005. (ENG.). 32p. (J). (gr. -1-2). 15.95 (978-0-87483-572-4(0)) August Hse. Pubs., Inc.

Harrison, Hannah E. Bernice Gets Carried Away. 2015. (Illus.). 32p. (J). (gr. -1-k). 17.99 (978-0-8037-3916-1(8), Dial Bks) Penguin Young Readers Group.

Harrison, Jo. The Jewellery Box Fairies. 2013. (Illus.). 24p. pap. 19.82 (978-1-4772-5112-6(X)) AuthorHouse.

Harrison, Lisi. Best Friends for Never. 2008. (Clique Novels Ser.). 197p. 20.00 (978-1-60686-290-2(1)) Perfection Learning Corp.

Hartt-Sussman, Heather. Nana's Summer Surprise. Graham, Georgia, illus. 2013. 32p. (J). (gr. -1-1). 17.95 (978-1-77049-324-7(7), Tundra Bks.) Tundra Bks. CAN. Dist: Penguin Random Hse. LLC.

Harvey, Alex. Olivia & the Kite Party. Spaziante, Patrick, illus. 2012. (Olivia Ready-To-Read Level 1 Ser.). lib. bdg. 13.55 (978-0-606-26360-3(8)) Turtleback.

Harvey, Jacqueline. Clementine Rose & the Birthday Emergency. 2016. (Clementine Rose Ser.: 10). (Illus.). 160p. (J). (gr. 1-3). 8.99 (978-0-85798-516-3(7)) Random Hse. Australia AUS. Dist: Independent Pubs. Group.

Hawa, Christine Elias. Joy the Girl How Never Smiled. 2011. 32p. pap. 16.19 (978-1-4634-3636-0(X)) AuthorHouse.

Haworth, Margaret. When Daddy Goes Away: Rusty Books. Edwards, Paul, illus. l.t. ed. 2003. (Books That Help Ser.: Vol. 2). 34p. (J). (gr. -1-5). pap. 9.95 (978-0-9740313-1-6(3)) Haworth, Margaret.

Hedgman, Janis. Party in the Garden. 2009. (Illus.). 52p. pap. (978-1-84748-514-4(6)) Athena Pr.

Heible, Beverly. A Christmas Party on River Row. 2012. 98p. 22.95 (978-1-62709-018-6(5)) America Star Bks.

Heim, Alastair. No Tooting at Tea. Not, Sara, illus. 2017. (ENG.). 40p. (J). (gr. -1-3). 17.99 (978-0-544-77474-2(4), 1637141, Clarion Bks.) HarperCollins Pubs.

Helms, Rhonda. Promposal. 2015. (ENG., Illus.). 224p. (YA). (gr. 7). pap. 9.99 (978-1-4814-2231-4(6), Simon Pulse) Simon Pulse.

Hill, Eric. Happy New Year, Spot! 2016. (Spot Ser.). (ENG., Illus.). 10p. (J). (-k). bds. 6.99 (978-0-14-137009-5(2), Warne) Penguin Young Readers Group.

—Spot's Birthday Party. Hill, Eric, illus. 2007. (Spot Ser.). (ENG., Illus.). 24p. (J). (gr. -1 — 1). bds. 9.99 (978-0-399-24770-5(X), Warne) Penguin Young Readers Group.

Hinkler Books, ed. The Little Princess Tea Party. 2012. 40p. (J). 19.99 (978-1-74308-402-1(1)) Hinkler Bks. Pty, Ltd. AUS. Dist: Ideals Pubns.

Hlad, Carole. Daisy's Dance Party: (from the Amanda's Cats Series) 2011. 24p. pap. 15.99 (978-1-4628-8006-5(1)) Xlibris Corp.

Ho, Jannie, illus. Violet Rose & the Surprise Party. 2016. (Violet Rose Ser.). (ENG.). 52p. (J). (gr. -1-3). 8.99 (978-0-7636-8917-9(3)) Candlewick Pr.

Hodgson, Mona. The Princess Twins & the Tea Party, 1 vol. Olson, Julie, illus. 2016. (I Can Read! / Princess Twins Ser.). (ENG.). 32p. (J). pap. 4.99 (978-0-310-75038-3(5)) Zonderkidz.

Hoffman, Mary Ann. Piñata Party, 1 vol. 2006. (Neighborhood Readers Ser.). (ENG.). 8p. (gr. k-1). pap. 5.15 (978-1-4042-5720-7(9), 3cbc62ae-3463-4fde-9ff0-2cb45541f68b, Rosen Classroom) Rosen Publishing Group, Inc., The.

Holabird, Katharine. Angelina's Perfect Party. Craig, Helen, illus. 2011. (Angelina Ballerina Ser.). (ENG.). 24p. (J). (gr. -1-1). 17.44 (978-0-448-45617-1(6)) Penguin Young Readers Group.

Holden, Pam. Pass It On, 1 vol. Hawley, Kelvin, illus. 2009. (Red Rocket Readers Ser.). (ENG.). 20p. (gr. 2-2). pap. (978-1-877363-66-5(9), Red Rocket Readers) Flying Start Bks.

—The Rainbow Party, 1 vol. Whimp, Pauline, illus. 2009. (Red Rocket Readers Ser.). (ENG.). 20p. pap. (978-1-877363-82-5(0)) Flying Start Bks.

—Sally Snip Snap's Party, 1 vol. Storey, Jim, illus. 2009. (Red Rocket Readers Ser.). (ENG.). 19p. (gr. 2-1). pap. (978-1-877363-57-3(X), Red Rocket Readers) Flying Start Bks.

—The Surprise Visitor, 1 vol. Hoit, Richard, illus. 2009. (Red Rocket Readers Ser.). (ENG.). 21p. (gr. 2-2). pap. (978-1-877363-85-6(5)) Flying Start Bks.

Holm, Jennifer L. & Holm, Matthew. Babymouse #18: Happy Birthday, Babymouse. Holm, Jennifer L. & Holm, Matthew, illus. 2014. (Babymouse Ser.: 18). (ENG., Illus.). 96p. (J). (gr. 2-5). pap. 6.99 (978-0-307-93161-0(7)) Penguin Random Hse. LLC.

—Happy Birthday, Babymouse. 2014. (Babymouse Ser.: 18). lib. bdg. 17.20 (978-0-606-35567-4(7)) Turtleback.

Holmes, Steve, illus. Animales Marinos: Mezcla y Diviertete. 2005. (Mezcla y Diviertete Ser.). (SPA.). 5p. (J). (gr. -1-7). (978-970-718-291-2(1), Silver Dolphin en Español) Advanced Marketing, S. de R. L. de C. V.

Holt, Kimberly Willis. Piper Reed, Party Planner. Davenier, Christine, illus. 2011. (Piper Reed Ser.: 3). (ENG.). 176p. (J). (gr. 3-6). pap. 9.99 (978-0-312-61677-9(5), 900076848) Square Fish.

Holub, Joan & Williams, Suzanne. Cinderella Stays Late. 2014. (Grimmtastic Girls Ser.: 1). lib. bdg. 16.00 (978-0-606-35395-3(X)) Turtleback.

Homberg, Ruth, adapted by. The Best Ball. 2017. (Illus.). 24p. (J). (978-1-5182-3608-2(1)) Random Hse., Inc.

Hook, Jacqueline A. You're Going to Be a Flower Girl. 2005. (J). per. (978-0-9664783-3-4(9)) Jacqueline Beverly Hills.

Hooks, Gwendolyn. Block Party, 1 vol. Ng-Benitez, Shirley, illus. 2017. (Confetti Kids Ser.: 3). (ENG.). 32p. (J). (gr. 1-5). 14.95 (978-1-62014-341-4(0), leelowbooks) Lee & Low Bks., Inc.

—Pet Costume Party: A Pet Club Story, 1 vol. Byrne, Mike, illus. 2011. (Pet Club Ser.). (ENG.). 32p. (J). (gr. 1-2). pap. 6.25 (978-1-4342-3053-9(8), 114653); lib. bdg. 22.65 (978-1-4342-2513-9(5), 113346) Capstone. (Stone Arch Bks.).

—Pets at the Party: A Pet Club Story. Byrne, Mike, illus. 2010. (Pet Club Ser.). (ENG.). 32p. (J). (gr. 1-2). pap. 6.25 (978-1-4342-2796-6(0), 114063, Stone Arch Bks.) Capstone.

Hooray for Halloween. 2016. (Curious George Ser.). (ENG., Illus.). 24p. (J). (gr. -1-3). 9.99 (978-0-544-69956-4(4), 1627726, Clarion Bks.) HarperCollins Pubs.

Hordos, Sandra. Marissa Plans a Princess Tea Party. Allen, Joshua, illus. 2010. 28p. pap. 12.49 (978-1-4520-2557-5(6)) AuthorHouse.

Hosford, Kate. Big Birthday. Clifton-Brown, Holly, illus. 2012. (Carolrhoda Picture Bks.). (ENG.). 32p. (J). (gr. k-2). lib. bdg. 16.95 (978-0-7613-5410-9(7)) Lerner Publishing Group.

Howe, James. Houndsley & Catina. Gay, Marie-Louise, illus. 2007. 36p. (J). (gr. k-2). lib. bdg. 12.65 (978-0-7569-8141-9(7)) Perfection Learning Corp.

—Houndsley & Catina & the Birthday Surprise: Candlewick Sparks. Gay, Marie-Louise, illus. (ENG.). 48p. (J). (gr. k-4). 2013. (Candlewick Sparks Ser.). pap. 5.99 (978-0-7636-6639-2(4)) 2006. (Houndsley & Catina Ser.: 2). 16.99 (978-0-7636-2405-7(5)) Candlewick Pr.

—Houndsley & Catina & the Quiet Time: Candlewick Sparks. Gay, Marie-Louise, illus. 2013. (Candlewick Sparks Ser.). (ENG.). 48p. (J). (gr. k-4). pap. 5.99 (978-0-7636-6863-1(X)) Candlewick Pr.

Huber, Mike. Evette's Invitation. Cowman, Joseph, illus. 2014. (ENG.). 32p. (gr. -1). 15.95 (978-1-60554-212-6(1)) Redleaf Pr.

Hudgens, Melica, illus. Flim Flam & Other Such Gobbledygook. 2015. (J). 14.99 (978-1-4621-1684-3(1)) Cedar Fort, Inc./CFI Distribution.

Hundal, Nancy. Twilight Fairies, 1 vol. Kilby, Don, illus. 2006. (ENG.). 32p. (J). (gr. k-3). per. 4.95 (978-1-55041-961-0(7), 01caf117-4f3d-4b67-b220-705bcbbd3fb0) Fitzhenry & Whiteside, Ltd. CAN. Dist: Firefly Bks., Ltd.

Huntley, Tex. Adventures with Grandpa! Petrossi, Fabrizio, illus. 2018. (J). (978-1-5444-0086-0(1), Golden Bks.) Random Hse. Children's Bks.

Hutchins, Hazel. Robyn's Party-in-the-Park. Cathcart, Yvonne, illus. 2005. 59p. (J). lib. bdg. 12.00 (978-1-4242-1203-3(0)) Fitzgerald Bks.

—Robyn's Party in the Park. Cathcart, Yvonne, illus. 2005. (Formac First Novels Ser.: 31). (ENG.). 64p. (J). (gr. 2-5). 14.95 (978-0-88780-663-6(5), 663); 4.95 (978-0-88780-662-9(7), 662) Formac Publishing Co., Ltd. CAN. Dist: Formac Lorimer Bks. Ltd.

Hutchinson, Shaun David. Fml. 2013. (ENG.). 304p. (YA). (gr. 9). pap. 9.99 (978-1-4424-3287-1(X)); (Illus.). 17.99 (978-1-4424-8318-7(0)) Simon Pulse. (Simon Pulse).

Idle, Molly. Tea Rex. 2013. (Rex Book Ser.). (Illus.). 40p. (J). (gr. -1-k). 18.99 (978-0-670-01430-9(3), Viking Books for Young Readers) Penguin Young Readers Group.

Imagine That Publishing Ltd. Princess Party a Scratch & Sketch Adventure! 2018. (Dover Kids Activity Books: Fantasy Ser.). (ENG.). 80p. (J). (gr. 1-4). 12.99 (978-0-486-82904-3(9), 829049) Dover Pubns., Inc.

Inches, Alison. La Quinceañera. Aikins, Dave, illus. 2006. (Dora la Exploradora Ser.). (SPA.). 24p. (J). (gr. -1-3). pap. 3.99 (978-1-4169-2462-3(0), Libros Para Ninos) Libros Para Ninos.

Iversen, Jeremy. Rush. 2011. (ENG.). 272p. (YA). (gr. 9). pap. 11.99 (978-1-4424-2400-5(1), Simon Pulse) Simon Pulse.

Izquierdo, Ana, tr. Caritas Felices: Winnie-the-Pooh. 2007. (Disney Winnie the Pooh (SilverDolphin) Ser.). (SPA., Illus.). 10p. (J). (gr. -1). bds. (978-970-718-393-3(4), Silver Dolphin en Español) Advanced Marketing, S. de R. L. de C. V.

Jackson, Armitra L. Eating Safe with Ace & Mace! 2007. 44p. per. 15.95 (978-1-4327-1255-6(1)) Outskirts Pr., Inc.

James, Helen Foster. Daddy's Girl. Corke, Estelle, illus. 2017. (ENG.). 32p. (J). (gr. -1-2). 15.99 (978-0-8249-5681-3(8)) Worthy Publishing.

JohnsonMargaret. Parties & Presents: Three Short Stories Level 2 Elementary/Lower-Intermediate. 2010. (Cambridge Experience Readers Ser.). (ENG., Illus.). 62p. pap. 14.75 (978-84-8323-836-3(5)) Cambridge Univ. Pr.

Johnston, Annie Fellows. The Little Colonel's House Party. 2018. (ENG., Illus.). 158p. (YA). (gr. 7-12). pap. (978-93-5297-430-6(1)) Alpha Editions.

—The Little Colonel's House Party. 2017. (ENG., Illus.). (J). 23.95 (978-1-374-96551-5(0)) Capital Communications, Inc.

—The Little Colonel's House Party. Meynell, Louis, illus. 2007. 176p. per. (978-1-4065-3514-3(1)) Dodo Pr.

Johnston, Tony. Laugh-Out-Loud Baby. Gammell, Stephen, illus. 2012. (ENG.). 32p. (J). (gr. -1-3). 16.99 (978-1-4424-1380-1(8), Simon & Schuster Bks. For Young Readers) Simon & Schuster/Paula Wiseman Bks.

JONAS #8: Prep School Party. 2010. 128p. pap. 4.99 (978-1-4231-2673-7(4)) Disney Pr.

Jones, Janey Louise. The Snow Fairy. Poh, Jennie, illus. 2018. (Superfairies Ser.). (ENG.). 56p. (J). (gr. k-3). lib. bdg. 23.99 (978-1-5158-2424-4(1), 137400, Picture Window Bks.) Capstone.

Judge, Chris. The Snow Beast. Judge, Chris, illus. 2015. (ENG., Illus.). 32p. (J). (gr. -1-3). 17.99 (978-1-4677-9313-1(2), a711d3a5-9c18-4a5e-a4f5-dd8ef98bb756) Lerner Publishing Group.

Jules, Jacqueline. Abuela's Birthday. Smith, Kim, illus. 2015. (Sofia Martinez Ser.). (ENG.). 32p. (J). (gr. k-2). lib. bdg. 21.32 (978-1-4795-5775-2(7), 126807, Picture Window Bks.) Capstone.

—El Cumpleaños de la Abuela. Smith, Kim, illus. 2018. (Sofia Martinez en Español Ser.). (SPA.). 32p. (J). (gr. k-2). lib. bdg. 21.32 (978-1-5158-2443-5(8), 137546, Picture Window Bks.) Capstone.

—Sofia's Party Shoes. Smith, Kim, illus. 2018. (Sofia Martinez Ser.). (ENG.). 32p. (J). (gr. k-2). lib. bdg. 21.32 (978-1-5158-2336-0(9), 137017, Picture Window Bks.) Capstone.

Julius, Jessica. A New Reindeer Friend. 2015. lib. bdg. 13.55 (978-0-606-36680-9(6)) Turtleback.

Kane, Kim. Ginger Green Is Absolutely MAD for Birthday Parties (Mostly), Volume 1. Davis, Jon, illus. 2019. (Ginger Green Ser.: 1). (ENG.). 144p. (J). (gr. k-2). pap. 8.99 (978-1-76050-105-1(0)) Hardie Grant Children?s Publishing AUS. Dist: Independent Pubs. Group.

Kann, Victoria. The Royal Tea Party. 2014. (Pinkalicious I Can Read Ser.). (J). lib. bdg. 13.55 (978-0-606-35473-8(5)) Turtleback.

Kargman, Jill & Karasyov, Carrie. Bittersweet Sixteen. 2006. (YA). (gr. 7-12). (ENG.). 240p. 15.99

(978-0-06-077844-6(X)); 230p. lib. bdg. 16.89 (978-0-06-077845-3(8)) HarperCollins Pubs.

Kayler, Ralph. The Tea Party in the Tree Tops. 2009. 48p. pap. 19.49 (978-1-4389-8000-3(0)) AuthorHouse.

Keene, Carolyn. Pool Party Puzzler. Francis, Peter, illus. 2015. (Nancy Drew Clue Book Ser.: 1). (ENG.). 96p. (J). (gr. 1-4). 17.99 (978-1-4814-3896-4(4), Aladdin) Simon & Schuster Children's Publishing.

Keithley, Laura Lee. Ellie's Big Day. Holliday, Holly, illus. 2008. 40p. pap. 24.95 (978-1-60672-474-3(6)) America Star Bks.

Kerr, Judith. The Crocodile under the Bed. 2015. (ENG., Illus.). 32p. (J). pap. 7.99 (**978-0-00-758677-6(9)**, HarperCollins Children's Bks.) HarperCollins Pubs. Ltd. GBR. Dist: HarperCollins Pubs.

Khan, Hana. Taylor's Birthday Party. Kemble, Mai S., illus. 2008. (J). (978-1-60108-048-6(4)) Red Cygnet Pr.

Khan, Rukhsana. Big Red Lollipop. Blackall, Sophie, illus. 2010. (ENG.). 40p. (J). (gr. -1-3). 18.99 (978-0-670-06287-4(1), Viking Books for Young Readers) Penguin Young Readers Group.

Kimmelman, Leslie. A Valentine for Frankenstein. Banks, Timothy, illus. 2018. (ENG.). 32p. (J). (gr. k-3). 17.99 (978-1-5124-3129-2(X), 167d90ab-668e-49b7-9865-a741925f37aa, Carolrhoda Bks.) Lerner Publishing Group.

Kimpton, Diana. A Surprise for Princess Ellie. Finlay, Lizzie, illus. 6th rev. ed. 2006. (ENG.). 96p. (gr. 1-4). pap. 3.99 (978-0-7868-4875-1(8)) Hyperion Pr.

Kincaid, Jamaica. Party: A Mystery. CortÁs, Ricardo, illus. 2019. (ENG.). 32p. (J). 17.95 (978-1-61775-716-7(0)) Akashic Bks.

Kinra, Richa, illus. The Princess Panda Tea Party: A Cerebral Palsy Fairy Tale. 2014. 45p. (J). pap. 14.95 (978-1-61599-219-5(7)) Loving Healing Pr., Inc.

Kirby, Stan. Captain Awesome Gets a Hole-In-One. O'Connor, George, illus. 2014. (Captain Awesome Ser.: 12). (ENG.). 128p. (J). (gr. k-4). pap. 5.99 (978-1-4814-1431-9(3), Little Simon) Little Simon.

Kirk, David. Happy Heartwood Day. 2005. (Illus.). (J). (978-1-4156-3888-0(8), Grosset & Dunlap) Penguin Publishing Group.

—Miss Spider's Tea Party. 2018. (ENG., Illus.). 32p. (J). (gr. -1-3). 19.95 (978-0-935112-13-9(8)) Callaway Editions, Inc.

—Miss Spider's Tea Party. unabr. ed. 2008. (Scholastic Bookshelf Ser.). (ENG., Illus.). (J). (gr. -1-3). 18.95 (978-0-545-02979-7(1)) Scholastic, Inc.

Kirk, David & Scholastic / LeapFrog. Miss Spider's Tea Party. 2008. (J). 13.99 (978-1-59319-934-0(1)) LeapFrog Enterprises, Inc.

Kirkland, Kim M. Mi Mi's Mini Tea Party. Swope, Brenda, illus. 2011. 28p. pap. 24.95 (978-1-4512-8099-9(8)) America Star Bks.

Klein, Abby. Halloween Parade. McKinley, John, illus. 2009. (Ready, Freddy! Reader List No. 3). 32p. (J). (978-0-545-14174-1(5)) Scholastic, Inc.

Kleinberg, Naomi. Abby's Pink Party (Sesame Street) Brannon, Tom, illus. 2011. (ENG.). 12p. (J). (gr. k — 1). bds. 6.99 (978-0-307-92956-3(6), Random Hse. Bks. for Young Readers) Random Hse. Children's Bks.

Kline, Trish & Donev, Mary. It's a Party! KA Reader 2. 2007. (Illus.). 32p. (J). per. 20.00 (978-0-9717234-3-6(5)) Ghost Hunter Productions.

Knight, Chris. Piggy's Party. 2011. (Illus.). 36p. (gr. 1-2). pap. 17.07 (978-1-4520-9585-1(X)) AuthorHouse.

Kole MacLean, Christine. Mary Margaret Running Scared. 2010. 152p. pap. 14.98 (978-0-557-24676-2(8)) Lulu Pr., Inc.

Kosara, Victoria. Graduation Party. Durk, Jim, illus. 2010. (J). pap. (978-0-545-23400-9(X)) Scholastic, Inc.

Krakower, Harold. Sugarland: Volume 2 Trouble in Sugarland. 2009. 28p. pap. 12.50 (978-1-4490-1880-1(7)) AuthorHouse.

Krishnaswami, Uma. The Big Party. 2006. (Early Explorers Ser.). (J). pap. (978-1-4108-6133-7(3)) Benchmark Education Co.

Krulik, Nancy & Burwasser, Amanda. Someone's Got a Screw Loose. Moran, Mike, illus. 2018. (Project Droid Ser.: 6). (ENG.). 112p. (J). (gr. 1-3). 13.99 (978-1-5107-2664-2(0), Sky Pony Pr.) Skyhorse Publishing Co., Inc.

Ku, Grace. When Grace Was. 2009. 24p. pap. 12.99 (978-1-4389-9945-6(3)) AuthorHouse.

Lach, Will. Norman Rockwell's a Day in the Life of a Girl. Rockwell, Norman, illus. 2017. (ENG.). 60p. (J). (gr. -1-3). 16.95 (978-0-7892-1290-0(0), 791290, Abbeville Kids) Abbeville Pr., Inc.

Laird, Judie. Jane's Special Day. 2009. 16p. pap. 8.95 (978-1-4490-1199-4(3)) AuthorHouse.

Lansky, Bruce. Polar BRRR Delivers. Wummer, Amy, illus. 2010. 10p. (J). bds. 6.99 (978-1-4169-9318-6(5)) Meadowbrook Pr.

Larsen, Angela. Travel to Tomorrow: Book One of the Fifties Chix Series. 2011. (ENG.). 260p. 14.95 (978-1-60746-817-2(4)) FastPrncil, Inc.

Lasota, Mary. Kitty Piper, Angel Cat, Book 3, A Surprise for Ashley. 2011. 48p. (gr. 1-2). pap. 11.66 (978-1-4634-1031-5(X)) AuthorHouse.

Lawson, Jennifer. The Secret Tea Party at the Zoo. 2010. (Illus.). 34p. pap. 19.95 (978-0-557-13707-7(1)) Lulu Pr., Inc.

Leedy, Loreen. Crazy Like a Fox: A Simile Story. 2009. (ENG., Illus.). 32p. (J). (gr. -1-3). 7.99 (978-0-8234-2248-7(8)) Holiday Hse., Inc.

Lester, Helen. Happy Birdday, Tacky! Munsinger, Lynn, illus. 2017. (Tacky the Penguin Ser.). (ENG.). 32p. (J). (gr. -1-3). pap. 7.99 (978-1-328-74057-1(9), 1677031, Clarion Bks.) HarperCollins Pubs.

Lewis, J. Patrick & Zappitello, Beth. First Dog's White House Christmas. Bowers, Tim, illus. 2010. (ENG.). 32p. (J). (gr. 1-4). 15.95 (978-1-58536-503-6(3), 202197) Sleeping Bear Pr.

Lewman, David. Branch's Bunker Birthday. Batson, Alan, illus. 2018. (J). (978-1-5444-0208-6(2), Golden Bks.) Random Hse. Children's Bks.

Lindner, Brooke. Diego's Halloween Party. Mawhinney, Art, illus. 2008. (Go, Diego, Go! Ser.). (ENG.). 16p. (J). (gr. -1-k). bds. 5.99 (978-1-4169-5497-2(X), Simon Spotlight/Nickelodeon) Simon Spotlight/Nickelodeon.

The live dolls' party Days. 2007. (Illus.). 160p. (J). lib. bdg. 59.00 (978-1-60304-010-5(2)) Dollworks.

Loggia, Wendy. Aurora: The Perfect Party. Studio IBOIX Staff, illus. 2012. (Disney Princess Ser.). (ENG.). 96p. (J). (gr. 2-6). lib. bdg. 31.36 (978-1-59961-181-5(3), 5182, Chapter Bks.) Spotlight.

Lokaisingh, Jasmine. The Tales of Mme. Bovarie Vache & Mr. P. Huggins: In Huggsie's Birthday. 2011. 16p. 8.32 (978-1-4520-4071-4(0)) AuthorHouse.

Look, Lenore. Alvin Ho: Allergic to Birthday Parties, Science Projects, & Other Man-Made Catastrophes. Pham, LeUyen, illus. 2011. (Alvin Ho Ser.: 3). 192p. (J). (gr. 1-4). 7.99 (978-0-375-87369-0(4), Yearling) Random Hse. Children's Bks.

Low, Dene. The Entomological Tales of Augustus T. Percival. Corace, Jen, illus. 2009. (ENG.). 208p. (J). (gr. 6-8). 18.69 (978-0-547-15250-9(7)) Houghton Mifflin Harcourt Publishing Co.

Lyles, Whitney. Party Games. 2012. (Romantic Comedies Ser.). (ENG.). 304p. (YA). (gr. 7). pap. 14.99 (978-1-4424-6060-7(1), Simon Pulse) Simon Pulse.

Lynn, Tammy. Happy Birthday Puppy: An I See Puppy Book. Stewart, Elaine, ed. Lynn, Tammy, illus. 2006. (Illus.). 12p. (J). bds. 6.99 (978-0-9774277-0-3(6), 0-9774277-0-6) I See Puppy, LLP.

Lyon, Tammie, illus. Eloise Throws a Party! Ready-To-Read Level 1. 2008. (Eloise Ser.). (ENG.). 32p. (J). (gr. -1-1). pap. 4.99 (978-1-4169-6172-7(0), Simon Spotlight) Simon Spotlight.

Lytle, Robert A. Pirate Party. Williams, Bill, illus. 2006. (Mackinac Passage Ser.). 258p. (J). (gr. 4-7). pap. 9.95 (978-0-9749412-5-7(5)) EDCO Publishing, Inc.

Mack, Paulette. Cookout at Grandma's House: The Adventures of Mielle & Cheeky. 2006. (ENG., Illus.). 24p. per. 10.95 (978-1-59800-998-9(2)) Outskirts Pr., Inc.

Mackall, Dandi Daley. Natalie & the Downside-Up Birthday, 1 vol. Blakeslee, Lys, illus. 2009. (That's Nat! Ser.: 4). (ENG.). 96p. (J). (gr. 1-4). pap. 4.99 (978-0-310-71569-6(5)) Zonderkidz.

Maed, Mary Ann Graziani. Filled to Capacity. 2008. 56p. pap. 24.50 (978-0-615-16077-1(8)) Wishing Star Children's Bks.

Malbrough, Mike. Marigold Finds the Magic Words. Malbrough, Mike, illus. 2019. (Illus.). 40p. (J). (gr. -1-2). 17.99 (978-1-5247-3743-6(7)) Flamingo Bks.

Malone, Jen & Nall, Gail. You're Invited. 2015. (Mix Ser.). (ENG., Illus.). 336p. (J). (gr. 4-8). 17.99 (978-1-4814-3197-2(8), Aladdin) Simon & Schuster Children's Publishing.

—You're Invited Too. 2016. (Mix Ser.). (ENG., Illus.). 304p. (J). (gr. 4-8). pap. 7.99 (978-1-4814-3199-6(4), Aladdin) Simon & Schuster Children's Publishing.

Mandy, Stanley. Bella: The Birthday Party. Mandy, Stanley, illus. 2010. (ENG., Illus.). 32p. (J). (gr. -1-k). 9.95 (978-1-58925-850-1(9)) Tiger Tales.

Mansfield, Katherine. The Garden Party. l.t. ed. 2006. pap. (978-1-84702-354-4(1)) Echo Library.

Manushkin, Fran. Daddy Can't Dance. Lyon, Tammie, illus. 2018. (Katie Woo Ser.). (ENG.). 32p. (J). (gr. k-2). lib. bdg. 21.32 (978-1-5158-2266-0(4), 136885, Picture Window Bks.) Capstone.

—Katie's Lucky Birthday, 1 vol. Lyon, Tammie, illus. 2011. (Katie Woo Ser.). (ENG.). 32p. (J). (gr. k-2). pap. 5.95 (978-1-4048-6612-6(4), 114671); lib. bdg. 21.32 (978-1-4048-6514-3(4), 114210) Capstone. (Picture Window Bks.).

Margolis, Leslie. We Are Party People. 2018. (ENG.). 304p. (J). pap. 7.99 (978-1-250-17725-4(1), 900158350) Square Fish.

Marshall, Wendy. The O'Clocks: Mr. O'Clock Goes to A Party. 2008. 40p. pap. 18.49 (978-1-4389-2403-8(8)) AuthorHouse.

Masino, Brian. Cabbage Patch Kids: We Are All Best Friends. Karl, Linda, illus. 2006. (J). pap. (978-0-439-76820-7(9)) Scholastic, Inc.

Mason, Jane B. & Stephens, Sarah Hines. Snowfall Surprise. 2009. (Candy Apple Ser.: 21). (ENG.). 144p. (J). (gr. 3-7). 5.99 (978-0-545-10067-0(4), Scholastic Paperbacks) Scholastic, Inc.

Maxson, H. A. & Young, Claudia H. Tea Party at Chestertown. Kosits, Andrew, illus. 2003. (Magical History Tours Ser.). 55p. (J). per. 8.95 (978-0-9741713-0-2(1)) Bay Oak Pubs., Ltd.

McCafferty, Megan. Jessica Darling's It List 3: The (Totally Not) Guaranteed Guide to Stressing, Obsessing & Second-Guessing. 2015. (Jessica Darling's It List Ser.: 3). (ENG.). 224p. (J). (gr. 3-7). 30.99 (978-0-316-33324-5(7), Poppy) Little, Brown Bks. for Young Readers.

McClure, Wendy. The Princess & the Peanut Allergy. Lyon, Tammie, illus. 2012. (J). (978-1-61913-127-9(7)) Weigl Pubs., Inc.

—The Princess & the Peanut Allergy. Lyon, Tammie, illus. 2019. (ENG.). 32p. (J). (gr. -1-3). pap. 7.99 (978-0-8075-6619-0(5), 807566195) Whitman, Albert & Co.

McConduit, Denise Walter. D. J. & the Debutante Ball, 1 vol. Henriquez, Emile F., illus. 2004. (D. J. Ser.). (ENG.). 32p. (J). (gr. k-3). 16.99 (978-1-58980-173-8(3), Pelican Publishing) Arcadia Publishing.

McCormick, Michelle. Priscilla Willa, Party Planner. 2013. (ENG.). 94p. (YA). pap. 9.95 (978-1-4787-1444-6(1)) Outskirts Pr., Inc.

—Priscilla Willa, Party Planner: Night at the Haunted Hotel. 2013. (ENG.). 108p. (YA). pap. 9.95 (978-1-4787-0890-2(5)) Outskirts Pr., Inc.

McCranie, Stephen. Mal & Chad: Belly Flop! McCranie, Stephen, illus. 3rd ed. 2012. (Mal & Chad Ser.: 3). (ENG., Illus.). 224p. (J). (gr. 3-7). pap. 10.99 (978-0-399-25658-5(X), Philomel Bks.) Penguin Young Readers Group.

Mcdonald, Megan. Jessica Finch in Pig Trouble. 2014. (Judy Moody & Friends Ser.: 1). (Illus.). 60p. (J). lib. bdg. 14.75 (978-0-606-35162-1(0)) Turtleback.

McDonald, Megan. Judy Moody & Friends: Jessica Finch in Pig Trouble. Madrid, Erwin, illus. 2014. (Judy Moody & Friends Ser.: 1). (ENG.). 64p. (J). (gr. -1-1). pap. 5.99 (978-0-7636-7027-6(8)) Candlewick Pr.

—Judy Moody & the Right Royal Tea Party. Reynolds, Peter H., illus. (Judy Moody Ser.: 14). (ENG.). 160p. (J). (gr. 1-4). 2019. pap. 5.99 (978-1-5362-0332-5(7)) 2018. 15.99 (978-0-7636-9567-5(X)) Candlewick Pr.

McElroy, Jean. Let's Count 1 2 3! 2011. (ENG., Illus.). 12p. (J). (gr. -1 — 1). 4.99 (978-1-4424-1198-2(8), Little Simon) Little Simon.

McFarlane, Susannah. In the Dark. 2015. 122p. (J). (978-1-61067-445-4(6)) Kane Miller.

—In the Dark: EJ12 Girl Hero. 2016. 128p. (J). pap. 5.99 (978-1-61067-383-9(2)) Kane Miller.

McGee, Warner, illus. Monster Halloween Party. 2007. (Backyardigans Ser.). (ENG.). 14p. (J). (gr. -1-k). bds. 6.99 (978-1-4169-3435-6(9), Simon Spotlight/Nickelodeon) Simon Spotlight/Nickelodeon.

Mcgill, Leslie. Hero. 2015. (Cap Central Ser.: 6). (YA). lib. bdg. 20.80 (978-0-606-37403-3(5)) Turtleback.

McGrath, Barbara Barbieri. Birthday Counting. Tagel, Peggy, illus. 2017. (First Celebrations Ser.: 7). 12p. (J). (— 1). bds. 6.99 (978-1-58089-537-8(9)) Charlesbridge Publishing, Inc.

McNair, Barbara. Tea Parties with Grandm. Hogan, Eric, illus. 2009. 48p. pap. 24.95 (978-1-60749-617-5(8)) America Star Bks.

McNamara, Margaret. Sylva & the Fairy Ball. 2013. (Fairy Bell Sisters Ser.: 1). (J). lib. bdg. 14.75 (978-0-606-31796-2(1)) Turtleback.

Meadows, Daisy. Belle the Birthday Fairy. 2012. (Rainbow Magic — Special Edition Ser.). lib. bdg. 17.20 (978-0-606-23726-0(7)) Turtleback.

—Eva the Enchanted Ball Fairy. 2012. (Rainbow Magic — the Princess Fairies Ser.: 7). lib. bdg. 14.75 (978-0-606-26175-3(3)) Turtleback.

—A Fairyland Costume Ball. 2012. (Rainbow Magic — Scholastic Reader Ser.). lib. bdg. 13.55 (978-0-606-26235-4(0)) Turtleback.

Meddaugh, Susan. Martha on the Case. 2010. (Martha Speaks Ser.). (ENG., Illus.). 112p. (J). (gr. 1-4). pap. 5.99 (978-0-547-21055-1(8)) Houghton Mifflin Harcourt Publishing Co.

—Pool Party. 2011. (Martha Speaks Ser.). (ENG., Illus.). 24p. (J). (gr. -1-3). pap. 3.99 (978-0-547-43882-5(6)) Houghton Mifflin Harcourt Publishing Co.

—Summer Fun, 3 bks. in 1. 2013. (Martha Speaks Ser.). (ENG., Illus.). 72p. (J). (gr. -1-3). pap. 7.99 (978-0-547-97025-7(0)) Houghton Mifflin Harcourt Publishing Co.

Mei, Michael. The Goofy Gourmet: Let's Cook Today! 2008. (J). pap. 12.95 (978-0-9800752-1-2(1)) Big Company, LLC, The.

Meister, Cari. Tiny the Birthday Dog. Davis, Rich, illus. 2013. (Tiny Ser.). 32p. (J). (gr. k-1). pap. 4.99 (978-0-448-46478-7(0), Penguin Young Readers) Penguin Young Readers Group.

—Tiny the Birthday Dog. 2013. (Penguin Young Readers: Level 1 Ser.). lib. bdg. 13.55 (978-0-606-31706-1(6)) Turtleback.

Metzger, Steve. Princess Kitty. Okstad, Ella, illus. 2017. (ENG.). 32p. (J). (gr. -1-3). 17.99 (978-0-06-230662-3(6), HarperCollins) HarperCollins Pubs.

Michalak, Jamie. Joe & Sparky, Party Animals! Remkiewicz, Frank, illus. (Candlewick Sparks Ser.). (ENG.). 48p. (J). (gr. k-4). 2018. pap. 5.99 (978-1-5362-0327-1(0)) 2017. 15.99 (978-0-7636-8206-4(3)) Candlewick Pr.

Micinilio, Leanne Plein. Tia's Troubles: The First in a series of Tia's Adventures. 2011. 40p. pap. 16.99 (978-1-4490-4695-8(9)) AuthorHouse.

Miller, Marie. Party Time, 1 vol. 2006. (Neighborhood Readers Ser.). (ENG.). 8p. (gr. k-1). pap. 5.15 (978-1-4042-6706-0(9), 4015b93f-9d69-4b30-bbc4-3fc5280b507b, Rosen Classroom) Rosen Publishing Group, Inc., The.

Milway, Alex. Pigsticks & Harold & the Tuptown Thief. Milway, Alex, illus. 2015. (Pigsticks & Harold Ser.). (ENG., Illus.). 80p. (J). (gr. k-4). 12.99 (978-0-7636-7809-8(0)) Candlewick Pr.

Mitchell, Pratima. Raju's Ride. Waterhouse, Stephen, illus. 2005. (ENG.). 24p. (J). lib. bdg. 23.65 (978-1-59646-726-2(6)) Dingles & Co.

Miyakoshi, Akiko. The Tea Party in the Woods. Miyakoshi, Akiko, illus. 2015. (ENG., Illus.). 32p. (J). (gr. -1-2). 19.99 (978-1-77138-107-9(8)) Kids Can Pr., Ltd. CAN. Dist: Hachette Bk. Group.

Moonheart, Ella. Kitty's Magic 6: Sooty the Birthday Cat. 2018. (Kitty's Magic Ser.). (ENG., Illus.). 128p. (J). 15.99 (978-1-68119-911-5(4), 900191748, Bloomsbury Children's Bks.) Bloomsbury Publishing USA.

Morgan, Anna & Turkienicz, Rachael. My Worst/Best Sleepover Party, 1 vol. 2007. (ENG., Illus.). 122p. (J). (gr. 2-5). pap. 7.95 (978-1-897187-20-3(3)) Second Story Pr. CAN. Dist: Orca Bk. Pubs. USA.

Morrow, Barbara Olenyik. Mr. Mosquito Put on His Tuxedo. Goembel, Ponder, illus. 2009. (ENG.). 32p. (J). (gr. -1-3). 16.95 (978-0-8234-2072-8(8)) Holiday Hse., Inc.

Moulton, Mark K. A Royal Wedding. Good, Karen H., illus. 2007. (ENG.). 32p. (J). (gr. k-3). 14.99 (978-0-8249-8677-3(6), Ideals Pubns.) Worthy Publishing.

Moulton, Mark Kimball. One Enchanted Evening. Crouch, Karen Hillard, illus. 2003. 32p. (J). 14.95 (978-0-8249-5480-2(7), Ideals Pubns.) Worthy Publishing.

Muecke, Anne. The Dinosaurs' Night Before Christmas. Hale, Nathan, illus. 2008. (ENG.). 36p. (J). (gr. -1-3). 18.99 (978-0-8118-6322-3(0)) Chronicle Bks. LLC.

Muncaster, Harriet. Isadora Moon Has a Birthday. 2018. (Isadora Moon Ser.: 4). (ENG., Illus.). 128p. (J). (gr. 1-4). 6.99 (978-0-399-55835-1(7)); 14.99 (978-0-399-55833-7(0)) Random Hse. Children's Bks. (Random Hse. Bks. for Young Readers).

Munoz, Norma. Los Cuentos de la Casa del Arbol. Olson, John & Olson, Johan, illus. rev. ed. 2005. (Castillo de la Lectura Blanca Ser.). (SPA & ENG.). 72p. (J). (gr. -1-3). pap. 6.95 (978-970-20-0124-9(2)) Castillo, Ediciones, S. A. de C. V. MEX. Dist: Macmillan.

Murray, Marjorie Dennis. Halloween Night. 2010. (ENG., Illus.). 40p. (J). (gr. k-4). 9.99 (978-0-06-201293-7(2), Greenwillow Bks.) HarperCollins Pubs.

Myracle, Lauren. Awesome Blossom: A Flower Power Book. 2013. (Flower Power Ser.). (ENG.). 272p. (J). (gr. 3-7). pap. 7.95 (978-1-4197-0791-9(4), 694403); (YA). (gr. 4-8). 17.95 (978-1-4197-0405-5(2), 694401) Abrams, Inc. (Amulet Bks.).

Neuschwander, Cindy. Sir Cumference & All the King's Tens. Geehan, Wayne, illus. 2009. (Sir Cumference Ser.). 32p. (J). (gr. 3-7). 16.95 (978-1-57091-727-1(2)) Charlesbridge Publishing, Inc.

Nickelodeon Staff. Party Time! 2013. (Spongebob Squarepants Step into Reading Ser.). lib. bdg. 13.55 (978-0-606-32221-8(3)) Turtleback.

Night, P. J. Don't Drink the Punch! 2012. (You're Invited to a Creepover Ser.: 11). (ENG.). 160p. (J). (gr. 3-7). pap. 6.99 (978-1-4424-5287-9(0), Simon Spotlight) Simon Spotlight.

—Don't Move a Muscle! 2016. (You're Invited to a Creepover Ser.: 21). (ENG., Illus.). 160p. (J). (gr. 3-7). pap. 6.99 (978-1-4814-2922-1(1), Simon Spotlight) Simon Spotlight.

—The House Next Door. 2013. (You're Invited to a Creepover Ser.: 16). (ENG., Illus.). 160p. (J). (gr. 3-7). pap. 6.99 (978-1-4424-8233-3(8), Simon Spotlight) Simon Spotlight.

—The House Next Door. 2013. (Creepover Ser.: 16). lib. bdg. 17.20 (978-0-606-32323-9(6)) Turtleback.

—No Trick-Or-Treating! 2012. (Creepover Ser.: 9). lib. bdg. 17.20 (978-0-606-26337-5(3)) Turtleback.

—Your Worst Nightmare. 2013. (Creepover Ser.: 17). lib. bdg. 17.20 (978-0-606-32324-6(4)) Turtleback.

Nolen, Jerdine. Bradford Street Buddies: Block Party Surprise. Henninger, Michelle, illus. 2015. (ENG.). 48p. (J). (gr. 1-4). pap. 4.99 (978-0-544-35863-8(5), 1587297, Clarion Bks.) HarperCollins Pubs.

North, Laura. Cinderella's Big Foot. Remphry, Martin, illus. 2014. (Tadpoles: Fairytale Twists Ser.). (ENG.). 32p. (J). (gr. 1-2). (978-0-7787-0440-9(8)); pap. (978-0-7787-0448-5(3)) Crabtree Publishing Co.

Nurse, Lesley D. The Tale of Greedy Reeby. 2013. 82p. pap. 16.99 (978-0-9797699-6-2(5)) 7Seven Spark Publishing.

Nyirenda, Vukani G. The Wise Old Tortoise & the Monkey. 2011. 24p. pap. 15.99 (978-1-4568-9133-6(2)) Xlibris Corp.

Ochoa, Mary Lou. Andy's Arctic Party. 2009. 20p. pap. 9.14 (978-1-4269-0943-6(8)) Trafford Publishing.

O'Connell, Rebecca. Baby Party. Poole, Susie, illus. 2017. (ENG.). 24p. (J). (gr. -1 — 1). bds. 7.99 (978-0-8075-0514-4(5), 807505145) Whitman, Albert & Co.

O'Connor, Jane. Fancy Day in Room 1-A. 2012. (Fancy Nancy - I Can Read! Ser.). (J). lib. bdg. 13.55 (978-0-606-26259-0(8)) Turtleback.

—Fancy Nancy: Super Secret Surprise Party. 2015. (I Can Read Level 1 Ser.). (ENG., Illus.). 32p. (J). (gr. -1-3). 16.99 (978-0-06-226979-9(8), HarperCollins) HarperCollins Pubs.

—Fancy Nancy: Super Secret Surprise Party. Glasser, Robin Preiss, illus. 2015. (I Can Read Level 1 Ser.). (ENG.). 32p. (J). (gr. -1-3). pap. 5.99 (978-0-06-226978-2(X), HarperCollins) HarperCollins Pubs.

—Fancy Nancy & the Fabulous Fashion Boutique. Glasser, Robin Preiss, illus. 2010. (Fancy Nancy Ser.). (ENG.). 32p. (J). (gr. -1-3). 17.99 (978-0-06-123592-4(X)); lib. bdg. 18.89 (978-0-06-123593-1(8)) HarperCollins Pubs. (HarperCollins).

—Fancy Nancy Big Book. Glasser, Robin Preiss, illus. 2009. (Fancy Nancy Ser.). (ENG.). 32p. (J). (gr. -1-3). pap. 24.99 (978-0-06-171944-8(7), HarperFestival) HarperCollins Pubs.

—Fancy Nancy: Bonjour, Butterfly. Glasser, Robin Preiss, illus. (Fancy Nancy Ser.). (ENG.). 32p. (J). (gr. -1-2). 2012. 10.99 (978-0-06-221053-1(X)) 2008. 17.99 (978-0-06-123588-7(1)) HarperCollins Pubs. (HarperCollins).

—Fancy Nancy Collector's Quintet. 2009. (I Can Read Level 1 Ser.). (ENG., Illus.). (J). (gr. k-3). 19.99 (978-0-06-171905-9(6), HarperCollins) HarperCollins Pubs.

—Fancy Nancy: Fanciest Doll in the Universe. Glasser, Robin Preiss, illus. 2013. (Fancy Nancy Ser.). (ENG.). 32p. (J). (gr. -1-3). 17.99 (978-0-06-170384-3(2)); lib. bdg. 18.89 (978-0-06-170385-0(0)) HarperCollins Pubs. (HarperCollins).

—Fancy Nancy: Jojo & the Twins. Glasser, Robin Preiss, illus. 2018. (My First I Can Read Ser.). (ENG.). 32p. (J). (gr. -1-3). 16.99 (978-0-06-237805-7(8)); pap. 4.99 (978-0-06-237804-0(X)) HarperCollins Pubs. (HarperCollins).

—Fancy Nancy: Nancy Clancy: My Secret Diary. Glasser, Robin Preiss, illus. 2015. (Nancy Clancy Ser.). (ENG.). 144p. (J). (gr. 1-5). pap. 11.99 (978-0-06-234983-5(X), HarperCollins) HarperCollins Pubs.

—Fancy Nancy: Tea for Two. Glasser, Robin Preiss, illus. 2012. (Fancy Nancy Ser.). (ENG.). 24p. (J). (gr. -1-3). pap. 4.99 (978-0-06-123597-9(0), HarperFestival) HarperCollins Pubs.

—Fancy Nancy: Tea Parties. Glasser, Robin Preiss, illus. 2009. (Fancy Nancy Ser.). (ENG.). 40p. (J). (gr. -1-2). 13.99 (978-0-06-180174-7(7), HarperCollins) HarperCollins Pubs.

—Super Secret Surprise Party. 2015. (Fancy Nancy - I Can Read! Ser.). (J). lib. bdg. 13.55 (978-0-606-36947-3(3)) Turtleback.

—Tea for Two. Glasser, Robin Preiss, illus. 2012. (Fancy Nancy Picture Bks.). (J). lib. bdg. 13.55 (978-0-606-23577-8(9)) Turtleback.

Oliver, Charles Folkes. Little Willy & the Party Animals. 2011. (Illus.). 20p. (gr. -1). pap. 14.99 (978-1-4567-5138-8(7)) AuthorHouse.

Olson, Nancy. Thanksgiving at Grandma's. Marino, Michael F., illus. 2009. 24p. pap. 10.95 (978-1-4251-8909-9(1)) Trafford Publishing.

Orme, Helen. She's My Friend Now. 2008. (Siti's Sisters Ser.). (ENG., Illus.). 36p. pap. (978-1-84167-740-8(X)) Ransom Publishing Ltd.

Pack, Sherri. Little Cat, 1 vol. 2009. 20p. pap. 24.95 (978-1-60813-706-0(6)) America Star Bks.

Pankiw, Dr Mary & Pankiw, Mary. Misilla Mouse. 2011. 32p. pap. (978-1-4269-5476-4(X)) Trafford Publishing (UK) Ltd.

Park, Barbara. Junie B. Jones #27: Dumb Bunny. Brunkus, Denise, illus. 2009. (Junie B. Jones Ser.: 27). (ENG.). 128p. (J). (gr. 1-4). 5.99 (978-0-375-83810-1(4), Random Hse. Bks. for Young Readers) Random Hse. Children's Bks.

Park, Linda Sue. Xander's Panda Party. Phelan, Matt, illus. (ENG.). 40p. (J). (gr. -1-3). 2017. pap. 8.99 (978-1-328-74058-8(7), 1677033) 2013. 16.99 (978-0-547-55865-3(1), 1453620) HarperCollins Pubs. (Clarion Bks.).

Pascual, Dennis Mark. The Adventures of Dj the Butterfly & Friends Series Presents Dj's Birthday Party. 2012. 20p. pap. 10.15 (978-1-105-35838-8(0)) Lulu Pr., Inc.

Patron, Susan. Lucky Breaks. Phelan, Matt, illus. 2009. (ENG.). 192p. (J). (gr. 3-7). 16.99 (978-1-4169-3998-6(9), Atheneum Bks. for Young Readers) Simon & Schuster Children's Publishing.

Paul, Miranda. Blobfish Throws a Party. Caton, Margret, illus. 2017. (ENG.). 32p. (J). (gr. -1-3). 16.99 (978-1-4998-0422-5(9)) Little Bee Books Inc.

Pearl, Alexa. Tales of Sasha 8: Showtime! Sordo, Paco, illus. 2018. (Tales of Sasha Ser.: 8). (ENG.). 112p. (J). (gr. k-3). 16.99 (978-1-4998-0605-2(1)); pap. 5.99 (978-1-4998-0604-5(3)) Little Bee Books Inc.

Peek, Merle & Giblin, James Cross. Mary Wore Her Red Dress & Henry Wore His Green Sneakers Book & Cd, 1 vol. 2006. (ENG., Illus.). 32p. (J). (gr. -1-k). audio compact disk 12.99 (978-0-618-75249-2(8), 100531, Clarion Bks.) HarperCollins Pubs.

Peeler, Penny. The Adventures of Spike & Sally. 2011. 52p. pap. 15.99 (978-1-4568-9981-3(3)) Xlibris Corp.

Perelman, Helen. The Sugar Ball. Waters, Erica-Jane, illus. 2013. (Candy Fairies Ser.: 6). (ENG.). 128p. (J). (gr. 2-5). 15.99 (978-1-4424-6498-8(4), Simon & Schuster/Paula Wiseman Bks.) Simon & Schuster/Paula Wiseman Bks.

Perkins, T. J. In the Grand Scheme of Things: A Kim & Kelly Mystery. 2007. (Illus.). 151p. (YA). 10.99 (978-0-9777538-4-0(0)) GumShoe Press.

Peschke, Marci. Party Queen, 1 vol. Mourning, Tuesday, illus. 2013. (Kylie Jean Ser.). (ENG.). 112p. (J). (gr. 1-3). lib. bdg. 22.65 (978-1-4048-7582-1(4), 119874, Picture Window Bks.) Capstone.

Pesson, Lauren. My Little Kappa Delta. 2006. (J). 15.00 (978-0-9779594-0-2(6)) Lauren Elizabeth Design.

Pitchford, Dean. The Big One-Oh. 2009. 208p. (J). (gr. 3-7). 7.99 (978-0-14-241292-3(9), Puffin Books) Penguin Young Readers Group.

Potter, Ellen. The Squatchicorns (Big Foot & Little Foot #3), Vol. 3. Sala, Felicita, illus. 2019. (Big Foot & Little Foot Ser.). (ENG.). 144p. (J). (gr. 1-4). pap. 6.99 (978-1-4197-3701-5(5), 1200903, Amulet Bks.) Abrams, Inc.

Powell, Gail. The Adventures of Harold J. Kat. 2008. 40p. pap. 16.99 (978-1-4259-6334-7(X)) AuthorHouse.

Preller, James. Jigsaw Jones: the Case of the Disappearing Dinosaur. 2017. (Jigsaw Jones Mysteries Ser.). (ENG., Illus.). 96p. (J). pap. 6.99 (978-1-250-11088-6(2), 900169776) Feiwel & Friends.

The Presents: Individual Title Six-Packs. (Sails Literacy Ser.). 16p. (gr. k-18). 27.00 (978-0-7635-4444-7(2)) Rigby Education.

Press, J. The Doodles of Sam Dibble. 2013. (Doodles of Sam Dibble Ser.: 1). lib. bdg. 14.75 (978-0-606-29777-6(4)) Turtleback.

Pretty Princess- Royal Party. 2005. (J). bds. (978-1-4194-0061-2(4)) Paradise Pr., Inc.

Prom Girl. 2nd ed. 2003. (J). pap. 8.95 (978-0-9726917-0-3(7)) Prom Girl Publishing. Inc.

Publications International Ltd. Staff. Play A Sound Video Fifi's Painting Party. 2008. 24p. 19.98 (978-1-4127-9435-0(8), PIL Kids) Publications International, Ltd.

Raschka, Chris. New York Is English, Chattanooga Is Creek. Raschka, Chris, illus. 2018. (ENG., Illus.). 40p. (J). (gr. -1-2). 11.99 (978-1-5344-3371-7(6), Atheneum Bks. for Young Readers) Simon & Schuster Children's Publishing.

Raven, Margot Theis. America's White Table. Benny, Mike, illus. 2005. (ENG.). 32p. (J). (gr. 1-4). 16.95 (978-1-58536-216-5(6), 202046) Sleeping Bear Pr.

Reichert, Amy. While Mama Had a Quick Little Chat. Boiger, Alexandra, illus. 2005. (ENG.). 40p. (J). (gr. -1-2). 19.99 (978-0-689-85170-4(7), Atheneum/Richard Jackson Bks.) Simon & Schuster Children's Publishing.

Reisfeld, Randi. No Strings Attached: CC (Cape Cod); Partiers Preferred. 2013. (ENG., Illus.). 624p. (YA). (gr. 9). pap. 9.99 (978-1-4424-5978-6(6), Simon Pulse) Simon Pulse.

Reisner, Molly. Dora's Princess Party. Aikins, Dave, illus. 2009. (Dora the Explorer Ser.). (ENG.). 12p. (J). (gr. -1-1). 6.99 (978-1-4169-9045-1(3), Simon Spotlight/Nickelodeon) Simon Spotlight/Nickelodeon.

Rey, H. A. Curious George Costume Party/Jorge el Curioso Va a una Fiesta de Disfraces: Bilingual English-Spanish. 2012. (Curious George Ser.). (ENG., Illus.). 24p. (J). (gr. -1-3). pap. 4.99 (978-0-547-86575-1(9), 1503625, Clarion Bks.) HarperCollins Pubs.

—Curious George Dance Party/Jorge el Curioso el Baile: Bilingual English-Spanish. 2013. (Curious George TV Ser.). (ENG., Illus.). 24p. (J). (gr. -1-3). pap. 4.99 (978-0-547-96822-3(1), 1521358, Clarion Bks.) HarperCollins Pubs.

—Curious George Pinata Party/Jorge el Curioso y la Pinata: Bilingual English-Spanish. 2009. (Curious George TV Ser.).Tr. of Curious George Pinata Party. (ENG., Illus.). 24p. (J). (gr. -1-3). pap. 4.99 (978-0-547-23830-2(4), 1084078, Clarion Bks.) HarperCollins Pubs.

Rey, H. A. & Rey, Margret. Curious George & the Pizza Party. 2010. (Curious George Ser.). (ENG., Illus.). 24p. (J). (gr. -1-3). 14.99 (978-0-547-23211-9(X), 1082701, Clarion Bks.) HarperCollins Pubs.

Rickman, Jeanie Parker. The Rising Star Ball. Taylor, Jennifer, illus. 2006. 32p. per. 17.95 (978-1-59858-201-7(1)) Dog Ear Publishing, LLC.

Rippin, Sally. The Best Party Ever. 2014. (ENG., Illus.). 48p. (J). pap. 4.99 (978-1-61067-261-0(5)) Kane Miller.

—The Birthday Mix-Up. Fukuoka, Aki, illus. 2013. (Billie B. Brown Ser.). (ENG.). 43p. (J). (978-1-61067-232-0(1)) Kane Miller.

—The Birthday Mix-Up: Billie B. Brown. 2014. (ENG., Illus.). 48p. (J). pap. 4.99 (978-1-61067-182-8(1)) Kane Miller.

—The Robot Blues. 2014. (ENG., Illus.). 48p. (J). pap. 4.99 (978-1-61067-124-8(4)) Kane Miller.

Rivas, Spelile. The Cucuy Stole My Cascarones / el Coco Me Robó Los Cascarones. Baeza Ventura, Gabriela, tr. Cervantes, Valeria, illus. 2013. (SPA & ENG.). 32p. (J). 17.95 (978-1-55885-771-1(0), Piñata Books) Arte Publico Pr.

Roberts, LaDawna. The Haunted Birthday Party. 2007. 48p. per. 16.95 (978-1-4241-8723-2(0)) America Star Bks.

Roberts, Scott. Patty Cake & Friends. 2006. (ENG., Illus.). 96p. pap. 12.95 (978-1-59362-030-1(6), 9cfda446-4ce9-4eff-99ca-b17a0b6a9b30) Slave Labor Bks.

Robertson, Charmaine. The Burrito Party, 1 vol. 2016. (Rosen REAL Readers: Social Studies Nonfiction / Fiction: Myself, My Community, My World Ser.). (ENG.). 8p. (gr. k-1). pap. 5.46 (978-1-5081-2497-9(3), bb339f6a-1491-4cb6-a606-19b1270721e2, Rosen Classroom) Rosen Publishing Group, Inc., The.

Robinson, Hilary. Ted's Party Bus. 2009. (ENG., Illus.). 24p. (J). pap. (978-0-7787-3901-2(5)); lib. bdg. (978-0-7787-3870-1(1)) Crabtree Publishing Co.

Roddy-Worsham, Clara. Bear Baby's Birthday Gift. 2013. 24p. 24.95 (978-1-4626-9940-7(5)) America Star Bks.

Roper, Robert, illus. Happy Birthday, Dora! 2010. (Dora the Explorer Ser.). (ENG.). 14p. (J). (gr. -1-k). bds. 6.99 (978-1-4424-0333-8(0), Simon Spotlight/Nickelodeon) Simon Spotlight/Nickelodeon.

Rosa-Mendoza, Gladys. It's My Birthday!/Es Mi Cumpleanos! Simard, Remy, illus. 2006. (Englishspanish Foundations Ser.). (ENG & SPA.). 20p. (J). (gr. -1-k). bds. 6.95 (978-1-931398-17-6(8)) Me+Mi Publishing.

Rosenberg, Madelyn. How to Behave at a Tea Party. Ross, Heather, illus. 2014. (ENG.). 32p. (J). (gr. -1-3). 17.99 (978-0-06-227926-2(2), Tegen, Katherine Bks) HarperCollins Pubs.

Ross, Darien. The Carr House Cats at Christmas. 2012. 36p. pap. 18.41 (978-1-4669-4794-8(2)) Trafford Publishing.

Roth, Jonathan. Party Crashers, 2. 2019. (Beep & Bob Ser.). (ENG.). 128p. (J). (gr. 2-4). 15.59 (978-1-64310-827-8(1)) Penworthy Co., LLC, The.

—Party Crashers. Roth, Jonathan, illus. 2018. (Beep & Bob Ser.: 2). (ENG., Illus.). 128p. (J). (gr. 1-4). 16.99 (978-1-4814-8856-3(2)); pap. 6.99 (978-1-4814-8855-6(4)) Simon & Schuster Children's Publishing. (Aladdin).

Rouillard, Wendy W. Barnaby's Tree House. 2005. (Illus.). 30p. (J). (978-0-9651070-4-4(3)) Barnaby & Co.

Roza, Greg. The Peanut Butter Party, 1 vol. 2006. (Neighborhood Readers Ser.). (ENG., Illus.). 12p. (gr. 1-2). pap. 5.90 (978-1-4042-6827-2(8), c84f875d-6805-4541-95d8-f5f3794dbb5d, Rosen Classroom) Rosen Publishing Group, Inc., The.

Rubin, Adam. Fiesta Secreta de Pizza. Salmieri, Daniel, illus. 2015. 40p. (J). (gr. -1-k). 8.99 (978-0-14-751560-5(2), Puffin Books) Penguin Young Readers Group.

—Secret Pizza Party. Salmieri, Daniel, illus. 2013. 40p. (J). (gr. -1-2). 18.99 (978-0-8037-3947-5(8), Dial Bks) Penguin Young Readers Group.

Russell, Rachel Renée. Dork Diaries 2: Tales from a Not-So-Popular Party Girl. Russell, Rachel Renée, illus. 2010. (Dork Diaries: 2). (ENG., Illus.). 288p. (J). (gr. 4-8). 14.99 (978-1-4169-8008-7(3), Aladdin) Simon & Schuster Children's Publishing.

—Tales from a Not-So-Happy Heartbreaker. 2013. (Dork Diaries: 6). lib. bdg. 25.75 (978-0-606-32424-3(0)) Turtleback.

—Tales from a Not-So-Popular Party Girl. 2010. (Dork Diaries: 2). lib. bdg. 25.75 (978-0-606-32420-5(8)) Turtleback.

Russell, Rachel Renée, et al. Tales from a Not-So-Popular Party Girl. 2010. (ENG.). pap. (978-1-4424-4042-5(2), Aladdin Paperbacks) Simon & Schuster Children's Publishing.

Ryan, Pam Muñoz. Mice & Beans. Cepeda, Joe, illus. 2005. (gr. -1-3). lib. bdg. 17.00 (978-0-7569-5089-7(9)) Perfection Learning Corp.

Rylant, Cynthia. Annie & Snowball & the Dress-Up Birthday. 2008. (Annie & Snowball Ready-To-Read Ser.). lib. bdg. 13.55 (978-1-4178-1126-7(9)) Turtleback.

—Annie & Snowball & the Dress-Up Birthday: Ready-To-Read Level 2. Stevenson, Suçie & Stevenson, Suçie, illus. (Annie & Snowball Ser.: 1). (ENG.). 40p. (J). (gr. k-2). 2008. pap. 4.99 (978-1-4169-1459-4(5)) 2007. 17.99 (978-1-4169-0938-5(9)) Simon Spotlight. (Simon Spotlight).

—Brownie & Pearl Step Out. Biggs, Brian, illus. 2009. (Brownie & Pearl Ser.). (ENG.). 24p. (J). (gr. -1-3). 16.99 (978-1-4169-8632-4(4), Beach Lane Bks.) Beach Lane Bks.

—Brownie & Pearl Step Out: Ready-To-Read Pre-Level 1. Biggs, Brian, illus. 2014. (Brownie & Pearl Ser.). (ENG.). 24p. (J). (gr. -1-k). 17.99 (978-1-4814-0314-6(1)); pap. 4.99 (978-1-4814-0313-9(3)) Simon Spotlight. (Simon Spotlight).

Saldana, Rene. Dale, Dale, Dale / Hit It, Hit It, Hit It: Una Fiesta de Numeros / a Fiesta of Numbers. Flores, Carolyn Dee, illus. 2014. (ENG & SPA.). (J). 17.95 (978-1-55885-782-7(6), Piñata Books) Arte Publico Pr.

Salzano, Tammi. Truck Party. Wood, Hannah, illus. 2011. (ENG.). 20p. (J). bds. 7.95 (978-1-58925-865-5(7)) Tiger Tales.

Sattler, Jennifer. Dollop & Mrs. Fabulous. 2019. (ENG., Illus.). 32p. (J). (gr. -1-2). lib. bdg. 20.99 (978-0-399-55336-3(3), Knopf Bks. for Young Readers) Random Hse. Children's Bks.

Sauer, Tammi. I Love Cake! Starring Rabbit, Porcupine, & Moose. Rozelaar, Angie, illus. 2016. (ENG.). 40p. (J). (gr. -1-3). 17.99 (978-0-06-227894-4(0), HarperCollins) HarperCollins Pubs.

Saunders, Karen. Suzy P, Forever Me. 2015. (Suzy P. Ser.). (ENG.). 352p. (J). (gr. 4-7). pap. 10.99 (978-1-78370-163-6(3)) Bonnier Publishing GBR. Dist: Independent Pubs. Group.

Scanlon, Liz Garton. Happy Birthday, Bunny! Graegin, Stephanie, illus. 2013. (ENG.). 32p. (J). (gr. -1-3). 19.99 (978-1-4424-0287-4(3), Beach Lane Bks.) Beach Lane Bks.

Schertle, Alice. Little Blue Truck's Halloween: A Halloween Book for Kids. McElmurry, Jill, illus. 2016. (Little Blue Truck Ser.). (ENG.). 16p. (J). (— 1). bds. 13.99 (978-0-544-77253-3(9), 1636990, Clarion Bks.) HarperCollins Pubs.

Scholastic. Peppa's Halloween Party (Peppa Pig), 1 vol. EOne, illus. 2016. (ENG.). 24p. (J). (gr. -1-k). pap. 5.99 (978-0-545-92543-3(6)) Scholastic, Inc.

Schreiber, Ellen. Magic of the Moonlight, 2. 2012. (Full Moon Ser.: 2). (ENG.). 256p. (YA). (gr. 8-12). pap. 9.99 (978-0-06-198656-7(9), Tegen, Katherine Bks) HarperCollins Pubs.

Schroeder, Lisa. Frosting & Friendship. 2013. (ENG., Illus.). 224p. (J). (gr. 3-7). 15.99 (978-1-4424-7396-6(7), Aladdin) Simon & Schuster Children's Publishing.

Scieszka, Jon & Barnett, Mac. Battle Bunny. Myers, Matt, illus. 2013. (ENG.). 32p. (J). (gr. k-4). 16.99 (978-1-4424-4673-1(0), Simon & Schuster Bks. For Young Readers) Simon & Schuster Bks. For Young Readers.

Seltzer, Eric. Party Pigs! 2019. (Ready-To-Read Ser.). (ENG.). 32p. (J). (gr. k-1). 13.96 (978-0-87617-998-7(7)) Penworthy Co., LLC, The.

—Party Pigs! Ready-To-Read Pre-Level 1. Disbury, Tom, illus. 2019. (Ready-To-Read Ser.). (ENG.). 32p. (J). (gr. -1-k). 17.99 (978-1-5344-2879-9(8)); pap. 4.99 (978-1-5344-2878-2(X)) Simon Spotlight. (Simon Spotlight).

Sendak, Maurice. Bumble-Ardy. Sendak, Maurice, illus. 2011. (ENG., Illus.). 40p. (J). 17.95 (978-0-06-205198-1(9), HarperCollins) HarperCollins Pubs.

Shea, Therese. At the Luau, 1 vol. 2006. (Neighborhood Readers Ser.). (ENG.). 16p. (gr. 1-2). pap. 6.50 (978-1-4042-7002-2(7), 0bce0e25-2e2b-46cc-bd07-323051aab55b, Rosen Classroom) Rosen Publishing Group, Inc., The.

Sheinmel, Courtney. The Kindness Club: Designed by Lucy. 2018. (Kindness Club Ser.). (ENG.). 224p. (J). pap. 7.99 (978-1-68119-899-6(1), 900191667, Bloomsbury Children's Bks.) Bloomsbury Publishing USA.

Shields, Carol Diggory. Saturday Night at the Dinosaur Stomp. Nash, Scott, illus. 2008. (ENG.). 32p. (J). (gr. -1-3). pap. 7.99 (978-0-7636-3887-0(0)) Candlewick Pr.

Silver, Gail. Mindful Bea & the Worry Tree. Hollbacher, Franziska, illus. 2019. 32p. (J). (978-1-4338-2954-3(1), Magination Pr.) American Psychological Assn.

Silverhardt, Lauryn. A Surprise Party. Yee, Josie, illus. 2003. (Dora the Explorer Ser.). (ENG.). 22p. (J). bds. 4.99 (978-0-689-85483-5(8), Simon Spotlight/Nickelodeon) Simon Spotlight/Nickelodeon.

Sloan, Brian. A Really Nice Prom Mess. 2008. (ENG., Illus.). 316p. (YA). (gr. 9-12). pap. 8.99 (978-1-4169-5389-0(2), Simon & Schuster Bks. For Young Readers) Simon & Schuster Bks. For Young Readers.

Smith, Adelene Keeler. Sophie Gets Curtains! Yamyamin, Floyd Ryan, illus. 2010. (ENG.). 28p. pap. 12.99 (978-1-4520-8943-0(4)) AuthorHouse.

Smith, Audrey. The Halloween Misfits. 2004. 23p. (J). pap. 9.95 incl. audio compact disk (978-0-9722673-4-2(4)) Audrey Productions.

Smith, Emma Bland. Pop-Up Movie Theater. Marlin, Lissy, illus. 2018. (Maddy Mcguire, CEO Ser.). (ENG.). 112p. (J). (gr. 2-5). lib. bdg. 38.50 (978-1-5321-3186-8(0), 28467, Calico Chapter Bks.) ABDO Publishing Co.

Smith, Rosemary. Lizzie Goes to Tea. 2013. 32p. pap. 12.50 (978-1-62212-338-4(7), Strategic Bk. Publishing) Strategic Book Publishing & Rights Agency (SBPRA).

Soto, Gary. Chato & the Party Animals. Guevara, Susan, illus. (Chato Ser.). 28.95 incl. audio compact disk (978-1-59112-920-2(6)); 25.95 incl. audio (978-1-59112-460-3(3)); 28.95 incl. audio compact disk (978-1-59112-920-2(6)); pap. 39.95 incl. audio compact disk (978-1-59112-921-9(4)); pap. 37.95 incl. audio (978-1-59112-461-0(1)) Live Oak Media.

—Chato & the Party Animals. Guevara, Susan, illus. 2004. 32p. (J). (gr. -1-3). reprint ed. pap. 8.99 (978-0-14-240032-6(7), Puffin Books) Penguin Young Readers Group.

—Chato & the Party Animals. Guevara, Susan, illus. 2004. (Chato Ser.). (gr. -1-3). 17.00 (978-0-7569-2921-3(0)) Perfection Learning Corp.

—Chato y Los Amigos Pachangueros. Guevara, Susan, illus. 2004. 32p. (J). (gr. -1-3). reprint ed. pap. 8.99 (978-0-14-240033-3(5), Puffin Books) Penguin Young Readers Group.

Spohn, Kate. Turtle & Snake's Spooky Halloween. Spohn, Kate, illus. 2003. (Easy-to-Read Ser.). (Illus.). 32p. (J). (gr. -1-3). 11.65 (978-0-7569-1949-8(5)) Perfection Learning Corp.

Stanek, Robert, pseud. Have a Surprise Party. 2009. (Bugville Critters Ser.: No. 13). (ENG., Illus.). 52p. (J). 14.95 (978-1-57545-209-8(X), Reagent Pr. Bks. for Young Readers) RP Media.

Starks-Johnson, Annie. Dottie's Surprise Birthday Party. 2009. 24p. pap. 11.49 (978-1-4389-4866-9(2)) AuthorHouse.

Starr, Meg. Alicia's Happy Day, 1 vol. Hu, Ying-Hwa, illus. (ENG.). 32p. (J). 2007. (gr. k-3). pap. 6.95 (978-1-59572-116-7(9)) 2003. pap. 5.95 (978-1-932065-06-0(7)) 2003. (gr. -1-3). 15.95 (978-1-887734-85-1(6)) Star Bright Bks., Inc.

—Alicia's Happy Day (Spanish/English), 1 vol. Fiol, Maria, tr. Van Wright, Cornelius & Hu, Ying-Hwa, illus. 2007. (ENG.). 32p. (J). (gr. -1-3). 15.95 (978-1-59572-115-0(0)) Star Bright Bks., Inc.

Stern, A. J. Miss Fortune, 7 vols. Marts, Doreen Mulryan, illus. 2012. (Frankly, Frannie Ser.: 7). 128p. (J). (gr. 1-3). pap. 6.99 (978-0-448-45748-2(2), Grosset & Dunlap) Penguin Young Readers Group.

Sticker Dolly Dressing Parties (Revised) 2017. (Sticker Dolly Dressing Ser.). (ENG.). (J). pap. 9.99 (978-0-7945-3784-5(7), Usborne) EDC Publishing.

Stilton, Thea & Schaffer, Andrea. The Royal Ball. Pellizzari, Barbara et al, illus. 2017. 108p. (J). (978-1-338-18275-0(7)) Scholastic, Inc.

Stine, R. L. The Birthday Party of No Return. 2012. (Goosebumps HorrorLand: Hall of Horrors Ser.: 6). lib. bdg. 17.20 (978-0-606-23932-5(4)) Turtleback.

—Fear Street Super Thriller. 2015. (Fear Street Ser.). (ENG.). 592p. (YA). (gr. 7-12). pap. 12.99 (978-1-250-07693-9(5), 900152585, St. Martin's Griffin) St. Martin's Pr.

Stone, Kate. Bunnies for Tea. 2013. (ENG., Illus.). 10p. (J). bds. 8.99 (978-1-4494-2887-7(8)) Andrews McMeel Publishing.

—Happy Birthday, Mouse! 2014. (ENG.). 16p. (J). bds. 5.99 (978-1-4494-4387-0(7)) Andrews McMeel Publishing.

Studio Mouse Staff. Pooh & Roo. 2008. (ENG., Illus.). 36p. (J). (gr. -1). 7.99 (978-1-59069-420-6(1)) Studio Mouse LLC.

Sullivan, Kevin & Goldman, Leslie. Anne's Babysitting Blues. 2010. (Anne of Green Gables for Young Readers Ser.). (ENG.). 64p. (J). (gr. 2-4). pap. 4.95 (978-0-9736803-1-7(8)) Davenport Pr. CAN. Dist: Independent Pubs. Group.

Swenson, Jamie A. A Fall Ball for All. Fedele, Chiara, illus. 2018. (ENG.). 32p. (J). (gr. k-2). 19.99 (978-1-5124-9803-5(3), 58a720c8-25c5-494b-baa5-616ae97cfa71, Millbrook Pr.) Lerner Publishing Group.

Tada, Hiroshi. Who's There. Perry, Mia, tr. 2009. 24p. 11.95 (978-1-74126-350-3(6)) R.I.C. Pubns. AUS. Dist: SCB Distributors.

Taylor, Chloë. Dressed to Frill. Zhang, Nancy, illus. 2015. (Sew Zoey Ser.: 12). (ENG.). 176p. (J). (gr. 3-7). pap. 7.99 (978-1-4814-2930-6(2), Simon Spotlight) Simon Spotlight.

Tebow, Tim. Bronco & Friends: a Party to Remember. Chapman, Jane, illus. 2021. (Bronco & Friends Ser.: 1). 40p. (J). (gr. -1-2). 17.99 (978-0-593-23204-0(6), WaterBrook Pr.) Crown Publishing Group, The.

Tegen, Katherine. Dracula & Frankenstein Are Friends. Cushman, Doug, illus. 2003. 32p. (J). (gr. -1-3). 15.99 (978-0-06-000115-5(1)) HarperCollins Pubs.

Terry, Anne. Honest Bob, the Dog, Has a Tea Party. 2013. 30p. pap. 9.83 (978-1-62884-761-1(1)) Speedy Publishing LLC.

Thaler, Mike. Friday the 13th from the Black Lagoon. Lee, Jared, illus. 2016. (Black Lagoon Adventures Set 4 Ser.). (ENG.). 64p. (J). (gr. 2-6). lib. bdg. 31.36 (978-1-61479-604-6(1), 24337, Chapter Bks.) Spotlight.

—The Pool Party from the Black Lagoon. Lee, Jared D., illus. 2016. 64p. (J). pap. (978-0-545-85073-5(8)) Scholastic, Inc.

—The Spring Dance from the Black Lagoon. Lee, Jared, illus. 2009. 62p. (J). (978-0-545-07223-6(9)) Scholastic, Inc.

—The Spring Dance from the Black Lagoon, 1 vol. Lee, Jared, illus. 2012. (Black Lagoon Adventures Ser.: No. 2). (ENG.). 64p. (J). (gr. 2-6). 31.36 (978-1-59961-963-7(6), 3607, Chapter Bks.) Spotlight.

Thompson, Yvonne. Miss Tilly's Party. Krecskay, Stephen, illus. 2004. (J). per. (978-0-9749561-0-7(4)) My Sunshine Bks.

Tice, Kimberly & Litvack, Venita. Lou Know What to Do Birthday Party, Vol. 3. Kerry, illus. 2017. (Lou Knows What to Do Ser.). (ENG.). 23p. (J). (gr. -1-5). pap. 10.95 (978-1-944882-16-7(2)) Boys Town Pr.

Trapani, Iza. Haunted Party. Trapani, Iza, illus. (Illus.). 28p. (J). 2010. (gr. -1-2). pap. 7.95 (978-1-58089-247-6(7)) 2009. (ENG., (gr. k-3). 22.44 (978-1-58089-246-9(9)) Charlesbridge Publishing, Inc.

Trimble, Marcia. Liberty Cafe Is Open. Hayden, Jennifer, illus. 2006. (J). pap. 895.00 (978-1-891577-91-8(3)); 32p. lib. bdg. 15.95 (978-1-891577-90-1(5)) Images Pr.

Turner, Jill. Percival's Party. Townsend, Peter, illus. 2003. (J). pap. 12.95 (978-1-74047-235-7(7)) Book Co. Publishing Pty, Ltd., The AUS. Dist: Penton Overseas, Inc.

Tuttle, Mark. Lexi's Tea Party. Combs, Bradley, illus. 2011. 32p. pap. 24.95 (978-1-4560-9919-0(1)) America Star Bks.

Valentin, Karen. Block Party. 2009. 32p. (J). (gr. -1-3). 6.95 (978-1-60349-017-7(5), Marimba Bks.) Just Us Bks., Inc.

Van Genechten, Guido. Ricky's Birthday. 2012. (ENG.). 24p. (J). (gr. -1-k). 16.95 (978-1-60537-119-1(X)) Clavis Publishing.

Vernon, Ursula. Hamster Princess: Whiskerella. 2018. (Hamster Princess Ser.: 5). (Illus.). 256p. (J). (gr. 3-7). 14.99 (978-0-399-18655-4(7), Dial Bks) Penguin Young Readers Group.

Vinci, Victoria. A Party for Piper: Practicing the P Sound, 1 vol. 2016. (Rosen Phonics Readers Ser.). (ENG., Illus.). 8p. (J). (gr. -1-2). pap. (978-1-5081-3071-0(X), 16420d36-b6aa-43dc-b665-5954ea5266bb, Rosen Classroom) Rosen Publishing Group, Inc., The.

Volker, Kerstin. Lilly's Birthday Party. 2003. (Funny Friends Lift-and-Learn Bks.). (Illus.). 14p. (J). 5.99 (978-1-59384-022-8(5)) Parklane Publishing.

Wallace, Nancy Elizabeth. Tell-A-Bunny, 0 vols. 2013. (ENG., Illus.). 36p. (J). (gr. 1-3). 7.99 (978-0-7614-5369-7(5), 9780761453697, Two Lions) Amazon Publishing.

Warne, Jude. The Girls Who Go to Parties. 2017. (Crushing Ser.). (ENG.). 192p. (YA). (gr. 5-12). lib. bdg. 31.42 (978-1-68076-716-2(X), 25380, Epic Escape) EPIC Pr.

Watson, Jane Werner. Walt Disney's Cinderella's Friends. 2017. (Illus.). (J). (978-1-5182-4598-5(6), Golden Bks.) Random Hse. Children's Bks.

Watt, Fiona. Complete Book of First Experiences. rev. ed. 2011. (First Experiences Ser.). 144p. (J). ring bd. 19.99 (978-0-7945-2948-2(8), Usborne) EDC Publishing.

Watt, Mélanie & Watt, Mélanie. Scaredy Squirrel Has a Birthday Party, 0 vols. Watt, Mélanie & Watt, Mélanie, illus. (ENG., Illus.). 32p. (J). (gr. -1-3). 2014. pap. 7.99 (978-1-55453-716-7(9)) 2011. 16.99 (978-1-55453-468-5(2)) Kids Can Pr., Ltd. CAN. Dist: Hachette Bk. Group.

Weeks, Sarah. Lizzy Mctizzy & the Busy Dizzy Day. Wildish, Lee, illus. 2019. (ENG.). 32p. (J). (gr. -1-3). 17.99 (978-0-06-244205-5(8), HarperCollins) HarperCollins Pubs.

—Oggie Cooder, Party Animal, 2. 2011. (ENG.). 176p. (J). (gr. 2-5). pap. 6.99 (978-0-439-92796-3(X), Scholastic Paperbacks) Scholastic, Inc.

Weinberg, Jennifer Liberts. Happy Birthday, Mike! 2014. (Step into Reading Level 2 Ser.). lib. bdg. 13.55 (978-0-606-36006-7(9)) Turtleback.

Welch-Biggs, Susan. Your Magical Party. 2008. (ENG.). 36p. per. 21.99 (978-1-4257-9181-0(6)) Xlibris Corp.

Wells, Carolyn. Patty at Home. 2007. (ENG.). 204p. per. 12.95 (978-1-4218-3321-7(2)) 1st World Publishing, Inc.

Wells, Rosemary. Bunny Party. 2003. (Max & Ruby Ser.). (Illus.). 32p. (J). (gr. -1-k). pap. 7.99 (978-0-14-250162-7(X), Puffin Books) Penguin Young Readers Group.

West, C. The Adventures of Ice Cream & Honey Buns: It's a Party. 2012. 24p. pap. 14.93 (978-1-4669-4665-1(2)) Trafford Publishing.

West, Kasie. Maybe This Time. 2019. (ENG., Illus.). 368p. (YA). (gr. 7-7). 17.99 (978-1-338-21008-8(4)) Scholastic, Inc.

Weston Woods Staff, creator. Chato & the Party Animals. 2011. 38.75 (978-0-439-84581-6(5)) 2011. 18.95 (978-0-439-73984-9(5)) 2004. 29.95 (978-1-55592-703-5(3)) Weston Woods Studios, Inc.

—Three Cheers for Catherine the Great. 2011. 18.95 (978-0-439-80506-3(6)) Weston Woods Studios, Inc.

—Three Cheers for Catherine the Great! 2011. 38.75 (978-0-439-78620-1(7)) Weston Woods Studios, Inc.

Westover, Gail. Mrs Mouse's Garden Party in Giggleswick Village. Daly, Karen Anne, illus. 2012. 26p. pap. 9.95 (978-0-9821507-9-5(2)) Thistlewood Publishing.

Wheeler, Lisa. Boogie Knights. Siegel, Mark, illus. 2008. (ENG.). 40p. (J). (gr. -1-3). 16.99 (978-0-689-87639-4(4), Atheneum/Richard Jackson Bks.) Simon & Schuster Children's Publishing.

White, Toni. Ridge Street Prom. 2008. 182p. pap. 12.96 (978-1-4357-1966-8(2)) Lulu Pr., Inc.

Willems, Mo. Elephant & Piggie: Happy Pig Day. 2015. (CHI.). (J). (978-7-5125-0741-8(0)) International Culture Publishing Corp.

—Happy Pig Day!-An Elephant & Piggie Book. 2011. (Elephant & Piggie Book Ser.: 15). (ENG., Illus.). 64p. (J). (gr. -1-k). 9.99 (978-1-4231-4342-0(6), Hyperion Books for Children) Disney Publishing Worldwide.

—I Am Invited to a Party!-An Elephant & Piggie Book. rev. ed. 2007. (Elephant & Piggie Book Ser.). (ENG., Illus.). 64p. (J). (gr. -1-k). 9.99 *(978-1-4231-0687-6(3)*, Hyperion Books for Children) Disney Publishing Worldwide.

Wilson, Karma. Bear Snores On. Chapman, Jane, illus. 2005. (Bear Bks.). (ENG.). 34p. (J). (gr. -1-k). bds. 7.99 *(978-1-4169-0272-0(4)*, Little Simon) Little Simon.

Wilson, Wendy. Just Desserts. 2007. 53p. pap. 16.95 *(978-1-4241-9285-4(4))* America Star Bks.

Wing, Natasha. The Night Before My Birthday. Wummer, Amy, illus. 2014. (Night Before Ser.). 32p. (J). (gr. -1-k). 5.99 *(978-0-448-48000-8(X)*, Grosset & Dunlap) Penguin Young Readers Group.

—The Night Before My Birthday. 2014. (Night Before Ser.). lib. bdg. 14.75 *(978-0-606-34133-2(1))* Turtleback.

Winkler, Henry & Oliver, Lin. Fake Snakes & Weird Wizards #4. Garrett, Scott, illus. 2015. (Here's Hank Ser.: 4). (ENG.). 128p. (J). (gr. 1-3). 6.99 *(978-0-448-48252-1(5)*, Penguin Workshop) Penguin Young Readers Group.

Winnie the Pooh: Party in the Wood. 2011. 32p. pap. 4.99 *(978-1-4231-5386-3(3))* Disney Pr.

Wood, Maryrose. The Incorrigible Children of Ashton Place: Book I: the Mysterious Howling. Klassen, Jon, illus. 2015. (Incorrigible Children of Ashton Place Ser.: 1). (ENG.). 288p. (J). (gr. 3-7). pap. 7.99 *(978-0-06-236693-1(9)*, Balzer & Bray) HarperCollins Pubs.

—The Incorrigible Children of Ashton Place: The Mysterious Howling Howlin G, Bk. I. Klassen, Jon, illus. 2010. (Incorrigible Children of Ashton Place Ser.: 1). (ENG.). 272p. (J). (gr. 3-7). 16.99 *(978-0-06-179105-5(9)*, Balzer & Bray) HarperCollins Pubs.

Wright, Jason F. Penny's Christmas Jar Party. Sowards, Ben, illus. 2009. 32p. (J). 17.95 *(978-1-60641-167-4(5)*, Shadow Mountain) Shadow Mountain Publishing.

Yasuda, Anita. Crazy Clues. Harpster, Steve, illus. 2013. (Dino Detectives Ser.). (ENG.). 32p. (J). (gr. 1-2). pap. 5.95 *(978-1-4342-6200-4(6)*, 123494, Stone Arch Bks.) Capstone.

Yasuda, Anita & Harpster, Steve. The Crazy Clues. 2013. (Dino Detectives Ser.). (ENG.). 32p. (J). (gr. 1-2). pap. 35.70 *(978-1-4342-6226-4(X)*, 20031, Stone Arch Bks.) Capstone.

Yolen, Jane. How Do Dinosaurs Say Happy Birthday? Teague, Mark, illus. 2011. (ENG.). 12p. (J). (gr. -1-k). bds. 7.99 *(978-0-545-15353-9(0)*, Blue Sky Pr., The) Scholastic, Inc.

Yorinks, Arthur. Flappy & Scrappy. 2010. (I Can Read Level 2 Ser.). (ENG., Illus.). 48p. (J). (gr. k-3). pap. 4.99 *(978-0-06-205913-0(0)*, HarperCollins) HarperCollins Pubs.

Zann, Tara. Wild Child: Forest's First Birthday Party. Widdowson, Dan, illus. 2017. (Wild Child Ser.: 3). (ENG.). 128p. (J). pap. 5.99 *(978-1-250-10389-5(4)*, 900163649) Imprint IND. Dist: Macmillan.

PARTIES, POLITICAL

see Political Parties

PASSIONS

see Emotions

PASSIVE RESISTANCE

see also Boycotts; Nonviolence

Aronson, Marc & Budhos, Marina. Sugar Changed the World: A Story of Magic, Spice, Slavery, Freedom, & Science. 2010. (ENG., Illus.). 176p. (YA). (gr. 7-18). 21.99 *(978-0-618-57492-6(1)*, 100422, Clarion Bks.) HarperCollins Pubs.

O'Brien, Anne Sibley & O'Brien, Perry Edmond. After Gandhi: One Hundred Years of Nonviolent Resistance. 2018. (Illus.). 224p. (J). (gr. 5). pap. 11.99 *(978-1-58089-130-1(6))* Charlesbridge Publishing, Inc.

Stanley, Diane. Resist! Peaceful Acts That Changed Our World. 2020. (ENG., Illus.). 48p. (J). (gr. 2-5). 18.99 *(978-0-8234-4487-8(2)*, Neal Porter Bks) Holiday Hse., Inc.

Terp, Gail. Nonviolent Resistance in the Civil Rights Movement, 1 vol. 2015. (Stories of the Civil Rights Movement Ser.). (ENG., Illus.). 48p. (J). (gr. 4-8). 35.64 *(978-1-62403-882-2(4)*, 18134) ABDO Publishing Co.

PASSOVER

Adler, David A. The Story of Passover. Weber, Jill, illus. (ENG.). 32p. (J). (gr. -1-3). 2015. 7.99 *(978-0-8234-3304-9(8))* 2014. 15.99 *(978-0-8234-2902-8(4))* Holiday Hse., Inc.

Aloian, Molly. Passover. 2009. (Celebrations in My World Ser.). (ENG., Illus.). 32p. (J). (gr. 1-3). pap. *(978-0-7787-4311-8(X))* Crabtree Publishing Co.

Balsley, Tilda. Lotsa Matzah. Gutierrez, Akemi, illus. 2013. (ENG.). 12p. (J). (gr. -1 — 1). bds. 5.99 *(978-0-7613-6629-4(6)*, 58ea0a1f-53e7-4293-ad89-8abbed9a0df4, Kar-Ben Publishing) Lerner Publishing Group.

Berger, Barry W. Passover Haggadah. Hall, Melanie W., illus. 2004. 36p. *(978-0-9674319-3-2(X))* Messianic Perspectives.

Bullard, Lisa. Sarah's Passover. Basaluzzo, Constanza, illus. 2012. (Holidays & Special Days Ser.: 24p. (J). (gr. k-2). pap. 39.62 *(978-0-7613-9245-3(9))*; (ENG.). pap. 8.99 *(978-0-7613-8582-0(7)*, 38f96a77-b14e-412f-85a2-36ccf8407dd7) Lerner Publishing Group. (Millbrook Pr.).

Cohen, Joan Freeman & Freeman, Jonathan M. In Every Generation: A Model Seder Haggadah. 2005. (J). *(978-0-87441-731-9(7))* Behrman Hse., Inc.

Cohen, Tina. Pesach What & Why? 2005. 36p. 14.99 *(978-1-4116-6454-8(X))* Lulu Pr., Inc.

dePaola, Tomie. My First Passover. dePaola, Tomie, illus. 2015. (Illus.). 14p. (J). (gr. -1 — 1). bds. 6.99 *(978-0-448-44791-9(6)*, Grosset & Dunlap) Penguin Young Readers Group.

Fishman, Cathy Goldberg. Passover. Reeves, Jeni, illus. 2006. (On My Own Holidays Ser.). (ENG.). 48p. (gr. 2-4). per. 6.95 *(978-1-57505-695-1(X)*, First Avenue Editions) Lerner Publishing Group.

Fishman, Cathy Goldberg & Hall, Melanie W. On Passover. 2003. (Illus.). 28p. (J). (gr. k-4). reprint ed. 16.00 *(978-0-7567-6988-8(4))* DIANE Publishing Co.

Gillespie, Katie. Passover. 2015. (Let's Celebrate American Holidays Ser.). (ENG.). (J). lib. bdg. 27.13 *(978-1-4896-3629-4(3)*, AV2 by Weigl) Weigl Pubs., Inc.

Grack, Rachel. Passover. 2018. (Celebrating Holidays Ser.). (ENG., Illus.). 24p. (J). (gr. k-3). lib. bdg. 26.95 *(978-1-62617-790-1(2)*, Blastoff! Readers) Bellwether Media.

Hayes, Amy. Celebrate Passover. 2015. (J). *(978-1-62713-478-1(6))* Cavendish Square Publishing LLC.

Heiligman, Deborah. Holidays Around the World: Celebrate Passover: With Matzah, Maror, & Memories. 2017. (Holidays Around the World Ser.). (Illus.). 32p. (J). (gr. 1-3). pap. 7.99 *(978-1-4263-2745-2(5)*, National Geographic Kids) Disney Publishing Worldwide.

House, Behrman. Family (and Frog!) Haggadah. 2017. (ENG., Illus.). 56p. (J). pap. 7.95 *(978-0-87441-937-5(9)*, 01a23756-84a1-4b2b-9027-0eeaa26ac7f9) Behrman Hse., Inc.

—Frogs in the Bed. 2014. (ENG., Illus.). 32p. (J). (gr. -1-3). pap. 9.95 *(978-0-87441-913-9(1)*, 72e7894b-91b5-4149-ac9e-6d05a037621b) Behrman Hse., Inc.

Kropf, Latifa Berry. It's Seder Time! Cohen, Tod, illus. Cohen, Tod, photos by. 2004. (ENG.). 24p. (J). (gr. -1-1). 12.95 *(978-1-58013-092-9(5)*, Kar-Ben Publishing) Lerner Publishing Group.

Lehman-Wilzig, Tami. Passover Around the World. Wolf, Elizabeth, illus. 2007. (ENG.). 48p. (J). (gr. 3-5). per. 8.99 *(978-1-58013-215-2(4)*, 7321458e-f18d-4157-a73c-0a949abfef41, Kar-Ben Publishing) Lerner Publishing Group.

Leon, Carol Boyd. Dayenu! A Passover Haggadah for Families & Children. Connelly, Gwen, illus. 2008. 32p. (J). (gr. 1-3). 16.95 incl. audio compact disk *(978-1-60280-041-0(3))*; pap. 8.95 incl. audio compact disk *(978-1-60280-039-7(1))*; spiral bd. 16.95 incl. audio compact disk *(978-1-60280-040-3(5))*; bds. 24.95 incl. audio compact disk *(978-1-60280-042-7(1))* Ktav Publishing Hse., Inc.

Lupo, Tamar. Passover. 2006. (American Holidays Ser.). (Illus.). 24p. (J). (gr. 3-7). lib. bdg. 24.45 *(978-1-59036-462-8(7))*; per. 8.95 *(978-1-59036-465-9(1))* Weigl Pubs., Inc.

Pirotta, Saviour. Passover, 1 vol. 2007. (We Love Holidays (2008-2009) Ser.). (ENG., Illus.). 24p. (J). (gr. 2-2). lib. bdg. 26.27 *(978-1-4042-3707-0(0)*, 46ed88c3-7bac-405a-8a6b-b73e8c6f28f9, PowerKids Pr.) Rosen Publishing Group, Inc., The.

Polak, Monique. Passover: Festival of Freedom, 1 vol. 2016. (Orca Origins Ser.: 1). (ENG., Illus.). 72p. (J). (gr. 4-7). 24.95 *(978-1-4598-0990-1(4))* Orca Bk. Pubs. USA.

—Passover Family, 1 vol. 2018. (ENG., Illus.). 24p. (J). (gr. -1 — 1). bds. 9.95 *(978-1-4598-1852-1(0))* Orca Bk. Pubs. USA.

Ribowsky, Helene & Zlotowitz, Rachel. The Search Is On! Can You Find the Ten Pieces of Chametz? Black, Elisheva, illus. 2017. 31p. (J). *(978-1-4226-1870-7(6)*, ArtScroll Series) Mesorah Pubns., Ltd.

Richardson, Betsy. Easter, Passover & Festivals of Hope, Vol. 10. 2018. (Celebrating Holidays & Festivals Around the World Ser.). (Illus.). 112p. (J). (gr. 7). lib. bdg. 34.60 *(978-1-4222-4146-2(7))* Mason Crest.

Rossel, Seymour. The Storybook Haggadah. 2007. pap. 9.95 *(978-1-932687-59-0(9)*, Pitspopany Pr.) Simcha Media Group.

Schorr, Titus. We Celebrate Passover, 1 vol., 1. 2015. (Rosen REAL Readers: Social Studies Nonfiction / Fiction: Myself, My Community, My World Ser.). (ENG.). 12p. (J). (gr. k-1). pap. 6.33 *(978-1-5081-1785-8(3)*, d1c1bfcb-83b0-47fa-b1f7-fce4d36ca12a, Rosen Classroom) Rosen Publishing Group, Inc., The.

Silberg, Francis Barry. The Story of Passover. Britt, Stephanie McFetridge, illus. 2017. (ENG.). 24p. (J). (gr. -1-k). bds. 6.99 *(978-0-8249-1652-7(2))* Worthy Publishing.

Soban Biniashvili, Freidele Galya. I Love Matzah. Scudamore, Angelika, illus. 2020. (ENG.). 12p. (J). (gr. -1 — 1). bds. 6.99 *(978-1-5415-5727-7(1)*, a7835eeb-2098-456a-9610-5e8ac84aa51c, Kar-Ben Publishing) Lerner Publishing Group.

Sollish, Ari. Touch of Passover - French (Pessa'h Sur le Bout des Doigts) 2013. (Touch & Feel Ser.). (ENG & FRE.). (J). bds. 9.95 *(978-0-8266-0024-0(7))* Kehot Pubn. Society.

Story of Passover. 2004. pap. 6.95 *(978-0-8249-6277-7(X)*, Ideals Pubns.) Worthy Publishing.

Traditional. Dayenu! a Favorite Passover Song. Latimer, Miriam, illus. 2012. (ENG.). 14p. (J). (gr. -1 — 1). bds. 7.99 *(978-0-545-31236-3(1)*, Cartwheel Bks.) Scholastic, Inc.

Webster, Christine. How to Draw Passover Symbols. 2009. (Kid's Guide to Drawing Ser.). 24p. (gr. 3-3). 47.90 *(978-1-61511-039-1(9)*, PowerKids Pr.) Rosen Publishing Group, Inc., The.

PASSOVER—FICTION

Akselrad, January & Young, Jennifer. Matzah & Miracles: A Passover Musical & Chapter Book. Palagonia, Peter, illus. 2012. (ENG.). 88p. (J). 15.00 *(978-0-9822134-8-3(4))* See The Wish.

Balsley, Tilda & Fischer, Ellen. Grover & Big Bird's Passover Celebration. Leigh, Tom, illus. 2013. (ENG.). 24p. (J). (gr. -1-1). 7.99 *(978-0-7613-8492-2(8)*, 75e3e8bc-1f18-4954-99c2-1899099d6436); lib. bdg. 16.99 *(978-0-7613-8491-5(X)*, fda19410-f407-428b-9e44-f0879de98943) Lerner Publishing Group. (Kar-Ben Publishing).

Barash, Chris. Is It Passover Yet? Psacharopulo, Alessandra, illus. 2015. (Celebrate Jewish Holidays Ser.). (ENG.). 32p. (J). (gr. -1-3). 16.99 *(978-0-8075-6330-4(7)*, 807563307) Whitman, Albert & Co.

Black, Joe. Afikomen Mambo. Prater, Linda, illus. 2011. (ENG.). 24p. (J). (gr. -1 — 1). pap. 8.95 *(978-0-7613-5639-4(8)*, 65275eb0-fee4-487a-b2b1-39cb1ab217c7, Kar-Ben Publishing) Lerner Publishing Group.

Clausman, Rachel. Miriam, Come Sit. 2011. 24p. pap. 11.32 *(978-1-4634-4812-7(0))* AuthorHouse.

Cohen, Deborah Bodin. Engineer Ari & the Passover Rush. Kober, Shahar, illus. 2015. (ENG.). 32p. (J). (gr. k-3). lib. bdg. 17.95 *(978-1-4677-3470-7(5))*; E-Book 27.99 *(978-1-4677-6201-4(6))* Lerner Publishing Group. (Kar-Ben Publishing).

Fireside, Bryna J. Private Joel & the Sewell Mountain Seder. Costello, Shawn, illus. 2008. (Passover Ser.). 47p. (J). (gr. 3-6). lib. bdg. 16.95 *(978-0-8225-7240-4(0)*, Kar-Ben Publishing) Lerner Publishing Group.

Gehl, Laura. And Then Another Sheep Turned Up. Adele, Amy, illus. 2015. (ENG.). 32p. (J). (gr. -1-3). E-Book 23.99 *(978-1-4677-1190-6(X)*, Kar-Ben Publishing) Lerner Publishing Group.

Goldin, Barbara Diamond. Passover Cowboy. Capaldi, Gina, illus. 2017. (ENG.). 32p. (J). 17.95 *(978-1-68115-527-2(3)*, 89f38416-194b-4a60-a3a2-721447b7c2b2) Behrman Hse., Inc.

Hannigan, Lynne. Sam's Passover. 2004. (Illus.). 32p. pap. 5.95 *(978-0-7136-4084-7(7)*, 93342, A&C Black) Bloomsbury Publishing Plc GBR. Dist: Consortium Bk. Sales & Distribution.

Hickman, Jessica. Alligator Seder. Elissambura, illus. 2020. (ENG.). 12p. (J). (gr. -1 — 1). bds. 6.99 *(978-1-5415-6041-3(8)*, 328acd50-3eca-4a22-a925-629f27e06cde, Kar-Ben Publishing) Lerner Publishing Group.

Ho, Jannie, illus. The Great Matzoh Hunt. 2010. 12p. (J). (gr. -1 — 1). bds. 7.99 *(978-0-8431-8969-8(X)*, Price Stern Sloan) Penguin Young Readers Group.

Kimmel, Eric A. Escape from Egypt. Stevanovic, Ivica, illus. 2015. (Scarlett & Sam Ser.). (ENG.). 168p. (J). (gr. 1-3). E-Book 23.99 *(978-1-4677-6207-6(5)*, Kar-Ben Publishing) Lerner Publishing Group.

King, Emily. Clopper & the Lost Boy, 1 vol. Olson, Ed, illus. 2009. 32p. (J). 12.99 *(978-0-8254-2946-0(3))* Kregel Pubns.

Kirkfield, Vivian. Pippa's Passover Plate. Weber, Jill, illus. 2019. 40p. (J). (gr. -1-3). 17.99 *(978-0-8234-4162-4(8))* Holiday Hse., Inc.

Koffsky, Ann. Kayla & Kugel's Almost-Perfect Passover. Koffsky, Ann, illus. 2016. (ENG., Illus.). 24p. (J). pap. 9.95 *(978-1-68115-508-1(7)*, 0906bbb7-cde0-459e-99ff-9087c1fb3317) Behrman Hse., Inc.

Lanton, Sandy. The Littlest Levine. Keay, Claire, illus. 2014. (ENG.). 24p. (J). (gr. -1-2). 7.95 *(978-0-7613-9046-6(4)*, b497aad7-f252-4a37-8c22-6411450d7d2b, Kar-Ben Publishing) Lerner Publishing Group.

Nelkin Wieder, Joy. The Passover Mouse. Kober, Shahar, illus. 2020. (ENG.). 32p. (J). (gr. -1-2). 20.99 *(978-1-9848-9552-3(4)*, Doubleday Bks. for Young Readers) Random Hse. Children's Bks.

Newman, Lesléa. A Sweet Passover. Slonim, David, illus. 2012. (ENG.). 40p. (J). (gr. -1-3). 17.95 *(978-0-8109-9737-0(1)*, 680501, Abrams Bks. for Young Readers) Abrams, Inc.

Newman, Leslea. Welcoming Elijah: A Passover Tale with a Tail. Gal, Susan, illus. 2020. 32p. (J). (gr. k-3). lib. bdg. 17.99 *(978-1-58089-882-9(3))* Charlesbridge Publishing, Inc.

Newman, Tracy. Around the Passover Table. Santos, Adriana, illus. 2019. (ENG.). 32p. (J). (gr. -1-3). 17.99 *(978-0-8075-0446-8(7)*, 807504467) Whitman, Albert & Co.

—Passover Is Coming! Garofoli, Viviana, illus. 2016. (ENG.). 12p. (J). (gr. -1 — 1). bds. 5.99 *(978-1-4677-5242-8(8)*, 6a3273e6-8c04-4222-8780-1c92ca1c3660); E-Book 23.99 *(978-1-4677-9610-1(7))* Lerner Publishing Group. (Kar-Ben Publishing).

O'Connell, Rebecca. Penina Levine Is a Hard-Boiled Egg. Lue Sue, Majella, illus. 2009. (ENG.). 192p. (J). (gr. 3-7). pap. 18.99 *(978-0-312-55026-4(X)*, 900055956) Square Fish.

Pearlman, Bobby. Passover Is Here! Passover Is Here! Desmoinaux, Christel, illus. 2005. (ENG.). 16p. (J). (gr. k-2). pap. 6.99 *(978-0-689-86587-9(2)*, Little Simon) Little Simon.

Peretz, I. L. & Goldin, Barbara Diamond. The Magician's Visit: A Passover Tale. Parker, Robert Andrew, illus. 2006. 28p. (J). (gr. 4-8). reprint ed. 15.00 *(978-1-4223-5408-7(3))*; pap. 5.00 *(978-1-4223-5400-1(8))* DIANE Publishing Co.

Portnoy, Mindy Avra. A Tale of Two Seders. Cis, Valeria, illus. 2010. (ENG.). 32p. (J). (gr. k-4). lib. bdg. 17.95 *(978-0-8225-9907-4(4))*; pap. 7.95 *(978-0-8225-9931-9(7)*, c5abecf4-d366-4d5a-bce9-17d3d9d9149f) Lerner Publishing Group. (Kar-Ben Publishing).

Rauchwerger, Diane Levin. Dinosaur on Passover. Wolff, Jason, illus. 2006. (ENG.). 24p. (J). (gr. -1-1). 15.95 *(978-1-58013-156-8(5))*; pap. 7.95 *(978-1-58013-161-2(1)*, cafad87e-3db8-4326-9bf7-529dce1248c6) Lerner Publishing Group. (Kar-Ben Publishing).

Rothenberg, Joan. Matzah Ball Soup. Rothenberg, Joan, illus. 2005. (Illus.). 29p. (J). (gr. -1-2). reprint ed. 15.00 *(978-0-7567-8930-5(3))* DIANE Publishing Co.

Rouss, Sylvia A. Sammy Spider's First Haggadah. Kahn, Katherine Janus, illus. 2007. (ENG.). 32p. (J). (gr. -1-3). per. 7.99 *(978-1-58013-230-5(8)*, a576058b-9534-4121-80bf-9ba351c5c0af, Kar-Ben Publishing) Lerner Publishing Group.

—Sammy Spider's Passover Shapes. Kahn, Katherine Janus, illus. 2017. (ENG.). 12p. (J). (gr. -1 — 1). bds. 5.99 *(978-1-4677-7970-8(9)*, ff930d1d-18ff-4e40-ae02-3260511dc5f1, Kar-Ben Publishing) Lerner Publishing Group.

Schotter, Roni. Passover Magic, 0 vols. Hafner, Marylin, illus. 2012. (ENG.). 34p. (J). (gr. -1-3). pap. 7.99 *(978-0-7614-5842-5(5)*, 9780761458425, Two Lions) Amazon Publishing.

Shulman, Lisa. The Matzo Ball Boy. Litzinger, Rosanne, illus. 2007. 32p. (J). (gr. -1-2). pap. 8.99 *(978-0-14-240769-1(0)*, Puffin Books) Penguin Young Readers Group.

Sollish, Ari. A Touch of Passover: A Touch & Feel Book. Becker, Boruch, illus. 2006. 12p. (J). bds. 7.95 *(978-0-8266-0021-9(2))* Merkos L'Inyonei Chinuch.

Strauss, Linda Leopold. A Different Kind of Passover. Tugeau, Jeremy, illus. 2017. (ENG.). 32p. (J). (gr. -1-3). E-Book 27.99 *(978-1-5124-2723-3(3)*, 9781512427233, Kar-Ben Publishing) Lerner Publishing Group.

Sussman, Joni Kibort. A Seder for Grover. Leigh, Tom, illus. 2019. (ENG.). 12p. (J). (gr. -1 — 1). bds. 5.99 *(978-1-5415-2921-2(9)*, 99abce9b-f8ff-42dd-9dcd-1f5227c19a10, Kar-Ben Publishing) Lerner Publishing Group.

Valder, Hayim. Di Vunderlikhe Ertseylung Fun Motl. Heler, Moti, illus. 2017. (YID.). 57p. (J). *(978-1-68091-169-5(4))* Kinder Shpiel USA, Inc.

PASTEL DRAWING

Bolte, Mari. Paint It: The Art of Acrylics, Oils, Pastels, & Watercolors, 1 vol. Ice, Dawn, illus. 2013. (Craft It Yourself Ser.). (ENG.). 144p. (J). (gr. 3-9). pap., pap., pap. 14.95 *(978-1-62370-009-6(4)*, 123602, Capstone Young Readers) Capstone.

Merberg, Julie & Bober, Suzanne. Dancing with Degas. 2003. (Mini Masters Ser.: 4). (ENG., Illus.). 22p. (J). (gr. -1-7). bds. 7.99 *(978-0-8118-4047-7(6))* Chronicle Bks. LLC.

Wood, Alix. Pastels, 1 vol. 2018. (Make a Masterpiece Ser.). (ENG.). 32p. (J). (gr. 3-4). pap. 11.50 *(978-1-5382-3581-2(1)*, 3801267e-44fe-473d-ae20-79b6da4c132e); lib. bdg. 28.27 *(978-1-5382-3593-5(5)*, d7c26d1d-7650-413d-ba73-5154893193c4) Stevens, Gareth Publishing LLLP.

PASTEL PAINTING

see Pastel Drawing

PASTELS

see Pastel Drawing

PASTEUR, LOUIS, 1822-1895

Ackerman, Jane. Louis Pasteur & the Founding of Microbiology. 2004. (Profiles in Science Ser.). (Illus.). 144p. (YA). (gr. 6-12). 26.95 *(978-1-931798-13-6(3))* Reynolds, Morgan Inc.

Alphin, Elaine Marie. Germ Hunter: A Story about Louis Pasteur. Verstraete, Elaine, illus. 2003. (Creative Minds Biography Ser.). 64p. (J). lib. bdg. 22.60 *(978-1-57505-179-6(6)*, Carolrhoda Bks.); (ENG.). (gr. 4-8). per. 9.99 *(978-0-87614-929-4(8)*, 136cda8a-5a1e-4dc9-9e0b-6b7431df4759) Lerner Publishing Group.

Ariel, A. D. Saving Lives the Story of Louis Pasteur. 2016. (Spring Forward Ser.). (J). (gr. 2). *(978-1-4900-9478-6(4))* Benchmark Education Co.

Dacquino, V. T. Louis Pasteur. 2011. (Early Connections Ser.). (J). *(978-1-61672-618-8(0))* Benchmark Education Co.

Dickmann, Nancy. Louis Pasteur: Germ Destroyer, 1 vol. 2015. (Superheroes of Science Ser.). (ENG., Illus.). 48p. (J). (gr. 6-6). pap. 15.05 *(978-1-4824-3141-4(6)*, 90c6c99a-0079-4ea0-9324-0dc84b350ca5) Stevens, Gareth Publishing LLLP.

Fandel, Jennifer. Louis Pasteur. 2003. (World Was Never the Same Ser.). (J). *(978-1-58417-266-6(5))* Lake Street Pubs.

Fandel, Jennifer & Barnett, Charles, III. Louis Pasteur & Pasteurization. Wilson, Keith, illus. 2007. (Inventions & Discovery Ser.). (ENG.). 32p. (J). (gr. 3-9). pap. 8.10 *(978-0-7368-7896-8(3)*, 93893, Capstone Pr.) Capstone.

Kjelle, Marylou Morano. Louis Pasteur: Fighter Against Contagious Disease. 2005. (Uncharted, Unexplored, & Unexplained Ser.). (Illus.). 48p. (J). (gr. 4-8). lib. bdg. 29.95 *(978-1-58415-363-4(6)*, 1244912) Mitchell Lane Pubs.

Vander Hook, Sue. Louis Pasteur: Groundbreaking Chemist & Biologist, 1 vol. 2011. (Essential Lives Set 6 Ser.). (ENG., Illus.). 112p. (J). (gr. 6-12). lib. bdg. 41.36 *(978-1-61714-783-8(4)*, 6731, Essential Library) ABDO Publishing Co.

Warren, Harvey. Louis Pasteur, Vol. 11. 2018. (Scientists & Their Discoveries Ser.). (Illus.). 96p. (J). (gr. 7). lib. bdg. 34.60 *(978-1-4222-4033-5(9))* Mason Crest.

Wasmer Smith, Linda. Louis Pasteur: Genius Disease Fighter, 1 vol. 2014. (Genius Scientists & Their Genius Ideas Ser.). (ENG.). 96p. (gr. 5-5). 29.60 *(978-0-7660-6575-8(8)*, 1caafcef-6933-4d89-a0a7-dfa51ab0bfd5); pap. 13.88 *(978-0-7660-6576-5(6)*, 1d5493be-8ec4-4f56-9eed-c81e0d260546) Enslow Publishing, LLC.

Zamosky, Lisa. Louis Pasteur & the Fight Against Germs, 1 vol. rev. ed. 2007. (Science: Informational Text Ser.). (ENG.). 32p. (gr. 3-6). pap. 12.99 *(978-0-7439-0588-6(1))* Teacher Created Materials, Inc.

PASTEUR, LOUIS, 1822-1895—FICTION

Malkus, Alida Sims. The Story of Louis Pasteur. Meadowcroft, Enid Lamonte, ed. Spier, Jo, illus. 2011. 190p. 42.95 *(978-1-258-05476-2(0))* Literary Licensing, LLC.

PASTIMES

see Amusements; Games; Recreation; Sports

PASTORS

see Clergy

PASTRY

Beery, Barbara. Pink Princess Cookbook, 1 vol. Snortum, Marty, photos by. 2006. (ENG., Illus.). 64p. (J). (gr. -1-3). spiral bd. 14.99 *(978-1-4236-0173-9(4))* Gibbs Smith, Publisher.

Patchett, Fiona, et al. Children's Book of Baking. Allman, Howard, photos by. 2007. (Children's Cooking Ser.). (ENG., Illus.). 96p. (J). 17.99 *(978-0-7945-1438-9(3)*, Usborne) EDC Publishing.

Price, Pamela S. Cool Pies & Tarts: Easy Recipes for Kids to Bake. 2010. (Cool Baking Ser.). (ENG.). 32p. (J). (gr. 3-6). 34.21 *(978-1-60453-778-9(7)*, 4610, Checkerboard Library) ABDO Publishing Co.

PATHOLOGICAL PSYCHOLOGY

see Psychology, Pathological

PATHOLOGY

see also Bacteriology; Immunity; Medicine

Allman, Toney. The Medical Examiner, 1 vol. 2006. (Crime Scene Investigations Ser.). (ENG., Illus.). 104p. (gr. 7-7). lib. bdg. 42.03 *(978-1-59018-912-2(4)*, ae2c1fbd-f357-4f86-b570-7728f1dbeb83, Lucent Pr.) Greenhaven Publishing LLC.

Brezina, Corona. Careers as a Medical Examiner. (Careers in Forensics Ser.). 64p. (gr. 5-5). 2009. 58.50 *(978-1-61511-799-4(7)*, Rosen Reference) 2008. (ENG., Illus.). (J). lib. bdg. 37.13 *(978-1-4042-1347-0(3)*, 5559df5e-914e-48e2-b6d6-18de6e33a566) Rosen Publishing Group, Inc., The.

Hyde, Natalie. What Is Germ Theory?, 1 vol. 2010. (Shaping Modern Science Ser.). (ENG.). 64p. (J). (gr. 5-8). pap. *(978-0-7787-7208-8(X))* Crabtree Publishing Co.

Jeffrey, Gary. Autopsies: Pathologists at Work. 2009. (Graphic Forensic Science Ser.). (ENG.). 48p. (YA). (gr. 5-5). 58.50 *(978-1-61512-941-6(3)*, Rosen Reference) Rosen Publishing Group, Inc., The.

Langwith, Jacqueline, ed. Birth Defects, 1 vol. 2010. (Perspectives on Diseases & Disorders Ser.). (ENG., Illus.). 160p. (gr. 10-12). 40.58 *(978-0-7377-4787-4(0)*, baa540fd-208f-428a-b5d0-181ab7e51e08, Greenhaven Publishing) Greenhaven Publishing LLC.

—Hepatitis, 1 vol. 2009. (Perspectives on Diseases & Disorders Ser.). (ENG., Illus.). 168p. (gr. 10-12). 45.93 *(978-0-7377-4553-5(3)*,

1529f0f6-85c1-4ad4-9786-3e750b974c71, Greenhaven Publishing) Greenhaven Publishing LLC.
Moe, Barbara. Coping with PMS (Premenstrual Syndrome) 2009. (Coping Ser.). 192p. (gr. 7-12). 63.90 *(978-1-61512-007-9(6))* Rosen Publishing Group, Inc., The.
—Coping with Tourette's Syndrome & Other Tic Disorders. 2009. (Coping Ser.). 192p. (gr. 7-12). 63.90 *(978-1-61512-016-1(5))* Rosen Publishing Group, Inc., The.
Newman, Michael E. Soft Tissue Sarcomas, 1 vol. 2011. (Cancer & Modern Science Ser.). (ENG.). 64p. (J). (gr. 5-5). lib. bdg. 37.13 *(978-1-4488-1307-0(7),* 80d736b2-7524-42c6-bca1-1a34d9b9c83c) Rosen Publishing Group, Inc., The.
Roza, Greg. What Happens When I Throw Up?, 1 vol. 2013. (My Body Does Strange Stuff! Ser.). (ENG., Illus.). 24p. (J). (gr. 1-2). pap. 9.15 *(978-1-4339-9353-4(8),* 920ff87f-1e87-4110-976a-284933b1750f); lib. bdg. 25.27 *(978-1-4339-9352-7(X),* 2bfe8121-ac3a-499b-a2c8-f15357a57e76) Stevens, Gareth Publishing LLLP.
Stair, Nancy L. Choosing a Career in Mortuary Science & the Funeral Industry. 2009. (World of Work Ser.). 64p. (gr. 5-5). 58.50 *(978-1-60854-333-5(1))* Rosen Publishing Group, Inc., The.
Stefoff, Rebecca. Forensics & Medicine, 1 vol. 2011. (Forensic Science Investigated Ser.). (ENG., Illus.). 80p. (gr. 5-7). lib. bdg. 36.93 *(978-0-7614-4143-4(3),* b44cc801-3e57-4872-aae2-88876aad0a36) Cavendish Square Publishing LLC.
Walker, Maryalice. Pathology. Noziglia, Carla Miller & Siegel, Jay A., eds. 2013. (Solving Crimes with Science: Forensics Ser.: 12). (Illus.). 112p. (J). (gr. 7-18). 22.95 *(978-1-4222-2872-2(X))* Mason Crest.
What Happens When I Throw Up? 2013. (My Body Does Strange Stuff! Ser.). 24p. (J). (gr. 1-3). pap. 48.90 *(978-1-4339-9354-1(6))* Stevens, Gareth Publishing LLLP.
Williams, Linda D. Forensics & Medicine. 2008. (J). *(978-0-7614-3079-7(2))* Marshall Cavendish.

PATRICK, SAINT, 373?-463?

Bilinsky, Cornelia Mary. Patrick & the Fire: A Legend about Saint Patrick. Coburn, Maggie, illus. 2017. 25p. (J). pap. *(978-0-8198-6037-8(9))* Pauline Bks. & Media.
dePaola, Tomie. Saint Patrick. 2019. (Illus.). 24p. (J). (— 1). bds. 7.99 *(978-0-8234-4235-5(7))* Holiday Hse., Inc.
Driscoll, Christ. And God Blessed the Irish: The Story of Patrick. Kelley, Patrick, illus. 2007. 59p. (J). (gr. 3-7). 14.95 *(978-1-929039-40-1(9))* Ambassador Bks., Inc.
Landau, Elaine. Celebrating St. Patrick's Day, 1 vol. 2012. (Celebrating Holidays Ser.). (ENG.). 48p. (gr. 3-3). 27.93 *(978-0-7660-4035-9(6),* 6b099526-2d3e-4bc0-82f5-f2aade72fe22, Enslow Elementary) Enslow Publishing, LLC.
Simms, George Otto. Saint Patrick: Ireland's Patron Saint. Rooney, David, illus. 3rd rev. ed. 2004. (Exploring Ser.). (ENG.). 104p. pap. 8.95 *(978-0-86278-749-3(1))* O'Brien Pr., Ltd., The. IRL. Dist: Dufour Editions, Inc.

PATRICK, SAINT, 373?-463?—FICTION

Smith, Sherry. The Wolf & the Shield: An Adventure with Saint Patrick. McNally, Nicholas, illus. 2016. 118p. (J). pap. *(978-0-8198-8356-8(5))* Pauline Bks. & Media.
Stengel, Joyce. St. Patrick & the Three Brave Mice, 1 vol. Leonhard, Herb, illus. 2009. (ENG.). 32p. (J). (gr. k-3). 16.99 *(978-1-58980-663-4(8),* Pelican Publishing) Arcadia Publishing.

PATRIOTIC SONGS

see National Songs

PATRIOTISM

ABDO Publishing Company Staff, et al. United We Stand, Set. 2003. (United We Stand Ser.: 4). (Illus.). (J). (gr. k-3). lib. bdg. 96.84 *(978-1-57765-876-4(0),* SandCastle) ABDO Publishing Co.
Adams, Michelle Medlock. What Is America? Wummer, Amy, illus. 2019. (What Is... ? Ser.). (ENG.). 22p. (J). (gr. -1-1). bds. 7.99 *(978-0-8249-1695-4(6),* Worthy Kids/Ideals) Worthy Publishing.
Amoroso, Cynthia. Patriotism. 2018. (Illus.). 24p. (J). *(978-1-4896-6075-6(5),* AV2 by Weigl) Weigl Pubs., Inc.
Borgert-Spaniol, Megan. Super Simple Presidents' Day Activities: Fun & Easy Holiday Projects for Kids. 2017. (Super Simple Holidays Ser.). (ENG., Illus.). 32p. (J). (gr. k-4). lib. bdg. 34.21 *(978-1-5321-1246-1(7),* 27633, Super SandCastle) ABDO Publishing Co.
Jackson, Cody. Pint-Sized Patriots. 2012. (J). 24.95 *(978-1-937084-51-6(5),* BQB Publishing) Boutique of Quality Books Publishing Co., Inc.
Kishel, Ann-Marie. U. S. Symbols. 2007. (First Step Nonfiction - Government Ser.). (ENG., Illus.). 24p. (gr. k-2). lib. bdg. 23.93 *(978-0-8225-6394-5(0),* Lerner Pubns.) Lerner Publishing Group.
LaMachia, John. So What Is Patriotism Anyway? 2009. (Student's Guide to American Civics Ser.). 48p. (gr. 5-8). 53.00 *(978-1-61511-240-1(5),* Rosen Reference) Rosen Publishing Group, Inc., The.
Manolis, Kay & Leslie, Tonya. Thomas Jefferson: A Life of Patriotism. 2007. (People of Character Ser.). (ENG., Illus.). 24p. (J). (gr. 2-5). lib. bdg. 26.95 *(978-1-60014-093-8(9))* Bellwether Media.
Peter, Val J. & Dowd, Tom. The Girls & Boys Town Book on Patriotism: Grades 7-12. 2004. 76p. pap. 25.95 *(978-1-889322-52-0(0),* 48-318T) Boys Town Pr.
Scheunemann, Pam. Patriotism. 2003. (United We Stand Ser.). (ENG., Illus.). 24p. (J). (gr. k-3). lib. bdg. 24.21 *(978-1-57765-880-1(9),* SandCastle) ABDO Publishing Co.
Stone, Tanya Lee. A Is for America: A Patriotic Alphabet Book. Kelley, Gerald, illus. 2011. 24p. (J). (gr. -1-k). mass mkt. 6.99 *(978-0-8431-9877-5(X),* Price Stern Sloan) Penguin Young Readers Group.
Stout, Carol A. Proud to Be an American, 1. 2004. (Illus.). 168p. pap. 6.95 *(978-1-886161-08-5(9))* Millennium Marketing & Publishing.
Warner, Roxie & Warner, Christian. Land of the Free, A to Z. Schartup, Adam, illus. 2014. (J). *(978-1-62086-801-0(6))* Amplify Publishing Group.
Webster, Christine. The Pledge of Allegiance. 2003. (Cornerstones of Freedom Ser.). (ENG., Illus.). 48p. (J). (gr. 4-6). 26.00 *(978-0-516-22674-3(6),* Children's Pr.) Scholastic Library Publishing.

PATRIOTISM—POETRY

Martin, Bill, Jr. & Sampson, Michael. I Pledge Allegiance. Raschka, Chris, illus. 2004. (ENG.). 40p. (J). (gr. 1-4). reprint ed. pap. 9.99 *(978-0-7636-2527-6(2))* Candlewick Pr.

PATTON, GEORGE S. (GEORGE SMITH), 1885-1945

Stanley, George E. George S. Patton: War Hero. Henderson, Meryl, illus. 2007. (Childhood of Famous Americans Ser.). (ENG.). 192p. (J). (gr. 3-7). pap. 7.99 *(978-1-4169-1547-8(8),* Simon & Schuster/Paula Wiseman Bks.) Simon & Schuster/Paula Wiseman Bks.
Sutcliffe, Jane. George S. Patton JR. 2006. (History Maker Bios Ser.). (Illus.). 48p. (J). (gr. 3-7). lib. bdg. 26.60 *(978-0-8225-2436-6(8),* Lerner Pubns.) Lerner Publishing Group.

PAUL, THE APOSTLE, SAINT

Dowley, Tim. Paul's Travels, 1 vol. 2010. (Candle Discovery Ser.). (Illus.). 28p. (J). (gr. 2-7). 14.99 *(978-0-8254-7383-8(7),* Candle Bks.) Lion Hudson PLC GBR. Dist: Kregel Pubns.
Fisher, Nancy. Take Your Students on a Cruise: Paul's Journeys Lesson Guide. Witte, Carol, ed. Hall, Beverly H., illus. 2004. 40p. (gr. 4-8). wbk. ed. 9.95 *(978-1-890947-00-2(8),* 308X) Rose Publishing.
Hartman, Bob & Gempf, Conrad. Paul, Man on a Mission: The Life & Letters of an Adventurer for Jesus, 1 vol. Smith, Dave, illus. 2017. (ENG.). 160p. (J). (gr. 4-6). pap. 11.99 *(978-0-7459-7739-3(1),* 00563eda-3515-415e-8848-9e40beb90637, Lion Children's) Lion Hudson PLC GBR. Dist: Baker & Taylor Publisher Services (BTPS).
Hill, Mary Lea. Saint Paul: The Thirteenth Apostle. Archambault, Matthew, illus. 2008. (Encounter the Saints Ser.: 22). 117p. (J). (gr. 3-7). per. 7.95 *(978-0-8198-7102-2(8))* Pauline Bks. & Media.
Hovland, Stephenie. Lydia Believes. Dorenkamp Repa, Michelle, illus. 2014. (Arch Bks.). (ENG.). 16p. (J). (gr. k-4). pap. 2.49 *(978-0-7586-4607-1(0))* Concordia Publishing Hse.
Jones, Rufus Matthew. St. Paul the Hero. 2007. (J). pap. *(978-1-59731-350-6(5))* Perennis, Sophia.
The Journey's of Paul. Date not set. (J). stu. ed., act. bk. ed. 1.49 *(978-0-88271-232-1(2),* 1748) Regina Pr., Malhame & Co.
Lumsden, Colin, illus. People in the Life of Paul. 2003. (Bible Colour & Learn Ser.). 32p. pap. 2.50 *(978-1-903087-50-3(3))* DayOne Pubns. GBR. Dist: Send The Light Distribution LLC.
—Story of Paul. 2003. (Bible Colour & Learn Ser.). 32p. pap. 2.50 *(978-1-903087-46-6(5))* DayOne Pubns. GBR. Dist: Send The Light Distribution LLC.
MacKenzie, Carine. Paul: The Wise Preacher. rev. ed. 2014. (Bible Time Ser.). (ENG.). 32p. (J). pap. 4.50 *(978-1-84550-382-6(1),* 1200487c-9f0a-420d-81cf-78ada5f91798) Christian Focus Pubns. GBR. Dist: Baker & Taylor Publisher Services (BTPS).
Miles, David. Paul Meets Jesus, 1 vol. 2016. (I Can Read! / Adventure Bible Ser.). (ENG., Illus.). 32p. (J). pap. 4.99 *(978-0-310-75076-5(8))* Zonderkidz.
Moore, Alan & Tavner, Gill. Paul of Tarsus. Donnelly, Karen, illus. 2014. (New Testament Ser.). (ENG.). 64p. pap. 7.95 *(978-1-906230-29-6(3))* Real Reads Ltd. GBR. Dist: Casemate Pubs. & Bk. Distributors, LLC.
Neeley, Deta Petersen & Neeley, Nathan Glen. Paul of Tarsus, V2: A Child's Story of the New Testament. 2011. 152p. 41.95 *(978-1-258-07519-4(9))* Literary Licensing, LLC.
Self, David. Saint Paul, 1 vol. Cockcroft, Jason, illus. 2009. 48p. (J). (gr. 2-7). 14.95 *(978-0-8254-7906-9(1),* Lion Children's) Lion Hudson PLC GBR. Dist: Kregel Pubns.
Selucky, Oldrich. Adventures of Saint Paul. Trouvé, Marianne Lorraine, tr. from CZE. Krejcova, Zdenka, illus. 2008. Orig. Title: Pavel, dobrudruh Viry. 96p. (J). (gr. 1-3). pap. *(978-0-8198-0786-1(9))* Pauline Bks. & Media.
Warner Press Kids, creator. Paul, a Servant of Jesus: Activity Book. 2008. 16p. (J). (gr. -1-3). pap. 11.34 *(978-1-59317-327-2(X))* Warner Pr., Inc.

PAUL, THE APOSTLE, SAINT—FICTION

Gormally, Eleanor. St Paul: The Man with the Letters. 2010. (ENG., Illus.). 32p. (J). pap. 16.95 *(978-1-84730-177-2(0))* Veritas Pubns. IRL. Dist: Casemate Pubs. & Bk. Distributors, LLC.
Hernandez, David. The Mighty Armor, 1 vol., 2. 2003. (Adventures of Toby Digz Ser.: 2). (ENG., Illus.). 96p. (YA). pap. 5.99 *(978-1-4003-0196-6(3),* Tommy Nelson) Nelson, Thomas Inc.

PAVLOVA, ANNA, 1885-1931

Allman, Barbara & Haas, Shelly O. Dance of the Swan: A Story about Anna Pavlova. 2006. (Creative Minds Biographies Ser.). (Illus.). 64p. (J). (gr. 4-8). lib. bdg. 22.60 *(978-1-57505-463-6(9))* Lerner Publishing Group.
Snyder, Laurel. Swan: The Life & Dance of Anna Pavlova. Morstad, Julie, illus. 2015. (ENG.). 52p. (J). (gr. 1-4). 17.99 *(978-1-4521-1890-1(6))* Chronicle Bks. LLC.

PEACE

see also Disarmament; Security, International; War

Agnew, Kate, ed. War & Peace: A Collection of Classic Poetry & Prose. 2011. (ENG.). 176p. (J). (gr. 7). 9.95 *(978-1-84046-570-9(0),* Wizard Books) Icon Bks., Ltd. GBR. Dist: Publishers Group West (PGW).
Center for Learning Staff. Justice & Peace. 2007. (Religion Ser.). 124p. (YA). spiral bd. 18.95 *(978-1-56077-795-3(8))* Center for Learning, The.
Darraj, Susan Muaddi. Mairead Corrigan & Betty Williams. 2006. (ENG., Illus.). 106p. (gr. 9-12). lib. bdg. 30.00 *(978-0-7910-9001-5(9),* P114508, Facts On File) Infobase Holdings, Inc.
Dawson, Eric David. Putting Peace First: 7 Commitments to Change the World. 2018. (Illus.). 160p. (J). (gr. 5). pap. 9.99 *(978-1-101-99733-8(8),* Viking Books for Young Readers) Penguin Young Readers Group.
Fish, Sandra Palmer. S E W for Peace. 2007. 48p. pap. 19.05 *(978-0-9722839-7-7(8))* Just Write Bks.
Friedman-Brunt, Elyse. Conflict Resolution in American History, Gr. 8: Lessons from the Past, Lessons for Today. Chandler, Terrence, illus. 2003. 48p. (YA). pap., wbk. ed. 19.95 *(978-1-878227-89-8(0))* Peace Education Foundation.
—Conflict Resolution in American History, Grade 8: Lessons from the Past, Lessons for Today. Chandler, Terrence, illus. 2003. 200p. pap., instr.'s training gde. ed. 29.95 *(978-1-878227-88-1(2))* Peace Education Foundation.
Gottfried, Ted. The Fight for Peace: A History of Antiwar Movements in America. 2005. (People's History Ser.). (ENG., Illus.). 136p. (gr. 5-12). lib. bdg. 33.26 *(978-0-7613-2932-9(3))* Lerner Publishing Group.
Haerens, Margaret, ed. World Peace, 1 vol. 2015. (Opposing Viewpoints Ser.). (ENG., Illus.). 248p. (gr. 10-12). 50.43 *(978-0-7377-7304-0(9),* 48a1ab28-44c5-4d2f-ae23-8ccf01e272c0, Greenhaven Publishing) Greenhaven Publishing LLC.
Harcourt School Publishers Staff. Leaders for Peace. 3rd ed. 2003. (Horizons Ser.). (Illus.). (J). (gr. 3). pap. 5.50 *(978-0-15-333278-4(6))* Harcourt Sch. Pubs.
Hess, Ingrid. Walk in Peace. 2009. (ENG.). 44p. (J). (gr. -1-k). pap. 13.99 *(978-0-8361-9469-2(1))* Herald Pr.
Hoffman, Mary. Lines in the Sand: New Writing on War & Peace. Lassiter, Rhiannon, ed. 2003. (ENG., Illus.). 288p. (J). (gr. 2-18). pap. 8.95 *(978-0-9729529-1-0(8))* Disinformation Co. Ltd., The.
Kerley, Barbara. A Little Peace. 2007. (Barbara Kerley Photo Inspirations Ser.). (Illus.). 32p. (J). (gr. -1-k). 16.95 *(978-1-4263-0086-8(7),* National Geographic Children's Bks.) Disney Publishing Worldwide.
Lampen, John. The Peace Kit. 2nd ed. 2007. (ENG., Illus.). 84p. per. *(978-0-85245-372-8(8))* Quaker Books.
Ogden, Charlie. Peace & War. 2017. (Our Values - Level 3 Ser.). (Illus.). 32p. (J). (gr. 5-6). *(978-0-7787-3738-4(1))* Crabtree Publishing Co.
Promoting Peace - Puppet Scripts Manual. 2005. (J). spiral bd. *(978-0-9768827-4-9(4))* Prevention Through Puppetry, Inc.
Promoting Peace - Student Workbook. 2005. (J). spiral bd. *(978-0-9768827-3-2(6))* Prevention Through Puppetry, Inc.
Radunsky, Vladimir. What Does Peace Feel Like? Radunsky, Vladimir, illus. 2004. (ENG., Illus.). 24p. (J). (gr. -1-3). 19.99 *(978-0-689-86676-0(3),* Atheneum Bks. for Young Readers) Simon & Schuster Children's Publishing.
Rivera, Sheila. Treaties & Resolutions. 2003. (World in Conflict-the Middle East Ser.). 32p. (gr. 4-8). 27.07 *(978-1-59197-420-8(8),* Abdo & Daughters) ABDO Publishing Co.
Robeson, Susan. Grandpa Stops a War: A Paul Robeson Story. Brown, Rod, illus. 2019. 32p. (J). (gr. k-4). 17.95 *(978-1-60980-882-2(7),* Triangle Square) Seven Stories Pr.
Selling, Rebecca. Plant a Seed of Peace. Rothshank, Brooke, illus. 2007. 115p. (J). (gr. 3-7). per. 15.99 *(978-0-8361-9397-8(0))* Faith & Life Pr.
Shah, Syeda Mieeha. Peace in My World. 2017. (ENG., Illus.). (J). (gr. -1-3). pap. 9.95 *(978-1-947825-34-5(8))* Yorkshire Publishing Group.
Short, Robyn & Williams, Nanon McKewn. Peace People. Bailey, Lindsey, illus. 2013. 38p. 18.95 *(978-0-9911148-2-5(5))* Goodmedia Communications, LLC.
Skoor, Susan. The Lion & the Lamb. Shipley, Marie, illus. 2003. (ENG.). (J). pap. 12.95 *(978-0-8309-1068-7(9))* Herald Publishing Hse.
Steele, Philip. Afghanistan: From War to Peace?, 1 vol. 2012. (Our World Divided Ser.). (ENG., Illus.). 48p. (J). (gr. 5-5). 34.47 *(978-1-4488-6030-2(X),* 1ea67c4c-2740-4170-b913-9c788a9bc782, Rosen Reference) Rosen Publishing Group, Inc., The.
Tor, Regina, et al. Growing Toward Peace. 2011. 90p. 38.95 *(978-1-258-02528-1(0))* Literary Licensing, LLC.
Walker, Niki. Why Do We Fight? Conflict, War, & Peace. 2019. (ENG., Illus.). 80p. (J). pap. 14.95 *(978-1-77147-354-5(1))* Owlkids Bks. Inc. CAN. Dist: Publishers Group West (PGW).
Walter, Virginia A. War & Peace: A Guide to Literature & New Media, Grades 4-8, 1 vol. 2006. (Children's & Young Adult Literature Reference Ser.). (ENG.). 288p. pap. 50.00 *(978-1-59158-271-7(7),* 900322242, Libraries Unlimited) ABC-CLIO, LLC.
Wilson, Janet, illus. One Peace: True Stories of Young Activists, 1 vol. 2008. (ENG.). 52p. (J). (gr. 4-7). 19.95 *(978-1-55143-892-4(5))* Orca Bk. Pubs. USA.
Winter, Jonah. Peaceful Heroes. Addy, Sean, illus. 2009. (J). pap. *(978-0-439-62308-7(1),* Levine, Arthur A. Bks.) Scholastic, Inc.
Yoder, Suzana E. Sensing Peace. 2010. (ENG., Illus.). 32p. (J). pap. 13.99 *(978-0-8361-9515-6(9))* Herald Pr.

PEACE—FICTION

Avignone, June. A Peek into the Secret Little Ones of Turtle Back Island. My Wolf Dog, illus. 2004. 40p. (J). pap. *(978-0-9654628-2-2(X))* Mill Street Forward, The.
Backer, Charles. Fireclaw. 2010. 288p. pap. 15.49 *(978-1-4520-1229-2(6))* AuthorHouse.
Baskwill, Jane. If Peace Is... Carter, Stephanie, illus. 2003. (J). 23p. pap. 7.95 *(978-1-59034-449-1(9));* 24p. (gr. 11-18). 15.95 *(978-1-59034-448-4(0))* Mondo Publishing.
Berenstain, Mike. The Berenstain Bears Blessed Are the Peacemakers, 1 vol. 2014. (Berenstain Bears/Living Lights: a Faith Story Ser.). (ENG.). 24p. (J). pap. 5.99 *(978-0-310-73481-9(9))* Zonderkidz.
Carter, Cathy. You Are My Very Best Friend: The Adventures of Mike & Gabe (in English & Spanish) 2012. 26p. 24.95 *(978-1-4626-7072-7(5))* America Star Bks.
Charters, Jane. The General. Foreman, Michael, illus. 2010. (ENG.). 48p. (J). (gr. k-3). 16.99 *(978-0-7636-4875-6(2),* Templar) Candlewick Pr.
Crawford, Quinton Douglass. Moochie the Soochie Visits the Peace People. 2007. (ENG.). 29p. 12.50 *(978-0-615-14879-3(4))* Crawford, Quinton Douglass.
Doodler, Todd H. Peas on Earth. 2012. (Illus.). 20p. (J). (gr. -1 — 1). 6.99 *(978-0-307-93088-0(2),* Robin Corey Bks.) Random Hse. Children's Bks.
Eshleman, Catherine, et al. Perry Passyflyer. 2012. 24p. pap. 17.99 *(978-1-4685-9571-0(7))* AuthorHouse.
Hoffelt, Jane. We Share One World. Husted, Marty, illus. 2004. 32p. (J). per. 15.95 *(978-0-9701907-8-9(6))* Illumination Arts Publishing Co., Inc.
Jacobson, John. The Quest: Adventure Story & Songs. Wilson, Roberta, illus. 2005. (ENG.). 48p. pap. 12.95 incl. audio compact disk *(978-1-4234-0019-6(4),* 09970931) Leonard, Hal Corp.
Katz, Karen. Can You Say Peace? 2016. (J). lib. bdg. 18.40 *(978-0-606-38444-5(8))* Turtleback.
Krall, Dan. The Great Lollipop Caper. Krall, Dan, illus. 2013. (ENG., Illus.). 48p. (J). (gr. -1-3). 16.99 *(978-1-4424-4460-7(6),* Simon & Schuster Bks. For Young Readers) Simon & Schuster Bks. For Young Readers.
Kriescher, Jeanette "Netty". A Big Message from a Little Book: A Color-Blind World. 2008. 25p. pap. 24.95 *(978-1-60563-376-3(3))* America Star Bks.
Lanagan, Margo. Tintinnabula. Cai, Rovina, illus. 2018. (ENG.). 24p. (J). (gr. k-2). 19.99 *(978-1-74297-525-2(9))* Little Hare Bks. AUS. Dist: Independent Pubs. Group.
LeBox, Annette. Peace Is an Offering. Graegin, Stephanie, illus. 2015. 40p. (J). (gr. -1-k). 17.99 *(978-0-8037-4091-4(3),* Dial Bks) Penguin Young Readers Group.
Linden, Dianne. Shimmerdogs, 1 vol. 2008. (ENG.). 176p. (J). pap. 10.95 *(978-1-897235-37-9(2))* Thistledown Pr., Ltd. CAN. Dist: Univ. of Toronto Pr.
McKee, David. Six Men. 2011. (ENG., Illus.). 44p. (J). (gr. -1-3). 16.95 *(978-0-7358-4050-8(4))* North-South Bks., Inc.
Mulder, Michelle. Yeny & the Children for Peace, 1 vol. 2008. (Kids' Power Book Ser.: 2). (ENG., Illus.). 118p. (J). (gr. 3-8). pap. 14.95 *(978-1-897187-45-6(9),* 1897187459) Second Story Pr. CAN. Dist: Orca Bk. Pubs. USA.
Norsgaard, E. Jaediker. How Krokken & Poppen Made Peace. 2008. 31p. pap. 24.95 *(978-1-60672-426-2(6))* America Star Bks.
Parr, todd. The Peace Book. (ENG.). (J). (gr. -1 — 1). 2017. Illus.). 22p. bds. 7.99 *(978-0-316-51077-6(7))* 2009. (Illus.). 32p. pap. 8.99 *(978-0-316-04349-6(4))* 2005. 32p. 14.99 *(978-0-316-05962-6(5))* Little, Brown Bks. for Young Readers.
—The Peace Book. Parr, todd, illus. 2019. (Todd Parr Picture Bks.). (ENG., Illus.). 32p. (J). (gr. -1-2). 31.36 *(978-1-5321-4377-9(X),* 31827, Picture Bk.) Spotlight.
Schaefer, Lola M. The Bear & the Star: A Winter & Holiday Book for Kids. Andersen, Bethanne, illus. 2019. (ENG.). 40p. (J). (gr. -1-3). 17.99 *(978-0-06-266037-4(3),* Greenwillow Bks.) HarperCollins Pubs.
Skelton, Vonda Skinner. Bitsy & the Mystery at Amelia Island. 2005. (Bitsy Burroughs Mysteries Ser.). 183p. (J). (gr. 3-7). per. 8.95 *(978-1-57072-307-0(9),* Silver Dagger Mysteries) Overmountain Pr.
Stella, Pilar. Seeking Serenity. Cummings, Maris, illus. 2008. (J). (gr. -1-3). pap. 17.95 *(978-1-60037-451-7(4))* Morgan James Publishing.
Stevens, Cat. Peace Train. Reynolds, Peter H., illus. 2021. (ENG.). 40p. (J). (gr. -1-3). 18.99 *(978-0-06-305399-1(3),* HarperCollins) HarperCollins Pubs.
Syed, Jaweria T. Enchantment Realm's First Adventure. 2012. 94p. 24.99 *(978-1-4771-1695-1(8));* pap. 15.99 *(978-1-4771-1694-4(X))* Xlibris Corp.
Tutu, Desmond & Abrams, Douglas Carlton. God's Dream. Pham, LeUyen, illus. 2010. (ENG.). 32p. (J). (— 1). bds. 8.99 *(978-0-7636-4742-1(X))* Candlewick Pr.
Woodson, Jacqueline. Peace, Locomotion. (ENG.). (J). 2010. 176p. (gr. 5-18). 8.99 *(978-0-14-241512-2(X),* Puffin Books) 2009. 144p. (gr. 4-6). 22.44 *(978-0-399-24655-5(X))* Penguin Young Readers Group.
Young, Lena. Karma: Reaping What We Sow. Tsai, Dora, illus. 2005. 26p. (J). pap. *(978-1-933554-00-6(2))* Primordia.

PEACE CORPS (U.S.)

Gallagher, Diane Shugrue, et al. Lives of Service: Stories from the Peace Corps. 2014. (Text Connections Ser.). (J). (gr. 6). *(978-1-4900-1524-8(8))* Benchmark Education Co.
Suen, Anastasia. El Cuerpo de Paz, 1 vol. 2003. (Organizaciones de Ayuda (Helping Organizations) Ser.). (SPA., Illus.). 24p. (J). (gr. 2-2). lib. bdg. 26.27 *(978-0-8239-6859-6(6),* d9b0e6ab-98c1-4565-8839-4925e72b2718) Rosen Publishing Group, Inc., The.
—El Cuerpo de Paz (the Peace Corps) 2009. (Organizaciones de ayuda (Helping Organizations) Ser.). (SPA.). 24p. (gr. 2-2). 42.50 *(978-1-60851-144-0(8),* Editorial Buenas Letras) Rosen Publishing Group, Inc., The.
—The Peace Corps. 2009. (Helping Organizations Ser.). 24p. (gr. 2-2). 42.50 *(978-1-61513-261-4(9),* PowerKids Pr.) Rosen Publishing Group, Inc., The.
Vandegrift, Tom. 24 New Moons. 2003. 429p. (YA). pap. 20.95 *(978-0-7414-1503-5(8))* Infinity Publishing.
Wimmer, Teresa. Peace Corps. 2016. (Agents of Government Ser.). (ENG.). 48p. (J). (gr. 4-7). pap. 12.00 *(978-1-62832-150-0(4),* 20850, Creative Paperbacks) Creative Co., The.

PEACOCKS

Bodden, Valerie. Le Paon. 2018. (Planète Animaux Ser.). (FRE., Illus.). 24p. (J). *(978-1-77092-395-9(0),* 19684) Creative Co., The.
—Peacocks. 2018. (Amazing Animals Ser.). (ENG., Illus.). 24p. (J). (gr. 1-3). pap. 8.99 *(978-1-62832-497-6(X),* 19631, Creative Paperbacks); *(978-1-60818-881-9(7),* 19633, Creative Education) Creative Co., The.
Borgert-Spaniol, Megan. Peacocks. 2013. (Animal Safari Ser.). (ENG., Illus.). 24p. (J). (gr. k-3). lib. bdg. 26.95 *(978-1-60014-914-6(6),* Blastoff! Readers) Bellwether Media.
Buckingham, Suzanne. Meet the Peacock. (Scales & Tails Ser.). 24p. (gr. 2-3). 2009. 42.50 *(978-1-60852-984-1(3))* 2008. (ENG., Illus.). (J). lib. bdg. 26.27 *(978-1-4042-4503-7(0),* 3b8a1693-538a-45d5-a5d7-9a2592c3a4fb) Rosen Publishing Group, Inc., The. (PowerKids Pr.).
Gish, Melissa. Peacocks. (Living Wild Ser.). (ENG., Illus.). 48p. (J). (gr. 4-7). 2017. pap. 12.00 *(978-1-62832-303-0(5),* 20618, Creative Paperbacks) 2016. *(978-1-60818-707-2(1),* 20620, Creative Education) Creative Co., The.
Lang, Elliott. Peafowls, Peacocks & Peahens Including Facts & Information about Blue, White, Indian & Green Peacocks Breeding, Owning, Keeping & Raising Pe. 2012. 140p. pap. *(978-0-9566269-9-8(8))* IMB Publishing.
Marsico, Katie. A Peachick Grows Up. 2007. (Scholastic News Nonfiction Readers Ser.). (ENG., Illus.). 24p. (J). (gr. 1-2). pap. 6.95 *(978-0-531-18699-2(7))* Scholastic Library Publishing.
Meister, Cari. Peacocks. 2015. (J). lib. bdg. 25.65 *(978-1-62031-168-4(2),* Bullfrog Bks.) Jump! Inc.
Pohl, Kathleen. Peacocks, 1 vol. 2007. (Animals I See at the Zoo Ser.). (ENG.). 24p. (gr. k-2). pap. 9.15 *(978-0-8368-8228-5(8),* c7bab42a-ee57-4126-9bcf-1185d448093d); (Illus.). lib. bdg.

24.67 (978-0-8368-8221-6(0), 9bb8d50c-8cee-4544-8066-468ef7d6063f) Stevens, Gareth Publishing LLLP. (Weekly Reader Leveled Readers).

—Peacocks / Pavos Reales, 1 vol. 2007. (Animals I See at the Zoo / Animales Que Veo en el Zoológico Ser.). (SPA & ENG.). 24p. (gr. k-2). pap. 9.15 (978-0-8368-8242-1(3), c677da4c-0504-4021-8e9e-65996fa26d62, Weekly Reader Leveled Readers) Stevens, Gareth Publishing LLLP.

Underwood, Deborah. Colorful Peacocks. 2006. (Pull Ahead Bks.). (Illus.). 32p. (J). (gr. 3-7). lib. bdg. 22.60 (978-0-8225-5930-6(7), Lerner Pubns.) Lerner Publishing Group.

PEACOCKS—FICTION

Brightwell, Beverly. Pea Key & Sam. 2012. 20p. pap. 24.95 (978-1-62709-200-5(5)) America Star Bks.

—Pea Key & Sam Go to the State Fair. 2013. 24p. pap. 24.95 (978-1-62709-261-6(7)) America Star Bks.

Chand, Emlyn. Poppy the Proud: A Bird Brain Book. Shaw, Sarah, illus. ed. 2012. (ENG.). 44p. (gr. k-3). 21.95 (978-1-62253-108-0(6)); pap. 10.95 (978-1-62253-120-2(5)) Evolved Publishing.

Curtis, Chary. Fancy & Brandy Peacock. 2005. (J). per. 9.99 (978-1-59879-030-6(7)) Lifevest Publishing, Inc.

Du Bois, Crystal L. God Made My Butt Big. 2012. 24p. pap. 14.93 (978-1-4669-0584-9(0)) Trafford Publishing.

Halverson, Barbara. Farm Friends Forever: Everyone Needs Friends. 2013. (ENG.). 27p. (J). pap. 13.95 (978-1-4787-1380-7(1)) Outskirts Pr., Inc.

Hodgkinson, Leigh. Limelight Larry. Hodgkinson, Leigh, illus. 2011. (ENG., Illus.). 32p. (J). (978-1-58925-102-1(4)) Tiger Tales.

Idle, Molly. Flora & the Peacocks. 2016. (Flora & Friends Ser.). (ENG., Illus.). 40p. (J). (gr. -1-k). 17.99 (978-1-4521-3816-9(8)) Chronicle Bks. LLC.

Johnson, Gillian. Thora & the Incredible Crystals. 2007. (Illus.). 272p. (978-0-207-20017-5(3)) HarperCollins Pubs. Australia.

Jules, Jacqueline. Feathers for Peacock. Cann, Helen, illus. 2016. 28p. (J). (gr. -1-3). 16.95 (978-1-937786-53-3(6), Wisdom Tales) World Wisdom, Inc.

Laminack, Lester L. Three Hens & a Peacock, 1 vol. Cole, Henry, illus. 2014. (ENG.). 32p. (J). (gr. -1-3). pap. 7.99 (978-1-56145-726-7(4)) Peachtree Publishing Co. Inc.

Long, Olivia. The Impossible Peacock. Long, Olivia, illus. Date not set. (Kaleidoscope Ser.). (Illus.). 32p. (J). (gr. -1-4). (978-1-880042-04-5(5)) Shelf-Life Bks.

Nugent, Carly. The Peacock Detectives. 2020. (ENG.). 288p. (J). (gr. 3-7). 16.99 (978-0-06-289670-4(9), HarperCollins) HarperCollins Pubs.

Peet, Bill. The Spooky Tail of Prewitt Peacock. 2015. 32p. pap. 9.00 (978-1-61003-499-9(6)) Center for the Collaborative Classroom.

Schexnayder, Paul, illus. In the Time of Shimmer & Light. 2018. (J). (978-1-946160-29-4(6)) Univ. of Louisiana at Lafayette Pr.

Weber, Roopa. Messy Penny. Szewczyk, Manda, illus. 2013. 38p. pap. 11.99 (978-0-9896966-2-3(6)) Karma Kollection LLC.

Woodson, Rick. Poodles & Thunderchicken. 2012. 40p. pap. 24.95 (978-1-4626-7531-9(X)) America Star Bks.

PEAFOWL

see Peacocks

PEANUTS

Bernard, Jan. Peanut Butter. 2016. (J). (978-1-4896-4537-1(3)) Weigl Pubs., Inc.

Best, B. J. Peanuts to Peanut Butter, 1 vol. 2016. (How It Is Made Ser.). (ENG., Illus.). 24p. (J). (gr. 1-1). pap. 9.22 (978-1-5026-2134-4(7), 20ab7766-9b9a-4091-aaf6-1ee3bd87a790); lib. bdg. 25.93 (978-1-5026-2136-8(3), 2415af4c-4ce7-4ec2-abb9-6e4bcf20bd2e) Cavendish Square Publishing LLC.

Della Casa, Chef Luca, contrib. by. No Peanuts, No Problem! Easy & Delecious Nut-Free Recipes for Kids with Allergies. 2016. (Allergy Aware Cookbooks Ser.). (ENG., Illus.). 32p. (J). (gr. 3-9). lib. bdg. 28.65 (978-1-4914-8054-0(8), 130553, Capstone Pr.) Capstone.

Driscoll, Laura. George Washington Carver: The Peanut Wizard. Weber, Jill, illus. 2003. (Smart about History Ser.). 32p. (J). (gr. k-4). mass mkt. 7.99 (978-0-448-43243-4(9), Grosset & Dunlap) Penguin Young Readers Group.

Eudy, P. D. PB & J Delight. 2010. 32p. pap. 14.78 (978-1-4520-0676-5(8)) AuthorHouse.

Heos, Bridget. From Peanuts to Peanut Butter. Coleman, Stephanie Fizer, illus. 2017. (Who Made My Lunch? Ser.). (ENG.). 24p. (J). (gr. 1-4). 20.95 (978-1-68151-123-8(1), 14653) Amicus.

McAneney, Caitlin. Peanut & Other Food Allergies, 1 vol. 2014. (Let's Talk about It Ser.). (ENG., Illus.). 24p. (J). (gr. 2-2). pap. 9.25 (978-1-4777-5807-6(0), 142e92e1-2a26-4bcc-877e-a0f5b9d737d3, PowerKids Pr.) Rosen Publishing Group, Inc., The.

Mckissack, Patricia & Mckissack, Fredrick. George Washington Carver: Scientist & Inventor, 1 vol. 2013. (Famous African Americans Ser.). (ENG., Illus.). 24p. (gr. k-2). lib. bdg. 25.27 (978-0-7660-4102-8(6), 8f37a16d-93f7-4b72-bd4b-c8b86043c47d, Enslow Elementary) Enslow Publishing, LLC.

Micucci, Charles. Life & Times of the Peanut. 2014. 16.95 (978-1-63419-716-8(X)) Perfection Learning Corp.

Nelson, Maria. I'm Allergic to Peanuts, 1 vol. 2014. (I'm Allergic Ser.). (ENG.). 24p. (J). (gr. 1-2). 24.27 (978-1-4824-0974-1(7), e2e7edfd-b5b1-4961-8dec-56d454bef84b); pap. 9.15 (978-1-4824-0975-8(5), c4d498fb-cdad-4826-b8ab-0885082f0e77) Stevens, Gareth Publishing LLLP.

Nelson, Robin. From Peanut to Peanut Butter. (Illus.). 24p. (J). (gr. k-3). 2012. (Start to Finish, Second Ser.: No. 2). (ENG.). pap. 7.99 (978-1-58013-969-4(8), fe8777ce-7b51-429b-bf4d-88881eec557c) 2004. (Start to Finish Ser.). 18.60 (978-0-8225-0944-8(X), Lerner Pubns.) Lerner Publishing Group.

—The Story of Peanut Butter: It Starts with Peanuts. 2021. (Step by Step Ser.). (ENG., Illus.). 24p. (J). (gr. -1-2). 26.65 (978-1-5415-9729-7(X), 028acf0b-eb8d-48f5-b2f3-d3537e5b5213, Lerner Pubns.) Lerner Publishing Group.

Nolan, Janet. PBandJ Hooray! 2016. (J). (978-1-4896-3870-0(9)) Weigl Pubs., Inc.

—PB&J Hooray! Your Sandwich's Amazing Journey from Farm to Table. Patton, Julia, illus. 2014. (ENG.). 32p. (J). (gr. -1-3). 17.99 (978-0-8075-6397-7(8), 807563978) Whitman, Albert & Co.

Sundance/Newbridge LLC Staff. From Peanuts to Peanut Butter. 2007. (Early Science Ser.). (gr. k-3). 18.95 (978-1-4007-6170-8(0)); pap. 6.10 (978-1-4007-6166-1(2)) Sundance/Newbridge Educational Publishing.

PEANUTS—FICTION

Baron, Charlie & Gamson, Alyse. Peanut Butter & Jelly. 2013. 12p. pap. 10.97 (978-1-62212-388-9(3), Strategic Bk. Publishing) Strategic Book Publishing & Rights Agency (SBPRA).

Blount-Jackson, Evetta. What? No Peanut Butter! 2011. 28p. pap. 14.50 (978-1-4634-0230-3(9)) AuthorHouse.

Border, Terry. Merry Christmas, Peanut! Border, Terry, illus. 2017. (Illus.). 32p. (J). (gr. -1-2). 17.99 (978-0-399-17621-0(7), Philomel Bks.) Penguin Young Readers Group.

Borsky, Mary. Benny Bensky & the Parrot-Napper. Hendry, Linda, illus. 2008. 128p. (J). (gr. 4-7). pap. 9.95 (978-0-88776-840-8(7), Tundra Bks.) Tundra Bks. CAN. Dist: Penguin Random Hse. LLC.

Fisher, Stacey & Paner, Amy, Illustrator. No Nuts for Nutty. 2008. 26p. 14.95 (978-0-615-19778-4(7)) Fisher-Paner Publishing.

Frame, Andrew Graham. Ein Stein: The Chipmunk Who Became an Engineer. 2011. 32p. pap. 13.95 (978-1-61204-009-7(8), Eloquent Bks.) Strategic Book Publishing & Rights Agency (SBPRA).

Graves, Mary. The Adventures of Peanut George. 2007. 72p. per. 19.95 (978-1-4241-8274-9(3)) America Star Bks.

Howard, Marie. Punkin & the Peanut. 2012. 30p. 24.95 (978-1-4626-7332-2(5)) America Star Bks.

Jacobs, Jessica. The Peanut Pickle: A Story about Peanut Allergy. Roslyn, Jacquelyn, illus. 2012. (ENG.). 48p. (J). (gr. -1-3). 14.95 (978-1-61608-672-5(6), 608672, Sky Pony Pr.) Skyhorse Publishing Co., Inc.

Ketch, Ann. There Goes Peanut Butter! Totire, Valerie, Illus. 2006. (ENG.). 12p. (gr. k-1). pap. 7.95 (978-1-57874-036-9(3), 74-036-3, Kaeden Bks.) Kaeden Corp.

King, Rosemary. Peanut Brittle. 2011. 28p. pap. 13.59 (978-1-4567-1444-4(9)) AuthorHouse.

Lewellyn, Natalie. Nutty to Meet You! Dr. Peanut Book #1. 2008. (Illus.). 32p. (J). 11.95 (978-0-9777082-0-8(9)) One Monkey Bks.

McClure, Wendy. The Princess & the Peanut Allergy. Lyon, Tammie, illus. 2012. (J). (978-1-61913-127-9(7)) Weigl Pubs., Inc.

—The Princess & the Peanut Allergy. Lyon, Tammie, illus. 2019. (ENG.). 32p. (J). (gr. -1-3). pap. 7.99 (978-0-8075-6619-0(5), 807566195) Whitman, Albert & Co.

Mehra, Heather & McManama, Kerry. Peanut-Free Tea for Three. Kline, Michael, illus. 2009. (J). (978-0-9822150-1-2(0)) Parent Perks, Inc.

Middleton, Shawn. Sam & the Peanut Butter Crackers. 2009. 32p. pap. 12.99 (978-1-4389-3400-6(9)) AuthorHouse.

Morrone Pedowitz, Laura. The Elephant Who Couldn't Eat Peanuts. 2009. 24p. pap. 11.49 (978-1-4389-4760-0(7)) AuthorHouse.

Nazareth, Melanie. Can I Have Some Cake Too? Lehner-Rhoades, Shirley, illus. 2013. 32p. (J). pap. 14.95 (978-1-935914-28-0(6)) River Sanctuary Publishing.

O'Connor, Jane. Peanut Butter & Jellyfish. 2015. (Fancy Nancy - I Can Read! Ser.). (J). lib. bdg. 13.55 (978-0-606-36479-9(X)) Turtleback.

One Pea, Two Pea, I Pee, You Pee. 2005. (J). bds. (978-0-9761228-0-7(4)) World of Imagination.

Paner, Amy & Fisher, Stacey. Nutty Scurries to School. 2008. 25p. 14.95 (978-0-615-23931-6(5)) Fisher-Paner Publishing.

Pangan, Catherine Hagerman. No Peanuts for Me! Warf, Gracie, illus. 2013. (ENG.). 30p. (J). (gr. -1-3). 14.95 (978-1-62086-433-3(9)) Amplify Publishing Group.

Schnitzlein, Danny. The Monster Who Ate My Peas, 1 vol. Faulkner, Matt, illus. 2010. 32p. (J). (gr. -1-3). pap. 7.95 (978-1-56145-533-1(4)) Peachtree Publishing Co. Inc.

Sofranac, Rodo. Polly & the Peanut Pull. 2013. (Illus.). 62p. pap. (978-1-939625-24-3(6)) Inkwell Books LLC.

Stanley, Mary. Bruno, Peanut & Me. 2011. (ENG.). 72p. pap. 7.99 (978-1-84840-103-7(5)) New Island Books IRL. Dist: Casemate Pubs. & Bk. Distributors, LLC.

Strasser, Stephanie. Pink Peanut Butter. 2010. 28p. 12.49 (978-1-4490-8383-0(8)) AuthorHouse.

Tait, Elena. The Day My Peanut Butter Lost Its Stick. Lee, Joe, illus. 2008. 24p. pap. 12.99 (978-1-4389-1936-2(0)) AuthorHouse.

Talbot, Rose. The Adventures of Peanut, the Sugar Glider. 2007. 80p. per. 15.99 (978-1-4257-9629-7(X)) Xlibris Corp.

Truscelli, John J. Can P B Find the Jelly? 2011. 24p. pap. 24.95 (978-1-4626-2666-3(1)) America Star Bks.

Whelahan, Marlene. Once upon a Peanut: A true Story... Killian, Sue, illus. 2009. 24p. pap. 12.99 (978-1-4389-5925-2(7)) AuthorHouse.

Wilson, Shannan. The Littlest Peanut: A Baby Book for the Teeny Tiny Ones. Cuniff, Joe, illus. 2011. 32p. 16.95 (978-1-61254-023-8(6)) Brown Books Publishing Group.

PEARL HARBOR (HAWAII), ATTACK ON, 1941

Allen, Thomas B. Remember Pearl Harbor: American & Japanese Survivors Tell Their Stories. 2015. (Remember Ser.). (Illus.). 64p. (J). (gr. 5-9). pap. 7.99 (978-1-4263-2248-8(8), National Geographic Kids) Disney Publishing Worldwide.

Anthony, Nathan & Gardner, Robert. The Attack on Pearl Harbor in United States History, 1 vol. 2014. (In United States History Ser.). (ENG., Illus.). 96p. (gr. 5-6). 31.61 (978-0-7660-5448-6(9), 448f0216-47c5-4c72-b923-7e644b6d516c) Enslow Publishing, LLC.

Benoit, Peter. The Attack on Pearl Harbor. 2013. (Cornerstones of Freedom™, Third Ser.). (ENG., Illus.). 64p. (J). pap. 8.95 (978-0-531-21959-1(3)); lib. bdg. 30.00 (978-0-531-23601-7(3)) Scholastic Library Publishing.

Bodden, Valerie. The Attack on Pearl Harbor. 2018. (Disasters for All Time Ser.). (ENG.). 48p. (J). (gr. 4-7). pap. 12.00 (978-1-62832-546-1(1), 19723, Creative Paperbacks) Creative Co., The.

Bowman, Chris. The Attack on Pearl Harbor. 2014. (Disaster Stories Ser.). (ENG., Illus.). 24p. (J). (gr. 3-8). 29.95 (978-1-62617-150-3(5), Black Sheep) Bellwether Media.

Burgan, Michael. The Attack on Pearl Harbor: U. S. Entry into World War II, 1 vol. 2012. (Perspectives On Ser.). (ENG., Illus.). 112p. (YA). (gr. 8-8). 42.64 (978-1-60870-448-4(3), 8295e9d5-7add-4634-94de-b5f45c295476) Cavendish Square Publishing LLC.

Darman, Peter, ed. Attack on Pearl Harbor: America Enters World War II, 1 vol. 2012. (World War II Ser.). (ENG., Illus.). 64p. (J). (gr. 6-6). lib. bdg. 37.13 (978-1-4488-9233-4(3), 09fbfaf9-e84a-4d0a-ba41-bb3c08bf4f91, Rosen Reference) Rosen Publishing Group, Inc., The.

Demuth, Patricia. What Was Pearl Harbor? 2013. (What Was... Ser.). lib. bdg. 16.00 (978-0-606-31686-6(8)) Turtleback.

Demuth, Patricia Brennan & Who HQ. What Was Pearl Harbor? Mantha, John, illus. 2013. (What Was? Ser.). 112p. (J). (gr. 3-7). pap. 7.99 (978-0-448-46462-6(4), Penguin Workshop) Penguin Young Readers Group.

Dougherty, Steve. Attack on Pearl Harbor: World War II Strikes Home in the USA. 2011. (J). pap. (978-0-545-32930-9(2)) Scholastic, Inc.

—Pearl Harbor: The U. S. Enters World War II. 2009. (24/7 Goes to War Ser.). (ENG.). 64p. (J). (gr. 5-8). lib. bdg. 22.44 (978-0-531-25525-4(5)) Scholastic Library Publishing.

—Pearl Harbor: the U. S. Enters World War II (24/7: Goes to War) 2009. (24/7: Goes to War Ser.). (ENG.). 64p. (J). (gr. 6-12). pap. 7.95 (978-0-531-25450-9(X), Watts, Franklin) Scholastic Library Publishing.

Dunn, Joe. The Bombing of Pearl Harbor, 1 vol. Wight, Joseph & Espinosa, Rod, illus. 2007. (Graphic History Ser.). (ENG.). 32p. (J). (gr. 3-8). 32.79 (978-1-60270-074-1(5), 9034, Graphic Planet - Fiction) Magic Wagon.

Edwards, Sue Bradford. Bombing of Pearl Harbor, 1 vol. 2015. (Essential Library of World War II Ser.). (ENG.). 112p. (YA). (gr. 6-12). 41.36 (978-1-62403-791-7(7), 17780, Essential Library) ABDO Publishing Co.

Fitzgerald, Stephanie. Pearl Harbor. 2017. (Eyewitness to World War II Ser.). (ENG., Illus.). 112p. (J). (gr. 5-9). lib. bdg. 38.65 (978-0-7565-5582-5(5), 135467, Compass Point Bks.) Capstone.

Freed, Kira. Surviving Pearl Harbor, 1 vol. 2015. (Surviving Disaster Ser.). (ENG., Illus.). 48p. (J). (gr. 5-6). 33.47 (978-1-4994-3649-5(1), 9dfc7861-bc93-4beb-839d-969f107fd9bc, Rosen Central) Rosen Publishing Group, Inc., The.

Garland, Sherry. Voices of Pearl Harbor, 1 vol. Johnson, Layne, illus. 2013. (Voices of History Ser.). (ENG.). 40p. (J). (gr. 3-3). 17.99 (978-1-4556-1609-1(5), Pelican Publishing) Arcadia Publishing.

Haugen, David M. & Musser, Susan, eds. The Attack on Pearl Harbor, 1 vol. 2011. (Perspectives on Modern World History Ser.). (ENG.). 216p. (gr. 10-12). 49.43 (978-0-7377-5004-1(9), a25b1323-9ec3-4766-b530-ad8a233914b6, Greenhaven Publishing) Greenhaven Publishing LLC.

Henzel, Cynthia Kennedy. The USS Arizona Story. 2017. (Famous Ships Ser.). (ENG., Illus.). 112p. (J). (gr. 6-12). lib. bdg. 41.36 (978-1-5321-1322-2(6), 27530, Essential Library) ABDO Publishing Co.

Johnson, Robin. Pearl Harbor. 2014. (Crabtree Chrome Ser.). (ENG., Illus.). 48p. (J). (gr. 2-2). (978-0-7787-1367-8(9)) Crabtree Publishing Co.

Krieg, Katherine. The Attack on Pearl Harbor: A History Perspectives Book. 2013. (Perspectives Library). (ENG., Illus.). 32p. (J). (gr. 4-8). 32.07 (978-1-62431-413-1(9), 202772); pap. 14.21 (978-1-62431-489-6(9), 202774) Cherry Lake Publishing.

Lassieur, Allison. The Attack on Pearl Harbor: An Interactive History Adventure. rev. ed. 2016. (You Choose: History Ser.). (ENG., Illus.). 112p. (J). (gr. 3-7). pap. 6.95 (978-1-5157-4260-9(1), 134013, Capstone Pr.) Capstone.

—The Attack on Pearl Harbor [Scholastic]: An Interactive History Adventure. 2009. (You Choose: History Ser.). 112p. (gr. 3-4). pap. 0.86 (978-1-4296-4046-6(4), Capstone Pr.) Capstone.

Loh-Hagan, Virginia. A Date Which Will Live in Infamy: Attack on Pearl Harbor. 2019. (Behind the Curtain Ser.). (ENG., Illus.). 32p. (J). (gr. 4-8). pap. 14.21 (978-1-5341-3998-5(2), 212821); lib. bdg. 32.07 (978-1-5341-4342-5(4), 212820) Cherry Lake Publishing. (45th Parallel Press).

Lowry, Lois. On the Horizon. Pak, Kenard, illus. 2020. (ENG.). 80p. (J). (gr. 5-7). 16.99 (978-0-358-12940-0(0), 1752988, Clarion Bks.) HarperCollins Pubs.

McNeese, Tim. The Attack on Pearl Harbor: America Enters World War II. 2004. (First Battles Ser.). (Illus.). 112p. (J). (gr. 6-12). 23.95 (978-1-883846-78-7(1), First Biographies) Reynolds, Morgan Inc.

Otfinoski, Steven. Day of Infamy: The Story of the Attack on Pearl Harbor. 2015. (Tangled History Ser.). (ENG., Illus.). 112p. (J). (gr. 3-9). pap. 6.95 (978-1-4914-7082-4(8), 129464, Capstone Pr.) Capstone.

—The Split History of the Attack on Pearl Harbor: A Perspectives Flip Book. 2018. (Perspectives Flip Books: Famous Battles Ser.). (ENG., Illus.). 64p. (J). (gr. 5-9). lib. bdg. 34.65 (978-0-7565-5691-4(0), 137036, Compass Point Bks.) Capstone.

Rice, Dona Herweck. You Are There! Pearl Harbor, December 7, 1941. 2nd rev. ed. 2016. (TIME(r): Informational Text Ser.). (ENG., Illus.). 32p. (gr. 6-8). pap. 10.99 (978-1-4938-3928-5(4)) Teacher Created Materials, Inc.

Ross, Stewart & Woodward, Joe. Pearl Harbor. 2011. (Place in History Ser.). (Illus.). 48p. (YA). (gr. 5-9). lib. bdg. 34.25 (978-1-84837-676-2(6)) Arcturus Publishing GBR. Dist: Black Rabbit Bks.

Russo, Kristin J. Viewpoints on the Attack on Pearl Harbor. 2018. (Perspectives Library: Viewpoints & Perspectives Ser.). (ENG., Illus.). 48p. (J). (gr. 5-8). lib. bdg. 39.21 (978-1-5341-2970-2(7), 211924) Cherry Lake Publishing.

Salisbury, Graham. Under the Blood-Red Sun. 2014. (Prisoners of the Empire Ser.: 1). (ENG.). 272p. (YA). (gr. 7-7). pap. 9.99 (978-0-385-38655-5(9), Ember) Random Hse. Children's Bks.

Samuels, Charlie. The Attack on Pearl Harbor, 1 vol., Vol. 1. 2013. (Turning Points in U. S. Military History Ser.). (ENG.). 48p. (J). (gr. 5-6). 34.61 (978-1-4824-0409-8(5), 24a85a65-96ca-4173-b00a-66c7a0e08511) Stevens, Gareth Publishing LLLP.

Swanson, Jennifer & Larson, Kirby. Pearl Harbor. McMorris, Kelley, illus. 2018. 106p. (J). (978-1-5444-0721-0(1)) Scholastic, Inc.

Uschan, Michael V. The Bombing of Pearl Harbor, 1 vol. 2003. (Landmark Events in American History Ser.). (ENG., Illus.). 48p. (gr. 5-8). lib. bdg. 33.67 (978-0-8368-5373-5(3), 520a4ee3-bdeb-4540-b404-a7b2fa061bcc, Gareth Stevens Secondary Library) Stevens, Gareth Publishing LLLP.

Uschan, Michael V. & Hudson Goff, Elizabeth. The Bombing of Pearl Harbor, 1 vol. 2005. (Graphic Histories Ser.). (ENG., Illus.). 32p. (gr. 3-3). pap. 11.50 (978-0-8368-6258-4(9), aba11a31-8eea-4cf9-ae78-676586a2f3ef); lib. bdg. 29.67 (978-0-8368-6206-5(6), f0871af5-fb9f-4de2-b656-7336def2ec00) Stevens, Gareth Publishing LLLP.

Wels, Susan. Pearl Harbor: America's Darkest Day. 2nd ed. 2006. (Illus.). 224p. 34.95 (978-1-887656-78-8(2)) Tehabi Bks.

White, Steve. Pearl Harbor: A Day of Infamy. (Graphic Battles of World War II Ser.). (ENG.). 48p. (gr. 5-5). 2009. (YA). 58.50 (978-1-61512-815-0(8), Rosen Reference) 2006. (Illus.). pap. 14.05 (978-1-4042-7428-0(6), 110479b3-feca-4fcf-bf25-417736034f2a) Rosen Publishing Group, Inc., The.

White, Steve D. Pearl Harbor: A Day of Infamy, 1 vol. Spahn, Jerrold, illus. 2007. (Graphic Battles of World War II Ser.). (ENG.). 48p. (YA). (gr. 5-5). lib. bdg. 37.13 (978-1-4042-0785-1(6), 30d5dd6e-eba7-4615-992a-9714f1d9620e) Rosen Publishing Group, Inc., The.

Whiting, Jim. The Story of the Attack on Pearl Harbor. 2005. (Monumental Milestones Ser.). (Illus.). 48p. (YA). (gr. 4-7). lib. bdg. 29.95 (978-1-58415-397-9(0)) Mitchell Lane Pubs.

Woog, Adam. Pearl Harbor. 2013. (Illus.). 96p. (J). lib. bdg. (978-1-60152-486-7(2)) ReferencePoint Pr., Inc.

Wukovits, John F. The Bombing of Pearl Harbor, 1 vol. 2011. (World History Ser.). (ENG.). 112p. (gr. 7-7). lib. bdg. 41.53 (978-1-4205-0330-2(8), d539e821-6330-440d-8f7f-a38ff5ca6493, Lucent Pr.) Greenhaven Publishing LLC.

Yomtov, Nel. The Attack on Pearl Harbor: December 7 1941, 1 vol. Campidelli, Maurizio, illus. 2014. (24-Hour History Ser.). (ENG.). 48p. (J). (gr. 3-9). pap. 8.95 (978-1-4329-9299-6(6), 124615); lib. bdg. 33.99 (978-1-4329-9293-4(7), 124610) Capstone. (Heinemann).

PEARL HARBOR (HAWAII), ATTACK ON, 1941—FICTION

Boyd, David. Pearl Harbor. Ng, Drew, illus. 2007. 48p. (J). lib. bdg. 23.08 (978-1-4242-1640-6(0)) Fitzgerald Bks.

Earle, Joan Zuber, mem. The Children of Battleship Row: Pearl Harbor 1940-1941. 2004. 136p. pap. 16.95 (978-1-57143-095-3(4)) RDR Bks.

Eaves, Victor Caleb. Vee's the Chapters of Expudict: Book One. 2008. 128p. pap. 12.00 (978-1-4389-3385-6(1)) AuthorHouse.

Gutman, Dan. Ted & Me. 2012. (Baseball Card Adventures Ser.). (ENG., Illus.). 208p. (J). (gr. 5-9). 15.99 (978-0-06-123487-3(7), HarperCollins) HarperCollins Pubs.

Hamilton, Elizabeth L. Surprise at Pearl Harbor. 2004. (Character Mystery Ser.: No. 2). (Illus.). 144p. (J). per. 9.95 (978-0-9754629-2-8(X), Character-in-Action) Quiet Impact, Inc.

Jenkins, Amanda. Mere Moments A Story of Pearl Harbor, the Day the Towers Fell. 2011. (Readers' & Writers' Genre Workshop Ser.). (J). pap. (978-1-4509-3019-2(0)) Benchmark Education Co.

Larson, Kirby. Hula for the Home Front. 2017. 176p. (J). (978-1-5182-5295-2(8), American Girl) American Girl Publishing, Inc.

Lemke, Donald & Lemke, Donald B. Captured off Guard: The Attack on Pearl Harbor, 1 vol. St. Aubin, Claude, illus. 2008. (Historical Fiction Ser.). (ENG.). 56p. (J). (gr. 3-6). pap. 6.25 (978-1-4342-0493-6(6), 94441, Stone Arch Bks.) Capstone.

Mazer, Harry. A Boy at War: A Novel of Pearl Harbor. 2004. (Illus.). 104p. (gr. 5-9). 16.00 (978-0-7569-4088-1(5)) Perfection Learning Corp.

Platt, Randall. Incommunicado. 2014. (ENG.). 336p. (J). (gr. 4-7). 14.95 (978-1-62914-646-1(3), Sky Pony Pr.) Skyhorse Publishing Co., Inc.

Salisbury, Graham. Under the Blood Red Sun. 246p. (YA). 22.00 (978-0-8446-7322-6(6)) Smith, Peter Pub., Inc.

Shimose Poe, Mayumi. Alice on the Island: A Pearl Harbor Survival Story. Forsyth, Matt, illus. 2019. (Girls Survive Ser.). (ENG.). 112p. (J). (gr. 3-7). pap. 7.95 (978-1-4965-8012-2(5), 139979, Stone Arch Bks.) Capstone.

Tarshis, Lauren. I Survived the Bombing of Pearl Harbor 1941. 2011. (I Survived Ser.: No. 4). lib. bdg. 14.75 (978-0-606-23744-4(5)) Turtleback.

—I Survived the Bombing of Pearl Harbor, 1941 (I Survived #4), 1 vol. Dawson, Scott, illus. 2011. (I Survived Ser.: 4). (ENG.). 112p. (J). (gr. 2-5). pap. 5.99 (978-0-545-20698-3(7), 49b44782-3a49-4716-a4c4-75402e52d8fb, Scholastic Paperbacks) Scholastic, Inc.

Uschan, Michael V. & Hudson Goff, Elizabeth. El Ataque a Pearl Harbor (the Bombing of Pearl Harbor), 1 vol. 2007. (Historias Gráficas (Graphic Histories) Ser.). (SPA.). 32p. (gr. 3-3). pap. 11.50 (978-0-8368-7899-8(X), 47009956-f6b2-400f-8bab-25404cabcd85); lib. bdg. 29.67 (978-0-8368-7892-9(2), 068cf5de-893a-4bc4-b37b-7afd6412b044) Stevens, Gareth Publishing LLLP.

PEARLS

Machajewski, Sarah. Pearls, 1 vol. 2015. (Gems: Nature's Jewels Ser.). (ENG., Illus.). 24p. (J). (gr. 2-3). pap. 9.15 (978-1-4824-2868-1(7), ea0d5f38-622c-4b79-87c4-a8e8119df4cf) Stevens, Gareth Publishing LLLP.

Morlock, Rachael. Diving for Pearls, 1 vol. 2017. (Gemstones of the World Ser.). (ENG.). 24p. (J). (gr. 3-3). 25.27 (978-1-5081-6422-7(3), 98d909b2-b9fe-40aa-80d5-0858362a8e0b, PowerKids Pr.) Rosen Publishing Group, Inc., The.

P Q R

PEARLS—FICTION

Grandma Pearl: A Story about Inner Beauty. 2008. (Illus.). 32p. (J). 17.95 *(978-0-9799021-1-6(8))* Aspire Publishing.

Ihara, Shigekatsu. Pokémon Diamond & Pearl Adventure!, Vol. 1. 2008. (ENG., Illus.). 188p. (J). (gr. k). pap. 9.99 *(978-1-4215-2286-9(1))* Viz Media.

—Pokémon Diamond & Pearl Adventure!, Vol. 2. 2008. (ENG., Illus.). 192p. (J). (gr. 1). pap. 9.99 *(978-1-4215-2287-6(X))* Viz Media.

Johnson, Julia. The Pearl Diver. Stacey International Staff, ed. Al-Fakhri, Patricia, illus. 2003. (ARA & ENG.). 240p. (J). (gr. 3-6). *(978-1-900988-62-9(3),* Stacey International) Stacey Publishing.

Kerven, Rosalind. Sparrow, the Crow & the Pearl. Williamson, Melanie, illus. 2005. (ENG.). 24p. (J). lib. bdg. 23.65 *(978-1-59646-754-5(1))* Dingles & Co.

Mau, Carol Demma. Wisdom from the Pearl Necklace. 2014. 138p. (J). pap. 11.99 *(978-1-4525-9012-7(5),* Balboa Pr.) Author Solutions, LLC.

McKenny, Stephanie L. Pearls of My Own. 2012. 102p. pap. 10.00 *(978-0-9705008-5-4(8))* J & J Publishing Co.

O'Dell, Scott. The Black Pearl. 2009. 9.00 *(978-0-7848-3610-1(8),* Everbind) Marco Bk. Co.

Saenz, Sandra C. Lot the Tot & the Beautiful Pearl. 2011. (ENG.). 24p. (gr. -1). pap. 16.99 *(978-1-4567-5385-6(1))* AuthorHouse.

Stilton, Gerónimo. The Enormouse Pearl Heist. 2012. (Geronimo Stilton Ser.: 51). lib. bdg. 18.40 *(978-0-606-26756-4(5))* Turtleback.

Tozier, Christopher. Olivia Brophie & the Pearl of Tagelus. 2013. (ENG.). 208p. (J). (gr. -1-12). pap. 12.95 *(978-1-56164-519-0(2))* Pineapple Pr., Inc.

Van Tassel, Mary A. Beach Ball's Discovery. 2013. 24p. pap. 24.95 *(978-1-4626-9698-7(8))* America Star Bks.

Wilson, Melissa Anne. Nalyn & the Indigo Pearl. 2008. (Illus.). 24p. (J). pap. 8.00 *(978-0-8059-7409-6(1))* Dorrance Publishing Co., Inc.

PEARY, ROBERT E. (ROBERT EDWIN), 1856-1920

Bedesky, Baron. Peary & Henson: The Race to the North Pole. 2006. (In the Footsteps of Explorers Ser.). (ENG., Illus.). 32p. (J). (gr. 4-7). lib. bdg. *(978-0-7787-2426-1(3))* Crabtree Publishing Co.

PEASANT ART

see Art Industries and Trade; Folk Art

PEASANTS

see also Agricultural Laborers; Sociology, Rural

Hiller, Sandra J. The Life of a Colonial Blacksmith, 1 vol. 2013. (Jr. Graphic Colonial America Ser.). (ENG., Illus.). 24p. (J). (gr. 2-3). pap. 11.60 *(978-1-4777-1433-1(2),* 590fe5ba-315d-489f-9490-b6565081c9a6); lib. bdg. 28.93 *(978-1-4777-1308-2(5),* 37ffb1ee-200e-4e53-9320-69c1eff09a28) Rosen Publishing Group, Inc., The. (PowerKids Pr.).

Hull, Robert. Peasant. 2009. (Illus.). 45p. (J). 32.80 *(978-1-59920-172-6(0))* Black Rabbit Bks.

Jeffrey, Gary. Rebellion & Revolt. Riley, Terry, illus. 2014. (Graphic Medieval History Ser.). (ENG.). 48p. (J). (gr. 5-5). *(978-0-7787-0399-0(1))* Crabtree Publishing Co.

The Life of a Colonial Blacksmith. 2013. (Jr. Graphic Colonial America Ser.). 24p. (J). (gr. 3-6). pap. 63.60 *(978-1-4777-1434-8(0),* PowerKids Pr.) Rosen Publishing Group, Inc., The.

Moening, Kate. Farmers. 2018. (Community Helpers Ser.). (ENG., Illus.). 24p. (J). (gr. k-3). lib. bdg. 26.95 *(978-1-62617-897-7(6),* Blastoff! Readers) Bellwether Media.

PEBBLES

see Rocks

PECCARIES

George, Jean Craighead. Summer Moon. 2003. (J). (gr. 3-7). 20.75 *(978-0-8446-7243-4(2))* Smith, Peter Pub., Inc.

Person, Stephen. Collared Peccary: Cactus-Eater. 2012. (America's Hidden Animal Treasures Ser.). 32p. (J). (gr. 2-7). lib. bdg. 28.50 *(978-1-61772-571-5(4))* Bearport Publishing Co., Inc.

Storad, Conrad J. Javelinas. 2008. (Early Bird Nature Bks.). (ENG., Illus.). 48p. (J). (gr. 2-5). 26.60 *(978-0-8225-7890-1(5))* Lerner Publishing Group.

PECOS BILL (LEGENDARY CHARACTER)

Braun, Eric & Bowman, James Cloyd. Pecos Bill Tames a Colossal Cyclone, 1 vol. Weber, Lisa K., illus. 2014. (American Folk Legends Ser.). (ENG.). 32p. (J). (gr. k-2). lib. bdg. 27.99 *(978-1-4795-5429-4(4),* 126077, Picture Window Bks.) Capstone.

Ferrell, David L. Pecos Bill, 1 vol. 2014. (Jr. Graphic American Legends Ser.). (ENG., Illus.). 24p. (J). (gr. 2-3). lib. bdg. 28.93 *(978-1-4777-7189-1(1),* 2f066cf9-5bda-427c-bba9-7b0c76977b73, PowerKids Pr.) Rosen Publishing Group, Inc., The.

Krensky, Stephen. Pecos Bill. 2008. pap. 40.95 *(978-0-8225-9296-9(7))* Lerner Publishing Group.

PEDAGOGY

see Education; Education—Study and Teaching; Teaching

PEDDLERS AND PEDDLING—FICTION

Chaconas, Dori. Pennies in a Jar, 1 vol. Lewin, Ted, illus. 2007. 36p. (J). (gr. 1-4). 16.95 *(978-1-56145-422-8(2))* Peachtree Publishing Co. Inc.

Derby, Sally. Two Fools & a Horse: An Orginal Tale, 1 vol. Rayevsky, Robert, illus. 2003. (ENG.). 32p. (J). (gr. k-3). 16.95 *(978-0-7614-5119-8(6))* Marshall Cavendish Corp.

Esphyr, Slobodkina & Slobodkina. Caps for Sale: A Tale of a Peddler, Some Monkeys & Their Monkey Business. 2014. (Reading Rainbow Bks). (ENG.). 48p. (J). 11.24 *(978-1-63245-155-2(7))* Lectorum Pubns., Inc.

Hunt, Mabel Leigh. The Peddler's Clock. Jones, Elizabeth Orton, illus. 2011. 30p. 35.95 *(978-1-258-09998-5(5))* Literary Licensing, LLC.

Leavey, Peggy Dymond. Growing up Ivy. 2010. (ENG.). 256p. (YA). (gr. 4-8). pap. 10.99 *(978-1-55488-723-1(2))* Dundurn Pr. CAN. Dist: Publishers Group West (PGW).

Merrill, Jean. The Pushcart War. 2006. (J). 1.25 *(978-1-4193-8348-9(5))* Recorded Bks., Inc.

Slobodkina, Esphyr. Caps for Sale: A Tale of a Peddler, Some Monkeys & Their Monkey Business. Slobodkina, Esphyr, illus. 2015. (ENG., Illus.). 48p. (J). (gr. -1-3). 17.99 *(978-0-201-09147-2(X))*; 75th ed. pap. 8.99 *(978-0-06-443143-9(6))* HarperCollins Pubs. (HarperCollins).

—Caps for Sale: A Tale of a Peddler, Some Monkeys & Their Monkey Businesss. Slobodkina, Esphyr, illus. 2008. (ENG., Illus.). 48p. (J). (gr. -1-3). lib. bdg. 17.89 *(978-0-06-025778-1(4),* HarperCollins) HarperCollins Pubs.

—Caps for Sale Board Book: A Tale of a Peddler, Some Monkeys & Their Monkey Business. Slobodkina, Esphyr, illus. 75th ed. 2015. (ENG., Illus.). 32p. (J). (gr. -1-3). bds. 8.99 *(978-0-06-147453-8(3),* HarperFestival) HarperCollins Pubs.

—Circus Caps for Sale. Slobodkina, Esphyr, illus. 2004. (Illus.). 40p. (J). (gr. -1-2). reprint ed. 17.00 *(978-0-7567-8345-7(3))* DIANE Publishing Co.

—Circus Caps for Sale. Slobodkina, Esphyr, illus. 2004. (ENG., Illus.). 48p. (J). (gr. -1-3). reprint ed. pap. 7.99 *(978-0-06-443793-6(0),* HarperCollins) HarperCollins Pubs.

—More Caps for Sale: Another Tale of Mischievous Monkeys Board Book. 2018. (ENG., Illus.). 32p. (J). (gr. -1-3). bds. 8.99 *(978-0-06-240560-9(8),* HarperFestival) HarperCollins Pubs.

Slobodkina, Esphyr & Sayer, Ann Marie Mulhearn. Caps for Sale & the Mindful Monkeys. Slobodkina, Esphyr, illus. 2017. (ENG., Illus.). 48p. (J). (gr. -1-3). 17.99 *(978-0-06-249988-2(2),* HarperCollins) HarperCollins Pubs.

—More Caps for Sale: Another Tale of Mischievous Monkeys. Slobodkina, Esphyr, illus. (ENG., Illus.). 40p. (J). (gr. -1-3). 2017. pap. 8.99 *(978-0-06-249957-8(2))* 2015. 18.99 *(978-0-06-240545-6(4))* HarperCollins Pubs. (HarperCollins).

Slobodkina, Esphyr & Slobodkina, E. Caps for Sale. 2015. (J). (gr. k-3). 17.20 *(978-0-8085-2604-9(9))* Turtleback.

Weston Woods Staff, creator. Caps for Sale. 2011. 18.95 *(978-0-439-72924-6(6))*; 38.75 *(978-0-439-72925-3(4))* Weston Woods Studios, Inc.

PEDIATRICS

see Children—Diseases; Children—Health and Hygiene

PEDIGREES

see Heraldry

PEER PRESSURE

Auer, Jim. Standing up to Peer Pressure: A Guide to Being True to You. Alley, R. W., illus. 2003. 32p. (J). per. 7.95 *(978-0-87029-375-7(3))* Abbey Pr.

Burstein, John. I Said No! Refusal Skills, 1 vol. 2009. (Slim Goodbody's Life Skills 101 Ser.). (ENG., Illus.). 32p. (J). (gr. 3-6). pap. *(978-0-7787-4805-2(7),* 1302928); lib. bdg. *(978-0-7787-4789-5(1),* 1302928) Crabtree Publishing Co.

Etingoff, Kim. Handling Peer Pressure. 2013. (Junior Martial Arts Ser.: 9). 32p. (J). (gr. 4-18). 19.95 *(978-1-4222-2736-7(7))* Mason Crest.

Evans, Lesli. But All My Friends Smoke: Cigarettes & Peer Pressure. 2009. (Illus.). 112p. (J). pap. 26.95 *(978-1-4222-1327-8(7),* 1291217) Mason Crest.

Feller, Robyn M. Everything You Need to Know about Peer Pressure. 2009. (Need to Know Library). 64p. (gr. 5-5). 58.50 *(978-1-60854-081-5(2))* Rosen Publishing Group, Inc., The.

Ferguson, Addy. What to Do When Your Friends Are Bullies, 1 vol. 2014. (Stand up: Bullying Prevention Ser.). (ENG.). 24p. (J). (gr. 2-3). lib. bdg. 26.27 *(978-1-4777-6877-8(7),* 03b4b271-f49d-4316-96a6-88b69ea395e2, PowerKids Pr.) Rosen Publishing Group, Inc., The.

Human Relations Media, prod. Clued in! on Saying No. 2005. (ENG.). 32p. (J). pap. 4.95 *(978-1-55548-051-6(9),* 675) Human Relations Media.

Juzwiak, Richard. Frequently Asked Questions about Peer Pressure, 1 vol. 2008. (FAQ: Teen Life Ser.). (ENG., Illus.). 64p. (YA). (gr. 5-6). lib. bdg. 37.13 *(978-1-4042-1805-5(X),* 42016b3a-20e2-4bc5-bd34-abe969908251) Rosen Publishing Group, Inc., The.

Lites, B. James & Lites, James R. Lessons in Peer Pressure For Kids All over the World. 2nd ed. 2006. (J). per. 13.95 *(978-0-9787674-1-9(1))* Aztec Bk. Publishing.

Mototsune, Kat. Image: Deal with It from the Inside Out. Shannon, Ben, illus. 2017. (Lorimer Deal with It Ser.). (ENG.). 32p. (J). (gr. 4-9). lib. bdg. 25.32 *(978-1-4594-1188-3(9),* 13e3cf56-eaaf-47e3-befd-c6f9c40ce8d4) James Lorimer & Co. Ltd., Pubs. CAN. Dist: Lerner Publishing Group.

—Image Deal with It: Deal with It from the Inside Out, 1 vol. Shannon, Ben, illus. 2007. (Lorimer Deal with It Ser.). (ENG.). 32p. (J). (gr. 4-6). pap. 12.95 *(978-1-55028-994-7(2),* 994) James Lorimer & Co. Ltd., Pubs. CAN. Dist: Formac Lorimer Bks. Ltd.

Slavens, Elaine. Peer Pressure: Deal with It Without Losing Your Cool, 1 vol. Shannon, Ben, illus. 2004. (Lorimer Deal with It Ser.). (ENG.). 32p. (J). (gr. 4-9). 12.95 *(978-1-55028-815-5(6),* 23f91d54-ec5f-4607-aa2e-bf652fcb36cd) James Lorimer & Co. Ltd., Pubs. CAN. Dist: Lerner Publishing Group.

Stephens, Ronald, ed. Peer Pressure & Relationships. 2014. (Safety First Ser.: 11). 48p. (J). (gr. 5-18). 20.95 *(978-1-4222-3050-3(3))* Mason Crest.

Straight Talk about Peer Pressure. (YA). (gr. 6-8). 69.95 *(978-1-55942-199-7(1),* 9241V9) Witcher Productions.

Webber, Diane. Scholastic Choices: Your Space. 2008. (Scholastic Choices Ser.). (ENG., Illus.). 112p. (YA). (gr. 8-12). pap. 8.95 *(978-0-531-14774-0(6),* Watts, Franklin) Scholastic Library Publishing.

World Book, Inc. Staff, contrib. by. Bullied by Friends. 2013. (J). *(978-0-7166-2072-3(3))* World Bk., Inc.

—Bullied to Belong. 2013. 48p. (J). *(978-0-7166-2076-1(6))* World Bk., Inc.

PEER PRESSURE—FICTION

Anhalt, Ariela. Freefall. 2011. (ENG.). 252p. (YA). (gr. 9). pap. 14.99 *(978-0-547-55216-3(5),* 1450661, Clarion Bks.) HarperCollins Pubs.

Brightwood, Laura, illus. Left Out. Brightwood, Laura, . 2006. (J). *(978-0-9779290-7-8(8))* 3-C Institute for Social Development.

Cabot, Meg. Pants on Fire. 2007. (J). (gr. 7-10). (ENG.). 272p. 16.99 *(978-0-06-088015-6(5))*; 260p. lib. bdg. 17.89 *(978-0-06-088016-3(3))* HarperCollins Pubs. (HarperTeen).

Carlson, Melody. The Day the Circus Came to Town. Butterfield, Ned, illus. 2004. 31p. (gr. -1-3). 14.99 *(978-1-58134-158-4(X))* Crossway.

Charles, Tami. Daphne Definitely Doesn't Do Fashion. Calo, Marcos, illus. 2018. (Daphne, Secret Vlogger Ser.). (ENG.). 96p. (J). (gr. 4-7). lib. bdg. 24.65 *(978-1-4965-6296-8(8),* 138022, Stone Arch Bks.) Capstone.

Christopher, Matt. Fairway Phenom. 2003. (ENG.). 144p. (J). (gr. 5-8). pap. 10.99 *(978-0-316-07551-0(5))* Little, Brown Bks. for Young Readers.

Cook, Julia. Peer Pressure Gauge, Volume 4. DuFalla, Anita, illus. 2013. (Building Relationships Ser.). (ENG.). 31p. (J). (gr. k-6). pap. 10.95 *(978-1-934490-48-8(2))* Boys Town Pr.

Cormier, Robert. The Chocolate War. 191p. (YA). (gr. 7-18). pap. 4.99 *(978-0-8072-1428-2(0),* Listening Library) Random Hse. Audio Publishing Group.

—The Chocolate War. 30th ed. 2004. (Chocolate War Ser.: 1). (ENG.). 272p. (YA). (gr. 7-12). pap. 10.99 *(978-0-375-82987-1(3),* Ember) Random Hse. Children's Bks.

Crane, Cheri J. Moment of Truth: A Novel. 2005. 238p. (YA). *(978-1-59156-727-1(0))* Covenant Communications.

Daniels, Cheri & Nicewander, Carol. Shadow Tail Meets the Gang. 2008. 24p. pap. 11.49 *(978-1-4389-3259-0(6))* AuthorHouse.

Emerson, Kevin. Carlos Is Gonna Get It. 2008. (J). pap. *(978-0-439-93526-5(1),* Levine, Arthur A. Bks.) Scholastic, Inc.

Friedman, Laurie. Honestly, Mallory! 2009. pap. 34.95 *(978-0-7613-4788-0(7))* Lerner Publishing Group.

—Honestly, Mallory! Pollak, Barbara, illus. (Mallory Ser.: 8). (ENG.). 160p. (J). (gr. 2-5). 2008. pap. 7.99 *(978-1-58013-840-6(3),* cbae7cde-0701-4e69-b123-1da3c7067db3, Darby Creek) 2007. 15.95 *(978-0-8225-6193-4(X),* Carolrhoda Bks.) Lerner Publishing Group.

Geragotelis, Brittany. What the Spell. (Life's a Witch Ser.). (ENG., Illus.). (YA). (gr. 9). 2014. 352p. pap. 9.99 *(978-1-4424-6707-1(X))* 2013. 336p. 16.99 *(978-1-4424-6815-3(7))* Simon & Schuster Bks. For Young Readers. (Simon & Schuster Bks. For Young Readers).

Gownley, Jimmy. True Things (Adults Don't Want Kids to Know) Gownley, Jimmy, illus. 2010. (Amelia Rules! Ser.). (ENG., Illus.). 176p. (J). (gr. 2-7). 19.99 *(978-1-4169-8611-9(1))*; pap. 12.99 *(978-1-4169-8609-6(X))* Simon & Schuster Children's Publishing. (Atheneum Bks. for Young Readers).

—The Tweenage Guide to Not Being Unpopular. Gownley, Jimmy, illus. 2010. (Amelia Rules! Ser.). (ENG., Illus.). 192p. (J). (gr. 2-7). pap. 12.99 *(978-1-4169-8608-9(1),* Atheneum Bks. for Young Readers) Simon & Schuster Children's Publishing.

Griffin, Adele. The Julian Game. 2011. (ENG.). 208p. (YA). (gr. 7-18). 7.99 *(978-0-14-241973-1(7),* Speak) Penguin Young Readers Group.

Hana's Year: Evaluation Guide. 2006. (J). *(978-1-55942-408-0(7))* Witcher Productions.

Hankins, M. Lil' Mikie Tells It Like It Is. 2007. 20p. per. 24.95 *(978-1-4137-0168-5(X))* America Star Bks.

Harrison, Lisi. P. S. I Loathe You. 2008. (Clique Novels Ser.). 208p. 20.00 *(978-1-60686-338-1(X))* Perfection Learning Corp.

Hole, Stian. Garmann's Street. 2010. (ENG., Illus.). 44p. (J). (gr. 1-5). 17.00 *(978-0-8028-5357-8(9),* Eerdmans Bks For Young Readers) Eerdmans, William B. Publishing Co.

Horrocks, Anita. What They Don't Know. braille ed. 2003. (J). (gr. 2). spiral bd. *(978-0-616-15267-6(1))* Canadian National Institute for the Blind/Institut National Canadien pour les Aveugles.

Juby, Susan. Getting the Girl: A Guide to Private Investigation, Surveillance, & Co Okery. 2010. (ENG.). 352p. (YA). (gr. 8). pap. 8.99 *(978-0-06-076528-6(3),* HarperTeen) HarperCollins Pubs.

Koja, Kathe. Buddha Boy. 2004. (ENG.). 128p. (YA). (gr. 7-11). reprint ed. 7.99 *(978-0-14-240209-2(5),* Speak) Penguin Young Readers Group.

—Buddha Boy. 2004. 117p. (gr. 3-7). 16.00 *(978-0-7569-3117-9(7))* Perfection Learning Corp.

Kropp, Paul. The Countess & Me, 1 vol. 2003. (ENG., Illus.). 32p. (YA). (gr. 6-8). pap. 8.95 *(978-1-55041-692-3(8),* 2c0c8a47-53b0-4129-ae17-c5326e906316) Fitzhenry & Whiteside, Ltd. CAN. Dist: Firefly Bks., Ltd.

Kucharski, Linda. Sneak the Sneaker. 2010. 44p. pap. 15.50 *(978-1-60911-487-9(6),* Eloquent Bks.) Strategic Book Publishing & Rights Agency (SBPRA).

Kushner, Elisabeth. The Purim Superhero. Byrne, Mike, illus. 2013. (ENG.). 32p. (J). (gr. -1-3). 8.99 *(978-0-7613-9062-6(6),* e21c8b88-429e-4a15-bf99-c61687205a7d, Kar-Ben Publishing) Lerner Publishing Group.

Larsen, Sharon G. The Parable of the Chocolate Chips. 2008. (J). *(978-1-59038-912-6(3))* Deseret Bk. Co.

Maloney, Brenna. Philomena's New Glasses. 2017. (Illus.). 40p. (J). (gr. -1-1). 17.99 *(978-0-425-28814-6(5),* Viking Books for Young Readers) Penguin Young Readers Group.

Margolis, Leslie. Fix. 2006. (ENG.). 256p. (YA). (gr. 9-12). pap. 7.99 *(978-1-4169-2456-2(6),* Simon Pulse) Simon Pulse.

Morgan, Amanda K. Secrets, Lies, & Scandals. (ENG.). (YA). (gr. 9). 2017. 368p. pap. 10.99 *(978-1-4814-4955-7(9))* 2016. (Illus.). 352p. 17.99 *(978-1-4814-4954-0(0))* Simon Pulse. (Simon Pulse).

Moss, Peggy. Our Friendship Rules, 1 vol. Imre Geis, Alissa, illus. (ENG.). (J). (gr. 2-6). 2007. 32p. 16.95 *(978-0-88448-291-8(X),* 884291) 2nd ed. 2017. 36p. pap. 9.95 *(978-0-88448-596-4(X),* 884596) Tilbury Hse. Pubs.

Nash, Andy. Melinda & Her Mule: For Kids Blessed with a Strong Will. 2008. (J). *(978-0-8127-0453-2(3))* Autumn Hse. Publishing Co.

Nigro, D. M. The Wolfman, the Shrink & the Eighth-Grade Election. 2006. 116p. (J). pap. 13.50 *(978-1-931201-66-7(8))* Twilight Times Bks.

Northrop, Michael. Trapped. 2011. (ENG.). 240p. (J). (gr. 7-10). 17.99 *(978-0-545-21012-6(7),* Scholastic Pr.) Scholastic, Inc.

Penn, Tony. The Misadventures of Michael McMichaels: The Creepy Campers, Vol. 3. Martin, Brian, illus. 2017. (Misadventures of Michael Mcmichaels Ser.: 3). (ENG.). 83p. (J). (gr. 1-6). pap. 7.95 *(978-1-944882-10-5(3))* Boys Town Pr.

Plum-Ucci, Carol. The Body of Christopher Creed: A Printz Honor Winner. 2008. (ENG., Illus.). 272p. (YA). (gr. 7). pap. 7.99 *(978-0-15-206386-3(2),* 1199120, Clarion Bks.) HarperCollins Pubs.

Polak, Monique. 121 Express, 1 vol. 2008. (Orca Currents Ser.). (ENG.). 144p. (J). (gr. 4-7). pap. 9.95 *(978-1-55143-976-1(X))* Orca Bk. Pubs. USA.

Rivadeneira, Caryn. The Wrong Shoes: A Book about Money & Self-Esteem. Ross, Graham, illus. 2018. 62p. (J). 14.99 *(978-1-5064-4681-3(7),* Beaming Books) 1517 Media.

Rountree, Wendy. Lost Soul. 2003. 87p. (J). pap. 19.95 *(978-1-59129-975-2(6))* America Star Bks.

Rowleym'Lin. Knights of Right, BK 3: The Warrior's Guard. 2010. 80p. (J). pap. 6.99 *(978-1-60641-240-4(X),* Shadow Mountain) Shadow Mountain Publishing.

Rowold, Shirley. Big Bear. 2010. 42p. pap. 15.50 *(978-1-60860-851-5(4),* Eloquent Bks.) Strategic Book Publishing & Rights Agency (SBPRA).

Salm, Arthur. Anyway* *a Story about Me with 138 Footnotes, 27 Exaggerations, & 1 Plate of Spaghetti. (ENG., Illus.). 192p. (J). (gr. 3-7). 2013. pap. 7.99 *(978-1-4424-2931-4(3))* 2012. 15.99 *(978-1-4424-2930-7(5))* Simon & Schuster Bks. For Young Readers. (Simon & Schuster Bks. For Young Readers).

Sauer, Tammi. Nugget & Fang. 2015. (Nugget & Fang Ser.). lib. bdg. 17.20 *(978-0-606-36825-4(6))* Turtleback.

—Nugget & Fang: Friends Forever — Or Snack Time? Slack, Michael, illus. 2013. (Nugget & Fang Ser.). (ENG.). 40p. (J). (gr. -1-3). 18.99 *(978-0-547-85285-0(1),* 1501493, Clarion Bks.) HarperCollins Pubs.

Schmatz, Pat. Mousetraps. Hauser, Bill, illus. 2008. (ENG.). 192p. (YA). (gr. 7-12). 17.95 *(978-0-8225-8657-9(6),* Carolrhoda Bks.) Lerner Publishing Group.

Schraff, Anne. The Petition. 2008. (Passages Ser.). 103p. (J). (gr. 4-6). lib. bdg. 13.95 *(978-0-7569-8391-8(6))* Perfection Learning Corp.

Schultz Nicholson, Lorna. Northern Star, 1 vol. 2006. (Lorimer Sports Stories Ser.). (ENG.). 112p. (J). (gr. 4-8). 16.95 *(978-1-55028-911-4(X),* 911) James Lorimer & Co. Ltd., Pubs. CAN. Dist: Formac Lorimer Bks. Ltd.

Spinelli, Jerry. Wringer. 2004. (ENG.). 256p. (J). (gr. 3-7). pap. 8.99 *(978-0-06-059282-0(6),* HarperCollins) HarperCollins Pubs.

Stampler, Ann Redisch. Where It Began. 2013. (ENG.). 384p. (YA). (gr. 7-12). 26.19 *(978-1-4424-2321-3(8))*; (gr. 9). pap. 9.99 *(978-1-4424-2322-0(6))* Simon Pulse. (Simon Pulse).

Strasser, Todd. American Terrorist. 2017. (YA). pap. *(978-1-4814-6134-4(6),* Simon & Schuster Bks. For Young Readers) Simon & Schuster Bks. For Young Readers.

Wilde, Jerry. Peace in the Halls: Stories & Activities to Manage Anger & Prevent School Violence. 2003. 112p. (YA). (gr. 4-12). pap. 9.95 *(978-0-9657610-4-8(5))* LGR Publishing, Inc.

Willson, Sarah. Hocus Focus. Wummer, Amy, illus. 2004. (Science Solves It! Ser.). (ENG.). 32p. (J). (gr. 1-3). pap. 5.99 *(978-1-57565-136-1(X),* a291c3a3-dfc2-47a4-93a8-acc3af9ffc3d, Kane Press) Astra Publishing Hse.

PEGASUS (GREEK MYTHOLOGY)

Pearce, Q. L. Pegasus, 1 vol. 2008. (Monsters Ser.). (ENG., Illus.). 48p. (gr. 4-8). lib. bdg. 36.83 *(978-0-7377-4082-0(5),* 24fb3b1b-1403-4936-8d4a-af7f8736769d, KidHaven Publishing) Greenhaven Publishing LLC.

Rose, Simon. Pegasus: The Myth & Science. 2015. (J). *(978-1-5105-0020-4(0))*; pap. *(978-1-5105-0269-7(6))* SmartBook Media, Inc.

PEKING (CHINA)

see Beijing (China)

PELE, 1940-2022

Brown, Monica. Pele, King of Soccer/Pele, el Rey Del Futbol: Bilingual English-Spanish. Gutierrez, Rudy, illus. 2008. (ENG.). 40p. (J). (gr. -1-3). 18.99 *(978-0-06-122779-0(X))* HarperCollins Español.

Buckley, James, Jr. & Who HQ. Who Was Pelé? Thomson, Andrew, illus. 2018. (Who Was? Ser.). 112p. (J). (gr. 3-7). 6.99 *(978-0-399-54261-9(2),* Penguin Workshop) Penguin Young Readers Group.

Cline-Ransome, Lesa. Young Pele: Soccer's First Star. Ransome, James E., illus. (ENG.). 40p. (J). (gr. -1-4). 2012. lib. bdg. 22.44 *(978-0-375-93599-2(1))* 2011. pap. 8.99 *(978-0-375-87156-6(X))* Random Hse. Children's Bks. (Dragonfly Bks.).

Collier Hillstrom, Laurie. Pelé: Soccer Superstar, 1 vol. 2007. (Twentieth Century's Most Influential Hispanics Ser.). (ENG., Illus.). 104p. (J). (gr. 7-10). lib. bdg. 39.08 *(978-1-4205-0023-3(6),* d96fc44f-fd97-40de-a05d-ebe3791f7bee, Lucent Pr.) Greenhaven Publishing LLC.

Gagne, Tammy. What It's Like to Be Pele. de la Vega, Eida, tr. 2011. (What It's Like to Be... = Que Se Sienta Al Ser... Ser.). (ENG & SPA., Illus.). 32p. (J). (gr. -1-2). lib. bdg. 25.70 *(978-1-58415-993-3(6))* Mitchell Lane Pubs.

Riner, Dax. Pelé. 2010. (Sports Heroes & Legends Ser.). (ENG., Illus.). 120p. (J). (gr. 5-12). lib. bdg. 30.60 *(978-0-7613-5368-3(2))* Lerner Publishing Group.

Simon, Eddy. Pelé: The King of Soccer. Brascaglia, Vincent, illus. 2017. (ENG.). 144p. (J). pap. 16.99 *(978-1-62672-755-7(4),* 900172778, First Second Bks.) Roaring Brook Pr.

PELICANS

Castro, Shirley. The Pelican Family Counting Book. Castro, Christopher, illus. 2006. (ENG.). (J). 15.00 *(978-0-9790307-0-3(6))* Castro, Shirley.

Cussen, Sarah. Those Peculiar Pelicans. Weaver, Steve, illus. 2005. (Those Amazing Animals Ser.). (ENG.). 58p. (J). (gr. -1-12). per. 11.95 *(978-1-56164-340-0(8))* Pineapple Pr., Inc.

Cussen, Sarah R. Those Peculiar Pelicans. Weaver, Steve, illus. Hammond, Roger, photos by. 2006. (Those Amazing Animals Ser.). (ENG.). 55p. (J). (gr. -1-12). lib. bdg. 14.95 *(978-1-56164-358-5(0))* Pineapple Pr., Inc.

Dabritz, Evelyn. It's Not Easy Being a Pelican. Hoffman, Isobel, illus. 2012. 32p. (J). *(978-1-930401-87-7(6))* Central Coast Bks./Pr.

Gish, Melissa. Living Wild: Pelicans. 2017. (Living Wild Ser.). (ENG., Illus.). 48p. (J). (gr. 5-7). pap. 13.99 *(978-1-62832-435-8(X),* 20202, Creative Paperbacks) Creative Co., The.

—Pelicans. 2017. (Living Wild Ser.). (ENG., Illus.). 48p. (J). (gr. 4-7). *(978-1-60818-832-1(9),* 20201, Creative Education) Creative Co., The.

Harris, Tim. Pelicans. 2008. (Nature's Children Ser.). (Illus.). 52p. (J). *(978-0-7172-6241-0(3))* Grolier, Ltd.

Kingston, Anna. The Life Cycle of a Pelican, 1 vol. 2011. (Nature's Life Cycles Ser.). (ENG., Illus.). 24p. (J). (gr. 2-3). pap. 9.15 *(978-1-4339-4684-4(X),* 796da8c3-a51f-460d-b3ce-bbcec3e44187); lib. bdg. 25.27 *(978-1-4339-4683-7(1),* 20f1c8ee-aa1c-407a-b7e1-d2c0162cdc30) Stevens, Gareth Publishing LLLP. (Gareth Stevens Learning Library).

Picayo, Mario. Brown Pelicans. 2016. (J). pap. *(978-1-934370-61-2(4))* Editorial Campana.

Pohl, Kathleen. Pelicans, 1 vol. 2007. (Let's Read about Animals Ser.). (ENG., Illus.). 24p. (gr. k-2). pap. 9.15 *(978-0-8368-7826-4(4),* bc409f12-0100-429f-8404-70314e87eb6e); lib. bdg. 24.67 *(978-0-8368-7819-6(1),* 695e46c7-149e-470f-8dd9-57c78eee4ab4) Stevens, Gareth Publishing LLLP. (Weekly Reader Leveled Readers).

—Pelicans / Pelícanos, 1 vol. 2007. (Let's Read about Animals / Conozcamos a Los Animales Ser.). (SPA & ENG., Illus.). 24p. (gr. k-2). lib. bdg. 24.67 *(978-0-8368-8008-3(0),* 2a884e6b-4632-4a46-8122-e93c6067ba9f, Weekly Reader Leveled Readers) Stevens, Gareth Publishing LLLP.

Stout, Frankie. Pelicans: Soaring the Seas. (Things with Wings Ser.). 24p. (gr. 2-3). 2009. 42.50 *(978-1-60854-354-0(4))* 2008. (ENG., Illus.). (J). lib. bdg. 26.27 *(978-1-4042-4497-9(2),* fe322131-4766-485a-8a78-c6968224238f) Rosen Publishing Group, Inc., The. (PowerKids Pr.).

Swan, Erin Pembrey. Pelicans, Cormorants, & Their Kin. 2003. (Animals in Order Ser.). (ENG., Illus.). 48p. (J). (gr. 4-6). pap. 6.95 *(978-0-531-16378-8(4),* Watts, Franklin) Scholastic Library Publishing.

PELICANS—FICTION

Bernay, Emma & Berne, Emma Carlson. Oil-Soaked Wings. Madrid, Erwin, illus. 2019. (Seaside Sanctuary Ser.). (ENG.). 112p. (J). (gr. 3-7). lib. bdg. 25.99 *(978-1-4965-7861-7(9),* 139400, Stone Arch Bks.) Capstone.

Castro, Shirley. The Pelican Family Series -- Telly's Story. Castro, Christopher, illus. 2008. 36p. (J). 15.00 *(978-0-9790307-1-0(4))* Castro, Shirley.

Dahl, Roald. The Giraffe & the Pelly & Me. Blake, Quentin, illus. 2009. (ENG.). 96p. (Orig.). (J). (gr. 3-7). 7.99 *(978-0-14-241384-5(4),* Puffin Books) Penguin Young Readers Group.

Deutsch, Neil. Rose & the Pelican. 2013. 32p. pap. 19.99 *(978-1-4817-0947-7(X))* AuthorHouse.

Dixon, Virginia. What Happened to Willie? Thomas, Tim, illus. 2007. 32p. (J). 16.00 *(978-0-9795386-0-5(2))* Grand Productions.

Erickson, John. The Case of the Dinosaur Birds. Holmes, Gerald L., illus. 2011. (Hank the Cowdog Ser.). (ENG.). 125p. (J). (gr. 3-6). pap. 5.99 *(978-1-59188-154-4(4))* Maverick Bks., Inc.

Fane, Judy B. Paddy the Pelican Survives the Storm. Alden, Carol, illus. 2010. 48p. pap. 16.50 *(978-1-60911-448-0(5),* Eloquent Bks.) Strategic Book Publishing & Rights Agency (SBPRA).

Froeber, Sarah & Mosher, Kim. Pelican & Pelicant. 2003. (Illus.). 36p. (J). 17.99 *(978-0-9744926-0-5(4))* Toucan Pr., Inc.

Gump, Granny. The Giraffe Who Went to School. 2011. 48p. pap. 21.99 *(978-1-4568-5805-6(X))* Xlibris Corp.

Halfmann, Janet. Pelican's Catch. Dacey, Bob & Bandelin, Debra, illus. (Smithsonian Oceanic Collection Ser.). (ENG.). 32p. (J). 2011. (gr. -1-3). 8.95 *(978-1-60727-657-9(7))* 2011. (gr. -1-3). 19.95 *(978-1-60727-656-2(9))* 2005. (gr. -1-2). 19.95 *(978-1-59249-310-4(6),* BC4026) 2005. (gr. -1-2). 9.95 *(978-1-59249-311-1(4),* PB4076) 2005. (gr. -1-2). 4.95 *(978-1-59249-286-2(X),* B4076) 2005. (gr. -1-2). 15.95 *(978-1-59249-287-9(8),* B4026) 2004. (gr. 2-7). 8.95 *(978-1-59249-309-8(2),* SC4026) 2004. (gr. -1-3). 6.95 *(978-1-59249-285-5(1),* S4026) Soundprints.

Harvey, Roland. On the River. 2016. (ENG.). 32p. (J). (gr. k-3). 17.99 *(978-1-76011-245-5(3))* Allen & Unwin AUS. Dist: Independent Pubs. Group.

Johnson, Rebecca. The Proud Pelican's Secret, 1 vol. 2005. (Animal Storybooks Ser.). (ENG., Illus.). 24p. (gr. k-2). lib. bdg. 24.67 *(978-0-8368-5974-4(X),* 054e0734-6e38-47d0-b79f-6e7b6a1d8a10, Gareth Stevens Learning Library) Stevens, Gareth Publishing LLLP.

Keiser, Frances R. Annie the River Otter: The Adventures of Pelican Pete. Keiser, Hugh M., illus. l.t. ed. 2006. (ENG.). 34p. (J). 19.99 *(978-0-9668845-4-8(X))* Sagaponack Bks.

Lease, Janice. Pellina the Pelican. 2008. 48p. pap. 19.95 *(978-0-9800762-1-9(8))* Cinnamon Ridge Publishing.

Renaud, Andrea. Sammy the Surfing Pelican Meets Steve the Surf Guru. l.t. ed. 2003. (Illus.). 32p. (J). per. *(978-0-9717041-3-8(9))* A Happy Friend, Inc.

Ryan, Mike. Mayda Saves the Day. Ralph, Karin, illus. 2004. 60p. (J). (gr. 1-5). 14.95 *(978-0-9701319-3-5(3))* Temenos Pr.

Rylant, Cynthia. The Turtle. McDaniels, Preston, illus. 2006. (Lighthouse Family Ser.). 47p. (J). (gr. -1-3). 11.65 *(978-0-7569-6611-9(6))* Perfection Learning Corp.

—The Turtle. McDaniels, Preston, illus. 2005. (Lighthouse Family Ser.: 4). (ENG.). 48p. (J). (gr. 1-5). 17.99 *(978-0-689-86244-1(X),* Simon & Schuster Bks. For Young Readers) Simon & Schuster Bks. For Young Readers.

Sargent, Dave & Sargent, David, Jr. Petie Pelican: Be Proud of Yourself, 20 vols., Vol. 14. Lenoir, Jane, illus. 2nd ed. 2003. (Feather Tales Ser.: 14). 42p. (J). lib. bdg. 20.95 *(978-1-56763-745-8(0))* Ozark Publishing.

Sprecher, John. Tori & Cassandra & the Pelican in Peril. Forrest, James, illus. l.t. ed. Date not set. (Special Kids "Special Message" Book Ser.: Vol. 3). 32p. (J). (gr. k-4). pap. 10.00 *(978-1-892186-02-7(0))* Anythings Possible, Inc.

Zschock, Martha. Hello, New Orleans! 2011. (Hello Ser.). (ENG., Illus.). 16p. (J). (gr. -1-k). bds. 9.99 *(978-1-933212-63-0(2),* Commonwealth Editions) Applewood Bks.

—Hello, San Francisco! 2012. (Hello Ser.). (ENG., Illus.). 16p. (J). (gr. -1-k). bds. 9.99 *(978-1-933212-65-4(9),* Commonwealth Editions) Applewood Bks.

PELTS

see Hides and Skins

PEN AND INK DRAWING

see Pen Drawing

PEN DRAWING

Corfee, Stephanie. Girl Plus Pen: Doodle, Draw, Color, & Express Your Individual Style. Corfee, Stephanie, illus. 2016. (Craft It Yourself Ser.). (ENG., Illus.). 144p. (J). (gr. 3-9). pap., pap., pap. 12.95 *(978-1-62370-596-1(7),* 130414, Capstone Young Readers) Capstone.

PENAL CODES

see Criminal Law

PENAL INSTITUTIONS

see Prisons

PENAL LAW

see Criminal Law

PENCIL DRAWING

Hanley, Cara. Anywhere, Anytime Art: Colored Pencil: A Playful Guide to Drawing with Colored Pencil on the Go! 2018. (Anywhere, Anytime Art Ser.). (ENG., Illus.). 128p. pap. 16.95 *(978-1-63322-494-0(5),* 301707, Walter Foster Jr) Quarto Publishing Group USA.

Saltzberg, Barney. Andrew Drew & Drew. 2012. (ENG., Illus.). 40p. (J). (gr. -1-1). 18.99 *(978-1-4197-0377-5(3),* 1014701, Abrams Appleseed) Abrams, Inc.

Top That! Kids, creator. Make Your Own Pencil Toppers. 2006. (Creative Studio Ser.). (Illus.). 48p. (J). (gr. -1-3). *(978-1-905359-86-8(1))* Top That! Publishing PLC.

PENGUINS

Adamson, Heather. Emperor Penguins. 2017. (Ocean Life up Close Ser.). (ENG., Illus.). 24p. (J). (gr. k-3). lib. bdg. 26.95 *(978-1-62617-641-6(8),* Blastoff! Readers) Bellwether Media.

Anderson, Jill. Emperor Penguins. 2007. (Wild Ones Ser.). (ENG., Illus.). 24p. (J). (gr. -1-1). 12.95 *(978-1-55971-972-8(9))*; pap. 6.95 *(978-1-55971-973-5(7))* Cooper Square Publishing Llc.

Arlington, Jane & Langdon, Sharon. Penguins. 2006. (J). 7.99 *(978-1-59939-032-1(9))* Cornerstone Pr.

—Penguins, 1 vol. (Amazing Animals Ser.). (ENG.). 48p. (gr. 3-5). 2009. pap. 11.50 *(978-1-4339-2018-9(2),* ad1d3ef8-409d-4385-9cc6-438a77882b47, Gareth Stevens Learning Library) 2008. (YA). lib. bdg. 30.67 *(978-0-8368-9101-0(5),* f54eb780-1368-43a1-9388-2730cabfa93d) Stevens, Gareth Publishing LLLP.

Arlon, Penelope & Gordon-Harris, Tory. Penguins. 2012. (J). lib. bdg. *(978-0-531-22956-9(4))* Scholastic, Inc.

Arrhenius, Ingela P., illus. Where's the Penguin? 2018. (Where's The Ser.). (ENG.). 10p. (J). (— 1). bds. 8.99 *(978-1-5362-0250-2(9))* Candlewick Pr.

Baggott, Stella. Flip, Flap, Flop. 2008. (Bath Bks). 8p. (J). 14.99 *(978-0-7945-2177-6(0),* Usborne) EDC Publishing.

Beer, Julie. Penguins vs. Puffins. 2017. (Illus.). 64p. (J). (gr. 1-3). 12.99 *(978-1-4263-2869-5(9),* National Geographic Kids) Disney Publishing Worldwide.

Bell, Samantha S. Penguins Are Awesome. 2018. (Animals Are Awesome Ser.). (ENG., Illus.). 32p. (J). (gr. 3-6). 32.80 *(978-1-63235-436-5(5),* 13814, 12-Story Library) Bookstaves, LLC.

Berger, Melvin & Berger, Gilda. Penguins. 2010. (Illus.). 16p. (J). *(978-0-545-16080-3(4))* Scholastic, Inc.

Best, B. J. Penguins, 1 vol. 2016. (Migrating Animals Ser.). (ENG., Illus.). 24p. (gr. 1-1). pap. 9.81 *(978-1-5026-2106-1(1),* 2badabe8-41d0-4191-8613-76c68ed2c3b1); lib. bdg. 27.36 *(978-1-5026-2108-5(8),* 81ce12ae-2b8e-4953-8661-a56e8413923d) Cavendish Square Publishing LLC.

Bodden, Valerie. Amazing Animals - Penguins. 2012. (Amazing Animals Ser.). (ENG.). 24p. (J). (gr. 1-4). 16.95 *(978-1-58341-810-9(5),* 22092, Creative Education) Creative Co., The.

—Amazing Animals: Penguins. 2011. (Amazing Animals Ser.). (ENG.). 24p. (J). (gr. 1-3). pap. 9.99 *(978-0-89812-743-0(2),* 22097, Creative Paperbacks) Creative Co., The.

—Penguins. 2015. (J). pap. *(978-1-62832-258-3(6),* Creative Paperbacks) Creative Co., The.

Bone, Emily & Watt, Fiona. Penguins. 2010. (Beginner's Nature Ser.). 32p. (J). pap. 7.99 *(978-0-7945-2581-1(4),* Usborne) EDC Publishing.

Books Are Fun 8 Title Animal Lives Set: Penguins. 2006. (J). *(978-1-59566-310-8(X))* QEB Publishing Inc.

Brannon, Cecelia H. Baby Penguins at the Zoo, 1 vol. 2015. (All about Baby Zoo Animals Ser.). (ENG.). 24p. (gr. k-1). pap. 10.35 *(978-0-7660-7150-6(2),* 262e1175-d809-4aeb-a97e-5f401d62af9e); (Illus.). lib. bdg. 24.27 *(978-0-7660-7152-0(9),* 675fbde3-4243-422a-bbee-59b870c91993) Enslow Publishing, LLC.

Brown Bear Books. Penguins. 2012. (Animal Families Ser.). (ENG., Illus.). 32p. (J). (gr. 3-6). 31.35 *(978-1-78121-005-5(5),* 16428) Brown Bear Bks.

Caswell, Deanna. Baby Penguins. 2020. (J). pap. *(978-1-62310-065-0(8))* Black Rabbit Bks.

Caviezel, Giovanni. Little Penguin. Rigo, Laura, illus. 2014. (Mini Look at Me Bks.). 10p. (J). (gr. -1 — 1). bds. 4.99 *(978-0-7641-6731-7(6))* Sourcebooks, Inc.

Child's Play, creator. Penguin. 2005. (ENG., Illus.). 12p. (J). (gr. -1-k). bds. *(978-0-85953-680-6(7))* Child's Play International Ltd.

Clark, Willow. Penguins: Life in the Colony, 1 vol. 2011. (Animal Families Ser.). (ENG.). 24p. (J). (gr. 1-1). pap. 9.25 *(978-1-4488-2606-3(3),* 0df6ab20-a3ac-4359-aa99-690e61aaa5d8); (Illus.). lib. bdg. 26.27 *(978-1-4488-2510-3(5),* 4da8f4af-57b1-4feb-9839-df2b9924f9ad) Rosen Publishing Group, Inc., The. (PowerKids Pr.).

—Penguins: Pingüinos: Life in the Colony: Vida en la Colonia, 1 vol. 2011. (Animal Families / Familias de Animales Ser.). (SPA & ENG., Illus.). 24p. (gr. 1-1). lib. bdg. 26.27 *(978-1-4488-3124-1(5),* e87d9dd5-6d9e-4295-b27a-a388703b54db, PowerKids Pr.) Rosen Publishing Group, Inc., The.

Cole, Carol A. La Dama de Los Pingüinos, 1 vol. Rogers, Sherry, illus. 2012. (SPA.). 32p. (J). (gr. k-1). pap. 11.95 *(978-1-62855-420-5(7),* ef322c54-f5bf-4f3b-aa6c-93335035e447) Arbordale Publishing.

—The Penguin Lady, 1 vol. Rogers, Sherry, illus. 2012. (ENG.). 32p. (J). (gr. -1-3). 17.95 *(978-1-60718-527-7(X))*; pap. 9.95 *(978-1-60718-536-9(9))* Arbordale Publishing.

Coleman, Miriam. Swimming with Penguins, 1 vol. 2009. (Flippers & Fins Ser.). (ENG., Illus.). 24p. (gr. 2-3). (J). pap. 9.25 *(978-1-4358-3245-9(0),* 1999a36f-c0ae-4c74-bdee-334d3b4db0c0, PowerKids Pr.); (YA). lib. bdg. 26.27 *(978-1-4042-8094-6(4),* 3cfc2156-393f-4842-8c62-40734bb84403) Rosen Publishing Group, Inc., The.

Cooper, Sharon Katz. When Penguins Cross the Ice: The Emperor Penguin Migration. Leonard, Tom, illus. 2015. (Extraordinary Migrations Ser.). (ENG.). 24p. (J). (gr. k-3). pap. 8.95 *(978-1-4795-6102-5(9),* 127831, Picture Window Bks.) Capstone.

—When Penguins Cross the Ice: The Emperor Penguin Migration. Leonard, Tom, illus. 2015. (Extraordinary Migrations Ser.). (ENG.). 24p. (J). (gr. k-3). lib. bdg. 27.32 *(978-1-4795-6078-3(2),* 127646, Picture Window Bks.) Capstone.

Costain, Meredith. Penguin, 1 vol. Hanna, Gary, illus. 2016. (Wild World Ser.). (ENG.). 32p. (J). (gr. 1-2). pap. 11.00 *(978-1-4994-8223-2(X),* 4b3004ef-906b-4898-8427-3992a6cc3b64, Windmill Bks.) Rosen Publishing Group, Inc., The.

Cussen, Sarah. Those Perky Penguins. Weaver, Steve, illus. 2011. (Those Amazing Animals Ser.). (ENG.). 56p. (J). (gr. -1-12). 14.95 *(978-1-56164-504-6(4))*; pap. 9.95 *(978-1-56164-505-3(2))* Pineapple Pr., Inc.

Daigle, Evelyne. The World of Penguins. Wright, Geneviève, tr. from FRE. Grenier, Daniel, illus. 2008. (ENG.). 48p. (J). (gr. 4-7). pap. 12.95 *(978-0-88776-947-4(0),* Tundra Bks.) Tundra Bks. CAN. Dist: Penguin Random Hse. LLC.

De La Bedoyere C. Why Why Why Cant Penguins Fly. 2008. 32p. pap. *(978-1-84810-000-8(0))* Miles Kelly Publishing, Ltd.

De la Bédoyère, Camilla. Penguins. 2010. (Remarkable Man & Beast Ser.). (Illus.). 48p. (J). (gr. 3-18). lib. bdg. 19.95 *(978-1-4222-1972-0(0))* Mason Crest.

—Why Why Why... Can't Penguins Fly? 2010. (Why Why Why Ser.). 32p. (J). (gr. 1-3). lib. bdg. 18.95 *(978-1-4222-1573-9(3))* Mason Crest.

—The Wild Life of Penguins, 1 vol. 2014. (Wild Side Ser.). (ENG.). 24p. (J). (gr. 2-2). lib. bdg. 26.27 *(978-1-4777-5502-0(0),* b10627a3-a5e4-4090-bc92-29f1be2ef707, Windmill Bks.) Rosen Publishing Group, Inc., The.

de le Bédoyère, Camilla. Egg to Penguin. 2010. (ENG., Illus.). 24p. (J). pap. *(978-1-84835-583-5(1))* QEB Publishing Inc.

Dinmont, Kerry. It's a Penguin! 2018. (Bumba Books (r) — Polar Animals Ser.). (ENG., Illus.). 24p. (J). (gr. -1-1). pap. 8.99 *(978-1-5415-2695-2(3),* 5fae717c-1cb1-4cc4-969e-42289fd6547f) Lerner Publishing Group.

Durrie, Karen. I Am a Penguin. 2012. (J). *(978-1-61913-229-0(X))*; pap. *(978-1-61913-230-6(3))* Weigl Pubs., Inc.

—Pingüino. 2013. (SPA.). (J). *(978-1-62127-573-2(6))* Weigl Pubs., Inc.

Early Macken, JoAnn. Penguins / Los Pinguinos, 1 vol. 2004. (Animals I See at the Zoo / Animales Que Veo en el Zoológico Ser.). (ENG & SPA., Illus.). 24p. (J). (gr. k-2). pap. 9.15 *(978-0-8368-4006-3(2),* 74d6e910-2d98-4e43-adf6-203bc5265399, Weekly Reader Leveled Readers) Stevens, Gareth Publishing LLLP.

Edwards, Roberta. Emperor Penguins. Schwartz, Carol, illus. 2007. (Penguin Young Readers, Level 3 Ser.). 48p. (J). (gr. 1-3). mass mkt. 4.99 *(978-0-448-44664-6(2),* Penguin Young Readers) Penguin Young Readers Group.

Emily Rose Townsend. Penguins [Scholastic]. 2009. (Polar Animals Ser.). 24p. (gr. k-1). pap. 0.34 *(978-1-4296-4224-8(6),* Pebble) Capstone.

Esbaum, Jill. Explore My World Penguins. 2014. (Explore My World Ser.). (Illus.). 32p. (J). (gr. -1-k). pap. 4.99 *(978-1-4263-1701-9(8),* National Geographic Kids) Disney Publishing Worldwide.

Ferri, Francesca, illus. Penguin & Friends: A Soft & Fuzzy Book Just for Baby! 2017. (Friends Cloth Bks.). (ENG.). 8p. (J). (gr. -1 — 1). 12.99 *(978-1-4380-0976-6(3))* Sourcebooks, Inc.

Franks, Katie. Penguins. 2014. (Zoo's Who's Who Ser.). (Illus.). 24p. (J). (gr. k-2). pap. 49.50 *(978-1-4777-6577-7(8),* PowerKids Pr.) Rosen Publishing Group, Inc., The.

Furstinger, Nancy. How Do Penguins Stay Warm? 2018. (Crazy Animal Facts Ser.). (ENG., Illus.). 32p. (J). (gr. 4-6). lib. bdg. 28.65 *(978-1-5435-4119-9(4),* 139073, Capstone Pr.) Capstone.

Gallagher, Debbie. Penguins, 1 vol. 2010. (Zoo Animals Ser.). (ENG.). 32p. (gr. 2-2). lib. bdg. 21.27 *(978-0-7614-4747-4(4),* 875ea76c-72cd-45dd-927c-58f786a873c1) Cavendish Square Publishing LLC.

Galvin, Laura Gates. Baby Penguin Waddles. 2011. (ENG.). 16p. (J). *(978-1-60727-616-6(X))* Soundprints.

Gish, Melissa. Penguin. 2019. (Spotlight on Nature Ser.). (ENG.). 32p. (J). (gr. 4-7). pap. 9.99 *(978-1-62832-747-2(2),* 19189, Creative Paperbacks) Creative Co., The.

Glaser, Rebecca. Penguins Waddle. 2016. (ENG., Illus.). 16p. (J). (gr. -1 — 1). bds. 7.99 *(978-1-68152-070-4(2),* 15819) Amicus.

Goldish, Meish. Emperor Penguin. 2018. (More SuperSized! Ser.). (ENG.). 24p. (J). (gr. k-3). 7.99 *(978-1-64280-079-1(1))* Bearport Publishing Co., Inc.

—Emperor Penguin: The World's Biggest Penguin. 2010. (More SuperSized! Ser.). (Illus.). 24p. (J). (gr. k-3). lib. bdg. 26.99 *(978-1-936087-29-7(4))* Bearport Publishing Co., Inc.

Gray, Susan H. Penguins Can't Fly. 2014. (Tell Me Why Library). (ENG., Illus.). 24p. (J). (gr. 2-5). 29.21 *(978-1-63188-010-0(1),* 205447) Cherry Lake Publishing.

Guiberson, Brenda Z. The Emperor Lays an Egg. Paley, Joan, illus. rev. ed. 2004. (ENG.). 32p. (J). (gr. -1-3). pap. 8.99 *(978-0-8050-7636-3(0),* 900024495) Square Fish.

Hall, Katharine. Osos Polares y Pingüinos: Un Libro de Comparaci�n y Contraste (Spanish Edition) 2014.Tr. of Polar Bears & Penguins: a Compare & Contrast Book. (SPA., Illus.). 32p. (J). (gr. 2-3). pap. 11.95 *(978-1-62855-227-0(1),* 93935288-1716-4142-a470-72278f59bb8c) Arbordale Publishing.

—Polar Bears & Penguins: a Compare & Contrast Book, 1 vol. 2014. (Compare & Contrast Ser.). (ENG., Illus.). 32p. (J). (gr. -1-3). 17.95 *(978-1-62855-209-6(3))* Arbordale Publishing.

Hall, Margaret. Penguins & Their Chicks: A 4D Book. rev. ed. 2018. (Animal Offspring Ser.). (ENG., Illus.). 24p. (J). (gr. -1-2). lib. bdg. 29.32 *(978-1-5435-0825-3(1),* 137588, Capstone Pr.) Capstone.

Hanel, Rachael. Penguins. 2008. (Living Wild Ser.). (Illus.). 46p. (J). (gr. 4-7). lib. bdg. 22.95 *(978-1-58341-658-7(7),* Creative Education) Creative Co., The.

Hastings, Derek. Penguins. 2019. (Creatures of the Ocean Ser.). (Illus.). 80p. (J). (gr. 12). lib. bdg. 34.60 *(978-1-4222-4307-7(9))* Mason Crest.

—Penguins - Pb: A Portrait of the Animal World. 2013. (Portrait of the Animal World Ser.). (Illus.). 72p. pap. 9.95 *(978-1-59764-325-2(4))* New Line Bks.

Hewett, Richard, illus. & photos by. A Penguin Chick Grows Up. Hewett, Richard, photos by. Hewett, Joan, photos by. 2004. (Baby Animals Ser.). 32p. (J). (gr. k-3). lib. bdg. 21.27 *(978-1-57505-200-7(8))* Lerner Publishing Group.

Hoff, Mary. Penguins. 2006. (Wild World of Animals Ser.). (Illus.). 31p. (J). 18.95 *(978-1-58341-435-4(5),* Creative Education) Creative Co., The.

Hoffman, Mary Ann. How Do Penguins Survive the Cold? (Look at Life Science Ser.). 24p. (gr. 3-3). 2009. 42.50 *(978-1-61511-214-2(6),* PowerKids Pr.) 2008. (ENG.). pap. 8.25 *(978-1-4042-8007-6(3),* de59ca1a-5467-4541-b88f-baa49615b15b, Rosen Classroom) Rosen Publishing Group, Inc., The.

Hollenbeck, Kathleen. Penguins Family: The Story of a Humboldt Penguin. Stegos, Daniel, illus. 2005. (ENG.). 32p. (J). (gr. -1-2). 4.95 *(978-1-59249-348-7(3),* B4077); pap. 6.95 *(978-1-59249-347-0(5),* S4027) Soundprints.

Hollenbeck, Kathleen & Smithsonian Institution Staff. Penguin's Family (la familia del Pinguino) 2008. (MUL.). 16p. 14.95 *(978-1-59249-850-5(7))* Soundprints.

Idzikowski, Lisa. How Penguins Grow Up, 1 vol. 2018. (Animals Growing Up Ser.). (ENG.). 24p. (gr. 1-2). 24.27 *(978-0-7660-9659-2(9),* bd265edd-b74e-4731-8ed0-2cf966a9e781) Enslow Publishing, LLC.

Jacquet, Luc. March of the Penguins: The Official Children's Book. Maison, Jérôme, photos by. 2005. (ENG., Illus.). 32p. (J). (gr. 2-17). per. 5.95 *(978-0-7922-6183-4(6),* National Geographic Children's Bks.) National Geographic Society.

James, Helen Foster. Discover Penguins. 2015. (21st Century Basic Skills Library: Splash! Ser.). (ENG., Illus.). 24p. (J). (gr. 2-4). 26.35 *(978-1-63362-603-4(2),* 206596) Cherry Lake Publishing.

Jaycox, Jaclyn. Penguins Are Awesome. 2019. (Polar Animals Ser.). (ENG., Illus.). 32p. (J). (gr. -1-2). pap. 7.95 *(978-1-9771-0995-8(0),* 140938, Pebble) Capstone.

Jenkins, Martin. The Emperor's Egg Big Book: Read & Wonder Big Book. Chapman, Jane, illus. 2003. (Read & Wonder Ser.). (ENG.). 32p. (J). (gr. k-3). pap. 27.99 *(978-0-7636-2233-6(8))* Candlewick Pr.

Johnson, Robin. Les Manchots. 2012. (FRE.). 32p. (J). pap. 9.95 *(978-2-89579-442-4(1))* Bayard Canada CAN. Dist: Crabtree Publishing Co.

Kalman, Bobbie. Life Cycle of an Emperors. 2008. (FRE.). 32p. (J). pap. 9.95 *(978-2-89579-201-7(1))* Bayard Canada Livres CAN. Dist: Crabtree Publishing Co.

Kalman, Bobbie & Johnson, Robin. El Ciclo de Vida del Pinguino Emperador. 2007. (Ciclos de Vida Ser.). (SPA., Illus.). 32p. (J). (gr. 3-7). lib. bdg. *(978-0-7787-8672-6(2))* Crabtree Publishing Co.

—El Ciclo de Vida Del Pinguino Emperador. 2007. (Libro de Bobbie Kalman Ser.). (SPA., Illus.). 32p. (J). *(978-1-4287-3238-4(1))* Crabtree Publishing Co.

—El Ciclo de Vida del Pinguino Emperador. rev. ed. 2007. (Ciclos de Vida Ser.). (SPA., Illus.). 32p. (J). (gr. 3-7). pap. *(978-0-7787-8718-1(4))* Crabtree Publishing Co.

—Endangered Penguins. 2007. (Earth's Endangered Animals Ser.). (ENG., Illus.). 32p. (J). (gr. 3-7). lib. bdg. *(978-0-7787-1863-5(8))*; (gr. -1-3). pap. *(978-0-7787-1909-0(X))* Crabtree Publishing Co.

—The Life Cycle of an Emperor Penguin. 2006. (Life Cycle Ser.). (ENG., Illus.). 32p. (J). (gr. -1-3). pap. *(978-0-7787-0704-2(0))* Crabtree Publishing Co.

Katz Cooper, Sharon. A Day in the Life of a Penguin: A 4D Book. 2018. (Day in the Life Ser.). (ENG., Illus.). 32p. (J). (gr. -1-2). lib. bdg. 29.99 *(978-1-5435-1517-6(7),* 137874, Capstone Pr.) Capstone.

Kawa, Katie. Baby Penguins, 1 vol. 2011. (Cute & Cuddly: Baby Animals Ser.). (Illus.). 24p. (gr. k-k). (ENG.). (J). pap. 9.15 *(978-1-4339-5532-7(6),* ad535690-27b5-4ba4-8c19-c5f29a24d720); (ENG., (J). lib. bdg. 25.27 *(978-1-4339-5530-3(X),* e41044a3-db0a-4e5f-9c1d-0588c1fecfad); 69.20 *(978-1-4339-6893-8(2))* Stevens, Gareth Publishing LLLP.

Kennington, Tammy. Penguins. 2014. (21st Century Skills Library: Exploring Our Oceans Ser.). (ENG., Illus.). 32p. (J). (gr. 3-6). 32.07 *(978-1-62431-605-0(0),* 203204) Cherry Lake Publishing.

Kolpin, Molly. Galapagos Penguins, 1 vol. 2012. (Endangered & Threatened Animals Ser.). (ENG., Illus.). 32p. (J). (gr. 3-9). lib. bdg. 28.65 *(978-1-4296-8431-6(3),* 118504) Capstone.

Landau, Elaine. Emperor Penguins: Animals of the Snow & Ice, 1 vol. 2010. (Animals of the Snow & Ice Ser.). (ENG., Illus.). 32p. (gr. 3-3). lib. bdg. 26.60 *(978-0-7660-3462-4(3),* f872c85c-9982-4cfb-8f03-3af76227c7dd) Enslow Publishing, LLC.

Lar Rieu, Barry, text. Penguin Paradise. 2007. (Illus.). 62p. (YA). per. 16.00 *(978-0-9660373-1-9(6))* Gallant Hse. Publishing.

Leigh, Autumn. A Penguin Colony, 1 vol. 2013. (Animal Groups Ser.). (ENG., Illus.). 24p. (J). (gr. 1-2). pap. 9.15 *(978-1-4339-8210-1(2),* edff01ef-3fa8-4eab-bc77-00626d9f5404); lib. bdg. 25.27 *(978-1-4339-8209-5(9),* 64041d81-0687-4dd2-9786-c1a475081147) Stevens, Gareth Publishing LLLP.

—A Penguin Colony / una Colonia de Pingüinos, 1 vol. 2013. (Animal Groups / Grupos de Animales Ser.). (ENG & SPA., Illus.). 24p. (gr. 1-2). 25.27 *(978-1-4339-8808-0(9),*

6a5f0933-67b3-4b1b-a7bc-acfcbe615e8b) Stevens, Gareth Publishing LLLP.

Lewis, Suzanne. A Penguin Named Patience: A Hurricane Katrina Rescue Story. Anchin, Lisa, illus. 2015. (ENG.). 24p. (J). (gr. 1-4). 15.95 *(978-1-58536-840-2(7)*, 203732) Sleeping Bear Pr.

L'Heureux, J. J. Good Day Book. 2006. spiral bd. *(978-0-9785892-0-2(3))* BrainStream.

Lindeen, Mary. Penguins. 2013. (ENG., Illus.). 24p. (J). lib. bdg. 25.65 *(978-1-62031-066-3(X))* Jump! Inc.

Ling, Mary & Dorling Kindersley Publishing Staff. Penguin. Fletcher, Neil & Williamson, Katie, photos by. 2007. (See How They Grow Ser.). (ENG., Illus.). 24p. (J). (gr. k-3). 16.19 *(978-0-7566-3371-4(0))* Dorling Kindersley Publishing, Inc.

Liu, Li. Penguins Have It All. 2017. (1-3Y Marine Life Ser.). (ENG., Illus.). 16p. (J). pap. 18.99 *(978-1-63437-624-2(2))* American Reading Co.

—What Penguins Need. 2011. (1-3Y Marine Life Ser.). (ENG., Illus.). 16p. (J). pap. 8.00 *(978-1-63437-690-7(0))* American Reading Co.

Lynch, Michelle. Penguin Baby. Washington, Joi, illus. 2012. (1G Science Ser.). (ENG.). 28p. (J). pap. 8.00 *(978-1-61406-167-0(X))* American Reading Co.

Lynch, Wayne. Penguins! The World's Coolest Birds. 2nd rev. ed. 2016. (ENG., Illus.). 80p. (J). (gr. 5-8). pap. 12.95 *(978-1-77085-858-9(X)*, 39cf011c-c461-473f-88bc-240c36fac087) Firefly Bks., Ltd.

Markle, Sandra. The Great Penguin Rescue: Saving the African Penguins. 2017. (Sandra Markle's Science Discoveries Ser.). (ENG., Illus.). 48p. (J). (gr. 4-6). 33.32 *(978-1-5124-1315-1(1)*, 13d008ae-882e-42e2-932f-9f3333384b00, Millbrook Pr.) Lerner Publishing Group.

—A Mother's Journey. Marks, Alan, illus. 32p. (J). (gr. -1-3). 2006. pap. 7.95 *(978-1-57091-622-9(5))* 2005. 16.95 *(978-1-57091-621-2(7))* Charlesbridge Publishing, Inc.

—A Mother's Journey. Marks, Alan, illus. 2006. (gr. 4-7). 16.95 *(978-0-7569-6967-7(0))* Perfection Learning Corp.

Marsh, Laura. National Geographic Readers: Cutest Animals Collection. 2014. (Readers Ser.). (Illus.). 128p. (J). (gr. 1-3). pap. 7.99 *(978-1-4263-1522-0(8)*, National Geographic Kids) Disney Publishing Worldwide.

Martin, Emmett. Penguins from Head to Tail, 1 vol. 2020. (Animals from Head to Tail Ser.). (ENG.). 24p. (J). (gr. k-2). pap. 9.15 *(978-1-5382-5526-1(X)*, e1c3aebd-bfc1-4eab-af86-00dbdcbf75fc) Stevens, Gareth Publishing LLLP.

Marzollo, Jean. Pierre the Penguin: A True Story. Regan, Laura, illus. 2010. (ENG.). 32p. (J). (gr. 1-4). 18.99 *(978-1-58536-485-5(1)*, 202193) Sleeping Bear Pr.

McLaughlin, Kari Massie. My Adventure with Penguins. 2009. (ENG.). 44p. (J). 8.99 *(978-1-59092-461-7(4))* Blue Forge Pr.

McNeil, Niki, et al. HOCPP 1123 Penguins. 2006. spiral bd. 16.00 *(978-1-60308-123-8(2))* In the Hands of a Child.

Meachen Rau, Dana. Adivina Quién Nada / Guess Who Swims, 1 vol. 2010. (Adivina Quién / Guess Who? Ser.). (ENG & SPA.). 32p. (gr. k-2). 25.50 *(978-0-7614-3483-2(6)*, 5cffc4e9-478f-4edd-b34d-88c1a1ade6b1) Cavendish Square Publishing LLC.

—Adivina Quién Nada (Guess Who Swims), 1 vol. 2010. (Adivina Quién (Guess Who?) Ser.). (SPA.). 32p. (gr. k-2). lib. bdg. 25.50 *(978-0-7614-3458-0(5)*, 1c6650ef-53d2-4485-8a78-8a3390c67a20) Cavendish Square Publishing LLC.

—Guess Who Swims, 1 vol. 2009. (Guess Who? Ser.). (ENG.). 32p. (gr. k-1). pap. 9.23 *(978-0-7614-3566-2(2)*, ccda0a4d-0cd8-44e5-b9c4-299a6d8318c1); lib. bdg. 25.50 *(978-0-7614-2974-6(3)*, 8934e38f-c926-4c45-925a-1edf5fb44664) Cavendish Square Publishing LLC.

Mettler, René. Der Pinguin. 2005. (Meyers Klien Kinderbibliothek Ser.). (GER., Illus.). spiral bd. 14.25 *(978-3-411-09611-4(X)*, MY611E) Langenscheidt Publishing Group.

Miller, Sara Swan. Emperor Penguins of the Antarctic. 2009. (Brrr! Polar Animals Ser.). 24p. (gr. 2-3). 42.50 *(978-1-61511-748-2(2)*, PowerKids Pr.); (ENG., Illus.). (J). pap. 9.25 *(978-1-4358-3146-9(2)*, 1291788, PowerKids Pr.); (ENG., Illus.). (J). lib. bdg. 26.27 *(978-1-4358-2742-4(2)*, 1291788) Rosen Publishing Group, Inc., The.

Moore Niver, Heather. 20 Fun Facts about Penguins, 1 vol. 2012. (Fun Fact File: Animals! Ser.). (ENG., Illus.). 32p. (J). (gr. 2-3). pap. 11.50 *(978-1-4339-6523-4(2)*, ec7e49fe-1a50-472b-8ca4-1b115afe98ec); lib. bdg. 27.93 *(978-1-4339-6521-0(6)*, 64b26bef-8f18-4d1c-b85a-3e7f03655755) Stevens, Gareth Publishing LLLP. (Gareth Stevens Learning Library).

Morgan, Sally. Penguins. 2004. (QEB Animal Lives Ser.). (Illus.). 32p. (J). lib. bdg. 18.95 *(978-1-59566-037-4(2))* QEB Publishing Inc.

Morgan, Sally & Teacher Created Resources Staff. Penguins. 2006. (Animal Lives Ser.). (ENG., Illus.). 32p. pap. 7.99 *(978-1-4206-8163-5(X))* Teacher Created Resources, Inc.

Murray, Julie. Penguin Chicks. 2017. (Baby Animals (Abdo Kids Junior) Ser.). (ENG., Illus.). 24p. (J). (gr. -1-2). lib. bdg. 31.36 *(978-1-5321-0005-5(1)*, 25096, Abdo Kids) ABDO Publishing Co.

—Penguins. 2016. (I Like Animals! Set 2 Ser.). (ENG., Illus.). 24p. (J). (gr. -1-2). lib. bdg. 31.36 *(978-1-68080-907-7(5)*, 23289, Abdo Kids) ABDO Publishing Co.

Murray, Laura K. Penguin. (Grow with Me Ser.). (ENG.). 32p. (J). (gr. 3-6). 2016. pap. 9.99 *(978-1-62832-164-7(4)*, 20874, Creative Paperbacks) 2015. (Illus.). *(978-1-60818-563-4(X)*, 20873, Creative Education) Creative Co., The.

Osborne, Mary Pope & Boyce, Natalie Pope. Penguins & Antarctica: A Nonfiction Companion to Magic Tree House Merlin Mission #12: Eve of the Emperor Penguin. Murdocca, Sal, illus. 2008. (Magic Tree House (R) Fact Tracker Ser.: 18). 128p. (J). (gr. 2-5). 6.99 *(978-0-375-84664-9(6)*, Random Hse. Bks. for Young Readers) Random Hse. Children's Bks.

Owen, Ruth. Penguin Chicks. 2012. (Water Babies Ser.). 24p. (J). (gr. -1-3). lib. bdg. 25.65 *(978-1-61772-602-6(8))* Bearport Publishing Co., Inc.

Penguins. (Eyes on Nature Ser.). 32p. (J). (gr. 1). pap. *(978-1-882210-61-9(1))* Action Publishing, Inc.

Perkins, Wendy. Penguin. 2011. (Amicus Readers. Animal Life Cycles (Level 2) Ser.). (ENG.). 24p. (J). (gr. 1-4). lib. bdg. 25.65 *(978-1-60753-158-6(5)*, 17066) Amicus.

Pringle, Laurence. Penguins! Strange & Wonderful. Henderson, Meryl Learnihan, illus. 2013. (Strange & Wonderful Ser.). (ENG.). 32p. (J). (gr. 2-5). pap. 9.95 *(978-1-62091-591-2(X)*, Astra Young Readers) Astra Publishing Hse.

Raatma, Lucia. Penguins. 2012. (Nature's Children Ser.). (ENG., Illus.). 48p. (J). pap. 6.95 *(978-0-531-21081-9(2))*; (gr. 3-5). lib. bdg. 28.00 *(978-0-531-20906-6(7))* Scholastic Library Publishing. (Children's Pr.).

Rake, Jody S. Emperor Penguins. 2019. (Penguins! Ser.). (ENG., Illus.). 24p. (J). (gr. -1-2). lib. bdg. 27.32 *(978-1-9771-0935-4(7)*, 140539, Pebble) Capstone.

—Gentoo Penguins. 2019. (Penguins! Ser.). (ENG., Illus.). 24p. (J). (gr. -1-2). lib. bdg. 27.32 *(978-1-9771-0936-1(5)*, 140541, Pebble) Capstone.

—King Penguins. 2019. (Penguins! Ser.). (ENG., Illus.). 24p. (J). (gr. -1-2). lib. bdg. 27.32 *(978-1-9771-0937-8(3)*, 140542, Pebble) Capstone.

—Little Penguins. 2019. (Penguins! Ser.). (ENG., Illus.). 24p. (J). (gr. -1-2). lib. bdg. 27.32 *(978-1-9771-0938-5(1)*, 140543, Pebble) Capstone.

—Rockhopper Penguins. 2019. (Penguins! Ser.). (ENG., Illus.). 24p. (J). (gr. -1-2). lib. bdg. 27.32 *(978-1-9771-0939-2(X)*, 140544, Pebble) Capstone.

Reher, Matt. Penguin Gets Away. 2014. (1G Marine Life Ser.). (ENG., Illus.). 28p. (J). pap. 8.00 *(978-1-63437-615-0(3))* American Reading Co.

Richmond, Ben. Baby Penguin's First Waddles. 2018. (First Discoveries Ser.). (Illus.). 32p. (J). (gr. -1-4). 16.95 *(978-1-4549-2701-3(1))* Sterling Publishing Co., Inc.

Riggs, Kate. Penguins. 2012. (Seedlings Ser.). (ENG.). 24p. (J). (gr. -1-k). 15.95 *(978-1-60818-279-4(7)*, 21997, Creative Education) Creative Co., The.

—Seedlings: Penguins. 2013. (Seedlings Ser.). (ENG.). 24p. (J). (gr. -1-k). pap. 10.99 *(978-0-89812-786-7(6)*, 22003, Creative Paperbacks) Creative Co., The.

Rudolph, Jessica. Rockhopper Penguin. 2016. (Weird but Cute Ser.). (ENG., Illus.). 24p. (J). (gr. -1-3). 26.99 *(978-1-62724-848-8(X))* Bearport Publishing Co., Inc.

Rustad, Martha E. H. A Baby Penguin Story, 1 vol. 2011. (Baby Animals Ser.). (ENG.). 24p. (J). (gr. -1-2). pap. 7.29 *(978-1-4296-7092-0(4)*, 116760, Capstone Pr.) Capstone.

Salomon, David. Penguins! 2017. (Step into Reading Ser.). (Illus.). 32p. (J). (gr. -1-1). pap. 5.99 *(978-1-5247-1560-1(3)*, Random Hse. Bks. for Young Readers) Random Hse. Children's Bks.

Santos, Rita. Emperor Penguins, 1 vol. 2019. (Life at the Poles Ser.). (ENG.). 24p. (gr. 2-2). pap. 10.35 *(978-1-9785-1209-2(0)*, dee7ead9-f2e4-48c6-a4b8-0153abf08def) Enslow Publishing, LLC.

Schafer, Kevin. Penguins 123. 2004. (Penguins Ser.). (ENG., Illus.). 32p. (J). (gr. -1 — 1). bds. 6.95 *(978-1-55971-906-3(0))* Cooper Square Publishing Llc.

—Penguins ABC. 2004. (Penguins Ser.). (ENG., Illus.). 32p. (J). (gr. -1 — 1). bds. 6.95 *(978-1-55971-905-6(2))* Cooper Square Publishing Llc.

Schreiber, Anne. National Geographic Readers: Penguins! 2009. (Readers Ser.). (Illus.). 32p. (J). (gr. 1-3). 4.99 *(978-1-4263-0426-2(9))*; (ENG., lib. bdg. 14.90 *(978-1-4263-0427-9(7))* Disney Publishing Worldwide. (National Geographic Kids).

Schuetz, Kari. Baby Penguins. 2013. (Super Cute! Ser.). (ENG., Illus.). 24p. (J). (gr. k-3). lib. bdg. 26.95 *(978-1-60014-931-3(6)*, Blastoff! Readers) Bellwether Media.

Schuh, Mari. Penguins. 2017. (Black & White Animals Ser.). (ENG., Illus.). 24p. (J). (gr. -1-2). lib. bdg. 22.65 *(978-1-5157-3371-3(8)*, 133367, Pebble) Capstone.

Schwartz, Carol & Edwards, Roberta. Emperor Penguins. Schwartz, Carol, illus. 2007. (All Aboard Science Reader Ser.). (Illus.). 48p. (gr. 1-3). 14.00 *(978-0-7569-8174-7(3))* Perfection Learning Corp.

Scott, Jonathan & Scott, Angela. Antarctica: Land of the Penguins: Band 10/White (Collins Big Cat) 2005. (Collins Big Cat Ser.). (ENG., Illus.). 32p. (J). (gr. 1-3). pap. 10.99 *(978-0-00-718640-2(1))* HarperCollins Pubs. Ltd. GBR. Dist: Independent Pubs. Group.

Sexton, Colleen. The Life Cycle of a Penguin. 2010. (Life Cycles Ser.). (ENG., Illus.). 24p. (J). (gr. k-3). lib. bdg. 26.95 *(978-1-60014-310-6(5)*, Blastoff! Readers) Bellwether Media.

Shulman, Lisa. How Penguins & Butterflies Grow, 6 vols., Set. 2004. (Phonics Readers Books 37-72 Ser.). (ENG.). 8p. (gr. k-1). pap. 35.70 *(978-0-7368-4053-8(2))* Capstone.

Sill, Cathryn. About Penguins: A Guide for Children, 1 vol. Sill, John, illus. 2nd rev. ed. 2013. (About... Ser.: 12). 48p. (J). (gr. -1-2). 7.95 *(978-1-56145-741-0(8))* Peachtree Publishing Co. Inc.

Sill, Cathryn P. About Penguins: A Guide for Children, 1 vol. Sill, John, illus. 2009. (ENG.). 48p. (J). (gr. -1-2). 15.95 *(978-1-56145-488-4(5))* Peachtree Publishing Co. Inc.

Simon, Seymour. Penguins. 2009. (ENG.). 32p. (J). (gr. k-4). pap. 7.99 *(978-0-06-446221-1(8)*, HarperCollins) HarperCollins Pubs.

—Penguins. 2009. (J). lib. bdg. 17.20 *(978-0-606-10540-8(9))* Turtleback.

Staff, Gareth Editorial Staff. Penguins, 1 vol. 2004. (All about Wild Animals Ser.). (ENG., Illus.). 32p. (gr. 2-4). lib. bdg. 28.67 *(978-0-8368-4186-2(7)*, 4b41d4b8-e9ca-4a51-89ba-a426d67d00c0, Gareth Stevens Learning Library) Stevens, Gareth Publishing LLLP.

Statts, Leo. Penguins. 2016. (Polar Animals Ser.). (ENG.). 24p. (J). (gr. -1-2). 49.94 *(978-1-68079-356-7(X)*, 22977, Abdo Zoom-Launch) ABDO Publishing Co.

Stefoff, Rebecca. Penguins, 1 vol. 2007. (Animal Ways Ser.). (ENG., Illus.). 112p. (gr. 6-6). lib. bdg. 38.36 *(978-0-7614-1743-9(5)*, 4e039e30-fbe3-411f-bc16-a0cf800133b5) Cavendish Square Publishing LLC.

Storm, Marysa. Penguins. 2020. (Awesome Animal Lives Ser.). (ENG.). 24p. (J). (gr. k-3). lib. bdg. *(978-1-62310-153-4(0)*, 14406, Bolt Jr.) Black Rabbit Bks.

Stout, Frankie. Penguins: Nature's Coolest Birds. (Things with Wings Ser.). 24p. (gr. 2-3). 2009. 42.50 *(978-1-60854-355-7(2))* 2008. (ENG., Illus.). (J). lib. bdg. 26.27 *(978-1-4042-4495-5(6)*, a6345127-6d1e-4d56-8759-cb3fe30885d6) Rosen Publishing Group, Inc., The. (PowerKids Pr.).

Swan, Erin Pembrey. Animals in Order: Penguins. 2003. (Animals in Order Ser.). (ENG.). 48p. (gr. 4-6). pap. 6.95 *(978-0-531-16660-4(0)*, Watts, Franklin) Scholastic Library Publishing.

Swanson, Diane. Penguins, 1 vol. 2004. (Welcome to the World of Animals Ser.). (ENG., Illus.). 32p. (gr. 2-4). lib. bdg. 26.67 *(978-0-8368-4025-4(9)*, fa00057b-805b-4c5c-99e1-c49d2ade5a8a, Gareth Stevens Learning Library) Stevens, Gareth Publishing LLLP.

—Welcome to the World of Penguins, 1 vol. 2003. (Welcome to the World Ser.: 0). (ENG., Illus.). 32p. (J). (gr. -1-2). pap. 7.95 *(978-1-55285-450-1(7)*, 1e594b91-ae51-4d84-b229-2574bc59ba12) Whitecap Bks., Ltd. CAN. Dist: Firefly Bks., Ltd.

Taylor, Barbara. Exploring Nature: Fantastic Penguins. 2014. (ENG., Illus.). 64p. (J). (gr. k-7). 12.99 *(978-1-84322-853-0(X)*, Armadillo) Anness Publishing GBR. Dist: National Bk. Network.

Taylor, Trace. Antarctic Penguins. 2012. (2G Marine Life Ser.). (ENG.). 12p. (J). (gr. k-2). pap. 8.00 *(978-1-59301-758-3(8))* American Reading Co.

Taylor, Trace & Sánchez, Lucía M. Pingüinos de la AntáRtida: Antarctic Penguins. 2015. (2G Animales Marinos Ser.). (ENG & SPA.). 12p. (J). (gr. k-2). pap. 8.00 *(978-1-61541-274-7(3))* American Reading Co.

Terp, Gail. Penguins. 2016. (Wild Animal Kingdom Ser.). (ENG.). 32p. (J). (gr. 4-6). pap. 9.99 *(978-1-64466-172-7(1)*, 10405); (Illus.). 31.35 *(978-1-68072-054-9(6)*, 10404) Black Rabbit Bks. (Bolt).

Ticktock Media, Ltd. Staff. What Do Penguins Do? 2008. (What Do Animals Do? Ser.). (ENG.). 10p. (J). (gr. k — 1). bds. 4.95 *(978-1-84696-792-4(9)*, TickTock Books) Octopus Publishing Group GBR. Dist: Independent Pubs. Group.

Trattles, Patricia. Emperor Penguins. 2006. (Pull Ahead Bks.). (Illus.). 32p. (J). (gr. -1). 22.60 *(978-0-8225-3484-6(3)*, Lerner Pubns.) Lerner Publishing Group.

Twine, Alice. Penguins. (Baby Animals Ser.). 24p. (gr. 1-1). 2009. 42.50 *(978-1-61511-494-8(7)*, PowerKids Pr.) 2008. (ENG., Illus.). (J). lib. bdg. 26.27 *(978-1-4042-4147-3(7)*, 90d08e82-f086-4f03-b145-4748b38b4fe3) Rosen Publishing Group, Inc., The.

—Penguins/Pinguinos. 2009. (Baby Animals/Animales bebé Ser.). (ENG & SPA.). 24p. (gr. 1-1). 42.50 *(978-1-61511-506-8(4)*, Editorial Buenas Letras) Rosen Publishing Group, Inc., The.

—Penguins/Pinguinos, 1 vol. Obregon, Jose Maria, tr. 2007. (Baby Animals / Animales Bebé Ser.). (ENG & SPA., Illus.). 24p. (J). (gr. 1-1). lib. bdg. 26.27 *(978-1-4042-7686-4(6)*, 4dfa9315-d932-464c-a472-4b247a549729) Rosen Publishing Group, Inc., The.

Ward, Finn. Penguins at the Zoo, 1 vol. 2015. (Zoo Animals Ser.). (ENG., Illus.). 24p. (J). (gr. k-k). pap. 9.15 *(978-1-4824-2605-2(6)*, d20682ad-7406-4fc5-bbb2-c957e6fabd87) Stevens, Gareth Publishing LLLP.

—Pingüinos / Penguins at the Zoo, 1 vol. 2015. (Animales Del Zoológico / Zoo Animals Ser.). (ENG & SPA.). 24p. (J). (gr. k-k). lib. bdg. 24.27 *(978-1-4824-3235-0(8)*, 9a0b9ad5-566f-47f7-aeff-3c886e7cb69b) Stevens, Gareth Publishing LLLP.

Waters, Kate. Penguins. 2009. (Illus.). 32p. (J). *(978-0-545-07232-8(8))* Scholastic, Inc.

Watt, Fiona. Hide-and-Seek Penguins. 2008. (Touchy-Feely Flap Bks). 10p. (J). bds. 16.99 *(978-0-7945-2339-8(0)*, Usborne) EDC Publishing.

—Penguins Luxury Touchy-Feely Board Book. 2010. (Luxury Touchy-Feely Board Bks). 10p. (J). bds. 15.99 *(978-0-7945-2586-6(5)*, Usborne) EDC Publishing.

Webb, Sophie. My Season with Penguins: An Antarctic Journal. 2004. (ENG., Illus.). 48p. (J). (gr. 5-7). reprint ed. pap. 5.95 *(978-0-618-43234-9(5)*, 410532, Clarion Bks.) HarperCollins Pubs.

Wendorff, Anne. Penguins. 2008. (Oceans Alive Ser.). (ENG., Illus.). 24p. (J). (gr. k-3). lib. bdg. 26.95 *(978-1-60014-206-2(0))* Bellwether Media.

West, David. Penguins & Other Birds, 1 vol. 2017. (Inside Animals Ser.). (ENG.). 24p. (J). (gr. 3-3). 26.27 *(978-1-5081-9388-3(6)*, 2a0a3a20-2d79-4ad8-89ba-a000e8970eb4); pap. 9.25 *(978-1-5081-9428-6(9)*, 827ae073-219f-452c-8d75-7576e2a2ba78) Rosen Publishing Group, Inc., The. (Windmill Bks.).

Westerskov, Kim, photos by. Penguins. 2004. (ENG., Illus.). 32p. (J). (gr. 4-4). pap. 7.47 net. *(978-0-7685-2111-5(4)*, Dominie Elementary) Savvas Learning Co.

Whitfield, David. Penguins. 2008. (Amazing Animals Ser.). (Illus.). 24p. (J). (gr. 2-4). pap. 8.95 *(978-1-59036-969-2(6))*; lib. bdg. 24.45 *(978-1-59036-968-5(8))* Weigl Pubs., Inc.

Wildlife Education. Penguins. 2007. (Illus.). 10p. (J). 5.99 *(978-1-932396-31-7(4)*, Critters Up Close) National Wildlife Federation.

Williams, Kathryn. National Geographic Readers: Hello, Penguin! (Pre-Reader) 2017. (Readers Ser.). (ENG., Illus.). 24p. (J). (gr. -1-k). lib. bdg. 13.90 *(978-1-4263-2896-1(6)*, National Geographic Kids) Disney Publishing Worldwide.

—National Geographic Readers: Hello, Penguin! (Prereader) 2017. (Readers Ser.). (Illus.). 24p. (J). (gr. -1-k). pap. 4.99 *(978-1-4263-2895-4(8)*, National Geographic Kids) Disney Publishing Worldwide.

World Book, Inc. Staff, contrib. by. Bob the Penguin. 2017. (Illus.). 31p. (J). *(978-0-7166-3527-7(5))* World Bk., Inc.

Young, Louise O. Penguin Comes Home. Elmore, Larry, illus. 2005. (Soundprints' Amazing Animal Adventures! Ser.). (ENG.). 32p. (J). (gr. -1-2). 19.95 *(978-1-59249-327-2(0)*, BC7108) Soundprints.

PENGUINS—FICTION

Abraham, M. K. Piko the Penguinaut. Jan, R. R., illus. 2012. 112p. (J). 12.95 *(978-1-937489-00-7(0))* StoryRobin Co.

Ackerley, Sarah. Patrick the Somnambulist. Ackerley, Sarah, illus. 2008. (ENG., Illus.). 32p. (J). (gr. -1 — 1). 14.95 *(978-1-933831-07-7(3))* Blooming Tree Pr.

Armstrong, Kim. Petunia in Manhattan. 2009. 50p. pap. 12.99 *(978-1-935436-97-3(X))* Rodaian Pr.

Ashdown, Rebecca. Bob & Flo. Ashdown, Rebecca, illus. 2015. (ENG., Illus.). 32p. (J). (gr. -1-3). 16.99 *(978-0-544-44430-0(2)*, 1597717, Clarion Bks.) HarperCollins Pubs.

—Bob & Flo Play Hide-And-Seek Board Book. 2017. (ENG., Illus.). 26p. (J). (— 1). bds. 7.99 *(978-0-544-85959-3(6)*, 1648584, Clarion Bks.) HarperCollins Pubs.

Atwater, Richard. Mr. Popper's Penguins. 2009. 160p. pap. 6.99 *(978-0-316-10616-0(X))* Little, Brown Bks. for Young Readers.

Atwater, Richard & Atwater, Florence. Mr. Popper's Penguins. Lawson, Robert, illus. 2020. 158p. pap. 18.95 *(978-4-87187-096-2(0))* Ishi Pr. International.

—Mr. Popper's Penguins. 2009. 9.00 *(978-0-7848-3295-0(1)*, Everbind) Marco Bk. Co.

Autrey, Nathan W. Purple Penguin Pumpkin Party. 2011. 42p. pap. 24.95 *(978-1-4560-8286-4(8))* America Star Bks.

Babypants, Caspar. Penguin on a Scooter. Endle, Kate, illus. 2018. 20p. (J). (— 1). bds. 9.99 *(978-1-63217-130-6(9)*, Little Bigfoot) Sasquatch Bks.

Bailey, Ella. One Day on Our Blue Planet: in the Antarctic. 2016. (One Day on Our Blue Planet Ser.). (ENG., Illus.). 32p. (J). (gr. -1-2). 16.95 *(978-1-909263-67-3(2))* Flying Eye Bks. GBR. Dist: Penguin Random Hse. LLC.

Bauer, Jutta. Madrechillona. 2nd ed. 2003. (Rosa y Manzana Ser.). (SPA., Illus.). 28p. (J). (gr. k-2). *(978-84-89804-36-4(2)*, LC30478) Lóguez Ediciones ESP. Dist: Lectorum Pubns., Inc.

Beggs, Melissa. Pompety-Pooh: Purplest Penguin in Zonkety Zoo. Laible, Steve William, ed. Almanstotter, Susanne, illus. 2013. 52p. pap. 12.95 *(978-0-9844784-9-1(3)*, Empire Holdings) Kodel Group, LLC, The.

Bennett, Eric. Noodles & Albie. Bannish, Liz, illus. 2014. (ENG.) (J). 17.95 *(978-1-937650-40-7(5))* Small Batch Bks.

Bentley, Tadgh. Little Penguin & the Lollipop. Bentley, Tadgh, illus. 2017. (ENG., Illus.). 40p. (J). (gr. -1-3). 17.99 *(978-0-06-256078-0(6)*, Balzer & Bray) HarperCollins Pubs.

—Little Penguin Gets the Hiccups. Bentley, Tadgh, illus. 2015. (ENG., Illus.). 40p. (J). (gr. -1-3). 17.99 *(978-0-06-233536-4(7)*, Balzer & Bray) HarperCollins Pubs.

—Little Penguin Gets the Hiccups Board Book. Bentley, Tadgh, illus. 2016. (ENG., Illus.). 34p. (J). (gr. -1 — 1). bds. 8.99 *(978-0-06-265224-9(9)*, Balzer & Bray) HarperCollins Pubs.

Berenstain, Stan & Berenstain, Jan. Nothing Ever Happens at the South Pole. Berenstain, Jan & Berenstain, Mike, illus. 2012. (ENG.). 40p. (J). (gr. -1-3). 10.99 *(978-0-06-207532-1(2)*, HarperCollins) HarperCollins Pubs.

Berg & Holland. Tamino Pingüino y el Asunto Del Huevo. 2004. (SPA., Illus.). 202p. (J). 17.99 *(978-84-261-3301-4(0))* Juventud, Editorial ESP. Dist: Lectorum Pubns., Inc.

Bernstein, Laurie & Helm, Joanna. Penny the Penguin Has Pku. 2012. 24p. pap. 17.99 *(978-1-4772-7226-8(7))* AuthorHouse.

Bogan, Paulette. Virgil & Owen. 2015. (ENG., Illus.). 32p. (J). (gr. k-3). 16.99 *(978-1-61963-372-8(8)*, 900135293, Bloomsbury USA Childrens) Bloomsbury Publishing USA.

Bollinger, Georgia G. The Penguins' Perilous Picnic. 2011. 32p. pap. 14.50 *(978-1-4634-2200-4(8))* AuthorHouse.

Book Buddy: Penguin with Story Book. Orig. Title: Child's Play. (Illus.). 10p. (J). (gr. -1-3). reprint ed. *(978-1-881469-45-2(X))* Safari, Ltd.

Bradley, Jeanette. Love, Mama. Bradley, Jeanette, illus. 2019. (ENG., Illus.). 28p. (J). bds. 7.99 *(978-1-250-24035-4(2)*, 900211506) Roaring Brook Pr.

Brooks, Erik. Polar Opposites, 0 vols. Brooks, Erik, illus. 2012. (ENG., Illus.). 32p. (J). (gr. k-3). 16.99 *(978-0-7614-5685-8(6)*, 9780761456858, Two Lions) Amazon Publishing.

Budge, Donald. Where Is My Butt? Parton, Daron, illus. 2019. 26p. (J). (gr. -1-2). bds. 7.95 *(978-1-4549-3447-9(6))* Sterling Publishing Co., Inc.

Burks, James. Bird & Squirrel on Ice: a Graphic Novel (Bird & Squirrel #2) Burks, James, illus. 2014. (Bird & Squirrel Ser.). (ENG., Illus.). 128p. (J). (gr. 2-5). pap. 10.99 *(978-0-545-56318-5(6)*, Graphix) Scholastic, Inc.

Burns, John. The Many Adventures of Pengey Penguin. Coles, James, illus. 2005. 207p. (J). per. 17.95 *(978-0-9774227-0-8(4))* San Francisco Story Works.

Buzzeo, Toni. One Cool Friend. 2014. (KOR.). 32p. (J). (gr. k-3). *(978-89-7938-087-3(9))* Dasan Publishing Hse.

—One Cool Friend. Small, David, illus. 2012. (ENG.). 32p. (J). (gr. k-3). 18.99 *(978-0-8037-3413-5(1)*, Dial Bks) Penguin Young Readers Group.

—One Cool Friend. Small, David, illus. 2015. DVD 59.95 *(978-0-545-67553-6(7))* Scholastic, Inc.

Caines-Floyd, Eydi. The Story of Wanton Desire. 2009. 64p. (J). pap. 26.49 *(978-1-4389-3156-2(5))* AuthorHouse.

Callahan, Susan. Always Right. 2012. 20p. pap. 15.99 *(978-1-4772-0424-5(5))* AuthorHouse.

Carr, Paul C. The Adventures of Three Cousins. 2006. 24.00 *(978-0-8059-9032-4(1))* Dorrance Publishing Co., Inc.

Caviezel, Giovanni. Little Penguin. Rigo, Laura, illus. 2010. (Look at Me Bks.). 10p. (J). (gr. -1 — 1). bds. 8.99 *(978-0-7641-6353-1(1))* Sourcebooks, Inc.

Chand, Emlyn. Courtney Saves Christmas. Giffin, Noelle, illus. 2012. 60p. 21.95 *(978-1-62253-114-1(0))* Evolved Publishing.

Chartier, Doris E. Ben's Desert Journey. 2009. 32p. pap. 14.49 *(978-1-4389-7756-0(5))* AuthorHouse.

Child's Play. What's up Penguin? Art. Cocoretto, illus. 2018. (What's Up? Ser.: 4). 12p. (J). bds. *(978-1-78628-154-8(6))* Child's Play International Ltd.

Chronicle Books. Baby Penguin: Finger Puppet Book. Huang, Yu-Hsuan, illus. 2018. (Baby Animal Finger Puppets Ser.: 11). (ENG.). 12p. (J). (gr. -1 — 1). 7.99 *(978-1-4521-6375-8(8))* Chronicle Bks. LLC.

Chronicle Books & ImageBooks. Little Penguin: Finger Puppet Book: (Finger Puppet Book for Toddlers & Babies, Baby Books for First Year, Animal Finger Puppets) 2008. (Little Finger Puppet Board Bks.: FING). (ENG., Illus.). 12p. (J). (gr. -1 — 1). bds. 7.99 *(978-0-8118-6355-1(7))* Chronicle Bks. LLC.

Clough, Lisa. Petal & Poppy & the Penguin. Briant, Ed, illus. 2014. (ENG.). 32p. (J). (gr. -1-3). pap. 4.99 *(978-0-544-13330-3(7)*, 1544663, Clarion Bks.) HarperCollins Pubs.

PQR

Colby, Carolyn. Penny Penguin: A Baby Penguin's Adventures on the Ice & Snow. Warren, Leonard, illus. 2011. 50p. 35.95 *(978-1-258-09986-2(1))* Literary Licensing, LLC.

Cole, Carol A. La Dama de Los Pingüinos, 1 vol. Rogers, Sherry, illus. 2012. (SPA.). 32p. (J). (gr. -1-3). 17.95 *(978-1-60718-697-7(7))* Arbordale Publishing.

Cosson, Kip. Ned Visits New York. 2006. (ENG., Illus.). 40p. (J). 16.95 *(978-0-9789384-0-6(2))* Kip Kids of New York.

Coudray, Jean-Luc. A Goofy Guide to Penguins: TOON Level 1. Coudray, Philippe, illus. 2016. 40p. (J). (gr. k-1). 12.95 *(978-1-935179-96-2(9))*, TOON Books) Astra Publishing Hse.

Creek, Silent. All the Ice of Afric. 2009. 160p. 22.95 *(978-1-4401-2118-0(4))* iUniverse, Inc.

Cuyler, Margery. Please Say Please! Penguin's Guide to Manners. Hillenbrand, Will, illus. 2005. (J). *(978-0-439-67874-2(9))* Scholastic, Inc.

Dahl, Michael. Penguin Misses Mom. Vidal, Oriol, illus. 2016. (Hello Genius Ser.). (ENG.). 20p. (J). (gr. -1 — 1). bds. 7.99 *(978-1-4795-8739-1(7)*, 131128, Picture Window Bks.) Capstone.

—Penguin Says Please, 1 vol. Vidal, Oriol, illus. 2012. (Hello Genius Ser.). (ENG.). 20p. (J). (gr. -1 — 1). bds. 7.99 *(978-1-4048-6788-8(0)*, 116226, Picture Window Bks.) Capstone.

Davies, Gill. I Won't Do That Today: A Story of Stubbornness, 1 vol. O'Neill, Robert, illus. 2009. (Let's Grow Together Ser.). (ENG.). 32p. (J). (gr. k-1). pap. 11.55 *(978-1-60754-765-5(1)*, 62d87be7-df60-4428-9805-3ce4fec02f4b); lib. bdg. 27.27 *(978-1-60754-758-7(9)*, bfe2b12c-188d-436b-b1d3-95775216b992) Rosen Publishing Group, Inc., The. (Windmill Bks.).

Doudna, Kelly. Penguin Suit. Chawla, Neena, illus. 2006. (Fact & Fiction Ser.). 24p. (J). pap. 48.42 *(978-1-59679-958-5(7))* ABDO Publishing Co.

Dunbar, Polly. Penguin. Dunbar, Polly, illus. 2010. (Tilly & Friends Ser.). (ENG., Illus.). 40p. (J). (gr. -1-3). pap. 7.99 *(978-0-7636-4972-2(4))* Candlewick Pr.

Duracell and the National Center for Missing & Exploited Children (NCMEC), creator. The Great Tomato Adventure: A Story about Smart Safety Choices. 2007. 0.00 *(978-0-9795307-0-8(9))* Duracell & the National Ctr. for Missing & Exploited Children (NCMEC).

Dyer, Heather. Tina & the Penguin. Levert, Mireille, illus. 2004. 32p. (J). (gr. k-3). pap. 5.95 *(978-1-55337-767-2(2))* Kids Can Pr., Ltd. CAN. Dist: Hachette Bk. Group.

Eaton, Maxwell, III. The Flying Beaver Brothers & the Evil Penguin Plan. 2012. (Flying Beaver Brothers Ser.: 1). lib. bdg. 17.20 *(978-0-606-23869-4(7))* Turtleback.

—The Flying Beaver Brothers & the Evil Penguin Plan: (a Graphic Novel) 2012. (Flying Beaver Brothers Ser.: 1). (Illus.). 96p. (J). (gr. 1-4). pap. 7.99 *(978-0-375-86447-6(4)*, Knopf Bks. for Young Readers) Random Hse. Children's Bks.

Edquist, Patrick. Zombie Penguins of the Antarctic. 2011. 40p. pap. 16.99 *(978-1-4567-6291-9(5))* AuthorHouse.

Emanuel, Effie Ann. The Penguin Party, 1 vol. 2009. 32p. pap. 24.95 *(978-1-60813-544-8(6))* America Star Bks.

Esposito, Tony. The Vagabond Penguin. 2010. 44p. 24.20 *(978-1-4269-4081-1(5))* Trafford Publishing.

Evans, Courtney. Percy the Penguin, 1 vol. 2010. 26p. pap. 24.95 *(978-1-4489-4881-9(9))* PublishAmerica, Inc.

Fenstermacher, Mary Wisham. Pablo Visits the Ocean. 2011. 60p. pap. 23.88 *(978-1-4634-6035-8(X))* AuthorHouse.

Ferry, Beth & Mundorff, Lisa. A Small Blue Whale. 2017. (ENG., Illus.). 32p. (J). (-k). 17.99 *(978-1-5247-1337-9(6))*; lib. bdg. 20.99 *(978-1-5247-1338-6(4))* Random Hse. Children's Bks. (Knopf Bks. for Young Readers).

Ford, Emily. Ten Playful Penguins. Julian, Russell, illus. 2015. (ENG.). 22p. (J). (gr. -1-k). bds. 12.99 *(978-0-545-79439-8(0)*, Cartwheel Bks.) Scholastic, Inc.

Freedman, Claire. The Lost Penguin: An Oliver & Patch Story. Hindley, Kate, illus. 2018. (ENG.). 32p. (J). 17.99 *(978-1-4711-1733-6(2))*; (gr. -1). 7.99 *(978-1-4711-1734-3(0))* Simon & Schuster, Ltd. GBR. (Simon & Schuster Children's). Dist: Simon & Schuster, Inc.

Friesen, Ray. Lookit!, Vol. 2. 2004. (YA). per. 4.95 *(978-0-9728177-3-8(5))* Don't Eat Any Bugs Prodns.

Fromental, Jean-Luc. 365 Penguins (Reissue) ed. 2017. (ENG., Illus.). 48p. (J). (gr. k-2). 17.99 *(978-1-4197-2917-1(9)*, 1213701, Abrams Bks. for Young Readers) Abrams, Inc.

Garbowska, Agata, et al. Gandy & Parker Escape the Zoo: An Illustrated Adventure. Garbowska, Agata, illus. 2013. (Illus.). 97p. pap. *(978-1-897472-82-8(X))* Golden Meteorite Pr.].

Garbowska, Agata, et al. Gandy & Parker Escape the Zoo: An Illustrated Adventure (Simplified Chinese Translation) 2015. (CHI., Illus.). 100p. pap. ***(978-1-897480-22-9(9))*** Golden Meteorite Pr. CAN. Dist: Lulu Pr., Inc.

Garden, Randa Sue. Penny the Penguin. 2003. 48p. per. 7.95 *(978-0-615-12322-6(8))* Garden, Randa.

Gates, Margo. The Little Penguin. Noschese, Kip, illus. 2019. (Let's Look at Animal Habitats (Pull Ahead Readers — Fiction) Ser.). (ENG.). 16p. (J). (gr. -1-1). pap. 8.99 *(978-1-5415-7308-6(0)*, b786be41-2e0e-4dfc-948a-bf60dfb28f46, Lerner Pubns.) Lerner Publishing Group.

Gevry, Claudine, illus. One Little Penguin & His Friends: A Pushing, Turning, Counting Book. 2012. (ENG.). 10p. (J). bds. *(978-1-84956-027-6(7))* Top That! Publishing PLC.

Glover, Clair. Fairy Penguin - the Penguin Who Loves to Play. 2013. 26p. pap. *(978-1-78222-119-7(0))* Paragon Publishing, Rothersthorpe.

Golub, Osu. Penguins Go for the Gold. 2009. 16p. pap. 10.00 *(978-1-4490-3907-3(3))* AuthorHouse.

Gough, Simon. I Can'T Fly & I Can'T Swim. 2011. (Illus.). 24p. pap. 11.44 *(978-1-4567-8063-0(8))* AuthorHouse.

Grant, Sharon. Mr. Special Visits Mrs. Precious' Class. 2004. (J). per. 9.95 *(978-1-59427-032-1(5))* Aglob Publishing.

Greene, Kristy. How Penguins Lost Their Flight. 2012. 20p. pap. 24.95 *(978-1-4626-7697-2(9))* America Star Bks.

Griffin, Esther M. Alex, the Lonely, Black-Footed Penguin. 2012. pap. 11.95 *(978-0-7414-7832-0(3))* Infinity Publishing.

Guest, Patrick. The Second Sky. Bentley, Jonathan, illus. 2019. (ENG.). 32p. (J). *(978-0-8028-5520-6(2)*, Eerdmans Bks For Young Readers) Eerdmans, William B. Publishing Co.

Hale, Bruce. Key Lardo: A Chet Gecko Mystery. Hale, Bruce, illus. 2007. (Chet Gecko Ser.: 12). (ENG., Illus.). 128p. (J). (gr. 3-7). pap. 7.99 *(978-0-15-205235-5(6)*, 1195772, Clarion Bks.) HarperCollins Pubs.

Hancocks, Helen. Penguin in Peril. Hancocks, Helen, illus. 2014. (ENG., Illus.). 32p. (J). (gr. -1-2). 18.99 *(978-0-7636-7159-4(2)*, Templar) Candlewick Pr.

Haylock, Heather. Granny McFlitter, the Champion Knitter. Chisholm, Lael, illus. 2018. (Granny McFlitter Ser.). 32p. (J). (gr. k-2). 16.99 *(978-0-14-377054-1(3))* Penguin Group New Zealand, Ltd. NZL. Dist: Independent Pubs. Group.

Heidenreich, Elke. Some Folk Think the South Pole's Hot: The Three Tenors Play the Antarctic. Buchholz, Quint, illus. 2004. (ENG.). 64p. (J). 17.95 *(978-1-56792-170-0(1))* Godine, David R. Pub.

Hinojosa, Francisco. Yanka, Yanka. Hinojosa, Francisco, illus. 2003. (SPA., Illus.). 44p. (J). (gr. k-3). pap. 10.95 *(978-968-19-0440-1(0))* Santillana USA Publishing Co., Inc.

Hollenbeck, Kathleen M. Penguin's Family: The Story of the a Humboldt Penguin. Stegos, Daniel J., illus. 2008. (ENG.). 32p. (J). (gr. -1-3). 19.95 *(978-1-59249-765-2(9))* Soundprints.

Hood, Morag. When Grandad Was a Penguin. 2018. (ENG., Illus.). 32p. (J). (gr. -1-k). pap. 14.99 *(978-1-5098-5097-6(X)*, 900326043, Two Hoots) Pan Macmillan GBR. Dist: Macmillan.

Horacek, Petr & Horacek, Petr. Blue Penguin. Horacek, Petr & Horacek, Petr, illus. 2016. (ENG., Illus.). 32p. (J). (gr. -1-2). 15.99 *(978-0-7636-9251-3(4))* Candlewick Pr.

Hub, Ulrich. Meet at the Ark at Eight. Mühle, Jörg & Mühle, Jörg, illus. 2012. (ENG.). 68p. (J). 12.00 *(978-0-8028-5410-0(9)*, Eerdmans Bks For Young Readers) Eerdmans, William B. Publishing Co.

Humphreys, Neil. Picking up a Penguin's Egg Really Got Me into Trouble. Cheng, Puay Koon, illus. 2014. (Abbie Rose & the Magic Suitcase Ser.). (ENG.). 24p. (J). (gr. -1 — 1). pap. 13.99 *(978-981-4484-18-3(0))* Marshall Cavendish International (Asia) Private Ltd. SGP. Dist: Independent Pubs. Group.

Hunt, Peter. The Fairy Penguin's Lesson & Other Tales. 2012. 44p. pap. 32.70 *(978-1-4797-4712-2(2))* Xlibris Corp.

Idle, Molly. Flora & the Penguin. 2014. (Flora & Friends Ser.). (ENG., Illus.). 40p. (J). (gr. -1-k). 16.99 *(978-1-4521-2891-7(X))* Chronicle Bks. LLC.

Innovative Kids Staff, creator. Playful Penguins. 2012. (ENG.). 6p. (J). (gr. -1 — 1). 14.99 *(978-1-60169-266-5(8))* Innovative Kids.

Iwasa, Megumi. Dear Professor Whale. Takabatake, Jun, illus. 2018. (ENG.). 104p. (J). (gr. k-3). 16.99 *(978-1-77657-206-9(8)*, 99e443a3-c963-40f9-861a-c55409bd2ce8) Gecko Pr. NZL. Dist: Lerner Publishing Group.

—Yours Sincerely, Giraffe. Takabatake, Jun, illus. 2017. (ENG.). 104p. (gr. k-3). (J). 16.99 *(978-1-927271-88-9(6)*, 4f529eba-51e5-4e27-8bb3-91fa7b989948); 9.99 *(978-1-77657-114-7(2))* Gecko Pr. NZL. Dist: Lerner Publishing Group.

Jadoul, Émile. All by Myself! 2012. (ENG.). 26p. (J). 14.00 *(978-0-8028-5411-7(7)*, Eerdmans Bks For Young Readers) Eerdmans, William B. Publishing Co.

Jamaldinian, Joe. Bob Winging It. Jamaldinian, Joe, illus. 2005. (Illus.). 32p. (J). 14.00 *(978-0-9786657-0-0(0))* Jamaldinian, Yousef.

Jeffers, Oliver. The Boy: His Stories & How They Came to Be. 2019. (ENG., Illus.). 168p. (J). (gr. -1-3). 40.00 *(978-0-593-11474-2(4)*, Philomel Bks.) Penguin Young Readers Group.

—Lost & Found. Jeffers, Oliver, illus. 2005. (ENG., Illus.). 32p. (J). (gr. -1-2). 18.99 *(978-0-399-24503-9(0)*, Philomel Bks.) Penguin Young Readers Group.

—Up & Down. Jeffers, Oliver, illus. 2010. (ENG., Illus.). 40p. (J). (gr. -1-2). 19.99 *(978-0-399-25545-8(1)*, Philomel Bks.) Penguin Young Readers Group.

John, Jory. Penguin Problems. Smith, Lane, illus. 2018. (ENG.). 32p. (J). (— 1). bds. 8.99 *(978-0-525-64575-7(6)*, Random Hse. Bks. for Young Readers) Random Hse. Children's Bks.

John Taylor, Jeannie St. Penguin's Special Christmas Tree. Lt. ed. 2012. 36p. (J). pap. *(978-1-4596-3452-7(7))* ReadHowYouWant.com, Ltd.

Johnson, Lori. The Prodigal Penguin. 2010. 20p. 13.95 *(978-1-4497-0252-6(X))* iUniverse, Inc.

Johnston, Johanna. Penguin's Way. Weisgard, Leonard, illus. 2015. 48p. 20.00 *(978-1-85124-427-0(1))* Bodleian Library GBR. Dist: Chicago Distribution Ctr.

Jonell, Bob. Penny the Chinstrap Penguin, 1 vol. Prince, Brian, illus. 2010. 22p. 24.95 *(978-1-4489-5334-9(0))* PublishAmerica, Inc.

Joyce, Melanie. Fly, Freddy, Fly. Seal, Julia, illus. 2014. (J). *(978-1-4351-5806-1(7))* Barnes & Noble, Inc.

Judge, Lita. Flight School. Judge, Lita, illus. 2019. (Flight School Ser.). (ENG., Illus.). 36p. (J). (gr. -1-k). bds. 8.99 *(978-1-5344-4481-2(5)*, Little Simon) Little Simon.

—Flight School. Judge, Lita, illus. 2014. (Flight School Ser.). (ENG., Illus.). 40p. (J). (gr. -1-3). 18.99 *(978-1-4424-8177-0(3)*, Atheneum Bks. for Young Readers) Simon & Schuster Children's Publishing.

—Penguin Flies Home. Judge, Lita, illus. 2019. (Flight School Ser.). (ENG., Illus.). 40p. (J). (gr. -1-3). 17.99 *(978-1-5344-1441-9(X)*, Atheneum Bks. for Young Readers) Simon & Schuster Children's Publishing.

Kemp, Dane. Imaginary Tales. 2011. 186p. pap. 24.95 *(978-1-4560-4686-6(1))* America Star Bks.

Kimmel, Elizabeth Cody. Mi Pinguino Oliver. Lewis, H. B., illus. 2004.Tr. of My Penguin Osbert. (SPA.). (J). 15.99 *(978-84-88342-68-3(3))* S.A. Kokinos ESP. Dist: Lectorum Pubns., Inc.

—My Penguin Osbert in Love: Midi Edition. Lewis, H. B., illus. 2010. (ENG.). 48p. (J). (gr. -1-3). 7.99 *(978-0-7636-5001-8(3))* Candlewick Pr.

Kitzing, Constanze V. Chilly Penguin. Kitzing, Constanze V., illus. 2018. (ENG., Illus.). 24p. (J). (gr. -1-k). bds. 8.99 *(978-1-78285-406-7(1)*, Barefoot Bks., Inc.

Klein, Judith Anne. Tuxedo Flyer. 2009. 28p. pap. 14.65 *(978-1-4490-0635-8(3))* AuthorHouse.

Krupinski, Tiffany J. Pangi the Penguin. 2011. 20p. pap. 24.95 *(978-1-4560-6074-9(0))* America Star Bks.

Kuo, Fifi. I Can Fly. 2018. (ENG., Illus.). 32p. (J). (gr. -1-3). 17.99 *(978-1-4998-0741-7(4))* Little Bee Books Inc.

—The Perfect Sofa. 2019. (ENG.). 32p. (J). (gr. -1-3). 17.99 *(978-1-4998-0742-4(2))* Little Bee Books Inc.

Lammers, Elizabeth A. & McKinney, Dan. The Tale of the Black Igloo: Another Adventure of Pepe & Pierre, 1 vol. Epstein, Gabriela, illus. 2010. 26p. pap. 24.95 *(978-1-60610-433-0(0))* PublishAmerica, Inc.

Latimer, Alex. Penguin's Hidden Talent, 1 vol. 2012. (ENG., Illus.). 32p. (J). (gr. -1-3). 15.95 *(978-1-56145-629-1(2))* Peachtree Publishing Co. Inc.

Lawton, Diana. Paulie the Penguin Meets Sammy the Seal. 2012. 30p. 24.95 *(978-1-4626-6782-6(1))* America Star Bks.

Lesley, Sharon. The Red Scarf & Other Stories. 2010. 165p. pap. 14.95 *(978-1-4457-6720-8(1))* Lulu Pr., Inc.

Lester, Helen. Tacky & the Haunted Igloo. Munsinger, Lynn, illus. 2015. (Tacky the Penguin Ser.). (ENG.). 32p. (J). 17.99 *(978-0-544-33994-1(0)*, 1584695, Clarion Bks.) HarperCollins Pubs.

—Tacky & the Winter Games: A Winter & Holiday Book for Kids. Munsinger, Lynn, illus. 2007. (Tacky the Penguin Ser.). (ENG.). 32p. (J). (gr. -1-3). 7.99 *(978-0-618-95674-6(3)*, 1021437, Clarion Bks.) HarperCollins Pubs.

—Tacky Goes to Camp. 2012. (Tacky the Penguin Ser.). lib. bdg. 17.20 *(978-0-606-23992-9(8))* Turtleback.

—Tacky the Penguin Board Book. Munsinger, Lynn, illus. 2008. (Tacky the Penguin Ser.). (ENG.). 32p. (J). (gr. -1-3). bds. 7.99 *(978-0-547-13344-7(8)*, 1048740, Clarion Bks.) HarperCollins Pubs.

—Tacky the Penguin Book & CD, 1 vol. Munsinger, Lynn, illus. 2006. (Tacky the Penguin Ser.). (ENG.). 32p. (J). (gr. -1-3). audio compact disk 12.99 *(978-0-618-73754-3(5)*, 489199, Clarion Bks.) HarperCollins Pubs.

—Tackylocks & the Three Bears. Munsinger, Lynn, illus. 2004. (Tacky the Penguin Ser.). (ENG.). 32p. (J). (gr. -1-3). pap. 7.99 *(978-0-618-43953-9(6)*, 439862, Clarion Bks.) HarperCollins Pubs.

Lewis, Jill. A Mom in a Million. Gulbis, Stephen, illus. 2005. 32p. (J). *(978-1-84458-368-3(6)*, Pavilion Children's Books) Pavilion Bks.

Little Bee Books. Kisses & Cuddles. 2015. (ENG., Illus.). 16p. (J). (gr. -1 — 1). bds. 5.99 *(978-1-4998-0151-4(3))* Little Bee Books Inc.

Logan, Christopher. Daphne. 2008. 145p. pap. 18.95 *(978-1-4357-5038-8(1))* Lulu Pr., Inc.

Lukachko, Mary Louise. Peter the Blue Penguin. 2012. 28p. pap. 24.95 *(978-1-4626-8186-0(7))* America Star Bks.

Lumry, Amanda & Hurwitz, Laura. South Pole Penguins. 2007. (Adventures of Riley Ser.). (Illus.). 36p. (J). (gr. -1-3). 15.95 *(978-0-9748411-5-1(3))*; lib. bdg. 18.95 *(978-0-9748411-8-2(8))* Eaglemont Pr.

MacIver, Juliette. Gwendolyn! Baynton, Terri Rose, illus. 2018. 32p. pap. 6.99 *(978-0-7333-3518-1(7))* ABC Bks. AUS. Dist: HarperCollins Pubs.

Martin, Mairead S. The Forgotten Little Penguin. 2013. 34p. pap. *(978-0-9576676-0-0(4))* Dream Cloud Bks.

Mattassi, Ezio. Pepito the Penguin, 1 vol. Mattassi, Ezio, illus. 2009. (Illus.). 15p. pap. 24.95 *(978-1-61582-731-2(5))* PublishAmerica, Inc.

Mayfield, Sue. I Can, You Can, Toucan! 2006. (Green Bananas Ser.). (ENG., Illus.). 48p. (J). (gr. -1-3). lib. bdg. *(978-0-7787-1032-5(7))* Crabtree Publishing Co.

Maynor, Megan. Ella & Penguin: a Perfect Match. Bonnet, Rosalinde, illus. 2017. (ENG.). 32p. (J). (gr. -1-3). 17.99 *(978-0-06-233089-5(6)*, HarperCollins) HarperCollins Pubs.

—Ella & Penguin Stick Together. Bonnet, Rosalinde, illus. 2016. (ENG.). 32p. (J). (gr. -1-3). 17.99 *(978-0-06-233088-8(8)*, HarperCollins) HarperCollins Pubs.

McAuliffe, Nichola. Attila, Loolagax & the Eagle. Collins, Ross, tr. Collins, Ross, illus. 2003. 128p. (J). pap. 10.99 *(978-0-7475-6499-7(X))* Bloomsbury Publishing Plc GBR. Dist: Independent Pubs. Group.

McGrath, Barbara Barbieri. Five Flying Penguins. Coleman, Stephanie Fizer, illus. 2018. (ENG.). 32p. (J). (gr. -1-2). lib. bdg. 12.99 *(978-1-58089-805-8(X))* Charlesbridge Publishing, Inc.

McGuinness, Jeff. Paddy the Penguin's Adventure. Starr, Lisa, illus. Lt. ed. 2006. 33p. (J). 27.95 *(978-1-59879-231-7(8))*; (gr. -1-3). per. 15.95 *(978-1-59879-229-4(6))* Lifevest Publishing, Inc.

McNamee, Kevin. My Brother the Frog. Morris, Alexander, illus. 2011. 24p. 19.95 *(978-1-61633-167-2(4))*; pap. 10.95 *(978-1-61633-159-7(3))* Guardian Angel Publishing, Inc.

Meadows, Daisy. Pia the Penguin Fairy. 2011. (J). (Rainbow Magic: Ocean Fairies Ser.: 3). (ENG.). 80p. (gr. 1-4). 17.44 *(978-0-545-27038-0(3))*; (Illus.). 63p. *(978-0-545-28873-6(8))* Scholastic, Inc.

Meschenmoser, Sebastian. Gordon & Tapir. 2016. (ENG., Illus.). 60p. (J). 18.95 *(978-0-7358-4253-3(1))* North-South Bks., Inc.

Messer, Claire. Grumpy Pants. Messer, Claire, illus. 2016. (ENG., Illus.). 32p. (J). (gr. -1-3). 16.99 *(978-0-8075-3075-7(1)*, 807530751) Whitman, Albert & Co.

Milbourne, Anna. How Big Is a Million? Rigliettti, Serena, illus. 2008. (J). *(978-0-545-11519-3(1))* Scholastic, Inc.

—How Big Was a Dinosaur? 2011. (Picture Books Ser.). 24p. (J). ring bd. 10.99 *(978-0-7945-3002-0(8)*, Usborne) EDC Publishing.

—How Deep Is the Sea? Rigliettti, Serena, illus. 2010. (Picture Bks). 24p. (J). 10.99 *(978-0-7945-2311-4(0))* EDC Publishing.

—How High Is the Sky? Rigliettti, Serena, illus. 2009. (Picture Bks). 24p. (J). (gr. -1). 10.99 *(978-0-7945-2273-5(4)*, Usborne) EDC Publishing.

Milne, J. E. The Adventures of Haole the Penguin: The Inner Game of Surfing. 2011. 264p. 25.95 *(978-1-4327-7160-7(4))*; pap. 13.95 *(978-1-4327-7142-3(6))* Outskirts Pr., Inc.

Minor, Florence. If You Were a Penguin. Minor, Wendell, illus. 2008. (ENG.). 32p. (J). (gr. -1-2). 19.99 *(978-0-06-113097-7(4)*, Tegen, Katherine Bks) HarperCollins Pubs.

Minor, Florence F. If You Were a Penguin. Minor, Wendell, illus. 2009. 32p. (J). (gr. -1-2). lib. bdg. 18.89 *(978-0-06-113098-4(2))* HarperCollins Pubs.

Mitchell, Lance B. The Penguin Adventures of Ping & Pong. 2008. 32p. pap. 24.95 *(978-1-60474-124-7(4))* America Star Bks.

Mitter, Matt. Penny Penguin. Brown, Jo, illus. 2010. (Snappy Fun Ser.). (ENG.). 10p. (J). bds. 7.99 *(978-0-7944-2014-7(1))* Reader's Digest Assn., Inc., The.

Monsell, Mary Elise. A Fish Named Yum Vol. IV: MR. PIN. 2007. 72p. (gr. 1-4). per. 8.95 *(978-0-595-47246-8(X)*, Backinprint.com) iUniverse, Inc.

—Mr Pin: The Chocolate Files. 2007. 68p. (gr. -1-3). per. 8.95 *(978-0-595-47318-2(0)*, Backinprint.com) iUniverse, Inc.

—The Mysterious Cases of Mr. Pin, Vol. I. 2007. 68p. (gr. -1-3). per. 8.95 *(978-0-595-47247-5(8)*, Backinprint.com) iUniverse, Inc.

—The Spy Who Came North from the Pole. 2007. 68p. (gr. -1-3). per. 8.95 *(978-0-595-47248-2(6)*, Backinprint.com) iUniverse, Inc.

Muldrow, Diane. How Do Penguins Play? Walker, David M., illus. 2011. (Little Golden Book Ser.). 24p. (J). (gr. -1-k). 5.99 *(978-0-375-86501-5(2)*, Golden Bks.) Random Hse. Children's Bks.

Murphy, Mary. I Like It When ... Board Book. Murphy, Mary, illus. 2005. (ENG., Illus.). 22p. (J). (gr. k — 1). bds. 7.99 *(978-0-15-205649-0(1)*, 1196986, Clarion Bks.) HarperCollins Pubs.

—I Like It When ... /Me Gusta Cuando ... Bilingual English-Spanish. Murphy, Mary, illus. 2008. (ENG., Illus.). 22p. (J). (gr. -1-k). bds. 7.99 *(978-0-15-206045-9(6)*, 1198156, Clarion Bks.) HarperCollins Pubs.

—Let's Go! 2005. (ENG., Illus.). 16p. (J). bds. 14.99 *(978-1-4052-1115-4(6))* Farshore GBR. Dist: Trafalgar Square Publishing.

One Cool Friend. 2014. pap. 16.99 *(978-0-545-67554-3(5))* Scholastic, Inc.

Ostermeyer, Tim. Snowball's Antarctic Adventures. 2011. (Illus.). 46p. (J). (gr. -1-3). 18.95 *(978-0-9794228-3-6(3))* Ostermeyer Photography.

Oxley, Jennifer & Aronson, Billy. Peg + Cat: The Penguin Problem. 2016. (Peg + Cat Ser.). (ENG., Illus.). 32p. (J). (gr. -1-2). 12.99 *(978-0-7636-9073-1(2)*, Candlewick Entertainment) Candlewick Pr.

Panpan, Alice. Antarctic Wings. 2011. 36p. pap. 21.99 *(978-1-4568-6210-7(3))* Xlibris Corp.

Parnell, Declan. Make Way for Penguins, 1 vol., 1. 2015. (Rosen REAL Readers: Social Studies Nonfiction / Fiction: Myself, My Community, My World Ser.). (ENG.). 8p. (J). (gr. k-1). pap. 5.46 *(978-1-5081-1884-8(1)*, d3d17b29-403e-49ca-ba77-6d47584814fc, Rosen Classroom) Rosen Publishing Group, Inc., The.

Pfister, Marcus. Penguin Pete. 2013. (Penguin Pete Ser.). (ENG., Illus.). 32p. (J). (gr. -1-3). 16.95 *(978-0-7358-4118-5(7))* North-South Bks., Inc.

—Penguin Pete & Pat. 2014. (Penguin Pete Ser.). (ENG., Illus.). 32p. (J). (gr. k-3). 14.95 *(978-0-7358-4155-0(1))* North-South Bks., Inc.

Pichon, Liz. Penguins. 2008. (J). *(978-0-545-08292-1(7)*, Orchard Bks.) Scholastic, Inc.

Pimot, Karen Hutchins. The Blue Penguin. Klanot, Makenna Karen, illus. 2008. 44p. pap. 14.95 *(978-1-934246-79-5(4))* Peppertree Pr., The.

Portis, Antoinette. A Penguin Story. Portis, Antoinette, illus. 2008. (ENG., Illus.). 40p. (J). (gr. -1-3). 17.99 *(978-0-06-145688-6(8)*, HarperCollins) HarperCollins Pubs.

Publications International Ltd. Staff, ed. Look & Find Surfs Up. 2007. (Illus.). 24p. (J). 7.10 *(978-1-4127-6836-8(5)*, PIL Kids) Publications International, Ltd.

Punter, Russell. Chilly Little Penguin. 2009. (First Reading Level 2 Ser.). 32p. (J). 6.99 *(978-0-7945-2424-1(9)*, Usborne) EDC Publishing.

Randall, Ronne. Snuggle up, Little Penguin! Church, Caroline Jayne, illus. 2003. (Little Friends Ser.). 14p. (J). 12.95 *(978-1-57145-919-0(7)*, Silver Dolphin Bks.) Readerlink Distribution Services, LLC.

Rees, Douglas. Uncle Pirate. Auth, Tony, illus. (ENG.). 112p. (J). (gr. 2-5). 2009. pap. 6.99 *(978-1-4169-4763-9(9))* 2008. 15.99 *(978-1-4169-4762-2(0))* McElderry, Margaret K. Bks. (McElderry, Margaret K. Bks.).

—Uncle Pirate to the Rescue. Auth, Tony, illus. 2010. (ENG.). 112p. (J). (gr. 2-5). pap. 6.99 *(978-1-4169-7505-2(5)*, McElderry, Margaret K. Bks.) McElderry, Margaret K. Bks.

Reyes, Nikki. An Unexpected Guest: It Started with a fish. It ended with a Friend. 2009. 48p. pap. 17.49 *(978-1-4363-9133-7(4))* Xlibris Corp.

Richardson, Justin & Parnell, Peter. And Tango Makes Three. Cole, Henry, illus. 2005. (ENG.). 32p. (J). (gr. -1-3). 18.99 *(978-0-689-87845-9(1)*, Simon & Schuster Bks. For Young Readers) Simon & Schuster Bks. For Young Readers.

Roberts, Daniel. The Penguin & the Polar Bear. 2009. 32p. pap. 14.95 *(978-1-4389-2845-6(9))* AuthorHouse.

Rosario, Joann. The PenguinThat Boom- Booms to a Ferret That Zoom- Zoomed. Rosario, Joann, illus. 2004. (Illus.). 28p. (J). (gr. -1-5). pap. 10.00 *(978-0-9758746-4-6(0)*, 1246169) J.G.R. Enterprises.

Ross, Melissa. Today I Am a Penguin. Ross, Melissa, illus. 2012. (Illus.). 24p. pap. 10.95 *(978-1-61633-306-5(5))* Guardian Angel Publishing, Inc.

Rossell, Judith. Oliver. Rossell, Judith, illus. 2012. (ENG., Illus.). 32p. (J). (gr. -1-2). 16.99 *(978-0-06-202210-3(5)*, HarperCollins) HarperCollins Pubs.

Ryan, Pam Muñoz. Tony Baloney: Buddy Trouble. Fotheringham, Ed, illus. 2013. 38p. (J). pap. *(978-0-545-48170-0(8))* Scholastic, Inc.

—Tony Baloney: Pen Pal. Fotheringham, Ed, illus. 2014. 39p. (J). pap. *(978-0-545-69227-4(X)*, Scholastic Pr.) Scholastic, Inc.

—Tony Baloney: School Rules. Fotheringham, Edwin, illus. 2012. 39p. (J). pap. *(978-0-545-48167-0(8))* Scholastic, Inc.

Rylant, Cynthia. Little Penguins. Robinson, Christian, illus. 2016. 40p. (J). (gr. -1-2). 18.99 *(978-0-553-50770-6(2)*, Schwartz & Wade Bks.) Random Hse. Children's Bks.

Sang, Franchesca Ho, compiled by. Wisdom of Penguins. 2006. (Illus.). 128p. (J). *(978-1-59258-254-9(0))* Hylas Publishing.

Sansone, V. K. A Daunting Quest for Quincy & Quigley. 2008. (ENG.). 32p. pap. 8.98 *(978-0-557-03594-6(5))* Lulu Pr., Inc.

Scott, Cavan & Alexander, Jim. Penguins of Madagascar: Operation Heist Vol. 2. Bartolini, Egle, illus. 2015. (Penguins of Madagascar Ser.: 2). (ENG.). 64p. (J). (gr. 1-4). pap. 6.99 *(978-1-78276-252-2(3))* Titan Bks. Ltd. GBR. Dist: Penguin Random Hse. LLC.

Scraper, Katherine. Pen Pal Penguin. Callen, Liz, illus. 2012. 8p. (J). *(978-0-7367-2639-9(X))* Zaner-Bloser, Inc.
—Save the Fairy Penguins. 2005. (J). pap. *(978-1-4108-4214-5(2))* Benchmark Education Co.
Server, David & Lanzing, Jackson. Penguins of Madagascar, Vol. 2. 2011. (ENG.). 52p. (J). pap. 6.95 *(978-1-936340-30-9(5),* 9781936340309) Ape Entertainment.
Sima, Jessie. Harriet Gets Carried Away. Sima, Jessie, illus. 2018. (ENG., Illus.). 48p. (J). (gr. -1-3). 18.99 *(978-1-4814-6911-1(8),* Simon & Schuster Bks. For Young Readers) Simon & Schuster Bks. For Young Readers.
Smith, Alex T. Mr. Penguin & the Fortress of Secrets, 1 vol. 2019. (Mr. Penguin Ser.: 2). (ENG., Illus.). 288p. (J). (gr. 3-7). 16.95 *(978-1-68263-130-0(3))* Peachtree Publishing Co. Inc.
—Mr. Penguin & the Lost Treasure. 2019. (Mr. Penguin Ser.: 1). (ENG., Illus.). 208p. (J). (gr. 3-7). 16.95 *(978-1-68263-120-1(6))* Peachtree Publishing Co. Inc.
Smith, Sarah, illus. Where's My Mommy? 2009. (J). *(978-0-7607-8404-4(3))* Barnes & Noble, Inc.
Sonneborn, Scott. Meet the South Police. Lozano, Omar, illus. 2015. (North Police Ser.). (ENG.). 32p. (J). (gr. k-2). lib. bdg. 21.32 *(978-1-4795-6486-6(9),* 128339, Picture Window Bks.) Capstone.
St-Laurent, Christina. Macaroni's Midnight Madness. 2011. 28p. pap. 15.99 *(978-1-4628-5427-1(3))* Xlibris Corp.
Stephens, Sarah. Pooches of Power!, 1 vol. Baltazar, Art, illus. 2011. (DC Super-Pets Ser.). (ENG.). 56p. (J). (gr. 1-3). pap. 4.95 *(978-1-4048-6620-1(5),* 114716, Stone Arch Bks.) Capstone.
Stepp, Shirley. Pongo Penguin's Whale of a Tale. 2012. 24p. 24.95 *(978-1-4626-5478-9(9))* America Star Bks.
Strasser, Todd. Is That an Angry Penguin in Your Gym Bag? 2009. (Is That...? Ser.). (ENG.). 208p. (J). (gr. 4-6). 18.69 *(978-0-439-77697-4(X))* Scholastic, Inc.
Straub-Martin, Susan M. Legends, Loves & Great Lakes. 2013. 28p. pap. 15.00 *(978-0-9830321-6-8(5))* Strauberry Studios.
Taylor, Sean. I Am Actually a Penguin. Matyjaszek, Kasia, illus. 2018. (ENG.). 32p. (J). (-k). 16.99 *(978-1-5362-0278-6(9),* Templar) Candlewick Pr.
Teckentrup, Britta. Up & Down. Teckentrup, Britta, illus. 2014. (ENG., Illus.). 28p. (J). (-k). 17.99 *(978-0-7636-7129-7(0),* Templar) Candlewick Pr.
Ted in a Red Bed Kid Kit. 2004. (Kid Kits Ser.). (Illus.). 10p. (J). bds. 9.95 *(978-1-58086-404-6(X))* EDC Publishing.
Toenies, Claudia. A Very Special Penguin. 2007. 36p. per. 16.99 *(978-1-4343-3074-1(5))* AuthorHouse.
Tomlinson, Jill. The Penguin Who Wanted to Find Out. Howard, Paul, illus. 2014. (ENG.). 96p. (J). (gr. -1-2). pap. 5.99 *(978-1-4052-7191-2(4))* Farshore GBR. Dist: HarperCollins Pubs.
Tomorrow, Tom. The Very Silly Mayor. 2009. (ENG., Illus.). 36p. (J). (gr. -1-3). pap. 16.99 *(978-1-935439-01-1(4))* Ig Publishing, Inc.
Toms, K. 10 Little Penguins Mini Book & Plush. 2009. 26p. pap. *(978-1-84879-065-0(1))* Make Believe Ideas.
Top That Publishing Staff, ed. One Little Penguin & His Friends: A Pushing, Turning, Counting Book. Gévry, Claudine, illus. 2007. 10p. (J). (gr. -1-3). bds. *(978-1-84666-268-3(0),* Tide Mill Pr.) Top That! Publishing PLC.
Top That!, creator. Shapes with Penny the Penguin. 2012. (Learn with Magnets Ser.). (ENG., Illus.). 10p. (J). (gr. -1). *(978-1-84956-671-1(2))* Top That! Publishing PLC.
Trussell-Cullen, Alan. The Lonely Penguin's Blog, 1 vol. rev. ed. 2013. (Literary Text Ser.). (ENG., Illus.). 28p. (gr. 2-3). pap. 9.99 *(978-1-4333-5559-2(0))* Teacher Created Materials, Inc.
Ullrich, Hortense. La Aventura de Lorenzo. (SPA.). (J). 7.95 *(978-958-04-7447-0(8))* Norma S.A. COL. Dist: Distribuidora Norma, Inc.
—La Prueba de Valor de Lorenzo. (SPA.). (J). 7.95 *(978-958-04-7069-4(3))* Norma S.A. COL. Dist: Distribuidora Norma, Inc.
Watt, Fiona. That's Not My Penguin. Wells, Rachel, illus. 2007. (Usborne Touchy-Feely Board Bks.). 8p. (gr. -1-k). bds. 7.99 *(978-0-7945-1810-3(9),* Usborne) EDC Publishing.
Watt, Mélanie & Watt, Mélanie. Augustine. Watt, Mélanie & Watt, Mélanie, illus. 2008. (ENG., Illus.). 32p. (J). (gr. -1-2). pap. 9.99 *(978-1-55453-268-1(X))* Kids Can Pr., Ltd. CAN. Dist: Hachette Bk. Group.
Weeks, Sarah. Without You. Duranceau, Suzanne, illus. 40p. (J). (gr. -1-2). 2007. (ENG.). pap. 7.99 *(978-0-06-113998-7(X),* HarperCollins) 2003. 16.99 *(978-0-06-027816-8(1),* Geringer, Laura Book) HarperCollins Pubs.
What I Learned from a Penguin. 2005. (YA). lib. bdg. 19.95 *(978-1-886565-42-5(2))* MindWorks Pr.
Willis, Jeanne. Penguin Pandemonium. 2013. (Awesome Animals Ser.). (ENG., Illus.). 192p. (J). (gr. 4-7). 21.19 *(978-1-4380-0301-6(3),* B.E.S. Publishing) Peterson's.
—Take Turns, Penguin! Birchall, Mark, illus. 2003. (Picture Bks.). 32p. (J). (gr. -1-3). 7.95 *(978-1-57505-493-3(0),* Carolrhoda Bks.) Lerner Publishing Group.
Wilson, Karma. Don't Be Afraid, Little Pip. Chapman, Jane, illus. 2009. (ENG.). 40p. (J). (gr. -1-2). 17.99 *(978-0-689-85987-8(2),* McElderry, Margaret K. Bks.) McElderry, Margaret K. Bks.
—What's in the Egg, Little Pip? Chapman, Jane, illus. 2010. (ENG.). 40p. (J). (gr. -1-3). 19.99 *(978-1-4169-4204-7(1),* McElderry, Margaret K. Bks.) McElderry, Margaret K. Bks.
—Where Is Home, Little Pip? Chapman, Jane, illus. 2008. (ENG.). 40p. (J). (gr. -1-3). 17.99 *(978-0-689-85983-0(X),* McElderry, Margaret K. Bks.) McElderry, Margaret K. Bks.
Wilson, Rosalee. Elijah the Penguin. 2007. 60p. pap. 16.95 *(978-0-9798154-8-5(7))* Living Waters Publishing Co.
Wisham Fenstermacher, Mary. Pablo Visits the Desert. 2010. 52p. pap. 22.49 *(978-1-4490-5180-8(4))* AuthorHouse.
Yoon, Salina. Penguin & Pinecone: A Friendship Story. 2014. (Penguin Ser.). (ENG., Illus.). 32p. (J). (gr. -1-1). bds. 8.99 *(978-0-8027-3731-1(5),* 900132665, Bloomsbury USA Childrens) Bloomsbury Publishing USA.
—Penguin & Pumpkin. 2014. (Penguin Ser.). (ENG., Illus.). 40p. (J). (gr. -1-1). 15.99 *(978-0-8027-3732-8(3),* 900134209); E-Book 6.39 *(978-0-8027-3770-0(6))* Bloomsbury Publishing USA. (Bloomsbury USA Childrens).
—Penguin Gets Dressed! Yoon, Salina, illus. 2010. (Illus.). 10p. bds. 7.95 *(978-1-60747-750-1(5),* Pickwick Pr.) Phoenix Bks., Inc.
—Penguin Gets Ready for Bed! Yoon, Salina, illus. 2010. (Illus.). 10p. bds. 7.95 *(978-1-60747-751-8(3),* Pickwick Pr.) Phoenix Bks., Inc.
—Penguin Goes to the Farm! Yoon, Salina, illus. 2010. (Illus.). 10p. bds. 7.95 *(978-1-60747-752-5(1),* Pickwick Pr.) Phoenix Bks., Inc.
—Penguin in Love. (Penguin Ser.). (ENG., Illus.). (J). (gr. -1-1). 2014. 34p. bds. 7.99 *(978-0-8027-3758-8(7),* 900135684) 2013. 40p. 14.99 *(978-0-8027-3600-0(9),* 900123419) Bloomsbury Publishing USA. (Bloomsbury USA Childrens).
—Penguin on Vacation. (Penguin Ser.). (ENG., Illus.). (J). (gr. -1-1). 2015. 34p. bds. 7.99 *(978-0-8027-3837-0(0),* 900142737) 2013. 40p. 14.99 *(978-0-8027-3397-9(2),* 900084821) Bloomsbury Publishing USA. (Bloomsbury USA Childrens).
—Penguin's Big Adventure. 2015. (Penguin Ser.). (ENG., Illus.). 40p. (J). (gr. -1-1). 14.99 *(978-0-8027-3828-8(1),* 900141990, Bloomsbury USA Childrens) Bloomsbury Publishing USA.
—Penguin's Christmas Wish. (Penguin Ser.). (ENG.). (J). 2017. 32p. bds. 7.99 *(978-1-68119-573-5(9),* 900178387) 2016. (Illus.). 40p. 14.99 *(978-1-68119-155-3(5),* 900160611) Bloomsbury Publishing USA. (Bloomsbury USA Childrens).
—Pingüino Enamorado. 2017. (SPA.). 36p. (J). (gr. k). 20.99 *(978-84-8470-545-1(5))* Corimbo, Editorial S.L. ESP. Dist: Lectorum Pubns., Inc.
Young, Louise. Penguin Comes Home. Elmore, Larry, illus. 2005. (Soundprints' Amazing Animal Adventures! Ser.). (ENG.). 32p. (J). (gr. -1-2). 9.95 *(978-1-59249-329-6(7),* PS7158) Soundprints.
Young, Louise O. Penguin Comes Home. Elmore, Larry, illus. (Amazing Animal Adventures Ser.). (ENG.). 36p. (J). (gr. -1-2). 2005. 2.95 *(978-1-59249-325-8(4),* S7158) 2005. 15.95 *(978-1-59249-324-1(6),* B7108) 2004. pap. 6.95 *(978-1-59249-326-5(2),* S7108) Soundprints.
Young, Louise O. & Elmore, Larry. Penguin Comes Home. 2005. (Soundprints' Amazing Animal Adventures! Ser.). (ENG., Illus.). 32p. (J). (gr. -1-3). 8.95 *(978-1-59249-328-9(9),* SC7108) Soundprints.
Young, Timothy. The Angry Little Puffin, 1 vol. 2014. (ENG., Illus.). 40p. (J). (gr. -1-3). 16.99 *(978-0-7643-4805-1(1),* 5183) Schiffer Publishing, Ltd.

PENICILLIN

Adams, Jonathan. Antibiotics, 1 vol. 2017. (Great Discoveries in Science Ser.). (ENG., Illus.). 128p. (YA). (gr. 9-9). 47.36 *(978-1-5026-2873-2(2),* 08dc9e32-7289-4f18-bac9-5204c659efdd) Cavendish Square Publishing LLC.
Bard, Jonathan & Bard, Mariel. Oops! It's Penicillin!, 1 vol. 2019. (Accidental Scientific Discoveries That Changed the World Ser.). (ENG.). 32p. (gr. 3-4). pap. 11.50 *(978-1-5382-3990-2(6),* e2fcd3bb-a5a1-4d9b-bf3e-b81c2a0ad711) Stevens, Gareth Publishing LLLP.
Rooney, Anne. Alexander Fleming & the Discovery of Penicillin. 2012. (Miracle Makers Ser.). (ENG., Illus.). 48p. (YA). (gr. 5-8). 27.95 *(978-1-4488-6035-7(0),* Rosen Reference) Rosen Publishing Group, Inc., The.

PENINSULAR WAR, 1807-1814—FICTION

Fortescue, W. J. The Drummer's Coat. 2007. 120p. 94.99 *(978-1-4280-7656-3(5));* per. 88.99 *(978-1-4280-7658-7(1))* IndyPublish.com.
Styles, Showell. The Flying Ensign: Greencoats Against Napoleon. 2003. (Budget Bks). Orig. Title: Greencoat Against Napoleon. (ENG.). 340p. (J). (gr. 7-9). pap. 14.95 *(978-1-883937-70-6(1))* Ignatius Pr.

PENITENTIARIES

see Prisons

PENN, WILLIAM, 1644-1718

Boothroyd, Jennifer. William Penn: A Life of Tolerance. 2006. (Pull Ahead Bks.). (Illus.). 32p. (J). (gr. 3-7). lib. bdg. 22.60 *(978-0-8225-6387-7(8),* Lerner Pubns.) Lerner Publishing Group.
Figley, Marty Rhodes. Who Was William Penn? And Other Questions about the Founding of Pennsylvania. 2012. (Six Questions of American History Ser.). (ENG.). 48p. (gr. 4-6). pap. 56.72 *(978-0-7613-9241-5(6))* Lerner Publishing Group.
Foster, Genevieve. The World of William Penn. 2008. (Illus.). 192p. (J). pap. *(978-1-893103-30-6(7))* Beautiful Feet Bks.
Hinman, Bonnie. The Life & Times of William Penn. 2006. (Profiles in American History Ser.). (Illus.). 48p. (J). (gr. 4-8). lib. bdg. 29.95 *(978-1-58415-433-4(0),* 1259521) Mitchell Lane Pubs.
Levy, Janey. William Penn: Shaping a Nation. (American History Milestones Ser.). 32p. 2009. (gr. 5-5). 47.90 *(978-1-61511-376-7(2))* 2009. (ENG.). (J). (gr. 5-5). lib. bdg. 28.93 *(978-1-4358-3016-5(4),* 24bd2188-de6c-4b3d-aa82-521f8e6f5069) 2009. (Illus.). (J). 60.00 *(978-1-4358-0196-7(2),* 1291824) 2008. (ENG., Illus.). (J). (gr. 5-5). pap. 10.00 *(978-1-4358-0195-0(4),* 513f85ca-cd43-44e9-a265-065502d0d251) Rosen Publishing Group, Inc., The. (PowerKids Pr.).
Marsh, Carole. William Penn. 2003. 12p. (gr. k-4). 2.95 *(978-0-635-02358-2(X))* Gallopade International.
Mountjoy, Shane. Philadelphia. 2007. (Colonial Settlements in America Ser.). (ENG., Illus.). 100p. (gr. 5-9). lib. bdg. 30.00 *(978-0-7910-9336-8(0),* P124648, Facts On File) Infobase Holdings, Inc.
Swain, Gwenyth. Freedom Seeker: A Story about William Penn. Harvey, Lisa, illus. 2003. (Creative Minds Biographies Ser.). 64p. (J). 22.60 *(978-1-57505-176-5(1),* Carolrhoda Bks.) Lerner Publishing Group.
William Penn's Peaceable Kingdom (NCHS) 52p. (J). (gr. 5-8). spiral bd., tchr.'s planning gde. ed. 11.50 *(978-0-382-40930-1(2))* Cobblestone Publishing Co.

PENNEY, J. C. (JAMES CASH), 1875-1971

Offutt, Jason. J. C. Penney: The Man with a Thousand Partners. 2017. (ENG., Illus.). 48p. (J). lib. bdg. 27.00 *(978-1-61248-208-8(2))* Truman State Univ. Pr.

PENNSYLVANIA

Bobek, Joanne R. A Day at Pond Snow. 2011. 16p. 8.47 *(978-1-4567-1706-3(5))* AuthorHouse.
Bodden, Valerie. Pennsylvania. 2010. (Let's Explore America Ser.). 24p. (J). (gr. k-2). 19.95 *(978-1-58341-836-9(9))* Creative Co., The.
Derkins, Susie. The Meltdown at Three Mile Island. 2009. (When Disaster Strikes! Ser.). 48p. (gr. 5-8). 53.00 *(978-1-60854-781-4(7),* Rosen Reference) Rosen Publishing Group, Inc., The.
Hart, Joyce. Pennsylvania, 1 vol. Santoro, Christopher, illus. 2004. (It's My State! (First Edition)(r) Ser.). (ENG.). 80p. (gr. 4-4). lib. bdg. 34.07 *(978-0-7614-1691-3(9),* d86182a8-be3d-4254-8ac5-4406b0a8ca8c) Cavendish Square Publishing LLC.
Hasan, Heather. Pennsylvania: Past & Present. 2009. (Illus.). 48p. (J). 70.50 *(978-1-4358-5581-6(7));* (ENG., (gr. 5-5). pap. 12.75 *(978-1-4358-5580-9(9),* 35b7a556-e825-4b0e-99de-16bb1160eec1); (ENG., (gr. 5-5). lib. bdg. 34.47 *(978-1-4358-5291-4(5),* ecd1a932-70b1-44a7-88cf-4e9316df10f2) Rosen Publishing Group, Inc., The. (Rosen Reference).
Jerome, Kate Boehm. Pennsylvania: What's So Great about This State?, 100 vols. 2011. (Arcadia Kids Ser.). (ENG.). 32p. (J). pap. 9.99 *(978-1-58973-021-2(6))* Arcadia Publishing.
Kane, Kristen. K Is for Keystone: A Pennsylvania Alphabet. Knorr, Laura, illus. 2003. (Discover America State by State Ser.). (ENG.). 40p. (J). (gr. 1-3). 17.95 *(978-1-58536-104-5(6),* 201979) Sleeping Bear Pr.
Kavanagh, James & Waterford Press Staff. Pennsylvania Birds: A Folding Pocket Guide to Familiar Species. Leung, Raymond, illus. 2017. (Wildlife & Nature Identification Ser.). (ENG.). 12p. (gr. 9). 7.95 *(978-1-58355-009-0(7))* Waterford Pr., Inc.
Lusted, Marcia Amidon. Pennsylvania: The Keystone State, 1 vol. 2009. (Our Amazing States Ser.). (ENG., Illus.). 24p. (J). (gr. 3-3). pap. 9.25 *(978-1-4358-3374-6(0),* cedfc6d9-7248-420a-9479-f42cd65d9d85, PowerKids Pr.) Rosen Publishing Group, Inc., The.
Marsh, Carole. My First Book about Pennsylvania. 2004. (Pennsylvania Experience! Ser.). (Illus.). 32p. (J). (gr. k-4). pap. 7.95 *(978-0-7933-9587-3(9))* Gallopade International.
—Pennsylvania Current Events Projects: 30 Cool, Activities, Crafts, Experiments & More for Kids to Do to Learn about Your State! 2003. (Pennsylvania Experience Ser.). 32p. (gr. k-8). pap. 5.95 *(978-0-635-02057-4(2),* Marsh, Carole Bks.) Gallopade International.
—Pennsylvania Geography Projects: 30 Cool, Activities, Crafts, Experiments & More for Kids to Do to Learn about Your State! 2003. (Pennsylvania Experience Ser.). 32p. (gr. k-5). pap. 5.95 *(978-0-635-01857-1(8),* Marsh, Carole Bks.) Gallopade International.
—Pennsylvania Government Projects: 30 Cool, Activities, Crafts, Experiments & More for Kids to Do to Learn about Your State! 2003. (Pennsylvania Experience Ser.). 32p. (gr. k-5). pap. 5.95 *(978-0-635-01957-8(4),* Marsh, Carole Bks.) Gallopade International.
—Pennsylvania Jeopardy! Answers & Questions about Our State! 2004. (Pennsylvania Experience! Ser.). (Illus.). 32p. (J). (gr. 3-8). pap. 7.95 *(978-0-7933-9588-0(7))* Gallopade International.
—Pennsylvania "Jography" A Fun Run Thru Our State! 2004. (Pennsylvania Experience! Ser.). (Illus.). 32p. (J). (gr. 3-8). pap. 7.95 *(978-0-7933-9589-7(5))* Gallopade International.
—Pennsylvania People Projects: 30 Cool, Activities, Crafts, Experiments & More for Kids to Do to Learn about Your State! 2003. (Pennsylvania Experience Ser.). 32p. (gr. k-5). pap. 5.95 *(978-0-635-02007-9(6),* Marsh, Carole Bks.) Gallopade International.
—Pennsylvania Symbols & Facts Projects: 30 Cool, Activities, Crafts, Experiments & More for Kids to Do to Learn about Your State! 2003. (Pennsylvania Experience Ser.). 32p. (gr. k-5). pap. 5.95 *(978-0-635-01907-3(8),* Marsh, Carole Bks.) Gallopade International.
—Pennsylvania's Big Activity Book. 2004. (Pennsylvania Experience! Ser.). (Illus.). 96p. (J). (gr. 2-6). pap. 9.95 *(978-0-7933-9590-3(9))* Gallopade International.
—The Proud Pennsylvania Coloring Book. 2004. (Pennsylvania Experience! Ser.). (Illus.). 32p. (J). (gr. k-2). pap. 3.95 *(978-0-7933-9591-0(7))* Gallopade International.
McNamara, Connie. My First University of Pittsburgh Words. 2004. (ENG.). (J). 11.95 *(978-0-9759703-2-4(1))* Shamrock Publishing, Inc.
Mercer, Henry C., et al. Color Me Pennsylvania: Our Heritage. 2007. (Illus.). 22p. (J). pap. 12.00 *(978-1-4223-1491-3(X))* DIANE Publishing Co.
El Meson en Belen (The Bethlehem Inn) (SPA.). (J). *(978-0-7899-0876-6(X),* 496235) Editorial Unilit.
Mis, M. S. How to Draw Pennsylvania's Sights & Symbols. 2009. (Kid's Guide to Drawing America Ser.). 32p. (gr. k-k). 50.50 *(978-1-61511-091-9(7),* PowerKids Pr.) Rosen Publishing Group, Inc., The.
Murray, Julie. Pennsylvania, 1 vol. 2006. (United States Ser.). (ENG., Illus.). 32p. (gr. 2-4). 27.07 *(978-1-59197-697-4(9),* Buddy Bks.) ABDO Publishing Co.
Noble, Trinka Hakes. One for All: A Pennsylvania Number Book. Papp, Lisa, illus. 2005. (America by the Numbers Ser.). (ENG.). 40p. (J). (gr. 1-3). 16.95 *(978-1-58536-200-4(X),* 202039) Sleeping Bear Pr.
—The Pennsylvania Reader. Darnell, K. L., illus. rev. ed. 2007. (State/Country Readers Ser.). (ENG.). 96p. (J). (gr. 1-4). 12.95 *(978-1-58536-320-9(0),* 202124) Sleeping Bear Pr.
Peters, Stephen & Hart, Joyce. Pennsylvania, 1 vol. 2nd rev. ed. 2009. (Celebrate the States (Second Edition) Ser.). (ENG.). 144p. (gr. 6-6). lib. bdg. 39.79 *(978-0-7614-3403-0(8),* 46fee572-0ef6-4d9b-b7ce-95855be7f74f) Cavendish Square Publishing LLC.
Somervill, Barbara A. Pennsylvannia. 2003. (From Sea to Shining Sea Ser.: 2). (ENG., Illus.). 80p. (J). 30.50 *(978-0-516-22388-9(7),* Children's Pr.) Scholastic Library Publishing.
Swain, Gwenyth. Pennsylvania. (J). 2012. lib. bdg. 25.26 *(978-0-7613-4553-4(1),* Lerner Pubns.) 2nd exp. rev. ed. 2003. (Illus.). 84p. (gr. 3-6). pap. 6.95 *(978-0-8225-4147-9(5))* Lerner Publishing Group.
Treasure Maps of Clarion County. 2004. per. 19.95 *(978-0-9743881-1-3(4))* Hufnagel Software.
Way, Jennifer. Pennsylvania/Pensilvania, 1 vol. Brusca, Maria Cristina, tr. 2005. (Bilingual Library of the United States of America Ser.: Set 2). (ENG & SPA., Illus.). 32p. (J). (gr. 2-2). lib. bdg. 28.93 *(978-1-4042-3103-0(X),* 2d27e7b3-427f-4be7-b271-4bdf274a4a71) Rosen Publishing Group, Inc., The.

PENNSYLVANIA—FICTION

Adams, Alane. The Circus Thief. Gallegos, Lauren, illus. 2018. (ENG.). 32p. (J). (gr. 1-2). 15.00 *(978-1-943006-75-5(X))* SparkPr. (a Bks.parks Imprint).
—The Coal Thief. Gallegos, Lauren, illus. 2015. (ENG.). 32p. (J). 15.00 *(978-1-940716-27-5(6))* SparkPr. (a Bks.parks Imprint).
Alender, Katie. The Dead Girls of Hysteria Hall. 2016. (ENG.). 329p. (YA). (gr. 7). 20.85 *(978-0-606-39121-4(5))* Turtleback.
Alexander, Yvonne. Adventure in Autou. 2012. 230p. pap. 15.99 *(978-1-62230-262-8(1))* Salem Author Services.
Alger, Horatio. Joe the Hotel Boy. 2006. pap. *(978-1-4065-0712-6(1))* Dodo Pr.
Altsheler, Joseph A. The Scouts of the Valley. (Young Trailers Ser.: Vol. 7). reprint ed. 2008. 272p. pap. 11.45 *(978-1-60597-237-4(1))* 2007. 276p. per. 14.95 *(978-1-60424-040-5(7))* Standard Publications, Inc. (Bk. Jungle).
—The Scouts of the Valley: A Story of Wyoming & the Chemung. 2005. (Young Trailers Ser.: Vol. 7). (J). reprint ed. 29.95 *(978-1-4218-1054-6(9));* 344p. pap. 14.95 *(978-1-4218-1154-3(5))* 1st World Publishing, Inc. (1st World Library - Literary Society).
—The Scouts of the Valley: A Story of Wyoming & the Chemung. 2007. (Young Trailers Ser.: Vol. 7). (ENG.). 284p. (J). reprint ed. pap. 21.99 *(978-1-4346-0327-2(X))* Creative Media Partners, LLC.
—The Scouts of the Valley: A Story of Wyoming & the Chemung. 2006. (Young Trailers Ser.: Vol. 7). (J). reprint ed. pap. *(978-1-4065-0821-5(7))* Dodo Pr.
—The Scouts of the Valley: A Story of Wyoming & the Chemung. 2007. (Young Trailers Ser.: Vol. 7). 208p. (J). reprint ed. per. *(978-1-4068-1685-3(X))* Echo Library.
—The Scouts of the Valley: A Story of Wyoming & the Chemung. 2004. (Young Trailers Ser.: Vol. 7). (J). reprint ed. pap. 27.95 *(978-1-4191-8163-4(7));* pap. 1.99 *(978-1-4192-8163-1(1))* Kessinger Publishing, LLC.
—The Scouts of the Valley (Webster's French Thesaurus Edition) 2008. (Young Trailers Ser.: Vol. 7). (FRE & ENG.). 360p. pap. 28.95 *(978-0-497-97888-4(1))* Icon Group International, Inc.
Anderson, Laurie Halse. Forge. (Seeds of America Trilogy Ser.). (ENG., Illus.). (J). (gr. 5-9). 2012. 320p. pap. 8.99 *(978-1-4169-6145-1(3))* 2010. 304p. 19.99 *(978-1-4169-6144-4(5))* Simon & Schuster Children's Publishing. (Atheneum Bks. for Young Readers).
—Prom. 2006. (ENG.). 240p. (YA). (gr. 7-18). reprint ed. 9.99 *(978-0-14-240570-3(1),* Speak) Penguin Young Readers Group.
Andrews, Jesse. Me & Earl & the Dying Girl. 2015. (CHI.). 320p. (YA). (gr. 9-17). pap. *(978-986-344-282-0(8))* Rye Field Publishing, Co.
—Me & Earl & the Dying Girl. 2015. lib. bdg. 20.80 *(978-0-606-37113-1(3))* Turtleback.
—Me & Earl & the Dying Girl (Revised Edition) rev. ed. 2015. (ENG.). 320p. (YA). (gr. 9-17). pap. 11.99 *(978-1-4197-1960-8(2),* 1003806) Abrams, Inc.
Armstrong, Cara. Moxie: The Dachshund of Fallingwater. 2010. (ENG., Illus.). 32p. (J). 19.95 *(978-1-933979-70-0(4),* bd3064bf-022b-413f-bb7d-524d0f769d68) Night Heron Media.
Ayres, Katherine. Macaroni Boy. 2004. 192p. (J). (gr. 3-7). per. 7.99 *(978-0-440-41884-9(4),* Yearling) Random Hse. Children's Bks.
Beaudoin, Sean. Going Nowhere Faster. 2008. (ENG.). 256p. (J). (gr. 7-17). pap. 13.99 *(978-0-316-01416-8(8))* Little, Brown Bks. for Young Readers.
Bender, Carrie. Hemlock Hill Hideaway: Whispering Brook Series #4. 2007. (Illus.). 168p. pap. 8.99 *(978-1-60126-022-2(9))* Masthof Pr.
—Timber Lane Cove. 2003. (ENG.). 144p. (YA). pap. 8.99 *(978-0-8361-9202-5(8))* Herald Pr.
Carlson, J. Kelley. Freeing Golden Eagle. 2007. 140p. 19.95 *(978-1-4327-0315-8(3));* per. 10.95 *(978-1-4327-0302-8(1))* Outskirts Pr., Inc.
Carvell, Marlene. Sweetgrass Basket. 2005. 256p. (J). (gr. 5-6). 17.99 *(978-0-525-47547-7(8),* Dutton Books for Young Readers) Penguin Young Readers Group.
Cassidy, Colette. DIVCO, the Little Milk Truck. 2007. (Illus.). 28p. (J). pap. 7.99 *(978-0-615-17346-7(2))* Redcay Publishing.
Church, Lorraine. Pencilvani. 2009. (Illus.). 32p. pap. 12.99 *(978-1-4389-2072-6(5))* AuthorHouse.
Cody, Matthew. Powerless. 2011. 288p. (J). (Supers of Noble's Green Ser.: 1). (gr. 3-7). 8.99 *(978-0-375-84489-8(9),* Yearling);1. (Supers of Noble Green Ser.). (ENG.). (gr. 4-6). lib. bdg. 18.69 *(978-0-375-95595-2(X),* Knopf Bks. for Young Readers) Random Hse. Children's Bks.
—Super. 2014. (Supers of Noble's Green Ser.: 2). (ENG.). 304p. (J). (gr. 3-7). 9.99 *(978-0-375-87291-4(4),* Yearling) Random Hse. Children's Bks.
Collins, Nafessa. Mrs. Precious & the Possum. 2012. 56p. (gr. -1). pap. 8.95 *(978-1-4759-1273-9(0))* iUniverse, Inc.
Connelly, Neil. The Miracle Stealer. 2010. (ENG.). 240p. (J). (gr. 9-18). 17.99 *(978-0-545-13195-7(2),* Levine, Arthur A. Bks.) Scholastic, Inc.
Connolly, Brian A. Hawk. 2007. 156p. 20.95 *(978-1-60264-030-6(0));* 160p. per. 13.95 *(978-1-60264-029-0(7))* Virtualbookworm.com Publishing, Inc.
Cook, Kajsa. Discoveries in the Shriver Family Attic: How a Woman & Her Children Dealt with the Battle of Gettysburg. 2009. (Illus.). 122p. (J). (gr. 4-8). pap. 8.95 *(978-1-57249-398-8(4),* White Mane Kids) White Mane Publishing Co., Inc.
Czerw, Nancy Carpenter. Itty & Bitty - On the Road. Berlin, Rose Mary, illus. 2008. (Itty & Bitty Ser.: 3). (ENG.). 32p. (J). (gr. -1-3). 16.95 *(978-0-9755618-4-3(7))* McWitty Pr., Inc.
Dana Kittendorf. Trail of Dreams. 2009. 136p. 21.95 *(978-1-4401-7787-3(2))* iUniverse, Inc.

P Q R

Darlington, Edgar B. P. The Circus Boys Across the Continent. 2005. 27.95 *(978-1-4218-1020-1(4))*; 212p. pap. 12.95 *(978-1-4218-1120-8(0))* 1st World Publishing, Inc. (1st World Library - Literary Society).
Dellasega, Cheryl. Nugri90 (Sadie), 0 vols. LaPierre, Karina, illus. 2012. (Bloggrls Ser.: 1). (ENG.). 192p. (YA). (gr. 7-12). pap. 9.99 *(978-0-7614-5396-3(2)*, 9780761453963, Skyscape) Amazon Publishing.
Deming, Sarah. Iris, Messenger. 2007. (ENG., Illus.). 224p. (J). (gr. 5-7). 16.00 *(978-0-15-205823-4(0)*, 1197496, Clarion Bks.) HarperCollins Pubs.
Douglas, Ryke Leigh. The Big Wheel. 2010. (Illus.). 21p. (J). pap. 15.95 *(978-1-4327-4495-3(X))* Outskirts Pr., Inc.
—Sam's Surprise. 2008. 28p. per. 12.95 *(978-1-4327-0850-4(3))* Outskirts Pr., Inc.
Dreistadt, Jessica R. Ashley & Tiana. 2009. 96p. pap. 10.00 *(978-0-578-02239-0(7))* Dreistadt, Jessica R.
D'Souza, Barbara. If We Were Snowflakes. 2018. (YA). pap. *(978-1-59719-091-6(8))* Pearlsong Pr.
Dudek, Mike. The Fairytale of the Morley Dog. 2007. (Illus.). 40p. (YA). spiral bd. 2.49 *(978-0-9740380-1-8(6))* Dudek, Mike.
Earl, Cheri Pray & Williams, Carol Lynch. Secret in Pennsylvania. 2009. (J). *(978-1-56145-477-8(X)*, Peachtree Junior) Peachtree Publishing Co. Inc.
Erskine, Kathryn. The Absolute Value of Mike. 2012. 272p. (J). (gr. 5-18). pap. 7.99 *(978-0-14-242101-7(4)*, Puffin Books) Penguin Young Readers Group.
—Quaking. 2007. (ENG.). 240p. (YA). (gr. 7-12). 22.44 *(978-0-399-24774-3(2))* Penguin Young Readers Group.
Faigen, Anne G. New World Waiting. 2006. iii, 188p. (J). pap. *(978-0-9744715-5-6(0))* Local History Co., The.
Federle, Tim. Better Nate Than Ever. 2014. lib. bdg. 18.40 *(978-0-606-35430-1(1))* Turtleback.
—Nate Expectations. (Nate Ser.). (ENG.). (J). (gr. 5). 2019. 272p. pap. 8.99 *(978-1-4814-0413-6(X))* 2018. (Illus.). 256p. 17.99 *(978-1-4814-0412-9(1))* Simon & Schuster Bks. For Young Readers. (Simon & Schuster Bks. For Young Readers).
Ficklin, Jonene H. The Garden Gate. 2005. (YA). 14.95 *(978-0-9761188-2-4(3))* Victor's Crown Publishing.
Franckowiak, Jon. When I Grow up I Want to be a Nittany Lion. 2008. 32p. pap. 9.95 *(978-0-9715415-0-4(7))* Franckowiak, Jon.
Freeman, Martha. Effie Starr Zook Has One More Question. 2019. (Penworthy Picks Middle School Ser.). (ENG.). 217p. (J). (gr. 4-5). 19.36 *(978-1-64310-940-4(5))* Penworthy Co., LLC, The.
—Effie Starr Zook Has One More Question. (ENG.). (J). (gr. 3-7). 2018. 240p. pap. 7.99 *(978-1-4814-7265-4(8))* 2017. (Illus.). 224p. 16.99 *(978-1-4814-7264-7(X))* Simon & Schuster/Paula Wiseman Bks. (Simon & Schuster/Paula Wiseman Bks.).
—Effie Starr Zook Has One More Question. 2018. lib. bdg. 18.40 *(978-0-606-40835-6(5))* Turtleback.
Gantos, Jack. Dead End in Norvelt. 2011. (Norvelt Ser.: 1). (ENG., Illus.). 352p. (J). (gr. 5-9). 19.99 *(978-0-374-37993-3(9)*, 900041629, Farrar, Straus & Giroux (BYR)) Farrar, Straus & Giroux.
—Dead End in Norvelt. 2013. (Norvelt Ser.: 1). (ENG., Illus.). 384p. (J). (gr. 5-9). pap. 9.99 *(978-1-250-01023-0(3)*, 900084760) Square Fish.
—Dead End in Norvelt. 2013. (J). lib. bdg. 18.40 *(978-0-606-31901-0(8))* Turtleback.
—From Norvelt to Nowhere. 2015. (J). lib. bdg. 18.40 *(978-0-606-37280-0(6))* Turtleback.
Garland, Sherry. Voices of Gettysburg, 1 vol. Hierstein, Judith, illus. 2010. (Voices of History Ser.). (ENG.). 40p. (J). (gr. 3-3). 17.99 *(978-1-58980-653-5(0)*, Pelican Publishing) Arcadia Publishing.
Gilbert, Joan. Mule Boy. Burke, Kathryn Schaar, illus. 2004. 248p. (YA). per. 12.95 *(978-0-930973-30-8(5))* Delaware &Lehigh National Heritage Corridor, Inc.
Glover, Dennis W. The Goat Farm. 2009. 32p. pap. 12.99 *(978-1-4490-1532-9(8))* AuthorHouse.
Grandpa Dennis, as told by. George Washington's Smallest Army: The Miracle Before Trenton. 2009. 216p. (J). pap. 17.49 *(978-1-4389-3147-0(6))* AuthorHouse.
Gregory, Kristiana. The Winter of Red Snow (Dear America) 2010. (Dear America Ser.). (ENG.). 192p. (J). (gr. 3-9). 12.99 *(978-0-545-23802-1(1)*, Scholastic Pr.) Scholastic, Inc.
Griffin, Paul. Saving Marty. 2018. (ENG.). 224p. (J). (gr. 5-9). 8.99 *(978-0-399-53908-4(5)*, Puffin Books) Penguin Young Readers Group.
Gurevich, Margaret. Gina's Balance. 2016. (What's Your Dream? Ser.). (ENG., Illus.). 96p. (J). (gr. 4-6). lib. bdg. 25.99 *(978-1-4965-3443-9(3)*, 132565) Capstone.
Haas, Jessie. Chase. 2007. 256p. (J). (gr. 5-9). lib. bdg. 17.89 *(978-0-06-112851-6(1))* HarperCollins Pubs.
Halse Anderson, Laurie. Forge. 2012. 18.00 *(978-1-61383-316-2(4))* Perfection Learning Corp.
—Forge. 2012. (Seeds of America Trilogy Ser.: 2). lib. bdg. 18.40 *(978-0-606-23680-5(5))* Turtleback.
—Prom. 2006. (YA). 1.25 *(978-1-4193-5096-2(X))* Recorded Bks., Inc.
Harlow, Joan Hiatt. Breaker Boy. 2017. (ENG., Illus.). 288p. (J). (gr. 3-7). 16.99 *(978-1-4814-6537-3(6)*, McElderry, Margaret K. Bks.) McElderry, Margaret K. Bks.
Harrell, Mary. The Mythmaker. 2018. (YA). pap. *(978-1-63051-500-3(0))*; (ENG., Illus.). 148p. (J). pap. 14.95 *(978-1-63051-503-4(5))* Chiron Pubns.
Higgins, Joanna. Waiting for the Queen: A Novel of Early America. 2013. (ENG.). 256p. (J). (gr. 4-10). 16.95 *(978-1-57131-700-1(7))* Milkweed Editions.
Horner, Doogie. This Might Hurt a Bit. 2019. (ENG., Illus.). 336p. (YA). (gr. 9). 18.99 *(978-1-5344-2717-4(1)*, Simon Pulse) Simon Pulse.
Hubler, Marsha. Southern Belle's Special Gift, 1 vol., 3. 2009. (Keystone Stables Ser.). (ENG.). 128p. (J). pap. 7.99 *(978-0-310-71794-2(9))* Zonderkidz.
—Summer Camp Adventure, 1 vol., 4. 2009. (Keystone Stables Ser.). (ENG.). 128p. (J). pap. 7.99 *(978-0-310-71795-9(7))* Zonderkidz.
Huffman, Nancy E. The Misadventures of Taylor R. Bailey. 2010. 112p. 23.99 *(978-1-4490-5791-6(8))*; pap. 13.99 *(978-1-4490-5790-9(X))* AuthorHouse.
Jacobs, Lily. The Littlest Bunny in Pennsylvania: An Easter Adventure. Dunn, Robert, illus. 2015. (Littlest Bunny Ser.). (ENG.). 32p. (J). (gr. -1-3). 9.99 *(978-1-4926-1177-6(8)*, Hometown World) Sourcebooks, Inc.
—The Littlest Bunny in Pittsburgh: An Easter Adventure. Dunn, Robert, illus. 2015. (Littlest Bunny Ser.). (ENG.). 32p. (J). (gr. -1-3). 9.99 *(978-1-4926-1183-7(2)*, Hometown World) Sourcebooks, Inc.
James, Eric. Santa's Sleigh Is on Its Way to Pennsylvania: A Christmas Adventure. Dunn, Robert, illus. 2015. (Santa's Sleigh Is on Its Way Ser.). (ENG.). 32p. (J). (gr. k-2). 12.99 *(978-1-4926-2745-6(3)*, Hometown World) Sourcebooks, Inc.
—Santa's Sleigh Is on Its Way to Pittsburgh: A Christmas Adventure. Dunn, Robert, illus. 2016. (Santa's Sleigh Is on Its Way Ser.). (ENG.). 32p. (J). (gr. k-2). 12.99 *(978-1-4926-4351-7(3)*, 9781492643517, Hometown World) Sourcebooks, Inc.
—The Spooky Express Pennsylvania. Piwowarski, Marcin, illus. 2017. (Spooky Express Ser.). (ENG.). 32p. (J). (gr. k-6). 9.99 *(978-1-4926-5392-9(6)*, Hometown World) Sourcebooks, Inc.
—The Spooky Express Pittsburgh. Piwowarski, Marcin, illus. 2017. (Spooky Express Ser.). (ENG.). 32p. (J). (gr. k-6). 9.99 *(978-1-4926-5394-3(2)*, Hometown World) Sourcebooks, Inc.
—Tiny the Pennsylvania Easter Bunny. 2018. (Tiny the Easter Bunny Ser.). (ENG.). 40p. (J). (gr. k-3). 9.99 *(978-1-4926-5957-0(6)*, Hometown World) Sourcebooks, Inc.
Jasper, Mark. Good Night Pittsburgh. Palmer, Ruth, illus. 2012. (Good Night Our World Ser.). (ENG.). 20p. (J). (gr. k — 1). bds. 9.95 *(978-1-60219-073-3(9))* Good Night Bks.
Jeffers, Sunni. Eyes on the Prize. 2009. (Tales from Grace Chapel Inn Ser.). (ENG.). 328p. pap. 13.99 *(978-0-8249-4787-3(8)*, Ideals Pubns.) Worthy Publishing.
Jordan, Cat. Eight Days on Planet Earth. 2017. (ENG.). 320p. (YA). (gr. 8). 17.99 *(978-0-06-257173-1(7)*, HarperTeen) HarperCollins Pubs.
Kay, Alan. Breaking the Rules. 2007. (Young Heroes of History Ser.: 7). 149p. (J). pap. 7.95 *(978-1-57249-389-6(5)*, White Mane Kids) White Mane Publishing Co., Inc.
Kay, Alan N. Crossroads at Gettysburg. 2005. (Young Heroes of History Ser.: 6). (Illus.). 166p. (J). (gr. 3-7). per. 7.95 *(978-1-57249-359-9(3)*, White Mane Kids) White Mane Publishing Co., Inc.
Keay, Ben. Perfect Solution. Hsu, Florence, illus. 2009. (YA). *(978-1-933791-09-8(8))* Finial Publishing.
Kelaita, Lynda. Some Houses Are White. 2009. 32p. pap. 10.95 *(978-1-935125-44-0(3))* Robertson Publishing.
Kelly, David A. Ballpark Mysteries Super Special #4: the World Series Kids. Meyers, Mark, illus. 2019. (Ballpark Mysteries Ser.: 4). (ENG.). 128p. (J). (gr. 1-4). pap. 5.99 *(978-0-525-57895-6(1)*, Random Hse. Bks. for Young Readers) Random Hse. Children's Bks.
Knopp, Sue, creator. Study Guide for Wolf Journal: A Novel. 2005. 60p. per. 7.95 *(978-1-58939-827-6(0))* Virtualbookworm.com Publishing, Inc.
Koraido, Beth S. Summers with Grampa Gus. 2008. 63p. pap. 19.95 *(978-1-60703-384-4(4))* America Star Bks.
Landis, Matthew. The Not So Boring Letters of Private Nobody. 2019. (ENG.). 320p. (J). (gr. 5-9). 8.99 *(978-0-7352-2799-6(3)*, Puffin Books) Penguin Young Readers Group.
Little Farm down the Lane, Bk. III. 2005. pap. 10.99 *(978-1-59781-702-8(3))* Salem Author Services.
Lois, Lowry. Crow Call. 2011. (J). (gr. -1-2). 29.95 incl. audio compact disk *(978-0-545-29674-8(9))* Weston Woods Studios, Inc.
Lokko, CNN. Adventures of Elizabeth Sam. 2012. 280p. pap. *(978-9964-70-151-2(9))* Afram Pubns. Ghana, Ltd.
Lubar, David. Sleeping Freshmen Never Lie. 2007. (ENG.). 288p. (YA). (gr. 7-18). 11.99 *(978-0-14-240780-6(1)*, Speak) Penguin Young Readers Group.
Lupica, Mike. The Underdogs. 2012. (ENG.). 304p. (J). (gr. 5-18). pap. 8.99 *(978-0-14-242139-0(1)*, Puffin Books) Penguin Young Readers Group.
Macor, Jim. Frazier Fir, A Christmas Fable. Macor, Jim, illus. 2007. (Illus.). 32p. (J). 17.95 *(978-0-9785551-3-9(9))* Zuber Publishing.
Marsh, Carole. The Mystery in Chocolate Town: Hershey, Pennsylvania. (Real Kids, Real Places Ser.). (Illus.). (J). 2009. 143p. lib. bdg. 18.99 *(978-0-635-07025-8(1)*, Marsh, Carole Mysteries) 2007. 145p. (gr. 2-8). 14.95 *(978-0-635-06389-2(1))* Gallopade International.
—The Mystery in Chocolate Town Hershey, Pennsylvania. 2007. (Real Kids, Real Places Ser.). (Illus.). 145p. (J). (gr. 2-8). per. 7.99 *(978-0-635-06333-5(6))* Gallopade International.
Martin, Joanna F. Betsey's Wishes. 2010. (Illus.). 255p. (J). (gr. 3-6). 9.80 *(978-0-7399-2424-2(9))* Rod & Staff Pubs., Inc.
Matson, Morgan. Second Chance Summer. 2013. (ENG.). 496p. (YA). (gr. 7). pap. 12.99 *(978-1-4169-9068-0(2)*, Simon & Schuster Bks. For Young Readers) Simon & Schuster Bks. For Young Readers.
—Second Chance Summer. 2012. (ENG.). 480p. (YA). (gr. 7). 19.99 *(978-1-4169-9067-3(4))* Simon & Schuster, Inc.
Mazeroski, Kelly. Maz, You're Up! Lauso, Judith, illus. 2010. 24p. (J). pap. 12.95 *(978-0-936340-18-0(5))* Historical Society of Western Pennsylvania.
McGough, Michael R. The Lincoln Inn. 2004. (Illus.). 108p. (YA). per. 14.95 *(978-1-57747-108-0(3))* Thomas Pubns.
McKain, Susan & Swann, Sandy. Tugger & Mini-Mew. 2011. 32p. pap. 15.95 *(978-1-4634-4920-9(8))* AuthorHouse.
Morgan, Melissa J. Grace's Twist #3. 2005. (Camp Confidential Ser.: 3). (ENG.). 160p. (J). (gr. 3-7). mass mkt. 4.99 *(978-0-448-43875-7(5)*, Grosset & Dunlap) Penguin Young Readers Group.
—Natalie's Secret #1, 1. 2005. (Camp Confidential Ser.: 1). (ENG.). 160p. (J). (gr. 3-7). 5.99 *(978-0-448-43737-8(6)*, Grosset & Dunlap) Penguin Young Readers Group.
Mostoller, Marcia. Emma's Summer Camp Dilemm. 2011. 64p. pap. 19.95 *(978-1-4626-2814-8(1))* America Star Bks.
Mullarkey, John & Mullarkey, Lisa. Johnstown Flood: An Up2U Historical Fiction Adventure, 1 vol. Martin, Dana, illus. 2013. (Up2U Adventures Ser.). (ENG.). 80p. (J). (gr. 2-5). lib. bdg. 35.64 *(978-1-61641-967-7(9)*, 15217, Calico Chapter Bks.) ABDO Publishing Co.
Otis, James. Stephen of Philadelphi: A Story of Penn's Colony. 2007. 144p. per. 9.95 *(978-0-9790876-5-3(1))* Living Bks. Pr.
Paulsen, Gary. Woods Runner. 2011. (ENG.). 176p. (YA). (gr. 7). pap. 9.99 *(978-0-375-85908-3(X)*, Lamb, Wendy Bks.) Random Hse. Children's Bks.
Price, Bc. Mabel & Her Litter Of. 2008. 132p. pap. 12.00 *(978-0-615-20692-9(1))* BCP Pubns.
Quick, Matthew. Boy21. 2013. (ENG.). 272p. (YA). (gr. 7-17). pap. 11.99 *(978-0-316-12796-7(5))* Little, Brown Bks. for Young Readers.
Richards, Jame. Three Rivers Rising. 2011. (ENG.). 304p. (YA). (gr. 7). pap. 8.99 *(978-0-375-85369-2(3)*, Ember) Random Hse. Children's Bks.
Richter, Conrad. The Light in the Forest: Illustrated by Warren Chappell. Chappell, Warren, illus. 2005. (Everyman's Library Children's Classics Ser.). (ENG.). 176p. (J). (gr. 5-7). 15.95 *(978-1-4000-4426-9(X)*, Everyman's Library) Knopf Doubleday Publishing Group.
Rosensweig, Jay B. & Repka, Janice. The Stupendous Dodgeball Fiasco. Dibley, Glin, illus. 2012. 181p. (J). (gr. 4-6). 21.19 *(978-0-525-47346-6(7))* Penguin Young Readers Group.
Ruby, Lois. Rebel Spirits. 2013. 292p. (YA). *(978-0-545-55282-0(6))* Scholastic, Inc.
Ryan, Pam Muñoz. Echo, 1 vol. 2015. (ENG., Illus.). 592p. (J). (gr. 5-9). 19.99 *(978-0-439-87402-1(5)*, Scholastic Pr.) Scholastic, Inc.
—Echo (Unabridged Edition), 1 vol. unabr. ed. 2015. (ENG.). (J). (gr. 5-9). 4p. audio compact disk 39.99 *(978-0-545-78836-6(6))*; Vol. 8. audio compact disk 79.99 *(978-0-545-78837-3(4))* Scholastic, Inc.
Salerni, Dianne K. The Caged Graves. 2014. (ENG.). 336p. (YA). (gr. 7). pap. 10.99 *(978-0-544-33622-3(4)*, 1584168, Clarion Bks.) HarperCollins Pubs.
Schlitz, Laura Amy. The Hired Girl. 2017. (ENG.). 400p. (J). (gr. 5-9). pap. 11.99 *(978-0-7636-9450-0(9))* Candlewick Pr.
—The Hired Girl. l.t. ed. 2020. (ENG.). pap. 15.99 *(978-1-4328-7417-9(9))* Thorndike Pr.
—The Hired Girl. 2018. lib. bdg. 22.10 *(978-0-606-40389-4(2))* Turtleback.
Serrano, Tina. The Catfish Caper. 2011. 54p. pap. 16.95 *(978-1-4560-6590-4(4))* America Star Bks.
Seyfert, Ella Maie. Amish Moving Day. Jones, Henrietta, illus. 2011. 132p. 40.95 *(978-1-258-01315-8(0))* Literary Licensing, LLC.
Shepard, Sara. Killer. 2010. (Pretty Little Liars Ser.: 6). (YA). lib. bdg. 20.85 *(978-0-606-12278-8(3))* Turtleback.
—Pretty Little Liars Bind-Up #1: Pretty Little Liars & Flawless. 2014. (Pretty Little Liars Ser.). (ENG.). 656p. (YA). (gr. 9). pap. 10.99 *(978-0-06-232292-0(3)*, HarperTeen) HarperCollins Pubs.
Siegrist, Bonnie. Little Farm down the Lane -Book IV. 2007. pap. 10.99 *(978-1-60034-912-6(9))* Salem Author Services.
Siegrist, Bonnie Bedi. Little Farm down the Lane Book V. 2008. 124p. pap. 11.99 *(978-1-60647-848-6(6))* Salem Author Services.
Skurzynski, Gloria. Good-Bye, Billy Radish. 2013. (ENG., Illus.). 152p. (J). (gr. 3-7). pap. 13.99 *(978-1-4814-0158-6(0)*, Simon & Schuster Bks. For Young Readers) Simon & Schuster Bks. For Young Readers.
Smith-Ready, Jeri. This Side of Salvation. 2014. (ENG., Illus.). 384p. (YA). (gr. 9). 17.99 *(978-1-4424-3948-1(3)*, Simon Pulse) Simon Pulse.
Smith, William D. Becoming a Superhero: Adventures of an American Superhero. 2008. 128p. per. 13.95 *(978-1-4327-2071-1(6))* Outskirts Pr., Inc.
Sonnenblick, Jordan. Curveball: the Year I Lost My Grip. (ENG.). 304p. 2014. (J). (gr. 7). pap. 10.99 *(978-0-545-32070-2(4)*, Scholastic Paperbacks) 2012. E-Book 17.99 *(978-0-545-39311-9(6))* Scholastic, Inc.
—Zen & the Art of Faking It. 2010. (ENG.). 272p. (J). (gr. 7-12). 9.99 *(978-0-439-83709-5(X)*, Scholastic Paperbacks) Scholastic, Inc.
Spinelli, Jerry. Love, Stargirl. 2009. (Stargirl Ser.: 2). (ENG.). 288p. (YA). (gr. 7). pap. 9.99 *(978-0-375-85644-0(7)*, Ember) Random Hse. Children's Bks.
Stauffer, Sharon. Cornfield Baby: And Other Nature Surprises. 2003. (Illus.). 179p. 8.40 *(978-0-7399-2314-6(5)*, 2344) Rod & Staff Pubs., Inc.
Sullivan, Paul. Breaker at Dawn. 2010. (J). pap. *(978-0-88092-705-5(4))* Royal Fireworks Publishing Co.
Sully, Katherine. Night-Night Pennsylvania. Poole, Helen, illus. 2016. (Night-Night Ser.). (ENG.). 20p. (J). (gr. -1-1). bds. 9.99 *(978-1-4926-4219-0(3)*, 9781492642190, Hometown World) Sourcebooks, Inc.
—Night-Night Pittsburgh. Poole, Helen, illus. 2017. (Night-Night Ser.). (ENG.). 20p. (J). (gr. -1-1). bds. 9.99 *(978-1-4926-5479-7(5)*, Hometown World) Sourcebooks, Inc.
Taschek, Karen. The the Risen Horse. 2010. (ENG.). 248p. (YA). (gr. 7-18). pap. 15.95 *(978-0-8263-4837-1(8)*, P198426) Univ. of New Mexico Pr.
Thomas, Kara. The Darkest Corners. 2017. 352p. (YA). (gr. 9). pap. 9.99 *(978-0-553-52148-1(9)*, Ember) Random Hse. Children's Bks.
Vinsh, Aara J. Ben, the Miracle Horse, 1 vol. 2010. 193p. pap. 24.95 *(978-1-4489-7591-4(3))* America Star Bks.
Wagner, Lloyd S. Ghosts at Gettysburg: An Oliver Family Adventure. 2007. 144p. 21.95 *(978-0-595-70995-3(8))*; per. 11.95 *(978-0-595-46877-5(2))* iUniverse, Inc.
Walkup, Jennifer. Second Verse. 2013. 270p. pap. 15.95 *(978-1-935462-87-3(3))*; (ENG.). 200p. (YA). (gr. 7-12). pap. 11.95 *(978-1-935462-85-9(7))* Luminis Bks., Inc.
Weeks, Sarah. Pie (Scholastic Gold) 2013. (ENG.). 192p. (J). (gr. 3-7). pap. 7.99 *(978-0-545-27012-0(X)*, Scholastic Paperbacks) Scholastic, Inc.
Welch, Sheila Kelly. The Shadowed Unicorn. 2011. 192p. (gr. -1). pap. 12.95 *(978-1-4502-6991-9(5))* iUniverse, Inc.
Weston Woods Staff, creator. Crow Call. 2011. 38.75 *(978-0-545-37494-1(4))*; 18.95 *(978-0-545-37493-4(6))* Weston Woods Studios, Inc.
Wolk, Lauren. Wolf Hollow. (ENG.). (J). (gr. 5). 2018. 320p. 8.99 *(978-1-101-99484-9(3)*, Puffin Books) 2016. 304p. 18.99 *(978-1-101-99482-5(7)*, Dutton Books for Young Readers) Penguin Young Readers Group.
—Wolf Hollow. 2018. lib. bdg. 19.65 *(978-0-606-40877-6(0))* Turtleback.

PENNSYLVANIA—HISTORY

Boehm Jerome, Kate. Pittsburgh & the State of Pennsylvania: Cool Stuff Every Kid Should Know. 2011. (Arcadia Kids Ser.). (ENG., Illus.). 48p. (J). (gr. 3-6). pap. 11.99 *(978-1-4396-0095-5(3))* Arcadia Publishing.
Boothroyd, Jennifer. William Penn: A Life of Tolerance. 2006. (Pull Ahead Bks.). (Illus.). 32p. (J). (gr. 3-7). lib. bdg. 22.60 *(978-0-8225-6387-7(8)*, Lerner Pubns.) Lerner Publishing Group.
Chang, Kirsten. The Liberty Bell. 2018. (Symbols of American Freedom Ser.). (ENG., Illus.). 24p. (J). (gr. k-3). lib. bdg. 26.95 *(978-1-62617-884-7(4)*, Blastoff! Readers) Bellwether Media.
Christianson, Gregory. Gettysburg: Kids Who Did the Impossible. 2019. (ENG., Illus.). 144p. (J). pap. 19.95 *(978-1-61121-399-7(1))* Savas Beatie.
Epstein, Brad M. Pittsburgh Steelers 101. 2010. (ENG., Illus.). 24p. (J). bds. *(978-1-60730-124-0(5)*, 101 Bk.) Michaelson Entertainment.
Evdokimoff, Natasha. Pennsylvania. 2011. (Guide to American States Ser.). (Illus.). 48p. (YA). (gr. 3-6). 29.99 *(978-1-61690-810-2(6))* Weigl Pubs., Inc.
—Pennsylvania: The Keystone State. 2016. (J). *(978-1-4896-4929-4(8))* Weigl Pubs., Inc.
Ferut, Michael. Gettysburg. 2014. (Scariest Places on Earth Ser.). (ENG., Illus.). 24p. (J). (gr. 3-7). lib. bdg. 26.95 *(978-1-60014-995-5(2)*, Torque Bks.) Bellwether Media.
Figley, Marty Rhodes. Who Was William Penn? And Other Questions about the Founding of Pennsylvania. 2012. (Six Questions of American History Ser.). (ENG.). 48p. (gr. 4-6). pap. 56.72 *(978-0-7613-9241-5(6))* Lerner Publishing Group.
Fox, Arthur B. Pittsburgh During the American Civil War 1860-1865. 2004. (Illus.). 236p. pap. 29.95 *(978-0-9760563-0-0(5)*, 7526S) Mechling Bookbindery.
Friesen, Helen Lepp. Pennsylvania: The Keystone State. 2012. (J). *(978-1-61913-395-2(4))*; pap. *(978-1-61913-396-9(2))* Weigl Pubs., Inc.
Galchefski, Christina, compiled by. Coloring the Pieces of Luzerne County 2003. (Illus.). 36p. (J). 4.00 *(978-0-937537-12-1(8))* Wyoming Historical & Geological Society.
Gamble, Adam & Jasper, Mark. Good Night Pennsylvania. 2013. (Good Night Our World Ser.). (ENG., Illus.). 20p. (J). (— 1). bds. 9.95 *(978-1-60219-074-0(7))* Good Night Bks.
Grey, Rochelle, text. My RiverPlace on the Schuylkill Coloring Book. 2006. (Illus.). 12p. (J). *(978-0-9785538-0-7(2))* RiverPlace Development Corp.
Gunderson, Jessica. Pennsylvania. 2009. (This Land Called America Ser.). 32p. (YA). (gr. 3-6). 19.95 *(978-1-58341-791-1(5))* Creative Co., The.
Hamilton, John. Pennsylvania, 1 vol. 2016. (United States of America Ser.). (ENG., Illus.). 48p. (J). (gr. 5-9). 34.21 *(978-1-68078-340-7(8)*, 21665, Abdo & Daughters) ABDO Publishing Co.
Harshman, Marc & Egan Smucker, Anna. Fallingwater: the Building of Frank Lloyd Wright's Masterpiece. Pham, LeUyen, illus. 2017. (ENG.). 40p. (J). 21.99 *(978-1-59643-718-0(9)*, 900075229) Roaring Brook Pr.
Hart, Joyce & Hantula, Richard. Pennsylvania, 1 vol. 2nd rev. ed. 2011. (It's My State! (Second Edition)(r) Ser.). (ENG.). 80p. (gr. 4-4). lib. bdg. 34.07 *(978-1-60870-058-5(5)*, 9547320c-641d-4b01-bfa3-9d2c0391d89d) Cavendish Square Publishing LLC.
Hart, Joyce, et al. Pennsylvania: The Keystone State, 1 vol. 3rd rev. ed. 2014. (It's My State! (Third Edition)(r) Ser.). (ENG., Illus.). 80p. (gr. 4-4). 35.93 *(978-1-5026-0015-8(3)*, 9fd3bec3-c38d-4085-8dde-d3eecc2866a7) Cavendish Square Publishing LLC.
Hinman, Bonnie. Pennsylvania: William Penn & the City of Brotherly Love. 2006. (Building America Ser.). (Illus.). 48p. (J). (gr. 3-7). lib. bdg. 29.95 *(978-1-58415-463-1(2))* Mitchell Lane Pubs.
Hooks, Gwendolyn. Ona Judge Outwits the Washingtons: An Enslaved Woman Fights for Freedom. Agoussoye, Simone, illus. 2019. (ENG.). 40p. (J). (gr. 3-6). 18.95 *(978-1-5435-1280-9(1)*, 137745, Capstone Editions) Capstone.
Jerome, Kate B. Lucky to Live in Pennsylvania. 2017. (Arcadia Kids Ser.). (ENG., Illus.). 32p. (J). 16.99 *(978-0-7385-2772-7(6))* Arcadia Publishing.
—The Wise Animal Handbook Pennsylvania. 2017. (Arcadia Kids Ser.). (ENG., Illus.). 32p. (J). 16.99 *(978-0-7385-2840-3(4))* Arcadia Publishing.
Kellaher, Karen. Pennsylvania (a True Book: My United States) (Library Edition) 2018. (True Book (Relaunch) Ser.). (ENG., Illus.). 48p. (J). (gr. 3-5). 31.00 *(978-0-531-23576-8(9)*, Children's Pr.) Scholastic Library Publishing.
Korman, Susan. P Is for Philadelphia. 2018. (ENG., Illus.). 64p. 19.95 *(978-1-59213-107-5(7))* Temple Univ. Pr.
Leathers, Daniel. The Johnstown Flood 1889. 2007. (Natural Disasters Ser.). (Illus.). 32p. (J). (gr. 1-4). lib. bdg. 25.70 *(978-1-58415-570-6(1))* Mitchell Lane Pubs.
Levy, Janey. William Penn: Shaping a Nation. (American History Milestones Ser.). 32p. 2009. (gr. 5-5). 47.90 *(978-1-61511-376-7(2))* 2009. (ENG.). (J). (gr. 5-5). lib. bdg. 28.93 *(978-1-4358-3016-5(4)*, 24bd2188-de6c-4b3d-aa82-521f8e6f5069) 2009. (Illus.). (J). 60.00 *(978-1-4358-0196-7(2)*, 1291824) 2008. (ENG., Illus.). (J). (gr. 5-5). pap. 10.00 *(978-1-4358-0195-0(4)*, 513f85ca-cd43-44e9-a265-065502d0d251) Rosen Publishing Group, Inc., The. (PowerKids Pr.).
Lewis, Noah & Graham, Loretta. Edward Ned Hector. 2005. (ENG., Illus.). 36p. per. 19.99 *(978-1-4208-6817-3(9))* AuthorHouse.
Lusted, Marcia Amidon. Pennsylvania: The Keystone State, 1 vol. 2009. (Our Amazing States Ser.). (ENG., Illus.). 24p. (J). (gr. 3-3). lib. bdg. 26.27 *(978-1-4042-8124-0(X)*, 7cb5591d-7370-497d-9111-c6fc17e8ba98, PowerKids Pr.) Rosen Publishing Group, Inc., The.
Magsamen, Sandra. I Love Pennsylvania: An ABC Adventure. 2016. (ABC Adventure Ser.). (ENG., Illus.). 40p. (J). (gr. -1-5). 12.99 *(978-1-4926-2839-2(5)*, Hometown World) Sourcebooks, Inc.
Marciniak, Kristin. What's Great about Pennsylvania? 2014. (Our Great States Ser.). (ENG., Illus.). 32p. (J). (gr. 2-5). lib.

bdg. 26.65 *(978-1-4677-3334-2(2)*, a4579b20-2efe-4745-870f-b7120553614a, Lerner Pubns.) Lerner Publishing Group.
Marsh, Carole. Exploring Pennsylvania Through Project-Based Learning: Geography, History, Government, Economics & More. 2016. (Pennsylvania Experience Ser.). (ENG.). (J). pap. 9.99 *(978-0-635-12362-6(2))* Gallopade International.
—Pennsylvania History Projects: 30 Cool, Activities, Crafts, Experiments & More for Kids to Do to Learn about Your State! 2003. (Pennsylvania Experience Ser.). 32p. (gr. k-5). pap. 5.95 *(978-0-635-01807-6(1)*, Marsh, Carole Bks.) Gallopade International.
Martin, Iain C. Gettysburg: The True Account of Two Young Heroes in the Greatest Battle of the Civil War. 2013. (ENG., Illus.). 208p. (YA). (gr. 6-6). 16.95 *(978-1-62087-532-2(2)*, 620532, Sky Pony Pr.) Skyhorse Publishing Co., Inc.
Meachen Rau, Dana. Pennsylvania, 1 vol. 2005. (Portraits of the States Ser.). (ENG., Illus.). 32p. (gr. 3-5). pap. 11.50 *(978-0-8368-4652-2(4)*, 64589718-1c63-41a7-bc4f-565e3b8e3179); lib. bdg. 28.67 *(978-0-8368-4633-1(8)*, 7f9ce50c-1d9d-4ff0-bd5b-0fca9815bff2) Stevens, Gareth Publishing LLLP. (Gareth Stevens Learning Library).
Micklos, John & Micklos, John, Jr. Washington's Crossing the Delaware & the Winter at Valley Forge: Through Primary Sources, 1 vol. 2013. (American Revolution Through Primary Sources Ser.). (ENG., Illus.). 48p. (J). (gr. 4-6). pap. 11.53 *(978-1-4644-0190-9(X)*, c759c386-064d-4048-9796-e54bc92199cf) Enslow Publishing, LLC.
Micklos, John, Jr., et al. Pennsylvania: The Keystone State, 1 vol. 4th ed. 2019. (It's My State! (Fourth Edition)(r) Ser.). (ENG.). 80p. (J). (gr. 4-4). lib. bdg. 35.93 *(978-1-5026-4238-7(7)*, 7af2bdc8-064e-41d4-bc58-fa818ae1999c) Cavendish Square Publishing LLC.
Mis, Melody S. The Colony of Pennsylvania: A Primary Source History. 2009. (Primary Source Library of the Thirteen Colonies & the Lost Colony Ser.). 24p. (gr. 3-4). 42.50 *(978-1-60854-153-9(3)*, PowerKids Pr.) Rosen Publishing Group, Inc., The.
Moore, Noreen. Reaching Tidewater: Life on the Delaware Canal. 2004. (Illus.). v, 92p. (J). pap. 5.95 *(978-1-57249-358-2(5)*, White Mane Kids) White Mane Publishing Co., Inc.
Mountjoy, Shane. Philadelphia. 2007. (Colonial Settlements in America Ser.). (ENG., Illus.). 100p. (gr. 5-9). lib. bdg. 30.00 *(978-0-7910-9336-8(0)*, P124648, Facts On File) Infobase Holdings, Inc.
Murphy, Jim. An American Plague: A Newbery Honor Award Winner. 2003. (ENG., Illus.). 176p. (J). (gr. 5-7). tchr. ed. 21.99 *(978-0-395-77608-7(2)*, 111936, Clarion Bks.) HarperCollins Pubs.
Noble, Trinka Hakes. Little Pennsylvania. Brett, Jeannie, illus. 2010. (Little State Ser.). (ENG.). 20p. (J). (gr. -1-1). bds. 9.95 *(978-1-58536-506-7(8)*, 202247) Sleeping Bear Pr.
Prentzas, G. S. The Colony of Pennsylvania, 1 vol. 2005. (Primary Sources of the Thirteen Colonies & the Lost Colony Ser.). (ENG., Illus.). 64p. (gr. 4-6). per. 12.95 *(978-1-4042-0673-1(6)*, 53def993-ba85-44b6-b3c3-adb5d6fa902e) Rosen Publishing Group, Inc., The.
—A Primary Source History of the Colony of Pennsylvania. (Primary Sources of the Thirteen Colonies & the Lost Colony Ser.). 64p. 2009. (gr. 5-8). 58.50 *(978-1-60851-887-6(6))* 2005. (ENG., Illus.). (YA). (gr. 4-6). lib. bdg. 37.13 *(978-1-4042-0433-1(4)*, aa629a19-1052-4a6c-b98a-2f67be41d62b) Rosen Publishing Group, Inc., The.
Rajczak, Michael. Haunted! Gettysburg, 1 vol. 2013. (History's Most Haunted Ser.). 32p. (J). (gr. 3-4). (ENG.). 29.27 *(978-1-4339-9248-3(5)*, ee47b6a8-c165-442c-a1b1-34b4edabafaf); (ENG.). pap. 11.50 *(978-1-4339-9249-0(3)*, 62fb7a90-651a-4e7f-b0e6-59a90b379399); pap. 63.00 *(978-1-4339-9250-6(7))* Stevens, Gareth Publishing LLLP.
Richards, Marlee. The Johnstown Flood: Core Events of Deadly Disaster, 1 vol. 2014. (What Went Wrong? Ser.). (ENG., Illus.). 32p. (J). (gr. 3-6). pap. 7.95 *(978-1-4765-5131-9(6)*, 124450) Capstone.
Robinson, Hilda & Kunkel, Jeff. Didn't We Have Fun! Robinson, Hilda, illus. 2012. (Illus.). 48p. (J). 19.95 *(978-1-933987-17-0(0)*, Crickhollow Bks.) Great Lakes Literary, LLC.
Schiel, Katy. The Whiskey Rebellion: An Early Challenge to America's New Government. (Life in the New American Nation Ser.). 32p. (gr. 4-4). 2009. 47.90 *(978-1-61514-289-7(4))* 2003. (ENG., Illus.). pap. 10.00 *(978-0-8239-4262-6(7)*, ccdb6263-16e0-4fcf-891d-08b22fad56f1) 2003. (ENG., Illus.). lib. bdg. 29.13 *(978-0-8239-4044-8(6)*, 45767c13-023c-49f0-98c7-a918ad520b87, Rosen Reference) Rosen Publishing Group, Inc., The.
Somervill, Barbara A. America the Beautiful: Pennsylvania (Revised Edition) 2014. (America the Beautiful, Third Ser. (Revised Edition) Ser.). (ENG., Illus.). 144p. (J). lib. bdg. 40.00 *(978-0-531-28289-2(9))* Scholastic Library Publishing.
Spender, Nick. George Washington & the Winter at Valley Forge, 1 vol. 2011. (Graphic Heroes of the American Revolution Ser.). (ENG.). 24p. (J). (gr. 3-3). pap. 9.15 *(978-1-4339-6014-7(1)*, 212546e8-51ff-4148-864f-6777e830450c, Gareth Stevens Learning Library); (Illus.). lib. bdg. 26.60 *(978-1-4339-6174-8(1)*, a7d37558-8404-4d5a-9b25-9d6db992cc36) Stevens, Gareth Publishing LLLP.
Spinelli, Jerry. Knots in My Yo-Yo Strong. Gentieu, Penny, photos by. 2014. (Illus.). 158p. pap. 11.00 *(978-1-61003-375-6(2))* Center for the Collaborative Classroom.
Swain, Gwenyth. Freedom Seeker: A Story about William Penn. Harvey, Lisa, illus. 2003. (Creative Minds Biographies Ser.). 64p. (J). 22.60 *(978-1-57505-176-5(1)*, Carolrhoda Bks.) Lerner Publishing Group.
Varonka, Steve. Hard Coal Times Vol. 3: Early Coal Transportation. 2004. (Illus.). 24p. (YA). 4.72 *(978-0-9709630-5-5(X))* Coal Hole Productions.
Waring, Kerry Jones, et al. Pennsylvania. 2015. lib. bdg. *(978-1-62712-766-0(6))* Cavendish Square Publishing LLC.
Way, Jennifer. Pennsylvania. 2009. (Bilingual Library of the United States of America Ser.). (ENG & SPA.). 32p. (gr. 2-2). 47.90 *(978-1-60853-382-4(4)*, Editorial Buenas Letras) Rosen Publishing Group, Inc., The.
Ziff, John. Northeast: New Jersey, New York, Pennsylvania, Vol. 19. 2015. (Let's Explore the States Ser.). (Illus.). 64p. (J). (gr. 5). 23.95 *(978-1-4222-3329-0(4))* Mason Crest.

PENOLOGY

see Prisons

PEOPLE WITH DISABILITIES

see also People with Mental Disabilities; Sick

Adams, Colleen. The Courage of Helen Keller. 2009. (Reading Room Collection 2 Ser.). 24p. (gr. 3-4). 42.50 *(978-1-60851-992-7(9)*, PowerKids Pr.) Rosen Publishing Group, Inc., The.
Andrysek, Jan & Mihailidis, Alex. New Hands, New Life: Robots, Prostheses & Innovation. 2017. (ENG., Illus.). 64p. (J). (gr. 4-7). 19.95 *(978-1-77085-969-2(1)*, 088fb460-e1de-4a59-be35-3beb1e456576); pap. 9.95 *(978-1-77085-991-3(8)*, 88034609-fa56-46cb-818b-9241f613a4a8) Firefly Bks., Ltd.
Apel, Melanie Ann. Let's Talk about Being in a Wheelchair. 2009. (Let's Talk Library). 24p. (gr. 2-3). 42.50 *(978-1-60853-438-8(3)*, PowerKids Pr.) Rosen Publishing Group, Inc., The.
Barasch, Lynne. Knockin' on Wood: Starring Peg Leg Bates. 2004. (ENG., Illus.). 32p. (J). 16.95 *(978-1-58430-170-7(8))* Lee & Low Bks., Inc.
Beale, Brian A. My Name Is Colin: ... & this Is Who I Am. 2010. 24p. 17.95 *(978-1-4520-3298-6(X))* AuthorHouse.
Bender, Lionel. Explaining Blindness. 2009. (Explaining... Ser.). 48p. (gr. 7-12). 37.10 *(978-1-59920-310-2(3))* Black Rabbit Bks.
Beyer, Mark. Stevie Wonder. 2009. (Rock & Roll Hall of Famers Ser.). 112p. (gr. 5-8). 63.90 *(978-1-60852-475-4(2)*, Rosen Reference) Rosen Publishing Group, Inc., The.
Boggs-Johnson, Stefanie. I See You, Little Naomi. 2014. (J). pap. 11.99 *(978-0-578-91579-1(0))* Stefanie Boggs-Johnson.
Borrelli, Kristin K. Sometimes I Make Noises. 2012. 24p. (-18). pap. 24.95 *(978-1-4626-9527-0(2))* America Star Bks.
Bowers, Matt. Team Sports at the Paralympics. 2020. (Paralympic Sports Ser.). (ENG.). 32p. (J). (gr. 2-4). pap. 9.99 *(978-1-68152-558-7(5)*, 10757) Amicus.
Brocker, Susan. Shockwave: Vision Without Sight. 2007. (Shockwave: Life Science & Medicine Ser.). (ENG., Illus.). 36p. (J). (gr. 4-6). lib. bdg. 25.00 *(978-0-531-17769-3(6)*, Children's Pr.) Scholastic Library Publishing.
Busic, Valerie. Jason's First Day. OI Foundation, ed. Meyers, Jeff, illus. Lt. ed. 2004. 48p. per. 8.50 *(978-0-9642189-4-9(1))* Osteogenesis Imperfecta Foundation.
Butler, Darren J. Helen Keller: Leader Without Sight or Sound. 2012. (Illus.). 108p. (J). pap. *(978-1-59421-083-9(7))* Seacoast Publishing, Inc.
Carillo, Christina Martin. Come Smile with Me. 2011. 40p. pap. 24.95 *(978-1-4560-8297-0(3))* America Star Bks.
Carolina Canines for Service & Nowak, Pat. A Job for Arabella. Baumgardner, Mary Alice, illus. 2007. 56p. (J). per. *(978-0-9800070-0-8(3))* Carolina Canines for Service Inc.
Crayton, Lisa A. The Fight for Disability Rights, 1 vol. 2019. (Activism in Action: a History Ser.). (ENG.). 112p. (gr. 8-8). pap. 18.65 *(978-1-5081-8543-7(3)*, bb82ffb1-dd1b-4878-bd65-7ea56ed96fd7) Rosen Publishing Group, Inc., The.
Crosetto, Alice, et al. Disabilities & Disorders in Literature for Youth: A Selective Annotated Bibliography for K-12. 2009. (Literature for Youth Ser.: 12). (ENG.). 400p. (J). (gr. -1-12). 117.00 *(978-0-8108-5977-7(7))* Scarecrow Pr., Inc.
Derke, Connie Butterfield. Mommy Has 1 Foot: Learning about Numbers - Learning about People. Smith, Tracy, illus. 2003. (Kayla's Learning Books). 24p. (J). (gr. 1-6). pap. 5.95 *(978-0-9747063-0-6(2))* Derke, Connie.
Doering Tourville, Amanda. Friends with Disabilities, 4 vols., Set. Sorra, Kristin, illus. Incl. My Friend Has ADHD. Flaherty, Terry. lib. bdg. 26.65 *(978-1-4048-5749-0(4)*, 102486); My Friend Has Autism. lib. bdg. 26.65 *(978-1-4048-5750-6(8)*, 102487); My Friend Has Dyslexia. lib. bdg. 26.65 *(978-1-4048-5752-0(4)*, 102489); (Illus.). (J). (gr. k-3). (Friends with Disabilities Ser.). (ENG.). 24p. 2010. 114.60 o.p. *(978-1-4048-6004-9(5)*, 169217, Picture Window Bks.) Capstone.
Donahue, Mary P. Coping When a Parent Has a Disability, 1 vol. 2018. (Coping Ser.). (ENG., Illus.). 112p. (J). (gr. 7-7). pap. 19.24 *(978-1-5081-7895-8(X)*, 7fddbc8b-f2f1-4845-baf4-26eefefef95a) Rosen Publishing Group, Inc., The.
Dudley Gold, Susan. The Americans with Disabilities Act, 1 vol. 2011. (Landmark Legislation Ser.). (ENG.). 128p. (YA). (gr. 8-8). 42.64 *(978-1-60870-039-4(9)*, 24829109-95ce-4bd0-9ddf-91d199d64035) Cavendish Square Publishing LLC.
Dwight, Laura. Brothers & Sisters, 1 vol. (ENG., Illus.). 32p. (J). 2012. pap. 7.95 *(978-1-59572-364-2(1))* 2005. (gr. -1-3). 15.95 *(978-1-887734-80-6(5))* Star Bright Bks., Inc.
Eboch, M. M., ed. Self-Advocacy & Disability Rights, 1 vol. 2018. (Introducing Issues with Opposing Viewpoints Ser.). (ENG.). 120p. (gr. 7-10). lib. bdg. 43.63 *(978-1-5345-0425-7(7)*, 4131721d-e21b-4113-9506-9165ba6030fb, Greenhaven Publishing) Greenhaven Publishing LLC.
Esherick, Joan. Breaking down Barriers: Youth with Physical Challenges. 2003. (Youth with Special Needs Ser.). (Illus.). 127p. (YA). (gr. 7). pap. 14.95 *(978-1-4222-0420-7(0))* Mason Crest.
—Guaranteed Rights: The Legislation That Protects Youths with Special Needs. 2003. (Youth with Special Needs Ser.). (Illus.). 127p. (YA). (gr. 7). pap. 14.95 *(978-1-4222-0423-8(5))* Mason Crest.
—The Journey Toward Recovery: Youth with Brain Injury. 2003. (Youth with Special Needs Ser.). (Illus.). 127p. (YA). (gr. 7). pap. 14.95 *(978-1-4222-0425-2(1))* Mason Crest.
—The Laws That Protect Youth with Special Needs. Albers, Lisa et al, eds. 2014. (Living with a Special Need Ser.: 16). 128p. (J). (gr. 7-18). 25.95 *(978-1-4222-3039-8(2))* Mason Crest.
—Physical Challenges. Albers, Lisa et al, eds. 2014. (Living with a Special Need Ser.: 16). 128p. (J). (gr. 7-18). 25.95 *(978-1-4222-3041-1(4))* Mason Crest.
Flath, Camden. Kids with Special Needs: IDEA (Individuals with Disabilities Education Act), 11 vols., Set. Incl. Finding My Voice: Kids with Speech Impairment. Stewart, Sheila. (Illus.). (YA). (gr. 5-18). lib. bdg. 19.95 *(978-1-4222-1722-1(1))*; Hidden Child: Kids with Autism. Stewart, Sheila. (Illus.). (YA). (gr. 5-18). lib. bdg. 19.95 *(978-1-4222-1724-5(8))*; I Can Do It! Kids with Physical Challenges. Stewart, Sheila. (Illus.). (YA). (gr. 5-18). lib. bdg. 19.95 *(978-1-4222-1723-8(X))*; Listening with Your Eyes: Kids Who Are Deaf & Hard of Hearing. Stewart, Sheila. (Illus.). (J). (gr. 5-18). lib. bdg. 19.95 *(978-1-4222-1717-7(5))*; My Name Is Not Slow: Kids with Intellectual Disabilities. Stewart, Sheila. (YA). (gr. 5-18). lib. bdg. 19.95 *(978-1-4222-1718-4(3))*; Seeing with Your Fingers: Kids with Blindness & Visual Impairment. Stewart, Sheila. (Illus.). (YA). (gr. 7-18). lib. bdg. 19.95 *(978-1-4222-1716-0(7))*; Sick All the Time: Kids with Chronic Illness. Chastain, Zachary. (YA). (gr. 5-18). lib. bdg. 19.95 *(978-1-4222-1719-1(1))*; Speed Racer: Kids with Attention-Deficit/Hyperactivity Disorder. Stewart, Sheila. (YA). (gr. 5-18). lib. bdg. 19.95 *(978-1-4222-1721-4(3))*; What's Wrong with My Brain? Kids with Brain Injury. Stewart, Sheila. (YA). (gr. 5-18). lib. bdg. 19.95 *(978-1-4222-1725-2(6))*; Why Can't I Learn Like Everyone Else? Kids with Learning Disabilities. Stewart, Sheila. (YA). (gr. 5-18). lib. bdg. 19.95 *(978-1-4222-1726-9(4))*; 2010. (Illus.). 48p. 2011. Set lib. bdg. 219.45 *(978-1-4222-1727-6(2))* Mason Crest.
Fukumoto, Jan. It's Hard Not to Stare: Helping Children Understand Disabilities. Huff, Tim, illus. 2013. 38p. pap. *(978-1-927355-28-2(1))* BayRidge Bks.
Gibson, Karen Bush. Ways to Help Children with Disabilities: A Guide to Giving Back. 2010. (How to Help Ser.). (Illus.). 48p. (J). (gr. 4-8). lib. bdg. 29.95 *(978-1-58415-916-2(2))* Mitchell Lane Pubs.
Goldish, Meish. Everything You Need to Know about Dyslexia. 2009. (Need to Know Library). 64p. (gr. 5-5). 58.50 *(978-1-60854-066-2(9))* Rosen Publishing Group, Inc., The.
—Surf Dog Miracles. 2012. (Dog Heroes Ser.). 32p. (J). (gr. 2-7). lib. bdg. 28.50 *(978-1-61772-577-7(3))* Bearport Publishing Co., Inc.
Green, Joanne. The Story of Thumper the Cleft-Affected Bunny. 2008. (Illus.). 56p. pap. *(978-1-897512-14-2(7))* Saga Bks.
Grillo, Marcela D. Disabilities, Sexual Health, & Consent, 1 vol. 2019. (Equal Access: Fighting for Disability Protections Ser.). (ENG.). 64p. (gr. 5-5). 36.13 *(978-1-5081-8382-2(1)*, 501020e9-22c1-4c22-80bb-7d727f2c1e80) Rosen Publishing Group, Inc., The.
Hale, Natalie. Oh, Brother! Growing up with a Special Needs Sibling. Sternberg, Kate, tr. Sternberg, Kate, illus. 2004. 48p. (J). pap. 9.95 *(978-1-59147-061-8(7)*, Magination Pr.) American Psychological Assn.
—Oh Brother! Growing up with a Special Needs Sibling. Sternberg, Kate, illus. 2004. (ENG.). 48p. (J). 14.95 *(978-1-59147-060-1(9)*, Magination Pr.) American Psychological Assn.
Haugen, David M. & Musser, Susan, eds. Disabilities, 1 vol. 2014. (Teen Rights & Freedoms Ser.). (ENG., Illus.). 200p. (gr. 10-12). lib. bdg. 43.63 *(978-0-7377-6995-1(5)*, 621e652d-504c-4250-8179-a14fa3c38604, Greenhaven Publishing) Greenhaven Publishing LLC.
Hayes, Amy. Disability Rights Movement, 1 vol. 2016. (Civic Participation: Working for Civil Rights Ser.). (ENG.). 32p. (J). (gr. 5-5). 27.93 *(978-1-4994-2850-6(2)*, 11418b13-56a9-42b7-9044-72493a97ed13); pap. 11.00 *(978-1-4994-2679-3(8)*, 5f623ea1-c85b-4eaa-93d9-26563fb55eaa) Rosen Publishing Group, Inc., The. (PowerKids Pr.).
Health Physically Challenged. (J). *(978-0-8136-9354-5(3))* Modern Curriculum Pr.
Herman, Gail & Who HQ. What Are the Paralympic Games? Thomson, Andrew, illus. 2020. (What Was? Ser.). 112p. (J). (gr. 3-7). 5.99 *(978-1-5247-9262-6(4))*; lib. bdg. 15.99 *(978-1-5247-9263-3(2))* Penguin Young Readers Group. (Penguin Workshop).
Hoge, Robert. Ugly. 2016. (ENG., Illus.). 208p. (J). (gr. 3-7). 16.99 *(978-0-425-28775-0(0)*, Viking Books for Young Readers) Penguin Young Readers Group.
Hucks, Doris. I Am a Shining Star. 2011. 36p. pap. 18.00 *(978-1-4634-1916-5(3))* AuthorHouse.
Johnson, Nerissa & Parra, Angelo. Teen Reflections, Then & Now. 2011. (Readers' & Writers' Genre Workshop Ser.). (YA). pap. *(978-1-4509-3025-3(5))* Benchmark Education Co.
Kennedy, Leola. There's a Reason. 2012. 82p. pap. *(978-1-77069-445-3(5))* Word Alive Pr.
Kluth, Paula & Schwarz, Patrick. Pedro's Whale, 1 vol. 2010. (Illus.). 32p. (J). 18.95 *(978-1-59857-160-8(5))* Brookes Publishing.
Kovatch, Sarah. Special Helpers. 2005. (Illus.). 16p. (J). *(978-0-7367-2854-6(6))* Zaner-Bloser, Inc.
Larabie, Gayle. Is My Dad Still My Dad? 2005. (Illus.). 32p. (J). *(978-1-55306-873-0(4))* Essence Publishing.
Leavitt, Amie Jane. Helping People with Disabilities & Special Needs Through Service Learning, 1 vol. 2014. (Service Learning for Teens Ser.). (ENG., Illus.). 80p. (J). (gr. 7-7). 37.80 *(978-1-4777-7965-1(5)*, 94b83274-be84-4c13-8f11-081438d7515b, Rosen Young Adult) Rosen Publishing Group, Inc., The.
Levete, Sarah. Explaining Deafness. 2009. (Explaining... Ser.). 48p. (gr. 7-12). 37.10 *(978-1-59920-313-3(8))* Black Rabbit Bks.
Lewis, Wendy. Sabrina, the Girl with a Hole in Her Heart. 2011. 16.95 *(978-0-615-47819-7(0))* Two Dolphins Publishing Group.
Libal, Autumn. My Name Isn't Slow: Youth with Mental Retardation. 2003. (Youth with Special Needs Ser.). (Illus.). 127p. (YA). (gr. 7). pap. 14.95 *(978-1-4222-0426-9(X))* Mason Crest.
—The Ocean Inside: Youth Who Are Deaf & Hard of Hearing. 2003. (Youth with Special Needs Ser.). (Illus.). 127p. (YA). (gr. -1). pap. 14.95 *(978-1-4222-0427-6(8))* Mason Crest.
Libal, Joyce. Finding My Voice: Youth with Speech Impairment. 2003. (Youth with Special Needs Ser.). (Illus.). 127p. (YA). pap. 14.95 *(978-1-4222-0422-1(7))* Mason Crest.
MacRae, Sloan. Respecting the Contributions of Disabled Americans, 1 vol. 2012. (Stop Bullying Now! Ser.). (ENG., Illus.). 24p. (J). (gr. 2-3). pap. 9.25 *(978-1-4488-7518-4(8)*, a71b26b5-91c4-4830-b0ca-26cedc62dc2c); lib. bdg. 26.27 *(978-1-4488-7445-3(9)*, 1f99b0be-878b-4678-9634-d12c67c78749) Rosen Publishing Group, Inc., The. (PowerKids Pr.).
Manson, Ainslie. Boy in Motion: Rick Hansen's Story. Benoit, Renne, illus. 2009. (ENG.). 48p. (J). (gr. k-3). pap. 12.00 *(978-1-55365-427-8(7)*, Greystone Kids) Greystone Books Ltd. CAN. Dist: Publishers Group West (PGW).
Marks, Elizabeth. Growing Together Across the Autism Spectrum: A Kid's Guide to Living with, Learning from, & Loving a Parent with Autism Spectrum Disorder. Marks, Elizabeth, illus. 2015. (ENG., Illus.). 47p. (J). pap. 19.95 *(978-1-942197-08-9(X))* Autism Asperger Publishing Co.
Martin, Mabel. Talking with Hands. Witmer, Ruth, illus. 2007. (Little Jewel Book Ser.). 24p. (J). (gr. 2). pap. 2.70 *(978-0-7399-2394-8(3))* Rod & Staff Pubs., Inc.
Mcclelland, Grace. The Gift of Grace. 2012. (ENG.). (J). pap. 20.00 *(978-1-4507-2003-8(X))* Independent Pub.
McIntosh, Kenneth & Walker, Ida. Youth with Cultural/Language Differences: Interpreting an Alien World. 2009. (Helping Youth with Mental, Physical, & Social Challenges Ser.). (Illus.). 128p. (YA). (gr. 7-18). lib. bdg. 24.95 *(978-1-4222-0141-1(4))* Mason Crest.
Mecum, Shelly & Chun, Peggy. Watercolor Cat. 2007. 48p. 14.95 *(978-1-56647-838-0(3))* Mutual Publishing LLC.
Meyer, Donald & Vadasy, Patricia F. Living with a Brother or Sister with Special Needs: A Book for Sibs. 2nd exp. rev. ed. 2003. (ENG., Illus.). 144p. (C). (gr. -1-18). pap. 24.95 *(978-0-295-97547-4(4))* Univ. of Washington Pr.
Meyer, Donald J., ed. Sibling Slam Book. 2005. (ENG., Illus.). 186p. pap. 15.95 *(978-1-890627-52-2(6))* Woodbine Hse.
Mikayla. Our Friend Mikayla. Resh, Kimberly, ed. 2007. (Illus.). 48p. (J). (gr. k-3). 14.95 *(978-1-4243-0734-0(1))* Independent Publisher Services.
Miller, Vivian. Grandma's Mercedes. 2010. 36p. pap. 15.49 *(978-1-4520-1710-5(7))* AuthorHouse.
Mitchell Haugen, Hayley, ed. People with Disabilities, 1 vol. 2011. (Social Issues Firsthand Ser.). (ENG.). 112p. (gr. 10-12). lib. bdg. 39.93 *(978-0-7377-4798-0(6)*, a0eada2f-b561-4ec7-af95-362a6b657aea, Greenhaven Publishing) Greenhaven Publishing LLC.
Monahan, Finn. Know Your Spectrum! An Autism Creative Writing Workbook for Teens. 2019. 288p. pap. 29.95 *(978-1-78592-435-4(4)*, 696742) Kingsley, Jessica Pubs. GBR. Dist: Hachette UK Distribution.
Neild, Piper. No One Is Like Sarah, 1 vol., 1. 2015. (Rosen REAL Readers: Social Studies Nonfiction / Fiction: Myself, My Community, My World Ser.). (ENG.). 8p. (J). (gr. k-1). pap. 5.46 *(978-1-5081-1665-3(2)*, 728b057a-1b59-4fb6-8976-8e7d84621760, Rosen Classroom) Rosen Publishing Group, Inc., The.
Nichols, Susan. Confronting Ableism, 1 vol. 2017. (Speak up! Confronting Discrimination in Your Daily Life Ser.). (ENG.). 64p. (YA). (gr. 7-7). pap. 13.95 *(978-1-5383-8160-1(5)*, a3e6e41b-f131-4c18-965d-c90516f31bf6) Rosen Publishing Group, Inc., The.
Olin, Nicki. God Made Me Special, Just Like You! 2012. 28p. pap. 12.95 *(978-1-61244-061-3(4))* Halo Publishing International.
Oxtra, Cristina. Stephen Hawking: Get to Know the Man Behind the Theory. 2019. (People You Should Know Ser.). (ENG., Illus.). 32p. (J). (gr. 3-6). pap. 7.95 *(978-1-5435-7468-5(8)*, 140908); lib. bdg. 27.99 *(978-1-5435-7186-8(7)*, 140437) Capstone.
Perron, Brigitte. I'm a Champ. 2010. 32p. 14.95 *(978-1-4269-1176-7(9))* Trafford Publishing.
—Je suis Grand. 2010. (FRE.). 36p. 16.95 *(978-1-4269-1173-6(4))* Trafford Publishing.
—Je Suis un Vainqueur. 2010. (FRE.). 32p. pap. 14.95 *(978-1-4269-1153-8(X))* Trafford Publishing.
Phillips, Karen, ed. What about You? 2009. (Illus.). 50p. (J). (gr. 3). 16.95 *(978-1-59174-612-6(4))* Klutz.
Poole, H. W. Disability & Families, Vol. 12. 2016. (Families Today Ser.). (Illus.). 48p. (J). (gr. 5). 20.95 *(978-1-4222-3614-7(5))* Mason Crest.
Pope, Ellen Dittman. Friends with a Difference. Dixon, Carol, illus. 2009. (J). *(978-0-929915-92-0(5))* Headline Bks., Inc.
Ratto, Linda Lee. (dis) Ability. 2004. (YA). per. 16.95 *(978-0-9748508-2-5(9))* Power Pr.
Roland, James. Disability Discrimination. 2018. (Discrimination in Society Ser.). (ENG.). 80p. (YA). (gr. 6-12). 39.93 *(978-1-68282-381-1(4))* ReferencePoint Pr., Inc.
Romero, Libby. DK Life Stories: Helen Keller. Ager, Charlotte, illus. 2019. (DK Life Stories Ser.). (ENG.). 128p. (J). (gr. 3-7). pap. 5.99 *(978-1-4654-7474-2(9)*, DK Children) Dorling Kindersley Publishing, Inc.
Rouss, Sylvia A. A Circle of Smiles: A Story about Beit Issie Shapiro, Israel's Leading Organization in the Field of Disability. 2010. (J). pap. *(978-0-9829273-1-1(2))* IGI Pr.
Rue, Nancy N. Lucy Out of Bounds, 1 vol. 2016. (Faithgirlz / a Lucy Novel Ser.: 2). (ENG.). 224p. (J). pap. 7.99 *(978-0-310-75505-0(0))* Zonderkidz.
Sabin, Ellen. The Special Needs Acceptance Book: Being a Friend to Someone with Special Needs. 2007. (Illus.). 64p. (J). 17.95 *(978-0-9759868-5-1(6))* Watering Can.
Sabin, Ellen & Driscoll, Patricia. The Healing Heroes Book: Braving the Changes When Someone You Love Is Wounded in Service. 2012. (ENG., Illus.). 64p. (J). spiral bd. 19.95 *(978-0-9826416-0-6(5))* Watering Can.
Schaefer, Lola M. Some Kids Are Blind: Revised Edition. rev. ed. 2008. (Understanding Differences Ser.). (ENG., Illus.). 24p. (J). (gr. -1-2). pap. 6.29 *(978-1-4296-1774-1(8)*, 94821, Pebble) Capstone.
—Some Kids Use Wheelchairs: A 4D Book. 2018. (Understanding Differences Ser.). (ENG., Illus.). 24p. (J). (gr. -1-2). lib. bdg. 29.32 *(978-1-5435-0998-4(3)*, 137671, Capstone Pr.) Capstone.
—Some Kids Use Wheelchairs: Revised Edition. rev. ed. 2008. (Understanding Differences Ser.). (ENG., Illus.). 24p. (J). (gr. -1-2). per. 6.29 *(978-1-4296-1776-5(4)*, 94823, Pebble) Capstone.
—Some Kids Wear Leg Braces: A 4D Book. 2018. (Understanding Differences Ser.). (ENG., Illus.). 24p. (J). (gr.

-1-2). lib. bdg. 29.32 (978-1-5435-0999-1(1), 137672, Capstone Pr.) Capstone.

—Some Kids Wear Leg Braces: Revised Edition. rev. ed. 2008. (Understanding Differences Ser.). (ENG., Illus.). 24p. (J). (gr. -1-2). pap. 6.29 (978-1-4296-1777-2(2), 94825) Capstone.

Schultz Nicholson, Lorna. Fighting for Gold: The Story of Canada's Sledge Hockey Paralympic Gold. 2009. (Recordbooks Ser.). (ENG., Illus.). 128p. (YA). (gr. 8-12). 16.95 (978-1-55277-031-3(1)) James Lorimer & Co. Ltd., Pubs. CAN. Dist: Casemate Pubs. & Bk. Distributors, LLC.

Sotomayor, Sonia. Just Ask! Be Different, Be Brave, Be You. López, Rafael & López, Rafael, illus. 2019. (ENG.). 32p. (J). (gr. -1-3). 17.99 (978-0-525-51412-1(0), Philomel Bks.) Penguin Young Readers Group.

Souder, Patricia. Blindness & Vision Impairment. Albers, Lisa et al, eds. 2014. (Living with a Special Need Ser.: 16). 128p. (J). (gr. 7-18). 25.95 (978-1-4222-3030-5(9)) Mason Crest.

Souder, Patti. A Different Way of Seeing: Youth with Visual Impairments & Blindness. 2003. (Youth with Special Needs Ser.). (Illus.). 127p. (YA). (gr. 7). pap. 14.95 (978-1-4222-0418-4(9)) Mason Crest.

Steininger-Moore, Cheryl A. Blue Tooth Sleuth. Schafer, Holden J., illus. 2013. 26p. 16.50 (978-1-61314-141-0(6)); (J). pap. 9.99 (978-1-61314-142-7(4), Innovo Pr.) Innovo Publishing, LLC.

Stewart, Gail B. Alexandra Scott: Champion for Cancer Research, 1 vol. 2006. (Young Heroes Ser.). (ENG., Illus.). 64p. (gr. 4-8). lib. bdg. 30.38 (978-0-7377-3613-7(5), 56ce8cb2-a3ac-4708-9117-c8dbe06ec0c7, KidHaven Publishing) Greenhaven Publishing LLC.

Stewart, Nancy. Katrina & Winter: Partners in Courage. 2012. 24p. 19.95 (978-1-61633-242-6(5)); pap. 11.95 (978-1-61633-243-3(3)) Guardian Angel Publishing, Inc.

Stewart, Sheila. Finding My Voice: Kids with Speech Impairment. 2009. (Kids with Special Needs Ser.). 48p. (YA). (gr. 5-18). pap. 7.95 (978-1-4222-1925-6(9)) Mason Crest.

—I Can Do It! Kids with Physical Challenges. 2009. (Kids with Special Needs Ser.). 48p. (YA). (gr. 5-18). pap. 7.95 (978-1-4222-1926-3(7)) Mason Crest.

—Listening with Your Eyes: Kids Who Are Deaf & Hard of Hearing. 2009. (Kids with Special Needs Ser.). 48p. (YA). (gr. 5-18). pap. 7.95 (978-1-4222-1920-1(8)) Mason Crest.

—My Name Is Not Slow: Kids with Intellectual Disabilities. 2009. (Kids with Special Needs Ser.). 48p. (YA). (gr. 5-18). pap. 7.95 (978-1-4222-1921-8(6)) Mason Crest.

Stewart, Sheila & Flath, Camden. I Can Do It! Kids with Physical Challenges. 2010. (Kids with Special Needs Ser.). (Illus.). 48p. (YA). (gr. 5-18). lib. bdg. 19.95 (978-1-4222-1723-8(X)) Mason Crest.

Sundquist, Josh. We Should Hang Out Sometime: Embarrassingly, a True Story. 2016. (ENG.). 352p. (YA). (gr. 7-17). pap. 10.99 (978-0-316-25100-6(3)) Little, Brown Bks. for Young Readers.

Thornton, Denise. Physical Disabilities: The Ultimate Teen Guide. 2007. (It Happened to Me Ser.: 17). (ENG., Illus.). 176p. (gr. 8-12). 69.00 (978-0-8108-5300-3(0)) Scarecrow Pr., Inc.

Turner, Amanda. Helping Those with Disabilities. 2019. (Careers Making a Difference Ser.). (Illus.). 80p. (J). (gr. 12). lib. bdg. 34.60 (978-1-4222-4259-9(5)) Mason Crest.

Whelahan, Marlene Verno. My Best Friend's Sister... A True Story. 2010. 20p. 12.99 (978-1-4389-8729-3(3)) AuthorHouse.

PEOPLE WITH DISABILITIES—BIOGRAPHY

All about Me: Growing up with Turner Syndrome & Nonverbal Learning Disabilities. 2004. (J). lib. bdg. 14.95 (978-0-9759850-0-7(0)); per. (978-0-9759850-1-4(9)) Maple Leaf Ctr.

Burcaw, Shane. Not So Different: What You Really Want to Ask about Having a Disability. Carr, Matt, illus. 2017. (ENG.). 40p. (J). 19.99 (978-1-62672-771-7(6), 900172893) Roaring Brook Pr.

Donaldson, Madeline. Louis Braille. 2008. pap. 52.95 (978-0-8225-9393-5(9)) Lerner Publishing Group.

Edwards, Karen. Christopher Reeve: A Real-Life Superhero. 2005. (Illus.). 32p. (J). (978-0-669-51411-7(X)) Great Source Education Group, Inc.

Eggleton, Jill. Up to the Challenge. 2007. (Connectors Ser.). (gr. 2-5). pap. (978-1-877453-21-2(8)) Global Education Systems Ltd.

Hollingsworth, Tamara. Helen Keller: A New Vision, 1 vol. 2nd rev. ed. 2013. (TIME for KIDS(r): Informational Text Ser.). (ENG., Illus.). 48p. (J). (gr. 4-5). lib. bdg. 29.96 (978-1-4807-1115-0(2)) Teacher Created Materials, Inc.

Lauren, Jill. That's Like Me!, 1 vol. 2009. (ENG.). 32p. (J). (gr. k-3). 17.95 (978-1-59572-207-2(6)) Star Bright Bks., Inc.

Lobb, Nancy. 16 Extraordinary Americans with Disabilities. 2nd ed. 2007. (16 Extraordinary Ser.). (Illus.). 139p. (J). (gr. 3-7). tchr. ed., per. 25.00 (978-0-8251-6278-7(5)) Walch Education.

Manson, Ainslie. Roll On: Rick Hansen Wheels Around the World, 1 vol. Lightburn, Ron, illus. 2013. (ENG.). 40p. (J). (gr. k-5). pap. 10.95 (978-1-77100-268-4(9), Greystone Kids) Greystone Books Ltd. CAN. Dist: Publishers Group West (PGW).

Mills, Nathan & Peck, Audrey. Helen Keller: Miracle Child, 1 vol. 2012. (Rosen Readers Ser.). (ENG., Illus.). 24p. (J). (gr. 1-2). pap. 8.25 (978-1-4488-8824-5(7), 4870d10f-4237-4f28-bc91-622475a3a847, Rosen Classroom) Rosen Publishing Group, Inc., The.

Moore, Sherry. Jason's #16 Dream. 2005. 48p. pap. 16.95 (978-1-4137-6878-7(4)) America Star Bks.

Mueller, Pamela Bauer. Aloha Crossing. 2008. (Aloha Set Ser.: 2). (ENG., Illus.). 176p. (J). (gr. 3-7). pap. 8.99 (978-0-9685097-9-1(7)) Pinata Publishing CAN. Dist: Independent Pubs. Group.

Ninteau, Sherrie. Rick's Story-the Story of Rick Hoyt. 2009. (J). 14.95 (978-1-934878-87-3(1)) Amplify Publishing Group.

O'Brien, John A. Who Was Helen Keller? Harrison, Nancy, illus. 2003. (Who Was... ? Ser.). 107p. (J). (gr. 3-7). 12.65 (978-0-7569-1596-4(1)) Perfection Learning Corp.

Packard, Mary. Beating the Odds: A Chapter Book. 2004. (True Tales Ser.). (ENG.). 48p. (J). 22.50 (978-0-516-23731-2(4), Children's Pr.) Scholastic Library Publishing.

Peck, Audrey. Helen Keller: Miracle Child, 1 vol. 2012. (Beginning Biographies Ser.). (ENG., Illus.). 24p. (J). (gr. 1-2). 26.27 (978-1-4488-8593-0(0), 01d48232-e725-4281-a3eb-1235e4a32875, PowerKids Pr.) Rosen Publishing Group, Inc., The.

Powers, J. L. Colors of the Wind: The Story of Blind Artist & Champion Runner George Mendoza. Mendoza, George, illus. 2014. (J). 18.95 (978-1-930900-73-8(2)) Purple Hse. Pr.

Quinlan, Don. Rick Hansen: A Life in Motion, 1 vol. 2013. (ENG.). 72p. (J). (978-1-55455-195-8(1)) Fitzhenry & Whiteside, Ltd.

—Rick Hansen: A Life in Motion, 1 vol. 2013. (Larger Than Life Ser.). (ENG.). 72p. (J). (gr. 3-5). pap. 6.95 (978-1-55455-196-5(X), 625001e0-90aa-479f-8158-30718ca7c73e) Fitzhenry & Whiteside, Ltd. CAN. Dist: Firefly Bks., Ltd.

Reeves, Jordan & Reeves, Jen Lee. Born Just Right. 2019. (Jeter Publishing Ser.). (ENG., Illus.). 160p. (J). (gr. 4-8). 17.99 (978-1-5344-2838-6(0), Aladdin) Simon & Schuster Children's Publishing.

Sandler, Michael. Jean Driscoll: Dream Big, Work Hard! 2006. (Defining Moments Ser.). (Illus.). 32p. (J). (gr. 2-5). lib. bdg. 25.27 (978-1-59716-268-5(X)) Bearport Publishing Co., Inc.

Senker, Cath. Stephen Hawking. 2015. (Against the Odds Biographies Ser.). (ENG., Illus.). 48p. (J). (gr. 3-6). 35.99 (978-1-4846-2466-1(1), 129624, Heinemann) Capstone.

Sutcliffe, Jane. Helen Keller. 2009. (History Maker Biographies Ser.). (gr. k-2). 27.93 (978-0-7613-4223-6(0), Lerner Pubns.) Lerner Publishing Group.

Thompson, Laurie Ann. Emmanuel's Dream: The True Story of Emmanuel Ofosu Yeboah. Qualls, Sean, illus. 2015. 40p. (J). (gr. -1-3). 18.99 (978-0-449-81744-5(X), Schwartz & Wade Bks.) Random Hse. Children's Bks.

Woog, Adam. Emmanuel Ososu Yeboah: Champion for Ghana's Disabled, 1 vol. 2006. (Young Heroes Ser.). (ENG., Illus.). 48p. (gr. 4-8). lib. bdg. 37.33 (978-0-7377-3614-4(3), 74f9b232-19ff-4f94-a52b-32600548d1ae, KidHaven Publishing) Greenhaven Publishing LLC.

PEOPLE WITH DISABILITIES—EDUCATION

Benson, Kerry Elizabeth. ADA & Your Rights at School & Work, 1 vol. 2019. (Equal Access: Fighting for Disability Protections Ser.). (ENG.). 64p. (gr. 5-5). pap. 13.95 (978-1-5081-8327-3(9), 807f97a8-3fff-4ab9-97b4-d137896f3dfb) Rosen Publishing Group, Inc., The.

Bryant, John E. Taking Speech Disorders to School. Schader, Karen, ed. Dineen, Tom, illus. 2004. (Special Kids in School Ser.: Sixteenth). (J). per. 11.95 (978-1-891383-24-3(8), 70016) JayJo Bks., LLC.

Duckworth, Katie. Education. 2004. (Children's Rights Ser.). (J). lib. bdg. 27.10 (978-1-58340-419-5(8)) Black Rabbit Bks.

O'Brien, John A. Who Was Helen Keller? Harrison, Nancy, illus. 2003. (Who Was... ? Ser.). 107p. (J). (gr. 3-7). 12.65 (978-0-7569-1596-4(1)) Perfection Learning Corp.

Spencer, Leslie. Social Stories for Children with Disabilities. 2011. 28p. pap. 24.95 (978-1-4560-2202-0(4)) America Star Bks.

PEOPLE WITH DISABILITIES—FICTION

Abdullah, Shaila & Abdullah, Aanyah. My Friend Suhana: A Story of Friendship & Cerebral Palsy. 2014. 30p. pap. 14.95 (978-1-61599-211-9(1)) Loving Healing Pr., Inc.

Akbarpour, Ahmad. Good Night, Commander, 1 vol. Mixter, Helen & Eskandani, Shadi, trs. Zahedi, Morteza, illus. 2010. (ENG.). 24p. (J). (gr. 1-3). 17.95 (978-0-88899-989-4(5)) Groundwood Bks. CAN. Dist: Publishers Group West (PGW).

Alborghetti, Marci. The Miracle of the Myrrh. Blondon, Herve, illus. 2003. (J). 16.95 (978-0-87946-249-9(3), 708) ACTA Pubns.

Armstrong, Gregory D. The Day Buddy Flew. 2013. 42p. (J). 21.99 (978-0-578-12191-8(3)) Armstrong, Greg.

—Don't Laugh at Me. 2013. 32p. 21.99 (978-0-578-12368-4(1)) Armstrong, Greg.

Arno, Ronni. Molly in the Middle. 2017. (Mix Ser.). (ENG.). 240p. (J). (gr. 4-8). 17.99 (978-1-4814-8032-1(4)); (Illus.). pap. 7.99 (978-1-4814-8031-4(6)) Simon & Schuster Children's Publishing. (Aladdin).

Arnold, David. Kids of Appetite. 2017. (ENG.). 368p. (YA). (gr. 9). pap. 10.99 (978-0-14-751366-3(9), Speak) Penguin Young Readers Group.

—Kids of Appetite. 2017. lib. bdg. 22.10 (978-0-606-40491-4(0)) Turtleback.

Artists with developmental disabilities. Disabled Fables, 1 vol. 2005. (ENG., Illus.). 32p. (J). (gr. 1-18). 19.95 (978-1-932065-97-8(0)) Star Bright Bks., Inc.

Asare, Meshack. Sosu's Call. Asare, Meshack, illus. 2006. (ENG., Illus.). 40p. (J). (gr. k-4). 11.99 (978-1-929132-21-8(2)) Kane Miller.

Atkins, Ben. The Breakaway Kid. Woods, Vanessa, illus. 2nd rev. ed. 2005. (ENG.). 32p. (J). per. 8.00 (978-0-9768653-0-8(0)) Summer Day Publishing, LLC.

Auch, M. J. One-Handed Catch. 2009. (ENG.). 272p. (J). (gr. 5-9). pap. 12.99 (978-0-312-53575-9(9), 900054755) Square Fish.

Auch, Mary Jane. One-Handed Catch. 2009. 272p. (J). (gr. 5-9). pap. 6.99 (978-0-312-58002-5(9)) Square Fish.

Avi. Prairie School. Farnsworth, Bill, illus. 2003. (I Can Read Level 4 Ser.). (ENG.). 48p. (J). (gr. 3-4). pap. 4.99 (978-0-06-051318-4(7), HarperCollins) HarperCollins Pubs.

—Prairie School. Farnsworth, Bill, illus. 2003. (I Can Read Bks.). 47p. (gr. 3-7). 14.00 (978-0-7569-1452-3(3)) Perfection Learning Corp.

Balardo, Sharon. I Am Abel. James-Thomson, Tammy, illus. 2012. (ENG.). 24p. pap. 17.99 (978-1-4772-7798-0(6)) AuthorHouse.

Balliett, Blue. The Danger Box. 2012. (ENG.). 320p. (J). (gr. 4-7). pap. 7.99 (978-0-439-85210-4(2), Scholastic Paperbacks) Scholastic, Inc.

Banister, Katie Rodriguez & Banister, Steve. Aunt Katie's Visit: A Child's First Book on Disabilities. Whitfield, Eric T., illus. 2003. (J). 16.99 (978-0-9744908-0-9(6)) Access-4-All, Inc.

Baratz-Logsted, Lauren. Crazy Beautiful. 2011. (ENG.). 204p. (YA). (gr. 7). pap. 12.95 (978-0-547-40310-6(0), 1428146, Clarion Bks.) HarperCollins Pubs.

Barchers, Suzanne I. Kate & Gail, 1 vol. rev. ed. 2011. (Phonics Ser.). (ENG., Illus.). 16p. (gr. k-2). 6.99 (978-1-4333-2907-4(7)) Teacher Created Materials, Inc.

—On a Walk with Ren, 1 vol. rev. ed. 2011. (Phonics Ser.). (ENG., Illus.). 16p. (gr. k-1). 6.99 (978-1-4333-2417-8(2)) Teacher Created Materials, Inc.

Barnes, Bobbie Jo. The Message. 2012. 24p. pap. 24.95 (978-1-4626-9047-3(5)) America Star Bks.

Barrett, Granny Rita. The Adventures on Granny's Fun-Ee Farm: Book 1. 2012. 20p. pap. 14.00 (978-1-4772-8356-1(0)) AuthorHouse.

Barrett, Kendra J., et al. Yes I Can! A Girl & Her Wheelchair. Lemay, Violet, illus. 2018. 32p. (J). (978-1-4338-2869-0(3), Magination Pr.) American Psychological Assn.

Barta, Jeralyn. Rolling with Life. 2010. 24p. pap. 15.99 (978-1-4490-6862-2(6)) AuthorHouse.

Bee, Stevie J. Cross Your Heart. 2009. 216p. 25.50 (978-1-60860-133-2(1), Eloquent Bks.) Strategic Book Publishing & Rights Agency (SBPRA).

Benjamin, Irwin H. The Legend of Toad Torrington. 2011. 24p. pap. 12.79 (978-1-4634-3746-6(3)) AuthorHouse.

Berk, Josh. The Dark Days of Hamburger Halpin. 2011. 256p. (YA). (gr. 7). pap. 8.99 (978-0-375-84625-0(5), Ember) Random Hse. Children's Bks.

Best, Cari. My Three Best Friends & Me, Zulay. Brantley-Newton, Vanessa, illus. 2015. (ENG.). 40p. (J). (gr. -1-3). 19.99 (978-0-374-38819-5(9), 900031513, Farrar, Straus & Giroux (BYR)) Farrar, Straus & Giroux.

Bevins, Rose. Coming to Terms. 2004. (Cover-To-Cover Books). (Illus.). 64p. pap. 9.00 (978-0-7891-6018-8(8)); 56p. (J). (gr. 1-4). lib. bdg. 16.95 (978-0-7569-1371-7(3)) Perfection Learning Corp.

Bingham, Kelly. Formerly Shark Girl. 2013. (ENG.). 352p. (YA). (gr. 7). 16.99 (978-0-7636-5362-0(4)) Candlewick Pr.

—Shark Girl. (ENG., Illus.). 288p. (YA). (gr. 7). 2010. pap. 9.99 (978-0-7636-4627-1(X))1. 2007. 16.99 (978-0-7636-3207-6(4)) Candlewick Pr.

Black, Chuck. Rise of the Fallen: Wars of the Realm, Book 2. 2015. (Wars of the Realm Ser.: 2). (ENG.). 320p. (YA). (gr. 7). pap. 13.00 (978-1-60142-504-1(X), Multnomah Bks.) Crown Publishing Group, The.

Bloor, Edward. Tangerine. (ENG.). 320p. (gr. 5-7). 2007. (YA). 18.00 (978-0-15-201246-5(X), 1189264) 2006. (Illus.). (J). pap. 9.99 (978-0-15-205780-0(3), 252998) HarperCollins Pubs. (Clarion Bks.).

Blos, Joan W. Brothers of the Heart: A Story of the Old Northwest, 1837-1838. 2008. (ENG.). 176p. (J). (gr. 3-7). pap. 5.99 (978-1-4169-7561-8(6), Simon & Schuster/Paula Wiseman Bks.) Simon & Schuster/Paula Wiseman Bks.

Boies, Jennifer. Bonnie Butterfly. 2010. 20p. pap. 11.99 (978-1-4490-4913-3(3)) AuthorHouse.

Boles, Jim. Ivan the Invacar Helps Big Dog. Cunningham, Bob, illus. 2012. 56p. pap. 19.95 (978-0-9845983-5-9(9)) People Ink Pr.

Borrelli, Theresa "Terrie". Why Is Jamie Different? 2012. 24p. pap. 24.95 (978-1-4137-9883-8(7)) America Star Bks.

Bowen, Julie. Sometimes I Can't Talk Well. 2013. 32p. pap. 13.99 (978-1-4624-0575-6(4), Inspiring Voices) Author Solutions, LLC.

Bowling, Dusti. Insignificant Events in the Life of a Cactus. (Life of a Cactus Ser.: 1). (J). (gr. 3-7). 2019. 288p. pap. 8.99 (978-1-4549-3299-4(6)) 2017. 272p. 16.95 (978-1-4549-2345-9(8)) Sterling Publishing Co., Inc.

Bowman, Crystal. Jake's New Friend, 1 vol. 2008. (I Can Read! / the Jake Ser.). (ENG., Illus.). 32p. (J). pap. 4.99 (978-0-310-71678-5(0)) Zonderkidz.

Bradley, Kimberly Brubaker. The War That Saved My Life. (ENG.). (J). (gr. 4-7). 2016. 352p. 9.99 (978-0-14-751048-8(1), Puffin Books) 2015. 320p. 17.99 (978-0-8037-4081-5(6), Dial Bks) Penguin Young Readers Group.

—The War That Saved My Life. 2016. (J). lib. bdg. 19.65 (978-0-606-38843-6(5)) Turtleback.

Bray, Libba. Going Bovine. 2010. (ENG.). 496p. (YA). (gr. 9). pap. 14.99 (978-0-385-73398-4(4), Ember) Random Hse. Children's Bks.

Brenna, Beverley. Something to Hang on To. 2009. (ENG.). 176p. (J). pap. 12.95 (978-1-897235-57-7(7)) Thistledown Pr., Ltd. CAN. Dist: Univ. of Toronto Pr.

Brown, Donna. Crippled Like Me. 2009. 36p. pap. 14.75 (978-1-60693-986-4(6), Eloquent Bks.) Strategic Book Publishing & Rights Agency (SBPRA).

Brown, Glenys. We Can All Be Good at Something. 2017. (ENG., Illus.). 38p. (J). pap. 25.05 (978-1-4990-9764-1(6)) Xlibris Corp.

Brown, Irene Bennett. Before the Lark. 2011. (ENG.). 208p. (J). (gr. 4-6). pap. 18.95 (978-0-89672-727-4(0), P193202) Texas Tech Univ. Pr.

Brudos, Susan E. & Rubino, Alisa A., illus. Wayne's Trail. 2004. (J). pap. (978-0-932991-62-1(9)) Place In The Woods, The.

Bryant, Louella. Two Tracks in the Snow. Fargo, Todd, illus. l.t. ed. 2004. (Turtle Bks.). 32p. (J). lib. bdg. 15.95 (978-0-944727-46-1(8)); per. 9.95 (978-0-944727-45-4(X)) Jason & Nordic Pubs. (Turtle Bks.).

Bundschuh, Rick. Burned: A Novel, 1 vol. 2014. (Faithgirlz / Soul Surfer Ser.: 2). (ENG.). 128p. (J). pap. 7.99 (978-0-310-74555-6(1)) Zonderkidz.

—Clash: A Novel, 1 vol. 2014. (Faithgirlz / Soul Surfer Ser.: 1). (ENG.). 128p. (J). pap. 7.99 (978-0-310-74582-2(9)) Zonderkidz.

Bundy, Tamara. Walking with Miss Millie. 2018. 240p. (J). (gr. 5). 8.99 (978-0-399-54457-6(7), Puffin Books) Penguin Young Readers Group.

Bunker, Lisa. Felix Yz. (ENG.). 288p. (J). (gr. 5-9). 2018. 8.99 (978-0-425-28851-1(X), Puffin Books) 2017. 16.99 (978-0-425-28850-4(1), Viking Books for Young Readers) Penguin Young Readers Group.

Burnett, Frances. The Secret Garden. 2012. (Illus.). 304p. (978-1-4351-4212-1(8)) Barnes & Noble, Inc.

—The Secret Garden. Robinson, Charles, illus. 2011. 304p. (J). (978-1-4351-3344-0(7)) Barnes & Noble, Inc.

—The Secret Garden, 1 vol. Simon, Ute, illus. 2011. (Calico Illustrated Classics Ser.: No. 3). (ENG.). 112p. (J). (gr. 2-5). 38.50 (978-1-61641-108-4(2), 4023, Calico Chapter Bks.) ABDO Publishing Co.

—The Secret Garden: A Young Reader's Edition of the Classic Story. 2005. 332p. 29.95 (978-1-4218-0619-8(3), 1st World Library - Literary Society) 1st World Publishing, Inc.

—The Secret Garden: A Young Reader's Edition of the Classic Story. (J). 22.95 (978-0-8488-0692-7(1)) Amereon Ltd.

—The Secret Garden: A Young Reader's Edition of the Classic Story. 2004. (Illus.). (J). (gr. 1-4). spiral bd. (978-0-616-14565-4(9)); spiral bd. (978-0-616-14566-1(7)) Canadian National Institute for the Blind/Institut National Canadien pour les Aveugles.

—The Secret Garden: A Young Reader's Edition of the Classic Story. 2005. 132p. per. 5.95 (978-1-4209-2229-5(7)) Digireads.com Publishing.

—The Secret Garden: A Young Reader's Edition of the Classic Story. 2004. reprint ed. pap. 28.95 (978-1-4179-2544-5(2)); pap. 1.99 (978-1-4192-8193-8(3)) Kessinger Publishing, LLC.

—The Secret Garden: A Young Reader's Edition of the Classic Story. (English As a Second Language Bk.). (Illus.). 92p. pap. 4.46 net. (978-0-582-53417-9(8)) Longman Publishing Group.

—The Secret Garden: A Young Reader's Edition of the Classic Story. 2005. (ENG.). 24.95 (978-1-55742-519-5(1)); pap. 15.95 (978-1-55742-524-9(8)) Wildside Pr., LLC.

—The Secret Garden: With a Discussion of Compassion. Lauter, Richard, illus. 2003. (Values in Action Illustrated Classics Ser.). 191p. (J). (978-1-59203-037-8(8)) Learning Challenge, Inc.

Burnett, Frances Hodgson. The Secret Garden. Moore, Inga, illus. 2010. (ENG.). 272p. (J). (gr. 1-4). pap. 19.99 (978-0-7636-4732-2(2)) Candlewick Pr.

—The Secret Garden. 2003. (Illus.). 288p. (gr. 12-18). mass mkt. 5.95 (978-0-451-52883-4(2), Signet) Penguin Publishing Group.

—The Secret Garden. 2013. (Vintage Children's Classics Ser.). (ENG.). 384p. (J). (gr. 4-7). pap. 12.99 (978-0-09-957295-4(8)) Penguin Random Hse. GBR. Dist: Independent Pubs. Group.

—The Secret Garden. 2008. (Puffin Classics Ser.). (Illus.). 368p. (J). (gr. 3-7). 8.99 (978-0-14-132106-6(7), Puffin Books) Penguin Young Readers Group.

—The Secret Garden. 2003. (Modern Library Classics Ser.). 288p. (J). (gr. 3-7). pap. 10.00 (978-0-8129-6998-6(7), Modern Library) Random House Publishing Group.

—The Secret Garden: Special Edition with Tasha Tudor Art & Bonus Materials. Tudor, Tasha, illus. 100th anniv. ed. 2010. (ENG.). 384p. (J). (gr. 4-18). reprint ed. pap. 9.99 (978-0-06-440188-3(X), HarperCollins) HarperCollins Pubs.

Callender, Kacen. This Is Kind of an Epic Love Story. 2019. (ENG.). 304p. (YA). (gr. 9). pap. 10.99 (978-0-06-282023-5(0), Balzer & Bray) HarperCollins Pubs.

Callender, Kheryn. This Is Kind of an Epic Love Story. 2018. (ENG.). 304p. (YA). (gr. 9). 17.99 (978-0-06-282022-8(2), Balzer & Bray) HarperCollins Pubs.

Carillo, Christina. Life Can Be A Smile. 2010. 30p. pap. 21.99 (978-1-4500-2848-6(9)) Xlibris Corp.

Carl, Dave. Super Cyclist. Mack, Kathryn, illus. 2010. (ENG.). (J). pap. 12.00 (978-0-9785160-8-6(7)) Etcetera Pr. LLC.

Carol Hersh. Handy Sandy. Baker, David, illus. 2011. 28p. pap. 24.95 (978-1-4560-8991-7(9)) America Star Bks.

Carrier, Therese & Carrier, Stephen. Josiah's School Fun Day. Hatfield, Tommy, illus. 2007. 29p. (J). 16.95 (978-0-9797648-0-6(7)) Carrier, Therese.

Carter, Jimmy & Carter, Amy. The Little Baby Snoogle- Fleejer. 2014. (ENG., Illus.). 24p. 19.95 (978-1-55728-671-0(X), P240466) Univ. of Arkansas Pr.

Cate, Shari. The Dreams of King Neb. 2013. 16p. pap. 7.95 (978-1-4497-9970-0(1), WestBow Pr.) Author Solutions, LLC.

Cervantes, J. C. Rick Riordan Presents the Fire Keeper (a Storm Runner Novel, Book 2) 2020. 24p. (J). (gr. 3-7). pap. 7.99 (978-1-368-04237-6(6), Riordan, Rick) Disney Publishing Worldwide.

—Rick Riordan Presents the Fire Keeper (a Storm Runner Novel, Book 2) Rodriguez, Irvin, illus. 2019. 20p. (J). (gr. 3-7). 16.99 **(978-1-368-04188-1(4)**, Rick Riordan Presents) Disney Publishing Worldwide.

—Rick Riordan Presents the Storm Runner. 2019. (Storm Runner Ser.: 1). 24p. (J). (gr. 3-7). pap. 7.99 (978-1-368-02360-3(6), Riordan, Rick) Disney Publishing Worldwide.

—Rick Riordan Presents the Storm Runner (a Storm Runner Novel, Book 1) 2018. 20p. (J). (gr. 3-7). 16.99 (978-1-368-01634-6(0), Riordan, Rick) Disney Publishing Worldwide.

Chartier, Brent & Jones, Patrick. Collateral Damage. 2015. (Support & Defend Ser.). (ENG.). 128p. (YA). (gr. 6-12). pap. 7.99 (978-1-4677-8091-9(X), aa18a38c-207a-4040-b2b0-3605af3fe712, Darby Creek) Lerner Publishing Group.

Chillemi, Stacey. My Daddy Has Epilepsy. 2007. (ENG., Illus.). 64p. (J). per. 34.50 (978-1-4303-0220-9(8)) Lulu Pr., Inc.

Christopher, Matt. The Great Quarterback Switch. 2008. (New Matt Christopher Sports Library). 144p. (J). (gr. 4-6). lib. bdg. 26.60 (978-1-59953-216-5(6)) Norwood Hse. Pr.

Clark, Shawnie. Wonder Wheels. 2017. (ENG., Illus.). (J). (gr. k-6). 17.99 (978-1-365-86141-3(4)) Lulu Pr., Inc.

—Wonder Wheels Dyslexic Font. 2017. (ENG., Illus.). (J). (gr. k-6). 17.99 (978-1-365-86143-7(0)) Lulu Pr., Inc.

Clements, Andrew. Things Not Seen. 2004. 272p. (J). (gr. 5-18). reprint ed. pap. 8.99 (978-0-14-240076-0(9), Puffin Books) Penguin Young Readers Group.

—Things Not Seen. 2004. 251p. (gr. 5-9). 17.00 (978-0-7569-2599-4(1)) Perfection Learning Corp.

—Things Not Seen. 2004. 256p. (J). (gr. 4-7). pap. 38.00 incl. audio (978-1-4000-9014-3(8), Listening Library) Random Hse. Audio Publishing Group.

Cocca-Leffler, Maryann. Janine & the Field Day Finish. 2018. (2019 Av2 Fiction Ser.). (ENG.). 32p. (J). (gr. -1-2). lib. bdg. 34.28 (978-1-4896-8269-7(4), AV2 by Weigl) Weigl Pubs., Inc.

Coolidge, Susan. What Katy Did. 2013. (ENG., Illus.). 200p. (J). 15.00 (978-1-84135-843-7(6)) Award Pubns. Ltd. GBR. Dist: Parkwest Pubns., Inc.

—What Katy Did. Ledyard, Addie, illus. 2013. 132p. pap. (978-1-909735-03-3(5)) Aziloth Bks.

—What Katy Did. 2012. 246p. pap. (978-1-78139-262-1(5)) Benediction Classics.

—What Katy Did. 2017. (ENG., Illus.). (J). (gr. 4-6). pap. 9.90 (978-1-366-50696-2(0)) Blurb, Inc.

—What Katy Did. 2016. (ENG., Illus.). (J). 26.95 (978-1-359-87966-0(8)) 2015. (ENG., Illus.). (J). (gr. 2-4).

25.95 (978-1-297-62709-5(1)) 2012. 302p. pap. 29.75 (978-1-286-07372-8(3)) 2012. 300p. pap. 29.75 (978-1-286-00091-5(2)) 2011. 290p. (gr. 3-7). pap. 28.75 (978-1-179-65265-8(7)) 2010. (ENG.). 282p. (gr. 3-7). pap. 28.75 (978-1-177-27477-7(9)) 2010. 302p. pap. 29.75 (978-1-145-74830-9(9)) 2008. 164p. (gr. 4-7). 25.99 (978-0-554-28634-1(3)) 2007. (ENG.). 144p. pap. 18.99 (978-1-4346-5943-9(7)) 2007. (ENG.). 160p. pap. 21.99 (978-1-4346-5944-6(5)) Creative Media Partners, LLC.

—What Katy Did. 2007. (ENG.). 148p. per. (978-1-4065-1527-5(2)) Dodo Pr.

—What Katy Did. (Dover Children's Evergreen Classics Ser.). (ENG.). (J). 2018. 176p. pap. 5.99 (978-0-486-82252-5(4), 822524) 2006. (Illus.). 160p. (gr. 3-8). per. 6.95 (978-0-486-44760-5(X)) Dover Pubns., Inc.

—What Katy Did. 2007. (ENG.). 104p. per. (978-1-4068-4855-7(7)) Echo Library.

—What Katy Did. 2010. (Illus.). 92p. (gr. 3-7). pap. 19.99 (978-1-153-74507-9(0)) 2009. 104p. pap. 6.40 (978-0-217-53637-0(9)) General Bks. LLC.

—What Katy Did. 2010. 132p. pap. (978-1-4076-5115-6(3)) HardPr.

—What Katy Did. Ledyard, Addie, illus. 284p. 2010. 35.16 (978-1-163-85079-4(9)) 2010. pap. 23.16 (978-1-163-77965-1(2)) 2007. 43.95 (978-0-548-53870-8(0)) 2007. per. 28.95 (978-0-548-48700-6(6)) Kessinger Publishing, LLC.

—What Katy Did. 2017. (Virago Modern Classics,What Katy Did Ser.). (ENG.). 208p. (J). (gr. 4-6). 11.99 (978-0-349-00959-9(7), Virago Press) Little, Brown Book Group Ltd. GBR. Dist: Hachette Bk. Group.

—What Katy Did. 2013. (Vintage Children's Classics Ser.). (Illus.). 256p. (J). (gr. 4-7). pap. 12.99 (978-0-09-957312-8(1)) Penguin Random Hse. GBR. Dist: Independent Pubs. Group.

—What Katy Did. 2007. (ENG.). 192p. pap. 12.45 (978-1-60424-403-8(8), Bk. Jungle) Standard Publications, Inc.

—What Katy Did. 144p. 2018. (ENG., Illus.). (J). 19.99 (978-1-5154-3178-7(9)) 2010. pap. 4.99 (978-1-61720-100-4(6)) Wilder Pubns., Corp.

—What Katy Did. 2011. 162p. (gr. 3-7). pap. (978-3-8424-6664-7(1)) tredition Verlag.

—What Katy Did: Illustrated by Susan Hellard. Hellard, Susan, illus. 2016. (Alma Junior Classics Ser.). (ENG.). 246p. (J). pap. 9.99 (978-1-84749-607-2(5), 331109) Alma Classics GBR. Dist: Bloomsbury Publishing Plc.

Coolidge, Susan & Ledyard, Addie. What Katy Did. 2010. (ENG.). 292p. pap. 28.75 (978-1-172-34659-2(3)) Creative Media Partners, LLC.

Cormier, Robert. Heroes. 2006. (York Notes Ser.). (ENG., Illus.). 112p. pap. (978-1-4058-3559-6(1)) Pearson Education, Ltd.

Coy, John. Gap Life. 2016. (ENG.). 224p. (YA). 24.99 (978-1-250-08895-6(X), 900158526) Feiwel & Friends.

Craik, Maria Dinah. The Little Lame Prince. 2008. 120p. 24.99 (978-0-554-21709-3(0)) 2006. 124p. pap. 18.99 (978-1-4264-0755-0(6)) 2006. 118p. pap. 19.99 (978-1-4264-0739-0(4)) Creative Media Partners, LLC.

—The Little Lame Prince. 2007. 128p. pap. 9.95 (978-1-60424-390-1(2), Bk. Jungle) Standard Publications, Inc.

Crawford, Brittany. I Sit in a Wheelchair but I Will Be Okay! 2010. 26p. pap. 12.50 (978-1-60911-200-4(8), Eloquent Bks.) Strategic Book Publishing & Rights Agency (SBPRA).

Creech, Sharon. Granny Torrelli Makes Soup. 2012. (ENG., Illus.). 160p. (J). (gr. 3-7). reprint ed. pap. 9.99 (978-0-06-440960-5(0), HarperCollins) HarperCollins Pubs.

—Granny Torrelli Makes Soup. Raschka, Chris, illus. 2004. (Joanna Cotler Bks.). 141p. (gr. 3-7). 17.00 (978-0-7569-4604-3(2)) Perfection Learning Corp.

Crockett-Blassingame, Linda, illus. See the Ocean. 2006. 32p. (J). 14.95 (978-0-9778143-0-5(0)) Inclusive Books LLC.

Cunningham, Julia. Burnish Me Bright. 2008. (J). (gr. 3-7). 23.75 (978-0-8446-6252-7(6)) Smith, Peter Pub., Inc.

Cushman, Karen. Alchemy & Meggy Swann. 2020. (ENG.). 192p. (J). (gr. 3-7). pap. 7.99 (978-0-358-09749-5(5), 1747606, Clarion Bks.) HarperCollins Pubs.

Daines, Julie. Unraveled: A Tale of True Love. 2014. 192p. (J). pap. 14.99 (978-1-62108-627-7(5)) Covenant Communications, Inc.

DeBear, Kirsten. Toby & Tutter Therapy Dogs. Dwight, Laura, photos by. 2012. (ENG., Illus.). 32p. (J). 17.95 (978-0-9847812-0-1(X)) Toby & Tutter Publishing.

Defelice, Cynthia. The Light on Hogback Hill. 2008. (ENG.). 128p. (J). (gr. 3-7). pap. 7.99 (978-1-4169-8691-1(X), Simon & Schuster/Paula Wiseman Bks.) Simon & Schuster/Paula Wiseman Bks.

DeGross, Monalisa. Donavan's Double Trouble. Bates, Amy, illus. 192p. (J). (gr. 2-5). 2008. lib. bdg. 16.89 (978-0-06-077294-9(8)) 2007. (ENG.). 16.99 (978-0-06-077293-2(X)) HarperCollins Pubs. (Amistad).

DeHart, Leslie Marie. Paloma: The Lilly Fairy, 1 vol. 2010. 50p. pap. 16.95 (978-1-4489-6818-3(6)) America Star Bks.

Delle Donne, Elena. Full-Court Press. (Hoops Ser.: 2). (ENG.). (J). (gr. 3-7). 2019. 176p. pap. 7.99 (978-1-5344-1235-4(2)) 2018. (Illus.). 160p. 17.99 (978-1-5344-1234-7(4)) Simon & Schuster Bks. For Young Readers. (Simon & Schuster Bks. For Young Readers).

Demonia, Lori. Leah's Voice. Turchan, Monique, illus. 2012. 28p. pap. 12.95 (978-1-61244-089-7(4)) Halo Publishing International.

Denman, K. L. Spiral, 1 vol. 2008. (Orca Soundings Ser.). (ENG.). (YA). (gr. 8-12). 112p. 16.95 (978-1-55143-932-7(8)); 128p. pap. 9.95 (978-1-55143-930-3(1)) Orca Bk. Pubs. USA.

DeWoskin, Rachel. Blind. 2014. 416p. (YA). (gr. 7). 17.99 (978-0-670-78522-3(9), Viking Books for Young Readers) Penguin Young Readers Group.

Dodson, Merilee. Kids from Critter Cove. Gregor, Terri, illus. 2007. 48p. per. 24.95 (978-1-4137-2644-2(5)) America Star Bks.

Dorris, Michael. Sees Behind Trees. 104p. (J). (gr. 4-6). pap. 4.95 (978-0-8072-1516-6(3), Listening Library) Random Hse. Audio Publishing Group.

Doti, James. Jimmy Finds His Voice. Mertins, Lisa, illus. 2013. (J). 14.95 (978-1-935204-47-3(5)) Salem Author Services.

Doyle, Marissa. Courtship & Curses. 2013. (ENG.). 368p. (YA). (gr. 9-13). pap. 19.99 (978-1-250-02744-3(6), 900098317) Square Fish.

Draper, Sharon M. Out of My Heart. 2021. (Out of My Mind Ser.). (ENG., Illus.). 352p. (J). (gr. 5). 18.99 (978-1-6659-0216-8(7), Atheneum/Caitlyn Dlouhy Books) Simon & Schuster Children's Publishing.

—Out of My Mind. 2012. (CHI & ENG.). 304p. (J). (gr. 5-8). pap. (978-986-6104-13-8(3)) DaskoviK, Izdatel'sko-torgovaja korporacija.

—Out of My Mind. 2009. 9.00 (978-0-7848-3780-1(5), Everbind) Marco Bk. Co.

—Out of My Mind. (Out of My Mind Ser.). (ENG., Illus.). (J). (gr. 5). 2012. 320p. pap. 9.99 (978-1-4169-7171-9(8)) 2010. 304p. 19.99 (978-1-4169-7170-2(X)) Simon & Schuster Children's Publishing. (Atheneum Bks. for Young Readers).

—Out of My Mind. 2012. lib. bdg. 20.85 (978-0-606-25672-8(5)) Turtleback.

Duey, Kathleen & Bale, Karen A. Swamp: Louisiana 1851. 2016. (Survivors Ser.). (ENG., Illus.). 160p. (J). (gr. 3-7). pap. 6.99 (978-1-4814-2783-8(0), Aladdin) Simon & Schuster Children's Publishing.

—Swamp: Louisiana 1851. 2016. (Survivors Ser.). (ENG., Illus.). 160p. (J). (gr. 3-7). 17.99 (978-1-4814-2784-5(9), Simon & Schuster/Paula Wiseman Bks.) Simon & Schuster/Paula Wiseman Bks.

Duff, Justin. Wishing Well. 2012. 32p. pap. 21.99 (978-1-4771-2099-6(8)) Xlibris Corp.

Dungy, Lauren & Dungy, Tony. You Can Be a Friend. Mazellan, Ron, illus. 2011. (ENG.). 32p. (J). (gr. -1-2). 17.99 (978-1-4169-9771-9(7), Little Simon Inspirations) Little Simon Inspirations.

Durfee, Jody Wind. Hadley-Hadley Benson. 2013. (ENG.). 144p. (J). pap. 11.99 (978-1-62108-151-7(6)) Covenant Communications, Inc.

Dwight, Laura. We Can Do It!, 1 vol. 2005. (ENG., Illus.). 32p. (J). pap. 5.95 (978-1-59572-033-7(2)) Star Bright Bks., Inc.

Eames, Brian. The Dagger Quick. (Dagger Chronicles Ser.). (ENG., (J). (gr. 3-7). 2013. Illus.). 352p. pap. 6.99 (978-1-4424-8368-2(7)) 2011. 336p. 15.99 (978-1-4424-2311-4(0)) Simon & Schuster/Paula Wiseman Bks. (Simon & Schuster/Paula Wiseman Bks.).

—The Dagger X. 2013. (Dagger Chronicles Ser.). (ENG.). 368p. (J). (gr. 3-7). 15.99 (978-1-4424-6855-9(6), Simon & Schuster Bks. For Young Readers) Simon & Schuster Bks. For Young Readers.

—The Dagger X. 2013. (Dagger Chronicles Ser.). (ENG., Illus.). 368p. (J). (gr. 3-7). pap. 6.99 (978-1-4424-6856-6(4), Simon & Schuster/Paula Wiseman Bks.) Simon & Schuster/Paula Wiseman Bks.

Easley, Sean. The Hotel Between. 2018. (ENG., Illus.). 352p. (J). (gr. 4-7). 19.99 (978-1-5344-1697-0(8), Simon & Schuster Bks. For Young Readers) Simon & Schuster Bks. For Young Readers.

—The Key of Lost Things. 2020. (ENG.). 400p. (J). (gr. 4-7). pap. 8.99 (978-1-5344-3788-3(6), Simon & Schuster Bks. For Young Readers) Simon & Schuster Bks. For Young Readers.

Edward, J. P. The Outsider. 2012. 24p. pap. 24.95 (978-1-4626-7213-4(2)) America Star Bks.

Eggleton, Jill. Tony's Dad. Hawley, Kelvin, illus. 2003. (Rigby Sails Sailing Solo Ser.). (ENG.). 24p. (gr. 1-2). pap. 9.05 (978-0-7578-3975-7(4)) Rigby Education.

Elkeles, Simone. Leaving Paradise. 2007. 23.30 (978-1-4177-8393-9(1)) Turtleback.

—Return to Paradise. 2010. (Leaving Paradise Novel Ser.: 2). (ENG.). 312p. (YA). (gr. 9-12). pap. 9.95 (978-0-7387-1868-2(8), 0738718688, Flux) North Star Editions.

—Return to Paradise. 2010. lib. bdg. 20.80 (978-0-606-14994-5(5)) Turtleback.

Elliott, Rebecca. Just Because. 2014. (ENG., Illus.). 12p. (J). (gr. k-2). bds. 6.99 (978-0-7459-6460-7(5), 2011181e-2b68-4ada-991c-9f5da2a12562, Lion Children's) Lion Hudson PLC GBR. Dist: Baker & Taylor Publisher Services (BTPS).

Enfield, Tyler. Wrush. 2010. 206p. (J). pap. 9.95 (978-1-934572-38-2(1), Emerald) Emerald Bk. Co.

Farley, Grant. Bones of a Saint. 2021. 288p. (YA). (gr. 9). 18.99 (978-1-64129-117-0(6), Soho Teen) Soho Pr., Inc.

Ferris, Jean. Of Sound Mind. 2004. (ENG.). 224p. (YA). (gr. 7). reprint ed. pap. 11.99 (978-0-374-45584-2(8), 900022579, Farrar, Straus & Giroux (BYR)) Farrar, Straus & Giroux.

—Of Sound Mind. 2004. 215p. (YA). (gr. 7). 14.60 (978-0-7569-2970-1(9)) Perfection Learning Corp.

Field, Jenepher. The Cloth Covered Notebook: That Was My Mother's Story. 2010. (ENG., Illus.). 97p. pap. 11.99 (978-0-9826781-6-9(9)) Etcetera Pr. LLC.

Fiona Fox Staff, ed. The Secret Garden. 2012. (ENG., Illus.). 64p. 15.00 (978-1-84135-837-6(1)) Award Pubns. Ltd. GBR. Dist: Parkwest Pubns., Inc.

Flake, Sharon G. Pinned. 2014. (ENG.). 240p. (YA). (gr. 9-9). pap. 10.99 (978-0-545-05733-2(7), Scholastic Pr.) Scholastic, Inc.

Fleming, Bryn. Jasper & Willie: Wildfire. 2015. (Range Riders Ser.). (ENG.). 130p. (J). 28.99 (978-1-941821-92-3(8)); pap. 9.99 (978-1-941821-71-8(5)) West Margin Pr. (West Winds Pr.).

Fletcher, Tom. The Christmasaurus. Devries, Shane, illus. 2018. (ENG.). 384p. (J). (gr. 3-7). 13.99 (978-1-5247-7330-4(1), Random Hse. Bks. for Young Readers) Random Hse. Children's Bks.

Flood, Nancy Bo. I Will Dance. Swaney, Julianna, illus. 2020. (ENG.). 48p. (J). (gr. -1-3). 18.99 (978-1-5344-3061-7(X), Atheneum Bks. for Young Readers) Simon & Schuster Children's Publishing.

Foreman, Michael. Seal Surfer. Foreman, Michael, illus. 2007. (ENG., Illus.). 32p. (J). (gr. k-4). pap. 12.99 (978-1-84270-578-0(4)) Andersen Pr. GBR. Dist: Independent Pubs. Group.

Fortmeyer, Kendra. Hole in the Middle. 2019. (ENG.). 360p. (YA). (gr. 9). pap. 10.99 (978-1-64129-033-3(1), Soho Teen) Soho Pr., Inc.

Fournier, Kevin Mark. Sandbag Shuffle. 2007. (ENG.). 240p. (gr. 8-13). per. 12.95 (978-1-897235-22-5(4)) Thistledown Pr., Ltd. CAN. Dist: Univ. of Toronto Pr.

Fox, Nita. Captain Benjamin Dale. Wallace, Andrea, illus. 2008. 32p. (J). (gr. -1-3). pap. 5.99 (978-0-9816107-0-2(6)) Fox's Den Publishing.

Franco, Karen. Just Hold My Hand. 2013. 48p. pap. (978-1-4602-0616-4(9)) FriesenPress.

Franklin, Miriam Spitzer. Extraordinary. (ENG.). (J). (gr. 2-7). 2017. 268p. pap. 12.99 (978-1-5107-1180-8(5)) 2015. 256p. 14.99 (978-1-63220-402-8(9)) Skyhorse Publishing Co., Inc. (Sky Pony Pr.).

Friend, Natasha. How We Roll. 2019. (ENG.). 272p. (YA). pap. 10.99 (978-1-250-30881-8(X), 900164411) Square Fish.

Frizzell, Colin. Chill, 1 vol. 2006. (Orca Soundings Ser.). (ENG.). 128p. (YA). (gr. 8-12). per. 9.95 (978-1-55143-507-7(1)) Orca Bk. Pubs. USA.

Fudge, Benjamin. Enrique Speaks with His Hands. Edmonson, Tim, illus. 2008. (ENG.). 32p. (J). (gr. -1-3). 16.95 (978-0-9800649-3-3(7)) Hilton Publishing Co.

Fussell, Sandy. Samurai Kids #2: Owl Ninja. James, Rhian Nest, illus. 2011. (Samurai Kids Ser.: 2). (ENG.). 272p. (J). (gr. 4-7). 15.99 (978-0-7636-5003-2(X)) Candlewick Pr.

Gaffney, Ellen. Wings for a Flower. Gaffney, Ellen, illus. 2013. (Illus.). 32p. (J). 16.95 (978-0-9882212-6-0(8)) Three Bean Pr.

Gallo, Donald R., ed. Owning It: Stories about Teens with Disabilities. 2010. (ENG., Illus.). 224p. (YA). (gr. 7). mass mkt. 7.99 (978-0-7636-4661-5(X)) Candlewick Pr.

Gantos, Jack. What Would Joey Do? 2004. (Joey Pigza Ser.). 229p. (J). (gr. 5-9). 13.65 (978-0-7569-2597-0(5)) Perfection Learning Corp.

—What Would Joey Do? 2014. (Joey Pigza Ser.: 3). (ENG.). 256p. (J). (gr. 5-9). pap. 8.99 (978-1-250-06169-0(5), 900142031) Square Fish.

Gehret, Jeanne. The Don't-Give-Up Kid: And Learning Disabilities. LaDuca, Michael, illus. 4th ed. 2009. (Coping Ser.). (ENG.). 32p. (J). (gr. 1-3). 17.95 (978-0-9821982-0-9(5)) Verbal Images Pr.

Geraldine Anderson. Bev's Amazing Adventures: The Kitten. 2012. 28p. pap. 24.95 (978-1-4626-7386-5(4)) America Star Bks.

Getzinger, Donna. Special. 2004. 108p. (J). pap. 7.95 (978-0-87714-530-1(X)) i-5 Publishing LLC.

Gianferrari, Maria. Hello Goodbye Dog. 2017. (ENG., Illus.). 40p. (J). 18.99 (978-1-62672-177-7(7), 900141433) Roaring Brook Pr.

Giff, Patricia Reilly. All the Way Home. 2003. (ENG., Illus.). 176p. (J). (gr. 3-7). pap. 7.99 (978-0-440-41182-6(3), Yearling) Random Hse. Children's Bks.

Gillmore, Inez Haynes. Maida's Little Shop. 2017. (ENG., Illus.). (J). pap. 9.99 (978-1-366-50746-4(0)) Blurb, Inc.

—Maida's Little Shop. 2017. (ENG., Illus.). (J). 23.95 (978-1-374-82488-1(7)); pap. 13.95 (978-1-374-82487-4(9)) Capital Communications, Inc.

—Maida's Little Shop. 2007. (ENG.). 158p. pap. 19.99 (978-1-4346-1156-7(6)); 172p. pap. 21.99 (978-1-4346-1227-4(9)) Creative Media Partners, LLC.

Gordon, Kathy L. I'm not sick, I have a Handicap. 2011. 24p. (gr. 1-2). pap. 11.32 (978-1-4567-5660-4(5)) AuthorHouse.

Grabenstein, Chris. I Funny: A Middle School Story. Patterson, James, ed. Park, Laura, illus. 2012. 303p. (J). 11.99 (978-0-316-22638-7(6), 1351607) Little Brown & Co.

Gray, John. Keller's Heart. Brickell, Shanna, illus. 2019. (ENG.). 40p. (J). (gr. -1). 12.99 (978-1-64060-174-1(0)) Paraclete Pr., Inc.

Green, Amy. Escape from Riddler's Pass, Vol. 2. 2011. (ENG., Illus.). 176p. (J). pap. 7.99 (978-1-59317-433-0(0)) Warner Pr., Inc.

Green, Tim. Lost Boy. (ENG.). (J). (gr. 3-7). 2016. 320p. pap. 9.99 (978-0-06-231709-4(1)) 2015. 304p. 16.99 (978-0-06-231708-7(3)) HarperCollins Pubs. (HarperCollins).

Greene, Janice. No Way to Run, 1 vol. unabr. ed. 2010. (Q Reads Ser.). (ENG.). 32p. (YA). (gr. 9-12). pap. 8.50 (978-1-61651-184-5(2)) Saddleback Educational Publishing, Inc.

Greene, Joanne. Lippy the Lion. 2006. (ENG., Illus.). 64p. per. (978-1-894936-67-5(1)) Saga Bks.

Griffin, Paul. The Orange Houses. 2011. (ENG.). 160p. (YA). (gr. 9-12). 22.44 (978-0-8037-3346-6(1), Dial) Penguin Publishing Group.

—The Orange Houses. 2011. 176p. (YA). (gr. 9-18). 8.99 (978-0-14-241982-3(6), Speak) Penguin Young Readers Group.

Griswold, Melissa. Friends, Like You. Fisher, Cynthia, illus. abr. ed. 2007. 32p. (J). 15.00 (978-0-9797287-3-0(8)) Mainstream Ctr., Schl. for the Deaf, The.

—Friends, Like You: Children's Activity Book. Fisher, Cynthia, illus. 2007. 16p. (J). (978-0-9797287-4-7(6)) Mainstream Ctr., Schl. for the Deaf, The.

Guerrero, Tanya. How to Make Friends with the Sea. 2020. (ENG.). 368p. (J). 16.99 (978-0-374-31199-5(4), 900197455, Farrar, Straus & Giroux (BYR)) Farrar, Straus & Giroux.

Gutman, Dan. The Million Dollar Putt. 2007. 69p. (J). (gr. 3-7). 13.65 (978-0-7569-8281-2(2)) Perfection Learning Corp.

Hagman, Harvey. Majesty from Assateague, 1 vol. 2009. (ENG., Illus.). 80p. (J). pap. 8.95 (978-0-87033-552-5(9), 3670, Cornell Maritime Pr./Tidewater Pubs.) Schiffer Publishing, Ltd.

Hale, Marian. The Truth about Sparrows. 2007. (ENG.). 288p. (YA). (gr. 6-8). pap. 11.99 (978-0-312-37133-3(0), 900044661) Square Fish.

Halliday, John. Shooting Monarchs. 2007. (ENG.). 144p. (YA). (gr. 8). pap. 8.95 (978-1-4169-5559-7(3), McElderry, Margaret K. Bks.) McElderry, Margaret K. Bks.

Hambrick, Sharon. Tommy's Race. Manning, Maurie J., illus. 2004. (Fig Street Kids Ser.). 95p. (J). (gr. 1-2). 7.49 (978-1-59166-286-0(9)) BJU Pr.

Harkness, Karen. Coralee's Best Run Yet. 2007. (Illus.). 40p. (J). per. 7.99 net. (978-0-9800934-0-7(6)) H&W Publishing Inc.

Harper Bowron, Leah. Colorblind: A Novel. 2017. (ENG.). 184p. (YA). pap. 16.95 (978-1-943006-08-3(3)) SparkPr. (a Bks.parks Imprint).

Harris, Donna. Ruff Life. 2011. 240p. pap. 17.99 (978-1-4567-5081-7(X)) AuthorHouse.

Harris, Loretta. The Inside Struggle. 2007. 30p. (YA). 1.99 (978-0-9786681-3-6(8)) Triumphant Living Enterprises, Inc.

Hartman, Carrie. Child of Mine. 2007. (ENG., Illus.). 32p. (J). lib. bdg. 11.99 (978-1-934277-12-6(6)) Marn Green Publishing, Inc.

Haskell, Merrie. Handbook for Dragon Slayers. 2013. (ENG.). 336p. (J). (gr. 3-7). 16.99 (978-0-06-200816-9(1), HarperCollins) HarperCollins Pubs.

Hayward, Mark Brauner. I See Without My Eyes. Hartman, Nancy Lee, illus. 2009. 32p. pap. 12.99 (978-1-4343-3823-5(1)) AuthorHouse.

Hebron, Yvette C. Ross. Cherry Blossom Kids & the Three-legged Dog. 2007. (Illus.). 48p. (J). 18.95 (978-0-9774982-0-8(4)) Steveedee Publishing Co.

Hege, Lynnita Rae. Dan & God's Gifts. Hackman, Evelyn, illus. 2016. (ENG.). 110p. (J). 6.25 (978-0-7399-2520-1(2)) Rod & Staff Pubs., Inc.

Henry, April. Count All Her Bones. 2018. (Girl, Stolen Ser.: 2). (ENG.). 256p. (YA). pap. 12.99 (978-1-250-15874-1(5), 900156292) Square Fish.

Henry, Heather French. Las Zapatas Magicas de Claire. 2007. (Claire's Everyday Adventures Ser Ser.). (SPA & ENG., Illus.). 32p. (J). (gr. k-4). pap. 9.95 (978-1-932824-03-2(0)) Cubbie Blue Publishing.

Herbauts, Anne, creator. What Color Is the Wind? 2016. (Illus.). 48p. (J). (gr. k). pap. 21.95 (978-1-59270-221-3(X)) Enchanted Lion Bks., LLC.

Herrera, Juan Felipe. Featherless: Desplumado (English & Spanish Edition), 1 vol. Cuevas, Ernesto, Jr., illus. 2013.Tr. of Desplumado. (ENG.). 32p. (J). (gr. k-3). pap. 11.95 (978-0-89239-303-9(3), leelowcbp) Lee & Low Bks., Inc.

—SkateFate. 2015. (ENG.). 128p. (YA). (gr. 8). pap. 9.99 (978-0-06-143289-7(X), HarperTeen) HarperCollins Pubs.

Hervey, Cheston & Doane, Darren. Kill the Dragon, Get the Girl. 2017. 188p. (J). pap. (978-1-59128-188-7(1)) Canon Pr.

Hines, Anna Grossnickle. Gramma's Walk. Hines, Anna Grossnickle, illus. 2016. (ENG., Illus.). (J). (gr. -1-3). 18.95 (978-1-930900-66-0(X)) Purple Hse. Pr.

Holman, Nedra. Beautiful Queen. Velitchenko, Olga, illus. 2008. 40p. (J). (978-1-4363-5461-5(7)) Xlibris Corp.

Hong, Nari, illus. Days with Dad. 2017. (ENG.). 40p. (J). (gr. -1-3). 16.95 (978-1-59270-233-6(3)) Enchanted Lion Bks., LLC.

Hostetter, Joyce Moyer. Comfort, 2. 2011. (Bakers Mountain Stories Ser.: 2). (ENG.). 312p. (J). (gr. 4-7). pap. 9.99 (978-1-59078-895-0(8), Calkins Creek) Highlights Pr., c/o Highlights for Children, Inc.

Hubler, Marsha. Leading the Way, 1 vol., 5. 2010. (Keystone Stables Ser.). (ENG., Illus.). 128p. (J). pap. 7.99 (978-0-310-71796-6(5)) Zonderkidz.

—The Long Ride Home, 1 vol., 8. 2010. (Keystone Stables Ser.). (ENG.). 144p. (J). pap. 7.99 (978-0-310-71692-1(6)) Zonderkidz.

—Summer Camp Adventure, 1 vol., 4. 2009. (Keystone Stables Ser.). (ENG.). 128p. (J). pap. 7.99 (978-0-310-71795-9(7)) Zonderkidz.

Hughes, Jack. Dachy's Deaf, 1 vol. 2014. (Dinosaur Friends Ser.). (ENG., Illus.). 32p. (J). (gr. 2-3). lib. bdg. 28.93 (978-1-4777-9222-3(8), e1aac8da-fff2-43c8-90f3-04b22316cff1, Windmill Bks.) Rosen Publishing Group, Inc., The.

Hugo, Victor. The Hunchback of Notre Dame: Illusrtrated Edition, 1 vol. 2011. (Calico Illustrated Classics Ser.: No. 4). (ENG., Illus.). 112p. (J). (gr. 2-5). 38.50 (978-1-61641-614-0(9), 4043, Calico Chapter Bks.) ABDO Publishing Co.

The Hunchback of Notre Dame. (Read-Along Ser.). (J). 7.99 incl. audio (978-1-55723-992-1(4)) Walt Disney Records.

Ikuwa, Robert Lono. The Face of Her King. 2007.Tr. of Ke Alo o Kona Moi. (ENG & HAW.). (J). lib. bdg. (978-0-9773495-3-1(5)) Na Kamalei Koolauloa Early Education Program.

Irick, Angela. Ashley Wins the First Day of School. 2012. 16p. pap. 15.99 (978-1-4772-7182-7(1)) AuthorHouse.

Jackson, Alisha. Noah's Fire Engine. 2011. 16p. 9.00 (978-1-4567-2977-6(2)) AuthorHouse.

Jasnoch, Dorothy. Frankie the Bunny: Newfound Friends. Korzeniowski, Samson O., ed. Jasnoch, Dorothy, illus. 2013. (Illus.). 28p. 17.99 (978-1-937752-15-6(1)) Owl About Bks. Pubs.

John, Antony. Five Flavors of Dumb. 2011. (ENG.). 368p. (YA). (gr. 7-18). 8.99 (978-0-14-241943-4(5), Speak) Penguin Young Readers Group.

Johnson, Harriet McBryde. Accidents of Nature. rev. ed. 2006. (ENG.). 240p. (YA). (gr. 7-12). 21.99 (978-0-8050-7634-9(4), 900024489, Holt, Henry & Co. Bks. For Young Readers) Holt, Henry & Co.

—Accidents of Nature. rev. l.t. ed. 2007. (Thorndike Literacy Bridge Ser.). 273p. (YA). (gr. 7-12). 22.95 (978-0-7862-9182-3(6)) Thorndike Pr.

Johnson, Lois Walfrid. Mystery of the Missing Map. 2009. (J). 8.99 (978-0-88062-283-7(0)) Mott Media.

Johnston, Julie. Hero of Lesser Causes. pap. 6.95 (978-0-7737-5850-6(X)) Stoddart Kids CAN. Dist: Fitzhenry & Whiteside, Ltd.

Jordan, Sherryl. The Raging Quiet. 2018. (ENG.). 272p. (YA). (gr. 9-7). pap. 17.99 (978-1-5344-4119-4(0), Simon Pulse) Simon Pulse.

—The Raging Quiet. l.t. ed. 2005. 416p. 22.95 (978-0-7862-7313-3(5), Large Print Pr.) Thorndike Pr.

Jung, Jin-Ho. Look Up! Kim, Mi Hyun, tr. 2018. (ENG.). 32p. (J). (gr. -1-3). 7.99 (978-0-8234-4013-9(3)) Holiday Hse., Inc.

Kats, Jewel. Cinderella's Magical Wheelchair: An Empowering Fairy Tale. Kinra, Richa, illus. 2012. (J). 24p. 29.95 (978-1-61599-113-6(1)); 20p. pap. 16.95 (978-1-61599-112-9(3)) Loving Healing Pr., Inc.

—Miss Popular Steals the Show: Girls in Wheelchairs Rule! Stenton, Murray, illus. 2014. 37p. (J). pap. 14.95 (978-1-61599-236-2(7)) Loving Healing Pr., Inc.

Kaufman, Sashi. Wired Man & Other Freaks of Nature. 2016. (ENG.). 264p. (YA). (gr. 9-12). 17.99 (978-1-4677-8563-1(6), 993090f4-4dbe-49de-98b1-080d77fec992, Carolrhoda Lab™) Lerner Publishing Group.

Kehoe, Amanda. TJ & His Wheelable Chair. 2016. (ENG., Illus.). 34p. pap. 14.95 (978-1-78612-399-2(1), 18a49070-c91c-411d-8624-aa633b8ca199) Austin Macauley Pubs. Ltd. GBR. Dist: Baker & Taylor Publisher Services (BTPS).

P
Q
R

Kelly, Erin Entrada. Hello, Universe. Roxas, Isabel, illus. 2018. (ENG.). 320p. (J). (gr. 3-7). 8.99 *(978-0-06-287750-5(X)*, Greenwillow Bks.) HarperCollins Pubs.

—Hello, Universe. 2018. lib. bdg. 17.20 *(978-0-606-41021-2(X))* Turtleback.

—Hello, Universe: A Newbery Award Winner. Roxas, Isabel, illus. (ENG.). (J). (gr. 3-7). 2020. 352p. pap. 9.99 *(978-0-06-241416-8(X))* 2017. 320p. 16.99 *(978-0-06-241415-1(1))* HarperCollins Pubs. (Greenwillow Bks.).

Kelly, Lynne. Song for a Whale. 2020. (Penworthy Picks YA Fiction Ser.). (ENG.). 298p. (J). (gr. 6-8). 19.96 *(978-1-64697-227-2(9))* Penworthy Co., LLC, The.

—Song for a Whale. 2019. (ENG.). (J). (gr. 3-7). 304p. 8.99 *(978-1-5247-7026-6(4)*, Yearling); (Illus.). 320p. 17.99 *(978-1-5247-7023-5(X)*, Delacorte Bks. for Young Readers) Random Hse. Children's Bks.

Kemmerer, Brigid. Call It What You Want. (ENG.). 384p. (YA). 2020. pap. 10.99 *(978-1-68119-812-5(6)*, 900187431) 2019. 18.99 *(978-1-68119-809-5(6)*, 900187438) Bloomsbury Publishing USA. (Bloomsbury Young Adult).

Kennedy, J. Aday. Buster Bear & Uncle B. Movshina, Marina, illus. 2012. 20p. pap. 10.95 *(978-1-61633-235-8(2))* Guardian Angel Publishing, Inc.

Kent, Renee Holmes. Robyn Flies Home, Vol. 4. 2004. (Adventures in Misty Falls Ser.: Vol. 4). (Illus.). 100p. (gr. 4-7). pap. 4.99 *(978-1-56309-764-5(8)*, N007106, New Hope Pubs.) Iron Stream Media.

Kent, Rose. Rocky Road. 2012. (ENG.). 304p. (J). (gr. 4-6). 21.19 *(978-0-375-86344-8(3)*, Knopf Bks. for Young Readers); (gr. 3-7). 7.99 *(978-0-375-86345-5(1)*, Yearling) Random Hse. Children's Bks.

Kephart, Beth. Wild Blues. Sulit, William, illus. (ENG.). (J). (gr. 5-9). 2019. 352p. pap. 9.99 *(978-1-4814-9154-9(7))* 2018. 336p. 17.99 *(978-1-4814-9153-2(9)*, Atheneum/Caitlyn Dlouhy Books) Simon & Schuster Children's Publishing.

Keplinger, Kody. Run. (ENG.). 304p. (YA). (gr. 9). 2017. pap. 10.99 *(978-0-545-83114-7(8)*, Scholastic Paperbacks) 2016. 17.99 *(978-0-545-83113-0(X)*, Scholastic Pr.) Scholastic, Inc.

Ketchen, Susan. Born That Way. 2009. (ENG.). 176p. (YA). (gr. 7-10). pap. 12.95 *(978-0-88982-254-2(9))* Oolichan Bks. CAN. Dist: Univ. of Toronto Pr.

Keyes, Daniel. Flores para Algernon. 2003. (SPA.). 224p. (J). *(978-84-483-0262-7(1))* Acento Editorial.

Khan, Rukhsana. King for a Day, 1 vol. Krömer, Christiane, illus. (ENG.). 32p. (J). 2019. (gr. 1-5). pap. 10.95 *(978-1-64379-056-5(0)*, leelowbooks) 2014. 17.95 *(978-1-60060-659-5(8))* Lee & Low Bks., Inc.

Kimmel, Elizabeth Cody. Mary Ingalls on Her Own. 2007. (Little House Sequel Ser.). (ENG.). 192p. (J). (gr. 3-7). 17.99 *(978-0-06-000905-2(5)*, HarperCollins) HarperCollins Pubs.

Kingsley, Linda Kurtz. Bringing up Sophie. Kingsley, Linda Kurtz, illus. 2010. (Illus.). 32p. (J). lib. bdg. 15.95 *(978-0-944727-25-6(5)*, Turtle Bks.) Jason & Nordic Pubs.

—Bringing up Sophie. 2009. (Illus.). 32p. (J). pap. 9.95 *(978-0-944727-24-9(7)*, Turtle Bks.) Jason & Nordic Pubs.

—Signs of Jays. Kingsley, Linda Kurtz, illus. 2008. (Illus.). 32p. (J). (ENG.). lib. bdg. 15.95 *(978-0-944727-23-2(9))*; pap. 9.95 *(978-0-944727-22-5(0))* Jason & Nordic Pubs. (Turtle Bks.).

Kinra, Richa, illus. The Princess Panda Tea Party: A Cerebral Palsy Fairy Tale. 2014. 45p. (J). pap. 14.95 *(978-1-61599-219-5(7))* Loving Healing Pr., Inc.

Kinsella, Audrey. Dingle: The Helpful Ice Cream Cone Delivery Dog. 2010. 24p. 14.49 *(978-1-4490-8362-5(5))* AuthorHouse.

Kinsey-Warnock, Natalie. Lumber Camp Library. Bernardin, James, illus. 2003. (ENG.). 96p. (J). (gr. 2-5). pap. 4.99 *(978-0-06-444292-3(6)*, HarperCollins) HarperCollins Pubs.

Klimo, Kate. Dog Diaries #10: Rolf, Vol. 10. Jessell, Tim, illus. 2017. (Dog Diaries: 10). (ENG.). 160p. (J). (gr. 2-5). pap. 8.99 *(978-0-399-55128-4(X)*, Random Hse. Bks. for Young Readers) Random Hse. Children's Bks.

Knox, Dahk. Zander, Friend of the Se. 2008. 32p. pap. 7.95 *(978-1-58275-229-7(X))* Black Forest Pr.

Kobliner, Beth & Shaw, Jacob. Jacob's Eye Patch. Feiffer, Jules, illus. 2013. (ENG.). 32p. 18.00 *(978-1-4767-3732-4(0))* Simon & Schuster.

Konigsburg, E. L. The View from Saturday. 280p. (YA). (gr. 5-18). pap. 4.95 *(978-0-8072-1511-1(2)*, Listening Library) Random Hse. Audio Publishing Group.

Kositchek, Gloria. Dream Prom, 1 vol. 2009. 174p. pap. 24.95 *(978-1-4489-9632-2(5))* America Star Bks.

Kraemer, Lillian Rosa. The Wheelchair Adventures of Jeannie & the Wallpaper Children. Drown, Eleanor J., illus. 2011. 150p. 40.95 *(978-1-258-08936-8(X))* Literary Licensing, LLC.

Kravitz, Danny. Tommy Mcknight & the Great Election. 2016. (Presidential Politics Ser.). (ENG., Illus.). 96p. (J). (gr. 3-6). lib. bdg. 26.65 *(978-1-4965-2585-7(X)*, 130712, Stone Arch Bks.) Capstone.

Kuhns, Jennifer. Hailey's Dream. Sneed, Patty, illus. 2013. 32p. pap. 13.95 *(978-0-9846811-8-1(3))* Shalako Pr.

Kumin, Maxine. Lizzie! Gilbert, Elliott, illus. 2014. 160p. (J). (gr. 4-7). 21.95 *(978-1-60980-518-0(6)*, Triangle Square) Seven Stories Pr.

Laird, Elizabeth. Red Sky in the Morning. 2012. (ENG.). 192p. (J). (gr. 3-10). pap. 12.95 *(978-1-60846-153-0(X))* Haymarket Bks.

Laird, Elizabeth & Davison, Roz. Jungle School. Sim, David, illus. 2006. (Green Bananas Ser.). (ENG.). 48p. (J). (gr. -1-3). *(978-0-7787-1042-4(4))* Crabtree Publishing Co.

Langston, Laura. Stepping Out, 1 vol. 2016. (Orca Limelights Ser.). (ENG.). 144p. (J). (gr. 4-7). pap. 9.95 *(978-1-4598-0895-9(9))* Orca Bk. Pubs. USA.

Lawrence, Iain. The Giant-Slayer. 2012. (ENG.). 304p. (J). (gr. 4-6). lib. bdg. 18.69 *(978-0-385-90393-6(6)*, Delacorte Pr.) Random Hse. Children's Bks.

Lewis, Beverly. In Jesse's Shoes: Appreciating Kids with Special Needs. Nikiel, Laura Gibbons, illus. 2007. (ENG.). 32p. (J). (gr. -1-4). 11.99 *(978-0-7642-0313-8(4))* Bethany Hse. Pubs.

LeZotte, Ann Clare. Show Me a Sign (Show Me a Sign, Book 1), 1 vol., Vol. 1. (Show Me a Sign Ser.). (ENG.). (J). (gr. 3-7). 2021. 304p. pap. 8.99 *(978-1-338-25582-9(7))* 2020. 288p. 18.99 *(978-1-338-25581-2(9)*, Scholastic Pr.) Scholastic, Inc.

—T4. 2008. (ENG.). 112p. (J). (gr. 5-7). 14.99 *(978-0-547-04684-6(7)*, 1034970, Clarion Bks.) HarperCollins Pubs.

Limb, Lisa. The Wishing Wheelchair. 2009. 40p. pap. 16.99 *(978-1-4389-4205-6(2))* AuthorHouse.

Liu, Carol & Caldarone, Marybeth Sidoti. Arlene on the Scene. 2010. 206p. (J). (gr. 3-5). pap. 7.95 *(978-1-934572-54-2(3))* Emerald Bk. Co.

Loewen, Ann E. Fast for My Feet. 2013. 176p. *(978-1-4602-3384-9(0))* FriesenPress.

Lois, Lowry. Gathering Blue. unabr. ed. 2004. (Middle Grade Cassette Librariestm Ser.). 224p. (J). (gr. 5-9). pap. 38.00 incl. audio *(978-0-8072-0989-9(9)*, S YA 250 SP, Listening Library) Random Hse. Audio Publishing Group.

—Gathering Blue. 2013. (Giver Quartet Ser.: 2). lib. bdg. 20.85 *(978-0-606-31673-6(6))* Turtleback.

Long, Susan Hill. The Magic Mirror: Concerning a Lonely Princess, a Foundling Girl, a Scheming King & a Pickpocket Squirrel. 2016. (ENG., Illus.). 320p. (J). (gr. 3-7). 16.99 *(978-0-553-51134-5(3)*, Knopf Bks. for Young Readers) Random Hse. Children's Bks.

Look, Lenore. Ruby Lu, Empress of Everything. Wilsdorf, Anne, illus. 2007. 164p. (gr. 1-5). 16.00 *(978-0-7569-8113-6(1))* Perfection Learning Corp.

—Ruby Lu, Empress of Everything. Wilsdorf, Anne, illus. 2006. (Ruby Lu Ser.). (ENG.). 176p. (J). (gr. 1-5). 17.99 *(978-0-689-86460-5(4)*, Atheneum Bks. for Young Readers) Simon & Schuster Children's Publishing.

Lord, Cynthia. Rules. 2007. (CHI.). 264p. (J). (gr. 4-7). pap. *(978-957-570-875-7(X))* Eastern Publishing Co., Ltd., The.

—Rules. 2009. 8.44 *(978-0-7848-2921-9(7)*, Everbind) Marco Bk. Co.

—Rules. 2008. (Illus.). 200p. (gr. 4-7). 17.00 *(978-0-7569-8283-6(9))* Perfection Learning Corp.

—Rules. (J). 2008. 77.49 *(978-1-4361-5837-4(0))* 2007. 220.75 *(978-1-4281-5209-0(1))* 2007. 87.75 *(978-1-4281-5214-4(8))* 2007. 89.75 *(978-1-4281-5212-0(1))* 2007. 74.75 *(978-1-4281-5208-3(3))* 2007. (SPA.). 72.75 *(978-1-4281-5210-6(5))* Recorded Bks., Inc.

—Rules. rev. l.t. ed. 2007. (Literacy Bridge Middle Reader Ser.). 191p. (J). (gr. 4-7). 23.95 *(978-0-7862-9559-3(7))* Thorndike Pr.

—Rules. 2008. lib. bdg. 17.20 *(978-1-4178-2956-9(7))* Turtleback.

—Rules (Scholastic Gold), 1 vol. (ENG.). (J). (gr. 4-7). 2008. 224p. pap. 8.99 *(978-0-439-44383-8(0)*, Scholastic Paperbacks) 2006. 208p. 19.99 *(978-0-439-44382-1(2)*, Scholastic Pr.) Scholastic, Inc.

Lovelace, Eloise. Elvin's Friends. 2012. 20p. pap. 17.99 *(978-1-4685-7615-3(1))* AuthorHouse.

Lowry, Lois. Gathering Blue. (Giver Quartet Ser.: 2). (ENG.). 256p. (YA). (gr. 7). 2013. pap. 11.99 *(978-0-547-90414-6(2)*, 1510989) 2012. 19.99 *(978-0-547-99568-7(7)*, 1525434) HarperCollins Pubs. (Clarion Bks.).

—The Windeby Puzzle: History & Story. 2023. (ENG., Illus.). 224p. (J). (gr. 5). 19.99 *(978-0-358-67250-0(3)*, Clarion Bks.) HarperCollins Pubs.

Luning, Barbara. The Quilted Zoo. 2008. 28p. pap. 15.99 *(978-1-4363-1778-8(9))* Xlibris Corp.

Lupica, Mike. Million-Dollar Throw. 2010. (ENG.). 272p. (J). (gr. 5-18). 8.99 *(978-0-14-241558-0(8)*, Puffin Books) Penguin Young Readers Group.

—Million-Dollar Throw. 2010. (Million Dollar Sports Ser.). lib. bdg. 18.40 *(978-0-606-25316-1(5))* Turtleback.

Macri, Rebecca. Pip: A Very Special Little Caterpillar. 2010. 32p. (J). 16.95 *(978-1-886057-61-6(3))* Warren Publishing, Inc.

Madden, Kerry. Gentle's Holler. 2007. (Maggie Valley Ser.). 237p. (gr. 4-7). 17.00 *(978-0-7569-8090-0(9))* Perfection Learning Corp.

Maddox, Jake. Ice Rink Rookie. Wood, Katie, illus. 2018. (Jake Maddox Girl Sports Stories Ser.). (ENG.). 72p. (J). (gr. 3-6). lib. bdg. 25.32 *(978-1-4965-5848-0(0)*, 136933, Stone Arch Bks.) Capstone.

Maguire, Gregory. Missing Sisters. 2009. 192p. (J). 16.99 *(978-0-06-123204-6(1))*; (ENG.). (gr. 3-7). pap. 6.99 *(978-0-06-123203-9(3)*, HarperCollins) HarperCollins Pubs.

Mahony, Mary. School is Not for Me, Jeremy James Conor McGee. Frederick, Sarah, illus. 2009. (J). pap. 7.95 *(978-0-9658879-4-6(4))* Redding Pr.

Martelli, Dawn. Like Me. Wharton, Jennifer Heyd, illus. 2004. (J). *(978-1-893516-01-4(6))* Our Child Pr.

Martin, Mary S. Don't Call Me Different. Brubacher, Marilyn, illus. 2016. (ENG.). 190p. (J). pap. 8.25 *(978-0-7399-2539-3(3))* Rod & Staff Pubs., Inc.

Martin, Rafe. Birdwing. 2007. (ENG.). 384p. (J). (gr. 7-12). pap. 7.99 *(978-0-439-21168-0(9)*, Levine, Arthur A. Bks.) Scholastic, Inc.

Martone, Ginny. Trouble at Big Bear Falls. 2011. 90p. pap. 19.95 *(978-1-4626-2558-1(4))* America Star Bks.

Massey, David. Taken. 2014. (ENG.). 320p. (YA). (gr. 9). 18.99 *(978-0-545-66128-7(5)*, Chicken Hse., The) Scholastic, Inc.

McBay, Bruce & Heneghan, James. Waiting for Sarah. 2004. 170p. (gr. 7). 17.95 *(978-0-7569-4567-1(4))* Perfection Learning Corp.

Mcelfresh, Lynn. Strong Deaf. 2012. 130p. 18.95 *(978-1-60898-126-7(6))*; pap. 9.95 *(978-1-60898-127-4(4))* namelos llc.

McGlen, Tim. Antonino's Impossible Dream. Touliatou, Sophia, illus. 2019. 32p. (J). (gr. -1-3). 17.99 *(978-1-5064-4933-3(6)*, Beaming Books) 1517 Media.

McGovern, Cammie. Say What You Will. 2015. (ENG.). 368p. (YA). (gr. 9). pap. 9.99 *(978-0-06-227111-2(3)*, HarperTeen) HarperCollins Pubs.

—A Step Toward Falling. 2016. (ENG.). 384p. (YA). (gr. 9). pap. 9.99 *(978-0-06-227114-3(8)*, HarperTeen) HarperCollins Pubs.

—A Step Toward Falling. 2016. (YA). lib. bdg. 20.85 *(978-0-606-39483-3(4))* Turtleback.

Messer, Celeste M. The Gift. 2004. (Adventures of Andi O'Malley Ser.). (Illus.). 82-92p. (J). (gr. 4-7). 4.95 *(978-0-9702171-3-4(7))* AshleyAlan Enterprises.

Meyers, Ann Marie. Up in the Air. 2013. 244p. (J). 22.99 *(978-1-939967-03-9(1)*, Jolly Fish Pr.) North Star Editions.

Michelinie, David, et al. Freemind - The Origin. 2003. (Freemind Ser.). (Illus.). 112p. 14.95 *(978-0-9744225-0-3(9))* Future Comics.

Mikaelsen, Ben. Petey. 2010. (ENG.). 256p. (J). (gr. 3-7). pap. 7.99 *(978-1-4231-3174-8(6))* Hyperion Bks. for Children.

—Petey. 2011. 8.32 *(978-0-7848-3604-0(3)*, Everbind) Marco Bk. Co.

—Stranded. rev. ed. 2010. (ENG.). 288p. (J). (gr. 3-7). pap. 7.99 *(978-1-4231-3362-9(5))* Hyperion Bks. for Children.

Miles, Ellen. Honey. 2009. 75p. (J). *(978-1-60744-367-4(8))* Scholastic, Inc.

Miller-Lachmann, Lyn. Gringolandia. 2009. (ENG.). 288p. (gr. 7-17). 18.95 *(978-1-931896-49-8(6))* Curbstone Pr.

Miller, Sarah. Miss Spitfire: Reaching Helen Keller. (ENG.). (J). (gr. 5-7). 2010. 256p. pap. 8.99 *(978-1-4424-0851-7(0))* 2007. 240p. 17.99 *(978-1-4169-2542-2(2))* Simon & Schuster Children's Publishing. (Atheneum Bks. for Young Readers).

Miranda, Conchita. Yago's Heartbeat. Brokenbrow, Jon, tr. Carretero, Mónica, illus. 2011. (Light (Cuento de Luz) Ser.). 42p. (J). (gr. k-3). 15.95 *(978-84-938240-3-7(8))* Cuento de Luz SL ESP. Dist: Publishers Group West (PGW).

Modesto, Michelle. Revenge & the Wild. 2016. (ENG.). 384p. (YA). (gr. 9). 17.99 *(978-0-06-236615-3(7)*, Balzer & Bray) HarperCollins Pubs.

Montgomery, L. M. Kilmeny of the Orchard. 2018. (ENG., Illus.). 118p. (J). (gr. 4-7). pap. *(978-93-5297-106-0(X))* Alpha Editions.

—Kilmeny of the Orchard. 2010. 146p. pap. 16.95 *(978-1-60444-108-6(9))* IndoEuropeanPublishing.com.

—Kilmeny of the Orchard. 2018. (ENG., Illus.). 124p. (J). (gr. 4-7). 14.99 *(978-1-5154-3231-9(9))* Wilder Pubns., Corp.

—Kilmeny of the Orchard. 2019. (ENG.). (J). 122p. pap. 7.99 *(978-1-7018-6677-5(3))*; 248p. pap. 11.99 *(978-1-6999-8624-0(X))*; 248p. pap. 15.99 *(978-1-6967-9912-6(0))*; 248p. pap. 15.99 *(978-1-6949-7534-8(7))*; 248p. pap. 15.99 *(978-1-6910-9073-0(5))*; 332p. pap. 19.99 *(978-1-6862-7332-2(0))*; 376p. pap. 25.00 *(978-1-0895-1503-6(0))*; 122p. pap. 9.99 *(978-1-0805-1773-2(1))*; 332p. pap. 19.99 *(978-1-0776-9765-2(1))*; 252p. pap. 18.99 *(978-1-0830-6207-9(7))*; 252p. pap. 15.99 *(978-1-0803-9449-4(4))*; 332p. pap. 19.99 *(978-1-0859-0762-0(7))*; 252p. pap. 18.99 *(978-1-0784-0836-3(X))*; 334p. pap. 19.99 *(978-1-0727-4932-5(7))*; 252p. pap. 15.99 *(978-1-0761-2348-0(1))*; 252p. pap. 15.99 *(978-1-0974-8816-2(0))*; 230p. pap. 13.99 *(978-1-0989-2774-5(5))*; 376p. pap. 22.99 *(978-1-0997-7222-1(2))*; 166p. pap. 12.99 *(978-1-0705-1744-5(5))*; 252p. pap. 15.99 *(978-1-0934-3789-8(8))*; 252p. pap. 16.99 *(978-1-0917-4648-0(6))*; 252p. pap. 14.99 *(978-1-7969-7320-4(3))* Independently Published.

—Kilmeny of the Orchard. 2019. (ENG.). (J). 112p. pap. 15.99 *(978-1-7077-9097-5(3))*; 84p. pap. 5.99 *(978-1-7036-1459-6(3))* Independently Published.

Montgomery, Lucy Maud. Kilmeny of the Orchard. 2019. (ENG.). 264p. (J). (gr. 4-7). 25.95 *(978-0-469-78399-7(0))*; pap. 15.95 *(978-0-469-78398-0(2))* Creative Media Partners, LLC. (Wentworth Pr.).

Montgomery, Ross. Max & the Millions. 2018. 265p. (J). pap. *(978-1-5247-1887-9(4))* Earthscan Canada.

—Max & the Millions. 2018. (ENG.). 272p. (J). (gr. 3-7). 16.99 *(978-1-5247-1884-8(X)*, Lamb, Wendy Bks.) Random Hse. Children's Bks.

Moskowitz, Hannah. Invincible Summer. 2011. (ENG.). 288p. (YA). (gr. 9-18). pap. 9.99 *(978-1-4424-0751-0(4)*, Simon Pulse) Simon Pulse.

Munsch, Robert. Zoom! Martchenko, Michael, illus. 2019. (ENG.). 32p. (J). pap. 7.99 *(978-0-7791-1432-0(9))* Scholastic Canada, Ltd. CAN. Dist: Publishers Group West (PGW).

Murdock, Catherine Gilbert. The Book of Boy: A Newbery Honor Award Winner. 2018. (ENG., Illus.). 288p. (J). (gr. 3-7). 16.99 *(978-0-06-268620-6(8)*, Greenwillow Bks.) HarperCollins Pubs.

Murillo, Vinicio. Roderick Roach. 2013. 50p. pap. 10.95 *(978-1-62516-018-8(6)*, Strategic Bk. Publishing) Strategic Book Publishing & Rights Agency (SBPRA).

My Uncle Has Wheels. 2005. (J). 8.00 *(978-0-9767077-1-4(3))* Carson, Tracy.

Nichol, Tim. Stephen Harris in Trouble: A Dyspraxic Drama in Several Clumsy Acts. 2003. 144p. (J). pap. 21.95 *(978-1-84310-134-5(3)*, 695197) Kingsley, Jessica Pubs. GBR. Dist: Hachette UK Distribution.

Nijkamp, Marieke. Unbroken: 13 Stories Starring Disabled Teens. 2018. (ENG.). 320p. (YA). 18.99 *(978-0-374-30650-2(8)*, 900176128, Farrar, Straus & Giroux (BYR)) Farrar, Straus & Giroux.

North, Sharon Rae. My Brand New Leg. 2003. (Illus.). 40p. (J). per. 11.95 *(978-0-9741544-0-4(7)*, Baby Faye Bks.) Northstar Entertainment Group, LLC.

Novel Units. The View from Saturday Novel Units Student Packet. 2019. (ENG.). (J). pap. 13.99 *(978-1-56137-936-1(0)*, Novel Units, Inc.) Classroom Library Co.

—The Weirdo Novel Units Student Packet. 2019. (ENG.). (J). pap., stu. ed. 13.99 *(978-1-56137-815-9(1)*, Novel Units, Inc.) Classroom Library Co.

Oakes, Stephanie. The Sacred Lies of Minnow Bly. 2015. (ENG.). 400p. (YA). (gr. 9). 17.99 *(978-0-8037-4070-9(0)*, Dial Bks) Penguin Young Readers Group.

O'Donnell, Liam. Ginger Leads the Way. Diefendorf, Cathy, illus. (Pet Tales Ser.). (ENG.). 32p. (J). (gr. -1-2). 2005. 4.95 *(978-1-59249-358-6(0)*, 1B023) 2005. 2.95 *(978-1-59249-359-3(9)*, 1B024) 2004. 9.95 *(978-1-59249-360-9(2)*, 1B025) Soundprints.

Oliveira, Luis. Children of Hope 2. 2008. (ENG.). 74p. pap. 15.95 *(978-0-615-19723-4(X))* Desktop Prepress Services.

O'Neill, Kaney. Dream & Reach. 2003. (Illus.). 29p. (J). pap. *(978-0-9747797-0-6(9))* ONeill, Gene & Assoc.

Palacio, R. J. Auggie & Me: Three Wonder Stories. 2015. (Wonder Ser.). (ENG.). 320p. (J). (gr. 3-7). 16.99 *(978-1-101-93485-2(9))*; lib. bdg. 19.99 *(978-1-101-93486-9(7))* Random Hse. Children's Bks. (Knopf Bks. for Young Readers).

—We're All Wonders. 2017. (Wonder Ser.). (ENG., Illus.). 32p. (J). (gr. -1-3). 18.99 *(978-1-5247-6649-8(6)*, Knopf Bks. for Young Readers) Random Hse. Children's Bks.

—Wonder. 2015. (JPN.). 420p. (J). *(978-4-593-53495-1(X))* Holp Shuppan, Publishing.

—Wonder. 2017. (Illus.). 341p. (J). *(978-1-5247-6446-3(9))* Knopf, Alfred A. Inc.

—Wonder. 2012. (Wonder Ser.). (ENG.). 320p. (J). (gr. 3-7). 17.99 *(978-0-375-86902-0(6))*; lib. bdg. 19.99 *(978-0-375-96902-7(0))* Random Hse. Children's Bks. (Knopf Bks. for Young Readers).

—Wonder. l.t. ed. 2013. (ENG.). 482p. 23.99 *(978-1-4104-5741-7(9))* Thorndike Pr.

—Wonder. 2012. lib. bdg. 29.40 *(978-0-606-36646-5(6))* Turtleback.

—The Wonder Journal. 2015. (Wonder Ser.). (ENG.). 176p. (J). (gr. 3-7). 12.99 *(978-0-553-49907-0(6)*, Knopf Bks. for Young Readers) Random Hse. Children's Bks.

—Wonder: la Historia de Julián / the Julian Chapter: a Wonder Story. 2015. (SPA.). 160p. (J). (gr. 3-7). pap. 9.95 *(978-607-31-3242-8(5)*, Nube De Tinta) Penguin Random House Grupo Editorial ESP. Dist: Penguin Random Hse. LLC.

Patterson, James. House of Robots: Robot Revolution. Neufeld, Juliana, illus. 2017. (House of Robots Ser.: 3). (ENG.). 336p. (J). (gr. 3-7). 13.99 *(978-0-316-34958-1(5)*, Jimmy Patterson) Little Brown & Co.

Patterson, James & Grabenstein, Chris. I Even Funnier: A Middle School Story. Park, Laura, illus. (I Funny Ser.: 2). (ENG.). 368p. (J). (gr. 3-7). 2017. pap. 8.99 *(978-0-316-20695-2(4))* 2013. 13.99 *(978-0-316-20697-6(0))* Little Brown & Co. (Jimmy Patterson).

—I Funny: A Middle School Story. Park, Laura, illus. (I Funny Ser.: 1). (ENG.). 320p. (J). (gr. 3-7). 2015. pap. 8.99 *(978-0-316-20692-1(X))* 2013. 13.99 *(978-0-316-32200-3(8))* 2012. 34.99 *(978-0-316-20693-8(8)*, 1351607) Little Brown & Co. (Jimmy Patterson).

—I Funny: School of Laughs. Tejido, Jomike, illus. 2017. 299p. (J). *(978-0-316-50853-7(5))* Little Brown & Co.

—I Funny TV: A Middle School Story. Park, Laura, illus. 2015. (I Funny Ser.: 4). (ENG.). 336p. (J). (gr. 3-7). 13.99 *(978-0-316-30109-1(4)*, Jimmy Patterson) Little Brown & Co.

—I Totally Funniest: A Middle School Story. Park, Laura, illus. 2015. (J). 320p. *(978-0-316-26161-6(0))*; (I Funny Ser.: 3). (ENG.). 336p. (gr. 3-7). 13.99 *(978-0-316-40593-5(0)*, Jimmy Patterson) Little Brown & Co.

Pellegrin, Leeann. Hey I'm Alex. Rolf, Heidi, illus. 2012. 26p. pap. 12.95 *(978-1-61244-049-1(5))* Halo Publishing International.

Pemberton, Teresa. Trissy's New Shoes. 2013. 32p. pap. 13.95 *(978-1-4497-9337-1(1)*, WestBow Pr.) Author Solutions, LLC.

Peretti, Paola. The Distance Between Me & the Cherry Tree. Muir, Denise, tr. 2020. (ENG., Illus.). 224p. (J). (gr. 3-7). pap. 7.99 *(978-1-5344-3963-4(3)*, Atheneum Bks. for Young Readers) Simon & Schuster Children's Publishing.

Perez, Annette. My Brain Won't Float Away / Mi cerebro no va a salir Flotando. Herranz Brooks, Jacqueline, tr. Fundora, Yolanda V., illus. 2007. (ENG & SPA.). 32p. (J). 19.95 *(978-0-9725611-2-9(9)*, Campanita Bks.) Editorial Campana.

Petrillo, Genevieve. Keep Your Ear on the Ball, 1 vol. Lyon, Lea, illus. 2007. (ENG.). 32p. (J). (gr. -1-3). 16.95 *(978-0-88448-296-3(0))* Tilbury Hse. Pubs.

Phyllarry (Rittmueller), Kathryn. Beauregart the Bear. 2009. (ENG., Illus.). 64p. (J). 12.95 *(978-0-943972-80-0(9))* Homestead Publishing.

Piper, Deb. From A— to Zulinski. 2008. (J). pap. *(978-0-88092-713-0(5))*; lib. bdg. *(978-0-88092-712-3(7))* Royal Fireworks Publishing Co.

Polacco, Patricia. The Junkyard Wonders. Polacco, Patricia, illus. 2010. (ENG., Illus.). 48p. (J). (gr. 1-4). 18.99 *(978-0-399-25078-1(6)*, Philomel Bks.) Penguin Young Readers Group.

Porter, Pamela. The Crazy Man, 1 vol. 2006. (ENG.). 176p. (J). (gr. 4-7). pap. 12.99 *(978-0-88899-695-4(0))* Groundwood Bks. CAN. Dist: Publishers Group West (PGW).

Powell, Randy. Tribute to Another Dead Rock Star. 2003. (ENG.). 224p. (YA). (gr. 7-12). pap. 15.99 *(978-0-374-47968-8(2)*, 900021239, Farrar, Straus & Giroux (BYR)) Farrar, Straus & Giroux.

Prince-Stokes, Cathy. The Story of Peabo, 1 vol. Edsall, Steven, illus. 2009. 35p. pap. 24.95 *(978-1-61582-732-9(3))* America Star Bks.

Purkapile, Susan & Peck, Amy. Mumbles the Bumble Bee: The Bee Who Couldn't Buzz. Ducommun, Barbara, illus. 2008. (J). *(978-1-930596-87-0(1))* Amherst Pr.

Reagan, Marianne & Reagan, John. It's Okay to Be Me. 2013. 28p. pap. 24.95 *(978-1-63004-045-1(2))* America Star Bks.

Reichert, Paul. The Lemonade Ripple: A Sweet Story of Kindness & Charity. 2012. (ENG., Illus.). 40p. (J). (gr. -1-k). 12.95 *(978-1-61608-701-2(3)*, 608701, Sky Pony Pr.) Skyhorse Publishing Co., Inc.

Reynolds, Jason. As Brave As You. (ENG.). 432p. (J). (gr. 5). 2017. pap. 8.99 *(978-1-4814-1591-0(3)*, Atheneum Bks. for Young Readers) 2016. (Illus.). 19.99 *(978-1-4814-1590-3(5)*, Atheneum/Caitlyn Dlouhy Books) Simon & Schuster Children's Publishing.

Rice, Linda. Rhino's Special Ears, 1 vol. 2010. 30p. pap. 24.95 *(978-1-61582-178-5(3))* PublishAmerica, Inc.

Richardson, Faith. Tree Root & River Rat. 2003. (Illus.). 248p. (J). 21.95 *(978-0-9744989-4-2(7))*; pap. 12.95 *(978-0-9744989-5-9(5))* Fox Song Bks.

Ridling, Carole. The Homerun Kid. 2011. 24p. pap. 11.32 *(978-1-4567-4998-9(6))* AuthorHouse.

Rivera, Lassen. Mi Silla de Ruedas. Alvarez, Mrinali, illus. 2006. (SPA.). 28p. 8.95 *(978-0-8477-1568-8(X))* Univ. of Puerto Rico Pr.

Roberts McKinnon, Hannah. The Properties of Water. 2010. (ENG.). 176p. (YA). (gr. 5-9). 28.99 *(978-0-374-36145-7(2)*, 900049781, Farrar, Straus & Giroux (BYR)) Farrar, Straus & Giroux.

Robinson, Gary. Tribal Journey. 2013. (PathFinders Ser.). (ENG.). 96p. (YA). (gr. 8-12). pap. 9.95 *(978-1-939053-01-5(3)*, 7th Generation) BPC.

Rocklin, Joanne. Fleabrain Loves Franny. (ENG.). (J). (gr. 3-7). 2015. 281p. pap. 8.95 *(978-1-4197-1676-8(X)*, 1073803)

2014. 288p. 16.95 *(978-1-4197-1068-1(0)*, 1073801) Abrams, Inc. (Amulet Bks.).
Roos, Stephen. The Gypsies Never Came. 2010. (ENG., Illus.). 128p. (J). (gr. 3-7). pap. 7.99 *(978-1-4424-2940-6(2)*, Simon & Schuster Bks. For Young Readers) Simon & Schuster Bks. For Young Readers.
Rose, Marilyn C. Kylie Gets a Cochlear Implant. 2013. 32p. pap. 13.00 *(978-1-62516-170-3(0)*, Strategic Bk. Publishing) Strategic Book Publishing & Rights Agency (SBPRA).
Rosenswelg, Jay B. & Repka, Janice. The Stupendous Dodgeball Fiasco. Dibley, Glin, illus. 2012. 181p. (J). (gr. 4-6). 21.19 *(978-0-525-47346-6(7))* Penguin Young Readers Group.
Roth, Judith L. & Rothshank, Brooke, illus. Julia's Words. 2008. (J). (gr. -1-3). pap. 12.99 *(978-0-8361-9417-3(9))* Herald Pr.
Sachar, Louis. The Cardturner. 2011. (ENG.). 352p. (YA). (gr. 7). pap. 9.99 *(978-0-385-73663-3(0)*, Ember) Random Hse. Children's Bks.
—The Cardturner. 2011. lib. bdg. 20.85 *(978-0-606-23428-3(4))* Turtleback.
—Small Steps. 2008. (Readers Circle Ser.). 257p. (gr. 5-9). 20.00 *(978-0-7569-9130-2(7))* Perfection Learning Corp.
—Small Steps. (ENG.). (YA). (gr. 7-9). 2008. (Holes Ser.: 2). 288p. pap. 10.99 *(978-0-385-73315-1(1)*, Ember) 2006. 272p. lib. bdg. 26.19 *(978-0-385-90333-2(2)*, Delacorte Pr.) Random Hse. Children's Bks.
—Small Steps. rev. l.t. ed. 2006. 339p. 23.95 *(978-0-7862-8297-5(5))* Thorndike Pr.
Salisbury, Linda G. The Mysterious Jamestown Suitcase: A Bailey Fish Adventure. Grotke, Christopher A., illus. 2006. (Bailey Fish Adventures Ser.). 191p. (J). (gr. 3-7). per. 8.95 *(978-1-881539-43-8(1))* Tabby Hse. Bks.
Sanford, Agnes. Melissa & the Little Red Book. Heinen, Sandy, illus. (J). (gr. 1-6). pap. 3.95 *(978-0-910924-81-8(3))* Macalester Park Publishing Co., Inc.
Savage, J. Scott. Land Keep. 2009. (Farworld Ser.: Bk. 2). 432p. (YA). (gr. 5-18). 18.95 *(978-1-60641-164-3(0)*, Shadow Mountain) Shadow Mountain Publishing.
Say, Allen. Silent Days, Silent Dreams. Say, Allen, illus. 2017. (ENG., Illus.). 64p. (J). (gr. 3-7). 24.99 *(978-0-545-92761-1(7)*, Levine, Arthur A. Bks.) Scholastic, Inc.
Schnee, Silke. Prince Noah & the School Pirates. Sistig, Heike, illus. 2016. (Prince Noah Book Ser.). (ENG.). 32p. (J). 16.00 *(978-0-87486-765-7(7))* Plough Publishing Hse.
Schneider, Maxwell. Do You Hear Me? Laughs for the Hard of Hearing by the Hard of Hearing, 1. 2003. (Illus.). 138p. per. 8.95 *(978-0-9727520-0-8(5)*, B555) Harris Communications, Inc.
Schneider, Robyn. The Beginning of Everything. (ENG.). 352p. (YA). (gr. 8). 2014. pap. 11.99 *(978-0-06-221714-1(3))* 2013. 17.99 *(978-0-06-221713-4(5))* HarperCollins Pubs. (Tegen, Katherine Bks).
Scott, Rosanna. Peter & Friends at Camp. Fargo, Todd, illus. l.t. ed. 2006. (Turtle Books). 32p. (J). (gr. k-4). pap. 9.95 *(978-0-944727-51-5(4))*; lib. bdg. 15.95 *(978-0-944727-52-2(2))* Jason & Nordic Pubs. (Turtle Bks.).
Sedgwick, Marcus. She Is Not Invisible. 2015. (ENG.). 240p. (YA). (gr. 7). pap. 11.99 *(978-1-250-05698-6(5)*, 900139107) Square Fish.
Seki, Sunny. Yuko-Chan & the Daruma Doll: The Adventures of a Blind Japanese Girl Who Saves Her Village - Bilingual English & Japanese Text. 2012. (Illus.). 32p. (J). (gr. -1-3). 15.95 *(978-4-8053-1187-5(8))* Tuttle Publishing.
Selznick, Brian. Wonderstruck, 1 vol. Selznick, Brian, illus. 2011. (ENG., Illus.). 640p. (J). (gr. 4-7). 29.99 *(978-0-545-02789-2(6)*, Scholastic Pr.) Scholastic, Inc.
Shonka, Maria. The Snail with Two Slippers. Sanchez, Evan, illus. 2011. 40p. pap. 24.95 *(978-1-60836-786-3(X))* America Star Bks.
Silverstein, Karol Ruth. Cursed. 2019. (Illus.). 336p. (YA). (gr. 7). lib. bdg. 17.99 *(978-1-58089-940-6(4)*, Charlesbridge Teen) Charlesbridge Publishing, Inc.
Smith-Armand, Kristie. Diamond in the Rough: More Fun Adventures with Abby Diamond. 2010. 256p. pap. 16.95 *(978-1-4502-4618-7(4))* iUniverse, Inc.
Smith, D. James. Probably the World's Best Story about a Dog & Th. 2010. (ENG., Illus.). 240p. (J). (gr. 4-7). pap. 11.99 *(978-1-4424-2194-3(0)*, Atheneum Bks. for Young Readers) Simon & Schuster Children's Publishing.
—Probably the World's Best Story about a Dog & the Girl Who Loved Me. 2011. (ENG.). 256p. (J). pap. 5.99 *(978-1-4169-9652-1(4)*, Atheneum Bks. for Young Readers) Simon & Schuster Children's Publishing.
Smith, Yolonda L. Differently Able Me. 2011. 24p. pap. 15.99 *(978-1-4568-4650-3(7))* Xlibris Corp.
Snader, Elisa Linovitz. The Wheelchair. Robb, Kimberly Gewerth, illus. 2008. (ENG.). 24p. pap. 12.50 *(978-1-4343-6234-6(5))* AuthorHouse.
Souliere, Lisa. Toasters Are Easy, School Not So Much. Rockwell, Joanna, illus. 2012. 20p. pap. 10.95 *(978-1-60976-654-2(7)*, Strategic Bk. Publishing) Strategic Book Publishing & Rights Agency (SBPRA).
Sovern, Megan Jean. The Meaning of Maggie. 2015. (ENG.). 232p. (J). (gr. 3-7). pap. 7.99 *(978-1-4521-2876-4(6))* Chronicle Bks. LLC.
Spencer, Leslie. Social Stories for Children with Disabilities, 1 vol. 2010. 46p. 24.95 *(978-1-4512-0917-4(7))* PublishAmerica, Inc.
Spitz, Clarita. Enrique Tiene Cinco Anos. 2014. (SPA.). 48p. (J). (gr. 2-3). pap. 14.99 *(978-958-30-4161-7(0))* Panamericana Editorial COL. Dist: Lectorum Pubns., Inc.
Spurlock, Cathy. Toby, the Two-Toed Tiger. 2008. 24p. pap. 24.95 *(978-1-60563-108-0(6))* America Star Bks.
Stahler, David, Jr. The Seer. 2008. 320p. (J). pap. 6.99 *(978-0-06-052290-2(9)*, Eos) HarperCollins Pubs.
Stamm, Linda J. Lilly & Zander: A Children's Story about Equine-Assisted Activities. Whitaker, Suzanne, illus. 2014. (J). pap. *(978-1-938313-03-5(8))* Graphite Pr.
Stenton, Murray, illus. My Brother Is Special: A Sibling with Cerebral Palsy. 2016. (J). pap. *(978-1-61599-309-3(6))* Loving Healing Pr., Inc.
Stevens, Eric. Skateboard Sonar, 1 vol. Sandoval, Gerardo, illus. 2010. (Sports Illustrated Kids Graphic Novels Ser.). (ENG.). 56p. (J). (gr. 3-8). 26.65 *(978-1-4342-1910-7(0)*, 102369); pap. 7.19 *(978-1-4342-2295-4(0)*, 103164) Capstone. (Stone Arch Bks.).
Stevenson, Robin. A Thousand Shades of Blue, 1 vol. 2008. (ENG.). 240p. (YA). (gr. 8-12). pap. 12.95 *(978-1-55143-921-1(2))* Orca Bk. Pubs. USA.
Stinson, Kathy. What Happened to Ivy, 1 vol. 2012. (ENG.). 120p. (YA). (gr. 7-10). pap. 11.95 *(978-1-926920-81-8(3))* Second Story Pr. CAN. Dist: Orca Bk. Pubs. USA.
Stratton-Porter, Gene. Freckles. (J). reprint ed. lib. bdg. 24.95 *(978-0-89190-949-1(4)*, Rivercity Pr.) Amereon Ltd.
—Freckles. l.t. ed. 2007. (ENG.). 248p. pap. 22.99 *(978-1-4264-5654-1(9))* Creative Media Partners, LLC.
—Freckles. 2006. 236p. (YA). 19.95 *(978-1-934169-32-2(3))*; pap. 8.95 *(978-1-934169-33-9(1))* Norilana Bks.
—Wonder, Hope, Love, & Loss: The Selected Novels of Gene Stratton-Porter. 2015. (ENG.). 784p. (gr. 6-6). pap. 17.99 *(978-1-63220-320-5(0)*, Sky Pony Pr.) Skyhorse Publishing Co., Inc.
Stuve-Bodeen, Stephanie. Babu's Song. Boyd, Aaron, illus. 2003. (ENG.). 32p. (J). 16.95 *(978-1-58430-058-8(2))* Lee & Low Bks., Inc.
Suen, Anastasia. Helping Sophia, 1 vol. Ebbeler, Jeffrey, illus. 2007. (Main Street School~ Kids with Character Ser.). (ENG.). 32p. (J). (gr. -1-4). 32.79 *(978-1-60270-030-7(3)*, 11261, Looking Glass Library) Magic Wagon.
Sumner, Jamie. Roll with It. 2019. (Roll with It Ser.). (ENG., Illus.). 256p. (J). (gr. 5). 19.99 *(978-1-5344-4255-9(3)*, Atheneum Bks. for Young Readers) Simon & Schuster Children's Publishing.
Sundquist, Josh. Love & First Sight. 2017. (ENG.). 288p. (YA). (gr. 7-17). 17.99 *(978-0-316-30535-8(9))* Little, Brown Bks. for Young Readers.
Swaney, Kathleen M. William's in a Wheelchair. Wysong, Ryan, illus. 2008. 24p. pap. 24.95 *(978-1-60703-447-6(6))* America Star Bks.
Tada, Joni Eareckson & Jensen, Steve. The Meanest Teacher. 2005. (Darcy & Friends Ser.). 144p. (gr. 3-6). pap. 5.99 *(978-1-58134-256-7(X)*, Crossway Bibles) Crossway.
—The Mission Adventure. 2005. (Darcy & Friends Ser.). 143p. (gr. 3-6). pap. 5.99 *(978-1-58134-257-4(8)*, Crossway Bibles) Crossway.
Taylor, Theodore. Timothy of the Cay. 2007. (ENG., Illus.). 176p. (J). (gr. 5-7). pap. 7.99 *(978-0-15-206320-7(X)*, 1198928, Clarion Bks.) HarperCollins Pubs.
—The Weirdo. 2006. (Illus.). 292p. (gr. 7-12). 18.00 *(978-0-7569-6752-9(X))* Perfection Learning Corp.
Terry, Trueman & Trueman. Stuck in Neutral. 2014. (ENG.). 128p. (J). (gr. 8-12). 13.24 *(978-1-63245-299-3(5))* Lectorum Pubns., Inc.
Thomas, Leah. Wild & Crooked. 2019. (ENG.). 448p. (YA). 18.99 *(978-1-5476-0002-1(0)*, 900194772, Bloomsbury Young Adult) Bloomsbury Publishing USA.
Tolley, Diane Stringham & Tolley, Diane Stringam. Carving Angels. 2011. 121p. (J). 12.99 *(978-1-59955-944-5(7)*, Bonneville Bks.) Cedar Fort, Inc./CFI Distribution.
Tomos, Angharad. Y Llipryn Llwyd. 2005. (WEL., Illus.). 48p. pap. *(978-0-86243-095-5(X))* Y Lolfa.
Tooke, Wes. King of the Mound: My Summer with Satchel Paige. (ENG.). 160p. (J). (gr. 3-7). 2013. pap. 7.99 *(978-1-4424-3347-2(7))* 2012. (Illus.). 17.99 *(978-1-4424-3346-5(9))* Simon & Schuster Bks. For Young Readers. (Simon & Schuster Bks. For Young Readers).
Trueman, Terry. Life Happens Next. 2012. (Stuck in Neutral Ser.: 3). (ENG.). 144p. (YA). (gr. 9). 17.99 *(978-0-06-202803-7(0)*, HarperTeen) HarperCollins Pubs.
—Stuck in Neutral. 2012. (Stuck in Neutral Ser.: 1). (ENG.). 144p. (YA). (gr. 8-18). pap. 9.99 *(978-0-06-447213-5(2)*, HarperTeen) HarperCollins Pubs.
Trufant, Robert & Mullins, Tinnesha. Angel Fingers Series: Na'dyd Goes to School. 2004. (Angel Fingers Ser.). (Illus.). 19p. (J). (gr. -1-2). 14.95 *(978-0-9760160-0-7(1))* Mullins Pubns. & Apparel, LLC.
Uhlberg, Myron. The Printer, 1 vol. Sorensen, Henri, illus. 32p. (J). (gr. -1-3). 2009. pap. 8.99 *(978-1-56145-483-9(4))* 2003. 16.95 *(978-1-56145-221-7(1))* Peachtree Publishing Co. Inc.
Van Draanen, Wendelin. The Running Dream. 2011. (ENG.). 352p. (YA). (gr. 7-18). 18.99 *(978-0-375-86667-8(1)*, Knopf Bks. for Young Readers) Random Hse. Children's Bks.
Vaught, Susan. Super Max & the Mystery of Thornwood's Revenge. (ENG.). (J). (gr. 3-7). 2018. 368p. pap. 8.99 *(978-1-4814-8684-2(5))* 2017. (Illus.). 352p. 16.99 *(978-1-4814-8683-5(7))* Simon & Schuster/Paula Wiseman Bks. (Simon & Schuster/Paula Wiseman Bks.).
—Super Max & the Mystery of Thornwood's Revenge. 2018. lib. bdg. 19.65 *(978-0-606-41467-8(3))* Turtleback.
Veenendall, Jennifer. Arnie & His School Tools: Simple Sensory Solutions That Build Success. 2008. (ENG., Illus.). 47p. (J). (gr. 1-7). 18.95 *(978-1-934575-15-4(1))* Autism Asperger Publishing Co.
—Why Does Izzy Cover Her Ears? Dealing with Sensory Overload. 2009. (Illus.). 39p. (J). 18.95 *(978-1-934575-46-8(1))* Autism Asperger Publishing Co.
Venkatraman, Padma. A Time to Dance. 2015. 336p. (YA). (gr. 7). pap. 12.99 *(978-0-14-751440-0(1)*, Penguin Books) Penguin Young Readers Group.
Vision, Mutiya Sahar. Disabilities. Alcantara, Ignacio, illus. 2009. 32p. 17.00 *(978-0-9659538-9-4(0))* Von Curtis Publishing.
Vogelaar, Alie. One Day at a Time, Margreet. VanBrugge, Jeanne, tr. from DUT. Kramer, Jaap, illus. 2004. Orig. Title: Elke Dag Genoeg, Margreet. 124p. *(978-0-9670728-6-9(7))* Early Foundations Pubs.
Voigt, Cynthia. Izzy, Willy-Nilly. 2005. (ENG.). 336p. (YA). (gr. 7). mass mkt. 8.99 *(978-1-4169-0339-0(9)*, Simon Pulse) Simon Pulse.
Vrabel, Beth. A Blind Guide to Normal. (ENG.). (J). (gr. 3-7). 2018. 304p. pap. 7.99 *(978-1-5107-2733-5(7))* 2016. 272p. 16.99 *(978-1-5107-0228-8(8))* Skyhorse Publishing Co., Inc. (Sky Pony Pr.).
—A Blind Guide to Stinkville. 2015. (ENG.). 264p. (J). (gr. 2-7). 16.99 *(978-1-63450-157-6(8)*, Sky Pony Pr.) Skyhorse Publishing Co., Inc.
Wait, Lea. Wintering Well. 2006. (ENG., Illus.). 192p. (J). (gr. 3-7). pap. 8.99 *(978-0-689-85647-1(4)*, McElderry, Margaret K. Bks.) McElderry, Margaret K. Bks.
Walker, D. S. Delightfully Different. 2010. 160p. (gr. -1). 22.95 *(978-1-4502-6051-0(9))*; pap. 12.95 *(978-1-4502-6050-3(0))* iUniverse, Inc.
Wallace, Bill. The Legend of Thunderfoot. 2007. (ENG.). 160p. (J). (gr. 3-7). pap. 7.99 *(978-1-4169-0692-6(4)*, Simon & Schuster/Paula Wiseman Bks.) Simon & Schuster/Paula Wiseman Bks.
Walsh, Patrick M., Jr. Who Says Timmy Can't Play: The Derby: A Timmy Wallings Story. McGriff, Aaron, ed. WFM Services, illus. 2011. 135p. (J). *(978-0-9842929-3-6(4))* Daddy Bean Bks.
Walters, Eric. My Name Is Blessing. Fernandes, Eugenie, illus. 2013. 32p. (J). (gr. 1-4). 17.95 *(978-1-77049-301-8(8)*, Tundra Bks.) Tundra Bks. CAN. Dist: Penguin Random Hse. LLC.
—Rebound, 1 vol. 2014. (ENG.). 236p. (J). (gr. 5-8). pap. 12.95 *(978-1-55455-309-9(1)*, fd5a7380-0086-473a-bb10-9ba74a7fcde) Fitzhenry & Whiteside, Ltd. CAN. Dist: Firefly Bks., Ltd.
Waters, Terrance D. I f I Y: A Novel Based on a True Story. 2008. 148p. 26.00 *(978-1-4251-3496-9(3))* Trafford Publishing.
Watson, C. G. The Absoluteness of Nothing. 2017. (ENG.). 272p. (YA). (gr. 9). pap. 10.99 *(978-1-4814-3185-9(4)*, Simon Pulse) Simon Pulse.
Webb, Amy. When Charley Met Emma. Liddiard, Merrilee, illus. 2019. (Charley & Emma Stories Ser.). 32p. (J). (gr. -1-k). 16.99 *(978-1-5064-4872-5(0)*, Beaming Books) 1517 Media.
Wess, Robert, illus. & photos by. Friends at Work & Play. Wess, Robert, photos by. Bunnett, Rochelle, photos by. 2003. 32p. (J). 14.95 *(978-0-9660884-2-7(5))*; pap. *(978-0-9660884-1-0(7))* Our Kids Pr.
West, Jacqueline. The Collectors. 2018. (ENG.). 384p. (J). (gr. 3-7). 16.99 *(978-0-06-269169-9(4)*, Greenwillow Bks.) HarperCollins Pubs.
—The Collectors. 2019. (ENG.). 400p. (J). (gr. 3-7). pap. 7.99 *(978-0-06-269170-5(8)*, Greenwillow Bks.) HarperCollins Pubs.
Whelan, Gloria. Forgive the River, Forgive the Sky. 2004. 96p. (J). pap. 8.00 *(978-0-8028-5256-4(4))* Eerdmans, William B. Publishing Co.
Williams, Sean. Impossible Music. 2019. (ENG.). 320p. (YA). (gr. 9). 17.99 *(978-0-544-81620-6(X)*, 1642320, Clarion Bks.) HarperCollins Pubs.
Winkelmann, Mary. Wheels. 2012. 66p. (gr. 10-12). pap. 10.43 *(978-1-4669-5560-8(0))* Trafford Publishing.
Withers, Pam. Daredevil Club, 1 vol. 2006. (Orca Currents Ser.). (ENG.). (J). 128p. (gr. 4-7). per. 9.95 *(978-1-55143-614-2(0))*; 102p. (gr. 6-8). 26.19 *(978-1-55143-618-0(3))* Orca Bk. Pubs. USA.
Wonder/365 Days of Wonder Boxed Set, 2 vols., Set. 2014. (Wonder Ser.). (ENG.). 432p. (J). (gr. 3-7). 31.98 *(978-0-553-49906-3(8)*, Knopf Bks. for Young Readers) Random Hse. Children's Bks.
Wood, Gail. Lizzie & the Big Lake Mystery. 2015. (Illus.). ix, 93p. (J). pap. *(978-1-57249-416-9(6)*, White Mane Kids) White Mane Publishing Co., Inc.
Yoo, Paula. Good Enough. 2012. (ENG.). 336p. (YA). (gr. 8). pap. 7.99 *(978-0-06-079090-5(3)*, HarperTeen) HarperCollins Pubs.
Young, Suzanne. All in Pieces. (ENG.). (YA). (gr. 9). 2017. 288p. pap. 11.99 *(978-1-4814-1884-3(X))* 2016. (Illus.). 272p. 17.99 *(978-1-4814-1883-6(1))* Simon Pulse. (Simon Pulse).
Zajac, Kristen K. Ebeneezer's Cousin. Houdeshell, Jennifer Thomas, illus. 2013. 24p. 19.95 *(978-1-61633-440-6(1))* Guardian Angel Publishing, Inc.

PEOPLE WITH DISABILITIES—REHABILITATION

Wright, Rebecca. Ups & Downs: Elementary Monologues That Explore Emotions. 2016. (ENG.). 192p. (J). pap. 15.95 *(978-1-56608-209-9(9)*, Meriwether Publishing) Meriwether Publishing, Ltd.

PEOPLE WITH MENTAL DISABILITIES

see also Mental Illness; Mentally Ill

Berlatsky, Noah, ed. Mental Illness, 1 vol. 2016. (Opposing Viewpoints Ser.). (ENG.). 224p. (gr. 10-12). 50.43 *(978-0-7377-7512-9(2)*, 99c51291-5a81-4127-b824-92b5bec464eb); pap. 34.80 *(978-0-7377-7513-6(0)*, 9233fd78-38f4-4ff0-a53e-9b77a30925e7) Greenhaven Publishing LLC. (Greenhaven Publishing).
Bowman-Kruhm, Mary. Everything You Need to Know about down Syndrome. 2009. (Need to Know Library). 64p. (gr. 5-5). 58.50 *(978-1-60854-065-5(0))* Rosen Publishing Group, Inc., The.
Fisher, Sherry. Amanda, Just the Way I Am. 2008. (ENG.). 24p. pap. 11.49 *(978-1-4343-1235-8(6))* AuthorHouse.
Landau, Jennifer, ed. Teens Talk about Learning Disabilities & Differences. 2017. (Teen Voices: Real Teens Discuss Real Problems Ser.). (Illus.). 64p. (J). (gr. 12-17). 77.70 *(978-1-5081-7636-7(1))* Rosen Publishing Group, Inc., The.
Lauren, Jill. That's Like Me!, 1 vol. 2009. (ENG.). 32p. (J). (gr. k-3). pap. 7.95 *(978-1-59572-208-9(4))* Star Bright Bks., Inc.
Libal, Autumn. Intellectual Disabilities. Albers, Lisa et al, eds. 2014. (Living with a Special Need Ser.: 16). 128p. (J). (gr. 7-18). 25.95 *(978-1-4222-3037-4(6))* Mason Crest.
Martin, Michael J. Teen Depression. 2004. (Illus.). 96p. (YA). (gr. 7-12). per. 32.45 *(978-1-59018-502-5(1)*, Lucent Bks.) Cengage Gale.
McIntosh, Kenneth & Livingston, Phyllis. Youth with Conduct Disorder: In Trouble with the World. 2007. (Helping Youth with Mental, Physical, & Social Disabilities Ser.). (Illus.). 128p. (YA). pap. 14.95 *(978-1-4222-0440-5(5))* Mason Crest.
Parent, Lauren. I'm Different but I'm Special. Parent, Lauren, illus. l.t. ed. 2006. (Illus.). 21p. (J). (gr. -1-3). per. 10.99 *(978-1-59879-259-1(8))* Lifevest Publishing, Inc.
Rosenberg, Marsha Sarah. Coping When a Brother or Sister Is Autistic. 2009. (Coping Ser.). 192p. (gr. 7-12). 63.90 *(978-1-61511-986-8(8))* Rosen Publishing Group, Inc., The.
Skotko, Brian & Levine, Susan. Fasten Your Seatbelt: A Crash Course on down Syndrome for Brothers & Sisters. 2008. (ENG., Illus.). 192p. (J). (gr. 4-10). pap. 18.95 *(978-1-890627-86-7(0))* Woodbine Hse.
Stewart, Sheila & Flath, Camden. My Name Is Not Slow: Kids with Intellectual Disabilities. 2010. (Kids with Special Needs Ser.). 48p. (YA). (gr. 5-18). lib. bdg. 19.95 *(978-1-4222-1718-4(3))* Mason Crest.
Whelahan, Marlene Verno. My Best Friend's Sister... A True Story. 2010. 20p. 12.99 *(978-1-4389-8729-3(3))* AuthorHouse.
Yoshida, Yuko. How to Be Yourself in a World That's Different: An Asperger Syndrome Study Guide for Adolescents. 2006. (Illus.). 112p. (C). pap. 17.95 *(978-1-84310-504-6(7)*, 693652) Kingsley, Jessica Pubs. GBR. Dist: Hachette UK Distribution.

PEOPLE WITH MENTAL DISABILITIES—FICTION

Acorn, Alesa. Diary of the Beloved Book One: The Hidden. 2011. 512p. 31.95 *(978-1-4634-0276-1(7))*; pap. 21.95 *(978-1-4634-0274-7(0))* AuthorHouse.
Avis, Heather. Different — A Great Thing to Be! Mensinga, Sarah, illus. 2021. 40p. (J). (gr. -1-2). 12.99 *(978-0-593-23265-1(8)*, WaterBrook Pr.) Crown Publishing Group, The.
Bowen, Fred. Perfect Game, 1 vol. 2013. (Fred Bowen Sports Story Ser.: 18). (Illus.). 144p. (J). (gr. 2-6). pap. 6.95 *(978-1-56145-625-3(X))* Peachtree Publishing Co. Inc.
Byars, Betsy. The Summer of the Swans. 2008. (Puffin Modern Classics Ser.). (Illus.). 129p. (gr. 4). 16.00 *(978-0-7569-8944-6(2))* Perfection Learning Corp.
—Summer of the Swans, the (Puffin Modern Classics) 2004. (Puffin Modern Classics Ser.). 144p. (J). (gr. 3-7). pap. 7.99 *(978-0-14-240114-9(5)*, Puffin Books) Penguin Young Readers Group.
Cartaya, Pablo. Marcus Vega Doesn't Speak Spanish. 2018. (ENG.). 272p. (J). (gr. 5). 17.99 *(978-1-101-99726-0(5)*, Viking Books for Young Readers) Penguin Young Readers Group.
Chase, L. P. Today Is Tuesday. 2006. (J). pap. 9.00 *(978-0-87426-069-4(8))* Whitmore Publishing Co.
Choldenko, Gennifer. One-Third Nerd. Ceulemans, Eglantine, illus. 2020. (ENG.). 224p. (J). (gr. 3-7). pap. 8.99 *(978-1-5247-1891-6(2)*, Yearling) Random Hse. Children's Bks.
Curtis, Christopher Paul. Bucking the Sarge. 2006. (ENG.). 288p. (YA). (gr. 7-7). reprint ed. mass mkt. 8.99 *(978-0-440-41331-8(1)*, Laurel Leaf) Random Hse. Children's Bks.
Fontes, Justine. Benito Runs. 2011. (Surviving Southside Ser.). (ENG.). 104p. (YA). (gr. 6-12). lib. bdg. 27.99 *(978-0-7613-6151-0(0)*, 1e02666c-1414-4f2b-9c03-e05b4294b401, Darby Creek) Lerner Publishing Group.
Gamache, Line. Hello, Me Pretty. Cochrane, KerryAnn, tr. 2007. (ENG., Illus.). 64p. per. 15.00 *(978-1-894994-23-1(X))* Conundrum Pr. CAN. Dist: Consortium Bk. Sales & Distribution.
Gehret, Jeanne. The Don't-Give-Up Kid: And Learning Differences. DePauw, Sandra A., illus. 3rd rev. ed. 2003. 40p. (J). (gr. 1-5). pap. 9.95 *(978-1-884281-10-5(9))* Verbal Images Pr.
Goelman, Ari. The Innocence Treatment. 2018. (ENG.). 272p. (YA). pap. 17.99 *(978-1-250-18082-7(1)*, 900176503) Square Fish.
Green, Jack. The Microchip Kid. 2011. 52p. pap. 16.95 *(978-1-4560-8494-3(1))* America Star Bks.
Hamilton, Kersten. In the Forests of the Night, 2. 2013. (Goblin Wars Ser.). (ENG.). 288p. (YA). (gr. 7-12). 24.94 *(978-0-547-43560-2(6)*, Clarion Bks.) HarperCollins Pubs.
Hesse, Karen. Wish on a Unicorn. 2009. (ENG.). 128p. (J). (gr. 3-7). pap. 16.99 *(978-0-312-37611-6(1)*, 9780312376116) Square Fish.
Hill, Genita. My Very Special Brother. McCall, William L., illus. 2007. 40p. per. 24.95 *(978-1-4241-8852-9(0))* America Star Bks.
Holt, Kimberly Willis. My Louisiana Sky. 208p. (YA). (gr. 5-18). 4.99 *(978-0-8072-8291-5(X)*, Listening Library) Random Hse. Audio Publishing Group.
—My Louisiana Sky. 2011. (ENG.). 224p. (J). (gr. 4-7). pap. 8.99 *(978-0-312-66095-6(2)*, 900070608) Square Fish.
Hubler, Marsha. Blue Ribbon Champ, 1 vol., 6. rev. ed. 2010. (Keystone Stables Ser.). (ENG.). 112p. (J). pap. 7.99 *(978-0-310-71797-3(3))* Zonderkidz.
Hyde, Catherine Ryan. The Year of My Miraculous Reappearance. 2009. (ENG.). 240p. (YA). (gr. 7). pap. 10.99 *(978-0-375-83261-1(0)*, Knopf Bks. for Young Readers) Random Hse. Children's Bks.
Kats, Jewel. Hansel & Gretel: A Fairy Tale with a Down Syndrome Twist. Lenart, Claudia, illus. 2014. 37p. (J). *(978-1-61599-251-5(0))* Loving Healing Pr., Inc.
Krukar, Jeff, et al. Melting Down: A Comic for Kids with Asperger's Disorder & Challenging Behavior (the Orp Library) 2013. 74p. pap. 12.99 *(978-1-939418-20-3(8))* Writer of the Round Table Pr.
Lange, Erin Jade. Dead Ends. 2013. (ENG.). 304p. E-Book 7.99 *(978-1-61963-081-9(8)*, Bloomsbury USA Childrens) Bloomsbury Publishing USA.
Lean, Sarah. A Dog Called Homeless. 2012. (ENG.). 208p. (J). (gr. 3-7). 16.99 *(978-0-06-212220-9(7)*, Tegen, Katherine Bks) HarperCollins Pubs.
Lewis, Beverly. In Jesse's Shoes: Appreciating Kids with Special Needs. Nikiel, Laura Gibbons, illus. 2007. (ENG.). 32p. (J). (gr. -1-4). 11.99 *(978-0-7642-0313-8(4))* Bethany Hse. Pubs.
Long, Tyler. Wires, 1 vol. Fleming, Christopher, illus. 2009. 28p. pap. 24.95 *(978-1-60836-217-2(5))* America Star Bks.
Lytton, Deborah. Silence. 2015. (ENG.). 320p. (YA). (gr. 7). 17.99 *(978-1-60907-945-1(0)*, 5125977, Shadow Mountain) Shadow Mountain Publishing.
Mackall, Dandi Daley. The Silence of Murder. 2012. 336p. (YA). (gr. 9). pap. 10.99 *(978-0-375-87293-8(0)*, Ember) Random Hse. Children's Bks.
McGill, Justin. Friends Forever, Signed Jeremy E. 2007. 48p. per. 16.95 *(978-1-4241-8794-2(X))* America Star Bks.
Morpurgo, Michael. Private Peaceful. 2006. 18.00 *(978-0-7569-6630-0(2))* Perfection Learning Corp.
—Private Peaceful. 2006. (YA). 1.25 *(978-1-4193-2976-0(6))* Recorded Bks., Inc.
—Private Peaceful. 2006. (ENG., Illus.). 224p. (J). (gr. 7-12). per. 8.99 *(978-0-439-63653-7(1)*, Scholastic Paperbacks) Scholastic, Inc.
Morton, Clay & Morton, Gail. Why Johnny Doesn't Flap: NT Is OK! Merry, Alex, illus. 2015. 32p. (J). 17.95 *(978-1-84905-721-9(4)*, 693892) Kingsley, Jessica Pubs. GBR. Dist: Hachette UK Distribution.

Newton, Nikki. Just Like You. Newton, Naiya, illus. 2008. (ENG.). 26p. per. 15.99 *(978-1-4257-6386-2(3))* Xlibris Corp.
Nolan, Han. A Face in Every Window. 2008. (ENG., Illus.). 276p. (YA). (gr. 7). pap. 15.95 *(978-0-15-206418-1(4),* 1199206, Clarion Bks.) HarperCollins Pubs.
Novel Units. To Kill a Mockingbird Novel Units Student Packet. 2019. (ENG.). (YA). pap. 13.99 *(978-1-56137-307-9(9),* NU3079SP, Novel Units, Inc.) Classroom Library Co.
Nuzum, K. A. A Small White Scar. 2008. (ENG.). 208p. (J). (gr. 5). pap. 8.99 *(978-0-06-075641-3(1),* HarperCollins) HarperCollins Pubs.
Sarno, Melissa. Just under the Clouds. 2019. (ENG.). 256p. (J). (gr. 3-7). pap. 8.99 *(978-1-5247-2011-7(9),* Yearling) Random Hse. Children's Bks.
Schnee, Silke. Prince Noah & the School Pirates. Sistig, Heike, illus. 2016. (Prince Noah Book Ser.). (ENG.). 32p. (J). 16.00 *(978-0-87486-765-7(7))* Plough Publishing Hse.
—The Prince Who Was Just Himself. Sistig, Heike, illus. 2015. (Prince Noah Book Ser.). 32p. (J). (gr. -1-4). 16.00 *(978-0-87486-682-7(0))* Plough Publishing Hse.
Sheldon, Kaylene Kauwila. A Day with Makana. 2007.Tr. of I Kekahi la me Makana. (ENG & HAW., Illus.). 19p. (J). lib. bdg. *(978-0-9773495-2-4(7))* Na Kamalei Koolauloa Early Education Program.
Simon, Scott. Sunnyside Plaza. 2020. (ENG.). 208p. (J). (gr. 3-17). 16.99 *(978-0-316-53120-7(0))* Little, Brown Bks. for Young Readers.
Sommer, Bill & Tilghman, Natalie Haney. A 52-Hertz Whale. 2015. (ENG.). 200p. (YA). (gr. 8-12). E-Book 27.99 *(978-1-4677-8811-3(2),* Carolrhoda Labක) Lerner Publishing Group.
Spain, Susan Rosson. The Deep Cut, 0 vols. 2014. (ENG.). 228p. (J). (gr. 5-7). pap. 9.99 *(978-1-4778-4768-8(5),* 9781477847688, Two Lions) Amazon Publishing.
—The Deep Cut, 1 vol. 2006. (ENG., Illus.). 224p. (J). (gr. 5-9). 16.99 *(978-0-7614-5316-1(4))* Marshall Cavendish Corp.
Vazquez, Tiziana & Llano, Gabriella. In My World: Down Syndrome. 2013. 108p. 23.99 *(978-1-4772-9274-7(8));* pap. 14.95 *(978-1-4772-9188-7(1))* AuthorHouse.
Williams, Michael. Now Is the Time for Running. 2013. (ENG.). 240p. (YA). (gr. 7-17). pap. 10.99 *(978-0-316-07788-0(7))* Little, Brown Bks. for Young Readers.
Wood, June Rae. The Man Who Loved Clowns. 2005. (ENG.). 224p. (J). (gr. 3-7). 8.99 *(978-0-14-240422-5(5),* Puffin Books) Penguin Young Readers Group.
—The Man Who Loved Clowns. 2005. 224p. (gr. 3-7). 16.00 *(978-0-7569-5516-8(5))* Perfection Learning Corp.
Wright, Betty Ren. The Dollhouse Murders (35th Anniversary Edition) Nickolls, Leo, illus. 35th ed. 2019. 160p. (J). (gr. 3-7). pap. 8.99 *(978-0-8234-3984-3(4))* Holiday Hse., Inc.
—The Dollhouse Murders (35th Anniversary Edition) 35th ed. 2018. 160p. (J). (gr. 3-7). 17.99 *(978-0-8234-4030-6(3))* Holiday Hse., Inc.
Yates, Alma J. Sammy's Song: A Novel. 2005. 272p. (J). *(978-1-59156-945-9(1))* Covenant Communications.

PEOPLE'S DEMOCRACIES

see Communist Countries

PEOPLE'S REPUBLIC OF CHINA

see China

PERCEPTION

see also Self-perception

Alaina, Maria. Patterns in Nature, 1 vol. 2011. (Wonder Readers Early Level Ser.). (ENG.). 16p. (gr. -1-1). (J). pap. 6.25 *(978-1-4296-7815-5(1),* 117987); pap. 35.94 *(978-1-4296-8138-4(1),* Capstone Pr.) Capstone.
Alexander, Emmett. Sort It by Size, 1 vol. 2015. (Sort It Out! Ser.). (ENG., Illus.). 24p. (J). (gr. k-1). pap. 9.15 *(978-1-4824-2573-4(4),* a84356cb-8115-4a18-9a57-6d0bdb071a8d) Stevens, Gareth Publishing LLLP.
Apel, Melanie Ann. Let's Talk about Feeling Confused. 2009. (Let's Talk Library). 24p. (gr. 2-3). 42.50 *(978-1-60853-439-5(1),* PowerKids Pr.) Rosen Publishing Group, Inc., The.
Bartowski, Amy. Shapes at the Store: Identify & Describe Shapes. 2013. (InfoMax Math Readers Ser.). (ENG.). 16p. (J). (gr. k-1). pap. 42.00 *(978-1-4777-1974-9(1));* (Illus.). pap. 7.00 *(978-1-4777-1973-2(3),* d5bb1654-c839-4cc9-9a38-be92101c6087) Rosen Publishing Group, Inc., The. (Rosen Classroom).
Bluemel Oldfield, Dawn. Patterns at the Seashore. 2014. (Math Blast!: Seeing Patterns All Around Ser.). (ENG.). 32p. (J). (gr. -1-3). lib. bdg. 28.50 *(978-1-62724-335-3(6))* Bearport Publishing Co., Inc.
Burstein, John. Patterns: What's on the Wall?, 1 vol. 2003. (Math Monsters(tm) Ser.). (ENG., Illus.). 24p. (J). (gr. k-3). lib. bdg. 23.67 *(978-0-8368-3816-9(5),* 0733a693-f036-41b1-b427-79065a52fe8b, Weekly Reader Leveled Readers) Stevens, Gareth Publishing LLLP.
Burton, Margie, et al. Looking Down. 2011. (Early Connections Ser.). (J). *(978-1-61672-260-9(6))* Benchmark Education Co.
Carr, Aaron. Animal Patterns. 2011. (J). *(978-1-61690-590-3(5)); (978-1-61690-945-1(5))* Weigl Pubs., Inc.
—Diseños de Animales. 2012. (SPA.). (J). *(978-1-61913-204-7(4))* Weigl Pubs., Inc.
—Diseños de Las Plantas. 2012. (SPA.). (J). *(978-1-61913-207-8(9))* Weigl Pubs., Inc.
Clark Sawyer, J. Patterns in the Snow. 2015. (J). lib. bdg. 28.50 *(978-1-62724-340-7(2))* Bearport Publishing Co., Inc.
Cleary, Brian P. A-B-A-B-A: A Book of Pattern Play. Gable, Brian, illus. 2010. (Math Is CATegorical (r) Ser.). (ENG.). 32p. (J). (gr. k-3). lib. bdg. 16.95 *(978-0-8225-7880-2(8))* Lerner Publishing Group.
Coan, Sharon. Message Received!, 1 vol. rev. ed. 2014. (Science: Informational Text Ser.). (ENG., Illus.). 24p. (gr. 1-2). pap. 9.99 *(978-1-4807-4565-0(0))* Teacher Created Materials, Inc.
Cobb, Vicki. On Stage. 2008. pap. 52.95 *(978-0-8225-9450-5(1))* Lerner Publishing Group.
Corcorane, Ann. Patterns Everywhere. 2011. (Wonder Readers Emergent Level Ser.). (ENG.). (gr. -1-1). 8p. (J). pap. 6.25 *(978-1-4296-7869-8(0),* 118201); 16p. pap. 35.94 *(978-1-4296-8137-7(3))* Capstone. (Capstone Pr.).
Davies, Ann. Fun Size. (Illus.). 40p. (J). 19.95 *(978-1-85479-230-3(X))* O'Mara, Michael Bks., Ltd. GBR. Dist: Trans-Atlantic Pubns., Inc.
Deen, Marilyn. Finding Patterns, 1 vol. 2011. (Wonder Readers Fluent Level Ser.). (ENG.). 16p. (J). (gr. -1-2). pap. 6.25 *(978-1-4296-7919-0(0),* 118251, Capstone Pr.) Capstone.
Domiano, Gloria. Ship Shapes: Identify & Describe Shapes. 2013. (Rosen Math Readers Ser.). (ENG.). 16p. (J). (gr. k-1). pap. 42.00 *(978-1-4777-1666-3(1));* (Illus.). pap. 7.00 *(978-1-4777-1665-6(3),* 009e772f-1da8-472c-9149-9c657f2b92ae) Rosen Publishing Group, Inc., The. (Rosen Classroom).
Felix, Rebecca. Patterns at the Zoo. 2015. (21st Century Basic Skills Library: Patterns All Around Ser.). (ENG., Illus.). 24p. (J). (gr. k-3). pap. 12.79 *(978-1-63188-935-6(4),* 206001) Cherry Lake Publishing.
—Patterns in Food. 2015. (21st Century Basic Skills Library: Patterns All Around Ser.). (ENG., Illus.). 24p. (J). (gr. k-3). pap. 12.79 *(978-1-63188-936-3(2),* 206005) Cherry Lake Publishing.
—Patterns in Sports. 2015. (21st Century Basic Skills Library: Patterns All Around Ser.). (ENG., Illus.). 24p. (gr. k-3). 26.35 *(978-1-63188-921-9(4),* 206008) Cherry Lake Publishing.
—Patterns in the City. 2015. (21st Century Basic Skills Library: Patterns All Around Ser.). (ENG.). 24p. (J). (gr. k-3). pap. 12.79 *(978-1-63188-938-7(9),* 206013) Cherry Lake Publishing.
—Patterns on the Farm. 2015. (21st Century Basic Skills Library: Patterns All Around Ser.). (ENG., Illus.). 24p. (J). (gr. k-3). pap. 12.79 *(978-1-63188-939-4(7),* 206017) Cherry Lake Publishing.
Freese, Joan. Un Desfile de PATRONES (PATTERNS on Parade), 1 vol. 2007. (Las Matemáticas en Nuestro Mundo - Nivel 1 (Math in Our World - Level 1) Ser.). (SPA.). 24p. (gr. 1-1). pap. 9.15 *(978-0-8368-8500-2(7),* 1d993209-c1ae-4b43-9f67-094b3cc85401); (Illus.). lib. bdg. 24.67 *(978-0-8368-8491-3(4),* 00cb2fa9-861a-4892-9594-3a52633787cb) Stevens, Gareth Publishing LLLP. (Weekly Reader Leveled Readers).
—PATTERNS on Parade, 1 vol. 2007. (Math in Our World - Level 1 Ser.). (ENG., Illus.). 24p. (gr. 1-1). pap. 9.15 *(978-0-8368-8482-1(5),* 2d5a9cb7-147c-4eda-97a3-5f9a36938805); lib. bdg. 24.67 *(978-0-8368-8473-9(6),* 6f51b3eb-24ff-430e-b55f-43ec61f82411) Stevens, Gareth Publishing LLLP. (Weekly Reader Leveled Readers).
Frisch-Schmoll, Joy. In & Out, 1 vol. 2013. (Exploring Opposites Ser.). (ENG., Illus.). 24p. (J). (gr. -1-2). pap. 7.29 *(978-1-62065-897-0(6),* 121808, Capstone Pr.) Capstone.
—In & Out. 2013. (Exploring Opposites Ser.). (ENG.). 24p. (J). (gr. k-1). pap. 43.74 *(978-1-62065-898-7(4),* 19449, Capstone Pr.) Capstone.
Goldstone, Bruce. I See a Pattern Here. Goldstone, Bruce, illus. 2015. (ENG., Illus.). 32p. (J). (gr. 2-5). 18.99 *(978-0-8050-9209-7(9),* 900066056, Holt, Henry & Co. Bks. For Young Readers) Holt, Henry & Co.
Gordon, Sharon. Arriba, Abajo / up, Down, 1 vol. 2008. (Exactamente lo Opuesto / Just the Opposite Ser.). (ENG & SPA., Illus.). 24p. (gr. k-1). lib. bdg. 25.50 *(978-0-7614-2449-9(0),* 9075ad88-93a7-4103-b890-72201cb69161) Cavendish Square Publishing LLC.
Hoban, Tana. Black & White. 2007. (ENG., Illus.). 16p. (J). (gr. -1 — 1). pap. 7.99 *(978-0-06-117211-3(1),* Greenwillow Bks.) HarperCollins Pubs.
—Black White: A High Contrast Book for Newborns. Hoban, Tana, illus. 2017. (ENG., Illus.). 36p. (J). (gr. -1 — 1). bds. 9.99 *(978-0-06-265690-2(2),* Greenwillow Bks.) HarperCollins Pubs.
Jason Fulford, Tamara Shopsin. Find Colors: Published in Association with the Whitney Museum of American Art. 2018. (ENG., Illus.). 28p. (gr. -1 — 1). bds. 14.95 *(978-0-7148-7659-7(3))* Phaidon Pr., Inc.
Jeffries, Joyce. Big & Small, 1 vol. 2013. (Dinosaur School Ser.). (ENG., Illus.). 24p. (J). (gr. k-k). pap. 9.15 *(978-1-4339-8084-8(3),* 9275d23c-ca29-426b-813b-13b52b4563b5); lib. bdg. 25.27 *(978-1-4339-8083-1(5),* c3bde0ec-060d-4464-934b-5ce83129e8bb) Stevens, Gareth Publishing LLLP.
—Near & Far, 1 vol. 2013. (Dinosaur School Ser.). (ENG., Illus.). 24p. (J). (gr. k-k). 25.27 *(978-1-4339-8099-2(1),* d9a354b0-5893-4bb9-bb54-a7722ef8b4e9); pap. 9.15 *(978-1-4339-8100-5(9),* 85691c94-6485-4ded-a823-d37f17da1024) Stevens, Gareth Publishing LLLP.
—Shapes at School: Identify & Describe Shapes. 2013. (Rosen Math Readers Ser.). (ENG.). 16p. (J). (gr. k-1). pap. 42.00 *(978-1-4777-1588-8(6));* (Illus.). pap. 7.00 *(978-1-4777-1587-1(8),* cdde6fe1-fedf-4181-8dc0-84012927b2bf) Rosen Publishing Group, Inc., The. (Rosen Classroom).
—Which Is Different?, 1 vol. 2013. (Dinosaur School Ser.). (ENG., Illus.). 24p. (gr. k-k). 25.27 *(978-1-4339-8103-6(3),* b86ab109-0e9e-4ae3-98f1-86dfa672d2a0); pap. 9.15 *(978-1-4339-8104-3(1),* 83546d08-f5d3-4b72-bf39-a65f81985139) Stevens, Gareth Publishing LLLP.
Kalman, Bobbie. How Are They the Same? 2011. (ENG.). 16p. (J). pap. *(978-0-7787-9581-0(0))* Crabtree Publishing Co.
—¿Qué Aspecto Tiene? 2008. (SPA.). 24p. (J). lib. bdg. *(978-0-7787-8723-5(0))* Crabtree Publishing Co.
—¿Qué Sigue? 2008. (SPA.). 24p. (J). lib. bdg. *(978-0-7787-8727-3(3))* Crabtree Publishing Co.
—What Comes Next? 2007. (Looking at Nature Ser.). (ENG., Illus.). 24p. (J). (gr. -1-2). pap. *(978-0-7787-3339-3(4))* Crabtree Publishing Co.
Kennedy Shea, Bobby. Patterns with Pandas, 1 vol. 2013. (Animal Math Ser.). (ENG.). 24p. (J). (gr. 1-2). pap. 9.15 *(978-1-4339-9319-0(8),* c05f70c0-c50a-4c4f-bcb1-6a5ab18aee27); (Illus.). lib. bdg. 25.27 *(978-1-4339-9318-3(X),* ff6b0c97-0f78-40e9-a979-00b688142e6e) Stevens, Gareth Publishing LLLP.
Look at Mealtime. (Look at Me Ser.). (Illus.). (J). bds. 5.95 *(978-0-590-24863-1(4))* Scholastic, Inc.
Lowery, Lawrence F. Look & See. 2nd ed. 2004. (J). per. *(978-0-9762724-9-6(0))* Educational Research & Applications, LLC.
Markovics, Joyce L. Patterns in the Jungle. 2014. (Math Blast!: Seeing Patterns All Around Ser.). (ENG.). 32p. (J). (gr. -1-3). lib. bdg. 28.50 *(978-1-62724-338-4(0))* Bearport Publishing Co., Inc.
McGrath, Barbara Barbieri. Teddy Bear Patterns. Nihoff, Tim, illus. 2013. (McGrath Math Ser.: 4). 32p. (J). (gr. -1-3). (ENG.). pap. 8.99 *(978-1-58089-423-4(2));* lib. bdg. 16.95 *(978-1-58089-422-7(4))* Charlesbridge Publishing, Inc.
Mealtime. 2003. (J). per. *(978-1-57657-893-3(3))* Paradise Pr., Inc.
Mineo, Tyrone. Near & Far with Birds, 1 vol. 2011. (Animal Math Ser.). (ENG., Illus.). 24p. (J). (gr. 1-2). pap. 9.15 *(978-1-4339-5668-3(3),* bf2936c9-0864-4981-92fd-2a46ae340bb1); lib. bdg. 25.27 *(978-1-4339-5666-9(7),* ce602309-563a-44c7-8edb-938292ef62c3) Stevens, Gareth Publishing LLLP.
Mitten, Luana K. Arriba y abajo (under & Over) 2009. (Conceptos (Concepts) Ser.). (ENG & SPA., Illus.). 24p. (J). (gr. k-2). lib. bdg. 22.79 *(978-1-60694-572-8(6))* Rourke Educational Media.
—Dentro y fuera (in & Out) 2009. (Conceptos (Concepts) Ser.). (ENG & SPA., Illus.). 24p. (J). (gr. k-2). lib. bdg. 22.79 *(978-1-60694-573-5(4))* Rourke Educational Media.
National Geographic Kids. National Geographic Kids Look & Learn: Match! 2011. (ENG., Illus.). 24p. (J). (gr. -1-k). bds. 7.99 *(978-1-4263-0871-0(X),* National Geographic Kids) Disney Publishing Worldwide.
—What in the World? Fun-Tastic Photo Puzzles for Curious Minds. 2014. (Illus.). 48p. (J). (gr. 3-7). 16.99 *(978-1-4263-1517-6(1),* National Geographic Kids) Disney Publishing Worldwide.
Penn, M. W. It's a Pattern!, 1 vol. 2011. (Pebble Math Ser.). (ENG.). 24p. (J). (gr. -1-2). pap. 6.29 *(978-1-4296-7067-8(3),* 116749); (gr. k-1). pap. 37.74 *(978-1-4296-7071-5(1),* 16670) Capstone. (Pebble).
Picthall, Chez, des. Flowers. 2015. (Illus.). 10p. (J). bds. 9.99 *(978-1-907604-76-8(6))* Award Pubns. Ltd. GBR. Dist: Parkwest Pubns., Inc.
—Spots & Dots. 2015. (Illus.). 10p. (J). bds. 9.99 *(978-1-909763-02-9(0))* Award Pubns. Ltd. GBR. Dist: Parkwest Pubns., Inc.
Pizza, Andy J. & Miller, Sophie. Invisible Things. 2023. (ENG., Illus.). 52p. (J). (gr. k-3). 17.99 *(978-1-7972-1520-4(5))* Chronicle Bks. LLC.
Randolph, Joanne. What I Look Like When I Am Confused. (Let's Look at Feelings Ser.).Tr. of What I Look Like When I am Confused. 24p. (gr. k-1). 2009. 42.50 *(978-1-61514-239-2(8))* 2003. (ENG., Illus.). 26.27 *(978-1-4042-2510-7(2),* 4a5710a6-e38f-4f39-b9a1-6504fcd94e20) Rosen Publishing Group, Inc., The. (PowerKids Pr.).
—What I Look Like When I am Confused / Cómo me veo cuando estoy Confundido. 2009. (Let's Look at Feelings / un vistazo a los sentimientos Ser.). (ENG & SPA.). 24p. (gr. k-1). 42.50 *(978-1-61514-246-0(0),* Editorial Buenas Letras) Rosen Publishing Group, Inc., The.
Rauen, Amy. Vamos a Encontrar lo Más Corto y lo Más Largo (Finding Shortest & Longest), 1 vol. 2008. (Matemáticas para Empezar (Getting Started with Math) Ser.). (SPA.). 16p. (gr. k-1). pap. 6.30 *(978-0-8368-8997-0(5),* 39b1fe38-e780-47d3-bb74-446b0fa25f41); (Illus.). lib. bdg. 21.67 *(978-0-8368-8992-5(4),* 8576efdd-56dd-41f9-b23c-60a1bfa2b984) Stevens, Gareth Publishing LLLP. (Weekly Reader Leveled Readers).
Rivera, Sheila. In & Out. 2004. (First Step Nonfiction Ser.). (J). pap. 3.95 *(978-0-8225-5353-3(8),* Lerner Pubns.) Lerner Publishing Group.
—Near & Far. 2004. (First Step Nonfiction Ser.). (J). pap. 3.95 *(978-0-8225-5354-0(6),* Lerner Pubns.) Lerner Publishing Group.
—Over & Under. 2004. (First Step Nonfiction Ser.). (J). pap. 3.95 *(978-0-8225-5350-2(3),* Lerner Pubns.) Lerner Publishing Group.
Rozines Roy, Jennifer & Roy, Gregory. Patterns in Nature, 1 vol. 2008. (Math All Around Ser.). (ENG., Illus.). 32p. (gr. 2-2). pap. 9.23 *(978-0-7614-3407-8(0),* d044acb2-663a-4d38-a27f-0740235eb622) Cavendish Square Publishing LLC.
Shea, Bobby Kennedy. Patterns with Pandas. 2013. (Animal Math Ser.). 24p. (J). (gr. 1-3). pap. 48.90 *(978-1-4339-9320-6(1))* Stevens, Gareth Publishing LLLP.
Smith, A. G. Visual Illusions Stained Glass Coloring Book. 2008. (Dover Design Coloring Bks.). (ENG., Illus.). 32p. (gr. 3-8). pap. 6.99 *(978-0-486-46563-0(2),* 465632) Dover Pubns., Inc.
Steffora, Tracey. Patterns at the Museum, 1 vol. 2011. (Math Around Us Ser.). (ENG.). 24p. (J). (gr. -1-1). pap. 6.29 *(978-1-4329-4931-0(4),* 114830, Heinemann) Capstone.
Stockland, Patricia M. Loops: Repeat, Repeat! Sanchez, Sr., illus. 2018. (Code It! Ser.). (ENG.). 24p. (C). (gr. 1-3). lib. bdg. 33.99 *(978-1-68410-390-4(8),* 140365) Cantata Learning.
Strait, Mark, et al. HearBuilder Auditory Memory Software Program: Home Edition. 2011. cd-rom 69.95 net. *(978-1-60723-007-6(0))* Super Duper Pubns.
—HearBuilder Auditory Memory Software Program: Professional Edition. 2011. cd-rom 149.95 net. *(978-1-60723-006-9(2))* Super Duper Pubns.
Tuxworth, Nicola. Funny Faces. 2015. (Illus.). 20p. (J). (gr. -1-12). bds. 6.99 *(978-1-86147-358-5(3),* Armadillo) Anness Publishing GBR. Dist: National Bk. Network.
—Patterns: Learn-a-Word Book. 2016. (Illus.). 20p. (J). (gr. -1-12). bds. 6.99 *(978-1-86147-462-9(8),* Armadillo) Anness Publishing GBR. Dist: National Bk. Network.
Wilcox, Charlotte. The Iroquois. 2006. (Native American Histories Ser.). (ENG., Illus.). 56p. (gr. 3-6). lib. bdg. 27.93 *(978-0-8225-2637-7(9),* Lerner Pubns.) Lerner Publishing Group.
World Book, Inc. Staff, contrib. by. Nature's Patterns. 2010. (J). *(978-0-7166-7740-6(7))* World Bk., Inc.

PERCEPTION—FICTION

Bryant, Gerry. Metamorphosed: Sun's Gift. 2006. (ENG.). 116p. (YA). 20.95 *(978-0-595-67412-1(7));* pap. 10.95 *(978-0-595-36729-0(1))* iUniverse, Inc.
Condon, Bill. The Simple Things. 2015. (ENG., Illus.). 168p. (J). (gr. 3-5). 9.99 *(978-1-74331-724-2(7))* Allen & Unwin AUS. Dist: Independent Pubs. Group.
Cook, Julia. I Just Want to Do It My Way! My Story about Staying on Task & Asking for Help!, Volume 5. De Weerd, Kelsey, illus. 2012. (Best Me I Can Be Ser.). (ENG.). 31p. (J). (gr. k-6). pap. 11.95 *(978-1-934490-43-3(1))* Boys Town Pr.
Diggle, David Mark. Bella: Shares Her Sticky Plan. Preuss, Sarah Louise, illus. 2011. 24p. (J). pap. *(978-0-9871658-9-3(5))* Diggle de Doo Productions Pty, Ltd.
Gates, Margo. Mia Can See Patterns. Herring, Carol, illus. 2019. (Science All Around Me (Pull Ahead Readers — Fiction) Ser.). (ENG.). 16p. (J). (gr. -1-1). pap. 8.99 *(978-1-5415-7334-5(X),* 650ab410-cd4b-4d14-85f3-8f036213e2e0, Lerner Pubns.) Lerner Publishing Group.
Holden, Pam. Dinosaur Hunters, 1 vol. Storey, Jim & Hawley, Kelvin, illus. 2009. (Red Rocket Readers Ser.). (ENG.). 16p. (gr. 2-2). pap. *(978-1-877363-59-7(6),* Red Rocket Readers) Flying Start Bks.
Knudsen, Michelle. Big Mean Mike. Magoon, Scott, illus. 2012. (ENG.). 40p. (J). (gr. -1-3). 15.99 *(978-0-7636-4990-6(2))* Candlewick Pr.
Margulies, Paul. What Julianna Could See, 1 vol. Zonneveld, Famke, illus. 2004. 32p. (J). 11.95 *(978-0-88010-515-6(1))* SteinerBooks, Inc.
Moss, Marissa. Amelia's Boredom Survival Guide. Moss, Marissa, illus. 2013. (Amelia Ser.). (ENG., Illus.). 64p. (J). (gr. 2-5). pap. 7.99 *(978-1-4424-8369-9(5),* Simon & Schuster/Paula Wiseman Bks.) Simon & Schuster/Paula Wiseman Bks.
Norac, Carl. My Daddy Is a Giant. Godon, Ingrid, illus. 2005. (ENG.). 32p. (J). (gr. -1-3). 16.00 *(978-0-618-44399-4(1),* 100372, Clarion Bks.) HarperCollins Pubs.
—My Daddy Is a Giant: For Everyone Who Has the Best Daddy in the World. Godon, Ingrid, illus. 2004. 32p. (J). (SPA & ENG.). pap. *(978-1-84444-372-7(8));* (ENG & TGL.). pap. *(978-1-84444-373-4(6));* (ENG & TWI.). pap. *(978-1-84444-376-5(0));* (ENG & URD.). pap. *(978-1-84444-377-2(9));* (ENG & VIE.). pap. *(978-1-84444-378-9(7));* (YOR & ENG.). pap. *(978-1-84444-379-6(5));* (SOM & ENG.). pap. *(978-1-84444-371-0(X));* (ENG & KOR.). pap. *(978-1-84444-300-0(0));* (ALB & ENG.). pap. *(978-1-84444-351-2(5));* (ENG & BEN.). pap. *(978-1-84444-353-6(1));* (ENG & BUL.). pap. *(978-1-84444-354-3(X));* (ENG & CHI.). pap. *(978-1-84444-355-0(8));* (ENG & CHI.). pap. *(978-1-84444-356-7(6));* (ENG & HRV.). pap. *(978-1-84444-357-4(4));* (FRE & ENG.). pap. *(978-1-84444-359-8(0));* (ITA & ENG.). pap. *(978-1-84444-363-5(9));* (ENG & JPN.). pap. *(978-1-84444-364-2(7));* (ENG & KUR.). pap. *(978-1-84444-365-9(5));* (ENG & SNA.). pap. *(978-1-84444-370-3(1));* (ENG & RUS.). pap. *(978-1-84444-369-7(8));* (ENG, PAN & MUL.). pap. *(978-1-84444-366-6(3))* Mantra Lingua.
Norac, Carl & Gordon, Ingrid. My Daddy Is a Giant: For Everyone Who Has the Best Daddy in the World. 2004. (Illus.). 32p. (J). (ENG & ARA.). pap. *(978-1-84444-352-9(3));* (ENG & PER., pap. *(978-1-84444-358-1(2));* (GER & ENG., pap. *(978-1-84444-360-4(4));* (ENG & GUJ., pap. *(978-1-84444-361-1(2));* (TUR & ENG., pap. *(978-1-84444-375-8(2));* (POL & ENG., pap. *(978-1-84444-367-3(1));* (POR & ENG., pap. *(978-1-84444-368-0(X));* (ENG & TAM., pap. *(978-1-84444-374-1(4));* (ENG & HIN., pap. *(978-1-84444-362-8(0))* Mantra Lingua.
ón, Raúl. Imagine! ón, Raúl, illus. 2018. (ENG., Illus.). 48p. (J). (gr. -1-3). 17.99 *(978-1-4814-6273-0(3),* Simon & Schuster/Paula Wiseman Bks.) Simon & Schuster/Paula Wiseman Bks.
Rizvi, Sobia. Zebra Stripes. 2011. 24p. pap. 15.99 *(978-1-4653-4618-6(X))* Xlibris Corp.
Rogers, Alan. En Forme de Bateau. 2003. (Little Giants Ser.). (FRE., Illus.). 16p. (J). (gr. -1-k). 5.95 *(978-1-58728-177-8(5),* Two-Can Publishing) T&N Children's Publishing.
Shannon, George. White Is for Blueberry. Dronzek, Laura, illus. 2005. 40p. (J). (gr. -1). lib. bdg. 17.89 *(978-0-06-029276-8(8));* (ENG.). 17.99 *(978-0-06-029275-1(X),* Greenwillow Bks.) HarperCollins Pubs.
Shively, Julie. What Belongs? Kurtz, John, illus. 2004. (Baby Looney Toons Ser.). (ENG.). 16p. (J). 6.95 *(978-0-8249-6561-7(2),* Ideals Pubns.) Worthy Publishing.
Wenzel, Brendan. They All Saw a Cat. 2017. (CHI.). (J). (gr. -1-k). *(978-7-5502-9169-0(1))* Jinghua Publishing House.
—They All Saw a Cat. 2018. (My Arabic Library). (ARA.). 44p. (J). (gr. -1-k). pap. 7.99 *(978-1-338-26772-3(8))* Scholastic, Inc.
Wenzel, Brendan, illus. A Stone Sat Still. 2019. (ENG.). 56p. (J). (gr. -1-k). 17.99 *(978-1-4521-7318-4(4))* Chronicle Bks. LLC.
—They All Saw a Cat. 2016. (Brendan Wenzel Ser.). (ENG.). 44p. (J). (gr. -1-k). 16.99 *(978-1-4521-5013-0(3))* Chronicle Bks. LLC.

PERCUSSION INSTRUMENTS

see also names of percussion instruments, e.g. Drums

Fyffe, Daniel. Indoor Percussion Ensembles & Drum Corps. 2009. (Team Spirit! Ser.). 64p. (gr. 6-6). 53.00 *(978-1-60853-270-4(4))* Rosen Publishing Group, Inc., The.
Ganeri, Anita. Drums & Percussion Instruments. 2011. (ENG., Illus.). 32p. (J). pap. 10.95 *(978-1-77092-030-9(7))* Saunders Bk. Co. CAN. Dist: RiverStream Publishing.
Kenney, Karen Latchana. Striking Sounds. Heinsz, Joshua, illus. 2019. (Physics of Music Ser.). (ENG.). 24p. (J). (gr. k-2). lib. bdg. 33.99 *(978-1-68410-343-0(6),* 140263) Cantata Learning.
Landau, Elaine. Are the Drums for You? 2010. (Ready to Make Music Ser.). (ENG.). 40p. (gr. 4-6). lib. bdg. 27.93 *(978-0-7613-5426-0(3),* Lerner Pubns.) Lerner Publishing Group.
Nunn, Daniel. Percussion, 1 vol. 2011. (Instruments & Music Ser.). (ENG.). 24p. (J). (gr. -1-1). pap. 6.29 *(978-1-4329-5067-5(3),* 115120, Heinemann) Capstone.

PERFORMING ARTS
see also Theater
also art forms performed on stage or screen, e.g. Ballet
All the World's a Stage! Individual Title Six-Packs. (Action Packs Ser.). 104p. (gr. 3-5). 44.00 *(978-0-7635-8406-1(1))* Rigby Education.
Backstage Pass, 6 Packs. (Bookweb Ser.). 32p. (gr. 4-18). 34.00 *(978-0-7635-3737-1(3))* Rigby Education.
Beall, Pamela Conn & Nipp, Susan Hagen. Wee Sing & Move. Klein, Nancy & Guida, Liisa, illus. 2009. (Wee Sing Ser.). 64p. (J). (gr. -1-2). 10.99 *(978-0-8431-8959-9(2),* Price Stern Sloan) Penguin Young Readers Group.
The Britannica Guide to the Visual & Performing Arts, 32 vols. 2015. (Britannica Guide to the Visual & Performing Arts Ser.). (ENG.). 216-280p. (YA). (gr. 9-10). 761.44 *(978-1-68048-199-0(1),* 8c8513a2-5cc8-48a2-b8fc-3f0b1de629c7, Britannica Educational Publishing) Rosen Publishing Group, Inc., The.
Capaccio, George. Advertising & Marketing in Theater, 1 vol. 2017. (Exploring Theater Ser.). (ENG.). 96p. (YA). (gr. 7-7). pap. 20.99 *(978-1-5026-3430-6(9),* ac3bb200-766c-43cb-bb86-efa25b4f99f6); lib. bdg. 44.50 *(978-1-5026-2999-9(2),* e0024756-f406-4e49-93e5-d9e59cc2c8c4) Cavendish Square Publishing LLC.
Cohn, Jessica. On the Job in the Theatre. Scheuer, Lauren, illus. 2016. (Core Content Social Studies — on the Job Ser.). (ENG.). 32p. (J). (gr. 2-5). lib. bdg. 26.65 *(978-1-63440-113-5(1),* b0afd95a-d25a-421b-9e7a-867039762333) Red Chair Pr.
Dowd, Olympia. A Young Dancer's Apprenticeship. 2003. (Illus.). 128p. (J). (gr. 7-18). pap. 14.95 *(978-0-7613-1898-9(4),* Twenty-First Century Bks.) Lerner Publishing Group.
Emmer, Rae. Drama Club: Club de Teatro, 1 vol. 2003. (School Activities / Actividades Escolares Ser.). (SPA & ENG., Illus.). 24p. (J). (gr. 1-2). lib. bdg. 26.27 *(978-0-8239-6898-5(7),* 603cc202-b4a2-4b05-8ca1-578610268561) Rosen Publishing Group, Inc., The.
Encyclopaedia Britannica, Inc. Staff, compiled by. The Arts. 2003. (Britannica Learning Library). (Illus.). (gr. 2-5). 14.95 *(978-1-59339-004-4(1),* 049905-EN-REF) Encyclopaedia Britannica, Inc.
Fraser, Fil. Alberta's Camelot Vol. 1: Culture & the Arts in the Lougheed Years, 1 vol. rev. ed. 2003. (ENG., Illus.). 240p. (gr. 4). pap. 21.95 *(978-1-55105-393-6(4),* b68aa00a-507c-4312-bdb5-5db28975287d) Lone Pine Publishing USA.
Hill, Z. B. Performing Arts. 2014. (Art Today! Ser.: 10). 64p. (J). (gr. 7-18). 23.95 *(978-1-4222-3174-6(7))* Mason Crest.
Hobbs, Mike. Entertainment. 2013. (Young Entrepreneurs' Club Ser.). 48p. (gr. 5-11). 37.10 *(978-1-59920-921-0(7))* Black Rabbit Bks.
Kallen, Stuart A. Careers in Entertainment. 2017. (Exploring Careers Ser.). (ENG.). 80p. (YA). (gr. 5-12). *(978-1-68282-198-5(6))* ReferencePoint Pr., Inc.
Mason, Antony. Performing Arts. 2004. (Culture Encyclopedia Ser.). (Illus.). 40p. (YA). (gr. 5-18). lib. bdg. 19.95 *(978-1-59084-481-6(5))* Mason Crest.
Meyer, Susan. Performing & Creating Speeches, Demonstrations, & Collaborative Learning Experiences with Cool New Digital Tools, 1 vol. 2013. (Way Beyond PowerPoint: Making 21st Century Presentations Ser.). (ENG.). 48p. (J). (gr. 6-6). 34.41 *(978-1-4777-1837-7(0),* 557e924e-9671-41a9-b113-a871abfc9a8a); pap. 12.75 *(978-1-4777-1851-3(6),* 90bf3a32-fd43-4a63-aab7-cac627201f94f) Rosen Publishing Group, Inc., The. (Rosen Reference).
Performing & Creating Speeches, Demonstrations, & Collaborative Learning Experiences with Cool New Digital Tools. 2013. (Way Beyond PowerPoint: Making 21st Century Presentations Ser.). 48p. (J). (gr. 5-8). pap. 70.50 *(978-1-4777-1852-0(4),* Rosen Reference) Rosen Publishing Group, Inc., The.
Performing Arts. 2010. (Career Launcher Ser.). 168p. (J). (gr. 9-18). pap. 14.95 *(978-0-8160-7975-9(7),* Checkmark Bks.) Infobase Holdings, Inc.
Pinky & the Brain in Bubba Bo Bob Brain. (Illus.). 32p. (J). (gr. -1-18). pap. 7.89 incl. audio *(978-1-56826-759-3(2),* KR2) Rhino Entertainment Co, A Warner Music Group Co.
Reeves, Diane Lindsey. Arts & Communication. 2017. (Bright Futures Press: World of Work Ser.). (ENG., Illus.). 32p. (J). (gr. 4-7). lib. bdg. 32.07 *(978-1-5341-0170-8(5),* 210150) Cherry Lake Publishing.
Woodland, Faith. Entertainment. 2018. (J). *(978-1-5105-3552-7(7))* SmartBook Media, Inc.

PERFORMING ARTS—BIOGRAPHY
Triumph Books Staff. Austin Mahone: Startin' Something Spectacular. 2013. (ENG.). 112p. (J). (gr. 4-7). pap. 12.95 *(978-1-60078-915-1(3))* Triumph Bks.

PERFORMING ARTS—FICTION
Binding, Tim. Sylvie & the Songman. 2011. (ENG.). 352p. (J). (gr. 4-6). lib. bdg. 22.44 *(978-0-385-75159-9(1),* Yearling) Random Hse. Children's Bks.
Charon Aldredge. Kiddie Rhythms the Show. 2010. 16p. pap. 15.00 *(978-1-4269-1970-1(0))* Trafford Publishing.
Cowley, Joy. Smarty Pants & the Talent Show. 2009. pap. 8.25 *(978-1-60559-241-1(2))* Hameray Publishing Group, Inc.
Denise, Anika & Gomez, Lorena Alvarez. Starring Carmen! 2017. (ENG., Illus.). 32p. (J). (gr. k-2). 16.95 *(978-1-4197-2321-6(9),* 1143501, Abrams Bks. for Young Readers) Abrams, Inc.
deRubertis, Barbara. Alexander Anteater's Amazing Act. Alley, R. W., illus. 2010. (Animal Antics a to Z Ser.). 32p. (J). (gr. -1-3). pap. 7.95 *(978-1-57565-300-6(1),* d44efd10-d888-4efd-8d00-5080695f7eb1, Kane Press) Astra Publishing Hse.
Eulberg, Elizabeth. Take a Bow. 2012. 280p. (YA). pap. *(978-0-545-43982-4(5))* Scholastic, Inc.
Garber, Stephanie. Finale. 2019. (Illus.). 478p. (YA). *(978-1-250-23197-0(3))* St. Martin's Pr.
—Finale: A Caraval Novel. 2019. (Caraval Ser.: 3). (ENG., Illus.). 496p. (YA). 19.99 *(978-1-250-15766-9(8),* 900185295) Flatiron Bks.
Garber, Stephanie & Davies, Rhys. Finale. 2019. (Illus.). 478p. (YA). *(978-1-250-24386-7(6))* St. Martin's Pr.
Harris, Lee. Carla & the Great Talent Show. 2009. 80p. pap. 10.00 *(978-1-60860-515-6(9),* Strategic Bk. Publishing) Strategic Book Publishing & Rights Agency (SBPRA).
Henkes, Kevin. Wemberly Worried. 2003. (Illus.). (J). (gr. -1-2). audio compact disk 28.95 *(978-1-59112-360-6(7))* Live Oak Media.
Holabird, Katharine. A Day at Miss Lilly's. Craig, Helen, illus. 2007. (Angelina Ballerina Ser.). (ENG.). 24p. (J). (gr. -1-1). pap. 4.99 *(978-0-448-44548-9(4),* Grosset & Dunlap) Penguin Publishing Group.
Kain, P. G. Dramatic Pause. 2012. (Commercial Breaks Ser.: 3). (ENG.). 288p. (J). (gr. 4-9). pap. 6.99 *(978-1-4169-9788-7(1),* Aladdin) Simon & Schuster Children's Publishing.
Ketchum, Liza. The Life Fantastic: A Novel in Three Acts. 2017. (ENG.). 256p. (YA). 17.99 *(978-1-4405-9876-0(2),* Simon Pulse) Simon Pulse.
McCully, Emily Arnold. 1, 2, 3, Pull! 2022. (I Like to Read Ser.). (Illus.). 32p. (J). (gr. -1-3). 15.99 *(978-0-8234-4509-7(7))* Holiday Hse., Inc.
Moskowitz, Hannah. Not Otherwise Specified. 2015. (ENG., Illus.). 304p. (YA). (gr. 9). pap. 12.99 *(978-1-4814-0595-9(0),* Simon Pulse) Simon Pulse.
Noel, Alyson. Unrivaled. 2017. (Beautiful Idols Ser.: 1). (ENG.). 448p. (YA). (gr. 9). pap. 9.99 *(978-0-06-232453-5(5),* Tegen, Katherine Bks) HarperCollins Pubs.
Noël, Alyson. Unrivaled: A Beautiful Idols Novel. 2016. 420p. (YA). *(978-0-06-245840-7(X))* HarperCollins Pubs.
Perelman, Helen. The Chocolate Rose. Waters, Erica-Jane, illus. 2013. (Candy Fairies Ser.: 11). (ENG.). 128p. (J). (gr. 2-5). pap. 5.99 *(978-1-4424-5299-2(4),* Aladdin) Simon & Schuster Children's Publishing.
—The Chocolate Rose. Waters, Erica-Jane, illus. 2013. (Candy Fairies Ser.: 11). (ENG.). 128p. (J). (gr. 2-5). 15.99 *(978-1-4424-6499-5(2),* Simon & Schuster/Paula Wiseman Bks.) Simon & Schuster/Paula Wiseman Bks.
Reisfeld, Randi. All Access. rev. ed. 2007. (ENG.). 288p. (gr. 7-12). pap. 8.99 *(978-1-4231-0503-9(6))* Hyperion Pr.
Rennison, Louise. A Midsummer Tights Dream. 2013. (Misadventures of Tallulah Casey Ser.: 2). (ENG.). 272p. (YA). (gr. 8). pap. 9.99 *(978-0-06-179938-9(6),* HarperTeen) HarperCollins Pubs.
—Withering Tights. 2012. (Misadventures of Tallulah Casey Ser.: 1). (ENG.). 304p. (YA). (gr. 8). pap. 8.99 *(978-0-06-179933-4(5),* HarperTeen) HarperCollins Pubs.
Robinson, Craig & Mansbach, Adam. Jake the Fake Keeps It Real. Knight, Keith, illus. 2018. (Jake the Fake Ser.: 1). 160p. (J). (gr. 3-7). 7.99 *(978-0-553-52354-6(6),* Yearling) Random Hse. Children's Bks.
Ross, Dev. We Both Read-Oh No! We're Doing a Show! Johnson, Meredith, illus. 2011. 44p. (J). 9.95 *(978-1-60115-255-8(8));* pap. 5.99 *(978-1-60115-256-5(6))* Treasure Bay, Inc.
Rushton, Rosie. I Think I'll Just Curl up & Die. 2005. 176p. (J). pap. 5.99 *(978-0-7868-5188-1(0))* Hyperion Bks. for Children.
Snowflake Day! 2014. (Daniel Tiger's Neighborhood Ser.). (ENG., Illus.). 14p. (J). (gr. -1-k). bds. 5.99 *(978-1-4814-1771-6(1),* Simon Spotlight) Simon Spotlight.
Sugg, Zoe. Girl Online: Going Solo: The Third Novel by Zoella. 2017. (Girl Online Book Ser.: 3). (ENG.). 336p. (gr. 7). pap. 17.99 *(978-1-5011-6212-1(8),* Atria Bks.) Simon & Schuster.
Weston Woods Staff, creator. The Clown of God. 2011. 18.95 *(978-0-545-08632-5(9));* 29.95 *(978-0-545-08638-7(8))* Weston Woods Studios, Inc.
—Scrambled States of America Talent Show. 2011. 38.75 *(978-0-545-34954-3(0));* 18.95 *(978-0-545-34618-4(5))* Weston Woods Studios, Inc.
Whittemore, Jo. D Is for Drama. 2012. (Mix Ser.). (ENG.). 272p. (J). (gr. 4-8). pap. 6.99 *(978-1-4424-4152-1(6),* Aladdin) Simon & Schuster Children's Publishing.
Wiles, Deborah. The Aurora County All-Stars. 2009. (ENG., Illus.). 256p. (J). (gr. 2-5). pap. 7.99 *(978-0-15-206626-0(8),* 1063363, Clarion Bks.) HarperCollins Pubs.

PERFUMES
Loh-Hagan, Virginia. Odor Tester. 2015. 32p. (J). pap. 9.95 *(978-1-63470-053-5(8))* Cherry Lake Publishing.

PERIODIC LAW
Adair, Rick. Beryllium. (Understanding the Elements of the Periodic Table Ser.). 48p. (gr. 6-6). 2009. 53.00 *(978-1-60854-634-3(9),* Rosen Reference) 2007. (ENG., Illus.). (YA). lib. bdg. 34.47 *(978-1-4042-1003-5(2),* 253718bb-fea0-412b-a6fc-e532d76e9e14) Rosen Publishing Group, Inc., The.
Belval, Brian. Gold, 1 vol. 2006. (Understanding the Elements of the Periodic Table Ser.). (ENG., Illus.). 48p. (J). (gr. 6-6). lib. bdg. 34.47 *(978-1-4042-0708-0(2),* acb3bba9-0a0b-4004-89de-a4ca12590ed3) Rosen Publishing Group, Inc., The.
—Silver. 2009. (Understanding the Elements of the Periodic Table Ser.). 48p. (gr. 6-6). 53.00 *(978-1-60854-682-4(9),* Rosen Reference) Rosen Publishing Group, Inc., The.
Congdon, Lisa. The Illustrated Encyclopedia of the Elements: The Powers, Uses, & Histories of Every Atom in the Universe. 2021. (ENG., Illus.). 148p. (J). (gr. 5-10). 22.99 *(978-1-4521-6159-4(3))* Chronicle Bks. LLC.
Crabtree Publishing Company Staff & Jackson, Tom. Introducing the Periodic Table. 2012. (ENG., Illus.). 32p. (J). *(978-0-7787-4230-2(0));* pap. *(978-0-7787-4234-0(2))* Crabtree Publishing Co.
Dingle, Adrian, et al. Basher Science: the Complete Periodic Table: All the Elements with Style! 2015. (Basher Science Ser.). (ENG., Illus.). 192p. (J). (gr. 5-9). pap. 11.99 *(978-0-7534-7197-5(3),* 900139963, Kingfisher) Roaring Brook Pr.
Gray, Leon. The Basics of the Periodic Table, 1 vol. 2013. (Core Concepts Ser.). (ENG., Illus.). 96p. (J). (gr. 7-7). 39.77 *(978-1-4777-2712-6(4),* e0456570-78dd-48da-b62e-0430e5c58d37) Rosen Publishing Group, Inc., The.
Green, Joey. The Electric Pickle: 50 Experiments from the Periodic Table, from Aluminum to Zinc. 2017. (ENG., Illus.). 272p. pap. 19.99 *(978-1-61373-959-4(1))* Chicago Review Pr., Inc.
Griffin, Mary. The Periodic Table, 1 vol. 2018. (Look at Chemistry Ser.). (ENG.). 32p. (gr. 2-2). lib. bdg. 28.27 *(978-1-5382-3014-5(3),* 342f1b57-5120-4baa-a8b1-561472436d30) Stevens, Gareth Publishing LLLP.
Hasan, Heather. Aluminum. 2009. (Understanding the Elements of the Periodic Table Ser.). 48p. (gr. 6-6). 53.00 *(978-1-60854-629-9(2),* Rosen Reference) Rosen Publishing Group, Inc., The.
—Fluorine, 1 vol. 2007. (Understanding the Elements of the Periodic Table Ser.). (ENG., Illus.). 48p. (YA). (gr. 6-6). lib. bdg. 34.47 *(978-1-4042-1005-9(9),* 7922f476-db26-4afb-8039-b149129cd8ec) Rosen Publishing Group, Inc., The.
—Iron. (Understanding the Elements of the Periodic Table Ser.). 48p. (gr. 6-6). 2009. 53.00 *(978-1-60854-658-9(6),* Rosen Reference) 2004. (ENG., Illus.). (J). lib. bdg. 34.47 *(978-1-4042-0157-6(2),* e1658c8f-8a65-443f-a32a-eed843113fb5) Rosen Publishing Group, Inc., The.
—Nitrogen. (Understanding the Elements of the Periodic Table Ser.). 48p. (gr. 6-6). 2009. 53.00 *(978-1-60854-673-2(X),* Rosen Reference) 2004. (ENG., Illus.). (J). lib. bdg. 34.47 *(978-1-4042-0158-3(0),* 57f380f6-ef74-4377-9e82-1205b541f60e) Rosen Publishing Group, Inc., The.
Holt, Rinehart and Winston Staff. Holt Science & Technology Chapter 12: Physical Science: Periodic Table. 5th ed. 2004. (Illus.). pap. 12.86 *(978-0-03-030404-0(0))* Holt McDougal.
Johanson, Paula. Lithium. 2009. (Understanding the Elements of the Periodic Table Ser.). 48p. (gr. 6-6). 53.00 *(978-1-60854-661-9(6),* Rosen Reference) Rosen Publishing Group, Inc., The.
Kean, Sam. The Disappearing Spoon: And Other True Tales of Rivalry, Adventure, & the History of the World from the Periodic Table of the Elements (Young Readers Edition) 2018. (ENG., Illus.). 240p. (J). E-Book *(978-0-316-38824-5(6))* Little Brown & Co.
—The Disappearing Spoon: And Other True Tales of Rivalry, Adventure, & the History of the World from the Periodic Table of the Elements (Young Readers Edition) 2019. (ENG., Illus.). 240p. (J). (gr. 5-17). pap. 9.99 *(978-0-316-38827-6(0))* Little, Brown Bks. for Young Readers.
Lew, Kristi. Argon. (Understanding the Elements of the Periodic Table Ser.). 48p. (gr. 6-6). 2009. 53.00 *(978-1-60854-632-9(2),* Rosen Reference) 2008. (ENG., Illus.). (YA). lib. bdg. 34.47 *(978-1-4042-1409-5(7),* 88a5c957-259a-4261-bab3-b96dc4542ae9) Rosen Publishing Group, Inc., The.
Mapua, Jeff. Phosphorus, 1 vol. 2018. (Exploring the Elements Ser.). (ENG.). 48p. (gr. 6-6). 29.60 *(978-1-9785-0368-7(7),* 55e459a9-ea68-409e-8b46-fbbd861bc4ad) Enslow Publishing, LLC.
McCormick, Anita Louise. Gold, 1 vol. 2018. (Exploring the Elements Ser.). (ENG.). 48p. (gr. 6-6). 29.60 *(978-1-9785-0365-6(2),* d9d4dfb2-982d-4ac0-a6ba-43ecc335a686) Enslow Publishing, LLC.
—Mercury, 1 vol. 2018. (Exploring the Elements Ser.). (ENG.). 48p. (gr. 6-6). 29.60 *(978-1-9785-0367-0(9),* 6d336cea-2075-4202-a961-939d6695f765) Enslow Publishing, LLC.
McKinney, Donna B. Carbon, 1 vol. 2018. (Exploring the Elements Ser.). (ENG.). 48p. (gr. 6-6). 29.60 *(978-0-7660-9905-0(9),* 7c8196e7-2170-4744-a3ea-77a6006ad597) Enslow Publishing, LLC.
—Lead, 1 vol. 2018. (Exploring the Elements Ser.). (ENG.). 48p. (gr. 6-6). 29.60 *(978-1-9785-0366-3(0),* 064925dc-5e14-49f1-a702-27a36ec3494b) Enslow Publishing, LLC.
Mullins, Matt. The Elements. 2011. (True Bk Ser.). (ENG., Illus.). 48p. (J). pap. 6.95 *(978-0-531-26585-7(4));* lib. bdg. 29.00 *(978-0-531-26323-5(1))* Scholastic Library Publishing. (Children's Pr.).
Roza, Greg. Arsenic. 2009. (Understanding the Elements of the Periodic Table Ser.). 48p. (gr. 6-6). 53.00 *(978-1-60854-633-6(0),* Rosen Reference) Rosen Publishing Group, Inc., The.
—Calcium. (Understanding the Elements of the Periodic Table Ser.). 48p. (gr. 6-6). 2009. 53.00 *(978-1-60854-641-1(1),* Rosen Reference) 2007. (ENG., Illus.). (J). lib. bdg. 34.47 *(978-1-4042-1963-2(3),* b39da23e-6765-4876-ad8e-db7c0f7cbf67) Rosen Publishing Group, Inc., The.
—Chromium. 2009. (Understanding the Elements of the Periodic Table Ser.). 48p. (gr. 6-6). 53.00 *(978-1-60854-644-2(6),* Rosen Reference) Rosen Publishing Group, Inc., The.
—Potassium. (Understanding the Elements of the Periodic Table Ser.). 48p. (gr. 6-6). 2009. 53.00 *(978-1-60854-678-7(0),* Rosen Reference) 2007. (ENG., Illus.). (J). lib. bdg. 34.47 *(978-1-4042-1964-9(1),* daef1ae6-a17b-4835-aa92-3374ba140a42) Rosen Publishing Group, Inc., The.
—Titanium. (Understanding the Elements of the Periodic Table Ser.). 48p. (gr. 6-6). 2009. 53.00 *(978-1-60854-688-6(8),* Rosen Reference) 2008. (ENG., Illus.). (J). lib. bdg. 34.47 *(978-1-4042-1412-5(7),* f5a085d8-d8db-45f1-9787-51fd7ec16487) Rosen Publishing Group, Inc., The.
—Zirconium. 2009. (Understanding the Elements of the Periodic Table Ser.). 48p. (gr. 6-6). 53.00 *(978-1-60854-690-9(X),* Rosen Reference); (ENG., Illus.). (J). lib. bdg. 34.47 *(978-1-4358-5070-5(X),* 277471dc-42dc-412b-95a1-4abd8d69c00c) Rosen Publishing Group, Inc., The.
Saucerman, Linda. Carbon. 2009. (Understanding the Elements of the Periodic Table Ser.). 48p. (gr. 6-6). 53.00 *(978-1-60854-642-8(X),* Rosen Reference) Rosen Publishing Group, Inc., The.
—Chlorine. (Understanding the Elements of the Periodic Table Ser.). 48p. (gr. 6-6). 2009. 53.00 *(978-1-60854-643-5(8),* Rosen Reference) 2007. (ENG., Illus.). (J). lib. bdg. 34.47 *(978-1-4042-1962-5(5),* ba602ca4-ac89-4035-885b-35b176322ccc) Rosen Publishing Group, Inc., The.
—Hydrogen. 2009. (Understanding the Elements of the Periodic Table Ser.). 48p. (gr. 6-6). 53.00 *(978-1-60854-656-5(X),* Rosen Reference) Rosen Publishing Group, Inc., The.
—Hydrogen: The Fuel for Life, 1 vol. 2004. (Understanding the Elements of the Periodic Table Ser.). (ENG., Illus.). 48p. (J). (gr. 6-6). lib. bdg. 34.47 *(978-1-4042-0156-9(4),* cf4b7d7e-df0e-4fab-9a1f-a39cb165bdae) Rosen Publishing Group, Inc., The.
Slade, Suzanne. Elements & the Periodic Table. (Library of Physical Science Ser.). 24p. (gr. 4-4). 2009. 42.50 *(978-1-60853-781-5(1))* 2006. (ENG., Illus.). (J). pap. 7.05 *(978-1-4042-2165-9(4),* 12b7d39b-ae6a-4168-bcb2-5e211fb06894) Rosen Publishing Group, Inc., The. (PowerKids Pr.).
Stefoff, Rebecca. The Four Elements & the Periodic Table, 1 vol. 2014. (Is It Science? Ser.). (ENG.). 48p. (gr. 5-5). lib. bdg. 32.64 *(978-1-62712-518-5(3),* 0e82c831-24fa-4462-bc4d-606c650dae32) Cavendish Square Publishing LLC.
Thomas, Michele. Oxygen. (Understanding the Elements of the Periodic Table Ser.). 48p. (gr. 6-6). 2009. 53.00 *(978-1-60854-674-9(8),* Rosen Reference) 2004. (ENG., Illus.). (J). lib. bdg. 34.47 *(978-1-4042-0159-0(9),* 34b8d032-3294-4022-8df9-dd110427ec84) Rosen Publishing Group, Inc., The.
—Sodium. 2009. (Understanding the Elements of the Periodic Table Ser.). 48p. (gr. 6-6). 53.00 *(978-1-60854-685-5(3),* Rosen Reference) Rosen Publishing Group, Inc., The.
Tobler, Elise. Sulfur, 1 vol. 2018. (Exploring the Elements Ser.). (ENG.). 48p. (gr. 6-6). 29.60 *(978-1-9785-0371-7(7),* 231c6cb5-35a5-4b20-8202-cf4e1392a756) Enslow Publishing, LLC.
—Zinc, 1 vol. 2018. (Exploring the Elements Ser.). (ENG.). 48p. (gr. 6-6). 29.60 *(978-1-9785-0372-4(5),* f3bd18f3-bc54-4f3a-b974-1e41031e3ea3) Enslow Publishing, LLC.
Understanding the Elements of the Periodic Table: Set 1, 10 vols. 2004. (Understanding the Elements of the Periodic Table Ser.). (ENG., Illus.). 48p. (gr. 6-6). lib. bdg. 172.35 *(978-1-4042-0348-8(6),* d3d5c161-e240-483f-a7e6-0409b8522447) Rosen Publishing Group, Inc., The.
Understanding the Elements of the Periodic Table: Set 3, 8 vols. Incl. Beryllium. Adair, Rick. (YA). lib. bdg. 34.47 *(978-1-4042-1003-5(2),* 253718bb-fea0-412b-a6fc-e532d76e9e14); Boron. Adair, Rick. (YA). lib. bdg. 34.47 *(978-1-4042-1004-2(0),* df3dc210-2227-44f7-898c-754d4d1df429); Fluorine. Hasan, Heather. (YA). lib. bdg. 34.47 *(978-1-4042-1005-9(9),* 7922f476-db26-4afb-8039-b149129cd8ec); Lithium. Johanson, Paula. (YA). lib. bdg. 34.47 *(978-1-4042-0940-4(9),* 452086a0-f090-48ec-9b08-2f7a75671d3b); Magnesium. Willett, Edward. (J). lib. bdg. 34.47 *(978-1-4042-1007-3(5),* a0ea4dd6-4be1-4e2c-ba3a-654391f51024); Neon. Willett, Edward. (YA). lib. bdg. 34.47 *(978-1-4042-1008-0(3),* 6cc39afa-2efe-401b-b608-9ce063a747ca); (Illus.). 48p. (gr. 6-6). 2007. (Understanding the Elements of the Periodic Table Ser.). (ENG.). 2006. Set lib. bdg. 137.88 *(978-1-4042-1043-1(1),* df73e275-4cb6-49b6-a0ba-195c5802ede9) Rosen Publishing Group, Inc., The.
Wiker, Benjamin, et al. The Mystery of the Periodic Table. 2003. (Living History Library). (ENG., Illus.). 170p. (J). (gr. 4-6). pap. 15.95 *(978-1-883937-71-3(X))* Ignatius Pr.
Willett, Edward. Magnesium. 2009. (Understanding the Elements of the Periodic Table Ser.). 48p. (gr. 6-6). 53.00 *(978-1-60854-664-0(0),* Rosen Reference) Rosen Publishing Group, Inc., The.
Wu, Ronald W. Carbon, 1 vol. 2004. (Understanding the Elements of the Periodic Table Ser.). (ENG., Illus.). 48p. (J). (gr. 6-6). lib. bdg. 34.47 *(978-1-4042-0155-2(6),* c4ef2ad6-c99a-4df6-b06b-b792eff82280) Rosen Publishing Group, Inc., The.
Zannos, Susan. Dmitri Mendeleyev & the Periodic Table. 2004. (Uncharted, Unexplored, & Unexplained Ser.). (Illus.). 48p. (J). (gr. 4-8). lib. bdg. 29.95 *(978-1-58415-267-5(2))* Mitchell Lane Pubs.

PERIODIC TABLE OF ELEMENTS
see Periodic Law

PERIODICALS
see also Newspapers
Baczynski, Kristyna. Read All about It! 10 Mini-Magazines to Make & Share. 2019. (ENG.). 48p. (J). (gr. 2-6). pap. 17.99 *(978-1-78627-404-5(3),* King, Laurence Publishing) Orion Publishing Group, Ltd. GBR. Dist: Hachette Bk. Group.
Birch, Ian. Iconic Magazine Covers: The Inside Stories Told by the People Who Made Them. 2018. (ENG., Illus.). 256p. 49.95 *(978-0-2281-0117-8(4),* 58f31083-8d63-4d3e-bdf1-0547990f02bb) Firefly Bks., Ltd.
Bodden, Valerie. Print & Subscription Sources. 2012. (Research for Writing Ser.). (ENG.). 48p. (J). (gr. 4-7). 23.95 *(978-1-60818-205-3(3),* 21953, Creative Education) Creative Co., The.
Chase, Aimee. One Question a Day for Kids: a Three-Year Journal: Create Your Own Personal Time Capsule. 2017. (One Question a Day Ser.). (ENG., Illus.). 368p. (J). 16.99 *(978-1-250-16651-7(9),* 900187160) St. Martin's Pr.
Guidone, Lisa M. What Happens at a Magazine?, 1 vol. 2008. (Where People Work Ser.). (ENG.). 24p. (gr. k-2). (J). lib. bdg. 24.67 *(978-0-8368-9275-8(5),* 5e3b7db5-2e00-4863-900c-8b998b9014c6); pap. 9.15 *(978-0-8368-9374-8(3),* 9effed73-7d63-4777-879b-18c94b64338e) Stevens, Gareth Publishing LLLP. (Weekly Reader Leveled Readers).
—What Happens at a Magazine? / ¿Qué Pasa en la Editorial de una Revista?, 1 vol. 2008. (Where People Work / ¿dónde Trabaja la Gente? Ser.). 24p. (gr. k-2). (ENG & SPA.). (J). lib. bdg. 24.67 *(978-0-8368-9281-9(X),* 4da684eb-8de0-4abb-9903-4397e909a1a9); (SPA & ENG.). pap. 9.15 *(978-0-8368-9380-9(8),* 5df060bf-7f7c-4b8c-b3d9-9e037b3b02e9) Stevens, Gareth Publishing LLLP. (Weekly Reader Leveled Readers).
Hamilton, John. Magazines, 1 vol. 2005. (Straight to the Source Ser.). (ENG., Illus.). 32p. (gr. k-6). 27.07 *(978-1-59197-546-5(8),* Checkerboard Library) ABDO Publishing Co.

In the News - The Election of Barak Obama: Race & Politics in America Set 5, 12 vols. Incl. Biofuels: Sustainable Energy in the 21st Century. Johanson, Paula. lib. bdg. 37.13 (978-1-4358-3584-9(0), 2cb1e4ee-621c-4dc3-831b-e4ea33bb5375); Election of Barack Obama: Race & Politics in America. Porterfield, Jason. lib. bdg. 37.13 (978-1-4358-3586-3(7), 78d62377-d582-4bf4-ba75-c91e7b718843); Illegal Immigration & Amnesty: Open Borders & National Security. Levy, Janey. lib. bdg. 37.13 (978-1-4358-3583-2(2), abfac7e0-03a2-401d-a399-95b132c4f399); Same-Sex Marriage: The Debate. Nagle, Jeanne. lib. bdg. 37.13 (978-1-4358-3582-5(4), 15aa3d3d-769f-45a5-a392-d8436f222377); Superbugs: The Rise of Drug-Resistant Germs. Watson, Stephanie. lib. bdg. 37.13 (978-1-4358-3585-6(9), 4059a9ef-83f8-4ce4-b01c-fc1d1cd0133f); (YA). (gr. 6-6). 2010. (In the News Ser.). (ENG., Illus.). 64p. 2009. Set lib. bdg. 222.78 (978-1-4358-3612-9(X), 8aadd19b-d43d-46fd-bfad-85954d1ebf27) Rosen Publishing Group, Inc., The.

Littler, Courtney. Interview with My Grandma: An Interactive Journal to Investigate Our Family History. 2018. (ENG., Illus.). 96p. (J). spiral bd. 9.99 (978-1-250-19057-4(6), 900192488) St. Martin's Pr.

Petley, Julian. Newspapers & Magazines. 2003. (Media Wise Ser.). (Illus.). 64p. (J). lib. bdg. 28.50 (978-1-58340-258-0(6)) Black Rabbit Bks.

Rocha, Toni L. Careers in Magazine Publishing. 2009. (Career Resource Library). 192p. (gr. 7-12). 63.90 (978-1-60853-399-2(9)) Rosen Publishing Group, Inc., The.

PERKINS, FRANCES, 1882-1965

Krull, Kathleen. The Only Woman in the Photo: Frances Perkins & Her New Deal for America. Bye, Alexandra, illus. 2020. (ENG.). 48p. (J). (gr. -1-3). 19.99 (978-1-4814-9151-8(2), Simon & Schuster Bks. For Young Readers) Simon & Schuster Bks. For Young Readers.

PERRY, MATTHEW CALBRAITH, 1794-1858

Blumberg, Rhoda. Commodore Perry in the Land of the Shogun. 2003. (Illus.). 144p. (gr. 3-7). 20.00 (978-0-7569-1440-0(X)) Perfection Learning Corp.

—Commodore Perry in the Land of the Shogun: A Newbery Honor Award Winner. 2003. (ENG., Illus.). 144p. (J). (gr. 3-18). pap. 9.99 (978-0-06-008625-1(4), HarperCollins) HarperCollins Pubs.

McNeese, Tim. The Perry Expedition & the Opening of Japan. 2012. (J). 35.00 (978-1-60413-924-2(2), Facts On File) Infobase Holdings, Inc.

Wittner, David G. Commodore Matthew Perry & the Perry Expedition to Japan. 2009. (Library of American Lives & Times Ser.). 112p. (gr. 5-5). 69.20 (978-1-60853-474-6(X)) Rosen Publishing Group, Inc., The.

PERSEUS (GREEK MYTHOLOGY)

Harkins, Susan Sales & Harkins, William H. Perseus. 2007. (Profiles in Greek & Roman Mythology Ser.). (Illus.). 48p. (J). (gr. 4-7). lib. bdg. 29.95 (978-1-58415-558-4(2)) Mitchell Lane Pubs.

Hepplewhite, Peter & Salariya, David. The Adventures of Perseus. Bergin, Mark, illus. 2013. 32p. (J). (978-1-4351-5119-2(4)) Barnes & Noble, Inc.

Jeffrey, Gary. Perseus Slays the Gorgon Medusa, 1 vol. 2012. (Graphic Mythical Heroes Ser.). (ENG., Illus.). 24p. (J). (gr. 3-3). 26.60 (978-1-4339-7523-3(8), c0d35dcb-84da-4b5c-825b-76b6337e2a24); pap. 9.15 (978-1-4339-7524-0(6), 9879f403-5f4d-43cf-bb4c-3b34178afb55) Stevens, Gareth Publishing LLLP.

McCaughrean, Geraldine. Perseus. 2005. (Heroes Ser.). (ENG., Illus.). 160p. (J). (gr. -1-7). 17.95 (978-0-8126-2735-0(0)) Cricket Bks.

Roesser, Blanche. The Story of Perseus. 1 vol. 2015. (Stories in the Stars Ser.). (ENG., Illus.). 24p. (J). (gr. 1-2). 24.27 (978-1-4824-2683-0(8), c474c835-92b6-4301-a844-88ac2424fce7) Stevens, Gareth Publishing LLLP.

Storrie, Paul D. Perseus: The Hunt for Medusa's Head [a Greek Myth]. Yeates, Thomas, illus. 2015. (Graphic Myths & Legends Ser.). (ENG.). 48p. (gr. 4-8). 21.32 (978-1-4677-5984-7(8), Lerner Digital) Lerner Publishing Group.

Weiss, Lynne. Perseus & Medusa, 1 vol., 1. 2013. (Jr. Graphic Myths: Greek Heroes Ser.). (ENG., Illus.). 24p. (J). (gr. 2-3). 28.93 (978-1-4777-6232-5(9), b07c4739-482d-434f-8e94-236b120300f4, PowerKids Pr.) Rosen Publishing Group, Inc., The.

PERSIAN GULF WAR, 1991

Calvert, John. The Arabian Peninsula in the Age of Oil. 2009. (Making of the Middle East Ser.). (Illus.). 88p. (YA). (gr. 3-7). lib. bdg. 22.95 (978-1-4222-0172-5(4)) Mason Crest.

Cruden, Alexander, ed. The Persian Gulf War, 1 vol. 2011. (Perspectives on Modern World History Ser.). (ENG., Illus.). 232p. (gr. 10-12). lib. bdg. 45.73 (978-0-7377-5261-8(0), 41ca0fb5-e6d4-4a07-a421-b8c4bf6bf5ea, Greenhaven Publishing) Greenhaven Publishing LLC.

Dongweck, James. The Goblin's Story. Bixby, Sean, illus. 2013. (J). (978-0-9719632-2-1(3)) Golden Monkey Publishing, LLC.

George, Enzo. The Persian Gulf War: War Against Iraqi Aggression, 1 vol. 2014. (Voices of War Ser.). (ENG.). 48p. (gr. 4-4). 33.07 (978-1-62712-876-6(X), 2a86fb05-d506-4b39-aedd-838dd1521e6d) Cavendish Square Publishing LLC.

Gunderson, Cory Gideon. U. N. Weapons Inspectors. 2003. (World in Conflict-the Middle East Ser.). 32p. (gr. 4-8). 27.07 (978-1-59197-414-7(3), Abdo & Daughters) ABDO Publishing Co.

Hillstrom, Laurie Collier. War in the Persian Gulf: From Operation Desert Storm to Operation Iraqi Freedom Reference Library, 4 vols. Incl. War in the Persian Gulf: Biographies. Hillstrom, Kevin. 320p. 129.00 (978-0-7876-6564-7(9)); War in the Persian Gulf Almanac: From Operation Desert Storm to Operation Iraqi Freedom. Carnagie, Julie, ed. 224p. 129.00 (978-0-7876-6563-0(0)); (J). (War in the Persian Gulf Reference Library). (ENG., Illus.). 208p. 2004. 348.00 (978-0-7876-6562-3(2), GML10504-182625, UXL) Cengage Gale.

Lowery, Zoe. Key Figures of the Wars in Iraq & Afghanistan, 1 vol. 2015. (Biographies of War Ser.). (ENG., Illus.). 112p. (J). (gr. 7-8). 35.47 (978-1-68048-066-5(9), 9ca29243-4569-4a9e-b3fe-531790e167d9, Britannica Educational Publishing) Rosen Publishing Group, Inc., The.

Martin, Michael. The Persian Gulf War: Saddam's Failed Invasion. 2004. (History's Great Defeats Ser.). (ENG.). (J). (gr. 7-10). 30.85 (978-1-59018-428-8(9), Lucent Bks.) Cengage Gale.

Murdico, Suzanne J. The Gulf War. (War & Conflict in the Middle East Ser.). 64p. (gr. 5-5). 2009. 58.50 (978-1-60854-737-1(X)) 2003. (ENG., Illus.). lib. bdg. 37.13 (978-0-8239-4551-1(0), bb4b8520-4d6f-4bf5-b07e-0fbd7f99c637) Rosen Publishing Group, Inc., The.

Perritano, John. Desert Storm. 2010. (America at War Ser.). 32p. (J). 27.00 (978-0-531-23210-1(7), Watts, Franklin) Scholastic Library Publishing.

Peterson, J. E. Tensions in the Gulf, 1978-1991. 2007. (Making of the Middle East Ser.). (Illus.). 88p. (J). (gr. 3-7). lib. bdg. 22.95 (978-1-4222-0175-6(9)) Mason Crest.

Rice, Earle. Overview of the Persian Gulf War 1990. 2008. (Monumental Milestones Ser.). (Illus.). 48p. (YA). (gr. 4-7). lib. bdg. 29.95 (978-1-58415-696-3(1)) Mitchell Lane Pubs.

Yasuda, Anita. The Gulf War. 2017. (J). (978-1-5105-3512-1(8)) SmartBook Media, Inc.

Zeinert, Karen & Miller, Mary. The Brave Women of the Gulf Wars: Operation Desert Storm & Operation Iraqi Freedom. 2005. (Women at War Ser.). (ENG., Illus.). 96p. (J). (gr. 7-12). 30.60 (978-0-7613-2705-9(3), Millbrook Pr.) Lerner Publishing Group.

Zwier, Lawrence J. & Weltig, Matthew S. The Persian Gulf & Iraqi Wars. 2005. (Chronicle of America's Wars Ser.). (Illus.). 96p. (J). (gr. 3-7). lib. bdg. 27.93 (978-0-8225-0848-9(6)) Lerner Publishing Group.

PERSONAL APPEARANCE

see Beauty, Personal; Grooming for Men

PERSONAL DEVELOPMENT

see Personality; Success

PERSONAL FINANCE

see Finance, Personal

PERSONAL GROOMING

see Beauty, Personal; Grooming for Men

PERSONAL IDENTITY

see Identity (Psychology); Personality

PERSONAL LIBERTY

see Liberty

PERSONALITY

see also Identity (Psychology); Individuality

Allman, Toney. Understanding Personality. 2017. (ENG.). 80p. (J). (gr. 5-12). (978-1-68282-277-7(X)) ReferencePoint Pr., Inc.

Becker, H. The Personality Quiz Book for You & Your BFFs: Learn All about Your Friends! 2017. (ENG., Illus.). 112p. (J). (gr. 5-8). pap. 7.99 (978-1-4926-5324-0(1)) Sourcebooks, Inc.

—The Personality Quiz Book Just for You: Learn All about You! 2017. (ENG., Illus.). 112p. (J). (gr. 5-8). pap. 8.99 (978-1-4926-5321-9(7)) Sourcebooks, Inc.

Berry, Joy. Help Me Be Good Being Selfish. Bartholomew, illus. 2010. (Help Me Be Good Ser.). (ENG.). 32p. (J). (gr. -1-2). pap. 4.99 (978-1-60577-133-5(3)) Berry, Joy Enterprises.

Brownlie, Marion. Spirit of Self. 2013. 36p. pap. (978-0-9875551-5-1(4)) Aurora House.

Carlson, Daniel & Rosen, Michael J. Just My Type: Understanding Personality Profiles. 2016. (ENG., Illus.). 80p. (YA). (gr. 6-12). E-Book 51.99 (978-1-4677-9579-1(8), Twenty-First Century Bks.) Lerner Publishing Group.

Feist, Jess, et al. Theories of Personality. 2020. (Illus.). xx, 639p. (J). (978-1-260-17576-9(6)) McGraw-Hill Higher Education.

Foster, Joanne. Bust Your BUTS: Tips for Teens Who Procrastinate. 2017. (ENG.). 168p. pap. 18.95 (978-1-935067-33-7(8)) Gifted UnLtd., LLC.

Greenspon, Thomas S. What to Do When Good Enough Isn't Good Enough: The Real Deal on Perfectionism. 2007. (ENG., Illus.). 144p. (YA). (gr. 4-8). pap. 15.99 (978-1-57542-234-3(4), 1195) Free Spirit Publishing Inc.

Hodgson, David. The Buzz: A Practical Confidence Builder for Teenagers, 1 vol. 2nd ed. 2015. (ENG., Illus.). 176p. (C). pap. 14.95 (978-1-84590-998-7(4)) Crown Hse. Publishing LLC.

Johnson, Kevin, et al. Find Your Fit: Unlock God's Unique Design for Your Talents, Spiritual Gifts, & Personality. rev. ed. 2018. (ENG., Illus.). 256p. (YA). pap. 14.99 (978-0-7642-3135-3(9)) Bethany Hse. Pubs.

—Find Your Fit Discovery Workbook: Discover Your Unique Design. rev. ed. 2018. (ENG., Illus.). 48p. (YA). pap. 7.99 (978-0-7642-3136-0(7)) Bethany Hse. Pubs.

Jones, Steven. Journey to Excellence: An Introduction to E4. 2003. 75p. (YA). per. 19.99 (978-0-9729798-0-1(8)) Keytochange Publishing, Inc.

Kalman, Bobbie. Today Is a Great Day! 2010. (My World Ser.). (ENG.). 16p. (J). (gr. k-3). (978-0-7787-9506-3(3)); pap. (978-0-7787-9531-5(4)) Crabtree Publishing Co.

Lewis, Barbara A. What Do You Stand For? For Kids: a Guide to Building Character. 2005. (ENG., Illus.). 176p. (J). (gr. 3-7). pap. 17.99 (978-1-57542-174-2(7), 617) Free Spirit Publishing Inc.

Miller, Reagan. Step Forward with Optimism. 2016. (Step Forward! Ser.). (ENG., Illus.). 24p. (J). (gr. 1-4). (978-0-7787-2780-4(7)) Crabtree Publishing Co.

Nelms, Davis Kenyon. Inner-Fire Kindling: Simple Exercises for the Permanent Establishment of Fulfilling Thoughts. 2004. (Illus.). 128p. per. 19.95 (978-0-9654169-7-9(6)) Billings Worldwide Brain.

Obregón, José María. Lionel Messi. 2009. (World Soccer Stars / Estrellas del fútbol mundial Ser.). (ENG & SPA.). 24p. (gr. 2-2). 42.50 (978-1-60854-848-4(1), Editorial Buenas Letras) Rosen Publishing Group, Inc., The.

Potts, Francesca. What's Your Personality? Facts, Trivia, & Quizzes. 2017. (Mind Games Ser.). (ENG., Illus.). 32p. (J). (gr. 2-5). lib. bdg. 27.99 (978-1-5124-3413-2(2), 403c6b2f-5025-423c-ad2a-9e3f00147151, Lerner Pubns.) Lerner Publishing Group.

Richardson, Tanya Carroll. Zen Teen: 40 Ways to Stay Calm When Life Gets Stressful. 2018. (ENG.). 240p. (gr. 7-17). pap. 15.99 (978-1-58005-782-0(9), Seal Pr.) Basic Bks.

Robertson, Rachel. Beginners Are Brave. 2020. (ENG., Illus.). 32p. (J). (gr. 3-7). 17.95 (978-1-60554-600-1(3)) Redleaf Pr.

Rule the World: 119 Shortcuts to Total World Domination. 2011. (Illus.). 180p. (J). (gr. 3-7). 16.99 (978-1-59174-849-6(6)) Klutz.

Welbourn, Shannon. Step Forward with Grit. 2016. (Step Forward! Ser.). (ENG., Illus.). 24p. (J). (gr. 1-4). (978-0-7787-2767-5(X)) Crabtree Publishing Co.

Williams, Jane A. A Bluestocking Guide - Building a Personal Model for Success: Companion Workbook to Richard J. Maybury's Uncle Eric Talks about Personal, Career, & Financial Security. Daniels, Kathryn, ed. 2004. (Bluestocking Guide Ser.). (ENG.). 47p. (YA). pap. 10.95 (978-0-942617-39-9(8)) Bluestocking Pr.

PERSONALITY—FICTION

Alafaci, Marie. Zelda's Big Adventure. McG, Shane, illus. 2017. (ENG.). 32p. (J). (gr. -1-3). 16.99 (978-1-328-66081-7(8), 1667182, Clarion Bks.) HarperCollins Pubs.

Bowen, Fred. The Final Cut, 1 vol. rev. ed. 2009. (Fred Bowen Sports Story Ser.: 8). (Illus.). 103p. (J). (gr. 2-6). pap. 6.99 (978-1-56145-510-2(5)) Peachtree Publishing Co. Inc.

—Soccer Team Upset, 1 vol. 2009. (Fred Bowen Sports Story Ser.: 10). 128p. (J). (gr. 2-6). pap. 6.99 (978-1-56145-495-2(8)) Peachtree Publishing Co. Inc.

—T. J. 's Secret Pitch, 1 vol. rev. ed. 2009. (Fred Bowen Sports Story Ser.: 2). (Illus.). 96p. (J). (gr. 2-6). pap. 6.95 (978-1-56145-504-1(0)) Peachtree Publishing Co. Inc.

Crouch, Cheryl. Troo Makes a Big Splash, 1 vol. Zimmer, Kevin, illus. 2011. (I Can Read! / Rainforest Friends Ser.). (ENG.). 32p. (J). (gr. -1-2). pap. 4.99 (978-0-310-71810-9(4)) Zonderkidz.

Dane Rehagen. How Katie Got Her Meow. 2010. 42p. pap. 15.00 (978-1-4251-8664-7(5)) Trafford Publishing.

Delessert, Etienne. Spartacus the Spider. 2010. (ENG., Illus.). 32p. (J). (gr. 1-3). 17.95 (978-1-56846-213-4(1), 22062, Creative Editions) Creative Co., The.

Denise, Susan Denise. The Little Lazy Lizard. 2008. 16p. pap. 24.95 (978-1-60474-502-3(9)) America Star Bks.

Errico, Daniel. The Journey of the Noble Gnarble. Turrill, Tiffany, illus. 2013. (ENG.). 32p. (J). (gr. -1-k). 16.95 (978-1-62087-732-6(5), 620732, Sky Pony Pr.) Skyhorse Publishing Co., Inc.

Fortson, Sarah Glenn. This Cowgirl Ain't Kiddin' about the Potty. Cox, Russ, illus. 2019. (ENG.). 40p. (J). 16.99 (978-1-4413-3165-6(4), 2a1167a3-f124-440f-ad6c-6d68081d6fc8) Peter Pauper Pr. Inc.

Gutman, Dan. The Million Dollar Strike. 2006. 176p. (J). (gr. 3-7). 13.65 (978-0-7569-7023-9(7)) Perfection Learning Corp.

Halvorson, Marilyn. Blue Moon. 2004. (Orca Soundings Ser.). 109p. (gr. 4-7). 19.95 (978-0-7569-4285-4(3)) Perfection Learning Corp.

Hart, Christine. Best Laid Plans, 1 vol. 2009. (Lorimer SideStreets Ser.). (ENG.). 152p. (YA). (gr. 9-12). 8.99 (978-1-55277-446-5(5), 5f4ae532-66f5-4cdc-b9fc-5239acc5b7b6); 26.19 (978-1-55277-447-2(3), 447) James Lorimer & Co. Ltd., Pubs. CAN. Dist: Lerner Publishing Group, Children's Plus, Inc.

Keller, Elinoar & Peleg Segal, Naama. Just Like I Wanted. Gordon-Noy, Aya, illus. 2015. (ENG.). 26p. (J). 17.00 (978-0-8028-5453-7(2), Eerdmans Bks For Young Readers) Eerdmans, William B. Publishing Co.

Kimmel, Elizabeth Cody. The Reinvention of Moxie Roosevelt. (ENG.). (J). 2011. 256p. (gr. 5-18). 6.99 (978-0-14-241870-3(6), Puffin Books) 2010. 208p. (gr. 6-8). 21.19 (978-0-8037-3303-9(8)) Penguin Young Readers Group.

Law, Felicia. Benjamin the Bear: A Tale of Selfishness, 1 vol. Spoor, Mike, illus. 2010. (Animal Fair Values Ser.). (ENG.). 32p. (J). (gr. 2-2). pap. 11.55 (978-1-60754-915-4(8), 7b5f4636-a441-4563-8151-76252a2ee4d2); lib. bdg. 27.27 (978-1-60754-905-5(0), 53ce3a90-a02e-4799-adfb-c91c07e9314c) Rosen Publishing Group, Inc., The. (Windmill Bks.).

Legrand, Claire. The Cavendish Home for Boys & Girls. Watts, Sarah, illus. 2012. (ENG.). 352p. (J). (gr. 5). 17.99 (978-1-4424-4291-7(3), Simon & Schuster Bks. For Young Readers) Simon & Schuster Bks. For Young Readers.

Levine, Rhoda. Three Ladies Beside the Sea. Gorey, Edward, illus. 2010. (ENG.). 40p. (J). (gr. k-4). 17.95 (978-1-59017-354-1(6), NYR Children's Collection) New York Review of Bks., Inc., The.

Lewis-Cook, Ashley. Beautiful Me! 2012. (Illus.). 16p. pap. 15.99 (978-1-4772-1291-2(4)) AuthorHouse.

Parker, David & Lyon, Tammie. ¡Soy Optimista! Lyon, Tammie, illus. 2011. (SPA., Illus.). (J). (978-0-545-27356-5(0)) Scholastic, Inc.

Paul, Chris. Long Shot: Never Too Small to Dream Big. Morrison, Frank, illus. 2009. (ENG.). 32p. (J). (gr. -1-3). 19.99 (978-1-4169-5079-0(6), Simon & Schuster Bks. For Young Readers) Simon & Schuster Bks. For Young Readers.

Potter, Ellen. Olivia Kidney Secret Beneath City. 2009. (ENG.). 336p. (J). (gr. 3-7). 9.99 (978-0-14-241263-3(5), Puffin Books) Penguin Young Readers Group.

Robberecht, Thierry. Sam's New Friend. Goossens, Philippe, illus. 2008. (ENG.). 32p. (J). (gr. -1-3). 12.00 (978-0-618-91448-7(X), 1014548, Clarion Bks.) HarperCollins Pubs.

Rodgers, Mary. Freaky Friday. 2003. (ENG.). 176p. (J). (gr. 5-18). pap. 7.99 (978-0-06-057010-1(5), HarperCollins) HarperCollins Pubs.

—Freaky Friday. 2003. (J). (gr. 7-12). 17.20 (978-0-613-68424-8(9)) Turtleback.

Rodgers, Mary, ed. Freaky Friday. 145p. (J). (gr. 4-6). pap. 4.95 (978-0-8072-1390-2(X), Listening Library) Random Hse. Audio Publishing Group.

Rodriguez, Alex. Out of the Ballpark. Morrison, Frank, illus. 2012. (ENG.). 32p. (J). (gr. -1-3). pap. 8.99 (978-0-06-115196-5(3), HarperCollins) HarperCollins Pubs.

Salm, Arthur. Anyway* *a Story about Me with 138 Footnotes, 27 Exaggerations, & 1 Plate of Spaghetti. 2013. (ENG., Illus.). 192p. (J). (gr. 3-7). pap. 7.99 (978-1-4424-2931-4(3), Simon & Schuster Bks. For Young Readers) Simon & Schuster Bks. For Young Readers.

Schirmer, Jodi L. Dear Deer Friend. 2008. 24p. pap. 11.95 (978-1-4327-2540-2(8)) Outskirts Pr., Inc.

Scraper, Katherine. Remember the Rules. 2006. (Early Explorers Ser.). (J). pap. (978-1-4108-6031-6(0)) Benchmark Education Co.

Skye, Obert. Choke. 2010. (Pillage Ser.: 2). (ENG., Illus.). 336p. (YA). (gr. 7). 17.99 (978-1-60641-653-2(7), 5040458, Shadow Mountain) Shadow Mountain Publishing.

Tarter, Mildred. Rexis! Where Are You! 2010. 24p. pap. 16.49 (978-1-4389-6874-2(4)) AuthorHouse.

Wilhelm, Hans. Pelican & Pelican't. 2007. (Illus.). (J). (978-0-545-00910-2(3)) Scholastic, Inc.

Zackery, Gary D. & Borgstedt, John. Stephen. 2011. 108p. 22.45 (978-1-4567-2712-3(5)); pap. 16.00 (978-1-4567-2711-6(7)) AuthorHouse.

PERSONNEL MANAGEMENT—VOCATIONAL GUIDANCE

Freedman, Jeri. Careers in Human Resources, 1 vol. 2013. (Essential Careers Ser.). (ENG.). 80p. (YA). (gr. 6-6). 37.47 (978-1-4777-1791-2(9), 7d8275a0-bbee-4a20-8260-3bc6464a30e0) Rosen Publishing Group, Inc., The.

PERSONNEL SERVICE IN EDUCATION

see Educational Counseling

PERSPECTIVE

see also Drawing

Burmeister, AimeeLeigh. Perspective for Kids Volume One Introduction to Perspective. 2010. (ENG.). 40p. pap. 26.00 (978-0-557-68821-0(3)) Lulu Pr., Inc.

Colins, Luke. Draw Funny 3-D Pictures! 24p. (J). 2020. pap. (978-1-62310-134-3(4)) 2019. (ENG.). (gr. 2-4). pap. 9.99 (978-1-64466-072-0(5), 13005, Hi Jinx) Black Rabbit Bks.

Levy, Janey. Renaissance Paintings: Using Perspective to Represent Three-Dimensional Objects, 1 vol. (Math for the REAL World Ser.). 32p. 2009. (ENG., Illus.). (gr. 5-6). pap. 10.00 (978-1-4042-5115-1(4), 4edb657e-f25d-4c96-94d1-fcb8fd7410a1) 2009. (gr. 4-5). 47.90 (978-1-60851-416-8(1), PowerKids Pr.) 2004. (ENG., Illus.). (J). (gr. 5-6). lib. bdg. 28.93 (978-1-4042-2926-6(4), d74fba5b-a79f-4ac2-b2b6-0fe322b4823d, PowerKids Pr.) Rosen Publishing Group, Inc., The.

PERSUASION (RHETORIC)

see Public Speaking; Rhetoric

PERU

Annabelle Alpaca Travels to Peru. 2005. (J). per. 7.99 (978-0-9746409-1-4(3)) O'Neill, Jan.

Brewer, Paul. The Lima Embassy Siege & Latin American Terrorists, 1 vol. 2005. (Terrorism in Today's World Ser.). (ENG., Illus.). 48p. (gr. 5-8). pap. 15.05 (978-0-8368-6564-6(2), 55ff82aa-c50c-43fd-b75a-54f3ff449287); lib. bdg. 33.67 (978-0-8368-6557-8(X), 225651b4-88d9-4146-9786-36c6f8c709ab) Stevens, Gareth Publishing LLLP. (Gareth Stevens Secondary Library).

Crespi, Jess. Exploring Peru with the Five Themes of Geography. (Library of the Western Hemisphere Ser.). 24p. 2009. (gr. 4-4). 42.50 (978-1-60853-929-1(6), PowerKids Pr.) 2004. (ENG., Illus.). (gr. 3-4). pap. 8.25 (978-0-8239-4636-5(3), 54790ebe-5533-4844-811b-8269ea79b80a) Rosen Publishing Group, Inc., The.

De Capua, Sarah. Peru, 1 vol. 2006. (Discovering Cultures Ser.). (ENG.). 48p. (gr. 3-4). 31.21 (978-0-7614-1796-5(6), 313377dc-22e2-4efd-b78e-55e36abaf59c) Cavendish Square Publishing LLC.

Erlic, Lily. Peru. 2018. (Illus.). 32p. (J). (978-1-4896-7512-5(4), AV2 by Weigl) Weigl Pubs., Inc.

Fajardo, Sara Andrea. In a Peruvian City, 1 vol. 2003. (Child's Day Ser.). (ENG., Illus.). 32p. (gr. 2-2). 32.64 (978-0-7614-1408-7(8), 0e7d0db9-65f3-4035-bfba-1b0c8fa2eb67) Cavendish Square Publishing LLC.

Falconer, Kieran & Quek, Lynette. Peru, 1 vol. 2nd rev. ed. 2007. (Cultures of the World (Second Edition)(r) Ser.). (ENG., Illus.). 144p. (gr. 5-5). lib. bdg. 49.79 (978-0-7614-2068-2(1), 13434fe9-7cfe-45ec-9de2-834ec5e9804f) Cavendish Square Publishing LLC.

Falconer, Kieran, et al. Peru, 1 vol. 3rd rev. ed. 2016. (Cultures of the World (Third Edition)(r) Ser.). (ENG., Illus.). 144p. (gr. 5-5). lib. bdg. 48.79 (978-1-5026-1843-6(5), 4e39c7bb-e2c2-4db6-baef-e617beaac19c) Cavendish Square Publishing LLC.

Fazzi, Cindy. How to Draw Peru's Sights & Symbols. 2009. (Kid's Guide to Drawing the Countries of the World Ser.). 48p. (gr. 4-4). 53.00 (978-1-61511-121-3(2), PowerKids Pr.) Rosen Publishing Group, Inc., The.

Johnson, Robin & Kalman, Bobbie. Spotlight on Peru, 1 vol. 2008. (Spotlight on my Country Ser.). (ENG., Illus.). 32p. (J). (gr. 3-7). pap. (978-0-7787-3482-6(X)) Crabtree Publishing Co.

Klepeis, Alicia Z. Peru. 2019. (Country Profiles Ser.). (ENG., Illus.). 32p. (J). (gr. 3-8). lib. bdg. 27.95 (978-1-62617-962-2(X), Blastoff! Discovery) Bellwether Media.

Levy, Janey. 20 Fun Facts about Machu Picchu, 1 vol., Vol. 1. 2013. (Fun Fact File: World Wonders! Ser.). (ENG.). 32p. (J). (gr. 2-3). 27.93 (978-1-4824-0452-4(4), 5d192fa9-9a4e-425a-9e29-757dd21c731f); pap. 11.50 (978-1-4824-0455-5(9), fc34126f-d6a2-4f29-b5d8-02f4bdced4af) Stevens, Gareth Publishing LLLP.

Lewin, Ted. Lost City: The Discovery of Machu Picchu. Lewin, Ted, illus. 2012. (ENG., Illus.). 48p. (J). (gr. 2-5). pap. 8.99 (978-0-14-242580-0(X), Puffin Books) Penguin Young Readers Group.

Mann, Elizabeth. Machu Picchu: The Story of the Amazing Inkas & Their City in the Clouds. Crehore, Amy, illus. 2006. (Wonders of the World Book Ser.). (ENG.). 48p. (J). (gr. 4-8). pap. 12.95 (978-1-931414-10-4(6), 685c9027-b79d-4729-9ed1-9a351327e933) Mikaya Pr.

Markovics, Joyce L. Peru. 2016. (Countries We Come From Ser.). (ENG., Illus.). 32p. (J). (gr. -1-3). 28.50 (978-1-944102-73-9(6)) Bearport Publishing Co., Inc.

Márquez, Herón. Peru in Pictures. 2nd rev. expurg. ed. 2004. (Visual Geography Series, Second Ser.). (ENG., Illus.). 80p. (gr. 5-12). 31.93 *(978-0-8225-1999-7(2))* Lerner Publishing Group.

Raum, Elizabeth. Machu Picchu. 2014. (Ancient Wonders Ser.). (ENG., Illus.). 32p. (J). (gr. 2-5). 28.50 *(978-1-60753-468-6(1)*, 15924) Amicus.

Sheen, Barbara. Foods of Peru, 1 vol. 2010. (Taste of Culture Ser.). (ENG.). 64p. (gr. 3-6). lib. bdg. 36.83 *(978-0-7377-5346-2(3)*, f318cdf1-91ce-403b-9f33-4c240b618d69, KidHaven Publishing) Greenhaven Publishing LLC.

Shields, Charles J. Peru. (South America Today Ser.). 64p. 2009. (Illus.). (J). (gr. 4-7). 21.95 *(978-1-4222-0639-3(4))* 2007. (YA). (gr. 7-18). pap. 9.95 *(978-1-4222-0706-2(4))* Mason Crest.

Weakland, Mark. Scooby-Doo! & the Ruins of Machu Picchu: The Hidden City Howler. Brizuela, Dario, illus. 2018. (Unearthing Ancient Civilizations with Scooby-Doo! Ser.). (ENG.). 32p. (J). (gr. 3-6). lib. bdg. 27.99 *(978-1-5157-7514-0(3)*, 135894, Capstone Pr.) Capstone.

PERU—ANTIQUITIES

Croy, Anita. Who Built Machu Picchu?, 1 vol. 2017. (Mysteries in History: Solving the Mysteries of the Past Ser.). (ENG.). 48p. (gr. 5-5). lib. bdg. 33.07 *(978-1-5026-2796-4(5)*, bcab9f74-ea01-483a-8f0d-1789eb0668cf) Cavendish Square Publishing LLC.

Hansen, Grace. Machu Picchu. 2017. (World Wonders Ser.). (ENG., Illus.). 24p. (J). (gr. -1-2). lib. bdg. 32.79 *(978-1-5321-0442-8(1)*, 26568, Abdo Kids) ABDO Publishing Co.

Leaf, Christina. Machu Picchu: The Lost Civilization. 2017. (Abandoned Places Ser.). (ENG., Illus.). 24p. (J). (gr. 3-7). lib. bdg. 26.95 *(978-1-62617-696-6(5)*, Torque Bks.) Bellwether Media.

Nagelhout, Ryan. Ancient Inca Technology, 1 vol. 2016. (Spotlight on the Maya, Aztec, & Inca Civilizations Ser.). (ENG., Illus.). 32p. (J). (gr. 4-6). pap. 12.75 *(978-1-4994-1953-5(8)*, 2614cf0c-21f8-46a4-8e76-675d0d814904, PowerKids Pr.) Rosen Publishing Group, Inc., The.

Peterson, Sheryl. Machu Picchu. 2005. (Ancient Wonders of the World Ser.). (Illus.). 32p. (J). (gr. 4-7). lib. bdg. 18.95 *(978-1-58341-357-9(X)*, Creative Education) Creative Co., The.

Regas, Ricard & Cañagueral, Albert. The Secrets of Ancient Ritual Sites: The Citadel of Machu Picchu & Stonehenge, 1 vol. 2017. (Secrets of History Ser.). (ENG.). 96p. (YA). (gr. 8-8). pap. 20.99 *(978-1-5026-3443-6(0)*, e496d876-6f02-4f14-b587-a73d1a5dda7d); lib. bdg. 44.50 *(978-1-5026-3274-6(8)*, 645aa15a-981b-44de-8508-e29d91844390) Cavendish Square Publishing LLC.

Richardson, G. Machu Picchu. 2018. (Structural Wonders of the World Ser.). (ENG.). 24p. (J). (gr. 2-5). lib. bdg. 28.55 *(978-1-4896-8169-0(8)*, AV2 by Weigl) Weigl Pubs., Inc.

Richardson, Gillian & Kissock, Heather. Machu Picchu. 2012. (J). 27.13 *(978-1-61913-250-4(8))*; pap. 12.95 *(978-1-61913-256-6(7))* Weigl Pubs., Inc.

Riggs, Kate. Machu Picchu. 2009. (Places of Old Ser.). 24p. (J). (gr. 1-5). lib. bdg. 24.25 *(978-1-58341-709-6(5)*, Creative Education) Creative Co., The.

Ryback, Carol. The Lost City. 2020. (J). pap. *(978-1-64290-722-3(7))* Teacher Created Materials, Inc.

Stine, Megan & Who HQ. Where Is Machu Picchu? O'Brien, John, illus. 2018. (Where Is? Ser.). 112p. (J). (gr. 3-7). 7.99 *(978-0-515-15961-5(1)*, Penguin Workshop) Penguin Young Readers Group.

PERU—FICTION

Anderson, Geraldine. Bev's Amazing Adventures Book Ii: The Girl from Peru. 2013. 20p. pap. 24.95 *(978-1-62709-129-9(7))* America Star Bks.

Anthony, Horowitz. Evil Star. 2007. (Gatekeepers Ser.: 2). 318p. lib. bdg. 19.65 *(978-1-4177-7663-4(3))* Turtleback.

Booher, Brock. The Charity Chip. 2015. pap. 16.99 *(978-1-4621-1669-0(8))* Cedar Fort, Inc./CFI Distribution.

Brown, Monica. Lola Levine & the Vacation Dream. 2017. (Lola Levine Ser.: 5). (J). lib. bdg. 16.00 *(978-0-606-40222-4(5))* Turtleback.

Carson, John E. & Carson, Marlene R. The Wire Forest of Peru. 2007. (Ramblin' Rose Ser.). 205p. (YA). (gr. 8-12). per. 8.99 *(978-0-9776043-9-5(X))* Aspirations Media, Inc.

Church, Anna. Hug-A-Bug Travels to Peru. Church, Anna & Taylor, Nicole, illus. 2013. 44p. pap. 12.00 *(978-0-9831449-4-6(X))* Mighty Lion Ventures.

Cosgrove, Matt. A Stack of Alpacas. Cosgrove, Matt, illus. 2020.Tr. of Stack of Alpacas. (ENG., Illus.). 24p. (J). (gr. -1-k). 14.99 *(978-1-338-71622-1(0)*, Scholastic Pr.) Scholastic, Inc.

Diaz, Katacha. Carolina's Gift: A Story of Peru. Landolt, Gredna, illus. 2003. (ENG.). 32p. (J). (gr. k-3). 15.95 *(978-1-56899-695-0(0)*, B8005) Soundprints.

Eby, Wes. Jungle Jeopardy. 2006. 56p. 7.75 *(978-0-8341-2228-4(6))* Beacon Hill Pr. of Kansas City.

Evans, Richard Paul. Michael Vey 2: Rise of the Elgen. (Michael Vey Ser.: 2). (ENG., Illus.). 352p. (YA). (gr. 7). 2013. pap. 12.99 *(978-1-4424-7510-6(2))* 2012. 19.99 *(978-1-4424-5414-9(8))* Simon Pulse/Mercury Ink. (Simon Pulse/Mercury Ink).

Finnish, V. K. The Society's Traitor. Oshida, Tim, illus. 2012. (The Discoveries of Arthur Grey ser.: 1). (ENG.). 298p. (J). (gr. 4-8). 27.99 *(978-0-9852202-0-4(1))* Panama Hat Publishing, Ltd.

Garcia, Randolph. The Steamer Trunk Adventures #2: The Ghosts of Machu Picchu. 2006. (ENG.). 88p. per. 16.95 *(978-1-4241-1843-4(3))* PublishAmerica, Inc.

Hamilton, Martha & Weiss, Mitch. The Stolen Smell. Wrenn, Tom, illus. 2007. (Story Cove Ser.). (ENG.). 32p. (J). (gr. -1-3). 4.95 *(978-0-87483-838-1(X))* August Hse. Pubs., Inc.

Jensen, Kathryn. Splash! 2012. 194p. 29.95 *(978-1-4489-6574-8(8))* America Star Bks.

Kain, Wallace M. The Red Column: A Young Woman's Capture, Imprisonment & Escape in the Amazon Jungle. 2006. (YA). per. 12.95 *(978-0-9742148-1-8(7))* Inkberry Pr.

Lacey, Josh. Island of Thieves. 2013. (ENG.). 240p. (J). (gr. 5-7). pap. 7.99 *(978-0-544-10485-3(4)*, 1540794, Clarion Bks.) HarperCollins Pubs.

Martinez-Neal, Juana. Zonia's Rain Forest. Martinez-Neal, Juana, illus. 2021. (ENG.). 40p. (J). (gr. -1-3). 17.99 *(978-1-5362-0845-0(0))* Candlewick Pr.

mercedes cecilia. Kusikiy A Child from Taquile, Peru. mercedes cecilia & mercedes cecilia, illus. 2011. (Illus.). (J). pap. 24.99 *(978-0-9844079-9-6(5))* Keepers of Wisdom and Peace Bks.

Mitchell, Sara. Carlos & Diego: A Tale from Peru, 1 vol. Vasquez, Natalia, illus. 2016. (ENG.). 24p. (J). pap. 9.95 *(978-1-927244-57-9(9))* Flying Start Bks. NZL. Dist: Flying Start Bks.

—Carlos & Diego (Big Book Edition) A Tale from Peru, 1 vol. Vasquez, Natalia, illus. 2016. (ENG.). 24p. (J). pap. *(978-1-927244-67-8(6))* Flying Start Bks.

Oshida, Tim, illus. The Society's Traitor. 2nd ed. 2015. (The Discoveries of Arthur Grey ser.: 1). (ENG.). 304p. (J). (gr. 4-8). 27.99 *(978-1-943317-00-4(3))* Panama Hat Publishing, Ltd.

Packard, Albert. Cavern of Babel. Boyles, Shawn, illus. 2006. (J). per. 14.95 *(978-0-9790652-0-0(8))* Diamond Triple C Ranch.

Paris, Harper. The Mystery Across the Secret Bridge. Calo, Marcos, illus. 2015. (Greetings from Somewhere Ser.: 7). (ENG.). 128p. (J). (gr. k-4). pap. 6.99 *(978-1-4814-2367-0(3)*, Little Simon) Little Simon.

Patterson, James. Treasure Hunters: Quest for the City of Gold. Neufeld, Juliana, illus. 2018. (Treasure Hunters Ser.: 5). (ENG.). 384p. (J). (gr. 3-7). 14.99 *(978-0-316-34955-0(0)*, Jimmy Patterson) Little Brown & Co.

Rosenberg, Michael. Chilly Goes to Peru. 2018. (ENG., Illus.). 32p. (J). (gr. k-6). pap. 13.95 *(978-1-948260-06-0(9))* Strategic Book Publishing & Rights Agency (SBPRA).

Russell, Elaine. Martin Mcmillan & the Lost Inca City. Cornell du Houx, Emily M. D., illus. 2005. 128p. (gr. 5-18). pap. 10.00 *(978-1-882190-86-7(6))* Solon Ctr. for Research & Publishing.

Simpson, Joe & Bembibre, Cecilia. Tocando el Vacío, 1 vol. 2014. (SPA., Illus.). 64p. pap., stu. ed. 15.00 incl. audio compact disk *(978-84-9848-133-4(3))* Edinumen, Editorial ESP. Dist: Cambridge Univ. Pr.

VanArsdale, Anthony, illus. The Khipu & the Final Key. 2017. (Boxcar Children Great Adventure Ser.: 5). (ENG.). 144p. (J). (gr. 2-5). 12.99 *(978-0-8075-0681-3(8)*, 119189763); 6.99 *(978-0-8075-0682-0(6)*, 119189763) Random Hse. Children's Bks. (Random Hse. Bks. for Young Readers).

PERU—HISTORY

Baicker, Karen. Conquistador: Francisco Pizarro Ravages the Inca Empire. 2011. (J). pap. *(978-0-545-32940-8(X))* Scholastic, Inc.

Benge, Janet & Benge, Geoff. Klaus-Dieter John: Hope in the Land of the Incas. 2014. (Illus.). 224p. (J). pap. 11.99 *(978-1-57658-755-3(X))* YWAM Publishing.

Burgan, Michael. Peru (Enchantment of the World) (Library Edition) 2018. (Enchantment of the World. Second Ser.). (ENG., Illus.). 144p. (J). (gr. 5-9). lib. bdg. 40.00 *(978-0-531-23591-1(2)*, Children's Pr.) Scholastic Library Publishing.

Burling, Alexis. The Destruction of the Inca Civilization, 1 vol. 2017. (Bearing Witness: Genocide & Ethnic Cleansing Ser.). (ENG.). 64p. (J). (gr. 6-6). 36.13 *(978-1-5081-7738-8(4)*, e5aab7b6-ef29-4c4b-8ea4-d984f3683002); pap. 13.95 *(978-1-5081-7869-9(0)*, c6322d3a-b131-4b41-803e-c7e3897f0e25) Rosen Publishing Group, Inc., The. (Rosen Young Adult).

Clapper, Nikki Bruno. Let's Look at Peru. 2018. (Let's Look at Countries Ser.). (ENG., Illus.). 24p. (J). (gr. -1-2). lib. bdg. 27.32 *(978-1-5157-9915-3(8)*, 136921, Capstone Pr.) Capstone.

DiConsiglio, John. Francisco Pizarro: Destroyer of the Inca Empire. 2008. (Wicked History Ser.). (ENG., Illus.). 128p. (J). 31.00 *(978-0-531-18551-3(6)*, Watts, Franklin) Scholastic Library Publishing.

Hessel-Mial, Michael. How STEM Built the Incan Empire, 1 vol. 2019. (How STEM Built Empires Ser.). (ENG.). 80p. (gr. 7-7). pap. 16.30 *(978-1-7253-4146-3(8)*, 8e00ab78-4c0f-4950-9a94-e3ae4af76b2e) Rosen Publishing Group, Inc., The.

Hinman, Bonnie. We Visit Peru. 2010. (Your Land & My Land Ser.). (Illus.). 64p. (J). (gr. 3-6). lib. bdg. 33.95 *(978-1-58415-886-8(7))* Mitchell Lane Pubs.

Hoogenboom, Lynn. Francisco Pizarro. 2009. (Primary Source Library of Famous Explorers Ser.). 24p. (gr. 4-4). 42.50 *(978-1-60854-121-8(5)*, PowerKids Pr.) Rosen Publishing Group, Inc., The.

—Francisco Pizarro: A Primary Source Biography, 1 vol. 2005. (Primary Source Library of Famous Explorers Ser.). (ENG., Illus.). 24p. (YA). (gr. 4-4). lib. bdg. 26.27 *(978-1-4042-3038-5(6)*, 95430adb-f0c1-40d6-92c8-2deb73222514) Rosen Publishing Group, Inc., The.

Hoyle, R. L. Peru. (SPA., Illus.). 260p. pap. 39.95 *(978-84-261-1060-0(0)*, JV800) Juventud, Editorial ESP. Dist: Continental Bk. Co., Inc.

Johnson, Robin & Kalman, Bobbie. Conoce Perú. 2009. (SPA.). 32p. (J). *(978-0-7787-8194-3(1))*; (gr. 2-5). pap. *(978-0-7787-8214-8(X))* Crabtree Publishing Co.

Kaspar, Anna. A Look at Pluto & Other Dwarf Planets, 1 vol. 2007. (Astronomy Now! Ser.). (ENG., Illus.). 24p. (YA). (gr. 2-3). lib. bdg. 26.27 *(978-1-4042-3824-4(7)*, 1cf8028f-d4c3-4751-9b44-778c3cd11f24) Rosen Publishing Group, Inc., The.

Leaf, Christina. Machu Picchu: The Lost Civilization. 2017. (Abandoned Places Ser.). (ENG., Illus.). 24p. (J). (gr. 3-7). lib. bdg. 26.95 *(978-1-62617-696-6(5)*, Torque Bks.) Bellwether Media.

Markovics, Joyce L. Perú. 2019. (Los Países de Donde Venimos/Countries We Come From Ser.). (SPA., Illus.). 32p. (J). (gr. k-3). 19.95 *(978-1-64280-232-0(8))* Bearport Publishing Co., Inc.

Meinking, Mary. Machu Picchu, 1 vol. 2014. (Digging up the Past Ser.). (ENG., Illus.). 112p. (YA). (gr. 6-12). lib. bdg. 41.36 *(978-1-62403-234-9(6)*, 1300, Essential Library) ABDO Publishing Co.

Morlock, Theresa. Ancient Inca Geography, 1 vol. 2016. (Spotlight on the Maya, Aztec, & Inca Civilizations Ser.). (ENG.). 32p. (J). (gr. 4-6). pap. 12.75 *(978-1-4994-1943-6(0)*, fc9a90ca-8182-45f3-a779-b64a90ea6d20, PowerKids Pr.) Rosen Publishing Group, Inc., The.

National Geographic Learning. Reading Expeditions (Social Studies: Civilizations Past to Present): Peru. 2007. (Nonfiction Reading & Writing Workshops Ser.). (ENG., Illus.). 24p. (J). pap. 15.95 *(978-0-7922-4538-4(5))* CENGAGE Learning.

Nussbaum, Ben. Inka Terraces. rev. ed. 2018. (Smithsonian: Informational Text Ser.). (ENG., Illus.). 32p. (J). (gr. 4-8). pap. 11.99 *(978-1-4938-6710-3(5))* Teacher Created Materials, Inc.

O'Brien, Cynthia. Explore with Francisco Pizarro. 2015. (Travel with the Great Explorers Ser.). (ENG., Illus.). 32p. (J). (gr. 4-5). *(978-0-7787-1700-3(3))* Crabtree Publishing Co.

Owings, Lisa. Peru. 2011. (Exploring Countries Ser.). (ENG., Illus.). 32p. (J). (gr. 3-7). lib. bdg. 27.95 *(978-1-60014-621-3(X))* Bellwether Media.

Ramen, Fred. Francisco Pizarro: The Exploration of Peru & the Conquest of the Inca. 2009. (Library of Explorers & Exploration Ser.). 112p. (gr. 5-8). 66.50 *(978-1-60853-603-0(3)*, Rosen Reference) Rosen Publishing Group, Inc., The.

Schmidt, Gary D. Martin de Porres: The Rose in the Desert. Diaz, David, illus. 2012. (ENG.). 32p. (J). (gr. 1-4). lib. bdg. 19.99 *(978-0-547-61218-8(4)*, 1464622, Clarion Bks.) HarperCollins Pubs.

Shields, Charles J. Peru, Vol. 13. Henderson, James D., ed. 2015. (Discovering South America: History, Politics, & Culture Ser.). (Illus.). 64p. (J). (gr. 7). lib. bdg. 22.95 *(978-1-4222-3302-3(2))* Mason Crest.

Sonneborn, Liz. Pizarro: Conqueror of the Mighty Incas, 1 vol. 2009. (Great Explorers of the World Ser.). (ENG., Illus.). 112p. (gr. 6-7). 35.93 *(978-1-59845-128-3(6)*, ce5cbabd-8cf7-41e3-9f9d-207cc7f6e5da) Enslow Publishing, LLC.

Steele, Philip. Step into the Inca World. 2006. (ENG., Illus.). 64p. (J). (gr. 4-7). pap. 6.99 *(978-1-84476-304-7(8))* Anness Publishing GBR. Dist: National Bk. Network.

Thomas, Emma. The Inca Tomb. 2011. (History Detectives Ser.). (ENG.). 32p. (J). (gr. 4-7). spiral bd. 9.95 *(978-1-84898-187-4(2)*, TickTock Books) Octopus Publishing Group GBR. Dist: Independent Pubs. Group.

Wood, Alix. Uncovering the Culture of Ancient Peru, 1 vol., 1. 2015. (Archaeology & Ancient Cultures Ser.). (ENG.). 32p. (J). (gr. 5-6). pap. 11.00 *(978-1-5081-4667-4(5)*, 78b283ed-340a-4b52-937c-f87ceba62979, PowerKids Pr.) Rosen Publishing Group, Inc., The.

World Book, Inc. Staff, contrib. by. The Enduring Mystery of Machu Picchu. 2015. (Illus.). 48p. (J). *(978-0-7166-2675-6(6))* World Bk., Inc.

—The Mysteries in the Nazca Desert. 2015. (Illus.). 48p. (J). *(978-0-7166-2676-3(4))* World Bk., Inc.

Zronik, John Paul & Zronik, John. Francisco Pizarro: Journeys Through Peru & South America, 1 vol. 2005. (In the Footsteps of Explorers Ser.). (ENG., Illus.). 32p. (J). (gr. -1-9). pap. *(978-0-7787-2447-6(6))* Crabtree Publishing Co.

PESTICIDE POLLUTION

see Pesticides—Environmental Aspects

PESTICIDES—ENVIRONMENTAL ASPECTS

Hile, Lori. Rachel Carson: Environmental Pioneer, 1 vol. 2014. (Women in Conservation Ser.). (ENG., Illus.). 48p. (J). (gr. 3-6). pap. 8.99 *(978-1-4846-0476-2(8)*, 126607, Heinemann) Capstone.

Landau, Jennifer. Pesticides & Your Body, 1 vol. 2012. (Incredibly Disgusting Environments Ser.). (ENG., Illus.). 48p. (J). (gr. 5-8). pap. 12.75 *(978-1-4488-8422-3(5)*, 53235dcc-8c20-4626-8c78-23b270fd51d5); lib. bdg. 34.47 *(978-1-4488-8413-1(6)*, 995c8df4-862c-45dc-a419-6ceaf8fccb19) Rosen Publishing Group, Inc., The. (Rosen Reference).

PESTS

see Fungi; Insect Pests; Parasites; Zoology, Economic

PETER, THE APOSTLE, SAINT

Bahamon, Claire. Peter Fished the Springs of Galilee. Sampson, Anne, ed. Cinelli, Lisa, illus. 2015. (ENG.). 32p. (J). pap. 7.99 *(978-0-9961139-0-8(8))* Donkey's Quest Pr.

Brennan, Gerald T. The Man Who Never Died: The Life & Adventures of St. Peter, the First Pope. 2005. (Illus.). 87p. (J). (gr. 3-7). per. 11.95 *(978-1-933184-09-8(4))* Sophia Institute Pr.

Lumsden, Colin, illus. Story of Peter. 2003. (Bible Colour & Learn Ser.). 32p. pap. 2.50 *(978-1-903087-45-9(7))* DayOne Pubns. GBR. Dist: Send The Light Distribution LLC.

MacKenzie, Carine. Peter: The Apostle. rev. ed. 2014. (Bible Time Ser.). (ENG., Illus.). 32p. (J). (gr. -1-2). pap. 4.50 *(978-1-84550-170-9(5)*, 80c4387a-c27c-44a9-bc5c-ce7ca9509e17) Christian Focus Pubns. GBR. Dist: Baker & Taylor Publisher Services (BTPS).

—Peter: The Fisherman. rev. ed. 2014. (Bible Time Ser.). (ENG., Illus.). 32p. (J). (gr. -1-2). pap. 4.50 *(978-1-84550-171-6(3)*, b3045b02-859c-4e9f-97f5-f5ed34fffd6f) Christian Focus Pubns. GBR. Dist: Baker & Taylor Publisher Services (BTPS).

Moore, Alan & Tavner, Gill. Simon Peter. Donnelly, Karen, illus. 2014. (New Testament Ser.). (ENG.). 64p. pap. 7.95 *(978-1-906230-26-5(9))* Real Reads Ltd. GBR. Dist: Casemate Pubs. & Bk. Distributors, LLC.

Willoughby, R. Peter Goes Feet First! Buckley, Joel, illus. 2004. 64p. pap. *(978-1-85999-766-6(X))* Scripture Union.

—Peter Strides Out. Buckley, Joel, illus. 2004. 64p. pap. *(978-1-84427-022-4(X))* Scripture Union.

PETER PAN (FICTITIOUS CHARACTER)—FICTION

Adams, Jennifer. Peter Pan: A BabyLit(TM) Adventure Primer, 1 vol. Oliver, Alison, illus. 2018. (BabyLit Ser.). 22p. (J). (— 1). bds. 9.99 *(978-1-4236-4860-4(9))* Gibbs Smith, Publisher.

Barrie, J. Peter Pan. 2020. (ENG.). 128p. (J). pap. 19.99 *(978-1-6781-4623-8(4))* Lulu Pr., Inc.

Barrie, J. M. Peter Pan. Leffler, Silke, illus. 2016. (ENG.). 176p. 25.00 *(978-0-7358-4259-5(0))* North-South Bks., Inc.

—Peter Pan. Bedford, Francis Donkin & Rackham, Arthur, illus. 2015. (Word Cloud Classics Ser.). (ENG.). 272p. pap. 14.99 *(978-1-62686-392-7(X)*, Canterbury Classics) Printers Row Publishing Group.

—Peter Pan. Bedford, F. D., illus. 2004. (Modern Library Classics Ser.). 192p. (J). (gr. 3-7). pap. 10.95 *(978-0-8129-7297-9(X)*, Modern Library) Random House Publishing Group.

—Peter Pan. 2013. (Puffin Chalk Ser.). 224p. (J). (gr. 3-7). pap. 7.99 *(978-0-14-750865-2(7)*, Puffin Books) Penguin Young Readers Group.

—Peter Pan. 2018. 224p. (J). (gr. 3). 19.95 *(978-0-241-35992-1(9)*, Puffin) Penguin Bks., Ltd. GBR. Dist: Independent Pubs. Group.

—Peter Pan. 2003. (Aladdin Classics Ser.). (ENG.). 256p. (J). (gr. 3-7). pap. 7.99 *(978-0-689-86691-3(7)*, Aladdin) Simon & Schuster Children's Publishing.

—Peter Pan, 1 vol. Tenney, Shawna J. C., illus. 2010. (Calico Illustrated Classics Ser.: No. 1). (ENG.). 112p. (J). (gr. 2-5). 38.50 *(978-1-60270-710-8(3)*, 3973, Calico Chapter Bks.) ABDO Publishing Co.

—Peter Pan: Or the Boy Who Would Not Grow up - a Fantasy in Five Acts. 2006. (Modern Plays Ser.). (ENG., Illus.). 192p. (gr. 4-7). per. 15.95 *(978-0-413-73550-8(8)*, 900071970, Methuen Drama) Bloomsbury Publishing Plc GBR. Dist: Macmillan.

—Peter Pan: Peter & Wendy & Peter Pan in Kensington Gardens. 2004. (Illus.). 272p. (gr. 12-18). 12.00 *(978-0-14-243793-3(X)*, Penguin Classics) Penguin Publishing Group.

—Peter Pan (MinaLima Edition) (Illustrated with Interactive Elements) MinaLima Ltd., MinaLima, illus. 2015. (ENG.). 256p. 32.50 *(978-0-06-236222-3(4)*, Harper) HarperCollins Pubs.

Barrie, J. M. & Barrie, J. M. Peter Pan. 2009. (Puffin Classics Ser.). (Illus.). 240p. (J). (gr. 5-7). 7.99 *(978-0-14-132257-5(8)*, Puffin Books) Penguin Young Readers Group.

Barrie, James Matthew. The Complete Adventures of Peter Pan Includes: The Little White Bird, Peter Pan in Kensington Gardens(Illustrated) & Peter. Rackham, Arthur & Bedford, F. D., illus. 2013. 326p. *(978-1-78139-361-1(3))* Benediction Classics.

—Peter & Wendy. 2013. (Cambridge Library Collection - Fiction & Poetry Ser.). (ENG., Illus.). 302p. 83.99 *(978-1-108-06034-9(X))* Cambridge Univ. Pr.

—Peter Pan. 2008. 124p. (gr. 5-18). 23.95 *(978-1-60664-889-6(6))*; pap. 10.95 *(978-1-60664-007-4(0))* Aegypan.

—Peter Pan. (SPA.). 191p. 15.95 *(978-84-206-3689-4(4))* Alianza Editorial, S. A. ESP. Dist: Distribooks, Inc.

—Peter Pan. 2005. 112p. per. 6.95 *(978-1-933652-07-8(1))* Bed Bks.

—Peter Pan. Date not set. (C). pap. *(978-0-7593-9877-1(1)*, Cengage Learning) CENGAGE Learning.

—Peter Pan. Cowley, Joy, ed. Jang, Yeong-seon, illus. 2015. (World Classics Ser.). (ENG.). 32p. (gr. k-4). 26.65 *(978-1-925246-19-3(1))*; 7.99 *(978-1-925246-71-1(X))*; 26.65 *(978-1-925246-45-2(0))* ChoiceMaker Pty. Ltd., The AUS. (Big and SMALL). Dist: Lerner Publishing Group.

—Peter Pan. Jang, Yeong-seon, illus. 2015. (World Classics Ser.). (ENG.). 32p. (J). (gr. k-4). 27.99 *(978-1-925186-71-0(7)*, 68033772-4b22-4594-b508-2cc9c61895ea); pap. 7.99 *(978-1-925186-65-9(2)*, 76d77fd9-e2f3-40ca-9ebe-3ef0b02658a5) ChoiceMaker Pty. Ltd., The AUS. (Big and SMALL). Dist: Lerner Publishing Group.

—Peter Pan. 2018. (ENG., Illus.). 140p. (J). (gr. 3-7). pap. 8.89 *(978-1-7271-5851-9(2))* CreateSpace Independent Publishing Platform.

—Peter Pan. 2005. 96p. per. 4.95 *(978-1-4209-2538-8(5))* Digireads.com Publishing.

—Peter Pan. 2006. pap. *(978-1-4065-0949-6(3))* Dodo Pr.

—Peter Pan. 2020. (ENG.). 148p. (J). (gr. 3-7). pap. *(978-1-77426-117-0(0))* East India Publishing Co.

—Peter Pan. 2009. 276p. (gr. 3-7). pap. *(978-1-4068-9291-8(2))* Echo Library.

—Peter Pan. Bustelo, Gabriela, tr. Vicente, Fernando, illus. 2006. (Alfaguara Infantil y Juvenil Ser.). 229p. (J). (gr. 4-7). pap. *(978-970-770-677-4(5))* Ediciones Alfaguara.

—Peter Pan. 2009. (Folio Junior Ser.: Vol. 62893). (FRE.). (J). (gr. 4-7). pap. *(978-2-07-062893-3(0))* Gallimard, Editions.

—Peter Pan. pap. 16.95 *(978-2-07-051627-8(X))* Gallimard, Editions FRA. Dist: Distribooks, Inc.

—Peter Pan. (ENG.). (J). pap. *(978-0-340-71498-0(0))* Hodder & Stoughton.

—Peter Pan. (J). (gr. 3-7). 2020. (ENG.). 170p. pap. 9.87 *(978-1-6542-8283-7(9))* 2019. (ENG.). 338p. pap. 36.99 *(978-1-7068-6567-4(8))* 2019. (ENG.). 336p. pap. 14.99 *(978-1-6996-1397-9(4))* 2019. (ENG.). 450p. pap. 25.99 *(978-1-6967-1742-7(6))* 2019. (ENG.). 336p. pap. 14.99 *(978-1-7018-0827-0(7))* 2019. (ENG.). 450p. pap. 25.99 *(978-1-6947-4628-3(3))* 2019. (ENG.). 336p. pap. 19.99 *(978-1-6907-1235-0(X))* 2019. (ENG.). 286p. pap. 21.99 *(978-1-6933-8515-5(5))* 2019. (ENG.). 220p. pap. 13.99 *(978-1-0898-7279-5(8))* 2019. (GSW.). 130p. pap. 7.00 *(978-1-6872-7104-4(6))* 2019. (ENG.). 460p. pap. 29.99 *(978-1-0895-1508-1(1))* 2019. (ENG.). 220p. pap. 13.99 *(978-1-0830-0549-6(9))* 2019. (ENG.). 336p. pap. 21.99 *(978-1-0825-4857-4(X))* 2019. (ENG.). 288p. pap. 19.99 *(978-1-0799-2247-9(4))* 2019. (ENG.). 286p. pap. 18.99 *(978-1-0792-1332-4(5))* 2019. (ENG.). 220p. pap. 16.99 *(978-1-0774-0822-7(6))* 2019. (ENG.). 460p. pap. 25.99 *(978-1-0997-7224-5(9))* 2019. (ENG.). 286p. pap. 16.99 *(978-1-0988-2863-9(1))* 2019. (ENG.). 450p. pap. 25.99 *(978-1-0968-5311-4(6))* 2019. (ENG.). 290p. pap. 16.99 *(978-1-7965-5860-9(5))* 2019. (ENG.). 88p. pap. 7.80 *(978-1-7951-0633-7(6))* 2018. (ENG., Illus.). 144p. pap. 10.99 *(978-1-7918-8182-5(3))* Independently Published.

—Peter Pan. 2020. (ENG.). 128p. (J). (gr. 3-7). pap. 18.99 *(978-1-6780-0338-8(7))* Lulu Pr., Inc.

—Peter Pan. 2019. (ENG.). 154p. (J). (gr. 3-7). *(978-3-7340-7307-6(3))*; pap. *(978-3-7340-7306-9(5))* Outlook Verlagsgesellschaft mbH.

—Peter Pan. Barrie, James Matthew, ed. Bedford, F. D. & Rackham, Arthur, illus. 2009. (ENG.). 287p. *(978-1-905716-40-1(0)*, Collector's Library, The) Pan Macmillan.

—Peter Pan. 160p. pap. *(978-1-85471-231-8(4))* Penguin Bks., Ltd.

PQR

—Peter Pan. 2013. (Vintage Children's Classics Ser.). (Illus.). 256p. (J). (gr. 4-7). pap. 10.99 *(978-0-09-957304-3(0))* Penguin Random Hse. GBR. Dist: Independent Pubs. Group.
—Peter Pan. (ENG., (J). 2018. Illus.). 166p. (gr. 3-7). 24.37 *(978-1-7317-0454-2(2))* 2018. (Illus.). 166p. (gr. 3-7). pap. 12.30 *(978-1-7317-0455-9(0))* 2018. 166p. (gr. 3-7). pap. 5.68 *(978-1-7317-0017-9(2))* 2018. (Illus.). 166p. (gr. 3-7). 12.46 *(978-1-7317-0016-2(4))* 2018. (Illus.). 166p. (gr. 3-7). 12.99 *(978-1-61382-278-4(2))* 2018. (Illus.). 166p. (gr. 3-7). pap. 5.99 *(978-1-61382-280-7(4))* 2013. (Illus.). 166p. (gr. 3-7). pap. 8.99 *(978-1-61382-503-7(X))* 2010. (Illus.). 14.99 *(978-1-61382-749-9(0))* Simon & Brown.
—Peter Pan. 2017. (ENG., Illus.). 216p. (YA). (gr. 7-12). pap. *(978-93-87164-42-0(X))* Speaking Tiger Publishing.
—Peter Pan. l.t. ed. 2003. (Perennial Bestsellers Ser.). (ENG.). 248p. (J). 29.95 *(978-0-7862-5263-3(4))* Thorndike Pr.
—Peter Pan. 2003. (Aladdin Classics Ser.). 228p. (gr. 3-7). lib. bdg. 18.40 *(978-0-613-86964-5(8))* Turtleback.
—Peter Pan: A Bed Book First Edition Classic. 2005. 112p. 12.95 *(978-1-933652-30-6(6))* Bed Bks.
—Peter Pan: An Illustrated Classic for Kids & Young Readers (Excellent for Bedtime & Young Readers) eMusic, Tom, ed. Friday, Arthur, illus. 2013. 38p. pap. 6.99 *(978-1-62321-067-0(4))* Tommye-music Corp. DBA Tom eMusic.
—Peter Pan: Complete & Unabridged. Barrie, James Matthew, illus. 2005. (Illus.). 176p. reprint ed. pap. 17.00 *(978-0-7567-9445-3(5))* DIANE Publishing Co.
—Peter Pan: The Original Tale of Neverland. Jaramillo, Raquel, illus. Jaramillo, Raquel, photos by. unabr. ed. 2003. 135p. (YA). (gr. 5-8). reprint ed. 25.00 *(978-0-7567-6883-6(7))* DIANE Publishing Co.
—Peter Pan - the Original Classic Edition. 2011. pap. *(978-1-74244-781-0(3)*, Tebbo) Emereo Pty Ltd.
—Peter Pan & Wendy. 2018. (ENG., Illus.). 142p. (J). (gr. 2-7). pap. 39.99 *(978-1-7181-1853-9(8))* Independently Published.
—Peter Pan & Wendy. 2010. 224p. pap. 19.95 *(978-0-557-36915-7(0))* Lulu Pr., Inc.
—Peter Pan & Wendy. 2013. (ENG.). 172p. (YA). 14.95 *(978-1-940849-05-8(5))* Murine Pubns.
—Peter Pan & Wendy. Foreman, Michael, illus. 2003. (Chrysalis Childrens Classics Ser.). 176p. (YA). pap. *(978-1-84365-039-3(8)*, Pavilion Children's Books) Pavilion Bks.
—Peter Pan & Wendy: Centenary Edition. Ingpen, Robert R., illus. 2004. (ENG.). 216p. (J). *(978-1-897035-12-2(8)*, Blue Heron Bks.) Raincoast Bk. Distribution.
—Peter Pan, by J. M. Barrie - the Original Classic Edition. 2011. mass mkt. *(978-1-74244-961-6(1)*, Tebbo) Emereo Pty Ltd.
—Peter Pan in Kensington Gardens. (J). 18.95 *(978-0-8488-0427-5(9))* Amereon Ltd.
—Peter Pan in Kensington Gardens. 2013. 123p. reprint ed. lthr. 69.00 *(978-0-7426-2518-1(4))* Classic Bks.
—Peter Pan in Kensington Gardens. 2006. pap. *(978-1-4065-0950-2(7))* Dodo Pr.
—Peter Pan in Kensington Gardens. unabr. ed. 2012. (Illus.). 147p. 39.99 *(978-1-4622-8152-7(4))* Repressed Publishing LLC.
—Peter Pan in Kensington Gardens. 2009. 108p. (gr. -1-18). pap. 9.95 *(978-1-60664-381-5(9))* Rodgers, Alan Bks.
—Peter Pan in Kensington Gardens & Peter & Wendy. 2009. 120p. pap. 7.99 *(978-1-4209-3191-4(1))* Digireads.com Publishing.
—Peter Pan y Wendy. Garrido, Felipe, tr. Pacheco, Gabriel, illus. 2018.Tr. of Peter Pan & Wendy. (SPA.). 240p. (J). (gr. 4-7). pap. 19.00 *(978-607-8469-40-6(1))* Nostra Ediciones MEX. Dist: Independent Pubs. Group.
—Tommy & Grizel. 2006. (Illus.). pap. *(978-1-4065-0954-0(X))* Dodo Pr.
Barrie, James Matthew & Bedford, F. D. Peter Pan. 2012. (Illus.). 200p. *(978-1-4351-4201-5(2))* Barnes & Noble, Inc.
Barrie, James Matthew & Edens, Cooper. Peter Pan. (SPA.). 174p. 26.95 *(978-84-666-0760-5(9))* Ediciones B ESP. Dist: Spanish Pubs., LLC.
Barrie, James Matthew & Ladybird Books Staff. Peter Pan. Wilkinson, Annie, illus. 2015. (Ladybird Classics Ser.). 72p. (J). (gr. k-3). 11.99 *(978-1-4093-1222-2(4))* Penguin Bks., Ltd. GBR. Dist: Independent Pubs. Group.
Braswell, Liz. Straight on till Morning-A Twisted Tale. 2020. (Twisted Tale Ser.). (ENG.). 496p. (YA). (gr. 7-12). 17.99 *(978-1-4847-8130-2(9)*, Disney-Hyperion) Disney Publishing Worldwide.
Disney Books. Peter Pan ReadAlong Storybook & CD. 2013. (Read-Along Storybook & CD Ser.). (ENG., Illus.). 32p. (J). (gr. -1-k). pap. 6.99 *(978-1-4231-8034-0(8)*, Disney Press Books) Disney Publishing Worldwide.
—World of Reading: Disney Classic Characters Level 1 Boxed Set: Level 1, Set. 2017. (World of Reading Ser.). (ENG., Illus.). 192p. (J). (gr. 1-3). 12.99 *(978-1-4847-9921-5(6)*, Disney Press Books) Disney Publishing Worldwide.
Jenny Press Staff. Peter Pan. 2016. (Illus.). 24p. (J). (gr. -1-12). pap. 7.99 *(978-1-86147-815-3(1)*, Armadillo) Anness Publishing GBR. Dist: National Bk. Network.
McCaughrean, Geraldine. Peter Pan de Rojo Escarlata. Gonzalez-Gallarza, Isabel, tr. Wyatt, David, illus. 2006. 296p. (J). (gr. 5-8). 17.95 *(978-958-704-467-6(3))* Ediciones Alfaguara ESP. Dist: Santillana USA Publishing Co., Inc.
—Peter Pan in Scarlet. Fischer, Scott M., illus. (ENG.). 320p. (J). (gr. 4-9). 2008. pap. 8.99 *(978-1-4169-1809-7(4))* 2006. 19.99 *(978-1-4169-1808-0(6))* McElderry, Margaret K. Bks. (McElderry, Margaret K. Bks.).
Peter Pantm. 2003. (J). 173.68 *(978-0-06-056911-2(5))* HarperCollins Pubs.
Publications International Ltd. Staff, ed. Peter Pan. 2007. (SPA.). (J). 3.98 *(978-1-4127-8878-6(1))* Publications International, Ltd.
Randolph, Grace. Muppet Peter Pan. Mebberson, Amy, illus. 2010. (Muppet Show Ser.). (ENG.). 112p. (J). pap. 9.99 *(978-1-60886-507-9(X))* BOOM! Studios.
Randolph, Grace & Barks, Carl. Muppet Peter Pan. Mebberson, Amy, illus. 2010. (Muppet Show Ser.). (ENG.). 112p. (J). 24.99 *(978-1-60886-531-4(2))* BOOM! Studios.
RH Disney. Peter Pan Step into Reading (Disney Peter Pan) RH Disney, illus. 2013. (Step into Reading Ser.). (ENG., Illus.). 32p. (J). (gr. -1-1). 5.99 *(978-0-7364-3114-9(4)*, RH/Disney) Random Hse. Children's Bks.
—Walt Disney's Peter Pan (Disney Classic) Dempster, Al, illus. 2007. (Little Golden Book Ser.). (ENG.). 24p. (J). (gr. -1-2). 5.99 *(978-0-7364-0238-5(1)*, Golden/Disney) Random Hse. Children's Bks.
Sabuda, Robert, illus. Peter Pan: Peter Pan. 2008. (ENG.). 16p. (J). 39.99 *(978-0-689-85364-7(5)*, Little Simon) Little Simon.
Sterne, Laurence. The Life & Opinions of Tristram Shandy, Gentleman. 2015. (Vintage Classics Ser.). 624p. pap. 13.95 *(978-0-09-951915-7(1))* Penguin Random Hse. GBR. Dist: Independent Pubs. Group.

PETER RABBIT (FICTITIOUS CHARACTER)—FICTION

Berry, Ron. Can You Make Peter Rabbit Giggle? Sharp, Chris, illus. 2012. 10p. (J). bds. 10.99 *(978-0-8249-1418-9(X)*, Ideals Pubns.) Worthy Publishing.
Burgess, Thornton W. Mother West Wind How Stories. 2017. (ENG., Illus.). (J). pap. *(978-0-649-14658-1(1))* Trieste Publishing Pty Ltd.
—Mother West Wind 'How' Stories. 2008. 108p. (gr. -1-3). 22.95 *(978-1-60664-893-3(4))*; pap. 9.95 *(978-1-60664-012-8(7))* Aegypan.
—Mrs Peter Rabbit. 2006. 120p. (gr. -1-3). 22.95 *(978-1-59818-464-8(4))* Aegypan.
Calumus, Bic-. The Tale of Peter Rabbit, the Original Latin Version, C 777 B C Faithfully Translated by Bic-Calamus. 2009. 48p. pap. 9.95 *(978-1-60693-626-9(3)*, Eloquent Bks.) Strategic Book Publishing & Rights Agency (SBPRA).
Flor Ada, Alma. Dear Peter Rabbit. Tryon, Leslie, illus. 2006. (Stories to Go! Ser.). (J). (gr. k-3). 12.65 *(978-0-7569-7322-3(8))* Perfection Learning Corp.
Ladybird. The Peter Rabbit Club Activity Book: Level 2. 2017. (Ladybird Readers Ser.). (ENG.). 16p. (J). (gr. k-2). 4.99 *(978-0-241-29799-5(0))* Penguin Bks., Ltd. GBR. Dist: Independent Pubs. Group.
Potter, Beatrix. The Complete Adventures of Peter Rabbit R/I. 2007. (Peter Rabbit Ser.). (ENG., Illus.). 80p. (J). (gr. -1-2). 17.99 *(978-0-7232-5916-9(X)*, Warne) Penguin Young Readers Group.
—Hello, Peter! 2012. (Peter Rabbit Ser.). (ENG.). 10p. (J). (gr. -1-k). bds. 6.99 *(978-0-7232-6744-7(6)*, Warne) Penguin Young Readers Group.
—Jeremy Fisher Rocks Out. 2015. (Peter Rabbit Animated Ser.). (ENG., Illus.). 32p. (J). (gr. -1-1). 16.19 *(978-1-4844-5560-9(6))* Penguin Young Readers Group.
—Miniature World of Peter Rabbit 12 Copy Mini Drawer R/I, 12 vols. 2007. (Peter Rabbit Ser.). (ENG., Illus.). 780p. (J). (gr. -1-2). pap. 21.99 *(978-0-7232-5785-1(X)*, Warne) Penguin Young Readers Group.
—My First Year: Peter Rabbit Baby Book. 2006. (Peter Rabbit Ser.). (ENG.). 48p. (gr. k-12). 14.99 *(978-0-7232-5683-0(7)*, Warne) Penguin Young Readers Group.
—The Original Peter Rabbit Presentation Box 1-23 R/I, 23 vols., Set. 2006. (Peter Rabbit Ser.). (ENG., Illus.). 1388p. (J). (gr. -1-2). 170.00 *(978-0-7232-5763-9(9)*, Warne) Penguin Young Readers Group.
—The Peter Rabbit & Friends Treasury. Potter, Beatrix, illus. 2006. (Illus.). 240p. (J). (gr. k-4). reprint ed. 20.00 *(978-1-4223-5452-0(0))* DIANE Publishing Co.
—Peter Rabbit & the Pumpkin Patch. Palmer, Ruth, illus. 2013. (Peter Rabbit Ser.). (ENG.). 32p. (J). (gr. -1-2). pap. 4.99 *(978-0-7232-7124-6(0)*, Warne) Penguin Young Readers Group.
—Peter Rabbit Book & Toy. 2006. (Peter Rabbit Ser.). (ENG., Illus.). 70p. (J). (gr. -1 — 1). 17.99 *(978-0-7232-5356-3(0)*, Warne) Penguin Young Readers Group.
—Peter Rabbit Finger Puppet Book. 2011. (Peter Rabbit Ser.). (ENG., Illus.). 14p. (J). (gr. -1 — 1). bds. 12.99 *(978-0-7232-6639-6(5)*, Warne) Penguin Young Readers Group.
—Peter Rabbit Large Shaped Board Book. 2008. (Peter Rabbit Ser.). (ENG., Illus.). 12p. (J). (gr. -1 — 1). bds. 8.99 *(978-0-7232-5956-5(9)*, Warne) Penguin Young Readers Group.
—Peter Rabbit Rainbow Shapes & Colors. Potter, Beatrix, illus. 2006. (Peter Rabbit Seedlings Ser.). (ENG., Illus.). 10p. (J). (gr. k-18). bds. 5.99 *(978-0-7232-5722-6(1)*, Puffin) Penguin Publishing Group.
—Peter Rabbit Touch & Feel. 2005. (Peter Rabbit Ser.). (ENG., Illus.). 12p. (J). (gr. -1-k). 12.99 *(978-0-7232-5578-9(4)*, Warne) Penguin Young Readers Group.
—Sgeulachd Pheadair Rabaid. MacDonald, James, 1st, tr. from ENG. Potter, Beatrix, illus. 2008.Tr. of Tale of Peter Rabbit. (GAE., Illus.). 84p. *(978-0-9552326-3-3(5))* Grace Note Pubns.
—The Tale of Peter Rabbit. 2013. (Children's Classics Ser.). (ENG., Illus.). 46p. pap. 9.99 *(978-1-909676-49-7(7)*, Sovereign) Bollinger, Max GBR. Dist: Lightning Source UK, Ltd.
—The Tale of Peter Rabbit. Hague, Michael, illus. 2003. 29p. (J). (gr. 2-5). reprint ed. 16.00 *(978-0-7567-6968-0(X))* DIANE Publishing Co.
—The Tale of Peter Rabbit. (Peter Rabbit Naturally Better Ser.). (ENG.). (J). (gr. -1-2). 2009. 72p. 7.99 *(978-0-7232-6392-0(2))* 2007. (Illus.). 24p. bds. 8.99 *(978-0-7232-5793-6(0))* 2004. (Illus.). 32p. mass mkt. 5.99 *(978-0-448-43521-3(7))* Penguin Young Readers Group. (Warne).
—The Tale of Peter Rabbit. McPhail, David, illus. 2014. (ENG.). 28p. (J). (gr. -1 — 1). bds. 6.99 *(978-0-545-65096-0(8)*, Cartwheel Bks.) Scholastic, Inc.
—The Tale of Peter Rabbit. (Illus.). 12p. 4.95 *(978-1-58989-271-2(2))*; 6p. (J). bds. 3.95 *(978-1-58989-201-9(1))* Thurman Hse., LLC.
—The Tale of Peter Rabbit: A Sound Story Book. 2013. (Peter Rabbit Ser.). (ENG., Illus.). 10p. (J). (gr. -1-2). 16.99 *(978-0-7232-6856-7(8)*, Warne) Penguin Young Readers Group.
Thompson, Emma. The Christmas Tale of Peter Rabbit. Taylor, Eleanor, illus. 2013. (Peter Rabbit Ser.). (ENG.). 72p. (J). (gr. -1-2). 20.00 *(978-0-7232-7694-4(3)*, Warne) Penguin Young Readers Group.
Thompson, Emma, et al. Sgeulachd Eile Mu Pheader Rabaid. Taylor, Eleanor, illus. 2012.Tr. of Further Tale of Peter Rabbit. (GLA.). 80p. (J). *(978-1-907676-12-3(0))* Grace Note Pubns.

PETROLEUM

see also Gasoline

Adams, Kenneth. Oil Drilling & Fracking, 1 vol. 2017. (Earth's Environment in Danger Ser.). (ENG.). 24p. (J). (gr. 3-3). 25.27 *(978-1-5383-2543-8(8)*, bc341ff5-0d52-4ae7-b83f-a51866a83ccc); pap. 9.25 *(978-1-5383-2613-8(2)*, 364a11bf-7be9-4933-8ca9-df809146ff17) Rosen Publishing Group, Inc., The. (PowerKids Pr.).
Benoit, Peter. The BP Oil Spill. 2011. (J). pap. *(978-0-531-29029-3(8))* Children's Pr., Ltd.
—The BP Oil Spill. 2011. (True Bks.). 48p. (J). (gr. 3-5). lib. bdg. 29.00 *(978-0-531-20630-0(0)*, Children's Pr.) Scholastic Library Publishing.
Bethea, Nikole Brooks. Oil & Coal. 2013. (Explorer Library: Language Arts Explorer Ser.). (ENG.). 32p. (gr. 4-8). pap. 14.21 *(978-1-61080-922-1(X)*, 202569); (Illus.). 32.07 *(978-1-61080-897-2(5)*, 202567); (Illus.). E-Book 49.21 *(978-1-61080-972-6(6)*, 202570) Cherry Lake Publishing.
Centore, Michael. Oil & Gas in the Arctic. 2017. (Exploring the Polar Regions Today Ser.: Vol. 8). (ENG., Illus.). 64p. (J). (gr. 7-12). 23.95 *(978-1-4222-3869-1(5))* Mason Crest.
Cunningham, Kevin. Gasoline. 2008. (21st Century Skills Library: Global Products Ser.). (ENG., Illus.). 32p. (gr. 4-8). lib. bdg. 32.07 *(978-1-60279-121-3(X)*, 200097) Cherry Lake Publishing.
Ditchfield, Christin. Oil. 2003. (True Bks.). (ENG., Illus.). 48p. (J). (gr. 3-5). pap. 6.95 *(978-0-516-29367-7(2)*, Children's Pr.) Scholastic Library Publishing.
Doeden, Matt. Finding Out about Coal, Oil, & Natural Gas. 2014. (Searchlight Books (tm) — What Are Energy Sources? Ser.). (ENG., Illus.). 40p. (J). (gr. 3-5). pap. 9.99 *(978-1-4677-4553-6(7)*, 2177fc50-1e4b-447f-a68e-161ee90ed5b8) Lerner Publishing Group.
Edwards, Ron, et al. Oil & Gas, 1 vol. 2004. (Rocks, Minerals, & Resources Ser.). (ENG., Illus.). 32p. (J). pap. *(978-0-7787-1444-6(6))*; lib. bdg. *(978-0-7787-1412-5(8))* Crabtree Publishing Co.
Friedman, Lauri S., ed. The B. P. Oil Spill, 1 vol. 2011. (Writing the Critical Essay: an Opposing Viewpoints Guide Ser.). (ENG., Illus.). 128p. (gr. 7-12). 39.93 *(978-0-7377-5833-7(3)*, 5a741e56-329f-47b8-92de-e9b3a9e50581, Greenhaven Publishing) Greenhaven Publishing LLC.
Goldish, Meish. Oil Spill: Deepwater Horizon. 2017. (Eco-Disasters Ser.). (ENG.). 32p. (J). (gr. 2-7). 19.95 *(978-1-68402-226-7(6))* Bearport Publishing Co., Inc.
Goldstein, Margaret J. Fuel under Fire: Petroleum & Its Perils. 2015. (ENG., Illus.). 104p. (YA). (gr. 6-12). lib. bdg. 34.65 *(978-1-4677-3831-6(X)*, 72203b6a-a8bc-4544-aac7-de71de14e056); E-Book 51.99 *(978-1-4677-8802-1(3))* Lerner Publishing Group. (Twenty-First Century Bks.).
Graham, Ian. From Crude Oil to Fast Food: An Energy Journey Through the World of Heat. 2015. (Energy Journeys Ser.). (ENG., Illus.). 48p. (J). (gr. 3-6). 35.99 *(978-1-4846-0885-2(2)*, 127969, Heinemann) Capstone.
Haerens, Margaret, ed. Offshore Drilling, 1 vol. 2010. (Opposing Viewpoints Ser.). (ENG., Illus.). 248p. (gr. 10-12). 50.43 *(978-0-7377-4779-9(X)*, 021ad570-9be3-45f7-bed6-15f6db2f449c); pap. 34.80 *(978-0-7377-4780-5(3)*, 95c3bf4c-9ff2-46c0-9710-9ee286ddf7f1) Greenhaven Publishing LLC. (Greenhaven Publishing).
—Oil, 1 vol. 2010. (Global Viewpoints Ser.). (ENG., Illus.). 224p. (gr. 10-12). 47.83 *(978-0-7377-4719-5(6)*, e410e347-0135-42c8-9772-1db08d3c8a4d); pap. 32.70 *(978-0-7377-4720-1(X)*, 6ce8ccef-a2e8-4a2e-9c2a-a046ae75ccff) Greenhaven Publishing LLC. (Greenhaven Publishing).
hal, marcovitz. Is Offshore Oil Drilling Worth the Risks? 2011. (Illus.). 96p. (J). lib. bdg. 41.27 *(978-1-60152-143-9(X))* ReferencePoint Pr., Inc.
Haugen, David M., ed. The B. P. Oil Spill, 1 vol. 2011. (At Issue Ser.). (ENG.). 112p. (gr. 10-12). 41.03 *(978-0-7377-5568-8(7)*, b39fe2f5-3de5-4f21-8e33-2b07156ca183); pap. 28.80 *(978-0-7377-5569-5(5)*, 6d1a6d21-c7c8-4a54-a75a-5409c71f3a64) Greenhaven Publishing LLC. (Greenhaven Publishing).
Hicks, Terry Allan. The Pros & Cons of Oil, 1 vol. 2014. (Economics of Energy Ser.). (ENG.). 80p. (YA). (gr. 7-7). lib. bdg. 37.36 *(978-1-62712-927-5(8)*, 912365eb-b9d1-474d-a322-2d3d46dcf5da) Cavendish Square Publishing LLC.
Manatt, Kathleen. Searching for Oil. 2007. (21st Century Skills Library: Power Up! Ser.). (ENG.). 32p. (gr. 4-8). pap. 14.21 *(978-1-60279-100-8(7)*, 200661); (Illus.). lib. bdg. 32.07 *(978-1-60279-043-8(4)*, 200057) Cherry Lake Publishing.
marcovitz, hal. How Serious a Threat Is Climate Change? 2011. (Illus.). 96p. (YA). lib. bdg. 41.27 *(978-1-60152-142-2(1))* ReferencePoint Pr., Inc.
McCage, Crystal, ed. Oil, 1 vol. 2006. (Fueling the Future Ser.). (ENG., Illus.). 144p. (gr. 10-12). lib. bdg. 46.23 *(978-0-7377-3588-8(0)*, 4fe44769-d770-4596-b7e5-10d25b4d811c, Greenhaven Publishing) Greenhaven Publishing LLC.
McClure, Jason & Willis, John. Oil. 2017. (Illus.). 24p. (J). *(978-1-5105-1401-0(5))* SmartBook Media, Inc.
Mooney, Carla. Oil Spills & Offshore Drilling. 2011. (Compact Research Ser.). 96p. (YA). (gr. 5-18). lib. bdg. 41.27 *(978-1-60152-141-5(3))* ReferencePoint Pr., Inc.
Nelson, Drew. Life on an Oil Rig, 1 vol. 2013. (Extreme Jobs in Extreme Places Ser.). (ENG., Illus.). 32p. (gr. 3-4). 29.27 *(978-1-4339-8497-6(0)*, 6de8ab69-adde-47cf-bb2a-80a9f3be93f3); pap. 11.50 *(978-1-4339-8498-3(9)*, 68055e5f-de44-4445-a6a2-ad6fc2cd1d85) Stevens, Gareth Publishing LLLP. (Gareth Stevens Learning Library).
Orr, Tamra B. BP Oil Spill & Energy Policy. 2017. (Perspectives Library: Modern Perspectives Ser.). (ENG., Illus.). 32p. (J). (gr. 4-7). lib. bdg. 32.07 *(978-1-63472-864-5(5)*, 209882) Cherry Lake Publishing.
Parker, Steve. Oil, Vol. 12. 2015. (North American Natural Resources Ser.). (Illus.). 64p. (J). (gr. 7). 23.95 *(978-1-4222-3386-3(3))* Mason Crest.
Pipe, Jim. Oil. 2010. (J). 28.50 *(978-1-59604-211-7(7))* Black Rabbit Bks.
Rae, Alison. Oil, Plastics, & Power. 2010. (Development Without Damage Ser.). (YA). (gr. 5-9). 34.25 *(978-1-59920-251-8(4))* Black Rabbit Bks.
Rajczak Nelson, Kristen. How Oil Is Formed, 1 vol. 2016. (From the Earth: How Resources Are Made Ser.). (ENG.). 32p. (J). (gr. 3-4). pap. 11.50 *(978-1-4824-4721-7(5)*, 223ac55f-3d16-4d15-b13e-abf6458128f0) Stevens, Gareth Publishing LLLP.
Redmond, Jim. Oil Makes Gasoline Power. 2003. (From Resource to Energy Source Ser.). (J). *(978-1-58417-292-5(4))*; pap. *(978-1-58417-293-2(2))* Lake Street Pubs.
Scherer, Lauri S., ed. Oil, 1 vol. 2013. (Introducing Issues with Opposing Viewpoints Ser.). (ENG., Illus.). 144p. (gr. 7-10). lib. bdg. 43.63 *(978-0-7377-6279-2(9)*, c5ab830c-358d-4b13-af42-927e5d19b708, Greenhaven Publishing) Greenhaven Publishing LLC.
Schuh, Mari. Sugars & Fats. 2012. (What's on Myplate? Ser.). (ENG.). 24p. (J). (gr. k-1). pap. 43.74 *(978-1-4296-9423-0(8)*, 18616, Capstone Pr.) Capstone.
Wyler, Rose & McSpadden, Warren W. Oil Comes to Us. Luyko, Th. D., illus. 2011. 32p. pap. 35.95 *(978-1-258-10512-9(8))* Literary Licensing, LLC.
Zemlicka, Shannon. Del Petroleo a la Gasolina. 2006. (De Principio a Fin Ser.). (SPA., Illus.). 24p. (J). (gr. 3-7). lib. bdg. 18.60 *(978-0-8225-6496-6(3)*, Ediciones Lerner) Lerner Publishing Group.
—Del petroleo a la gasolina (from Oil to Gas) 2006. (De Principio a Fin (Start to Finish) Ser.). (Illus.). 24p. (J). (gr. -1-3). per. 5.95 *(978-0-8225-6633-5(8)*, Ediciones Lerner) Lerner Publishing Group.
—From Oil to Gas. 2003. (From Start to Finish Ser.). (Illus.). 24p. (J). 18.60 *(978-0-8225-0718-5(8)*, Lerner Pubns.) Lerner Publishing Group.

PETROLEUM—FICTION

Bottoms, Bud. Davey & the GOM Giant Oil Monster. 2008. (Illus.). 39p. (J). (gr. -1-5). per. 14.95 *(978-0-9795444-1-5(6))* Summerland Publishing.

PETROLEUM—HISTORY

Gardner, Timothy. Oil. 2009. (Diminishing Resources Ser.). (Illus.). 111p. (J). lib. bdg. 28.95 *(978-1-59935-117-9(X))* Reynolds, Morgan Inc.
Marrin, Albert. Black Gold: The Story of Oil in Our Lives. 2013. (ENG.). 192p. (YA). (gr. 7). pap. 15.99 *(978-0-375-85968-7(3)*, Knopf Bks. for Young Readers) Random Hse. Children's Bks.

PETROLEUM AS FUEL

Bickerstaff, Linda. Oil Power of the Future: New Ways of Turning Petroleum into Energy. 2009. (Library of Future Energy Ser.). 64p. (gr. 5-5). 58.50 *(978-1-60853-628-3(9))* Rosen Publishing Group, Inc., The.
Graham, Ian. From Crude Oil to Fast Food: An Energy Journey Through the World of Heat. 2015. (Energy Journeys Ser.). (ENG., Illus.). 48p. (J). (gr. 3-6). 35.99 *(978-1-4846-0885-2(2)*, 127969, Heinemann) Capstone.
Knight, M. J. Why Should I Walk More Often? 2009. (One Small Step Ser.). (YA). (gr. 2-5). 28.50 *(978-1-59920-268-6(9))* Black Rabbit Bks.

PETROLEUM INDUSTRY AND TRADE

Alkire, Jessie. Oil Energy: Putting Oil to Work. 2018. (Earth's Energy Innovations Ser.). (ENG., Illus.). 24p. (J). (gr. k-4). lib. bdg. 32.79 *(978-1-5321-1573-8(3)*, 29000, Super SandCastle) ABDO Publishing Co.
Bolden, Tonya. Searching for Sarah Rector: The Richest Black Girl in America. 2014. (ENG., Illus.). 80p. (J). (gr. 3-7). 24.99 *(978-1-4197-0846-6(5)*, 672501, Abrams Bks. for Young Readers) Abrams, Inc.
Bowman, Chris. Oil Field Worker. 2014. (Dangerous Jobs Ser.). (ENG., Illus.). 24p. (J). (gr. 3-7). lib. bdg. 26.95 *(978-1-62617-111-4(4)*, Torque Bks.) Bellwether Media.
Bright, Michael. From Oil Rig to Gas Pump. 2016. (Source to Resource Ser.). (ENG., Illus.). 32p. (J). (gr. 3-6). *(978-0-7787-2706-4(8))* Crabtree Publishing Co.
Calvert, John. The Arabian Peninsula in the Age of Oil. 2009. (Making of the Middle East Ser.). (Illus.). 88p. (YA). (gr. 3-7). lib. bdg. 22.95 *(978-1-4222-0172-5(4))* Mason Crest.
Centore, Michael. Oil & Gas in the Arctic. 2017. (Exploring the Polar Regions Today Ser.: Vol. 8). (ENG., Illus.). 64p. (J). (gr. 7-12). 23.95 *(978-1-4222-3869-1(5))* Mason Crest.
Dalton, Anna. Examining Oil Spills. 2015. (ENG., Illus.). 48p. (J). lib. bdg. 24.95 net. *(978-1-934545-65-2(1))* Oliver Pr., Inc.
Gardner, Timothy. Oil. 2009. (Diminishing Resources Ser.). (Illus.). 111p. (J). lib. bdg. 28.95 *(978-1-59935-117-9(X))* Reynolds, Morgan Inc.
Gunderson, Cory Gideon. The Need for Oil. 2003. (World in Conflict-the Middle East Ser.). 32p. (gr. 4-8). 27.07 *(978-1-59197-417-8(8)*, Abdo & Daughters) ABDO Publishing Co.
Hicks, Terry Allan. The Pros & Cons of Oil, 1 vol. 2014. (Economics of Energy Ser.). (ENG.). 80p. (YA). (gr. 7-7). lib. bdg. 37.36 *(978-1-62712-927-5(8)*, 912365eb-b9d1-474d-a322-2d3d46dcf5da) Cavendish Square Publishing LLC.
Holdren, Annie C. Building an Offshore Oil Rig. 2020. (Sequence Amazing Structures Ser.). (ENG.). 32p. (J). (gr. 2-5). lib. bdg. *(978-1-68151-833-6(3)*, 10713) Amicus.
Hyde, Natalie. Oil & Pipelines. 2019. (Get Informed — Stay Informed Ser.). (Illus.). 48p. (J). (gr. 5-6). *(978-0-7787-5334-6(4))*; pap. *(978-0-7787-5348-3(4))* Crabtree Publishing Co.
Idzikowski, Lisa, ed. Pipelines & Politics, 1 vol. 2017. (At Issue Ser.). (ENG.). 152p. (YA). (gr. 10-12). 41.03 *(978-1-5345-0203-1(3)*, 3ef39f67-1b88-41ae-8054-a92f8f4f1243) Greenhaven Publishing LLC.
Jarrow, Jesse. Oil, Steel, & Railroads: America's Big Businesses in the Late 1800s. (America's Industrial Society in the 19th Century Ser.). 32p. (gr. 4-4). 2009. 47.90 *(978-1-61511-337-8(1))* 2003. (ENG., Illus.). pap. 10.00 *(978-0-8239-4276-3(7)*, a40b88e8-1561-410a-b257-646a9dc4260d) Rosen Publishing Group, Inc., The.

Labrecque, Ellen. Drilling & Fracking. 2017. (21st Century Skills Library: Global Citizens: Environmentalism Ser.). (ENG., Illus.). 32p. (J). (gr. 4-7). lib. bdg. 32.07 *(978-1-63472-868-3(8)*, 209898) Cherry Lake Publishing.

Lankford, Ronald D., Jr., ed. Foreign Oil Dependence, 1 vol. 2012. (At Issue Ser.). (ENG.). 136p. (gr. 10-12). lib. bdg. 41.03 *(978-0-7377-6177-1(6)*, 34a1042a-8699-4d18-a913-0644cc3bea50, Greenhaven Publishing) Greenhaven Publishing LLC.

Miller, Debra A., ed. Oil, 1 vol. 2010. (Current Controversies Ser.). (ENG.). 224p. (gr. 10-12). 48.03 *(978-0-7377-4919-9(9)*, e47eee70-e221-4fe1-ac26-45cd578a4ab2); pap. 33.00 *(978-0-7377-4920-5(2)*, 9d85d746-7b75-44bb-a07c-f1c81193fa5c) Greenhaven Publishing LLC. (Greenhaven Publishing).

Pipe, Jim. Oil. 2010. (J). 28.50 *(978-1-59604-211-7(7))* Black Rabbit Bks.

Rajczak Nelson, Kristen. How Oil Is Formed, 1 vol. 2016. (From the Earth: How Resources Are Made Ser.). (ENG.). 32p. (J). (gr. 3-4). pap. 11.50 *(978-1-4824-4721-7(5)*, 223ac55f-3d16-4d15-b13e-abf6458128f0) Stevens, Gareth Publishing LLLP.

Spilsbury, Richard & Spilsbury, Louise. The Oil Industry, 1 vol. 2011. (Development or Destruction? Ser.). (ENG.). 48p. (YA). (gr. 5-5). pap. 12.75 *(978-1-4488-6998-5(6)*, ea90e5f1-7b5d-4d59-bcf7-4b0b2d26ba15); lib. bdg. 34.47 *(978-1-4488-6991-6(9)*, 19065d3c-d2a0-4da3-b638-8465c27057f5) Rosen Publishing Group, Inc., The.

Stone, Adam. The Deepwater Horizon Oil Spill. 2014. (Disaster Stories Ser.). (ENG., Illus.). 24p. (J). (gr. 3-8). 29.95 *(978-1-62617-152-7(1)*, Black Sheep) Bellwether Media.

Thomas, William David. Oil Rig Worker, 1 vol. 2011. (Dirty & Dangerous Jobs Ser.). (ENG.). 32p. (gr. 3-3). 31.21 *(978-1-60870-173-5(5)*, 597527f2-f539-44f7-8d03-1fe67e38e0d3) Cavendish Square Publishing LLC.

PETROLEUM INDUSTRY AND TRADE—FICTION

Dixon, Franklin. Running on Fumes. 2005. 150p. (J). lib. bdg. 16.92 *(978-1-4242-0384-0(8))* Fitzgerald Bks.

Winfield, Arthur M. Rover Boys in the Land of Luck or Stirr. 2006. pap. 30.95 *(978-1-4286-4101-3(7))* Kessinger Publishing, LLC.

PETROLEUM INDUSTRY AND TRADE—VOCATIONAL GUIDANCE

Horn, Geoffrey M. Oil Rig Roughneck, 1 vol. 2008. (Cool Careers: Adventure Careers Ser.). (ENG., Illus.). 32p. (gr. 3-3). pap. 11.50 *(978-0-8368-8890-4(1)*, 7f520cd3-6496-4d38-b995-b0e61e790670); lib. bdg. 28.67 *(978-0-8368-8883-6(9)*, cd9679ef-c36c-4e8b-a054-583fbba6e3df) Stevens, Gareth Publishing LLLP.

PETS

see also Domestic Animals

also names of animals, e.g. Cats; Dogs

Abbott, Simon. Pop & Play: Pets. 2014. (ENG., Illus.). 10p. (J). (gr. -1-k). bds. 8.99 *(978-0-7534-7156-2(6)*, 900126009, Kingfisher) Roaring Brook Pr.

About Pets Staff. Hamsters. 2003. (Illus.). 64p. pap. 4.95 *(978-0-7434-4542-9(2))* ibooks, Inc.

—Tropical Fish. 2003. (Illus.). 64p. pap. 4.95 *(978-0-7434-4543-6(0))* ibooks, Inc.

Accord Publishing, Accord. Stick to It: Pets: A Magnetic Puzzle Book. 2010. (ENG.). 14p. (J). (gr. -1). bds. 16.99 *(978-0-7407-9726-2(3))* Andrews McMeel Publishing.

Adelman, Beth. Dogs & Cats: Saving Our Precious Pets. 2017. (Protecting the Earth's Animals Ser.: Vol. 8). (ENG.). 64p. (YA). (gr. 5-8). 23.95 *(978-1-4222-3875-2(X))* Mason Crest.

Agusta, Autum. Rita & Rascal. 2013. 116p. (gr. 2-4). 22.25 *(978-1-4669-6973-5(3))*; pap. 12.25 *(978-1-4669-6971-1(7))* Trafford Publishing.

All about Pets, 12 vols. 2016. (All about Pets Ser.). 24p. (ENG.). (gr. k-1). lib. bdg. 145.62 *(978-0-7660-7488-0(9)*, 96a4cce4-592b-4543-bef7-23ed96114555); (gr. 1-k). pap. 56.10 *(978-0-7660-7963-2(5))* Enslow Publishing, LLC.

All My Pets. (Girls' World Ser.). 16p. (J). *(978-2-7643-0142-5(1))* Phidal Publishing, Inc./Editions Phidal, Inc.

All My Pets: What's New? (Girls' Activity Kit Ser.). (J). *(978-2-7643-0213-2(4))* Phidal Publishing, Inc./Editions Phidal, Inc.

Amstutz, Lisa J. Hamsters. 2018. (Our Pets Ser.). (ENG., Illus.). 24p. (J). (gr. -1-2). lib. bdg. 22.65 *(978-1-5435-0159-9(1)*, 137100, Pebble) Capstone.

—Our Pets. 2018. (Our Pets Ser.). (ENG.). 24p. (J). (gr. -1-2). 135.90 *(978-1-5435-0183-4(4)*, 27574, Pebble) Capstone.

Antol, Jenna. "Do" The Once Forgotten Little Bunny Who Grew to Become a World Record Holder. 2012. (ENG.). 36p. (J). pap. 14.95 *(978-1-4787-1593-1(6))* Outskirts Pr., Inc.

Armadillo. Let's Look & See: Pets. 2014. (ENG., Illus.). 24p. (J). (gr. k-2). bds. 6.99 *(978-1-86147-378-3(8)*, Armadillo) Anness Publishing GBR. Dist: National Bk. Network.

Arnez, Lynda. We Take Care of Pets, 1 vol. 2019. (We Can Be Responsible! Ser.). (ENG.). 24p. (gr. k-k). pap. 9.15 *(978-1-5382-3930-8(2)*, 95af594b-f697-4737-b1ac-37b252c90e70) Stevens, Gareth Publishing LLLP.

Aronson, Virginia & Szejko, Allyn. Iguana Invasion! Exotic Pets Gone Wild in Florida. 2010. (ENG.). 69p. (J). (gr. -1-12). 16.95 *(978-1-56164-468-1(4))* Pineapple Pr., Inc.

Atlantic, Leonard. We Play with Pets!, 1 vol. 2017. (Ways to Play Ser.). (ENG.). 24p. (gr. k-k). pap. 9.15 *(978-1-4824-6357-6(1)*, 83478db0-a5a7-425e-843d-7596e30c5cfd) Stevens, Gareth Publishing LLLP.

Autrey, Jacquelyn & Yeager, Alice. U.S. Presidents & Their Animal Friends. Passarella, Jennie, illus. 2004. 32p. (J). *(978-1-59421-005-1(5))* Seacoast Publishing, Inc.

Bailey, Debbie. My Pet. Huszar, Susan, photos by. 3rd ed. 2003. (Talk-About-Bks.: 18). (ENG., Illus.). 16p. (J). (gr. -1 — 1). bds. 6.95 *(978-1-55037-816-0(3)*, 9781550378160) Annick Pr., Ltd. CAN. Dist: Publishers Group West (PGW).

Baker, Charles F., ed. Pets: Cats, Dogs, Horses, & Camels, Too! 2005. (ENG., Illus.). 32p. (J). (gr. 1-5). 17.95 *(978-0-8126-7925-0(3))* Cobblestone Pr.

Beck, Angela. Guinea Pigs: Keeping & Caring for Your Pet, 1 vol. 2013. (Keeping & Caring for Your Pet Ser.). (ENG.). 72p. (gr. 6-7). lib. bdg. 31.93 *(978-0-7660-4184-4(0)*, 410a5a47-9e6a-4489-9af2-0c4b77b74e03) Enslow Publishing, LLC.

Beck, Isabel L., et al. Trophies Kindergarten: Pet Day. 2003. (Trophies Ser.). (gr. k-6). 13.80 *(978-0-15-329519-5(8))* Harcourt Schl. Pubs.

Beer, Julie. Pet Records. 2020. (Illus.). 208p. (J). (gr. 3-7). pap. 14.99 *(978-1-4263-3735-2(3))*; (ENG., lib. bdg. 24.90 *(978-1-4263-3736-9(1))* Disney Publishing Worldwide. (National Geographic Kids).

Bennett, Mia. Ferrets, 1 vol. 2017. (Our Weird Pets Ser.). (ENG.). 24p. (J). (gr. 3-3). 25.27 *(978-1-5081-5416-7(3)*, 6b346bcd-5358-4d2e-89a7-da0d5ac4686e, PowerKids Pr.) Rosen Publishing Group, Inc., The.

Berger, Melvin & Berger, Gilda. Pets. 2009. (Scholastic True or False Ser.: 6). (ENG.). 48p. (J). (gr. k-3). pap. 16.19 *(978-0-545-00396-4(2))* Scholastic, Inc.

Berman, Ruth. My Pet Dog. Hustace, Billy, photos by. 2005. (All about Pets Ser.). (Illus.). 64p. (gr. 2-6). lib. bdg. 22.60 *(978-0-8225-2259-1(4))* Lerner Publishing Group.

Bernay, Emma & Berne, Emma Carlson. My Pets, Your Pets, Our Pets. Stevanovic, Tanja, illus. 2018. (How Are We Alike & Different? Ser.). (ENG.). 24p. (J). (gr. -1-2). lib. bdg. 33.99 *(978-1-68410-240-2(5)*, 138444) Cantata Learning.

Besel, Tucker. Build Your Own Bug Bot. Gould, Grant, illus. 2018. (Bot Maker Ser.). (ENG.). 24p. (J). (gr. 4-6). lib. bdg. *(978-1-68072-321-2(9)*, 12068, Hi Jinx) Black Rabbit Bks.

—Build Your Own Bug Bot. 2018. (Bot Maker Ser.). (ENG.). (J). (gr. 3-7). pap. 8.95 *(978-1-68072-645-9(5))* Hi Jinx Pr.

Beylon, Cathy. At the Pet Shop. 2004. (Dover Animal Coloring Bks.). (ENG., Illus.). 32p. (J). (gr. -1-2). pap. 3.99 *(978-0-486-43644-9(6)*, 436446) Dover Pubns., Inc.

—Favorite Pets. 2007. (Dover Nature Coloring Book Ser.). (ENG., Illus.). 32p. (J). (gr. -1-8). 2.95 *(978-0-486-45641-6(2))* Dover Pubns., Inc.

—I Love Pets Coloring Book. 2014. (ENG.). 64p. (J). (gr. -1-3). pap. 3.99 *(978-0-486-77964-5(5)*, 779645) Dover Pubns., Inc.

Bicknell, Joanna. Googlies: Pet Pals. 2006. (Illus.). 12p. (gr. -1). per. *(978-1-84610-296-7(0))* Make Believe Ideas.

Big Cats Are Not Pets! 2013. (When Pets Attack! Ser.). 32p. (J). (gr. 3-6). pap. 63.00 *(978-1-4339-9275-9(2))* Stevens, Gareth Publishing LLLP.

Biniok, Janice. Adopting a Pet. 2011. (J). 34.95 *(978-1-932904-73-4(5))* Eldorado Ink.

—Guinea Pigs. 2009. (Illus.). 112p. (J). 14.95 *(978-1-932904-37-6(9))* Eldorado Ink.

—Rabbits. 2009. (Illus.). 112p. (J). 14.95 *(978-1-932904-40-6(9))* Eldorado Ink.

Birney, Betty G. Humphrey's World of Pets. 2013. (Humphrey Ser.). (ENG.). 224p. (J). (gr. 3-7). 12.99 *(978-0-14-750953-6(X)*, Puffin Books) Penguin Young Readers Group.

Bjorklund, Ruth. Lizards, 1 vol. 2009. (Great Pets Ser.). (ENG.). 48p. (gr. 3-3). lib. bdg. 32.64 *(978-0-7614-2997-5(2)*, 58f52f39-1129-4c55-90b7-5d18bc7db540) Cavendish Square Publishing LLC.

Blackie. Mels -A-Bob. 2012. 20p. pap. 17.99 *(978-1-4685-9661-8(6))* AuthorHouse.

Bodden, Valerie. Guinea Pigs. 2009. (My First Look at: Pets Ser.). (J). (gr. 1-5). 24.25 *(978-1-58341-723-2(0)*, Creative Education) Creative Co., The.

Boone, Eugene. The Big Book of Pet Names: More Than 10,000 Pet Names - Includes Celebrity Pet Names - the Most Complete Guide to Pet Names & Meanings. 2004. (Illus.). 412p. pap. 15.95 *(978-0-930865-54-2(5))* RSVP Pr.

Boothroyd, Jennifer. How I Care for My Pet. 2014. (First Step Nonfiction — Responsibility in Action Ser.). (ENG., Illus.). 24p. (J). (gr. k-2). lib. bdg. 23.99 *(978-1-4677-3632-9(5)*, 1bfa63a6-a290-44ed-b65e-ade4e020a9c6, Lerner Pubns.) Lerner Publishing Group.

Bozzo, Linda. Mi Primera Mascota Pequeña / My First Guinea Pig & Other Small Pets, 1 vol. 2008. (Mi Primera Mascota / My First Pet Library from the American Humane Association Ser.).Tr. of My First Guinea Pig & Other Small Pets. (ENG & SPA., Illus.). 32p. (gr. k-2). lib. bdg. 26.60 *(978-0-7660-3037-4(7)*, 78016b3a-2170-4186-a96d-7d122388fd48) Enslow Publishing, LLC.

Brainard, Jason. Is a Fish a Good Pet for Me?, 1 vol. 2019. (Best Pet for Me Ser.). (ENG.). 24p. (J). (gr. 3-3). pap. 9.25 *(978-1-7253-0104-7(0)*, 7cd6a09c-4977-4e13-a7c2-e3a45df89329, PowerKids Pr.) Rosen Publishing Group, Inc., The.

—Is a Hamster a Good Pet for Me?, 1 vol. 2019. (Best Pet for Me Ser.). (ENG.). 24p. (J). (gr. 3-3). 25.27 *(978-1-7253-0114-6(8)*, 0e78559d-efdd-43f3-abfa-6a6e92680520, PowerKids Pr.) Rosen Publishing Group, Inc., The.

Britton, Tamara L. Rottweilers, 1 vol. 2013. (Dogs Ser.). (ENG.). 24p. (J). (gr. 3-6). lib. bdg. 31.36 *(978-1-61783-591-9(9)*, 5256, Checkerboard Library) ABDO Publishing Co.

Brownlee, Christen. Beware of (Prairie) Dog! A Pet Swap Goes Viral. 2011. (J). pap. *(978-0-545-32805-0(5))* Scholastic, Inc.

—Cute, Furry, & Deadly: Diseases You Can Catch from Your Pet! 2007. (24/7: Science Behind the Scenes Ser.). (ENG., Illus.). 64p. (J). (gr. 9-12). pap. 7.95 *(978-0-531-18737-1(3)*, Watts, Franklin) Scholastic Library Publishing.

Burke Battistini, Maryanne. Lacey's Story: A Little Tale That Wags. 2009. 72p. pap. 24.99 *(978-1-4389-8874-0(5))* AuthorHouse.

Burstein, John. Slim Goodbody's Inside Guide to Pets, 10 vols., Set. Incl. Birds. lib. bdg. 28.67 *(978-0-8368-8953-6(3)*, 618b18f0-911f-425b-912f-4a7fd3ebcc8d); Cats. lib. bdg. 28.67 *(978-0-8368-8954-3(1)*, 61ead312-e436-49bf-8b71-85e732c52976); Dogs. lib. bdg. 28.67 *(978-0-8368-8955-0(X)*, ef08d55f-ef44-4b6b-ba86-d67f0b5e8d8c); Goldfish. (J). lib. bdg. 28.67 *(978-0-8368-8956-7(8)*, 6f1e608c-cfa4-44bc-9b6c-ebe4694c2c68); Guinea Pigs. (J). lib. bdg. 28.67 *(978-0-8368-8957-4(6)*, 712a00da-0c1f-4762-ac8f-0409a5513541); Rabbits. lib. bdg. 28.67 *(978-0-8368-8958-1(4)*, 6a9236b4-f006-4141-90a2-7f87be512c9e); (Illus.). (gr. 3-5). (Slim Goodbody's Inside Guide to Pets Ser.). (ENG.). 32p. 2008. Set lib. bdg. 143.35 *(978-0-8368-8952-9(5)*, a4555c7b-3247-4396-8396-0df1269aea7b, Gareth Stevens Learning Library) Stevens, Gareth Publishing LLLP.

Burton, Jeffrey. Laugh Out Loud I Ruff Jokes. 2017. (Laugh Out Loud Ser.). (ENG., Illus.). 208p. (J). (gr. k-2). pap. 6.99 *(978-1-5344-0029-0(X)*, Little Simon) Little Simon.

Burton, Jeffrey & Naundorff, Brittany. Laugh Out Loud. 2017. (Illus.). *(978-1-5379-7454-5(8)*, Little Simon) Little Simon.

Burton, Margie, et al. Caring for Our Pets. 2011. (Early Connections Ser.). (J). *(978-1-61672-251-7(7))* Benchmark Education Co.

Cammarata, Jan. Karli's Kritters. 2009. (ENG.). 24p. pap. 12.00 *(978-1-4389-6726-4(8))* AuthorHouse.

Cantor, Don & Cantor, Michael. The Perfect Pet: Finding a pet that is dear to your Heart. Martin, McDonald, illus. 2010. 30p. (J). pap. 9.95 *(978-0-9823906-6-5(1))* Wiggles Pr.

Carr, Aaron. Ferret. 2014. (Illus.). 24p. (J). *(978-1-62127-292-2(3))* Weigl Pubs., Inc.

—Frog. 2014. (Illus.). 24p. (J). *(978-1-62127-293-9(1))* Weigl Pubs., Inc.

—Frogs. 2017. (World Languages Ser.). (ENG.). 24p. (J). (gr. k-2). lib. bdg. 35.70 *(978-1-4896-6624-6(9)*, AV2 by Weigl) Weigl Pubs., Inc.

—Guinea Pig. 2014. (Illus.). 24p. (J). *(978-1-62127-294-6(X))* Weigl Pubs., Inc.

—Hamster. 2011. (J). *(978-1-61690-923-9(4))*; *(978-1-61690-569-9(7))* Weigl Pubs., Inc.

—Hermit Crab. 2014. (J). *(978-1-4896-3098-8(8))* Weigl Pubs., Inc.

—Iguana. 2014. (Illus.). 24p. (J). *(978-1-62127-295-3(8))* Weigl Pubs., Inc.

—Rat. 2014. (J). *(978-1-4896-3102-2(X))* Weigl Pubs., Inc.

—Salamander. 2014. (J). *(978-1-4896-3106-0(2))* Weigl Pubs., Inc.

Carraway, Rose. Fun Frogs, 1 vol. 2012. (Pet Corner Ser.). (ENG.). 24p. (J). (gr. k-k). pap. 9.15 *(978-1-4339-6287-5(X)*, ed333917-b43b-412a-9bd2-fb9903c5d249); lib. bdg. 25.27 *(978-1-4339-6285-1(3)*, d485c0ce-6f4b-404f-8a3c-0e94aefd9e09) Stevens, Gareth Publishing LLLP.

—Fun Frogs / Ranas Saltarinas, 1 vol. 2012. (Pet Corner / Rincón de Las Mascotas Ser.). (SPA & ENG.). 24p. (J). (gr. k-k). lib. bdg. 25.27 *(978-1-4339-6637-8(9)*, 26d11162-cec2-45f7-8f1f-c0f804174ddf) Stevens, Gareth Publishing LLLP.

—Marvelous Mice, 1 vol. 2012. (Pet Corner Ser.). (ENG.). 24p. (J). (gr. k-k). pap. 9.15 *(978-1-4339-6299-8(3)*, 78825e48-7cb5-4b89-ba20-f4f3464ef63c); lib. bdg. 25.27 *(978-1-4339-6297-4(7)*, b9d13ec9-b71b-417f-890c-c36c34c6df79) Stevens, Gareth Publishing LLLP.

—Marvelous Mice / Ratones Maravillosos, 1 vol. 2012. (Pet Corner / Rincón de Las Mascotas Ser.). (SPA & ENG., Illus.). 24p. (J). (gr. k-k). lib. bdg. 25.27 *(978-1-4339-6643-9(3)*, 720c3665-fb82-48fb-a998-e437f6eeea74) Stevens, Gareth Publishing LLLP.

—Slithering Snakes, 1 vol. 2012. (Pet Corner Ser.). (ENG., Illus.). 24p. (J). (gr. k-k). pap. 9.15 *(978-1-4339-6303-2(5)*, 9fcd5eaf-ff5d-459e-853e-da7bd85612a8); lib. bdg. 25.27 *(978-1-4339-6301-8(9)*, 6d0fe6d8-2634-4256-ac5f-5f405e629b40) Stevens, Gareth Publishing LLLP.

—Slithering Snakes / Serpientes Resbaladizas, 1 vol. 2012. (Pet Corner / Rincón de Las Mascotas Ser.). (SPA & ENG.). 24p. (J). (gr. k-k). lib. bdg. 25.27 *(978-1-4339-6645-3(X)*, 7f28b1c0-6bf7-497a-8128-6298b83294c1) Stevens, Gareth Publishing LLLP.

—Terrific Turtles, 1 vol. 2012. (Pet Corner Ser.). (ENG., Illus.). 24p. (J). (gr. k-k). pap. 9.15 *(978-1-4339-6311-7(6)*, fb854867-ac66-4842-a000-00341ea1021e); lib. bdg. 25.27 *(978-1-4339-6309-4(4)*, 38801156-4bf0-47e7-b864-818ae0c37555) Stevens, Gareth Publishing LLLP.

—Terrific Turtles / Tortugas Asombrosas, 1 vol. 2012. (Pet Corner / Rincón de Las Mascotas Ser.). (SPA & ENG.). 24p. (J). (gr. k-k). lib. bdg. 25.27 *(978-1-4339-6647-7(6)*, 43d01710-5eaa-45b9-a6fb-88b8d9c8f7be) Stevens, Gareth Publishing LLLP.

Casado, Dami. Los Ruidos de Las Mascotas. 2005. (SPA.). 12p. 7.99 *(978-84-272-8293-3(1))* Molino, Editorial ESP. Dist: Santillana USA Publishing Co., Inc.

Chapman, J. Pet Pals: Learning the P Sound. 2009. (PowerPhonics Ser.). 24p. (gr. 1-1). 39.90 *(978-1-60851-467-0(6)*, PowerKids Pr.) Rosen Publishing Group, Inc., The.

Charlesworth, Liza. Meet Our Class Pets. Smith, Ian, illus. 2017. 16p. (J). *(978-1-338-18028-2(2))* Scholastic, Inc.

Chin, Amanda. Pet's Playground: Playing Safe in a Dog-And-Cat World. Feldman, Luke, illus. 2009. 104p. (J). pap. 11.95 *(978-1-58326-115-6(X))* American Animal Hospital Assn. Pr.

Christian, Cheryl. Who Lives Here? PETS: Hmong/English, 1 vol. Dwight, Laura, photos by. 2012. (ENG., Illus.). 24p. (J). 5.95 *(978-1-59572-352-9(8))* Star Bright Bks., Inc.

—Who Lives Here? PETS: Portugese/English, 1 vol. Dwight, Laura, photos by. 2012. (ENG., Illus.). 24p. (J). 5.95 *(978-1-59572-353-6(6))* Star Bright Bks., Inc.

—Who Lives Here? PETS: Spanish/English, 1 vol. Dwight, Laura, photos by. 2012. (ENG., Illus.). 32p. (J). bds. 5.95 *(978-1-59572-349-9(8))* Star Bright Bks., Inc.

—Who Lives Here? Pets Photoflaps: English, 1 vol. Dwight, Laura, photos by. 2012. (ENG., Illus.). 32p. (J). bds. 5.95 *(978-1-59572-264-5(5))* Star Bright Bks., Inc.

Coates, Jennifer. Lizards. 2009. (Illus.). 112p. (J). 14.95 *(978-1-932904-39-0(5))* Eldorado Ink.

—Snakes. 2009. (Illus.). 112p. (J). 14.95 *(978-1-932904-41-3(7))* Eldorado Ink.

Collard, Sneed B. Sneed B. Collard III's Most Fun Book Ever about Lizards. 2012. (ENG., Illus.). 48p. (J). (gr. 4-7). 22.44 *(978-1-58089-324-4(4))* Charlesbridge Publishing, Inc.

Collard, Sneed B., III. Sneed B. Collard III's Most Fun Book Ever about Lizards. 2012. (ENG., Illus.). 48p. (J). (gr. 4-7). pap. 8.99 *(978-1-58089-325-1(2))* Charlesbridge Publishing, Inc.

Collard, Sneed B., III & Collard, Sneed B. Insects: The Most Fun Bug Book Ever. 2017. (Illus.). 48p. (J). (gr. 4-7). lib. bdg. 17.99 *(978-1-58089-642-9(1))* Charlesbridge Publishing, Inc.

Color All About: A Giant Coloring Book about Loving Our Pets: Pets. 2004. (Illus.). 36p. (J). *(978-1-59949-002-1(1))* Food Marketing Consultants, Inc.

Colson, Rob. The Pet to Get: Rat. 2017. (Pet to Get Ser.). (ENG., Illus.). 32p. (J). (gr. 4-6). pap. 12.99 *(978-0-7502-8929-0(5)*, Wayland) Hachette Children's Group GBR. Dist: Hachette Bk. Group.

Connolly, Randy, et al. Poison Ivy, Pets & People: Scratching the Poison Ivy, Oak & Sumac Itch. 2005. (10thingstoknow about ... Ser.). (Illus.). 104p. pap. 9.95 *(978-0-9722400-1-7(2))* 2Lakes Publishing.

Connors, Kathleen. What's It Like to Be the President's Pet?, 1 vol. 2014. (White House Insiders Ser.). (ENG.). 24p. (J). (gr. 2-3). 24.27 *(978-1-4824-1105-8(9)*, 943bbde3-9474-462b-b23a-078c1452866c) Stevens, Gareth Publishing LLLP.

Coppendale, Jane. The Ultimate Pet Guide. 2007. (J). spiral bd. *(978-1-59566-500-3(5))* QEB Publishing Inc.

Coppendale, Jean. Puppy. 2004. (QEB You & Your Pet Ser.). (Illus.). 32p. (J). lib. bdg. 15.95 *(978-1-59566-051-0(8))* QEB Publishing Inc.

Craats, Rennay. Caring for Your Frog. 2005. (Caring for Your Pet Ser.). (Illus.). 32p. (J). (gr. 4-7). per. 9.95 *(978-1-59036-218-1(7))*; lib. bdg. 26.00 *(978-1-59036-198-6(9))* Weigl Pubs., Inc.

—Caring for Your Gecko. (Caring for Your Pet Ser.). (Illus.). 32p. (J). 2005. (gr. -1-3). lib. bdg. 26.00 *(978-1-59036-119-1(9))* 2004. per. 9.95 *(978-1-59036-154-2(7))* Weigl Pubs., Inc.

—Caring for Your Snake. (Caring for Your Pet Ser.). (Illus.). 32p. (J). 2005. (gr. 4-7). per. 9.95 *(978-1-59036-216-7(0))* 2004. lib. bdg. 26.00 *(978-1-59036-196-2(2))* Weigl Pubs., Inc.

—Gecko. 2009. (My Pet Ser.). (Illus.). 32p. (J). (gr. 3-5). pap. 9.95 *(978-1-60596-099-9(3))*; lib. bdg. 26.00 *(978-1-60596-098-2(5))* Weigl Pubs., Inc.

Craats, Rennay & Gillespie, Katie. Gecko. 2015. (J). *(978-1-4896-2958-6(0))* Weigl Pubs., Inc.

Cunningham, Alan Blain, compiled by. Goodbye My Good Friend: Memories of Lost Animal Companions & Loved Ones. 2007. (ENG., Illus.). 112p. per. 15.95 *(978-0-9777072-2-5(9))* Agreka Bks., LLC.

Dalpra-Berman, Gina. Remembering Pets: A Book for Children Who Have Lost a Special Friend. Schneider, Barbara Hoss, illus. 2010. (ENG.). 30p. (gr. -1-3). 14.95 *(978-1-885003-68-3(4))* Reed, Robert D. Pubs.

Day, Trevor. Pets Parents Hate! [Scholastic]: Animal Life Cycles. 2011. (Extreme! Ser.). 32p. pap. 1.00 *(978-1-4296-6487-5(8)*, Capstone Pr.) Capstone.

Denzer, Barbara. The Kids Guide to Petiquette: The Inside Scoop on Pet Behavior. 2007. (J). 7.95 *(978-0-9744749-2-2(4))* Crazy Pet Pr., The.

Denzer, Barbara & Denzer, Missy. The Crazy Kids Guide to Cooking for Your Pet: Recipes, Jokes, Pet Care Tips & Fun Things to Do with Your Pet Featuring the Back Bones of Character. Rodriguez, Manny, illus. 2004. 64p. (J). (gr. k-7). 12.95 *(978-0-9744749-0-8(8))* Crazy Pet Pr., The.

Deverell, Christine. Pop-up Pets. Deverell, Richard & King, Chris, illus. 2005. 12p. (J). (gr. k-4). reprint ed. 20.00 *(978-0-7567-8776-9(9))* DIANE Publishing Co.

Dils, Tracey E. My Pets & Me 1, 2, 3: A Pets Counting Book. 2015. (1, 2, 3 Count with Me Ser.). (ENG., Illus.). 24p. (J). (gr. k-2). lib. bdg. 19.95 *(978-1-60753-716-8(8)*, 15248) Amicus.

Dittemore, Mindie. Keeping Chickens: A Kid's Guide to Everything You Need to Know about Breeds, Coops, Behavior, Eggs, & More! 2019. (ENG., Illus.). 256p. (J). (gr. 2-8). pap. 17.99 *(978-1-5107-4583-4(1)*, Sky Pony Pr.) Skyhorse Publishing Co., Inc.

DK. Ultimate Sticker Book: Pets. 2017. (Ultimate Sticker Book Ser.). (ENG.). 32p. (J). (gr. k-2). pap. 6.99 *(978-1-4654-6200-8(7)*, DK Children) Dorling Kindersley Publishing, Inc.

Dobson, Starr. My Goat Gertrude, 1 vol. Dodwell, Dayle, illus. 2011. (ENG.). 32p. (J). (gr. 1-3). 18.95 *(978-1-55109-861-6(X)*, 5db2ae4a-49d6-4eb5-97dd-9d63ae6008a5) Nimbus Publishing, Ltd. CAN. Dist: Baker & Taylor Publisher Services (BTPS).

Domnauer, Teresa. Peculiar Pets. 2006. (Extreme Readers: Level 1 Ser.). (Illus.). 32p. (J). (gr. -1-3). 11.60 *(978-0-7569-6838-0(0))* Perfection Learning Corp.

Donohue, Moira Rose. Kangaroo to the Rescue! And More True Stories of Amazing Animal Heroes. 2015. (NGK Chapters Ser.). 112p. (J). (gr. 3-7). pap. 5.99 *(978-1-4263-1913-6(4)*, National Geographic Kids) Disney Publishing Worldwide.

Driscoll, Laura. Presidential Pets. Slade, Christian, illus. 2009. (ENG.). 64p. (J). (gr. 1-3). 17.44 *(978-0-448-45250-0(2)*, Grosset & Dunlap) Penguin Publishing Group.

Early Macken, JoAnn. Kittens, 1 vol. 2003. (Let's Read about Pets Ser.). (ENG., Illus.). 24p. (gr. k-2). pap. 9.15 *(978-0-8368-3846-6(7)*, 930fec1a-5b64-4073-ae23-25e44c940e25, Weekly Reader Leveled Readers) Stevens, Gareth Publishing LLLP.

—Parakeets, 1 vol. 2003. (Let's Read about Pets Ser.). (ENG., Illus.). 24p. (gr. k-2). pap. 9.15 *(978-0-8368-3847-3(5)*, 765c0ccd-fb94-4107-bf92-df31f2b3c5cb, Weekly Reader Leveled Readers) Stevens, Gareth Publishing LLLP.

—Puppies, 1 vol. 2003. (Let's Read about Pets Ser.). (ENG., Illus.). 24p. (gr. k-2). pap. 9.15 *(978-0-8368-3848-0(3)*, ebf1e473-4f12-4966-bf5a-4647bdec0ced, Weekly Reader Leveled Readers) Stevens, Gareth Publishing LLLP.

Eck, Kristin. Animals in My House. 2004. (Look-And-Learn Books). (J). lib. bdg. 8.95 *(978-1-4042-2701-9(6)*, PowerKids Pr.) Rosen Publishing Group, Inc., The.

Edwards, Nicola. A Pet. 2003. (Saying Goodbye to Ser.). (Illus.). 32p. (J). (gr. -1-2). lib. bdg. 16.95 *(978-1-932333-19-0(3))* Chrysalis Education.

Ellis, Carol. Hamsters & Gerbils, 1 vol. 2008. (Great Pets Ser.). (ENG.). 48p. (gr. 3-3). lib. bdg. 32.64 *(978-0-7614-2999-9(9)*, b14a73f6-8f91-4e72-b5db-008882003ca2) Cavendish Square Publishing LLC.

Emminizer, Theresa. Is a Cat a Good Pet for Me?, 1 vol. 2019. (Best Pet for Me Ser.). (ENG.). 24p. (J). (gr. 3-3). 25.27

PQR

(978-1-7253-0098-9(2), 4df78702-e478-4ca1-83aa-60fce1961e17, PowerKids Pr.) Rosen Publishing Group, Inc., The.

Faust, Daniel R. Weird Inventions for Your Pet, 1 vol. 2018. (Wild & Wacky Inventions Ser.). (ENG.). 32p. (gr. 4-5). 28.27 (978-1-5382-2075-7(X), 9aa5cde8-36f7-43f2-b6d1-f571d5a72d20) Stevens, Gareth Publishing LLLP.

Feldman, Thea. A Parrot in the Painting: The Story of Frida Kahlo & Bonito (Ready-To-Read Level 2) Sanson, Rachel, illus. 2018. (Tails from History Ser.). (ENG.). 32p. (J). (gr. k-2). 17.99 (978-1-5344-2230-8(7)); pap. 4.99 (978-1-5344-2229-2(3)) Simon Spotlight. (Simon Spotlight).

Ferguson, Jennifer. Unwanted Litter. 2010. 68p. pap. 37.37 (978-1-4535-3471-7(7)) Xlibris Corp.

Fiedler, Heidi. Wacky Things Pets Do — Volume 1: Weird & Amazing Things Pets Do! Sorte, Marta, illus. 2018. (Wacky Things Ser.). (ENG.). 32p. (J). (gr. 3-5). lib. bdg. 27.99 (978-1-60058-788-7(7), 9e6d677a-4b7f-46be-89f6-aea3814d14fa, Walter Foster Jr) Quarto Publishing Group USA.

—Wacky Things Pets Do — Volume 2: Weird & Amazing Things Pets Do! Sorte, Marta, illus. 2018. (Wacky Things Ser.). (ENG.). 32p. (J). (gr. 3-5). lib. bdg. 27.99 (978-1-60058-789-4(5), f92d0cbe-aa86-4eb9-a5bd-98fd6505342d, Walter Foster Jr) Quarto Publishing Group USA.

Fields, Hannah. Is a Guinea Pig a Good Pet for Me? 2019. (Best Pet for Me Ser.). (ENG.). 24p. (gr. 3-3). 49.50 (978-1-7253-0109-2(1), PowerKids Pr.) Rosen Publishing Group, Inc., The.

Fiorella, Christina. My Boy Kyle. 2010. 20p. 13.99 (978-1-4520-6519-9(5)) AuthorHouse.

Fleury, Rick & Staehr, Linda. Rainbows for Buckerou. 2013. (ENG.). 26p. pap. 10.95 (978-1-4497-8775-2(4), WestBow Pr.) Author Solutions, LLC.

Foran, Jill. Caring for Your Dog. Marshall, Diana & Nault, Jennifer, eds. 2003. (Caring for Your Pet Ser.). (Illus.). 32p. (J). pap. 9.95 (978-1-59036-063-7(X)) Weigl Pubs., Inc.

—Caring for Your Guinea Pig. 2004. (Caring for Your Pet Ser.). (Illus.). 32p. (J). per. 9.95 (978-1-59036-151-1(2)); lib. bdg. 26.00 (978-1-59036-116-0(4)) Weigl Pubs., Inc.

—Caring for Your Hamster. Marshall, Diana & Nault, Jennifer, eds. 2003. (Caring for Your Pet Ser.). (Illus.). 32p. (J). pap. 9.95 (978-1-59036-066-8(4)) Weigl Pubs., Inc.

—Caring for Your Rabbit. Marshall, Diana & Nault, Jennifer, eds. 2003. (Caring for Your Pet Ser.). (Illus.). 32p. (J). pap. 9.95 (978-1-59036-064-4(8)) Weigl Pubs., Inc.

Foran, Jill & Gillespie, Katie. Guinea Pig. 2015. (J). (978-1-4896-2962-3(9)) Weigl Pubs., Inc.

Fortuna, Lois. Caring for a Pet, 1 vol. 2015. (We Can Do It! Ser.). (ENG., Illus.). 24p. (J). (gr. k-k). pap. 9.15 (978-1-4824-3795-9(3), 657b6870-80bf-40f4-bebe-a53921cf57a6) Stevens, Gareth Publishing LLLP.

Franco, Michou. Can I Have a Pet Crocodile?, 1 vol. 2018. (That's Not a Pet! Ser.). (ENG.). 24p. (gr. k-k). 24.27 (978-1-5382-1780-1(5), 0ebec76a-6544-4ed1-ac07-f8adc6d1fece) Stevens, Gareth Publishing LLLP.

—Can I Have a Pet Eagle?, 1 vol. 2018. (That's Not a Pet! Ser.). (ENG.). 24p. (gr. k-k). 24.27 (978-1-5382-1784-9(8), 3b6e676b-f6b9-41a2-81a3-05d5014796c5) Stevens, Gareth Publishing LLLP.

—Can I Have a Pet Elephant?, 1 vol. 2018. (That's Not a Pet! Ser.). (ENG.). 24p. (gr. k-k). 24.27 (978-1-5382-1788-7(0), f6449710-a185-4425-b2dc-f0c1d44204bb) Stevens, Gareth Publishing LLLP.

Frattini, Stephane. Face-to-Face with the Cat. Klein, Jean-Louis & Hubert, Marie-Luce, illus. 2004. (Face to Face Ser.). 28p. (J). 9.95 (978-1-57091-454-6(0)) Charlesbridge Publishing, Inc.

Fretland VanVoorst, Jenny. Therapy Cats, Dogs, & Rabbits. 2013. (We Work! Animals with Jobs Ser.). 24p. (J). (gr. -1-3). lib. bdg. 25.65 (978-1-61772-895-2(0)) Bearport Publishing Co., Inc.

Funny Faces: Wacky Pets. (J). (978-1-86091-113-2(7), 91) Standard International Print Group Inc.

Gagne, Tammy. Care for a Pet Hedgehog. 2009. (How to Convince Your Parents You Can ... Ser.). 32p. (J). (gr. 1-4). 25.70 (978-1-58415-798-4(4)) Mitchell Lane Pubs.

—Care for a Wolfdog. 2009. (How to Convince Your Parents You Can ... Ser.). 32p. (J). (gr. 1-4). 25.70 (978-1-58415-796-0(8)) Mitchell Lane Pubs.

—Caring for Rabbits: A 4D Book. 2018. (Expert Pet Care Ser.). (ENG., Illus.). 24p. (J). (gr. 1-3). lib. bdg. 27.99 (978-1-5435-2743-8(4), 138201, Capstone Pr.) Capstone.

—Expert Pet Care. 2018. (Expert Pet Care Ser.). (ENG.). 24p. (J). (gr. 1-3). 167.94 (978-1-5435-2762-9(0), 28247, Capstone Pr.) Capstone.

Gale Research Inc. Animal Rights: Pets. 2018. (Animal Rights & Welfare Ser.). (ENG., Illus.). 256p. 51.00 (978-1-4103-8113-2(7)) Cengage Gale.

Galvin, Laura & McCune, Jamie. I Love My Pet. 2011. (ENG.). 16p. (J). 6.95 (978-1-60727-286-1(5)) Soundprints.

Gardeski, Christina Mia. Hamsters: Questions & Answers. 2016. (Pet Questions & Answers Ser.). (ENG., Illus.). 24p. (J). (gr. -1-2). lib. bdg. 27.32 (978-1-5157-0352-5(5), 131986, Capstone Pr.) Capstone.

—Pet Questions & Answers. 2016. (Pet Questions & Answers Ser.). (ENG.). 24p. (J). (gr. -1-2). lib. bdg., lib. bdg., lib. bdg. 163.92 (978-1-5157-0713-4(X), Capstone Pr.) Capstone.

Garwood, Mary. Pawprints upon My Heart II: The Journey Continues. 2004. 132p. (J). per. 11.95 (978-0-9714086-3-0(7)) Tarbutton Pr.

George, Chris. Pets Are Fun, 1 vol. 2017. (Early Concepts Ser.). (ENG.). 24p. (gr. 1-1). pap. 9.25 (978-1-5081-6221-6(2), c1d664fb-2e76-4643-a7ff-8f79f83deb15, PowerKids Pr.) Rosen Publishing Group, Inc., The.

George, Jean Craighead. The Tarantula in My Purse & 172 Other Wild Pets: True-Life Stories to Read Aloud. Cowdrey, Richard, illus. 2019. (ENG.). 144p. (J). (gr. 3-7). reprint ed. pap. 9.99 (978-0-06-446201-3(3), HarperCollins) HarperCollins Pubs.

Gintrac, Brigitte. Let's Play with Lou. 2010. 24p. pap. 15.95 (978-1-4389-5243-7(0)) AuthorHouse.

Glaser, Rebecca. Bunnies Hop. 2017. (Amicus Ink Board Bks.). (Illus.). 14p. (J). (gr. -1 — 1). bds. 7.99 (978-1-68152-199-2(7), 14730) Amicus.

—Fish Swim. 2017. (Amicus Ink Board Bks.). (Illus.). 14p. (J). (gr. -1 — 1). bds. 7.99 (978-1-68152-198-5(9), 14729) Amicus.

—Kittens Pounce. 2017. (Amicus Ink Board Bks.). (Illus.). 14p. (J). (gr. -1 — 1). bds. 7.99 (978-1-68152-197-8(0), 14728) Amicus.

—Puppies Chase. 2017. (Amicus Ink Board Bks.). (Illus.). 14p. (J). (gr. -1 — 1). bds. 7.99 (978-1-68152-196-1(2), 14727) Amicus.

Graham Gaines, Ann. Kids Top 10 Pet Reptiles & Amphibians, 1 vol. 2014. (American Humane Association Top 10 Pets for Kids Ser.). (ENG.). 48p. (gr. 3-4). 26.93 (978-0-7660-6645-8(2), 1652e1e3-e698-4316-9202-08f032713417); pap. 11.53 (978-0-7660-6646-5(0), c3e68103-d434-40c6-bfbd-f6d39f1b52d4, Enslow Elementary) Enslow Publishing, LLC.

—Kids Top 10 Small Mammal Pets, 1 vol. 2014. (American Humane Association Top 10 Pets for Kids Ser.). (ENG.). 48p. (gr. 3-4). 26.93 (978-0-7660-6650-2(9), f9e54a01-448b-4020-a7eb-89e4fc22f5ff); pap. 11.53 (978-0-7660-6651-9(7), 91b75ee7-ee96-485b-a367-c17108750adc, Enslow Elementary) Enslow Publishing, LLC.

Graubart, Norman D. Mi Hmster / My Hamster, 1 vol., 1. Green, Christina, ed. 2013. (¡Las Mascotas Son Geniales! / Pets Are Awesome! Ser.). (SPA & ENG.). 24p. (J). (gr. 1-2). 26.27 (978-1-4777-3313-4(2), eeef79c3-b099-4739-a66a-40328bc499fc, PowerKids Pr.) Rosen Publishing Group, Inc., The

—Mi Tortuga / My Turtle, 1 vol., 1. Green, Christina, ed. 2013. (¡Las Mascotas Son Geniales! / Pets Are Awesome! Ser.). (SPA & ENG.). 24p. (J). (gr. 1-2). 26.27 (978-1-4777-3316-5(7), d6e9d08e-9e3f-42c2-a1e2-88811687d4c1, PowerKids Pr.) Rosen Publishing Group, Inc., The.

—My Hamster, 1 vol., 1. 2013. (Pets Are Awesome! Ser.). (ENG.). 24p. (J). (gr. 1-2). 26.27 (978-1-4777-2868-0(6), 65e78c68-1779-4f64-9c23-3220d574e86a, PowerKids Pr.) Rosen Publishing Group, Inc., The.

—My Turtle, 1 vol., 1. 2013. (Pets Are Awesome! Ser.). (ENG.). 24p. (J). (gr. 1-2). 26.27 (978-1-4777-2869-7(4), 7b4bf9fc-f983-47e3-a8c3-3e755f4e187c, PowerKids Pr.) Rosen Publishing Group, Inc., The.

Gray, Elizabeth. A Giraffe for a Pet, 1 vol. Valente, Christa, illus. 2010. 16p. 24.95 (978-1-4489-6515-1(2)) PublishAmerica, Inc.

Graziano, John, illus. Woof! Funny Pet Stories. 2012. 96p. (J). pap. (978-0-545-38687-6(X)) Ripley Entertainment, Inc.

Great Pets, 10 vols., Set. Incl. Hamsters & Gerbils. Ellis, Carol. 2008. lib. bdg. 32.64 (978-0-7614-2999-9(9), b14a73f6-bf91-4e72-b5db-008882003ca2); Lizards. Bjorklund, Ruth. 2009. lib. bdg. 32.64 (978-0-7614-2997-5(2), 58f52f39-1129-4c55-90b7-5d18bc7db540); Parrots. Haney, Johannah. 2009. lib. bdg. 32.64 (978-0-7614-2998-2(0), c575f812-b500-4651-af4c-2749e9e3738e); Small Dogs. Hart, Joyce. 2009. lib. bdg. 32.64 (978-0-7614-2995-1(6), 4f5d3d2d-9ec9-4c98-81c0-751eea4f189c); Snakes. Hart, Joyce. 2009. lib. bdg. 32.64 (978-0-7614-2996-8(4), cbcd11b0-5a23-44bc-a513-3a076c8f5d8f); 48p. (gr. 3-3). (Great Pets Ser.). (ENG.). 2009. Set lib. bdg. 163.20 (978-0-7614-2994-4(8), 9c6ac3b9-db69-437b-8a36-81408ee951e8); Set lib. bdg. 163.20 (978-0-7614-2706-3(6), 622debca-bfed-4ebd-b0d4-3f22f1f79990) Cavendish Square Publishing LLC. (Cavendish Square).

Green, Gail. The Kids' Guide to Projects for Your Pet, 1 vol. 2012. (Kids' Guides). (ENG.). 32p. (J). (gr. 3-9). lib. bdg. 28.65 (978-1-4296-7662-5(0), 117259, Capstone Pr.) Capstone.

Greening, Rosie. Touch & Sparkle: Pets. 2016. (ENG.). 12p. (J). (gr. -1 — 1). bds. 6.99 (978-1-78598-131-9(5)) Make Believe Ideas GBR. Dist: Scholastic, Inc.

Greenwell, Jessica. Pets Sticker Book. 2011. (First Sticker Books Ser.). 16p. (J). pap. 6.99 (978-0-7945-2995-6(X), Usborne) EDC Publishing.

Greve, Meg & Sturm, Jeanne. Mi Mascota: Pet Tricks. 2008. (ENG & SPA., Illus.). 24p. (J). 19.44 (978-1-60472-507-0(9)) Rourke Educational Media.

Grossi, Craig. Craig & Fred Young Readers' Edition: A Marine, a Stray Dog, & How They Rescued Each Other. 2017. (ENG., Illus.). 256p. (J). (gr. 3). 16.99 (978-0-06-269335-8(2), HarperCollins) HarperCollins Pubs.

Gunderson, Megan M. Scottish Deerhounds, 1 vol. 2013. (Dogs Ser.). (ENG.). 24p. (J). (gr. 3-6). lib. bdg. 31.36 (978-1-61783-592-6(7), 5258, Checkerboard Library) ABDO Publishing Co.

—Whippets, 1 vol. 2013. (Dogs Ser.). (ENG.). 24p. (J). (gr. 3-6). lib. bdg. 31.36 (978-1-61783-593-3(5), 5260, Checkerboard Library) ABDO Publishing Co.

Gunzi, Christiane. My Early Learning Library: Pets. 2nd rev. ed. 2015. (ENG., Illus.). 34p. (J). bds. 7.99 (978-1-906572-13-6(5)) Award Pubns. Ltd. GBR. Dist: Parkwest Pubns., Inc.

Hamilton, Lynn. Caring for Your Bird. 2003. (Caring for Your Pet Ser.). (Illus.). 32p. (J). (gr. -1-3). lib. bdg. 26.00 (978-1-59036-037-8(0)) Weigl Pubs., Inc.

—Caring for Your Ferret. (Caring for Your Pet Ser.). (Illus.). 32p. (J). 2007. per. 9.95 (978-1-59036-150-4(4)) 2004. lib. bdg. 26.00 (978-1-59036-115-3(6)) Weigl Pubs., Inc.

—Caring for Your Fish. 2005. (Caring for Your Pet Ser.). (Illus.). 32p. (J). (gr. 4-7). lib. bdg. 26.00 (978-1-59036-035-4(4)) Weigl Pubs., Inc.

—Caring for Your Turtle. 2004. (Caring for Your Pet Ser.). (Illus.). 32p. (J). per. 9.95 (978-1-59036-153-5(9)) Weigl Pubs., Inc.

—Ferret. 2009. (My Pet Ser.). (Illus.). 32p. (J). (gr. 3-5). pap. 9.95 (978-1-60596-097-5(7)); lib. bdg. 26.00 (978-1-60596-096-8(9)) Weigl Pubs., Inc.

—Turtle. 2009. (My Pet Ser.). (Illus.). 32p. (J). (gr. 3-5). lib. bdg. 26.00 (978-1-60596-088-3(8)) Weigl Pubs., Inc.

—Turtle: My Pet. 2009. (Illus.). 32p. (J). pap. 9.95 (978-1-60596-089-0(6)) Weigl Pubs., Inc.

Hamilton, Lynn & Gillespie, Katie. Ferret. 2015. (J). (978-1-4896-2954-8(8)) Weigl Pubs., Inc.

—Turtle. 2015. (J). (978-1-4896-2974-6(2)) Weigl Pubs., Inc.

Hamilton, Lynn A. Caring for Your Bird. Marshall, Diana & Nault, Jennifer, eds. 2003. (Caring for Your Pet Ser.). (Illus.). 32p. (J). pap. 9.95 (978-1-59036-067-5(2)) Weigl Pubs., Inc.

—Caring for Your Fish. Kissock, Heather & Marshall, Diana, eds. 2003. (Caring for Your Pet Ser.). (Illus.). 32p. (J). pap. 9.95 (978-1-59036-065-1(6)) Weigl Pubs., Inc.

—Caring for Your Turtle. 2005. (Caring for Your Pet Ser.). (Illus.). 32p. (J). (gr. -1-3). lib. bdg. 26.00 (978-1-59036-118-4(0)) Weigl Pubs., Inc.

Hammond, Charmaine. Toby, the Pet Therapy Dog, Says Be a Buddy, Not a Bully. 2013. (ENG., Illus.). 34p. (J). pap. 12.99 (978-0-9836045-4-9(1)) Youngs, Bettie Bks.

—Toby, the Pet Therapy Dog, Says Be a Buddy Not a Bully. Prevec, Rose Anne, illus. 2013. (ENG.). (J). pap. 12.95 (978-0-9836045-5-6(X), Kendahl Hse. Pr.) Youngs, Bettie Bks.

Haney, Johannah. Ferrets, 1 vol. 2010. (Great Pets Ser.). (ENG.). 48p. (gr. 3-3). lib. bdg. 32.64 (978-0-7614-4153-3(0), f4a76042-c3d7-4687-bf16-72dbb123949d) Cavendish Square Publishing LLC.

Harasymiw, Mark. Alligators Are Not Pets! 2013. (When Pets Attack! Ser.). (Illus.). 32p. (J). (gr. 3-6). pap. 63.00 (978-1-4339-9280-3(9)) Stevens, Gareth Publishing LLLP.

Harasymiw, Mark J. Alligators Are Not Pets!, 1 vol. 2013. (When Pets Attack! Ser.). (ENG., Illus.). 32p. (J). (gr. 3-4). 29.27 (978-1-4339-9278-0(7), e3c9caad-b3f3-4b2f-9516-eec5aa59fa1e); pap. 11.50 (978-1-4339-9279-7(5), 09af0552-6ff2-4263-85d2-90002020ede1) Stevens, Gareth Publishing LLLP.

Harpan, Gaile. True Puppy Tails. 2010. 24p. pap. 12.95 (978-1-936343-26-3(6)) Peppertree Pr., The.

Harrington, Jane. Extreme Pets. 2007. (ENG., Illus.). 164p. (J). (gr. 2-5). pap., instr.'s hndbk. ed. 12.99 (978-0-439-82948-9(8)) Scholastic, Inc.

Harrison, Megan Bernadette. Fears, Tears, & Laughter: The Adventures of Kitty Tom & Blossom Book Two, 1 vol. 2010. 48p. pap. 24.95 (978-1-4489-9314-7(8)) PublishAmerica, Inc.

Harrison, Paul. My Pet. 2011. (Window on the World Ser.). (Illus.). 32p. (978-1-84089-662-6(0)) Zero to Ten, Ltd.

Hart, Joyce. Snakes, 1 vol. 2009. (Great Pets Ser.). (ENG.). 48p. (gr. 3-3). lib. bdg. 32.64 (978-0-7614-2996-8(4), cbcd11b0-5a23-44bc-a513-3a076c8f5d8f) Cavendish Square Publishing LLC.

Harte, May. Hide-and-Seek Pets. 2004. (Hide-And-Seek Books). (J). lib. bdg. 21.25 (978-1-4042-2815-3(2), PowerKids Pr.) Rosen Publishing Group, Inc., The.

—Hide & Seek Pets. 2009. (Tough Toddler Bks). 16p. (gr. k-k). 42.50 (978-1-60854-572-8(5), PowerKids Pr.) Rosen Publishing Group, Inc., The.

Head, Honor. Cats & Kittens. 2007. (QEB Know Your Pet Ser.). (Illus.). 32p. lib. bdg. 19.95 (978-1-59566-217-0(0)) QEB Publishing Inc.

—Horses & Ponies. 2007. (QEB Know Your Pet Ser.). (Illus.). 32p. (J). lib. bdg. 19.95 (978-1-59566-219-4(7)) QEB Publishing Inc.

Healing Your Heart When Your Animal Friend Is Gone: A Children's Pet Bereavement Workbook. 2004. (J). 14.95 (978-0-9748512-0-4(5)) Bree's Gift Publishing.

Heighton, Mary Beth & Laskey, Andrew. What I Do When You're Not Home, 1 vol. 2009. 38p. pap. 24.95 (978-1-60813-167-9(X)) America Star Bks.

Heinemann Educational Ltd. Publishing Staff. The Wild Side of Pets Package. 2004. pap. 243.00 (978-1-4109-1387-6(2)) Harcourt Schl. Pubs.

Heneghan, Judith. Love Your Hamster, 1 vol. 2013. (Your Perfect Pet Ser.). (ENG., Illus.). 32p. (gr. 3-3). 29.93 (978-1-4777-0186-7(9), 0cbd72e6-7a50-4e01-9cc7-bdd37874d2f8); pap. 11.00 (978-1-4777-0200-0(8), c54c4c8a-82b8-4d4c-83e1-60eae41102fe) Rosen Publishing Group, Inc., The. (Windmill Bks.).

Heos, Bridget. Do You Really Want a Guinea Pig? Longhi, Katya, illus. 2015. (Do You Really Want a Pet? Ser.). (ENG.). 24p. (J). (gr. 1-4). lib. bdg. 19.95 (978-1-60753-749-6(4), 15279) Amicus.

—Do You Really Want a Lizard? Longhi, Katya, illus. 2015. (Do You Really Want a Pet? Ser.). (ENG.). 24p. (J). (gr. 1-4). lib. bdg. 19.95 (978-1-60753-750-2(8), 15280) Amicus.

—Do You Really Want a Turtle? Longhi, Katya, illus. 2015. (Do You Really Want a Pet? Ser.). (ENG.). 24p. (J). (gr. 1-3). 19.95 (978-1-60753-752-6(4)) Amicus Learning.

—Make Money! Be a Pet Sitter. Fabbri, Daniele, illus. 2013. (Make Money! Ser.). (ENG.). 24p. (J). (gr. 1-4). lib. bdg. 27.10 (978-1-60753-362-7(6), 16279) Amicus.

Herglotz, Pam Herglotz. Ichabod & the Chipmunks. 2010. 40p. pap. 17.91 (978-0-557-19218-2(8)) Lulu Pr., Inc.

Herriot, James. James Herriot's Treasury for Children: Warm & Joyful Tales by the Author of All Creatures Great & Small. Brown, Ruth & Barrett, Peter, illus. 2014. (ENG.). 272p. (J). (gr. -1-3). 25.99 (978-1-250-05813-3(9), 900139655, St. Martin's Griffin) St. Martin's Pr.

Hibbert, Clare. Hamster. 2004. (Illus.). 32p. (J). lib. bdg. 27.10 (978-1-58340-433-1(3)) Black Rabbit Bks.

Holden, Pam. Look after Pets, 1 vol. 2015. (ENG., Illus.). 16p. (-1). pap. (978-1-77654-115-7(4), Red Rocket Readers) Flying Start Bks.

HOP, LLC. Hooked on Animals Pets Super Activity Kit. 2006. (J). (gr. -1). 9.99 (978-1-933863-20-7(X)) HOP, LLC.

How to Choose a Pet: Individual Title Six-Packs. (Discovery World Ser.). 24p. (gr. 1-2). 33.00 (978-0-7635-8475-7(4)) Rigby Education.

Hughes, Catherine D. Little Kids First Big Book of Pets. 2019. (National Geographic Little Kids First Big Bks.). (Illus.). 128p. (J). (gr. -1-k). 14.99 (978-1-4263-3470-2(2)); (ENG., lib. bdg. 24.90 (978-1-4263-3471-9(0)) Disney Publishing Worldwide. (National Geographic Kids).

Hunt, James. I Have a New Puppy! Now What? A Puppy Survival Guide for Kids. Dickens, Christina, illus. 2007. (Fireman James & Flame Ser.). 40p. (J). (gr. 1-3). 14.99 (978-0-9769401-0-4(8)) Hunt, J. L. Publishing.

Hyland, Tony & Scarborough, Kate. Killer Pets. 2012. (Fast Facts Ser.). (ENG.). 32p. (gr. 4-6). pap. 28.50 (978-1-59771-327-6(9)) Sea-To-Sea Pubns.

Idzikowski, Lisa, ed. Ethical Pet Ownership: Puppy Mills, Rescue Pets, & Exotic Animal Trade, 1 vol. 2018. (At Issue Ser.). (ENG.). 128p. (gr. 10-12). 41.03 (978-1-5345-0379-3(X), d8029ed0-1b83-4a66-b330-f5d1ea2f5d8d) Greenhaven Publishing LLC.

Ikids Staff & Francis, Guy. Pets. 2009. (ENG., Illus.). 10p. (J). (gr. -1-1). 15.99 (978-1-58476-940-8(8)) Innovative Kids.

Ipcizade, Catherine. BIG Pets. 2010. (Big Ser.). (ENG.). 24p. (J). (gr. -1-2). lib. bdg. 27.32 (978-1-4296-3997-2(0), 102607, Capstone Pr.) Capstone.

Jacobs, Pat. Unusual Pet Pals. 2018. (Pet Pals Ser.). (Illus.). 32p. (J). (gr. 3-3). (978-0-7787-5730-6(7)) Crabtree Publishing Co.

Jeffrey, Laura S. Choosing a Hamster, Gerbil, Guinea Pig, Rabbit, Ferret, Mouse, or Rat: How to Choose & Care for a Small Mammal, 1 vol. 2013. (American Humane Association Pet Care Ser.). (ENG.). 48p. (gr. 3-3). pap. 11.53 (978-1-4644-0217-3(5), 09cd07e0-95e5-4041-ad02-62463cf3eb9c, Enslow Elementary); lib. bdg. 27.93 (978-0-7660-4082-3(8), d3d8843b-30fd-47f5-897a-ead7dd0b568e) Enslow Publishing, LLC.

Jenkins, Steve, et al. The True Adventures of Esther the Wonder Pig. Doerrfeld, Cori, illus. 2018. (ENG.). 40p. (J). (gr. -1-3). 17.99 (978-0-316-55476-3(6)) Little, Brown Bks. for Young Readers.

Johnson, J. Angelique. Getting a Pet, Step by Step, 1 vol. 2011. (Step-By-Step Stories Ser.). (ENG.). 32p. (J). (gr. -1-2). lib. bdg. 29.99 (978-1-4296-6024-2(4), 114968, Capstone Pr.) Capstone.

Johnson, Jinny. Guinea Pig. 2014. (My New Pet Ser.). (ENG.). 24p. (J). (gr. k-3). lib. bdg. 28.50 (978-1-62588-029-1(4), 17353) Black Rabbit Bks.

—Hamster & Gerbil. 2014. (My New Pet Ser.). (ENG.). 24p. (J). (gr. k-3). lib. bdg. 28.50 (978-1-62588-030-7(8), 17354) Black Rabbit Bks.

Jojo. Landon Wants a Puppy. 2009. 68p. pap. 26.99 (978-1-4389-4656-6(2)) AuthorHouse.

Jones, Tammy. Big Pet, Little Pet. 2009. (Sight Word Readers Set A Ser.). (J). 3.49 net. (978-1-60719-153-7(9)) Newmark Learning LLC.

—My Pet. 2009. (Sight Word Readers Set A Ser.). (J). 3.49 net. (978-1-60719-145-2(8)) Newmark Learning LLC.

Kadylak, Shirley. Cody's New Pet. 2012. 32p. pap. 15.95 (978-1-4497-5986-5(6), WestBow Pr.) Author Solutions, LLC.

Kain, Kathleen. All about Pets. Miyake, Yoshi, illus. 2004. (Treasure Tree Ser.). 32p. (J). (978-0-7166-1626-9(2)) World Bk., Inc.

Kaleta, Don. Puppy Scents: The Kids' Guide to Puppy Care. Habel, Helen, illus. 2010. (ENG.). 72p. (J). pap. 17.95 (978-0-615-39881-5(2)) Kaleta Publishing, LLC.

Kalman, Bobbie. Baby Pets. 2012. (ENG., Illus.). 24p. (J). (978-0-7787-4075-9(7)); pap. (978-0-7787-4080-3(3)) Crabtree Publishing Co.

—My Big & Small Pets. 2010. (My World Ser.). (ENG., Illus.). 16p. (J). (gr. k-2). (978-0-7787-9426-4(1)); pap. (978-0-7787-9470-7(9)) Crabtree Publishing Co.

Kalman, Bobbie & MacAulay, Kelley. Les Cochons D'Inde. 2011. (FRE., Illus.). 32p. (J). pap. 9.95 (978-2-89579-391-5(3)) Bayard Canada CAN. Dist: Crabtree Publishing Co.

—Guinea Pigs. Crabtree, Marc, illus. Crabtree, Marc, photos by. 2003. (Pet Care Ser.). (ENG.). 32p. (J). lib. bdg. (978-0-7787-1755-3(0)) Crabtree Publishing Co.

Kawa, Katie. Furry Hamsters, 1 vol. 2011. (Pet Corner Ser.). (ENG., Illus.). 24p. (J). (gr. k-k). pap. 9.15 (978-1-4339-5605-8(5), 5fe63841-806b-4856-99fc-19415c35593b); lib. bdg. 25.27 (978-1-4339-5603-4(9), edd6b58d-53ac-40b5-a221-7a8233a14891) Stevens, Gareth Publishing LLLP.

—Furry Hamsters / Hámsteres Peludos, 1 vol. 2011. (Pet Corner / Rincón de Las Mascotas Ser.). (SPA & ENG., Illus.). 24p. (J). (gr. k-k). lib. bdg. 25.27 (978-1-4339-5607-2(1), a4fca469-fb30-4cf5-98e4-6618de2641e0) Stevens, Gareth Publishing LLLP.

Khan, Sarah. Pets Lift-the-Flap. 2005. (Luxury Lift-the-Flap Learners Ser.). 16p. (J). (gr. 1-18). 11.95 (978-0-7945-0914-9(2), Usborne) EDC Publishing.

Kobasa, Paul A. Pet Animals. 2018. (J). (978-0-7166-3574-1(7)) World Bk., Inc.

Korté, Steve. DC Super-Pets Character Encyclopedia, 1 vol. Baltazar, Art, illus. 2013. (DC Super-Pets Ser.). (ENG.). 128p. (J). (gr. 1-3). 26.60 (978-1-4795-2030-5(6), 123734, Stone Arch Bks.) Capstone.

Kramer, Nash. How Many Pets Do You Have? 2012. (Level C Ser.). (ENG., Illus.). 16p. (J). (gr. k-2). pap. 7.95 (978-1-927136-20-1(2), 19417) RiverStream Publishing.

Krull, Kathleen. Writers & Their Pets. Lemay, Violet, illus. 2019. 192p. (J). (gr. 2-5). 14.95 (978-1-947458-52-9(3), 805852) Duo Pr. LLC.

Ladybird. Favourite Pets - Read It Yourself with Ladybird Level 1. 2016. (Read It Yourself with Ladybird Ser.). (ENG.). 32p. (J). 5.99 (978-0-241-23734-2(3)); (gr. 2-4). pap. 9.99 (978-0-241-23732-8(7)) Penguin Bks., Ltd. GBR. Dist: Independent Pubs. Group.

Lawrence-Loughlin, Amy. For the Love of Gus: A True Rescue to Riches Tale. 2012. 36p. pap. 15.49 (978-1-4669-5371-0(3)) Trafford Publishing.

Leavitt, Amie Jane. Care for a Pet Sugar Glider. 2009. (How to Convince Your Parents You Can ... Ser.). (Illus.). 32p. (J). (gr. 1-4). lib. bdg. 25.70 (978-1-58415-800-4(X)) Mitchell Lane Pubs.

Lee, Lynne. Bramble'S Story. 2009. 60p. pap. 19.99 (978-1-60693-427-2(9), Eloquent Bks.) Strategic Book Publishing & Rights Agency (SBPRA).

Less, Emma. Veterinarians. 2018. (Real-Life Superheroes Ser.). (ENG.). 16p. (J). (gr. k-2). pap. 7.99 (978-1-68152-283-8(7), 14922) Amicus.

Let's Get a Pet! 2017. (Let's Get a Pet! Ser.). 24p. (gr. 1-2). pap. 48.90 (978-1-5382-0201-2(8)); (ENG.). lib. bdg. 145.62 (978-1-5382-0200-5(X), e0c2f892-99e7-4a64-b571-20d410a39381) Stevens, Gareth Publishing LLLP.

Lim, Annalees. Pet Crafts, 1 vol., 1. 2015. (Creating Creature Crafts Ser.). (ENG., Illus.). 24p. (J). (gr. 2-3). pap. 11.60 *(978-1-5081-9109-4(3),* 7d2a62e2-840c-4fd0-b437-802140aba4d6, Windmill Bks.) Rosen Publishing Group, Inc., The.

Linde, Barbara M. Snakes Are Not Pets!, 1 vol. 2013. (When Pets Attack! Ser.). (Illus.). 32p. (J). (gr. 3-4). (ENG.). 29.27 *(978-1-4339-9298-8(1),* f9e659de-fa0b-49f0-8978-37d6333e3a4e); pap. 63.00 *(978-1-4339-9300-8(7))* Stevens, Gareth Publishing LLLP.

Liss-Levinson, Nechama & Baskette, Molly Phinney. Remembering My Pet: A Kid's Own Spiritual Workbook for When a Pet Dies. 2007. (ENG., Illus.). 48p. (gr. 3-7). wbk. ed. 25.99 *(978-1-59473-221-8(3),* e54bc3ac-bfcd-40c5-b873-0ad427384ad1, Skylight Paths Publishing) LongHill Partners, Inc.

Litwiller, Hannah. The Young Adult Guide's Pet Ownership: Everything You Need to Know about Raising Your First Pet. 2018. (ENG.). 164p. (YA). pap. 19.95 *(978-1-62023-572-0(2),* 913ca08f-8b6a-44cc-9a9c-ddbc471014d7) Atlantic Publishing Group, Inc.

Lodien, Jennie, des. Cat Tales. 2004. (Illus.). 48p. (YA). ring bd. 16.95 *(978-0-9746341-8-0(2))* Chin & A Pr.

—A Doggie Diary: The story of our Dog. 2003. (Illus.). 48p. (YA). ring bd. 16.95 *(978-0-9746341-7-3(4))* Chin & A Pr.

—Life on a Leash: My Dog's Story. 2003. (Illus.). 48p. (YA). ring bd. 16.95 *(978-0-9746341-6-6(6))* Chin & A Pr.

Loh-Hagan, Virginia. Pet Food Tester. 2016. (Odd Jobs Ser.). (ENG., Illus.). 32p. (J). (gr. 4-8). 32.07 *(978-1-63471-096-1(7),* 208495, 45th Parallel Press) Cherry Lake Publishing.

Lollis, Sylvia & Hogan, Joyce W. Should We Have Pets? A Persuasive Text. 2003. (Illus.). 32p. (J). pap. 6.00 *(978-1-59034-044-8(2))* Mondo Publishing.

Lomberg, Michelle. Caring for Your Horse. 2004. (Caring for Your Pet Ser.). (Illus.). 32p. (J). (gr. 4-7). per. 9.95 *(978-1-59036-152-8(0));* lib. bdg. 26.00 *(978-1-59036-117-7(2))* Weigl Pubs., Inc.

—Caring for Your Spider. 2004. (Caring for Your Pet Ser.). (Illus.). 32p. (J). (gr. 4-7). per. 9.95 *(978-1-59036-155-9(5));* lib. bdg. 26.00 *(978-1-59036-120-7(2))* Weigl Pubs., Inc.

—Horse. 2009. (My Pet Ser.). (Illus.). 32p. (J). (gr. 3-5). pap. 9.95 *(978-1-60596-093-7(4));* lib. bdg. 26.00 *(978-1-60596-092-0(6))* Weigl Pubs., Inc.

—Spider. 2009. (My Pet Ser.). (Illus.). 32p. (J). (gr. 3-5). pap. 9.95 *(978-1-60596-095-1(0));* lib. bdg. 26.00 *(978-1-60596-094-4(2))* Weigl Pubs., Inc.

Lomberg, Michelle & Gillespie, Katie. Spider. 2015. (J). *(978-1-4896-2970-8(X))* Weigl Pubs., Inc.

Lord, Cynthia. Borrowing Bunnies: A Surprising True Tale of Fostering Rabbits. Mitchell, Hazel, illus. Bald, John, photos by. 2019. (ENG.). 40p. (J). 17.99 *(978-0-374-30841-4(1),* 900186026, Farrar, Straus & Giroux (BYR)) Farrar, Straus & Giroux.

Love, Ann & Drake, Jane. Talking Tails: The Incredible Connection Between People & Their Pets. Slavin, Bill, illus. 80p. (J). (gr. 4-7). 2012. pap. 9.95 *(978-1-77049-359-9(X))* 2010. 22.95 *(978-0-88776-884-2(9))* Tundra Bks. CAN. (Tundra Bks.). Dist: Penguin Random Hse. LLC.

Lowenstein Niven, Felicia. Learning to Care for Reptiles & Amphibians, 1 vol. 2010. (Beginning Pet Care with American Humane Ser.). (ENG.). 48p. (gr. 3-3). 27.93 *(978-0-7660-3194-4(2),* 35b8272f-1772-4790-8fa3-b5d12cf8ecc0, Enslow Elementary) Enslow Publishing, LLC.

—Learning to Care for Small Mammals, 1 vol. 2010. (Beginning Pet Care with American Humane Ser.). (ENG.). 48p. (gr. 3-3). 27.93 *(978-0-7660-3195-1(0),* c4dbf867-2297-430e-9662-e07b36f64229, Enslow Elementary) Enslow Publishing, LLC.

Lunis, Natalie. Furry Ferrets. 2009. (Peculiar Pets Ser.). (Illus.). 24p. (YA). (gr. 2-5). lib. bdg. 26.99 *(978-1-59716-860-1(2))* Bearport Publishing Co., Inc.

—Green Iguanas. 2009. (Peculiar Pets Ser.). (Illus.). 24p. (YA). (gr. 2-5). lib. bdg. 26.99 *(978-1-59716-863-2(7))* Bearport Publishing Co., Inc.

MacAulay, Kelley, et al. Les Lapins. 2011. (Petit Monde Vivant (Small Living World) Ser.: No. 78). (FRE., Illus.). 32p. (J). pap. 9.95 *(978-2-89579-372-4(7))* Bayard Canada Livres CAN. Dist: Crabtree Publishing Co.

Maher, Jack. Animal Instincts. 2011. (J). pap. *(978-0-531-22560-8(7))* Scholastic, Inc.

Make Believe Ideas, Ltd., creator. Pets & Puppies Pack. 2007. (Touch & Sparkle Ser.). (Illus.). (gr. -1-k). per., bds. *(978-1-84610-692-7(3))* Make Believe Ideas.

Make Your Own Pom Pom Pets. 2004. (Fun Kits Ser.). (Illus.). 48p. (J). *(978-1-84229-861-9(5))* Top That! Publishing PLC.

Maloney, Brenna. 125 Animals That Changed the World. 2019. (Illus.). 112p. (J). (gr. 3-7). pap. 12.99 *(978-1-4263-3277-7(7),* National Geographic Kids) Disney Publishing Worldwide.

Mansfield, Carol M. Jake & Jebadiah Visit the Veterinarian, 1 vol. 2010. 22p. pap. 24.95 *(978-1-4489-2548-3(7))* PublishAmerica, Inc.

Markovics, Pearl. My Favorite Pets. 2019. (My Favorite Things Ser.). (ENG., Illus.). 16p. (J). (gr. -1-1). 6.99 *(978-1-64280-389-1(8))* Bearport Publishing Co., Inc.

Mascotas. 2005. (Collection Abre Tus Ojos, Collection Eye Openers Ser.) Tr. of Pets. (SPA.). (J). (gr. k-2). 6.95 *(978-950-11-0899-6(6))* Sigmar ARG. Dist: Iaconi, Mariuccia Bk. Imports.

Mason, Paul. Caring for Critters. 2011. (ENG.). 24p. (J). pap. *(978-0-7787-7870-7(3));* (gr. 3-6). *(978-0-7787-7848-6(7))* Crabtree Publishing Co.

Matthews, Derek. Escucha y Aprende - Mascotas. 2005. (Escucha y Aprende Ser.). (SPA., Illus.). 10p. (J). (gr. -1-k). *(978-970-718-299-8(7),* Silver Dolphin en Español) Advanced Marketing, S. de R. L. de C. V.

McAneney, Caitie. Is a Bird a Good Pet for Me?, 1 vol. 2019. (Best Pet for Me Ser.). (ENG.). 24p. (J). (gr. 3-3). pap. 9.25 *(978-1-7253-0092-7(3),* a03ee3a8-213d-4667-b9cc-90f4d3ce535e, PowerKids Pr.) Rosen Publishing Group, Inc., The.

McBride, Anne. Hamsters, Vol. 12. 2016. (Understanding & Caring for Your Pet Ser.). (Illus.). 128p. (J). (gr. 5). 25.95 *(978-1-4222-3699-4(4))* Mason Crest.

McDonnell, Patrick. The Mutts Diaries. 2014. (Mutts Kids Ser.: 1). (ENG., Illus.). 224p. (J). pap. 9.99 *(978-1-4494-5870-6(X))* Andrews McMeel Publishing.

McKay, Sindy. We Both Read Bilingual Edition-About Pets/Acerca de las Mascotas. 2015.Tr. of Acerca de Las Mascotas. (ENG & SPA., Illus.). 44p. (J). (gr. 1-2). pap. 5.99 *(978-1-60115-062-2(8))* Treasure Bay, Inc.

McKenzie, Rosemarie. Cupcakes for Penny. 2011. 28p. pap. 15.99 *(978-1-4568-2335-1(3))* Xlibris Corp.

Mead, Wendy. Kids Top 10 Pet Birds, 1 vol. 2014. (American Humane Association Top 10 Pets for Kids Ser.). (ENG.). 48p. (gr. 3-4). 26.93 *(978-0-7660-6625-0(8),* 0738492e-f0e0-4f5f-ae4e-cb71b2e9a845); pap. 11.53 *(978-0-7660-6626-7(6),* f8b8dc80-7fd8-441d-8a07-19b705db96d5, Enslow Elementary) Enslow Publishing, LLC.

Meister, Cari. Birds. 2014. (Illus.). 24p. (J). lib. bdg. 25.65 *(978-1-62031-120-2(8),* Bullfrog Bks.) Jump! Inc.

—Cats. 2014. (Illus.). 24p. (J). lib. bdg. 25.65 *(978-1-62031-121-9(6),* Bullfrog Bks.) Jump! Inc.

—Dogs. 2014. (Illus.). 24p. (J). lib. bdg. 25.65 *(978-1-62031-122-6(4),* Bullfrog Bks.) Jump! Inc.

—Fish. 2014. (Illus.). 24p. (J). lib. bdg. 25.65 *(978-1-62031-123-3(2),* Bullfrog Bks.) Jump! Inc.

—Guinea Pigs. 2014. (Illus.). 24p. (J). lib. bdg. 25.65 *(978-1-62031-127-1(5),* Bullfrog Bks.) Jump! Inc.

—Hamsters. 2014. (Illus.). 24p. (J). lib. bdg. 25.65 *(978-1-62031-124-0(0),* Bullfrog Bks.) Jump! Inc.

—Rabbits. 2014. (Illus.). 24p. (J). lib. bdg. 25.65 *(978-1-62031-125-7(9),* Bullfrog Bks.) Jump! Inc.

—Turtles. 2014. (Illus.). 24p. (J). lib. bdg. 25.65 *(978-1-62031-126-4(7),* Bullfrog Bks.) Jump! Inc.

Melanie Z. Kato the True Story of a Siamese Cat. 2012. 28p. 24.95 *(978-1-4626-6919-6(0))* America Star Bks.

Mellion, Nicole. Liam's Pets. Filipina, Monika, illus. 2017. (Text Connections Guided Close Reading Ser.). (J). (gr. 1). *(978-1-4900-1802-7(6))* Benchmark Education Co.

Mi. Mi's Pets. 2012. 20p. pap. 13.77 *(978-1-4669-4019-2(0))* Trafford Publishing.

Miles, Ellen. Guide to Puppies. 2013. (Puppy Place Ser.). lib. bdg. 16.00 *(978-0-606-31503-6(9))* Turtleback.

—Kitty Corner: Guide to Kittens. 2013. (Kitty Corner Ser.). lib. bdg. 16.00 *(978-0-606-31502-9(0))* Turtleback.

Miles, Lisa. Origami Pets, 1 vol. 2013. (Amazing Origami Ser.). 32p. (J). (gr. 2-3). (ENG.). pap. 11.50 *(978-1-4339-9657-3(X),* 6e6f4732-641b-4de2-acaa-eceb8d590065); pap. 63.00 *(978-1-4339-9658-0(8));* (ENG., Illus.). lib. bdg. 29.27 *(978-1-4339-9656-6(1),* 40adfff3-6af6-4f2f-b379-6f2ebb735abe) Stevens, Gareth Publishing LLLP.

Miller, Pat. A Pet for Every Person. 2007. (Illus.). 24p. (J). *(978-1-60213-016-6(7),* Upstart Bks.) Highsmith Inc.

Mills, Nathan & Jamison, Linc. Caring for My Pet, 1 vol. 2012. (Rosen Readers Ser.). (ENG., Illus.). 16p. (J). (gr. k-k). pap. 7.00 *(978-1-4488-8710-1(0),* 28103ea8-e5db-4724-8300-8a8ae00e5757, Rosen Classroom) Rosen Publishing Group, Inc., The.

Minden, Cecilia. Sam & Jen Get a Pet. 2018. (Little Blossom Stories Ser.). (ENG., Illus.). 16p. (J). (gr. -1-2). pap. 11.36 *(978-1-5341-2398-4(9),* 210583, Cherry Blossom Press) Cherry Lake Publishing.

Mitchell Lane Publishers Inc. Staff. How to Convince Your Parents You Can..., 10 vols., Set. 2009. (J). (gr. 1-4). lib. bdg. 257.00 *(978-1-58415-664-2(3))* Mitchell Lane Pubs.

Moberg, Julia. Presidential Pets: The Weird, Wacky, Little, Big, Scary, Strange Animals That Have Lived in the White House. 2012. 96p. pap. 14.95 *(978-1-60734-471-1(8))* Charlesbridge Publishing, Inc.

—Presidential Pets: the Weird, Wacky, Little, Big, Scary, Strange Animals That Have Lived in the White House. Jeff Albrecht Studios, Jeff Albrecht, illus. 2016. 96p. (J). (gr. 3-7). pap. 9.95 *(978-1-62354-086-9(0))* Charlesbridge Publishing, Inc.

Moore, Elizabeth. Taking Care of a Pet, 1 vol. 2011. (Wonder Readers Emergent Level Ser.). (ENG.). 8p. (gr. -1-1). (J). pap. 6.25 *(978-1-4296-7847-6(X),* 118160); pap. 35.94 *(978-1-4296-8234-3(5),* Capstone Pr.) Capstone.

Moore Niver, Heather. Ostriches Are Not Pets!, 1 vol. 2013. (When Pets Attack! Ser.). (ENG.). 32p. (J). (gr. 3-4). 29.27 *(978-1-4339-9283-4(3),* 49ae0d97-6fc9-4c70-b1cc-e71b0b57002e); pap. 11.50 *(978-1-4339-9284-1(1),* ee3d7371-2cfd-4742-b0cb-7ca9547bce11) Stevens, Gareth Publishing LLLP.

Murray, Julie. Birds. 2019. (Pet Care Ser.). (ENG., Illus.). 24p. (J). (gr. 1-1). pap. 8.95 *(978-1-64185-664-5(5),* 1641856645, Abdo Zoom-Dash) ABDO Publishing Co.

National Geographic Kids. Look & Learn: Pets. 2018. (Look & Learn Ser.). (Illus.). 24p. (J). (gr. -1-k). bds. 6.99 *(978-1-4263-2992-0(X),* National Geographic Kids) Disney Publishing Worldwide.

—National Geographic Kids 125 True Stories of Amazing Pets: Inspiring Tales of Animal Friendship & Four-Legged Heroes, Plus Crazy Animal Antics. 2014. (Illus.). 112p. (J). (gr. 3-7). pap. 12.99 *(978-1-4263-1459-9(0),* National Geographic Kids) Disney Publishing Worldwide.

National Geographic Staff. National Geographic Kids: 125 True Stories of Amazing Pets. 2014. lib. bdg. 24.50 *(978-0-606-35574-2(X))* Turtleback.

Nelson, Maria. I'm Allergic to Pets, 1 vol. 2014. (I'm Allergic Ser.). (ENG.). 24p. (J). (gr. 1-2). 24.27 *(978-1-4824-0979-6(8),* 03dac294-a68a-4662-a886-0cf489c937ca) Stevens, Gareth Publishing LLLP.

Nelson, Robin. Pet Frog. 2003. (First Step Nonfiction). (Illus.). 24p. (J). (gr. k-2). lib. bdg. 18.60 *(978-0-8225-1271-4(8))* Lerner Publishing Group.

—Pet Hamster. 2003. (First Step Nonfiction). (Illus.). 24p. (J). (gr. k-2). lib. bdg. 18.60 *(978-0-8225-1269-1(6))* Lerner Publishing Group.

Olson, Elsie. Pet Rescue. 2017. (Animal Rights Ser.). (ENG., Illus.). 32p. (J). (gr. 3-6). lib. bdg. 32.79 *(978-1-5321-1260-7(2),* 27577, Checkerboard Library) ABDO Publishing Co.

Olsson, Elizabeth. The Tiny Pink House. 2010. 24p. 19.95 *(978-1-4520-1203-2(2))* AuthorHouse.

Orcutt, Cherie. A Beautiful Husky Needs a Home. Frongia, Daniela, illus. 2012. 32p. pap. 21.00 *(978-1-4685-7156-1(7))* AuthorHouse.

Ormiston, Rickey. My Dog Wiggles. 2010. 20p. 11.49 *(978-1-4490-9824-7(X))* AuthorHouse.

Ostriches Are Not Pets! 2013. (When Pets Attack! Ser.). 32p. (J). (gr. 3-6). pap. 63.00 *(978-1-4339-9285-8(X))* Stevens, Gareth Publishing LLLP.

O'Sullivan, Elizabeth. Sugar Gliders. 2008. (Early Bird Nature Bks.). (ENG.). 48p. (gr. 2-5). 26.60 *(978-0-8225-7891-8(3))* Lerner Publishing Group.

Our Weird Pets, 12 vols. 2017. (Our Weird Pets Ser.). 24p. (ENG.). (gr. 3-3). 151.62 *(978-1-4994-3496-5(0),* f3b80280-edac-45e5-9b4b-44731df402be); (gr. 7-8). pap. 49.50 *(978-1-5081-5433-4(3))* Rosen Publishing Group, Inc., The. (PowerKids Pr.).

Owen, Ruth. Icky House Invaders. 2011. (Up Close & Gross Ser.). 24p. (YA). (gr. 2-5). lib. bdg. 26.99 *(978-1-61772-124-3(7))* Bearport Publishing Co., Inc.

Pearce, Sue & Quin, Caroline. Pets. 2004. (Activities for 3-5 Year Olds Ser.). (Illus.). 32p. pap. 11.00 *(978-1-897675-38-0(0))* Brilliant Pubns. GBR. Dist: Parkwest Pubns., Inc.

Pearson, Marie. Pet Groomer. 2019. (Jobs with Animals Ser.). (ENG., Illus.). 32p. (J). (gr. 4-6). pap. 7.95 *(978-1-5435-6049-7(0),* 140094); lib. bdg. 28.65 *(978-1-5435-5787-9(2),* 139744) Capstone.

Perry, Sondra. The Most Unusual Pet Ever, Henry Our Great Blue Heron & His Adventures 2nd Edition. Byer, Janice, illus. 2014. 49p. 18.95 *(978-1-62652-432-3(7))* Salem Author Services.

Pet Day: Individual Title Six-Packs. (gr. k-1). 23.00 *(978-0-7635-8826-7(1))* Rigby Education.

Pet Day at School, 6 Packs. (Story Steps Ser.). (gr. k-2). 32.00 *(978-0-7635-9606-4(X))* Rigby Education.

Pet Dictionary: An a to Z of Animal Companions. 2005. (Illus.). 64p. (J). pap. *(978-0-439-75459-0(3))* Scholastic, Inc.

Pets: Individual Title Six-Packs. (Literatura 2000 Ser.). (gr. k-1). 28.00 *(978-0-7635-0062-7(3))* Rigby Education.

Pickett, Robert & Pickett, Justine, illus. Cat. Pickett, Robert & Pickett, Justine, photos by. 2004. 32p. (J). lib. bdg. 27.10 *(978-1-58340-431-7(7))* Black Rabbit Bks.

—Dog. Pickett, Robert & Pickett, Justine, photos by. 2004. 32p. (J). lib. bdg. 27.10 *(978-1-58340-430-0(9))* Black Rabbit Bks.

Piney Grove Elementary School (Kernsville, N.C.) Staff & Scholastic, Inc. Staff, contrib. by. A Kid for Jack: A True Story. 2012. (Illus.). 28p. *(978-0-545-51574-0(2))* Scholastic, Inc.

Playful Pets. (Flip Flap Fun Book Ser.). 10p. (J). bds. *(978-2-7643-0182-1(0))* Phidal Publishing, Inc./Editions Phidal, Inc.

Pomerance, Diane. Animal Companions: Your Friends, Teachers & Guides. Mier, Vanessa, illus. 2003. 9.95 *(978-0-9708500-2-7(6))* Polaire Pubns.

Priddy, Roger. Bright Baby Touch & Feel Perfect Pets. 2006. (Bright Baby Touch & Feel Ser.). (ENG., Illus.). 10p. (J). (gr. -1 — 1). bds. 4.95 *(978-0-312-49860-3(8),* 900041829) St. Martin's Pr.

—Funny Faces: Vampire Pets. 2014. (Funny Faces Ser.). (ENG.). 10p. (J). (gr. -1-1). bds. 8.99 *(978-0-312-51721-2(1),* 900132619) St. Martin's Pr.

Puchalski, Robin. Foo Foo the Shih Poo: My First Day Home. 2012. 20p. pap. 24.95 *(978-1-4626-6625-6(6))* America Star Bks.

Purple Walrus & Other Perfect Pets: 6 Each of 1 Anthology, 6 vols. (Wildcats Ser.). 32p. (gr. 2-8). *(978-0-322-00575-4(2))* Wright Group/McGraw-Hill.

Rabe, Tish. Oh, the Pets You Can Get! All about Our Animal Friends. Ruiz, Aristides & Mathieu, Joe, illus. 2005. (Cat in the Hat's Learning Library). (ENG.). 48p. (J). (gr. -1-3). 9.99 *(978-0-375-82278-0(X),* Random Hse. Bks. for Young Readers) Random Hse. Children's Bks.

Rajczak Nelson, Kristen. Sequential Words with Your Pets, 1 vol. 2013. (Write Right! Ser.). (Illus.). 24p. (J). (gr. 2-3). (ENG.). pap. 9.15 *(978-1-4339-9078-6(4),* 74ac8c57-a2ea-48f6-8da8-1a6d5c3cd83c); (ENG., lib. bdg. 25.27 *(978-1-4339-9077-9(6),* cfdc2aaa-e604-441a-9f1f-5291d3c438fc); (SPA & ENG., pap. 48.90 *(978-1-4339-9079-3(2),* 1358360) Stevens, Gareth Publishing LLLP.

Rake, Jody Sullivan. Why Rabbits Eat Poop & Other Gross Facts about Pets. 2012. (Gross Me Out Ser.). (ENG.). 24p. (gr. 1-2). pap. 41.70 *(978-1-4296-8378-4(3),* Capstone Pr.) Capstone.

Randolph, Joanne. Classroom Pets, 12 vols., Set. Incl. Fish. lib. bdg. 26.27 *(978-1-4042-3681-3(3),* ae488853-c828-467e-a777-b7fa2b84bd43); Guinea Pigs. lib. bdg. 26.27 *(978-1-4042-3676-9(7),* b46088c2-a14f-402e-8365-ad0f5bbd7b35); Rabbits. lib. bdg. 26.27 *(978-1-4042-3680-6(5),* 677ff52e-bb45-46e3-9322-fd2ba4f6e629); Snakes. lib. bdg. 26.27 *(978-1-4042-3679-0(1),* a3440aa5-262a-4d5b-bd82-05bd08f7de04); Tarantulas. lib. bdg. 26.27 *(978-1-4042-3678-3(3),* d606a576-9005-425a-a0a2-968259d1afd7); Turtles. lib. bdg. 26.27 *(978-1-4042-3677-6(5),* 08610ce0-8943-482b-bc7f-aa563c1e7c3b); (Illus.). 24p. (J). (gr. 2-3). (Classroom Pets Ser.). (ENG.). 2006. Set lib. bdg. 157.62 *(978-1-4042-3608-0(2),* 783c73fc-de18-49f7-be64-e197652cc3b7, PowerKids Pr.) Rosen Publishing Group, Inc., The.

Ransom, Candice. Terrier Trouble! And More True Stories of Animals Behaving Badly. 2017. (NGK Chapters Ser.). (Illus.). 112p. (J). (gr. 3-7). pap. 5.99 *(978-1-4263-2899-2(0),* National Geographic Kids) Disney Publishing Worldwide.

Rayner, Matthew. Cat, 1 vol. 2004. (I Am Your Pet Ser.). (ENG., Illus.). 32p. (gr. 2-4). lib. bdg. 28.67 *(978-0-8368-4102-2(6),* fd6457df-0cd2-4595-819b-9a7246033922, Gareth Stevens Learning Library) Stevens, Gareth Publishing LLLP.

—Dog, 1 vol. 2004. (I Am Your Pet Ser.). (ENG., Illus.). 32p. (gr. 2-4). lib. bdg. 28.67 *(978-0-8368-4103-9(4),* 378dbf9a-383e-4710-8531-47366a54cefc, Gareth Stevens Learning Library) Stevens, Gareth Publishing LLLP.

—Hamster, 1 vol. 2004. (I Am Your Pet Ser.). (ENG., Illus.). 32p. (gr. 2-4). lib. bdg. 28.67 *(978-0-8368-4104-6(2),* 37c756b9-f51e-4337-97ea-f0d80bfffc82, Gareth Stevens Learning Library) Stevens, Gareth Publishing LLLP.

—I Am Your Pet, 4 bks. Incl. Cat. lib. bdg. 28.67 *(978-0-8368-4102-2(6),* fd6457df-0cd2-4595-819b-9a7246033922); Dog. lib. bdg. 28.67 *(978-0-8368-4103-9(4),* 378dbf9a-383e-4710-8531-47366a54cefc); Hamster. lib. bdg. 28.67 *(978-0-8368-4104-6(2),* 37c756b9-f51e-4337-97ea-f0d80bfffc82); Rabbit. lib. bdg. 28.67 *(978-0-8368-4105-3(0),* cdf60275-a42d-44e6-be6a-275b66efedb4); 32p. (gr. 2-4)., Gareth Stevens Learning Library (Illus.). 2004. Set lib. bdg. 93.32 o.p. *(978-0-8368-4101-5(8));* Set lib. bdg. 47.86 o.p. *(978-0-8368-8384-8(5))* Stevens, Gareth Publishing LLLP.

—Rabbit, 1 vol. 2004. (I Am Your Pet Ser.). (ENG., Illus.). 32p. (gr. 2-4). lib. bdg. 28.67 *(978-0-8368-4105-3(0),* cdf60275-a42d-44e6-be6a-275b66efedb4, Gareth Stevens Learning Library) Stevens, Gareth Publishing LLLP.

Rebman, Nick. We Take Care of Pets. 2019. (Activities We Do Ser.). (ENG., Illus.). 16p. (J). (gr. k-1). pap. 7.95 *(978-1-64185-872-4(9),* 1641858729, Focus Readers) North Star Editions.

Reid, Siuna A. Reptiles Are Cool- Understanding My Tortoise. Lodge, Vivienne E., ed. 2013. (Illus.). 76p. pap. *(978-0-9576568-2-6(3))* Siuna A Reid.

Reilly, Cherie Brooks. Feathered & Furry Friends at the Farm. 2012. 108p. (gr. -1). pap. 11.92 *(978-1-4669-4095-6(6))* Trafford Publishing.

Ring, Susan. Caring for Your Cat. Kissock, Heather & Marshall, Diana, eds. 2003. (Caring for Your Pet Ser.). (Illus.). 32p. (J). pap. 9.95 *(978-1-59036-062-0(1))* Weigl Pubs., Inc.

Ripley's Entertainment Inc. Woof! Graziano, John, illus. 2012. (Ripley's Shout Outs Ser.: 3). (ENG.). 96p. (J). (gr. 2-5). pap. 4.99 *(978-0-545-38077-5(4))* Scholastic, Inc.

Rizzi, Kathleen. Who Lives Here? Pets (Arabic/Eng) (Arabic Edition) (Arabic & English Edition) 2012. (ARA., Illus.). 24p. (J). bds. 5.95 *(978-1-59572-351-2(X))* Star Bright Bks., Inc.

Rober, Harold. Getting a Pet. 2017. (Bumba Books (r) — Fun Firsts Ser.). (ENG., Illus.). 24p. (J). (gr. -1-1). 26.65 *(978-1-5124-2553-6(2),* 5ddc1ea3-2a2e-4785-afd3-5fcb66f1ca2d); E-Book 39.99 *(978-1-5124-2749-3(7));* E-Book 39.99 *(978-1-5124-3674-7(7),* 9781512436747); E-Book 4.99 *(978-1-5124-3675-4(5),* 9781512436754) Lerner Publishing Group. (Lerner Pubns.).

—I Love Hermit Crabs. 2016. (Bumba Books (r) — Pets Are the Best Ser.). (ENG., Illus.). 24p. (J). (gr. -1-1). lib. bdg. 26.65 *(978-1-5124-1418-9(2),* 15a1b6c1-c491-48e6-8a4d-1b3bf0733a58, Lerner Pubns.) Lerner Publishing Group.

Roberts, Heulwen. Anifeiliaid Anwes. 2005. (WEL., Illus.). 16p. pap. *(978-1-85644-778-2(2))* CAA.

Robinson, Joanna Jarc. Philip & Penny Learn about Pronouns. Hu, Caroline, illus. 2014. (Language Builders Ser.). (ENG.). 32p. (J). (gr. 2-4). lib. bdg. 25.27 *(978-1-59953-670-5(6))* Norwood Hse. Pr.

Romaine, Claire. Matemáticas con Mascotas / Math with Pets, 1 vol. de la Vega, Eida, tr. 2016. (¡Matemáticas en Todas Partes! / Math Is Everywhere! Ser.). (ENG & SPA.). 24p. (gr. k-k). lib. bdg. 24.27 *(978-1-4824-5216-7(2),* 5adaf151-1e5b-44b4-afab-ead628a673aa) Stevens, Gareth Publishing LLLP.

Ross, Daisy. Peter's Pets, 1 vol. 2012. (InfoMax Readers Ser.). (ENG., Illus.). 16p. (J). (gr. k-k). pap. 7.00 *(978-1-4488-8929-7(4),* 31705a41-dfa8-43d7-b2dc-34f015f8c727, Rosen Classroom) Rosen Publishing Group, Inc., The.

Ross, Michael Elsohn. Indoor Zoo. Seeley, Tim, illus. 2003. (You Are the Scientist Ser.). 48p. (J). (gr. 3-6). lib. bdg. 23.93 *(978-0-87614-621-7(3))* Lerner Publishing Group.

Ross, Tony. Mascotas. 2006. (Little Princess Ser.).Tr. of Pets. (SPA.). (J). (gr. -1-k). bds. 7.95 *(978-968-19-1485-1(6),* AT33279) Lectorum Pubns., Inc.

—Mascotas: La Pequena Princesa. 2006. (SPA., Illus.). 14p. (gr. -1-k). bds. *(978-84-372-2400-8(4))* Altea, Ediciones, S.A. - Grupo Santillana.

Roswell, Jackie. Gerbils. 2017. (Illus.). 128p. (J). *(978-1-4222-3691-8(9))* Mason Crest.

Rowe, Brooke. What Pet Should You Get? 2015. (Best Quiz Ever Ser.). (ENG., Illus.). 32p. (J). (gr. 4-8). 32.07 *(978-1-63470-034-4(1),* 206808) Cherry Lake Publishing.

Rudy, Maggie. I Wish I Had a Pet. Rudy, Maggie, illus. 2014. (ENG., Illus.). 40p. (J). (gr. -1-3). 17.99 *(978-1-4424-5332-6(X),* Beach Lane Bks.) Beach Lane Bks.

Rustad, Martha E. H. Je Compte Par 2 les Bébés Animaux. 2016. (1, 2, 3 Compte Avec Moi Ser.). (FRE., Illus.). 24p. (J). (gr. k-2). *(978-1-77092-349-2(7),* 17624) Amicus.

Ryan, Victoria. When Your Pet Dies: A Healing Handbook for Kids. Ryan, Victoria & Alley, R. W., illus. 2003. (Elf-Help Books for Kids). 32p. (J). per. 7.95 *(978-0-87029-376-4(1))* Abbey Pr.

Salzano, Tammi J., et al. Animal Friends. 2009. (Illus.). 32p. (J). *(978-0-545-13901-4(5))* Scholastic, Inc.

Sandy Creek (Firm) Staff, contrib. by. My First Book of Pets: Learn about Dogs, Cats, Lizards, & More with Fun Facts! 2016. (Illus.). 51p. (J). *(978-1-4351-6527-4(6))* Barnes & Noble, Inc.

Schafer, Susan. Invasive Mammals, 1 vol. 2016. (Invasive Species Ser.). (ENG.). 48p. (gr. 4-4). 33.07 *(978-1-5026-1832-0(X),* 956ebcc0-c427-44ec-b32a-e8eae0dc4f73) Cavendish Square Publishing LLC.

Schuh, Mari. Turtles. 2018. (Spot Pets Ser.). (ENG.). 16p. (J). (gr. -1-2). pap. 7.99 *(978-1-68152-291-3(8),* 14959) Amicus.

Schwab Marzolf, Julie. Big Cats Are Not Pets!, 1 vol. 2013. (When Pets Attack! Ser.). (ENG.). 32p. (J). (gr. 3-4). 29.27 *(978-1-4339-9273-5(6),* 11d275bc-5d34-4ed3-9ef1-ec34257106fc); pap. 11.50 *(978-1-4339-9274-2(4),* 51711e0a-0298-4840-8502-61d25ce90fab) Stevens, Gareth Publishing LLLP.

—Gross Things about Your Pets, 1 vol. 2012. (That's Gross! Ser.). (ENG., Illus.). 24p. (J). (gr. 2-3). 25.27

(978-1-4339-7119-8(4), 8dda6000-881c-4f81-b005-85b026d0a591); pap. 9.15 (978-1-4339-7120-4(8), 1bd8be6f-b00c-40d8-800b-9f098978bd67) Stevens, Gareth Publishing LLLP. (Gareth Stevens Learning Library).

Sexton, Colleen. Caring for Your Turtle. 2010. (Pet Care Library). (ENG., Illus.). 24p. (J). (gr. 2-5). lib. bdg. 26.95 (978-1-60014-472-1(1), Blastoff! Readers) Bellwether Media.

Shaw, Lucy K. Ethical Pet Ownership, 1 vol. 2019. (Ethical Living Ser.). (ENG.). 64p. (J). (gr. 6-6). 36.13 (978-1-5081-8061-6(X), 31bec12b-a767-47cc-aca9-9e82f7972d74) Rosen Publishing Group, Inc., The.

Shea, Therese M. Is a Turtle a Good Pet for Me? 2019. (Best Pet for Me Ser.). (ENG.). 24p. (gr. 3-3). 49.50 (978-1-7253-0121-4(0), PowerKids Pr.) Rosen Publishing Group, Inc., The.

Siemens, Jared. Ferret. 2017. (Illus.). 24p. (J). (978-1-5105-0560-5(1)) SmartBook Media, Inc.

Sigurdsson, Rev. Rupert. A Lifetime of Pets, 1 vol. 2010. 63p. pap. 19.95 (978-1-4489-5803-0(2)) America Star Bks.

Silverstein, Alvin, et al. Beautiful Birds. 2003. (What a Pet! Ser.). (Illus.). 48p. (gr. 5-8). lib. bdg. 23.90 (978-0-7613-2513-0(1), Millbrook Pr.) Lerner Publishing Group.

—Boas & Pythons: Cool Pets!, 1 vol. 2012. (Far-Out & Unusual Pets Ser.). (ENG., Illus.). 48p. (gr. 3-3). 27.93 (978-0-7660-3878-3(5), 88b54025-586d-452d-b348-7bcba32b25c8); pap. 11.53 (978-1-4644-0129-9(2), 7dbbf2f2-ad1c-48d5-9fe2-570fbc050858) Enslow Publishing, LLC. (Enslow Elementary).

—Creepy Crawlies. 2003. (What a Pet! Ser.). (ENG., Illus.). 48p. (gr. 3-6). lib. bdg. 23.93 (978-0-7613-2511-6(5), Millbrook Pr.) Lerner Publishing Group.

—Curious Cats. 2003. (What a Pet! Ser.). (ENG., Illus.). 48p. (gr. 3-6). lib. bdg. 23.93 (978-0-7613-2512-3(3), Millbrook Pr.) Lerner Publishing Group.

—Hairless Dogs: Cool Pets!, 1 vol. 2012. (Far-Out & Unusual Pets Ser.). (ENG., Illus.). 48p. (gr. 3-3). pap. 11.53 (978-1-4644-0124-4(1), 13d2fc58-b4da-4dff-81ed-3ad78d67aed5, Enslow Elementary) Enslow Publishing, LLC.

—Hermit Crabs: Cool Pets!, 1 vol. 2011. (Far-Out & Unusual Pets Ser.). (ENG., Illus.). 48p. (gr. 3-3). lib. bdg. 27.93 (978-0-7660-3684-0(7), 6d2c18be-dd3c-4d38-a2a2-833f82e14ac2) Enslow Publishing, LLC.

—Poison Dart Frogs: Cool Pets!, 1 vol. 2012. (Far-Out & Unusual Pets Ser.). (ENG., Illus.). 48p. (gr. 3-3). 27.93 (978-0-7660-3881-3(5), 8a27b532-a487-4beb-8281-6b61cf31ad11); pap. 11.53 (978-1-4644-0126-8(8), 28bd4360-9a70-46c4-b587-77176a13c2d9) Enslow Publishing, LLC. (Enslow Elementary).

—Rats: Cool Pets!, 1 vol. 2012. (Far-Out & Unusual Pets Ser.). (ENG., Illus.). 48p. (gr. 3-3). pap. 11.53 (978-1-4644-0127-5(6), 3222b4c8-0319-4c26-9c41-798f3e2f957e, Enslow Elementary) Enslow Publishing, LLC.

—Tarantulas: Cool Pets!, 1 vol. 2012. (Far-Out & Unusual Pets Ser.). (ENG., Illus.). 48p. (gr. 3-3). 27.93 (978-0-7660-3883-7(1), ab1664d0-c445-4b40-b542-9de363ab4bcf); pap. 11.53 (978-1-4644-0128-2(4), 5e073838-cca2-4500-b75b-9e5dba74d480) Enslow Publishing, LLC. (Enslow Elementary).

Simon, Elizabeth. Caring for Your Iguana. 2005. (Caring for Your Pet Ser.). (Illus.). 32p. (J). per. 9.95 (978-1-59036-215-0(2)); (gr. 4-7). lib. bdg. 26.00 (978-1-59036-195-5(4)) Weigl Pubs., Inc.

—Caring for Your Rat. (Caring for Your Pet Ser.). (Illus.). 32p. (J). 2005. (gr. 4-7). per. 9.95 (978-1-59036-217-4(9)) 2004. lib. bdg. 26.00 (978-1-59036-197-9(0)) Weigl Pubs., Inc.

Simonds, Lucy. People & Pets. 2007. (Trackers-Math Ser.). (gr. 2-5). pap. 5.00 (978-1-59055-920-8(7)) Pacific Learning, Inc.

Sjonger, Rebecca & Kalman, Bobbie. Gerbils. Crabtree, Marc, illus. Crabtree, Marc, photos by. 2003. (Pet Care Ser.). (ENG.). 32p. (J). lib. bdg. (978-0-7787-1752-2(6)) Crabtree Publishing Co.

—Hamsters. Crabtree, Marc, illus. Crabtree, Marc, photos by. 2003. (Pet Care Ser.). (ENG.). 32p. (J). lib. bdg. (978-0-7787-1753-9(4)) Crabtree Publishing Co.

—Mice, 1 vol. Crabtree, Marc, illus. Crabtree, Marc, photos by. 2003. (Pet Care Ser.). (ENG.). 32p. (J). pap. (978-0-7787-1786-7(0)); lib. bdg. (978-0-7787-1754-6(2)) Crabtree Publishing Co.

—Puppies. 2003. (Pet Care Ser.). (ENG., Illus.). 32p. (J). lib. bdg. (978-0-7787-1751-5(8)) Crabtree Publishing Co.

Sjonger, Rebecca, et al. Les Souris. 2011. (Petit Monde Vivant (Small Living World) Ser.: No. 77). (FRE., Illus.). 32p. (J). pap. 9.95 (978-2-89579-371-7(9)) Bayard Canada Livres CAN. Dist: Crabtree Publishing Co.

Smalley, Carol Parenzan. Care for a Pet Hamster. 2009. (How to Convince Your Parents You Can ... Ser.). 32p. (J). (gr. 1-4). 25.70 (978-1-58415-804-2(2)) Mitchell Lane Pubs.

Sparling, Rebecca. Gerbils. 2009. (Illus.). 112p. (J). 14.95 (978-1-932904-36-9(0)) Eldorado Ink.

Spears, James. National Geographic Kids Everything Pets: Furry Facts, Photos, & Fun-Unleashed! 2013. (National Geographic Kids Everything Ser.). 64p. (J). (gr. 3-7). (ENG.). lib. bdg. 21.90 (978-1-4263-1363-9(2)); (Illus.). pap. 12.95 (978-1-4263-1362-2(4)) Disney Publishing Worldwide. (National Geographic Kids).

Stark, Kristy. Fantastic Kids: Care for Animals. 2018. (TIME for KIDS(r): Informational Text Ser.). (ENG., Illus.). 12p. (J). (gr. k-1). 7.99 (978-1-4258-4952-8(0)) Teacher Created Materials, Inc.

—Niños Fantásticos: Cuidar a Los Animales. rev. ed. 2019. (TIME for KIDS(r): Informational Text Ser.). (SPA., Illus.). 12p. (gr. k-1). 7.99 (978-1-4258-2689-5(X)) Teacher Created Materials, Inc.

Starosta, Paul. Face-to-Face with the Hamster. 2004. (Illus.). 25p. (J). 9.95 (978-1-57091-456-0(7)) Charlesbridge Publishing, Inc.

Stevenson, Sharry. Gibby's Story. 2012. 36p. pap. 18.41 (978-1-4669-3322-4(4)) Trafford Publishing.

Steward, Martha. Darby's Story: The Life of an Adopted Dog. 2009. 36p. pap. 15.95 (978-1-4490-2775-9(X)) AuthorHouse.

Stoltman, Joan. My First Bird, 1 vol. 2017. (Let's Get a Pet! Ser.). (ENG.). 24p. (J). (gr. 1-2). pap. 9.15 (978-1-4824-6437-5(3), d80f1d2e-0fb9-49a1-9f46-8b09bd063f63) Stevens, Gareth Publishing LLLP.

—My First Cat, 1 vol. 2017. (Let's Get a Pet! Ser.). (ENG.). 24p. (gr. 1-2). pap. 9.15 (978-1-4824-6445-0(4), 03debabb-aea7-4283-9100-8a0f4b98f02d) Stevens, Gareth Publishing LLLP.

—My First Dog, 1 vol. 2017. (Let's Get a Pet! Ser.). (ENG.). 24p. (gr. 1-2). pap. 9.15 (978-1-4824-6449-8(7), 98095814-eaf8-49b5-a9ee-00c20ddaa56b) Stevens, Gareth Publishing LLLP.

Stone, Kelly P. What Do Pets Do When They Go up to Heaven?, 1 vol. Stone, Kelly P. & Stone, Joyce M., illus. 2009. 13p. pap. 24.95 (978-1-61546-212-4(0)) America Star Bks.

Sullivant, Holly. Hamsters. 2009. (Illus.). 112p. (J). 14.95 (978-1-932904-38-3(7)) Eldorado Ink.

Tanguy. Can I Keep It? Small Pets Guide: 39 Cool, Easy-To-Care-for Insects, Reptiles, Mammals, Amphibians, & More. 2020. (ENG., Illus.). 168p. (J). pap. 16.99 (978-1-62008-391-8(4), 3918Ca, CompanionHouse Bks.) Fox Chapel Publishing Co., Inc.

Terry, Paul. Top 10 for Kids Pets. 2015. (ENG., Illus.). 96p. (J). (gr. 3-6). pap. 9.95 (978-1-77085-527-4(0), 0ed1ef0d-020f-4ba7-adeb-97321ae099a3) Firefly Bks., Ltd.

Thomas, Isabel. Pet Projects. 2015. (Pet Projects Ser.). (ENG.). 32p. (J). (gr. 3-5). 122.60 (978-1-4109-8068-7(5), 23674) Capstone.

—Slinky's Guide to Caring for Your Snake, 1 vol. Peterson, Rick, illus. 2014. (Pets' Guides). (ENG.). 32p. (J). (gr. 1-3). 29.99 (978-1-4846-0263-8(3), 126314); pap. 7.99 (978-1-4846-0270-6(6), 126320) Capstone. (Heinemann).

—Squeak's Guide to Caring for Your Pet Rats or Mice, 1 vol. Peterson, Rick, illus. 2014. (Pets' Guides). (ENG.). 32p. (J). (gr. 1-3). pap. 7.99 (978-1-4846-0271-3(4), 126321, Heinemann) Capstone.

Thomas, Pat. I Miss My Pet: A First Look at When a Pet Dies. Harker, Lesley, illus. 2012. (First Look At... Ser.). (ENG.). 32p. (J). (gr. k-2). pap. 7.99 (978-1-4380-0188-3(6)) Sourcebooks, Inc.

Toliver, Marilyn. Marcellus Really Wants a Pet. 2012. 28p. pap. 16.09 (978-1-4669-0090-5(3)) Trafford Publishing.

Tracy, Kathleen. The Frog in Our Class. 2011. (Randy's Corner Ser.). (Illus.). 32p. (J). (gr. -1-2). lib. bdg. 25.70 (978-1-58415-977-3(4)) Mitchell Lane Pubs.

Tuxworth, Nicola. Pets. 2015. (Illus.). 20p. (J). (gr. -1-12). bds. 6.99 (978-1-86147-647-0(7), Armadillo) Anness Publishing GBR. Dist: National Bk. Network.

Van Der Linden, Elly. The Little Hamster, 114 vols. Lavreys, Debbie, illus. 2007. (ENG.). 12p. (gr. -1-k). (978-0-86315-605-2(3)) Floris Bks.

Velasquez, Maria. Pet Parade. Mooney, Alyssa, illus. 2007. (J). pap. 21.00 (978-0-15-379895-5(5)) Houghton Mifflin Harcourt School Pubs.

Verdick, Elizabeth. Tails Are Not for Pulling. Heinlen, Marieka, illus. 2005. (ENG.). (J). (Best Behavior(r) Paperback Ser.). 40p. (gr. 4-7). pap. 11.99 (978-1-57542-181-0(X), 990); (Best Behavior(r) Board Book Ser.: Bk. 3). 26p. (gr. 3 — 1). bds. 9.99 (978-1-57542-180-3(1), 989) Free Spirit Publishing Inc.

Vincenti, Catherine, ed. & illus. Pet Pals Grades 3-4: A Spanish-English Workbook. Vincenti, Catherine, illus. 2003.Tr. of Mascotas Companeros. (SPA.). 34p. wbk. ed. 3.00 (978-0-941246-21-7(3), Humane Society Pr.) National Assn. for Humane & Environmental Education.

—Pet Pals Grades 5-6: A Spanish-English Workbook. Vincenti, Catherine, illus. 2003.Tr. of Mascotas Companeros. (SPA.). 34p. wbk. ed. 3.00 (978-0-941246-22-4(1), Humane Society Pr.) National Assn. for Humane & Environmental Education.

—Pet Pals Grades K-2: A Spanish-English Workbook. Vincenti, Catherine, illus. 2003.Tr. of Mascotas Companeros. (SPA.). 34p. (J). wbk. ed. 3.00 (978-0-941246-20-0(5), Humane Society Pr.) National Assn. for Humane & Environmental Education.

Vink, Amanda. Is a Dog a Good Pet for Me? 2019. (Best Pet for Me Ser.). (ENG.). 24p. (gr. 3-3). 49.50 (978-1-7253-0101-6(6), PowerKids Pr.) Rosen Publishing Group, Inc., The.

Walker, Niki & Kalman, Bobbie. Kittens, 1 vol. 2003. (Pet Care Ser.). (ENG., Illus.). 32p. (J). pap. (978-0-7787-1782-9(8)) Crabtree Publishing Co.

Wallace, Bruce & Make Believe Ideas Staff. Pets. 2005. (Touch & Sparkle Ser.). (Illus.). 12p. (gr. -1-k). bds. (978-1-905051-01-4(8)) Make Believe Ideas.

Webb, Cheryl Renee. Do Pets & Other Animals Go to Heaven? How to Recover from the Loss of an Animal Friend. 2003. (Illus.). 108p. per. 15.95 (978-0-9726363-0-8(7)) Brite Bks.

West, David. Animals in the Home. 2013. (Nora the Naturalist's Animals Ser.). 24p. (gr. k-3). 28.50 (978-1-62588-005-5(7)) Black Rabbit Bks.

—Pets in the Home. West, David, illus. 2014. (Nora the Naturalist's Animals Ser.). (Illus.). 24p. (J). (gr. k-3). pap. 8.95 (978-1-62588-052-9(9)) Black Rabbit Bks.

When Pets Attack!, 12 vols. 2013. (When Pets Attack! Ser.). 32p. (J). (gr. 3-4). (ENG.). 175.62 (978-1-4339-9677-1(4), ffdf9b5f-abb7-427e-b75a-47d3b81d5bb1); pap. 378.00 (978-1-4339-9742-6(8)); pap. 63.00 (978-1-4339-9741-9(X)) Stevens, Gareth Publishing LLLP.

Where Is My Pet?, 6 Packs. (Chiquilibros Ser.). (gr. k-1). 23.00 (978-0-7635-0438-0(6)) Rigby Education.

Wilberforce, Bert. Can I Have a Pet Giraffe?, 1 vol. 2018. (That's Not a Pet! Ser.). (ENG.). 24p. (gr. k-k). 24.27 (978-1-5382-1792-4(9), c01caf04-6522-4ba5-a8ba-89b27a22399a) Stevens, Gareth Publishing LLLP.

—Can I Have a Pet Gorilla?, 1 vol. 2018. (That's Not a Pet! Ser.). (ENG.). 24p. (gr. k-k). 24.27 (978-1-5382-1796-2(1), 04d42cff-0eb4-4a58-b61c-0581da3dfaa3) Stevens, Gareth Publishing LLLP.

—Can I Have a Pet Polar Bear?, 1 vol. 2018. (That's Not a Pet! Ser.). (ENG.). 24p. (gr. k-k). 24.27 (978-1-5382-1800-6(3), 688efb45-2257-4e50-9257-632fdb7a50e8) Stevens, Gareth Publishing LLLP.

William H. Sadlier Staff. Good Pets: Big Book, Vol. 3. 2005. (Emergent Library: Vol. 1). (gr. -1-1). 24.00 net. (978-0-8215-8910-6(5)) Sadlier, William H. Inc.

Willow Creek Press, creator. What Pets Teach Us: Life's Lessons Learned from Our Best Friends. 2006. (ENG., Illus.). 32p. (J). (gr. -1-1). 12.95 (978-1-59543-393-0(7)) Willow Creek Pr., Inc.

Wilson, Paula M. Cute & Unusual Pets. 2018. (Cute & Unusual Pets Ser.). (ENG.). 32p. (J). (gr. 3-9). 122.60 (978-1-5435-3060-5(5), 28513, Capstone Pr.) Capstone.

Wittrock, Jeni. Pet Hermit Crabs up Close. 2015. (Pets up Close Ser.). (ENG., Illus.). 24p. (J). (gr. -1-2). lib. bdg. 27.32 (978-1-4914-2109-3(6), 127592, Capstone Pr.) Capstone.

World Book, Inc. Staff, contrib. by. Can Cats Swim Even If They Don't Like Water? World Book Answers Your Questions about Pets & Other Animals. 2019. (Illus.). 96p. (J). (978-0-7166-3825-4(8)) World Bk., Inc.

—Green Anoles & Other Pet Lizards. 2009. (J). (978-0-7166-1368-8(9)) World Bk., Inc.

—Hamsters & Other Pet Rodents. 2009. (J). (978-0-7166-1370-1(0)) World Bk., Inc.

—World of Pets. 2010. (J). (978-0-7166-7745-1(8)) World Bk., Inc.

Yoyo Books, creator. Pets. 2011. (ENG., Illus.). 10p. (gr. -1-k). bds. (978-94-6151-208-6(2)) YoYo Bks.

Zondervan Staff. Cats, Dogs, Hamsters, & Horses, 1 vol. 2010. (I Can Read! / Made by God Ser.). (ENG., Illus.). 32p. (J). (gr. -1-2). pap. 4.99 (978-0-310-72009-6(5)) Zonderkidz.

Zullo, Allan. Bad Pets Save Christmas! 2012. 139p. (J). pap. (978-0-545-61229-6(2)) Scholastic, Inc.

—Miracle Pets: True Tales of Courage & Survival. 2011. 122p. (978-0-545-25507-3(4)) Scholastic, Inc.

PETS—FICTION

Abbott, Rosalind. A Pet for Me. Seltzer, Jerry, illus. 2013. 24p. (J). 16.95 (978-1-60131-155-9(9), Castlebridge Bks.) Big Tent Bks.

Ada, Alma Flor. Daniel's Pet. Karas, G. Brian, illus. 2003. (Green Light Readers Level 1 Ser.). (ENG.). 24p. (J). (gr. -1-3). pap. 4.99 (978-0-15-204865-5(0), 1194691, Clarion Bks.) HarperCollins Pubs.

Adams, Jean Ekman. When Dogs Dream. 2013. 32p. (J). 15.95 (978-1-933855-84-4(3), Rio Nuevo Pubs.) Rio Nuevo Pubs.

Adamson, Ged. Shark Dog! 2017. (ENG., Illus.). 40p. (J). (gr. -1-3). 17.99 (978-0-06-245713-4(6), HarperCollins) HarperCollins Pubs.

Ahlberg, Allan & Amstutz, Andre. Funnybones: the Pet Shop: A Funnybones Story. 2018. (Funnybones Ser.: 2). (Illus.). 32p. (J). (gr. -1-k). pap. 12.99 (978-0-14-137870-1(0)) Penguin Bks., Ltd. GBR. Dist: Independent Pubs. Group.

Albee, Sarah. Off to Bed. Ebert, Len, illus. 2006. (Step-By-Step Readers Ser.). (J). pap. (978-1-59939-060-4(4), Reader's Digest Young Families, Inc.) Studio Fun International.

Alexander, Lori. Backhoe Joe. Cameron, Craig, illus. 2014. (ENG.). 40p. (J). (gr. -1-3). 16.99 (978-0-06-225015-5(9), HarperCollins) HarperCollins Pubs.

Alvarez, Jennifer Lynn. The Pet Washer. 2nd ed. 2012. (ENG.). 171p. (J). (gr. 3-7). pap. 8.99 (978-0-9848484-5-4(2)) Dreamcatcher Bks.

Amateau, Gigi. Chancey: Horses of the Maury River Stables. 2010. (Horses of the Maury River Ser.: 1). (ENG., Illus.). 256p. (J). (gr. 4-7). pap. 8.99 (978-0-7636-4523-6(0)) Candlewick Pr.

Amdahl Elco, Anita & Weikert Stelmach, Katherine. Who Is in That Shell? Patch, Michael, illus. 2012. 130p. (J). pap. 13.50 (978-0-9883568-0-1(5)) Inkwell Books LLC.

Anderson, Laurie Halse. New Beginnings, 13 vols., 13. 2012. (Vet Volunteers Ser.: 13). (ENG.). 192p. (J). (gr. 3-7). 7.99 (978-0-14-241675-4(4), Puffin) Penguin Young Readers Group.

—Treading Water. 2014. (Vet Volunteers Ser.: 16). (ENG.). 192p. (J). (gr. 3-7). pap. 7.99 (978-0-14-241678-5(9), Puffin Books) Penguin Young Readers Group.

Arguello, John. Ophelia & the Pet Peeve. 2009. 24p. pap. 12.99 (978-1-4389-9197-9(5)) AuthorHouse.

Arnold, Tedd. Fly Guy's Ninja Christmas (Fly Guy #16) Arnold, Tedd, illus. 2016. (Fly Guy Ser.: 16). (ENG., Illus.). 32p. (J). (gr. -1-2). 6.99 (978-0-545-66277-2(X), Cartwheel Bks.) Scholastic, Inc.

—A Pet for Fly Guy. Arnold, Tedd, illus. 2014. (Fly Guy Ser.). (ENG., Illus.). 32p. (J). (gr. -1-3). 16.99 (978-0-545-31615-6(4), Orchard Bks.) Scholastic, Inc.

—There Was an Old Lady Who Swallowed Fly Guy (Fly Guy #4) Arnold, Tedd, illus. 2007. (Fly Guy Ser.: 4). (ENG., Illus.). 32p. (J). (gr. -1-3). 6.99 (978-0-439-63906-4(9), Cartwheel Bks.) Scholastic, Inc.

Arruzza, Rick. No Descanso Para Sparky. Newton, Pilar, illus. 2004. (SPA.). 24p. (J). mass mkt. 7.95 (978-0-9744509-3-3(6)) Three Spots Productions.

—No Rest for Sparky. Newton, Pilar, illus. 2004. 24p. (J). mass mkt. 7.95 (978-0-9744509-2-6(8)) Three Spots Productions.

Arsenault, Isabelle. Colette's Lost Pet. 2017. (Mile End Kids Story Ser.: 1). (Illus.). 48p. (J). (gr. -1-3). 17.99 **(978-1-101-91759-6(8)**, Tundra Bks.) Tundra Bks. CAN. Dist: Penguin Random Hse. LLC.

Asch, Frank. The Ghost of P. S. 42. Kanzler, John, illus. 2014. (Class Pets Ser.). (ENG.). 96p. (J). (gr. 2-5). pap. 13.99 (978-1-4814-3624-3(4), Simon & Schuster/Paula Wiseman Bks.) Simon & Schuster/Paula Wiseman Bks.

Ashman, Linda. Take Your Pet to School Day. Kaufman, Suzanne, illus. 2019. 40p. (J). (gr. -1-2). 17.99 (978-1-5247-6559-0(7)); (ENG.). 20.99 (978-1-5247-6560-6(0)) Random Hse. Children's Bks. (Random Hse. Bks. for Young Readers).

Auerbach, Annie. Meet Boulder the Construction-Bot. 2013. (Transformers Passport to Reading Ser.). (J). lib. bdg. 13.55 (978-0-606-32274-4(4)) Turtleback.

Aulbach, Kathy. Flower Sprouts: Let's have a Fest! 2009. 29p. 15.95 (978-0-615-21683-6(8)) Flower Sprouts.

Averbeck, Jim. Two Problems for Sophia. Ismail, Yasmeen, illus. 2018. (Sophia Bks.). (ENG.). 40p. (J). (gr. -1-3). 17.99 (978-1-4814-7788-8(9), McElderry, Margaret K. Bks.) McElderry, Margaret K. Bks.

AZ Books Staff. My Pets. Yaroshevich, Angelica, ed. 2012. (Open the Book-I Am Alive Ser.). (ENG.). 8p. (J). (— 1). bds. 5.95 (978-1-61889-045-0(X)) AZ Bks. LLC.

Baby Pets: Chunky photo Book. 2006. (J). bds. 3.99 (978-1-934004-01-2(4)) Byeway Bks.

Baglio, Ben M. Come Back, Buddy! 2004. (Illus.). 118p. (J). pap. (978-0-439-68883-3(3)) Scholastic, Inc.

—Help Find Honey! 2006. (Pet Finders Club Ser.: Vol. 10). (Illus.). 157p. (J). (978-0-439-87143-3(3)) Scholastic, Inc.

—Max Is Missing. 2005. (Pet Finders Club Ser.: Vol. 2). (Illus.). 126p. (J). pap. (978-0-439-68884-0(1)) Scholastic, Inc.

Baker, Courtney. The Perfect Pet. Snider, Jackie, illus. 2003. (Hello Reader! Ser.). (J). pap. (978-0-439-47111-4(7)) Scholastic, Inc.

Baltazar, Art & Aureliani, Franco. Super-Pets!, 1 vol. Baltazar, Art, illus. 2013. (Superman Family Adventures Ser.). (ENG., Illus.). 32p. (J). (gr. 1-3). 22.60 (978-1-4342-4792-6(9), 121574, Stone Arch Bks.) Capstone.

Banerjee, Anjali. Seaglass Summer. 2011. (ENG.). 176p. (J). (gr. 4-6). lib. bdg. 22.44 (978-0-385-90555-8(6), Lamb, Wendy Bks.); (Illus.). (gr. 3-7). pap. 7.99 (978-0-375-84399-0(X), Yearling) Random Hse. Children's Bks.

Barkley, Callie. Ellie the Flower Girl. Bishop, Tracy, illus. 2016. (Critter Club Ser.: 14). (ENG.). 128p. (J). (gr. k-4). pap. 6.99 (978-1-4814-6718-6(2), Little Simon) Little Simon.

—Marion & the Secret Letter. Bishop, Tracy, illus. 2017. (Critter Club Ser.: 16). (ENG.). 128p. (J). (gr. k-4). pap. 6.99 (978-1-4814-8702-3(7), Little Simon) Little Simon.

—Marion & the Secret Letter. 2017. (Critter Club Ser.: 16). lib. bdg. 16.00 (978-0-606-39739-1(6)) Turtleback.

Barroux, Stephane, illus. My Goldfish. 2009. 36p. (J). (gr. -1-2). 15.00 (978-0-8028-5334-9(X), Eerdmans Bks For Young Readers) Eerdmans, William B. Publishing Co.

Bartoletti, Susan Campbell. Nobody's Diggier Than a Dog. Giacobbe, Beppe, illus. 2005. (ENG.). 40p. (gr. -1-17). 15.99 (978-0-7868-1824-2(7)) Hyperion Pr.

Barton, Byron. My Bus Board Book. Barton, Byron, illus. 2015. (ENG., Illus.). 38p. (J). (gr. -1 — 1). bds. 8.99 (978-0-06-228738-0(9), Greenwillow Bks.) HarperCollins Pubs.

Beck, Sharon. The Fish in Our Class. 2011. (Randy's Corner Ser.). (Illus.). 32p. (J). (gr. -1-2). lib. bdg. 25.70 (978-1-58415-978-0(2)) Mitchell Lane Pubs.

Beck, W. H. Malcolm at Midnight. Lies, Brian, illus. 2015. (ENG.). 272p. (J). (gr. 3-7). pap. 7.99 (978-0-544-33666-7(6), 1584188, Clarion Bks.) HarperCollins Pubs.

Bell, Samantha. The Perfect Pet, 1 vol. 2013. (SPA., Illus.). 32p. (J). (gr. k-1). pap. 11.95 (978-1-60718-701-1(9), 7762f99b-3f03-429d-809c-56bd3d3036bc) Arbordale Publishing.

Bellisario, Gina. Mighty Pet Sitter. von Innerebner, Jessika, illus. 2018. (Ellie Ultra Ser.). (ENG.). 128p. (J). (gr. 1-3). lib. bdg. 25.99 (978-1-4965-5238-9(5), 136263, Stone Arch Bks.) Capstone.

Bennett, Kelly. No a Norman: La Historia de un Pececito Dorado. Jones, Noah Z., illus. 2016. (SPA.). 32p. (J). (gr. -1-3). 6.99 (978-0-7636-8906-3(8)) Candlewick Pr.

—Not Norman: A Goldfish Story. Jones, Noah Z., illus. 2008. (ENG.). 32p. (J). (gr. -1-3). pap. 7.99 (978-0-7636-2763-8(1)) Candlewick Pr.

Bentley, Catherine & Bentley, Dawn. Hoppy Goes to School. Huerta, Catherine, illus. 2006. (Pet Tales Ser.). (ENG.). 32p. (J). 2.95 (978-1-59249-558-0(3)) Soundprints.

Bentley, Dawn. Hoppy Goes to School. Huerta, Catherine, illus. 2006. (ENG.). 32p. (J). pap. 9.95 (978-1-59249-559-7(1)); (gr. -1-3). 4.95 (978-1-59249-556-6(7)) Soundprints.

Berenstain, Jan & Berenstain, Mike. The Berenstain Bears' Really Big Pet Show. Berenstain, Jan & Berenstain, Mike, illus. 2008. (Berenstain Bears Ser.). (Illus.). 32p. (J). (gr. -1-2). 8.99 (978-0-06-057406-2(2), HarperFestival) HarperCollins Pubs.

—The Berenstain Bears' Really Big Pet Show. Berenstain, Jan & Mike, illus. 2008. (Berenstain Bears Ser.). (ENG.). 32p. (J). (gr. -1-2). pap. 3.99 (978-0-06-057390-4(2), HarperFestival) HarperCollins Pubs.

Bernstein, Ariel. Warren & Dragon Weekend with Chewy. Malbrough, Mike, illus. 2018. (Warren & Dragon Ser.: 2). 96p. (J). (gr. k-3). 5.99 (978-0-425-28849-8(8), Puffin Books) Penguin Young Readers Group.

Berry, Lynne. Pig & Pug. Correll, Gemma, illus. 2015. (ENG.). 40p. (J). (gr. -1-3). 16.99 (978-1-4814-2131-7(X), Simon & Schuster Bks. For Young Readers) Simon & Schuster Bks. For Young Readers.

Beyers, Kathryn. Babe's Vacation. 2012. 32p. pap. 17.49 (978-1-4771-5671-1(2)) Xlibris Corp.

Biedrzycki, David. Me & My Dragon. Biedrzycki, David, illus. 2011. (Me & My Dragon Ser.). (ENG., Illus.). 40p. (J). (gr. -1-3). 18.99 (978-1-58089-278-0(7)) Charlesbridge Publishing, Inc.

—Me & My Dragon: Christmas Spirit. Biedrzycki, David, illus. 2015. (Me & My Dragon Ser.). (ENG., Illus.). 40p. (J). (gr. -1-3). lib. bdg. 17.95 (978-1-58089-622-1(7)) Charlesbridge Publishing, Inc.

—Me & My Dragon: Scared of Halloween. Biedrzycki, David, illus. 2013. (Me & My Dragon Ser.). (Illus.). 32p. (J). (gr. -1-3). pap. 7.99 (978-1-58089-659-7(6)) Charlesbridge Publishing, Inc.

—Mi Dragón y Yo. Biedrzycki, David, illus. 2014. (Illus.). 32p. (J). (gr. -1-3). pap. 7.95 (978-1-58089-574-3(3)); lib. bdg. 17.95 (978-1-58089-693-1(6)) Charlesbridge Publishing, Inc.

Bird, Benjamin. Supergirl's Pet Problem! Levins, Tim, illus. 2015. (Amazing Adventures of Superman! Ser.). (ENG.). 32p. (J). (gr. k-2). pap. 3.95 (978-1-4795-6523-8(7), 128511, Stone Arch Bks.) Capstone.

Birney, Betty G. Humphrey's Pet Show Panic. Burris, Priscilla, illus. 2018. (Humphrey's Tiny Tales Ser.: 7). (ENG.). 96p. (J). (gr. k-3). 6.99 (978-1-5247-3718-4(6), Puffin Books) Penguin Young Readers Group.

—Humphrey's Pet Show Panic. 2018. (Humphrey's Tiny Tales Ser.: 7). lib. bdg. 14.75 (978-0-606-40887-5(8)) Turtleback.

—Humphrey's Treasure Hunt Trouble. Burris, Priscilla, illus. 2017. (Humphrey's Tiny Tales Ser.: 6). (ENG.). 96p. (J). (gr. k-3). 6.99 (978-0-14-751462-2(2), Puffin Books) Penguin Young Readers Group.

The check digit for ISBN-10 appears in parentheses after the full ISBN-13

—Life According to Og the Frog. 2019. (Og the Frog Ser.: 1). (ENG.). 192p. (J). (gr. 3-7). 7.99 *(978-1-5247-3996-6(0),* Puffin Books) Penguin Young Readers Group.

—Secrets According to Humphrey. 2015. (According to Humphrey Ser.: 10). lib. bdg. 16.00 *(978-0-606-36600-7(8))* Turtleback.

Blabey, Aaron. Pig the Star. 2018. (Pig the Pug Ser.). (ENG., Illus.). 32p. (J). (gr. -1-k). 14.99 *(978-1-338-28021-0(X),* Scholastic Pr.) Scholastic, Inc.

Black, Angie. Adopting Jake. Lucas, Diane, illus. 2010. 32p. pap. 12.95 *(978-1-935268-47-5(3))* Halo Publishing International.

Blackidge, Barbara. Lucky: My Story. 2010. 24p. (J). pap. 12.95 *(978-1-934449-64-6(4))* Legacy Publishing Services, Inc.

Blake, Linda. My Pet Rabbit. 2012. 24p. 24.95 *(978-1-4626-6187-9(4))* America Star Bks.

Blake, Quentin. Loveykins. 2003. (ENG., Illus.). 32p. (J). (gr. -1-3). 15.95 *(978-1-56145-282-8(3))* Peachtree Publishing Co. Inc.

Blance, Ellen & Cook, Tony. Monster Buys a Pet. Date not set. (Illus.). 40p. pap. 129.15 *(978-0-582-19311-6(7))* Addison-Wesley Longman, Ltd. GBR. Dist: Trans-Atlantic Pubns., Inc.

Blevins, Wiley. Max Has a Fish. Clanton, Ben, illus. 2012. (Penguin Young Readers, Level 1 Ser.). (ENG.). 32p. (J). (gr. k-1). pap. 5.99 *(978-0-448-46158-8(7),* Penguin Young Readers) Penguin Young Readers Group.

—Max Has a Fish. 2012. (Penguin Young Readers: Level 1 Ser.). lib. bdg. 13.55 *(978-0-606-26640-6(2))* Turtleback.

Bloncourt, N. Fanny Flies to France. 2019. (Fanny Ser.). (Illus.). 40p. (J). (gr. -1-12). 20.00 *(978-1-943876-49-5(5))* G Arts LLC.

Blume, Erma Hill. Tattle-Tale Pete. 2012. 28p. pap. 24.95 *(978-1-62709-097-1(5))* America Star Bks.

Boelts, Maribeth. Before You Were Mine. Walker, David, illus. 2008. (J). (gr. -1-3). 27.95 incl. audio *(978-0-8045-6961-3(4));* 29.95 incl. audio compact disk *(978-0-8045-4184-8(1))* Spoken Arts, Inc.

Boland, Janice. Zippers. Pfeiffer, Judith, illus. 2003. (Books for Young Learners). (ENG.). 8p. (J). pap. 15.00 *(978-1-57274-700-5(5),* BB2220, Bks. for Young Learners) Owen, Richard C. Pubs., Inc.

Bollman, Anne. Help Find Frank. 2018. (Illus.). 40p. (J). (gr. -1-2). 16.95 *(978-1-4549-2678-8(3))* Sterling Publishing Co., Inc.

Bolton, Robin. Sunny Goes Out to Play. 2011. 28p. pap. 12.03 *(978-1-4634-2530-2(9))* AuthorHouse.

Bonnell, Kris. Pets for Us. 2007. (J). pap. 5.95 *(978-1-933727-50-9(0))* Reading Reading Bks., LLC.

—We Love Pets. 2007. (J). pap. 5.95 *(978-1-933727-56-1(X))* Reading Reading Bks., LLC.

Bourgeois, Paulette. Franklin Wants a Pet. Clark, Brenda, illus. 2013. (Franklin Ser.). (ENG.). 32p. (J). (gr. -1-3). pap. 6.99 *(978-1-77138-004-1(7))* Kids Can Pr., Ltd. CAN. Dist: Hachette Bk. Group.

Bove, Candace Scobie. Calypso: A Day in the Life of a Puppy. 2012. 24p. 24.95 *(978-1-4626-4122-2(9))* America Star Bks.

Bradmon, Karen. Goldie: A Fishtale of Adventure. 2008. 22p. pap. 24.95 *(978-1-60672-472-9(X))* America Star Bks.

Braun, Eric. Taking Care of Your Centaur. 2019. (Caring for Your Magical Pets Ser.). (ENG., Illus.). 24p. (J). (gr. 2-4). pap. 8.99 *(978-1-64466-088-1(1),* 12925); (gr. 4-6). lib. bdg. *(978-1-68072-909-2(8),* 12924) Black Rabbit Bks. (Hi Jinx).

—Taking Care of Your Dragon. 2019. (Caring for Your Magical Pets Ser.). (ENG., Illus.). 24p. (J). (gr. 2-4). pap. 8.99 *(978-1-64466-089-8(X),* 12929); (gr. 4-6). lib. bdg. *(978-1-68072-910-8(1),* 12928) Black Rabbit Bks. (Hi Jinx).

—Taking Care of Your Griffin. 2019. (Caring for Your Magical Pets Ser.). (ENG., Illus.). 24p. (J). (gr. 2-4). pap. 8.99 *(978-1-64466-090-4(3),* 12933); (gr. 4-6). lib. bdg. *(978-1-68072-911-5(X),* 12932) Black Rabbit Bks. (Hi Jinx).

—Taking Care of Your Phoenix. 2019. (Caring for Your Magical Pets Ser.). (ENG., Illus.). (J). (gr. 4-6). lib. bdg. *(978-1-68072-912-2(8),* 12936, Hi Jinx) Black Rabbit Bks.

—Taking Care of Your Sea Monster. 2019. (Caring for Your Magical Pets Ser.). (ENG., Illus.). 24p. (J). (gr. 2-4). pap. 8.99 *(978-1-64466-093-5(8),* 12945); (gr. 4-6). lib. bdg. *(978-1-68072-914-6(4),* 12944) Black Rabbit Bks. (Hi Jinx).

—Taking Care of Your Unicorn. 2019. (Caring for Your Magical Pets Ser.). (ENG., Illus.). 24p. (J). (gr. 2-4). pap. 8.99 *(978-1-64466-092-8(X),* 12941); (gr. 4-6). lib. bdg. *(978-1-68072-913-9(6),* 12940) Black Rabbit Bks. (Hi Jinx).

Bremauntz, M. The Adventures of Marcela & Little Joey: Little Joey Loves Bugs. 2010. 32p. 17.25 *(978-1-4269-4417-8(9))* Trafford Publishing.

Brett, Jan. Annie & the Wild Animals. Brett, Jan, illus. 2012. (Illus.). 32p. (J). (gr. -1-k). 18.99 *(978-0-399-16104-9(X),* G.P. Putnam's Sons Books for Young Readers) Penguin Young Readers Group.

Brett, Jan, illus. Annie & the Wild Animals Book & CD. 2012. (ENG.). 32p. (J). (gr. -1-3). audio 10.99 *(978-0-547-85082-5(4),* 1501067, Clarion Bks.) HarperCollins Pubs.

Brewer, Elly. Jerry & the Jannans. 2006. 320p. (J). (gr. 4-7). pap. 11.99 *(978-0-7475-8213-7(0))* Bloomsbury Publishing Plc GBR. Dist: Independent Pubs. Group.

Brezinova, Ivona. To Have a Dog. Deisadze, Zaur, illus. 2007. (POL & ENG.). 32p. (J). pap. 12.95 *(978-1-60195-106-9(X))* International Step by Step Assn.

Brodsky, Kathy. Just Sniffing Around. Bennett, Cameron, illus. 2009. (ENG.). 40p. 19.99 *(978-0-578-03620-5(7))* Helpingwords.

Brown, Marc. Arthur & the School Pet. 2005. (Step into Reading Sticker Bks.). (Illus.). 24p. 14.00 *(978-0-7569-5571-7(8))* Perfection Learning Corp.

—Arthur & the School Pet. 2003. (Step into Reading Ser.). (ENG., Illus.). 24p. (J). (gr. k-3). pap. 5.99 *(978-0-375-81001-5(3),* Random Hse. Bks. for Young Readers) Random Hse. Children's Bks.

—Arthur & the School Pet. 2003. (Arthur Step into Reading Ser.). (gr. -1-2). lib. bdg. 13.55 *(978-0-613-57492-1(3))* Turtleback.

—Arthur's New Puppy. (Arthur Adventure Ser.). (J). (gr. k-3). 7.98 incl. audio NewSound, LLC.

Brown, Peter. Children Make Terrible Pets. 2010. (Starring Lucille Beatrice Bear Ser.: 1). (ENG., Illus.). 40p. (J). (gr. -1-3). 18.99 *(978-0-316-01548-6(2))* Little, Brown Bks. for Young Readers.

Bruel, Nick. Bad Kitty School Daze (paperback Black-And-white Edition) 2014. (Bad Kitty Ser.). (ENG., Illus.). 176p. (J). (gr. 2-5). pap. 6.99 *(978-1-250-03947-7(9),* 900123378) Square Fish.

Buggs, Michael A. Tabard. Buggs, Michael A., illus. (Illus.). 64p. (Orig.). (J). (gr. 2-6). pap. 15.00 *(978-0-9657723-0-3(6))* Mogul Comics.

Burchette, Ruby J. The Dog Went to School, 1 vol. 2010. 48p. pap. 16.95 *(978-1-4489-4962-5(9))* America Star Bks.

Burkhart, Jessica. Bella's Birthday Unicorn. Ying, Victoria, illus. 2014. (Unicorn Magic Ser.: 1). (ENG.). 144p. (J). (gr. 1-4). pap. 6.99 *(978-1-4424-9822-8(6),* Aladdin) Simon & Schuster Children's Publishing.

—The Hidden Treasure. Ying, Victoria, illus. 2015. (Unicorn Magic Ser.: 4). (ENG.). 112p. (J). (gr. 1-4). pap. 6.99 *(978-1-4424-9829-7(3),* Aladdin) Simon & Schuster Children's Publishing.

—Where's Glimmer? Ying, Victoria, illus. 2014. (Unicorn Magic Ser.: 2). (ENG.). 144p. (J). (gr. 1-4). pap. 6.99 *(978-1-4424-9824-2(2),* Aladdin) Simon & Schuster Children's Publishing.

Burlingham, Abigail. Best Friends, 1 vol. Everitt-Stewart, Andy, illus. 2009. (Stories to Grow With Ser.). (ENG.). 24p. (J). (gr. 1-2). 27.27 *(978-1-60754-475-3(X),* 865a1417-c6c5-4b2c-8520-30a151879845); pap. 9.15 *(978-1-60754-476-0(8),* b38080d8-5904-4490-a44b-62f66fe45156) Rosen Publishing Group, Inc., The. (Windmill Bks.).

Cabral, Jeane. Bad Dog Ben. 2009. (Jeane Cabral Bks.). (Illus.). (J). bds. 12.99 *(978-1-934650-05-9(6))* Just For Kids Pr., LLC.

Calmenson, Stephanie. May I Pet Your Dog? The How-To Guide for Kids Meeting Dogs (and Dogs Meeting Kids) Ormerod, Jan, illus. 2007. (ENG.). 32p. (J). (gr. -1-3). 13.99 *(978-0-618-51034-4(6),* 100806, Clarion Bks.) HarperCollins Pubs.

Camacho, Norma I. Mikey/Jackster. 2011. 48p. (gr. 4-6). pap. 9.89 *(978-1-4669-0155-1(1))* Trafford Publishing.

Campbell, Rod. Dear Zoo. 2005. (Dear Zoo & Friends Ser.). (ENG., Illus.). 20p. (J). (gr. -1-k). 15.99 *(978-0-689-87751-3(X),* Little Simon) Little Simon.

—Dear Zoo. 2004. (BEN & ENG., Illus.). 16p. (J). bds. *(978-1-84444-169-5(4))* Mantra Lingua.

—Dear Zoo. Campbell, Rod, illus. 2004. (Illus.). 16p. (J). (RUS & ENG.). bds. *(978-1-84444-178-5(4));* (CHI & ENG., bds. *(978-1-84444-171-6(7));* (VIE & ENG., bds. *(978-1-84444-183-9(0));* (CHI & ENG., bds. *(978-1-84444-170-9(9));* (ENG & ARA., bds. *(978-1-84444-168-6(7));* (ENG & SOM., bds. *(978-1-84444-180-8(6));* (ENG & PER., bds. *(978-1-84444-172-3(5));* (ENG & FRE., bds. *(978-1-84444-173-0(3));* (URD & ENG., bds. *(978-1-84444-182-2(2));* (ENG & TUR., bds. *(978-1-84444-181-5(4));* (ENG & ALB., bds. *(978-1-84444-167-9(9));* (ENG & SPA., bds. *(978-1-84444-179-2(2));* (ENG & POR., bds. *(978-1-84444-177-8(6));* (ENG & PAN., bds. *(978-1-84444-176-1(8));* (ENG & HIN., bds. *(978-1-84444-175-4(X));* (ENG & GUJ., bds. *(978-1-84444-174-7(1))* Mantra Lingua.

—Dear Zoo. Campbell, Rod, illus. 2019. (Dear Zoo & Friends Ser.). (ENG., Illus.). 24p. (J). (— 1). 17.99 *(978-1-5344-6012-6(8),* Little Simon) Little Simon.

—Dear Zoo: A Lift-The-Flap Book. Campbell, Rod, illus. 25th ed. 2007. (Dear Zoo & Friends Ser.). (ENG., Illus.). 18p. (J). (gr. -1 — 1). bds. 7.99 *(978-1-4169-4737-0(X),* Little Simon) Little Simon.

—Dear Zoo Animal Shapes. Campbell, Rod, illus. 2016. (Dear Zoo & Friends Ser.). (ENG., Illus.). 20p. (J). (gr. -1 — 1). bds. 6.99 *(978-1-4814-8069-7(3),* Little Simon) Little Simon.

Candlewick Press. Peppa Pig & the Great Vacation. 2014. (Peppa Pig Ser.). (ENG.). 32p. (J). (-k). 14.99 *(978-0-7636-6986-7(5),* Candlewick Entertainment) Candlewick Pr.

Capucilli, Alyssa Satin. Biscuit's Pet & Play Christmas: A Touch & Feel Book: a Christmas Holiday Book for Kids. Schories, Pat & Young, Mary O'Keefe, illus. 2006. (Biscuit Ser.). (ENG.). 12p. (J). (gr. -1 — 1). bds. 9.99 *(978-0-06-009470-6(2),* HarperFestival) HarperCollins Pubs.

—Biscuit's Pet & Play Farm Animals: A Touch & Feel Book: an Easter & Springtime Book for Kids. Schories, Pat, illus. 2018. (Biscuit Ser.). (ENG.). 12p. (J). (gr. -1 — 1). bds. 8.99 *(978-0-06-249052-0(4),* HarperFestival) HarperCollins Pubs.

Carbone, Courtney. Palace Pets: Snuggle Buddies. 2014. (Step into Reading Level 2 Ser.). lib. bdg. 13.55 *(978-0-606-35193-5(0))* Turtleback.

—Snuggle Buddies (Disney Princess: Palace Pets) RH Disney, illus. 2014. (Step into Reading Ser.). (ENG.). 32p. (J). (gr. -1-1). 5.99 *(978-0-7364-3155-2(1),* RH/Disney) Random Hse. Children's Bks.

Carlisle, Samantha. The Day Sam Lost Lucky. 2009. (Illus.). 52p. pap. 13.95 *(978-1-4327-2412-2(6))* Outskirts Pr., Inc.

Carney, Larry, adapted by. Silly Farm. 2010. (ENG., Illus.). 24p. (J). pap. 6.95 *(978-1-60072-156-4(7))* PC Treasures, Inc.

Carson, Jeanelle. Lexi Lou Meets Jadie Bear. 2010. 36p. pap. 15.49 *(978-1-4520-9449-6(7))* AuthorHouse.

Carter, Tammy. My Friend, Dinner. 2013. 28p. pap. 24.95 *(978-1-4241-0629-5(X))* America Star Bks.

Carvajal, Victor. Chipana. (SPA.). (YA). (gr. 5-8). pap. 7.95 *(978-958-04-5044-3(7),* NR3753) Norma S.A. COL. Dist: Lectorum Pubns., Inc., Distribuidora Norma, Inc.

Cassany, Mia & Casal, Mikel. Frankfurt. 2018. (ENG., Illus.). 32p. (J). (gr. -1-k). 14.99 *(978-1-84976-579-4(0),* 1325401) Tate Publishing, Ltd. GBR. Dist: Abrams, Inc.

Ceville, Laura. My Dog, Jack. 2013. 24p. pap. 8.99 *(978-1-938768-25-5(6))* Gypsy Pubns.

Chall, Marsha Wilson. Pick a Pup. Henry, Jed, illus. 2011. (ENG.). 32p. (J). (gr. -1-k). 19.99 *(978-1-4169-7961-6(1),* McElderry, Margaret K. Bks.) McElderry, Margaret K. Bks.

Charlesworth, Liza. The Best Pet: An Animal Friends Reader. Smith, Ian, illus. 2015. 16p. (J). *(978-0-545-85961-5(1))* Scholastic, Inc.

Chicatelli, Joy. Bailey's Heartstrings. Rottinger, Amy, illus. 2011. 28p. pap. 12.95 *(978-1-935268-96-3(1))* Halo Publishing International.

Child, Lauren. A Dog with Nice Ears: Featuring Charlie & Lola. Child, Lauren, illus. 2018. (Charlie & Lola Ser.). (ENG., Illus.). 32p. (J). (gr. -1-2). 17.99 *(978-1-5362-0036-2(0))* Candlewick Pr.

Chimenti, Maureen. The Day My Pet Went to Heaven. 2008. 44p. pap. 17.99 *(978-1-4389-3271-2(5))* AuthorHouse.

Chimes, Lisa. My First Kitten. Burke, Tina, illus. 2016. (ENG.). 32p. (J). 10.99 *(978-1-61067-517-8(7))* Kane Miller.

Christopher, Matt. Soccer 'Cats: You Lucky Dog. Vasconcellos, Daniel, illus. 8th ed. 2003. (ENG.). 64p. (J). (gr. 1-4). pap. 8.99 *(978-0-316-73805-7(0))* Little, Brown Bks. for Young Readers.

—You Lucky Dog. Vasconcellos, Daniel, illus. 2003. (Soccer Cats Ser.: Bk. 8). 49p. (J). (gr. 2-4). 12.65 *(978-0-7569-3907-6(0))* Perfection Learning Corp.

Clara Mulholland. Naughty Miss Bunny. 2007. 128p. per. 10.95 *(978-1-4218-3938-7(5),* 1st World Library - Literary Society) 1st World Publishing, Inc.

Clark, Sandra. My Tears Count Too. 2009. 84p. pap. 28.99 *(978-1-4389-8357-8(3))* AuthorHouse.

Climo, Liz. Rory the Dinosaur Wants a Pet. 2016. (ENG., Illus.). 40p. (J). (gr. -1-3). 16.99 *(978-0-316-27729-7(0))* Little, Brown Bks. for Young Readers.

Coe, Victoria J. Fenway & Hattie & the Evil Bunny Gang. 2018. (Fenway & Hattie Ser.: 2). (ENG.). 208p. (J). (gr. 3-7). 8.99 *(978-1-101-99634-8(X),* Puffin Books) Penguin Young Readers Group.

—Fenway & Hattie up to New Tricks. 2019. (Fenway & Hattie Ser.: 3). (ENG.). 208p. (J). (gr. 3-7). 7.99 *(978-1-5247-3785-6(2),* Puffin Books) Penguin Young Readers Group.

Cohen, Lettie. Lila's New Pet. 2013. 20p. pap. 17.99 *(978-1-4817-0109-9(6))* AuthorHouse.

Collins, Ellen M. My Book: Fun Favorite Stories. 2010. 68p. pap. 26.99 *(978-1-4490-5236-2(3))* AuthorHouse.

Cook, Sonya Correll. Quest for a Family Pet: The Adventures of Nique, Nick, & Nelle. Transou, Devora & Watkins, Karen, illus. 2008. (ENG.). 24p. pap. 11.49 *(978-1-4343-5043-5(6))* AuthorHouse.

Cooney, Doug. The Beloved Dearly. DiTerlizzi, Tony, illus. 2003. (ENG.). 192p. (J). (gr. 3-7). pap. 8.99 *(978-0-689-86354-7(3),* Simon & Schuster Bks. For Young Readers) Simon & Schuster Bks. For Young Readers.

Coons, Anita. Graze, Gaze & Saddle Days. 2005. (Illus.). 144p. (J). per. 10.95 *(978-1-59713-003-5(6))* Goose River Pr.

Cooper, D. C. Rascal the Baby Squirrel. 2013. 32p. *(978-1-4602-2658-2(5))* FriesenPress.

Corderoy, Tracey. Fairy Tale Pets. Martin, Jorge, illus. 2017. (ENG.). 32p. (J). (gr. -1-2). 16.99 *(978-1-68010-064-8(5))* Tiger Tales.

—Fairy Tale Pets. Martin, Jorge, illus. 2017. (ENG.). 32p. (J). pap. *(978-1-84869-442-2(3))* Tiger Tales.

Cordone Warner, Debra. Henry's Daily Walk. 2010. 56p. pap. 24.99 *(978-0-557-60667-2(5))* Lulu Pr., Inc.

Corlyn, Ron. The House That Grew. 2013. 24p. pap. 24.95 *(978-1-63000-118-6(X))* America Star Bks.

Coven, Wanda. Heidi Heckelbeck & the Tie-Dyed Bunny. 2014. (Heidi Heckelbeck Ser.: 10). lib. bdg. 16.00 *(978-0-606-35429-5(8))* Turtleback.

Coville, Bruce. Jeremy Thatcher, Dragon Hatcher: A Magic Shop Book. Lippincott, Gary A., illus. 20th ed. 2007. (Magic Shop Book Ser.: 2). (ENG.). 176p. (J). (gr. 5-7). pap. 7.99 *(978-0-15-206252-1(1),* 1198750, Clarion Bks.) HarperCollins Pubs.

Coxon, Michele. Have You Fed the Cat? Spanish/English Bilingual Edition. 2004. (ENG., Illus.). 32p. (J). 15.95 *(978-1-59572-001-6(4));* pap. 5.95 *(978-1-59572-002-3(2))* Star Bright Bks., Inc.

Crossno, Frances M. Cole's Perfect Puppy. Perfect Puppies Book One. 2016. (ENG., Illus.). 98p. (J). pap. 14.95 *(978-1-5069-0168-8(9))* First Edition Design Publishing.

Crow, Melinda Melton. Little Lizard's New Pet, 1 vol. Rowland, Andrew, illus. 2011. (Little Lizards Ser.). (ENG.). 32p. (J). (gr. -1-1). pap. 6.25 *(978-1-4342-3049-2(X),* 114649, Stone Arch Bks.) Capstone.

Cynthia, Rylant. Every Living Thing. 2014. (ENG.). 96p. (J). (gr. 5-9). 10.24 *(978-1-63245-336-5(3))* Lectorum Pubns., Inc.

Dadey, Debbie. The Secret Sea Horse. Avakyan, Tatevik, illus. 2013. (Mermaid Tales Ser.: 6). (ENG.). 112p. (J). (gr. 1-4). 17.99 *(978-1-4424-8261-6(3));* pap. 6.99 *(978-1-4424-8260-9(5))* Simon & Schuster Children's Publishing. (Aladdin).

Dale, Jay. My Pets. Richards, Kirsten, illus. 2012. (Wonder Words Ser.). (ENG.). 16p. (J). (gr. k-2). pap. 36.94 *(978-1-4296-8887-1(4),* 18339, Capstone Pr.) Capstone.

Dale, Jay & Scott, Kay. My Pets, 1 vol. Richards, Kirsten, illus. 2012. (Wonder Words Ser.). (ENG.). 16p. (J). (gr. k-2). pap. 6.99 *(978-1-4296-8886-4(6),* 119946, Capstone Pr.) Capstone.

Dapre, Alan. Porridge the Tartan Cat & the Pet Show Show-Off, 28 vols. Somina, Yuliya, illus. 2018. (Porridge the Tartan Cat Ser.: 6). 152p. (J). pap. 6.95 *(978-1-78250-360-6(9),* Kelpies) Floris Bks. GBR. Dist: Consortium Bk. Sales & Distribution.

Darling, Nina. Pet Shop Talk: A Grooming for Max, 1 vol. 2009. 27p. pap. 24.95 *(978-1-60813-646-9(9))* America Star Bks.

Davies, Katie. The Great Rabbit Rescue. Shaw, Hannah, illus. 2011. (Great Critter Capers Ser.). (ENG.). 224p. (J). (gr. 3-7). 12.99 *(978-1-4424-2064-9(2),* Beach Lane Bks.) Beach Lane Bks.

Davis, Jim. Garfield Gets in a Pickle. 2012. (Garfield Ser.: 54). lib. bdg. 25.75 *(978-0-606-26835-6(9))* Turtleback.

Dawson, Brianog Brady. Danny's Pesky Pet. Connor, Michael, tr. Connor, Michael, illus. 2003. (Pandas Ser.: 25). (ENG.). 64p. (J). pap. 11.00 *(978-0-86278-803-2(X))* O'Brien Pr., Ltd., The IRL. Dist: Dufour Editions, Inc.

de Rham, Mickey. Hey Bossie, You're a Spokescow! Gusterson, Leigh, illus. 2004. 24p. (J). 9.95 *(978-0-9755216-0-1(8))* Plaidswede Publishing.

Dean, James & Dean, Kimberly. Pete the Cat: a Pet for Pete. Dean, James, illus. 2014. (My First I Can Read Ser.). (ENG., Illus.). 32p. (J). (gr. -1-3). pap. 5.99 *(978-0-06-230379-0(1),* HarperCollins) HarperCollins Pubs.

—Pete the Cat & the Tip-Top Tree House. Dean, James, illus. 2017. (My First I Can Read Ser.). (ENG., Illus.). 32p. (J). (gr. -1-3). pap. 4.99 *(978-0-06-240431-2(8),* HarperCollins) HarperCollins Pubs.

Dennis, Elizabeth. Marigold Fairy Makes a Friend: Ready-To-Read Level 1. Smillie, Natalie, illus. 2018. (Flower Wings Ser.: 2). (ENG.). 24p. (J). (gr. -1-1). 17.99 *(978-1-5344-1174-6(7));* pap. 4.99 *(978-1-5344-1173-9(9))* Simon Spotlight. (Simon Spotlight).

dePaola, Tomie. Little Grunt & the Big Egg: A Prehistoric Fairy Tale. 2007. 29.95 incl. audio compact disk *(978-0-8045-4158-9(2));* 27.95 incl. audio *(978-0-8045-6944-6(4))* Spoken Arts, Inc.

—Pancakes for Breakfast. 2018. lib. bdg. 18.40 *(978-0-606-41211-7(5))* Turtleback.

Diamond, Lorraine. I Want a Camel for a Pet, 1 vol. 2009. 13p. pap. 24.95 *(978-1-61546-425-8(5))* America Star Bks.

Diamond, Shendl, illus. & text. The True Story of Critter Angels by Yani. Diamond, Shendl, text. 2005. (J). 15.95 *(978-0-9764724-3-8(0))* LikeMinds Pr.

DiPucchio, Kelly. Gilbert Goldfish Wants a Pet. Shea, Bob, illus. 2011. 32p. (J). (gr. -1-k). 18.99 *(978-0-8037-3394-7(1),* Dial Bks) Penguin Young Readers Group.

DiTerlizzi, Angela. Some Pets. Wenzel, Brendan, illus. 2016. (ENG.). 32p. (J). (gr. -1-3). 18.99 *(978-1-4814-4402-6(6),* Beach Lane Bks.) Beach Lane Bks.

Dmaples. Big Dog, Little Puppy. 2012. 28p. pap. 19.99 *(978-1-4685-6064-0(6))* AuthorHouse.

Dominguez, Angela. Maria Had a Little Llama / María Tenía una Llamita: Bilingual. Dominguez, Angela, illus. 2013.Tr. of Maria Had a Little Llama. (SPA., Illus.). 32p. (J). (gr. -1-2). 19.99 *(978-0-8050-9333-9(8),* 900070912, Holt, Henry & Co. Bks. For Young Readers) Holt, Henry & Co.

Downie, David. David & Jacko. Tatsi, Andreanna, tr. Seroya, Tea, illus. 2012. 52p. pap. *(978-1-922159-24-3(7));* pap. *(978-1-922159-15-1(8))* Blue Peg Publishing.

—David & Jacko. Ivanova, Kalina, tr. Seroya, Tea, illus. 2012. 52p. pap. *(978-1-922159-01-4(8))* Blue Peg Publishing.

—David & Jacko. Seroya, Tea, illus. 2012. 52p. pap. *(978-1-922159-99-1(9))* Blue Peg Publishing.

Drescher, Henrik. Love the Beastie: A Spin-And-Play Book. 2011. (ENG., Illus.). 11p. (J). (gr. -1-3). 12.95 *(978-0-7611-6109-7(0),* 16109) Workman Publishing Co., Inc.

Dubois, Rikki Marie-José Grenier. Muffy Was Fluffy. 2012. 28p. pap. 24.95 *(978-1-62709-167-1(X))* America Star Bks.

Duchene-Marshall, Michele A. Shirley's Red Satin Shoes. Marshall, Alan David, ed. Ousley, Clayton Gerard, photos by. l.t. ed. 2003. (Illus.). 17p. (J). spiral bd. 10.00 *(978-0-9761675-1-8(4))* Storybook Acres.

Dullaart, Alberta M. Snowy Black & White. 2010. 20p. 10.49 *(978-1-4520-1385-5(3))* AuthorHouse.

Duncan-Pauley, Chadney. A Bull's Paradise. 2009. (ENG.). 32p. pap. 15.60 *(978-0-557-17660-1(3))* Lulu Pr., Inc.

Dvok, Eduard & Dvorák, Eduard. Bobek, the Cat with a Pompon Tail. Dvorák, Jaroslav, illus. 2010. 52p. pap. 17.00 *(978-1-60911-734-4(4),* Eloquent Bks.) Strategic Book Publishing & Rights Agency (SBPRA).

Dyckman, Ame. You Don't Want a Unicorn! Climo, Liz, illus. 2017. (ENG.). 40p. (J). (gr. -1-3). 18.99 *(978-0-316-34347-3(1))* Little, Brown Bks. for Young Readers.

Easton, Marilyn. New Girl in Town. 2013. (LEGO Friends Chapter Bks.: 1). lib. bdg. 14.75 *(978-0-606-31548-7(9))* Turtleback.

Eaton, Jason Carter. How to Train a Train. Rocco, John, illus. (ENG.). (J). 2016. 28p. (-k). bds. 7.99 *(978-0-7636-8899-8(1))* 2013. 48p. (gr. -1-3). 18.99 *(978-0-7636-6307-0(7))* Candlewick Pr.

Edgin, Brenda. Little Winston & His Big Adventures in Natchez: New Home near the Woods. 2011. 16p. 12.99 *(978-1-4567-3639-2(6))* AuthorHouse.

Edwards, Sal A. A Forever Family: Living in the Big House. 2012. 42p. (-18). pap. 17.45 *(978-1-4624-0329-5(8),* Inspiring Voices) Author Solutions, LLC.

Edwards, Sonia. Noson y Llygaid Llachar. 2005. (WEL., Illus.). 88.0p. pap. 4.99 *(978-0-84323-400-5(9))* Gomer Pr. GBR. Dist: Gomer Pr.

Egea, Marcelo. Sobe, the Cat That Thinks He's a Dog. 2012. 24p. pap. 15.99 *(978-1-4691-5925-6(2))* Xlibris Corp.

Elliott, David. This Orq. (He #1!) Nichols, Lori, illus. 2016. (ENG.). 40p. (J). (gr. -1-2). 16.95 *(978-1-62979-336-8(1),* Astra Young Readers) Astra Publishing Hse.

—This Orq. (He Say UGH!) Nichols, Lori, illus. 2015. (ENG.). 40p. (J). (gr. -1-2). 16.95 *(978-1-62091-789-3(0),* Astra Young Readers) Astra Publishing Hse.

Elliott, Rebecca. Baxter Is Missing: a Branches Book (Owl Diaries #6) Elliott, Rebecca, illus. 2017. (Owl Diaries: 6). (ENG., Illus.). 80p. (J). (gr. k-2). pap. 6.99 *(978-1-338-04284-9(X))* Scholastic, Inc.

—Eva's New Pet: a Branches Book (Owl Diaries #15) Elliott, Rebecca, illus. 2021. (Owl Diaries: 15). (ENG., Illus.). 80p. (J). (gr. k-2). pap. 5.99 *(978-1-338-74537-5(9))* Scholastic, Inc.

—Eva's New Pet: a Branches Book (Owl Diaries #15) (Library Edition) Elliott, Rebecca, illus. 2021. (Owl Diaries: 15). (ENG., Illus.). 80p. (J). (gr. k-2). lib. bdg. 24.99 *(978-1-338-74538-2(7))* Scholastic, Inc.

Emma Treehouse Ltd. My Pets. Davis, Caroline, illus. 2007. (Easy Flaps Ser.). 10p. (J). (gr. -1). bds. 6.95 *(978-1-58925-824-2(X))* Tiger Tales.

Erickson, Carol. Not a Used Dog, at All. 2009. 32p. pap. 14.49 *(978-1-4389-5204-8(X))* AuthorHouse.

Evans, Cathy. Halo & the Rainbows. 2013. 36p. pap. 16.95 *(978-1-4624-0704-0(8),* Inspiring Voices) Author Solutions, LLC.

Exelby, Kathy. My Dog Harpo: The Biggest Kid I Know. Wall Darby, Colleen, illus. 2007. (J). per. 20.00 *(978-1-932583-39-7(4))* Bates Jackson Engraving Co., Inc.

Faciana, Michelle. Snickers' Day Out. 2010. (ENG.). 18p. (J). pap. 9.99 *(978-1-4490-5216-4(9))* AuthorHouse.

Faris, Stephanie. Piper Morgan to the Rescue. Fleming, Lucy, illus. 2016. (Piper Morgan Ser.: 3). (ENG.). 112p. (J). (gr. 1-4). 16.99 *(978-1-4814-5715-6(2),* Simon & Schuster/Paula Wiseman Bks.) Simon & Schuster/Paula Wiseman Bks.

Farnsley, Kathleen. This Little Piggy Named Pony. 2008. 24p. pap. 12.99 *(978-1-4389-2659-9(6))* AuthorHouse.

Fay, Nancy Cartnick. I Wanted a Puppy - Not Fish! 2012. 24p. pap. 15.99 *(978-1-4691-7535-5(5))* Xlibris Corp.

Feiffer, Jules. A Room with a Zoo. Feiffer, Jules, illus. 2007. (ENG., Illus.). 192p. (gr. 2-7). per. 7.99 (978-0-7868-3703-8(9), di Capua, Michael Bks.) Hyperion Bks. for Children.

Fensham, Elizabeth. My Dog Gets a Job. 2019. (My Dog Ugly Ser.: 2). (ENG., Illus.). 192p. (J). (gr. 3-7). pap. 7.99 (978-1-4926-8089-5(3)) Sourcebooks, Inc.

Fergus, Maureen. Buddy & Earl Go to School, 1 vol. Sookocheff, Carey, illus. 2017. (Buddy & Earl Ser.: 4). (ENG.). 32p. (J). (gr. k-2). 16.95 (978-1-55498-927-0(2)) Groundwood Bks. CAN. Dist: Publishers Group West (PGW).

Ferry, Beth. Land Shark. Mantle, Ben, illus. 2015. (ENG.). 36p. (J). (gr. -1-k). 16.99 (978-1-4521-2458-2(2)) Chronicle Bks. LLC.

Finch, Kate. A Big Surprise (Pet Hotel #2) 2013. (Pet Hotel Ser.: 2). lib. bdg. 14.75 (978-0-606-31985-0(9)) Turtleback.

—On with the Show! Gurney, John, illus. 2014. 76p. (J). (978-1-4242-5954-0(1)) Scholastic, Inc.

—On with the Show! 2014. (Pet Hotel Ser.: 4). lib. bdg. 14.75 (978-0-606-35201-7(5)) Turtleback.

Fine, Dvm. Too Many Pets & Not Enough Homes! 2012. 24p. pap. 12.56 (978-1-4669-0248-0(5)) Trafford Publishing.

Finkbeiner, Betty Ladley. Pepper's Forever Home. Alonso, Marvin, illus. 2013. (ENG.). 24p. pap. 10.99 (978-1-4797-6982-7(7)) Xlibris Corp.

Finzi, Ama. At Baba's House. 2011. 36p. pap. 16.46 (978-1-4269-7095-5(1)) Trafford Publishing.

Fisher, C. R. The Adventures of Sam Fisher: It's Ruff to Be A Puppy. 2008. 64p. pap. 19.49 (978-1-4389-2040-5(7)) AuthorHouse.

Flamburis, Georgia M. How Karis' Kitten Got Its Name. 2012. 34p. pap. 9.99 (978-0-615-47908-8(1)) Flamburis, Georgia.

Flor Ada, Alma. Daniel's Pet. 2003. (Green Light Readers Level 1 Ser.). (gr. -1-2). 13.50 (978-0-613-64481-5(6)) Turtleback.

Forde, Catherine. Slippy. 2012. (Stoke Books Titles Ser.). 72p. (J). (gr. 5-8). pap. 7.95 (978-1-78112-032-3(3)); pap. 45.32 (978-0-7613-9223-1(8)); lib. bdg. 22.60 (978-1-78112-031-6(5)) Stoke Bks.

Foreman, Michael. El Lorito Pelon. Diego, Rapi & Flores, Martha, illus. 2008. (SPA.). 30p. (J). (gr. 1-3). 15.99 (978-1-930332-56-0(4)) Lectorum Pubns., Inc.

Fox, Paula. La habitación de Mauricio. 2003. (SPA., Illus.). 96p. (J). (gr. 3-5). (978-84-279-3457-3(2), NG4695) Noguer y Caralt Editores, S. A. ESP. Dist: Lectorum Pubns., Inc.

Franciosi, Pete. Dusty Wants A Kitty. 2011. 23p. 14.95 (978-1-4327-7596-4(0)) Outskirts Pr., Inc.

Fraser, Ian. Life with Mammoth, 0 vols. Fraser, Mary Ann, illus. (Ogg & Bob Ser.: 2). (ENG.). 64p. (J). 2013. (gr. k-3). pap. 9.99 (978-1-4778-1615-8(1), 9781477816158) 2012. (gr. 1-3). 14.99 (978-0-7614-5722-0(4), 9780761457220) Amazon Publishing. (Two Lions).

—Meet Mammoth, 0 vols. Fraser, Mary Ann, illus. 2013. (Ogg & Bob Ser.: 1). (ENG.). 64p. (J). (gr. 1-3). pap. 9.99 (978-1-4778-1617-2(8), 9781477816172, Two Lions) Amazon Publishing.

Freedman, Claire. Don't Wake the Yeti! Ranucci, Claudia, illus. 2017. (ENG.). 32p. (J). (gr. -1-3). 17.99 (978-0-8075-1690-4(2), 807516902) Whitman, Albert & Co.

Friedman, Laurie. Mallory vs. Max. Schmitz, Tamara, illus. 2006. (Mallory Ser.: 3). (ENG.). 160p. (J). (gr. 2-5). per. 7.99 (978-1-57505-863-4(4), a9938cdb-4867-42f6-9747-88b51dffd127, Darby Creek) Lerner Publishing Group.

—Ruby Valentine & the Sweet Surprise. Avril, Lynne, illus. 2014. (Ruby Valentine Ser.). (ENG.). 32p. (J). (gr. k-3). 16.95 (978-0-7613-8873-9(7), 7491b02d-c3ff-421c-a33c-6400cf28d745, Carolrhoda Bks.) Lerner Publishing Group.

Fruchter, Jason, illus. Remembering Blue Fish. 2017. (Daniel Tiger's Neighborhood Ser.). (ENG.). 24p. (J). (gr. -1-2). pap. 4.99 (978-1-5344-0095-5(8), Simon Spotlight) Simon Spotlight.

Gallagher, Diana G. A No-Sneeze Pet, 1 vol. Puglisi, Adriana & Puglisi, Adriana, illus. 2013. (Pet Friends Forever Ser.). (ENG.). 88p. (J). (gr. 1-3). pap. 5.95 (978-1-4795-1862-3(X), 123500); lib. bdg. 25.99 (978-1-4048-7499-2(2), 119542) Capstone. (Picture Window Bks.).

Galvin, Laura Gates. My First Pet. Schwaeber, Barbie Heit & Halpenny, Karen, eds. 2008. (ENG., Illus.). 24p. (J). (gr. -1). 4.99 (978-1-59069-654-5(9)) Studio Mouse LLC.

Ganz, Yaffa. Raise a Rabbit, Grow a Goose. Klineman, Harvey, illus. 2008. 30p. 14.99 (978-1-59826-235-3(1)) Feldheim Pubs.

Gardiner, C. Pirate Betty of Wigan. 2013. 12p. pap. 10.60 (978-1-291-30672-9(2)) Lulu Pr., Inc.

Garis, Howard R. The Curlytops & Their Pets: Or, Uncle Toby's Strange Collection. 2017. (ENG., Illus.). (J). 23.95 (978-1-374-93100-8(4)); pap. 13.95 (978-1-374-93099-5(7)) Capital Communications, Inc.

Garland, Taylor. Celebrate the Season: the Twelve Pets of Christmas. 2017. (Celebrate the Season Ser.: 2). (ENG.). 176p. (J). (gr. 3-7). pap. 6.99 (978-0-316-47253-1(0)) Little, Brown Bks. for Young Readers.

Gee, Randi. Everybody Has a Cat Named Molly. 2010. 32p. pap. 15.50 (978-0-557-27671-4(3)) Lulu Pr., Inc.

George, Jean Craighead, et al. Crowbar: The Smartest Bird in the World. Minor, Wendell, illus. 2021. (ENG.). 32p. (J). (gr. -1-3). 17.99 (978-0-06-000257-2(3), Tegen, Katherine Bks) HarperCollins Pubs.

Giancamilli, Vanessa. Patches Finds a Home. Hatala, Dan, illus. 2006. (Pet Tales Ser.). (ENG.). 32p. (J). (gr. -1-3). 4.95 (978-1-59249-639-6(3)); pap. 2.95 (978-1-59249-640-2(7)) Soundprints.

Gilbert, Frances. I Love Pink! Unten, Eren, illus. 2017. (Step into Reading Ser.). 32p. (J). (gr. -1-1). 5.99 (978-1-101-93737-2(8), Random Hse. Bks. for Young Readers) Random Hse. Children's Bks.

Gilman, Grace. Dixie & the Best Day Ever. 2014. (I Can Read Level 1 Ser.). (ENG., Illus.). 32p. (J). (gr. -1-3). pap. 4.99 (978-0-06-208659-4(6), HarperCollins) HarperCollins Pubs.

Glaser, Karina Yan. The Vanderbeekers to the Rescue. 2019. (Vanderbeekers Ser.: 3). (ENG., Illus.). 368p. (J). (gr. 3-7). 17.99 (978-1-328-57757-3(0), 1728478, Clarion Bks.) HarperCollins Pubs.

Glazer, Maryann. The Adventures of Teddy Bark-Lee: Teddy Goes to the Doctor. 2009. 28p. pap. 13.99 (978-1-4490-2836-7(5)) AuthorHouse.

Glesener, Loretta. Bringing Back Dinner Time. 2011. 40p. pap. 24.95 (978-1-4560-4221-9(1)) America Star Bks.

Golden Books, illus. PAW Patrol Little Golden Book Library (PAW Patrol) Itty-Bitty Kitty Rescue; Puppy Birthday!; Pirate Pups; All-Star Pups!; Jurassic Bark!, 5 vols. 2017. (Little Golden Book Ser.). (ENG.). 120p. (J). (-k). 24.95 (978-1-5247-6412-8(4), Golden Bks.) Random Hse. Children's Bks.

Gomes, Linda Nunes. Special Words: A Story about Multicultural Families & Their Pets. Levine, Lenora D., illus. 2007. (YA). per. 12.99 (978-1-934400-02-9(5)) Rock Village Publishing.

Good Dog... Not So Good Dog. 2007. (J). (978-0-9793568-1-0(4)) Merlin, Debbi.

Goodner, David & Thomas, Louis. Ginny Goblin Cannot Have a Monster for a Pet. 2019. (ENG., Illus.). 40p. (J). (gr. -1-3). 17.99 (978-0-544-76416-3(1), 1635201, Clarion Bks.) HarperCollins Pubs.

Gorbachev, Valeri. The Best Cat. Gorbachev, Valeri, illus. 2010. (Illus.). 32p. (J). (gr. -1-2). 15.99 (978-0-7636-3675-3(4)) Candlewick Pr.

—Cats Are Cats. 2019. (I Like to Read Ser.). (Illus.). 32p. (J). (gr. -1-3). pap. 7.99 (978-0-8234-4524-0(0)) Holiday Hse., Inc.

Gotsch, Connie. Belle's Star. Cogan, John, illus. 2009. (Belle Ser.: 1). (ENG.). 136p. (J). (-1). pap. 8.99 (978-1-932926-01-9(1)) Artemesia Publishing, LLC.

—Belle's Trial. Cogan, John, illus. 2010. (Belle Ser.: 2). (ENG.). 152p. (J). (gr. 5-1). pap. 8.99 (978-1-932926-12-5(7), Kinkajou Pr.) Artemesia Publishing, LLC.

Granger, Barbara. Down to Earth with a Bump. 2009. (Illus.). 40p. pap. 16.99 (978-1-4389-1211-0(0)) AuthorHouse.

Gréban, Quentin. Woolly & Me, 1 vol. 2018. (ENG., Illus.). 32p. (J). (gr. -1-2). 16.95 (978-0-88448-636-7(2), 884636) Tilbury Hse. Pubs.

Green, D. L. Zeke Meeks vs the Pain-In-the-Neck Pets, 1 vol. Alves, Josh, illus. 2014. (Zeke Meeks Ser.). (ENG.). 128p. (J). (gr. 2-4). 22.65 (978-1-4795-2166-1(3), 123881, Picture Window Bks.) Capstone.

Greenberg, Mike & Greenberg, Stacy Steponate. Mvp: Most Valuable Puppy. Pang, Bonnie, illus. 2018. (ENG.). 32p. (J). (gr. -1-3). 17.99 (978-1-4814-8931-7(3), Aladdin) Simon & Schuster Children's Publishing.

Greenwood, Grace. History of My Pets by Grace Greenwood [Pseud.], with Engravings from Designs by Billings. 2006. 128p. per. 16.99 (978-1-4255-0870-8(7)) Michigan Publishing.

Griffis, Molly. The Buffalo in the Mall. Doner, Kim, illus. 32p. 8.95 (978-1-57168-635-0(5)) Eakin Pr.

Grindley, Sally. Captain Pepper's Pets. Parkins, David, illus. 2004. 48p. (J). pap. (978-0-7534-1042-4(7), Kingfisher) Roaring Brook Pr.

Griner, Jack. Archibald My Pet Pig. Knudson, Dana, illus. 2011. pap. 8.95 (978-0-9836081-1-0(3)) Canoed Sun Publishing, LLC.

Grubman, Bonnie. How Do You Get a Mouse to Smile?, 1 vol. Van Wright, Cornelius, illus. 2009. (ENG.). 32p. (J). (gr. -1-3). pap. 6.50 (978-1-59572-167-9(3)) Star Bright Bks., Inc.

Gutierrez-Haley, Lisa. The New Pet: Adventures of Hayden & Jace. 2011. 20p. pap. 24.95 (978-1-4626-1872-9(3)) America Star Bks.

Gutman, Dan. My Weird School: Class Pet Mess! Paillot, Jim, illus. 2017. (I Can Read Level 2 Ser.). (ENG.). 32p. (J). (gr. -1-3). pap. 4.99 (978-0-06-236746-4(3), HarperCollins) HarperCollins Pubs.

Hahn, Brian. It's Not the Yellow Fever. 2013. 20p. pap. 24.95 (978-1-62709-969-1(7)) America Star Bks.

Hall, Kirsten. Slider's Pet: All about Nature. Luedecke, Bev, illus. 2004. (Beastieville Ser.). (J). 19.50 (978-0-516-22898-3(6), Children's Pr.) Scholastic Library Publishing.

Hamilton, Patricia D. Peaches the Private Eye Poodle: Finding Dipsey Doodle. 2008. 32p. pap. 13.50 (978-1-60693-276-6(4), Eloquent Bks.) Strategic Book Publishing & Rights Agency (SBPRA).

—Peaches the Private Eye Poodle: Finding Foster a Home. 2010. 36p. (gr. -1-3). pap. 13.50 (978-1-60911-108-3(7), Eloquent Bks.) Strategic Book Publishing & Rights Agency (SBPRA).

Hanning, Jacob. Mommy's Little Helper: That's Me. 2012. 28p. pap. 24.95 (978-1-4626-5649-3(8)) America Star Bks.

Hano, Patricia. Tyler Meets the Moon. 2010. 28p. pap. 11.99 (978-1-60911-189-2(3), Eloquent Bks.) Strategic Book Publishing & Rights Agency (SBPRA).

Hanson, Sandy. A Camel's Story, I Met the Lamb. 2012. 62p. 24.99 (978-1-61996-615-4(8)); pap. 14.99 (978-1-61996-614-7(X)) Salem Author Services.

Hanson, Shelley. K9 Crew Beginnings. 2004. 160p. (J). per. 9.99 (978-0-9752887-0-2(9)) Tail Wagging Productions.

Hapka, Catherine, pseud. Dolphin School: Echo's New Pet. 2017. (ENG., Illus.). 107p. (J). pap. 4.99 (978-1-338-05374-6(4)) Scholastic, Inc.

Harley, Stephen. The Christmastime Dog Rescue. 2013. (ENG.). 24p. pap. 19.99 (978-1-4624-0774-3(9), Inspiring Voices) Author Solutions, LLC.

Harmon, Minnie. Golden's Routine. 2010. 28p. pap. 15.99 (978-1-4500-3321-3(0)) Xlibris Corp.

Harper, Aimee. Crystal (Dream Dogs, Book 4), Book 4. 2010. (Dream Dogs Ser.: Bk. 4). (ENG., Illus.). 112p. (J). (gr. -1-3). 5.99 (978-0-00-732037-0(X)) HarperCollins Pubs. Ltd. GBR. Dist: Independent Pubs. Group.

—Nugget (Dream Dogs, Book 3), Book 3. 2010. (Dream Dogs Ser.: Bk. 3). (ENG., Illus.). 112p. (J). (gr. -1-3). 6.99 (978-0-00-732036-3(1)) HarperCollins Pubs. Ltd. GBR. Dist: Independent Pubs. Group.

Harrington, Claudia. Book 1: Otis the Very Large Dog. Syed, Anoosha, illus. 2016. (Hank the Pet Sitter Ser.). (ENG.). 32p. (J). (gr. -1-3). lib. bdg. 32.79 (978-1-62402-187-9(5), 24553, Calico Chapter Bks) Magic Wagon.

—Book 4: Elmer the Very Sneaky Sheep. Syed, Anoosha, illus. 2016. (Hank the Pet Sitter Ser.). (ENG.). 32p. (J). (gr. -1-3). lib. bdg. 32.79 (978-1-62402-190-9(5), 24559, Calico Chapter Bks) Magic Wagon.

Harrington, Jenna. Katie Mcginty Wants a Pet! Simpson, Finn, illus. 2015. (ENG.). 32p. (J). (gr. -1-2). 16.99 (978-1-58925-192-2(X)) Tiger Tales.

Harris, Robie H. Goodbye Mousie. Ormerod, Jan, illus. 2004. (ENG.). 32p. (J). (gr. -1-3). reprint ed. 9.99 (978-0-689-87134-4(1), Aladdin) Simon & Schuster Children's Publishing.

Harrison, Megan Bernadette. The Adventures of Kitty Tom & Blossom: Book One. 2009. 36p. pap. 24.95 (978-1-60749-257-3(1)) America Star Bks.

Hay, Sam. Flight of the Pummeled Parakeet. 2015. (Undead Pets Ser.: 6). lib. bdg. 16.00 (978-0-606-38405-6(7)) Turtleback.

—Flight of the Pummeled Parakeet #6. Cooper, Simon, illus. 2015. (Undead Pets Ser.: 6). (ENG.). 120p. (J). (gr. 1-3). 5.99 (978-0-448-47800-5(5), Grosset & Dunlap) Penguin Young Readers Group.

—Gasp of the Ghoulish Guinea Pig. 2016. (Undead Pets Ser.: 7). lib. bdg. 16.00 (978-0-606-38406-3(5)) Turtleback.

—Goldfish from Beyond the Grave. 2015. (Undead Pets Ser.: 4). lib. bdg. 16.00 (978-0-606-36220-7(7)) Turtleback.

—Rise of the Zombie Rabbit #5. Cooper, Simon, illus. 2015. (Undead Pets Ser.: 5). (ENG.). 112p. (J). (gr. 1-3). 5.99 (978-0-448-47799-2(8), Grosset & Dunlap) Penguin Young Readers Group.

Hays, Anna Jane. The Pup Speaks Up. Petrone, Valeria, illus. 2003. (Step into Reading Ser.). 32p. (gr. -1-1). 14.00 (978-0-7569-1696-1(8)) Perfection Learning Corp.

—The Pup Speaks Up. Petrone, Valeria, illus. 2003. (Step into Reading Ser.). 32p. (J). (gr. -1-1). pap. 4.99 (978-0-375-81232-3(6), Random Hse. Bks. for Young Readers) Random Hse. Children's Bks.

HB Staff. The Perfect Pet. 97th ed. 2003. (First-Place Reading Ser.). (gr. 1-18). pap. 16.50 (978-0-15-308133-0(3)) Harcourt Schl. Pubs.

Heder, Thyra. Alfie: (the Turtle That Disappeared) 2017. (ENG., Illus.). 48p. (J). (gr. -1-3). 18.99 (978-1-4197-2529-6(7), 1165701, Abrams Bks. for Young Readers) Abrams, Inc.

Heiligman, Deborah. Fun Dog, Sun Dog, 0 vols. Bowers, Tim, illus. 2012. (ENG.). 34p. (J). (gr. -1-2). pap. 7.99 (978-0-7614-5836-4(0), 9780761458364, Two Lions) Amazon Publishing.

Here Kitty. 2005. 32p. (J). 12.99 (978-0-9758709-3-8(9), A.W.A. Gang) Journey Stone Creations, LLC.

Hermes, Patricia. Emma Dilemma & the New Nanny, 0 vols. Carter, Abby, illus. 2012. (Emma Dilemma Ser.: 1). (ENG.). 114p. (J). (gr. 3-6). pap. 6.99 (978-0-7614-5619-3(8), 9780761456193, Two Lions) Amazon Publishing.

—Emma Dilemma, the Nanny, & the Secret Ferret, 0 vols. 2012. (Emma Dilemma Ser.: 5). (ENG., Illus.). 146p. (J). (gr. 3-6). 15.99 (978-0-7614-5650-6(3), 9780761456506, Two Lions) Amazon Publishing.

Herrera, Juan Felipe. Featherless: Desplumado (English & Spanish Edition), 1 vol. Cuevas, Ernesto, Jr., illus. 2013.Tr. of Desplumado. (ENG.). 32p. (J). (gr. k-3). pap. 11.95 (978-0-89239-303-9(3), leelowcbp) Lee & Low Bks., Inc.

Hess, Mary Rand & Greig, Steve. The One & Only Wolfgang: From Pet Rescue to One Big Happy Family, 1 vol. Sarell, Nadja, illus. 2019. (ENG.). 32p. (J). 17.99 (978-0-310-76823-4(3)) Zonderkidz.

Hicks, Kelli. Maddie's Pet Peeve. 2015. (Rourke's Beginning Chapter Bks.). (ENG.). 48p. (gr. 1-3). 25.64 (978-1-63430-372-9(5), 9781634303729) Rourke Educational Media.

Hietpas, Polly. Hello Rosie Cat. 2009. 16p. pap. 8.49 (978-1-4490-0283-1(8)) AuthorHouse.

Hileman, Jane & Pitt, Marilyn. Come with Me. Bianchi, John, illus. 2016. (1G Potato Chip Bks.). (ENG.). 12p. (J). (gr. k-1). pap. 8.00 (978-1-61541-162-7(3)) American Reading Co.

Hill, Meggan. Nico & Lola: Kindness shared between a boy & a dog. 2009. 32p. (J). (978-0-615-23040-5(7)) Genuine Prints, LLC.

Hillert, Margaret. Dear Dragon Gets a Pet. Jack Pullan, illus. 2015. (Beginning-To-Read Ser.). (ENG.). 32p. (J). (gr. k-2). pap. 13.26 (978-1-60357-791-5(2)) Norwood Hse. Pr.

—Dear Dragon Gets a Pet. Pullan, Jack, illus. 2015. (BeginningtoRead Ser.). (ENG.). 32p. (J). (gr. k-2). lib. bdg. 22.60 (978-1-59953-706-1(0)) Norwood Hse. Pr.

Hobbie, Holly. A Cat Named Swan. 2017. (Illus.). 32p. (J). (gr. -1-2). 17.99 (978-0-553-53744-4(X), Random Hse. Bks. for Young Readers) Random Hse. Children's Bks.

Hobbs, Constance. Bugsy's Special Event. 2008. 64p. pap. 10.50 (978-0-9556783-7-0(4)) Hobbs, Constance GBR. Dist: Lulu Pr., Inc.

Hock, Dan. The Afternoon Auction: An Iggy & Igor Mystery. 2004. (Illus.). 48p. (J). per. 4.99 (978-0-9754046-0-7(1)) Anticipation Pr.

Hodge, A. D. Bubbles & Boundaries. 2013. 32p. (978-1-4602-2858-6(8)) FriesenPress.

Hoena, Blake A. Ack's New Pet, 1 vol. Harpster, Steve, illus. 2014. (Eek & Ack Early Chapter Bks.). (ENG.). 32p. (J). (gr. k-2). lib. bdg. 22.65 (978-1-4342-6406-0(8), 123886, Stone Arch Bks.) Capstone.

Hoffman, Mary Ann. A Parrot for Pam, 1 vol. 2006. (Neighborhood Readers Ser.). (ENG.). 8p. (gr. k-1). pap. 5.15 (978-1-4042-5690-3(3), 75199843-5e0f-402b-b6b1-1a68bd5ea1bf, Rosen Classroom) Rosen Publishing Group, Inc., The.

Holland, Frances. Ryan's Praying Mantis, 1 vol. 2009. 19p. pap. 24.95 (978-1-60749-432-4(9)) PublishAmerica, Inc.

Homberg, Ruth. The Best Ball (Disney Palace Pets: Whisker Haven Tales) RH Disney, illus. 2017. (Step into Reading Ser.). (ENG.). 24p. (J). (gr. -1-1). pap. 4.99 (978-0-7364-3596-3(4), RH/Disney) Random Hse. Children's Bks.

Homberg, Ruth, adapted by. The Best Ball. 2017. (Illus.). 24p. (J). (978-1-5182-3608-2(1)) Random Hse., Inc.

Hooks, Gwendolyn. The Best Trick: A Pet Club Story, 1 vol. Byrne, Mike, illus. 2010. (Pet Club Ser.). (ENG.). 32p. (J). (gr. 1-2). 22.65 (978-1-4342-2052-3(4), 102782, Stone Arch Bks.) Capstone.

—The Cat Food Mystery: A Pet Club Story, 1 vol. Byrne, Mike, illus. 2011. (Pet Club Ser.). (ENG.). 32p. (J). (gr. 1-2). pap. 6.25 (978-1-4342-3051-5(1), 114651, Stone Arch Bks.) Capstone.

—Find the Cat! A Pet Club Story. Byrne, Mike, illus. 2010. (Pet Club Ser.). (ENG.). 32p. (J). (gr. 1-2). pap. 6.25 (978-1-4342-2795-9(2), 114062, Stone Arch Bks.) Capstone.

—The Lucky Charm: A Pet Club Story, 1 vol. Byrne, Mike, illus. 2011. (Pet Club Ser.). (ENG.). 32p. (J). (gr. 1-2). pap. 6.25 (978-1-4342-3052-2(X), 114652, Stone Arch Bks.) Capstone.

—The Noisy Night: A Pet Club Story, 1 vol. Byrne, Mike, illus. 2010. (Pet Club Ser.). (ENG.). 32p. (J). (gr. 1-2). 22.65 (978-1-4342-2049-3(4), 102781); pap. 6.25 (978-1-4342-2793-5(6), 114060) Capstone. (Stone Arch Bks.).

—Pet Club. Byrne, Mike, illus. 2013. (Pet Club Ser.). (ENG.). 32p. (J). (gr. -1-1). 135.90 (978-1-4342-8841-7(2), 21113, Stone Arch Bks.) Capstone.

—Pet Costume Party: A Pet Club Story, 1 vol. Byrne, Mike, illus. 2011. (Pet Club Ser.). (ENG.). 32p. (J). (gr. 1-2). pap. 6.25 (978-1-4342-3053-9(8), 114653); lib. bdg. 22.65 (978-1-4342-2513-9(5), 113346) Capstone. (Stone Arch Bks.).

—The Pet Wash: A Pet Club Story, 1 vol. Byrne, Mike, illus. 2011. (Pet Club Ser.). (ENG.). 32p. (J). (gr. 1-2). pap. 6.25 (978-1-4342-3054-6(6), 114654); lib. bdg. 22.65 (978-1-4342-2514-6(3), 113347) Capstone. (Stone Arch Bks.).

—Pets at the Party: A Pet Club Story. Byrne, Mike, illus. 2010. (Pet Club Ser.). (ENG.). 32p. (J). (gr. 1-2). pap. 6.25 (978-1-4342-2796-6(0), 114063, Stone Arch Bks.) Capstone.

Hope, Laura Lee. Bunny Brown & His Sister Sue. 2005. 188p. pap. 11.95 (978-1-4218-1165-9(0), 1st World Library - Literary Society) 1st World Publishing, Inc.

Housel, Debra. Charlotte's Web: An Instructional Guide for Literature. rev. ed. 2015. (Great Works). (ENG., Illus.). 72p. (gr. 3-5). pap. 9.99 (978-1-4807-6995-3(9)) Shell Educational Publishing.

Howard, Arthur. Hoodwinked. Howard, Arthur, illus. 2005. (ENG., Illus.). 32p. (J). (gr. -1-3). pap. 7.00 (978-0-15-205386-4(7), 1196217, Clarion Bks.) HarperCollins Pubs.

Howe, James. Bunnicula Meets Edgar Allan Crow. Fortune, Eric, illus. (Bunnicula & Friends Ser.). (ENG.). 160p. (J). (gr. 3-7). 2008. pap. 7.99 (978-1-4169-1473-0(0)) 2006. 17.99 (978-1-4169-1458-7(7)) Simon & Schuster Children's Publishing. (Atheneum Bks. for Young Readers).

Howland, Naomi. The Better-Than-Best Purim, 0 vols. 2012. (ENG.). 32p. (J). (gr. -1-2). 16.99 (978-0-7614-6203-3(1), 9780761462033, Two Lions) Amazon Publishing.

Hubbard, Sharron/Y. Link & Rosie's Pets. Schleihs, Kristin, illus. 2007. (J). bds. (978-0-9762434-3-4(1)) Link & Rosie Pr.

Hughes, Emily C. Ponies Love Pets! 2017. (My Little Pony Leveled Readers Ser.). (ENG.). 32p. (J). (gr. -1-3). lib. bdg. 31.36 (978-1-5321-4096-9(7), 26969) Spotlight.

—Ponies Love Pets! 2014. (Passport to Reading Level 1 Ser.). (J). lib. bdg. 13.55 (978-0-606-35298-7(8)) Turtleback.

Hull, Rod. Dr. Potts, My Pets Have Spots! Latimer, Miriam, illus. 2017. (ENG.). 32p. (J). (gr. -1-2). pap. 9.99 (978-1-78285-324-4(3)) Barefoot Bks., Inc.

Hurst, Christine. Symphony Smythe Wants a Pet. 2013. (Illus.). 50p. pap. (978-0-473-26322-5(X)) Prickly Cat Publishing.

Hurwitz, Johanna. Amazing Monty. McGrory, Anik, illus. 2013. (Monty Ser.: 3). (ENG.). 112p. (J). (gr. k-4). pap. 5.99 (978-0-7636-6561-6(4)) Candlewick Pr.

Husband Haddow, Barbara. One More Than Enough. 2011. 34p. pap. (978-1-77067-260-4(5)) FriesenPress.

Hutton, John. Pets: Baby Unplugged. Kang, Andrea, illus. 2011. (Baby Unplugged Ser.). (ENG.). 14p. (J). (— 1). bds. 7.99 (978-1-936669-02-8(1)) Blue Manatee Press.

Ignato, Shirley. Wing ding my Chameleon. 2011. 20p. (gr. -1). pap. 12.74 (978-1-4634-1342-2(4)) AuthorHouse.

Impey, Rose & Dhami, Narinder. Mega Sleepover 2 (the Sleepover Club), No. 2. 2010. (Sleepover Club Ser.). (ENG.). 280p. (gr. 2-4). 9.99 (978-0-00-710903-6(2), HarperCollins Children's Bks.) HarperCollins Pubs. Ltd. GBR. Dist: HarperCollins Pubs.

Ireland, Justina. Zach Lopez vs. the Shadow Cats. Champion, Tyler, illus. 2018. (Devils' Pass Ser.). (ENG.). 128p. (J). (gr. 4-8). lib. bdg. 25.99 (978-1-4965-6524-2(X), 138524, Stone Arch Bks.) Capstone.

Ishida, Sanae. Chibi Samurai Wants a Pet: An Adventure with Little Kunoichi the Ninja Girl. 2017. (Little Kunoichi the Ninja Girl Ser.). (Illus.). 32p. (J). (gr. -1-2). 16.99 (978-1-63217-117-7(1), Little Bigfoot) Sasquatch Bks.

J, Granny. Pinky Gets a New Puppy: Pinky Frink's Adventures. 2012. (ENG.). 36p. pap. 17.99 (978-1-105-86479-7(0)) Lulu Pr., Inc.

Jacobs, Paul DuBois & Swender, Jennifer. The Bow-Wow Bus. Laberis, Stephanie, illus. 2017. (Animal Inn Ser.: 3). (ENG.). 112p. (J). (gr. 2-5). pap. 5.99 (978-1-4814-6229-7(6), Simon & Schuster/Paula Wiseman Bks.) Simon & Schuster/Paula Wiseman Bks.

—Bright Lights, Big Kitty! Laberis, Stephanie, illus. 2017. (Animal Inn Ser.: 4). (ENG.). 112p. (J). (gr. 2-5). pap. 5.99 (978-1-4814-6232-7(6), Aladdin) Simon & Schuster Children's Publishing.

—Whooooo Done It? Laberis, Stephanie, illus. 2018. (Animal Inn Ser.: 5). (ENG.). 96p. (J). (gr. 2-5). 17.99 (978-1-4814-9963-7(7)); pap. 5.99 (978-1-4814-9962-0(9)) Simon & Schuster Children's Publishing. (Aladdin).

Jane, Pamela. Winky Blue Goes Wild! Tilley, Debbie, illus. 2003. 64p. (J). 13.95 (978-1-59034-588-7(6)); pap. (978-1-59034-589-4(4)) Mondo Publishing.

Javernick, Ellen. The Birthday Pet, 0 vols. O'Malley, Kevin, illus. 2012. (ENG.). 34p. (J). (gr. -1-2). pap. 9.99 (978-0-7614-6238-5(4), 9780761462385, Two Lions) Amazon Publishing.

Jeffers, Oliver. This Moose Belongs to Me. Jeffers, Oliver, illus. 2012. (ENG., Illus.). 32p. (J). (gr. -1-2). 19.99 (978-0-399-16103-2(1), Philomel Bks.) Penguin Young Readers Group.

Jenkins, Amanda. George & Grace Find an Egg. Zolotic, Aleksander, illus. 2017. (Text Connections Guided Close Reading Ser.). (J). (gr. 2). (978-1-4900-1846-1(8)) Benchmark Education Co.

Jenkins, Emily. Cinco Criaturas. Cortes, Eunice, tr. Bogacki, Tomek, illus. 2003. (Picture Bks.).Tr. of Five Creatures. (SPA.). (J). (978-970-690-648-9(7)) Planeta Mexicana Editorial S. A. de C. V.

Jennings, Patrick. We Can't All Be Rattlesnakes. (J). 2011. (ENG.). 144p. (gr. 3-7). pap. 9.99 *(978-0-06-082117-3(5)*, HarperCollins) 2009. 121p. lib. bdg. 16.89 *(978-0-06-082116-6(7))* HarperCollins Pubs.

Jobe, Lisa. Can I Keep It? 2019. (ENG., Illus.). 32p. (J). 17.99 *(978-1-62414-696-1(1)*, 900198607) Page Street Publishing Co.

Joey & Scout. 2004. (Illus.). (J). 7.95 *(978-0-9753704-0-7(5))* MYHRECO.

Johnson, Angela. Julius. Pilkey, Dav, illus. 2015. 32p. pap. 7.00 *(978-1-61003-548-4(8))* Center for the Collaborative Classroom.

Johnson, Myrna. I Still Want a Pet. 2016. (ENG., Illus.). (gr. k-6). pap. 12.00 *(978-1-62288-157-4(5))* Austin, Stephen F. State Univ. Pr.

Johnson, Sandi. Harold the Hopping Hamster. Johnson, Britt, ed. Sturgeon, Bobbi, illus. l.t. ed. 2003. (ENG.). 34p. (J). (gr. k-5). pap. 12.99 *(978-1-929063-91-8(1)*, 322) Moons & Stars Publishing For Children.

Jones, Molly. Something in the Air. Welch, Sheila Kelly, illus. 2005. (J). *(978-1-893516-03-8(2))* Our Child Pr.

Juan, Ana. The Pet Shop Revolution. 2011. (J). pap. *(978-0-545-12811-7(0)*, Levine, Arthur A. Bks.) Scholastic, Inc.

Julie, Aunt. Paddieduck! Julie, A Little Girl from Texas. 2011. 56p. (gr. 2-4). pap. 8.95 *(978-1-4269-2584-9(0))* Trafford Publishing.

Kagiliery, Theodore. Angelo & Peter. 2012. 32p. pap. 19.99 *(978-1-4772-2893-7(4))* AuthorHouse.

Kalomas, Alice & Kerr, Lenora. Sir Wrinkles Goes to School. Utomo, Gabhor, illus. 2005. (J). 16.95 *(978-0-9766639-1-1(0))* Sir Wrinkles Pr.

Kankey, Andrew T. Penelope & Mrs Grace: A Swine Mystery. 2011. 80p. 17.95 *(978-1-4575-0531-7(2))* Dog Ear Publishing, LLC.

Karst, Patrice. The Invisible Leash: An Invisible String Story about the Loss of a Pet. Lew-Vriethoff, Joanne, illus. 2019. (Invisible String Ser.: 3). (ENG.). 32p. (J). (gr. -1-3). 18.99 *(978-0-316-52485-8(9))* Little, Brown Bks. for Young Readers.

Kats, Jewel. Jenny & Her Dog Both Fight Cancer: A Tale of Chemotherapy & Caring. 2015. (Illus.). 32p. (J). pap. *(978-1-61599-279-9(0))* Loving Healing Pr., Inc.

Katz, Karen. Where Is Baby's Puppy? A Lift-The-Flap Book. Katz, Karen, illus. 2011. (ENG., Illus.). 14p. (J). (gr. -1 — 1). bds. 7.99 *(978-1-4169-8684-3(7)*, Little Simon) Little Simon.

Kaufman Orloff, Karen. I Wanna Iguana. Catrow, David, illus. 2004. 32p. (J). (gr. -1-3). 18.99 *(978-0-399-23717-1(8)*, G.P. Putnam's Sons Books for Young Readers) Penguin Young Readers Group.

Kawai, Ritsuko. Hamtaro Postcard Book. Kawai, Ritsuko, illus. 2003. (Hamtaro Ser.). (ENG., Illus.). 24p. (J). pap. 7.95 *(978-1-56931-845-4(X))* Viz Media.

Kear, Nicole C. The Fix-It Friends: Wish You Were Here. Dockray, Tracy, illus. 2017. (Fix-It Friends Ser.: 4). (ENG.). 160p. (J). pap. 7.99 *(978-1-250-08670-9(1)*, 900157581) Imprint IND. Dist: Macmillan.

Keats, Ezra Jack. Pet Show! (J). (gr. -1-3). pap. 12.95 incl. audio Weston Woods Studios, Inc.

Keene, Carolyn. Pets on Parade. Francis, Peter, illus. 2016. (Nancy Drew Clue Book Ser.: 6). (ENG.). 96p. (J). (gr. 1-4). pap. 5.99 *(978-1-4814-5823-8(X)*, Aladdin) Simon & Schuster Children's Publishing.

Kellogg, Steven. The Mysterious Tadpole. Kellogg, Steven, illus. 25th anniv. ed. 2004. (Illus.). 40p. (J). (gr. k-3). reprint ed. pap. 8.99 *(978-0-14-240140-8(4)*, Puffin Books) Penguin Young Readers Group.

Kennedy Center, The. Unleashed: The Lives of White House Pets. Hoyt, Ard, illus. 2011. (ENG.). 112p. (J). (gr. 2-5). pap. 5.99 *(978-1-4169-4862-9(7)*, Simon & Schuster Bks. For Young Readers) Simon & Schuster Bks. For Young Readers.

Kerr, Mike. Mike & a Lynx Named Kitty. Vitt, Karren, illus. 2nd rev. ed. 2006. 112p. per. 13.50 *(978-1-931195-36-2(6))* KiwE Publishing, Ltd.

Kessler, Kathryn. Marvin Discovers Snow. 2010. 36p. (J). pap. 15.77 *(978-1-4520-0590-4(7))* AuthorHouse.

King, Zelda. The Class Surprise, 1 vol. 2006. (Neighborhood Readers Ser.). (ENG.). 16p. (gr. 1-2). pap. 6.50 *(978-1-4042-6994-1(0)*, ce91d7dc-161e-4b30-94f8-41fcf95a8609, Rosen Classroom) Rosen Publishing Group, Inc., The.

Kirby, Lee. Super Turbo & the Fire-Breathing Dragon. O'Connor, George, illus. 2017. (Super Turbo Ser.: 5). (ENG.). 128p. (J). (gr. k-4). 16.99 *(978-1-4814-9997-2(1))*; pap. 5.99 *(978-1-4814-9996-5(3))* Little Simon. (Little Simon).

—Super Turbo Protects the World. O'Connor, George, illus. 2017. (Super Turbo Ser.: 4). (ENG.). 128p. (J). (gr. k-4). 16.99 *(978-1-4814-9994-1(7))*; pap. 6.99 *(978-1-4814-9993-4(9))* Little Simon. (Little Simon).

—Super Turbo Saves the Day! O'Connor, George, illus. 2016. (Super Turbo Ser.: 1). (ENG.). 128p. (J). (gr. k-4). 17.99 *(978-1-4814-8885-3(6))*; pap. 5.99 *(978-1-4814-8884-6(8))* Little Simon. (Little Simon).

—Super Turbo vs. the Flying Ninja Squirrels. O'Connor, George, illus. 2016. (Super Turbo Ser.: 2). (ENG.). 128p. (J). (gr. k-4). 17.99 *(978-1-4814-8888-4(0))*; pap. 5.99 *(978-1-4814-8887-7(2))* Little Simon. (Little Simon).

—Super Turbo vs. the Pencil Pointer. O'Connor, George, illus. 2017. (Super Turbo Ser.: 3). (ENG.). 128p. (J). (gr. k-4). pap. 5.99 *(978-1-4814-9438-0(4)*, Little Simon) Little Simon.

—Super Turbo vs. Wonder Pig. O'Connor, George, illus. 2018. (Super Turbo Ser.: 6). (ENG.). 128p. (J). (gr. k-4). 16.99 *(978-1-5344-1182-1(8))*; pap. 6.99 *(978-1-5344-1181-4(X))* Little Simon. (Little Simon).

Klein, Abby. Stop That Hamster! McKinley, John, illus. 2008. (Ready, Freddy! Ser.: Bk. 12). 95p. (gr. -1-3). 16.00 *(978-0-7569-8300-0(2))* Perfection Learning Corp.

Koeppel, Ruth. Nick Jr. Wonder Pets Adventures: Book & Magnetic Playset. 2009. 16p. (J). bds. 14.99 *(978-0-7944-1769-7(8))* Reader's Digest Assn., Inc., The.

Korté, Steve. Ace: The Origin of Batman's Dog. Baltazar, Art, illus. 2017. (DC Super-Pets Origin Stories Ser.). (ENG.). 48p. (gr. 1-3). lib. bdg. 25.32 *(978-1-4965-5138-2(9)*, 136162, Stone Arch Bks.) Capstone.

Koster, Amy Sky. Cuddly Princess Pals. 2014. lib. bdg. 13.55 *(978-0-606-35552-0(9))* Turtleback.

Krensky, Stephen. My Pet Tree, Albert. Hobai, Ioana, illus. 2016. (J). *(978-0-7680-8372-9(9))* SAE Intl.

—Paul Bunyan. Orback, Craig, illus. 2007. (On My Own Folklore Ser.). (ENG.). 48p. (J). (gr. 2-4). per. 7.99 *(978-0-8225-6479-9(3)*, bd620386-6b18-48ef-82bc-69b02315f5be, First Avenue Editions) Lerner Publishing Group.

Krinsky, Ed. Pip, Veronica & the Harmonica. Evans, Casey, illus. 2013. 32p. pap. 13.00 *(978-1-62516-945-7(0)*, Strategic Bk. Publishing) Strategic Book Publishing & Rights Agency (SBPRA).

Kruse, Anne. Takota's Dream. 2010. pap. 16.99 *(978-0-578-05291-5(1))* Sisterhaus Publishing.

Kruse, Donald W. Gorilla Soup! 2012. 48p. pap. 12.95 *(978-1-59663-862-4(1)*, Castle Keep Pr.) Rock, James A. & Co. Pubs.

—Gorilla Soup! Crank, Donny, illus. 2017. (ENG.). (J). (gr. k-5). pap. 14.95 *(978-0-9981972-2-7(X))* Zaccheus Entertainment Co.

La Rue, Coco. A New Pig in Town. May, Kyla, illus. 2013. 127p. (J). pap. *(978-0-545-46607-3(5))* Scholastic, Inc.

LaFaye, A. No Frogs in School. Ceulemans, Eglantine, illus. 2018. 32p. (J). (gr. -1-2). 16.95 *(978-1-4549-2698-6(8))* Sterling Publishing Co., Inc.

Laird, Lisa J. I'm the Only One Who Loves Cliff the Goat. 2009. 48p. pap. 19.49 *(978-1-4389-5660-2(6))* AuthorHouse.

Lam, Thao. My Cat Looks Like My Dad. 2019. (ENG., Illus.). 32p. (J). 17.95 *(978-1-77147-351-4(7))* Owlkids Bks. Inc. CAN. Dist: Publishers Group West (PGW).

Lambert, George J. 8 Boys & 8 Beasts, 1 vol. Lambert, Celeste, illus. 2010. 24p. 24.95 *(978-1-4489-5901-3(2))* PublishAmerica, Inc.

Lane, Nickel. The Ferret Crusaders: Quest of the Wish A Pod. 2nd ed. 2004. 73p. (J). per. 8.49 *(978-1-4116-0459-9(8))* Lulu Pr., Inc.

Lawson, Sue. Ferret Boy. (Illus.). 256p. pap. *(978-0-7344-0465-7(4)*, Lothian Children's Bks.) Hachette Australia.

Layne, Steven. Play with Puppy, 1 vol. Hoyt, Ard, illus. 2018. (ENG.). 32p. (J). (gr. -1-3). 16.99 *(978-1-4556-2374-7(1)*, Pelican Publishing) Arcadia Publishing.

Lee, Spike & Lee, Tonya Lewis. Please, Puppy, Please. Nelson, Kadir, illus. 2005. (ENG.). 32p. (J). (gr. -1-3). 18.99 *(978-0-689-86804-7(9)*, Simon & Schuster Bks. For Young Readers) Simon & Schuster Bks. For Young Readers.

Lehman, Seth. The Color Pets. 2006. (Illus.). 52p. (J). 7.00 net. *(978-0-9787986-0-4(0))* 4All Ages LLC.

Lennon, Margie. Snowball's Sheepdog Adventures: Summer. 2012. 24p. pap. 14.99 *(978-1-4685-4655-2(4))* AuthorHouse.

Leonardo, Cory. The Simple Art of Flying. 2019. (ENG., Illus.). 384p. (J). (gr. 3-7). 17.99 *(978-1-5344-2099-1(1)*, Aladdin) Simon & Schuster Children's Publishing.

Light, Steven. Have You Seen My Monster? Light, Steve, illus. 2015. (ENG.). 48p. (J). (-k). 16.99 *(978-0-7636-7513-4(X))* Candlewick Pr.

Lindgren, Barbro. Julia Wants a Pet. Dyssegaard, Elisabeth Kallick, tr. Eriksson, Eva, illus. 2003. 32p. (J). (gr. -1 — 1). 15.00 *(978-91-29-65940-5(X))* R & S Bks. SWE. Dist: Macmillan.

Little Airplane Productions & Fogarty, Alexandria, illus. Baby Beaver Rescue. 2009. (Wonder Pets! Ser.). (ENG.). 24p. (J). (gr. -1-2). pap. 3.99 *(978-1-4169-8499-3(2)*, Simon Spotlight/Nickelodeon) Simon Spotlight/Nickelodeon.

Little, Celeste. Scales. Motz, Mike, illus. 2012. 24p. (J). 12.95 *(978-1-60131-116-0(8))* Big Tent Bks.

Little, Jean. Emma's Strange Pet. 2004. (I Can Read Level 3 Ser.). (ENG., Illus.). 64p. (J). (gr. k-3). pap. 4.99 *(978-0-06-444259-6(4)*, HarperCollins) HarperCollins Pubs.

—Emma's Strange Pet. Plecas, Jennifer, illus. 2003. (I Can Read Bks.). 64p. (J). (gr. k-3). 15.99 *(978-0-06-028350-6(5))* HarperCollins Pubs.

Lockard, Donna Lee. Sasha the Tortoise's Summer Vacation. 2013. (ENG.). 36p. (J). pap. 19.95 *(978-1-4787-0938-1(3))* Outskirts Pr., Inc.

Loewen, Nancy. Good-Bye, Jeepers: What to Expect When Your Pet Dies, 1 vol. Lyles, Christopher, illus. 2011. (Life's Challenges Ser.). (ENG.). 24p. (J). (gr. 2-3). lib. bdg. 26.65 *(978-1-4048-6680-5(9)*, 115032, Picture Window Bks.) Capstone.

Loggins, Kenny. Moose N' Me. Nash, Joshua, illus. 2013. 32p. (J). (gr. -1-3). 14.95 *(978-0-578-07552-5(0))* Charlesbridge Publishing, Inc.

Lombardi, Kristine. The Grumpy Pets. 2016. (ENG., Illus.). 32p. (J). (gr. k-2). 14.95 *(978-1-4197-1888-5(6)*, 1094801, Abrams Bks. for Young Readers) Abrams, Inc.

Long, Ethan. Me & My Big Mouse, 0 vols. 2014. (ENG.). 32p. (J). (gr. -1-2). 16.99 *(978-1-4778-4728-2(6)*, 9781477847282, Two Lions) Amazon Publishing.

Long, Olivia. The Boy & the Dog. Long, Olivia, illus. Date not set. (Pets & Their People Ser.). (Illus.). 32p. (J). (gr. k-5). *(978-1-880042-07-6(X))* Shelf-Life Bks.

—Diary of a Dog. Long, Olivia, illus. Date not set. (Pets & Their People Ser.). (Illus.). 32p. (J). (gr. -1-4). 9.95 *(978-1-880042-06-9(1)*, SL12456) Shelf-Life Bks.

—Too Many Kittens. Long, Olivia, illus. Date not set. (Pets & Their People Ser.). (Illus.). 32p. (J). (gr. -1-4). *(978-1-880042-09-0(6))* Shelf-Life Bks.

Lopresti, Tony. My Cat. Johnson, Deborah C., illus. 2012. 24p. pap. 13.99 *(978-0-9838018-6-3(X))* 4RV Pub.

Lord, Cynthia. Jelly Bean. 2014. (Shelter Pet Squad Ser.: 1). lib. bdg. 16.00 *(978-0-606-36063-0(8))* Turtleback.

Louise, Zanni. Tiggy & the Magic Paintbrush: a Pet Called Nibbles, Volume 2. 2018. (Tiggy & the Magic Paintbrush Ser.: 2). (ENG., Illus.). 32p. (J). (gr. k-2). pap. 9.99 *(978-1-76068-041-1(9))* Little Hare Bks. AUS. Dist: Independent Pubs. Group.

Luke, Melinda. The Green Dog. Manning, Jane K., illus. 2006. (Science Solves It Ser.). 32p. (J). pap. 7.99 *(978-0-15-356581-6(0))* Houghton Mifflin Harcourt School Pubs.

Luthardt, Kevin. Peep!, 1 vol. (Illus.). 36p. (J). (gr. -1-k). 2012. pap. 7.95 *(978-1-56145-682-6(9))* 2003. 15.95 *(978-1-56145-046-6(4))* Peachtree Publishing Co. Inc.

Lyle-Soffe, Shari. Shoo Cat. Foster, Jack, illus. 2010. 16p. pap. 9.95 *(978-1-61633-033-0(3))* Guardian Angel Publishing, Inc.

Mack, Phillip. Missy Finds a Home. 2005. v, 93p. pap. 14.00 *(978-1-4120-6681-5(6))* Trafford Publishing.

Maithya, Susan M. Struffel Cares: Struffel's New Pet. 2012. 40p. pap. 20.99 *(978-1-4772-3323-8(7))* AuthorHouse.

Man-Kong, Mary. I Can Be a Pet Vet (Barbie) An, Jiyoung, illus. 2010. (Step into Reading Ser.). (ENG.). 32p. (J). (gr. -1-1). pap. 5.99 *(978-0-375-86581-7(0)*, Random Hse. Bks. for Young Readers) Random Hse. Children's Bks.

Mantchev, Lisa. Strictly No Elephants. Yoo, Taeeun, illus. 2015. (ENG.). 32p. (J). (gr. -1-3). 18.99 *(978-1-4814-1647-4(2)*, Simon & Schuster Bks. For Young Readers) Simon & Schuster Bks. For Young Readers.

Marinsky, Jane. Just Perfect. Marinsky, Jane, illus. 2012. (ENG., Illus.). 32p. (J). (gr. k). 16.95 *(978-1-56792-428-2(X))* Godine, David R. Pub.

Marsoli, Lisa Ann. Dinos are Big Babies & Dylan's Pets. Smitherton, Jeb, illus. 2005. (J). bds. 19.99 *(978-0-9767325-7-0(2))* Toy Quest.

—Dylan's Pets from A to Z. Santat, Dan, illus. 2005. (J). bds. 14.99 *(978-0-9767325-1-8(3))* Toy Quest.

Martin, Stephen W. Charlotte & the Rock. Cotterill, Samantha, illus. 2017. (ENG.). 32p. (J). (-k). 18.99 *(978-1-101-99389-7(8)*, Dial Bks) Penguin Young Readers Group.

Massey, Jane, illus. Mascotas. (Coloca y Siente). (SPA.). 10p. (J). (gr. k-2). bds. *(978-968-5308-66-3(7)*, Silver Dolphin en Español) Advanced Marketing, S. de R. L. de C. V.

Mather, David. A Frog in the House. 2011. 32p. (gr. 1-2). 16.95 *(978-0-9819307-9-4(4))*; pap. 9.95 *(978-0-9819307-8-7(6))* Raven Productions, Inc.

Mathews, Madge. Amelia Asks May I Have A Pet. Cook, Laurie, illus. 2008. 24p. (J). 3.99 *(978-0-9796536-1-2(4)*, EPI Kid Bks.) EPI Bks.

Matson, Erik. Robobattlepets - Home Invasion. 2012. 144p. pap. 7.99 *(978-0-9841187-6-2(4))* Asteroid Publishing.

Mayer, Mercer. Just One More Pet. 2013. (Little Critter Ser.). (J). lib. bdg. 13.55 *(978-0-606-31791-7(0))* Turtleback.

—Just Pick Us, Please! 2017. (Little Critter: I Can Read! Ser.). (Illus.). 32p. (J). lib. bdg. 13.55 *(978-0-606-40406-8(6))* Turtleback.

—These Are My Pets. 2019. (Step into Reading Ser.). (ENG.). 32p. (J). (gr. -1-1). pap. 5.99 *(978-1-9848-3099-9(6))*; lib. bdg. 12.99 *(978-1-9848-9495-3(1))* Random Hse. Children's Bks. (Random Hse. Bks. for Young Readers).

McCann, Jesse L., et al. Crisis of Infinite Kryptos, 1 vol. 2014. (Krypto the Superdog Ser.). (ENG., Illus.). 32p. (J). (gr. 1-3). 22.60 *(978-1-4342-6471-8(8)*, 124153, Stone Arch Bks.) Capstone.

McCardie, Amanda. Our Very Own Dog: Taking Care of Your First Pet. Rubbino, Salvatore, illus. 2017. (ENG.). 32p. (J). (gr. -1-2). 15.99 *(978-0-7636-8948-3(3))* Candlewick Pr.

McCarty, Peter. Hondo & Fabian. McCarty, Peter, illus. 2007. (ENG., Illus.). 40p. (J). (gr. -1-1). per. 8.99 *(978-0-312-36747-3(3)*, 900042352) Square Fish.

McCombie, Karen. My Big (Strange) Happy Family. Monks, Lydia, illus. 2009. (J). pap. *(978-0-385-73597-1(9)*, Yearling) Random Hse. Children's Bks.

McDonald, Brenda. How Do You Love A Big Dog? 2007. 18.00 *(978-0-8059-7314-3(1))* Dorrance Publishing Co., Inc.

Mcdonald, Megan. Triple Pet Trouble. 2015. (Judy Moody & Friends Ser.: 6). (Illus.). 60p. (J). lib. bdg. 14.75 *(978-0-606-36872-8(8))* Turtleback.

Mcdonnell, Patrick. The Mutts Diaries. 2016. (ENG., Illus.). 226p. (J). (gr. 3-7). 29.99 *(978-1-4494-7380-8(6))* Andrews McMeel Publishing.

—Year of Yesh. 2016. lib. bdg. 33.05 *(978-0-606-39185-6(1))* Turtleback.

McGhee, Holly M. Matylda, Bright & Tender. 2017. (ENG.). 224p. (J). (gr. 3-7). 16.99 *(978-0-7636-8951-3(3))* Candlewick Pr.

McGill, Erin. I Do Not Like Al's Hat. McGill, Erin, illus. 2017. (ENG., Illus.). 32p. (J). (gr. -1-3). 17.99 *(978-0-06-245576-5(1)*, Greenwillow Bks.) HarperCollins Pubs.

McGreal, Sue. Jimmy Fox's Great Pet Adventure. 2013. 68p. pap. *(978-1-78299-607-1(9))* FeedARead.com.

McKay, Hilary. Lulu & the Rabbit Next Door. 2014. (Lulu Ser.: 4). (J). lib. bdg. 14.75 *(978-0-606-41566-8(1))* Turtleback.

—Lulu & the Rabbit Next Door. Lamont, Priscilla, illus. 2014. (Lulu Ser.: 4). (ENG.). 112p. (J). (gr. 1-5). 13.99 *(978-0-8075-4816-5(2)*, 807548162) Whitman, Albert & Co.

McKinlay, Meg. Duck for a Day. Rudge, Leila, illus. 2012. (ENG.). 96p. (J). (gr. 2-4). 12.99 *(978-0-7636-5784-0(0))* Candlewick Pr.

McLean, Claire. Bo & the Ghosts of the White House Pets. 2012. 88p. pap. 17.95 *(978-1-4626-7416-9(X))* America Star Bks.

McNeely Schultz, Geri. Kristie's Excellent Adventures: A Visit to the Fridge. Bertolami, Vince, illus. 2013. (ENG.). 40p. (J). pap. 9.99 *(978-1-935766-88-9(0))* Windy City Pubs.

McOmber, Rachel B., ed. McOmber Phonics Storybooks: Ben Has a Pet. rev. ed. (Illus.). (J). *(978-0-944991-26-8(2))* Swift Learning Resources.

McPhail, David. Crash! the Cat. (I Like to Read Ser.). (ENG.). 32p. (J). (gr. -1-3). 2018. 7.99 *(978-0-8234-3982-9(8))* 2016. (Illus.). 16.95 *(978-0-8234-3649-1(7))* Holiday Hse., Inc.

—Dot & Bob. McPhail, David, illus. 2008. (Green Light Readers Ser.). (ENG., Illus.). 24p. (J). (gr. -1-1). pap. 5.99 *(978-0-15-206541-6(5)*, 1199496, Clarion Bks.) HarperCollins Pubs.

McQuinn, Anna. Lola Gets a Cat. Beardshaw, Rosalind, illus. (Lola Reads Ser.: 5). (ENG.). 28p. (J). (-k). 2018. pap. 7.99 *(978-1-58089-845-4(9))* 2017. lib. bdg. 15.99 *(978-1-58089-736-5(3))* Charlesbridge Publishing, Inc.

—Lola Quiere un Gato. Beardshaw, Rosalind, illus. 2019. (Lola Reads Ser.: 5). (SPA.). 28p. (J). (-k). 16.99 *(978-1-58089-670-2(7))* Charlesbridge Publishing, Inc.

—Lola Quiere un Gato / Lola Gets a Cat. Beardshaw, Rosalind, illus. 2019. (Lola Reads Ser.: 5).Tr. of Lola Gets a Cat. 28p. (J). (-k). pap. 7.99 *(978-1-58089-988-8(9))* Charlesbridge Publishing, Inc.

Meadows, Daisy. Bella the Bunny Fairy. Ripper, Georgie, illus. 2008. (Rainbow Magic — the Pet Fairies Ser.). 65p. (gr. 7). lib. bdg. 14.75 *(978-1-4178-2996-5(6))* Turtleback.

—Georgia the Guinea Pig Fairy. Ripper, Georgie, illus. 2008. (Rainbow Magic — the Pet Fairies Ser.). 65p. (gr. 3). lib. bdg. 14.75 *(978-1-4178-2997-2(4))* Turtleback.

—Katie the Kitten Fairy. Ripper, Georgie, illus. 2008. 65p. (J). pap. *(978-0-545-13320-3(3))* Scholastic, Inc.

—Katie the Kitten Fairy. Ripper, Georgie, illus. 2008. (Rainbow Magic — the Pet Fairies Ser.). 65p. (gr. 1-4). lib. bdg. 14.75 *(978-1-4178-2999-6(0))* Turtleback.

—Molly the Goldfish Fairy. Ripper, Georgie, illus. 2008. (Rainbow Magic — the Pet Fairies Ser.). 68p. (gr. -1-3). lib. bdg. 14.75 *(978-1-4178-3001-5(8))* Turtleback.

—Penny the Pony Fairy. 2008. (Rainbow Magic — the Pet Fairies Ser.). lib. bdg. 14.75 *(978-1-4178-3008-4(5))* Turtleback.

—Pet Fairies to the Rescue! 2013. (Rainbow Magic — Scholastic Reader Ser.). lib. bdg. 13.55 *(978-0-606-31510-4(1))* Turtleback.

Meagher, Ed. D. Zach & His Dog: A Story of Bonding, Love, & Loss for Children & Adults to Share Together. 2009. 56p. pap. 23.99 *(978-1-4389-4228-5(1))* AuthorHouse.

Messner, Kate. Marty McGuire Has Too Many Pets! 2015. (Marty Mcguire Ser.: 3). lib. bdg. 16.00 *(978-0-606-37021-9(8))* Turtleback.

Michiko Florence, Debbi. Jasmine Toguchi, Flamingo Keeper. Vukovic, Elizabet, illus. 2018. (Jasmine Toguchi Ser.: 4). (ENG.). 128p. (J). pap. 5.99 *(978-0-374-30837-7(3)*, 900185590, Farrar, Straus & Giroux (BYR)) Farrar, Straus & Giroux.

Miles, Ellen. Jake. 2018. 85p. (J). (gr. 1-4). 16.36 *(978-1-64310-123-1(4))* Penworthy Co., LLC, The.

—Maggie & Max (the Puppy Place #10) Maggie & Max. 2008. (Puppy Place Ser.: 10). (ENG.). 96p. (J). (gr. 2-5). 5.99 *(978-0-545-03456-2(6)*, Scholastic Paperbacks) Scholastic, Inc.

—Molly. 2013. (Puppy Place Ser.: 31). lib. bdg. 14.75 *(978-0-606-32385-7(6))* Turtleback.

—Pugsley. 2008. 81p. (J). *(978-0-545-09948-6(X))* Scholastic, Inc.

Mills, Claudia. Mason Dixon: Pet Disasters. Francis, Guy, illus. 2012. (Mason Dixon Ser.: 1). (ENG.). 176p. (J). (gr. 4-7). 6.99 *(978-0-375-87274-7(4)*, Yearling) Random Hse. Children's Bks.

—Pet Disasters, 1. Francis, Guy, illus. 2012. (Mason Dixon Ser.). (ENG.). 176p. (J). (gr. 4-6). lib. bdg. 21.19 *(978-0-375-96873-0(3)*, Knopf Bks. for Young Readers) Random Hse. Children's Bks.

Milo, Margaret D. Matthew Pet Adventure. 2012. 24p. 24.95 *(978-1-4626-6850-2(X))* America Star Bks.

Montgomery, Lewis B. The Case of the Amazing Zelda, Vol. 4. Wummer, Amy, illus. 2009. (Milo & Jazz Mysteries Ser.). 96p. (J). (gr. k-3). 22.60 *(978-1-57565-298-6(6))* Astra Publishing Hse.

—The Case of the Amazing Zelda. Wummer, Amy, illus. 2012. (Milo & Jazz Mysteries Ser.: Vol. 4). (ENG.). (J). (gr. 2-4). pap. 20.95 incl. audio compact disk *(978-1-4301-1209-9(3))* Live Oak Media.

—The Case of the Amazing Zelda (Book 4) Wummer, Amy, illus. 2009. (Milo & Jazz Mysteries Ser.). 96p. (J). (gr. 2-6). pap. 6.99 *(978-1-57565-296-2(X)*, 5d25f054-5ef2-4513-9e71-ec29da4fff54, Kane Press) Astra Publishing Hse.

—The Case of the Poisoned Pig (Book 2), No. 2. Wummer, Amy, illus. 2009. (Milo & Jazz Mysteries Ser.). 96p. (J). (gr. 2-6). pap. 6.99 *(978-1-57565-286-3(2)*, dccfda40-f72a-4587-96f6-a30894d647f4, Kane Press) Astra Publishing Hse.

Montgomery, R. A. Space Pup. Newton, Keith, illus. 2014. (ENG.). 80p. (J). (gr. 2-2). pap. 8.99 *(978-1-937133-43-6(5))* Chooseco LLC.

Morningforest, Chris & Raymond, Rebecca. Taking Care of Funny Pets. 2006. (ENG.). 36p. (J). pap. 15.43 *(978-1-4116-7710-4(2))* Lulu Pr., Inc.

Moroney, Trace. The Things I Love about Pets. 2019. (Things I Love about Ser.). (ENG.). 10p. (J). (— 1). bds. 8.99 *(978-1-76068-127-2(X))* Bonnier Publishing GBR. Dist: Independent Pubs. Group.

Morpurgo, Michael. Snakes & Ladders. Kober, Shahar, illus. 2013. (Red Bananas Ser.). (ENG.). 48p. (J). (gr. -1-2). pap. 17.44 *(978-1-4052-6081-7(5))* Farshore GBR. Dist: Children's Plus, Inc.

Morris, J. E. Flubby Is Not a Good Pet! Morris, J. E., illus. (Flubby Ser.). (Illus.). 32p. (J). 2020. (gr. k-2). 5.99 *(978-1-5247-9078-3(8))* 2019. (gr. -1-3). 9.99 *(978-1-5247-8776-9(0))* Penguin Young Readers Group. (Penguin Workshop).

Morris, Kyle. Watching the Puppy Grow. 2017. (Text Connections Guided Close Reading Ser.). (J). (gr. 1). *(978-1-4900-1805-8(0))* Benchmark Education Co.

Morrison, Cathy. I Want a Pet. 2012. (ENG., Illus.). 32p. (J). *(978-1-58925-113-7(X))* Tiger Tales.

Mortensen, Lori. The Cat That Disappeared, 1 vol. Simard, Rémy, illus. 2010. (My First Graphic Novel Ser.). (ENG.). 32p. (J). (gr. k-2). pap. 6.25 *(978-1-4342-2282-4(9)*, 103152, Stone Arch Bks.) Capstone.

—The Class Pet. 2016. (Spring Forward Ser.). (J). (gr. 1). *(978-1-4900-2228-4(7))* Benchmark Education Co.

Moyer, Anna B. Her Name Is Sophi. 2013. 28p. pap. 16.09 *(978-1-4669-7275-9(0))* Trafford Publishing.

Mubiru, Betha. Muzinge the Bird. 2004. (Illus.). 16p. pap. *(978-9970-02-447-6(7))* Fountain Pubs. Ltd. UGA. Dist: Michigan State Univ. Pr.

Muench-Williams, Heather. I Want a Pet. Teeple, Jackie, illus. l.t. ed. 2006. 12p. (J). (gr. -1-k). pap. 10.95 *(978-1-57332-353-6(5)*, HighReach Learning, Incorporated) Carson-Dellosa Publishing, LLC.

Mulholland, Clara. Naughty Miss Bunny. 2007. 128p. 25.95 *(978-1-4218-3838-0(9)*, 1st World Library - Literary Society) 1st World Publishing, Inc.

Mullican, Judy. Taking Care of Pets. Ruminski, Jeff, illus. l.t. ed. 2004. (HRL Big Book Ser.). 8p. (J). (gr. -1-1). pap. 10.95 *(978-1-57332-278-2(4))*; pap. 10.95 *(978-1-57332-279-9(2))*; pap. 10.95 *(978-1-57332-278-2(4))* Carson-Dellosa Publishing, LLC. (HighReach Learning, Incorporated).

Murphy, Nancy K. Rv Adventures by Sweetie, Miss Bell, Pierce & Sadie: By Sweetie Miss Bell, Pierce & Sad. 2011. 50p. pap. 15.99 *(978-1-4653-4158-7(7))* Xlibris Corp.

Murray, Caryn Eve. Philomena's Homecoming: The (mostly) true story of a New York prairie dog's search for a Family. 2010. 48p. pap. 8.95 *(978-1-4502-2769-8(4))* iUniverse, Inc.

Murray, Diana. Grimelda & the Spooktacular Pet Show. Ross, Heather, illus. 2017. (ENG.). 40p. (J). (gr. -1-3). 16.99 *(978-0-06-226449-7(4),* Tegen, Katherine Bks) HarperCollins Pubs.

Murray, Martine. Henrietta: There's No One Better. 2010. (Henrietta Ser.). (ENG., Illus.). 96p. (J). (gr. k-2). pap. 10.99 *(978-1-74114-718-6(2))* Allen & Unwin AUS. Dist: Independent Pubs. Group.

—Henrietta: There's No One Better. 2006. (Illus.). 88p. (J). 9.99 *(978-0-439-80749-4(2),* Levine, Arthur A. Bks.) Scholastic, Inc.

Muthu, Antony M. Athim. 2008. 48p. pap. 19.49 *(978-1-4389-3074-9(7))* AuthorHouse.

Myers, Don. My Life with Roger. 2009. (Illus.). 49p. (J). pap. 12.95 *(978-1-4327-3873-0(9))* Outskirts Pr., Inc.

Myers, Martha. Nibbles, the Mostly Mischievous Monkey. 2003. (Julius & Friends Ser.: Vol. 10). (Illus.). 91p. (J). 6.99 *(978-0-8163-1947-3(2))* Pacific Pr. Publishing Assn.

Myracle, Lauren. Friends of a Feather. Henry, Jed, illus. 2015. (Life of Ty Ser.: 3). (ENG.). 144p. (J). (gr. 1-4). 7.99 *(978-0-14-242320-2(3),* Puffin Books) Penguin Young Readers Group.

Namm, Diane. Pick a Pet. Suárez, Maribel, illus. 2004. (My First Reader Ser.). (ENG.). 32p. (J). 18.50 *(978-0-516-24417-4(5),* Children's Pr.) Scholastic Library Publishing.

Nash, Andy. Marcus & His Monkey: For Kids Blessed with Popularity. 2010. (J). *(978-0-8127-0452-5(5))* Autumn Hse. Publishing Co.

—Tatum & Her Tiger: For Kids Blessed with Passion. 2007. (Illus.). (J). 9.99 *(978-0-8127-0451-8(7))* Autumn Hse. Publishing Co.

Naylor, Phyllis Reynolds. Patches & Scratches, 0 vols. Ramsey, Marcy, illus. 2012. (Simply Sarah Ser.: 3). (ENG.). 80p. (J). (gr. 1-3). pap. 7.99 *(978-0-7614-5731-2(3),* 9780761457312, Two Lions) Amazon Publishing.

Nees, Susan. Class Pets. 2013. (Missy's Super Duper Royal Deluxe Ser.: 2). (ENG., Illus.). 80p. (J). (gr. k-2). pap. 4.99 *(978-0-545-43852-0(7))* Scholastic, Inc.

—Class Pets. 2013. (Missy's Super Duper Royal Deluxe Ser.: 2). lib. bdg. 14.75 *(978-0-606-31980-5(8))* Turtleback.

Neumeyer, P. & Gorey, E. The Donald Boxed Set. 2012. 48p. (J). *(978-0-7649-6130-4(6))* Pomegranate Communications, Inc.

Nicklaus, Terry. Schweppe. 2012. 24p. pap. 15.99 *(978-1-4771-4565-4(6))* Xlibris Corp.

Niemann, Christoph. The Pet Dragon: A Story about Adventure, Friendship, & Chinese Characters. Niemann, Christoph, illus. 2008. (ENG., Illus.). 40p. (J). (gr. -1-3). 18.99 *(978-0-06-157776-5(6),* Greenwillow Bks.) HarperCollins Pubs.

Nino, Carl. The Perfect Pet. Grott, Isabella, illus. 2017. (Family Time Ser.). (ENG.). 24p. (gr. -1-2). pap. 9.95 *(978-1-68342-755-1(6),* 9781683427551) Rourke Educational Media.

No Trouble at All! Individual Title Six-Packs. (Action Packs Ser.). 120p. (gr. 3-5). 44.00 *(978-0-7635-8397-2(9))* Rigby Education.

Norris II, Charles H. Fat Little Ugly Friend. 2008. 12p. per. 24.95 *(978-1-4241-9222-9(6))* America Star Bks.

Novel Units. Jeremy Thatcher, Dragon Hatcher Novel Units Student Packet. 2019. (Magic Shop Bks.). (ENG.). (J). pap., stu. ed., wbk. ed. 13.99 *(978-1-56137-878-4(X),* Novel Units, Inc.) Classroom Library Co.

Noyes, William H., Jr. Mittens. 2008. 36p. pap. 24.95 *(978-1-4241-9440-7(7))* America Star Bks.

Numan, Aisha. The Chameleon Pet. 2003. (Illus.). 52p. (gr. -1-3). pap. *(978-9966-46-682-2(7))* Heinemann Kenya, Limited (East African Educational Publishers Ltd E.A.E.P.) KEN. Dist: Michigan State Univ. Pr.

Nuurali, Siman. Sadiq & the Pet Problem. Sarkar, Anjan, illus. 2019. (Sadiq Ser.). (ENG.). 64p. (J). (gr. 1-3). pap. 6.95 *(978-1-5158-4568-3(0),* 141156, Picture Window Bks.) Capstone.

O'Donnell, Liam. Winston in the City. (ENG., Illus.). 32p. (J). (gr. -1-2). 9.95 *(978-1-59249-449-1(8),* 1B033) Soundprints.

—Winston in the City. Hatala, Dan, illus. 2005. (Pet Tales Ser.). (ENG.). 32p. (J). (gr. -1-2). pap. 2.95 *(978-1-59249-448-4(X),* 1B032) Soundprints.

—Winston in the City. Hatala, Dan, illus. 2005. (Pet Tales Ser.). (ENG.). 32p. (J). (gr. -1 — 1). 4.95 *(978-1-59249-447-7(1),* 1B031) Soundprints.

Offill, Jenny. Sparky! Appelhans, Chris, illus. 2014. (ENG.). 40p. (J). (gr. -1-3). 16.99 *(978-0-375-87023-1(7),* Schwartz & Wade Bks.) Random Hse. Children's Bks.

Ogden, Charles. Nod's Limbs. Carton, Rick, illus. 2007. (Edgar & Ellen Ser.: 6). (ENG.). 224p. (J). (gr. 3-7). 24.99 *(978-1-4169-1501-0(X),* Simon & Schuster/Paula Wiseman Bks.) Simon & Schuster/Paula Wiseman Bks.

—Pet's Revenge. Carton, Rick, illus. 2006. (Edgar & Ellen Ser.: 4). (ENG.). 192p. (J). (gr. 3-7). 23.99 *(978-1-4169-1408-2(0),* Simon & Schuster/Paula Wiseman Bks.) Simon & Schuster/Paula Wiseman Bks.

O'Grady, Patricia. The Naughty Ones. 2010. 24p. pap. 12.99 *(978-1-4520-2502-5(9))* AuthorHouse.

Old Cat & the Kitten. 2014. (ENG., Illus.). 128p. (J). (gr. 3-7). pap. 6.99 *(978-1-4814-1938-3(2),* Aladdin) Simon & Schuster Children's Publishing.

Oliveto, Michelle. My Dog the Faker. 2012. 24p. 24.95 *(978-1-4560-2194-8(X))* America Star Bks.

O'Neal, Shaquille. Little Shaq: Star of the Week. Taylor, Theodore, III, illus. 2016. (ENG.). 80p. (J). 9.99 *(978-1-61963-879-2(7),* 900150926, Bloomsbury USA Childrens) Bloomsbury Publishing USA.

Owens, Connie S. Missing Maggie: The Death of a Pet. 2003. (J). pap. 5.99 *(978-1-59317-007-3(6))* Warner Pr., Inc.

P. I. Kids. Palace Pets First Look & Find - O/P. 2015. (ENG.). 16p. (J). *(978-1-4508-8634-5(5),* 1450886345) Publications International, Ltd.

—Palace Pets Little Pop up Song Book O/P. 2014. (ENG.). 10p. (J). *(978-1-4508-8635-2(3),* 1450886353) Publications International, Ltd.

Palatini, Margie. The Perfect Pet. Whatley, Bruce, illus. 2003. 32p. (J). (gr. -1-2). 16.99 *(978-0-06-000108-7(9))* HarperCollins Pubs.

Papp, Lisa. Madeline Finn & the Shelter Dog. 2019. (ENG., Illus.). 32p. (J). (gr. -1-3). 17.95 *(978-1-68263-075-4(7))* Peachtree Publishing Co. Inc.

Paraskevas, Betty. Peter Pepper's Pet Spectacular. Paraskevas, Michael, illus. 2007. 32p. (J). (gr. 2-6). pap. 14.95 *(978-1-60095-257-9(7))* Carson-Dellosa Publishing, LLC.

Parish, Peggy. No More Monsters for Me! 2003. 22.95 *(978-0-673-75926-9(1))* Celebration Pr.

Parker, Emma. Pet Day. 2010. (Illus.). pap. *(978-1-877561-28-3(2))* First Edition Ltd.

Patchett, Mary Elwyn. Ajax: Golden Dog of the Australian Bush. Tansley, Eric, illus. 2011. 172p. 42.95 *(978-1-258-01103-1(4))* Literary Licensing, LLC.

Patton, Julia. Drat That Fat Cat! 2018. (2019 Av2 Fiction Ser.). (ENG.). 32p. (J). (gr. -1-2). lib. bdg. 34.28 *(978-1-4896-8257-4(0),* AV2 by Weigl) Weigl Pubs., Inc.

—Drat That Fat Cat! Patton, Julia, illus. 2016. (ENG., Illus.). 32p. (J). (gr. -1-3). 16.99 *(978-0-8075-1713-0(5),* 807517135) Whitman, Albert & Co.

Pearl, B. B. Poerava's Heaven. 2011. (Illus.). 88p. pap. 12.85 *(978-1-4567-8985-5(6))* AuthorHouse.

Pearson, Peter. How to Walk a Dump Truck. Catusanu, Mircea, illus. 2019. (ENG.). 40p. (J). (gr. -1-3). 17.99 *(978-0-06-232063-6(7),* HarperCollins) HarperCollins Pubs.

Peet, Joy. Sophia's Flutterfly. 2008. 19p. pap. 24.95 *(978-1-60610-806-2(9))* America Star Bks.

Pennypacker, Sara. Pax. Klassen, Jon, illus. 2016. (ENG.). (J). (gr. 3-3). 16.99 *(978-0-06-245703-5(9))* Blackstone Audio, Inc.

—Pax. Klassen, Jon, illus. (Pax Ser.). (ENG.). (J). (gr. 3-7). 2019. 304p. pap. 8.99 *(978-0-06-237702-9(7))* 2016. 288p. 17.99 *(978-0-06-237701-2(9))* HarperCollins Pubs. (Balzer & Bray).

—Pax. 2017. (SPA.). lib. bdg. 29.35 *(978-0-606-40010-7(9))* Turtleback.

—Pax, Journey Home. Klassen, Jon, illus. 2021. 246p. (J). *(978-0-06-314400-2(X)); (978-0-06-320674-8(9))* Addison Wesley.

—Pax, Journey Home. Klassen, Jon, illus. (Pax Ser.). (ENG.). (J). (gr. 3-7). 2023. 272p. pap. 9.99 *(978-0-06-293036-1(2))* 2021. 272p. E-Book *(978-0-06-293037-8(0),* 9780062930378) 2021. 256p. 17.99 *(978-0-06-293034-7(6))* HarperCollins Pubs. (Balzer & Bray).

—Pax. una Historia de Paz y Amistad / Pax. 2017. (SPA.). 304p. (J). (gr. 3-7). pap. 16.95 *(978-84-15594-95-6(X),* Nube De Tinta) Penguin Random House Grupo Editorial ESP. Dist: Penguin Random Hse. LLC.

Pet Stories Set 2 800888, 3 vols. 2005. (J). pap. *(978-1-59794-063-4(1))* Environments, Inc.

Pet Stories Set 800887, 3 vols. 2005. (J). pap. *(978-1-59794-062-7(3))* Environments, Inc.

Pet Tales!, 8 vols. 2017. (Pet Tales! Ser.). 24p. (ENG.). (gr. 1-1). 101.08 *(978-1-5081-5794-6(4),* 2debed44-5801-455f-9978-eaeb2e8d9876); (gr. 4-6). pap. 33.00 *(978-1-5081-5771-7(5))* Rosen Publishing Group, Inc., The. (PowerKids Pr.).

Peters, Kathryn. A Pet for Elizabeth Rose. Peters, Kathryn, illus. l.t. ed. 2005. (Illus.). 42p. (J). 8.99 *(978-0-9752647-9-9(6))* Proton Arts.

Petrucha, Stefan & Pendleton, Thomas. Prey. 2008. (Wicked Dead Ser.). (ENG.). 208p. (J). (gr. 7-18). pap. 9.99 *(978-0-06-113853-9(3),* HarperTeen) HarperCollins Pubs.

The Pets: Individual Title Six-Packs. (Sails Literacy Ser.). 16p. (gr. k-18). 27.00 *(978-0-7635-4420-1(5))* Rigby Education.

Pets Board Book Set 800792, 6. 2005. (J). bds. *(978-1-59794-022-1(4))* Environments, Inc.

Pett, Mark. Lizard from the Park. Pett, Mark, illus. 2015. (ENG., Illus.). 40p. (J). (gr. -1-3). 18.99 *(978-1-4424-8321-7(0),* Simon & Schuster Bks. For Young Readers) Simon & Schuster Bks. For Young Readers.

Philip, Simon. I Don't Know What to Call My Cat. Bailey, Ella, illus. 2017. (ENG.). 32p. (J). (gr. -1-3). 16.99 *(978-0-544-97143-1(4),* 1662675, Clarion Bks.) HarperCollins Pubs.

Picayo, Mario. A Very Smart Cat: Una Gata Muy Inteligente. Fundora, Yolanda V., illus. 2008. (SPA & ENG.). 32p. (J). *(978-1-934370-00-1(2))* Editorial Campana.

Pinkney, Brian. Puppy Truck. Pinkney, Brian, illus. 2019. (ENG., Illus.). 40p. (J). (gr. k-3). 17.99 *(978-1-5344-2687-0(6))* Simon & Schuster Children's Publishing.

Pinson, Mignon L. My Two Best Friends Are Hamsters. 2010. 24p. 12.99 *(978-1-4520-3309-9(9))* AuthorHouse.

Pintozzi, Nick. Bentley & the Great Fire. Pintozzi, Nick et al, illus. 2004. 16.95 *(978-0-9749465-2-8(4))* BentDaiSha.

Pitt, Marilyn & Hileman, Jane. Let Me In. Bianchi, John, illus. 2016. (1G Potato Chip Bks.). (ENG.). 12p. (J). (gr. k-1). pap. 8.00 *(978-1-61541-168-9(2))* American Reading Co.

—The Storm. Bianchi, John, illus. 2017. (1G Potato Chip Bks.). (ENG.). 12p. (J). (gr. k-1). pap. 9.60 *(978-1-61541-232-7(8))* American Reading Co.

Pitt, Marilyn & Sánchez, Lucía M. ¡Arriba! Bianchi, John, illus. 2010. (1G Libros Papas Fritas Ser.).Tr. of Get Up. (SPA & ENG.). 12p. (J). (gr. k-1). pap. 8.00 *(978-1-61541-084-2(8))* American Reading Co.

Pittar, Gill. Milly, Molly & the Ferryman. Morrell, Cris, illus. 2004. 28p. pap. *(978-1-86972-004-9(0))* Milly Molly Bks.

Polak, Monique. Finding Elmo, 1 vol. 2007. (Orca Currents Ser.). (ENG.). 128p. (J). (gr. 4-7). per. 9.95 *(978-1-55143-686-9(8))* Orca Bk. Pubs. USA.

—Forensics Squad Unleashed, 1 vol. 2016. (ENG.). 208p. (J). (gr. 4-7). pap. 10.95 *(978-1-4598-0979-6(3))* Orca Bk. Pubs. USA.

Porter, Gary. Duffy: The Tale of a Terrier. 2011. (Illus.). 256p. (J). 22.95 *(978-1-59298-369-8(3))* Beaver's Pond Pr., Inc.

Porter, Lisa. Billy & Froggy. 2011. 24p. pap. 12.79 *(978-1-4634-3528-8(2))* AuthorHouse.

Posner-Sanchez, Andrea, illus. Dog Days. 2016. 22p. (J). *(978-1-5182-3229-9(9))* Random Hse., Inc.

Potash, Mildred. Millie & Cupcake. 2013. (ENG.). 24p. (J). pap. 10.95 *(978-1-4787-0997-8(9))* Outskirts Pr., Inc.

Poydar, Nancy. Fish School. 2009. (ENG., Illus.). 32p. (J). (gr. -1-3). 16.95 *(978-0-8234-2140-4(6))* Holiday Hse., Inc.

Preller, James. Jigsaw Jones: the Case of the Best Pet Ever. 2017. (Jigsaw Jones Mysteries Ser.). (ENG., Illus.). 96p. (J). pap. 6.99 *(978-1-250-11093-0(9),* 900169788) Feiwel & Friends.

Procter, Diann. It Happened in the Goldfish Bowl. Procter, Bill, illus. 2007. 28p. pap. 24.95 *(978-1-4241-8357-9(X))* America Star Bks.

Provencher, Rose-Marie. Slithery Jake. Carter, Abby, illus. 2004. (ENG.). 32p. (J). 15.99 *(978-0-06-623820-3(X))* HarperCollins Pubs.

Provensen, Alice. A Day in the Life of Murphy. Provensen, Alice, illus. 2003. (ENG., Illus.). 40p. (J). (gr. -1-3). 19.99 *(978-0-689-84884-1(6),* Simon & Schuster Bks. For Young Readers) Simon & Schuster Bks. For Young Readers.

Publications International Ltd. Staff. First Look & Find Wonder Pets. 2008. 16p. (J). bds. 9.98 *(978-1-4127-9394-0(7),* PIL Kids) Publications International, Ltd.

Publications International Ltd. Staff, ed. Handy Manny. 2008. 16p. (J). bds. 9.98 *(978-1-4127-9373-5(4),* PIL Kids) Publications International, Ltd.

—Wonder Pets: Save the Baby Kitten. 2008. (J). bds. 10.98 *(978-1-4127-9198-4(7))* Publications International, Ltd.

Punnett, Dick. Name Patty's Pets: A Talk-along Book. Punnett, Yvonne, ed. 2nd ed. 2005. (Talk-Along Bks.). (Illus.). 32p. (J). pap. 6.99 *(978-0-9657211-5-8(9))* Tomoka Pr.

Ralston, Carole. Light in the Forest. 2012. 24p. 24.95 *(978-1-4626-6283-8(8))* America Star Bks.

Rand, Emily. A Dog Day. 2015. (ENG., Illus.). 26p. (gr. -1 — 1). 18.95 *(978-1-84976-290-8(2),* 1668301) Tate Publishing, Ltd. GBR. Dist: Abrams, Inc.

Random House. Nickelodeon 5-Minute Christmas Stories (Nickelodeon) Random House, illus. 2017. (ENG., Illus.). 160p. (J). (gr. -1-2). 12.99 *(978-1-5247-6398-5(5),* Random Hse. Bks. for Young Readers) Random Hse. Children's Bks.

Rankine-Van Wassenhoven, Jacqueline. A Little Honey for Serge. 2009. 16p. pap. 9.00 *(978-1-4490-0810-9(0))* AuthorHouse.

Rasheed, Winona. Smiles & Frowns Through Animal Town's Storybook. 2008. 55p. pap. 13.70 *(978-1-4357-4617-6(1))* Lulu Pr., Inc.

Ray Charles Lockamy, Inez Eason. The Adventures of Tracks & Cookout. 2010. 40p. pap. *(978-1-4269-2159-9(4))* Trafford Publishing (UK) Ltd.

Rebai, Tara. Sarah Sue Smith: A Crooked Wharf Adventure. 2010. 52p. pap. 22.49 *(978-1-4520-7165-7(9))* AuthorHouse.

Reed, Tom. Pookus & Buckie: A Children's Book Based on a True Story. Carter, Sandy Lewis, illus. l.t. ed. 2005. 36p. (J). per. 11.95 *(978-0-9749725-4-1(1),* 10000, Lonestar Abilene Publishing) LoneStar Abilene Publishing, LLC.

Reiche, Dietlof & Brownjohn, John. Freddy in Peril: Book Two in the Golden Hamster Saga. Cepeda, Joe, illus. 2004. 202p. (J). pap. *(978-0-439-64984-1(6))* Scholastic, Inc.

Rennich, Lori. When Cooper Got to Heaven. 2011. 28p. pap. 21.99 *(978-1-4568-6199-5(9))* Xlibris Corp.

Resnicoff, Stan. Stanley, the Seal of Approval. 2012. (ENG.). (J). pap. *(978-1-4675-1535-1(3))* Independent Pub.

Reul, Sarah Lynne. Pet the Pets: A Lift-The-Flap Book. Reul, Sarah Lynne, illus. 2018. (ENG., Illus.). 18p. (J). (gr. -1 — 1). bds. 8.99 *(978-1-5344-0939-2(4),* Little Simon) Little Simon.

Reynolds, Judy. A Blue Jay's Choice. 2010. 72p. pap. 10.49 *(978-1-4520-6455-0(5))* AuthorHouse.

RH Disney. Tutu Terrific! (Disney Palace Pets: Whisker Haven Tales) Wu, Vivien, illus. 2016. (Little Golden Book Ser.). (ENG.). 24p. (J). (-k). 4.99 *(978-0-7364-3504-8(2),* Golden/Disney) Random Hse. Children's Bks.

Rice, Dona Herweck & Thompson, Chad. Old Mother Hubbard. 2009. (Early Literacy Ser.). (ENG., Illus.). 16p. (gr. k-1). 19.99 *(978-1-4333-1478-0(9))* Teacher Created Materials, Inc.

Richardson, Lin Douglas. The Meaning of Me. 2011. 28p. pap. 24.95 *(978-1-4626-2891-9(5))* America Star Bks.

Ries, Lori. Aggie & Ben: Three Stories. Dormer, Frank W., illus. 2006. (Aggie & Ben Ser.). (ENG.). 48p. (J). (gr. -1-1). lib. bdg. 18.69 *(978-1-57091-594-9(6))* Charlesbridge Publishing, Inc.

—Good Dog, Aggie. Dormer, Frank W., illus. (Aggie & Ben Ser.). (ENG.). 48p. (J). (gr. -1-3). 2012. pap. 5.95 *(978-1-57091-646-5(2))* 2009. 12.95 *(978-1-57091-645-8(4))* Charlesbridge Publishing, Inc.

—Tita y Ben. Dormer, Frank W. & Dormer, Frank W., illus. 2010. (SPA.). 48p. (J). (gr. -1-3). 13.95 *(978-1-57091-934-3(8))* Charlesbridge Publishing, Inc.

—Tita y Ben. Dormer, Frank W., illus. 2010. (SPA.). 48p. (J). (gr. -1-3). pap. 6.99 *(978-1-57091-935-0(6))* Charlesbridge Publishing, Inc.

Rieser, Karen. A Cat with Three Tales. 2013. 48p. pap. 8.95 *(978-1-937260-93-4(3))* Sleepytown Pr.

Rippin, Sally. The New Friend: Hey Jack! 2014. (ENG., Illus.). 48p. (J). pap. 4.99 *(978-1-61067-125-5(2))* Kane Miller.

Ritz, C. Tiger's World: Growing Up. 2013. 72p. pap. *(978-1-77097-596-5(9))* FriesenPress.

Robare, Jay, illus. Pets in Heaven Activity Book: Children's Companion Book to: Do Pets & Other Animals Go to Heaven? 2003. 86p. (J). per. 12.95 *(978-0-9726363-1-5(5),* 6315) Brite Bks.

Robbins, Jacqui. The New Girl ... & Me. Phelan, Matt, illus. 2006. (ENG.). 32p. (J). (gr. -1-2). 19.99 *(978-0-689-86468-1(X),* Atheneum/Richard Jackson Bks.) Simon & Schuster Children's Publishing.

Roberton, Fiona. A Tale of Two Beasts. 2015. (ENG., Illus.). 32p. (J). pap. 12.99 *(978-1-61067-361-7(1))* Kane Miller.

Roberts, Victoria. Best Pet Ever. Allwright, Deborah, illus. 2011. (ENG.). 32p. pap. 7.95 *(978-1-58925-432-9(5))* Tiger Tales.

Robinson, Hilary. La Sorprendente Mascota del Señor Pérez. Archbold, Tim, illus. 2005. (Lectores Relampago / Lightning Readers: Level 3 Ser.). (SPA.). 32p. (J). (gr. 1-2). 16.19 *(978-0-7696-4061-7(3))* School Specialty, Incorporated.

Robinson, Hilary & Archbold, Tim. Mr. Smith's Surprising Pet, Grades 1 - 2, Level 3. 2005. (Lightning Readers: Level 3 Ser.). (ENG., Illus.). 32p. (gr. 1-2). 16.19 *(978-0-7696-4021-1(4))* School Specialty, Incorporated.

Roddy, Lee. The City Bear's Adventures. 2008. (D. J. Dillon Adventure Ser.: No. 2). (J). 7.99 *(978-0-88062-266-0(0))* Mott Media.

Rogers, Jewels. The Princess & the Rabbit. 2011. 28p. pap. 12.50 *(978-1-4567-5171-5(9))* AuthorHouse.

Roland, Timothy. Monkey Me & the Pet Show. 2014. (Monkey Me Ser.: 2). lib. bdg. 14.75 *(978-0-606-35359-5(3))* Turtleback.

Ross, Tony. I Want a Cat! Ross, Tony, illus. 2008. (ENG., Illus.). 32p. (J). (gr. -1-k). pap. 12.99 *(978-1-84270-691-6(8))* Andersen Pr. GBR. Dist: Independent Pubs. Group.

—Rita's Rhino. Ross, Tony, illus. 2015. (ENG., Illus.). 32p. (J). (gr. -1-3). E-Book 27.99 *(978-1-4677-6319-6(5))* Lerner Publishing Group.

Rosseter, Patrick W. Grampa Pat's Little Animal Tales. 2008. 88p. pap. 10.99 *(978-1-60647-466-2(9))* Salem Author Services.

Rostoker-Gruber, Karen. Ferret Fun, 0 vols. de Tagyos, Paul Rátz, illus. 2012. (ENG.). 32p. (J). (gr. k-3). 17.99 *(978-0-7614-5817-3(4),* 9780761458173, Two Lions) Amazon Publishing.

Roundtree, Beth. Wilhamina Constance Winston Churchill Ingersol & the Cat. 2012. 24p. pap. 10.99 *(978-1-4624-0389-9(1),* Inspiring Voices) Author Solutions, LLC.

Rowe, Helen, illus. Fun with Pets: A Pop-Up Book. 2016. (ENG.). 12p. (J). (gr. -1-k). bds. 8.99 *(978-1-4998-0300-6(1))* Little Bee Books Inc.

Rowe, W. W. Jerry's Mastery. 2017. (ENG.). 103p. (YA). (gr. 8-17). pap. 8.95 *(978-1-936012-80-0(4))* Larson Pubns.

Roy, Ron. The Canary Caper. Gurney, John, illus. unabr. ed. 2004. (A to Z Mysteries Ser.: No. 3). 80p. (J). (gr. k-3). pap. 17.00 incl. audio *(978-0-8072-1705-4(0),* S FTR 271 SP, Listening Library) Random Hse. Audio Publishing Group.

—A to Z Mysteries: Collection #1, No. 1. Gurney, John Steven, illus. 2010. (to Z Mysteries Ser.: Nos. 1-4). (ENG.). 384p. (J). (gr. 1-4). 9.99 *(978-0-375-85946-5(2),* Random Hse. Bks. for Young Readers) Random Hse. Children's Bks.

Russell, Bill. Bruno the Red Ear Slider. 2013. 24p. pap. 24.95 *(978-1-62709-547-1(0))* America Star Bks.

Russell, Rachel Renée. Dork Diaries 10: Tales from a Not-So-Perfect Pet Sitter. Russell, Rachel Renée, illus. 2015. (Dork Diaries: 10). (ENG., Illus.). 320p. (J). (gr. 4-8). 13.99 *(978-1-4814-5704-0(7),* Aladdin) Simon & Schuster Children's Publishing.

—Tales from a Not-So-Perfect Pet Sitter. Russell, Rachel Renée, illus. 2015. (Dork Diaries: 10). (ENG., Illus.). 320p. (J). (gr. 4-8). lib. bdg. 25.75 *(978-0-606-37923-6(1))* Turtleback.

Rylant, Cynthia. Annie & Snowball & the Pink Surprise: Ready-To-Read Level 2. Stevenson, Suçie & Stevenson, Suçie, illus. (Annie & Snowball Ser.: 4). (ENG.). 40p. (J). (gr. k-2). 2010. pap. 4.99 *(978-1-4169-1462-4(5))* 2008. 17.99 *(978-1-4169-0941-5(9))* Simon Spotlight. (Simon Spotlight).

—Annie & Snowball & the Wintry Freeze: Ready-To-Read Level 2. Stevenson, Suçie & Stevenson, Suçie, illus. (Annie & Snowball Ser.: 8). (ENG.). 40p. (J). (gr. k-2). 2011. pap. 4.99 *(978-1-4169-7206-8(4))* 2010. 17.99 *(978-1-4169-7205-1(6))* Simon Spotlight. (Simon Spotlight).

—Henny, Penny, Lenny, Denny, & Mike. Austin, Mike, illus. 2017. (ENG.). 40p. (J). (gr. -1-4). 17.99 *(978-1-4814-4523-8(5),* Beach Lane Bks.) Beach Lane Bks.

—Henry & Mudge & the Funny Lunch: Ready-To-Read Level 2. Bracken, Carolyn, illus. 2005. (Henry & Mudge Ser.: 24). (ENG.). 40p. (J). (gr. k-2). pap. 4.99 *(978-0-689-83444-8(6),* Simon Spotlight) Simon Spotlight.

Sands, Kathryn Ann. How Chili Willie Got His Name. 2013. 24p. pap. 17.99 *(978-1-4817-0641-4(1))* AuthorHouse.

Sandstrom, Heather. Brenda Badbroom & the Very Best Pet Yet. 2008. 28p. pap. 14.99 *(978-1-4389-0324-8(3))* AuthorHouse.

Santat, Dan. Sidekicks: a Graphic Novel. Santat, Dan, illus. 2011. (ENG., Illus.). 224p. (J). (gr. 3-7). pap. 12.99 *(978-0-439-29819-3(9),* Graphix) Scholastic, Inc.

Santillo, LuAnn. Steve & Pete. Santillo, LuAnn, ed. 2003. (Half-Pint Kids Readers Ser.). (Illus.). 7p. (J). (gr. -1-1). pap. 1.00 *(978-1-59256-103-2(9))* Half-Pint Kids, Inc.

—The Vet. Santillo, LuAnn, ed. 2003. (Half-Pint Kids Readers Ser.). (Illus.). 7p. (J). (gr. -1-1). pap. 1.00 *(978-1-59256-123-0(3))* Half-Pint Kids, Inc.

Sarah's Pet: Level L, 6 vols. 128p. (gr. 2-3). 41.95 *(978-0-7699-0990-5(6))* Shortland Pubns. (U. S. A.) Inc.

Sargent, Dave & Sargent, Pat. A Puppy for Bobby/un cachorro para Robertito, 10 vols. Robinson, Laura, illus. 2004. (Learn to Read Ser.: 10). (ENG & SPA.). 18p. (J). pap. 10.95 *(978-1-56763-982-7(8))* Ozark Publishing.

—Puppy for Bobby/un cachorro para Robertito, 10, 11. Robinson, Laura, illus. 2004. (Learn to Read Ser.: 10). (ENG & SPA.). 18p. (J). lib. bdg. 19.95 *(978-1-56763-981-0(X))* Ozark Publishing.

Satchwell, Sm. Len Stories. 2012. (Illus.). 24p. pap. 19.82 *(978-1-4685-0478-1(9))* AuthorHouse.

Sauer, Tammi. Me Want Pet! Shea, Bob, illus. 2012. (ENG.). 40p. (J). (gr. -1-3). 19.99 *(978-1-4424-0810-4(3),* Simon & Schuster/Paula Wiseman Bks.) Simon & Schuster/Paula Wiseman Bks.

Saumier, Chantelle. Vinnie! Star of the Show. 2013. 40p. *(978-1-4602-3098-5(1)); pap. (978-1-4602-1741-2(1))* FriesenPress.

Sayles, Kristi. Jacob's Monkey-the Trouble with Lying. 2005. 38p. (J). pap. 10.29 *(978-1-4116-6429-6(9))* Lulu Pr., Inc.

Sazaklis, John. Deep-Sea Duel, 1 vol. Baltazar, Art, illus. 2012. (DC Super-Pets Ser.). (ENG.). 56p. (J). (gr. 1-3). pap. 4.95 *(978-1-4048-7662-0(6),* 120249, Stone Arch Bks.) Capstone.

Scanlon, Michael. How We Met! Little Airplane Productions Staff, illus. 2010. (Wonder Pets! Ser.). (ENG.). 24p. (J). pap. 3.99 *(978-1-4424-0654-4(2),* Simon Spotlight/Nickelodeon) Simon Spotlight/Nickelodeon.

Schiavone, Fabio. Ben Makes a Mess: Practicing the Short E Sound, 1 vol. 2016. (Rosen Phonics Readers Ser.). (ENG., Illus.). 8p. (J). (gr. -1-2). pap. *(978-1-5081-3089-5(2),* 298a60e0-a30c-4e63-be00-ce92e89cabbe, Rosen Classroom) Rosen Publishing Group, Inc., The.

Schlangen, D. V. M. Zoe's Good-Bye. 2005. (Illus.). 32p. (J). 17.95 *(978-1-59298-110-6(0))* Beaver's Pond Pr., Inc.

Schnitt, Deborah. Petey's Angel. 2012. 25.95 *(978-0-7414-7845-0(5));* pap. 18.95 *(978-0-7414-7844-3(7))* Infinity Publishing.

Scholastic, Inc. Staff. Dear Mrs. Larue. 2005. (ENG.). (J). pap. 550.00 *(978-0-439-70787-9(0),* Sidekicks TM) Scholastic, Inc.

Scott, Brandon James. The Big Pet Story. 2013. (Justin Time Ser.). (ENG., Illus.). 36p. (J). (gr. -1-3). 15.95 (978-1-59702-041-1(9)) Immedium.

Seagreaves, Kelly E. The Best Pet. Zoller, Jayson D., illus. l.t. ed. 2004. 29p. (J). lib. bdg. 14.95 (978-1-932338-56-0(X)); per. 8.99 (978-1-932338-53-9(5)) Lifevest Publishing, Inc.

Sebring, Ruthie. Charlie, Itty's Guinea Pig, 1 vol. 2010. 30p. 24.95 (978-1-4489-4391-3(4)) PublishAmerica, Inc.

Seignobosc, Francoise. Springtime for Jeanne-Marie. 2004. (Illus.). (J). mass mkt. 9.99 (978-0-9740599-3-8(5)) Omnibus Publishing.

Selfors, Suzanne. Wedgie & Gizmo. Fisinger, Barbara, illus. 2017. (Wedgie & Gizmo Ser.: 1). (ENG.). 176p. (J). (gr. 3-7). 13.99 (978-0-06-244763-0(7), Tegen, Katherine Bks) HarperCollins Pubs.

—Wedgie & Gizmo vs. the Toof. 2018. (Wedgie & Gizmo Ser.: 2). (ENG., Illus.). 192p. (J). (gr. 3-7). 12.99 (978-0-06-244765-4(3), Tegen, Katherine Bks) HarperCollins Pubs.

Selig, Josh. Go, Wonder Pets! Little Airplane Productions, illus. 2008. (Wonder Pets! Ser.). (ENG.). 26p. (J). bds. 5.99 (978-1-4169-4723-3(X), Simon Spotlight/Nickelodeon) Simon Spotlight/Nickelodeon.

Seuling, Barbara. Robert & the Attack of the Giant Tarantula. Brewer, Paul, illus. 2003. (Oh No, It's Robert Ser.). (ENG.). 64p. (J). pap. 3.99 (978-0-439-23545-7(6), Scholastic Paperbacks) Scholastic, Inc.

Seuss. What Pet Should I Get? (Beginner Books(R) Ser.). (ENG.). (J). (gr. -1-2). 2019. 40p. lib. bdg. 12.99 (978-0-525-70736-3(0)) 2019. (Illus.). 40p. 9.99 (978-0-525-70735-6(2)) 2015. (Illus.). 48p. 17.99 (978-0-553-52426-0(7)) Random Hse. Children's Bks. (Random Hse. Bks. for Young Readers).

Seuss, Dr. What Pet Should I Get? 2015. 48p. (J). lib. bdg. 30.60 (978-0-606-37381-4(0)) Turtleback.

Sexton, Bethany. Big Dog, Little Dog, Fish. Briggs Johnson, Chloe, illus. 2015. (ENG.). 17.95 (978-1-59298-862-4(8)) Beaver's Pond Pr., Inc.

S.H., Addan. Guardabosque Del Ano 3000: Canis Familiaris Evolucion. 2004. (SPA., Illus.). 340p. pap. (978-1-84401-133-9(X)) Athena Pr.

Shadow. 2006. (J). (978-1-933343-17-4(6)) Stabenfeldt Inc.

Shah, Yasmin. Abby & the Feather Quest. 2010. (Illus.). 48p. pap. 10.49 (978-1-4343-9839-0(0)) AuthorHouse.

Shan Shan, Kathryn. Everyday Circus. Wilson, Lynda Farrington, illus. 2013. 48p. pap. 10.97 (978-1-939896-01-8(0)) Levity Pr.

Shaw, Ellie. Together Again. 2012. 24p. pap. 24.95 (978-1-4626-6427-6(X)) America Star Bks.

Shephard, H. Ferebee. Jonathan & Roscoe. 2011. 24p. pap. 14.39 (978-1-4634-4881-3(3)) AuthorHouse.

Shepherd, Donna J. & Foster, Jack. Where Is Salami. 2011. (Illus.). 16p. pap. 9.95 (978-1-61633-147-4(X)) Guardian Angel Publishing, Inc.

Siems, Thomas F. The Dangerous Pet. Blye, Steven G., illus. 2009. (ENG.). 46p. pap. 21.99 (978-1-4415-3454-5(7)) Xlibris Corp.

Sima, Jessie. Spencer's New Pet. Sima, Jessie, illus. 2019. (ENG., Illus.). 56p. (J). (gr. -1-3). 17.99 (978-1-5344-1877-6(6), Simon & Schuster Bks. For Young Readers) Simon & Schuster Bks. For Young Readers.

Singleton, Linda Joy. A Cat Is Better. Martin, Jorge, illus. 2017. (ENG.). 32p. (J). (gr. -1-3). 16.99 (978-1-4998-0278-8(1)) Little Bee Books Inc.

Sky Koster, Amy. The Knight Night Guard (Disney Palace Pets: Whisker Haven Tales) RH Disney, illus. 2016. (Step into Reading Ser.). (ENG.). 24p. (J). (gr. -1-1). 4.99 (978-0-7364-3450-8(X), RH/Disney) Random Hse. Children's Bks.

Smith, Alex T. Mr. Penguin & the Fortress of Secrets, 1 vol. 2019. (Mr. Penguin Ser.: 2). (ENG., Illus.). 288p. (J). (gr. 3-7). 16.95 (978-1-68263-130-0(3)) Peachtree Publishing Co. Inc.

Smith, Emma Bland. Pet Camp. Marlin, Lissy, illus. 2018. (Maddy Mcguire, CEO Ser.). (ENG.). 112p. (J). (gr. 2-5). lib. bdg. 38.50 (978-1-5321-3185-1(2), 28465, Calico Chapter Bks.) ABDO Publishing Co.

Smith, Sindy. Ervin & Alma's Little Mouse House. 2013. 38p. 24.95 (978-1-63004-209-7(9)); 40p. pap. 24.95 (978-1-62709-189-3(0)) America Star Bks.

Snyder, Sandy. There's Only One I in Charlie. Ferrenburg, Susie, illus. 2011. 48p. pap. 24.95 (978-1-4626-4086-7(9)) America Star Bks.

Snyder, Sharon J. Zeus Comes Home. 2012. 20p. pap. 24.95 (978-1-4626-5860-2(1)) America Star Bks.

Sommer, Carl. Tied up in Knots Read-along 2003. (Another Sommer-Time Story Ser.). (Illus.). 48p. (J). lib. bdg. 23.95 incl. audio (978-1-57537-753-7(5)) Advance Publishing, Inc.

—Tied up in Knots Read-along. Budwine, Greg, illus. 2003. (Another Sommer-Time Story Ser.). (ENG.). 48p. (J). lib. bdg. 23.95 incl. audio compact disk (978-1-57537-703-2(9)) Advance Publishing, Inc.

Spellmeyer, William. Ick-n-Pog: How it all Began Book 1. 2010. 104p. pap. 12.99 (978-1-4251-9236-5(X)) Trafford Publishing.

Spiegelman, Nadja. Zig & Wikki in Something Ate My Homework: Toon Books Level 3. Loeffler, Trade, illus. (Toon Ser.). (ENG.). 40p. (J). (gr. -1-3). 2013. pap. 7.99 (978-1-935179-38-2(1)) 2010. 12.95 (978-1-935179-02-3(0)) Astra Publishing Hse. (Toon Books).

Spiegelman, Nadja & Loeffler, Trade. Zig & Wikki in Something Ate My Homework. 2013. (Toon Books Level 3 Ser.). lib. bdg. 14.75 (978-0-606-32252-2(3)) Turtleback.

Spinelli, Eileen. Moe Mctooth: An Alley Cat's Tale. Bronson, Linda, illus. 2003. (ENG.). 32p. (J). (gr. -1-3). tchr. ed. 15.00 (978-0-618-11760-4(1), 111073, Clarion Bks.) HarperCollins Pubs.

Spitz, Eleanor. Phoenix the Rising Star. 2013. 26p. pap. 11.95 (978-1-61244-223-5(4)) Halo Publishing International.

Spitz, Mary Y. Mint's Christmas Message. Pierce, Joanne Y., illus. 2003. 32p. 14.95 (978-0-9724570-0-2(3)) Mother Moose Pr.

Spooky Pet, 6 vols., Set D,Pack. (Smart Start Ser.). (gr. k-1). 23.00 (978-0-7635-0455-7(6)) Rigby Education.

Starling, Landa. If You Sleep with a Cat on Your Head. Formelio, Lorri, illus. 2008. 27p. pap. 24.95 (978-1-60703-318-9(6)) America Star Bks.

Staunton, Ted. Morgan's Pet Plot, 1 vol. Slavin, Bill, illus. 2003. (Formac First Novels Ser.: 24). (ENG.). 64p. (J). (gr. 1-5). 4.95 (978-0-88780-587-5(6), 587); 14.95 (978-0-88780-588-2(4), 588) Formac Publishing Co., Ltd. CAN. Dist: Formac Lorimer Bks. Ltd.

Stephens, Kat. Where Did Gypsy Go? 2010. 32p. (gr. -1). 15.50 (978-1-4490-8008-2(1)) AuthorHouse.

Stern, A. J. Doggy Day Care, 2 vols. Marts, Doreen Mulryan, illus. 2010. (Frankly, Frannie Ser.: 2). 128p. (J). (gr. 1-3). pap. 4.99 (978-0-448-45350-7(9), Grosset & Dunlap) Penguin Young Readers Group.

Stine, R. L. The Great Smelling Bee, 2. Park, Trip, illus. 2011. (Rotten School Ser.: No. 2). (ENG.). 128p. (J). (gr. 2-6). 31.36 (978-1-59961-826-5(5), 13129, Chapter Bks.) Spotlight.

—Little Shop of Hamsters. 2010. (Goosebumps HorrorLand Ser.: 14). lib. bdg. 17.20 (978-0-606-10559-0(X)) Turtleback.

—The Lizard of Oz. 2016. 135p. (J). (978-1-338-10392-2(X)) Scholastic, Inc.

Stock, Lisa. Perfect Pets. 2014. (DK Reader Level 2 Ser.). lib. bdg. 13.55 (978-0-606-35731-9(9)) Turtleback.

Studio Mouse Staff. Pet Friends. rev. ed. 2008. (ENG.). 12p. (J). 12.99 (978-1-59069-611-8(5)) Studio Mouse LLC.

Sullivan, Mary. Ball Board Book. 2015. (ENG., Illus.). 32p. (J). (— 1). bds. 7.99 (978-0-544-31361-3(5), 1581629, Clarion Bks.) HarperCollins Pubs.

Summers, Darien. The Mischievous Hare. 2009. (Illus.). 48p. pap. 9.95 (978-1-4327-4602-5(2)) Outskirts Pr., Inc.

Summers, Terry. Peter Wanted a Pet. Kai, illus. 2012. 26p. 24.95 (978-1-4626-6120-6(3)) America Star Bks.

Surovec, Yasmine. My Pet Human. 2016. (ENG.). 108p. (J). (gr. 1-5). 16.00 (978-0-606-39282-2(3)) Turtleback.

Swain, Cynthia. Can We Have a Pet? 2006. (Early Explorers Ser.). (J). pap. (978-1-4108-6037-8(X)) Benchmark Education Co.

Swann, Sandy & McKain, Susan. Tugger: The Pretzel Pup. Anderson, Regina, illus. 2010. (ENG.). 36p. pap. 16.99 (978-1-4490-8499-8(0)) AuthorHouse.

Taeschner, Jacquelin. Boss. 2005. pap. 32.50 (978-1-4208-7369-6(5)) AuthorHouse.

Taylor Kent, Derek. El Perro con Sombrero: A Bilingual Doggy Tale. Henry, Jed, illus. unabr. ed. 2015. (SPA.). 40p. (J). (gr. -1-2). 19.99 (978-0-8050-9989-8(1), 900129320, Holt, Henry & Co. Bks. For Young Readers) Holt, Henry & Co.

Taylor, Thomas. The Pets You Get. Reynolds, Adrian, illus. 2013. (ENG.). 32p. (J). (gr. -1-3). 16.95 (978-1-4677-1143-2(8), 6b92e368-27d7-4535-bc74-f4d91d824681) Lerner Publishing Group.

TenNapel, Doug. Tommysaurus Rex: a Graphic Novel. 2013. (ENG., Illus.). 144p. (J). (gr. 4-7). pap. 12.99 (978-0-545-48383-4(2), Graphix) Scholastic, Inc.

Tesler, Ellen. Maggie Adopts a Rescue Dog. 2013. 24p. pap. 17.99 (978-1-4817-0570-7(9)) AuthorHouse.

Thaler, Mike. The New Puppy from the Black Lagoon. Lee, Jared D., illus. 2017. 64p. (J). (978-1-338-24461-8(2)) Scholastic, Inc.

The Guide Dog, Thelma. For the Love of My Pet. Hartley, Joshua, illus. 2012. (ENG.). 26p. (gr. k-5). pap. 14.95 (978-1-61448-338-0(8)) Morgan James Publishing.

Things That Go! (Flip Flap Fun Book Ser.). 10p. (J). bds. (978-2-89393-933-9(3)) Phidal Publishing, Inc./Editions Phidal, Inc.

Thorpe, Kiki. Never Girls #11: into the Waves (Disney: the Never Girls) Christy, Jana, illus. 2016. (Never Girls Ser.: 11). (ENG.). 128p. (J). (gr. 1-4). 6.99 (978-0-7364-3525-3(5), RH/Disney) Random Hse. Children's Bks.

Thyroff, Brad. Albert & Freddie. Gillen, Rosemarie, illus. 2013. 24p. pap. 9.99 (978-1-61286-190-6(3)) Avid Readers Publishing Group.

Tidd, Louise Vitellaro. La Mejor Mascota. Handelman, Dorothy, photos by. 2007. (Lecturas para niños de verdad - Nivel 2 (Real Kids Readers - Level 2) Ser.).Tr. of Best Pet Yet. (SPA., Illus.). 32p. (J). (gr. -1-3). per. 5.95 (978-0-8225-7804-8(2), Ediciones Lerner) Lerner Publishing Group.

Tortorich, Vinnie. Monty: A Friendship Can Lead to a Miracle 2004. (Illus.). 36p. (J). 16.95 (978-0-9762854-0-3(1), 2500) National Horseman Publishing Inc., The.

Tracy, Kathleen. The Hamster in Our Class. 2011. (Randy's Corner Ser.). (Illus.). 32p. (J). (gr. -1-2). lib. bdg. 25.70 (978-1-58415-980-3(4)) Mitchell Lane Pubs.

—The Turtle in Our Class. 2011. (Randy's Corner Ser.). (Illus.). 32p. (J). (gr. -1-2). lib. bdg. 25.70 (978-1-58415-979-7(0)) Mitchell Lane Pubs.

Truesdell, Charlotte White. Steinway Kitty. 2010. 16p. 8.49 (978-1-4490-5922-4(8)) AuthorHouse.

Ulrich, George. Mrs. Picasso's Polliwog: A Mystery. Ulrich, George, illus. 2003. (Illus.). 32p. pap. 7.95 (978-1-891577-84-0(0)); (J). (gr. -1-7). lib. bdg. 15.95 (978-1-891577-83-3(2)) Images Pr.

Urbanovic, Jackie. Duck & Cover: An Easter & Springtime Book for Kids. Urbanovic, Jackie, illus. 2009. (Max the Duck Ser.: 3). (ENG., Illus.). 32p. (J). (gr. -1-2). 17.99 (978-0-06-121444-8(2), HarperCollins) HarperCollins Pubs.

Uy, Katherine Nepomuceno. Teeny Tiny People & Pets. 2012. 60p. pap. 31.99 (978-1-4691-5710-8(1)) Xlibris Corp.

Van Allsburg, Chris. The Misadventures of Sweetie Pie. Van Allsburg, Chris, illus. 2014. (ENG., Illus.). 32p. (J). (gr. -1-3). 18.99 (978-0-547-31582-9(1), 1415338, Clarion Bks.) HarperCollins Pubs.

van de Vendel, Edward. The Dog That Nino Didn't Have. van Hertbruggen, Anton, illus. 2015. (ENG.). 34p. (J). 17.00 (978-0-8028-5451-3(6), Eerdmans Bks For Young Readers) Eerdmans, William B. Publishing Co.

Venable, Colleen A. F. Raining Cats & Detectives. Yue, Stephanie, illus. 2012. (Guinea Pig, Pet Shop Private Eye Ser.: 5). lib. bdg. 17.15 (978-0-606-26631-4(3)) Turtleback.

Verrett, Michael. It Followed Me Home Can I Keep It? 2010. 35p. pap. 10.00 (978-0-557-28827-4(4)) Lulu Pr., Inc.

—It Followed Me Home Can I Keep It? (full Color) 2010. 35p. pap. 19.00 (978-0-557-29796-2(6)) Lulu Pr., Inc.

Victoria, Roberts. The Best Pet Ever. Deborah, Allwright, illus. 2010. (ENG.). 32p. (J). (gr. -1-2). 15.95 (978-1-58925-089-5(3)) Tiger Tales.

Viorst, Judith. Lulu & the Brontosaurus. Smith, Lane, illus. (Lulu Ser.). (ENG.). 128p. (J). (gr. 1-5). 2012. pap. 8.99 (978-1-4169-9962-1(0)) 2010. 19.99 (978-1-4169-9961-4(2)) Simon & Schuster Children's Publishing. (Atheneum Bks. for Young Readers).

—Lulu & the Brontosaurus. 2012. (Lulu Ser.: 1). lib. bdg. 18.40 (978-0-606-23676-8(7)) Turtleback.

Viselman, Kenn. Li'l Pet Hospital: The Great Race. 2003. 32p. pap. 3.99 (978-0-06-054840-7(1), Harper Entertainment) HarperCollins Pubs.

Voake, Charlotte. Melissa's Octopus & Other Unsuitable Pets. Voake, Charlotte, illus. 2015. (ENG., Illus.). 32p. (J). (gr. -1-2). 16.99 (978-0-7636-7481-6(8)) Candlewick Pr.

Wallace, Bill. Goosed! Rogers, Jacqueline, illus. 2004. (ENG.). 128p. (J). (gr. 2-4). pap. 7.99 (978-0-689-86681-4(X), Aladdin) Simon & Schuster Children's Publishing.

Walthers, Joanie. The Fish Smuggler. Walthers, Don, illus. 2013. (ENG.). 24p. (J). 19.95 (978-1-4787-1167-4(1)) Outskirts Pr., Inc.

Watkins, Constance L. Happy Was His Name. 2011. 24p. (gr. 1-2). pap. 11.75 (978-1-4634-0421-5(2)) AuthorHouse.

Webb, Holly. Alone in the Night. Williams, Sophy, illus. 2017. 126p. (J). (978-1-5182-5346-1(6)) Tiger Tales.

—The Kitten Nobody Wanted & Other Tales. Williams, Sophy, illus. 2017. (Pet Rescue Adventures Ser.). (ENG.). 384p. (J). (gr. 1-4). pap. 10.99 (978-1-68010-405-9(5)) Tiger Tales.

—The Lost Puppy. Williams, Sophy, illus. 2016. (Pet Rescue Adventures Ser.). (ENG.). 128p. (J). (gr. 1-4). pap. 4.99 (978-1-58925-491-6(0)) Tiger Tales.

—The Missing Kitten & Other Tales. Williams, Sophy, illus. 2018. (Pet Rescue Adventures Ser.). (ENG.). 384p. (J). (gr. 1-4). pap. 10.99 (978-1-68010-415-8(2)) Tiger Tales.

—The Rescued Puppy. Williams, Sophy, illus. 2017. 124p. (J). (978-1-5182-4904-4(3)) Tiger Tales.

—Sammy the Shy Kitten. Williams, Sophy, illus. 2017. 127p. (J). (978-1-5182-4902-0(7)) Tiger Tales.

—The Scruffy Puppy. Williams, Sophy, illus. 2016. (Pet Rescue Adventures Ser.). (ENG.). 128p. (J). (gr. 1-4). pap. 4.99 (978-1-58925-490-9(2)) Tiger Tales.

—Sky the Unwanted Kitten. Williams, Sophy, illus. 2016. 122p. (J). (978-0-545-16624-9(1)) Tiger Tales.

—The Tiniest Puppy. Williams, Sophy, illus. 2017. 126p. (J). (978-1-5182-4905-1(1)) Tiger Tales.

Webb, Ryan. Buddy: Dog of the Smoky Mountains. 2013. (Illus.). 34p. (J). pap. 12.00 (978-0-9847836-3-2(6)) Celtic Cat Publishing.

Weir, Patricia. My Kitty & Me. 2008. 20p. per. 24.95 (978-1-60441-908-5(3)) America Star Bks.

Wells, Rosemary. Ivy Takes Care. LaMarche, Jim, illus. 2015. (ENG.). 208p. (J). (gr. 3-7). pap. 6.99 (978-0-7636-7660-5(8)) Candlewick Pr.

Wendling, Nathalie & Glatzmayer, Thomas. Melanie & Tommy Have Two Pet Rats & One Syndrome. 2010. 48p. pap. (978-1-926582-67-2(5)) Insomniac Pr.

Wensley, Walter F. Yorkie. 2011. 44p. pap. 19.50 (978-1-4634-3185-3(6)) AuthorHouse.

Weston Woods Staff, creator. Children Make Terrible Pets. 2011. 29.95 (978-0-545-40221-7(2)) Weston Woods Studios, Inc.

—Corduroy. 2011. 18.95 (978-0-545-14078-2(1)); 29.95 (978-0-545-14916-7(9)); 38.75 (978-0-545-14080-5(3)) Weston Woods Studios, Inc.

—Crictor. 2011. 38.75 (978-0-545-23361-3(5)); 18.95 (978-0-545-23360-6(7)) Weston Woods Studios, Inc.

—Hondo & Fabian. 2011. 38.75 (978-0-545-14959-4(2)); 18.95 (978-0-545-14958-7(4)) Weston Woods Studios, Inc.

—Millions of Cats Weston Woods. 2011. 29.95 (978-0-439-73496-7(7)); 18.95 (978-0-439-72840-9(1)); 38.75 (978-0-439-72842-3(8)) Weston Woods Studios, Inc.

—Pet Show! 2011. 38.75 (978-0-439-72866-9(5)); 18.95 (978-0-439-72865-2(7)); 29.95 (978-0-439-73506-3(8)) Weston Woods Studios, Inc.

Whalley, Jim. Baby's First Bank Heist. Collins, Stephen, illus. 2019. (ENG.). 32p. (J). 17.99 (978-1-5476-0062-5(4), 900196647, Bloomsbury Children's Bks.) Bloomsbury Publishing USA.

Wheeler, Lisa. The Pet Project: Cute & Cuddly Vicious Verses. OHora, Zachariah, illus. 2013. (ENG.). 40p. (J). (gr. -1-3). 19.99 (978-1-4169-7595-3(0), Atheneum Bks. for Young Readers) Simon & Schuster Children's Publishing.

Wheeler, Mary A. Over the Edge. 2010. 373p. pap. 16.95 (978-1-4327-5994-0(9)) Outskirts Pr., Inc.

Which Pet Measures Up? 2003. (J). per. (978-1-932524-02-4(9)) Region 4 Education Service Ctr.

Whimsy. Benny's Pets. Meadow, Amy, illus. 2005. 32p. (J). 15.95 (978-0-9702675-0-4(9)) World of Whimsy Productions, LLC.

Whiteside, Andy. Valentino Finds a Home, 1 vol. Hnatov, Catherine, illus. 2012. (ENG.). (J). 32p. 15.95 (978-1-59572-284-3(X)); 24p. pap. 5.95 (978-1-59572-286-7(6)) Star Bright Bks., Inc.

Wiebe, Trina. Lizards Don't Wear Lip Gloss. Sarrazin, Marisol, illus. 2004. (Abby & Tess Pet-Sitters Ser.). 91p. 15.95 (978-0-7569-3425-5(7)) Perfection Learning Corp.

Willems, Mo. The Pigeon Wants a Puppy! 2008. (Pigeon Ser.). (ENG., Illus.). 40p. (J). (gr. -1-k). 17.99 (978-1-4231-0960-0(0), Hyperion Books for Children) Disney Publishing Worldwide.

Williams, Eula. Loving Danger. Branch Jr., Robert F., illus. 2012. 20p. pap. 24.95 (978-1-4626-6954-7(9)) America Star Bks.

Williams, Rozanne Lanczak. How Can I Get a Pet? Reid, Mick, illus. 2006. (Learn to Write Ser.). 8p. (J). (gr. k-2). pap. (978-1-59198-290-6(1), 6184) Creative Teaching Pr., Inc.

—How Can I Get a Pet? Maio, Barbara & Faulkner, Stacey, eds. Reid, Mick, illus. 2006. (J). per. 6.99 (978-1-59198-363-7(0)) Creative Teaching Pr., Inc.

Williams, T. E. Fluffy!! 2011. 24p. 16.25 (978-1-4520-3743-1(4)) AuthorHouse.

Willis, Jeanne. The Pet Person. Ross, Tony, illus. 2015. (ENG.). 32p. (J). (-k). pap. 9.99 (978-1-78344-242-3(5)) Andersen Pr. GBR. Dist: Independent Pubs. Group.

Wing, Natasha. The Night Before the New Pet. 2016. (Night Before Ser.). lib. bdg. 14.75 (978-0-606-38418-6(9)) Turtleback.

Winkler, Henry & Oliver, Lin. Day of the Iguana. 2004. (Hank Zipzer Ser.: No. 3). 160p. (J). (gr. 2-6). pap. 29.00 incl. audio (978-1-4000-9008-2(3), Listening Library) Random Hse. Audio Publishing Group.

—How to Scare the Pants off Your Pets, 3. 2013. (Ghost Buddy Ser.: 3). (ENG.). 176p. (J). (gr. 4-6). 18.69 (978-0-545-29884-1(9)) Scholastic, Inc.

—A Short Tale about a Long Dog. 2014. (Here's Hank Ser.: 2). lib. bdg. 16.00 (978-0-606-34143-1(9)) Turtleback.

—A Short Tale about a Long Dog #2, No. 2. Garrett, Scott, illus. 2014. (Here's Hank Ser.: 2). (ENG.). 128p. (J). (gr. 1-3). 6.99 (978-0-448-47998-9(2), Penguin Workshop) Penguin Young Readers Group.

—Stop That Frog! 2014. (Here's Hank Ser.: 3). lib. bdg. 16.00 (978-0-606-36161-3(8)) Turtleback.

—Stop That Frog! #3. Garrett, Scott, illus. 2014. (Here's Hank Ser.: 3). 128p. (J). (gr. 1-3). 6.99 (978-0-448-48152-4(9), Penguin Workshop) Penguin Young Readers Group.

Wise, William. Christopher Mouse: The Tale of a Small Traveler. Benson, Patrick, illus. 2006. (ENG.). 160p. (YA). (gr. 2-5). per. 8.99 (978-1-58234-708-0(5), 900039046, Bloomsbury USA Childrens) Bloomsbury Publishing USA.

Wolczyk, Deborah R. Maisie - the Dress up Cat. 2010. 76p. pap. 24.99 (978-1-4520-7681-2(2)) AuthorHouse.

Wolf, Carol A. Foggy Dog Discovers Christmas. 2012. (ENG.). 40p. (J). pap. 16.46 (978-1-4669-6253-8(4)) Trafford Publishing.

Wrecks, Billy. Super-Pets! (DC Super Friends) Beavers, Ethen, illus. 2016. (Little Golden Book Ser.). (ENG.). 24p. (J). (gr. -1-k). 5.99 (978-0-553-53923-3(X), Golden Bks.) Random Hse. Children's Bks.

Yaccarino, Dan. Journey to the Center of Town. 2017. (Class Pet Squad Ser.: 1). (J). lib. bdg. 17.20 (978-0-606-39943-2(7)) Turtleback.

—New Pet. Yaccarino, Dan, illus. 2003. (ENG., Illus.). 40p. (J). (gr. -1-2). pap. 4.99 (978-0-7868-1429-9(2)) Hyperion Pr.

Yager, Jan. The Reading Rabbit. Lyman, Mitzi, illus. 32p. (J). 2014. (ENG.). 25.95 (978-1-938998-00-3(6)) 2013. pap. 17.95 (978-1-938998-01-0(4)) Hannacroix Creek Bks., Inc.

Yolen, Jane. How Do Dinosaurs Choose Their Pets? Teague, Mark, illus. 2016. (ENG.). 40p. (J). (gr. -1-k). 18.99 (978-1-338-03278-9(X), Blue Sky Pr., The) Scholastic, Inc.

Young, Amy. A Unicorn Named Sparkle. Young, Amy, illus. 2018. (Unicorn Named Sparkle Ser.: 1). (ENG., Illus.). 32p. (J). bds. 9.99 (978-0-374-30872-8(1), 900187523, Farrar, Straus & Giroux (BYR)) Farrar, Straus & Giroux.

—A Unicorn Named Sparkle: A Picture Book. Young, Amy, illus. 2016. (Unicorn Named Sparkle Ser.: 1). (ENG., Illus.). 40p. (J). 16.99 (978-0-374-30185-9(9), 900140948, Farrar, Straus & Giroux (BYR)) Farrar, Straus & Giroux.

Young, Jessica. Pet-Rified. Sécheret, Jessica, illus. 2017. (Finley Flowers Ser.). (ENG.). 128p. (J). (gr. 1-3). lib. bdg. 25.32 (978-1-4795-9805-2(4), 133580, Picture Window Bks.) Capstone.

—Pet This Book. Wiseman, Daniel, illus. 2018. (ENG.). 32p. (J). 15.99 (978-1-68119-507-0(0), 900175607, Bloomsbury Children's Bks.) Bloomsbury Publishing USA.

Young, Judy. A Pet for Miss Wright. Wesson, Andrea, illus. 2011. (ENG.). 32p. (J). (gr. 1-4). lib. bdg. 15.95 (978-1-58536-509-8(2), 202202) Sleeping Bear Pr.

Youngs, Kendahl Brooke. Kendahl Gets a Puppy. 2012. (ENG.). (J). pap. 13.95 (978-0-9836045-8-7(4), Kendahl Hse. Pr.) Youngs, Bettie Bks.

Zambak Çucok Publishing Staff, ed. The Rainbow: Niloya 1. 2016. (J). pap. 4.99 (978-1-4621-1862-5(3), Horizon Pubs.) Cedar Fort, Inc./CFI Distribution.

Zeltser, David. Stinker. Patton, Julia, illus. 2017. (ENG.). 32p. (J). (gr. -1-3). 17.99 (978-1-5124-1792-0(0), 9c00f0f8-e843-47ee-b9cf-1f5a39a683d1, Carolrhoda Bks.) Lerner Publishing Group.

Zsikai-Spiker, Lisa Marie. Buster & Snoopy. Schimmelman, Alex, illus. 2012. 24p. 24.95 (978-1-4626-7112-0(8)) America Star Bks.

Zuill, Andrea & Zuill, Andrea. Business Pig. 2018. (Illus.). 32p. (J). (gr. -1-2). 16.95 (978-1-4549-2684-9(8)) Sterling Publishing Co., Inc.

Zullo, Allan. Bad Pets: On the Loose! 2012. 125p. (J). pap. (978-0-545-46041-5(7)) Scholastic, Inc.

PHANTOM OF THE OPERA (FICTITIOUS CHARACTER)—FICTION

Behling, Steve. Iron Man: Invasion of the Space Phantoms. 2016. (Mighty Marvel Chapter Bks.). (J). lib. bdg. 16.00 (978-0-606-38305-9(0)) Turtleback.

—Iron Man: Invasion of the Space Phantoms. Pham, Khoi & Sotomayor, Chris, illus. 2018. (Mighty Marvel Chapter Bks.). (ENG.). 128p. (J). (gr. 2-7). lib. bdg. 31.36 (978-1-5321-4217-8(X), 28554, Chapter Bks.) Spotlight.

Coker, Lauren. The Phantom's Lullaby: A Novel. 2008. 332p. pap. 19.95 (978-0-595-47695-4(3)) iUniverse, Inc.

Francis, Pauline, retold by. The Phantom of the Opera, 1 vol. 2010. (Essential Classics - Horror Ser.). (ENG., Illus.). 56p. pap. (978-0-237-54095-1(9)) Evans Brothers, Ltd.

Knighton, Kate, retold by. Phantom of the Opera. 2008. (Young Reading Series 2 Gift Bks). 64p. (J). 8.99 (978-0-7945-2082-3(0), Usborne) EDC Publishing.

PHANTOMS

see Apparitions; Ghosts

PHARMACEUTICAL CHEMISTRY

see also Drugs; Materia Medica; Pharmacy; Poisons

Field, Jon Eben. Medicine Cabinet Chemistry, 1 vol. 2011. (Chemtastrophe! Ser.). (ENG.). 32p. (J). (gr. 5-8). pap. (978-0-7787-5304-9(2)); lib. bdg. (978-0-7787-5287-5(9)) Crabtree Publishing Co.

Kendrick, Karolyn. Chemistry in Medicine: Set Of 6. 2010. (Navigators Ser.). (J). pap. 48.00 net. (978-1-4108-6233-4(X)) Benchmark Education Co.

—Chemistry in Medicine: Text Pairs. 2008. (Bridges/Navigators Ser.). (J). (gr. 5). 81.00 (978-1-4108-8410-7(4)) Benchmark Education Co.

Romero, Libby. Medical Chemistry. 2006. (J). pap. (978-1-4108-6499-4(5)) Benchmark Education Co.

PHARMACOPOEIAS

see Materia Medica

PHARMACY

see also Botany, Medical; Drugs; Materia Medica; Pharmaceutical Chemistry

Ballard, Carol. The Search for Cures from the Rain Forest, 1 vol. 2005. (Science Quest Ser.). (ENG., Illus.). 32p. (J). (gr. 4-6). lib. bdg. 28.67 (978-0-8368-4554-9(4),

9d72a50d-defe-4099-abb6-74e7245766cd, Gareth Stevens Learning Library) Stevens, Gareth Publishing LLLP.

Chambers, Catherine. Living Forever: the Pharmaceutical Industry, 1 vol. 2012. (Big-Buck Business Ser.). (ENG., Illus.). 48p. (J). (gr. 6-6). 34.60 *(978-1-4339-7755-8(9)*, 075d49db-8040-4b43-a4c3-fb0fd305c6f6); pap. 15.05 *(978-1-4339-7756-5(7)*, a13ec7a8-2766-46b3-9a82-91dfb422d010) Stevens, Gareth Publishing LLLP. (Gareth Stevens Secondary Library).

Gill, Monica K. Biopharmaceuticals, 1 vol. 2015. (Biotechnology Revolution Ser.). (ENG., Illus.). 184p. (J). (gr. 10-10). lib. bdg. 41.35 *(978-1-62275-582-0(0)*, 49805248-22ea-453f-a487-402c072deefb, Britannica Educational Publishing) Rosen Publishing Group, Inc., The.

Miller, Malinda. The Pharmaceutical Industry: Better Medicine for the 21st Century. 2010. (New Careers for the 21st Century Ser.). 64p. (YA). (gr. 7-18). lib. bdg. 22.95 *(978-1-4222-1819-8(8))* Mason Crest.

Rodger, Ellen. Top Secret Science in Medicine. 2019. (Top Secret Science Ser.). 48p. (J). (gr. 5-5). *(978-0-7787-5994-2(6))*; pap. *(978-0-7787-6032-0(4))* Crabtree Publishing Co.

Sayler, Mary Harwell. Prescription Pain Relievers. 2010. (Understanding Drugs Ser.). (ENG., Illus.). 112p. (gr. 9-12). 34.95 *(978-1-60413-549-7(2)*, P459470, Facts On File) Infobase Holdings, Inc.

Walker, Ida. Sedatives & Hypnotics: Deadly Downers. 2012. (J). pap. *(978-1-4222-2459-5(7))* Mason Crest.

—Sedatives & Hypnotics: Deadly Downers. Henningfield, Jack E., ed. 2012. (Illicit & Misused Drugs Ser.). 128p. (J). (gr. 7). 24.95 *(978-1-4222-2440-3(6))* Mason Crest.

PHARMACY—VOCATIONAL GUIDANCE

Miller, Malinda. The Pharmaceutical Industry: Better Medicine for the 21st Century. 2010. (New Careers for the 21st Century Ser.). 64p. (YA). (gr. 7-18). pap. 9.95 *(978-1-4222-2040-5(0))* Mason Crest.

PHEASANTS—FICTION

Meierhenry, Mark, et al. The Mystery of the Pheasants. 2012. (Mystery Ser.). (ENG., Illus.). 44p. (J). 14.95 *(978-0-9845041-9-0(2)*, P240881) South Dakota Historical Society Pr.

Minnema, Cheryl. Johnny's Pheasant. Flett, Julie, illus. 2019. (ENG.). 32p. (J). (gr. -1-3). 16.95 *(978-1-5179-0501-9(X))* Univ. of Minnesota Pr.

PHELPS, MICHAEL, 1985-

Fishman, Jon M. Michael Phelps. 2017. (Sports All-Stars Ser.). (ENG.). 32p. (J). (gr. 2-5). 12.99 *(978-1-5124-5400-0(1)*, Lerner Pubns.); 39.99 *(978-1-5124-5398-0(6)*, Lerner Pubns.); (Illus.). pap. 9.99 *(978-1-5124-5401-7(X)*, c7692f5e-3c98-491b-9751-34f1c4f6d4dd); (Illus.). lib. bdg. 29.32 *(978-1-5124-5396-6(X)*, c4231634-53a0-4a1e-af58-63f53e4c480a, Lerner Pubns.); (Illus.). E-Book 42.65 *(978-1-5124-5397-3(8)*, Lerner Pubns.) Lerner Publishing Group.

Goldish, Meish. Michael Phelps: Anything Is Possible! 2009. (Defining Moments Ser.). (Illus.). 32p. (YA). (gr. 2-5). lib. bdg. 28.50 *(978-1-59716-855-7(6))* Bearport Publishing Co., Inc.

Hansen, Grace. Michael Phelps. 2016. (Olympic Biographies Ser.). (ENG., Illus.). 24p. (J). (gr. -1-2). lib. bdg. 32.79 *(978-1-68080-945-9(8)*, 23355, Abdo Kids) ABDO Publishing Co.

Kennedy, Mike. Michael Phelps, 1 vol. 2009. (People We Should Know (Second Series) Ser.). (ENG.). 48p. (J). (gr. 3-5). pap. 11.50 *(978-1-4339-2151-3(0)*, c10eb56c-5cde-4362-a61e-2c47cff7d4b5); lib. bdg. 33.67 *(978-1-4339-1950-3(8)*, 9c4d1374-f328-4c9d-9fa4-58c0d6e8c363) Stevens, Gareth Publishing LLLP. (Gareth Stevens Learning Library).

Lajiness, Katie. Michael Phelps. 2016. (Big Buddy Olympic Biographies Ser.). (ENG., Illus.). 32p. (J). (gr. 2-5). lib. bdg. 34.21 *(978-1-68078-555-5(9)*, 23597, Big Buddy Bks.) ABDO Publishing Co.

Markovics, Joyce L. Michael Phelps. 2017. (Amazing Americans: Olympians Ser.). (ENG., Illus.). 24p. (J). (gr. -1-3). 26.99 *(978-1-68402-239-7(8))* Bearport Publishing Co., Inc.

McDowell, Pamela. Michael Phelps. 2014. (Illus.). 24p. (J). *(978-1-62127-391-2(1))* Weigl Pubs., Inc.

Michael Phelps. rev. ed. 2009. (Amazing Athletes Ser.). (gr. 2-5). pap. 6.95 *(978-0-7613-4138-3(2)*, First Avenue Editions) Lerner Publishing Group.

Nagelhout, Ryan. Michael Phelps: Greatest Swimmer of All Time, 1 vol. 2017. (Breakout Biographies Ser.). (ENG.). 32p. (J). (gr. 4-5). pap. 11.00 *(978-1-5081-6066-3(X)*, 259e5eaa-0b6e-4931-9277-78a8f6e5c59e, PowerKids Pr.) Rosen Publishing Group, Inc., The.

Phelps, Michael & Abrahamson, Alan. How to Train with a T. Rex & Win 8 Gold Medals. Jenkins, Ward, illus. 2009. (ENG.). 32p. (J). (gr. -1-3). 19.99 *(978-1-4169-8669-0(3)*, Simon & Schuster Bks. For Young Readers) Simon & Schuster Bks. For Young Readers.

Scheff, Matt. Michael Phelps. 2016. (Olympic Stars Ser.). (ENG., Illus.). 32p. (J). (gr. 3-9). lib. bdg. 32.79 *(978-1-68078-561-6(3)*, 23805, SportsZone) ABDO Publishing Co.

Sheen, Barbara. Michael Phelps, 1 vol. 2010. (People in the News Ser.). (ENG.). 96p. (gr. 7-7). 41.03 *(978-1-4205-0282-4(4)*, baa1dc84-fa5c-4cf4-a1db-87fa9a125f47, Lucent Pr.) Greenhaven Publishing LLC.

Torsiello, David P. Michael Phelps: Swimming for Olympic Gold, 1 vol. 2009. (Hot Celebrity Biographies Ser.). (ENG., Illus.). 48p. (gr. 5-7). pap. 11.53 *(978-0-7660-3630-7(8)*, 6e3a4df6-ddb2-4b4a-8123-96488a794dc2); lib. bdg. 27.93 *(978-0-7660-3591-1(3)*, ac24e243-5636-4b37-b61f-51163b4b62ec) Enslow Publishing, LLC.

Zuehlke, Jeffrey. Michael Phelps. 2005. (First Step Nonfiction Ser.). (Illus.). 32p. (J). (gr. 2-5). per. 5.95 *(978-0-8225-2631-5(X))*; (gr. 3-7). lib. bdg. 23.93 *(978-0-8225-2431-1(7))* Lerner Publishing Group.

—Michael Phelps (Revised Edition) 2009. pap. 40.95 *(978-0-7613-4777-4(1))* Lerner Publishing Group.

PHILADELPHIA (PA.)

Ashley, Susan. The Liberty Bell, 1 vol. 2004. (Places in American History Ser.). (ENG., Illus.). 24p. (YA). (gr. 2-4). lib. bdg. 24.67 *(978-0-8368-4141-1(7)*, e704d18f-590d-4eb1-9031-afc9d9257503, Weekly Reader Leveled Readers) Stevens, Gareth Publishing LLLP.

Douglas, Lloyd G. The Liberty Bell. 2003. (Welcome Bks.). (Illus.). 24p. (J). 19.00 *(978-0-516-25852-2(4)*, Children's Pr.) Scholastic Library Publishing.

—Welcome Books: Liberty Bell. 2003. (Welcome Bks.). (ENG., Illus.). 24p. (J). (gr. -1-2). pap. 4.95 *(978-0-516-27875-9(4)*, Children's Pr.) Scholastic Library Publishing.

Eldridge, Alison & Eldridge, Stephen. The Liberty Bell: An American Symbol, 1 vol. 2012. (All about American Symbols Ser.). (ENG.). 24p. (gr. -1-1). 25.27 *(978-0-7660-4059-5(3)*, 0d12a906-9890-419d-a9e6-66d158e6537c, Enslow Publishing) Enslow Publishing, LLC.

Gamble, Adam. Good Night Philadelphia. Stevenson, Harvey, illus. 2006. (Good Night Our World Ser.). (ENG.). 20p. (J). (gr. k — 1). bds. 9.95 *(978-0-9777979-4-3(5))* Good Night Bks.

James, Lincoln. Making History: The Liberty Bell, 1 vol. 2005. (Content-Area Literacy Collections). (ENG.). 24p. (gr. 3-4). pap. 8.85 *(978-1-4042-5587-6(7)*, 9da605d6-4ef8-4d56-9135-f7e98974d5be) Rosen Publishing Group, Inc., The.

Jango-Cohen, Judith. The Liberty Bell. 2003. (Pull Ahead Books — American Symbols Ser.). (ENG., Illus.). 32p. (J). (gr. k-3). pap. 7.99 *(978-0-8225-3754-0(0)*, 10dda843-6754-45da-b70b-a61749669699, First Avenue Editions) Lerner Publishing Group.

Silate, Jennifer. The Liberty Bell, 1 vol. 2005. (Primary Sources of American Symbols Ser.). (ENG., Illus.). 24p. (J). (gr. 3-3). lib. bdg. 26.27 *(978-1-4042-2687-6(7)*, 63263e67-6bed-4b81-8eda-1c3a62718d92) Rosen Publishing Group, Inc., The.

PHILADELPHIA (PA.)—FICTION

Barr, Jennifer Robin. Goodbye, Mr. Spalding. 2019. 272p. (J). (gr. 4-7). 18.95 *(978-1-68437-178-5(3)*, Calkins Creek) Highlights Pr., c/o Highlights for Children, Inc.

Brown, Philip. Franky Franklyn's Philadelphia Adventure. 2011. 108p. 21.99 *(978-1-4567-5423-5(8))*; pap. 10.99 *(978-1-4567-1269-3(1))* AuthorHouse.

Cox, Judy. Mrs. Millie Goes to Philly!, 0 vols. Mathieu, Joe, illus. 2013. (ENG.). 32p. (J). (gr. -1-2). pap. 9.99 *(978-1-4778-1680-6(1)*, 9781477816806, Two Lions) Amazon Publishing.

Davis, Anthony C. I Ain't Lying. 2008. 112p. pap. 19.95 *(978-1-60474-087-5(6))* America Star Bks.

Edgeworth, Maria. Rosamond: With Other Tales. by Maria Edgeworth. 2006. 388p. per. 26.99 *(978-1-4255-4076-0(7))* Michigan Publishing.

Extreme Danger. 2007. 15.00 *(978-0-7569-7603-3(0))* Perfection Learning Corp.

Griffin, Wiley Chase. Chase the Shark: Flies Like a Bird. 2010. 28p. pap. 12.50 *(978-1-4520-5173-4(9))* AuthorHouse.

Grocki, Jennifer. From A to Zamboni, the Alphabet Hockey Style! Flyers Edition. Lendway, Andy, illus. 2007. 32p. (J). 16.95 *(978-0-9793833-0-4(7))* Team Kidz, Inc.

Halley, Marilyn. Apple-Green Eyes. 2005. pap. 8.00 *(978-0-8059-6681-7(1))* Dorrance Publishing Co., Inc.

Halse Anderson, Laurie. Fever 1793. 2014. (ENG.). 272p. (J). 12.24 *(978-1-63245-124-8(7))* Lectorum Pubns., Inc.

Holm, Jennifer L. The Creek. 2003. 240p. (J). (gr. 7-18). 15.99 *(978-0-06-000133-9(X))*; 16.89 *(978-0-06-000134-6(8))* HarperCollins Pubs.

Jacobs, Lily. The Littlest Bunny in Philadelphia: An Easter Adventure. Dunn, Robert, illus. 2015. (Littlest Bunny Ser.). (ENG.). 32p. (J). (gr. -1-3). 9.99 *(978-1-4926-1180-6(8)*, Hometown World) Sourcebooks, Inc.

James, Eric. Santa's Sleigh Is on Its Way to Philadelphia: A Christmas Adventure. Dunn, Robert, illus. 2016. (Santa's Sleigh Is on Its Way Ser.). (ENG.). 32p. (J). (gr. k-2). 12.99 *(978-1-4926-4350-0(5)*, 9781492643500, Hometown World) Sourcebooks, Inc.

—The Spooky Express Philadelphia. Piwowarski, Marcin, illus. 2017. (Spooky Express Ser.). (ENG.). 32p. (J). (gr. k-6). 9.99 *(978-1-4926-5393-6(4)*, Hometown World) Sourcebooks, Inc.

—Tiny the Philadelphia Easter Bunny. 2018. (Tiny the Easter Bunny Ser.). (ENG.). 40p. (J). (gr. k-3). 9.99 *(978-1-4926-5958-7(4)*, Hometown World) Sourcebooks, Inc.

Johnson, Maureen. The Key to the Golden Firebird. 2004. (ENG.). 304p. (J). (gr. 7-18). 15.99 *(978-0-06-054138-5(5))* HarperCollins Pubs.

Kelly, David A. Ballpark Mysteries #9: the Philly Fake. Meyers, Mark, illus. 2014. (Ballpark Mysteries Ser.: 9). (ENG.). 112p. (J). (gr. 1-4). 6.99 *(978-0-307-97785-4(4)*, Random Hse. Bks. for Young Readers) Random Hse. Children's Bks.

—The Philly Fake. 2014. (Ballpark Mysteries Ser.: Bk. 9). lib. bdg. 14.75 *(978-0-606-35566-7(9))* Turtleback.

Kientz, Chris & Hockensmith, Steve. Claws & Effect. Nielsen, Lee, illus. 2016. (Secret Smithsonian Adventures Ser.: 2). 64p. (gr. 4-7). pap. 10.95 *(978-1-58834-567-7(X)*, Smithsonian Bks.) Smithsonian Institution Scholarly Pr.

Mark, Jessica & Mark, Rebecca. Sky the Fly Explores Philadelphia. 2013. 28p. pap. 11.00 *(978-1-4349-3272-3(9)*, RoseDog Bks.) Dorrance Publishing Co., Inc.

Marsh, Carole. The Mystery on the Underground Railroad. 2009. (Real Kids, Real Places Ser.). (Illus.). 146p. (J). lib. bdg. 18.99 *(978-0-635-06991-7(1)*, Marsh, Carole Mysteries) Gallopade International.

—The Mystery on the Underground Railroad (Hardcover) 2003. 160p. (gr. 2-8). 14.95 *(978-0-635-02110-6(2))* Gallopade International.

Mohsenian, Javad. 9/11 Children. 2006. (ENG.). 128p. per. 10.95 *(978-0-7414-3218-6(8))* Infinity Publishing.

Mulubah, Sr. Denise's Pet Dove. 2009. 36p. pap. 16.99 *(978-1-4389-7536-8(8))* AuthorHouse.

Neri, G. Ghetto Cowboy (the Inspiration for Concrete Cowboy) Watson, Jesse Joshua, illus. 2013. (ENG.). 224p. (J). (gr. 5). pap. 7.99 *(978-0-7636-6453-4(7))* Candlewick Pr.

Osborne, Mary Pope. To the Future, Ben Franklin! Ford, A. G., illus. 2019. (Magic Tree House (R) Ser.: 32). (J). (gr. 1-4). 96p. 13.99 *(978-0-525-64832-1(1))*; (ENG.). 112p. lib. bdg. 16.99 *(978-0-525-64833-8(X))* Random Hse. Children's Bks. (Random Hse. Bks. for Young Readers).

Ostow, Micol. GoldenGirl. 2009. (Bradford Ser.). (ENG.). 224p. (YA). (gr. 9-18). pap. 9.99 *(978-1-4169-6118-5(6)*, Simon Pulse) Simon Pulse.

Ribay, Randy. After the Shot Drops. 2020. (ENG.). 336p. (YA). (gr. 9). pap. 15.99 *(978-0-358-10806-1(3)*, 1748879, Clarion Bks.) HarperCollins Pubs.

Rinaldi, Ann. Finishing Becca: A Story about Peggy Shippen & Benedict Arnold. 2004. (Great Episodes Ser.). (ENG.). 384p. (YA). (gr. 7-8). pap. 17.95 *(978-0-15-205079-5(5)*, 1195340, Clarion Bks.) HarperCollins Pubs.

Rubin, Sarah. The Impossible Clue. 2017. 293p. (J). pap. *(978-0-545-94272-0(1)*, Chicken Hse., The) Scholastic, Inc.

Skewes, John & Mullin, Michael. Larry Gets Lost in Philadelphia. Skewes, John, illus. 2013. (Larry Gets Lost Ser.). (ENG., Illus.). 32p. (J). (gr. -1-2). 17.99 *(978-1-57061-792-8(9)*, Little Bigfoot) Sasquatch Bks.

Smallman, Steve. Santa Is Coming to Philadelphia. Dunn, Robert, illus. 2nd ed. 2019. (Santa Is Coming... Ser.). (ENG.). 40p. (J). (gr. -1-3). 12.99 *(978-1-7282-0094-1(6)*, Hometown World) Sourcebooks, Inc.

Smith, Roland. Independence Hall. (I, Q Ser.: Bk. 1). (ENG., 312p. (YA). (gr. 6-8). 2009. illus.). 15.95 *(978-1-58536-468-8(1)*, 202188) 2008. pap. 12.99 *(978-1-58536-325-4(1)*, 202289) Sleeping Bear Pr.

Spinelli, Jerry. Eggs. 2008. (ENG., Illus.). 240p. (J). (gr. 3-7). pap. 8.99 *(978-0-316-16647-8(2))* Little, Brown Bks. for Young Readers.

Sully, Katherine. Night-Night Philadelphia. Poole, Helen, illus. 2017. (Night-Night Ser.). (ENG.). 20p. (J). (gr. -1-1). bds. 9.99 *(978-1-4926-4774-4(8)*, 9781492647744, Hometown World) Sourcebooks, Inc.

Vivian, Siobhan. Same Difference. 2014. (ENG.). 304p. (YA). (gr. 7-7). pap. 10.99 *(978-0-545-75802-4(5))* Scholastic, Inc.

Zschock, Martha. Hello, Philadelphia! 2011. (Hello Ser.). (ENG., Illus.). 16p. (J). (gr. -1-k). bds. 9.99 *(978-1-933212-64-7(0)*, Commonwealth Editions) Applewood Bks.

PHILADELPHIA (PA.)—HISTORY

ABC Travel Guides for Kids-Philadelphia. 2004. (J). per. 12.95 *(978-0-9760047-0-7(4))* Rosenberger, Matthew.

Boehm Jerome, Kate. Philadelphia & the State of Pennsylvania: Cool Stuff Every Kid Should Know. 2011. (Arcadia Kids Ser.). (ENG., Illus.). 48p. (J). (gr. 3-6). pap. 11.99 *(978-1-4396-0094-8(5))* Arcadia Publishing.

Britton, Tamara L. Independence Hall. 2003. (Symbols, Landmarks & Monuments Set 1 Ser.). 32p. (gr. k-6). 27.07 *(978-1-57765-853-5(1)*, Checkerboard Library) ABDO Publishing Co.

Chang, Kirsten. The Liberty Bell. 2018. (Symbols of American Freedom Ser.). (ENG., Illus.). 24p. (J). (gr. k-3). pap. 7.99 *(978-1-61891-470-5(7)*, 12123, Blastoff! Readers) Bellwether Media.

Cheung, Shu Pui, et al. Walking on Solid Ground. Wei, Deborah & Kodish, Debora, eds. Chau, Ming, photos by. 2004. (ENG & CHI., Illus.). 64p. (J). pap. 12.95 *(978-0-9644937-4-2(8)*, 09644937-4-8) Philadelphia Folklore Project.

Danis Drouot, Lucile, illus. Philadelphia Monsters: A Search & Find Book. 2018. (ENG.). 22p. (J). (gr. -1). bds. 9.99 *(978-2-924734-09-4(6))* City Monsters Bks. CAN. Dist: Publishers Group West (PGW).

Epstein, Brad. Philadelphia Eagles 101. 2010. (Illus.). 24p. (J). bds. *(978-1-60730-123-3(7)*, 101 Bk.) Michaelson Entertainment.

Figley, Marty Rhodes. Prisoner for Liberty. Orback, Craig, illus. (On My Own History Ser.). (ENG.). 48p. (gr. 2-4). 2009. (J). pap. 8.99 *(978-0-8225-9022-4(0)*, 71b3881b-9399-4d9c-a66b-0223c579b66b, First Avenue Editions) 2008. lib. bdg. 25.26 *(978-0-8225-7280-0(X)*, Millbrook Pr.) Lerner Publishing Group.

—Salvar a la Campana de la Libertad. Lepp, Kevin, illus. 2005. (Yo Solo - Historia (on My Own - History) Ser.). (SPA.). 48p. (J). (gr. 3-7). lib. bdg. 25.26 *(978-0-8225-3094-7(5)*, Ediciones Lerner); (gr. 2-5). per. 6.95 *(978-0-8225-3095-4(3))* Lerner Publishing Group.

—Salvar a la Campana de la Libertad; Saving the Liberty Bell. 2008. pap. 40.95 *(978-0-7613-3933-5(7))* Lerner Publishing Group.

—Saving the Liberty Bell. Lepp, Kevin, illus. 2004. (On My Own History Ser.). (ENG.). 48p. (J). (gr. 2-4). pap. 8.99 *(978-1-57505-696-8(8)*, 910d2276-4910-411d-bd61-133c42e06133, First Avenue Editions) Lerner Publishing Group.

Figley, Mary Rhodes. Prisoner for Liberty. 2009. pap. 40.95 *(978-0-7613-4796-5(8))* Lerner Publishing Group.

Hess, Debra. The Liberty Bell, 1 vol. 2008. (Symbols of America Ser.). (ENG.). 40p. (gr. 3-3). pap. 9.23 *(978-0-7614-3391-0(0)*, af9316c8-f6a9-47dc-8f4b-2dafafd22aad) Cavendish Square Publishing LLC.

Hopper, Whitney. I Visit the Liberty Bell, 1 vol. 2016. (Symbols of Our Country Ser.). (ENG., Illus.). 24p. (J). (gr. 1-1). pap. 9.25 *(978-1-4994-2732-5(8)*, 5a1749f2-87a7-406b-a79b-61fa716fbca5, PowerKids Pr.) Rosen Publishing Group, Inc., The.

Kelly, Elaine A. & Carl, Jean R. Among the Buildings That Touch the Sky: Philadelphia. Noone, Cathleen L., illus. 2009. *(978-0-578-06873-2(7))* Kelly, Elaine A.

Kopp, Megan. Liberty Bell with Code. 2012. (AV2 American Icons Ser.). (ENG., Illus.). 24p. (J). pap. 12.95 *(978-1-61913-301-3(6))*; lib. bdg. 27.13 *(978-1-61913-078-4(5))* Weigl Pubs., Inc. (AV2 by Weigl).

Lloyd, Sandra Mackenzie, ed. Patriots, Pirates, Heroes & Spies: Stories from Historic Philadelphia. 2012. (ENG., Illus.). 192p. 11.95 *(978-0-9855319-0-4(8))* Historic Philadelphia, Inc.

Mattern, Joanne. The Liberty Bell: History's Silent Witness. 2017. (Core Content Social Studies — Let's Celebrate America Ser.). (ENG., Illus.). 32p. (J). (gr. 2-5). pap. 8.99 *(978-1-63440-235-4(9)*, 28ed5c3f-ee1c-4654-af96-f22535bc1256); lib. bdg. 26.65 *(978-1-63440-225-5(1)*, 0b005936-2891-4184-8159-c5ba8f4d5d28) Red Chair Pr.

—Philadelphia. 2018. (Illus.). 24p. (J). *(978-1-4896-9466-9(8)*, AV2 by Weigl) Weigl Pubs., Inc.

McDonald, Megan. Saving the Liberty Bell. 2005. (ENG., Illus.). 32p. (J). (gr. k-3). 19.99 *(978-0-689-85167-4(7)*, Atheneum/Richard Jackson Bks.) Simon & Schuster Children's Publishing.

Mountjoy, Shane. Philadelphia. 2007. (Colonial Settlements in America Ser.). (ENG., Illus.). 100p. (gr. 5-9). lib. bdg. 30.00 *(978-0-7910-9336-8(0)*, P124648, Facts On File) Infobase Holdings, Inc.

National Geographic Learning. Reading Expeditions (Social Studies: Voices from America's Past): Colonial Life. 2007. (Avenues Ser.). (ENG., Illus.). 40p. (J). pap. 21.95 *(978-0-7922-8678-3(2))* CENGAGE Learning.

Orr, Tamra B. The Liberty Bell: Introducing Primary Sources. 2016. (Introducing Primary Sources Ser.). (ENG., Illus.). 32p. (J). (gr. -1-2). lib. bdg. 28.65 *(978-1-4914-8224-7(9)*, 130686, Capstone Pr.) Capstone.

Randolph, Ryan. Betsy Ross: The American Flag, & Life in a Young America. 2009. (Library of American Lives & Times Ser.). 112p. (gr. 5-5). 69.20 *(978-1-60853-473-9(1))* Rosen Publishing Group, Inc., The.

Roberts, Russell. Philadelphia. 2009. (Class Trip Ser.). (Illus.). 48p. (J). (gr. 2-5). lib. bdg. 29.95 *(978-1-58415-807-3(7))* Mitchell Lane Pubs.

Rustad, Martha E. H. Can We Ring the Liberty Bell? Poling, Kyle, illus. 2014. (Cloverleaf Books (tm) — Our American Symbols Ser.). (ENG.). 24p. (J). (gr. k-2). pap. 8.99 *(978-1-4677-4467-6(0)*, b17becb7-9a69-4951-8e08-465b29f5a72b, Millbrook Pr.) Lerner Publishing Group.

Sedlacek, Jan Gill. Colors of a City: Philadelphia. Oudinot, Wanda & Baum, Kipley, photos by. 2012. (Illus.). 46p. (J). pap. 14.00 *(978-0-9836878-7-0(0))* Aperture Pr., LLC.

Smith, Robin Wayne. If You Got It, a Truck Brought It. Smith, Robin Wayne, illus. 2012. (Illus.). 20p. pap. 6.00 *(978-0-615-63721-1(3))* Bright Tyke Creations LLC.

Wyner, Zach. On the Hardwood: Philadelphia 76ers. 2013. (On the Hardwood Ser.). (ENG., Illus.). 48p. (gr. 3-8). pap. 8.95 *(978-1-61570-831-4(6))* Scobre Pr. Corp.

Zschock, Martha. Journey Around Philadelphia from a to Z. 2006. (Journeys Ser.). (ENG., Illus.). 32p. (J). (gr. 1-6). 17.95 *(978-1-933212-28-9(4)*, Commonwealth Editions) Applewood Bks.

PHILADELPHIA (PA.)—HISTORY—FICTION

Alger, Horatio. Jack's Ward. 2005. 28.95 *(978-1-4218-1454-4(4))*; 260p. pap. 13.95 *(978-1-4218-1554-1(0))* 1st World Publishing, Inc. (1st World Library - Literary Society).

—Jack's Ward. 2006. pap. *(978-1-4065-0711-9(3))* Dodo Pr.

—Jack's Ward: Or, The Boy Guardian. 2006. 176p. pap. 19.99 *(978-1-4264-0882-3(X))*; (ENG.). 168p. pap. 21.99 *(978-1-4264-0863-2(3))* Creative Media Partners, LLC.

—Timothy Crump's Ward. 2005. 27.95 *(978-1-4218-1451-3(X))*; 220p. pap. 12.95 *(978-1-4218-1551-0(6))* 1st World Publishing, Inc. (1st World Library - Literary Society).

Bender, Albert C. More 'Kids in the Alley' Tales. 2011. (Illus.). 200p. pap. 16.95 *(978-1-4327-7174-4(4))* Outskirts Pr., Inc.

Blackwood, Gary. Curiosity. 2015. 336p. (J). (gr. 4-7). 8.99 *(978-0-14-242448-3(X)*, Puffin Books) Penguin Young Readers Group.

Coleman, Evelyn. Shadows on Society Hill. 2007. (American Girl Mysteries Ser.). (ENG., Illus.). 192p. (J). (gr. 4-7). 10.95 *(978-1-59369-163-9(7)*, American Girl) American Girl Publishing, Inc.

Haislip, Phyllis Hall. Lili's Gift: A Civil War Healer's Story. 2008. (ENG., Illus.). 204p. (J). pap. 8.95 *(978-1-57249-392-6(5)*, White Mane Kids) White Mane Publishing Co., Inc.

Noble, Trinka Hakes. The Scarlet Stockings Spy. Papp, Robert, illus. 2004. (Tales of Young Americans Ser.). (ENG.). 48p. (J). (gr. 1-4). 16.95 *(978-1-58536-230-1(1)*, 202055) Sleeping Bear Pr.

PHILADELPHIA (PA.)—INDEPENDENCE HALL

see Independence Hall (Philadelphia, Pa.)

PHILADELPHIA PHILLIES (BASEBALL TEAM)

Frisch, Aaron. Philadelphia Phillies. 2009. (World Series Champions Ser.). (Illus.). 23p. (J). (gr. 2-3). 24.25 *(978-1-58341-693-8(5)*, Creative Education) Creative Co., The.

Gilbert, Sara. Philadelphia Phillies. 2013. (World Series Champions Ser.). (ENG.). 24p. (J). (gr. 1-4). pap. 7.99 *(978-0-89812-821-5(8)*, 21858, Creative Paperbacks); (Illus.). 25.65 *(978-1-60818-270-1(3)*, 21857, Creative Education) Creative Co., The.

Goodman, Michael E. The Story of the Philadelphia Phillies. 2011. (J). 35.65 *(978-1-60818-051-6(4)*, Creative Education) 2007. (Illus.). 48p. (YA). (gr. 4-7). lib. bdg. 32.80 *(978-1-58341-497-2(5))* Creative Co., The.

Jackson, Dave. Philadelphia Phillies, 1 vol. 2015. (Inside MLB Ser.). (ENG., Illus.). 48p. (J). (gr. 3-6). lib. bdg. 34.21 *(978-1-62403-480-0(2)*, 17123, SportsZone) ABDO Publishing Co.

Kelley, K. C. Philadelphia Phillies. 2019. (Major League Baseball Teams Ser.). (ENG.). 32p. (J). (gr. 2-5). lib. bdg. 35.64 *(978-1-5038-2834-6(4)*, 212641) Child's World, Inc, The.

—Philadelphia Phillies. 2016. (Illus.). 32p. (J). *(978-1-4896-5944-6(7)*, AV2 by Weigl) Weigl Pubs., Inc.

Lajiness, Katie. Philadelphia Eagles. 2016. (NFL's Greatest Teams Set 3 Ser.). (ENG., Illus.). 32p. (J). (gr. 2-5). lib. bdg. 34.21 *(978-1-68078-538-8(9)*, 23639, Big Buddy Bks.) ABDO Publishing Co.

MacRae, Sloan. The Philadelphia Phillies. 24p. (J). 2012. 49.50 *(978-1-4488-5150-8(5))* 2011. (ENG.). (gr. 2-3). pap. 9.25 *(978-1-4488-5149-2(1)*, 7191bf9c-384e-4548-bcde-c00fa2598de8) 2011. (ENG.). (gr. 2-3). lib. bdg. 26.27 *(978-1-4488-5008-2(8)*, 02f21102-d9dd-4e29-bb1c-b0695eaf981b) Rosen Publishing Group, Inc., The. (PowerKids Pr.).

Savage, Jeff. Ryan Howard. 2008. (Amazing Athletes Ser.). (Illus.). 32p. (J). (gr. 3-7). lib. bdg. 23.93 *(978-0-8225-8833-7(1)*, Lerner Pubns.) Lerner Publishing Group.

Stewart, Mark. The Philadelphia Phillies. 2012. (Team Spirit Ser.). 48p. (J). (gr. 3-6). lib. bdg. 29.27 *(978-1-59953-492-3(4))* Norwood Hse. Pr.

Tometich, Annabelle. Superstars of the Philadelphia Phillies. 2014. (Pro Sports Superstars - MLB Ser.). (ENG.). 24p. (J).

(gr. 1-4). lib. bdg. 27.10 *(978-1-60753-595-9(5)*, 16011) Amicus.

PHILANTHROPISTS

Basen, Ryan. Dwight Howard: Gifted & Giving Basketball Star, 1 vol. 2010. (Sports Stars Who Give Back Ser.). (ENG., Illus.). 128p. (gr. 5-6). 35.93 *(978-0-7660-3586-7(7)*, 20c5f538-d007-43e7-8f80-8de0c4362d5b) Enslow Publishing, LLC.

—Kyle Busch: Gifted & Giving Racing Star, 1 vol. 2010. (Sports Stars Who Give Back Ser.). (ENG., Illus.). 128p. (gr. 5-6). 35.93 *(978-0-7660-3589-8(1)*, 9c0a02b2-e85e-4fb8-9293-7cb8a7eb8ad0) Enslow Publishing, LLC.

Belmonte, Kevin. A Journey Through the Life of William Wilberforce: The Abolitionist Who Changed the Face of a Nation. 2007. (Illus.). 122p. *(978-0-89221-671-0(9))* New Leaf Publishing Group.

Benge, Janet & Benge, Geoff. Heroes of History - William Wilberforce: Take up the Fight. 2015. (ENG.). 218p. (YA). pap. 11.99 *(978-1-62486-057-7(5))* Emerald Bks.

Capua, Sarah De. Andrew Carnegie. 2007. (21st Century Skills Library: Life Skills Biographies Ser.). (Illus.). 48p. (gr. 4-8). lib. bdg. 34.93 *(978-1-60279-067-4(1)*, 200038) Cherry Lake Publishing.

De Lorenzo, Dawn. Peanut Butter & Jelly Possibilities: Youthful Inspirations. 2004. 96p. (J). (gr. 5-18). per. 12.95 *(978-0-9745190-0-5(6))* Crysalis Publishing, Inc.

Edge, Laura Bufano. Andrew Carnegie. 2004. (Lerner Biographies Ser.). (Illus.). 128p. (J). (gr. 6-12). lib. bdg. 27.93 *(978-0-8225-4965-9(4))* Lerner Publishing Group.

Gilliam, Scott. Andrew Carnegie: Industrial Giant & Philanthropist, 1 vol. 2009. (Essential Lives Set 3 Ser.). (ENG., Illus.). 112p. (YA). (gr. 6-12). lib. bdg. 41.36 *(978-1-60453-521-1(0)*, 6671, Essential Library) ABDO Publishing Co.

Gitlin, Marty. David Wright: Gifted & Giving Baseball Star, 1 vol. 2010. (Sports Stars Who Give Back Ser.). (ENG., Illus.). 128p. (gr. 5-6). 35.93 *(978-0-7660-3588-1(3)*, e7c8379c-84ba-428e-bef2-5940fbb3e36a) Enslow Publishing, LLC.

Kent, Zachary A. Andrew Carnegie: Industrialist & Philanthropist, 1 vol. 2014. (Legendary American Biographies Ser.). (ENG.). 96p. (gr. 6-6). pap. 13.88 *(978-0-7660-6436-2(0)*, 699940b5-73e2-48a5-829d-05a6f6a0215d) Enslow Publishing, LLC.

Moening, Kate. Melinda Gates: Philanthropist. 2020. (Women Leading the Way Ser.). (ENG., Illus.). 24p. (J). (gr. k-3). pap. 7.99 *(978-1-61891-797-3(8)*, 12582, Blastoff! Readers) Bellwether Media.

Orr, Tamra B. Oprah Winfrey. 2019. (ENG., Illus.). 32p. (J). 26.50 *(978-1-62469-428-8(4))* Purple Toad Publishing, Inc.

Parker, Lewis K. Andrew Carnegie & the Steel Industry. 2009. (American Tycoons Ser.). 24p. (gr. 3-3). 42.50 *(978-1-61511-388-0(6)*, PowerKids Pr.) Rosen Publishing Group, Inc., The.

Rajczak Nelson, Kristen. Andrew Carnegie & the Steel Industry, 1 vol. 2016. (Great Entrepreneurs in U. S. History Ser.). (ENG., Illus.). 32p. (J). (gr. 5-5). pap. 12.75 *(978-1-4994-2115-6(X)*, 86a635c6-2e46-4123-87f9-cf147087a193, PowerKids Pr.) Rosen Publishing Group, Inc., The.

Rappoport, Ken. Dale Earnhardt, Jr.: A Car Racer Who Cares, 1 vol. 2011. (Sports Stars Who Care Ser.). (ENG., Illus.). 48p. (gr. 3-3). pap. 11.53 *(978-1-59845-228-0(2)*, 16318e05-32bb-496d-9928-f51f33930119, Enslow Elementary); lib. bdg. 27.93 *(978-0-7660-3777-9(0)*, b854be65-d423-40f6-a010-24d9cca3be80) Enslow Publishing, LLC.

—David Wright: A Baseball Star Who Cares, 1 vol. 2011. (Sports Stars Who Care Ser.). (ENG., Illus.). 48p. (gr. 3-3). pap. 11.53 *(978-1-59845-229-7(0)*, 68ec2bed-6a13-44f7-99f1-9dcd892ddb91, Enslow Elementary); lib. bdg. 27.93 *(978-0-7660-3775-5(4)*, 3c698fc6-9a19-47c2-a321-0925828ad54d) Enslow Publishing, LLC.

Robinson, Tom. Ben Roethlisberger: Gifted & Giving Football Star, 1 vol. 2010. (Sports Stars Who Give Back Ser.). (ENG., Illus.). 128p. (gr. 5-6). lib. bdg. 35.93 *(978-0-7660-3590-4(5)*, 36739868-90b7-4937-adf6-368d2576a931) Enslow Publishing, LLC.

Roselius, J. Chris. David Beckham: Gifted & Giving Soccer Star, 1 vol. 2010. (Sports Stars Who Give Back Ser.). (ENG., Illus.). 128p. (gr. 5-6). lib. bdg. 35.93 *(978-0-7660-3587-4(5)*, e2f976aa-b6d9-4695-8418-0e59441985d5) Enslow Publishing, LLC.

Small, Cathleen. Melinda Gates: Philanthropist & Education Advocate, 1 vol. 2017. (Leading Women Ser.). (ENG.). 112p. (YA). (gr. 7-7). 41.64 *(978-1-5026-2707-0(8)*, a4b2b610-dab1-4807-adfd-e693276b757a) Cavendish Square Publishing LLC.

Sorensen, Lita. Mark Zuckerberg & Priscilla Chan: Top Couple in Tech & Philanthropy, 1 vol. 2018. (Influential Lives Ser.). (ENG.). 128p. (gr. 7-7). 40.27 *(978-1-9785-0345-8(8)*, d6eb6c78-4a06-4e93-acb1-860d86f0e963) Enslow Publishing, LLC.

Torres, John A. Shaun White: A Snowboarder & Skateboarder Who Cares, 1 vol. 2014. (Sports Stars Who Care Ser.). (ENG.). 48p. (gr. 3-3). pap. 11.53 *(978-1-4644-0535-8(2)*, f6a156ac-e19d-4d94-a5e6-73fe0c308035); lib. bdg. 27.93 *(978-0-7660-4295-7(2)*, 59117e52-bea6-4351-9be7-d013097c7ace) Enslow Publishing, LLC. (Enslow Elementary).

Waxman, Laura Hamilton. W. K. Kellogg. 2006. (History Maker Biographies Ser.). (Illus.). 48p. (J). (gr. 3-7). lib. bdg. 26.60 *(978-0-8225-6578-9(1)*, Lerner Pubns.) Lerner Publishing Group.

Wilner, Barry. Peyton Manning: A Football Star Who Cares, 1 vol. 2011. (Sports Stars Who Care Ser.). (ENG., Illus.). 48p. (gr. 3-3). pap. 11.53 *(978-1-59845-232-7(0)*, 69363360-41a2-44fa-9ac7-cf2b7e62bef1, Enslow Elementary); lib. bdg. 27.93 *(978-0-7660-3774-8(6)*, 904203d0-a579-49e7-b708-5ede16594e7f) Enslow Publishing, LLC.

—Tom Brady: A Football Star Who Cares, 1 vol. 2011. (Sports Stars Who Care Ser.). (ENG., Illus.). 48p. (gr. 3-3). pap. 11.53 *(978-1-59845-233-4(9)*, 86e96d2a-0393-47d4-b140-51f576bc23f5, Enslow Elementary); lib. bdg. 27.93 *(978-0-7660-3773-1(8)*, 592597ac-1e52-4ea6-9817-e8b59b577bb4) Enslow Publishing, LLC.

Yasuda, Anita. Hannah Taylor. 2011. 24p. (YA). (gr. 2-4). *(978-1-77071-646-9(7))*; pap. *(978-1-77071-650-6(5))* Weigl Educational Pubs. Ltd.

—Hannah Taylor. Ma Vie. Karvonen, Tanjah, tr. from ENG. 2011. (FRE., Illus.). 24p. (YA). (gr. 2-4). *(978-1-77071-434-2(0))* Weigl Educational Pubs. Ltd.

PHILANTHROPY

see Gifts; Social Service

PHILIP II, KING OF SPAIN, 1527-1598

Hilliam, David. Philip II: King of Spain & Leader of the Counter-Reformation. 2009. (Rulers, Scholars, & Artists of the Renaissance Ser.). 112p. (gr. 5-8). 66.50 *(978-1-60852-944-5(4)*, Rosen Reference) Rosen Publishing Group, Inc., The.

PHILIPPINE ISLANDS

see Philippines

PHILIPPINES

Anderson, Corey. Kumusta, Philippines. 2019. (Countries of the World Ser.). (ENG., Illus.). 48p. (J). (gr. 4-8). pap. 17.07 *(978-1-5341-5091-1(9)*, 213671); lib. bdg. 39.21 *(978-1-5341-4805-5(1)*, 213670) Cherry Lake Publishing.

Corrigan, Jim. Filipino Immigration. 2005. (Changing Face of North America Ser.). (Illus.). 112p. (YA). lib. bdg. 24.95 *(978-1-59084-684-1(2))* Mason Crest.

Daniels-Cowart, Catrina. Philippines. 2019. (Asian Countries Today Ser.). (Illus.). 96p. (J). (gr. 12). lib. bdg. 34.60 *(978-1-4222-4269-8(2))* Mason Crest.

Fazzi, Cindy. How to Draw the Philippines's Sights & Symbols. 2009. (Kid's Guide to Drawing the Countries of the World Ser.). 48p. (gr. 4-4). 53.00 *(978-1-61511-128-2(X)*, PowerKids Pr.) Rosen Publishing Group, Inc., The.

Franchino, Vicky. It's Cool to Learn about Countries: Philippines. 2010. (Explorer Library: Social Studies Explorer Ser.). (ENG., Illus.). 48p. (gr. 4-8). lib. bdg. 34.93 *(978-1-60279-834-2(6)*, 200534) Cherry Lake Publishing.

Goldsworthy, Steve. Philippines. 2014. (J). *(978-1-4896-3062-9(7))* Weigl Pubs., Inc.

Gray, Shirley W. The Philippines. 2003. (True Bks.). (ENG.). 48p. (J). (gr. 3-5). pap. 6.95 *(978-0-516-27775-2(8)*, Children's Pr.) Scholastic Library Publishing.

Gray, Shirley Wimbish. The Philippines. 2003. (True Bks.). (ENG., Illus.). 48p. (J). 25.00 *(978-0-516-24212-5(1)*, Children's Pr.) Scholastic Library Publishing.

Italia, Bob. The Philippines. 2003. (Countries Set 4 Ser.). 40p. (gr. k-6). 27.07 *(978-1-57765-842-9(6)*, Checkerboard Library) ABDO Publishing Co.

Jimenez, Gidget Roceles. All about the Philippines: Stories, Songs, Crafts & Games for Kids. Dandan-Albano, Corazon, illus. 64p. (J). (gr. 3-6). 2017. 14.95 *(978-0-8048-4848-0(3))* 2015. (ENG.). 16.95 *(978-0-8048-4072-9(5))* Tuttle Publishing.

Kalman, Bobbie. Spotlight on the Philippines. 2011. (Spotlight on My Country Ser.: No. 18). (ENG.). 32p. (J). (gr. k-3). pap. *(978-0-7787-3489-5(7))* Crabtree Publishing Co.

Longworth, Holly. The Philippines. 2015. (Countries We Come From Ser.). (ENG., Illus.). 32p. (J). (gr. k-3). lib. bdg. 28.50 *(978-1-62724-855-6(2))* Bearport Publishing Co., Inc.

Mattern, Joanne. Philippines, 1 vol. 2017. (Exploring World Cultures (First Edition) Ser.). (ENG.). 32p. (gr. 3-3). pap. 12.16 *(978-1-5026-3019-3(2)*, 54c361e3-d9a4-4057-8659-9db1cabc7fc4) Cavendish Square Publishing LLC.

Orr, Tamra. Filipino Heritage. 2018. (21st Century Junior Library: Celebrating Diversity in My Classroom Ser.). (ENG., Illus.). 24p. (J). (gr. 2-4). pap. 12.79 *(978-1-5341-0835-6(1)*, 210704); lib. bdg. 30.64 *(978-1-5341-0736-6(3)*, 210703) Cherry Lake Publishing.

Otfinoski, Steven. World War II Infantrymen: An Interactive History Adventure. 2013. (You Choose: World War II Ser.). (ENG., Illus.). 112p. (J). (gr. 3-7). pap. 6.95 *(978-1-62065-716-4(3)*, 121702, Capstone Pr.) Capstone.

Romulo, Liana. Filipino Celebrations: A Treasury of Feasts & Festivals. Dandan-Albano, Corazon, illus. 2012. 48p. (J). (gr. k-4). 16.95 *(978-0-8048-3821-4(6))* Tuttle Publishing.

—My First Book of Tagalog Words: An ABC Rhyming Book of Filipino Language & Culture. Laurel, Jaime, illus. 2018. (My First Words Ser.). 32p. (J). (gr. -1-3). 10.99 *(978-0-8048-5014-8(3))* Tuttle Publishing.

Schraff, Anne. Philippines. 2009. pap. 52.95 *(978-0-7613-4731-6(3))* Lerner Publishing Group.

Sexton, Colleen A. Philippines in Pictures. 2006. (Visual Geography Series, Second Ser.). (ENG., Illus.). 80p. (gr. 5-12). 31.93 *(978-0-8225-2677-3(8))* Lerner Publishing Group.

Sheen, Barbara. Foods of the Philippines, 1 vol. 2006. (Taste of Culture Ser.). (ENG., Illus.). 64p. (gr. 3-6). lib. bdg. 32.08 *(978-0-7377-3454-6(X)*, ba9e0497-5997-49f9-ba0e-94df1ed43e15, KidHaven Publishing) Greenhaven Publishing LLC.

Tope, Lily Rose, et al. Philippines, 1 vol. 3rd rev. ed. 2012. (Cultures of the World (Third Edition)(r) Ser.). (ENG., Illus.). 144p. (gr. 5-5). lib. bdg. 48.79 *(978-1-60870-993-9(0)*, c81b5809-c73b-4dbf-9042-f1a85eca4e1b) Cavendish Square Publishing LLC.

PHILIPPINES—FICTION

Blaine, John. The Golden Skull: Rick Brant Science Adventure Story. 2011. 224p. 44.95 *(978-1-258-09873-5(3))* Literary Licensing, LLC.

Cruz, Marie Miranda. Everlasting Nora. 2018. 287p. (YA). *(978-1-250-31468-0(2)*, Starscape) Doherty, Tom Assocs., LLC.

Daniel, Zoe. Angel: Through My Eyes - Natural Disaster Zones. White, Lyn, ed. 2019. (Through My Eyes Ser.). (ENG.). 192p. (J). (gr. 6-9). pap. 15.99 *(978-1-76011-377-3(8))* Allen & Unwin AUS. Dist: Independent Pubs. Group.

de la Paz, Myrna J. Abadeha: The Philippine Cinderella, 1 vol. Tang, Youshan, illus. 2014. (Cinderella Ser.). (ENG.). 32p. (J). (gr. 1-4). pap. 11.95 *(978-1-885008-44-2(9)*, leelowshens, Shen's Bks.) Lee & Low Bks., Inc.

Galang, M. Evelina. Angel de la Luna & the 5th Glorious Mystery. 2013. (ENG.). 304p. (J). (gr. 6). pap. 16.95 *(978-1-56689-333-6(X))* Coffee Hse. Pr.

Gourlay, Candy. Tall Story. 2012. (ENG.). 304p. (J). (gr. 5). 8.99 *(978-0-385-75233-6(4)*, Yearling) Random Hse. Children's Bks.

Guerrero, Tanya. How to Make Friends with the Sea. 2020. (ENG.). 368p. (J). 16.99 *(978-0-374-31199-5(4)*, 900197455, Farrar, Straus & Giroux (BYR)) Farrar, Straus & Giroux.

Hargrave, Kiran Millwood. The Island at the End of Everything. 2018. (ENG.). 256p. (J). (gr. 5). lib. bdg. 19.99 *(978-0-553-53533-4(1)*, Knopf Bks. for Young Readers) Random Hse. Children's Bks.

The Jesus Jeepney. 2007. 32p. pap. 4.50 *(978-0-8341-2276-5(6)*, 083-412-2766) Beacon Hill Pr. of Kansas City.

Koehler, Hanne Lore & Laraya-Coutts, Corie. A Tale of a Malipayon Warrior. 2010. 128p. 21.95 *(978-1-4502-1344-8(8))*; pap. 11.95 *(978-1-4502-1346-2(4))* iUniverse, Inc.

Lazo Gilmore, Dorina K. Cora Cooks Pancit. Valiant, Kristi, illus. 2014. (ENG.). 32p. (J). (gr. -1-3). 17.95 *(978-1-885008-35-0(X))*; (gr. k-4). pap. 11.95 *(978-1-885008-48-0(1)*, leelowshens) Lee & Low Bks., Inc. (Shen's Bks.).

Lennon, Andrew J. & Lennon, Jeffrey L. Things Can Get Better. 2010. 20p. 12.95 *(978-1-4490-9454-6(6))* AuthorHouse.

Polacco, Patricia. Tucky Jo & Little Heart. Polacco, Patricia, illus. 2015. (ENG., Illus.). 48p. (J). (gr. -1-3). 19.99 *(978-1-4814-1584-2(0)*, Simon & Schuster Bks. For Young Readers) Simon & Schuster Bks. For Young Readers.

Ralphson, G. Harvey. Boy Scouts in the Philippines. 2007. 112p. per. *(978-1-4068-3729-2(6))* Echo Library.

Ray, Keri. The Saving Journey. 2009. 48p. pap. 10.49 *(978-1-4389-5008-2(X))* AuthorHouse.

Ribay, Randy. Patron Saints of Nothing. 2019. (ENG., Illus.). 352p. (YA). (gr. 9). 19.99 *(978-0-525-55491-2(2)*, Kokila) Penguin Young Readers Group.

Romeu, Emma. Naufragio en las Filipinas. 2003.Tr. of Shipwrecked in the Philippines. (SPA., Illus.). 162p. (J). (gr. 5-8). pap. 9.95 *(978-968-19-0555-2(5))* Santillana USA Publishing Co., Inc.

Romulo, Liana. Filipino Friends. Dandan-Albano, Corazon, illus. 2006. 32p. (J). (gr. 1-3). 15.95 *(978-0-8048-3822-1(4))* Tuttle Publishing.

Schraff, Anne. Something Dreadful down Below, 1 vol. unabr. ed. 2010. (Q Reads Ser.). (ENG.). 32p. (YA). (gr. 9-12). pap. 8.50 *(978-1-61651-205-7(9))* Saddleback Educational Publishing, Inc.

Sia, Cress. The Bamboo Dance. Butler, Lisa, illus. 2011. (ENG.). 32p. (J). (gr. -1-3). 12.99 *(978-0-615-48984-1(2))* Hartlyn Kids Media, LLC.

Villanueva, Gail D. My Fate According to the Butterfly. 2019. (ENG.). 240p. (J). (gr. 3-7). 17.99 *(978-1-338-31050-4(X)*, Scholastic Pr.) Scholastic, Inc.

PHILOLOGY

see Language and Languages

PHILOSOPHERS

Abboud, Tony. Al Kindi: The Father of Arab Philosophy. 2009. (Great Muslim Philosophers & Scientists of the Middle Ages Ser.). 112p. (gr. 6-6). 66.50 *(978-1-61513-176-1(0)*, Rosen Reference) Rosen Publishing Group, Inc., The.

Anderson, Margaret J. & Stephenson, Karen F. Aristotle: Genius Philosopher & Scientist, 1 vol. 2014. (Genius Scientists & Their Genius Ideas Ser.). (ENG.). 96p. (gr. 5-5). (J). 29.60 *(978-0-7660-6535-2(9)*, 459c9f5a-2af5-44aa-bf25-accba6b3ee96); pap. 13.88 *(978-0-7660-6536-9(7)*, ac311030-e0fa-4387-98d2-2507ddcf9eaf) Enslow Publishing, LLC.

Bowen, Richard. Socrates: Greek Philosopher. 2013. (People of Importance Ser.: 21). (Illus.). 32p. (J). (gr. 4-18). 19.95 *(978-1-4222-2857-9(6))* Mason Crest.

Carew-Miller, Anna. Confucius: Great Chinese Philosopher. 2004. (Great Names Ser.). (Illus.). 32p. (J). (gr. 3-18). lib. bdg. 19.95 *(978-1-59084-149-5(2))* Mason Crest.

Cates, David. Karl Marx: Philosopher & Revolutionary, 1 vol. 2011. (Essential Lives Set 7 Ser.). (ENG., Illus.). 112p. (YA). (gr. 6-12). lib. bdg. 41.36 *(978-1-61783-005-1(4)*, 6749, Essential Library) ABDO Publishing Co.

Coakley, Louis C. & Karamanides, Dimitra. Pythagoras: Mathematician & Mystic, 1 vol. 2015. (Greatest Greek Philosophers Ser.). (ENG., Illus.). 112p. (J). (gr. 7-8). 38.80 *(978-1-4994-6132-9(1)*, ecf0f4c9-b0e9-4345-a709-89fab1ccae09, Rosen Young Adult) Rosen Publishing Group, Inc., The.

Coddington, Andrew. Henry David Thoreau: Writer of the Transcendentalist Movement, 1 vol. 2016. (Great American Thinkers Ser.). (ENG.). 128p. (YA). (gr. 9-9). 47.36 *(978-1-5026-1928-0(8)*, c7412a25-5d57-4984-96fe-10de8f021b02) Cavendish Square Publishing LLC.

Conklin, Wendy & Lee, Gisela. Confucius: Chinese Philosopher, 1 vol. rev. ed. 2007. (Social Studies: Informational Text Ser.). (ENG.). 32p. (gr. 4-8). pap. 11.99 *(978-0-7439-0437-7(0))* Teacher Created Materials, Inc.

Demi. Confucius: The Heart of China, 1 vol. 2018. (ENG., Illus.). 48p. (J). (gr. 3-12). 21.00 *(978-1-62014-193-9(0)*, leelowshens) Lee & Low Bks., Inc.

Demi & Demi. Al-Ghazali. 2015. (ENG., Illus.). 48p. (J). pap. 24.95 *(978-1-941610-12-1(9)*, P473973) Fons Vitae of Kentucky, Inc.

Dhillon, Natasha C. & Lim, Jun. Socrates: The Father of Ethics & Inquiry, 1 vol. 2015. (Greatest Greek Philosophers Ser.). (ENG.). 112p. (J). (gr. 7-8). 38.80 *(978-1-4994-6134-3(8)*, 4581f937-e9a9-4dbb-95d1-36a58e935818, Rosen Young Adult) Rosen Publishing Group, Inc., The.

DK. Children's Book of Philosophy: An Introduction to the World's Great Thinkers & Their Big Ideas. 2015. (DK Children's Book Of Ser.). (ENG., Illus.). 144p. (J). (gr. 3-7). 19.99 *(978-1-4654-2923-0(9)*, DK Children) Dorling Kindersley Publishing, Inc.

Duignan, Brian, ed. The Britannica Guide to the World's Most Influential People (Print/Ebook Combo Set) Print/Ebook Combo Set. 64 vols. Incl. 100 Most Influential Philosophers of All Time. (ENG.). 368p. (YA). (gr. 10-10). 2010. 113.18 *(978-1-61530-072-3(4)*, 247aac42-c737-4e0d-8e4a-b7306f082367); (Britannica Guide to the World's Most Influential People Ser.). (ENG.). 336-384p. 2010. 905.44 *(978-1-61530-165-2(8)*, ea8db089-fd00-4db0-8986-b9239413f7c8) Rosen Publishing Group, Inc., The.

Escalera, Manuel Silva. Cassandrita y Los Sabios: De Los 10 Mandamientos y Filosofia. 2012. (SPA.). 108p. (gr. -1). pap. 14.95 *(978-1-4772-0516-7(0))* AuthorHouse.

Gordon, Susan. Montesquieu: The French Philosopher Who Shaped Modern Government. 2009. (Philosophers of the Enlightenment Ser.). 112p. (gr. 5-8). 66.50 *(978-1-60851-166-2(9)*, Rosen Reference) Rosen Publishing Group, Inc., The.

Gow, Mary. The Great Philosopher: Plato & His Pursuit of Knowledge, 1 vol. 2010. (Great Minds of Ancient Science & Math Ser.). (ENG.). 128p. (gr. 4-6). 35.93 *(978-0-7660-3119-7(5)*, db65f425-a3cc-4994-8d27-e361a49ca90e) Enslow Publishing, LLC.

—The Great Thinker: Aristotle & the Foundations of Science, 1 vol. 2010. (Great Minds of Ancient Science & Math Ser.). (ENG.). 128p. (gr. 4-6). 35.93 *(978-0-7660-3121-0(7)*, ec09824d-bd32-4caa-b787-f641068f33b5) Enslow Publishing, LLC.

Hall, Derek, ed. Philosophy, Invention, & Engineering. 2009. (FAYFT: Great Scientists Ser.). 64p. (gr. 4-10). 39.95 *(978-1-933834-48-1(X))* Brown Bear Bks.

Harkins, Susan Sales & Harkins, William H. The Life & Times of Pythagoras. 2007. (Biography from Ancient Civilizations Ser.). (Illus.). 48p. (J). (gr. 4-8). lib. bdg. 29.95 *(978-1-58415-545-4(0))* Mitchell Lane Pubs.

Isle, Mick. Aristotle: Pioneering Philosopher & Founder of the Lyceum. 2009. (Library of Greek Philosophers Ser.). 112p. (gr. 6-6). 66.50 *(978-1-60853-658-0(0)*, Rosen Reference) Rosen Publishing Group, Inc., The.

Jones, Viola & Hasan, Heather. Archimedes: Innovative Mathematician, Engineer, & Inventor, 1 vol. 2015. (Greatest Greek Philosophers Ser.). (ENG., Illus.). 112p. (J). (gr. 7-8). 38.80 *(978-1-4994-6124-4(0)*, d67ff58c-961f-4a84-8672-79fea36ce271, Rosen Young Adult) Rosen Publishing Group, Inc., The.

Klepeis, Alicia. Pythagoras. 2017. (Junior Biography From Ancient Civilization Ser.). (Illus.). 48p. (J). (gr. 4-6). 29.95 *(978-1-68020-032-4(1))* Mitchell Lane Pubs.

Lim, Bridget & Viegas, Jennifer. Al-Kindi, 1 vol. 2016. (Physicians, Scientists, & Mathematicians of the Islamic World Ser.). (ENG.). 112p. (J). (gr. 6-6). 38.80 *(978-1-5081-7138-6(6)*, 16c5a865-6c6f-4d09-a0b4-06fba0154646) Rosen Publishing Group, Inc., The.

Lusted, Marcia. Plato. 2017. (Junior Biography From Ancient Civilization Ser.). 48p. (J). (gr. 4-6). 29.95 *(978-1-68020-026-3(7))* Mitchell Lane Pubs.

Martin. Dietrich Bonhoeffer. 2011. (Champion of Freedom Ser.). (gr. 7-12). 28.95 *(978-1-59935-169-8(2))* Reynolds, Morgan Inc.

Miller, Anna Carew & Carew-Miller, Anna. Confucius: Great Chinese Philosopher. 2013. (People of Importance Ser.: 21). (Illus.). 32p. (J). (gr. 4-18). 19.95 *(978-1-4222-2845-6(2))* Mason Crest.

Nagle, Jeanne, ed. Top 101 Philosophers, 1 vol., 1. 2013. (People You Should Know Ser.). (ENG.). 152p. (YA). (gr. 8-8). 38.84 *(978-1-62275-132-7(9)*, f41ca296-4894-4261-907e-22a62e0d0742) Rosen Publishing Group, Inc., The.

Philosophers of the Enlightenment, 12 vols. 2005. (Philosophers of the Enlightenment Ser.). (ENG., Illus.). (YA). (gr. 5-8). 238.80 *(978-1-4042-0620-5(5)*, bb27505d-81b2-463d-a566-9c01f8296bcb, Rosen Reference) Rosen Publishing Group, Inc., The.

Rodríguez, Ricardo. Walter Benjamin -Salida de Emergencia. 2005. (SPA.). 116p. (YA). *(978-958-30-1598-4(9))* Panamericana Editorial.

Roscoe, Kelly & Isle, Mick. Aristotle: The Father of Logic, 1 vol. 2015. (Greatest Greek Philosophers Ser.). (ENG.). 112p. (J). (gr. 7-8). 38.80 *(978-1-4994-6126-8(7)*, 2bbe47fc-070e-4c62-b4c9-ea47550e0b0e, Rosen Young Adult) Rosen Publishing Group, Inc., The.

Rosenberg, Aaron. Thomas Hobbes: An English Philosopher in the Age of Reason. (Philosophers of the Enlightenment Ser.). 112p. (gr. 5-8). 2009. 66.50 *(978-1-60851-167-9(7)*, Rosen Reference) 2005. (ENG., Illus.). (J). lib. bdg. 39.80 *(978-1-4042-0419-5(9)*, efb4c242-d7b1-4f93-828a-cbfed93074a5) Rosen Publishing Group, Inc., The.

Rössig, Wolfgang. Karl Marx. 2009. (Profiles in Economics Ser.). 112p. (YA). lib. bdg. 28.95 *(978-1-59935-132-2(3))* Reynolds, Morgan Inc.

Santillian, Beatriz & Randall, Bernard. Solon: Athenian Statesman & Poet, 1 vol. 2017. (Leaders of the Ancient World Ser.). (ENG., Illus.). 112p. (J). (gr. 6-6). 38.80 *(978-1-5081-7493-6(8)*, 9e229bc7-da52-47ff-8710-b22f9277c86a, Rosen Young Adult) Rosen Publishing Group, Inc., The.

Sharafeddine, Fatima. The Amazing Discoveries of Ibn Sina, 1 vol. Ali, Intelaq, illus. 2015. (ENG.). 32p. (J). (gr. 2-6). 17.95 *(978-1-55498-710-8(5))* Groundwood Bks. CAN. Dist: Publishers Group West (PGW).

Sherman, Patrice. John Locke: Philosopher of the Enlightenment, 1 vol. rev. ed. 2012. (Social Studies: Informational Text Ser.). (ENG.). 32p. (gr. 4-8). pap. 11.99 *(978-1-4333-5014-6(9))* Teacher Created Materials, Inc.

Taylor, Diane C. The Renaissance Thinkers: With History Projects for Kids. 2018. (the Renaissance for Kids Ser.). (ENG., Illus.). 112p. (J). (gr. 5-10). 22.95 *(978-1-61930-692-9(1)*, 3c9390fe-bce0-49a7-bc51-b4d53654767b) Nomad Pr.

Tent, M. B. W., ed. Gottfried Wilhelm Leibniz: The Polymath Who Brought Us Calculus. 2011. (ENG., Illus.). 260p. (C). 42.95 *(978-1-4398-9222-0(9)*, K14134) AK Peters, Ltd.

Tracy, Kathleen. The Life & Times of Confucius. 2004. (Biography from Ancient Civilizations Ser.). (Illus.). 48p. (J). (gr. 4-8). lib. bdg. 29.95 *(978-1-58415-246-0(X))* Mitchell Lane Pubs.

Trouvé, Marianne Lorraine. Saint Thomas Aquinas: Missionary of Truth. Morrison, Cathy, illus. 2015. 137p. (J). pap. 8.95 *(978-0-8198-9026-9(X))* Pauline Bks. & Media.

Urbina, Manuel Iván. Sören Kierkegaard -la conciencia de un Desesperado. 2005. (SPA.). 128p. (YA). *(978-958-30-1701-8(9))* Panamericana Editorial.

Viegas, Jennifer. William James: American Philosopher, Psychologist, & Theologian. 2009. (Library of American Thinkers Ser.). 112p. (gr. 6-6). 66.50 *(978-1-60853-517-0(7),* Rosen Reference) Rosen Publishing Group, Inc., The.

Whiting, Jim. The Life & Times of Plato. 2006. (Biography from Ancient Civilizations Ser.). (Illus.). 48p. (J). (gr. 3-7). lib. bdg. 29.95 *(978-1-58415-507-2(8),* 1259591) Mitchell Lane Pubs.

PHILOSOPHERS' STONE

see Alchemy

PHILOSOPHY

see also Belief and Doubt; Ethics; God; Good and Evil; Humanism; Knowledge, Theory of; Logic; Mind and Body; Psychology; Universe

also general subjects with the subdivision Philosophy, e.g. History—Philosophy, etc.

Carr, Aaron. Opuestos. 2013. (Ninos y la Ciencia Ser.). (SPA., Illus.). 24p. (J). (gr. -1-3). lib. bdg. 27.13 *(978-1-62127-611-1(2),* AV2 by Weigl) Weigl Pubs., Inc.

Cherenfant, Sabine, ed. Presentism: Reexamining Historical Figures Through Today's Lens, 1 vol. 2018. (At Issue Ser.). (ENG.). 128p. (gr. 10-12). 41.03 *(978-1-5345-0381-6(1),* fc1d0958-bb26-42be-9567-218594c9886a) Greenhaven Publishing LLC.

Dayton, Connor. Water. 2014. (Four Elements Ser.). (Illus.). 32p. (J). (gr. k-3). pap. 60.00 *(978-1-4777-9265-0(1))* Windmill Bks.

DK. Children's Book of Philosophy: An Introduction to the World's Great Thinkers & Their Big Ideas. 2015. (DK Children's Book Of Ser.). (ENG., Illus.). 144p. (J). (gr. 3-7). 19.99 *(978-1-4654-2923-0(9),* DK Children) Dorling Kindersley Publishing, Inc.

Earth, 1 vol. 2014. (Four Elements Ser.). (ENG.). 32p. (J). (gr. 3-3). pap. 11.00 *(978-1-4777-9273-5(2),* c694e598-90ea-41c0-b096-d083fc44b28a, Windmill Bks.) Rosen Publishing Group, Inc., The.

Fakhouri, Shoua. Ibn Sina: Level 13. 2019. (Collins Big Cat Ser.). (ENG.). 32p. (J). (gr. 4-6). pap. 8.99 *(978-0-00-829944-6(7))* HarperCollins Pubs. Ltd. GBR. Dist: Independent Pubs. Group.

Fire. 2014. (Four Elements Ser.). (Illus.). 32p. (J). (gr. k-3). pap. 60.00 *(978-1-4777-9269-8(4))* Windmill Bks.

Flynn, Sarah Wassner. This Book Is Cute: The Soft & Squishy Science & Culture of Aww. 2019. (Illus.). 112p. (J). (gr. 3-7). pap. 12.99 *(978-1-4263-3294-4(7));* (ENG., lib. bdg. 22.90 *(978-1-4263-3295-1(5))* Disney Publishing Worldwide. (National Geographic Kids).

Franco, Eloise. The Young Look. 2003. (Illus.). 168p. (gr. 3-7). 5.95 *(978-0-87516-294-2(0),* Devorss Pubns.) DeVorss & Co.

Gunderson, Jessica. How Long? Wacky Ways to Compare Length, 1 vol. Sinkovec, Igor, illus. 2013. (Wacky Comparisons Ser.). (ENG.). 24p. (J). (gr. -1-2). pap. 8.95 *(978-1-4795-1914-9(6),* 123621, Picture Window Bks.) Capstone.

Hill, Z. B. Optimism & Self-Confidence. Croft, Cindy, ed. 2014. (Causes & Effects of Emotions Ser.: 13). 64p. (J). (gr. 7-18). 23.95 *(978-1-4222-3076-3(7))* Mason Crest.

Honders, Christine. Understanding Points of View: Perspective-Taking, 1 vol. 2019. (Spotlight on Social & Emotional Learning Ser.). (ENG.). 24p. (gr. 4-6). 27.93 *(978-1-7253-0702-5(2),* 7a4e71e8-0da6-4694-a355-9b82cf89a49e, PowerKids Pr.) Rosen Publishing Group, Inc., The.

Houk, Katherine. The Little Book of Sticky Isms. 2010. (ENG.). 32p. 15.00 *(978-0-557-67022-2(5))* Lulu Pr., Inc.

Krishnamurti, Jiddu. Que Estas Haciendo con Tu Vida: Comentarios Sobre el Vivir para Jovenes. 2003. (Teen Bks. on Living: Vol. 1). (SPA., Illus.). 240p. *(978-84-7556-277-3(9),* 1500) Oceano Difusion Editorial, S. A.

Lehmann, Devra. Spinoza: The Outcast Thinker. 2014. (Illus.). xvii, 269p. (J). *(978-1-60898-180-9(0))* namelos llc.

Lightner, Laura. FirstFires. Messina, Linda, illus. 2008. 27p. (J). 31.99 *(978-1-4363-4542-2(1))* Xlibris Corp.

Markowitz-Meredith, Susan. What Is Form? 2009. (Get Art Smart Ser.). (ENG., Illus.). 24p. (J). (gr. k-4). lib. bdg. *(978-0-7787-5124-3(4));* (gr. 1-3). pap. *(978-0-7787-5138-0(4))* Crabtree Publishing Co.

McCurrach, Moriah. Kids Without Limits: You can be anything you want to Be! 2007. 52p. per. 9.95 *(978-0-595-46425-8(4))* iUniverse, Inc.

Morrison, Matthew. Big Questions: Incredible Adventures in Thinking. 2011. (ENG., Illus.). 204p. (J). (gr. 4-8). pap. 7.95 *(978-1-84046-670-6(7))* Icon Bks., Ltd. GBR. Dist: Publishers Group West (PGW).

Nelson, S. D. Greet the Dawn: The Lakota Way. 2012. (ENG., Illus.). 48p. 18.95 *(978-0-9845041-6-9(8),* P233293, South Dakota State Historical Society Pr.) South Dakota Historical Society Pr.

Phelan, J. W. Philosophy: Themes & Thinkers. 2005. (Cambridge International Examinations Ser.). (ENG., Illus.). 354p. (gr. 8-12). pap. 45.29 *(978-0-521-53742-1(8))* Cambridge Univ. Pr.

Philosophie: Scholastik, Logik, Metaphysik: Einblick in Modelle und Schulen der Philosophie. (Duden-Schuelerduden Ser.). (GER.). 492p. (YA). 27.95 *(978-3-411-02206-9(X))* Bibliographisches Institut & F. A. Brockhaus AG DEU. Dist: Continental Bk. Co., Inc.

Playing with Plato: The Republic as a Lens into Popular Culture. 2004. (YA). per. *(978-1-932948-05-9(8))* Student Pr. Initiative.

Ruggiero, Adriane, ed. Confucianism, 1 vol. 2005. (Religions & Religious Movements Ser.). (ENG.). 240p. (gr. 10-12). lib. bdg. 48.03 *(978-0-7377-2567-4(2),* 20026055-437f-45d7-a365-174d3826aba7, Greenhaven Publishing) Greenhaven Publishing LLC.

Seidman, David. What If I'm an Atheist? A Teen's Guide to Exploring a Life Without Religion. 2015. (ENG., Illus.). 256p. (YA). (gr. 7). pap. 12.99 *(978-1-58270-406-7(6))* Simon Pulse/Beyond Words.

Simpson, Deb. Pink Place Paperback. 2010. 32p. pap. 18.50 *(978-0-557-47673-2(9))* Lulu Pr., Inc.

Stark, Kristy. Life in Numbers. 2018. (TIME for KIDS(r): Informational Text Ser.). (ENG., Illus.). 12p. (J). (gr. k-1). 7.99 *(978-1-4258-4948-1(2))* Teacher Created Materials, Inc.

—La vida en números: Tus favoritos (Life in Numbers: Our Favorites) (Spanish Version) (Level K) rev. ed. 2019. (TIME for KIDS(r): Informational Text Ser.). (SPA., Illus.). 12p. (gr. k-1). 7.99 *(978-1-4258-2685-7(7))* Teacher Created Materials, Inc.

Teague Meyer, Terry. Optimism. 2013. (7 Character Strengths of Highly Successful Students Ser.). 64p. (J). (gr. 5-8). pap. 77.70 *(978-1-4488-9562-5(6));* (ENG.). (gr. 6-6). 37.12 *(978-1-4488-9545-8(6),* a7c55dec-5e8f-406e-a3eb-82fca6b94191); (ENG.). (gr. 6-6). pap. 13.95 *(978-1-4488-9561-8(8),* 703d9cba-817c-42a2-8e6b-04735ce0f2bc) Rosen Publishing Group, Inc., The.

Walker, Robert. Live It: Optimism. 2009. (ENG., Illus.). 32p. (J). (gr. 3-6). lib. bdg. *(978-0-7787-4887-8(1))* Crabtree Publishing Co.

Watts, Alan. The Fish Who Found the Sea. Le, Khoa, illus. 2020. (ENG.). 32p. (J). 17.99 *(978-1-68364-289-3(9),* 900220032) Sounds True, Inc.

Weakland, Mark. Football Opposites, 1 vol. 2013. (SI Kids Rookie Bks.). (ENG., Illus.). 32p. (J). (gr. -1-2). lib. bdg. 27.99 *(978-1-4296-9960-0(4),* 120667) Capstone.

—How Heavy? Wacky Ways to Compare Weight, 1 vol. Bolton, Bill, illus. 2013. (Wacky Comparisons Ser.). (ENG.). 24p. (J). (gr. -1-2). pap. 8.95 *(978-1-4795-1912-5(X),* 123619, Picture Window Bks.) Capstone.

—How Tall? Wacky Ways to Compare Height, 1 vol. Sinkovec, Igor, illus. 2013. (Wacky Comparisons Ser.). (ENG.). 24p. (J). (gr. -1-2). pap. 8.95 *(978-1-4795-1913-2(8),* 123620, Picture Window Bks.) Capstone.

Windsor, Susan, illus. Animals by Design: Exploring Unique Creature Features. 2018. 125p. (J). pap. *(978-1-946246-12-7(3))* Institute for Creation Research.

PHILOSOPHY, ANCIENT

Roscoe, Kelly & Isle, Mick. Aristotle: The Father of Logic, 1 vol. 2015. (Greatest Greek Philosophers Ser.). (ENG.). 112p. (J). (gr. 7-8). 38.80 *(978-1-4994-6126-8(7),* 2bbe47fc-070e-4c62-b4c9-ea47550e0b0e, Rosen Young Adult) Rosen Publishing Group, Inc., The.

PHILOSOPHY, GREEK

see Philosophy, Ancient

PHILOSOPHY, MORAL

see Ethics

PHILOSOPHY, ROMAN

see Philosophy, Ancient

PHILOSOPHY AND RELIGION

see also Religion—Philosophy

Watts, Alan. The Fish Who Found the Sea. Le, Khoa, illus. 2020. (ENG.). 32p. (J). 17.99 *(978-1-68364-289-3(9),* 900220032) Sounds True, Inc.

PHILOSOPHY OF RELIGION

see Religion—Philosophy

PHOENICIA

Reece, Katherine E. The Phoenicians: The Mysterious Sea People. 2004. (Ancient Civilizations Ser.). (Illus.). 48p. (gr. 4-8). lib. bdg. *(978-1-59515-236-7(9))* Rourke Educational Media.

PHONETICS

see also Speech; Voice

Acorn's Gold Mine. 2004. (J). cd-rom 39.00 *(978-1-890265-12-0(8))* Janelle Pubns., Inc.

Activity Worksheets. 2004. (J). spiral bd. 29.95 *(978-1-886441-64-4(2))* Zoo-phonics, Inc.

The Adventures of Tutankhamen: Level T. Group 2, 6 vols. (Sunshine Ser.). 48p. 44.95 *(978-0-7802-4175-6(4))* Wright Group/McGraw-Hill.

Akers, Martin & Benchmark Education Co., LLC Staff. Fran Grabs It. 2015. (BuildUp Ser.). (J). (gr. 1). *(978-1-4900-0719-9(9))* Benchmark Education Co.

—A Night Hunt for Food. 2015. (BuildUp Ser.). (J). (gr. 1). *(978-1-4900-0735-9(0))* Benchmark Education Co.

Al Circo, Al Circo! 2003. 35.50 *(978-0-8136-8083-5(2));* stu. ed. 35.50 *(978-0-8136-8081-1(6))* Modern Curriculum Pr.

Alfarrimas Phonics Kit. (J). (gr. k). 767.22 *(978-0-7362-2629-5(X))* CENGAGE Learning.

Alinas, Marv. Clark the Clam: The Sound of CL. 2017. (Consonant Blends Ser.). (ENG.). 24p. (J). (gr. -1-2). lib. bdg. 32.79 *(978-1-5038-1938-2(8),* 211535) Child's World, Inc, The.

—Crazy Crayons: The Sound of CR. 2017. (Consonant Blends Ser.). (ENG.). 24p. (J). (gr. -1-2). lib. bdg. 32.79 *(978-1-5038-1934-4(5),* 211538) Child's World, Inc, The.

Alliteration Configuration. 2006. (Illus.). 60p. (J). 24.99 *(978-0-9790434-0-6(9))* Jamiram Publishing.

Alphabet & Phonemic Awareness Activity Cards (OCR) 2004. (J). 14.95 *(978-1-56911-192-5(8))* Learning Resources, Inc.

Alphasnaps & Snapphonics: Snapphonics Big Book: Eek! Squeak! A Leak! 2003. 36.95 *(978-0-673-60206-0(0))* Celebration Pr.

Alphasnaps & Snapphonics: Snapphonics Big Book: Scat the Cat. 2003. 36.95 *(978-0-673-60207-7(9))* Celebration Pr.

Alphasnaps & Snapphonics: Snapphonics Package With 4 Big Books. 2003. 499.95 *(978-0-673-59265-1(0))* Celebration Pr.

Amoroso, Cynthia & Noyed, Bob. It Is Friday: The Sound of FR. 2017. (Consonant Blends Ser.). (ENG.). 24p. (J). (gr. -1-2). lib. bdg. 32.79 *(978-1-5038-1936-8(1),* 211539) Child's World, Inc, The.

Ancient Man of the Ice: Level T. Group 2, 6 vols. (Sunshine Ser.). 48p. 44.95 *(978-0-7802-4182-4(7))* Wright Group/McGraw-Hill.

Anin, Ravi & Benchmark Education Co., LLC Staff. In Our Town. 2015. (BuildUp Ser.). (J). (gr. 1). *(978-1-4900-0737-3(7))* Benchmark Education Co.

Anin, Ravi, et al. In Our Town - Ray Makes a Choice - a Room for Moose: BuildUp Unit 9 Lap Book. Anderson, Nicola, illus. 2015. (Build up Core Phonics Ser.). (J). (gr. 1). *(978-1-4900-2608-4(8))* Benchmark Education Co.

The Ants & the Grasshopper: R-Controlled Review: Level C, 6 vols. (Wright Skills Ser.). 16p. (gr. k-3). 26.50 *(978-0-322-01501-2(4))* Wright Group/McGraw-Hill.

Arita, Vera. Animals Sing Aloha. Louie, Ron, illus. 2009. (ENG.). 20p. (J). (gr. -1-1). bds. 7.95 *(978-1-933067-29-2(2))* Beachhouse Publishing, LLC.

Astroword: Complete CD-ROM & Lab Pack Sets. 2003. 1849.95 *(978-0-7652-0909-2(8));* 499.95 *(978-0-7652-0907-8(1))* Modern Curriculum Pr.

Astroword: Module 1-Phonemic Awareness (K-1) 2003. *(978-0-7652-0577-3(7))* Modern Curriculum Pr.

Astroword: Module 10-Vowel Digraphs & Diphthongs (1-3) 2003. 166.95 net. *(978-0-7652-0831-6(8))* Modern Curriculum Pr.

Astroword: Module 12-Base Words & Endings (2-6) 2003. 55.50 net. *(978-0-7652-0589-6(0))* Modern Curriculum Pr.

Astroword: Module 13-Compound Words (2-6) 2003. 55.50 net. *(978-0-7652-0590-2(4))* Modern Curriculum Pr.

Astroword: Module 14-Suffixes (2-6) 2003. 55.50 net. *(978-0-7652-0591-9(2));* 158.95 net. *(978-0-7652-0835-4(0))* Modern Curriculum Pr.

Astroword: Module 15-Prefixes (2-6) 2003. 55.50 net. *(978-0-7652-0592-6(0));* 158.95 net. *(978-0-7652-0836-1(9))* Modern Curriculum Pr.

Astroword: Module 6-Consonant Blends & Digraphs (1-2) 2003. 166.95 net. *(978-0-7652-0825-5(3))* Modern Curriculum Pr.

Astroword: Module 7-Long Vowels A, I (1-3) 2003. 166.95 net. *(978-0-7652-0826-2(1))* Modern Curriculum Pr.

Astroword: Module 8-Long Vowels I, O (1-3) 2003. 166.95 net. *(978-0-7652-0828-6(8))* Modern Curriculum Pr.

Astroword: Module 9-Long Vowels E, U (1-3) 2003. 166.95 net. *(978-0-7652-0829-3(6))* Modern Curriculum Pr.

Ballard, Peg. Chad Checks: The Sound of CH. 2017. (Consonant Blends Ser.). (ENG.). 24p. (J). (gr. -1-2). lib. bdg. 32.79 *(978-1-5038-1932-0(9),* 211534) Child's World, Inc, The.

—Shoes: The Sound of SH. 2017. (Consonant Blends Ser.). (ENG.). 24p. (J). (gr. -1-2). lib. bdg. 32.79 *(978-1-5038-1929-0(9),* 211541) Child's World, Inc, The.

—This & That: The Sound of TH. 2017. (Consonant Blends Ser.). (ENG.). 24p. (J). (gr. -1-2). lib. bdg. 32.79 *(978-1-5038-1930-6(2),* 211542) Child's World, Inc, The.

Baron, L. A Day with My Dad: Learning the D Sound. 2009. (PowerPhonics Ser.). 24p. (gr. 1-1). 39.90 *(978-1-60851-429-8(3),* PowerKids Pr.) Rosen Publishing Group, Inc., The.

Battiston, I. My Red Rose: Learning the R Sound. 2009. (PowerPhonics Ser.). 24p. (gr. 1-1). 39.90 *(978-1-60851-462-5(5),* PowerKids Pr.) Rosen Publishing Group, Inc., The.

The Battle of Bowling Street: Level 4, 6 vols. (Fluency Strand Ser.). (gr. 4-8). 45.00 *(978-1-4045-1224-5(1))* Wright Group/McGraw-Hill.

Beginning Consonants (Gr. K-1) 2003. (J). *(978-1-58232-037-3(3))* ECS Learning Systems, Inc.

Benchmark Education Company, LLC Staff, compiled by. BuildUp Phonics Skill Bag Set. 2006. (Phonics Ser.). (J). 2169.00 *(978-1-4108-6365-2(4))* Benchmark Education Co.

—Phonics Poetry Posters. 2008. (Phonics Ser.). (J). (gr. k-1). 289.00 *(978-1-4108-8450-3(3))* Benchmark Education Co.

—Phonological Awareness. 2005. pap. 47.00 *(978-1-4108-5064-5(1))* Benchmark Education Co.

—SpiralUp Phonics Lesson Resources. 2005. (Phonics Ser.). spiral bd. 470.00 *(978-1-4108-5832-0(4))* Benchmark Education Co.

—SpiralUp Phonics Skill Bag Set. 2006. (Phonics Ser.). (J). spiral bd. 825.00 *(978-1-4108-6366-9(2))* Benchmark Education Co.

—SpiralUp Phonics Support Tools. 2005. (Phonics Ser.). spiral bd. 180.00 *(978-1-4108-5833-7(2))* Benchmark Education Co.

—Start up Phonics Readers Add to Pack: Set Of 26. 2004. (Phonics Ser.). (J). pap. 98.00 *(978-1-4108-1500-2(5))* Benchmark Education Co.

—Start up Phonics Readers Set. ed. 2004. (Phonics Ser.). (J). spiral bd., instr.'s gde. ed. 575.00 *(978-1-4108-1489-0(0))* Benchmark Education Co.

Benjamin, Joseph, et al. Ten Red Hens - Get up, Meg! - Dan & Ed: StartUp Unit 6 Lap Book. Pike, Carol et al, illus. 2015. (Start up Core Phonics Ser.). (J). (gr. k). *(978-1-4900-2595-7(2))* Benchmark Education Co.

Bennett, Liza & Benchmark Education Co., LLC Staff. I Am Sam. 2015. (StartUp Ser.). (J). (gr. k). *(978-1-4900-0686-4(9))* Benchmark Education Co.

—I See. 2015. (StartUp Ser.). (J). (gr. k). *(978-1-4900-0687-1(7))* Benchmark Education Co.

Bennett, Liza & Ling, Lei. I Am Sam - I See - I See Nat: StartUp Unit 2 Lap Book. Palacios, Sara et al, illus. 2015. (Start up Core Phonics Ser.). (J). (gr. k). *(978-1-4900-2591-9(X))* Benchmark Education Co.

Benton, Celia & Benchmark Education Co., LLC Staff. Use It to Pull. 2015. (StartUp Ser.). (J). (gr. k). *(978-1-4900-0711-3(3))* Benchmark Education Co.

Bergen, Lara Rice. Phonics Comics: the Fearless Four - Level 2. Semple, Dave, illus. 2007. (ENG.). 24p. (J). (gr. 1-17). per. 3.99 *(978-1-58476-564-6(X))* Innovative Kids.

Blends & Digraphs (Gr. 1-2) 2003. (J). *(978-1-58232-109-7(4))* ECS Learning Systems, Inc.

Blevins, Wiley. Can You See It?, 6 vols., Set. 2003. (Phonics Readers 1-36 Ser.). (ENG.). 8p. (gr. k-1). pap. 29.70 *(978-0-7368-3191-8(6))* Capstone.

—Mapping the World, 6 vols., Set. 2004. (Phonics Readers Books 37-72 Ser.). (ENG.). 8p. (gr. k-1). pap. 35.70 *(978-0-7368-4075-0(3))* Capstone.

—Meat-Eating Plants, 6 vols., Set. 2004. (Phonics Readers Books 37-72 Ser.). (ENG.). 8p. (gr. k-1). pap. 35.70 *(978-0-7368-4065-1(6))* Capstone.

Blue Collection. (Elefonetica Ser.). (SPA.). (gr. 1-2). 373.22 *(978-0-7362-0795-9(3))* CENGAGE Learning.

Bradshaw, Georgine & Wrighton, Charlene. Basic Kit - Kindergarten. Clark, Irene, illus. 2005. Orig. Title: Basic Kit II. (J). 249.95 *(978-1-886441-31-6(6))* Zoo-phonics, Inc.

—Kindergarten Zoo-per Kit. Clark, Irene, illus. 2005. (J). 499.95 *(978-1-886441-34-7(0),* ZOP4219) Zoo-phonics, Inc.

—Preschool Zoo-per Kit. Clark, Irene, illus. 2005. (J). 449.95 *(978-1-886441-32-3(4),* ZOP4218) Zoo-phonics, Inc.

Brighter Child, compiled by. Phonics. 2006. (ENG., Illus.). 54p. (gr. -1-2). 2.99 *(978-0-7696-4749-4(9),* 0769647499, Brighter Child) Carson-Dellosa Publishing, LLC.

Brown, Jamal. Dora's Dolls: Practicing the d Sound, 1 vol. 2016. (Rosen Phonics Readers Ser.). (ENG.). 8p. (J). (gr. -1-2). pap. *(978-1-5081-3259-2(3),* be4917e2-614c-4349-9e3e-a610c7e08e22, Rosen Classroom) Rosen Publishing Group, Inc., The.

—The Eye Exam: Practicing the GZ Sound, 1 vol. 2016. (Rosen Phonics Readers Ser.). (ENG., Illus.). 12p. (J). (gr. -1-2). pap. *(978-1-5081-3603-3(3),* c4ae6ecc-2e07-47ee-b592-fdbfb6639c20, Rosen Classroom) Rosen Publishing Group, Inc., The.

—I Can Paint: Practicing the AI Sound, 1 vol. 2016. (Rosen Phonics Readers Ser.). (ENG.). 8p. (J). (gr. -1-2). pap. *(978-1-5081-3184-7(8),* f1274c1c-c889-480a-9d4a-d2077b879bb6, Rosen Classroom) Rosen Publishing Group, Inc., The.

—I See a Bee: Practicing the Ee Sound, 1 vol. 2016. (Rosen Phonics Readers Ser.). (ENG.). 8p. (J). (gr. -1-2). pap. *(978-1-5081-3328-5(X),* 0e73a5ec-d1f8-469f-a55e-a5ca086958de, Rosen Classroom) Rosen Publishing Group, Inc., The.

—The Lost Lion: Practicing the l Sound, 1 vol. 2016. (Rosen Phonics Readers Ser.). (ENG., Illus.). 8p. (J). (gr. -1-2). pap. *(978-1-5081-3100-7(7),* d3dd6af7-0523-4d6e-9a7d-e66c2331a990, Rosen Classroom) Rosen Publishing Group, Inc., The.

—Mr. Fox can fix it! Practicing the KS Sound, 1 vol. 2016. (Rosen Phonics Readers Ser.). (ENG., Illus.). 12p. (J). (gr. -1-2). pap. *(978-1-5081-3554-8(1),* 69a9b242-c1f7-4fba-a52e-f26feb2d324d, Rosen Classroom) Rosen Publishing Group, Inc., The.

Buitres En La Playa: Little Books, Level 4, Vol. 19. 2003. (Fonolibros Ser.). (SPA.). 25.50 *(978-0-7652-0096-9(1))* Modern Curriculum Pr.

Callella, Kim. Build-a-Skill Instant Books Short & Long Vowels. Shiotsu, Vicky & Faulkner, Stacey, eds. Campbell, Jenny & Tom, Darcy, illus. 2007. (J). 4.99 *(978-1-59198-412-2(2))* Creative Teaching Pr., Inc.

Campbell, Barbara. Lets Build Something: A Story Book/Coloring Book/Workbook. 2009. 64p. pap. 14.95 *(978-0-692-00349-7(5))* Mumford Institute.

Un Canguro en la Cocina! Little Books, Level 10, Vol. 2. 2003. (Fonolibros Ser.). (SPA.). 25.50 *(978-0-7652-0111-9(9))* Modern Curriculum Pr.

Carson Dellosa Education, compiled by. Phonics for Kindergarten, Grade K. 2010. (Home Workbooks Ser.: 12). (ENG.). 64p. (gr. k-k). pap. 4.49 *(978-1-60418-774-8(3),* 104343) Carson-Dellosa Publishing, LLC.

Carson-Dellosa Publishing Staff. Phonics for First Grade. 2010. (Home Workbooks Ser.: 11). (ENG.). 64p. (gr. 1-1). pap. 4.49 *(978-1-60418-785-4(9),* 104354) Carson-Dellosa Publishing, LLC.

Carson, J. Visiting the Vet: Learning the V Sound. 2009. (PowerPhonics Ser.). 24p. (gr. 1-1). 39.90 *(978-1-60851-476-2(5),* PowerKids Pr.) Rosen Publishing Group, Inc., The.

Cartwright, Stephen. Usborne Phonics Flashcards: Dog. Cartwright, Stephen, illus. 2007. (Usborne Flashcards Ser.). (Illus.). 48p. (J). (gr. -1-k). 9.99 *(978-0-7945-1516-4(9),* Usborne) EDC Publishing.

La Casa de Abuelito. 2003. (SPA., Illus.). 35.50 *(978-0-8136-8526-7(5))* Modern Curriculum Pr.

Cernak, Kim. Build-a-Skill Instant Books Consonant Blends & Digraphs. Shiotsu, Vicky & Faulkner, Stacey, eds. Campbell, Jenny & Tom, Darcy, illus. 2007. (J). 4.99 *(978-1-59198-410-8(6))* Creative Teaching Pr., Inc.

Classification (Gr. 1-2) 2003. (J). *(978-1-58232-040-3(3))* ECS Learning Systems, Inc.

Cleary, Brian P. The Bug in the Jug Wants a Hug. Miskimins, Jason, illus. 2009. (Sounds Like Reading (r) Ser.: 1). (ENG.). (gr. -1-2). pap. 39.62 *(978-0-7613-4700-2(3))* Lerner Publishing Group.

—Chips & Cheese & Nana's Knees: What Is Alliteration? Goneau, Martin, illus. 2015. (Words Are CATegorical (r) Ser.). (ENG.). 32p. (J). (gr. 2-5). lib. bdg. 17.95 *(978-1-4677-2649-8(4),* fc165dc4-e09c-4b51-8843-f79941bde702, Millbrook Pr.) Lerner Publishing Group.

—The Clown in the Gown Drives the Car with the Star. Miskimins, Jason, illus. 2009. (Sounds Like Reading (r) Ser.: 8). (ENG.). (gr. -1-2). pap. 39.62 *(978-0-7613-4707-1(0))* Lerner Publishing Group.

—The Frail Snail on the Trail. Miskimins, Jason, illus. 2009. (Sounds Like Reading (r) Ser.: 4). (ENG.). (gr. -1-2). pap. 39.62 *(978-0-7613-4703-3(8))* Lerner Publishing Group.

—The Nice Mice in the Rice. Miskimins, Jason, illus. 2009. (Sounds Like Reading (r) Ser.: 3). (ENG.). (gr. -1-2). pap. 39.62 *(978-0-7613-4702-6(X))* Lerner Publishing Group.

—Stop, Drop, & Flop in the Slop. Miskimins, Jason, illus. 2009. (Sounds Like Reading (r) Ser.: 2). (ENG.). (gr. -1-2). pap. 39.62 *(978-0-7613-4701-9(1))* Lerner Publishing Group.

—The Thing on the Wing Can Sing. Miskimins, Jason, illus. 2009. (Sounds Like Reading (r) Ser.: 5). (ENG.). (gr. -1-2). pap. 39.62 *(978-0-7613-4704-0(6))* Lerner Publishing Group.

—Whose Shoes Would You Choose. Miskimins, Jason, illus. 2009. (Sounds Like Reading (r) Ser.: 6). (ENG.). (gr. -1-2). pap. 39.62 *(978-0-7613-4705-7(4))* Lerner Publishing Group.

Cochran, Kate & Benchmark Education Co., LLC Staff. A Room for Moose. 2015. (BuildUp Ser.). (J). (gr. 1). *(978-1-4900-0739-7(3))* Benchmark Education Co.

Cochran, Kate, et al. Why Kittens Hide - Pete Mule's Hat - a Snail in May: BuildUp Unit 6 Lap Book. Piwowarski, Marcin et al, illus. 2015. (Build up Core Phonics Ser.). (J). (gr. 1). *(978-1-4900-2605-3(3))* Benchmark Education Co.

Coleccion A, Level A. (De Canciones A Cuentos Ser.). (SPA.). (gr. k-18). 444.07 *(978-1-56334-873-0(X))* CENGAGE Learning.

Coleccion B, Level B. (De Canciones A Cuentos Ser.). (SPA.). (gr. 1-18). 434.56 *(978-1-56334-991-1(4))* CENGAGE Learning.

Coleccion C, Level C. (De Canciones A Cuentos Ser.). (SPA.). (gr. 2-18). 406.81 *(978-0-7362-0440-8(7))* CENGAGE Learning.

Cole's Notes: Long Vowel o, CVCe Pattern: Level B, 6 vols. (Wright Skills Ser.). 16p. (gr. k-3). 17.95 *(978-0-322-03101-2(X))* Wright Group/McGraw-Hill.

Collins Big Cat. Phonics for Letters & Sounds Set 1. 2018. (Collins Big Cat Ser.). (ENG.). pap. 315.00

(978-0-00-827985-1(3)) HarperCollins Pubs. Ltd. GBR. Dist: Independent Pubs. Group.

Collins Easy Learning. Phonics Flashcards: Ideal for Home Learning. 2017. (Collins Easy Learning Preschool Ser.). (ENG.). 52p. (J). (gr. -1). 8.99 (978-0-00-820105-0(6)) HarperCollins Pubs. Ltd. GBR. Dist: Independent Pubs. Group.

—Phonics Quick Quizzes Ages 5-7: Ideal for Home Learning. 2017. (Collins Easy Learning KS1 Ser.). (ENG., Illus.). 32p. (J). (gr. k-2). pap. 6.99 (978-0-00-821244-5(9)) HarperCollins Pubs. Ltd. GBR. Dist: Independent Pubs. Group.

Come & Get It: Consonant l: Level A, 6 vols. (Wright Skills Ser.). 12p. (gr. k-3). 17.95 (978-0-322-03116-6(8)) Wright Group/McGraw-Hill.

Come on, Dot: Short Vowel o: Level A, 6 vols. (Wright Skills Ser.). 12p. (gr. k-3). 17.95 (978-0-322-03112-8(5)) Wright Group/McGraw-Hill.

Complete Phonics Readers Program. (Phonics Readers Ser.). (gr. k-2). 1322.95 (978-0-7368-4098-9(2), Red Brick Learning) Capstone.

Complete Program, Set D. 2004. (Phonics Readers Books 37-72 Ser.). (ENG.). 8p. (gr. k-1). pap. 428.40 (978-0-7368-4090-3(7)) Capstone.

Consonants (Gr. K-1) 2003. (J). (978-1-58232-108-0(6)) ECS Learning Systems, Inc.

Corner Store. (J). 21.95 (978-0-8136-4337-3(6)) Modern Curriculum Pr.

Crane, Kathy Dickerson. Phonics - The Gerbil Plays Guitar on the Girafee, Bk. 3. Klistoff, Lorin & Coan, Sharon, eds. McMahon, Kelly, illus. 2004. (Phonics (Teacher Created Resources) Ser.). (ENG.). 176p. pap. 17.99 (978-0-7439-3017-8(7)) Teacher Created Resources, Inc.

Cuando Seamos Grandes: Little Books. Level 12, Vol. 4. 2003. (Fonolibros Ser.). 35.50 (978-0-7652-0113-3(5)) Modern Curriculum Pr.

Cuentos de la Luna: Little Books, Level 20, Vol. 12. 2003. (Fonolibros Ser.). 34.95 (978-0-7652-0122-5(4)) Modern Curriculum Pr.

Dan & the Fan: Consonants d, f, n, p; Short Vowel a word families: Level A, 6 vols. (Wright Skills Ser.). 12p. (gr. k-3). 17.95 (978-0-322-01446-6(8)) Wright Group/McGraw-Hill.

Davies, Aysha & Benchmark Education Co., LLC Staff. Lunch for Patch. 2015. (BuildUp Ser.). (J). (gr. 1). (978-1-4900-0723-6(7)) Benchmark Education Co.

de Diaz, Rosario Ahumada. Juguemos a Leer: Libro de Lectura. (SPA.). (J). 6.95 (978-968-24-1220-2(X), TRM391) Trillas Editorial, S. A. MEX. Dist: Continental Bk. Co., Inc.

Delgado, Ben & Benchmark Education Co., LLC Staff. Big Bus. 2015. (BuildUp Ser.). (J). (gr. 1). (978-1-4900-0717-5(2)) Benchmark Education Co.

Den of Thieves: Level 6, 6 vols. (Fluency Strand Ser.). (gr. 4-8). 45.00 (978-1-4045-1238-2(1)) Wright Group/McGraw-Hill.

Un Desastre Monumental Vol. 12: Little Books, Level 4. 2003. (Fonolibros Ser.). 25.50 (978-0-7652-0089-1(9)) Modern Curriculum Pr.

Did You Know? Big Book: Level L. Group 1. (Sunshine Ser.). 24p. 36.50 (978-0-322-00334-7(2)) Wright Group/McGraw-Hill.

Diego, John & Benchmark Education Co., LLC Staff. Go Slow, Go Fast. 2015. (BuildUp Ser.). (J). (gr. 1). (978-1-4900-0731-1(8)) Benchmark Education Co.

—Grace & Ace. 2015. (BuildUp Ser.). (J). (gr. 1). (978-1-4900-0727-4(X)) Benchmark Education Co.

Diego, John, et al. Go Slow, Go Fast - Read a USA Time Line - High in the Sky: BuildUp Unit 7 Lap Book. 2015. (Build up Core Phonics Ser.). (J). (gr. 1). (978-1-4900-2606-0(1)) Benchmark Education Co.

Discovering Phonics. 2005. (ENG., Illus.). (J). (978-0-9774310-7-6(X)) Educational Tools, Inc.

DK. DK Workbooks: Spelling, Second Grade: Learn & Explore. 2015. (DK Workbooks Ser.). (ENG.). 60p. (J). (gr. 1-3). pap. 6.99 (978-1-4654-2912-4(3), DK Children) Dorling Kindersley Publishing, Inc.

—DK Workbooks: Spelling, Third Grade: Learn & Explore. 2015. (DK Workbooks Ser.). (ENG.). 60p. (J). (gr. 2-4). pap. 6.99 (978-1-4654-2913-1(1), DK Children) Dorling Kindersley Publishing, Inc.

Donde Viven? Little Books, Level 8, Vol. 14. 2003. (Fonolibros Ser.). 25.50 (978-0-7652-0091-4(0)) Modern Curriculum Pr.

Don't Scratch, Max! (Consonant x), Level K. 2003. ("Plaid" Phonics & Stories Libraries). (gr. k-1). 34.95 (978-0-8136-9126-8(5)) Modern Curriculum Pr.

Douglas, Vincent & Blevins, Wiley. Money, 6, Set. 2004. (Phonics Readers Books 37-72 Ser.). (ENG.). 8p. (gr. k-1). pap. 35.70 (978-0-7368-4052-1(4)) Capstone.

Dr Awkward: Level 6, 6 vols. (Fluency Strand Ser.). (gr. 4-8). 45.00 (978-1-4045-1239-9(X)) Wright Group/McGraw-Hill.

En Busca de Bravo: Little Books, Level 12, Vol. 27. 2003. (Fonolibros Ser.). 35.50 (978-0-7652-0106-5(2)) Modern Curriculum Pr.

En el Bano, 6, Pack. (Chiquilibros Ser.). (SPA.). (gr. k-1). 23.00 (978-0-7635-8616-4(1)) Rigby Education.

En el Supermercado, 6, Pack. (Chiquilibros Ser.). (SPA.). (gr. k-1). 23.00 (978-0-7635-8617-1(X)) Rigby Education.

En la Playa, 6, Pack. (Chiquilibros Ser.). (SPA.). (gr. k-1). 23.00 (978-0-7635-8618-8(8)) Rigby Education.

Esa Mosca! Little Books, Level 3, Vol. 15. 2003. (Fonolibros Ser.). 25.50 (978-0-7652-0092-1(9)) Modern Curriculum Pr.

Esparza, Thomas, Jr., prod. Esther's Playhouse, Disk C. 2004. (Illus.). (J). cd-rom (978-1-879817-44-9(6), Children) Star Light Pr.

Evan-Moor Educational Publishers. Basic Phonics Skills Level A. 2004. (Basic Phonics Skills Ser.). (ENG., Illus.). 288p. (J). (gr. -1-k). pap., tchr. ed. 29.99 (978-1-55799-966-5(X)) Evan-Moor Educational Pubs.

—Basic Phonics Skills Level B. 2004. (Basic Phonics Skills Ser.). (ENG., Illus.). 288p. (J). (gr. k-1). pap., tchr. ed. 29.99 (978-1-55799-967-2(8), EMC 3319) Evan-Moor Educational Pubs.

—Basic Phonics Skills Level C. 2004. (Basic Phonics Skills Ser.). (ENG., Illus.). 288p. (J). (gr. 1-2). pap., tchr. ed. 29.99 (978-1-55799-968-9(6), EMC 3320) Evan-Moor Educational Pubs.

—Basic Phonics Skills Level D. 2004. (Basic Phonics Skills Ser.). (ENG., Illus.). 288p. (J). (gr. 2-3). pap., tchr. ed. 29.99 (978-1-55799-969-6(4), EMC 3321) Evan-Moor Educational Pubs.

—Phonics Centers Grades 1-2. 2004. (Take It to Your Seat: Phonics Centers Ser.). (ENG., Illus.). 192p. (J). (gr. 1-2). pap., tchr. ed. 24.99 (978-1-55799-982-5(1), EMC 3329) Evan-Moor Educational Pubs.

—Phonics Centers Grades K-1. 2004. (Take It to Your Seat: Phonics Centers Ser.). (ENG., Illus.). 192p. (J). (gr. k-1). pap., tchr. ed. 24.99 (978-1-55799-981-8(3), EMC 3328) Evan-Moor Educational Pubs.

—Phonics Centers Grades Pre-K-K. 2004. (Take It to Your Seat: Phonics Centers Ser.). (ENG., Illus.). 192p. (J). (gr. -1-k). pap., tchr. ed. 24.99 (978-1-55799-980-1(5), EMC 3327) Evan-Moor Educational Pubs.

The Farm: Individual Title Six-Packs. (Chiquilibros Ser.). (gr. k-1). 23.00 (978-0-7635-0413-7(0)) Rigby Education.

The Farm: Individual Title Two-Packs. (Chiquilibros Ser.). (gr. -1-1). 12.00 (978-0-7635-8529-7(7)) Rigby Education.

Fast Forward! 2003. (Fast Forward! Ser.). Level C. (J). (gr. 1-18). stu. ed., per. 7.95 (978-1-58830-779-8(4))Level D. (J). (gr. 2-18). stu. ed., per. 67.95 (978-1-58830-334-9(9))Level D. (J). (gr. 2-18). stu. ed., per. 7.95 (978-1-58830-780-4(8))Level A. tchr. ed., per., tchr.'s training gde. ed. 39.95 (978-1-58830-783-5(2))Level A. (J). (gr. 1-18). stu. ed., per. 7.95 (978-1-58830-777-4(8))Level B. tchr. ed., per., tchr.'s training gde. ed. 39.95 (978-1-58830-784-2(0))Level B. (J). (gr. 1-18). stu. ed., per. 7.95 (978-1-58830-778-1(6))Level E. (J). (gr. 1-18). stu. ed., per. 7.95 (978-1-58830-781-1(6))Level E. (J). (gr. 2-18). stu. ed., per. 67.95 (978-1-58830-335-6(7))Level F. (J). (gr. 2-18). stu. ed., per. 67.95 (978-1-58830-336-3(5))Level F. (J). (gr. 2-18). stu. ed., per. 7.95 (978-1-58830-782-8(4)) Metropolitan Teaching & Learning Co.

Feldman, Jean. Dr Jean Variety Pack. 2007. (J). (gr. -1-3). pap. 56.87 incl. audio compact disk (978-1-59198-719-2(9)) Creative Teaching Pr., Inc.

Fenner, M. On My Block: Learning the BL Sound. 2009. (PowerPhonics Ser.). 24p. (gr. 1-1). 39.90 (978-1-60851-464-9(1), PowerKids Pr.) Rosen Publishing Group, Inc., The.

Flip, Flap, & Fluff: Family Blends: Level B, 6 vols. (Wright Skills Ser.). 16p. (gr. k-3). 17.95 (978-0-322-01459-6(X)) Wright Group/McGraw-Hill.

Flynn, Cam & Benchmark Education Co., LLC Staff. Mark Sees the Stars. 2015. (BuildUp Ser.). (J). (gr. 1). (978-1-4900-0734-2(2)) Benchmark Education Co.

—Paul Takes a Walk. 2015. (BuildUp Ser.). (J). (gr. 1). (978-1-4900-0741-0(5)) Benchmark Education Co.

Flynn, Cam, et al. Mark Sees the Stars - a Night Hunt for Food - Red Bird Chirps: BuildUp Unit 8 Lap Book. Filipina, Monika et al, illus. 2015. (Build up Core Phonics Ser.). (J). (gr. 1). (978-1-4900-2607-7(X)) Benchmark Education Co.

Fonolibros Series: Complete Stage One. 2003. (SPA.). 1230.95 (978-0-7652-1052-4(5)) Modern Curriculum Pr.

Fonolibros Series: Complete Stage Two. 2003. (SPA.). 895.50 (978-0-7652-1053-1(3)) Modern Curriculum Pr.

Fowler, Allan. Sound-a-Likes: Homonyms & Phonics, 4 bks., Set. Cafferata, Sue, illus. (J). (gr. k-4). lib. bdg. 73.80 (978-1-56674-901-5(8)) Forest Hse. Publishing Co., Inc.

The Fox: Consonants q, x, z; -ack, -ick, -ill word families: Level A, 6 vols. (Wright Skills Ser.). 12p. (gr. k-3). 17.95 (978-0-322-01456-5(5)) Wright Group/McGraw-Hill.

Gale, John E. Speedyread: A Phonics-Based Reading & Spelling Program. 2005. 353p. ring bd. 275.00 (978-0-9777683-0-1(9)) Mirror Pond Publishing.

Gallagher, Carole M. Little ABC Phonics Workbook. 2006. 283p. (J). 14.50 (978-0-9702197-1-8(7)) Gallagher, Carole M.

Garcia, Isabella. Cow on theTown: Practicing the OW Sound, 1 vol. 2016. (Rosen Phonics Readers Ser.). (ENG., Illus.). 12p. (J). (gr. -1-2). pap. (978-1-5081-3566-1(5), 2fded99f-5e3c-41b4-9e99-516255391e23, Rosen Classroom) Rosen Publishing Group, Inc., The.

—Fred Goes Fishing: Practicing the F Sound, 1 vol. 2016. (Rosen Phonics Readers Ser.). (ENG., Illus.). 8p. (J). (gr. -1-2). pap. (978-1-5081-3077-2(9), 57979073-4860-4ef3-9ab2-15e58fd59c50, Rosen Classroom) Rosen Publishing Group, Inc., The.

—Fun in the Sun: Practicing the Short U Sound, 1 vol. 2016. (Rosen Phonics Readers Ser.). (ENG.). 8p. (J). (gr. -1-2). pap. (978-1-5081-3297-4(6), 438e1d1c-79b9-4bfe-a334-b98d431f5a79, Rosen Classroom) Rosen Publishing Group, Inc., The.

—The Goat in my Boat: Practicing the OA Sound, 1 vol. 2016. (Rosen Phonics Readers Ser.). (ENG., Illus.). 8p. (J). (gr. -1-2). pap. (978-1-5081-3008-6(6), 72329619-1565-46f8-ab6d-79859dfe2576, Rosen Classroom) Rosen Publishing Group, Inc., The.

—Our Yard Sale: Practicing the Y Sound, 1 vol. 2016. (Rosen Phonics Readers Ser.). (ENG.). 12p. (J). (gr. -1-2). pap. (978-1-5081-3214-1(3), 43d5400b-7198-41dd-9255-bb51edcc7ec8, Rosen Classroom) Rosen Publishing Group, Inc., The.

—Tiny Toys: Practicing the T Sound, 1 vol. 2016. (Rosen Phonics Readers Ser.). (ENG.). 8p. (J). (gr. -1-2). pap. (978-1-5081-3247-9(X), 748ec251-b9f7-4e4e-a4f8-1bf2ac15ce25, Rosen Classroom) Rosen Publishing Group, Inc., The.

—What is that Noise? Practicing the OI Sound, 1 vol. 2016. (Rosen Phonics Readers Ser.). (ENG.). 12p. (J). (gr. -1-2). pap. (978-1-5081-3590-6(8), 2ef121a7-a0db-42dc-b4b9-d1320410cea2, Rosen Classroom) Rosen Publishing Group, Inc., The.

—Ziggy the Zebra: Practicing the Z Sound, 1 vol. 2016. (Rosen Phonics Readers Ser.). (ENG., Illus.). 12p. (J). (gr. -1-2). pap. (978-1-5081-3042-0(6), 3139a32c-a6d0-480a-b6a4-1a80349336fe, Rosen Classroom) Rosen Publishing Group, Inc., The.

El Gato Que Rompio las Reglas: Little Books, Level 18, Vol. 7. 2003. (Fonolibros Ser.). 35.50 (978-0-7652-0117-1(8)) Modern Curriculum Pr.

Gaydos, Nora. Now I'm Reading! Slide, See & Say Flashcards - 50 Short Vowel Words! 2011. (ENG., Illus.). 25p. (J). (gr. -1-2). 9.99 (978-1-60169-074-6(6)) Innovative Kids.

—Phonics Comics: Pony Tales - Level 1. Hamilton, Pamela, illus. 2007. (ENG.). 24p. (J). (gr. 1-17). per. 3.99 (978-1-58476-553-0(4)) Innovative Kids.

Gifford, Myrna. Talking & Walking: A Read-and-Sing Book. Cooper, Frances, illus. 2005. 12p. (J). 9.95 (978-0-9720763-9-5(5)) Action Factor, Inc.

—Two Little Letters: A Read-and-Sing Book. Cooper, Frances, illus. 2005. 12p. (J). 9.95 (978-0-9720763-8-8(7)) Action Factor, Inc.

—What's That Sound? A Read-and-Sing Book. Cooper, Frances, illus. 2003. 12p. (J). 9.95 (978-0-9720763-3-3(6)) Action Factor, Inc.

Gifford, Myrna Ross. Outlaws: A Read-and-Sing Book. Cooper, Frances, illus. 2005. 12p. (J). 9.95 (978-0-9754618-1-5(8)) Action Factor, Inc.

—Silent E: A Read-and-Sing Book. Cooper, Frances, illus. 2005. 12p. (J). 9.95 (978-0-9754618-0-8(X)) Action Factor, Inc.

Giglio, Judy. Dreaming of Great Ideas, 6 vols., Set. 2004. (Phonics Readers Books 37-72 Ser.). (ENG.). 8p. (gr. k-1). pap. 35.70 (978-0-7368-4064-4(8)) Capstone.

—Sounds & How We Hear Them, 6 vols., Set. 2004. (Phonics Readers Books 37-72 Ser.). (ENG.). 8p. (gr. k-1). pap. 35.70 (978-0-7368-4069-9(9)) Capstone.

Goldish. Lights, Camera, Action: Small Books X6 (Discovery Phonics), Level B. 2003. ("Plaid" Phonics & Stories Libraries). (gr. 2-3). 38.50 (978-0-8136-9147-3(8)) Modern Curriculum Pr.

Gomez, Sonia & Benchmark Education Co., LLC Staff. It Can Fit! 2015. (StartUp Ser.). (J). (gr. k). (978-1-4900-0690-1(7)) Benchmark Education Co.

Green Collection. (Elefonetica Ser.). (SPA.). (gr. 1-2). 324.85 (978-0-7362-0784-3(8)) CENGAGE Learning.

Green, Lila & Benchmark Education Co., LLC Staff. Mr. Dan Has a Plan. 2015. (BuildUp Ser.). (J). (gr. 1). (978-1-4900-0713-7(X)) Benchmark Education Co.

Green, Lila, et al. Mr. Dan Has a Plan - We Can Fix It! - a Big Job: BuildUp Unit 1 Lap Book. Chambers, Nick, illus. 2015. (Build up Core Phonics Ser.). (J). (gr. 1). (978-1-4900-2600-8(2)) Benchmark Education Co.

Grizzly & the Bumble-bee: Big Book: Level K. Group 1. (Sunshine Ser.). 16p. 36.50 (978-0-7802-5789-4(8)) Wright Group/McGraw-Hill.

Group/McGraw-Hill, Wright. Phonics & Word Study Complete Kits: Phonics & Word Study: Level A. (gr. k-3). 339.95 (978-0-322-03871-4(5)) Wright Group/McGraw-Hill.

—Phonics & Word Study Complete Kits: Phonics & Word Study: Level B. (gr. k-3). 429.50 (978-0-322-03872-1(3)) Wright Group/McGraw-Hill.

—Sunshine: Early Emergent - Group 3: 1 Each of 4 Student Books: Level A. (Sunshine Ser.). 16.95 (978-0-322-03707-6(7)) Wright Group/McGraw-Hill.

—Sunshine: Early Emergent - Group 3: 1 Each of 4 Student Books: Level C. (Sunshine Ser.). 16.95 (978-0-322-03709-0(3)) Wright Group/McGraw-Hill.

—Sunshine: Early Emergent - Group 3:1 Each of 4 Student Books: Level B. (Sunshine Ser.). 16.95 (978-0-322-03708-3(5)) Wright Group/McGraw-Hill.

—The Wright Skills: Level A Sets - 1 Each of 40 Titles (includes Short Vowels) (Wright Skills Ser.). (gr. k-3). (978-0-322-03873-8(1)) Wright Group/McGraw-Hill.

—The Wright Skills: Level A Sets - 6 Each of 40 Titles (includes Short Vowels) (Wright Skills Ser.). (gr. k-3). 730.50 (978-0-322-03874-5(X)) Wright Group/McGraw-Hill.

—The Wright Skills: Level A Sets - Short Vowels only: 1 Each of 19 Titles. (Wright Skills Ser.). (gr. k-3). 56.95 (978-0-322-06473-7(2)) Wright Group/McGraw-Hill.

—The Wright Skills: Level A Sets - Short Vowels only: 6 Each of 19 Titles. (Wright Skills Ser.). (gr. k-3). 122.95 (978-0-322-06474-4(0)) Wright Group/McGraw-Hill.

—The Wright Skills: Level B Sets - 1 Each of 40 Titles (includes long Vowels) (Wright Skills Ser.). (gr. k-3). 143.95 (978-0-322-03878-3(2)) Wright Group/McGraw-Hill.

—The Wright Skills: Level B Sets - 6 Each of 40 Titles (includes long Vowels) (gr. k-3). 860.50 (978-0-322-03880-6(4)) Wright Group/McGraw-Hill.

Guardians of the Garden: Level 3, 6 vols. (Fluency Strand Ser.). (gr. 4-8). 45.00 (978-1-4045-1218-4(7)) Wright Group/McGraw-Hill.

Guille-Marrett, Emily & Raby, Charlotte. Collins Big Cat Phonics for Letters & Sounds - Sound Walk: Band 00/Lilac. Gurrea, Susana, illus. 2018. (Collins Big Cat Phonics Ser.). (ENG.). 16p. (J). (— 1). pap. 6.99 (978-0-00-825127-7(4)) HarperCollins Pubs. Ltd. GBR. Dist: Independent Pubs. Group.

Hands on Consonant Sounds (Gr. K-1) 2003. (J). (978-1-58232-115-8(9)) ECS Learning Systems, Inc.

Hands on Sight Words (Gr. 1-2) 2003. (J). (978-1-58232-118-9(3)) ECS Learning Systems, Inc.

Hands on Vowel Sounds (Gr. 1-2) 2003. (J). (978-1-58232-116-5(7)) ECS Learning Systems, Inc.

Hap & the Hat: Consonant h: Level A, 6 vols. (Wright Skills Ser.). 12p. (gr. k-3). 17.95 (978-0-322-03110-4(9)) Wright Group/McGraw-Hill.

Harcourt School Publishers Staff. Collections: Phonics Activity Book. 2003. (First-Place Reading Ser.). (Illus.). (gr. k-6). 6.90 (978-0-15-313423-4(2)) Harcourt Schl. Pubs.

—Decodable Book, Bk. 17. 3rd ed. 2003. (Trophies Ser.). pap. 7.00 (978-0-15-326764-2(X)) Harcourt Schl. Pubs.

Hasbrouck, Ph.D., Jan, contrib. by. Quick Phonics Assessment. 2007. spiral bd. 200.00 (978-1-4108-6802-2(8)) Benchmark Education Co.

Hassan, Miriam & Benchmark Education Co., LLC Staff. Gabe, Kate, Dave. 2015. (StartUp Ser.). (J). (gr. k). (978-1-4900-0708-3(3)) Benchmark Education Co.

—Go up, up, Up. 2015. (StartUp Ser.). (J). (gr. k). (978-1-4900-0696-3(6)) Benchmark Education Co.

—Win, Win, Win! 2015. (StartUp Ser.). (J). (gr. k). (978-1-4900-0701-4(6)) Benchmark Education Co.

Hassan, Miriam, et al. Win, Win, Win! - I Am Lin - Jim & Jan: StartUp Unit 7 Lap Book. Palacios, Sara, illus. 2015. (Start up Core Phonics Ser.). (J). (gr. k). (978-1-4900-2596-4(0)) Benchmark Education Co.

HB Staff. Fantastic Phonics Practice!, 40 bks., Set. 97th ed. 2003. (Harcourt Title I Reading Programs Ser.). (gr. 1-18). pap. 130.20 (978-0-15-309070-7(7)) Harcourt Schl. Pubs.

Headway Level D Real Phonics Workbook A. (J). (gr. 2). (978-0-89688-294-2(2), 88-294) SRA/McGraw-Hill.

Headway Level F Real Phonic Workbook. (J). (gr. 3). (978-0-89688-295-9(0), 88-295) SRA/McGraw-Hill.

Hidden Pictures Phonics (Gr. 1-2) 2003. (J). (978-1-58232-064-9(0)) ECS Learning Systems, Inc.

Hinkler Books Staff, ed. Phonics. 2009. (ENG.). 24p. (J). 9.99 (978-0-8249-1400-4(7), Ideals Pubns.) Worthy Publishing.

Hirsh, Mia & Benchmark Education Co., LLC Staff. Cat in a Cap. 2015. (StartUp Ser.). (J). (gr. k). (978-1-4900-0693-2(1)) Benchmark Education Co.

—Val Is a Vet. 2015. (StartUp Ser.). (J). (gr. k). (978-1-4900-0706-9(7)) Benchmark Education Co.

Hogenkamp, S. My Birthday: Learning the IR Sound. 2009. (PowerPhonics Ser.). 24p. (gr. 1-1). 39.90 (978-1-60851-460-1(9), PowerKids Pr.) Rosen Publishing Group, Inc., The.

Hollander, Cass. Keeping Fit, 6 vols., Set. 2004. (Phonics Readers Books 37-72 Ser.). (ENG.). 8p. (gr. k-1). pap. 35.70 (978-0-7368-4058-3(3)) Capstone.

Hooked on Phonics - Get Ready to Read - Letter Names. 2005. (J). (gr. -1-18). 99.99 (978-1-931020-46-6(9)) HOP, LLC.

Hooked on Phonics - Get Ready to Read - Letter Sounds. 2005. (J). (gr. -1-18). 99.99 (978-1-931020-47-3(7)) HOP, LLC.

HOP, LLC. Hooked on Phonics Beginning Reading with Bible Stories. 2006. 29.99 (978-1-931020-80-0(9)) HOP, LLC.

—Hooked on Phonics Learn to Read (Kindergarten & First Grade) 2006. 139.99 (978-1-931020-95-4(7)) HOP, LLC.

—Hooked on Phonics Reading Comprehension. 2006. 64p. 3.79 (978-1-933863-94-8(3)) HOP, LLC.

—Hooked on Phonics Word Games. 2006. 64p. 3.79 (978-1-933863-93-1(5)) HOP, LLC.

HOP LLC Staff. Hooked on Phonics - Learn to Read Kindergarten. 2005. (J). (gr. k-18). 69.99 (978-1-931020-29-9(9)) HOP, LLC.

—Hooked on Phonics - Learn to Read Second Grade. 2005. (J). (gr. 2-18). 69.99 (978-1-931020-31-2(0)) HOP, LLC.

HOP LLC Staff, ed. Hooked on Phonics - Learn to Read First Grade. 2005. (J). (gr. 1-18). 69.99 (978-1-931020-30-5(2)) HOP, LLC.

La Hora de Comer, 6 Packs. (Chiquilibros Ser.). (SPA.). (gr. k-1). 23.00 (978-0-7635-8590-7(4)) Rigby Education.

Hsu, Kim & Benchmark Education Co., LLC Staff. Read a USA Time Line. 2015. (BuildUp Ser.). (J). (gr. 1). (978-1-4900-0732-8(6)) Benchmark Education Co.

Huggles Can Jungle: Level A. Group 1. (Sunshine Ser.). 8p. 20.95 (978-0-7802-5707-8(3)) Wright Group/McGraw-Hill.

I Can Say S. (Illus.). 160p. 19.95 (978-0-937857-88-5(2), 1478) Speech Bin, Inc., The.

I'm Learning My Phonics. 2004. (Flash Card + Music CD Learning Kits Ser.). (Illus.). 20p. 18.99 (978-1-894677-61-5(7)) Kidzup Productions.

J My Name Is Jess: Take-Home Book. 2005. (Emergent Library: Vol. 2). (YA). (gr. -1-1). 12.60 (978-0-8215-7265-8(2)) Sadlier, William H. Inc.

Jake's Big Day: Long Vowel a, CVCe Pattern: Level B, 6 vols. (Wright Skills Ser.). 16p. (gr. k-3). 17.95 (978-0-322-01465-7(4)) Wright Group/McGraw-Hill.

Joe's Toe: Long o Digraphs: Level B, 6 vols. (Wright Skills Ser.). 16p. (gr. k-3). 26.50 (978-0-322-01480-0(8)) Wright Group/McGraw-Hill.

Jog to the Dam: Consonants g, h, j; Short Vowel o word families: Level A, 6 vols. (Wright Skills Ser.). 12p. (gr. k-3). 17.95 (978-0-322-01448-0(4)) Wright Group/McGraw-Hill.

Johnson, Bruce. We Read Phonics-A Day at the Zoo. Johnson, Meredith, illus. 2012. 32p. (J). 9.95 (978-1-60115-349-4(X)); pap. 4.99 (978-1-60115-350-0(3)) Treasure Bay, Inc.

Johnson, Juliette. Birthday Thief: Practicing the Unvoiced TH Sound, 1 vol. 2016. (Rosen Phonics Readers Ser.). (ENG.). 12p. (J). (gr. -1-2). pap. (978-1-5081-3236-3(4), dd12a3ed-fdee-4f86-9c9a-5a5c24b48d75, Rosen Classroom) Rosen Publishing Group, Inc., The.

—I Have Another Brother: Practicing the Voiced TH Sound, 1 vol. 2016. (Rosen Phonics Readers Ser.). (ENG., Illus.). 12p. (J). (gr. -1-2). pap. (978-1-5081-3557-9(6), 5bd176f0-e5a1-42fb-bd1b-c84b32421d8a, Rosen Classroom) Rosen Publishing Group, Inc., The.

—The King & the Ring: Practicing the Ng Sound, 1 vol. 2016. (Rosen Phonics Readers Ser.). (ENG., Illus.). 12p. (J). (gr. -1-2). pap. (978-1-5081-3118-2(X), d5580e62-3b10-45d2-bc17-fd4f51922dff, Rosen Classroom) Rosen Publishing Group, Inc., The.

—We Love to Learn: Practicing the I Sound, 1 vol. 2016. (Rosen Phonics Readers Ser.). (ENG.). 8p. (J). (gr. -1-2). pap. (978-1-5081-3279-0(8), 92ade07b-fa95-4553-874b-55dd7bdb550f, Rosen Classroom) Rosen Publishing Group, Inc., The.

Johnson, Tiffany & Benchmark Education Co., LLC Staff. I. 2015. (StartUp Ser.). (J). (gr. k). (978-1-4900-0684-0(2)) Benchmark Education Co.

—Kids Have Fun. 2015. (StartUp Ser.). (J). (gr. k). (978-1-4900-0704-5(0)) Benchmark Education Co.

Johnson, Tiffany, et al. Kids Have Fun - Yes, Cubs! - Val Is a Vet: StartUp Unit 8 Lap Book. Leonidou, Niki, illus. 2015. (Start up Core Phonics Ser.). (J). (gr. k). (978-1-4900-2597-1(9)) Benchmark Education Co.

Jones, Shelley V. & Gunn, Barbara. Read Well Magazine Unit 20: Slanted Text. 2003. (Read Well Level K Ser.). (Illus.). 8p. (J). (978-1-59318-104-8(3)) Cambium Education, Inc.

—Shells on the Shore: Read Well Level K Unit 14 Storybook. Jerde, Susan, illus. 2003. (Read Well Level K Ser.). 20p. (J). (978-1-57035-685-8(8), 55546) Cambium Education, Inc.

Jones, Tambor & Benchmark Education Co., LLC Staff. Cole & Rose. 2015. (BuildUp Ser.). (J). (gr. 1). (978-1-4900-0726-7(1)) Benchmark Education Co.

Jordan, Sara & Brudzynski, Jack. Funky Phonics Learn to Read. 2004. (Funky Phonics Learn to Read Ser.: 2). (ENG., Illus.). 64p. (J). pap. 15.95 (978-1-55386-011-2(X), 155386011X) Jordan, Sara Publishing.

Kalar, Bonnie. At Dawn. Spreen, Kathe, illus. Date not set. 8p. (J). (gr. -1-2). pap. (978-1-891619-24-3(1)) Corona Pr.

—At the Lake. Spreen, Kathe, illus. Date not set. 12p. (J). (gr. -1-2). pap. (978-1-891619-34-2(9)) Corona Pr.

—At the Pond. Spreen, Kathe, illus. Date not set. 8p. (J). (gr. -1-2). pap. (978-1-891619-07-6(1)) Corona Pr.

—At the Zoo. Spreen, Kathe, illus. Date not set. 8p. (J). (gr. -1-2). pap. (978-1-891619-18-2(7)) Corona Pr.

—Beth & Thad. Spreen, Kathe, illus. Date not set. 12p. (J). (gr. -1-2). pap. (978-1-891619-17-5(9)) Corona Pr.

—The Bird & the Shirt. Spreen, Kathe, illus. Date not set. 12p. (J). (gr. -1-2). pap. (978-1-891619-30-4(6)) Corona Pr.

—Burt. Spreen, Kathe, illus. Date not set. 8p. (J). (gr. -1-2). pap. (978-1-891619-31-1(4)) Corona Pr.

—Chuck & the Chick. Spreen, Kathe, illus. Date not set. 8p. (J). (gr. -1-2). pap. (978-1-891619-16-8(0)) Corona Pr.

—The Clown. Spreen, Kathe, illus. Date not set. 12p. (J). (gr. -1-2). pap. (978-1-891619-22-9(5)) Corona Pr.

—The Cook & the Crook. Spreen, Kathe, illus. Date not set. 12p. (J). (gr. -1-2). pap. (978-1-891619-29-8(2)) Corona Pr.

—The Crows. Spreen, Kathe, illus. Date not set. 8p. (J). (gr. -1-2). pap. (978-1-891619-28-1(4)) Corona Pr.

—A Dream. Spreen, Kathe, illus. Date not set. 12p. (J). (gr. -1-2). pap. (978-1-891619-23-6(3)) Corona Pr.

—Early Phonetic Readers - Set A, 5 bks., Set. Spreen, Kathe, illus. Incl. Bob. pap. (978-1-891619-01-4(2)); Cat & the Ant. pap. (978-1-891619-02-1(0)); Gus on the Bus. pap. (978-1-891619-03-8(9)); Hen & the Jet. pap. (978-1-891619-05-2(5)); Tim & Kim. pap. (978-1-891619-04-5(7)); 8p. (J). (gr. -1-2). 1998. (Illus.). 8.25 (978-1-891619-00-7(4)) Corona Pr.

—Early Phonetic Readers - Set B, 5 bks., Set. Spreen, Kathe, illus. Incl. At the Pond. pap. (978-1-891619-07-6(1)); Fran & the Doll. pap. (978-1-891619-09-0(8)); Fred. pap. (978-1-891619-10-6(1)); Stan & His Sled. pap. (978-1-891619-08-3(X)); Trip. pap. (978-1-891619-11-3(X)); 8p. (J). (gr. -1-2). (Illus.). 8.25 (978-1-891619-06-9(3)) Corona Pr.

—Early Phonetic Readers - Set C, 20 bks., Set. Spreen, Kathe, illus. Incl. At Dawn. 8p. pap. (978-1-891619-24-3(1)); At the Zoo. 8p. pap. (978-1-891619-18-2(7)); Beth & Thad. 12p. pap. (978-1-891619-17-5(9)); Bird & the Shirt. 12p. pap. (978-1-891619-30-4(6)); Bright Light. 8p. 5.25 hd (978-1-891619-32-8(2)); Burt. 8p. pap. (978-1-891619-31-1(4)); Chuck & the Chick. 8p. pap. (978-1-891619-16-8(0)); Clown. 12p. pap. (978-1-891619-22-9(5)); Cook & the Crook. 12p. pap. (978-1-891619-29-8(2)); Crows. 8p. pap. (978-1-891619-28-1(4)); Dream. 12p. pap (978-1-891619-23-6(3)); Gail Sails. 12p. pap. (978-1-891619-20-5(9)); Gay & Jay Play. 8p. pap. (978-1-891619-19-9(5)); Jack. 12p. pap. (978-1-891619-13-7(6)); Joan's Coat. 12p. pap. (978-1-891619-21-2(7)); Josh & the Fish. 8p. pap. (978-1-891619-14-4(4)); Lew & His New Cap. 8p. pap. (978-1-891619-27-4(6)); Mark at the Farm. 12p. pap. (978-1-891619-25-0(X)); Scouts. 8p. pap. (978-1-891619-26-7(8)); Sheep & the Bee. 8p. pap. (978-1-891619-15-1(2)); (J). (gr. -1-2). (Illus.). 38.50 (978-1-891619-12-0(8)) Corona Pr.

—Early Phonetic Readers - Set D, 3 bks., Set. Spreen, Kathe, illus. Incl. At the Lake. 12p. pap. (978-1-891619-34-2(9)); Mike. 8p. pap. (978-1-891619-35-9(7)); Rose & the Mole. 12p. pap. (978-1-891619-36-6(5)); (J). (gr. -1-2). (Illus.). 6.25 (978-1-891619-33-5(0)) Corona Pr.

—Early Phonetic Readers - Set E, 7 bks., set. Spreen, Kathe, illus. Incl. Ann Paints & Plays. pap. (978-1-891619-40-3(3)); Clair at Home. pap. (978-1-891619-44-1(6)); Good Day. pap. (978-1-891619-41-0(1)); Kirk & the Deer. pap. (978-1-891619-43-4(8)); Miss Lane's Class. pap. (978-1-891619-38-0(1)); Neal Camps Out. pap. (978-1-891619-39-7(X)); Trip to the Beach. pap. (978-1-891619-42-7(X)); 12p. (J). (gr. -1-2). (Illus.). Set pap. 14.50 (978-1-891619-37-3(3)) Corona Pr.

—Fran & the Doll. Spreen, Kathe, illus. Date not set. 8p. (J). (gr. -1-2). pap. (978-1-891619-09-0(8)) Corona Pr.

—Fred. Spreen, Kathe, illus. Date not set. 8p. (J). (gr. -1-2). pap. (978-1-891619-10-6(1)) Corona Pr.

—Gail Sails. Spreen, Kathe, illus. Date not set. 12p. (J). (gr. -1-2). pap. (978-1-891619-20-5(9)) Corona Pr.

—Gay & Jay Play. Spreen, Kathe, illus. Date not set. 8p. (J). (gr. -1-2). pap. (978-1-891619-19-9(5)) Corona Pr.

—Joan's Coat. Spreen, Kathe, illus. Date not set. 12p. (J). (gr. -1-2). pap. (978-1-891619-21-2(7)) Corona Pr.

—Lew & His New Cap. Spreen, Kathe, illus. Date not set. 8p. (J). (gr. -1-2). pap. (978-1-891619-27-4(6)) Corona Pr.

—Mark at the Farm. Spreen, Kathe, illus. Date not set. 12p. (J). (gr. -1-2). pap. (978-1-891619-25-0(X)) Corona Pr.

—Mike. Spreen, Kathe, illus. Date not set. 8p. (J). (gr. -1-2). pap. (978-1-891619-35-9(7)) Corona Pr.

—Rose & the Mole. Spreen, Kathe, illus. Date not set. 12p. (J). (gr. -1-2). pap. (978-1-891619-36-6(5)) Corona Pr.

—The Sheep & the Bee. Spreen, Kathe, illus. Date not set. 8p. (J). (gr. -1-2). pap. (978-1-891619-15-1(2)) Corona Pr.

—Stan & His Sled. Spreen, Kathe, illus. Date not set. 8p. (J). (gr. -1-2). pap. (978-1-891619-08-3(X)) Corona Pr.

—The Trip. Spreen, Kathe, illus. Date not set. 8p. (J). (gr. -1-2). pap. (978-1-891619-11-3(X)) Corona Pr.

Karsten, Dylan. At the Museum: Practicing the YOO Sound, 1 vol. 2016. (Rosen Phonics Readers Ser.). (ENG.). 12p. (J). (gr. -1-2). pap. (978-1-5081-3238-7(0), 5703a5c6-a20d-44a7-8b2f-e43f72e43931, Rosen Classroom) Rosen Publishing Group, Inc., The.

—Dad's Day Off: Practicing the D Sound, 1 vol. 2016. (Rosen Phonics Readers Ser.). (ENG., Illus.). 8p. (J). (gr. -1-2). pap. (978-1-5081-3081-9(7), fdafcd2e-e350-4cad-9316-8cadc55886fb, Rosen Classroom) Rosen Publishing Group, Inc., The.

—I Can Measure It: Practicing the Zh Sound, 1 vol. 2016. (Rosen Phonics Readers Ser.). (ENG.). 12p. (J). (gr. -1-2). pap. (978-1-5081-3599-9(1), e0040e6c-7534-4d45-a01f-da7617e4f252, Rosen Classroom) Rosen Publishing Group, Inc., The.

—A Job in a Shop: Practicing the Short o Sound, 1 vol. 2016. (Rosen Phonics Readers Ser.). (ENG.). 8p. (J). (gr. -1-2). pap. (978-1-5081-3257-8(7), 8fa390e7-a48c-4f83-b4bc-b787ef68ef78, Rosen Classroom) Rosen Publishing Group, Inc., The.

—My Coach: Practicing the OA Sound, 1 vol. 2016. (Rosen Phonics Readers Ser.). (ENG.). 8p. (J). (gr. -1-2). pap. (978-1-5081-3188-5(0), 563596c8-51a1-432b-861c-25009265b96d, Rosen Classroom) Rosen Publishing Group, Inc., The.

—No Sleep for the Queen: Practicing the EE Sound, 1 vol. 2016. (Rosen Phonics Readers Ser.). (ENG., Illus.). 8p. (J). (gr. -1-2). pap. (978-1-5081-3147-2(3), 654cb723-91ab-483b-a023-fa4eae7207a1, Rosen Classroom) Rosen Publishing Group, Inc., The.

—Things in Spring: Practicing the NG Sound, 1 vol. 2016. (Rosen Phonics Readers Ser.). (ENG.). 12p. (J). (gr. -1-2). pap. (978-1-5081-3298-1(4), 45b085b1-6b56-4c67-a5c3-caa7ef05962a, Rosen Classroom) Rosen Publishing Group, Inc., The.

Katschke, Judy. Phonics Comics. Baumann, Marty, illus. 2006. (ENG.). 24p. (J). (gr. 1-17). per. 3.99 (978-1-58476-411-3(2), IKIDS) Innovative Kids.

Kertell, Lynn Maslen. Bob Books - First Stories Box Set | Phonics, Ages 4 & up, Kindergarten (Stage 1: Starting to Read), 1 vol. Sullivan, Dana, illus. 2015. (Bob Bks.). (ENG.). 12p. (J). (gr. -1-1). pap., pap., pap. 17.99 (978-0-545-73409-7(6)) Scholastic, Inc.

Khatri, Meeta. Can You Sound Out with Me? 2012. (ENG.). 35p. (J). pap. 14.95 (978-1-4327-8618-2(0)) Outskirts Pr., Inc.

Kindergarten Review 1.1: Take-Home Version. 2004. (Scott Foresman Reading Ser.). (gr. 1-18). stu. ed. 48.00 (978-0-328-02543-5(7)) Addison-Wesley Educational Pubs., Inc.

King, Amber. Carrot Cake: Practicing the Hard C - K Sound, Vol. 1. 2016. (Rosen Phonics Readers Ser.). (ENG.). 8p. (J). (gr. -1-2). pap. (978-1-5081-3261-5(5), 5a7fc36e-cf49-4f0f-baff-2a04a98bfa26, Rosen Classroom) Rosen Publishing Group, Inc., The.

—Fan in Autumn: Practicing the AU Sound, 1 vol. 2016. (Rosen Phonics Readers Ser.). (ENG.). 12p. (J). (gr. -1-2). pap. (978-1-5081-3283-7(6), e01018ea-eefd-4975-902f-26c4ab10aff2, Rosen Classroom) Rosen Publishing Group, Inc., The.

—It's a Shark: Practicing the SH Sound, 1 vol. 2016. (Rosen Phonics Readers Ser.). (ENG.). 12p. (J). (gr. -1-2). pap. (978-1-5081-3228-8(3), b9f95e6e-0c2d-439b-8aac-95c39a8fe327, Rosen Classroom) Rosen Publishing Group, Inc., The.

—The Toad in My Tent: Practicing the T Sound, 1 vol. 2016. (Rosen Phonics Readers Ser.). (ENG., Illus.). 8p. (J). (gr. -1-2). pap. (978-1-5081-3069-7(8), 3b923d54-e696-4678-9a2a-aa8908222f57, Rosen Classroom) Rosen Publishing Group, Inc., The.

Kozyrev, Joann. Sound Bites: Pronunciation Activities. 2004. (ENG.). 256p. (C). pap. 40.95 (978-0-618-25972-4(4), 330538) Thomson ELT.

Kratky, Lada, et al. Alphachant Phonics K: Phonics Kit. 2003. (Summer School Ser.). (ENG.). (C). (gr. -1-k). pap. 1568.95 (978-0-7362-2020-0(8)) CENGAGE Learning.

Kumon. My Book Rhyming Words Long Vowels. 2007. (Kumon Workbooks Ser.). (ENG., Illus.). 80p. pap. 7.95 (978-1-933241-37-1(3)) Kumon Publishing North America, Inc.

Ladybird. BBC Earth: Dangerous Journeys Activity Book: Level 4. 2017. (Ladybird Readers Ser.). (ENG.). 16p. (J). (gr. k-2). 4.99 (978-0-241-29872-5(5)) Penguin Bks., Ltd. GBR. Dist: Independent Pubs. Group.

Ladybird I'm Ready for Phonics: Say the Sounds. 2016. (Ladybird I'm Ready Ser.). (ENG., Illus.). 48p. (J). (gr. -1-1). pap. 11.99 (978-0-241-21598-2(6)) Penguin Bks., Ltd. GBR. Dist: Independent Pubs. Group.

Lane, Tracy & Benchmark Education Co., LLC Staff. A Snail in May. 2015. (BuildUp Ser.). (J). (gr. 1). (978-1-4900-0730-4(X)) Benchmark Education Co.

Lane, Tracy, et al. Shade Lake - Cole & Rose - Grace & Ace: BuildUp Unit 5 Lap Book. Chambers, Nick & Battuz, Christine, illus. 2015. (Build up Core Phonics Ser.). (J). (gr. 1). (978-1-4900-2604-6(5)) Benchmark Education Co.

LaRosa, Paula & Benchmark Education Co., LLC Staff. I Am Pat. 2015. (StartUp Ser.). (J). (gr. k). (978-1-4900-0691-8(5)) Benchmark Education Co.

—Time to Tug. 2015. (StartUp Ser.). (J). (gr. k). (978-1-4900-0710-6(5)) Benchmark Education Co.

LaRosa, Paula, et al. Time to Tug - Use a Mule - Can He See Me? StartUp Unit 10 Lap Book. 2015. (Start up Core Phonics Ser.). (J). (gr. k). (978-1-4900-2599-5(5)) Benchmark Education Co.

Las Estaciones: Individual Title Two-Packs. (Chiquilibros Ser.). (SPA.). (gr. -1-1). 12.00 (978-0-7635-8563-1(7)) Rigby Education.

Laurence, Jo. How to Be a Wizard at Phonics. 48p. (J). (gr. 1-4). pap. (978-1-875739-64-6(5)) Wizard Bks.

Lectura en Familia: Spanish Phonics Grade 1 Combo. (SPA.). (gr. 1-18). 200.04 (978-0-7362-1490-2(9)) CENGAGE Learning.

Lectura en Familia: Spanish Phonics Grade 2 Combo. (SPA.). (gr. 2-18). 114.18 (978-0-7362-1491-9(7)) CENGAGE Learning.

Lee, Etrulia R. Phonics Is My Way Series, 21 bks. Incl. Blake the Duck. 24p. (gr. -1-2). 1994. pap. (978-1-884876-09-7(9)); Dill. 20p. (gr. -1-2). 1995. pap. (978-1-884876-03-5(X)); Footprints in the Sand. 32p. (gr. k-2). 1994. pap. (978-1-884876-19-6(6)); Horse on a Porch. 36p. (gr. k-2). 1994. pap. (978-1-884876-15-8(3)); I Can Jump. 16p. (gr. -1-2). 1994. pap. (978-1-884876-01-1(3)); I Like to Dream. 32p. (gr. k-2). 1994. pap. (978-1-884876-11-0(0)); Jam, Ham & Yams. 20p. (gr. -1-2). 1994. pap. (978-1-884876-02-8(1)); Mel. 20p. (gr. -1-2). 1994. pap. (978-1-884876-07-3(2)); Mel Is Back. 32p. (gr. k-2). 1994. pap. (978-1-884876-13-4(7)); Mel's Store. 36p. (gr. k-2). 1994. pap. (978-1-884876-21-9(8)); Red Beans & Rice. 32p. (gr. k-2). 1994. pap. (978-1-884876-20-2(X)); Skates & Grapes. 24p. (gr. k-2). 1994. pap. (978-1-884876-12-7(9)); Space Trip. 24p. (gr. k-2). 1994. pap. (978-1-884876-18-9(8)); Stuff. 20p. (gr. k-2). 1994. pap. (978-1-884876-17-2(X)); Team. 24p. (gr. -1-2). 1994. pap. (978-1-884876-08-0(0)); Tiff & His Bone. 28p. (gr. -1-2). 1994. pap. (978-1-884876-04-2(8)); Train Ride. 20p. (gr. -1-2). 1994. pap. (978-1-884876-10-3(2)); Wake up Time. 20p. (gr. -1-2). 1994. pap. What Would You Say? 24p. (gr. k-2). 1994. pap. (978-1-884876-14-1(5)); Zip-a-Zap Zing. 32p. (gr. k-2). 1994. pap. (978-1-884876-16-5(1)); (Illus.). (J). 149.95 (978-1-884876-00-4(5)) Chamike Pubs.

Lee, Kim & Benchmark Education Co., LLC Staff. Pop! Pop! Pop! 2015. (StartUp Ser.). (J). (gr. k). (978-1-4900-0692-5(3)) Benchmark Education Co.

Lee, Kim, et al. Pop! Pop! Pop! - Cat in a Cap - Hot, Hot, Hot: StartUp Unit 4 Lap Book. Filipina, Monika et al, illus. 2015. (Start up Core Phonics Ser.). (J). (gr. k). (978-1-4900-2593-3(6)) Benchmark Education Co.

Lee, Quinlan B. Star Wars Phonics Boxed Set #2 (Star Wars) 2015. (Star Wars Ser.). (ENG.). 16p. (J). (gr. -1-k). 12.99 (978-0-545-84045-3(7)) Scholastic, Inc.

Lee, Wan & Benchmark Education Co., LLC Staff. A Fish Wish. 2015. (BuildUp Ser.). (J). (gr. 1). (978-1-4900-0722-9(9)) Benchmark Education Co.

El Leon Ruge: Little Books, Level 12, 28. 2003. (Fonolibros Ser.). 35.50 (978-0-7652-0107-2(0)) Modern Curriculum Pr.

Let's Read — Letter Sounds. 2003. 16p. (J). 3.79 (978-1-58792-050-9(6)) Trend Enterprises, Inc.

Let's Read Big Book, 3 bks., Set, Level B. (Phonics & Friends Ser.). (gr. -1-2). 14.76 (978-0-7362-1064-5(4)) CENGAGE Learning.

Letters & Sounds, Level A. Incl. Headway Level A Thinking Book. (978-0-89688-280-5(2), 88-280); Level A. suppl. ed. (978-0-89688-774-9(X), 88-774); Level A. suppl. ed. (J). (gr. k-6). pap., stu. ed., act. bk. ed. (978-0-89688-274-4(8), 88-274) Open Court Publishing Co.

Level a Big Book Program. (Phonics & Friends Ser.). (gr. -1-2). 651.23 (978-0-7362-0355-5(9)) CENGAGE Learning.

Level E Classroom Set. (Phonics & Friends Ser.). (gr. -1-2). 682.59 (978-0-7362-0601-3(9)) CENGAGE Learning.

Level E Let's Read Little Book Set. (Phonics & Friends Ser.). (gr. -1-2). 14.76 (978-0-7362-1068-3(7)) CENGAGE Learning.

Level F Classroom Set. (Phonics & Friends Ser.). (gr. -1-2). 682.59 (978-0-7362-0644-0(2)) CENGAGE Learning.

Level F Let's Read Little Book Set. (Phonics & Friends Ser.). (gr. -1-2). 14.76 (978-0-7362-1069-0(5)) CENGAGE Learning.

Levels E-F Super Classroom Set. (Phonics & Friends Ser.). (gr. -1-2). 1204.58 (978-0-7362-0596-2(9)) CENGAGE Learning.

Lewis, Ethan. Be Quiet! Practicing the KW Sound, 1 vol. 2016. (Rosen Phonics Readers Ser.). (ENG.). 12p. (J). (gr. -1-2). pap. (978-1-5081-3304-9(2), c29be1e8-8c08-4fe0-8965-ed433b91ed58, Rosen Classroom) Rosen Publishing Group, Inc., The.

—The Big Dig: Practicing the Short I Sound, 1 vol. 2016. (Rosen Phonics Readers Ser.). (ENG., Illus.). 8p. (J). (gr. -1-2). pap. (978-1-5081-3096-3(5), 867e3ec4-ec84-4505-9755-cf109698afb4, Rosen Classroom) Rosen Publishing Group, Inc., The.

—Brice Flies a Kite: Practicing the IE Sound, 1 vol. 2016. (Rosen Phonics Readers Ser.). (ENG.). 8p. (J). (gr. -1-2). pap. (978-1-5081-3226-4(7), cdf78cc2-d806-4149-af9f-1e4e90d11d30, Rosen Classroom) Rosen Publishing Group, Inc., The.

—Elaine Takes a Train: Practicing the AI Sound, 1 vol. 2016. (Rosen Phonics Readers Ser.). (ENG., Illus.). 8p. (J). (gr. -1-2). pap. (978-1-5081-3016-1(7), 0788067d-7589-4594-ba43-3ee73b179be9, Rosen Classroom) Rosen Publishing Group, Inc., The.

—Let's Do Chores: Practicing the Ch Sound, 1 vol. 2016. (Rosen Phonics Readers Ser.). (ENG.). 12p. (J). (gr. -1-2). pap. (978-1-5081-3234-9(8), 71b10b44-0e2b-4612-a399-5177fa1832c2, Rosen Classroom) Rosen Publishing Group, Inc., The.

—Sheena Shops for Shoes: Practicing the SH Sound, 1 vol. 2016. (Rosen Phonics Readers Ser.). (ENG., Illus.). 12p. (J). (gr. -1-2). pap. (978-1-5081-3049-9(3), fb9a2927-0958-408f-8674-9969308e450f, Rosen Classroom) Rosen Publishing Group, Inc., The.

—Treasure Hunt: Practicing the Zh Sound, 1 vol. 2016. (Rosen Phonics Readers Ser.). (ENG., Illus.). 12p. (J). (gr. -1-2). pap. (978-1-5081-3572-2(X), b6419b0e-4dc6-45c9-be4c-4d00d1b63a6e, Rosen Classroom) Rosen Publishing Group, Inc., The.

—What is the Weather? Practicing the Voiced TH Sound, 1 vol. 2016. (Rosen Phonics Readers Ser.). (ENG.). 12p. (J). (gr. -1-2). pap. (978-1-5081-3581-4(9), 8ce4854c-a4e8-45bd-9e86-a31c533d62d3, Rosen Classroom) Rosen Publishing Group, Inc., The.

—Yuki to the Rescue: Practicing the Yoo Sound, 1 vol. 2016. (Rosen Phonics Readers Ser.). (ENG., Illus.). 12p. (J). (gr. -1-2). pap. (978-1-5081-3058-1(2), d7dbb70a-faa1-4fae-b9c0-9f78f0464bd2, Rosen Classroom) Rosen Publishing Group, Inc., The.

Lewis, Samantha & Benchmark Education Co., LLC Staff. I Am Lib. 2015. (StartUp Ser.). (J). (gr. k). (978-1-4900-0702-1(4)) Benchmark Education Co.

Ling, Lei & Benchmark Education Co., LLC Staff. A Home for Moles. 2015. (StartUp Ser.). (J). (gr. k). (978-1-4900-0709-0(1)) Benchmark Education Co.

—I See Nat. 2015. (StartUp Ser.). (J). (gr. k). (978-1-4900-0688-8(5)) Benchmark Education Co.

Lloyd, Sue & Wernham, Sara. Stories: Join Our Adventures & Learn Your Sounds. Stephen, Lib, illus. 2008. (ENG.). 80p. (J). 31.75 (978-1-84414-081-7(4), Jolly Learning) Jolly Learning, Ltd. GBR. Dist: American International Distribution Corp.

Lluch, Alex A. Let's Leap Ahead Phonics. 2012. 80p. (J). (gr. -1). spiral bd. 9.95 (978-1-936061-74-7(0)) WS Publishing.

—Let's Leap Ahead: Phonics, Colors & More Play & Learn! Phonics, Colors & More Play & Learn! 2013. (Illus.). 126p. (J). (gr. -1). pap. 7.95 (978-1-61351-071-1(3)) WS Publishing.

Long Vowels (Gr. 1-2) 2003. (J). (978-1-58232-111-0(6)) ECS Learning Systems, Inc.

Los animales se Acostaron: Individual Title-Six Packs. (Chiquilibros Ser.). (SPA.). (gr. k-1). 23.00 (978-0-7635-8623-2(4)) Rigby Education.

Los Tres Deseos: Little Books, Level 20, Vol. 8. 2003. (Fonolibros Ser.). 34.95 (978-0-7652-0118-8(6)) Modern Curriculum Pr.

MacDonald, Kimber. The Misfits, Level 3. Swain, Wilson, illus. 2006. (ENG.). 24p. (J). (gr. 1-17). per. 3.99 (978-1-58476-421-2(X), IKIDS) Innovative Kids.

Mackinnon, Mairi. Phonics Workbook 3. 2013. (Very First Reading Workbooks Ser.). 32p. (J). pap. 7.99 (978-0-7945-3191-1(1), Usborne) EDC Publishing.

—Phonics Workbook 4. 2013. (Very First Reading Workbooks Ser.). 32p. (J). pap. 7.99 (978-0-7945-3192-8(X), Usborne) EDC Publishing.

Madu, Abraham. The Road to take to School Is the Phonics Way: Companion Book for Students. 2003. 98p. pap. 11.95 (978-0-595-27748-3(9)) iUniverse, Inc.

Mairi, Mackinnon. Phonics Workbook 1. 2012. (Very First Reading Workbooks Ser.). 36p. (J). pap. 7.99 (978-0-7945-3115-7(6), Usborne) EDC Publishing.

—Phonics Workbook 2. 2012. (Very First Reading Workbooks Ser.). 36p. (J). pap. 7.99 (978-0-7945-3116-4(4), Usborne) EDC Publishing.

La Manana: Individual Title Two-Packs. (Chiquilibros Ser.). (SPA.). (gr. -1-1). 12.00 (978-0-7635-8551-8(3)) Rigby Education.

Mann, Elsa & Benchmark Education Co., LLC Staff. Hot, Hot, Hot. 2015. (StartUp Ser.). (J). (gr. k). (978-1-4900-0694-9(X)) Benchmark Education Co.

—Jim & Jan. 2015. (StartUp Ser.). (J). (gr. k). (978-1-4900-0703-8(2)) Benchmark Education Co.

Mapaches Y Mapachitos: Little Books, Level 14, Vol. 22. 2003. (Fonolibros Ser.). 34.95 (978-0-7652-0100-3(3)) Modern Curriculum Pr.

Marcel Meringue: Level 2, 6 vols. (Fluency Strand Ser.). (gr. 4-8). 45.00 (978-1-4045-1212-2(8)) Wright Group/McGraw-Hill.

Marks, Melanie. Phonics Comics: Spooky Sara - Level 3, Level 3. Ball, Victoria, illus. 2006. (ENG.). 24p. (J). (gr. 1-17). per. 3.99 (978-1-58476-473-1(2), IKIDS) Innovative Kids.

—Phonics Comics: Super Sam - Level 3: Issue 1. Collins, Daryll, illus. 2006. (ENG.). 24p. (J). (gr. 1-17). per. 3.99 (978-1-58476-420-5(1), IKIDS) Innovative Kids.

Marrow, Lesley Mandel & Vacca, Richard T. Sadlier Phonics: Level A. 2001st rev. ed. 2004. (Sadlier Phonics Reading Program). (Illus.). 344p. (gr. 1-18). pap., stu. ed. 9.00 net. (978-0-8215-7001-2(3)) Sadlier, William H. Inc.

—Sadlier Phonics: Level B Grade 2. 2004. (Phonics Pre K-C(3) & Word Study D(4)-F(6) Ser.: Vol. 4). (Illus.). 336p. (gr. 2-18). pap., tchr. ed. 64.00 net. (978-0-8215-7012-8(9)) Sadlier, William H. Inc.

—Sadlier Phonics: Level C Grade 3. 2001st ed. 2004. (Sadlier Phonics Reading Program). (Illus.). 336p. (gr. 3-18). pap., tchr. ed. 64.00 net. (978-0-8215-7013-5(7)) Sadlier, William H. Inc.

—Sadlier Phonics: Level K. 2004. (Sadlier Phonics (Pre K-Level C) Ser.). (Illus.). 232p. (gr. k-18). pap., stu. ed. 9.00 net. (978-0-8215-7000-5(5)) Sadlier, William H. Inc.

—Sadlier Phonics/Reading: Level B. 2004. (Phonics Pre K-C(3) & Word Study D(4)-F(6) Ser.: Vol. 4). (Illus.). 240p. (gr. 2-18). pap., stu. ed. 9.00 net. (978-0-8215-7002-9(1)) Sadlier, William H. Inc.

—Sadlier Phonics/Reading: Level C. 2001st rev. ed. 2004. (Sadlier Phonics Reading Program). (Illus.). 224p. (gr. 3-18). pap., stu. ed. 9.00 net. (978-0-8215-7003-6(X)) Sadlier, William H. Inc.

Martinez, Jeny. A Walk in the Park. 2011. 32p. pap. 21.99 (978-1-4568-5229-0(9)) Xlibris Corp.

Max Is Sick: Consonants q, x, z; -ack, -ick, -ill word families: Level A, 6 vols. (Wright Skills Ser.). 12p. (gr. k-3). 17.95 (978-0-322-01457-2(3)) Wright Group/McGraw-Hill.

McAdams Moore, Carol. Phonics Comics: Cave Dave - Level 1. Dammer, Mike, illus. 2007. (ENG.). 24p. (J). (gr. 1-17). per. 3.99 (978-1-58476-552-3(6)) Innovative Kids.

McConnell, S. Let's Bring Mom Breakfast: Learning the BR Sound. 2009. (PowerPhonics Ser.). 24p. (gr. 1-1). 39.90 (978-1-60851-455-7(2), PowerKids Pr.) Rosen Publishing Group, Inc., The.

McConochie, Jennifer. Shape & Say. 2009. 172p. pap. 29.99 (978-1-4269-1401-0(6)) Trafford Publishing.

McCutcheon, Randall, et al. Glencoe Speech, Student Edition. 3rd ed. 2004. (Ntc: Speech Comm Matters Ser.). (ENG., Illus.). 605p. (gr. 9-12). stu. ed. 123.68 (978-0-07-861618-1(2), 0078616182) McGraw-Hill Education.

McGraw-Hill Staff. Listen!Listen!Letter Sounds in Rhymes Complt Set. (gr. k-1). 210.95 (978-0-322-02636-0(9)) Wright Group/McGraw-Hill.

McKay, Sindy. We Read Phonics-I Want to Be a Cowboy! Raglin, Tim, illus. 2012. 32p. (J). 9.95 (978-1-60115-351-7(1)); pap. 4.99 (978-1-60115-352-4(X)) Treasure Bay, Inc.

MCP Phonics & Stories Library, 20 bks. 2003. (J). Level C. instr.'s training gde. ed. 52.95 (978-0-7652-0542-1(4))Level A. instr.'s training gde. ed. 52.95 (978-0-7652-0532-2(7))Level B. instr.'s training gde. ed. 52.95 (978-0-7652-0537-7(8)) Modern Curriculum Pr.

Medias, 6 vols., Pack. (Chiquilibros Ser.). (SPA.). (gr. k-1). 23.00 (978-0-7635-8595-2(5)) Rigby Education.

Meow-Meow Gets Out: Diphthongs ou, ow: Level B, 6 vols. (Wright Skills Ser.). 16p. (gr. k-3). 26.50 (978-0-322-01484-8(0)) Wright Group/McGraw-Hill.

Metz, L. On the Job: Learning the O Sound. 2009. (PowerPhonics Ser.). 24p. (gr. 1-1). 39.90 (978-1-60851-466-3(8), PowerKids Pr.) Rosen Publishing Group, Inc., The.

Mi Casa: Individual Title Six-Packs. (Literatura 2000 Ser.). (SPA.). (gr. 1-2). 28.00 (978-0-7635-1071-8(8)) Rigby Education.

Mischel, Jenny Ann. Animal Alphabet. Bell-Myers, Darcy, illus. 2006. (J). bds. (978-0-9769239-0-9(4)) Perfect 4 Preschool.

Modern Staff. Day at Our Dairy Farm. (J). (gr. k-1). 38.95 (978-0-8136-1358-1(2)) Modern Curriculum Pr.

Monaghan, Jennifer. The Illustrated Phonics Booklet. 2012. (ENG.). (J). pap. (978-1-4675-2946-4(X)) Independent Pub.

Un Monstruo Debajo de la Cama: Little Books, Level 28. 2003. (Fonolibros Ser.: Vol. 9). 39.50 (978-0-7652-0119-5(4)) Modern Curriculum Pr.

Moore, M. Meet My Mom: Learning the M Sound. 2009. (PowerPhonics Ser.). 24p. (gr. 1-1). 39.90 (978-1-60851-459-5(5), PowerKids Pr.) Rosen Publishing Group, Inc., The.

Moreau, Maryellen Rooney & Welch, Brian Scott. Talk to Write, Write to Learn Manual: A Teachers' Manual for Differentiated Instruction & Tiered Intervention. 2007. pap. 65.00 (978-0-9761393-9-3(1)) Mindwing Concepts, Inc.

Mortimer, Susan. Alphabet Island Phonics 2B. 2004. (J). pap. 7.99 (978-1-931292-06-1(X)) Eagle's Wings Educational Materials.

Moskal, G. Family Fun: Learning the F Sound. 2009. (PowerPhonics Ser.). 24p. (gr. 1-1). 39.90 (978-1-60851-441-0(2), PowerKids Pr.) Rosen Publishing Group, Inc., The.

—I Like Winter: Learning the ER Sound. 2009. (PowerPhonics Ser.). 24p. (gr. 1-1). 39.90 (978-1-60851-451-9(X), PowerKids Pr.) Rosen Publishing Group, Inc., The.

Moya, Rafael. A Gift for Lily: Practicing the Short I Sound, 1 vol. 2016. (Rosen Phonics Readers Ser.). (ENG.). 8p. (J). (gr. -1-2). pap. (978-1-5081-3263-9(1), d4d2cd2d-3206-44c7-a8ad-fd0ccbf53162, Rosen Classroom) Rosen Publishing Group, Inc., The.

—Chad's Chickens: Practicing the Ch Sound, 1 vol. 2016. (Rosen Phonics Readers Ser.). (ENG., Illus.). 12p. (J). (gr. -1-2). pap. (978-1-5081-3055-0(8), ea17404f-58fb-4959-a21d-288f41c22027, Rosen Classroom) Rosen Publishing Group, Inc., The.

—The Moose in the Zoo: Practicing the Long Oo Sound, 1 vol. 2016. (Rosen Phonics Readers Ser.). (ENG.). 12p. (J). (gr. -1-2). pap. (978-1-5081-3332-2(8), 0165df4a-e2c6-4cf1-b09a-0b73e766be75, Rosen Classroom) Rosen Publishing Group, Inc., The.

—Nina's Noisy: Practicing the N Sound, 1 vol. 2016. (Rosen Phonics Readers Ser.). (ENG., Illus.). 8p. (J). (gr. -1-2). pap. (978-1-5081-3093-2(0), df801bf8-0171-44dc-bf45-b9853403e391, Rosen Classroom) Rosen Publishing Group, Inc., The.

—Rain Showers: Practicing the OW Sound, 1 vol. 2016. (Rosen Phonics Readers Ser.). (ENG.). 12p. (J). (gr. -1-2). pap. (978-1-5081-3593-7(2), a3a72dfb-b824-4ec6-960d-aec75683436e, Rosen Classroom) Rosen Publishing Group, Inc., The.

—Rocky's Road Trip: Practicing the R Sound, 1 vol. 2016. (Rosen Phonics Readers Ser.). (ENG., Illus.). 8p. (J). (gr. -1-2). pap. (978-1-5081-3098-7(1), 9ff24797-6ce1-437f-a2e1-288d5eed7632, Rosen Classroom) Rosen Publishing Group, Inc., The.

—We Play Sports: Practicing the or Sound, 1 vol. 2016. (Rosen Phonics Readers Ser.). (ENG.). 8p. (J). (gr. -1-2). pap. (978-1-5081-3199-1(6), 50f385e7-58e3-4da6-915c-d8ffc739f9eb, Rosen Classroom) Rosen Publishing Group, Inc., The.

Mr Hoot's Room: Variant Vowel Review: Level C, 6 vols. (Wright Skills Ser.). 16p. (gr. k-3). 26.50 (978-0-322-01504-3(9)) Wright Group/McGraw-Hill.

Mrs Patches & Her Fudge: Silent Consonants: Level C, 6 vols. (Wright Skills Ser.). 16p. (gr. k-3). 26.50 (978-0-322-01503-6(0)) Wright Group/McGraw-Hill.

Mrs. Sheep's Garden (18), Vol. 18. (Early Intervention Levels Ser.). 5.31 (978-0-7362-0607-5(8)) CENGAGE Learning.

My First Sight Words (Gr. K-1) 2003. (J). (978-1-58232-090-8(X)) ECS Learning Systems, Inc.

Nickelodeon Staff, ed. Phonics - Spongebob Squarepants. 2010. (Write, Slide & Learn Ser.). 14p. (J). (gr. -1-1). 9.99 (978-1-74184-520-4(3), Ideals Pubns.) Worthy Publishing.

Night Mare Trip: Level 5, 6 vols. (Fluency Strand Ser.). (gr. 4-8). 45.00 (978-1-4045-1230-6(6)) Wright Group/McGraw-Hill.

No Sweat! Short e Digraph: Level B, 6 vols. (Wright Skills Ser.). 16p. (gr. k-3). 26.50 (978-0-322-01477-0(8)) Wright Group/McGraw-Hill.

Noyed, Bob & Amoroso, Cynthia. What & Where: The Sound of WH. 2017. (Consonant Blends Ser.). (ENG.). 24p. (J). (gr. -1-2). lib. bdg. 32.79 (978-1-5038-1931-3(0), 211543) Child's World, Inc, The.

Nutria, Nutria: Student Book. 2003. 33.95 (978-0-8136-8075-0(1)) Modern Curriculum Pr.

Ocho Amigos en Total: Little Books, Level 4, Vol. 2525. 2003. (Fonolibros Ser.). 25.50 (978-0-7652-0104-1(6)) Modern Curriculum Pr.

Ochoa, Louisa & Benchmark Education Co., LLC Staff. Know about Storms. 2015. (BuildUp Ser.). (J). (gr. 1). (978-1-4900-0740-3(7)) Benchmark Education Co.

Ochoa, Louisa, et al. Know about Storms - Paul Takes a Walk - City Lights: BuildUp Unit 10 Lap Book. Jennings, Sarah, illus. 2015. (Build up Core Phonics Ser.). (J). (gr. 1). (978-1-4900-2609-1(6)) Benchmark Education Co.

Olo: Level 6, 6 vols. (Fluency Strand Ser.). (gr. 4-8). 45.00 (978-1-4045-1237-5(3)) Wright Group/McGraw-Hill.

Once, Twice, Boom: Level 7, 6 vols. (Fluency Strand Ser.). (gr. 4-8). 45.00 (978-1-4045-1240-5(3)) Wright Group/McGraw-Hill.

Orange Collection. (Elefonetica Ser.). (SPA.). (gr. 1-2). 296.76 (978-0-7362-0790-4(2)) CENGAGE Learning.

Orphan Train: Medial Digraphs: Level C, 6 vols. (Wright Skills Ser.). 16p. (gr. k-3). 26.50 (978-0-322-01498-5(0)) Wright Group/McGraw-Hill.

Orshoski, Paul. We Read Phonics-Who Took the Cookbook? Light, Kelly, illus. 2012. 32p. (J). 9.95 (978-1-60115-347-0(3)); pap. 4.99 (978-1-60115-348-7(1)) Treasure Bay, Inc.

Out of the Computer: Level 6, 6 vols. (Fluency Strand Ser.). (gr. 4-8). 45.00 (978-1-4045-1235-1(7)) Wright Group/McGraw-Hill.

Out of the Sunless Land: Level T. Group 2, 6 vols. (Sunshine Ser.). 48p. 44.95 (978-0-7802-4186-2(X)) Wright Group/McGraw-Hill.

Padilla, Mara & Benchmark Education Co., LLC Staff. High in the Sky. 2015. (BuildUp Ser.). (J). (gr. 1). (978-1-4900-0733-5(4)) Benchmark Education Co.

—A Sled Club. 2015. (BuildUp Ser.). (J). (gr. 1). (978-1-4900-0718-2(0)) Benchmark Education Co.

La Paleteria: Individual Title Two-Packs. (Chiquilibros Ser.). (SPA.). (gr. -1-1). 12.00 (978-0-7635-8554-9(8)) Rigby Education.

Panec, D. J. Riddle Rhymes (We Both Read - Level Pk-K) 2016. (We Both Read Level Pk-K Ser.). (ENG., Illus.). 42p. (J). 9.95 (978-1-60115-277-0(9)) Treasure Bay, Inc.

Papil: Level T. Group 1, 6 vols. (Sunshine Ser.). 48p. 44.95 (978-0-7802-5600-2(X)) Wright Group/McGraw-Hill.

Parker, Helen. Wipe Clean Phonics. 2007. (Wipe Clean Ser.). (Illus.). 12p. (J). bds. (978-1-84610-583-8(8)) Make Believe Ideas.

El Pastel de Javier: Little Books, Level 16, Vol. 3. 2003. (Fonolibros Ser.). 25.50 (978-0-7652-0112-6(7)) Modern Curriculum Pr.

El Pato Atascado: Little Books, Level 10, Vol. 20. 2003. (Fonolibros Ser.). 25.50 (978-0-7652-0098-3(8)) Modern Curriculum Pr.

Paws, Jaws, & Claws: Variant Vowels al, au, aw: Level B, 6 vols. (Wright Skills Ser.). 16p. (gr. k-3). 26.50 (978-0-322-01482-4(4)) Wright Group/McGraw-Hill.

Phonemic Awareness, Level 1. 2003. (Illus.). (J). spiral bd. (978-1-58605-822-7(3), LeapFrog Schl. Hse.) LeapFrog Enterprises, Inc.

Phonemic Awareness Pack. (Phonemic Awareness Pack Ser.). (gr. -1-k). 523.57 incl. audio compact disk (978-0-7362-0899-4(2)) CENGAGE Learning.

Phonemic Awareness Pack with Tapes. (Phonemic Awareness Pack Ser.). (gr. -1-k). 538.88 (978-0-7362-0900-7(X)) CENGAGE Learning.

Phonic Books. Phonic Books Magic Belt: Decodable Books for Older Readers (CVC, Consonant Blends & Consonant Teams) 2014. (Phonic Books Intervention Decodables Ser.). (ENG., Illus.). 192p. (J). (gr. 4-7). 79.00 (978-1-78369-242-2(1), Phonic Bks.) DK.

Phonic Books. Phonic Books Talisman 1: Decodable Books for Older Readers (Alternative Vowel Spellings) 2014. (Phonic Books Intervention Decodables Ser.). (ENG., Illus.). 200p. (J). (gr. 4-7). 69.00 **(978-1-78369-244-6(8)**, Phonic Bks.) DK.

Phonics. 2004. (Scott Foresman Reading Ser.). (gr. k-18). suppl. ed., wbk. ed. 1.95 (978-0-328-02433-9(3)); (gr. k-6). tchr. ed., wbk. ed. 48.00 (978-0-673-61433-9(6)); (gr. k-6). wbk. ed. 5.25 (978-0-673-61428-5(X)); (gr. 1-18). suppl. ed., wbk. ed. 48.00 (978-0-673-61430-8(1)); (gr. 2-18). suppl. ed., wbk. ed. 48.00 (978-0-673-61431-5(X)); (gr. 3-18). tchr. ed., wbk. ed. 48.00 (978-0-673-61432-2(8)) Addison-Wesley Educational Pubs., Inc.

Phonics. 2004. (Help with Homework Ser.). 32p. (J). (gr. k-2). wbk. ed. 3.99 (978-1-904586-15-9(5)) Byeway Bks.

Phonics 3-4. 2003. (Gold Stars Workbook Ser.). (Illus.). 32p. (J). 2.98 (978-1-4054-1192-9(9)) Parragon, Inc.

Phonics 4-5. 2003. (Illus.). 32p. (J). 2.98 (978-1-4054-1193-6(7)) Parragon, Inc.

Phonics 5-6. 2003. (Gold Stars Workbook Ser.). (Illus.). 32p. (J). 2.98 (978-1-4054-1194-3(5)) Parragon, Inc.

Phonics 6-7. 2003. (Gold Stars Workbook Ser.). (Illus.). 32p. (J). 2.98 (978-1-4054-1195-0(3)) Parragon, Inc.

Phonics & Word Study Complete Kits: Phonics & Word Study: Level C. (gr. k-3). 333.95 (978-0-322-01644-6(4)) Wright Group/McGraw-Hill.

Phonics & Word Study Core Kits: Phonics & Word Study: Level A. (gr. k-3). 153.50 (978-0-322-01641-5(X)) Wright Group/McGraw-Hill.

Phonics & Word Study Core Kits: Phonics & Word Study: Level B. (gr. k-3). 185.50 (978-0-322-01643-9(6)) Wright Group/McGraw-Hill.

Phonics & Word Study Core Kits: Phonics & Word Study: Level C. (gr. k-3). 153.50 (978-0-322-01645-3(2)) Wright Group/McGraw-Hill.

Phonics Decodable Reader 1. 2004. (Scott Foresman Reading Ser.). (gr. 1-18). suppl. ed. 3.35 (978-0-673-65172-3(X)) Addison-Wesley Educational Pubs., Inc.

Phonics Decodable Reader 2. 2004. (Scott Foresman Reading Ser.). (gr. 1-18). suppl. ed. 3.35 (978-0-673-65173-0(8)) Addison-Wesley Educational Pubs., Inc.

Phonics Decodable Reader 3. 2004. (Scott Foresman Reading Ser.). (gr. 1-18). suppl. ed. 3.35 (978-0-673-65174-7(6)) Addison-Wesley Educational Pubs., Inc.

Phonics Decodable Reader 33-41. 2004. (Scott Foresman Reading Ser.). (gr. 1-18). suppl. ed. 7.75 (978-0-673-65180-8(0)) Addison-Wesley Educational Pubs., Inc.

Phonics Decodable Reader 42-50. 2004. (Scott Foresman Reading Ser.). (gr. 1-18). suppl. ed. 7.75 (978-0-673-65181-5(9)) Addison-Wesley Educational Pubs., Inc.

Phonics Decodable Reader 5. 2004. (Scott Foresman Reading Ser.). (gr. 1-18). suppl. ed. 3.35 (978-0-673-65176-1(2)) Addison-Wesley Educational Pubs., Inc.

Phonics Plus Staff. Phonics Plus. 2nd ed. Bk. D. (J). 9.55 (978-0-8136-0394-0(3))Bk. E. tchr. ed. 9.55 (978-0-8136-0395-7(1))Bk. F. (J). 9.55 (978-0-8136-0396-4(X)) Modern Curriculum Pr.

Phonics Practice Book. (De Canciones A Cuentos Ser.). (SPA.). (gr. 1-18). 9.13 (978-1-56334-895-2(0)) CENGAGE Learning.

Phonics Puzzles (Gr. 1) 2003. (J). (978-1-58232-047-2(0)) ECS Learning Systems, Inc.

Phonics Readers. (Phonics Readers 1-36 Ser.). (ENG.). 8p. (gr. k-1). Bks. 1-36, Set C. 2003. pap. 356.40 (978-0-7368-3225-0(4))Set E. 2004. pap. 428.40 (978-0-7368-4092-7(3))Set F. 2004. pap. 428.40 (978-0-7368-4094-1(X)) Capstone.

Phonics Readers Big Books. 2005. (J). pap. 95.00 (978-1-58970-687-3(0)) Lakeshore Learning Materials.

Phonics Readers Bks. 1-36, Set: A Complete Program. 2003. (Phonics Readers 1-36 Ser.). (ENG.). 8p. (gr. k-1). pap. 387.35 (978-0-7368-3221-2(1)) Capstone.

Phonics Readers Bookshelf Collection, 36 bks., Set. 2004. (gr. 1-18). 594.00 (978-0-328-00401-0(4)); (gr. 2-18). 495.00 (978-0-328-00402-7(2)); (gr. 3-18). 495.00 (978-0-328-00403-4(0)) Addison-Wesley Educational Pubs., Inc.

Phonics Readers Student Books. 2005. (J). pap. 29.95 (978-1-58970-685-9(4)) Lakeshore Learning Materials.

Phonics Songs & Rhymes Flip Chart. 2004. (gr. 1-18). suppl. ed. 109.15 (978-0-673-59716-8(4)) Addison-Wesley Educational Pubs., Inc.

Phonics Take-Home Readers. 2004. (Scott Foresman Reading Ser.). (gr. 3-18). 48.00 (978-0-673-61260-1(0)) Addison-Wesley Educational Pubs., Inc.

Pigs & Dogs Play Ball: Consonants b, w; Short Vowel i word families: Level A, 6 vols. (Wright Skills Ser.). 12p. (gr. k-3). 17.95 (978-0-322-01450-3(6)) Wright Group/McGraw-Hill.

The Pink Tent: Final Blends -nd, -nk, -nt: Level B, 6 vols. (Wright Skills Ser.). 16p. (gr. k-3). 17.95 (978-0-322-01462-6(X)) Wright Group/McGraw-Hill.

La Pizzeria, 2 Packs. (Chiquilibros Ser.). (SPA.). (gr. -1-1). 12.00 (978-0-7635-8555-6(6)) Rigby Education.

Places to Visit, Places to See: Take-Home Book. 2005. (Lee Bennett Hopkins Worlds of Poetry Classroom Library). (YA). (gr. k-3). 13.50 (978-0-8215-0568-7(8)) Sadlier, William H. Inc.

Popovic, Novak. I Hear with My Ears: Practicing the EER Sound, 1 vol. 2016. (Rosen Phonics Readers Ser.). (ENG.). 12p. (J). (gr. -1-2). pap. (978-1-5081-3584-5(3), 9c4c6c9e-dbb6-47d0-ba23-fd5e91aa92f4, Rosen Classroom) Rosen Publishing Group, Inc., The.

—In the Wild: Practicing the W Sound, 1 vol. 2016. (Rosen Phonics Readers Ser.). (ENG.). 12p. (J). (gr. -1-2). pap. (978-1-5081-3224-0(0), 49ee3b6e-3ea1-4e48-9cc4-cb1885d66ddb, Rosen Classroom) Rosen Publishing Group, Inc., The.

—Mike Likes Pie: Practicing the IE Sound, 1 vol. 2016. (Rosen Phonics Readers Ser.). (ENG., Illus.). 8p. (J). (gr. -1-2). pap. (978-1-5081-3047-5(7), 65a0821b-2902-4985-8228-ae2e35744661, Rosen Classroom) Rosen Publishing Group, Inc., The.

—Pen Pals: Practicing the P Sound, 1 vol. 2016. (Rosen Phonics Readers Ser.). (ENG.). 8p. (J). (gr. -1-2). pap. (978-1-5081-3250-9(X), 8c4d4a1f-f70f-4e26-839b-4d297d5dd086, Rosen Classroom) Rosen Publishing Group, Inc., The.

Powell, Marie. Dan Can! Cartwright, Amy, illus. 2016. (Word Families Ser.). (ENG.). 16p. (J). (gr. k-2). lib. bdg. 17.95 (978-1-60753-924-7(1), 15537) Amicus.

—Go to Bed, Ted! Cartwright, Amy, illus. 2016. (Word Families Ser.). (ENG.). 16p. (J). (gr. k-2). lib. bdg. 17.95 (978-1-60753-927-8(6), 15540) Amicus.

—The Map Trap. Cartwright, Amy, illus. 2016. (Word Families Ser.). (ENG.). 16p. (J). (gr. k-2). lib. bdg. 17.95 (978-1-60753-928-5(4), 15541) Amicus.

—Nab the Crab. 2013. (Word Families Ser.). (ENG.). 16p. (J). (gr. k-2). lib. bdg. 25.65 (978-1-60753-513-3(0), 16231) Amicus.

—Out for Trout. 2013. (Word Families Ser.). (ENG.). 16p. (J). (gr. k-2). lib. bdg. 25.65 (978-1-60753-514-0(9), 16232) Amicus.

—Stop, Pop! Cartwright, Amy, illus. 2016. (Word Families Ser.). (ENG.). 16p. (J). (gr. k-2). lib. bdg. 17.95 (978-1-60753-925-4(X), 15538) Amicus.

—What Good Is an A? 2015. (Vowels Ser.). (ENG., Illus.). 16p. (J). (gr. k-2). 17.95 (978-1-60753-708-3(7), 15238) Amicus.

—When, Jen? Cartwright, Amy, illus. 2016. (Word Families Ser.). (ENG.). 16p. (J). (gr. k-2). lib. bdg. 17.95 (978-1-60753-926-1(8), 15539) Amicus.

—Win, Min! Cartwright, Amy, illus. 2016. (Word Families Ser.). (ENG.). 16p. (J). (gr. k-2). lib. bdg. 17.95 (978-1-60753-929-2(2), 15542) Amicus.

Publications International Ltd. Staff, ed. Kindergarten Boot Camp. 2010. (J). 20.98 (978-1-4508-0069-3(6)) Publications International, Ltd.

—My First Phonics Dictionary. 2011. (Illus.). 96p. (J). 8.98 (978-1-4508-1480-5(8)) Phoenix International Publications, Inc.

Puedes Subir: Little Books, Level 3, 8. 2003. (Fonolibros Ser.). 25.50 (978-0-7652-0085-3(6)) Modern Curriculum Pr.

Puedo Salir? Student Book. 2003. 35.50 (978-0-8136-8099-6(9)) Modern Curriculum Pr.

Pulse Fun with Phonics. 2006. cd-rom 4.99 (978-1-60245-039-4(0)) GDL Multimedia, LLC.

Purcell, Susan. Goldilocks, 1 vol. 2017. (Fairy-Tale Phonics Ser.). (ENG.). 24p. (J). (gr. 1-1). 26.27 (978-1-5081-9376-0(2), c4669a1e-c0e2-49cb-83c1-22b5fdf64649); pap. 9.25 (978-1-5081-9447-7(5), a562a763-aaad-476d-a9fd-706d9e57e7fe) Rosen Publishing Group, Inc., The. (Windmill Bks.).

Quake: Level 4, 6 vols. (Fluency Strand Ser.). (gr. 4-8). 45.00 (978-1-4045-1226-9(8)) Wright Group/McGraw-Hill.

Que Es Eso? Little Books, Level 3, Vol. 26. 2003. (Fonolibros Ser.). 25.50 (978-0-7652-0105-8(4)) Modern Curriculum Pr.

Que Es Una Linea? Little Books, Level 6, 3. 2003. 25.50 (978-0-7652-0079-2(1)) Modern Curriculum Pr.

Que Gato! Little Books, Level 16, Vol. 5. 2003. (Fonolibros Ser.). 35.50 (978-0-7652-0114-0(3)) Modern Curriculum Pr.

Que quiere Beto? Individual Title-Six Packs. (Chiquilibros Ser.). (SPA.). (gr. k-1). 23.00 (978-0-7635-8610-2(2)) Rigby Education.

Que Soy? Little Books, Level 4, 9. 2003. (Fonolibros Ser.). 25.50 (978-0-7652-0086-0(4)) Modern Curriculum Pr.

Queen Jelly Bean: Vowel Digraph Review: Level C, 6 vols. (Wright Skills Ser.). 16p. (gr. k-3). 26.50 (978-0-322-01499-2(9)) Wright Group/McGraw-Hill.

Quit It! Consonant q: Level A, 6 vols. (Wright Skills Ser.). 12p. (gr. k-3). 17.95 (978-0-322-03122-7(2)) Wright Group/McGraw-Hill.

Rasinski, Timothy V. Daily Word Ladders: Grades 4-6. 2005. (Daily Word Ladders Ser.). (ENG., Illus.). 112p. (gr. 4-6). pap. 15.99 (978-0-439-77345-4(8), Teaching Resources) Scholastic, Inc.

Read & Spell with Zoo-phonics. 2004. (J). cd-rom 29.95 (978-1-886441-46-0(4)) Zoo-phonics, Inc.

Read & Spell with Zoo=Phonics Guide for CD-ROM. 2004. (J). 14.95 (978-1-886441-45-3(6)) Zoo-phonics, Inc.

Reading at Home: Phonics Grade 1 Combo. (gr. 1-18). 517.92 (978-0-7362-1401-8(1)) CENGAGE Learning.

Reading at Home: Phonics Grade 2 Combo. (gr. 2-18). 368.64 (978-0-7362-1402-5(X)) CENGAGE Learning.

Reading Rods Phonemic Awareness Activity Book. 2003. (J). pap. 4.95 (978-1-56911-117-8(0)) Learning Resources, Inc.

Reading Rods Phonemic Awareness Activity Cards, Set 2. 2003. (J). 19.95 (978-1-56911-113-0(8)) Learning Resources, Inc.

Reading Rods Readers: Phonics Foundation 1 Classpack. 2003. (J). per. 249.95 (978-1-56911-575-6(3)) Learning Resources, Inc.

Reading Rods Readers: Phonics Foundation 2 Classpack. 2003. (J). per. 249.95 (978-1-56911-576-3(1)) Learning Resources, Inc.

Reading Rods Readers: Phonics Foundation Set 1. 2003. (J). pap. 44.95 (978-1-56911-121-5(9)) Learning Resources, Inc.

Reading Rods Readers: Phonics Foundation Set 2. 2003. (J). pap. 44.95 (978-1-56911-122-2(7)) Learning Resources, Inc.

El Rio Crece: Little Books, Level 16. 2003. (Fonolibros Ser.). 35.50 (978-0-7652-0110-2(0)) Modern Curriculum Pr.

Ristuccia, Christine & Ristuccia, James. The Entire World of S & Z Instructional Workbook: A Comprehensive Approach to Remediate Frontal & Lateral Lisps. l.t. ed. 2003. (Illus.). 208p. (J). per. 34.99 (978-0-9723457-4-3(4)) Say It Right.

Robinson, Lisa & Benchmark Education Co., LLC Staff. Can He See Me? 2015. (StartUp Ser.). (J). (gr. k). (978-1-4900-0712-0(1)) Benchmark Education Co.

—I Zip to My Job. 2015. (StartUp Ser.). (J). (gr. k). (978-1-4900-0707-6(5)) Benchmark Education Co.

Robinson, Lisa, et al. Mr. Max - Gabe, Kate, & Dave - a Home for Moles: StartUp Unit 9 Lap Book. Czernichowska, Joanna, illus. 2015. (Start up Core Phonics Ser.). (J). (gr. k). (978-1-4900-2598-8(7)) Benchmark Education Co.

Rogers, Jane & Benchmark Education Co., LLC Staff. Get Well, Red Hen! 2015. (BuildUp Ser.). (J). (gr. 1). (978-1-4900-0716-8(4)) Benchmark Education Co.

Rogers, Jane, et al. Get Well, Red Hen! - Big Bus - a Sled Club: BuildUp Unit 2 Lap Book. Anderson, Nicola & Greenhead, Bill, illus. 2015. (Build up Core Phonics Ser.). (J). (gr. 1). (978-1-4900-2601-5(0)) Benchmark Education Co.

Roman, Douglas T. How to Learn Phonics: Students' Workbook with More Than 3,000 Words to Make Good Readers. 2013. 160p. pap. 54.35 (978-1-4669-8556-8(9)) Trafford Publishing.

Rooney Moreau, Maryellen & Welch, Brian Scott. Talk to Write, Write to Learn Kit. 2007. pap. 199.95 (978-0-9769527-5-6(0)) Mindwing Concepts, Inc.

Rosario, Sherwin, illus. Meet the Vowels. 2005. 12p. (J). bds. 7.99 (978-0-9767008-2-1(4)) Preschool Prep Co.

Rose, Emma. Energy Every Day, 6 vols., Set. 2004. (Phonics Readers Books 37-72 Ser.). (ENG.). 8p. (gr. k-1). pap. 35.70 (978-0-7368-4086-6(9)) Capstone.

Rosen, Rachel, et al. Sit, Sit, Sit - I Can Fit! - I Am Pat: StartUp Unit 3 Lap Book. 2015. (Start up Core Phonics Ser.). (J). (gr. k). (978-1-4900-2592-6(8)) Benchmark Education Co.

Russo, Gina & Benchmark Education Co., LLC Staff. A Big Job. 2015. (BuildUp Ser.). (J). (gr. 1). (978-1-4900-0715-1(6)) Benchmark Education Co.

A Saludar Y A Celebrar: Little Books, Level 4, Vol. 23. 2003. (Fonolibros Ser.). (SPA.). 25.50 (978-0-7652-0101-0(1)) Modern Curriculum Pr.

Sandviks HOP, Inc. Staff. Discover Reading: Baby Edition. 2007. 39.99 (978-1-60143-760-0(9)) HOP, LLC.

—Discover Reading Toddler Edition. 2007. 39.99 (978-1-60143-765-5(X)) HOP, LLC.

—Hooked on English. 2007. 199.99 (978-1-60143-752-5(8)) HOP, LLC.

—Hooked on First Grade. 2007. 39.99 (978-1-60143-750-1(1)) HOP, LLC.

Sandviks HOP, Inc. Staff, contrib. by. Hooked on Second Grade Super Workbook. 2007. 320p. (J). pap. 12.99 (978-1-60143-468-5(5)) HOP, LLC.

Santillo, LuAnn. Fun with Phonemes. Santillo, LuAnn, ed. 2004. (Half-Pint Readers Ser.). (Illus.). 36p. (J). (gr. -1-1). pap. 11.95 (978-1-59256-129-2(2)) Half-Pint Kids, Inc.

—Lots More Fun with Phonemes. Santillo, LuAnn, ed. 2004. (Half-Pint Readers Ser.). (Illus.). 36p. (J). (gr. -1-1). pap. 11.95 (978-1-59256-131-5(4)) Half-Pint Kids, Inc.

—More Fun with Phonemes. Santillo, LuAnn, ed. 2004. (Half-Pint Readers Ser.). (Illus.). 36p. (J). (gr. -1-1). pap. 11.95 (978-1-59256-130-8(6)) Half-Pint Kids, Inc.

Santos, D. Friends: Learning the FR Sound. 2009. (PowerPhonics Ser.). 24p. (gr. 1-1). 39.90 (978-1-60851-442-7(0), PowerKids Pr.) Rosen Publishing Group, Inc., The.

—I Can Draw: Learning the DR Sound. 2009. (PowerPhonics Ser.). 24p. (gr. 1-1). 39.90 (978-1-60851-446-5(3), PowerKids Pr.) Rosen Publishing Group, Inc., The.

—My New Glasses: Learning the GL Sound. 2009. (PowerPhonics Ser.). 24p. (gr. 1-1). 39.90 (978-1-60851-461-8(7), PowerKids Pr.) Rosen Publishing Group, Inc., The.

Sarkisian, K. You Need Your Nose: Learning the N Sound. 2009. (PowerPhonics Ser.). 24p. (gr. 1-1). 39.90 (978-1-60851-482-3(X), PowerKids Pr.) Rosen Publishing Group, Inc., The.

Saxton, Brenda, illus. Reading Pals: Alphabet Recognition Gr. Pre K-K. 2007. (J). per. 6.99 (978-1-59198-435-1(1)) Creative Teaching Pr., Inc.

Scat! Said the Cat: Big Book: Level D. Group 1. (Sunshine Ser.). 8p. 20.95 (978-0-7802-5734-4(0)) Wright Group/McGraw-Hill.

Schiavone, Fabio. A Unicorn is Born: Practicing the OR Sound, 1 vol. 2016. (Rosen Phonics Readers Ser.). (ENG., Illus.). 8p. (J). (gr. -1-2). pap. (978-1-5081-3028-4(0), 235e675c-f518-4750-ab0f-55f57427577f, Rosen Classroom) Rosen Publishing Group, Inc., The.

—I Grow a Garden: Practicing the Hard G Sound, 1 vol. 2016. (Rosen Phonics Readers Ser.). (ENG.). 8p. (J). (gr. -1-2). pap. (978-1-5081-3268-4(2), 3330d40c-238e-4ec8-b0a5-41c98bc25dd9, Rosen Classroom) Rosen Publishing Group, Inc., The.

—Ravi's Robot: Practicing the R Sound, 1 vol. 2016. (Rosen Phonics Readers Ser.). (ENG.). 8p. (J). (gr. -1-2). pap. (978-1-5081-3277-6(1), ae1f8eb3-4952-4dc0-b8dd-210616f93264, Rosen Classroom) Rosen Publishing Group, Inc., The.

—Smelly Skunks: Practicing the S Sound, 1 vol. 2016. (Rosen Phonics Readers Ser.). (ENG.). 8p. (J). (gr. -1-2). pap. (978-1-5081-3272-1(0), 200df40b-919b-4f2a-b373-80b8317995b4, Rosen Classroom) Rosen Publishing Group, Inc., The.

—Stars in the Dark: Practicing the AR Sound, 1 vol. 2016. (Rosen Phonics Readers Ser.). (ENG., Illus.). 12p. (J). (gr. -1-2). pap. (978-1-5081-3022-2(1), e7a8b94d-d1b0-43b2-99c3-38ab85e457ab, Rosen Classroom) Rosen Publishing Group, Inc., The.

—Theo Gives Thanks: Practicing the Unvoiced TH Sound, 1 vol. 2016. (Rosen Phonics Readers Ser.). (ENG., Illus.). 12p. (J). (gr. -1-2). pap. (978-1-5081-3059-8(0),

6c, Rosen Classroom) Rosen Publishing Group, Inc., The.
schn),* Cartwheel Bks.) Scholastic, Inc.
Scholastic, Inc. Staff & C s, 6 vols., Set. 2003. (Phonics Readers 1-36 Ser.). (ENG.). 8p. (gr. k-1). pap. 29.70 *(978-0-7368-318(4))* School Zone Publishing Co.
School Zone Publishing.))* School Zone Publishing Co.
School Zone Publishing Company Staff. . (Illus.). (J). 19.99 incl. audio compact disk *(978-0-88743-96(3))* Addison-Wesley Educational Pubs., Inc. (Scott Foresman).
Set B Complete Program. 2003. (Phonics Readers 1-36 Ser.). (ENG.). 8p. (gr. s. 2003. (Kids Can Learn with Franklin Ser.). (ENG., Illus.). 32p. (J). (gr. . (Kids Can Learn with Franklin Ser.). (ENG., Illus.). 32p. (J). (gr. 1-R Sound. 2009. (PowerPhonics Ser.). 24p. (gr. 1-1). 39.90 *(978-1-60851-430-4(7),* PowerKids Pr.) Rosen Publishing Group, Inc., The.
Shelly's Shell: Digraph sh: Level B, 6 vols. (Wright Skills Ser.). 16p. (gr. k-3). 17.95 *(978-0-322-0147. Faulkner, Stacey, ed. Campbell, Jenny & Tom, Darcy, illus. 2007. (J). 4.99 *(978-1-59198-41.
Shopping: Big Book: Level A. (Sunshine Ser.). 8p. 20.95 *(978-0-7802-5710-8(3))* Wright Group/McGraw-Hill.
Short & L Phonics: Read-Alone Phonics Stories. 2003. (Summer School Ser.). (ENG.). (C). (gr. -1-k). pap. 21.95 *(978-0-7362-2007-1(0))* CENGAGE Learning.
—Avenues .
The Silly Supper: Medial Consonants: Level C, 6 vols. (Wright Skills Ser.). 16p. (gr. k-3). 26.50 *(978-0-322-01491-6(3))* Wright Group/McGraw-Hill.
S))* Center for the Collaborative Classroom.
SIPPS Beginning))* Center for the Collaborative Classroom.
SIPPS Beginning))* Center for the Collaborative Classroom.
SIPPS Beginning Sound Wall Cards. 2004. *(978-1-57621-454-1(0))* Center for the Collaborative Classroom.
S: Big Book: Level M. Group 1. (Sunshine Ser.). 24p. 36.50 *(978-0-7802-5 Sound. 2009. (PowerPhonics Ser.). 24p. (gr. 1-1). 39.90 *(978-1-60851-434-2(X),* PowerKids Pr.) Rosen Publishing Group, Inc., The.
Snake at the Lake: Long Vowel Review: Level C, 6 vols. (Wright Skills Ser.). 16p. (gr. k-3). 26.50 *(978-0-322-0149: Practicing the J Sound, 1 vol. 2016. (Rosen Phonics Readers Ser.). (ENG., Illus.). 8p. (J). (gr. -1-2). pap. *(978-1-5081-30 4b0, Rosen Classroom) Rosen Publishing Group, Inc., The.
—Man Sound, 1 vol. 2016. (Rosen Phonics Readers Ser.). (ENG., Illus.). 8p. (J). (gr. -1-2). pap. *(978-1-5081-3067-cf60, Rosen Classroom) Rosen Publishing Group, Inc., The.
—The Sad Seal: Practicing the S Sound, 1 vol. 2016. (Rosen Phonics Readers Ser.). (ENG., Illus.). 8p. (J). (gr. -1-2). pap. *(978-1-5081-309 e5, Rosen Classroom) Rosen Publishing Group, Inc., The.
—Up at Bat: Practicing the Short A Sound, 1 vol. 2016. (Rosen Phonics Readers Ser.). (ENG.). 8p. (J). (gr. -1-2). pap. *(978-1-5081-325 82, Rosen Classroom) Rosen Publishing Group, Inc., The.
—Zebras & Zookeepers: Practicing the Z Sound, 1 vol. 2016. (Rosen Phonics Readers Ser.). (ENG.). 12p. (J). (gr. -1-2). pap. *(978-1-5081-322 6f, Rosen Classroom) Rosen Publishing Group, Inc., The.
So, Level B. 2003. ("Plaid" Phonics & Stories Libraries). (gr. 2-3). 38.50 *(978-0-8136-91, illus. 2015. (Start up Core Phonics Ser.). (J). (gr. k). *(978-1-4900-259: Level B, 6 vols. (Wright Skills Ser.). 16p. (gr. k-3). 17.95 *(978-0-322-0146: Plain Text. 2004. (Read Well Level K Ser.). (Illus.). 8p. (J). *(978-1-57035-743-5(9))* Cambium Education, Inc.
—Read Well Magazine Unit 13: Slanted Text. 2004. (Read Well Level K Ser.). (Illus.). 8p. (J). *(978-1-57035-769-5(2))* Cambium Education, Inc.
—Read Well Magazine Unit 14: Slanted Text. 2004. (Read Well Level K Ser.). (Illus.). 8p. (J). *(978-1-57035-698-8(X))* Cambium Education, Inc.
—Read Well Magazine Unit 16: Plain Text. 2004. (Read Well Level K Ser.). (Illus.). 8p. (J). *(978-1-57035-746-6(3))* Cambium Education, Inc.
—Read Well Magazine Unit 17: Plain Text. 2003. (Read Well Level K Ser.). (Illus.). 8p. (J). *(978-1-57035-747-3(1))* Cambium Education, Inc.
—Read Well Magazine Unit 18: Plain Text. 2004. (Read Well Level K Ser.). (Illus.). 8p. (J). *(978-1-57035-748-0(X))* Cambium Education, Inc.
—Read Well Magazine Unit 18: Slanted Text. 2003. (Read Well Level K Ser.). (Illus.). 8p. (J). *(978-1-59318-102-4(7))* Cambium Education, Inc.
—Read Well Magazine Unit 19: Plain Text. 2003. (Read Well Level K Ser.). (Illus.). 8p. (J). *(978-1-57035-749-7(8))* Cambium Education, Inc.
—Read Well Magazine Unit 19: Slanted Text. 2003. (Read Well Level K Ser.). (Illus.). 8p. (J). *(978-1-59318-103-1(5))* Cambium Education, Inc.
—Read Well Magazine Unit 2: Plain Text. 2003. (Read Well Level K Ser.). (Illus.). 8p. (J). *(978-1-57035-733-6(1))* Cambium Education, Inc.
—Read Well Magazine Unit 2: Slanted Text. 2003. (Read Well Level K Ser.). (Illus.). 8p. (J). *(978-1-57035-783-1(8))* Cambium Education, Inc.
—Read Well Magazine Unit 20: Plain Text. 2003. (Read Well Level K Ser.). (Illus.). 8p. (J). *(978-1-57035-775-6(7))* Cambium Education, Inc.
—Read Well Magazine Unit 3: Plain Text. 2003. (Read Well Level K Ser.). (Illus.). 8p. (J). *(978-1-57035-734-3(X))* Cambium Education, Inc.
—Read Well Magazine Unit 3: Slanted Text. 2003. (Read Well Level K Ser.). (Illus.). 8p. (J). *(978-1-57035-784-8(6))* Cambium Education, Inc.
—Read Well Magazine Unit 4: Plain Text. 2003. (Read Well Level K Ser.). (Illus.). 8p. (J). *(978-1-57035-732-9(3))* Cambium Education, Inc.
—Read Well Magazine Unit 4: Slanted Text. 2003. (Read Well Level K Ser.). (Illus.). 8p. (J). *(978-1-57035-785-5(4))* Cambium Education, Inc.
—Read Well Magazine Unit 5: Plain Text. 2003. (Read Well Level K Ser.). (Illus.). 8p. (J). *(978-1-57035-736-7(6))* Cambium Education, Inc.
—Read Well Magazine Unit 5: (2))* Cambium Education, Inc.
—Read Well Magazine Unit 6: Plain Text. 2003. (Read Well Level K Ser.). (Illus.). 8p. (J). *(978-1-57035-737-4(4))* Cambium Education, Inc.
—Read Well Magazine Unit 6: Slanted Text. 2003. (Read Well Level K Ser.). (Illus.). 8p. (J). *(978-1-57035-787-9(0))* Cambium Education, Inc.
—Read Well Magazine Unit 7: Plain Text. 2003. (Read Well Level K Ser.). (Illus.). 8p. (J). *(978-1-57035-738-1(2))* Cambium Education, Inc.
—Read Well Magazine Unit 8: Plain Text. 2003. (Read Well Level K Ser.). (Illus.). 8p. (J). *(978-1-57035-726-8(9))* Cambium Education, Inc.
—Read Well Magazine Unit 8: Slanted Text. 2003. (Read Well Level K Ser.). (Illus.). 8p. (J). *(978-1-57035-789-3(7))* Cambium Education, Inc.
—Read Well Magazine Unit 9: Plain Text. 2003. (Read Well Level K Ser.). (Illus.). 8p. (J). *(978-1-57035-739-8(0))* Cambium Education, Inc.
—Read Well Magazine Unit 9: Slanted Text. 2003. (Read Well Level K Ser.). (Illus.). 8p. (J). *(978-1-57035-790-9(0))* Cambium Education, Inc.
—Rescue Workers: Read Well Level K Unit 11 Storybook. Zillis, Tom, illus. 2003. (Read Well Level K Ser.). 20p. (J). *(978-1-57035-682-7(3),* 55511) Cambium Education, Inc.
—Spiders: Read Well Level K Unit 1 Storybook. Shupe, Bobbi & Crum, Anna-Maria, illus. 2003. (Read Well Level K Ser.). 20p. (J). *(978-1-57035-673-5(4))* Cambium Education, Inc.
—Spiders: Unit 1 Read Well Level K Teacher's Storybook. Shupe, Bobbi & Crum, Anna-Maria, illus. 2003. (Read Well Level K Ser.). 20p. (J). *(978-1-57035-696-4(3))* Cambium Education, Inc.
—Student Workbook 1 (Plain Text) Units 1-9 Plus Review Unit. 2003. (Read Well Level K Ser.). (Illus.). 104p. (J). *(978-1-59318-166- Text) Units 1-9 Plus Review Unit. 2003. (Read Well Level K Ser.). (Illus.). 104p. (J). *(978-1-59318-169-7(8))* Cambium Education, Inc.
—Student Workbook 2 (Plain Text) Units 10-18 Plus Review Unit. 2003. (Read Well Level K Ser.). (Illus.). 104p. (J). *(978-1-59318-167-t Text) Units 10-18 Plus Review Unit. 2003. (Read Well Level K Ser.). (Illus.). 104p. (J). *(978-1-59318-170-3(1))* Cambium Education, Inc.
St t. Starfall Education, ed. 2004. (ENG., Illus.). 8p. (J). pap. *(978-1-59577-00 at. Starfall Education, ed. 2004. (ENG., Illus.). 8p. (J). pap. *(978-1-59577-00 o: Level B, 6 vols. (Wright Skills Ser.). 16p. (gr. k-3). 26.50 *(978-0-322-0148: Level B, 6 vols. (Wright Skills Ser.). 16p. (gr. k-3). 26.50 *(978-0-322-03: Level 7, 6 vols. (Fluency Strand Ser.). (gr. 4-8). 45.00 *(978-1-4045-124.
Student Pack. (Cuentacuentos Ser.). (SPA.). (gr. k-18). 83.31 *(978-1-56334-798-6(9))* CENGAGE Learning.
Su))* Wright Group/McGraw-Hill.
Sunshine: Early Emergent - Group))* Wright Group/McGraw-Hill.
Sunshine: Early Emergent - Group))* Wright Group/McGraw-Hill.
Sunshine: Early Emergent - Group 2: 1 Each of 8 Student Books: Level))* Wright Group/McGraw-Hill.
Sunshine: Early Emergent - Group 2: 1 Each of 8 Student Books: Level B. ())* Wright Group/McGraw-Hill.
Sunshine: Early Emergent - Group 2: 1 Each of 8 Student Books: Level C. ())* Wright Group/McGraw-Hill.
Sunshine: Early Emergent - Nonfiction 1: 1 Each of 4 Student Books: Level A. (Sunshine Ser.). 16.95 *(978-0-7802-3763-6(3))* Wright Group/McGraw-Hill.
Sunshine: Early Emergent - (2))* Wright Group/McGraw-Hill.
Sunshine: Early Emergent: L Sound. 2009. (PowerPhonics Ser.). 24p. (gr. 1-1). 39.90 *(978-1-60851-439-7(0),* PowerKids Pr.) Rosen Publishing Group, Inc., The.
Tat Is Sad: Consonant d: Level A, 6 vols. (Wright Skills Ser.). 12p. (gr. k-3). 17.95 *(978-0-322-03105-0(2))* Wright Group/McGraw-Hill.
Terror Bear Canyon: Level 5, 6 vols. (Fluency Strand Ser.). (gr. 4-8). 45.00 *(978-1-4045-1225-2(X))* Wright Group/McGraw-Hill.
Tes.
Thomas, M. Summer at the Beach: Learning the EA Sound. 2009. (PowerPhonics Ser.). 24p. (gr. 1-1). 39.90 *(978-1-60851-472-4(2),* PowerKids Pr.) Rosen Publishing Group, Inc., The.
Thompson, : Practicing the V Sound, 1 vol. 2016. (Rosen Phonics Readers Ser.). (ENG., Illus.). 12p. (J). (gr. -1-2). pap. *(978-1-5081-30 4, Rosen Classroom) Rosen Publishing Group, Inc., The.
—At the Whale? Practicing the WH Sound, 1 vol. 2016. (Rosen Phonics Readers Ser.). (ENG.). 12p. (J). (gr. -1-2). pap. *(978-1-5081-323 82, Rosen Classroom) Rosen Publishing Group, Inc., The.
—Bi Sound, 1 vol. 2016. (Rosen Phonics Readers Ser.). (ENG.). 8p. (J). (gr. -1-2). pap. *(978-1-5081-325 d84, Rosen Classroom) Rosen Publishing Group, Inc., The.
—Cat & Rat: Practicing the Short a Sound, 1 vol. 2016. (Rosen Phonics Readers Ser.). (ENG., Illus.). 8p. (J). (gr. -1-2). pap. *(978-1-5081-307 7f, Rosen Classroom) Rosen Publishing Group, Inc., The.
—In the Sound, 1 vol. 2016. (Rosen Phonics Readers Ser.). (ENG.). 12p. (J). (gr. -1-2). pap. *(978-1-5081-359 fc, Rosen Classroom) Rosen Publishing Group, Inc., The.
—The Moon Is My Balloon: Practicing the Long Oo Sound, 1 vol. 2016. (Rosen Phonics Readers Ser.). (ENG., Illus.). 12p. (J). (gr. -1-2). pap. *(978-1-5081-31 86, Rosen Classroom) Rosen Publishing Group, Inc., The.
—Our Car Trip: Practicing the AR Sound, 1 vol. 2016. (Rosen Phonics Readers Ser.). (ENG.). 12p. (J). (gr. -1-2). pap. *(978-1-5081-32 f18, Rosen Classroom) Rosen Publishing Group, Inc., The.
—Paul Makes Sauce: Practicing the AU Sound, 1 vol. 2016. (Rosen Phonics Readers Ser.). (ENG., Illus.). 12p. (J). (gr. -1-2). pap. *(978-1-5081-31 ba, Rosen Classroom) Rosen Publishing Group, Inc., The.
Th s: Level C, 6 vols. (Wright Skills Ser.). 16p. (gr. k-3). 26.50 *(978-0-322-0149.
Thud! Thump! Thud! Digraph th: Level B, 6 vols. (Wright Skills Ser.). 16p. (gr. k-3). 17.95 *(978-0-322-0147: Level T. Group 1, 6 vols. (Sunshine Ser.). 48p. 44.95 *(978-0-7802-5602-6(6))* Wright Group/McGraw-Hill.
To Catch a Thief: Level 3, 6 vols. (Fluency Strand Ser.). (gr. 4-8). 45.00 *(978-1-4045-1219-1(5))* Wright Group/McGraw-Hill.
To : Level 4, 6 vols. (Fluency Strand Ser.). (gr. 4-8). 45.00 *(978-1-4045-1223-8(: Level B, 6 vols. (Wright Skills Ser.). 16p. (gr. k-3). 17.95 *(978-0-322-0147: Level 5, 6 vols. (Fluency Strand Ser.). (gr. 4-8). 45.00 *(978-1-4045-1231-3(4))* Wright Group/McGraw-Hill.
Up in a Tree: Level D. Group 1. (Sunshine Ser.). 8p. 20.95 *(978-0-7802-573 Skills Guide. (Sunshine Skills Guides). 25.95 *(978-0-7802-9: Level A, 6 vols. (Wright Skills Ser.). 12p. (gr. k-3). 17.95 *(978-0-322-0311 I Sound. 2009. (PowerPhonics Ser.). 24p. (gr. 1-1). 39.90 *(978-1-60851-469-4(2),* PowerKids Pr.) Rosen Publishing Group, Inc., The.
—What I Think: Learning the TH Sound. 2009. (PowerPhonics Ser.). 24p. (gr. 1-1). 39.90 *(978-1-60851-47 e: Long Vowel i, CVCe Pattern: Level B, 6 vols. (Wright Skills Ser.). 16p. (gr. k-3). 17.95 *(978-0-322-0146 Sound, 1 vol. 2016. (Rosen Phonics Readers Ser.). (ENG.). 8p. (J). (gr. -1-2). pap. *(978-1-5081-32 ac, Rosen Classroom) Rosen Publishing Group, Inc., The.
—My Mother is a Dancer: Practicing the ER Sound, 1 vol. 2016. (Rosen Phonics Readers Ser.). (ENG., Illus.). 12p. (J). (gr. -1-2). pap. *(978-1-5081-30 ab, Rosen Classroom) Rosen Publishing Group, Inc., The.
—Yummy & Yucky: Practicing the y Sound, 1 vol. 2016. (Rosen Phonics Readers Ser.). (ENG., Illus.). 12p. (J). (gr. -1-2). pap. *(978-1-5081-30 31, Rosen Classroom) Rosen Publishing Group, Inc., The.

Wait for Me: Take-Home Book. 2005. (Emergent Library: Vol. 2). (YA). (gr. -1-1). 12.60 *(978-0-8215-7261-0(X))* Sadlier, William H. Inc.

Wake Up! Long Vowel a, CVCe Pattern: Level B, 6 vols. (Wright Skills Ser.). 16p. (gr. k-3). 17.95 *(978-0-322-03129-6(X))* Wright Group/McGraw-Hill.

Walker, Whitney. The Bat in the Barn: Practicing the B Sound, 1 vol. 2016. (Rosen Phonics Readers Ser.). (ENG., Illus.). 8p. (J). (gr. -1-2). pap. *(978-1-5081-3075-8(2),* 385f63d7-74ed-48e5-8e9c-ff88db4aa892, Rosen Classroom) Rosen Publishing Group, Inc., The.

—Brooke can Cook: Practicing the Short OO Sound, 1 vol. 2016. (Rosen Phonics Readers Ser.). (ENG., Illus.). 12p. (J). (gr. -1-2). pap. *(978-1-5081-3600-2(9),* f841693d-6f3e-43a6-8402-d2a982393c6c, Rosen Classroom) Rosen Publishing Group, Inc., The.

—The Family Farm: Practicing the F Sound, 1 vol. 2016. (Rosen Phonics Readers Ser.). (ENG.). 8p. (J). (gr. -1-2). pap. *(978-1-5081-3256-1(9),* e2f63dc5-01d8-4584-b9eb-7e752d526ac2, Rosen Classroom) Rosen Publishing Group, Inc., The.

—Max Packs a Box: Practicing the Ks Sound, 1 vol. 2016. (Rosen Phonics Readers Ser.). (ENG.). 12p. (J). (gr. -1-2). pap. *(978-1-5081-3575-3(4),* 414596fb-c20f-497f-99d4-3ebc02b4d2da, Rosen Classroom) Rosen Publishing Group, Inc., The.

—Valentine's Vet Visit: Practicing the V Sound, 1 vol. 2016. (Rosen Phonics Readers Ser.). (ENG.). 12p. (J). (gr. -1-2). pap. *(978-1-5081-3216-5(X),* d0dbd96a-c83b-4c88-aa30-1a0c4e8ddf90, Rosen Classroom) Rosen Publishing Group, Inc., The.

—Winter Weather: Practicing the Er Sound, 1 vol. 2016. (Rosen Phonics Readers Ser.). (ENG.). 12p. (J). (gr. -1-2). pap. *(978-1-5081-3195-3(3),* 6f11c615-ab03-493d-b9d7-5c892bc971db, Rosen Classroom) Rosen Publishing Group, Inc., The.

Wax, Wendy. Phonics Comics: Clara the Klutz - Level 2. Sullivan, Mary, illus. 2007. (ENG.). 24p. (J). (gr. 1-17). per. 3.99 *(978-1-58476-565-3(8))* Innovative Kids.

We Can! Level A: Consonant W. (Wright Skills Ser.). 12p. (gr. k-3). 17.95 *(978-0-322-03114-2(1))* Wright Group/McGraw-Hill.

Weil, Ann. Ice Skating. Fletcher, Rusty, illus. 2004. (Elements of Reading: Phonics Ser.). 16p. pap. 40.00 *(978-0-7398-9010-3(7))* Houghton Mifflin Harcourt Supplemental Pubs.

Weiss, Bobbi J. G. & Weiss, David Cody. Phonic Comics - Hiro Dragon Warrior: Fight or Flight Level 2, Issue 3. 2011. (ENG., Illus.). 24p. (J). (gr. 1-17). pap. 3.99 *(978-1-60169-111-8(4))* Innovative Kids.

Wernham, Sara & Lloyd, Sue. Jolly Phonics Activity Book 4: Ai, J, Oa, Ie, Ee, Or, 7 vols. Wade, Sarah, illus. 2010. (Jolly Phonics Activity Books, Set 1-7 Ser.). (ENG.). 7p. (J). pap. *(978-1-84414-156-2(X))* Jolly Learning, Ltd.

When the Alligator Came to Class: Short a; Consonants c, p; Blends cl, cr, scr, pl, spl, Level A. 2003. ("Plaid" Phonics & Stories Libraries). (gr. 1-2). 38.50 *(978-0-8136-9141-1(9))* Modern Curriculum Pr.

Wilkens, Karen & Benchmark Education Co., LLC Staff. ABC. 2015. (StartUp Ser.). (J). (gr. k). *(978-1-4900-0683-3(4))* Benchmark Education Co.

—I Like. 2015. (StartUp Ser.). (J). (gr. k). *(978-1-4900-0685-7(0))* Benchmark Education Co.

William H. Sadlier Staff. J My Name Is Jess. 2005. (Emergent Library: Vol. 2). (gr. -1-1). 24.00 net. *(978-0-8215-8935-9(0))* Sadlier, William H. Inc.

—Looking at Lizards: Big Book, Vol. 2. 2005. (Emergent Library: Vol. 1). (gr. -1-1). 24.00 net. *(978-0-8215-8906-9(7))* Sadlier, William H. Inc.

—Wait for Me. 2005. (Emergent Library: Vol. 2). (gr. -1-1). 24.00 net. *(978-0-8215-8931-1(8))* Sadlier, William H. Inc.

—Wake up, Sleepyheads!, Vol. 2. 2005. (Early Library). (gr. k-2). 24.00 net. *(978-0-8215-8955-7(5))* Sadlier, William H. Inc.

Williams, Richie. There's a Bear with a Pear! 2006. (Illus.). 32p. (J). 19.50 *(978-0-9777100-0-3(9))* Geoscience Information Services.

Winget, Kerry. Differential Processing Training Program Acoustic Linguistic Tasks. 2007. per. 32.95 *(978-0-7606-0723-7(0))* LinguiSystems, Inc.

—Differential Processing Training Program Acoustic Tasks. 2007. per. 32.95 *(978-0-7606-0722-0(2))* LinguiSystems, Inc.

—Differential Processing Training Program Linguistic Tasks. 2007. per. 32.95 *(978-0-7606-0724-4(9))* LinguiSystems, Inc.

Word Families. 2005. (J). *(978-1-60015-010-4(1))* Steps To Literacy, LLC.

Word Wall Words. 2004. (gr. k-18). suppl. ed. 39.70 *(978-0-673-62182-5(0));* (gr. 1-18). suppl. ed. 220.50 *(978-0-673-62183-2(9));* (gr. 2-18). suppl. ed. 220.50 *(978-0-673-62184-9(7));* (gr. 3-18). suppl. ed. 220.50 *(978-0-673-62185-6(5))* Addison-Wesley Educational Pubs., Inc.

A World Worth Keeping: Level T, Group 1, 6 vols. (Sunshine Ser.). 48p. 44.95 *(978-0-7802-6092-4(9))* Wright Group/McGraw-Hill.

The Wrecks: Level T, Group 2, 6 vols. (Sunshine Ser.). 48p. 44.95 *(978-0-7802-4177-0(0))* Wright Group/McGraw-Hill.

Wrestle Mania: Magazine Anthology: Level 5, 6 vols. (Comprehension Strand Ser.). (gr. 4-8). 54.00 *(978-0-322-06036-4(2))* Wright Group/McGraw-Hill.

The Wright Skills: Level B Sets - Long vowels only: 1 Each of 6 Titles. (gr. k-3). 17.95 *(978-0-322-01934-8(6))* Wright Group/McGraw-Hill.

The Wright Skills: Level B Sets - Long vowels only: 6 Each of 6 Titles. (gr. k-3). 109.50 *(978-0-322-01935-5(4))* Wright Group/McGraw-Hill.

The Wright Skills: Level C Sets - 1 Each of 16 Titles. (gr. k-3). 69.95 *(978-0-322-00734-5(8))* Wright Group/McGraw-Hill.

The Wright Skills: Level C Sets - 6 Each of 16 Titles. (gr. k-3). 322.95 *(978-0-322-00813-7(1))* Wright Group/McGraw-Hill.

Wrighton, Charlene & Bradshaw, Georgine. Basic Kit - Preschool. Clark, Irene, illus. 2005. Orig. Title: Basis Kit l. (J). 249.95 *(978-1-886441-30-9(8))* Zoo-phonics, Inc.

Yamile Y Yo Vol. 21: Little Books, Level 12. 2003. (Fonolibros Ser.). 34.95 *(978-0-7652-0099-0(6))* Modern Curriculum Pr.

Yip & Yap: Consonant y: Level A, 6 vols. (Wright Skills Ser.). 12p. (gr. k-3). 17.95 *(978-0-322-03120-3(6))* Wright Group/McGraw-Hill.

Yo Se Nadar! Little Books, Level 2, Vol. 18. 2003. (Fonolibros Ser.). 25.50 *(978-0-7652-0095-2(3))* Modern Curriculum Pr.

York. Phonics, Level A. 2004. (Steck-Vaughn Phonics Ser.). (ENG.). 416p. (gr. 1-1). tchr. ed., spiral bd. 64.50 *(978-0-7398-9140-7(5))* Houghton Mifflin Harcourt Publishing Co.

Young, Lee. Gabby Gets: Practicing the Hard G Sound, 1 vol. 2016. (Rosen Phonics Readers Ser.). (ENG., Illus.). 8p. (J). (gr. -1-2). pap. *(978-1-5081-3087-1(6),* 465717cb-bffd-4c49-a35d-5449bce295f2, Rosen Classroom) Rosen Publishing Group, Inc., The.

—Hers or His? Practicing the H Sound, 1 vol. 2016. (Rosen Phonics Readers Ser.). (ENG.). 8p. (J). (gr. -1-2). pap. *(978-1-5081-3265-3(8),* 0095d20e-e7ad-4f5a-8e88-e01d68e799f1, Rosen Classroom) Rosen Publishing Group, Inc., The.

—The Little Poodle: Practicing the UL Sound, 1 vol. 2016. (Rosen Phonics Readers Ser.). (ENG., Illus.). 12p. (J). (gr. -1-2). pap. *(978-1-5081-3569-2(X),* eaf43e6e-e3fd-4ba4-afd8-3987369675c1, Rosen Classroom) Rosen Publishing Group, Inc., The.

—The Lucky Bug: Practicing the Short U Sound, 1 vol. 2016. (Rosen Phonics Readers Ser.). (ENG., Illus.). 8p. (J). (gr. -1-2). pap. *(978-1-5081-3097-0(3),* b6f33d42-7557-4891-86a8-dfade26e53d1, Rosen Classroom) Rosen Publishing Group, Inc., The.

—Nico's New Net: Practicing the N Sound, 1 vol. 2016. (Rosen Phonics Readers Ser.). (ENG.). 8p. (J). (gr. -1-2). pap. *(978-1-5081-3274-5(7),* 3fe00bb8-c9fd-40cf-bb73-1bfe0918908b, Rosen Classroom) Rosen Publishing Group, Inc., The.

—The Queen's Question: Practicing the KW Sound, 1 vol. 2016. (Rosen Phonics Readers Ser.). (ENG., Illus.). 12p. (J). (gr. -1-2). pap. *(978-1-5081-3124-3(4),* 0d4ec4e8-40b1-4493-b6b0-e390b9a90caa, Rosen Classroom) Rosen Publishing Group, Inc., The.

—Troy's Choice: Practicing the Oi Sound, 1 vol. 2016. (Rosen Phonics Readers Ser.). (ENG., Illus.). 12p. (J). (gr. -1-2). pap. *(978-1-5081-3562-3(2),* 8fafc86e-fe76-44a0-8a22-f7697b556c16, Rosen Classroom) Rosen Publishing Group, Inc., The.

—Walter the Whale: Practicing the WH Sound, 1 vol. 2016. (Rosen Phonics Readers Ser.). (ENG., Illus.). 12p. (J). (gr. -1-2). pap. *(978-1-5081-3051-2(5),* e7425059-7a5a-49c0-949f-2f81af0b4764, Rosen Classroom) Rosen Publishing Group, Inc., The.

—Where Is the Exit? Practicing the Gz Sound, 1 vol. 2016. (Rosen Phonics Readers Ser.). (ENG.). 12p. (J). (gr. -1-2). pap. *(978-1-5081-3587-6(8),* c6a20efe-b8fd-40c5-90b6-a4a191a40406, Rosen Classroom) Rosen Publishing Group, Inc., The.

Zoboomafoo: Beginning Phonics. 2003. 32p. pap., wbk. ed. 14.95 incl. cd-rom *(978-1-57791-020-6(6));* pap., wbk. ed. 14.95 incl. cd-rom *(978-1-57791-021-3(4))* Brighter Minds Children's Publishing.

Zone Zoomers: Level 2, 6 vols. (Fluency Strand Ser.). (gr. 4-8). 45.00 *(978-1-4045-1213-9(6))* Wright Group/McGraw-Hill.

Zoo-phonics Quick Tests for the Classroom. 2004. cd-rom *(978-1-886441-41-5(3))* Zoo-phonics, Inc.

PHONICS

see Phonetics

PHONOGRAPH

see also Sound—Recording and Reproducing

Bell, Samantha S. Before Streaming Music. 2020. (What Did We Do? Ser.). (ENG., Illus.). 32p. (J). (gr. 2-3). pap. 9.95 *(978-1-64493-124-0(9),* 1644931249); lib. bdg. 31.35 *(978-1-64493-045-8(5),* 1644930455) North Star Editions. (Focus Readers).

Top That. Fun Kits Play the REC. 2008. *(978-1-84666-594-3(9))* Top That! Publishing PLC.

World Windows 3 (Social Studies): Thomas Edison: Content Literacy, Nonfiction Reading, Language & Literacy. 2011. (World Windows Ser.). (Illus.). 16p. (J). pap. 10.95 *(978-1-133-49279-5(7))* Cengage Heinle.

PHONOLOGY

see Phonetics

PHOTOGRAPHERS

Anderson, Christopher C. L. Margaret Bourke-White: Adventurous Photographer. 2005. (Great Life Stories Ser.). (ENG., Illus.). 127p. (J). (gr. 6-8). 30.50 *(978-0-531-12405-5(3),* Watts, Franklin) Scholastic Library Publishing.

Anderson, William. Les Kelly. Kelly, Leslie A., illus. Date not set. (J). (gr. 3-7). Vol. 1. 9.99 *(978-0-06-440851-6(5))* Vol. 2. 9.99 *(978-0-06-440850-9(7))* HarperCollins Pubs.

Armstrong, Jennifer. Photo by Brady: A Picture of the Civil War. 2005. (ENG., Illus.). 160p. (J). (gr. 4-9). 22.99 *(978-0-689-85785-0(3),* Atheneum Bks. for Young Readers) Simon & Schuster Children's Publishing.

—Photo by Brady: A Picture of the Civil War. 2013. (ENG., Illus.). 128p. (J). pap. 11.95 *(978-0-689-85786-7(1),* Simon & Schuster/Paula Wiseman Bks.) Simon & Schuster/Paula Wiseman Bks.

Baxter, Kathleen & McConnell, Robert L., contrib. by. Civil War Witness: Mathew Brady's Photos Reveal the Horrors of War, 1 vol. 2013. (Captured History Ser.). (ENG., Illus.). 64p. (J). (gr. 5-9). 35.32 *(978-0-7565-4693-9(1),* 123110, Compass Point Bks.) Capstone.

Blumenthal, Deborah. Polka Dot Parade: A Book about Bill Cunningham. D'yans, Masha, illus. 2018. (ENG.). 40p. (J). (gr. -1-3). 17.99 *(978-1-4998-0664-9(7))* Little Bee Books Inc.

Braun, Marta. Muybridge & the Riddle of Locomotion. 2013. (ENG., Illus.). 24p. (J). (gr. 4-12). 19.95 *(978-1-77085-229-7(8),* 73ced1c6-a6aa-444c-af06-f8079265a71d) Firefly Bks., Ltd.

Bueno, Julián David. Henry Cartier - Bresson- el azar y el Instante. 2005. (SPA.). 132p. (YA). *(978-958-30-1704-9(3))* Panamericana Editorial.

Burgan, Michael. Shadow Catcher: How Edward S. Curtis Documented American Indian Dignity & Beauty. 2015. (Captured History Ser.). (ENG., Illus.). 64p. (J). (gr. 5-9). pap. 8.95 *(978-0-7565-4998-5(1),* 127808, Compass Point Bks.) Capstone.

Cerullo, Mary M. Journey to Shark Island: A Shark Photographer's Close Encounters, 1 vol. Rotman, Jeffrey L., illus. Rotman, Jeffrey L., photos by. 2014. (Shark Expedition Ser.). (ENG.). 40p. (J). (gr. 5-9). lib. bdg. 32.65 *(978-0-7565-4887-2(X),* 124954, Compass Point Bks.) Capstone.

Cornell, Kari. Mathew Brady Records the Civil War. 2017. (Defining Images Ser.). (ENG., Illus.). 112p. (J). (gr. 6-12). lib. bdg. 41.36 *(978-1-5321-1016-0(2),* 25608, Essential Library) ABDO Publishing Co.

Crabtree, Marc. Meet My Neighbor, the Photographer. 2013. (ENG., Illus.). 24p. (J). *(978-0-7787-0873-5(X));* pap. *(978-0-7787-0877-3(2))* Crabtree Publishing Co.

Dallas, Justin & Rissman, Rebecca. Fashion Photographer: The Coolest Jobs on the Planet, 1 vol. 2014. (Coolest Jobs on the Planet Ser.). (ENG., Illus.). 48p. (J). (gr. 5-8). 35.32 *(978-1-4109-6641-4(0),* 126142); pap. 8.99 *(978-1-4109-6647-6(X),* 126146) Capstone. (Raintree).

goodall, lian. Photographing Greatness: The Story of Karsh. 2007. (Stories of Canada Ser.: 11). (ENG., Illus.). 96p. (J). 21.99 *(978-1-894917-34-6(0),* Napoleon & Co.) Dundurn Pr. CAN. Dist: Publishers Group West (PGW).

Hollihan, Kerrie Logan. Reporting under Fire: 16 Daring Women War Correspondents & Photojournalists. 2014. (Women of Action Ser.: 9). (ENG., Illus.). 256p. (YA). (gr. 7). 19.95 *(978-1-61374-710-0(1))* Chicago Review Pr., Inc.

King, David C. Dorothea Lange: Photographer of the People: Photographer of the People. 2009. (ENG., Illus.). 88p. (C). (gr. 6-18). lib. bdg. 180.00 *(978-0-7656-8154-6(4),* Y181941) Routledge.

Loney, Andrea. Take a Picture of Me, James Van der Zee!, 1 vol. Mallett, Keith, illus. 2017. (ENG.). 40p. (J). (gr. 2-7). 20.95 *(978-1-62014-260-8(0),* leelowbooks) Lee & Low Bks., Inc.

Martin, Jacqueline Briggs. Snowflake Bentley: A Caldecott Award Winner. Azarian, Mary, illus. 2009. (ENG.). 32p. (J). (gr. -1-3). pap. 8.99 *(978-0-547-24829-5(6),* 1100744, Clarion Bks.) HarperCollins Pubs.

Murray, Stuart A. P. Mathew Brady: Photographer of Our Nation: Photographer of Our Nation. 2009. (ENG., Illus.). 83p. (gr. 6-18). lib. bdg. 180.00 *(978-0-7656-8151-5(X),* Y182957) Routledge.

Nardo, Don. Edward S. Curtis Chronicles Native Nations. 2017. (Defining Images Ser.). (ENG.). 112p. (J). (gr. 6-12). 59.93 *(978-1-68078-800-6(0),* 26201); (Illus.). lib. bdg. 41.36 *(978-1-5321-1015-3(4),* 25606) ABDO Publishing Co. (Essential Library).

—Mathew Brady: The Camera Is the Eye of History, 1 vol. 2008. (Americans: the Spirit of a Nation Ser.). (ENG., Illus.). 128p. (gr. 5-6). lib. bdg. 35.93 *(978-0-7660-3023-7(7),* 4d1b9ae1-c55c-413b-81b3-7343482ad868) Enslow Publishing, LLC.

Nash, Eric Peter. Ansel Adams: The Spirit of Wild Places, Vol. 8. 2018. (American Artists Ser.). 144p. (J). (gr. 7). 35.93 *(978-1-4222-4155-4(6))* Mason Crest.

Novesky, Amy. Imogen: The Mother of Modernism & Three Boys. Congdon, Lisa, illus. 2012. (ENG.). 32p. (J). (gr. -1-3). 16.95 *(978-1-937359-32-4(8),* 1331101, Cameron Books) Cameron + Co.

Plain, Nancy. Light on the Prairie: Solomon D. Butcher, Photographer of Nebraska's Pioneer Days. 2012. (ENG., Illus.). 128p. (YA). pap. 16.95 *(978-0-8032-3520-5(8),* Bison Bks.) Univ. of Nebraska Pr.

Quintero, Isabel. Photographic: The Life of Graciela Iturbide. Peña, Zeke, illus. 2018. (ENG.). 96p. (YA). (gr. 7-17). 19.95 *(978-1-947440-00-5(4),* 1317401) Getty Pubns.

Quintero, Isabel & Iturbide, Graciela. Photographic: The Life of Graciela Iturbide. Peña, Zeke, illus. 2017. (J). *(978-1-60606-557-0(2),* J. Paul Getty Museum) Getty Pubns.

Robinson, Fiona. The Bluest of Blues: Anna Atkins & the First Book of Photographs. 2019. (ENG., Illus.). 48p. (J). (gr. 1-4). 19.99 *(978-1-4197-2551-7(3),* 1102901, Abrams Bks. for Young Readers) Abrams, Inc.

Rosenstock, Barb. Dorothea's Eyes: Dorothea Lange Photographs the Truth. Dubois, Gerard, illus. 2016. (ENG.). 40p. (J). (gr. 2-5). 18.99 *(978-1-62979-208-8(X),* Calkins Creek) Highlights Pr., c/o Highlights for Children, Inc.

Rubiano, Roberto. Robert Capa -Imágenes de Guerra. 2005. (SPA.). 168p. (YA). *(978-958-30-1905-0(4))* Panamericana Editorial.

Schulke, Flip. Witness to Our Times: My Life As a Photojournalist. 2003. (ENG., Illus.). 160p. (J). (gr. 7-18). 19.95 *(978-0-8126-2682-7(6))* Cricket Bks.

Show Me America, 5 vols., Set. Incl. Dorothea Lange: Photographer of the People: Photographer of the People. King, David C. 88p. (C). 2009. lib. bdg. 180.00 *(978-0-7656-8154-6(4),* Y181941); George Catlin: Painter of Indian Life: Painter of Indian Life. Worth, Richard. 80p. (C). 2009. lib. bdg. 180.00 *(978-0-7656-8152-2(8),* Y182314); John Trumbull: Painter of the Revolutionary War: Painter of the Revolutionary War. Murray, Stuart A. P. 83p. (C). 2008. lib. bdg. 180.00 *(978-0-7656-8150-8(1),* Y182501); Lewis Hine: Photographer of Americans at Work: Photographer of Americans at Work. Worth, Richard. 80p. (C). 2009. lib. bdg. 180.00 *(978-0-7656-8153-9(6),* Y182862); Mathew Brady: Photographer of Our Nation: Photographer of Our Nation. Murray, Stuart A. P. 83p. 2009. lib. bdg. 180.00 *(978-0-7656-8151-5(X),* Y182957); (Illus.). (gr. 6-18). (ENG.). 2009. Set lib. bdg. 165.00 *(978-0-7656-8149-2(8),* Y183560) Routledge.

Somervill, Barbara A. Wildlife Photographer. (21st Century Skills Library: Cool STEAM Careers Ser.). (ENG., Illus.). 32p. (gr. 4-7). 2015. (J). 32.07 *(978-1-63362-569-3(9),* 206460) 2008. lib. bdg. 32.07 *(978-1-60279-300-2(X),* 200139) Cherry Lake Publishing.

Stark, Kristy. En el Trabajo: Fotógrafo: Valor Posicional. rev. ed. 2018. (Mathematics in the Real World Ser.). (SPA., Illus.). 32p. (J). (gr. 2-3). pap. 10.99 *(978-1-4258-2858-5(2))* Teacher Created Materials, Inc.

—On the Job: Photographer: Place Value (Grade 2) 2018. (Mathematics in the Real World Ser.). (ENG., Illus.). 32p. (J). (gr. 2-3). pap. 10.99 *(978-1-4258-5741-7(8))* Teacher Created Materials, Inc.

Sullivan, George. Berenice Abbott, Photographer: An Independent Vision. 2006. (ENG., Illus.). 176p. (J). (gr. 5-7). 20.00 *(978-0-618-44026-9(7),* 100362, Clarion Bks.) HarperCollins Pubs.

Tanaka, Kazumi. Kazumi Tanaka: Words & Works. 2003. (Illus.). 104p. 14.95 *(978-1-878607-84-3(7))* Kent Gallery.

Thomas, William David. Wildlife Photographer, 1 vol. 2008. (Cool Careers: Adventure Careers Ser.). (ENG., Illus.). 32p. (gr. 3-3). pap. 11.50 *(978-0-8368-8892-8(8),* f411b758-f08a-4667-9f16-d1763a457d18); lib. bdg. 28.67 *(978-0-8368-8885-0(5),* 3e0a9aa4-db8f-4082-a587-e37c2419f096) Stevens, Gareth Publishing LLLP.

Weatherford, Carole Boston. Gordon Parks: How the Photographer Captured Black & White America. Christoph, Jamey, illus. 2015. (ENG.). 32p. (J). (gr. -1-3). 16.99 *(978-0-8075-3017-7(4),* 807530174) Whitman, Albert & Co.

Weston Woods Staff, creator. Snowflake Bentley. 2011. 18.95 *(978-0-545-31414-5(3));* 38.75 *(978-0-545-31415-2(1))* Weston Woods Studios, Inc.

Worth, Richard. Lewis Hine: Photographer of Americans at Work: Photographer of Americans at Work. 2009. (ENG., Illus.). 80p. (C). (gr. 6-18). lib. bdg. 180.00 *(978-0-7656-8153-9(6),* Y182862) Routledge.

PHOTOGRAPHY

see also Cameras; Nature Study

About Face: Portraits of Activism. 2004. (YA). per. *(978-1-932948-06-6(6))* Student Pr. Initiative.

Anderson, Rane. Taking Photos from Space (Grade 3) rev. ed. 2018. (Smithsonian: Informational Text Ser.). (ENG., Illus.). 32p. (J). (gr. 3-4). pap. 11.99 *(978-1-4938-6685-4(0))* Teacher Created Materials, Inc.

Bankston, John. Louis Daguerre & the Story of the Daguerreotype. 2004. (Uncharted, Unexplored, & Unexplained Ser.). (Illus.). 48p. (J). (gr. 4-8). lib. bdg. 29.95 *(978-1-58415-247-7(8))* Mitchell Lane Pubs.

Bartlett, Karen T. A Kid's Guide to Chicago. Brown, Don, illus. 2010. 64p. (J). pap. 16.95 *(978-1-934907-03-0(0))* Twin Lights Pubs., Inc.

Beardsley, Kurt. Under Saharan Skies. 2004. (Illus.). 96p. per. 25.00 *(978-0-9761103-0-9(X),* 1000) International Vaquero Productions.

Blumenthal, Deborah. Polka Dot Parade: A Book about Bill Cunningham. D'yans, Masha, illus. 2018. (ENG.). 40p. (J). (gr. -1-3). 17.99 *(978-1-4998-0664-9(7))* Little Bee Books Inc.

Bodden, Valerie. Photography. 2008. (Media Sources Ser.). (J). pap. 9.95 *(978-0-89812-531-3(6));* (Illus.). 24p. lib. bdg. 24.25 *(978-1-58341-558-0(0))* Creative Co., The. (Creative Education).

Bohn, Klaus. Healthy Me: I Love Fruit, I Love Veggies. Bohn, Klaus, illus. 2012. (ENG., Illus.). 44p. (J). pap. *(978-1-77143-034-0(6),* CCB Publishing) CCB Publishing.

Boswell, Kelly. Research Visual Primary Sources: Photographs, Paintings, Video, & More! 2019. (Primary Source Pro Ser.). (ENG., Illus.). 24p. (J). (gr. 1-3). pap. 7.95 *(978-1-9771-0513-4(0),* 139916, Capstone Pr.) Capstone.

Burgan, Michael. Exposing Hidden Worlds: How Jacob Riis' Photos Became Tools for Social Reform. 2017. (Captured History Ser.). (ENG., Illus.). 64p. (J). (gr. 5-9). lib. bdg. 35.32 *(978-0-7565-5618-1(X),* 135804, Compass Point Bks.) Capstone.

—The Hindenburg in Flames: How a Photograph Marked the End of the Airship. 2016. (Captured World History Ser.). (ENG., Illus.). 64p. (J). (gr. 5-9). lib. bdg. 35.32 *(978-0-7565-5441-5(1),* 132576, Compass Point Bks.) Capstone.

Carroll, Henry. Be a Super Awesome Photographer. 2019. (ENG., Illus.). 64p. (J). (gr. 2-6). 14.99 *(978-1-78627-420-5(5),* King, Laurence Publishing) Orion Publishing Group, Ltd. GBR. Dist: Hachette Bk. Group.

Chapel, Jamie Moore & Eberhardt, Nancy Chapel. ¿Qué Es Diferente ... ¿Qué Es lo Mismo? 2013. 34p. pap. 10.00 *(978-1-939054-14-2(1))* Rowe Publishing.

Coll-Seck, Jayden. My Mom Shows Me Old Photos, 1 vol., 1. 2015. (Rosen REAL Readers: Social Studies Nonfiction / Fiction: Myself, My Community, My World Ser.). (ENG.). 8p. (J). (gr. k-1). pap. 5.46 *(978-1-5081-1689-9(X),* 84e3867f-2b71-46da-8e79-17552ba4fcfe, Rosen Classroom) Rosen Publishing Group, Inc., The.

Crabtree, Marc. Meet My Neighbor, the Photographer. 2013. (ENG., Illus.). 24p. (J). *(978-0-7787-0873-5(X));* pap. *(978-0-7787-0877-3(2))* Crabtree Publishing Co.

Dallas, Justin & Rissman, Rebecca. Fashion Photographer: The Coolest Jobs on the Planet, 1 vol. 2014. (Coolest Jobs on the Planet Ser.). (ENG., Illus.). 48p. (J). (gr. 5-8). 35.32 *(978-1-4109-6641-4(0),* 126142); pap. 8.99 *(978-1-4109-6647-6(X),* 126146) Capstone. (Raintree).

Dell, Pamela. Man on the Moon: How a Photograph Made Anything Seem Possible, 1 vol. 2010. (Captured History Ser.). (ENG.). 64p. (J). (gr. 5-7). pap. 8.95 *(978-0-7565-4447-8(5),* 115528, Compass Point Bks.) Capstone.

Digital Photo Activity Kit Deluxe Vivitar 3700 series Lab-10. 2005. (J). cd-rom 1790.00 *(978-1-933229-02-7(0))* APTE, Inc.

Digital Photo Activity Kit Deluxe Vivitar 3700 series Lab-15. 2005. (J). cd-rom 2610.00 *(978-1-933229-03-4(9))* APTE, Inc.

Digital Photo Activity Kit Deluxe Vivitar 3700 series Lab-20. 2005. (J). 3260.00 *(978-1-933229-04-1(7))* APTE, Inc.

Digital Photo Activity Kit Deluxe Vivitar 3700 series Lab-25. 2005. (J). 3924.00 *(978-1-933229-05-8(5))* APTE, Inc.

Digital Photo Activity Kit Deluxe Vivitar 3700 series Lab-30. 2005. (J). 4585.00 *(978-1-933229-06-5(3))* APTE, Inc.

Digital Photo Activity Kit Deluxe Vivitar 3700 series Lab-35. 2005. (J). 5239.00 *(978-1-933229-07-2(1))* APTE, Inc.

Digital Photo Activity Kit Deluxe Vivitar 3700 series Lab-5. 2005. (J). cd-rom 648.95 *(978-1-933229-01-0(2))* APTE, Inc.

Digital Photo Activity Kit Deluxe Vivitar 3700 Series school Version. 2005. (J). cd-rom 133.95 *(978-1-933229-00-3(4))* APTE, Inc.

Digital Photo Activity Kit Deluxe Vivitar 5300 series Lab- 2005. (J). 1759.95 *(978-1-933229-09-6(8))* APTE, Inc.

Digital Photo Activity Kit Deluxe Vivitar 5300 series Lab-10. 2005. (J). 3469.99 *(978-1-933229-10-2(1))* APTE, Inc.

Digital Photo Activity Kit Deluxe Vivitar 5300 series Lab-15. 2005. (J). 5129.95 *(978-1-933229-11-9(X))* APTE, Inc.

Digital Photo Activity Kit Deluxe Vivitar 5300 series Lab-25. 2005. (J). 8123.90 *(978-1-933229-12-6(8))* APTE, Inc.

Digital Photo Activity Kit Deluxe Vivitar 5300 series Lab-30. 2005. (J). 9624.95 *(978-1-933229-14-0(4))* APTE, Inc.
Digital Photo Activity Kit Deluxe Vivitar 5300 series Lab-35. 2005. (J). 11119.95 *(978-1-933229-15-7(2))* APTE, Inc.
Digital Photo Activity Kit Deluxe Vivitar 5300 series Single. 2005. (J). 359.99 *(978-1-933229-08-9(X))* APTE, Inc.
Dutcher, Jim. National Geographic Kids Chapters: Living with Wolves! True Stories of Adventures with Animals. 2016. (NGK Chapters Ser.). (Illus.). 112p. (J). (gr. 3-7). pap. 5.99 *(978-1-4263-2563-2(0)*, National Geographic Kids) Disney Publishing Worldwide.
Dyan, Penelope. By the Sea — -A Kid's Guide to Valletta, Malt. Weigand, John D., photos by. 2011. (Illus.). 38p. pap. 11.95 *(978-1-935630-55-5(5))* Bellissima Publishing, LLC.
—High on a Hill! a Kid's Guide to Innsbruck, Austri. Weigand, John D., photos by. 2011. (Illus.). 40p. pap. 12.95 *(978-1-935630-76-0(8))* Bellissima Publishing, LLC.
—Steam Train! All the Way to Canterbury, England. Weigand, John D., photos by. 2011. (Illus.). 40p. pap. 11.95 *(978-1-935630-75-3(X))* Bellissima Publishing, LLC.
Elton, Candice & Elton, Richard. My Family Album. 2003. (Illus.). 32p. (J). spiral bd. 19.95 *(978-1-58685-323-5(6))* Gibbs Smith, Publisher.
—My Vacation Album: Includes: Reusable Camera, Film, Batteries & Glue Stick. Lee, Fran, illus. 2003. (ENG.). 28p. (J). spiral bd. 19.95 *(978-1-58685-280-1(9))* Gibbs Smith, Publisher.
Essential Photography. 2004. (I-Quest Ser.). (Illus.). 48p. (J). per. *(978-1-84229-744-5(9))* Top That! Publishing PLC.
Fandel, Jennifer. Picture Yourself Writing Nonfiction: Using Photos to Inspire Writing. 2011. (See It, Write It Ser.). (ENG.). 32p. (gr. 3-4). pap. 47.70 *(978-1-4296-7208-5(0)*, Capstone Pr.) Capstone.
Fast, Suellen M. America's Daughters. Fast, Suellen M., photos by. (Illus.). 100p. (Orig.). (J). (gr. k-18). pap. 19.00 *(978-0-935281-13-2(4))* Daughter Culture Pubns.
Fretland VanVoorst, Jenny. Photography. 2016. (Artist's Studio Ser.). (Illus.). 24p. (J). (gr. k-2). lib. bdg. 25.65 *(978-1-62031-283-4(2)*, Bullfrog Bks.) Jump! Inc.
Furgang, Adam. Snap & Share: Exploring the Potential of Instagram & Other Photo & Video Apps, 1 vol. 2014. (Digital & Information Literacy Ser.). (ENG., Illus.). 48p. (J). (gr. 5-5). 33.47 *(978-1-4777-7934-7(5)*, 4af8ec55-21f8-43aa-beaf-760ecdc7ab2b, Rosen Reference) Rosen Publishing Group, Inc., The.
Gardner, Jane P. Photo Science, Vol. 11. Lewin, Russ, ed. 2015. (Science 24/7 Ser.). (Illus.). 48p. (J). (gr. 5). 20.95 *(978-1-4222-3413-6(4))* Mason Crest.
Gerard, James H. The Blue Marble: How a Photograph Revealed Earth's Fragile Beauty, 1 vol. 2014. (Captured World History Ser.). (ENG., Illus.). 64p. (J). (gr. 5-9). pap. 8.95 *(978-0-7565-4788-2(1)*, 124530, Compass Point Bks.) Capstone.
Gladstone, James. Earthrise: Apollo 8 & the Photo That Changed the World. Lundy, Christy, illus. 2018. (ENG.). 32p. (J). (gr. 2-5). 16.95 *(978-1-77147-316-3(9))* Owlkids Bks. Inc. CAN. Dist: Publishers Group West (PGW).
Greenagel, Frank L., photos by. Think Like a Photographer! How to Take Better Pictures Than Anyone in Your Family. 2006. (Illus.). (J). *(978-1-59336-766-4(X))* Mondo Publishing.
Hamilton, John. Astrophotography. 2018. (Digital Photography Ser.). (ENG., Illus.). 48p. (J). (gr. 5-9). lib. bdg. 34.21 *(978-1-5321-1585-1(7)*, 28746, Abdo & Daughters) ABDO Publishing Co.
—Fashion Photography. 2018. (Digital Photography Ser.). (ENG., Illus.). 48p. (J). (gr. 5-9). lib. bdg. 34.21 *(978-1-5321-1586-8(5)*, 28748, Abdo & Daughters) ABDO Publishing Co.
—Outdoor Photography. 2018. (Digital Photography Ser.). (ENG.). 48p. (J). (gr. 5-9). lib. bdg. 34.21 *(978-1-5321-1587-5(3)*, 28750, Abdo & Daughters) ABDO Publishing Co.
—Portrait Photography. 2018. (Digital Photography Ser.). (ENG., Illus.). 48p. (J). (gr. 5-9). lib. bdg. 34.21 *(978-1-5321-1589-9(X)*, 28754, Abdo & Daughters) ABDO Publishing Co.
—Sports Photography. 2018. (Digital Photography Ser.). (ENG.). 48p. (J). (gr. 5-9). lib. bdg. 34.21 *(978-1-5321-1590-5(3)*, 28756, Abdo & Daughters) ABDO Publishing Co.
Handler, Daniel. Girls Standing on the Lawn. Kalman, Maira, illus. 2014. (ENG.). 64p. (gr. 5-17). 14.95 *(978-0-87070-908-1(9))* Museum of Modern Art.
Honovich, Nancy. National Geographic Kids Guide to Photography: Tips & Tricks on How to Be a Great Photographer from the Pros & Your Pals at My Shot. 2015. (Illus.). 160p. (J). (gr. 3-7). pap. 14.99 *(978-1-4263-2066-8(3)*, National Geographic Kids) Disney Publishing Worldwide.
Horne, Ronald William. Forgotten Faces: A Window into Our Immigrant Past (5x8-Clr-BW) 2004. (Illus.). 120p. per. 24.95 *(978-0-9747395-1-9(0)*, FF5x8ClrBW) Personal Genesis Publishing.
Janovich, Leah. Patty's Pictures. Billin-Frye, Paige, illus. 2010. 16p. (J). *(978-0-545-24820-4(5))* Scholastic, Inc.
Jarrow, Gail. Spooked! How a Radio Broadcast & the War of the Worlds Sparked the 1938 Invasion of America. 2018. (Illus.). 144p. (J). (gr. 5-9). 22.99 *(978-1-62979-776-2(6)*, Calkins Creek) Highlights Pr., c/o Highlights for Children, Inc.
Kallen, Stuart A. Photography, 1 vol. 2007. (Eye on Art Ser.). (ENG., Illus.). 112p. (gr. 7-7). lib. bdg. 41.03 *(978-1-59018-986-3(8)*, 91e172da-5853-4dfe-a8e1-d1d3f410f7df, Lucent Pr.) Greenhaven Publishing LLC.
Lightning Bolt Books: Famous Places, 18 vols., Set. Incl. Empire State Building. Bullard, Lisa. (gr. 1-3). 2009. 30.65 *(978-0-8225-9404-8(8)*, 8c2ca64f-d960-4383-871a-b5472e0846ea); Grand Canyon. Zuehlke, Jeffrey. (gr. 1-3). 2010. lib. bdg. 30.65 *(978-0-7613-4261-8(3)*, 238a878d-885b-4076-995c-18d9da4b43c8); Great Lakes. Piehl, Janet. (gr. 1-3). 2010. lib. bdg. 30.65 *(978-0-7613-4456-8(X)*, e8b06c85-9697-4c81-b791-02d3ea168e06); Lincoln Memorial. Nelson, Kristin L. (gr. k-2). 2010. lib. bdg. 25.26 *(978-0-7613-6018-6(2))*; Mount Rushmore. Jango-Cohen, Judith. (gr. k-2). 2010. lib. bdg. 25.26 *(978-0-7613-6021-6(2))*; Washington Monument. Nelson, Kristin L. (gr. k-2). 2010. lib. bdg. 25.26 *(978-0-7613-6019-3(0))*; Yellowstone National Park. Piehl, Janet. (gr. 1-3). 2010. lib. bdg. 30.65 *(978-0-7613-4455-1(1)*, 46efe48e-7059-41ba-bc38-c619b757a09b); (Illus.). 32p. (J). 2009. Set lib. bdg. 454.68 *(978-0-8225-9403-1(X)*, Lerner Pubns.) Lerner Publishing Group.
Lüsted, Marcia Amidon. For People Who Are Good with a Camera, 1 vol. 2016. (Cool Careers Without College Ser.). (ENG., Illus.). 104p. (J). (gr. 7-7). 41.12 *(978-1-5081-7276-5(5)*, 5b2c7460-af4f-4de0-bb72-c4061a16afd7) Rosen Publishing Group, Inc., The.
Mauro, Paul & Melton, H. Keith. Crime Scene & Surveillance Photography. 2004. (Detective Academy Ser.). (Illus.). 48p. (J). *(978-0-439-57182-1(0))* Scholastic, Inc.
McDougall, Carol & LaRamee-Jones, Shanda. Baby Look, 1 vol. 2012. (Baby Steps Ser.). (ENG., Illus.). 12p. (J). (gr. -1 — 1). bds. 8.95 *(978-1-55109-937-8(3)*, 07551a77-cf7c-46ee-9a51-ad85e9ec62ef) Nimbus Publishing, Ltd. CAN. Dist: Baker & Taylor Publisher Services (BTPS).
Mosley, Kim, text. Workbook for Black & White Photography, 1 vol. 3rd ed. 2005. (ENG.). 48p. (C). *(978-0-9663215-1-7(0))* Mosley, Kim.
Nash, Eric Peter. Ansel Adams: The Spirit of Wild Places, Vol. 8. 2018. (American Artists Ser.). 144p. (J). (gr. 7). 35.93 *(978-1-4222-4155-4(6))* Mason Crest.
Omoth, Tyler. Busting Boredom with Technology. 2017. (Boredom Busters Ser.). (ENG., Illus.). 32p. (J). (gr. 3-9). lib. bdg. 28.65 *(978-1-5157-4705-5(0)*, 134344, Capstone Pr.) Capstone.
Orr, Tamra. Image Sharing. 2019. (21st Century Skills Library: Global Citizens: Social Media Ser.). (ENG., Illus.). 32p. (J). (gr. 4-7). pap. 14.21 *(978-1-5341-3964-0(8)*, 212685); lib. bdg. 32.07 *(978-1-5341-4308-1(4)*, 212684) Cherry Lake Publishing.
Oxlade, Chris. Cameras: How They Work, Film, Digital, Filters, Effects - With 9 Easy-to-Do Experiments & 230 Exciting Pictures. 2016. (Illus.). 64p. (J). (gr. -1-12). 12.99 *(978-1-86147-663-0(9)*, Armadillo) Anness Publishing GBR. Dist: National Bk. Network.
Photography. (Make It Work Ser.). 42p. (J). (gr. 4-8). pap. *(978-1-882210-43-5(3))* Action Publishing, Inc.
Publications International Ltd. Staff, ed. Itsy Bitsy Spider. 2010. 12p. (J). bds. 3.98 *(978-1-60553-147-2(2))* Publications International, Ltd.
Rabbat, Suzy. Post It! Sharing Photos with Friends & Family. 2012. (Explorer Junior Library: Information Explorer Junior Ser.). (ENG., Illus.). 24p. (gr. 1-4). (J). pap. 12.79 *(978-1-61080-659-6(X)*, 202269); 32.07 *(978-1-61080-485-1(6)*, 202095) Cherry Lake Publishing.
—Using Digital Images. 2010. (Explorer Library: Information Explorer Ser.). (ENG., Illus.). 32p. (gr. 4-8). lib. bdg. 32.07 *(978-1-60279-954-7(7)*, 200633) Cherry Lake Publishing.
Rausch, Monica. George Eastman & the Camera, 1 vol. 2007. (Inventors & Their Discoveries Ser.). (ENG., Illus.). 24p. (gr. 2-4). pap. 9.15 *(978-0-8368-7730-4(6)*, 080c6546-48ca-40c8-a874-4d71baadf4fd); lib. bdg. 24.67 *(978-0-8368-7499-0(4)*, 18b8cd49-1810-4207-a067-c514c70c0b92) Stevens, Gareth Publishing LLLP. (Weekly Reader Leveled Readers).
Ringstad, Arnold. NASA Takes Photography into Space. 2017. (Defining Images Ser.). (ENG., Illus.). 112p. (J). (gr. 6-12). lib. bdg. 41.36 *(978-1-5321-1017-7(0)*, 25610, Essential Library) ABDO Publishing Co.
Sanderson, Krystyna. Light at Ground Zero: St. Paul's Chapel After 9/11. Bustard, Ned, ed. 2003. (Illus.). 120p. per. 11.99 *(978-0-9658798-4-2(4))* Square Halo Bks.
Sandmann, Alexa & Baxter, Kathleen. Captured History, 4 vols., Set. Incl. Birmingham 1963: How a Photograph Rallied Civil Rights Support. Tougas, Shelley. lib. bdg. 35.32 *(978-0-7565-4398-3(3)*, 113897); Migrant Mother: How a Photograph Defined the Great Depression. Nardo, Don. (Illus.). lib. bdg. 35.32 *(978-0-7565-4397-6(5)*, 113896); (J). (gr. 5-7). (Captured History Ser.). (ENG.). 64p. 2010. 105.96 o.p. *(978-0-7565-4399-0(1)*, 170685, Compass Point Bks.) Capstone.
Schaub, Stephen, photos by. Through a Glass Darkly: Photographs by Stephen M. Schaub. 2004. (ENG & FRE., Illus.). 60p. 65.00 *(978-0-9669079-1-9(4))* Indian Hill Gallery of Fine Photography.
Senior, Kathryn, et al. Photography. (Make It Work! Ser.). (Illus.). 48p. (J). pap. 7.99 *(978-0-590-24913-3(4))*; pap. 16.99 *(978-0-590-24912-6(6))* Scholastic, Inc.
Skerry, Brian & Zoehfeld, Kathleen Weidner. National Geographic Kids Chapters: the Whale Who Won Hearts: And More True Stories of Amazing Animal Adventures. 2014. (NGK Chapters Ser.). (Illus.). 112p. (J). (gr. 3-7). pap. 5.99 *(978-1-4263-1520-6(1)*, National Geographic Kids) Disney Publishing Worldwide.
Skog, Jason. Taking the Shot. 2012. (Photography for Teens Ser.). (ENG.). 48p. (J). (gr. 5-9). lib. bdg. 29.99 *(978-0-7565-4490-4(4)*, 115735, Compass Point Bks.) Capstone.
Skog, Jason & Kalz, Jill. Displaying the Shot. 2012. (Photography for Teens Ser.). (ENG.). 48p. (J). (gr. 5-9). 29.99 *(978-0-7565-4491-1(2)*, 115736, Compass Point Bks.) Capstone.
Smith-Llera, Danielle. Lunch Counter Sit-Ins: How Photographs Helped Foster Peaceful Civil Rights Protests. 2018. (Captured History Ser.). (ENG., Illus.). 64p. (J). (gr. 5-9). lib. bdg. 35.32 *(978-0-7565-5878-9(6)*, 138646, Compass Point Bks.) Capstone.
—Serena vs. Venus: How a Photograph Spotlighted the Fight for Equality. 2017. (Captured History Sports Ser.). (ENG., Illus.). 64p. (J). (gr. 5-9). lib. bdg. 35.32 *(978-0-7565-5529-0(9)*, 134414, Compass Point Bks.) Capstone.
Spence, Kelly. Maker Projects for Kids Who Love Photography. 2016. (Be a Maker! Ser.). (ENG.). 32p. (J). (gr. 5-9). *(978-0-7787-2578-7(2))* Crabtree Publishing Co.
Spencer, Jeffrey. Building for the Ages: Omaha's Architectural Landmarks. 2003. (Illus.). 208p. (YA). lib. bdg. 39.95 *(978-0-9745410-1-3(X))* Omaha Bks.
Stanton, Brandon. Little Humans. Stanton, Brandon, photos by. 2014. (ENG., Illus.). 40p. (J). (gr. -1-1). 19.99 *(978-0-374-37456-3(2)*, 900123448, Farrar, Straus & Giroux (BYR)) Farrar, Straus & Giroux.
Stark, Kristy. En el Trabajo: Fotógrafo: Valor Posicional. rev. ed. 2018. (Mathematics in the Real World Ser.). (SPA., Illus.). 32p. (J). (gr. 2-3). pap. 10.99 *(978-1-4258-2858-5(2))* Teacher Created Materials, Inc.
—On the Job: Photographer: Place Value (Grade 2) 2018. (Mathematics in the Real World Ser.). (ENG., Illus.). 32p. (J). (gr. 2-3). pap. 10.99 *(978-1-4258-5741-7(8))* Teacher Created Materials, Inc.
Stewart, Gail B. The Crime Scene Photographer, 1 vol. 2008. (Crime Scene Investigations Ser.). (ENG., Illus.). 104p. (gr. 7-7). lib. bdg. 42.03 *(978-1-4205-0036-3(8)*, 340b9f2d-f6fa-4019-b5f0-769c2ac446f6, Lucent Pr.) Greenhaven Publishing LLC.
Stuckey, Rachel. Get into Photography. 2016. (Get-into-It Guides). (ENG.). 32p. (J). (gr. 3-6). *(978-0-7787-2643-2(6))* Crabtree Publishing Co.
Thompson, Gary. Digital Photography & Your PC: A Guide to Using Your PC to Create Your Own Personalized Photo Albums. 2003. (Illus.). 166p. (YA). spiral bd. 29.95 *(978-0-9749763-0-3(X))* Guiding Horizons.
Thomson, Ruth. Photos Framed: a Fresh Look at the World's Most Memorable Photographs. 2014. (ENG., Illus.). 64p. (J). (gr. 5). 18.99 *(978-0-7636-7154-9(1))* Candlewick Pr.
Tress, Arthur, photos by. Facing Up: Tress: Facing Up. ltd. ed. 2004. (ENG & FRE., Illus.). 1250.00 *(978-0-9761396-7-6(7)*, Tress-LE1) Top Choice Pr., LLC.
Turnbull, Stephanie. Cool Stuff to Photograph. 2015. (ENG., Illus.). 32p. (J). pap. 9.95 *(978-1-77092-224-2(5))* RiverStream Publishing.
—Photography. 2015. (Try This! Ser.). (ENG., Illus.). 24p. (J). (gr. 3-6). 27.10 *(978-1-62588-374-2(9)*, 17448) Black Rabbit Bks.
Turnbull, Stephaniel. Cool Stuff to Photograph. 2014. (Cool Stuff Ser.). 32p. (gr. 2-5). 31.35 *(978-1-62588-190-8(8))* Black Rabbit Bks.
VanVoorst, Jenny Fretland. La Fotografía. 2016. (El Estudio del Artista (Artist's Studio)).Tr. of Photography. (SPA., Illus.). 24p. (J). lib. bdg. 25.65 *(978-1-62031-324-4(3)*, Bullfrog Bks.) Jump! Inc.
Ventura, Marne. The 12 Most Influential Photographs of All Time. 2018. (Most Influential Ser.). (ENG., Illus.). 32p. (J). (gr. 3-6). 32.80 *(978-1-63235-412-9(8)*, 13749, 12-Story Library) Bookstaves, LLC.
Walters, John. Sportswriting & Sports Photography, Vol. 10. Ferrer, Al, ed. 2015. (Careers off the Field Ser.). (Illus.). 64p. (J). (gr. 7). lib. bdg. 23.95 *(978-1-4222-3273-6(5))* Mason Crest.
Wanless, Harold R. Book of Aerial Stereo Photographs, 10 bks., Set. (Illus.). (J). (gr. 7-12). spiral bd. 13.50 *(978-0-8331-1703-8(3)*, 589) Hubbard Scientific, Inc.
Weatherford, Carole Boston. Dorothea Lange. 2018. (2019 Av2 Fiction Ser.). (ENG.). 32p. (J). lib. bdg. 34.28 *(978-1-4896-8255-0(4)*, AV2 by Weigl) Weigl Pubs., Inc.
Webber, Diane. Shot & Framed: Photographers at the Crime Scene. 2007. (24/7: Science Behind the Scenes Ser.). (ENG., Illus.). 64p. (YA). (gr. 9-12). 29.00 *(978-0-531-12063-7(5)*, Watts, Franklin) Scholastic Library Publishing.
Wood, Alix. Be a Director of Photography: Make Every Shot Count, 1 vol. 2017. (Moviemakers' Film Club Ser.). (ENG.). 32p. (J). (gr. 4-5). 27.93 *(978-1-5383-2274-1(9)*, 7a14555c-3ccd-4887-8fb8-f15170b1b4bd); pap. 11.00 *(978-1-5383-2370-0(2)*, 7360409f-d6b8-4089-a129-8677f5698c5a) Rosen Publishing Group, Inc., The. (PowerKids Pr.).

PHOTOGRAPHY, AERIAL

see Aerial Photography

PHOTOGRAPHY—AESTHETICS

see Photography, Artistic

PHOTOGRAPHY, ARTISTIC

Bower, John. Lingering Spirit: A Photographic Tribute to Indiana's Fading, Forlorn, & Forgotten Places. 2003. (Illus.). 144p. per. 22.00 *(978-0-9745186-0-2(3))* Studio Indiana.
Burkhard, Balthasar. Click, Said the Camera. 2006. (Illus.). 42p. pap. 30.00 *(978-3-907044-56-8(8))* Lars Muller Pubs. CHE. Dist: Springer.
Finger, Brad. 13 Photos Children Should Know. 2011. (13 Children Should Know Ser.). (ENG., Illus.). 48p. (J). (gr. 3-7). 14.95 *(978-3-7913-7047-7(2))* Prestel Verlag GmbH & Co KG. DEU. Dist: Penguin Random Hse. LLC.
Fulford, Jason & Shopsin, Tamara. This Equals That. Fulford, Jason & Shopsin, Tamara, illus. 2014. (Illus.). 80p. (J). (gr. 3-7). 19.95 *(978-1-59711-288-8(7)*, e7e22b10-8d87-4780-b06b-4ca20d91302b) Aperture Foundation, Inc.
Kallas, Randi & Dougherty, Mike, eds. Rochester, Minnesota: A Visual & Historic Journey. 2003. (Illus.). 136p. pap. 24.95 *(978-0-9659875-3-0(1))* Riggott, Dean Photography.
Lynch, Marietta & Perry, Patricia. No More Monkeys: A Photographic Version of the Children's Finger Game. (Orig.). (J). (gr. -1-3). pap. 2.95 *(978-0-9610962-0-5(9))* Lynch, Marietta & Patricia Perry.
Quintero, Isabel. Photographic: The Life of Graciela Iturbide. Peña, Zeke, illus. 2018. (ENG.). 96p. (YA). (gr. 7-17). 19.95 *(978-1-947440-00-5(4)*, 1317401) Getty Pubns.
Quintero, Isabel & Iturbide, Graciela. Photographic: The Life of Graciela Iturbide. Peña, Zeke, illus. 2017. (J). *(978-1-60606-557-0(2)*, J. Paul Getty Museum) Getty Pubns.

PHOTOGRAPHY—FICTION

Alphin, Elaine Marie. Picture Perfect. 2003. (ENG., Illus.). 256p. (YA). (gr. 5-12). 15.95 *(978-0-8225-0535-8(5)*, c127bed3-b5f7-4f26-be27-1bd20d565a98, Carolrhoda Bks.) Lerner Publishing Group.
Arcos, Carrie. We Are All That's Left. 2018. 400p. (YA). (gr. 7). 17.99 *(978-0-399-17554-1(7)*, Philomel Bks.) Penguin Young Readers Group.
Avi. The Seer of Shadows. 2009. (ENG.). 224p. (J). (gr. 4-7). pap. 7.99 *(978-0-06-000017-2(1)*, HarperCollins) HarperCollins Pubs.
Bailer, Darice. Railroad!, Level 3: A Story of the Transcontinental Railroad. Farnsworth, Bill, illus. 3rd ed. 2004. (Soundprints' Read-and-Discover Ser.). (ENG.). 48p. (J). (gr. 1-4). pap. 3.95 *(978-1-59249-017-2(4)*, S2007) Soundprints.
Bauer, Joan. Thwonk. 2005. 224p. (YA). (gr. 7-7). pap. 7.99 *(978-0-14-240429-4(2)*, Speak) Penguin Young Readers Group.
—Thwonk. 2005. 215p. (gr. 7-12). 18.00 *(978-0-7569-5782-7(6))* Perfection Learning Corp.
Bentley, Sue. Picture Perfect #13. Swan, Angela, illus. 2014. (Magic Kitten Ser.: 13). (ENG.). 128p. (J). (gr. 1-3). 5.99 *(978-0-448-46796-2(8)*, Grosset & Dunlap) Penguin Young Readers Group.
Bernard, Janice. The Gum. 2011. 40p. pap. 21.99 *(978-1-4568-6487-3(4))* Xlibris Corp.
Bick, Ilsa J. The Sin-Eater's Confession. 2014. (ENG., Illus.). 296p. (YA). (gr. 9-12). pap. 9.95 *(978-1-4677-3705-0(4)*, d1d2a2d6-a315-4ec1-843c-4b7c1da54080, Carolrhoda Lab™) Lerner Publishing Group.
Breisacher, Cathy. Petunia Pepper's Picture Day. Elden, Christian, illus. 2010. 32p. (J). 14.99 *(978-1-59317-397-5(0))* Warner Pr., Inc.
Cangilla-McAdam, Claudia. Maria's Mysterious Mission. Crum, Anna-Maria, illus. 2007. 32p. (J). (gr. 3-7). 12.95 *(978-1-56579-588-4(1))* Fielder, John Publishing.
Carter, Brooke. The Unbroken Hearts Club, 1 vol. 2019. (Orca Soundings Ser.). (ENG.). 160p. (YA). (gr. 8-12). pap. 9.95 *(978-1-4598-2061-6(4))* Orca Bk. Pubs. USA.
Chatel, Kim. A Talent for Quiet. Chatel, Kim, photos by. 2009. (Illus.). 32p. pap. 10.95 *(978-1-935137-56-6(5))* Guardian Angel Publishing, Inc.
Cheese, Please! Individual Title Six-Packs. (Story Steps Ser.). (gr. k-2). 29.00 *(978-0-7635-9589-0(6))* Rigby Education.
Cross, Julie & Perini, Mark. Halfway Perfect. 2015. 384p. (YA). (gr. 8-12). pap. 9.99 *(978-1-4022-9719-9(X)*, 9781402297199) Sourcebooks, Inc.
Cunliffe, John. Postman Pat Takes a Photo. (ENG., Illus.). 20p. (J). 11.99 *(978-0-340-73712-5(3))* Hodder & Stoughton GBR. Dist: Trafalgar Square Publishing.
Curious George Dinosaur Tracks (Reader Level 1) 2011. (Curious George TV Ser.). (ENG., Illus.). 24p. (J). (gr. -1-3). pap. 4.99 *(978-0-547-43888-7(5)*, 1433465, Clarion Bks.) HarperCollins Pubs.
Da Costa, Deborah. Hanukkah Moon. Mosz, Gosia, illus. 2007. (Hanukkah Ser.). 32p. (J). (gr. -1-3). 17.95 *(978-1-58013-244-2(8)*, Kar-Ben Publishing) Lerner Publishing Group.
Desai Hidier, Tanuja. Born Confused. 2014. (ENG.). 512p. (YA). (gr. 9). pap. 13.99 *(978-0-545-66451-6(9)*, PUSH) Scholastic, Inc.
Devlin, Calla. Right Where You Left Me. 2017. (ENG., Illus.). 256p. (YA). (gr. 9). 17.99 *(978-1-4814-8699-6(3)*, Atheneum Bks. for Young Readers) Simon & Schuster Children's Publishing.
Doudna, Kelly. Goat Cheese. Haberstroh, Anne, illus. 2006. (Fact & Fiction Ser.). 24p. (J). pap. 48.42 *(978-1-59679-938-7(2))* ABDO Publishing Co.
Dwyer, Cynthia. Can You See Me Now? Schuepbach, Lynnette, illus. 2006. 24p. (J). 12.95 *(978-0-9677685-8-8(6))* Grannie Annie Family Story Celebration, The.
Echols, Jennifer. Perfect Couple. 2015. (Superlatives Ser.). (ENG., Illus.). 336p. (YA). (gr. 9). pap. 12.99 *(978-1-4424-7448-2(3)*, Simon Pulse) Simon Pulse.
Enderle, Dotti. Tell No One!, 1 vol. McWilliam, Howard, illus. 2009. (Ghost Detectors Ser.: No. 1). (ENG.). 80p. (J). (gr. 2-5). 35.64 *(978-1-60270-692-7(1)*, 8804, Calico Chapter Bks.) ABDO Publishing Co.
Fields, Jan. Chase the Chupacabra, 1 vol. Brundage, Scott, illus. 2014. (Monster Hunters Ser.). (ENG.). 80p. (J). (gr. 2-5). 35.64 *(978-1-62402-044-5(5)*, 1523, Calico Chapter Bks.) ABDO Publishing Co.
—Hunt for Sewer Gators, 1 vol. Brundage, Scott, illus. 2014. (Monster Hunters Ser.). (ENG.). 80p. (J). (gr. 2-5). 35.64 *(978-1-62402-045-2(3)*, 1525, Calico Chapter Bks.) ABDO Publishing Co.
—Search for Bigfoot, 1 vol. Brundage, Scott, illus. 2014. (Monster Hunters Ser.). (ENG.). 80p. (J). (gr. 2-5). 35.64 *(978-1-62402-046-9(1)*, 1527, Calico Chapter Bks.) ABDO Publishing Co.
—Tame Tahoe Tessie, 1 vol. Brundage, Scott, illus. 2014. (Monster Hunters Ser.). (ENG.). 80p. (J). (gr. 2-5). 35.64 *(978-1-62402-047-6(X)*, 1529, Calico Chapter Bks.) ABDO Publishing Co.
Geras, Adèle. Cecily's Portrait. 2009. (Historical House Ser.). 169p. (YA). (gr. 5-18). pap. 5.99 *(978-0-7945-2334-3(X)*, Usborne) EDC Publishing.
Gibaldi, Lauren. Autofocus. 2016. (ENG.). 352p. (YA). (gr. 9). 17.99 *(978-0-06-230223-6(X)*, HarperTeen) HarperCollins Pubs.
Gutknecht, Allison. Never Wear Red Lipstick on Picture Day: (and Other Lessons I've Learned) Lewis, Stevie, illus. 2014. (ENG.). 176p. (J). (gr. 2-5). 16.99 *(978-1-4814-2959-7(0)*, Aladdin) Simon & Schuster Children's Publishing.
Gutman, Dan. Flashback Four #1: the Lincoln Project. 2016. (Flashback Four Ser.: 1). (ENG.). 240p. (J). (gr. 3-7). 16.99 *(978-0-06-237441-7(9)*, HarperCollins) HarperCollins Pubs.
—Flashback Four #3: the Pompeii Disaster. (Flashback Four Ser.: 3). (ENG.). (J). (gr. 3-7). 2019. 272p. pap. 7.99 *(978-0-06-237445-5(1))* 2018. 256p. 16.99 *(978-0-06-237444-8(3))* HarperCollins Pubs. (HarperCollins).
—Flashback Four #4: the Hamilton-Burr Duel. 2019. (Flashback Four Ser.: 4). (ENG., Illus.). 240p. (J). (gr. 3-7). 16.99 *(978-0-06-237447-9(8)*, HarperCollins) HarperCollins Pubs.
—Ms. Joni Is a Phony! Paillot, Jim, illus. 2017. 105p. (J). *(978-1-5182-3403-3(8))* Harper & Row Ltd.
—My Weirdest School #7: Ms. Joni Is a Phony! Paillot, Jim, illus. 2017. (My Weirdest School Ser.: 7). (ENG.). 112p. (J). (gr. 1-5). pap. 4.99 *(978-0-06-242929-2(9)*, HarperCollins) HarperCollins Pubs.
Jaden, Denise. Never Enough. 2012. (ENG.). 400p. (YA). (gr. 9). pap. 9.99 *(978-1-4424-2907-9(0)*, Simon Pulse) Simon Pulse.
Keene, Carolyn. Hidden Pictures. 2020. (Nancy Drew Diaries: 19). (ENG.). 192p. (J). (gr. 3-7). pap. 6.99 *(978-1-5344-2102-8(5)*, Simon & Schuster/Paula Wiseman Bks.) Simon & Schuster/Paula Wiseman Bks.
Kelley, Marty. Campground Creature. 2018. (Molly Mac Ser.). (ENG., Illus.). 56p. (J). (gr. k-2). pap. 4.95

(978-1-5158-2389-6(X), 137204); lib. bdg. 22.65 *(978-1-5158-2385-8(7)*, 137200) Capstone. (Picture Window Bks.).

Kernan, Elizabeth. Patty's Pictures, 1 vol. 2006. (Neighborhood Readers Ser.). (ENG.). 12p. (gr. k-1). pap. 5.90 *(978-1-4042-6471-7(X)*, ee545f66-6b81-4a35-8abe-dd574071ee79, Rosen Classroom) Rosen Publishing Group, Inc., The.

Larson, Kirby. The Fences Between Us: The Diary of Piper Davis. 2010. (Illus.). 313p. (J). pap. *(978-0-545-27094-6(4))* Scholastic, Inc.

Lemke, Donald & Lemke, Donald B. Captured off Guard: The Attack on Pearl Harbor, 1 vol. St. Aubin, Claude, illus. 2008. (Historical Fiction Ser.). (ENG.). 56p. (J). (gr. 3-6). pap. 6.25 *(978-1-4342-0493-6(6)*, 94441, Stone Arch Bks.) Capstone.

Maas, Susan Thogerson. Picture Imperfect. 2015. 228p. (J). pap. *(978-1-941720-10-3(2))* Ashberry Lane.

Mason, Jane B. & Stephens, Sarah Hines. Now You See Me..., 4. 2010. (Poison Apple Ser.: 4). (ENG.). 176p. (J). (gr. 6-8). 18.69 *(978-0-545-21513-8(7))* Scholastic, Inc.

McIntosh, Kenneth. Close-Up: Forensic Photography. 2009. (J). pap. 24.95 *(978-1-4222-1455-8(9))* Mason Crest.

—Close-Up: Forensic Photography, 5 vols. Sanborn, Casey, illus. 2007. (Crime Scene Club Ser.: Bk. 5). 144p. (YA). (gr. 9-12). lib. bdg. 24.95 *(978-1-4222-0251-7(8))* Mason Crest.

McNamara, Margaret. Class Picture Day: Ready-To-Read Level 1. Gordon, Mike, illus. 2011. (Robin Hill School Ser.). (ENG.). 32p. (J). (gr. -1-1). pap. 4.99 *(978-1-4169-9173-1(5)*, Simon Spotlight) Simon Spotlight.

Menchin, Scott. Goodnight Selfie. Collet-Derby, Pierre, illus. 2015. (ENG.). 32p. (J). (gr. -1-3). 16.99 *(978-0-7636-3182-6(5))* Candlewick Pr.

Meyer, Carolyn. Girl with a Camera: Margaret Bourke-White, Photographer: a Novel. 2017. (ENG., Illus.). 352p. (J). (gr. 5-9). 17.95 *(978-1-62979-584-3(4)*, Calkins Creek) Highlights Pr., c/o Highlights for Children, Inc.

Mills, Charles. The Bandit of Benson Park. 2003. (Honors Club Story Ser.: Vol. 1). 127p. (J). *(978-0-8163-1977-0(4))* Pacific Pr. Pubns.

Nees, Susan. Missy's Super Duper Royal Deluxe: Picture Day. 2013. (Missy's Super Duper Royal Deluxe Ser.: 1). (ENG., Illus.). 80p. (J). (gr. k-2). pap. 4.99 *(978-0-545-43851-3(9))* Scholastic, Inc.

—Picture Day. 2013. (Missy's Super Duper Royal Deluxe Ser.: 1). lib. bdg. 14.75 *(978-0-606-31979-9(4))* Turtleback.

Perkins, Lynne Rae. Pictures from Our Vacation. Perkins, Lynne Rae, illus. 2007. (Illus.). 32p. (J). (gr. k-3). 17.89 *(978-0-06-085098-2(1))*; (ENG., 17.99 *(978-0-06-085097-5(3))* HarperCollins Pubs. (Greenwillow Bks.).

Rey, H. A. Curious George: Dinosaur Tracks/Jorge el Curioso Huellas de Dinosaurio: Bilingual English-Spanish. 2011. (Curious George TV Ser.). (ENG., Illus.). 24p. (J). (gr. -1-3). pap. 4.99 *(978-0-547-55798-4(1)*, 1453316, Clarion Bks.) HarperCollins Pubs.

Rosen, Robert. The Family Photo. de Polonia, Nina, illus. 2017. (Family Time Ser.). (ENG.). 24p. (gr. -1-2). pap. 9.95 *(978-1-68342-764-3(5)*, 9781683427643) Rourke Educational Media.

Schroeder, Lisa. Mia's Golden Bird. 2014. (Charmed Life Ser.: 2). lib. bdg. 16.00 *(978-0-606-35850-7(1))* Turtleback.

Scotton, Rob. Russell & the Lost Treasure. Scotton, Rob, illus. 2006. (ENG., Illus.). 32p. (J). (gr. -1-2). 19.99 *(978-0-06-059851-8(4)*, HarperCollins) HarperCollins Pubs.

Shea, Therese. Carmen's Photo Album, 1 vol. 2006. (Neighborhood Readers Ser.). (ENG.). 12p. (gr. 1-2). pap. 5.90 *(978-1-4042-6795-4(6)*, cd9ce055-4067-420a-a40f-2dab1a5bac4e, Rosen Classroom) Rosen Publishing Group, Inc., The.

Sher, Emil. Young Man with Camera. Wyman, David, photos by. 2015. (ENG., Illus.). 240p. (YA). (gr. 7). 17.99 *(978-0-545-54131-2(X)*, Levine, Arthur A. Bks.) Scholastic, Inc.

Snyder, Karen. Safari Smooches. LaGrange, Tiffany, illus. 2011. 24p. pap. 12.95 *(978-1-936343-95-9(9))* Peppertree Pr., The.

Sonnenblick, Jordan. Curveball: the Year I Lost My Grip. (ENG.). 304p. 2014. (J). (gr. 7). pap. 10.99 *(978-0-545-32070-2(4)*, Scholastic Paperbacks) 2012. E-Book 17.99 *(978-0-545-39311-9(6))* Scholastic, Inc.

Tatulli, Mark. Desmond Pucket & the Mountain Full of Monsters. 2014. (Desmond Pucket Ser.: 2). (ENG.). 240p. (J). 13.99 *(978-1-4494-3549-3(1))* Andrews McMeel Publishing.

Taylor, Debbie A. Sweet Music in Harlem, 1 vol. Morrison, Frank, illus. 2004. (ENG.). 32p. (J). (gr. 1-4). pap. 11.95 *(978-1-62014-080-2(2)*, leelowbooks) Lee & Low Bks., Inc.

Ticktock. Snapped by Sam! 2013. (I Love Reading Phonics: Level 5 Ser.). (ENG.). 24p. (J). (gr. k-3). 16.19 *(978-1-84898-775-3(7)*, TickTock Books) Octopus Publishing Group GBR. Dist: Children's Plus, Inc.

Toliver, K. S. Pam Brown Is Picture Perfect!! 2008. 28p. pap. 12.95 *(978-1-4327-2058-2(9))* Outskirts Pr., Inc.

Townley, Roderick. The Red Thread: A Novel in Three Incarnations. 2012. (ENG.). 304p. (YA). (gr. 7). pap. 14.99 *(978-1-4169-0895-1(1)*, Atheneum Bks. for Young Readers) Simon & Schuster Children's Publishing.

Tracy, Kristen. Project (un)Popular Book #1. 2017. (Project (un)Popular Ser.: 1). (ENG.). 336p. (J). (gr. 5). 8.99 *(978-0-553-51051-5(7)*, Yearling) Random Hse. Children's Bks.

Vivian, Siobhan. A Little Friendly Advice. 2015. (ENG.). 256p. (YA). (gr. 6-7). pap. 9.99 *(978-0-545-75801-7(7)*, PUSH) Scholastic, Inc.

Walters, Eric. Northern Exposures, 1 vol. 2008. (ENG.). 208p. (J). (gr. 4-7). pap. 11.95 *(978-1-55455-107-1(2)*, dab1355d-4a34-44b3-be1a-b77fedf71038) Trifolium Bks., Inc. CAN. Dist: Firefly Bks., Ltd.

Ylvisaker, Anne. The Luck of the Buttons. 2012. (ENG., Illus.). 240p. (J). (gr. 3-7). pap. 8.99 *(978-0-7636-6061-1(2))* Candlewick Pr.

Young, Brigit. Worth a Thousand Words. 2020. (ENG.). 304p. (J). pap. 7.99 *(978-1-250-30875-7(5)*, 900177859) Square Fish.

PHOTOGRAPHY—HISTORY

Aller, Susan Bivin. George Eastman. 2003. (History Maker Biographies Ser.). (ENG., Illus.). 48p. (gr. 3-6). lib. bdg. 27.93 *(978-0-8225-0200-5(3))* Lerner Publishing Group.

Bankston, John. Louis Daguerre & the Story of the Daguerreotype. 2004. (Uncharted, Unexplored, & Unexplained Ser.). (Illus.). 48p. (J). (gr. 4-8). lib. bdg. 29.95 *(978-1-58415-247-7(8))* Mitchell Lane Pubs.

Buckley, Annie. Photography. 2008. (21st Century Skills Innovation Library: Innovation in Entertainment Ser.). (ENG., Illus.). 32p. (gr. 4-8). lib. bdg. 32.07 *(978-1-60279-221-0(6)*, 200152) Cherry Lake Publishing.

Burgan, Michael. Breaker Boys: How a Photograph Helped End Child Labor, 1 vol. 2011. (Captured History Ser.). (ENG.). 64p. (J). (gr. 5-7). pap. 8.95 *(978-0-7565-4510-9(2)*, 116899, Compass Point Bks.) Capstone.

Colby, Jennifer. Black & White Photographs to Instagram. 2019. (21st Century Junior Library: Then to Now Tech Ser.). (ENG.). 24p. (J). (gr. 2-5). pap. 12.79 *(978-1-5341-5010-2(2)*, 213347); (Illus.). lib. bdg. 30.64 *(978-1-5341-4724-9(1)*, 213346) Cherry Lake Publishing.

James, Sara. Photography. 2014. (Art Today! Ser.: 10). 64p. (J). (gr. 7-18). 23.95 *(978-1-4222-3175-3(5))* Mason Crest.

Mattern, Joanne. George Eastman & Photographic Film. 2004. (Uncharted, Unexplored, & Unexplained Ser.). (Illus.). 48p. (J). (gr. 4-8). lib. bdg. 29.95 *(978-1-58415-258-3(3))* Mitchell Lane Pubs.

Murray, Stuart A. P. Mathew Brady: Photographer of Our Nation: Photographer of Our Nation. 2009. (ENG., Illus.). 83p. (gr. 6-18). lib. bdg. 180.00 *(978-0-7656-8151-5(X)*, Y182957) Routledge.

Nagelhout, Ryan. The Problem with Early Cameras, 1 vol. 2015. (Bloopers of Invention Ser.). (ENG., Illus.). 24p. (J). (gr. 2-3). pap. 9.15 *(978-1-4824-2756-1(7)*, eca58c12-e78a-45ac-a1cb-7f4a7dd18572) Stevens, Gareth Publishing LLLP.

Pobst, Sandy. The Camera, 1 vol. 2004. (Great Inventions Ser.). (ENG., Illus.). 48p. (gr. 5-8). lib. bdg. 33.67 *(978-0-8368-5801-3(8)*, b240881f-f2e4-4e4a-900a-588fdd92fda7, Gareth Stevens Secondary Library) Stevens, Gareth Publishing LLLP.

Sabelko, Rabecca & Sabelko, Rebecca. The Camera. 2019. (Inventions That Changed the World Ser.). (ENG., Illus.). 32p. (J). (gr. 3-8). pap. 8.99 *(978-1-61891-510-8(X)*, 12160, Blastoff! Discovery) Bellwether Media.

Sabelko, Rebecca. The Camera. 2019. (Inventions That Changed the World Ser.). (ENG., Illus.). 32p. (J). (gr. 3-8). lib. bdg. 27.95 *(978-1-62617-967-7(0)*, Blastoff! Discovery) Bellwether Media.

Stefoff, Rebecca. The Camera, 1 vol. 2008. (Great Inventions Ser.). (ENG., Illus.). 144p. (YA). (gr. 8-8). lib. bdg. 45.50 *(978-0-7614-2596-0(9)*, 6fa1fc62-d69a-4b5f-9058-4c37d0dbcb9d) Cavendish Square Publishing LLC.

Vallencourt, Margaret. The History of Photography, 1 vol. 2015. (Britannica Guide to the Visual & Performing Arts Ser.). (ENG.). 216p. (J). (gr. 9-10). 47.59 *(978-1-68048-073-3(1)*, c03c6bc7-7f29-4fae-a2cb-3fefdec2f299, Britannica Educational Publishing) Rosen Publishing Group, Inc., The.

PHOTOGRAPHY, JOURNALISTIC

see Photojournalism

PHOTOGRAPHY—VOCATIONAL GUIDANCE

Somervill, Barbara A. Wildlife Photographer. 2015. (21st Century Skills Library: Cool STEAM Careers Ser.). (ENG., Illus.). 32p. (J). (gr. 4-7). 32.07 *(978-1-63362-569-3(9)*, 206460) Cherry Lake Publishing.

Sommers, Michael A. Wildlife Photographers: Life Through a Lens, 1 vol. 2003. (Extreme Careers Ser.). (ENG., Illus.). 64p. (YA). (gr. 5-5). 37.13 *(978-0-8239-3638-0(4)*, a63bd0b8-9562-4a8a-8bf9-18d51d2f1e8d) Rosen Publishing Group, Inc., The.

PHOTOGRAPHY OF ANIMALS

see also Animal Painting and Illustration

Burkhard, Balthasar. Click, Said the Camera. 2006. (Illus.). 42p. pap. 30.00 *(978-3-907044-56-8(8))* Lars Muller Pubs. CHE. Dist: Springer.

Earhart, Kristin, ed. Life-Size Zoo: From Tiny Rodents to Gigantic Elephants, an Actual Size Animal Encyclopedia. 2009. (ENG., Illus.). 48p. (gr. -1). 17.95 *(978-1-934734-20-9(9))* Seven Footer Pr.

Kalman, Bobbie. It Looks Like a Dog. 2011. (ENG.). 16p. (J). lib. bdg. *(978-0-7787-9546-9(2))*; pap. *(978-0-7787-9571-1(3))* Crabtree Publishing Co.

Leach, Michael & Lland, Meriel. Wildlife Watcher Guide: Animal Tracking - Photography Skills - Fieldcraft - Safety - Footprint Indentification - Camera Traps - Making a Blind - Night-TimeTracking. 2016. (ENG., Illus.). 96p. (J). (gr. 5-8). pap. 9.95 *(978-1-77085-742-1(7)*, ee0bff71-5743-4c7f-8f17-3144370a2a3e) Firefly Bks., Ltd.

L'Heureux, J. J. Good Day Book. 2006. spiral bd. *(978-0-9785892-0-2(3))* BrainStream.

Somervill, Barbara A. Wildlife Photographer. 2008. (21st Century Skills Library: Cool Careers Ser.). (ENG., Illus.). 32p. (gr. 4-8). lib. bdg. 32.07 *(978-1-60279-300-2(X)*, 200139) Cherry Lake Publishing.

Sommers, Michael. Wildlife Photographers: Life Through a Lens. 2009. (Extreme Careers Ser.). 64p. (gr. 5-5). 58.50 *(978-1-61512-421-3(7)*, Rosen Reference) Rosen Publishing Group, Inc., The.

Thomas, William David. Wildlife Photographer, 1 vol. 2008. (Cool Careers: Adventure Careers Ser.). (ENG., Illus.). 32p. (gr. 3-3). pap. 11.50 *(978-0-8368-8892-8(8)*, f411b758-f08a-4667-9f16-d1763a457d18); lib. bdg. 28.67 *(978-0-8368-8885-0(5)*, 3e0a9aa4-db8f-4082-a587-e37c2419f096) Stevens, Gareth Publishing LLLP.

Watts, Gillian & Watts, Gillian. Creatures Close Up. Martin, Philippe & Martin, Philippe, photos by. 2016. (ENG., Illus.). 64p. (J). (gr. 3-7). pap. 9.95 *(978-1-77085-782-7(6)*, eff6fabf-8d39-4625-b752-a5c974d852e2) Firefly Bks., Ltd.

PHOTOGRAPHY OF NATURE

see Nature Photography

PHOTOJOURNALISM

Burgan, Michael. Ali's Knockout Punch: How a Photograph Stunned the Boxing World. 2017. (Captured History Sports Ser.). (ENG., Illus.). 64p. (J). (gr. 5-9). lib. bdg. 35.32 *(978-0-7565-5527-6(2)*, 134410, Compass Point Bks.) Capstone.

—Olympic Gold 1936: How the Image of Jesse Owens Crushed Hitler's Evil Myth. 2017. (Captured History Sports Ser.). (ENG., Illus.). 64p. (J). (gr. 5-9). lib. bdg. 35.32 *(978-0-7565-5528-3(0)*, 134413, Compass Point Bks.) Capstone.

Elish, Dan. Inside the Situation Room: How a Photograph Showed America Defeating Osama Bin Laden. 2018. (Captured History Ser.). (ENG., Illus.). 64p. (J). (gr. 5-9). lib. bdg. 35.32 *(978-0-7565-5879-6(4)*, 138647, Compass Point Bks.) Capstone.

Hamilton, John. Photojournalism. 2018. (Digital Photography Ser.). (ENG., Illus.). 48p. (J). (gr. 5-9). lib. bdg. 34.21 *(978-1-5321-1588-2(1)*, 28752, Abdo & Daughters) ABDO Publishing Co.

Koh, Frederick. The 10 Most Compelling News Images. 2008. (J). 14.99 *(978-1-55448-533-8(9))* Scholastic Library Publishing.

Linde, Barbara & Benchmark Education Co. Staff. Opinions about Matthew Brady. 2014. (Text Connections Ser.). (J). (gr. 5). *(978-1-4900-1380-0(6))* Benchmark Education Co.

Miller, Derek. Vietnam & the Rise of Photojournalism, 1 vol. 2018. (Fourth Estate: Journalism in North America Ser.). (ENG.). 112p. (gr. 8-8). lib. bdg. 44.50 *(978-1-5026-3483-2(X)*, 04bd1665-281b-46bb-a1c6-79510fb6022c) Cavendish Square Publishing LLC.

PHOTOPLAYS

see Motion Picture Plays

PHOTOSYNTHESIS

Andersen, Jill. Plants Need Light, 1 vol. 2016. (Rosen REAL Readers: STEM & STEAM Collection). (ENG.). 8p. (gr. k-1). pap. 5.46 *(978-1-5081-2386-6(1)*, d6604804-4507-4839-a131-4294e3f4b2a0, Rosen Classroom) Rosen Publishing Group, Inc., The.

Bang, Molly & Chisholm, Penny. Living Sunlight: How Plants Bring the Earth to Life. Bang, Molly, illus. 2009. (ENG., Illus.). 40p. (J). (gr. -1-3). 19.99 *(978-0-545-04422-6(7)*, Blue Sky Pr., The) Scholastic, Inc.

Davis, Barbara J. & Voege, Debra. How Do Plants Get Food? 2009. (Science in the Real World Ser.). (ENG., Illus.). 32p. (gr. 4-6). 28.00 *(978-1-60413-468-1(2)*, P173440, Chelsea Clubhse.) Infobase Holdings, Inc.

Duling, Kaitlyn. The Sun & Plant. 2019. (Power of the Sun Ser.). (ENG.). 32p. (gr. 3-3). 63.48 *(978-1-5026-4675-0(7))* Cavendish Square Publishing LLC.

—The Sun & Plants, 1 vol. 2019. (Power of the Sun Ser.). (ENG.). 32p. (gr. 3-3). pap. 11.58 *(978-1-5026-4674-3(9)*, e40f5afa-98f9-4418-8fd5-4c3b2ef89b15) Cavendish Square Publishing LLC.

Goldsworthy, Kaite. Producers. 2016. (Illus.). 24p. (J). *(978-1-4896-5779-4(7))* 2011. (J). (gr. 4-6). pap. 12.95 *(978-1-61690-716-7(9)*, AV2 by Weigl) 2011. (Illus.). 24p. (YA). (gr. 2-5). 27.13 *(978-1-61690-710-5(X))* Weigl Pubs., Inc.

Juettner, Bonnie. Photosynthesis. 2005. (KidHaven Science Library). (ENG., Illus.). 48p. (J). (gr. 3-7). lib. bdg. 27.50 *(978-0-7377-2350-2(5)*, Greenhaven Pr., Inc.) Cengage Gale.

Kalman, Bobbie. La Fotosíntesis: De la Luz Del Sol Al Alimento. 2006. (Cambios Que Suceden en la Naturaleza Ser.). (SPA., Illus.). 32p. (J). (gr. 3-7). pap. *(978-0-7787-8386-2(3))* Crabtree Publishing Co.

—La Fotosintesis: De la Luz del Sol al Alimento. 2006. (Cambios Que Suceden en la Naturaleza Ser.). (SPA., Illus.). 32p. (J). (gr. 3-7). lib. bdg. *(978-0-7787-8372-5(3))* Crabtree Publishing Co.

—How Do Living Things Find Food? 2010. (Introducing Living Things Ser.). (ENG.). 24p. (J). (gr. 1-4). pap. *(978-0-7787-3258-7(4))*; lib. bdg. *(978-0-7787-3234-1(7))* Crabtree Publishing Co.

—Photosynthesis: Changing Sunlight into Food. (ENG.). 32p. (J). 2008. *(978-0-7787-7717-5(0))* 2005. (Illus.). (gr. -1-3). pap. *(978-0-7787-2308-0(9))* Crabtree Publishing Co.

Kalman, Bobbie & Sjonger, Rebecca. Photosynthesis: Changing Sunlight into Food. 2008. (ENG.). 32p. (J). *(978-0-7787-7716-8(2))* Crabtree Publishing Co.

Latham, Donna. Respiration & Photosynthesis. rev. ed. 2016. (Sci-Hi: Life Science Ser.). (ENG.). 48p. (J). (gr. 6-10). pap. 8.99 *(978-1-4109-8632-0(2)*, 134718, Raintree) Capstone.

Lawrence, Ellen. Cooking with Sunshine: How Plants Make Food. 2012. (Science Slam: Plant-Ology Ser.). 24p. (J). (gr. -1-3). lib. bdg. 26.99 *(978-1-61772-586-9(2))* Bearport Publishing Co., Inc.

—How Plants Clean the Air. 2014. (Science Slam: Plant-Ology Ser.). (ENG.). 24p. (J). (gr. -1-3). lib. bdg. 26.99 *(978-1-62724-305-6(4))* Bearport Publishing Co., Inc.

Maloof, Torrey. Photosynthesis, 1 vol. 2015. (Science: Informational Text Ser.). (ENG., Illus.). 32p. (gr. 3-4). pap. 11.99 *(978-1-4807-4640-4(1))* Teacher Created Materials, Inc.

O'Donnell, Liam. Understanding Photosynthesis with Max Axiom, Super Scientist, 1 vol. Dominguez, Richard & Barnett, Charles, III, illus. 2007. (Graphic Science Ser.). (ENG.). 32p. (J). (gr. 3-9). per. 8.10 *(978-0-7368-7893-7(9)*, 1264938, Capstone Pr.) Capstone.

—Understanding Photosynthesis with Max Axiom Super Scientist: 4D an Augmented Reading Science Experience. Dominguez, Richard & Dominguez, Richard, illus. 2018. (Graphic Science 4D Ser.). (ENG.). 32p. (J). (gr. 3-9). pap. 7.95 *(978-1-5435-2963-0(1)*, 138563); lib. bdg. 36.65 *(978-1-5435-2952-4(6)*, 138541) Capstone. (Capstone Pr.).

O'Donnell, Liam & Barnett, Charles, III. Cómo Comprender la Fotosíntesis con Max Axiom, Supercientifico. Dominguez, Richard, illus. 2013. (Ciencia Gráfica Ser.). (SPA.). 32p. (J). (gr. 3-9). pap. 8.10 *(978-1-62065-984-7(0)*, 121945) Capstone.

Silverstein, Alvin, et al. Photosynthesis. 2007. (Science Concepts, Second Ser.). (Illus.). 80p. (YA). (gr. 5-9). lib. bdg. 31.93 *(978-0-8225-6798-1(9))* Lerner Publishing Group.

Spiro, Ruth. Baby Loves Thermodynamics! Chan, Irene, illus. 2017. (Baby Loves Science Ser.: 3). 22p. (J). (— 1). bds. 8.99 *(978-1-58089-768-6(1))* Charlesbridge Publishing, Inc.

Staub, Frank. Photosynthesis. 2003. (World of Wonder Ser.). (Illus.). 32p. (J). lib. bdg. *(978-1-58341-265-7(4)*, Creative Education) Creative Co., The.

Wells, Robert E. Why Do Elephants Need the Sun? 2012. (J). 34.28 *(978-1-61913-142-2(0))* Weigl Pubs., Inc.

—Why Do Elephants Need the Sun? Wells, Robert E., illus. 2012. (Wells of Knowledge Science Ser.). (ENG., Illus.). 32p. (J). (gr. -1-3). pap. 8.99 *(978-0-8075-9082-9(7)*, 807590827) Whitman, Albert & Co.

PHYSICAL CHEMISTRY

see Chemistry, Physical and Theoretical

PHYSICAL CULTURE

see Physical Education and Training

PHYSICAL EDUCATION AND TRAINING

see also Athletics; Coaching (Athletics); Exercise; Games; Gymnastics; Health Education; Physical Fitness; Sports

also names of kinds of exercises, e.g. Fencing; Judo

Abramovitz, Melissa. Skiing, 1 vol. 2014. (Science Behind Sports Ser.). (ENG., Illus.). 120p. (gr. 7-7). lib. bdg. 41.03 *(978-1-4205-1155-0(6)*, 4adae9a8-ded1-46c2-b289-d551c5568a73, Lucent Pr.) Greenhaven Publishing LLC.

Becker, Helaine. Skateboarding Science. 2008. (Sports Science Ser.). (ENG., Illus.). 32p. (J). (gr. 4-6). pap. *(978-0-7787-4553-2(8))*; lib. bdg. *(978-0-7787-4536-5(8))* Crabtree Publishing Co.

Bloom, Paul. Rules in the Gym, 1 vol. 2015. (School Rules Ser.). (ENG., Illus.). 24p. (J). (gr. k-k). pap. 9.15 *(978-1-4824-2645-8(5)*, 3c827ece-e30a-4f54-b2dc-39089dd24228) Stevens, Gareth Publishing LLLP.

Boudreau, Hélène. Swimming Science. 2008. (Sports Science Ser.). (ENG., Illus.). 32p. (J). (gr. 4-6). pap. *(978-0-7787-4555-6(4))*; lib. bdg. *(978-0-7787-4538-9(4))* Crabtree Publishing Co.

Bow, James. Baseball Science. 2008. (Sports Science Ser.). (ENG., Illus.). 32p. (J). (gr. 4-6). pap. *(978-0-7787-4551-8(1))* Crabtree Publishing Co.

—Cycling Science. 2008. (Sports Science Ser.). (ENG., Illus.). 32p. (J). (gr. 4-6). pap. *(978-0-7787-4552-5(X))*; lib. bdg. *(978-0-7787-4535-8(X))* Crabtree Publishing Co.

Bow, Patricia. Tennis Science. 2008. (Sports Science Ser.). (ENG., Illus.). 32p. (J). (gr. 4-6). pap. *(978-0-7787-4556-3(2))*; lib. bdg. *(978-0-7787-4539-6(2))* Crabtree Publishing Co.

Brezina, Corona. What Happens to Your Body When You Are Weight Training, 1 vol. 2009. (How & Why of Exercise Ser.). (ENG., Illus.). 48p. (YA). (gr. 5-6). 34.47 *(978-1-4358-5307-2(5)*, b68470d3-4667-43bc-8c01-673df1a355c1) Rosen Publishing Group, Inc., The.

Chaline, Eric. Martial Arts for Athletic Conditioning. 2003. (Martial & Fighting Arts Ser.). (Illus.). 96p. (J). (gr. 7-18). lib. bdg. *(978-1-59084-397-0(5))* Mason Crest.

Compton, Leanne, et al. Jump Start 7 & 8: Health & Physical Education. 2007. 336p. pap. 41.00 incl. cd-rom *(978-0-521-70156-3(2))* Cambridge Univ. Pr.

Davis, Barbara. 404 Deskside Activities for Energetic Kids. 2006. (SmartFun Activity Bks.). (ENG., Illus.). 168p. (gr. -1-5). pap. 14.95 *(978-0-89793-467-1(9))*; spiral bd. 19.95 *(978-0-89793-468-8(7))* Turner Publishing Co. (Hunter Hse.).

Day, Erin. Up & down in Gym Class, 1 vol. 2017. (Opposites at School Ser.). (ENG.). 24p. (J). (gr. 1-1). 25.27 *(978-1-5081-6351-0(0)*, b771a4c1-e35c-4741-9b41-1ce4301f6f41, PowerKids Pr.) Rosen Publishing Group, Inc., The.

Dintiman, George Blough. Speed Improvement for Young Athletes: How to Sprint Faster in Your Sport in 30 Workouts. rev. ed. 2006. (Illus.). 153p. pap. 17.95 *(978-0-938074-26-7(1))* National Assn. of Speed & Explosion.

DiPrimio, Pete. The World of CrossFit. 2014. 48p. (gr. 4-8). 29.95 *(978-1-61228-552-8(X))* Mitchell Lane Pubs.

Entrenamiento Deportivo Series, 10 vols., Set. 2003. (Entrenamiento Deportivo (Sports Training) Ser.). (SPA., Illus.). (J). (gr. 1-2). 131.35 *(978-0-8239-6913-5(4)*, 154d9ebf-6dad-4f9f-9bdb-fe9c2363efd5, Editorial Buenas Letras) Rosen Publishing Group, Inc., The.

Ferguson, creator. Coaches & Fitness Professionals. 2nd rev. ed. 2008. (Ferguson's Careers in Focus Ser.). (ENG.). 188p. (gr. 6-12). 32.95 *(978-0-8160-7284-2(1)*, P179088, Ferguson Publishing Company) Infobase Holdings, Inc.

Fridell, Ron. Sports Technology. 2009. pap. 52.95 *(978-0-7613-4785-9(2))* Lerner Publishing Group.

Gallagher, R., et al. Addysg Gorfforol Trwy Ddiagramau: Llawlyfr Adolygu TGAU. 2005. (WEL., Illus.). 92p. pap. *(978-1-85644-562-7(3))* CAA.

Gigliotti, Jim. STEM in Sports. 2015. (STEM in Sports Ser.). (Illus.). 64p. (J). (gr. 7). 23.95 *(978-1-4222-3233-0(6))* Mason Crest.

Glass, Maya. The Marching Book, 1 vol. 2003. (Let's Get Moving Ser.). (ENG., Illus.). 24p. (J). (gr. k-k). lib. bdg. 26.27 *(978-1-4042-2516-9(1)*, 22698639-29ab-4ea5-852f-4d5ec77464c0, PowerKids Pr.) Rosen Publishing Group, Inc., The.

Goodstein, Madeline. Sports Science Fair Projects, 1 vol. 2015. (Prize-Winning Science Fair Projects Ser.). (ENG.). 128p. (gr. 7-7). lib. bdg. 38.93 *(978-0-7660-7026-4(3)*, 3e3997a0-ca8c-4617-b8a2-0586ef09d1e4) Enslow Publishing, LLC.

Harcourt School Publishers Staff. Harcourt Physical Education Posters, Grades 3-6. 3rd ed. 2003. (Illus.). 55.20 *(978-0-15-339102-6(2))* Harcourt Schl. Pubs.

Hardman, Lizabeth. Baseball, 1 vol. 2010. (Science Behind Sports Ser.). (ENG., Illus.). 104p. (gr. 7-7). 41.03 *(978-1-4205-0262-6(X)*, 2ad0694b-75cf-472c-90b3-2e0343ff4d39, Lucent Pr.) Greenhaven Publishing LLC.

Hyde, Natalie. Soccer Science. 2008. (Sports Science Ser.). (ENG., Illus.). 32p. (J). (gr. 4-6). pap. *(978-0-7787-4554-9(6))* Crabtree Publishing Co.

James, Rob. AS/A Level Physical Education: Skills Acquisition & Sports Psychology. 2010. (ENG.). 204p. pap. 13.95 *(978-1-4441-1545-1(6))* Hodder Education Group GBR. Dist: Trans-Atlantic Pubns., Inc.

Kassebaum, Danica. Underwater Training (Grade 3) rev. ed. 2018. (Smithsonian: Informational Text Ser.). (ENG., Illus.).

32p. (J). (gr. 3-4). pap. 11.99 *(978-1-4938-6682-3(6))* Teacher Created Materials, Inc.

Kortemeier, Todd. 12 Ways to Improve Athletic Performance. 2017. (Healthy Living Ser.). (ENG., Illus.). 32p. (J). (gr. 3-6). 32.80 *(978-1-63235-369-6(5)*, 11847); pap. 9.95 *(978-1-63235-387-0(3)*, 11855) Bookstaves, LLC. (12-Story Library).

Lasslett, Sally, et al. Jump Start 9 & 10: Health & Physical Education. 2007. pap. 32.95 incl. cd-rom *(978-0-521-70167-9(8))* Cambridge Univ. Pr.

Lewis, Daniel. Fitness, Personal Care Services & Education, Vol. 10. 2018. (Careers in Demand for High School Graduates Ser.). 112p. (J). (gr. 7). lib. bdg. 34.60 *(978-1-4222-4140-0(8))* Mason Crest.

Massad, Diane Patterson. Hang On! The Kidskills International Training Series. 2004. (Kidskills America Training Ser.). (ENG., Illus.). (YA). spiral bd. 12.95 *(978-0-9710641-9-5(9))* Kidskills International.

—Making Muscles! The Kidskills America Training Series. 2004. (Kidskills America Training Ser.). (Illus.). 75p. (J). spiral bd. 12.95 *(978-0-9710641-6-4(4))* Kidskills International.

—Up & Over! The Kidskills America Training Series. 2004. (Kidskills America Training Ser.). (Illus.). 75p. (J). spiral bd. 12.95 *(978-0-9710641-5-7(6)*, Kidskills America) Kidskills International.

Middlewood, G. & Debenham, A. 43 Team-Building Activities. 2007. 64p. per. *(978-1-903853-57-3(5))* Brilliant Pubns.

Morris, Ann. That's Our Gym Teacher! Linenthal, Peter, illus. Linenthal, Peter, photos by. 2003. (That's Our School Ser.). (ENG.). 32p. (gr. k-3). lib. bdg. 22.60 *(978-0-7613-2403-4(8)*, Millbrook Pr.) Lerner Publishing Group.

Thompson, Graham. Physical Education: Anatomy & Exercise Physiology. 2010. (ENG.). 204p. pap. 13.95 *(978-1-4441-1540-6(5))* Hodder Education Group GBR. Dist: Trans-Atlantic Pubns., Inc.

Verdick, Elizabeth & Lisovskis, Marjorie. Reach: A Board Book about Curiosity. 2013. (Happy Healthy Baby(r) Ser.). (ENG., Illus.). 24p. (J). (— 1). bds. 7.99 *(978-1-57542-424-8(X))* Free Spirit Publishing Inc.

Wiggins-James, Nesta. AS/A-Level Physical Education: Historical Factors & Contemporary Issues. 2010. (ENG.). 204p. pap. 13.95 *(978-1-4441-1544-4(8))* Hodder Education Group GBR. Dist: Trans-Atlantic Pubns., Inc.

Yancey, Diane. Basketball, 1 vol. 2011. (Science Behind Sports Ser.). (ENG.). 112p. (gr. 7-7). 41.03 *(978-1-4205-0293-0(X)*, 0ef36af5-eeb1-40ad-a31d-7be850b204e0, Lucent Pr.) Greenhaven Publishing LLC.

PHYSICAL FITNESS

Aliotti, Johnny. Johnny's Simple Dumbbell Workout. 2004. spiral bd. 14.95 *(978-0-9740600-1-9(1))*; (Illus.). 102p. per. 13.95 *(978-0-9740600-0-2(3))* ProTips(TM) Media.

Arzón, Robin. Strong Mama. Sonda, Addy Rivera, illus. 2022. (ENG.). 40p. (J). (gr. -1-3). 17.99 *(978-0-316-29994-7(4))* Little, Brown Bks. for Young Readers.

at, The Experts at Gold's Gym. Find Balance with Yoga & Pilates, 1 vol. 2018. (Gold's Gym Guide to Fitness Ser.). (ENG.). 48p. (YA). (gr. 7-7). lib. bdg. 29.60 *(978-1-9785-0658-9(9)*, eb89acfd-1e64-4b52-aef3-794915ad0d96) Enslow Publishing, LLC.

—Make a Fitness Plan, 1 vol. 2018. (Gold's Gym Guide to Fitness Ser.). (ENG.). 48p. (YA). (gr. 7-7). lib. bdg. 29.60 *(978-1-9785-0655-8(4)*, 4f026f35-5afd-4da1-8c6f-0135fd11112a) Enslow Publishing, LLC.

—Take the Cardio Challenge, 1 vol. 2018. (Gold's Gym Guide to Fitness Ser.). (ENG.). 48p. (YA). (gr. 7-7). lib. bdg. 29.60 *(978-1-9785-0657-2(0)*, 71c3dceb-601b-4edd-99a1-ee160cc38423) Enslow Publishing, LLC.

—Train for Strength, 1 vol. 2018. (Gold's Gym Guide to Fitness Ser.). (ENG.). 48p. (YA). (gr. 7-7). lib. bdg. 29.60 *(978-1-9785-0656-5(2)*, cb6b5512-279c-4ae3-8d3c-6352153efcac) Enslow Publishing, LLC.

Berger, Melvin & Berger, Gilda. Kicking, Running, & Stretching. 2007. (Illus.). 32p. (J). pap. *(978-0-439-02449-5(8))* Scholastic, Inc.

Berton, Judy & Guimond, Rick. Do a Dance Picture Book. 2006. (Illus.). (J). spiral bd. 8.95 *(978-0-9761051-1-4(X))* Kidrich Corp.

Bodden, Valerie. Being Fit. 2015. (Healthy Plates Ser.). (ENG.). 24p. (J). (gr. 1-4). pap. 9.99 *(978-1-62832-106-7(7)*, 21201, Creative Paperbacks); *(978-1-60818-506-1(0)*, 21200, Creative Education) Creative Co., The.

Borgert-Spaniol, Megan. Keeping Fit. 2012. (Eating Right with Myplate Ser.). (ENG., Illus.). 24p. (J). (gr. k-3). lib. bdg. 26.95 *(978-1-60014-758-6(5)*, Blastoff! Readers) Bellwether Media.

Brezina, Corona. What Happens to Your Body When You Are Weight Training, 1 vol. 2009. (How & Why of Exercise Ser.). (ENG., Illus.). 48p. (YA). (gr. 5-6). 34.47 *(978-1-4358-5307-2(5)*, b68470d3-4667-43bc-8c01-673df1a355c1) Rosen Publishing Group, Inc., The.

Burgan, Michael. Health Careers in Sports, Vol. 10. Ferrer, Al, ed. 2015. (Careers off the Field Ser.). (Illus.). 64p. (J). (gr. 7). lib. bdg. 23.95 *(978-1-4222-3268-2(9))* Mason Crest.

Burkhead, Frank, Jr. Sports Ministry for Christ. 2005. 49p. (YA). per. 10.25 *(978-0-9770043-5-5(X))* New Global Publishing.

Burton, Margie, et al. Your Body. 2011. (Early Connections Ser.). (J). *(978-1-61672-549-5(4))* Benchmark Education Co.

Canino, Kate. Maintaining a Healthy Weight, 1 vol. 2010. (Healthy Habits Ser.). (ENG., Illus.). 64p. (YA). (gr. 5-5). pap. 13.95 *(978-1-4488-0609-6(7)*, 654e0307-1d2f-44d4-bf9e-5eeb53271969); lib. bdg. 37.13 *(978-1-4358-9439-6(1)*, e999b1dd-7402-449e-882f-3a766ad0a71c) Rosen Publishing Group, Inc., The. (Rosen Reference).

Carle, Eric. De la Cabeza a Los Pies: From Head to Toe (Spanish Edition) Carle, Eric, illus. 2007.Tr. of From Head to Toe. (SPA., Illus.). 32p. (J). (gr. -1-3). pap. 9.99 *(978-0-06-051313-9(6))* HarperCollins Español.

—From Head to Toe Big Book. Carle, Eric, illus. 2007. (ENG., Illus.). 32p. (J). (gr. -1-k). pap. 24.99 *(978-0-06-111972-9(5)*, HarperFestival) HarperCollins Pubs.

Carleton, Kate. What Happens to Your Body When You Cycle, 1 vol. 2009. (How & Why of Exercise Ser.). (ENG., Illus.). 48p. (YA). (gr. 5-6). 34.47 *(978-1-4358-5308-9(3)*, ae369987-67b7-4f81-9290-2fdcf8c7a562) Rosen Publishing Group, Inc., The.

Clark, Rosalyn. Why We Exercise. 2018. (Bumba Books (r) — Health Matters Ser.). (ENG., Illus.). 24p. (J). (gr. -1-1). lib. bdg. 26.65 *(978-1-5124-8295-9(1)*, 214d4c86-6d89-4422-914d-dab32ba2e6f8, Lerner Pubns.) Lerner Publishing Group.

Coan, Sharon. Good for Me: Play & Exercise. 2nd rev. ed. 2015. (TIME for KIDS(r): Informational Text Ser.). (ENG., Illus.). 12p. (J). (gr. -1-k). 7.99 *(978-1-4938-2152-5(0))* Teacher Created Materials, Inc.

Crest, Mason. Fitness. 2019. (Health & Nutrition Ser.). (Illus.). 80p. (J). (gr. 12). lib. bdg. 34.60 *(978-1-4222-4218-6(8))* Mason Crest.

Crockett, Kyle A. Nutrition for Achievement in Sports & Academics. Borus, Joshua, ed. 2013. (Understanding Nutrition: a Gateway to Physical & Mental Health Ser.). (Illus.). 48p. (J). (gr. 5-18). pap. 9.95 *(978-1-4222-2990-3(4))*; 19.95 *(978-1-4222-2884-5(3))* Mason Crest.

Dahn Healer School. Home Massage Therapy Book 1: Heal Yourself & Your Loved Ones, 2 vols. 2004. (Dahnhak, the Way to Perfect Health Ser.: Vol. 2). (Illus.). 142p. per. 17.95 *(978-0-9720282-9-5(3))* Healing Society, Inc.

Day, Erin. Up & down in Gym Class, 1 vol. 2017. (Opposites at School Ser.). (ENG.). 24p. (J). (gr. 1-1). 25.27 *(978-1-5081-6351-0(0)*, b771a4c1-e35c-4741-9b41-1ce4301f6f41, PowerKids Pr.) Rosen Publishing Group, Inc., The.

Dee, Janet. A Practical Guide to Everyday Health & Well Being. 2005. (J). 9.95 *(978-0-9768403-1-2(6))* Wings Above.

Dinmont, Kerry. David's New Bike: A Book about Being Active. 2017. (My Day Readers Ser.). (ENG.). 24p. (J). (gr. -1-2). lib. bdg. 32.79 *(978-1-5038-2023-4(8)*, 211857) Child's World, Inc, The.

DiPrimio, Pete. The World of CrossFit. 2014. 48p. (gr. 4-8). 29.95 *(978-1-61228-552-8(X))* Mitchell Lane Pubs.

Doeden, Matt. Stay Fit! How You Can Get in Shape. 2009. pap. 52.95 *(978-0-7613-4687-6(2))* Lerner Publishing Group.

—Stay Fit! How You Can Get in Shape. Desrocher, Jack, illus. 2008. (Health Zone Ser.). 64p. (YA). (gr. 4-7). lib. bdg. 30.60 *(978-0-8225-7553-5(1))* Lerner Publishing Group.

El-Hewie, Mohamed F. Essentials of Weightlifting & Strength Training. 2nd rev. exp. ed. 2005. (Illus.). 700p. lib. bdg. 85.00 *(978-0-9719581-9-7(X))* Shaymaa Publishing Corp.

Evans, Lynette. Shockwave: Move Your Bones. 2007. (Shockwave: the Human Experience Ser.). (ENG., Illus.). 36p. (J). (gr. 3-5). 25.00 *(978-0-531-17761-7(0)*, Children's Pr.) Scholastic Library Publishing.

Fisher, Beverly. Mental Toughness for Personal Fitness: Workbook for Life 2004. (Illus.). 64p. pap. 10.99 *(978-0-9745066-0-9(5))* Sports In Mind.

Fitness for the Mind & Body, 8 vols. 2014. (Fitness for the Mind & Body Ser.). (ENG.). 192p. (YA). (gr. 8-8). lib. bdg. 165.88 *(978-1-4777-8170-8(6)*, 283115cb-1d85-41c9-a99e-1896ffd99810, Rosen Young Adult) Rosen Publishing Group, Inc., The.

Furgang, Kathy. Having Healthful Habits & Tener hábitos Sanos: 6 English, 6 Spanish Adaptations. 2011. (ENG & SPA.). (J). 97.00 net. *(978-1-4108-5710-1(7))* Benchmark Education Co.

Gagne, Tammy. African Dance Trends. 2014. (Illus.). 48p. (J). (gr. 4-8). 29.95 *(978-1-61228-557-3(0))* Mitchell Lane Pubs.

Gifford, Clive. Sports. 2010. (Healthy Lifestyles Ser.). 48p. (J). 35.65 *(978-1-60753-088-6(0))* Amicus Learning.

Gilliam, Thomas & Neill, Jane. Move It. Lose It. Live Healthy: Achieve a Healthier Workplace One Employee at a Time! 2004. (J). per. 19.95 *(978-0-9762703-0-0(7))* Gilliam, T. & Associates, LLC.

Gogerly, Liz. Exercise. Gordon, Mike, illus. 2008. (Looking after Me Ser.). (ENG.). 32p. (J). (gr. -1-3). pap. *(978-0-7787-4118-3(4))* Crabtree Publishing Co.

Goodbody, Slim & Burstein, John. A Million Moves: Keeping Fit. 2008. (Slim Goodbody's Lighten Up! Ser.). (ENG., Illus.). 32p. (J). (gr. 3-7). pap. *(978-0-7787-3930-2(9))*; lib. bdg. *(978-0-7787-3912-8(0))* Crabtree Publishing Co.

Greathouse, Lisa. Find Your Sport, 1 vol. 2011. (Science: Informational Text Ser.). (ENG., Illus.). 32p. (gr. 3-4). pap. 11.99 *(978-1-4333-3090-2(3))* Teacher Created Materials, Inc.

—Get Moving, 1 vol. 2011. (Science: Informational Text Ser.). (ENG.). 32p. (gr. 3-4). pap. 11.99 *(978-1-4333-3089-6(X))* Teacher Created Materials, Inc.

—Healthy Habits, Healthy You, 1 vol. 2011. (Science: Informational Text Ser.). (ENG., Illus.). 32p. (gr. 3-4). pap. 11.99 *(978-1-4333-3091-9(1))* Teacher Created Materials, Inc.

Green, Emily K. Keeping Fit. 2006. (Blastoff! Readers Ser.). (ENG., Illus.). 24p. (J). (gr. k-3). lib. bdg. 24.95 *(978-1-60014-006-8(8))* Bellwether Media.

—Keeping Fit. 2011. (Blastoff! Readers: New Food Guide Pyramid Ser.). (Illus.). 24p. (J). pap. 5.95 *(978-0-531-25853-8(X)*, Children's Pr.) Scholastic Library Publishing.

Harcourt School Publishers Staff. Be Active! Cardiovascular Flipchart. 2nd ed. 2003. (Illus.). (J). (gr. 1-6). 9.20 *(978-0-15-340983-7(5))* Harcourt Schl. Pubs.

—Be Active! Flexibility Flipchart. 2nd ed. 2003. (Illus.). (J). (gr. 1-6). 9.20 *(978-0-15-340981-3(9))* Harcourt Schl. Pubs.

—Be Active! Movement Flipchart. 2nd ed. 2003. (Illus.). (J). 9.20 *(978-0-15-340982-0(7))* Harcourt Schl. Pubs.

—Be Active! Strength Flipchart. 2nd ed. 2003. (Illus.). (J). (gr. 1-6). 9.20 *(978-0-15-340980-6(0))* Harcourt Schl. Pubs.

—Be Active! Program: Health & Fitness. 4th ed. 2004. (Illus.). (gr. k-2). 311.60 *(978-0-15-341407-7(3))*; (gr. 3-6). 314.90 *(978-0-15-341408-4(1))* Harcourt Schl. Pubs.

—Health & Fitness: Activity Book. 4th ed. 2003. (gr. -1). pap., act. bk. ed. 4.80 *(978-0-15-341170-0(8))* Harcourt Schl. Pubs.

—Health & Fitness: Resources for Spanish Speakers. 4th ed. 2004. (SPA.). (gr. 1). pap. 20.00 *(978-0-15-341180-9(5))*; (gr. 2). pap. 20.00 *(978-0-15-341181-6(3))*; (gr. 3). pap. 25.40 *(978-0-15-341182-3(1))*; (gr. 4). pap. 25.40 *(978-0-15-341183-0(X))*; (gr. 5). pap. 25.40 *(978-0-15-341184-7(8))*; (gr. 6). pap. 25.40 *(978-0-15-341185-4(6))* Harcourt Schl. Pubs.

—Health & Fitness 5-Pack: Activity Book. 4th ed. 2003. (gr. -1). act. bk. ed. 23.70 *(978-0-15-341171-7(6))* Harcourt Schl. Pubs.

—Health & Fitness, Grade 3-6. 4th ed. 2003. pap., tchr. ed. 88.20 *(978-0-15-341101-4(5))* Harcourt Schl. Pubs.

—Health & Fitness, Grade K-2. 4th ed. 2003. pap., tchr. ed. 84.80 *(978-0-15-341100-7(7))* Harcourt Schl. Pubs.

Hau, Stephanie. I Can Live To 100! Secrets Just for Kids. Hau, Joseph, illus. 2005. 60p. (J). per. 9.95 *(978-0-9767324-0-2(8)*, Kids Can) Proactive Publishing.

Head, Honor. Keeping Fit. 2013. (Let's Read & Talk about Ser.). (ENG., Illus.). 32p. (J). (gr. 2-5). 28.50 *(978-1-59771-396-2(1))* Sea-To-Sea Pubns.

Heart E Heart & Friends Activity Book: Have Fun the Healthy Way. 2004. (J). per. 11.95 *(978-0-9762703-2-4(3))* Gilliam, T. & Associates, LLC.

Heart E Heart & Friends Storybook for Children Ages 2 to 4 Years Old: A Children's Way to a Healthy Lifestyle. 2004. (J). per. 5.95 *(978-0-9762703-1-7(5))* Gilliam, T. & Associates, LLC.

Hill, Z. B. Endurance & Cardio Training. Hart, Diane H., ed. 2014. (Integrated Life of Fitness Ser.). 64p. (J). (gr. 7-18). pap. 11.95 *(978-1-4222-3198-2(4))*; 23.95 *(978-1-4222-3160-9(7))* Mason Crest.

Hoeft, Jen. FUNdamental Fitness: Playground Exercises for Grownups. 1. 2004. 144p. per. 19.95 *(978-0-9762868-0-6(7))* Read Publishing.

Hoena, Blake. Stretchy Shapes! Straight, Curved, & Twisty. Thomas, Glenn, illus. 2018. (Creative Movement Ser.). (ENG.). 24p. (J). (gr. -1-2). lib. bdg. 33.99 *(978-1-68410-245-7(6)*, 138435) Cantata Learning.

Hopwood, Lolly & Kusters, YoYo. Move! Flowers, Luke, illus. 2016. (ENG.). 32p. (J). (gr. -1-1). bds. 12.99 *(978-0-7611-8733-2(2)*, 18733) Workman Publishing Co., Inc.

Hovius, Christopher. Fitness & Nutrition. McDonnell, Mary Ann & Forman, Sara, eds. 2013. (Young Adult's Guide to the Science of Health Ser.: 15). 128p. (J). (gr. 7-18). 24.95 *(978-1-4222-2809-8(6))* Mason Crest.

Hunt, C. J. The Perfect Human Diet: The Doctor-Proven Solution for the Health & the Life You Deserve. Hunt, C. J., ed. 2nd ed. 2015. (ENG.). 9.99 *(978-0-9630377-2-5(2))* Hunt Thompson Media.

Hunt, Jamie. Getting Stronger, Getting Fit: The Importance of Exercise. 2010. (Kids & Obesity Ser.). (Illus.). 48p. (YA). lib. bdg. 19.95 *(978-1-4222-1709-2(4))* Mason Crest.

Hunt, Sara. Stay Fit: Your Guide to Staying Active. 2011. (Healthy Me Ser.). (ENG.). 32p. (J). (gr. 3-4). pap. 50.14 *(978-1-4296-7294-8(3)*, 16812, Capstone Pr.) Capstone.

Hurst, Brooklynn. Fitness for Teens: Getting you Motivated for Life by Providing Principles for Healthy Living. 2nd exp. l.t. ed. 2004. (ENG., Illus.). 108p. (YA). spiral bd. 20.00 *(978-0-9746262-3-9(6))* Achieving Corporate Excellence, Inc.

James, Sara. Flexibility & Agility. Hart, Diane H., ed. 2014. (Integrated Life of Fitness Ser.). 64p. (J). (gr. 7-18). pap. 11.95 *(978-1-4222-3200-2(X))*; 23.95 *(978-1-4222-3162-3(3))* Mason Crest.

—Yoga & Pilates. Hart, Diane H., ed. 2014. (Integrated Life of Fitness Ser.). (Illus.). 64p. (J). (gr. 7-18). pap. 11.95 *(978-1-4222-3204-0(2))*; 23.95 *(978-1-4222-3166-1(6))* Mason Crest.

Johnson, Haley S. Amazing Human Feats of Endurance. 2018. (Superhuman Feats Ser.). (ENG., Illus.). 32p. (J). (gr. 4-6). lib. bdg. 28.65 *(978-1-5435-4123-6(2)*, 139077, Capstone Pr.) Capstone.

Jorgensen, Katrina. Football Fuel: Recipes for Before, During, & after the Big Game. 2015. (Football Cookbooks Ser.). (ENG.). 48p. (J). (gr. 3-9). lib. bdg. 31.99 *(978-1-4914-2135-2(5)*, 127618) Capstone.

Kallio, Jamie. 12 Ways to Stay Active & Fit. 2017. (Healthy Living Ser.). (ENG., Illus.). 32p. (J). (gr. 3-6). pap. 9.95 *(978-1-63235-389-4(X)*, 11857, 12-Story Library) Bookstaves, LLC.

—12 Ways to Stay Active & Fit. 2017. (J). *(978-1-62143-513-6(X))* Pr. Room Editions LLC.

Kawa, Katie. Staying Fit with Sports!, 1 vol. 2013. (Rosen Readers Ser.). (ENG.). 24p. (J). (gr. 3-3). pap. 8.25 *(978-1-4777-2590-0(3)*, ffcab87a-9029-4d6e-9ccd-e440bb9234e8); pap. 49.50 *(978-1-4777-2592-4(X))* Rosen Publishing Group, Inc., The. (Rosen Classroom).

Kray, Peter. The Monster. 2003. 91p. per. 12.95 *(978-0-9715715-1-8(1))* Greenleaf Book Group.

Lee, Ilchi. Meridian Exercise for Self-Healing Book 1: Classified by Common Symptoms, 2 vols. 2003. (Dahnhak, the Way to Perfect Health Ser.: Vol. 1). (Illus.). 151p. per. 17.95 *(978-0-9720282-7-1(7))* Healing Society, Inc.

—Meridian Exercise for Self-Healing Book 2: Classified by Common Symptoms, 2 vols., Vol. 2. 2003. (Dahnhak, the Way to Perfect Health Ser.: 2). (Illus.). 193p. per. 17.95 *(978-0-9720282-8-8(5))* Healing Society, Inc.

Libal, Autumn. Exercise for Fitness & Weight Loss. Garcia, Victor, ed. 2014. (Understanding Obesity Ser.: 10). (Illus.). 104p. (J). (gr. 7-18). lib. bdg. 24.95 *(978-1-4222-3060-2(0))* Mason Crest.

Lockspeiser, Nancy Flanders. Flexible You: 21 Stretches a Day for a 9-Lives Body: a Cat's Quick Guide to Stretching & Self-Massage. Lockspeiser, Nancy Flanders, illus. 2004. (Illus.). 48p. spiral bd. 14.94 *(978-0-9752922-0-4(X))* Catamount Publishing LLC.

Mapua, Jeff. Basketball for Fun & Fitness, 1 vol. 2019. (Sports for Fun & Fitness Ser.). (ENG.). 32p. (gr. 3-3). pap. 11.53 *(978-1-9785-1329-7(1)*, cf17b5ca-9f14-4a8e-97ee-0df840d370a9) Enslow Publishing, LLC.

—Martial Arts for Fun & Fitness, 1 vol. 2019. (Sports for Fun & Fitness Ser.). (ENG.). 32p. (gr. 3-3). pap. 11.53 *(978-1-9785-1341-9(0)*, 6cb453a7-887b-4976-a482-58981ba76c5a) Enslow Publishing, LLC.

Maring, Therese Kauchak. A Smart Girl's Guide: Sports & Fitness: How to Use Your Body & Mind to Play & Feel Your Best. Roe, Monika, illus. 2018. (American Girl(r) Wellbeing Ser.). (ENG.). 112p. (J). pap. 12.99 *(978-1-68337-062-8(7))* American Girl Publishing, Inc.

Massad, Diane. Go! STOP Go! Vol. 3: The Kidskills America Training Series. 2004. (Kidskills America Training Ser.: Three). (Illus.). 75p. (J). spiral bd. 12.95 *(978-0-9710641-3-3(X))* Kidskills International.

Massad, Diane P. Moving Right Along! The Kidskills America Training Series. 2004. (Kidskills America Training Ser.: 2). (Illus.). 71p. (J). spiral bd. 12.95 *(978-0-9710641-2-6(1)*, Kidskills America) Kidskills International.

McIntosh, J. S. Elite Forces Selection. 2010. (Special Forces Ser.). 64p. (YA). (gr. 7-18). lib. bdg. 22.95 *(978-1-4222-1839-6(2))* Mason Crest.

McMillan, Charla & Weinress, Jonathan. Power up for Fitness: Exercise for Playing Stronger & Running Longer. 2018. (Let's Move Ser.). (ENG., Illus.). 32p. (J). (gr. 1-3). pap. 4.99 *(978-1-63440-411-2(4)*, e8330bbc-196f-4fa3-a953-74e538b159a6); lib. bdg. 19.99 *(978-1-63440-409-9(2)*, 71a4cee5-64d7-4089-b97e-667b1c39c46e) Red Chair Pr.

Meiners, Cheri J. Grow Strong! A Book about Healthy Habits. Allen, Elizabeth, illus. 2016. (Being the Best Me(r) Ser.). (ENG.). 40p. (J). (gr. -1-2). pap. 11.99 *(978-1-63198-085-5(8))* Free Spirit Publishing Inc.

Meter, Pete O. & Meter, Pete. Walk the Walk: The Kid's Book of Pedometer Challenges. 2008. (ENG., Illus.). 56p. (J). (gr. 4). spiral bd. 12.95 *(978-1-60433-048-9(1)*, Applesauce Pr.) Cider Mill Pr. Bk. Pubs., LLC.

Nagle, Jeanne. What Happens to Your Body When You Swim, 1 vol. 2009. (How & Why of Exercise Ser.). (ENG., Illus.). 48p. (YA). (gr. 5-6). 34.47 *(978-1-4358-5309-6(1)*, 5e299e4e-3890-4064-b215-9557e7d5e8f2) Rosen Publishing Group, Inc., The.

National Geographic Learning. Reading Expeditions (Science: the Human Body): Keeping Fit. 2006. (Nonfiction Reading & Writing Workshops Ser.). (ENG., Illus.). 32p. (J). pap. 18.95 *(978-0-7922-8863-3(7))* CENGAGE Learning.

Pappas, Diane H., et al. Why I Need Exercise. Estrada, Ric, illus. 2007. (J). pap. *(978-0-545-01428-1(X))* Scholastic, Inc.

Payment, Simone. What Happens to Your Body When You Run, 1 vol. 2009. (How & Why of Exercise Ser.). (ENG., Illus.). 48p. (YA). (gr. 5-6). 34.47 *(978-1-4358-5306-5(7)*, 213c9029-6f61-4a48-aaf4-30866cae4c4f) Rosen Publishing Group, Inc., The.

Peters, Celeste A. Health. 2016. (J). *(978-1-5105-2237-4(9))* SmartBook Media, Inc.

Potts, Sue. Get Fit with Video Workouts. 2014. (ENG., Illus.). 48p. (J). (gr. 4-8). 29.95 *(978-1-61228-550-4(3))* Mitchell Lane Pubs.

Reeves, Diane Lindsey. Making Choices for a Healthy Body. 2018. (21st Century Junior Library: Smart Choices Ser.). (ENG., Illus.). 24p. (J). (gr. k-2). lib. bdg. 30.64 *(978-1-5341-0790-8(8)*, 210919) Cherry Lake Publishing.

—Making Choices for My Healthy Body. 2018. (21st Century Junior Library: Smart Choices Ser.). (ENG., Illus.). 24p. (J). (gr. k-2). pap. 12.79 *(978-1-5341-0889-9(0)*, 210920) Cherry Lake Publishing.

Rice, Dona Herweck. Keeping Fit with Sports, 1 vol. 2nd rev. ed. 2011. (TIME for KIDS(r): Informational Text Ser.). (ENG.). 20p. (gr. 1-2). 6.99 *(978-1-4333-3596-9(4))* Teacher Created Materials, Inc.

—Mantenerse en Forma con Deportes. 2nd rev. ed. 2012. (TIME for KIDS(r): Informational Text Ser.). (SPA.). 20p. (gr. 1-2). 6.99 *(978-1-4333-4429-9(7))* Teacher Created Materials, Inc.

—Mantenerse Sano. 2nd rev. ed. 2012. (TIME for KIDS(r): Informational Text Ser.).Tr. of Staying Healthy. (SPA., Illus.). 20p. (gr. 1-2). 8.99 *(978-1-4333-4428-2(9))* Teacher Created Materials, Inc.

—Physical Feats & Failures. 2nd rev. ed. 2012. (TIME for KIDS(r): Informational Text Ser.). (ENG.). 48p. (gr. 4-6). pap. 13.99 *(978-1-4333-4870-9(5))* Teacher Created Materials, Inc.

—Staying Healthy, 1 vol. 2nd rev. ed. 2011. (TIME for KIDS(r): Informational Text Ser.). (ENG.). 20p. (gr. 1-2). 8.99 *(978-1-4333-3595-2(6))* Teacher Created Materials, Inc.

Rissman, Rebecca. Fit Girl: Yoga for Fitness & Flexibility. 2015. (Yoga for You Ser.). (ENG.). 64p. (J). (gr. 4-8). lib. bdg. 35.32 *(978-1-4914-2120-8(7)*, 127603) Capstone.

Rissman, Rebecca & Smith, Sian. Getting Exercise, 1 vol. 2012. (Take Care of Yourself! Ser.). (ENG.). 24p. (gr. -1-1). 23.32 *(978-1-4329-6710-9(X))*; pap. 6.29 *(978-1-4329-6717-8(7))* Capstone. (Heinemann).

Ritchie, Scot. See How We Move! A First Book of Health & Well-Being. Ritchie, Scot, illus. 2018. (ENG., Illus.). 32p. (J). (gr. -1-2). 19.99 *(978-1-77138-967-9(2))* Kids Can Pr., Ltd. CAN. Dist: Hachette Bk. Group.

Rodomista, Kim. 101 Cool Pool Games for Children: Fun & Fitness for Swimmers of All Levels. Patterson, Robin, illus. 2006. (SmartFun Activity Bks.). (ENG.). 160p. (J). (gr. -1). per. 17.99 *(978-0-89793-483-1(0)*, Hunter Hse.) Turner Publishing Co.

Royston, Angela. Why Do I Run? 2012. (My Body Ser.). (ENG., Illus.). 24p. (gr. k-4). pap. 7.95 *(978-1-77092-000-2(5))* Saunders Bk. Co. CAN. Dist: RiverStream Publishing.

Rustad, Martha E. H. I Stay Active. 2017. (Healthy Me Ser.). (ENG., Illus.). 24p. (J). (gr. -1-2). lib. bdg. 22.65 *(978-1-5157-3982-1(1)*, 133881, Pebble) Capstone.

Schmidt, Debra. Careers in Sports & Fitness. 2016. (Exploring Careers Ser.). (ENG., Illus.). 80p. (J). (gr. 5-12). 38.60 *(978-1-60152-814-8(0))* ReferencePoint Pr., Inc.

Schuh, Mari. Get Moving!, 1 vol. 2012. (What's on Myplate? Ser.). (ENG., Illus.). 24p. (J). (gr. -1-2). pap. 7.29 *(978-1-4296-9414-8(9)*, 120402, Capstone Pr.) Capstone.

Scott, Celicia. Sports & Fitness. Hart, Diane H., ed. 2014. (Integrated Life of Fitness Ser.). 64p. (J). (gr. 7-18). pap. 11.95 *(978-1-4222-3201-9(8))*; 23.95 *(978-1-4222-3163-0(1))* Mason Crest.

—Weight Lifting & Strength Building. Hart, Diane H., ed. 2014. (Integrated Life of Fitness Ser.). 64p. (J). (gr. 7-18). pap. 11.95 *(978-1-4222-3203-3(4))*; 23.95 *(978-1-4222-3165-4(8))* Mason Crest.

Selwyn, Josephine. How Can I Get Fit? 2012. (Level E Ser.). (ENG., Illus.). 16p. (J). (gr. k-2). pap. 7.95 *(978-1-927136-43-0(1)*, 19409) RiverStream Publishing.

Senker, Cath. Exercise & Play, 1 vol. 2007. (Healthy Choices Ser.). (ENG., Illus.). 24p. (J). (gr. 1-2). lib. bdg. 26.27 (978-1-4042-4305-7(4), 311ab516-b2a5-4f67-8124-5eac72dbcc0a, PowerKids Pr.) Rosen Publishing Group, Inc., The.

Shryer, Donna & Forschmiedt, Jodi. Peak Performance: Sports Nutrition, 1 vol. 2010. (Food & You Ser.). (ENG.). 32p. (gr. 5-5). 31.21 (978-0-7614-4366-7(5), ded32e69-994c-4789-a057-5cd5acf06a56) Cavendish Square Publishing LLC.

Sjonger, Rebecca. Do Your Bit to Be Physically Fit! 2015. (Healthy Habits for a Lifetime Ser.). (ENG., Illus.). 24p. (J). (gr. 2-2). (978-0-7787-1879-6(4)) Crabtree Publishing Co.

—Hop, Throw, & Play: Build Your Skills Every Day! 2016. (ENG., Illus.). 24p. (J). (978-0-7787-2349-3(6)) Crabtree Publishing Co.

Slim Goodbody's Good Health Guides, 12 vols. 2007. (Slim Goodbody's Good Health Guides). (ENG.). 32p. (gr. 3-5). lib. bdg. 172.02 (978-0-8368-7738-0(1), 1c079a8f-1701-42ca-8997-f78c4733277b, Gareth Stevens Learning Library) Stevens, Gareth Publishing LLLP.

Smith-Richard, Dean. Softball & Baseball for Fun & Fitness, 1 vol. 2019. (Sports for Fun & Fitness Ser.). (ENG.). 32p. (gr. 3-3). pap. 11.53 (978-1-9785-1349-5(6), 46282a83-25eb-4637-be2d-1051c4321ad7) Enslow Publishing, LLC.

Smithyman, Kathryn & Kalman, Bobbie. Active Kids: Fun Ways to Be Active. 2003. (Kid Power Ser.). (ENG., Illus.). 32p. (J). (gr. 3). pap. (978-0-7787-1275-6(3)); lib. bdg. (978-0-7787-1253-4(2)) Crabtree Publishing Co.

Spilsbury, Louise. Get Active! 2010. (Crabtree Connections Ser.). (ENG.). 24p. (J). (gr. 3-6). (978-0-7787-9941-2(7)); pap. (978-0-7787-9963-4(8)) Crabtree Publishing Co.

Sports & Fitness (Gr. PreK-5) 2003. (J). (978-1-58232-026-7(8)) ECS Learning Systems, Inc.

Steck-Vaughn Company, creator. Fitness. 2009. (Fact Matters: Healthy Bodies Ser.). (Illus.). 32p. pap. 8.67 (978-1-4190-5469-3(4)) Heinemann-Raintree.

Strauss, Greg. Eleven Minute Workout: Total Fitness in 11 Minutes a Day. 2003. (Illus.). 124p. per. 11.00 (978-0-9744568-0-5(2), EMW:0974456802) Motion Fitness LLC.

Tecco, Betsy Dru. Food for Fuel: The Connection Between Food & Physical Activity. (Library of Nutrition Ser.). 48p. 2009. (gr. 5-8). 53.00 (978-1-60853-766-2(8), Rosen Reference) 2007. (ENG., Illus.). (gr. 5-8). per. 12.75 (978-1-4042-1635-8(9), 030297f5-d816-480a-aa89-080d24465e77) 2004. (Illus.). (J). lib. bdg. 26.50 (978-1-4042-0303-7(6)) Rosen Publishing Group, Inc., The.

Viardi, Debbie & Vilardi, Deborah. Amazing Human Feats of Strength. 2018. (Superhuman Feats Ser.). (ENG., Illus.). 32p. (J). (gr. 4-6). lib. bdg. 28.65 (978-1-5435-4124-3(0), 139078, Capstone Pr.) Capstone.

Vogel, Elizabeth. A Hacer Ejercicio!, 1 vol. 2003. (Limpieza y Salud Todo el día (Clean & Healthy All Day Long) Ser.). (SPA., Illus.). 24p. (J). (gr. 1-1). lib. bdg. 22.27 (978-0-8239-6614-1(3), 9bd33a9c-2734-43d7-bbdd-8a442927e522, Editorial Buenas Letras) Rosen Publishing Group, Inc., The.

—Let's Exercise = a Hacer Ejercicio, 1 vol. 2003. (Clean & Healthy All Day Long / Limpieza y Salud Todo el Día Ser.). (ENG & SPA., Illus.). 24p. (J). (gr. 1-1). lib. bdg. 22.27 (978-0-8239-6615-8(1), af680680-8d47-4ec9-b3c4-6017bcd5509c, Editorial Buenas Letras) Rosen Publishing Group, Inc., The.

—Let's Exercise / ¡A hacer Ejercicio! 2009. (Clean & Healthy All Day Long / Limpieza y salud todo el día Ser.). (SPA.). 24p. (gr. 1-1). 37.50 (978-1-61511-871-7(3), Editorial Buenas Letras) Rosen Publishing Group, Inc., The.

White, Andrea & Mimi, Vance. Tummies on the Run. Shepperson, Rob, illus. 2012. 32p. pap. 11.95 (978-1-60898-134-2(7)) namelos llc.

Willis, Laurie, ed. Exercise & Fitness, 1 vol. 2013. (Issues That Concern You Ser.). (ENG., Illus.). 120p. (gr. 7-10). lib. bdg. 43.63 (978-0-7377-6293-8(4), 44843ba3-2904-46cb-a245-a9f980026fdb, Greenhaven Publishing) Greenhaven Publishing LLC.

PHYSICAL GEOGRAPHY

see also Climate; Earth (Planet); Earthquakes; Geophysics; Glaciers; Ice; Icebergs; Lakes; Meteorology; Mountains; Ocean; Rivers; Tides; Volcanoes; Winds

ABDO Publishing Company Staff. Continents. 2003. (Continents Ser.). (ENG.). 32p. (gr. k-4). (978-1-57765-957-0(0), Buddy Bks.) ABDO Publishing Co.

Anderson, Sheila. Plateaus. 2008. (First Step Nonfiction - Landforms Ser.). (ENG., Illus.). 24p. (gr. k-2). lib. bdg. 23.93 (978-0-8225-8592-3(8), Lerner Pubns.) Lerner Publishing Group.

Believe It Or Not!, Ripleys, compiled by. Ripley Twists PB: Extreme Earth. 2018. (Twist Ser.: 5). (ENG.). 48p. (J). pap. 7.99 (978-1-60991-228-4(4)) Ripley Entertainment, Inc.

Benchmark Education Co., LLC. Physical & Human Geography. 2014. (PRIME Ser.). (J). (gr. 6-8). pap. (978-1-4509-9502-3(0)) Benchmark Education Co.

Benchmark Education Company, LLC Staff, compiled by. Cactus & Canyons & Regions. 2005. spiral bd. 225.00 (978-1-4108-5805-4(7)) Benchmark Education Co.

Britannica, Learning Library. Planet Earth. 2003. (Illus.). 64p. 14.95 (978-1-59339-032-7(7)) Encyclopaedia Britannica, Inc.

Coote, Roger. Earth. 2003. (Knowledge Masters Ser.). (Illus.). 32p. (YA). pap. incl. cd-rom (978-1-903954-11-9(8), Pavilion Children's Books) Pavilion Bks.

Dayton, Connor. Rock Formations. 2009. (Rocks & Minerals Ser.). 24p. (gr. 2-3). 42.50 (978-1-60852-502-7(3), PowerKids Pr.) Rosen Publishing Group, Inc., The.

De Agostini, Jim. People & Their Quality of Life, 1 vol. 2004. (Atlases of the Earth & Its Resources Ser.). (ENG., Illus.). 80p. (gr. 6-8). lib. bdg. 37.67 (978-0-8368-5618-7(X), 65ec49a1-ead6-4d53-b0a7-9a3130611536, World Almanac Library) Stevens, Gareth Publishing LLLP.

DeCristofano, Carolyn. National Geographic Kids Ultimate Space Atlas. 2017. 160p. (J). (gr. 3-7). (ENG.). lib. bdg. 22.90 (978-1-4263-2803-9(6)); (Illus.). pap. 12.99 (978-1-4263-2802-2(8)) Disney Publishing Worldwide. (National Geographic Kids).

Gall, Susan B., ed. Junior Worldmark Encyclopedia of Physical Geography, 5 vols. 2003. (Illus.). (J). (978-0-7876-6267-7(4)); (978-0-7876-6633-0(5)); (978-0-7876-6266-0(6)); (978-0-7876-6269-1(0)); (978-0-7876-6268-4(2)) Cengage Gale. (UXL).

Gilbert, Sara. Les Canyons. 2018. (Vive la Terre! Ser.). (FRE., Illus.). 24p. (J). (978-1-77092-399-7(3), 19688) Creative Co., The.

—Canyons. 2018. (Earth Rocks! Ser.). (ENG., Illus.). 24p. (J). (gr. 1-4). (978-1-60818-891-8(4), 19513, Creative Education) Creative Co., The.

—Earthquakes. 2018. (Earth Rocks! Ser.). (ENG., Illus.). 24p. (J). (gr. 1-4). pap. 9.99 (978-1-62832-507-2(0), 19511, Creative Paperbacks) Creative Co., The.

Green, Emily K. Forests. 2006. (Learning about the Earth Ser.). (ENG., Illus.). 24p. (J). (gr. k-3). lib. bdg. 26.95 (978-1-60014-036-5(X)) Bellwether Media.

Griffin, Mary. Los Lugares Más Altos de la Tierra (Earth's Highest Places), 1 vol. 2014. (Lugares Extremos de la Tierra (Earth's Most Extreme Places) Ser.). (SPA.). 24p. (J). (gr. 2-3). 24.27 (978-1-4824-1917-7(3), 727ba9bd-2d57-4ff9-9dc1-0bb40e83c64b) Stevens, Gareth Publishing LLLP.

Grucella, Cali. A Look at Landforms, 1 vol. 2008. (Real Life Readers Ser.). (ENG.). 8p. (gr. k-1). pap. 5.15 (978-1-4042-7983-4(0), 54b461fb-a470-4470-9168-937fe5e8cf6f, Rosen Classroom) Rosen Publishing Group, Inc., The.

Harcourt School Publishers Staff. Horizons: States & Regions. 3rd ed. 2003. (Harcourt School Publishers Horizons Ser.). (ENG., Illus.). 584p. (gr. 3-4). pupil's gde. ed. 83.95 (978-0-15-320942-0(9)) Harcourt Schl. Pubs.

—Horizons 2003 Vol. 1: States & Regions. 3rd ed. 2003. (Harcourt School Publishers Horizons Ser.). (ENG.). 600p. (gr. 3-4). tchr. ed. 161.50 (978-0-15-320944-4(5)) Harcourt Schl. Pubs.

Holt, Rinehart and Winston Staff. Holt Science & Technology Chapter 2: Earth Science: Maps & Models of the Earth. 5th ed. 2004. (Illus.). pap. 12.86 (978-0-03-030271-8(4)) Holt McDougal.

Junior Worldmark Encyclopedia of Physical Geography, 5 vols. 2003. (ENG., Illus.). 832p. (J). 458.00 (978-0-7876-6265-3(8), UXL) Cengage Gale.

Kalman, Bobbie. ¿Qué le Da Forma a la Tierra? 2009. (SPA.). 32p. (J). (978-0-7787-8240-7(9)); pap. (978-0-7787-8257-5(3)) Crabtree Publishing Co.

Lerner Publishing Group Staff, ed. Time Nature's Wonders: The Science & Splendor of Earth's Most Fascinating Places. 2008. (Time Inc. Home Entertainment Library-Bound Titles Ser.). (ENG.). 128p. (gr. 5-12). lib. bdg. 39.93 (978-0-7613-4228-1(1), Twenty-First Century Bks.) Lerner Publishing Group.

Lewis, J. Patrick. Earth & You - A Closer View: Nature's Features. Canyon, Christopher, illus. 2004. (Sharing Nature with Children Book Ser.). 36p. (J). (gr. -1-3). 16.95 (978-1-58469-016-0(X)) Take Heart Pubns.

Looye, Juliette, text. I Live on an Island. 2004. (Illus.). 16p. (J). pap. (978-0-7367-1936-0(9)) Zaner-Bloser, Inc.

Mattern, Joanne. Sand, Silt, & Mud & the Rock Cycle, 1 vol. 2005. (Shaping & Reshaping of Earth's Surface Ser.). (ENG., Illus.). 24p. (J). (gr. 4-4). pap. 9.25 (978-1-4358-3263-3(9), a5f6d661-716c-4f5f-acd7-1c05fc05ab25, PowerKids Pr.) Rosen Publishing Group, Inc., The.

Meachen Rau, Dana. Land, 1 vol. 2009. (Earth Matters Ser.). (ENG.). 32p. (gr. 1-2). lib. bdg. 25.50 (978-0-7614-3043-8(1), 36cf1a21-dca9-464d-afc8-08f3bdb3e081) Cavendish Square Publishing LLC.

—La Tierra / Land, 1 vol. 2010. (Nuestro Planeta Es Importante / Earth Matters Ser.). (ENG & SPA.). 32p. (gr. 1-2). lib. bdg. 25.50 (978-0-7614-3490-0(9), ea2a66cf-4ec8-4429-a4ca-a787b0833168) Cavendish Square Publishing LLC.

—La Tierra (Land), 1 vol. 2010. (Nuestro Planeta Es Importante (Earth Matters) Ser.). (SPA.). 32p. (gr. 1-2). lib. bdg. 25.50 (978-0-7614-3465-8(8), 3f7ae062-a253-46fa-8968-d58667160e61) Cavendish Square Publishing LLC.

Moignot, Daniel, illus. Atlas of the Earth. 2012. (ENG.). 36p. (J). (gr. -1-k). spiral bd. 19.99 (978-1-85103-406-2(4)) Moonlight Publishing, Ltd. GBR. Dist: Independent Pubs. Group.

Nadeau, Isaac. Peninsulas, 1 vol. 2005. (Library of Landforms Ser.). (ENG., Illus.). 24p. (J). (gr. 3-4). lib. bdg. 26.27 (978-1-4042-3125-2(0), 3c93878f-ea66-4fc5-beae-966d60c373e1) Rosen Publishing Group, Inc., The.

Nagel, Rob. UXL Encyclopedia of Landforms & Other Geologic Features, 3 vols. 2003. (Illus.). xxvii, 314p. (J). (978-0-7876-7670-4(5)); (978-0-7876-7672-8(1)); (978-0-7876-7671-1(3)) Cengage Gale. (UXL).

National Geographic Learning. Reading Expeditions (Social Studies: the Land Around Us): Coasts. 2007. (Nonfiction Reading & Writing Workshops Ser.). (ENG., Illus.). 32p. (J). pap. 18.95 (978-0-7922-4563-6(6)) CENGAGE Learning.

—Reading Expeditions (Social Studies: the Land Around Us): Plains. 2007. (Nonfiction Reading & Writing Workshops Ser.). (ENG., Illus.). 32p. (J). pap. 18.95 (978-0-7922-4564-3(4)) CENGAGE Learning.

S. P. C. K. Stories from the History of Sweden. 2006. pap. 29.50 (978-1-4101-0922-4(4)) Fredonia Bks.

Samuels, Charlie. Mapping the Physical World. 2017. (Mapping in the Modern World Ser.). (ENG.). 32p. (J). (gr. 5-5). (978-0-7787-3236-5(3)); pap. (978-0-7787-3242-6(8)) Crabtree Publishing Co.

Soll, Karen. Highest Places on the Planet. 2016. (Extreme Earth Ser.). (ENG., Illus.). 24p. (J). (gr. -1-2). lib. bdg. 27.32 (978-1-4914-8342-8(3), 130812, Capstone Pr.) Capstone.

—Lowest Places on the Planet. 2016. (Extreme Earth Ser.). (ENG., Illus.). 24p. (J). (gr. -1-2). lib. bdg. 27.32 (978-1-4914-8343-5(1), 130813, Capstone Pr.) Capstone.

Taylor, Barbara. Understanding Landforms. 2007. (Geography Skills/Watts Ser.). (Illus.). 46p. (J). (gr. 4-7). lib. bdg. 32.80 (978-1-59920-049-1(X)) Black Rabbit Bks.

Twist, Clint. Extreme Earth. 2010. (Ripley Twists Ser.). (Illus.). 48p. (J). (gr. 3-18). lib. bdg. 19.95 (978-1-4222-1829-7(5), 1318258) Mason Crest.

Twist, Clint, et al. Extreme Earth. 2009. (Ripley Twists Ser.). (Illus.). 48p. (J). (gr. 3-18). pap. 8.95 (978-1-4222-2067-2(2), 1318258) Mason Crest.

Van Gorp, Lynn. Investigating Landforms, 1 vol. rev. ed. 2007. (Science: Informational Text Ser.). (ENG., Illus.). 32p. (gr. 4-6). pap. 12.99 (978-0-7439-0557-2(1)) Teacher Created Materials, Inc.

White, Nancy. Using Earth's Underground Heat. 2018. (Going Green Ser.). (ENG.). 32p. (J). (gr. 2-7). 7.99 (978-1-64280-074-6(0)) Bearport Publishing Co., Inc.

World Book, Inc. Staff, contrib. by. Earth's Features. 2010. (J). (978-0-7166-7738-3(5)) World Bk., Inc.

Zuravicky, Orli. Map Math: Learning about Latitude & Longitude Using Coordinate Systems, 1 vol. 2010. (Math for the REAL World Ser.). (ENG.). 32p. (gr. 5-6). pap. 10.00 (978-1-4042-5133-5(2), 6fe8d50d-49cd-4352-a9d0-83948f8ab6a8, PowerKids Pr.) Rosen Publishing Group, Inc., The.

PHYSICAL GEOGRAPHY—NORTH AMERICA

Harcourt School Publishers Staff. Horizons: Texas Edition. 3rd ed. 2003. (Illus.). (gr. 4). 70.10 (978-0-15-320181-3(9)) Harcourt Schl. Pubs.

—Horizons: US History. 3rd ed. 2003. (Harcourt School Publishers Horizons Ser.). (ENG., Illus.). 826p. (gr. 5-5). pupil's gde. ed. 93.85 (978-0-15-320182-0(7)) Harcourt Schl. Pubs.

PHYSICAL STAMINA

see Physical Fitness

PHYSICAL THERAPY—VOCATIONAL GUIDANCE

Amidon Lusted, Marcia. Jump-Starting a Career in Physical Therapy & Rehabilitation, 1 vol. 2013. (Health Care Careers in 2 Years Ser.). (ENG.). 80p. (YA). (gr. 7-7). 38.41 (978-1-4777-1695-3(5), a6197c57-317a-4168-a682-f79c8038b5d5) Rosen Publishing Group, Inc., The.

Flath, Camden. Therapy Jobs in Educational Settings: Speech, Physical, Occupational & Audiology. 2010. (New Careers for the 21st Century Ser.). (Illus.). 64p. (YA). (gr. 7-18). pap. 9.95 (978-1-4222-2047-4(8)) Mason Crest.

Kassnoff, David. Working As a Physical Therapist in Your Community, 1 vol. 2015. (Careers in Your Community Ser.). (ENG., Illus.). 80p. (J). (gr. 7-8). 37.47 (978-1-4994-6109-1(7), 60bcc1a8-3e40-41a3-9029-4901fcdb4a1b, Rosen Young Adult) Rosen Publishing Group, Inc., The.

PHYSICAL TRAINING

see Physical Education and Training

PHYSICALLY CHALLENGED PEOPLE

see People with Disabilities

PHYSICALLY DISABLED PEOPLE

see People with Disabilities

PHYSICALLY HANDICAPPED

see People with Disabilities

PHYSICIANS

see also Women Physicians

also names of specialists, e.g. Surgeons

Alexander, Lori. A Sporting Chance: How Ludwig Guttmann Created the Paralympic Games. Drummond, Allan, illus. 2020. (ENG.). 128p. (J). (gr. 3-7). 17.99 (978-1-328-58079-5(2), 1728624, Clarion Bks.) HarperCollins Pubs.

Anderson, Catherine Corley. John F. Kennedy. 2005. (Just the Facts Biographies Ser.). (ENG., Illus.). 112p. (gr. 5-12). lib. bdg. 27.93 (978-0-8225-2643-8(3), Lerner Pubns.) Lerner Publishing Group.

Askew, Amanda & Crowson, Andrew. Doctor. 2012. (ENG., Illus.). 24p. (gr. 1-3). pap. 7.95 (978-1-926853-47-5(4)) Saunders Bk. Co. CAN. Dist: RiverStream Publishing.

Bailey, Diane. Physics. 2017. (Illus.). 64p. (J). (978-1-4222-3554-6(8)) Mason Crest.

Bankston, John. Joseph Lister & the Story of Antiseptics. 2004. (Uncharted, Unexplored, & Unexplained Ser.). (Illus.). 48p. (J). (gr. 4-8). lib. bdg. 29.95 (978-1-58415-262-0(1)) Mitchell Lane Pubs.

Bell, Samantha. Doctor. Bane, Jeff, illus. 2017. (My Early Library: My Friendly Neighborhood Ser.). (ENG.). 24p. (J). (gr. k-1). lib. bdg. 30.64 (978-1-63472-829-4(7), 209742) Cherry Lake Publishing.

—Sports Medicine Doctor. 2015. (21st Century Skills Library: Cool STEAM Careers Ser.). (ENG., Illus.). 32p. (J). (gr. 4-7). pap. 14.21 (978-1-63362-654-6(7), 206441) Cherry Lake Publishing.

Bellamy, Adam. This Is My Doctor, 1 vol. 2016. (All about My World Ser.). (ENG., Illus.). 24p. (gr. k-1). pap. 10.35 (978-0-7660-8098-0(6), 51f275d5-b56c-4504-a875-775e4b3cb479) Enslow Publishing, LLC.

Benge, Janet & Benge, Geoff. Klaus-Dieter John: Hope in the Land of the Incas. 2014. (Illus.). 224p. (J). pap. 11.99 (978-1-57658-755-3(X)) YWAM Publishing.

Bennett, Howard J. Lions Aren't Scared of Shots: A Story for Children about Visiting the Doctor. Weber, Michael S., illus. 2006. 32p. (J). (gr. -1-3). 14.95 (978-1-59147-473-9(6), 441A473, Magination Pr.) American Psychological Assn.

—Lions Aren't Scared of Shots: A Story for Children about Visiting the Doctor. Weber, M. S., illus. 2006. 32p. (J). (gr. -1-3). per. 9.95 (978-1-59147-474-6(4), 441A474, Magination Pr.) American Psychological Assn.

BENSON, Mary Rubec. Follow the Warrior's Path: Life Story of Ohiyesa Better Known As Dr. Eastman. 2003. (YA). pap. 14.95 (978-0-89992-155-6(8)) Council for Indian Education.

Boothroyd, Jennifer. All about Doctors. 2020. (Sesame Street (r) Loves Community Helpers Ser.). (ENG., Illus.). 32p. (J). (gr. -1-2). 29.32 (978-1-5415-8996-4(3), 75616dc5-c76b-4563-ac0b-9b0753f6df94, Lerner Pubns.) Lerner Publishing Group.

Boyd, Nicole. A Doctor's Busy Day. 2009. (Reading Room Collection 2 Ser.). 24p. (gr. 3-4). 42.50 (978-1-60851-952-1(X), PowerKids Pr.) Rosen Publishing Group, Inc., The.

Brill, Marlene Targ. Doctors. 2005. (Pull Ahead Bks.). (Illus.). 32p. (J). lib. bdg. 22.60 (978-0-8225-1689-7(6)) Lerner Publishing Group.

Brinker, Spencer. At the Doctor's Office. 2019. (I Spy Ser.). (ENG., Illus.). 16p. (J). (gr. -1-1). 6.99 (978-1-64280-396-9(0)) Bearport Publishing Co., Inc.

Brooks, Felicity. Daisy Doctor. Litchfield, Jo, illus. 2005. 24p. (J). pap. 6.95 (978-0-7945-0724-4(7), Usborne) EDC Publishing.

Brown, Don. Up & Down: The Adventures of John Jeffries, First American to Fly. Brown, Don, illus. 2018. (Illus.). 40p. (J). (gr. 1-4). 16.99 (978-1-58089-812-6(2)) Charlesbridge Publishing, Inc.

Bryant, Jen. A River of Words: The Story of William Carlos Williams. Sweet, Melissa, illus. 2008. (ENG.). 34p. (J). (gr. 4-7). 17.50 (978-0-8028-5302-8(1), Eerdmans Bks For Young Readers) Eerdmans, William B. Publishing Co.

Charles, Audrey. I Can Be a Doctor, 1 vol. 2017. (I Can Be Anything! Ser.). (ENG.). 24p. (gr. k-k). pap. 9.15 (978-1-4824-6317-0(2), 725e5c0c-4bd5-4bab-9510-5b2c94415840) Stevens, Gareth Publishing LLLP.

Christy, Lee Louis. I Go to Work as a Doctor. 2003. (I Go to Work As Ser.). (Illus.). (J). (978-1-58417-042-6(5)); pap. (978-1-58417-107-2(3)) Lake Street Pubs.

Civardi, Anne. Going to the Doctor. rev. ed. 2005. 16p. (J). pap. 4.95 (978-0-7945-1004-6(3), Usborne) EDC Publishing.

Clark, Sarah Kartchner. Doctors Then & Now, 1 vol. rev. ed. 2006. (Social Studies: Informational Text Ser.). (ENG.). 32p. (gr. 2-3). pap. 11.99 (978-0-7439-9373-9(X)) Teacher Created Materials, Inc.

Coan, Sharon. Trabajadores Que Me Cuidan. 2nd rev. ed. 2016. (TIME for KIDS(r): Informational Text Ser.). (SPA., Illus.). 12p. (gr. -1-k). 7.99 (978-1-4938-3028-2(7)) Teacher Created Materials, Inc.

Crabtree, Marc. Meet My Neighbor, the Doctor. 2013. (ENG., Illus.). 24p. (J). (978-0-7787-0871-1(3)); pap. (978-0-7787-0875-9(6)) Crabtree Publishing Co.

Dawson, Patricia A. A Doctor's Job, 1 vol. 2014. (Community Workers Ser.). (ENG.). 24p. (gr. 1-1). pap. 9.23 (978-1-62712-991-6(X), 9f9e2b2a-3cb3-40de-8ac9-bb33d4a2ff58); lib. bdg. 25.93 (978-1-62712-990-9(1), a26900eb-6b69-43cf-bb3b-f2a4f167d3b6) Cavendish Square Publishing LLC.

La Doctora, 2 Pack. (Chiquilibros Ser.). (SPA.). (gr. -1-1). 12.00 (978-0-7635-8564-8(5)) Rigby Education.

Doering Tourville, Amanda. Whose Tools Are These?, 1 vol. 2011. (Community Helper Mysteries Ser.). (ENG.). 24p. (J). (gr. -1-2). lib. bdg. 27.32 (978-1-4296-6081-5(3), 115012, Capstone Pr.) Capstone.

Driscoll, Laura. I Want to Be a Doctor. Echeverri, Catalina, illus. 2018. 31p. (J). (978-1-5444-0496-7(4)) Harper & Row Ltd.

Dyan, Penelope. The Place of Tales — - a Kid's Guide to Canterbury, Kent, England. Weigand, John, photos by. 2011. (Illus.). 40p. pap. 12.95 (978-1-935630-66-1(0)) Bellissima Publishing, LLC.

Elford, Jole Shack. William Harvey & the Mechanics of the Heart. 2005. (Illus.). 141p. (YA). (gr. 6-10). reprint ed. 28.00 (978-0-7567-9712-6(8)) DIANE Publishing Co.

Farndon, John. Quacks & con Artists: The Dubious History of Doctors. Dean, Venitia, illus. 2017. (Sickening History of Medicine Ser.). (ENG.). 32p. (J). (gr. 3-6). E-Book 42.65 (978-1-5124-3635-8(6), 9781512436358); E-Book 4.99 (978-1-5124-3636-5(4), 9781512436365); E-Book 42.65 (978-1-5124-2712-7(8)) Lerner Publishing Group. (Hungry Tomato (r)).

Flor Ada, Alma & Campoy, F. Isabel, contrib. by. Voces. (Literature Collection of Puertas Al Sol Ser.).Tr. of Voices. (SPA.). 32p. (J). (gr. k-6). pap. 13.95 (978-1-59437-707-5(3)) Santillana USA Publishing Co., Inc.

Foy, Debbie. Medical Pioneers, 1 vol. 2011. (20th Century Lives Ser.). (ENG.). 32p. (YA). (gr. 5-5). lib. bdg. 30.27 (978-1-4488-3293-4(4), 04c6096a-be82-42cf-b07c-1a3345d29a2d) Rosen Publishing Group, Inc., The.

Goldish, Meish. Doctors to the Rescue. 2011. (Work of Heroes: First Responders in Action Ser.). 32p. (YA). (gr. 1-4). lib. bdg. 28.50 (978-1-61772-285-1(5)) Bearport Publishing Co., Inc.

Gow, Mary. The Greatest Doctor of Ancient Times: Hippocrates & His Oath, 1 vol. 2009. (Great Minds of Ancient Science & Math Ser.). (ENG., Illus.). 128p. (gr. 4-6). lib. bdg. 35.93 (978-0-7660-3118-0(7), 30478f77-2521-40b0-aa72-91b30d0cfb273) Enslow Publishing, LLC.

Gregory, Josh. What Do They Do? Doctors. 2010. (Community Connections: What Do They Do? Ser.). (ENG., Illus.). 24p. (gr. 2-5). lib. bdg. 29.21 (978-1-60279-805-2(2), 200500) Cherry Lake Publishing.

Griffin, Lydia. Susan Anderson: Colorado's Doc Susie. 2010. (ENG., Illus.). 72p. (J). pap. 8.95 (978-0-86541-108-1(5)) Filter Pr., LLC.

Hapka, Cathy, pseud. My Little Doctor Bag Book. Sharp, Paul, illus. 2005. (J). (978-1-57151-754-8(5)) Playhouse Publishing.

Harcourt School Publishers Staff. Your Health Reader: The Doctor. 3rd ed. 2003. (Illus.). pap. 9.40 (978-0-15-338776-0(9)) Harcourt Schl. Pubs.

Harrison, Lorraine. Doctors on the Job. 2017. (Jobs in Our Community Ser.). 24p. (gr. k-k). pap. 49.50 (978-1-5345-2138-4(0)) Cengage Gale.

—Doctors on the Job, 1 vol. 2016. (Jobs in Our Community Ser.). (ENG.). 24p. (J). (gr. 1-1). 26.23 (978-1-5345-2139-1(9), 4af63693-ac8a-4683-83d7-63df87fdb939); pap. 9.25 (978-1-5345-2137-7(2), 63d86029-c35d-427e-973c-95a428abf3d8) Greenhaven Publishing LLC. (KidHaven Publishing).

Haxton, Jason. Andrew Taylor Still: Father of Osteopathic Medicine. 2016. (ENG., Illus.). 48p. (J). 27.00 (978-1-61248-174-6(4)) Truman State Univ. Pr.

Heath, Erin. Doctors in Our Community, 1 vol. 2009. (On the Job Ser.). (ENG.). 24p. (J). (gr. 1-1). pap. 9.25 (978-1-4358-2454-6(7), c6203f97-123b-4fb3-941e-950d32eee473); (Illus.). lib. bdg. 26.27 (978-1-4042-8070-0(7), bcca58ee-cd1d-474d-97dd-86e7074d5669) Rosen Publishing Group, Inc., The. (PowerKids Pr.).

Heos, Bridget. Doctors in My Community. Moran, Mike, illus. 2018. (Meet a Community Helper (Early Bird Stories (tm))

PQR

Ser.). (ENG.). 24p. (J). (gr. k-2). 29.32 *(978-1-5415-2023-3(8)*, 87c72431-b3ba-4913-97ee-6a21e990877d, Lerner Pubns.) Lerner Publishing Group.

—Let's Meet a Doctor. Moran, Mike, illus. 2013. (Cloverleaf Books (tm) — Community Helpers Ser.). (ENG.). 24p. (J). (gr. k-2). pap. 8.99 *(978-1-4677-0801-2(1)*, dc885535-9338-4ad2-863e-161ead0d6259, Millbrook Pr.) Lerner Publishing Group.

Herweck, Diana. All in a Day's Work: ER Doctor, 1 vol. 2nd rev. ed. 2013. (TIME for KIDS(r): Informational Text Ser.). (ENG., Illus.). 64p. (J). (gr. 4-8). lib. bdg. 31.96 *(978-1-4333-7429-6(3))* Teacher Created Materials, Inc.

—ER Doctor, 1 vol. 2nd rev. ed. 2013. (TIME for KIDS(r): Informational Text Ser.). (ENG., Illus.). 64p. (J). (gr. 4-8). pap. 14.99 *(978-1-4333-4906-5(X))* Teacher Created Materials, Inc.

Hoena, Blake A. The Doctor's Office: A 4D Book. rev. ed. 2018. (Visit To... Ser.). (ENG., Illus.). 24p. (J). (gr. -1-2). lib. bdg. 29.32 *(978-1-5435-0827-7(8)*, 137590, Capstone Pr.) Capstone.

Honders, Christine. What's It Really Like to Be a Doctor?, 1 vol. 2019. (Jobs Kids Want Ser.). (ENG.). 24p. (gr. 1-2). 25.27 *(978-1-5383-4982-3(5)*, 06580438-3cda-45e4-b699-68a7197bb10a, PowerKids Pr.) Rosen Publishing Group, Inc., The.

Hunsaker, Jennifer. Physical Therapists. 2017. (Careers in Healthcare Ser.: Vol. 13). (ENG., Illus.). 64p. (YA). (gr. 7-12). 23.95 *(978-1-4222-3803-5(2))* Mason Crest.

Jankowski, Connie. Hippocrates: Making the Way for Medicine, 1 vol. rev. ed. 2017. (Science: Informational Text Ser.). (ENG.). 32p. (gr. 3-6). pap. 12.99 *(978-0-7439-0596-1(2))* Teacher Created Materials, Inc.

Juarez, Christine. Hector P. Garcia. 2016. (Great Hispanic & Latino Americans Ser.). (ENG., Illus.). 24p. (J). (gr. -1-2). lib. bdg. 24.65 *(978-1-5157-1891-8(3)*, 132590, Capstone Pr.) Capstone.

Kenan, Tessa. Hooray for Doctors! 2017. (Bumba Books (r) — Hooray for Community Helpers! Ser.). (ENG., Illus.). 24p. (J). (gr. -1-1). 26.65 *(978-1-5124-3350-0(0)*, 231e4c3e-e3db-4040-80ab-e6763aae106d, Lerner Pubns.); pap. 8.99 *(978-1-5124-5550-2(4)*, 82dda8c0-7290-42d6-8499-c76bec0dbb60) Lerner Publishing Group.

—¡Que Vivan Los Doctores! (Hooray for Doctors!) 2018. (Bumba Books (r) en Español — ¡Que Vivan Los Ayudantes Comunitarios! (Hooray for Community Helpers!) Ser.). (SPA., Illus.). 24p. (J). (gr. -1-1). 26.65 *(978-1-5124-9758-8(4)*, 7be13b88-c109-4100-83fa-1133931089ea, Ediciones Lerner) Lerner Publishing Group.

Kidder, Tracy. Mountains Beyond Mountains (Adapted for Young People) The Quest of Dr. Paul Farmer, a Man Who Would Cure the World. 2014. (ENG.). (YA). (gr. 7). lib. bdg. 19.60 *(978-1-68065-029-7(7))* Perfection Learning Corp.

Kidder, Tracy & French, Michael. Mountains Beyond Mountains (Adapted for Young People) The Quest of Dr. Paul Farmer, a Man Who Would Cure the World. 2014. (ENG.). 288p. (YA). (gr. 7). pap. 9.99 *(978-0-385-74319-8(X)*, Ember) Random Hse. Children's Bks.

King, Aven. A Doctor's Tools, 1 vol. 2015. (Community Helpers & Their Tools Ser.). (ENG., Illus.). 24p. (J). (gr. 2-3). pap. 9.25 *(978-1-4994-0838-6(2)*, 0d1de156-fa5b-4681-a017-74289ecacbe6, PowerKids Pr.) Rosen Publishing Group, Inc., The.

Klar, Jeremy & Lily, Henrietta M. Josef Mengele, 1 vol., 1. 2015. (Holocaust Ser.). (ENG., Illus.). 112p. (J). (gr. 7-7). 38.80 *(978-1-5081-7047-1(9)*, 235b5638-0a52-4682-847f-b5852fc56307, Rosen Young Adult) Rosen Publishing Group, Inc., The.

Kummer, Pat. Sports Medicine Doctor. 2008. (21st Century Skills Library: Cool Careers Ser.). (ENG., Illus.). 32p. (gr. 4-8). lib. bdg. 32.07 *(978-1-60279-302-6(6)*, 200141) Cherry Lake Publishing.

Laks Gorman, Jacqueline. Doctors, 1 vol. 2010. (People in My Community (Second Edition) Ser.). (ENG.). 24p. (J). (gr. k-2). pap. 9.15 *(978-1-4339-3804-7(9)*, 775e6237-e96b-4d09-9720-e2099fafb242); lib. bdg. 25.27 *(978-1-4339-3803-0(0)*, c75f5605-0fdc-46cf-a6c1-b15db9d6a0c3) Stevens, Gareth Publishing LLLP.

Less, Emma. Doctors. 2018. (Real-Life Superheroes Ser.). (ENG.). 16p. (J). (gr. k-2). pap. 7.99 *(978-1-68152-275-3(6)*, 14914) Amicus.

Liebman, Dan & Liebman, Dan. I Want to Be a Doctor. 2nd rev. ed. 2018. (I Want to Be Ser.). (ENG., Illus.). 24p. (J). (gr. -1-2). pap. 3.99 *(978-0-2281-0096-6(8)*, f730093c-676d-4d14-b6b1-b60220a10e46) Firefly Bks., Ltd.

Lim, Bridget & Ramen, Fred. Albucasis: The Father of Modern Surgery, 1 vol. 2016. (Physicians, Scientists, & Mathematicians of the Islamic World Ser.). (ENG.). 112p. (gr. 6-6). 38.80 *(978-1-5081-7140-9(8)*, ba3e970d-391d-4ae9-979e-46d783ada49f) Rosen Publishing Group, Inc., The.

Louie, Ai-Ling. Yo-Yo & Yeou-Cheng Ma, Finding Their Way: Amazing Asian Americans. Peng, Cathy, illus. 2012. (Biographies of Amazing Asian Americans Ser.: 2). (ENG.). 48p. (J). pap. 16.99 *(978-0-9787465-0-6(3))* Dragoneagle Pr.

Lusted, Marcia. Hippocrates. 2017. (Junior Biography From Ancient Civilization Ser.). (gr. 4-6). 29.95 *(978-1-68020-030-0(5))* Mitchell Lane Pubs.

Marsico, Katie. The Doctor, 1 vol. 2012. (Colonial People Ser.). (ENG.). 48p. (gr. 4-4). 34.07 *(978-1-60870-412-5(2)*, 9c3e868d-1a34-4ae0-aa47-edca7c340aed) Cavendish Square Publishing LLC.

Martin, Oscar, Jr., creator. Doctors I.t. ed. 2003. (Illus.). 25p. (J). E-Book 19.95 incl. cd-rom *(978-0-9748416-5-6(X))* Build Your Story.

Mattern, Joanne. I Use Math at the Doctor's, 1 vol. 2005. (I Use Math Ser.). (ENG., Illus.). 24p. (gr. k-2). pap. 9.15 *(978-0-8368-4861-8(6)*, bea58154-7045-4edd-9bb6-08bb716625dc); lib. bdg. 24.67 *(978-0-8368-4854-0(3)*, a403b2d9-c09e-4792-8130-00e071f1c673) Stevens, Gareth Publishing LLLP. (Weekly Reader Leveled Readers).

Meachen Rau, Dana. Doctors, 1 vol. 2008. (Tools We Use Ser.). (ENG.). 32p. (gr. k-1). pap. 9.23 *(978-0-7614-3291-3(4)*, 1c40dbed-a5da-43c7-a1db-caf83702980c); (Illus.). lib. bdg. 25.50 *(978-0-7614-2659-2(0)*, 1c41e19e-e5dd-440d-b4a5-2c6e6bd2fb63) Cavendish Square Publishing LLC.

—Los Doctores / Doctors, 1 vol. 2009. (Instrumentos de Trabajo / Tools We Use Ser.). (ENG & SPA., Illus.). 32p. (gr. k-2). lib. bdg. 25.50 *(978-0-7614-2824-4(0)*, 0e80f18c-a7f7-4ed1-a7ce-aa4cd164cb2a) Cavendish Square Publishing LLC.

—Los Doctores (Doctors), 1 vol. 2009. (Instrumentos de Trabajo (Tools We Use) Ser.). (SPA., Illus.). 32p. (gr. k-2). lib. bdg. 25.50 *(978-0-7614-2799-5(6)*, 0489dfa7-b17d-49f5-86df-f85d36e15380) Cavendish Square Publishing LLC.

Messner, Kate. Dr. Fauci: How a Boy from Brooklyn Became America's Doctor. Bye, Alexandra, illus. 2021. (ENG.). 48p. (J). (gr. -1-3). 17.99 *(978-1-6659-0243-4(4)*, Simon & Schuster Bks. For Young Readers) Simon & Schuster Bks. For Young Readers.

Miller, Connie Colwell. I'll Be a Doctor. Baroncelli, Silvia, illus. 2016. (When I Grow Up Ser.). (ENG.). 24p. (J). (gr. 1-4). lib. bdg. 20.95 *(978-1-60753-760-1(5)*, 15572) Amicus.

—Médecin. Baroncelli, Silvia, illus. 2016. (Plus Tard, Je Serai... Ser.). (FRE.). 24p. (J). (gr. 1-4). *(978-1-77092-354-6(3)*, 17617) Amicus.

Murray, Julie. Doctors, 1 vol. 2015. (My Community: Jobs Ser.). (ENG., Illus.). 24p. (J). (gr. -1-2). 31.36 *(978-1-62970-912-3(3)*, 18282, Abdo Kids) ABDO Publishing Co.

Owen, Ann & Picture Window Books Staff. Keeping You Healthy: A Book about Doctors, 1 vol. Thomas, Eric, illus. 2003. (Community Workers Ser.). (ENG.). 24p. (J). (gr. -1-3). per. 8.95 *(978-1-4048-0479-1(X)*, 92654, Picture Window Bks.) Capstone.

Parks, Peggy J. Doctor. 2003. (Exploring Careers Ser.). (ENG., Illus.). 48p. (J). (gr. 3-5). 27.50 *(978-0-7377-1484-5(0)*, Kidhaven) Cengage Gale.

QEB Start Reading & Talking National Book Stores Edition: First Experiences: Going to the Doctor. 2006. (J). per. *(978-1-59566-253-8(7))* QEB Publishing Inc.

Raines, Christie. My Trip to the Hospital. 2012. (ENG.). 24p. (J). pap. 15.95 *(978-1-4327-9423-1(X))* Outskirts Pr., Inc.

Rameck, Hunt, et al. We Beat the Street: How a Friendship Pact Led to Success. 2014. (ENG.). 208p. (J). 12.24 *(978-1-63245-093-7(3))* Lectorum Pubns., Inc.

Ramen, Fred. Albucasis (Abu al-Qasim Al-Zahrawi) Renowned Muslim Surgeon of the Tenth Century. 2009. (Great Muslim Philosophers & Scientists of the Middle Ages Ser.). 112p. (gr. 6-6). 66.50 *(978-1-61513-178-5(7)*, Rosen Reference) Rosen Publishing Group, Inc., The.

Ready, Dee. Dentists Help. 2013. (Our Community Helpers Ser.). (ENG.). 24p. (J). (gr. k-1). pap. 37.74 *(978-1-62065-842-0(9)*, 19417, Pebble) Capstone.

—Doctors Help. 2013. (Our Community Helpers Ser.). (ENG.). 24p. (J). (gr. k-1). pap. 38.74 *(978-1-62065-844-4(5)*, 19418, Pebble) Capstone.

Ready, Dee & Ready, Dee. Dentists Help, 1 vol. 2013. (Our Community Helpers Ser.). (ENG.). 24p. (J). (gr. -1-2). pap. 6.29 *(978-1-62065-841-3(0)*, 121785, Pebble) Capstone.

—Doctors Help, 1 vol. 2013. (Our Community Helpers Ser.). (ENG.). 24p. (J). (gr. -1-2). pap. 6.29 *(978-1-62065-843-7(7)*, 121786, Capstone Pr.) Capstone.

Rich, Mari. Medicine, Vol. 10. Gilmore, Malinda & Pouson, Mel, eds. 2016. (Black Achievement in Science Ser.). (Illus.). 64p. (J). (gr. 7). 23.95 *(978-1-4222-3561-4(0))* Mason Crest.

Rivera, Sheila. Doctor. 2005. (First Step Nonfiction — Work People Do Ser.). (ENG., Illus.). 8p. (J). (gr. k-2). pap. 5.99 *(978-0-8225-5357-1(0)*, e718aa0d-e8f5-4fff-883f-feb74b8911ed) Lerner Publishing Group.

Rogers, Amy B. Que Hacen Los Doctores? / What Do Doctors Do?, 1 vol. 2015. (Ayudantes de la Comunidad / Helping the Community Ser.). (ENG & SPA.). 24p. (J). (gr. 1-1). 25.27 *(978-1-4994-0620-7(7)*, ab9fe87c-2a0e-463b-ab26-16e23876c4b6, PowerKids Pr.) Rosen Publishing Group, Inc., The.

—What Do Doctors Do?, 1 vol. 2015. (Helping the Community Ser.). (ENG., Illus.). 24p. (J). (gr. 1-1). pap. 9.25 *(978-1-4994-0617-7(7)*, f51330b3-fce2-4fc8-a625-2bd42193db2f, PowerKids Pr.) Rosen Publishing Group, Inc., The.

Rogers, Lisa. 16 Words: William Carlos Williams & the Red Wheelbarrow. Groenink, Chuck, illus. 2019. 40p. (J). (gr. -1-3). 17.99 *(978-1-5247-2016-2(X)*, Schwartz & Wade Bks.) Random Hse. Children's Bks.

Schuh, Mari. Dentists. 2018. (Community Helpers Ser.). (ENG., Illus.). 24p. (J). (gr. k-3). pap. 7.99 *(978-1-61891-305-0(0)*, 12091, Blastoff! Readers) Bellwether Media.

Sharafeddine, Fatima. The Amazing Discoveries of Ibn Sina. 1 vol. Ali, Intelaq, illus. 2015. (ENG.). 32p. (J). (gr. 2-6). 17.95 *(978-1-55498-710-8(5))* Groundwood Bks. CAN. Dist: Publishers Group West (PGW).

Shepherd, Jodie. A Day with Doctors. 2012. (ENG., Illus.). 32p. (J). lib. bdg. 23.00 *(978-0-531-28950-1(8))* Scholastic Library Publishing.

Siemens, Jared. Doctors. 2016. (Illus.). 24p. (J). *(978-1-5105-2103-2(8))* SmartBook Media, Inc.

—Doctors. 2015. (Illus.). 24p. (J). *(978-1-4896-3641-6(2))* Weigl Pubs., Inc.

Simon, Samantha. Physician Assistants. 2017. (Careers in Healthcare Ser.: Vol. 13). (ENG., Illus.). 64p. (YA). (gr. 7-12). 23.95 *(978-1-4222-3804-2(0))* Mason Crest.

Spielman, Gloria. Janusz Korczak's Children. Archambault, Matthew, illus. 2007. (Kar-Ben for Older Readers Ser.). (ENG.). 40p. (J). (gr. 3-7). lib. bdg. 17.95 *(978-1-58013-255-8(3)*, Kar-Ben Publishing) Lerner Publishing Group.

Spitz, Michael. Life As a Doctor in the Civil War, 1 vol. 2017. (Life As... Ser.). (ENG.). 32p. (gr. 3-3). pap. 11.58 *(978-1-5026-3035-3(4)*, e11411b3-38c4-4f65-a99a-a2e86b7df7dd) Cavendish Square Publishing LLC.

Stefoff, Rebecca. Forensics & Medicine, 1 vol. 2011. (Forensic Science Investigated Ser.). (ENG., Illus.). 80p. (gr. 5-7). lib. bdg. 36.93 *(978-0-7614-4143-4(3)*, b44cc801-3e57-4872-aae2-88876aad0a36) Cavendish Square Publishing LLC.

Stratton, Connor. Working at a Hospital. 2020. (People at Work Ser.). (ENG., Illus.). 16p. (J). (gr. k-1). pap. 7.95 *(978-1-64493-094-6(3)*, 1644930943); lib. bdg. 25.64 *(978-1-64493-015-1(3)*, 1644930153) North Star Editions. (Focus Readers).

Suen, Anastasia. Doctors Without Borders. 2009. (Helping Organizations Ser.). 24p. (gr. 2-2). 42.50 *(978-1-61513-258-4(9)*, PowerKids Pr.) Rosen Publishing Group, Inc., The.

—Médicos sin Fronteras (Doctors Without Borders) 2009. (Organizaciones de ayuda (Helping Organizations) Ser.). (SPA.). 24p. (gr. 2-2). 42.50 *(978-1-60851-147-1(2)*, Editorial Buenas Letras) Rosen Publishing Group, Inc., The.

Thalhamer, Ellen Viola. Let's Play Doctor: I Love to Pretend! 2010. 36p. pap. 15.99 *(978-1-4490-7487-6(1))* AuthorHouse.

Waxman, Laura Hamilton. Doctor Tools. 2019. (Bumba Books (r) — Community Helpers Tools of the Trade Ser.). (ENG., Illus.). 24p. (J). (gr. -1-1). pap. 8.99 *(978-1-5415-7350-5(1)*, 6dd445e8-da17-486e-82f2-274b5a65e1e8, Lerner Pubns.) Lerner Publishing Group.

Whiting, Jim. The Life & Times of Hippocrates. 2006. (Biography from Ancient Civilizations Ser.). (Illus.). 48p. (J). (gr. 3-7). lib. bdg. 29.95 *(978-1-58415-512-6(4)*, 1259600) Mitchell Lane Pubs.

Wood, Alix. Mystery in the Morgue: Be a Pathologist. 2017. (Crime Solvers Ser.). 48p. (gr. 6-6). pap. 84.30 *(978-1-5382-0621-8(8))* Stevens, Gareth Publishing LLLP.

Yomtov, Nel. Epidemiologist. 2013. (21st Century Skills Library: Cool STEM Careers Ser.). (ENG., Illus.). 32p. (gr. 4-8). (J). pap. 14.21 *(978-1-62431-031-7(1)*, 202481); 32.07 *(978-1-62431-007-2(9)*, 202479) Cherry Lake Publishing.

Yount, Lisa. William Harvey: Genius Discoverer of Blood Circulation, 1 vol. 2014. (Genius Scientists & Their Genius Ideas Ser.). (ENG.). 96p. (gr. 5-5). 29.60 *(978-0-7660-6585-7(5)*, 005874db-0bc8-4e0d-919b-6ecdc9526208); pap. 13.88 *(978-0-7660-6586-4(3)*, b4cc6cf1-56c7-45d0-9986-84a18e3e2341) Enslow Publishing, LLC.

PHYSICIANS—FICTION

Aguirre, Ann. Vanguard: A Razorland Companion Novel. 2018. (Razorland Trilogy Ser.: 4). (ENG.). 368p. (YA). pap. 15.99 *(978-1-250-15867-3(2)*, 900185525) Square Fish.

Alcott, Louisa. Les Quatre Filles du Docteur March.Tr. of Little Women. (FRE.). (J). pap. 19.95 *(978-2-07-051516-5(8))* Gallimard, Editions FRA. Dist: Distribooks, Inc.

Anderson, Laurie Halse. Manatee Blues, No. 4. 2008. (Vet Volunteers Ser.: 4). (ENG.). 144p. (J). (gr. 3-7). 7.99 *(978-0-14-241084-4(5)*, Puffin Books) Penguin Young Readers Group.

Aryal, Aimee. Hello, Doc! 2008. (J). 14.95 *(978-1-934878-47-7(2))* Amplify Publishing Group.

Bacon, Joy. Oliver Bean, Doctors Aren't Mean! Edward J Russell Elementary School Students, illus. 2007. (ENG.). 32p. (J). (gr. 4-7). pap. 8.95 *(978-0-9792371-1-9(4))* Keene Publishing.

Bailey, Leslie J. Jacub's Journey. DeBroeck, Sarah, illus. 2011. 28p. pap. 24.95 *(978-1-4560-9951-0(5))* America Star Bks.

Banks, Steven. Spongebob Goes to the Doctor. Saunders, Zina, illus. 2005. 22p. (J). lib. bdg. 15.00 *(978-1-4242-0976-7(5))* Fitzgerald Bks.

Barchers, Suzanne I. Kip Gets Sick, 1 vol. rev. ed. 2011. (Phonics Ser.). (ENG., Illus.). 16p. (J). (gr. k-1). 6.99 *(978-1-4333-2422-2(9))* Teacher Created Materials, Inc.

BBC. 12 Doctors, 12 Stories, 13 vols. gif. ed. 2014. (ENG.). 592p. (YA). pap. 24.99 *(978-0-14-135971-7(4)*, 80d7606a-7a15-47d7-8a01-0e08801c7795) Penguin Bks., Ltd. GBR. Dist: Diamond Comic Distributors, Inc.

Beaty, Andrea. Doctor Ted. Lemaitre, Pascal, illus. 2008. (ENG.). 32p. (J). (gr. -1-3). 19.99 *(978-1-4169-2820-1(0)*, McElderry, Margaret K. Bks.) McElderry, Margaret K. Bks.

Beinstein, Phoebe & A and J Studios Staff. Di "Aaaa"! Dora Va al Médico. 2008. (Dora la Exploradora Ser.). (SPA & ENG., Illus.). 24p. (J). (gr. -1-2). pap. 3.99 *(978-1-4169-5492-7(9)*, Libros Para Ninos) Libros Para Ninos.

—Say Ahhh! Dora Goes to the Doctor. 2008. (Dora the Explorer Ser.: 26). (ENG., Illus.). 24p. (J). (gr. -1-2). pap. 3.99 *(978-1-4169-5430-9(9)*, Simon Spotlight/Nickelodeon) Simon Spotlight/Nickelodeon.

Bender, Carol. The Doctor's Little Stowaway. 2009. 28p. pap. 13.99 *(978-1-4490-3711-6(9))* AuthorHouse.

Benenfeld, Rikki. I Go to the Doctor. Benenfeld, Rikki, illus. 2004. (Toddler Experience Ser.). (ENG., Illus.). 32p. (J). lib. bdg. 11.95 *(978-1-929628-15-5(3))* Hachai Publishing.

Beobi & the Magic Coloring Book A Visit to the Doctor. 2005. (J). 3.99 *(978-0-9743847-3-3(9))* Cohn, Tricia.

Brewer, Jo Ann. The Little Girl No One Wanted. 2011. 48p. pap. 15.99 *(978-1-4568-6581-8(1))* Xlibris Corp.

Brooks, Felicity. Daisy the Doctor. Litchfield, Jo, illus. 2008. (Jobs People Do Ser.). 23p. (J). (gr. 4-7). pap. 6.99 *(978-0-7945-2214-8(9)*, Usborne) EDC Publishing.

Brown, Emma. Shady Bay Buddies: Archie Goes to the Doctor. 2017. (ENG., Illus.). 32p. (J). pap. 12.95 *(978-1-78249-544-4(4)*, Cico Kidz) Ryland Peters & Small GBR. Dist: WIPRO.

Brown, Mary. An Ear for Graci. 2011. 16p. 8.99 *(978-1-4520-9702-2(X))* AuthorHouse.

Bryant, Cathy. The Doctor Said I Have Leukemi. Bunker, Thomas, illus. 2012. 24p. pap. 24.95 *(978-1-4560-6929-2(2))* America Star Bks.

By Kaleena Ma. Glasses for Me? Oh No! Dawn Phillips, illus. 2009. 40p. pap. 18.49 *(978-1-4389-5418-9(2))* AuthorHouse.

Capucilli, Alyssa Satin. Biscuit Visits the Doctor. Schories, Pat, illus. 2008. (Biscuit Ser.). (ENG.). 24p. (J). (gr. -1-1). pap. 4.99 *(978-0-06-112843-1(0)*, HarperFestival) HarperCollins Pubs.

Chambers, Cindy. Beamer Learns the Signs of a Stroke & How to Help. 2013. 28p. pap. 14.95 *(978-1-4575-1725-9(6))* Dog Ear Publishing, LLC.

Chase, L. P. Today Is Tuesday. 2006. (J). pap. 9.00 *(978-0-87426-069-4(8))* Whitmore Publishing Co.

Chwast, Seymour. Dr. Dolittle. Chwast, Seymour, illus. 2015. (ENG., Illus.). 40p. (J). (gr. 4-7). 18.99 *(978-1-56846-258-5(1)*, 20825, Creative Editions) Creative Co., The.

Civardi, Anna. Going to the Doctor Sticker Book. 2009. (First Experiences Sticker Book Ser.). 16p. (J). pap. 6.99 *(978-0-7945-2572-9(5)*, Usborne) EDC Publishing.

Civardi, Anne. Going to the Hospital. 2009. (First Experiences Sticker Bks). 18p. (J). pap. 6.99 *(978-0-7945-2431-9(1)*, Usborne) EDC Publishing.

—Going to the Hospital. Bates, Michelle, ed. Cartwright, Stephen, illus. rev. ed. 2005. (Usborne First Experiences Ser.). 16p. (J). (gr. -1-3). per. 4.99 *(978-0-7945-1006-0(X)*, Usborne) EDC Publishing.

Cole, Joanna. My Friend the Doctor. Chambliss, Maxie, illus. 2005. (ENG.). 32p. (J). (gr. -1 — 1). 7.99 *(978-0-06-050500-4(1)*, HarperFestival) HarperCollins Pubs.

Compestine, Ying Chang. Revolution Is Not a Dinner Party. 2009. (ENG.). 272p. (J). (gr. 6-8). pap. 10.99 *(978-0-312-58149-7(1)*, 900062006) Square Fish.

Coolidge, Susan. Clover. 2017. (ENG., Illus.). (J). 23.95 *(978-1-374-96593-5(6))* Capital Communications, Inc.

—Clover. 2016. (ENG., Illus.). (J). 26.95 *(978-1-359-71234-9(8))* Creative Media Partners, LLC.

Cousineau, Craig S. Skippy & Oaf Explore the Battles of the Immune System. 2010. (ENG., Illus.). 180p. (J). (gr. 2-4). pap. 9.95 *(978-1-933255-56-9(0))* DNA Pr.

Cowley, Joy. Poor Sore Hungry Giant. 2009. pap. 8.25 *(978-1-60559-237-4(4))* Hameray Publishing Group, Inc.

Cronin, A. J. The Citadel. 2017. (ENG., Illus.). (J). 32.56 *(978-1-5280-6237-4(X))*; pap. 16.57 *(978-1-334-89985-0(1))* Forgotten Bks.

Cushman, Karen. Matilda Bone. 2020. (ENG.). 192p. (J). (gr. 3-7). pap. 7.99 *(978-0-358-09752-5(5)*, 1747612, Clarion Bks.) HarperCollins Pubs.

—Matilda Bone. unabr. ed. 2004. (Middle Grade Cassette Librariestm Ser.). 176p. (J). (gr. 5-9). pap. 36.00 incl. audio *(978-0-8072-1725-2(5)*, S YA 252 SP, Listening Library) Random Hse. Audio Publishing Group.

Davis, David Denton. Polly's Promise: A Story about Thriving Rather Than Simply Surviving... Turning Apparent Disability into Gifted Ability. 2013. 80p. pap. 21.95 *(978-1-4787-0275-7(3))* Outskirts Pr., Inc.

DeFelice, Cynthia. The Apprenticeship of Lucas Whitaker. 2007. (ENG.). 160p. (J). (gr. 5-9). per. 16.99 *(978-0-374-40014-9(8)*, 900042005) Square Fish.

Depken, Kristen L. I Can Be a Baby Doctor. 2013. (Barbie Step into Reading Level 2 Ser.). lib. bdg. 13.55 *(978-0-606-26968-1(1))* Turtleback.

Derubertis, Barbara. Izzy Impala's Imaginary Illnesses. 2010. pap. 45.32 *(978-0-7613-6511-2(7))* Astra Publishing Hse.

deRubertis, Barbara & DeRubertis, Barbara. Izzy Impala's Imaginary Illnesses. Alley, R. W., illus. 2012. (Animal Antics A to Z Ser.). 32p. (J). (gr. 2 — 1). cd-rom 7.95 *(978-1-57565-402-7(4))* Astra Publishing Hse.

Dietrich, Christopher & Character Building Studio (Firm) Staff. Doc on Call. 2015. (Illus.). (J). *(978-1-4847-2292-3(2))* Disney Publishing Worldwide.

Donaldson, Julia. Zog & the Flying Doctors. Scheffler, Axel, illus. 2017. (ENG.). 32p. (J). (gr. -1-3). 17.99 *(978-1-338-13417-9(5)*, Levine, Arthur A. Bks.) Scholastic, Inc.

Draper, Sharon M. November Blues. 2009. (Jericho Trilogy Ser.). (ENG.). 400p. (YA). (gr. 7). mass mkt. 8.99 *(978-1-4169-0699-5(1)*, Simon Pulse) Simon Pulse.

Dumas, Kim Foster. Gator Gets a Nose Bleed. 2012. 24p. 24.95 *(978-1-4626-4239-7(X))* America Star Bks.

Elchgar, Yasmin. Noonoo the Doctor. 2013. 20p. pap. 13.77 *(978-1-4907-1037-2(X))* Trafford Publishing.

Electra, Agnes. Medical School for Children: Part I. 2011. 46p. pap. 18.00 *(978-0-60911-756-6(5)*, Eloquent Bks.) Strategic Book Publishing & Rights Agency (SBPRA).

Evans, Jan. Repetitive Rhonda. 2007. (Illus.). 29p. (J). 18.95 *(978-0-9720176-7-1(4))* Breath & Shadows Productions.

Faulkerson, President & CEO Jeffery, Founder. IT's GOOD to BE GOLDEN: Golden Innovations. 2008. 30p. 14.95 *(978-0-615-19351-9(X))* PRACTICAL SOLUTIONS Writing, Editing, Consulting.

—IT's GOOD to BE GOLDEN: the Story of Henry the Heart. 2008. 19p. 14.95 *(978-0-615-19350-2(1))* PRACTICAL SOLUTIONS Writing, Editing, Consulting.

Fontana, Shea & Nee, Chris. Smitten with a Kitten. 2016. (Doc Mcstuffins Ser.). (ENG., Illus.). 24p. (J). (gr. -1-1). 17.44 *(978-1-4844-8806-5(7))* Disney Pr.

Freeman, Don. Corduroy Goes to the Doctor (lg Format) McCue, Lisa, illus. 2005. (Corduroy Ser.). 14p. (J). (gr. -1 — 1). bds. 6.99 *(978-0-670-06031-3(3)*, Viking Books for Young Readers) Penguin Young Readers Group.

Ganz, Yaffa. The Travels & Tales of Dr. Emanuel J. Mitzva. 2003. (J). 15.99 *(978-1-58330-581-2(5))* Feldheim Pubs.

Gay, Michel. Bibunde. 2003. (SPA.). 40p. *(978-84-8470-043-2(7))* Corimbo, Editorial S.L.

—Doctor Bibunde. 2003. (SPA.). 134p. *(978-84-8470-045-6(3))* Corimbo, Editorial S.L.

Gaydos, Nora. Now I'm Growing! - A Visit to the Doctor. Gutierrez, Akemi, illus. 2011. (ENG.). 30p. (J). (gr. -1-17). 8.99 *(978-1-60169-153-8(X))* Innovative Kids.

Going to the Doctor: Individual Title Six-Packs. (gr. -1-2). 27.00 *(978-0-7635-9450-3(4))* Rigby Education.

Golden Books. The Doctor Is in! (Bubble Guppies) Unten, Eren, illus. 2012. (Little Golden Book Ser.). (ENG.). 24p. (J). (gr. k-k). 4.99 *(978-0-307-97588-1(6)*, Golden Bks.) Random Hse. Children's Bks.

Greene, Kathi. Betty Gets Ready for the Doctor. 2009. (ENG.). 28p. pap. 15.00 *(978-1-4389-4936-9(7))* AuthorHouse.

Greensill, Rowina Anne. James Goes to Play School. 2010. (Illus.). 28p. pap. 12.49 *(978-1-4490-7039-7(6))* AuthorHouse.

Griffith, Christina. Why Jubilee & Ashanti go to the Doctor? 2011. 28p. pap. 13.54 *(978-1-4269-7069-6(2))* Trafford Publishing.

Guerra, S. F. Billy the Kid Is Not Crazy, 0 vols. 2013. (ENG.). 224p. (J). (gr. 2-6). 16.99 *(978-1-4778-1732-2(8)*, 9781477817322, Two Lions) Amazon Publishing.

Hands, Nikki. Lilly Bunny Goes to the Doctor. 2011. 28p. pap. 24.95 *(978-1-4626-3638-9(1))* America Star Bks.

Hansell, Donna. The Adventures of Kirbey the Kidney. 2012. 20p. pap. 11.59 *(978-1-4669-4527-2(3))* Trafford Publishing.

Harlow, Joan Hiatt. Breaker Boy. 2017. (ENG., Illus.). 288p. (J). (gr. 3-7). 16.99 *(978-1-4814-6537-3(6)*, McElderry, Margaret K. Bks.) McElderry, Margaret K. Bks.

Hewitt, Franz. Monster Doctor, M. D. 2010. 40p. pap. 18.49 *(978-0-557-53188-2(8))* Lulu Pr., Inc.

Horne, Jay. Published Youth Volume Two. 2010. 61p. pap. 10.99 *(978-0-557-30674-9(4))* Lulu Pr., Inc.

Howard, Cheryl Lynne. Captured by Love: A Wild Horse Story Based on Psalm 139. 2011. 48p. pap. 11.00 *(978-1-4567-1822-0(3))* AuthorHouse.

Hurley, Crystal. The Witch with an Itch. 2008. 24p. pap. 24.95 *(978-1-60703-339-4(9))* America Star Bks.

Hutchings, Paul. Halloween Tails. 2012. 24p. pap. 24.95 *(978-1-4626-7106-9(3))* America Star Bks.

Jansson, Tove. Moomin & the Golden Tail. 2014. (Moomin Ser.). (ENG., Illus.). 56p. (J). (gr. 4-7). pap. 9.95 *(978-1-77046-133-8(7)*, 900125201) Drawn & Quarterly Pubns. CAN. Dist: Macmillan.

Jenisch, Betty. Rennie. 2007. 9.00 *(978-0-8059-8947-2(1))* Dorrance Publishing Co., Inc.

Jensen, Patricia. I Am Sick. Hantel, Johanna, illus. 2005. (My First Reader Ser.). (ENG.). 32p. (J). (gr. k-1). lib. bdg. 18.50 *(978-0-516-24878-3(2)*, Children's Pr.) Scholastic Library Publishing.

Jones, Wendy Lou. Bastian - Defender of Golden Downs. 2013. 234p. pap. 10.95 *(978-0-9777110-3-1(X))* Royal Knight Inc.

Kennedy, Cam, illus. Dr Jekyll & Mr Hyde: RL Stevenson's Strange Case. 2008. (ENG.). 48p. (YA). (gr. 7). pap. 11.95 *(978-0-88776-882-8(2)*, Tundra Bks.) Tundra Bks. CAN. Dist: Penguin Random Hse. LLC.

Klein, Adria F. Max Goes to the Doctor. Gallagher-Cole, Mernie, illus. 2007. (Read-It! Readers: the Life of Max Ser.). (ENG.). 24p. (J). (gr. -1-2). per. 3.95 *(978-1-4048-3686-0(1)*, 94290, Picture Window Bks.) Capstone.

—Max Va Al Doctor. Lozano, Clara, tr. Gallagher-Cole, Mernie, illus. 2008. (Read-It! Readers en Español: la Vida de Max Ser.). (SPA.). 24p. (J). (gr. -1-3). per. 3.95 *(978-1-4048-4584-8(4)*, 94929, Picture Window Bks.) Capstone.

Kramer, Paul M. Are You Afraid of the Doctor? 2016. (ENG.). 32p. 15.95 *(978-0-9819745-3-8(8))* Aloha Wellness Pubs.

Kristen, Mantooth. Danny Goes to the Doctor. Kristen, Mantooth, illus. 2007. (Illus.). 24p. (J). 10.00 *(978-0-9800580-0-0(7))* Ballyhoo Printing.

Krumrey, Melanie. Bagels, Buddy, & Me: A Story about Gluten Intolerance & Celiac Disease. 2007. (Illus.). 40p. (J). per. 14.95 *(978-0-9797703-0-2(0))* Mustard Seed Pr.

Lange, Willem. Favor Johnson: A Christmas Story. Dodson, Bert, illus. 2009. (ENG.). 32p. (J). (gr. 1-3). 16.95 *(978-1-59373-082-6(9))* Bunker Hill Publishing, Inc.

Lewellyn, Natalie. Nutty to Meet You! Dr. Peanut Book #1. 2008. (Illus.). 32p. (J). 11.95 *(978-0-9777082-0-8(9))* One Monkey Bks.

London, Jonathan. Froggy Goes to the Doctor. 2004. (Illus.). (J). (gr. k-3). spiral bd. *(978-0-616-14585-2(3))*; spiral bd. *(978-0-616-14586-9(1))* Canadian National Institute for the Blind/Institut National Canadien pour les Aveugles.

—Froggy Goes to the Doctor. Remkiewicz, Frank, illus. 2004. (Froggy Ser.). 32p. (J). (gr. -1-k). pap. 7.99 *(978-0-14-240193-4(5)*, Puffin Books) Penguin Young Readers Group.

—Froggy Goes to the Doctor. 2004. (Froggy Ser.). (J). (gr. -1-18). 1.25 *(978-1-4025-3420-1(5))* Recorded Bks., Inc.

MacDonald, George. The History of Gutta-Percha Willie. 2006. 116p. per. 9.95 *(978-1-59818-578-2(0))* Aegypan.

Man-Kong, Mary. My Visit to the Doctor. Riley, Kellee, illus. 2017. (J). *(978-1-5182-2648-9(5))* Random Hse., Inc.

Marie, Jill Jana. Balloon Blessing. Zamboni, David, illus. 2008. 28p. pap. 12.95 *(978-0-9820479-7-2(5))* Peppertree Pr., The.

Marsh, Carole. The Adventure Diaries of Dharma, the Dedicated Doctor!, 3 vols. 2003. 48p. (J). (gr. 1-4). pap. 5.95 *(978-0-635-01157-2(3))* Gallopade International.

Mcdonald, Megan. Judy Moody, M. D. The Doctor Is In! 2018. (Judy Moody Ser.: 5). lib. bdg. 16.00 *(978-0-606-41195-0(X))* Turtleback.

McGinnis, Mindy. A Madness So Discreet. 2015. (ENG.). 384p. (YA). (gr. 9). 17.99 *(978-0-06-232086-5(6)*, Tegen, Katherine Bks) HarperCollins Pubs.

McQuinn, Anna. Leo Gets a Checkup. Hearson, Ruth, illus. 2018. (Leo Can! Ser.). (ENG.). 24p. (J). (— 1). lib. bdg. 9.99 *(978-1-58089-891-1(2))* Charlesbridge Publishing, Inc.

Meister, Cari. The Shivery Shark, 1 vol. Harpster, Steve, illus. 2011. (Ocean Tales Ser.). (ENG.). 32p. (J). (gr. 2-3). lib. bdg. 22.65 *(978-1-4342-3200-7(X)*, 114964, Stone Arch Bks.) Capstone.

Middleton Gray, Family Np. Maddie Goes to the Nurse Practitioner. 2008. 32p. pap. 13.50 *(978-1-4389-0220-3(4))* AuthorHouse.

Miles, Talaythea L. Fly, My Lupus Butterfly, Fly. 2012. 24p. pap. 14.93 *(978-1-4669-1504-6(8))* Trafford Publishing.

Morgan, Nicola. Fleshmarket. 2003. (ENG.). 272p. (J). (gr. 7-17). pap. 9.99 *(978-0-340-85557-7(6))* Hachette Children's Group GBR. Dist: Hachette Bk. Group.

Nakagawa, Masafumi. Dr. Mouse's Mission. Perry, Mia Lynn, tr. Yamawaki, Yuriko, illus. 2007. (R. I. C. Story Chest Ser.). 27p. (J). (gr. -1-1). 14.95 incl. audio compact disk *(978-1-74126-051-9(5))* R.I.C. Pubns. AUS. Dist: SCB Distributors.

Nicol, Lisa. Dr Boogaloo & the Girl Who Lost Her Laughter. 2019. (Illus.). 192p. (J). (gr. 2-4). 9.99 *(978-1-76089-236-4(X)*, Puffin) Penguin Random Hse. AUS. Dist: Independent Pubs. Group.

Novel Units. Dr. Jekyll & Mr. Hyde Novel Units Student Packet. 2019. (ENG.). (YA). (gr. 9-12). pap., stu. ed. 13.99 *(978-1-58130-785-6(3)*, Novel Units, Inc.) Classroom Library Co.

Oxenbury, Helen. Con el Medico (At the Doctor's) (SPA.). 24p. (J). 7.95 *(978-84-261-1998-8(0))* Juventud, Editorial ESP. Dist: AIMS International Bks., Inc.

Palmer, Robin. Girl vs. Superstar, 1. 2010. (Yours Truly, Lucy B. Parker Ser.: 1). 224p. (J). (gr. 6-8). 21.19 *(978-0-14-241500-9(6))* Penguin Young Readers Group.

Parkinson, Curtis. Death in Kingsport. 2007. 224p. (YA). (gr. 7-9). per. 11.95 *(978-0-88776-827-9(X)*, Tundra Bks.) Tundra Bks. CAN. Dist: Penguin Random Hse. LLC.

Pasternak, Boris Leonidovich. Doktor Zivago. 32.95 *(978-5-04-004105-3(5))* Dksmo-Press, Izdatel'skaja firma RUS. Dist: Distribooks, Inc.

Patrick, Wellman. Mr. Duz Goes to the Doctor. Sam, Kagan, illus. 2007. 24p. (J). 5.95 *(978-0-9796226-6-3(2))* MrDuz.com.

Peacock, Shane. The Dark Missions of Edgar Brim: Monster. 2019. (Dark Missions of Edgar Brim Ser.: 2). 288p. (YA). (gr. 7). pap. 9.99 *(978-0-7352-6273-7(X)*, Penguin Teen) PRH Canada Young Readers CAN. Dist: Penguin Random Hse. LLC.

PI, Kids. Custom Frame Doc Mcstuffins- O/P. 2015. (ENG.). 12p. (J). *(978-1-4508-9350-3(3)*, 1450893503) Publications International, Ltd.

Pinkwater, Daniel M. Mrs. Noodlekugel & Four Blind Mice. Stower, Adam, illus. 2013. (Mrs. Noodlekugel Ser.: 2). (ENG.). 96p. (J). (gr. k-4). 14.99 *(978-0-7636-5054-4(4))* Candlewick Pr.

Posner-Sanchez, Andrea. Boomer Gets His Bounce Back (Disney Junior: Doc Mcstuffins) RH Disney, illus. 2013. (Little Golden Book Ser.). (ENG.). 24p. (J). (-k). 5.99 *(978-0-7364-3143-9(8)*, Golden/Disney) Random Hse. Children's Bks.

—Shake Your Tail Feathers (Disney Junior: Doc Mcstuffins) RH Disney, illus. 2015. (Little Golden Book Ser.). (ENG.). 24p. (J). (-k). 4.99 *(978-0-7364-3274-0(4)*, Golden/Disney) Random Hse. Children's Bks.

Pressler, Mirjam. Malka. Murdoch, Brian, tr. 2005. 280p. (YA). (gr. 7-12). 13.65 *(978-0-7569-5217-4(4))* Perfection Learning Corp.

Publications International Ltd. Staff, ed. Elmo Goes to the Doctor. 2010. 14p. (J). bds. 16.98 *(978-1-4127-4609-0(4))* Phoenix International Publications, Inc.

Rader, Jared. Sandy's Dream. Meyers, Sarah, illus. 2007. 16p. (J). (gr. -1-3). 10.99 *(978-1-59879-398-7(5))* Lifevest Publishing, Inc.

Rahnama, Seyed Javad. Minty Ear. 2011. (Illus.). 20p. pap. 14.11 *(978-1-4567-8188-0(X))* AuthorHouse.

Ramthun, Bonnie. The White Gates. 2008. (ENG.). 256p. (J). (gr. 6-8). lib. bdg. 22.44 *(978-0-375-94554-0(7))* Random House Publishing Group.

Random House & Roper, Robert. Dora Goes to the Doctor/Dora Goes to the Dentist (Dora the Explorer) Random House, illus. 2013. (Pictureback(R) Ser.). (ENG., Illus.). 32p. (J). (gr. -1-2). 5.99 *(978-0-449-81771-1(7)*, Random Hse. Bks. for Young Readers) Random Hse. Children's Bks.

Rebello, Gleeson & Harisiades, Jamie. Darebone's Big Break. 2013. (Illus.). 38p. (J). pap. 14.95 *(978-0-9829256-7-6(0))* SDP Publishing.

—Darebone's Big Break (Hardcover) 2013. (Illus.). 38p. (J). 19.95 *(978-0-9889381-4-4(6))* SDP Publishing.

Reuterstrand, Siri. Ellis Goes to the Doctor. Wik, Jenny, illus. 2012. (ENG.). 24p. (J). (gr. -1-k). 12.95 *(978-1-61608-662-6(9)*, 608662, Sky Pony Pr.) Skyhorse Publishing Co., Inc.

Rigby Education Staff, ed. Going to the Doctor. (Illus.). 8p. (J). bds. 3.95 *(978-0-7635-6427-8(3)*, 764273C99) Rigby Education.

Rinaldi, Ann. An Acquaintance with Darkness. 2005. (Great Episodes Ser.). (ENG.). 384p. (YA). (gr. 7-8). pap. 9.99 *(978-0-15-205387-1(5)*, 1196220, Clarion Bks.) HarperCollins Pubs.

—An Acquaintance with Darkness. 2005. (Great Episodes Ser.). 374p. (gr. 7-12). 18.00 *(978-0-7569-5040-8(6))* Perfection Learning Corp.

Rocheleau, Nicole. Ollie Ollie in Come Free! 2006. 76p. pap. 16.95 *(978-1-4241-0433-8(5))* PublishAmerica, Inc.

Rohrer, Kim. The Adventures of Little Dooey: The Doctor. 2012. 24p. pap. 9.95 *(978-0-9848050-7-5(9)*, Little Creek Bks.) Jan-Carol Publishing, INC.

Roper, Robert. Dora Goes to the Doctor. 2013. (Dora the Explorer 8X8 Ser.). lib. bdg. 14.75 *(978-0-606-32216-4(7))* Turtleback.

Rose, Marilyn C. Kylie Gets a Cochlear Implant. 2013. 32p. pap. 13.00 *(978-1-62516-170-3(0)*, Strategic Bk. Publishing) Strategic Book Publishing & Rights Agency (SBPRA).

Rose, Mary. Dolphin Readers Starter. Doctor, Doctor. International Edition. Wright, Craig, ed. 2010. (ENG., Illus.). 20p. 5.00 *(978-0-19-440075-6(1))* Oxford Univ. Pr., Inc.

Salenas, Bobbi. Cinderella Latina - Cinicienta Latina. La Madrid, Enriquee, tr. Salenas, Bobbi, illus. 2003. (SPA., Illus.). (YA). (gr. 3-12). 19.95 *(978-0-934925-06-8(2))* Pinata Pubns.

Sanschagrin, Joceline. Caillou at the Doctor. Brignaud, Pierre, illus. 3rd ed. 2013. (Step by Step Ser.). (ENG.). 24p. (J). (gr. -1-k). bds. 5.99 *(978-2-89718-058-4(7))* Caillouet, Gerry.

Sargent, Dave & Sargent, Pat. Gus: (Slate Grullo) Be Thankful, 30 vols., Vol. 32. Lenoir, Jane, illus. 2003. (Saddle up Ser.: Vol. 32). 42p. (J). lib. bdg. 23.60 *(978-1-56763-693-2(4))*; pap. 10.95 *(978-1-56763-694-9(2))* Ozark Publishing.

Scarry, Richard. Richard Scarry's Nicky Goes to the Doctor. 2014. lib. bdg. 14.75 *(978-0-606-35561-2(8))* Turtleback.

Scarry, Richard & Golden Books Staff. Richard Scarry's Nicky Goes to the Doctor. 2014. (Pictureback(R) Ser.). (Illus.). 24p. (J). (gr. -1-2). pap. 4.99 *(978-0-307-11842-4(8)*, Random Hse. Bks. for Young Readers) Random Hse. Children's Bks.

Schauer, M., et al. Rip, M. D. 2010. (ENG., Illus.). 88p. pap. 12.99 *(978-0-60699-369-9(0)*, 699369) Fantagraphics Bks.

Scotton, Rob. Splat the Cat Goes to the Doctor: Includes More Than 30 Stickers! Scotton, Rob, illus. 2014. (Splat the Cat Ser.). (ENG., Illus.). 24p. (J). (gr. -1-3). pap. 4.99 *(978-0-06-211588-1(X)*, HarperFestival) HarperCollins Pubs.

Shaw, Helen. Five Cents Worth, 1 vol. rev. ed. 2013. (Literary Text Ser.). (ENG., Illus.). 32p. (J). (gr. 3-4). pap. 11.99 *(978-1-4333-5642-1(2))* Teacher Created Materials, Inc.

Smith, Leone. Jasmine Finds a Doctor. Smith, Marcelle, illus. 2011. 30p. pap. 12.50 *(978-1-61204-042-4(X)*, Strategic Bk. Publishing) Strategic Book Publishing & Rights Agency (SBPRA).

Steig, William. Doctor de Soto. Steig, William, illus. 2010. (ENG., Illus.). 32p. (J). (gr. -1-3). pap. 8.99 *(978-0-312-61189-7(7)*, 900065535) Square Fish.

Stevenson, Robert Louis. Classic Starts(r): the Strange Case of Dr. Jekyll & Mr. Hyde: Retold from the Robert Louis Stevenson Original. Akib, Jamel, illus. 2006. (Classic Starts(r) Ser.). 160p. (J). (gr. 2-4). 6.95 *(978-1-4027-2667-5(8)*, 1252057) Sterling Publishing Co., Inc.

—Dr. Jekyll & Mr. Hyde. 2008. (Bring the Classics to Life Ser.). (ENG., Illus.). 72p. (gr. 4-12). pap., act. bk. ed. 10.95 *(978-0-931334-50-4(0)*, EDCTR-402B) EDCON Publishing Group.

—Dr. Jekyll & Mr. Hyde Graphic Novel. 2010. (Illustrated Classics Ser.). (ENG., Illus.). 64p. (YA). (gr. 4-12). per. 11.95 *(978-1-56254-894-0(8))* Saddleback Educational Publishing, Inc.

—The Strange Case of Dr. Jekyll & Mr. Hyde. (Classics Illustrated Ser.). (Illus.). 52p. (YA). pap. 4.95 *(978-1-57209-008-8(1))* Classics International Entertainment, Inc.

—The Strange Case of Dr. Jekyll & Mr. Hyde. Andrews, Gary, illus. 2008. (Fast Track Classics Ser.). (ENG.). 48p. pap. 10.00 *(978-1-4190-5082-4(6))* Steck-Vaughn.

—The Strange Case of Dr. Jekyll & Mr. Hyde (Quality Library Classics) 2008. (YA). pap. 14.95 *(978-1-57545-703-1(2))* RP Media.

Stevenson, Robert Louis & Venable, Alan. The Strange Case of Dr. Jekyll & Mr. Hyde. 2005. (Classic Literature Ser.). 108p. pap. 9.95 *(978-1-4105-0119-6(1))*; pap., E-Book 69.00 incl. audio compact disk *(978-1-4105-0117-2(5))* Building Wings LLC.

Stine, R. L. The Five Masks of Dr. Screem: Special Edition (Goosebumps Hall of Horrors #3), 1 vol. 2011. (Goosebumps Hall of Horrors Ser.: 3). (ENG.). 192p. (J). (gr. 3-7). pap. 7.99 *(978-0-545-28936-8(X)*, Scholastic Paperbacks) Scholastic, Inc.

Stockham, Jess, illus. Doctor. 2011. (First Time Ser.). 24p. (J). (gr. 2-2). pap. *(978-1-84643-334-4(7))* Child's Play International Ltd.

Swanson Sateren, Shelley. Max & Zoe at the Doctor, 1 vol. Sullivan, Mary, illus. 2013. (Max & Zoe Ser.). (ENG.). 32p. (J). (gr. k-2). pap. 5.19 *(978-1-4048-8060-3(7)*, 121736, Picture Window Bks.) Capstone.

Thaler, Mike. The Dentist from the Black Lagoon. Lee, Jared D., illus. 2014. (Black Lagoon Ser.). (ENG.). 32p. (J). (gr. -1-4). 31.36 *(978-1-61479-197-3(X)*, 3637, Picture Bk.) Spotlight.

Van Wyk, Tasja. Twins: Meet the Doctor. 2011. (Illus.). 28p. pap. 13.78 *(978-1-4567-7813-2(7))* AuthorHouse.

Venkatraman, Padma. Climbing the Stairs. 2010. (ENG., Illus.). 254p. (YA). (gr. 7-18). 10.99 *(978-0-14-241490-3(5)*, Speak) Penguin Young Readers Group.

Vern, Jules. The Field of Ice: Part II of the Adventures of Captain Hatteras. 2007. (ENG.). 154p. pap. 19.99 *(978-1-4264-3591-1(6))* Creative Media Partners, LLC.

Vernon, Louise A. Key to the Prison. Eitzen, Allan, illus. 2nd ed. 2003. (Louise A. Vernon Ser.). (ENG.). 146p. (YA). (gr. 4-9). pap. 8.99 *(978-0-8361-1698-4(4))* Herald Pr.

Walden, Pamela Charlene. Puff Bear Goes to the Hospital. 2013. 44p. pap. 9.99 *(978-1-62839-470-2(6))* Salem Author Services.

Walley, Keith. An Angel to Guide Me. 2011. (ENG.). 33p. pap. 12.99 *(978-1-105-68254-4(4))* Lulu Pr., Inc.

Ward, C. L. Portia the Porcupine Visits the Doctor. 2010. 36p. pap. 16.95 *(978-1-4490-9230-6(6))* AuthorHouse.

Warwick, J. M. An Open Vein. 2007. (YA). per. 12.95 *(978-1-933963-96-9(4))* Grove Creek Publishing, LLC.

Watt, Fiona. Complete Book of First Experiences. rev. ed. 2011. (First Experiences Ser.). 144p. (J). ring bd. 19.99 *(978-0-7945-2948-2(8)*, Usborne) EDC Publishing.

Weinberg, Jennifer Liberts. Doc Mcstuffins: Blame It on the Rain. 2014. (World of Reading Ser.). (J). lib. bdg. 13.55 *(978-0-606-35909-2(5))* Turtleback.

Weston Woods Staff, creator. Doctor de Soto. 2011. (SPA.). 38.75 *(978-0-439-78365-1(8))*; 29.95 *(978-0-439-73624-4(2))* Weston Woods Studios, Inc.

Whelan, Gloria. Listening for Lions. 2006. (ENG.). 208p. (J). (gr. 5-9). pap. 9.99 *(978-0-06-058176-3(X)*, HarperCollins) HarperCollins Pubs.

—Listening for Lions. 2007. 194p. (gr. 5-9). 16.00 *(978-0-7569-7800-6(9))* Perfection Learning Corp.

White, Paul. Jungle Doctor in Slippery Places. 2011. (Flamingo Fiction 9-13s Ser.). (ENG., Illus.). 160p. (J). (gr. 4-7). pap. 8.99 *(978-1-84550-298-0(1)*, 2d5341c8-b7a7-41d9-9f98-f018ae7cd7c8) Christian Focus Pubns. GBR. Dist: Baker & Taylor Publisher Services (BTPS).

—Jungle Doctor Meets a Lion. 2011. (Flamingo Fiction 9-13s Ser.). (ENG., Illus.). 176p. (J). 8.99 *(978-1-84550-392-5(9)*, 0590f404-45d7-4593-b5b3-7e20994a2ae9) Christian Focus Pubns. GBR. Dist: Baker & Taylor Publisher Services (BTPS).

—Jungle Doctor on the Hop. 2015. (Flamingo Fiction 9-13s Ser.). (ENG., Illus.). 160p. (J). (gr. 4-7). per. 8.99 *(978-1-84550-297-3(3)*, d66d650a-5d06-4ed6-9f8e-bb803656ca4a) Christian Focus Pubns. GBR. Dist: Baker & Taylor Publisher Services (BTPS).

—Jungle Doctor Pulls a Leg. rev. ed. 2008. (Flamingo Fiction 9-13s Ser.). (ENG., Illus.). 176p. (J). 8.99 *(978-1-84550-389-5(9)*, 202e638e-2686-475c-9905-e26560541b03) Christian Focus Pubns. GBR. Dist: Baker & Taylor Publisher Services (BTPS).

—Jungle Doctor Spots a Leopard. rev. ed. 2008. (Flamingo Fiction 9-13s Ser.). (ENG., Illus.). 176p. (J). (gr. 5-7). per. 8.99 *(978-1-84550-301-7(5)*, 19e1be96-5b42-4620-a898-bc67dd924342) Christian Focus Pubns. GBR. Dist: Baker & Taylor Publisher Services (BTPS).

—Jungle Doctor Stings a Scorpion. rev. ed. 2008. (Flamingo Fiction 9-13s Ser.). (ENG., Illus.). 160p. (J). 8.99 *(978-1-84550-390-1(2)*, 365d3eb7-29af-4f22-ba6a-32a6c0f815de) Christian Focus Pubns. GBR. Dist: Baker & Taylor Publisher Services (BTPS).

Whitney, A. D. T. Patience Strong's Outings by Mrs a D T Whitney. 2006. 236p. per. 20.99 *(978-1-4255-2007-6(3))* Michigan Publishing.

Wiggins, D. L. Where Dreams Are Born. Carter, Kelly, illus. 2012. 26p. (J). 16.95 *(978-1-60131-128-3(1)*, Castlebridge Bks.) Big Tent Bks.

Winslow, Justin, illus. El Perro y el Gato. Winslow, Justin, . 2010.Tr. of Perro y el Gato: la Nieve. (SPA.). 28p. 3.99 *(978-0-9828167-3-8(1))* Home Box Office, Inc.

Wolfe, Bradley W. Upside Downside Up. 2009. (ENG.). 144p. 27.99 *(978-0-557-11670-6(8))* Lulu Pr., Inc.

Wright, Unasue Sellers. Dr. Chubby. 2013. 32p. pap. 13.95 *(978-1-4497-8931-2(5)*, WestBow Pr.) Author Solutions, LLC.

Young, Judy. Digger & Daisy Go to the Doctor. Sullivan, Dana, illus. 2014. (Digger & Daisy Ser.). (ENG.). 32p. (J). (gr. k-2). 9.99 *(978-1-58536-845-7(8)*, 203674); pap. 5.99 *(978-1-58536-846-4(6)*, 203728) Sleeping Bear Pr.

—Digger et Daisy Vont Au Docteur (Digger & Daisy Go to the Doctor) Sullivan, Dana, illus. 2016. (Digger & Daisy Ser.). (FRE.). 32p. (J). (gr. k-2). 12.95 *(978-1-62753-949-4(2)*, 204172) Sleeping Bear Pr.

—Digger y Daisy Van Al Médico (Digger & Daisy Go to the Doctor) Sullivan, Dana, illus. 2016. (Digger & Daisy Ser.). (SPA.). 32p. (J). (gr. k-2). 9.99 *(978-1-62753-953-1(0)*, 204176) Sleeping Bear Pr.

PHYSICISTS

Allman, Toney. J. Robert Oppenheimer: Theoretical Physicist, Atomic Pioneer. 2005. (Giants of Science Ser.). (ENG., Illus.). 64p. (J). (gr. 3-7). lib. bdg. 28.35 *(978-1-56711-889-6(5)*, Blackbirch Pr., Inc.) Cengage Gale.

Anderson, Margaret J. Isaac Newton: Greatest Genius of Science, 1 vol. 2014. (Genius Scientists & Their Genius Ideas Ser.). (ENG.). 96p. (gr. 5-5). (J). 29.60 *(978-0-7660-6570-3(7)*, c024e73b-77b0-49dd-8539-2348f721f97e); pap. 13.88 *(978-0-7660-6571-0(5)*, f7079f7b-165a-4d7b-8a01-007b93f6769d) Enslow Publishing, LLC.

Berne, Jennifer. On a Beam of Light: A Story of Albert Einstein (Albert Einstein Book for Kids, Books about Scientists for Kids, Biographies for Kids, Kids Science Books) Radunsky, Vladimir, illus. 2016. (Illustrated Biographies by Chronicle Bks.). (ENG.). 56p. (J). (gr. k-3). pap. 7.99 *(978-1-4521-5211-0(X))* Chronicle Bks. LLC.

Bingham, Derick. Michael Faraday: Spiritual Dynamo. rev. ed. 2010. (Trail Blazers Ser.). (ENG.). 176p. (J). pap. 8.99 *(978-1-84550-156-3(X)*, db106938-6a73-4099-8ed5-872cea02fb78) Christian Focus Pubns. GBR. Dist: Baker & Taylor Publisher Services (BTPS).

Bodden, Valerie. Marie Curie: Chemist & Physicist. 2017. (Women in Science Ser.). (ENG., Illus.). 112p. (J). (gr. 6-12). lib. bdg. 41.36 *(978-1-5321-1041-2(3)*, 25658, Essential Library) ABDO Publishing Co.

—Nuclear Physicist Chien-Shiung Wu. 2016. (STEM Trailblazer Bios Ser.). (ENG., Illus.). 32p. (J). (gr. 2-5). 26.65 *(978-1-5124-0786-0(0)*, bc397cd0-0220-433e-8b54-50739c954f80, Lerner Pubns.) Lerner Publishing Group.

Bortz, Fred. Laws of Motion & Isaac Newton, 1 vol. 2013. (Revolutionary Discoveries of Scientific Pioneers Ser.). (ENG., Illus.). 80p. (J). (gr. 6-6). 38.41 *(978-1-4777-1808-7(7)*, 874ae16c-2d37-4d79-a8df-bb2a415e1f52) Rosen Publishing Group, Inc., The.

Brallier, Jess M. Who Was Albert Einstein? Parker, Robert Andrew, illus. 2003. (Who Was... ? Ser.). 105p. (gr. 4-7). 15.00 *(978-0-7569-1586-5(4))* Perfection Learning Corp.

Brezina, Corona. Galileo Galilei, 1 vol. 2017. (Leaders of the Scientific Revolution Ser.). (ENG., Illus.). 112p. (J). (gr. 8-8). 38.80 *(978-1-5081-7468-4(7)*, ca95b1f4-3867-438d-95c3-243ae8c0d1f3, Rosen Young Adult) Rosen Publishing Group, Inc., The.

Brown, Don. Odd Boy Out: Young Albert Einstein. 2008. (ENG., Illus.). 32p. (J). (gr. -1-3). pap. 8.99 *(978-0-547-01435-7(X)*, 1030950, Clarion Bks.) HarperCollins Pubs.

Coates, Eileen S. The Curies' Research with Radiation, 1 vol. 2018. (STEM Milestones: Historic Inventions & Discoveries Ser.). (ENG.). 24p. (gr. 3-3). 25.27 *(978-1-5383-4356-2(8)*, 71325f2e-1e93-474e-8b00-55a2d4904440, PowerKids Pr.) Rosen Publishing Group, Inc., The.

Cooperman, Stephanie. Chien-Shiung Wu: Pioneering Physicist & Atomic Researcher, 1 vol. 2003. (Women Hall of Famers in Mathematics & Science Ser.). (ENG., Illus.). 112p. (gr. 5-8). lib. bdg. 39.80 *(978-0-8239-3875-9(1)*, 69423929-57f1-4b93-a63d-76efe3c3c2db, Rosen Reference) Rosen Publishing Group, Inc., The.

Cooperman, Stephanie H. Chien-Shiung Wu: Pioneering Physicist & Atomic Researcher. 2009. (Women Hall of Famers in Mathematics & Science Ser.). 112p. (gr. 5-8). 63.90 *(978-1-60854-810-1(4)*, Rosen Reference) Rosen Publishing Group, Inc., The.

Cornell, Kari. Theoretical Physicist Stephen Hawking. 2016. (STEM Trailblazer Bios Ser.). (ENG., Illus.). 32p. (J). (gr. 2-5). 26.65 *(978-1-4677-9528-9(3)*, 73d57c91-05df-4980-82c7-559911b3b49e, Lerner Pubns.) Lerner Publishing Group.

Culp, Jennifer. Neil DeGrasse Tyson, 1 vol. 2014. (Great Science Writers Ser.). (ENG., Illus.). 112p. (J). (gr. 7-7). 38.80 *(978-1-4777-7691-9(5)*, be204f99-ab43-4c05-8351-d4966a76b067) Rosen Publishing Group, Inc., The.

Dakers, Diane. Albert Einstein: Forging the Path of Modern Physics. 2013. (ENG., Illus.). 112p. (J). *(978-0-7787-1188-9(9))*; pap. *(978-0-7787-1190-2(0))* Crabtree Publishing Co.

Delano, Marfe Ferguson. Genius: A Photobiography of Albert Einstein. 2015. (Photobiographies Ser.). 64p. (J). (gr. 5-9). pap. 7.99 *(978-1-4263-2219-8(4)*, National Geographic Kids) Disney Publishing Worldwide.

Demuth, Patricia Brennan. Who Was Galileo? 2019. (Who HQ Ser.). (ENG.). 112p. (J). (gr. 2-4). 16.36 *(978-1-64310-814-8(X))* Penworthy Co., LLC, The.

—Who Was Galileo? 2015. (Who Was... ? Ser.). lib. bdg. 16.00 *(978-0-606-36594-9(X))* Turtleback.

Demuth, Patricia Brennan & Who HQ. Who Was Galileo? O'Brien, John, illus. 2015. (Who Was? Ser.). 112p. (J). (gr. 3-7). 5.99 *(978-0-448-47985-9(0)*, Penguin Workshop) Penguin Young Readers Group.

Devera, Czeena. Albert Einstein. Bane, Jeff, illus. 2018. (My Early Library: My Itty-Bitty Bio Ser.). (ENG.). 24p. (J). (gr.

PQR

k-1). lib. bdg. 30.64 *(978-1-5341-2886-6(7),* 211588) Cherry Lake Publishing.

DiPrimio, Peter. Neil Degrasse Tyson. 2015. (ENG., Illus.). 32p. (J). 26.50 *(978-1-62469-090-7(4))* Purple Toad Publishing, Inc.

Doeden, Matt. Albert Einstein: Relativity Rock Star. 2020. (Gateway Biographies Ser.). (ENG., Illus.). 48p. (J). (gr. 4-8). pap. 11.99 *(978-1-5415-8885-1(1),* 59af402d-2595-43ea-a3ed-b530aef54dcc); lib. bdg. 31.99 *(978-1-5415-7743-5(4),* 0301db16-7b69-45be-b0d2-41de3eb21e49) Lerner Publishing Group. (Lerner Pubns.).

—Theoretical Physicist Brian Greene. 2015. (STEM Trailblazer Bios Ser.). (ENG., Illus.). 32p. (J). (gr. 2-5). lib. bdg. 26.65 *(978-1-4677-5790-4(X),* 8f30562c-ffa6-409c-8e88-86f83dd8f060, Lerner Pubns.) Lerner Publishing Group.

Dolz, Jordi Bayarri. Albert Einstein & the Theory of Relativity. Dolz, Jordi Bayarri, illus. 2020. (Graphic Science Biographies Ser.). (ENG., Illus.). 40p. (J). (gr. 5-8). 30.65 *(978-1-5415-7823-4(6),* b97e8b89-c1fb-4f38-9932-ecae0f607b31, Graphic Universe™) Lerner Publishing Group.

—Isaac Newton & the Laws of Motion. Dolz, Jordi Bayarri, illus. 2020. (Graphic Science Biographies Ser.). (ENG., Illus.). 40p. (J). (gr. 5-8). 30.65 *(978-1-5415-7824-1(4),* f4e739d4-966f-428f-b673-126f76a0245c, Graphic Universe™) Lerner Publishing Group.

Feldman, Thea. Katherine Johnson. 2019. (Ready-To-Read Ser.). (ENG.). 47p. (J). (gr. 2-3). 13.89 *(978-1-64310-883-4(2))* Penworthy Co., LLC, The.

—Katherine Johnson. Petersen, Alyssa, illus. 2017. 47p. (J). *(978-1-5182-5284-6(2),* Simon Spotlight) Simon Spotlight.

—Katherine Johnson: Ready-To-Read Level 3. Petersen, Alyssa, illus. 2017. (You Should Meet Ser.). (ENG.). 48p. (J). (gr. 1-3). 17.99 *(978-1-5344-0341-3(8));* pap. 4.99 *(978-1-5344-0340-6(X))* Simon Spotlight. (Simon Spotlight).

Forman, Lillian E. Albert Einstein: Physicist & Genius, 1 vol. 2009. (Essential Lives Set 3 Ser.). (ENG., Illus.). 112p. (YA). (gr. 6-12). lib. bdg. 41.36 *(978-1-60453-524-2(5),* 6677, Essential Library) ABDO Publishing Co.

Frisch, Aaron. Albert Einstein. 2005. (Genius Ser.). (Illus.). 48p. (J). (gr. 5-9). lib. bdg. 21.95 *(978-1-58341-328-9(6),* Creative Education) Creative Co., The.

Gagne, Tammy. Physicist. 2020. (J). *(978-1-7911-1692-7(2),* AV2 by Weigl) Weigl Pubs., Inc.

Gianopoulos, Andrea & Barnett, Charles, III. Isaac Newton & the Laws of Motion, 1 vol. Miller, Phil, illus. 2007. (Inventions & Discovery Ser.). (ENG.). 32p. (J). (gr. 3-9). pap. 8.10 *(978-0-7368-7899-9(8),* 93895, Capstone Pr.) Capstone.

Gigliotti, Jim. Who Was Stephen Hawking? 2019. (Who HQ Ser.). (ENG.). 106p. (J). (gr. 2-3). 16.36 *(978-0-87617-488-3(8))* Penworthy Co., LLC, The.

Gigliotti, Jim & Who HQ. Who Was Stephen Hawking? Copeland, Gregory, illus. 2019. (Who Was? Ser.). 112p. (J). (gr. 3-7). 5.99 *(978-0-451-53248-0(1),* Penguin Workshop) Penguin Young Readers Group.

Goldenstern, Joyce. Albert Einstein: Genius of the Theory of Relativity, 1 vol. 2014. (Genius Scientists & Their Genius Ideas Ser.). (ENG.). 96p. (gr. 5-5). 29.60 *(978-0-7660-6515-4(4),* fbc0d8fb-434d-4399-8a19-0f2134aa9bf1); pap. 13.88 *(978-0-7660-6516-1(2),* 5ec6765a-d33b-4935-bf86-59ba3beccad3) Enslow Publishing, LLC.

Goldstein, Margaret J. Astronaut & Physicist Sally Ride. 2018. (STEM Trailblazer Bios Ser.). (ENG., Illus.). 32p. (J). (gr. 2-5). 26.65 *(978-1-5415-0009-9(1),* 0a678350-1fa6-471a-80d7-c4b325e81ef4, Lerner Pubns.) Lerner Publishing Group.

Graham, Ian. You Wouldn't Want to Be Sir Isaac Newton! A Lonely Life You'd Rather Not Lead. 2013. (You Wouldn't Want To Ser.). lib. bdg. 20.80 *(978-0-606-31632-3(9))* Turtleback.

Graubart, Norman D. Neil DeGrasse Tyson: Spokesperson for Science, 1 vol. 2015. (Exceptional African Americans Ser.). (ENG.). 24p. (gr. 3-4). pap. 10.35 *(978-0-7660-6666-3(5),* 4f431ac1-d04d-466e-b0cc-c36d694d6603); (Illus.). 24.27 *(978-0-7660-6668-7(1),* 4d47699a-0e5b-4ac0-9650-762b51d9bd45) Enslow Publishing, LLC.

Hanson-Harding, Alexandra. Albert Einstein, 1 vol., 1. 2015. (Britannica Beginner Bios Ser.). (ENG., Illus.). 32p. (J). (gr. 2-3). pap. 13.90 *(978-1-5081-0060-7(8),* 3465d3b7-e568-4898-8b4a-da217ef8cbd1, Britannica Educational Publishing) Rosen Publishing Group, Inc., The.

Haynie, Rachel & Cook, Trahern. First, You Explore: The Story of Young Charles Townes 2014. (Young Palmetto Bks.). (ENG., Illus.). 40p. 29.95 *(978-1-61117-343-7(4),* P231851) Univ. of South Carolina Pr.

Hightower, Paul W. Galileo: Astronomer & Physicist, 1 vol. rev. ed. 2009. (Great Minds of Science Ser.). (ENG., Illus.). 128p. (gr. 5-6). lib. bdg. 35.93 *(978-0-7660-3008-4(3),* d3d0248b-d7f8-431d-81f8-dafe2d9cce0f) Enslow Publishing, LLC.

—Galileo: Genius Astronomer, 1 vol. 2014. (Genius Scientists & Their Genius Ideas Ser.). (ENG.). 96p. (gr. 5-5). 29.60 *(978-0-7660-6560-4(X),* 69763ae1-4d15-453a-9bb4-e9386fe2c62f); pap. 13.88 *(978-0-7660-6561-1(8),* bd39ac1a-e886-4184-9b20-b47e44844f5b) Enslow Publishing, LLC.

Hilliam, Rachel. Galileo Galilei: Father of Modern Science. (Rulers, Scholars, & Artists of the Renaissance Ser.). 112p. (gr. 5-8). 2009. 66.50 *(978-1-60852-941-4(X),* Rosen Reference) 2004. (ENG., Illus.). (J). lib. bdg. 39.80 *(978-1-4042-0314-3(1),* b392ef11-048c-40fb-b80a-082fe0ff8755) Rosen Publishing Group, Inc., The.

Hollihan, Kerrie Logan. Isaac Newton & Physics for Kids: His Life & Ideas with 21 Activities. 2009. (For Kids Ser.: 30). (Illus.). 144p. (J). (gr. 4-7). pap. 20.99 *(978-1-55652-778-4(0))* Chicago Review Pr., Inc.

Indovino, Shaina. Women in Physics. Lee-Karlon, Ann, ed. 2013. (Major Women in Science Ser.: 10). 64p. (J). (gr. 7-18). 22.95 *(978-1-4222-2930-9(0))* Mason Crest.

Isaac Newton: Organizing the Universe. 2004. (Great Scientists Ser.). (Illus.). 144p. (YA). (gr. 6-12). 26.95 *(978-1-931798-01-3(X))* Reynolds, Morgan Inc.

James, Emily. Albert Einstein. 2017. (Great Scientists & Inventors Ser.). (ENG., Illus.). 24p. (J). (gr. -1-2). lib. bdg. 27.32 *(978-1-5157-3884-8(1),* 133787, Capstone Pr.) Capstone.

Johnson, Katherine. Reaching for the Moon: The Autobiography of NASA Mathematician Katherine Johnson. (ENG., Illus.). (J). (gr. 5). 2020. 272p. pap. 8.99 *(978-1-5344-4084-5(4))* 2019. 256p. 17.99 *(978-1-5344-4083-8(6))* Simon & Schuster Children's Publishing. (Atheneum Bks. for Young Readers).

Kamberg, Mary-Lane. Stephen Hawking, 1 vol. 2014. (Great Science Writers Ser.). (ENG., Illus.). 112p. (J). (gr. 7-7). 38.80 *(978-1-4777-7683-4(4),* e79ad039-6fbb-4d47-acac-1d756ff4ae2f) Rosen Publishing Group, Inc., The.

Kleiner, Mariela. Meet Einstein. Garofoli, Viviana, illus. 2011. 28p. (J). (gr. -1-1). lib. bdg. *(978-0-615-31579-9(8))* Meet Bks., LLC.

Krull, Kathleen. Albert Einstein. Kulikov, Boris, illus. 2015. (Giants of Science Ser.). 144p. (J). (gr. 3-7). 8.99 *(978-0-14-751464-6(9),* Puffin Books) Penguin Young Readers Group.

—Isaac Newton. Kulikov, Boris, illus. 2008. (Giants of Science Ser.). 128p. (J). (gr. 3-7). 7.99 *(978-0-14-240820-9(4),* Puffin Books) Penguin Young Readers Group.

Krull, Kathleen & Brewer, Paul. Starstruck: The Cosmic Journey of Neil DeGrasse Tyson. Morrison, Frank, illus. 2018. 48p. (J). (gr. -1-3). 17.99 *(978-0-399-55024-9(0));* (ENG.). lib. bdg. 20.99 *(978-0-399-55025-6(9))* Random Hse. Children's Bks. (Crown Books For Young Readers).

Lakin, Patricia. Albert Einstein: Genius of the Twentieth Century (Ready-To-Read Level 3) Daniel, Alan & Daniel, Lea, illus. 2005. (Ready-To-Read Stories of Famous Americans Ser.). (ENG.). 48p. (J). (gr. 1-3). pap. 4.99 *(978-0-689-87034-7(5),* Simon Spotlight) Simon Spotlight.

Lassieur, Allison. Albert Einstein: Genius of the Twentieth Century. 2005. (Great Life Stories Ser.). (ENG., Illus.). 127p. (J). (gr. 6-8). 30.50 *(978-0-531-12401-7(0),* Watts, Franklin) Scholastic Library Publishing.

Lee, T. S. The Stephen Hawking Story: The First Stephen Hawking Comic Biography. 2010. 179p. (J). pap. 14.95 *(978-0-9819542-9-5(4))* DASANBOOKS.

LeVine, Harry, III. The Great Explainer: The Story of Richard Feynman. 2009. (Profiles in Science Ser.). (Illus.). 144p. (J). (gr. 7-10). 28.95 *(978-1-59935-113-1(7),* 1309604) Reynolds, Morgan Inc.

Lin, Yoming S. Isaac Newton & Gravity, 1 vol. 2011. (Eureka! Ser.). (ENG., Illus.). 24p. (YA). (gr. 2-3). lib. bdg. 26.27 *(978-1-4488-5032-7(0),* 045846db-34e4-4764-b472-196b83ca9a9e) Rosen Publishing Group, Inc., The.

Loh-Hagan, Virginia. The Real Albert Einstein. 2018. (History Uncut Ser.). (ENG., Illus.). 32p. (J). (gr. 4-8). lib. bdg. 32.07 *(978-1-5341-2953-5(7),* 211856, 45th Parallel Press) Cherry Lake Publishing.

—Sally Ride. Bane, Jeff, illus. 2018. (Mi Mini Biografía (My Itty-Bitty Bio): My Early Library). (ENG.). 24p. (J). (gr. k-1). pap. 12.79 *(978-1-5341-0808-0(4),* 210596); lib. bdg. 30.64 *(978-1-5341-0709-0(6),* 210595) Cherry Lake Publishing.

—Shirley Ann Jackson. Bane, Jeff, illus. 2018. (Mi Mini Biografía (My Itty-Bitty Bio): My Early Library). (ENG.). 24p. (J). (gr. k-1). pap. 12.79 *(978-1-5341-0812-7(2),* 210612); lib. bdg. 30.64 *(978-1-5341-0713-7(4),* 210611) Cherry Lake Publishing.

MacLeod, Elizabeth. Marie Curie. Mantha, John, illus. 2009. (Kids Can Read Ser.). (ENG.). 32p. (J). (gr. 1-3). 11.99 *(978-1-55453-297-1(3))* Kids Can Pr., Ltd. CAN. Dist: Hachette Bk. Group.

Mara, Wil. DK Life Stories: Albert Einstein. Ager, Charlotte, illus. 2019. (DK Life Stories Ser.). (ENG.). 128p. (J). (gr. 3-7). pap. 5.99 *(978-1-4654-7570-1(2),* DK Children) Dorling Kindersley Publishing, Inc.

Marsh, Carole. Albert Einstein. 2003. 12p. (gr. k-4). 2.95 *(978-0-635-02352-0(0))* Gallopade International.

Marsico, Katie. Genius Physicist Albert Einstein. 2017. (STEM Trailblazer Bios Ser.). (ENG., Illus.). 32p. (J). (gr. 2-5). pap. 8.99 *(978-1-5124-5629-5(2),* 685e23f9-f418-4d20-994e-52d6dfa6a710) Lerner Publishing Group.

Mattern, Joanne & Santrey, Laurence. Albert Einstein, Creative Genius. Beier, Ellen, illus. 2005. 45p. (J). pap. *(978-0-439-80152-2(4))* Scholastic, Inc.

May, Andrew. Albert Einstein: Scientist, 1 vol. 2016. (History Makers Ser.). (ENG., Illus.). 144p. (J). (gr. 9-9). 47.36 *(978-1-5026-2441-3(9),* fb5ee328-811f-405d-bae1-c6c77f7ac235) Cavendish Square Publishing LLC.

McLeese, Don. Albert Einstein. 2005. (Inventores Famosos Ser.). (SPA & ENG., Illus.). 24p. (J). 22.79 *(978-1-59515-673-0(9))* Rourke Educational Media.

McPherson, Stephanie Sammartino. Albert Einstein. 2004. (History Maker Bios Ser.). (Illus.). 48p. (J). (gr. 3-5). lib. bdg. 26.60 *(978-0-8225-0350-7(6))* Lerner Publishing Group.

Meltzer, Brad. I Am Albert Einstein. Eliopoulos, Christopher, illus. 2014. (Ordinary People Change the World Ser.). 40p. (J). (gr. k-4). 15.99 *(978-0-8037-4084-6(0),* Dial Bks) Penguin Young Readers Group.

Meltzer, Milton. Albert Einstein: A Biography. 2007. (ENG., Illus.). 48p. (J). (gr. 1-5). 16.95 *(978-0-8234-1966-1(5))* Holiday Hse., Inc.

Meyer, Susan. Isaac Newton, 1 vol. 2017. (Leaders of the Scientific Revolution Ser.). (ENG., Illus.). 112p. (J). (gr. 8-8). 38.80 *(978-1-5081-7470-7(9),* 66a1cb61-49f7-483d-9294-4756e72496bc, Rosen Young Adult) Rosen Publishing Group, Inc., The.

Miklowitz, Gloria D. Albert Einstein. 2004. (ENG., Illus.). 32p. (J). (gr. 2-5). pap. 5.97 net. *(978-0-7685-1212-0(3),* Dominie Elementary) Savvas Learning Co.

Milani, Alice. Marie Curie: A Life of Discovery. Milani, Alice, illus. 2019. (ENG., Illus.). 208p. (YA). (gr. 9-12). pap. 14.99 *(978-1-5415-7286-7(6),* a623d3f9-7a12-4621-89ae-d0b1969b7646); lib. bdg. 33.32 *(978-1-5415-2817-8(4),* 0808a15c-bea9-462c-b2d4-e9601cf1155b) Lerner Publishing Group. (Graphic Universe™).

Novelli, Luca. Newton & the Antigravity Formula. 2017. (Flashes of Genius Ser.). (ENG., Illus.). 112p. (J). (gr. 2). pap. 9.99 *(978-1-61373-861-0(7))* Chicago Review Pr., Inc.

O'Donnell, Kerri. Galileo: Man of Science. 2009. (Reading Room Collection 2 Ser.). 24p. (gr. 3-4). 42.50 *(978-1-60851-964-4(3),* PowerKids Pr.) Rosen Publishing Group, Inc., The.

—Sir Isaac Newton: Using the Laws of Motion to Solve Problems, 1 vol. (Math for the REAL World Ser.). 32p. (gr. 5-5). 2009. (ENG., Illus.). pap. 10.00 *(978-1-4042-6079-5(X),* ce33957a-c41c-4955-bcc4-d67057e0f665) 2009. 47.90 *(978-1-60851-366-6(1),* PowerKids Pr.) 2006. (ENG., Illus.). (YA). lib. bdg. 28.93 *(978-1-4042-3363-8(6),* f0654ff1-b3f5-49ff-b288-9b7bdf626c27) Rosen Publishing Group, Inc., The.

Panchyk, Richard. Galileo for Kids: His Life & Ideas, 25 Activities. 2005. (For Kids Ser.: 17). (Illus.). 184p. (J). (gr. 4). pap. 19.99 *(978-1-55652-566-7(4))* Chicago Review Pr., Inc.

Pascal, Janet B. & Who HQ. Who Was Isaac Newton? Foley, Tim, illus. 2014. (Who Was? Ser.). 112p. (J). (gr. 3-7). pap. 5.99 *(978-0-448-47913-2(3),* Penguin Workshop) Penguin Young Readers Group.

Pohlen, Jerome. Albert Einstein & Relativity for Kids: His Life & Ideas with 21 Activities & Thought Experiments. 2012. (For Kids Ser.: 45). (Illus.). 144p. (J). (gr. 4). pap. 18.99 *(978-1-61374-028-6(X))* Chicago Review Pr., Inc.

Riddolls, Tom. Sally Ride: The First American Woman in Space. 2010. (Crabtree Groundbreaker Biographies Ser.). (ENG., Illus.). 112p. (J). pap. *(978-0-7787-2550-3(2));* (gr. 5-8). lib. bdg. *(978-0-7787-2541-1(3))* Crabtree Publishing Co.

Robeson, Teresa. Queen of Physics: How Wu Chien Shiung Helped Unlock the Secrets of the Atom. Huang, Rebecca, illus. 2019. (People Who Shaped Our World Ser.: 6). 48p. (J). (gr. k). 17.99 *(978-1-4549-3220-8(1))* Sterling Publishing Co., Inc.

Romero, Libby. National Geographic Readers: Albert Einstein. 2016. (Readers Bios Ser.). (Illus.). 48p. (J). (gr. 1-3). pap. 4.99 *(978-1-4263-2536-6(3),* National Geographic Kids) Disney Publishing Worldwide.

Sally Ride: Life on a Mission. 2014. (Real-Life Story Ser.). (ENG., Illus.). 160p. (J). (gr. 3-7). 18.99 *(978-1-4424-8854-0(9),* Aladdin) Simon & Schuster Children's Publishing.

Sarantou, Katlin. Stephen Hawking. Bane, Jeff, illus. 2019. (My Early Library: My Itty-Bitty Bio Ser.). (ENG.). 24p. (J). (gr. k-1). pap. 12.79 *(978-1-5341-4989-2(9),* 213263); lib. bdg. 30.64 *(978-1-5341-4703-4(9),* 213262) Cherry Lake Publishing.

Senker, Cath. Stephen Hawking. 2015. (Against the Odds Biographies Ser.). (ENG., Illus.). 48p. (J). (gr. 3-6). 35.99 *(978-1-4846-2466-1(1),* 129624, Heinemann) Capstone.

Sherman, Josepha. J. J. Thomson & the Discovery of Electrons. 2005. (Uncharted, Unexplored, & Unexplained Ser.). (Illus.). 48p. (J). (gr. 4-8). lib. bdg. 29.95 *(978-1-58415-370-2(9))* Mitchell Lane Pubs.

Simons, Lisa M. Bolt. Marie Curie: Physicist & Chemist. 2018. (STEM Scientists & Inventors Ser.). (ENG., Illus.). 24p. (J). (gr. 1-3). lib. bdg. 27.99 *(978-1-5435-0643-3(7),* 137406, Capstone Pr.) Capstone.

Slade, Suzanne. Albert Einstein: Scientist & Genius. Schultz, Jolene, illus. 2007. (Biographies Ser.). (ENG.). 24p. (gr. k-3). 25.99 *(978-1-4048-3730-0(2),* Picture Window Bks.) Capstone.

Snedden, Robert. Stephen Hawking: Master of the Cosmos, 1 vol. 2015. (Superheroes of Science Ser.). (ENG., Illus.). 48p. (J). (gr. 6-6). pap. 15.05 *(978-1-4824-3157-5(2),* 4bfc9a62-08bb-4b95-908b-a8dca73830d7) Stevens, Gareth Publishing LLLP.

Spiller, Sara. Lise Meitner. Bane, Jeff, illus. 2018. (My Early Library: My Itty-Bitty Bio Ser.). (ENG.). 24p. (J). (gr. k-1). lib. bdg. 30.64 *(978-1-5341-2883-5(2),* 211576) Cherry Lake Publishing.

Stiefel, Chana. Sky High. 2011. (J). *(978-0-531-22558-5(5))* Scholastic, Inc.

Stine, Megan. Who Was Sally Ride? 2013. (Who Was... ? Ser.). lib. bdg. 16.00 *(978-0-606-31683-5(3))* Turtleback.

Stine, Megan & Who HQ. Who Was Sally Ride? Hammond, Ted, illus. 2013. (Who Was? Ser.). 112p. (J). (gr. 3-7). pap. 6.99 *(978-0-448-46687-3(2),* Penguin Workshop) Penguin Young Readers Group.

Sullivan, Anne Marie. Sir Isaac Newton: Famous English Scientist. (Illus.). 32p. (J). 2013. (People of Importance Ser.: 21). (gr. 4-18). 19.95 *(978-1-4222-2856-2(8))* 2004. (Great Names Ser.). (gr. 3-18). lib. bdg. 19.95 *(978-1-59084-139-6(5))* Mason Crest.

Venezia, Mike. Getting to Know the World's Greatest Inventors & Scientists: Lise Meitner. Venezia, Mike, illus. 2010. (Getting to Know the World's Greatest Inventors & Scientists Ser.). (ENG., Illus.). 32p. (J). (gr. 3-4). pap. 6.95 *(978-0-531-20776-5(5),* Children's Pr.) Scholastic Library Publishing.

—Lise Meitner: Had the Right Vision about Nuclear Fission. Venezia, Mike, illus. 2009. (Getting to Know the World's Greatest Inventors & Scientists Ser.). (ENG., Illus.). 32p. (J). (gr. 2-5). 28.00 *(978-0-531-23702-1(8))* Scholastic Library Publishing.

—Luis Alvarez (Getting to Know the World's Greatest Inventors & Scientists) Venezia, Mike, illus. 2010. (Getting to Know the World's Greatest Inventors & Scientists Ser.). (ENG., Illus.). 32p. (J). (gr. 3-4). pap. 6.95 *(978-0-531-20777-2(3),* Children's Pr.) Scholastic Library Publishing.

—Stephen Hawking: Cosmologist Who Gets a Big Bang Out of the Universe. Venezia, Mike, illus. 2009. (Getting to Know the World's Greatest Inventors & Scientists Ser.). (ENG., Illus.). 32p. (J). (gr. 2-5). 28.00 *(978-0-531-23728-1(1))* Scholastic Library Publishing.

Wade McCormick, Lisa. Albert Einstein, 1 vol. 2014. (Great Science Writers Ser.). (ENG., Illus.). 112p. (J). (gr. 7-7). 38.80 *(978-1-4777-7687-2(7),* e96f5ed4-f362-4b1c-bd77-a320a960a83e) Rosen Publishing Group, Inc., The.

Weir, Jane. Max Planck: Uncovering the World of Matter, 1 vol. rev. ed. 2007. (Science: Informational Text Ser.). (ENG.). 32p. (gr. 3-6). pap. 12.99 *(978-0-7439-0568-8(7))* Teacher Created Materials, Inc.

Wyckoff, Edwin Brit. The Man Who Invented the Laser: The Genius of Theodore H. Maiman, 1 vol. 2013. (Genius Inventors & Their Great Ideas Ser.). (ENG.). 48p. (gr. 3-3). pap. 11.53 *(978-1-4644-0208-1(6),* d3f32df7-a703-4e06-bfc3-45b4864f0bc1); (Illus.). 27.93 *(978-0-7660-4138-7(7),* 101a9735-0fa2-47eb-928c-e7705772b974) Enslow Publishing, LLC. (Enslow Elementary).

Yasuda, Anita. Albert Einstein. 2013. (J). *(978-1-62127-305-9(9));* pap. *(978-1-62127-311-0(3))* Weigl Pubs., Inc.

Yomtov, Nel. Chien-Shiung Wu: Nuclear Physicist. 2017. (Women in Science Ser.). (ENG., Illus.). 112p. (J). (gr. 6-12). lib. bdg. 41.36 *(978-1-5321-1046-7(4),* 25668, Essential Library) ABDO Publishing Co.

Zannos, Susan. Michael Faraday & the Discovery of Electromagnetism. 2004. (Uncharted, Unexplored, & Unexplained Ser.). (Illus.). 48p. (J). (gr. 4-8). lib. bdg. 29.95 *(978-1-58415-307-8(5))* Mitchell Lane Pubs.

PHYSICISTS—FICTION

AZ Books, creator. Little Physicist. 2012. (Millions of Inventions Ser.). (ENG., Illus.). 16p. (J). (gr. 1-3). pap. 5.95 *(978-1-61889-303-1(3))* AZ Bks. LLC.

Jacobs, Edgar P. Atlantis Mystery. 2012. (Blake & Mortimer Ser.: 12). (Illus.). 72p. (J). (gr. 5-12). pap. 15.95 *(978-1-84918-107-5(1))* CineBook GBR. Dist: National Bk. Network.

—Blake & Mortimer Vol. 17: the Secret of the Swordfish Part 3. 2014. (Blake & Mortimer Ser.: 17). (Illus.). 64p. pap. 15.95 *(978-1-84918-174-7(8))* CineBook GBR. Dist: National Bk. Network.

—The Mystery of the Great Pyramid. (Blake & Mortimer Ser.: 2). (Illus.). Pt. 1. 2007. 72p. pap. 15.95 *(978-1-905460-37-3(6))*Pt. 2. 2008. 56p. pap. 15.95 *(978-1-905460-38-0(4))* CineBook GBR. Dist: National Bk. Network.

—S. O. S. Meteors. 2009. (Blake & Mortimer Ser.: 6). (Illus.). 64p. pap. 15.95 *(978-1-905460-97-7(X))* CineBook GBR. Dist: National Bk. Network.

—The Secret of the Swordfish. 2013. (Blake & Mortimer Ser.: 16). (Illus.). 64p. pap. 15.95 *(978-1-84918-161-7(6))* CineBook GBR. Dist: National Bk. Network.

Sente, Yves. The Sarcophagi of the Sixth Coninent, Pt. 1, Vol. 9. Juillard, André, illus. 2011. (Blake & Mortimer Ser.: 9). 64p. (J). (gr. -1-12). pap. 15.95 *(978-1-84918-067-2(9))* CineBook GBR. Dist: National Bk. Network.

Sente, Yves & Juillard, Andre. The Gondwana Shrine. 2012. (Blake & Mortimer Ser.: 11). (Illus.). 64p. pap. 15.95 *(978-1-84918-094-8(6))* CineBook GBR. Dist: National Bk. Network.

—The Oath of the Five Swords, Vol. 18. 2014. (Blake & Mortimer Ser.: 18). (Illus.). 72p. pap. 15.95 *(978-1-84918-191-4(8))* CineBook GBR. Dist: National Bk. Network.

—The Sarcophagi of the Sixth Continent, Pt. 2. 2011. (Blake & Mortimer Ser.: 10). (Illus.). 64p. pap. 15.95 *(978-1-84918-077-1(6))* CineBook GBR. Dist: National Bk. Network.

PHYSICS

see also Astrophysics; Chemistry, Physical and Theoretical; Dynamics; Electricity; Electronics; Geophysics; Gravitation; Hydrostatics; Light; Liquids; Magnetism; Matter; Mechanics; Music—Acoustics and Physics; Nuclear Physics; Optics; Quantum Theory; Radiation; Radioactivity; Relativity (Physics); Sound; Thermodynamics

Alaina, Maria. Estimating. 2011. (Wonder Readers Early Level Ser.). (ENG.). 16p. (gr. -1-1). pap. 35.94 *(978-1-4296-8085-1(7),* Capstone Pr.) Capstone.

Bailey, Gerry & Law, Felicia. Energy & Movement. 2015. (Stone Age Science Ser.). (ENG., Illus.). 32p. (J). (gr. 4-5). lib. bdg. *(978-0-7787-1888-8(3))* Crabtree Publishing Co.

Barr, George. Sports Science for Young People. 2011. (Dover Science for Kids Ser.). (ENG., Illus.). 176p. (J). (gr. 3-8). pap. 11.95 *(978-0-486-26527-8(7),* 265277) Dover Pubns., Inc.

Basher, Simon. Basher Science: Extreme Physics. Basher, Simon, illus. 2013. (Basher Science Ser.). (ENG., Illus.). 64p. (J). (gr. 5-9). pap. 9.99 *(978-0-7534-6956-9(1),* 900088071, Kingfisher) Roaring Brook Pr.

Basiswissen Mathematik zur Physik. (Duden Abiturhilfen Ser.). (GER.). 96p. (YA). (gr. 11-13). *(978-3-411-04841-0(7))* Bibliographisches Institut & F. A. Brockhaus AG DEU. Dist: International Bk. Import Service, Inc.

Benchmark Education Company, LLC Staff, compiled by. Physical Science. 2006. spiral bd. 145.00 *(978-1-4108-6945-6(8))* 2006. spiral bd. 140.00 *(978-1-4108-6936-4(9))* 2006. spiral bd. 170.00 *(978-1-4108-6930-2(X))* 2006. spiral bd. 115.00 *(978-1-4108-6922-7(9))* 2005. spiral bd. 385.00 *(978-1-4108-5439-1(6))* 2005. spiral bd. 180.00 *(978-1-4108-3845-2(5))* 2005. spiral bd. 335.00 *(978-1-4108-3844-5(7))* 2005. spiral bd. 145.00 *(978-1-4108-5869-6(3))* 2005. spiral bd. 385.00 *(978-1-4108-5868-9(5))* 2005. spiral bd. 110.00 *(978-1-4108-3864-3(1))* 2005. spiral bd. 750.00 *(978-1-4108-5438-4(8))* 2005. spiral bd. 400.00 *(978-1-4108-4517-7(6))* 2005. spiral bd. 140.00 *(978-1-4108-3917-6(6))* 2005. spiral bd. 280.00 *(978-1-4108-3916-9(8))* 2005. spiral bd. 50.00 *(978-1-4108-3871-1(4))* Benchmark Education Co.

—Science Theme: Physical Science. 2005. spiral bd. 220.00 *(978-1-4108-5310-3(1))* Benchmark Education Co.

Best, Arthur. Mass & Weight, 1 vol. 2018. (Properties of Matter Ser.). (ENG.). 24p. (J). (gr. 1-1). pap. 9.22 *(978-1-5026-4224-0(7),* 958bc6c7-67ef-4264-9965-236e6200c1a9) Cavendish Square Publishing LLC.

Bingaman, Jay. Physical Science Student Lab Manual. Matthews, Douglas L., ed. 2003. (Illus.). stu. ed., per., wbk. ed. *(978-1-931680-30-1(2),* Expert Systems for Teachers) Teaching Point, Inc.

Bodden, Valerie. Baseball. 2016. (Making the Play Ser.). (ENG.). 24p. (J). (gr. 1-4). lib. bdg. 9.99 *(978-1-60818-653-2(9),* 20480, Creative Education) Creative Co., The.

—Basketball. 2016. (Making the Play Ser.). (ENG.). 24p. (J). (gr. 1-4). lib. bdg. 9.99 *(978-1-60818-654-9(7)*, 20483, Creative Education) Creative Co., The.

—Golf. 2016. (Making the Play Ser.). (ENG.). 24p. (J). (gr. 1-4). lib. bdg. 9.99 *(978-1-60818-655-6(5)*, 20486, Creative Education) Creative Co., The.

—Soccer. 2016. (Making the Play Ser.). (ENG., Illus.). 24p. (J). (gr. 1-4). lib. bdg. 9.99 *(978-1-60818-657-0(1)*, 20492, Creative Education) Creative Co., The.

Boothroyd, Jennifer. Give It a Push! Give It a Pull! A Look at Forces. 2010. (Lightning Bolt Books (r) — Exploring Physical Science Ser.). (ENG., Illus.). 32p. (J). (gr. 1-3). pap. 9.99 *(978-0-7613-6056-8(5)*, 5acdca6c-74bd-48de-a57d-b1b856d8b855) Lerner Publishing Group.

Brezina, Corona. Discovering Relativity, 1 vol. 2014. (Scientist's Guide to Physics Ser.). (ENG.). 112p. (J). (gr. 7-7). 39.80 *(978-1-4777-8006-0(8)*, baa0f5d0-eb60-433b-804f-adbe40fc51aa, Rosen Young Adult) Rosen Publishing Group, Inc., The.

Brown Bear Books. Mechanics. 2011. (Introducing Physics Ser.). (ENG.). 64p. (J). (gr. 8-11). lib. bdg. 39.95 *(978-1-936333-09-7(0)*, 16506) Brown Bear Bks.

Brown, Jordan D. The Innings & Outs of Baseball: Ready-To-Read Level 3. Downey, Dagney, illus. 2015. (Science of Fun Stuff Ser.). (ENG.). 48p. (J). (gr. 1-3). 17.99 *(978-1-4814-2862-0(4))*; pap. 4.99 *(978-1-4814-2861-3(6))* Simon Spotlight. (Simon Spotlight).

—The Thrills & Chills of Amusement Parks: Ready-To-Read Level 3. Borgions, Mark, illus. 2015. (Science of Fun Stuff Ser.). (ENG.). 48p. (J). (gr. 1-3). pap. 4.99 *(978-1-4814-2858-3(6)*, Simon Spotlight) Simon Spotlight.

Burton, Margie, et al. What Floats? What Sinks? 2011. (Early Connections Ser.). (J). *(978-1-61672-547-1(8))* Benchmark Education Co.

—What Pushes? What Pulls? 2011. (Early Connections Ser.). (J). *(978-1-61672-548-8(6))* Benchmark Education Co.

Cientificos! 8: Ciencias Fisicas. (SPA.). (J). 55.00 *(978-958-04-6347-4(6))* Norma S.A. COL. Dist: Distribuidora Norma, Inc.

Cleary, Brian P. On the Scale, a Weighty Tale. Gable, Brian, illus. 2010. (Math Is CATegorical (r) Ser.). (ENG.). 32p. (J). (gr. k-3). pap. 7.99 *(978-1-58013-845-1(4)*, b48d6f41-79fa-4546-8bd9-fb9a013c034b, Millbrook Pr.) Lerner Publishing Group.

—On the Scale, A Weighty Tale. 2010. pap. 39.62 *(978-0-7613-6997-4(X))* Lerner Publishing Group.

Contemporary Discourse in the Field of Physics, 10 vols., Set. 2005. (Contemporary Discourse in the Field of Physics Ser.). (ENG.). (YA). (gr. 10-12). lib. bdg. 205.65 *(978-1-4042-0630-4(2)*, e4e7bd71-af20-43c9-a63f-f487d84e8a7b) Rosen Publishing Group, Inc., The.

Cooke, Andy & Martin, Jean. Spectrum Physics Class Book. 2004. (Spectrum Key Stage 3 Science Ser.). (ENG., Illus.). 182p. pap. 33.65 *(978-0-521-54923-3(X))* Cambridge Univ. Pr.

Curran, Greg. Physics. 2005. (Illus.). 1p. (gr. 9-12). pap. 15.99 *(978-1-56414-768-4(1)*, Career Pr.) Red Wheel/Weiser.

Curry, Don L. What Is Mass? (Rookie Read-About Science: Physical Science: Previous Editions) Senisi, Ellen B., photos by. 2005. (Rookie Read-About Science Ser.). (ENG., Illus.). 32p. (J). (gr. 1-2). pap. 4.95 *(978-0-516-24666-6(6)*, Children's Pr.) Scholastic Library Publishing.

Cutnell, John D. Test Bank to Accompany Physics. 6th ed. 2004. 516p. (YA). *(978-0-471-23124-0(X))* Wiley, John & Sons, Inc.

Earth & Moon, 6 vols. (Sunshinetm Science Ser.). 24p. (gr. 1-2). 31.50 *(978-0-7802-0293-1(7))*; 36.95 *(978-0-7802-0544-4(8))* Wright Group/McGraw-Hill.

Fakhruddin, Hasan. Physics Demos & Hands-ons. 2006. 188p. pap. 23.30 *(978-1-4116-8162-0(2))* Lulu Pr., Inc.

Farndon, John & Graham, Ian. Discovering Science. 2010. (Science Library). 40p. (J). (gr. 3-18). lib. bdg. 19.95 *(978-1-4222-1548-7(2))* Mason Crest.

Ferrie, Chris. ABCs of Physics. 2017. (Baby University Ser.: 0). (Illus.). 26p. (J). (gr. -1-k). bds. 9.99 *(978-1-4926-5624-1(0))* Sourcebooks, Inc.

—General Relativity for Babies. 2017. (Baby University Ser.: 0). (Illus.). 24p. (J). (gr. -1-k). bds. 9.99 *(978-1-4926-5626-5(7))* Sourcebooks, Inc.

—Newtonian Physics for Babies. 2017. (Baby University Ser.: 0). (Illus.). 24p. (J). (gr. -1-k). bds. 9.99 *(978-1-4926-5620-3(8))* Sourcebooks, Inc.

—Statistical Physics for Babies. 2018. (Baby University Ser.: 0). (Illus.). 24p. (J). (gr. -1-k). bds. 9.99 *(978-1-4926-5627-2(5))* Sourcebooks, Inc.

Field, Andrea R., ed. The Science of Physics, 1 vol. 2011. (Introduction to Physics Ser.). (ENG.). 80p. (YA). (gr. 8-8). lib. bdg. 35.29 *(978-1-61530-676-3(5)*, 2e82a06a-c170-4b5a-94a7-d48778a33d96) Rosen Publishing Group, Inc., The.

Galat, Joan Marie. Stories of the Aurora: The Myths & Facts of the Northern Lights, 1 vol. Bennett, Lorna, illus. 2016. (Dot to Dot in the Sky Ser.). (ENG.). 68p. (J). (gr. 6-8). pap. 16.95 *(978-1-77050-210-9(6)*, 363f7059-8083-4c12-bc05-b9443887aa62) Whitecap Bks., Ltd. CAN. Dist: Firefly Bks., Ltd.

Gardner, Jane P. Physics: Investigate the Forces of Nature. Carbaugh, Samuel, illus. 2014. (Inquire & Investigate Ser.). (ENG.). 128p. (J). (gr. 6-10). 21.95 *(978-1-61930-227-3(6)*, 88c7c30a-ba1c-4ed3-93b6-494a82b32d6b) Nomad Pr.

Gardner, Robert. Solids, Liquids, & Gases Experiments Using Water, Air, Marbles, & More: One Hour or Less Science Experiments, 1 vol. 2012. (Last-Minute Science Projects Ser.). (ENG., Illus.). 48p. (gr. 5-6). 27.93 *(978-0-7660-3962-9(5)*, 3c0ba31a-d01e-4f25-9776-287319b424eb) Enslow Publishing, LLC.

Gareth Stevens Vital Science: Physical Science, 8 vols. 2007. (Gareth Stevens Vital Science Library: Physical Science Ser.). (ENG.). 48p. (gr. 5-8). lib. bdg. 118.68 *(978-0-8368-8083-0(8)*, 5a39a16b-fc73-431c-a76c-1384c154f2ac, Gareth Stevens Secondary Library) Stevens, Gareth Publishing LLLP.

Gaughan, Richard. Gravitational Waves Explained, 1 vol. 2018. (Mysteries of Space Ser.). (ENG.). 80p. (gr. 7-7). 38.93 *(978-1-9785-0456-1(X)*, 4f4e3f8e-0f57-4696-b05b-efd6625e7be9) Enslow Publishing, LLC.

—Physics in Your Everyday Life, 1 vol. 2019. (Real World Science Ser.). (ENG.). 64p. (gr. 6-6). 36.27 *(978-1-9785-0761-6(5)*, b86f57a2-7cc6-4340-b96b-eee9c6de34ff) Enslow Publishing, LLC.

—Wormholes Explained, 1 vol. 2018. (Mysteries of Space Ser.). (ENG.). 80p. (gr. 7-7). 38.93 *(978-0-7660-9965-4(2)*, 50898e31-3da7-4939-83fc-32809f8340db) Enslow Publishing, LLC.

Goodstein, Madeline. Sports Science Fair Projects, 1 vol. 2015. (Prize-Winning Science Fair Projects Ser.). (ENG.). 128p. (gr. 7-7). lib. bdg. 38.93 *(978-0-7660-7026-4(3)*, 3e3997a0-ca8c-4617-b8a2-0586ef09d1e4) Enslow Publishing, LLC.

Green, Dan & Basher, Simon. Basher Science: Physics: Why Matter Matters! Basher, Simon, illus. 2008. (Basher Science Ser.). (ENG., Illus.). 128p. (J). (gr. 5-9). pap. 9.99 *(978-0-7534-6214-0(1)*, 900053352, Kingfisher) Roaring Brook Pr.

Grey-Tomlinson, Marlene. Collins Exploring Physics - Workbook: Grade 9 for Jamaica. 2017. (ENG.). 48p. pap. 7.99 *(978-0-00-825208-3(4))* HarperCollins Pubs. Ltd. GBR. Dist: Independent Pubs. Group.

Hantula, Richard. Science at Work in Auto Racing, 1 vol. 2012. (Sports Science Ser.). (ENG.). 32p. (gr. 5-5). 31.21 *(978-1-60870-586-3(2)*, e8cf5b7a-a03d-4530-bc2a-b5579dbfa329) Cavendish Square Publishing LLC.

—Science at Work in Baseball, 1 vol. 2012. (Sports Science Ser.). (ENG., Illus.). 32p. (gr. 5-5). 31.21 *(978-1-60870-587-0(0)*, bc01afcb-7914-46a9-bae2-d8056c8aa3ea) Cavendish Square Publishing LLC.

—Science at Work in Basketball, 1 vol. 2012. (Sports Science Ser.). (ENG.). 32p. (gr. 5-5). 31.21 *(978-1-60870-588-7(9)*, 6918e43a-da7a-40ab-a9cf-a80636e88ab0) Cavendish Square Publishing LLC.

—Science at Work in Football, 1 vol. 2012. (Sports Science Ser.). (ENG.). 32p. (gr. 5-5). 31.21 *(978-1-60870-589-4(7)*, 3e3dc6ec-72cb-4d84-9d76-d69e4eec2797) Cavendish Square Publishing LLC.

—Science at Work in Snowboarding, 1 vol. 2012. (Sports Science Ser.). (ENG., Illus.). 32p. (gr. 5-5). 31.21 *(978-1-60870-590-0(0)*, b05c251f-239a-4c4e-8fca-343df2eff231) Cavendish Square Publishing LLC.

—Science at Work in Soccer, 1 vol. 2012. (Sports Science Ser.). (ENG., Illus.). 32p. (gr. 5-5). 31.21 *(978-1-60870-591-7(9)*, d3228d60-012c-4dd1-b500-64e8212a2270) Cavendish Square Publishing LLC.

Harris, Tim. Physical Science, 1 vol. 2015. (Science Q & A Ser.). (ENG., Illus.). 32p. (gr. 3-3). pap. 11.58 *(978-1-5026-0624-2(0)*, e21cf389-153c-4cb0-8c33-727efb3e7cd3) Cavendish Square Publishing LLC.

Hauptman, John & Bahng, E. J. Children Doing Physics: How to Foster the Natural Scientific Instincts in Children. 2nd ed. 2019. (ENG.). 358p. pap. 118.95 *(978-1-5165-4886-6(8)*, P625349) Cognella, Inc.

Hoffmann, Sara E. Staying Still. 2012. (First Step Nonfiction — Balance & Motion Ser.). (ENG., Illus.). 8p. (J). (gr. k-2). pap. 5.99 *(978-1-4677-0515-8(2)*, 186fa4fa-ced3-47a1-8cb1-b61af1ba65cb) Lerner Publishing Group.

Holics, László. 300 Creative Physics Problems with Solutions. 2010. (Illus.). 538p. 115.00 *(978-1-84331-869-9(5)*, 1843318695) Anthem Pr. GBR. Dist: Two Rivers Distribution.

Holman. Science Spectacular: Physics: Enhanced Online Edition. 4th ed. 2004. 17.26 *(978-0-03-037157-8(0))* Holt McDougal.

—Science Spectacular: Physics: Online Edition Upgrade. 4th ed. 2004. 31.93 *(978-0-03-037177-6(5))* Holt McDougal.

Holt, Rinehart and Winston Staff. Holt Physics: Premier Online Edition. 6th ed. 2005. 19.93 *(978-0-03-040089-6(9))* Holt McDougal.

—Holt Science & Technology. 4th ed. 2004. (Holt Science & Technology Ser.). (ENG., Illus.). 816p. (gr. 8-8). 92.70 *(978-0-03-073168-6(2))* Houghton Mifflin Harcourt Publishing Co.

—Holt Science & Technology: Physical Science. 5th ed. 2004. tchr. ed. 128.80 *(978-0-03-066482-3(9))* Holt McDougal.

—Holt Science & Technology: Physical Science: Enhanced Online Edition. 4th ed. 2004. 17.26 *(978-0-03-037152-3(X))* Holt McDougal.

—Holt Science & Technology Chapter 1: Physical Science: The World of Physical Science. 5th ed. 2004. (Illus.). pap. 12.86 *(978-0-03-030356-2(7))* Holt McDougal.

—Holt Science & Technology Chapter 7: Physical Science: Forces in Fluids. 5th ed. 2004. (Illus.). pap. 12.86 *(978-0-03-030386-9(9))* Holt McDougal.

—Holt Science & Technology Chapter 8: Physical Science: Work & Machines. 5th ed. 2004. (Illus.). pap. 12.86 *(978-0-03-030391-3(5))* Holt McDougal.

—Holt Science & Technology Online Edition. 5th ed. 2004. 15.93 *(978-0-03-030581-8(0))*; 15.93 *(978-0-03-030582-5(9))*; 15.93 *(978-0-03-030583-2(7))*; 15.93 *(978-0-03-030586-3(1))*; 15.93 *(978-0-03-030591-7(8))*; 15.93 *(978-0-03-030594-8(2))*; 15.93 *(978-0-03-030606-8(X))*; 15.93 *(978-0-03-030603-7(5))*; 15.93 *(978-0-03-030604-4(3))*; 15.93 *(978-0-03-030596-2(9))*; 15.93 *(978-0-03-030597-9(7))*; 15.93 *(978-0-03-030598-6(5))*; 15.93 *(978-0-03-030599-3(3))*; 15.93 *(978-0-03-030601-3(9))*; 15.93 *(978-0-03-030602-0(7))* Holt McDougal.

—Holt Science Spectrum: A Physical Approach - Spanish Study Guide. 4th ed. Date not set. pap. 11.20 *(978-0-03-068273-5(8))* Holt McDougal.

—Holt Science Spectrum Chptr. 7: Solutions. 4th ed. Date not set. (Illus.). pap. 11.20 *(978-0-03-068584-2(2))* Holt McDougal.

—Holt Science Spectrum Chptr. 11: Forces. 4th ed. Date not set. pap. 11.20 *(978-0-03-068583-5(4))* Holt McDougal.

—Physics: Premier Online Edition. 6th ed. Date not set. 83.93 *(978-0-03-036843-1(X))* Holt McDougal.

—Physics: Science Special - Assessments. 4th ed. 2004. (SPA.). pap. 11.20 *(978-0-03-068333-6(5))* Holt McDougal.

—Science Spectrum: Physics Math Skills. 4th ed. 2004. pap., wbk. ed. 11.13 *(978-0-03-067084-8(5))* Holt McDougal.

Hughes, Susan. Is It Heavy or Light? 2012. (ENG., Illus.). 24p. (J). *(978-0-7787-2048-5(9))*; pap. *(978-0-7787-2055-3(1))* Crabtree Publishing Co.

Hutton, Sarah. Cool Physics: Filled with Fantastic Facts for Kids of All Ages. Weighill, Damien, illus. 2017. (Cool Ser.). (ENG.). 112p. (J). (gr. 5). 15.99 *(978-1-84365-324-0(9)*, Pavilion Children's Books) Pavilion Bks. GBR. Dist: HarperCollins Pubs.

Integrated Physics & Chemistry, Chapter 1, Activities. 2005. (Illus.). 22p. (YA). pap. 5.00 *(978-1-59476-173-7(6))* Paradigm Accelerated Curriculum.

Integrated Physics & Chemistry Chapter 1, Text. 2005. Orig. Title: (Key Topics. (Illus.). 34p. (YA). pap. 7.00 *(978-1-59476-161-4(2))* Paradigm Accelerated Curriculum.

Integrated Physics & Chemistry, Chapter 10, Activities. 2005. (Illus.). 32p. (YA). pap. 5.00 *(978-1-59476-182-9(5))* Paradigm Accelerated Curriculum.

Integrated Physics & Chemistry, Chapter 10, Text. 2005. (Illus.). 68p. (YA). pap. 7.00 *(978-1-59476-170-6(1))* Paradigm Accelerated Curriculum.

Integrated Physics & Chemistry, Chapter 11, Activities. 2005. (Illus.). 40p. (YA). pap. 5.00 *(978-1-59476-183-6(3))* Paradigm Accelerated Curriculum.

Integrated Physics & Chemistry, Chapter 11, Text. 2005. (Illus.). 64p. (YA). pap. 7.00 *(978-1-59476-171-3(X))* Paradigm Accelerated Curriculum.

Integrated Physics & Chemistry, Chapter 12, Activities. 2005. (Illus.). 32p. (YA). pap. 5.00 *(978-1-59476-184-3(1))* Paradigm Accelerated Curriculum.

Integrated Physics & Chemistry, Chapter 12, Text. 2005. (Illus.). 66p. (YA). pap. 7.00 *(978-1-59476-172-0(8))* Paradigm Accelerated Curriculum.

Integrated Physics & Chemistry, Chapter 2, Activities. 2005. (Illus.). 42p. (YA). pap. 5.00 *(978-1-59476-174-4(4))* Paradigm Accelerated Curriculum.

Integrated Physics & Chemistry, Chapter 2, Text. 2005. (Illus.). 66p. (YA). pap. 7.00 *(978-1-59476-162-1(0))* Paradigm Accelerated Curriculum.

Integrated Physics & Chemistry, Chapter 3 Activities. 2005. (Illus.). 32p. (YA). pap. 5.00 *(978-1-59476-175-1(2))* Paradigm Accelerated Curriculum.

Integrated Physics & Chemistry, Chapter 3, Text. 2005. (Illus.). 66p. (YA). pap. 7.00 *(978-1-59476-163-8(9))* Paradigm Accelerated Curriculum.

Integrated Physics & Chemistry, Chapter 4, Text. 2005. (Illus.). 64p. (YA). pap. 7.00 *(978-1-59476-164-5(7))* Paradigm Accelerated Curriculum.

Integrated Physics & Chemistry, Chapter 5, Activities. 2005. (Illus.). 32p. (YA). pap. 5.00 *(978-1-59476-177-5(9))* Paradigm Accelerated Curriculum.

Integrated Physics & Chemistry, Chapter 5, Text. 2005. (Illus.). 64p. (YA). pap. 7.00 *(978-1-59476-165-2(5))* Paradigm Accelerated Curriculum.

Integrated Physics & Chemistry, Chapter 6, Activities. 2005. (Illus.). 32p. (YA). pap. 5.00 *(978-1-59476-178-2(7))* Paradigm Accelerated Curriculum.

Integrated Physics & Chemistry, Chapter 6, Text. 2005. (Illus.). 64p. (YA). pap. 7.00 *(978-1-59476-166-9(3))* Paradigm Accelerated Curriculum.

Integrated Physics & Chemistry, Chapter 7, Activities. 2005. (Illus.). 32p. (YA). pap. 5.00 *(978-1-59476-179-9(5))* Paradigm Accelerated Curriculum.

Integrated Physics & Chemistry, Chapter 7, Text. 2005. (Illus.). 66p. (YA). pap. 7.00 *(978-1-59476-167-6(1))* Paradigm Accelerated Curriculum.

Integrated Physics & Chemistry, Chapter 8, Activities. 2005. (Illus.). 32p. (YA). pap. 5.00 *(978-1-59476-180-5(9))* Paradigm Accelerated Curriculum.

Integrated Physics & Chemistry, Chapter 8, Text. 2005. (Illus.). 64p. (YA). pap. 7.00 *(978-1-59476-168-3(X))* Paradigm Accelerated Curriculum.

Integrated Physics & Chemistry, Chapter 9, Activities. 2005. (Illus.). 32p. (YA). pap. 5.00 *(978-1-59476-181-2(7))* Paradigm Accelerated Curriculum.

Integrated Physics & Chemistry, Chapter 9, Text. 2005. (Illus.). 68p. (YA). pap. 7.00 *(978-1-59476-169-0(8))* Paradigm Accelerated Curriculum.

Integrated Physics & Chemistry, Full Course Kit, 25 bks. 2005. (Illus.). 7969p. (YA). 169.00 *(978-1-59476-187-4(6))* Paradigm Accelerated Curriculum.

Integrated Physics & Chemistry, Teacher's Resource Kit with CD. 2005. (Illus.). 439p. (YA). pap. 25.00 *(978-1-59476-185-0(X))* Paradigm Accelerated Curriculum.

Johnson, Rose. Discoveries in Physics That Changed the World, 1 vol. 2014. (Scientific Breakthroughs Ser.). (ENG.). 48p. (J). (gr. 6-6). 33.47 *(978-1-4777-8603-1(1)*, 5a2a04c1-1d5c-4044-a937-38164a4795e8, Rosen Reference) Rosen Publishing Group, Inc., The.

Jorden, Tyler. Physics Animated! Martins, Elsa, illus. 2019. (ENG.). 14p. (J). (gr. k-2). bds. 14.99 *(978-1-64170-132-7(3)*, 550132) Familius LLC.

Keller, R W. Physics Level I Laboratory Workbook. 2005. (Real Science-4-Kids Ser.). (Illus.). 56p. (J). (gr. 3-7). per. 23.95 *(978-0-9749149-5-4(9))* Gravitas Pubns., Inc.

Keller, Rebecca W. Physics Level I. 2005. (Real Science-4-Kids Ser.). (Illus.). 65p. (J). (gr. 3-6). 24.95 *(978-0-9749149-4-7(0))* Gravitas Pubns., Inc.

—Pre-Level I Physics Laboratory Workbook. 2009. 126p. pap. 23.95 *(978-0-9823163-2-0(1))* Gravitas Pubns., Inc.

Kelly, Lynne. Simple Concepts in Physics: Sound & Light. (Illus.). 88p. (J). (gr. 5-6). pap. *(978-1-875739-69-1(6))* Wizard Bks.

Lancaster, Juliana. PBIS- Lift, Spin, Drop & Fall. 2005. pap., stu. ed. 8.00 *(978-1-58591-564-4(5))* It's About Time, Herff Jones Education Div.

Lawrence, Carol. Water. Zito, Francesco, illus. 2018. (Baby Explorer Ser.). (ENG.). 24p. (J). (gr. -1 — 1). bds. 6.99 *(978-0-8075-0517-5(X)*, 080750517X) Whitman, Albert & Co.

Lawrence, Ellen. Water. 2013. (Science Slam: FUN-Damental Experiments Ser.). (Illus.). 24p. (J). (gr. -1-3). lib. bdg. 26.99 *(978-1-61772-736-8(9))* Bearport Publishing Co., Inc.

Leavitt, Amie Jane. Physical Computing & Makerspaces, 1 vol. 2014. (Digital & Information Literacy Ser.). (ENG., Illus.). 48p. (J). (gr. 6-6). 33.47 *(978-1-4777-7659-9(1)*, 9a8cefaa-02d7-422c-aaf0-b540a0ebe6db, Rosen Reference) Rosen Publishing Group, Inc., The.

Lemonwood, A. C. Jumbo Minds' Science ABCs - ABCs of Physics: ABCs of Physics. 2015. (Illus.). 60p. (J). (gr. -1-12). pap. 9.99 *(978-1-944049-13-3(4))* Jumbo Minds, Inc.

Lerner Publishing Group Staff. Lightning Bolt Books: Exploring Physical Science, 6 vols., Set. 2011. (J). (gr. k-2). lib. bdg. 151.56 *(978-0-7613-7482-4(5))* Lerner Publishing Group.

LernerClassroom Editors. Early Bird Physics Teaching Guide. 2009. pap. 7.95 *(978-0-8225-5540-7(9))* Lerner Publishing Group.

LernerClassroom Editors, ed. Teaching Guide for Lbb / Exploring Physical Science. 2010. pap. 5.95 *(978-0-7613-6693-5(8))* Lerner Publishing Group.

Letts Cambridge, Igcse. Cambridge IGCSE Physics Revision Guide. 2nd rev. ed. 2017. (Illus.). 144p. (YA). (gr. 9-11). pap. 16.99 *(978-0-00-821033-5(0))* HarperCollins Pubs. Ltd. GBR. Dist: Independent Pubs. Group.

The Library of Physics, 6 vols. 2004. (Library of Physics Ser.). (ENG.). (YA). (gr. 7-7). lib. bdg. 103.41 *(978-1-4042-0381-5(8)*, e2a35b70-91ac-4578-b0e5-aa1a1ba2ebeb) Rosen Publishing Group, Inc., The.

Lindeen, Mary. Color & Shape. 2017. (Beginning-To-Read Ser.). (ENG.). 32p. (J). (gr. k-2). pap. 13.26 *(978-1-68404-101-5(5))*; (Illus.). 22.60 *(978-1-59953-882-2(2))* Norwood Hse. Pr.

Lord, Roberta. Reflections: English Version. 2003. 200p. 9.95 net. *(978-1-931934-23-7(1))* Back Yard Pub.

Manolis, Kay. Density. 2008. (First Science Ser.). (ENG., Illus.). 24p. (J). (gr. 2-5). lib. bdg. 26.95 *(978-1-60014-224-6(9))* Bellwether Media.

Marquardt, Meg. Stem in Auto Racing. 2017. (STEM in Sports Ser.). (ENG., Illus.). 48p. (J). (gr. 3-6). lib. bdg. 34.21 *(978-1-5321-1346-8(3)*, 27644, SportsZone) ABDO Publishing Co.

Mastering Physics, 12 vols. 2014. (Mastering Physics Ser.). (ENG.). 48p. (J). (gr. 8-8). lib. bdg. 198.42 *(978-1-5026-0300-5(4)*, 0ce3055a-8d7b-42d6-9859-d5ced4e664a7, Cavendish Square) Cavendish Square Publishing LLC.

Mattern, Joanne. Focus on Inertia. 2017. (Hands-On STEM Ser.). (ENG., Illus.). 32p. (J). (gr. 2-3). pap. 9.95 *(978-1-63517-348-2(5)*, 1635173485); lib. bdg. 31.35 *(978-1-63517-283-6(7)*, 1635172837) North Star Editions. (Focus Readers).

McClanahan, Ben. Northern Lights. 2018. (Natural Phenomena Ser.). (ENG., Illus.). 32p. (J). (gr. 3-5). pap. 9.95 *(978-1-64185-012-4(4)*, 1641850124); lib. bdg. 31.35 *(978-1-63517-910-1(6)*, 1635179106) North Star Editions. (Focus Readers).

McDougal-Littell Publishing Staff. Electricity & Magnetism 2005. 2004. (McDougal Littell Middle School Science Ser.). (ENG., Illus.). 64p. (gr. 6-8). lib. bdg., stu. ed. 21.80 *(978-0-618-33440-7(8)*, 2-01027) Great Source Education Group, Inc.

—Matter & Energy. 2004. (McDougal Littell Middle School Science Ser.). (ENG., Illus.). 64p. (gr. 6-8). lib. bdg. 21.80 *(978-0-618-33444-5(0)*, 2-01031) Great Source Education Group, Inc.

—Modules: Physical Science. 2004. (McDougal Littell Science Ser.). (ENG.). 48p. (gr. 6-8). pap., lab manual ed. 15.30 *(978-0-618-43729-0(0)*, 2-01222) Great Source Education Group, Inc.

—Modules: Physical Science - Motion & Forces PE. 2004. (McDougal Littell Science Ser.). (ENG.). 64p. (gr. 6-8). pap., lab manual ed. 15.30 *(978-0-618-43733-7(9)*, 2-01226) Great Source Education Group, Inc.

—Modules: Physical Science, Matter & Energy. 2004. (McDougal Littell Science Ser.). (ENG.). 48p. (gr. 6-8). pap., lab manual ed. 15.30 *(978-0-618-43732-0(0)*, 2-01225) Great Source Education Group, Inc.

—Waves, Sound & Light. 2004. (McDougal Littell Science Ser.). (ENG.). 64p. (gr. 6-8). pap., lab manual ed. 15.30 *(978-0-618-43736-8(3)*, 2-01229) Great Source Education Group, Inc.

—Waves, Sound, & Light. 2004. (McDougal Littell Middle School Science Ser.). (ENG., Illus.). 64p. (gr. 6-8). lib. bdg. 21.80 *(978-0-618-33446-9(7)*, 2-01033) Great Source Education Group, Inc.

McDougal-Littell Publishing Staff, creator. Motion & Forces. 2005. (McDougal Littell Science Ser.). (Illus.). 176p. (gr. 6-12). lib. bdg. *(978-0-618-33442-1(4)*, 2-01029) Holt McDougal.

McGraw Hill. Glencoe Physical IScience, Grade 8, Reading Essentials, Student Edition. 2004. (Physical Science Ser.). (ENG., Illus.). 448p. (gr. 8-8). stu. ed., per., wbk. ed. 24.88 *(978-0-07-866089-4(0)*, 0078660890) McGraw-Hill Education.

—Glencoe Physical IScience Modules: Waves, Sound, & Light, Grade 8, Laboratory Manual, Student Edition. 2004. (GLEN SCI: SOUND & LIGHT Ser.). (ENG., Illus.). 48p. (gr. 6-8). stu. ed., spiral bd., lab manual ed. 7.12 *(978-0-07-867322-1(4)*, 0078673224) McGraw-Hill Education.

—Glencoe Physical IScience, Reinforcement & Study Guide, Student Edition. 2004. (Physical Science Ser.). (ENG.). 104p. (gr. 8-8). stu. ed., spiral bd., pupil's gde. ed. 8.72 *(978-0-07-866091-7(2)*, 0078660912) McGraw-Hill Education.

—Glencoe Science: Waves, Sound, & Light, Student Edition. 2nd ed. 2004. (GLEN SCI: SOUND & LIGHT Ser.). (ENG., Illus.). 192p. (gr. 6-8). stu. ed. 38.36 *(978-0-07-861776-8(6)*, 0078617766) McGraw-Hill Education.

McPartland, Randall. Understanding Quantum Physics. 2015. (J). lib. bdg. *(978-1-62713-433-0(6))* Cavendish Square Publishing LLC.

Moore, Rob. Why Do Balls Bounce?, 1 vol. 2010. (Solving Science Mysteries Ser.). 24p. (ENG.). (J). (gr. 4-5). pap. 9.25 *(978-1-61531-910-7(7)*, 2ae3f95e-e84c-4308-993f-1437134e63c6, PowerKids Pr.);

(Illus.). (J). 49.50 (978-1-61531-911-4(5), 1307162, PowerKids Pr.); (ENG., Illus.). (YA). (gr. 4-5). lib. bdg. 26.27 (978-1-61531-889-6(5), 3efae534-857c-4e61-b464-5310dbb9e276) Rosen Publishing Group, Inc., The.

Moreau, Nancy. Physics: Physical Setting STAReview. 2003. (ENG., Illus.). 397p. (YA). per. 15.95 (978-0-935487-76-3(X), STAReviews) N&N Publishing Co., Inc.

Mouton, M. J. Richie Doodles: The Brilliance of a Young Richard Feynman. Cuevas, Jezreel S., illus. 2018. (Tiny Thinkers Ser.). 24p. (J). (gr. k-3). 16.95 (978-0-9983147-1-6(4), Secular Media Group) Rare Bird Bks.

Murphy, John, ed. Physics: Understanding the Properties of Matter & Energy, 1 vol. 2014. (Study of Science Ser.). (ENG., Illus.). 120p. (J). (gr. 8-8). 37.82 (978-1-62275-418-2(2), 292cbc2c-0212-417c-97ef-643b8d615e64) Rosen Publishing Group, Inc., The.

Nagelhout, Ryan. The Science of Football, 1 vol. 2015. (Sports Science Ser.). (ENG.). 32p. (J). (gr. 4-5). pap. 11.00 (978-1-4994-1066-2(2), e0428f42-2fc3-43bd-a698-48cfd4214cb5, PowerKids Pr.) Rosen Publishing Group, Inc., The.

National Geographic Learning. Language, Literacy & Vocabulary - Reading Expeditions (Physical Science): What Is Matter? 2007. (ENG., Illus.). 36p. (J). pap. 20.95 (978-0-7922-5442-3(2)) CENGAGE Learning.

Nelson, Beth. Science Spectacular Physics: Enhanced Online Edition. 6th ed. Date not set. cd-rom 87.33 (978-0-03-040014-8(7)) Holt McDougal.

Newland, Sonya. Doodle Yourself Smart... Physics. 2012. (Doodle Bks.). (ENG., Illus.). 128p. pap. 12.95 (978-1-60710-439-1(3), Thunder Bay Pr.) Readerlink Distribution Services, LLC.

Nikolo, Martin. Physics for the Rest of Us. 2003. (Illus.). 280p. pap. 79.95 (978-0-9741638-0-2(5)) Copernicus Pr.

Nsrc. Science & Technology for Children Books: Ecosystems. 2004. (Illus.). 64p. (J). (978-1-933008-05-9(9)) Smithsonian Science Education Ctr. (SSEC).

—Science & Technology for Children Books: Floating & Sinking. 2004. (Illus.). 64p. (J). (978-1-933008-07-3(5)) Smithsonian Science Education Ctr. (SSEC).

—Science & Technology for Children Books: Magnets & Motors. 2004. (Illus.). 64p. (J). (978-1-933008-10-3(5)) Smithsonian Science Education Ctr. (SSEC).

O'Connell, Diane. Strong Force: The Story of Physicist Shirley Ann Jackson. 2006. (ENG., Illus.). 128p. per. 19.95 (978-0-309-09553-2(0), Joseph Henry Pr.) National Academies Pr.

Oxlade, Chris. Solids: An Investigation, 1 vol. 2007. (Science Investigations Ser.). (ENG., Illus.). 32p. (YA). (gr. 4-5). lib. bdg. 30.27 (978-1-4042-4284-5(8), 1d8e4ccd-ba54-42dd-910e-b2454e999dc0) Rosen Publishing Group, Inc., The.

Oxlade, Chris, et al, eds. The Usborne Illustrated Dictionary of Physics. 2nd rev. ed. 2004. (Illustrated Dictionaries Ser.). (ENG., Illus.). 1p. (YA). (gr. 7-18). pap. 12.95 (978-0-7460-3796-6(1)) EDC Publishing.

Paris, Stephanie. Vroom! Speed & Acceleration, 1 vol. 2nd rev. ed. 2013. (TIME for KIDS(r): Informational Text Ser.). (ENG., Illus.). 64p. (J). (gr. 4-8). lib. bdg. 31.96 (978-1-4333-7437-1(4)) Teacher Created Materials, Inc.

Peters, Katie. Changing Water. 2019. (Science All Around Me (Pull Ahead Readers — Nonfiction) Ser.). (ENG., Illus.). 16p. (J). (gr. -1-1). pap. 8.99 (978-1-5415-7332-1(3), 118cc92f-3cfa-4c1d-b740-17b5aa8cccf2); lib. bdg. 27.99 (978-1-5415-5847-2(2), 3d1a77ca-d9c8-4745-b9b6-eba71b7f4550) Lerner Publishing Group. (Lerner Pubns.).

Peterson, Megan Cooley. Scooby-Doo! a Science of Electricity Mystery: The Mutant Crocodile. Comia, Christian, illus. 2017. (Scooby-Doo Solves It with S. T. E. M. Ser.). (ENG.). 32p. (J). (gr. 3-6). pap. 7.95 (978-1-5157-3702-5(0), 133671, Capstone Pr.) Capstone.

Randolph, Joanne. Liquids in My World, 1 vol. 2005. (My World of Science Ser.). (ENG., Illus.). 24p. (J). (gr. k-2). lib. bdg. 22.27 (978-1-4042-3285-3(0), 8a401747-0f5d-476c-a91e-f2a2fe9c080a, PowerKids Pr.) Rosen Publishing Group, Inc., The.

—Solids in My World, 1 vol. (Journeys Ser.). (ENG.). 24p. (gr. k-2). 2006. pap. 7.05 (978-1-4042-8422-7(2), 66e9452a-b99f-4744-9968-fc3be2d6b4dc, Rosen Classroom) 2005. (Illus.). (J). lib. bdg. 22.27 (978-1-4042-3283-9(4), 9f6abeb4-f08f-43be-b170-fe2c8f6e47fa, PowerKids Pr.) Rosen Publishing Group, Inc., The.

Regan, Lisa. Physics Is Out of This World, 1 vol. 2016. (Amazing World of Science & Math Ser.). (ENG.). 48p. (gr. 5-5). pap. 15.05 (978-1-4824-4982-2(X), d0dac4ba-c73a-4557-90d2-c2993184a43d) Stevens, Gareth Publishing LLLP.

Reinke, Beth Bence. Measuring Volume. Petelinsek, Kathleen, illus. 2014. (Explorer Junior Library: Math Explorer Junior Ser.). (ENG.). 24p. (J). (gr. 1-4). 32.07 (978-1-62431-651-7(4), 203116) Cherry Lake Publishing.

Richards, Roy. En Movimiento. (Coleccion 101 Trucos Cientificos). (SPA., Illus.). (J). (gr. 3-5). pap. (978-950-724-176-5(0), LMA8753) Lumen ARG. Dist: Lectorum Pubns., Inc.

Riley, Peter D. Checkpoint Physics. 2005. (Illus.). 192p. pap. 47.50 (978-0-7195-8069-7(2)) Hodder Education Group GBR. Dist: Trans-Atlantic Pubns., Inc.

Rivera, Sheila. Is It Heavy or Light? 2005. (First Step Nonfiction — Properties of Matter Ser.). (ENG., Illus.). 8p. (J). (gr. k-2). pap. 5.99 (978-0-8225-5408-0(9), caaa5a79-5228-4565-8d2d-894c45bf05bc) Lerner Publishing Group.

Rookie Read-About Science: Physical Science, 6 bks., Set. Incl. What Is Density? Barkan, Joanne. lib. bdg. 20.50 (978-0-516-23618-6(0)); Will It Float or Sink? Stewart, Melissa. lib. bdg. 17.44 (978-0-516-24955-1(X), Children's Pr.); (Illus.). 32p. (J). (gr. 1-2). 2006. 117.00 o.p. (978-0-516-25417-3(0), Children's Pr.) Scholastic Library Publishing.

Rosinsky, Natalie M. & Picture Window Books Staff. Imanes: Atraen y Rechazan, 1 vol. Robledo, Sol, tr. Boyd, Sheree, illus. 2007. (Ciencia Asombrosa Ser.).Tr. of Magnets: Pulling Together & Pushing Apart. (SPA.). 24p. (J). (gr. k-4). 27.32 (978-1-4048-3220-6(3), 93771, Picture Window Bks.) Capstone.

Ryan, Lawrie, et al. Physics. 2003. (ENG., Illus.). 80p. pap. (978-0-7487-6801-1(7)) Nelson Thornes Ltd.

Science & Technology for Children Books, Ecosystems Set, 8 vols. 2004. (Illus.). (J). (978-1-933008-17-2(2)) Smithsonian Science Education Ctr. (SSEC).

Science & Technology for Children Books, Floating & Sinking Set, 8 vols. 2004. (Illus.). 64p. (J). (978-1-933008-19-6(9)) Smithsonian Science Education Ctr. (SSEC).

Science & Technology for Children Books, Magnets & Motors Set, 8 vols. 2004. (Illus.). 64p. (J). (978-1-933008-22-6(9)) Smithsonian Science Education Ctr. (SSEC).

The Science of Energy. 2016. (Illus.). 48p. (J). (978-1-4222-3513-3(0)) Mason Crest.

Sian revision gears at Work. 2004. (Science in A Nutshell Ser.). (J). (978-1-59242-037-7(0)) Delta Education, LLC.

Sian revision pulley Power. 2004. (J). (978-1-59242-061-2(3)) Delta Education, LLC.

Sian Solids. 2004. (J). (978-1-59242-073-5(7)) Delta Education, LLC.

Smith, Ben. Why Does This Float? 2012. (Level D Ser.). (ENG., Illus.). 16p. (J). (gr. k-2). pap. 7.95 (978-1-927136-39-3(3), 19465) RiverStream Publishing.

Solway, Andrew. Energy & Matter. 2010. (21st Century Science Ser.). (ENG.). 112p. (YA). (gr. 9-12). 42.80 (978-1-933834-72-6(2), 16383) Brown Bear Bks.

Sonneborn, Liz. Forces in Nature: Understanding Gravitational, Electrical, & Magnetic Force, 1 vol. 2004. (Library of Physics Ser.). (ENG., Illus.). 48p. (YA). (gr. 7-7). lib. bdg. 34.47 (978-1-4042-0332-7(X), d0f8cf35-a5f6-499b-a0bc-3bcc348c9259) Rosen Publishing Group, Inc., The.

Sootin, Harry. Experiments with MacHines & Matter. Aloise, Frank, illus. 2012. 96p. 38.95 (978-1-258-23744-8(X)); pap. 23.95 (978-1-258-24341-8(5)) Literary Licensing, LLC.

Spilsbury, Richard. Investigating Forces & Motion. 2018. (Investigating Science Challenges Ser.). (ENG., Illus.). 32p. (J). (gr. 4-4). (978-0-7787-4205-0(9)); pap. (978-0-7787-4253-1(9)) Crabtree Publishing Co.

Spiro, Ruth. Baby Loves Quantum Physics! Chan, Irene, illus. 2017. (Baby Loves Science Ser.: 4). 22p. (J). (— 1). bds. 8.99 (978-1-58089-769-3(X)) Charlesbridge Publishing, Inc.

Spyglass Books-Physical Science Complete Set. (Spyglass Books: Physical Science Ser.). (gr. 1-2). 119.58 (978-0-7565-0785-5(5), Compass Point Bks.) Capstone.

Stewart, Melissa. Energy in Motion. 2006. (Rookie Read-About Science Ser.). (ENG., Illus.). 32p. (J). (gr. 1-2). pap. 4.95 (978-0-516-23736-7(5), Children's Pr.) Scholastic Library Publishing.

—Will It Float or Sink? 2006. (Rookie Read-About Science: Physical Science Ser.). (ENG., Illus.). 32p. (J). (gr. 1-2). lib. bdg. 17.44 (978-0-516-24955-1(X), Children's Pr.) Scholastic Library Publishing.

Stockley, Corinne, et al. Illustrated Dictionary of Physics. Johnson, Fiona, illus. 2007. (Illustrated Dictionaries Ser.). 128p. (J). (gr. 4-7). pap. 12.99 (978-0-7945-1561-4(4), Usborne) EDC Publishing.

Strauss, Michael J. Investigating the Natural World of Chemistry with Kids: Experiments, Writing, & Drawing Activities for Learning Science. 2012. 226p. pap. 25.95 (978-1-61233-155-3(6)) Universal Pubs.

The Basics of Electronics: Core Concepts: Physics: Set 3, 20 vols. 2014. (Core Concepts Ser.). (ENG.). 96p. (YA). (gr. 7-7). 397.70 (978-1-4777-7772-5(5), 73e28560-3f39-4959-8b53-8737bd174ad5) Rosen Publishing Group, Inc., The.

The Scientist's Guide to Physics: Set 2, 8 vols. 2014. (Scientist's Guide to Physics Ser.). (ENG.). 112p. (YA). (gr. 7-7). lib. bdg. 159.20 (978-1-4777-8059-6(9), fcb9ab36-0882-489d-9c45-ff44324b1c9d, Rosen Young Adult) Rosen Publishing Group, Inc., The.

Usborne Books Staff, ed. Illustrated Dictionary of Physics. rev. ed. 2004. (Illustrated Dictionaries Ser.). (Illus.). 128p. (J). (gr. 7-18). lib. bdg. 20.95 (978-1-58086-283-7(7)) EDC Publishing.

VanCleave, Janice Pratt. Even More of Janice Vancleave's Wild, Wacky, & Weird Physics Experiments, 1 vol. 2017. (Janice VanCleave's Wild, Wacky, & Weird Science Experiments Ser.). (ENG.). 64p. (gr. 5-5). 38.47 (978-1-4994-6690-4(0), cd94f232-f1d4-4c85-b62b-4d661c064174, Rosen Central) Rosen Publishing Group, Inc., The.

VanVoorst, Jenny Fretland. Bicycles. 2016. (Early Physics Fun). (Illus.). 24p. (J). (gr. 2-5). lib. bdg. (978-1-62031-314-5(6), Pogo) Jump! Inc.

—Boomerangs. 2016. (Early Physics Fun). 24p. (J). (gr. 2-5). lib. bdg. (978-1-62031-315-2(4), Pogo) Jump! Inc.

—Hula Hoops. 2016. (Early Physics Fun). (Illus.). 24p. (J). (gr. 2-5). lib. bdg. (978-1-62031-316-9(2), Pogo) Jump! Inc.

—Paper Airplanes. 2016. (Early Physics Fun). 24p. (J). (gr. 2-5). lib. bdg. (978-1-62031-317-6(0), Pogo) Jump! Inc.

—Slides. 2016. (Illus.). 24p. (J). (gr. 2-5). lib. bdg. (978-1-62031-318-3(9), Pogo) Jump! Inc.

—Trampolines. 2016. (Early Physics Fun). (Illus.). 24p. (J). (gr. 2-5). lib. bdg. (978-1-62031-319-0(7), Pogo) Jump! Inc.

Vilardi, Debbie. What Are Clouds Made Of? 2019. (Science Questions Ser.). (ENG., Illus.). 24p. (J). (gr. 1-1). pap. 8.95 (978-1-64185-585-3(1), 1641855851) North Star Editions.

—What Are Clouds Made Of? 2018. (Science Questions Ser.). (ENG., Illus.). 24p. (J). (gr. k-3). lib. bdg. 31.36 (978-1-5321-6214-5(6), 30211, Pop! Cody Koala) Pop!

Vogel, Julia. Weight. 2018. (Illus.). 24p. (J). (978-1-4896-5886-9(6), AV2 by Weigl) Weigl Pubs., Inc.

Walker, Sally M. Investigating Matter. 2011. (Searchlight Books (tm) — How Does Energy Work? Ser.). (ENG., Illus.). (gr. 3-5). 40p. (J). pap. 9.99 (978-0-7613-7875-4(8), c14848eb-749d-4a42-89aa-34d6242a337a); pap. 51.01 (978-0-7613-8409-0(X)) Lerner Publishing Group.

—Libros de Energia para Madrugadores; Early Bird Energy: Complete Set. 2008. pap. 316.95 (978-1-58013-301-2(0)) Lerner Publishing Group.

—Sound. King, Andy, photos by. 2005. (Early Bird Energy Ser.). (Illus.). 48p. (J). (gr. 3-7). lib. bdg. 25.26 (978-0-8225-2634-6(4), Lerner Pubns.) Lerner Publishing Group.

Walliman, Dominic. Professor Astro Cat's Space Rockets. Newman, Ben, illus. 2018. (ENG.). 32p. (J). (gr. k-2). 13.99 (978-1-911171-94-2(1)) Flying Eye Bks. GBR. Dist: Penguin Random Hse. LLC.

Weir, Jane. Isaac Newton & the Laws of the Universe, 1 vol. rev. ed. 2007. (Science: Informational Text Ser.). (ENG.). 32p. (gr. 3-6). pap. 12.99 (978-0-7439-0574-9(1)) Teacher Created Materials, Inc.

Weir, Kirsten & Brent, Lynnette. States of Matter, 1 vol. 2008. (Why Chemistry Matters Ser.). (ENG., Illus.). 32p. (J). (gr. 3-7). pap. (978-0-7787-4251-7(2)) Crabtree Publishing Co.

What Floats? Big Book: Level C. 8p. 20.95 (978-0-322-00370-5(9)) Wright Group/McGraw-Hill.

Wick, Walter. A Ray of Light. Wick, Walter, illus. 2019. (ENG., Illus.). 40p. (J). (gr. 1-3). 19.99 (978-0-439-16587-7(3), Scholastic Pr.) Scholastic, Inc.

Willett, Edward. The Basics of Quantum Physics: Understanding the Photoelectric Effect & Line Spectra, 1 vol. 2004. (Library of Physics Ser.). (ENG., Illus.). 48p. (YA). (gr. 7-7). lib. bdg. 34.47 (978-1-4042-0334-1(6), daccd3a4-a34f-4933-8cc1-fc881d39010c) Rosen Publishing Group, Inc., The.

Williams, Gareth, et al. New Physics for You. 2nd ed. 2006. (ENG., Illus.). 400p. (YA). pap., stu. ed. 54.50 (978-0-7487-8328-1(8)) Nelson Thornes Ltd. GBR. Dist: Trans-Atlantic Pubns., Inc.

World Book, Inc. Staff, contrib. by. Encyclopedia of Matter & Energy. 2013. (Illus.). 245p. (J). (978-0-7166-7521-1(8)) World Bk., Inc.

Wynne, Patricia J. & Silver, Donald M. My First Book about Physics. 2019. (Dover Science for Kids Coloring Bks.). (ENG.). 48p. (J). (gr. 3-6). pap. 5.99 (978-0-486-82614-1(7), 826147) Dover Pubns., Inc.

Zac Newton Investigates Fabulous Forces. 2018. (J). (978-0-7166-4057-8(0)) World Bk., Inc.

Zubek, Adeline. Heavy or Light?, 1 vol. 2019. (All about Opposites Ser.). (ENG.). 24p. (gr. k-k). pap. 9.15 (978-1-5382-3722-9(9), fca8bd9d-12b6-45f2-a6b9-c5b4f6aa23e9) Stevens, Gareth Publishing LLLP.

Zuchora-Walske, Christine. We're the Center of the Universe! Science's Biggest Mistakes about Astronomy & Physics. 2014. (Science Gets It Wrong Ser.). (ENG., Illus.). 32p. (J). (gr. 4-6). lib. bdg. 26.65 (978-1-4677-3663-3(5), 5ba1d614-30d8-4032-bed1-0faf23fb880e, Lerner Pubns.) Lerner Publishing Group.

PHYSICS, ASTRONOMICAL

see Astrophysics

PHYSICS—EXPERIMENTS

Ace Academics, ed. Physics: A Whole Course in a Box! 2007. (Exambusters Ser.). 384p. (gr. 7-18). 12.95 (978-1-881374-87-9(4), Exambusters) Ace Academics, Inc.

Almukahhal, Raja. Physics Laboratory Experiments for the Gifted: Middle & High School. 2005. (Illus.). 90p. (978-0-910609-51-7(9)) Gifted Education Pr.

Bobrowsky, Matthew, et al. Using Physical Science Gadgets & Gizmos, Grades 9-12: Phenomenon-Based Learning. 2014. (ENG., Illus.). 169p. pap. 59.99 (978-1-936959-36-5(4), P234616) National Science Teachers Assn.

Bonnet, Robert L. & Keen, Dan. Home Run! Science Projects with Baseball & Softball, 1 vol. 2009. (Score! Sports Science Projects Ser.). (ENG., Illus.). 104p. (gr. 5-6). lib. bdg. 35.93 (978-0-7660-3365-8(1), dba14f41-8d17-48fa-a413-92e4bc29a7a0) Enslow Publishing, LLC.

Braun, Eric. Joe-Joe the Wizard Brews up Solids, Liquids, & Gases, 1 vol. Boyden, Robin, illus. 2012. (In the Science Lab Ser.). (ENG.). 24p. (J). (gr. k-3). pap. 9.95 (978-1-4048-7238-7(8), 118177, Picture Window Bks.) Capstone.

Brown, Jordan D. Science Stunts: Fun Feats of Physics. Owsley, Anthony, illus. 2016. 80p. (J). (gr. 3-7). 16.95 (978-1-62354-064-7(X)) Charlesbridge Publishing, Inc.

Cobb, Vicki. I Fall Down. Gorton, Julia, illus. 2004. (ENG.). 40p. (J). (gr. -1-3). 18.99 (978-0-688-17842-0(1), HarperCollins) HarperCollins Pubs.

Davies, Kate. What's Physics All About? 2010. (Science Stories Ser.). 96p. (YA). (gr. 3-18). pap. 10.99 (978-0-7945-2118-9(5), Usborne) EDC Publishing.

Farndon, John. Experimenting with Physics, 1 vol. 2009. (Experimenting with Science Ser.). (ENG.). 104p. (gr. 5-5). lib. bdg. 38.36 (978-0-7614-3929-5(3), bdfadb4c-4e0d-4c1e-82ef-7f54c8eb74ab) Cavendish Square Publishing LLC.

Gardner, Robert. Physics Experiments in Your Own Light Box, 1 vol. 2015. (Design, Build, Experiment Ser.). (ENG., Illus.). 128p. (gr. 7-7). lib. bdg. 38.93 (978-0-7660-6958-9(3), 5b695160-3928-48f7-b053-106f2fc21807) Enslow Publishing, LLC.

Gardner, Robert & Conklin, Joshua. Experiments for Future Engineers, 1 vol. 2016. (Experiments for Future STEM Professionals Ser.). (ENG.). 128p. (gr. 6-6). 38.93 (978-0-7660-7853-6(1), c2dd6370-5739-446b-9a3d-0cf16e8f454f) Enslow Publishing, LLC.

—Experiments for Future Physicists, 1 vol. 2016. (Experiments for Future STEM Professionals Ser.). (ENG.). 128p. (gr. 6-6). 38.93 (978-0-7660-7855-0(8), ca937114-9d1c-44a7-b5b9-894d03ceeee1) Enslow Publishing, LLC.

Gardner, Robert & Shortelle, Dennis. Slam Dunk! Science Projects with Basketball, 1 vol. 2009. (Score! Sports Science Projects Ser.). (ENG., Illus.). 104p. (gr. 5-6). lib. bdg. 35.93 (978-0-7660-3366-5(X), 3a1ecb7c-3db4-4917-9411-3322e74f5780) Enslow Publishing, LLC.

Gardner, Robert, et al. Ace Your Physical Science Project: Great Science Fair Ideas, 1 vol. 2009. (Ace Your Physics Science Project Ser.). (ENG., Illus.). 128p. (J). (gr. 5-6). lib. bdg. 35.93 (978-0-7660-3225-5(6), 9b932f2c-8b79-482c-a7a7-89f386b3f7ab) Enslow Publishing, LLC.

Goodstein, Madeline. Goal! Science Projects with Soccer, 1 vol. 2009. (Score! Sports Science Projects Ser.). (ENG., Illus.). 104p. (gr. 5-6). lib. bdg. 35.93 (978-0-7660-3106-7(3), 4e2da253-e69d-416f-a848-a59dec36c85f) Enslow Publishing, LLC.

Hollihan, Kerrie Logan. Isaac Newton & Physics for Kids: His Life & Ideas with 21 Activities. 2009. (For Kids Ser.: 30). (Illus.). 144p. (J). (gr. 4-7). pap. 20.99 (978-1-55652-778-4(0)) Chicago Review Pr., Inc.

Low, A. M. Popular Scientific Recreations - Science. 2006. 292p. per. (978-1-4067-9717-6(0), Hesperides Pr.) Read Bks.

McGraw Hill. Glencoe Physical IScience, Grade 8, Laboratory Activities Manual, Student Edition. 2004. (Physical Science Ser.). (ENG., Illus.). 216p. (gr. 8-8). stu. ed., per., lab manual ed. 8.44 (978-0-07-866084-9(X), 007866084X) McGraw-Hill Education.

Mercer, Bobby. Junk Drawer Physics: 50 Awesome Experiments That Don't Cost a Thing. 2014. (Junk Drawer Science Ser.: 1). (ENG., Illus.). 208p. (J). (gr. 4). pap. 16.99 (978-1-61374-920-3(1)) Chicago Review Pr., Inc.

Merrill, Amy French. Everyday Physical Science Experiments with Solids. 2009. (Science Surprises Ser.). 24p. (gr. 3-3). 42.50 (978-1-60853-064-9(7), PowerKids Pr.) Rosen Publishing Group, Inc., The.

Oxlade, Chris. Hands-on Science Projects: Physics. 2008. (ENG., Illus.). 64p. (J). (gr. 4-7). pap. 7.99 (978-1-84476-620-8(9)) Anness Publishing GBR. Dist: National Bk. Network.

Ryckman, Tatiana. Investigating Matter Through Modeling, 1 vol. 2019. (Science Investigators Ser.). (ENG.). 48p. (gr. 5-5). pap. 13.93 (978-1-5026-5249-2(8), fc4c65d7-1fe8-4df9-b53c-875ab9fd5bae) Cavendish Square Publishing LLC.

Slade, Suzanne. Cool Physics Activities for Girls. 2012. (Girls Science Club Ser.). (ENG.). 32p. (gr. 3-4). pap. 47.70 (978-1-4296-8520-7(4), Capstone Pr.); (J). pap. 8.19 (978-1-4296-8022-6(9), 118354) Capstone.

Taylor-Butler, Christine. Think Like a Scientist in the Gym. 2011. (Explorer Junior Library: Science Explorer Junior Ser.). (ENG., Illus.). 32p. (gr. 4-8). lib. bdg. 32.07 (978-1-61080-163-8(6), 201096) Cherry Lake Publishing.

Thiel, Kristin. Investigating Forces & Motion Through Modeling, 1 vol. 2019. (Science Investigators Ser.). (ENG.). 48p. (J). (gr. 5-5). pap. 13.93 (978-1-5026-5243-0(9), 8765dffd-7790-459e-a224-3f5aac28a4be) Cavendish Square Publishing LLC.

VanCleave, Janice. More of Janice VanCleave's Wild, Wacky, & Weird Physics Experiments, 1 vol. 2016. (Janice VanCleave's Wild, Wacky, & Weird Science Experiments Ser.). (ENG., Illus.). 64p. (J). (gr. 5-5). pap. 14.53 (978-1-4994-6553-2(X), 7838fae0-2783-4b81-a7e1-2e1762d9d3bf, Rosen Young Adult) Rosen Publishing Group, Inc., The.

VanCleave, Janice Pratt. Janice Vancleave's Crazy, Kooky, & Quirky Physics Experiments, 1 vol. 2018. (Janice VanCleave's Crazy, Kooky, & Quirky Science Experiments Ser.). (ENG.). 64p. (gr. 5-5). 38.47 (978-1-5081-8094-4(6), f84e0f2f-e70e-4cb4-a34a-7294e30236dc, Rosen Reference) Rosen Publishing Group, Inc., The.

—Janice VanCleave's Wild, Wacky, & Weird Physics Experiments, 1 vol. 2016. (Janice VanCleave's Wild, Wacky, & Weird Science Experiments Ser.). (ENG.). 64p. (J). (gr. 5-5). pap. 14.53 (978-1-4777-8977-3(4), 94f9a9a5-8103-4513-a7e3-2552962aa058, Rosen Reference) Rosen Publishing Group, Inc., The.

—Many More of Janice VanCleave's Wild, Wacky, & Weird Physics Experiments, 1 vol. 2017. (Janice VanCleave's Wild, Wacky, & Weird Science Experiments Ser.). (ENG., Illus.). 64p. (J). (gr. 5-5). pap. 14.53 (978-1-4994-3955-7(5), 7b8737be-45cd-405a-8c9d-3a174660eca6) Rosen Publishing Group, Inc., The.

Williams, Zella. Experiments with Physical Science. (Do-It-Yourself Science Ser.). 24p. (gr. 2-3). 2009. 47.90 (978-1-61512-189-2(7), PowerKids Pr.) 2007. (ENG., Illus.). (J). lib. bdg. 28.93 (978-1-4042-3659-2(7), 033aea5c-3b2b-4ab3-80d2-5f52678098b9) Rosen Publishing Group, Inc., The.

Wood, Alix. Backyard Physics Experiments, 1 vol. 2018. (Backyard Scientist Ser.). (ENG.). 32p. (gr. 3-3). 27.93 (978-1-5383-3745-5(2), a9b24d08-1b5b-4d14-92ab-cfc86bf95b7a, PowerKids Pr.) Rosen Publishing Group, Inc., The.

PHYSICS—HISTORY

Atkinson, Mary. Schockwave: the Earth Is Flat! 2007. (Shockwave: Science in Practice Ser.). (ENG., Illus.). 36p. (J). (gr. 3-5). 25.00 (978-0-531-17580-4(4), Children's Pr.) Scholastic Library Publishing.

Bendick, Jeanne. Archimedes & the Door of Science: Immortals of Science. 2011. 154p. (gr. 5-8). 41.95 (978-1-258-01488-9(2)) Literary Licensing, LLC.

Bodden, Valerie. Nuclear Physicist Chien-Shiung Wu. 2016. (STEM Trailblazer Bios Ser.). (ENG., Illus.). 32p. (J). (gr. 2-5). 26.65 (978-1-5124-0786-0(0), bc397cd0-0220-433e-8b54-50739c954f80, Lerner Pubns.) Lerner Publishing Group.

Brown Bear Books. Physical Sciences. 2009. (Great Scientists Ser.). (ENG.). 64p. (J). (gr. 8-11). 39.95 (978-1-933834-46-7(3), 16494) Brown Bear Bks.

Graham, Ian. You Wouldn't Want to Be Sir Isaac Newton! A Lonely Life You'd Rather Not Lead. 2013. (You Wouldn't Want To Ser.). lib. bdg. 20.80 (978-0-606-31632-3(9)) Turtleback.

Meyer, Susan. Isaac Newton, 1 vol. 2017. (Leaders of the Scientific Revolution Ser.). (ENG., Illus.). 112p. (J). (gr. 8-8). 38.80 (978-1-5081-7470-7(9), 66a1cb61-49f7-483d-9294-4756e72496bc, Rosen Young Adult) Rosen Publishing Group, Inc., The.

Nittany, Paul M. Isaac Newton, Vol. 11. 2018. (Scientists & Their Discoveries Ser.). (Illus.). 96p. (J). (gr. 7). lib. bdg. 34.60 (978-1-4222-4031-1(2)) Mason Crest.

Oxlade, Chris. Hands-on Science Projects: Physics. 2008. (ENG., Illus.). 64p. (J). (gr. 4-7). pap. 7.99 (978-1-84476-620-8(9)) Anness Publishing GBR. Dist: National Bk. Network.

Rain, Derrick. Albert Einstein, Vol. 11. 2018. (Scientists & Their Discoveries Ser.). (Illus.). 96p. (J). (gr. 7). lib. bdg. 34.60 (978-1-4222-4024-3(X)) Mason Crest.

Renn, Jürgen, ed. Einstein's Annalen Papers: The Complete Collection 1901 - 1922. 2005. (ENG., Illus.). 590p. 166.95 (978-3-527-40564-0(X), Wiley-VCH) Wiley, John & Sons, Inc.

Shoup, Kate. Quantum Mechanics, 1 vol. 2018. (Great Discoveries in Science Ser.). (ENG.). 128p. (gr. 9-9). 47.36 *(978-1-5026-4382-7(0),* dfcdaa75-ba66-4478-ab6b-880a36ca8e5c) Cavendish Square Publishing LLC.

PHYSICS, TERRESTRIAL

see Geophysics

PHYSICS—VOCATIONAL GUIDANCE

Ferguson, creator. Mathematics & Physics. 2nd rev. ed. 2008. (Ferguson's Careers in Focus Ser.). (ENG.). 202p. (gr. 6-12). 32.95 *(978-0-8160-7274-3(4),* P179081, Ferguson Publishing Company) Infobase Holdings, Inc.

Gagne, Tammy. Physicist. 2020. (J). *(978-1-7911-1692-7(2),* AV2 by Weigl) Weigl Pubs., Inc.

Indovino, Shaina. Women in Physics. Lee-Karlon, Ann, ed. 2013. (Major Women in Science Ser.: 10). 64p. (J). (gr. 7-18). 22.95 *(978-1-4222-2930-9(0))* Mason Crest.

Publishing, Ferguson, creator. Mathematics & Physics. 2003. (Ferguson's Careers in Focus Ser.). (ENG., Illus.). 192p. (gr. 6-12). 29.95 *(978-0-89434-413-8(7),* P053165, Ferguson Publishing Company) Infobase Holdings, Inc.

PHYSIOGRAPHY

see Physical Geography

PHYSIOLOGICAL CHEMISTRY

see Biochemistry

PHYSIOLOGISTS

Bosarge, Jerusha. Inventing Ott: The Legacy of Arthur C. Guyton. 2005. (Illus.). 120p. (J). (gr. 3-7). 10.95 *(978-1-893062-78-6(3))* Quail Ridge Pr., Inc.

Elford, Jole Shack. William Harvey & the Mechanics of the Heart. 2005. (Illus.). 141p. (YA). (gr. 6-10). reprint ed. 28.00 *(978-0-7567-9712-6(8))* DIANE Publishing Co.

Saunders, Barbara R. Ivan Pavlov: Exploring the Mysteries of Behavior, 1 vol. 2006. (Great Minds of Science Ser.). (ENG., Illus.). 112p. (gr. 5-6). lib. bdg. 35.93 *(978-0-7660-2506-6(3),* f32f06bd-23c8-462e-b4f6-042ab111870d) Enslow Publishing, LLC.

Tracy, Kathleen. Friedrich Miescher & the Story of Nucleic Acid. 2005. (Uncharted, Unexplored, & Unexplained Ser.). (Illus.). 48p. (J). (gr. 4-8). lib. bdg. 29.95 *(978-1-58415-369-6(5))* Mitchell Lane Pubs.

Yount, Lisa. William Harvey: Genius Discoverer of Blood Circulation, 1 vol. 2014. (Genius Scientists & Their Genius Ideas Ser.). (ENG.). 96p. (gr. 5-5). pap. 13.88 *(978-0-7660-6586-4(3),* b4cc6cf1-56c7-45d0-9986-84a18e3e2341) Enslow Publishing, LLC.

PHYSIOLOGY

see also Anatomy; Blood; Body Temperature; Bones; Cells; Digestion; Growth; Nervous System; Nutrition; Old Age; Reproduction; Respiration; Senses and Sensation

also names of organs, e.g. Heart

Abbott, Simon, illus. 100 Questions about the Human Body: And All the Answers Too! 2019. (100 Questions Ser.). (ENG.). 48p. (J). 7.99 *(978-1-4413-3101-4(8),* ea01589f-e28b-4ef0-b339-1865856b3f87) Peter Pauper Pr. Inc.

Amsel, Sheri. The Everything KIDS' Human Body Book: All You Need to Know about Your Body Systems - from Head to Toe! 2012. (Everything(r) Kids Ser.). (ENG., Illus.). 160p. pap. 9.99 *(978-1-4405-5659-3(8))* Adams Media Corp.

Andrews, Barbara. The Respiratory System. 2006. (J). pap. *(978-1-4108-6511-3(8))* Benchmark Education Co.

Arbuthnott, Gill. What Makes Your Body Work? Mones, Marc, illus. 2016. (ENG.). 64p. (J). *(978-0-7787-2241-0(4))* Crabtree Publishing Co.

Bailey, Gerry. Body & Health, 1 vol. 2009. (Simply Science Ser.). (ENG., Illus.). 32p. (J). (gr. 3-5). lib. bdg. 28.67 *(978-1-4339-0030-3(0),* 5c843853-9c63-44c6-964e-ba0cd95c9e23) Stevens, Gareth Publishing LLLP.

Bailey, Jacqui. What Happens When Your Heart Beats?, 1 vol. 2008. (How Your Body Works (2008) Ser.). (ENG., Illus.). 32p. (J). (gr. 3-3). lib. bdg. 30.27 *(978-1-4042-4430-6(1),* 98f7125e-6fa6-4096-81ac-83db2cce9f05, PowerKids Pr.) Rosen Publishing Group, Inc., The.

Ballard, Carol. How Your Body Moves, 1 vol. 2010. (Your Body at Work Ser.). (ENG.). 32p. (YA). (gr. 2-4). lib. bdg. 29.27 *(978-1-4339-4100-9(7),* 32636265-b7b0-4c92-aef1-05a09c05d789) Stevens, Gareth Publishing LLLP.

—How Your Brain Works, 1 vol. 2010. (Your Body at Work Ser.). (ENG.). 32p. (YA). (gr. 2-4). lib. bdg. 29.27 *(978-1-4339-4103-0(1),* d8b72d18-bb80-4dfa-8ff4-7f3f37446067) Stevens, Gareth Publishing LLLP.

—The Skeleton & Muscles. 2005. (Exploring the Human Body Ser.). (ENG., Illus.). 32p. (J). (gr. 3-6). lib. bdg. 27.80 *(978-0-7377-3022-7(6),* Greenhaven Pr., Inc.) Cengage Gale.

Benbow, Ann & Mably, Colin. Sensational Human Body Science Projects, 1 vol. 2010. (Real Life Science Experiments Ser.). (ENG., Illus.). 48p. (gr. 3-3). lib. bdg. 27.93 *(978-0-7660-3149-4(7),* f43b4cf3-f2e3-4245-87d5-828cf077ff6d) Enslow Publishing, LLC.

Bethune, Helen. Why Does My Heart Pump?, 1 vol. 2010. (Solving Science Mysteries Ser.). (ENG., Illus.). 24p. (gr. 4-5). (J). pap. 9.25 *(978-1-4488-0404-7(3),* 891e44e4-0bba-48c7-b72b-5391a4c60ade, PowerKids Pr.); (YA). 26.27 *(978-1-4488-0403-0(5),* 8df5a368-ff67-4611-a852-2a2f537f552e) Rosen Publishing Group, Inc., The.

Biskup, Agnieszka. Stopping Runaway Trains: Superman & the Science of Strength. 2016. (Superman Science Ser.). (ENG., Illus.). 32p. (J). (gr. 3-9). lib. bdg. 27.99 *(978-1-5157-0914-5(0),* 132212, Stone Arch Bks.) Capstone.

Braun, Eric. Awesome, Disgusting, Unusual Facts about the Human Body. 24p. (J). 2019. (Illus.). pap. *(978-1-68072-753-1(2))* 2018. (ENG.). (gr. 4-6). pap. 8.99 *(978-1-64466-306-6(6),* 12519, Hi Jinx) Black Rabbit Bks.

Brett, Flora. Your Circulatory System Works! 2015. (Your Body Systems Ser.). (ENG., Illus.). 24p. (J). (gr. 1-3). lib. bdg. 27.99 *(978-1-4914-2063-8(4),* 127541, Capstone Pr.) Capstone.

—Your Digestive System Works! 2015. (Your Body Systems Ser.). (ENG., Illus.). 24p. (J). (gr. 1-3). lib. bdg. 27.99 *(978-1-4914-2064-5(2),* 127542, Capstone Pr.) Capstone.

—Your Muscular System Works! 2015. (Your Body Systems Ser.). (ENG., Illus.). 24p. (J). (gr. 1-3). lib. bdg. 27.99 *(978-1-4914-2065-2(0),* 127543, Capstone Pr.) Capstone.

—Your Nervous System Works! 2015. (Your Body Systems Ser.). (ENG., Illus.). 24p. (J). (gr. 1-3). lib. bdg. 27.99 *(978-1-4914-2066-9(9),* 127544, Capstone Pr.) Capstone.

—Your Respiratory System Works! 2015. (Your Body Systems Ser.). (ENG., Illus.). 24p. (J). (gr. 1-3). lib. bdg. 27.99 *(978-1-4914-2067-6(7),* 127545, Capstone Pr.) Capstone.

Buchanan, Shelly. Animal Senses. 2015. (Science: Informational Text Ser.). (ENG.). 32p. (J). (gr. 3-5). pap. 11.99 *(978-1-4807-4678-7(9))* Teacher Created Materials, Inc.

Burstein, John. The Mighty Muscular & Skeletal Systems: How Do My Bones & Muscles Work? 2009. (Slim Goodbody's Body Buddies Ser.). (ENG., Illus.). 32p. (J). (gr. 3-5). lib. bdg. *(978-0-7787-4419-1(1))* Crabtree Publishing Co.

Calabresi, Linda. Human Body. 2008. (Insiders Ser.). (ENG., Illus.). 64p. (J). (gr. 3-7). 19.99 *(978-1-4169-3861-3(3),* Simon & Schuster Bks. For Young Readers) Simon & Schuster Bks. For Young Readers.

Capicola, Anthony. Spit & Phlegm. 2017. (Your Body at Its Grossest Ser.). 24p. (gr. 1-2). pap. 48.90 *(978-1-4824-6473-3(X))* Stevens, Gareth Publishing LLLP.

Centore, Michael. Water. 2017. (Illus.). 64p. (J). *(978-1-4222-3746-5(X))* Mason Crest.

Chambers, Catherine. See for Yourself: Body Science. 2010. (Crabtree Connections Ser.). (ENG.). 24p. (J). (gr. 3-6). *(978-0-7787-9950-4(6))*; pap. *(978-0-7787-9972-6(7))* Crabtree Publishing Co.

Chang, Heidi. The Skin on Your Body, 1 vol. 2014. (Let's Find Out! the Human Body Ser.). (ENG.). 32p. (J). (gr. 2-3). 26.06 *(978-1-62275-644-5(4),* 65bf5023-1670-455e-b071-52819e4e26ba, Britannica Educational Publishing) Rosen Publishing Group, Inc., The.

Claybourne, Anna. Smelly Farts & Other Body Horrors. 2014. (Disgusting & Dreadful Science Ser.). (ENG., Illus.). 32p. (J). (gr. 3-3). *(978-0-7787-1404-0(7))* Crabtree Publishing Co.

Cohen, Robert Z. The Stomach & Intestines in Your Body, 1 vol. 2014. (Let's Find Out! the Human Body Ser.). (ENG.). 32p. (J). (gr. 2-3). 26.06 *(978-1-62275-632-2(0),* 9e4d3f18-f613-4fce-b6a2-d35b937dcfda, Britannica Educational Publishing) Rosen Publishing Group, Inc., The.

Copons, Jaume & Copons, Jaume. Everything I Know about Poop. Gali, Merce & Gali, Merce, illus. 2018. (ENG.). 28p. (J). (gr. k-2). 12.95 *(978-0-2281-0083-6(6),* b0327fe1-7ef6-4f47-8d3e-9faa915df042) Firefly Bks., Ltd.

Crispin, Sam. Vomit! 2017. (Your Body at Its Grossest Ser.). 24p. (gr. 1-2). pap. 48.90 *(978-1-4824-6481-8(0))* Stevens, Gareth Publishing LLLP.

Daniels, Patricia. Ultimate Bodypedia: An Amazing Inside-Out Tour of the Human Body. 2014. (ENG.). 272p. (J). (gr. 3-7). lib. bdg. 33.90 *(978-1-4263-1722-4(0),* National Geographic Children's Bks.) Disney Publishing Worldwide.

deMarin, Layne. Everybody Moves. 2011. (Wonder Readers Fluent Level Ser.). (ENG.). 16p. (gr. -1-2). pap. 35.94 *(978-1-4296-8086-8(5),* Capstone Pr.) Capstone.

DK. First Human Body Encyclopedia. 2018. (DK First Reference Ser.). (ENG., Illus.). 128p. (J). (gr. 2-5). 17.99 *(978-1-4654-4348-9(7),* DK Children) Dorling Kindersley Publishing, Inc.

—Knowledge Encyclopedia Human Body! 2017. (DK Knowledge Encyclopedias Ser.). (ENG., Illus.). 208p. (J). (gr. 4-7). 24.99 *(978-1-4654-6239-8(2),* DK Children) Dorling Kindersley Publishing, Inc.

—Mi Primer Libro Del Cuerpo/My First Body Board Book. 2005. (My First Ser.).Tr. of My First Body Board Book. (Illus.). 36p. (J). (gr. -1 — 1). bds. 6.99 *(978-0-7566-1501-7(1),* DK Children) Dorling Kindersley Publishing, Inc.

—Pocket Genius: Human Body: Facts at Your Fingertips. 2016. (Pocket Genius Ser.: 10). (ENG., Illus.). 160p. (J). (gr. 3-7). pap. 6.99 *(978-1-4654-4588-9(9),* DK Children) Dorling Kindersley Publishing, Inc.

Emerson, Charles P. & Betts, George Herbert. Living at Our Best, Book: Habits of Right Living Series. 2011. 338p. 50.95 *(978-1-258-08164-5(4))* Literary Licensing, LLC.

Enslow, Brian. My Body, 1 vol. 2010. (All about My Body Ser.). (ENG., Illus.). 24p. (-1). pap. 10.35 *(978-1-59845-172-6(3),* a7ffed72-9a41-4dc3-86be-76d9114d28d0); (gr. -1-1). 25.27 *(978-0-7660-3811-0(4),* 9e24dbe6-2f48-46ee-83fe-c1281ab66ada) Enslow Publishing, LLC. (Enslow Publishing).

Farnsworth, Vesta J. The House We Live in or the Making of the Body. 2004. reprint ed. pap. 24.95 *(978-1-4179-2036-5(X))* Kessinger Publishing, LLC.

Felix, Rebecca. Keeping Cool in Summer. 2014. (21st Century Basic Skills Library: Let's Look at Summer Ser.). (ENG., Illus.). 24p. (J). (gr. k-3). 26.35 *(978-1-63137-597-2(0),* 205171) Cherry Lake Publishing.

Furgang, Kathy. My Brain. 2009. (My Body Ser.). 24p. (gr. 3-3). 42.50 *(978-1-61514-686-4(5),* PowerKids Pr.) Rosen Publishing Group, Inc., The.

Galvin, Laura Gates. Human Body A to Z. MacDonald, Judy, illus. 2012. (ENG.). 40p. 9.95 *(978-1-60727-296-0(2))* Soundprints.

Glass, Maya. The Jumping Book. 2009. (Let's Get Moving Ser.). 24p. (gr. k-k). 42.50 *(978-1-61514-228-6(2),* PowerKids Pr.) Rosen Publishing Group, Inc., The.

—The Jumping Book / Saltar. 2009. (Let's Get Moving / Diviértete en movimiento Ser.). (ENG & SPA.). 24p. (gr. k-1). 42.50 *(978-1-61514-234-7(7),* Editorial Buenas Letras) Rosen Publishing Group, Inc., The.

Goddard, Jolyon. Inside the Human Body, 1 vol. 2011. (Invisible Worlds Ser.). (ENG.). 48p. (gr. 4-4). 31.21 *(978-0-7614-4190-8(5),* bac1ae7e-9604-452a-a723-f2f78473d084) Cavendish Square Publishing LLC.

Gomdori Co & Han, Hyun-dong. Survive! Inside the Human Body, Vol. 2: The Circulatory System. 2013. (ENG., Illus.). 180p. (J). (gr. 2). pap. 17.95 *(978-1-59327-472-6(6))* No Starch Pr., Inc.

—Survive! Inside the Human Body, Vol. 3: The Nervous System. 2013. (ENG., Illus.). 184p. (J). (gr. 2). pap. 17.95 *(978-1-59327-473-3(4))* No Starch Pr., Inc.

Green, Jen. Inside Animals, 1 vol. 2011. (Invisible Worlds Ser.). (ENG.). 48p. (gr. 4-4). 31.21 *(978-0-7614-4195-3(6),* b441287e-76af-48d8-82ac-6501f1bfad70) Cavendish Square Publishing LLC.

Guerber, Hélène Adeline. Yourself & Your House Wonderful. 2012. 330p. pap. 13.50 *(978-1-936639-24-3(6))* St. Augustine Academy Pr.

Gunzi, Christane & Picthall, Chez. My Early Learning Library: My Body. Murrell, Deborah, ed. 2015. (ENG., Illus.). 34p. (J). bds. 7.99 *(978-1-906572-22-8(4))* Award Pubns. Ltd. GBR. Dist: Parkwest Pubns., Inc.

Hansen, Grace. Skeletal System. 2018. (Beginning Science: Body Systems Ser.). (ENG., Illus.). 24p. (J). (gr. -1-2). lib. bdg. 32.79 *(978-1-5321-8189-4(2),* 29851, Abdo Kids) ABDO Publishing Co.

Haslam, Andrew, et al. Body. (Make It Work! Ser.). (Illus.). 48p. (J). pap. 15.95 *(978-0-590-24333-9(0))*; pap. 7.99 *(978-0-590-24614-9(3))* Scholastic, Inc.

Hipp, Earl. Fighting Invisible Tigers: Stress Management for Teens. 4th ed. 2019. (ENG., Illus.). 144p. (J). pap. 14.99 *(978-1-63198-435-8(7),* 84358) Free Spirit Publishing Inc.

Holden, Arianne. It's Fun to Learn about My Body: A Busy Picture Book Full of Fabulous Facts & Things to Do! 2016. (Illus.). 32p. (J). (gr. -1-12). pap. 9.99 *(978-1-86147-730-9(9))* Anness Publishing, Inc.

Holden, Pam. Going Up, 1 vol. Hawley, Kelvin, illus. 2009. (Red Rocket Readers Ser.). (ENG.). 16p. (gr. -1-1). pap. *(978-1-877363-18-4(9),* Red Rocket Readers) Flying Start Bks.

Holmes, Kirsty Louise. Why Do I Poo? 2018. (Why Do I? Ser.). (Illus.). 24p. (J). (gr. 3-4). *(978-0-7787-5144-1(9))* Crabtree Publishing Co.

Hutmacher, Kimberly M. Your Nose Never Stops Growing & Other Cool Human Body Facts. 2019. (Mind-Blowing Science Facts Ser.). (ENG., Illus.). 32p. (J). (gr. 4-6). lib. bdg. 28.65 *(978-1-5435-5766-4(X),* 139722) Capstone.

Hyde, Natalie. Human Body Mysteries Revealed. 2010. (ENG., Illus.). 32p. (J). pap. *(978-0-7787-7430-3(9))*; (gr. 4-7). lib. bdg. *(978-0-7787-7415-0(5))* Crabtree Publishing Co.

Jennings, Ken. The Human Body. Lowery, Mike, illus. 2015. (Ken Jennings' Junior Genius Guides). (ENG.). 160p. (J). (gr. 3-5). pap. 9.99 *(978-1-4814-0173-9(4),* Little Simon) Little Simon.

Johnson, Rebecca L. Ultra-Organized Cell Systems. 2008. pap. 52.95 *(978-0-8225-9384-3(X))* Lerner Publishing Group.

—Ultra-Organized Cell Systems. Desrocher, Jack & Fairman, Jennifer, illus. 2007. (Microquests Ser.). (ENG.). 48p. (gr. 3-5). lib. bdg. 29.27 *(978-0-8225-7138-4(2),* Millbrook Pr.) Lerner Publishing Group.

Jones, Peter. The Complete Guide to the Human Body. 2015. (Illus.). 144p. (J). *(978-1-4351-6167-2(X))* Barnes & Noble, Inc.

Jones, Rebecca, illus. My Body. 2018. (First Explorers Ser.). (ENG.). 10p. (J). (— 1). bds. 8.95 *(978-1-4549-2942-0(1))* Sterling Publishing Co., Inc.

Kalman, Bobbie. Warm-Blooded or Cold-Blooded? 2008. (Big Science Ideas Ser.). (ENG., Illus.). 32p. (J). (gr. 1-4). pap. *(978-0-7787-3301-0(7))* Crabtree Publishing Co.

Kenney, Karen Latchana. Extreme Longevity: Discovering Earth's Oldest Organisms. 2018. (ENG., Illus.). 104p. (YA). (gr. 6-12). 37.32 *(978-1-5124-8372-7(9),* b3b547fc-4921-45c2-a6e2-72a8d836f162, Twenty-First Century Bks.) Lerner Publishing Group.

Kirk, Bill. The Ins & Outs of Air: The Sum of Our Parts Series. 2013. (GER., Illus.). 24p. pap. 10.95 *(978-1-61633-391-1(X))* Guardian Angel Publishing, Inc.

Kolpin, Molly. Why Do I Burp? 2015. (My Silly Body Ser.). (ENG., Illus.). 24p. (J). (gr. -1-2). lib. bdg. 27.32 *(978-1-4914-2105-5(3),* 127589, Capstone Pr.) Capstone.

—Why Do I Hiccup? 2015. (My Silly Body Ser.). (ENG., Illus.). 24p. (J). (gr. -1-2). lib. bdg. 27.32 *(978-1-4914-2106-2(1),* 127588, Capstone Pr.) Capstone.

—Why Do I Sneeze? 2015. (My Silly Body Ser.). (ENG., Illus.). 24p. (J). (gr. -1-2). lib. bdg. 27.32 *(978-1-4914-2108-6(8),* 127591, Capstone Pr.) Capstone.

—Why Do I Yawn? 2015. (My Silly Body Ser.). (ENG., Illus.). 24p. (J). (gr. -1-2). lib. bdg. 27.32 *(978-1-4914-2107-9(X),* 127590, Capstone Pr.) Capstone.

Lawrence, Ellen. Wet, Blue, & Good for You. 2016. (Drip, Drip, Drop: Earth's Water Ser.). (ENG., Illus.). 24p. (J). (gr. -1-3). 26.99 *(978-1-943553-25-9(4))* Bearport Publishing Co., Inc.

Lennon, Liz. Our Special World: My Body. 2018. (Our Special World Ser.). (ENG., Illus.). 24p. (J). (gr. -1-k). pap. 9.99 *(978-1-4451-4895-3(1),* Franklin Watts) Hachette Children's Group GBR. Dist: Hachette Bk. Group.

Libra, Anna. Why Does My Head Hurt? An Inside Look at the Nervous System. 2003. (J). pap. *(978-1-58417-065-5(4))* Lake Street Pubs.

—Why Does My Stomach Ache? An Inside Look at the Digestive System. 2003. (J). lib. bdg. *(978-1-58417-005-1(0))* Lake Street Pubs.

Lowell, Barbara. Bodily Functions. 2018. (Amazing Human Body Ser.). (ENG.). 32p. (gr. 2-7). 9.95 *(978-1-68072-681-7(1))*; (J). (gr. 4-6). pap. 9.99 *(978-1-64466-234-2(5),* 12195); (Illus.). (J). (gr. 4-6). lib. bdg. *(978-1-68072-387-8(1),* 12194) Black Rabbit Bks. (Bolt).

—Les Fonctions Corporelles. 2018. (incroyable Corps Humain Ser.). (FRE.). 32p. (J). (gr. 4-6). *(978-1-77092-447-5(7),* 12438, Bolt) Black Rabbit Bks.

—Las Funciones Corporales. 2018. (Asombroso Cuerpo Humano Ser.). (SPA., Illus.). 32p. (J). (gr. 4-6). lib. bdg. *(978-1-68072-957-3(8),* 12420, Bolt) Black Rabbit Bks.

Macaulay, David. The Way We Work. 2008. (ENG., Illus.). 336p. (J). (gr. 5-7). 35.00 *(978-0-618-23378-6(4),* 590582, Clarion Bks.) HarperCollins Pubs.

Margulies, Sheldon. The Fascinating Body: How It Works. 2004. (ENG., Illus.). 424p. (J). pap. 43.95 *(978-1-57886-076-0(8))* Scarecrow Pr., Inc.

Marsico, Katie. I Burp. 2015. (Tell Me Why Library). (ENG., Illus.). 24p. (gr. 2-5). 29.21 *(978-1-63188-992-9(3),* 205880) Cherry Lake Publishing.

Martin, Ruth. Little Explorers: My Amazing Body. Sanders, Allan, illus. 2015. (Little Explorers Ser.). (ENG.). 18p. (J). (gr. -1-3). 10.99 *(978-1-4998-0040-1(1))* Little Bee Books Inc.

Martineau, Susan. Respecting Others. 2011. (Positive Steps Ser.). (ENG.). 32p. (J). (gr. 2-5). lib. bdg. 31.35 *(978-1-59920-493-2(2),* 19342, Smart Apple Media) Black Rabbit Bks.

Mason, Paul. Your Growling Guts & Dynamic Digestive System. 2015. (Your Brilliant Body! Ser.). (ENG., Illus.). 32p. (J). (gr. 4-5). lib. bdg. *(978-0-7787-2197-0(3))* Crabtree Publishing Co.

Maynard, Christopher, et al. How Your Body Works. 2004. (Knowledge Masters Plus Ser.). (Illus.). 32p. (YA). pap. incl. cd-rom *(978-1-903954-44-7(4),* Pavilion Children's Books) Pavilion Bks.

Meister, Cari. Totally Wacky Facts about the Human Body. 2016. (Mind Benders Ser.). (ENG., Illus.). 112p. (J). (gr. 3-6). lib. bdg. 23.99 *(978-1-4914-8359-6(8),* 130826, Capstone Pr.) Capstone.

Miller, Derek. Eyes, Ears, & Noses, 1 vol. 2018. (Animal Structures Ser.). (ENG.). 24p. (J). (gr. 1-1). pap. 9.22 *(978-1-5026-4180-9(1),* 0126d668-9e73-4ab6-9472-4cc62dadd307) Cavendish Square Publishing LLC.

My Body Does Strange Stuff!, 12 vols. 2013. (My Body Does Strange Stuff! Ser.). 24p. (J). (gr. 1-2). (ENG.). 151.62 *(978-1-4339-9673-3(1),* 865b90b3-4674-43e8-ad3c-ab72732d4f97); pap. 48.90 *(978-1-4339-9763-1(0))*; pap. 293.40 *(978-1-4339-9764-8(9))* Stevens, Gareth Publishing LLLP.

Nagelhout, Ryan. The Heart & Blood in Your Body, 1 vol. 2014. (Let's Find Out! the Human Body Ser.). (ENG.). 32p. (J). (gr. 2-3). 26.06 *(978-1-62275-640-7(1),* 77894d9a-817d-43c3-ae06-4792237da99f, Britannica Educational Publishing) Rosen Publishing Group, Inc., The.

—How Pigeons & Other Animals Sense Magnetic Fields, 1 vol. 2015. (Superior Animal Senses Ser.). (ENG., Illus.). 24p. (J). (gr. 3-4). pap. 9.25 *(978-1-4994-0992-5(3),* 635d5109-0afb-41ee-9280-02a9f566a421, PowerKids Pr.) Rosen Publishing Group, Inc., The.

Parker, Steve. Human Body. 2013. (Illus.). 48p. (J). *(978-1-4351-5091-1(0))* Barnes & Noble, Inc.

—What about the Human Body. 2008. 40p. pap. *(978-1-84810-070-1(1))* Miles Kelly Publishing, Ltd.

Perish, Patrick. Disgusting Bodily Functions. 2014. (Totally Disgusting Ser.). (ENG.). 24p. (J). (gr. 3-7). 26.95 *(978-1-62617-129-9(7),* Epic Bks.) Bellwether Media.

Pimentel, Annette Bay. My Stomach. Alberini, Teresa, illus. 2015. (Inside My Body Ser.). (ENG.). 24p. (J). (gr. 1-4). lib. bdg. 19.95 *(978-1-60753-758-8(3),* 15288) Amicus.

Podesto, Martine. The Body, 1 vol. 2008. (My Science Notebook Ser.). (ENG., Illus.). 104p. (YA). (gr. 4-5). lib. bdg. 33.67 *(978-0-8368-9212-3(7),* 63c0610b-0e9e-45b9-8329-89604dfbf439) Stevens, Gareth Publishing LLLP.

Rake, Jody Sullivan. Speed, Strength, & Stealth: Animal Weapons & Defenses. 2012. (Animal Weapons & Defenses Ser.). (ENG.). 32p. (gr. 1-2). pap. 47.70 *(978-1-4296-8503-0(4),* Capstone Pr.); (J). (gr. 3-9). pap. 8.10 *(978-1-4296-8010-3(5),* 118342) Capstone.

Rice, Christopher. My First Body Book. (Illus.). (J). pap. 22.99 *(978-0-590-24611-8(9))* Scholastic, Inc.

Riehecky, Janet. Teeth, Claws, & Jaws: Animal Weapons & Defenses, 1 vol. 2012. (Animal Weapons & Defenses Ser.). (ENG.). 32p. (J). (gr. 3-9). pap. 8.10 *(978-1-4296-8012-7(1),* 118344) Capstone.

Riley, Ange Belle Chandler. The House in Which You Live. 2005. reprint ed. pap. 24.95 *(978-1-4191-3533-0(3))* Kessinger Publishing, LLC.

Rinder, Lenore. Bones & Skin. Oszkay, Zulay, tr. Date not set.Tr. of Huesos y Piel. (J). (gr. -1-7). pap. 5.00 *(978-0-9678778-1-5(4),* 002) Child Scope Productions.

Ripley's Believe It Or Not! Ripley Twists: Human Body PORTRAIT EDN. 2014. (Twist Ser.). (ENG., Illus.). 48p. (J). 12.95 *(978-1-893951-84-6(7))* Ripley Entertainment, Inc.

Romain, Trevor & Verdick, Elizabeth. Stress Can Really Get on Your Nerves. Mark, Steve, illus. rev. ed. 2018. (Laugh & Learn(r) Ser.). (ENG.). 104p. (J). (gr. 3-8). pap. 10.99 *(978-1-63198-245-3(1),* 82453) Free Spirit Publishing Inc.

Rose, Simon. The Brain: All about the Nervous System. 2017. (Illus.). 32p. (J). *(978-1-5105-0893-4(7))* SmartBook Media, Inc.

—Lungs: All about the Respiratory System. 2017. (Illus.). 32p. (J). *(978-1-5105-0896-5(1))* SmartBook Media, Inc.

—Stomach: All about the Digestive System. 2017. (Illus.). 32p. (J). *(978-1-5105-0887-3(2))* SmartBook Media, Inc.

Royston, Angela. What Do You Know about Human & Animal Bodies?, 1 vol. 2017. (Test Your Science Skills Ser.). (ENG.). 32p. (J). (gr. 5-5). 29.27 *(978-1-5383-2213-0(7),* 8db546ad-7725-450d-9370-eabff5026844); pap. 12.75 *(978-1-5383-2306-9(0),* 017fe1bc-681f-4fe0-9245-3473a4949623) Rosen Publishing Group, Inc., The. (PowerKids Pr.).

Rushworth, Gary. Body Systems: Human Cells: Text Pairs. 2008. (Bridges/Navigators Ser.). (J). (gr. 5). 81.00 *(978-1-4108-8406-0(6))* Benchmark Education Co.

—Body Systems: Skeletal & Muscular: Text Pairs. 2008. (Bridges/Navigators Ser.). (J). (gr. 5). 81.00 *(978-1-4108-8408-4(2))* Benchmark Education Co.

Russo, Kristin J. Human Body Facts or Fibs. 2018. (Facts or Fibs? Ser.). (ENG., Illus.). 32p. (J). (gr. 3-9). pap. 7.95 *(978-1-5435-0207-7(5),* 137129, Capstone Pr.) Capstone.

Samuels, Charlie. Astonishing Bodies. 2012. (ENG.). 32p. (J). *(978-0-7787-8006-9(6))*; pap. *(978-0-7787-8011-3(2))* Crabtree Publishing Co.

Scherrer, David L. & Klepacki, Linda M. Celebrating Changes: Everything You Always Wanted to Know about Sex in Middle School. 2004. (Worth Waiting for Ser.). 176p. (YA). (gr. 11-18). 19.99 *(978-0-7814-4077-6(7),* 0781440777) Cook, David C.

Schnell, Lisa K. Human Body Systems. 2018. (Human Machine Ser.). (ENG., Illus.). 32p. (J). (gr. 3-6). lib. bdg. 32.79 *(978-1-64156-433-5(4),* 9781641564335) Rourke Educational Media.

Scholastic. Knees & Toes! (Rookie Toddler) 2009. (Rookie Toddler Ser.). (ENG., Illus.). 14p. (J). (gr. -1 — 1). bds. 6.95

P Q R

(978-0-531-24546-0(2), Children's Pr.) Scholastic Library Publishing.

Seidlitz, Lauri. Human Body. 2007. (Life Science (Weigl Hardcover) Ser.). (Illus.). 32p. (J). (gr. 4-7). lib. bdg. 26.00 *(978-1-59036-705-6(7))*; per. 9.95 *(978-1-59036-706-3(5))* Weigl Pubs., Inc.

Shaffer, Jody Jensen. My Heart. Alberini, Teresa, illus. 2015. (Inside My Body Ser.). (ENG.). 24p. (J). (gr. 1-4). lib. bdg. 19.95 *(978-1-60753-755-7(9)*, 15285) Amicus.

—My Lungs. Alberini, Teresa, illus. 2015. (Inside My Body Ser.). (ENG.). 24p. (J). (gr. 1-4). lib. bdg. 19.95 *(978-1-60753-756-4(7)*, 15286) Amicus.

—My Muscles. Alberini, Teresa, illus. 2015. (Inside My Body Ser.). (ENG.). 24p. (J). (gr. 1-4). lib. bdg. 19.95 *(978-1-60753-757-1(5)*, 15287) Amicus.

Shier, David N., et al. Hole's Essentials of Human Anatomy & Physiology with OLC bind-In Card. 8th rev. ed. 2003. 640p. (J). (gr. 6-12). 123.75 *(978-0-07-293224-9(4)*, 9780072932249) Glencoe/McGraw-Hill.

Silver, Donald M. & Wynne, Patricia J. The Body Book. 2008. (ENG.). 128p. (gr. 3-6). pap. 18.99 *(978-0-545-04873-6(7)*, Teaching Resources) Scholastic, Inc.

Silverstein, Alvin & Silverstein, Virginia. Snot, Poop, Vomit, & More: The Yucky Body Book, 1 vol. 2010. (Yucky Science Ser.). (ENG., Illus.). 48p. (gr. 5-7). 27.93 *(978-0-7660-3318-4(X)*, 34b8304a-020d-4522-a074-1614fcc6195d) Enslow Publishing, LLC.

Slack, Michael H., illus. Gross Body Science, 5 vols., Set. Incl. Clot & Scab: Gross Stuff about Your Scrapes, Bumps, & Bruises. Lew, Kristi. lib. bdg. 29.27 *(978-0-8225-8965-5(6))*; Crust & Spray: Gross Stuff in Your Eyes, Ears, Nose, & Throat. Larsen, C. S. lib. bdg. 29.27 *(978-0-8225-8964-8(8))*; Hawk & Drool: Gross Stuff in Your Mouth. Donovan, Sandy. lib. bdg. 29.27 *(978-0-8225-8966-2(4))*; Itch & Ooze: Gross Stuff on Your Skin. Lew, Kristi & Lewandowski, Laura C. lib. bdg. 29.27 *(978-0-8225-8963-1(X))*; Rumble & Spew: Gross Stuff in Your Stomach & Intestines. Donovan, Sandy. lib. bdg. 29.27 *(978-0-8225-8899-3(4))*; (Illus.). 48p. (gr. 3-5). 2009. Set lib. bdg. 146.35 *(978-0-8225-8898-6(6)*, Millbrook Pr.) Lerner Publishing Group.

Smith, Sian & Guillain, Charlotte. How Does My Body Work?, 1 vol. 2011. (ENG.). 24p. (J). (gr. -1-1). 26.65 *(978-1-4329-5349-2(4)*, 116061, Heinemann) Capstone.

Sohn, Emily. Human Body. 2019. (IScience Ser.). (ENG., Illus.). 32p. (J). (gr. 3-4). pap. 13.26 *(978-1-68404-379-8(4))* Norwood Hse. Pr.

Spilsbury, Louise. Head-to-Toe Body Questions. 2010. (Crabtree Connections Ser.). (ENG.). 24p. (J). (gr. 3-6). *(978-0-7787-9954-2(9))*; pap. *(978-0-7787-9976-4(X))* Crabtree Publishing Co.

—What Is the Structure of an Animal?, 1 vol., 1. 2013. (Let's Find Out! Life Science Ser.). (ENG.). 32p. (gr. 2-3). 27.04 *(978-1-62275-246-1(5)*, 287e9b80-28bb-41bc-a250-34ddba45ec22) Rosen Publishing Group, Inc., The.

Steele, Philip. My Body. 2009. (Now We Know About... Ser.). (ENG., Illus.). 24p. (J). (gr. k-3). pap. *(978-0-7787-4738-3(7))* Crabtree Publishing Co.

Steele, Philip & Goldsmith, Mike. My Body. 2009. (ENG., Illus.). 24p. (J). (gr. k-4). lib. bdg. *(978-0-7787-4721-5(2))* Crabtree Publishing Co.

Stewart, Melissa. How Is My Brain Like a Supercomputer? And Other Questions about the Human Body. Bull, Peter, illus. 2014. (Good Question! Ser.). (ENG.). 32p. (J). (gr. 1). pap. 5.95 *(978-1-4549-0681-0(2))* Sterling Publishing Co., Inc.

Stout, Frankie. Nature's Strongest Animals. (Extreme Animals Ser.). 24p. (gr. 2-3). 2009. 42.50 *(978-1-61512-382-7(2))* 2008. (ENG., Illus.). (J). lib. bdg. 26.27 *(978-1-4042-4158-9(2)*, 25a9ab25-dabf-4d27-8301-56e761dc443a) Rosen Publishing Group, Inc., The. (PowerKids Pr.).

Swanson, Jennifer. Building with Poop, 1 vol. 2017. (Power of Poop Ser.). (ENG.). 32p. (gr. 3-4). pap. 11.52 *(978-0-7660-9108-5(2)*, e815bab0-7468-415b-a1e0-eacd992e53a7) Enslow Publishing, LLC.

Taylor, Julia V. The Body Image Workbook for Teens: Activities to Help Girls Develop a Healthy Body Image in an Image-Obsessed World. 2014. (ENG.). 200p. (YA). (gr. 6-12). pap. 21.95 *(978-1-62625-018-5(9)*, 30185) New Harbinger Pubns.

Tu Cuerpo: Conoce Por Dentro. 2007. (Titles in Spanish Ser.). (SPA., Illus.). 15p. (J). (gr. -1). bds. 12.99 *(978-0-7460-8386-4(6)*, Usborne) EDC Publishing.

Tyler, Madeline. Why Do I Sneeze? 2018. (Why Do I? Ser.). (Illus.). 24p. (J). (gr. 3-4). *(978-0-7787-5145-8(7))* Crabtree Publishing Co.

Walker, Denise. Cells & Life Processes. 2007. (Basic Biology Ser.). (Illus.). 48p. (YA). (gr. 5-9). lib. bdg. 34.25 *(978-1-58340-988-6(2))* Black Rabbit Bks.

Walker, Richard. Human Body. 2006. (Kingfisher Knowledge Ser.). (Illus.). 64p. (J). *(978-0-7534-1317-3(5)*, Kingfisher) Roaring Brook Pr.

Walliman, Dominic. Professor Astro Cat's Human Body Odyssey. Newman, Ben, illus. 2018. (ENG.). 64p. (J). (gr. 2-5). 24.00 *(978-1-911171-91-1(7))* Flying Eye Bks. GBR. Dist: Penguin Random Hse. LLC.

Way, Jennife. The Hopping Book / Brincar en un Pie. 2009. (Let's Get Moving / Diviértete en movimiento Ser.). (SPA.). 24p. (gr. k-1). 42.50 *(978-1-61514-233-0(9)*, Editorial Buenas Letras) Rosen Publishing Group, Inc., The.

Way, Jennifer. The Hopping Book. 2009. (Let's Get Moving Ser.). 24p. (gr. k-k). 42.50 *(978-1-61514-227-9(4)*, PowerKids Pr.) Rosen Publishing Group, Inc., The.

World Book, Inc. Staff, contrib. by. The Digestive & Urinary Systems. 2013. (J). *(978-0-7166-1843-0(5))* World Bk., Inc.

—Explore & Learn-Me & My Body. 2008. (J). *(978-0-7166-3021-0(4))* World Bk., Inc.

—The Human Body. 2019. (Illus.). 96p. (J). *(978-0-7166-3728-8(6))* World Bk., Inc.

—My Body. 2007. (J). *(978-0-7166-7727-7(X))* World Bk., Inc.

—The Respiratory System. 2013. (Illus.). 32p. (J). *(978-0-7166-1847-8(8))* World Bk., Inc.

Wynne, Patricia J. & Silver, Donald M. My First Human Body Book. 2009. (Dover Science for Kids Coloring Bks.). (ENG., Illus.). 32p. (J). (gr. 1-5). pap. 3.99 *(978-0-486-46821-1(6)*, 468216) Dover Pubns., Inc.

Zelinger, Laurie & Zelinger, Jordan. Please Explain Anxiety to Me! Simple Biology & Solutions for Children & Parents. Sabella, Elisa, illus. 2010. 38p. 32.95 *(978-1-61599-051-1(8))*; 40p. pap. 21.95 *(978-1-61599-029-0(1))* Loving Healing Pr., Inc.

PHYSIOLOGY, COMPARATIVE

Adamson, Heather. Animals with Speed. 2010. (Amicus Readers. Our Animal World (Level 1) Ser.). (ENG.). 24p. (J). (gr. k-2). lib. bdg. 25.65 *(978-1-60753-007-7(4)*, 17162) Amicus.

Bedoyere, Camilla & Bedoyere, Camilla. Fastest & Slowest. 2010. (Animal Opposites Ser.). (ENG., Illus.). 32p. (J). (gr. -1-3). pap. 5.95 *(978-1-55407-809-7(1)*, 59ccdcef-29bb-4aa0-ae05-48ce7fe86876) Firefly Bks., Ltd.

PHYSIOLOGY OF PLANTS

see Plant Physiology

PHYTOGEOGRAPHY

see Plant Distribution

PIANISTS

Batten, Jack. Oscar Peterson: The Man & His Jazz. 2012. (Illus.). 192p. (J). (gr. 5). 19.95 *(978-1-77049-269-1(0)*, Tundra Bks.) Tundra Bks. CAN. Dist: Penguin Random Hse. LLC.

Engle, Margarita. Dancing Hands: How Teresa Carreño Played the Piano for President Lincoln. López, Rafael & López, Rafael, illus. 2019. (ENG.). 40p. (J). (gr. -1-3). 18.99 *(978-1-4814-8740-5(X))* Simon & Schuster Children's Publishing.

Harrah, Madge. Blind Boone: Piano Prodigy. 2004. (Trailblazers Biographies Ser.). (Illus.). 112p. (J). (gr. 5-9). lib. bdg. 30.60 *(978-1-57505-057-7(9))* Lerner Publishing Group.

Kaufmann, Anne. Glenn Gould: Sketches of Solitude. Koci, Rudin, illus. 2013. *(978-0-9868657-9-4(6))* Brownridge Publishing.

Lang Lang, Lang. Lang Lang: Playing with Flying Keys. 2010. 256p. (J). (gr. 3-7). mass mkt. 7.99 *(978-0-440-42284-6(1)*, Laurel Leaf) Random Hse. Children's Bks.

Shichtman, Sandra H. & Indenbaum, Dorothy. The Joy of Creation: The Story of Clara Schumann. 2011. (Classical Composers Ser.). (Illus.). 159p. lib. bdg. 28.95 *(978-1-59935-123-0(4))* Reynolds, Morgan Inc.

PIANISTS—FICTION

Beard, Sarah. Porcelain Keys. 2014. pap. 15.99 *(978-1-4621-1396-5(6)*, Horizon Pubs.) Cedar Fort, Inc./CFI Distribution.

Blake, Ashley Herring. How to Make a Wish. 2018. (ENG.). 352p. (YA). (gr. 9). pap. 11.99 *(978-1-328-86932-6(6)*, 1696697, Clarion Bks.) HarperCollins Pubs.

—How to Make a Wish. 2018. lib. bdg. 20.85 *(978-0-606-40996-4(3))* Turtleback.

Coveleskie, Sally, et al. Henry the Steinway & the Piano Recital. Friedman, Laura, illus. 2003. (Henry the Steinway Ser.: Vol. 1). 32p. (J). (gr. k-3). *(978-1-931721-05-9(X))* Night Heron Media.

de Brunhoff, Laurent. Babar Raconte le Pianiste. (Babar Ser.). (FRE., Illus.). 48p. (J). (gr. -1-3). 19.95 *(978-0-7859-8822-9(X))* French & European Pubns., Inc.

Hunt, Julie. KidGlovz. Newman, Dale, illus. 2017. (ENG.). 288p. (J). (gr. 3-7). 19.99 *(978-1-74237-852-7(8))* Allen & Unwin AUS. Dist: Independent Pubs. Group.

Perdue, Gillian. Conor's Concert. Connor, Michael, illus. 2003. (Pandas Ser.: 26). (ENG.). 64p. (J). pap. 11.00 *(978-0-86278-847-6(1))* O'Brien Pr., Ltd., The IRL. Dist: Casemate Pubs. & Bk. Distributors, LLC.

Weston, Rhonda. Playing to Distraction. 2011. 48p. pap. 16.95 *(978-1-4560-4076-5(6))* America Star Bks.

Zarr, Sara. The Lucy Variations. 2014. (ENG.). 336p. (YA). (gr. 7-17). pap. 17.99 *(978-0-316-20500-9(1))* Little, Brown Bks. for Young Readers.

PIANO

Barden, Christine H., et al. Music for Little Mozarts Little Mozarts Perform the Nutcracker: 8 Favorites Form Tchaikovsky's Nutcracker Suite. 2007. (Music for Little Mozarts Ser.). (ENG.). 24p. (J). pap. 7.99 *(978-0-7390-4822-1(8))* Alfred Publishing Co., Inc.

Congratulations: Grade 2 Piano. 9.95 *(978-1-85909-813-4(4)*, Warner Bros. Pubns.) Alfred Publishing Co., Inc.

Ganeri, Anita. Pianos & Keyboards. 2011. (ENG., Illus.). 32p. (J). pap. 10.95 *(978-1-77092-031-6(5))* Saunders Bk. Co. CAN. Dist: RiverStream Publishing.

Green, Dan & Harrod, Elisa. How to Improve at Playing Piano. 2010. (ENG.). 48p. (J). pap. *(978-0-7787-3601-1(6))*; lib. bdg. *(978-0-7787-3579-3(6))* Crabtree Publishing Co.

Healy, Nick. The Piano. 2005. (What in the World Ser.). (Illus.). 48p. (J). (gr. 5-9). lib. bdg. 21.95 *(978-1-58341-376-0(6)*, Creative Education) Creative Co., The.

Liszt, Franz. Danse Macabre & Other Piano Transcriptions. Glover, Daniel, ed. 2013. (Dover Classical Piano Music Ser.). (ENG.). 208p. pap. 16.95 *(978-0-486-49731-0(3)*, 497313) Dover Pubns., Inc.

Phoenix Books Staff, illus. Thomas' Piano Book. 2014. 14p. (J). bds. 12.98 *(978-1-4508-6584-5(4)*, 1450865844) Phoenix International Publications, Inc.

Piano Accompaniment. 2003. (Share the Music Ser.). (gr. k-18). *(978-0-02-295579-3(8))*; (gr. 1-18). *(978-0-02-295580-9(1))*; (gr. 2-18). *(978-0-02-295581-6(X))*; (gr. 3-18). *(978-0-02-295582-3(8))*; (gr. 4-18). *(978-0-02-295583-0(6))*; (gr. 5-18). *(978-0-02-295584-7(4))*; (gr. 6-18). *(978-0-02-295585-4(2))* Macmillan/McGraw-Hill Schl. Div.

Riggs, Kate. Piano. 2014. (Making Music Ser.). (ENG.). 24p. (J). (gr. 1-4). pap. 9.99 *(978-0-89812-948-9(6)*, 21534, Creative Paperbacks) Creative Co., The.

Rusch, Elizabeth. The Music of Life: Bartolomeo Cristofori & the Invention of the Piano. Priceman, Marjorie, illus. 2017. (ENG.). 48p. (J). (gr. -1-3). 19.99 *(978-1-4814-4484-2(0))* Simon & Schuster Children's Publishing.

Sebba, Jane. Abracadabra Piano 3 Vol. 3: Graded Pieces for the Young Pianist. 2004. (ENG., Illus.). 48p. pap. 7.95 *(978-0-7136-3726-7(9)*, 93115, A&C Black) Bloomsbury Publishing Plc GBR. Dist: Consortium Bk. Sales & Distribution.

PIANO—INSTRUCTION AND STUDY

Alexander, Dennis, et al. Alfred's Premier Piano Course: Performance 3. Manus, Morton, ed. 2007. (Alfred's Premier Piano Course Ser.). (Illus.). 32p. pap. 6.95 *(978-0-7390-4743-9(4))* Alfred Publishing Co., Inc.

—Premier Piano Course Assignment Book: Level 1A-6. 2007. (Premier Piano Course Ser.). (ENG.). 80p. pap. 6.95 *(978-0-7390-4877-1(5))* Alfred Publishing Co., Inc.

—Premier Piano Course Lesson Book, Bk 3. 2007. (Premier Piano Course Ser.: Bk 3). (ENG., Illus.). 48p. pap. 8.99 *(978-0-7390-4639-5(X))* Alfred Music.

—Premier Piano Course Technique, Bk 1A, Bk. 1A. 2008. (Premier Piano Course Ser.: Bk 1A). (ENG., Illus.). 32p. pap. 9.99 *(978-0-7390-4543-5(1))* Alfred Publishing Co., Inc.

—Premier Piano Course Theory, Bk 3. 2007. (Premier Piano Course Ser.: Bk 3). (ENG., Illus.). 32p. pap. 9.99 *(978-0-7390-4750-7(7))* Alfred Publishing Co., Inc.

Barden, Christine H., et al. My First Pop Songs, Bk 1: Eleven Favorite Pop Songs for the Beginning Pianist. 2008. (My First... Ser.: Bk 1). (ENG., Illus.). 24p. pap. 8.99 *(978-0-7390-5101-6(6))* Alfred Publishing Co., Inc.

—My First Pop Songs, Bk 2: Eleven Favorite Pop Songs for the Beginning Pianist. 2008. (My First... Ser.: Bk 2). (ENG., Illus.). 24p. pap. 7.95 *(978-0-7390-5102-3(4))* Alfred Publishing Co., Inc.

Barden, Christine H., et al. Alfred's Kid's Piano Course Notespeller, Bk 1 And 2: Music Reading Activities That Make Learning Even Easier! 2012. (Alfred's Kid's Piano Course Ser.: Bk 1 & 2). (ENG.). 48p. pap. 8.99 *(978-0-7390-9245-3(6))* Alfred Publishing Co., Inc.

Burnam, Edna Mae. Step by Step Piano Course - Book 6. 2005. (ENG.). 64p. pap. 10.99 *(978-1-4234-3591-4(5)*, 00414847) Willis Music Co.

—Write It Right - Book 5 Bk. 5: Written Lessons Designed to Correlate Exactly with Edna Mae Burnam's Step by Step/Later Elementary. 2005. (ENG., Illus.). 24p. pap. 5.99 *(978-1-4234-3603-4(2)*, 00404477) Willis Music Co.

Celik, Vladislav. You Too Can Play Piano & Organ Without Teacher, Vol. 1. (Music Instructional Ser.). (Illus.). 96p. (J). pap. 12.95 incl. audio *(978-0-9624062-1-8(X))* Music Institute of California.

Dyke, Sylvie. Piano Music Made Easy. 2012. (illus.). 28p. pap. *(978-1-78148-794-5(4))* Grosvenor Hse. Publishing Ltd.

Elliot, K. & Gimmell, K. Piano Course Book 1. rev. ed. 2008. (Music Ser.). 32p. (J). pap. 7.99 *(978-0-7945-1539-3(8)*, Usborne) EDC Publishing.

Marks, Anthony. Easy Piano Classics. Rogers, Kirsteen, ed. Whatmore, Candice, illus. 2007. (Easy Piano Classics Ser.). 64p. (J). 18.99 *(978-0-7945-1273-6(9)*, Usborne) EDC Publishing.

Marshall, Karen & Hammond, Heather. Get Set! Piano - Get Set! Piano Pieces Book 2. 2014. (Get Set! Ser.). (ENG., Illus.). 24p. (J). pap. 11.95 *(978-1-4081-9278-8(0))* HarperCollins Pubs. Ltd. GBR. Dist: Independent Pubs. Group.

—Get Set! Piano - Get Set! Piano Tutor Book 2. 2014. (Get Set! Ser.). (ENG., Illus.). 48p. (J). pap. 12.95 *(978-1-4081-9307-5(8))* HarperCollins Pubs. Ltd. GBR. Dist: Independent Pubs. Group.

Matz, Carol. Learn to Play Piano with Strawberry Shortcake: A "Berry" Fun Introduction to the Piano for Young Beginners. 2007. (ENG., Illus.). 24p. (J). (gr. -1-3). pap. 7.95 *(978-0-7390-4958-7(5))* Alfred Publishing Co., Inc.

Musgrave, Paul Christopher & Musgrave, Machiko Yamane. Doctor Mozart Music Theory Workbook Level 3: In-Depth Piano Theory Fun for Children's Music Lessons & HomeSchooling - For Beginners Learning a Musical Instrument. 2012. (Illus.). 48p. pap. *(978-0-9881688-0-0(4))* April Avenue Music.

Patrick Green, Ann. Piano Music for Little Fingers: Book 2. 2nd ed. 2012. (Dover Classical Piano Music for Beginners Ser.). (ENG.). 48p. (J). (gr. -1-4). pap. 7.95 *(978-0-486-48825-7(X)*, 48825X) Dover Pubns., Inc.

Philipp, Lillie H. Piano Technique: Tone, Touch, Phrasing & Dynamics. 2010. (Dover Books on Music: Piano Ser.). (ENG., Illus.). 96p. (gr. 7-18). reprint ed. pap. 10.95 *(978-0-486-24272-9(2)*, 242722) Dover Pubns., Inc.

Rejino, Mona. Just for Kids: HLSPL Composer Showcase NFMC 2014-2016 Selection Elementary Level. 2011. (ENG.). 24p. pap. 7.99 *(978-1-61774-200-2(7)*, 00296840) Leonard, Hal Corp.

Sebba, Jane. Abracadabra Piano, Bk. 1. Edwards, Gunvor & Felstead, Cathie, illus. (ENG.). 48p. (J). pap. *(978-0-7136-3724-3(2)*, 93113, A&C Black) Bloomsbury Publishing Plc.

Sembos, Evangelos C. Solo Piano for Children. 2008. 48p. pap. 16.95 *(978-1-4357-1537-0(3))* Lulu Pr., Inc.

Tunstall, Tricia. Note by Note: A Celebration of the Piano Lesson. 2009. (ENG.). 224p. pap. 15.99 *(978-1-4165-4051-9(2))* Simon & Schuster.

Wedgwood, Pam. More Up-Grade! Grades 0-1. 2003. (Faber Edition: up-Grade! Ser.). (ENG.). 24p. (gr. k-1). pap. 11.99 *(978-0-571-51956-9(3))* Faber & Faber, Ltd. GBR. Dist: Alfred Publishing Co., Inc.

—Up-Grade! Piano: Grades 0-1. 2003. (Faber Edition: up-Grade! Ser.). (ENG.). 24p. (gr. k-1). pap. 11.99 *(978-0-571-51737-4(4))* Faber & Faber, Ltd. GBR. Dist: Alfred Publishing Co., Inc.

PIANO MUSIC

Adolphe, Bruce. Piano Puzzlers: Thirty Popular Melodies & Folk Tunes in the Styles of Famous Composers. 2004. 42p. 21.95 *(978-0-9701249-2-0(9))* PollyRhythm Productions.

Baker, Ed. Blues Riffs for Piano. Date not set. 30p. (YA). pap. 14.95 incl. audio *(978-0-89524-928-9(6))* Cherry Lane Music Co.

Bergerac. A First Book of Classical Music for the Beginning Pianist: With Downloadable MP3s. 2014. (Dover Classical Piano Music for Beginners Ser.). (ENG.). 48p. (gr. -1). pap. 7.95 *(978-0-486-78009-2(0)*, 780090) Dover Pubns., Inc.

Dutkanicz, David. Big Book of Beginner's Piano Classics: 57 Favorite Pieces in Easy Piano Arrangements. 2017. (Dover Classical Piano Music for Beginners Ser.). (ENG.). 96p. (gr. -1). pap. 16.95 *(978-0-486-81266-3(9)*, 812669) Dover Pubns., Inc.

Faber, Nancy, et al. BigTime Piano Kids' Songs - Level 4. 2012. (ENG.). 40p. pap. 8.99 *(978-1-61677-629-9(3)*, 00420325) Faber Piano Adventures(r).

Feldstein, Sandy & Clark, Larry. Arietta - Clarinet/Bass Clarinet Solo w/ Piano Acc. w/ CD. 2005. (YA). pap. 9.95 *(978-1-932895-18-6(3))* PlayinTime Productions, Inc.

—Arietta - Flute/Oboe Solo w/ Pianio Acc & CD. 2005. (YA). pap. 9.95 *(978-1-932895-17-9(5))* PlayinTime Productions, Inc.

—Arietta - Trombone/Bariton/Bassoon Solo w/ Piano Acc. W/CD. 2005. (YA). pap. 9.95 *(978-1-932895-23-0(X))* PlayinTime Productions, Inc.

—Arietta - Trumpet/Baritone Solo w/ Piano Acc. W/CD. 2005. (YA). pap. 9.95 *(978-1-932895-21-6(3))* PlayinTime Productions, Inc.

—Arietta - Tuba Solo w/Piano Acc. w/ CD. 2005. (YA). pap. 9.95 *(978-1-932895-24-7(8))* PlayinTime Productions, Inc.

—Arietta- Keyboard Percussion Solo w/Piano Acc. W/CD. 2005. (YA). pap. *(978-1-932895-25-4(6))* PlayinTime Productions, Inc.

—Arrietta - Alto Sax/Bari Sax Solo w/ Piano Acc. w/ CD. 2005. (YA). pap. 9.95 *(978-1-932895-19-3(1))* PlayinTime Productions, Inc.

—Bacarolle - Flute/Oboe Solo with Piano Acc. W/CD. 2005. (YA). pap. *(978-1-932895-87-2(6))* PlayinTime Productions, Inc.

—Bacarolle - Tenor Sax Solo with Piano Acc. W/CD. 2005. (YA). pap. 10.95 *(978-1-932895-90-2(6))* PlayinTime Productions, Inc.

—Barbara Allen - Alto Sax/Bari. Sax Solo with Piano Acc. W/CD. 2005. (YA). pap. 9.95 *(978-1-932895-59-9(0))* PlayinTime Productions, Inc.

—Barbara Allen - Clarinet/Bass Clarinet Solo with Piano Acc. W/CD. 2005. (YA). pap. 9.95 *(978-1-932895-58-2(2))* PlayinTime Productions, Inc.

—Barbara Allen - Flute/Oboe Solo with Piano Acc. W/CD. 2005. (YA). pap. 9.95 *(978-1-932895-57-5(4))* PlayinTime Productions, Inc.

—Barbara Allen - Horn in F Solo with Piano Acc. W/CD. 2005. (YA). pap. 9.95 *(978-1-932895-62-9(0))* PlayinTime Productions, Inc.

—Barbara Allen - Keyboard Percussion Solo with Piano Acc. W/CD. 2005. (YA). pap. 9.95 *(978-1-932895-65-0(5))* PlayinTime Productions, Inc.

—Barbara Allen - Tenor Sax Solo with Piano Acc. W/CD. 2005. (YA). pap. 9.95 *(978-1-932895-60-5(4))*; pap. 9.95 *(978-1-932895-61-2(2))* PlayinTime Productions, Inc.

—Barbara Allen - Trombone/Baritone/Bassoon Solo with Piano Acc. W/CD. 2005. (YA). pap. 9.95 *(978-1-932895-63-6(9))* PlayinTime Productions, Inc.

—Barbara Allen - Tuba Solo with Piano Acc. W/CD. 2005. (YA). pap. 9.95 *(978-1-932895-64-3(7))* PlayinTime Productions, Inc.

—Barcarolle - Alto Sax. /Bari. Sax Solo with Piano Acc. 2005. (YA). pap. 10.95 incl. audio compact disk *(978-1-932895-89-6(2))* PlayinTime Productions, Inc.

—Barcarolle - Clarinet/Bass Clarinet Solo with Piano Acc. 2005. (YA). pap. 10.95 incl. audio compact disk *(978-1-932895-88-9(4))* PlayinTime Productions, Inc.

—Barcarolle - Keyboard Percussion Solo with Piano Acc. 2005. (YA). pap. 10.95 incl. audio compact disk *(978-1-932895-95-7(7))* PlayinTime Productions, Inc.

—Barcarolle - Snare Drum Solo with Piano Acc. 2005. (YA). pap. 10.95 *(978-1-932895-96-4(5))* PlayinTime Productions, Inc.

—Barcarolle - Tuba Solo with Piano Acc. 2005. (YA). pap. 10.95 incl. audio compact disk *(978-1-932895-94-0(9))* PlayinTime Productions, Inc.

—Barcarolle -Trombone/Baritone/Bassoon Solo with Piano Acc. 2005. (YA). pap. 10.95 incl. audio compact disk *(978-1-932895-93-3(0))* PlayinTime Productions, Inc.

—Barcarolle-Trumpet/Baritone Solo with Piano Acc. 2005. (YA). pap. 10.95 incl. audio compact disk *(978-1-932895-91-9(4))* PlayinTime Productions, Inc.

—Fafare Minuet - Keyboard Percussion Solo with Piano Acc. W/CD. 2005. (YA). pap. 9.95 *(978-1-932895-55-1(8))* PlayinTime Productions, Inc.

—Fanfare & Minuet -Flute/Oboe Solo with Piano Acc. W/CD. 2005. (YA). pap. 9.95 *(978-1-932895-47-6(7))* PlayinTime Productions, Inc.

—Fanfare Minuet - Alto Sax/Bari. Sax Solo with Piano Acc. W/CD. 2005. (YA). pap. 9.95 *(978-1-932895-49-0(3))* PlayinTime Productions, Inc.

—Fanfare Minuet - Clarinet/Bass Clarinet Solo with Piano Acc. 2005. (YA). pap. 9.95 incl. audio compact disk *(978-1-932895-48-3(5))* PlayinTime Productions, Inc.

—Fanfare Minuet - Horn in F Solo with Piano Acc. 2005. (YA). pap. 9.95 incl. audio compact disk *(978-1-932895-52-0(3))* PlayinTime Productions, Inc.

—Fanfare Minuet - Snare Drim Solo with Piano Acc. 2005. (YA). pap. incl. audio compact disk *(978-1-932895-56-8(6))* PlayinTime Productions, Inc.

—Fanfare Minuet - Tenor Sax Solo with Piano Acc. 2005. (YA). pap. 9.95 incl. audio compact disk *(978-1-932895-50-6(7))* PlayinTime Productions, Inc.

—Fanfare Minuet - Tuba Solo with Piano Acc. W/CD. 2005. (YA). pap. 9.95 *(978-1-932895-54-4(X))* PlayinTime Productions, Inc.

—The Fifers - Alto Sax. /Bari. Sax Solo with Piano Acc. 2005. (YA). pap. 10.95 incl. audio compact disk *(978-1-932895-79-7(5))* PlayinTime Productions, Inc.

—The Fifers - Clarinet/Bass Clarinet Solo with Piano Acc. W/CD. 2005. (YA). pap. 10.95 *(978-1-932895-78-0(7))* PlayinTime Productions, Inc.

—The Fifers - Flute/Oboe Solo with Piano Acc. 2005. (YA). pap. 10.95 incl. audio compact disk *(978-1-932895-77-3(9))* PlayinTime Productions, Inc.

—The Fifers - Horn in F Solo with Piano Acc. 2005. (YA). pap. 10.95 incl. audio compact disk *(978-1-932895-82-7(5))* PlayinTime Productions, Inc.

—The Fifers - Keyboard Percussion Solo with Piano Acc. 2005. (YA). pap. 10.95 incl. audio compact disk *(978-1-932895-85-8(X))* PlayinTime Productions, Inc.

—The Fifers - Snare Drum Solo with Piano Acc. W/CD. 2005. (YA). pap. 10.95 *(978-1-932895-86-5(8))* PlayinTime Productions, Inc.

—The Fifers - Tenor Sax. Solo with Piano Acc. 2005. (YA). pap. 10.95 incl. audio compact disk *(978-1-932895-80-3(9))* PlayinTime Productions, Inc.

—The Fifers - Trombone/Baritone/Bassoon Solo with Piano Acc. 2005. (YA). pap. 10.95 incl. audio compact disk *(978-1-932895-83-4(3))* PlayinTime Productions, Inc.
—The Fifers - Tuba Solo with Piano Acc. 2005. (YA). pap. 10.95 incl. audio compact disk *(978-1-932895-84-1(1))* PlayinTime Productions, Inc.
—Horn in F Solo with Piano Acc. 2005. (YA). pap. 10.95 incl. audio compact disk *(978-1-932895-92-6(2))* PlayinTime Productions, Inc.
—Scherzando - Flute Solo with Piano Acc. w/CD. 2005. (YA). pap. 9.95 *(978-1-932895-26-1(4))* PlayinTime Productions, Inc.
—Scherzando -Horn in F Solo with Piano Acc. W/CD. 2005. (YA). pap. 9.95 *(978-1-932895-31-5(0))* PlayinTime Productions, Inc.
—Schezando - Clarinet/Bass Clarinet Solo with Piano acc. W/CD. 2005. (YA). pap. 9.95 *(978-1-932895-27-8(2))* PlayinTime Productions, Inc.
—Sensational Snare - Snare Drum Solo with Piano Acc. W/cd. 2005. (YA). pap. 9.95 *(978-1-932895-36-0(1))* PlayinTime Productions, Inc.
—Snarendipity - Snare Drum Solo with Piano Acc. W/CD. 2005. (YA). pap. 9.95 *(978-1-932895-66-7(3))* PlayinTime Productions, Inc.
—Sonatina - Alto Sax/Bari. Sax Solo with Piano Acc. W/CD. 2005. (YA). pap. 10.95 *(978-1-932895-69-8(8))* PlayinTime Productions, Inc.
—Sonatina - Clarinet/Bass Clarinet Solo with Piano Acc. W/CD. 2005. (YA). pap. 10.95 *(978-1-932895-68-1(X))* PlayinTime Productions, Inc.
—Sonatina - Flute/Oboe Solo with Piano Acc. W/CD. 2005. (YA). pap. *(978-1-932895-67-4(1))* PlayinTime Productions, Inc.
—Sonatina - Horn in F Solo with Piano Acc. W/CD. 2005. (YA). pap. 10.95 *(978-1-932895-72-8(8))* PlayinTime Productions, Inc.
—Sonatina - Keyboard Percussion Solo with Piano Acc. W/CD. 2005. (YA). pap. 10.95 *(978-1-932895-75-9(2))* PlayinTime Productions, Inc.
—Sonatina - Snare Drum Solo with Piano Acc. W/CD. 2005. (YA). pap. 10.95 *(978-1-932895-76-6(0))* PlayinTime Productions, Inc.
—Sonatina - Tenor Sax Solo with Piano Acc. W/CD. 2005. (YA). pap. 10.95 *(978-1-932895-70-4(1))* PlayinTime Productions, Inc.
—Sonatina - Trombone/Baritone/Bassoon Solo with Piano Acc. W/CD. 2005. (YA). pap. 10.95 *(978-1-932895-73-5(6))* PlayinTime Productions, Inc.
—Sonatina - Trumpet/Baritone Solo with Piano Acc. W/CD. 2005. (YA). pap. 10.95 *(978-1-932895-71-1(X))* PlayinTime Productions, Inc.
—Sonatina - Tuba Solo with Piano Acc. W/CD. 2005. (YA). pap. 10.95 *(978-1-932895-74-2(4))* PlayinTime Productions, Inc.
—Variations on a Theme by Greig -Flute Solo w/Piano Acc. W/CD. 2005. (YA). pap. 9.95 *(978-1-932895-37-7(X))* PlayinTime Productions, Inc.
—Variations on a Theme by Greig - Alto Sax/Bari. Sax Solo with Piano Acc. W/CD. 2005. (YA). pap. 9.95 *(978-1-932895-39-1(6))* PlayinTime Productions, Inc.
—Variations on a Theme by Greig - Clarinet/Bass Clarinet Solo with Piano Acc. W/CD. 2005. (YA). pap. 9.95 *(978-1-932895-38-4(8))* PlayinTime Productions, Inc.
—Variations on a Theme by Greig - Keyboard Percussion Solo with Piano Acc. W/CD. 2005. (YA). pap. 9.95 *(978-1-932895-45-2(0))* PlayinTime Productions, Inc.
—Variations on a Theme by Greig - Snare Drum Solo with Piano Acc. W/CD. 2005. (YA). pap. 9.95 *(978-1-932895-46-9(9))* PlayinTime Productions, Inc.
—Variations on a Theme by Greig - Trombone/Baritone/Basson Solo with Piano Acc. W/CD. 2005. (YA). pap. 9.95 *(978-1-932895-43-8(4))* PlayinTime Productions, Inc.
—Variations on a Theme by Greig - Trumpet/Baritone Solo with Piano Acc. W/CD. 2005. (YA). pap. 9.95 *(978-1-932895-41-4(8))* PlayinTime Productions, Inc.
—Variations on a Theme by Greig - Tuba Solo with Piano Acc. W/CD. 2005. (YA). pap. 9.95 *(978-1-932895-44-5(2))* PlayinTime Productions, Inc.
—Variations on the theme by Greig - Horn in F Solo with Piano Acc. W/CD. 2005. (YA). pap. 9.95 *(978-1-932895-42-1(6))* PlayinTime Productions, Inc.
—Variatons on a theme by Greig- Tenor Sax Solo with Piano Acc. W/CD. 2005. (YA). pap. 9.95 *(978-1-932895-40-7(X))* PlayinTime Productions, Inc.
Finn, Cheryl. Beanstalk's Basics for Piano: Theory Book Book 1, Bk. 1. 2005. (ENG.). 48p. pap. 11.99 *(978-0-87718-045-6(8),* 00406440) Willis Music Co.
—Beanstalk's Basics for Piano: Theory Book Book 2, Bk. 2. 2005. (ENG.). 48p. pap. 10.99 *(978-0-87718-046-3(6),* 00406441) Willis Music Co.
—Beanstalk's Basics for Piano: Theory Book Book 3, Bk. 3. 2005. (ENG.). 48p. pap. 6.95 *(978-0-87718-047-0(4),* 00406445) Willis Music Co.
—Beanstalk's Basics for Piano: Theory Book Book 4, Bk. 4. 2005. (ENG.). 48p. pap. 6.95 *(978-0-87718-048-7(2),* 00406446) Willis Music Co.
—Beanstalk's Basics for Piano: Theory Book Preparatory Book A, Bk. A. 2005. (ENG.). 44p. pap. 11.99 *(978-0-87718-043-2(1),* 00406438) Willis Music Co.
—Beanstalk's Basics for Piano: Theory Book Preparatory Book B, Vol. Prep B. 2005. (ENG.). 40p. pap. 10.99 *(978-0-87718-044-9(X),* 00406439) Willis Music Co.
Finn, Cheryl, et al. Beanstalk's Basics for Piano Bk. A: Lesson Book Preparatory Book A. 2005. (ENG.). 48p. pap. 13.99 *(978-0-87718-037-1(7),* 00406415) Willis Music Co.
—Beanstalk's Basics for Piano Bk. B: Lesson Book Preparatory Book B. 2005. (ENG.). 48p. pap. 13.99 *(978-0-87718-038-8(5),* 00406416) Willis Music Co.
Hal Leonard Corp. Staff, creator. Teaching Little Fingers to Play More Broadway Songs: Mid to Later Elementary Level. 2012. (ENG.). 32p. pap. 12.99 incl. audio compact disk *(978-1-4584-1768-8(9),* 00416929) Willis Music Co.
Ingkavet, Andrew. Play Piano for Kids: Penguins Don't Play Piano, but You Can! 2012. (ENG.). pap. *(978-1-4675-3174-0(X))* Independent Pub.
Jones, Edward Huws, ed. Unbeaten Tracks for Trumpet. 2003. (Faber Edition: Unbeaten Tracks Ser.). (ENG.). 32p. (gr. 4-7). pap. 13.99 *(978-0-571-52005-3(7))* Faber & Faber, Ltd. GBR. Dist: Alfred Publishing Co., Inc.
Lowe, Marilyn & Gordon, Edwin. Music Moves for Piano. 2004. (J). Bk. 1. 56p. 17.95 *(978-1-57999-343-6(5),* G-6439)Bk. 2. 55p. 17.95 *(978-1-57999-345-0(1),* G-6441) G I A Pubns., Inc.
—Music Moves for Piano Preparatory Book. 2004. 36p. (J). 14.95 *(978-1-57999-341-2(9),* G-6437) G I A Pubns., Inc.
Lowe, Marilyn, et al. Music Moves for Piano Boogies & Blues. 2004. 30p. (J). 7.95 *(978-1-57999-349-8(4),* G-6445) G I A Pubns., Inc.
Marks, A. Easy Piano Tunes. 2004. (Easy Tunes Ser.). (Illus.). 32p. (J). pap. 8.95 *(978-0-7945-0474-8(4))* EDC Publishing.
—Piano Tunes for Children. 2004. (Easy Tunes Ser.). (Illus.). 32p. (J). pap. 8.95 *(978-0-7945-0459-5(0))* EDC Publishing.
Marshall, Karen & Hammond, Heather. Get Set! Piano - Get Set! Piano Pieces Book 2. 2014. (Get Set! Ser.). (ENG., Illus.). 24p. (J). pap. 11.95 *(978-1-4081-9278-8(0))* HarperCollins Pubs. Ltd. GBR. Dist: Independent Pubs. Group.
—Get Set! Piano - Get Set! Piano Tutor Book 2. 2014. (Get Set! Ser.). (ENG., Illus.). 48p. (J). pap. 12.95 *(978-1-4081-9307-5(8))* HarperCollins Pubs. Ltd. GBR. Dist: Independent Pubs. Group.
Milne, Elissa. More Little Peppers: A Vibrant Collection of Compositions Written Especially for the Young Performer. 2004. (Faber Edition: Little Peppers Ser.). (ENG.). 999p. pap. 11.99 *(978-0-571-52314-6(5))* Faber & Faber, Ltd. GBR. Dist: Alfred Publishing Co., Inc.
More What Else Can I Play: Piano Grade 1. (gr. 1). 6.95 *(978-1-85909-523-2(2),* Warner Bros. Pubns.) Alfred Publishing Co., Inc.
More What Else Can I Play: Piano Grade 2. (gr. 2). 6.95 *(978-1-85909-524-9(0),* Warner Bros. Pubns.) Alfred Publishing Co., Inc.
Music. Gr 6 Stm Te/Piano Accomp. 2003. (Share the Music Ser.). (gr. 6-18). *(978-0-02-295593-9(3))* Macmillan/McGraw-Hill Schl. Div.
Okun, Milton, ed. Christmas Carols for Piano Duet. 63p. (YA). pap. 14.95 *(978-0-89524-948-7(0),* 02505651) Cherry Lane Music Co.
—From a Distance & Twenty-Four Other Easy Listening Favorites for Easy Piano. 119p. (Orig.). (YA). pap. 12.95 *(978-0-89524-871-8(9),* 02505508) Cherry Lane Music Co.
PI Kids. Thomas & Friends: Thomas' Piano Book. 2014. (ENG., Illus.). 12p. (J). bds. 21.99 *(978-1-4127-4552-9(7),* 1359) Phoenix International Publications, Inc.
Publications International Ltd. Staff, ed. Disney Princess: Royal Recital. 2011. 14p. (J). bds. 17.98 *(978-1-4508-1006-7(3))* Phoenix International Publications, Inc.
—Minnie Mouse: Pretty Piano Play-Along: Piano Book. 2013. (Illus.). 14p. (J). (gr. k-3). bds. 18.98 *(978-1-4508-6770-2(7),* a4f2852b-3a90-4b10-ac4c-e802ee4cfa50) Phoenix International Publications, Inc.
—Nickelodeon Dora the Explorer: Follow the Music. 2011. 14p. (J). 18.98 *(978-1-4508-0712-8(7))* Phoenix International Publications, Inc.
—Nickelodeon Dora the Explorer: Follow the Music: Piano Book. 2013. 14p. (J). bds. 16.98 *(978-1-4508-6380-3(9),* 355bc6ba-2b76-413c-bb3d-3975072deb9b) Phoenix International Publications, Inc.
—Princess Songs Play & Learn. 2010. 24p. (J). 12.98 *(978-1-4508-0113-3(7))* Phoenix International Publications, Inc.
Rocherolle, Eugénie R. Keyboard Capers. 2004. (Composer Spotlight Ser.). (ENG., Illus.). 28p. pap. 7.99 *(978-0-7579-1897-1(2))* Alfred Publishing Co., Inc.
Ruth, Anita, ed. Lorie Line - Music from the Heart: Greatest Cover Hits. 2004. (ENG.). 116p. pap. 34.95 *(978-1-891195-12-9(3),* 00306577) Leonard, Hal Corp.
Spivak, Samuel. Children's Cowboy Songs for Piano. Barbelle, illus. 2011. 28p. 35.95 *(978-1-258-06408-2(1))* Literary Licensing, LLC.
Tansman, Alexandre. Alexandre Tansman: Je Joue Pour Papa: Douze Morceaux Tres Faciles et en Grosses Notes. 2007. (ENG.). 28p. pap. 16.95 *(978-1-4234-2730-8(0),* 50564798) Leonard, Hal Corp.
Tokarjewa, Viktorija. Der Pianist: Erzaehlungen. (GER.). 176p. *(978-3-257-06139-0(0))* Diogenes Verlag AG CHE. Dist: International Bk. Import Service, Inc.
Turner, Barrie Carson. Classic FM — Classics for Children: A Great Collection of Well-Known Classics Arranged for Grade 1 — 2 Level Piano. 2011. (Faber Edition: Classic FM Ser.). (ENG.). 999p. pap., pap. 13.80 *(978-0-571-53578-1(X))* Faber Music, Ltd. GBR. Dist: Alfred Publishing Co., Inc.
Turner, Gary. Piano Method for Young Beginners, Book 1. Stewart, James, illus. 2006. (Young Beginner Giant Coloring Bks.). 44p. pap. incl. audio compact disk *(978-1-86469-098-9(4))* LearnToPlayMusic.com Pty Ltd.
Twelsiek, Monika, ed. Animals: 30 Easy Piano Pieces for Children. 2009. (ENG.). 48p. pap. 16.99 *(978-3-7957-5874-5(2),* 49017635) Schott Music Corp.

PICASSO, PABLO, 1881-1973

Bernier-Grand, Carmen T. Picasso: I the King, Yo el Rey, 0 vols. Diaz, David, illus. 2012. (ENG.). 64p. (YA). (gr. 9-12). 19.99 *(978-0-7614-6177-7(9),* 9780761461777) Amazon Publishing.
Fandel, Jennifer. Pablo Picasso. (Odysseys in Artistry Ser.). (Illus.). (J). 2016. (ENG.). 80p. (gr. 7-10). *(978-1-60818-720-1(9),* 20662) 2005. 48p. (gr. 5-9). lib. bdg. 21.95 *(978-1-58341-331-9(6))* Creative Co., The. (Creative Education).
Flor Ada, Alma & Campoy, F. Isabel, contrib. by. Sonrisas. (Literature Collection of Puertas Al Sol Ser.). (SPA.). 32p. (J). (gr. k-6). pap. 13.95 *(978-1-59437-701-3(4))* Santillana USA Publishing Co., Inc.
Hyde, Margaret, ed. Picasso for Kids, 1 vol. 2nd rev. ed. 2008. (Great Art for Kids Ser.). (ENG., Illus.). 14p. (J). (gr. k-k). bds. 8.95 *(978-1-58980-659-7(X),* Pelican Publishing) Arcadia Publishing.
Hyde, Margaret E., ed. Picasso for Kids, 1 vol. 2004. (Great Art for Kids Ser.). (ENG., Illus.). 12p. (J). 8.95 *(978-1-58980-205-6(5),* Pelican Publishing) Arcadia Publishing.
Jacobson, Rick. Picasso: Soul on Fire. Jacobson, Rick & Fernandez, Laura, illus. 2011. (ENG.). 32p. (J). (gr. 5-18). pap. 8.95 *(978-1-77049-263-9(1),* Tundra Bks.) Tundra Bks. CAN. Dist: Penguin Random Hse. LLC.
Kelley, True & Who HQ. ¿Quién Fue Pablo Picasso? Kelley, True, illus. 2012. (¿Quién Fue? Ser.). (Illus.). 112p. (J). (gr. 3-7). pap. 6.99 *(978-0-448-46175-5(7),* Penguin Workshop) Penguin Young Readers Group.
—Who Was Pablo Picasso? Kelley, True, illus. 2009. (Who Was? Ser.). (ENG., Illus.). 103p. (J). (gr. 3-7). pap. 5.99 *(978-0-448-44987-6(0),* Penguin Workshop) Penguin Young Readers Group.
Lebscky, Ibi. Pablito. Cardoni, Paolo, illus. (Coleccion Seran Famosos).Tr. of Little Pablo Picasso. (SPA.). 28p. (J). (gr. 2-4). 14.95 *(978-84-233-1265-8(8))* Ediciones Destino ESP. Dist: AIMS International Bks., Inc.
Lemay, Violet, illus. 100 Pablo Picassos. 2015. 32p. (J). (gr. k-5). 14.99 *(978-1-938093-32-6(1),* 809332) Duo Pr. LLC.
Lomberg, Michelle. Pablo Picasso. 2016. (J). *(978-1-4896-4625-5(6))* Weigl Pubs., Inc.
Lowery, Linda. Pablo Picasso. 2006. (Yo Solo Biografías Ser.). (SPA., Illus.). 48p. (J). (gr. 3-7). lib. bdg. 23.93 *(978-0-8225-6259-7(6),* Ediciones Lerner) Lerner Publishing Group.
Mason, Antony. El Arte Moderno: En los Tiempos de Picasso. 2005. (Arte Alrededor del Mundo Ser.). (Illus.). 48p. (J). (gr. 4-7). pap. 9.95 *(978-85-7416-240-9(X))* Callis Editora Ltda BRA. Dist: Independent Pubs. Group.
Nichols, Catherine. Pablo Picasso. (Primary Source Library of Famous Artists Ser.). 32p. (gr. 3-4). 2009. 42.50 *(978-1-60854-103-4(7))* 2005. (ENG., Illus.). (J). lib. bdg. 27.60 *(978-1-4042-2764-4(4),* b4a8853a-9a38-454a-8e0e-b86278de3848) Rosen Publishing Group, Inc., The. (PowerKids Pr.).
Pablo Picasso. 2006. (J). pap. 6.95 *(978-0-8225-6624-3(9),* Ediciones Lerner) Lerner Publishing Group.
Penrose, Antony & Picasso, Pablo. The Boy Who Bit Picasso. 2011. (ENG., Illus.). 48p. (J). (gr. k-2). 17.95 *(978-0-8109-9728-8(2),* Abrams Bks. for Young Readers) Abrams, Inc.
Richardson, Adele. Pablo Picasso. 2016. (Odysseys in Artistry Ser.). (ENG., Illus.). 80p. (J). (gr. 7-10). pap. 15.99 *(978-1-62832-316-0(7),* 20660, Creative Paperbacks) Creative Co., The.
Rollyson, Carl. Pablo Picasso: A Biography for Beginners. 2009. 88p. pap. 9.95 *(978-1-4401-3247-6(X))* iUniverse, Inc.
Spence, David. Picasso. 2010. (Great Artists & Their World Ser.). 48p. 32.80 *(978-1-84898-315-1(8))* Black Rabbit Bks.
—Picasso: Una Revolucion en el Arte. (Coleccion Grandes Artistas).Tr. of Picasso: Breaking the Rules of Art. (SPA.). 226p. (YA). (gr. 5-8). 12.76 *(978-84-8211-134-6(5))* Celeste Ediciones, S.A. ESP. Dist: Lectorum Pubns., Inc.
Stephens, Pamela Geiger. Dropping in on Picasso. McNeill, Jim, illus. 2004. 32p. (J). 15.95 *(978-1-56290-325-1(X))* Crystal Productions.
Venezia, Mike. Pablo Picasso (Revised Edition) (Getting to Know the World's Greatest Artists) Venezia, Mike, illus. 2014. (Getting to Know the World's Greatest Artists Ser.). (ENG., Illus.). 40p. (J). (gr. 3-4). pap. 7.95 *(978-0-531-22537-0(2),* Children's Pr.) Scholastic Library Publishing.
Vila, Carmen. Tracy Knows Picasso: Children's Art History Read-Along Book. (Illus.). 24p. (J). (gr. 1-6). incl. audio *(978-0-9635047-0-8(3))* VILA Group, Inc., The.

PICASSO, PABLO, 1881-1973—FICTION

Anholt, Laurence. Picasso & the Girl with a Ponytail: An Art History Book for Kids. 2007. (Anholt's Artists Books for Children Ser.). (ENG., Illus.). 32p. (J). (gr. k-3). pap. 9.99 *(978-0-7641-3853-9(7))* Sourcebooks, Inc.
Picasso, Pablo. Birds & Other Animals: With Pablo Picasso. Gartner, Maya, ed. 2017. (First Concepts with Fine Artists Ser.). (ENG., Illus.). 30p. (gr. -1 — 1). bds. 9.95 *(978-0-7148-7418-0(3))* Phaidon Pr., Inc.
Ploss, Skip. If Picasso Were a Fish. Ploss, Skip, illus. 2006. (Illus.). 40p. (gr. k-2). 15.99 *(978-1-4116-9220-6(9))* Lulu Pr., Inc.
Scott, Elaine. Secrets of the Cirque Medrano. 2008. (Illus.). 216p. (J). (gr. 5-9). 15.95 *(978-1-57091-712-7(4))* Charlesbridge Publishing, Inc.
—The Spanish Web: An Encounter with Picasso. 2004. (Art Encounters Ser.). (J). 15.95 *(978-0-8230-0410-2(4));* pap. 6.99 *(978-0-8230-0413-3(9))* Watson-Guptill Pubns., Inc.

PICKETT, BILL, APPROXIMATELY 1860-1932

Sanford, William R. & Green, Carl R. Bill Pickett: Courageous African-American Cowboy, 1 vol. 2013. (Courageous Heroes of the American West Ser.). (ENG., Illus.). 48p. (J). (gr. 5-7). 25.27 *(978-0-7660-4001-4(1),* c9d15464-f7c9-41fa-bd21-8bf27ee9da30) Enslow Publishing, LLC.

PICKLING

see Canning and Preserving

PICNICKING

At the Lake: KinderReaders Individual Title Six-Packs. (Kinderstarters Ser.). 8p. (gr. -1-1). 21.00 *(978-0-7635-8663-8(3))* Rigby Education.
Benjamin, Tina. Let's Have a Picnic, 1 vol. 2015. (Let's Go Outdoors! Ser.). (ENG., Illus.). 24p. (J). (gr. k-k). pap. 9.15 *(978-1-4824-2625-0(0),* 89d5c6fa-27ee-4e29-9547-c794b5377f86) Stevens, Gareth Publishing LLLP.
Claire, Linda. Picnics: Figuras Tridimensionales. rev. ed. 2019. (Mathematics in the Real World Ser.). (SPA., Illus.). 20p. (J). (gr. k-1). 8.99 *(978-1-4258-2835-6(3))* Teacher Created Materials, Inc.
—Your World: Picnics: 3-D Shapes (Kindergarten) 2018. (Mathematics in the Real World Ser.). (ENG., Illus.). 20p. (J). (gr. k-1). 8.99 *(978-1-4258-5628-1(4))* Teacher Created Materials, Inc.
La Excursion (The Picnic) (Granja Oso de Miel Ser.). (SPA., Illus.). (J). bds. 4.99 *(978-0-7899-0608-3(2),* 495050) Editorial Unilit.
Meachen Rau, Dana & Vargus, Nanci Reginelli. At a Picnic, 1 vol. 2008. (Fun Time Ser.). (ENG., Illus.). 24p. (gr. k-1). lib. bdg. 25.50 *(978-0-7614-2607-3(8),* 5bb67d7f-6019-44c7-a008-38aa0a00c0b8, Cavendish Square) Cavendish Square Publishing LLC.
—En el Picnic (at the Picnic), 1 vol. 2009. (Tiempo de la Diversión (Fun Time) Ser.). (SPA., Illus.). 24p. (gr. k-1). lib. bdg. 25.50 *(978-0-7614-2779-7(1),* 13634c26-34be-44d8-880e-acbfb4af0a09) Cavendish Square Publishing LLC.
Moore, Richard. It's Time for a Picnic, 1 vol. 2017. (It's Time Ser.). (ENG.). 24p. (J). (gr. 1-1). 25.27 *(978-1-5081-6363-3(4),* 38d1e140-7612-4904-bc9f-64acc10ee457, PowerKids Pr.) Rosen Publishing Group, Inc., The.
The Special Ride: Individual Title Six-Packs. 16p. (gr. 2-18). 35.00 *(978-0-7635-9377-3(X))* Rigby Education.

PICNICKING—FICTION

Adeney, Anne. Five Teddy Bears. Shimmen, Cathy, illus. 2008. (Tadpoles Ser.). (ENG.). 24p. (J). (gr. -1-k). pap. *(978-0-7787-3884-8(1));* lib. bdg. *(978-0-7787-3853-4(1))* Crabtree Publishing Co.
Agha-Khan, Aliyar. Cyrus & Kaleo Go Rock Hunting. 2012. 32p. pap. 12.99 *(978-1-4634-1567-9(2))* AuthorHouse.
Bagnoli, Christine. Miguel's Family Picnic, 1 vol. 2006. (Neighborhood Readers Ser.). (ENG.). 16p. (gr. 1-2). pap. 6.50 *(978-1-4042-7006-0(X),* 177b5ffe-840f-4d2a-915e-fb5f9fd5ef22, Rosen Classroom) Rosen Publishing Group, Inc., The.
Beckford, Lois. The Interesting Pen Pal. 2010. 44p. pap. 21.99 *(978-1-4415-0878-2(3))* Xlibris Corp.
Bell, Rebecca. Rebekah Armstronge. 2012. 48p. pap. 21.99 *(978-1-4772-2136-5(0))* AuthorHouse.
Bollinger, Georgia G. The Penguins' Perilous Picnic. 2011. 32p. pap. 14.50 *(978-1-4634-2200-4(8))* AuthorHouse.
Bond, Rebecca. Pig & Goose & the First Day of Spring. Bond, Rebecca, illus. 2017. (Illus.). 48p. (J). (gr. k-3). lib. bdg. 12.99 *(978-1-58089-594-1(8))* Charlesbridge Publishing, Inc.
Brendler, Carol. The Pickwicks' Picnic: A Counting Adventure. Kurilla, Renée, illus. 2017. (ENG.). 40p. (J). (gr. -1-3). 16.99 *(978-0-544-83958-8(7),* 1646081, Clarion Bks.) HarperCollins Pubs.
Bunting, Eve. A Picnic in October. Carpenter, Nancy, illus. 2004. (ENG.). 32p. (J). (gr. -1-3). reprint ed. pap. 7.99 *(978-0-15-205065-8(5),* 1195297, Clarion Bks.) HarperCollins Pubs.
Burningham, John. Picnic. Burningham, John, illus. 2014. (ENG., Illus.). 32p. (J). (-k). 17.99 *(978-0-7636-6945-4(8))* Candlewick Pr.
Carr, Elias. Ava & the Skimpy Picnic: A Book about Sharing. Garton, Michael, illus. 2016. (Frolic First Faith Ser.). 32p. (J). (gr. -1-k). 12.99 *(978-1-5064-1051-7(0),* Sparkhouse Family) 1517 Media.
—Ava y el Picnic Raquitico. Garton, Michael, illus. 2016. (SPA.). (J). *(978-1-5064-2095-0(8))* 1517 Media.
Cleveland, Marie. Jason's Giant Dilemma: A Storybook Land Adventure. 2007. 76p. per. 19.95 *(978-1-4241-7811-7(8))* America Star Bks.
Condon, Bill. Planet Puzzle, 1 vol. rev. ed. 2013. (Literary Text Ser.). (ENG., Illus.). 28p. (gr. 2-3). pap. 9.99 *(978-1-4333-5562-2(0))* Teacher Created Materials, Inc.
Cowan, Charlotte. Moose with Loose Poops. Neal, Penelope, illus. 2008. (Dr. Hippo Ser.). (ENG.). 32p. (J). (gr. -1-2). 17.95 *(978-0-9753516-5-9(6))* Hippocratic Pr., The.
Cronin, Doreen. Click, Clack, Quackity-Quack. 2005. (Click Clack Book Ser.). (ENG., Illus.). 24p. (J). (gr. -1-3). 18.99 *(978-0-689-87715-5(3),* Atheneum Bks. for Young Readers) Simon & Schuster Children's Publishing.
—Click, Clack, Quackity-Quack: A Typing Adventure. Lewin, Betsy, illus. 2008. (Click Clack Book Ser.). (ENG.). 14p. (J). (gr. -1-k). 14.99 *(978-1-4169-5517-7(8),* Little Simon) Little Simon.
—Click, Clack, Quackity-Quack: An Alphabetical Adventure. Lewin, Betsy, illus. 2006. (Doreen Cronin: Click-Clack & More Ser.). (ENG.). (J). (gr. k-5). lib. bdg. 31.36 *(978-1-59961-089-4(2),* 5417, Picture Bk.) Spotlight.
Davis, Catherine. Abby & Alex Feel Their Hearts' Little. 2006. 57p. pap. 16.95 *(978-1-4241-4586-7(4))* PublishAmerica, Inc.
DiTerlizzi, Tony & DiTerlizzi, Angela. Yummy Trip! DiTerlizzi, Tony, illus. 2010. (Adventure of Meno Ser.: 3). (ENG., Illus.). 48p. (J). (gr. -1-k). 9.99 *(978-1-4169-7150-4(5),* Simon & Schuster Bks. For Young Readers) Simon & Schuster Bks. For Young Readers.
Dotlich, Rebecca. Peanut & Pearl's Picnic Adventure. Alley, R. W., illus. 2008. (My First I Can Read Ser.). (ENG.). 32p. (J). (gr. -1 — 1). pap. 4.99 *(978-0-06-054922-0(X),* HarperCollins) HarperCollins Pubs.
Elder, Elizabeth. When I'm with You. Mansmann, Leslie, illus. 2003. (ENG.). 32p. (J). 15.95 *(978-0-9671662-8-5(4))* Islandport Pr., Inc.
Etting, Tali. Max's Amazing Adventure. 2011. (Illus.). 32p. 14.09 *(978-1-4567-7251-2(1))* AuthorHouse.
Fellure, Kathy Boyd. Mr Snowman Ate Our Picnic Lunch. 2010. (ENG.). 36p. pap. 16.95 *(978-0-557-79684-7(9))* Lulu Pr., Inc.
Flor Ada, Alma. Celebrate Fourth of July with Champ, the Scamp. Mazali, Gustavo, illus. 2006. (Cuentos para Celebrar / Stories to Celebrate Ser.). 30p. (J). (gr. k-6). per. 11.95 *(978-1-59820-131-4(X))* Santillana USA Publishing Co., Inc.
Florence, Debbi Michiko. Dorothy & Toto the Disappearing Picnic. Roe, Monika, illus. 2016. (Dorothy & Toto Ser.). (ENG.). 40p. (J). (gr. k-2). lib. bdg. 21.32 *(978-1-4795-8704-9(4),* 130953) Capstone.
Flowerpot Press, contrib. by. Sockheadz: Picnic. 2013. (ENG., Illus.). 20p. (J). (gr. -1-k). 8.99 *(978-1-77093-616-4(5))* Flowerpot Children's Pr. Inc. CAN. Dist: Cardinal Pubs. Group.
George, Joshua. Tiny Town Picnic Fun. Ribbon, Lemon, illus. 2018. (Soft Felt Play Bks.). (ENG.). 10p. (J). (gr. -1-k). bds. 9.99 *(978-1-78700-386-6(8))* Top That! Publishing PLC GBR. Dist: Independent Pubs. Group.
Geraldi, Michele J. Pennies at Piper Park. 2009. 24p. pap. 12.99 *(978-1-4389-2829-6(7))* AuthorHouse.
Giurco, Diane. The Adventures of Willy & Nilly. 2008. (Illus.). 32p. pap. 14.49 *(978-1-4389-1134-2(3))* AuthorHouse.
Glass, Graeme. A Bee's Kiss. Trone, Jo, illus. 2012. 60p. pap. 21.50 *(978-1-61897-383-2(5),* Strategic Bk. Publishing) Strategic Book Publishing & Rights Agency (SBPRA).
Glennon, Michelle. My Big Green Teacher: Taking the Green Road. Glennon, Michelle, illus. 2008. (Illus.). 32p. (J). 19.95 *(978-0-9796625-7-7(5))* GDG Publishing.

Goode, Diane. The Most Perfect Spot. Goode, Diane, illus. 2006. (ENG., Illus.). 32p. (J). (gr. -1-3). 16.99 *(978-0-06-072697-3(0))* HarperCollins Pubs.

Goodrich, C. C. Barnabee: At the Picnic. 2009. (Illus.). 32p. pap. 13.99 *(978-1-4389-8388-2(3))* AuthorHouse.

Gupta, Jennifer. Silly Turtle! That's Not on the Menu! 2008. 28p. pap. 13.99 *(978-1-4343-9183-4(3))* AuthorHouse.

Harris, Robie. What's So Yummy? All about Eating Well & Feeling Good. Westcott, Nadine Bernard, illus. 2014. (Let's Talk about You & Me Ser.). (ENG.). 40p. (J). (-k). 17.99 *(978-0-7636-3632-6(0))* Candlewick Pr.

Holden, Pam. A Quick Picnic, 1 vol. Ross, Christine, illus. 2009. (Red Rocket Readers Ser.). (ENG.). 16p. (gr. -1-1). pap. *(978-1-877363-22-1(7)*, Red Rocket Readers) Flying Start Bks.

Holub, Joan. Picnic! A Day in the Park (Ready-To-Read Pre-Level 1) Terry, Will, illus. 2008. (Ant Hill Ser.). (ENG.). 24p. (J). (gr. -1-k). pap. 4.99 *(978-1-4169-5133-9(4)*, Simon Spotlight) Simon Spotlight.

Honigsberg, Peter John. Too Much Picnic. Jones, Ryan, illus. 2006. 32p. (J). 16.95 *(978-1-57143-154-7(3))* RDR Bks.

Jacqueline, Thomas. Birthday Picnic. 2010. 24p. pap. 9.99 *(978-0-88144-493-3(6))* Yorkshire Publishing Group.

Jennings, Sharon, et al, adapted by. Franklin's Picnic. 2006. (Kids Can Read Ser.). (ENG., Illus.). 32p. (J). (gr. 1-2). 3.95 *(978-1-55337-715-3(X))*; 14.95 *(978-1-55337-714-6(1))* Kids Can Pr., Ltd. CAN. Dist: Hachette Bk. Group.

Judson, Clara Ingram. Mary Jane: Her Book. 2007. 88p. per. *(978-1-4065-4677-4(1))* Dodo Pr.

Jumbo & the Stranger. 2004. (J). per. 15.99 *(978-0-9744205-5-4(7))* Golden Eagle Publishing Hse., Inc.

Kennedy, Anne Vittur. The Farmer's Away! Baa! Neigh! Kennedy, Anne Vittur, illus. 2014. (ENG., Illus.). 32p. (J). (-k). 15.99 *(978-0-7636-6679-8(3))* Candlewick Pr.

Kennedy, Jimmy. The Teddy Bears' Picnic. Day, Alexandra, illus. 2015. (Classic Board Bks.). (ENG.). 34p. (J). (gr. -1-k). bds. 8.99 *(978-1-4814-2274-1(X)*, Little Simon) Little Simon.

Khing, T. T. Where Is the Cake? 2010. (ENG & DUT., Illus.). 32p. (J). (gr. -1-3). pap. 7.95 *(978-0-8109-8924-5(7))* UK Abrams Bks. for Young Readers.

Krishnaswami, Uma. The Ants Have a Picnic. 2006. (Early Explorers Ser.). (J). pap. *(978-1-4108-6115-3(5))* Benchmark Education Co.

Kruusval, Catarina. Franny's Friends. Sandin, Joan, tr. from SWE. 2008. (Illus.). 32p. (J). (gr. -1-1). 16.00 *(978-91-29-66836-0(0))* R & S Bks. SWE. Dist: Macmillan.

Levy, Janey. The Piggles Picnic, 1 vol. 2006. (Neighborhood Readers Ser.). (ENG.). 12p. (gr. k-1). pap. 5.90 *(978-1-4042-6455-7(8)*, 4dffa697-ee25-4c5a-8f8a-87630102bce9, Rosen Classroom) Rosen Publishing Group, Inc., The.

Lies, Brian. Bats at the Beach. 2006. (Bat Book Ser.). (ENG., Illus.). 32p. (J). (gr. -1-3). 18.99 *(978-0-618-55744-8(X)*, 529911, Clarion Bks.) HarperCollins Pubs.

Lovell, H. N. Wootie's Delightful Picnic. 2006. (J). pap. 12.95 *(978-0-9761182-4-4(6))* Alpha Run Pr., LLC.

Lucy's Picnic. 2006. (J). *(978-0-9764719-3-6(0))* MiceWorks.

Mack, Jeff. Good News, Bad News. 2012. (ENG., Illus.). 40p. (J). (gr. -1-1). 16.99 *(978-1-4521-0110-1(8))* Chronicle Bks. LLC.

McCully, Emily Arnold. Picnic. McCully, Emily Arnold, illus. 2003. (Illus.). 32p. (J). (gr. -1-k). 16.89 *(978-0-06-623855-5(2))* HarperCollins Pubs.

—Picnic. 2003. (ENG., Illus.). 32p. (J). (gr. -1-k). 17.99 *(978-0-06-623854-8(4)*, HarperCollins) HarperCollins Pubs.

Mello, Alondra. Alanora's Magic Tree: Alanora's Spirit Journey. 2007. 48p. per. 12.97 *(978-1-932344-77-6(2))* Thornton Publishing, Inc.

Mendicino, Ellen, et al. Zuko the Zany Dog. 2013. 70p. pap. 9.99 *(978-0-9890288-0-6(1))* Mindstir Media.

Michaels, Evan. Tressa & Dan's Picnic at the Zoo. 2010. (Illus.). 34p. (J). pap. 19.95 *(978-0-9826865-0-8(1))* Win Enterprises LLC.

Miles, Ryan. The Picnic Nightmare. 2012. 24p. pap. 24.95 *(978-1-4512-7153-9(0))* America Star Bks.

Murphy, Stuart J. Freda Organiza una Merienda. 2011. (I See I Learn Ser.: 18). (Illus.). 32p. (J). (-k). 14.95 *(978-1-58089-488-3(7))* Charlesbridge Publishing, Inc.

—Freda Plans a Picnic. 2010. (I See I Learn Ser.: 2). (Illus.). 32p. (J). (gr. -1-k). 14.95 *(978-1-58089-456-2(9))*; pap. 6.95 *(978-1-58089-457-9(7))* Charlesbridge Publishing, Inc.

Myott, Lanita. RJ Saves the Day. 2003. 19p. 11.16 *(978-1-4116-0354-7(0))* Lulu Pr., Inc.

Nash, Andy. Tatum & Her Tiger: For Kids Blessed with Passion. 2007. (Illus.). (J). 9.99 *(978-0-8127-0451-8(7))* Autumn Hse. Publishing Co.

Nelson, Jim. Crosstown Crush. 2005. 82p. Vol. 1, Bk. 1. (YA). pap. 9.00 *(978-1-4116-5266-8(5))* Vol. 1,Bk. 2. (ENG.). pap. 9.00 *(978-1-4116-6654-2(2))* Lulu Pr., Inc.

Paterson, Brian. Zigby - the Picnic. Paterson, Brian, illus. 2006. (ENG., Illus.). 16p. (J). (gr. -1). bds. 6.99 *(978-0-00-717421-8(7)*, HarperCollins Children's Bks.) HarperCollins Pubs. Ltd. GBR. Dist: Trafalgar Square Publishing.

Patty & Pop's Picnic: Take-Home Book. 2005. (Emergent Library: Vol. 2). (YA). (gr. -1-1). 12.60 *(978-0-8215-7262-7(8))* Sadlier, William H. Inc.

Phillipps, J. C. The Simples Love a Picnic. Phillipps, J. C., illus. 2014. (ENG., Illus.). 32p. (J). (gr. -1-3). 16.99 *(978-0-544-16667-7(1)*, 1551093, Clarion Bks.) HarperCollins Pubs.

The Picnic, 6 Packs. (gr. k-1). 23.00 *(978-0-7635-8836-6(9))* Rigby Education.

Piggy Toes Press Staff. All the Way's I Love You Mini. Downing, Julie, illus. 2005. (ENG.). 10p. (J). 4.95 *(978-1-58117-437-3(3)*, Intervisual/Piggy Toes) Bendon, Inc.

Pittar, Gill. Milly, Molly & the Picnic. Morrell, Cris, illus. 2005. 28p. (gr. -1). pap. *(978-1-86972-045-2(8))* Milly Molly Bks.

Polacco, Patricia. Picnic at Mudsock Meadow. 2009. (ENG.). 32p. (J). (gr. k-3). pap. 7.99 *(978-0-14-241392-0(5)*, Puffin Books) Penguin Young Readers Group.

Rathmann, Peggy. The Day the Babies Crawled Away. Rathmann, Peggy, illus. 2003. (Illus.). 40p. (J). (gr. -1-k). 18.99 *(978-0-399-23196-4(X)*, G.P. Putnam's Sons Books for Young Readers) Penguin Young Readers Group.

Reid, Hunter. Let's Have a Picnic! Hinton, Stephanie, illus. 2016. (Fluorescent Pop! Ser.). (ENG.). 14p. (J). (gr. -1-k). bds. 5.99 *(978-1-4998-0220-7(X))* Little Bee Books Inc.

Ricci, Christine. Dora's Picnic. Hall, Susan, illus. 2003. (Ready-to-Read Ser.: Vol. 1). (ENG.). 24p. (J). pap. 3.99 *(978-0-689-85238-1(X)*, Simon Spotlight/Nickelodeon) Simon Spotlight/Nickelodeon.

Rigby Education Staff. Headline News. (Sails Literacy Ser.). (Illus.). 16p. (gr. 1-2). 27.00 *(978-0-7635-9930-0(1)*, 699301C99) Rigby Education.

Ritchey, Kate. A Perfect Picnic. 2013. (Mickey & Friends World of Reading Ser.). (J). lib. bdg. 13.55 *(978-0-606-31753-5(8))* Turtleback.

Rosenthal, Betsy R. Porcupine's Picnic: Who Eats What? Capizzi, Giusi, illus. 2017. (ENG.). 32p. (J). (gr. -1-2). 19.99 *(978-1-4677-9519-7(4)*, 35b32061-ef3d-44ab-b216-87a602614795); E-Book 30.65 *(978-1-5124-2840-7(X))* Lerner Publishing Group. (Millbrook Pr.).

Santillo, LuAnn. The Picnic. Santillo, LuAnn, ed. 2003. (Half-Pint Kids Readers Ser.). (Illus.). 7p. (J). (gr. -1-1). pap. 1.00 *(978-1-59256-090-5(3))* Half-Pint Kids, Inc.

—The Trip. Santillo, LuAnn, ed. 2003. (Half-Pint Kids Readers Ser.). (Illus.). 7p. (J). (gr. -1-1). pap. 1.00 *(978-1-59256-057-8(1))* Half-Pint Kids, Inc.

Sargent-Barker, Erika. Living with a Legend. 2012. 32p. pap. 16.95 *(978-1-4626-9618-5(X))* America Star Bks.

Scholastic, Inc. Staff & Silver, Ivy. Time for a Picnic. 2011. (Scholastic Reader: Level 1 Ser.: 4). (ENG.). 32p. (J). (gr. -1-1). 16.19 *(978-0-545-20057-8(1))* Scholastic, Inc.

Shakespeare, Nancy. Benjamin the Bear Goes on a Picnic. Clouette, Katie, illus. 2013. (Benjamin the Bear Ser.). (ENG.). (J). (gr. -1-3). 14.95 *(978-1-62086-314-5(6))* Amplify Publishing Group.

Simont, Marc. The Stray Dog: A Caldecott Honor Award Winner. Simont, Marc, illus. 2003. (ENG., Illus.). 32p. (J). (gr. -1-3). pap. 8.99 *(978-0-06-443669-4(1)*, HarperCollins) HarperCollins Pubs.

Smith, B. M. My Very Own Picnic Basket: An Evan & Cassie Adventure. 2012. 28p. pap. 24.95 *(978-1-4626-7551-7(4))* America Star Bks.

Smythe, Katie. The Summer Picnic, 1 vol. 2015. (Rosen REAL Readers: STEM & STEAM Collection). (ENG.). 8p. (gr. k-1). pap. 5.46 *(978-1-4994-9557-7(9)*, 4f01c03b-4d63-44a7-8e71-9fbfe3d720ec, Rosen Classroom) Rosen Publishing Group, Inc., The.

Snowden, Gary. The Lost Treasure of Hawkins Cave. Pierce Clark, Donna, illus. 2013. 112p. pap. 7.99 *(978-1-938768-10-1(8))* Gypsy Pubns.

Song, Mika. Picnic with Oliver. 2018. (ENG., Illus.). 32p. (J). (gr. -1-3). 17.99 *(978-0-06-242950-6(7)*, HarperCollins) HarperCollins Pubs.

Spencer, Hannah. With All Best Wishes, Mrs Butterbean. 2008. 28p. pap. 13.50 *(978-1-60693-138-7(5)*, Eloquent Bks.) Strategic Book Publishing & Rights Agency (SBPRA).

Squires, Ricky. Lily & Ike, 1 vol. 2010. 32p. 24.95 *(978-1-4512-9308-1(9))* PublishAmerica, Inc.

Stanek, Robert, pseud. Have a Backyard Picnic. 2009. (Bugville Critters Ser.: No. 14). (ENG., Illus.). 52p. (J). 14.95 *(978-1-57545-210-4(3)*, Reagent Pr. Bks. for Young Readers) RP Media.

Stone, Jessica J. Picnic at the Zoo. 2011. 24p. 11.32 *(978-1-4567-4386-4(4))* AuthorHouse.

Studio Mouse Staff. Pooh & Piglet. 2008. (ENG., Illus.). 36p. (J). (gr. -1). 7.99 *(978-1-59069-419-0(8))* Studio Mouse LLC.

Su, Lucy. Make a Picnic. Su, Lucy, illus. 2003. (Kitten & Baby Kitten Ser.). (Illus.). 32p. (YA). *(978-1-85602-445-7(8)*, Pavilion Children's Books) Pavilion Bks.

Thompson, Lauren. Mouse's First Summer. Erdogan, Buket, illus. 2013. (Classic Board Bks.). (ENG.). 34p. (J). (gr. -1 — 1). bds. 8.99 *(978-1-4424-5842-0(9)*, Little Simon) Little Simon.

—Mouse's First Summer. Erdogan, Buket, illus. 2014. (J). *(978-1-4351-5506-0(8))* Simon & Schuster.

Twin Sisters(r) Staff. Five Little Skunks. 2010. (J). (gr. k-2). pap. 4.99 *(978-1-59922-509-8(3))* Twin Sisters IP, LLC.

Underwood, Barbara J. Paula's Pickle Picnic. Pfeiffer, Judith, illus. 2006. (ENG.). 20p. (gr. 1-3). pap. 8.95 *(978-1-57874-293-6(5)*, Kaeden Bks.) Kaeden Corp.

—Paula's Pickle Picnic (6 Pack) Pfeiffer, Judith, illus. 2006. (ENG.). 20p. (gr. 1-3). pap. *(978-1-57874-294-3(3)*, Kaeden Bks.) Kaeden Corp.

Ungerer, Tomi. The Mellops Strike Oil. 2011. (ENG., Illus.). 32p. (gr. -1-2). 12.95 *(978-0-7148-6249-1(5))* Phaidon Pr., Inc.

Usher, Sam. Sun. Usher, Sam, illus. 2018. (Seasons Quartet Ser.). (ENG., Illus.). 40p. (J). (gr. -1-2). 16.99 *(978-0-7636-9949-9(7)*, Templar) Candlewick Pr.

Van Stockum, Hilda. A Day on Skates: The Story of a Dutch Picnic. Van Stockum, Hilda, illus. 2007. (Illus.). 40p. (J). (gr. 1). 19.95 *(978-1-932350-18-0(7))* Bethlehem Bks.

Wax, Wendy. Picnic Day! Artful Doodlers, illus. 2006. 24p. (J). lib. bdg. 15.00 *(978-1-4242-0952-1(8))* Fitzgerald Bks.

Wells, Bridget & Wells, Alexis. Mason & Molly: Picnic. 2010. 12p. 13.00 *(978-1-4269-3469-8(6))* Trafford Publishing.

William H. Sadlier Staff. Patty & Pop's Picnic. 2005. (Emergent Library: Vol. 2). (gr. -1-1). 24.00 net. *(978-0-8215-8932-8(6))* Sadlier, William H. Inc.

Williams, David K. The Picnic. Ovresat, Laura, illus. 2006. (Green Light Readers Level 1 Ser.). (ENG.). 24p. (J). (gr. -1-3). pap. 4.99 *(978-0-15-205782-4(X)*, 1197377, Clarion Bks.) HarperCollins Pubs.

—The Picnic. Ovresat, Laura, illus. 2006. (Green Light Readers Level 1 Ser.). (gr. -1-1). 13.95 *(978-0-7569-7209-7(4))* Perfection Learning Corp.

Williams, Rozanne. A Picnic. 2017. (Learn-To-Read Ser.). (ENG., Illus.). (J). pap. 3.49 *(978-1-68310-322-6(X))* Pacific Learning, Inc.

Willis, Lisa M. The Bug's Picnic. 2008. 28p. pap. 24.95 *(978-1-60563-389-3(5))* America Star Bks.

Yeoman, John. The Bear's Water Picnic. Blake, Quentin, illus. 2011. (ENG.). 40p. (J). (gr. k-k). pap. 12.99 *(978-1-84939-004-0(5))* Andersen Pr. GBR. Dist: Independent Pubs. Group.

Young, Lauren. Ally M. & Ally G. Rooney, Sandra, illus. 2006. 20p. (J). 9.95 *(978-1-4120-8518-2(7))* Trafford Publishing.

Young, Polly G. Pokey Pig's Picnic. Raymond, Janet Y., illus. 2007. (J). pap. 15.00 *(978-0-8059-7298-6(6))* Dorrance Publishing Co., Inc.

PICTOGRAPHS

see Picture-Writing

PICTORIAL WORKS

see Pictures

PICTURE BOOKS

see also Stories without Words

Abernethy, Jean. Fergus & the Night Before Christmas. 2018. (ENG., Illus.). 40p. 15.95 *(978-1-57076-896-5(X))* Trafalgar Square Bks.

Abnett, Dan. Dreamworks Classics: Game On!, Vol. 3. Gallant, S., illus. 2016. (DreamWorks Classics Ser.: 3). (ENG.). 64p. (J). (gr. 3-7). pap. 6.99 *(978-1-78276-248-5(5))* Titan Bks. Ltd. GBR. Dist: Penguin Random Hse. LLC.

Abrams, Pam. Now I Eat My ABC's. Wolf, Bruce, illus. 2004. (ENG.). 8p. (J). (gr. -1 — 1). bds. 7.99 *(978-0-439-64942-1(0)*, Cartwheel Bks.) Scholastic, Inc.

Accord Publishing, Accord. Where Does Love Come From? Kirkova, Milena, illus. 2012. (ENG.). 18p. (J). bds. 5.99 *(978-1-4494-2884-6(3))* Andrews McMeel Publishing.

Acreman, Hayley. Found You Rabbit! Acreman, Hayley, illus. 2011. (ENG., Illus.). 34p. (J). (gr. k-2). pap. 9.95 *(978-1-905762-87-3(9))* Parthian Bks. GBR. Dist: Independent Pubs. Group.

Adams, Ben. Chico Plays Hide & Seek. Cameron, Craig, illus. 2013. (Googly Eyes Ser.). (ENG.). 12p. (J). (gr. -1-k). bds. 6.99 *(978-1-84322-280-4(9)*, Armadillo) Anness Publishing GBR. Dist: National Bk. Network.

—The Pig with the Curliest Tail. Cameron, Craig, illus. 2013. (Googly Eyes Ser.). 12p. (J). (gr. -1-k). bds. 6.99 *(978-1-84322-618-5(9)*, Armadillo) Anness Publishing GBR. Dist: National Bk. Network.

—Polly the Farm Puppy. Cameron, Craig, illus. 2013. (Googly Eyes Ser.). 12p. (J). (gr. -1-k). bds. 6.99 *(978-1-84322-319-1(8)*, Armadillo) Anness Publishing GBR. Dist: National Bk. Network.

Adams, Chris. Dan the Biggest Dump Truck. Briggs-Greenberg, Ruthie, illus. 2017. 40p. (J). (gr. -1-2). 15.95 *(978-1-63076-056-4(0))* Muddy Boots Pr.

Adams, Jennifer. Alice in Wonderland: A BabyLit(TM) Colors Primer, 1 vol. Oliver, Alison, illus. 2012. (BabyLit Ser.). 22p. (J). (gr. k-1). bds. 11.99 *(978-1-4236-2477-6(7))* Gibbs Smith, Publisher.

—Around the World in 80 Days: A BabyLit(TM) Transportation Primer, 1 vol. Oliver, Alison, illus. 2018. (BabyLit Ser.). 22p. (J). (— 1). bds. 9.99 *(978-1-4236-4746-1(7))* Gibbs Smith, Publisher.

—A Christmas Carol: A BabyLit(TM) Colors Primer, 1 vol. Oliver, Alison, illus. 2012. (BabyLit Ser.). 22p. (J). (gr. k-1). bds. 11.99 *(978-1-4236-2575-9(7))* Gibbs Smith, Publisher.

—Dracula: A BabyLit(TM) Counting Primer, 1 vol. Oliver, Alison, illus. 2012. (BabyLit Ser.). 22p. (J). (gr. k-1). bds. 11.99 *(978-1-4236-2480-6(7))* Gibbs Smith, Publisher.

—Edgar Gets Ready for Bed: Inspired by Edgar Allan Poe's the Raven, 1 vol. Stucki, Ron, illus. 2015. (Edgar the Raven Ser.). 22p. (J). (— 1). 11.99 *(978-1-4236-4175-9(2))* Gibbs Smith, Publisher.

—Edgar Gets Ready for Bed: a BabyLit(TM) Book: Inspired by Edgar Allan Poe's the Raven, 1 vol. Stucki, Ron, illus. 2014. (ENG.). 32p. (J). 16.99 *(978-1-4236-3528-4(0))* Gibbs Smith, Publisher.

—Jane Eyre: A BabyLit(TM) Counting Primer, 1 vol. Oliver, Alison, illus. 2012. 22p. (J). (gr. k-1). bds. 9.99 *(978-1-4236-2474-5(2))* Gibbs Smith, Publisher.

—A Midsummer Night's Dream: A BabyLit(TM) Fairies Primer, 1 vol. Oliver, Alison, illus. 2016. (BabyLit Ser.). 22p. (J). (— 1). bds. 11.99 *(978-1-4236-4181-0(7))* Gibbs Smith, Publisher.

—Moby Dick: A BabyLit(TM) Ocean Primer, 1 vol. Oliver, Alison, illus. 2013. (BabyLit Ser.). 22p. (J). (gr. k-1). bds. 9.99 *(978-1-4236-3204-7(4))* Gibbs Smith, Publisher.

—Pride & Prejudice: A BabyLit(TM) Counting Primer, 1 vol. Oliver, Alison, illus. 2011. 22p. (J). (gr. k-1). bds. 9.99 *(978-1-4236-2202-4(2))* Gibbs Smith, Publisher.

—Sense & Sensibility: A BabyLit(TM) Opposites Primer, 1 vol. Oliver, Alison, illus. 2013. 22p. (J). (gr. k-1). bds. 9.99 *(978-1-4236-3170-5(6))* Gibbs Smith, Publisher.

—Wuthering Heights: A BabyLit(TM) Weather Primer, 1 vol. Oliver, Alison, illus. 2013. 22p. (J). (gr. k-1). bds. 9.99 *(978-1-4236-3173-6(0))* Gibbs Smith, Publisher.

Adams, Pam, illus. The Farmer in the Dell. 2013. (Classic Books with Holes 8x8 with CD Ser.). (ENG.). 16p. (J). (gr. -1). *(978-1-84643-624-6(9))* Child's Play International Ltd.

Adams, Sarah. Gary & Ray. 2012. (Illus.). 36p. (J). pap. *(978-1-84780-260-6(5)*, White Lion Publishing) Quarto Publishing Group UK.

Adams, Wayne. Laci the Ladybug. Kern, Shelly, illus. 2012. 16p. pap. 24.95 *(978-1-4626-7615-6(4))* America Star Bks.

Adams, William J. Hate That Thunder/Odio Ese Trueno, 1 vol. Stiglich, Tom, illus. 2007. (Mandy & Andy Bks.). (ENG & SPA.). 49p. (J). (gr. k-2). per. 10.95 *(978-0-9772757-1-7(X))* Mandy & Andy Bks., Inc.

Adamson, Ged. Ava & the Rainbow (Who Stayed) 2018. (ENG., Illus.). 40p. (J). (gr. -1-3). 18.99 *(978-0-06-267080-9(8)*, HarperCollins) HarperCollins Pubs.

Adamson, Jean. Topsy & Tim: First Sleepover. 2016. (Topsy & Tim Ser.). (ENG., Illus.). 32p. (J). (gr. -1-k). pap. 9.99 *(978-0-241-18970-2(5))* Penguin Bks., Ltd. GBR. Dist: Independent Pubs. Group.

—Topsy & Tim Go for Gold. Worsley, Belinda & Adamson, Gareth, illus. 2016. (Topsy & Tim Ser.). (ENG.). 32p. (J). (gr. -1-1). pap. 9.99 *(978-1-4093-0946-8(0))* Penguin Bks., Ltd. GBR. Dist: Independent Pubs. Group.

—Topsy & Tim: Go on Holiday. 2017. (Topsy & Tim Ser.). (Illus.). 32p. (J). (gr. -1-1). pap. 9.99 *(978-0-241-28255-7(1))* Penguin Bks., Ltd. GBR. Dist: Independent Pubs. Group.

—Topsy & Tim: Have Their Eyes Tested. 2017. (Topsy & Tim Ser.). (Illus.). 32p. (J). (gr. -1-1). pap. 9.99 *(978-0-241-28254-0(3))* Penguin Bks., Ltd. GBR. Dist: Independent Pubs. Group.

Adewoyin, Beverly. Inside the Mommie Pond. 2013. (ENG.). 28p. (J). pap. 11.95 *(978-1-4327-9703-4(4))* Outskirts Pr., Inc.

Adler, David A. Money Madness. Miller, Edward, illus. 2009. (ENG.). 32p. (J). (gr. -1-3). pap. 7.99 *(978-0-8234-2272-2(0))* Holiday Hse., Inc.

—A Picture Book of John F. Kennedy. Casilla, Robert, illus. 2018. (Picture Book Biography Ser.). (ENG.). 32p. (J). (gr. -1-3). 7.99 *(978-0-8234-4048-1(6))* Holiday Hse., Inc.

Adler, David A. & Adler, Michael S. A Picture Book of Cesar Chavez. Olofsdotter, Marie, illus. 2018. (Picture Book Biography Ser.). 32p. (J). (gr. -1-3). pap. 7.99 *(978-0-8234-4058-0(3))* Holiday Hse., Inc.

—A Picture Book of Harry Houdini. Collins, Matt, illus. 2010. (Picture Book Biography Ser.). (ENG.). 32p. (J). (gr. k-3). pap. 7.99 *(978-0-8234-2302-6(6))* Holiday Hse., Inc.

AG Ferrari, A. G. I Like My Bike. 2019. (I Like to Read Ser.). (Illus.). 32p. (J). (gr. -1-3). 15.99 *(978-0-8234-4097-9(4))* Holiday Hse., Inc.

Aguada, Kaira Pérez. Julia the Raindrop / la Gota Julia: A Windy Day / un día de Viento. 2019. (ENG & SPA., Illus.). 44p. (J). (gr. k-2). pap. 10.95 *(978-0-89556-285-2(5))* Gateways Bks. & Tapes.

—Two Amazing Cats / Dos Gatos Maravillosos. 2020. (ENG, SPA & MUL., Illus.). 44p. (J). (gr. k-2). pap. 11.95 *(978-0-89556-286-9(3))* Gateways Bks. & Tapes.

Aguirre, Zuriñe & Aguirre, Zuriñe. Sardines of Love. Aguirre, Zuriñe & Aguirre, Zuriñe, illus. 2016. (Child's Play Library). (Illus.). 36p. (J). *(978-1-84643-726-7(1))* Child's Play International Ltd.

Ah-Koon, Didier. Minions: Banana!, Vol. 1. Renaud, Collin, illus. 2015. (Minions Ser.: 1). (ENG.). 48p. (J). (gr. 1-4). 14.99 *(978-1-78276-557-8(3))* Titan Bks. Ltd. GBR. Dist: Penguin Random Hse. LLC.

Ajmera, Maya, et al. Music Everywhere! 2014. (Global Fund for Children Bks.). (ENG., Illus.). 32p. (J). (gr. -1-3). pap. 7.95 *(978-1-57091-937-4(2))* Charlesbridge Publishing, Inc.

Aki. The Nature Girls. Aki, illus. 2019. (ENG., Illus.). 32p. (J). 16.99 *(978-1-62779-621-7(5)*, 900156982, Holt, Henry & Co. Bks. For Young Readers) Holt, Henry & Co.

—The Weather Girls. Aki, illus. 2018. (ENG., Illus.). 32p. (J). 17.99 *(978-1-62779-620-0(7)*, 900156981, Holt, Henry & Co. Bks. For Young Readers) Holt, Henry & Co.

Akiona, Micalynn. My Mom Can Do Anything. 2011. 28p. pap. 15.99 *(978-1-4568-2006-0(0))* Xlibris Corp.

Alaimo, Rino. Like a Shooting Star. 2017. (ENG., Illus.). 32p. (J). (gr. -1-1). 16.99 *(978-1-944822-80-4(1)*, 552280) Familius LLC.

Albee, Sarah. The Bunny Hop (Sesame Street) Swanson, Maggie, illus. 2015. (Little Golden Book Ser.). (ENG.). 24p. (J). (-k). 4.99 *(978-0-553-50798-0(2)*, Golden Bks.) Random Hse. Children's Bks.

—Elmo's 12 Days of Christmas. Swanson, Maggie, illus. 2015. (Little Golden Book Ser.). (ENG.). 24p. (J). (-k). 5.99 *(978-0-553-52430-7(5)*, Golden Bks.) Random Hse. Children's Bks.

—Elmo's Tricky Tongue Twisters. Swanson, Maggie, illus. 2016. 24p. (J). *(978-1-4806-9705-8(2)*, Golden Bks.) Random Hse. Children's Bks.

—The Monsters on the Bus (Sesame Street) Ewers, Joe, illus. 2013. (Little Golden Book Ser.). 24p. (J). (-k). 5.99 *(978-0-307-98058-8(8)*, Golden Bks.) Random Hse. Children's Bks.

Albers, Josef. Squares & Other Shapes: With Josef Albers. 2016. (ENG., Illus.). 30p. (gr. -1 — 1). bds. 12.95 *(978-0-7148-7256-8(3))* Phaidon Pr., Inc.

Alborozo. The Acrobat. 2016. (Child's Play Library). (Illus.). 32p. (J). pap. *(978-1-84643-633-8(8))* Child's Play International Ltd.

Albrecht, Ed D. I Won't Take the Mark: A Bible Book & Contract for Children. 2014. (ENG., Illus.). 42p. (J). 25.00 *(978-0-9882802-1-2(3))* Virtue Pr.

Album, Jenny. Bea Gives up Her Dummy: The Book That Makes Children Want to Move on from Dummies! Keay, Claire, illus. 2015. (ENG.). 50p. (J). pap. *(978-0-9926167-3-1(5))* Little Boo Publishing.

Alcraft, Rob. Collins Big Cat Phonics for Letters & Sounds - How Not to Be Eaten: Band 05/Green, Bd. 6. 2018. (Collins Big Cat Phonics Ser.). (ENG., Illus.). 24p. (J). pap. 6.99 *(978-0-00-825175-8(4))* HarperCollins Pubs. Ltd. GBR. Dist: Independent Pubs. Group.

Alderton, David. I Love Cats & Kittens. 2014. (Illus.). 120p. (J). pap. *(978-1-4351-5533-6(5))* Barnes & Noble, Inc.

Aldridge, Ethan M. Estranged. Aldridge, Ethan M., illus. 2018. (ENG., Illus.). 224p. (J). (gr. 3-7). 21.99 *(978-0-06-265387-1(3))*; pap. 13.99 *(978-0-06-265386-4(5))* HarperCollins Pubs. (Quill Tree Bks.).

Alegria, Ricardo. Make a Face. Kuvarzina, Anya, illus. 2017. (ENG.). 32p. (J). (-k). 15.99 *(978-1-57687-850-7(3)*, powerHouse Bks.) powerHse. Bks.

Alemagna, Beatrice. The Bug Next Door. David, Annette, tr. 2012. (ENG., Illus.). 40p. (gr. -1-4). 12.95 *(978-0-7148-6356-6(4))* Phaidon Pr., Inc.

—Child of Glass. 2019. (Illus.). 52p. (gr. 1-5). 18.95 *(978-1-59270-303-6(8))* Enchanted Lion Bks., LLC.

—On a Magical Do-Nothing Day. Alemagna, Beatrice, illus. 2017. (ENG., Illus.). 48p. (J). (gr. -1-3). 18.99 *(978-0-06-265760-2(7)*, HarperCollins) HarperCollins Pubs.

Alko, Selina, illus. My Fathers World. 2006. 36p. (J). 14.99 *(978-0-7847-1440-9(1)*, 04075) Standard Publishing.

Allabach, P. R. Dragon & Captain. Turnbloom, Lucas, illus. 2015. (ENG.). 32p. (J). (gr. k-2). 17.95 *(978-1-936261-33-8(2))* Flashlight Pr.

Allan, Jo, illus. Hide-And-Seek Hettie: The Highland Cow Who Can't Hide!, 30 vols. 2018. 24p. (J). 11.95 *(978-1-78250-508-2(3)*, Kelpies) Floris Bks. GBR. Dist: Consortium Bk. Sales & Distribution.

—Hungry Hettie: The Highland Cow Who Won't Stop Eating!, 30 vols. 2010. 24p. (J). (gr. -1-1). 11.95 *(978-0-86315-779-0(3))* Floris Bks. GBR. Dist: Consortium Bk. Sales & Distribution.

Allcroft, Britt, et al. Thomas & the Buzzy Bees. 2017. (Illus.). 23p. (J). *(978-1-5182-3651-8(0))* Random Hse., Inc.

Allen, Constance. Peekaboo, Elmo! (Sesame Street) Prebenna, David, illus. 2014. (Big Bird's Favorites Board Bks.). (ENG.). 24p. (J). (— 1). bds. 4.99 *(978-0-449-81483-3(1)*, Random Hse. Bks. for Young Readers) Random Hse. Children's Bks.

The check digit for ISBN-10 appears in parentheses after the full ISBN-13

Allen, Debbie. Dancing in the Wings. Nelson, Kadir, illus. 2003. (ENG.). 32p. (J). (gr. -1-3). 8.99 *(978-0-14-250141-2(7),* Puffin Books) Penguin Young Readers Group.

Allen, Elaine Ann. Olly Explores 7 Wonders of the Chesapeake Bay, 1 vol. Nash, Kelli, illus. 2015. (ENG.). 32p. (J). (gr. -1-3). 16.99 *(978-0-7643-4938-6(4),* 6693) Schiffer Publishing, Ltd.

Allen, Kathryn Madeline. A Kiss Means I Love You. Futran, Eric, photos by. 2016. (ENG., Illus.). 16p. (J). (gr. -1 — 1). bds. 8.99 *(978-0-8075-4189-0(3),* 0807541893) Whitman, Albert & Co.

—This Book. Doyle, Lizzy, illus. 2018. (ENG.). 24p. (J). (gr. -1 — 1). bds. 9.99 *(978-0-8075-7881-0(9),* 807578819) Whitman, Albert & Co.

Allen, Pat. The Field by the Sea. 2010. 20p. 21.50 *(978-1-4457-3405-7(2))* Lulu Pr., Inc.

Allen, Traudi. The Squeaky Door. 2012. 40p. pap. 16.95 *(978-1-4525-0826-9(7))* Balboa Pr.

Allepuz, Anuska. That Fruit Is Mine! 2018. (Illus.). 32p. (J). *(978-1-4063-7548-0(9))* Whitman, Albert & Co.

Altes, Marta. No! 2011. (Child's Play Library). (Illus.). 32p. (J). *(978-1-84643-417-4(3))* Child's Play International Ltd.

Alvarez, Lourdes M. My First Book Alphabet. Brooks, David, illus. 2005. (My First Book Ser.). 9p. (J). (gr. -1-17). bds. 3.95 *(978-1-933050-08-9(X))* Sweetwater Pr.

—My First Book Colors. Brooks, David, illus. 2005. (My First Book Ser.). 9p. (J). (gr. -1-1). bds. 3.95 *(978-1-933050-07-2(1))* Sweetwater Pr.

—My First Book Numbers. Brooks, David, illus. 2005. (My First Book Ser.). 9p. (J). (gr. -1-1). bds. 3.95 *(978-1-933050-06-5(3))* Sweetwater Pr.

—My First Book Shapes. Brooks, David, illus. 2005. (My First Book Ser.). 9p. (J). (gr. -1-1). bds. 3.95 *(978-1-933050-11-9(X))* Sweetwater Pr.

Amato, Max. Perfect. 2019. (ENG., Illus.). 48p. (J). (gr. -1-k). 16.99 *(978-0-545-82931-1(3),* Scholastic Pr.) Scholastic, Inc.

Ambatchew, Daniel. Mimi Mystery. 2012. (Illus.). 39p. pap. 10.95 *(978-9988-647-83-4(2))* Sub-Saharan Pubs. & Traders GHA. Dist: African Bks. Collective, Ltd.

American Museum of Natural History, American Museum. Camouflage. 2016. (Science for Toddlers Ser.). (Illus.). 18p. (J). (gr. -1). bds. 7.95 *(978-1-4549-2079-3(3))* Sterling Publishing Co., Inc.

America's Test Kitchen Kids & Frost, Maddie. A Is for Artichoke: A Foodie Alphabet from Artichoke to Zest. 2018. (ENG., Illus.). 26p. (J). (gr. -1-k). bds. 9.99 *(978-1-4926-7003-2(0))* Sourcebooks, Inc.

—1 2 3 the Farm & Me. 2018. (ENG., Illus.). 24p. (J). (gr. -1-k). bds. 9.99 *(978-1-4926-7004-9(9))* Sourcebooks, Inc.

Amery, H. & Cartwright, S. Three Little Pigs. 2004. (First Stories Ser.). 16p. (J). pap. 4.99 *(978-0-7945-0609-4(7))* EDC Publishing.

Amery, Heather. Three Little Pigs. Tyler, Jenny, ed. 2004. (Usborne First Stories Ser.). (Illus.). 16p. (J). (gr. -1). lib. bdg. 12.95 *(978-1-58086-623-1(9),* Usborne) EDC Publishing.

Amnesty International. Dreams of Freedom. 2015. (ENG., Illus.). 48p. (J). (gr. 1-4). 19.99 *(978-1-84780-453-2(5),* 312305, Frances Lincoln Children's Bks.) Quarto Publishing Group UK GBR. Dist: Hachette UK Distribution.

Anastasio, Dina. Mickey & the Beanstalk (Disney Classic) Golden Books, illus. 2018. (Little Golden Book Ser.). (ENG.). 24p. (J). (-k). 5.99 *(978-0-7364-3785-1(1),* Golden/Disney) Random Hse. Children's Bks.

Andersen, Hans Christian. The Emperor's New Clothes. Yim, Gyeong-mi, illus. 2015. (World Classics Ser.). (ENG.). 32p. (J). (gr. k-4). 27.99 *(978-1-925186-10-9(5),* 75c94028-5d52-40d8-85fe-c11393e6dcc2); 7.99 *(978-1-925186-04-8(0),* f7f3027b-8239-449e-aa31-981bdabfe701) ChoiceMaker Pty. Ltd., The AUS. (Big and SMALL). Dist: Lerner Publishing Group.

—The Princess & the Pea. Christy, Jana, illus. 2013. (Little Golden Book Ser.) Tr. of Prindsessen Paa Aerten. 24p. (J). (-k). 5.99 *(978-0-307-97951-3(2),* Golden Bks.) Random Hse. Children's Bks.

Andersen, Hans Christian. & Kusama, Yayoi. The Little Mermaid: A Fairy Tale of Infinity & Love Forever. 2016. (ENG., Illus.). 96p. 45.00 *(978-87-92877-59-8(1))* Louisana Museum of Modern Art DNK. Dist: D.A.P./Distributed Art Pubs.

Anderson, Airlie. Cat's Colours. Anderson, Airlie, illus. 2016. (Child's Play Library). (Illus.). 32p. (J). pap. *(978-1-84643-760-1(1))* Child's Play International Ltd.

Anderson-Craig, Danielle. The Magic of We. Dooling, Carly, illus. 2018. (ENG.). 40p. (J). 17.95 *(978-0-9964016-3-0(6))* Third Man Books.

—The Magic of We: Paperback. Dooling, Carly, illus. 2019. (ENG.). 40p. (J). pap. 14.95 *(978-0-9974578-6-5(4))* Third Man Books.

Anderson, Doug. Hadley & the Bean. 2004. (Illus.). (J). 16.95 *(978-1-59404-038-2(9))* Peanut Butter Publishing.

Anderson, Hans Christian. The Little Christmas Tree: With an Advent Calendar Just for You! Downer, Maggie, illus. 2015. (ENG.). 10p. (J). (gr. k-3). bds. 7.99 *(978-1-86147-291-5(9),* Armadillo) Anness Publishing GBR. Dist: National Bk. Network.

—The Little Match Girl. 2017. (ENG., Illus.). 32p. (J). (gr. 1). 18.99 *(978-1-62972-359-4(2),* 5182575, Shadow Mountain) Shadow Mountain Publishing.

Anderson Jr., John F. My Hearing Loss & Me: We Get along Most of the Time. Bushell, William, illus. 2004. (ENG.). 44p. pap. 24.00 *(978-1-4120-0308-7(3))* Trafford Publishing.

Anderson, M. T. Me, All Alone, at the End of the World. Hawkes, Kevin, illus. 2017. (ENG.). 48p. (J). (gr. 1-4). 14.99 *(978-0-7636-8902-5(5))* Candlewick Pr.

Anderson, Richard. A Home Run for Bunny. Purnell, Gerald, illus. 2013. (ENG.). (J). (gr. -1-3). 16.95 *(978-0-9855417-2-9(5))* Inspire Every Child dba Illumination Arts.

Anderson, Ted, et al. My Little Pony: Friendship Is Magic Volume 15 Vol. 15. Price, Andy & Fleecs, Tony, illus. 2018. (My Little Pony Ser.: 15). (ENG.). 120p. (J). (gr. 4-7). pap. 17.99 *(978-1-68405-357-5(9))* Idea & Design Works, LLC.

Anderson, William T. Almanzo Picture Book Biography. Date not set. (Illus.). 40p. (J). (gr. -1-3). 15.99 *(978-0-06-028975-1(9));* pap. 5.99 *(978-0-06-443684-7(5));* lib. bdg. 16.89 *(978-0-06-028976-8(7))* HarperCollins Pubs.

Andreae, Giles. I Love My Daddy [board Book]. Dodd, Emma, illus. 2014. (ENG.). 26p. (J). (gr. -1 — 1). bds. 7.99 *(978-1-4231-9970-0(7))* Hyperion Bks. for Children.

—Mad about Mega Beasts! 2015. (Mad About Ser.). (ENG., Illus.). 32p. (J). (gr. -1-k). pap. 9.99 *(978-1-4083-2936-8(0),* Orchard Bks.) Hachette Children's Group GBR. Dist: Hachette Bk. Group.

—Morris the Mankiest Monster. McIntyre, Sarah, illus. 2011. 32p. (J). (gr. -1-k). pap. 14.95 *(978-0-552-55935-5(0))* Transworld Publishers Ltd. GBR. Dist: Independent Pubs. Group.

—My Little World of Happy, 9 vols. 2013. (World of Happy Ser.). (ENG., Illus.). 90p. (J). (— 1). bds. 15.99 *(978-1-4052-6082-4(3))* Farshore GBR. Dist: Independent Pubs. Group.

Andrews, Alexa. At the Beach. Keimig, Candice, illus. 2013. (Penguin Young Readers, Level 1 Ser.). 32p. (J). (gr. k-1). pap. 4.99 *(978-0-448-46471-8(3),* Penguin Young Readers) Penguin Young Readers Group.

Andrews, Julie & Hamilton, Emma Walton. A Fairy Merry Christmas. 2012. (Passport to Reading Level 1 Ser.). (J). lib. bdg. 14.75 *(978-0-606-26692-5(5))* Turtleback.

Andrews McMeel Publishing, Andrews McMeel. Hop, Pop, & Play. 2014. (ENG.). 12p. (J). bds. 5.99 *(978-1-4494-6053-2(4))* Andrews McMeel Publishing.

Anfousse, Ginette & Sarrazin, Marisol. Polo et le Garde-Manger. 2003. (Polo Ser.). (FRE., Illus.). 32p. (J). (gr. -1-3). bds. *(978-2-89021-601-3(2))* Diffusion du livre Mirabel (DLM).

Angleberger, Tom. Bach to the Rescue!!! How a Rich Dude Who Couldn't Sleep Inspired the Greatest Music Ever. Eliopolous, Chris, illus. 2019. (ENG.). 40p. (J). (gr. -1-3). 17.99 *(978-1-4197-3164-8(5),* 1194301, Abrams Bks. for Young Readers) Abrams, Inc.

Anholt, Laurence. The Magical Garden of Claude Monet. 2007. (Anholt's Artists Books for Children Ser.). (ENG., Illus.). 32p. (J). (gr. k-3). pap. 9.99 *(978-0-7641-3855-3(3))* Sourcebooks, Inc.

Anthony, Michelle. The Big God Story, 1 vol. Godbey, Cory, illus. 2010. (ENG.). 36p. (J). 12.99 *(978-1-4347-6454-6(0),* 106521) Cook, David C.

Anthony, Ross. Please Don't Step on the Ants. Anthony, Ross, illus. 2006. (ENG, CHI, SPA & JPN., Illus.). (J). per. *(978-0-9727894-4-8(8))* Arizona Blueberry Studios.

Appel, Dee. The Friends in My Garden. Francour, Kathleen, photos by. Date not set. (Tiny Times Board Book Ser.). (Illus.). 10p. (J). bds. 5.99 *(978-0-7369-0564-0(2))* Harvest Hse. Pubs.

—Let's Play Dress Up. Francour, Kathleen, photos by. Date not set. (Tiny Times Board Book Ser.). (Illus.). 10p. (J). bds. 5.99 *(978-0-7369-0563-3(4))* Harvest Hse. Pubs.

Apple, Sam. The Saddest Toilet in the World. Ricks, Sam, illus. 2016. (ENG.). 32p. (J). (gr. -1-2). 18.99 *(978-1-4814-5122-2(7),* Aladdin) Simon & Schuster Children's Publishing.

April, Elyse & Ryan, Regina Sara. Stand Up! The Courage to Care. Oglesby, Maria, illus. 2016. (Family & World Health Ser.). (ENG.). 32p. (J). pap. 9.95 *(978-1-942493-17-4(7))* Hohm Pr.

Archer, Claire. Wolf Spiders, 1 vol. 2014. (Spiders (Abdo Kids) Ser.). (ENG.). 24p. (J). (gr. k-2). lib. bdg. 32.79 *(978-1-62970-076-2(2),* 1655, Abdo Kids) ABDO Publishing Co.

Ardwin, Juanita. Remember When, 1 vol. 2009. 40p. pap. 19.95 *(978-1-4489-2008-2(6))* PublishAmerica, Inc.

Arhoj, Anders. Catch Me: a Sneak-And-Find Book (Search & Find Books for Kids, Interactive Dog Books for Kids, Interactive Toddler Book) 2019. (Find Me, Catch Me Ser.). (ENG., Illus.). 40p. (J). (gr. k-3). 17.99 *(978-1-4521-6649-0(8))* Chronicle Bks. LLC.

Armadillo. Let's Count 123: A Very First Number Book. 2015. (Illus.). 48p. (J). (gr. -1-12). bds. 9.99 *(978-1-86147-659-3(0),* Armadillo) Anness Publishing GBR. Dist: National Bk. Network.

—Let's Look & See: Animals. 2014. (ENG., Illus.). 24p. (J). (gr. k-2). bds. 6.99 *(978-1-86147-376-9(1),* Armadillo) Anness Publishing GBR. Dist: National Bk. Network.

—Let's Look & See: Pets. 2014. (ENG., Illus.). 24p. (J). (gr. k-2). bds. 6.99 *(978-1-86147-378-3(8),* Armadillo) Anness Publishing GBR. Dist: National Bk. Network.

—Things That Go! Tractors Trucks Trains Planes Helicopters Balloons Ships Ferries Boats Bicycles Motorcycles Cars. 2016. (Illus.). 48p. (J). (gr. -1-12). bds. 9.99 *(978-1-86147-693-7(0),* Armadillo) Anness Publishing GBR. Dist: National Bk. Network.

Armadillo Press Staff. Alphabet. 2018. (Illus.). 24p. (J). (gr. -1-12). bds. 6.99 *(978-1-86147-664-7(7),* Armadillo) Anness Publishing GBR. Dist: National Bk. Network.

—My Book of Baby Animals: A Fun-Packed Picture & Puzzle Book for Little Ones. 2016. (Illus.). 48p. (J). (gr. -1-12). bds. 9.99 *(978-1-86147-662-3(0),* Armadillo) Anness Publishing GBR. Dist: National Bk. Network.

—My Very First Box of Books: A Set of Six Exciting Picture Books, 6 vols. 2018. (Illus.). 72p. (J). (gr. -1-12). bds. 14.99 *(978-1-86147-739-2(2),* Armadillo) Anness Publishing GBR. Dist: National Bk. Network.

Armadillo Publishing Staff. Words - Let's Look & See. 2015. (ENG., Illus.). 24p. (J). (gr. -1-12). bds. 6.99 *(978-1-86147-485-8(7),* Armadillo) Anness Publishing GBR. Dist: National Bk. Network.

Armitage, Ronda. A Mighty Bitey Creature. Dyson, Nikki, illus. 2018. (ENG.). 40p. (J). (gr. -1-2). 17.99 *(978-0-7636-9878-2(4))* Candlewick Pr.

Armstrong, Ashley Sage-Taylor. The Adventures of Starlight & Sunny: Building a Dream , How to Focus & Make Your Dreams Come to Life, with Positive Conscious Morals. Picture Boo. 2013. 52p. pap. *(978-1-927863-04-6(X))* Armstrong, Ashley.

—The Adventures of Starlight & Sunny: I Am Me ! Who Are You?, How to Find Good Quality Friends & Stand up for One Another, with Positive Morals, Pi. 2013. 52p. pap. *(978-1-927863-00-8(7))* Armstrong, Ashley.

—The Adventures of Starlight & Sunny: The Secret Valley , Book 2, How to Be Happy, to Find Inner Beauty & Peace, with Positive Conscious Morals, P. 2013. 52p. pap. *(978-0-9919517-9-6(4))* Armstrong, Ashley.

Armstrong, Jason. Chocolate Mixer. 2015. (ENG., Illus.). 32p. (J). 12.95 *(978-1-943274-91-8(6),* 9781943274918) Waldorf Publishing.

Armstrong, Jeannette. Dancing with the Cranes, 1 vol. Hall, Ron, illus. 2nd rev. ed. 2017. (ENG.). 24p. (J). (gr. 1-3). pap. 10.95 *(978-1-894778-70-1(7))* Theytus Bks., Ltd. CAN. Dist: Orca Bk. Pubs. USA.

Arnold, Nick, et al. Sticker Activity Atlas. (Illus.). 8p. (J). pap. 9.99 *(978-0-590-24921-8(5))* Scholastic, Inc.

Arnold, Ted. Fly Guy & the Alienzz. 2019. (Scholastic Readers Ser.). (SPA.). 29p. (J). (gr. k-1). 13.89 *(978-0-87617-739-6(9))* Penworthy Co., LLC, The.

Arnold, Tedd. Fly Guy & the Alienzz (Fly Guy #18) 2018. (Fly Guy Ser.: 18). (ENG., Illus.). 32p. (J). (gr. k-2). 6.99 *(978-0-545-66318-2(0),* Cartwheel Bks.) Scholastic, Inc.

Aromshtam, Marina. The Real Boat. Semykina, Victoria, illus. 2019. (ENG.). 64p. (J). (gr. k-3). 17.99 *(978-1-5362-0277-9(0),* Templar) Candlewick Pr.

Aronson, Billy. Melia & Jo. Oxley, Jennifer, illus. 2018. (ENG.). 48p. (J). (gr. -1-3). 17.99 *(978-1-328-91626-6(X),* 1701986, Clarion Bks.) HarperCollins Pubs.

Arruzza, Rick. El Paseo de Sparky. Newton, Pilar, illus. 2003. (SPA.). 24p. mass mkt. 7.95 *(978-0-9744509-1-9(X))* Three Spots Productions.

—Sparky's Walk. Newton, Pilar, illus. 2003. 24p. (J). mass mkt. 7.95 *(978-0-9744509-0-2(1))* Three Spots Productions.

Arsenault, Moira. Bubbles. 2011. 28p. pap. 15.99 *(978-1-4568-5057-9(1))* Xlibris Corp.

Artell, Mike. Hidden Picture Puzzlers. 2018. (Dover Kids Activity Bks.). (ENG.). 128p. (J). (gr. 2-5). pap. 10.99 *(978-0-486-82505-2(1),* 825051) Dover Pubns., Inc.

Arthur, Clint. Bleep Blop Bloop, 1. Schedeen, Minnie, illus. 2006. 24p. (J). per. 8.99 net. *(978-1-4276-0218-3(2))* Aardvark Global Publishing.

Asch, Frank. Mr. Maxwell's Mouse, 0 vols. Asch, Devin, illus. 2014. (ENG.). 32p. (J). (gr. k-4). pap. 8.95 *(978-1-77138-117-8(5))* Kids Can Pr., Ltd. CAN. Dist: Hachette Bk. Group.

Ashman, Linda. Just Another Morning. Muñoz, Claudio, illus. 2004. (ENG.). 32p. (J). (gr. -1-3). 15.99 *(978-0-06-029053-5(6))* HarperCollins Pubs.

Asim, Jabari. Boy of Mine. Pham, LeUyen, illus. 2010. (ENG.). 20p. (J). (gr. -1 — 1). bds. 8.99 *(978-0-316-73577-3(9))* Little, Brown Bks. for Young Readers.

—Girl of Mine. Pham, LeUyen, illus. 2010. (ENG.). 20p. (J). (gr. -1 — 1). bds. 7.99 *(978-0-316-73578-0(7))* Little, Brown Bks. for Young Readers.

Aston, Dianna Hutts. A Rock Is Lively. Long, Sylvia, illus. 2015. (Family Treasure Nature Encylopedias Ser.). (ENG.). 40p. (J). (gr. k-3). pap. 8.99 *(978-1-4521-4555-6(5))* Chronicle Bks. LLC.

Atherton, Isabel. Smelly Ghost. Straker, Bethany, illus. 2013. (ENG.). 32p. (J). (gr. -1-k). 14.95 *(978-1-62087-989-4(1),* 620989, Sky Pony Pr.) Skyhorse Publishing Co., Inc.

Atinuke. Baby Goes to Market. Brooksbank, Angela, illus. (ENG.). (J). 2019. 26p. (-k). bds. 8.99 *(978-1-5362-0552-7(4))* 2017. 32p. (gr. -1-2). 17.99 *(978-0-7636-9570-5(X),* 40028171753) Candlewick Pr.

Atkins, Adam. The Adventures of Shelley the Shuttlecock. 2018. (ENG., Illus.). 28p. (J). pap. 8.99 *(978-1-64133-282-8(4))* MainSpringBks.

Atkins, Jill. Toad Swims for his Life! Mostyn, David, illus. 2004. (ENG.). 24p. (J). lib. bdg. 23.65 *(978-1-59646-712-5(6))* Dingles & Co.

—Tortoise Races Home. Blake, Beccy, illus. 2009. (Tadpoles Ser.). (ENG.). 24p. (J). (gr. -1-2). pap. *(978-0-7787-3902-9(3))* Crabtree Publishing Co.

Atkinson, Cale. Sir Simon: Super Scarer. 2018. (Illus.). 48p. (J). (gr. -1-3). 17.99 *(978-1-101-91909-5(4),* Tundra Bks.) Tundra Bks. CAN. Dist: Penguin Random Hse. LLC.

—Where Oliver Fits. (Illus.). (J). (gr. -1-2). 2019. 38p. bds. 9.99 *(978-0-7352-6511-0(9))* 2017. 40p. 18.99 *(978-1-101-91907-1(8))* Tundra Bks. CAN. (Tundra Bks.). Dist: Penguin Random Hse. LLC.

Atteberry, Kevan. Bunnies!!! Board Book: An Easter & Springtime Book for Kids. Atteberry, Kevan, illus. 2018. (ENG., Illus.). 34p. (J). (gr. -1 — 1). bds. 7.99 *(978-0-06-274141-7(1),* HarperFestival) HarperCollins Pubs.

Atwood, Frederick D. Rocks & Minerals - Pb: A Portrait of the Natural World. 2013. (Portrait of the Natural World Ser.). (Illus.). 72p. pap. 9.95 *(978-1-59764-332-0(7))* New Line Bks.

Atwood, Margaret. Up in the Tree, 1 vol. 2010. (ENG., Illus.). 32p. (J). (gr. k-k). 19.95 *(978-1-55498-080-2(1))* Groundwood Bks. CAN. Dist: Publishers Group West (PGW).

Aulenback, Stephany. If I Wrote a Book about You. Holmes, Denise, illus. 2014. (ENG.). 32p. (J). (gr. -1-3). 16.95 *(978-1-927018-46-0(3),* 9781927018460) Simply Read Bks. CAN. Dist: Ingram Publisher Services.

Austin, Mike. Monsters Love School. Austin, Mike, illus. 2014. (ENG., Illus.). 40p. (J). (gr. -1-3). 18.99 *(978-0-06-228618-5(8),* HarperCollins) HarperCollins Pubs.

Austin, Ruth. Hide Seek Stinky Sweet: a Little Book of Opposites: Board Book. 2018. (ENG., Illus.). 24p. (J). (gr. -1-k). bds. 12.95 *(978-1-946873-08-8(X))* Compendium, Inc., Publishing & Communications.

Author, Oxford. Oxford Picture Dictionary Content Area for Kids Teacher's Edition. 2nd ed. 2012. (Illus.). 376p. tchr. ed., spiral bd. 64.31 *(978-0-19-401780-0(X))* Oxford Univ. Pr., Inc.

Award, Anna. Mealtime: Teach Your Toddler Tab Book. 2017. (ENG., Illus.). 8p. (J). bds. 8.00 *(978-1-909763-24-1(1))* Award Pubns. Ltd. GBR. Dist: Parkwest Pubns., Inc.

—The Story of Goldilocks. 2012. 24p. (J). 9.95 *(978-1-84135-517-7(8))* Award Pubns. Ltd. GBR. Dist: Parkwest Pubns., Inc.

Award Publications Limited Staff, creator. My First Bumper Colouring Fun: ABC & 1 2 3. 2013. (ENG., Illus.). 32p. (J). (gr. -1-3). pap. 6.50 *(978-1-84135-997-7(1))* Award Pubns. Ltd. GBR. Dist: Parkwest Pubns., Inc.

Away in a Manger Coloring Book. 16p. (J). 1.89 *(978-0-7847-1260-3(3))* Standard Publishing.

Awdry, W. Dinos & Discoveries / Emily Saves the World. 2015. (Thomas & Friends 8X8 Ser.). lib. bdg. 14.75 *(978-0-606-36403-4(X))* Turtleback.

Ayer, Paula & Banyard, Antonia. Water Wow! A Visual Exploration. 2016. (Visual Exploration Ser.). (ENG., Illus.). 64p. (J). (gr. 3-7). pap. 12.95 *(978-1-55451-821-0(0))* Annick Pr., Ltd. CAN. Dist: Publishers Group West (PGW).

AZ Books, creator. What Shape? 2012. (Smarty Ser.). (ENG., Illus.). 10p. (J). (gr. -1 — 1). 9.95 *(978-1-61889-247-8(9))* AZ Bks. LLC.

Azadi, Azita. Thank You Sun. 2009. 32p. pap. 16.50 *(978-1-4269-2197-1(7))* Trafford Publishing.

Azore, Barbara. Wanda & the Frogs. Graham, Georgia, illus. 2012. 32p. (J). (gr. -1-1). pap. 7.95 *(978-1-77049-307-0(7),* Tundra Bks.) Tundra Bks. CAN. Dist: Penguin Random Hse. LLC.

—Wanda & the Wild Hair. Graham, Georgia, illus. 2012. 32p. (J). (gr. -1-2). pap. 7.95 *(978-1-77049-306-3(9),* Tundra Bks.) Tundra Bks. CAN. Dist: Penguin Random Hse. LLC.

—Wanda's Freckles. Graham, Georgia, illus. 2012. 24p. (J). (gr. -1-2). pap. 7.95 *(978-1-77049-308-7(5),* Tundra Bks.) Tundra Bks. CAN. Dist: Penguin Random Hse. LLC.

Baas, Thomas. The Flight of Mr. Finch. 2018. (ENG., Illus.). 40p. (J). 17.99 *(978-1-84976-590-9(1),* 1325301) Tate Publishing, Ltd. GBR. Dist: Hachette Bk. Group, Abrams, Inc.

Babsky, Irene. Playing with Words. 2009. (ENG., Illus.). 64p. (J). (gr. -1-3). pap. 7.99 *(978-1-84476-621-5(7))* Anness Publishing GBR. Dist: National Bk. Network.

Baby Shakespeare. (Illus.). 28p. (J). (gr. -1). pap. 21.95 incl. VHS *(978-1-892309-18-1(1))* Baby Einstein Co., LLC, The.

Bach, Nancy. Cristoforo Colombo e la Pasta Al Pomodoro - Christopher Columbus & the Pasta with Tomato Sauce: A Bilingual Picture Book (Italian-English Text) Lätti, Leo, illus. 2013. 30p. pap. *(978-1-938712-06-7(4))* Roxby Media Ltd.

—Galileo Galilei e la Torre Di Pisa - Galileo Galilei & the Pisa Tower: A Bilingual Picture Book about the Italian Astronomer (Italian-English Text) Lätti, Leo, illus. 2013. 26p. pap. *(978-1-938712-07-4(2))* Roxby Media Ltd.

Bader, Bonnie. My Little Golden Book about Martin Luther King Jr. Cornelison, Sue, illus. 2018. (Little Golden Book Ser.). 24p. (J). (gr. -1-3). 5.99 *(978-0-525-57870-3(6),* Golden Bks.) Random Hse. Children's Bks.

Baer, Edith. This Is the Way We Go to School. 2014. 17.00 *(978-1-63419-734-2(8))* Perfection Learning Corp.

Baer, Julien. The Book in the Book in the Book. Bailly, Simon, illus. 2019. 56p. (J). (gr. -1-3). 18.99 *(978-0-8234-4243-0(8))* Holiday Hse., Inc.

Baggott, Stella. Baby's Very First Bath Book. 2011. (Baby's Very First Ser.). 10p. (J). 9.99 *(978-0-7945-2972-7(0),* Usborne) EDC Publishing.

—Baby's Very First Touchy-Feely Book. 2010. (Baby's Very First Board Bks). 10p. (J). bds. 9.99 *(978-0-7945-2647-4(0),* Usborne) EDC Publishing.

Bailey, Catherine. Hypnosis Harry. Rich, Sarita, illus. 2016. 40p. (J). (gr. -1-k). 16.99 *(978-1-63450-171-2(3),* Sky Pony Pr.) Skyhorse Publishing Co., Inc.

Bailey, Linda. If Kids Ruled the World. Huyck, David, illus. 2014. (ENG.). 32p. (J). (gr. -1-2). 16.95 *(978-1-55453-591-0(3))* Kids Can Pr., Ltd. CAN. Dist: Hachette Bk. Group.

—If You Happen to Have a Dinosaur. Jack, Colin, illus. (J). 2017. 30p. (— 1). bds. 8.99 *(978-1-101-91891-3(8))* 2014. 40p. (gr. -1-2). 17.99 *(978-1-77049-568-5(1))* Tundra Bks. CAN. (Tundra Bks.). Dist: Penguin Random Hse. LLC.

—Stanley's Beauty Contest. Slavin, Bill, illus. 2009. (ENG.). 32p. (J). (gr. -1-2). 17.95 *(978-1-55453-318-3(X))* Kids Can Pr., Ltd. CAN. Dist: Hachette Bk. Group.

—Stanley's Wild Ride. Slavin, Bill, illus. 2008. (Stanley Ser.). (ENG.). 32p. (J). (gr. -1-2). pap. 8.99 *(978-1-55453-254-4(X))* Kids Can Pr., Ltd. CAN. Dist: Hachette Bk. Group.

—When Santa Was a Baby. Godbout, Geneviève, illus. 2017. 30p. (J). (— 1). bds. 9.99 *(978-1-101-91916-3(7),* Tundra Bks.) Tundra Bks. CAN. Dist: Penguin Random Hse. LLC.

Bajtlik, Jan. Alphadoodler: The Activity Book That Brings Letters to Life. 2016. (ENG., Illus.). 160p. (J). (gr. k-2). pap. 16.95 *(978-1-84976-405-6(0),* 1649003) Tate Publishing, Ltd. GBR. Dist: Abrams, Inc.

Baker, Adam. Maury C. Moose & the Forest Noel. 2014. (ENG., Illus.). 96p. (gr. 1-6). pap. 10.95 *(978-1-63047-054-8(6))* Morgan James Publishing.

Baker, Catherine. Collins Big Cat Phonics for Letters & Sounds - up on Deck: Band 01B/Pink B, Bd. 1B. Corke, Estelle, illus. 2018. (Collins Big Cat Phonics Ser.). (ENG.). 16p. (J). (gr. -1-k). pap. 6.99 *(978-0-00-825138-3(X))* HarperCollins Pubs. Ltd. GBR. Dist: Independent Pubs. Group.

Baker, Liza. Harold & the Purple Crayon: Under the Sea. 2003. (Festival Reader Ser.). (ENG., Illus.). 32p. (J). (gr. -1-2). pap. 3.99 *(978-0-06-000178-0(X),* HarperFestival) HarperCollins Pubs.

Baker, Stacy. Sammy's Secret. 2005. (J). lib. bdg. 19.95 *(978-1-933732-03-9(2))* Big Ransom Studio.

Baldwin, Christy. Remembering Wilma. Barnes, Sarah, illus. Lt. ed. 2005. 22p. (J). per. 9.95 *(978-0-9765072-0-8(X))* Tribute Bks.

Balet, Jan. Amos & the Moon. 2016. (ENG., Illus.). 24p. (J). 17.95 *(978-1-62326-052-1(3))* AMMO Bks., LLC.

—The Five Rollatinis. 2016. (ENG., Illus.). 24p. (J). 17.95 *(978-1-62326-053-8(1))* AMMO Bks., LLC.

Balla, Trace. Rockhopping. 2016. (ENG., Illus.). 80p. (J). (gr. 3-6). 18.99 *(978-1-76011-234-9(8))* Allen & Unwin AUS. Dist: Independent Pubs. Group.

Ballarini, Joe. A Babysitter's Guide to Monster Hunting #3: Mission to Monster Island. 2019. (Babysitter's Guide to Monsters Ser.: 3). (ENG., Illus.). 320p. (J). (gr. 3-7). 13.99 *(978-0-06-243790-7(9),* Tegen, Katherine Bks) HarperCollins Pubs.

Balsley, Tilda & Wyrick, Monica. Crabbing: A Lowcountry Family Tradition. 2016. (Young Palmetto Bks.). (ENG., Illus.). 32p. 18.99 *(978-1-61117-640-7(9),* P496413) Univ. of South Carolina Pr.

Baltazar, Art. Aw Yeah Comics Volume 2: Time for... Adventure! Vol. 2. Aureliani, Franco, illus. 2015. (Aw Yeah Comics Ser.: 2). 168p. (J). (gr. 3-7). pap. 12.99 *(978-1-61655-689-1(7),* Dark Horse Books) Dark Horse Comics.

Bancroft, Bronwyn. Why I Love Australia. Bancroft, Bronwyn, illus. 2016. (ENG., Illus.). 32p. (J). (gr. -1-k). 13.99 *(978-1-76012-512-7(1))* Little Hare Bks. AUS. Dist: Independent Pubs. Group.

Banks, Kate. Rumble Grumble ... Hush. Shin, Simone, illus. 2018. 40p. (J). (gr. -1-2). 17.99 *(978-1-101-94049-5(2),* Schwartz & Wade Bks.) Random Hse. Children's Bks.
Bar-el, Dan. Dreamboats. Wakelin, Kirsti Anne, illus. 2013. (ENG.). 44p. (J). (gr. -1-3). 17.95 *(978-1-897476-87-1(6))* Simply Read Bks. CAN. Dist: Ingram Publisher Services.
—A Fish Named Glub, 0 vols. Bisaillon, Josée, illus. 2014. (ENG.). 32p. (J). (gr. -1-3). 16.95 *(978-1-55453-812-6(2))* Kids Can Pr., Ltd. CAN. Dist: Hachette Bk. Group.
—It's Great Being a Dad. Perry, Gina, illus. 2017. 32p. (J). (gr. -1-3). 16.99 *(978-1-77049-605-7(X),* Tundra Bks.) Tundra Bks. CAN. Dist: Penguin Random Hse. LLC.
Barasch, Lynne. First Come the Zebra, 1 vol. 2005. (ENG., Illus.). 40p. (J). (gr. 1-4). pap. 12.95 *(978-1-62014-029-1(2),* leelowbooks) Lee & Low Bks., Inc.
Barash, Chris. Is It Rosh Hashanah Yet? Psacharopulo, Alessandra, illus. 2018. (Celebrate Jewish Holidays Ser.). (ENG.). 32p. (J). (gr. -1-3). 16.99 *(978-0-8075-3396-3(3),* 807533963) Whitman, Albert & Co.
Barber, Tom & Chapman, Lynne. Open Wide! 2004. (Illus.). 32p. 14.95 *(978-1-84458-241-9(8))* Avalon Publishing.
Barberi, Gladys. Pink Fire Trucks. Safar, Lina, illus. 2013.Tr. of Los Camiones de Bomberos de Color Rosado. 30p. (J). 16.95 *(978-1-60131-145-0(1))* Big Tent Bks.
Bardhan-Quallen, Sudipta. Tyrannosaurus Wrecks! A Preschool Story. OHora, Zachariah, illus. 2018. (ENG.). 32p. (J). (gr. -1 — 1). pap. 7.99 *(978-1-4197-3322-2(2),* 1051110, Abrams Appleseed) Abrams, Inc.
Barefoot Books. Fast & Slow. Teckentrup, Britta, illus. 2013. (ENG.). 16p. (J). (gr. -1-k). bds. 7.99 *(978-1-84686-952-5(8))* Barefoot Bks., Inc.
Barganier, Jeff S. The Crooked Tree. 2010. (ENG.). 24p. pap. 15.99 *(978-1-4500-4396-0(8))* Xlibris Corp.
Barker, Cordell. The Cat Came Back. 2017. (ENG., Illus.). 48p. (J). (gr. k-3). 19.95 *(978-1-77085-929-6(2),* 1b87e8cf-82b4-43af-beda-42e8330a3f67) Firefly Bks., Ltd.
Barklem, Jill. Adventures in Brambly Hedge. 2020. (Brambly Hedge Ser.). (ENG., Illus.). 128p. (J). 34.99 *(978-0-00-746145-5(3),* HarperCollins Children's Bks.) HarperCollins Pubs. Ltd. GBR. Dist: HarperCollins Pubs.
—A Year in Brambly Hedge. Barklem, Jill, illus. 2017. (ENG., Illus.). 128p. (J). 29.99 *(978-0-00-824117-9(1),* HarperCollins Children's Bks.) HarperCollins Pubs. Ltd. GBR. Dist: HarperCollins Pubs.
Barnard, Lucy. I'm Bigger Than You. Barnard, Lucy, illus. 2018. (Story Corner Ser.). (ENG., Illus.). 24p. (J). (gr. -1-k). lib. bdg. 19.99 *(978-1-68297-316-5(6),* 81e18a26-ec51-4e39-b930-ce0c534ecb52) QEB Publishing Inc.
Barnes, Lesley. Jill & Dragon. 2016. (ENG., Illus.). 32p. (J). (gr. k-2). 17.95 *(978-1-84976-340-0(2),* 1648001) Tate Publishing, Ltd. GBR. Dist: Hachette Bk. Group.
—Jill & Lion. 2017. (ENG., Illus.). 32p. (J). (gr. -1-2). 17.95 *(978-1-84976-437-7(9),* 1644401) Tate Publishing, Ltd. GBR. Dist: Hachette Bk. Group.
Barnes, Steve. Hector. 2012. (ENG., Illus.). 36p. (J). (gr. -1-5). 16.99 *(978-1-60887-070-7(7),* Earth Aware Editions) Mandala Publishing.
Barnham, Kay & Frost, Maddie. The Amazing Life Cycle of Plants. 2018. (ENG., Illus.). 32p. (J). (gr. k-3). 14.99 *(978-1-4380-5043-0(7))* Sourcebooks, Inc.
—The Great Big Water Cycle Adventure. 2018. (ENG., Illus.). 32p. (J). (gr. k-3). 10.99 *(978-1-4380-5044-7(5))* Sourcebooks, Inc.
—A Stroll Through the Seasons. 2018. (ENG., Illus.). 32p. (J). (gr. k-3). 10.99 *(978-1-4380-5041-6(0))* Sourcebooks, Inc.
Barrett, Philip. Where's Larry? Barrett, Philip, illus. 2012. (ENG., Illus.). 32p. (J). pap. 15.00 *(978-1-84717-276-1(8))* O'Brien Pr., Ltd., The IRL. Dist: Casemate Pubs. & Bk. Distributors, LLC.
Barroux. How Many Trees? 2018. (ENG., Illus.). 32p. (J). (gr. -1-k). pap. 7.99 *(978-1-4052-8055-6(7))* Farshore GBR. Dist: HarperCollins Pubs.
Barthe, Raquel M. Rigoberta y la Tormenta. 2018. 40p. (J). pap. 18.99 *(978-607-746-386-3(8))* Progreso, Editorial, S. A. MEX. Dist: Lectorum Pubns., Inc.
Bartlett, Alison. Erice the Reindeer. (ENG., Illus.). 32p. (J). *(978-0-340-65598-6(4))* Hodder & Stoughton.
Barton, Bethany. Give Bees a Chance. Barton, Bethany, illus. (Illus.). 40p. (J). (gr. -1-3). 2019. pap. 8.99 *(978-0-593-11372-1(1),* Puffin Books) 2017. 17.99 *(978-0-670-01694-5(2),* Viking Books for Young Readers) Penguin Young Readers Group.
Barton, Byron. My Bike Lap Book. 2016. (ENG., Illus.). 40p. (J). (gr. -1-3). bds. 12.99 *(978-0-06-233702-3(5),* Greenwillow Bks.) HarperCollins Pubs.
—My Bus. 2014. (ENG., Illus.). 40p. (J). (gr. -1-3). 16.99 *(978-0-06-228736-6(2),* Greenwillow Bks.) HarperCollins Pubs.
—My Car. Barton, Byron, illus. 2004. (ENG., Illus.). 40p. (J). (gr. -1-3). reprint ed. pap. 7.99 *(978-0-06-058940-0(X),* Greenwillow Bks.) HarperCollins Pubs.
—My Car Board Book. Barton, Byron, illus. 2003. (ENG., Illus.). 36p. (J). (gr. -1-3). bds. 9.99 *(978-0-06-056045-4(2),* Greenwillow Bks.) HarperCollins Pubs.
Baruzzi, Agnese. Hidden in Nature: Search, Find, & Count! 2018. (ENG., Illus.). 56p. (J). (gr. k). 14.95 *(978-1-4549-2937-6(5))* Sterling Publishing Co., Inc.
Bash, Sarah E. My Daddy Is Strong, Handsome, & Tall. 2009. 32p. pap. 12.99 *(978-1-4389-5470-7(0))* AuthorHouse.
Bashford, Helen. Perry Panda: A Story about Parental Depression. Skinner, Russell Scott, illus. 2017. 32p. (J). 19.95 *(978-1-78592-412-5(5),* 696669) Kingsley, Jessica Pubs. GBR. Dist: Hachette UK Distribution.
Batt, Tanya Robyn & Barefoot Books. Faery's Gift. Ceccoli, Nicoletta, illus. 2015. 32p. (J). (gr. -1-2). 10.99 *(978-1-78285-145-5(3))* Barefoot Bks., Inc.
Bauman, Amy. Farm Animal Sounds. 2010. 12p. (J). (gr. -1). 9.95 *(978-1-60747-708-2(4),* Pickwick Pr.) Phoenix Bks., Inc.
Baxter, Nicola. Head, Shoulders, Knees & Toes & Other Action Rhymes. Buckingham, Gabriella, illus. 2013. 16p. (J). (gr. -1-6). bds. 7.99 *(978-1-84322-829-5(7),* Armadillo) Anness Publishing GBR. Dist: National Bk. Network.
—Kaleidoscope Book: My First Book of Learning. Elliott, Rebecca, illus. 2013. (ENG.). 16p. (J). (gr. -1-12). bds. 16.99 *(978-1-84322-930-8(7),* Armadillo) Anness Publishing GBR. Dist: National Bk. Network.
—Learn to Count. Elliott, Rebecca, illus. 2013. (ENG.). 16p. (J). (gr. -1-2). bds. 17.99 *(978-1-84322-984-1(6),* Armadillo) Anness Publishing GBR. Dist: National Bk. Network.
—Learn to Tell Time: With Magnets to Use Again & Again! Elliott, Rebecca, illus. 2013. (ENG.). 16p. (J). (gr. -1-12). bds. 17.99 *(978-1-84322-638-3(3),* Armadillo) Anness Publishing GBR. Dist: National Bk. Network.
—The Mermaid & the Star. Rigby, Deborah, illus. 2025. 14p. (J). bds. *(978-1-84322-907-0(2),* Armadillo) Anness Publishing.
—My Ballet Theatre: Peek Inside the 3-D Windows. Chaffey, Samantha, illus. 2014. (ENG.). 24p. (J). (gr. -1-12). 16.99 *(978-1-84322-949-0(8),* Armadillo) Anness Publishing GBR. Dist: National Bk. Network.
—My First 200 Words: Learning Is Fun with Teddy the Bear! Lacome, Susie, illus. 2016. 24p. (J). (gr. -1-12). pap. 7.99 *(978-1-86147-759-0(7),* Armadillo) Anness Publishing GBR. Dist: National Bk. Network.
—My First Fairy Tales: Eight Exciting Picture Stories for Little Ones. Parry, Jo, illus. 2013. (ENG.). 16p. (J). (gr. -1-2). bds. 13.99 *(978-1-84322-991-9(9),* Armadillo) Anness Publishing GBR. Dist: National Bk. Network.
—My First Farmyard Tales: Eight Exciting Picture Stories for Little Ones. Lodge, Ali, illus. 2013. (ENG.). 16p. (J). (gr. -1-2). bds. 13.99 *(978-1-84322-990-2(0),* Armadillo) Anness Publishing GBR. Dist: National Bk. Network.
—My First Words: Nature. Lacome, Susie, illus. 2016. 24p. (J). (gr. -1-12). pap. 7.99 *(978-1-86147-770-5(8),* Armadillo) Anness Publishing GBR. Dist: National Bk. Network.
—My Perfect Doll's House: Peek Inside the 3D Windows. Chaffey, Samantha, illus. 2013. (ENG.). 12p. (J). (gr. k-4). 16.99 *(978-1-84322-924-7(2),* Armadillo) Anness Publishing GBR. Dist: National Bk. Network.
—Out & About: Name 200 Things in the World Around You! Lacome, Susie, illus. 2016. 24p. (J). (gr. -1-12). pap. 7.99 *(978-1-86147-777-4(5),* Armadillo) Anness Publishing GBR. Dist: National Bk. Network.
—Pull the Lever: Who's at Nursery? Lawson, Peter, illus. 2014. (ENG.). 8p. (J). (gr. -1-1). bds. 6.99 *(978-1-86147-393-6(1),* Armadillo) Anness Publishing GBR. Dist: National Bk. Network.
—Rhymes for Playtime Fun. Shuttleworth, Cathie, illus. 2013. (ENG.). 80p. (J). (gr. -1-k). pap. 9.99 *(978-1-84322-921-6(8))* Anness Publishing GBR. Dist: National Bk. Network.
—Shapes. Siewert, Pauline, illus. 2021. 5p. (J). (gr. -1-12). bds. 2.99 *(978-1-84322-782-3(7),* Armadillo) Anness Publishing GBR. Dist: National Bk. Network.
—Sing-Along Songs for Children: Join in with Your Free CD. Finn, Rebecca, illus. 2014. (ENG.). 12p. (J). (gr. -1-k). bds. 14.99 *(978-1-84322-892-9(0),* Armadillo) Anness Publishing GBR. Dist: National Bk. Network.
—The Starlight Ballerina. Jones, Deborah, illus. 2025. 14p. (J). bds. *(978-1-84322-885-1(8))* Anness Publishing.
—Tales from the Toy Box. Press, Jenny, illus. 2012. 80p. (J). (gr. k-4). pap. 9.99 *(978-1-84322-951-3(X))* Anness Publishing GBR. Dist: National Bk. Network.
—The Trouble with Tippers. Ball, Geoff, illus. 2012. (ENG.). 24p. (J). (gr. -1-k). pap. 6.99 *(978-1-84322-783-0(5),* Armadillo) Anness Publishing GBR. Dist: National Bk. Network.
—The Trouble with Trains. Ball, Geoff, illus. 2012. (ENG.). 24p. (J). (gr. -1-k). pap. 6.99 *(978-1-84322-785-4(1),* Armadillo) Anness Publishing GBR. Dist: National Bk. Network.
—The Trouble with Trucks. Ball, Geoff, illus. 2012. (ENG.). 24p. (J). (gr. -1-k). pap. 6.99 *(978-1-84322-786-1(X),* Armadillo) Anness Publishing GBR. Dist: National Bk. Network.
—3-Minute Animal Stories. Everitt-Stewart, Andy, illus. 2013. (ENG.). 80p. (J). (gr. -1-k). pap. 9.99 *(978-1-84322-978-0(1),* Armadillo) Anness Publishing GBR. Dist: National Bk. Network.
Baxter, Nicola & Adams, Ben. Freddie the Fish, Star of the Show. Cameron, Craig, illus. 2013. (Googly Eyes Ser.). 12p. (J). (gr. -1-k). bds. 6.99 *(978-1-84322-621-5(9),* Armadillo) Anness Publishing GBR. Dist: National Bk. Network.
Baxter, Nicola & Birkinshaw, Marie. A Treasury for Little Ones: Hours of Fun for Babies & Toddlers - Stories & Rhymes, Puzzles to Solve, & Things to Make & Do. Endersby, Frank, illus. 2014. 80p. (J). (gr. -1-6). 14.99 *(978-1-86147-368-4(0),* Armadillo) Anness Publishing GBR. Dist: National Bk. Network.
Baxter, Nicola & Cooper, Gill. Ballet Star: A Little Girl with a Big Dream... 2017. (Illus.). 14p. (J). (gr. -1-12). bds. 9.99 *(978-1-86147-853-5(4),* Armadillo) Anness Publishing GBR. Dist: National Bk. Network.
Beale, Madeline. Sarah's Happy Holidays. Goh, Douglas, illus. 2017. 24p. (J). 14.99 *(978-981-4751-88-9(X))* Marshall Cavendish International (Asia) Private Ltd. SGP. Dist: Independent Pubs. Group.
Beard, Lauren, illus. The Fairytale Hairdresser & Father Christmas. 2014. (Fairytale Hairdresser Ser.: 5). (ENG.). 32p. (J). (-k). pap. 12.99 *(978-0-552-57052-7(4))* Transworld Publishers Ltd. GBR. Dist: Independent Pubs. Group.
Bears for Kids: Amazing Pictures & Fun Fact Children Book. 2013. 32p. pap. 12.97 *(978-1-63022-034-1(5))* Speedy Publishing LLC.
Beaty, Andrea. Iggy Peck, Architect. Roberts, David, illus. 2010. (ENG.). 32p. (J). (gr. k-17). pap. 7.95 *(978-0-8109-8928-3(X))* UK Abrams Bks. for Young Readers.
Beauvais, Clémentine & Beauvais, Clémentine. Hello, Monster! Shearring, Maisie Paradise, illus. 2018. (ENG.). 28p. (J). (gr. k-3). 14.95 *(978-0-500-65170-4(1),* 565170) Thames & Hudson.
Beavington, Ruth. Edward Bear. 2012. (Illus.). 112p. (gr. 1-2). 19.95 *(978-1-84624-721-7(7))* Book Guild, Ltd. GBR. Dist: Trans-Atlantic Pubns., Inc.
Bechtold, Lisze. Buster the Very Shy Dog: More Adventures with Phoebe. 2018. (Illus.). 32p. (J). *(978-1-5444-0473-8(5))* Follett School Solutions.
Beck, Carolyn. Buttercup's Lovely Day. 2018. lib. bdg. 22.05 *(978-0-606-41266-7(2))* Turtleback.
Beck, Ian. The Christmas Story. 2005. (Illus.). 32p. (J). pap. 13.99 *(978-0-552-54937-0(1))* Transworld Publishers Ltd. GBR. Dist: Independent Pubs. Group.
Becker, Shelly. Even Superheroes Have Bad Days. Kaban, Eda, illus. 2016. (Superheroes Are Just Like Us Ser.). 40p. (J). (gr. -1-4). 17.99 *(978-1-4549-1394-8(0))* Sterling Publishing Co., Inc.
—Even Superheroes Make Mistakes. Kaban, Eda, illus. 2018. (Superheroes Are Just Like Us Ser.). 40p. (J). (gr. -1-4). 17.99 *(978-1-4549-2703-7(8))* Sterling Publishing Co., Inc.
Beckford, Lois. The Interesting Pen Pal. 2010. 44p. pap. 21.99 *(978-1-4415-0878-2(3))* Xlibris Corp.
Beckler, Bruce. My Daddy Is A Deputy Sheriff. Finney, Simone, illus. Lt. ed. 2004. 14p. (J). per. 5.59 *(978-0-9745210-4-6(3))* Myers Publishing Co.
—My Daddy Is A Fire Fighter: My Daddy Is A Fireman. Peek, Jeannette, illus. Lt. ed. 2004. 16p. (J). 5.59 *(978-0-9745210-8-4(6))* Myers Publishing Co.
—My Daddy Is a Police Officer: My Daddy Wears a Star. Finney, Simone, illus. Lt. ed. 2004. 14p. (J). per. 5.59 *(978-0-9745210-3-9(5))* Myers Publishing Co.
—My Daddy Is A Police Officer: Wears A Badge, 8 bks. Finney, Simone, illus. Lt. ed. 2004. 14p. (J). per. 5.59 *(978-0-9745210-2-2(7))* Myers Publishing Co.
—My Mommy Is A Deputy Sheriff. Finney, Simone, illus. Lt. ed. 2004. 14p. (J). 5.59 *(978-0-9745210-7-7(8))* Myers Publishing Co.
—My Mommy Is A Nurse. Peek, Jeannette, illus. Lt. ed. 2004. 20p. (J). 5.59 *(978-0-9745210-9-1(4))* Myers Publishing Co.
—My Mommy Is A Police Officer: My Mommy Wears A Badge. Finney, Simone, illus. Lt. ed. 2004. 14p. (J). per. 5.59 *(978-0-9745210-5-3(1))* Myers Publishing Co.
—My Mommy Is A Police Officer: My Mommy Wears A Star. Finney, Simone, illus. Lt. ed. 2004. 14p. (J). 5.59 *(978-0-9745210-6-0(X))* Myers Publishing Co.
Beckstrand, Karl. She Doesn't Want the Worms: A Mystery - with Online Secrets. Hollenbach, David, illus. Lt. ed. 2011. (Mini-Mysteries for Minors Ser.: 3).Tr. of Ella No Quiere Los Gusanos. (ENG.). 24p. (gr. -1-2). pap. 9.18 *(978-0-615-49278-0(9))* Premio Publishing & Gozo Bks., LLC.
Bedford, David. The Three Ninja Pigs. Moor, Becka, illus. 2016. (ENG.). 32p. (J). pap. 10.99 *(978-1-4711-2191-3(7),* Simon & Schuster Children's) Simon & Schuster, Ltd. GBR. Dist: Simon & Schuster, Inc.
Bednar, Martin. Sandy's Vision. 2006. (J). lib. bdg. 19.95 *(978-1-933732-15-2(6))* Big Ransom Studio.
Bee, William. And the Cars Go... Bee, William, illus. 2013. (ENG., Illus.). 32p. (J). (-k). 15.99 *(978-0-7636-6580-7(0))* Candlewick Pr.
—Migloo's Day. Bee, William, illus. 2015. (ENG., Illus.). 38p. (J). (gr. -1-2). 14.99 *(978-0-7636-7374-1(9))* Candlewick Pr.
—Stanley the Mailman, 1 vol. 2016. (Stanley Picture Bks.: 5). (ENG., Illus.). 32p. (J). (gr. -1-2). 14.95 *(978-1-56145-867-7(8))* Peachtree Publishing Co. Inc.
—Stanley's Diner, 1 vol. 2015. (Stanley Picture Bks.: 4). (ENG., Illus.). 32p. (J). (gr. -1-2). 14.99 *(978-1-56145-802-8(3))* Peachtree Publishing Co. Inc.
Beedie, Duncan. The Lumberjack's Beard. Beedie, Duncan, illus. 2017. (ENG., Illus.). 40p. (J). (gr. k-3). 16.99 *(978-0-7636-9649-8(8),* Templar) Candlewick Pr.
Beiser, Tim. Bradley Mcgogg: The Very Fine Frog. Berman, Rachel, illus. 2011. 24p. (J). (gr. k-k). pap. 7.95 *(978-1-77049-276-9(3),* Tundra Bks.) Tundra Bks. CAN. Dist: Penguin Random Hse. LLC.
—Little Chicken Duck. Slavin, Bill, illus. 2013. 24p. (J). (gr. -1-2). 17.95 *(978-1-77049-392-6(1),* Tundra Bks.) Tundra Bks. CAN. Dist: Penguin Random Hse. LLC.
Beisner, Monika. Fantastic Toys: A Catalog. 2019. (Illus.). 32p. (J). (-k). 17.95 *(978-1-68137-311-9(4),* NYR Children's Collection) New York Review of Bks., Inc., The.
Bell, Cece. Bee-Wigged. Bell, Cece, illus. 2017. (ENG., Illus.). 40p. (J). (gr. -1-3). 7.99 *(978-0-7636-9312-1(X))* Candlewick Pr.
—Sock Monkey Takes a Bath. Bell, Cece, illus. 2015. (Cece Bell's Sock Monkey Ser.). (ENG., Illus.). 32p. (J). (gr. -1-3). 14.00 *(978-0-7636-7759-6(0))* Candlewick Pr.
Bell, Davina & Colpoys, Allison. Under the Love Umbrella. 2020. (ENG., Illus.). 32p. (J). (gr. -1-1). 16.99 *(978-1-947534-97-1(1))* Scribe Pubns. AUS. Dist: Consortium Bk. Sales & Distribution.
Belli, Alfredo, illus. Speed Bonnie Boat: A Tale from Scottish History Inspired by the Skye Boat Song, 30 vols. 2017. (Traditional Scottish Tales Ser.). 24p. (J). 11.95 *(978-1-78250-367-5(6),* Kelpies) Floris Bks. GBR. Dist: Consortium Bk. Sales & Distribution.
Belshaw, Yvonne. Toby the Flying Cat. Sheldon, Tamia, illus. 2013. (ENG.). 28p. (J). (gr. -1-2). pap. 9.99 *(978-1-62395-495-6(9))* Xist Publishing.
BELTEI, Nadia. Emily's BOOKS: Coloring & Activity book, age Level: 2-3. 2010. 39p. pap. 19.99 *(978-0-557-32843-7(8))* Lulu Pr., Inc.
Ben-Barak, Idan. Do Not Lick This Book. Frost, Julian, illus. 2018. (ENG.). 40p. (J). 18.99 *(978-1-250-17536-6(4),* 900189389) Roaring Brook Pr.
Bender, Rebecca. Giraffe & Bird Together Again. 2018. (Giraffe & Bird Ser.: 4). (ENG., Illus.). 32p. (J). (gr. k-2). 17.95 *(978-1-77278-051-2(0))* Pajama Pr. CAN. Dist: Publishers Group West (PGW).
Benjamin, Floella. My Two Grandads. Chamberlain, Margaret, illus. 2019. (ENG.). 32p. (J). (gr. k-3). pap. 9.99 *(978-0-7112-4091-9(4),* 324891, Frances Lincoln Children's Bks.) Quarto Publishing Group UK GBR. Dist: Hachette UK Distribution.
Bennett, Elizabeth. I Love You to the Moon. Poh, Jennie, illus. 2014. (ENG.). 22p. (J). (gr. -1). bds. 8.95 *(978-1-58925-642-2(5))* Tiger Tales.
—It's Spring Time! Baccala, Gladys, illus. 2013. (ENG.). 16p. (J). (gr. -1). bds. 8.95 *(978-1-58925-639-2(5))* Tiger Tales.
Bennett, Jeffrey. Max Goes to Mars: A Science Adventure with Max the Dog. Okamoto, Alan, illus. 2015. (Science Adventures with Max the Dog Ser.). (ENG.). 32p. (J). (gr. 2-4). 15.00 *(978-1-937548-44-5(9))* Big Kid Science.
—Max Goes to the Space Station: A Science Adventure with Max the Dog. Carroll, Michael, illus. 2013. (Science Adventures with Max the Dog Ser.). (ENG.). 32p. (J). (gr. 2-4). 15.00 *(978-1-937548-28-5(7))* Big Kid Science.
Bennett, Leonie. Locket Out. Adams, Arlene, illus. 2004. (ENG.). 24p. (J). lib. bdg. 23.65 *(978-1-59646-688-3(X))* Dingles & Co.
—No Problem! Brown, Judy, illus. 2004. (ENG.). 16p. (J). lib. bdg. 23.65 *(978-1-59646-680-7(4))* Dingles & Co.
Benoit-Renard, Anne. Navani from Delhi. Rigaudie, Mylène, illus. 2014. (AV2 Fiction Readalong Ser.: Vol. 133). (ENG.). 32p. (J). (gr. -1-3). lib. bdg. 34.28 *(978-1-4896-2271-6(3),* AV2 by Weigl) Weigl Pubs., Inc.
Benson, Cindy. Chloe & Hairy Go to School. 2012. 32p. pap. 12.99 *(978-0-9855202-9-8(9))* Kids At Heart Publishing, LLC.
Bentley, Dawn. Gingerbread Man. 2005. (Holiday Sparklers Book Ser.). (ENG., Illus.). 10p. (J). 4.95 *(978-1-58117-163-1(3),* Intervisual/Piggy Toes) Bendon, Inc.
Bentley, Sue. Picture Perfect. 2014. (Magic Kitten Ser.: 13). lib. bdg. 14.75 *(978-0-606-35683-1(5))* Turtleback.
Bently, Peter. Dustbin Dad. Ayto, Russell, illus. 2013. (ENG.). 32p. (J). pap. 8.99 *(978-1-84738-874-2(4),* Simon & Schuster Children's) Simon & Schuster, Ltd. GBR. Dist: Simon & Schuster, Inc.
Berenstain, Jan & Berenstain, Mike. The Berenstain Bears: The Very First Easter, Vol. 1. 2019. (Berenstain Bears/Living Lights: a Faith Story Ser.). (ENG., Illus.). 24p. (J). pap. 4.99 *(978-0-310-76218-8(9))* Zonderkidz.
—The Berenstain Bears Truth about Gossip, 1 vol. 2018. (Berenstain Bears/Living Lights: a Faith Story Ser.). (ENG., Illus.). 32p. (J). bds. 3.99 *(978-0-310-76575-2(7))* Zonderkidz.
Berenstain, Jan & Berenstain, Stan. The Berenstain Bears Respect Each Other, 1 vol. 2018. (I Can Read! / Berenstain Bears / Living Lights: a Faith Story Ser.). (ENG., Illus.). 32p. (J). pap. 4.99 *(978-0-310-76009-2(7))* Zonderkidz.
Berenstain, Mike. The Berenstain Bears Stand up to Bullying, 1 vol. 2018. (Berenstain Bears/Living Lights: a Faith Story Ser.). (ENG., Illus.). 24p. (J). pap. 3.99 *(978-0-310-76445-8(9))* Zonderkidz.
—Berenstain Bears/Living Lights: The Berenstain Bears' Harvest Festival, 1 vol. 2015. (Berenstain Bears/Living Lights: a Faith Story Ser.). (ENG., Illus.). 24p. (J). pap. 4.99 *(978-0-310-74865-6(8))* Zonderkidz.
Berenstain, Stan. The Berenstain Bears Respect Each Other. 2019. (I Can Read Ser.). (ENG., Illus.). 32p. (J). (gr. k-1). 14.59 *(978-1-64310-905-3(7))* Penworthy Co., LLC, The.
Berenstain, Stan & Berenstain, Jan. Be Your Best Bear! Life Lessons from the Berenstain Bears. 2018. (Illus.). 192p. (J). (gr. -1-2). 12.99 *(978-0-525-57767-6(X),* Random Hse. Bks. for Young Readers) Random Hse. Children's Bks.
Beresford, Elisabeth. Deep Space Womble. (ENG., Illus.). 15p. (J). (gr. k-6). pap. *(978-0-340-74671-4(8))* Hodder & Stoughton.
—The Ghost of Wimbledon Common. (ENG., Illus.). 15p. (J). (gr. k-6). pap. *(978-0-340-73579-4(1))* Hodder & Stoughton.
—Tomsk to the Rescue. (ENG., Illus.). 15p. (J). (gr. k-6). pap. *(978-0-340-73581-7(3))* Hodder & Stoughton.
—The Wombles: Chaos on the Common. (ENG., Illus.). 16p. (J). (gr. k-6). pap. *(978-0-340-74674-5(2))* Hodder & Stoughton.
—Wombles Camping & Cloudberries. (ENG., Illus.). 15p. (J). (gr. k-6). pap. *(978-0-340-73584-8(8))* Hodder & Stoughton.
Berg, Brook. What Marion Taught Willis. Alberg, Nathan, illus. 2005. (J). 16.95 *(978-1-932146-31-8(8),* 1242215) Highsmith Inc.
Berger, Samantha. A Crankenstein Valentine. Santat, Dan, illus. 2014. (ENG.). 40p. (J). (gr. -1-3). 18.99 *(978-0-316-37638-9(8))* Little, Brown Bks. for Young Readers.
Bergman, Mara. Glitter Kitty. Monks, Lydia, illus. 2014. (ENG.). 32p. (J). 8.99 *(978-1-4711-2216-3(6),* Simon & Schuster Children's) Simon & Schuster, Ltd. GBR. Dist: Simon & Schuster, Inc.
Berne, Jennifer. Manfish: A Story of Jacques Cousteau (Jacques Cousteau Book for Kids, Children's Ocean Book, Underwater Picture Book for Kids) Puybaret, Eric, illus. 2015. (ENG.). 38p. (J). (gr. k-3). pap. 9.99 *(978-1-4521-4123-7(1))* Chronicle Bks. LLC.
Berning, Terri J. Grace Alone Is Enough, 1 vol. Arling, Jackie L., illus. 2010. 34p. 24.95 *(978-1-4512-9045-5(4))* PublishAmerica, Inc.
Berrios, Frank. Black Panther. Spaziante, Patrick, illus. 2018. (J). *(978-1-5444-0200-0(7),* Golden Bks.) Random Hse. Children's Bks.
—Black Panther Little Golden Book (Marvel: Black Panther) Spaziante, Patrick, illus. 2018. (Little Golden Book Ser.). (ENG.). 24p. (J). (-k). 5.99 *(978-1-5247-6388-6(8),* Golden Bks.) Random Hse. Children's Bks.
—Football with Dad: A Book for Dads & Kids. Biggs, Brian, illus. 2015. (Little Golden Book Ser.). 24p. (J). (-k). 5.99 *(978-0-385-37925-0(0),* Golden Bks.) Random Hse. Children's Bks.
Berry Byrd, Holly. Jingle & Joy. 2019. (ENG., Illus.). 10p. (J). (gr. -1-k). bds. 10.99 *(978-1-68052-128-3(4),* 1001211) Cottage Door Pr.
Berry, Cate. Penguin & Tiny Shrimp Don't Do Bedtime! Santoso, Charles, illus. 2018. (ENG.). 32p. (J). (gr. -1-3). 17.99 *(978-0-06-249153-4(9),* Balzer & Bray) HarperCollins Pubs.
Berube, Kate. Mae's First Day of School. 2018. (ENG., Illus.). 32p. (J). (gr. -1-2). 16.99 *(978-1-4197-2325-4(1),* 1107001, Abrams Bks. for Young Readers) Abrams, Inc.
Beskow, Elsa. Christopher's Garden, 24 vols. 2nd rev. ed. 2016. Orig. Title: Lasse-Liten I Trädgården. (Illus.). 32p. (J). 19.95 *(978-1-78250-349-1(8))* Floris Bks. GBR. Dist: Consortium Bk. Sales & Distribution.
—The Land of Long Ago, 23 vols. 2010. (Illus.). 32p. (J). (gr. -1-1). 17.95 *(978-0-86315-771-4(8))* Floris Bks. GBR. Dist: Consortium Bk. Sales & Distribution.
—Peter & Lotta's Adventure, 23 vols. 2nd rev. ed. 2016. (Illus.). 32p. (J). 17.95 *(978-1-78250-303-3(X))* Floris Bks. GBR. Dist: Consortium Bk. Sales & Distribution.
Best, Cari. Mabel Beecher: Future Teacher. Hunt, Lisa, illus. 2018. (ENG.). 32p. (J). (gr. -1 — 1). 16.99 *(978-1-5107-2071-8(5),* Sky Pony Pr.) Skyhorse Publishing Co., Inc.
Best Sisters Ever! 2016. (Illus.). (J). *(978-1-5182-2655-7(8))* Random Hse., Inc.
Bethel, Ellie. Michael Recycle Saves Christmas. Colombo, Alexandra, illus. 2010. (Michael Recycle Ser.). 32p. (J). (gr. 1-3). 15.99 *(978-1-60010-843-3(1),* 9781600108433) Idea & Design Works, LLC.
Bevan, Clare. Comet the Fairy Unicorn. 2015. (Mimi's Magical Fairy Friends Ser.: 3). (ENG., Illus.). 32p. (J). (gr. -1-2). pap.

10.99 *(978-1-4472-9424-5(6))* Pan Macmillan GBR. Dist: Independent Pubs. Group.

Bevans, Ph. D. Don't Do That, Harry! The Balloon Story. 2009. 20p. pap. 10.49 *(978-1-4490-2926-5(4))* AuthorHouse.

Beveridge, Dorothy. Counting Belize Frogs & Toads. Beveridge, Jim, photos by. 2012. (Illus.). 26p. pap. *(978-976-8142-47-4(2))* Producciones de la Hamaca.

Bhasin, Kamla. Malu Bhalu. 2022. (ENG., Illus.). 32p. (J). (gr. -1-k). pap. 11.99 ***(978-81-86896-01-3(5))*** Tulika Pubs. IND. Dist: Independent Pubs. Group.

Bianchi, Ms. The Sailor Who Loved to Draw. Bianchi, Ana, illus. 2018. (ENG.). 32p. (J). (gr. -1-8). 15.95 *(978-1-58423-711-2(2),* aa39c005-d909-4f65-825b-bd674742aeea) Gingko Pr., Inc.

Biddulph, Rob. Happy Hatchday (Dinosaur Juniors, Book 1) 2019. (Dinosaur Juniors Ser.: 1). (ENG.). 32p. (J). 17.99 *(978-0-00-832550-3(2),* HarperCollins Children's Bks.) HarperCollins Pubs. Ltd. GBR. Dist: HarperCollins Pubs.

—Odd Dog Out. Biddulph, Rob, illus. 2019. (ENG., Illus.). 32p. (J). (gr. -1-3). 17.99 *(978-0-06-236726-6(9),* HarperCollins) HarperCollins Pubs.

Bieber Domm, Kristin. Hatchling's Journey, 1 vol. Domm, Jeffrey, illus. 2003. (ENG.). 40p. (J). (gr. -1-3). pap. 10.95 *(978-1-55109-438-0(X),* f57d42de-ae15-4d0b-b10c-3384cc83a12d) Nimbus Publishing, Ltd. CAN. Dist: Baker & Taylor Publisher Services (BTPS).

Biedrzycki, David. Ace Lacewing, Bug Detective: the Big Swat. Biedrzycki, David, illus. 2012. (Ace Lacewing, Bug Detective Ser.). (Illus.). 44p. (J). (gr. k-4). pap. 8.95 *(978-1-57091-748-6(5))* Charlesbridge Publishing, Inc.

—Bad Bugs Are My Business. Biedrzycki, David, illus. 2011. (Ace Lacewing, Bug Detective Ser.). (Illus.). 44p. (J). (gr. k-4). pap. 8.95 *(978-1-57091-693-9(4))* Charlesbridge Publishing, Inc.

—Me & My Dragon. Biedrzycki, David, illus. 2011. (Me & My Dragon Ser.). (Illus.). 40p. (J). (gr. -1-3). pap. 7.95 *(978-1-58089-279-7(5))* Charlesbridge Publishing, Inc.

Big Picture 2010. (Big Picture Ser.). (ENG.). 24p. (gr. 1-2). pap. 333.60 *(978-1-4296-5829-4(0),* Capstone Pr.) Capstone.

Biggs, Mac Barnett; pictures by Brian. Noisy Night. 2017. (ENG., Illus.). 32p. (J). 18.99 *(978-1-59643-967-2(X),* 900126272) Roaring Brook Pr.

Big's Big Baby. (Looney Tunes Song & Sound Bks.). (Illus.). 16p. (J). (gr. -1-k). 7.98 *(978-0-7853-1608-4(6),* PI10) Publications International, Ltd.

Bilik-Franklin, MidiAna & Griffith, Indigo, photos by. The Carseat Tourist. 2006. (Illus.). (J). bds. 7.95 *(978-0-9772825-0-0(3))* Critter Camp Inc.

Billings, David. Louie the Buoy. 2010. 36p. pap. 16.99 *(978-1-4520-3010-4(3))* AuthorHouse.

Birdsong, Michelle. Sneasy the Greasy Babysits Abigail. 2009. 20p. pap. 7.32 *(978-1-4120-7205-2(0))* Trafford Publishing.

Biro, Val. Gumdrop Finds a Ghost. (ENG., Illus.). 27p. (J). *(978-0-340-71062-3(4));* pap. *(978-0-340-71063-0(2))* Hodder & Stoughton.

—Gumdrop Makes a Start. (ENG., Illus.). 27p. (J). *(978-0-340-71058-6(6));* pap. *(978-0-340-71059-3(4))* Hodder & Stoughton.

—Gumdrop's Merry Christmas. (ENG., Illus.). 26p. (J). *(978-0-340-71060-9(8))* Hodder & Stoughton.

Bishop, Sam. I Like Bees, I Don't Like Honey! Lumbers, Fiona, illus. 2018. (ENG.). 32p. (J). pap. 8.95 *(978-0-571-33419-3(9),* Faber & Faber Children's Bks.) Faber & Faber, Inc.

Bixley, Donovan. Nga Wira o Te Pahi (the Wheels on the Bus Maori Edition) 2022. (ENG., Illus.). 24p. (J). (gr. -1-k). pap. 17.99 *(978-1-86971-359-1(1))* Hachette Australia AUS. Dist: Hachette Bk. Group.

—Te Pamu o Koro Meketanara (Old Macdonald's Farm Maori Edition) 2022. (ENG., Illus.). 24p. (J). (gr. -1-k). pap. 17.99 *(978-1-86971-358-4(3))* Hachette Australia AUS. Dist: Hachette Bk. Group.

Bixley, Donovan, illus. Pussycat, Pussycat: Purrfect Nursery Rhymes. 2016. 24p. (J). (— 1). pap. 9.99 *(978-1-927262-28-3(3))* Upstart Pr. NZL. Dist: Independent Pubs. Group.

Bjorklund, Dane. Cattitude. 2016. (Illus.). 48p. (J). *(978-1-338-11148-4(5))* Scholastic, Inc.

Blabey, Aaron. Don't Call Me Bear! Blabey, Aaron, illus. 2019. (ENG., Illus.). 32p. (J). (gr. -1-k). 14.99 *(978-1-338-36002-8(7),* Scholastic Pr.) Scholastic, Inc.

Blackburn, Katie. Dozy Bear & the Secret of Food. Smythe, Richard, illus. 2018. (Dozy Bear Ser.). (ENG.). 32p. (J). pap. 9.95 *(978-0-571-33443-8(1),* Faber & Faber Children's Bks.) Faber & Faber, Inc.

—Scoot! Smith, Jim, illus. 2018. (ENG.). 32p. (J). pap. 9.95 *(978-0-571-33639-5(6),* Faber & Faber Children's Bks.) Faber & Faber, Inc.

Blackmore, Katherine, illus. Because of You, Mom. 2019. (J). 13.99 *(978-1-62972-520-8(X))* Deseret Bk. Co.

Blackstone, Stella. Bear Takes a Trip (Oso Se Va de Viaje) Harter, Debbie, illus. 2014. (ENG & SPA.). 32p. (J). (gr. k-1). pap. 7.99 *(978-1-84686-945-7(5))* Barefoot Bks., Inc.

—Bear's Birthday (L'Anniversaire de l'Ours) Harter, Debbie, illus. 2013. 24p. (J). (gr. k-1). pap. 6.99 *(978-1-84686-944-0(7))* Barefoot Bks., Inc.

—Bear's Birthday/El Cumpleanos de Oso. Harter, Debbie, illus. 2013. (ENG & SPA.). 24p. (J). (gr. k-1). 6.99 *(978-1-84686-943-3(9))* Barefoot Bks., Inc.

—Cleo & Caspar. Mockford, Caroline, illus. 2013. 24p. (J). pap. 6.99 *(978-1-78285-053-3(8))* Barefoot Bks., Inc.

—Cleo in the Snow. Mockford, Caroline, illus. 2013. 24p. (J). pap. 6.99 *(978-1-78285-055-7(4));* bds. 6.99 *(978-1-78285-054-0(6))* Barefoot Bks., Inc.

—Cleo on the Move. Mockford, Caroline, illus. 2013. 24p. (J). bds. 6.99 *(978-1-78285-056-4(2));* (gr. -1-k). pap. 6.99 *(978-1-78285-057-1(0))* Barefoot Bks., Inc.

—Cleo the Cat. Mockford, Caroline, illus. 2013. 24p. (J). (gr. -1-k). pap. 6.99 *(978-1-78285-051-9(1))* Barefoot Bks., Inc.

—Hip Shapes. Bell, Siobhan, illus. 2012. 24p. (J). (gr. -1-1). pap. 18.69 *(978-1-84686-762-0(2))* Barefoot Bks., Ltd. GBR. Dist: Children's Plus, Inc.

—Octopus Opposites. Bauer, Stephanie, illus. 2011. (ENG.). 32p. (J). (gr. -1-k). bds. 9.99 *(978-1-84686-591-6(3))* Barefoot Bks., Inc.

—Who Are You, Baby Kangaroo? Beaton, Clare, illus. 2005. (ENG.). 24p. (J). (gr. -1-2). bds. 6.99 *(978-1-905236-19-0(0))* Barefoot Bks., Inc.

—You & Me. Manna, Giovanni, illus. 2009. (ENG.). 32p. (J). 14.99 *(978-1-84686-336-3(8))* Barefoot Bks., Inc.

Blackstone, Stella & Scribens, Sunny. Baby's First Words. Engel, Christiane, illus. 2017. (ENG.). 30p. (J). (gr. -1-k). bds. 14.99 *(978-1-78285-321-3(9))* Barefoot Bks., Inc.

Blair, Beth L. & Ericsson, Jennifer A. The Everything Kids' Picture Puzzles Book: Hidden Pictures, Matching Games, Pattern Puzzles, & More! 2014. (Everything(r) Kids Ser.). (ENG.). 144p. pap. 15.99 *(978-1-4405-7067-4(1),* Everything) Adams Media Corp.

Blair, Rachael. Maya's Gossamer: A Gentle Guide on How to Manifest Virtues in Children. 2014. 80p. pap. 27.99 *(978-1-4525-8684-7(5),* Balboa Pr.) Author Solutions, LLC.

Blake, Quentin. Jack & Nancy: Celebrate Quentin Blake's 90th Birthday. 2013. (Illus.). 32p. (J). (gr. -1-k). pap. 14.99 *(978-1-84941-689-4(3),* Red Fox) Random House Children's Books GBR. Dist: Independent Pubs. Group.

—Three Little Monkeys. Clark, Emma Chichester, illus. 2017. (ENG.). 40p. (J). (gr. -1-3). 18.99 *(978-0-06-267067-0(0),* HarperCollins) HarperCollins Pubs.

Blanchette, Carol & Dugan, Jenifer. The Golden Forest: Exploring a Coastal California Ecosystem. 2017. (Long Term Ecological Research Ser.). (Illus.). 32p. (J). (gr. 2-5). 15.95 *(978-1-63076-180-6(X))* Muddy Boots Pr.

Blathwayt, Benedict. Bear's Adventure. 2016. (Illus.). 32p. (J). (gr. -1-k). pap. 9.99 *(978-1-78027-365-5(7),* 1780273657, Birlinn) Birlinn, Ltd. GBR. Dist: Casemate Pubs. & Bk. Distributors, LLC.

—The Little House by the Sea. 2015. (Illus.). 32p. (J). (gr. -1-k). pap. 10.95 *(978-1-78027-314-3(2))* Birlinn, Ltd. GBR. Dist: Casemate Pubs. & Bk. Distributors, LLC.

—Little Seal. 2017. (Illus.). 32p. (J). (gr. -1-k). pap. 9.99 *(978-1-78027-460-7(2))* Birlinn, Ltd. GBR. Dist: Casemate Pubs. & Bk. Distributors, LLC.

—Rally Car. 2017. (ENG., Illus.). 12p. (J). (— 1). 7.99 *(978-1-78027-366-2(5))* Birlinn, Ltd. GBR. Dist: Casemate Pubs. & Bk. Distributors, LLC.

—Tig & Tag. 2015. (Illus.). 32p. (J). (gr. -1-k). pap. 9.99 *(978-1-78027-312-9(6))* Birlinn, Ltd. GBR. Dist: Casemate Pubs. & Bk. Distributors, LLC.

Blazin' Hot: Picture Book (English) NL 9x9 with Snipe. 2007. (J). 5.99 *(978-1-933934-46-4(8))* Mighty Kids Media.

Bledsoe, Amanda. Chores, S'mores!, 1 vol. Perry, Jodi, ed. 2009. 28p. pap. 24.95 *(978-1-60703-605-0(3))* PublishAmerica, Inc.

—Chores S'mores, 1 vol. 2010. 26p. 24.95 *(978-1-4512-1507-6(X))* PublishAmerica, Inc.

Bleu, Kennedy. Cotter Otter in Treasure Water. Goembel, Ponder, illus. 2014. (ENG.). 24p. (J). pap. 24.95 *(978-1-63004-814-3(3))* America Star Bks.

Blight, Peter. The Lonely Giraffe. Terry, Michael, illus. 2006. (Bloomsbury Paperbacks Ser.). 32p. (J). (gr. -1-3). pap. 12.99 *(978-0-7475-7144-5(9))* Bloomsbury Publishing Plc GBR. Dist: Trafalgar Square Publishing.

Bloch, Serge. The Big Adventure of a Little Line. 2016. (ENG., Illus.). 88p. (J). (gr. 1-3). 19.95 *(978-0-500-65058-5(6),* 565058) Thames & Hudson.

Blume, Judy. The One in the Middle Is the Green Kangaroo. 39p. (J). (gr. k-3). pap. 3.99 *(978-0-8072-1337-7(3),* Listening Library) Random Hse. Audio Publishing Group.

Blyton, Enid. Stories Jesus Told. 2012. 24p. (J). 9.95 *(978-1-84135-745-4(6))* Award Pubns. Ltd. GBR. Dist: Parkwest Pubns., Inc.

—Story of Jesus. 2012. 24p. (J). 9.95 *(978-1-84135-744-7(8))* Award Pubns. Ltd. GBR. Dist: Parkwest Pubns., Inc.

Boddy, Gary. Giraffe's Holiday in Sydney. 2007. 23p. 19.95 *(978-1-84799-919-1(0))* Lulu Pr., Inc.

—This Cow These Cows. 2007. 31p. 21.00 *(978-1-84799-960-3(3))* Lulu Pr., Inc.

Bodecker, N. M. The Mushroom Center Disaster. Blegvad, Erik & Starr, Branka, illus. 2004. (ENG.). 48p. (J). reprint ed. *(978-1-931561-98-3(2))* MacAdam/Cage Publishing, Inc.

—Quimble Wood. Starr, Branka, illus. 2004. (ENG.). 32p. (J). reprint ed. *(978-1-931561-97-6(4))* MacAdam/Cage Publishing, Inc.

Boehne, Jacob A. Two Long Ears, 1 vol. 2016. (ENG., Illus.). 24p. (J). bds. 9.99 *(978-0-7643-5039-9(0),* 9780764350399) Schiffer Publishing, Ltd.

Boelts, Maribeth. A Bike Like Sergio's. Jones, Noah Z., illus. (ENG.). 40p. (J). (gr. k-3). 2018. 7.99 *(978-1-5362-0295-3(9))* 2016. 17.99 *(978-0-7636-6649-1(1))* Candlewick Pr.

Bogart, Jo Ellen. Big & Small, Room for All. Newland, Gillian, illus. 2017. 30p. (J). (— 1). bds. 8.99 *(978-0-14-319893-2(9),* Tundra Bks.) Tundra Bks. CAN. Dist: Penguin Random Hse. LLC.

—Count Your Chickens. Smith, Lori Joy, illus. 2017. 32p. (J). (-k). 16.99 *(978-1-77049-792-4(7),* Tundra Bks.) Tundra Bks. CAN. Dist: Penguin Random Hse. LLC.

Bolden, Tonya. Beautiful Moon. 2014. (ENG., Illus.). 32p. (J). (gr. -1-3). 16.95 *(978-1-4197-0792-6(2),* 679501, Abrams Bks. for Young Readers) Abrams, Inc.

Boldt, Claudia. Melvin the Luckiest Monkey. 2013. (ENG., Illus.). 32p. (J). (gr. -1-k). 14.95 *(978-1-84976-086-7(1))* Tate Publishing, Ltd. GBR. Dist: Hachette Bk. Group.

—The Mystery of the Missing Cake. 2018. (ENG., Illus.). 32p. (J). (gr. -1-3). 16.95 *(978-1-84976-485-8(9))* Tate Publishing, Ltd. GBR. Dist: Hachette Bk. Group.

—Odd Dog. 2012. (ENG., Illus.). 32p. (J). (gr. -1-1). 16.95 *(978-0-7358-4068-3(7))* North-South Bks., Inc.

—Outfoxed. 2016. (ENG., Illus.). 32p. (J). (gr. k-2). 16.95 *(978-1-84976-313-4(5),* 1666201) Tate Publishing, Ltd. GBR. Dist: Abrams, Inc.

Boldt, Mike. 123 Versus ABC. Boldt, Mike, illus. 2013. (ENG., Illus.). 32p. (J). (gr. -1-3). 17.99 *(978-0-06-210299-7(0),* HarperCollins) HarperCollins Pubs.

Bollman, Anne. Help Find Frank. 2018. (Illus.). 40p. (J). (gr. -1-2). 16.95 *(978-1-4549-2678-8(3))* Sterling Publishing Co., Inc.

Bond, Felicia. The Halloween Play. Bond, Felicia, illus. 2003. Orig. Title: The Halloween Performance. (Illus.). 32p. (J). (gr. -1-18). 6.99 *(978-0-06-054443-0(0))* HarperCollins Pubs.

Bond, Michael. The Paddington Treasury: Six Classic Bedtime Stories. Alley, R. W., illus. 2014. (Paddington Ser.). (ENG.). 160p. (J). (gr. -1-3). 21.99 *(978-0-06-231242-6(1),* HarperCollins) HarperCollins Pubs.

Bone, Emily. Seashore. 2018. (Young Beginners Ser.). (ENG.). 32p. (J). 4.99 *(978-0-7945-4031-9(7),* Usborne) EDC Publishing.

Bonilla, Rocío & Lethem, Mara. Max & the Superheroes. Bonilla, Rocío & Malet, Oriol, illus. 2018. (ENG.). 48p. (J). (gr. -1-3). lib. bdg. 14.99 *(978-1-58089-844-7(0))* Charlesbridge Publishing, Inc.

Bonnet, Rosalinde. Very First Words Christmas. 2011. (Very First Words Board Book Ser.). 24p. (J). ring bd. 6.99 *(978-0-7945-2937-6(2),* Usborne) EDC Publishing.

Bonnet, Rosalinde, illus. Alphabet Picture Book. 2011. (Alphabet Picture Book Ser.). 26p. (J). ring bd. 11.99 *(978-0-7945-2954-3(2),* Usborne) EDC Publishing.

Bonwill, Ann. Naughty Toes. Murfin, Teresa, illus. 2011. (ENG.). 32p. 15.95 *(978-1-58925-103-8(2));* pap. 7.95 *(978-1-58925-430-5(9))* Tiger Tales.

Boon, Emilie. Ella & Monkey at Sea. Boon, Emilie, illus. 2018. (Illus.). 32p. (J). (gr. -1-2). 16.99 *(978-0-7636-9233-9(6))* Candlewick Pr.

Booth, Anne. I Want a Friend. Proud, Amy, illus. 2017. (ENG.). 32p. (J). pap. 10.99 *(978-0-7459-7706-5(5),* d322e2dd-abd5-495f-bf57-6714fdca9910, Lion Children's) Lion Hudson PLC GBR. Dist: Baker & Taylor Publisher Services (BTPS).

Booth, Tom. Day at the Beach. Booth, Tom, illus. 2018. (Jeter Publishing Ser.). (ENG., Illus.). 40p. (J). (gr. -1-3). 19.99 *(978-1-5344-1105-0(4),* Aladdin) Simon & Schuster Children's Publishing.

Borando, Silvia. The Cat Book: A Minibombo Book. Borando, Silvia, illus. 2017. (Minibombo Ser.). (ENG., Illus.). 32p. (J). (-k). 9.99 *(978-0-7636-9472-2(X))* Candlewick Pr.

Borando, Silvia, et al. The White Book: A Minibombo Book. 2015. (Minibombo Ser.). (ENG., Illus.). 48p. (J). (gr. -1-k). 14.00 *(978-0-7636-8107-4(5))* Candlewick Pr.

Border, Terry. Snack Attack! Border, Terry, illus. 2019. (Illus.). 32p. (J). (gr. -1-2). 18.99 *(978-1-5247-4011-5(X),* Philomel Bks.) Penguin Young Readers Group.

Borgert-Spaniol, Megan. Math You Can Munch. 2018. (Super Simple Science You Can Snack On Ser.). (ENG., Illus.). 32p. (J). (gr. k-4). lib. bdg. 34.21 *(978-1-5321-1726-8(4),* 30740, Super SandCastle) ABDO Publishing Co.

Bosak, Susan V. Dream: A Tale of Wonder, Wisdom & Wishes. Dillon, Leo et al, illus. 2004. 40p. (J). *(978-1-896232-04-1(3),* TCP Pr.) Communication Project, The.

—A Little Something. McGaw, Laurie, illus. 2008. 32p. (J). *(978-1-896232-06-5(X),* TCP Pr.) Communication Project, The.

Bostrom, Kathleen Long. Count Your Blessings. Reed, Lisa, illus. 2017. (VeggieTales Ser.). (ENG.). 20p. (J). (gr. -1-k). bds. 7.99 *(978-0-8249-1664-0(6))* Worthy Publishing.

Botman, Loes, illus. Hello Animals, What Makes You Special?, 65 vols. 2015. (Hello Animals Ser.). 12p. (J). 9.95 *(978-1-78250-218-0(1))* Floris Bks. GBR. Dist: Consortium Bk. Sales & Distribution.

—Hello Animals, Where Do You Live?, 65 vols. 2015. (Hello Animals Ser.). 12p. (J). 9.95 *(978-1-78250-219-7(X))* Floris Bks. GBR. Dist: Consortium Bk. Sales & Distribution.

Bouchard, David & Bouchard, David. Nokum Is My Teacher, 1 vol. Sapp, Allen, illus. 2006. (ENG.). 32p. (J). (gr. 2-5). 24.95 *(978-0-88995-367-3(8),* 07eb83b6-4ced-4e78-a5bb-79378d37c75b) Red Deer Pr. CAN. Dist: Firefly Bks., Ltd.

Bourke, Nike & Danalis, Stella. What the Sky Knows. 2005. (Illus.). 32p. (J). *(978-0-7022-3501-6(6))* Univ. of Queensland Pr.

Bourne, Lars. Casper the Friendly Ghost Classics, Vol. 1. 2018. (ENG., Illus.). 144p. (J). pap. 19.99 *(978-1-945205-09-5(1),* 6f3c8c7d-7cb9-4da7-9e6e-6fe4a68f7ef1) American Mythology Productions.

Bové, Jennifer. I Wish I Was a Gorilla. 2018. (Illus.). 31p. (J). *(978-1-5444-0104-1(3))* Harper & Row Ltd.

Bowen, Anne. I Loved You Before You Were Born Board Book. Shed, Greg, illus. 2017. (ENG.). 30p. (J). (gr. -1 — 1). bds. 8.99 *(978-0-06-269094-4(9),* HarperFestival) HarperCollins Pubs.

Bowie, C. W. Busy Fingers. Willingham, Fred, illus. 2004. (ENG.). 28p. (J). (gr. -1 — 1). bds. 7.95 *(978-1-58089-048-9(2))* Charlesbridge Publishing, Inc.

Bowie, Sarah. Let's See Ireland! Bowie, Sarah, illus. 2016. (ENG., Illus.). 32p. (J). 21.00 *(978-1-84717-731-5(X))* O'Brien Pr., Ltd., The IRL. Dist: Casemate Pubs. & Bk. Distributors, LLC.

—We're Going to the Zoo! 2018. (ENG., Illus.). 32p. (J). 20.00 *(978-1-84717-949-4(5))* O'Brien Pr., Ltd., The IRL. Dist: Casemate Pubs. & Bk. Distributors, LLC.

Bowman, Crystal. My Christmas Stocking: Filled with God's Love, 1 vol. Gevry, Claudine, illus. 2015. (ENG.). 14p. (J). bds. 6.99 *(978-0-310-73823-7(7))* Zonderkidz.

Bowness, Kim. The Brave Engineers. 2007. (Illus.). 30p. (J). lib. bdg. 19.95 *(978-1-933732-36-7(9))* Big Ransom Studio.

Box, Su. Baby Jesus. East, Jacqueline, illus. 2014. (Bible Dial-A-Picture Bks.). (ENG.). 8p. (J). (gr. k-1). bds. 6.99 *(978-0-7641-6694-5(8))* Sourcebooks, Inc.

Boyd, Lizi. I Love Grandma. Boyd, Lizi, illus. 2009. (Super Sturdy Picture Bks.). (ENG., Illus.). 24p. (J). (gr. -1-k). 8.99 *(978-0-7636-3728-6(9))* Candlewick Pr.

—Who Loves Books? A Flip-Flap Book (Interactive Board Book for Toddlers, Mix & Match Animals) 2020. (ENG., Illus.). 18p. (J). (gr. -1 — 1). bds. 12.99 *(978-1-4521-7097-8(5))* Chronicle Bks. LLC.

Boyer, Crispin. So Cool! Sharks. 2019. (Cool/Cute Ser.). (Illus.). 32p. (J). (gr. -1-k). 6.99 *(978-1-4263-3361-3(7),* National Geographic Kids) Disney Publishing Worldwide.

Boyer, Mitch. Vivian the Dog Moves to the Big City. Boyer, Mitch, illus. 2017. (ENG., Illus.). 40p. (J). (gr. -1-3). 17.99 *(978-0-06-267327-5(0),* HarperCollins) HarperCollins Pubs.

Boylan, Susan. When Knife Married Fork. 2017. (ENG., Illus.). (gr. k-5). *(978-1-925590-71-5(2))* Vivid Publishing.

Boyle, Brian & Boyle, Pamela. Swim Bark Run. Hughes, Beth, illus. 2018. (ENG.). 32p. (J). (gr. -1-1). 16.99 *(978-1-5107-2696-3(9),* Sky Pony Pr.) Skyhorse Publishing Co., Inc.

Boynton, Sandra. Buenas Noches a Todos (the Going to Bed Book) Boynton, Sandra, illus. 2004.Tr. of Going to Bed Book. (SPA., Illus.). 16p. (J). (gr. -1-k). bds. 5.99 *(978-0-689-86652-4(6))* Simon & Schuster, Inc.

—Little Pookie. Boynton, Sandra, illus. 2017. (Little Pookie Ser.). (ENG., Illus.). 18p. (J). (gr. -1-k). bds. 6.99 *(978-1-4814-9768-8(5))* Simon & Schuster, Inc.

—Perritos (Doggies) Un Libro para Contar y Ladrar. Boynton, Sandra, illus. 2004.Tr. of Doggies. (SPA., Illus.). 16p. (J). (gr. -1-k). bds. 6.99 *(978-0-689-86303-5(9))* Simon & Schuster, Inc.

Bradford, Wade. There's a Dinosaur on the 13th Floor. Hawkes, Kevin, illus. 2018. (ENG.). 40p. (J). (gr. -1-3). 17.99 *(978-0-7636-8665-9(4))* Candlewick Pr.

Bradley, Jeanette. Love, Mama. Bradley, Jeanette, illus. 2019. (ENG., Illus.). 28p. (J). bds. 7.99 *(978-1-250-24035-4(2),* 900211506) Roaring Brook Pr.

Bradman, Tony. Flora the Fairy (Reading Ladder Level 1) Carlow, Emma, illus. 2nd ed. 2016. (Reading Ladder Level 1 Ser.). (ENG.). 48p. (gr. k-2). pap. 4.99 *(978-1-4052-8225-3(8),* Reading Ladder) Farshore GBR. Dist: HarperCollins Pubs.

—Mr. Wolf Bounces Back, 1 vol. Warburton, Sarah, illus. 2013. (After Happily Ever After Ser.). (ENG.). 56p. (J). (gr. 3-6). pap. 4.95 *(978-1-4342-6414-5(9),* 123898, Stone Arch Bks.) Capstone.

—Red Riding Hood Takes Charge, 1 vol. Warburton, Sarah, illus. 2013. (After Happily Ever After Ser.). (ENG.). 56p. (J). (gr. 3-6). pap. 4.95 *(978-1-4342-6413-8(0),* 123897, Stone Arch Bks.) Capstone.

Brandenberg, Franz. I Wish I Was Sick, Too! Aliki, illus. 2018. 40p. (J). (gr. -1-2). 16.95 *(978-1-68137-228-0(2),* NYR Children's Collection) New York Review of Bks., Inc., The.

Brandenburg, Jim. Face to Face with Wolves. 2018. (Face to Face with Animals Ser.). (Illus.). 32p. (J). (gr. 3-7). pap. 6.99 *(978-1-4263-3056-8(1),* National Geographic Kids) Disney Publishing Worldwide.

Brandenburg, Jim & Brandenburg, Judy. Face to Face with Wolves. 2010. (Face to Face (Paperback National Geographic) Ser.). (ENG.). (J). (gr. 2-5). lib. bdg. 17.55 *(978-1-62765-573-6(5))* Perfection Learning Corp.

Brandt, Lois & Vogel, Vin. Maddi's Fridge. 2014. (Illus.). 32p. (J). (gr. k-4). 17.95 *(978-1-936261-29-1(4))* Flashlight Pr.

Brandy. CAN & CAN't Believe in Themselves: Big Life Lessons for Little Kids. 2017. (Illus.). 169p. (J). (gr. -1 — 1). 13.99 *(978-981-4771-29-0(5))* Marshall Cavendish International (Asia) Private Ltd. SGP. Dist: Independent Pubs. Group.

—COULD & COULDN't Are Not Afraid of the Dark: Big Life Lessons for Little Kids. 2017. (Illus.). 345p. (J). 14.99 *(978-981-4771-30-6(9))* Marshall Cavendish International (Asia) Private Ltd. SGP. Dist: Independent Pubs. Group.

—WAS & WASN't Learn That It's Good to Win, but Its Ok to Lose: Big Life Lessons for Little Kids. 2017. (Illus.). 240p. (J). 14.99 *(978-981-4771-32-0(5))* Marshall Cavendish International (Asia) Private Ltd. SGP. Dist: Independent Pubs. Group.

—WILL & WON't Learn to Share: Big Life Lessons for Little Kids. 2017. (Illus.). 272p. (J). 14.99 *(978-981-4771-33-7(3))* Marshall Cavendish International (Asia) Private Ltd. SGP. Dist: Independent Pubs. Group.

Brannon, Pat. Has a Donkey Ever Brought You Breakfast in Bed? Demming, Karen, illus. 2012. 38p. pap. 10.00 *(978-1-938634-90-1(X))* Freedom of Speech Publishing, Inc.

Braud, Alexis. Parade, 1 vol. 2016. (ENG., Illus.). 32p. (J). (gr. -1-3). 16.99 *(978-1-4556-2148-4(X),* Pelican Publishing) Arcadia Publishing.

Bray, Darrell. I Remember Pop's General Store. 2013. 24p. pap. 24.95 *(978-1-63004-679-8(5))* America Star Bks.

Breisacher, Cathy. Cavekid Birthday. GARRIGUE, Roland, illus. 2019. 32p. (J). (gr. -1-3). lib. bdg. 16.99 *(978-1-58089-876-8(9))* Charlesbridge Publishing, Inc.

Brennan, Sarah. The Tale of Temujin. Harrison, Harry, illus. 2012. (ENG.). 32p. (J). *(978-1-937160-23-4(8))* Auspicious Times.

Brenner, Norm. The Leopard Who Lost His Spots. 2010. (ENG.). 28p. pap. 21.99 *(978-1-4535-2436-7(3))* Xlibris Corp.

Breslin, Theresa. The Dragon Stoorworm, 37 vols. Land, Matthew, illus. 2014. (Traditional Scottish Tales Ser.). 24p. (J). pap. 11.95 *(978-1-78250-117-6(7),* Kelpies) Floris Bks. GBR. Dist: Consortium Bk. Sales & Distribution.

—Mary, Queen of Scots: Escape from Lochleven Castle, 48 vols. Martinez, Teresa, illus. 2018. (Traditional Scottish Tales Ser.). 32p. (J). 14.95 *(978-1-78250-512-9(1),* Kelpies) Floris Bks. GBR. Dist: Consortium Bk. Sales & Distribution.

Brett, Jan. Armadillo Rodeo. Brett, Jan, illus. 2004. (Illus.). 32p. (J). (gr. -1-3). pap. 8.99 *(978-0-14-240125-5(0),* Puffin Books) Penguin Young Readers Group.

—Fritz & the Beautiful Horses. Brett, Jan, illus. 2016. (Illus.). 32p. (J). (-k). 18.99 *(978-0-399-17458-2(3),* G.P. Putnam's Sons Books for Young Readers) Penguin Young Readers Group.

—El Mitón. Brett, Jan, illus. 2017.Tr. of Mitten. (Illus.). 32p. (J). (gr. -1-3). pap. 9.99 *(978-0-425-29170-2(7),* Puffin Books) Penguin Young Readers Group.

—The Mitten. Brett, Jan, illus. 20th anniv. ed. 2009. (Illus.). 32p. (J). (gr. -1-k). 19.99 *(978-0-399-25296-9(7),* G.P. Putnam's Sons Books for Young Readers) Penguin Young Readers Group.

Brian, Janeen. I'm a Dirty Dinosaur. 2014. (ENG., Illus.). 22p. (J). 11.99 *(978-1-61067-296-2(8))* Kane Miller.

Bridge, Chris Helene. Read to Me! Bilingual. 2016. (ENG., Illus.). 32p. (J). pap. 9.95 *(978-1-942945-36-9(1),* 9b5bd1bf-e2c4-4b39-b79b-bddcb22ef19d) Night Heron Media.

Bridges, Shirin Yim. Ruby's Wish. Blackall, Sophie, illus. 2015. (ENG.). 36p. (J). (gr. 3-7). pap. 7.99 *(978-1-4521-4569-3(5))* Chronicle Bks. LLC.

Bridwell, Norman. Clifford's Family (Classic Storybook), 1 vol. Bridwell, Norman, illus. 2010. (ENG., Illus.). 32p. (J). (gr. -1-2). pap. 4.99 *(978-0-545-21585-5(4),* Cartwheel Bks.) Scholastic, Inc.

Bridwell, Norman, illus. Clifford Takes a Swim. 2016. (J). *(978-1-338-08716-1(9))* Scholastic, Inc.

Briers, Erica. Little Lamb to the Rescue. Boey, Stephanie, illus. 2004. (ENG.). 24p. (J). *(978-1-55168-257-0(5))* Fenn, H. B. & Co., Ltd.

Briggs, Korwin. The Invention Hunters Discover How Electricity Works. 2019. (ENG., Illus.). 48p. (J). E-Book (978-0-316-43686-1(0)) Little Brown & Co.

Bright, J. E. Splat the Cat & the Big Secret. 2018. 24p. (J). 13.89 (978-1-64310-115-6(3)) Penworthy Co., LLC, The.

Bright, Rachel. Benjamin & the Super Spectacles (the Wonderful World of Walter & Winnie) 2013. (Wonderful World of Walter & Winnie Ser.). (ENG., Illus.). 32p. (J). pap. 9.99 (978-0-00-744550-9(4), HarperCollins Children's Bks.) HarperCollins Pubs. Ltd. GBR. Dist: HarperCollins Pubs.

—The Squirrels Who Squabbled. Field, Jim, illus. 2019. (ENG.). 32p. (J). (gr. -1-k). 14.99 (978-1-338-53803-8(9), Scholastic Pr.) Scholastic, Inc.

British Museum of Natural History Staff, contrib. by. What Do Animals Eat Colouring Book. (Illus.). 8p. (J). (gr. -1-6). pap. 2.95 (978-0-565-00808-6(0)) Natural History Museum Pubns. GBR. Dist: Parkwest Pubns., Inc.

Britland, Jan. The Adventures of Rodger Dodger Dog. Swaim, Michael, illus. 2009. 40p. pap. 15.95 (978-1-936051-23-6(0)) Peppertree Pr., The.

Broekstra, Lorette. Bush Birthday. 2018. (ENG., Illus.). 24p. (J). (gr. -1-k). 12.99 (978-1-925267-05-1(9)) Allen & Unwin AUS. Dist: Independent Pubs. Group.

Bronstein, Christine. Stewie BOOM! & Princess Penelope: Handprints, Snowflakes & Playdates: Handprints, Snowflakes & Playdates. Young, Karen L., illus. 2018. (Stewie BOOM! Ser.). (ENG.). (J). (gr. -1-3). 36p. 22.50 (978-0-9972962-8-0(3)); 46p. pap. 9.99 (978-0-9972962-7-3(5)) Nothing But The Truth, LLC.

Brooke, L. Leslie. Johnny Crow's Picture Book. 2015. (ENG., Illus.). 192p. (J). (gr. k-3). pap. 14.99 (978-0-486-79598-0(5)) Dover Pubns., Inc.

—Ring o' Roses, a Nursery Rhyme Picture Book. Brooke, L. Leslie, illus. 2012. (Illus.). 102p. pap. 9.99 (978-1-61720-438-8(2)) Wilder Pubns., Corp.

Brooke, Susan Rich. World of Eric Carle: Sing Sound Book. 2018. (ENG., Illus.). 12p. (J). bds. 15.99 (978-1-5037-2205-7(8), 2509, PI Kids) Phoenix International Publications, Inc.

Brooks, David, illus. Animals. 2005. (My First Book Ser.). 9p. (J). (gr. -1-1). bds. 3.95 (978-1-933050-09-6(8)) Sweetwater Pr.

Brooks, F. & Litchfield, J. Picture Dictionary: A First Alphabetical Word Book. 2004. (Picture Dictionaries Ser.). 96p. (J). lib. bdg. 24.95 (978-1-58086-437-4(6)) EDC Publishing.

Brooks, Felicity. All You Need to Know Before You Start School. 2018. (ENG.). 26p. (J). 14.99 (978-0-7945-4042-5(2), Usborne) EDC Publishing.

—Brush Your Teeth, Max & Millie. 2011. (Toddler Bks). 24p. (J). ring bd. 7.99 (978-0-7945-2998-7(4), Usborne) EDC Publishing.

—Build a Picture Tractors Sticker Book. Lovell, Katie, illus. 2013. (Build a Picture Sticker Bks). 24p. (J). pap. 6.99 (978-0-7945-3319-9(1), Usborne) EDC Publishing.

—Take Turns, Max & Millie. 2011. (Toddler Bks). 24p. (J). ring bd. 7.99 (978-0-7945-3000-6(1), Usborne) EDC Publishing.

—Time for Bed, Max & Millie. 2011. (Toddler Bks). 24p. (J). ring bd. 7.99 (978-0-7945-3068-6(0), Usborne) EDC Publishing.

—Very First Animals Board Book. 2010. (Very First Words Board Bks). 10p. (J). bds. 6.99 (978-0-7945-2479-1(6), Usborne) EDC Publishing.

—Very First Numbers. 2009. (First Words Board Bks). 18p. (J). bds. 6.99 (978-0-7945-2354-1(4), Usborne) EDC Publishing.

Brooks, Felicity & Fearn, Katrina. First Dot-To-Dot Animals. 2013. (First Dot-To-Dot Ser.). 16p. (J). pap. 5.99 (978-0-7945-3198-0(9), Usborne) EDC Publishing.

Broom, Jenny. Animalium Poster Book. Scott, Katie, illus. 2017. (Welcome to the Museum Ser.). (ENG.). 56p. (J). (gr. 2-4). pap. 22.00 (978-0-7636-9318-3(9), Big Picture Press) Candlewick Pr.

Brosnan, Paris & Lerway, Paris. Billy Bee: Sugarplums & Honey. 2017. (ENG., Illus.). 27p. (J). pap. 13.95 (978-1-78710-075-6(8), 07536626-b42a-4a60-b991-ab346949fafb) Austin Macauley Pubs. Ltd. GBR. Dist: Baker & Taylor Publisher Services (BTPS).

Broutin & Stehr. Baldomero Va A la Escuela. (SPA.). 26p. (978-84-95150-47-9(6)) Corimbo, Editorial S.L.

Brown, Carron. En la Estación Espacial: Shine-A-light. Johnson, Bee, illus. 2019.Tr. of On the Space Station. (SPA.). (J). 12.99 (978-1-61067-913-8(X)) Kane Miller.

—Secretos Del Planeta Tierra: Shine-A-light. Robbins, Wesley, illus. 2019.Tr. of Secrets of Our Earth. (SPA.). (J). 12.99 (978-1-61067-911-4(3)) Kane Miller.

—Secrets of Our Earth. Robins, Wesley, illus. 2017. (ENG.). 36p. (J). 12.99 (978-1-61067-536-9(3)) Kane Miller.

—Space Station. Johnson, Bee, illus. 2016. (ENG.). 36p. (J). 12.99 (978-1-61067-411-9(1)) Kane Miller.

Brown, Emma. Shady Bay Buddies: Archie Goes to the Doctor. 2017. (ENG., Illus.). 32p. (J). pap. 12.95 (978-1-78249-544-4(4), Cico Kidz) Ryland Peters & Small GBR. Dist: WIPRO.

Brown, Janet. Jack & the Beanstalk: My First Reading Book. Morton, Ken, illus. 2015. (ENG.). 24p. (J). (gr. -1-12). pap. 6.99 (978-1-86147-474-2(1), Armadillo) Anness Publishing GBR. Dist: National Bk. Network.

Brown, Marc. Arthur's Perfect Christmas. 2004. (ENG., Illus.). 40p. (J). (gr. -1-1). pap. 6.99 (978-0-316-00130-4(9), Tingley, Megan Bks.) Little, Brown Bks. for Young Readers.

Brown, Margaret Wise. Goodnight Moon. Hurd, Clement, illus. 60th anniv. ed. 2007. (ENG.). 32p. (J). (gr. -1-3). pap. 8.99 (978-0-06-443017-3(0), HarperCollins) HarperCollins Pubs.

—Goodnight Moon. Hurd, Clement, illus. (J). pap. 32.75 incl. audio. (gr. -1-3). 24.95 incl. audio Weston Woods Studios, Inc.

—Goodnight Moon Board Book. Hurd, Clement, illus. 60th anniv. ed. 2007. (ENG.). 34p. (J). (gr. -1 — 1). bds. 8.99 (978-0-694-00361-7(1), HarperFestival) HarperCollins Pubs.

—Home for a Bunny: A Bunny Book for Kids. Williams, Garth, illus. 2012. (Little Golden Book Ser.). 24p. (J). (gr. k-k). 4.99 (978-0-307-93009-5(2), Golden Bks.) Random Hse. Children's Bks.

—A Home in the Barn. Pinkney, Jerry, illus. 2018. (ENG.). 32p. (J). (gr. -1-3). 19.99 (978-0-06-623787-9(4), HarperCollins) HarperCollins Pubs.

—Margaret Wise Brown's the Steam Roller. Staake, Bob, illus. (J). (978-1-5379-5883-5(6)) Follett School Solutions.

—Margaret Wise Brown's the Whispering Rabbit. Won, Annie, illus. 2017. (J). (978-1-5182-2278-8(1), Golden Bks.) Random Hse. Children's Bks.

Brown, Michelle Haney. My First Book of Japanese Words: An ABC Rhyming Book of Japanese Language & Culture. Padron, Aya, illus. 2017. (My First Words Ser.). 32p. (J). (gr. -1-3). 10.95 (978-0-8048-4953-1(6)) Tuttle Publishing.

Brown, Mick. From Round about Midnight until about Five! 2012. 60p. pap. 27.45 (978-1-4772-2701-5(6)) AuthorHouse.

Brown, Ruth. The Big Sneeze. Brown, Ruth, illus. 2011. (ENG., Illus.). 32p. (J). (gr. k-k). pap. 12.99 (978-1-84939-052-1(5)) Andersen Pr. GBR. Dist: Independent Pubs. Group.

—Greyfriars Bobby. Brown, Ruth, illus. 2013. (ENG., Illus.). 32p. (J). (gr. -1-k). pap. 12.99 (978-1-84939-632-5(9)) Andersen Pr. GBR. Dist: Independent Pubs. Group.

—Snail Trail. Brown, Ruth, illus. 2013. (ENG., Illus.). 20p. (J). (gr. -1-k). 12.99 (978-1-84939-252-5(8)) Andersen Pr. GBR. Dist: Independent Pubs. Group.

—Ten Seeds. Brown, Ruth, illus. 2013. (ENG., Illus.). 24p. (J). (gr. -1-k). 10.99 (978-1-84939-251-8(X)) Andersen Pr. GBR. Dist: Independent Pubs. Group.

Brown, Ruth, illus. The Christmas Mouse. 2013. (J). (978-1-4351-5021-8(X)) Barnes & Noble, Inc.

Brown, Ruth & Brown, Ken. Lion in the Long Grass. 2013. (Silver Tales Ser.). (ENG., Illus.). (J). (gr. -1-2). pap. (978-1-74352-445-9(5)) Hinkler Bks. Pty. Ltd.

Browne, Anthony. Hide & Seek. Browne, Anthony, illus. 2018. (ENG., Illus.). 32p. (J). (gr. -1-2). 17.99 (978-1-5362-0260-1(6)) Candlewick Pr.

Browne, Christopher. Mario. 2017. (ENG., Illus.). 40p. (J). (gr. -1-3). 17.99 (978-0-06-244113-3(2), Balzer & Bray) HarperCollins Pubs.

—Mario & the Dinosaurs. 2018. (ENG., Illus.). 40p. (J). (gr. -1-3). 17.99 (978-0-06-244115-7(9), Balzer & Bray) HarperCollins Pubs.

Browne, Mahogany L. Woke Baby. Ill, Theodore Taylor, illus. 2018. (ENG.). 32p. (J). 18.99 (978-1-62672-295-8(1), 900150273) Roaring Brook Pr.

Brownlow, Mike. Ten Little Dinosaurs. 2016. (Ten Little Ser.). (ENG., Illus.). 32p. (J). (gr. -1-k). pap. (978-1-4083-3401-0(1), Orchard Bks.) Hachette Children's Group GBR. Dist: Hachette Bk. Group.

Bruna, Dick. Farmer John's Seeds. 2004. (Illus.). 12p. pap. 5.99 (978-1-59226-191-8(4)) Big Tent Entertainment, Inc.

—Miffy the Artist Activity Book. 2018. (ENG., Illus.). 28p. (J). (gr. -1-k). pap. 12.95 (978-1-84976-578-7(2), 1315403) Tate Publishing, Ltd. GBR. Dist: Hachette Bk. Group.

—My Vest Is White. 2012. (ENG., Illus.). 28p. 7.95 (978-1-84976-075-1(6)) Tate Publishing, Ltd. GBR. Dist: Hachette Bk. Group.

—On My Scooter. 2013. (ENG., Illus.). 28p. (J). (gr. -1-1). 7.95 (978-1-84976-216-8(3)) Tate Publishing, Ltd. GBR. Dist: Hachette Bk. Group.

—The School. 2013. (ENG., Illus.). 28p. (J). (gr. -1-1). 7.95 (978-1-84976-215-1(5)) Tate Publishing, Ltd. GBR. Dist: Hachette Bk. Group.

Brundin, Anders & Dranger, Joanna Rubin. Dudley the Daydreamer. Perry, Frank, tr. from SWE. 2008. (ENG., Illus.). 32p. (J). (gr. k-2). pap. 12.95 (978-1-905341-10-8(5)) WingedChariot Pr. GBR. Dist: Independent Pubs. Group.

Brunellière, Lucie. Deep in the Ocean. 2019. (ENG., Illus.). 14p. (J). (gr. -1-k). bds. 15.99 (978-1-4197-3356-7(7), 1254910, Abrams Appleseed) Abrams, Inc.

Bruzzone, Catherine, et al. Spanish-English Picture Dictionary. 2011. (First Bilingual Picture Dictionaries Ser.). (ENG., Illus.). 48p. (J). (gr. 2-4). pap. 7.99 (978-0-7641-4661-9(0)) Sourcebooks, Inc.

Bryan, Ed, illus. The Three Little Pigs: a Nosy Crow Fairy Tale. 2016. (ENG.). 32p. (J). (gr. -1-2). 9.99 (978-0-7636-8655-0(7)) Candlewick Pr.

Bryan, Jennifer Liu. Hilda, A Very Loyal Goat. 2009. (ENG.). 36p. (J). 15.95 (978-0-9816265-1-2(3)) Next Chapter Pr.

Bryant, Ann. Tag. 2009. (ENG., Illus.). 24p. (J). pap. (978-0-7787-3900-5(7)); lib. bdg. (978-0-7787-3869-5(8)) Crabtree Publishing Co.

Buble, Brandee. Jayde the Jaybird. Liska, Eliska, illus. 2015. (One of a Kind Ser.: 2). (ENG.). 32p. (J). 15.95 (978-1-927018-69-9(2)) Simply Read Bks. CAN. Dist: Ingram Publisher Services.

—O'Shae the Octopus. Liska, Eliska, illus. 2014. (ENG.). 32p. (J). (gr. -1-3). 15.95 (978-1-927018-56-9(0)) Simply Read Bks. CAN. Dist: Ingram Publisher Services.

Buchwald, Claire. Are You Ready for Me? Hansen, Amelia, illus. 2009. (Sit! Stay! Read! Ser.). (ENG.). 24p. (J). (gr. k-1). pap. 7.95 (978-0-940719-08-8(8)) Gryphon Pr., The.

Buckingham, Gabriella, illus. The Wheels on the Bus & Other Action Rhymes. 2013. (ENG.). 16p. (J). (gr. -1-12). bds. 7.99 (978-1-84322-830-1(0), Armadillo) Anness Publishing GBR. Dist: National Bk. Network.

Buckley, Elizabeth & Keyes, Joan Ross. Oxford Picture Dictionary Content Area for Kids Workbook. 2nd ed. 2012. (ENG., Illus.). 184p. pap., wbk. ed. 18.70 (978-0-19-401779-4(6)) Oxford Univ. Pr., Inc.

Budney, Blossom. N Is for Nursery, 1 vol. Bobri, Vladimir, illus. 2018. 32p. 20.00 (978-1-85124-482-9(4)) Bodleian Library GBR. Dist: Chicago Distribution Ctr.

—What Is Round?, 1 vol. Bobri, Vladimir, illus. 2018. 32p. (J). 20.00 (978-1-85124-481-2(6)) Bodleian Library GBR. Dist: Chicago Distribution Ctr.

Buehner, Caralyn. Snowmen at Work. Buehner, Mark, illus. 2012. 32p. (J). (gr. -1-2). 18.99 (978-0-8037-3579-8(0), Dial Bks) Penguin Young Readers Group.

Buffalo, Tom And Tracey. Loganaes Big Night Out. 2008. 24p. pap. 11.99 (978-1-4389-1893-8(3)) AuthorHouse.

Buitrago, Jairo. Two White Rabbits, 1 vol. Amado, Elisa, tr. Yockteng, Rafael, illus. 2015. (ENG.). 56p. (J). (gr. k-2). 19.99 (978-1-55498-741-2(5)) Groundwood Bks. CAN. Dist: Publishers Group West (PGW).

—Walk with Me, 1 vol. Amado, Elisa, tr. Yockteng, Rafael, illus. 2017. (ENG.). 32p. (J). (gr. -1-1). 18.95 (978-1-55498-857-0(8)) Groundwood Bks. CAN. Dist: Publishers Group West (PGW).

Bulla, Clyde Robert. A Tree Is a Plant. Schuett, Stacey, illus. 2016. (Let's-Read-And-Find-Out Science 1 Ser.). (ENG.). 40p. (J). (gr. -1-3). pap. 7.99 (978-0-06-238210-8(1), HarperCollins) HarperCollins Pubs.

Bunn, Cullen. Terrible Lizard. Moss, Drew, illus. 2015. (ENG.). 136p. pap. 19.99 (978-1-62010-236-7(6), 9781620102367, Lion Forge) Oni Pr., Inc.

Bunting, Eve. Emma's Turtle. Winborn, Marsha, illus. 2014. (ENG.). 32p. (J). (gr. -1-3). pap. 6.99 (978-1-62091-735-0(1), Astra Young Readers) Astra Publishing Hse.

—My Special Day at Third Street School. Bloom, Suzanne, illus. 2009. (ENG.). 32p. (J). (gr. k-2). pap. 10.95 (978-1-59078-745-8(5), Astra Young Readers) Astra Publishing Hse.

—Peepers. Ransome, James E., illus. 2017. (ENG.). 32p. (J). (gr. -1-3). pap. 7.99 (978-1-328-74047-2(1), 1677001, Clarion Bks.) HarperCollins Pubs.

—Scary, Scary Halloween Gift Edition. Brett, Jan, illus. 2017. (ENG.). 40p. (J). (gr. -1-3). 8.99 (978-0-544-88034-4(X), 1651183, Clarion Bks.) HarperCollins Pubs.

—Yard Sale. Castillo, Lauren, illus. 2017. (ENG.). 32p. (J). (gr. -1-2). 7.99 (978-0-7636-9305-3(7)) Candlewick Pr.

Bunting, Philip. Sandcastle. 2019. (ENG., Illus.). 32p. (J). (gr. -1-1). 16.99 (978-1-76029-538-7(8)) Allen & Unwin AUS. Dist: Independent Pubs. Group.

Burach, Ross. Hi-Five Animals! (a Never Bored Book!) Burach, Ross, illus. 2018. (ENG., Illus.). 20p. (J). (gr. -1 — 1). bds. 6.99 (978-1-338-24567-7(8), Scholastic Pr.) Scholastic, Inc.

—I Am Not a Chair. 2017. (ENG., Illus.). 40p. (J). (gr. -1-3). 17.99 (978-0-06-236016-8(7), HarperCollins) HarperCollins Pubs.

Burgess, Matthew. Enormous Smallness: A Story of E. E. Cummings. Di Giacomo, Kris, illus. 2015. 64p. (J). (gr. -1-3). 17.95 (978-1-59270-171-1(X)) Enchanted Lion Bks., LLC.

Burks, James. Gabby & Gator. 2015. (ENG.). (J). (gr. 1-17). lib. bdg. 20.60 (978-1-62765-716-7(9)) Perfection Learning Corp.

Burks, James, creator. Gabby & Gator. 2020. (ENG., Illus.). 192p. (J). (gr. 1-17). pap. 11.00 (978-1-9753-1856-7(0), Yen Pr.) Yen Pr. LLC.

Burnett, Frances. Frances Hodgson Burnett's the Secret Garden. Barrager, Brigette, illus. 2017. (J). (978-1-5182-2305-1(2), Golden Bks.) Random Hse. Children's Bks.

Burnham, Janet Hayward. The Dragoness Mess. 2003. (Illus.). 32p. (J). (gr. k-1). pap. 12.95 (978-0-9740743-1-3(4)) My Little Jessie Pr.

Burningham, John. Mouse House. Burningham, John, illus. 2018. (ENG., Illus.). 32p. (J). (gr. -1-2). 16.99 (978-1-5362-0039-3(5)) Candlewick Pr.

—Mr. Gumpy's Outing. Date not set. (Illus.). (J). bds. 6.95 (978-0-8050-7373-7(6), Holt, Henry & Co. Bks. For Young Readers) Holt, Henry & Co.

—Picnic. Burningham, John, illus. 2014. (ENG., Illus.). 32p. (J). (-k). 17.99 (978-0-7636-6945-4(8)) Candlewick Pr.

Burns, Joanne. What Is Heaven Like? 2005. 35p. (J). 10.99 (978-1-4116-3360-5(1)) Lulu Pr., Inc.

Burow, Ginger. The Night That Was Christmas, 1 vol. 2009. 21p. pap. 24.95 (978-1-4489-9842-5(5)) America Star Bks.

Burrows, Fiona. Violet & Nothing. 2019. (Illus.). 32p. (J). 17.95 (978-1-925591-55-2(7)) Fremantle Pr. AUS. Dist: Independent Pubs. Group.

Burslem, Tobe. Bermendani. 2011. 28p. pap. 21.99 (978-1-4628-5490-5(7)) Xlibris Corp.

Burton, Robert. Wally A. Bow 21st Century Abow. 2010. 48p. 19.49 (978-1-4520-8046-8(1)) AuthorHouse.

Bush, Emilie P. Steamduck Learns to Fly! Petty, William Kevin, illus. 2012. 36p. pap. 11.95 (978-0-9849028-1-1(3)) Coal City Stories.

Bush, Zack. Made for Me. De Lauretis, Gregorio, illus. (ENG.). (J). (gr. -1-k). 2019. 20p. bds. 12.99 (978-1-64170-200-3(1), 550200) 2018. 32p. 16.99 (978-1-945547-69-0(3), 554769) Familius LLC.

Butterworth, Chris & Voake, Charlotte. The Things That I LOVE about TREES. 2018. (Illus.). 32p. (J). (978-1-4063-4940-5(2)) Candlewick Pr.

Butterworth, Nick. The Whisperer. Butterworth, Nick, illus. 2005. (ENG., Illus.). 32p. (gr. k-3). pap. 15.95 (978-0-00-712018-5(4), HarperCollins Children's Bks.) HarperCollins Pubs. Ltd. GBR. Dist: HarperCollins Pubs.

Button, Lana. My Teacher's Not Here! Battuz, Christine, illus. 2018. (ENG.). 32p. (J). (gr. -1-2). 16.99 (978-1-77138-356-1(9)) Kids Can Pr., Ltd. CAN. Dist: Hachette Bk. Group.

Buzzeo, Toni. But I Read It on the Internet! Yoshikawa, Sachiko, illus. 2013. 32p. (J). 17.95 (978-1-60213-062-3(0), Upstart Bks.) Highsmith Inc.

—Whose Boat? (a Guess-The-Job Book) Froese, Tom, illus. 2018. (Guess-The-Job Book Ser.). (ENG.). 16p. (J). (gr. -1 — 1). bds. 9.99 (978-1-4197-2835-8(0), 1195910, Abrams Appleseed) Abrams, Inc.

Byeway Books, creator. Colors. 2011. (My First Picture Fun Bks.). (ENG., Illus.). 24p. (gr. -1-k). bds. 5.99 (978-1-60176-021-0(3)) Byeway Bks.

—Rhymes. 2011. (My First Picture Fun Bks.). (ENG., Illus.). 24p. (J). (gr. -1). bds. 5.99 (978-1-60176-022-7(1)) Byeway Bks.

Byrne, Richard. This Book Just Stole My Cat! 2018. (CHI.). (J). (gr. -1-3). (978-986-189-843-8(3)) Grimm Cultural Ent., Co., Ltd.

Cabrera, Jane. Row, Row, Row Your Boat. 2016. (Jane Cabrera's Story Time Ser.). (ENG., Illus.). 24p. (J). (-k). bds. 7.99 (978-0-8234-3632-3(2)) Holiday Hse., Inc.

Cache, Dee. Captain Tugalong, 1 vol. 2009. (ENG., Illus.). 30p. (J). (gr. -1-3). 12.95 (978-0-87033-515-0(4), 3606, Cornell Maritime Pr./Tidewater Pubs.) Schiffer Publishing, Ltd.

Cafaro, Phyllis. The Legend of Captain McFinn & Friends. 2012. (ENG., Illus.). 24p. pap. 19.99 (978-0-9799283-1-4(1), 9780979928314) Captain McFinn and Friends LLC, McFinn Pr.

Cain, Marie Mowery. A Message for You. 2013. (Big Books, Blue Ser.). (ENG & SPA., Illus.). 16p. pap. 33.00 (978-1-59246-013-7(5)) Big Books, by George!

Caisley, Raewyn. Something Wonderful. Blair, Karen, illus. 2018. 32p. (J). (gr. -1-3). 13.99 (978-0-14-350666-9(8), Puffin) Penguin Random Hse. AUS. Dist: Independent Pubs. Group.

Calder, Alexander. One & Other Numbers: With Alexander Calder. 2017. (ENG., Illus.). 30p. (gr. -1 — 1). bds. 9.95 (978-0-7148-7510-1(4)) Phaidon Pr., Inc.

Cali, Davide. Cinderella & the Furry Slippers. Barbanegre, Raphaelle, illus. 2017. 32p. (J). (gr. -1-2). 17.99 (978-1-101-91898-2(5), Tundra Bks.) Tundra Bks. CAN. Dist: Penguin Random Hse. LLC.

—I Hate My Cats (a Love Story) (Cat Book for Kids, Picture Book about Pets) Pirolli, Anna, illus. 2018. (ENG.). 44p. (J). (gr. k-3). 15.99 (978-1-4521-6595-0(5)) Chronicle Bks. LLC.

Calver, Paul & Reynolds, Toby. First Sticker Art: in the Ocean: Use Stickers to Create 20 Cute Ocean Animals. Savva, Ksenya, illus. 2019. (First Sticker Art Ser.). (ENG.). 64p. (J). (gr. -1-2). pap. 9.99 (978-1-4380-1247-6(0)) Sourcebooks, Inc.

—First Sticker Art: Zoo Animals: Use Stickers to Create 20 Cute Zoo Animals. Savva, Ksenya, illus. 2019. (First Sticker Art Ser.). (ENG.). 64p. (J). (gr. -1-2). pap. 9.99 (978-1-4380-1248-3(9)) Sourcebooks, Inc.

Cameron, Becky. Wishing for a Dragon. 2019. (ENG., Illus.). 32p. (J). (gr. -1-k). pap. 9.99 (978-1-4449-3623-0(9)) Hachette Children's Group GBR. Dist: Hachette Bk. Group.

Campbell, Jen. Franklin's Flying Bookshop. Harnett, Katie, illus. 2017. (Franklin & Luna Ser.: 0). 32p. (J). (gr. -1-3). 17.95 (978-0-500-65109-4(4), 565109) Thames & Hudson.

Campbell, K. G. Lester's Dreadful Sweaters. Campbell, K. G., illus. 2012. (ENG., Illus.). 32p. (J). (gr. -1-3). 16.95 (978-1-55453-770-9(3)) Kids Can Pr., Ltd. CAN. Dist: Hachette Bk. Group.

Campbell, Rod. Dear Zoo. Campbell, Rod, illus. 2019. (Dear Zoo & Friends Ser.). (ENG., Illus.). 24p. (J). (— 1). 17.99 (978-1-5344-6012-6(8), Little Simon) Little Simon.

—Dear Zoo Animal Shapes. Campbell, Rod, illus. 2016. (Dear Zoo & Friends Ser.). (ENG., Illus.). 20p. (J). (gr. -1 — 1). bds. 6.99 (978-1-4814-8069-7(3), Little Simon) Little Simon.

Campbell, Wanda Gail. Little Buckets Full of Big Love. 2008. (Illus.). 48p. pap. 19.49 (978-1-4389-0688-1(9)) AuthorHouse.

Camping Caper: Picture Book (English) 8x8. 2007. (Illus.). (J). 5.99 (978-1-933934-64-8(6)) Mighty Kids Media.

Campisi, Stephanie. Luis & Tabitha. Mengert, Hollie, illus. 2018. (ENG.). 32p. (J). (gr. k-3). 16.99 (978-1-64170-040-5(8), 550040) Familius LLC.

Canby, Kelly. The Hole Story. 2018. (Illus.). 32p. (J). (gr. -1-k). 14.99 (978-1-925591-12-5(3)) Fremantle Pr. AUS. Dist: Independent Pubs. Group.

—Rodney. 2019. (Illus.). 32p. (J). (gr. -1-k). 17.95 (978-1-925815-32-0(3)) Fremantle Pr. AUS. Dist: Independent Pubs. Group.

Candau, Brittany. Box of Mixed Emotions. Maruyama, Jerrod, illus. 2015. (J). (978-1-4847-3220-5(0)) Disney Publishing Worldwide.

Candlewick Press. Peppa Pig & the Busy Day at School. Candlewick Press, illus. 2013. (Peppa Pig Ser.). (ENG., Illus.). 32p. (J). (-k). 12.99 (978-0-7636-6525-8(8), Candlewick Entertainment) Candlewick Pr.

—Peppa Pig & the Career Day. 2018. (Peppa Pig Ser.). (ENG., Illus.). 32p. (J). (-k). 12.99 (978-1-5362-0344-8(0), Candlewick Entertainment) Candlewick Pr.

—Peppa Pig & the I Love You Game. 2015. (Peppa Pig Ser.). (ENG.). 32p. (J). (-k). 14.99 (978-0-7636-8126-5(1), Candlewick Entertainment) Candlewick Pr.

Candy Cane Press, creator. Safe at Home! Indoor Safety. 2005. (ENG., Illus.). 14p. (J). (gr. -1-k). bds. 12.95 (978-0-8249-6592-1(2), Ideals Pubns.) Worthy Publishing.

—Safe at Play: Outdoor Safety. 2005. (ENG., Illus.). 14p. (J). (gr. -1-k). bds. 12.95 (978-0-8249-6593-8(0), Ideals Pubns.) Worthy Publishing.

Cane, Ella. My World. 2013. (My World Ser.). (ENG.). 24p. (J). (gr. -1-2). pap., pap., pap. 41.70 (978-1-4765-3683-5(X), 20175, Pebble) Capstone.

Canetti, Yanitzia. Colores escolares/School Colors: A World of Color. 2010. (ENG & SPA.). 24p. (J). pap. 6.99 (978-1-59835-272-6(5), BrickHouse Education) Cambridge BrickHouse, Inc.

—Colorful Shapes/Figuras de Colores: A World of Color. 2010. (SPA & ENG.). 24p. (J). pap. 6.99 (978-1-59835-278-8(4), BrickHouse Education) Cambridge BrickHouse, Inc.

—Colorful Sights Paisajes de Colores: A World of Color. 2010. (SPA & ENG.). 24p. (J). pap. 6.99 (978-1-59835-280-1(6), BrickHouse Education) Cambridge BrickHouse, Inc.

—Colors on Colors/Colores Sobre Colores: A World of Color. 2010. (SPA & ENG.). 24p. (J). pap. 6.99 (978-1-59835-276-4(8), BrickHouse Education) Cambridge BrickHouse, Inc.

—Tasty Colors/Colores de Sabores: A World of Color. 2010. (SPA & ENG.). 24p. (J). pap. 6.99 (978-1-59835-270-2(9), BrickHouse Education) Cambridge BrickHouse, Inc.

Canfield, Dorothy. Understood Betsy: Illustrated. 2017. (ENG., Illus.). (J). pap. 4.25 (978-1-68422-133-2(1)) Martino Fine Bks.

Canty, John. Heads & Tails. Canty, John, illus. 2018. (ENG., Illus.). 40p. (J). (-k). 17.99 (978-1-5362-0033-1(6)) Candlewick Pr.

Capucilli, Alyssa Satin. A Biscuit Collection: 3 Woof-Tastic Tales: 3 Biscuit Stories in 1 Padded Board Book! Schories, Pat, illus. 2017. (Biscuit Ser.). (ENG.). 30p. (J). (gr. -1 — 1). bds. 11.99 (978-0-06-274135-6(7), HarperFestival) HarperCollins Pubs.

—Biscuit's Pet & Play Farm Animals: A Touch & Feel Book: an Easter & Springtime Book for Kids. Schories, Pat, illus. 2018. (Biscuit Ser.). (ENG.). 12p. (J). (gr. -1 — 1). bds. 8.99 (978-0-06-249052-0(4), HarperFestival) HarperCollins Pubs.

Caravan, Jill. Pandas: A Portrait of the Animal World. 2nd rev. ed. 2012. (Portrait of the Animal World Ser.). (Illus.). 72p. 12.95 (978-1-59764-230-9(4)) New Line Bks.

Carbone, Courtney. Dragon Pox! (Shimmer & Shine) Cartobaleno, illus. 2018. (Little Golden Book Ser.). (ENG.). 24p. (J). (-k). 4.99 (978-1-5247-6798-3(0), Golden Bks.) Random Hse. Children's Bks.

Carbonell-Matela, Anna. Whitaker Farm. 2012. 24p. pap. 15.99 (978-1-4691-6352-9(7)) Xlibris Corp.

Carey, Anna. The Making of Mollie. 2016. (ENG.). 304p. (J). pap. 17.00 (978-1-84717-847-3(2)) O'Brien Pr., Ltd., The IRL. Dist: Casemate Pubs. & Bk. Distributors, LLC.

Carle, Eric. All about the Very Hungry Caterpillar. Carle, Eric, illus. 2018. (World of Eric Carle Ser.). (ENG., Illus.). 10p. (J).

(gr. k-k). bds. 9.99 *(978-1-5247-8588-8(1)*, Grosset & Dunlap) Penguin Young Readers Group.

—Calm with the Very Hungry Caterpillar. Carle, Eric, illus. 2019. (World of Eric Carle Ser.). (ENG., Illus.). 32p. (J). (-k). 9.99 *(978-1-5247-9218-3(7))* Penguin Young Readers Group.

—Eric Carle Classics: The Tiny Seed; Pancakes, Pancakes!; Walter the Baker. Carle, Eric, illus. 2011. (World of Eric Carle Ser.). (ENG., Illus.). 112p. (J). (gr. -1-2). 19.99 *(978-1-4424-3988-7(2)*, Simon & Schuster Bks. For Young Readers) Simon & Schuster Bks. For Young Readers.

—Have You Seen My Cat? 2012. (Eric Carle Ready-To-Read Ser.). lib. bdg. 13.55 *(978-0-606-26356-6(X))* Turtleback.

—House for Hermit Crab. Carle, Eric, illus. 2004. (World of Eric Carle Ser.). (ENG., Illus.). 32p. (J). (gr. k-3). bds. 8.99 *(978-0-689-87064-4(7)*, Little Simon) Little Simon.

—My Very First Book of Shapes. Carle, Eric, illus. 2005. (ENG., Illus.). 20p. (J). (gr. -1 — 1). bds. 6.99 *(978-0-399-24387-5(9))* Penguin Young Readers Group.

—Pancakes, Pancakes! Carle, Eric, illus. 2004. (World of Eric Carle Ser.). (ENG., Illus.). 32p. (J). (gr. -1-3). bds. 8.99 *(978-0-689-87148-1(1)*, Little Simon) Little Simon.

—La Semillita (the Tiny Seed) Romay, Alexis, tr. Carle, Eric, illus. 2016. (World of Eric Carle Ser.). (SPA., Illus.). 40p. (J). (gr. -1-3). 8.99 *(978-1-4814-7834-2(6)*, Libros Para Ninos) Libros Para Ninos.

—Thanks from the Very Hungry Caterpillar. 2017. (ENG., Illus.). 32p. (J). (-k). 8.99 *(978-0-515-15806-9(2))* Penguin Young Readers Group.

—The Tiny Seed. Carle, Eric, illus. 2005. (World of Eric Carle Ser.). (ENG., Illus.). 34p. (J). (gr. -1-k). bds. 8.99 *(978-0-689-87149-8(X)*, Little Simon) Little Simon.

—What's Your Favorite Food? 2019. (Eric Carle & Friends' What's Your Favorite Ser.: 4). (ENG., Illus.). 40p. (J). 18.99 *(978-1-250-29514-9(9)*, 900195178, Holt, Henry & Co. Bks. For Young Readers) Holt, Henry & Co.

Carlson, Nancy. Think Big! 2005. (Illus.). 28p. (J). (gr. -1-3). 15.95 *(978-1-57505-622-7(4)*, Carolrhoda Bks.) Lerner Publishing Group.

Carlton, Glenis. Four Snails & an Umbrella. 2016. (ENG., Illus.). 22p. (J). pap. 13.95 *(978-1-78612-331-2(2)*, fcf89cff-577e-4e8a-941a-c14ebec3a909) Austin Macauley Pubs. Ltd. GBR. Dist: Baker & Taylor Publisher Services (BTPS).

Carney, Charles. A Day Just for Daddies. 2011. (Illus.). 24p. (J). 15.99 *(978-1-60010-439-8(8))* Idea & Design Works, LLC.

Carpenter, Tad. I Say, You Say Colors! 2014. (ENG., Illus.). 18p. (J). (gr. -1 — 1). bds. 6.99 *(978-0-316-20072-1(7))* Little, Brown Bks. for Young Readers.

Carr, Jan. Greedy Apostrophe: A Cautionary Tale. Long, Ethan, illus. 2009. (ENG.). 32p. (J). (gr. 1-3). pap. 7.99 *(978-0-8234-2205-0(4))* Holiday Hse., Inc.

Carrington, Leonora. Leche Del Sueno. 2013. (SPA.). 46.95 *(978-607-16-1217-5(9))* Fondo de Cultura Economica USA.

—The Milk of Dreams. 2017. (Illus.). 56p. (J). (gr. 1-4). 18.95 *(978-1-68137-094-1(8)*, NYR Children's Collection) New York Review of Bks., Inc., The.

Carroll, Lewis, pseud. Alice in Wonderland Picture Book. Maraja, Libico, illus. 2013. (Children's Die-Cut Shape Book Ser.). (ENG.). 16p. (J). 10.95 *(978-1-59583-701-1(9))* Laughing Elephant.

—Lit for Little Hands: Alice's Adventures in Wonderland, Volume 2. Miles, David W., illus. 2018. (Lit for Little Hands Ser.: 2). (ENG.). 16p. (J). (gr. -1-1). bds. 12.99 *(978-1-945547-68-3(5)*, 554768) Familius LLC.

Carson-Dellosa Publishing Staff. Hidden Pictures, Grades PK - 1. 2010. (Home Workbooks Ser.: 6). (ENG.). 64p. (gr. -1-1). pap. 4.49 *(978-1-60418-770-0(0)*, 104339) Carson-Dellosa Publishing, LLC.

Carter, Amy. The Not So Wicked, Wicked Witch! 2009. 24p. pap. 15.95 *(978-1-4327-3781-8(3))* Outskirts Pr., Inc.

Carter, David A. Bugs at the Beach: Ready-To-Read Level 1. Carter, David A., illus. 2016. (David Carter's Bugs Ser.). (ENG., Illus.). 24p. (J). (gr. -1-1). pap. 4.99 *(978-1-4814-4050-9(0)*, Simon Spotlight) Simon Spotlight.

—One Red Dot: One Red Dot. 2005. (ENG., Illus.). 18p. (J). (gr. -1-3). 32.99 *(978-0-689-87769-8(2)*, Little Simon) Little Simon.

Cartwright, Shannon, illus. Alaska ABC, 40th Anniversary Edition. 40th anniv. ed. 2018. (Paws IV Ser.). 32p. (J). (gr. -1-2). pap. 11.99 *(978-1-63217-166-5(X)*, Little Bigfoot) Sasquatch Bks.

Casale, Roberto, illus. El Osito Binky. 2017.Tr. of Little Binky Bear. (J). 7.99 *(978-0-9986498-0-1(5))* Show N' Tell Publishing.

Casey, Dawn. A Lullaby for Little One. Fuge, Charles, illus. 2015. (ENG.). 32p. (J). (-k). 12.99 *(978-0-7636-7608-7(X))* Candlewick Pr.

Cassany, Mia & Casal, Mikel. Frankfurt. 2018. (ENG., Illus.). 32p. (J). (gr. -1-k). 14.99 *(978-1-84976-579-4(0)*, 1325401) Tate Publishing, Ltd. GBR. Dist: Abrams, Inc.

Cassidy, Sean. Good to Be Small, 1 vol. 2005. (ENG., Illus.). 32p. (J). (gr. -1-1). pap. 7.95 *(978-1-55041-699-2(5)*, 5873fc8c-d0f9-49ca-b5da-492804f35793) Fitzhenry & Whiteside, Ltd. CAN. Dist: Firefly Bks., Ltd.

Castle, Caroline. Snip Snap Croc. Castle, Caroline, illus. 2017. (Story Corner Ser.). (ENG., Illus.). 24p. (J). (gr. -1-k). lib. bdg. 19.99 *(978-1-68297-185-7(6)*, d39bf9ed-6b67-43d9-8fc6-0732feaa4f37) QEB Publishing Inc.

Castor, Daniel & Castor, Harriet. Wondaglop Plot. (ENG., Illus.). 61p. (J). pap. 6.99 *(978-0-340-63442-4(1))* Hodder & Stoughton GBR. Dist: Trafalgar Square Publishing.

Castro, Shirley. The Pelican Family Series — Stelly & the Sticky, Gooey Taffy. Castro, Christopher, illus. 2011. 36p. (J). 15.00 *(978-0-9790307-3-4(0))* Castro, Shirley.

Castrovilla, Selene. Revolutionary Rogues: John André & Benedict Arnold. O'Brien, John, illus. 2017. (ENG.). 48p. (J). (gr. 2-5). 17.95 *(978-1-62979-341-2(8)*, Calkins Creek) Highlights Pr., c/o Highlights for Children, Inc.

Cate, Annette LeBlanc. The Magic Rabbit. 2013. lib. bdg. 17.20 *(978-0-606-31601-9(9))* Turtleback.

Caudle, Ruth. Yvette, Annette & Renette. 2007. (Illus.). 32p. (J). 16.99 *(978-0-9793039-0-6(7))* Haiti World.

Caughill, Jeff. The Good Old Hockey Game. 2012. 28p. pap. *(978-1-105-58056-7(3))* Lulu.com.

Cavanaugh, Brian. Miracle of the Poinsettia (Milagro de la Flor de Nochebuena) Lopez-Platek, Carmen, tr. 2017. (ENG., Illus.). 32p. (J). pap. 12.95 *(978-0-8091-6779-1(4))* Paulist Pr.

Caviezel, Giovanni. Ballerina. Mesturini, C., illus. 2011. (Mini People Shape Bks.). 10p. (J). (gr. -1-1). bds. 5.99 *(978-0-7641-6436-1(8))* Sourcebooks, Inc.

—Builder. Mesturini, C., illus. 2011. (Mini People Shape Bks.). 10p. (J). (gr. -1-1). bds. 5.99 *(978-0-7641-6437-8(6))* Sourcebooks, Inc.

—Fire Fighter. Mesturini, C., illus. 2009. (Mini People Shape Bks.). 10p. (J). (gr. -1-1). bds. 5.99 *(978-0-7641-6220-6(9))* Sourcebooks, Inc.

Cawthorne, Nigel. Pirates: An Illustrated History. 2013. (Illus.). 144p. (J). *(978-1-4351-4657-0(3))* Metro Bks.

Cecil, Randy. Lucy. Cecil, Randy, illus. 2016. (ENG., Illus.). 144p. (J). (gr. k-3). 19.99 *(978-0-7636-6808-2(7))* Candlewick Pr.

Cenko, Doug. My Papa Is a Princess. 2018. (ENG., Illus.). 32p. (J). (gr. -1-2). 17.99 *(978-1-936669-70-7(6))* Blue Manatee Press.

Cerulli, Claudia. Ottavia e I Gatti Di Roma - Octavia & the Cats of Rome: A Bilingual Picture Book in Italian & English. Lätti, Leo, illus. 2013. 40p. pap. *(978-1-938712-11-1(0))* Roxby Media Ltd.

Cervone, Shannon. The Black Suitcase. Vene, Alessandro, illus. 2013. (ENG.). 32p. (J). 15.99 *(978-1-938501-08-1(X))* Turn the Page Publishing.

Chaban, Liz. Jules of the World: The California Caper. 2012. (ENG.). 40p. pap. 18.99 *(978-1-105-92248-0(0))* Lulu Pr., Inc.

Chabbert, Ingrid & Beal, Marjorie. In Shape. 2017. (ENG., Illus.). 18p. (J). bds. 14.95 *(978-1-58423-656-6(6)*, 09094aad-6275-4fc3-a2e0-63b4c11cd321) Gingko Pr., Inc.

Chadwick, Anita. Rosebuds Puppies. 2012. 20p. pap. 13.77 *(978-1-4669-1632-6(X))* Trafford Publishing.

Chalker Browne, Susan. Freddy's Hockey Hero, 1 vol. Rose, Hilda, illus. 2010. (ENG.). 32p. (J). (gr. k-3). *(978-1-897174-62-3(4))* Breakwater Bks., Ltd.

Challoner, Jack & Walshaw, Rodney. Rocks & Minerals: Crystals, Erosion, Geology, Fossils: With 19 Easy-To-Do Experiments & 400 Exciting Pictures. 2015. (Illus.). 64p. (J). (gr. -1-12). 12.99 *(978-1-86147-465-0(2)*, Armadillo) Anness Publishing GBR. Dist: National Bk. Network.

Chan, Marty. True Story. Bennett, Lorna, illus. 2009. (ENG.). 32p. (J). 9.95 *(978-0-9810449-0-3(5))* Ink Jockey, Inc. CAN. Dist: Univ. of Toronto Pr.

Chand, Emlyn. Ricky the Runt: A Bird Brain Book. Giffin, Noelle, illus. l.t. ed. 2013. (ENG.). 52p. (gr. k-3). pap. 10.95 *(978-1-62253-125-7(6))* Evolved Publishing.

—Vicky Finds a Valentine: Bird Brain Books. Giffin, Noelle, illus. ed. 2013. (ENG.). 50p. (gr. k-1). pap. 10.95 *(978-1-62253-116-5(7))* Evolved Publishing.

Chandler, Pauline. Mr. Rabbit the Farmer. Smith, Eric, illus. 2005. (ENG.). 24p. (J). lib. bdg. 23.65 *(978-1-59646-736-1(3))* Dingles & Co.

Chandler, Richy K. You Make Your Parents Super Happy! A Book about Parents Separating. Chandler, Richy K., illus. 2017. (Illus.). 40p. (J). 15.95 *(978-1-78592-414-9(1)*, 696704) Kingsley, Jessica Pubs. GBR. Dist: Hachette UK Distribution.

Chapeau, Chelsey. You Are Brave. Kriebel, Jacqueline, illus. 2017. 26p. pap. 11.99 *(978-1-943871-42-1(6))* Painted Gate Publishing.

Chapman, Jared, illus. T. Rex Time Machine: Dinos in De-Nile. 2019. (T. Rex Time Machine Ser.). (ENG.). 44p. (J). (gr. -1-k). 16.99 *(978-1-4521-6155-6(0))* Chronicle Bks. LLC.

Chapman, Pat. The Best Mum in the World. Chapman, Cat, illus. 2017. 32p. (J). (gr. -1-k). 14.99 *(978-1-927262-80-1(1))* Upstart Pr. NZL. Dist: Independent Pubs. Group.

Chappell, Billie-Jean & Williams, Frederick C. Happiness Colouring Book. Williams, Frederick C., illus. 2012. (Illus.). 36p. pap. *(978-0-9566564-2-1(0))* Dreamality Bks.

Chaput, Elaine. What Would You Do?, 1 vol. 2015. (ENG., Illus.). 32p. (J). mass mkt. 10.95 *(978-1-894717-48-9(1)*, 09b9c000-7b6b-4ee9-aed0-0f664070e9a4) Pemmican Pubns., Inc. CAN. Dist: Firefly Bks., Ltd.

Charles, Faustin. The Selfish Crocodile Anniversary Edition. Terry, Michael, illus. 20th anniv. ed. 2018. (Selfish Crocodile Ser.). (ENG.). 32p. (J). *(978-1-4088-8525-3(5)*, 337203, Bloomsbury Children's Bks.) Bloomsbury Publishing Plc.

Charon Aldredge. Kiddie Rhythms the Show. 2010. 16p. pap. 15.00 *(978-1-4269-1970-1(0))* Trafford Publishing.

Chase, Kit, illus. Little Sweet Pea, God Loves You, 1 vol. 2019. (ENG.). 32p. (J). 15.99 *(978-0-310-76699-5(0))* Zonderkidz.

Check, S. A., et al. Haunted Hijinks. Jourdan, Diego & Galligher, John, illus. 2019. (ENG.). 128p. (J). pap. 19.99 *(978-1-945205-17-0(2)*, 569b79fc-c4dc-495f-80a1-cae5adb305ab) American Mythology Productions.

Chedekel, Evelyn. The Fake Doughnut. Le, Loanne, illus. 2013. 24p. 16.95 *(978-0-9888974-0-3(7))* BugaBk. llc.

Chedru, Delphine. How Many Kisses? 2018. (Illus.). 32p. (J). (gr. -1-k). 12.95 *(978-0-500-65145-2(0)*, 565145) Thames & Hudson.

Cheetham, Stephen, illus. Off to the Park! 2014. (Tactile Bks.). 12p. (J). spiral bd. *(978-1-84643-502-7(1))* Child's Play International Ltd.

Chernesky, Felicia Sanzari. The Boy Who Said Nonsense. Anderson, Nicola, illus. 2016. (ENG.). 32p. (J). (gr. -1-3). 16.99 *(978-0-8075-5742-6(0)*, 807557420) Whitman, Albert & Co.

Chichester Clark, Emma. Bears Don't Read! Chichester Clark, Emma, illus. 2016. (Illus.). 32p. (J). 12.99 *(978-1-61067-366-2(2))* Kane Miller.

—Come to School Too, Blue Kangaroo! Chichester Clark, Emma, illus. 2013. (ENG., Illus.). 32p. (J). pap. 9.99 *(978-0-00-725868-0(2)*, HarperCollins Children's Bks.) HarperCollins Pubs. Ltd. GBR. Dist: HarperCollins Pubs.

—I'll Show You, Blue Kangaroo! (Blue Kangaroo) Chichester Clark, Emma, illus. 2019. (Blue Kangaroo Ser.). (ENG., Illus.). 32p. (J). pap. 6.99 *(978-0-00-826627-1(1)*, HarperCollins Children's Bks.) HarperCollins Pubs. Ltd. GBR. Dist: HarperCollins Pubs.

—It Was You, Blue Kangaroo (Blue Kangaroo) Chichester Clark, Emma, illus. 2018. (Blue Kangaroo Ser.). (ENG., Illus.). 32p. pap. 6.99 *(978-0-00-826626-4(3)*, HarperCollins Children's Bks.) HarperCollins Pubs. Ltd. GBR. Dist: HarperCollins Pubs.

—Plum & Rabbit & Me (Humber & Plum, Book 3), Book 3. Chichester Clark, Emma, illus. 2010. (Humber & Plum Ser.: 3). (ENG., Illus.). 32p. (J). (gr. -1-k). pap. 9.99 *(978-0-00-727325-6(8)*, HarperCollins Children's Bks.) HarperCollins Pubs. Ltd. GBR. Dist: HarperCollins Pubs.

Chiew, Suzanne. Friends to the Rescue. Pedler, Caroline, illus. 2016. (ENG.). 32p. (J). (gr. -1-2). 16.99 *(978-1-68010-007-5(6))* Tiger Tales.

Child Abuse Prevention Centre, Boost. I'M a Great Little Kid, Set. 2003. (I'm a Great Little Kid Ser.). (ENG., Illus.). 1p. (J). (gr. k-2). 99.95 *(978-1-896764-75-7(4))* Second Story Pr. CAN. Dist: Orca Bk. Pubs. USA.

—I'm a Great Little Kid, Set. 2003. (I'm a Great Little Kid Ser.). (ENG., Illus.). 1p. (J). (gr. k-2). pap. 49.95 *(978-1-896764-74-0(6))* Second Story Pr. CAN. Dist: Orca Bk. Pubs. USA.

Child, Lauren. Beware of the Storybook Wolves. 2012. (ENG., Illus.). 32p. (J). (gr. -1-k). pap. 9.99 *(978-1-4083-1480-7(0)*, Orchard Bks.) Hachette Children's Group GBR. Dist: Hachette Bk. Group.

—I Can't Stop Hiccuping! 2010. (Charlie & Lola Ser.). lib. bdg. 13.55 *(978-0-606-10629-0(4))* Turtleback.

—The New Small Person. Child, Lauren, illus. 2018. (ENG., Illus.). 32p. (J). (gr. -1-3). 8.99 *(978-0-7636-9974-1(8))* Candlewick Pr.

Child's Play. Emergency. Cocoretto, illus. alt. ed. 2017. (Wheels at Work (US Edition) Ser.: 4). (ENG.). 12p. (J). bds. *(978-1-78628-080-0(9))* Child's Play International Ltd.

—Spring. Busby, Ailie, illus. 2015. (Seasons Ser.: 4). 12p. (J). (gr. 1-1). spiral bd. *(978-1-84643-741-0(5))* Child's Play International Ltd.

—Summer. Busby, Ailie, illus. 2015. (Seasons Ser.: 4). 12p. (J). (gr. 1-1). spiral bd. *(978-1-84643-742-7(3))* Child's Play International Ltd.

—What's That Noise? CHOO! CHOO! Guess the Vehicle! Cocoretto, illus. 2015. (What's That Noise? Ser.: 4). 12p. (J). spiral bd. *(978-1-84643-746-5(6))* Child's Play International Ltd.

—What's That Noise? SNAP! SNAP! Guess the Animal! Cocoretto, illus. 2015. (What's That Noise? Ser.: 4). 12p. (J). spiral bd. *(978-1-84643-748-9(2))* Child's Play International Ltd.

—What's That Noise? TAP! TAP! Guess the Toy! Cocoretto, illus. 2015. (What's That Noise? Ser.: 4). 12p. (J). spiral bd. *(978-1-84643-747-2(4))* Child's Play International Ltd.

—What's That Noise? TOOT! TOOT! Guess the Instrument! Cocoretto, illus. 2015. (What's That Noise? Ser.: 4). 12p. (J). spiral bd. *(978-1-84643-749-6(0))* Child's Play International Ltd.

—What's up Tiger? Food. Cocoretto, illus. 2018. (What's Up? Ser.: 4). 12p. (J). bds. *(978-1-78628-157-9(0))* Child's Play International Ltd.

—Winter. Busby, Ailie, illus. 2015. (Seasons Ser.: 4). 12p. (J). (gr. 1-1). spiral bd. *(978-1-84643-745-8(8))* Child's Play International Ltd.

Chilton, Mark. Stinky Dog. 2018. (ENG., Illus.). 27p. (J). 23.95 *(978-1-78629-190-5(8)*, 965ac0ee-01c3-4512-ab74-c5b73ca2b0d5); pap. 14.95 *(978-1-5289-0873-3(2)*, 7d8ac463-f8a2-459a-a983-4db2029fbbcd) Austin Macauley Pubs. Ltd. GBR. Dist: Baker & Taylor Publisher Services (BTPS).

Chin, Jason. Redwoods. Chin, Jason, illus. 2009. (ENG., Illus.). 40p. (J). (gr. -1-3). 19.99 *(978-1-59643-430-1(9)*, 900054268) Roaring Brook Pr.

Chin, Oliver. Tales from the Chinese Zodiac: The 12 Year Box Set. 2017. (Tales from the Chinese Zodiac Ser.). (Illus.). 480p. (J). (gr. -1-3). pap. 179.95 *(978-1-59702-137-1(7))* Immedium.

Ching, Kai Yun & Li, Wai-Yant, illus. From the Stars in the Sky to the Fish in the Sea. 2017. 40p. (J). (gr. -1-3). 18.95 *(978-1-55152-709-3(X))* Arsenal Pulp Pr. CAN. Dist: Consortium Bk. Sales & Distribution.

Chissick, Michael. Seahorse's Magical Sun Sequences: How All Children (And Sea Creatures) Can Use Yoga to Feel Positive, Confident & Completely Included. Peacock, Sarah, illus. 2015. 48p. (J). 21.95 *(978-1-84819-283-6(5)*, 693880, Singing Dragon) Kingsley, Jessica Pubs. GBR. Dist: Hachette UK Distribution.

Chlebowski, Rachel. Dance! Hug! Sing! 2016. (Illus.). (J). *(978-1-5182-2423-2(7))* Random Hse., Inc.

—The Epic Trolls Sticker Book (DreamWorks Trolls) Golden Books, illus. 2016. (ENG.). 64p. (J). (gr. -1-2). pap. 12.99 *(978-0-399-55901-3(9)*, Golden Bks.) Random Hse. Children's Bks.

Chriscoe, Sharon. Bulldozer Dreams. Joven, John, illus. 2017. (ENG.). 32p. (J). (gr. -1-3). 16.99 *(978-0-7624-5966-7(2)*, Running Pr. Kids) Running Pr.

Christelow, Eileen. Five Little Monkeys Storybook Treasury/Cinco Monitos Coleccion de Oro: Bilingual English-Spanish. Christelow, Eileen, illus. 2012. (Five Little Monkeys Story Ser.). (ENG., Illus.). 192p. (J). (gr. -1-3). 12.99 *(978-0-547-74593-0(1)*, 1486369, Clarion Bks.) HarperCollins Pubs.

—Five Little Monkeys Trick-Or-Treat. Christelow, Eileen, illus. 2018. (Five Little Monkeys Story Ser.). (ENG., Illus.). 40p. (J). (gr. -1-3). pap. 7.99 *(978-1-328-86927-2(X)*, 1696687, Clarion Bks.) HarperCollins Pubs.

—Five Little Monkeys Trick-Or-Treat Board Book. Christelow, Eileen, illus. 2015. (Five Little Monkeys Story Ser.). (ENG., Illus.). 36p. (J). (— 1). bds. 7.99 *(978-0-544-43062-4(X)*, 1595737, Clarion Bks.) HarperCollins Pubs.

Christmas Stable, 1 vol. 2014. (Candle Tiny Tots Ser.). (ENG., Illus.). 16p. (J). 11.99 *(978-1-78128-122-2(X)*, adbd8aec-c73d-44fe-b60a-cb8587021262, Candle Bks.) Lion Hudson PLC GBR. Dist: Baker & Taylor Publisher Services (BTPS).

Churnin, Nancy. Irving Berlin: The Immigrant Boy Who Made America Sing. Sanchez, James Rey, illus. 2018. (ENG.). 32p. (J). (gr. 2-5). 17.99 *(978-1-939547-44-6(X)*, 1df1180d-2f36-4457-bfda-659435817043) Creston Bks.

Cioffi, Dom, illus. Digby & the Lake Monster. l.t. ed. 2006. 36p. (J). per. *(978-0-9745931-0-4(9))* Vermont Bookworks.

Clanton, Ben. Boo Who? Clanton, Ben, illus. (ENG., Illus.). 32p. (J). 2018. (-k). bds. 7.99 *(978-0-7636-9967-3(5))* 2017. (gr. -1-2). 15.99 *(978-0-7636-8824-0(X))* Candlewick Pr.

—Mo's Mustache. 2013. (ENG., Illus.). 32p. (J). (gr. -1-2). 16.99 *(978-1-77049-538-8(X)*, Tundra Bks.) Tundra Bks. CAN. Dist: Penguin Random Hse. LLC.

Clarion Books, Clarion. Five Silly Ghosts Board Book. Kushnir, Hilli, illus. 2018. (ENG.). 12p. (J). (— 1). bds. 6.99 *(978-1-328-86659-2(9)*, 1696027, Clarion Bks.) HarperCollins Pubs.

Clarke, Isabel. My Big Book of Words. Tulip, Jenny, illus. 2014. 40p. (J). (gr. -1-k). 12.99 *(978-1-86147-325-7(7)*, Armadillo) Anness Publishing GBR. Dist: National Bk. Network.

Clarke, Jane. How to Bathe Your Little Dino. Birkett, Georgie, illus. 2017. 16p. (J). bds. 8.99 *(978-1-61067-495-9(2))* Kane Miller.

—I'm Not Wearing That! Mostyn, David, illus. 2005. (ENG.). 24p. (J). lib. bdg. 23.65 *(978-1-59646-716-3(9))* Dingles & Co.

—Prince Albert's Birthday. Chatterton, Martin, illus. 2005. 24p. (J). lib. bdg. 23.65 *(978-1-59646-748-4(7))* Dingles & Co.

Clarke, Justine & Baysting, Arthur. The Gobbledygook Is Eating a Book. Jellett, Tom, illus. 2016. 32p. (J). (gr. -1-2). 13.99 *(978-0-14-350693-5(5))* Random Hse. Australia AUS. Dist: Independent Pubs. Group.

Clarke, Lyndia A. Tidy up Tommy. Clarke, Lyndia A., illus. 2005. (Illus.). (J). 1700.00 *(978-0-9762898-6-9(5))* LightHouse Pr.

Clarke, Maxine Beneba. The Patchwork Bike. Rudd, Van Thanh, illus. 2018. (ENG.). 40p. (J). (gr. 1-4). 16.99 *(978-1-5362-0031-7(X))* Candlewick Pr.

Clarke, Terreece M. Olivia's Potty Adventures! Hayden, Seitu, illus. 2018. (ENG.). 26p. (J). (gr. -1-k). 14.95 *(978-1-941958-40-7(0))* Cedar Grove Publishing.

Clarkson, Kelly. River Rose & the Magical Christmas. 2017. (ENG., Illus.). 32p. (J). (gr. -1-3). 19.99 *(978-0-06-269764-6(1)*, HarperCollins) HarperCollins Pubs.

Class 1-208. Pizza Place Ghost, 1 vol. Sur, Duendes Del, illus. 2013. (Scooby-Doo! Picture Clue Bks.). (ENG.). 24p. (J). (gr. k-2). lib. bdg. 31.36 *(978-1-61479-038-9(8)*, 13232) Spotlight.

Clayton, Coo & Soye, Alison. Maggie's Mittens. 2017. (Maggie Ser.). (ENG., Illus.). 36p. (J). (gr. -1-k). pap. 9.99 *(978-1-78530-148-3(9))* Black and White Publishing Ltd. GBR. Dist: Independent Pubs. Group.

Clayton, Dallas. An Awesome Book of Thanks!, 0 vols. Clayton, Dallas, illus. unabr. ed. 2010. (ENG.). 86p. (J). (gr. -1-2). 17.95 *(978-1-935597-37-7(X)*, 9781935597377, Two Lions) Amazon Publishing.

Cleave, Andrew. Snakes & Reptiles - Pb: A Portrait of the Animal World. 2013. (Portrait of the Animal World Ser.). (Illus.). 80p. pap. 9.95 *(978-1-59764-318-4(1))* New Line Bks.

Clement, Debbie. Red, White, & Blue. 2010. 19.95 *(978-0-578-06631-8(9))* Rainbows Within Reach.

Clement, Gary. The Great Poochini. 2004. (J). (gr. 1-4). spiral bd. *(978-0-616-03027-1(4))* Canadian National Institute for the Blind/Institut National Canadien pour les Aveugles.

Clerici, Lorenzo. The Dog Book: A Minibombo Book. Clerici, Lorenzo, illus. 2017. (Minibombo Ser.). (ENG., Illus.). 32p. (J). (-k). 9.99 *(978-0-7636-9487-6(8))* Candlewick Pr.

Climo, Liz. Rory the Dinosaur: Me & My Dad. 2015. (Illus.). 48p. (J). pap. *(978-0-316-26391-7(5))* Little Brown & Co.

Coat, Janik & Duisit, Bernard. What Are You Wearing Today? 2018. (Flip Flap Pop-Up Ser.: 0). (ENG., Illus.). 16p. (J). (gr. -1-3). 14.95 *(978-0-500-65143-8(4)*, 565143) Thames & Hudson.

Cocca-Leffler, Maryann. Rain Brings Frogs: A Little Book of Hope. Cocca-Leffler, Maryann, illus. 2011. (ENG., Illus.). 32p. (J). (gr. -1-2). 10.99 *(978-0-06-196106-9(X)*, HarperCollins) HarperCollins Pubs.

Cochran, Bruce. First Birthday Bear. 10p. (J). *(978-1-886386-35-8(8))* Trisar, Inc.

—First Pony: Blue. 10p. (J). *(978-1-886386-34-1(X))* Trisar, Inc.

—First Pony: Pink. 10p. (J). *(978-1-886386-33-4(1))* Trisar, Inc.

—It's the Big 1: Blue. 10p. (J). *(978-1-886386-37-2(4))* Trisar, Inc.

—It's the Big 1: Pink. 10p. (J). *(978-1-886386-36-5(6))* Trisar, Inc.

Cocoretto, illus. Peekaboo! in the Ocean! 2016. (Peekaboo! Ser.: 4). 12p. (J). spiral bd. *(978-1-84643-867-7(5))* Child's Play International Ltd.

Coe, Catherine. Collins Big Cat Phonics for Letters & Sounds - Look at Them Go: Band 02B/Red B, Bd. 2B. 2018. (Collins Big Cat Phonics Ser.). (ENG.). 16p. (J). (gr. -1-k). pap. 6.99 *(978-0-00-825152-9(5))* HarperCollins Pubs. Ltd. GBR. Dist: Independent Pubs. Group.

Coelho, Rogério. Boat of Dreams, 1 vol. 2017. (ENG., Illus.). 80p. (J). (gr. 2-17). 22.95 *(978-0-88448-528-5(5)*, 884528) Tilbury Hse. Pubs.

Cofer, Amadeus. Friendship Rules: How to Make & Keep Friends, 1. l.t. ed. 2004. (Illus.). 36p. (J). 14.00 *(978-1-932957-00-6(6))* Legacy Pubs.

Cole, Barbara H. Anna & Natalie, 1 vol. Himler, Ronald, illus. 2010. (ENG.). 32p. (J). pap. 6.95 *(978-1-59572-211-9(4))* Star Bright Bks., Inc.

Cole, Henry. One Little Bag: an Amazing Journey. Cole, Henry, illus. 2020. (ENG., Illus.). 48p. (J). (gr. -1-3). 18.99 *(978-1-338-35997-8(5)*, Scholastic Pr.) Scholastic, Inc.

Colleen, Marcie. Penguinaut! Yarlett, Emma, illus. 2018. (ENG.). 32p. (J). (gr. -1-k). 18.99 *(978-0-545-84884-8(9))* Scholastic, Inc.

Collier, Kelly. A Horse Named Steve. Collier, Kelly, illus. 2017. (Steve the Horse Ser.). (ENG., Illus.). 32p. (J). (gr. -1-3). 16.95 *(978-1-77138-736-1(X))* Kids Can Pr., Ltd. CAN. Dist: Hachette Bk. Group.

—Team Steve. Collier, Kelly, illus. 2018. (Steve the Horse Ser.). (ENG., Illus.). 40p. (J). (gr. -1-3). 16.99 *(978-1-77138-932-7(X))* Kids Can Pr., Ltd. CAN. Dist: Hachette Bk. Group.

Collins, Billy. Voyage. Romagna, Karen, illus. 2014. (ENG.). 32p. (J). (gr. 1-7). 16.95 *(978-1-59373-154-0(X))* Bunker Hill Publishing, Inc.

Collins, Pat Lowery. I Am a Dancer. Graham, Mark, illus. 2008. (Millbrook Picture Books Ser.). 30p. (J). (gr. 3-7). 22.60 *(978-0-8225-6369-3(X)*, Millbrook Pr.) Lerner Publishing Group.

Collins, Peggy. In the Garden. Collins, Peggy, illus. 2009. (ENG., Illus.). 40p. (J). 14.95 *(978-1-60433-026-7(0),* Applesauce Pr.) Cider Mill Pr. Bk. Pubs., LLC.

Collins, Ross. My Amazing Dad. 2014. (ENG., Illus.). 32p. (J). pap. 8.99 *(978-1-4711-2258-3(1),* Simon & Schuster Children's) Simon & Schuster, Ltd. GBR. Dist: Simon & Schuster, Inc.

Collins UK. Times Tables Quick Quizzes: Ages 5-7. 2017. (Collins Easy Learning KS1 Ser.). (ENG., Illus.). 32p. (J). (gr. k-3). pap. 6.95 *(978-0-00-821249-0(X))* HarperCollins Pubs. Ltd. GBR. Dist: Independent Pubs. Group.

Colorful Cars. 2017. (Colorful Cars Ser.). 24p. (gr. 4-6). pap. 24.75 *(978-1-5081-6178-3(X),* PowerKids Pr.) Rosen Publishing Group, Inc., The.

Colting, Fredrik & Medina, Melissa. Early Learning Guide to Homer's the Odyssey. Yun, Yeji, illus. 2017. (KinderGuides Early Learning Guide to Culture Classics Ser.). (ENG.). 48p. (J). 16.95 *(978-0-9988205-1-4(2))* Moppet Bks.

—Kinderguides Early Learning Guide to Herman Melville's Moby Dick. Rymenants, Stef, illus. 2018. (KinderGuides Early Learning Guide to Culture Classics Ser.). (ENG.). 50p. (J). 16.95 *(978-0-9988205-4-5(7))* Moppet Bks.

Colton, Nicola. A Dublin Fairytale. 2015. (ENG., Illus.). 32p. (J). 21.00 *(978-1-84717-774-2(3))* O'Brien Pr., Ltd., The IRL. Dist: Casemate Pubs. & Bk. Distributors, LLC.

Consentino, Ralph, illus. Peanut Bear: What's in the Forest? 2018. (ENG.). 24p. (J). bds. 7.99 *(978-1-68383-235-5(3))* Insight Editions.

Contraire, Bastien. Food: Hide & Sneak. 2018. (ENG., Illus.). 26p. (gr. -1 — 1). bds. 9.95 *(978-0-7148-7723-5(9))* Phaidon Pr., Inc.

—Vehicles: Hide & Sneak. 2017. (ENG., Illus.). 26p. (gr. -1 — 1). bds. 9.95 *(978-0-7148-7516-3(3))* Phaidon Pr., Inc.

Cook, David C. Publishing Staff & Tangvald, Christine. Josiah, the Boy King. 2004. (Pencil Fun Bks.: Vol. 10). 16p. (J). (gr. 1-4). pap. 9.90 *(978-1-55513-918-6(3),* 1555139183) Cook, David C.

Cook, Julia. Sorry, I Forgot to Ask! My Story about Asking Permission & Making an Apology! De Weerd, Kelsey, illus. 2012. (ENG.). 32p. 16.95 *(978-1-934490-29-7(6));*Volume 3. 31p. (J). pap. 10.95 *(978-1-934490-28-0(8))* Boys Town Pr.

—Table Talk: A Book about Table Manners, Volume 7. DuFalla, Anita, illus. 2016. (Building Relationships Ser.: Vol. 7). (ENG.). 31p. (J). (gr. k-6). pap. 10.95 *(978-1-934490-97-6(0))* Boys Town Pr.

Cool by the Pool: Picture Book (English) 8x8. 2007. (J). 5.99 *(978-1-933934-37-2(9))* Mighty Kids Media.

Cool by the Pool: Picture Book (English) NL 9x9 with Snipe. 2007. (J). 5.99 *(978-1-933934-47-1(6))* Mighty Kids Media.

Coombs, Kate. Goodnight Mr. Darcy: A BabyLit(TM) Parody Board Book, 1 vol. 2015. (ENG., Illus.). 22p. (J). bds. 9.99 *(978-1-4236-4177-3(9))* Gibbs Smith, Publisher.

Cooper, Chris, et al. Adventures of Puss in Boots: Cat about Town. 2016. (Adventures of Puss in Boots Ser.: 2). (Illus.). 64p. (J). (gr. 1-4). pap. 6.99 *(978-1-78585-332-6(5))* Titan Bks. Ltd. GBR. Dist: Penguin Random Hse. LLC.

Cooper, Jenny, illus. Do Your Ears Hang Low? 2017. (ENG.). 40p. (J). (gr. -1). 14.95 *(978-1-4549-1614-7(1))* Sterling Publishing Co., Inc.

Cooper, Kelly. If a Horse Had Words. Eldridge, Lucy, illus. 2018. 48p. (J). (gr. -1-3). 17.99 *(978-1-101-91872-2(1),* Tundra Bks.) Tundra Bks. CAN. Dist: Penguin Random Hse. LLC.

Coote, Maree. Andy Web Artist: Artist. Coote, Maree, illus. 2018. (ENG., Illus.). 24p. (J). (gr. k-2). 22.99 *(978-0-9924917-5-8(4))* Melbournestyle Bks. AUS. Dist: Independent Pubs. Group.

—Robyn Boid Architect: Architect. Coote, Maree, illus. 2018. (ENG., Illus.). 24p. (J). (gr. k-2). 22.99 *(978-0-9924917-4-1(6))* Melbournestyle Bks. AUS. Dist: Independent Pubs. Group.

Copons, Jaume. Alex & the Monsters: Restaurant Rescue! Warriner, David, tr. Fortuny, Liliana, illus. 2018. 145p. (J). (gr. 1). 9.99 *(978-2-924786-10-9(X),* CrackBoom! Bks.) Chouette Publishing CAN. Dist: Publishers Group West (PGW).

Coppo, Marianna. Petra. 2018. (ENG., Illus.). 48p. (J). (gr. -1-2). 17.99 *(978-0-7352-6267-6(5),* Tundra Bks.) Tundra Bks. CAN. Dist: Penguin Random Hse. LLC.

Copus, Julia. My Bed Is an Air Balloon. Jay, Alison, illus. 2018. (ENG.). 32p. 15.95 *(978-0-571-33484-1(9),* Faber & Faber Children's Bks.) Faber & Faber, Inc.

Corbalis, Judy. Get That Ball! 2018. (ENG., Illus.). 32p. (J). (-k). 19.99 *(978-1-78344-169-3(0))* Andersen Pr. GBR. Dist: Independent Pubs. Group.

Corderoy, Tracey. Fairy Tale Pets. Martin, Jorge, illus. 2017. (ENG.). 32p. (J). pap. *(978-1-84869-442-2(3))* Tiger Tales.

—It's Christmas! Warnes, Tim, illus. 2017. (ENG.). 32p. (J). (gr. -1-2). 16.99 *(978-1-68010-067-9(X))* Tiger Tales.

Corrigan, Kathleen. ABC, 1 vol. 2014. (Canadian Board Bks.). (ENG & FRE.). 20p. bds. 7.99 *(978-1-62370-223-6(2),* Capstone Young Readers) Capstone.

—123, 1 vol. 2014. (Canadian Board Bks.). (ENG & FRE.). 20p. bds. 7.99 *(978-1-62370-224-3(0),* Capstone Young Readers) Capstone.

Corse, Nicole. Pet Heroes. 2011. (Scholastic Reader, Level 3 Ser.). (ENG.). 32p. (J). (gr. 1-3). pap. 3.99 *(978-0-545-25837-1(5))* Scholastic, Inc.

Cortez, Tammy. AbbeyLoo & Gus the Talking Toad. 2015. (ENG., Illus.). 32p. 19.95 *(978-1-943093-11-3(3))* Primedia eLaunch LLC.

—AbbeyLoo & Gus the Talking Toad. Landry, Noemie Gionet, illus. 2015. (ENG.). 32p. (J). pap. 9.95 *(978-1-943274-38-3(X),* 9781943274383) Waldorf Publishing.

Cosentino, Ralph. Kitty Cones: the Purrfect Day. 2018. (ENG., Illus.). 32p. (J). 14.99 *(978-1-68383-239-3(6))* Insight Editions.

—Kitty Cones: What Makes Us Happy? 2018. (ENG., Illus.). 24p. (J). bds. 8.99 *(978-1-68383-237-9(X))* Insight Editions.

Cosmic. Superpower Dogs. 2019. (ENG., Illus.). 48p. (J). (gr. -1-3). 18.99 *(978-0-316-45359-2(5))* Little, Brown Bks. for Young Readers.

Cosneau, Olivia & Duisit, Bernard. How Do You Sleep? 2018. (Flip Flap Pop-Up Ser.: 0). (ENG., Illus.). 14p. (J). (gr. -1-2). 14.95 *(978-0-500-65144-5(2),* 565144) Thames & Hudson.

Cossons, Malcolm & Stevens, Neil. Dot to Dot... Dot Plans a Birthday Surprise. 2013. (Illus.). 32p. (J). (gr. -1-k). 15.95 *(978-0-500-65015-8(2),* 565015) Thames & Hudson.

Côté, Geneviève. Me & You. Côté, Geneviève, illus. 2009. (Piggy & Bunny Ser.). (ENG., Illus.). 32p. (J). (gr. -1-k). 16.99 *(978-1-55453-446-3(1))* Kids Can Pr., Ltd. CAN. Dist: Hachette Bk. Group.

Côté, Geneviève & Côté, Geneviève. Mr. King's Castle. Côté, Geneviève & Côté, Geneviève, illus. 2013. (Mr. King Ser.). (ENG., Illus.). 32p. (J). (gr. -1-2). 16.95 *(978-1-55453-972-7(2))* Kids Can Pr., Ltd. CAN. Dist: Hachette Bk. Group.

—Mr. King's Things. Côté, Geneviève & Côté, Geneviève, illus. 2012. (Mr. King Ser.). (ENG., Illus.). 32p. (J). (gr. -1-2). 16.95 *(978-1-55453-700-6(2))* Kids Can Pr., Ltd. CAN. Dist: Hachette Bk. Group.

Cotter, Bill. Don't Push the Button! 2013. (Illus.). 32p. (J). (gr. -1-3). 16.99 *(978-1-4022-8746-6(1),* Sourcebooks Jabberwocky) Sourcebooks, Inc.

—Don't Push the Button! A Halloween Treat. 2018. (Illus.). 22p. (J). (gr. -1-k). bds. 7.99 *(978-1-4926-6095-8(7),* Sourcebooks Jabberwocky) Sourcebooks, Inc.

—Don't Touch This Book! 2016. (Illus.). 28p. (J). (gr. -1-k). bds. 6.99 *(978-1-4926-4804-8(3),* 9781492648048, Sourcebooks Jabberwocky) Sourcebooks, Inc.

Cottringer, Anne. Hot Dog. Walker, Katherine, illus. 2005. (ENG.). 24p. (J). lib. bdg. 23.65 *(978-1-59646-738-5(X))* Dingles & Co.

Cottswold, Wooley. Rose & the Bald-Headed Elephant. 2009. (Illus.). 28p. (J). 16.95 *(978-0-9779064-0-6(X))* Archie Publishing.

Coudrille, Jonathon. Farmer Fisher's Russian Christmas. 2013. 42p. pap. *(978-1-908867-20-9(5))* FootSteps Pr.

Courgeon, Remi. Feather. Bedrick, Claudia Zoe, tr. 2017. (ENG., Illus.). 36p. (J). (gr. k-4). 17.95 *(978-1-59270-210-7(4))* Enchanted Lion Bks., LLC.

Courtney-Tickle, Jessica. Little Christmas Tree. Courtney-Tickle, Jessica, illus. 2018. (ENG., Illus.). 12p. (J). (-k). bds. 15.99 *(978-1-5362-0311-0(4),* Big Picture Press) Candlewick Pr.

Cousins, Lucy. Maisy Goes to a Wedding. Cousins, Lucy, illus. 2019. (Maisy Ser.). (ENG., Illus.). 32p. (J). (-k). 6.99 *(978-1-5362-0614-2(8))* Candlewick Pr.

—Maisy Goes to a Wedding. 2018. (Illus.). 32p. (J). *(978-1-4063-7851-1(8))* Candlewick Pr.

—Maisy Goes to a Wedding. 2019. (Maisy First Experiences Pic Bks). (ENG.). 26p. (J). (gr. k-1). 17.36 *(978-0-87617-298-8(2))* Penworthy Co., LLC, The.

—Maisy's Plane. Cousins, Lucy, illus. 2015. (Maisy Ser.). (ENG., Illus.). 18p. (J). (— 1). bds. 6.99 *(978-0-7636-7304-8(8))* Candlewick Pr.

—Splish, Splash, Ducky! Cousins, Lucy, illus. 2019. (ENG., Illus.). 28p. (J). (— 1). bds. 8.99 *(978-1-5362-0004-1(2))* Candlewick Pr.

Covello, Paul. Canada Animals. 2018. (ENG.). 30p. (J). (gr. -1-k). bds. 11.99 *(978-1-4434-5383-7(8),* HarperCollins) HarperCollins Pubs.

—Toronto ABC. 2014. (ENG., Illus.). 15p. (J). bds. 10.50 *(978-1-4434-3144-6(3),* Harper Trophy) HarperCollins Pubs.

Covington, Jean. Nanny Planted Love. (J). 2006. per. 11.99 *(978-1-933732-12-1(1))* 2005. lib. bdg. 19.95 *(978-0-9754728-9-7(5))* Big Ransom Studio.

Cowell, Cressida. Emily Brown: Emily Brown & the Thing. 2015. (Emily Brown Ser.). (ENG., Illus.). 32p. (J). (gr. -1-k). pap. 10.99 *(978-1-4449-2340-7(4))* Hachette Children's Group GBR. Dist: Hachette Bk. Group.

Cowell, Cressida & Mayhew, James. Emily Brown: Emily Brown & the Elephant Emergency. 2015. (Emily Brown Ser.). (ENG., Illus.). 32p. (J). (gr. -1-k). pap. 10.99 *(978-1-4449-2343-8(9))* Hachette Children's Group GBR. Dist: Hachette Bk. Group.

Cowley, Joy. Freddy Bear & the Big Bed. Webb, Philip, illus. 2017. (Freddy Bear Ser.). 20p. (J). (— 1). bds. 7.99 *(978-1-927262-96-2(8))* Upstart Pr. NZL. Dist: Independent Pubs. Group.

—Freddy Bear & the Toothpaste. Webb, Phillip, illus. 2017. (Freddy Bear Ser.). 20p. (J). (— 1). bds. 7.99 *(978-1-927262-97-9(6))* Upstart Pr. NZL. Dist: Independent Pubs. Group.

Cowling, Douglas. Vivaldi's Ring of Mystery. Fernandez, Laura & Jacobson, Rick, illus. 2004. (ENG.). 44p. (J). *(978-0-439-96904-8(2),* North Winds Pr) Scholastic Canada, Ltd.

Cox, Phil Roxbee, ed. Find the Duck. Cartwright, Stephen, illus. 2004. (Find It Board Bks.). (ENG.). 1p. (J). (gr. -1-18). bds. 3.95 *(978-0-7460-3821-5(6))* EDC Publishing.

Cox, Tracey M. Arachnabet- an Alphabet of Spiders. 2013. 20p. pap. 9.95 *(978-1-61633-362-1(6))* Guardian Angel Publishing, Inc.

Coy, John. My Mighty Journey: A Waterfall's Story. Schanilec, Gaylord, illus. 2019. (ENG.). 40p. (J). 18.95 *(978-1-68134-008-1(9))* Minnesota Historical Society Pr.

Coyle, Carmela Lavigna. Do Princesses Boogie? Gordon, Mike, illus. 2016. (Do Princesses Ser.). 26p. (J). (gr. -1-2). bds. 7.95 *(978-1-63076-159-2(1))* Taylor Trade Publishing.

COYLE, Gary. Wild Zoo Train. 2017. (Illus.). 32p. (J). (gr. -1-2). 15.95 *(978-1-63076-306-0(3))* Muddy Boots Pr.

Craig, Jenny. I Believe in Genevieve. Edelson, Wendy, illus. 2013. (ENG.). 40p. (J). (gr. -1-3). 16.95 *(978-1-62157-085-1(1),* Regnery Kids) Regnery Publishing.

Craig, Lindsey. Farmyard Beat. Brown, Marc, illus. 2012. 32p. (J). (gr. k-k). 6.99 *(978-0-307-93082-8(3),* Knopf Bks. for Young Readers) Random Hse. Children's Bks.

Crawford, Georgina. Archie-Parchie-Piddley-Poo. 2009. (Illus.). 24p. pap. 12.99 *(978-1-4389-7307-4(1))* AuthorHouse.

Cree, Tahara, text. Bonnie the Bee. 2012. (ENG., Illus.). 13p. pap. 5.00 *(978-0-9824964-3-5(5))* Creative Education & Publishing.

Creek, Lorie. Who Is This Jesus? A Hidden Picture Book. Creek, Chris, illus. 2012. (J). 18.99 *(978-1-60908-909-2(X))* Deseret Bk. Co.

Crews, Donald. Freight Train. 2010. (Illus.). (J). *(978-1-4351-1213-1(X))* Barnes & Noble, Inc.

—Freight Train/Tren de Carga: A Caldecott Honor Award Winner (Bilingual English-Spanish) Crews, Donald, illus. 2003. (ENG., Illus.). 24p. (J). (gr. -1-3). 17.99 *(978-0-06-056202-1(1))* HarperCollins Español.

—Freight Train/Tren de Carga: A Caldecott Honor Award Winner (Bilingual English-Spanish) Crews, Donald, illus. 2008. (ENG., Illus.). 24p. (J). (gr. -1-3). pap. 9.99 *(978-0-06-056204-5(8),* Greenwillow Bks.) HarperCollins Pubs.

—Freight Train/Tren de Carga Bilingual Board Book. 2016. (ENG., Illus.). 32p. (J). (gr. -1 — 1). bds. 8.99 *(978-0-06-245708-0(X),* Greenwillow Bks.) HarperCollins Pubs.

Croft, Malcolm. One Direction In 3D. 2015. (Y Ser.). (ENG., Illus.). 48p. (gr. 4). 12.95 *(978-1-78097-564-1(3))* Carlton Bks., Ltd. GBR. Dist: Two Rivers Distribution.

Cronin, Doreen. A Barnyard Collection: Click, Clack, Moo & More. Lewin, Betsy, illus. 2010. (Click Clack Book Ser.). (ENG.). 128p. (J). (gr. -1-3). 19.99 *(978-1-4424-1263-7(1),* Atheneum Bks. for Young Readers) Simon & Schuster Children's Publishing.

—Click, Clack, Moo. 2016. (Simon & Schuster Ready-To-Read Level 2 Ser.). (Illus.). (J). lib. bdg. 13.55 *(978-0-606-39751-3(5))* Turtleback.

—Click, Clack, Moo: Cows That Type. braille ed. 2004. (Illus.). (J). (gr. k-3). spiral bd. *(978-0-616-07227-1(9))* Canadian National Institute for the Blind/Institut National Canadien pour les Aveugles.

—Click, Clack, Surprise! 2019. (Ready-To-Read Ser.). (ENG.). 38p. (J). (gr. k-1). 13.96 *(978-0-87617-586-6(8))* Penworthy Co., LLC, The.

—Click, Clack, Surprise! Lewin, Betsy, illus. 2016. (Click Clack Book Ser.). (ENG.). 40p. (J). (gr. -1-3). 17.99 *(978-1-4814-7031-5(0),* Atheneum/Caitlyn Dlouhy Books) Simon & Schuster Children's Publishing.

—Click, Clack, Surprise! Lewin, Betsy, illus. 2020. (Doreen Cronin: Click, Clack & More Ser.). (ENG.). 40p. (J). (gr. -1-3). 31.36 *(978-1-5321-4468-4(7),* 35158, Picture Bk.) Spotlight.

—Diary of a Worm: Nat the Gnat. 2014. (I Can Read Level 1 Ser.). (ENG., Illus.). 32p. (J). (gr. -1-3). pap. 4.99 *(978-0-06-208707-2(X),* HarperCollins) HarperCollins Pubs.

—Duck for President. Lewin, Betsy, illus. 2004. (Click Clack Book Ser.). (ENG.). 32p. (J). (gr. -1-3). 19.99 *(978-0-689-86377-6(2),* Atheneum Bks. for Young Readers) Simon & Schuster Children's Publishing.

Cronin, Doreen & Simon and Schuster/LeapFrog Staff. Click, Clack, Moo: Cows That Type. Lewin, Betsy, illus. 2008. (J). 13.99 *(978-1-59319-936-4(8))* LeapFrog Enterprises, Inc.

Cross, Gillian. Sam Sorts It Out. Mier, Colin, illus. 2005. (ENG.). 24p. (J). lib. bdg. 23.65 *(978-1-59646-702-6(9))* Dingles & Co.

Cross, Ken. Who Is Pat Dump? 2009. 48p. pap. 21.99 *(978-1-4363-9568-7(2))* Xlibris Corp.

Crossley-Holland, Kevin. The Riddlemaster, 1 vol. Jorisch, Stéphane, illus. 2016. (ENG.). 32p. (J). (gr. 1-3). 16.95 *(978-1-926890-11-1(6))* Tradewind Bks. CAN. Dist: Orca Bk. Pubs. USA.

Crow, Melinda Melton. Truck Buddies, 1 vol. Rooney, Veronica, illus. 2009. (Truck Buddies Ser.). (ENG.). 32p. (J). (gr. -1-1). pap. 6.25 *(978-1-4342-1756-1(6),* 102228, Stone Arch Bks.) Capstone.

Cruz, Marie Miranda. Everlasting Nora: A Novel. 2018. (ENG.). 288p. (J). 16.99 *(978-0-7653-9459-0(6),* 900176815, Starscape) Doherty, Tom Assocs., LLC.

Cullimore, Stan. Alien Swap. Schon, Nick, illus. 2005. (ENG.). 24p. (J). lib. bdg. 23.65 *(978-1-59646-744-6(4))* Dingles & Co.

Cumming, Hannah. The Cloud. Cumming, Hannah, illus. 2010. (Child's Play Library). (Illus.). 32p. (J). (gr. 1-2). pap. *(978-1-84643-343-6(6))* Child's Play International Ltd.

—The Lost Stars. Cumming, Hannah, illus. 2011. (Child's Play Library). (Illus.). 32p. (J). *(978-1-84643-416-7(5))* Child's Play International Ltd.

Cummings, Troy. The Eensy Weensy Spider Freaks Out! (Big-Time!) Cummings, Troy, illus. 2015. (Illus.). 40p. (J). (gr. -1-2). 7.99 *(978-0-553-49672-7(7),* Dragonfly Bks.) Random Hse. Children's Bks.

Cummings, W. T. The Girl in the White Hat. 2017. (ENG., Illus.). 32p. (J). 14.95 *(978-0-486-81586-2(2),* 815862) Dover Pubns., Inc.

Cunliffe, John. Postman Pat & the Goat's Supper. (ENG., Illus.). 20p. (J). *(978-0-340-71437-9(9))* Hodder & Stoughton.

—Postman Pat Mends a Clock. (ENG., Illus.). 20p. (J). pap. 11.99 *(978-0-340-73718-7(2))* Hodder & Stoughton GBR. Dist: Trafalgar Square Publishing.

—Postman Pat Surprise Breakfast. (ENG., Illus.). 24p. (J). *(978-0-340-71433-1(6))* Hodder & Stoughton.

—Postman Pats Special Delivery Bind. (ENG., Illus.). 94p. (J). 22.99 *(978-0-340-71055-5(1))* Hodder & Stoughton GBR. Dist: Trafalgar Square Publishing.

Cunningham, S. C. Ginormous Joe's Broken Bark. 2009. 48p. pap. 21.90 *(978-1-4490-3116-9(1))* AuthorHouse.

Curious George: Sweet Dreams, Curious George. 2016. (Curious George Ser.). (ENG., Illus.). 24p. (J). (gr. -1-3). 4.99 *(978-0-544-50321-2(X),* 1604665, Clarion Bks.) HarperCollins Pubs.

Curious George Discovers Germs. 2015. (Curious George Ser.). (ENG., Illus.). 32p. (J). (gr. -1-3). 6.99 *(978-0-544-43066-2(2),* 1595741, Clarion Bks.) HarperCollins Pubs.

Curious George Discovers the Ocean. 2015. (Curious George Ser.). (ENG., Illus.). 32p. (J). (gr. -1-3). 6.99 *(978-0-544-43065-5(4),* 1595740, Clarion Bks.) HarperCollins Pubs.

Curious George Discovers the Rainbow. 2015. (Curious George Ser.). (ENG., Illus.). 32p. (J). (gr. -1-3). 6.99 *(978-0-544-43068-6(9),* 1595743, Clarion Bks.) HarperCollins Pubs.

Curious George Discovers the Senses. 2015. (Curious George Ser.). (ENG., Illus.). 32p. (J). (gr. -1-3). 6.99 *(978-0-544-50023-5(7),* 1604222, Clarion Bks.) HarperCollins Pubs.

Curious George Goes to the Beach. 2014. (Curious George Ser.). (ENG., Illus.). 24p. (J). (gr. -1-3). pap. 5.99 *(978-0-544-25001-7(X),* 1566524, Clarion Bks.) HarperCollins Pubs.

Curious George Makes a Valentine (Gir Level 2) 2017. (Curious George Ser.). (ENG., Illus.). 24p. (J). (gr. -1-3). pap. 4.99 *(978-1-328-69556-7(5),* 1671217, Clarion Bks.) HarperCollins Pubs.

Curious George Makes Pancakes. 2018. (Curious George Ser.). (ENG., Illus.). 24p. (J). (— 1). bds. 12.99 *(978-1-328-76461-4(3),* 1681069, Clarion Bks.) HarperCollins Pubs.

Curious George Ready for School. 2017. (Curious George Ser.). (ENG., Illus.). 14p. (J). (— 1). bds. 7.99 *(978-0-544-93120-6(3),* 1657523, Clarion Bks.) HarperCollins Pubs.

Currie, Robin. Baby Bible 123. 2005. (Baby Bible Ser.). (Illus.). 48p. (J). bds. 12.99 *(978-0-7814-3906-0(X),* 078143906X) Cook, David C.

Currie Santamaria, Jenni & Ross Keyes, Joan. Oxford Picture Dictionary Content Area for Kids English-Spanish Dictionary. 2nd ed. 2012. (ENG., Illus.). 208p. pap. 30.80 *(978-0-19-401777-0(X))* Oxford Univ. Pr., Inc.

Curry, Casey. I Remember You Today: An Interactive Picturebook for Children Dealing with the Loss of a Sibling or Parent. 2003. (Illus.). 24p. (J). wbk. ed. *(978-1-884878-15-2(6))* Annapolis Publishing Co.

Curtis, Joan Scott. The Number Fairy. 2012. (ENG.). (J). pap. 18.00 *(978-1-4675-5219-6(4))* Independent Pub.

Curto Family, The & Fischer, Rusty. One Little Christmas Tree. 2012. 26p. pap. 9.99 *(978-0-9840338-1-2(5))* Good Times at Home LLC.

Custer, Jason. Everyday Monsters. 2005. (J). lib. bdg. 19.95 *(978-0-9754728-3-5(6))* Big Ransom Studio.

Cutbill, Andy, illus. Albie & the Big Race. 2004. (ENG.). 32p. (J). pap. 9.99 *(978-0-00-712212-7(8))* HarperCollins Pubs. Ltd. GBR. Dist: Trafalgar Square Publishing.

Czekaj, Jef. Dog Rules. Czekaj, Jef, illus. 2016. (ENG., Illus.). 32p. (J). (gr. -1-3). 17.99 *(978-0-06-228018-3(X),* Balzer & Bray) HarperCollins Pubs.

Daciute, Evelina & Kiudulaite, Ausra. The Fox on the Swing. 2018. (Illus.). 48p. (J). (gr. 2-5). 16.95 *(978-0-500-65156-8(6),* 565156) Thames & Hudson.

Daddo, Andrew. When I Grow Up. Bentley, Jonathan, illus. 2017. 32p. 17.99 *(978-0-7333-3341-5(9))* ABC Bks. AUS. Dist: HarperCollins Pubs.

Dahl, Michael. Be a Star, Wonder Woman! Lozano, Omar, illus. 2017. (DC Super Heroes Ser.). (ENG.). 32p. (J). (gr. -1-2). 15.95 *(978-1-62370-875-7(3),* 135196, Stone Arch Bks.) Capstone.

—Monster Street Complete Set, Set. Ornia-Blanco, Miguel, illus. Incl. Two Heads Are Better Than One. (ENG., Illus.). 32p. (J). (gr. 1-3). 2010. lib. bdg. 23.99 *(978-1-4048-6067-4(3),* 103251, Picture Window Bks.); (Monster Street Ser.). (ENG.). Illus.). 32p. 2010. 71.97 o.p. *(978-1-4048-6352-1(4),* 15360, Picture Window Bks.) Capstone.

Daley, Lashon. Mr. Okra Sells Fresh Fruits & Vegetables, 1 vol. Henriquez, Emile, illus. 2016. (ENG.). 32p. (J). (gr. k-3). 16.99 *(978-1-4556-2112-5(9),* Pelican Publishing) Arcadia Publishing.

Daley, Matthew & Daley, Arlene. The Not-So Secret Society: Tale of the Gummy. Clark, Wook-Jin, illus. 2017. (ENG.). 128p. (J). (gr. 3). pap. 9.99 *(978-1-60886-997-8(0))* BOOM! Studios.

Daley, Michael J. Beach Socks, 1 vol. Corke, Estelle, illus. 2013. (ENG.). 10p. (J). bds. 6.99 *(978-1-59572-637-7(3))* Star Bright Bks., Inc.

Daly, Kathleen N. Jingle Bells. Miller, J. P., illus. 2015. (Little Golden Book Ser.). 24p. (J). (-k). 5.99 *(978-0-553-51112-3(2),* Golden Bks.) Random Hse. Children's Bks.

Damm, Antje. Waiting for Goliath. Damm, Antje, illus. 2017. (ENG., Illus.). 32p. (J). (gr. -1-3). 16.99 *(978-1-77657-141-3(X),* 43f581aa-63b3-4d70-9107-218650db8424) Gecko Pr. NZL. Dist: Lerner Publishing Group.

Damschroder, Scott. The Crazy Carnival Clown We Call Croc. 2006. (Illus.). 40p. (J). lib. bdg. 19.95 *(978-0-9754728-1-1(X))* Big Ransom Studio.

Dane Rehagen. How Katie Got Her Meow. 2010. 42p. pap. 15.00 *(978-1-4251-8664-7(5))* Trafford Publishing.

Danger Alert: Picture Book (English) 2006. (Illus.). 47p. (J). 5.99 *(978-1-933934-03-7(4))* Mighty Kids Media.

Danger Alert: Picture Book (English) 8x8. 2007. (J). 5.99 *(978-1-933934-39-6(5))* Mighty Kids Media.

Danger Alert: Picture Book (English) 9x9 with Snipe. 2007. (J). 5.99 *(978-1-933934-49-5(2))* Mighty Kids Media.

Danielsdottir, Sigrun. Your Body Is Awesome: Body Respect for Children. Bjarkadottir, Bjork, illus. 2014. 36p. (J). pap. 19.95 *(978-1-84819-228-7(2),* 694244, Singing Dragon) Kingsley, Jessica Pubs. GBR. Dist: Hachette UK Distribution.

Dardik, Helen, illus. The Story of Christmas. 2017. (ENG.). 24p. (J). (gr. -1 — 1). bds. 9.95 *(978-0-7624-6242-1(6),* Running Pr. Kids) Running Pr.

—The Story of Easter. 2019. (ENG.). 26p. (J). (gr. -1 — 1). bds. 9.95 *(978-0-7624-9269-5(4),* Running Pr. Kids) Running Pr.

Davenport, Andrew. Here Come the Teletubbies. 2004. (Illus.). (J). (gr. -1-2). spiral bd. *(978-0-616-03029-5(0));* spiral bd. *(978-0-616-04551-0(4))* Canadian National Institute for the Blind/Institut National Canadien pour les Aveugles.

Davenport, Maxine & Roberts, Cindy, illus. What Can You Spot? 2018. (J). *(978-1-4998-0737-0(6))* Little Bee Books Inc.

Davey, Owen, illus. Foxly's Feast. 2014. (ENG.). 32p. (J). (-k). 14.95 *(978-1-62914-608-9(0),* Sky Pony Pr.) Skyhorse Publishing Co., Inc.

David, Juliet. All Aboard with Noah, 1 vol. Canuso, Jackie & Canuso, Jackie, illus. 2016. (ENG.). 12p. (J). (gr. -1-k). 11.99 *(978-1-78128-249-6(8),* b8b47fdf-710b-4ba4-850d-be9857166e82, Candle Bks.) Lion Hudson PLC GBR. Dist: Baker & Taylor Publisher Services (BTPS).

—The Christmas Story, 1 vol. Ellis, Elina, illus. 2016. (99 Stories from the Bible Ser.). (ENG.). 24p. (J). (gr. k-3). 7.99 *(978-1-78128-282-3(X),* 6c214623-2042-49ba-85fc-363e557d832b, Candle Bks.) Lion Hudson PLC GBR. Dist: Baker & Taylor Publisher Services (BTPS).

—The Great Flood, 1 vol. Parry, Jo, illus. 2014. 12p. (J). bds. 3.99 *(978-1-85985-991-9(7),* Candle Bks.) Lion Hudson PLC GBR. Dist: Kregel Pubns.

Davidson, Rose. National Geographic Readers: Odd Animals (PreReader) 2019. (Readers Ser.). (Illus.). 24p. (J). (gr. -1-k).

pap. 4.99 *(978-1-4263-3339-2(0))*; (ENG., lib. bdg. 14.90 *(978-1-4263-3340-8(4))* Disney Publishing Worldwide. (National Geographic Kids).

Davidson, Susanna. Christmas Carol (Picture Book) 2007. (Picture Book Classics Ser.). 24p. (J). 9.99 *(978-0-7945-1894-3(X)*, Usborne) EDC Publishing.

—Cinderella Picture Book. 2015. (Picture Bks.). (ENG.). 24p. (J). 9.99 *(978-0-7945-3423-3(6)*, Usborne) EDC Publishing.

—Nutcracker with Music. 2012. (Picture Books with Music Ser.). 24p. (J). bds. 18.99 *(978-0-7945-2646-7(2)*, Usborne) EDC Publishing.

—Swan Lake with Music. 2012. (Picture Books with Music Ser.). 24p. (J). bds. 18.99 *(978-0-7945-3301-4(9)*, Usborne) EDC Publishing.

Davies, Beth. Rise of the Rogues. 2017. (Illus.). 48p. (J). *(978-1-5182-3600-6(6))* Dorling Kindersley Publishing, Inc.

Davies, Nicola. Deadly! The Truth about the Most Dangerous Creatures on Earth. Layton, Neal, illus. 2015. (Animal Science Ser.). (ENG.). 64p. (J). (gr. 3-7). pap. 7.99 *(978-0-7636-7971-2(2))* Candlewick Pr.

—I (Don't) Like Snakes. Lozano, Luciano, illus. 2018. (Read & Wonder Ser.). (ENG.). 32p. (J). (gr. k-4). 7.99 *(978-1-5362-0323-3(8))* Candlewick Pr.

—The Promise. Carlin, Laura, illus. (ENG.). 40p. (J). (gr. k-4). 2017. 9.99 *(978-0-7636-9303-9(0))* 2014. 18.99 *(978-0-7636-6633-0(5))* Candlewick Pr.

Davies, Stephen & Corr, Christopher. The Goggle-Eyed Goats. 2013. (ENG., Illus.). 32p. (J). (gr. -1-k). pap. 12.99 *(978-1-84939-312-6(5))* Andersen Pr. GBR. Dist: Independent Pubs. Group.

Dávila, Claudia. Super Red Riding Hood. Dávila, Claudia, illus. 2014. (ENG., Illus.). 32p. (J). (gr. -1-2). 16.95 *(978-1-77138-020-1(9))* Kids Can Pr., Ltd. CAN. Dist: Hachette Bk. Group.

Dávila, Valeria & López. Diary of a Fairy. Warriner, tr. Aguerrebehere, Laura, illus. 2018. (Dear Diary Ser.). 32p. (J). (gr. -1-1). 7.99 *(978-2-924786-65-9(7)*, CrackBoom! Bks.) Chouette Publishing CAN. Dist: Publishers Group West (PGW).

—Diary of a Monster. Warriner, tr. Aguerrebehere, Laura, illus. 2018. (Dear Diary Ser.). 32p. (J). (gr. -1-1). 7.99 *(978-2-924786-71-0(1)*, CrackBoom! Bks.) Chouette Publishing CAN. Dist: Publishers Group West (PGW).

—Diary of an Ogre. Warriner, tr. Aguerrebehere, Laura, illus. 2018. (Dear Diary Ser.). 32p. (J). (gr. -1-1). 7.99 *(978-2-924786-69-7(X)*, CrackBoom! Bks.) Chouette Publishing CAN. Dist: Publishers Group West (PGW).

Dávila, Valeria & López, Mónica. Diary of a Witch. Warriner, David, tr. Aguerrebehere, Laura, illus. 2018. (Dear Diary Ser.). 32p. (J). (gr. -1-1). 7.99 *(978-2-924786-67-3(3)*, CrackBoom! Bks.) Chouette Publishing CAN. Dist: Publishers Group West (PGW).

Davis, Anne. No Dogs Allowed!, No. 1. Davis, Anne, illus. 2011. (ENG., Illus.). 32p. (J). (gr. -1-3). 16.99 *(978-0-06-075353-5(6)*, HarperCollins) HarperCollins Pubs.

Davis, Caroline. Animals in the Water. 2009. (My First Noisy Bath Bks.). (ENG.). 8p. (J). (gr. -1-k). 6.99 *(978-0-7641-9591-4(3))* Sourcebooks, Inc.

—Diggers. Davis, Caroline, illus. 2010. (ENG., Illus.). 20p. (J). bds. *(978-1-4083-0785-4(5)*, Orchard Bks.) Hachette Children's Group GBR. Dist: Hachette Bk. Group.

—First Abc. 2012. (ENG., Illus.). 10p. (J). (gr. k-1). pap. 7.99 *(978-1-84322-772-4(X))* Anness Publishing GBR. Dist: National Bk. Network.

—First Opposites. 2012. (Illus.). 10p. (J). (gr. -1-1). bds. 7.99 *(978-1-84322-844-8(0)*, Armadillo) Anness Publishing GBR. Dist: National Bk. Network.

—First Pictures. 2012. (Illus.). 196p. (J). (gr. -1-12). bds. 7.99 *(978-1-84322-774-8(6)*, Armadillo) Anness Publishing GBR. Dist: National Bk. Network.

Davis, Jacky. I Love You, Bingo. Soman, David, illus. 2015. (Ladybug Girl Ser.). (ENG.). 32p. (J). (gr. 1-2). pap. 5.99 *(978-0-448-48756-4(X)*, Penguin Young Readers) Penguin Young Readers Group.

—Ladybug Girl Ready for Snow. Soman, David, illus. 2014. (Ladybug Girl Ser.). 14p. (J). (gr. -1 — 1). bds. 7.99 *(978-0-8037-4137-9(5)*, Dial Bks) Penguin Young Readers Group.

Davison, Roz. Jungle School. Laird, Elizabeth & Sim, David, illus. 2nd ed. 2016. (Reading Ladder Level 1 Ser.). (ENG.). 48p. (gr. k-2). pap. 7.99 *(978-1-4052-8226-0(6)*, Reading Ladder) Farshore GBR. Dist: Independent Pubs. Group, HarperCollins Pubs.

Dawnay, Gabby. A House for Mouse. Barrow, Alex, illus. 2018. (ENG.). 32p. (J). (gr. -1-2). 16.95 *(978-0-500-65137-7(X)*, 565137) Thames & Hudson.

—If I Had a Dinosaur. Barrow, Alex, illus. 2017. (If I Had A... Ser.: 0). (ENG.). 32p. (J). (gr. -1-2). 15.95 *(978-0-500-65099-8(3)*, 565099) Thames & Hudson.

—London Calls. Barrow, Alex, illus. 2015. (ENG.). 40p. (J). (gr. -1-2). 13.95 *(978-1-84976-230-4(9)*, 1669201) Tate Publishing, Ltd. GBR. Dist: Hachette Bk. Group.

Dawson, Eugene T. Little Valerie Wants to Grow Taller. 2009. 24p. pap. 14.95 *(978-1-4389-7002-8(1))* AuthorHouse.

Day, Alexandra. Carl & the Sick Puppy. 2012. (My Readers: Level 1 Ser.). (J). lib. bdg. 13.55 *(978-0-606-26121-0(4))* Turtleback.

de Anda, Diane. The Day Abuelo Got Lost: Memory Loss of a Loved Grandfather. Harris, Alleanna, illus. 2019. (ENG.). 32p. (J). (gr. -1-3). 16.99 *(978-0-8075-1492-4(6)*, 807514926) Whitman, Albert & Co.

de Beer, Hans. Nugget on Top of the World. 2015. (ENG., Illus.). 32p. (J). (gr. k-2). 17.95 *(978-0-7358-4242-7(6))* North-South Bks., Inc.

De Beer, Hans, pseud. Kleiner eisbar wohin fahrst Du. pap. 17.95 *(978-3-423-07954-9(1))* Deutscher Taschenbuch Verlag GmbH & Co KG DEU. Dist: Distribooks, Inc.

De la Bédoyère, Camilla. Where Is the Bear? Kelly, Richard, ed. Levey, Emma, illus. 2017. (ENG.). 24p. (J). pap. 9.95 *(978-1-78209-984-0(0))* Miles Kelly Publishing, Ltd. GBR. Dist: Parkwest Pubns., Inc.

de la Mare, Walter. Snow. Rabei, Carolina, illus. 2018. (Four Seasons of Walter de la Mare Ser.). (ENG.). 16p. bds. 7.95 *(978-0-571-33713-2(9)*, Faber & Faber Children's Bks.) Faber & Faber, Inc.

de Maeyer, Gregie. Juul. 2003. (SPA., Illus.). 204p. *(978-84-85334-90-2(6))* Lóguez Ediciones ESP. Dist: Lectorum Pubns., Inc.

De Roma, Giuseppino. Francis of Assisi. (Illus.). 31p. 7.95 *(978-1-875570-64-5(0))* St Pauls Pubns. AUS. Dist: St Pauls/Alba Hse. Pubs.

De Smet, Marian & Meijer, Marja. Encerrada: Anna's Tight Squeeze. Pacheco, Laura Emilia, tr. Uitgeverij, Clavis, illus. 2004. 28p. (J). 14.95 *(978-970-29-0665-0(2))* Santillana USA Publishing Co., Inc.

Dean, James. Pete the Cat & the Cool Caterpillar. 2018. (I Can Read Ser.). (ENG.). 32p. (J). (gr. -1-k). 13.89 *(978-1-64310-215-3(X))* Penworthy Co., LLC, The.

Dean, James & Dean, Kimberly. Pete the Cat & the Cool Caterpillar. Dean, James, illus. 2018. (I Can Read Level 1 Ser.). (ENG., Illus.). 32p. (J). (gr. -1-3). 17.99 *(978-0-06-267522-4(2))*; pap. 4.99 *(978-0-06-267521-7(4))* HarperCollins Pubs. (HarperCollins).

—Pete the Cat Treasury: Five Groovy Stories. Dean, James, illus. 2017. (Pete the Cat Ser.). (ENG., Illus.). 160p. (J). (gr. -1-3). 21.99 *(978-0-06-274036-6(9)*, HarperCollins) HarperCollins Pubs.

—Pete the Cat: Twinkle, Twinkle, Little Star. Dean, James, illus. 2014. (Pete the Cat Ser.). (ENG., Illus.). 32p. (J). (gr. -1-3). 9.99 *(978-0-06-230416-2(X)*, HarperCollins) HarperCollins Pubs.

—Pete the Cat's 12 Groovy Days of Christmas: A Christmas Holiday Book for Kids. Dean, James, illus. 2018. (Pete the Cat Ser.). (ENG., Illus.). 48p. (J). (gr. -1-3). 13.99 *(978-0-06-267527-9(3)*, HarperCollins) HarperCollins Pubs.

—Pete the Kitty & the Groovy Playdate. Dean, James, illus. 2018. (Pete the Cat Ser.). (ENG., Illus.). 40p. (J). (gr. -1-3). lib. bdg. 18.89 *(978-0-06-267541-5(9)*, HarperCollins) HarperCollins Pubs.

—Pete the Kitty: I Love Pete the Kitty. Dean, James, illus. 2017. (Pete the Cat Ser.). (ENG., Illus.). 24p. (J). (gr. -1 — 1). bds. 7.99 *(978-0-06-243581-1(7)*, HarperFestival) HarperCollins Pubs.

Dean, James, et al. Pete the Cat: Three Bite Rule. 2018. (Pete the Cat Ser.). (ENG., Illus.). 32p. (J). (gr. -1-3). 12.99 *(978-0-06-287260-9(5)*, HarperFestival) HarperCollins Pubs.

Dean, Kim & Dean, James, illus. Pete the Cat & the Missing Cupcakes. 2016. (J). *(978-0-605-95181-5(0))* Harper & Row Ltd.

DeDonato, Rick. Pipsie, Nature Detective: the Lunchnapper, 0 vols. Bishop, Tracy, illus. 2016. (Pipsie, Nature Detective Ser.). (ENG.). 40p. (J). (gr. -1-2). 17.99 *(978-1-5039-5061-0(1)*, 9781503950610, Two Lions) Amazon Publishing.

Degen, Bruce. Degen Picture Book. Date not set. (Illus.). 32p. (J). (gr. -1-1). 5.99 *(978-0-06-443579-6(2))* HarperCollins Pubs.

DeGregorio, Chieri & DeGregorio, Steve. Vehicles. 2019. (Kids' Picture Show Ser.). (Illus.). 16p. (J). (-k). bds. 7.99 *(978-1-5247-9076-9(1)*, Penguin Workshop) Penguin Young Readers Group.

deGroat, Diane. Roses Are Pink, Your Feet Really Stink. deGroat, Diane, illus. 2022. (ENG., Illus.). 32p. (J). (gr. -1-3). pap. 8.99 *(978-0-688-15220-8(1)*, HarperCollins) HarperCollins Pubs.

Delacre, Lulu. How Far Do You Love Me?, 1 vol. 2013. (ENG., Illus.). 32p. (J). 11.95 *(978-1-60060-882-7(5))* Lee & Low Bks., Inc.

DeLand, M. Maitland. The Great Katie Kate Discusses Diabetes. 2010. (Illus.). 32p. 14.95 *(978-1-60832-039-4(1)*, Greenleaf Book Group Pr.) Greenleaf Book Group.

—The Great Katie Kate Offers Answers about Asthma. 2011. (Illus.). 32p. 14.95 *(978-1-60832-074-5(X))* Greenleaf Book Group.

DeLand, M. Maitland. Baby Santa & the Lost Letters. 2011. (Illus.). 36p. (J). 14.95 *(978-1-60832-194-0(0))* Greenleaf Book Group.

Delaronde, Deborah L. Duck's Bay. Dawson, Sheldon, illus. 2004. 48p. (J). pap. *(978-1-894717-24-3(4)*, Spotlight Poets) Pemmican Pubns., Inc.

DeLong, Lucianne. Mrs. Mumford's Missing. Richoll, Stephanie, illus. 2013. (Saloman Sawdust's Snappy Stories Ser.). (ENG.). 24p. (J). 4.99 *(978-0-9833237-5-4(5))* Krullstone Publishing, LLC.

Demarest, Chris. Bus. 2017. (ENG., Illus.). 16p. (J). (— 1). bds. 6.99 *(978-0-544-87087-1(5)*, 1649083, Clarion Bks.) HarperCollins Pubs.

—Bus/el Autobús Board Book: Bilingual English-Spanish. 2017. (ENG., Illus.). 16p. (J). (— 1). bds. 4.99 *(978-0-544-99114-9(1)*, 1665902, Clarion Bks.) HarperCollins Pubs.

—Plane Board Book. 2017. (ENG., Illus.). 16p. (J). (— 1). bds. 6.99 *(978-0-544-97703-7(3)*, 1663472, Clarion Bks.) HarperCollins Pubs.

—Ship Board Book. 2017. (ENG., Illus.). 16p. (J). (— 1). bds. 6.99 *(978-0-544-97702-0(5)*, 1663470, Clarion Bks.) HarperCollins Pubs.

—Train. 2017. (ENG., Illus.). 16p. (J). (— 1). bds. 6.99 *(978-0-544-87608-8(3)*, 1651101, Clarion Bks.) HarperCollins Pubs.

Demarest, Jeannie. My Best Friend Troubles. 2009. 28p. pap. 21.99 *(978-1-4415-3236-7(6))* Xlibris Corp.

Dempsey, Kristy. Surfer Chick. Cole, Henry, illus. 2018. (ENG.). 32p. (J). (gr. -1-k). pap. 4.99 *(978-1-4197-2931-7(4)*, 689803, Abrams Bks. for Young Readers) Abrams, Inc.

Dencer, Christine. Misty. Meserve, Jessica, illus. 2015. (Stanley & Me Ser.: 1). (ENG.). 34p. (J). 12.95 *(978-1-927018-59-0(5))* Simply Read Bks. CAN. Dist: Ingram Publisher Services.

Denchfield, Nick & Denchdfield, Nick. Charlie Chick Finds an Egg. Parker, Ant, illus. 2017. (Charlie Chick Ser.: 5). (ENG.). 16p. (J). (gr. -1-k). 11.99 *(978-1-5098-2883-8(4)*, Campbell Bks.) Pan Macmillan GBR. Dist: Independent Pubs. Group.

Denis, Toni. How Do the Children Pray? Olds, Irene, illus. 2010. 16p. 10.99 *(978-1-4490-5164-8(2))* AuthorHouse.

Dennis, Elizabeth. Violet Fairy Gets Her Wings. Smillie, Natalie, illus. 2016. (J). *(978-1-5182-4501-5(3))* Simon & Schuster Children's Publishing.

dePaola, Tomie. Nana Upstairs & Nana Downstairs. unabr. ed. 2006. (J). (gr. k-3). pap. 19.95 incl. audio compact disk *(978-0-8045-4157-2(4))*; pap. 17.95 incl. audio *(978-0-8045-6943-9(6))* Spoken Arts, Inc.

—Strega Nona. dePaola, Tomie, illus. 2017. (Strega Nona Book Ser.). (ENG., Illus.). 36p. (J). (gr. -1-k). bds. 8.99 *(978-1-4814-8724-5(8)*, Little Simon) Little Simon.

—Tomie DePaola's the Quicksand Book. 2019. (ENG., Illus.). 32p. (J). (gr. -1-3). 17.99 *(978-0-8234-4237-9(3))* Holiday Hse., Inc.

—When Andy Met Sandy. 2018. lib. bdg. 16.00 *(978-0-606-40845-5(2))* Turtleback.

Depisco, Dorothea. Beetle Bugs Party: A Counting Book. Parry, Jo, illus. 2005. 10p. (J). (gr. -1-3). 10.95 *(978-1-58117-415-1(2)*, Intervisual/Piggy Toes) Bendon, Inc.

Depken, Kristen L. Rubble's Big Wish. Moore, Harry, illus. 2017. 17p. (J). *(978-1-5182-3644-0(8))* Random Hse., Inc.

Dergachov, Oleg. The Yellow Elves. Andryczyk, Mark, tr. from UKR. 2004. (Illus.). 14p. (J). pap. *(978-0-9735003-0-1(1))* StudioNib Publishing.

Desai, Naina. Fun Jungle. 2009. 28p. pap. 13.99 *(978-1-4490-2058-3(5))* AuthorHouse.

Deseret Book Company. Because of You. Dad. Keele, Kevin, illus. 2018. (J). 13.99 *(978-1-62972-561-1(7))* Deseret Bk. Co.

Deuchars, Marion. Bob the Artist. 2016. (ENG., Illus.). 32p. (J). (gr. -1-k). 15.95 *(978-1-78067-767-5(7)*, King, Laurence Publishing) Orion Publishing Group, Ltd. GBR. Dist: Hachette Bk. Group.

Deuchars, Marion, illus. Bob's Blue Period. 2018. (ENG.). 32p. (J). (gr. -1-k). 15.99 *(978-1-78627-070-2(6)*, King, Laurence Publishing) Orion Publishing Group, Ltd. GBR. Dist: Hachette Bk. Group.

deVet, L. J. Teddy's Christmas Wish. Zabarylo-Duma, Ewa, illus. 2013. (ENG.). 48p. (J). *(978-0-9873686-0-7(5))*; pap. *(978-0-9873686-1-4(3))* Print-Rite Publishers.

Devine, Monica. Kayak Girl. 2012. (ENG., Illus.). 32p. (J). pap. 13.95 *(978-1-60223-188-7(5))* Univ. of Alaska Pr.

Dewdney, Anna. Llama Llama Easter Egg. 2015. (Llama Llama Ser.). (Illus.). 14p. (J). (— 1). bds. 7.99 *(978-0-451-46982-3(8)*, Viking Books for Young Readers) Penguin Young Readers Group.

—Llama Llama Mad at Mama. 2009. (Illus.). (J). *(978-0-545-15933-3(4))* Scholastic, Inc.

Dhami, Narinder. Monster under the Stairs. Spoor, Mike, illus. 2005. (ENG.). 24p. (J). lib. bdg. 23.65 *(978-1-59646-718-7(5))* Dingles & Co.

—Samosa Thief. Blundell, Tony, illus. 2005. (ENG.). 24p. (J). lib. bdg. 23.65 *(978-1-59646-708-8(8))* Dingles & Co.

Diane, Rachel And Rebecca Sall. Mother Earth's Message. 2009. 28p. pap. 15.99 *(978-1-4363-8613-5(6))* Xlibris Corp.

Diaper Days Songs. (Baby Looney Tunes Song Bks.). (Illus.). 16p. (J). (gr. -1). 7.98 *(978-0-7853-1612-1(4)*, PI112) Publications International, Ltd.

DiCamillo, Kate. Great Joy (midi Edition) Ibatoulline, Bagram, illus. 2010. (ENG.). 32p. (J). (gr. -1-3). 12.00 *(978-0-7636-4996-8(1))* Candlewick Pr.

Dicamillo, Kate. Louise, the Adventures of a Chicken. Bliss, Harry, illus. 2009. (J). (gr. -1-2). 29.95 incl. audio compact disk *(978-1-4301-0688-3(3))* Live Oak Media.

DiCicco, Sue. Peek-a-Boo Baby. 2010. 12p. (J). (gr. -1). 9.95 *(978-1-60747-709-9(2)*, Pickwick Pr.) Phoenix Bks., Inc.

Dickins, Rosie. How the Leopard Got His Spots. 2018. (Picture Bks.). (ENG.). 24p. (J). 9.99 *(978-0-7945-4201-6(8)*, Usborne) EDC Publishing.

Dicmas, Courtney. Bathtime. Dicmas, Courtney, illus. 2014. (Wild! Ser.: 4). (Illus.). 14p. (J). (gr. k-k). spiral bd. *(978-1-84643-686-4(9))* Child's Play International Ltd.

—Bedtime. Dicmas, Courtney, illus. 2014. (Wild! Ser.: 4). (Illus.). 14p. (J). (gr. k-k). spiral bd. *(978-1-84643-687-1(7))* Child's Play International Ltd.

—Mealtime. Dicmas, Courtney, illus. 2014. (Wild! Ser.: 4). (Illus.). 14p. (J). (gr. k-k). spiral bd. *(978-1-84643-684-0(2))* Child's Play International Ltd.

—Playtime. Dicmas, Courtney, illus. 2014. (Wild! Ser.: 4). (Illus.). 14p. (J). (gr. k-k). spiral bd. *(978-1-84643-685-7(0))* Child's Play International Ltd.

Dieker, Wendy Strobel. Los Trenes. 2019. (Máquinas Poderosas Ser.). (SPA.). 16p. (J). (gr. -1-2). *(978-1-68151-888-6(0)*, 10833) Amicus.

Diesen, Deborah. The Perfect School Picture. Santat, Dan, illus. 2019. (ENG.). 32p. (J). (gr. k-2). pap. 4.99 *(978-1-4197-3509-7(8)*, 690903, Abrams Bks. for Young Readers) Abrams, Inc.

—Pout-Pout Fish: Back to School. Hanna, Dan, illus. 2019. (Pout-Pout Fish Paperback Adventure Ser.). (ENG.). 24p. (J). 5.99 *(978-0-374-31047-9(5)*, 900193159, Farrar, Straus & Giroux (BYR)) Farrar, Straus & Giroux.

—Pout-Pout Fish: Haunted House. Hanna, Dan, illus. 2019. (Pout-Pout Fish Paperback Adventure Ser.). (ENG.). 24p. (J). 5.99 *(978-0-374-31052-3(1)*, 900193164, Farrar, Straus & Giroux (BYR)) Farrar, Straus & Giroux.

Dillard, Sheri. Cowhide-And-Seek. Pauwels, Jess, illus. 2019. (ENG.). 32p. (J). (gr. -1-3). 17.99 *(978-0-7624-9184-1(1)*, Running Pr. Kids) Running Pr.

Dillon, Diane & Dillon, Leo, illus. Love & the Rocking Chair. 2019. (ENG.). 40p. (J). (gr. -1-k). 18.99 *(978-1-338-33265-0(1)*, Blue Sky Pr., The) Scholastic, Inc.

Dinosaurs. (Illus.). (J). (gr. -1-6). pap. 2.95 *(978-0-565-01078-2(6))* Natural History Museum Pubns. GBR. Dist: Parkwest Pubns., Inc.

Discovery Education. 2013. (Discovery Education Ser.). 32p. (J). (gr. 3-6). 1035.25 *(978-1-4777-1555-0(X))*; pap. 410.00 *(978-1-4777-2736-2(1))*; pap. 2460.00 *(978-1-4777-2737-9(X))* Rosen Publishing Group, Inc., The. (PowerKids Pr.).

Dismondy, Maria. The Fruit Salad Friend: Recipe for a True Friend. Selbert, Kathryn, illus. 2018. (ENG.). 32p. (J). (gr. 2-4). 10.95 *(978-0-9976085-2-6(8)*, b541c0ae-46bf-48a4-8a90-e846da42b66f, Cardinal Rule Pr.) Dismondy, Maria Inc.

Disney Books. Disney Baby: 100 First Words LifttheFlap. 2018. (ENG., Illus.). 12p. (J). (gr. -1 — 1). bds. 10.99 *(978-1-4847-1801-8(1)*, Disney Press Books) Disney Publishing Worldwide.

—Disney Baby: My First Easter. 2018. (ENG., Illus.). 12p. (J). (gr. -1 — 1). bds. 8.99 *(978-1-368-01116-7(0)*, Disney Press Books) Disney Publishing Worldwide.

—Disney Bunnies: Thumper's Hoppy Home: A Lift-The-Flap Board Book. 2018. (ENG., Illus.). 10p. (J). (gr. -1-k). bds. 8.99 *(978-1-4847-7371-0(3)*, Disney Press Books) Disney Publishing Worldwide.

—5-Minute Disney Classic Stories. 2018. (5-Minute Stories Ser.). (ENG., Illus.). 192p. (J). (gr. 1-3). 12.99 *(978-1-368-00676-7(0)*, Disney Press Books) Disney Publishing Worldwide.

—5-Minute Halloween Stories. 2018. (5-Minute Stories Ser.). (ENG., Illus.). 192p. (J). (gr. 1-3). 12.99 *(978-1-368-00257-8(9)*, Disney Press Books) Disney Publishing Worldwide.

—5-Minute Mickey Mouse Stories. 2018. (5-Minute Stories Ser.). (ENG., Illus.). 192p. (J). (gr. 1-3). 12.99 *(978-1-368-02235-4(9)*, Disney Press Books) Disney Publishing Worldwide.

Disney Editors. Olaf Loves... Everything! 2016. (Frozen 8X8 Ser.). lib. bdg. 14.75 *(978-0-606-39858-9(9))* Turtleback.

Dixon, Andy. Star Quest. Brooks, Felicity, ed. Harris, Nick, illus. 2006. (Usborne Fantasy Puzzle Bks.). 32p. (YA). (gr. 7). lib. bdg. 15.99 *(978-1-58086-906-5(8)*, Usborne) EDC Publishing.

Dixon, Pamela. A Windy Day Walk. Homer, Maree, illus. 2016. (ENG.). 32p. (J). (gr. 1-4). *(978-0-473-34486-3(6))* Lizzy Web Bks.

DK. Baby Faces. 2016. (Baby Sparkle Ser.). (ENG., Illus.). 14p. (J). (— 1). bds. 5.99 *(978-1-4654-4466-0(1)*, 1403588, DK Children) Dorling Kindersley Publishing, Inc.

—Baby Touch & Feel: Halloween. 2017. (Baby Touch & Feel Ser.). (ENG., Illus.). 14p. (J). (— 1). bds. 7.99 *(978-1-4654-6235-0(X)*, DK Children) Dorling Kindersley Publishing, Inc.

—Boys' Potty Time. 2010. (ENG., Illus.). 14p. (J). (gr. -1-k). bds. 9.99 *(978-0-7566-5884-7(5)*, DK Children) Dorling Kindersley Publishing, Inc.

—Buenas Noches, Bebe! / Good Night, Baby! 2004. (Soft-To-Touch Bks.).Tr. of Good Night, Baby! (Illus.). 18p. (J). (gr. -1-k). bds. 5.99 *(978-0-7566-0438-7(9)*, DK Children) Dorling Kindersley Publishing, Inc.

—Buenos Dias, Bebe! / Good Morning, Baby! 2004. (Soft-To-Touch Bks.).Tr. of Good Morning, Baby! (Illus.). 18p. (J). (gr. -1 — 1). bds. 5.99 *(978-0-7566-0437-0(0)*, DK Children) Dorling Kindersley Publishing, Inc.

—Crunch! Munch! Bunny. 2019. (Super Noisy Bks.). (ENG.). 12p. (J). (— 1). bds. 14.99 *(978-1-4654-7853-5(1)*, DK Children) Dorling Kindersley Publishing, Inc.

—Dinosaurs: a Visual Encyclopedia, 2nd Edition. 2nd ed. 2018. (DK Children's Visual Encyclopedias Ser.). (ENG., Illus.). 304p. (J). (gr. 4-7). 29.99 *(978-1-4654-7011-9(5))*; pap. 19.99 *(978-1-4654-6948-9(6))* Dorling Kindersley Publishing, Inc. (DK Children).

—Fire Truck. 2003. (Wheelie Bks.). (ENG., Illus.). 12p. (J). (gr. -1-k). bds. 8.99 *(978-0-7894-9712-3(3)*, DK Children) Dorling Kindersley Publishing, Inc.

—Human Body: a Visual Encyclopedia. 2018. (DK Children's Visual Encyclopedias Ser.). (ENG., Illus.). 256p. (J). (gr. 3-7). pap. 19.99 *(978-1-4654-7358-5(0)*, DK Children) Dorling Kindersley Publishing, Inc.

—Inventions: a Visual Encyclopedia. 2018. (DK Children's Visual Encyclopedias Ser.). (ENG., Illus.). 304p. (J). (gr. 3-7). 29.99 *(978-1-4654-5838-4(7)*, DK Children) Dorling Kindersley Publishing, Inc.

—Is It Warm Enough for Ice Cream? 2018. (ENG., Illus.). 18p. (J). (-k). bds. 9.99 *(978-1-4654-6786-7(6)*, DK Children) Dorling Kindersley Publishing, Inc.

—My Encyclopedia of Very Important Dinosaurs: Discover More Than 80 Prehistoric Creatures. 2018. (My Very Important Encyclopedias Ser.). (ENG., Illus.). 224p. (J). (gr. k-4). 18.99 *(978-1-4654-6848-2(X)*, DK Children) Dorling Kindersley Publishing, Inc.

—My First Touch & Feel Picture Cards: Things That Go. 2018. (My First Board Bks.). (ENG.). 17p. (J). (— 1). 9.99 *(978-1-4654-6812-3(9)*, DK Children) Dorling Kindersley Publishing, Inc.

—My First Trucks. 2015. (My First Board Bks.). (ENG.). 36p. (J). (gr. -1 — 1). bds. 5.99 *(978-1-4654-2904-9(2)*, DK Children) Dorling Kindersley Publishing, Inc.

—Nature's Deadliest Creatures Visual Encyclopedia. 2018. (DK Children's Visual Encyclopedias Ser.). (ENG.). 208p. (J). (gr. 3-7). 17.99 *(978-1-4654-5897-1(2)*, DK Children) Dorling Kindersley Publishing, Inc.

—Peek & Seek. Milner, Charlotte, illus. 2018. (ENG.). 18p. (J). (gr. -1-1). bds. 12.99 *(978-1-4654-6865-9(X)*, DK Children) Dorling Kindersley Publishing, Inc.

—Science: a Visual Encyclopedia. 2018. (DK Children's Visual Encyclopedias Ser.). (ENG., Illus.). 304p. (J). (gr. 3-7). 29.99 *(978-1-4654-7322-6(X)*, DK Children) Dorling Kindersley Publishing, Inc.

—Sophie la Girafe: Sophie's Big First Word Book. 2016. (Sophie la Girafe Ser.). (ENG., Illus.). 18p. (J). (gr. -1 — 1). bds. 9.99 *(978-1-4654-4494-3(7)*, DK Children) Dorling Kindersley Publishing, Inc.

DK & Woodward, John. The Dinosaur Book. 2018. (DK Our World in Pictures Ser.). (ENG., Illus.). 208p. (J). (gr. 4-7). 22.99 *(978-1-4654-7476-6(5)*, DK Children) Dorling Kindersley Publishing, Inc.

Dobbins, Jan. A Farmer's Life for Me. Huliska-Beith, Laura, illus. 2013. 24p. (J). (gr. k-3). pap. 6.99 *(978-1-84686-939-6(0))* Barefoot Bks., Inc.

Dobell, Darcy. The Oyster Who Looked at the Sky. 2008. (ENG., Illus.). 32p. 16.95 *(978-0-88982-250-4(6))* Oolichan Bks. CAN. Dist: Univ. of Toronto Pr.

Dodd, Emily. Ollie & the Otter: A Scottish Osprey Story, 30 vols. Harris-Jones, Kirsteen, illus. 2023. (Picture Kelpies Ser.). 24p. 11.95 *(978-1-78250-369-9(2)*, Kelpies) Floris Bks. GBR. Dist: Consortium Bk. Sales & Distribution.

Dodd, Emma. Counting. 2017. (Illus.). 12p. (J). (gr. -1-12). bds. 9.99 *(978-1-86147-839-9(9)*, Armadillo) Anness Publishing GBR. Dist: National Bk. Network.

—Dog & Friends: Shapes. 2017. (Illus.). 12p. (J). (gr. -1-12). bds. 9.99 *(978-1-86147-844-3(5)*, Armadillo) Anness Publishing GBR. Dist: National Bk. Network.

—Dog & Friends: Sounds. 2017. (Illus.). 12p. (J). (gr. -1-12). bds. 9.99 *(978-1-86147-841-2(0)*, Armadillo) Anness Publishing GBR. Dist: National Bk. Network.

—Forever. Dodd, Emma, illus. 2019. (Emma Dodd's Love You Bks.). (ENG., Illus.). 22p. (J). (— 1). bds. 10.99 *(978-1-5362-0812-2(4)*, Templar) Candlewick Pr.

P Q R

—On the Farm. 2017. (Illus.). 12p. (J). (gr. -1-12). bds. 9.99 *(978-1-86147-838-2(0)*, Armadillo) Anness Publishing GBR. Dist: National Bk. Network.

—Opposites. 2017. (Illus.). 12p. (J). (gr. -1-12). bds. 9.99 *(978-1-86147-843-6(7)*, Armadillo) Anness Publishing GBR. Dist: National Bk. Network.

—Playtime. 2017. (Illus.). 12p. (J). (gr. -1-1). bds. 9.99 *(978-1-86147-842-9(9)*, Armadillo) Anness Publishing GBR. Dist: National Bk. Network.

—Rainbow Fun. 2017. (Illus.). 12p. (J). (gr. -1-12). bds. 9.99 *(978-1-86147-840-5(2)*, Armadillo) Anness Publishing GBR. Dist: National Bk. Network.

Dodd, Emma, illus. Dog & Friends: Birthday. 2017. 12p. (J). (gr. -1-12). bds. 9.99 *(978-1-86147-836-8(4)*, Armadillo) Anness Publishing GBR. Dist: National Bk. Network.

—Dog & Friends: Busy Day. 2017. 12p. (J). (gr -1-12). bds. 9.99 *(978-1-86147-835-1(6)*, Armadillo) Anness Publishing GBR. Dist: National Bk. Network.

—Dog's 123: A Canine Counting Adventure! 2016. (ENG.). 14p. (J). (gr. -1-12). bds. 14.99 *(978-1-86147-698-2(1)*, Armadillo) Anness Publishing GBR. Dist: National Bk. Network.

—Dog's ABC: An Alphabet Adventure! 2016. 14p. (J). (gr. -1-12). bds. 14.99 *(978-1-86147-699-9(X)*, Armadillo) Anness Publishing GBR. Dist: National Bk. Network.

—Dog's Farmyard Friends: A Touch & Tickle Book - with Fun-To-Feel Flocking! 2016. (ENG.). 12p. (J). (gr. -1-1). bds. 14.99 *(978-1-86147-719-4(8)*, Armadillo) Anness Publishing GBR. Dist: National Bk. Network.

Doerrfeld, Cori. Wild Baby. Doerrfeld, Cori, illus. 2019. (ENG., Illus.). 32p. (J). (gr. -1-3). 17.99 *(978-0-06-269894-0(X)*, HarperCollins) HarperCollins Pubs.

Doherty, Gillian. 1001 Animales Que Buscar. 2004. (1001 Things to Spot Ser.).Tr. of 1001 Animals to Spot. (SPA., Illus.). (J). pap. 6.95 *(978-0-7460-5081-1(X))* EDC Publishing.

—1001 Things to Spot Long Ago. 2010. (1001 Things to Spot Ser.). 32p. (J). 9.99 *(978-0-7945-2731-0(0)*, Usborne) EDC Publishing.

Dolan, Elys. The Mystery of the Haunted Farm. Dolan, Elys, illus. 2016. (ENG., Illus.). 32p. (J). (gr. -1-3). 17.99 *(978-0-7636-8658-1(1))* Candlewick Pr.

Don, Lari. The Secret of the Kelpie, 30 vols. Longson, Philip, illus. 2022. (Traditional Scottish Tales Ser.). 32p. (J). pap. 14.95 *(978-1-78250-252-4(1)*, Kelpies) Floris Bks. GBR. Dist: Consortium Bk. Sales & Distribution.

—The Tale of Tam Linn, 30 vols. 2014. (Traditional Scottish Tales Ser.). (Illus.). 32p. (J). pap. 11.95 *(978-1-78250-134-3(7)*, Kelpies) Floris Bks. GBR. Dist: Consortium Bk. Sales & Distribution.

Don, Lari. The Treasure of the Loch Ness Monster, 30 vols. Ilincic, Natasa, illus. 2023. (Traditional Scottish Tales Ser.). 32p. (J). 14.95 ***(978-1-78250-480-1(X)***, Kelpies) Floris Bks. GBR. Dist: Consortium Bk. Sales & Distribution.

—The Treasure of the Loch Ness Monster, 30 vols. Ilincic, Nataea, illus. 2018. (Traditional Scottish Tales Ser.). (ENG.). 32p. (J). (gr. -1-2). 17.95 *(978-1-78250-485-6(0)*, Kelpies) Floris Bks. GBR. Dist: Consortium Bk. Sales & Distribution.

Don, Lari, et al. Little Red Riding Hood. Chauffrey, Celia, illus. 2012. 32p. (J). (gr. -1-3). 9.99 *(978-1-84686-768-2(1))* Barefoot Bks., Inc.

Donaldson, Connie & Polinko, Les. The Ganorch under the Porch. Polinko, Les, illus. 2013. (Illus.). 36p. pap. 9.95 *(978-0-9836682-3-7(X))* Hearthstone Rose.

Donaldson, Julia. Animal Music. Sharratt, Nick, illus. 2014. (ENG.). 24p. (J). (— 1). pap. 12.99 *(978-1-4472-1095-5(6)*, 900326066, Macmillan Children's Bks.) Pan Macmillan GBR. Dist: Macmillan.

—Chocolate Mousse for Greedy Goose. Sharratt, Nick, illus. 2015. (ENG.). 18p. (J). (-k). bds. 12.99 *(978-1-4472-8788-9(6)*, 900326058, Macmillan Children's Bks.) Pan Macmillan GBR. Dist: Macmillan.

—The Detective Dog. Ogilvie, Sara, illus. 2018. (ENG.). 32p. (J). 19.99 *(978-1-250-15676-1(9)*, 900185100, Holt, Henry & Co. Bks. For Young Readers) Holt, Henry & Co.

—The Flying Bath. Roberts, David, illus. 2016. (ENG.). 32p. (J). (gr. -1-k). pap. 9.99 *(978-1-4472-7711-8(2)*, Macmillan Children's Bks.) Pan Macmillan GBR. Dist: Independent Pubs. Group.

—Goat Goes to Playgroup, 8. Sharratt, Nick, illus. 2013. (ENG.). 32p. (J). (gr. -1-k). pap. 14.99 *(978-1-4472-1094-8(8)*, 900326068, Macmillan Children's Bks.) Pan Macmillan GBR. Dist: Macmillan.

—One Mole Digging a Hole. Sharratt, Nick, illus. 2015. (ENG.). 22p. (J). (-k). bds. 12.99 *(978-1-4472-8790-2(8)*, 900326060, Macmillan Children's Bks.) Pan Macmillan GBR. Dist: Macmillan.

—One Ted Falls Out of Bed. Currey, Anna, illus. (ENG.). (J). 2012. 26p. (gr. -1 — 1). bds. 12.99 *(978-1-4472-0995-9(8)*, 900326069) 2015. 32p. (— 1). pap. 14.99 *(978-1-4472-6614-3(5)*, 900326063) Pan Macmillan GBR. (Macmillan Children's Bks.). Dist: Macmillan.

—Reiver Rat: The Highway Rat in Scots. Robertson, James, tr. from ENG. Scheffler, Axel, illus. 2015. 32p. (J). (-k). pap. 10.99 *(978-1-84502-996-8(8)*, Itchy Coo) Black and White Publishing Ltd. GBR. Dist: Independent Pubs. Group.

—Room on the Broom. Scheffler, Axel, illus. 2012. (ENG.). 24p. (J). (— 1). bds. 7.99 *(978-0-8037-3841-6(2)*, Dial Bks) Penguin Young Readers Group.

—Room on the Broom in Scots. Robertson, James, tr. Scheffler, Axel, illus. 2014. 32p. (J). (-k). pap. 10.99 *(978-1-84502-753-7(1))* Black and White Publishing Ltd. GBR. Dist: Independent Pubs. Group.

—Rosie's Hat. Currey, Anna, illus. 2015. (ENG.). 32p. (J). (-k). pap. 14.99 *(978-1-4472-6612-9(9)*, 900326055, Macmillan Children's Bks.) Pan Macmillan GBR. Dist: Macmillan.

—Spinderella. Braun, Sebastien, illus. 2022. (ENG.). 32p. (J). (gr. -1-k). pap. 6.99 *(978-1-4052-8272-7(X))* Farshore GBR. Dist: HarperCollins Pubs.

—The Ugly Five. Scheffler, Axel, illus. 2018. (ENG.). 32p. (J). (gr. -1-3). 17.99 *(978-1-338-24953-8(3)*, Scholastic Pr.) Scholastic, Inc.

Donohue, Moira Rose. National Geographic Little Kids First Big Book of the Rain Forest. 2018. (Illus.). 128p. (J). (gr. -1-k). 14.99 *(978-1-4263-3171-8(1)*, National Geographic Kids) Disney Publishing Worldwide.

Doodler, Todd H. Peas on Earth. 2012. (Illus.). 20p. (J). (gr. -1 — 1). 6.99 *(978-0-307-93088-0(2)*, Robin Corey Bks.) Random Hse. Children's Bks.

Doolittle, Sara. Lillie's Smile. Locke, Margo, illus. 2011. 32p. (J). pap. 18.99 *(978-0-9827611-6-8(3)*, Catch the Spirit of Appalachia) Ammons Communications, Ltd.

Dopffer, Guillaume & Nicola, Baxter. My First 200 Words in French: Learning Is Fun with Teddy the Bear! Lacome, Susie, illus. 2016. 24p. (J). (gr. -1-12). pap. 7.99 *(978-1-86147-760-6(0)*, Armadillo) Anness Publishing GBR. Dist: National Bk. Network.

Dorfman, Craig. I Knew You Could! A Book for All the Stops in Your Life. Ong, Cristina, illus. 2003. (Little Engine That Could Ser.). 32p. (J). (gr. -1-2). 12.99 *(978-0-448-43148-2(3)*, Grosset & Dunlap) Penguin Young Readers Group.

Dorling Kindersley Publishing Staff. Dinosaur. 2016. (ENG., Illus.). 36p. (J). bds. *(978-0-241-23758-8(0))* Dorling Kindersley Publishing, Inc.

—Is It Warm Enough for Ice Cream? 2018. (ENG., Illus.). 18p. (J). bds. *(978-0-241-31305-3(8))* Dorling Kindersley Publishing, Inc.

—RHS How Does a Butterfly Grow? 2019. (Illus.). 18p. (J). bds. *(978-0-241-35546-6(X))* Dorling Kindersley Publishing, Inc.

Dotlich, Rebecca Kai. One Day, the End: Short, Very Short, Shorter-Than-Ever Stories. Koehler, Fred, illus. 2015. (ENG.). 32p. (J). (gr. -1-3). 17.99 *(978-1-62091-451-9(4)*, 1396728, Astra Young Readers) Astra Publishing Hse.

Dougherty, Brandi. The Littlest Valentine. Todd, Michelle, illus. 2017. (J). *(978-1-338-20702-6(4))* Scholastic, Inc.

Douglas, Rachel. "You're a Meany!" Drewes, Dan, illus. 2011. 13p. pap. 10.19 *(978-1-4567-8643-4(1))* AuthorHouse.

Dover, Ilana. The Talking MacHine: The Story of Alexander Graham Bell. 2012. 36p. pap. 17.49 *(978-1-4691-8328-2(5))* Xlibris Corp.

Dowley, Tim. Would You Like to Know? Collection: The Complete Collection, 1 vol. Reeves, Eira, illus. 2017. (Would You Like to Know? Ser.). (ENG.). 168p. (J). (gr. -1-k). pap. 13.99 *(978-1-78128-327-1(3)*, a912a5bd-f9fa-49a5-8213-deaf266f33b1, Candle Bks.) Lion Hudson PLC GBR. Dist: Baker & Taylor Publisher Services (BTPS).

—Would You Like to Know God?, 1 vol. Reeves, Eira, illus. 2016. (ENG.). 28p. (J). pap. 3.49 *(978-1-78128-275-5(7)*, 4e74f9c5-c4cb-4c61-865d-b8cfccc9a610, Candle Bks.) Lion Hudson PLC GBR. Dist: Baker & Taylor Publisher Services (BTPS).

Dowling, Paul. The Night Journey. 2003. 12p. (J). 9.95 *(978-1-57717-290-1(6))* New Line Bks.

Downer, Maggie, illus. Noah: My First Storybook. 2016. 48p. (J). (gr. -1-12). bds. 9.99 *(978-1-86147-776-7(7)*, Armadillo) Anness Publishing GBR. Dist: National Bk. Network.

Doyle, Malachy. King Donal's Secret. Watson, Richard, illus. 2005. (ENG.). 24p. (J). lib. bdg. 23.65 *(978-1-59646-740-8(1))* Dingles & Co.

—Rory's Lost His Voice. Semple, David, illus. 2005. (ENG.). 24p. (J). lib. bdg. 23.65 *(978-1-59646-714-9(2))* Dingles & Co.

Drake, Jennifer & Feltham, Sarah. Scotty's Postcards from Rome. 2012. (ENG., Illus.). 27p. (J). pap. 10.95 *(978-0-578-10548-2(9))* Drake Feltham Publishing.

Dreamworks Classics: Hide & Seek, Vol. 1. 2015. (DreamWorks Classics Ser.: 1). (ENG., Illus.). 64p. (J). (gr. 1-4). pap. 6.99 *(978-1-78276-246-1(9))* Titan Bks. Ltd. GBR. Dist: Penguin Random Hse. LLC.

Drehsen, Britta. Flip-O-saurus. Ball, Sara, illus. 2010. (ENG.). 22p. (J). (gr. -1-3). bds. 16.95 *(978-0-7892-1061-6(4)*, 791061, Abbeville Kids) Abbeville Pr., Inc.

Drescher, Daniela. Goodnight Sandman, 30 vols. 2018. Orig. Title: Als der Sandmann Fast Verschlafen Hätte. (Illus.). 26p. (J). 16.95 *(978-1-78250-525-9(3))* Floris Bks. GBR. Dist: Consortium Bk. Sales & Distribution.

—In the Land of Elves, 1 vol. 2nd rev. ed. 2016. Orig. Title: Im Zwergenland. (Illus.). 24p. (J). 15.95 *(978-1-78250-242-5(4))* Floris Bks. GBR. Dist: Consortium Bk. Sales & Distribution.

—Pippa & Pelle, 60 vols. 2nd rev. ed. 2019. (Pippa & Pelle Ser.). Orig. Title: Pippa und Pelle. (Illus.). 12p. (J). bds. 9.95 *(978-1-78250-617-1(9))* Floris Bks. GBR. Dist: Consortium Bk. Sales & Distribution.

—Pippa & Pelle in the Autumn Wind, 30 vols. 2017. (Pippa & Pelle Ser.). Orig. Title: Pippa und Pelle Im Brausewind. (Illus.). 12p. (J). 9.95 *(978-1-78250-442-9(7))* Floris Bks. GBR. Dist: Consortium Bk. Sales & Distribution.

—Pippa & Pelle in the Spring Garden, 30 vols. 2018. (Pippa & Pelle Ser.). Orig. Title: Pippa & Pelle Im Garten. (Illus.). 12p. (J). 9.95 *(978-1-78250-471-9(0))* Floris Bks. GBR. Dist: Consortium Bk. Sales & Distribution.

—What's Hiding in There?, 24 vols. 2008. Orig. Title: Was Raschelt Denn Da? (ENG., Illus.). 16p. (J). *(978-0-86315-634-2(7))* Floris Bks.

—What's Hiding in There: A Lift-The-Flap Book of Discovering Nature, 40 vols. 2nd rev. ed. 2016. Orig. Title: Was Raschelt Denn Da? (Illus.). 16p. (J). 17.95 *(978-1-78250-261-6(0))* Floris Bks. GBR. Dist: Consortium Bk. Sales & Distribution.

Drimmer, Stephanie Warren. Hey, Baby! A Collection of Pictures, Poems, & Stories from Nature's Nursery. 2017. (Illus.). 192p. (J). (gr. -1-k). 24.99 *(978-1-4263-2931-9(8)*, National Geographic Kids) Disney Publishing Worldwide.

Driscoll, Laura. I Want to Be a Doctor. Echeverri, Catalina, illus. 2018. (I Can Read Level 1 Ser.). (ENG.). 32p. (J). (gr. -1-3). 16.99 *(978-0-06-243241-4(9))*; pap. 4.99 *(978-0-06-243240-7(0))* HarperCollins Pubs. (HarperCollins).

Drops of Water. Date not set. 9.95 *(978-0-89868-291-5(6))*; pap. 3.95 *(978-0-89868-290-8(8))* ARO Publishing Co.

Drummond, Ree. Charlie the Ranch Dog: Where's the Bacon? Degroat, Diane, illus. 2013. (I Can Read Level 1 Ser.). (ENG.). 32p. (J). (gr. -1-3). pap. 4.99 *(978-0-06-221908-4(1)*, HarperCollins) HarperCollins Pubs.

—Charlie the Ranch Dog: Where's the Bacon? deGroat, Diane, illus. 2013. (I Can Read Level 1 Ser.). (ENG.). 32p. (J). (gr. -1-3). 16.99 *(978-0-06-221909-1(X)*, HarperCollins) HarperCollins Pubs.

—Little Ree #2: Best Friends Forever! Rogers, Jacqueline, illus. 2018. (Little Ree Ser.). (ENG.). 40p. (J). (gr. -1-3). 17.99 *(978-0-06-245319-8(X)*, HarperCollins) HarperCollins Pubs.

Druvert, Hélène. Mary Poppins up, up & Away. 2017. (ENG., Illus.). 36p. (J). (gr. k-4). 24.95 *(978-0-500-65104-9(3)*, 565104) Thames & Hudson.

Druvert, Hélène & Druvert, Hélène. Paris up, up & Away. 2016. (ENG., Illus.). 36p. (J). (gr. -1-1). 24.95 *(978-0-500-65059-2(4)*, 565059) Thames & Hudson.

Du Bois, Crystal L. God Made My Butt Big. 2012. 24p. pap. 14.93 *(978-1-4669-0584-9(0))* Trafford Publishing.

DuBois, Juli. The Happiness of Being Me: An A-Z Owners Manual, 1 vol. Zitnak, Allison Day, illus. 2009. 47p. pap. 24.95 *(978-1-60749-613-7(5))* America Star Bks.

Dubosarsky, Ursula. Too Many Elephants in This House. Joyner, Andrew, illus. 2017. 32p. (J). (gr. -1-k). 10.99 *(978-0-14-378539-2(7))* Random Hse. Australia AUS. Dist: Independent Pubs. Group.

Dudar, Judy. I Spy a Bunny, 1 vol. Rudnicki, Richard, illus. 2009. (ENG.). 32p. (J). (gr. -1-k). 17.95 *(978-1-55109-700-8(1)*, c7f6750d-91ca-4dd9-86b7-0cbc864d538f) Nimbus Publishing, Ltd. CAN. Dist: Baker & Taylor Publisher Services (BTPS).

Duddle, Jonny. The Pirates of Scurvy Sands. Duddle, Jonny, illus. 2018. (ENG., Illus.). 44p. (J). (gr. 1-4). 16.99 *(978-0-7636-9293-3(X)*, Templar) Candlewick Pr.

Dufek, Holly. Busy on the Farm: With Casey & Friends, 7 vols. Nunn, Paul E. & Kasun, Mike, illus. 2017. (Casey & Friends Ser.: 6). (ENG.). 32p. (J). (gr. k-3). 14.99 *(978-1-937747-79-4(4))* Octane Pr.

Duffield, Katy. Loud Lula. Boldt, Mike, illus. 2015. 32p. (J). *(978-1-4778-2785-7(4))* Amazon Publishing.

Duffield, Katy S. Loud Lula, 0 vols. Boldt, Mike, illus. 2015. (ENG.). 32p. (J). (gr. k-2). 17.99 *(978-1-4778-2776-5(5)*, 9781477827765, Two Lions) Amazon Publishing.

Dufft, Sanne. The Night Lion. Dufft, Sanne, illus. 2018. Orig. Title: Magnus und der Nachtlöwe. (ENG., Illus.). 32p. (J). (gr. -1-k). 15.95 *(978-1-77278-041-3(3))* Pajama Pr. CAN. Dist: Publishers Group West (PGW).

Dumbleton, Mike. Digger. Cowcher, Robin, illus. 2018. (ENG.). 32p. (J). (gr. k-3). 19.99 *(978-1-76029-673-5(2))* Allen & Unwin AUS. Dist: Independent Pubs. Group.

Dumont, Claire. Noel: An Unforgettable Night! Keshavarz, Mehrafarin, illus. 2017. (ENG.). 32p. (J). 14.95 *(978-0-8091-6780-7(8))* Paulist Pr.

Dunbar, Joyce. Do Dare Duck. 2015. (ENG., Illus.). 32p. (J). (-k). pap. 12.99 *(978-1-78008-024-6(7))* Transworld Publishers Ltd. GBR. Dist: Independent Pubs. Group.

Dunbar, Joyce & Varley, Susan. The Spring Rabbit. 2015. (ENG., Illus.). 32p. (J). (gr. -1-k). pap. 13.99 *(978-1-78344-078-8(3))* Andersen Pr. GBR. Dist: Independent Pubs. Group.

Dunn, Georgia. Lupin Leaps In: A Breaking Cat News Adventure, Volume 1. 2019. (Breaking Cat News Ser.: 1). (ENG., Illus.). 208p. (J). pap. 9.99 *(978-1-4494-9522-0(2))* Andrews McMeel Publishing.

Dunn, Jill. The ABC's of Going Green. Hill, Bodhi, illus. 2012. 64p. (J). 21.99 *(978-0-9852146-2-3(7))* AM Ink Publishing.

Dunn, Robert. There's Only One Scruffle. Dunn, Robert, illus. 2017. (Story Corner Ser.). (ENG., Illus.). 24p. (J). (gr. -1-k). lib. bdg. 19.99 *(978-1-68297-187-1(2)*, 96771075-1754-4164-ab82-ca4e8e72c4ca) QEB Publishing Inc.

Dunrea, Olivier. Jasper & Joop Board Book. Dunrea, Olivier, illus. 2014. (Gossie & Friends Ser.). (ENG., Illus.). 32p. (J). (— 1). bds. 7.99 *(978-0-544-17320-0(1)*, 1552169, Clarion Bks.) HarperCollins Pubs.

Dunston, Marc. The Magic of Giving, 1 vol. Cantrell, Katie, illus. 2010. (ENG.). 32p. (J). (gr. k-3). 16.99 *(978-1-58980-805-8(3)*, Pelican Publishing) Arcadia Publishing.

duopress labs. Do You Know a Superhero? Escudero, Jesus, illus. 2018. 22p. (J). (— 1). bds. 7.95 *(978-1-947458-24-6(8)*, 805824) Duo Pr. LLC.

—My First Lift-The-Flap Animal Book. Mullen, Amy, illus. 2018. (Natural World Ser.). 20p. (J). (gr. -1-1). bds. 9.95 *(978-1-946064-95-0(5)*, 806495) Duo Pr. LLC.

—Zoom! Beep! Vroom! Busy Cities. Cleland, Josh, illus. 2018. 22p. (J). (gr. -1 — 1). bds. 9.95 *(978-1-947458-27-7(2)*, 805827) Duo Pr. LLC.

duopress labs, concept. Hello, Ocean Friends. 2015. (High-Contrast Bks.). (Illus.). 20p. (J). (-k). bds. 7.99 *(978-1-938093-41-8(0)*, 809341) Duo Pr. LLC.

duopress labs & Margie & Jimbo. My Fridge: My First Book of Food. 2017. (Illus.). 20p. (J). (gr. -1-k). bds. 7.95 *(978-1-946064-00-4(9)*, 806400) Duo Pr. LLC.

Duren, Sheila Gregory. Pepper's Great Move! 2011. 28p. pap. 15.99 *(978-1-4568-6766-9(0))* Xlibris Corp.

Duvoisin, Roger. The House of Four Seasons. 2017. (Illus.). 40p. (J). (gr. -1-1). 18.95 *(978-1-68137-098-9(0)*, NYR Children's Collection) New York Review of Bks., Inc., The.

—Veronica. 2nd ed. 2016. (Illus.). 32p. 20.00 *(978-1-85124-245-0(7))* Bodleian Library GBR. Dist: Chicago Distribution Ctr.

Dwyer, Judy. Storybook Starters. (Illus.). (J). (gr. k-3). pap. *(978-1-876367-01-5(6))* Wizard Bks.

Dyan, Penelope. Some Bunny Loves You! 2013. 34p. pap. 11.95 *(978-1-61477-068-8(9))* Bellissima Publishing, LLC.

Dyckman, Ame. Misunderstood Shark: Friends Don't Eat Friends. Magoon, Scott, illus. 2019. (ENG.). 48p. (J). (gr. -1-k). 17.99 *(978-1-338-11388-4(7)*, Orchard Bks.) Scholastic, Inc.

Dynamo. Googly Eyes: Flipper the Seal Makes a Discovery! 2014. (ENG., Illus.). 12p. (J). (gr. -1-2). bds. 6.99 *(978-1-84322-905-6(6)*, Armadillo) Anness Publishing GBR. Dist: National Bk. Network.

—Googly Eyes: Goodnight, Benjy Bunny! 2014. (ENG., Illus.). 12p. (J). (gr. -1-12). bds. 6.99 *(978-1-84322-879-0(3)*, Armadillo) Anness Publishing GBR. Dist: National Bk. Network.

Dyson, Nikki, illus. 1,000 Things to Eat. 2015. (1,000 Pictures Ser.). (ENG.). 34p. (J). (gr. k-5). 14.99 *(978-0-7945-3406-6(6)*, Usborne) EDC Publishing.

Eakle, Janice. 3 A's & 3 B's All the Way to Z, 1 vol. Eakle, Tayah, illus. 2009. 36p. pap. 24.95 *(978-1-60813-739-8(2))* America Star Bks.

Earth Picture Book. 2009. 64p. 8.99 *(978-1-4231-2204-3(6))* Disney Pr.

Eastman, P. D. Ve, Perro. Ve! (Go, Dog. Go! Spanish Edition) Perdomo, Adolfo Perez, tr. from ENG. 2003. (Bright & Early Board Books(TM) Ser.).Tr. of Go, Dog, Go! (SPA., Illus.). 24p. (J). (— 1). bds. 4.99 *(978-0-375-82361-9(1)*, Random House Para Ninos) Random Hse. Children's Bks.

Easton, Marilyn. Eris to the Rescue. 2013. (LEGO Legends of Chima: Comic Reader Ser.: 3). lib. bdg. 13.55 *(978-0-606-32398-7(8))* Turtleback.

Eaton, Jason Carter. Great, Now We've Got Barbarians! Fearing, Mark, illus. 2017. (ENG.). 40p. (J). (gr. -1-3). 16.99 *(978-0-7636-6827-3(3))* Candlewick Pr.

—How to Train a Train. Rocco, John, illus. 2016. (ENG.). 28p. (J). (-k). bds. 7.99 *(978-0-7636-8899-8(1))* Candlewick Pr.

Eddy, Olympia. Mysterious View. 2010. 20p. pap. 13.99 *(978-1-60844-423-6(6))* Dog Ear Publishing, LLC.

Edens, Cooper. Edens Picture Book, No. 3. Day, Alexandra, illus. Date not set. (J). 14.99 *(978-0-06-205153-0(9))* HarperCollins Pubs.

Edgson, Alison, illus. The Magician's Apprentice. 2011. (Flip-Up Fairy Tales Ser.). 24p. (J). (gr. 2-2). *(978-1-84643-370-2(3))* Child's Play International Ltd.

Educational Adventures, creator. Blazin' Hot: Picture Book (Spanish) 9x9. 2006. (SPA., Illus.). (J). 5.99 *(978-0-9770455-4-9(4))* Mighty Kids Media.

—Cool by the Pool: Picture Book (Spanish) 9x9. 2007. (Illus.). (J). per. 5.99 *(978-1-933934-72-3(7))* Mighty Kids Media.

—Danger Alert: Picture Book (Spanish) 9x9. 2006. (Illus.). (J). 5.99 *(978-1-933934-04-4(2))* Mighty Kids Media.

—Free Wheelin' Picture Book (Spanish) w/ Snipe. 2006. (Illus.). (J). 5.99 *(978-0-9770455-6-3(0))* Mighty Kids Media.

—Poison Patrol: Picture Book (Spanish) 9x9. 2006. (Illus.). (J). 5.99 *(978-1-933934-00-6(X))* Mighty Kids Media.

—Street Smarts: Picture Book (Spanish) 9x9. 2007. (Illus.). (J). per. 5.99 *(978-1-933934-77-8(8))* Mighty Kids Media.

Edward, Justine. Shine. 2013. 28p. pap. 13.95 *(978-1-4525-7531-5(2)*, Balboa Pr.) Author Solutions, LLC.

Edwards, Caroline. Who Took Poppy's Skates? 2010. (ENG., Illus.). 24p. pap. *(978-1-84876-392-0(1))* Troubador Publishing Ltd.

Edwards, Josh. Pull-Out Christmas, 1 vol. Embleton-Hall, Chris, illus. 2014. (Candle Pull-Out Ser.). (ENG.). 10p. (J). (gr. -1-k). bds. 9.99 *(978-1-85985-999-5(2)*, 8e2d1272-478c-46e6-853b-8a5970c418b6, Lion Children's) Lion Hudson PLC GBR. Dist: Baker & Taylor Publisher Services (BTPS).

—Pull-Out David & Goliath, 1 vol. Embleton-Hall, Chris, illus. 2014. (Candle Pull-Out Ser.). (ENG.). 10p. (J). (gr. -1-k). bds. 9.99 *(978-1-85985-997-1(6)*, be674cf2-0724-4737-bc32-49e069ff7c54, Candle Bks.) Lion Hudson PLC GBR. Dist: Baker & Taylor Publisher Services (BTPS).

Edwards, Nicola. Mind Your Manners. Parker-Thomas, Feronia, illus. 2019. (J). 12.99 *(978-1-61067-811-7(7))* Kane Miller.

Eeles, Alex. Bedtime on the Farm Red Band. Ortu, Davide, illus. 2016. (Cambridge Reading Adventures Ser.). (ENG.). 16p. pap. 7.95 *(978-1-316-50081-1(0))* Cambridge Univ. Pr.

Ehlert, Lois. Growing Vegetable Soup Board Book. 2004. (ENG., Illus.). 32p. (J). (gr. -1-k). bds. 6.95 *(978-0-15-205055-9(8)*, 1195267, Clarion Bks.) HarperCollins Pubs.

Eisenberg, Rebecca & Kjesbo, Rynette. Cool in School Communication Game: Gb362. Lefebvre, Patrick, photos by. 2011. (Illus.). (J). 64.95 net. *(978-1-58650-994-1(2))* Super Duper Pubns.

Eisner, Fern. Saba's Room. 2009. 28p. pap. 15.99 *(978-1-4415-1843-9(6))* Xlibris Corp.

Elephants, It's Raining. Martha & Me. 2018. (ENG., Illus.). 80p. (J). (gr. -1-4). 16.95 *(978-0-500-65142-1(6)*, 565142) Thames & Hudson.

Eliot, T. S. Macavity: The Mystery Cat. Robins, Arthur, illus. 75th ed. 2016. (Old Possum Picture Bks.). (ENG.). 32p. (J). (-k). pap. 9.95 *(978-0-571-30813-2(9))* Faber & Faber, Inc.

—Macavity's Not There! A Lift-The-Flap Book. Robins, Arthur, illus. (Old Possum Picture Bks.). (ENG.). 16p. 2018. (J). bds. 8.00 *(978-0-571-33528-2(4))* 2017. 14.95 *(978-0-571-32863-5(6))* Faber & Faber, Inc.

Elliott, David. On the Wing. Stadtlander, Becca, illus. (ENG.). 32p. (J). (gr. -1-2). 2017. 6.99 *(978-0-7636-9302-2(2))* 2014. 16.99 *(978-0-7636-5324-8(1))* Candlewick Pr.

Elliott, George. The Boy Who Loved Bananas. Krystoforski, Andrej, illus. 2005. 32p. (J). (gr. -1-2). 15.95 *(978-1-55337-744-3(3))* Kids Can Pr., Ltd. CAN. Dist: Hachette Bk. Group.

Elliott, Odette. Sammy Goes Flying. McIntyre, Georgina, illus. 2011. (ENG.). 32p. (J). (gr. -1-k). pap. 15.99 *(978-1-84853-050-8(1))* Transworld Publishers Ltd. GBR. Dist: Independent Pubs. Group.

Elliott, Rebecca. Dalmatian in a Digger. 2017. (Fiction Picture Bks.). (ENG., Illus.). 32p. (J). (gr. k-2). lib. bdg. 27.99 *(978-1-5158-0684-4(7)*, Picture Window Bks.) Capstone.

—Noah's Noisy Animals, 1 vol. 2016. (ENG., Illus.). 5p. (J). (— 1). bds. 7.99 *(978-0-7459-6561-1(X)*, 88bbce0e-3f1c-4a69-90bd-47734452d124, Lion Children's) Lion Hudson PLC GBR. Dist: Baker & Taylor Publisher Services (BTPS).

—Not So Silent Night, 1 vol. 2016. (ENG., Illus.). 5p. (J). (— 1). bds. 7.99 *(978-0-7459-6560-4(1)*, 8b565f41-af2c-41ef-9334-eb623bb83f92, Lion Children's) Lion Hudson PLC GBR. Dist: Baker & Taylor Publisher Services (BTPS).

Ellis, Carson. Du Iz Tak? Ellis, Carson, illus. (ENG.). 48p. (J). (gr. -1-3). 2023. 9.99 *(978-1-5362-2352-1(2))* 2016. (Illus.). 18.99 *(978-0-7636-6530-2(4))* Candlewick Pr.

Ellis, Sarah. Ben over Night, 1 vol. LaFave, Kim, illus. 2005. (ENG.). 32p. (J). (gr. -1-1). 10.95 *(978-1-55041-807-1(6)*, 0e84cead-52c1-40e8-bd0e-975d5935d88e) Fitzhenry & Whiteside, Ltd. CAN. Dist: Firefly Bks., Ltd.

Elmquist, Laurie. Beach Baby, 1 vol. MacKay, Elly, illus. 2016. (ENG.). 24p. (J). (gr. -1 — 1). bds. 10.95 *(978-1-4598-0954-3(8))* Orca Bk. Pubs. USA.

Elschner, Géraldine & Elschner, Géraldine. The Cat & the Bird: A Children's Book Inspired by Paul Klee. 2012. (Children's Books Inspired by Famous Artworks Ser.). (ENG., Illus.). 32p. (J). (gr. -1-3). 14.95 *(978-3-7913-7099-6(5))* Prestel Verlag GmbH & Co KG. DEU. Dist: Penguin Random Hse. LLC.

—The Little Hippo: A Children's Book Inspired by Egyptian Art. Klauss, Anja, illus. 2014. (Children's Books Inspired by Famous Artworks Ser.). (ENG.). 32p. (J). (gr. -1-3). 14.95 *(978-3-7913-7167-2(3))* Prestel Verlag GmbH & Co KG DEU. Dist: Penguin Random Hse. LLC.

Elsohn Ross, Michael. Mama's Milk / Mamá Me Alimenta. Wolff, Ashley, illus. 2016. 24p. (J). (-k). bds. 7.99 *(978-0-553-53874-8(8),* Tricycle Pr.) Random Hse. Children's Bks.

Emberley, Barbara. One Wide River to Cross. 2015. (ENG., Illus.). 32p. 17.95 *(978-1-62326-059-0(0))* AMMO Bks., LLC.

—The Story of Paul Bunyan. 2015. (ENG., Illus.). 32p. 17.95 *(978-1-62326-062-0(0))* AMMO Bks., LLC.

Emberley, Ed. The Wing on a Flea. 2015. (ENG., Illus.). 48p. 17.95 *(978-1-62326-058-3(2))* AMMO Bks., LLC.

Emberley, Rebecca. Mice on Ice. Emberley, Ed, illus. 2013. (I Like to Read Ser.). (ENG.). 24p. (J). (gr. -1-3). pap. 7.99 *(978-0-8234-2908-0(3))* Holiday Hse., Inc.

Embleton-Hall, Chris. Noah's Amazing Ark: A Lift-The-Flap Adventure, 1 vol. 2017. (ENG., Illus.). 12p. (J). (gr. -1-k). 10.99 *(978-1-78128-317-2(6),* 42def216-dbb4-4fac-bddb-9605966ab6b3, Candle Bks.) Lion Hudson PLC GBR. Dist: Baker & Taylor Publisher Services (BTPS).

Empson, Jo. Never Ever. Empson, Jo, illus. 2013. (Child's Play Library). (ENG., Illus.). 32p. (J). *(978-1-84643-552-2(8))* Child's Play International Ltd.

—Rabbityness. Empson, Jo, illus. alt. ed. 2012. (Child's Play Library). (Illus.). 32p. (J). *(978-1-84643-482-2(3))* Child's Play International Ltd.

Engel, Christiane. ABC for Me: ABC Mindful Me, Volume 4. 2018. (ABC for Me Ser.: 4). (ENG., Illus.). 36p. (J). (gr. -1-1). bds. 16.95 *(978-1-63322-510-7(0),* 301672, Walter Foster Jr) Quarto Publishing Group USA.

Engel, Christiane, illus. Astronauts. 2018. (First Explorers Ser.). (ENG.). 10p. (J). (— 1). bds. 9.95 *(978-1-4549-2940-6(5))* Sterling Publishing Co., Inc.

Engelbreit, Mary. A Night of Great Joy, 1 vol. 2016. (ENG., Illus.). 32p. (J). 17.99 *(978-0-310-74354-5(0))* Zonderkidz.

Engledow, Dave. The Little Girl Who Didn't Want to Go to Bed. Engledow, Dave, illus. 2017. (ENG., Illus.). 40p. (J). (gr. -1-3). 17.99 *(978-0-06-242537-9(4),* HarperCollins) HarperCollins Pubs.

Ennis, Garth. ERF. 2013. (ENG., Illus.). 48p. (J). 14.99 *(978-0-615-62967-4(9),* d57c52ff-9a4a-4e4d-86b0-958135ffb198, Dynamite Entertainment) Dynamic Forces, Inc.

Esbaum, Jill. Explore My World Adorable Animals. 2017. (Explore My World Ser.). (Illus.). 96p. (J). (gr. -1-k). pap. 9.99 *(978-1-4263-2949-4(0),* National Geographic Kids) Disney Publishing Worldwide.

Esberger, Trudi. The Boy Who Lost His Bumble. Esberger, Trudi, illus. 2016. (Child's Play Library). (Illus.). 32p. (J). *(978-1-84643-661-1(3))* Child's Play International Ltd.

Esenwine, Matt Forrest. Flashlight Night. Koehler, Fred, illus. 2017. (ENG.). 32p. (J). (gr. -1-3). 16.95 *(978-1-62979-493-8(7),* Astra Young Readers) Astra Publishing Hse.

Esenwine, Matt Forrest & Bruss, Deborah. Don't Ask a Dinosaur. Chin, Louie, illus. 2018. (ENG.). 32p. (J). (gr. -1-2). 17.99 *(978-1-57687-841-5(4),* powerHouse Bks.) powerHse. Bks.

Esham, Barbara. Stacey Coolidge Fancy-Smancy Cursive Handwriting. Gordon, Mike, illus. 2018. (Adventures of Everyday Geniuses Ser.: 0). 32p. (J). (gr. -1-3). 17.99 *(978-1-4926-6996-8(2),* Little Pickle Pr.) Sourcebooks, Inc.

Esham, Barbara & Gordon, Carl. Mrs. Gorski I Think I Have the Wiggle Fidgets. Gordon, Mike, illus. 2018. (Adventures of Everyday Geniuses Ser.: 0). 32p. (J). (gr. -1-3). 17.99 *(978-1-4926-6997-5(0),* Little Pickle Pr.) Sourcebooks, Inc.

Esmaili, Roza. Zagros & Nature Force: Coloring Book. Sun Rise Illustration and Computer Animation Staff, illus. Date not set. 74p. (J). (gr. k-8). pap. 2.49 *(978-0-9656185-1-9(X))* Esmaili, Inc.

Estela, Lucy. Suri's Wall. Ottley, Matt, illus. 2018. 32p. (J). (gr. 1-5). 16.99 *(978-0-14-350596-9(3),* Puffin) Penguin Random Hse. AUS. Dist: Independent Pubs. Group.

Eszterhas, Suzi. Baby Animals Eating. 2018. (Baby Animals Ser.: 3). (ENG., Illus.). 24p. (J). (gr. -1-4). 14.95 *(978-1-77147-317-0(7))* Owlkids Bks. Inc. CAN. Dist: Publishers Group West (PGW).

Evans, Jane. How Are You Feeling Today Baby Bear? Exploring Big Feelings after Living in a Stormy Home. Jackson, Laurence, illus. 2014. 32p. (C). 18.95 *(978-1-84905-424-9(X),* 694274) Kingsley, Jessica Pubs. GBR. Dist: Hachette UK Distribution.

Evans, Kate. Don't Call Me Princess. 2018. (Illus.). 32p. (J). 12.95 *(978-1-78026-465-3(8))* New Internationalist Pubns., Ltd. GBR. Dist: Consortium Bk. Sales & Distribution.

Evanson, Ashley. London: A Book of Opposites. Evanson, Ashley, illus. 2015. (Hello, World Ser.). (Illus.). 16p. (J). (— 1). bds. 7.99 *(978-0-448-48916-2(3),* Penguin Workshop) Penguin Young Readers Group.

Everett, Forrest. Old MacDonald Had a Farm in Oregon. Sergeeva, Mary, illus. 2018. (Old MacDonald Had a Farm Regional Board Ser.). (ENG.). 16p. (J). (gr. k-3). bds. 12.99 *(978-1-64170-014-6(9),* 550014) Familius LLC.

Ewald, Wendy. America Border Culture Dreamer: The Young Immigrant Experience from a to Z. 2018. (ENG., Illus.). 64p. (J). (gr. 5-17). 18.99 *(978-0-316-48495-4(4))* Little, Brown Bks. for Young Readers.

Ewashen, Julie. Life in the Arctic with Nina & Nikita. 2013. 56p. pap. *(978-1-4602-2727-5(1))* FriesenPress.

Exactly Like Me. 2003. (J). per. 8.95 *(978-0-9746151-0-3(2))* Alta Retreat Ctr.

Eystad, Janet Lynn. What I Got into Last Summer. 2012. 28p. 24.95 *(978-1-4626-5316-4(2))* America Star Bks.

Eyuboglu, Melisa, illus. Angel in a Bubble. Eyuboglu, Melisa, . 2007. 28p. (J). 10.95 *(978-1-933090-48-1(0))* Guardian Angel Publishing, Inc.

Faber, Polly. Grab That Rabbit! Smith, Briony May, illus. 2018. (ENG.). 32p. (J). (gr. -1-k). pap. 9.99 *(978-1-84365-369-1(9),* Pavilion Children's Books) Pavilion Bks. GBR. Dist: HarperCollins Pubs.

Fabrikant, Amy. When Kayla Was Kyle. Levine, Jennifer, illus. 2013. 32p. pap. 8.95 *(978-1-61286-154-8(7))* Avid Readers Publishing Group.

Faces. Date not set. (Illus.). 40p. (J). 3.98 *(978-1-4054-0174-6(5))* Parragon, Inc.

Fagan, Cary. A Cage Went in Search of a Bird, 1 vol. Erfanian, Banafsheh, illus. 2017. (ENG.). 32p. (J). (gr. k-2). 18.95 *(978-1-55498-861-7(6))* Groundwood Bks. CAN. Dist: Publishers Group West (PGW).

—Little Blue Chair. Kloepper, Madeline, illus. 2017. 40p. (J). (gr. -1-2). 16.99 *(978-1-77049-755-9(2),* Tundra Bks.) Tundra Bks. CAN. Dist: Penguin Random Hse. LLC.

—What Are You Doing, Benny? Denton, Kady MacDonald, illus. 2019. 36p. (J). (gr. -1-2). 17.99 *(978-1-77049-857-0(5),* Tundra Bks.) Tundra Bks. CAN. Dist: Penguin Random Hse. LLC.

Fairgray, Richard & Burke, Alexander. Sweet Penny & the Lion. 2018. (ENG., Illus.). 32p. (J). (gr. -1-k). 16.99 *(978-1-5107-3484-5(8),* Sky Pony Pr.) Skyhorse Publishing Co., Inc.

Fakhouri, Shoua. Omar's First Day at School Pink B Band. Pérez, Moni, illus. 2016. (Cambridge Reading Adventures Ser.). (ENG.). 16p. pap. 7.95 *(978-1-316-60811-1(5))* Cambridge Univ. Pr.

Falafel, Olaf. Old MacDonald Heard a Fart. 2017. (ENG.). 32p. (J). 17.99 *(978-0-00-824279-4(8),* HarperCollins Children's Bks.) HarperCollins Pubs. Ltd. GBR. Dist: HarperCollins Pubs.

Falconer, Ian. Olivia. unabr. ed. 2004. (Classic Board Bks.). (ENG., Illus.). 34p. (J). (gr. -1-k). bds. 8.99 *(978-0-689-87472-7(3),* Atheneum Bks. for Young Readers) Simon & Schuster Children's Publishing.

—Olivia the Spy. Falconer, Ian, illus. 2017. (ENG., Illus.). 40p. (J). (gr. -1-3). 17.99 *(978-1-4814-5795-8(0),* Atheneum/Caitlyn Dlouhy Books) Simon & Schuster Children's Publishing.

Falconer, Ian, et al. Olivia & Her Great Adventures. Osterhold, Jared & Johnson, Shane L., illus. 2012. (J). *(978-1-4351-4316-6(7),* Simon Spotlight) Simon Spotlight.

Falsetto, Rita. A Cat's Furry Tale. 2011. 60p. pap. 31.99 *(978-1-4568-4802-6(X))* Xlibris Corp.

Falwell, Cathryn. Feast For 10. 2017. (ENG., Illus.). 32p. (J). (gr. -1-3). pap. 26.99 *(978-0-544-93030-8(4),* 1657477, Clarion Bks.) HarperCollins Pubs.

—Rainbow Stew, 1 vol. 2019. (ENG., Illus.). 32p. (J). (gr. -1-3). pap. 11.95 *(978-1-64379-057-2(9),* leelowbooks) Lee & Low Bks., Inc.

—Rainbow Stew, 1 vol. Falwell, Cathryn, illus. 2013. (ENG., Illus.). 32p. (J). 17.95 *(978-1-60060-847-6(7))* Lee & Low Bks., Inc.

Fantasia, Kathryn. Pass It On. Flanagan, Jeff, illus. 2009. 28p. pap. 18.65 *(978-1-4415-5446-8(7))* Xlibris Corp.

Farah, Mo, et al. Ready Steady Mo! 2017. (ENG., Illus.). 32p. (J). (gr. -1-k). pap. 8.99 *(978-1-4449-3407-6(4))* Hachette Children's Group GBR. Dist: Hachette Bk. Group.

Fardell, John. Jeremiah Jellyfish Flies High! Fardell, John, illus. 2011. (ENG., Illus.). 32p. (J). (gr. -1-k). pap. 13.99 *(978-1-84939-147-4(5))* Andersen Pr. GBR. Dist: Independent Pubs. Group.

Farish, Terry. Joseph's Big Ride. Daley, Ken, illus. 2017. (ENG.). 32p. (J). (gr. -1-2). pap. 9.95 *(978-1-55451-805-0(9))* Annick Pr., Ltd. CAN. Dist: Publishers Group West (PGW).

Farley, Charlie. A T-Wit for a T-Woo. Marlow, Layn, illus. 2019. (ENG.). 32p. (J). (gr. -1-k). 14.99 *(978-1-4083-4649-5(4));* pap. 9.99 *(978-1-4083-4650-1(8))* Hachette Children's Group GBR. (Orchard Bks.). Dist: Hachette Bk. Group.

Farley, Christin & Miles, Stephanie. Let's Count Florida. 2018. (ENG., Illus.). 20p. (J). (gr. -1-1). bds. 12.99 *(978-1-64170-020-7(3),* 550020) Familius LLC.

—Let's Count Montana: Numbers & Colors in the Treasure State. Kaliaha, Volha, illus. 2018. (Let's Count Regional Board Bks.). (ENG.). 20p. (J). (gr. -1 — 1). bds. 12.99 *(978-1-945547-87-4(1),* 554787) Familius LLC.

Farley, Robin. Mia: The Sweetest Valentine. 2012. (J). lib. bdg. 14.75 *(978-0-606-26872-1(3))* Turtleback.

—Mia & the Big Sister Ballet. 2012. (Mia I Can Read Bks.). (J). lib. bdg. 13.55 *(978-0-606-26282-8(2))* Turtleback.

Farnsworth, Bill, illus. The Great Stone Face. 2005. 32p. (J). pap. 8.00 *(978-0-8028-5292-2(0))* Eerdmans, William B. Publishing Co.

Farquharson, Jerome. Playtime to Bedtime: Memories That Last Forever... 2011. (Illus.). 24p. (J). pap. 10.95 *(978-0-615-45886-1(6))* JFAR Bks.

Farrell, Alison. Cycle City: (City Books for Kids, Find & Seek Books) 2018. (ENG., Illus.). 40p. (J). (gr. -1-k). 17.99 *(978-1-4521-6334-5(0))* Chronicle Bks. LLC.

—The Hike: (Nature Book for Kids, Outdoors-Themed Picture Book for Preschoolers & Kindergarteners) 2019. (ENG., Illus.). 56p. (J). (gr. -1-k). 17.99 *(978-1-4521-7461-7(X))* Chronicle Bks. LLC.

Faulkner, Nicholas. A Visual History of Ships & Navigation, 1 vol. 2016. (Visual History of the World Ser.). (ENG., Illus.). 96p. (J). (gr. 8-8). 38.80 *(978-1-4994-6594-5(7),* 6100f876-8ced-48ff-b09a-6b0a423d36a9) Rosen Publishing Group, Inc., The.

Faust, Lauren. My Little Pony: the Magic Begins, Vol. 1. 2013. (MLP Episode Adaptations Ser.). (Illus.). 112p. (J). (gr. 1-3). pap. 7.99 *(978-1-61377-754-1(X),* 9781613777541) Idea & Design Works, LLC.

Favorite, Deborah. The Tush People. Arinsberg, Norman, illus. (J). 11.95 *(978-0-9722514-0-2(5))* Tush People, The.

Featherstone, Ann, ed. A World of Kindness. Del Rizzo, Suzanne et al, illus. 2018. (World of... Values to Grow On Ser.: 1). (ENG.). 32p. (J). (gr. -1-1). 17.95 *(978-1-77278-050-5(2))* Pajama Pr. CAN. Dist: Publishers Group West (PGW).

Federman, Cassandra. This Is a Sea Cow. Federman, Cassandra, illus. 2019. (ENG., Illus.). 32p. (J). (gr. -1-3). 16.99 *(978-0-8075-7874-2(6),* 807578746) Whitman, Albert & Co.

Feelings. Date not set. 5.95 *(978-0-89868-345-5(9))* ARO Publishing Co.

Feeney, Tatyana. Socks for Mr Wolf: A Woolly Adventure Around Ireland. 2017. (ENG., Illus.). 32p. 23.00 *(978-1-84717-906-7(1))* O'Brien Pr., Ltd., The IRL. Dist: Casemate Pubs. & Bk. Distributors, LLC.

Fenske, Jonathan. Let's Play, Crabby!: an Acorn Book (a Crabby Book #2) Fenske, Jonathan, illus. 2019. (Crabby Book Ser.: 2). (ENG., Illus.). 48p. (J). (gr. -1-1). pap. 4.99 *(978-1-338-28155-2(0))* Scholastic, Inc.

Fentiman, David. The Adventures of BB-8. 2016. (Illus.). 47p. (J). *(978-1-5182-1848-4(2))* Dorling Kindersley Publishing, Inc.

Fergus, Maureen. Buddy & Earl Go Exploring, 1 vol. Sookocheff, Carey, illus. (Buddy & Earl Ser.: 2). (ENG.). 32p. (J). 2018. (gr. -1-2). 7.95 *(978-1-77306-120-7(8))* 2016. (gr. k-2). 16.95 *(978-1-55498-714-6(8))* Groundwood Bks. CAN. Dist: Publishers Group West (PGW).

—Buddy & Earl Go to School, 1 vol. Sookocheff, Carey, illus. 2017. (Buddy & Earl Ser.: 4). (ENG.). 32p. (J). (gr. k-2). 16.95 *(978-1-55498-927-0(2))* Groundwood Bks. CAN. Dist: Publishers Group West (PGW).

—The Day Dad Joined My Soccer Team. Lowery, Mike, illus. 2018. (ENG.). 32p. (J). (gr. -1-2). 16.99 *(978-1-77138-654-8(1))* Kids Can Pr., Ltd. CAN. Dist: Hachette Bk. Group.

—The Day Santa Stopped Believing in Harold. Atkinson, Cale, illus. 2016. 32p. (J). (gr. -1-3). 16.99 *(978-1-77049-824-2(9),* Tundra Bks.) Tundra Bks. CAN. Dist: Penguin Random Hse. LLC.

—The Reptile Club. Ellis, Elina, illus. 2018. (ENG.). 32p. (J). (gr. -1-2). 16.99 *(978-1-77138-655-5(X))* Kids Can Pr., Ltd. CAN. Dist: Hachette Bk. Group.

Fernandez, Joyce. Little Bird - Pajarito. 2010. 31p. 15.95 *(978-0-615-23709-1(6))* My Second Language Publishing, USA.

Ferrell, Sean. I Don't Like Koala. Santoso, Charles, illus. 2015. (ENG.). 40p. (J). (gr. -1-3). 17.99 *(978-1-4814-0068-8(1),* Atheneum Bks. for Young Readers) Simon & Schuster Children's Publishing.

Ferrie, Chris. Quantum Information for Babies. 2018. (Baby University Ser.: 0). (Illus.). 24p. (J). (gr. -1-k). bds. 9.99 *(978-1-4926-5630-2(5))* Sourcebooks, Inc.

—Quantum Physics for Babies. 2017. (Baby University Ser.: 0). (Illus.). 24p. (J). (gr. -1-k). bds. 9.99 *(978-1-4926-5622-7(4))* Sourcebooks, Inc.

—Statistical Physics for Babies. 2018. (Baby University Ser.: 0). (Illus.). 24p. (J). (gr. -1-k). bds. 9.99 *(978-1-4926-5627-2(5))* Sourcebooks, Inc.

—8 Little Planets. Doyle, Lizzy, illus. 2018. 18p. (J). (gr. -1-k). bds. 10.99 *(978-1-4926-7124-4(X))* Sourcebooks, Inc.

Ferrie, Chris & Florance, Cara. Evolution for Babies. 2018. (Baby University Ser.: 0). (Illus.). 24p. (J). (gr. -1-k). bds. 9.99 *(978-1-4926-7115-2(0))* Sourcebooks, Inc.

Ferrie, Chris & Kregenow, Julia. Astrophysics for Babies. 2018. (Baby University Ser.: 0). (Illus.). 24p. (J). (gr. -1-k). bds. 9.99 *(978-1-4926-7113-8(4))* Sourcebooks, Inc.

Ferry, Beth. Sealed with a Kiss. Tallec, Olivier, illus. 2019. (ENG.). 32p. (J). (gr. -1-3). 19.99 *(978-0-06-247577-0(0),* HarperCollins) HarperCollins Pubs.

Feuchter, Anke. Felix from Berlin. Durand, Élodie, illus. 2014. (AV2 Fiction Readalong Ser.: Vol. 126). (ENG.). 32p. (J). (gr. -1-3). lib. bdg. 34.28 *(978-1-4896-2277-8(2),* AV2 by Weigl) Weigl Pubs., Inc.

Fiedler, Heidi. Butterflies: A Close-Up Photographic Look Inside Your World. 2017. (Up Close Ser.). (ENG., Illus.). 32p. (J). (gr. k-6). lib. bdg. 27.99 *(978-1-942875-37-6(1),* 5a072f95-7e40-4275-ab31-c4be0206e021, Walter Foster Jr) Quarto Publishing Group USA.

—Sea Swimmers: A Close-Up Photographic Look Inside Your World. 2017. (Up Close Ser.). (ENG., Illus.). 32p. (J). (gr. k-6). lib. bdg. 27.99 *(978-1-942875-34-5(7),* dd816102-a195-4d1f-a62d-15f916573bab, Walter Foster Jr) Quarto Publishing Group USA.

Fields, Terri. Being Responsible. 2018. (I Wonder Ser.). (ENG., Illus.). 16p. (gr. -1-2). lib. bdg. 28.50 *(978-1-64156-184-6(X),* 9781641561846) Rourke Educational Media.

Fienberg, Anna, et al. Once Tashi Met a Dragon. 2014. (Tashi Ser.). (ENG., Illus.). 32p. (J). (gr. k-2). 16.99 *(978-1-74175-887-0(4))* Allen & Unwin AUS. Dist: Independent Pubs. Group.

Fierstein, Harvey. The Sissy Duckling: Book & CD. Cole, Henry, illus. 2014. (ENG.). 40p. (J). (gr. -1-3). pap. 10.99 *(978-1-4424-9817-4(X),* Little Simon) Little Simon.

Filipina, Monika. All about Cats. Filipina, Monika, illus. 2017. (Child's Play Library). (ENG., Illus.). 32p. (J). *(978-1-84643-934-6(5))* Child's Play International Ltd.

Filippis, Dina De. Mrs Nguyen's Garden. 2011. 28p. pap. 15.99 *(978-1-4568-3337-4(5))* Xlibris Corp.

Finch, Mary. The Little Red Hen. Slater, Kate, illus. 2018. (ENG.). 32p. (J). (gr. k-5). pap. 9.99 *(978-1-78285-041-0(4))* Barefoot Bks., Inc.

—Three Billy Goats Gruff PB W CD. 2016. (ENG., Illus.). 32p. (J). (gr. -1-1). 9.99 *(978-1-78285-305-3(7))* Barefoot Bks., Inc.

Finch, Mary & Messing, Debra. The Little Red Hen. Slater, Kate, illus. 2013. 32p. (J). (gr. -1-2). 16.99 *(978-1-84686-575-6(1));* 9.99 *(978-1-84686-751-4(7))* Barefoot Bks., Inc.

Finnan, Kristie. Mommy's High Heel Shoes. Achilles, Pat, illus. 2008. 32p. (J). 16.99 *(978-0-9817565-2-3(2))* Mommy Workshop Bks.

Firefly Books Staff. Bedtime. (ENG., Illus.). 10p. bds. *(978-1-55209-358-0(1))* Firefly Bks., Ltd.

Fischer, Jean. I Prayed for You, 1 vol. 2015. (ENG., Illus.). 20p. (J). bds. 8.99 *(978-0-7180-4987-4(X),* Tommy Nelson) Nelson, Thomas Inc.

—Little Book of Easter Blessings, 1 vol. 2018. (Precious Moments Ser.). (ENG., Illus.). 32p. (J). bds. 9.99 *(978-0-7180-9866-7(8),* Tommy Nelson) Nelson, Thomas Inc.

Fisher, Dorothy Canfield. Understood Betsy - Illustrated. Williamson, Ada C., illus. 2013. 112p. pap. 3.97 *(978-1-60386-582-1(9),* Merchant Bks.) Rough Draft Printing.

Fisher, Henry. When I Dream of ABC. 2014. (Illus.). (J). *(978-1-4351-5469-8(X))* Barnes & Noble, Inc.

—When I Dream of ABC. Fisher, Henry, illus. 2018. (Padded Board Bks.). (ENG., Illus.). 26p. (J). (gr. -1-1). bds. 9.99 *(978-1-78700-258-6(6))* Top That! Publishing PLC GBR. Dist: Independent Pubs. Group.

Fishman, Jon M. Cool Muscle Cars. 2018. (Lightning Bolt Books (r) — Awesome Rides Ser.). (ENG., Illus.). 24p. (J). (gr. 1-3). pap. 9.99 *(978-1-5415-2755-3(0),* 2bd2f678-3ffd-46ac-812a-a0ed0a3dd7eb); lib. bdg. 29.32 *(978-1-5415-1997-8(3),* 8b44eac6-a323-4a86-a112-8055a0ec8039, Lerner Pubns.) Lerner Publishing Group.

—Cool Pickup Trucks. 2018. (Lightning Bolt Books (r) — Awesome Rides Ser.). (ENG., Illus.). 24p. (J). (gr. 1-3). lib. bdg. 29.32 *(978-1-5415-1995-4(7),* e99c3422-3714-4f56-a361-4410153542fc, Lerner Pubns.) Lerner Publishing Group.

—Cool Self-Driving Cars. 2018. (Lightning Bolt Books (r) — Awesome Rides Ser.). (ENG., Illus.). 24p. (J). (gr. 1-3). pap. 9.99 *(978-1-5415-2757-7(7),* a0ffbc93-20aa-43ab-b7dd-95609d3e9e1b); lib. bdg. 29.32 *(978-1-5415-1999-2(X),* bf4251f0-9fd3-4f71-967c-f4c47c9a0ce5, Lerner Pubns.) Lerner Publishing Group.

—Cool Stock Cars. 2018. (Lightning Bolt Books (r) — Awesome Rides Ser.). (ENG., Illus.). 24p. (J). (gr. 1-3). pap. 9.99 *(978-1-5415-2759-1(3),* 795e8885-37fd-4826-98a5-dfa3c23f8ccd); lib. bdg. 29.32 *(978-1-5415-1993-0(0),* 0e10e735-0253-4e89-bba4-3e69a9a0d48e, Lerner Pubns.) Lerner Publishing Group.

Fitzgerald, D. M. The True Story of the Big Red Onion. Cudd, Savannah, illus. 2013. 36p. 18.99 *(978-0-9890288-7-5(9));* pap. 10.99 *(978-0-9890288-5-1(2))* Mindstir Media.

Fitzgerald, Joanne. Este Soy Yo y lo Que Me Rodea: This Is Me & Where I Am - Spanish Edition, 1 vol. Fitzgerald, Joanne, illus. 2008. (SPA., Illus.). 32p. (J). (gr. -1-k). pap. 7.95 *(978-1-55455-108-8(0),* 9a1566a6-3f62-4ad4-a66a-c502aee169ba) Fitzhenry & Whiteside, Ltd. CAN. Dist: Firefly Bks., Ltd.

—This Is Me & Where I Am, 1 vol. 2006. (ENG., Illus.). 32p. (J). (gr. -1-k). bds. 9.95 *(978-1-55041-786-9(X),* 65890fbd-9060-4bdc-be85-bfe4aa3b3d49) Fitzhenry & Whiteside, Ltd. CAN. Dist: Firefly Bks., Ltd.

Fitzpatrick, Joe. I Am So Awesome: Read with Me. Kummer, Mark, illus. 2014. (ENG.). 32p. (J). (gr. k-4). 7.99 *(978-1-4867-0005-9(5))* Flowerpot Children's Pr. Inc. CAN. Dist: Cardinal Pubs. Group.

Fitzpatrick, Marie-Louise. Owl Bat Bat Owl. Fitzpatrick, Marie-Louise, illus. 2017. (ENG., Illus.). 32p. (J). (gr. -1-2). 15.99 *(978-0-7636-9161-5(5))* Candlewick Pr.

Fleabite. 2004. (J). 14.95 *(978-0-9746710-0-0(2))* Terra Linda Publishing.

Fleck, Jay. Tilly & Tank. 2018. (Illus.). 48p. (J). (gr. -1-2). 17.99 *(978-1-101-91786-2(5),* Tundra Bks.) Tundra Bks. CAN. Dist: Penguin Random Hse. LLC.

Fleming, Denise. The Everything Book. Fleming, Denise, illus. rev. ed. 2004. (ENG., Illus.). 26p. (J). (— 1). bds. 9.99 *(978-0-8050-7709-4(X),* 900026642, Holt, Henry & Co. Bks. For Young Readers) Holt, Henry & Co.

Fletcher, Tom. There's a Monster in Your Book. Abbott, Greg, illus. (Who's in Your Book? Ser.). (ENG.). (J). 2018. 34p. (— 1). bds. 8.99 *(978-0-525-64578-8(0))* 2017. 32p. (gr. -1-2). 18.99 *(978-1-5247-6456-2(6))* Random Hse. Children's Bks. (Random Hse. Bks. for Young Readers).

Fletcher, Tom & Poynter, Dougie. The Dinosaur That Pooped a Planet! Parsons, Garry, illus. 2017. (Dinosaur That Ser.). (ENG.). 32p. (J). (gr. -1-3). 16.99 *(978-1-4814-9866-1(5),* Aladdin) Simon & Schuster Children's Publishing.

—The Dinosaur That Pooped Christmas! Parsons, Garry, illus. 2019. (Dinosaur That Ser.). (ENG.). 32p. (J). (gr. -1-3). 17.99 *(978-1-4814-9872-2(X),* Aladdin) Simon & Schuster Children's Publishing.

—The Dinosaur That Pooped the Past! Parsons, Garry, illus. 2018. (Dinosaur That Ser.). (ENG.). 32p. (J). (gr. -1-3). 16.99 *(978-1-4814-9868-5(1),* Aladdin) Simon & Schuster Children's Publishing.

Fliess, Sue. From Here to There. 2018. (2019 Av2 Fiction Ser.). (ENG.). 32p. (J). lib. bdg. 34.28 *(978-1-4896-8265-9(1),* AV2 by Weigl) Weigl Pubs., Inc.

—From Here to There. Engel, Christiane, illus. 2016. (ENG.). 32p. (J). (gr. -1-3). 16.99 *(978-0-8075-2622-4(3),* 807526223) Whitman, Albert & Co.

—How to Be a Pirate. Dyson, Nikki, illus. 2014. (Little Golden Book Ser.). 24p. (J). (-k). 5.99 *(978-0-449-81309-6(6),* Golden Bks.) Random Hse. Children's Bks.

—I'm a Ballerina! Chou, Joey, illus. 2015. (Little Golden Book Ser.). 24p. (J). (-k). 5.99 *(978-0-553-49758-8(8),* Golden Bks.) Random Hse. Children's Bks.

Flip Flaps Colours. 2014. (ENG., Illus.). 36p. 10.00 *(978-1-906572-79-2(8))* Award Pubns. Ltd. GBR. Dist: Parkwest Pubns., Inc.

Florian, Douglas. The Wonderful Habits of Rabbits. Sánchez, Sonia, illus. (ENG.) (J). (gr. -1-3). 2018. 26p. bds. 7.99 *(978-1-4998-0622-9(1))* 2016. 32p. 16.99 *(978-1-4998-0104-0(1))* Little Bee Books Inc.

Flouw, Benjamin. The Golden Glow. 2018. (ENG., Illus.). 48p. (J). (gr. -1-3). 17.99 *(978-0-7352-6412-0(0),* Tundra Bks.) Tundra Bks. CAN. Dist: Penguin Random Hse. LLC.

Flowerpot Press Staff, contrib. by. Sockheadz: Counting. 2013. (ENG., Illus.). 20p. (J). (gr. -1-k). 6.99 *(978-1-77093-594-5(0))* Flowerpot Children's Pr. Inc. CAN. Dist: Cardinal Pubs. Group.

—Sockheadz: First Words. 2013. (ENG., Illus.). 20p. (J). (gr. -1-k). 6.99 *(978-1-77093-595-2(9))* Flowerpot Children's Pr. Inc. CAN. Dist: Cardinal Pubs. Group.

Fluent Stage 3. 2005. (Little Celebrations Picture/Text & Literacy Cards Ser.). (J). (gr. k-3). 128.50 *(978-0-673-77359-3(0))* Celebration Pr.

Foce, Natalia, tr. from ENG. Jesus el Milagroso. Anderson, Jeff, illus. l.t. ed. 2009. Orig. Title: Jesus the Miracle Worker. (SPA & ENG.). 24p. (J). 3.49 *(978-1-932789-28-7(6))* Editorial Sendas Antiguas, LLC.

—Jesus Maestro. Anderson, Jeff, illus. l.t. ed. 2009. Orig. Title: Jesus the Teacher. (SPA & ENG.). 24p. (J). 3.49 *(978-1-932789-26-3(X))* Editorial Sendas Antiguas, LLC.

—Jesus Narrador. Anderson, Jeff, illus. l.t. ed. 2009. Orig. Title: Jesus the Storyteller. (SPA & ENG.). 24p. (J). 3.49 *(978-1-932789-25-6(1))* Editorial Sendas Antiguas, LLC.

—Jesus Niño. Anderson, Jeff, illus. l.t. ed. 2009. Orig. Title: Jesus the Child. (SPA & ENG.). 24p. (J). 3.49 *(978-1-932789-24-9(3))* Editorial Sendas Antiguas, LLC.

—Jesus Salvador. Anderson, Jeff, illus. l.t. ed. 2009. Orig. Title: Jesus the Saviour. (SPA & ENG.). 24p. (J). 3.49 *(978-1-932789-29-4(4))* Editorial Sendas Antiguas, LLC.

—Jesus Sanador. Anderson, Jeff, illus. l.t. ed. 2009. Orig. Title: Jesus the Healer. (SPA & ENG.). 24p. (J). 3.49 *(978-1-932789-27-0(8))* Editorial Sendas Antiguas, LLC.

Foges, Clare. Bathroom Boogie. Murphy, Al, illus. 2018. (ENG.). 32p. (J). 16.95 *(978-0-571-34045-3(8),* Faber & Faber Children's Bks.) Faber & Faber, Inc.

—Kitchen Disco. Murphy, Al, illus. 2017. (ENG.). 32p. (J). (-k). pap. 9.95 *(978-0-571-30788-3(4))* Faber & Faber, Inc.

Foley, Greg. Thank You Bear Board Book. Foley, Greg, illus. 2012. (ENG., Illus.). 30p. (J). (gr. -1-k). bds. 7.99 *(978-0-670-78507-0(5),* Viking Books for Young Readers) Penguin Young Readers Group.

Fontana, Shea. Big Splash! (DC Super Hero Girls) Doescher, Erik, illus. 2018. (Pictureback(R) Ser.). 24p. (J). (gr. -1-2). pap. 5.99 *(978-1-5247-6868-3(5),* Random Hse. Bks. for Young Readers) Random Hse. Children's Bks.

Foreman, Grindley -. La playa de Pedro. 2003. (SPA., Illus.). 32p. (J). (gr. 1-3). 19.99 *(978-84-261-3314-4(2))* Juventud, Editorial ESP. Dist: Lectorum Pubns., Inc.

Foreman, Michael. The Little Bookshop & the Origami Army! 2015. (Origami Girl Ser.). (ENG., Illus.). 32p. (J). (gr. -1-k). 16.99 *(978-1-78344-120-4(8))* Andersen Pr. GBR. Dist: Independent Pubs. Group.

—Moose. Foreman, Michael, illus. 2015. (ENG., Illus.). 32p. (J). (gr. -1-k). pap. 9.99 *(978-1-78344-101-3(1))* Andersen Pr. GBR. Dist: Independent Pubs. Group.

—Newspaper Boy & Origami Girl! Foreman, Michael, illus. 2013. (Origami Girl Ser.). (ENG., Illus.). 32p. (J). (gr. -1-k). 20.99 *(978-1-84939-451-2(2))* Andersen Pr. GBR. Dist: Independent Pubs. Group.

—One World. 2012. (ENG., illus.). 32p. (J). (gr. -1-k). pap. 12.99 *(978-1-84939-304-1(4))* Andersen Pr. GBR. Dist: Independent Pubs. Group.

—Superfrog & the Big Stink! Foreman, Michael, illus. 2014. (ENG., Illus.). 32p. (J). (gr. -1-k). pap. 9.99 *(978-1-78344-030-6(9))* Andersen Pr. GBR. Dist: Independent Pubs. Group.

Forler, Nan. Trampoline Boy. Arbona, Marion, illus. 2018. 48p. (J). (gr. -1-2). 17.99 *(978-1-77049-830-3(3),* Tundra Bks.) Tundra Bks. CAN. Dist: Penguin Random Hse. LLC.

Forte, Lauren, adapted by. The Best Video Game Ever. 2017. (ENG., Illus.). 32p. (J). pap. *(978-1-5344-1926-1(8),* Simon Spotlight) Simon Spotlight.

Foxe, Steve. Yawn! a Grumpy Cat Bedtime Story (Grumpy Cat) Laberis, Steph, illus. 2018. (Little Golden Book Ser.). 24p. (J). (-k). 4.99 *(978-1-5247-2055-1(0),* Golden Bks.) Random Hse. Children's Bks.

Franceschelli, Christopher. A Box of Blocks. Peski Studio, illus. 2017. (ENG.). 290p. (J). (gr. -1 — 1). bds. 50.00 *(978-1-4197-2818-1(0))* Abrams, Inc.

—Buildablock (an Abrams Block Book) 2017. (Abrams Block Book Ser.). (ENG., Illus.). 90p. (J). (gr. -1 — 1). bds. 17.99 *(978-1-4197-2569-2(6),* 1146310) Abrams, Inc.

—Hello, New York! Cosneau, Géraldine, illus. 2018. (Hello, Big City! Ser.). (ENG.). 46p. (J). (gr. -1 — 1). bds. 12.99 *(978-1-4197-2829-7(6),* 1184410) Abrams, Inc.

Francois, Saragine. The White Gorilla & the Three Chimpanzees a Day from the Zoo. 2011. 28p. pap. 14.99 *(978-1-4520-3190-3(8))* AuthorHouse.

Frank, Janet. Daddies: A Book for Dads & Kids. Gergely, Tibor, illus. 2011. (Little Golden Book Ser.). (ENG.). 24p. (J). (gr. -1-2). 5.99 *(978-0-375-86130-7(0),* Golden Bks.) Random Hse. Children's Bks.

Franks, Alison. On My Feet! 2013. 24p. pap. 28.03 *(978-1-4797-6958-2(4))* Xlibris Corp.

Frasconi, Antonio. The House That Jack Built: A Picture Book in Two Languages. 2017. (ENG., Illus.). 32p. 14.95 *(978-0-486-81646-3(X),* 81646X) Dover Pubns., Inc.

Frazee, Marla. The Boss Baby. Frazee, Marla, illus. 2016. (ENG., Illus.). 40p. (J). (gr. -1-3). pap. 7.99 *(978-1-4814-6981-4(9),* Beach Lane Bks.) Beach Lane Bks.

—Santa Claus: the World's Number One Toy Expert Board Book: A Christmas Holiday Book for Kids. Frazee, Marla, illus. 2018. (ENG., Illus.). 32p. (J). (— 1). bds. 7.99 *(978-1-328-48542-7(0),* 1715776, Clarion Bks.) HarperCollins Pubs.

Frazier, Craig. Sitting Board Book. Frazier, Craig, illus. 2019. (ENG., Illus.). 32p. (J). (gr. -1 — 1). bds. 7.99 *(978-0-06-279630-1(5),* HarperFestival) HarperCollins Pubs.

Fredrickson, Anne. The Baseball Brothers. 2008. lib. bdg. 12.95 *(978-0-615-20146-7(6))* Fredrickson, Anne.

Fredrickson, Lane. Monster Trouble! Robertson, Michael, illus. 2015. 32p. (J). (gr. -1-2). 16.95 *(978-1-4549-1345-0(2))* Sterling Publishing Co., Inc.

Free Wheelin' Picture Book (English) NL 9x9 with Snipe. 2007. (J). 5.99 *(978-1-933934-48-8(4))* Mighty Kids Media.

Freedman, Claire. Florence Frizzball. Massey, Jane, illus. 2018. (ENG.). 32p. (J). 7.99 *(978-1-4711-4454-7(2),* Simon & Schuster Children's) Simon & Schuster, Ltd. GBR. Dist: Simon & Schuster, Inc.

—The Lost Penguin: An Oliver & Patch Story. Hindley, Kate, illus. 2018. (ENG.). 32p. (J). 17.99 *(978-1-4711-1733-6(2));* (gr. -1). 7.99 *(978-1-4711-1734-3(0);* Simon & Schuster, Ltd. GBR. (Simon & Schuster Children's). Dist: Simon & Schuster, Inc.

—Where Snowflakes Fall. Macnaughton, Tina, illus. 2012. 24p. (J). *(978-1-4351-4321-0(3))* Barnes & Noble, Inc.

Freedman, Claire & Scott, Gavin. Cuddle Bear. 2013. (ENG.). (J). 26.99 *(978-1-61067-193-4(7))* Kane Miller.

Freeman, Don. Corduroy. 2014. (Corduroy Ser.). (Illus.). 34p. (J). (gr. -1 — 1). bds. 7.99 *(978-0-451-47079-9(6),* Viking Books for Young Readers) Penguin Young Readers Group.

—A Pocket for Corduroy. 2015. (Corduroy Ser.). (Illus.). 34p. (J). (— 1). bds. 8.99 *(978-0-451-47113-0(X),* Viking Books for Young Readers) Penguin Young Readers Group.

Freeman, Tor. Benji Bear's Busy Day. Freeman, Tor, illus. 2015. (ENG., Illus.). 18p. (J). (-k). bds. 17.99 *(978-1-5098-0111-4(1))* Pan Macmillan GBR. Dist: Independent Pubs. Group.

—Olive & the Big Secret. Freeman, Tor, illus. 2012. (ENG., Illus.). 32p. (J). (gr. -1-3). 15.99 *(978-0-7636-6149-6(X),* Templar) Candlewick Pr.

French, Jackie & Whatley, Bruce. Wombat Goes to School. 2020. (ENG.). 32p. pap. 7.99 *(978-0-7322-9903-3(9),* HarperCollins) HarperCollins Pubs.

French, Vivian. Cave-Baby & the Mammoth. Williams, Lisa, illus. 2010. 32p. pap. *(978-1-84089-635-0(3))* Zero to Ten, Ltd.

Fretz, Denette. I Want Your Smile, Crocodile, 1 vol. Urbanovic, Jackie, illus. 2018. (ENG.). 32p. (J). 17.99 *(978-0-310-75890-7(4))* Zonderkidz.

Freudig, Laura. Halfway Wild, 1 vol. Barry, Kevin, illus. 2016. (ENG.). 32p. (J). 17.95 *(978-1-934031-48-3(8),* 73f100ad-e4d5-44ec-9395-1c31bdb64c29) Islandport Pr., Inc.

Friester, Paul. Owl Howls Again! Goossens, Philippe, illus. 2015. (ENG.). 32p. (J). (gr. -1-1). 15.95 *(978-0-7358-4129-1(2))* North-South Bks., Inc.

Frohlich, Anja. Animals in the Outhouse. Kiss, Gergely, illus. 2012. (ENG.). 28p. (J). (gr. k-3). 16.95 *(978-1-61608-659-6(9),* 608659, Sky Pony Pr.) Skyhorse Publishing Co., Inc.

Fronis, Aly. This Little Reindeer. Flowers, Luke, illus. 2017. (ENG.). 16p. (J). (gr. -1-k). bds. 5.99 *(978-1-4998-0525-3(X))* Little Bee Books Inc.

Frost, Maddie. Once upon a Zzzz. Frost, Maddie, illus. 2018. (ENG., Illus.). 40p. (J). (gr. -1-3). 16.99 *(978-0-8075-6064-8(2),* 807560642) Whitman, Albert & Co.

Frost, Maddie, illus. Candy Apple Blessings, 1 vol. 2018. (Sweet Blessings Ser.). (ENG.). 20p. (J). bds. 8.99 *(978-1-4003-1779-0(7),* Tommy Nelson) Nelson, Thomas Inc.

—Indestructibles: Busy City: Chew Proof · Rip Proof · Nontoxic · 100% Washable (Book for Babies, Newborn Books, Safe to Chew) 2018. (Indestructibles Ser.). (ENG.). 12p. (J). (gr. -1 — 1). pap. 5.95 *(978-1-5235-0468-8(4),* 100468) Workman Publishing Co., Inc.

—Indestructibles: Hello, Farm! Chew Proof · Rip Proof · Nontoxic · 100% Washable (Book for Babies, Newborn Books, Safe to Chew) 2018. (Indestructibles Ser.). (ENG.). 12p. (J). (gr. -1 — 1). pap. 5.99 *(978-1-5235-0467-1(6),* 100467) Workman Publishing Co., Inc.

—Indestructibles: My Neighborhood: Chew Proof · Rip Proof · Nontoxic · 100% Washable (Book for Babies, Newborn Books, Safe to Chew) 2018. (Indestructibles Ser.). (ENG.). 12p. (J). (gr. -1 — 1). pap. 5.99 *(978-1-5235-0469-5(2),* 100469) Workman Publishing Co., Inc.

Frosty the Snowman: Songs of the Season: 5-Button Song Book. (Illus.). 10p. (J). (gr. -1-2). 7.98 *(978-0-7853-2067-8(9),* PI27) Publications International, Ltd.

Frucci, Pamela A. The Visit to my Great Great Grandfather. 2009. (ENG.). 24p. pap. 12.99 *(978-1-4363-7509-2(6))* Xlibris Corp.

Fuggle, Debbie. The Two Little Fir Trees. 2012. 28p. pap. 32.70 *(978-1-4691-3253-2(2))* Xlibris Corp.

Fujii, Hideaki. LBX: New Dawn Raisers, Vol. 1 Vol. 1: New Dawn Raisers. 2014. (Lbx Ser.: 1). (ENG., Illus.). 192p. (J). pap. 9.99 *(978-1-4215-7695-4(3))* Viz Media.

Fuller, Rachel, illus. Look at Me! 2009. (New Baby Ser.). 12p. (J). (gr. -1). spiral bd. *(978-1-84643-278-1(2))* Child's Play International Ltd.

Funk, Josh. The Case of the Stinky Stench. Kearney, Brendan, illus. 2017. (Lady Pancake & Sir French Toast Ser.: 2). 40p. (J). (gr. -1-3). 18.99 *(978-1-4549-1960-5(4))* Sterling Publishing Co., Inc.

—How to Code a Sandcastle. Palacios, Sara, illus. 2018. 44p. (J). (gr. -1-3). 18.99 *(978-0-425-29198-6(7),* Viking Books for Young Readers) Penguin Young Readers Group.

Furie, Matt. The Night Riders. (Illus.). 48p. (J). 2013. (gr. -1-3). 8.95 *(978-1-938073-72-4(X),* 54da59fb-b496-483f-a5f6-41367ed7cd06) 2012. 17.95 *(978-1-936365-56-2(1),* 2454ed7d-2dca-42de-ba36-428c14a0a599) McSweeney's Publishing.

Furman, Simon. Kung Fu Panda Collection: Ready, Set Po!, Vol. 1. Robinson, Lee et al, illus. 2016. (Kung Fu Panda Ser.: 1). 112p. (J). (gr. 1-4). pap. 12.99 *(978-1-78276-697-1(9))* Titan Bks. Ltd. GBR. Dist: Penguin Random Hse. LLC.

Fusek Peters, Andrew. The Ant & the Big Bad Bully Goat. Wadham, Anna, illus. 2010. (Traditional Tales with a Twist Ser.). 32p. (J). (gr. -1-2). *(978-1-84643-348-1(7))* Child's Play International Ltd.

—Bear & Turtle & the Great Lake Race. Edgson, Alison, illus. 2010. (Traditional Tales with a Twist Ser.). 32p. (J). (gr. -1-2). *(978-1-84643-347-4(9))* Child's Play International Ltd.

—The Talkative Tortoise. 2011. (Traditional Tales with a Twist Ser.). (Illus.). 32p. (J). *(978-1-84643-418-1(1))* Child's Play International Ltd.

G., Ashley. Critter Colors. G., Ashley, illus. 2015. (ENG., Illus.). 28p. (J). (gr. -1-k). bds. 7.99 *(978-1-4814-4218-3(X),* Little Simon) Little Simon.

Gaertner, Meg. A Spring Pond. 2020. (Spring Is Here Ser.). (ENG., Illus.). 16p. (J). (gr. k-1). pap. 7.95 *(978-1-64493-103-5(6),* 1644931036); lib. bdg. 25.64 *(978-1-64493-024-3(2),* 1644930242) North Star Editions. (Focus Readers).

Gaiman, Neil. Chu's Day at the Beach Board Book. Rex, Adam, illus. 2016. (ENG.). 36p. (J). (gr. -1 — 1). bds. 7.99 *(978-0-06-238124-8(5),* HarperFestival) HarperCollins Pubs.

Galbraith, Kathryn O. Arbor Day Square, 1 vol. Moore, Cyd, illus. 2016. 32p. (J). (gr. -1-3). pap. 7.99 *(978-1-56145-922-3(4))* Peachtree Publishing Co. Inc.

Galdone, Paul. Cinderella. Galdone, Paul, illus. 2013. (Folk Tale Classics Ser.). (ENG., Illus.). 48p. (J). (gr. -1-3). 9.99 *(978-0-547-98867-2(2),* 1524566, Clarion Bks.) HarperCollins Pubs.

Gale, Emily. Just Josie & the Number 7. Byrne, Mike, illus. 2010. (Picture Books Ser.). 25p. (J). (gr. -1-1). *(978-1-4075-9505-4(9))* Parragon, Inc.

—Just Josie & the Perfect Day. Byrne, Mike, illus. 2010. (Picture Books Ser.). 25p. (J). (gr. -1-1). *(978-1-4075-9506-1(7))* Parragon, Inc.

Galindo, Renata. The Cherry Thief. Galindo, Renata, illus. (Child's Play Library). (Illus.). 32p. (J). 2016. *(978-1-84643-651-2(6))* 2014. *(978-1-84643-652-9(4))* Child's Play International Ltd.

Gall, Chris. Dinotrux. 2012. (Dinotrux Ser.: 1). (ENG., Illus.). 32p. (J). (gr. -1-3). pap. 8.99 *(978-0-316-13392-0(2))* Little, Brown Bks. for Young Readers.

—Revenge of the Dinotrux. 2015. (Dinotrux Ser.: 2). (ENG., Illus.). 28p. (J). (gr. -1 — 1). bds. 6.99 *(978-0-316-40635-2(X))* Little, Brown Bks. for Young Readers.

Gallardo, Yuri Caravaca & Gallardo, Yuri Caravaca, eds. Houses & Apartments under 1000 Square Feet. 2013. (ENG., Illus.). 256p. pap. 24.95 *(978-1-77085-214-3(X),* 8883b036-2577-479d-bfb8-e1e6da76f691) Firefly Bks., Ltd.

Galloway, Fhiona, illus. Moo: A First Book of Counting. 2016. (J). *(978-1-5182-3185-8(3))* Tiger Tales.

Galvin, Laura Gates. Baby Duck Gets Lost. 2007. (Baby Animals Ser.). (ENG., Illus.). 16p. (gr. -1-k). 6.95 *(978-1-59249-747-8(0))* Soundprints.

Gamble, Adam & Jasper, Mark. Good Night Austin. Veno, Joe, illus. 2015. (Good Night Our World Ser.). (ENG.). 20p. (J). (— 1). bds. 9.95 *(978-1-60219-233-1(2))* Good Night Bks.

—Good Night Baby Dragons. Chan, Suwin, illus. 2018. (Good Night Our World Ser.). 20p. (J). (— 1). bds. 9.95 *(978-1-60219-511-0(0))* Good Night Bks.

—Good Night Boats. Veno, Joe, illus. 2016. (Good Night Our World Ser.). (ENG.). 20p. (J). (— 1). bds. 9.95 *(978-1-60219-500-4(5))* Good Night Bks.

—Good Night Campsite. Stevenson, Harvey, illus. 2018. (Good Night Our World Ser.). 20p. (J). (— 1). bds. 9.95 *(978-1-60219-514-1(5))* Good Night Bks.

—Good Night Fairies. Holder, Jimmy, illus. 2018. (Good Night Our World Ser.). 20p. (J). (— 1). bds. 9.95 *(978-1-60219-433-5(5))* Good Night Bks.

—Good Night Fish. Veno, Joe, illus. 2016. (Good Night Our World Ser.). (ENG.). 20p. (J). (— 1). bds. 9.95 *(978-1-60219-502-8(1))* Good Night Bks.

—Good Night Grand Canyon. Kelly, Cooper, illus. 2016. (Good Night Our World Ser.). (ENG.). 20p. (J). (— 1). bds. 9.95 *(978-1-60219-503-5(X))* Good Night Bks.

—Good Night Grandma. Stevenson, Harvey, illus. 2016. (ENG.). 20p. (J). (— 1). bds. 9.95 *(978-1-60219-409-0(2))* Good Night Bks.

—Good Night Idaho. Veno, Joe, illus. 2018. (Good Night Our World Ser.). 20p. (J). (— 1). bds. 9.95 *(978-1-60219-410-6(6))* Good Night Bks.

—Good Night Little Brother. Kelly, Cooper, illus. 2016. (Good Night Our World Ser.). (ENG.). 20p. (J). (— 1). bds. 9.95 *(978-1-60219-505-9(6))* Good Night Bks.

—Good Night Little Monsters. Kelly, Cooper, illus. 2017. (Good Night Our World Ser.). 20p. (J). (gr. -1 — 1). bds. 9.95 *(978-1-60219-489-2(0))* Good Night Bks.

—Good Night Little Sister. Stevenson, Harvey, illus. 2016. (Good Night Our World Ser.). (ENG.). 20p. (J). (— 1). bds. 9.95 *(978-1-60219-506-6(4))* Good Night Bks.

—Good Night Mommy. Kelly, Cooper, illus. 2015. (Good Night Our World Ser.). (ENG.). 20p. (J). (— 1). bds. 9.95 *(978-1-60219-230-0(8))* Good Night Bks.

—Good Night Museums. Kelly, Cooper, illus. 2018. (Good Night Our World Ser.). 20p. (J). (— 1). bds. 9.95 *(978-1-60219-576-9(5))* Good Night Bks.

—Good Night Nebraska. 2015. (Good Night Our World Ser.). (ENG., Illus.). 20p. (J). (— 1). bds. 9.95 *(978-1-60219-087-0(9))* Good Night Bks.

—Good Night New Mexico. Palmer, Ruth, illus. 2014. (Good Night Our World Ser.). (ENG.). 20p. (J). (— 1). bds. 9.95 *(978-1-60219-088-7(7))* Good Night Bks.

—Good Night Outer Banks. Veno, Joe, illus. 2018. (Good Night Our World Ser.). 20p. (J). (— 1). bds. 9.95 *(978-1-60219-604-9(4))* Good Night Bks.

—Good Night Snow. 2016. (Good Night Our World Ser.). (ENG., Illus.). 20p. (J). (— 1). bds. 9.95 *(978-1-60219-412-0(2))* Good Night Bks.

—Good Night Summer. Blackmore, Katherine, illus. 2017. (Good Night Our World Ser.). 20p. (J). (— 1). bds. 9.95 *(978-1-60219-440-3(8))* Good Night Bks.

—Good Night Whales. Stevenson, Harvey, illus. 2016. (Good Night Our World Ser.). (ENG.). 20p. (J). (— 1). bds. 9.95 *(978-1-60219-507-3(2))* Good Night Bks.

Gamonal, Dulce. Diego from Madrid. Audouin, Laurent, illus. 2014. (AV2 Fiction Readalong Ser.: Vol. 124). (ENG.). 32p. (J). (gr. -1-3). lib. bdg. 34.28 *(978-1-4896-2280-8(2),* AV2 by Weigl) Weigl Pubs., Inc.

Gardner, Louise, illus. Old MacDonald. 2004. 24p. (J). bds. 6.99 *(978-1-85854-901-9(9))* Brimax Books Ltd. GBR. Dist: Byeway Bks.

Gardner, Sally. Book of Princesses. (ENG., Illus.). 96p. (J). 19.95 *(978-1-85881-350-9(6),* Orion) Orion Publishing Group, Ltd. GBR. Dist: Trafalgar Square Publishing.

Garnett, Sandy, creator. The Rainbow Riders. 2011. (Rainbow Riders Ser.). (ENG., Illus.). 36p. 18.00 *(978-0-9822348-5-3(6),* Chelsea Pr.) Chelsea Multimedia.

Garson, Sarah. One, Two, Cockatoo! Garson, Sarah, illus. 2012. (ENG., Illus.). 32p. (J). (gr. k — 1). pap. 10.99 *(978-1-84270-944-3(5))* Andersen Pr. GBR. Dist: Independent Pubs. Group.

Garza, Armando N. Itty Bitty Saves the Day. 2007. (Illus.). 22p. (J). (gr. -1-3). 21.99 *(978-1-59879-482-3(5))* Lifevest Publishing, Inc.

Garza, Fabiola, illus. Coco. 2017. (J). *(978-1-5379-5892-7(5),* Golden Bks.) Random Hse. Children's Bks.

Gassman, Julie. You Get What You Get, 1 vol. Horne, Sarah, illus. 2013. (Little Boost Ser.). (ENG.). 32p. (J). (gr. -1-1). 14.95 *(978-1-4795-2157-9(4),* 123867, Picture Window Bks.) Capstone.

Gates, Susan. Mole Who was Scared of the Dark. Breakespeare, Andrew, illus. 2005. (ENG.). 24p. (J). lib. bdg. 23.65 *(978-1-59646-710-1(X))* Dingles & Co.

Gauch, Patricia Lee. Christina Katerina & the Box. Burns, Doris, illus. 2012. (ENG.). 48p. (J). (gr. -1-3). 9.99 *(978-1-59078-915-5(6),* Astra Young Readers) Astra Publishing Hse.

Gauthier, Elizabeth. A Bald Chimpanzee: An Adventure in ABCs. Gauthier, Elizabeth & Bonney, Joan, illus. 2012. (ENG.). 40p. (J). pap. 12.99 *(978-0-9833593-5-7(0),* Frog Legs Ink) Gauthier Pubns. Inc.

Gaven, Jim. Friends Find Fun for Food: All about Alliterations. 2013. 28p. pap. 24.95 *(978-1-63000-140-7(6))* America Star Bks.

Gay, Marie-Louise. Read Me a Story, Stella, 1 vol. 2013. (Stella & Sam Ser.: 7). (ENG., Illus.). 32p. (J). (gr. -1-k). 16.95 *(978-1-55498-216-5(2))* Groundwood Bks. CAN. Dist: Publishers Group West (PGW).

Gay, Susana & Gay, Owen. First Easter. 2019. (ENG., Illus.). 16p. (J). (gr. -1 — 1). bds. 6.99 *(978-0-8249-1685-5(9),* Worthy Kids/Ideals) Worthy Publishing.

Geillespie, Desiree & McKay-Fleming, Kimberly. Journey Through the Circle of Life: Un Voyage a Travers le Cercle de la Vie, 1 vol. 2015. (FRE., Illus.). 32p. (J). mass mkt. 10.95 *(978-1-894717-61-8(9),* f3dd9406-2a2f-471e-bdb5-494c19feaa01) Pemmican Pubns., Inc. CAN. Dist: Firefly Bks., Ltd.

Geisert, Arthur, creator. Thunderstorm. (ENG., Illus.). (J). 2015. 34p. (gr. k). 60.00 *(978-1-59270-170-4(1))* 2013. 32p. (gr. -1). 17.95 *(978-1-59270-133-9(7))* Enchanted Lion Bks., LLC.

Genaille, Cynthia & Wheeler, Jordan. Boog the Bug, 1 vol. Lucas, Diane, illus. 2015. (ENG.). 32p. (J). (gr. -1-k). mass mkt. 10.95 *(978-1-894717-46-5(5),* 6e78ea3c-8d38-4f29-9c90-ecef7a35c2d1) Pemmican Pubns., Inc. CAN. Dist: Firefly Bks., Ltd.

George, Joshua. Fame Mouse. 2017. (ENG., Illus.). 32p. (J). (gr. -1-k). pap. 10.99 *(978-1-78445-704-4(3))* Top That! Publishing PLC GBR. Dist: Independent Pubs. Group.

—Goodnight Bear. Ovocheva, Zhanna, illus. 2018. (Magic Flashlight Bks.). (ENG.). 10p. (J). bds. 9.99 *(978-1-78700-611-9(5))* Top That! Publishing PLC GBR. Dist: Independent Pubs. Group.

—Goodnight Lion. Ovocheva, Zhanna, illus. 2018. (Magic Flashlight Bks.). (ENG.). 10p. (J). bds. 9.99 *(978-1-78700-612-6(3))* Top That! Publishing PLC GBR. Dist: Independent Pubs. Group.

—Tiny Town Hide & Seek Counting. Ribbon, Lemon, illus. 2018. (Tiny Town Hide & Seek Board Bks.). (ENG.). 12p. (J). (-k). bds. 6.99 *(978-1-78700-379-8(5))* Top That! Publishing PLC GBR. Dist: Independent Pubs. Group.

—Tiny Town Hide & Seek Words. Ribbon, Lemon, illus. 2018. (Tiny Town Hide & Seek Board Bks.). (ENG.). 12p. (J). (-k). bds. 6.99 *(978-1-78700-380-4(9))* Top That! Publishing PLC GBR. Dist: Independent Pubs. Group.

—Tiny Whale. Pinillos, Puy, illus. 2018. (Picture Bks.). (ENG.). 32p. (J). (gr. -1-k). 16.99 *(978-1-78700-457-3(0))* Willow Tree Bks. GBR. Dist: Independent Pubs. Group.

George, K. Duck, Duck, Dinosaur: Perfect Pumpkin. Vidal, Oriol, illus. 2017. 32p. (J). *(978-1-5182-4363-9(0))* Harper & Row Ltd.

George, Kallie. Duck, Duck, Dinosaur: Snowy Surprise. Vidal, Oriol, illus. 2017. (My First I Can Read Ser.). (ENG.). 32p. (J). (gr. -1-3). 16.99 *(978-0-06-235319-1(5));* pap. 5.99 *(978-0-06-235318-4(7))* HarperCollins Pubs. (HarperCollins).

—Goodnight, Anne: Inspired by Anne of Green Gables. Godbout, Geneviève, illus. 2018. 40p. (J). (gr. -1-2). 17.99 *(978-1-77049-926-3(1),* Tundra Bks.) Tundra Bks. CAN. Dist: Penguin Random Hse. LLC.

—The Melancholic Mermaid. Halpin, Abigail, illus. 2011. (ENG.). 64p. (J). (gr. k-4). 16.95 *(978-1-897476-53-6(1))* Simply Read Bks. CAN. Dist: Ingram Publisher Services.

George, Lynn. The Leaf Pile, 1 vol. 2006. (Neighborhood Readers Ser.). (ENG.). 16p. (gr. 1-2). pap. 6.50 *(978-1-4042-7120-3(1),* eb28fcd8-46b5-4310-bbff-9d8e2396137c, Rosen Classroom) Rosen Publishing Group, Inc., The.

George, Sandy. Anika's Travel Diaries: The Lava Island Trip. 2012. 28p. pap. 17.99 *(978-1-4772-9297-6(7))* AuthorHouse.

Geraghty, Paul. Hoppameleon. Geraghty, Paul, illus. 2014. (Illus.). 32p. (J). (gr. -1-k). pap. 9.99 *(978-1-84939-773-5(2))* Andersen Pr. GBR. Dist: Independent Pubs. Group.

—Tortuga. 2013. (ENG., Illus.). 32p. (J). (gr. k-2). pap. 9.99 *(978-1-84939-557-1(8))* Andersen Pr. GBR. Dist: Independent Pubs. Group.

Gerlings, Rebecca. Ho-Ho-Hopeless Santa. Jennings, Sarah, illus. 2016. (ENG.). 32p. (J). 8.99 *(978-1-4711-4600-8(6),* Simon & Schuster Children's) Simon & Schuster, Ltd. GBR. Dist: Simon & Schuster, Inc.

Gerra, Laurent. Tying the Knot, Vol. 45. 2014. (Lucky Luke Ser.: 45). (Illus.). 48p. (J). (gr. -1-12). pap. 11.95 *(978-1-84918-188-4(8))* CineBook GBR. Dist: National Bk. Network.

Gerry, Lisa M. Explore My World: Weather. 2018. (Explore My World Ser.). (Illus.). 32p. (J). (gr. -1-k). pap. 4.99 *(978-1-4263-3155-8(X));* (ENG., lib. bdg. 14.90 *(978-1-4263-3156-5(8))* Disney Publishing Worldwide. (National Geographic Kids).

Gershator, Phillis. Listen, Listen. Jay, Alison, illus. 2008. (ENG.). 32p. (J). (gr. -1-2). bds. 14.99 *(978-1-84686-201-4(9))* Barefoot Bks., Inc.

Gershman, Regina. Animals from My Window. 2011. 24p. pap. 16.44 *(978-1-4634-2094-9(3))* AuthorHouse.

Gerstein, Mordicai. Mountains of Tibet. Gerstein, Mordicai, illus. 2013. (ENG., Illus.). 32p. (J). (gr. k-5). 14.99 *(978-1-78285-047-2(3))* Barefoot Bks., Inc.

Ghosh, Ronojoy. Ollie & the Wind. 2017. (Illus.). 32p. (J). (gr. k-2). 14.99 *(978-0-14-378506-4(0))* Random Hse. Australia AUS. Dist: Independent Pubs. Group.

The Ghost Ship. 2013. (Illus.). (J). *(978-1-4351-4725-6(1))* Barnes & Noble, Inc.

Gianferrari, Maria. Hawk Rising. 2018. (ENG., Illus.). 40p. (J). 18.99 *(978-1-62672-096-1(7),* 900135780) Roaring Brook Pr.

—Terrific Tongues! Liu, Jia, illus. 2018. 32p. (J). (gr. -1-3). 17.99 *(978-1-62091-784-8(X),* Astra Young Readers) Astra Publishing Hse.

Gibault, Thomas. Hotel Fantastic. Gibault, Thomas, illus. 2018. (ENG., Illus.). 32p. (J). (gr. -1-2). 16.99 *(978-1-77138-992-1(3))* Kids Can Pr., Ltd. CAN. Dist: Hachette Bk. Group.

Gibbes, Lesley. Quick As a Wink, Fairy Pink. Acton, Sara, illus. 2019. 32p. pap. 6.99 *(978-1-921504-87-7(0),* Working Title Pr.) HarperCollins Pubs. Australia AUS. Dist: HarperCollins Pubs.

Gibbons, Gail. Hurricanes! (New & Updated Edition) 2019. (Illus.). 32p. (J). (gr. -1-3). 18.99 *(978-0-8234-4157-0(1));* pap. 8.99 *(978-0-8234-4179-2(2))* Holiday Hse., Inc.

—Ice Cream: The Full Scoop. 2008. (ENG., Illus.). 32p. (J). (gr. -1-3). 7.99 *(978-0-8234-2155-8(4))* Holiday Hse., Inc.

—The Moon Book (New & Updated Edition) 2019. (Illus.). 32p. (J). (gr. -1-3). 18.99 *(978-0-8234-4324-6(8));* pap. 8.99 *(978-0-8234-4323-9(X))* Holiday Hse., Inc.

—Planes. 2019. (Illus.). 24p. (J). (— 1). bds. 7.99 *(978-0-8234-4154-9(7))* Holiday Hse., Inc.

Gibbs Smith. La Catrina: Emotions/Emociones, 1 vol. 2018. (SPA., Illus.). 22p. (J). (gr. -1-k). bds. 9.99 *(978-0-9861099-6-6(7))* Little Libros, LLC.

Gibby, Shauna. Follow the Prophet: A Flashlight Discovery Book. Beech, Bryan, illus. 2019. (J). 16.99 *(978-1-62972-576-5(5))* Deseret Bk. Co.

Giesler, Dagmar & Geisler, Dagmar. Max juega en la Arena. 2004. (Coleccion Max Max Ser.). (SPA.). (J). bds. 11.95 *(978-84-261-3295-6(2))* Juventud, Editorial ESP. Dist: Distribooks, Inc.

Gifford, Kathie Lee. The Gift That I Can Give for Little Ones, 1 vol. Seal, Julia, illus. 2018. (ENG.). 26p. (J). bds. 9.99 *(978-1-4002-0925-5(0)*, Tommy Nelson) Nelson, Thomas Inc.

Giles, Sophie, et al. My First Picture Dictionary. Burton, Terry & Hicks, Angela, illus. 2014. (ENG.). 125p. 17.50 *(978-1-84135-873-4(8))* Award Pubns. Ltd. GBR. Dist: Parkwest Pubns., Inc.

Gilleland, Linda. I Love You, Baby Deer. Irish, Leigh Ann, illus. 2012. (ENG.). 56p. 19.99 *(978-1-61254-025-2(2))* Brown Books Publishing Group.

Gillmor, Don. Fabuleuse Melodie De. Gay, Marie-Louise, illus. 2013. (ENG.). 44p. (J). (gr. -1-k). 16.95 *(978-2-923163-30-7(3))* La Montagne Secrete CAN. Dist: Independent Pubs. Group.

Gilman, Michelle. What Grandma Built. Sasky, Jazmin, illus. 2016. (ENG.). 32p. (J). pap. *(978-1-55017-753-4(2)*, a01fcb21-1f91-440d-be71-cb4c7c06d815) Harbour Publishing Co., Ltd.

Gilman, Phoebe. The Balloon Tree. 2004. (J). (gr. k-3). spiral bd. *(978-0-616-01650-3(6))* Canadian National Institute for the Blind/Institut National Canadien pour les Aveugles.

Gilmore, Dorina Lazo. A Stone in the Soup. Hires, Josh, illus. 2006. 39p. per. 15.00 *(978-0-938911-29-6(5))* Individualized Education Systems/Poppy Lane Publishing.

Gilmore, Rachna. The Flute, 1 vol. Biswas, Pulak, illus. 2012. (ENG.). 32p. (J). (gr. -1-k). 16.95 *(978-1-896580-57-9(2))* Tradewind Bks. CAN. Dist: Orca Bk. Pubs. USA.

Gingras, Charlotte. L' Ecuyere. DuBois, Gérard, illus. 2004. (Picture Bks.). (FRE.). 32p. (J). (gr. -1). *(978-2-89021-666-2(7))*; pap. *(978-2-89021-665-5(9))* Diffusion du livre Mirabel (DLM).

Gingrich, Callista. Christmas in America. Arciero, Susan, illus. 2015. (Ellis the Elephant Ser.: 5). (ENG.). 40p. (J). (gr. -1-3). 16.99 *(978-1-62157-345-6(1)*, Regnery Kids) Regnery Publishing.

Girel, Stephane, illus. Where Is the Frog? A Children's Book Inspired by Claude Monet. 2013. (Children's Books Inspired by Famous Artworks Ser.). (ENG.). 32p. (J). (gr. -1-3). 14.95 *(978-3-7913-7139-9(8))* Prestel Verlag GmbH & Co KG. DEU. Dist: Penguin Random Hse. LLC.

Giuliani, Alfred. Zootopia. Wu, Vivien, illus. 2016. (J). *(978-1-4806-9720-1(6)*, Golden Bks.) Random Hse. Children's Bks.

Giusti, Katiuscia. The Clean-Up Contest. 2014. (AV2 Animated Storytime Ser.: Vol. 29). (ENG., Illus.). 32p. (J). (gr. -1-3). lib. bdg. 29.99 *(978-1-4896-2299-0(3)*, AV2 by Weigl) Weigl Pubs., Inc.

Given, Cate. Cartwheeling. Hill-Peterson, Jodi, illus. 2006. (J). *(978-0-9790057-1-8(X))* Paws in the Sand Publishing.

Glass, Eleri. The Red Shoes. Spires, Ashley, illus. 2017. (ENG.). 40p. (J). (gr. -1-3). 8.99 *(978-1-927018-85-9(4))* Simply Read Bks. CAN. Dist: Ingram Publisher Services.

Gledhill, Carly. Monty & Sylvester a Tale of Everyday Super Heroes. 2019. (Monty & Sylvester Ser.). (ENG., Illus.). 32p. (J). (gr. -1-k). 16.99 *(978-1-4083-5174-1(9)*, Orchard Bks.) Hachette Children's Group GBR. Dist: Hachette Bk. Group.

Gleisner, Jenna Lee. Winter Solstice. 2018. (Welcoming the Seasons Ser.). (ENG.). 24p. (J). (gr. -1-2). lib. bdg. 32.79 *(978-1-5038-2391-4(1)*, 212234) Child's World, Inc, The.

Glencoe Staff. Make Your Mark '83, Level 2. (J). *(978-0-02-131620-5(1))* Macmillan Publishing Co., Inc.

Glori, Debi. Little Owl's Egg. Brown, Alison, illus. (ENG.). 32p. (J). 2018. bds. 7.99 *(978-1-68119-893-4(2)*, 900191670, Bloomsbury Children's Bks.) 2017. 16.99 *(978-1-68119-324-3(8)*, 900170041, Bloomsbury USA Childrens) Bloomsbury Publishing USA.

—The Tobermory Cat. 2013. (Illus.). 32p. (J). (gr. -1-k). pap. 10.95 *(978-1-78027-131-6(X))* Birlinn, Ltd. GBR. Dist: Casemate Pubs. & Bk. Distributors, LLC.

Gobert-Martin, Virginie. Whose Eyes Are These? Peirsman, Madeline, illus. 2017. (ENG.). 64p. (J). (gr. -1-k). 17.95 *(978-1-84976-506-0(5)*, 1306701) Tate Publishing, Ltd. GBR. Dist: Abrams, Inc.

Goetz, Steve. Old MacDonald Had a Boat. Kaban, Eda, illus. 2018. (ENG.). 44p. (J). (gr. -1-k). 16.99 *(978-1-4521-6505-9(X))* Chronicle Bks. LLC.

Goldberg, Leah. Room for Rent. 2017. (ENG., Illus.). 24p. (J). *(978-965-229-920-8(0))* Gefen Publishing Hse., Ltd.

Golden Books. Adventures with Grandpa! (PAW Patrol) Petrossi, Fabrizio, illus. 2018. (Little Golden Book Ser.). (ENG.). 24p. (J). (-k). 4.99 *(978-1-5247-6874-4(X)*, Golden Bks.) Random Hse. Children's Bks.

Goldman, Marcia. Lola Goes to School. 2016. (Lola Ser.). (ENG., Illus.). 32p. (J). (gr. -1-k). 16.95 *(978-1-939547-27-9(X)*, 75f727ac-b1dd-47ad-962f-4980043a392d) Creston Bks.

Goldman Marshall, Lauren. My Beautiful Bow: An Adoption Story. Marschell, Hannah, illus. 2010. 36p. pap. 14.95 *(978-1-60844-395-6(7))* Dog Ear Publishing, LLC.

Gomi, Taro. I Know Numbers! (Counting Books for Kids, Children's Number Books) 2017. (ENG., Illus.). 40p. (J). (gr. -1-k). 15.99 *(978-1-4521-5918-8(1))* Chronicle Bks. LLC.

—I Really Want to See You, Grandma: (Books for Grandparents, Gifts for Grandkids, Taro Gomi Book) 2018. (ENG., Illus.). 40p. (J). (gr. -1-k). 16.99 *(978-1-4521-6158-7(5))* Chronicle Bks. LLC.

—Little Plane: (Transportation Books for Toddlers, Board Book for Toddlers) 2019. (ENG., Illus.). 22p. (J). (gr. -1 — 1). bds. 6.99 *(978-1-4521-7450-1(4))* Chronicle Bks. LLC.

Good Night, Curious George. 2017. (ENG., Illus.). 12p. (J). (— 1). bds. 9.99 *(978-1-328-79591-5(8)*, 1685558, Clarion Bks.) HarperCollins Pubs.

The Good Samaritan. 2014. (Illus.). 24p. (J). *(978-1-84898-934-4(2)*, TickTock Books) Octopus Publishing Group.

Goodhart, Pippa. House that Jack Built. Parker, Andy, illus. 2004. (ENG.). 24p. (J). lib. bdg. 23.65 *(978-1-59646-700-2(2))* Dingles & Co.

—Just Imagine. Sharratt, Nick, illus. 2014. 32p. (J). 12.99 *(978-1-61067-343-3(3))* Kane Miller.

—What Will Danny Do Today? Usher, Sam, illus. 2016. (J). 11.99 *(978-1-61067-512-3(6))* Kane Miller.

Goodreau, Sarah. The World-Famous Book of Counting. Goodreau, Sarah, illus. 2018. (ENG., Illus.). 16p. (J). (gr. -1-2). bds. 18.99 *(978-0-7636-9894-2(6)*, Big Picture Press) Candlewick Pr.

Goodspeed, Judy. Saddle Up. 2007. (Illus.). 24p. (J). (ENG.). 14.99 *(978-0-9794660-7-6(5))*; 24.99 *(978-0-9794660-0-7(8))*; per. 12.99 *(978-0-9794660-1-4(6))* Dragonfly Publishing, Inc.

Gorbachev, V. Big Little Hippo. 2019. (ENG., Illus.). 22p. (J). (— 1). bds. 7.95 *(978-1-4549-3131-7(0))* Sterling Publishing Co., Inc.

Gorbachev, Valeri. Goldilocks & the Three Bears. 2019. (ENG.). 32p. (J). (gr. -1-2). pap. 8.95 *(978-0-7358-4335-6(X))* North-South Bks., Inc.

—Lost & Found Ducklings. 2019. (Illus.). 32p. (J). (-k). 17.99 *(978-0-8234-4107-5(5))* Holiday Hse., Inc.

Gordon, Gordon Coyle. Do Princesses Wear Hiking Boots? 2016. (Do Princesses Ser.). (Illus.). 32p. (J). (gr. -1-1). bds. 7.95 *(978-1-63076-164-6(8))* Taylor Trade Publishing.

Gordon, Lynn & Idle, Molly. Circus Fantastico: A Magnifying Mystery. 2010. (ENG., Illus.). 38p. (J). (gr. k-3). 16.99 *(978-0-7407-9199-4(0))* Andrews McMeel Publishing.

Gorgas, Paula Blais. The Perfect Purple Present. I.t. ed. 2007. (Illus.). 24p. (J). 24.99 *(978-0-9794660-4-5(0))*; per. 12.99 *(978-0-9794660-5-2(9))* Dragonfly Publishing, Inc.

Gottlieb, Suzanne. What Is Red? Bobri, Vladimir, illus. 2016. (ENG.). 24p. (J). 20.00 *(978-1-85124-458-4(1))* Bodleian Library GBR. Dist: Chicago Distribution Ctr.

Gourounas, Jean. Something's Fishy. 2017. (ENG., Illus.). 40p. (J). (gr. -1-1). 16.95 *(978-0-7148-7531-6(7))* Phaidon Pr., Inc.

Gove-Berg, Christie. Greta the Great-Horned Owl: A True Story of Rescue & Rehabilitation. 2019. (Wildlife Rescue Stories Ser.). (ENG., Illus.). 32p. (J). (gr. -1-3). 14.95 *(978-1-59193-815-6(5)*, Adventure Pubns.) AdventureKEEN.

Gozansky, Shana. My Art Book of Love. 2018. (ENG., Illus.). 48p. (gr. -1 — 1). bds. 18.95 *(978-0-7148-7718-1(2))* Phaidon Pr., Inc.

—My Art Book of Sleep. 2019. (ENG., Illus.). 48p. (gr. -1 — 1). bds. 18.95 *(978-0-7148-7865-2(0))* Phaidon Pr., Inc.

Graboff, Abner. There Was an Old Lady. 2018. (Illus.). 48p. 20.00 *(978-1-85124-494-2(8))* Bodleian Library GBR. Dist: Chicago Distribution Ctr.

—What Can Cats Do? Graboff, Abner, illus. 2018. (Illus.). 48p. 20.00 *(978-1-85124-493-5(X))* Bodleian Library GBR. Dist: Chicago Distribution Ctr.

Graham, Alistair. Full Moon Soup. Graham, Alistair, illus. 2003. (Full Moon Soup & Full Moon Afloat Ser.). (Illus.). 32p. (YA). pap. *(978-1-85602-071-8(1)*, Pavilion Children's Books) Pavilion Bks.

Graham, Bob. A Bus Called Heaven. Graham, Bob, illus. 2018. (ENG., Illus.). 40p. (J). (gr. -1-2). 7.99 *(978-1-5362-0294-6(0))* Candlewick Pr.

—The Silver Button. Graham, Bob, illus. 2013. (ENG., Illus.). 32p. (J). (gr. -1-1). 16.99 *(978-0-7636-6437-4(5))* Candlewick Pr.

—The Silver Button. Graham, Bob, illus. 2018. (ENG., Illus.). 32p. (J). (gr. -1-1). 7.99 *(978-1-5362-0144-4(8))* Candlewick Pr.

Graham, Cenesha. I Want to Help. 2011. 24p. pap. 14.56 *(978-1-4634-1803-8(5))* AuthorHouse.

Graham, Elspeth. Sandwich that Jack Made. Mould, Chris, illus. 2004. (ENG.). 24p. (J). lib. bdg. 23.65 *(978-1-59646-698-2(7))* Dingles & Co.

Graham, Ian. Flying Machines. Biesty, Stephen, illus. 2018. (Inside Vehicles Ser.). (ENG.). 16p. (J). (gr. k-3). 17.99 *(978-1-5362-0281-6(9)*, Templar) Candlewick Pr.

Graham, Judith A. The Didley-Doo's Go on an Adventure, 1 vol. 2009. 33p. pap. 24.95 *(978-1-60749-897-1(9))* America Star Bks.

Graham, Mark. Hello, I Am Fiona from Scotland. Sofilas, Mark, illus. 2014. (AV2 Fiction Readalong Ser.: Vol. 128). (ENG.). 32p. (J). (gr. -1-3). lib. bdg. 34.28 *(978-1-4896-2253-2(5)*, AV2 by Weigl) Weigl Pubs., Inc.

Graham, Oakley. Tiny Town What Did Busy Bunny Hear? Ribbon, Lemon, illus. 2018. (Tiny Town Touch & Trace Ser.). (ENG.). 10p. (J). (— 1). bds. 7.99 *(978-1-78700-378-1(7))* Top That! Publishing PLC GBR. Dist: Independent Pubs. Group.

Graham, Richard. The Cranky Caterpillar. 2017. (Illus.). 32p. (J). (gr. -1-4). 16.95 *(978-0-500-65108-7(6)*, 565108) Thames & Hudson.

Grahame, Kenneth & Williams, Nicholas. An Gwyns I'n Helyk. Shepard, Ernest H., illus. 2013. (COR.). 202p. pap. *(978-1-78201-029-6(7))* Evertype.

Grambling, Lois G. Can I Bring Woolly to the Library, Ms. Reeder? Love, Judy, illus. 2012. (Prehistoric Pets Ser.: 2). 32p. (J). (gr. k-3). pap. 7.95 *(978-1-58089-282-7(5))* Charlesbridge Publishing, Inc.

Grange, Emma. DK Braille: LEGO DUPLO: Farm. 2018. (DK Braille Bks.). (ENG.). 18p. (J). (-k). bds. 15.99 *(978-1-4654-6855-0(2)*, DK Children) Dorling Kindersley Publishing, Inc.

Grant, Carolyn E. Maggie's Neighborhood. 2009. 24p. pap. 11.99 *(978-1-4389-7230-5(X))* AuthorHouse.

Grant, Carrie and David. Elephant's Birthday Bells: Jump up & Join In. Busby, Ailie, illus. 2013. 32p. (J). pap. 7.99 *(978-1-61067-181-1(3))* Kane Miller.

—Lion's Speedy Sauce: Jump up & Join In. Busby, Ailie, illus. 2013. 32p. (J). pap. 7.99 *(978-1-61067-180-4(5))* Kane Miller.

Graphics, Section, illus. My Body: Explained & Illustrated. 2015. (ENG.). 48p. (J). (gr. 3-7). 24.95 *(978-3-89955-712-1(3))* Die Gestalten Verlag DEU. Dist: Ingram Publisher Services.

Gravett, Emily. Dogs. Gravett, Emily, illus. 2010. (ENG., Illus.). 32p. (J). (gr. -1-3). 19.99 *(978-1-4169-8703-1(7)*, Simon & Schuster Bks. For Young Readers) Simon & Schuster Bks. For Young Readers.

—Old Hat. Gravett, Emily, illus. 2018. (ENG., Illus.). 32p. (J). (gr. -1-3). 17.99 *(978-1-5344-0917-0(3)*, Simon & Schuster Bks. For Young Readers) Simon & Schuster Bks. For Young Readers.

Gray, Kes. Daisy: Really, Really. Sharratt, Nick, illus. 2016. (Daisy Picture Bks.: 2). 32p. (J). (gr. -1-k). pap. 11.99 *(978-1-78295-646-4(8)*, Red Fox) Random House Children's Books GBR. Dist: Independent Pubs. Group.

—Daisy: Tiger Ways. Sharratt, Nick, illus. 2016. (Daisy Picture Bks.: 6). 32p. (J). (gr. -1-k). pap. 11.99 *(978-1-78295-649-5(2)*, Red Fox) Random House Children's Books GBR. Dist: Independent Pubs. Group.

—Nuddy Ned. Parsons, Garry, illus. 2013. (ENG.). 32p. (J). (gr. -1-k). *(978-1-4088-3659-0(9)*, 161263, Bloomsbury Children's Bks.) Bloomsbury Publishing Plc.

—Oi Cat! Field, Jim, illus. 2019. (Oi Frog & Friends Ser.). (ENG.). 32p. (J). (gr. -1-k). 16.99 *(978-1-4449-3251-5(9))*; pap. 9.99 *(978-1-4449-3252-2(7))* Hachette Children's Group GBR. Dist: Hachette Bk. Group.

—Quick Quack Quentin. 2017. (ENG., Illus.). 32p. (J). (gr. -1-k). pap. 7.99 *(978-1-4449-1957-8(1))* Hachette Children's Group GBR. Dist: Hachette Bk. Group.

Gray, Libba Moore. Is There Room on the Feather Bed? 2004. (Illus.). (J). (gr. -1-2). spiral bd. *(978-0-616-03037-0(1))*; spiral bd. *(978-0-616-04555-8(7))* Canadian National Institute for the Blind/Institut National Canadien pour les Aveugles.

Gray Smith, Monique. My Heart Fills with Happiness, 1 vol. Flett, Julie, illus. 2016. (ENG.). 24p. (J). (gr. -1 — 1). bds. 12.95 *(978-1-4598-0957-4(2))* Orca Bk. Pubs. USA.

Greanias, Margaret Chiu. Maximillian Villainous. 2018. (ENG., Illus.). 40p. (J). (gr. -1-3). 16.99 *(978-0-7624-6297-1(3)*, Running Pr. Kids) Running Pr.

Gréban, Quentin. Woolly & Me, 1 vol. 2018. (ENG., Illus.). 32p. (J). (gr. -1-2). 16.95 *(978-0-88448-636-7(2)*, 884636) Tilbury Hse. Pubs.

Greder, Armin. The Mediterranean. 2018. (ENG., Illus.). 40p. (J). (gr. 3). 25.99 *(978-1-76063-095-9(0))* Allen & Unwin AUS. Dist: Independent Pubs. Group.

Green, Alison. The Fox in the Dark. Allwright, Deborah, illus. 2012. (ENG.). 32p. (J). (gr. -1-1). pap. 7.95 *(978-1-58925-437-4(6))* Tiger Tales.

Green, Jen. Big Fantastic Earth. 2016. (Illus.). 96p. (J). *(978-1-5182-1730-2(3))* Dorling Kindersley Publishing, Inc.

Green, Katie May. Seen & Not Heard. Green, Katie May, illus. 2015. (ENG., Illus.). 32p. (J). (gr. k-3). 15.99 *(978-0-7636-7612-4(8))* Candlewick Pr.

Green, Rebecca. How to Make Friends with a Ghost. 2017. (ENG., Illus.). 40p. (J). (gr. -1-3). 17.99 *(978-1-101-91901-9(9)*, Tundra Bks.) Tundra Bks. CAN. Dist: Penguin Random Hse. LLC.

Green, Ruth. Hedgehog Holidays. 2017. (ENG., Illus.). 32p. (J). (gr. k-3). 14.95 *(978-1-84976-484-1(0)*, 1306901) Tate Publishing, Ltd. GBR. Dist: Abrams, Inc.

Green, Ruth, illus. Stanley's Plan: The Birthday Surprise. 2015. (ENG.). 32p. (J). (gr. -1-3). 16.95 *(978-1-84976-305-9(4)*, 1637401) Tate Publishing, Ltd. GBR. Dist: Hachette Bk. Group.

Green, Sylvia. We're Hungry Too. Lorenzo, David & Lorenzo, David, illus. 2018. (ENG.). 32p. (J). pap. 12.99 *(978-0-281-07672-7(3)*, cfe04710-86c8-431b-8aba-e9564691aec3) SPCK Publishing GBR. Dist: Baker & Taylor Publisher Services (BTPS).

Greenberg, Carmel. Who Stole Pop Pop's Underwear? Jennings, Randy, illus. 2009. (ENG.). 46p. 16.99 *(978-0-615-20924-1(6)*, d1f87490-1e8c-4369-845e-33a85fc9fd96) Kicks and Giggles Today.

Greenberg, David E. The Ugly Brown Pear. 2010. 40p. pap. 12.96 *(978-0-557-28055-1(9))* Lulu Pr., Inc.

Greenberg, Nicki. Meerkat Choir. 2018. (ENG., Illus.). 32p. (J). (gr. -1-2). 17.99 *(978-1-76029-079-5(3))* Allen & Unwin AUS. Dist: Independent Pubs. Group.

—The Naughtiest Reindeer. 2014. (Naughtiest Reindeer Ser.). (ENG., Illus.). 32p. (J). (gr. -1-k). 15.99 *(978-1-74331-304-6(7))* Allen & Unwin AUS. Dist: Independent Pubs. Group.

Greenleaf, E. Who Wants to Nap? (Illus.). 32p. (J). (gr. 2-3). lib. bdg. 9.95 *(978-0-87783-050-4(9))* Oddo Publishing, Inc.

Gregorich, Barbara. The Big Race, Level 2. Hoffman, Joan, ed. 2nd ed. 2011. (ENG., Illus.). 16p. (J). (gr. -1-2). pap. 3.49 *(978-0-88743-018-3(X)*, a1a1ad43-3963-4c63-aa32-0d21b873d6d0) School Zone Publishing Co.

Gregson, Tyler Knott & Linden, Sarah. North Pole Ninjas: MISSION: Christmas! Thibodeau, Piper, illus. 2018. 32p. (J). (gr. -1-2). 10.99 *(978-1-5247-9079-0(6)*, Penguin Workshop) Penguin Young Readers Group.

Greig, Louise. The Island & the Bear, 50 vols. Nastanlieva, Vanya, illus. 2017. 24p. (J). 11.95 *(978-1-78250-368-2(4)*, Kelpies) Floris Bks. GBR. Dist: Consortium Bk. Sales & Distribution.

—The Night Box. Lindsay, Ashling, illus. 2018. (ENG.). 32p. (J). (gr. -1-3). 20.99 *(978-1-328-85093-5(5)*, 1693450, Clarion Bks.) HarperCollins Pubs.

Gresham, Xanthe. The Princess & the Pea. Clara, Miss, illus. 2013. 40p. (J). 17.99 *(978-1-84686-905-1(6))* Barefoot Bks., Inc.

Grey, Mini. Traction Man Is Here! 2012. lib. bdg. 18.40 *(978-0-606-26385-6(3))* Turtleback.

Griffith, Linda, illus. The Best Ever Ring Bearer: All the Best Things about Being in a Wedding. 2010. (ENG.). 24p. 10.99 *(978-1-4022-3818-5(5))* Sourcebooks, Inc.

—The Most Special Flower Girl: All the Best Things about Being in a Wedding. 2010. (ENG.). 24p. 10.99 *(978-1-4022-3817-8(7))* Sourcebooks, Inc.

Grill, William. Shackleton's Journey. 2014. (ENG., Illus.). 80p. (J). (gr. 2-2). 19.99 *(978-1-909263-10-9(9))* Flying Eye Bks. GBR. Dist: Penguin Random Hse. LLC.

Grillo, Trine. I'm Not Afraid of That. 2011. (Illus.). 44p. (J). pap. 18.99 *(978-1-59092-761-8(3))* Blue Forge Pr.

Grimard, Gabrielle. Lila & the Crow. 2018. (Illus.). 32p. (J). (gr. 1-4). pap. 9.95 *(978-1-55451-857-9(1))* Annick Pr., Ltd. CAN. Dist: Publishers Group West (PGW).

Grimm, Brothers. Little Red Riding Hood. Watts, Bernadette, illus. 2018. (ENG.). 32p. (J). (gr. -1-3). 17.95 *(978-0-7358-4303-5(1))* North-South Bks., Inc.

—Sleeping Beauty. Dusíková, Maja, illus. 2012. (ENG.). 32p. (J). (gr. -1-3). 17.95 *(978-0-7358-4087-4(3))* North-South Bks., Inc.

—Snow White: The Classic Edition. 2019. (Charles Santore Children's Classics Ser.). (ENG., Illus.). 64p. (J). 19.95 *(978-1-60433-853-9(9)*, Applesauce Pr.) Cider Mill Pr. Bk. Pubs., LLC.

Grimm, Jacob & Grimm, Wilhelm. Little Red Riding Hood. 2014. (ENG., Illus.). 28p. (J). (gr. -1-3). 16.95 *(978-3-89955-723-7(9))* Die Gestalten Verlag DEU. Dist: Ingram Publisher Services.

Grimm, Jacob and Wilhelm. The Magical Wishing Fish: The Classic Grimm's Tale of the Fisherman & His Wife, 30 vols. Koopmans, Loek, illus. 2018. Orig. Title: Het Wensvisje. 24p. (J). 16.95 *(978-1-78250-524-2(5))* Floris Bks. GBR. Dist: Consortium Bk. Sales & Distribution.

Grimm, Jeanette. Living with Grandma & Grandpa. 2010. 24p. pap. 15.99 *(978-1-4535-5573-6(0))* Xlibris Corp.

Grosset & Dunlap. Wheels on the Bus. Smath, Jerry, illus. 2016. (Pudgy Board Bks.). 18p. (J). (— 1). bds. 5.99 *(978-0-451-53270-1(8)*, Grosset & Dunlap) Penguin Young Readers Group.

Groves, Julia, illus. Animal Babies in the Forest! 2016. (Animal Babies Ser.: 4). 14p. (J). spiral bd. *(978-1-84643-878-3(0))* Child's Play International Ltd.

—Rainforest. 2018. (Child's Play Library). 36p. (J). (ENG.). *(978-1-84643-936-0(1))*; pap. *(978-1-84643-935-3(3))* Child's Play International Ltd.

Gruelle, Deb. Ten Little Night Stars, 1 vol. Murphy, Gabi, illus. 2018. (ENG.). 22p. (J). bds. 9.99 *(978-0-310-76212-6(X))* Zonderkidz.

Gruener, Nina. Kiki & Coco in Paris. 2011. (ENG., Illus.). 32p. (J). (gr. -1-3). 18.95 *(978-0-918684-50-9(1)*, 1331701) Abrams, Inc.

Guarnaccia, Steven. Cinderella: A Fashionable Tale. 2013. (ENG., Illus.). 32p. (J). (gr. -1-3). 19.95 *(978-1-4197-0986-9(0)*, 1068901, Abrams Bks. for Young Readers) Abrams, Inc.

Guendelsberger, Erin. Inky the Octopus: Bound for Glory. Leonard, David, illus. 2018. 32p. (J). (gr. k-6). 17.99 *(978-1-4926-5414-8(0))* Sourcebooks, Inc.

Guerras, Safia. Lou Lou. 2012. (Illus.). 40p. *(978-1-78132-021-1(7))*; pap. *(978-1-78132-019-8(5))* SilverWood Bks.

Guess Who? Christmas: A Flip-The-Flap Book. 2014. (ENG., Illus.). 6p. (J). (— 1). bds. 9.99 *(978-0-7459-6408-9(7)*, 6d672ab0-8922-4179-915d-ddd3f66f0cfd, Lion Children's) Lion Hudson PLC GBR. Dist: Baker & Taylor Publisher Services (BTPS).

Guettier, Bénédicte. At the Circus. 2011. (Funny Faces Ser.). (Illus.). 14p. bds. *(978-1-84089-678-7(7))* Zero to Ten, Ltd.

—Dinosaur Dinners. 2011. (Funny Faces Ser.). (Illus.). 14p. bds. *(978-1-84089-677-0(9))* Zero to Ten, Ltd.

Gugler, Laurel Dee. There's a Billy Goat in the Garden. Beaton, Clare, illus. 2003. (ENG.). 32p. (J). (gr. -1-2). 14.99 *(978-1-84148-089-3(4))* Barefoot Bks., Inc.

Guile, Gill, illus. Bear Picks a Pumpkin, 1 vol. 2018. (ENG.). 24p. (J). bds. 8.99 *(978-0-310-76621-6(4))* Zonderkidz.

Gunzi, Christiane. Colours. 2nd rev. ed. 2015. (ENG., Illus.). 34p. (J). bds. 7.99 *(978-1-906572-20-4(8))* Award Pubns. Ltd. GBR. Dist: Parkwest Pubns., Inc.

—Farm. 2nd rev. ed. 2015. (ENG., Illus.). 34p. (J). bds. 7.95 *(978-1-906572-28-0(3))* Award Pubns. Ltd. GBR. Dist: Parkwest Pubns., Inc.

—My Early Learning Library: Pets. 2nd rev. ed. 2015. (ENG., Illus.). 34p. (J). bds. 7.99 *(978-1-906572-13-6(5))* Award Pubns. Ltd. GBR. Dist: Parkwest Pubns., Inc.

—My Favourite Things. 2013. (Illus.). 6p. (J). bds. 7.95 *(978-1-907604-37-9(5))* Award Pubns. Ltd. GBR. Dist: Parkwest Pubns., Inc.

—My Lovely Day. 2013. (Illus.). 6p. (J). bds. 7.95 *(978-1-907604-36-2(7))* Award Pubns. Ltd. GBR. Dist: Parkwest Pubns., Inc.

—Opposites. Murrell, Deborah, ed. 2nd rev. ed. 2015. (ENG., Illus.). 34p. (J). bds. 7.99 *(978-1-906572-21-1(6))* Award Pubns. Ltd. GBR. Dist: Parkwest Pubns., Inc.

—Zoo. Zwemmer, Dominic, ed. 2015. (ENG., Illus.). 34p. (J). bds. 7.95 *(978-1-906572-30-3(5))* Award Pubns. Ltd. GBR. Dist: Parkwest Pubns., Inc.

—1 2 3. 2015. (Illus.). 34p. (J). bds. 7.99 *(978-1-906572-18-1(6))* Award Pubns. Ltd. GBR. Dist: Parkwest Pubns., Inc.

Gunzi, Christiane & Picthall, Chez. My Early Learning Library: My Body. Murrell, Deborah, ed. 2015. (ENG., Illus.). 34p. (J). bds. 7.99 *(978-1-906572-22-8(4))* Award Pubns. Ltd. GBR. Dist: Parkwest Pubns., Inc.

Gunzi, Christiane. Colours. 2015. (Illus.). 6p. (J). bds. 7.99 *(978-1-907604-95-9(2))* Award Pubns. Ltd. GBR. Dist: Parkwest Pubns., Inc.

—Little Ponies: A Feels Real Book to Touch & Share. 2015. (ENG., Illus.). 8p. (J). bds. 9.99 *(978-1-909763-10-4(1))* Award Pubns. Ltd. GBR. Dist: Parkwest Pubns., Inc.

—Numbers. 2015. (Illus.). 6p. (J). bds. 7.99 *(978-1-907604-94-2(4))* Award Pubns. Ltd. GBR. Dist: Parkwest Pubns., Inc.

—On the Farm. 2015. (ENG., Illus.). 8p. (J). bds. 9.99 *(978-1-909763-09-8(8))* Award Pubns. Ltd. GBR. Dist: Parkwest Pubns., Inc.

Gunzi, Christiane & Award, Anna. Cuddly Puppies. 2017. (ENG., Illus.). 8p. (J). bds. 9.00 *(978-1-909763-07-4(1))* Award Pubns. Ltd. GBR. Dist: Parkwest Pubns., Inc.

—Furry Kittens. 2017. (ENG., Illus.). 8p. (J). bds. 9.00 *(978-1-909763-08-1(X))* Award Pubns. Ltd. GBR. Dist: Parkwest Pubns., Inc.

Guridi. Once upon a Time. 2018. (ENG., Illus.). 32p. (J). (gr. -1-3). 17.95 *(978-1-84976-513-8(8)*, 1314101) Tate Publishing, Ltd. GBR. Dist: Abrams, Inc.

Gurney, Stella. Not so Silly Sausage. Million, Liz, illus. 2011. 32p. pap. *(978-1-84089-707-4(4))* Zero to Ten, Ltd.

Gürth, Per-Henrik & Gürth, Per-Henrik. Snowy Sports: Ready, Set, Play! Gürth, Per-Henrik & Gürth, Per-Henrik, illus. 2009. (ENG., Illus.). 24p. (J). (gr. -1-2). 14.95 *(978-1-55337-367-4(7))* Kids Can Pr., Ltd. CAN. Dist: Hachette Bk. Group.

P Q R

Guthrie, Woody. Enviarme a Ti, Level 2. Flor Ada, Alma, tr. Rosenberry, Vera, illus. 2003. (Dejame Leer Ser.). (SPA.). 8p. (J). (gr. -1-1). 6.50 *(978-0-673-36301-5(5)*, Good Year Bks.) Celebration Pr.

Gutman, Dan. Teamwork Trouble. Paillot, Jim, illus. 2018. 30p. (J). *(978-1-5444-0102-7(7))* Harper & Row Ltd.

Guttiere, Benedicte. When Christmas Comes. 2011. (Funny Faces Ser.). (Illus.). 14p. bds. *(978-1-84089-710-4(4))* Zero to Ten, Ltd.

Gyatso, Geshe Kelsang. What Is Buddhism? Buddhism for Children Level 3. 2013. (ENG., Illus.). 32p. (J). (gr. 4-6). 8.95 *(978-1-61606-023-7(9)*, 50ad0759-95f6-4d1a-a729-106832827ba7) Tharpa Pubns. USA.

Hagin, Karen. Jeremy, the Giraffe Who Was Afraid of Heights. 2005. (J). lib. bdg. 19.95 *(978-0-9754728-8-0(7))* Big Ransom Studio.

Hahm, Ji-seul. Prokofiev's Peter & the Wolf. Lupton, David, illus. 2016. (Music Storybooks Ser.). (ENG.). 44p. (J). (gr. 3-5). 29.32 *(978-1-925247-39-8(2)*, f25f94ec-ce49-43d6-8868-fb807d406b1b, Big and SMALL) ChoiceMaker Pty. Ltd., The AUS. Dist: Lerner Publishing Group.

Hailes, Ronald. The Pink Rabbit. 2009. 24p. pap. 10.96 *(978-1-4269-1456-0(3))* Trafford Publishing.

Hale, Bruce & Hoff, Syd. Syd Hoff's Danny & the Dinosaur & the New Puppy. Cutting, David, illus. 2015. 32p. (J). *(978-1-4806-8576-5(3))* Harper & Row Ltd.

Hale, Christy. Water Land: Land & Water Forms Around the World. Hale, Christy, illus. 2018. (ENG., Illus.). 32p. (J). 21.99 *(978-1-250-15244-2(5)*, 900183618) Roaring Brook Pr.

Hale, Shannon & Hale, Dean. The Princess in Black Takes a Vacation. Pham, LeUyen, illus. 2016. 87p. (J). *(978-1-5182-4386-8(X))* Candlewick Pr.

Hall, Hannah C. God Made the World. 2019. (Buck Denver Asks... What's in the Bible? Ser.). (ENG., Illus.). 24p. (J). (gr. -1 — 1). bds. 8.99 *(978-1-5460-1197-2(8)*, Jelly Telly Pr.) FaithWords.

Hallowell, George & Holub, Joan. Wagons Ho! Avril, Lynne, illus. 2014. (AV2 Fiction Readalong Ser.: Vol. 153). (ENG.). 32p. (J). (gr. -1-3). lib. bdg. 34.28 *(978-1-4896-2389-8(2)*, AV2 by Weigl) Weigl Pubs., Inc.

—Wagons Ho! Then & Now on the Oregon Trail. Avril, Lynne, illus. 2019. (ENG.). 32p. (J). (gr. -1-3). pap. 7.99 *(978-0-8075-8613-6(7)*, 807586137) Whitman, Albert & Co.

Halsey, Jacqueline & Muller, Carrie. The Terrible, Horrible, Smelly Pirate, 1 vol. Orchard, Eric, illus. 2008. (ENG.). 32p. (J). (gr. -1-k). pap. 11.95 *(978-1-55109-655-1(2)*, bf2280e6-ca5d-4964-be00-1c8b95c6a4ac) Nimbus Publishing, Ltd. CAN. Dist: Baker & Taylor Publisher Services (BTPS).

Hamernik, Cathy. What Do You See? 2008. 24p. pap. 16.50 *(978-1-60693-388-6(4)*, Strategic Bk. Publishing) Strategic Book Publishing & Rights Agency (SBPRA).

Hamilton, Benny. The Goat in the Coat. 2010. 36p. (J). pap. 21.95 *(978-1-4327-4884-5(X))* Outskirts Pr., Inc.

Hamilton, Kersten. Blue Boat. Petrone, Valeria, illus. 2016. (Red Truck & Friends Ser.). (ENG.). 30p. (J). (— 1). bds. 8.99 *(978-1-101-99853-3(9)*, Viking Books for Young Readers) Penguin Young Readers Group.

—Red Truck. Petrone, Valeria, illus. 2012. (Red Truck & Friends Ser.). 26p. (J). (gr. -1 — 1). bds. 8.99 *(978-0-670-01467-5(2)*, Viking Books for Young Readers) Penguin Young Readers Group.

—Yellow Copter. Petrone, Valeria, illus. 2016. (Red Truck & Friends Ser.). 26p. (J). (— 1). bds. 8.99 *(978-1-101-99796-3(6)*, Viking Books for Young Readers) Penguin Young Readers Group.

Hamilton, Virginia. The People Could Fly: The Picture Book. 2015. lib. bdg. 18.40 *(978-0-606-36377-8(7))* Turtleback.

—The People Could Fly: the Picture Book. Dillon, Leo & Dillon, Diane, illus. 32p. (J). (gr. -1-3). 2015. 7.99 *(978-0-553-50780-5(X)*, Dragonfly Bks.) 2004. 18.99 *(978-0-375-82405-0(7)*, Knopf Bks. for Young Readers) Random Hse. Children's Bks.

Hampson, Sarah. Dr. Coo & the Pigeon Protest. Reich, Kass, illus. 2018. (ENG.). 32p. (J). (gr. -1-2). 19.99 *(978-1-77138-361-5(5))* Kids Can Pr., Ltd. CAN. Dist: Hachette Bk. Group.

Hancocks, Helen. Penguin in Peril. Hancocks, Helen, illus. 2014. (ENG., Illus.). 32p. (J). (gr. -1-2). 18.99 *(978-0-7636-7159-4(2)*, Templar) Candlewick Pr.

Hannaford, Robert & Starke, Ruth. My Gallipoli. 2019. (Illus.). 48p. 17.99 *(978-1-921504-76-1(5)*, Working Title Pr.) HarperCollins Pubs. Australia AUS. Dist: HarperCollins Pubs.

Hannah, Vickie. There's A Schnoozle in My Closet. 2004. (J). lib. bdg. 19.95 *(978-0-9754728-4-2(4))* Big Ransom Studio.

Hansen, Grace. Little Activists, 6 vols., Set. 2018. (Little Activists: Endangered Species Ser.). (ENG.). 24p. (J). (gr. -1-2). lib. bdg. 196.74 *(978-1-5321-8197-9(3)*, 29853, Abdo Kids) ABDO Publishing Co.

Hansen, Nichole. Kids Count. Hansen, Tevin, illus. 2015. 44p. (J). pap. 9.49 *(978-1-941429-18-1(1))* Handersen Publishing.

Hansen, Tevin & Hansen, Nichole. The Thumb Book. Hansen, Tevin, illus. 2015. (ENG., Illus.). 48p. pap. 9.99 *(978-1-941429-21-1(1))* Handersen Publishing.

Hanson, Jean. The 5,000 Friends of Veronica Veetch. Parry, Launie, illus. 2017. (ENG.). 32p. (J). 17.95 *(978-1-934649-27-5(9))* Bailiwick Pr.

Harcourt School Publishers Staff. Horizons Big Book Collection. 2nd ed. 2003. (Illus.). (gr. 1). pap. 840.00 *(978-0-15-337573-6(6))*; (gr. 2). pap. 840.00 *(978-0-15-337581-1(7))* Harcourt Schl. Pubs.

—Horizons Big Book Collection Unit 1. 2nd ed. 2003. (Illus.). pap. 140.00 *(978-0-15-337574-3(4))*; pap. 140.00 *(978-0-15-337812-6(3))* Harcourt Schl. Pubs.

—Horizons Big Book Collection Unit 2. 2nd ed. 2003. (Illus.). pap. 140.00 *(978-0-15-337575-0(2))*; pap. 140.00 *(978-0-15-337813-3(1))* Harcourt Schl. Pubs.

—Horizons Big Book Collection Unit 3. 2nd ed. 2003. (Illus.). pap. 140.00 *(978-0-15-337577-4(9))*; pap. 140.00 *(978-0-15-337814-0(X))* Harcourt Schl. Pubs.

—Horizons Big Book Collection Unit 4. 2nd ed. 2003. (Illus.). pap. 140.00 *(978-0-15-337578-1(7))*; pap. 140.00 *(978-0-15-337815-7(8))* Harcourt Schl. Pubs.

—Horizons Big Book Collection Unit 5. 2nd ed. 2003. (Illus.). pap. 140.00 *(978-0-15-337579-8(5))*; (J). pap. 140.00 *(978-0-15-337816-4(6))* Harcourt Schl. Pubs.

—Horizons Big Book Collection Unit 6. 2nd ed. 2003. (Illus.). pap. 140.00 *(978-0-15-337580-4(9))*; pap. 140.00 *(978-0-15-337817-1(4))* Harcourt Schl. Pubs.

Hargreaves, Adam. Mr. Mischief & the Leprechaun. 2016. (Mr. Men & Little Miss Ser.). (ENG., Illus.). 32p. (J). (-k). pap. 4.99 *(978-0-8431-8376-4(4)*, Grosset & Dunlap) Penguin Young Readers Group.

Harman, Jax & Buckley, Jacs. A Big Fat Naughty Cat. 2016. (ENG.). 22p. (J). pap. 14.95 *(978-1-78612-470-8(X)*, 9d2d8474-82af-4f4e-8c26-805ae4e1bd20) Austin Macauley Pubs. Ltd. GBR. Dist: Baker & Taylor Publisher Services (BTPS).

Harper, Charise Mericle. Cupcake. Harper, Charise Mericle, illus. 2010. (ENG., Illus.). 32p. (J). (gr. -1-3). 14.99 *(978-1-4231-1897-8(9))* Hyperion Pr.

—Go! Go! Go! Stop! 2015. (ENG.). 32p. (J). (-k). bds. 7.99 *(978-0-553-53391-0(6)*, Knopf Bks. for Young Readers) Random Hse. Children's Bks.

Harper, Jamie. Miss Mingo Weathers the Storm. Harper, Jamie, illus. (Miss Mingo Ser.). (ENG., Illus.). 40p. (J). (gr. -1-3). 2017. 6.99 *(978-0-7636-9514-9(9))* 2012. 15.99 *(978-0-7636-4931-9(7))* Candlewick Pr.

HarperCollins Treasury of Picture Book Classics: A Child's First Collection. 2015. (ENG., Illus.). 464p. (J). (gr. -1-3). 35.00 *(978-0-06-242725-0(3)*, HarperCollins) HarperCollins Pubs.

Harriman, Marinell & Harriman, Robert. A Myriad of Minstrels. Harriman, Marinell & Harriman, Robert, illus. (Illus.). 32p. (Orig.). (J). (gr. 5-7). pap. 3.50 *(978-0-940920-00-2(X))* Drollery Pr.

Harris, Amber. Bingo Did It! Hoyt, Ard, illus. 2016. (Wisteria Jane Book Ser.). (ENG.). 32p. (J). (gr. -1-3). 16.95 *(978-1-60554-491-5(4))* Redleaf Pr.

Harris, Joel Chandler. Brer Rabbit & the Great Race. Smith, Lesley, illus. 2014. (ENG.). 24p. (J). pap. 6.95 *(978-1-84135-963-2(7))* Award Pubns. Ltd. GBR. Dist: Parkwest Pubns., Inc.

Harris, Robie H. Who?: a Celebration of Babies: A Celebration of Babies. Rosenberg, Natascha, illus. 2018. (ENG.). 20p. (J). (gr. -1 — 1). bds. 8.99 *(978-1-4197-2834-1(2)*, 1206110, Abrams Appleseed) Abrams, Inc.

Harrison, Paul. Billy on the Ball. Raga, Silvia, illus. 2010. 32p. pap. *(978-1-84089-634-3(5))* Zero to Ten, Ltd.

—Collins Big Cat Phonics for Letters & Sounds - It Is Hidden: Band 02B/Red B, Bd. 2B. 2018. (Collins Big Cat Phonics Ser.). (ENG., Illus.). 16p. (J). (gr. -1-k). pap. 7.99 *(978-0-00-825151-2(7))* HarperCollins Pubs. Ltd. GBR. Dist: Independent Pubs. Group.

—Collins Big Cat Phonics for Letters & Sounds - This Is My Kit: Band 02A/Red A, Bd. 2A. 2018. (Collins Big Cat Phonics Ser.). (ENG., Illus.). 16p. (J). (gr. -1-k). pap. 6.99 *(978-0-00-825146-8(0))* HarperCollins Pubs. Ltd. GBR. Dist: Independent Pubs. Group.

—Elephant Rides Again, 1 vol. Million, Liz, illus. 2009. (Get Ready Readers Ser.). (ENG.). 32p. (J). (gr. k-k). lib. bdg. 27.27 *(978-1-60754-259-9(5)*, 01ae3f53-b298-4352-a940-1e6a5639308b, Windmill Bks.) Rosen Publishing Group, Inc., The.

—Undersea Adventure. Nascimbeni, Barbara, illus. 2011. 32p. pap. *(978-1-84089-638-1(8))* Zero to Ten, Ltd.

Harrisson, Christopher. Make Buildings. Farmer, Charlotte, illus. 2016. (ENG.). 112p. (J). pap. 11.99 *(978-1-61067-410-2(3))* Kane Miller.

Hart, Caryl. Catch That Rat. McLaughlin, Tom, illus. 2013. (ENG.). 32p. (J). pap. 8.99 *(978-1-84738-931-2(7)*, Simon & Schuster Children's) Simon & Schuster, Ltd. GBR. Dist: Simon & Schuster, Inc.

—How to Catch a Dragon. Eaves, Ed, illus. 2014. (ENG.). 32p. pap. 8.99 *(978-0-85707-959-6(X)*, Simon & Schuster Children's) Simon & Schuster, Ltd. GBR. Dist: Simon & Schuster, Inc.

—How to Save a Superhero. Eaves, Ed, illus. 2018. (ENG.). 32p. (J). (gr. -1). 7.99 *(978-1-4711-4478-3(X)*, Simon & Schuster Children's) Simon & Schuster, Ltd. GBR. Dist: Simon & Schuster, Inc.

—Let's Go to the Farm! Tobia, Lauren, illus. 2018. (ENG.). 32p. (J). 11.99 *(978-1-61067-630-4(0))* Kane Miller.

—The Princess & the Presents. Warburton, Sarah, illus. 2014. (ENG.). 32p. (J). (gr. -1-2). 16.99 *(978-0-7636-7398-7(6))* Candlewick Pr.

—Whiffy Wilson. 2012. (ENG., Illus.). 32p. (J). (gr. -1-k). pap. 9.99 *(978-1-4083-0919-3(X)*, Orchard Bks.) Hachette Children's Group GBR. Dist: Hachette Bk. Group.

Hartmann, Annabelle. As Big As a Mountain. 2003. (ENG., Illus.). 32p. (YA). *(978-1-84365-001-0(0)*, Pavilion Children's Books) Pavilion Bks.

Harvey, Damian. Mr. Fox's Socks. Rescek, Sanja, illus. 2004. (ENG.). 16p. (J). lib. bdg. 23.65 *(978-1-59646-678-4(2))* Dingles & Co.

Harvey-Zahra, Lou. Through the Rainbow: A Waldorf Birthday Story for Children, 30 vols. Parrilli, Sara, illus. 2018. 32p. (J). 19.95 *(978-1-78250-507-5(5))* Floris Bks. GBR. Dist: Consortium Bk. Sales & Distribution.

Harwood, Beth. One Snowy Night. Ronchi, Susanna, illus. 2005. 12p. (J). *(978-1-84011-627-4(7))* Templar Publishing.

Haskamp, Steven, illus. Five Silly Monkeys. 2006. (ENG.). 12p. (J). (gr. -1-k). 12.95 *(978-1-58117-460-1(8)*, Intervisual/Piggy Toes) Bendon, Inc.

Hastings, Derek. Penguins - Pb: A Portrait of the Animal World. 2013. (Portrait of the Animal World Ser.). (Illus.). 72p. pap. 9.95 *(978-1-59764-325-2(4))* New Line Bks.

Hatkoff, Craig, et al. Winter's Tail: How One Little Dolphin Learned to Swim Again: How One Little Dolphin Learned to Swim Again. 2011. (ENG.). 40p. (J). (gr. -1-5). pap. 7.99 *(978-0-545-34830-0(7)*, Scholastic Paperbacks) Scholastic, Inc.

Haugen, Matt & Haugen, Marty. I Wanna Be a Dinosaur! Mirocha, Stephanie, illus. 2015. (ENG.). 32p. (J). (— 1). 16.95 *(978-1-57999-999-5(9))* G I A Pubns., Inc.

Haughom, Lisa, illus. People, Places & Things. 2010. (J). *(978-1-58865-541-7(5))* Kidsbooks, LLC.

Hawes, Alison. Collins Big Cat Phonics for Letters & Sounds - in the Fish Tank: Band 02A/Red A, Bd. 2A. John and Gus art, illus. 2018. (Collins Big Cat Phonics Ser.). (ENG.). 16p. (J). (gr. -1-k). pap. 6.99 *(978-0-00-825142-0(8))* HarperCollins Pubs. Ltd. GBR. Dist: Independent Pubs. Group.

—A Hot Day. Lee, Maxine, illus. 2016. (Cambridge Reading Adventures Ser.). (ENG.). 16p. pap. 7.95 *(978-1-316-60069-6(6))* Cambridge Univ. Pr.

—School Trip. Mould, Chris, illus. 2004. (ENG.). 24p. (J). lib. bdg. 23.65 *(978-1-59646-694-4(4))* Dingles & Co.

Hawkins, Colin & Hawkins, Jacqui. Witch Pigs. 2006. (Illus.). 32p. (J). (gr. 1-2). 19.99 *(978-0-224-06467-5(3)*, Jonathan Cape) Penguin Random Hse. GBR. Dist: Trafalgar Square Publishing.

Hawkins, Emily. Atlas of Miniature Adventures: A Pocket-Sized Collection of Small-scale Wonders - Because Bigger Isn't Always Better. Letherland, Lucy, illus. 2016. (Atlas Of Ser.). (ENG.). 64p. (J). 9.99 *(978-1-84780-909-4(X)*, Wide Eyed Editions) Quarto Publishing Group UK GBR. Dist: Littlehampton Bk Services, Ltd.

Hawley, Shane. ABC Death. Erkkinen, Joel, illus. 2018. (Button Poetry Ser.). (ENG.). 72p. (J). 16.00 *(978-1-943735-46-4(8))* Button Poetry.

Haworth, Katie. Terrible Tim! Hughes, Laura, illus. 2016. (ENG.). 32p. (J). (gr. -1-3). 16.99 *(978-1-4998-0137-8(8))* Little Bee Books Inc.

Hay, Sam. The Star in the Jar. Massini, Sarah, illus. 2018. (ENG.). 32p. (J). (gr. -1-3). 17.99 *(978-1-4926-6220-4(8)*, Sourcebooks Jabberwocky) Sourcebooks, Inc.

Hayes, Jennifer. Face to Face with Sharks. 2018. (Face to Face with Animals Ser.). (Illus.). 32p. (J). (gr. 3-7). pap. 6.99 *(978-1-4263-3259-3(9)*, National Geographic Kids) Disney Publishing Worldwide.

Hayes, Karel. The Autumn Visitors. 2015. (ENG., Illus.). 32p. (J). (gr. -1-3). 16.95 *(978-1-60893-454-6(3))* Down East Bks.

—The Spring Visitors. 2018. (Illus.). 32p. (J). (gr. -1-3). 17.95 *(978-1-60893-967-1(7))* Down East Bks.

Hayward, Linda. Noah's Ark. 2018. (Step into Reading Ser.). (ENG., Illus.). 32p. (J). (gr. -1-1). pap. 4.99 *(978-0-394-88716-6(6)*, Random Hse. Bks. for Young Readers) Random Hse. Children's Bks.

Haywood, John, ed. Everyday Life in the Ancient World. 2018. 256p. (J). (gr. -1-12). pap. 9.99 *(978-1-84477-021-2(4)*, Armadillo) Anness Publishing GBR. Dist: National Bk. Network.

Heapy, Teresa. Very Little Red Riding Hood. Heap, Sue, illus. 2014. (Very Little Ser.). (ENG.). 32p. (J). (gr. -1-3). 16.99 *(978-0-544-28000-7(8)*, 1570487, Clarion Bks.) HarperCollins Pubs.

Heart, Sandra. Pernanna & Yerbo, the Toe-Tamals Family & Friends. 2011. 44p. pap. 21.99 *(978-1-4568-3296-4(4))* Xlibris Corp.

Hedderwick, Mairi. Katie Morag & the Big Boy Cousins. 2010. (Katie Morag Ser.: 5). (Illus.). 32p. (J). (gr. k-2). pap. 12.99 *(978-1-84941-089-2(5)*, Red Fox) Random House Children's Books GBR. Dist: Independent Pubs. Group.

Hegarty, Patricia. The River. Clulow, Hanako, illus. 2016. (J). 12.99 *(978-1-61067-468-3(5))* Kane Miller.

Heidecker, Samie. Who's Looking at Whom? Christmas, 1 vol. 2010. 38p. 24.95 *(978-1-4489-4855-0(X))* PublishAmerica, Inc.

Heiligman, Deborah. From Caterpillar to Butterfly. Weissman, Bari, illus. 2015. (Let's-Read-And-Find-Out Science 1 Ser.). (ENG.). 32p. (J). (gr. -1-3). pap. 6.99 *(978-0-06-238183-5(0)*, HarperCollins) HarperCollins Pubs.

Heiman, Laura. My Favorite Michael. Keen, Sophie, illus. 2009. (J). (gr. -1-2). 32p. 15.95 *(978-1-58925-086-4(9))*; 24p. pap. 7.95 *(978-1-58925-419-0(8))* Tiger Tales.

Heling, Kathryn & Hembrook, Deborah. Clothesline Clues to Jobs People Do. Davies, Andy Robert, illus. 2014. (ENG.). 40p. (J). (gr. -1-2). pap. 7.95 *(978-1-58089-252-0(3))* Charlesbridge Publishing, Inc.

Hellen, N. Touch & Peek with Teddy & Me. 2003. (ENG., Illus.). 18p. (J). 9.99 *(978-1-85292-184-2(6)*, Campbell Bks.) Pan Macmillan GBR. Dist: Trafalgar Square Publishing.

Hello, Sunny Day! 2012. (ENG.). 36p. pap. 20.99 *(978-1-4490-0244-2(7))* AuthorHouse.

Hello!Lucky. My Dad Is Amazing! (a Hello!Lucky Book) 2018. (Hello!Lucky Book Ser.). (ENG., Illus.). 24p. (J). (gr. -1 — 1). bds. 8.99 *(978-1-4197-2961-4(6)*, 1212010) Abrams, Inc.

—Super Pooper & Whizz Kid: Potty Power! 2018. (Hello!Lucky Book Ser.). (ENG., Illus.). 24p. (J). (gr. -1 — 1). bds. 9.99 *(978-1-4197-3157-0(2)*, 1212201) Abrams, Inc.

Hello!Lucky & Moyle, Sabrina. My Mom Is Magical! (a Hello!Lucky Book) Moyle, Eunice, illus. 2018. (Hello!Lucky Book Ser.). (ENG.). 24p. (J). (gr. -1 — 1). bds. 7.99 *(978-1-4197-2962-1(4)*, 1212110) Abrams, Inc.

Hellsing, Lennart & Strøyer, Poul. The Cantankerous Crow. 2016. (ENG., Illus.). 28p. (J). (gr. k-1). 19.95 *(978-0-500-65079-0(9)*, 565079) Thames & Hudson.

Helman, Andrea. 1, 2, 3 Moose: An Animal Counting Book. Wolfe, Art, photos by. 2016. (Illus.). 20p. (J). (— 1). bds. 10.99 *(978-1-63217-032-3(9)*, Little Bigfoot) Sasquatch Bks.

Hemingway, Edward. Bad Apple: A Tale of Friendship. Hemingway, Edward, illus. 2015. (Illus.). 32p. (J). (gr. -1-k). 8.99 *(978-0-14-751748-7(6)*, Puffin Books) Penguin Young Readers Group.

Henderson, Robert. I See, I See. 2019. (ENG., Illus.). 48p. (J). (gr. -1-k). 17.99 *(978-1-4521-8334-3(1))* Chronicle Bks. LLC.

Hendra, Sue. Simon Sock. East, Nick, illus. 2019. (ENG.). 32p. (J). (gr. -1-k). pap. 9.99 *(978-1-4449-3681-0(6))* Hachette Children's Group GBR. Dist: Hachette Bk. Group.

Hendra, Sue & Linnet, Paul. Cake. Hendra, Sue, illus. 2019. (ENG., Illus.). 32p. (J). (gr. -1-3). 17.99 *(978-1-5344-2550-7(0)*, Aladdin) Simon & Schuster Children's Publishing.

—Keith the Cat with the Magic Hat. Hendra, Sue, illus. 2018. (ENG., Illus.). 32p. (J). (gr. -1-3). 14.99 *(978-1-4814-9035-1(4)*, Aladdin) Simon & Schuster Children's Publishing.

Hendricks, Brenda K. What's the Buzz, Bumbly Bee? Hendricks, Brenda K., illus. 2013. (Illus.). 30p. pap. 9.99 *(978-0-9826582-3-9(0))* Two Small Fish Pubns.

Hendry, Diana. You Can't Cuddle a Crocodile. Eaves, Ed, illus. 2020. (ENG.). 32p. (J). (gr. -1-k). 18.99 *(978-1-4449-2454-1(0))* Hachette Children's Group GBR. Dist: Hachette Bk. Group.

Heneghan, Judith. Brandon's So Bossy! Hughes, Jack, illus. 2016. (Dragon School Ser.). (ENG.). 32p. (J). (gr. -1-k). pap. *(978-0-7502-8357-1(2)*, Wayland) Hachette Children's Group GBR. Dist: Hachette Bk. Group.

—Dragon School: Ruby's SO Rude. 2016. (Dragon School Ser.). (ENG., Illus.). 32p. (J). (gr. -1-k). pap. *(978-0-7502-8356-4(4)*, Wayland) Hachette Children's Group GBR. Dist: Hachette Bk. Group.

Henkes, Kevin. Birds Board Book. Dronzek, Laura, illus. 2017. (ENG.). 32p. (J). (gr. -1 — 1). bds. 7.99 *(978-0-06-257305-6(5)*, Greenwillow Bks.) HarperCollins Pubs.

—A Box of Treats: Five Little Picture Books about Lilly & Her Friends: a Christmas Holiday Book Set for Kids. Henkes, Kevin, illus. 2004. (ENG., Illus.). 120p. (J). (gr. -1-k). pap. 14.99 *(978-0-06-073211-0(3)*, Greenwillow Bks.) HarperCollins Pubs.

—When Spring Comes Board Book: An Easter & Springtime Book for Kids. Dronzek, Laura, illus. 2018. (ENG.). 36p. (J). (gr. -1-k). bds. 7.99 *(978-0-06-274166-0(7)*, Greenwillow Bks.) HarperCollins Pubs.

Henry, Will. Wallace the Brave. 2017. (Wallace the Brave Ser.). (ENG., Illus.). 176p. (J). pap. 11.99 *(978-1-4494-8998-4(2))* Andrews McMeel Publishing.

Heos, Bridget. Mustache Baby Lap Board Book. Ang, Joy, illus. 2018. (Mustache Baby Ser.). (ENG.). 36p. (J). (— 1). bds. 12.99 *(978-1-328-91048-6(2)*, 1701056, Clarion Bks.) HarperCollins Pubs.

Heras, Theo. Our New Kittens. Carter, Alice, illus. 2018. (ENG.). 24p. (J). (gr. -1-1). 15.95 *(978-1-77278-060-4(X))* Pajama Pr. CAN. Dist: Publishers Group West (PGW).

—Where's Bunny? Benoit, Renné, illus. 2018. (Toddler Skill Builders Ser.: 3). (ENG.). 24p. (J). (gr. -1-k). 13.95 *(978-1-77278-043-7(X))* Pajama Pr. CAN. Dist: Publishers Group West (PGW).

Herder, Ronald. Great Works for Piano Four Hands. Herder, Ronald, ed. 2012. (Dover Music for Piano Ser.). (ENG.). 224p. pap. 22.95 *(978-0-486-40173-7(1))* Dover Pubns., Inc.

Herz, Henry. Alice's Magic Garden: Before the Rabbit Hole ... Hoopes, Natalie, illus. 2018. (ENG.). 32p. (J). (gr. -1-k). 16.99 *(978-1-64170-032-0(7)*, 550032) Familius LLC.

Herz, Henry, et al. Mabel & the Queen of Dreams, 1 vol. Woods, Lisa, illus. 2016. (ENG.). 32p. (J). 16.99 *(978-0-7643-5137-2(0)*, 7522) Schiffer Publishing, Ltd.

Hess, Mary Rand. Little Larry Goes to School. 2019. (Baby Animal Tales Ser.). (Illus.). 32p. (J). (gr. -1-k). 16.99 *(978-1-4263-3316-3(1)*, National Geographic Kids) Disney Publishing Worldwide.

Hest, Amy. Are You Sure, Mother Bear? Tobia, Lauren, illus. 2016. (ENG.). 32p. (J). (-k). 15.99 *(978-0-7636-7207-2(6))* Candlewick Pr.

—Charley's First Night. Oxenbury, Helen, illus. 2012. (ENG.). 32p. (J). (gr. -1-2). 15.99 *(978-0-7636-4055-2(7))* Candlewick Pr.

Heuninck, Ronald. Rain or Shine, 40 vols. 2nd rev. ed. 2014. Orig. Title: Buiten Spelen. (Illus.). 14p. (J). 9.95 *(978-1-78250-044-5(8))* Floris Bks. GBR. Dist: Consortium Bk. Sales & Distribution.

Hibbs, Gillian. Errol's Garden. Hibbs, Gillian, illus. 2018. (Child's Play Library). (Illus.). 32p. (J). pap. *(978-1-78628-084-8(1))*; *(978-1-78628-085-5(X))* Child's Play International Ltd.

—Errol's Garden. 2019. (ENG.). 28p. (J). (gr. k-1). 17.96 *(978-1-64310-964-0(2))* Penworthy Co., LLC, The.

—Tilly's Staycation. Hibbs, Gillian, illus. 2014. (Child's Play Library). (ENG., Illus.). 32p. (J). *(978-1-84643-601-7(X))* Child's Play International Ltd.

Hickox, Rebecca. Per & the Dala Horse. Gilbert, Yvonne, illus. 2003. 32p. (J). pap. 8.95 *(978-1-57534-034-0(8))* Skandisk, Inc.

Hicks, Barbara Jean. I Like Black & White. Prap, Lila, illus. 2006. 24p. (J). (gr. -1-3). 9.95 *(978-1-58925-056-7(7))* Tiger Tales.

Hicks, Kelli. I Can Prove It! Investigating Science. 2012. (My Science Library). (ENG.). 24p. (gr. 4-5). pap. 8.95 *(978-1-61810-244-7(3)*, 9781618102447) Rourke Educational Media.

Hicks, Linda Ashman. Just Another Amazing Morning. Date not set. 32p. (J). (gr. -1-3). pap. 5.99 *(978-0-06-443712-7(4))* HarperCollins Pubs.

Hicks, Robert Z. Tommie Turtle's Secret. Rolseth, Ruthie, illus. 2007. (ENG.). 40p. (J). 16.95 *(978-0-9792031-0-7(4))* R.Z. Enterprises of Florida.

Higgins, Carter. Bikes for Sale (Story Books for Kids, Books about Friendship, Preschool Picture Books) OHora, Zachariah, illus. 2019. (ENG.). 40p. (J). (gr. -1-k). 16.99 *(978-1-4521-5932-4(7))* Chronicle Bks. LLC.

Higginson, Sheila Sweeny. Drip, Drop! the Rain Won't Stop! Your Turn, My Turn Reader. Yee, Josie, illus. 2010. (Playskool Ser.). (ENG.). 24p. (J). (gr. -1-k). pap. 3.99 *(978-1-4169-9046-8(1)*, Simon Spotlight) Simon Spotlight.

Hilberts, Aly. The Shepherd Boy & the Christmas Gifts, 44 vols. Dufft, Sanne, illus. 2017. Orig. Title: Nathan, de Kleine Herder. 32p. (J). 17.95 *(978-1-78250-438-2(9))* Floris Bks. GBR. Dist: Consortium Bk. Sales & Distribution.

Hill, Cheryl E. R Is for Reading Books. Pierce, Dave G., illus. 2012. 56p. pap. 17.99 *(978-0-9859770-0-9(0))* N.O.A.H Bks.

Hill, Eric. Spot Goes to the Fire Station. 2017. (Spot Ser.). (Illus.). 14p. (J). (-k). bds. 6.99 *(978-0-14-137598-4(1)*, Warne) Penguin Young Readers Group.

—Spot Goes to the Swimming Pool. 2018. (Spot Ser.). (ENG., Illus.). 14p. (J). (-k). bds. 6.99 *(978-0-241-32708-1(3)*, Warne) Penguin Young Readers Group.

—Spot Says Please. Hill, Eric, illus. 2013. (Spot Ser.). (ENG., Illus.). 14p. (J). (gr. -1-k). bds. 6.99 *(978-0-7232-7832-0(6)*, Warne) Penguin Young Readers Group.

—Spot's Christmas. Hill, Eric, illus. 2004. (Spot Ser.). (ENG., Illus.). 12p. (J). (gr. -1 — 1). bds. 6.99 *(978-0-399-24320-2(8)*, Warne) Penguin Young Readers Group.

Hill, Janet. Miss Mink: Life Lessons for a Cat Countess. 2019. (Illus.). 48p. (J). (gr. -1-3). 17.99 *(978-1-77049-922-5(9)*, Tundra Bks.) Tundra Bks. CAN. Dist: Penguin Random Hse. LLC.

Hill, Kelly, illus. Anne's Colors: Inspired by Anne of Green Gables. 2018. (Anne of Green Gables Ser.). 20p. (J). (— 1). bds. 7.99 *(978-0-7352-6284-3(5)*, Tundra Bks.) Tundra Bks. CAN. Dist: Penguin Random Hse. LLC.

—Anne's Numbers: Inspired by Anne of Green Gables. 2018. (Anne of Green Gables Ser.). 22p. (J). (— 1). bds. 8.99 (978-0-7352-6285-0(3), Tundra Bks.) Tundra Bks. CAN. Dist: Penguin Random Hse. LLC.

Hill, Monica. Rin Tin Tin & the Lost Indian. Greene, Hamilton, illus. 2011. 28p. pap. 35.95 (978-1-258-00567-2(0)) Literary Licensing, LLC.

Hillenbrand, Will. Snowman's Story, 0 vols. 2014. (ENG., Illus.). 32p. (J). (gr. -1-2). 16.99 (978-1-4778-4787-9(1), 9781477847879, Two Lions) Amazon Publishing.

—Spring Is Here: A Bear & Mole Story. 2012. (Bear & Mole Ser.: 1). (ENG., Illus.). 32p. (J). (-k). pap. 7.99 (978-0-8234-2431-3(6)) Holiday Hse., Inc.

Hillenburg, Stephen. SpongeBob Comics: Book 1: Silly Sea Stories. 2017. (SpongeBob Comics Ser.). (ENG., Illus.). 112p. (J). (gr. 3-7). pap. 12.99 (978-1-4197-2319-3(7), 1151801) Abrams, Inc.

—SpongeBob Comics: Book 2: Aquatic Adventurers, Unite! 2017. (SpongeBob Comics Ser.). (ENG., Illus.). 112p. (J). (gr. 3-7). pap. 12.99 (978-1-4197-2320-9(0), 1151901) Abrams, Inc.

—SpongeBob Comics: Book 3: Tales from the Haunted Pineapple. 2017. (SpongeBob Comics Ser.). (ENG., Illus.). 112p. (J). (gr. 3-7). pap. 12.99 (978-1-4197-2560-9(2), 1152001, Amulet Bks.) Abrams, Inc.

Hills, Laila, illus. Animal Friends. 2017. (J). (978-1-62885-342-1(5)) Kidsbooks, LLC.

Hills, Tad. Rocket's Mighty Words (Oversized Board Book) Hills, Tad, illus. 2013. (Rocket Ser.). (ENG., Illus.). 22p. (J). (-k). bds. 10.99 (978-0-385-37233-6(7), Schwartz & Wade Bks.) Random Hse. Children's Bks.

Himmelman, John. Box Turtle. 2018. (Illus.). 32p. (J). (gr. -1-12). 15.95 (978-1-63076-331-2(4)) Taylor Trade Publishing.

Hinckley, Peter. Little Lacers: 123: Lace & Learn Your First Numbers! Kaliaha, Volha, illus. 2019. (Little Lacers Ser.). (ENG.). 14p. (J). (gr. -1-k). bds. 16.99 (978-1-64170-008-5(4), 550008) Familius LLC.

Hindley, Judy. Eyes, Nose, Fingers, & Toes: A First Book All about You. Granström, Brita, illus. 2004. (ENG.). 24p. (J). (gr. k-k). bds. 7.99 (978-0-7636-2383-8(0)) Candlewick Pr.

Hineman, Jonathan. Goodbye, Santa. Cruz, Cheryl, illus. 2013. 26p. (J). 16.95 (978-1-60131-172-6(9)) Big Tent Bks.

Hirschi, Ron. Ocean Seasons, 1 vol. Carlson, Kirsten., Illus. 2007. (ENG.). 32p. (J). (gr. k-4). pap. 10.95 (978-1-60718-863-6(5)) Arbordale Publishing.

Hirst, Daisy. Hilda & the Runaway Baby. Hirst, Daisy, illus. 2017. (ENG., Illus.). 32p. (J). (-k). 16.99 (978-0-7636-9490-6(8)) Candlewick Pr.

Hirst, Jo. A House for Everyone: A Story to Help Children Learn about Gender Identity & Gender Expression. Bardoff, Naomi, illus. 2018. 32p. (J). pap. 18.95 (978-1-78592-448-4(6), 696700) Kingsley, Jessica Pubs. GBR. Dist: Hachette UK Distribution.

History Speaks: Picture Books Plus Reader's Theater, 12 vols., Set. Incl. Ellen Craft's Escape from Slavery. Moore, Cathy. Braught, Mark, illus. (J). 2010. lib. bdg. 27.93 (978-0-7613-5875-6(7)); George Washington & the Story of the U. S. Constitution. Ransom, Candice. Reeves, Jeni, illus. 2011. 27.93 (978-0-7613-5877-0(3)); Little Rock Nine Stand up for Their Rights. Lucas, Eileen. Gustavson, Adam, illus. 2011. lib. bdg. 27.93 (978-0-7613-5874-9(9)); 48p. (gr. 2-4)., Millbrook Pr. 2011. Set lib. bdg. 335.16 (978-0-7613-5100-9(0)) Lerner Publishing Group.

Ho, Cammie. Butterfly Butterfly. 2016. (Life Cycle Bks.). (ENG., Illus.). 27p. (J). (gr. k-2). pap. 7.99 (978-1-943241-03-3(1)) Phonic Monic.

—Duckling Duckling. 2016. (Life Cycle Bks.). (ENG., Illus.). 33p. (J). (gr. k-2). pap. 7.99 (978-1-943241-00-2(7)) Phonic Monic.

—Ladybug Ladybug. 2016. (Life Cycle Bks.). (ENG., Illus.). 29p. (J). (gr. k-2). pap. 7.99 (978-1-943241-02-6(3)) Phonic Monic.

—Parrot Parrot. 2016. (Life Cycle Bks.). (ENG., Illus.). 31p. (J). (gr. k-2). pap. 7.99 (978-1-943241-04-0(X)) Phonic Monic.

—Tadpole Tadpole. 2016. (Life Cycle Bks.). (ENG., Illus.). 31p. (J). (gr. k-2). pap. 7.99 (978-1-943241-01-9(5)) Phonic Monic.

Ho, Jannie. Bear & Chicken. 2017. (ENG., Illus.). 40p. (J). (gr. -1-3). 16.99 (978-0-7624-6266-7(3), Running Pr. Kids) Running Pr.

Hoare, Ben. The Wonders of Nature. 2019. (DK Children's Anthologies Ser.). (ENG., Illus.). 224p. (J). (gr. 2-4). 21.99 (978-1-4654-8536-6(8), DK Children) Dorling Kindersley Publishing, Inc.

Hobbie, Holly. Gem. 2012. (ENG., Illus.). 32p. (J). (gr. -1-3). 16.99 (978-0-316-20334-0(3)) Little, Brown Bks. for Young Readers.

Hodakov, Levi. I Go to the Ohel. Rosenfeld, D. L. & Leverton, Yossi, eds. Benenfeld, Rikki, illus. 2011. (Toddler Experience Ser.). 32p. (J). 11.99 (978-1-929628-61-2(7)) Hachai Publishing.

Hodge, Deborah. Bear's Winter Party, 1 vol. Cinar, Lisa, illus. 2016. (ENG.). 32p. (J). (gr. k-2). 16.95 (978-1-55498-853-2(5)) Groundwood Bks. CAN. Dist: Publishers Group West (PGW).

Hodgkinson, Leigh. Goldilocks & Just One Bear. Hodgkinson, Leigh, illus. 2012. (ENG., Illus.). 32p. (J). (gr. -1-2). 16.99 (978-0-7636-6172-4(4)) Candlewick Pr.

Hoffman, Don. Abigail Is a Big Girl. Dakins, Todd, illus. 2nd ed. 2016. (Billy & Abby Ser.). (ENG.). 28p. (J). (gr. -1-k). pap. 3.99 (978-1-943154-03-6(1)) Peek-A-Boo Publishing.

—Billy Is a Big Boy. Dakins, Todd, illus. 2nd ed. 2016. (Billy & Abby Ser.). (ENG.). 28p. (J). (gr. -1-k). pap. 3.99 (978-1-943154-02-9(3)) Peek-A-Boo Publishing.

—A Counting Book with Billy & Abigail. Dakins, Todd, illus. 2nd ed. 2016. (Billy & Abby Ser.). (ENG.). 24p. (J). (gr. -1-k). pap. 3.99 (978-1-943154-08-1(2)) Peek-A-Boo Publishing.

—Good Morning, Good Night Billy & Abigail. Dakins, Todd, illus. 2nd ed. 2016. (Billy & Abby Ser.). (ENG.). 24p. (J). (gr. -1-k). pap. 3.99 (978-1-943154-09-8(0)) Peek-A-Boo Publishing.

—A Very Special Snowflake. Dakins, Todd, Illus. 2nd ed. 2016. (ENG.). 28p. (J). (gr. -1-k). pap. 3.99 (978-1-943154-01-2(5)) Peek-A-Boo Publishing.

Hoffman, Don & Palmer, Priscilla. Turbo & Tuxedo. Nadler, Anna, illus. 2016. (ENG.). 32p. (J). (gr. -1-k). pap. 3.99 (978-1-943154-04-3(X)) Peek-A-Boo Publishing.

Hoffman, E. T. A. The Nutcracker. Zwerger, Lisbeth, illus. 2016. (ENG.). 40p. (J). (gr. k-2). 19.95 (978-0-7358-4270-0(1)) North-South Bks., Inc.

Hoffmann, E. T. A. The Nutcracker. Innocenti, Roberto, illus. 2017. 136p. (J). (gr. 3-5). 29.99 (978-1-56846-313-1(8), 20176, Creative Editions) Creative Co., The.

Hofmann-Maniyar, Ariane. Ice in the Jungle. Hofmann-Maniyar, Ariane, illus. 2016. (Child's Play Library). (Illus.). 32p. (J). pap. (978-1-84643-730-4(X)) Child's Play International Ltd.

Hofmeyr, Dianne. Zeraffa Giraffa. Ray, Jane, illus. 2015. (ENG.). 40p. (J). pap. 9.99 (978-1-84780-661-1(9), Frances Lincoln Children's Bks.) Quarto Publishing Group UK GBR. Dist: Littlehampton Bk Services, Ltd.

Holabird, Katharine. Twinkle. Warburton, Sarah, illus. 2018. (Twinkle Ser.). (ENG.). 32p. (J). (gr. -1-2). 18.99 (978-1-5344-2915-4(8), Little Simon) Little Simon.

Holcomb, Carrie E., ed. Buggin' with Ruud. 2007. (Illus.). 48p. (J). per. 6.99 (978-0-696-23690-7(7)) Meredith Bks.

Holden, Arianne. It's Fun to Learn about Colors: A Busy Picture Book Full of Fabulous Facts & Things to Do! 2016. (Illus.). 32p. (J). (gr. -1-12). 9.99 (978-1-86147-710-1(4), Armadillo) Anness Publishing GBR. Dist: National Bk. Network.

—It's Fun to Learn about My Body: A Busy Picture Book Full of Fabulous Facts & Things to Do! 2016. (Illus.). 32p. (J). (gr. -1-12). pap. 9.99 (978-1-86147-730-9(9)) Anness Publishing, Inc.

Holden, Robert. The Pied Piper of Hamelin. Zak, Drahos, illus. 2004. 28p. (J). (gr. k-4). reprint ed. 15.00 (978-0-7567-7686-2(4)) DIANE Publishing Co.

Holl, Adelaide. The Rain Puddle. Duvoisin, Roger, illus. 2017. 36p. (J). 20.00 (978-1-85124-469-0(7)) Bodleian Library GBR. Dist: Chicago Distribution Ctr.

Holmes, Andy. If You Give a Boy a Bible. 2004. (Illus.). 32p. (J). 10.99 (978-0-8254-5513-1(8)) Kregel Pubns.

Holtz, Monica Stauber. Behind the Zoo: Find Out What the Animals Eat & Do at Irvine Park Zoo, Chippewa Falls, Wisconsin. Opatz, Shane, illus. Opatz, Shane, photos by. 2011. (J). (978-0-9837617-1-6(X)) Holtz Creative Enterprises.

Holub, Joan & Williams, Suzanne. Goldilocks Breaks in (Grimmtastic Girls #6) 6th ed. 2015. (Grimmtastic Girls Ser.: 6). (ENG.). 192p. (J). (gr. 3-7). pap. 5.99 (978-0-545-78394-1(1), Scholastic Paperbacks) Scholastic, Inc.

Homberg, Ruth, adapted by. The Best Ball. 2017. (Illus.). 24p. (J). (978-1-5182-3608-2(1)) Random Hse., Inc.

Hong, Seonna. Animus. 2005. (ENG., Illus.). 34p. (gr. -1-7). bds. 25.00 (978-0-9729388-5-3(0)) Baby Tattoo Bks.

Hood, Karen Jean Matsko. Angels, Angels Way up High. Whispering Pine Press International, ed. Alexandra Dzhiganskaya, illus. 2017. (Hood Picture Book Ser.). (J). bk. 2. pap. 15.95 (978-1-930948-09-9(3)) Vol. 2. 24.95 (978-1-930948-81-5(6)) Whispering Pine Pr. International, Inc.

Hood, Morag. Sophie Johnson, Unicorn Expert. Okstad, Ella, illus. 2018. (Sophie Johnson, Unicorn Expert Ser.). (ENG.). 32p. (J). (gr. -1-3). 17.99 (978-1-5344-3161-4(6), Aladdin) Simon & Schuster Children's Publishing.

—The Steves. 2018. (ENG.). 32p. (J). (gr. k-4). 15.99 (978-1-4926-6914-2(8), Sourcebooks Jabberwocky) Sourcebooks, Inc.

—When Grandad Was a Penguin. 2018. (ENG., Illus.). 32p. (J). (gr. -1-k). pap. 14.99 (978-1-5098-5097-6(X), 900326043, Two Hoots) Pan Macmillan GBR. Dist: Macmillan.

Hood, Susan. The Tooth Mouse. Nadeau, Janice, illus. 2012. (ENG.). 32p. (J). (gr. -1-2). 16.95 (978-1-55453-565-1(4)) Kids Can Pr., Ltd. CAN. Dist: Hachette Bk. Group.

Hoopmann, Kathy. Blue Bottle Mystery - the Graphic Novel: An Asperger Adventure. 2015. (Asperger Adventures Ser.). (ENG., Illus.). 68p. (J). 21.95 (978-1-84905-650-2(1), 693887) Kingsley, Jessica Pubs. GBR. Dist: Hachette UK Distribution.

Hope-Simpson, Lila. Fiddles & Spoons (pb) Journey of an Acadian Mouse, 1 vol. 2017. (ENG., Illus.). 32p. (J). (gr. 1-3). pap. 14.95 (978-1-77108-562-5(2), 0111bba3-b60b-4751-968b-82be0680d6b3) Nimbus Publishing, Ltd. CAN. Dist: Baker & Taylor Publisher Services (BTPS).

Hopgood, Tim. Walter's Wonderful Web: A First Book about Shapes. 2016. (ENG., Illus.). 32p. (J). 18.99 (978-0-374-30352-5(5), 900156325, Farrar, Straus & Giroux (BYR)) Farrar, Straus & Giroux.

Hopkins, Douglas. Princess June & the Shadow Pirates, 1 vol. 2007. (ENG., Illus.). 32p. (J). (gr. -1-2). per. (978-1-894294-88-1(2)) Breakwater Bks., Ltd.

Hopper, Ada. Out of Remote Control. Ross, Graham, illus. 2017. (DATA Set Ser.: 7). (ENG.). 128p. (J). (gr. k-4). 17.99 (978-1-4814-9192-1(X)); pap. 5.99 (978-1-4814-9191-4(1)) Little Simon. (Little Simon).

Horacek, Petr. The Fly. Horacek, Petr, illus. 2015. (ENG., Illus.). 32p. (J). (gr. -1-2). 14.99 (978-0-7636-7480-9(X)) Candlewick Pr.

—Jonathan & Martha. 2012. (ENG., Illus.). 40p. (gr. -1-1). 14.95 (978-0-7148-6351-1(3)) Phaidon Pr., Inc.

—Who Is the Biggest? Horacek, Petr, illus. 2019. (ENG., Illus.). 16p. (J). (— 1). bds. 8.99 (978-1-5362-0171-0(5)) Candlewick Pr.

Horacek, Petr & Horacek, Petr. Blue Penguin. Horacek, Petr & Horacek, Petr, illus. 2016. (ENG., Illus.). 32p. (J). (gr. -1-2). 15.99 (978-0-7636-9251-3(4)) Candlewick Pr.

—The Mouse Who Wasn't Scared. Horacek, Petr & Horacek, Petr, illus. 2018. (ENG., Illus.). 32p. (J). (-k). 15.99 (978-0-7636-9881-2(4)) Candlewick Pr.

Hore, Rosie. Big Picture Thesaurus IR. 2017. (Big Picture Books* Ser.). (ENG.). 40p. 14.99 (978-0-7945-3983-2(1), Usborne) EDC Publishing.

Horvath, James. Build, Dogs, Build: A Tall Tail. 2016. (I Can Read Level 1 Ser.). (ENG., Illus.). 32p. (J). (gr. -1-3). pap. 4.99 (978-0-06-235705-2(0), HarperCollins) HarperCollins Pubs.

—Dig, Dogs, Dig: A Construction Tail. Horvath, James, illus. 2013. (ENG., Illus.). 40p. (J). (gr. -1-3). 15.99 (978-0-06-218964-6(6), HarperCollins) HarperCollins Pubs.

Hosino, Ryuichi, illus. Disney: Pixar's Finding Nemo: Special Collectors Manga. 2016. (Disney Manga: Pixar's Finding Nemo Ser.). 176p. (J). (gr. 1-1). 15.99 (978-1-4278-5658-6(3), 9a07f0fd-50ef-4dfa-b4a5-6b40b95a43c9, TOKYOPOP Manga) TOKYOPOP, Inc.

Houran, Lori Haskins. My Little Golden Book about Dogs. Golden, Jess, illus. 2018. (Little Golden Book Ser.). 24p. (J). (-k). 4.99 (978-0-399-55813-9(6), Golden Bks.) Random Hse. Children's Bks.

Howard, Chloe. Stand Beautiful, 1 vol. Melmon, Deborah, illus. 2018. (ENG.). 32p. (J). 16.99 (978-0-310-76495-3(5)) Zonderkidz.

Howard, Ruth I. Crabby Crab. Hunter, Helen D., illus. 2004. (ENG.). 24p. (YA). pap. 9.00 (978-1-4120-1432-8(8)) Trafford Publishing.

Howard, Virginia. The Wind Plays Tricks. Chua, Charlene, illus. 2019. (ENG.). 32p. (J). (gr. -1-3). 16.99 (978-0-8075-8735-5(4), 807587354) Whitman, Albert & Co.

Howarth, Heidi. The Otter Who Loved to Hold Hands. Howarth, Daniel, illus. 2014. (J). (978-1-4351-5537-4(8)) Barnes & Noble, Inc.

Howarth, Jill. 1-2-3, You Love Me. 2017. (ENG., Illus.). 14p. (J). (gr. -1 — 1). bds. 7.99 (978-0-7624-6269-8(8), Running Pr. Kids) Running Pr.

Howarth, Jill, illus. The 12 Days of Christmas. 2018. (ENG.). 26p. (J). (gr. -1 — 1). bds. 7.99 (978-0-7624-9142-1(6), Running Pr. Kids) Running Pr.

Howe, James. Big Bob, Little Bob. Anderson, Laura Ellen, illus. 2016. (ENG.). 32p. (J). (gr. -1-1). 16.99 (978-0-7636-4436-9(6)) Candlewick Pr.

Howell, Gill. Selkie Child. Keen, Sophie, illus. 2005. (ENG.). 24p. (J). lib. bdg. 23.65 (978-1-59646-750-7(9)) Dingles & Co.

—Snow King. Cann, Helen, illus. 2005. (ENG.). 24p. (J). lib. bdg. 23.65 (978-1-59646-742-2(8)) Dingles & Co.

—Tortoise & the Baboon. Woody, illus. 2004. (ENG.). 16p. (J). lib. bdg. 23.65 (978-1-59646-686-9(3)) Dingles & Co.

Howes, Katey. Magnolia Mudd & Super Jumptastic Launc. 2018. (ENG., Illus.). 40p. (J). (gr. -1). 16.95 (978-1-4549-2174-5(9)) Sterling Publishing Co., Inc.

Hoyt, Charlene. Where the Leprechauns Hide. Fischer, Sandi, illus. 2007. (ENG.). 40p. per. 12.99 (978-0-9792258-9-5(2)) Bezalel Bks.

Hsu, Yi Ling. Typhoon Holidays: Taiwan. Cowley, Joy, ed. Kwag, Jin-yeong, illus. 2015. (Global Kids Storybooks Ser.). (ENG.). 32p. (gr. 1-4). 26.65 (978-1-925246-04-9(3)); 7.99 (978-1-925246-56-8(6)); 26.65 (978-1-925246-30-8(2)) ChoiceMaker Pty. Ltd., The AUS. (Big and SMALL). Dist: Lerner Publishing Group.

Hu, Vicky. The Muses: Greek Mythology (Mitologia Griega) 2009. 44p. pap. 21.99 (978-1-4415-3415-6(6)) Xlibris Corp.

Hubbard, Ben & Langley, Andrew. Adventures in Space. 2015. (Adventures in Space Ser.). (ENG.). 48p. (J). (gr. 4-6). 143.96 (978-1-4846-2518-7(8), 23580, Heinemann) Capstone.

Hubbard, Suzanna. The Lady Who Lived in a Car. Hubbard, Suzanna, illus. 2007. (ENG., Illus.). 32p. (J). (gr. k-2). pap. 6.99 (978-1-84458-055-2(5)) Pavilion Bks. GBR. Dist: Independent Pubs. Group.

Hubbell, Patricia. Cars: Rushing! Honking! Zooming!, 0 vols. Halsey, Megan & Addy, Sean, illus. 2012. (ENG.). 32p. (J). (gr. -1-1). pap. 7.99 (978-0-7614-5616-2(3), 9780761456162, Two Lions) Amazon Publishing.

Huber, Mike. The Amazing Erik. Cowman, Joseph, illus. 2014. (ENG.). 32p. (gr. -1). 15.95 (978-1-60554-209-6(1)) Redleaf Pr.

—Evette's Invitation. Cowman, Joseph, illus. 2014. (ENG.). 32p. (gr. -1). 15.95 (978-1-60554-212-6(1)) Redleaf Pr.

Huber, Raymond. Flight of the Honey Bee. Lovelock, Brian, illus. 2015. (Read & Wonder Ser.). (ENG.). 32p. (J). (gr. -1-2). 8.99 (978-0-7636-7648-3(9)) Candlewick Pr.

Hudson, Cheryl Willis. Hands Can Big Book. Bourke, John-Francis, photos by. 2012. (ENG., Illus.). 32p. (J). (gr. k-k). pap. 27.99 (978-0-7636-5819-9(7)) Candlewick Pr.

Huggins, Peter. Trosclair & the Alligator, 1 vol. Gardiner, Lindsey, illus. 2013. (ENG.). 32p. (J). pap. 7.95 (978-1-59572-640-7(3)) Star Bright Bks., Inc.

Hughes, Emily. Wild. 2013. (ENG., Illus.). 32p. (J). (gr. -1-2). 16.95 (978-1-909263-08-6(7)) Flying Eye Bks. GBR. Dist: Penguin Random Hse. LLC.

Hughes, John Ceiriog. All Through the Night. Boulton, Harold, tr. Alizadeh, Kate, illus. 2013. (ENG.). 24p. (J). (gr. -1-2). bds. 12.95 (978-1-927018-09-5(9)) Simply Read Bks. CAN. Dist: Ingram Publisher Services.

Hughes, Marghanita. Toffee at Home on the Farm. (Illus.). 20p. 13.95 (978-1-899827-50-3(1)) Scottish Children's Pr. GBR. Dist: Gatewood Pr.

Hughes, Mónica. Little Mouse Deer & the Crocodile. Moricuchi, Mique, illus. 2004. 24p. (J). lib. bdg. 23.65 (978-1-59646-684-5(7)) Dingles & Co.

—More Little Mouse Deer Tales. Clemenston, John, illus. 2005. 24p. (J). lib. bdg. 23.65 (978-1-59646-730-9(4)) Dingles & Co.

Hughes-Odgers, Kyle. One Thousand Trees. 2019. 32p. (J). 12.95 (978-1-925591-78-1(6)) Fremantle Pr. AUS. Dist: Independent Pubs. Group.

Hughes, Sarah Anne. Peterson Field Guide Coloring Books: Reptiles & Amphibians. 2nd ed. 2013. (Peterson Field Guide Color-In Bks.). (ENG., Illus.). 64p. 10.99 (978-0-544-02695-7(0), 1529290, Mariner Bks.) HarperCollins Pubs.

Hughes, Shirley. Alfie & Dad. Hughes, Shirley, illus. 2017. (Alfie Ser.). (ENG., Illus.). 32p. (J). (gr. -1-k). 22.99 (978-1-78230-066-3(X)) Penguin Random Hse. GBR. Dist: Independent Pubs. Group.

—Alfie & Dad. 2018. (Alfie Ser.). (Illus.). 32p. (J). (-k). pap. 14.99 (978-1-78295-691-4(3), Red Fox) Random House Children's Books GBR. Dist: Independent Pubs. Group.

—Alfie & His Very Best Friend. 2016. (Alfie Ser.). (ENG., Illus.). 32p. (J). (gr. -1-k). 19.99 (978-1-78230-061-8(9)) Penguin Random Hse. GBR. Dist: Independent Pubs. Group.

—Alfie & Mum. 2017. (Alfie Ser.). (Illus.). 32p. (J). (gr. -1-k). pap. 12.99 (978-1-78295-645-7(X), Red Fox) Random House Children's Books GBR. Dist: Independent Pubs. Group.

—Alfie at Nursery School. 2018. (ENG., Illus.). 32p. (J). (-k). 19.99 (978-1-78230-071-7(6)) Penguin Random Hse. GBR. Dist: Independent Pubs. Group.

—Alfie Gets in First. 2018. (Alfie Ser.). (Illus.). 30p. (J). (gr. -1-k). bds. 12.99 (978-1-78295-658-7(1), Red Fox) Random House Children's Books GBR. Dist: Independent Pubs. Group.

—Alfie Outdoors. 2016. (Alfie Ser.). (Illus.). 32p. (J). (-k). pap. 14.99 (978-1-78295-265-7(9), Red Fox) Random House Children's Books GBR. Dist: Independent Pubs. Group.

—Alfie's Christmas. 2016. (Alfie Ser.). (ENG., Illus.). 32p. (J). (gr. -1-k). 12.99 (978-1-78230-064-9(3)) Penguin Random Hse. GBR. Dist: Independent Pubs. Group.

—Jonadab & Rita. Hughes, Shirley, illus. 2010. (Alfie Ser.). (ENG., Illus.). 32p. (J). (gr. -1-k). pap. 11.99 (978-1-86230-313-3(4), Red Fox) Random House Children's Books GBR. Dist: Independent Pubs. Group.

—Lucy & Tom at School. 2018. (Lucy & Tom Ser.). (Illus.). 32p. (J). (gr. -1-k). pap. 12.99 (978-1-78295-659-4(X), Red Fox) Random House Children's Books GBR. Dist: Independent Pubs. Group.

—Lucy & Tom at the Seaside. 2016. (Illus.). 32p. (J). (-k). pap. 12.99 (978-1-78295-516-0(X), Red Fox) Random House Children's Books GBR. Dist: Independent Pubs. Group.

—Ruby in the Ruins. 2018. (Illus.). 32p. (J). (978-1-4063-7589-3(6)) Candlewick Pr.

Hughes, Susan. Bath Time. 2017. (Time To Ser.). (ENG., Illus.). 14p. (J). (gr. -1). bds. 7.99 (978-1-55451-947-7(0)) Annick Pr., Ltd. CAN. Dist: Publishers Group West (PGW).

—Nap Time. 2017. (ENG., Illus.). 14p. (J). (gr. -1). bds. 7.99 (978-1-55451-949-1(7)) Annick Pr., Ltd. CAN. Dist: Publishers Group West (PGW).

—Play Time. 2017. (ENG., Illus.). 14p. (J). (gr. -1). bds. 7.99 (978-1-55451-951-4(9)) Annick Pr., Ltd. CAN. Dist: Publishers Group West (PGW).

—Walking in the City with Jane: A Story of Jane Jacobs. Boivin, Valérie, illus. 2018. (ENG.). 36p. (J). (gr. 1-4). 18.99 (978-1-77138-653-1(3)) Kids Can Pr., Ltd. CAN. Dist: Hachette Bk. Group.

Hughes, Vi & Shefrin, Sima Elizabeth. Once upon a Bathtime, 1 vol. 2011. (ENG., Illus.). 32p. (J). (gr. -1-k). 17.95 (978-1-896580-54-8(8)) Tradewind Bks. CAN. Dist: Orca Bk. Pubs. USA.

Hulin, Rachel. Flying Henry. 2013. (ENG., Illus.). 40p. (J). (-k). 12.95 (978-1-57687-626-8(8), powerHouse Bks.) powerHse. Bks.

Hull, Maureen. Rainy Days with Bear. l.t. ed. 2012. 51p. (J). pap. (978-1-4596-3453-4(5)) ReadHowYouWant.com, Ltd.

Humphreys, Audrey. The Dragon Princess. 2012. 24p. pap. 24.99 (978-1-4691-6554-7(6)) Xlibris Corp.

Humphreys, Neil. I Trapped a Dolphin but It Really Wasn't My Fault. Cheng, Puay Koon, illus. 2013. (Abbie Rose & the Magic Suitcase Ser.). (ENG.). 24p. (J). (gr. -1 — 1). pap. 13.99 (978-981-4408-51-6(4)) Marshall Cavendish International (Asia) Private Ltd. SGP. Dist: Independent Pubs. Group.

—Picking up a Penguin's Egg Really Got Me into Trouble. Cheng, Puay Koon, illus. 2014. (Abbie Rose & the Magic Suitcase Ser.). (ENG.). 24p. (J). (gr. -1 — 1). pap. 13.99 (978-981-4484-18-3(0)) Marshall Cavendish International (Asia) Private Ltd. SGP. Dist: Independent Pubs. Group.

Hundal, Nancy. Twilight Fairies, 1 vol. Kilby, Don, illus. 2006. (ENG.). 32p. (J). (gr. k-3). per. 4.95 (978-1-55041-961-0(7), 01caf117-4f3d-4b67-b220-705bcbbd3fb0) Fitzhenry & Whiteside, Ltd. CAN. Dist: Firefly Bks., Ltd.

Hunnicutt, M. E. The Wedding Wonderful. 2013. 24p. pap. 24.95 (978-1-62709-035-3(5)) America Star Bks.

Huntley, Tex. Adventures with Grandpa! Petrossi, Fabrizio, illus. 2018. (J). (978-1-5444-0086-0(1), Golden Bks.) Random Hse. Children's Bks.

Hurd, Thacher. Mystery on the Docks 25th Anniversary Edition. Hurd, Thacher, illus. 25th anniv. ed. 2008. (ENG., Illus.). 32p. (J). (gr. -1-3). pap. 8.99 (978-0-06-443058-6(8), HarperCollins) HarperCollins Pubs.

—The Pea Patch Jig. Hurd, Thacher, illus. rev. ed. 2015. (ENG., Illus.). 40p. (J). (gr. k-3). 16.95 (978-1-939547-21-7(0), e65be881-f4b0-4c14-b47c-f22a2beec635) Creston Bks.

Hurry, Helen, illus. Peepo! Boo! Who Are You? 2014. (ENG.). 12p. (J). 17.00 (978-0-85707-679-3(5), Simon & Schuster Children's) Simon & Schuster, Ltd. GBR. Dist: Simon & Schuster, Inc.

Hurst, Carol Otis. Picture Books in the Classroom: Addressing Concepts & Skills throughout the Curriculum Through Literature Kindergarten through Grade 2 2004. (Illus.). 285p. cd-rom 29.95 (978-0-9748509-1-7(8)) Hurst, Carol Consultants.

Hurtado, Ernest R. Freddy the Unfixer. 2011. 28p. (J). pap. 21.99 (978-1-4568-0995-9(4)) Xlibris Corp.

Husar, Jaco & Husar, Stephane. Hello, I Am Lily from New York City. Rigaudie, Mylène, illus. 2014. (AV2 Fiction Readalong Ser.: Vol. 129). (ENG.). 32p. (J). (gr. -1-3). lib. bdg. 34.28 (978-1-4896-2259-4(4), AV2 by Weigl) Weigl Pubs., Inc.

Husar, Stephane. Hello, I Am Charlie from London. Robert, Yannick, illus. 2014. (AV2 Fiction Readalong Ser.: Vol. 127). (ENG.). 32p. (J). (gr. -1-3). lib. bdg. 34.28 (978-1-4896-2256-3(X), AV2 by Weigl) Weigl Pubs., Inc.

—Hello, I Am Max from Sydney. Sofilas, Mark, illus. 2014. (AV2 Fiction Readalong Ser.: Vol. 130). (ENG.). 32p. (J). (gr. -1-3). lib. bdg. 34.28 (978-1-4896-2250-1(0), AV2 by Weigl) Weigl Pubs., Inc.

—Paolo from Rome. Le Grand, Claire, illus. 2014. (AV2 Fiction Readalong Ser.: Vol. 134). (ENG.). 32p. (J). (gr. -1-3). lib. bdg. 34.28 (978-1-4896-2274-7(8), AV2 by Weigl) Weigl Pubs., Inc.

Huser, Glen. The Snuggly, 1 vol. Pavlović, Milan, illus. 2018. (ENG.). 32p. (J). (gr. k-2). 16.95 (978-1-55498-901-0(9)) Groundwood Bks. CAN. Dist: Publishers Group West (PGW).

HuskMitNavn, illus. The Wrong Book. 2018. (ENG.). 14p. (J). bds. 14.95 (978-1-58423-673-3(6), 2a00f5cc-f841-4c71-bc2d-b1df524a6413) Gingko Pr., Inc.

Hutchins, Pat. Rosie's Walk. 2009. 9.00 (978-0-7848-2915-8(2), Everbind) Marco Bk. Co.

Hutt, Sarah. Animals Are Delicious. 2016. (ENG., Illus.). 48p. (gr. -1 — 1). 17.95 *(978-0-7148-7144-8(3))* Phaidon Pr., Inc.

Hutton, John. Fiona's Friends. 2018. (ENG., Illus.). 14p. (J). (— 1). bds. 7.99 *(978-1-936669-68-4(4))* Blue Manatee Press.

—Fiona's Feelings. Cincinnati Zoo and Botanical Garden Staff, photos by. 2018. (ENG., Illus.). 14p. (J). (— 1). bds. 7.99 *(978-1-936669-65-3(X))* Blue Manatee Press.

—SHARE This Book. Brown, Christina, illus. 2018. (ENG.). 14p. (J). (— 1). bds. 7.99 *(978-1-936669-67-7(6))* Blue Manatee Press.

—Zzzookeeper. Cenko, Doug, illus. 2018. (ENG.). 32p. (J). (gr. -1-2). 17.99 *(978-1-936669-69-1(2))* Blue Manatee Press.

Huusmann, Thomas-Bo & Fables, Aesops. The Lion & the Mouse. 2013. 26p. pap. *(978-87-995724-4-1(3))* Huusmann, Thomas-Bo.

Huxley, Dee & Huxley, Tiffany. My Brother. Huxley, Oliver, illus. 2019. (ENG.). 32p. pap. 6.99 *(978-1-921504-95-2(1)*, Working Title Pr.) HarperCollins Pubs. Australia AUS. Dist: HarperCollins Pubs.

Hyman, Zachary. The Bambino & Me. Pullen, Zachary, illus. 2014. (ENG.). 48p. (J). (gr. 1-4). 17.99 *(978-1-77049-627-9(0)*, Tundra Bks.) Tundra Bks. CAN. Dist: Penguin Random Hse. LLC.

Icilda. God Made Me Perfect & Wonderful: To Do What? 2009. 28p. pap. 13.99 *(978-1-4490-4545-6(6))* AuthorHouse.

Icinori. Issun Boshi: The One-Inch Boy. 2014. (ENG., Illus.). 40p. (J). 19.95 *(978-3-89955-718-3(2))* Die Gestalten Verlag DEU. Dist: Ingram Publisher Services.

III, Maxwell Eaton. The Truth about Dolphins: Seriously Funny Facts about Your Favorite Animals. 2018. (Truth about Your Favorite Animals Ser.). (ENG., Illus.). 32p. (J). 17.99 *(978-1-62672-668-0(X)*, 900169985) Roaring Brook Pr.

Ikids Staff. Ibaby - Goodnight, Baby: Tuck All the Babies into Their Beds. Larranaga, Ana Martin, illus. 2006. (ENG.). 12p. (J). (gr. -1 — 1). 9.99 *(978-1-58476-482-3(1)*, IKIDS) Innovative Kids.

Imperato, Teresa. Colors All Around: A Turn & Pop Book. Petrone, Valeria, illus. 2005. (Turn & Pop Book Ser.). 10p. (J). bds. 5.95 *(978-1-58117-277-5(X)*, Intervisual/Piggy Toes) Bendon, Inc.

—Good Morning, Good Night! Mitchell, Melanie, illus. 2006. (ENG.). 12p. (J). (gr. -1-18). 9.95 *(978-1-58117-279-9(6)*, Intervisual/Piggy Toes) Bendon, Inc.

—How Many Ducks in a Row? A Turn & Pop Book. Petrone, Valeria, illus. 2005. 10p. (J). bds. 5.95 *(978-1-58117-278-2(8)*, Intervisual/Piggy Toes) Bendon, Inc.

Impey, Rose. Digger Disaster. Chatterton, Chris, illus. 2017. (Dino Diggers Ser.). (ENG.). 24p. (J). pap. *(978-1-4088-7244-4(7)*, 296265, Bloomsbury Children's Bks.) Bloomsbury Publishing Plc.

—Dumper Truck Danger. Chatterton, Chris, illus. 2018. (Dino Diggers Ser.). (ENG.). 24p. (J). pap. *(978-1-4088-7248-2(X)*, 296272, Bloomsbury Children's Bks.) Bloomsbury Publishing Plc.

—Ten Little Babies. Smee, Nicola, illus. 2011. (ENG.). 32p. (J). (gr. -1-k). *(978-1-4088-1118-4(9)*, 38990, Bloomsbury Children's Bks.) Bloomsbury Publishing Plc.

Ingham, Anne. The Ball Book. 2012. 28p. pap. 21.99 *(978-1-4691-8747-1(7))* Xlibris Corp.

Ingledew, Leah. Ugly Ollie. 2018. (ENG., Illus.). 34p. (J). pap. 15.95 *(978-1-78878-201-2(1)*, 4d451ea0-23bb-4cd7-8cfd-0ab2d390b4fa) Austin Macauley Pubs. Ltd. GBR. Dist: Baker & Taylor Publisher Services (BTPS).

Inglese, Judith. I Have a Friend. 2014. (ENG., Illus.). 40p. (J). 17.95 *(978-1-935874-22-5(5))* Satya Hse. Pubns.

Ingman, Bruce, illus. My Worst Book Ever! 2018. 64p. (J). (gr. k-5). 16.95 *(978-0-500-65090-5(X)*, 565090) Thames & Hudson.

Inkpen, Mick. Beachmoles & Bellvine. MC, ed. 2006. (Blue Nose Island Ser.: Bk. 2). (Illus.). 34p. (J). (gr. -1). 13.95 *(978-1-84456-225-1(5))* Hodder & Stoughton GBR. Dist: Trafalgar Square Publishing.

—Hide Me, Kipper. 2016. (Kipper Ser.). (ENG., Illus.). 32p. (J). (gr. -1-k). 7.99 *(978-1-4449-2977-5(1))* Hachette Children's Group GBR. Dist: Hachette Bk. Group.

—Kipper's Beach Ball. 2016. (Kipper Ser.). (ENG., Illus.). 32p. (J). (gr. -1-k). pap. 7.99 *(978-1-4449-2402-2(8))* Hachette Children's Group GBR. Dist: Hachette Bk. Group.

—One Year with Kipper. 2015. (ENG., Illus.). 32p. (J). (gr. -1-k). pap. 10.99 *(978-1-4449-1820-5(6))* Hodder & Stoughton GBR. Dist: Hachette Bk. Group.

Innovative Kids Staff, creator. Soft Shapes Photo Books: Tropical Fish. 2012. (ENG., Illus.). 8p. (J). (gr. -1 — 1). 10.99 *(978-1-60169-225-2(0))* Innovative Kids.

—Vehicles. 2012. (ENG., Illus.). 1p. (J). (gr. -1 — 1). 10.99 *(978-1-60169-224-5(2))* Innovative Kids.

Ipcar, Dahlov, illus. Black & White. 2015. (ENG.). 40p. (J). (gr. -1-2). 17.95 *(978-1-909263-44-4(3))* Flying Eye Bks. GBR. Dist: Penguin Random Hse. LLC.

Ipcizade, Catherine. 'Twas the Day Before Zoo Day, 1 vol. Hodson, Ben, illus. 2008. (Basic Math Operations Ser.). (ENG.). 32p. (J). (gr. -1-2). 17.95 *(978-1-60718-585-7(7))* Arbordale Publishing.

Irving Ed.D., Harry R. Un Image-Word D'Enfants et Livre Simple de Phrase: Version Francaise Catégories Primaires. 2010. 192p. pap. 51.53 *(978-1-4251-6396-9(3))* Trafford Publishing.

Isadora, Rachel. Say Hello! Isadora, Rachel, illus. 2010. (ENG., Illus.). 32p. (J). (gr. -1-k). 17.99 *(978-0-399-25230-3(4)*, G.P. Putnam's Sons Books for Young Readers) Penguin Young Readers Group.

Isis, Watalia. Ronald's Adventures Throught Time & Imagination. 2013. (Illus.). 40p. pap. *(978-0-9575371-8-7(2))* Starflower Pr.

Israel, Susan E. Be Just Me. 2012. 26p. pap. *(978-0-9827449-6-3(X))* Roxby Media Ltd.

Ives, Burl. Sailing on a Very Fine Day. Myers, Bernice & Myers, Lou, illus. 2011. 32p. pap. 35.95 *(978-1-258-04002-4(6))* Literary Licensing, LLC.

Ives, Frances. Maybe the Moon. 2019. (ENG., Illus.). 32p. (J). (gr. -1-k). pap. 9.99 *(978-1-910552-84-1(4))* O'Mara, Michael Bks., Ltd. GBR. Dist: Independent Pubs. Group.

Iwamura, Kazuo. Bedtime in the Forest. 2010. (ENG., Illus.). 32p. (J). (gr. -1-2). 19.95 *(978-0-7358-2310-5(3))* North-South Bks., Inc.

Iwamura, Kazuo & Yamashita, Haruo. Seven Little Mice Go to the Beach. 2012. (ENG., Illus.). 32p. (J). (gr. -1-1). 16.95 *(978-0-7358-4073-7(3))* North-South Bks., Inc.

Izumo, Rebecca. Colorful Race Cars, 1 vol. 2017. (Wonderful World of Colors Ser.). (ENG.). 24p. (gr. 1-1). pap. 9.25 *(978-1-5383-2095-2(9)*, d81ab878-673f-4dde-b482-0105f5f2803c, PowerKids Pr.) Rosen Publishing Group, Inc., The.

Jack, David M. The Treehouse Adventure. Brown, Christopher, illus. 2017. (Furnace Room Ser.: 2). 36p. (J). (gr. k-3). 21.33 *(978-0-692-81087-3(0))* BookBaby.

Jackson, Kathryn. Richard Scarry's the Animals' Merry Christmas. Scarry, Richard, illus. 2016. (J). *(978-1-5182-2103-3(3)*, Golden Bks.) Random Hse. Children's Bks.

Jackson, Max. 123, Anteater Stuck up a Tree: A Curious Counting Book. Jackson, Max, illus. 2019. (ENG., Illus.). 32p. (J). (— 1). 16.99 *(978-1-78055-531-7(8))* O'Mara, Michael Bks., Ltd. GBR. Dist: Independent Pubs. Group.

Jacobson, Ryan. Super Animal Powers: The Amazing Abilities of Animals. 2016. (Wildlife Picture Bks.). (ENG., Illus.). 32p. (J). (gr. -1-3). 12.95 *(978-1-59193-648-0(9)*, Adventure Pubns.) AdventureKEEN.

—What Eats That? Predators, Prey, & the Food Chain. 2017. (Wildlife Picture Bks.). (ENG., Illus.). 32p. (J). (gr. -1-3). 14.95 *(978-1-59193-749-4(3)*, Adventure Pubns.) AdventureKEEN.

Jahn, Benny. Ah-Choo - God Bless You. Scott, Chelsey, illus. 2009. 24p. pap. 11.95 *(978-1-60844-178-5(4))* Dog Ear Publishing, LLC.

James, Diane. Here We Go. 2004. (Jigsaw Rhymes Ser.). (ENG., Illus.). 12p. (J). (gr. -1-k). 9.95 *(978-1-58728-024-5(8)*, Two-Can Publishing) T&N Children's Publishing.

James, Simon. The Boy Who Went to Mars. James, Simon, illus. 2018. (ENG., Illus.). 32p. (J). (gr. -1-2). 16.99 *(978-0-7636-9598-9(X))* Candlewick Pr.

—Frog & Beaver. James, Simon, illus. 2018. (ENG., Illus.). 32p. (J). (gr. -1-2). 16.99 *(978-0-7636-9819-5(9))* Candlewick Pr.

Janousky, Peggy Robbins. Move It, Miss Macintosh! Lands, Meghan, illus. 2016. (ENG.). 32p. (J). (gr. -1-2). 9.95 *(978-1-55451-862-3(8))* Annick Pr., Ltd. CAN. Dist: Publishers Group West (PGW).

Janry, Tome, illus. Spirou & Fantasio in Moscow, Vol. 6. 2014. (Spirou & Fantasio Ser.: 6). 48p. (J). (gr. -1-12). pap. 11.95 *(978-1-84918-193-8(4))* CineBook GBR. Dist: National Bk. Network.

Jardine Stoddart, Heidi. Back to the Beach, 1 vol. 2009. (ENG., Illus.). 32p. (J). (gr. 1-3). 12.95 *(978-1-55109-702-2(8)*, d7c26c62-ea19-4d5f-bd53-296e3752f163) Nimbus Publishing, Ltd. CAN. Dist: Baker & Taylor Publisher Services (BTPS).

—East to the Sea, 1 vol. 2006. (ENG., Illus.). 32p. (J). (gr. -1-3). pap. 11.95 *(978-1-55109-577-6(7)*, 3cfbcb0f-f867-4d00-a28a-91cd0f76dc07) Nimbus Publishing, Ltd. CAN. Dist: Baker & Taylor Publisher Services (BTPS).

Jarman, Julia. Molly & the Giant. Sholto, Walker, illus. 2005. (ENG.). 24p. (J). lib. bdg. 23.65 *(978-1-59646-746-0(0))* Dingles & Co.

Jarvis. Tropical Terry. Jarvis, illus. 2019. (ENG., Illus.). 32p. (J). (-k). 16.99 *(978-1-5362-0546-6(X))* Candlewick Pr.

Jason Fulford, Tamara Shopsin. A Pile of Leaves: Published in Collaboration with the Whitney Museum of American Art. 2018. (ENG., Illus.). 24p. (gr. -1 — 1). bds. 18.95 *(978-0-7148-7720-4(4))* Phaidon Pr., Inc.

Jay, Alison. Bee & Me. Jay, Alison, illus. 2017. (Old Barn Bks.). (ENG., Illus.). 32p. (J). (-k). 17.99 *(978-0-7636-9010-6(4))* Candlewick Pr.

—Song of the Stars, 1 vol. 2015. (ENG., Illus.). 32p. (J). bds. 7.99 *(978-0-310-73630-1(7))* Zonderkidz.

Jay, Alison, illus. Bee & Me. 2017. (J). *(978-0-605-97081-6(5))* Candlewick Pr.

Jay, Larsen. What If Cows Could... ? 2005. (J). lib. bdg. 19.95 *(978-1-933732-01-5(6))* Big Ransom Studio.

Jeffers, Oliver. An Alphabet. Jeffers, Oliver, illus. 2017. (ENG., Illus.). 26p. (J). (— 1). bds. 9.99 *(978-0-399-54542-9(5)*, Philomel Bks.) Penguin Young Readers Group.

—Once upon an Alphabet: Short Stories for All the Letters. Jeffers, Oliver, illus. 2014. (ENG., Illus.). 112p. (J). (gr. -1-k). 26.99 *(978-0-399-16791-1(9)*, Philomel Bks.) Penguin Young Readers Group.

Jenkins, Martin. Exploring Space: from Galileo to the Mars Rover & Beyond. Biesty, Stephen, illus. 2017. (ENG.). 64p. (J). (gr. 3-7). 17.99 *(978-0-7636-8931-5(9))* Candlewick Pr.

—Fabulous Frogs. Hopgood, Tim, illus. 2018. (Read & Wonder Ser.). (ENG.). 32p. (J). (gr. k-3). 7.99 *(978-0-7636-9970-3(5))* Candlewick Pr.

Jenkins, Steve. Just a Second. Jenkins, Steve, illus. 2017. (ENG., Illus.). 32p. (J). (gr. -1-3). pap. 7.99 *(978-1-328-74086-1(2)*, 1677123, Clarion Bks.) HarperCollins Pubs.

Jenkyns, Brenda. Ever After. 2012. pap. 11.95 *(978-0-7414-7620-3(7))* Infinity Publishing.

Jennings, Linda. Duna y Dan. Chapman, Jane, illus. (SPA.). 28p. (J). (gr. k-1). *(978-84-8418-027-2(1)*, ZZ4481) Zendrera Zariquiey, Editorial ESP. Dist: Lectorum Pubns., Inc.

Jennings, Sharon, et al, adapted by. Franklin's Picnic. 2006. (Kids Can Read Ser.). (ENG., Illus.). 32p. (J). (gr. 1-2). 14.95 *(978-1-55337-714-6(1))* Kids Can Pr., Ltd. CAN. Dist: Hachette Bk. Group.

Jennings, Sharon, et al. Franklin the Detective. Gagnon, Céleste, illus. 2004. 32p. (J). pap. *(978-0-439-41822-5(4))* Scholastic, Inc.

Jenny Press Staff. Peter Pan. 2016. (Illus.). 24p. (J). (gr. -1-12). pap. 7.99 *(978-1-86147-815-3(1)*, Armadillo) Anness Publishing GBR. Dist: National Bk. Network.

Jensen, Bonnie Rickner. A Very Merry Christmas Prayer: A Sweet Poem of Gratitude for Holiday Joys, Family Traditions, & Baby Jesus, 1 vol. 2015. (Time to Pray Ser.). (ENG., Illus.). 24p. (J). bds. 8.99 *(978-0-7180-3053-7(2)*, Tommy Nelson) Nelson, Thomas Inc.

Jian, Li. The Horse & the Mysterious Drawing: A Story in English & Chinese (Stories of the Chinese Zodiac) 2013. (Stories of the Chinese Zodiac Ser.). (ENG., Illus.). 42p. (gr. -1-3). 16.95 *(978-1-60220-984-8(7))* Shanghai Pr.

—Ming's Adventure with the Terracotta Army: A Terracotta Army General 'Souvenir' Comes Alive & Swoops Ming Away! Wert, Yijin, tr. 2013. (ENG., Illus.). 42p. (gr. -1-3). 16.95 *(978-1-60220-983-1(9))* Shanghai Pr.

—The Snake Goddess Colors the World: A Chinese Tale Told in English & Chinese. Jian, Li, illus. 2013. (Stories of the Chinese Zodiac Ser.). (ENG., Illus.). 42p. (gr. -1-3). 16.95 *(978-1-60220-982-4(0))* Shanghai Pr.

Jin, Nayoung. Shooting Star Rider. Côté, Geneviève, illus. 2017. (ENG.). 36p. (J). (gr. -1-3). 16.95 *(978-1-77229-020-2(3))* Simply Read Bks. CAN. Dist: Ingram Publisher Services.

Job. Yakari & Nanabozo. Derib, illus. 2014. (Yakari Ser.: 11). 48p. (J). (gr. -1-12). pap. 11.95 *(978-1-84918-177-8(2))* CineBook GBR. Dist: National Bk. Network.

Job Joris & Marieke. Who Did That? a Whodunit for Children. 2018. (Illus.). 32p. (J). (gr. -1). 15.95 *(978-2-924786-38-3(X)*, CrackBoom! Bks.) Chouette Publishing CAN. Dist: Publishers Group West (PGW).

Jocelyn, Marthe. Over Under. Slaughter, Tom, illus. 2005. 24p. (J). (gr. k-k). 15.99 *(978-0-88776-708-1(7)*, Tundra Bks.) Tundra Bks. CAN. Dist: Penguin Random Hse. LLC.

—Sam Sorts. 2017. (Illus.). 32p. (J). (gr. -1-2). 16.99 *(978-1-101-91805-0(5)*, Tundra Bks.) Tundra Bks. CAN. Dist: Penguin Random Hse. LLC.

John, Jory. Come Home Already! Davies, Benji, illus. 2017. (ENG.). 32p. (J). (gr. -1-3). 19.99 *(978-0-06-237097-6(9)*, 118990985, HarperCollins) HarperCollins Pubs.

—Penguin Problems. Smith, Lane, illus. 2018. (ENG.). 32p. (J). (— 1). bds. 8.99 *(978-0-525-64575-7(6)*, Random Hse. Bks. for Young Readers) Random Hse. Children's Bks.

John, Margaret. Little Belly Monster Makes a Pizza. Kim, Sarah, illus. 2011. 36p. pap. *(978-0-9869424-0-2(5))* Belly Productions, Inc.

John Taylor, Jeannie St. Penguin's Special Christmas Tree. l.t. ed. 2012. 36p. (J). pap. *(978-1-4596-3452-7(7))* ReadHowYouWant.com, Ltd.

Johnson, Crockett. Harold's Imagination: 3 Adventures with the Purple Crayon. Johnson, Crockett, illus. 2018. (ENG., Illus.). 208p. (J). (gr. -1-3). 19.99 *(978-0-06-283945-9(4)*, HarperCollins) HarperCollins Pubs.

—Time for Spring. Johnson, Crockett, illus. 2016. (ENG., Illus.). 40p. (J). (gr. -1-3). 14.99 *(978-0-06-243033-5(5)*, HarperCollins) HarperCollins Pubs.

Johnson, D. B. Henry Hikes to Fitchburg. 2006. (Henry Book Ser.). (ENG., Illus.). 32p. (J). (gr. -1-3). reprint ed. 8.99 *(978-0-618-73749-9(9)*, 488706, Clarion Bks.) HarperCollins Pubs.

Johnson, Dennis. The Tree That Went Sailing. 2009. (J). pap. *(978-1-61623-539-0(X))* Independent Pub.

—The Tree That Went Sailing: (Based on a true story - Palm Beach, Florida) 2009. (ENG.). 40p. pap. 21.99 *(978-1-4415-0181-3(9))* Xlibris Corp.

Johnson, Michael G. & Johnson, Michael G. Iroquois: People of the Longhouse. 2013. (ENG., Illus.). 160p. 35.00 *(978-1-77085-218-1(2)*, a3d5f8cc-6d1b-4288-8207-96ecb55419a0) Firefly Bks., Ltd.

Johnson, Myrna. Cool Cat Says Hear the Story Here. 2018. (ENG., Illus.). 32p. pap. 12.00 *(978-1-62288-179-6(6)*, P563682) Austin, Stephen F. State Univ. Pr.

—Cool Cats Carry Canes. 2014. (ENG., Illus.). 32p. (gr. -1-3). pap. 12.00 *(978-1-62288-088-1(9)*, P472924) Austin, Stephen F. State Univ. Pr.

Johnston, Jan. Amélie the Most Amazing Butterfly: I Do So Love Being a Butterfly ... 2013. (Illus.). 24p. pap. 17.99 *(978-1-4817-8018-6(2))* AuthorHouse.

—Lisa Finds a Playful Tree Elf: No! I Am Not a Fairy! 2013. (Illus.). 24p. pap. 17.99 *(978-1-4817-8020-9(4))* AuthorHouse.

Johnston, Johanna. Whale's Way. Weisgard, Leonard, illus. 2015. 48p. 20.00 *(978-1-85124-428-7(X))* Bodleian Library GBR. Dist: Chicago Distribution Ctr.

Johnston, Tony. Loving Hands. Bates, Amy June, illus. 2018. (ENG.). 32p. (J). (gr. -1-1). 16.99 *(978-0-7636-7993-4(3))* Candlewick Pr.

Jonas, Debbie Sue. The Key Lime Candies Clubt in Two Turtles' Tales. 2012. 44p. pap. 17.49 *(978-1-4691-5283-7(5))* Xlibris Corp.

Jones, Bryony. Where's Santa? Whelon, Chuck, illus. 2015. (ENG.). 32p. (J). (gr. k-3). 12.99 *(978-1-4814-0619-2(1)*, Aladdin) Simon & Schuster Children's Publishing.

Jones, Ceri Wyn. Ruck in the Muck. 2015. (ENG., Illus.). 32p. (J). pap. 8.95 *(978-1-78562-067-6(3))* Gomer Pr. GBR. Dist: Casemate Pubs. & Bk. Distributors, LLC.

Jones, Christianne C. Lacey Walker, Nonstop Talker, 1 vol. Watson, Richard, illus. 2013. (Little Boost Ser.). (ENG.). 32p. (J). (gr. -1-1). 14.95 *(978-1-4795-2156-2(6)*, 123866, Picture Window Bks.) Capstone.

—Lucía Villar Habla Sin Parar. Aparicio Publishing LLC, Aparicio Publishing, tr. Watson, Richard, illus. (Pasito a Pasito Ser.).Tr. of Lacey Walker, Nonstop Talker. (SPA.). 32p. (J). (gr. -1-1). 2020. pap. 9.95 *(978-1-5158-6083-9(3)*, 142361) 2019. lib. bdg. 23.99 *(978-1-5158-4734-2(9)*, 141332) Capstone. (Picture Window Bks.).

Jones, Janey Louise. Princess Poppy: the Sleepover. 2016. (Princess Poppy Picture Bks.). (ENG., Illus.). 32p. (J). (gr. -1-k). pap. 11.99 *(978-0-552-57069-5(9))* Transworld Publishers Ltd. GBR. Dist: Independent Pubs. Group.

Jones, Kristy. The Adventures of Ziggy the Trucker Dog. 2010. (ENG.). 24p. pap. 15.99 *(978-1-4500-8751-3(5))* Xlibris Corp.

Jones, Nicholas. Pandora's Feather. 2017. (ENG., Illus.). 20p. (J). pap. 14.95 *(978-1-78554-790-4(9)*, 6319e61b-3e44-42d7-a0cc-a29be2521928) Austin Macauley Pubs. Ltd. GBR. Dist: Baker & Taylor Publisher Services (BTPS).

Jones, Pip. The Chocolate Monster. Hughes, Laura, illus. 2019. (Ruby Roo Ser.: 2). (ENG.). 32p. pap. 9.95 *(978-0-571-32751-5(6)*, Faber & Faber Children's Bks.) Faber & Faber, Inc.

Jones, Rebecca, illus. My Body. 2018. (First Explorers Ser.). (ENG.). 10p. (J). (— 1). bds. 8.95 *(978-1-4549-2942-0(1))* Sterling Publishing Co., Inc.

Jones, Sarah. Ears, Nose, Eyes... Surprise! 2018. (ROYGBaby Ser.). (ENG., Illus.). 14p. (J). (— 1). bds. 7.99 *(978-1-936669-62-2(5))* Blue Manatee Press.

Jones, Sonia. Yoga Poga Shmoga! Dakins, Todd, illus. 2016. (ENG.). 36p. (J). (gr. k-2). pap. 3.99 *(978-1-943154-32-6(5)*, See-Saw Publishing) Peek-A-Boo Publishing.

—Yoga Poga Shmoga! Dakins, Todd, illus. 2016. (ENG.). 36p. (J). (gr. k-2). 7.95 *(978-1-943154-33-3(3)*, See-Saw Publishing) Peek-A-Boo Publishing.

Jones, Tammy. My Pet. 2009. (Sight Word Readers Set A Ser.). (J). 3.49 net. *(978-1-60719-145-2(8))* Newmark Learning LLC.

—My Town. 2009. (Sight Word Readers Set A Ser.). (J). *(978-1-60719-147-6(4))* Newmark Learning LLC.

—We Go to School. 2009. (Sight Word Readers Set A Ser.). (J). 3.49 net. *(978-1-60719-146-9(6))* Newmark Learning LLC.

—We Have Fruit. 2009. (Sight Word Readers Set A Ser.). (J). *(978-1-60719-136-0(9))* Newmark Learning LLC.

—We Like Birthdays. 2009. (Sight Word Readers Set A Ser.). (J). 3.49 net. *(978-1-60719-149-0(0))* Newmark Learning LLC.

—What Has Stripes? 2009. (Sight Word Readers Set A Ser.). (J). 3.49 net. *(978-1-60719-151-3(2))* Newmark Learning LLC.

Joosse, Barbara. Sail Away Dragon. Cecil, Randy, illus. 2017. (Girl & Dragon Bks.). (ENG.). 32p. (J). (gr. -1-2). 15.99 *(978-0-7636-7313-0(7))* Candlewick Pr.

Jordan, Apple, adapted by. The Right Track. 2017. (Illus.). 24p. (J). *(978-1-5182-3645-7(6))* Random Hse., Inc.

Jorden, Brooke. Lit for Little Hands: the Secret Garden, Volume 4. Miles, David, illus. 2019. (Lit for Little Hands Ser.: 4). (ENG.). 16p. (J). (gr. -1-1). bds. 12.99 *(978-1-64170-105-1(6)*, 550105) Familius LLC.

—100 First Words for Little Geeks. Kershner, Kyle, illus. 2018. (100 First Words Ser.). (ENG.). 20p. (J). (gr. -1 — 1). bds. 9.99 *(978-1-945547-95-9(2)*, 554795) Familius LLC.

Jorden, Tyler. Physics Animated! Martins, Elsa, illus. 2019. (ENG.). 14p. (J). (gr. k-2). bds. 14.99 *(978-1-64170-132-7(3)*, 550132) Familius LLC.

Jorgensen, Norman. Last Viking Returns. Foley, James, illus. 2018. (Last Viking Ser.). 32p. (J). (gr. -1-k). 12.95 *(978-1-925163-16-2(4))* Fremantle Pr. AUS. Dist: Independent Pubs. Group.

Josiah, Iris. Tiny Bird. 2012. (Illus.). 28p. (J). pap. *(978-0-9572728-4-2(7))* Tiny Island Pr.

—Tiny Goat. 2012. (Illus.). 28p. (J). pap. *(978-0-9572728-2-8(0))* Tiny Island Pr.

—Tiny Goat's Alphabet Book. 2015. (Illus.). 40p. (J). pap. *(978-0-9572728-7-3(1))* Tiny Island Pr.

—Tiny Hen. 2012. (Illus.). 28p. (J). pap. *(978-0-9572728-3-5(9))* Tiny Island Pr.

—Tiny Hen's Alphabet Book. 2015. (Illus.). 40p. (J). pap. *(978-0-9572728-8-0(X))* Tiny Island Pr.

—Tiny Pig. 2012. (Illus.). 28p. (J). pap. *(978-0-9572728-1-1(2))* Tiny Island Pr.

—Tiny Pig's Alphabet Book. 2015. (Illus.). 40p. (J). pap. *(978-0-9572728-6-6(3))* Tiny Island Pr.

—Tiny Rabbit. 2012. (Illus.). 28p. (J). pap. *(978-0-9572728-0-4(4))* Tiny Island Pr.

—Tiny Rabbit's Alphabet Book. 2015. (Illus.). 40p. (J). pap. *(978-0-9572728-5-9(5))* Tiny Island Pr.

Jovanovic, Katarina. The King Has Goat Ears, 1 vol. Béha, Phillippe, illus. 2008. (ENG.). 32p. (J). (gr. -1-k). 16.95 *(978-1-896580-22-7(X))* Tradewind Bks. CAN. Dist: Orca Bk. Pubs. USA.

Joyce, William. The Sandman: The Story of Sanderson Mansnoozie. Joyce, William, illus. 2012. (Guardians of Childhood Ser.). (ENG., Illus.). 48p. (J). (gr. -1-3). 19.99 *(978-1-4424-3042-6(7)*, Atheneum Bks. for Young Readers) Simon & Schuster Children's Publishing.

Judge, Chris. The Great Explorer. 2012. (ENG., Illus.). 32p. (J). (gr. -1-2). pap. 13.99 *(978-1-84939-401-7(6))* Andersen Pr. GBR. Dist: Independent Pubs. Group.

Judge, Chris & Wickham, Mark. Brian & the Vikings. 2014. (ENG., Illus.). 32p. (J). pap. 14.00 *(978-1-84717-687-5(9))* O'Brien Pr., Ltd., The IRL. Dist: Casemate Pubs. & Bk. Distributors, LLC.

Jugran, Jan. Baby Dolphins. Larranaga, Ana Martin, illus. 2006. (ENG.). 6p. (J). (gr. -1 — 1). 14.99 *(978-1-58476-490-8(2)*, IKIDS) Innovative Kids.

Jullien, Jean. This Is Not a Book. 2016. (ENG., Illus.). 32p. (gr. -1 — 1). bds. 16.95 *(978-0-7148-7112-7(5))* Phaidon Pr., Inc.

—Why the Face? 2018. (ENG., Illus.). 32p. (gr. -1 — 1). bds. 16.95 *(978-0-7148-7719-8(0))* Phaidon Pr., Inc.

Kaiser, Lori. George Washington. Kaiser, Lori, illus. 2012. (Illus.). 26p. pap. *(978-0-9836651-7-5(6))* Roxby Media Ltd.

Kala & Kol. Where Your Love Is: For Peace Is in This Place. 2012. 60p. pap. 31.99 *(978-1-4691-5926-3(0))* Xlibris Corp.

Kaldor, Connie. A Duck in New York City. Fil & Julie, Connie, illus. 2005. (ENG.). 36p. (J). (gr. -1-2). 16.95 *(978-2-923163-02-4(8))* La Montagne Secrete CAN. Dist: Independent Pubs. Group.

—A Poodle in Paris. Fil & Julie, Connie, illus. 2006. (ENG.). 36p. (J). (gr. -1-2). 16.95 *(978-2-923163-12-3(5))* La Montagne Secrete CAN. Dist: Independent Pubs. Group.

Kallevig, Christine P. Nature Fold-along Stories: Quick & Easy Origami Tales about Plants & Animals. 2009. (ENG., Illus.). 80p. (Orig.). (J). (gr. k-8). pap. 11.95 *(978-0-9628769-2-9(5))* Storytime Ink International.

Kalman, Maira. Looking at Lincoln. Kalman, Maira, illus. 2017. (ENG., Illus.). 48p. (J). (gr. k-3). pap. 8.99 *(978-0-14-751798-2(2)*, Puffin Books) Penguin Young Readers Group.

Kalomas, Alice & Kerr, Lenora. Sir Wrinkles. Utomo, Gabhor, illus. 2005. (J). 14.95 *(978-0-9766639-0-4(2))* Sir Wrinkles Pr.

Kamke, Bridget. The Story of the Infinipede. Ospital, Geneveive, illus. 2003. (J). 19.95 *(978-0-9744306-0-7(9))* You Can Do It! Productions.

Kane, Kim. Esther's Rainbow. Acton, Sara, illus. 2015. (ENG.). 32p. (J). (gr. -1-k). 16.99 *(978-1-925266-28-3(1))* Allen & Unwin AUS. Dist: Independent Pubs. Group.

Kaneko, Yuki. Into the Snow. Saito, Masamitsu, illus. 2016. (ENG.). 32p. (J). (gr. -1-2). 16.95 *(978-1-59270-188-9(4))* Enchanted Lion Bks., LLC.

Kang, Anna. I Am Not Scared. Weyant, Christopher, illus. 2017. (You Are Not Small Ser.: 3). (ENG.). 32p. (J). (gr. -1-2). 17.99 *(978-1-5039-3745-1(3)*, 9781503937451, Two Lions) Amazon Publishing.

—Will You Help Me Fall Asleep? Weyant, Christopher, illus. 2018. (ENG.). 40p. (J). (gr. -1-3). 17.99 *(978-0-06-239685-3(4)*, HarperCollins) HarperCollins Pubs.
Kangaroo at the Zoo IR. 2017. (Phonics Readers Ser.). (ENG.). (J). pap. 6.99 *(978-0-7945-3716-6(2)*, Usborne) EDC Publishing.
Kann, Victoria. Pinkalicious: 5-Minute Pinkalicious Stories: Includes 12 Pinkatastic Stories! Kann, Victoria, illus. 2017. (Pinkalicious Ser.). (ENG., Illus.). 192p. (J). (gr. -1-3). 12.99 *(978-0-06-256697-3(0)*, HarperCollins) HarperCollins Pubs.
—Pinkalicious & the New Teacher. Kann, Victoria, illus. 2014. (Pinkalicious Ser.). (ENG., Illus.). 24p. (J). (gr. -1-3). pap. 6.99 *(978-0-06-218913-4(1)*, HarperFestival) HarperCollins Pubs.
—Pinkalicious: Apples, Apples, Apples! Kann, Victoria, illus. 2016. (Pinkalicious Ser.). (ENG., Illus.). 24p. (J). (gr. -1-3). pap. 5.99 *(978-0-06-241079-5(2)*, HarperFestival) HarperCollins Pubs.
—Pinkalicious: Flower Girl. Kann, Victoria, illus. 2013. (Pinkalicious Ser.). (ENG., Illus.). 24p. (J). (gr. -1-3). pap. 3.99 *(978-0-06-218766-6(X)*, HarperFestival) HarperCollins Pubs.
—Pinkalicious: Pinkie Promise. Kann, Victoria, illus. 2011. (I Can Read Level 1 Ser.). (ENG., Illus.). 32p. (J). (gr. -1-3). 17.99 *(978-0-06-192888-8(7))*; pap. 4.99 *(978-0-06-192887-1(9))* HarperCollins Pubs. (HarperCollins).
Kantor, Susan. What Is Soft? Barker, Erin, illus. 2018. (ENG.). 14p. (J). (— 1). bds. 7.99 *(978-1-936669-63-9(3))* Blue Manatee Press.
Kao, Sleepless. Duet. 2015. (ENG., Illus.). 34p. (J). (gr. -1-3). 16.95 *(978-1-897476-76-5(0))* Simply Read Bks. CAN. Dist: Ingram Publisher Services.
Kaplan, Arie. The Threat of Thanos (Marvel Avengers) Clester, Shane, illus. 2018. (Little Golden Book Ser.). (ENG.). 24p. (J). (-k). 5.99 *(978-1-5247-6856-0(1)*, Golden Bks.) Random Hse. Children's Bks.
Kartinyeri, Doris. Bush Games & Knucklebones. McInerney, Kunyi June-Anne, illus. 2003. 32p. (J). pap. *(978-1-875641-81-9(5))* Magabala Bks.
Kates, Bobbi. We're Different, We're the Same (Sesame Street) Mathieu, Joe, illus. 2017. (ENG.). 40p. (J). (gr. -1-2). 9.99 *(978-1-5247-7056-3(6)*, Random Hse. Bks. for Young Readers) Random Hse. Children's Bks.
Katirgis, Jane. Baby Forest Animals, 1 vol. 2010. (All about Baby Animals Ser.). (ENG., Illus.). 24p. (-1). pap. 10.35 *(978-1-59845-161-0(8)*, 0f99b719-28d8-45ef-a7f3-ab1a9e7bb23d, Enslow Publishing) Enslow Publishing, LLC.
Katschke, Judy. Shrek the Third. 2007. (Illus.). (J). *(978-0-696-23947-2(7))* Meredith Bks.
Katz, Andrew & Léveillé-Trudel, Juliana. How to Catch a Bear Who Loves to Read. Sherman, Joseph, illus. 2018. (ENG.). 32p. (J). (gr. -1). 15.95 *(978-2-924786-47-5(9)*, CrackBoom! Bks.) Chouette Publishing CAN. Dist: Publishers Group West (PGW).
Katz, Karen. Baby's Big Busy Book. Katz, Karen, illus. 2017. (ENG., Illus.). 12p. (J). (gr. -1 — 1). bds. 14.99 *(978-1-4814-8830-3(9)*, Little Simon) Little Simon.
—Princess Baby. Katz, Karen, illus. 2012. (Princess Baby Ser.). (Illus.). 30p. (J). (gr. k-k). 7.99 *(978-0-307-93146-7(3)*, Schwartz & Wade Bks.) Random Hse. Children's Bks.
—Princess Baby, Night-Night. Katz, Karen, illus. 2014. (Princess Baby Ser.). (ENG., Illus.). 28p. (J). (— 1). bds. 7.99 *(978-0-385-37848-2(3)*, Schwartz & Wade Bks.) Random Hse. Children's Bks.
—Where Is Baby's Belly Button? 2005. (CHI.). 12p. (J). 6.95 *(978-986-7517-72-2(5))* Shan Jen Publishing Co., Ltd. TWN. Dist: Chinasprout, Inc.
—Where Is Baby's Belly Button? Anniversary Edition/Lap Edition. Katz, Karen, illus. anniv. ed. 2009. (ENG., Illus.). 14p. (J). (gr. -1 — 1). bds. 12.99 *(978-1-4169-8733-8(9)*, Little Simon) Little Simon.
—Where Is Baby's Home? A Karen Katz Lift-The-Flap Book. Katz, Karen, illus. 2017. (ENG., Illus.). 14p. (J). (gr. -1 — 1). bds. 6.99 *(978-1-5344-0088-7(5)*, Little Simon) Little Simon.
Kaufman, Elliott, photos by. Numbers Everywhere. 2013. (ENG., Illus.). 32p. (J). (gr. -1-1). 12.95 *(978-0-7892-1157-6(2)*, 791157, Abbeville Kids) Abbeville Pr., Inc.
Kean, Edward. Howdy Doody's Lucky Trip. McNaught, Harry, illus. 2011. 30p. 35.95 *(978-1-258-02772-8(0))* Literary Licensing, LLC.
Keefe, Alicia. An Incredible Journey. NOAA Fisheries, West Coast Region (U.S.), ed. Gladnick, Anke, illus. 2018. (ENG.). 47p. (J). (gr. 2). pap. 13.00 *(978-0-16-094604-2(2)*, 003-017-0573-9, National Marine Fisheries Service) United States Government Printing Office.
Kellerhals-Stewart, Heather. Skookum Sal, Birling Gal. Blaine, Janice, illus. unabr. ed. 2003. (ENG.). 32p. (J). *(978-1-55017-285-0(9)*, 1e2eff2c-7cc2-442f-ab71-ac66903cba23) Harbour Publishing Co., Ltd.
Kelley, Marty. Almost Everybody Farts. (Everybody Farts Ser.). (J). (gr. -1). 2019. 28p. bds. 8.99 *(978-1-4549-3430-1(1))* 2017. (Illus.). 32p. 12.95 *(978-1-4549-1954-4(X))* Sterling Publishing Co., Inc.
Kellogg, Steven. The Missing Mitten Mystery. Kellogg, Steven, illus. 2004. (Picture Puffins Ser.). (Illus.). (gr. -1-3). 17.00 *(978-0-7569-2581-9(9))* Perfection Learning Corp.
Kelly, John. Can I Join Your Club? Laberis, Steph, illus. 2017. (ENG.). 32p. (J). *(978-1-84869-435-4(0))* Kane Miller.
—Fixer the Robot. 2019. (ENG., Illus.). 32p. (J). 16.95 *(978-0-571-33636-4(1)*, Faber & Faber Children's Bks.) Faber & Faber, Inc.
—Hibernation Hotel. Brenlla, Laura, illus. 2017. (ENG.). 32p. (J). *(978-1-84869-675-4(2))* Tiger Tales.
Kelly, Sharon L. C. M. Coco's Vineyard Vacation: Double Fun on Martha's Vineyard. Galbraith, Alison L., illus. 2005. 40p. (J). 16.95 *(978-0-9766283-0-9(9))* Secret Garden Bookworks.
Keltie, Helen. The Mysterious Lake: Otriana. 2013. 68p. pap. 8.99 *(978-1-4525-0949-5(2)*, Balboa Pr.) Author Solutions, LLC.
Kendall, Jane. Tennessee Rose. 2012. (Horse Diaries: 9). lib. bdg. 18.40 *(978-0-606-26554-6(6))* Turtleback.
Kendall, Penny. Sleepy Baby. 2011. (Illus.). 14p. bds. *(978-1-84089-609-1(4))* Zero to Ten, Ltd.
—Socks. 2011. (Illus.). 14p. bds. *(978-1-84089-608-4(6))* Zero to Ten, Ltd.
Kenison, Misti. The Lost Race Car: A Fox & Goat Mystery, 1 vol. 2018. (Fox & Goat Mysteries Ser.: 2). (ENG., Illus.). 28p. (J). bds. 12.99 *(978-0-7643-5599-8(6)*, 16098) Schiffer Publishing, Ltd.
—The Missing Bouncy Ball: A Fox & Goat Mystery, 1 vol. 2018. (Fox & Goat Mysteries Ser.: 1). (ENG., Illus.). 28p. (J). bds. 12.99 *(978-0-7643-5600-1(3)*, 16097) Schiffer Publishing, Ltd.
Kennedy, Anne Vittur. The Farmer's Away! Baa! Neigh! Kennedy, Anne Vittur, illus. 2014. (ENG., Illus.). 32p. (J). (-k). 15.99 *(978-0-7636-6679-8(3))* Candlewick Pr.
—Go Baby! Go Dog! Kennedy, Anne Vittur, illus. 2018. (ENG., Illus.). 20p. (J). (gr. -1 — 1). bds. 7.99 *(978-0-8075-2971-3(0)*, 807529710) Whitman, Albert & Co.
—One Spring Lamb, 1 vol. 2016. (ENG., Illus.). 20p. (J). bds. 8.99 *(978-0-7180-8782-1(8)*, Tommy Nelson) Nelson, Thomas Inc.
Kennedy, Kim. Pirate Pete. Kennedy, Doug & Kennedy, Roy D., illus. 2010. (ENG.). 40p. (J). (gr. -1-3). pap. 8.95 *(978-0-8109-8923-8(9))* Abrams, Inc.
Kennedy, Pamela. Night-Night, Bunny. Keay, Claire, illus. 2017. (ENG.). 16p. (J). (gr. -1-k). bds. 7.99 *(978-0-8249-1660-2(3))* Worthy Publishing.
—We Wish You a Merry Christmas! Reed, Lisa, illus. 2017. (VeggieTales Ser.). (ENG.). 16p. (J). (gr. -1-k). bds. 12.99 *(978-0-8249-1663-3(8))* Worthy Publishing.
—You Can Do It, Bunny. Keay, Claire, illus. 2018. (ENG.). 18p. (J). (gr. -1-k). bds. 7.99 *(978-0-8249-1669-5(7))* Worthy Publishing.
Kenney, Cindy. Veggie Tales I Can! And So Can You!, 1 vol. 2004. (Big Idea Books / VeggieTales Ser.). (ENG., Illus.). (J). bds. 12.99 *(978-0-310-70893-3(1))* Zonderkidz.
Kent, Lorna, illus. At the Beach. 2004. 8p. (J). bds. 3.99 *(978-1-85854-087-0(9))* Brimax Books Ltd. GBR. Dist: Byeway Bks.
Kerbel, Deborah. Sun Dog. Del Rizzo, Suzanne, illus. 2018. (ENG.). 32p. (J). (gr. k-2). 17.95 *(978-1-77278-038-3(3))* Pajama Pr. CAN. Dist: Publishers Group West (PGW).
Kerley, Barbara. Portland Baby. Cleland, Josh, illus. 2017. (Local Baby Bks.). (ENG.). 22p. (J). (gr. -1 — 1). bds. 8.95 *(978-1-946064-05-9(X)*, 806405) Duo Pr. LLC.
Kernahan, Maria. R Is for Rocky Mountains. Schafbuch, Michael, illus. 2017. (ENG.). 56p. (J). (gr. -1-k). bds. 9.95 *(978-1-942402-46-6(5)*, b4b42ae7-d425-495c-a90b-11ddf96d8ba3) Dry Climate Studios.
Kerr, Judith. Goose in a Hole. Kerr, Judith, illus. 2005. (ENG., Illus.). 40p. (J). (gr. k-2). 15.99 *(978-0-00-720793-0(X))* HarperCollins Pubs. Ltd. GBR. Dist: Independent Pubs. Group.
—The Great Granny Gang: Band 11/Lime (Collins Big Cat) Kerr, Judith, illus. 2019. (Collins Big Cat Ser.). (ENG., Illus.). 36p. (J). (gr. k-2). pap. 9.99 *(978-0-00-832090-4(X))* HarperCollins Pubs. Ltd. GBR. Dist: Independent Pubs. Group.
—Katinka's Tail. 2018. (ENG.). 32p. (J). 17.99 *(978-0-00-826912-8(2)*, HarperCollins Children's Bks.) HarperCollins Pubs. Ltd. GBR. Dist: HarperCollins Pubs.
—Mog & the Baby & Other Stories. 2019. (ENG.). 112p. (J). pap. 12.99 *(978-0-00-832652-4(5)*, HarperCollins Children's Bks.) HarperCollins Pubs. Ltd. GBR. Dist: HarperCollins Pubs.
—Mog the Forgetful Cat Book & Toy Gift Set, 1 vol. Kerr, Judith, illus. 2020. (ENG., Illus.). 40p. 19.99 *(978-0-00-826214-3(4)*, HarperCollins Children's Bks.) HarperCollins Pubs. Ltd. GBR. Dist: HarperCollins Pubs.
—Mog's Christmas. Kerr, Judith, illus. 2019. (ENG., Illus.). 30p. (J). bds. 7.99 *(978-0-00-834764-2(6)*, HarperCollins Children's Bks.) HarperCollins Pubs. Ltd. GBR. Dist: HarperCollins Pubs.
—My First Mog Books. Kerr, Judith, illus. 2019. (ENG., Illus.). 40p. (J). bds. 8.99 *(978-0-00-834765-9(4)*, HarperCollins Children's Bks.) HarperCollins Pubs. Ltd. GBR. Dist: HarperCollins Pubs.
—The Tiger Who Came to Tea. 2006. pap. *(978-0-06-052468-5(5))* HarperCollins Canada, Ltd.
Kershner, Kyle. 100 First Words for Little Artists, Volume 3. 2019. (100 First Words Ser.: 3). (ENG., Illus.). 20p. (J). (gr. -1-3). bds. 9.99 *(978-1-64170-128-0(5)*, 550128) Familius LLC.
Kerven, Rosalind. Sparrow, the Crow & the Pearl. Williamson, Melanie, illus. 2005. (ENG.). 24p. (J). lib. bdg. 23.65 *(978-1-59646-754-5(1))* Dingles & Co.
Kessler, Leonard P. Mr. Pine's Purple House. Kessler, Leonard P., illus. 40th anniv. ed. 2005. (Illus.). 64p. (J). 16.00 *(978-1-930900-32-5(5))* Purple Hse. Pr.
Khan, Aliyah. The Adventures of Solomon Spider: Solomon Sees the City. 2011. 28p. (gr. -1 — 1). pap. 14.09 *(978-1-4490-1546-6(8))* AuthorHouse.
Khan, Hena. Golden Domes & Silver Lanterns: A Muslim Book of Colors. Amini, Mehrdokht, illus. 2015. (Muslim Book of Concepts Ser.). (ENG.). 32p. (J). (gr. -1-k). pap. 7.99 *(978-1-4521-4121-3(5))* Chronicle Bks. LLC.
—Night of the Moon: A Muslim Holiday Story. Paschkis, Julie, illus. 2018. (ENG.). 36p. (J). (gr. -1-k). pap. 7.99 *(978-1-4521-6896-8(2))* Chronicle Bks. LLC.
Khan, Sara. My First Book about the Qur'an. Lodge, Alison, illus. 2017. 26p. (J). (gr. -1-k). bds. 9.95 *(978-0-86037-618-7(4))* Kube Publishing Ltd. GBR. Dist: Consortium Bk. Sales & Distribution.
Kheiriyeh, Rashin, illus. Two Parrots. 2014. (ENG.). 32p. (J). (gr. k-3). 17.95 *(978-0-7358-4171-0(3)*, 9780735841710) North-South Bks., Inc.
Khing, T. T. Where Is the Cake? 2010. (ENG & DUT., Illus.). 32p. (J). (gr. -1-3). pap. 7.95 *(978-0-8109-8924-5(7))* UK Abrams Bks. for Young Readers.
Khzouz, Medlaine. Suzie Time. 2011. 24p. pap. 15.99 *(978-1-4568-7454-4(3))* Xlibris Corp.
Kids, National Geographic. Weird but True Animals. 2018. (Weird but True Ser.). (Illus.). 208p. (J). (gr. 3-7). pap. 8.99 *(978-1-4263-2981-4(4)*, National Geographic Kids) Disney Publishing Worldwide.
Kilgus, Walter C. Bess Takes a Ride. Howarth, Craig, illus. 2008. (ENG.). 36p. pap. 17.49 *(978-1-4257-8807-0(6))* Xlibris Corp.
Killen, Nicola. Bobo & Co. Colours. Killen, Nicola, illus. 2017. (ENG., Illus.). 10p. (J). bds. *(978-1-4088-8001-2(6)*, 298891, Bloomsbury Children's Bks.) Bloomsbury Publishing Plc.
—Bobo & Co. Numbers. Killen, Nicola, illus. 2017. (ENG., Illus.). 10p. (J). bds. *(978-1-4088-8002-9(4)*, 298892, Bloomsbury Children's Bks.) Bloomsbury Publishing Plc.
—I Got a Crocodile. 2013. (ENG., Illus.). 32p. (J). 15.99 *(978-0-85707-577-2(2))* Simon & Schuster, Ltd. GBR. Dist: Simon & Schuster, Inc.
Kim, Byung-Gyu & Hao, K. T. The 100th Customer. Ferri, Giuliano, illus. 2005. (ENG.). 32p. (J). (gr. -1-17). 15.95 *(978-1-933327-03-7(0))* Purple Bear Bks., Inc.
Kim, Cecil. I Can't Sleep: Imagination - Bedtime. Cowley, Joy, ed. Bisaillon, Josee, illus. 2015. (Step up - Creative Thinking Ser.). (ENG.). 32p. (gr. -1-2). 26.65 *(978-1-925246-13-1(2))*; 26.65 *(978-1-925246-39-1(6))*; 7.99 *(978-1-925246-65-0(5))* ChoiceMaker Pty. Ltd., The AUS. (Big and SMALL). Dist: Lerner Publishing Group.
—One Little Bean: Observation - Life Cycle. Cowley, Joy, ed. Dattola, Chiara, illus. 2015. (Step up - Creative Thinking Ser.). (ENG.). 32p. (gr. -1-2). 26.65 *(978-1-925246-12-4(4))*; 26.65 *(978-1-925246-38-4(8))*; 7.99 *(978-1-925246-64-3(7))* ChoiceMaker Pty. Ltd., The AUS. (Big and SMALL). Dist: Lerner Publishing Group.
Kim, Soo-hyeon. There It Is! Observation - Objects. Cowley, Joy, ed. Lee, Hyeon-joo, illus. 2015. (Step up - Creative Thinking Ser.). (ENG.). 32p. (gr. -1-2). 7.99 *(978-1-925246-61-2(2))*; 26.65 *(978-1-925246-35-3(3))*; 26.65 *(978-1-925246-09-4(4))* ChoiceMaker Pty. Ltd., The AUS. (Big and SMALL). Dist: Lerner Publishing Group.
—What Does the Bee See? Observation - Parts & Whole. Cowley, Joy, ed. Jo, Eun-hwa, illus. 2015. (Step up - Creative Thinking Ser.). (ENG.). 32p. (gr. -1-2). 26.65 *(978-1-925246-08-7(6))*; 7.99 *(978-1-925246-60-5(4))*; 26.65 *(978-1-925246-34-6(5))* ChoiceMaker Pty. Ltd., The AUS. (Big and SMALL). Dist: Lerner Publishing Group.
—What Does the Bee See? Observation - Parts & Whole. Jo, Eun-hwa, illus. 2015. (Step up — Creative Thinking Ser.). (ENG.). 32p. (J). (gr. -1-2). 7.99 *(978-1-925186-54-3(7)*, 6f7803c3-9de4-4443-902a-381936fa2bc6, Big and SMALL) ChoiceMaker Pty. Ltd., The AUS. Dist: Lerner Publishing Group.
Kimberly. Ocean Friends "Sing-A-Long" 2009. (ENG.). 28p. pap. 13.99 *(978-1-4415-3386-9(3))* Xlibris Corp.
Kimmel, Eric A. Joha Makes a Wish: A Middle Eastern Tale, 0 vols. Rayyan, Omar, illus. 2013. (ENG.). 40p. (J). (gr. -1-3). pap. 7.99 *(978-1-4778-1687-5(9)*, 9781477816875, Two Lions) Amazon Publishing.
—Los Tres Cabritos, 0 vols. Ramirez Rodenas, Marta, tr. Gilpin, Stephen, illus. 2012. (SPA.). 32p. (J). (gr. k-2). pap. 22.44 *(978-0-7614-5961-3(8)*, 9780761459613, Amazon Children's Publishing) Amazon Publishing.
Kimmelman, Leslie. Everybody Bonjours! McMenemy, Sarah, illus. 2015. 40p. (J). (gr. -1-2). pap. 7.99 *(978-0-553-50782-9(6)*, Dragonfly Bks.) Random Hse. Children's Bks.
Kimura, Yuichi. On the Seesaw Bridge. Hata, Kowshiro, illus. 2011. (ENG.). 36p. (J). (gr. -1-3). 14.95 *(978-1-935654-18-6(7)*, Vertical) Kodansha America, Inc.
Kinast, Susan. Play from A to Z. 2006. (J). lib. bdg. 19.95 *(978-1-933732-11-4(3))* Big Ransom Studio.
King, Anthea. Where Do Butterflies Go ... ?? 2013. 32p. pap. *(978-1-4602-1743-6(8))* FriesenPress.
King, Trey. Sidekick Showdown! Wang, Sean, illus. 2016. (J). *(978-1-5182-2744-8(9))* Scholastic, Inc.
Kinkade, Thomas, illus. Away in a Manger. 2005. 32p. (J). 16.99 *(978-0-06-078730-1(9))* Zonderkidz.
Kirby, Lee. Super Turbo vs. the Pencil Pointer. O'Connor, George, illus. 2017. (Super Turbo Ser.: 3). (ENG.). 128p. (J). (gr. k-4). pap. 5.99 *(978-1-4814-9438-0(4)*, Little Simon) Little Simon.
Kirk, Bill. The Ins & Outs of Air: The Sum of Our Parts Series. 2013. (GER., Illus.). 24p. pap. 10.95 *(978-1-61633-391-1(X))* Guardian Angel Publishing, Inc.
Kirk, Daniel. Home Sweet Home. 2013. (ENG., Illus.). 40p. (J). (gr. 1-4). pap. 7.95 *(978-1-4197-1049-0(4))* UK Abrams Bks. for Young Readers.
—Library Mouse: A Museum Adventure. 2012. (ENG., Illus.). 32p. (J). (gr. -1-3). 18.99 *(978-1-4197-0173-3(8)*, 1007501, Abrams Bks. for Young Readers) Abrams, Inc.
—Museum Adventure. 2012. (ENG., Illus.). 32p. (J). (gr. k-2). pap. 7.95 *(978-1-4197-0318-8(8))* UK Abrams Bks. for Young Readers.
—A Prayer for the Animals. 2018. (ENG., Illus.). 40p. (J). (gr. -1-3). 17.99 *(978-1-4197-3199-0(8)*, 1157301, Abrams Bks. for Young Readers) Abrams, Inc.
Kirkby, Joanne & Cooper, Sharon, illus. Mosaic Picture Sticker Book. 2015. (Mosaic Sticker Bks.). (ENG.). 24+12p. (J). (gr. k-5). pap. 10.99 *(978-0-7945-3015-0(X)*, Usborne) EDC Publishing.
Kirkfield, Vivian. Pippa's Passover Plate. Weber, Jill, illus. 2019. 40p. (J). (gr. -1-3). 17.99 *(978-0-8234-4162-4(8))* Holiday Hse., Inc.
Kirkland, Kim M. Car Cars Go Zoom Zoom Zoom. 2012. 24p. pap. 24.95 *(978-1-4626-6926-4(3))* America Star Bks.
Kitamura, Satoshi. Pot-San's Tabletop Tales. Kitamura, Satoshi, illus. 2013. (ENG., Illus.). 32p. (J). (gr. -1-k). 22.99 *(978-1-84939-378-2(8))* Andersen Pr. GBR. Dist: Independent Pubs. Group.
—When Sheep Can't Sleep (Cuando los Borregos no Pueden Dormir) (SPA.). (J). (gr. 1-6). 19.95 *(978-84-372-6605-3(X))* Santillana USA Publishing Co., Inc.
Kitten. (Buggy Buddies Ser.). (Illus.). (J). (gr. -1). bds. *(978-1-56021-350-5(7)*, 201) W.J. Fantasy, Inc.
Kizer, Linda M. Plug, the Lonely Little Fire Hydrant. 2009. 60p. pap. 26.99 *(978-1-4490-2873-2(X))* AuthorHouse.
Klaassen, Sandra. Peg & Uan: Making Friends, 52 vols. 2017. (Illus.). 14p. (J). 9.95 *(978-1-78250-441-2(9)*, Kelpies) Floris Bks. GBR. Dist: Consortium Bk. Sales & Distribution.
—Peg the Little Sheepdog, 44 vols. 2015. (Illus.). 32p. (J). 11.95 *(978-1-78250-181-7(9)*, Kelpies) Floris Bks. GBR. Dist: Consortium Bk. Sales & Distribution.
Kleinberg, Naomi. Elmo's Christmas Snowman (Sesame Street) Brannon, Tom, illus. 2013. (ENG.). 12p. (J). (— 1). bds. 6.99 *(978-0-449-81257-0(X)*, Random Hse. Bks. for Young Readers) Random Hse. Children's Bks.
—The Runaway Egg (Sesame Street) Mathieu, Joe, illus. 2018. (Pictureback(R) Ser.). (ENG.). 24p. (J). (gr. -1-2). pap. 6.99 *(978-1-5247-6905-5(3)*, Random Hse. Bks. for Young Readers) Random Hse. Children's Bks.
Kleven, Elisa. Sun Bread. 2004. (Illus.). 32p. (J). (gr. -1-k). reprint ed. pap. 8.99 *(978-0-14-240073-9(4)*, Puffin Books) Penguin Young Readers Group.
Klutz Editors, contrib. by. Shrinky Dinks Refill, Pack. (ENG.). 8p. 8.95 *(978-1-57054-585-6(5))* Klutz.
Knapman, Timothy. Can't Catch Me! Ciraolo, Simona, illus. 2017. (ENG.). 32p. (J). (-k). 15.99 *(978-0-7636-9496-8(7))* Candlewick Pr.
—A Monster Moved In! Schauer, Loretta, illus. 2015. (ENG.). 32p. (J). (gr. -1-2). 16.99 *(978-1-58925-176-2(8))* Tiger Tales.
—Superhero Dad. Berger, Joe, illus. 2018. (ENG.). 26p. (J). (-k). bds. 8.99 *(978-0-7636-9951-2(9))* Candlewick Pr.
Knapp, Andrew. Let's Find Momo! A Hide-And-Seek Board Book. 2017. (Find Momo Ser.: 3). (ENG., Illus.). 24p. (J). (-k). bds. 9.99 *(978-1-59474-958-2(2))* Quirk Bks.
Knapp, Artie. Little Otter Learns to Swim. 2018. (ENG., Illus.). 32p. (J). (gr. 1-4). 15.95 *(978-0-8214-2340-0(1))* Ohio Univ. Pr.
Knudsen, Michelle. Marilyn's Monster. Phelan, Matt, illus. 2017. (ENG.). (J). (gr. -1-3). lib. bdg. 17.20 *(978-0-606-39844-2(9))* Turtleback.
Koch, Joann. Annie's World. 2009. 20p. (J). pap. 9.95 *(978-1-4327-4063-4(6))* Outskirts Pr., Inc.
Koehler, L. Ah Choo O/P. 2016. (ENG., Illus.). 40p. (J). (gr. k-2). 14.95 *(978-1-4549-1415-0(7))* Sterling Publishing Co., Inc.
Kohara, Kazuno. Here Comes Jack Frost. Kohara, Kazuno, illus. 2011. (ENG., Illus.). 32p. (J). (gr. -1-1). pap. 9.99 *(978-0-312-60446-2(7)*, 900076478) Square Fish.
Konishi, Noriyuki. YO-KAI WATCH, Vol. 6, Vol. 6. 2016. (Yo-Kai Watch Ser.: 6). (ENG., Illus.). 192p. (J). pap. 9.99 *(978-1-4215-9217-6(7))* Viz Media.
—YO-KAI WATCH, Vol. 7, Vol. 7. 2017. (Yo-Kai Watch Ser.: 7). (ENG., Illus.). 176p. (J). pap. 9.99 *(978-1-4215-9218-3(5))* Viz Media.
—YO-KAI WATCH, Vol. 9, Vol. 9. 2018. (Yo-Kai Watch Ser.: 9). (ENG., Illus.). 184p. (J). pap. 9.99 *(978-1-4215-9753-9(5))* Viz Media.
Koniver, Laura. From the Ground Up. Koniver, Laura, illus. 2012. (Illus.). 44p. (J). pap. 16.99 *(978-1-937848-03-3(5))* Do Life Right, Inc.
Könnecke, Ole. Sports Are Fantastic Fun! Könnecke, Ole, illus. 2018. (ENG., Illus.). 56p. (J). (gr. -1-k). 19.99 *(978-1-77657-201-4(7)*, 4bb59a55-4dc5-4cec-a2a1-54ead8ff0079) Gecko Pr. NZL. Dist: Lerner Publishing Group.
Kontinen, Satu. Mokomaki. 2017. (ENG., Illus.). 32p. (J). (-k). 14.95 *(978-1-57687-805-7(8)*, powerHouse Bks.) powerHse. Bks.
Koopmans, Loek. The Pancake That Ran Away, 1 vol. 2nd rev. ed. 2015. Orig. Title: Een Dikke Vette Pannenkoek. (Illus.). 24p. (J). 16.95 *(978-1-78250-176-3(2))* Floris Bks. GBR. Dist: Consortium Bk. Sales & Distribution.
Kooser, Ted. The Bell in the Bridge. Root, Barry, illus. 2016. 32p. (J). (gr. 1-4). 16.99 *(978-0-7636-6481-7(2))* Candlewick Pr.
Koralek, Jenny. The Coat of Many Colors. Baynes, Pauline, illus. 2004. 32p. (J). 16.00 *(978-0-8028-5277-9(7))* Eerdmans, William B. Publishing Co.
Koren, Robert. The Moon in the Man. 2010. 28p. pap. 15.99 *(978-1-4535-3946-0(8))* Xlibris Corp.
Korr, Mary. Winston the water Dog: Portuguese water dog tales book One. 2009. 40p. pap. 17.49 *(978-1-4415-8406-9(4))* Xlibris Corp.
Kove, Torill. My Grandmother Ironed the King's Shirts. 2017. (ENG., Illus.). 32p. (J). (gr. 2-5). 16.95 *(978-1-77085-967-8(5)*, 319c0f4a-7322-463c-80c3-3b4624c58445) Firefly Bks., Ltd.
Kovecses, Anna. One Thousand Things. 2015. (Learn with Little Mouse Ser.). (ENG., Illus.). 80p. (J). (-k). 17.99 *(978-1-84780-607-9(4)*, 313737, Wide Eyed Editions) Quarto Publishing Group UK GBR. Dist: Hachette UK Distribution.
Kralapp, Karl E. Fish Food. Kralapp, Karl E., illus. (Illus.). 28p. 2018. (ENG.). (J). 14.99 *(978-1-948365-37-6(5))* 2013. pap. 9.99 *(978-1-937165-62-8(0))* Orange Hat Publishing.
Kranowitz, Asher. Absolutely No Dogs Allowed. Abrams, Annette, illus. 2016. (ENG.). 32p. (J). pap. 14.95 *(978-1-935567-58-5(6))* Sensory Resources.
Kranz, Linda. Where I Belong. 2016. (Illus.). 32p. (J). (gr. -1-1). 12.95 *(978-1-63076-066-3(8))* Taylor Trade Publishing.
Krasner, Justin. Crinkle, Crinkle, Little Star. Yarlett, Emma, illus. 2017. (ENG.). 16p. (J). (gr. -1 — 1). 12.95 *(978-1-5235-0120-5(0)*, 100120) Workman Publishing Co., Inc.
Kratt, Chris & Kratt, Martin. Wild in Africa! (Wild Kratts) Fruchter, Jason, illus. 2016. (Little Golden Book Ser.). 24p. (J). (-k). 5.99 *(978-1-101-93862-1(5)*, Golden Bks.) Random Hse. Children's Bks.
Kraul, Walter. Astronomy for Young & Old: A Beginner's Guide to the Visible Sky, 20 vols. Maclean, Christian, tr. Kamerl, Dazze, illus. 2014. Orig. Title: Erscheinungen Am Sternenhimmel: Die Bewegungen der Gestirne Beobachten und Verstehen. 144p. pap. 24.95 *(978-1-78250-046-9(4))* Floris Bks. GBR. Dist: Consortium Bk. Sales & Distribution.
Kraulis, Julie. A Pattern for Pepper. 2017. (Illus.). 40p. (J). (gr. k-4). 16.99 *(978-1-101-91756-5(3)*, Tundra Bks.) Tundra Bks. CAN. Dist: Penguin Random Hse. LLC.
—Whimsy's Heavy Things. Kraulis, Julie, illus. 2013. (Illus.). 32p. (J). (gr. -1-1). 17.99 *(978-1-77049-403-9(0)*, Tundra Bks.) Tundra Bks. CAN. Dist: Penguin Random Hse. LLC.
Krause, Ute. Oscar & the Very Hungry Dragon. Krause, Ute, illus. 2015. (ENG., Illus.). 32p. (J). (gr. -1-2). 8.95 *(978-0-7358-4230-4(2))* North-South Bks., Inc.
Krauss, Ruth. Bears. Sendak, Maurice, illus. 2005. (ENG.). 24p. (J). 21.99 *(978-0-06-027994-3(X)*, HarperCollins) HarperCollins Pubs.
—The Carrot Seed. Johnson, Crockett, illus. 60th anniv. ed. 2004. (ENG.). 32p. (J). (gr. -1-3). lib. bdg. 17.89 *(978-0-06-023351-8(6)*, HarperCollins) HarperCollins Pubs.
Krebs, Laurie. Riding on a Caravan. Cann, Helen, illus. 2017. (ENG.). 32p. (J). (gr. k-5). pap. 9.99 *(978-1-78285-344-2(8))* Barefoot Bks., Inc.

Kredensor, Diane. Buck's Tooth. Kredensor, Diane, illus. 2015. (Pix Ser.). (ENG., Illus.). 64p. (J). (gr. 1-4). 12.99 *(978-1-4814-2382-3(7),* Aladdin) Simon & Schuster Children's Publishing.

Krishna, McArthur. What Would It Be Like? 2016. (ENG., Illus.). 34p. (J). (gr. 2-4). 17.99 *(978-0-692-58721-8(7),* Little Adventures) Amberjack Publishing Co.

Kronenberg, Kat. Dream Big. 2017. (ENG., Illus.). 48p. (gr. -1-5). 15.95 *(978-1-62634-347-4(0))* Greenleaf Book Group.

Kronheim, Joseph Martin. My First Picture Book. 2007. (Illus.). 56p. per. *(978-1-4065-3654-6(7))* Dodo Pr.

Kropp, Joseph P. Nathan Meets His Monsters. Johnston, Phillip, illus. 2012. 34p. 16.95 *(978-1-890905-59-0(3));* pap. 9.95 *(978-1-890905-58-3(5))* Day to Day Enterprises.

Krudwig, Vickie L., creator. Silly Circles Sketch Pad. 2004. (Illus.). 50p. (J). spiral bd. *(978-0-9700127-2-2(1))* Harmony Hse. Art Studio.

Krulik, Nancy. Ice-Cream Dreams. Martinez, Heather, illus. 2004. 22p. (J). lib. bdg. 15.00 *(978-1-4242-0975-0(7))* Fitzgerald Bks.

Krull, Kathleen. A Kids' Guide to the American Revolution. DiVito, Anna, illus. 2018. (Kids' Guide to American History Ser.: 2). (ENG.). 224p. (J). (gr. 3-7). 16.99 *(978-0-06-238110-1(5));* pap. 6.99 *(978-0-06-238109-5(1))* HarperCollins Pubs. (HarperCollins).

Kruse, Donald W. Gorilla Soup! 2012. 48p. pap. 12.95 *(978-1-59663-862-4(1),* Castle Keep Pr.) Rock, James A. & Co. Pubs.

—Gorilla Soup! Crank, Donny, illus. 2017. (ENG.). (J). (gr. k-5). pap. 14.95 *(978-0-9981972-2-7(X))* Zaccheus Entertainment Co.

Kubart, Tim. Oopsie-Do! Richmond, Lori, illus. 2018. (ENG.). 32p. (J). (gr. -1-3). 17.99 *(978-0-06-257303-2(9),* HarperCollins) HarperCollins Pubs.

Kubler, Annie, illus. Dress Up! 2012. (Mix & Match Babies Ser.). (ENG.). 12p. (J). bds. *(978-1-84643-485-3(8))* Child's Play International Ltd.

—Itsy, Bitsy Spider: American Sign Language. 2005. (Sign & Singalong Ser.). (ENG.). 12p. (J). (gr. k-k). bds. *(978-1-904550-43-3(6))* Child's Play International Ltd.

—Teddy Bear, Teddy Bear: American Sign Language. 2005. (Sign & Singalong Ser.). (ENG.). 12p. (J). (gr. k-1). bds. *(978-1-904550-40-2(1))* Child's Play International Ltd.

—Twinkle, Twinkle, Little Star: American Sign Language. 2005. (Sign & Singalong Ser.). (ENG.). 12p. (J). (gr. k-k). bds. *(978-1-904550-42-6(8))* Child's Play International Ltd.

Kubler, Annie & Adams, Pam. Down by the Station. 2005. 16p. (J). bds. *(978-0-85953-457-4(X))* Child's Play International Ltd.

KUBU. Farm Friends: A Visit to the Farm. 2016. (Kubu Ser.: 2). (Illus.). 32p. (J). (gr. -1-2). pap. 5.99 *(978-1-57826-475-9(8),* Hatherleigh Pr.) Hatherleigh Co., Ltd., The.

Kuenzler, Lou. Not yet Zebra. Woolf, Julia, illus. 2018. (ENG.). 32p. (J). (gr. -1-1). 16.95 *(978-0-571-34288-4(4),* Faber & Faber Children's Bks.) Faber & Faber, Inc.

Kuiling, Monica. Merci Mister Dash! Melo, Esperança, illus. 2011. 32p. (J). (gr. -1-2). 17.95 *(978-0-88776-964-1(0),* Tundra Bks.) Tundra Bks. CAN. Dist: Penguin Random Hse. LLC.

Kumon Publishing, ed. My Book of Amazing Tracing. 2012. (Illus.). 80p. (J). pap. 7.95 *(978-4-7743-0007-8(1))* Kumon Publishing North America, Inc.

Kunhardt, Dorothy. Now Open the Box. Kunhardt, Dorothy, illus. 2013. (Illus.). 60p. (J). (gr. -1-2). 16.95 *(978-1-59017-708-2(8),* NYR Children's Collection) New York Review of Bks., Inc., The.

Kunnas, Mauri. Goodnight, Mr. Clutterbuck. Timbers, Jill, tr. Kunnas, Mauri, illus. 2017. (Illus.). 36p. (J). (gr. -1-3). 18.00 *(978-0-914671-76-3(6),* Elsewhere Editions) Steerforth Pr.

Kuo, Julia. Everyone Eats. 2012. (ENG., Illus.). 22p. (J). (gr. -1). 9.95 *(978-1-897476-74-1(4))* Simply Read Bks. CAN. Dist: Ingram Publisher Services.

Kushner, Tony. Brundibar. Sendak, Maurice, illus. 2003. (ENG.). 56p. (J). (gr. 5-9). 24.99 *(978-0-7868-0904-2(3))* Little, Brown Bks. for Young Readers.

Kusugak, Michael. The Littlest Sled Dog, 1 vol. Krykorka, Vladyana, illus. 2010. (ENG.). 32p. (J). (gr. -1-k). pap. 12.95 *(978-1-55469-174-6(5))* Orca Bk. Pubs. USA.

Kutschbach, Doris. Art Detective: Spot the Difference! 2013. (ENG., Illus.). 48p. (J). (gr. 3-7). 14.95 *(978-3-7913-7104-7(5))* Prestel Verlag GmbH & Co KG. DEU. Dist: Penguin Random Hse. LLC.

Kwant, Admar. Pip the Gnome's Bedtime. 72 vols. 2017. (Illus.). 12p. (J). 9.95 *(978-1-78250-413-9(3))* Floris Bks. GBR. Dist: Consortium Bk. Sales & Distribution.

Lacey, Minna. Big Book of Big Machines. 2010. (Big Book of Big Machines Ser.). 14p. (J). 13.99 *(978-0-7945-2764-8(7),* Usborne) EDC Publishing.

Lachenmeyer, Nathaniel. Octopus Escapes! Dormer, Frank W., illus. 2018. 32p. (J). (-k). lib. bdg. 16.99 *(978-1-58089-795-2(9))* Charlesbridge Publishing, Inc.

Lachner, Dorothea. Santa Claus & the Christmas Surprise, 30 vols. Dusíl/2kovi1/2, Maja, illus. 2018. Orig. Title: Ein Geschenk Vom Nikolaus. 28p. (J). 17.95 *(978-1-78250-543-3(1))* Floris Bks. GBR. Dist: Consortium Bk. Sales & Distribution.

Ladybird. Ladybird First Favourite Tales Goldilocks & the Three Bears. 2015. (First Favourite Tales Ser.). (Illus.). 32p. (J). (-k). 8.99 *(978-1-4093-0629-0(1))* Penguin Bks., Ltd. GBR. Dist: Independent Pubs. Group.

—Ladybird I'm Ready for School! 2016. (Ladybird I'm Ready Ser.). (ENG., Illus.). 48p. (J). (— 1). pap. 11.99 *(978-0-241-21597-5(8))* Penguin Bks., Ltd. GBR. Dist: Independent Pubs. Group.

—On the Farm - Read It Yourself with Ladybird Level 2. 2016. (Read It Yourself with Ladybird Ser.). (ENG., Illus.). 32p. (J). (gr. 2-4). 5.99 *(978-0-241-23731-1(9))* Penguin Bks., Ltd. GBR. Dist: Independent Pubs. Group.

—The Peter Rabbit Club Activity Book: Level 2. 2017. (Ladybird Readers Ser.). (ENG.). 16p. (J). (gr. k-2). 4.99 *(978-0-241-29799-5(0))* Penguin Bks., Ltd. GBR. Dist: Independent Pubs. Group.

—Snow White - Ladybird Readers Level 3. 2018. (Ladybird Readers Ser.). (Illus.). 64p. (J). (gr. k-2). pap. 8.99 *(978-0-241-31955-0(2))* Penguin Bks., Ltd. GBR. Dist: Independent Pubs. Group.

—The Wizard of Oz. 2016. (First Favourite Tales Ser.). (Illus.). 32p. (J). (gr. -1-k). 8.99 *(978-0-7232-9219-7(1))* Penguin Bks., Ltd. GBR. Dist: Independent Pubs. Group.

Ladybird, Ladybird. Snow White & Rose Red. 2016. (Ladybird Tales Ser.). (Illus.). 48p. (J). (gr. k-2). 9.99 *(978-0-7232-9447-4(X))* Penguin Bks., Ltd. GBR. Dist: Independent Pubs. Group.

Lafortune, Claude. The Wonderful Story of Christmas. gif. ed. 2003. (Illus.). 24p. *(978-2-89507-438-0(0))* Novalis Publishing.

Lagonegro, Melissa. Beauty & the Beast. 2017. (Illus.). 24p. (J). *(978-1-5182-3646-4(4))* Random Hse., Inc.

—Beauty & the Beast Big Golden Book (Disney Beauty & the Beast) RH Disney, illus. 2017. (Big Golden Book Ser.). (ENG.). 48p. (J). (gr. -1-2). 9.99 *(978-0-7364-3575-8(1),* Golden/Disney) Random Hse. Children's Bks.

—Beauty & the Beast Deluxe Step into Reading (Disney Beauty & the Beast) RH Disney, illus. 2017. (Step into Reading Ser.). (ENG.). 24p. (J). (gr. -1-1). pap. 5.99 *(978-0-7364-3594-9(8),* RH/Disney) Random Hse. Children's Bks.

Lagrange, Tiffany. My Abc Blue Book. LaGrange, Tiffany, illus. 2008. 32p. pap. 12.95 *(978-1-934246-38-2(7))* Peppertree Pr., The.

Lallemand, Orianne. The Blue Bird's Palace. Hénaff, Carole, illus. 2016. (ENG.). 32p. (J). (gr. k-5). 16.99 *(978-1-84686-885-6(8))* Barefoot Bks., Inc.

Lam, Thao. Wallpaper. 2018. (ENG., Illus.). 32p. (J). (gr. -1-3). 18.95 *(978-1-77147-283-8(9))* Owlkids Bks. Inc. CAN. Dist: Publishers Group West (PGW).

Lambe, Mona. Yintin Tales. 2013. (Illus.). 60p. pap. *(978-0-9576015-0-5(6))* Moyin Bks.

Lambert, Jonny. The Great Aaa-Ooo! 2016. (ENG., Illus.). 32p. (J). *(978-1-84869-275-6(7))* Tiger Tales.

—Jonny Lambert's Animal 123. Lambert, Jonny, illus. 2018. (Jonny Lambert Illustrated Ser.). (ENG., Illus.). 24p. (J). (— 1). bds. 12.99 *(978-1-4654-7845-0(0),* DK Children) Dorling Kindersley Publishing, Inc.

Laminack, Lester L. The Sunsets of Miss Olivia Wiggins, 1 vol. Bergum, Constance R., illus. rev. ed. 2018. 32p. (J). (gr. 1-4). pap. 8.95 *(978-1-68263-063-1(3))* Peachtree Publishing Co. Inc.

Lamont, Priscilla. Nursery Rhyme Crimes: Little Bo Peep. 2012. (Illus.). 24p. (J). pap. *(978-1-84780-354-2(7),* White Lion Publishing) Quarto Publishing Group UK.

Landers, Ace. Revenge of the Sith. White, Dave, illus. 2015. (J). *(978-1-4806-9629-7(3))* Scholastic, Inc.

Lang, Heather. Anybody's Game: Kathryn Johnston, the First Girl to Play Little League Baseball. Puglesi, Cecilia, illus. 2018. (She Made History Ser.). (ENG.). 32p. (J). (gr. -1-3). 16.99 *(978-0-8075-0379-9(7),* 807503797) Whitman, Albert & Co.

—Fearless Flyer: Ruth Law & Her Flying Machine. ón, Raul, illus. 2016. (ENG.). 40p. (J). (gr. 2-5). 16.95 *(978-1-62091-650-6(9),* Calkins Creek) Highlights Pr., c/o Highlights for Children, Inc.

Langen, Annette. Felix Travels Back in Time. Droop, Constanza, illus. 2004. 40p. (J). 14.99 *(978-1-59384-032-7(2))* Parklane Publishing.

Langford, Jane. Hero. Vince, Dawn, illus. 2005. (ENG.). 24p. (J). lib. bdg. 23.65 *(978-1-59646-720-0(7))* Dingles & Co.

—An Old Red Hat. Axworthy, Anni, illus. 2004. (ENG.). 24p. (J). lib. bdg. 23.65 *(978-1-59646-676-0(6))* Dingles & Co.

Lanning, Andrea J. The Imposturous Egg. Lanning, Andrea J., illus. Corcacas, Maria, photos by. 2012. (Illus.). 32p. *(978-0-9571677-0-4(9));* pap. *(978-0-9571677-4-2(1))* Ginnal Creatives Ltd.

Lansky, Bruce. Early Birdy Gets the Worm. Wummer, Amy, illus. 2010. 10p. (J). bds. 6.99 *(978-1-4169-9316-2(9))* Meadowbrook Pr.

—Monkey See, Monkey Do at the Zoo. Wummer, Amy, illus. 2010. 10p. (J). bds. 6.99 *(978-1-4169-9317-9(7))* Meadowbrook Pr.

—Polar BRRR Delivers. Wummer, Amy, illus. 2010. 10p. (J). bds. 6.99 *(978-1-4169-9318-6(5))* Meadowbrook Pr.

LaRochelle, David. Isle of You. Kim, Jaime, illus. 2018. (ENG.). 32p. (J). (gr. -1-2). 16.99 *(978-0-7636-9116-5(X))* Candlewick Pr.

Larsen, Andrew. The Bagel King. Nichols, Sandy, illus. 2018. (ENG.). 32p. (J). (gr. -1-2). 16.99 *(978-1-77138-574-9(X))* Kids Can Pr., Ltd. CAN. Dist: Hachette Bk. Group.

—In the Tree House. Petricic, Dušan, illus. (ENG.). 32p. (J). (gr. -1-2). 2018. pap. 7.99 *(978-1-5253-0017-2(2))* 2013. 16.95 *(978-1-55453-635-1(9))* Kids Can Pr., Ltd. CAN. Dist: Hachette Bk. Group.

Larsen, Kirsten. It's Sharing Day! Zalme, Ron, illus. 2007. (SPA & ENG.). (J). pap. *(978-0-439-92237-1(2),* Scholastic) Scholastic, Inc.

Larsen, Mylisa & Raff, Anna. If I Were a Kangaroo. 2017. (Illus.). 32p. (J). (— 1). 18.99 *(978-0-451-46958-8(5),* Viking Books for Young Readers) Penguin Young Readers Group.

Lasky, Kathryn. Untitled Historical #1: Picturebook Series. 2005. 32p. (J). 15.49 *(978-0-7868-2436-6(0));* (ENG.). 14.99 *(978-0-7868-0503-7(X))* Hyperion Pr.

—Untitled Historical #2: Picturebook Series. 2005. 32p. (J). 15.49 *(978-0-7868-2437-3(9));* (ENG.). 14.99 *(978-0-7868-0504-4(8))* Hyperion Pr.

—Untitled Historical #3: Picturebook Series. 2005. 32p. (J). 15.49 *(978-0-7868-2438-0(7));* (ENG.). 14.99 *(978-0-7868-0505-1(6))* Hyperion Pr.

Latimer, Alex. Woolf. Latimer, Patrick, illus. 2017. (ENG.). 32p. (J). (gr. k-2). pap. 9.99 *(978-1-84365-340-0(0),* Pavilion Children's Books) Pavilion Bks. GBR. Dist: HarperCollins Pubs.

Laufer, Tiffany A. The Porch Dream. 2009. (Bellaboo & Friends Ser.). (Illus.). 32p. 15.99 *(978-0-9820088-2-9(1))* Bellaboozle Books, Inc.

Laughing Elephant Staff, ed. By the Sea: Shape Book. 2013. (Children's Die-Cut Shape Book Ser.). (ENG., Illus.). 16p. (J). 10.95 *(978-1-59583-702-8(7))* Laughing Elephant.

Lavelle, David. Collins Big Cat Phonics for Letters & Sounds - Get Set for Fun: Band 02B/Red B, Bd. 2B. 2018. (Collins Big Cat Phonics Ser.). (ENG.). 16p. (J). (gr. -1-k). pap. 6.99 *(978-0-00-825150-5(9))* HarperCollins Pubs. Ltd. GBR. Dist: Independent Pubs. Group.

Lavie, Oren. The Bear Who Wasn't There: And the Fabulous Forest. Erlbruch, Wolf, illus. 2016. (ENG.). 48p. (J). (gr. -1-2). 17.95 *(978-1-61775-490-6(0),* Black Sheep) Akashic Bks.

Law, Jessica. A Hole in the Bottom of the Sea. McDonald, Jill, illus. 2013. (ENG.). 24p. (J). (gr. k-3). pap. 6.99 *(978-1-84686-948-8(X))* Barefoot Bks., Inc.

Lawler, Janet. Winter Cats. Smietanka, Ela, illus. 2019. (ENG.). 32p. (J). (gr. -1-3). 16.99 *(978-0-8075-9124-6(6),* 807591246) Whitman, Albert & Co.

Lawrence, Carol. Leaves. Zito, Francesco, illus. 2018. (Baby Explorer Ser.). (ENG.). 24p. (J). (gr. -1 — 1). bds. 6.99 *(978-0-8075-0516-8(1),* 807505161) Whitman, Albert & Co.

Lawrence, Donna. The Miracle of Susie the Puppy That Changed the Law. Coble, Lynn Berner, ed. Cappoen, Jennifer Tipton, illus. 2012. 54p. 24.95 *(978-0-9846724-2-4(7))* Paws and Claws Publishing, LLC.

—Susie's Tale Hand with Paw We Changed the Law. Coble, Lynn Berner, ed. Cappoen, Jennifer Tipton, illus. 2012. 64p. 24.95 *(978-0-9846724-1-7(9))* Paws and Claws Publishing, LLC.

Lawson, JonArno. Leap! Bisaillon, Josée, illus. 2017. (ENG.). 32p. (J). (gr. -1-2). 16.99 *(978-1-77138-678-4(9))* Kids Can Pr., Ltd. CAN. Dist: Hachette Bk. Group.

—Over the Rooftops, under the Moon. Kazemi, Nahid, illus. 2019. (ENG.). 56p. (J). 17.95 *(978-1-59270-262-6(7))* Enchanted Lion Bks., LLC.

—Uncle Holland, 1 vol. Nelson, Natalie, illus. 2017. (ENG.). 32p. (J). (gr. k-2). 17.95 *(978-1-55498-929-4(9))* Groundwood Bks. CAN. Dist: Publishers Group West (PGW).

Lazo, Dorina. Children of the San Joaquin Valley. Hires, Josh, photos by. 2005. (Illus.). 35p. (YA). (gr. 7-12). pap. 15.00 *(978-0-938911-28-9(7))* Individualized Education Systems/Poppy Lane Publishing.

Le Jars, David. Uno, Dos, Hola y Adios. 2004. (Hablemos Ser.).Tr. of One, Two, Hello & Goodbye to You. (SPA., Illus.). 24p. (J). (gr. -1-k). 9.95 *(978-1-58728-948-4(2),* Two-Can Publishing) T&N Children's Publishing.

Leannah, Michael. Goodnight Whispers. Torrent, Dani, illus. 2018. (ENG.). 32p. (J). (gr. k-3). 16.99 *(978-1-64170-031-3(9),* 550031) Familius LLC.

Learning Fun, Early & Priddy, Roger. Things That Go. 2010. (ENG., Illus.). 20p. (J). bds. *(978-1-84915-141-2(5),* Priddy Bks.) St. Martin's Pr.

Leblond, Michaël. Pajamarama - Carnival: Make it Move with Magic Stripes! Bertrand, Frédérique, illus. 2017. 22p. (J). (gr. k-4). pap. 16.95 *(978-0-500-65125-4(6),* 565125) Thames & Hudson.

Leblond, Michaël & Bertrand, Frédérique. Pajamarama - Fever: Make It Move with Magic Stripes! 2017. (Illus.). 22p. (J). (gr. k-5). pap. 16.95 *(978-0-500-65115-5(9),* 565115) Thames & Hudson.

Lebost, Diana. Mr. Kite & the Perilous Flight: Izzy & Daisy. Ersoz, Sahin, illus. 2013. 88p. pap. 18.95 *(978-0-9912023-5-5(X))* Pep & Olie Publishing.

Lee, Edith. Romeo & Julie Square. 2012. 28p. pap. *(978-0-9881235-0-2(9))* Bound Publishing.

Lee, G. I Want My Kitty Cat Tv! Scott, E., illus. 2012. 24p. pap. 24.95 *(978-1-4626-6610-2(8))* America Star Bks.

Lee, Gia. Hurricane Hound. Davis, Jason, illus. 2011. 40p. pap. 24.95 *(978-1-4560-9743-1(1))* America Star Bks.

Lee, Ji-yeong. Tchaikovsky's Swan Lake. Pacheco, Gabriel, illus. 2016. (Music Storybooks Ser.). (ENG.). 44p. (J). (gr. 3-5). pap. 9.99 *(978-1-925247-11-4(2),* 9f5264d9-18d9-44d5-80a4-89189b93ca5a, Big and SMALL) ChoiceMaker Pty. Ltd., The AUS. Dist: Lerner Publishing Group.

Lee, Mary R. Island Dog Books. 2009. 32p. (J). 20.99 *(978-1-4363-0351-4(6))* Xlibris Corp.

Leedy, Loreen. Step by Step. 2018. (ENG., Illus.). (J). (— 1). 30p. bds. 7.99 *(978-0-8234-4023-8(0));* 32p. 17.99 *(978-0-8234-3939-3(9))* Holiday Hse., Inc.

Leese, Vickie. When God Created Little Girls... 2011. 22p. pap. 17.99 *(978-1-61379-521-7(1))* Salem Author Services.

Lefebvre, Jason. Too Much Glue. Retz, Zac, illus. 2013. (ENG.). 32p. (J). (gr. k-2). 17.95 *(978-1-936261-27-7(8))* Flashlight Pr.

Légaré, Gisèle & L'Heureux. Good Night! Brignaud, Pierre, illus. 2006. (Hand in Hand Ser.). (ENG.). 24p. (J). (gr. -1-k). 5.95 *(978-2-89450-588-5(4))* Caillouet, Gerry.

Leighton, Noreen. Mr Tilly & the Christmas Lights. Wilson, Lorna, illus. 2013. 38p. pap. *(978-0-9573315-7-0(6))* Tatterdemalion Blue.

—Mr Tilly & the Halloween Mystery. Wilson, Lorna, illus. 2013. 42p. pap. *(978-0-9573315-6-3(8))* Tatterdemalion Blue.

Leist, Christina. Jack the Bear. 2009. (ENG., Illus.). 40p. (J). (gr. -1-3). 16.95 *(978-1-894965-97-2(3))* Simply Read Bks. CAN. Dist: Ingram Publisher Services.

Lemke, Horst, illus. Places & Faces. 32p. (J). (gr. -1). 14.95 *(978-0-87592-041-2(1))* Scroll Pr., Inc.

Leng, Qin, illus. Not Just Another Princess Story. 2015. (ENG.). 62p. (J). 16.95 *(978-1-927018-57-6(9))* Simply Read Bks. CAN. Dist: Ingram Publisher Services.

L'Engle, Madeleine. The Other Dog. Davenier, Christine, illus. 2018. (ENG.). 48p. (J). (gr. -1-k). 17.99 *(978-1-4521-7189-0(0))* Chronicle Bks. LLC.

Lennon, Liz. Our Special World: My Body. 2018. (Our Special World Ser.). (ENG., Illus.). 24p. (J). (gr. -1-k). pap. 9.99 *(978-1-4451-4895-3(1),* Franklin Watts) Hachette Children's Group GBR. Dist: Hachette Bk. Group.

—Our Special World: My Friends. 2018. (Our Special World Ser.). (ENG., Illus.). 24p. (J). (gr. -1-k). 12.99 *(978-1-4451-4899-1(4),* Franklin Watts) Hachette Children's Group GBR. Dist: Hachette Bk. Group.

Lenski, Lois. The Little Airplane. 2015. (Illus.). 32p. (J). (-k). bds. 6.99 *(978-0-385-39208-2(7),* Random Hse. Bks. for Young Readers) Random Hse. Children's Bks.

Leonard, Dion. Gobi for Little Ones: The Race for Home, 1 vol. Manuzak, Lisa, illus. 2018. (ENG.). 24p. (J). bds. 9.99 *(978-0-7180-7530-9(7),* Tommy Nelson) Nelson, Thomas Inc.

Lerner Publishing Group Staff. History Speaks: Picture Books Plus Reader's Theater, 6 vols., Set. 2011. (J). (gr. 2-4). lib. bdg. 167.58 *(978-0-7613-7483-1(3))* Lerner Publishing Group.

Leshem-Pelly, Miri. Scribble & Author. 2017. (ENG., Illus.). 32p. (J). 12.99 *(978-1-61067-575-8(4))* Kane Miller.

Lester, Alison. Yikes! 25th Anniversary Edition: In Seven Wild Adventures, Who Would You Be? 75th ed. 2019. (ENG., Illus.). 32p. (J). (gr. -1-2). 19.99 *(978-1-76052-861-4(7))* Allen & Unwin AUS. Dist: Independent Pubs. Group.

Lester, Sharon. The Boy Who Wouldn't Sit Still!, Vol. 2. Smith, Jeff, illus. 2nd ed. 2011. 40p. (J). 15.95 *(978-0-9802302-2-2(5))* Privileged Communications, LLC.

Let's Say Our Numbers. 2007. (Simple First Words Ser.). (Illus.). 14p. (J). *(978-1-84332-520-8(9))* Priddy Bks.

Lettice, Jenna. The 12 Days of Thanksgiving. Madden, Colleen, illus. 2018. (12 Days Of Ser.). 24p. (J). (gr. -1-2). pap. 4.99 *(978-1-5247-6658-0(5),* Random Hse. Bks. for Young Readers) Random Hse. Children's Bks.

Leung, Hilary. Will Sheep Sleep? 2018. (ENG., Illus.). 38p. (J). (gr. -1 — 1). bds. 7.99 *(978-1-338-21562-5(0),* Cartwheel Bks.) Scholastic, Inc.

Leung, Peyton. The Pirate Girl's Treasure: An Origami Adventure. Leung, Hilary, illus. 2012. (ENG.). 32p. (J). (gr. -1-3). 16.95 *(978-1-55453-660-3(X))* Kids Can Pr., Ltd. CAN. Dist: Hachette Bk. Group.

Levandowski, Barbara. The Adventures of Muffin & Alexander: The Please & Thank You Tea Party. 2012. 36p. pap. 18.41 *(978-1-4669-6246-0(1))* Trafford Publishing.

LeVerrier, Renee. The Four Friends. 2011. (Illus.). 44p. (J). pap. 18.99 *(978-1-59092-762-5(1))* Blue Forge Pr.

Levin, Jack E. & Levin, Norma R. My Dog Spot. Levin, Jack E. & Levin, Norma R., illus. 2016. (ENG., Illus.). 40p. (J). (gr. -1-3). 17.99 *(978-1-4814-6907-4(X),* Aladdin) Simon & Schuster Children's Publishing.

Levine, Arthur & Kath, Katie. What a Beautiful Morning. 2016. (ENG., Illus.). 40p. (J). (gr. -1-1). 16.95 *(978-0-7624-5906-3(9),* Running Pr. Kids) Running Pr.

Levine, Gail Carson. Betsy Who Cried Wolf. Nash, Scott, illus. 2005. (ENG.). 40p. (J). (gr. -1-3). reprint ed. pap. 7.99 *(978-0-06-443640-3(3),* HarperCollins) HarperCollins Pubs.

Levison, Jesse. U Is for Underwear. 2014. (ENG., Illus.). 28p. (J). (-k). bds. 9.95 *(978-1-57687-690-9(X),* powerHouse Bks.) powerHse. Bks.

Levy, Marv. Go Cubs Go! Baseball's Never Give up Story. 2017. (ENG., Illus.). 47p. (J). 18.95 *(978-0-9966742-7-0(6))* Ascend Bks., LLC.

Lewellyn, Claire. Starting Life Ladybug. Mendez, Simon, illus. 2004. (Starting Life Ser.). (ENG.). 24p. (J). (gr. k-3). 16.95 *(978-1-55971-892-9(7))* Cooper Square Publishing Llc.

Lewin, Ted. I See & See. 2016. (I Like to Read Ser.). (ENG., Illus.). 32p. (J). (gr. -1-3). 7.99 *(978-0-8234-3545-6(8))* Holiday Hse., Inc.

Lewis, Anne Margaret. Tears of Mother Bear. Fritz, Kathleen Cheney, illus. 2012. 32p. (J). (gr. -1-3). pap. 8.95 *(978-1-934133-62-0(0),* Mackinac Island Press, Inc.) Charlesbridge Publishing, Inc.

Lewis, Jan. Baby's First Book of Prayers. 2013. (Illus.). 24p. (J). (gr. -1-12). bds. 6.99 *(978-1-86147-340-0(0),* Armadillo) Anness Publishing GBR. Dist: National Bk. Network.

—Baby's First Stories of Jesus. 2015. (Illus.). 24p. (J). (gr. -1-2). bds. 6.99 *(978-1-86147-415-5(6),* Armadillo) Anness Publishing GBR. Dist: National Bk. Network.

—Farm. 2015. (Illus.). 24p. (J). (gr. -1-k). bds. 6.99 *(978-1-86147-635-7(3),* Armadillo) Anness Publishing GBR. Dist: National Bk. Network.

—First Fairy Tales: Puss in Boots. 2015. (ENG., Illus.). 24p. (J). (gr. -1-12). bds. 6.99 *(978-1-86147-626-5(4),* Armadillo) Anness Publishing GBR. Dist: National Bk. Network.

—First Fairy Tales Aladdin & the Lamp. 2013. (Illus.). 24p. (J). (gr. -1-12). bds. 6.99 *(978-1-86147-337-0(0),* Armadillo) Anness Publishing GBR. Dist: National Bk. Network.

—First Fairy Tales Goldilocks & the Three Bears. 2013. (Illus.). 24p. (J). (gr. -1-12). bds. 6.99 *(978-1-86147-332-5(X),* Armadillo) Anness Publishing GBR. Dist: National Bk. Network.

—First Fairy Tales Little Red Riding Hood. 2013. (Illus.). 24p. (J). (gr. -1-12). bds. 6.99 *(978-1-86147-336-3(2),* Armadillo) Anness Publishing GBR. Dist: National Bk. Network.

—First Fairy Tales Snow White. 2013. (Illus.). 24p. (J). (gr. -1-12). bds. 6.99 *(978-1-86147-335-6(4),* Armadillo) Anness Publishing GBR. Dist: National Bk. Network.

—Look & Learn with Little Dino: Colour Fun. Lewis, Jan, illus. 2014. (ENG., Illus.). 24p. (J). (gr. -1-2). bds. 6.99 *(978-1-86147-380-6(X),* Armadillo) Anness Publishing GBR. Dist: National Bk. Network.

—My First Words. 2015. (ENG., Illus.). 24p. (J). (gr. -1 — 1). bds. 6.99 *(978-1-86147-498-8(9),* Armadillo) Anness Publishing GBR. Dist: National Bk. Network.

—My Treasure Box of Fairy Tales: Classic Stories Retold in Six Charming Boardbooks, 6 vols. 2018. (Illus.). 72p. (J). (gr. -1-12). bds. 14.99 *(978-1-86147-845-0(3),* Armadillo) Anness Publishing GBR. Dist: National Bk. Network.

Lewis, Jan, illus. ABC: Turn the Wheels; Find the Words. 2016. 10p. (J). (gr. -1-12). bds. 14.99 *(978-1-86147-712-5(0),* Armadillo) Anness Publishing GBR. Dist: National Bk. Network.

—Ask Me about Colours: Lift the Flaps & Find the Answers! 2016. 14p. (J). (gr. -1-12). 10.99 *(978-1-86147-775-0(9),* Armadillo) Anness Publishing GBR. Dist: National Bk. Network.

—At School. 2017. 14p. (J). (gr. -1-12). 11.99 *(978-1-86147-726-2(0),* Armadillo) Anness Publishing GBR. Dist: National Bk. Network.

—Fairy Palace: You Are Invited to a Party in the Fairy Palace! 2015. 10p. (J). (gr. k-3). bds. 7.99 *(978-1-86147-315-8(X),* Armadillo) Anness Publishing GBR. Dist: National Bk. Network.

—First Fairy Tales: Cinderella. 2013. (ENG.). 24p. (J). (gr. -1-k). bds. 6.99 *(978-1-86147-334-9(6),* Armadillo) Anness Publishing GBR. Dist: National Bk. Network.

—First Fairy Tales: Sleeping Beauty. 2013. (ENG.). 24p. (J). (gr. -1-k). bds. 6.99 *(978-1-86147-338-7(9),* Armadillo) Anness Publishing GBR. Dist: National Bk. Network.

—Look & Learn with Little Dino: Action Words. 2014. (ENG.). 24p. (J). (gr. k-2). bds. 6.99 *(978-1-86147-382-0(6),* Armadillo) Anness Publishing GBR. Dist: National Bk. Network.

—Look & Learn with Little Dino: Busy Day. 2014. (ENG.). 24p. (J). (gr. k-2). bds. 6.99 *(978-1-86147-379-0(6),* Armadillo) Anness Publishing GBR. Dist: National Bk. Network.

P
Q
R

—Look & Learn with Little Dino: Count 123. 2014. (ENG.). 24p. (J). (gr. -1-1). bds. 6.99 *(978-1-86147-381-3(8),* Armadillo) Anness Publishing GBR. Dist: National Bk. Network.

—My First 123. 2014. (ENG.). 24p. (J). (gr. -1-k). bds. 6.99 *(978-1-86147-371-4(0),* Armadillo) Anness Publishing GBR. Dist: National Bk. Network.

—My First 123: Learn to Count from 1 To 100! 2015. 48p. (J). (gr. -1-12). pap. 9.99 *(978-1-86147-425-4(3),* Armadillo) Anness Publishing GBR. Dist: National Bk. Network.

—My First ABC. 2014. (ENG.). 24p. (J). (gr. -1-k). bds. 6.99 *(978-1-86147-372-1(9),* Armadillo) Anness Publishing GBR. Dist: National Bk. Network.

—My First ABC: Learn the Alphabet with 300 Words & Pictures. 2016. 48p. (J). (gr. -1-12). pap. 9.99 *(978-1-86147-728-6(7),* Armadillo) Anness Publishing GBR. Dist: National Bk. Network.

—My First Animals. 2014. (ENG.). 24p. (J). (gr. -1-k). bds. 6.99 *(978-1-86147-373-8(7),* Armadillo) Anness Publishing GBR. Dist: National Bk. Network.

—My First Bible Stories: Adam & Eve, Noah's Ark, Moses, Joseph, David & Goliath, Jesus. 2016. 48p. (J). (gr. -1-12). bds. 9.99 *(978-1-86147-737-8(6),* Armadillo) Anness Publishing GBR. Dist: National Bk. Network.

—My First Colours. 2014. (ENG.). 24p. (J). (gr. -1-k). bds. 6.99 *(978-1-86147-374-5(5),* Armadillo) Anness Publishing GBR. Dist: National Bk. Network.

—My First Learning Library: 3 Great Books: First Abc First 123 First Words, 3 vols. 2014. (ENG.). 72p. (J). (gr. -1-1). bds. 9.99 *(978-1-86147-387-5(7),* Armadillo) Anness Publishing GBR. Dist: National Bk. Network.

—Performance. 2012. (First Time Ser.). 24p. (J). *(978-1-84643-487-7(4))* Child's Play International Ltd.

—The Princess & the Pea. 2015. 24p. (J). (gr. -1-12). bds. 6.99 *(978-1-86147-467-4(9),* Armadillo) Anness Publishing GBR. Dist: National Bk. Network.

—Santa's Christmas Box of Books: A Festive Box of Fun Picture Books. 2017. (ENG.). 1p. (J). (gr. -1-12). bds. 14.99 *(978-1-86147-738-5(4),* Armadillo) Anness Publishing GBR. Dist: National Bk. Network.

—Santa's Workshop: The Inside Story! 2015. 10p. (J). (gr. k-4). bds. 7.99 *(978-1-86147-314-1(1),* Armadillo) Anness Publishing GBR. Dist: National Bk. Network.

—Words: Turn the Wheels, Find the Pictures. 2015. 10p. (J). (gr. -1-12). bds. 14.99 *(978-1-86147-660-9(4),* Armadillo) Anness Publishing GBR. Dist: National Bk. Network.

—123: Turn the Wheels - Learn to Count! 2015. 10p. (J). (gr. -1-12). bds. 14.99 *(978-1-86147-661-6(2),* Armadillo) Anness Publishing GBR. Dist: National Bk. Network.

Lewis, Jill. Ug-A-Lug: Four Cavemen & a Prehistoric Pencil. Rickerty, Simon, illus. 2014. (ENG.). 32p. (J). 16.99 *(978-1-4711-1728-2(6))* Simon & Schuster, Ltd. GBR. Dist: Simon & Schuster, Inc.

Lewis, K. s. & Lewis, K. S. Happiness: A Charlie Travel Adventure Story. 2009. (ENG.). 24p. 21.20 *(978-0-557-12094-9(2))* Lulu Pr., Inc.

Li, Jian. The Water Dragon: A Chinese Legend - Retold in English & Chinese (Stories of the Chinese Zodiac) 2012. (Stories of the Chinese Zodiac Ser.). (Illus.). 42p. (gr. -1-3). 16.95 *(978-1-60220-978-7(2))* Shanghai Pr.

Li, Maggie. The Amazing Human Body Detectives. 2015. (ENG., Illus.). 32p. (J). (gr. 2-4). 15.99 *(978-1-84365-297-7(8),* Pavilion Children's Books) Pavilion Bks. GBR. Dist: HarperCollins Pubs.

Li-Qiong, Yu. A New Year's Reunion: A Chinese Story. Cheng-Liang, Zhu, illus. 2013. (ENG.). 40p. (J). (gr. -1-2). 7.99 *(978-0-7636-6748-1(X))* Candlewick Pr.

Lie, Bjorn R. Slush Mountain. 2016. (Illus.). 32p. (J). (gr. -1-3). 16.95 *(978-1-927018-82-8(X))* Simply Read Bks. CAN. Dist: Ingram Publisher Services.

Lies, Brian. Got to Get to Bear's! 2018. (ENG., Illus.). 32p. (J). (gr. -1-3). 17.99 *(978-0-544-94882-2(3),* 1660304, Clarion Bks.) HarperCollins Pubs.

Light, John. The Flower. Evans, Lisa, illus. 2011. (Child's Play Library). (ENG.). 32p. (J). *(978-1-84643-070-1(4))* Child's Play International Ltd.

Light, Steve. Builders & Breakers. Light, Steve, illus. 2018. (ENG., Illus.). 40p. (J). (gr. -1-2). 17.99 *(978-0-7636-9872-0(5))* Candlewick Pr.

—The Bunny Burrow Buyer's Book: A Tale of Rabbit Real Estate. 2016. (ENG., Illus.). 16p. (J). (gr. -1-3). 19.95 *(978-1-57687-752-4(3),* powerHouse Bks.) powerHse. Bks.

Lightburn, Sandra. Pumpkin People, 1 vol. Lightburn, Ron, illus. 2008. (ENG.). 32p. (J). (gr. -1-k). 17.95 *(978-1-55109-681-0(1),* 13b97ce6-9128-4c3d-bb24-cd1b6efa4608) Nimbus Publishing, Ltd. CAN. Dist: Baker & Taylor Publisher Services (BTPS).

Lin, Kelly Jenkins. Mr. Astley's Blueberries. Fiddy, Samantha Lane, illus. 2012. 36p. pap. 12.95 *(978-0-615-67849-8(1))* Three Flower Farm Pr.

Linden, Joanne. Ben & Zip: Two Short Friends. Goldsmith, Tom, illus. 2014. (ENG.). 32p. (J). (gr. -1-k). 16.95 *(978-1-936261-28-4(6))* Flashlight Pr.

Lindsay, Andrew. Nana & Poppa. 2018. (ENG., Illus.). 26p. (J). *(978-1-5289-2404-7(5));* pap. *(978-1-5289-2405-4(3))* Austin Macauley Pubs. Ltd.

Lindsay, Courtney B. ABC Scream, It's Halloween! 2010. 48p. 17.99 *(978-1-4520-3889-6(9))* AuthorHouse.

Lindsay, Elizabeth. Socks. Sharratt, Nick, illus. 2018. 32p. (J). (— 1). pap. 12.99 *(978-0-552-57221-7(7))* Transworld Publishers Ltd. GBR. Dist: Independent Pubs. Group.

Linenthal, Peter. Look at the Animals. 2006. (Illus.). 18p. (J). (gr. -1 — 1). bds. 8.99 *(978-0-525-47582-8(6),* Dutton Books for Young Readers) Penguin Young Readers Group.

Linn, Susie. Old MacDonald Had a Farm. Crisp, Dan, illus. 2019. (Counting to Ten Bks.). (ENG.). 22p. (J). 9.99 *(978-1-78700-978-3(5))* Top That! Publishing PLC GBR. Dist: Independent Pubs. Group.

—Princesses. 2016. (My First Sticker Book Ser.). (ENG.). (J). pap. *(978-1-78445-768-6(X))* Top That! Publishing PLC.

—Ten Little Mermaids. Ellis, Lauren, illus. 2018. (Counting to Ten Bks.). (ENG.). 20p. (J). (gr. -1-1). bds. 10.99 *(978-1-78700-375-0(2))* Top That! Publishing PLC GBR. Dist: Independent Pubs. Group.

—Ten Little Unicorns. Hunt, Brad, illus. 2018. (Counting to Ten Bks.). (ENG.). 20p. (J). (gr. -1-1). bds. 10.99 *(978-1-78700-376-7(0))* Top That! Publishing PLC GBR. Dist: Independent Pubs. Group.

Lionni, Leo. The Greentail Mouse. 2013. (Illus.). 32p. (J). (gr. -1-2). pap. 8.99 *(978-0-307-98151-6(7),* Dragonfly Bks.) Random Hse. Children's Bks.

—Pezzettino. 2012. (Illus.). 40p. (J). (gr. -1-3). pap. 8.99 *(978-0-307-92999-0(X),* Dragonfly Bks.) Random Hse. Children's Bks.

—Swimmy. 2017. (ENG., Illus.). 32p. (J). (gr. -1-2). 8.99 *(978-0-399-55550-3(1),* Dragonfly Bks.) Random Hse. Children's Bks.

—What? 2014. (ENG., Illus.). 16p. (J). (— 1). bds. 6.99 *(978-0-385-75406-4(X),* Knopf Bks. for Young Readers) Random Hse. Children's Bks.

—Where? 2014. (ENG., Illus.). 16p. (J). (— 1). bds. 5.99 *(978-0-385-75407-1(8),* Knopf Bks. for Young Readers) Random Hse. Children's Bks.

—Who? 2014. (ENG., Illus.). 16p. (J). (— 1). bds. 6.99 *(978-0-385-75405-7(1),* Knopf Bks. for Young Readers) Random Hse. Children's Bks.

Lippman, Peter. Mini House: the Land of Dinosaurs. 2012. (Mini House Ser.). (ENG., Illus.). 11p. 11.95 *(978-0-7611-6598-9(3),* 16598) Workman Publishing Co., Inc.

Litchfield, Jo, illus. First Picture 123. 2005. (First Picture Board Books Ser.). 16p. (J). 11.95 *(978-0-7945-0939-2(8),* Usborne) EDC Publishing.

Little Bear, Shena. How the lone wolf got her Name. 2008. 80p. pap. 9.95 *(978-0-578-00171-5(3))* Stone Castle Publishing.

Little Gestalten, Little, ed. Goliath: The Boy Who Was Different. Abadía, Ximo, illus. 2019. (ENG.). 48p. 19.95 *(978-3-89955-826-5(X))* Die Gestalten Verlag DEU. Dist: Ingram Publisher Services.

Little Golden Book Christmas Stories. 2015. (Illus.). 224p. (J). (-k). 12.99 *(978-0-553-52227-3(2),* Golden Bks.) Random Hse. Children's Bks.

Little Red Riding Hood. 2017. (Picture Bks.). (ENG.). (J). 9.99 *(978-0-7945-3723-4(5),* Usborne) EDC Publishing.

Little Red Riding Pooh: A Fairy Tale Friend a Board Book & Plush Figure. 2004. (Pooh's Fairy Tale Theater Ser.). 12p. (J). 6.99 *(978-0-7364-2239-0(0),* RH/Disney) Random Hse. Children's Bks.

Littledale, Richard. The Littlest Star. Kolanovic, Dubravka, illus. 2016. (ENG.). 32p. (J). pap. 10.99 *(978-0-7459-7695-2(6),* ca685c5d-9c95-4fbe-bd68-fcc0809e303b, Lion Children's) Lion Hudson PLC GBR. Dist: Baker & Taylor Publisher Services (BTPS).

Lively, Kevin. Disney Parks Presents: Jungle Cruise: Animals! 2018. (Disney Parks Presents Ser.). (ENG., Illus.). 20p. (J). (gr. -1 — 1). bds. 7.99 *(978-1-368-03931-4(6),* Disney Press Books) Disney Publishing Worldwide.

Llewellyn, Claire. It's Fun to Learn about Sizes: A Busy Picture Book Full of Fabulous Facts & Things to Do! 2016. (Illus.). 32p. (J). (gr. -1-12). 9.99 *(978-1-86147-761-3(9),* Armadillo) Anness Publishing GBR. Dist: National Bk. Network.

—It's Fun to Learn about Sums: A Busy Picture Book Full of Fabulous Facts & Things to Do! 2016. (Illus.). 32p. (J). (gr. -1-12). 9.99 *(978-1-86147-762-0(7),* Armadillo) Anness Publishing GBR. Dist: National Bk. Network.

—It's Fun to Learn about Words: A Busy Picture Book Full of Fabulous Facts & Things to Do! 2016. (Illus.). 32p. (J). (gr. -1-12). 9.99 *(978-1-86147-743-9(0),* Armadillo) Anness Publishing GBR. Dist: National Bk. Network.

Lloyd, Jennifer. The Best Thing about Kindergarten. Leng, Qin, illus. 2013. (ENG.). 36p. (J). (gr. -1-1). 16.95 *(978-1-897476-82-6(5))* Simply Read Bks. CAN. Dist: Ingram Publisher Services.

—Ella's Umbrellas. Spires, Ashley, illus. 2017. 36p. (J). (gr. -1-3). 8.99 *(978-1-77229-010-3(6))* Simply Read Bks. CAN. Dist: Ingram Publisher Services.

—Looking for Loons. Wakelin, Kirsti Anne, illus. 2017. 32p. (J). (gr. -1-3). 8.99 *(978-1-77229-015-8(7))* Simply Read Bks. CAN. Dist: Ingram Publisher Services.

—Murilla Gorilla & the Hammock Problem. Lee, Jacqui, illus. 2014. (Murilla Gorilla Ser.: 3). (ENG.). 42p. (J). (gr. -1-3). 9.95 *(978-1-927018-47-7(1))* Simply Read Bks. CAN. Dist: Ingram Publisher Services.

—Murilla Gorilla & the Lost Parasol. Lee, Jacqui, illus. 2013. (Murilla Gorilla Ser.: 2). (ENG.). 42p. (J). (gr. -1-3). 9.95 *(978-1-927018-23-1(4))* Simply Read Bks. CAN. Dist: Ingram Publisher Services.

Lloyd-Jones, Sally. My Merry Christmas (padded Board Book) Gianassi, Sara, illus. 2017. (ENG.). 20p. (J). (gr. -1-k). bds. 12.99 *(978-1-4336-4895-3(4),* 005790558, B&H Kids) B&H Publishing Group.

Lloyd, Sam, illus. Inspector Croc Investigates. 2014. (J). *(978-1-4351-5627-2(7))* Barnes & Noble, Inc.

Lobel, Anita. Potatoes, Potatoes. 2004. 40p. (J). 16.89 *(978-0-06-051818-9(9));* 15.99 *(978-0-06-023927-5(1));* lib. bdg. 16.89 *(978-0-06-023928-2(X))* HarperCollins Pubs.

Lock, Deborah. Wild Baby Animals. 2016. (Illus.). 48p. (J). *(978-1-5182-1132-4(1))* Dorling Kindersley Publishing, Inc.

Lodge, Jo. Little Roar's Red Boots. 2013. (Little Roar Ser.). (ENG., Illus.). 20p. (J). (gr. -1-k). 8.99 *(978-1-4449-0482-6(5))* Hachette Children's Group GBR. Dist: Hachette Bk. Group.

—Little Roar's Round Balloon. 2013. (Little Roar Ser.). (ENG., Illus.). 20p. (J). (gr. -1-k). 5.99 *(978-1-4449-0483-3(3))* Hachette Children's Group GBR. Dist: Hachette Bk. Group.

Loehr, Mallory. I'm a Unicorn. Chou, Joey, illus. 2018. (Little Golden Book Ser.). 24p. (J). (-k). 5.99 *(978-1-5247-1512-0(3),* Golden Bks.) Random Hse. Children's Bks.

Loewen, Nancy. Baby Wants Mama, 0 vols. Meimon, Deborah, illus. 2013. (ENG.). 24p. (J). (gr. -1-k). 14.99 *(978-1-4778-1651-6(8),* 9781477816516, Two Lions) Amazon Publishing.

Loggins, Kenny. Moose N' Me. Nash, Joshua, illus. 2013. 32p. (J). (gr. -1-3). 14.95 *(978-0-578-07552-5(0))* Charlesbridge Publishing, Inc.

Lolley, Sarah. Emily & the Mighty Om. Kao, Sleepless, illus. 2014. 40p. (J). (gr. -1-3). 16.95 *(978-1-897476-35-2(3))* Simply Read Bks. CAN. Dist: Ingram Publisher Services.

Lomp, Stephan. Indestructibles: Bebé, Vamos a Comer! / Baby, Let's Eat! Chew Proof · Rip Proof · Nontoxic · 100% Washable (Book for Babies, Newborn Books, Safe to Chew) 2018. (Indestructibles Ser.). (SPA., Illus.). 12p. (J). (gr. -1 — 1). pap. 5.99 *(978-1-5235-0318-6(1),* 100318) Workman Publishing Co., Inc.

Lomp, Stephan, illus. Indestructibles: Baby, Let's Eat! Chew Proof · Rip Proof · Nontoxic · 100% Washable (Book for Babies, Newborn Books, Safe to Chew) 2018. (Indestructibles Ser.). (ENG.). 12p. (J). (gr. -1 — 1). pap. 5.99 *(978-1-5235-0207-3(X),* 100207) Workman Publishing Co., Inc.

—Indestructibles: Home Sweet Home: Chew Proof · Rip Proof · Nontoxic · 100% Washable (Book for Babies, Newborn Books, Safe to Chew) 2018. (Indestructibles Ser.). (ENG.). 12p. (J). (gr. -1 — 1). pap. 5.99 *(978-1-5235-0208-0(8),* 100208) Workman Publishing Co., Inc.

—Indestructibles: Love You, Baby: Chew Proof · Rip Proof · Nontoxic · 100% Washable (Book for Babies, Newborn Books, Safe to Chew) 2017. (Indestructibles Ser.). (ENG.). 12p. (J). (gr. -1 — 1). pap. 5.99 *(978-1-5235-0122-9(7),* 100122) Workman Publishing Co., Inc.

London, Jonathan. Froggy Builds a Tree House. 2013. (Froggy Ser.). 32p. (J). (-k). pap. 7.99 *(978-0-14-242533-6(8),* Puffin Books) Penguin Young Readers Group.

—Froggy Builds a Tree House. 2013. (Froggy Ser.). lib. bdg. 17.20 *(978-0-606-30518-1(1))* Turtleback.

—Froggy's Birthday Wish. Remkiewicz, Frank, illus. 2016. (Froggy Ser.). 32p. (J). (-k). 7.99 *(978-0-14-751799-9(0),* Puffin Books) Penguin Young Readers Group.

—Froggy's Worst Playdate. Remkiewicz, Frank, illus. 2015. (Froggy Ser.). 32p. (J). (gr. -1-k). 8.99 *(978-0-14-242229-8(0),* Puffin Books) Penguin Young Readers Group.

—Here Comes Doctor Hippo: A Little Hippo Story. Eduar, Gilles, illus. 2013. (Little Hippo Story Ser.). (ENG.). 32p. (J). (gr. -1-k). pap. 6.95 *(978-1-62091-595-0(2),* Astra Young Readers) Astra Publishing Hse.

—Otters Love to Play. So, Meilo, illus. (Read & Wonder Ser.). (ENG.). 32p. (J). (gr. k-4). 2018. 7.99 *(978-1-5362-0324-0(6))* 2016. 17.99 *(978-0-7636-6913-3(X))* Candlewick Pr.

Long, Ethan. Big Cat. (I Like to Read Ser.). (ENG.). (J). (gr. -1-3). 2017. 32p. 4.99 *(978-0-8234-3881-5(3))* 2016. (Illus.). 24p. 7.99 *(978-0-8234-3539-5(3))* Holiday Hse., Inc.

—Me & My Big Mouse, 0 vols. 2014. (ENG.). 32p. (J). (gr. -1-2). 16.99 *(978-1-4778-4728-2(6),* 9781477847282, Two Lions) Amazon Publishing.

—Snickerdoodle Takes the Cake. 2017. *(978-0-8234-3926-3(7))* Holiday Hse., Inc.

Long, Melinda & Wyrick, Monica. Art Smart, Science Detective: The Case of the Sliding Spaceship. 2018. (Young Palmetto Bks.). (ENG., Illus.). 64p. pap. 12.99 *(978-1-61117-935-4(1),* P599510) Univ. of South Carolina Pr.

Longstaff, Abie. The Fairytale Hairdresser & Sleeping Beauty. Beard, Lauren, illus. 2014. (Fairytale Hairdresser Ser.: 3). 32p. (J). (-k). pap. 12.99 *(978-0-552-56755-8(8))* Transworld Publishers Ltd. GBR. Dist: Independent Pubs. Group.

Longworth, Holly. The Philippines. 2015. (Countries We Come From Ser.). (ENG., Illus.). 32p. (J). (gr. k-3). lib. bdg. 28.50 *(978-1-62724-855-6(2))* Bearport Publishing Co., Inc.

Looney Tunes Talk Back to the Movies. (Looney Tunes Song & Sound Bks.). (Illus.). 24p. (J). (gr. -1-6). 14.98 *(978-0-7853-1253-6(6),* PI5) Publications International, Ltd.

Lore, Erin, illus. Timmy the Dragon. I.t. ed. 2007. 32p. (J). 8.95 *(978-0-9741562-7-9(2))* Yarrow Pr.

Lorenz Books Staff, creator. Patterns, 12 vols. 2006. (Learn-A-Word Picture Bks.). (ENG., Illus.). 12p. (J). (gr. -1-k). bds. 6.99 *(978-0-7548-1460-3(2))* Anness Publishing GBR. Dist: National Bk. Network.

Lorton, Barbara. Sidney Seagull Marks Lighthouses & Buoys of the Chesapeake. 2013. (Illus.). 28p. pap. 16.99 *(978-1-4582-1055-5(3),* Abbott Pr.) Author Solutions, LLC.

Love, Pamela. A Cub Explores. Sykes, Shannon, illus. 2004. (ENG.). 32p. (J). (gr. -1-17). 15.95 *(978-0-89272-593-9(1))* Down East Bks.

Lovvorn, Ann R. Chocolate Puddles. Reece, James A., illus. 2010. 36p. pap. 15.49 *(978-1-4520-5158-1(5))* AuthorHouse.

Low, J. H. The Hyena & the Monster. 2016. (ENG., Illus.). 32p. (J). 14.99 *(978-981-4721-69-1(7))* Marshall Cavendish International (Asia) Private Ltd. SGP. Dist: Independent Pubs. Group.

—The Lazy Hyena. 2016. (ENG., Illus.). 32p. (J). 14.99 *(978-981-4721-70-7(0))* Marshall Cavendish International (Asia) Private Ltd. SGP. Dist: Independent Pubs. Group.

—Lost in the Gardens. Low, J. H., illus. 2015. (ENG., Illus.). 48p. (J). 14.99 *(978-981-4677-10-3(8))* Marshall Cavendish International (Asia) Private Ltd. SGP. Dist: Independent Pubs. Group.

—There Is Nothing Buried Here. 2016. (ENG., Illus.). 32p. (J). 14.99 *(978-981-4721-67-7(0))* Marshall Cavendish International (Asia) Private Ltd. SGP. Dist: Independent Pubs. Group.

—A Thief in the Night. 2016. (ENG., Illus.). 32p. (J). 14.99 *(978-981-4721-68-4(9))* Marshall Cavendish International (Asia) Private Ltd. SGP. Dist: Independent Pubs. Group.

Lowell, Susan. Josefina Javelina: A Hairy Tale. MacPherson, Bruce, illus. 2005. (ENG.). 32p. (J). (gr. -1-3). 15.95 *(978-0-87358-790-7(1))* Cooper Square Publishing Llc.

—The Tortoise & the Jackrabbit: La Tortuga y la Liebre. Harris, Jim, illus. 2004. (New Bilingual Picture Book Ser.). (ENG.). 32p. (J). (gr. -1-3). pap. 7.95 *(978-0-87358-869-0(X))* Cooper Square Publishing Llc.

Loyie, Larry. The Gathering Tree, 1 vol. Holmlund, Heather D., illus. 2nd ed. 2005. (ENG.). 48p. (J). (gr. 1-3). pap. 18.95 *(978-1-894778-42-8(1))* Theytus Bks., Ltd. CAN. Dist: Orca Bk. Pubs. USA.

Ltd., Nelvana, illus. Ranger Rob: a Campfire Story. 2018. (ENG.). 24p. (J). (gr. -1-1). 3.99 *(978-2-924786-43-7(6),* CrackBoom! Bks.) Chouette Publishing CAN. Dist: Publishers Group West (PGW).

—Ranger Rob: Nature Quest. 2018. (ENG.). 24p. (J). (gr. -1-1). 3.99 *(978-2-924786-41-3(X),* CrackBoom! Bks.) Chouette Publishing CAN. Dist: Publishers Group West (PGW).

Lucas, David. Christmas at the Toy Museum. Lucas, David, illus. 2012. (ENG., Illus.). 32p. (J). (gr. -1-2). 15.99 *(978-0-7636-5868-7(5))* Candlewick Pr.

—The Robot & the Bluebird. 2008. (ENG., Illus.). 32p. (J). (-k). pap. 14.99 *(978-1-84270-732-6(9))* Andersen Pr. GBR. Dist: Independent Pubs. Group.

Ludwig, Trudy. My Secret Bully. Marble, Abigail, illus. 2015. 32p. (J). (gr. 1-4). 8.99 *(978-0-553-50940-3(3),* Dragonfly Bks.) Random Hse. Children's Bks.

Ludwig VanDerwater, Amy. Dreaming of You. DeWitt, Aaron, illus. 2018. (ENG.). 32p. (J). (gr. -1-k). 17.95 *(978-1-62979-212-5(8),* Astra Young Readers) Astra Publishing Hse.

Luftner, Kai. Lily Loves. Drews, Judith, illus. 2012. (ENG.). 32p. (J). (gr. -1-3). 16.95 *(978-1-897476-94-9(9))* Simply Read Bks. CAN. Dist: Ingram Publisher Services.

Lund, Deb. Monsters on Machines. Neubecker, Robert, illus. 2017. (ENG.). 40p. (J). (gr. -1-3). pap. 6.99 *(978-0-544-92783-4(4),* 1657204, Clarion Bks.) HarperCollins Pubs.

Lund, Evelyn. It Happened on Alphabet Street. 2003. (ENG., Illus.). 32p. (J). pap. 12.95 *(978-1-878044-50-1(8),* Wild Rose) Mayhaven Publishing, Inc.

Luongo, Ruth E. Beautiful, Big & Bright: The Journey of Sunny Sunflower Seed. 2004. (ENG.). 48p. pap. 16.99 *(978-1-4116-1161-0(6))* Lulu Pr., Inc.

Lutz, Barbara. My Cat. 2011. 28p. pap. 15.99 *(978-1-4628-4512-5(6))* Xlibris Corp.

Lynch, Jennifer. Livi & Grace. 2019. (ENG., Illus.). (gr. -1-1). 14.95 *(978-1-62634-591-1(0))* Greenleaf Book Group.

Lyon, George Ella. What Forest Knows. 2014. (ENG., Illus.). 40p. (J). (gr. -1-3). 19.99 *(978-1-4424-6775-0(4),* Atheneum Bks. for Young Readers) Simon & Schuster Children's Publishing.

Macalino, Damien. What If an Alligator Ate an Avalanche. Paj, Eduardo, illus. 2013. 32p. pap. 10.00 *(978-0-9836303-8-8(0))* Crystal Mosaic Bks.

MacDonald, Alan & Ladybird Books Staff. The Magic Porridge Pot. 2015. (First Favourite Tales Ser.). (Illus.). 32p. (J). (-k). 8.99 *(978-1-4093-0954-3(1))* Penguin Bks., Ltd. GBR. Dist: Independent Pubs. Group.

Macdonald, Fiona. Inca Town. Mark, Bergin, illus. 2017. (Time Traveler's Guide Ser.). 48p. (gr. 3-7). 37.10 *(978-1-911242-01-7(6))* Book Hse. GBR. Dist: Black Rabbit Bks.

MacGregor, Roy. The Highest Number in the World. Després, Geneviève, illus. 2014. 32p. (J). (gr. 1-4). 17.99 *(978-1-77049-575-3(4),* Tundra Bks.) Tundra Bks. CAN. Dist: Penguin Random Hse. LLC.

MacIver, Juliette. Gwendolyn! Baynton, Terri Rose, illus. 2018. 32p. pap. 6.99 *(978-0-7333-3518-1(7))* ABC Bks. AUS. Dist: HarperCollins Pubs.

Mack, Jeff. Hush Little Polar Bear: A Picture Book. Mack, Jeff, illus. 2013. (ENG., Illus.). 36p. (J). (gr. -1-1). bds. 7.99 *(978-1-59643-945-0(9),* 900123718) Roaring Brook Pr.

Mackay, Janis. The Selkie Girl, 30 vols. Mhasane, Ruchi, illus. 2014. (Traditional Scottish Tales Ser.). 32p. (J). pap. 11.95 *(978-1-78250-130-5(4),* Kelpies) Floris Bks. GBR. Dist: Consortium Bk. Sales & Distribution.

Mackenzie, Carin. David el Luchador Valiente Foce, Natalia, tr. Apps, Fred, illus. I.t. ed. 2004. (Biblewise Ser.). (SPA.). 32p. (J). pap. 4.50 *(978-1-932789-18-8(9),* bd04170e-10f9-4622-9342-cefa1ee482f9, CF4Kids) Christian Focus Pubns. GBR. Dist: Baker & Taylor Publisher Services (BTPS).

Mackenzie, Carine. Daniel, el Príncipe que Oraba Foce, Natalia, tr. Apps, Fred, illus. I.t. ed. 2004. (Biblewise Ser.). (SPA.). 32p. (J). pap. 4.50 *(978-1-932789-19-5(7),* 1434af2d-43fa-41db-bc9e-13acdb88436d, CF4Kids) Christian Focus Pubns. GBR. Dist: Baker & Taylor Publisher Services (BTPS).

—La Historia de Pablo — Viajes de Aventura, 1. Foce, Natalia, tr. Apps, Fred, illus. I.t. ed. 2004. (Biblewise Ser.). Orig. Title: Journeys of Adventure — the Story of Paul. (SPA.). 32p. (J). pap. 4.50 *(978-1-932789-23-2(5),* efac6dff-4e7f-4558-9d9d-e2637b85f563, CF4Kids) Christian Focus Pubns. GBR. Dist: Baker & Taylor Publisher Services (BTPS).

—Jose el Sonador de Dios Foce, Natalia, tr. Apps, Fred, illus. I.t. ed. 2004. (Biblewise Ser.). (SPA.). 32p. (J). pap. 4.50 *(978-1-932789-16-4(2),* 45545360-0975-4e2b-93f4-605e93caf8c0, CF4Kids) Christian Focus Pubns. GBR. Dist: Baker & Taylor Publisher Services (BTPS).

—El Nacimiento de Jesús: El Niño Prometido, 1. Foce, Natalia, tr. Apps, Fred, illus. I.t. ed. 2004. (Biblewise Ser.). Orig. Title: The Birth of Jesus — the Promised Child. (SPA.). 32p. (J). pap. 4.50 *(978-1-932789-20-1(0),* f4652f8c-e9f5-4524-a9d9-78b84dc0b3bb, CF4Kids) Christian Focus Pubns. GBR. Dist: Baker & Taylor Publisher Services (BTPS).

—El Plan de Rescate: La Historia de Noe, 1. Foce, Natalia, tr. Apps, Fred, illus. I.t. ed. 2004. (Biblewise Ser.). Orig. Title: The Rescue Plan. (SPA.). 32p. (J). pap. 4.50 *(978-1-932789-15-7(4),* 4c0355ad-bd8f-4f33-abfe-1edc64f1ecef, CF4Kids) Christian Focus Pubns. GBR. Dist: Baker & Taylor Publisher Services (BTPS).

—La Resurrección: Jesús Está Vivo, 1. Foce, Natalia, tr. Apps, Fred, illus. I.t. ed. 2004. (Biblewise Ser.). Orig. Title: The Resurrection — Jesus Is Alive. (SPA.). 32p. (J). pap. 4.50 *(978-1-932789-21-8(9),* dc3ffeed-60b5-4a2d-b0e4-8f6331fa9528, CF4Kids) Christian Focus Pubns. GBR. Dist: Baker & Taylor Publisher Services (BTPS).

—Samuel, el Niño que Escuchaba. Foce, Natalia, tr. Apps, Fred, illus. I.t. ed. 2004. (Biblewise Ser.). (SPA.). 32p. (J). pap. 4.50 *(978-1-932789-17-1(0),* f2437bbe-4496-4d7f-b872-9ab2be341cfc, CF4Kids) Christian Focus Pubns. GBR. Dist: Baker & Taylor Publisher Services (BTPS).

—Sara y Abraham: La maravillosa Promesa. Foce, Natalia C., tr. Apps, Fred, illus. 2004. (Biblewise Ser.). Orig. Title: Sarah & Abraham - the Wonderful Promise. (SPA.). 32p. (J). pap. 4.50 *(978-1-932789-14-0(6),* ba8079af-ab18-4cb4-ac1d-753741e1619b, CF4Kids) Christian Focus Pubns. GBR. Dist: Baker & Taylor Publisher Services (BTPS).

—Saúl — el Milagro en el Camino, 1. Foce, Natalia, tr. Apps, Fred, illus. I.t. ed. 2004. (Biblewise Ser.). Orig. Title: Saul —

the Miracle on the Road. (SPA.). 32p. (J). pap. 4.50 *(978-1-932789-22-5(7),* 989958f2-14a9-4571-8fbf-bbc02893e8b7, CF4Kids) Christian Focus Pubns. GBR. Dist: Baker & Taylor Publisher Services (BTPS).

MacKey, Esther L. Meet Mickey. 2012. 28p. pap. 7.95 *(978-1-937260-18-7(6))* Sleepytown Pr.

Mackey, Stephen. Pushka. 2013. (ENG., Illus.). 240p. (J). (gr. -1-k). pap. 8.99 *(978-1-4449-0135-1(4))* Hodder & Stoughton GBR. Dist: Hachette Bk. Group.

Mackintosh, David. There's a Bug on My Arm That Won't Let Go. Mackintosh, David, illus. 2020. (ENG., Illus.). 32p. (J). pap. 6.99 *(978-0-00-835797-9(8),* HarperCollins Children's Bks.) HarperCollins Pubs. Ltd. GBR. Dist: HarperCollins Pubs.

—What's up Mumu? Mackintosh, David, illus. 2015. (ENG., Illus.). 32p. (J). 17.99 *(978-0-00-812469-4(8),* HarperCollins Children's Bks.) HarperCollins Pubs. Ltd. GBR. Dist: HarperCollins Pubs.

MacLachlan, Patricia. Chicken Talk. Krosoczka, Jarrett J., illus. 2019. (ENG.). 32p. (J). (gr. -1-3). 17.99 *(978-0-06-239864-2(4),* Tegen, Katherine Bks) HarperCollins Pubs.

Maclaine, James. Big Picture Book of General Knowledge IR. 2018. (Big Picture Books* Ser.). (ENG.). 32p. 14.99 *(978-0-7945-3960-3(2),* Usborne) EDC Publishing.

—Miss Molly's School of Manners. 2019. (ENG.). 32ppp. (J). 14.99 *(978-0-7945-4199-6(2),* Usborne) EDC Publishing.

Maclear, Kyo. The Fog. Pak, Kenard, illus. 2017. 48p. (J). (gr. -1-3). 17.99 *(978-1-77049-492-3(8),* Tundra Bks.) Tundra Bks. CAN. Dist: Penguin Random Hse. LLC.

—Julia, Child. Morstad, Julie, illus. 32p. (J). (gr. -1-2). 2018. pap. 7.99 *(978-0-7352-6401-4(5))* 2014. 17.99 *(978-1-77049-449-7(9))* Tundra Bks. CAN. (Tundra Bks.). Dist: Penguin Random Hse. LLC.

—The Liszts. Sardà, Júlia, illus. 2016. (ENG.). 40p. (J). (gr. k-4). 16.99 *(978-1-77049-496-1(0),* Tundra Bks.) Tundra Bks. CAN. Dist: Penguin Random Hse. LLC.

—Virginia Wolf. Arsenault, Isabelle, illus. 2012. (ENG.). 32p. (J). (gr. -1-3). 16.99 *(978-1-55453-649-8(9))* Kids Can Pr., Ltd. CAN. Dist: Hachette Bk. Group.

—Yak & Dove. Shapiro, Esmé, illus. 2017. 56p. (J). (gr. -1-3). 18.99 *(978-1-77049-494-7(4),* Tundra Bks.) Tundra Bks. CAN. Dist: Penguin Random Hse. LLC.

MacMillan, Kathy. Nita's First Signs, Volume 1. Brezzi, Sara, illus. 2018. (Little Hands Signing Ser.: 1). (ENG.). 12p. (J). (gr. -1 — 1). bds. 14.99 *(978-1-945547-67-6(7),* 554767) Familius LLC.

Macomber, Debbie & Carney, Mary Lou. The Truly Terribly Horrible Sweater... That Grandma Knit. Nguyen, Vincent, illus. 2009. (ENG.). 32p. (J). (gr. -1-2). 16.99 *(978-0-06-165093-2(5),* HarperCollins) HarperCollins Pubs.

Macri, Giancarlo & Zanotti, Carolina. The Wall: A Timeless Tale. Vallarino, Elisa & Sacco, Mauro, illus. 2019. (ENG.). 40p. (J). 16.99 *(978-1-64124-038-3(5),* 0383) Fox Chapel Publishing Co., Inc.

Mader, Roger. Tiptop Cat. Mader, Roger, illus. 2014. (ENG., Illus.). 40p. (J). (gr. -1-3). 17.99 *(978-0-544-14799-7(5),* 1547591, Clarion Bks.) HarperCollins Pubs.

Madhu, Kailash. The Wise Tree & Meu: Mind & Spirit. 2012. 108p. pap. 40.81 *(978-1-4669-2744-5(5))* Trafford Publishing.

Madinabeitia Manso, Susana. In Winter / en Invierno. Hanako Momohara, Emily, illus. 2018. (Seasons/Estaciones Ser.). (ENG.). 14p. (J). (— 1). bds. 7.99 *(978-1-936669-66-0(8))* Blue Manatee Press.

Madson, Trish. 12 Little Elves Visit California, Volume 3. Han, Sadie, illus. 2017. (12 Little Elves Ser.: 3). (ENG.). 32p. (J). (gr. -1-1). 16.99 *(978-1-945547-11-9(1),* 554711) Familius LLC.

—12 Little Elves Visit Colorado, Volume 5. Kung, Chorkung, illus. 2018. (12 Little Elves Ser.: 5). (ENG.). 32p. (J). (gr. k-3). 16.99 *(978-1-64170-041-2(6),* 550041) Familius LLC.

—12 Little Elves Visit Montana, Volume 6. Kung, Chorkung, illus. 2018. (12 Little Elves Ser.: 6). (ENG.). 32p. (J). (gr. k-3). 16.99 *(978-1-64170-042-9(4),* 550042) Familius LLC.

—12 Little Elves Visit Oregon, Volume 4. Han, Sadie, illus. 2017. (12 Little Elves Ser.: 4). (ENG.). 32p. (J). (gr. -1-1). 16.99 *(978-1-945547-10-2(3),* 554710) Familius LLC.

Magabala Books, Magabala. Australian Babies. 2005. (Illus.). 10p. (J). bds. *(978-1-875641-92-5(0))* Magabala Bks.

Magee, Wes. Little Dragon. Warburton, Sarah, illus. 2004. (ENG.). 24p. (J). lib. bdg. 23.65 *(978-1-59646-690-6(1))* Dingles & Co.

Magsamen, Sandra. Beecause I Love You. Magsamen, Sandra, illus. 2017. (Made with Love Ser.). (ENG., Illus.). 14p. (J). (— 1). bds. 7.99 *(978-1-338-11090-6(X),* Cartwheel Bks.) Scholastic, Inc.

—I Love to Gobble You Up! Magsamen, Sandra, illus. 2018. (Made with Love Ser.). (ENG., Illus.). 10p. (J). (gr. -1 — 1). bds. 7.99 *(978-1-338-11092-0(6),* Cartwheel Bks.) Scholastic, Inc.

—I Love You Snow Much. Magsamen, Sandra, illus. 2017. (Made with Love Ser.). (ENG., Illus.). 10p. (J). (— 1). bds. 7.99 *(978-1-338-11086-9(1),* Cartwheel Bks.) Scholastic, Inc.

—Peep, Peep, I Love You! Magsamen, Sandra, illus. 2018. (ENG., Illus.). 10p. (J). (gr. -1 — 1). bds. 8.99 *(978-1-338-24314-7(4),* Cartwheel Bks.) Scholastic, Inc.

Mairi, Mackinnon. Phonics Workbook 1. 2012. (Very First Reading Workbooks Ser.). 36p. (J). pap. 7.99 *(978-0-7945-3115-7(6),* Usborne) EDC Publishing.

—Phonics Workbook 2. 2012. (Very First Reading Workbooks Ser.). 36p. (J). pap. 7.99 *(978-0-7945-3116-4(4),* Usborne) EDC Publishing.

Malam, John. Greek Town. Antram, David, illus. 2017. (Time Traveler's Guide Ser.). 48p. (gr. 3-7). 37.10 *(978-1-911242-00-0(8))* Book Hse. GBR. Dist: Black Rabbit Bks.

Malnor, Carol L. On Kiki's Reef, 1 vol. Hunner, Trina L., illus. 2014. (ENG.). 32p. (J). (gr. k-4). 16.95 *(978-1-58469-476-2(9),* Dawn Pubns.) Sourcebooks, Inc.

Malone, Cheryl Lawton. Elephants Walk Together. 2018. (2019 Av2 Fiction Ser.). (ENG.). 32p. (J). lib. bdg. 34.28 *(978-1-4896-8261-1(9),* AV2 by Weigl) Weigl Pubs., Inc.

—Elephants Walk Together. Masseva, Bistra, illus. 2017. (ENG.). 32p. (J). (gr. -1-3). 16.99 *(978-0-8075-1960-8(X),* 080751960X) Whitman, Albert & Co.

Malouf, Ranya. Blue Fish's Secret Wish. 2011. (ENG.). 32p. pap. *(978-9963-610-72-3(2))* Rimal Pubns.

Mamada, Mineko. Which Is Round? Which Is Bigger? Mamada, Mineko, illus. 2013. (ENG., Illus.). 24p. (J). (gr. -1-1). 16.95 *(978-1-55453-973-4(0))* Kids Can Pr., Ltd. CAN. Dist: Hachette Bk. Group.

Mandell, B. B. Samanthasaurus Rex. Kaufman, Suzanne, illus. 2016. (ENG.). 32p. (J). (gr. -1-3). 17.99 *(978-0-06-234873-9(6),* Balzer & Bray) HarperCollins Pubs.

Manderly, Lorin. Lilith Celebrates Lammas. Drewes, Dan, illus. 2010. 36p. pap. 15.50 *(978-1-4520-2689-3(0))* AuthorHouse.

Mandracchia, Charles, creator. A Wacky Wonder World. Lt. ed. 2005. (Illus.). 24p. (J). 13.95 *(978-0-9721957-1-3(8))* Mandracchia, Charles.

Mangual, C. Ines. Bug Battle! Spaziante, Patrick, illus. 2017. 20p. (J). *(978-1-5182-2750-9(3))* Random Hse., Inc.

Mann, Brooke Malia, illus. Miracles of Jesus. 2019. (J). 16.99 *(978-1-62972-522-2(6))* Deseret Bk. Co.

Mansfield, Andy. See the Stripes. Mansfield, Andy, illus. 2018. (ENG., Illus.). 14p. (J). (gr. -1-2). 15.00 *(978-0-7636-9895-9(4))* Candlewick Pr.

Manson, Beverlie, illus. The Little Mermaid. 2017. 24p. (J). (gr. -1-12). pap. 7.99 *(978-1-86147-826-3(3),* Armadillo) Anness Publishing GBR. Dist: National Bk. Network.

Manuel Reeves, Emily. Fiona Flamingo Has Lost Her Pink. 2013. 20p. pap. 10.00 *(978-0-9821506-1-0(X))* Reeves, Emily.

Manushkin, Fran. Happy in Our Skin. Tobia, Lauren, illus. (ENG.). 32p. (J). 2018. (gr. -1-1). 7.99 *(978-0-7636-9972-7(1))* 2015. (-k). 17.99 *(978-0-7636-7002-3(2))* Candlewick Pr.

—Katie Woo: Star Writer. Lyon, Tammie, illus. 2013. (Katie Woo: Star Writer Ser.). (ENG.). 32p. (J). (gr. k-2). 116.60 *(978-1-4048-8082-5(8),* 19487); pap., pap., pap. 35.70 *(978-1-4795-1991-0(X),* 20074) Capstone. (Picture Window Bks.).

Marchus, Linda. The Gorilla Who Wanted to Dance. Marchus, Linda, illus. 2003. (Illus.). 32p. (J). lib. bdg. 15.95 *(978-0-9723122-1-9(8))* Wee Read Publishing.

Marcus, Leonard S. Ways of Telling: Conversations on the Art of the Picture Book. 2005. (Illus.). 247p. reprint ed. 30.00 *(978-0-7567-9704-1(7))* DIANE Publishing Co.

Margrave, David R. When Fur & Feather Get Together. Wyly, Kim, illus. 2018. (ENG.). 32p. (J). 11.99 *(978-1-945507-72-4(1))* Carpenter's Son Publishing.

Marie, K. Misty Blue: The Kloudsville Series. Bundoc, Oliver Kryzz, illus. 2018. (Kloudsville Ser.: 1). (ENG.). 36p. 21.99 *(978-0-9989541-1-0(X))* BookBaby.

Marie, Lynne. Hedgehog Goes to Kindergarten. Kennedy, Anne, illus. 2011. (J). pap. *(978-0-545-29874-2(1))* Scholastic, Inc.

Marinaro, Stacy. Nap Time. 2009. 34p. pap. 16.50 *(978-0-557-06881-4(9))* Lulu Pr., Inc.

Marineau, Michèle. Wash On! Gauthier, Manon, illus. 2018. (ENG.). 40p. (J). (gr. k-2). 16.95 *(978-1-77278-018-5(9))* Pajama Pr. CAN. Dist: Publishers Group West (PGW).

Marino, Gianna. I Am the Mountain Mouse. 2016. (Illus.). 40p. (J). (-k). bds. 16.99 *(978-0-451-46955-7(0),* Viking Books for Young Readers) Penguin Young Readers Group.

—Night Animals. Marino, Gianna, illus. 2015. (Illus.). 32p. (J). (gr. -1-k). 18.99 *(978-0-451-46954-0(2),* Viking Books for Young Readers) Penguin Young Readers Group.

Marley, Bob & Marley, Cedella. Get up, Stand Up. Cabuay, John Jay, illus. 2019. (Bob Marley by Chronicle Bks.). (ENG.). 36p. (J). (gr. -1-k). 16.99 *(978-1-4521-7172-2(6))* Chronicle Bks. LLC.

Marley, Cedella. One Love: (Multicultural Childrens Book, Mixed Race Childrens Book, Bob Marley Book for Kids, Music Books for Kids) Newton, Vanessa, illus. 2011. (Marley Ser.). (ENG.). 32p. (J). (gr. -1 — 1). 16.99 *(978-1-4521-0224-5(4))* Chronicle Bks. LLC.

Marovic, Mason A. Divorce & Me. 2009. 44p. pap. 21.99 *(978-1-4363-9171-9(7))* Xlibris Corp.

Marsh, Carole. The Mystery at Grizzly Graveyard. 2014. (Real Kids, Real Places Ser.: Vol. 3). (ENG., Illus.). 158p. (J). (gr. 3-5). pap. 7.99 *(978-0-635-11187-6(X),* Marsh, Carole Mysteries) Gallopade International.

—The Mystery at Rattlesnake Ridge. 2014. (Wildlife Mysteries Ser.). (ENG., Illus.). 158p. (J). (gr. 2-9). pap. 7.99 *(978-0-635-11188-3(8),* Marsh, Carole Bks.) Gallopade International.

Marshall, Natalie. Jungle. 2019. (ENG.). 12p. (J). (gr. -1 — 1). bds. 9.99 *(978-1-4380-5070-6(4))* Sourcebooks, Inc.

—Millie-Mae: In Winter. 2014. (Illus.). (J). *(978-1-4351-5613-5(7))* Barnes & Noble, Inc.

Martell, Hazel Mary. Roman Town. Mark, Bergin, illus. 2017. (Time Traveler's Guide Ser.). 48p. (gr. 3-7). 37.10 *(978-1-911242-02-4(4))* Book Hse. GBR. Dist: Black Rabbit Bks.

Martí, Meritxell. Grow, Baby, Grow! Watch Baby Grow Month by Month! Salomo, Xavier, illus. 2019. (ENG.). 18p. (J). (gr. k-2). 24.99 *(978-1-64170-100-6(5),* 550100) Familius LLC.

Martin, Jacqueline Briggs. Bim, Bam, Bop ... & Oona. Day, Larry, illus. 2019. (ENG.). 32p. (J). 16.95 *(978-1-5179-0395-4(5))* Univ. of Minnesota Pr.

Martin, Susi. Animal 123. 2014. (ENG., Illus.). 32p. (J). (gr. -1-2). 9.95 *(978-1-77085-454-3(1),* 90ea0ac2-942c-4806-9d10-0e55bb143cc8) Firefly Bks., Ltd.

Martinez-Neal, Juana. Alma & How She Got Her Name. Martinez-Neal, Juana, illus. 2018. (ENG., Illus.). 32p. (J). (gr. -1-3). 17.99 *(978-0-7636-9355-8(3))* Candlewick Pr.

Martins, Isabel Minhos. The World in a Second. Carvalho, Bernardo, illus. 2015. 56p. (J). (gr. -1-3). 18.95 *(978-1-59270-157-5(4))* Enchanted Lion Bks., LLC.

Martins, Isabel Minhós & Martins, Isabel Minhós. Coming & Going. Carvalho, Bernardo, illus. 2014. (ENG.). 48p. (gr. k-17). 16.95 *(978-1-84976-161-1(2))* Tate Publishing, Ltd. GBR. Dist: Abrams, Inc.

Marvel Press Book Group, Marvel Press. World of Reading: This Is Miles Morales. 2018. (World of Reading Ser.). (ENG., Illus.). 32p. (J). (gr. 1-3). pap. 4.99 *(978-1-368-02863-9(2))* Marvel Worldwide, Inc.

Marvin, Dan. But I Don't Eat Ants. Fry, Kelly, illus. 2017. (ENG.). 32p. (J). (gr. -1-2). 16.99 *(978-1-57687-837-8(6),* powerHouse Bks.) powerHse. Bks.

Marzo, Bridget, illus. Tiz & Ott's Big Draw. 2015. (ENG.). 32p. (J). (gr. -1-3). 15.95 *(978-1-84976-310-3(0),* 1646501) Tate Publishing, Ltd. GBR. Dist: Hachette Bk. Group.

Marzollo, Jean. Funny Frog. 2012. (I Spy — Scholastic Ser.). lib. bdg. 13.55 *(978-0-606-23969-1(3))* Turtleback.

—Mama Mama/Papa Papa Flip Board Book. Regan, Laura, illus. 2003. (ENG.). 32p. (J). (gr. -1 — 1). bds. 7.99 *(978-0-06-051915-5(0),* HarperFestival) HarperCollins Pubs.

Maskell, Hazell. Very First Words. 2009. (First Words Board Bks). 18p. (J). bds. 6.99 *(978-0-7945-2052-6(9),* Usborne) EDC Publishing.

Mason, Margaret H. These Hands. Cooper, Floyd, illus. 2015. (ENG.). 32p. (J). (gr. -1-3). 7.99 *(978-0-544-55546-4(5),* 1610453, Clarion Bks.) HarperCollins Pubs.

Massenot, Véronique. The Dreaming Giant: A Children's Book Inspired by Wassily Kandinsky. Nille, Peggy, illus. 2017. (Children's Books Inspired by Famous Artworks Ser.). (ENG.). 32p. (J). (gr. -1-3). 14.95 *(978-3-7913-7279-2(3))* Prestel Verlag GmbH & Co KG. DEU. Dist: Penguin Random Hse. LLC.

—The Great Wave: A Children's Book Inspired by Hokusai. Pilorget, Bruno, illus. 2011. (Children's Books Inspired by Famous Artworks Ser.). (ENG.). 32p. (J). (gr. -1-3). 14.95 *(978-3-7913-7058-3(8))* Prestel Verlag GmbH & Co KG. DEU. Dist: Penguin Random Hse. LLC.

—Journey on a Cloud: A Children's Book Inspired by Marc Chagall. Mansot, Elise, illus. 2011. (Children's Books Inspired by Famous Artworks Ser.). (ENG.). 32p. (J). (gr. -1-3). 14.95 *(978-3-7913-7057-6(X))* Prestel Verlag GmbH & Co KG. DEU. Dist: Penguin Random Hse. LLC.

Massenot, Véronique & Hie, Vanessa. The Three Musicians: A Children's Book Inspired by Pablo Picasso. 2013. (Children's Books Inspired by Famous Artworks Ser.). (ENG., Illus.). 32p. (J). (gr. -1-3). 14.95 *(978-3-7913-7151-1(7))* Prestel Verlag GmbH & Co KG. DEU. Dist: Penguin Random Hse. LLC.

Massey, Claire. My Brother & Me. 2018. (ENG., Illus.). 26p. (J). (gr. 1-5). pap. *(978-1-5289-2443-6(6))* Austin Macauley Pubs. Ltd.

Matheson, Anne. I Love to Sing. Cutting, David A., illus. 2014. (ENG.). 32p. (J). (gr. 1-5). 7.99 *(978-1-4867-0001-1(2))* Flowerpot Children's Pr. Inc. CAN. Dist: Cardinal Pubs. Group.

Matheson, Christie. Bird Watch. Matheson, Christie, illus. 2019. (ENG., Illus.). 48p. (J). (gr. -1-3). 17.99 *(978-0-06-239340-1(5),* Greenwillow Bks.) HarperCollins Pubs.

Mathias, Irene. The Short Straw. Uhren, Anja, illus. 2017. (ENG.). 30p. (J). (gr. -1-4). 14.99 *(978-1-941429-77-8(7))* Handersen Publishing.

Matisse, Henri. Blue & Other Colors: With Henri Matisse. 2016. (ENG., Illus.). 30p. (gr. -1 — 1). bds. 12.95 *(978-0-7148-7142-4(7))* Phaidon Pr., Inc.

Matthews, Caitlin & Barefoot Books. Fireside Stories: Tales for a Winter's Eve. Cann, Helen, illus. 2015. 96p. (J). (gr. 2-6). 19.99 *(978-1-78285-251-3(4))* Barefoot Bks., Inc.

Matthews, Gail. Simonie & the Dance Contest. Hinch, Ali, illus. 2019. (ENG.). 36p. (J). (gr. 1-3). pap. 10.95 *(978-1-77227-224-6(8))* Inhabit Media Inc. CAN. Dist: Consortium Bk. Sales & Distribution.

Matyjaszek, Kasia, illus. This Bonny Baby: A Mirror Board Book, 96 vols. 2017. 12p. (J). 9.95 *(978-1-78250-465-8(6),* Kelpies) Floris Bks. GBR. Dist: Consortium Bk. Sales & Distribution.

Maurer, Ashley, illus. Jennie Jenkins. 2015. (First Steps in Music Ser.). (ENG.). 32p. (J). (— 1). 17.95 *(978-1-62277-139-4(7))* G I A Pubns., Inc.

Mavrikis, Peter. Classic Warships. 2014. (Illus.). 48p. (J). *(978-1-4351-5368-4(5))* Barnes & Noble, Inc.

May, Tallulah, adapted by. Crystal Heart Kisses. 2016. (Illus.). (J). *(978-1-5182-3830-7(0))* Little, Brown Bks. for Young Readers.

Mayaprua, Alejandro Taish. Nantu & Auju: How the Moon & the Potoo Bird Came to Be. Youth of the Achuar Tribe of Ecuador, illus. 2005. (J). 15.95 *(978-0-9745477-0-1(0))* Arutam Pr.

Mayer, Mercer. All That I Can Be (Little Critter) An Inspirational Gift for Kids. 2017. (Pictureback(R) Ser.). (Illus.). 48p. (J). (gr. -1-2). 5.99 *(978-0-399-55377-6(0),* Random Hse. Bks. for Young Readers) Random Hse. Children's Bks.

—Fair Play. 2012. (Big Little Critter Ser.: 1). (ENG., Illus.). 98p. (J). 12.95 *(978-1-60746-763-2(1),* Premiere) FastPrncil, Inc.

—Helping Out. 2012. (Big Little Critter Ser.: 2). (ENG., Illus.). 96p. (J). 12.95 *(978-1-60746-071-8(8),* Premiere) FastPrncil, Inc.

—It's Bedtime, Little Critter! (Little Critter) 2018. (Illus.). 48p. (J). (gr. -1-2). pap. 5.99 *(978-1-5247-6900-0(2),* Random Hse. Bks. for Young Readers) Random Hse. Children's Bks.

—Just Me & My Mom/Just Me & My Dad (Little Critter) Mayer, Mercer, illus. 2014. (Pictureback(R) Ser.). (Illus.). 48p. (J). (gr. -1-2). 4.99 *(978-0-385-37175-9(6),* Random Hse. Bks. for Young Readers) Random Hse. Children's Bks.

—Little Critter: Just a Special Thanksgiving. Mayer, Mercer, illus. 2015. (Little Critter Ser.). (ENG., Illus.). 24p. (J). (gr. -1-3). pap. 4.99 *(978-0-06-147811-6(3),* HarperFestival) HarperCollins Pubs.

Mayfield, Anthony. Alexander Anthony Finds a Great Love. Samuka, illus. 2004. (ENG.). 42p. (gr. 2-5). per. 12.99 *(978-1-4134-3778-2(8))* Xlibris Corp.

Mayhew, James. Katie & the Bathers. 2016. (Katie Ser.). (ENG., Illus.). 32p. (J). (gr. k-17). pap. 9.99 *(978-1-4083-3189-7(6),* Orchard Bks.) Hachette Children's Group GBR. Dist: Hachette Bk. Group.

—Katie & the Dinosaurs. 2014. (Katie Ser.). (ENG., Illus.). 32p. (J). (gr. -1-k). 9.99 *(978-1-4083-3191-0(8))* Hodder & Stoughton GBR. Dist: Hachette Bk. Group.

—Katie & the Spanish Princess. 2015. (Katie Ser.). (ENG., Illus.). 32p. (J). (gr. -1-k). pap. 11.99 *(978-1-4083-3242-9(6))* Hodder & Stoughton GBR. Dist: Hachette Bk. Group.

—Katie: Katie & the Mona Lisa. 2016. (Katie Ser.). (ENG., Illus.). 32p. (J). (gr. -1-k). pap. 10.99 *(978-1-4083-3194-1(2),* Orchard Bks.) Hachette Children's Group GBR. Dist: Hachette Bk. Group.

—Katie: Katie's London Christmas. 2016. (Katie Ser.). (ENG., Illus.). 32p. (J). (gr. -1-k). pap. 10.99 *(978-1-4083-2642-8(6),* Orchard Bks.) Hachette Children's Group GBR. Dist: Hachette Bk. Group.

Mayhew, James & McQuillan, Mary. Katie & the British Artists. 2015. (Katie Ser.). (ENG., Illus.). 32p. (J). (gr. -1-k). 9.99 *(978-1-4083-3190-3(X))* Hodder & Stoughton GBR. Dist: Hachette Bk. Group.

—Katie & the Waterlily Pond. 2015. (Katie Ser.). (ENG., Illus.). 32p. (J). (gr. -1-k). pap. 10.99 *(978-1-4083-3245-0(0))* Hodder & Stoughton GBR. Dist: Hachette Bk. Group.

Mayhew, James & Wildish, Lee. Katie & the Starry Night. 2015. (Katie Ser.). (ENG., Illus.). 32p. (J). (gr. -1-k). pap. 9.99 *(978-1-4083-3243-6(4),* Orchard Bks.) Hachette Children's Group GBR. Dist: Hachette Bk. Group.

Mazur, Gabrielle. Boppy & Me. Collins, Linda, illus. 2013. 38p. 14.97 *(978-1-4507-3897-2(4))* Bush Publishing Inc.

—Boppy & Me. Collins, Linda, illus. 2013. 38p. pap. 12.95 *(978-1-4507-3906-1(7))* Bush Publishing Inc.

McAllister, Margaret. Emily & the Lamb. Vince, Dawn, illus. 2005. (ENG.). 24p. (J). lib. bdg. 23.65 *(978-1-59646-756-9(8))* Dingles & Co.

McAnulty, Stacy. Brave. Lew-Vriethoff, Joanne, illus. 2017. (ENG.). 32p. (J). (gr. -1-3). 17.99 *(978-0-7624-5782-3(1),* Running Pr. Kids) Running Pr.

—Sun! One in a Billion. Lewis, Stevie, illus. 2018. (Our Universe Ser.: 2). (ENG.). 40p. (J). 18.99 *(978-1-250-19932-4(8),* 900194804, Holt, Henry & Co. Bks. For Young Readers) Holt, Henry & Co.

McBain, Chani. No Such Thing As Nessie! A Loch Ness Monster Adventure, 30 vols. Harris-Jones, Kirsteen, illus. 2013. (ENG.). 32p. (J). pap. 11.95 *(978-0-86315-953-4(2),* Kelpies) Floris Bks. GBR. Dist: Consortium Bk. Sales & Distribution.

McBeth, T. L. Robot in Love. McBeth, T. L., illus. 2018. (ENG., Illus.). 40p. (J). 17.99 *(978-1-250-18593-8(9),* 900191448, Holt, Henry & Co. Bks. For Young Readers) Holt, Henry & Co.

McBratney, Sam. Guess How Much I Love You Padded Board Book. Jeram, Anita, illus. 2019. (Guess How Much I Love You Ser.). (ENG.). 30p. (J). (— 1). bds. 10.99 *(978-1-5362-1062-0(5))* Candlewick Pr.

McCanna, Tim. Boing! A Very Noisy ABC. Martin, Jorge, illus. 2018. (ENG.). 32p. (J). (gr. -1-3). 17.99 *(978-1-4814-8755-9(8),* Simon & Schuster/Paula Wiseman Bks.) Simon & Schuster/Paula Wiseman Bks.

McCarthy, Jenna. Lola's Rules for Friendship. Palacios, Sara, illus. 2017. (ENG.). 32p. (J). (gr. -1-3). 17.99 *(978-0-06-225018-6(3),* Balzer & Bray) HarperCollins Pubs.

McCarthy, Laura. My Daddy Can Too!!! 2011. 24p. pap. 28.03 *(978-1-4568-3778-5(8))* Xlibris Corp.

McCarthy, Meghan. My Little Pony: Twilight's Kingdom. 2017. (MLP Episode Adaptations Ser.). (Illus.). 144p. (J). (gr. 1-3). pap. 7.99 *(978-1-68405-064-2(2))* Idea & Design Works, LLC.

McCarthy, Meghan & Larson, Mitch. My Little Pony: When Cutie Calls. 2014. (MLP Episode Adaptations Ser.: 1). (Illus.). 128p. (J). (gr. 1-3). pap. 7.99 *(978-1-61377-830-2(9),* 9781613778302) Idea & Design Works, LLC.

McCarthy, Michael. The Story of Daniel in the Lions' Den. Ferri, Giuliano, illus. 2003. 32p. (J). (gr. 1-3). 16.99 *(978-1-84148-209-5(9))* Barefoot Bks., Inc.

McCarthy, Rebecca. A Very Special Mama's Day. Artful Doodlers Ltd. Staff, illus. 2013. (Zoobies! Ser.). (ENG.). 24p. (J). (gr. -1-1). 17.44 *(978-0-448-46316-2(4))* Penguin Young Readers Group.

McCartney, Tania. Peas in a Pod. Snerling, Tina, illus. 2015. (ENG.). 32p. (J). (gr. -1-2). 17.95 *(978-1-921966-71-2(8))* Exisle Publishing Pty Ltd. AUS. Dist: Two Rivers Distribution.

McCleary, Stacey. I Give You the World. Saldana, Carmen, illus. 2018. (ENG.). 32p. (J). (gr. -1-2). 16.99 *(978-1-68010-082-2(3))* Tiger Tales.

McClintock. Little Princess Picture Book. Date not set. (Illus.). 40p. (J). (gr. -1-3). pap. 4.99 *(978-0-06-443539-0(3))* HarperCollins Pubs.

McCloud, Carol & Butzke, Caryn. Bucket Filling from a to Z: The Key to Being Happy. Zimmer, Glenn, illus. 2017. 32p. (J). (gr. -1-4). pap. 9.95 *(978-0-9974864-3-8(0),* Bucket Fillosophy) Cardinal Rule Pr.

McClure, Nikki. Apple. 2019. (ENG.). 30p. (J). (gr. -1-k). bds. 8.99 *(978-1-4197-3631-5(0),* 692110, Abrams Appleseed) Abrams, Inc.

—Mama, Is It Summer Yet? 2018. (ENG., Illus.). 30p. (J). (gr. -1 — 1). bds. 9.99 *(978-1-4197-2828-0(8),* 1202510, Abrams Appleseed) Abrams, Inc.

McConnell, Lynn. Grandma's Tree. 2009. 24p. pap. 11.49 *(978-1-4389-8069-0(8))* AuthorHouse.

McCool, Ben, et al. Grumpy Cat & Pokey, Vol. 3. 2017. (ENG., Illus.). 104p. (J). 12.99 *(978-1-5241-0246-3(6),* 8497b40c-b311-44ea-aa3e-ee1aa918532a, Dynamite Entertainment) Dynamic Forces, Inc.

McCranie, Stephen. Mal & Chad: Belly Flop! McCranie, Stephen, illus. 3rd ed. 2012. (Mal & Chad Ser.: 3). (ENG., Illus.). 224p. (J). (gr. 3-7). pap. 10.99 *(978-0-399-25658-5(X),* Philomel Bks.) Penguin Young Readers Group.

McCue, L. Hide Away Husky. 2016. (HideAway Pets Bks.). (ENG., Illus.). 32p. (J). (gr. -1-2). 9.95 *(978-1-4549-1812-7(8))* Sterling Publishing Co., Inc.

McCully, Emily Arnold. First Snow. McCully, Emily Arnold, illus. 2003. (ENG., Illus.). 32p. (J). (gr. -1-3). 17.99 *(978-0-06-623852-4(8),* HarperCollins) HarperCollins Pubs.

McCurry, Kristen. Pick a Picture, Write an Opinion!, 1 vol. 2014. (Little Scribe Ser.). (ENG., Illus.). 32p. (J). (gr. -1-2). lib. bdg. 27.99 *(978-1-4765-4240-9(6),* 124347, Capstone Pr.) Capstone.

McDermott, Mustafa Yusuf. Muslim Nursery Rhymes. rev. ed. 2015. (ENG., Illus.). 29p. (J). 14.95 *(978-0-86037-563-0(3))* Kube Publishing Ltd. GBR. Dist: Consortium Bk. Sales & Distribution.

McDonald, Avril. The Wolf & the Shadow Monster, 1 vol. Minina, Tatiana, illus. 2016. (Feel Brave Ser.). (ENG.). 32p. (J). pap. 12.95 *(978-1-78583-018-1(X))* Crown Hse. Publishing LLC.

McDonald, Jill. Hello, World! Dinosaurs. 2018. (Hello, World! Ser.). (Illus.). 26p. (J). (— 1). bds. 8.99 *(978-1-5247-1934-0(X),* Doubleday Bks. for Young Readers) Random Hse. Children's Bks.

—Hello, World! Solar System. 2016. (Hello, World! Ser.). (Illus.). 26p. (J). (— 1). bds. 8.99 *(978-0-553-52103-0(9),* Doubleday Bks. for Young Readers) Random Hse. Children's Bks.

—Hello, World! Weather. 2016. (Hello, World! Ser.). (Illus.). 26p. (J). (— 1). bds. 8.99 *(978-0-553-52101-6(2),* Doubleday Bks. for Young Readers) Random Hse. Children's Bks.

McDonnell, Rory. Up or Down?, 1 vol. 2019. (All about Opposites Ser.). (ENG.). 24p. (gr. k-k). 24.27 *(978-1-5382-3736-6(9),* ccf7ee8d-a6d9-497b-909d-97dbc1554093) Stevens, Gareth Publishing LLLP.

McGillivray, Dave & Feehrer, Nancy. Dream Big: A True Story of Courage & Determination. Himler, Ron, illus. 2018. (ENG.). 32p. (J). 16.95 *(978-1-61930-618-9(2),* d6b095db-9a57-41d0-968d-ef8d7bc7dbef) Nomad Pr.

McGrath, Barbara Barbieri. Teddy Bear Addition. Nihoff, Tim, illus. 2014. (McGrath Math Ser.: 5). 32p. (J). (gr. -1-3). pap. 7.95 *(978-1-58089-425-8(9))* Charlesbridge Publishing, Inc.

McGrath, Jennifer. The Snow Knows, 1 vol. Bisaillon, Josée, illus. 2016. (ENG.). 32p. (J). (gr. -1-k). 22.95 *(978-1-77108-441-3(3),* 19104a78-5d06-46f7-9cd1-abbb54d26bd8) Nimbus Publishing, Ltd. CAN. Dist: Baker & Taylor Publisher Services (BTPS).

McGraw, Royal, et al. Grumpy Cat, Vol. 1. 2016. (ENG., Illus.). 104p. (J). 12.99 *(978-1-60690-796-2(4),* 7edde535-7787-4551-8b26-f7a8a64f9bc5, Dynamite Entertainment) Dynamic Forces, Inc.

McGreevy, Anne Kelly. Liliana Loretta Larue. Desrochers, Fache, illus. 2017. (ENG.). 28p. (J). pap. 8.95 *(978-1-68350-069-8(5))* Morgan James Publishing.

McGrellis, Barbara. Love Never Fails. 2013. 24p. pap. 10.99 *(978-1-4624-0745-3(5),* Inspiring Voices) Author Solutions, LLC.

McKain, Kelly. The Haunted Shipwreck. Johansson, Cecilia, illus. 2004. (Mermaid Rock Ser.). 48p. (J). *(978-0-439-62647-7(1))* Scholastic, Inc.

McKay, Elizabeth. Wee Granny's Magic Bag & the Pirates, 1 vol. Bogade, Maria, illus. 2018. 32p. (J). 11.95 *(978-1-78250-475-7(3),* Kelpies) Floris Bks. GBR. Dist: Consortium Bk. Sales & Distribution.

McKee, Brett. Monsters Don't Cry. Burfoot, Ella, illus. 2012. (ENG.). 32p. (J). (gr. -1-k). 19.99 *(978-1-84939-291-4(9))* Andersen Pr. GBR. Dist: Independent Pubs. Group.

McKee, Brett & McKee, David. George's Invisible Watch. McKee, David, illus. 2013. (Illus.). 32p. (J). (gr. -1-k). pap. 8.99 *(978-1-84270-864-4(3))* Andersen Pr. GBR. Dist: Independent Pubs. Group.

McKee, David. The Adventures of King Rollo. 2016. (ENG., Illus.). 128p. (J). (-k). 19.99 *(978-1-78344-468-7(1))* Andersen Pr. GBR. Dist: Independent Pubs. Group.

—Denver. McKee, David, illus. 2012. (ENG., Illus.). 32p. (J). (gr. -1-k). pap. 10.99 *(978-1-84939-389-8(3))* Andersen Pr. GBR. Dist: Independent Pubs. Group.

—Elmer & Aunt Zelda. McKee, David, illus. 2017. (Elmer Ser.). (ENG., Illus.). 32p. (J). (gr. -1-3). 17.99 *(978-1-5124-3945-8(2),* 5760b89f-74a3-4fee-bcab-186c1b37be5d) Lerner Publishing Group.

—Elmer & the Flood. McKee, David, illus. 2015. (Elmer Ser.). (ENG., Illus.). 32p. (J). (gr. -1-3). E-Book 27.99 *(978-1-4677-9314-8(0))* Lerner Publishing Group.

—Elmer & the Race. McKee, David, illus. 2016. (Elmer Ser.). (ENG., Illus.). 32p. (J). (gr. -1-3). 17.99 *(978-1-5124-1624-4(X),* 648b377c-7450-48f1-a53b-ea9b1626bb7f) Lerner Publishing Group.

—Elmer & the Rainbow. 2016. (Elmer Ser.). (ENG., Illus.). 30p. (J). (-k). bds. 13.99 *(978-1-78344-424-3(X))* Andersen Pr. GBR. Dist: Independent Pubs. Group.

—Elmer & Wilbur. 2018. (Elmer Ser.). (ENG., Illus.). 26p. (J). (-k). bds. 9.99 *(978-1-78344-530-1(0))* Andersen Pr. GBR. Dist: Independent Pubs. Group.

—Elmer's Colours (English-Polish), 1 vol. 2010. (Elmer Ser.). (ENG., Illus.). 16p. (J). (gr. k — 1). bds. 8.95 *(978-1-84059-531-4(0))* Milet Publishing.

—Elmer's Day. 2018. (Elmer Ser.). (ENG., Illus.). 10p. (J). (— 1). bds. 9.99 *(978-1-78344-608-7(0))* Andersen Pr. GBR. Dist: Independent Pubs. Group.

—Elmer's Day, 1 vol. 2010. (Elmer Ser.). (ENG., Illus.). 16p. (J). (gr. k — 1). bds. 8.95 *(978-1-84059-532-1(9))* Milet Publishing.

—Elmer's New Friend. 2003. (ENG., Illus.). 11p. (J). 8.99 *(978-1-84270-034-1(0))* Andersen Pr. GBR. Dist: Trafalgar Square Publishing.

—Isabel's Noisy Tummy. McKee, David, illus. 2013. (Illus.). 32p. (J). (gr. -1-k). pap. 10.99 *(978-1-84939-689-9(2))* Andersen Pr. GBR. Dist: Independent Pubs. Group.

—Melric & the Dragon. 2016. (Melric Ser.: 4). (ENG., Illus.). 32p. (J). (-k). pap. 13.99 *(978-1-78344-210-2(7))* Andersen Pr. GBR. Dist: Independent Pubs. Group.

—Melric & the Petnapping. McKee, David, illus. 2014. (Melric Ser.). (ENG., Illus.). 32p. (J). (gr. -1-k). 16.99 *(978-1-78344-008-5(2))* Andersen Pr. GBR. Dist: Independent Pubs. Group.

—Melric the Magician Who Lost His Magic. McKee, David, illus. 2013. (Melric Ser.). (ENG., Illus.). 32p. (J). (gr. -1-k). pap. 12.99 *(978-1-84939-525-0(X));* 16.99 *(978-1-84939-439-0(3))* Andersen Pr. GBR. Dist: Independent Pubs. Group.

—Two Can Toucan. 40th ed. 2017. (ENG., Illus.). 32p. (J). (-k). 15.99 *(978-1-78344-480-9(0))* Andersen Pr. GBR. Dist: Independent Pubs. Group.

McKellar, Danica. Bathtime Mathtime. Padrón, Alicia, illus. 2018. (McKellar Math Ser.). 20p. (J). (-k). bds. 8.99 *(978-1-101-93394-7(1),* Crown Books For Young Readers) Random Hse. Children's Bks.

—Ten Magic Butterflies. Bricking, Jen, illus. (McKellar Math Ser.). (J). 2019. 38p. (— 1). bds. 8.99 *(978-1-101-93385-5(2))* 2018. (ENG.). 40p. (gr. -1-1). 17.99 *(978-1-101-93382-4(8))* Random Hse. Children's Bks. (Crown Books For Young Readers).

McKendry, Sam. Are You Ticklish? Mitchell, Melanie, illus. 2006. (ENG.). 12p. (J). (gr. -1-18). bds. 10.95 *(978-1-58117-376-5(8),* Intervisual/Piggy Toes) Bendon, Inc.

McKernan, Wendy. The Thing I Say I Saw Last Night: A Christmas Story. Bzymek, Izabela, illus. 2011. 32p. (J). *(978-0-9866204-0-9(8));* pap. *(978-0-9866204-1-6(6))* Little Dragon Publishing.

McLaughlin, Eoin. The Hug. Dunbar, Polly, illus. 2019. (Hedgehog & Friends Ser.). (ENG.). 56p. (J). 15.95 *(978-0-571-34875-6(0),* Faber & Faber Children's Bks.) Faber & Faber, Inc.

McLaughlin, Julie. Hungry Mr. Gator. McKay, Ann Marie, illus. 2005. (J). 15.99 *(978-0-933101-24-1(4))* Legacy Pubns.

McLaughlin, Tom. The Story Machine. 2015. (ENG., Illus.). 32p. (J). (gr. -1-1). 12.99 *(978-1-4088-3934-8(2),* 234931, Bloomsbury Children's Bks.) Bloomsbury Publishing Plc GBR. Dist: Macmillan.

McLean, Wendy & Book Company Staff. Follow an Elf. Worthington, Leonie, illus. 2003. (Sparkle Bk.). 10p. (J). bds. 8.95 *(978-1-74047-314-9(0))* Book Co. Publishing Pty, Ltd., The AUS. Dist: Penton Overseas, Inc.

McLellan, Stephanie Simpson. Leon's Song, 1 vol. Bonder, Dianna, illus. 2004. (ENG.). 32p. (J). (gr. -1-3). *(978-1-55041-813-2(0))* Fitzhenry & Whiteside, Ltd.

McLelland, Kate. Isla & Pickle: Best Friends, 30 vols. 2017. (Isla & Pickle Ser.). (Illus.). 24p. (J). 11.95 *(978-1-78250-421-4(4),* Kelpies) Floris Bks. GBR. Dist: Consortium Bk. Sales & Distribution.

—Isla & Pickle: the Highland Show, 25 vols. 2018. (Isla & Pickle Ser.). (Illus.). 24p. (J). pap. 11.95 *(978-1-78250-509-9(1),* Kelpies) Floris Bks. GBR. Dist: Consortium Bk. Sales & Distribution.

McLoughlin Brothers, McLoughlin Brothers. Baby's Opera (HC) A Book of Old Rhymes with New Dresses. 2012. (Applewood Bks.). (ENG., Illus.). 64p. (J). (gr. k-1). 14.95 *(978-1-4290-8033-0(7))* Applewood Bks.

McMullan, Kate. I'm Cool! McMullan, Jim, illus. 2015. (ENG.). 40p. (J). (gr. -1-3). 18.99 *(978-0-06-230629-6(4),* Balzer & Bray) HarperCollins Pubs.

McNamee, Kevin. If I Could Be Anything. Movshina, Marina, illus. 2009. 16p. pap. 9.95 *(978-1-61633-011-8(2))* Guardian Angel Publishing, Inc.

—Just for Today. Movshina, Marina, illus. 2012. 16p. pap. 9.95 *(978-1-61633-314-0(6))* Guardian Angel Publishing, Inc.

MCP Staff. Zelda's Zipper. 2003. (J). 38.95 *(978-0-8136-1323-9(X))* Modern Curriculum Pr.

McPhail, David. Big Brown Bear's Birthday Surprise. 2018. (ENG., Illus.). 32p. (J). (gr. -1-3). pap. 3.99 *(978-1-328-89578-3(5),* 1699659, Clarion Bks.) HarperCollins Pubs.

—The Blue Door, 1 vol. 2003. (First Flight Level 2 Ser.). (ENG., Illus.). 32p. (J). (gr. -1-1). pap. 4.95 *(978-1-55041-802-6(5),* e00e64fc-e139-4123-a087-796c57062883) Fitzhenry & Whiteside, Ltd. CAN. Dist: Firefly Bks., Ltd.

—Brothers/Hermanos: Bilingual English-Spanish. McPhail, David, illus. 2017. (ENG., Illus.). 28p. (J). (— 1). bds. 4.99 *(978-0-544-91586-2(0),* 1655576, Clarion Bks.) HarperCollins Pubs.

—Pig Pig Meets the Lion. McPhail, David, illus. 2012. (Illus.). pap. 15.95 *(978-0-60734-080-5(1));* (ENG., 32p. (J). (gr. -1-3). 15.95 *(978-1-58089-358-9(9))* Charlesbridge Publishing, Inc.

Mead, Purnima. Bibia Meets Gripper. Kerber, Kathy, illus. 2013. (ENG.). 24p. pap. 12.45 *(978-1-4497-9751-5(2),* WestBow Pr.) Author Solutions, LLC.

Meadows, Daisy. Natalie the Christmas Stocking Fairy. 2014. (Rainbow Magic — Special Edition Ser.). lib. bdg. 17.20 *(978-0-606-36055-5(7))* Turtleback.

Meddaugh, Susan. Martha Says It with Flowers. 2010. (Martha Speaks Ser.). (ENG., Illus.). 32p. (J). (gr. -1-3). 12.99 *(978-0-547-21058-2(2))* Houghton Mifflin Harcourt Publishing Co.

Medina, Meg. Mango, Abuela, & Me. Dominguez, Angela, illus. (ENG.). 32p. (J). (gr. k-3). 2017. 7.99 *(978-0-7636-9513-2(0))* 2015. 17.99 *(978-0-7636-6900-3(8))* Candlewick Pr.

Medina, Melissa & Colting, Fredrik. Kinderguides Early Learning Guide to Shakespeare's Romeo & Juliet. Buurlage, Marijke, illus. 2018. (KinderGuides Early Learning Guide to Culture Classics Ser.). (ENG.). 50p. (J). 16.95 *(978-0-9988205-3-8(9))* Moppet Bks.

Medina, Tony. I & I Bob Marley, 1 vol. Watson, Jesse Joshua, illus. 2009. (ENG.). 48p. (J). (gr. 3-8). pap. 12.95 *(978-1-62014-030-7(6),* leelowbooks) Lee & Low Bks., Inc.

Mellen, Wynette. What Do You See? Rasmussen, Jennifer, illus. 2012. 42p. (J). pap. 9.95 *(978-0-9839957-4-6(5))* Freundship Pr., LLC.

Melling, David. How to Hug with Hugless Douglas. 2016. (Hugless Douglas Ser.). (ENG., Illus.). 14p. (J). (gr. -1-k). 9.99 *(978-1-4449-2408-4(7))* Hachette Children's Group GBR. Dist: Hachette Bk. Group.

—Hugless Douglas & the Big Sleepover. 2013. (ENG., Illus.). 32p. (J). *(978-1-58925-116-8(4))* Tiger Tales.

Melmed, Laura Krauss. Daddy, Me, & the Magic Hour. Rich, Sarita, illus. 2018. (ENG.). 32p. (J). (gr. -1-k). 16.99 *(978-1-5107-0791-7(3),* Sky Pony Pr.) Skyhorse Publishing Co., Inc.

Melmon, Deborah. Pups of the Spirit, 1 vol. 2015. (ENG., Illus.). 22p. (J). bds. 9.99 *(978-0-310-74798-7(8))* Zonderkidz.

Melnychuck, Karen & Melnychuck, Sofia. Art Saguaros. Melnychuck, Karen, ed. Melnychuck, Sofia, illus. 2016. (ENG., Illus.). 24p. (J). pap. 12.99 *(978-0-9859171-5-9(6),* PinkPowerful Bks.) PinkPowerful LLC.

Melton, Lexi. Buck Toothed Charlie & Other Stories. 2010. 72p. pap. 34.99 *(978-1-4490-6183-8(4))* AuthorHouse.

Melvin, Alice. The World of Alice Melvin: Me & You: A Book of Opposites. 2018. (ENG., Illus.). 20p. (J). (gr. -1 — 1). 9.99 *(978-1-84976-585-5(5),* 1325110) Tate Publishing, Ltd. GBR. Dist: Abrams, Inc.

—The World of Alice Melvin: My Day: A Book of Actions. 2018. (ENG., Illus.). 20p. (J). 9.99 *(978-1-84976-586-2(3),* 1325210) Tate Publishing, Ltd. GBR. Dist: Abrams, Inc.

Meneely, Starr. What a Lovely Sound! 2013. (Illus.). 32p. pap. *(978-0-9575371-3-2(1))* Starflower Pr.

Merberg, Julie. Baby's First Eames: From Art Deco to Zaha Hadid. Aki, illus. 2018. (ENG.). 24p. (J). (gr. -1 — 1). bds. 11.99 *(978-1-941367-39-1(9))* Downtown Bookworks.

Mercer, Graham. The Secret Cave. 2009. (ENG.). 52p. pap. 10.50 *(978-1-4092-9055-1(7))* Lulu Pr., Inc.

Merrie Melodies. (Looney Tunes Song & Sound Bks.). (Illus.). 24p. (J). (gr. -1-5). 14.98 *(978-0-7853-1249-9(8),* PI4) Publications International, Ltd.

Merritt, Kate, illus. Indestructibles: Baby Babble: a Book of Baby's First Words: Chew Proof · Rip Proof · Nontoxic · 100% Washable (Book for Babies, Newborn Books, Safe to Chew) 2012. (Indestructibles Ser.). (ENG.). 12p. (J). (gr. -1 — 1). pap. 5.95 *(978-0-7611-6880-5(X),* 16880) Workman Publishing Co., Inc.

—Indestructibles: Baby Faces: a Book of Happy, Silly, Funny Faces: Chew Proof · Rip Proof · Nontoxic · 100% Washable (Book for Babies, Newborn Books, Safe to Chew) 2012. (Indestructibles Ser.). (ENG.). 12p. (J). (gr. -1 — 1). pap. 5.99 *(978-0-7611-6881-2(8),* 16881) Workman Publishing Co., Inc.

Merry Christmas, Curious George. 2017. (Curious George Ser.). (ENG., Illus.). 24p. (J). (gr. -1-3). pap. 5.99 *(978-1-328-69558-1(1),* 1671221, Clarion Bks.) HarperCollins Pubs.

Merry, Margaret. The Lonely Digger. 2009. 72p. pap. 21.50 *(978-1-60860-144-8(7),* Strategic Bk. Publishing) Strategic Book Publishing & Rights Agency (SBPRA).

Meschenmoser, Sebastian. Mr. Squirrel & the Moon. 2015. (ENG., Illus.). 48p. (J). (gr. -1-1). 18.95 *(978-0-7358-4156-7(X))* North-South Bks., Inc.

Messaoudi, Michele. My Mum is a Wonder. 2016. (ENG., Illus.). 24p. (J). (gr. -1). 8.95 *(978-0-86037-298-1(7))* Kube Publishing Ltd. GBR. Dist: Consortium Bk. Sales & Distribution.

Messer, Claire. Lazybones. Messer, Claire, illus. 2018. (ENG., Illus.). 32p. (J). (gr. -1-3). 16.99 *(978-0-8075-4402-0(7),* 807544027) Whitman, Albert & Co.

Metzger, Steve. I Love You All Year Long. Keay, Claire, illus. 2009. 20p. (J). (gr. -1-k). 8.95 *(978-1-58925-847-1(9))* Tiger Tales.

Meyers, Carly J. J. Michael's Superheroes. Bruner, Garth, illus. 2013. 28p. (J). pap. *(978-0-8425-2845-0(8),* BYU Creative Works) Brigham Young Univ.

Miceli, Mary Anne. Confessor's Animal Wartime Blues. 2009. 56p. pap. 31.99 *(978-1-4415-2867-4(9))* Xlibris Corp.

Michael, Bedwin, 1 vol. David, Amanda, illus. 2009. (ENG.). 46p. 24.95 *(978-1-60813-258-4(7))* America Star Bks.

Michalak, Jamie. Fizzy's Lunch Lab: Escape from Greasy World. Lunch Lab, LLC., illus. 2015. (Fizzy's Lunch Lab Ser.). (ENG.). 48p. (J). (gr. 1-4). pap. 5.99 *(978-0-7636-7546-2(6),* Candlewick Entertainment) Candlewick Pr.

—Joe & Sparky, Party Animals! Remkiewicz, Frank, illus. (Candlewick Sparks Ser.). (ENG.). 48p. (J). (gr. k-4). 2018. pap. 5.99 *(978-1-5362-0327-1(0))* 2017. 15.99 *(978-0-7636-8206-4(3))* Candlewick Pr.

Mike, Nadia. The Muskox & the Caribou, 1 vol. Campeau, Tamara, illus. 2018. (ENG.). 32p. (J). (gr. k-2). 16.95 *(978-1-77227-163-8(2))* Inhabit Media Inc. CAN. Dist: Consortium Bk. Sales & Distribution.

Milbourne, Anna. Sunny Day (Picture Book) 2008. (Picture Bks). 24p. (J). 9.99 *(978-0-7945-2117-2(7),* Usborne) EDC Publishing.

—Under the Sea. Shimmen, Cathy, illus. 2007. (Picture Bks). 32p. (J). 9.99 *(978-0-7945-1801-1(X),* Usborne) EDC Publishing.

—Where Do Baby Animals Come From? 2012. (Picture Bks). 24p. (J). bds. 10.99 *(978-0-7945-3284-0(5),* Usborne) EDC Publishing.

Miles, David W. Book. Hoopes, Natalie, illus. 2015. (ENG.). 32p. (J). (gr. -1-3). 16.95 *(978-1-939629-65-4(9),* 552965) Familius LLC.

—Unicorn (and Horse) Mengert, Hollie, illus. 2018. (ENG.). 48p. (J). (gr. k-3). 16.99 *(978-1-945547-76-8(6),* 554776) Familius LLC.

Miles, Stephanie. Mommy Loves Me: The Book That Comes with a Hug! Miles, David W., illus. 2018. (ENG.). 10p. (J). (gr. -1 — 1). bds. 12.99 *(978-1-945547-94-2(4),* 554794) Familius LLC.

Miles, Stephanie & Farley, Christin. C Is for Colorado. Kaliaha, Volha, illus. 2018. (ABC Regional Board Bks.). (ENG.). 20p. (J). (gr. -1 — 1). bds. 12.99 *(978-1-945547-86-7(3),* 554786) Familius LLC.

Milet Publishing. My First Bilingual Book-Numbers (English-Italian), 1 vol. 2010. (My First Bilingual Book Ser.). (ENG & ITA., Illus.). 24p. (J). (gr. k — 1). bds. 8.99 *(978-1-84059-543-7(4))* Milet Publishing.

—My First Bilingual Book-Numbers (English-Spanish), 1 vol. 2010. (My First Bilingual Book Ser.). (ENG & SPA., Illus.). 24p. (J). (gr k — 1). bds. 8.99 *(978-1-84059-545-1(0))* Milet Publishing.

Milet Publishing Staff. Clothes, 1 vol. 2014. (My First Bilingual Book Ser.). (ENG., Illus.). 20p. (J). (— 1). bds. 7.99 *(978-1-84059-865-0(4));* bds. 8.99 *(978-1-84059-870-4(0))* Milet Publishing.

—Clothes - My First Bilingual Book, 1 vol. 2014. (My First Bilingual Book Ser.). (ENG., Illus.). 20p. (J). (— 1). bds. 8.99 *(978-1-84059-860-5(3));* bds. 8.99 *(978-1-84059-864-3(6));* bds. 8.99 *(978-1-84059-867-4(0));* bds. 8.99 *(978-1-84059-873-5(5))* Milet Publishing.

—Colors, 1 vol. 2010. (My First Bilingual Book Ser.). (ENG & SPA., Illus.). 24p. (J). (gr. k — 1). bds. 8.99 *(978-1-84059-539-0(6))* Milet Publishing.

—Colours, 1 vol. 2010. (My First Bilingual Book Ser.). (ENG., Illus.). 24p. (J). (gr. k — 1). bds. 7.99 *(978-1-84059-563-5(9))* Milet Publishing.

—Colours - My First Bilingual Book, 1 vol. 2010. (My First Bilingual Book Ser.). (ENG & ITA., Illus.). 24p. (J). (gr. k — 1). bds. 8.99 *(978-1-84059-537-6(X));* bds. 7.99 *(978-1-84059-565-9(5));* bds. 8.99 *(978-1-84059-538-3(8))* Milet Publishing.

—Jobs Empregos, 1 vol. 2012. (My First Bilingual Book Ser.). (ENG., Illus.). 24p. (J). (gr. k — 1). bds. 7.99 *(978-1-84059-709-7(7))* Milet Publishing.

—Music, 1 vol. 2012. (My First Bilingual Book Ser.). (ENG & POR., Illus.). 24p. (J). (gr. k — 1). bds. 8.99 *(978-1-84059-724-0(0))* Milet Publishing.

—Music - My First Bilingual Book, 1 vol. 2012. (My First Bilingual Book Ser.). (ENG., Illus.). 24p. (J). (gr. k — 1). bds. 7.99 *(978-1-84059-725-7(9))* Milet Publishing.

—My Bilingual Book - Sight, 1 vol. 2014. (My Bilingual Book Ser.). (ENG., Illus.). 24p. (J). (gr. -1-k). 9.95 *(978-1-84059-801-8(8))* Milet Publishing.

—My Bilingual Book - Smell, 1 vol. 2014. (My Bilingual Book Ser.). (ENG & CHI., Illus.). 24p. (J). (gr. -1-k). 9.95 *(978-1-84059-806-3(9))* Milet Publishing.

—My Bilingual Book-Hearing, 1 vol. 2014. (My Bilingual Book Ser.). (ENG., Illus.). 24p. (J). (gr. -1-k). 9.95 *(978-1-84059-779-0(8));* 9.95 *(978-1-84059-785-1(2));* 9.95 *(978-1-84059-774-5(7))* Milet Publishing.

—My Bilingual Book-Hearing (English-Arabic), 1 vol. 2014. (My Bilingual Book Ser.). (ENG & ARA., Illus.). 24p. (J). (gr. -1-k). 9.95 *(978-1-84059-772-1(0))* Milet Publishing.

—My Bilingual Book-Hearing (English-Bengali), 1 vol. 2014. (My Bilingual Book Ser.). (ENG & BEN., Illus.). 24p. (J). (gr. -1-k). 9.95 *(978-1-84059-773-8(9))* Milet Publishing.

—My Bilingual Book-Hearing (English-Farsi), 1 vol. 2014. (My Bilingual Book Ser.). (ENG., Illus.). 24p. (J). (gr. -1-k). 9.95 *(978-1-84059-775-2(5))* Milet Publishing.

—My Bilingual Book-Hearing (English-French), 1 vol. 2014. (My Bilingual Book Ser.). (ENG & FRE., Illus.). 24p. (J). (gr. -1-k). 9.95 *(978-1-84059-776-9(3))* Milet Publishing.

—My Bilingual Book-Hearing (English-German), 1 vol. 2014. (My Bilingual Book Ser.). (ENG & GER., Illus.). 24p. (J). (gr. -1-k). 9.95 *(978-1-84059-777-6(1))* Milet Publishing.

—My Bilingual Book-Hearing (English-Italian), 1 vol. 2014. (My Bilingual Book Ser.). (ENG & ITA., Illus.). 24p. (J). (gr. -1-k). 9.95 *(978-1-84059-778-3(X))* Milet Publishing.

—My Bilingual Book-Hearing (English-Polish), 1 vol. 2014. (My Bilingual Book Ser.). (ENG & POR., Illus.). 24p. (J). (gr. -1-k). 9.95 *(978-1-84059-780-6(1))* Milet Publishing.

—My Bilingual Book-Hearing (English-Portuguese), 1 vol. 2014. (My Bilingual Book Ser.). (ENG & POR., Illus.). 24p. (J). (gr. -1-k). 9.95 *(978-1-84059-781-3(X))* Milet Publishing.

—My Bilingual Book-Hearing (English-Russian), 1 vol. 2014. (My Bilingual Book Ser.). (ENG & RUS., Illus.). 24p. (J). (gr. -1-k). 9.95 *(978-1-84059-782-0(8))* Milet Publishing.

—My Bilingual Book-Hearing (English-Somali), 1 vol. 2014. (My Bilingual Book Ser.). (ENG., Illus.). 24p. (J). (gr. -1-k). 9.95 *(978-1-84059-783-7(6))* Milet Publishing.

—My Bilingual Book-Hearing (English-Urdu), 1 vol. 2014. (My Bilingual Book Ser.). (ENG., Illus.). 24p. (J). (gr. -1-k). 9.95 *(978-1-84059-786-8(0))* Milet Publishing.

—My Bilingual Book-Hearing (English-Vietnamese), 1 vol. 2014. (My Bilingual Book Ser.). (ENG., Illus.). 24p. (J). (gr. -1-k). 9.95 *(978-1-84059-787-5(9))* Milet Publishing.

—My Bilingual Book-Sight, 1 vol. 2014. (My Bilingual Book Ser.). (ENG., Illus.). 24p. (J). (gr. -1-k). 9.95 *(978-1-84059-795-0(X))* Milet Publishing.

—My Bilingual Book-Sight (English-Bengali), 1 vol. 2014. (My Bilingual Book Ser.). (ENG & BEN., Illus.). 24p. (J). (gr. -1-k). 9.95 *(978-1-84059-789-9(5))* Milet Publishing.

—My Bilingual Book-Sight (English-Chinese), 1 vol. 2014. (My Bilingual Book Ser.). (ENG & CHI., Illus.). 24p. (J). (gr. -1-k). 9.95 *(978-1-84059-790-5(9))* Milet Publishing.

—My Bilingual Book-Sight (English-Farsi), 1 vol. 2014. (My Bilingual Book Ser.). (ENG., Illus.). 24p. (J). (gr. -1-k). 9.95 *(978-1-84059-791-2(7))* Milet Publishing.

—My Bilingual Book-Sight (English-French), 1 vol. 2014. (My Bilingual Book Ser.). (ENG & FRE., Illus.). 24p. (J). (gr. -1-k). 9.95 *(978-1-84059-792-9(5))* Milet Publishing.

—My Bilingual Book-Sight (English-German), 1 vol. 2014. (My Bilingual Book Ser.). (ENG & GER., Illus.). 24p. (J). (gr. -1-k). 9.95 *(978-1-84059-793-6(3))* Milet Publishing.

—My Bilingual Book-Sight (English-Italian), 1 vol. 2014. (My Bilingual Book Ser.). (ENG & ITA., Illus.). 24p. (J). (gr. -1-k). 9.95 *(978-1-84059-794-3(1))* Milet Publishing.

—My Bilingual Book-Sight (English-Polish), 1 vol. 2014. (My Bilingual Book Ser.). (ENG & POR., Illus.). 24p. (J). (gr. -1-k). 9.95 *(978-1-84059-796-7(8))* Milet Publishing.

—My Bilingual Book-Sight (English-Portuguese), 1 vol. 2014. (My Bilingual Book Ser.). (ENG & POR., Illus.). 24p. (J). (gr. -1-k). 9.95 *(978-1-84059-797-4(6))* Milet Publishing.

—My Bilingual Book-Sight (English-Russian), 1 vol. 2014. (My Bilingual Book Ser.). (ENG & RUS., Illus.). 24p. (J). (gr. -1-k). 9.95 *(978-1-84059-798-1(4))* Milet Publishing.

—My Bilingual Book-Sight (English-Somali), 1 vol. 2014. (My Bilingual Book Ser.). (ENG., Illus.). 24p. (J). (gr. -1-k). 9.95 *(978-1-84059-799-8(2))* Milet Publishing.

—My Bilingual Book-Sight (English-Spanish), 1 vol. 2014. (My Bilingual Book Ser.). (ENG & SPA., Illus.). 24p. (J). (gr. -1-k). 9.95 *(978-1-84059-800-1(X))* Milet Publishing.

—My Bilingual Book-Sight (English-Urdu), 1 vol. 2014. (My Bilingual Book Ser.). (ENG., Illus.). 24p. (J). (gr. -1-k). 9.95 *(978-1-84059-802-5(6))* Milet Publishing.

—My Bilingual Book-Sight (English-Vietnamese), 1 vol. 2014. (My Bilingual Book Ser.). (ENG., Illus.). 24p. (J). (gr. -1-k). 9.95 *(978-1-84059-803-2(4))* Milet Publishing.

—My Bilingual Book-Smell, 1 vol. 2014. (My Bilingual Book Ser.). (ENG., Illus.). 24p. (J). (gr. -1-k). 9.95 *(978-1-84059-811-7(5))* Milet Publishing.

—My Bilingual Book-Smell (English-Arabic), 1 vol. 2014. (My Bilingual Book Ser.). (ENG & ARA., Illus.). 24p. (J). (gr. -1-k). 9.95 *(978-1-84059-804-9(2))* Milet Publishing.

—My Bilingual Book-Smell (English-Bengali), 1 vol. 2014. (My Bilingual Book Ser.). (ENG & BEN., Illus.). 24p. (J). (gr. -1-k). 9.95 *(978-1-84059-805-6(0))* Milet Publishing.

—My Bilingual Book-Smell (English-Farsi), 1 vol. 2014. (My Bilingual Book Ser.). (ENG., Illus.). 24p. (J). (gr. -1-k). 9.95 *(978-1-84059-807-0(7))* Milet Publishing.

—My Bilingual Book-Smell (English-Italian), 1 vol. 2014. (My Bilingual Book Ser.). (ENG & ITA., Illus.). 24p. (J). (gr. -1-k). 9.95 *(978-1-84059-810-0(7))* Milet Publishing.

—My Bilingual Book-Smell (English-Urdu), 1 vol. 2014. (My Bilingual Book Ser.). (ENG., Illus.). 24p. (J). (gr. -1-k). 9.95 *(978-1-84059-818-6(2))* Milet Publishing.

—My First Bilingual Book - Clothes, 1 vol. 2014. (My First Bilingual Book Ser.). (ENG., Illus.). 20p. (J). (— 1). bds. 7.99 *(978-1-84059-869-8(7));* bds. 7.99 *(978-1-84059-863-6(8));* bds. 7.99 *(978-1-84059-861-2(1));* bds. 7.99 *(978-1-84059-859-9(X));* bds. 8.99 *(978-1-84059-866-7(2));* bds. 7.99 *(978-1-84059-858-2(1));* bds. 7.99 *(978-1-84059-872-8(7));* bds. 7.99 *(978-1-84059-871-1(9));* bds. 8.99 *(978-1-84059-862-9(X));* bds. 7.99 *(978-1-84059-868-1(9))* Milet Publishing.

—My First Bilingual Book - Numbers, 1 vol. 2010. (My First Bilingual Book Ser.). (ENG., Illus.). 24p. (J). (gr. k — 1). bds. 7.99 *(978-1-84059-546-8(9));* bds. 8.99 *(978-1-84059-542-0(6))* Milet Publishing.

P
Q
R

—My First Bilingual Book - Plants, 1 vol. 2014. (My First Bilingual Book Ser.). (ENG & GER., Illus.). 20p. (J). (— 1). bds. 8.99 *(978-1-84059-879-7(4))*; bds. 7.99 *(978-1-84059-887-2(5))*; bds. 7.99 *(978-1-84059-885-8(9))*; bds. 8.99 *(978-1-84059-874-2(3))*; bds. 7.99 *(978-1-84059-883-4(2))*; bds. 8.99 *(978-1-84059-876-6(X))* Milet Publishing.

—My First Bilingual Book - Plants (English-Farsi), 1 vol. 2014. (My First Bilingual Book Ser.). (ENG., Illus.). 20p. (J). (— 1). bds. 7.99 *(978-1-84059-877-3(8))* Milet Publishing.

—My First Bilingual Book - Plants (English-Korean), 1 vol. 2014. (My First Bilingual Book Ser.). (ENG., Illus.). 20p. (J). (— 1). bds. 7.99 *(978-1-84059-881-0(6))* Milet Publishing.

—My First Bilingual Book - School, 1 vol. 2014. (My First Bilingual Book Ser.). (ENG & POR., Illus.). 20p. (J). (— 1). bds. 7.99 *(978-1-84059-899-5(9))*; bds. 7.99 *(978-1-84059-891-9(3))*; bds. 8.99 *(978-1-84059-894-0(8))*; bds. 8.99 *(978-1-84059-905-3(7))*; bds. 7.99 *(978-1-84059-895-7(6))*; bds. 7.99 *(978-1-84059-903-9(0))*; bds. 7.99 *(978-1-84059-893-3(X))*; bds. 7.99 *(978-1-84059-892-6(1))* Milet Publishing.

—My First Bilingual Book - School (English-Korean), 1 vol. 2014. (My First Bilingual Book Ser.). (ENG., Illus.). 20p. (J). (— 1). bds. 7.99 *(978-1-84059-897-1(2))* Milet Publishing.

—My First Bilingual Book - School (English-Somali), 1 vol. 2014. (My First Bilingual Book Ser.). (ENG., Illus.). 20p. (J). (— 1). bds. 8.99 *(978-1-84059-901-5(4))* Milet Publishing.

—My First Bilingual Book - Tools, 1 vol. 2014. (My First Bilingual Book Ser.). (ENG & GER., Illus.). 20p. (J). (— 1). bds. 7.99 *(978-1-84059-911-4(1))*; bds. 7.99 *(978-1-84059-918-3(9))*; bds. 7.99 *(978-1-84059-919-0(7))*; bds. 7.99 *(978-1-84059-916-9(2))*; bds. 7.99 *(978-1-84059-906-0(5))*; bds. 7.99 *(978-1-84059-907-7(3))*; bds. 7.99 *(978-1-84059-920-6(0))*; bds. 7.99 *(978-1-84059-914-5(6))* Milet Publishing.

—My First Bilingual Book - Tools - English, 1 vol. 2014. (My First Bilingual Book Ser.). (ENG., Illus.). 20p. (J). (— 1). bds. 7.99 *(978-1-84059-921-3(9))* Milet Publishing.

—My First Bilingual Book - Tools - Ferramentas, 1 vol. 2014. (My First Bilingual Book Ser.). (ENG & POR., Illus.). 20p. (J). (— 1). bds. 7.99 *(978-1-84059-915-2(4))* Milet Publishing.

—My First Bilingual Book - Tools (English-Somali), 1 vol. 2014. (My First Bilingual Book Ser.). (ENG., Illus.). 20p. (J). (— 1). bds. 7.99 *(978-1-84059-917-6(0))* Milet Publishing.

—My First Bilingual Book - Vehicles, 1 vol. 2014. (My First Bilingual Book Ser.). (ENG., Illus.). 20p. (J). (— 1). bds. 7.99 *(978-1-84059-925-1(1))*; bds. 8.99 *(978-1-84059-937-4(5))*; bds. 7.99 *(978-1-84059-933-6(2))*; bds. 7.99 *(978-1-84059-929-9(4))*; bds. 8.99 *(978-1-84059-924-4(3))*; bds. 7.99 *(978-1-84059-935-0(9))* Milet Publishing.

—My First Bilingual Book - Vehicles (English-Russian), 1 vol. 2014. (My First Bilingual Book Ser.). (ENG., Illus.). 20p. (J). (— 1). bds. 7.99 *(978-1-84059-932-9(4))* Milet Publishing.

—My First Bilingual Book-Music (English-Russian), 1 vol. 2012. (My First Bilingual Book Ser.). (ENG., Illus.). 24p. (J). (gr. k — 1). bds. 7.99 *(978-1-84059-726-4(7))* Milet Publishing.

—My First Bilingual Book-Music (English-Somali), 1 vol. 2012. (My First Bilingual Book Ser.). (ENG., Illus.). 24p. (J). (gr. k — 1). bds. 8.99 *(978-1-84059-727-1(5))* Milet Publishing.

—My First Bilingual Book-Opposites, 1 vol. 2012. (My First Bilingual Book Ser.). (ENG., Illus.). 24p. (J). (gr. k — 1). bds. 8.99 *(978-1-84059-734-9(8))* Milet Publishing.

—Numbers - My First Bilingual Book, 60 vols. 2010. (My First Bilingual Book Ser.). (ENG., Illus.). 24p. (J). (gr. k — 1). bds. 8.99 *(978-1-84059-544-4(2))*; bds. 8.99 *(978-1-84059-541-3(8))* Milet Publishing.

—Opposites, 1 vol. 2012. (My First Bilingual Book Ser.). (ENG., Illus.). 24p. (J). (gr. k — 1). bds. 8.99 *(978-1-84059-735-6(6))* Milet Publishing.

—Plants - My First Bilingual Book, 1 vol. 2014. (My First Bilingual Book Ser.). (ENG & FRE., Illus.). 20p. (J). (— 1). bds. 8.99 *(978-1-84059-878-0(6))*; bds. 7.99 *(978-1-84059-888-9(3))*; bds. 7.99 *(978-1-84059-880-3(8))*; bds. 7.99 *(978-1-84059-875-9(1))*; bds. 7.99 *(978-1-84059-882-7(4))*; bds. 7.99 *(978-1-84059-886-5(7))*; bds. 7.99 *(978-1-84059-889-6(1))*; bds. 8.99 *(978-1-84059-884-1(0))* Milet Publishing.

—School, 1 vol. 2014. (My First Bilingual Book Ser.). (ENG & ITA., Illus.). 20p. (J). (— 1). bds. 7.99 *(978-1-84059-896-4(4))* Milet Publishing.

—School - My First Bilingual Book, 1 vol. 2014. (My First Bilingual Book Ser.). (ENG., Illus.). 20p. (J). (— 1). bds. 7.99 *(978-1-84059-904-6(9))*; bds. 7.99 *(978-1-84059-890-2(5))*; bds. 8.99 *(978-1-84059-900-8(6))*; bds. 8.99 *(978-1-84059-902-2(2))* Milet Publishing.

—School - My First Bilingual Book (Szkola), 1 vol. 2014. (My First Bilingual Book Ser.). (ENG & POR., Illus.). 20p. (J). (— 1). bds. 7.99 *(978-1-84059-898-8(0))* Milet Publishing.

—Sight - English-Arabic, 1 vol. 2014. (My Bilingual Book Ser.). (ENG & ARA., Illus.). 24p. (J). (gr. -1-k). 9.95 *(978-1-84059-788-2(7))* Milet Publishing.

—Smell / Das Riechen, 1 vol. 2014. (My Bilingual Book Ser.). (ENG & GER., Illus.). 24p. (J). (gr. -1-k). 9.95 *(978-1-84059-809-4(3))* Milet Publishing.

—Smell (English-French), 1 vol. 2014. (My Bilingual Book Ser.). (ENG & FRE., Illus.). 24p. (J). (gr. -1-k). 9.95 *(978-1-84059-808-7(5))* Milet Publishing.

—Tools, 1 vol. 2014. (My First Bilingual Book Ser.). (ENG & ITA., Illus.). 20p. (J). (— 1). bds. 7.99 *(978-1-84059-912-1(X))* Milet Publishing.

—Tools - My First Bilingual Book, 1 vol. 2014. (My First Bilingual Book Ser.). (ENG., Illus.). 20p. (J). (— 1). bds. 7.99 *(978-1-84059-909-1(X))*; bds. 7.99 *(978-1-84059-913-8(8))*; bds. 7.99 *(978-1-84059-908-4(1))* Milet Publishing.

—Tools (English-French), 1 vol. 2014. (My First Bilingual Book Ser.). (ENG & FRE., Illus.). 20p. (J). (— 1). bds. 7.99 *(978-1-84059-910-7(3))* Milet Publishing.

—Vehicles, 1 vol. 2014. (My First Bilingual Book Ser.). (ENG & ITA., Illus.). 20p. (J). (— 1). bds. 7.99 *(978-1-84059-928-2(6))*; bds. 8.99 *(978-1-84059-922-0(7))*; bds. 7.99 *(978-1-84059-934-3(0))* Milet Publishing.

—Vehicles - My First Bilingual Book, 1 vol. 2014. (My First Bilingual Book Ser.). (ENG., Illus.). 20p. (J). (— 1). bds. 7.99 *(978-1-84059-923-7(5))*; bds. 7.99 *(978-1-84059-936-7(7))*; bds. 8.99 *(978-1-84059-926-8(X))*; bds. 8.99 *(978-1-84059-931-2(6))*; bds. 8.99 *(978-1-84059-930-5(8))* Milet Publishing.

—Vehicles (English-German), 1 vol. 2014. (My First Bilingual Book Ser.). (ENG & GER., Illus.). 20p. (J). (— 1). bds. 8.99 *(978-1-84059-927-5(8))* Milet Publishing.

Milford, Diana Viola. Fuzzum & Wuzzum, 1 vol. 2010. 34p. pap. 24.95 *(978-1-4489-9168-6(4))* PublishAmerica, Inc.

Milgrim, David. Moo Bird. 2016. (Illus.). 32p. (J). *(978-1-5182-0400-5(7))* Scholastic, Inc.

—Moo Bird (Scholastic Reader, Level 1) Milgrim, David, illus. 2015. (Scholastic Reader, Level 1 Ser.). (ENG., Illus.). 32p. (J). (gr. -1-1). pap. 3.99 *(978-0-545-82502-3(4))* Scholastic, Inc.

Millard, Bart. I Can Only Imagine for Little Ones: A Friendship with Jesus Now & Forever, 1 vol. Collina, Sumiti, illus. 2018. (ENG.). 24p. (J). bds. 9.99 *(978-1-4003-2201-5(4))*, Tommy Nelson) Nelson, Thomas Inc.

Millard, Glenda. Pea Pod Lullaby. King, Stephen Michael, illus. 2018. (ENG.). 40p. (J). (gr. -1-2). 16.99 *(978-1-5362-0197-0(9))* Candlewick Pr.

Miller, Arthur. Jane's Blanket. Parker, Al, illus. 2017. (ENG.). 64p. (J). (gr. -1-3). 24.95 *(978-3-89955-786-2(7))* Die Gestalten Verlag DEU. Dist: Ingram Publisher Services.

—Jane's Blanket. Al, Parker, illus. 2015. (ENG.). 64p. pap. 9.99 *(978-0-486-79682-6(5)*, 796825) Dover Pubns., Inc.

Miller, Connie Colwell. I'll Be a Police Officer. Baroncelli, Silvia, illus. 2018. (When I Grow Up Ser.). (ENG.). 24p. (J). (gr. 1-4). *(978-1-68151-398-0(6)*, 15053) Amicus.

Miller, Janet. DuckDumB. 2010. 32p. pap. 21.95 *(978-0-557-57669-2(5))* Lulu Pr., Inc.

Miller, Kerri. My Twin & Me - Fun with Twin Brothers & Sisters. 2013. (Illus.). 20p. pap. *(978-0-9576753-0-8(5))* Hot Tub Publishing, Ltd.

Miller, Mona. Poppy & Branch's Big Adventure. 2017. (Illus.). 32p. (J). *(978-1-5182-3647-1(2))* Random Hse., Inc.

Miller, Pat Zietlow. Wherever You Go. 2015. (ENG., Illus.). 32p. (J). (gr. -1-3). 17.99 *(978-0-316-40002-2(5))* Little, Brown Bks. for Young Readers.

Miller, Philip J. We All Sing with the Same Voice. 2005. (ENG., Illus.). 40p. (J). (gr. -1-2). reprint ed. pap. 8.99 *(978-0-06-073900-3(2)*, HarperCollins) HarperCollins Pubs.

Miller, Tim. What's Cooking, Moo Moo? Miller, Tim, illus. 2018. (Moo Moo & Mr. Quackers Book Ser.). (ENG., Illus.). 32p. (J). (gr. -1-3). 17.99 *(978-0-06-241441-0(0)*, Balzer & Bray) HarperCollins Pubs.

Millett, Peter. The Great Escape White Band. Belli, Alfredo, illus. 2016. (Cambridge Reading Adventures Ser.). (ENG.). 24p. pap. 8.80 *(978-1-107-55158-9(7))* Cambridge Univ. Pr.

Milligan, Bryce. Brigid's Cloak. Cann, Helen, illus. 2005. 32p. (J). (gr. k-17). pap. 9.00 *(978-0-8028-5297-7(1)*, Eerdmans Bks For Young Readers) Eerdmans, William B. Publishing Co.

Mills, Alan. The Hungry Goat. Graboff, Abner, illus. 2019. 52p. 20.00 *(978-1-85124-503-1(0))* Bodleian Library GBR. Dist: Chicago Distribution Ctr.

Milne, A. A. Winnie the Pooh & the Wrong Bees. Shepard, E. H., illus. 2016. (ENG.). 48p. (J). 9.99 *(978-1-4052-8132-4(4))* Farshore GBR. Dist: HarperCollins Pubs.

Minchin, Adele. The Caravan Club. 2003. 224p. pap. 12.00 *(978-0-7043-4978-0(7))* Women's Pr., Ltd., The GBR. Dist: Trafalgar Square Publishing.

Minchin, Tim. When I Grow Up. Antony, Steve, illus. 2018. (ENG.). 32p. (J). pap. *(978-1-4071-8043-4(6))* Scholastic, Inc.

Mini My First Picture Dictiona. 2004. (Early Learning Ser.). 18p. (J). bds. 2.99 *(978-1-85854-832-6(2))* Brimax Books Ltd. GBR. Dist: Byeway Bks.

Minor, Wendell. Pumpkin Heads. Minor, Wendell, illus. 2021. (Illus.). 32p. (J). (gr. -1-2). lib. bdg. 11.99 *(978-1-58089-935-2(8))* Charlesbridge Publishing, Inc.

Mireles, Ashley Marie. Little Fingers Ballet. Skomorokhova, Olga, illus. 2019. (ENG.). 10p. (J). (gr. -1-k). bds. 16.99 *(978-1-64170-155-6(2)*, 550155) Familius LLC.

Mitchell, David L. A Fun, Cool & Colorful Read: " A Picture Book for Children to Learn Great New Words" 2009. (ENG.). 44p. pap. 21.99 *(978-1-4363-9551-9(8))* Xlibris Corp.

Mitchell, Melanie, illus. Good Morning, Good Night Bilingual: Buenos Dias! Buenas Noches! 2005. (ENG & SPA.). 12p. (J). 9.95 *(978-1-58117-389-5(X)*, Intervisual/Piggy Toes) Bendon, Inc.

Mitchell, Pratima. Raju's Ride. Waterhouse, Stephen, illus. 2005. (ENG.). 24p. (J). lib. bdg. 23.65 *(978-1-59646-726-2(6))* Dingles & Co.

Mitchell, Robin & Steedman, Judith. Snowy & Chinook. 2005. (ENG., Illus.). 22p. (J). (gr. -1-3). 15.95 *(978-0-9688768-9-3(7))* Simply Read Bks. CAN. Dist: Ingram Publisher Services.

Mitter, Matt. Sesame Street: Guess Who, Easter Elmo! Mathieu, Joe, illus. 2nd ed. 2018. (Guess Who! Book Ser.). (ENG.). 10p. (J). (gr. -1-k). 10.99 *(978-0-7944-4197-5(1)*, Studio Fun International) Printers Row Publishing Group.

Mitton, Tony. Amazing Machines: First Numbers. Parker, Ant, illus. 2018. (Amazing Machines Ser.). (ENG.). 22p. (J). bds. 9.99 *(978-0-7534-7440-2(9)*, 900192346, Kingfisher) Roaring Brook Pr.

—Amazing Machines: First Words. Parker, Ant, illus. 2018. (Amazing Machines Ser.). (ENG.). 22p. (J). bds. 9.99 *(978-0-7534-7439-6(5)*, 900192345, Kingfisher) Roaring Brook Pr.

—Terrific Trains. 2017. (Amazing Machines Ser.). (ENG.). 20p. (J). bds. 6.99 *(978-0-7534-7372-6(0)*, 900178406, Kingfisher) Roaring Brook Pr.

—Twist & Hop, Minibeast Bop! 2017. (ENG., Illus.). 32p. (J). (gr. -1-k). pap. 7.99 *(978-1-4083-3687-8(1)*, Orchard Bks.) Hachette Children's Group GBR. Dist: Hachette Bk. Group.

Miura, Taro. Hello, Love! (Board Books for Baby, Baby Books on Love an Friendship) 2018. (ENG., Illus.). 22p. (J). (gr. -1 — 1). bds. 6.99 *(978-1-4521-7087-9(8))* Chronicle Bks. LLC.

Miyares, Daniel. Night Out. 2018. (Illus.). 40p. (J). (gr. -1-3). 17.99 *(978-1-5247-6572-9(4))*; (ENG., lib. bdg. 20.99 *(978-1-5247-6573-6(2))* Random Hse. Children's Bks. (Schwartz & Wade Bks.).

—Pardon Me! Miyares, Daniel, illus. 2014. (ENG., Illus.). 40p. (J). (gr. -1-3). 19.99 *(978-1-4424-8997-4(9)*, Simon & Schuster Bks. For Young Readers) Simon & Schuster Bks. For Young Readers.

Miyazaki, Hayao. Howl's Moving Castle Picture Book. 2005. (Howl's Moving Castle Picture Book Ser.). (ENG., Illus.). 184p. (J). 19.99 *(978-1-4215-0090-4(6))* Viz Media.

MJ Illustrations (Group) Staff, contrib. by. Marshall to the Rescue! 2016. (Illus.). (J). *(978-1-4806-9669-3(2)*, Golden Bks.) Random Hse. Children's Bks.

Moerbeek, Kees. Cinderella: My Secret Scrapbook Diary. Moerbeek, Kees, illus. 2011. (My Secret Scrapbook Diary Ser.). (Illus.). 10p. (J). *(978-1-84643-450-1(5))* Child's Play International Ltd.

—Puss in Boots: My Secret Scrapbook Diary. 2014. (My Secret Scrapbook Diary Ser.). (Illus.). 10p. (J). *(978-1-84643-592-8(7))* Child's Play International Ltd.

—The Ugly Duckling: My Secret Scrapbook Diary. 2014. (My Secret Scrapbook Diary Ser.). (Illus.). 10p. (J). *(978-1-84643-593-5(5))* Child's Play International Ltd.

Mole in a Hole IR. 2017. (Phonics Readers Ser.). (ENG.). (J). pap. 6.99 *(978-0-7945-3715-9(4)*, Usborne) EDC Publishing.

Moller, Jonathan R. Bath Time: Picture Book. l.t. ed. 2003. (Illus.). 71p. pap. 19.95 *(978-0-9740169-0-0(X))* Lemonflavor Productions.

Molloy, Tom. Everything but the Beach: A Slice of Manchester Life. 2012. (ENG., Illus.). 192p. (J). pap. 9.60 *(978-1-291-15817-5(0))* Lulu Pr., Inc.

Molver, Luke W. Shaka Rising: A Legend of the Warrior Prince. Molver, Luke W., illus. 2018. (African Graphic Novel Ser.). (ENG., Illus.). 96p. (J). (gr. 6). pap. 16.99 *(978-1-946498-98-4(X)*, Story Pr. Africa) Catalyst Pr. LLC.

Momenceau, Amandine. Mother Fox & Her Cubs. 2016. (ENG., Illus.). 48p. (J). (gr. -1-2). 19.95 *(978-0-500-65089-9(6)*, 565089) Thames & Hudson.

Monaco, Gérard Lo. A Sea Voyage: A Pop-Up Story about All Sorts of Boats. 2016. (ENG., Illus.). 8p. (J). (gr. k-2). 29.95 *(978-0-500-65088-2(8)*, 565088) Thames & Hudson.

A Monarch Universe CD: Children's Picture Book. 2007. (J). cd-rom 22.95 *(978-0-9800222-2-3(3))* UPfirst.com Bks.

Mondesir, Ketly. Tyrese & the Three Dogs Plus a Cat. 2009. (ENG.). 32p. pap. 21.99 *(978-1-4257-8694-6(4))* Xlibris Corp.

Moniz, Michael. The Boy & the Whale. 2013. (ENG., Illus.). 36p. (J). (gr. -1-3). 16.95 *(978-1-927018-14-9(5))* Simply Read Bks. CAN. Dist: Ingram Publisher Services.

—The Cardinal & the Crow. 2015. (Illus.). 235p. (J). 16.95 *(978-1-927018-58-3(7))* Simply Read Bks. CAN. Dist: Ingram Publisher Services.

Moniz, Michael, illus. Wazzyjump. 2017. (ENG.). 40p. (J). (gr. -1-2). 8.99 *(978-1-77229-017-2(3))* Simply Read Bks. CAN. Dist: Ingram Publisher Services.

Moniz, Tomas. Collaboration: Ways We Work Together. Dornadic, Alicia, illus. 2018. (ENG.). 38p. (J). 14.95 *(978-1-84935-312-0(3))* AK Pr. GBR. Dist: Consortium Bk. Sales & Distribution.

Montana, Hannah. Live from London. 2010. (Hannah Montana on Tour Ser.: No. 4). 80p. (gr. 2-5). pap. 3.99 *(978-1-4231-1815-2(4))* Disney Pr.

Montardre, Hélène. The Cat & the Dog. 2003. (Illus.). 8p. (J). bds. 7.95 *(978-1-58728-483-0(9)*, Two-Can Publishing) T&N Children's Publishing.

—Night & Day. 2003. (Illus.). 8p. (J). bds. 7.95 *(978-1-58728-481-6(2)*, Two-Can Publishing) T&N Children's Publishing.

Montgomery, Margaret, illus. The Adventures of Anna Banana Shoeshine: Anna Banana Takes a Bath. 2006. 40p. (J). *(978-1-930401-49-5(3))* Central Coast Bks./Pr.

Mook-Sang, Jennifer. Captain Monty Takes the Plunge. Starin, Liz, illus. 2017. (ENG.). 32p. (J). (gr. -1-2). 16.99 *(978-1-77138-626-5(6))* Kids Can Pr., Ltd. CAN. Dist: Hachette Bk. Group.

Moore, Brian L. The Story Behind Santa Sacks. Mulligan, Todd, illus. 2004. 32p. *(978-0-9732651-0-1(8))* Hills-n-Hollows Publishing.

Moore, David. National Geographic Science 1-2 (Earth Science: Land & Water): Explore on Your Own: the Island That Formed in One Day. 2009. (Illus.). 12p. (C). pap. 8.95 *(978-0-7362-5522-6(2))* National Geographic School Publishing, Inc.

Moore, Natalia. The Wolf Who Learned to Be Good. Moore, Natalia, illus. 2017. (ENG., Illus.). 32p. (J). (gr. -1-3). 16.99 *(978-0-8075-9204-5(8)*, 807592048) Whitman, Albert & Co.

Moore Niver, Heather. Picture Books, 1 vol. 2018. (Let's Learn about Literature Ser.). (ENG.). 24p. (gr. 1-2). 24.27 *(978-0-7660-9747-6(1)*, 8c8a4a02-6627-47d5-97af-d2f9a7ba2942) Enslow Publishing, LLC.

Mora, Pat. Agua Agua Agua, Level 2. Flor Ada, Alma, tr. Ortega, Jose, illus. 3rd ed. 2003. (Dejame Leer Ser.). (SPA.). 16p. (J). (gr. -1-1). 6.50 *(978-0-673-36292-6(2)*, Good Year Bks.) Celebration Pr.

—Book Fiesta! Celebrate Children's Day/Book Day; Celebremos el Dia de Los Ninos/el Dia de Los Libros. 2016. (ENG., Illus.). 40p. (J). (gr. -1-3). pap. 9.99 *(978-0-06-128878-4(0)*, HarperCollins) HarperCollins Pubs.

Moreillon, Judi. Vamos a Leer. Mercado, Mary M., tr. from ENG. Teis, Kyra, illus.Tr. of Read to Me. (SPA.). 12p. (J). 2005. bds. 6.95 *(978-1-59572-015-3(4))* 2004. 6.95 *(978-1-932065-50-3(4))* Star Bright Bks., Inc.

Morgan, Michaela. Band of Friends. Price, Nick, illus. 2005. (ENG.). 24p. (J). lib. bdg. 23.65 *(978-1-59646-734-7(7))* Dingles & Co.

—Mouse with No Name. Mikhail, Jess, illus. 2004. (ENG.). 24p. (J). lib. bdg. 23.65 *(978-1-59646-682-1(0))* Dingles & Co.

—Shy Shark. Gomez, Elena, illus. 2005. (ENG.). 24p. (J). lib. bdg. 23.65 *(978-1-59646-722-4(3))* Dingles & Co.

Morgan, Ruth. Big Liam, Little Liam. Archbold, Tim, illus. 2005. (ENG.). 24p. (J). lib. bdg. 23.65 *(978-1-59646-728-6(2))* Dingles & Co.

—Jess & the Bean Root. Vagnozzi, Barbara, illus. 2005. (ENG.). 24p. (J). lib. bdg. 23.65 *(978-1-59646-732-3(0))* Dingles & Co.

Morgan, Sally. Collins Big Cat Phonics for Letters & Sounds - Living Fossils: Band 07/Turquoise, Bd. 7. Kundu, Kunal, illus. 2018. (Collins Big Cat Phonics Ser.). (ENG.). 24p. (J). (gr. 1-2). pap. 9.99 *(978-0-00-825180-2(0))* HarperCollins Pubs. Ltd. GBR. Dist: Independent Pubs. Group.

Morgand, Virginie. Achoo! 2016. (ENG., Illus.). 36p. (J). (gr. -1 — 1). 16.95 *(978-1-84976-376-9(3)*, 1648501) Tate Publishing, Ltd. GBR. Dist: Abrams, Inc.

—3, 2, 1, Go! 2018. (Illus.). 48p. (J). (gr. -1-1). 14.95 *(978-0-500-65154-4(X)*, 565154) Thames & Hudson.

Moroney, Trace. The Things I Love about Pets. 2019. (Things I Love about Ser.). (ENG.). 10p. (J). (— 1). bds. 8.99 *(978-1-76068-127-2(X))* Bonnier Publishing GBR. Dist: Independent Pubs. Group.

—When I'm Feeling Scared. 2019. (Feelings Ser.). (ENG.). 24p. (J). (— 1). 10.99 *(978-1-76068-068-8(0))* Bonnier Publishing GBR. Dist: Independent Pubs. Group.

Morpurgo, Michael. Coming Home. Hyndman, Kerry, illus. 2018. (ENG.). 32p. (J). (gr. -1-2). 17.99 *(978-1-5362-0042-3(5))* Candlewick Pr.

Morris, Jackie. The Seal Children. rev. ed. 2019. (ENG., Illus.). 32p. (J). (gr. k-3). 18.99 *(978-1-910959-47-3(2))* Otter-Barry Bks. GBR. Dist: Independent Pubs. Group.

Morris, Kim Ely. Through the Eyes of Love. 2009. (ENG., Illus.). 24p. pap. 14.99 *(978-1-4389-6756-1(X))* AuthorHouse.

Morris, Richard T. This Is a Moose. 2014. (ENG., Illus.). 48p. (J). (gr. -1-3). 18.99 *(978-0-316-21360-8(8))* Little, Brown Bks. for Young Readers.

Morris, Suzanne. A Trapezoid Is Not a Dinosaur! Morris, Suzanne, illus. 2019. (Illus.). 32p. (J). (gr. k-3). pap. 7.99 *(978-1-58089-580-4(8))* Charlesbridge Publishing, Inc.

Morstad, Julie. How To. 2013. (Illus.). 36p. (J). (gr. -1-3). 16.95 *(978-1-897476-57-4(4))* Simply Read Bks. CAN. Dist: Ingram Publisher Services.

—Today. 2016. (Illus.). 40p. (J). (gr. -1-3). 16.95 *(978-1-927018-68-2(4))* Simply Read Bks. CAN. Dist: Ingram Publisher Services.

Mortimer, Rachael. Red Riding Hood & the Sweet Little Wolf. Pichon, Liz, illus. 2013. (ENG.). 32p. 12.95 *(978-1-58925-117-5(2))* Tiger Tales.

—The Three Billy Goats Fluff. Pichon, Liz, illus. 2013. (ENG.). 32p. (J). (gr. -1-2). pap. 7.95 *(978-1-58925-439-8(2))* Tiger Tales.

Mortmain, Beatrice. I Help at Grandpa's House, 1 vol. Aguilera, Aurora, illus. 2017. (Ways I Help Ser.). (ENG.). 24p. (J). (gr. 1-1). pap. 9.25 *(978-1-5081-5677-2(8)*, cd8f6c2b-f4e1-4dff-beab-5ff7686e0238, PowerKids Pr.) Rosen Publishing Group, Inc., The.

Morton, Sasha. Collins Big Cat Phonics for Letters & Sounds - Cubs: Band 02A/Red A, Bd. 2A. 2018. (Collins Big Cat Ser.). (ENG., Illus.). 16p. (J). pap. 6.99 *(978-0-00-823021-0(8))* HarperCollins Pubs. Ltd. GBR. Dist: Independent Pubs. Group.

Moser, Lisa. A Friendship Yarn. Demidova, Olga, illus. 2019. (ENG.). 32p. (J). (gr. -1-3). 16.99 *(978-0-8075-0762-9(8)*, 807507628) Whitman, Albert & Co.

Moses, Anne E. Gatos Musikos: A Secret Told by the Moon. 2013. (Illus.). 58p. 24.95 *(978-1-4575-2189-8(X))* Dog Ear Publishing, LLC.

Moses, Brian. The Frog Olympics. 2017. (ENG., Illus.). 32p. (J). (gr. -1-k). pap. 9.99 *(978-0-7502-9683-0(6)*, Wayland) Hachette Children's Group GBR. Dist: Hachette Bk. Group.

Moss, Patricia Crocker. Dillie's Encounter with the Bucket Man. 2010. 36p. pap. 21.99 *(978-1-4535-4460-0(7))* Xlibris Corp.

Mostoller, Marcia. Poor William Dill. 2011. 28p. pap. 24.95 *(978-1-4626-0835-5(3))* America Star Bks.

Mother Goose Programs, prod. What's the BIG Idea? Shapes & Spaces Librarian Manual. 2008. 70p. pap. *(978-0-9753985-9-3(8))* Mother Goose Programs.

Mountbatten-Windsor, Sarah & York, Sarah. Tea for Ruby. 2012. lib. bdg. 18.40 *(978-0-606-26884-4(7))* Turtleback.

Muir, Nicola. Baba Didi & the Godwits Fly, 1 vol. Hayward, Annie, illus. 2013. (ENG.). 32p. (J). (gr. k-4). 8.95 *(978-1-78026-130-0(6))* New Internationalist Pubns., Ltd. GBR. Dist: Consortium Bk. Sales & Distribution.

Mullen, Amy. Colors of New England: Explore the Colors of Nature. Kids Will Love Discovering the Colors of New England with Vivid & Beautiful Art, from the Purple Northern Blazing Star to the Green Mallard Duck. 2017. (Naturally Local Ser.). (ENG., Illus.). 20p. (J). (gr. -1-k). bds. 8.95 *(978-1-938093-99-9(2)*, 809399) Duo Pr. LLC.

Mullen, Diane C. One Little Lot: The 1-2-3s of an Urban Garden. Vidal, Oriol, illus. 2020. 32p. (J). (gr. -1-2). lib. bdg. 16.99 *(978-1-58089-889-8(0))* Charlesbridge Publishing, Inc.

Muller, Gerda. The Gerda Muller Seasons Gift Collection: Spring, Summer, Autumn & Winter, 4 vols. 2018. (Seasons Board Bks.). (Illus.). 48p. 30.00 *(978-1-78250-473-3(7))* Floris Bks. GBR. Dist: Consortium Bk. Sales & Distribution.

—A Year Around the Great Oak, 24 vols. 2nd rev. ed. 2019. Orig. Title: Unser Baum. (ENG., Illus.). 40p. (J). 18.95 *(978-1-78250-602-7(0))* Floris Bks. GBR. Dist: Consortium Bk. Sales & Distribution.

Mullin, René. Aibītir. 2013. (ENG., Illus.). 40p. (J). pap. 7.95 *(978-0-85640-917-2(0))* Blackstaff Pr., Ltd. GBR. Dist: Casemate Pubs. & Bk. Distributors, LLC.

Mumford, Martha. The Royal Baby's Big Red Bus Tour of London. Grey, Ada, illus. 2016. (ENG.). 32p. (J). *(978-1-4088-6896-6(2)*, 282146, Bloomsbury Children's Bks.) Bloomsbury Publishing Plc.

Munsch, Robert. Angela's Airplane. Martchenko, Michael, illus. (Classic Munsch Ser.). (ENG.). 24p. (J). (gr. k-2). 2018. 6.95 *(978-1-77321-076-6(9))* 2016. bds. 7.99 *(978-1-55451-829-6(6))* Annick Pr., Ltd. CAN. Dist: Publishers Group West (PGW).

—L' Anniversaire. Martchenko, Michael, illus. 2003. (Droles D'Histories Ser.).Tr. of Moira's Birthday. (FRE.). 24p. (J). (gr. k-18). pap. *(978-2-89021-114-8(2))* Diffusion du livre Mirabel (DLM).

—The Boy in the Drawer. Martchenko, Michael, illus. 2019. (Classic Munsch Ser.). 28p. (J). (gr. k-2). pap. 6.95 *(978-1-77321-102-2(1))*; (ENG.). 19.95 *(978-1-77321-103-9(X))* Annick Pr., Ltd. CAN. Dist: Publishers Group West (PGW).

—The Dark. Martchenko, Michael, illus. 2019. (Classic Munsch Ser.). (ENG.). 32p. (J). 19.95 *(978-1-77321-105-3(6))*; pap. 6.95 *(978-1-77321-104-6(8))* Annick Pr., Ltd. CAN. Dist: Publishers Group West (PGW).

—David's Father. Martchenko, Michael, illus. 2018. (Classic Munsch Ser.). 32p. (J). (gr. k-2). 6.95 *(978-1-77321-078-0(5))* Annick Pr., Ltd. CAN. Dist: Publishers Group West (PGW).

—Le Dodo. Martchenko, Michael, illus. 2003. (Droles D'Histories Ser.).Tr. of Mortimer. (FRE.). 24p. (J). (gr. k-18). pap. *(978-2-89021-055-4(3))* Diffusion du livre Mirabel (DLM).

—The Enormous Suitcase. Martchenko, Michael, illus. 2019. (ENG.). 32p. (J). pap. 7.99 *(978-1-4431-6318-7(X))* Scholastic Canada, Ltd. CAN. Dist: Publishers Group West (PGW).

—The Fire Station. Martchenko, Michael, illus. (Classic Munsch Ser.). (ENG.). 24p. (J). 2018. (gr. k-2). 19.95 *(978-1-77321-081-0(5))* 5th ed. 2012. (gr. -1-k). bds. 7.99 *(978-1-55451-423-6(1)*, 9781554514236) Annick Pr., Ltd. CAN. Dist: Publishers Group West (PGW).

—I Have to Go! Martchenko, Michael, illus. 2019. (Classic Munsch Ser.). 24p. (J). 19.95 *(978-1-77321-107-7(2))*; (ENG.). pap. 7.95 *(978-1-77321-106-0(4))* Annick Pr., Ltd. CAN. Dist: Publishers Group West (PGW).

—Jonathan Cleaned up ... Then He Heard a Sound. Martchenko, Michael, illus. 2018. (Classic Munsch Ser.). (ENG.). 32p. (J). (gr. k-2). 7.95 *(978-1-77321-088-9(2))* Annick Pr., Ltd. CAN. Dist: Publishers Group West (PGW).

—Look at Me! Martchenko, Michael, illus. 2021. (ENG.). 32p. (J). pap. 7.99 *(978-0-545-99431-6(4))* Scholastic Canada, Ltd. CAN. Dist: Publishers Group West (PGW).

—Love You Forever. McGraw, Sheila, illus. 2018. (ENG.). 32p. (J). (gr. -1-1). bds. 8.95 *(978-0-2281-0104-8(2)*, 93279bc2-9280-4ed0-8e4f-216516529c98) Firefly Bks., Ltd.

—Love You Forever Pop-Up Edition. McGraw, Sheila, illus. 2017. (ENG.). 14p. (J). (gr. -1-1). 29.95 *(978-1-77085-965-4(9)*, a9e2dca8-f177-424e-8b80-a3c02dd73a41) Firefly Bks., Ltd.

—Moira's Birthday. Martchenko, Michael, illus. 2019. (Classic Munsch Ser.). 32p. (J). pap. 6.95 *(978-1-77321-108-4(0))* Annick Pr., Ltd. CAN. Dist: Publishers Group West (PGW).

—Mortimer. Martchenko, Michael, illus. 2018. (Classic Munsch Ser.). 24p. (J). (gr. k-2). 6.95 *(978-1-77321-082-7(3))* Annick Pr., Ltd. CAN. Dist: Publishers Group West (PGW).

—Much More Munsch! (Combined Volume) A Robert Munsch Collection. Martchenko, Michael et al, illus. 2019. (ENG.). 184p. (J). 26.99 *(978-0-439-93571-5(7))* Scholastic Canada, Ltd. CAN. Dist: Publishers Group West (PGW).

—Mud Puddle. Petričić, Dusan, illus. 2019. (Classic Munsch Ser.). 32p. (J). (gr. k-2). (ENG.). pap. 7.95 *(978-1-77321-110-7(2))*; 19.95 *(978-1-77321-111-4(0))* Annick Pr., Ltd. CAN. Dist: Publishers Group West (PGW).

—Murmel, Murmel, Murmel. Martchenko, Michael, illus. 2018. (Classic Munsch Ser.). (ENG.). 32p. (J). (gr. k-2). 6.95 *(978-1-77321-084-1(X))* Annick Pr., Ltd. CAN. Dist: Publishers Group West (PGW).

—Pigs. Martchenko, Michael, illus. (Classic Munsch Ser.). (J). (gr. -1-2). 2018. (ENG.). 32p. 19.95 *(978-1-77321-032-2(7))* 2018. 32p. pap. 7.95 *(978-1-77321-031-5(9))* 2014. (ENG.). 26p. bds. 7.99 *(978-1-55451-628-5(5)*, 9781554516285) Annick Pr., Ltd. CAN. Dist: Publishers Group West (PGW).

—Purple, Green & Yellow. Desputeaux, Hélène & Desputeaux, Hélène, illus. 2018. (Classic Munsch Ser.). (ENG.). 32p. (J). (gr. -1-2). 19.95 *(978-1-77321-034-6(3))* Annick Pr., Ltd. CAN. Dist: Publishers Group West (PGW).

—Purple, Green & Yellow. Desputeaux, Hélène, illus. 2018. (Classic Munsch Ser.). 36p. (J). (gr. -1-2). pap. 7.95 *(978-1-77321-033-9(5))* Annick Pr., Ltd. CAN. Dist: Publishers Group West (PGW).

—Roar! Martchenko, Michael, illus. 2019. (ENG.). 32p. (J). pap. 7.99 *(978-0-545-98020-3(8))* Scholastic Canada, Ltd. CAN. Dist: Publishers Group West (PGW).

—The Sandcastle Contest. Martchenko, Michael, illus. 2021. (ENG.). 32p. (J). (gr. k-3). pap. 7.99 *(978-0-439-95590-4(4))* Scholastic Canada, Ltd. CAN. Dist: Publishers Group West (PGW).

—Show & Tell. Martchenko, Michael, illus. 2019. (Classic Munsch Ser.). (ENG.). 32p. (J). 19.95 *(978-1-77321-113-8(7))* Annick Pr., Ltd. CAN. Dist: Publishers Group West (PGW).

—Something Good. Martchenko, Michael, illus. 2018. (Classic Munsch Ser.). 32p. (J). (gr. k-2). 7.95 *(978-1-77321-086-5(6))* Annick Pr., Ltd. CAN. Dist: Publishers Group West (PGW).

—Thomas' Snowsuit. Martchenko, Michael, illus. 2018. (Classic Munsch Ser.). (ENG.). 32p. (J). (gr. -1-2). 19.95 *(978-1-77321-038-4(6))*; pap. 7.95 *(978-1-77321-037-7(8))* Annick Pr., Ltd. CAN. Dist: Publishers Group West (PGW).

—Wait & See. Martchenko, Michael, illus. 2019. (Classic Munsch Ser.). 28p. (J). 19.95 *(978-1-77321-115-2(3))* Annick Pr., Ltd. CAN. Dist: Publishers Group West (PGW).

—50 below Zero. Martchenko, Michael, illus. (Classic Munsch Ser.). (J). 2019. 24p. 19.95 *(978-1-77321-101-5(3))* 2019. 24p. pap. 6.95 *(978-1-77321-100-8(5))* 3rd ed. 2013. (ENG.). 22p. (gr. -1-k). bds. 7.99 *(978-1-55451-532-5(7)*, 9781554515325) Annick Pr., Ltd. CAN. Dist: Publishers Group West (PGW).

Muntean, Michaela. Elmo Can... Taste! Touch! Smell! See! Hear! (Sesame Street) Swanson, Maggie, illus. 2013. (Big Bird's Favorites Board Bks.). (ENG.). 24p. (J). (— 1). bds. 4.99 *(978-0-307-98078-6(2)*, Random Hse. Bks. for Young Readers) Random Hse. Children's Bks.

Murphy, Julie. Gilly's Treasure. Fontano, Jay, illus. 2016. (ENG.). 14.99 *(978-1-4621-1845-8(3)*, Sweetwater Bks.) Cedar Fort, Inc./CFI Distribution.

Murphy, Lorna. Maisie's Mountain. 2013. (Illus.). 40p. pap. *(978-0-9568866-2-2(X))* Bluebudgie Publishing.

Murphy, Stuart J. Emma's Friendwich. 2010. (I See I Learn Ser.: 1). (Illus.). 32p. (J). (gr. -1-k). pap. 6.95 *(978-1-58089-451-7(8))* Charlesbridge Publishing, Inc.

—Freda Plans a Picnic. 2010. (I See I Learn Ser.: 2). (Illus.). 32p. (J). (gr. -1-k). pap. 6.95 *(978-1-58089-457-9(7))* Charlesbridge Publishing, Inc.

—Percy Plays It Safe. 2010. (I See I Learn Ser.: 4). (Illus.). 32p. (J). (gr. -1-k). pap. 6.95 *(978-1-58089-453-1(4))* Charlesbridge Publishing, Inc.

Murray, Alison. Hare & Tortoise. Murray, Alison, illus. 2016. (ENG., Illus.). 32p. (J). (-k). 18.99 *(978-0-7636-8721-2(9))* Candlewick Pr.

Murray, Diana. Groggle's Monster Valentine. Langley, Bats, illus. 2017. (Groggle's Monster Bks.). (ENG.). 32p. (J). (gr. -1-k). 9.99 *(978-1-5107-0508-1(2)*, Sky Pony Pr.) Skyhorse Publishing Co., Inc.

Murray, Stuart. Submarines. 2014. (Illus.). 48p. (J). *(978-1-4351-5371-4(5))* Barnes & Noble, Inc.

Murray, Tamsyn. Snug as a Bug. Abbot, Judi, illus. 2013. (ENG.). 32p. (J). *(978-0-85707-108-8(4))* Barnes & Noble, Inc.

—Snug as a Bug. Abbot, Judi, illus. 2014. (ENG.). 32p. (J). (gr. -1). pap. 8.99 *(978-0-85707-109-5(2))* Simon & Schuster, Ltd. GBR. Dist: Simon & Schuster, Inc.

—Snug As a Bug. Abbot, Judi & Gaviraghi, Giuditta, illus. 2013. (ENG.). 30p. (J). *(978-1-4351-4731-7(6))* Barnes & Noble, Inc.

Musgrave, Ruth A. National Geographic Kids Little Kids First Board Book: Animals on the Go. 2019. (First Board Bks.). (Illus.). 26p. (J). (gr. -1 — 1). bds. 7.99 *(978-1-4263-3312-5(9)*, National Geographic Kids) Disney Publishing Worldwide.

Muszynski, Julie. Henley in Hollywood. 2015. (Illus.). 56p. 20.00 *(978-0-9905320-0-2(3))* G Arts LLC.

Mutch, Ian. More & More & More. 2019. (Illus.). 32p. (J). (gr. k-2). 17.95 *(978-1-925591-54-5(9))* Fremantle Pr. AUS. Dist: Independent Pubs. Group.

My First 100 Words in Spanish/English. 2003. 32p. (J). 11.95 *(978-0-7525-7769-2(7))* Parragon, Inc.

My First Book of Trucks. 2004. (Illus.). 18p. (J). bds. 5.99 *(978-1-85854-431-1(9))* Brimax Books Ltd. GBR. Dist: Byeway Bks.

Myers, Tim J. & Myers, Priscilla. Full of Empty. Sorge, Rebecca, illus. 2016. (ENG.). 32p. (J). (gr. -1-3). 16.95 *(978-1-942934-35-6(1)*, 553435) Familius LLC.

Nadel, Carolina. Daddy's Home. Nadel, Carolina, illus. 2012. (Illus.). 32p. (J). 19.95 *(978-0-9792761-4-9(4))* Mookind Pr.

Nagara, Innosanto. A Is for Activist. Nagara, Innosanto, illus. 2012. (ENG., Illus.). 28p. bds. 15.00 *(978-0-9883448-9-1(0))* Kupu Kupu Pr.

Naish, Sarah & Jefferies, Rosie. Callum Kindly & the Very Weird Child: A Story about Sharing Your Home with a New Child. Evans, Megan, illus. 2017. (Therapeutic Parenting Bks.). (ENG.). 32p. (C). pap. 17.95 *(978-1-78592-300-5(5)*, 696531) Kingsley, Jessica Pubs. GBR. Dist: Hachette UK Distribution.

Nanji, Shenaaz. An Alien in My House. 1 vol. McLeod, Chum, illus. 2003. (ENG.). 24p. (J). (gr. -1-3). 15.95 *(978-1-896764-77-1(0))* Second Story Pr. CAN. Dist: Orca Bk. Pubs. USA.

Naoshi. Ice Cream Work. Naoshi, illus. 2015. (ENG., Illus.). 40p. (J). (gr. -1-k). 14.95 *(978-0-9834917-3-6(9))* Overcup Pr.

Nastanlieva, Vanya. Mo & Beau. 2015. (Illus.). 36p. (J). (gr. -1-3). 15.95 *(978-1-927018-63-7(3))* Simply Read Bks. CAN. Dist: Ingram Publisher Services.

—The New Arrival. 2017. (ENG., Illus.). 1p. (J). (gr. -1-3). 8.99 *(978-1-77229-009-7(2))* Simply Read Bks. CAN. Dist: Ingram Publisher Services.

—The New Arrival. Nastanlieva, Vanya, illus. 2013. (ENG., Illus.). 32p. (J). (gr. -1-3). 16.95 *(978-1-927018-13-2(7))* Simply Read Bks. CAN. Dist: Ingram Publisher Services.

National Geographic Kids. National Geographic Kids Baby Animals Sticker Activity Book. 2018. (NG Sticker Activity Bks.). 56p. (J). (gr. -1-k). pap. 6.99 *(978-1-4263-3020-9(0)*, National Geographic Kids) Disney Publishing Worldwide.

—National Geographic Kids Look & Learn: Count! 2011. (Illus.). 24p. (J). (gr. -1-k). bds. 6.99 *(978-1-4263-0891-8(4)*, National Geographic Kids) Disney Publishing Worldwide.

—National Geographic Kids Look & Learn: Match! 2011. (ENG., Illus.). 24p. (J). (gr. -1-k). bds. 7.99 *(978-1-4263-0871-0(X)*, National Geographic Kids) Disney Publishing Worldwide.

—National Geographic Little Kids First Big Book Collector's Set: Animals, Dinosaurs, Why?, 3 vols., Set. 2014. (National Geographic Little Kids First Big Bks.). (ENG.). 384p. (J). (gr. -1-k). pap. 44.85 *(978-1-4263-2010-1(8)*, National Geographic Kids) Disney Publishing Worldwide.

—Weird but True Animals. 2018. (Weird but True Ser.). (ENG., Illus.). 208p. (J). (gr. 3-7). lib. bdg. 17.90 *(978-1-4263-2982-1(2)*, National Geographic Kids) Disney Publishing Worldwide.

National Geographic Learning. Windows on Literacy Step up (Science: Animals Around Us): a Dog's Life. 2007. (ENG., Illus.). 8p. (J). pap. 9.95 *(978-0-7922-8480-2(1))* National Geographic School Publishing, Inc.

Natural History. (Illus.). (J). (gr. -1-6). pap., act. bk. ed. 2.95 *(978-0-565-00857-4(9))* Natural History Museum Pubns. GBR. Dist: Parkwest Pubns., Inc.

Natus, Uwe. The Creation of the World. Geisler, Dagmar, illus. 2016. (ENG.). 28p. (J). (gr. -1-3). 14.99 *(978-1-5064-0883-5(4)*, Sparkhouse Family) 1517 Media.

Nazeer, Tasnim & Publishing, Greenbirdbooks Childrens. Allah's Gifts. Frongia, Daniela, illus. 2012. 26p. pap. *(978-0-9562141-7-1(7))* Greenbird Bks.

Nazran, Govinder, illus. Aladdin. 2017. 24p. (J). (gr. -1-12). pap. 7.99 *(978-1-86147-819-1(4)*, Armadillo) Anness Publishing GBR. Dist: National Bk. Network.

Neasi, Barbara J. Como Yo. Hantel, Johanna, illus. 2003. (Rookie Reader Español Ser.).Tr. of Just Like Me. (SPA.). 32p. (J). (gr. k-2). pap. 4.95 *(978-0-516-27795-0(2)*, Children's Pr.) Scholastic Library Publishing.

Nedelcu, Ovi. Just Like Daddy. 2015. (ENG., Illus.). 32p. (J). (gr. -1-2). 17.95 *(978-1-57687-756-2(6)*, powerHouse Bks.) powerHse. Bks.

Negley, Keith. Mary Wears What She Wants. Negley, Keith, illus. 2019. (ENG., Illus.). 48p. (J). (gr. -1-3). 18.99 *(978-0-06-284679-2(5)*, Balzer & Bray) HarperCollins Pubs.

Negrescolor, Joan. Animal City: (Animal Books for Kids, Children's Nature Books) 2018. (ENG., Illus.). 40p. (J). (gr. -1-k). 18.99 *(978-1-4521-7029-9(0))* Chronicle Bks. LLC.

Nelid, Piper. My Father Teaches Overseas, 1 vol., 1. 2015. (Rosen REAL Readers: Social Studies Nonfiction / Fiction: Myself, My Community, My World Ser.). (ENG.). 12p. (J). (gr. k-1). pap. 6.33 *(978-1-5081-1734-6(9)*, d4266005-f8eb-42c4-85d4-9a30481b04c5, Rosen Classroom) Rosen Publishing Group, Inc., The.

Nellist, Glenys. God Made Mommy Special, 1 vol. Corke, Estelle, illus. 2018. (ENG.). 20p. (J). bds. 9.99 *(978-0-310-76233-1(2))* Zonderkidz.

—'Twas the Evening of Christmas, 1 vol. Selivanova, Elena, illus. 2017. ('Twas Ser.). (ENG.). 32p. (J). 17.99 *(978-0-310-74553-2(5))* Zonderkidz.

Nelson, Dianne Elizabeth. By Here. 2009. 32p. pap. 14.49 *(978-1-4490-0366-1(4))* AuthorHouse.

Nelson, Scott. Mulch the Lawnmower. 2006. (Illus.). 32p. 15.98 *(978-0-9745715-4-6(7))* KRBY Creations, LLC.

Nelson, Thomas. Big Trucks: A Touch-And-Feel Book, 1 vol. 2018. (ENG., Illus.). 12p. (J). bds. 9.99 *(978-1-4003-1058-6(X)*, Tommy Nelson) Nelson, Thomas Inc.

—Daddy Loves You So Much, 1 vol. 2015. (ENG., Illus.). 20p. (J). bds. 9.99 *(978-0-529-12335-0(5)*, Tommy Nelson) Nelson, Thomas Inc.

—Go to Sleep, Sheep!, 1 vol. 2018. (Bedtime Barn Ser.). (ENG., Illus.). 20p. (J). bds. 8.99 *(978-1-4003-1027-2(X)*, Tommy Nelson) Nelson, Thomas Inc.

—Mommy Loves You So Much, 1 vol. 2015. (ENG., Illus.). 20p. (J). bds. 9.99 *(978-0-529-12338-1(X)*, Tommy Nelson) Nelson, Thomas Inc.

Nesbitt, Kenn. More Bears! Cummings, Troy, illus. 2010. 32p. (J). (gr. k-3). 14.99 *(978-1-4022-3835-2(5)*, Sourcebooks Jabberwocky) Sourcebooks, Inc.

Neumann, Casey. Chase's Loose Tooth! (PAW Patrol) Random House, illus. 2018. (Pictureback(R) Ser.). (ENG.). 24p. (J). (gr. -1-2). pap. 6.99 *(978-1-5247-7271-0(2)*, Random Hse. Bks. for Young Readers) Random Hse. Children's Bks.

New York City Ballet. The Nutcracker. Docampo, Valeria, illus. 2018. (Classic Board Bks.). (ENG.). 38p. (J). (gr. -1-3). bds. 8.99 *(978-1-5344-2843-0(7)*, Little Simon) Little Simon.

Newby-Tynes, Claudia. His Love Flows. 2012. 28p. pap. 24.95 *(978-1-4626-8270-6(7))* America Star Bks.

Newell, Peter. The Rocket Book. 2016. (Peter Newell Children's Bks.). (ENG., Illus.). 52p. (J). (gr. 2-6). 9.95 *(978-0-8048-4742-1(8))* Tuttle Publishing.

Newman, Lesléa & Bates, Amy June. Gittel's Journey: An Ellis Island Story. 2019. (ENG., Illus.). 48p. (J). (gr. k-3). 18.99 *(978-1-4197-2747-4(8)*, 1152401, Abrams Bks. for Young Readers) Abrams, Inc.

Newman, Marlene. Myron's Magic Cow. 2005. (Illus.). 40p. (J). 16.99 *(978-1-84148-495-2(4))* Barefoot Bks., Inc.

Newman, Robin. No Peacocks! A Feathered Tale of Three Mischievous Foodies. Ewald, Chris, illus. 2018. (ENG.). 32p. (J). (gr. -1-3). 16.99 *(978-1-5107-1480-9(4)*, Sky Pony Pr.) Skyhorse Publishing Co., Inc.

Newmark Learning, compiled by. Sight Word Readers 12 copy set with Rack Set A. 2009. (Sight Word Readers Set A Ser.). (J). 1095.12 net. *(978-1-60719-159-9(8))* Newmark Learning LLC.

Nichols, Travis. Fowl Play: A Mystery Told in Idioms! (Detective Books for Kids, Funny Children's Books) 2017. (ENG., Illus.). 40p. (J). (gr. k-3). pap. 7.99 *(978-1-4521-6435-9(5))* Chronicle Bks. LLC.

Nicholson, Caitlin Dale. Niwîchihâw / I Help, 1 vol. Morin-Neilson, Leona, tr. 2018. (Nôhkom Ser.: 2). (CRE., Illus.). 24p. (J). (gr. k-2). 12.99 *(978-1-77306-116-0(X))* Groundwood Bks. CAN. Dist: Publishers Group West (PGW).

Nicholson, Melissa. Prissy & Pop Deck the Halls: A Christmas Holiday Book for Kids. Nicholson, Melissa, illus. 2016. (ENG., Illus.). 32p. (J). (gr. -1-3). 17.99 *(978-0-06-243996-3(0)*, HarperCollins) HarperCollins Pubs.

Nick, Barbara. Bella the Dragon. Steckler, Elaine, illus. 2013. 36p. pap. 11.75 *(978-1-938078-05-7(5))* Catto Creations, LLC.

Nickelodeon Staff, ed. Words - Dora the Explorer. 2010. (Write, Slide & Learn Ser.). 14p. (J). (gr. -1-1). 9.99 *(978-1-74184-519-8(X)*, Ideals Pubns.) Worthy Publishing.

Nicklin, Linda & Nicklin, Flip. Face to Face with Whales. 2010. (Face to Face with Animals Ser.). (Illus.). 32p. (J). (gr. 3-7). pap. 6.95 *(978-1-4263-0697-6(0)*, National Geographic Kids) Disney Publishing Worldwide.

Nicol, Scott Thomas. Dr. Jim & the Special Stethoscope. Youngblood, David W., illus. 2010. (Adventures of Dr. Jim Ser.). 32p. (J). pap. 12.95 *(978-0-9830355-7-2(1)*, Creative Hse. Kids Pr.) Bourgeois Media & Consulting.

Nicoll, David. Bean at the Fair. 2012. 24p. pap. 15.99 *(978-1-4691-4706-2(8))* Xlibris Corp.

—Bean on the Farm. 2012. 24p. pap. 15.99 *(978-1-4691-7837-0(0))* Xlibris Corp.

Nicoll, Helen & Pienkowski, Jan. Meg & Mog. 2004. (Meg & Mog Ser.). (Illus.). 30p. (J). (gr. -1-k). bds. 14.99 *(978-0-14-138059-9(4)*, Puffin) Penguin Bks., Ltd. GBR. Dist: Independent Pubs. Group.

Niehaus, Rebecca. The Birth of a Kitten. 2011. 48p. pap. 19.99 *(978-1-4567-6556-9(6))* AuthorHouse.

Nielsen, Gwyn English. Torey the Turkey Goes Skiing. 2003. (Illus.). 24p. (Orig.). (gr. -1-4). pap. 5.99 *(978-0-9660726-0-0(X))* C.G.S. Pr.

Nielsen, Susin. Princess Puffybottom ... & Darryl. Mueller, Olivia Chin, illus. 2019. 32p. (J). (gr. -1-2). 17.99 *(978-1-101-91925-5(6)*, Tundra Bks.) Tundra Bks. CAN. Dist: Penguin Random Hse. LLC.

Nieminen, Lotta. Cookies! An Interactive Recipe Book. 2018. (Cook in a Book Ser.). (ENG., Illus.). 16p. (gr. -1 — 1). bds. 19.95 *(978-0-7148-7773-0(5))* Phaidon Pr., Inc.

Nille, Peggy, illus. Hidden in the Jungle: A Search & Find Book. 2018. (ENG.). 26p. (J). 12.99 *(978-1-4413-2653-9(7)*, a8e10753-1eec-46d4-9f64-c8a19eef4b3b) Peter Pauper Pr. Inc.

Nilsen, Anna. My Mum's Best. Dodd, Emma, illus. 2011. 24p. bds. *(978-1-84089-679-4(5))* Zero to Ten, Ltd.

—Puzzle Heroes: People's Planet. Smith, Dave, illus. 2019. (Puzzle Heroes Ser.). (ENG.). 32p. (J). (gr. 3-7). pap. 11.99 *(978-1-4451-2135-2(2)*, Franklin Watts) Hachette Children's Group GBR. Dist: Hachette Bk. Group.

Nilsson, Ulf. Little Sister Rabbit Gets Lost. 46 vols. Beard, Susan, tr. Eriksson, Eva, illus. 2017. Orig. Title: Nar Lilla Syster Kanin Gick Alldeles Vilse. 32p. (J). 17.95 *(978-1-78250-377-4(3))* Floris Bks. GBR. Dist: Consortium Bk. Sales & Distribution.

No Laughing Matter. 2003. (Illus.). pap. 7.60 *(978-0-7398-7531-5(0))* Steck-Vaughn.

No Laughing Matter, 6 vols. (Ragged Island Mysteriestm Ser.). 161p. (gr. 5-7). 42.50 *(978-0-322-01653-8(3))* Wright Group/McGraw-Hill.

Noakes, Polly. The Very Long Sleep. Noakes, Polly, illus. 2018. (Child's Play Library). (Illus.). 32p. (J). pap. *(978-1-78628-128-9(7))*; *(978-1-78628-127-2(9))* Child's Play International Ltd.

Noll, Elizabeth. Coding in Transportation. 2018. (Coding Is Everywhere Ser.). (ENG., Illus.). 24p. (J). (gr. k-3). lib. bdg. 26.95 *(978-1-62617-835-9(6)*, Blastoff! Readers) Bellwether Media.

Nolte, Nancy. Richard Scarry's the Gingerbread Man. Scarry, Richard, illus. 2015. (Little Golden Book Ser.). 24p. (J). (-k). 5.99 *(978-0-385-37619-8(7)*, Golden Bks.) Random Hse. Children's Bks.

Nordqvist, Sven. Findus Plants Meatballs, 27 vols. Large, Nathan, tr. Nordqvist, Sven, illus. 2013. (Children's Classics Ser.). (Illus.). 32p. (J). (gr. -1-3). 19.95 *(978-1-907359-29-3(X))* Hawthorn Pr. GBR. Dist: Independent Pubs. Group.

Nordqvist, Sven. Findus Rules the Roost, 24 vols. 2018. (Fundus & Pettson Ser.: 10). (Illus.). 28p. (J). (gr. 2-4). 19.99 **(978-1-907359-87-3(7))** Hawthorn Pr. GBR. Dist: Independent Pubs. Group.

Norman, Kim. Ten on the Sled. Woodruff, Liza, illus. 2014. (ENG.). 24p. (J). (— 1). bds. 7.95 *(978-1-4549-1191-3(3))* Sterling Publishing Co., Inc.

North, Merry. My Grandma & Me: A Picture, Play & Tote Book. 2004. 10p. (J). (gr. -1-18). bds. 5.99 *(978-1-57151-724-1(3))* Playhouse Publishing.

Norton, Tamra. Bearubs & Flutterberries. 2008. (Bearubs Ser.). pap. 3.99 *(978-0-9796008-1-4(2))* Lindsley, David Studio.

—Bearubs Clydes New Job. 2008. (Bearubs Ser.). 32p. pap. 3.99 *(978-0-9796008-2-1(0))* Lindsley, David Studio.

—Meet Bearubs. 2008. (Bearubs Ser.). 32p. pap. 3.99 *(978-0-9796008-0-7(4))* Lindsley, David Studio.

Novel Units. Donde Viven Los Monstruos (Where the Wild Things Are) Novel Units Teacher Guide. 2019. (ENG.). (J). pap. 12.99 *(978-1-56137-544-8(6)*, NU5725, Novel Units, Inc.) Classroom Library Co.

Novesky, Amy. Love Is a Truck. Gillingham, Sara, illus. 2016. (ENG.). 24p. (J). (gr. -1-1). bds. 13.99 *(978-1-937359-86-7(7)*, 1330001) Abrams, Inc.

—Love Is a Tutu. Gillingham, Sara, illus. 2016. (ENG.). 24p. (J). (gr. -1-k). bds. 13.99 *(978-1-937359-81-2(6)*, 1330101, Cameron Kids) Cameron + Co.

—Me, Frida. Diaz, David, illus. 2015. (ENG.). 32p. (J). (gr. k-2). pap. 9.95 *(978-1-4197-1516-7(X)*, 679403, Abrams Bks. for Young Readers) Abrams, Inc.

Novick, Mary. The Big Book of Animals & Bugs. Hale, Jenny, illus. (Double Delights Ser.). (ENG.). 32p. (J). pap. *(978-1-877003-38-7(7))* Little Hare Bks. AUS. Dist: HarperCollins Pubs. Australia.

Novotny-Hunter, Jana. A Bear Hug at Bedtime. Widdowson, Kay, illus. 2017. (Child's Play Library). 32p. (J). (ENG.). *(978-1-84643-987-2(6))*; pap. *(978-1-84643-988-9(4))* Child's Play International Ltd.

Noyes, Deborah. Red Butterfly: How a Princess Smuggled the Secret of Silk Out of China. Blackall, Sophie, illus. 2019. (ENG.). 32p. (J). (gr. 1-4). 7.99 *(978-1-5362-0376-9(9))* Candlewick Pr.

Numeroff, Laura. The Best Mouse Cookie Padded Board Book. Bond, Felicia, illus. 2018. (If You Give... Ser.). (ENG.). 24p. (J). (gr. -1 — 1). bds. 10.99 *(978-0-06-284483-5(0)*, HarperFestival) HarperCollins Pubs.

—Happy Easter, Mouse! An Easter & Springtime Book for Kids. Bond, Felicia, illus. 2019. (If You Give... Ser.). (ENG.). 24p. (J). (gr. -1 — 1). bds. 7.99 *(978-0-694-01422-4(2)*, HarperFestival) HarperCollins Pubs.

Nutkis, Phyllis. When the World Was Quiet. Argoff, Patti, illus. 2003. (ENG.). 28p. (J). pap. 11.95 *(978-1-929628-14-8(5))* Hachai Publishing.

Nye, Naomi Shihab. Baby Radar. Carpenter, Nancy, illus. 2003. 32p. (J). lib. bdg. 16.89 *(978-0-688-15949-8(4))* HarperCollins Pubs.

Oaks, Kristen M. My Home Can Be a Holy Place. Burr, Dan, illus. 2015. (J). 18.99 *(978-1-62972-099-9(2))* Deseret Bk. Co.

Oaks, Kristen M. & Phillips, JoAnn. The Testimony Glove. Burr, Dan, illus. 2010. 31p. (J). (gr. -1-4). 17.99 *(978-1-60641-151-3(9))* Deseret Bk. Co.

Obed, Ellen Bryan. Twelve Kinds of Ice. McClintock, Barbara, illus. 2015. (ENG.). 64p. (J). (gr. 1-4). 6.99 *(978-0-544-55554-9(6)*, 1610460, Clarion Bks.) HarperCollins Pubs.

O'Brien, Eileen. This Little Piggy. Tyler, Jenny, ed. Edward, Linda, illus. 2004. (Carry-Me Bks.). 16p. (J). 5.95 *(978-0-7945-0125-9(7)*, Usborne) EDC Publishing.

O'Brien, Melanie. Pat Them Gently. Runnells, Treesha, illus. 2006. (ENG.). 10p. (J). (gr. -1-3). bds. 8.95 *(978-1-58117-462-5(4)*, Intervisual/Piggy Toes) Bendon, Inc.

O'Callaghan, Joanne. Found in Melbourne. Song, Kori, illus. 2018. (ENG.). 36p. (J). (gr. -1-1). 19.99 *(978-1-76052-341-1(0))* Allen & Unwin AUS. Dist: Independent Pubs. Group.

O'Conaill, Seamus. Spuds & the Spider. Archimede, Daniele, illus. 2018. (ENG.). 32p. (J). pap. 16.00 *(978-0-7171-7995-4(8))* Gill Bks. IRL. Dist: Casemate Pubs. & Bk. Distributors, LLC.

O'Connor, Jane. Budding Ballerina. 2013. (Fancy Nancy Picture Bks.). (J). lib. bdg. 13.55 *(978-0-606-32158-7(6))* Turtleback.

—Fancy Nancy: Apples Galore! Glasser, Robin Preiss, illus. 2013. (I Can Read Level 1 Ser.). (ENG.). 32p. (J). (gr. -1-3). pap. 4.99 *(978-0-06-208310-4(4)*, HarperCollins) HarperCollins Pubs.

—Fancy Nancy: Budding Ballerina. Glasser, Robin Preiss, illus. 2013. (Fancy Nancy Ser.). (ENG.). 24p. (J). (gr. -1-3). pap. 4.99 *(978-0-06-208628-0(6)*, HarperFestival) HarperCollins Pubs.

—Fancy Nancy & the Fall Foliage. 2014. (Fancy Nancy Ser.). (ENG., Illus.). 24p. (J). (gr. -1-3). pap. 4.99 *(978-0-06-208630-3(8)*, HarperFestival) HarperCollins Pubs.

—Fancy Nancy: Apples Galore! Glasser, Robin Preiss, illus. 2013. (I Can Read Level 1 Ser.). (ENG.). 32p. (J). (gr. -1-3). 16.99 *(978-0-06-208311-1(2)*, HarperCollins) HarperCollins Pubs.

—Fancy Nancy: Nancy Clancy Sees the Future, 3 vols. Glasser, Robin Preiss, illus. 2013. (Nancy Clancy Ser.: 3). (ENG.). 128p. (J). (gr. 1-5). 9.99 *(978-0-06-208297-8(3)*, HarperCollins) HarperCollins Pubs.

—Fancy Nancy: Puppy Party. Glasser, Robin Preiss, illus. 2013. (Fancy Nancy Ser.). (ENG.). 24p. (J). (gr. -1-3). pap. 3.99 (978-0-06-208627-3(8), HarperFestival) HarperCollins Pubs.

—Fancy Nancy Storybook Treasury. Glasser, Robin Preiss, illus. 2013. (Fancy Nancy Ser.). (ENG.). 192p. (J). (gr. -1-3). 11.99 (978-0-06-211978-0(8), HarperFestival) HarperCollins Pubs.

—Fancy Nancy's Elegant Easter: An Easter & Springtime Book for Kids. Glasser, Robin Preiss, illus. 2009. (Fancy Nancy Ser.). (ENG.). 16p. (J). (gr. -1-3). pap. 6.99 (978-0-06-170379-9(6), HarperFestival) HarperCollins Pubs.

—Fancy Nancy's Perfectly Posh Paper Doll Book. Glasser, Robin Preiss, illus. 2009. (Fancy Nancy Ser.). (ENG.). 16p. (J). (gr. -1-3). pap. 6.99 (978-0-06-187328-7(4), HarperFestival) HarperCollins Pubs.

Ohi, Ruth. Me & My Brother. 2007. (ENG., Illus.). 24p. (J). (gr. -1-k). 19.95 (978-1-55451-092-4(9), 9781554510924) Annick Pr., Ltd. CAN. Dist: Publishers Group West (PGW).

Old MacDonald. (J). 46.95 (978-0-8136-8807-7(8)) Modern Curriculum Pr.

Old MacDonald. (J). (gr. k-3). (978-0-663-46485-2(4), MD7225) Silver, Burdett & Ginn, Inc.

O'Leary, Sara. This Is Sadie. Morstad, Julie, illus. (J). 2018. 30p. (— 1). bds. 8.99 (978-0-7352-6324-6(8)) 2015. 32p. (gr. -1-2). 17.99 (978-1-77049-532-6(0)) Tundra Bks. CAN. (Tundra Bks.). Dist: Penguin Random Hse. LLC.

O'leary, Sara. When I Was Small. Morstad, Julie, illus. 2012. (ENG.). 32p. (J). (gr. -1-3). 16.95 (978-1-897476-38-3(8)) Simply Read Bks. CAN. Dist: Ingram Publisher Services.

—When You Were Small. Morstad, Julie, illus. 2017. 40p. (J). (gr. -1-3). 8.99 (978-1-77229-008-0(4)) Simply Read Bks. CAN. Dist: Ingram Publisher Services.

O'Leary, Sara. Where You Came From. Morstad, Julie, illus. 2020. (ENG.). 40p. (J). (gr. -1-3). 8.99 (978-1-77229-016-5(5)) Simply Read Bks. CAN. Dist: Ingram Publisher Services.

Oliver, Alison. Be Bold, Baby: Oprah. Oliver, Alison, illus. 2018. (Be Bold, Baby Ser.). (ENG., Illus.). 20p. (J). (— 1). bds. 9.99 (978-1-328-51990-0(2), 1720771, Clarion Bks.) HarperCollins Pubs.

Oliver, Martin. Off with Their Heads! Pinder, Andrew, illus. 2017. (Buster Reference Ser.). (ENG.). 128p. (J). (gr. 3-7). pap. 8.99 (978-1-78055-465-5(6)) O'Mara, Michael Bks., Ltd. GBR. Dist: Independent Pubs. Group.

Oliver, Narelle. Tide Pool Secrets. Oliver, Narelle, illus. 2017. (ENG., Illus.). 32p. (J). (gr. -1-2). 18.99 (978-0-7636-9159-2(3)) Candlewick Pr.

Olsen, Jan Z. Mat Man on the Go. Delaney, Molly, illus. 2010. (ENG.). stu. ed. 13.75 (978-1-934825-39-6(5)) Handwriting Without Tears.

Olsen, Sylvia. Yetsa's Sweater, 1 vol. Larson, Joan, illus. 2013. (ENG.). 40p. (J). (gr. 1-3). 12.95 (978-1-55039-202-9(6)) Sono Nis Pr. CAN. Dist: Orca Bk. Pubs. USA.

Omary, Rachel, illus. Animals in Dari. I.t. ed. 2003. 4p. (J). spiral bd. 10.95 (978-0-9740535-3-0(8)) Knight Publishing.

—Animals in Farsi. I.t. ed. 2003. 4p. (J). spiral bd. 10.95 (978-0-9740535-4-7(6)) Knight Publishing.

—Animals in Pashto. I.t. ed. 2003. 4p. (J). spiral bd. 10.95 (978-0-9740535-5-4(4)) Knight Publishing.

One Cool Friend. 2014. pap. 16.99 (978-0-545-67554-3(5)) Scholastic, Inc.

O'Neal, Jayce. Crazy Circus World. 2009. (Illus.). 40p. (978-1-55452-372-6(9)) Essence Publishing.

O'Neill, Elizabeth & McPherson, Missie. Alfred Visits New York City. 2003. (Illus.). 24p. (J). pap. 12.00 (978-1-4120-1338-3(0)) Funny Bone Bks.

O'Neill, Michael Patrick. Fishy Friends: A Journey Through the Coral Kingdom. O'Neill, Michael Patrick, photos by. 2003. (Illus.). 64p. (J). 19.95 (978-0-9728653-0-2(6)) Batfish Bks.

Ong, Gelyn. The Forest Fable. 2013. (Illus.). 54p. (J). (gr. -1-2). 19.99 (978-981-4408-56-1(5)) Marshall Cavendish International (Asia) Private Ltd. SGP. Dist: Independent Pubs. Group.

Oram, Hiawyn. In the Attic. Kitamura, Satoshi, illus. 2012. (ENG.). 28p. (J). (gr. -1-k). pap. 13.99 (978-1-84939-298-3(6)) Andersen Pr. GBR. Dist: Independent Pubs. Group.

Oroma Alikor-Adele. The Lonely Bugerfly. 2010. 28p. pap. 21.99 (978-1-4535-6225-3(7)) Xlibris Corp.

Orsolini, Laura. Maddalena. 2016. (Illus.). 36p. (J). (gr. -1-3). 16.95 (978-1-77229-007-3(6)) Simply Read Bks. CAN. Dist: Ingram Publisher Services.

Oskarsson, Bárdur. The Flat Rabbit. 2014. (ENG., Illus.). 40p. (J). (gr. -1-4). 17.95 (978-1-77147-059-9(3), Owlkids) Owlkids Bks. Inc. CAN. Dist: Publishers Group West (PGW).

Ostrowski, Jay & Ostrowski, Bodie. Someone: A Story of Acceptance. 2018. (ENG., Illus.). 20p. (J). (gr. -1 — 1). 15.99 (978-1-62872-969-6(4), Arcade Publishing) Skyhorse Publishing Co., Inc.

Oswald, Helen. Cat & Dog. Waring, Zoe, illus. 2016. (ENG.). 32p. (J). (gr. -1-1). pap. 8.99 (978-1-78445-286-5(6)) Top That! Publishing PLC GBR. Dist: Independent Pubs. Group.

—Cat & Dog. Waring, Zoe, illus. 2018. (Picture Bks.). (ENG.). 32p. (J). (gr. -1-k). 16.99 (978-1-78700-455-9(4)) Willow Tree Bks. GBR. Dist: Independent Pubs. Group.

O'Toole, Janet. On the Farm: Lift the Flaps to Find Out about Farms! Adams, Ben, illus. 2013. 16p. (J). (gr. -1-12). bds. 6.99 (978-1-84322-794-6(0), Armadillo) Anness Publishing GBR. Dist: National Bk. Network.

O'Toole, Janet & Anness Publishing Staff. First Words: Lift the Flaps to Find Out about Words! Adams, Ben, illus. 2013. 16p. (J). (gr. -1-12). bds. 6.99 (978-1-84322-795-3(9), Armadillo) Anness Publishing GBR. Dist: National Bk. Network.

—Vehicles: Lift the Flaps to Find Out about Vehicles! Adams, Ben, illus. 2013. 16p. (J). (gr. -1-12). bds. 6.99 (978-1-84322-728-1(2), Armadillo) Anness Publishing GBR. Dist: National Bk. Network.

O'Toole, Patrick. Alphabetimals Picture Dictionary. 2014. (Dover Alphabet Coloring Bks.). (ENG.). 144p. (J). (gr. -1). pap. 6.99 (978-0-486-49180-6(3), 491803) Dover Pubns., Inc.

Over in the Meadow. (J). (gr. 1). stu. ed. 23.50 (978-0-8136-0271-4(8)) Modern Curriculum Pr.

Owen, Hyun Jung. Hodder Cambridge Primary Science Story Book C Foundation Stage Dinosaur Adventure, Bk. C. 2019. (ENG., Illus.). 16p. (gr. k-k). pap. 6.40 (978-1-5104-4865-0(9)) Hodder Education Group GBR. Dist: Ingram Publisher Services.

Owen, Lucy. Boo-A-Bog in the Park. 2016. (ENG., Illus.). 36p. (J). pap. 8.95 (978-1-78562-169-7(6)) Gomer Pr. GBR. Dist: Casemate Pubs. & Bk. Distributors, LLC.

Owen, Ruth. All about Families. 2017. (First Words & Pictures Ser.). (ENG., Illus.). 32p. (J). (gr. -1-2). lib. bdg. 29.32 (978-1-911341-81-9(2), 22a2695d-0a73-4e5f-bff3-7932776f5954) Ruby Tuesday Books Limited GBR. Dist: Lerner Publishing Group.

—1 2 3 Numbers & Counting. 2017. (First Words & Pictures Ser.). (ENG., Illus.). 32p. (J). (gr. -1-2). lib. bdg. 29.32 (978-1-911341-79-6(0), 62c09a34-c296-472f-b1da-ad22bf4a4ebf) Ruby Tuesday Books Limited GBR. Dist: Lerner Publishing Group.

Owens, Katherine. Tree Seasons Ball, 1 bk. I.t. ed. 2004. (Illus.). 40p. (J). per. 19.99 (978-0-9760419-0-0(1), TREESEASONSBALL) ThatsMyLife Co.

Oxford, ed. Oxford Picture Dictionary Content Area for Kids Reproducible Collection Pack Pack. 2nd ed. 2012. (ENG.). 333.30 (978-0-19-401784-8(2)) Oxford Univ. Pr., Inc.

Oxford Picture Dictionary Content Area for Kids English-Spanish Dictionary Student Pack. 2012. (ENG.). pap. 45.10 (978-0-19-401788-6(5)) Oxford Univ. Pr., Inc.

Oxford Picture Dictionary: Content Areas for Kids E-Book. 2nd ed. 2013. (ENG.). 13.70 (978-0-19-401795-4(8)) Oxford Univ. Pr., Inc.

Oxley, Jennifer & Aronson, Billy. Peg + Cat: the Sleepover. 2018. (Peg + Cat Ser.). (ENG.). 24p. (J). (gr. -1-2). 5.99 (978-1-5362-0345-5(9), Candlewick Entertainment) Candlewick Pr.

Pachek, Mary C. Isabella & the Merry Mouse House: A Christmas Story Coloring Book. Noad, Jordan, illus. 2009. 34p. pap. 14.49 (978-1-4389-8467-4(7)) AuthorHouse.

Painted Daisies Inc. Staff & Borgatti, Katherine. Shermit's Adventure to Sprinkle Island. Painted Daisies Inc. Staff, illus. 2010. (ENG., Illus.). 32p. (J). 15.95 (978-0-615-34491-1(7)) Painted Daisies Inc.

Paiva, Johannah Gilman. Is There a Monster in My Closet? Read with Me. Grey, James, ed. Long, Paulette Rich, illus. 2014. (ENG.). 32p. (J). (gr. -1-3). 7.99 (978-1-4867-0002-8(0)) Flowerpot Children's Pr. Inc. CAN. Dist: Cardinal Pubs. Group.

Paiva, Johannah Gilman, ed. Zoo Friends. 2013. (Illus.). 20p. (J). bds. 8.99 (978-1-77093-629-4(7)) Flowerpot Children's Pr. Inc. CAN. Dist: Cardinal Pubs. Group.

Palatini, Margie. Untitled Picture Book. 2005. 32p. (J). 14.99 (978-0-7868-0323-1(1)) Hyperion Pr.

Palmer, Priscilla & Hoffman, Don. Tony the Ferry Riding Pigeon. Goldberger, Dylan, illus. 2016. (ENG.). 32p. (J). (gr. k-2). pap. 3.99 (978-1-943154-05-0(8)) Peek-A-Boo Publishing.

Pan, Hui-Mei. Piggy in My Pocket. 2004. (Illus.). 14p. (J). bds. 5.95 (978-1-887734-96-7(1)) Star Bright Bks., Inc.

—Piggy in My Pocket: Spanish/English, 1 vol. 2004. (ENG., Illus.). 32p. (J). bds. 5.95 (978-1-932065-11-4(3)) Star Bright Bks., Inc.

—What's in Grandma's Grocery Bag?, 1 vol. 2004. (ENG., Illus.). 32p. (J). bds. 6.25 (978-1-887734-97-4(X)) Star Bright Bks., Inc.

Paniaq, Herve. Takannaaluk, 1 vol. Amattaujuq (Amaktauyok), Germaine, illus. 2018. (Inuit Folktales Ser.). (ENG.). 32p. (J). (gr. 1-3). 16.95 (978-1-77227-181-2(0)) Inhabit Media Inc. CAN. Dist: Consortium Bk. Sales & Distribution.

Panpan, Alice. Antarctic Wings. 2011. 36p. pap. 21.99 (978-1-4568-6210-7(3)) Xlibris Corp.

Paratore, Coleen Murtagh. The Big Book about Being Big. Fennell, Clare, illus. 2019. 40p. (J). (gr. -1-2). 17.99 (978-1-4926-9684-1(6), Little Pickle Pr.) Sourcebooks, Inc.

Park, Jeonghyeon. What Shall We Do? 2019. (ENG., Illus.). 40p. (J). 15.95 (978-1-927018-87-3(0)) Simply Read Bks. CAN. Dist: Ingram Publisher Services.

Park, Kyubyong & Amen, Henry J. My First Book of Korean Words: An ABC Rhyming Book of Korean Language & Culture. Padron, Aya, illus. 2017. (My First Words Ser.). 32p. (J). (gr. -1-3). 10.95 (978-0-8048-4940-1(4)) Tuttle Publishing.

Park, Mac. Sky High: d-Bot Squad 2. Hart, James, illus. 2018. (D-Bot Squad Ser.: 2). (ENG.). 80p. (J). (gr. k-2). pap. 7.99 (978-1-76029-598-1(1)) Allen & Unwin AUS. Dist: Independent Pubs. Group.

Parker, Amy. Night Night, Jungle, 1 vol. Allyn, Virginia, illus. 2018. (Night Night Ser.). (ENG.). 20p. (J). bds. 9.99 (978-0-7180-9086-9(1), Tommy Nelson) Nelson, Thomas Inc.

—Night Night, Sleepytown, 1 vol. Allyn, Virginia, illus. 2018. (Night Night Ser.). (ENG.). 20p. (J). bds. 9.99 (978-1-4003-1003-6(2), Tommy Nelson) Nelson, Thomas Inc.

Parker, Ant & Denchfield, Nick. Charlie Chick, 1. 2014. (Charlie Chick Ser.). (ENG., Illus.). 400p. (J). 12.99 (978-1-4472-5764-6(2)) Pan Macmillan GBR. Dist: Independent Pubs. Group.

Parker, Danny. Perfect. Blackwood, Freya, illus. (ENG.). 32p. (J). 2018. (gr. -1-k). 10.99 (978-1-76050-140-2(9)) 2017. (— 1). 16.99 (978-1-921894-84-8(9)) Little Hare Bks. AUS. Dist: Independent Pubs. Group.

Parker, Emma. At the Circus. 2010. (Illus.). 20p. pap. (978-1-877561-52-8(5)) First Edition Ltd.

—At the Farm. 2010. (Illus.). pap. (978-1-877547-94-2(8)) First Edition Ltd.

—Bath Time. 2010. (Illus.). pap. (978-1-877547-83-6(2)) First Edition Ltd.

—Blah the Bacteria. 2010. (Illus.). pap. (978-1-877547-46-1(8)) First Edition Ltd.

—The Butterfly on the Subway. 2010. (Illus.). pap. (978-1-877547-81-2(6)) First Edition Ltd.

—Can Your Dog? 2010. (Illus.). pap. (978-1-877547-96-6(4)) First Edition Ltd.

—Captain Gold. 2010. (Illus.). pap. (978-1-877561-26-9(6)) First Edition Ltd.

—The Carousel. 2010. (Illus.). 16p. pap. (978-1-877561-73-3(8)) First Edition Ltd.

—Cat on the High Seas. 2010. (Illus.). 16p. pap. (978-1-877561-75-7(4)) First Edition Ltd.

—Cecil the Caterpillar. 2010. (Illus.). pap. (978-1-877547-95-9(6)) First Edition Ltd.

—Chuck the Chilli. 2010. (Illus.). pap. (978-1-877547-92-8(1)) First Edition Ltd.

—Dancing Class. 2010. (Illus.). pap. (978-1-877561-05-4(3)) First Edition Ltd.

—Davey Dory. 2010. (Illus.). 20p. pap. (978-1-877561-58-0(4)) First Edition Ltd.

—Delia Dynamite. 2010. (Illus.). 24p. pap. (978-1-877561-35-1(5)) First Edition Ltd.

—The Fluffiest Chicken. 2010. (Illus.). pap. (978-1-877561-13-9(4)) First Edition Ltd.

—The Frog That Did Not Like Water. 2010. (Illus.). pap. (978-1-877547-93-5(X)) First Edition Ltd.

—The Fruity Girls. 2010. (Illus.). pap. (978-1-877561-11-5(8)) First Edition Ltd.

—Granny Odd Legs. 2010. (Illus.). pap. (978-1-877547-86-7(7)) First Edition Ltd.

—Groat & the Coat. 2010. (Illus.). pap. (978-1-877547-99-7(9)) First Edition Ltd.

—How Many Fish? 2010. (Illus.). pap. (978-1-877561-10-8(X)) First Edition Ltd.

—How Shall I Get to School Today? 2010. (Illus.). pap. (978-1-877547-84-3(0)) First Edition Ltd.

—Jack & the Beanstalk. 2010. (Illus.). 24p. pap. (978-1-877561-49-8(5)) First Edition Ltd.

—Karaoke Colin. 2010. (Illus.). 20p. pap. (978-1-877561-34-4(7)) First Edition Ltd.

—The Lightning Game. 2010. (Illus.). 24p. pap. (978-1-877561-55-9(X)) First Edition Ltd.

—The Lucky Pearl. 2010. (Illus.). 20p. pap. (978-1-877561-18-4(5)) First Edition Ltd.

—Lulu & the Seed. 2010. (Illus.). pap. (978-1-877547-82-9(4)) First Edition Ltd.

—The Magic Show. 2010. (Illus.). pap. (978-1-877561-23-8(1)) First Edition Ltd.

—The Magic Snow Globe. 2010. (Illus.). pap. (978-1-877561-30-6(4)) First Edition Ltd.

—Missy Hip Hoppo. 2010. (Illus.). 16p. pap. (978-1-877561-56-6(8)) First Edition Ltd.

—The Monkey in the Tree. 2010. (Illus.). pap. (978-1-877547-91-1(3)) First Edition Ltd.

—Mr Grumpy Bunny. 2010. (Illus.). pap. (978-1-877561-22-1(3)) First Edition Ltd.

—The Naughty Puppy. 2010. (Illus.). pap. (978-1-877547-89-8(1)) First Edition Ltd.

—The Not So Scary Scarecrow. 2010. (Illus.). pap. (978-1-877547-88-1(3)) First Edition Ltd.

—One Leg Ned. 2010. (Illus.). pap. (978-1-877561-12-2(6)) First Edition Ltd.

—Pet Day. 2010. (Illus.). pap. (978-1-877561-28-3(2)) First Edition Ltd.

—Robot Tim. 2010. (Illus.). 20p. pap. (978-1-877561-54-2(1)) First Edition Ltd.

—Safari Adventure. 2010. (Illus.). pap. (978-1-877561-29-0(0)) First Edition Ltd.

—Sam the Traveling Snail. 2010. (Illus.). pap. (978-1-877561-19-1(3)) First Edition Ltd.

—Sebastian the Ant. 2010. (Illus.). pap. (978-1-877561-14-6(2)) First Edition Ltd.

—Skipping Sally. 2010. (Illus.). pap. (978-1-877561-24-5(X)) First Edition Ltd.

—Snafu & the Shoes. 2010. (Illus.). pap. (978-1-877561-00-9(2)) First Edition Ltd.

—The Snowman Olympics. 2010. (Illus.). 20p. pap. (978-1-877561-36-8(3)) First Edition Ltd.

—Sooty the Stink Bomb. 2010. (Illus.). pap. (978-1-877561-15-3(0)) First Edition Ltd.

—The Space Rocket. 2010. (Illus.). pap. (978-1-877547-87-4(5)) First Edition Ltd.

—The Spaghetti Tree. 2010. (Illus.). pap. (978-1-877561-02-3(9)) First Edition Ltd.

—Splat & the Hat. 2010. (Illus.). pap. (978-1-877561-04-7(5)) First Edition Ltd.

—Square Sidney. 2010. 16p. pap. (978-1-877561-31-3(2)) First Edition Ltd.

—Summer Camp. 2010. (Illus.). pap. (978-1-877561-27-6(4)) First Edition Ltd.

—The Wedding Day. 2010. (Illus.). 16p. pap. (978-1-877561-51-1(7)) First Edition Ltd.

—What a Hullabaloo. 2010. 20p. pap. (978-1-877561-32-0(0)) First Edition Ltd.

—The Wickedest Witch. 2010. (Illus.). pap. (978-1-877561-17-7(7)) First Edition Ltd.

Parker, Emma & Renaud, Marguerite. Chatterbox Caz. 2010. (Illus.). 16p. pap. (978-1-877561-77-1(0)) First Edition Ltd.

—Dragon Bowling. 2010. (Illus.). 24p. pap. (978-1-877561-82-5(7)) First Edition Ltd.

—Hedgehogs. 2010. (Illus.). 16p. pap. (978-1-877561-80-1(0)) First Edition Ltd.

—The Honey Bee Race. 2010. (Illus.). 16p. pap. (978-1-877561-78-8(9)) First Edition Ltd.

Parker, Marjorie Blain. Psst! I Love You. Hanson, Sydney, illus. (Snuggle Time Stories Ser.: 7). (J). 2018. 22p. (— 1). bds. 8.95 (978-1-4549-2705-1(4)) 2017. (ENG.). 32p. (gr. -1-k). 9.95 (978-1-4549-1721-2(0)) Sterling Publishing Co., Inc.

Parker, Sandy. What Day Is Today? Hofher, Cathy, illus. I.t. ed. 2003. 24p. (gr. k-1). 13.95 (978-0-9643462-3-9(0), 10, Just Think Bks.) Canary Connect Pubns.

Parnell, Declan. Mr. Wilson Is Our Crossing Guard, 1 vol., 1. 2015. (Rosen REAL Readers: Social Studies Nonfiction / Fiction: Myself, My Community, My World Ser.). (ENG.). 8p. (J). (gr. k-1). pap. 5.46 (978-1-5081-1704-9(7), 20bbe29d-2d08-4aeb-b5f1-68b83f790019, Rosen Classroom) Rosen Publishing Group, Inc., The.

Parr, todd. Be Who You Are. 2016. (ENG., Illus.). 32p. (J). (gr. -1-1). 18.99 (978-0-316-26523-2(3)) Little, Brown Bks. for Young Readers.

—The Daddy Book. 2015. (ENG., Illus.). 20p. (J). (gr. -1 — 1). bds. 7.99 (978-0-316-25784-8(2)) Little, Brown Bks. for Young Readers.

—Love the World. 2019. (ENG., Illus.). 22p. (J). (gr. -1 — 1). bds. 7.99 (978-0-316-45716-3(7)) Little, Brown Bks. for Young Readers.

—Love the World. Parr, todd, illus. 2019. (Todd Parr Picture Bks.). (ENG., Illus.). 32p. (J). (gr. -1-2). 31.36 (978-1-5321-4376-2(1), 31826, Picture Bk.) Spotlight.

—The Mommy Book. 2016. (ENG., Illus.). 20p. (J). (gr. -1 — 1). bds. 7.99 (978-0-316-33774-8(9)) Little, Brown Bks. for Young Readers.

—Otto Goes to School. 2013. (Passport to Reading Level 1 Ser.). (ENG., Illus.). 32p. (J). (gr. -1-1). 4.99 (978-0-316-22931-9(8)) Little, Brown Bks. for Young Readers.

Parry, Alan & Parry, Linda. The Herald Angels. 2003. (Illus.). 16p. 9.99 (978-1-85608-253-2(9)) Hunt, John Publishing Ltd. GBR. Dist: Send The Light Distribution LLC.

—Look for the Rainbow: Look Through the Telescope, Lift the Flaps, Work the Puzzles, See the Pop-Ups, & Enjoy Hours of Fun with Noah. 2003. (Illus.). 14p. 12.99 (978-1-85608-212-9(1)) Hunt, John Publishing Ltd. GBR. Dist: Send The Light Distribution LLC.

Parry, Jo. Sleep, Little Pup. Parry, Jo, illus. 2017. (Story Corner Ser.). (ENG., Illus.). 24p. (J). (gr. -1-k). lib. bdg. 19.99 (978-1-68297-183-3(X), bb617383-c35d-4db3-9614-b0dc5129f56c) QEB Publishing Inc.

Pasquali, Elena. Two-Minute Bedtime Stories. Smee, Nicola, illus. 2010. (Two-Minute Stories Ser.). (ENG.). 48p. (J). (gr. -1-k). 12.99 (978-0-7459-6079-1(0)) Lion Hudson PLC GBR. Dist: Independent Pubs. Group.

Patel, Sanjay & Haynes, Emily. Ganesha's Sweet Tooth. 2015. (ENG., Illus.). 40p. (J). (gr. -1-3). pap. 7.99 (978-1-4521-4556-3(3)) Chronicle Bks. LLC.

Patricelli, Leslie. Bigger! Bigger! Patricelli, Leslie, illus. 2018. (ENG., Illus.). 32p. (J). (-k). 15.99 (978-0-7636-7930-9(5)) Candlewick Pr.

—Binky. Patricelli, Leslie, illus. 2005. (Leslie Patricelli Board Bks.). (ENG., Illus.). 24p. (J). (— 1). bds. 7.99 (978-0-7636-2364-7(4)) Candlewick Pr.

—Blankie. Patricelli, Leslie, illus. 2005. (Leslie Patricelli Board Bks.). (ENG., Illus.). 24p. (J). (— 1). bds. 7.99 (978-0-7636-2363-0(6)) Candlewick Pr.

—Higher! Higher! Patricelli, Leslie, illus. 2010. (Leslie Patricelli Board Bks.). (ENG., Illus.). 30p. (J). (-k). bds. 7.99 (978-0-7636-4433-8(1)) Candlewick Pr.

Patrick, Denise Lewis. MaDear's Old Green House. Sadler, Sonia Lynn, illus. 2004. 32p. (J). (gr. k-3). 16.95 (978-0-940975-55-2(6), Sankofa Bks.) Just Us Bks., Inc.

Patrick, Kat. Doodle Cat Is Bored. Marriott, Lauren, illus. 2017. (Doodle Cat Ser.). 32p. (J). (978-1-925321-88-3(6)) Scribe Pubns. AUS. Dist: Consortium Bk. Sales & Distribution.

Patterson, C. Marie. Little Dinky's Love for Basketball. 2009. 24p. pap. 15.99 (978-1-4415-1255-0(1)) Xlibris Corp.

Patterson, Ellie. Michael Recycle & Bootleg Peg. Colombo, Alexandra, illus. 2014. (Michael Recycle Ser.). 28p. (J). (gr. 1-3). 17.99 (978-1-61377-708-4(6), 9781613777084) Idea & Design Works, LLC.

Patterson, James. The Candies Save Christmas. Elkerton, Andy, illus. 2017. (Candies Ser.). (ENG.). 24p. (J). (gr. -1 — 1). bds. 7.99 (978-0-316-43576-5(7), Jimmy Patterson) Little Brown & Co.

Patterson, Rebecca. Nightbear. 2014. (ENG., Illus.). 32p. (J). (-k). pap. 11.99 (978-1-78008-008-6(5)) Transworld Publishers Ltd. GBR. Dist: Independent Pubs. Group.

Paul, Alison. The Plan. Lehman, Barbara, illus. 2015. (ENG.). 32p. (J). (gr. -1-3). 17.99 (978-0-544-28333-6(3), 1571292, Clarion Bks.) HarperCollins Pubs.

Paul, Ann Whitford. Fiesta Fiasco. Long, Ethan, illus. 2012. pap. 18.95 (978-1-4301-1099-6(6)) Live Oak Media.

Paula, Cristina De. Sweet Pomchu. 2011. 28p. pap. 15.99 (978-1-4568-5816-2(5)) Xlibris Corp.

Pearce, Philippa. Amy's Three Best Things. Craig, Helen, illus. 2013. (ENG.). 40p. (J). (gr. -1-3). 15.99 (978-0-7636-6314-8(X)) Candlewick Pr.

Pearlman, Robb. Pink Is for Boys. Kaban, Eda, illus. 2018. (ENG.). 40p. (J). (gr. -1-3). 18.99 (978-0-7624-6247-6(7), Running Pr. Kids) Running Pr.

Pearse, Asha, illus. Wizard of Oz. 2017. (10 Minute Classics Ser.). (ENG.). 32p. (J). (gr. 1-4). 16.99 (978-1-4867-1221-2(5), 341fccfd-893b-4e64-bc14-77b725bee85d) Flowerpot Pr.

—Wizard of Oz. 2017. (ENG.). 32p. (J). (gr. 1-5). (978-1-4867-1269-4(X)) Flowerpot Children's Pr. Inc.

—Wizard of Oz. 2014. (ENG.). 16p. (J). (gr. -1-4). 7.99 (978-1-4867-0009-7(8)) Flowerpot Children's Pr. Inc. CAN. Dist: Cardinal Pubs. Group.

Pearson, Luke. Hilda & the Stone Forest: Hilda Book 5. 2018. (Hildafolk Ser.: 5). (ENG., Illus.). 64p. (J). (gr. 3-7). pap. 10.99 (978-1-911171-71-3(2)) Flying Eye Bks. GBR. Dist: Penguin Random Hse. LLC.

Pellegrini, Isabelle. Eva from Stockholm. Picard, Charline, illus. 2014. (AV2 Fiction Readalong Ser.: Vol. 125). (ENG.). 32p. (J). (gr. -1-3). lib. bdg. 34.28 (978-1-4896-2265-5(9), AV2 by Weigl) Weigl Pubs., Inc.

Pelley, Kathleen T. & Harper, Ruth E. Happy Mamas. 2016. (ENG., Illus.). 30p. 14.95 (978-1-58760-160-6(5), P544297, CWLA Pr.) Child Welfare League of America, Inc.

Penado, Martha. Eggstinkt. 2008. 32p. pap. 24.95 (978-1-60610-906-9(5)) America Star Bks.

Pendziwol, Jean E. No Dragons for Tea. 2004. (Illus.). (J). (gr. k-3). spiral bd. (978-0-616-01756-2(1)); spiral bd. (978-0-616-01755-5(3)) Canadian National Institute for the Blind/Institut National Canadien pour les Aveugles.

—Once upon a Northern Night, 1 vol. Arsenault, Isabelle, illus. 2013. (ENG.). 36p. (J). (gr. k-2). 17.95 (978-1-55498-138-0(7)) Groundwood Bks. CAN. Dist: Publishers Group West (PGW).

Penn, Mw. Sidney the Silly Who Only Eats 6. Tommer, Sarah, illus. 2013. 36p. pap. 13.95 (978-0-9840425-7-9(1)) MathWord Pr., LLC.

Penna, Natalie. Sooty the Bear: Honey Bees. 2018. (ENG., Illus.). 25p. pap. 14.95 (978-1-78823-719-2(6), 8433f32a-d76d-4edb-b813-e809bc5a01ba) Austin Macauley Pubs. Ltd. GBR. Dist: Baker & Taylor Publisher Services (BTPS).

Penrose, Antony. Miró's Magic Animals. 2016. (ENG., Illus.). 48p. (J). (gr. -1-2). 14.95 (978-0-500-65066-0(7), 565066) Thames & Hudson.

#People Date not set. (I Can Draw Ser.). 32p. (J). 4.98 (978-1-4054-0020-6(X)) Parragon, Inc.

Percival, Tom. Perfectly Norman. 2018. (Big Bright Feelings Ser.). (ENG., Illus.). 32p. (J). 17.99 (978-1-68119-785-2(5),

900186965, Bloomsbury Children's Bks.) Bloomsbury Publishing USA.

Perez-Martinez, Irella. Suyensita & Her Adventures. 2011. 48p. pap. 21.99 *(978-1-4568-5767-7(3))* Xlibris Corp.

Perkins, Myrna. What Makes Honey? Perkins, William C. & Perkins, Lori L., illus. 32p. (Orig.). (J). (gr. -1-3). pap. 3.95 *(978-0-937729-03-8(5))* Markins Enterprises.

Perkins, T. J. Four Little Witches, 1 vol. Pinero, Eimi, illus. 2015. (ENG.). 40p. (J). 12.99 *(978-0-7643-4943-0(0)*, 6691, Red Feather) Schiffer Publishing, Ltd.

Perry, Robert. Down at the Seaweed Cafe. Guzek, Greta, illus. unabr. ed. 2010. (ENG.). 32p. (J). pap. 9.95 *(978-0-88971-246-1(8)*, d81e6a73-3fa8-4ade-abf2-e74b316542bc) Nightwood Editions CAN. Dist: Harbour Publishing Co., Ltd.

—The Ferryboat Ride. Guzek, Greta, illus. 2017. (ENG.). 20p. (J). bds. 9.95 *(978-0-88971-340-6(5)*, 8cdb6fe9-780a-47da-970b-f97975872ddb) Nightwood Editions CAN. Dist: Harbour Publishing Co., Ltd.

Pesenti, Antonia. Rhyme Flies. 2018. (ENG., Illus.). 40p. (gr. -1 — 1). bds. 14.95 *(978-0-7148-7639-9(9))* Phaidon Pr., Inc.

Pessin-Whedbee, Brook. Who Are You? The Kid's Guide to Gender Identity. Bardoff, Naomi, illus. 2016. 40p. (J). 18.95 *(978-1-78592-728-7(0)*, 696300) Kingsley, Jessica Pubs. GBR. Dist: Hachette UK Distribution.

Petek-Markic, Zdenka. Birds. 2012. 52p. pap. 19.97 *(978-1-61897-694-9(X)*, Strategic Bk. Publishing) Strategic Book Publishing & Rights Agency (SBPRA).

Peterson, Mary. Snail Has Lunch. Peterson, Mary, illus. 2016. (Pix Ser.). (ENG., Illus.). 64p. (J). (gr. 1-4). 12.99 *(978-1-4814-5302-8(5)*, Aladdin) Simon & Schuster Children's Publishing.

Petrlik, Andrea, illus. Hansel & Gretel. 2006. (Flip-Up Fairy Tales Ser.). 24p. (J). (gr. 1-2). *(978-1-904550-73-0(8))* Child's Play International Ltd.

—Shoo, Fly! 2008. (J). *(978-0-545-03046-5(3))* Scholastic, Inc.

Petrone, Epp. Anna's Teeth. Maiste, Piia, illus. 2013. 94p. pap. *(978-9949-511-27-3(5))* Petrone Print.

Pfeffer, Wendy. From Seed to Pumpkin. Hale, James Graham, illus. 2015. (Let's-Read-And-Find-Out Science 1 Ser.). (ENG.). 40p. (J). (gr. -1-3). pap. 7.99 *(978-0-06-238185-9(7)*, HarperCollins) HarperCollins Pubs.

—From Tadpole to Frog. Keller, Holly, illus. 2015. (Let's-Read-And-Find-Out Science 1 Ser.). (ENG.). 32p. (J). (gr. -1-3). pap. 6.99 *(978-0-06-238186-6(5)*, HarperCollins) HarperCollins Pubs.

—Light Is All Around Us. Meisel, Paul, illus. (Let's-Read-And-Find-Out Science 2 Ser.). (ENG.). 40p. (J). (gr. -1-3). 2015. pap. 6.99 *(978-0-06-238190-3(3))* 2014. 17.99 *(978-0-06-029121-1(4))* HarperCollins Pubs. (HarperCollins).

—What's It Like to Be a Fish? Keller, Holly, illus. 2015. (Let's-Read-And-Find-Out Science 1 Ser.). (ENG.). 32p. (J). (gr. -1-3). pap. 6.99 *(978-0-06-238199-6(7)*, HarperCollins) HarperCollins Pubs.

Pfister, Marcus. Good Night, Little Rainbow Fish. 2017. (Rainbow Fish Ser.: 1). (ENG., Illus.). 12p. (J). (gr. -1-k). bds. 10.95 *(978-0-7358-4285-4(X))* North-South Bks., Inc.

—Penguin Pete & Pat. 2014. (Penguin Pete Ser.). (ENG., Illus.). 32p. (J). (gr. k-3). 14.95 *(978-0-7358-4155-0(1))* North-South Bks., Inc.

—The Rainbow Fish & the Sea Monsters' Cave. 2015. (Rainbow Fish Ser.). (ENG., Illus.). 32p. (J). pap. 9.95 *(978-3-314-01733-9(2))* North-South Bks., Inc.

—The Rainbow Fish Opposites. 2013. (Rainbow Fish Ser.). (ENG., Illus.). 12p. (J). (gr. -1-1). bds. 7.95 *(978-0-7358-4146-8(2))* North-South Bks., Inc.

—Rainbow Fish to the Rescue! 2015. (Rainbow Fish Ser.). Tr. of Regenbogenfisch, Komm Hilf Mir! (ENG., Illus.). 32p. (J). pap. 10.95 *(978-3-314-01574-8(7))* North-South Bks., Inc.

—You Can't Win Them All, Rainbow Fish. (ENG., Illus.). 32p. (J). (gr. -1-2). 2018. (Rainbow Fish Ser.: 1). pap. 10.95 *(978-0-7358-4305-9(8))* 2017. 18.95 *(978-0-7358-4287-8(6))* North-South Bks., Inc.

Phelps, Piki Nestares. The Art of Falconry. 2009. (ENG.). 34p. pap. 14.99 *(978-1-4415-5421-5(1))* Xlibris Corp.

Phillips, Clifton C. We Are Children of Eden. 2011. 28p. pap. 9.99 *(978-1-61286-010-7(9))* Avid Readers Publishing Group.

Phillips, Gina & Martin, Stuart. Ants & Caterpillars. 2003. (Busy Bugs Ser.). 12p. (J). bds. 14.95 *(978-1-74047-240-1(3))* Book Co. Publishing Pty, Ltd., The AUS. Dist: Penton Overseas, Inc.

Phillips, Jillian. The World Around Us! Hearing. 2010. (Dover Science for Kids Coloring Bks.). (ENG., Illus.). 32p. (J). (gr. k-3). pap. 4.99 *(978-0-486-47730-5(4)*, 477304) Dover Pubns., Inc.

—The World Around Us! Seeing. 2010. (Dover Science for Kids Coloring Bks.). (ENG., Illus.). 32p. (J). (gr. k-3). pap. 4.99 *(978-0-486-47731-2(2)*, 477312) Dover Pubns., Inc.

Phoenix International Staff, illus. Write-and-Erase Look & Find(r) Disney: Packed with 'Find 'Ems & Picture Puzzles! Look, Circle, Wipe Clean, & Play Again! 2014. 20p. (J). bds. *(978-1-4508-8033-6(9)*, 1450880339) Phoenix International Publications, Inc.

PI Kids. Disney Baby: ABCs First Look & Find. The Disney Storybook Art Team, illus. 2017. (ENG.). 16p. (J). bds. 12.99 *(978-1-5037-2177-7(9)*, 2499, PI Kids) Phoenix International Publications, Inc.

—Disney Baby: Head to Toe! Head, Shoulders, Knees & Toes Sound Book. 2017. (ENG., Illus.). 20p. (J). bds. 18.99 *(978-1-5037-2567-6(7)*, 2607, PI Kids) Phoenix International Publications, Inc.

—Disney Pixar Cars 3: Lightning & Friends Sound Book. 2017. (ENG., Illus.). 12p. (J). bds. 14.99 *(978-1-5037-1521-9(3)*, 2308, PI Kids) Phoenix International Publications, Inc.

—Disney Pixar Finding Dory: Going Home Sound Book. The Disney Storybook Art Team, illus. 2016. (ENG.). 12p. (J). bds. 21.99 *(978-1-5037-0940-9(X)*, 2127, PI Kids) Phoenix International Publications, Inc.

—Disney Pixar Incredibles 2: Elastigirl to the Rescue! Sound Book. 2018. (ENG., Illus.). 12p. (J). bds. 14.99 *(978-1-5037-3047-2(6)*, 2733, PI Kids) Phoenix International Publications, Inc.

—Disney Pixar Incredibles 2: Look & Find. 2018. (ENG., Illus.). 24p. (J). 10.99 *(978-1-5037-3044-1(1)*, 2731, PI Kids) Phoenix International Publications, Inc.

—Disney Princess: Storytime with Belle. 2017. (ENG., Illus.). 12p. (J). bds. 21.99 *(978-1-5037-2198-2(1)*, 2505, PI Kids) Phoenix International Publications, Inc.

—Marvel Avengers: Look & Find. Mawhinney, Art, illus. 2018. (ENG.). 24p. (J). 10.99 *(978-1-5037-3405-0(6)*, 2827, PI Kids) Phoenix International Publications, Inc.

—Marvel: Sound Storybook Treasury. 2017. (ENG., Illus.). 34p. (J). 29.99 *(978-1-5037-1386-4(5)*, 2275, PI Kids) Phoenix International Publications, Inc.

—Nickelodeon PAW Patrol: Ready, Set, Rescue! Sound Book. 2018. (ENG., Illus.). 12p. (J). bds. 14.99 *(978-1-5037-3118-9(9)*, 2739, PI Kids) Phoenix International Publications, Inc.

PI Kids. Thomas & Friends: On Time with Thomas. 2016. (ENG., Illus.). 12p. 21.99 *(978-1-5037-1436-6(5)*, 2294, PI Kids) Phoenix International Publications, Inc.

PI Kids. World of Eric Carle: Animals All Around Sound Book. 2017. (ENG., Illus.). 12p. (J). bds. 21.99 *(978-1-5037-2204-0(X)*, 2508, PI Kids) Phoenix International Publications, Inc.

Pichon, Liz. Bored Bill. Pichon, Liz, illus. 2006. (Illus.). 32p. (J). (gr. -1-3). 15.95 *(978-1-58925-053-6(2))* Tiger Tales.

Picthall, Chez. Baby Animals. 2015. (Illus.). 10p. (J). bds. 7.99 *(978-1-906572-07-5(0))* Award Pubns. Ltd. GBR. Dist: Parkwest Pubns., Inc.

—Bedtime. Hewett, Angela, illus. 2015. 10p. (J). bds. 11.99 *(978-1-909763-43-2(8))* Award Pubns. Ltd. GBR. Dist: Parkwest Pubns., Inc.

—Flip Flaps Zoo. 2015. (Illus.). 18p. (J). bds. 9.99 *(978-1-907604-53-9(7))* Award Pubns. Ltd. GBR. Dist: Parkwest Pubns., Inc.

—My Top 100 Racers. 2015. (ENG., Illus.). 12p. (J). pap. 7.99 *(978-1-907604-80-5(4))* Award Pubns. Ltd. GBR. Dist: Parkwest Pubns., Inc.

Picthall, Chez, creator. Flip Flaps Shapes. 2014. (ENG., Illus.). 32p. 10.00 *(978-1-906572-80-8(1))* Award Pubns. Ltd. GBR. Dist: Parkwest Pubns., Inc.

Picthall, Chez, des. Flowers. 2015. (Illus.). 10p. (J). bds. 9.99 *(978-1-907604-76-8(6))* Award Pubns. Ltd. GBR. Dist: Parkwest Pubns., Inc.

—Spots & Dots. 2015. (Illus.). 10p. (J). bds. 9.99 *(978-1-909763-02-9(0))* Award Pubns. Ltd. GBR. Dist: Parkwest Pubns., Inc.

Picture, Play & Tote Counter Display. (J). *(978-1-57151-726-5(X))* Playhouse Publishing.

Piers, Helen. Long Neck & Thunder Foot. Foreman, Michael, illus. 2013. (ENG.). 32p. (J). (gr. -1-k). pap. 8.99 *(978-1-84939-482-6(2))* Andersen Pr. GBR. Dist: Independent Pubs. Group.

Pilkey, Dav. Dragon's Merry Christmas: an Acorn Book (Dragon #5) Pilkey, Dav, illus. 2020. (Dragon Ser.: 5). (ENG., Illus.). 64p. (J). (gr. k-2). pap. 4.99 *(978-1-338-34752-4(7))* Scholastic, Inc.

—The Paperboy. 2015. 32p. pap. 7.00 *(978-1-61003-556-9(9))* Center for the Collaborative Classroom.

Pinder, Eric. Cat in the Clouds. 2017. (ENG., Illus.). 32p. (J). (gr. 1-3). 29.99 *(978-1-4671-3848-2(7)*, History Pr., The) Arcadia Publishing.

Pinfold, Levi. Black Dog. Pinfold, Levi, illus. 2012. (ENG., Illus.). 32p. (J). (gr. -1-3). 17.99 *(978-0-7636-6097-0(3)*, Templar) Candlewick Pr.

Pinkwater, Daniel M. Four Different Stories. 2018. (ENG.). 240p. (gr. 3-9). pap. 16.95 *(978-0-486-82260-0(5)*, 822605) Dover Pubns., Inc.

Pinky & the Brain. (Look & Find Bks.). (Illus.). 24p. (J). (gr. k-5). 7.98 *(978-0-7853-1607-7(8)*, PI11) Publications International, Ltd.

Piper, Sophie. The Angel & the Dove: A Story for Easter, 1 vol. Stephenson, Kristina, illus. 2010. 32p. (J). 12.99 *(978-0-8254-7897-0(9)*, Lion Children's) Lion Hudson PLC GBR. Dist: Kregel Pubns.

Piper, Watty. The Little Engine That Could. Hauman, George and Doris, illus. 2015. (Little Engine That Could Ser.). 26p. (J). (gr. -1 — 1). bds. 11.99 *(978-0-448-48731-1(4)*, Grosset & Dunlap) Penguin Young Readers Group.

Pippin-Mathur, Courtney. Dragons Rule, Princesses Drool! Pippin-Mathur, Courtney, illus. 2017. (ENG., Illus.). 40p. (J). (gr. -1-3). 17.99 *(978-1-4814-6138-2(9)*, Little Simon) Little Simon.

Pirc, Jerri J. Kate & Caboodle. Smith, Janie, illus. 2015. pap. *(978-0-473-32583-1(7))* Pirc, Jerri J.

Pirotta, Saviour. Puss in Boots. Newson, Karl, illus. 2017. (Once upon a Time ... Ser.). (ENG.). 24p. (J). (gr. -1-k). lib. bdg. 19.99 *(978-1-68297-171-0(6)*, 7efd6415-b533-4b0d-88bd-cefd0a7956a9) QEB Publishing Inc.

Pittar, Gill. Milly, Molly & Alf. 2005. 28p. *(978-1-86972-018-6(0))* Milly Molly Bks.

—Milly, Molly & Aunt Maude. 2004. 28p. *(978-1-86972-014-8(8))* Milly Molly Bks.

—Milly, Molly & Different Dads. 2004. 28p. *(978-1-86972-019-3(9))* Milly Molly Bks.

—Milly, Molly & Sock Heaven. 2004. 28p. *(978-1-86972-015-5(6))* Milly Molly Bks.

—Milly, Molly & Special Friends. 2004. 28p. *(978-1-86972-017-9(2))* Milly Molly Bks.

Piven, Hanoch. My Dog Is As Smelly As Dirty Socks: And Other Funny Family Portraits. Piven, Hanoch, illus. 2012. (Illus.). 40p. (J). (gr. -1-3). pap. 8.99 *(978-0-307-93089-7(0)*, Dragonfly Bks.) Random Hse. Children's Bks.

Platt, Christine. Summer in Savannah. 2019. (Ana & Andrew Ser.). (ENG., Illus.). 32p. (J). (gr. 2-2). pap. 9.95 *(978-1-64494-258-1(5)*, 1644942585, Calico Kid) ABDO Publishing Co.

Platt, Richard & Biesty, Stephen. Man-of-War. (Illus.). (J). pap. 21.95 *(978-0-590-74610-6(3))* Scholastic, Inc.

Podd, Gloria. A Royal Runt. 2013. 20p. pap. 24.95 *(978-1-63004-012-3(6))* America Star Bks.

Poelman, Heidi. Courageous People Who Changed the World, Volume 1. Kershner, Kyle, illus. 2018. (People Who Changed the World Ser.: 1). (ENG.). 16p. (J). (gr. -1-k). bds. 9.99 *(978-1-945547-75-1(8)*, 554775) Familius LLC.

—Inventors Who Changed the World. Kershner, Kyle, illus. 2018. (People Who Changed the World Ser.). (ENG.). 20p. (J). (gr. -1-3). bds. 9.99 *(978-1-64170-035-1(1)*, 550035) Familius LLC.

Poison Patrol: Picture Book 8x8. 2007. (J). 5.99 *(978-1-933934-40-2(9))* Mighty Kids Media.

Poison Patrol: Picture Book (English) 9x9 with Snipe. 2007. (J). 5.99 *(978-1-933934-50-1(6))* Mighty Kids Media.

Pollard, Mary Jean. Octrina the Octopus. 2011. 28p. pap. 15.99 *(978-1-4568-4778-4(3))* Xlibris Corp.

Ponti, Claude. En El Coche. 2003. (SPA.). 32p. 15.95 *(978-84-95150-08-0(5))* Corimbo, Editorial S.L. ESP. Dist: Distribooks, Inc.

—Hiznobyuti. Waters, Alyson, tr. Ponti, Claude, illus. 2018. (Illus.). 35p. (J). (gr. k-4). 18.00 *(978-0-914671-90-9(1)*, Elsewhere Editions) Steerforth Pr.

Ponzi, Emiliano. The Journey of the Penguin. 2015. (Illus.). 96p. (gr. 2-12). 18.00 *(978-0-14-310785-9(2)*, Penguin Bks.) Penguin Publishing Group.

Poole, Susie. A Christmas Journey. Poole, Susie, illus. 2014. (ENG., Illus.). 48p. (gr. -1-3). 12.99 *(978-1-4336-8343-5(1)*, 005617204, B&H Kids) B&H Publishing Group.

Popper, Garry. Ali in Egypt. Johnson, Andi, illus. 2004. 36p. (gr. -1-7). 4.00 *(978-1-84161-078-8(X))* Ravette Publishing, Ltd. GBR. Dist: Parkwest Pubns., Inc.

—Billy Joe in the U. S. A. Johnson, Andi, illus. 2004. 36p. (gr. -1-7). 4.00 *(978-1-84161-053-5(4))* Ravette Publishing, Ltd. GBR. Dist: Parkwest Pubns., Inc.

—James & Jemma in Great Britain. Johnson, Andi, illus. 2004. 36p. (gr. -1-7). 4.00 *(978-1-84161-054-2(2))* Ravette Publishing, Ltd. GBR. Dist: Parkwest Pubns., Inc.

—Keito in Japan. Johnson, Andi, illus. 2004. 36p. (gr. -1-7). 4.00 *(978-1-84161-058-0(5))* Ravette Publishing, Ltd. GBR. Dist: Parkwest Pubns., Inc.

—Kez in Australia. Johnson, Andi, illus. 2004. 36p. (gr. -1-7). 4.00 *(978-1-84161-055-9(0))* Ravette Publishing, Ltd. GBR. Dist: Parkwest Pubns., Inc.

—Lena & Peter in Germany. Johnson, Andi, illus. 2004. 36p. (gr. -1-7). 4.00 *(978-1-84161-060-3(7))* Ravette Publishing, Ltd. GBR. Dist: Parkwest Pubns., Inc.

—Li & Lilly May in China. Johnson, Andi, illus. 2004. 36p. (gr. -1-7). 4.00 *(978-1-84161-057-3(7))* Ravette Publishing, Ltd. GBR. Dist: Parkwest Pubns., Inc.

—Mario in Italy. Johnson, Andi, illus. 2004. 36p. (gr. -1-7). 4.00 *(978-1-84161-059-7(3))* Ravette Publishing, Ltd. GBR. Dist: Parkwest Pubns., Inc.

—Mina in India. Johnson, Andi, illus. 2004. 36p. (gr. -1-7). 4.00 *(978-1-84161-079-5(8))* Ravette Publishing, Ltd. GBR. Dist: Parkwest Pubns., Inc.

—Paul in France. Johnson, Andi, illus. 2004. 36p. (gr. -1-7). 4.00 *(978-1-84161-056-6(9))* Ravette Publishing, Ltd. GBR. Dist: Parkwest Pubns., Inc.

popular, Cancionero. Juguemos en el bosque. 2004. (SPA., Illus.). 28p. (J). (gr. k-18). pap. 6.50 *(978-980-257-282-3(9))* Ekare, Ediciones VEN. Dist: Iaconi, Mariuccia Bk. Imports.

Posada, Jorge. Sí, Puedes (Play Ball!) ón, Raúl, illus. 2010. (SPA.). 32p. (J). (gr. 1-5). 8.99 *(978-1-4169-9826-6(8)*, Simon & Schuster/Paula Wiseman Bks.) Simon & Schuster/Paula Wiseman Bks.

Posner-Sanchez, Andrea. Meet Maui (Disney Moana) The Disney Storybook Art Team, illus. 2017. (Pictureback(R) Ser.). (ENG.). 24p. (J). (gr. -1-2). pap. 4.99 *(978-0-7364-3738-7(X)*, RH/Disney) Random Hse. Children's Bks.

Potter, Beatrix. The Tale of Peter Rabbit. 2013. (Children's Classics Ser.). (ENG., Illus.). 46p. pap. 9.99 *(978-1-909676-49-7(7)*, Sovereign) Bollinger, Max GBR. Dist: Lightning Source UK, Ltd.

—The Tale of Peter Rabbit, 5 vols. 110th ed. 2012. (Peter Rabbit Ser.). (ENG., Illus.). 72p. (J). (gr. -1-2). 8.99 *(978-0-7232-6769-0(3)*, Warne) Penguin Young Readers Group.

—The Tale of Squirrel Nutkin. 2013. (Children's Classics Ser.). (ENG., Illus.). 46p. pap. 9.99 *(978-1-909676-06-0(3)*, Sovereign) Bollinger, Max GBR. Dist: Lightning Source UK, Ltd.

Potter, Giselle. Tell Me What to Dream About. Potter, Giselle, illus. 2015. (Illus.). 40p. (J). (gr. -1-2). 17.99 *(978-0-385-37423-1(2)*, Schwartz & Wade Bks.) Random Hse. Children's Bks.

Powell, Amy. Hope Music. Farley, Katherine, illus. 2006. 32p. (J). (gr. -1-3). per. 12.00 *(978-0-9773608-4-0(9))* Shiny Red Ball Publishing.

Prasadam-Halls, Smriti. Kiss It Better. Massini, Sarah, illus. 2017. (ENG.). 26p. (J). bds. 7.99 *(978-1-68119-164-5(4)*, 900161040, Bloomsbury USA Childrens) Bloomsbury Publishing USA.

Pratt, Pierre. Marcel et Andre. 2003. (Picture Bks.). (FRE., Illus.). 32p. (J). (gr. -1). *(978-2-89021-633-4(0))* Diffusion du livre Mirabel (DLM).

Preston-Gannon, Frann. Deep Deep Sea. 2014. (ENG., Illus.). 14p. (J). (-k). bds. 7.99 *(978-1-84365-268-7(4)*, Pavilion Children's Books) Pavilion Bks. GBR. Dist: HarperCollins Pubs.

—Sloth Slept On. 2019. (ENG.). 30p. (J). (gr. -1). bds. 7.95 *(978-1-4549-3449-3(2))* Sterling Publishing Co., Inc.

Price, Jesse. Dad. 2008. 28p. pap. 15.99 *(978-1-4363-1489-3(5))* Xlibris Corp.

Price, M. J. Momot. Grandma & Grandpa Are Retiring. 2013. 32p. pap. 24.95 *(978-1-63000-966-3(0))* America Star Bks.

Priddy Books Staff. Kids Can Time. 2003. (J). bds. *(978-0-312-49171-0(9)*, Priddy Bks.) St. Martin's Pr.

Priddy, Roger. Bright Baby Touch & Feel Easter. 2012. (Bright Baby Touch & Feel Ser.). (ENG., Illus.). 10p. (J). (gr. -1 — 1). bds. 4.95 *(978-0-312-51375-7(5)*, 900082318) St. Martin's Pr.

—Changing Picture Book: Dinosaur Galore! 2018. (Changing Picture Ser.). (ENG., Illus.). 10p. (J). bds. 9.99 *(978-0-312-52658-0(X)*, 900185564) St. Martin's Pr.

—Lift-The-Flap Tab: on the Go. 2014. (Lift-The-Flap Tab Bks.). (ENG., Illus.). 16p. (J). (gr. -1 — 1). bds. 8.99 *(978-0-312-51731-1(9)*, 900132617) St. Martin's Pr.

—Little Friends: All You Need Is Love: A Lift the Flaps Book. 2017. (Little Friends Ser.). (ENG., Illus.). 10p. (J). bds. 8.99 *(978-0-312-52147-9(2)*, 900178605) St. Martin's Pr.

—My Big Seek-And-Find Book: With Wipe-Clean Pen! 2018. (Seek-And-Find Ser.). (ENG., Illus.). 56p. (J). spiral bd. 12.99 *(978-0-312-52224-7(X)*, 900175689) St. Martin's Pr.

—Wipe Clean: Pen Control. 2012. (Wipe Clean Learning Bks.). (ENG., Illus.). 26p. (J). (gr. -1-1). bds. 8.95 *(978-0-312-51395-5(X)*, 900082334) St. Martin's Pr.

The Princess & the Magic Locket. (My Tooth Is Loose!). (Illus.). 32p. (J). *(978-1-4054-1022-9(1))* Parragon, Inc.

Pringle, Laurence. Octopuses! Strange & Wonderful. Henderson, Meryl Learnihan, illus. 2015. (Strange & Wonderful Ser.). (ENG.). 32p. (J). (gr. 2-5). 17.99 *(978-1-59078-928-5(8)*, Astra Young Readers) Astra Publishing Hse.

Pritchard, Gabby. Omar in Trouble Orange Band. Pérez, Moni, illus. 2016. (Cambridge Reading Adventures Ser.). (ENG.). 16p. pap. 7.95 *(978-1-316-50329-4(1))* Cambridge Univ. Pr.

Prokofiev, Sergei. Sergei Prokofiev's Peter & the Wolf: With a Fully-Orchestrated & Narrated CD. Malone, Peter, illus. 2004. (ENG.). 40p. (J). (gr. -1-2). 19.99 *(978-0-375-82430-2(8)*, Knopf Bks. for Young Readers) Random Hse. Children's Bks.

Propes, Chrysti Carol. I Am Here. Bostrom, Laura, illus. 3rd ed. 2013. 32p. 24.95 *(978-0-9790791-9-1(5))* Fig & The Vine, LLC, The.

Publications International Ltd. Staff. My 1St Libraries Winnie the Pooh. 2011. 10p. (J). bds. 13.98 *(978-1-4508-0870-5(0))* Phoenix International Publications, Inc.

Publications International Ltd. Staff, ed. Disney Pixar Picture Puzzle. 2010. 128p. (J). spiral bd. 12.98 *(978-1-60553-132-8(4))* Phoenix International Publications, Inc.

—Disney Princess Picture Puzzles. 2010. 128p. (J). pap. 13.98 *(978-1-60553-131-1(6))* Phoenix International Publications, Inc.

—I Can Be a Princess: Picture Book. 2014. 22p. (J). bds. 4.98 *(978-1-4508-8582-9(9)*, 1450885829) Publications International, Ltd.

—Look & Find - Captain America: The First Avenger. 2011. 24p. (J). 3.75 net. *(978-1-4508-1877-3(3))* Phoenix International Publications, Inc.

—Mickey Mouse Clubhouse. 2010. 128p. (J). pap. 12.98 *(978-1-60553-129-8(4)*, PIL Kids) Publications International, Ltd.

Puchner, Willy. ABC of Fantastic Princess. 2015. (ENG., Illus.). 64p. (J). (gr. -1-2). 19.95 *(978-0-7358-4198-7(5))* North-South Bks., Inc.

Puck. Babies Around the World: A Board Book about Diversity That Takes Tots on a Fun Trip Around the World from Morning to Night. Lemay, Violet, illus. 2017. (Babies Around the World Ser.). 20p. (J). (gr. -1 — 1). bds. 7.95 *(978-1-938093-87-6(9)*, 809387) Duo Pr. LLC.

—Bookstore Babies. Lemay, Violet, illus. 2019. 22p. (J). bds. 7.95 *(978-1-947458-50-5(7)*, 805850) Duo Pr. LLC.

—One to Ten L. A. 2016. (ENG., Illus.). 22p. (J). (gr. k-k). bds. 9.95 *(978-1-938093-49-4(6)*, 809349) Duo Pr. LLC.

Puck & Stollberg, Jon. Totally Epic, True & Wacky Soccer Facts & Stories. 2017. (Illus.). 156p. (J). (gr. 3-7). pap. 12.95 *(978-1-938093-81-4(X))* Duo Pr. LLC.

Pugsley, Kate. Mermaid Dreams. 2019. (Illus.). 32p. (J). (gr. -1-2). 17.99 *(978-0-7352-6491-5(0)*, Tundra Bks.) Tundra Bks. CAN. Dist: Penguin Random Hse. LLC.

Pulley, Kelly. The Cycling Wangdoos. Pulley, Kelly, illus. 2011. (Illus.). 32p. (J). (gr. -1-3). 16.95 *(978-0-9820812-1-1(9)*, Frog Legs Ink) Gauthier Pubns. Inc.

—The Cycling Wangdoos, 1 vol. 2017. (ENG., Illus.). 32p. (J). 16.99 *(978-0-7643-5406-9(X)*, 7845) Schiffer Publishing, Ltd.

Punter, Russell. Flamingo Plays Bingo. 2019. (Phonics Readers Ser.). (ENG.). 24ppp. (J). pap. 6.99 *(978-0-7945-4396-9(0)*, Usborne) EDC Publishing.

—Kitty Kat, Kitty Kat Where Have You Been - London. 2018. (Picture Bks.). (ENG.). 24p. (J). 9.99 *(978-0-7945-3970-2(X)*, Usborne) EDC Publishing.

—Pirate Stories for Little Children. 2015. (Stories for Little Children Gift Bks.). (ENG.). 176p. (J). 19.99 *(978-0-7945-2260-5(2)*, Usborne) EDC Publishing.

Purcell, Susan. Letters, 1 vol. 2018. (My Book Of Ser.). (ENG.). 24p. (gr. k-1). 26.27 *(978-1-5081-9599-3(4)*, 5333a151-c9bc-4135-93ad-9bb05e45bfc7, Windmill Bks.) Rosen Publishing Group, Inc., The.

—Words, 1 vol. 2018. (My Book Of Ser.). (ENG.). 24p. (gr. k-1). 26.27 *(978-1-5081-9655-6(9)*, 809c7c4b-3bab-4f2a-ad2f-176f664fe929, Windmill Bks.) Rosen Publishing Group, Inc., The.

Quansah, Carol-Ann. The Garden. 2010. 40p. pap. 22.65 *(978-1-4535-1345-3(0))* Xlibris Corp.

Quattlebaum, Mary. Jo MacDonald Had a Garden. Bryant, Laura J., illus. 2013. 26p. (J). (gr. -1-3). bds. 7.95 *(978-1-58469-225-6(1)*, Dawn Pubns.) Sourcebooks, Inc.

—Jo MacDonald Saw a Pond. Bryant, Laura J., illus. 2013. 26p. (J). (gr. -1 — 1). bds. 7.95 *(978-1-58469-224-9(3)*, Dawn Pubns.) Sourcebooks, Inc.

Quayle, Susan. Mouse's Best Day Ever: Children's Reflexology to Soothe Sore Teeth & Tums. Muldoon, Melissa, illus. 2016. 44p. 18.95 *(978-1-84819-315-4(7)*, 694042, Singing Dragon) Kingsley, Jessica Pubs. GBR. Dist: Hachette UK Distribution.

Quinlan, Patricia. Tiger Flowers, 1 vol. Wilson, Janet, illus. 2005. (ENG.). 32p. (J). (gr. -1-1). per. 6.95 *(978-1-55005-139-1(3)*, 31efd12b-4515-439e-a8a0-35d9d702d286) Trifolium Bks., Inc. CAN. Dist: Firefly Bks., Ltd.

Quinn, Jason. The Beautiful Game: Survival. Sharma, Lalit Kumar, illus. 2017. (Campfire Graphic Novels Ser.: 9). 160p. (J). (gr. 5). pap. 12.99 *(978-93-81182-11-6(6)*, Campfire) Steerforth Pr.

Rabe, Tish. I Love You, Grandma! Hitch, David, illus. 2016. (Little Golden Book Ser.). 24p. (J). (-k). 5.99 *(978-1-101-93455-5(7)*, Golden Bks.) Random Hse. Children's Bks.

Rabei, Carolina. Crunch! Rabei, Carolina, illus. 2016. (Child's Play Library). (Illus.). 36p. (J). pap. *(978-1-84643-732-8(6))* Child's Play International Ltd.

Rabouin, Rochelle. Shapes Friends. 2009. (ENG.). 52p. 24.99 *(978-1-4363-8329-5(3))*; pap. 15.99 *(978-1-4363-8328-8(5))* Xlibris Corp.

Raczka, Bob. Beware! Day, Larry, illus. 2019. 32p. (J). (gr. -1-2). lib. bdg. 15.99 *(978-1-58089-683-2(9))* Charlesbridge Publishing, Inc.

Radford, James & Wooders, Dave. Adventures on the Queen Mary: ... tales of a Teenage Crew Member! 2015. (ENG., Illus.). 274p. pap. 25.00 *(978-0-692-54554-6(9))* Perfect Page, The.

Radford, Sheri. Penelope & the Humongous Burp. Lt. ed. 2012. 64p. (J). pap. *(978-1-4596-3451-0(9))* ReadHowYouWant.com, Ltd.

Radford, Tracey. Brian the Lion Goes into Space. 2018. (ENG., Illus.). 32p. (J). 16.95 *(978-1-78249-576-5(2)*, 1782495762, CICO Books) Ryland Peters & Small GBR. Dist: WIPRO.

Raeside, Adrian. The Rainbow Bridge: A Visit to Pet Paradise. 2012. (Illus.). 32p. (J). *(978-1-55017-584-4(X)*, 7ef54ede-1b36-4e71-80d3-cb552e04a644) Harbour Publishing Co., Ltd.

Rahim, Yasmeen. Hassan & Aneesa Celebrate Eid. Burgess, Omar, illus. 2018. 24p. (J). pap. 5.99 *(978-0-86037-698-9(2))* Kube Publishing Ltd. GBR. Dist: Consortium Bk. Sales & Distribution.

—Hassan & Aneesa Go to Madrasa. Burgess, Omar, illus. 2016. (Hassan & Aneesa Ser.). (ENG.). 16p. (J). pap. 5.99 *(978-0-86037-459-6(9))* Kube Publishing Ltd. GBR. Dist: Consortium Bk. Sales & Distribution.

—Hassan & Aneesa Go to Masjid. Burgess, Omar, illus. 2016. (Hassan & Aneesa Ser.). 28p. (J). pap. 5.99 *(978-0-86037-521-0(8))* Kube Publishing Ltd. GBR. Dist: Consortium Bk. Sales & Distribution.

Rainville, Doris L., creator. The Girl Who Never Let Her Mother Brush Her Hair. Lt. ed. 2003. (Illus.). 24p. (J). per. 7.95 *(978-0-9744879-0-8(2))* Magical Creations.

—The Power of Love. Lt. ed. 2003. (Illus.). 24p. (J). per. 7.95 *(978-0-9744879-1-5(0))* Magical Creations.

Raisinghani, Jaya. I Will Always Know. 2013. 16p. pap. 17.00 *(978-1-4669-3491-7(3))* Trafford Publishing.

Raisner Glass, Beth. Blue-Ribbon Dad. Moore, Margie, illus. 2011. (ENG.). 32p. (J). (gr. k-2). 15.95 *(978-0-8109-9727-1(4)*, 674101, Abrams Bks. for Young Readers) Abrams, Inc.

Rajan, Lisa. Tara Binns: Big Idea Engineer: Band 14/Ruby (Collins Big Cat) 2019. (Collins Big Cat Tara Binns Ser.). (ENG., Illus.). 48p. (J). (gr. 3-4). 10.99 *(978-0-00-830658-8(3))* HarperCollins Pubs. Ltd. GBR. Dist: Independent Pubs. Group.

Ramsay, Betsy. Cecil Centipede's Career. Christman, Therese, illus. 2005. 25p. (J). per. 19.99 *(978-1-4208-7870-7(0))* AuthorHouse.

Randall, Emma, illus. Over the River & Through the Wood. 2018. 32p. (J). (gr. -1-2). 17.99 *(978-0-515-15765-9(1)*, Penguin Workshop) Penguin Young Readers Group.

—The Twelve Days of Christmas. 2017. 32p. (J). (gr. -1-2). 16.99 *(978-0-515-15763-5(5)*, Penguin Workshop) Penguin Young Readers Group.

Randall, Ronne. The Little Red Hen. 2015. (First Favourite Tales Ser.). (Illus.). 32p. (J). (-k). 8.99 *(978-1-4093-0958-1(4))* Penguin Bks., Ltd. GBR. Dist: Independent Pubs. Group.

Random House. Pokémon Storybook Treasury (Pokémon) Random House, illus. 2018. (ENG., Illus.). 96p. (J). (gr. -1-2). 9.99 *(978-1-5247-7259-8(3)*, Random Hse. Bks. for Young Readers) Random Hse. Children's Bks.

—Sea Patrol to the Rescue! (PAW Patrol) Lovett, Nate, illus. 2018. (Pictureback(R) Ser.). (ENG.). 24p. (J). (gr. -1-2). pap. 5.99 *(978-1-5247-6875-1(8)*, Random Hse. Bks. for Young Readers) Random Hse. Children's Bks.

—Spring Is Everywhere! (Nickelodeon) Random House, illus. 2017. (ENG., Illus.). 96p. (J). (gr. -1-2). 9.99 *(978-1-5247-0067-6(3)*, Random Hse. Bks. for Young Readers) Random Hse. Children's Bks.

—You Can Be a Soccer Player (Barbie) 2018. (Step into Reading Ser.). (ENG., Illus.). 24p. (J). (gr. -1-1). pap. 5.99 *(978-1-5247-6911-6(8)*, Random Hse. Bks. for Young Readers) Random Hse. Children's Bks.

Random House Staff. Meet the Wish Sitters! (Maryoku Yummy) Random House Staff, illus. 2011. (Pictureback Favorites Ser.). (ENG., Illus.). 16p. (J). (gr. -1-1). 16.19 *(978-0-375-87125-2(X))* Random House Publishing Group.

Rankin, Heather & Rankin, Heather. All It Takes Is One Friend. 2012. 46p. pap. *(978-0-9878945-0-2(1))* Our Farm Bks.

Rankin, Joan & Hartmann, Wendy. The African Orchestra. 2019. (ENG., Illus.). 32p. (J). (gr. 1-2). pap. 8.95 *(978-1-56656-025-2(X)*, Crocodile Bks.) Interlink Publishing Group, Inc.

Ransom, Jeanie Franz. What Really Happened to Humpty? Axelsen, Stephen, illus. 2010. (Nursery-Rhyme Mysteries Ser.: 1). (ENG.). 40p. (J). (gr. 1-4). pap. 7.95 *(978-1-58089-391-6(0))* Charlesbridge Publishing, Inc.

Rapkin, Mickey. It's Not a Bed, It's a Time Machine. Martinez, Teresa, illus. 2019. (It's Not a Book Series, It's an Adventure Ser.). (ENG.). 32p. (J). 17.99 *(978-1-250-16762-0(0)*, 900187570) Imprint IND. Dist: Macmillan.

Raschka, Chris. New Shoes. 2018. (ENG., Illus.). 32p. (J). (gr. -1-3). 17.99 *(978-0-06-265752-7(6)*, Greenwillow Bks.) HarperCollins Pubs.

Rassi, Lee. Capital Heroes. 2008. (Illus.). 56p. pap. 23.99 *(978-1-4343-8208-5(7))* AuthorHouse.

Ray, Cindy & Kids Write On, creators. The Stapler Caper: You Write the Story. 2008. (ENG., Illus.). 28p. (J). 16.95 *(978-0-615-23574-5(3))* Kids Write On, LLC.

Ray, Jane. Cinderella. Ray, Jane, illus. 2012. (ENG., Illus.). 12p. (J). (gr. k-4). 19.99 *(978-0-7636-6175-5(9))* Candlewick Pr.

Ray, Mary Lyn. Go to Sleep, Little Farm Padded Board Book. Neal, Christopher Silas, illus. 2015. (ENG.). 38p. (J). (— 1). bds. 8.99 *(978-0-544-57916-3(X)*, 1613308, Clarion Bks.) HarperCollins Pubs.

—Goodnight, Good Dog Padded Board Book. Malone, Rebecca, illus. 2018. (ENG.). 30p. (J). (— 1). bds. 8.99 *(978-1-328-85242-7(3)*, 1694366, Clarion Bks.) HarperCollins Pubs.

Read-It! Readers - Gus the Hedgehog. 2005. (Read-It! Readers: Gus the Hedgehog Ser.). (ENG., Illus.). 32p. (gr. k-3). 79.96 *(978-1-4048-0995-6(3)*, Picture Window Bks.) Capstone.

Read It! Readers: Folk Tales, 6 vols. 2005. (Read-It! Readers: Folk Tales Ser.). (ENG., Illus.). 32p. (gr. k-3). 59.97 *(978-1-4048-0999-4(6)*, Picture Window Bks.) Capstone.

Reader, Gwendolin. The Life Cycle of A Snowman. 2010. 24p. pap. 12.50 *(978-1-4520-7686-7(3))* AuthorHouse.

Reagan, Jean. How to Surprise a Dad: A Book for Dads & Kids. Wildish, Lee, illus. 2019. (How to Ser.). (ENG.). 26p. (J). (— 1). bds. 8.99 *(978-1-9848-4959-5(X)*, Knopf Bks. for Young Readers) Random Hse. Children's Bks.

Recob, Amy. The BugaBees: Friends with Food Allergies. 2009. (Illus.). 32p. (J). *(978-1-59298-279-0(4))* Beaver's Pond Pr., Inc.

Redford, Alison. The Boy Who Built a Wall Around Himself. Simpson, Kara, illus. 2015. 32p. (J). 17.95 *(978-1-84905-683-0(8)*, 693905) Kingsley, Jessica Pubs. GBR. Dist: Hachette UK Distribution.

Reece, Colleen L. & DeMarco, Julie Reece. God Loves You Whoever You Are. Snider, K. C., illus. 2011. 20p. pap. 10.95 *(978-1-61633-183-2(6))* Guardian Angel Publishing, Inc.

Reed, Liz & Reed, Jimmy. Sweet Success. Reed, Liz & Reed, Jimmy, illus. 2018. (ENG., Illus.). 40p. (J). (gr. -1-3). 17.99 *(978-0-06-240360-5(5)*, HarperCollins) HarperCollins Pubs.

Reed, Lynn Rowe. Benny Shark Goes to Friend School. Montijo, Rhode, illus. 2017. (ENG.). 32p. (J). (gr. -1-2). 17.99 *(978-1-4778-2803-8(6)*, 9781477828038, Two Lions) Amazon Publishing.

Rees, Guy Parker. Tom & Millie: Whizzy Busy People. 2014. (ENG., Illus.). 32p. (J). (gr. -1-k). pap. 10.99 *(978-1-4083-1552-1(1))* Hodder & Stoughton GBR. Dist: Hachette Bk. Group.

Regan, Dian Curtis. Space Boy & His Dog. Neubecker, Robert, illus. 2015. (Space Boy Ser.). (ENG.). 32p. (J). (gr. -1-2). 16.95 *(978-1-59078-955-1(5)*, Astra Young Readers) Astra Publishing Hse.

Regan, Patrick. The Nutcracker. Kuricheva, Natasha, illus. 2016. (ENG.). 26p. (J). bds. 9.99 *(978-1-4494-5586-6(7))* Andrews McMeel Publishing.

Reich, J. J. Deer Dad: Kampp Tales Outdoor Adventures. Johnathan, Kuehl, illus. 2006. (BAT.). 32p. (J). *(978-0-9762971-0-9(8))* Outdoor Originals LLC.

Reid, Camilla. Lulu Loves Numbers. Busby, Ailie, illus. 2015. (ENG.). 12p. (J). (gr. -1-1). bds. 8.99 *(978-1-4088-4957-6(7)*, 900143539, Bloomsbury Children's Bks.) Bloomsbury Publishing USA.

—Lulu Loves Nursery. Busby, Ailie, illus. 2013. (Lulu Ser.). (ENG.). 32p. (J). (gr. -1-k). pap. *(978-1-4088-2819-9(7)*, 142106, Bloomsbury Children's Bks.) Bloomsbury Publishing Plc.

—Lulu Loves Shapes. Busby, Ailie, illus. 2015. (Lulu Ser.). (ENG.). 12p. (J). (gr. -1-1). bds. *(978-1-4088-4958-3(5)*, 233927, Bloomsbury Children's Bks.) Bloomsbury Publishing Plc.

Reidy, Jean. Pup 681: A Sea Otter Rescue Story. Crowley, Ashley, illus. 2019. (ENG.). 40p. (J). 17.99 *(978-1-250-11450-1(0)*, 900171459, Holt, Henry & Co. Bks. For Young Readers) Holt, Henry & Co.

Reilly, Michael. Monster Sandwich. 2009. 50p. (J). pap. 31.99 *(978-1-4415-0056-4(1))* Xlibris Corp.

Renauld, Laura. Porcupine's Pie. Poh, Jennie, illus. 2018. (Woodland Friends Ser.). 32p. (J). 16.99 *(978-1-5064-3180-2(1)*, Beaming Books) 1517 Media.

Rennocks, Sam. Under the Sea ABC. 2018. (Padded Board Bks.). (ENG., Illus.). 28p. (J). (gr. -1-k). bds. 9.99 *(978-1-78700-452-8(X))* Top That! Publishing PLC GBR. Dist: Independent Pubs. Group.

Renyi Bilingual Picture Dictionaries, 12 vols., Set. Date not set. (Illus.). 2304p. 244.40 *(978-1-55674-937-4(9))* Forest Hse. Publishing Co., Inc.

Revenge of the Tune Squad. Date not set. (Space Jam Eye Illusion Bks.). (Illus.). 24p. (J). (gr. 1-6). pap. 2.95 *(978-1-56144-889-0(3)*, SJM032) Modern Publishing.

Rey, H. A. Busy Days with Curious George. 2017. (Curious George Ser.). (ENG., Illus.). 208p. (J). (gr. -1-3). 11.99 *(978-1-328-69598-7(0)*, 1671312, Clarion Bks.) HarperCollins Pubs.

—Curious George Discovers the Sun. 2015. (Curious George Ser.). (ENG., Illus.). 32p. (J). (gr. -1-3). pap. 6.99 *(978-0-544-43067-9(0)*, 1595742, Clarion Bks.) HarperCollins Pubs.

—Curious George Makes a Valentine (CGTV Reader) 2017. (Curious George Ser.). (ENG., Illus.). 24p. (J). (gr. -1-3). 12.99 *(978-1-328-69557-4(3)*, 1671219, Clarion Bks.) HarperCollins Pubs.

—Curious George's Box of Books. 2018. (Curious George Ser.). (ENG., Illus.). 80p. (J). (— 1). pap. 18.99 *(978-1-328-79895-4(X)*, 1685686, Clarion Bks.) HarperCollins Pubs.

—Get Well, Curious George. 2017. (Curious George Ser.). (ENG., Illus.). 24p. (J). (gr. -1-3). 14.99 *(978-0-544-97750-1(5)*, 1663693, Clarion Bks.) HarperCollins Pubs.

Reynolds, Luke. If My Love Were a Fire Truck: A Daddy's Love Song. Mack, Jeff, illus. 2018. 26p. (J). (— 1). bds. 7.99 *(978-0-525-58066-9(2)*, Doubleday Bks. for Young Readers) Random Hse. Children's Bks.

Reynolds, Peter H. Peter Reynolds Creatrilogy Box Set (Dot, Ish, Sky Color), 3 vols. 2012. (Creatrilogy Ser.). (ENG.). 96p. (J). (gr. k-4). 45.00 *(978-0-7636-6327-8(1))* Candlewick Pr.

RH Disney. Sleeping Beauty & the Good Fairies (Disney Classic) RH Disney, illus. 2018. (Little Golden Book Ser.). (ENG., Illus.). 24p. (J). (-k). 4.99 *(978-0-7364-3771-4(1)*, Golden/Disney) Random Hse. Children's Bks.

Rhymes, Wriggly. No Place Like Home. 2013. (ENG., Illus.). 40p. pap. 11.00 *(978-1-78035-602-0(1)*, Fastprint Publishing) Upfront Publishing Ltd. GBR. Dist: Printondemand-worldwide.com.

Rice, Inez. The March Wind. Bobri, Vladimir, illus. 2017. 32p. (J). 20.00 *(978-1-85124-461-4(1))* Bodleian Library GBR. Dist: Chicago Distribution Ctr.

Richards, Dan. The Problem with Not Being Scared of Monsters. Neubecker, Robert, illus. 2014. (ENG.). 32p. (J). (gr. -1-3). 15.95 *(978-1-62091-024-5(1)*, Astra Young Readers) Astra Publishing Hse.

Richards, Josie Aleardi. Grandma's Just Not Herself. Rowland, Lauri, illus. 2010. 36p. pap. 13.95 *(978-1-60911-236-3(9)*, Eloquent Bks.) Strategic Book Publishing & Rights Agency (SBPRA).

Richardson, Deborra. Treasures at the Museum. 2011. (Illus.). 64p. (J). pap. 5.99 *(978-0-9824945-1-6(3))* Elevator Group, The.

Rickards, Lynne. Skye the Puffling: A Baby Puffin's Adventure, 30 vols. Mitchell, Jon, illus. 2016. 32p. (J). pap. 11.95 *(978-1-78250-255-5(6)*, Kelpies) Floris Bks. GBR. Dist: Consortium Bk. Sales & Distribution.

—Skye the Puffling: A Wee Puffin Board Book, 30 vols. Mitchell, Jon, illus. 2018. 12p. (J). 9.95 *(978-1-78250-487-0(7)*, Kelpies) Floris Bks. GBR. Dist: Consortium Bk. Sales & Distribution.

Rider, Cynthia. Chatterbox Turtle. Petrlik, Andrea, illus. 2004. (ENG.). 24p. (J). lib. bdg. 23.65 *(978-1-59646-696-8(0))* Dingles & Co.

Ries, Lori. Aggie the Brave. Dormer, Frank W., illus. 2012. (Aggie & Ben Ser.). (ENG.). 48p. (J). (gr. -1-3). pap. 5.95 *(978-1-57091-636-6(5))* Charlesbridge Publishing, Inc.

Rigo, Laura. Little Duckling. 2011. (Mini Look at Me Bks.). (Illus.). 10p. (J). bds. 8.99 *(978-0-7641-6425-5(2))* Sourcebooks, Inc.

—Little Pony. 2011. (Look at Me Bks.). (Illus.). 10p. (J). (gr. -1). bds. 8.99 *(978-0-7641-6448-4(1))* Sourcebooks, Inc.

—Little Reindeer. 2011. (Mini Look at Me Bks.). (Illus.). 10p. (J). (gr. -1). bds. 7.99 *(978-0-7641-6450-7(3))* Sourcebooks, Inc.

Rigo, Laura, illus. Little Elephant. 2011. (Look at Me Bks.). 10p. (J). (gr. -1). bds. 8.99 *(978-0-7641-6426-2(0))* Sourcebooks, Inc.

Riley Guertin, Annemarie. How the Finch Got His Colors. Garcia, Helena Perez, illus. 2018. (ENG.). 32p. (J). (gr. k-3). 16.99 *(978-1-945547-77-5(4)*, 554777) Familius LLC.

Ringbom, Antonia & Wiklund, Alison. The Hiding Hyena. 2nd ed. 2007. (YA). *(978-0-9789617-1-8(4))* H.B.P., Inc.

Rinker, Sherri Duskey. Celebrate You! Kang, A. N., illus. 2019. (ENG.). 40p. (J). (gr. -1-3). 17.99 *(978-0-06-256402-3(1)*, Balzer & Bray) HarperCollins Pubs.

Risom, Ole. I Am a Bunny. Scarry, Richard, illus. 2004. (Golden Sturdy Book Ser.). (ENG.). 26p. (J). (gr. -1 — 1). bds. 7.99 *(978-0-375-82778-5(1)*, Golden Bks.) Random Hse. Children's Bks.

Rissman, Rebecca. Simple Machines: Real Size Science, 1 vol. 2013. (Real Size Science Ser.). (ENG.). 24p. (J). (gr. -1-1). pap. 6.95 *(978-1-4329-7884-6(5)*, 122824, Heinemann) Capstone.

Ritchie, Alison. The Tortoise & the Hare. Noj, Nahta, illus. 2015. (ENG.). 32p. (J). (-k). 15.99 *(978-0-7636-7601-8(2)*, Templar) Candlewick Pr.

Ritchie, Scot. The Everything Kids' More Puzzles Book: From Mazes to Hidden Pictures - & Hours of Fun in Between. 2010. (Everything(r) Kids Ser.). (ENG., Illus.). 144p. pap. 15.99 *(978-1-4405-0647-5(7))* Adams Media Corp.

Rivas, H. J. Word Sag: A Bedtime Story. 2012. 24p. pap. 15.99 *(978-1-4691-5661-3(X))* Xlibris Corp.

Rizzi, Kathleen. What's in My Dresser?, 1 vol. Riggs, Jenna, illus. 2013. (ENG.). 32p. (J). bds. 7.99 *(978-1-59572-165-5(7))* Star Bright Bks., Inc.

Rml. An Interesting Crew. 2012. 16p. (-18). pap. 15.99 *(978-1-4772-8699-9(3))* AuthorHouse.

Robaard, Jedda. George the Bilby Chef & the Raspberry Muffin Surprise. 2019. (ENG.). 32p. (J). (gr. -1-k). 12.99 *(978-1-76006-711-3(3))* Little Hare Bks. AUS. Dist: Independent Pubs. Group.

—The Little Rabbit Who Lost Her Hop. 2018. (ENG.). 12p. (J). (gr. -1-k). bds. 7.99 *(978-1-4998-0683-0(3))* Little Bee Books Inc.

Robbins, Heather Roan. Talulla Bear's Bedtime Book: A Sleepytime Tale. 2016. (ENG., Illus.). 32p. (J). (gr. 8-2). 14.95 *(978-1-78249-379-2(4)*, 1782493794, CICO Books) Ryland Peters & Small GBR. Dist: WIPRO.

Robert, Na'ima B. Ramadan Moon. Adl, Shirin, illus. 2015. (ENG.). 32p. (J). (gr. -1-1). pap. 9.99 *(978-1-84780-206-4(0)*, 316238, Frances Lincoln Children's Bks.) Quarto Publishing Group UK GBR. Dist: Hachette UK Distribution.

Roberts, Daniel. The Ghost of Froggy's Swamp. 2012. 36p. pap. 18.99 *(978-1-4772-0316-3(8))* AuthorHouse.

—The Good Night Book: A Book of Animal Sounds. 2009. 36p. pap. 16.99 *(978-1-4389-8278-6(X))* AuthorHouse.

—Mouse & His Balloon. 2011. 32p. pap. 14.95 *(978-1-4634-2090-1(0))* AuthorHouse.

—The Naughty Dog. 2010. 32p. 14.95 *(978-1-4490-8344-1(7))* AuthorHouse.

—Young Pep Squad Mysteries. 2011. 36p. pap. 16.99 *(978-1-4567-9640-2(2))* AuthorHouse.

Roberts, Lynn. Little Red: A Fizzingly Funny Fairy Tale. Roberts, David, illus. 2017. (ENG.). 40p. (J). (gr. k-2). pap. 9.99 *(978-1-84365-328-8(1)*, Pavilion Children's Books) Pavilion Bks. GBR. Dist: HarperCollins Pubs.

Roberts, Melva J. Mrs Moon's Pond. 2011. 28p. pap. 21.99 *(978-1-4628-4613-9(0))* Xlibris Corp.

Roberts, Phyllis. Teeny Tiny Star. 2007. (Illus.). 30p. (J). lib. bdg. 19.95 *(978-1-933732-40-4(7))* Big Ransom Studio.

Roberts, Tony. Turquie the Turkey. 2011. 28p. pap. 15.99 *(978-1-4568-5969-5(2))* Xlibris Corp.

Robertson, David A. When We Were Alone, 1 vol. Flett, Julie, illus. 2016. (ENG.). 32p. (J). (gr. 1-3). *(978-1-55379-673-2(X)*, HighWater Pr.) Portage & Main Pr.

Robertson, James. Katie's a Tae Z: An Alphabet for Wee Folk. Sutherland, Karen, illus. 2014. 20p. (J). (-k). bds. 12.99 *(978-1-84502-754-4(X))* Black and White Publishing Ltd. GBR. Dist: Independent Pubs. Group.

Robinson, Casey W. Iver & Ellsworth. Larson, Melissa, illus. 2018. (ENG.). 40p. (J). (gr. k-2). 18.99 *(978-0-9990249-1-1(4))* Ripple Grove Pr.

Robinson, Hilary. Beauty & the Pea, 1 vol. Sanfilippo, Simona, illus. 2013. (ENG.). 32p. (J). pap. *(978-0-7787-1159-9(5))* Crabtree Publishing Co.

—Cinderella & the Beanstalk, 1 vol. Sanfilippo, Simona, illus. 2013. (ENG.). 32p. (J). pap. *(978-0-7787-1161-2(7))* Crabtree Publishing Co.

—Hansel, Gretel, & the Ugly Duckling. Sanfilippo, Simona, illus. 2013. (ENG.). 32p. (J). pap. *(978-0-7787-1166-7(8))* Crabtree Publishing Co.

—Rapunzel & the Billy Goats, 1 vol. Sanfilippo, Simona, illus. 2013. (ENG.). 32p. (J). pap. *(978-0-7787-1158-2(7))* Crabtree Publishing Co.

—Ted's Party Bus. 2009. (ENG., Illus.). 24p. (J). pap. *(978-0-7787-3901-2(5))*; lib. bdg. *(978-0-7787-3870-1(1))* Crabtree Publishing Co.

Robson, Kirsteen. Mosaic Sticker Flowers. 2015. (Mosaic Sticker Bks.). (ENG.). 20+10p. (J). (gr. k-5). pap. 9.99 *(978-0-7945-3545-2(3)*, Usborne) EDC Publishing.

Roca, Nuria. Fall. Curto, Rosa M., illus. 2004. (Seasons Ser.). 36p. (J). (gr. -1-2). pap. 8.99 *(978-0-7641-2729-8(2))* Sourcebooks, Inc.

—El Invierno. 2004. (Estaciones / Seasons Ser.).Tr. of Winter. (SPA., Illus.). 36p. (J). (gr. k-3). 21.19 *(978-0-7641-2732-8(2)*, B.E.S. Publishing) Peterson's.

—La Primavera (Spring) 2004. (Estaciones / Seasons Ser.).Tr. of Spring. (SPA., Illus.). 36p. (J). (gr. k-3). 22.44 *(978-0-7641-2734-2(9)*, B.E.S. Publishing) Peterson's.

Roche, Jackie, illus. The Derby Ram. 2010. (First Steps in Music Ser.). (ENG.). 32p. (J). (gr. -1-k). 17.95 *(978-1-57999-783-0(X))* G I A Pubns., Inc.

Roche, Maite. My First Pictures of Jesus. 2012. (ENG.). 14p. (J). 6.99 *(978-1-58617-651-8(X))* Ignatius Pr.

Rock, Lois. A Gift for Baby's Christening, 1 vol. Rescek, Sanja, illus. 2014. (ENG.). 48p. (J). (— 1). 7.99 *(978-0-7459-6490-4(7)*, 57dc4a6c-0fd3-48a6-bad6-1f19af0ba00c, Lion Children's) Lion Hudson PLC GBR. Dist: Baker & Taylor Publisher Services (BTPS).

Rockwell, Anne. Bugs Are Insects. Jenkins, Steve, illus. 2015. (Let's-Read-And-Find-Out Science 1 Ser.). (ENG.). 40p. (J). (gr. -1-3). pap. 7.99 *(978-0-06-238182-8(2)*, HarperCollins) HarperCollins Pubs.

—Zoo Day. Rockwell, Lizzy, illus. 2018. (My First Experience Book Ser.). (ENG.). 32p. (J). (gr. -1-3). 7.99 *(978-1-4814-2735-7(0)*, Aladdin) Simon & Schuster Children's Publishing.

—Zoo Day. Rockwell, Lizzy, illus. 2017. (My First Experience Book Ser.). (ENG.). 32p. (J). (gr. -1-3). 17.99 *(978-1-4814-2734-0(2)*, Simon & Schuster/Paula Wiseman Bks.) Simon & Schuster/Paula Wiseman Bks.

Rodriguez, Patty & Stein, Ariana. Cuauhtemoc: Shapes/Formas, 1 vol. Reyes, Citlali, illus. 2018.Tr. of Spanish. (SPA.). 22p. (J). (gr. -1-k). bds. 9.99 *(978-0-9861099-3-5(2))* Little Libros, LLC.

—Un Elefante: Numbers / Numeros: Numbers- Numeros, 1 vol. Reyes, Citlali, illus. 2018.Tr. of Spanish. 22p. (J). (gr. -1-k). bds. 9.99 *(978-0-9861099-4-2(0))* Little Libros, LLC.

—Guadalupe: First Words/Primeras Palabras, 1 vol. Reyes, Citlali, illus. 2018. 22p. (J). bds. 9.99 *(978-0-9861099-0-4(8))* Little Libros, LLC.

—Life of/la Vida de Celia, 1 vol. Reyes, Citlali, illus. 2018. (SPA.). 22p. (J). (gr. -1-k). bds. 9.99 *(978-0-9861099-5-9(9))* Little Libros, LLC.

—The Life of/la Vida de Selena, 1 vol. Reyes, Citlali, illus. 2018. (SPA.). 22p. (J). (gr. -1-k). bds. 9.99 *(978-0-9861099-9-7(1)*, Lil' Libros) Little Libros, LLC.

—La Llorona: Counting down / Contando Hacia Atras: Counting down - Contando Hacia Atras, 1 vol. Reyes, Citlali, illus. 2018. (ENG.). 22p. (J). bds. 9.99 *(978-0-9861099-2-8(4))* Little Libros, LLC.

—Lucha Libre: Anatomy / Anatomia: Anatomy - Anatomia, 1 vol. Reyes, Citlali, illus. 2018. (ENG.). 22p. (J). bds. 9.99 *(978-0-9861099-1-1(6))* Little Libros, LLC.

—Zapata: Colors / Colores, 1 vol. Reyes, Citlali, illus. 2018. 22p. (J). bds. 9.99 *(978-1-4951-2657-4(9))* Little Libros, LLC.

Rodriguez, Rachel Victoria. Through Georgia's Eyes. Paschkis, Julie, illus. rev. ed. 2006. (ENG.). 32p. (J). (gr. k-3). 19.99 *(978-0-8050-7740-7(5)*, 900031594, Holt, Henry & Co. Bks. For Young Readers) Holt, Henry & Co.

Roffey, M. First Words Indoors. 2003. (Illus.). 12p. (J). 3.99 *(978-1-85292-227-6(3)*, Campbell Bks.) Pan Macmillan GBR. Dist: Trafalgar Square Publishing.

Rogers, Alan. Le Vent Tourne! 2003. (Little Giants Ser.). (FRE., Illus.). 16p. (J). (gr. -1-k). 5.95 *(978-1-58728-179-2(1)*, Two-Can Publishing) T&N Children's Publishing.

Rogers, Andy. The Puppy Brothers Adventures with Forest Friends - Children's Picture Book for Ages 3 To 8. 2013. 38p. pap. 10.00 *(978-1-63022-036-5(1))* Speedy Publishing LLC.

Rogers, Jacqueline. Goblin Moon. Rogers, Jacqueline, illus. 2019. (ENG., Illus.). 32p. (J). (gr. -1-3). 17.99 *(978-0-06-279229-7(6)*, HarperCollins) HarperCollins Pubs.

Rohmann, Eric. A Kitten Tale. 2012. 32p. (J). (gr. -1-2). pap. 8.99 *(978-0-307-97774-8(9)*, Dragonfly Bks.) Random Hse. Children's Bks.

Rohner, Dorothia, illus. Effie's Image. 2006. 32p. (J). (gr. -1-3). 17.95 *(978-0-9759829-5-2(8))* Prairieland Pr.

ROI Visual, R. O. I., illus. Robocar Poli: Storm Rescue: Storm Rescue. 2018. (Robocar Poli Ser.). 24p. (J). (gr. -1-1). pap. 3.99 *(978-2-924786-86-4(X)*, CrackBoom! Bks.) Chouette Publishing CAN. Dist: Publishers Group West (PGW).

Roi Visual, Roi, illus. Robocar Poli: Race Against Time: Race Against Time. 2018. (Robocar Poli Ser.). 24p. (J). (gr. -1-1). pap. 3.99 *(978-2-924786-88-8(6)*, CrackBoom! Bks.) Chouette Publishing CAN. Dist: Publishers Group West (PGW).

Rokus, Patti. A Savior Is Born: Rocks Tell the Story of Christmas, 1 vol. 2018. (ENG., Illus.). 32p. (J). 17.99 *(978-0-310-76496-0(3))* Zondervan.

Rooks, Elizabeth. Where Does Santa Go on Vacation after Christmas? 2012. 24p. pap. 17.99 *(978-1-4772-6535-2(X))* AuthorHouse.

Roop, Connie & Roop, Peter. Our Solar System. 2016. (Science for Toddlers Ser.: 1). (Illus.). 26p. (J). (gr. -1 — 1). bds. 8.99 *(978-1-4549-1418-1(1)*, 1404673) Sterling Publishing Co., Inc.

Root, Andrew. Hamsters Don't Fight Fires! Olien, Jessica, illus. 2017. (ENG.). 40p. (J). (gr. -1-3). 17.99 *(978-0-06-245294-8(0)*, HarperCollins) HarperCollins Pubs.

Root, Phyllis. Creak! Said the Bed. Dunnick, Regan, illus. 2015. (ENG.). 32p. (J). (gr. -1-3). 7.99 *(978-0-7636-7969-9(0))* Candlewick Pr.

—Rattletrap Car Big Book. Barton, Jill, illus. 2009. (ENG.). 40p. (J). (gr. -1-3). pap. 27.99 *(978-0-7636-4139-9(1))* Candlewick Pr.

Rosa-Mendoza, Gladys. Animals at the Farm/Animales de la Granja. Wolff, Jason, illus. 2004. (English-Spanish Foundations Ser.). (SPA & ENG.). 20p. (J). (gr. -1). bds. 6.95 *(978-1-931398-13-8(5))* Me+Mi Publishing.

—Cars, Trucks & Planes/Carros, Camiones y Aviones. Tugeau, Jeremy, illus. 2004. (English-Spanish Foundations Ser.). (SPA & ENG.). 20p. (J). (gr. -1). bds. 6.95 *(978-1-931398-14-5(3))* Me+Mi Publishing.

—Lupe Lupita, Where Are You?/Lupe Lupita, Donde Estas? Ochoa, Ana, illus. 2005. (English-Spanish Foundations Ser.). (SPA & ENG.). 20p. (J). (gr. -1). bds. 6.95 *(978-1-931398-16-9(X))* Me+Mi Publishing.

Roscoe, Charlie. The Red Prince. Cole, Tom Clohosy, illus. 2016. (ENG.). 32p. (J). (-k). 16.99 *(978-0-7636-8912-4(2)*, Templar) Candlewick Pr.

Rose, Nancy. The Secret Life of Squirrels. 2014. (ENG., Illus.). 32p. (J). (gr. -1-3). 18.99 *(978-0-316-37027-1(4))* Little, Brown Bks. for Young Readers.

Rosen, Aaron & Watts, Riley. Where's Your Creativity? Maijala, Marika, illus. 2018. (ENG.). 32p. (J). (gr. -1-k). 16.95 *(978-1-84976-509-1(X))* Tate Publishing, Ltd. GBR. Dist: Hachette Bk. Group.

Rosen, Michael. Aesop's Fables, 1 vol. Hacikyan, Talleen, illus. 2013. (ENG.). 32p. (J). (gr. 1-3). 16.95 *(978-1-896580-81-4(5))* Tradewind Bks. CAN. Dist: Orca Bk. Pubs. USA.

—Send for a Superhero! McEwen, Katharine, illus. 2014. (ENG.). 40p. (J). (gr. -1-2). 16.99 *(978-0-7636-6438-1(3))* Candlewick Pr.

Rosenberg, Madelyn. Take Care. Gregori, Giuliana, illus. 2018. (ENG.). 24p. (J). (gr. -1-3). 12.99 *(978-0-8075-7732-5(4),* 807577324) Whitman, Albert & Co.

Rosenthal, Amy Krouse. I Wish You More. Lichtenheld, Tom, illus. 2015. (ENG.). 40p. (J). (gr. k-3). 14.99 *(978-1-4521-2699-9(2))* Chronicle Bks. LLC.

Rosenthal, Amy Krouse & Rosenthal, Paris. Dear Girl, A Celebration of Wonderful, Smart, Beautiful You! Hatam, Holly, illus. 2017. (ENG.). 40p. (J). (gr. -1-3). 17.99 *(978-0-06-242250-7(2),* HarperCollins) HarperCollins Pubs.

Ross, Mandy & Ladybird Books Staff. Little Red Riding Hood. 2015. (First Favourite Tales Ser.). (Illus.). 32p. (J). (-k). 8.99 *(978-1-4093-0631-3(3))* Penguin Bks., Ltd. GBR. Dist: Independent Pubs. Group.

Ross, Thea. Lucy Loves Winter. 2004. 16p. (J). bds. 4.99 *(978-1-59384-077-8(2))* Parklane Publishing.

Ross, Tony. Goldilocks & the Three Bears. 2016. (ENG., Illus.). 10p. (J). (-k). bds. 9.99 *(978-1-78344-409-0(6))* Andersen Pr. GBR. Dist: Independent Pubs. Group.

—I Want My Dinner! 2018. (Little Princess Ser.). (ENG., Illus.). 32p. (J). (-k). pap. 9.99 *(978-1-78344-581-3(5))* Andersen Pr. GBR. Dist: Independent Pubs. Group.

—I Want My Potty! (ENG., Illus.). (J). (-k). 2018. (Little Princess Ser.: 1). 32p. pap. 11.99 *(978-1-78344-632-2(3))* 2017. 20p. bds. 13.99 *(978-1-78344-544-8(0))* Andersen Pr. GBR. Dist: Independent Pubs. Group.

Ross, Tony & Ross, Tony. Goldilocks & the Three Bears. 40th ed. 2017. (ENG., Illus.). 32p. (J). (-k). 15.99 *(978-1-78344-469-4(X))* Andersen Pr. GBR. Dist: Independent Pubs. Group.

Rosselson, Leon. Tom the Whistling Wonder. Haslam, John, illus. 2005. (ENG.). 24p. (J). lib. bdg. 23.65 *(978-1-59646-758-3(4))* Dingles & Co.

Roth, Anthony H. Little Anthony Doesn't Want to Eat His Dinner. 2012. 26p. 24.95 *(978-1-4626-5776-6(1))* America Star Bks.

Roth, Carol. Five Little Ducklings Go to School. Julian, Sean, illus. 2019. (ENG.). 32p. (J). (gr. -1-2). pap. 8.95 *(978-0-7358-4346-2(5))* North-South Bks., Inc.

—The Little School Bus. Paparone, Pamela, illus. (ENG.). 32p. (J). (gr. -1-1). 2012. 22.44 *(978-0-7358-1646-6(8))* 2004. pap. 8.95 *(978-0-7358-1905-4(X))* North-South Bks., Inc.

Roth, Carol & Julian, Sean. Five Little Ducklings Go to Bed. 2013. (Illus.). 32p. (J). pap. *(978-0-7358-4153-6(5))* North-South Bks., Inc.

Roth, Penny S. Chickenfriend. Busse, Alyssa, illus. 2018. (ENG.). 32p. (J). (gr. -1). pap. 12.95 *(978-1-943027-27-9(7),* 164283) Electric Moon Publishing.

Roth, Sarra J. Not the Quitting Kind. Bishop, Tracy, illus. 2014. (ENG.). 32p. (J). 16.99 *(978-1-4413-1415-4(6),* 1449d677-112d-4408-b198-ea19b3cef1c3) Peter Pauper Pr. Inc.

Rotner, Shelley. All Kinds of People. 2018. (Illus.). 24p. (J). (— 1). bds. 7.99 *(978-0-8234-3972-0(0))* Holiday Hse., Inc.

Roussey, Christine. My Funny Bunny. 2019. (ENG., Illus.). 32p. (J). (gr. -1-1). 16.99 *(978-1-4197-3618-6(3),* 1271001, Abrams Bks. for Young Readers) Abrams, Inc.

Rowand, Phyllis. It Is Night. Dronzek, Laura, illus. 2014. (ENG.). 32p. (J). (gr. -1-3). 16.99 *(978-0-06-225024-7(8),* Greenwillow Bks.) HarperCollins Pubs.

Rowe, Amanda. If There Never Was a You. Skomorokhova, Olga, illus. 2019. (ENG.). 20p. (J). (gr. -1 — 1). bds. 12.99 *(978-1-64170-111-2(0),* 550111) Familius LLC.

Rowe, Thereza. Hearts: Toon Books Level 1. Rowe, Thereza, illus. 2014. (ENG., Illus.). 32p. (J). (gr. -1-3). 12.95 *(978-1-935179-59-7(4),* TOON Books) Astra Publishing Hse.

—In the Woods. 2017. (Illus.). 40p. (J). (gr. -1-3). 16.95 *(978-0-500-65105-6(1),* 565105) Thames & Hudson.

—Mister Pip. 2016. (ENG., Illus.). 32p. (J). (gr. -1-k). 16.95 *(978-1-84976-382-0(8),* 1648201) Tate Publishing, Ltd. GBR. Dist: Abrams, Inc.

Rowland, Lucy. Gecko's Echo. Rimmington, Natasha, illus. 2017. (ENG.). 32p. (J). *(978-1-4088-5949-0(1),* 267679, Bloomsbury Children's Bks.) Bloomsbury Publishing Plc.

—Pirate Pete & His Smelly Feet. Chambers, Mark, illus. 2017. (ENG.). 32p. (J). (gr. -1-1). 17.99 *(978-1-5098-1776-4(X),* Macmillan Children's Bks.) Pan Macmillan GBR. Dist: Independent Pubs. Group.

Roy, Philip. Jellybean Mouse. Torrey Balsara, Andrea, illus. 2014. (ENG.). 32p. 11.95 *(978-1-55380-344-7(2))* Ronsdale Pr. CAN. Dist: SPD-Small Pr. Distribution.

—Mouse Pet. Torrey Balsara, Andrea, illus. 2015. (ENG.). 32p. 12.95 *(978-1-55380-443-7(0))* Ronsdale Pr. CAN. Dist: SPD-Small Pr. Distribution.

Roy, Ronald. Turkey Trouble on the National Mall. 2012. (Capital Mysteries Ser.: 14). lib. bdg. 14.75 *(978-0-606-26809-7(X))* Turtleback.

Rubin, Adam. Big Bad Bubble. Salmieri, Daniel, illus. 2017. (ENG.). 40p. (J). (gr. -1-3). pap. 9.99 *(978-0-544-92782-7(6),* 1657202, Clarion Bks.) HarperCollins Pubs.

—Big Bad Bubble. Salmieri, Daniel, illus. 2017. (ENG.). (J). (gr. -1-3). lib. bdg. 18.40 *(978-0-606-39829-9(5))* Turtleback.

—Those Darn Squirrels Fly South. Salmieri, Daniel, illus. 2015. (ENG.). 32p. (J). (gr. -1-3). 8.99 *(978-0-544-55545-7(7),* 1610412, Clarion Bks.) HarperCollins Pubs.

Rubino, Michael. Bang! How We Came to Be. 2011. (Illus.). 69p. (J). (gr. -1-12). pap. 17.00 *(978-1-61614-472-2(6))* Prometheus Bks., Pubs.

Rubow, Carol. God Loves You. 2010. (Illus.). 32p. (J). (gr. -1). 12.99 *(978-0-7586-1855-9(7))* Concordia Publishing Hse.

—God Loves You Mini Book. 2010. 32p. (J). (gr. -1). pap. 2.49 *(978-0-7586-1856-6(5))* Concordia Publishing Hse.

Rue, Leonard Lee. Wolves - PB: A Portrait of the Animal World. 2013. (Portrait of the Animal World Ser.). (Illus.). 80p. pap. 9.95 *(978-1-59764-326-9(2))* New Line Bks.

Rueda, Claudia. Hungry Bunny. 2018. (Bunny Interactive Picture Bks.). (ENG., Illus.). 64p. (J). (gr. -1-k). 15.99 *(978-1-4521-6255-3(7))* Chronicle Bks. LLC.

Ruiz, John. The Squirrel, the Eagle & the Red Hawk. 2012. 32p. pap. 21.99 *(978-1-4691-7970-4(9))* Xlibris Corp.

Rumbaugh, Melinda. Somebunny Loves You! 2019. (ENG., Illus.). 18p. (J). (gr. -1-k). bds. 9.99 *(978-0-8249-1687-9(5),* Worthy Kids/Ideals) Worthy Publishing.

Runnells, Treesha. Forest Friends: A Fold-Out Fun Book. Runnells, Treesha, illus. 2005. (Fold-Out Fun Ser.). (Illus.). 10p. (J). 4.95 *(978-1-58117-275-1(3),* Intervisual/Piggy Toes) Bendon, Inc.

—Safari Friends: Fold-Out Fun. Runnells, Treesha, illus. 2005. (Fold-Out Fun Ser.). (Illus.). 10p. (J). 4.95 *(978-1-58117-276-8(1),* Intervisual/Piggy Toes) Bendon, Inc.

Russell, Natalie. Donkey's Busy Day. Russell, Natalie, illus. 2009. (Illus.). 32p. (J). (gr. k-k). pap. 11.95 *(978-0-7475-9547-2(X))* Bloomsbury Publishing Plc GBR. Dist: Independent Pubs. Group.

—Home Sweet Hamish. 2008. (Bloomsbury Paperbacks Ser.). (Illus.). 32p. (J). (gr. -1-2). pap. 10.95 *(978-0-7475-8319-6(6))* Bloomsbury Publishing Plc GBR. Dist: Independent Pubs. Group.

Russo, Marisabina. The Bunnies Are Not in Their Beds. Russo, Marisabina, illus. 2013. (Illus.). 40p. (J). (gr. -1-2). 7.99 *(978-0-307-98126-4(6),* Dragonfly Bks.) Random Hse. Children's Bks.

Rustrian, Edvin E. The Adventures of Timmy & Jay. 2010. 24p. pap. 15.99 *(978-1-4535-3792-3(9))* Xlibris Corp.

Ryan, Darlene & Manchester, Peter. Kisses, Kisses, Kisses. 2004. (Illus.). 24p. (J). *(978-1-55131-092-3(9))* Univ. of New Brunswick, Dept. of Graphic Services.

Ryan, Tom. A Giant Man from a Tiny Town: A Story of Angus MacAskill, 1 vol. Hoyt, Christopher, illus. 2018. (ENG.). 32p. (J). (gr. -1-k). 22.95 *(978-1-77108-654-7(8),* 30748773-4b07-43a8-a6e7-b868399e986e) Nimbus Publishing, Ltd. CAN. Dist: Baker & Taylor Publisher Services (BTPS).

Rylant, Cynthia. Let's Go Home: The Wonderful Things about a House. Halperin, Wendy Anderson, illus. 2005. (ENG.). 32p. (J). (gr. -1-3). 9.99 *(978-1-4169-0839-5(0),* Simon & Schuster Bks. For Young Readers) Simon & Schuster Bks. For Young Readers.

—The Stars Will Still Shine. Beeke, Tiphanie, illus. 2005. (ENG.). 40p. (J). (gr. -1-3). 17.99 *(978-0-06-054639-7(5),* HarperCollins) HarperCollins Pubs.

Ryski, Dawid. My Four Seasons. 2017. (ENG., Illus.). 32p. (J). (gr. -1-3). 19.95 *(978-3-89955-784-8(0))* Die Gestalten Verlag DEU. Dist: Ingram Publisher Services.

Sabatier-Morel, Francoise & Pellegrini, Isabelle. Marie from Paris. Camcam, Princesse, illus. 2014. (AV2 Fiction Readalong Ser.: Vol. 131). (ENG.). 32p. (J). (gr. -1-3). lib. bdg. 34.28 *(978-1-4896-2262-4(4),* AV2 by Weigl) Weigl Pubs., Inc.

Sachs, Andrew. Teddybear Tales. 2013. (Illus.). 32p. (J). (gr. -1-1). 5.99 *(978-1-84322-811-0(4),* Armadillo) Anness Publishing GBR. Dist: National Bk. Network.

Sadler, Judy Ann. Nothing Happens in This Book. Vigg, illus. 2018. (ENG.). 40p. (J). (gr. -1-2). 16.99 *(978-1-77138-737-8(8))* Kids Can Pr., Ltd. CAN. Dist: Hachette Bk. Group.

Sadler, Marilyn & Comstock, Eric. Charlie Piechart & the Case of the Missing Hat. Comstock, Eric, illus. 2016. (Charlie Piechart Ser.). (ENG., Illus.). 40p. (J). (gr. -1-3). 17.99 *(978-0-06-237056-3(1),* HarperCollins) HarperCollins Pubs.

Saillard, Remi, illus. Funny Machines for George the Sheep: A Children's Book Inspired by Leonardo Da Vinci. 2014. (Children's Books Inspired by Famous Artworks Ser.). (ENG.). 32p. (J). (gr. -1-3). 14.95 *(978-3-7913-7166-5(5))* Prestel Verlag GmbH & Co KG. DEU. Dist: Penguin Random Hse. LLC.

Sakai, Komako. Emily's Balloon. 2015. (ENG., Illus.). 44p. (J). (gr. -1-7). pap. 7.99 *(978-1-4521-4567-9(9))* Chronicle Bks. LLC.

Sakmar-Sullivan, Eva M. Willie the Taxi Cat, 1 vol. 2013. (ENG., Illus.). 32p. (J). 16.99 *(978-0-7643-4436-7(6),* 4755) Schiffer Publishing, Ltd.

Sala, Laurenne. You Made Me a Dad. Malbrough, Mike, illus. 2019. (ENG.). 32p. (J). (gr. -1-3). 15.99 *(978-0-06-239694-5(3),* HarperCollins) HarperCollins Pubs.

—You Made Me a Mother. Glasser, Robin Preiss, illus. 2016. (ENG.). 32p. (J). (gr. -1-3). 16.99 *(978-0-06-235886-8(3),* HarperCollins) HarperCollins Pubs.

Salten, Felix. Bambi. 2017. (GER., Illus.). (J). (gr. 3-6). pap. *(978-3-7448-3019-5(5))* Books on Demand GmbH.

—Bambi. 2019. (Clydesdale Classics Ser.). 218p. (J). (-5). pap. 5.99 *(978-1-949846-05-8(9))* Clydesdale Pr., LLC.

Saltzberg, Barney. Dog & Rabbit. Saltzberg, Barney, illus. 2019. (Illus.). 48p. (J). (gr. -1-2). lib. bdg. 14.99 *(978-1-62354-107-1(7))* Charlesbridge Publishing, Inc.

—Enough Is Enough! Saltzberg, Barney, illus. 2018. (ENG., Illus.). 32p. (J). (gr. -1-k). 16.99 *(978-1-939547-42-2(3),* 152caa52-2579-43f5-b008-cab6309601bb) Creston Bks.

Salzano, Tammi. One Little Blueberry. Whelan, Kat, illus. 2011. (ENG.). 22p. (J). (gr. -1-k). 12.95 *(978-1-58925-859-4(2))* Tiger Tales.

Sammarco, Teresa "T". The What If Book. Curley, Carol, illus. 2013. (J). lib. bdg. 16.95 *(978-1-59598-236-0(1))* HenschelHAUS Publishing, Inc.

Sammurtok, Nadia. Siuluk: the Last Tuniq, 1 vol. Nix, Rob, illus. 2018. (ENG.). 28p. (J). (gr. 1-3). 10.95 *(978-1-77227-178-2(0))* Inhabit Media Inc. CAN. Dist: Consortium Bk. Sales & Distribution.

Sams, Carl R. Lost in the Woods: A Photographic Fantasy. Sams, Carl R. & Stoick, Jean, photos by. 2004. (ENG., Illus.). (J). 19.95 *(978-0-9671748-8-4(0))* Sams, II, Carl R. Photography, Inc.

Sandall, Ellie. Everybunny Count! Sandall, Ellie, illus. 2018. (ENG., Illus.). 32p. (J). (gr. -1-3). 17.99 *(978-1-5344-0014-6(1),* McElderry, Margaret K. Bks.) McElderry, Margaret K. Bks.

Sandburg, Carl. The Wedding Procession of the Rag Doll & the Broom Handle & Who Was in It. Pincus, Harriet, illus. 2017. (ENG.). 32p. 16.95 *(978-0-486-81585-5(4),* 815854) Dover Pubns., Inc.

Sanderson, Ruth. The Crystal Mountain. 2019. (Ruth Sanderson Collection). (ENG., Illus.). 32p. (J). (gr. 1-2). pap. 8.95 *(978-1-56656-007-8(1),* Crocodile Bks.) Interlink Publishing Group, Inc.

—The Golden Mare, the Firebird, & the Magic Ring. 2019. (Ruth Sanderson Collection). (ENG., Illus.). 32p. (J). (gr. 1-2). pap. 8.95 *(978-1-56656-066-5(7),* Crocodile Bks.) Interlink Publishing Group, Inc.

Santamaria, Jenni & Ross Keyes, Joan. Oxford Picture Dictionary Content Area for Kids English Dictionary. 2nd ed. 2012. (ENG., Illus.). 200p. pap. 30.80 *(978-0-19-401775-6(3))* Oxford Univ. Pr., Inc.

Santore, Charles. Velveteen Rabbit Hardcover: The Classic Edition. 2013. (Charles Santore Children's Classics Ser.). (ENG., Illus.). 48p. (J). (gr. -1). 19.95 *(978-1-60433-277-3(8),* Applesauce Pr.) Cider Mill Pr. Bk. Pubs., LLC.

—William the Curious: Knight of the Water Lilies: the Classic Edition. 2014. (Charles Santore Children's Classics Ser.). (ENG., Illus.). 44p. (J). (gr. -1). 16.95 *(978-1-60433-474-6(6))* Cider Mill Pr. Bk. Pubs., LLC.

Sarell, Nadja, illus. Little Dove & the Story of Easter, 1 vol. 2019. (ENG.). 22p. (J). bds. 7.99 *(978-0-310-76668-1(0))* Zonderkidz.

Sassi, Laura. Goodnight, Ark, 1 vol. Chapman, Jane, illus. 2015. (ENG.). 24p. (J). bds. 8.99 *(978-0-310-74938-7(7))* Zonderkidz.

—Goodnight, Manger, 1 vol. Chapman, Jane, illus. 2015. (ENG.). 32p. (J). 17.99 *(978-0-310-74556-3(X))* Zonderkidz.

Sauer, Cat. Gwendolyn the Ghost. Jankowski, Daniel, illus. l.t. ed. 2006. (Brown Bag Bedtime Bks.: 1). 29p. (J). (gr. -1-2). 16.95 incl. audio compact disk *(978-0-9704460-9-1(8))* Writer's Ink. Studios, Inc.

Sauer, Tammi. Go Fish! Waring, Zoe, illus. 2018. (ENG.). 40p. (J). (gr. -1 — 1). 14.99 *(978-0-06-242155-5(7),* HarperCollins) HarperCollins Pubs.

—Me Want Pet! Shea, Bob, illus. 2012. (ENG.). 40p. (J). (gr. -1-3). 19.99 *(978-1-4424-0810-4(3),* Simon & Schuster/Paula Wiseman Bks.) Simon & Schuster/Paula Wiseman Bks.

Savage, Doug. Laser Moose & Rabbit Boy: Disco Fever. 2017. (Laser Moose & Rabbit Boy Ser.: 2). (ENG., Illus.). 144p. (J). pap. 9.99 *(978-1-4494-8687-7(8))* Andrews McMeel Publishing.

Savage, Sarah. Are You a Boy or Are You a Girl? Fisher, Fox, illus. 2017. 32p. (J). 18.95 *(978-1-78592-267-1(X),* 696461) Kingsley, Jessica Pubs. GBR. Dist: Hachette UK Distribution.

Savage, Stephen. Little Tug. Savage, Stephen, illus. 2015. (ENG., Illus.). 34p. (J). (gr. -1-1). bds. 10.99 *(978-1-62672-124-1(6),* 900138367) Roaring Brook Pr.

Savary, Fabien & Vadeboncoeur, Isabelle. Caillou: Los Contrarios. Tipeo, illus. 2004. (Caillou Ser.).Tr. of What's the Difference? (SPA.). 12p. (J). (gr. -1 — 1). bds. 4.95 *(978-1-58728-348-2(4))* Cooper Square Publishing Llc.

Saxby, Claire. Emu. Byrne, Graham, illus. 2015. (ENG.). 32p. (J). (gr. k-3). 16.99 *(978-0-7636-7479-3(6))* Candlewick Pr.

Saxon, Victoria. Big Trouble in Little Rodentia. 2016. (Illus.). (J). *(978-1-5182-0883-6(5))* Random House Children's Books.

Scarry, Patsy. Richard Scarry's the Bunny Book. Scarry, Richard, illus. 2015. (Big Golden Book Ser.). 32p. (J). (-k). 9.99 *(978-0-385-39090-3(4),* Golden Bks.) Random Hse. Children's Bks.

Scarry, Richard. Richard Scarry's Best Bunny Book Ever! Scarry, Richard, illus. 2014. (Illus.). 80p. (J). (-k). 7.99 *(978-0-385-38467-4(X),* Golden Bks.) Random Hse. Children's Bks.

—Richard Scarry's Best Nursery Tales Ever. 2014. (Illus.). 72p. (J). (gr. -1-2). 16.99 *(978-0-385-37533-7(6),* Golden Bks.) Random Hse. Children's Bks.

—Richard Scarry's Busy, Busy World. Scarry, Richard, illus. 2015. (Illus.). 96p. (J). (gr. -1-2). 16.99 *(978-0-385-38480-3(7),* Golden Bks.) Random Hse. Children's Bks.

—Richard Scarry's Cars. 2015. (Illus.). 24p. (J). (— 1). bds. 4.99 *(978-0-385-38926-6(4),* Golden Bks.) Random Hse. Children's Bks.

—Richard Scarry's Nicky Goes to the Doctor. 2014. lib. bdg. 14.75 *(978-0-606-35561-2(8))* Turtleback.

—Richard Scarry's the Animals of Farmer Jones. 2018. (Illus.). 26p. (J). (— 1). bds. 7.99 *(978-1-101-93833-1(1),* Golden Bks.) Random Hse. Children's Bks.

—Richard Scarry's What Do People Do All Day? 2015. (Illus.). 96p. (J). (gr. -1-2). 17.99 *(978-0-553-52059-0(8),* Golden Bks.) Random Hse. Children's Bks.

Schaefer, Lola M. An Island Grows. 2006. (ENG., Illus.). 40p. (J). (gr. -1-3). 17.99 *(978-0-06-623930-9(3),* Greenwillow Bks.) HarperCollins Pubs.

Schaub, Michelle. Finding Treasure: A Collection of Collections. Saldana, Carmen, illus. 2019. 32p. (J). (gr. -1-3). lib. bdg. 16.99 *(978-1-58089-875-1(0))* Charlesbridge Publishing, Inc.

Scheffler, Axel. Noisy Farm. 2014. (ENG., Illus.). 10p. (J). (gr. -1-k). 23.95 *(978-0-230-76680-8(3))* Pan Macmillan GBR. Dist: Independent Pubs. Group.

—The New Friend. 2017. (ENG., Illus.). 32p. (J). pap. *(978-0-85763-874-8(2))* Candlewick Pr.

Schertle, Alice. Little Blue Truck Leads the Way. McElmurry, Jill, illus. 2009. (ENG.). 40p. (J). (gr. -1-3). 18.99 *(978-0-15-206389-4(7),* 1199129, Clarion Bks.) HarperCollins Pubs.

—Very Hairy Bear. Phelan, Matt, illus. 2012. lib. bdg. 17.20 *(978-0-606-26605-5(4))* Turtleback.

Scheyder, S. Jane. One More Thing. Scheyder, Jacob P., illus. 2013. (ENG.). 42p. (J). pap. 7.99 *(978-0-9830318-6-4(X))* Andres & Blanton.

Schmid, Paul. Little Bear Dreams. 2018. (ENG., Illus.). 40p. (gr. -1 — 1). 17.95 *(978-0-7148-7724-2(7))* Phaidon Pr., Inc.

Schmidt, Jacqueline. Patchwork Goes under Cover. 2014. (Patchwork Adventures Ser.). (ENG., Illus.). 32p. (J). (gr. -1-2). 17.95 *(978-1-57687-717-3(5),* powerHouse Bks.) powerHse. Bks.

Schnee-Bosch, Penny. Mommy Always Comes Back. Bosch, David, illus. 2013. 40p. pap. 13.95 *(978-0-9727993-6-2(2))* Athanata Arts, Ltd.

Schneider, Judy. But Not Quite. Weeks, Mary, illus. 2004. (J). 19.95 *(978-1-59404-005-4(2))* Peanut Butter Publishing.

Schneider, Marine, illus. I Am Life. 2017. (ENG.). 48p. (J). (gr. -1-3). 19.95 *(978-3-89955-793-0(X))* Die Gestalten Verlag DEU. Dist: Ingram Publisher Services.

Scholastic. George Catches a Cold (Peppa Pig) EOne, illus. 2015. (Geronimo Stilton Cavemice Ser.). (ENG.). 24p. (J). (gr. 2-5). E-Book 7.99 *(978-1-338-05805-5(3))* Scholastic, Inc.

Scholastic, Inc. Staff, contrib. by. The World of Harry Potter: Harry Potter Poster Book. 2011. (Illus.). 125p. (J). pap. *(978-0-545-31482-4(8))* Scholastic, Inc.

Schomer-Wendel, Gretchen & Schomer, Adam Anthony. All Around Town, 1 vol. Renthrope, Damon, illus. 2009. (Becka & the Big Bubble Ser.). (ENG.). 32p. (J). (gr. 1-2). pap. 11.55 *(978-1-60754-105-9(X),* 40ba8d14-355a-4eed-8c80-5dccc55d9e6f, Windmill Bks.) Rosen Publishing Group, Inc., The.

School Zone Staff. Big Hidden Pictures & More. 2019. (ENG.). 320p. (J). (gr. k-2). pap. 13.99 *(978-1-60159-258-3(2),* 3280724e-3904-4601-88f6-cd53873b8ceb) School Zone Publishing Co.

—My First Dot-To-Dots. 2019. (ENG.). 48p. (J). (gr. -1-k). pap. 3.49 *(978-1-60159-246-0(9),* 4c933749-1158-4705-a72c-69190a279aba) School Zone Publishing Co.

—My First Hidden Pictures. 2019. (ENG.). 48p. (J). (gr. -1-k). pap. 3.49 *(978-1-60159-251-4(5),* ec4d1ede-7109-447f-b1f3-b541099c6f62) School Zone Publishing Co.

Schrey, Sophie. Follow Me: Play for Little Hands. Sheridan, Lucie, illus. 2019. (Play for Little Hands Ser.). (ENG.). 14p. (J). (— 1). bds. 9.99 *(978-1-910552-80-3(1))* O'Mara, Michael Bks., Ltd. GBR. Dist: Independent Pubs. Group.

Schuh, Mari. Buses: A 4D Book. 2018. (Transportation Ser.). (ENG., Illus.). 24p. (J). (gr. -1-2). lib. bdg. 24.65 *(978-1-9771-0142-6(9),* 138316, Pebble) Capstone.

—Swimming. 2019. (Spot Sports Ser.). (ENG.). 16p. (J). (gr. -1-1). pap. 7.99 *(978-1-68152-439-9(2),* 11025) Amicus.

—Tae Kwon Do. 2019. (Spot Sports Ser.). (ENG.). 16p. (J). (gr. -1-1). pap. 7.99 *(978-1-68152-440-5(6),* 11026) Amicus.

Schwartz, Amy. Things That Make Me Happy. 2017. (100 Things Ser.). (ENG., Illus.). 24p. (J). (gr. -1 — 1). bds. 7.95 *(978-1-4197-2367-4(7),* 1045010, Abrams Appleseed) Abrams, Inc.

Schwartz, Roslyn. The Mole Sisters & the Blue Egg. 2019. (Mole Sisters Ser.). (Illus.). 32p. (J). bds. 7.99 *(978-1-77321-219-7(2))* Annick Pr., Ltd. CAN. Dist: Publishers Group West (PGW).

—The Mole Sisters & the Question. 2019. (Mole Sisters Ser.). (ENG., Illus.). 32p. (J). (gr. -1-k). bds. 7.99 *(978-1-77321-224-1(9))* Annick Pr., Ltd. CAN. Dist: Publishers Group West (PGW).

—The Mole Sisters & the Rainy Day. 2019. (Mole Sisters Ser.). (ENG., Illus.). 32p. (J). (gr. -1-k). bds. 7.99 *(978-1-77321-229-6(X))* Annick Pr., Ltd. CAN. Dist: Publishers Group West (PGW).

—The Mole Sisters & the Wavy Wheat. 2019. (Mole Sisters Ser.). (ENG., Illus.). 32p. (J). (gr. -1-k). bds. 7.99 *(978-1-77321-214-2(1))* Annick Pr., Ltd. CAN. Dist: Publishers Group West (PGW).

Schwarz, Viviane. Counting with Tiny Cat. Schwarz, Viviane, illus. (ENG., Illus.). (J). (-k). 2018. 24p. bds. 7.99 *(978-0-7636-9821-8(0))* 2017. 32p. 14.99 *(978-0-7636-9462-3(2))* Candlewick Pr.

Schweizer, Chris. The Crogan Adventures: Catfoot's Vengeance. 2015. (Crogan Adventures Ser.: 1). (ENG., Illus.). 200p. (J). pap. 17.99 *(978-1-62010-203-9(X),* 9781620102039, Lion Forge) Oni Pr., Inc.

Scieszka, Jon. Math Curse. Smith, Lane, illus. 2011. (J). (gr. 1-4). 29.95 *(978-0-545-13458-3(7))* Weston Woods Studios, Inc.

—The True Story of the Three Little Pigs 25th Anniversary Edition. Smith, Lane, illus. 25th anniv. ed. 2014. 32p. (J). (gr. k-3). 18.99 *(978-0-451-47195-6(4),* Viking Books for Young Readers) Penguin Young Readers Group.

Scollon, Bill. The Big Case (Disney Zootopia) The Disney Storybook Art Team, illus. 2016. (Step into Reading Ser.). (ENG.). 32p. (J). (gr. -1-1). 5.99 *(978-0-7364-3456-0(9),* RH/Disney) Random Hse. Children's Bks.

Scott-Dixon, Valerie. My Fuzzy Wuzzy Hair. 2012. 32p. pap. 24.95 *(978-1-4626-6426-9(1))* America Star Bks.

Scott, Foresman and Company Staff. Work & Play, Big & Little, You & Me. (J). 18.82 *(978-0-673-21373-0(0),* Scott Foresman) Addison Wesley Schl.

Scott, Margaret. Jimmy Gets a Pet Passport. 2018. (ENG., Illus.). 36p. (J). (gr. 1-5). *(978-1-5289-2440-5(1));* pap. *(978-1-5289-2439-9(8))* Austin Macauley Pubs. Ltd.

Scott, MaryJo. Corduroy's Colors. McCue, Lisa, illus. 2016. (Corduroy Ser.). 14p. (J). (— 1). bds. 5.99 *(978-0-451-47247-2(0),* Viking Books for Young Readers) Penguin Young Readers Group.

Scotton, Rob. Splat the Cat: Oopsie-Daisy. 2014. (Splat the Cat Ser.). (ENG., Illus.). 24p. (J). (gr. -1-3). pap. 5.99 *(978-0-06-211585-0(5),* HarperFestival) HarperCollins Pubs.

—Splat the Cat Takes the Cake. 2012. (Splat the Cat: I Can Read Ser.). (J). lib. bdg. 13.55 *(978-0-606-23582-2(5))* Turtleback.

Scribens, Sunny. My Friend Robot! Skipp, Hui, illus. 2017. (ENG.). 32p. (J). (gr. -1-1). 16.99 *(978-1-78285-322-0(7))* Barefoot Bks., Inc.

Scudamore, Angelika. Noah's Ark Animal ABCs, 1 vol. 2018. (ENG., Illus.). 28p. (J). bds. 9.99 *(978-0-310-76700-8(8))* Zonderkidz.

Seabag-Montefiore, Mary. Black Beauty (Picture Book) Marks, Alan, illus. 2008. (Picture Book Classics Ser.). 24p. (J). 9.99 *(978-0-7945-2250-6(5),* Usborne) EDC Publishing.

Seal, Glenda. The Birth of Billy Bird. 2016. (ENG., Illus.). 56p. (J). pap. *(978-1-910077-95-5(X))* 2QT, Ltd. (Publishing).

Seaworthy, Oscar. Port Side Pirates. 2008. (ENG., Illus.). 32p. (J). 9.99 *(978-1-84686-153-6(5));* 6.99 *(978-1-84686-205-2(1))* Barefoot Bks., Inc.

Sebe, Masayuki. Let's Count To 100! Sebe, Masayuki, illus. 2014. (ENG., Illus.). 24p. (J). (gr. -1-2). 7.95 *(978-1-55453-813-3(0))* Kids Can Pr., Ltd. CAN. Dist: Hachette Bk. Group.

Sebring Lowrey, Janette. Where Is the Poky Little Puppy? Tenggren, Gustaf, illus. 2015. (Little Golden Book Ser.). 24p.

(J). (-k). 5.99 *(978-0-375-84750-9(2)*, Golden Bks.) Random Hse. Children's Bks.

Sedacca, Luisa M. Gigi's Magic Carpet Ride: Travels with Gigi. 2009. (ENG.). 24p. pap. 15.99 *(978-1-4500-0547-0(0))* Xlibris Corp.

Seder, Rufus Butler. ABC Animals!: a Scanimation Picture Book. 2016. (Scanimation Ser.). (ENG., Illus.). 16p. (J). (gr. -1-k). 19.95 *(978-0-7611-7782-1(5)*, 17782) Workman Publishing Co., Inc.

Segel, Robert G. Machine Gun Inventors: A Military History Coloring Book. Pajot, Lauren, illus. 2016. 16p. 4.95 *(978-0-9823918-2-2(X))* Chipotle Publishing, LLC.

Sehlin, Gunhild. Mary's Little Donkey, 30 vols. Muller, Helene, illus. 2016. 32p. (J). 17.95 *(978-1-78250-294-4(7))* Floris Bks. GBR. Dist: Consortium Bk. Sales & Distribution.

Selbert, Kathryn, illus. Ye Cannae Shove Yer Granny off a Bus: A Favourite Scottish Rhyme with Moving Parts, 20 vols. 2018. (Scottish Rhymes Ser.). 12p. (J). 9.95 *(978-1-78250-478-8(8)*, Kelpies) Floris Bks. GBR. Dist: Consortium Bk. Sales & Distribution.

Selznick, Brian. Baby Monkey, Private Eye. 2018. (CHI.). (J). (gr. -1-3). *(978-957-08-5160-1(0))* Linking Publishing Co., Ltd.

Selznick, Brian & Serlin, David. Baby Monkey, Private Eye. Selznick, Brian, illus. 2018. (ENG., Illus.). 192p. (J). (gr. -1-3). 16.99 *(978-1-338-18061-9(4)*, Scholastic Pr.) Scholastic, Inc.

Sendak, Maurice. Donde Viven los Monstruos. 2003. (SPA., Illus.). 40p. (J). (gr. k-3). 12.95 *(978-84-372-2185-4(4))* Altea, Ediciones, S.A. - Grupo Santillana ESP. Dist: Santillana USA Publishing Co., Inc.

—In the Night Kitchen. 2009. (Illus.). 40p. 19.00 *(978-0-7569-9298-9(2))* Perfection Learning Corp.

—In the Night Kitchen: A Caldecott Honor Award Winner. Sendak, Maurice, illus. 25th anniv. rev. ed. 2023. (ENG., Illus.). 40p. (J). (gr. -1-3). 18.95 *(978-0-06-026668-4(6))*; pap. 9.95 *(978-0-06-443436-2(2))* HarperCollins Pubs. (HarperCollins).

—Pierre: A Cautionary Tale in Five Chapters & a Prologue. Sendak, Maurice, illus. 2018. (ENG., Illus.). 48p. (J). (gr. -1-3). pap. 7.95 *(978-0-06-285442-1(9)*, HarperCollins) HarperCollins Pubs.

—Where the Wild Things Are: A Caldecott Award Winner. Sendak, Maurice, illus. 25th anniv. ed. 2012. (ENG., Illus.). 48p. (J). (gr. -1-3). 21.99 *(978-0-06-025492-6(0))*; pap. 8.95 *(978-0-06-443178-1(9))* HarperCollins Pubs. (HarperCollins).

Sender, Ana. The Cottingley Fairies. 2019. (ENG., Illus.). 48p. (J). (gr. -1-2). 17.95 *(978-0-7358-4338-7(4))* North-South Bks., Inc.

Senior, Nicola. Wolfie's Secret. 2019. (ENG., Illus.). 32p. pap. 9.95 *(978-0-571-33124-6(6)*, Faber & Faber Children's Bks.) Faber & Faber, Inc.

Senior, Olive. Anna Carries Water, 1 vol. James, Laura, illus. 2014. (ENG.). 40p. (J). (gr. 1-3). 18.95 *(978-1-896580-60-9(2))* Tradewind Bks. CAN. Dist: Orca Bk. Pubs. USA.

Senior, Suzy. Tales from Christmas Wood. Gray, James Newman, illus. 2015. (ENG.). 32p. (J). pap. 9.99 *(978-0-7459-6546-8(6)*, af064aa2-f291-4bb4-8b6c-132f9f1e1dde, Lion Children's) Lion Hudson PLC GBR. Dist: Baker & Taylor Publisher Services (BTPS).

Sergeyeva, Marina. Nikki & Nick Are Great Friends to Pick. Sergeyeva, Marina, illus. 2012. (Illus.). 34p. 19.95 *(978-0-9834735-4-1(4))* Leo Publishing.

Sermons, Faye. No Ordinary Cat. Becket, Nancy, illus. 2009. 40p. pap. 16.99 *(978-1-4389-6242-9(8))* AuthorHouse.

Server, Lee. Lions - Pb: A Portrait of the Animal World. 2013. (Portrait of the Animal World Ser.). (Illus.). 72p. pap. 9.95 *(978-1-59764-331-3(9))* New Line Bks.

—Tigers - Pb: A Portrait of the Animal World. 2013. (Portrait of the Animal World Ser.). (Illus.). 72p. pap. 9.95 *(978-1-59764-319-1(X))* New Line Bks.

Sesame Workshop, Sesame, et al. Sesame Street Let's Cook! 2015. (Sesame Street Ser.). (ENG., Illus.). 128p. (gr. -1-k). 19.99 *(978-0-544-45436-1(7)*, 1599082, Harvest) HarperCollins Pubs.

Seuss. Dr. Seuss's Happy Birthday, Baby! Gerardi, Jan, illus. 2009. (Dr. Seuss Nursery Collection). (ENG.). 12p. (J). (— 1). 11.99 *(978-0-375-84621-2(2)*, Random Hse. Bks. for Young Readers) Random Hse. Children's Bks.

—Gerald Mcboing Boing. Crawford, Mel, illus. 2017. (Classic Seuss Ser.). (ENG.). 40p. (J). (gr. k-4). 16.99 *(978-1-5247-1635-6(9)*, Random Hse. Bks. for Young Readers) Random Hse. Children's Bks.

—Gerald Mcboing Boing. Seuss, illus. 2004. (Little Golden Book Ser.). (ENG., Illus.). 24p. (J). (gr. -1-2). 5.99 *(978-0-375-82721-1(8)*, Golden Bks.) Random Hse. Children's Bks.

—The Many Mice of Mr. Brice. McKie, Roy, illus. 2015. (Big Bright & Early Board Book Ser.). 24p. (J). (— 1). bds. 7.99 *(978-0-553-49733-5(2)*, Random Hse. Bks. for Young Readers) Random Hse. Children's Bks.

—Would You Rather Be a Bullfrog? 2014. (Big Bright & Early Board Book Ser.). (ENG., Illus.). 24p. (J). (— 1). bds. 6.99 *(978-0-385-37515-3(8)*, Random Hse. Bks. for Young Readers) Random Hse. Children's Bks.

Seven, John & Christy, Jana. Happy Punks 1 2 3: A Counting Story. 2013. (Wee Rebel Ser.). (ENG., Illus.). 32p. (gr. -1). bds. 15.95 *(978-1-933149-67-7(1))* Manic D Pr.

Sewell, Matt. The Atlas of Amazing Birds: (fun, Colorful Watercolor Paintings of Birds from Around the World with Unusual Facts, Ages 5-10, Perfect Gift for Young Birders & Naturalists) 2019. (ENG., Illus.). 160p. (J). (gr. k-5). 19.95 *(978-1-61689-857-1(7))* Princeton Architectural Pr.

Seyderhelm, Amanda. Isaac & the Red Jumper. Scott, Ann, illus. 2013. 26p. pap. *(978-0-9572146-1-3(8))* HARK Pubns.

Shah, Sapna Jaiswal. Sapna Aunty's Hindi Book of Colors: Rang. 2004. (HIN.). (J). 8.00 *(978-0-9741686-0-9(2))* 3N Media Group.

Shand, Jennifer. Why Do Tractors Have Such Big Tires? Stem. Fabbri, Daniele, illus. 2014. (ENG.). 20p. (J). (gr. k-4). 8.99 *(978-1-4867-0382-1(8))* Flowerpot Children's Pr. Inc. CAN. Dist: Cardinal Pubs. Group.

Shannon, David. Roy Digs Dirt. Shannon, David, illus. 2020. (ENG., Illus.). 40p. (J). (gr. -1-k). 17.99 *(978-1-338-25101-2(5)*, Blue Sky Pr., The) Scholastic, Inc.

Shapur, Mira. Singer & the Paint. Shapur, Fredun, illus. 2017. (ENG.). 32p. (J). (gr. -1-17). 16.95 *(978-1-84976-475-9(1)*, 1652201) Tate Publishing, Ltd. GBR. Dist: Abrams, Inc.

Sharp, Lani. Has Anyone Seen the Creature? 2016. (ENG., Illus.). 24p. pap. 9.95 *(978-1-78554-396-8(2)*, 2b175d46-ee31-4189-8e2c-2bdce7d4690c) Austin Macauley Pubs. Ltd. GBR. Dist: Baker & Taylor Publisher Services (BTPS).

Sharpe, Jemima. Mr Moon Wakes Up. Sharpe, Jemima, illus. 2016. (Child's Play Library). (Illus.). 32p. (J). pap. *(978-1-84643-693-2(1))* Child's Play International Ltd.

Sharpe, Katie & Sharpe, Tony. Wake up Sun. 2008. (ENG.). 26p. pap. 14.99 *(978-1-4389-2897-5(1))* AuthorHouse.

Shaskan, Trisha Speed. Meteorite or Meteor-Wrong? Case 2. Shaskan, Stephen, illus. 2018. (Q & Ray Ser.). (ENG.). 48p. (J). (gr. 2-5). pap. 9.99 *(978-1-5415-1047-0(X)*, 447b5341-8871-4bd0-9db7-4c80dbc326c4, Graphic Universe™) Lerner Publishing Group.

Shattil, Wendy, et al, photos by. Sierra Babies. 2013. (Illus.). 26p. (J). 8.95 *(978-1-56037-557-9(4))* Farcountry Pr.

Shava, Ryder. Mr. Ramirez Is My Teacher, 1 vol., 1. 2015. (Rosen REAL Readers: Social Studies Nonfiction / Fiction: Myself, My Community, My World Ser.). (ENG.). 8p. (J). (gr. k-1). pap. 5.46 *(978-1-5081-1710-0(1)*, 547d12e6-f150-4590-8eea-b69a6136296c, Rosen Classroom) Rosen Publishing Group, Inc., The.

Shaw-MacKinnon, Margaret. Tiktala, 1 vol. Gal, Laszlo, illus. 2005. (ENG.). 32p. (J). (gr. 1-4). per. 9.95 *(978-1-55005-143-8(1)*, e1d19284-7c03-4f56-a262-c414345d9bdb) Fitzhenry & Whiteside, Ltd. CAN. Dist: Firefly Bks., Ltd.

Shaw, Mary. Brady Brady & the Cleanup Hitters. Temple, Chuck, illus. 2008. 32p. (J). pap. *(978-1-897169-11-7(6))* Brady Brady, Inc.

Shaw, Nancy E. Sheep in a Shop Board Book. Apple, Margot, illus. 2017. (Sheep in a Jeep Ser.). (ENG.). 28p. (J). (— 1). bds. 7.99 *(978-1-328-70286-9(3)*, 1672394, Clarion Bks.) HarperCollins Pubs.

Shea, Bob. Buddy & the Bunnies in: Don't Play with Your Food! 2014. (ENG., Illus.). 40p. (J). (gr. -1-3). 16.99 *(978-1-4231-6807-2(0))* Hyperion Bks. for Children.

—Dinosaur vs. Bedtime. Shea, Bob, illus. 2011. (Dinosaur vs. Book Ser.: 1). (ENG., Illus.). 30p. (J). (gr. -1-k). bds. 6.99 *(978-1-4231-3788-7(4))* Hyperion Pr.

Shealy, Dennis R. I'm a Bulldozer. 2015. (Little Golden Book Ser.). (Illus.). 24p. (J). (-k). 5.99 *(978-0-553-49683-3(2)*, Golden Bks.) Random Hse. Children's Bks.

—I'm a Monster Truck. Staake, Bob, illus. 2011. (Little Golden Book Ser.). 24p. (J). (gr. -1-2). 5.99 *(978-0-375-86132-1(7)*, Golden Bks.) Random Hse. Children's Bks.

—My Little Golden Book about Dinosaurs. Laberis, Steph, illus. 2017. (Little Golden Book Ser.). 24p. (J). (-k). 5.99 *(978-0-385-37861-1(0)*, Golden Bks.) Random Hse. Children's Bks.

Shearring, Maisie Paradise. The Happy Prince: A Tale by Oscar Wilde. 2017. (ENG., Illus.). 48p. (J). (gr. k-5). 14.95 *(978-0-500-65111-7(6)*, 565111) Thames & Hudson.

Sheckels, Astrid, illus. Nic & Nellie, 1 vol. 2013. (ENG.). 36p. (J). (gr. 1-4). 17.95 *(978-1-934031-52-0(6)*, d981927c-4686-4e6f-bbee-9d134ce68c96) Islandport Pr., Inc.

Sheehan, Peter. Willy Wagtail grows Up. 2010. 32p. pap. 19.99 *(978-1-4461-3281-4(1))* Lulu Pr., Inc.

Shepherd, Donna J. Sully's Topsy Tale. Collier, Kevin Scott, illus. 2010. 20p. pap. 10.95 *(978-1-61633-047-7(3))* Guardian Angel Publishing, Inc.

Shepherd, Jessica. Grandma. 2014. (Child's Play Library). (Illus.). 32p. (J). *(978-1-84643-602-4(8))* Child's Play International Ltd.

Shepherd, Jodie. A Sweet Christmas on Sesame Street (Sesame Street) A Scratch & Sniff Story. Brannon, Tom, illus. 2018. (ENG.). 24p. (J). (gr. -1-2). 9.99 *(978-0-525-58133-8(2)*, Random Hse. Bks. for Young Readers) Random Hse. Children's Bks.

Sheppard, Markette. My Rainy Day Rocket Ship. Palmer, Charly, illus. 2020. (ENG.). 32p. (J). (gr. -1-3). 17.99 *(978-1-5344-6177-2(9)*, Simon & Schuster Bks. For Young Readers) Simon & Schuster Bks. For Young Readers.

Sheth, Kashmira. Tiger in My Soup, 1 vol. Ebbeler, Jeffrey, illus. 2015. 32p. (J). (gr. -1-3). pap. 7.99 *(978-1-56145-890-5(2))* Peachtree Publishing Co. Inc.

Shields, Gillian. When the World Was Waiting for You. Currey, Anna, illus. 2018. (ENG.). 26p. (J). bds. 9.99 *(978-1-5476-0033-5(0)*, 900196018, Bloomsbury Children's Bks.) Bloomsbury Publishing USA.

Shin, Ami. Mice in the City: London. 2018. (Mice in the City Ser.: 0). (Illus.). 32p. (J). (gr. k-5). 19.95 *(978-0-500-65129-2(9)*, 565129) Thames & Hudson.

—Mice in the City: New York. 2018. (Mice in the City Ser.: 0). (Illus.). 32p. (J). (gr. k-5). 19.95 *(978-0-500-65128-5(0)*, 565128) Thames & Hudson.

Shin, Yujin, illus. My Magical Unicorn. 2019. (My Magical Friends Ser.). (ENG.). 8p. (J). (gr. -1 — 1). bds. 8.99 *(978-1-4197-3729-9(5)*, 1277910) Abrams, Inc.

Shipton, Paul. Clown School. Blake, Beccy, illus. 2005. (ENG.). 24p. (J). lib. bdg. 23.65 *(978-1-59646-752-1(5))* Dingles & Co.

Short, Robyn & Williams, Nanon McKewn. Peace People. Bailey, Lindsey, illus. 2013. 38p. 18.95 *(978-0-9911148-2-5(5))* Goodmedia Communications, LLC.

Shraya, Vivek. The Boy & the Bindi. Perera, Rajni, illus. 2016. 38p. (J). (gr. -1-3). 17.95 *(978-1-55152-668-3(9))* Arsenal Pulp Pr. CAN. Dist: Consortium Bk. Sales & Distribution.

Siber, Kate. National Parks of the USA. Turnham, Chris, illus. 2018. (National Parks of the USA Ser.: 1). (ENG.). 112p. (J). (gr. 1-4). 30.00 *(978-1-84780-976-6(6)*, 302819, Wide Eyed Editions) Quarto Publishing Group UK GBR. Dist: Hachette UK Distribution.

Siddals, Mary McKenna. Compost Stew: An a to Z Recipe for the Earth. Wolff, Ashley, illus. 2014. 40p. (J). (gr. -1-2). 8.99 *(978-0-385-75538-2(4)*, Dragonfly Bks.) Random Hse. Children's Bks.

Sierra, Judy. Mind Your Manners, B. B. Wolf. 2012. lib. bdg. 18.40 *(978-0-606-26784-7(0))* Turtleback.

—Suppose You Meet a Dinosaur: a First Book of Manners. Bowers, Tim, illus. 2016. 40p. (J). (gr. -1-2). 7.99 *(978-1-101-93250-6(3)*, Dragonfly Bks.) Random Hse. Children's Bks.

Sif, Birgitta. Oliver. Sif, Birgitta, illus. 2012. (ENG., Illus.). 40p. (J). (gr. -1-3). 17.99 *(978-0-7636-6247-9(X))* Candlewick Pr.

Silver Dolphin en Español Editors. Tesoro de Libros de Calcomanias Princesas. 2004. (Disney Calcomanias Ser.). (SPA., Illus.). 72p. (J). pap. *(978-970-718-106-9(0)*, Silver Dolphin en Español) Advanced Marketing, S. de R. L. de C. V.

Silver, Gail. Peace, Bugs, & Understanding: An Adventure in Sibling Harmony. Ly, Youme Nguyen, illus. 2014. 48p. (J). (gr. -1-3). 16.95 *(978-1-937006-63-1(8)*, Plum Blossom Bks.) Parallax Pr.

Silver, Skye. Baby Play. 2019. (ENG., Illus.). 16p. (J). (gr. -1-k). bds. 7.99 *(978-1-78285-728-0(1))* Barefoot Bks., Inc.

Silverstein, Shel. Lafcadio, the Lion Who Shot Back. Silverstein, Shel, illus. 2013. (ENG., Illus.). 112p. (J). (gr. -1-3). 17.99 *(978-0-06-025675-3(3)*, HarperCollins) HarperCollins Pubs.

—Lafcadio, the Lion Who Shot Back. 2009. (CHI., Illus.). (J). *(978-7-5442-4521-0(7))* Nanhai Publishing Co.

Silvestro, Annie. The Christmas Tree Who Loved Trains: A Christmas Holiday Book for Kids. Zakimi, Paola, illus. 2018. (ENG.). 32p. (J). (gr. -1-3). 17.99 *(978-0-06-256168-8(5)*, HarperCollins) HarperCollins Pubs.

Sim, Stephanie. Copycat. 2016. (Illus.). 32p. (J). (gr. -1-2). 16.95 *(978-1-927018-76-7(5))* Simply Read Bks. CAN. Dist: Ingram Publisher Services.

Simard, Danielle. The Little Word Catcher, 1 vol. Côté, Geneviève & Côté, Geneviève, illus. 2008. (ENG.). 32p. (J). (gr. 1-3). 14.95 *(978-1-897187-44-9(0))* Second Story Pr. CAN. Dist: Orca Bk. Pubs. USA.

Simee. Giggles Feel Good, 1 vol. 2010. 18p. pap. 24.95 *(978-1-4489-4878-9(9))* PublishAmerica, Inc.

Simmonds, Posy. Baker Cat. 2015. (ENG., Illus.). 32p. (J). (gr. -1-k). pap. 11.99 *(978-1-78344-105-1(4))* Andersen Pr. GBR. Dist: Independent Pubs. Group.

—Fred. 2014. (ENG., Illus.). 32p. (J). (-k). pap. 9.99 *(978-1-78344-029-0(5))* Andersen Pr. GBR. Dist: Independent Pubs. Group.

Simms, Albert Clint. My Values & Morales Treasury. 2011. 114p. 32.50 *(978-1-257-16162-1(8))* Lulu Pr., Inc.

Simon, Annette. Robot Zombie Frankenstein! Simon, Annette, illus. 2012. (ENG., Illus.). 40p. (J). (gr. -1-3). 16.99 *(978-0-7636-5124-4(9))* Candlewick Pr.

Simon, Francesca. The Goat Cafe. Broadley, Leo, illus. 2019. (ENG.). 32p. 16.95 *(978-0-571-32867-3(9)*, Faber & Faber Children's Bks.) Faber & Faber, Inc.

—Horrid Henry: Horrid Henry's Gold Medal Games: Colouring, Puzzles & Activities. 2017. (Horrid Henry Ser.). (ENG., Illus.). 24p. (J). (gr. 1-3). pap. 8.99 *(978-1-5101-0127-2(6)*, Orion Children's Bks.) Hachette Children's Group GBR. Dist: Hachette Bk. Group.

Simon, Jenne, adapted by. The Magic Charm Chase. 2016. (Little Charmers Ser.). (ENG., Illus.). 24p. (J). (gr. -1-1). 16.19 *(978-1-4844-8691-7(9))* Scholastic, Inc.

Simon, Seymour. Water. 2017. (ENG., Illus.). 40p. (J). (gr. 1-5). 17.99 *(978-0-06-247055-3(8))*; pap. 7.99 *(978-0-06-247054-6(X))* HarperCollins Pubs. (HarperCollins).

Simont, Marc. The Stray Dog: A Caldecott Honor Award Winner. Simont, Marc, illus. 2003. (ENG., Illus.). 32p. (J). (gr. -1-3). pap. 8.99 *(978-0-06-443669-4(1)*, HarperCollins) HarperCollins Pubs.

Simpson, Caroll. The First Beaver, 1 vol. 2015. (Coastal Spirit Tales Ser.). (ENG., Illus.). 32p. (J). (gr. 1-3). pap. 12.95 *(978-1-77203-062-4(7))* Heritage Hse. CAN. Dist: Orca Bk. Pubs. USA.

Simpson, Dana. Today I'll Be a Unicorn. 2018. (Phoebe & Her Unicorn Ser.). (ENG., Illus.). 12p. (J). bds. 7.99 *(978-1-4494-8999-1(0))* Andrews McMeel Publishing.

Simpson McLellan, Stephanie. Leon's Song, 1 vol. Bonder, Dianna, illus. 2005. (ENG.). 32p. (J). (gr. -1-2). pap. 7.95 *(978-1-55041-815-6(7)*, ddd0d308-43e9-4d5f-a98a-385ec719b937) Fitzhenry & Whiteside, Ltd. CAN. Dist: Firefly Bks., Ltd.

Sims, Lesley & Sims, Lesley. Stories from Around the World for Children. 2013. (Picture Bks). 128p. (J). ring bd. 18.99 *(978-0-7945-3210-9(1)*, Usborne) EDC Publishing.

Singh, Lee. The Greatest Opposites Book on Earth. Frost, Tom, illus. 2017. (ENG.). 16p. (J). (gr. -1-2). bds. 18.99 *(978-0-7636-9554-5(8)*, Big Picture Press) Candlewick Pr.

Singh, Neha. I Need to Pee. 2018. (ENG., Illus.). 32p. (J). (gr. k-3). pap. 8.99 *(978-0-14-344293-6(7)*, Puffin) Penguin Bks. India PVT, Ltd IND. Dist: Independent Pubs. Group.

Sis, Peter. Fire Truck Board Book. Sis, Peter, illus. 2004. (ENG., Illus.). 28p. (J). (gr. -1-1). bds. 6.99 *(978-0-06-056259-5(5)*, Greenwillow Bks.) HarperCollins Pubs.

Sisson, Stephanie Roth. Spring after Spring: How Rachel Carson Inspired the Environmental Movement. Sisson, Stephanie Roth, illus. 2018. (ENG., Illus.). 40p. (J). 18.99 *(978-1-62672-819-6(4)*, 900174864) Roaring Brook Pr.

Sitzenstock, Gabriele. Raising Puppy. 2006. (J). spiral bd. 12.95 *(978-1-59872-721-0(4))* Instant Pub.

Skewes, John. Larry Loves Boston! A Larry Gets Lost Book. 2016. (Larry Gets Lost Ser.). (Illus.). 20p. (J). (— 1). bds. 10.99 *(978-1-63217-047-7(7)*, Little Bigfoot) Sasquatch Bks.

—Larry Loves Washington, DC! A Larry Gets Lost Book. 2016. (Larry Gets Lost Ser.). (Illus.). 20p. (J). (— 1). bds. 10.99 *(978-1-63217-048-4(5)*, Little Bigfoot) Sasquatch Bks.

Skorpen, Liesel Moak. Outside My Window. Mayer, Mercer, illus. 2004. 32p. (J). (gr. -1-3). 16.89 *(978-0-06-050775-6(6))* HarperCollins Pubs.

Slate, Joseph. Miss Bindergarten Stays Home from Kindergarten. Wolff, Ashley, illus. 2004. 40p. (J). (gr. -1-k). reprint ed. pap. 8.99 *(978-0-14-230127-2(2)*, Puffin Books) Penguin Young Readers Group.

Slater, David Michael. The Bored Book. Keith, Doug, illus. 2017. (ENG.). 32p. (J). (gr. -1-3). 8.99 *(978-1-77229-018-9(1))* Simply Read Bks. CAN. Dist: Ingram Publisher Services.

Slater, Kate. Magpie's Treasure. Slater, Kate, illus. 2012. (ENG., Illus.). 32p. (J). (gr. -1 — 1). pap. 10.99 *(978-1-84939-075-0(4))* Andersen Pr. GBR. Dist: Independent Pubs. Group.

Slavin, Bill. Who Broke the Teapot?! 2016. (Illus.). 32p. (J). (gr. -1-2). 16.99 *(978-1-77049-833-4(8)*, Tundra Bks.) Tundra Bks. CAN. Dist: Penguin Random Hse. LLC.

Slenzak, Miller. I Can Be a Pilot, 1 vol. 2018. (I Can Be Anything! Ser.). (ENG.). 24p. (gr. k-k). 24.27 *(978-1-5382-1764-1(3)*, 5fc5352a-d821-4054-85dc-b5c19cb0bc0a) Stevens, Gareth Publishing LLLP.

Slobodkin, Louis & Slobodkin, Florence. Too Many Mittens / a Good Place to Hide / the Little Mermaid Who Could Not Sing. 2017. (Dover Children's Classics Ser.). (ENG., Illus.). 112p. pap. 14.99 *(978-0-486-81588-6(9)*, 815889) Dover Pubns., Inc.

Smale, Denise L. What If the Sun Didn't Rise. Smale, Denise L. & Blowars, Ryan, illus. 2011. 32p. pap. 24.95 *(978-1-4560-5032-0(X))* America Star Bks.

Smart, Jamie. Where's the Doctor? 2017. (Illus.). 40p. (YA). pap. 9.99 *(978-1-4059-0904-4(8)*, 14ba51f7-18af-45aa-bc80-7ed27d625b1a) Penguin Bks., Ltd. GBR. Dist: Diamond Comic Distributors, Inc.

Smart Start Pencil Skills: Numbers. 2017. (ENG., Illus.). 64p. (J). pap. 8.00 *(978-1-907604-90-4(1))* Award Pubns. Ltd. GBR. Dist: Parkwest Pubns., Inc.

Smiley, Jess Smart. Upside down (Book Two): a Hat Full of Spells. 2015. (Illus.). 192p. (J). (gr. 4-7). pap. 14.99 *(978-1-60309-371-2(0)*, 9781603093712) Top Shelf Productions.

Smith, Ben Bailey. Bear Moves. Akyuz, Sav, illus. 2018. (ENG.). 40p. (J). (-k). 15.99 *(978-0-7636-9831-7(8)*, Candlewick Entertainment) Candlewick Pr.

Smith, Brendan Powell. The Christmas Story: The Brick Bible for Kids. 2012. (Illus.). 32p. (J). (gr. -1-k). 12.95 *(978-1-62087-173-7(4)*, 620173, Sky Pony Pr.) Skyhorse Publishing Co., Inc.

Smith Bresciani, Cathleen & Eldredge, Richard. Sassafrass Jones & the Search for a Forever Home. 2013. 54p. 24.99 *(978-0-578-12084-3(4))* Misfit Mouse.

Smith, Danna. Springtime Babies. Fisher, Takako, illus. 2018. (Little Golden Book Ser.). 24p. (J). (-k). 4.99 *(978-1-5247-1516-8(6)*, Golden Bks.) Random Hse. Children's Bks.

Smith, Fiona Veitch. David & the Grumpy King. 2015. (ENG., Illus.). 32p. (J). pap. 9.00 *(978-0-281-07459-4(3)*, f04c046f-17f8-45da-9c83-05b030a2cae9) SPCK Publishing GBR. Dist: Baker & Taylor Publisher Services (BTPS).

—David & the Kingmaker. 2015. (ENG., Illus.). 32p. (J). pap. 9.00 *(978-0-281-07456-3(9)*, ea304135-b524-489c-88dd-82434b078562) SPCK Publishing GBR. Dist: Baker & Taylor Publisher Services (BTPS).

—David & the Lonely Prince. 2015. (ENG., Illus.). 32p. (J). pap. 9.00 *(978-0-281-07458-7(5)*, 3d4fc4fe-ccc3-44cb-8925-e5e0f050cffd) SPCK Publishing GBR. Dist: Baker & Taylor Publisher Services (BTPS).

—David & the Never-Ending Kingdom. 2015. (ENG., Illus.). 32p. (J). pap. 9.00 *(978-0-281-07460-0(7)*, a8eeb260-d770-4e6e-a775-c807ad6348cc) SPCK Publishing GBR. Dist: Baker & Taylor Publisher Services (BTPS).

—Joseph & the Jealous Brothers. 2016. (ENG., Illus.). 32p. (J). pap. 12.99 *(978-0-281-07469-3(0)*, 3f67d757-302a-428a-9f25-c9504186fcf4) SPCK Publishing GBR. Dist: Baker & Taylor Publisher Services (BTPS).

—Joseph & the Lying Lady. 2016. (ENG., Illus.). 32p. (J). pap. 9.00 *(978-0-281-07470-9(4)*, 59d8279c-fad6-4d42-921c-7f06b72bf0e9) SPCK Publishing GBR. Dist: Baker & Taylor Publisher Services (BTPS).

—Joseph & the Rainbow Robe. 2016. (ENG., Illus.). 32p. (J). pap. 12.99 *(978-0-281-07468-6(2)*, fe2a3c7a-048d-450b-80a4-4b9b1c275f40) SPCK Publishing GBR. Dist: Baker & Taylor Publisher Services (BTPS).

Smith, Jane. It's Halloween, Chloe Zoe! Smith, Jane, illus. 2017. (Chloe Zoe Ser.). (ENG., Illus.). 32p. (J). (gr. -1-3). 12.99 *(978-0-8075-1210-4(9)*, 807512109) Whitman, Albert & Co.

Smith, Jim. Future Ratboy & the Quest for the Missing Thingy (Future Ratboy) 2017. (Future Ratboy Ser.: 3). (ENG., Illus.). 256p. (J). (gr. 2-4). pap. 5.99 *(978-1-4052-8398-4(X))* Farshore GBR. Dist: HarperCollins Pubs.

Smith, Kim. Back to the Future. 2018. (Illus.). 44p. (J). *(978-1-68369-044-3(3))* Quirk Bks.

Smith, Kim, illus. Back to the Future: The Classic Illustrated Storybook. 2018. (Pop Classics Ser.: 4). 40p. (J). (gr. -1-3). 18.99 *(978-1-68369-023-8(0))* Quirk Bks.

—Buffy the Vampire Slayer: A Picture Book. 2018. (Pop Classics Ser.: 5). 40p. (J). (gr. -1-3). 18.99 *(978-1-68369-069-6(9))* Quirk Bks.

Smith, Lesley, illus. Great Big Enormous Turnip. Smith, Lesley, . 2012. (ENG.). 32p. (J). pap. 6.50 *(978-1-84135-192-6(X))* Award Pubns. Ltd. GBR. Dist: Parkwest Pubns., Inc.

Smith, Linda. Smith Picture Book. Date not set. (Illus.). 32p. (J). (gr. -1-3). 5.99 *(978-0-06-443621-2(7))* HarperCollins Pubs.

Smith, Lori Joy. Good Morning Book. 2017. (Illus.). 24p. (J). (gr. -1-k). 12.95 *(978-1-77229-004-2(1))* Simply Read Bks. CAN. Dist: Ingram Publisher Services.

—The Goodnight Book. 2014. (ENG., Illus.). 24p. (J). (gr. -1-k). 12.95 *(978-1-927018-42-2(0)*, 9781927018422) Simply Read Bks. CAN. Dist: Ingram Publisher Services.

—I Love You Like ... 2018. (ENG., Illus.). 32p. (J). (gr. -1-3). 16.95 *(978-1-77147-157-2(3))* Owlkids Bks. Inc. CAN. Dist: Publishers Group West (PGW).

Smith, Michael W. Nighty Night & Good Night, 1 vol. 2018. (Nurturing Steps Ser.). (ENG., Illus.). 22p. (J). bds. 9.99 *(978-0-310-76941-5(8))* Zonderkidz.

Smith, Michael W. & Nawrocki, Mike. Nighty Night & Good Night, 1 vol. 2018. (Nurturing Steps Ser.). (ENG., Illus.). 24p. (J). 12.99 *(978-0-310-76701-5(6))* Zonderkidz.

Smith, Miranda. What's Inside? McLelland, Kate, illus. 2019. (ENG.). 12p. (J). (gr. -1-k). 21.99 *(978-1-4052-8863-7(9)*, Red Shed) Farshore GBR. Dist: Independent Pubs. Group, HarperCollins Pubs.

Smith, Nikki. Five Little Speckled Frogs Activity Guide. 2010. 66p. pap. 10.00 *(978-0-557-36823-5(5))* Lulu Pr., Inc.

Smith, Sarah. The Butterfly House. 2014. (ENG., Illus.). 32p. (gr. k-17). 19.95 *(978-1-84976-205-2(8))* Tate Publishing, Ltd. GBR. Dist: Abrams, Inc.

—Home & Dry. Smith, Sarah, illus. 2017. (Child's Play Library). (Illus.). 32p. (J). pap. *(978-1-84643-756-4(3))* Child's Play International Ltd.

Smith, Sherri. Where's the Baby??? 2012. (ENG.). 39p. pap. 11.95 *(978-1-4327-9609-9(7))* Outskirts Pr., Inc.

Smith, Suzanne & Taylor, Lindsay. Doodle Girl & the Monkey Mystery. Maurri, Marnie, illus. 2016. (ENG.). 32p. (J). pap. 9.99 *(978-1-4711-2318-4(9),* Simon & Schuster Children's) Simon & Schuster, Ltd. GBR. Dist: Simon & Schuster, Inc.

Smith, Wade. Smitty Tackles Bullying. Little, James, illus. 2017. (ENG.). 24p. (J). 19.95 *(978-1-942945-49-9(3),* 64f42c16-b1e5-447e-a6e2-426622b69688) Night Heron Media.

Smothers, Ethel Footman. Auntee Edna. Clay, Wil, illus. 2004. 32p. (J). (ENG.). pap. 8.00 *(978-0-8028-5246-5(7));* 16.00 *(978-0-8028-5154-3(1))* Eerdmans, William B. Publishing Co.

Snider, Grant. What Color Is Night? 2019. (ENG., Illus.). 44p. (J). (gr. -1 — 1). 15.99 *(978-1-4521-7992-6(1))* Chronicle Bks. LLC.

—What Sound Is Morning? 2020. (ENG., Illus.). 48p. (J). (gr. -1 — 1). 15.99 *(978-1-4521-7993-3(X))* Chronicle Bks. LLC.

Sobel, June. B Is for Bulldozer Lap Board Book: A Construction ABC. Iwai, Melissa, illus. 2018. (ENG.). 32p. (J). (— 1). bds. 12.99 *(978-1-328-77052-3(4),* 1681071, Clarion Bks.) HarperCollins Pubs.

—The Goodnight Train Lap Board Book. Huliska-Beith, Laura, illus. 2017. (Goodnight Train Ser.). (ENG.). 30p. (J). (— 1). bds. 12.99 *(978-1-328-76438-6(9),* 1681068, Clarion Bks.) HarperCollins Pubs.

Sobrino, Javier. Me Gusta. Villamuza, Noemí, tr. Villamuza, Noemí, illus. (SPA.). 28p. 20.99 *(978-84-88342-35-5(7))* S.A. Kokinos ESP. Dist: Lectorum Pubns., Inc.

—Night Sounds, 1 vol. Amado, Elisa, tr. Urberuaga, Emilio, illus. 2013. (ENG.). 36p. (J). (gr. -1-1). 16.95 *(978-1-55498-332-2(0))* Groundwood Bks. CAN. Dist: Publishers Group West (PGW).

Sofer, Barbara. Ilan Ramon: Israel's First Astronaut. 2004. (General Jewish Interest Ser.). (J). pap. 6.95 *(978-0-929371-49-8(6))* Lerner Publishing Group.

—Shabbat Shalom: Israel's First Astronaut. 2004. (Illus.). 12p. (J). 16.95 *(978-0-930494-91-9(1),* Kar-Ben Publishing) Lerner Publishing Group.

Sollinger, Emily. Dinotrux to the Rescue! 2016. (Dinotrux Passport Reading Level 1 Ser.). (J). lib. bdg. 13.55 *(978-0-606-38320-2(4))* Turtleback.

Sommer, Carl. Can You Help Me Find My Smile? Budwine, Greg, illus. 2003. (Another Sommer-Time Story Ser.). (ENG.). 48p. (J). (gr. 1-4). 16.95 incl. audio compact disk *(978-1-57537-507-6(9))* Advance Publishing, Inc.

—I Am a Lion! 2003. (Another Sommer-Time Story Ser.). (Illus.). 48p. (J). (gr. k-4). lib. bdg. 23.95 incl. audio *(978-1-57537-759-9(4))* Advance Publishing, Inc.

—I Am a Lion! Budwine, Greg, illus. 2003. (Another Sommer-Time Story Ser.). (ENG.). 48p. (J). (gr. k-4). lib. bdg. 23.95 incl. audio compact disk *(978-1-57537-709-4(8))* Advance Publishing, Inc.

—I Am a Lion! 2003. (Another Sommer-Time Story Ser.). (Illus.). 48p. (J). (gr. 1-4). 16.95 incl. audio *(978-1-57537-558-8(3))* Advance Publishing, Inc.

—I Am a Lion! Budwine, Greg, illus. 2003. (Another Sommer-Time Story Ser.). (ENG.). 48p. (J). (gr. 1-4). 16.95 incl. audio compact disk *(978-1-57537-509-0(5))* Advance Publishing, Inc.

—If Only I Were. . . 2003. (Another Sommer-Time Story Ser.). (Illus.). 48p. (J). (gr. 1-4). 16.95 incl. audio *(978-1-57537-551-9(6))* Advance Publishing, Inc.

—If Only I Were. . . James, Kennon, illus. 2003. (Another Sommer-Time Story Ser.). (ENG.). 48p. (J). 16.95 incl. audio compact disk *(978-1-57537-502-1(8))* Advance Publishing, Inc.

—King of the Pond. 2003. (Another Sommer-Time Story Ser.). (Illus.). 48p. (J). (gr. k-4). lib. bdg. 23.95 incl. audio *(978-1-57537-766-7(7));* (gr. 1-4). 16.95 incl. audio *(978-1-57537-565-6(6))* Advance Publishing, Inc.

—King of the Pond. Budwine, Greg, illus. 2003. (Another Sommer-Time Story Ser.). (ENG.). 48p. (J). (gr. k-4). lib. bdg. 23.95 incl. audio compact disk *(978-1-57537-716-2(0));* (gr. 1-4). 16.95 incl. audio compact disk *(978-1-57537-516-8(8))* Advance Publishing, Inc.

—Light Your Candle. 2003. (Another Sommer-Time Story Ser.). (Illus.). 48p. (J). (gr. k-4). lib. bdg. 23.95 incl. audio compact disk *(978-1-57537-768-1(3));* 16.95 incl. audio *(978-1-57537-567-0(2))* Advance Publishing, Inc.

—Light Your Candle. James, Kennon, illus. 2003. (Another Sommer-Time Story Ser.). 48p. (J). (ENG.). 16.95 incl. audio compact disk *(978-1-57537-518-2(4));* lib. bdg. 23.95 incl. audio compact disk *(978-1-57537-718-6(7))* Advance Publishing, Inc.

—The Little Red Train. 2003. (Another Sommer-Time Story Ser.). (Illus.). 48p. (J). (gr. k-4). lib. bdg. 23.95 incl. audio *(978-1-57537-764-3(0))* Advance Publishing, Inc.

—The Little Red Train. James, Kennon, illus. 2003. (Another Sommer-Time Story Ser.). (ENG.). 48p. (J). (gr. k-3). 16.95 incl. audio compact disk *(978-1-57537-014-9(X));* lib. bdg. 23.95 incl. audio compact disk *(978-1-57537-714-8(4))* Advance Publishing, Inc.

—The Little Red Train. 2003. (Another Sommer-Time Story Ser.). (Illus.). 48p. (J). (gr. 1-4). 16.95 incl. audio compact disk *(978-1-57537-514-4(1));* 16.95 incl. audio *(978-1-57537-563-2(X))* Advance Publishing, Inc.

—Mayor for a Day. 2003. (Another Sommer-Time Story Ser.). (Illus.). 48p. (J). (gr. 1-4). 16.95 incl. audio *(978-1-57537-562-5(1))* Advance Publishing, Inc.

—Mayor for a Day. Westbrook, Dick, illus. 2003. (Another Sommer-Time Story Ser.). (ENG.). 48p. (J). (gr. k-4). lib. bdg. 23.95 incl. audio compact disk *(978-1-57537-713-1(6));* (gr. 1-4). 16.95 incl. audio compact disk *(978-1-57537-513-7(3))* Advance Publishing, Inc.

—No Longer a Dilly Dally, 1 bk. 2003. (Another Sommer-Time Story Ser.). (Illus.). 48p. (J). 16.95 incl. audio *(978-1-57537-550-2(8))* Advance Publishing, Inc.

—No Longer a Dilly Dally, 11 vols. James, Kennon, illus. 2003. (Another Sommer-Time Story Ser.). (ENG.). 48p. (J). (gr. 1-4). 16.95 incl. audio compact disk *(978-1-57537-501-4(X))* Advance Publishing, Inc.

—No One Will Ever Know. Westbrook, Dick, illus. 2003. (Another Sommer-Time Story Ser.). (ENG.). 48p. (J). (gr. 1-4). 16.95 incl. audio compact disk *(978-1-57537-506-9(0))* Advance Publishing, Inc.

—The Sly Fox & the Chicks. 2003. (Another Sommer-Time Story Ser.). (Illus.). 48p. (J). (gr. 1-4). 16.95 incl. audio *(978-1-57537-553-3(2))* Advance Publishing, Inc.

—The Sly Fox & the Chicks. James, Kennon, illus. 2003. (Another Sommer-Time Story Ser.). (ENG.). 48p. (J). 16.95 incl. audio compact disk *(978-1-57537-504-5(4))* Advance Publishing, Inc.

—Tied up in Knots. Budwine, Greg, illus. 2003. (Another Sommer-Time Story Ser.). (ENG.). 48p. (J). 16.95 incl. audio compact disk *(978-1-57537-503-8(6))* Advance Publishing, Inc.

—Tied up in Knots. 2003. (Another Sommer-Time Story Ser.). (Illus.). 48p. (J). (gr. 1-4). 16.95 incl. audio *(978-1-57537-552-6(4))* Advance Publishing, Inc.

—The Ugly Caterpillar. 2003. (Another Sommer-Time Story Ser.). (Illus.). 48p. (J). (gr. 1-4). 16.95 incl. audio *(978-1-57537-564-9(8))* Advance Publishing, Inc.

—The Ugly Caterpillar. Budwine, Greg, illus. 2003. (Another Sommer-Time Story Ser.). 48p. (J). (gr. 1-4). 16.95 incl. audio compact disk *(978-1-57537-515-1(X))* Advance Publishing, Inc.

—You Move You Lose. 2003. (Another Sommer-Time Story Ser.). (Illus.). 48p. (J). (gr. 1-4). 16.95 incl. audio *(978-1-57537-554-0(0))* Advance Publishing, Inc.

—You Move You Lose. James, Kennon, illus. 2003. (Another Sommer-Time Story Ser.). (ENG.). 48p. (J). (gr. 1-4). 16.95 incl. audio compact disk *(978-1-57537-505-2(2))* Advance Publishing, Inc.

—Your Job Is Easy. James, Kennon, illus. 2003. (Another Sommer-Time Story Ser.). (ENG.). 48p. (J). (gr. -1-4). 9.95 *(978-1-57537-018-7(2));* (gr. 1-4). 16.95 incl. audio compact disk *(978-1-57537-517-5(6));* (gr. 2-4). lib. bdg. 16.95 *(978-1-57537-067-5(0))* Advance Publishing, Inc.

—Your Job Is Easy. 2003. (Another Sommer-Time Story Ser.). (Illus.). 48p. (J). (gr. 1-4). 16.95 incl. audio *(978-1-57537-566-3(4))* Advance Publishing, Inc.

Sonder, Ben. Parrots: A Portrait of the Animal World. 2012. (Portrait of the Animal World Ser.). (Illus.). 72p. 12.95 *(978-1-59764-270-5(3))* New Line Bks.

—Parrots - Pb: A Portrait of the Animal World. 2013. (Portrait of the Animal World Ser.). (Illus.). 72p. pap. 9.95 *(978-1-59764-330-6(0))* New Line Bks.

Sookocheff, Carey. Solutions for Cold Feet & Other Little Problems. (Illus.). (J). 2018. 38p. (— 1). bds. 9.99 *(978-0-7352-6464-9(3))* 2016. 48p. (gr. -1-3). 16.99 *(978-1-77049-873-0(7))* Tundra Bks. CAN. (Tundra Bks.). Dist: Penguin Random Hse. LLC.

Sorenson, Ashley. Color Blocked. Miles, David W., illus. 2017. (ENG.). 40p. (J). (gr. -1-1). 16.99 *(978-1-944822-82-8(8),* 552282) Familius LLC.

Sornson, Bob. The Juice Box Bully: Empowering Kids to Stand up for Others. 2010. (Illus.). 32p. (J). (gr. k-5). pap. 10.95 *(978-1-933916-72-9(9))* Early Learning Foundation, LLC.

Sowa, Marzena. That Night, a Monster ... 2018. (ENG., Illus.). 40p. (J). (gr. 1-5). 12.95 *(978-1-941250-30-3(0),* odod bks.) Uncivilized Bks.

Spalding, Andrea. Dance Baby Dance, 1 vol. 2009. (ENG., Illus.). 24p. (J). (gr. -1 — 1). bds. 9.95 *(978-1-55469-079-4(X))* Orca Bk. Pubs. USA.

Spalding, Andrea & Scow, Alfred. Secret of the Dance, 1 vol. Gait, Darlene, illus. 2009. (ENG.). 32p. (J). (gr. -1-k). 10.95 *(978-1-55469-129-6(X))* Orca Bk. Pubs. USA.

Spanyol, Jessica. Clive & His Art. Spanyol, Jessica, illus. 2016. (All about Clive Ser.: 4). (Illus.). 14p. (J). spiral bd. *(978-1-84643-883-7(7))* Child's Play International Ltd.

—Clive & His Babies. Spanyol, Jessica, illus. 2016. (All about Clive Ser.). (Illus.). 14p. (J). spiral bd. *(978-1-84643-882-0(9))* Child's Play International Ltd.

—Clive & His Bags. Spanyol, Jessica, illus. 2016. (All about Clive Ser.). (Illus.). 14p. (J). spiral bd. *(978-1-84643-884-4(5))* Child's Play International Ltd.

—Clive & His Hats. Spanyol, Jessica, illus. 2016. (All about Clive Ser.). (Illus.). 14p. (J). spiral bd. *(978-1-84643-885-1(3))* Child's Play International Ltd.

—Clive Is a Librarian. Spanyol, Jessica, illus. 2017. (Clive's Jobs Ser.: 4). (Illus.). 14p. (J). spiral bd. *(978-1-84643-989-6(2))* Child's Play International Ltd.

—Clive Is a Nurse. Spanyol, Jessica, illus. 2017. (Clive's Jobs Ser.: 4). (Illus.). 14p. (J). spiral bd. *(978-1-84643-991-9(4))* Child's Play International Ltd.

—Clive Is a Teacher. Spanyol, Jessica, illus. 2017. (Clive's Jobs Ser.: 4). (Illus.). 14p. (J). spiral bd. *(978-1-84643-990-2(6))* Child's Play International Ltd.

—Clive Is a Waiter. Spanyol, Jessica, illus. 2017. (Clive's Jobs Ser.: 4). (Illus.). 14p. (J). spiral bd. *(978-1-84643-992-6(2))* Child's Play International Ltd.

Sparkes, Amy. Ellie's Magic Wellies. East, Nick, illus. 2017. (ENG.). 32p. (J). (gr. -1-k). pap. 7.99 *(978-1-4052-7379-4(8))* Farshore GBR. Dist: HarperCollins Pubs.

—Once upon a Wish. Ogilvie, Sara, illus. 2017. (ENG.). 32p. (J). (gr. -1-k). pap. 9.99 *(978-1-84941-661-0(3),* Red Fox) Random House Children's Books GBR. Dist: Independent Pubs. Group.

Sparrow, Kerry Lyn. Sleep, Sheep! Perreault, Guillaume, illus. 2018. (ENG.). 32p. (J). (gr. -1-2). 16.99 *(978-1-77138-796-5(3))* Kids Can Pr., Ltd. CAN. Dist: Hachette Bk. Group.

Speechley, Michael. The All New Must Have Orange 430. 2018. 32p. (J). (gr. k-1). 24.99 *(978-0-14-378897-3(3),* Viking Adult) Penguin Publishing Group.

Speight, Peter. Wally the Whale Says: To Be Safe on a Bike. 2015. (ENG., Illus.). 18p. (J). pap. *(978-1-78222-438-9(6))* Paragon Publishing, Rothersthorpe.

Spenceley, Annabel, illus. Beauty & the Beast. 2017. 24p. (J). (gr. -1-12). pap. 7.99 *(978-1-86147-817-7(8),* Armadillo) Anness Publishing GBR. Dist: National Bk. Network.

—Cinderella. 2016. 24p. (J). (gr. -1-12). pap. 7.99 *(978-1-86147-813-9(5),* Armadillo) Anness Publishing GBR. Dist: National Bk. Network.

Sper, Emily. Follow the Yarn: A Book of Colors. Sper, Emily, illus. 2016. (ENG., Illus.). 24p. (J). (gr. -1 — 1). bds. 7.99 *(978-0-9754902-8-0(1),* 9780975490280) Jump Pr.

Spergel, Heather. Cloud City: A Child's Journey Through Bereavement. Stylou, Georgia, illus. 2013. (ENG.). 40p. (J). 15.95 *(978-1-938501-45-6(4))* Turn the Page Publishing.

—Gabi Babaroni on Broadway. Vene, Alessandro, illus. 2013. (ENG.). 32p. (J). 18.99 *(978-1-938501-29-6(2))* Turn the Page Publishing.

—NiNi Spergelini: Guitar-Ific! Perla, Brian, illus. 2013. (NiNi Spergelini Ser.: 1). (ENG.). 32p. (J). 18.99 *(978-0-9832148-5-4(9))* Turn the Page Publishing.

Sperring, Mark. Little Hugs from Little Loves. Frost, Maddie, illus. 2019. (ENG.). 24p. (J). (gr. -1 — 1). bds. 7.99 *(978-0-316-48433-6(4))* Little, Brown Bks. for Young Readers.

—The Littlest Things Give the Loveliest Hugs. Frost, Maddie, illus. 2018. (ENG.). 32p. (J). (gr. -1-3). 17.99 *(978-0-316-48434-3(2))* Little, Brown Bks. for Young Readers.

—The Naughty Naughty Baddies. Tazzyman, David, illus. 2017. (ENG.). 32p. (J). *(978-1-4088-4973-6(9),* 246729, Bloomsbury Children's Bks.) Bloomsbury Publishing Plc.

Spigarelli, Jane. Oxford Picture Dictionary Third Edition: Low-Beginning Workbook. 3rd ed. 2017. (ENG.). 272p. pap., wbk. ed. 24.20 *(978-0-19-451124-7(3))* Oxford Univ. Pr., Inc.

Spilsbury, Louise. Racism & Intolerance. Kai, Hanane, illus. 2018. (ENG.). 32p. (J). (gr. 1-2). 9.99 *(978-1-4380-5022-5(4))* Sourcebooks, Inc.

Spinelli, Eileen. Miss Fox's Class Earns a Field Trip. Kennedy, Anne, illus. 2018. (Miss Fox's Class Ser.). (ENG.). 32p. (J). (gr. -1-3). 7.99 *(978-0-8075-5170-7(8),* 807551708) Whitman, Albert & Co.

—Miss Fox's Class Gets It Wrong. Kennedy, Anne, illus. 2018. (Miss Fox's Class Ser.). (ENG.). 32p. (J). (gr. -1-3). 7.99 *(978-0-8075-5173-8(2),* 807551732) Whitman, Albert & Co.

—Miss Fox's Class Shapes Up. Kennedy, Anne, illus. 2018. (Miss Fox's Class Ser.). (ENG.). 32p. (J). (gr. -1-3). 7.99 *(978-0-8075-5172-1(4),* 807551724) Whitman, Albert & Co.

—Nora's Ark, 1 vol. Hilb, Nora, illus. 2018. (ENG.). 24p. (J). bds. 8.99 *(978-0-310-76144-0(1))* Zonderkidz.

—Now It Is Winter. DePalma, Mary Newell, illus. 2004. 32p. (J). 16.00 *(978-0-8028-5244-1(0))* Eerdmans, William B. Publishing Co.

—Peace Week in Miss Fox's Class. Kennedy, Anne, illus. 2018. (Miss Fox's Class Ser.). (ENG.). 32p. (J). (gr. -1-3). 8.99 *(978-0-8075-6390-8(0),* 807563900) Whitman, Albert & Co.

Spires, Ashley. Edie's Ensembles. 2014. (Illus.). 32p. (J). (gr. -1-3). 17.99 *(978-1-77049-490-9(1),* Tundra Bks.) Tundra Bks. CAN. Dist: Penguin Random Hse. LLC.

—Larf. Spires, Ashley, illus. 2012. (ENG., Illus.). 32p. (J). (gr. -1-2). 16.95 *(978-1-55453-701-3(0))* Kids Can Pr., Ltd. CAN. Dist: Hachette Bk. Group.

—The Most Magnificent Thing, 0 vols. Spires, Ashley, illus. 2013. (ENG., Illus.). 32p. (J). (gr. -1-2). 18.99 *(978-1-55453-704-4(5))* Kids Can Pr., Ltd. CAN. Dist: Hachette Bk. Group.

—Over-Scheduled Andrew. 2016. (Illus.). 32p. (J). (gr. -1-3). 16.99 *(978-1-77049-484-8(7),* Tundra Bks.) Tundra Bks. CAN. Dist: Penguin Random Hse. LLC.

—Penguin & the Cupcake. 2nd ed. 2014. (ENG., Illus.). 32p. (J). (gr. -1-3). 16.95 *(978-1-927018-45-3(5))* Simply Read Bks. CAN. Dist: Ingram Publisher Services.

Spizzirri, Linda, ed. Cats of the Wild. (Illus.). 32p. (J). (gr. 1-8). pap. 4.98 incl. audio *(978-0-86545-045-5(5))* Spizzirri Pr., Inc.

—Endangered Species. (Illus.). 32p. (J). (gr. 1-8). pap. 4.98 incl. audio *(978-0-86545-041-7(2))* Spizzirri Pr., Inc.

Sports Illustrated for Kids Editors. My First Book of Soccer: Mostly Everything Explained about the Game. 2017. (ENG., Illus.). 48p. (J). (gr. -1-1). 11.99 *(978-1-68330-002-1(5))* Sports Illustrated For Kids.

Spudvilas, Anne. Swan Lake. 2019. (ENG.). 48p. (J). (gr. 5-9). 19.99 *(978-1-74331-845-4(6))* Allen & Unwin AUS. Dist: Independent Pubs. Group.

Spurr, Elizabeth. In the Snow, 1 vol. Oliphant, Manelle, illus. 2017. (In the Weather Ser.). 22p. (J). (gr. -1 — 1). bds. 6.99 *(978-1-56145-855-4(4))* Peachtree Publishing Co. Inc.

Squires, Patricia. Enter Here. 2008. 62p. (J). 41.99 *(978-1-4257-7867-5(4))* Xlibris Corp.

Sretaw. Homonym Hunt. 2010. 24p. pap. 28.03 *(978-1-4500-5228-3(2))* Xlibris Corp.

Srinivasan, Divya. Little Owl's Colors. Srinivasan, Divya, illus. 2015. (Little Owl Ser.). (Illus.). 18p. (J). (— 1). bds. 7.99 *(978-0-451-47456-8(2),* Viking Books for Young Readers) Penguin Young Readers Group.

Stahl, Jon. The Dragons Eat Noodles on Tuesdays. Bentley, Tadgh, illus. 2019. (ENG.). 40p. (J). (gr. -1-3). 17.99 *(978-1-338-12551-1(6),* Scholastic Pr.) Scholastic, Inc.

Staller, Mary J. Meet Sandy Gull. 2007. (ENG.). 24p. pap. 10.00 *(978-1-4251-3171-5(9))* Trafford Publishing.

Stanek, Gerald. Sarah 'n' Dippity. Stanek, Joyce Huntington, illus. 2004. (ENG.). 28p. (J). 14.95 *(978-0-9747417-0-3(1))* Shiver Hill Bks.

Stanké, Claudie. Les Bisous. Malépart, Céline, illus. 2004. (Picture Bks.). (FRE.). 32p. (J). (gr. -1). *(978-2-89021-694-5(2));* pap. *(978-2-89021-693-8(4))* Diffusion du livre Mirabel (DLM).

Stanley, Mandy. First Words. 2018. (Kingfisher Board Bks.). (ENG.). 10p. (J). bds. 4.99 *(978-0-7534-7464-8(6),* 900192051, Kingfisher) Roaring Brook Pr.

—On the Farm. 2018. (Kingfisher Board Bks.). (ENG.). 10p. (J). bds. 4.99 *(978-0-7534-7447-1(6),* 900192010, Kingfisher) Roaring Brook Pr.

Starishevsky, Jill. My Body Belongs to Me: A Book about Body Safety. Padron, Angela, illus. 2014. (ENG.). 32p. (J). (gr. -1-3). 15.99 *(978-1-57542-461-3(4))* Free Spirit Publishing Inc.

Stark, Ulf. The Yule Tomte & the Little Rabbits: A Christmas Story for Advent, 15 vols. Beard, Susan, tr. Eriksson, Eva, illus. 2014. 104p. (J). 24.95 *(978-1-78250-136-7(3))* Floris Bks. GBR. Dist: Consortium Bk. Sales & Distribution.

Starr, Ringo, pseud. Octopus's Garden. Cort, Ben, illus. 2014. (ENG.). 32p. (J). (gr. -1-3). 19.99 *(978-1-4814-0362-7(1),* Aladdin) Simon & Schuster Children's Publishing.

Stauffer, Lisa Lowe. Two by Two, 1 vol. Scudamore, Angelika, illus. 2018. (ENG.). 18p. (J). bds. 8.99 *(978-0-310-76273-7(1))* Zonderkidz.

Steers, Billy. Tractor Mac Harvest Time. 2017. (Tractor Mac Ser.). (ENG., Illus.). 24p. (J). pap. 5.99 *(978-0-374-30600-7(1),* 900173474, Farrar, Straus & Giroux (BYR)) Farrar, Straus & Giroux.

Stehr, Frederic. Bim Bam Boom. Stehr, Frederic, illus. 2018. (ENG., Illus.). 26p. (J). (gr. -1-k). bds. 12.99 *(978-1-77657-136-9(3),* 00827d5b-f865-496f-8cd5-fb14ec1be5f9) Gecko Pr. NZL. Dist: Lerner Publishing Group.

Stein, David Ezra. Dinosaur Kisses. Stein, David Ezra, illus. 2014. (ENG., Illus.). 34p. (J). (-k). bds. 7.99 *(978-0-7636-7389-5(7))* Candlewick Pr.

—Ice Boy. Stein, David Ezra, illus. 2017. (ENG., Illus.). 40p. (J). (gr. -1-2). 15.99 *(978-0-7636-8203-3(9))* Candlewick Pr.

—Ice Boy. 2017. (Illus.). 32p. (J). *(978-1-4063-7691-3(4))* Candlewick Pr.

Stein, Joshua David. Brick: Who Found Herself in Architecture. 2018. (ENG., Illus.). 40p. (gr. -1-k). 16.95 *(978-0-7148-7631-3(3))* Phaidon Pr., Inc.

—Can I Eat That? 2016. (ENG., Illus.). 40p. 16.95 *(978-0-7148-7110-3(9))* Phaidon Pr., Inc.

Steiner, Nancy. On This Night: The Steps of the Seder in Rhyme. Leff, Tova, illus. 2013. (ENG.). 32p. (J). 11.99 *(978-1-929628-51-3(X))* Hachai Publishing.

Stephens, Helen. The Big Adventure of the Smalls. Stephens, Helen, illus. 2012. (ENG., Illus.). 32p. (J). (gr. -1-3). 15.99 *(978-1-4424-5058-5(4),* Aladdin) Simon & Schuster Children's Publishing.

Stephenson, Kristina. Sir Charlie Stinky Socks: the Really Big Adventure (Sir Charlie Stinky Socks) 2015. (Sir Charlie Stinky Socks Ser.). (ENG., Illus.). 32p. (J). (gr. -1-k). pap. 7.99 *(978-1-4052-7768-6(8))* Farshore GBR. Dist: HarperCollins Pubs.

Sterling Children's, Sterling. Clothes/la Ropa. 2016. (Say & Play Ser.). (ENG., Illus.). 28p. (J). (— 1). bds. 4.95 *(978-1-4549-1997-1(3))* Sterling Publishing Co., Inc.

—Food/Los Alimentos. 2016. (Say & Play Ser.). (ENG., Illus.). 28p. (J). (— 1). bds. 4.95 *(978-1-4549-1998-8(1))* Sterling Publishing Co., Inc.

Stern, Beth. Yoda Gets a Buddy. Crane, Devin, illus. 2015. (ENG.). 32p. (J). (gr. -1-3). 17.99 *(978-1-4814-6969-2(X),* Aladdin) Simon & Schuster Children's Publishing.

Sternberg, Julie. Puppy, Puppy, Puppy. Koehler, Fred, illus. 2017. (ENG.). 32p. (J). (-k). 16.95 *(978-1-62979-466-2(X),* Astra Young Readers) Astra Publishing Hse.

Sterry, Paul. Insects - Pb: A Portrait of the Animal World. 2013. (Portrait of the Animal World Ser.). (Illus.). 72p. pap. 9.95 *(978-1-59764-324-5(6))* New Line Bks.

Stevens, Beverly. This Dog Team Lives in the House. 2005. (Illus.). 32p. (J). pap. 9.95 *(978-1-57833-317-2(2))* Todd Communications.

Stevens, Liza. Not Today, Celeste! A Dog's Tale about Her Human's Depression. 2016. (Illus.). 36p. (J). 17.95 *(978-1-78592-008-0(1),* 693958) Kingsley, Jessica Pubs. GBR. Dist: Hachette UK Distribution.

Stevenson, Charles. The Adventures of the Glo-Worm Family. 2012. (ENG., Illus.). 34p. pap. 9.99 *(978-1-78035-338-8(3),* Fastprint Publishing) Upfront Publishing Ltd. GBR. Dist: Printondemand-worldwide.com.

Stewart, H. E. The Patched Heart: A Gift of Friendship & Caring, 1 vol. 2010. (ENG., Illus.). 32p. (J). (gr. 1-3). 19.95 *(978-0-9693852-5-7(0))* Tudor Hse. GBR. Dist: Orca Bk. Pubs. USA.

Stewart, James. There's a Hole in My Garden. Stewart, James, illus. 2018. (ENG., Illus.). 32p. (J). (gr. -1-3). 16.99 *(978-0-8075-7855-1(X),* 080757855X) Whitman, Albert & Co.

Stewart, Lizzy. There's a Tiger in the Garden. Stewart, Lizzy, illus. 2018. (ENG., Illus.). 40p. (J). (gr. -1-3). 17.99 *(978-1-328-79183-2(1),* 1685033, Clarion Bks.) HarperCollins Pubs.

—There's a Tiger in the Garden. 2016. (ENG., Illus.). (J). 40p. pap. 9.99 *(978-1-84780-807-3(7));* 32p. 18.99 *(978-1-84780-806-6(9))* Quarto Publishing Group UK GBR. (Frances Lincoln Children's Bks.). Dist: Littlehampton Bk Services, Ltd.

Stewart, Melissa. Caterpillar to Butterfly. 2016. (Science for Toddlers Ser.). (Illus.). 24p. (J). (gr. -1 — 1). bds. 8.99 *(978-1-4549-1406-8(8))* Sterling Publishing Co., Inc.

Stewart, Pat. Invisible Bugs Magic Picture Book. 2003. (Dover Little Activity Bks.). (ENG., Illus.). 16p. (J). (gr. -1-2). pap. 1.50 *(978-0-486-42635-8(1))* Dover Pubns., Inc.

Stickley, Lisa. Handstand. (ENG., Illus.). 32p. (J). (gr. -1-1). 2019. pap. 9.99 *(978-1-84365-345-5(1))* 2016. 14.99 *(978-1-84365-312-7(5))* Pavilion Bks. GBR. (Pavilion). Dist: Independent Pubs. Group.

Stier, Catherine. When a Kid Like Me Fights Cancer. Chang, Angel, illus. 2019. (ENG.). 32p. (J). (gr. -1-3). 16.99 *(978-0-8075-6391-5(9),* 807563919) Whitman, Albert & Co.

Stifflemire, Beth Ann & Terry, Barbara. Mr. Waldorf Travels to the Huge Russia the Spectacular World of Waldorf. 2016. (Spectacular World of Waldorf Ser.: 4). (ENG., Illus.). 32p. (J). pap. 12.95 *(978-1-943274-42-0(8),* 9781943274420) Waldorf Publishing.

Stiles, Dan. Today I'm Going to Wear ... 2014. (ENG., Illus.). 16p. (J). (gr. -1-2). bds. 9.95 *(978-1-57687-718-0(3),* powerHouse Bks.) powerHse. Bks.

Still, Teresa B. Tessa Has Two Homes. 2009. 28p. pap. 14.99 *(978-1-4389-8202-1(X))* AuthorHouse.

Stilton, Gerónimo. Rescue Rebellion. 2015. (Geronimo Stilton Spacemice Ser.: 5). lib. bdg. 17.20 *(978-0-606-37775-1(1))* Turtleback.

Stilton, Gerónimo & Pizzelli, Anna. The Underwater Planet. Facciotto, Giuseppe & Verzini, Daniele, illus. 2016. 113p. (J). *(978-1-5182-0303-9(5))* Scholastic, Inc.

Stimson, Joan. Brave Lion, Scared Lion. Rubio, Esther, tr. Rutherford, Meg, illus. (J). (gr. k-1). pap. *(978-0-590-90985-3(1),* SO3690) Scholastic, Inc.

—The Dinosaur Next Door. 2009. (ENG., Illus.). 24p. (J). pap. *(978-0-7787-3904-3(X));* lib. bdg. *(978-0-7787-3873-2(6))* Crabtree Publishing Co.

Stinson, Kathy. The Dog Who Wanted to Fly. Scott, Brandon James, illus. 2019. 36p. (J). (gr. -1-1). 17.95 *(978-1-77321-280-7(X))* Annick Pr., Ltd. CAN. Dist: Publishers Group West (PGW).

—Harry & Walter. Leng, Qin, illus. 2018. (ENG.). 32p. (J). (gr. k-2). pap. 9.95 *(978-1-55451-801-2(6))* Annick Pr., Ltd. CAN. Dist: Publishers Group West (PGW).

—Red Is Best. Lewis, Robin Baird, illus. 6th ed. 2011. 24p. (J). (gr. -1 — 1). bds. 7.99 *(978-1-55451-364-2(2),* 9781554513642) Annick Pr., Ltd. CAN. Dist: Publishers Group West (PGW).

Stockdale, Sean & Strick, Alex. Max the Champion. Asquith, Ros, illus. 2014. (ENG.). 32p. (J). pap. 8.99 *(978-1-84780-519-5(1),* White Lion Publishing) Quarto Publishing Group UK GBR. Dist: Littlehampton Bk Services, Ltd.

Stockham, Jess. The Big Red Rock, 1 vol. Stockham, Jess, illus. 2018. (Child's Play Library). (Illus.). 32p. (J). *(978-1-78628-003-9(5));* pap. *(978-1-78628-002-2(7))* Child's Play International Ltd.

Stockham, Jess, illus. The Boy Who Cried Wolf. 2011. (Flip-Up Fairy Tales Ser.). 24p. (J). *(978-1-84643-407-5(6))* Child's Play International Ltd.

—Dentist. 2011. (First Time Ser.). 24p. (J). (gr. 2-2). pap. *(978-1-84643-335-1(5))* Child's Play International Ltd.

—Doctor. 2011. (First Time Ser.). 24p. (J). (gr. 2-2). pap. *(978-1-84643-334-4(7))* Child's Play International Ltd.

—Hospital. 2011. (First Time Ser.). 24p. (J). (gr. 2-2). pap. *(978-1-84643-336-8(3))* Child's Play International Ltd.

—Moving Day! 2011. (Helping Hands Ser.). 24p. (J). *(978-1-84643-414-3(9))* Child's Play International Ltd.

—Recycling! 2011. (Helping Hands Ser.). 24p. (J). *(978-1-84643-415-0(7))* Child's Play International Ltd.

—Shopping! 2011. (Helping Hands Ser.). 24p. (J). *(978-1-84643-412-9(2))* Child's Play International Ltd.

—Vet. 2011. (First Time Ser.). 24p. (J). (gr. 2-2). pap. *(978-1-84643-337-5(1))* Child's Play International Ltd.

Stoh, Emily. Roger Meets Sam. Stoh, Judy, illus. 2009. 24p. pap. 9.95 *(978-1-935105-41-1(8))* Avid Readers Publishing Group.

Stokes, Brenda. Bella's Blessings. 2012. (ENG., Illus.). 50p. (J). (gr. -1-3). 17.95 *(978-1-897476-61-1(2))* Simply Read Bks. CAN. Dist: Ingram Publisher Services.

Stone, Tiffany. Teatime. Van Der Linde, Jori, illus. 2017. 32p. (J). 15.95 *(978-1-927018-67-5(6))* Simply Read Bks. CAN. Dist: Ingram Publisher Services.

Stortz, Diane. I Am: The Names of God for Little Ones, 1 vol. Le Feyer, Diane, illus. 2018. (ENG.). 24p. (J). bds. 9.99 *(978-1-4003-1079-1(2),* Tommy Nelson) Nelson, Thomas Inc.

The Story Orchestra: the Nutcracker: Press the Note to Hear Tchaikovsky's Music, Volume 2. 2017. (Story Orchestra Ser.: 2). (ENG., Illus.). 24p. (J). (gr. 1-4). 24.99 *(978-1-78603-068-9(3),* 317609, Frances Lincoln Children's Bks.) Quarto Publishing Group UK GBR. Dist: Hachette Bk. Group.

Stott, Ann. Want to Play Trucks? Graham, Bob, illus. 2018. (ENG.). 32p. (J). (gr. -1-2). 17.99 *(978-0-7636-8173-9(3))* Candlewick Pr.

Strachan, Linda. Hamish Mchaggis & the Edinburgh Adventure. Collins, Sally J., illus. 2005. (Hamish Mchaggis Ser.). 26p. (J). per. 9.00 *(978-0-9546701-7-7(5))* GW Publishing GBR. Dist: Gatewood Pr.

—Hamish Mchaggis & the Ghost of Glamis. Collins, Sally J., illus. 2005. (Hamish Mchaggis Ser.). 26p. (J). per. 9.00 *(978-0-9546701-9-1(1))* GW Publishing GBR. Dist: Gatewood Pr.

—Hamish Mchaggis & the Search for the Loch Ness Monster. Collins, Sally J., illus. 2005. 32p. (J). pap. 9.00 *(978-0-9546701-5-3(9))* GW Publishing GBR. Dist: Gatewood Pr.

Stranaghan, Crystal. The 13th Floor: Colouring Outside the Lines. Bzymek, Izabela, illus. 2012. 34p. (-18). *(978-1-926691-25-1(3))* Gumboot Bks.

Street Smarts: Picture Book 9x9 with Snipe. 2006. (Illus.). (J). 5.99 *(978-1-933934-17-4(4))* Mighty Kids Media.

Street Smarts: Picture Book (English) 8x8. 2006. (Illus.). (J). 5.99 *(978-1-933934-16-7(6))* Mighty Kids Media.

Stringer, Beverly. Joe the Dancing Spider. 2004. (ENG., Illus.). 26p. pap. 13.50 *(978-1-4120-2020-6(4))* Trafford Publishing.

Style Guide, illus. Super Team. 2016. (PJ Masks Ser.). (ENG.). 16p. (J). (gr. -1-3). pap. 5.99 *(978-1-4814-8978-2(X),* Simon Spotlight) Simon Spotlight.

Sudo, Kumiko. Coco-Chan's Kimono. Sudo, Kumiko, illus. 2010. (ENG., Illus.). 32p. (J). (gr. k-2). 16.95 *(978-1-933308-26-5(5))* Breckling Pr.

Suhay, Lisa. Pardon Me, It's Ham, Not Turkey. Barcita, Pamela, illus. 2007. (J). (gr. -1-3). 17.95 *(978-1-933982-01-4(2))* Bumble Bee Publishing.

Sullivan-Fraser, Deannie. Johnny & the Gypsy Moth, 1 vol. Rose, Hilda, illus. 2009. (ENG.). 32p. (J). (gr. k-5). *(978-1-897174-40-1(3))* Breakwater Bks., Ltd.

Sullivan, Kevin & Morgan, Elizabeth. Anne's New Home. 2010. (Anne of Green Gables Picture Bks.). (ENG.). 32p. (J). (gr. k-2). pap. 4.95 *(978-0-9736803-7-9(7))* Davenport Pr. CAN. Dist: Independent Pubs. Group.

Sullivan, Kyle. Don't Eat Me, Chupacabra! / No Me Comas, Chupacabra! A Delicious Story with Digestible Spanish Vocabulary. Sullivan, Derek, illus. 2018. (Hazy Dell Press Monster Ser.). (ENG.). 30p. (J). (gr. k-1). bds. 13.95 *(978-0-9965787-7-6(3))* Hazy Dell Pr.

—Hush Now, Banshee! A Not-So-Quiet Counting Book. Sullivan, Derek, illus. 2018. (Hazy Dell Press Monster Ser.). 30p. (J). (gr. k-1). bds. 13.95 *(978-0-9965787-5-2(7))* Hazy Dell Pr.

Sutcliffe, Charlie. Zubert. 2014. (ENG., Illus.). 32p. (J). (gr. -1-3). 18.95 *(978-1-84976-121-5(3))* Tate Publishing, Ltd. GBR. Dist: Abrams, Inc.

Sutherland, Lilli. Jasper at Plumrose Farm. 2016. (ENG., Illus.). 25p. (J). pap. 13.95 *(978-1-78612-614-6(1),* 4375b497-e400-4b09-8651-7b3faeac1554) Austin Macauley Pubs. Ltd. GBR. Dist: Baker & Taylor Publisher Services (BTPS).

Sutton, Benn. Hedgehug's Halloween. Pinto, Dan, illus. 2013. (ENG.). 40p. (J). (gr. -1-3). 9.99 *(978-0-06-196104-5(3),* HarperCollins) HarperCollins Pubs.

Swain, Gwenyth. I Wonder as I Wander. Himler, Ronald, illus. 2005. 32p. (J). (gr. k-3). pap. 8.00 *(978-0-8028-5298-4(X),* Eerdmans Bks For Young Readers) Eerdmans, William B. Publishing Co.

Sweeney, Linda Booth. When the Snow Falls. Christy, Jana, illus. 2017. 32p. (J). (-k). 16.99 *(978-0-399-54720-1(7),* G.P. Putnam's Sons Books for Young Readers) Penguin Young Readers Group.

Sweet Dreams Lullabies. (Baby Looney Tunes Song Bks.). (Illus.). 16p. (J). (gr. -1). 7.98 *(978-0-7853-1613-8(2),* PI13) Publications International, Ltd.

Swenlin, Brian & Bardekoff, Jennifer. Magical Mermaids! Aikins, Dave, illus. 2017. 24p. (J). *(978-1-5182-3609-9(X))* Random Hse., Inc.

Swerling, Lisa & Lazar, Ralph. The Sky Is the Limit: A Celebration of All the Things You Can Do (Graduation Book for Kids, Preschool Graduation Gift, Toddler Book) 2020. (ENG., Illus.). 60p. (J). (gr. -1-17). 14.99 *(978-1-4521-7982-7(4))* Chronicle Bks. LLC.

Swift, Gayle H. & Swift, Casey Anne. Abc, Adoption & Me. Griffin, Paul, illus. 2013. 36p. pap. 13.99 *(978-0-9856762-8-5(0))* WRB Pub.

Swinney, Nicola Jane. I Love Horses & Ponies. 2014. (Illus.). 120p. (J). pap. *(978-1-4351-5535-0(1))* Barnes & Noble, Inc.

Swirnow, Linda. What's New at the Zoo? A PhotoPhOnics (c)Reader. 2009. 32p. pap. 12.99 *(978-1-4490-2218-1(9))* AuthorHouse.

Szymanski, Lois. Wild Colt, 1 vol. 2012. (ENG., Illus.). 40p. (J). 16.99 *(978-0-7643-3975-2(3),* 4445) Schiffer Publishing, Ltd.

Tafuri, Nancy. All Kinds of Kisses. 2014. (ENG., Illus.). 26p. (J). (gr. -1 — 1). bds. 7.99 *(978-0-316-12236-8(X))* Little, Brown Bks. for Young Readers.

—Daddy Hugs. 2014. (ENG., Illus.). 32p. (J). (gr. -1-1). 17.00 *(978-0-316-22923-4(7))* Little, Brown Bks. for Young Readers.

Talbott, Shawn M. Springtime Robins. 2006. (J). lib. bdg. 19.95 *(978-1-933732-05-3(9))* Big Ransom Studio.

Tallarico, Tony. Ultimate Hidden Pictures: Under the Sea. 2003. (Ultimate Hidden Pictures Ser.). (Illus.). 48p. (J). (gr. -1-3). mass mkt. 5.99 *(978-0-8431-0266-6(7),* Price Stern Sloan) Penguin Young Readers Group.

Tallec, Olivier, illus. Who Done It? 2015. (Who Done It? Ser.). (ENG.). 32p. (J). (gr. -1-k). 15.99 *(978-1-4521-4198-5(3))* Chronicle Bks. LLC.

Tam-McMillan, Gianni. Your Journey Through the Airport. 2012. 28p. pap. 21.99 *(978-1-4797-2112-2(3))* Xlibris Corp.

Tanco, Miguel. Mom & Me, Me & Mom (Mother Daughter Gifts, Mother Daughter Books, Books for Moms, Motherhood Books) 2019. (You & Me, Me & You Ser.). (ENG., Illus.). 36p. (J). (gr. -1-k). 12.99 *(978-1-4521-7190-6(4))* Chronicle Bks. LLC.

—You & Me, Me & You. 2017. (You & Me, Me & You Ser.). (ENG., Illus.). 36p. (J). (gr. -1-k). 12.99 *(978-1-4521-4486-3(9))* Chronicle Bks. LLC.

—You & Me, Me & You: Brothers: (Kids Books for Siblings, Gift for Brothers) 2018. (You & Me, Me & You Ser.). (ENG., Illus.). 40p. (J). (gr. -1-k). 12.99 *(978-1-4521-6548-6(3))* Chronicle Bks. LLC.

Tankard, Jeremy. Sleepy Bird. Tankard, Jeremy, illus. 2018. (ENG., Illus.). 32p. (J). (gr. -1-k). 16.99 *(978-1-338-15785-7(X),* Scholastic Pr.) Scholastic, Inc.

Tanner, Martha. And God Said. 2011. 28p. pap. 13.75 *(978-1-4567-3691-0(4))* AuthorHouse.

Taplin, Sam. Noisy Orchestra. 2013. (Noisy Bks). 10p. (J). ring bd. 19.99 *(978-0-7945-3334-2(5),* Usborne) EDC Publishing.

Tarore, Martha. The Runaway Bubble. 2011. (ENG.). 35p. (J). pap. 16.95 *(978-1-4327-5898-1(5))* Outskirts Pr., Inc.

Tarpley, Natasha Anastasia. I Love My Hair! Lewis, E. B., illus. 2014. 32p. pap. 7.00 *(978-1-61003-348-0(5))* Center for the Collaborative Classroom.

Tarpley, Todd. Beep! Beep! Go to Sleep! Rocco, John, illus. 2015. (ENG.). 40p. (J). (gr. -1-3). 17.99 *(978-0-316-25443-4(6))* Little, Brown Bks. for Young Readers.

Tasmanian Devil. (Looney Tunes Look & Find Bks.). (Illus.). 24p. (J). (gr. -1-5). 7.98 *(978-0-7853-1186-7(6),* PI1) Publications International, Ltd.

Tavares, Matt. Mudball. Tavares, Matt, illus. 2011. (ENG., Illus.). 32p. (J). (gr. 1-4). pap. 7.99 *(978-0-7636-4136-8(7))* Candlewick Pr.

—Red & Lulu. Tavares, Matt, illus. 2017. (ENG., Illus.). 40p. (J). (gr. -1-2). 17.99 *(978-0-7636-7733-6(7))* Candlewick Pr.

Taylor, Dereen. Alien Adventure: Peek Inside the Pop-Up Windows! Hutchinson, Tim, illus. 2015. (ENG.). 12p. (J). (gr. 1-3). 16.99 *(978-1-86147-487-2(3),* Armadillo) Anness Publishing GBR. Dist: National Bk. Network.

—The Dragon's Magic Wish. Hutchinson, Tim, illus. 2012. 12p. (J). (gr. 1-6). 16.99 *(978-1-84322-856-1(4))* Anness Publishing GBR. Dist: National Bk. Network.

—The Fairy Midnight Surprise Party. Stone, Lyn, illus. 2012. 12p. (J). (gr. 1-6). 16.99 *(978-1-84322-763-2(0))* Anness Publishing GBR. Dist: National Bk. Network.

—Journey to the World of the Dinosaurs: Peek Inside the Pop-Up Windows! Kavanagh, Peter, illus. 2014. (ENG.). 12p. (J). (gr. 2-7). 16.99 *(978-1-86147-319-6(2),* Armadillo) Anness Publishing GBR. Dist: National Bk. Network.

—The Lost Treasure of the Jungle Temple: Peek Inside the 3D Windows! Hutchinson, Tim, illus. 2013. (ENG.). 12p. (J). (gr. 1-8). 16.99 *(978-1-84322-822-6(X),* Armadillo) Anness Publishing GBR. Dist: National Bk. Network.

—The Mystery of the Vampire Boy: Dare You Peek Through the Pop-Up Windows? Spoor, Mike, illus. 2014. 12p. (J). (gr. k-5). 16.99 *(978-1-86147-410-0(5),* Armadillo) Anness Publishing GBR. Dist: National Bk. Network.

—Paulo & the Football Thieves: Peek Inside the Pop-Up Windows! Hutchinson, Tim, illus. 2014. 12p. (J). (gr. -1-12). 16.99 *(978-1-86147-409-4(1),* Armadillo) Anness Publishing GBR. Dist: National Bk. Network.

—Robo-Pup to the Rescue! Hutchinson, Tim, illus. 2013. (ENG.). 12p. (J). (gr. 1-8). 16.99 *(978-1-84322-821-9(1),* Armadillo) Anness Publishing GBR. Dist: National Bk. Network.

—Rosie Rides to the Rescue: Peek Inside the Pop-Up Windows! Stone, Lyn, illus. 2015. (ENG.). 12p. (J). (gr. -1-4). 16.99 *(978-1-86147-488-9(1),* Armadillo) Anness Publishing GBR. Dist: National Bk. Network.

—Trapped in the Witch's Lair: Peek Inside the Pop-Up Windows! Catchpole, Diana, illus. 2014. (ENG.). 12p. (J). (gr. 2-7). 16.99 *(978-1-86147-320-2(6),* Armadillo) Anness Publishing GBR. Dist: National Bk. Network.

Taylor, Helen. Kakapo Dance. 2019. 14p. (J). (— 1). bds. 10.99 *(978-0-14-377222-4(8))* Penguin Group New Zealand, Ltd. NZL. Dist: Independent Pubs. Group.

Taylor, Thomas. Little Mouse & the Big Cupcake. Barton, Jill, illus. 2017. (ENG.). 24p. (J). (— 1). bds. 6.95 *(978-1-910716-32-8(4))* Boxer Bks., Ltd. GBR. Dist: Sterling Publishing Co., Inc.

Taylor, Trace & Sánchez, Lucía M. Pingüinos de la AntáRtida: Antarctic Penguins. 2015. (2G Animales Marinos Ser.). (ENG & SPA.). 12p. (J). (gr. k-2). pap. 8.00 *(978-1-61541-274-7(3))* American Reading Co.

Taylor Trade Publish. Meet Ranger Rick Jr: Critter Crafts & Recipes. 2016. (Ranger Rick: Animal Fun for Young Children Ser.). (Illus.). 32p. (J). (gr. -1-1). pap. 5.99 *(978-0-63076-210-0(5))* Taylor Trade Publishing.

Taz TV. (Looney Tunes Song & Sound Bks.). (Illus.). 16p. (J). (gr. -1-k). 7.98 *(978-0-7853-1609-1(4),* PI9) Publications International, Ltd.

Teckentrup, Britta. Bee: a Peek-Through Picture Book. 2017. (ENG., Illus.). 32p. (J). (gr. -1-2). 17.99 *(978-1-5247-1526-7(3),* Doubleday Bks. for Young Readers) Random Hse. Children's Bks.

—Fish Everywhere. Teckentrup, Britta, illus. 2019. (Animals Everywhere Ser.). (ENG., Illus.). 32p. (J). (gr. 1-4). 17.99 *(978-1-5362-0625-8(3),* Big Picture Press) Candlewick Pr.

—The Memory Tree. 2014. (ENG., Illus.). 32p. (J). (gr. -1-k). pap. 9.99 *(978-1-4083-2634-3(5))* Hodder & Stoughton GBR. Dist: Hachette Bk. Group.

Teckentrup, Britta, illus. Get Out of My Bath! 2015. (ENG.). 24p. (J). (gr. -1-2). 16.99 *(978-0-7636-8006-0(0))* Candlewick Pr.

—My Book of Opposites. 2014. (J). *(978-1-4351-5678-4(1))* Barnes & Noble, Inc.

Tedder, Elizabeth, illus. Alphabet & Numbers in a New Way. 2011. 32p. pap. 35.95 *(978-1-258-06357-3(3))* Literary Licensing, LLC.

Tekavec, Heather. Stop, Thief! Pratt, Pierre, illus. 2014. (ENG.). 32p. (J). (gr. -1-2). 16.95 *(978-1-77138-012-6(8))* Kids Can Pr., Ltd. CAN. Dist: Hachette Bk. Group.

Tekiela, Stan. C Is for Cardinal, 1 vol. 2016. (ENG., Illus.). 64p. (J). (-k). 8.95 *(978-1-59193-533-9(4),* Adventure Pubns.) AdventureKEEN.

—Our Love of Owls. 2018. (Our Love of Wildlife Ser.). (ENG., Illus.). 48p. 9.95 *(978-1-59193-813-2(9),* Adventure Pubns.) AdventureKEEN.

Terry, Donna. Whose Toes Are Those? 2009. 24p. pap. 11.99 *(978-1-4490-0009-7(6))* AuthorHouse.

Tesoro de Libros de Calcomanías V. 2004. (Disney Calcomanias Ser.). (SPA., Illus.). 72p. (J). pap. *(978-970-718-105-2(2),* Silver Dolphin en Español) Advanced Marketing, S. de R. L. de C. V.

Tewee, Laqaixit. Winterbloom & the Magical Swan: Book 1 Discovery of the Moon Treasure. 2012. 68p. pap. 31.99 *(978-1-4653-9933-5(X))* Xlibris Corp.

Tey, Priscilla. In-Between Things. Tey, Priscilla, illus. 2018. (ENG., Illus.). 40p. (J). (gr. -1-3). 16.99 *(978-0-7636-8983-4(1))* Candlewick Pr.

Thaler, Mike. The Custodian from the Black Lagoon. Lee, Jared, illus. 2014. (Black Lagoon Ser.). (ENG.). 32p. (J). (gr. -1-4). lib. bdg. 31.36 *(978-1-61479-196-6(1),* 3636, Picture Bk.) Spotlight.

Thalhamer, Ellen Viola. Let's Play Cashier: I Love to Pretend! 2011. 36p. pap. 15.49 *(978-1-4490-7488-3(X))* AuthorHouse.

Thatcher, Stephanie. Polly Does NOT Want a Cracker. 2020. (Illus.). 32p. (J). (gr. k-2). 9.99 *(978-1-988516-59-2(5))* Upstart Pr. NZL. Dist: Independent Pubs. Group.

Thayer, Robert Scott. Kobee Manatee: Shipwreck Sea Friends. Gallegos, Lauren, illus. 2017. (ENG.). 32p. (J). (gr. k-2). 16.99 *(978-0-9971239-3-7(1))* Thompson Mill Pr.

The Beatles. Yellow Submarine. Edelmann, Heinz, illus. 2018. (ENG.). 40p. (J). (gr. 2-5). 15.99 *(978-1-5362-0145-1(6))* Candlewick Pr.

The Book Company, ed. Home. (Sparkle Bks.). (ENG.). 10p. (J). bds. 4.99 *(978-1-74047-330-9(2))* Book Co. Publishing Pty, Ltd., The AUS. Dist: Penton Overseas, Inc.

The Brothers Grimm, The Brothers. Snow White & Rose Red. Vivanco, Kelly, illus. 2014. (ENG.). 40p. (J). (gr. -1-4). 17.95 *(978-1-927018-34-7(X))* Simply Read Bks. CAN. Dist: Ingram Publisher Services.

The Ciletti Publishing Group. Story Time Cafe Maisy's Blue Bath Set. The Ciletti Publishing Group, illus. 2010. (Illus.). (J). 24.95 *(978-0-917665-71-4(6))* Ciletti Publishing Group, Inc., The.

The Metropolitan Museum of Art. The Christmas Story [Deluxe Edition]. deluxe ed. 2017. (ENG., Illus.). 32p. (J). (gr. -1-2). 19.95 *(978-1-4197-2307-0(3),* 668502, Abrams Bks. for Young Readers) Abrams, Inc.

The Trustees of the British Museum, illus. 123: Early Learning at the Museum. 2018. (Early Learning at the Museum Ser.). (ENG.). 22p. (J). (— 1). bds. 7.99 *(978-1-5362-0267-0(3))* Candlewick Pr.

The Wiggles, The. The Wiggles Emma!: Emma's New Glasses Storybook. 2017. (Wiggles Ser.). (ENG.). 24p. (J). (gr. -1-k). 11.99 *(978-1-76040-687-5(2))* Bonnier Publishing GBR. Dist: Independent Pubs. Group.

Thomas, B. K. Logs. Thomas, B. K., illus. 2013. (Illus.). 36p. 24.95 *(978-1-4512-2170-1(3))* America Star Bks.

Thomas, Glenn. Little Flowers Can't Talk. 2012. 40p. pap. 32.70 *(978-1-4691-6004-7(8))* Xlibris Corp.

Thomas-Logan, Sharon. The Miracles of Jesus Christ. 2009. 24p. pap. 12.99 *(978-1-4389-4615-3(5))* AuthorHouse.

Thomas Nelson Publishing Staff. Grandma Kisses, 1 vol. 2015. (ENG., Illus.). 20p. (J). bds. 9.99 *(978-0-7180-3659-1(X),* Tommy Nelson) Nelson, Thomas Inc.

Thomas, Rebecca L. A to Zoo: Subject Access to Children's Picture Books, 1 vol. 10th rev. ed. 2018. (Children's & Young Adult Literature Reference Ser.). (ENG.). 1656p. 115.00 *(978-1-4408-3434-9(2),* 794340, Libraries Unlimited) Bloomsbury Publishing USA.

Thomas, Shelley Moore. No, No, Kitten! Nichols, Lori, illus. 2015. (ENG.). 40p. (J). (gr. -1-2). 16.95 *(978-1-62091-631-5(2),* Astra Young Readers) Astra Publishing Hse.

Thomas, Valerie. Winnie's Big Bad Robot. Paul, Korky, illus. 2015. (ENG.). 32p. *(978-0-19-273874-5(7))* Oxford Univ. Pr.

Thompson, Carol. Rain. Thompson, Carol, illus. 2014. (Whatever the Weather Ser.: 4). (Illus.). 12p. (J). (gr. k-k). spiral bd. *(978-1-84643-683-3(4))* Child's Play International Ltd.

—Snow. Thompson, Carol, illus. 2014. (Whatever the Weather Ser.). (Illus.). 12p. (J). (gr. k-k). spiral bd. *(978-1-84643-681-9(8))* Child's Play International Ltd.

—Sun. Thompson, Carol, illus. 2014. (Whatever the Weather Ser.). (Illus.). 12p. (J). (gr. k-k). spiral bd. *(978-1-84643-680-2(X))* Child's Play International Ltd.

—Wind. Thompson, Carol, illus. 2014. (Whatever the Weather Ser.). (Illus.). 12p. (J). (gr. k-k). spiral bd. *(978-1-84643-682-6(6))* Child's Play International Ltd.

Thompson, Lauren. Cuaquito (Little Quack) Anderson, Derek, illus. 2010. (SPA.). 34p. (J). (gr. -1-1). bds. 8.99 *(978-1-4169-9894-5(2),* Libros Para Ninos) Libros Para Ninos.

Thompson, Sophie. Zoo Boy & the Jewel Thieves. Ashdown, Rebecca, illus. 2017. (Zoo Boy Ser.). (ENG.). 192p. (J). pap. 8.50 *(978-0-571-32520-7(3),* Faber & Faber Children's Bks.) Faber & Faber, Inc.

Thompson, Vivian L. Kimo Makes Music. Nomura, Beverly, photos by. 2005. (ENG., Illus.). 24p. pap. 14.99 *(978-1-4120-1137-2(X))* Trafford Publishing.

Thong, Roseanne. Round Is a Mooncake: A Book of Shapes. Lin, Grace, illus. 2014. (ENG.). 40p. (J). (gr. -1-k). 7.99 *(978-1-4521-3644-8(0))* Chronicle Bks. LLC.

—Round Is a Tortilla: A Book of Shapes. Parra, John, illus. 2015. (Latino Book of Concepts Ser.). (ENG.). 40p. (J). (gr. -1-k). 7.99 *(978-1-4521-4568-6(7))* Chronicle Bks. LLC.

Thorup, Bryce. Doctor Matthews' Family Christmas. Muller, Ruth, illus. 2005. (J). 18.95 *(978-0-9765964-1-7(5))* Round Tower Pr.

—Two Birthdays. Muller, Daniel, illus. 2005. (J). 18.95 *(978-0-9765964-0-0(7))* Round Tower Pr.

Tibo, Gilles. Au Boulot les Animaux. 2004. (FRE., Illus.). (J). (gr. -1-k). spiral bd. *(978-0-616-11146-8(0))* Canadian National Institute for the Blind/Institut National Canadien pour les Aveugles.

Tiere der Nacht. (GER.). *(978-3-411-09261-1(0))* Bibliographisches Institut & F. A. Brockhaus AG DEU. Dist: i. b. d., Ltd.

Tierney, Tom. Legendary Baseball Stars. 81st ed. 2009. (Dover Paper Dolls Ser.). (ENG.). 32p. (J). (gr. 4-5). 9.99 *(978-0-486-24846-2(1))* Dover Pubns., Inc.

Tiger Tales Staff, ed. Animals Go. Emily, Bolam, illus. 2010. (Touch, Look, & Learn! Ser.). (ENG.). 10p. (J). (gr. -1). bds. 5.95 *(978-1-58925-854-9(1))* Tiger Tales.

Tilby, Ginny. You Should, You Should! 2017. (ENG., Illus.). 32p. (J). (gr. -1-1). pap. 6.99 *(978-1-945547-54-6(5),* 554754) Familius LLC.

Tildes, Phyllis Limbacher. Bunny's Big Surprise. Tildes, Phyllis Limbacher, illus. 2020. (Illus.). 32p. (J). (-k). lib. bdg. 16.99 *(978-1-58089-684-9(7))* Charlesbridge Publishing, Inc.

Timmers, Leo. Franky. Timmers, Leo, illus. 2016. (ENG., Illus.). 40p. (J). (gr. -1-2). E-Book 26.65 *(978-1-77657-054-6(5),* 9781776570546); E-Book 26.65 *(978-1-77657-053-9(7))* Gecko Pr. NZL. Dist: Lerner Publishing Group.

—Gus's Garage. Timmers, Leo, illus. 2017. (ENG., Illus.). 32p. (gr. -1-k). (J). 16.99 *(978-1-77657-092-8(8),* 972546ee-c75c-40e3-b578-20e22695b85e); 9.99 *(978-1-77657-094-2(4))* Gecko Pr. NZL. Dist: Lerner Publishing Group.

Timothy, Ering. Frog Belly Rat F & G. 2003. (J). bds. 16.99 *(978-0-7636-2248-0(6))* Candlewick Pr.

Tischler, Tracey. Heroes in the Sandbox. 2009. 28p. pap. 13.95 *(978-1-4490-5502-8(8))* AuthorHouse.

Tischner, Lukasz. Milosz & the Problem of Evil. Bill, Stanley, tr. 2015. (ENG.). 272p. (C). pap. 34.95 *(978-0-8101-3177-4(3))* Northwestern Univ. Pr.

Titan Comics, Titan. Dragons Riders of Berk: Underworld, Vol. 6. 2015. (Riders of Berk Ser.). (ENG., Illus.). 64p. (J). (gr. 3-7). pap. 6.99 *(978-1-78276-081-8(4))* Titan Bks. Ltd. GBR. Dist: Penguin Random Hse. LLC.

To the Extreme [Really Good Stuff]. 2010. (To the Extreme Ser.). 32p. pap. 79.50 *(978-1-4296-5362-6(0),* Capstone Pr.) Capstone.

Todd, Barbara. Edward & the Eureka Lucky Wish Company. Storms, Patricia, illus. 2009. 32p. (J). (gr. -1-2). 16.95 *(978-1-55453-264-3(7))* Kids Can Pr., Ltd. CAN. Dist: Hachette Bk. Group.

Toft, Barbara. Complete Guides Animals. 2012. (ENG.). 144p. (J). *(978-1-4351-4403-3(1))* Barnes & Noble, Inc.

Toft, Kim Michelle. The World That We Want. 2005. (Illus.). 32p. (J). (gr. -1 — 1). pap. 6.95 *(978-1-58089-115-8(2));* bds. 16.95 *(978-1-58089-114-1(4))* Charlesbridge Publishing, Inc.

Tone, Satoe. Where the Heart Is. 2017. (Illus.). 32p. (J). (gr. -1-3). 15.95 *(978-1-77229-006-6(8))* Simply Read Bks. CAN. Dist: Ingram Publisher Services.

Toole, Anne. Crystal Cadets Vol. 1. O'Neill, K., illus. 2016. (ENG.). 128p. (J). pap. 12.99 *(978-1-941302-16-3(5),* 7e636ac5-2ec6-4bab-be53-c19c34c9ab48, Lion Forge) Oni Pr., Inc.

Tooth, Lucy. Star the Tooth Fairy Wants to Know If You Need Braces? 2009. 36p. 16.95 *(978-0-557-07542-3(4))* Lulu Pr., Inc.

Toothman, Sherry. I'm Okay, Mommy. Toothman, Lindsey, illus. 2007. 20p. per. 24.95 *(978-1-4241-8733-1(8))* America Star Bks.

Tornqvist, Marit. Charlie's Magical Carnival, 28 vols. 2018. Orig. Title: Fabiens Feest. (Illus.). 32p. (J). 17.95 *(978-1-78250-460-3(5))* Floris Bks. GBR. Dist: Consortium Bk. Sales & Distribution.

Torres, J. Checkers & Dot at the Beach. Lum, J., illus. 2013. (Checkers & Dot Ser.: 4). 16p. (J). (— 1). bds. 7.95 *(978-1-77049-444-2(8),* Tundra Bks.) Tundra Bks. CAN. Dist: Penguin Random Hse. LLC.

—Checkers & Dot on the Farm. Lum, J., illus. 2013. (Checkers & Dot Ser.: 3). 16p. (J). (— 1). bds. 7.95 *(978-1-77049-443-5(X),* Tundra Bks.) Tundra Bks. CAN. Dist: Penguin Random Hse. LLC.

Torrey, Richard. My Dog, Bob. 2018. (ENG., Illus.). 32p. (J). (gr. -1-3). pap. 6.99 *(978-0-8234-4470-0(8))* Holiday Hse., Inc.

Tougas, Chris. Mechanimals, 1 vol. 2012. (ENG., Illus.). 32p. (J). (gr. -1-k). 14.95 *(978-1-4598-0273-5(X))* Orca Bk. Pubs. USA.

—Tinkle, Tinkle, Little Star. Tougas, Chris, illus. 2018. (ENG., Illus.). 24p. (J). (gr. -1 — 1). bds. 9.99 *(978-1-77138-839-9(0))* Kids Can Pr., Ltd. CAN. Dist: Hachette Bk. Group.

Tracy, Joe. Arnie the Imagination Boy. 2011. 24p. pap. 15.99 *(978-1-4568-9135-0(9))* Xlibris Corp.

Tran, Phuoc Thi Minh. My First Book of Vietnamese Words: An ABC Rhyming Book of Vietnamese Language & Culture. Nguyen, Dong & Nguyen, Hop Thi, illus. 2017. (My First Words Ser.). 32p. (J). (gr. -1-3). 10.95 *(978-0-8048-4907-4(2))* Tuttle Publishing.

Trapani, Iza. Vole & Troll. Trapani, Iza, illus. 2019. (Illus.). 32p. (J). (-k). lib. bdg. 15.99 *(978-1-58089-885-0(8))* Charlesbridge Publishing, Inc.

Trasler, Janee. Big Chickie, Little Chickie. 2016. (ENG., Illus.). 24p. (J). (gr. -1 — 1). bds. 8.99 *(978-0-06-234231-7(2),* HarperFestival) HarperCollins Pubs.

Treahy, Iona & Ladybird Books Staff. Jack & the Beanstalk. 2015. (First Favourite Tales Ser.). (ENG., Illus.). 32p. (J). (-k). 8.99 *(978-1-4093-0959-8(2))* Penguin Bks., Ltd. GBR. Dist: Independent Pubs. Group.

Tremblay, Marc. Le Petit Frere du Chaperon Rouge. Fil et al, illus. 2004. (était une Fois Ser.). (FRE.). 24p. (J). (gr. -1). pap. *(978-2-89021-698-3(5))* Diffusion du livre Mirabel (DLM).

Tremblay, Patrick. Poor, Poor Jack. 2010. (ENG.). 40p. pap. 26.00 *(978-0-557-25375-3(6))* Lulu Pr., Inc.

Tripp, Valerie. Camille's Mermaid Tale. Thai, Thu, illus. 2017. 100p. (J). *(978-1-5182-4321-9(5),* American Girl) American Girl Publishing, Inc.

Troupe, Thomas Kingsley. Staying Safe at School. Uno, Kat, illus. 2019. (School Rules Ser.). (ENG.). 24p. (J). (gr. k-2). pap. 8.95 *(978-1-5158-4065-7(4),* 140059, Picture Window Bks.) Capstone.

Trumbauer, Lisa. The Great Reindeer Rebellion. Ho, Jannie, illus. 2014. 32p. (J). (gr. -1). pap. 6.95 *(978-1-4549-1356-6(8))* Sterling Publishing Co., Inc.

Trzpil, M. Bear Who Loved to Dance - O/P. 2016. (ENG., Illus.). 32p. (J). (gr. -1-1). pap. 8.99 *(978-1-78445-245-2(9))* Top That! Publishing PLC GBR. Dist: Independent Pubs. Group.

Tsiang, Sarah. Sugar & Snails. Wimmer, Sonja, illus. 2018. 32p. (J). (gr. k-2). 18.95 *(978-1-77321-005-6(X))* Annick Pr., Ltd. CAN. Dist: Publishers Group West (PGW).

Tsurumi, Andrea. Accident! 2017. (ENG., Illus.). 48p. (J). (gr. -1-3). 18.99 *(978-0-544-94480-0(1),* 1659175, Clarion Bks.) HarperCollins Pubs.

Ttofa, Juliette. The Boat Star: A Story about Loss. 2017. (Nurturing Emotional Resilience Storybooks Ser.). (ENG., Illus.). 38p. pap. 15.95 *(978-1-138-30882-4(X),* Y367695) Routledge.

—The Boy Who Longed to Look at the Sun: A Story about Self-Care. 2017. (Nurturing Emotional Resilience Storybooks Ser.). (ENG., Illus.). 16p. pap. 15.95 *(978-1-138-30892-3(7),* Y367706) Routledge.

—The Day the Sky Fell In: A Story about Finding Your Element. 2017. (Nurturing Emotional Resilience Storybooks Ser.). (ENG., Illus.). 28p. pap. 15.95 *(978-1-138-30888-6(9),* Y367702) Routledge.

—The Girl Who Collected Her Own Echo: A Story about Friendship. 2017. (Nurturing Emotional Resilience Storybooks Ser.). (ENG., Illus.). 28p. pap. 15.95 *(978-1-138-30889-3(7),* Y367703) Routledge.

—The Tale of Two Fishes: A Story about Resilient Thinking. 2017. (Nurturing Emotional Resilience Storybooks Ser.). (ENG., Illus.). 20p. pap. 15.95 *(978-1-138-30884-8(6),* Y367697) Routledge.

Tucker, Stephen. Jack & the Beanstalk, 2 vols. Sharratt, Nick, illus. 2016. (Lift-The-Flap Fairy Tales Ser.). (ENG.). 24p. (J). (gr. -1-k). bds. 12.99 *(978-1-5098-1714-6(X))* Pan Macmillan GBR. Dist: Independent Pubs. Group.

—The Three Little Pigs, 2 vols. Sharratt, Nick, illus. 2016. (Lift-The-Flap Fairy Tales Ser.). (ENG.). 24p. (J). (gr. -1-k). bds. 11.99 *(978-1-5098-1713-9(1))* Pan Macmillan GBR. Dist: Independent Pubs. Group.

Tudor, Tasha. A Tale for Easter. Tudor, Tasha, illus. 2004. (ENG., Illus.). 32p. (J). (gr. -1-3). 7.99 *(978-0-689-86694-4(1),* Aladdin) Simon & Schuster Children's Publishing.

Tugwood, Wendy. I Love You Too, I Love You Three. McGraw, Sheila & McGraw, Sheila, illus. 2016. (ENG.). 24p. (J). (gr. -1-1). 14.95 *(978-1-77085-784-1(2),* c8159125-9b73-4780-bdf1-62f545bb9ceb) Firefly Bks., Ltd.

Tullet, Hervé. Say Zoop! (Toddler Learning Book, Preschool Learning Book, Interactive Children's Books) 2017. (Press Here by Herve Tullet Ser.). (ENG., Illus.). 64p. (J). (gr. -1-k). 15.99 *(978-1-4521-6473-1(8))* Chronicle Bks. LLC.

Tullet, Hervé & Tullet, Hervé. The Countryside Game. 2013. (ENG., Illus.). 14p. 12.95 *(978-0-7148-6074-9(3))* Phaidon Pr., Inc.

—The Game of Lines. 2015. (ENG., Illus.). 14p. (gr. -1-17). 12.95 *(978-0-7148-6873-8(6))* Phaidon Pr., Inc.

—The Game of Tops & Tails. 2015. (ENG., Illus.). 14p. (gr. -1-17). 12.95 *(978-0-7148-6874-5(4))* Phaidon Pr., Inc.

—The Trail Game. 2015. (ENG., Illus.). 14p. (gr. -1-17). 12.95 *(978-0-7148-6876-9(0))* Phaidon Pr., Inc.

Turkowski, Einar, illus. Houses Floating Home. 2016. (ENG.). 32p. (J). (gr. -1-3). 16.95 *(978-1-59270-183-4(3))* Enchanted Lion Bks., LLC.

Turner, Matthew Paul. When God Made Light. Catrow, David, illus. 2018. (ENG.). 48p. (J). (gr. -1-2). 11.99 *(978-1-60142-920-9(7),* Convergent Bks.) Crown Publishing Group, The.

Turner-Rahman, Gregory. Ellabug. 2009. 40p. pap. 12.95 *(978-1-935290-09-4(6))* Diversion Pr.

Turner, Sarah E. The Littlest Monkey, 1 vol. 2010. (ENG., Illus.). 32p. (J). (gr. 1-3). pap. 9.95 *(978-1-55039-174-9(7))* Sono Nis Pr. CAN. Dist: Orca Bk. Pubs. USA.

Turpin, Nick. Molly Is New. Raga, Silvia, illus. 2010. 32p. pap. *(978-1-84089-650-3(7))* Zero to Ten, Ltd.

Tuxworth, Nicola. Baby Animals. 2015. (Illus.). 20p. (J). (gr. -1-12). bds. 6.99 *(978-1-86147-357-8(5),* Armadillo) Anness Publishing GBR. Dist: National Bk. Network.

—Clothes. 2014. (Illus.). 20p. (J). (gr. -1 — 1). bds. 6.99 *(978-1-84322-861-5(0),* Armadillo) Anness Publishing GBR. Dist: National Bk. Network.

—Colours. 2014. (Illus.). 20p. (J). (gr. -1-12). bds. 6.99 *(978-1-84322-749-6(5),* Armadillo) Anness Publishing GBR. Dist: National Bk. Network.

—Funny Faces. 2015. (Illus.). 20p. (J). (gr. -1-12). bds. 6.99 *(978-1-86147-358-5(3),* Armadillo) Anness Publishing GBR. Dist: National Bk. Network.

—Messy. 2016. (Illus.). 20p. (J). (gr. -1-k). bds. 6.99 *(978-1-86147-690-6(6),* Armadillo) Anness Publishing GBR. Dist: National Bk. Network.

—Mix & Match. 2016. (Learn-a-Word Book Ser.). (Illus.). 20p. (J). (gr. -1-2). bds. 6.99 *(978-1-84322-862-2(9),* Armadillo) Anness Publishing GBR. Dist: National Bk. Network.

—Nature. 2015. (Illus.). 20p. (J). (gr. -1-12). bds. 6.99 *(978-1-86147-411-7(3),* Armadillo) Anness Publishing GBR. Dist: National Bk. Network.

—Numbers. 2015. (Learn-a-Word Book Ser.). (Illus.). 20p. (J). (gr. -1-2). bds. 6.99 *(978-1-84322-750-2(9),* Armadillo) Anness Publishing GBR. Dist: National Bk. Network.

—Patterns: Learn-a-Word Book. 2016. (Illus.). 20p. (J). (gr. -1-12). bds. 6.99 *(978-1-86147-462-9(8),* Armadillo) Anness Publishing GBR. Dist: National Bk. Network.

—Peekaboo! 2016. (Illus.). 20p. (J). (gr. -1-12). bds. 6.99 *(978-1-86147-477-3(6),* Armadillo) Anness Publishing GBR. Dist: National Bk. Network.

—Puppies. 2013. (ENG.). 12p. (J). (gr. -1-12). bds. 6.99 *(978-0-7548-2210-3(9))* Anness Publishing GBR. Dist: National Bk. Network.

—Shapes. 2015. (Illus.). 20p. (J). (gr. -1-12). bds. 6.99 *(978-1-86147-648-7(5),* Armadillo) Anness Publishing GBR. Dist: National Bk. Network.

—Splish Splash. 2013. (ENG.). 12p. (J). (gr. -1 — 1). bds. 6.99 *(978-0-7548-2211-0(7))* Anness Publishing GBR. Dist: National Bk. Network.

Tuxworth, Nicole. Kittens. 2015. (Illus.). 20p. (J). (gr. -1 — 1). bds. 6.99 *(978-1-86147-384-4(2),* Armadillo) Anness Publishing GBR. Dist: National Bk. Network.

Twintig, Gus. The Clock Without a Face: A Gus Twintig Mystery. 2010. (Illus.). 30p. (J). (gr. 2-18). bds. 19.95 *(978-1-934781-71-5(1),* 57ce4b2f-3c83-44ed-891c-1ae966831e7a) McSweeney's Publishing.

Twiss, Jill. The Someone New. Keller, E. G., illus. 2019. (ENG.). 32p. (J). (gr. -1-3). 18.99 *(978-0-06-293374-4(4),* HarperCollins) HarperCollins Pubs.

Twohy, Mike. Oops, Pounce, Quick, Run! An Alphabet Caper. Twohy, Mike, illus. 2016. (ENG., Illus.). 32p. (J). (gr. -1-3). 17.99 *(978-0-06-237700-5(0),* Balzer & Bray) HarperCollins Pubs.

Tyler, Michael. The Skin You Live In. Csicsko, David Lee, illus. 2005. (ENG.). 32p. (J). (gr. k-2). 15.95 *(978-0-9759580-0-1(3))* Chicago Children's Museum.

Tyrrell, Melissa. The Gingerbread Man. McMullen, Nigel, illus. 2005. (Fairytale Friends Ser.: Vol. 8). 12p. (J). (gr. -1-k). bds. 5.95 *(978-1-58117-154-9(4),* Intervisual/Piggy Toes) Bendon, Inc.

Tyson, Leigh Ann. Good Night, Little Dragons. 2012. (Little Golden Book Ser.). (Illus.). 24p. (J). (gr. k-k). 5.99 *(978-0-307-92957-0(4),* Golden Bks.) Random Hse. Children's Bks.

Uegaki, Chieri. Hana Hashimoto, Sixth Violin. Leng, Qin, illus. 2014. (ENG.). 32p. (J). (gr. -1-3). 18.99 *(978-1-894786-33-1(5))* Kids Can Pr., Ltd. CAN. Dist: Hachette Bk. Group.

—Ojiichan's Gift. Simms, Genevieve, illus. 2019. (ENG.). 32p. (J). (gr. -1-2). 19.99 *(978-1-77138-963-1(X))* Kids Can Pr., Ltd. CAN. Dist: Hachette Bk. Group.

Ulkutay Design Group Staff & Random House Children's Books Staff, contrib. by. My Book of Kittens. 2016. (Illus.). (J). *(978-1-4806-9710-2(9),* Golden Bks.) Random Hse. Children's Bks.

Underwood, Deborah. The Loud Book! Padded Board Book. Liwska, Renata, illus. 2015. (ENG.). 32p. (J). (— 1). bds. 8.99 *(978-0-544-43064-8(6),* 1595739, Clarion Bks.) HarperCollins Pubs.

—Ogilvy. McBeth, T. L., illus. 2019. (ENG.). 40p. (J). 18.99 *(978-1-250-15176-6(7),* 900183400, Holt, Henry & Co. Bks. For Young Readers) Holt, Henry & Co.

Ungaro, Marley. Darling Dozen of the Deep. 2012. (ENG.). (J). pap. 24.99 *(978-1-4675-4418-4(3))* Independent Pub.

Ungerer, Tomi. Crictor. (J). (gr. -1-3). pap. 12.95 incl. audio Weston Woods Studios, Inc.

—The Mellops Go Spelunking. 2015. (ENG., Illus.). 32p. (gr. -1-k). 14.95 *(978-0-7148-6971-1(6))* Phaidon Pr., Inc.

Unknown. Doctor Who: the Illustrated Adventures. 2018. (Illus.). 208p. (J). 24.99 *(978-1-4059-2722-2(4),* 9e24d6ee-13a7-488a-9b01-fde0026bb671) Penguin Bks., Ltd. GBR. Dist: Diamond Comic Distributors, Inc.

Unwin, Shelly. You're Five! Battersby, Katherine, illus. 2018. (ENG.). 32p. (J). (-k). 9.99 *(978-1-76029-131-0(5))* Allen & Unwin AUS. Dist: Independent Pubs. Group.

—You're Four! Battersby, Katherine, illus. 2018. (ENG.). 32p. (J). (-k). 9.99 *(978-1-76029-130-3(7))* Allen & Unwin AUS. Dist: Independent Pubs. Group.

—You're One! Battersby, Katherine, illus. 2019. (ENG.). 26p. (J). (— 1). bds. 7.99 *(978-1-9848-9245-4(2),* Doubleday Bks. for Young Readers) Random Hse. Children's Bks.

—You're Two! Battersby, Katherine, illus. 2019. (ENG.). 26p. (J). (— 1). bds. 7.99 *(978-1-9848-9247-8(9),* Doubleday Bks. for Young Readers) Random Hse. Children's Bks.

Upjohn, Rebecca. Lily & the Paper Man, 1 vol. Benoit, Renné, illus. 2007. (ENG.). 24p. (J). (gr. k-3). 15.95 *(978-1-897187-19-7(X))* Second Story Pr. CAN. Dist: Orca Bk. Pubs. USA.

Urban, Linda. Little Red Henry. Valentine, Madeline, illus. 2015. (ENG.). 40p. (J). (gr. -1-3). 16.99 *(978-0-7636-6176-2(7))* Candlewick Pr.

USCCB Department of Justice, Peace, and Human Development. Green Street Park. 2015. (ENG., Illus.). 32p. (J). (gr. k-3). pap. 7.95 *(978-0-8294-4099-7(2))* Loyola Pr.

V., Larry. Larry Bendeco Johannes Von Sloop: Read with Me. K., Mark, illus. 2014. (ENG.). 32p. (J). (gr. k-5). 7.99 *(978-1-4867-0000-4(4))* Flowerpot Children's Pr. Inc. CAN. Dist: Cardinal Pubs. Group.

Vaid, Stephen. Moo's Walk. 2010. (Illus.). 28p. pap. *(978-0-7552-1236-1(3))* Authors OnLine, Ltd.

Vaisberg, Diego & DGPH Stufio Staff. Dino. Vaisberg, Diego & DGPH Stufio Staff, illus. 2018. (ENG., Illus.). 40p. (J). (gr. k-3). 15.99 *(978-1-5362-0280-9(0),* Templar) Candlewick Pr.

Valckx, Catharina. Bruno: Some of the More Interesting Days in My Life So Far. Hubesch, Nicolas, illus. 2017. (ENG.). 96p. (J). (gr. k-4). 19.99 *(978-1-77657-124-6(X),* c354b005-7a6e-498c-a928-d07919dcc79f) Gecko Pr. NZL. Dist: Lerner Publishing Group.

Valentin, Karen. Allie's World: Abuela & Abuelo Move: Abuela & Abuelo Move. 2009. 32p. 6.95 *(978-1-60349-021-4(3),* Marimba Bks.) Just Us Bks., Inc.

Valentine Davies Estate & Hill, Susanna Leonard. Miracle on 34th Street: A Storybook Edition of the Christmas Classic. Newman Gray, James, illus. 2018. (ENG.). 32p. (J). 17.99 *(978-1-4926-6986-9(5))* Sourcebooks, Inc.

Valério, Geraldo & Valério, Geraldo. Canadian Animals in Colour. 2019. (Canadian Concepts Ser.: 3). (ENG., Illus.). 22p. (J). (gr. -1-1). bds. 9.95 *(978-1-77147-388-0(6))* Owlkids Bks. Inc. CAN. Dist: Publishers Group West (PGW).

Van Allsburg, Chris. The Wreck of the Zephyr. 2014. 32p. pap. 9.00 *(978-1-61003-222-3(5))* Center for the Collaborative Classroom.

—The Wreck of the Zephyr 30th Anniversary Edition. Van Allsburg, Chris, illus. 30th anniv. ed. 2013. (ENG., Illus.). 32p. (J). (gr. -1-3). 18.99 *(978-0-544-05005-1(3),* 1532468, Clarion Bks.) HarperCollins Pubs.

Van Camp, Katie. CookieBot! Agnew, Lincoln, illus. 2011. (Harry & Horsie Adventures Ser.: 2). (ENG.). 32p. (J). (gr. -1-1). 16.99 *(978-0-06-197445-8(5),* Balzer & Bray) HarperCollins Pubs.

Van der Merwe, Avril. Once upon a Rhinoceros. Greeff, Heidi-Kate, illus. 2018. (ENG.). 16p. pap. 7.50 *(978-1-4859-0037-5(9))* Penguin Random House South Africa ZAF. Dist: Casemate Pubs. & Bk. Distributors, LLC.

Van Doorn, Sandra. Paper Hearts. 2014. (ENG., Illus.). 32p. (J). (gr. -1-3). 16.95 *(978-1-927018-41-5(2),* 9781927018415) Simply Read Bks. CAN. Dist: Ingram Publisher Services.

Van Fleet, Matthew. Dog. 2007. (ENG., Illus.). 20p. (J). (gr. -1-2). 24.99 *(978-1-4169-4137-8(1),* Simon & Schuster/Paula Wiseman Bks.) Simon & Schuster/Paula Wiseman Bks.

van Lieshout, Maria. I Sleep in a Big Bed: (Milestone Books for Kids, Big Kid Books for Young Readers. 2018. (Big Kid Power Ser.). (ENG., Illus.). 24p. (J). (gr. -1 — 1). 9.99 *(978-1-4521-6290-4(5))* Chronicle Bks. LLC.

VanSickle, Vikki. If I Had a Gryphon. Atkinson, Cale, illus. (J). 2018. 30p. (— 1). bds. 9.99 *(978-0-7352-6465-6(1))* 2016. 32p. (gr. -1-2). 16.99 *(978-1-77049-809-9(5))* Tundra Bks. CAN. (Tundra Bks.). Dist: Penguin Random Hse. LLC.

Vasiliu, Mircea. A Day at the Beach. 2007. (Illus.). 36p. (J). 7.95 *(978-1-59091-068-9(0))* Eastern National.

Vasquez, Paula. Lily Wool, 1 vol. 2017. (ENG., Illus.). 40p. (J). (gr. k-3). 14.99 *(978-1-4236-4728-7(9))* Gibbs Smith, Publisher.

Velikanje, Kathryn. Zebras Paint Themselves Rainbow. Hovhannisyan, Nune, illus. 2013. 58p. pap. 12.28 *(978-1-939896-02-5(9))* Levity Pr.

Velthuijs, Max. The Little Boy & the Big Fish. 2018. (ENG., Illus.). 32p. (J). (gr. -1-3). 17.95 *(978-0-7358-4309-7(0))* North-South Bks., Inc.

—Where Is Frog? 2017. (ENG., Illus.). 14p. (J). (gr. -1-k). bds. 8.95 *(978-0-2281-0002-7(X),* f160cafb-5292-4031-b9d3-ebd20c041d70) Firefly Bks., Ltd.

Verde, Susan. I Am Yoga. 2017. (I Am Bks.). (ENG., Illus.). 24p. (J). (gr. -1 — 1). bds. 8.95 *(978-1-4197-2697-2(8),* 1191610, Abrams Appleseed) Abrams, Inc.

Verhille, Alexandre & Tavernier, Sarah, illus. Recordmania: Atlas of the Incredible. 2018. (ENG.). 48p. 14.95 *(978-3-89955-814-2(6))* Die Gestalten Verlag DEU. Dist: Ingram Publisher Services.

Vernick, Shirley. I Love You, Michigan Baby. Bergin, Molly, illus. 2018. (ENG.). 22p. (J). (gr. -1-k). bds. 8.99 *(978-1-946064-96-7(3),* 806496) Duo Pr. LLC.

Verrept, Paul. El Pequeno Soldado. Bourgeois, Elodie, tr. Verrept, Paul, illus. 2004. (SPA., Illus.). 26p. (J). (gr. -1-3). 17.99 *(978-84-261-3306-9(1))* Juventud, Editorial ESP. Dist: Lectorum Pubns., Inc.

Verrett, Michael. It Followed Me Home Can I Keep It? (full Color) 2010. 35p. pap. 19.00 *(978-0-557-29796-2(6))* Lulu Pr., Inc.

—The White Alligator (paper Back) 2010. 116p. pap. 17.30 *(978-0-557-28042-1(7))* Lulu Pr., Inc.

Viau, Nancy. Just One Thing!, 1 vol. Young, Timothy, illus. 2016. (ENG.). 144p. (gr. 3-6). 12.99 *(978-0-7643-5162-4(1),* 7556) Schiffer Publishing, Ltd.

Vickers, Roy Henry & Budd, Robert. One Eagle Soaring. 2018. (First West Coast Bks.: 2). (Illus.). 20p. (J). bds. *(978-1-55017-828-9(8),* 75bb6098-eb13-47f7-b260-09aa207b64e6) Harbour Publishing Co., Ltd.

—Sockeye Silver, Saltchuck Blue. Vickers, Roy Henry, illus. 2019. (First West Coast Bks.: 3). (ENG., Illus.). 20p. (J). bds. *(978-1-55017-870-8(9),* 520ce3c0-4f6a-4af7-9ce5-9d7f6dd08fa5) Harbour Publishing Co., Ltd.

Vickery-Bharadwaj, Janice. Valentino & His Friends: It's Magic! 2012. 28p. pap. 12.99 *(978-1-4691-7709-0(9))* Xlibris Corp.

Vidal, Séverine. Mega Mouse. Barroux, Stephane, illus. 2015. (Mega Hero Bks.). (ENG.). 28p. (J). (gr. k-2). pap. 6.95 *(978-1-77085-655-4(2),* 3a743630-56f7-453e-b7f4-f6b26b3e506e) Firefly Bks., Ltd.

—Mega Wolf. Barroux, Stephane, illus. 2015. (Mega Hero Bks.). (ENG.). 28p. (J). (gr. k-2). pap. 6.95 *(978-1-77085-653-0(6),* 5eae0766-a768-4c00-beb0-29163ed714c0) Firefly Bks., Ltd.

Virjan, Emma J. What This Story Needs Is a Hush & a Shush. 2016. (Pig in a Wig Book Ser.). (ENG., Illus.). 40p. (J). (gr. -1-3). 9.99 *(978-0-06-241528-8(X),* HarperCollins) HarperCollins Pubs.

—What This Story Needs Is a Munch & a Crunch. 2016. (Pig in a Wig Book Ser.). (ENG., Illus.). 40p. (J). (gr. -1-3). 9.99 *(978-0-06-241529-5(8),* HarperCollins) HarperCollins Pubs.

Viva, Frank. Outstanding in the Rain. 2015. (Illus.). 32p. (J). (gr. -1-3). 18.00 *(978-0-316-36627-4(7))* Little, Brown Bks. for Young Readers.

Voake, Charlotte. Melissa's Octopus & Other Unsuitable Pets. Voake, Charlotte, illus. 2015. (ENG., Illus.). 32p. (J). (gr. -1-2). 16.99 *(978-0-7636-7481-6(8))* Candlewick Pr.

Voake, Steve. Insect Detective. Voake, Charlotte, illus. 2015. 32p. pap. 7.00 *(978-1-61003-407-4(4))* Center for the Collaborative Classroom.

—Insect Detective. 2012. (Read & Wonder Ser.). lib. bdg. 17.20 *(978-0-606-23802-1(6))* Turtleback.

—Insect Detective: Read & Wonder. Voake, Charlotte, illus. 2012. (Read & Wonder Ser.). (ENG.). 32p. (J). (gr. -1-3). pap. 7.99 *(978-0-7636-5816-8(2))* Candlewick Pr.

Volant, Iris. Under the Canopy: Trees Around the World. Alonso, Cynthia, illus. 2018. (ENG.). 56p. (J). (gr. 2). 19.95 *(978-1-911171-42-3(9))* Flying Eye Bks. GBR. Dist: Penguin Random Hse. LLC.

Volke, Gordon. Big World Activity Sticker Book, Vol. 2. 2004. (Illus.). 16p. 7.25 *(978-1-84161-130-3(1))* Ravette Publishing, Ltd. GBR. Dist: Parkwest Pubns., Inc.

von Olfers, Sibylle. My First Snow Children, 30 vols. 2018. (Illus.). 12p. (J). bds. 9.95 *(978-1-78250-523-5(7))* Floris Bks. GBR. Dist: Consortium Bk. Sales & Distribution.

Vuillamy, Clara. The Bear with Sticky Paws Won't Go to Bed. Vuillamy, Clara, illus. 2010. (ENG., Illus.). 32p. (J). (gr. -1-2). 15.95 *(978-1-58925-087-1(7))* Tiger Tales.

Vuillamy, Clara. Bear with Sticky Paws Goes to School. Vuillamy, Clara, illus. 2010. (ENG., Illus.). 32p. pap. 7.95 *(978-1-58925-424-4(4))* Tiger Tales.

Waber, Bernard. The House on East 88th Street. 2022. (Lyle the Crocodile Ser.). (ENG., Illus.). 48p. (J). (gr. -1-3). tchr. ed. 19.99 *(978-0-395-18157-7(7),* 597493, Clarion Bks.) HarperCollins Pubs.

—Lyle, Lyle, Crocodile. 2022. (Lyle the Crocodile Ser.). (ENG., Illus.). 48p. (J). (gr. -1-3). tchr. ed. 19.99 *(978-0-395-16995-7(X),* 597524, Clarion Bks.) HarperCollins Pubs.

Wacker, Eileen. Silver Bunny & the Secret of Fort Chop. 2014. (ENG., Illus.). 40p. (J). 10.99 *(978-1-938806-11-7(5),* df7802a6-7c03-48e6-93cd-01a54df1e379) Oncekids.

Waddell, Martin. Something So Big. Canty, Charlotte, illus. 2004. (ENG.). 24p. (J). lib. bdg. 23.65 *(978-1-59646-706-4(1))* Dingles & Co.

Wadhwa, Vick. A New Take on ABCs - S Is for Smiling Sunrise: An Alphabet Book of Goodness, Beauty, & Wonder [Free Audio-Book Download Included]. Artists, Various, illus. I.t. ed. 2014. 32p. (J). 16.95 *(978-1-940229-12-6(X))* WordsBright.

Wagner, Anke. Help, I Don't Want a Babysitter! Behl, Anne-Kathrin, illus. 2015. (ENG.). 32p. (J). (gr. -1-2). 17.95 *(978-0-7358-4214-4(0))* North-South Bks., Inc.

Wagner, Veronica. Disney Mickey & the Roadster Racers: Go, Go, Go! Look & Find. The Disney Storybook Art Team, illus. 2017. (ENG.). 16p. (J). bds. 12.99 *(978-1-5037-2298-9(8),* 2531, PI Kids) Phoenix International Publications, Inc.

—Sound Storybook Treasury Disney Princess Bedtime. 2017. (ENG., Illus.). 34p. (J). 29.99 *(978-1-5037-1869-0(1),* 2413, PI Kids) Phoenix International Publications, Inc.

Wagstaff, Janiel M. Stella: Poet Extraordinaire. 2018. (ENG.). 32p. (gr. k-3). pap. 7.99 *(978-1-338-26478-4(8))* Scholastic, Inc.

Wahl, Phoebe. Sonya's Chickens. (Illus.). 32p. (J). (gr. -1-3). 2018. pap. 7.99 *(978-1-77049-790-0(0))* 2015. 17.99 *(978-1-77049-789-4(7))* Tundra Bks. CAN. (Tundra Bks.). Dist: Penguin Random Hse. LLC.

Wahler, Pat & Nielsen, Sheree K. Midnight, the One-Eyed Cat. Dimmett, Janelle, illus. 2018. (ENG.). 32p. (J). (gr. -1-k). 16.95 *(978-0-9963901-9-4(7))* TreeHse. Publishing Group.

Waldman, David K. How Teddy Bears Find Their Homes. Danner, Maggie, illus. 2nd ed. 2015. (ENG.). 154p. (gr. k-2). pap. 38.40 *(978-0-945522-02-7(9))* BookBaby.

Waldman, Debby. A Sack Full of Feathers, 1 vol. Revell, Cindy, illus. 2007. (ENG.). 32p. (J). (gr. -1-k). 9.95 *(978-1-55143-863-4(1))* Orca Bk. Pubs. USA.

Walker, Anna. I Love Birthdays. Walker, Anna, illus. 2010. (ENG., Illus.). 32p. (J). (gr. -1-1). 9.99 *(978-1-4169-8320-0(1),* Simon & Schuster Bks. For Young Readers) Simon & Schuster Bks. For Young Readers.

—I Love My Mom. Walker, Anna, illus. 2010. (ENG., Illus.). 32p. (J). (gr. -1-1). 9.99 *(978-1-4169-8318-7(X),* Simon & Schuster Bks. For Young Readers) Simon & Schuster Bks. For Young Readers.

Walker, B. Mr Peeze, Say Something Else Please! 2011. 28p. pap. 15.99 *(978-1-4568-2937-7(8))* Xlibris Corp.

Wallace, Chad. The Mouse & the Meadow, 1 vol. 2014. (Illus.). 32p. (J). (gr. k-4). 16.95 *(978-1-58469-481-6(5),* Dawn Pubns.) Sourcebooks, Inc.

Wallace, Ian. The Huron Carol, 1 vol. 2013. (ENG., Illus.). 32p. (J). (gr. k). 14.95 *(978-1-55498-394-0(0))* Groundwood Bks. CAN. Dist: Publishers Group West (PGW).

Wallner, S. J. Hans & the Golden Stirrup. (Illus.). 48p. (J). (gr. 2-3). lib. bdg. 10.95 *(978-0-87783-016-0(9));* pap. 3.94 *(978-0-87783-093-1(2))* Oddo Publishing, Inc.

Walsch, Neale Donald. The Little Soul & the Earth: I'm Somebody! Riccio, Frank, illus. 2005. 32p. (J). 20.00 *(978-1-57174-451-7(7))* Hampton Roads Publishing Co., Inc.

Walser, David. Meg & the Romans. Pienkowski, Jan, illus. 2017. 32p. (J). (-k). pap. 11.99 *(978-0-241-29875-6(X))* Penguin Bks., Ltd. GBR. Dist: Independent Pubs. Group.

Walsh, Aly. My Mum Says Blah Blah Blah. Walsh, Marilyn, illus. 2012. 30p. pap. 15.97 *(978-1-61204-854-3(4),* Strategic Bk. Publishing) Strategic Book Publishing & Rights Agency (SBPRA).

Walsh, Joanna. Did You Ever See? 2016. (ENG., Illus.). 32p. (J). (gr. k-4). 16.95 *(978-1-84976-349-3(6),* 1674301) Tate Publishing, Ltd. GBR. Dist: Abrams, Inc.

Walsh, Liza Gardner. Do Fairies Bring the Spring. Mitchell, Hazel, illus. 2019. 22p. (J). (gr. -1-12). 8.95 *(978-1-60893-660-1(0))* Down East Bks.

—How Do Fairies Have Fun in the Sun? Mitchell, Hazel, illus. 2019. 22p. (J). (gr. -1 — 1). 8.95 *(978-1-60893-661-8(9))* Down East Bks.

Walters, Eric. Hope Springs. Fernandes, Eugenie, illus. 2014. 32p. (J). (gr. 1-4). 17.99 *(978-1-77049-530-2(4),* Tundra Bks.) Tundra Bks. CAN. Dist: Penguin Random Hse. LLC.

—My Name Is Blessing. Fernandes, Eugenie, illus. 2013. 32p. (J). (gr. 1-4). 17.95 *(978-1-77049-301-8(8),* Tundra Bks.) Tundra Bks. CAN. Dist: Penguin Random Hse. LLC.

Walters, Eric, compiled by. From the Heart of Africa: A Book of Wisdom. 2018. (Illus.). 40p. (J). (gr. 1-4). 17.99 *(978-1-77049-719-1(6),* Tundra Bks.) Tundra Bks. CAN. Dist: Penguin Random Hse. LLC.

Wan, Joyce. You Are My Merry Little Christmas. Wan, Joyce, illus. 2016. (ENG., Illus.). 14p. (J). (— 1). bds. 6.99 *(978-0-545-88093-0(9),* Cartwheel Bks.) Scholastic, Inc.

Wang, Holman. Great Job, Dad! 2019. (Great Job Ser.: 1). (Illus.). 32p. (J). (gr. -1-2). 16.99 *(978-0-7352-6410-6(4),* Tundra Bks.) Tundra Bks. CAN. Dist: Penguin Random Hse. LLC.

—Great Job, Mom! 2019. (Great Job Ser.: 2). (Illus.). 32p. (J). (gr. -1-2). 16.99 *(978-0-7352-6408-3(2),* Tundra Bks.) Tundra Bks. CAN. Dist: Penguin Random Hse. LLC.

Wang, Margaret. Eency Weency Spider. Rueda, Claudia, illus. 2006. (ENG.). 22p. (J). (gr. -1-3). bds. 10.95 *(978-1-58117-418-2(7),* Intervisual/Piggy Toes) Bendon, Inc.

—Postcards from Kitty. Silver-Thompson, Pattie, illus. 2005. 12p. (J). (gr. -1-3). 9.95 *(978-1-58117-427-4(5),* Intervisual/Piggy Toes) Bendon, Inc.

Wang, Ruowen. To Share One Moon. Xu, Wei & Zheng, Xiaoyan, illus. 2008. 32p. (J). (gr. 2-4). *(978-0-9738799-5-7(5))* Kevin & Robin Bks., Ltd.

Warburg, Sandol Stoddard. The Thinking Book. 2016. (ENG., Illus.). 24p. 14.95 *(978-1-62326-088-0(4))* AMMO Bks., LLC.

Ward, Helen. The King of Birds. 2018. (ENG., Illus.). 40p. (J). (gr. -1-3). 17.95 *(978-1-56792-625-5(8))* Godine, David R. Pub.

—Moon Dog. 2005. (Illus.). 40p. (J). *(978-1-84011-864-3(4))* Templar Publishing.

Ward, Nick. The Tadpole Prince. 2003. (Illus.). 32p. (YA). *(978-1-84365-016-4(9),* Pavilion Children's Books) Pavilion Bks.

Waring, Geoff. Oscar & the Bird: A Book about Electricity. Waring, Geoff, illus. 2011. (Start with Science Ser.). (ENG., Illus.). 32p. (J). (gr. -1-3). pap. 7.99 *(978-0-7636-5302-6(0))* Candlewick Pr.

—Oscar & the Snail: A Book about Things That We Use. Waring, Geoff, illus. 2011. (Start with Science Ser.). (ENG., Illus.). 32p. (J). (gr. -1-3). pap. 6.99 *(978-0-7636-5303-3(9))* Candlewick Pr.

Waring, Zoe. No Hugs for Porcupine. 2017. (ENG., Illus.). 32p. (J). (gr. -1-1). 16.99 *(978-0-7624-6225-4(6),* Running Pr. Kids) Running Pr.

Warren, Rick. God's Great Love for You, 1 vol. Saunders, Chris, illus. 2017. (ENG.). 32p. (J). 17.99 *(978-0-310-75247-9(7))* Zonderkidz.

Watanabe, Kaori. I Love You (My First Taggies Book) Watanabe, Kaori, illus. 2004. (My First Taggies Book Ser.). (ENG., Illus.). 8p. (J). (gr. -1 — 1). 12.99 *(978-0-439-64947-6(1),* Cartwheel Bks.) Scholastic, Inc.

Watkins, Kathleen. Pigín of Howth. Suggs, Margarate A., illus. 2017. (ENG.). 64p. (J). 28.00 *(978-0-7171-6972-6(3))* Gill Bks. IRL. Dist: Casemate Pubs. & Bk. Distributors, LLC.

Watkins, Ross. Dad's Camera. Anelli, Liz, illus. 2018. (ENG.). 40p. (J). (gr. k-4). 16.99 *(978-1-5362-0138-3(3))* Candlewick Pr.

Watson, Hannah. 1,000 Things in Nature. 2018. (1,000 Pictures Ser.). (ENG.). 34p. 14.99 *(978-0-7945-4119-4(4),* Usborne) EDC Publishing.

Watson, Jacqueline. Six Frogs on a Log! 2004. 43p. pap. 24.95 *(978-1-4137-2986-3(X))* PublishAmerica, Inc.

Watson, Jane Werner. Animal Friends. Williams, Garth, illus. 2016. (Little Golden Book Ser.). 24p. (J). (gr. -1-k). 5.99 *(978-0-553-53642-3(7),* Golden Bks.) Random Hse. Children's Bks.

Watson, Tom. & Long, Ethan, illus. Stick Dog Slurps Spaghetti. 2016. 238p. (J). *(978-0-06-245857-5(4))* Harper & Row Ltd.

Watt, Fiona. Baby's Very First Noisy Book Jungle. 2017. (Picture Bks.). (ENG.). 10p. (J). 15.99 *(978-0-7945-3986-3(6),* Usborne) EDC Publishing.

—Este No Es Mi Tren. rev. ed. 2004. (Titles in Spanish Ser.).Tr. of That's Not My Train. 32p. (J). 12.99 *(978-1-58086-585-2(2))* EDC Publishing.

—Polar Bears. Chiara, Francesca De, illus. 2010. (Luxury Touchy-Feely Board Bks). 10p. (J). bds. 15.99 *(978-0-7945-2544-6(X),* Usborne) EDC Publishing.

—Rainy Day Stroller Book. Baggott, Stella, illus. 2010. 8p. (J). 7.99 *(978-0-7945-2850-8(3),* Usborne) EDC Publishing.

—Seaside Stroller Book. Baggott, Stella, illus. 2010. 8p. (J). 7.99 *(978-0-7945-2810-2(4),* Usborne) EDC Publishing.

—That's Not My Dragon... Wells, Rachel, illus. 2006. (Usborne Touchy-Feely Bks.). 10p. (J). (gr. -1-k). bds. 7.99 *(978-0-7945-1285-9(2),* Usborne) EDC Publishing.

—That's Not My Dragon. rev. ed. 2011. (Touchy-Feely Board Bks). 10p. (J). ring bd. 8.99 *(978-0-7945-3092-1(3),* Usborne) EDC Publishing.

—That's Not My Prince. Wells, Rachel, illus. 2013. (Usborne Touchy-Feely Board Bks.). (ENG.). 10p. (J). 9.99 *(978-0-7945-2838-6(4),* Usborne) EDC Publishing.

—That's Not My Santa. rev. ed. 2012. (Touchy-Feely Board Bks). 10p. (J). bds. 8.99 *(978-0-7945-3310-6(8),* Usborne) EDC Publishing.

Watt, Fiona & Wells, Rachel. Gatitos. 2004. (SPA.). 10p. (J). 11.95 *(978-0-7460-5091-0(7))* EDC Publishing.

Watt, Mélanie. Scaredy Squirrel. 2011. (J). (gr. -1-3). 29.95 *(978-0-545-32740-4(7));* 18.95 *(978-0-545-32752-7(0));*Set. 38.75 *(978-0-545-32759-6(8))* Weston Woods Studios, Inc.

Watt, Mélanie & Watt, Mélanie. Chester's Back! Watt, Mélanie & Watt, Mélanie, illus. 2013. (Chester Ser.). (ENG., Illus.). 32p. (J). (gr. -1-3). 9.99 *(978-1-55453-461-6(5))* Kids Can Pr., Ltd. CAN. Dist: Hachette Bk. Group.

—Have I Got a Book for You! Watt, Mélanie & Watt, Mélanie, illus. 2013. (ENG., Illus.). 32p. (J). (gr. k-4). pap. 9.99 *(978-1-55453-483-8(6))* Kids Can Pr., Ltd. CAN. Dist: Hachette Bk. Group.

—Scaredy Squirrel at Night. Watt, Mélanie & Watt, Mélanie, illus. 2009. (Scaredy Squirrel Ser.). (ENG., Illus.). 32p. (J). (gr. -1-3). 16.99 *(978-1-55453-288-9(4))* Kids Can Pr., Ltd. CAN. Dist: Hachette Bk. Group.

—Scaredy Squirrel Has a Birthday Party. Watt, Mélanie & Watt, Mélanie, illus. 2011. (ENG., Illus.). 32p. (J). (gr. -1-3). 16.99 *(978-1-55453-468-5(2))* Kids Can Pr., Ltd. CAN. Dist: Hachette Bk. Group.

Watts, Bernadette. The Golden Plate. 2014. (ENG., Illus.). 32p. (J). 17.95 *(978-0-7358-4175-8(6))* North-South Bks., Inc.

—Peter's Tree, 36 vols. 2015. (Illus.). 34p. 17.95 *(978-1-78250-178-7(9))* Floris Bks. GBR. Dist: Consortium Bk. Sales & Distribution.

Watts, Bernadette & Grimm, Jacob and Wilhelm. The Enchanted Nightingale: The Classic Grimm's Tale of Jorinda & Joringel, 34 vols. 2017. Orig. Title: Jorinde und Joringel. (Illus.). 32p. (J). 17.95 *(978-1-78250-436-8(2))* Floris Bks. GBR. Dist: Consortium Bk. Sales & Distribution.

Weakly, Chris A. Toby the Little Switch Engine. 2012. 24p. 24.95 *(978-1-4626-4884-9(3))* America Star Bks.

Weatherford, Carole Boston. Freedom on the Menu: The Greensboro Sit-Ins. Lagarrigue, Jerome Lagarrigue, illus. 2007. 32p. (J). (gr. -1-3). pap. 8.99 *(978-0-14-240894-0(8),* Puffin Books) Penguin Young Readers Group.

Weaver, A. J. Big Cats, Little Cats. Budgen, Tim, illus. 2013. 32p. pap. *(978-1-909423-03-9(3))* Bks. to Treasure.

Webb, Holly. The Rescued Puppy. Williams, Sophy, illus. 2017. 124p. (J). *(978-1-5182-4904-4(3))* Tiger Tales.

Webb, Sarah & Ranson, Claire. Sally Go Round the Stars: Favourite Rhymes from an Irish Childhood. McCarthy, Steve, illus. 2014. (ENG.). 64p. (J). pap. 17.00 *(978-1-84717-675-2(5))* O'Brien Pr., Ltd., The IRL. Dist: Casemate Pubs. & Bk. Distributors, LLC.

Webb, Steve. Happy Zappa Cat. Le Huche, Magali, illus. 2014. (ENG.). 32p. 15.99 *(978-0-85707-620-5(5),* Simon & Schuster Children's) Simon & Schuster, Ltd. GBR. Dist: Simon & Schuster, Inc.

Webber, Helen. Webber Quartet, 4 Vols. deluxe ed. (J). (gr. k-6). 35.00 *(978-0-8392-3070-0(2))* Astor-Honor, Inc.

Webster, Christy. Fast As the Flash! Doescher, Erik, illus. 2018. 24p. (J). *(978-1-5444-0227-7(9))* Random Hse., Inc.

—Fast As the Flash! 2018. (Step into Reading Level 2 Ser.). lib. bdg. 14.75 *(978-0-606-40932-2(7))* Turtleback.

—Fast As the Flash! (DC Super Friends) Doescher, Erik, illus. 2018. (Step into Reading Ser.). (ENG.). 24p. (J). (gr. -1-1). pap. 5.99 *(978-1-5247-6864-5(2),* Random Hse. Bks. for Young Readers) Random Hse. Children's Bks.

—A Is for Awful: a Grumpy Cat ABC Book (Grumpy Cat) Laberis, Steph, illus. 2017. (Little Golden Book Ser.). 24p. (J). (gr. -1-1). 5.99 *(978-0-399-55783-5(0),* Golden Bks.) Random Hse. Children's Bks.

Webster, Jean. Papaíto-Piernas-Largas. (SPA.). (YA). (gr. 5-8). pap. *(978-950-08-1515-4(X),* AA7255) Atlantida ARG. Dist: Lectorum Pubns., Inc.

Wedge, Chris. Bunny: A Picture Book Adapted from the Animated Film. Wedge, Chris, illus. 2004. (Illus.). 30p. (J). (gr. k-4). reprint ed. 19.00 *(978-0-7567-7460-8(8))* DIANE Publishing Co.

Wehr, Julian. Snow White. 2004. (Illus.). 14p. (J). pap. 12.95 *(978-0-9748093-0-4(6))* Wehr Animations.

Weidenbach, Kristin. Meet Banjo Paterson. Hancock, James Gulliver, illus. 2015. (Meet... Ser.: Bk. 7). (ENG.). 32p. (J). (gr. -1-k). 21.99 *(978-0-85798-008-3(4))* Random Hse. Australia AUS. Dist: Independent Pubs. Group.

Weidner, Teri, illus. Sleep, Baby, Sleep. 2009. 20p. (J). (gr. -1-k). 8.95 *(978-1-58925-843-3(6))* Tiger Tales.

Weigand, Jessica. I Have a Monster under My Bed. 2009. 20p. pap. 10.49 *(978-1-4389-7503-0(1))* AuthorHouse.

Weiser, Florence, illus. Twinkle, Twinkle, Little Star: A Light-Up Bedtime Book. 2017. (ENG.). 10p. (J). (gr. -1 — 1). bds. 10.99 *(978-0-7624-6182-0(9),* Running Pr. Kids) Running Pr.

Weiskal, N. J. C Is for the Christ Child. 2009. 32p. pap. 8.00 *(978-1-935125-55-6(9))* Robertson Publishing.

Weiskal, N. j. & Weiskal, N. J. The Skittery Kitten & the Scaredy Cat. Weiskal, N. J., illus. 2009. (Illus.). 36p. pap. 8.00 *(978-1-935125-59-4(1))* Robertson Publishing.

Weiss, Ellen. Simba's Moon. Cuddy, Robin, illus. Date not set. (ENG.). 32p. (J). (gr. -1-2). 12.99 *(978-0-7868-3267-5(3))* Disney Pr.

Welcome Home, Bear: A Book of Animal Habitats. 2015. (Illus.). 32p. (J). (— 1). 16.99 *(978-0-385-75375-3(6),* Knopf Bks. for Young Readers) Random Hse. Children's Bks.

Wellesley, Rosie. The Very Hungry Hedgehog. 2018. (ENG., Illus.). 32p. (J). (gr. -1-k). 9.99 *(978-1-84365-353-0(2),* Pavilion Children's Books) Pavilion Bks. GBR. Dist: HarperCollins Pubs.

—The Wide Awake Hedgehog. 2016. (ENG., Illus.). 32p. (J). (gr. -1-k). 9.99 *(978-1-84365-309-7(5),* Pavilion Children's Books) Pavilion Bks. GBR. Dist: HarperCollins Pubs.

Wellington, Monica. Dear Ballerina. 2019. (Illus.). 40p. (J). (-k). 17.99 *(978-0-8234-3932-4(1))* Holiday Hse., Inc.

Wells, E. A. The Butterfly Weed Patch. 2012. 32p. pap. *(978-1-105-50787-8(4))* Lulu.com.

Wells, Mark & Wells, Meagan. Tommy's Lost Tooth. Wells, Mark, illus. 2011. (Illus.). 28p. pap. 11.99 *(978-1-61170-020-6(5))* Robertson Publishing.

Wells, Rosemary. Fiona's Little Accident. Wells, Rosemary, illus. (Felix & Fiona Ser.). (ENG., Illus.). 32p. (J). (gr. k-3). 2019. 5.99 *(978-1-5362-0895-5(7))* 2018. 14.99 *(978-0-7636-8982-7(3))* Candlewick Pr.

—Max & Ruby's Bedtime Book. 2015. (Max & Ruby Ser.). (Illus.). 48p. (J). (gr. -1-k). 8.99 *(978-0-14-751746-3(X),* Puffin Books) Penguin Young Readers Group.

—Sleep, My Bunny. Wells, Rosemary, illus. 2018. (ENG., Illus.). 24p. (J). (-k). 14.99 *(978-0-7636-9262-9(X))* Candlewick Pr.

Welsh, Karen Leis. Frolicking Friends. 2012. (Illus.). 44p. pap. 21.99 *(978-1-4685-6422-8(6))* AuthorHouse.

Welton, Jude. Tomas Loves... A Rhyming Book about Fun, Friendship - & Autism. Telford, Jane, illus. 2015. 32p. 17.95 *(978-1-84905-544-4(0),* 693420) Kingsley, Jessica Pubs. GBR. Dist: Hachette UK Distribution.

Weninger, Brigitte. Happy Birthday, Davy! Tharlet, Eve, illus. 2nd rev. ed. 2015. (ENG.). 32p. (J). (gr. -1-2). 15.95 *(978-0-7358-4224-3(8))* North-South Bks., Inc.

—Happy Easter, Davy! Tharlet, Eve, illus. 2014. (ENG.). 32p. (J). (gr. k-3). 15.95 *(978-0-7358-4161-1(6))* North-South Bks., Inc.

—Merry Christmas, Davy! Tharlet, Eve, illus. 2014. (ENG.). 32p. (J). (gr. k-2). 15.95 *(978-0-7358-4186-4(1))* North-South Bks., Inc.

Werner Watson, Jane. The Fuzzy Duckling. Provensen, Martin & Provensen, Alice, illus. 2015. (Little Golden Book Ser.). (ENG.). 24p. (J). (-k). 5.99 *(978-0-553-52213-6(2),* Golden Bks.) Random Hse. Children's Bks.

Wesley, Gloria Ann. Abigail's Wish, 1 vol. Rudnicki, Richard, illus. 2016. (ENG.). 32p. (J). (gr. 1-3). 22.95 *(978-1-77108-439-0(1),* defd3a5e-1b53-4362-8bd4-703fa1483fd1) Nimbus Publishing, Ltd. CAN. Dist: Baker & Taylor Publisher Services (BTPS).

West, Colin. Have You Seen the Crocodile? Read & Share. West, Colin, illus. 2003. (Read & Share Ser.). (ENG., Illus.). 32p. (J). (gr. -1-3). pap. 3.99 *(978-0-7636-0862-0(9))* Candlewick Pr.

Weston, Robert Paul. Sakura's Cherry Blossoms. Saburi, Misa, illus. 2018. 40p. (J). (gr. -1-2). 17.99 *(978-1-101-91874-6(8),* Tundra Bks.) Tundra Bks. CAN. Dist: Penguin Random Hse. LLC.

Wezeman, Phyllis Vos & Liechty, Anna L. Tell Me a Story: 30 Children's Sermons Based on Best-Loved Books. 2005. (New Brown Bag Ser.). (Illus.). 96p. pap. 12.00 *(978-0-8298-1635-8(6))* Pilgrim Pr., The/United Church Pr.

Whale Mail. 2003. (J). spiral bd. 9.95 *(978-0-89610-126-5(6))* Island Heritage Publishing.

Whamond, Dave. Rosie's Glasses. Whamond, Dave, illus. 2018. (ENG., Illus.). 32p. (J). (gr. -1-2). 19.99 *(978-1-77138-991-4(5))* Kids Can Pr., Ltd. CAN. Dist: Hachette Bk. Group.

Wheeler, Lisa. Even Monsters Go to School. Van Dusen, Chris, illus. 2019. (ENG.). 32p. (J). (gr. -1-3). 17.99 *(978-0-06-236642-9(4),* Balzer & Bray) HarperCollins Pubs.

—Mater's Backward ABC Book (Disney/Pixar Cars 3) Hashimoto, Satoshi, illus. 2017. (ENG.). 48p. (J). (-k). 9.99 *(978-0-7364-3818-6(1),* RH/Disney) Random Hse. Children's Bks.

—Ugly Pie. Solomon, Heather, illus. 2014. (ENG.). 32p. (J). (gr. -1-3). pap. 7.99 *(978-0-544-23961-6(X),* 1565437, Clarion Bks.) HarperCollins Pubs.

When I Go. 2003. (Illus.). (J). bds. 7.98 *(978-0-7525-8657-1(2))* Parragon, Inc.

Where Is Curious George? Around the Town: A Look-And-Find Bo. 2015. (Curious George Ser.). (ENG., Illus.). 32p. (J). (gr. -1-3). 9.99 *(978-0-544-38072-1(X),* 1591847, Clarion Bks.) HarperCollins Pubs.

White, Howard. The Airplane Ride. Guzek, Greta, illus. unabr. ed. 2006. (ENG.). 32p. (J). 16.95 *(978-0-88971-224-9(7),* 43db8bfb-f228-4671-91c4-7604289a9785) Nightwood Editions CAN. Dist: Harbour Publishing Co., Ltd.

Whitford Paul, Ann. Fiesta Fiasco. 2012. 29.95 *(978-1-4301-1100-9(3))* Live Oak Media.

Whitley, Jeremy. Get over Yourself, Vol. 2. 2013. (ENG., Illus.). 128p. (J). pap. 14.95 *(978-0-9859652-4-2(X),* e56f8563-fa69-4329-9ae3-6c4a31782008) Action Lab Entertainment.

Whitman, Nancy C. Counting Petals: Using Flowers of Hawaii. Chong, Luther, photos by. 2009. (Illus.). 31p. (J). *(978-1-4363-8562-6(8))* Xlibris Corp.

Whittingham, Jane. A Good Day for Ducks. Tuazon, Noel, illus. 2018. (ENG.). 24p. (J). (gr. -1-k). 16.95 *(978-1-77278-061-1(8))* Pajama Pr. CAN. Dist: Publishers Group West (PGW).

Whybrow, Ian. Say Hello to the Animals! Warnes, Tim, illus. 2017. 20p. (J). *(978-1-4351-6512-0(8))* Barnes & Noble, Inc.

—Say Hello to the Snowy Animals! Eaves, Edward, illus. 2012. (J). *(978-0-7607-9675-7(0))* Barnes & Noble, Inc.

—Tim, Ted & the Pirates. Ayto, Russell, illus. 2014. (ENG.). 32p. (J). 17.99 *(978-0-00-755930-5(5),* HarperCollins Children's Bks.) HarperCollins Pubs. Ltd. GBR. Dist: HarperCollins Pubs.

—Where's Tim's Ted? It's Time for Bed! Ayto, Russell, illus. 2014. (ENG.). 32p. (J). 17.99 *(978-0-00-755929-9(1),* HarperCollins Children's Bks.) HarperCollins Pubs. Ltd. GBR. Dist: HarperCollins Pubs.

Whybrow, Ian, et al. Owain A'r Cloc. 2005. (WEL., Illus.). 20.0p. 6.99 *(978-1-84323-366-4(5))* Gomer Pr. GBR. Dist: Gomer Pr.

Widgen, Susan. A Caring Deed for Becky. Novak, Steven, illus. 2012. 36p. pap. 8.99 *(978-1-60820-579-0(7))* MLR Pr., LLC.

Widmark, Martin. The House of Lost & Found, 20 vols. Dziubak, Emilia, illus. 2018. Orig. Title: Huset Som Vaknade. 40p. (J). 17.95 *(978-1-78250-542-6(3))* Floris Bks. GBR. Dist: Consortium Bk. Sales & Distribution.

Wieder, Stefanie Paige. Baby Food. 2019. (ENG., Illus.). 16p. (J). (gr. -1-k). bds. 7.99 *(978-1-78285-730-3(3))* Barefoot Bks., Inc.

Wiesner, David. Tuesday: A Caldecott Award Winner. 2011. (ENG., Illus.). 32p. (J). (gr. -1-3). pap. 8.99 *(978-0-395-87082-2(8),* 111994, Clarion Bks.) HarperCollins Pubs.

Wigden, Susan. I Want to Learn to Dance. Franzese, Nora Tapp, illus. 2012. 36p. pap. 11.99 *(978-1-60820-725-1(0))* MLR Pr., LLC.

Wilcox, Leah. Waking Beauty. Monks, Lydia, illus. 2011. 32p. (J). (gr. -1-k). pap. 7.99 *(978-0-14-241538-2(3),* Puffin Books) Penguin Young Readers Group.

Wild, Margaret & Gamble, Kim. First Day. 2017. (ENG.). 32p. (J). (gr. k-2). pap. 13.99 *(978-1-76029-391-8(1))* Allen & Unwin AUS. Dist: Independent Pubs. Group.

Wilde, Oscar. The Selfish Giant. Bowman, Jeanne, illus. 2019. (ENG.). 32p. (J). (gr. k-3). 17.99 *(978-1-64170-126-6(9),* 550126) Familius LLC.

Wilder, Laura Ingalls. A Little House Picture Book Treasury: Six Stories of Life on the Prairie. Graef, Renee, illus. 2017. (Little House Picture Book Ser.). (ENG.). 208p. (J). (gr. -1-3). 24.99 *(978-0-06-247077-5(9),* HarperCollins) HarperCollins Pubs.

Wilhelm, Hans. Pigs in a Blanket (Board Books for Toddlers, Bedtime Stories, Goodnight Board Book) Salcedo, Erica, illus. 2019. (Pigs in A Ser.). (ENG.). 14p. (J). (gr. -1 — 1). bds. 9.99 *(978-1-4521-6451-9(7))* Chronicle Bks. LLC.

Wilkes, Ruth. Dancing Fruit Put on a Show! Cross, James, illus. 2013. 48p. 18.99 *(978-1-62314-797-6(2))* Willow Publishing.

Wilkins, James Francis. The Queen & Mr Brown: A Day for Dinosaurs. 2015. (Queen & Mr Brown Ser.). (ENG., Illus.). 48p. (J). (gr. k-2). pap. 11.99 *(978-0-565-09354-9(1))* Natural History Museum Pubns. GBR. Dist: Independent Pubs. Group.

—The Queen & Mr Brown: a Night in the Natural History Museum. 2016. (Queen & Mr Brown Ser.). (ENG., Illus.). 48p. (J). (gr. -1-2). 17.99 *(978-0-565-09376-1(2))* Natural History Museum Pubns. GBR. Dist: Independent Pubs. Group.

—The Queen & Mr Brown: Meet the Rats. (Queen & Mr Brown Ser.). (ENG., Illus.). 48p. (J). (gr. k-2). 2019. pap. 12.99 *(978-0-565-09446-1(7))* 2017. 17.99 *(978-0-565-09438-6(6))* Natural History Museum Pubns. GBR. Dist: Independent Pubs. Group.

Wilkins, Nalini. Doby's First Christmas. Robb, Jonathan, illus. 2012. 28p. pap. 12.50 *(978-1-62212-777-1(3),* Strategic Bk. Publishing) Strategic Book Publishing & Rights Agency (SBPRA).

Willems, Mo. Don't Let the Pigeon Drive the Bus! 2003. (Pigeon Ser.). (ENG., Illus.). 40p. (J). (gr. -1-k). 17.99 *(978-0-7868-1988-1(X),* Hyperion Books for Children) Disney Publishing Worldwide.

—Knuffle Bunny: a Cautionary Tale. 2004. (Knuffle Bunny Ser.). (ENG., Illus.). 40p. (J). (gr. -1-k). 17.99 *(978-0-7868-1870-9(0),* Hyperion Books for Children) Disney Publishing Worldwide.

—The Pigeon Has Feelings, Too! 2005. (Pigeon Ser.). (ENG., Illus.). 12p. (J). (gr. -1-k). bds. 6.99 *(978-0-7868-3650-5(4),* Hyperion Books for Children) Disney Publishing Worldwide.

—The Pigeon Loves Things That Go! 2005. (Pigeon Ser.). (ENG., Illus.). 12p. (J). (gr. -1-k). bds. 6.99 *(978-0-7868-3651-2(2),* Hyperion Books for Children) Disney Publishing Worldwide.

Willems, Mo, illus. Don't Let the Pigeon Drive the Bus! 2005. 40p. (J). *(978-1-84428-013-1(6))* Walker Bks. Australia Pty, Ltd.

William H. Sadlier Staff. Stop by a Pond. 2005. (Early Library). (gr. k-2). 24.00 net. *(978-0-8215-8942-7(3))* Sadlier, William H. Inc.

Williams, Brenda. Home for a Penguin, Home for a Whale. Beghelli, Annalisa, illus. 2019. (ENG.). 32p. (J). (gr. -1-3). 16.99 *(978-1-78285-743-3(5))* Barefoot Bks., Inc.

—Outdoor Opposites. Oldfield, Rachel, illus. 2015. (Barefoot Singalongs Ser.). (ENG.). 32p. (J). (gr. -1-2). pap. 10.99 *(978-1-78285-095-3(3))* Barefoot Bks., Inc.

Williams, Chase. The Tale of the Beaver. 2012. 36p. pap. 21.99 *(978-1-4691-7984-1(9))* Xlibris Corp.

Williams, Emma Louise. Harry the Hedgehog Loses His Favorite Sock. 2012. 20p. pap. 7.99 *(978-1-939076-00-7(5))* Wiggies, Piggy.

—What's That Smell Monkey? williams, Emma Louise, illus. 2012. 12p. pap. 7.99 *(978-1-939076-07-6(2))* Wiggies, Piggy.

Williams-Garcia, Rita. Bottle Cap Boys on Royal Street. 2009. (Illus.). 32p. (J). 16.95 *(978-1-60349-030-6(2),* Marimba Bks.) Just Us Bks., Inc.

Williams, Garth. Baby Farm Animals. 2016. (Illus.). 26p. (J). (gr. -1-k). bds. 7.99 *(978-0-553-53632-4(X),* Golden Bks.) Random Hse. Children's Bks.

—Bunnies' ABC. Williams, Garth, illus. 2015. (Little Golden Book Ser.). (Illus.). 24p. (J). (-k). 4.99 *(978-0-385-39128-3(5),* Golden Bks.) Random Hse. Children's Bks.

Williams, Margery. The Velveteen Rabbit. Berg, Maria, illus. 2018. (ENG.). 36p. (J). (gr. k-5). 24.95 *(978-1-60025-124-5(2))* Bassett, Maurice.

—The Velveteen Rabbit. 2017. (ENG., Illus.). (J). (gr. k-2). pap. 4.95 *(978-1-68422-087-8(4))* Martino Fine Bks.

—The Velveteen Rabbit. 2018. (ENG., Illus.). 24p. (J). 9.99 *(978-1-5154-2926-5(1))* Wilder Pubns., Corp.

—Velveteen Rabbit. Nicholson, William, illus. ed. 2022. (ENG.). 48p. (J). (gr. -1-k). pap. 8.99 *(978-1-4052-1054-6(0))* Farshore GBR. Dist: HarperCollins Pubs.

Williams, Renee Pierce. Buck the Good Doog. 2012. 28p. pap. 15.99 *(978-1-4691-5325-4(4))* Xlibris Corp.

Williams, Walter. The Bicycle Garden. 2013. 40p. pap. 6.99 *(978-0-9890698-0-9(X))* Fernwood & Hedges Bks.

Williamson, Jennifer. Timmy the Tow Truck, 6 vols. Williamson, Alan, 8th, illus. 2005. 28p. (J). pap. *(978-0-9771678-1-4(X))* Theee Hole Punch Publishing.

Williamson, Karen. My Little Story of Christmas. Enright, Amanda, illus. 2014. (ENG.). 20p. (J). (gr. -1-k). E-Book 3.99 *(978-1-78128-153-6(X),* Candle Bks.) Lion Hudson PLC GBR. Dist: Independent Pubs. Group.

Williamson, Melanie, illus. The Wheels on the Bus. 2014. (Barefoot Singalongs Ser.). (ENG.). 24p. (J). (gr. -1-1). pap. 10.99 *(978-1-84686-788-0(6))* Barefoot Bks., Inc.

Willis, Jeanne. Caterpillar Dreams. Ross, Tony, illus. 2013. (ENG.). 32p. (J). (gr. -1-k). pap. 8.99 *(978-1-84939-025-5(8))* Andersen Pr. GBR. Dist: Independent Pubs. Group.

—Chicken Clicking. Ross, Tony, illus. 2015. (Online Safety Picture Bks.). (ENG.). 32p. (J). (gr. -1-k). pap. 14.99 *(978-1-78344-161-7(5))* Andersen Pr. GBR. Dist: Independent Pubs. Group.

—Dr Xargle's Book of Earth Tiggers. Ross, Tony, illus. 2012. (ENG.). 28p. (J). (gr. -1-k). pap. 11.99 *(978-1-84939-297-6(8))* Andersen Pr. GBR. Dist: Independent Pubs. Group.

—Dr Xargle's Book of Earthlets. Ross, Tony, illus. 2012. (ENG.). 28p. (J). (gr. -1-k). pap. 12.99 *(978-1-84939-292-1(7))* Andersen Pr. GBR. Dist: Independent Pubs. Group.

—Mammoth Pie. Ross, Tony, illus. 2013. (ENG.). 32p. (J). (gr. -1-k). pap. 8.99 *(978-1-84270-757-9(4))* Andersen Pr. GBR. Dist: Independent Pubs. Group.

—Mayfly Day. Ross, Tony, illus. 2012. (ENG.). 32p. (J). (gr. -1-k). pap. 10.99 *(978-1-84270-606-0(3))* Andersen Pr. GBR. Dist: Independent Pubs. Group.

—Prince Charmless. Ross, Tony, illus. 2014. (ENG.). 32p. (J). (gr. -1-k). pap. 14.99 *(978-1-84939-778-0(3))* Andersen Pr. GBR. Dist: Independent Pubs. Group.

—We're Going to a Party! Ross, Tony, illus. 2015. (ENG.). 16p. (J). (-k). pap. 14.99 *(978-1-84939-456-7(3))* Andersen Pr. GBR. Dist: Independent Pubs. Group.

—Who's in the Loo? Reynolds, Adrian, illus. 10th ed. 2016. (ENG.). 12p. (J). (— 1). bds. 9.99 *(978-1-78344-420-5(7))* Andersen Pr. GBR. Dist: Independent Pubs. Group.

Wilson Sr., Tyrone L. The Spectacle of Lights. Livingston, Tim, illus. 2012. (ENG.). 44p. pap. 15.99 *(978-1-4691-7514-0(2))* Xlibris Corp.

Wilson, Troy. Little Red Reading Hood & the Misread Wolf. Campana, Ilaria, illus. 2019. (ENG.). 32p. (J). (gr. -1-3). 17.99 *(978-0-7624-9266-4(X),* Running Pr. Kids) Running Pr.

—Perfect Man, 1 vol. Griffiths, Dean, illus. 2005. (ENG.). 32p. (J). (gr. 1-3). per. 9.95 *(978-1-55143-435-3(0))* Orca Bk. Pubs. USA.

Wing, Natasha. The Night Before Class Picture Day. Wummer, Amy, illus. 2016. (Night Before Ser.). 32p. (J). (-k). bds. 4.99 *(978-0-448-48902-5(3),* Grosset & Dunlap) Penguin Young Readers Group.

—The Night Before My First Communion. Wummer, Amy, illus. 2018. (Night Before Ser.). 32p. (J). (-k). pap. 5.99 *(978-1-5247-8619-9(5),* Grosset & Dunlap) Penguin Young Readers Group.

—The Night Before the New Pet. Wummer, Amy, illus. 2016. (Night Before Ser.). (ENG.). 32p. (J). (-k). pap. 5.99

(978-0-448-48903-2(1), Grosset & Dunlap) Penguin Young Readers Group.

Winstanley, Nicola. How to Give Your Cat a Bath: In Five Easy Steps. Martz, John, illus. 2019. (How to Cat Bks.). 40p. (J). (gr. -1-2). 17.99 *(978-0-7352-6354-3(X)*, Tundra Bks.) Tundra Bks. CAN. Dist: Penguin Random Hse. LLC.

—The Pirate's Bed. James, Matt, illus. 2015. 32p. (J). (gr. -1-2). 17.99 *(978-1-77049-616-3(5)*, Tundra Bks.) Tundra Bks. CAN. Dist: Penguin Random Hse. LLC.

Winters, Kari-Lynn. No-Matter-What Friend, 1 vol. Pratt, Pierre, illus. 2014. (ENG.). 32p. (J). (gr. 1-3). 16.95 *(978-1-896580-83-8(1))* Tradewind Bks. CAN. Dist: Orca Bk. Pubs. USA.

—On My Bike, 1 vol. Leist, Christina, illus. 2017. (On My ... Ser.: 2). (ENG.). 24p. (J). (gr. -1-k). bds. 12.95 *(978-1-926890-13-5(2))* Tradewind Bks. CAN. Dist: Orca Bk. Pubs. USA.

—On My Skis, 1 vol. Leist, Christina, illus. 2017. (On My ... Ser.: 3). (ENG.). 24p. (J). (gr. -1-k). bds. 12.95 *(978-1-926890-03-6(5))* Tradewind Bks. CAN. Dist: Orca Bk. Pubs. USA.

—On My Swim, 1 vol. Leist, Christina, illus. 2018. (On My ... Ser.: 4). (ENG.). 24p. (J). (gr. -1-k). 12.95 *(978-1-926890-16-6(7))* Tradewind Bks. CAN. Dist: Orca Bk. Pubs. USA.

Wirth, Beverly. Flowers from Seeds: A Garden Parable. 2012. 40p. pap. 16.99 *(978-1-4624-0101-7(5)*, Inspiring Voices) Author Solutions, LLC.

Wise Brown, Margaret. The Golden Egg Book. Weisgard, Leonard, illus. 2015. (Little Golden Book Ser.). 24p. (J). (-k). 4.99 *(978-0-385-38476-6(9)*, Golden Bks.) Random Hse. Children's Bks.

Wishinsky, Frieda. Maggie Can't Wait, 1 vol. Griffiths, Dean, illus. 2009. (ENG.). 32p. (J). (gr. -1-1). 17.95 *(978-1-55455-103-3(X)*, b93c1bd4-e847-4eb4-a342-031efc5ebcf4) Fitzhenry & Whiteside, Ltd. CAN. Dist: Firefly Bks., Ltd.

Witek, Jo. Hello in There! A Big Sister's Book of Waiting. 2013. (Growing Hearts Ser.). (ENG., Illus.). 28p. (J). (gr. -1 — 1). 18.99 *(978-1-4197-0371-3(4)*, 1037007, Abrams Appleseed) Abrams, Inc.

Wolcott, P. A. The Fox, the Badger, & the Bunny: A Dales Tale. Wolcott, K. Hannah, ed. Schweitzer, Patty, illus. 2009. 20p. pap. 24.95 *(978-1-60749-525-3(2))* America Star Bks.

Wolfe, Jane. Cheeky Frog. Benham, Tors, illus. 2016. 8p. (J). (gr. -1-12). bds. 6.99 *(978-1-84322-718-2(5)*, Armadillo) Anness Publishing GBR. Dist: National Bk. Network.

—Crazy Cow. Benham, Tors, illus. 2013. 8p. (J). (gr. -1-k). bds. 6.99 *(978-1-84322-775-5(4)*, Armadillo) Anness Publishing GBR. Dist: National Bk. Network.

—Dizzy Duck. Benham, Tors, illus. 2016. 8p. (J). (gr. -1-12). bds. 6.99 *(978-1-84322-719-9(3)*, Armadillo) Anness Publishing GBR. Dist: National Bk. Network.

—Happy Cat. Benham, Tors, illus. 2016. 8p. (J). (gr. -1-k). bds. 6.99 *(978-1-84322-720-5(7)*, Armadillo) Anness Publishing GBR. Dist: National Bk. Network.

—Hungry Horse. Benham, Tors, illus. 2016. 8p. (J). (gr. -1-12). bds. 6.99 *(978-1-84322-721-2(5)*, Armadillo) Anness Publishing GBR. Dist: National Bk. Network.

—Messy Pig. Benham, Tors, illus. 2013. 8p. (J). (gr. -1-k). bds. 6.99 *(978-1-84322-777-9(0)*, Armadillo) Anness Publishing GBR. Dist: National Bk. Network.

—Noisy Dog. Benham, Tors, illus. 2013. 8p. (J). (gr. -1-k). bds. 6.99 *(978-1-84322-779-3(7)*, Armadillo) Anness Publishing GBR. Dist: National Bk. Network.

—Pull the Lever: Who Does What? Benham, Tors, illus. 2014. (ENG.). 8p. (J). (gr. -1-2). bds. 6.99 *(978-1-86147-392-9(3)*, Armadillo) Anness Publishing GBR. Dist: National Bk. Network.

—Pull the Lever: Who's in Here? Benham, Tors, illus. 2014. (ENG.). 8p. (J). (gr. -1-2). bds. 6.99 *(978-1-86147-394-3(X)*, Armadillo) Anness Publishing GBR. Dist: National Bk. Network.

—Sleepy Sheep. Benham, Tors, illus. 2013. 8p. (J). (gr. -1-k). bds. 6.99 *(978-1-84322-778-6(9)*, Armadillo) Anness Publishing GBR. Dist: National Bk. Network.

Wolfer, Dianne. Nanna's Button Tin. Potter, Heather, illus. 2018. (ENG.). 32p. (J). (gr. -1-1). 15.99 *(978-0-7636-8096-1(6))* Candlewick Pr.

Wood, A. J. The Christmas Hat. Kneen, Maggie, illus. 2004. (ENG.). 24p. (J). *(978-1-55168-267-9(2))* Fenn, H. B. & Co., Ltd.

Wood, Alix. Pen & Ink, 1 vol. 2018. (Make a Masterpiece Ser.). (ENG.). 32p. (J). (gr. 3-4). pap. 11.50 *(978-1-5382-3580-5(3)*, 3907e391-ce1e-40d4-815a-6833c345c84b); lib. bdg. 28.27 *(978-1-5382-3592-8(7)*, 5b5eda5b-69d6-4557-871e-dc218597a9cb) Stevens, Gareth Publishing LLLP.

Wood, Audrey. The Napping House Board Book. Wood, Don, illus. 2015. (ENG.). 32p. (J). (— 1). bds. 9.99 *(978-0-544-60225-0(0)*, 1616872, Clarion Bks.) HarperCollins Pubs.

Wood, Barbie. The Adventure of Mookin Munchkin. Klick, Gloria, illus. 2013. 32p. pap. 24.95 *(978-1-63004-041-3(X))* America Star Bks.

Wood, Jacqueline & Wood, Jakki. Baby Parade. 2003. (ENG., Illus.). 32p. (J). 14.95 *(978-0-7112-2065-2(4))* Fleming, Randall.

Wood, Ramona. Now Caitlin Can: A Donated Organ Helps a Child Get Well. 2004. (Illus.). 32p. (J). 16.00 *(978-0-9758622-0-9(0))* ABC Pr.

Woods-Whitaker, Kim. Elijah's Big Imagination: A Ball of an Adventure. 2010. 20p. 11.49 *(978-1-4490-1518-3(2))* AuthorHouse.

Woodward, Antonia. The Promised One: The Wonderful Story of Easter. Woodward, Antonia, illus. 2017. (ENG., Illus.). 32p. (J). pap. 10.99 *(978-0-7459-7679-2(4)*, 57148a3b-2061-41ef-9826-6a34cd27ea72, Lion Children's) Lion Hudson PLC GBR. Dist: Baker & Taylor Publisher Services (BTPS).

Woodward, Caroline. Singing Away the Dark. Morstad, Julie, illus. 2017. 44p. (J). (gr. -1-3). 16.95 *(978-1-77229-019-6(X))* Simply Read Bks. CAN. Dist: Ingram Publisher Services.

Workman Publishing. Eyelike Stickers: Kittens. 2018. (Eyelike Stickers Ser.). (ENG., Illus.). 12p. (J). (gr. k-7). 6.95 *(978-1-5235-0274-5(6)*, 100274) Workman Publishing Co., Inc.

—Eyelike Stickers: Puppies. 2018. (Eyelike Stickers Ser.). (ENG., Illus.). 12p. (J). (gr. k-7). 6.95 *(978-1-5235-0294-3(0)*, 100294) Workman Publishing Co., Inc.

—Paint by Sticker Kids: Beautiful Bugs: Create 10 Pictures One Sticker at a Time! (Kids Activity Book, Sticker Art, No Mess Activity, Keep Kids Busy) 2018. (Paint by Sticker Ser.). (ENG., Illus.). 44p. (J). (gr. k-7). 9.95 *(978-1-5235-0295-0(9)*, 100295) Workman Publishing Co., Inc.

Wormell, Chris. Eric!.. The Hero? 2013. (Illus.). 32p. (J). (gr. -1-k). pap. 15.99 *(978-1-84941-284-1(7)*, Red Fox) Random House Children's Books GBR. Dist: Independent Pubs. Group.

Wormell, Christopher. Scruffy Bear & the Lost Ball. 2014. (Illus.). 32p. (J). (-k). pap. 16.99 *(978-1-84941-546-0(3)*, Red Fox) Random House Children's Books GBR. Dist: Independent Pubs. Group.

Wotton, Joy. My First Word Book: Pictures & Words to Start Toddlers Reading & to Help Pre-Schoolers Develop Vocabulary Skills. Tulip, Jenny, illus. 2012. 200p. (J). (gr. -1-12). 9.99 *(978-1-84322-617-8(0)*, Armadillo) Anness Publishing GBR. Dist: National Bk. Network.

Wrecks, Billy. Shark Attack! Doescher, Erik, illus. 2017. 24p. (J). *(978-1-5182-2649-6(3))* Random Hse., Inc.

Wren, Jenny, illus. Night Animals. 2017. (First Explorers Ser.). (ENG.). 10p. (J). (— 1). bds. 8.95 *(978-1-4549-2657-3(0))* Sterling Publishing Co., Inc.

Wright, Kelly. The Bluebell Wood. 2018. (ENG., Illus.). 28p. (J). 23.95 *(978-1-78848-022-2(8)*, 47ea17a3-7ec3-4c2d-b329-0bc824f11a88); pap. 14.95 *(978-1-78848-021-5(X)*, 33977408-63aa-4e19-942e-c5df4b951712) Austin Macauley Pubs. Ltd. GBR. Dist: Baker & Taylor Publisher Services (BTPS).

Wu, Faye-Lynn. My First Book of Chinese Words: An ABC Rhyming Book of Chinese Language & Culture. Padron, Aya, illus. 2017. (My First Words Ser.). 32p. (J). (gr. -1-3). 10.95 *(978-0-8048-4941-8(2))* Tuttle Publishing.

Wykes, Reece. I Dare You. 2017. (ENG., Illus.). 32p. (J). (-k). 23.99 *(978-1-78344-537-0(8))* Andersen Pr. GBR. Dist: Independent Pubs. Group.

Wynbeek Rikkers, Doris. Little Jesus, Little Me, 1 vol. 2017. (ENG., Illus.). 14p. (J). bds. 6.99 *(978-0-310-76177-8(8))* Zonderkidz.

Wynne-Jones, Tim. Pounce de Leon, 1 vol. Tapia, Alfredo, illus. 2014. (ENG.). 32p. (J). (gr. -1-2). pap. 9.95 *(978-0-88995-510-3(7)*, cb934c96-990c-4b71-ab00-657f78d17b5a) Red Deer Pr. CAN. Dist: Firefly Bks., Ltd.

X-Men. 2003. (J). *(978-1-57657-859-9(3))* Paradise Pr., Inc.

Yamada, Miho. Miyako from Tokyo. Camcam, Princesse, illus. 2014. (AV2 Fiction Readalong Ser.: Vol. 132). (ENG.). 32p. (J). (gr. -1-3). lib. bdg. 34.28 *(978-1-4896-2268-6(3)*, AV2 by Weigl) Weigl Pubs., Inc.

Yamashita, Haruo. Seven Little Mice Go to School. Iwamura, Kazuo, illus. 2011. (ENG.). 32p. (J). (gr. -1-k). 17.95 *(978-0-7358-4012-6(1))* North-South Bks., Inc.

Yankey, Lindsey. Bluebird. 2014. (ENG., Illus.). 36p. (J). (gr. -1-3). 17.95 *(978-1-927018-33-0(1))* Simply Read Bks. CAN. Dist: Ingram Publisher Services.

Yarrow, Peter & Lipton, Lenny. Puff, the Magic Dragon. Puybaret, Eric, illus. 2010. 32p. (J). (gr. k-2). 9.95 *(978-1-4027-7216-0(5))* Sterling Publishing Co., Inc.

Yates, Irene. Ladybird First Favourite Tales the Enormous Turnip. 2015. (First Favourite Tales Ser.). (Illus.). 32p. (J). (-k). 9.99 *(978-1-4093-0957-4(6))* Penguin Bks., Ltd. GBR. Dist: Independent Pubs. Group.

Yates, Louise. Dog Loves Fairy Tales. 2016. (Illus.). 32p. (J). pap. 13.99 *(978-1-78295-593-1(3)*, Red Fox) Random House Children's Books GBR. Dist: Independent Pubs. Group.

—Toad & I. 2016. (Illus.). 32p. (J). (gr. k-2). pap. 12.99 *(978-1-78008-105-2(7))* Transworld Publishers Ltd. GBR. Dist: Independent Pubs. Group.

Yayo, illus. Pikiq, 1 vol. 2017. (ENG.). 32p. (J). (gr. -1-k). 16.95 *(978-1-926890-05-0(1))* Tradewind Bks. CAN. Dist: Orca Bk. Pubs. USA.

Yeoman, John. All the Year Round. Blake, Quentin, illus. 2019. (ENG.). 32p. (J). (gr. k-2). pap. 16.99 *(978-1-78344-613-1(7))* Andersen Pr. GBR. Dist: Independent Pubs. Group.

—The Bear's Water Picnic. Blake, Quentin, illus. 2011. (ENG.). 40p. (J). (gr. k-k). pap. 12.99 *(978-1-84939-004-0(5))* Andersen Pr. GBR. Dist: Independent Pubs. Group.

—The Heron & the Crane. Blake, Quentin, illus. 2011. (ENG.). 32p. (J). (gr. -1-k). pap. 13.99 *(978-1-84939-200-6(5))* Andersen Pr. GBR. Dist: Independent Pubs. Group.

—Mouse Trouble. Blake, Quentin, illus. 2011. (ENG.). 32p. (J). (gr. -1-k). pap. 12.99 *(978-1-84939-201-3(3))* Andersen Pr. GBR. Dist: Independent Pubs. Group.

—Sixes & Sevens. Blake, Quentin, illus. 2012. (ENG.). 32p. (J). (gr. -1-k). pap. 11.99 *(978-1-84939-308-9(7))* Andersen Pr. GBR. Dist: Independent Pubs. Group.

Yeoman, John & Blake, Quentin. The Fabulous Foskett Family Circus. 2014. (ENG., Illus.). 32p. (J). (gr. -1-k). 19.99 *(978-1-84939-564-9(0))* Andersen Pr. GBR. Dist: Independent Pubs. Group.

Yeoman, John & Quentin, Blake. Up with Birds! 2013. (ENG., Illus.). 32p. (J). (gr. k-2). pap. 11.99 *(978-1-84939-651-6(5))* Andersen Pr. GBR. Dist: Independent Pubs. Group.

Yerxa, Leo. Ancient Thunder, 1 vol. 2012. (ENG., Illus.). 40p. (J). (gr. -1-k). 12.99 *(978-1-55498-127-4(1))* Groundwood Bks. CAN. Dist: Publishers Group West (PGW).

Ying, Victoria. Meow! Ying, Victoria, illus. 2017. (ENG., Illus.). 32p. (J). (gr. -1-3). 15.99 *(978-0-06-244096-9(9)*, HarperCollins) HarperCollins Pubs.

Yip, Mingmei. Grandma Panda's China Storybook: Legends, Traditions, & Fun. 2013. (ENG., Illus.). 32p. (J). (gr. -1-3). 15.95 *(978-0-8048-4149-8(7))* Tuttle Publishing.

Yolen, Jane. A Bear Sat on My Porch Today: (Story Books for Kids, Childrens Books with Animals, Friendship Books, Inclusivity Book) Alexander, Rilla, illus. 2018. (ENG.). 32p. (J). (gr. -1-k). 17.99 *(978-1-4521-0249-8(X))* Chronicle Bks. LLC.

—How Do Dinosaurs Learn to Read? Teague, Mark, illus. 2018. (ENG.). 40p. (J). (gr. -1-k). 18.99 *(978-1-338-23301-8(7)*, Blue Sky Pr., The) Scholastic, Inc.

Yolen, Jane & Stemple, Heidi E. A Kite for Moon, 1 vol. Phelan, Matt, illus. 2019. (ENG.). 32p. (J). 17.99 *(978-0-310-75642-2(1))* Zonderkidz.

Young, Cybèle. Nancy Knows. 2017. (Illus.). 32p. (J). (— 1). bds. 8.99 *(978-1-101-91892-0(6)*, Tundra Bks.) Tundra Bks. CAN. Dist: Penguin Random Hse. LLC.

Young, Cybèle & Young, Cybèle. Nancy Knows. 2014. (Illus.). 40p. (J). (gr. -1-2). 17.99 *(978-1-77049-482-4(0)*, Tundra Bks.) Tundra Bks. CAN. Dist: Penguin Random Hse. LLC.

Young, Sarah. Jesus Calling: The Story of Christmas, 1 vol. Longhi, Katya, illus. 2018. (Jesus Calling(r) Ser.). (ENG.). 32p. (J). 17.99 *(978-1-4002-1029-9(1)*, Tommy Nelson) Nelson, Thomas Inc.

—Jesus Calling Little Book of Prayers, 1 vol. Farias, Carolina, illus. 2018. (Jesus Calling(r) Ser.). (ENG.). 26p. (J). bds. 8.99 *(978-0-7180-9753-0(X)*, Tommy Nelson) Nelson, Thomas Inc.

Young, Timothy. If You Give the Puffin a Muffin, 1 vol. 2018. (ENG., Illus.). 32p. (J). 16.99 *(978-0-7643-5552-3(X)*, 9846) Schiffer Publishing, Ltd.

Young, Timothy, illus. Do Not Open the Box, 1 vol. 2016. (ENG.). 32p. (J). 16.99 *(978-0-7643-5043-6(9)*, 6805) Schiffer Publishing, Ltd.

Younger, Mary. You're Not A Ladybird You've Got No Spots. 2011. (Illus.). 24p. 14.09 *(978-1-4567-7082-2(9))* AuthorHouse.

Yoyo Books, creator. Numbers. 2011. (Baby's First Library). (ENG., Illus.). 40p. (gr. -1-k). bds. *(978-94-6033-702-4(3))* YoYo Bks.

Yu, Jennifer. Talking Flower Garden: A Series of Ricky's Secret Friends, vols. 6, vol. 5. Yu, Jennifer, illus. 2018. (Ricky's Secret Friends Picturebook Ser.). (ENG & CHI., Illus.). (gr. 1-6). 49.95 *(978-0-9787591-1-7(7))* Direct World Publishing.

—Texas Animal Ranch: Ricky's Secret Friends Series, vols. 6, vol. 2. Yu, Jennifer, illus. 2018. (Ricky's Secret Friends Picturebook Ser.: 6). (ENG & CHI., Illus.). (gr. 1-4). 49.95 *(978-0-9787591-2-4(5))* Direct World Publishing.

Yuly, Toni. Cat Nap. 2017. (ENG., Illus.). 32p. (J). bds. 9.99 *(978-1-250-11261-3(3)*, 900170501) Feiwel & Friends.

Yun, Yeo-rim. Liang's Treasure: China. Cowley, Joy, ed. Choi, Yang-sook, illus. 2015. (Global Kids Storybooks Ser.). (ENG.). 32p. (gr. 1-4). 26.65 *(978-1-925246-05-6(1))*; 7.99 *(978-1-925246-57-5(4))*; 26.65 *(978-1-925246-31-5(0))* ChoiceMaker Pty. Ltd., The AUS. (Big and SMALL). Dist: Lerner Publishing Group.

Yundt, Katherine. Thankful Tonight. 2018. (ENG., Illus.). 22p. (J). bds. 12.99 *(978-1-4621-2239-4(6))* Cedar Fort, Inc./CFI Distribution.

Zeltser, David. Codzilla. Chapman, Jared, illus. 2019. (ENG.). 40p. (J). (gr. -1-3). 17.99 *(978-0-06-257067-3(6)*, HarperCollins) HarperCollins Pubs.

Zeman, Ludmila, illus. & retold by. Sindbad's Secret: From the Tales of the Thousand & One Nights. Zeman, Ludmila, retold by. 2011. 32p. (J). (gr. 1-4). pap. 9.95 *(978-1-77049-265-3(8)*, Tundra Bks.) Tundra Bks. CAN. Dist: Penguin Random Hse. LLC.

Zeppa, Talaylin. Teddy the Tub. 2011. 32p. pap. 32.70 *(978-1-4568-6908-3(6))* Xlibris Corp.

Zimmerman, Andrea & Clemesha, David. Digger Man. Zimmerman, Andrea, illus. 2016. (Digger Man Ser.: 1). (ENG., Illus.). 32p. (J). bds. 8.99 *(978-1-62779-444-2(1)*, 900150728, Holt, Henry & Co. Bks. For Young Readers) Holt, Henry & Co.

Zion, Gene. Harry the Dirty Dog. Graham, Margaret Bloy, illus. 50th anniv. ed. 2006. (ENG.). 32p. (J). (gr. -1-3). 18.99 *(978-0-06-026865-7(4)*, HarperCollins) HarperCollins Pubs.

Zoehfeld, Kathleen Weidner. What Lives in a Shell? Davie, Helen K., illus. 2015. (Let's-Read-And-Find-Out Science 1 Ser.). (ENG.). 32p. (J). (gr. -1-3). pap. 6.99 *(978-0-06-238196-5(2)*, HarperCollins) HarperCollins Pubs.

Zommer, Yuval. The Big Book of the Blue. 2018. (Big Book Ser.: 0). (ENG., Illus.). 64p. (J). (gr. -1-3). 19.95 *(978-0-500-65119-3(1)*, 565119) Thames & Hudson.

—Big Brown Bear's Cave. Zommer, Yuval, illus. 2018. (ENG., Illus.). 32p. (J). (gr. -1-2). 16.99 *(978-0-7636-9646-7(3)*, Templar) Candlewick Pr.

Zonderkidz. Bedtime Collection: 20 Favorite Bible Stories & Prayers, 1 vol. 2018. (Beginner's Bible Ser.). (ENG., Illus.). 128p. (J). 13.99 *(978-0-310-76328-4(2))* Zonderkidz.

—Let's Meet Jesus, 1 vol. 2018. (Beginner's Bible Ser.). (ENG., Illus.). 16p. (J). bds. 9.99 *(978-0-310-76003-0(8))* Zonderkidz.

Zou, Bridgette. Norman & the Nom Nom Factory. Zou, Bridgette, illus. 2018. (ENG., Illus.). 32p. (J). (gr. -1-3). 18.99 *(978-1-63592-032-1(9)*, 00d60042-dd2f-441d-be65-12b6d9ed49dc, Astra Young Readers) Astra Publishing Hse.

Zucchelli-Romer, Claire. TouchThinkLearn: Wiggles: (Childrens Books Ages 1-3, Interactive Books for Toddlers, Board Books for Toddlers) 2018. (Touch Think Learn Ser.). (ENG., Illus.). 26p. (J). (gr. -1 — 1). bds. 15.99 *(978-1-4521-6475-5(4))* Chronicle Bks. LLC.

Zuckerman, Linda. The Day Is Waiting, 1 vol. Freeman, Don, illus. 2015. (ENG.). 32p. (J). 9.99 *(978-0-310-74054-4(1))* Zonderkidz.

Zuppardi, Sam. Things to Do with Dad. Zuppardi, Sam, illus. 2017. (ENG., Illus.). 32p. (J). (gr. -1-3). 16.99 *(978-0-7636-8146-3(6))* Candlewick Pr.

—Things to Do with Dad. 2017. (Illus.). 32p. (J). pap. *(978-1-4063-7694-4(9))* Candlewick Pr.

Zur Muehlen, Nersel. Monkey in the Mirror. Sanchez, Sara, illus. 2012. 56p. pap. 14.95 *(978-0-9829224-2-2(6))* BPM Research LLC.

23andMe Inc. You Share Genes with Me. Killoran, Ariana, illus. 2016. (ENG.). 18p. (J). (gr. -1-k). bds. 9.99 *(978-0-9891537-0-6(3)*, 1330810) Abrams, Inc.

PICTURE FRAMES AND FRAMING

Beauvais, Den & creator. Alien Parade Pt. 1: Animated Flip Book. Beauvais, Den, creator. 2004. (Illus.). (YA). per. 4.25 *(978-0-9745213-1-2(0))* Dragonfly Entertainment.

PICTURE GALLERIES

see Art Museums

PICTURE POSTERS

see Posters

PICTURE-WRITING

see also Cave Paintings; Hieroglyphics

Award, Anna. Moses in the Bulrushes: See the Picture & Say the Word. 2012. (ENG., Illus.). 24p. (J). pap. 6.50 *(978-1-84135-602-0(6))* Award Pubns. Ltd. GBR. Dist: Parkwest Pubns., Inc.

Cortland, D J. A Week of Weather: Learning to Collect & Record Data on a Pictograph. 2004. (Math Big Bookstm Ser.). (ENG., Illus.). 8p. (gr. k-1). 29.95 *(978-0-8239-7630-0(0))* Rosen Publishing Group, Inc., The.

Paplow, Paula. Hands upon the Rock. 2013. 48p. 19.99 *(978-0-9884268-0-1(3))* Little Cottonwood River Bks.

PICTURES

see also Cartoons and Comics; Portraits

Cocca, Lisa Colozza. Pictographs. 2013. (Explorer Junior Library: Math Explorer Junior Ser.). (ENG.). 24p. (gr. 1-4). pap. 12.79 *(978-1-61080-938-2(6)*, 202633); (Illus.). 32.07 *(978-1-61080-913-9(0)*, 202631) Cherry Lake Publishing.

Furgang, Adam. Searching Online for Image, Audio, & Video Files, 1 vol. 2009. (Digital & Information Literacy Ser.). (ENG., Illus.). 48p. (YA). (gr. 6-6). lib. bdg. 33.47 *(978-1-4358-5318-8(0)*, b4f69062-0f30-48d6-8f79-c901d282a33b) Rosen Publishing Group, Inc., The.

Greene, Joshua M. The Littlest Giant: The Story of Vamana. 2014. (ENG., Illus.). 32p. (gr. -1). 16.99 *(978-1-60887-303-6(X))* Mandala Publishing.

Group/McGraw-Hill, Wright. Picture This! 6 Each of 1 Anthology, 6 vols. (Wildcats Ser.). 32p. (gr. 2-8). *(978-0-322-05627-5(6))* Wright Group/McGraw-Hill.

Harrison, Paul. The Brilliant Book of 3D Thrillers: Get Ready for the Ultimate 3d Adventure! 2012. (ENG., Illus.). 96p. (J). pap. 9.95 *(978-1-84837-875-9(0)*, e0fcc238-c4e3-4bab-94e5-fa676923f79e) Arcturus Publishing GBR. Dist: Baker & Taylor Publisher Services (BTPS).

Naish, Sarah. Ellie Jelly & the Massive Mum Meltdown: A Story about When Parents Lose Their Temper & Want to Put Things Right. Grimshaw, Kath, illus. 2018. (ENG.). 32p. (J). 19.95 *(978-1-78592-516-0(4)*, 696827) Kingsley, Jessica Pubs. GBR. Dist: Hachette UK Distribution.

Paragon Publishing Staff, ed. Words. 2003. (J). per. *(978-1-884907-41-8(5))* Paradise Pr., Inc.

Parragon Staff, ed. Words. Date not set. (Illus.). (J). bds. 5.98 *(978-0-7525-8559-8(2))* Parragon, Inc.

Rabbat, Suzy. Using Digital Images. 2010. (Explorer Library: Information Explorer Ser.). (ENG., Illus.). 32p. (gr. 4-8). lib. bdg. 32.07 *(978-1-60279-954-7(7)*, 200633) Cherry Lake Publishing.

PICTURES, HUMOROUS

see Cartoons and Comics

PIERCE, FRANKLIN, 1804-1869

DiConsiglio, John. Encyclopedia of Presidents: Franklin Pierce. 2004. (Encyclopedia of Presidents Ser.). (ENG., Illus.). 112p. (YA). (gr. 5-9). 34.00 *(978-0-516-24235-4(0))* Scholastic Library Publishing.

King, David C. Franklin Pierce, 1 vol. 2010. (Presidents & Their Times Ser.). (ENG.). 96p. (gr. 6-6). 36.93 *(978-0-7614-3624-9(3)*, 02121b27-1f59-43c2-b172-1ac50cc9c213) Cavendish Square Publishing LLC.

Lazo, Caroline Evensen. Franklin Pierce. 2007. (Presidential Leaders Ser.). (Illus.). 112p. (J). (gr. 3-7). lib. bdg. 29.27 *(978-0-8225-1492-3(3)*, Twenty-First Century Bks.) Lerner Publishing Group.

Rumsch, BreAnn. Franklin Pierce, 1 vol. 2016. (United States Presidents *2017 Ser.). (ENG., Illus.). 40p. (J). (gr. 2-5). 35.64 *(978-1-68078-112-0(X)*, 21841, Big Buddy Bks.) ABDO Publishing Co.

Venezia, Mike. Franklin Pierce: Fourteenth President. Venezia, Mike, illus. 2005. (Getting to Know the U. S. Presidents Ser.). (ENG., Illus.). 32p. (J). (gr. 3-7). lib. bdg. 28.00 *(978-0-516-22619-4(3)*, Children's Pr.) Scholastic Library Publishing.

Zamora, Dulce. How to Draw the Life & Times of Franklin Pierce. (Kid's Guide to Drawing the Presidents of the United States of America Ser.). 32p. (gr. 4-4). 2009. 50.50 *(978-1-61511-137-4(9)*, PowerKids Pr.) 2005. (ENG.). (YA). 30.27 *(978-1-4042-2991-4(4)*, 891fb2eb-8678-46c5-89ea-bbe363fddea6) Rosen Publishing Group, Inc., The.

PIGEONS

Barclay, Marjorie. Flutter: A Very Special Pigeon. 2010. 40p. 24.99 *(978-1-4520-6362-1(1))* AuthorHouse.

Dunn, Joeming & Dunn, Ben. Cher Ami: WWI Homing Pigeon, 1 vol. 2011. (Famous Firsts: Animals Making History Ser.). (ENG., Illus.). 32p. (J). (gr. 3-8). 32.79 *(978-1-61641-639-3(4)*, 7208, Graphic Planet - Fiction) Magic Wagon.

Emminizer, Theresa. Raising Pigeons, 1 vol. 2019. (Unusual Farm Animals Ser.). (ENG.). 24p. (gr. 2-3). pap. 9.25 *(978-1-7253-0906-7(8)*, abd0fadc-15dc-49f4-a93a-5e792287c262, PowerKids Pr.) Rosen Publishing Group, Inc., The.

Fretland VanVoorst, Jenny. Homing Pigeons. 2013. (We Work! Animals with Jobs Ser.). 24p. (J). (gr. -1-3). lib. bdg. 25.65 *(978-1-61772-900-3(0))* Bearport Publishing Co., Inc.

Gagne, Tammy. Care for a Racing Pigeon. 2009. (How to Convince Your Parents You Can ... Ser.). 32p. (J). (gr. 1-4). 25.70 *(978-1-58415-801-1(8))* Mitchell Lane Pubs.

Lajiness, Katie. Homing Pigeons: Navigation All-Stars. 2018. (Awesome Animal Powers Ser.). (ENG., Illus.). 32p. (J). (gr. 2-5). lib. bdg. 34.21 *(978-1-5321-1499-1(0)*, 28852, Big Buddy Bks.) ABDO Publishing Co.

Piehl, Janet. Let's Look at Pigeons. 2015. (Lightning Bolt Books (r) — Animal Close-Ups Ser.). (ENG., Illus.). 32p. (J). (gr. 1-3). E-Book 42.65 *(978-1-5124-1055-6(1)*, 9781512410556, Lerner Pubns.) Lerner Publishing Group.

Roza, Greg. Your Neighbor the Pigeon, 1 vol. 2011. (City Critters Ser.). (ENG., Illus.). 24p. (J). (gr. 2-3). pap. 9.25 *(978-1-4488-5133-1(5)*, 1d4a7d75-6980-48e7-9a5e-2712330cb2c2); lib. bdg. 27.27 *(978-1-61533-384-4(3)*, c6087039-2c17-4b6a-8a2d-002a8b7840c0) Rosen Publishing Group, Inc., The. (Windmill Bks.).

Thomas, Isabel. Pigeon: City Safari, 1 vol. 2014. (City Safari Ser.). (ENG., Illus.). 24p. (J). (gr. k-2). lib. bdg. 25.99 *(978-1-4329-8806-7(9)*, 124774, Heinemann) Capstone.

Willis, Danny. Why Pigeons? a Young Boy Discovers Gods Masterpieces. 2009. 40p. pap. 16.95 *(978-1-60860-314-5(8)*, Strategic Bk. Publishing) Strategic Book Publishing & Rights Agency (SBPRA).

PIGEONS—FICTION

Arthur, Anne. The Pigeon with the Sticky Stuck Neck. Liebman, Simean, illus. 2004. (J). per. 7.99 *(978-0-9753320-0-9(7))* Riverbank Publishing.

Barnes, Kenneth Edward. A Children's Story Collection. 2011. 216p. (gr. 1-2). 24.59 *(978-1-4634-2864-8(2))* AuthorHouse.

Bauman Wispe, Lisa. Fritter's Spring: A Pocono Rabbit's Tale. 2010. pap. 11.95 *(978-0-7414-5796-7(2))* Infinity Publishing.

Bennett, Virginia. The Pigeon Tale. Hardy, E. Stuart, illus. 2007. 48p. per. *(978-1-4065-4810-5(3))* Dodo Pr.

Bliss, Harry. Luke on the Loose. 2014. (Toon Books Level 2 Ser.). lib. bdg. 14.75 *(978-0-606-32101-3(2))* Turtleback.

—Luke on the Loose: Toon Books Level 2. Bliss, Harry, illus. (Toon Ser.). (ENG., Illus.). 32p. (J). (gr. -1-3). 2014. pap. 7.99 *(978-1-935179-36-8(5)*, 9781935179368, Toon Books) 2009. 12.99 *(978-1-935179-00-9(4)*, TOON Books) Astra Publishing Hse.

Brazauski, Vickie. Tweeter the Peachick A True Story, 1 vol. 2010. 26p. 24.95 *(978-1-4489-4257-2(8))* PublishAmerica, Inc.

Davies, Nicola. King of the Sky. Carlin, Laura, illus. 2017. (ENG.). 48p. (J). (gr. -1-3). 18.99 *(978-0-7636-9568-2(8))* Candlewick Pr.

Dolan, Penny. Plip & Plop. Smith, Lisa, illus. 2004. (Read-It! Readers Ser.). (J). lib. bdg. 18.60 *(978-1-4048-0551-4(6)*, Picture Window Bks.) Capstone.

Freeman, Don. Fly High, Fly Low. Freeman, Don, illus. 2007. (Illus.). 56p. (gr. -1-3). 18.00 *(978-0-7569-8001-6(1))* Perfection Learning Corp.

—Fly High, Fly Low (50th Anniversary Ed.) 50th anniv. ed. 2007. (Illus.). 64p. (J). (gr. -1-k). 8.99 *(978-0-14-240817-9(4)*, Puffin Books) Penguin Young Readers Group.

Frossard, Claire, illus. Emma's Journey. Frossard, Etienne, photos by. 2010. (ENG.). 56p. (J). (gr. -1-3). 17.95 *(978-1-59270-099-8(3))* Enchanted Lion Bks., LLC.

Gall, Ginnie. The Great Pigeon Race. Griffin, Don, illus. 2008. 28p. per. 24.95 *(978-1-4241-9457-5(1))* America Star Bks.

Greenham, Caz. The Adventures of Eric Seagull. Homfray, Nick, illus. 2013. 40p. pap. *(978-1-78132-093-8(4))* SilverWood Bks.

Haddow, Swapna. Dave Pigeon (Racer!) World Book Day 2023 Author. Dempsey, Sheena, illus. 2018. (Dave Pigeon Ser.). (ENG.). 160p. (J). pap. 9.95 *(978-0-571-33690-6(6)*, Faber & Faber Children's Bks.) Faber & Faber, Inc.

Hamilton, Kersten. The Ire of Iron Claw: Gadgets & Gears, Book 2. Hamilton, James, illus. 2016. (Gadgets & Gears Ser.: 2). (ENG.). 192p. (J). (gr. 3-7). pap. 6.99 *(978-0-544-66854-6(5)*, 1625480, Clarion Bks.) HarperCollins Pubs.

Healey, Richard (Dick). Holly the Christmas Dove. 2005. 36p. (J). 13.28 *(978-1-4116-5496-9(X))* Lulu Pr., Inc.

Hub, Ulrich. Meet at the Ark at Eight. Mühle, Jörg & Mühle, Jörg, illus. 2012. (ENG.). 68p. (J). 12.00 *(978-0-8028-5410-0(9)*, Eerdmans Bks For Young Readers) Eerdmans, William B. Publishing Co.

Hughes, Cheryl. Jackson, the Pigeon Who Was Afraid of Heights. 2008. 44p. pap. 16.99 *(978-1-4389-2143-3(8))* AuthorHouse.

Jerry, Spinelli. Wringer. 2014. (ENG.). 256p. (J). (gr. 8-12). 13.24 *(978-1-63245-323-5(1))* Lectorum Pubns., Inc.

Kassel, Roger de. Mr P & the Silver Red Bag. 2013. (ENG., Illus.). 12p. pap. 7.00 *(978-1-78035-536-8(X)*, Fastprint Publishing) Upfront Publishing Ltd. GBR. Dist: Printondemand-worldwide.com.

—Mr P & the Sticky Gum. 2013. (ENG., Illus.). 12p. pap. 7.00 *(978-1-78035-537-5(8)*, Fastprint Publishing) Upfront Publishing Ltd. GBR. Dist: Printondemand-worldwide.com.

Kay, L. M. Frederick's Birthday Surprise. 2009. 36p. pap. 24.95 *(978-1-60836-944-7(7))* America Star Bks.

Lloyd, Elizabeth. Piggyon. 2009. (Illus.). 36p. pap. 16.99 *(978-1-4490-2654-7(0))* AuthorHouse.

Macaulay, David. Angelo. 2006. (ENG., Illus.). 48p. (J). (gr. -1-3). reprint ed. pap. 6.95 *(978-0-618-69336-8(X)*, 490582, Clarion Bks.) HarperCollins Pubs.

McDonald, Jody. Who Is in the Egg? 2010. 28p. pap. 28.03 *(978-1-4500-8840-4(6))* Xlibris Corp.

Mellon, Gray. The Weird Worlds of Willoughby Wren Wren & the Pigeons. 2010. 196p. pap. *(978-1-907652-06-6(X))* Grosvenor Hse. Publishing Ltd.

Molloy, Mary. The Search for Monty. 2005. (ENG.). 100p. (J). pap. 9.60 *(978-1-4116-4505-9(7))* Lulu Pr., Inc.

Murray, Diana. City Shapes. Collier, Bryan, illus. 2016. (ENG.). 40p. (J). (gr. -1-3). 18.99 *(978-0-316-37092-9(4))* Little, Brown Bks. for Young Readers.

Naylor, Phyllis Reynolds. Cuckoo Feathers, 0 vols. Ramsey, Marcy, illus. 2012. (Simply Sarah Ser.: 2). (ENG.). 96p. (J). (gr. 1-4). pap. 7.99 *(978-0-7614-5541-7(8)*, 9780761455417, Two Lions) Amazon Publishing.

Novel Units. Wringer Novel Units Teacher Guide. 2019. (ENG.). (J). pap., tchr. ed. 12.99 *(978-1-58130-676-7(8)*, Novel Units, Inc.) Classroom Library Co.

O'Connor, Barbara. On the Road to Mr. Mineo's. 2014. (ENG., Illus.). 208p. (J). (gr. 3-7). pap. 10.99 *(978-1-250-03993-4(2)*, 900123696) Square Fish.

Power, Barry. The First Ice Pigeon of London. 2009. 80p. pap. 10.49 *(978-1-4490-3070-4(X))* AuthorHouse.

Redmond, Shirley Raye. Pigeon Hero! Ettlinger, Doris, illus. 2005. (Ready-to-Read Ser.). 31p. (gr. k-2). 14.00 *(978-0-7569-5560-1(2))* Perfection Learning Corp.

—Pigeon Hero! Ettlinger, Doris, illus. 2003. (Ready-To-Reads Ser.). (ENG.). 32p. (J). lib. bdg. 11.89 *(978-0-689-85487-3(0)*, Aladdin Library) Simon & Schuster Children's Publishing.

—Pigeon Hero! Ready-To-Read Level 2. Ettlinger, Doris, illus. 2003. (Ready-To-Read Ser.). (ENG.). 32p. (J). (gr. k-2). pap. 4.99 *(978-0-689-85486-6(2)*, Simon Spotlight) Simon Spotlight.

Richmond, Lori. Pax & Blue. Richmond, Lori, illus. 2017. (ENG., Illus.). 32p. (J). (gr. -1-3). 17.99 *(978-1-4814-5132-1(4)*, Simon & Schuster/Paula Wiseman Bks.) Simon & Schuster/Paula Wiseman Bks.

Rudge, Leila. Gary. Rudge, Leila, illus. 2016. (ENG., Illus.). 32p. (J). (gr. -1-2). 16.99 *(978-0-7636-8954-4(8))* Candlewick Pr.

Sargent, Dave & Sargent, David M., Jr. Pammie Pigeon: Keep Your Cool, 19 vols., Vol. 12. Lenoir, Jane, illus. 2003. (Feather Tales Ser.: 12). 42p. (J). pap. 10.95 *(978-1-56763-742-7(6))*; 2nd ed. lib. bdg. 20.95 *(978-1-56763-741-0(8))* Ozark Publishing.

—Penny Penguin: Be Kind to Others, 20 vols., Vol. 13. Lenoir, Jane, illus. 2nd ed. 2003. (Feather Tales Ser.: 13). 42p. (J). lib. bdg. 20.95 *(978-1-56763-743-4(4))* Ozark Publishing.

Shalev, Michal. How to Be Famous. Shalev, Michal, illus. 2016. (ENG., Illus.). 32p. (J). (gr. -1-1). E-Book 26.65 *(978-1-77657-057-7(X)*, 9781776570577); E-Book 9.99 *(978-1-77657-045-4(6)*, 9781776570454); E-Book 26.65 *(978-1-77657-047-8(2))* Gecko Pr. NZL. Dist: Lerner Publishing Group.

Slater, Dashka. The Antlered Ship. Fan, Terry & Fan, Eric, illus. 2017. (ENG.). 48p. (J). (gr. -1-3). 17.99 *(978-1-4814-5160-4(X)*, Beach Lane Bks.) Beach Lane Bks.

Spinelli, Jerry. Wringer: A Newbery Honor Award Winner. 2018. (ENG.). 256p. (J). (gr. 3-7). pap. 9.99 *(978-0-06-440578-2(8)*, HarperCollins) HarperCollins Pubs.

Stolz, Mary. Pigeon Flight. Tinkelman, Murray, illus. 2012. 62p. 36.95 *(978-1-258-25234-2(1))*; pap. 21.95 *(978-1-258-25387-5(9))* Literary Licensing, LLC.

Sudbury, Dave. King of Rome. Saefkow, Hans, illus. 2008. (ENG.). 32p. (J). (gr. -1-3). 17.95 *(978-1-894965-94-1(9))* Simply Read Bks. CAN. Dist: Ingram Publisher Services.

Thompson, Kimberly. Toulouse Tangled up in Lights. Easey, Chris, illus. 2011. 64p. (J). 19.95 *(978-0-9818976-1-5(4))* Little Pigeon Bks.

Van Dixhorn, Brenda. The Pigeon Books: An Instructional Guide for Literature. rev. ed. 2015. (Great Works). (ENG., Illus.). 72p. (gr. k-3). pap. 9.99 *(978-1-4807-6992-2(4))* Shell Educational Publishing.

Watson, J. A. Pigeon Problems: An Urban Bird Researcher's Journal. 2018. (Science Squad Ser.). (ENG., Illus.). 192p. (J). (gr. 3-4). lib. bdg. 28.50 *(978-1-63163-187-0(X)*, 163163187X, Jolly Fish Pr.) North Star Editions.

—Pigeon Problems: An Urban Bird Researcher's Journal. Olbey, Arpad, illus. 2018. (Science Squad Ser.). (ENG.). 192p. (J). (gr. 3-4). pap. 9.99 *(978-1-63163-188-7(8)*, 1631631888, Jolly Fish Pr.) North Star Editions.

Weathers, Marion. Henry Baldpate & His Treetop Friends. 2008. 24p. pap. 24.95 *(978-1-60672-923-6(3))* America Star Bks.

Webster, Andrea K. Pigeon in the Park. 2012. 28p. pap. 19.99 *(978-1-4772-2530-1(7))* AuthorHouse.

Weston Woods Staff, creator. The Pigeon Finds a Hot Dog. 2011. 38.75 *(978-0-545-26298-9(4))* Weston Woods Studios, Inc.

Willems, Mo. Don't Let the Pigeon Finish This Activity Book!-Pigeon Series. 2012. (Pigeon Ser.: 8). (ENG., Illus.). 272p. (J). (gr. -1 — 1). pap. 19.99 *(978-1-4231-3310-0(2)*, Hyperion Books for Children) Disney Publishing Worldwide.

—Don't Let the Pigeon Stay up Late! 2006. (Pigeon Ser.). (ENG., Illus.). 40p. (J). (gr. -1-k). 17.99 *(978-0-7868-3746-5(2)*, Hyperion Books for Children) Disney Publishing Worldwide.

—Don't Let the Pigeon Stay Up Late! 2011. (J). (gr. -1-2). 29.95 *(978-0-545-32735-0(0))*; pap. 18.95 incl. audio compact disk *(978-0-545-32791-6(1))*;Set. pap. 38.75 incl. audio compact disk *(978-0-545-32792-3(X))* Weston Woods Studios, Inc.

—The Duckling Gets a Cookie!? (Pigeon Series) Willems, Mo, illus. 2012. (ENG., Illus.). 40p. (J). (gr. -1-k). 17.99 *(978-1-4231-5128-9(3)*, Hyperion Books for Children) Disney Publishing Worldwide.

—¡la Paloma Encuentra un Perro Caliente! 2011. (ENG., Illus.). 40p. (J). (gr. -1-k). pap. 9.99 *(978-1-4231-4051-1(6)*, Hyperion Books for Children) Disney Publishing Worldwide.

—¡No Dejes Que la Paloma Conduzca el Autobus! 2011.Tr. of Don't Let the Pigeon Drive the Bus. (ENG., Illus.). 40p. (J). (gr. -1-k). pap. 7.99 *(978-1-4231-4052-8(4)*, Hyperion Books for Children) Disney Publishing Worldwide.

—The Pigeon Finds a Hot Dog! 2004. (Pigeon Ser.). (ENG., Illus.). 40p. (J). (gr. -1-k). 17.99 *(978-0-7868-1869-3(7)*, Hyperion Books for Children) Disney Publishing Worldwide.

—The Pigeon Has Feelings, Too! 2005. (Pigeon Ser.). (ENG., Illus.). 12p. (J). (gr. -1-k). bds. 6.99 *(978-0-7868-3650-5(4)*, Hyperion Books for Children) Disney Publishing Worldwide.

—The Pigeon HAS to Go to School! 2019. (Pigeon Ser.). (ENG.). 40p. (J). (gr. -1-k). 17.99 *(978-1-368-04645-9(2)*, Hyperion Books for Children) Disney Publishing Worldwide.

—The Pigeon Loves Things That Go! 2005. (Pigeon Ser.). (ENG., Illus.). 12p. (J). (gr. -1-k). bds. 6.99 *(978-0-7868-3651-2(2)*, Hyperion Books for Children) Disney Publishing Worldwide.

—Pigeon Needs a Bath!, the-Pigeon Series. 2014. (Pigeon Ser.: 9). (ENG., Illus.). 40p. (J). (gr. -1-k). 17.99 *(978-1-4231-9087-5(4)*, Hyperion Books for Children) Disney Publishing Worldwide.

—The Pigeon Wants a Puppy! 2008. (Pigeon Ser.). (ENG., Illus.). 40p. (J). (gr. -1-k). 17.99 *(978-1-4231-0960-0(0)*, Hyperion Books for Children) Disney Publishing Worldwide.

—The Pigeon Will Ride the Roller Coaster! 2022. (ENG., Illus.). 40p. (J). (gr. -1-k). 17.99 *(978-1-4549-4686-1(5)*, Union Square Pr.) Sterling Publishing Co., Inc.

Willems, Mo, illus. The Pigeon Will Ride the Roller Coaster! 2022. (J). **(978-1-4549-4816-2(7))** Sterling Publishing Co., Inc.

Willems, Mo & Scieszka, Jon, narrated by. Don't Let the Pigeon Drive the Bus! 2011. (J). (gr. -1-1). 29.95 *(978-0-545-13453-8(6))* Weston Woods Studios, Inc.

Willems, Mo & Willems, Trixie, narrated by. The Pigeon Finds a Hot Dog! 2011. (J). (gr. -1-1). 29.95 *(978-0-545-23795-6(5))*; 18.95 *(978-0-545-26297-2(6))* Weston Woods Studios, Inc.

Wyeth, Sharon Dennis. Message in the Sky Bk. 3: Corey's Underground Railroad Diary. 2003. (My America Ser.). (ENG.). 112p. (J). 10.95 *(978-0-439-37057-8(4)*, Scholastic Pr.) Scholastic, Inc.

Yang, Belle. Always Come Home to Me. Yang, Belle, illus. 2007. (ENG., Illus.). 32p. (J). (gr. -1-3). 16.99 *(978-0-7636-2899-4(9))* Candlewick Pr.

Yang, Belle & Williams, Marcia. Archie's War: My Scrapbook of the First World War. Williams, Marcia, illus. 2007. (ENG., Illus.). 48p. (J). (gr. 3-7). 18.99 *(978-0-7636-3532-9(4))* Candlewick Pr.

Yardley, Liz. The Firefly Legacy - Book Vii. Yardley, Liz, illus. 2013. (Illus.). 314p. pap. *(978-0-9872013-2-4(8))* BlueFlower Bks.

PIGGLE-WIGGLE, MRS. (FICTITIOUS CHARACTER)—FICTION

MacDonald, Betty. Hello, Mrs. Piggle-Wiggle. Boiger, Alexandra, illus. 2007. (ENG.). 176p. (J). (gr. 3-7). pap. 7.99 *(978-0-06-440149-4(9)*, HarperCollins) HarperCollins Pubs.

—Hello, Mrs. Piggle Wiggle. Boiger, Alexandra, illus. 2007. (ENG.). 176p. (J). (gr. 3-7). 16.99 *(978-0-397-31715-8(8)*, HarperCollins) HarperCollins Pubs.

—Mrs. Piggle-Wiggle. Boiger, Alexandra, illus. rev. ed. 2007. (ENG.). 144p. (J). (gr. 3-7). 16.99 *(978-0-397-31712-7(3))*; pap. 8.99 *(978-0-06-440148-7(0))* HarperCollins Pubs. (HarperCollins).

—Mrs. Piggle-Wiggle's Magic. Boiger, Alexandra, illus. 2007. (ENG.). 192p. (J). (gr. 3-7). pap. 6.99 *(978-0-06-440151-7(0)*, HarperCollins) HarperCollins Pubs.

MacDonald, Betty & Canham, Anne MacDonald. Happy Birthday, Mrs. Piggle-Wiggle. Boiger, Alexandra, illus. 2008. (ENG.). 208p. (J). (gr. 3-7). pap. 7.99 *(978-0-06-072814-4(0)*, HarperCollins) HarperCollins Pubs.

MacDonald, Betty Bard. Happy Birthday, Mrs. Piggle-Wiggle. Boiger, Alexandra, illus. 2007. (Mrs. Piggle-Wiggle Ser.). 193p. (J). (gr. 3-7). lib. bdg. 16.89 *(978-0-06-072813-7(2))* HarperCollins Pubs.

—Hello, Mrs Piggle Wiggle. unabr. ed. 2004. 125p. (J). (gr. 2-5). pap. 29.00 incl. audio *(978-0-8072-1184-7(2)*, S YA 1018 SP, Listening Library) Random Hse. Audio Publishing Group.

—Mrs. Piggle-Wiggle's Magic. 2004. (Illus.). 144p. (J). (gr. 2-5). pap. 29.00 incl. audio *(978-1-4000-9001-3(6)*, Listening Library) Random Hse. Audio Publishing Group.

PIGLET (FICTITIOUS CHARACTER)—FICTION

Champier, Jacqueline. The Little Piggy Goes South. 2012. 28p. pap. 19.99 *(978-1-4772-8976-1(3))* AuthorHouse.

Chronicle Books. Baby Piglet: Finger Puppet Book (Pig Puppet Book, Piggy Book for Babies, Tiny Finger Puppet Books) Huang, Yu-Hsuan, illus. 2019. (Baby Animal Finger Puppets Ser.: 15). (ENG.). 12p. (J). (gr. -1 — 1). 7.99 *(978-1-4521-7078-7(9))* Chronicle Bks. LLC.

Johnson, Carole. Pennie the Piglet. 2007. 60p. per. 16.95 *(978-1-4241-7019-7(2))* America Star Bks.

Milne, A. A. Winnie the Pooh: Piglet Meets Heffalump. Shepard, E. H., illus. 2016. (ENG.). 48p. (J). 9.99 *(978-1-4052-8134-8(0))* Farshore GBR. Dist: HarperCollins Pubs.

Studio Mouse Staff. Pooh & Piglet. 2008. (ENG., Illus.). 36p. (J). (gr. -1). 7.99 *(978-1-59069-419-0(8))* Studio Mouse LLC.

Taylor, W. Y. This Little Piggy Goes Green. 2009. (ENG.). 12p. bds. 3.95 *(978-1-58117-925-5(1)*, Intervisual/Piggy Toes) Bendon, Inc.

Winnie the Pooh. The Close-up Day. 2010. 16p. 5.99 *(978-1-4231-3096-3(0))* Disney Pr.

PIGMENTATION

see Animals—Color; Human Skin Color

PIGS

Adele, Gloria. My Wild Backyard: Wild Hogs. 2012. 32p. pap. 21.99 *(978-1-4771-4129-8(4))* Xlibris Corp.

Albright, Rosie. Pig Detectives, 1 vol. 2012. (Animal Detectives Ser.). (ENG.). 24p. (J). (gr. 1-1). pap. 9.25 *(978-1-4488-6262-7(0)*, 28aabfda-9b11-4108-b69e-be75a618072f); (Illus.). 26.27 *(978-1-4488-6151-4(9)*, 5b125778-ba3e-481e-9587-026655b93b0c) Rosen Publishing Group, Inc., The. (PowerKids Pr.).

Alexander, Carol. The Big Squeal: A True Story about a Homeless Pig's Search for Life, Liberty & the Pursuit of Happiness. 2013. (ENG., Illus.). 32p. (J). pap. 16.00 *(978-1-61009-112-1(4)*, Acorn) Oak Tree Publishing.

—The Big Squeal: A True Story about a Homeless Pig's Search for Life, Liberty & the Pursuit of Happiness. Kalpart Designs, illus. 2012. (ENG.). 24p. (J). 24.00 *(978-1-61009-036-0(5)*, Acorn) Oak Tree Publishing.

Arnold, Quinn M. Pigs. 2017. (Seedlings Ser.). (ENG., Illus.). 24p. (J). (gr. -1-k). *(978-1-60818-787-4(X)*, 20137, Creative Education) Creative Co., The.

—Seedlings: Pigs. 2017. (Seedlings Ser.). (ENG., Illus.). 24p. (J). (gr. -1-1). pap. 10.99 *(978-1-62832-395-5(7)*, 20135, Creative Paperbacks) Creative Co., The.

Aspen-Baxter, Linda & Kissock, Heather. Cerdos. 2012. (SPA.). (J). *(978-1-61913-190-3(0))* Weigl Pubs., Inc.

Austin, Richard, photos by. Pocket Piggies Colors! Featuring the Teacup Pigs of Pennywell Farm. 2014. (ENG., Illus.). 22p. (J). (gr. -1 — 1). bds. 5.95 *(978-0-7611-7980-1(1)*, 17980) Workman Publishing Co., Inc.

Beck, Angela. Guinea Pigs: Keeping & Caring for Your Pet, 1 vol. 2013. (Keeping & Caring for Your Pet Ser.). (ENG.). 72p. (gr. 6-7). pap. 11.53 *(978-1-4644-0299-9(X)*, 1db5c74a-e033-4982-b366-9b4cf3da1cb8) Enslow Publishing, LLC.

Beck, Isabel L., et al. Trophies Kindergarten: My Pig. 2003. (Trophies Ser.). (gr. k-6). 13.80 *(978-0-15-329535-5(X))* Harcourt Schl. Pubs.

Blake, Kevin. Feral Pigs: Chomp, Chomp! 2015. (They Don't Belong: Tracking Invasive Species Ser.). (ENG., Illus.). 32p. (J). (gr. 2-7). lib. bdg. 28.50 *(978-1-62724-829-7(3))* Bearport Publishing Co., Inc.

Boothroyd, Jennifer. Meet a Baby Pig. 2016. (Lightning Bolt Books (r) — Baby Farm Animals Ser.). (ENG., Illus.). 32p. (J). (gr. 1-3). 29.32 *(978-1-5124-0799-0(2)*, 91e19929-380e-43e6-9441-5bdaf30b49bf, Lerner Pubns.) Lerner Publishing Group.

Borgert-Spaniol, Megan. Warthogs. 2012. (Animal Safari Ser.). (ENG., Illus.). 24p. (J). (gr. k-3). lib. bdg. 26.95 *(978-1-60014-770-8(4)*, Blastoff! Readers) Bellwether Media.

Braidich, S. Little Pigs, Big Pigs: Learning the Short I Sound. 2009. (PowerPhonics Ser.). 24p. (gr. 1-1). 39.90 *(978-1-60851-456-4(0)*, PowerKids Pr.) Rosen Publishing Group, Inc., The.

Carr, Aaron. Potbellied Pig. 2014. (Illus.). 24p. (J). *(978-1-62127-296-0(6))* Weigl Pubs., Inc.

Carraway, Rose. Pigs on the Farm, 1 vol. 2012. (Farm Animals Ser.). (Illus.). 24p. (gr. k-k). (ENG.). (J). 25.27 *(978-1-4339-7360-4(X)*, 7136315f-d7eb-45e0-8c99-22948c85be7c); (ENG., (J). pap. 9.15 *(978-1-4339-7361-1(8)*, a19d9ea9-7bd1-4405-b5ff-69ab09650b20); 69.20 *(978-1-4339-8056-5(8))* Stevens, Gareth Publishing LLLP.

—Pigs on the Farm / Cerdos de Granja, 1 vol. 2012. (Farm Animals / Animales de Granja Ser.). (SPA & ENG., Illus.). 24p. (J). (gr. k-k). lib. bdg. 25.27 *(978-1-4339-7402-1(9)*, b638697d-049a-48db-bbfd-f1c29d1bdb2a) Stevens, Gareth Publishing LLLP.

Chester, John. Saving Emma the Pig. Meyer, Jennifer L., illus. 2019. (Biggest Little Farm Ser.). (ENG.). 40p. (J). 20.99 *(978-1-250-18779-6(6)*, 900191877) Feiwel & Friends.

Conner, Mac. Ambrose. 2011. 24p. pap. *(978-1-4269-6578-4(8))* Trafford Publishing (UK) Ltd.

Dicker, Katie. Pigs. 2014. (Farm Animals Ser.). (Illus.). 24p. (gr. 2-5). 28.50 *(978-1-62588-023-9(5))* Black Rabbit Bks.

Dieker, Wendy. Pigs. 2012. (Illus.). 24p. (J). lib. bdg. 25.65 *(978-1-62031-005-2(8))* Jump! Inc.

Doubleday Entertainment USA - Pigs: Down on the Farm. 2006. (J). per. 6.95 *(978-1-59566-228-6(6))* QEB Publishing Inc.

Early Macken, JoAnn. Pigs, 1 vol. 2nd rev. ed. 2009. (Animals That Live on the Farm (Second Edition) Ser.). (ENG.). 24p. (J). (gr. 1-1). pap. 9.15 *(978-1-4339-2468-2(4)*, d588f8ab-12dc-4d17-b221-8d2c28e996dc); lib. bdg. 25.27 *(978-1-4339-2399-9(8)*, 52936b91-0503-4614-aacc-5cfd9bdfe742) Stevens, Gareth Publishing LLLP. (Weekly Reader Leveled Readers).

—Pigs / Los Cerdos, 1 vol. (Animals That Live on the Farm / Animales Que Viven en la Granja (First Edition) Ser.). 24p. (gr. 1-1). 2004. (SPA & ENG., Illus.). pap. 9.15 *(978-0-8368-4296-8(0)*, 43a0d930-aec4-4353-b2c8-0137ea42750a, Weekly Reader Leveled Readers) 2004. (SPA & ENG., Illus.). lib. bdg. 23.67 *(978-0-8368-4289-0(8)*, e8838688-a9b4-4e86-944c-200f23298997) 2nd rev. ed. 2009. (ENG & SPA.). (J). pap. 9.15 *(978-1-4339-2475-0(7)*, 1bd4a59d-5a7c-44d9-ae76-f12ac172a1bb, Weekly Reader Leveled Readers) 2nd rev. ed. 2009. (ENG & SPA.). (J). lib. bdg. 25.27 *(978-1-4339-2431-6(5)*, 4cca6b43-628b-499a-8e00-b83e8e7a0e93) Stevens, Gareth Publishing LLLP.

Elora, Grace. Piglets. 2011. (Cute & Cuddly: Baby Animals Ser.). (Illus.). 24p. (J). (gr. k-2). 69.20 *(978-1-4339-6152-6(0))*; (ENG., (J). lib. bdg. 25.27 *(978-1-4339-4515-1(0)*, 1c0fbeda-02ad-498b-a86d-139a46f6f0bd) Stevens, Gareth Publishing LLLP.

Fretland VanVoorst, Jenny. Pig Detectives. 2013. (We Work! Animals with Jobs Ser.). 24p. (J). (gr. -1-3). lib. bdg. 25.65 *(978-1-61772-899-0(3))* Bearport Publishing Co., Inc.

Gaertner, Meg. Piglets. 2019. (Animal Babies Ser.). (ENG., Illus.). 16p. (J). (gr. k-1). 25.64 *(978-1-64185-749-9(8)*, 1641857498, Focus Readers) North Star Editions.

Gibbs, Maddie. Pigs, 1 vol. 2014. (Farmyard Friends Ser.). (ENG., Illus.). 24p. (J). (gr. 1-2). lib. bdg. 25.27 *(978-1-4994-0168-4(X)*, 4e825543-4eb6-4820-aa7c-1fa30d99c292, PowerKids Pr.) Rosen Publishing Group, Inc., The.

Glaser, Rebecca. Pigs Oink. 2016. (Illus.). 14p. (J). (gr. -1 — 1). bds. 7.99 *(978-1-68152-128-2(8)*, 15820) Amicus.

Gorski-Sterner, Gail. The Adventures of Isabelle the Lost Pot Belly Pig: Based on a True Story. 2011. 36p. (gr. -1). pap. 19.99 *(978-1-4520-9040-5(8))* AuthorHouse.

Green, Emily K. Pigs. 2007. (Farm Animals Ser.). (ENG., Illus.). 24p. (J). (gr. k-3). lib. bdg. 26.95 *(978-1-60014-068-6(8))* Bellwether Media.

Hansen, Grace. Warthog. 2017. (African Animals (Abdo Kids Jumbo) Ser.). (ENG., Illus.). 24p. (J). (gr. -1-2). lib. bdg. 32.79 *(978-1-5321-0422-0(7)*, 26548, Abdo Kids) ABDO Publishing Co.

Harasymiw, R. P. Problem Solving with Pigs, 1 vol. 2013. (Animal Math Ser.). (ENG.). 24p. (J). (gr. 1-2). pap. 9.15 *(978-1-4339-9324-4(4)*, 5d0db16d-001a-4fe5-a268-8051cf8d7637); (Illus.). lib. bdg. 25.27 *(978-1-4339-9323-7(6)*, c3c3704c-7c10-4e54-99b1-070f7fc39daf) Stevens, Gareth Publishing LLLP.

Harasymiw, Raymond. Problem Solving with Pigs. 2013. (Animal Math Ser.). 24p. (J). (gr. 1-3). pap. 48.90 *(978-1-4339-9325-1(2))* Stevens, Gareth Publishing LLLP.

Hendrix, Emilia. Pigs & Piglets, 1 vol. 2015. (Animal Family Ser.). (ENG., Illus.). 24p. (J). (gr. k-k). pap. 9.15 *(978-1-4824-3783-6(X)*, 48594dc2-f1c5-4870-8572-66da75162d73) Stevens, Gareth Publishing LLLP.

Howard, Nancy S. Mischief in Tuscany. Running Wild in a Famous Italian Painting. Ediz. Illustrata. 2008. (ENG., Illus.). 48p. 17.95 *(978-88-7461-094-5(7))* Mandragora ITA. Dist: National Bk. Network.

Hudak, Heather C. Pigs. 2006. (Farm Animals Ser.). (Illus.). 24p. (J). (gr. 3-7). lib. bdg. 24.45 *(978-1-59036-425-3(2))*; per. 8.95 *(978-1-59036-432-1(5))* Weigl Pubs., Inc.

Jeffrey, Gary. Terminator Pig. 2017. (Graphic Prehistoric Animals Ser.). (ENG., Illus.). 32p. (J). (gr. 5-8). 31.35 *(978-1-62588-412-1(5)*, 19281, Smart Apple Media) Black Rabbit Bks.

Kalman, Bobbie. Baby Pigs. 2010. (ENG., Illus.). 24p. (J). *(978-0-7787-3962-3(7))*; pap. *(978-0-7787-3981-4(3))* Crabtree Publishing Co.

Kalman, Bobbie, contrib. by. Les Bébés Cochons. 2013. (FRE.). 24p. (J). pap. 9.95 *(978-2-89579-482-0(0))* Bayard Canada Livres CAN. Dist: Crabtree Publishing Co.

King-Smith, Dick. All Pigs Are Beautiful with Audio: Read, Listen, & Wonder. Jeram, Anita, illus. 2008. (Read, Listen, & Wonder Ser.). (ENG.). 32p. (J). (gr. -1-3). pap. 8.99 *(978-0-7636-3866-5(8))* Candlewick Pr.

Kishel, Ann-Marie. Pigs & Piglets. 2006. (First Step Nonfiction — Animal Families Ser.). (ENG., Illus.). 8p. (J). (gr. k-2). pap. 5.99 *(978-0-8225-5651-0(0)*, 6f57410a-c284-4c9a-9a81-c631f07abd59) Lerner Publishing Group.

Kissock, Heather & Aspen-Baxter, Linda. Pigs. 2011. (J). 27.13 *(978-1-61690-928-4(5))* Weigl Pubs., Inc.

Leaf, Christina. Baby Pigs. 2014. (Super Cute! Ser.). (ENG., Illus.). 24p. (J). (gr. k-3). lib. bdg. 26.95 *(978-1-60014-975-7(8)*, Blastoff! Readers) Bellwether Media.

Leighton, Christina. Pigs. 2018. (Animals on the Farm Ser.). (ENG., Illus.). 24p. (J). (gr. k-3). lib. bdg. 26.95 (978-1-62617-725-3(2), Blastoff! Readers) Bellwether Media.

Ling, Mary & Dorling Kindersley Publishing Staff. See How They Grow - Pig. Senior, Helen, illus. Ling, Bill, photos by. 2007. (See How They Grow Ser.). (ENG.). 96p. (J). (gr. k-3). 16.19 (978-0-7566-3018-8(5)) Dorling Kindersley Publishing, Inc.

Lunis, Natalie. Potbellied Pigs. 2009. (Peculiar Pets Ser.). (Illus.). 24p. (YA). (gr. 2-5). lib. bdg. 26.99 (978-1-59716-862-5(9)) Bearport Publishing Co., Inc.

MacLean, Kerry Lee. Peaceful Piggy Yoga. MacLean, Kerry Lee, illus. 2014. (ENG., Illus.). 32p. (J). (gr. -1-3). 7.99 (978-0-8075-6383-0(8), 807563838) Whitman, Albert & Co.

Martin, Emmett. Pigs from Head to Tail, 1 vol. 2020. (Animals from Head to Tail Ser.). (ENG.). 24p. (gr. k-2). pap. 9.15 (978-1-5382-5538-4(3), 4617d794-aaaf-4687-b699-f3ac2aa9523f) Stevens, Gareth Publishing LLLP.

McNeil, Niki, et al. HOCPP 1125 Pigs. 2006. spiral bd. 16.00 (978-1-60308-125-2(9)) In the Hands of a Child.

Meachen Rau, Dana. Adivina Quién Gruñe / Guess Who Grunts, 1 vol. 2009. (Adivina Quién / Guess Who? Ser.). (ENG & SPA.). 32p. (gr. k-2). 25.50 (978-0-7614-3481-8(X), 8f14b7df-3640-41e3-9d20-a5ee80ad182c) Cavendish Square Publishing LLC.

—Adivina Quién Gruñe (Guess Who Grunts), 1 vol. 2010. (Adivina Quién (Guess Who?) Ser.). (SPA.). 32p. (gr. k-2). lib. bdg. 25.50 (978-0-7614-3455-9(0), 8311737c-76de-4199-83a6-0e81482e749f) Cavendish Square Publishing LLC.

—Guess Who Grunts, 1 vol. 2009. (Guess Who? Ser.). (ENG.). 32p. (gr. k-1). pap. 9.23 (978-0-7614-3561-7(1), e2bd0185-3f08-4d40-a0ac-3d0e3da4bebe); lib. bdg. 25.50 (978-0-7614-2906-7(9), 0a8f4823-c6cb-4a5a-ae51-895f67248d94) Cavendish Square Publishing LLC.

Mercer, Abbie. Pigs on a Farm, 1 vol. 2009. (Barnyard Animals Ser.). (ENG.). 24p. (J). (gr. 1-1). pap. 9.25 (978-1-4042-8067-0(7), ec77cb2d-9ef2-4f80-8f03-6140feb7f516); (Illus.). lib. bdg. 26.27 (978-1-4042-8053-3(7), 0553ab6a-f416-486e-b734-8397c3dc418e) Rosen Publishing Group, Inc., The. (PowerKids Pr.).

Miller, Dave. Dogs, Frogs, & Hogs. 2006. (ENG., Illus.). (J). 3.00 (978-0-932859-88-4(7)) Apologetics Pr., Inc.

Minden, Cecilia. Farm Animals: Pigs. 2009. (21st Century Junior Library: Farm Animals Ser.). (ENG., Illus.). 24p. (gr. 2-4). lib. bdg. 29.21 (978-1-60279-542-6(8), 200275) Cherry Lake Publishing.

—Pig. 2018. (Learn about Animals Ser.). (ENG., Illus.). 16p. (J). (gr. -1-2). pap. 11.36 (978-1-5341-2394-6(6), 210571) Cherry Lake Publishing.

Murray, Julie. Piglets. 2018. (Baby Animals (Abdo Kids Junior) Ser.). (ENG., Illus.). 24p. (J). (gr. -1-2). lib. bdg. 31.36 (978-1-5321-8167-2(1), 29891, Abdo Kids) ABDO Publishing Co.

—Pigs, 1 vol. 2015. (Farm Animals (Abdo Kids Junior) Ser.). (ENG., Illus.). 24p. (J). (gr. -1-2). 31.36 (978-1-62970-942-0(5), 18262, Abdo Kids) ABDO Publishing Co.

National Geographic Kids & Beer, Julie. Piglets vs. Pugs. 2018. (ENG., Illus.). 64p. (J). (gr. 1-4). 17.99 (978-1-4263-3176-3(2)) National Geographic Society.

Nelson, Robin. Pigs. 2009. (First Step Nonfiction - Farm Animals Ser.). (ENG., Illus.). 24p. (gr. k-2). 23.93 (978-0-7613-4059-1(9), Lerner Pubns.) Lerner Publishing Group.

Nye, Kimara. The Four Little Pigs. Bruchnalski, Marcin, illus. 2019. (Early Bird Readers — Purple (Early Bird Stories (tm)) Ser.). (ENG.). 32p. (J). (gr. k-3). 30.65 (978-1-5415-4227-3(4), 60cefd4f-6003-46ef-a1b5-4f0a01fafd6e); pap. 9.99 (978-1-5415-7422-9(2), 22486836-c7a2-484e-b99a-2e87d84aedc9) Lerner Publishing Group. (Lerner Pubns.).

Older, Jules. Pig. Severance, Lyn, illus. 2004. 32p. (J). (gr. k-3). 16.95 (978-0-88106-109-3(3)) Charlesbridge Publishing, Inc.

Olivia's ABC. 2014. (ENG., Illus.). 30p. (J). (gr. -1-k). bds. 8.99 (978-1-4814-2192-8(1), Atheneum Bks. for Young Readers) Simon & Schuster Children's Publishing.

Orr, Tamra. Care for a Potbellied Pig. 2008. (How to Convince Your Parents You Can ... Ser.). (Illus.). 32p. (YA). (gr. 1-4). lib. bdg. 25.70 (978-1-58415-661-1(9)) Mitchell Lane Pubs.

Otfinoski, Steven. Pigs & Hogs, 1 vol. 2010. (Animals, Animals Ser.). (ENG.). 48p. (gr. 5-5). 32.64 (978-0-7614-3971-4(4), 9ed01665-c2ac-4e1c-bbe6-d923e1944206) Cavendish Square Publishing LLC.

Owen, Ruth. Warthogs, 1 vol., 1. 2013. (Dr. Bob's Amazing World of Animals Ser.). (ENG.). 32p. (J). (gr. 2-3). 31.27 (978-1-4777-9044-1(6), ec90f20f-7abd-452c-986a-f6fee018057f, Windmill Bks.) Rosen Publishing Group, Inc., The.

Pigs. Date not set. (Old MacDonald Stickers Ser.). (Illus.). 16p. (J). 5.98 (978-0-7525-9968-7(2)) Parragon, Inc.

Randolph, Joanne. My Friend the Potbellied Pig, 1 vol. 2010. (Curious Pet Pals Ser.). (ENG.). 24p. (J). (gr. 2-3). lib. bdg. 27.27 (978-1-60754-975-8(1), d9e75ccf-1c31-4408-aa1b-65e22e4acdc9); (Illus.). pap. 9.15 (978-1-60754-982-6(4), 9517186a-7b50-4218-bf00-a02585a80f44) Rosen Publishing Group, Inc., The. (Windmill Bks.).

Ray, Hannah. Pigs. 2006. (Down on the Farm Ser.). (Illus.). 24p. (J). (gr. 4-7). lib. bdg. 15.95 (978-1-59566-181-4(6)) QEB Publishing Inc.

Reasoner, Charles. Ooink! 2009. (Lift & Learn Ser.). (Illus.). 10p. (J). (gr. -1-k). 10.99 (978-1-934650-12-7(9)) Just For Kids Pr., LLC.

Rockwood, Leigh. Pigs Are Smart! 2010. (Illus.). 24p. (J). 49.50 (978-1-4358-9835-6(4), PowerKids Pr.); (ENG., (gr. 2-3). pap. 9.25 (978-1-4358-9834-9(6), 9792a7d5-528f-4dd2-8441-2000c340d5ab, PowerKids Pr.); (ENG., (gr. 2-3). lib. bdg. 26.27 (978-1-4358-9373-3(5), 16ff760c-8af2-45fa-a30a-db9f903d2995) Rosen Publishing Group, Inc., The.

Schuetz, Kari. Warthogs & Banded Mongooses. 2019. (Animal Tag Teams Ser.). (ENG., Illus.). 24p. (J). (gr. k-3). lib. bdg. 26.95 (978-1-62617-958-5(1), Blastoff! Readers) Bellwether Media.

Scieszka, Jon. The True Story of the 3 Little Pigs. Smith, Lane, illus. 2011. (J). (gr. -1-3). 29.95 (978-0-545-09457-3(7)); 18.95 (978-0-545-09459-7(3)) Weston Woods Studios, Inc.

Searl, Duncan. Pigs. 2006. (Smart Animals! Ser.). (Illus.). 32p. (J). (gr. 2-5). lib. bdg. 28.50 (978-1-59716-164-0(0)) Bearport Publishing Co., Inc.

Sexton, Colleen. Piglets. 2008. (Watch Animals Grow Ser.). (ENG., Illus.). 24p. (J). (gr. k-3). lib. bdg. 26.95 (978-1-60014-169-0(2)) Bellwether Media.

Siemens, Jared. Pigs. 2018. pap. (978-1-4896-9537-6(0), AV2 by Weigl) Weigl Pubs., Inc.

—Potbellied Pig. 2017. (Illus.). 24p. (J). (978-1-5105-0575-9(X)) SmartBook Media, Inc.

Silverstein, Alvin, et al. Potbellied Pigs: Cool Pets!, 1 vol. 2011. (Far-Out & Unusual Pets Ser.). (ENG., Illus.). 48p. (gr. 3-3). lib. bdg. 27.93 (978-0-7660-3687-1(1), 34fbae45-b0d3-4575-a2d9-6ef56a82fff6) Enslow Publishing, LLC.

Statts, Leo. Pigs. 2016. (Farm Animals Ser.). (ENG., Illus.). 24p. (J). (gr. -1-2). lib. bdg. 31.36 (978-1-68079-906-4(1), 24116, Abdo Zoom-Launch) ABDO Publishing Co.

Stiefel, Chana. Pigs on the Family Farm, 1 vol. 2013. (Animals on the Family Farm Ser.). (ENG.). 24p. (gr. k-2). pap. 10.35 (978-1-4644-0359-0(7), 49f744b9-9cd6-4e5f-85a6-a48f4a445688, Enslow Elementary); lib. bdg. 25.27 (978-0-7660-4208-7(1), 8e746535-9a6a-416b-8021-e126dff70cde) Enslow Publishing, LLC.

Stone, Tanya Lee. Pigs. 2003. (Wild Wild World Ser.). 24p. (YA). 24.94 (978-1-56711-819-3(4), Blackbirch Pr., Inc.) Cengage Gale.

Tait, Leia. Caring for Your Potbellied Pig. 2006. (Caring for Your Pet Ser.). (Illus.). 32p. (J). (gr. 3-7). lib. bdg. 26.00 (978-1-59036-474-1(0)) Weigl Pubs., Inc.

Thatcher, Henry. Wild Boars & Teacup Pigs, 1 vol., 1. 2014. (Big Animals, Small Animals Ser.). (ENG.). 32p. (J). (gr. 2-3). 28.93 (978-1-4777-6097-0(0), 7a0dd1bf-b5d4-4132-bd56-9ad2af6a712b, PowerKids Pr.) Rosen Publishing Group, Inc., The.

Top That Publishing Staff, ed. Wacky Pig. 2004. (Wacky Animals Ser.). (Illus.). 10p. (J). pap. (978-1-84510-090-2(5)) Top That! Publishing PLC.

Walden, Katherine. Warthogs. 2009. (Safari Animals Ser.). 24p. (gr. 1-1). 42.50 (978-1-60852-963-6(0)); (ENG.). (J). lib. bdg. 26.27 (978-1-4358-2688-5(4), 4fafb23b-a3e9-4544-8676-d0d1eab4824c) Rosen Publishing Group, Inc., The. (PowerKids Pr.).

Wendt, Jennifer. Showing Pigs at the Fair, 1 vol. 2018. (Blue Ribbon Animals Ser.). (ENG.). 24p. (gr. 2-3). lib. bdg. 24.27 (978-1-5382-2930-9(7), 2fcb2e9a-cbe9-4e12-b9e8-b4de1f4d0e32) Stevens, Gareth Publishing LLLP.

Wilsdon, Christina. Pigs, 1 vol. 2009. (Amazing Animals Ser.). (ENG.). 48p. (J). (gr. 3-5). pap. 11.50 (978-1-4339-2126-1(X), 6a407828-f272-4ca3-88ff-dbf7f1731b6e, Gareth Stevens Learning Library); lib. bdg. 30.67 (978-0-8368-9122-5(8), fde8cbe0-2e85-4371-9d5c-8782c9fb675a) Stevens, Gareth Publishing LLLP.

Wilson, Paula M. Mini Pigs. 2018. (Cute & Unusual Pets Ser.). (ENG., Illus.). 32p. (J). (gr. 3-9). lib. bdg. 28.65 (978-1-5435-3058-2(3), 138630, Capstone Pr.) Capstone.

Wood, Alix. Mini Pigs, 1 vol. 2016. (Mini Animals Ser.). (ENG., Illus.). 32p. (J). (gr. 2-3). pap. 11.00 (978-1-4994-8155-6(1), 916b5d77-c6ce-4cce-a529-9c6c5896e7e2, Windmill Bks.) Rosen Publishing Group, Inc., The.

Woods, Sadie. We Take Care of the Pigs, 1 vol. 2017. (I Live on a Farm Ser.). (ENG.). 24p. (J). (gr. 1-1). 25.27 (978-1-5081-6334-3(0), 2a7bcbda-7079-45cc-8fc8-307cf93df44c, PowerKids Pr.) Rosen Publishing Group, Inc., The.

PIGS—FICTION

Acevedo, Ari. Juan Bobo Sends the Pig to Mass. Wrenn, Tom, illus. 2008. (Story Cove Ser.). (SPA & ENG.). 24p. (J). (gr. -1-3). pap. 4.95 (978-0-87483-883-1(5)) August Hse. Pubs., Inc.

Ackerman, Jill. This Little Piggy: a Hand-Puppet Board Book. Berg, Michelle, illus. 2007. (Little Scholastic Ser.). (ENG.). 6p. (J). (gr. -1 — 1). bds. 12.99 (978-0-545-03038-0(2)) Scholastic, Inc.

Adams, Alison. The Three Little Pigs: Classic Tales Edition. Greenhead, Bill, illus. 2011. (Classic Tales Ser.). (J). (978-1-936258-71-0(4)) Benchmark Education Co.

Adams, Ben. The Pig with the Curliest Tail. Cameron, Craig, illus. 2013. (Googly Eyes Ser.). 12p. (J). (gr. -1-k). bds. 6.99 (978-1-84322-618-5(9), Armadillo) Anness Publishing GBR. Dist: National Bk. Network.

Adams, Jean Ekman. Clarence & the Purple Horse Bounce into Town. Adams, Jean Ekman, illus. 2003. (ENG., Illus.). 32p. (J). (gr. -1-3). 15.95 (978-0-87358-826-3(6), Rising Moon Bks. for Young Readers) Northland Publishing.

Adventures of the Robber Pig: Level J, 6 vols. (Leveled Books). 128p. (gr. 2-3). 41.95 (978-0-7699-0987-5(6)) Shortland Pubns. (U. S. A.) Inc.

Aguayo, Sal. The Tiny Telepaths: A Continuing Saga, 1 vol. 2010. 62p. pap. 19.95 (978-1-4489-5212-0(3)) America Star Bks.

Aina, Olaiya E. Ijapa, the Lion, & the Boar. 2010. 20p. 13.80 (978-1-4269-3183-3(2)) Trafford Publishing.

Albee, Sarah. Where Is Pig? Velez, Walter, illus. 2006. (Step-By-Step Readers Ser.). (J). pap. (978-1-59939-056-7(6), Reader's Digest Young Families, Inc.) Studio Fun International.

Alexander, Lloyd. The Book of Three. 2006. (Chronicles of Prydain Ser.: 1). (ENG., Illus.). 224p. (J). (gr. 3-7). pap. 7.99 (978-0-8050-8048-3(1), 900038435) Square Fish.

All Pull Together, 6 vols., Pack. (gr. -1-2). 23.00 (978-0-7635-8789-5(3)) Rigby Education.

Amery & Cartwright. Curly the Pig Kid Kit. 2007. (Kid Kits Ser.). (Illus.). 10p. (J). (gr. -1). bds. 12.99 (978-1-60130-009-6(3), Usborne) EDC Publishing.

Amery, H. Where's Curly? Cartwright, Stephen, illus. 2004. (Treasury of Farmyard Tales Ser.). 16p. (J). (gr. 1-18). pap. 7.95 (978-0-7945-0514-1(7)); lib. bdg. 15.95 (978-1-58086-563-0(1)) EDC Publishing.

Amery, H. & Cartwright, S. Three Little Pigs. 2004. (First Stories Ser.). 16p. (J). pap. 4.99 (978-0-7945-0609-4(7)) EDC Publishing.

Amery, Heather. Curly the Pig Board Book. Cartwright, Stephen, illus. 2004. (Young Farmyard Tales Board Books Ser.). 10p. (J). bds. 3.95 (978-0-7945-0468-7(X), Usborne) EDC Publishing.

—Three Little Pigs. Tyler, Jenny, ed. 2004. (Usborne First Stories Ser.). (Illus.). 16p. (J). (gr. -1). lib. bdg. 12.95 (978-1-58086-623-1(9), Usborne) EDC Publishing.

Anderson, Derek. Ten Hungry Pigs: An Epic Lunch Adventure. Anderson, Derek, illus. 2016. (ENG., Illus.). 40p. (J). (gr. -1-k). 17.99 (978-0-545-16848-9(1)) Scholastic, Inc.

Anderson, Lena & Sandin, Joan. Hedgehog, Pig, & the Sweet Little Friend. Sandin, Joan, tr. from SWE. 2007. (Illus.). 32p. (J). (gr. -1-1). 16.00 (978-91-29-66742-4(9)) R & S Bks. SWE. Dist: Macmillan.

Andrews, Roxanna. The Adventures of Super Pig. 2006. (Illus.). 68p. (J). 15.95 (978-1-59879-232-4(6)) Lifevest Publishing, Inc.

Arinola Awokoya. The Adventures of High Jumper. 2009. 112p. pap. 14.99 (978-1-4269-1792-9(9)) Trafford Publishing.

Artell, Mike. Three Little Cajun Pigs. Harris, Jim, illus. 2006. 32p. (J). (gr. k-3). 18.99 (978-0-8037-2815-8(8), Dial Bks) Penguin Young Readers Group.

Astley, Neville & Baker, Mark. Peppa's Easter Egg Hunt. 2016. (Illus.). (J). (978-1-5182-0103-5(2)) Scholastic, Inc.

—The Pumpkin Contest. 2018. (Illus.). (J). (978-1-5444-0652-7(5)) Scholastic, Inc.

Atlas, Ron. Ten Pigs Fiddling. Flint, Stacie, illus. 2006. (ENG.). 32p. (J). (gr. -1-k). 16.00 (978-0-9630243-8-1(8), 1249130) Amberwood Pr.

—Ten Pigs Fiddling. Flint, Stacie, illus. 2nd rev. ed. 2006. (ENG.). 32p. (J). (gr. -1-k). 17.95 (978-0-9630243-3-6(7)) Amberwood Pr.

Auerbach, Annie. I Can Be Anything! (Peppa Pig) EOne, illus. 2018. (ENG.). 16p. (J). (gr. -1-k). bds. 7.99 (978-1-338-22883-0(8)) Scholastic, Inc.

—Princess Peppa (Peppa Pig) EOne, illus. 2017. (ENG.). 32p. (J). (gr. -1-k). 8.99 (978-0-545-62786-3(9)) Scholastic, Inc.

Axelrod, Amy. Pigs at Odds: Fun with Math & Games. McGinley-Nally, Sharon, illus. 2003. (ENG.). 40p. (J). (gr. -1-4). 8.99 (978-0-689-86144-4(3), Aladdin) Simon & Schuster Children's Publishing.

Ayres, Pam. Piggo & the Fork Lift Truck. (Illus.). 32p. (978-0-563-36310-1(X)) BBC Worldwide.

Bader, Bonnie. Pig-Piggy-Pigs. 2015. (Penguin Young Readers, Level 2 Ser.). (ENG., Illus.). 32p. (J). (gr. 1-2). pap. 4.99 (978-0-448-48221-7(5), Penguin Young Readers) Penguin Young Readers Group.

Bajaj, Subash, illus. The Three Little Pigs. 2010. (J). (978-1-60617-135-6(6)) Teaching Strategies, LLC.

Baker, E. D. Magic Animal Rescue 4: Maggie & the Flying Pigs. 2017. (ENG., Illus.). 128p. (J). 16.99 (978-1-68119-489-9(9), 900175461); pap. 5.99 (978-1-68119-485-1(6), 900175433) Bloomsbury Publishing USA. (Bloomsbury USA Childrens).

Baker, Nancy Scott. Peggy Sue at the Pony Barn. Reese, Shelbye J., illus. 2009. (ENG.). 24p. pap. 15.99 (978-1-4415-6593-8(0)) Xlibris Corp.

Barchers, Suzanne I. How Big Is Kip?, 1 vol. rev. ed. 2011. (Phonics Ser.). (ENG., Illus.). 16p. (gr. k-1). 6.99 (978-1-4333-2410-9(5)) Teacher Created Materials, Inc.

Barkley, Callie. Ellie & the Good-Luck Pig. Riti, Marsha, illus. 2015. (Critter Club Ser.: 10). (ENG.). 128p. (J). (gr. k-4). pap. 6.99 (978-1-4814-2402-8(5), Little Simon) Little Simon.

Barnum, Richard. Squinty the Comical Pig. 2004. reprint ed. pap. 15.95 (978-1-4191-4865-1(6)); pap. 1.99 (978-1-4192-4865-8(0)) Kessinger Publishing, LLC.

—Squinty the Comical Pig Illustrated Edit. 2006. (Illus.). pap. (978-1-4065-0921-2(3)) Dodo Pr.

Bas, Merce Escardo I. The Three Little Pigs/Los Tres Cerditos. 2006. (Bilingual Fairy Tales Ser.: BILI). (ENG., Illus.). 32p. (J). (gr. -1-7). pap. 7.99 (978-0-8118-5064-3(1)) Chronicle Bks. LLC.

Bassede, Francine. Dia con los Cerditos. (Buenas Noches Ser.). (SPA.). (J). (gr. 1-3). 8.95 (978-958-04-5626-1(7)) Norma S.A. COL. Dist: Lectorum Pubns., Inc., Distribuidora Norma, Inc.

Bean, Margo Cronbaugh. Buffaloed Badger. Perry, Aumi Kauffman, illus. 2012. 24p. 19.95 (978-1-61633-239-6(5)); pap. 11.95 (978-1-61633-240-2(9)) Guardian Angel Publishing, Inc.

Beaton, Clare & Blackstone, Stella. How Big Is a Pig? Beaton, Clare, illus. 2004. (ENG., Illus.). 24p. (J). (gr. -1-k). pap. 6.99 (978-1-84148-702-1(3)) Barefoot Bks., Inc.

Bender, Carol. Picky Eater, That Peter. 2011. 25p. (J). 24.95 (978-1-4327-7055-6(1)) Outskirts Pr., Inc.

Bennicke, Rune Brandt. The Mystery Hat. Jensen, Jakob Hjort, illus. 2014. (ENG.). 32p. (J). (gr. -1-k). 16.95 (978-1-62914-621-8(8), Sky Pony Pr.) Skyhorse Publishing Co., Inc.

Bergen, Lara. Tutu Twins. Pastel, Elyse & Pastel, Elyse, illus. 2008. (ENG.). 24p. (J). (gr. k-17). per. 3.99 (978-1-58476-615-5(8)) Innovative Kids.

Berry, Lynne. Pig & Pug. Correll, Gemma, illus. 2015. (ENG.). 40p. (J). (gr. -1-3). 16.99 (978-1-4814-2131-7(X), Simon & Schuster Bks. For Young Readers) Simon & Schuster Bks. For Young Readers.

Between the Lions - Early Literacy Kit - Huff & Puff, 2 bks., 1 cass. 2005. (Between the Lions Ser.). (Illus.). (J). VHS 29.95 (978-1-59375-283-5(0), WG38613) WGBH Boston Video.

Biddle, Charles, Jr. The Three Little Pigs. Malak, Annabel, illus. 2011. (ENG.). 16p. pap. 12.95 (978-2-89558-409-4(5), 9782895584094) Editions Alexandre Stanke CAN. Dist: Baker & Taylor Publisher Services (BTPS).

Bigler, Stephanie, et al. Sir Francis Bacon & the Wolves of Isle Royale: A Little Pig's Big Adventure. 2008. 24p. pap. 13.99 (978-1-4389-1524-1(1)) AuthorHouse.

Bills, Taylor, illus. Three Little Pigs. 2009. 24p. (J). 12.95 (978-0-9776845-0-2(4)) 3D Alley, Inc.

Blabey, Aaron. Pig the Star. 2018. (Pig the Pug Ser.). (ENG., Illus.). 32p. (J). (gr. -1-k). 14.99 (978-1-338-28021-0(X), Scholastic Pr.) Scholastic, Inc.

Black, Michael Ian. A Pig Parade Is a Terrible Idea. Hawkes, Kevin, illus. 2010. (ENG.). 40p. (J). (gr. -1-3). 19.99 (978-1-4169-7922-7(0), Simon & Schuster Bks. For Young Readers) Simon & Schuster Bks. For Young Readers.

Blackford, Andy. The Three Little Pigs & the New Neighbor. Zlatic, Tomislav, illus. 2014. (Tadpoles: Fairytale Twists Ser.). (ENG.). 32p. (J). (gr. 1-2). (978-0-7787-0447-8(5)); pap. (978-0-7787-0482-9(3)) Crabtree Publishing Co.

Blackstone, Stella. Cerdota Grandota. Beaton, Clare, illus. 2003.Tr. of How Big Is a Pig. 24p. (J). (gr. k-2). pap. 6.99 (978-1-84148-926-1(3)) Barefoot Bks., Inc.

Bland, Nick, illus. King Pig. 2013. (J). pap. (978-0-545-67013-5(6)) Scholastic, Inc.

Bloker Cantrell, Jeannette, et al. The Summer of Joanie & Bobo. 2012. 72p. pap. 12.00 (978-1-4349-1759-1(2)) Dorrance Publishing Co., Inc.

Bloser, Cheryl. Little Mouse & the Muddy Feet. 2012. 28p. pap. 9.99 (978-0-9836771-1-6(5)) Mindstir Media.

Bond, Rebecca. Pig & Goose & the First Day of Spring. Bond, Rebecca, illus. 2017. (Illus.). 48p. (J). (gr. k-3). lib. bdg. 12.99 (978-1-58089-594-1(8)) Charlesbridge Publishing, Inc.

Book Company Staff. Who Am I: Pig. 2003. (Board Bks.). (Illus.). (J). bds. 10.95 (978-1-74047-309-5(4)) Book Co. Publishing Pty, Ltd., The AUS. Dist: Penton Overseas, Inc.

Boonen, Stefan. When Pigs Fly! Loufane, illus. 2004. 32p. (J). 6.95 (978-1-58925-384-1(1)) Tiger Tales.

Bowater, Alan. A Pig Called Pete, 1 vol. Pascoe, Pete, illus. 2009. (Pig Called Pete Ser.). (ENG.). 32p. (J). (gr. 1-2). 27.27 (978-1-60754-558-3(6), 666020cf-7837-4b2a-b12e-20b4a79ed0be); pap. 11.55 (978-1-60754-559-0(4), cb0d11a6-5d4a-4d60-b1ce-61000758511e) Rosen Publishing Group, Inc., The. (Windmill Bks.).

—A Pig Called Pete Meets a Cat Called Kitty, 1 vol. Pascoe, Pete, illus. 2009. (Pig Called Pete Ser.). (ENG.). 32p. (J). (gr. 1-2). 27.27 (978-1-60754-561-3(6), c0dc3532-dd69-4c5c-b589-4605b6ad1a8d); pap. 11.55 (978-1-60754-562-0(4), a093fe7e-f194-4109-9998-d945cb3dcf94) Rosen Publishing Group, Inc., The. (Windmill Bks.).

—A Pig Called Pete Meets a Cow Called Carlotta, 1 vol. Pascoe, Pete, illus. 2009. (Pig Called Pete Ser.). (ENG.). 32p. (J). (gr. 1-2). 27.27 (978-1-60754-567-5(5), 7bce1ef7-d77b-4cb3-a277-3fcd6edfd4dc); pap. 11.55 (978-1-60754-568-2(3), 575eefbf-ad67-411e-b7df-705b6a6f7410) Rosen Publishing Group, Inc., The. (Windmill Bks.).

—A Pig Called Pete Meets a Dog Called Doug, 1 vol. Pascoe, Pete, illus. 2009. (Pig Called Pete Ser.). (ENG.). 32p. (J). (gr. 1-2). 27.27 (978-1-60754-564-4(0), 56bd013a-538d-45f2-b896-7506c1bc8e25); pap. 11.55 (978-1-60754-565-1(9), 7ca69340-a347-4013-8075-5a7bc3ea5c33) Rosen Publishing Group, Inc., The. (Windmill Bks.).

—A Pig Called Pete Meets a Sheep Called Sean, 1 vol. Pascoe, Pete, illus. 2009. (Pig Called Pete Ser.). (ENG.). 32p. (J). (gr. 1-2). 27.27 (978-1-60754-570-5(5), 8b646817-e167-43ce-8f24-7259135fe187); pap. 11.55 (978-1-60754-571-2(3), 41e4b4d7-04af-4691-87e0-bd9043543e3f) Rosen Publishing Group, Inc., The. (Windmill Bks.).

Boynton. Bath Time! 2007. 10p. pap. 7.95 (978-0-7611-4780-0(2)) Workman Publishing Co., Inc.

Boynton, Sandra. Happy Birthday, Little Pookie. Boynton, Sandra, illus. 2017. (Little Pookie Ser.). (ENG., Illus.). 18p. (J). (gr. -1-k). bds. 6.99 (978-1-4814-9770-1(7)) Simon & Schuster, Inc.

—Merry Christmas, Little Pookie. Boynton, Sandra, illus. 2018. (Little Pookie Ser.). (ENG., Illus.). 18p. (J). (gr. -1-k). bds. 6.99 (978-1-5344-3724-1(X)) Simon & Schuster, Inc.

Bradman, Tony. The Three Little Pigs Go Camping, 1 vol. Warburton, Sarah, illus. 2014. (After Happily Ever After Ser.). (ENG.). 56p. (J). (gr. 3-6). lib. bdg. 25.99 (978-1-4342-7952-1(9), 124700, Stone Arch Bks.) Capstone.

Brave M.A., Kathryn A. & Lavin, Paul J. A Fit ting Fairy Tale. 2006. 60p. pap. 16.95 (978-1-4241-2992-8(3)) PublishAmerica, Inc.

Breathed, Berkeley. Pete & Pickles. Breathed, Berkeley, illus. 2008. (ENG., Illus.). 48p. (J). (gr. -1-k). 17.99 (978-0-399-25082-8(4), Philomel Bks.) Penguin Young Readers Group.

Briley, Randy W. Big Pigs & Sock Dances. 2013. 36p. pap. 10.99 (978-0-9896269-2-7(X)) Raven Mad Studios.

Brooke, L. Leslie. The Story of the Three Little Pig & Other Shorts Works. l.t. ed. 2007. 70p. 18.99 (978-1-4346-1999-0(0)) Creative Media Partners, LLC.

Brooks, Nan, illus. This Little Piggy. 2004. (J). 11.99 (978-1-890647-10-0(1)) TOMY International, Inc.

Brooks, Walter R. Freddy & the Ignormus, 4 vols. 2003. (Freddy the Pig Ser.). (J). 57.75 (978-0-7887-2996-6(9), 40878) Recorded Bks., Inc.

—Freddy Goes to Florida. Wiese, Kurt, illus. 2012. (ENG.). 224p. (YA). (gr. 4-13). 11.99 (978-1-59020-741-3(6), 1452703, Amulet Bks.) Abrams, Inc.

—Freddy the Detective. Wiese, Kurt, illus. 2010. (ENG.). 272p. (YA). (gr. 4-13). 11.99 (978-1-59020-418-4(2), 1453803, Amulet Bks.) Abrams, Inc.

Brown, Carron, ed. The Three Little Pigs & Little Red Riding Hood: Two Tales & Their Histories, 1 vol. 2009. (World of Fairy Tales Ser.). (ENG., Illus.). 32p. (J). (gr. 1-2). pap. 11.55 (978-1-60754-641-2(8), f11044f7-61ec-4d84-b6c3-6bebc70efb3a); lib. bdg. 27.27 (978-1-60754-640-5(X), dd97079b-c28b-4ca3-abf6-5e8b46ef1003) Rosen Publishing Group, Inc., The. (Windmill Bks.).

Brown, E. Jane. Pinkie. 2005. 76p. pap. 10.00 (978-1-4116-3115-1(3)) Lulu Pr., Inc.

Brown, Janet. Three Little Pigs (Floor Book) My First Reading Book. Morton, Ken, illus. 2015. (ENG.). 24p. (J). (gr. -1-1). pap. 6.99 (978-1-86147-396-7(6), Armadillo) Anness Publishing GBR. Dist: National Bk. Network.

Bryan, Ed, illus. The Three Little Pigs: a Nosy Crow Fairy Tale. 2016. (ENG.). 32p. (J). (gr. -1-2). 9.99 (978-0-7636-8655-0(7)) Candlewick Pr.

Bryant, Ann. Tag. 2009. (ENG., Illus.). 24p. (J). pap. (978-0-7787-3900-5(7)); lib. bdg. (978-0-7787-3869-5(8)) Crabtree Publishing Co.

Bryson, Brenda. The Adventures of Roo & Winston. 2007. (ENG.). 82p. pap. *(978-1-4357-0145-8(3))* Lulu Pr., Inc.

Burgo, Ann & Shelton, Sherry. A Parable of the Three Little Pigs. 2009. 32p. pap. 14.49 *(978-1-4490-0577-1(2))* AuthorHouse.

Burke, Bob. The Third Pig Detective Agency: The Complete Casebook. 2015. (ENG.). 432p. 8.99 *(978-0-00-747940-5(9)*, Friday Project) HarperCollins Pubs. Ltd. GBR. Dist: HarperCollins Pubs.

Butler, Ellis Parker. Pigs Is Pigs & Other Favorites. 2004. reprint ed. pap. 20.95 *(978-1-4179-2471-4(3))* Kessinger Publishing, LLC.

Candlewick Press. Peppa Pig & the Busy Day at School. Candlewick Press, illus. 2013. (Peppa Pig Ser.). (ENG., Illus.). 32p. (J). (-k). 12.99 *(978-0-7636-6525-8(8)*, Candlewick Entertainment) Candlewick Pr.

—Peppa Pig & the Camping Trip. 2016. (Peppa Pig Ser.). (ENG., Illus.). 32p. (J). (-k). 14.99 *(978-0-7636-8741-0(3)*, Candlewick Entertainment) Candlewick Pr.

—Peppa Pig & the Career Day. 2018. (Peppa Pig Ser.). (ENG., Illus.). 32p. (J). (-k). 12.99 *(978-1-5362-0344-8(0)*, Candlewick Entertainment) Candlewick Pr.

—Peppa Pig & the Day at Snowy Mountain. 2014. (Peppa Pig Ser.). (ENG., Illus.). 32p. (J). (-k). 12.99 *(978-0-7636-7455-7(9)*, Candlewick Entertainment) Candlewick Pr.

—Peppa Pig & the Easter Rainbow. 2017. (Peppa Pig Ser.). (ENG., Illus.). 32p. (J). (-k). 14.99 *(978-0-7636-9438-8(X)*, Candlewick Entertainment) Candlewick Pr.

—Peppa Pig & the Great Vacation. 2014. (Peppa Pig Ser.). (ENG.). 32p. (J). (-k). 14.99 *(978-0-7636-6986-7(5)*, Candlewick Entertainment) Candlewick Pr.

—Peppa Pig & the Halloween Costume. 2018. (Peppa Pig Ser.). (ENG., Illus.). 32p. (J). (-k). 14.99 *(978-1-5362-0060-7(3)*, Candlewick Entertainment) Candlewick Pr.

—Peppa Pig & the I Love You Game. 2015. (Peppa Pig Ser.). (ENG.). 32p. (J). (-k). 14.99 *(978-0-7636-8126-5(1)*, Candlewick Entertainment) Candlewick Pr.

—Peppa Pig & the Lost Christmas List. Candlewick Press, illus. 2012. (Peppa Pig Ser.). (ENG., Illus.). 32p. (J). (gr. k-k). 12.99 *(978-0-7636-6276-9(3)*, Candlewick Entertainment) Candlewick Pr.

—Peppa Pig & the Perfect Day. 2013. (Peppa Pig Ser.). (ENG., Illus.). 8p. (J). (gr. -1-2). 17.99 *(978-0-7636-6825-9(7)*, Candlewick Entertainment) Candlewick Pr.

—Peppa Pig & the Silly Sniffles. 2018. (Peppa Pig Ser.). (ENG., Illus.). 32p. (J). (-k). 12.99 *(978-1-5362-0343-1(2)*, Candlewick Entertainment) Candlewick Pr.

—Peppa Pig & the Treasure Hunt. 2015. (Peppa Pig Ser.). (ENG.). 32p. (J). (-k). 12.99 *(978-0-7636-7703-9(5)*, Candlewick Entertainment) Candlewick Pr.

—Peppa Pig & the Year of Family Fun. 2016. (Peppa Pig Ser.). (ENG., Illus.). 10p. (J). (gr. -1-2). 17.99 *(978-0-7636-8739-7(1)*, Candlewick Entertainment) Candlewick Pr.

—Peppa Pig's Pop-Up Princess Castle. Entertainment One, Entertainment, illus. 2017. (Peppa Pig Ser.). (ENG.). 6p. (J). (gr. -1-2). 24.99 *(978-0-7636-9734-1(6)*, Candlewick Entertainment) Candlewick Pr.

Candlewick Press Editors. Peppa Pig & the Busy Day at School. 2014. (Peppa Pig Ser.). lib. bdg. 16.00 *(978-0-606-35154-6(X))* Turtleback.

—Peppa Pig & the Great Vacation. 2015. (Peppa Pig Ser.). lib. bdg. 16.00 *(978-0-606-36857-5(4))* Turtleback.

—Peppa Pig & the I Love You Game. 2016. (Peppa Pig Ser.). (ENG.). 32p. (J). (gr. -1-1). 16.00 *(978-0-606-39091-0(X))* Turtleback.

—Peppa Pig & the Muddy Puddles. 2014. (Peppa Pig Ser.). lib. bdg. 16.00 *(978-0-606-35153-9(1))* Turtleback.

—Peppa Pig & the Vegetable Garden. 2015. (Peppa Pig Ser.). lib. bdg. 16.00 *(978-0-606-36856-8(6))* Turtleback.

Candlewick Press Staff. Peppa Pig & the Backyard Circus. 2017. (Peppa Pig Ser.). (ENG., Illus.). 32p. (J). (gr. -1-2). 12.99 *(978-0-7636-9437-1(1)*, Candlewick Entertainment) Candlewick Pr.

Capstone Press Staff. The Three Little Pigs. Blecha, Aaron, illus. 2009. (Graphic Spin Ser.). (ENG.). 40p. (J). (gr. 3-6). pap. 5.95 *(978-1-4342-1395-2(1)*, 95685, Stone Arch Bks.) Capstone.

Carbone, Courtney. Princess Peppa & the Royal Ball. 2018. (Scholastic Readers Ser.). (ENG.). 32p. (J). (gr. -1-k). 13.89 *(978-1-64310-234-4(6))* Penworthy Co., LLC, The.

—Princess Peppa & the Royal Ball (Peppa Pig: Scholastic Reader, Level 1), 1 vol. (Scholastic Reader, Level 1 Ser.). (ENG., 32p. (J). 2017. Illus.). (gr. -1-k). pap. 4.99 *(978-1-338-18258-3(7))* 2005. (gr. 2-5). E-Book 7.99 *(978-1-338-19011-3(3))* Scholastic, Inc.

—The Safety First! EOne, illus. 2018. (Scholastic Reader, Level 1 Ser.). (ENG.). 32p. (J). (gr. -1-k). pap. 4.99 *(978-1-338-22882-3(X))* Scholastic, Inc.

—The Safety First! (Peppa Pig: Level 1 Reader) EOne, illus. 2015. (ENG.). 32p. (J). (gr. -1-k). E-Book 8.99 *(978-1-338-29114-8(9))* Scholastic, Inc.

Carlson, Nancy. Get up & Go! 2008. (Illus.). 32p. (J). (gr. -1-k). pap. 8.99 *(978-0-14-241064-6(0)*, Puffin Books) Penguin Young Readers Group.

—Get up & Go! 2008. (Illus.). (gr. -1-3). 16.00 *(978-0-7569-8922-4(1))* Perfection Learning Corp.

—Louanne Pig in Making the Team. 2005. (Louanne Pig Ser.). (Illus.). 32p. (J). (gr. k-2). lib. bdg. 15.95 *(978-1-57505-914-3(2))* Lerner Publishing Group.

—Louanne Pig in Making the Team, 2nd Edition. rev. ed. 2005. (Nancy Carlson Picture Bks.). (ENG., Illus.). 32p. (J). (gr. k-2). per. 9.99 *(978-1-57505-997-6(5)*, ca8535c9-f160-4c84-88fe-d762f191e5d3, Carolrhoda Bks.) Lerner Publishing Group.

—Louanne Pig in the Mysterious Valentine. rev. ed. 2004. (Carolrhoda Picture Books Ser.). (Illus.). 32p. (J). (gr. k-2). 15.95 *(978-1-57505-671-5(2))* Lerner Publishing Group.

—Louanne Pig in the Mysterious Valentine, 2nd Edition. 2nd rev. ed. 2004. (Nancy Carlson Picture Bks.). (ENG., Illus.). 32p. (J). (gr. k-2). per. 9.99 *(978-1-57505-722-4(0)*, 996de222-b558-480f-94ac-14e4e20b0b97, Carolrhoda Bks.) Lerner Publishing Group.

—Louanne Pig in the Perfect Family. 2nd rev. ed. 2004. (Nancy Carlson's Neighborhood Ser.). (ENG., Illus.). 32p. (J). (gr. k-2). 15.95 *(978-1-57505-611-1(9))* Lerner Publishing Group.

—Louanne Pig in the Talent Show. 2005. (Louanne Pig Ser.). (Illus.). 32p. (J). (gr. -1-3). lib. bdg. 15.95 *(978-1-57505-915-0(0))* Lerner Publishing Group.

—Louanne Pig in Witch Lady. 2006. (Illus.). 32p. (J). (gr. -1-3). lib. bdg. 15.95 *(978-0-8225-6196-5(4)*, Carolrhoda Bks.) Lerner Publishing Group.

—Louanne Pig in Witch Lady, 2nd Edition. Carlson, Nancy, illus. 2nd rev. ed. 2006. (Nancy Carlson Picture Bks.). (ENG., Illus.). 32p. (J). (gr. k-2). per. 9.99 *(978-0-8225-6197-2(2)*, 475f80c0-3a3c-4067-973b-9f16b2201a07, Carolrhoda Bks.) Lerner Publishing Group.

—Louanne Pig Series, 3 bks. (Illus.). (J). (gr. k-3). pap. 44.95 incl. audio *(978-0-87499-474-2(8))* Live Oak Media.

Cartwright, Stephen, illus. Three Little Pigs. 2006. (First Stories Sticker Bks.). 16p. (J). (gr. -1-3). pap. 6.99 *(978-0-7945-1386-3(7)*, Usborne) EDC Publishing.

Caviezel, Giovanni. Little Pig. Rigo, Laura, illus. 2010. (Mini Look at Me Bks.). 10p. (J). (gr. -1 — 1). bds. 8.99 *(978-0-7641-6355-5(8))* Sourcebooks, Inc.

Cazet, Denys. Will You Read to Me? Cazet, Denys, illus. 2007. (ENG., Illus.). 32p. (J). (gr. -1-1). 16.99 *(978-1-4169-0935-4(4)*, Atheneum/Richard Jackson Bks.) Simon & Schuster Children's Publishing.

Cerasi, Chris. The Angry Birds Movie: Too Many Pigs. 2016. (I Can Read Level 2 Ser.). (ENG., Illus.). 32p. (J). (gr. -1-3). pap. 4.99 *(978-0-06-245334-1(3)*, HarperCollins) HarperCollins Pubs.

—Too Many Pigs. 2016. (I Can Read! Level 1 Ser.). (J). lib. bdg. 13.55 *(978-0-606-38186-4(4))* Turtleback.

Chace, Rebecca. June Sparrow & the Million-Dollar Penny. Schwartz, Kacey, illus. 2017. (ENG.). 352p. (J). (gr. 3-7). 16.99 *(978-0-06-246498-9(1)*, Balzer & Bray) HarperCollins Pubs.

Chandler, Andrew & Chandler, Amanda. Gertrude & Abigail: The Adventures Thereof. 2006. 35p. (J). 18.90 *(978-1-4116-7572-8(X))* Lulu Pr., Inc.

Charlesworth, Liza. Pig Wants a Peach: An Animal Friends Reader. Smith, Ian, illus. 2015. 16p. (J). pap. *(978-0-545-85965-3(4))* Scholastic, Inc.

Chesterfield, Sadie. Let's Make a Snowman! 2007. (Peppa Pig Ser.). 24p. (J). pap. 6.99 *(978-0-06-117367-7(3)*, Harper Entertainment) HarperCollins Pubs.

Chin, Oliver. The Year of the Pig: Tales from the Chinese Zodiac. Alcorn, Jeremiah, illus. 2018. (Tales from the Chinese Zodiac Ser.). (ENG.). 40p. (J). (gr. -1-3). 15.95 *(978-1-59702-143-2(1))* Immedium.

Chocolate, Debbi. Pigs Can Fly! The Adventures of Harriet Pig & Friends. Tryon, Leslie, illus. 2004. 64p. (J). 15.95 *(978-0-8126-2706-0(7))* Cricket Bks.

Clark, Nicole K. Pigment the Rainbow Pig. Clark, Nicole K., illus. Date not set. (Illus.). (J). (gr. -1-2). *(978-1-892176-18-9(1))* PremaNations Publishing.

Clem, Margaret H. Elbert ein Swine, Genius Pig. Clem, Margaret H., illus. 2003. (ENG., Illus.). 32p. (J). (gr. k-4). pap. 6.95 *(978-1-878044-12-9(5))* Mayhaven Publishing, Inc.

Cloke, Rene, illus. The Three Little Pigs. 2012. (ENG.). 24p. pap. 6.50 *(978-1-84135-544-3(5))* Award Pubns. Ltd. GBR. Dist: Parkwest Pubns., Inc.

Cocca-Leffler, Maryann. A Homemade Together Christmas. Cocca-Leffler, Maryann, illus. 2015. (ENG., Illus.). 32p. (J). (gr. -1-3). 16.99 *(978-0-8075-3366-6(1)*, 807533661) Whitman, Albert & Co.

Considine-Johnson, Joan. Olivia Makes Memories. Spaziante, Patrick, illus. 2015. (J). *(978-1-4806-9185-8(2)*, Simon Spotlight) Simon Spotlight.

Cook, Sherry & Johnson, Terri. Pressure Pete, 26 vols. Kuhn, Jesse, illus. l.t. ed. 2006. (Quirkles — Exploring Phonics through Science Ser.: 16). 32p. (J). 7.99 *(978-1-933815-15-2(9)*, Quirkles, The) Creative 3, LLC.

Cook, Teri Ann. The Adventures of Mrs. Patsy's Farm: A Gift! Is a Gift! Is a Gift!, 1 vol. 2009. 24p. pap. 24.95 *(978-1-60749-549-9(X))* America Star Bks.

Cooke, James. Pink Pig in a Boat. 2004. 59p. pap. 16.95 *(978-1-4137-4338-8(2))* America Star Bks.

Cosgrove, Stephen. Jalopy. 2011. (Orig.). (J). *(978-0-86592-797-1(9))* Rourke Enterprises, Inc.

Costello, David Hyde. Little Pig Joins the Band. Costello, David Hyde, illus. 2014. (Illus.). 32p. (J). (gr. -1-3). pap. 7.95 *(978-1-58089-265-0(5))* Charlesbridge Publishing, Inc.

—Little Pig Joins the Band. Costello, David Hyde, illus. 2012. (Illus.). 29.95 incl. audio compact disk *(978-1-4301-1139-9(9))* Live Oak Media.

—Little Pig Joins the Band. 2014. (ENG.). (J). (gr. -1-3). lib. bdg. 18.55 *(978-1-62765-428-9(3))* Perfection Learning Corp.

—Little Pig Saves the Ship. Costello, David Hyde, illus. 2017. (Illus.). 32p. (J). (gr. -1-2). 14.99 *(978-1-58089-715-0(0))* Charlesbridge Publishing, Inc.

Coulman, Valerie. When Pigs Fly. l.t. ed. 2012. 63p. (J). pap. *(978-1-4596-3455-8(1))* ReadHowYouWant.com, Ltd.

Cowley, Joy. Mrs. Wishy-Washy's Farm. Fuller, Elizabeth, illus. (ENG.). 32p. (J). (gr. -1-k). 2006. 8.99 *(978-0-14-240299-3(0)*, Puffin Books) 2003. 17.99 *(978-0-399-23872-7(7)*, Philomel Bks.) Penguin Young Readers Group.

Cox, Phil Roxbee. Big Pig on a Dig. Tyler, Jenny, ed. Cartwright, Stephen, illus. rev. ed. 2006. (Phonics Readers Ser.). 16p. (J). (gr. -1-3). pap. 6.99 *(978-0-7945-1501-0(0)*, Usborne) EDC Publishing.

Cox, Rhonda. Pigs Peek. Cox, Rhonda, photos by. 2003. (ENG., Illus.). 12p. (J). pap. 15.00 *(978-1-57274-698-5(X)*, BB2180, Bks. for Young Learners) Owen, Richard C. Pubs., Inc.

Coxe, Molly. Princess Pig. 2018. (Bright Owl Bks.). (Illus.). 40p. (J). (gr. -1-2). pap. 6.99 *(978-1-57565-979-4(4)*, 1349fd5e-e9d9-4c7a-b8c9-e9f69e3c4360); lib. bdg. 17.99 *(978-1-57565-978-7(6)*, 95fbd3b3-968c-4313-9d96-307237a342f5) Astra Publishing Hse. (Kane Press).

Croteau, Marie-Danielle. Fred & the Pig Race. Cummins, Sarah, tr. St-Aubin, Bruno, illus. 2007. (Formac First Novels Ser.). (ENG.). 64p. (gr. 2-5). 14.95 *(978-0-88780-733-6(X)*, 733); (J). (gr. 1-5). 5.95 *(978-0-88780-731-2(3)*, 8cd27fa0-c52d-4f80-b205-213b035c3951) Formac Publishing Co., Ltd. CAN. Dist: Formac Lorimer Bks. Ltd., Lerner Publishing Group.

Crump, Fred, Jr. The Three Little Brown Piggies. 2007. (Illus.). 32p. (J). 12.95 *(978-1-934056-21-9(9))* UMI (Urban Ministries, Inc.).

Crump Jr., Fred. The Three Little Brown Piggies. 2007. (Illus.). 32p. (J). pap. 9.95 *(978-1-932715-83-5(5))* UMI (Urban Ministries, Inc.).

Cullen, Lisa Anne. Three Wild Pigs: A Carolina Folktale. 2018. (Young Palmetto Bks.). (ENG., Illus.). 32p. 18.99 *(978-1-61117-944-6(0)*, P599432) Univ. of South Carolina Pr.

Dahl, Michael. Pig Takes a Bath, 1 vol. Vidal, Oriol, illus. 2010. (Hello Genius Ser.). (ENG.). 20p. (J). (gr. -1 — 1). bds. 7.99 *(978-1-4048-5729-2(X)*, 102306, Picture Window Bks.) Capstone.

Dakos, Kalli. Our Principal Promised to Kiss a Pig. 2018. (2019 Av2 Fiction Ser.). (ENG.). 32p. (J). lib. bdg. 34.28 *(978-1-4896-8275-8(9)*, AV2 by Weigl) Weigl Pubs., Inc.

Dakos, Kalli & DesMarteau, Alicia. Our Principal Promised to Kiss a Pig. DiRocco, Carl, illus. (ENG.). 32p. (J). 2017. (gr. -1-3). pap. 7.99 *(978-0-8075-6635-0(7)*, 807566357) 2004. (gr. 2-5). 16.99 *(978-0-8075-6629-9(2))* Whitman, Albert & Co.

Davies, Gill & Freeman, Tina. Two Naughty Piglets. 2004. (Tales from Yellow Barn Farm Ser.). (Illus.). 24p. (J). 3.99 *(978-1-85854-325-3(8))* Brimax Books Ltd. GBR. Dist: Byeway Bks.

Davis, Donald. The Pig Who Went Home on Sunday: An Appalachian Folktale. Mazzucco, Jennifer, illus. 2007. (ENG.). 40p. (J). (gr. -1-3). 8.95 *(978-0-87483-851-0(7))* August Hse. Pubs., Inc.

De Kockere, Geert. Piglet Bo Can Do Anything! van Hemeldonck, Tineke, illus. 2015. (ENG.). 32p. (J). (gr. -1-k). 16.99 *(978-1-63220-600-8(5)*, Sky Pony Pr.) Skyhorse Publishing Co., Inc.

—Piglet Bo Is Not Scared! van Hemeldonck, Tineke, illus. 2015. (ENG.). 32p. (J). (gr. -1-k). 16.99 *(978-1-63450-182-8(9)*, Sky Pony Pr.) Skyhorse Publishing Co., Inc.

Dean, James. Pete the Cat's Train Trip. 2015. (Pete the Cat I Can Read Ser.). (J). lib. bdg. 13.55 *(978-0-606-36967-1(8))* Turtleback.

Degman, Lori. Norbert's Big Dream. Bucci, Marco, illus. 2016. (ENG.). 32p. (J). (gr. k-3). 16.99 *(978-1-58536-959-1(4)*, 204108) Sleeping Bear Pr.

deRubertis, Barbara & DeRubertis, Barbara. Hanna Hippo's Horrible Hiccups. Alley, R. W., illus. 2012. (Animal Antics A to Z Ser.). 32p. (J). (gr. 2 — 1). cd-rom 7.95 *(978-1-57565-401-0(6))* Astra Publishing Hse.

Desmet, Sara. Scared Silly. Desmet, Sara, illus. 2006. (Illus.). 32p. (J). (gr. -1-3). 15.95 *(978-1-60108-009-7(3))* Red Cygnet Pr.

Dicamillo, Kate. Mercy Watson: Something Wonky This Way Comes. 2011. 16.00 *(978-1-61383-049-9(1))* Perfection Learning Corp.

DiCamillo, Kate. Mercy Watson Boxed Set: Adventures of a Porcine Wonder: Books 1-6, 6 vols. Van Dusen, Chris, illus. 2011. (Mercy Watson Ser.). (ENG.). 496p. (J). (gr. k-3). pap. 39.99 *(978-0-7636-5709-3(3))* Candlewick Pr.

—Mercy Watson Fights Crime. Van Dusen, Chris, illus. (Mercy Watson Ser.: 3). (ENG.). 80p. (J). (gr. k-3). 2010. pap. 6.99 *(978-0-7636-4952-4(X))* 2006. 15.99 *(978-0-7636-2590-0(6))* Candlewick Pr.

Dicamillo, Kate. Mercy Watson Fights Crime. 2010. (Mercy Watson Ser.: Bk. 3). lib. bdg. 16.00 *(978-0-606-14927-3(9))* Turtleback.

—Mercy Watson Goes for a Ride. 2012. 16.00 *(978-1-61383-702-3(X))* Perfection Learning Corp.

DiCamillo, Kate. Mercy Watson Goes for a Ride. Van Dusen, Chris, illus. (Mercy Watson Ser.: 2). (ENG.). 80p. (J). (gr. k-3). 2009. pap. 6.99 *(978-0-7636-4505-2(2))* 2006. 15.99 *(978-0-7636-2332-6(6))* Candlewick Pr.

Dicamillo, Kate. Mercy Watson Goes for a Ride. 2009. (Mercy Watson Ser.: Bk. 2). lib. bdg. 16.00 *(978-0-606-06699-0(3))* Turtleback.

DiCamillo, Kate. Mercy Watson: Princess in Disguise. Van Dusen, Chris, illus. (Mercy Watson Ser.: 4). (ENG.). 80p. (J). (gr. k-3). 2010. pap. 6.99 *(978-0-7636-4951-7(1))* 2007. 15.99 *(978-0-7636-3014-0(4))* Candlewick Pr.

—Mercy Watson: Something Wonky This Way Comes. Van Dusen, Chris, illus. (Mercy Watson Ser.: 6). (ENG.). 96p. (J). (gr. k-3). 2011. pap. 6.99 *(978-0-7636-5232-6(6))* 2009. 15.99 *(978-0-7636-3644-9(4))* Candlewick Pr.

—Mercy Watson Thinks Like a Pig. Van Dusen, Chris, illus. (Mercy Watson Ser.: 5). (ENG.). 80p. (J). (gr. k-3). 2011. pap. 6.99 *(978-0-7636-5231-9(8))* 2008. 15.99 *(978-0-7636-3265-6(1))* Candlewick Pr.

—Mercy Watson to the Rescue. Van Dusen, Chris, illus. (Mercy Watson Ser.: 1). (ENG.). 80p. (J). (gr. k-3). 2009. pap. 6.99 *(978-0-7636-4504-5(4))* 2005. 15.99 *(978-0-7636-2270-1(2))* Candlewick Pr.

Dicamillo, Kate. Mercy Watson to the Rescue. 2009. (Mercy Watson Ser.: Bk. 1). lib. bdg. 16.00 *(978-0-606-06704-1(3))* Turtleback.

DiCamillo, Kate. A Piglet Named Mercy. Van Dusen, Chris, illus. 2019. (Mercy Watson Ser.). (ENG.). 32p. (J). (gr. -1-2). 18.99 *(978-0-7636-7753-4(1))* Candlewick Pr.

Disney Books. Gravity Falls: Once upon a Swine. 2014. (Gravity Falls Chapter Book Ser.: 2). (ENG., Illus.). 112p. (J). (gr. 1-3). pap. 4.99 *(978-1-4847-1140-8(8)*, Disney Press Books) Disney Publishing Worldwide.

Disney Press Staff. Once upon a Swine. 2014. (Gravity Falls Ser.: 2). (J). lib. bdg. 14.75 *(978-0-606-35916-0(8))* Turtleback.

DK. The Three Little Pigs. Di Lernia, Giuseppe, illus. 2019. (Storytime Lap Bks.). (ENG.). 30p. (J). (-k). bds. 14.99 *(978-1-4654-7848-1(5)*, DK Children) Dorling Kindersley Publishing, Inc.

Dockery, Marie F. The Three Billy Goats Gruff Find Jesus & the Three Little Souls. 2008. 52p. pap. 12.99 *(978-1-60647-605-5(X))* Salem Author Services.

Dodd, Melissa. Santa Sheds, 1 vol. 2009. 17p. pap. 24.95 *(978-1-60749-208-5(3))* America Star Bks.

Dompierre, Judith. I See Pigs Everywhere, 1 vol. 2010. 28p. pap. 29.95 *(978-1-4489-8838-9(1))* America Star Bks.

Dotlich, Rebecca Kai. Mama Loves. Brown, Kathryn, illus. 2004. 32p. (J). (gr. -1-2). lib. bdg. 15.89 *(978-0-06-029408-3(6))* HarperCollins Pubs.

Dougherty, Jane L. Pig Party. 2008. 36p. pap. 24.95 *(978-1-4241-9045-4(2))* America Star Bks.

Dougherty, John. There's a Pig up My Nose! Hughes, Laura, illus. 2017. (ENG.). 32p. (J). (gr. -1-k). pap. 7.99 *(978-1-4052-7716-7(5))* Farshore GBR. Dist: HarperCollins Pubs.

Dowley-Wise, Justine. A Pig Called Harriet. 2008. (ENG.). 112p. pap. 31.99 *(978-1-4389-3388-7(6))* AuthorHouse.

Doyle, Malachy. Big Pig. Bendall-Brunello, John, illus. 2006. (ENG.). 32p. (J). (gr. -1-k). pap. 9.99 *(978-0-689-87485-7(5))* Simon & Schuster, Ltd. GBR. Dist: Simon & Schuster, Inc.

The Dreamer: (Inspirational Story, Picture Book for Children, Books about Perseverance) 2018. (ENG., Illus.). 52p. (J). (gr. -1-k). 16.99 *(978-1-4521-5608-8(5))* Chronicle Bks. LLC.

Dubé, Pierrette. The Little Pig, the Bicycle, & the Moon. Orbie, illus. 2018. (ENG.). 40p. (J). (gr. -1-3). 17.99 *(978-1-5344-1472-3(X)*, McElderry, Margaret K. Bks.) McElderry, Margaret K. Bks.

Dufresne, Michèle. Dinner Time. 2005. (Gilbert the Pig Chapter Ser.). (J). pap. 7.67 *(978-1-58453-298-9(X))* Pioneer Valley Bks.

—Gilbert the Pig Chapter Books (Illustrated) 2005. (J). pap. 29.33 *(978-1-58453-296-5(3))* Pioneer Valley Bks.

Edminister, David. Pork Chop. 2010. (Illus.). 36p. (J). pap. 15.95 *(978-1-4327-5345-0(2))* Outskirts Pr., Inc.

Elchgar, Yasmin. Noonoo the Doctor. 2013. 20p. pap. 13.77 *(978-1-4907-1037-2(X))* Trafford Publishing.

Elliot, David. Henry's Map. Elliot, David, illus. 2013. (Illus.). 40p. (J). (gr. -1-3). 18.99 *(978-0-399-16072-1(8)*, Philomel Bks.) Penguin Young Readers Group.

—Oink. Elliot, David, illus. 2019. (ENG., Illus.). 32p. (J). (gr. -1-k). 16.99 *(978-1-77657-214-4(9)*, 796c305c-57d0-4b54-bc60-7ef027c12b6e) Gecko Pr. NZL. Dist: Lerner Publishing Group.

Elliott, Linda. When Little Pinkie Gets Her Wings. Switzer, Bobbi, illus. 2007. 28p. per. 11.95 *(978-1-59800-871-5(4))* Outskirts Pr., Inc.

Elora, Grace. Cute & Cuddly: Baby Animals, 6 vols., Set. Incl. Bear Cubs. lib. bdg. 25.27 *(978-1-4339-4499-4(5)*, db254a93-30e1-44ca-aeba-8d53ddd44dc1); Bunnies. 25.27 *(978-1-4339-4503-8(7)*, 8f3a3374-c087-465c-9eee-da1def1fb6be); Foals. lib. bdg. 25.27 *(978-1-4339-4507-6(X)*, c12bca36-5e74-49e8-b9d3-c099efb6d70d); Kittens. lib. bdg. 25.27 *(978-1-4339-4511-3(8)*, e416c840-947a-446f-9ee1-77bc3c50d456); Piglets. lib. bdg. 25.27 *(978-1-4339-4515-1(0)*, 1c0fbeda-02ad-498b-a86d-139a46f6f0bd); Puppies. lib. bdg. 25.27 *(978-1-4339-4519-9(3)*, f36090c1-7818-4469-9255-8e5bf7f67846); (J). (gr. k-k). (Cute & Cuddly: Baby Animals Ser.). (ENG., Illus.). 24p. 2011. Set lib. bdg. 75.81 *(978-1-4339-4946-3(6)*, 0ced8a30-b1e6-40cc-a7a1-0d4d4ceb1b06) Stevens, Gareth Publishing LLLP.

Emmett, Jonathan. The Princess & the Pig. Bernatene, Poly, illus. 2011. (ENG.). 32p. (J). (gr. k-8). 17.99 *(978-0-8027-2334-5(9)*, 900076370, Bloomsbury USA Childrens) Bloomsbury Publishing USA.

Erickson, John. The Case of the Missing Bird Dog. Holmes, Gerald L., illus. 2011. (Hank the Cowdog Ser.: No. 40). (ENG.). 126p. (J). (gr. 3-6). pap. 5.99 *(978-1-59188-140-7(4))* Maverick Bks., Inc.

Escardo Bas, Mercè. Los Tres Cerditos. Joan, Pere, illus. 2003. (SPA.). 24p. *(978-84-246-1939-8(0)*, GL30510) La Galera, S.A. Editorial ESP. Dist: Lectorum Pubns., Inc.

Evans, Claire. The Three Little Superpigs. Evans, Claire, illus. 2018. (Three Little Superpigs Ser.). (ENG., Illus.). 40p. (J). (gr. -1-k). 16.99 *(978-1-338-24545-5(7)*, Scholastic Pr.) Scholastic, Inc.

—The Three Little Superpigs: Once upon a Time. Evans, Claire, illus. 2019. (Three Little Superpigs Ser.). (ENG., Illus.). 40p. (J). (gr. -1-k). 14.99 *(978-1-338-24548-6(1)*, Scholastic Pr.) Scholastic, Inc.

Evans, Cordelia. Olivia & the Easter Egg Hunt. 2013. (Olivia 8x8 Ser.). lib. bdg. 14.75 *(978-0-606-27062-5(0))* Turtleback.

—Olivia & the Fancy Party. 2014. (Olivia 8x8 Ser.). lib. bdg. 13.55 *(978-0-606-35762-3(9))* Turtleback.

Fairley, Melissa. Ding! Dong! Harland, Jackie, illus. 2011. (ENG.). 12p. (J). (gr. -1-k). 15.95 *(978-1-84898-362-5(X)*, TickTock Books) Octopus Publishing Group GBR. Dist: Independent Pubs. Group.

Fairy Tales- Three little Pigs. 2005. (J). bds. *(978-1-4194-0044-5(4))* Paradise Pr., Inc.

Falconer, Ian. Olivia. 2004. (Olivia Ser.). (J). (gr. k-3). (FRE., Illus.). spiral bd. *(978-0-616-14599-9(3))*; spiral bd. *(978-0-616-07232-5(5))*; spiral bd. *(978-0-616-07233-2(3))* Canadian National Institute for the Blind/Institut National Canadien pour les Aveugles.

—Olivia. 2009. (Los Especiales de A la Orilla del Viento Ser.). (SPA.). 32p. (J). 13.99 *(978-968-16-6346-9(2))* Fondo de Cultura Económcia.

—Olivia. Mlawer, Teresa, tr. 2004. (Olivia Ser.). (SPA., Illus.). (J). (gr. k-2). 16.00 *(978-1-930332-20-1(3)*, LC5675) Lectorum Pubns., Inc.

—Olivia. unabr. ed. 2004. (Classic Board Bks.). (ENG., Illus.). 34p. (J). (gr. -1-k). bds. 8.99 *(978-0-689-87472-7(3)*, Atheneum Bks. for Young Readers) Simon & Schuster Children's Publishing.

—Olivia: Book & CD. Falconer, Ian, illus. 2009. (ENG., Illus.). 40p. (J). (gr. -1-3). 15.99 *(978-1-4169-8034-6(2)*, Atheneum Bks. for Young Readers) Simon & Schuster Children's Publishing.

—Olivia ... & the Missing Toy. Falconer, Ian, illus. 2003. (ENG., Illus.). 42p. (J). (gr. -1-3). 19.99 *(978-0-689-85291-6(6)*, Atheneum Bks. for Young Readers) Simon & Schuster Children's Publishing.

—Olivia & the Fairy Princesses. 2013. (CHI.). 40p. (J). (gr. -1-2). *(978-986-189-389-1(X))* Grimm Cultural Ent., Co., Ltd.

—Olivia & the Fairy Princesses. Falconer, Ian, illus. 2012. (ENG., Illus.). 40p. (J). (gr. -1-3). 19.99 *(978-1-4424-5027-1(4)*, Atheneum Bks. for Young Readers) Simon & Schuster Children's Publishing.

—Olivia fait son Cirque. (Olivia Ser.). 29.95 *(978-2-02-051642-6(X))* Editions du Seuil FRA. Dist: Distribooks, Inc.

—Olivia Forma una Banda. Mlawer, Teresa, tr. from ENG. Falconer, Ian, illus. 2007. (SPA., Illus.). 39p. (J). (gr. -1-3). 17.99 *(978-1-933032-23-8(5))* Lectorum Pubns., Inc.

—Olivia Forms a Band. Falconer, Ian, illus. 2006. (ENG., Illus.). 50p. (J). (gr. -1-3). 19.99 *(978-1-4169-2454-8(X)*, Atheneum Bks. for Young Readers) Simon & Schuster Children's Publishing.

—Olivia Forms a Band: Book & CD. Falconer, Ian, illus. 2009. (ENG., Illus.). 50p. (J). (gr. -1-3). 14.99 *(978-1-4169-8037-7(7)*, Atheneum Bks. for Young Readers) Simon & Schuster Children's Publishing.

—Olivia Goes to Venice. Falconer, Ian, illus. 2010. (ENG., Illus.). 48p. (J). (gr. -1-2). 19.99 *(978-1-4169-9674-3(5)*, Atheneum Bks. for Young Readers) Simon & Schuster Children's Publishing.

—Olivia Helps with Christmas. Falconer, Ian, illus. 2013. (Classic Board Bks.). (ENG., Illus.). 40p. (J). (gr. -1-2). bds. 7.99 *(978-1-4424-9446-6(8)*, Atheneum Bks. for Young Readers) Simon & Schuster Children's Publishing.

—Olivia sait Compter. (Olivia Ser.). 18.95 *(978-2-02-056487-8(4))* Editions du Seuil FRA. Dist: Distribooks, Inc.

—Olivia Saves the Circus. 2004. (Olivia Ser.). (J). (gr. k-2). spiral bd. *(978-0-616-11111-6(8))*; spiral bd. *(978-0-616-11110-9(X))* Canadian National Institute for the Blind/Institut National Canadien pour les Aveugles.

—Olivia Saves the Circus. Falconer, Ian, illus. 2010. (Classic Board Bks.). (ENG., Illus.). 36p. (J). (gr. -1-2). bds. 8.99 *(978-1-4424-1287-3(9)*, Atheneum Bks. for Young Readers) Simon & Schuster Children's Publishing.

—Olivia the Spy. Falconer, Ian, illus. 2017. (ENG., Illus.). 40p. (J). (gr. -1-3). 17.99 *(978-1-4814-5795-8(0)*, Atheneum/Caitlyn Dlouhy Books) Simon & Schuster Children's Publishing.

—Olivia y Las Princesas. 2012. (SPA., Illus.). 32p. (J). (gr. -1-1). 17.99 *(978-1-933032-82-5(0))* Lectorum Pubns., Inc.

Falconer, Ian & Simon and Schuster/LeapFrog Staff. Olivia. 2008. (Olivia Ser.). (J). 11.99 *(978-1-59319-990-6(2))* LeapFrog Enterprises, Inc.

Falconer, Ian, et al. Olivia & Her Great Adventures. Osterhold, Jared & Johnson, Shane L., illus. 2012. (J). *(978-1-4351-4316-6(7)*, Simon Spotlight) Simon Spotlight.

Falk, Barbara Bustetter. Gardener Pig. 2007. (ENG.). 38p. pap. 15.99 *(978-1-4257-2957-8(6))* Xlibris Corp.

Farhat, Michael. Adventures of the Eastside Pigs: Produced by Funnybook Factory. Chan, Carol, ed. 2012. 40p. pap. 19.99 *(978-1-4669-0289-3(2))* Trafford Publishing.

Farnsworth-Simpson, Patricia Ann. Flick the Karate Pig. 2008. 163p. pap. 16.50 *(978-1-4357-2843-1(2))* Lulu Pr., Inc.

Farrell, Liam. The True Story of the Three Little Pigs & the Big Bad Wolf. 2nd rev. ed. 2012. (ENG.). 192p. (J). pap. 13.95 *(978-1-85635-955-9(7))* Mercier Pr., Ltd., The IRL. Dist: Dufour Editions, Inc.

Fenske, Jonathan. A Pig, a Fox, & a Box. 2019. 32p. (J). (gr. k-2). 4.99 *(978-0-593-09464-8(6)*, Penguin Workshop) Penguin Young Readers Group.

—A Pig, a Fox, & Stinky Socks. 2019. (ENG., Illus.). 32p. (J). (gr. k-2). 4.99 *(978-0-593-09597-3(9)*, Penguin Workshop) Penguin Young Readers Group.

—A Pig, a Fox, & Stinky Socks. 2018. (Penguin Young Readers Ser.). (ENG.). 32p. (J). (gr. -1-1). 13.89 *(978-1-64310-420-1(9))* Penworthy Co., LLC, The.

—A Pig, a Fox, & Stinky Socks. 2017. (Penguin Young Readers Level 2 Ser.). lib. bdg. 13.55 *(978-0-606-39771-1(X))* Turtleback.

Ferguson, J. M. Bubbles the Little Pig. 1 vol. 2008. (ENG.). 44p. 24.95 *(978-1-60474-229-9(1))* America Star Bks.

Field, Matthew S. The Three Pigs, Business School, & Wolf Hash Stew. Hedderich, Tom, illus. 2006. (ENG.). (J). 19.95 *(978-0-9761528-1-9(9))* Matting Leah Publishing Co.

The Fight on the Hill: Individual Title Six-Pack. (Story Steps Ser.). (gr. k-2). 23.00 *(978-0-7635-9837-2(2))* Rigby Education.

Filipek, Nina. The Three Little Pigs. O'Toole, Jeanette, illus. 2009. (Fairy Tale Firsts Ser.). 12p. (J). (gr. -1-k). bds. 11.40 *(978-1-60754-693-1(0))* Windmill Bks.

Fisher, Karin, adapted by. Pig, Pig, & Pig: The Classic Fable of the Three Little Pigs, Retold in One-syllable Words. 2003. (J). pap. 7.95 *(978-0-9744343-0-8(2)*, SA-303) Bright Solutions for Dyslexia, LLC.

Fisher, Tina Mollie. Pig's Big Adventure. 2012. 42p. pap. 20.45 *(978-1-4497-5020-6(6)*, WestBow Pr.) Author Solutions, LLC.

Flor Ada, Alma. Dear Peter Rabbit. Tryon, Leslie, illus. 2006. (Stories to Go! Ser.). (J). (gr. k-3). 12.65 *(978-0-7569-7322-3(8))* Perfection Learning Corp.

Florian, Douglas. Pig & Cat Are Pals. 2018. (I Like to Read Ser.). (ENG., Illus.). 32p. (J). (gr. -1-3). 7.99 *(978-0-8234-3938-6(0))* Holiday Hse., Inc.

—Pig & Cat Are Pals. 2019. (I Like to Read Ser.). (ENG.). 29p. (J). (gr. k-1). 17.96 *(978-0-87617-958-1(8))* Penworthy Co., LLC, The.

—Pig Is Big on Books. 2015. (I Like to Read Ser.). (ENG., Illus.). 24p. (J). (gr. -1-3). 7.99 *(978-0-8234-3424-4(9))* Holiday Hse., Inc.

The Flying Pig & the Daredevil Dog: Individual Title Six-Packs. (Action Packs Ser.). 104p. (gr. 3-5). 44.00 *(978-0-7635-2985-7(0))* Rigby Education.

Folgueira, Rodrigo. Ribbit! Bernatene, Poly, illus. 2013. (ENG.). 40p. (J). (gr. -1-k). 16.99 *(978-0-307-98146-2(0)*, Knopf Bks. for Young Readers) Random Hse. Children's Bks.

Forte, Lauren. Olivia Goes to the Library. 2013. (Olivia Ready-To-Read Level 1 Ser.). lib. bdg. 13.55 *(978-0-606-35186-7(8))* Turtleback.

—Olivia Helps Mother Nature. 2014. (Olivia Ready-To-Read Level 1 Ser.). lib. bdg. 13.55 *(978-0-606-35452-3(2))* Turtleback.

—Olivia Makes Memories. 2015. (Olivia 8x8 Ser.). lib. bdg. 13.55 *(978-0-606-37868-0(5))* Turtleback.

French, Vivian. Pig in Love. Archbold, Tim, illus. 2005. 32p. (J). lib. bdg. 9.00 *(978-1-4242-0889-0(0))* Fitzgerald Bks.

French, Vivian & Melling. Iggy Pig's Skippy Day. (ENG., Illus.). 42p. (J). pap. *(978-0-340-71360-0(7))* Hodder & Stoughton.

Fuentes, Marco. Houses for the Three Pigs. 2016. (Spring Forward Ser.). (J). (gr. k). *(978-1-4900-3730-1(6))* Benchmark Education Co.

Gal, Susan. Day by Day. 2012. (ENG., Illus.). 40p. (J). (gr. k-4). E-Book *(978-0-375-98433-4(X)*, Knopf Bks. for Young Readers) Random Hse. Children's Bks.

Galdone, Paul & Galdone, Joanna C. The Three Little Pigs. Galdone, Paul, illus. 2011. (Paul Galdone Nursery Classic Ser.). (ENG., Illus.). 48p. (J). (gr. -1-3). 9.99 *(978-0-547-37020-0(2)*, 1423303, Clarion Bks.) HarperCollins Pubs.

—The Three Little Pigs Book & Cd. 1 vol. Galdone, Paul, illus. 2006. (Paul Galdone Nursery Classic Ser.). (ENG., Illus.). 48p. (J). (gr. -1-3). audio compact disk 10.99 *(978-0-618-73277-7(2)*, 100519, Clarion Bks.) HarperCollins Pubs.

Gallion, Sue Lowell. Pug & Pig Trick-Or-Treat. Wan, Joyce, illus. 2017. (Pug & Pig Ser.). (ENG.). 40p. (J). (gr. -1-3). 18.99 *(978-1-4814-4977-9(X)*, Beach Lane Bks.) Beach Lane Bks.

—Pug Meets Pig. Wan, Joyce, illus. 2016. (Pug & Pig Ser.). (ENG.). 40p. (J). (gr. -1-3). 18.99 *(978-1-4814-2066-2(6)*, Beach Lane Bks.) Beach Lane Bks.

Gallo, Tina. Olivia Plays Soccer. 2013. (Olivia Ready-To-Read Level 1 Ser.). lib. bdg. 13.55 *(978-0-606-32060-3(1))* Turtleback.

—Olivia Wishes on a Star. 2014. (Olivia 8x8 Ser.). lib. bdg. 13.55 *(978-0-606-36118-7(9))* Turtleback.

—The Three Little Pigs: A Wheel-Y Silly Fairy Tale. Bryne, Kelly, illus. 2011. (Little Simon Sillies Ser.). (ENG.). 14p. (J). (gr. -1-1). 6.99 *(978-1-4424-2107-3(X)*, Little Simon) Little Simon.

Galloway, Shannon. The Little Pig That Was Afraid of the Mud. Woodard, Dana, illus. 2007. (J). (gr. -1-3). per. 12.99 *(978-1-59879-244-7(X))* Lifevest Publishing, Inc.

Galvin, Laura. Baby Pig Time to Play. 2008. (Smithsonian Baby Animals Ser.). (ENG., Illus.). 16p. (J). (gr. -1-k). 13.95 *(978-1-59249-788-1(8))* Soundprints.

Galvin, Laura Gates. Baby Pig Time to Play. 2008. (ENG., Illus.). 16p. (J). (gr. -1-k). 6.95 *(978-1-59249-787-4(X))* Soundprints.

Garis, Howard R. Curly & Floppy Twistytail. 2011. 130p. 24.95 *(978-1-4638-9713-0(8))*; pap. 10.95 *(978-1-60664-569-7(2))* Rodgers, Alan Bks.

Gaudet, Mary Kate. Peppa Pig: Coloring & Activity Book & Crayons. 2007. (Peppa Pig Ser.). 32p. (J). pap. 4.99 *(978-0-06-117374-5(6)*, Harper Entertainment) HarperCollins Pubs.

Gay, Marie-Louise. The Three Little Pigs. 1 vol. 2nd ed. 2004. (ENG., Illus.). 32p. (J). (gr. -1-1). pap. 8.95 *(978-0-88899-639-8(X))* Groundwood Bks. CAN. Dist: Publishers Group West (PGW).

Geisert, Arthur, creator. The Giant Seed. 2012. (Stories Without Words Ser.). (ENG., Illus.). 32p. (J). (gr. -1-3). 14.95 *(978-1-59270-115-5(9))* Enchanted Lion Bks., LLC.

—Ice. 2011. (Stories Without Words Ser.). (ENG., Illus.). 32p. (J). (gr. -1-2). 14.95 *(978-1-59270-098-1(5))* Enchanted Lion Bks., LLC.

George, Susie. Let's Go on a Treasure Hunt. 2007. (Peppa Pig Ser.). 24p. (J). pap. 3.99 *(978-0-06-117363-9(0)*, Harper Entertainment) HarperCollins Pubs.

Gibson, Carol Ann. Loopy. 2003. pap. 16.00 *(978-0-8059-6096-9(1))* Dorrance Publishing Co., Inc.

Gonzalo, Angela. The Pig, Bear, & the Pear: The Pear Meets the Pig & Bear. 2013. 44p. pap. 17.45 *(978-1-4624-0576-3(2)*, Inspiring Voices) Author Solutions, LLC.

Graban, Virginia M. & Rasmussen, Jude. 3 Pigs Move On: Pigs on the Road, Pigs in Africa. 2005. (ENG.). 50p. pap. 15.99 *(978-1-4134-1508-7(3))* Xlibris Corp.

Grant, Nicola. Don't Be So Nosy, Posy! Warnes, Tim, illus. 2004. 32p. (J). tchr. ed. 15.95 *(978-1-58925-036-9(2))* Tiger Tales.

Grant, Vicki. Pigboy. 2007. (Orca Currents Ser.). 101p. (gr. 5). 19.95 *(978-0-7569-8067-2(4))* Perfection Learning Corp.

Gravett, Emily. Wolf Won't Bite! Gravett, Emily, illus. 2012. (ENG., Illus.). 32p. (J). (gr. -1-1). 19.99 *(978-1-4424-2763-1(9)*, Simon & Schuster Bks. For Young Readers) Simon & Schuster Bks. For Young Readers.

Graziani, Mary. Fat Pigs Fly! 2007. 24p. per. 24.95 *(978-1-4241-8344-9(8))* America Star Bks.

Greene, Stephanie. Pig Pickin'. 0 vols. Mathieu, Joe, illus. 2013. (Moose & Hildy Ser.: 3). (ENG.). 68p. (J). (gr. 1-3). pap. 9.99 *(978-1-4778-1684-4(4)*, 9781477816844, Two Lions) Amazon Publishing.

Griffin, Adele & Sheinmel, Courtney. Agnes & Clarabelle. 2018. (Read & Bloom Ser.). (J). lib. bdg. 17.20 *(978-0-606-41069-4(4))* Turtleback.

Griffin, Paul. Saving Marty. 2018. (ENG.). 224p. (J). (gr. 5-9). 8.99 *(978-0-399-53908-4(5)*, Puffin Books) Penguin Young Readers Group.

Griner, Jack. Archibald My Pet Pig. Knudson, Dana, illus. 2011. pap. 8.95 *(978-0-9836081-1-0(3))* Canoed Sun Publishing, LLC.

Griswell, Kim T. Rufus Goes to School. Valeri, Gorbachev, illus. 2013. 32p. (J). (gr. -1-1). 16.95 *(978-1-4549-0416-8(X))* Sterling Publishing Co., Inc.

Guarnaccia, Steven. The Three Little Pigs: An Architectural Tale. 2010. (ENG., Illus.). 32p. (J). (gr. -1-2). 24.99 *(978-0-8109-8941-2(7)*, 682901, Abrams Bks. for Young Readers) Abrams, Inc.

Guess, Catherine Ritch. Rudy & the Magic Sleigh. 2006. (Rudy the Red Pig Ser.). (ENG., Illus.). 32p. 14.95 *(978-1-933341-18-7(1))* CRM.

—Rudy el Puerco Rojo. 2006. (SPA & ENG., Illus.). 32p. 14.95 *(978-1-933341-21-7(1))* CRM.

—Rudy the Red Pig. Haynes, Jason & Oke, Rachel, illus. 2006. (ENG.). 32p. (J). 13.95 *(978-1-933341-13-2(0))* CRM.

Guibert, Emmanuel. A Beautiful Cow. 2014. (Ariol Ser.: 4). (J). lib. bdg. 24.50 *(978-0-606-35103-4(5))* Turtleback.

—Happy as a Pig... 2013. (Ariol Ser.: 3). (J). lib. bdg. 24.50 *(978-0-606-32310-9(4))* Turtleback.

Gulemetova, Maria. Beyond the Fence. Gulemetova, Maria, illus. 2018. (Child's Play Library). (Illus.). 36p. (J). *(978-1-84643-931-5(0))*; pap. *(978-1-84643-930-8(2))* Child's Play International Ltd.

Gunderson, Jessica. No Lie, Pigs (and Their Houses) Can Fly! The Story of the Three Little Pigs As Told by the Wolf. Bernardini, Cristian, illus. 2016. (Other Side of the Story Ser.). (ENG.). 24p. (J). (gr. -1-3). lib. bdg. 27.99 *(978-1-4795-8621-9(8)*, 130443, Picture Window Bks.) Capstone.

Haley, Carrie. The Three Little Female Pigs. 2010. (ENG.). 32p. pap. 17.49 *(978-1-4269-3028-7(3))* Trafford Publishing.

Hamilton, Elizabeth L. Pansy Pig's Patience Pit. 2004. (Character Critters Ser.: No. 7). (Illus.). 32p. (J). per. 5.95 *(978-0-9754629-3-5(8)*, Character-in-Action) Quiet Impact, Inc.

Harrington, Claudia. Book 2: Pickles the Very Hungry Pig. Syed, Anoosha, illus. 2016. (Hank the Pet Sitter Ser.). (ENG.). 32p. (J). (gr. -1-3). lib. bdg. 32.79 *(978-1-62402-188-6(3)*, 24555, Calico Chapter Bks) Magic Wagon.

Harris, Brooke. This Little Piggy. Ledger, Bill, illus. 2010. (Rising Readers Ser.). (J). 3.49 *(978-1-60719-696-9(4))* Newmark Learning LLC.

Harrison, Paul. Three Blind Mice Team up with the Three Little Pigs. Epelbaum, Mariano, illus. 2016. (Fairy Tale Mix-Ups Ser.). (ENG.). 24p. (J). (gr. k-2). lib. bdg. 23.99 *(978-1-4109-8301-5(3)*, 132996, Raintree) Capstone.

Hartley, Alicia Byrd. I Like Being Me. Abbott, Amory, illus. 2012. (ENG.). 24p. pap. 15.50 *(978-1-4772-9088-0(5))* AuthorHouse.

Harvey, Alex. Olivia & the Kite Party. Spaziante, Patrick, illus. 2012. (Olivia Ready-To-Read Level 1 Ser.). lib. bdg. 13.55 *(978-0-606-26360-3(8))* Turtleback.

Haskamp, Steve, illus. Este Cerdito. 2005.Tr. of This Little Piggy. (SPA & ENG.). 22p. (J). 9.95 *(978-1-58117-328-4(8)*, Intervisual/Piggy Toes) Bendon, Inc.

Hawkins, Brett, illus. A Triune Tale of Diminutive Swine. 2012. pap. 15.00 *(978-0-9854699-0-0(0))* Rockshow Comedy, Inc.

Hawkins, Colin & Hawkins, Jacqui. Witch Pigs. 2006. (Illus.). 32p. (J). (gr. 1-2). 19.99 *(978-0-224-06467-5(3)*, Jonathan Cape) Penguin Random Hse. GBR. Dist: Trafalgar Square Publishing.

Hearne, Betsy. Wishes, Kisses, & Pigs. 2003. (ENG.). 144p. (J). (gr. 3-7). pap. 6.99 *(978-0-689-86347-9(0)*, Simon & Schuster/Paula Wiseman Bks.) Simon & Schuster/Paula Wiseman Bks.

Heiney, Sue P. Zig the Pig Goes to School. Charles, Akins, illus. l.t. ed. 2004. 32p. (J). 7.00 *(978-0-9761700-0-6(0))* Zig the Pig.

Helakoski, Leslie. Big Pigs. 2014. (ENG., Illus.). 32p. (J). (gr. -1-2). 16.95 *(978-1-62091-023-8(3)*, Astra Young Readers) Astra Publishing Hse.

Herman, Gail. Peppa Pig & Her Best Friend. 2007. (My First I Can Read Bks.). 32p. (J). pap. 3.99 *(978-0-06-117305-9(3)*, Harper Trophy) HarperCollins Pubs.

Hickerson, Joel, illus. ImagineLand's Bubble Gum Trouble, Vol. 1. l.t. ed. 2004. 32p. (J). *(978-0-9765038-0-4(8))* Imagineland, Ltd.

Hillert, Margaret. The Three Little Pigs. Dorenkamp, Michelle, illus. 2016. (BeginningtoRead Ser.). (ENG.). 32p. (J). (-2). lib. bdg. 22.60 *(978-1-59953-789-4(3))* Norwood Hse. Pr.

—Los Tres Cerditos. Jack Pullan & Dorenkamp, Michelle, illus. 2017. (BeginningtoRead Ser.).Tr. of Three Little Pigs. (ENG & SPA.). 32p. (J). (-2). 22.60 *(978-1-59953-852-5(0))* Norwood Hse. Pr.

Hillert, Margaret, et al. Los Tres Cerditos. Dorenkamp, Michelle, illus. 2018. (BeginningtoRead Ser.). (SPA.). 32p. (J). (gr. -1-2). lib. bdg. 22.60 *(978-1-59953-956-0(X))* Norwood Hse. Pr.

Hinkler Studios Staff., ed. Three Little Pigs. 2011. (Fairytale Pop-Ups Ser.). 12p. (J). 12.99 *(978-1-74185-086-4(X))* Hinkler Bks. Pty. Ltd. AUS. Dist: Ideals Pubns.

Hobbie, Holly. Toot & Puddle. (Toot & Puddle Ser.: 1). (ENG., Illus.). 32p. (J). (gr. -1-3). 2010. 8.99 *(978-0-316-08080-4(2))* 2007. 18.99 *(978-0-316-16702-4(9))* Little, Brown Bks. for Young Readers.

—Toot & Puddle: Let It Snow. 2016. (Toot & Puddle Ser.: 11). (ENG.). 32p. (J). (gr. -1-3). 8.99 *(978-0-316-35224-6(1))* Little, Brown Bks. for Young Readers.

—Toot & Puddle: You Are My Sunshine. 2010. (Toot & Puddle Ser.: 3). (ENG., Illus.). 32p. (J). (gr. -1-3). pap. 8.99 *(978-0-316-16703-1(7))* Little, Brown Bks. for Young Readers.

Holden, Pam. Huff & Puff!. 1 vol. Storey, Jim, illus. 2009. (Red Rocket Readers Ser.). (ENG.). 16p. (gr. 2-2). pap. *(978-1-877363-58-0(8)*, Red Rocket Readers) Flying Start Bks.

Hollaway, David. Quigley Mccormick: And the Curse of the Polka Dotted Pig. 3 vols. l.t. ed. 2005. (Illus.). 156p. (J). (gr. -1-3). per. 15.95 *(978-1-933211-54-1(7))* Quackenworth Publishing.

Housel, Debra. Charlotte's Web: An Instructional Guide for Literature. rev. ed. 2015. (Great Works). (ENG., Illus.). 72p. (gr. 3-5). pap. 9.99 *(978-1-4807-6995-3(9))* Shell Educational Publishing.

Howell, Julie Ann. Mrs Owl's Nest of Rhymes. LaGrange, Tiffany, illus. 2008. 24p. pap. 12.95 *(978-0-9818683-8-7(X))* Peppertree Pr., The.

Hulst, W. G. van de & Hulst, Willem G. van de, illus. The Pig under the Pew. 2014. (J). *(978-1-928136-10-1(9))* Inheritance Pubns.

Hupf, Zetta & Hupf, Mitchell. Henry Goes to the Park. 1 vol. Hupf, Zetta, illus. 2009. (Illus.). 33p. pap. 24.95 *(978-1-61546-279-7(1))* America Star Bks.

Imperato, Teresa. This Little Piggy. Haskamp, Steve, illus. 2006. (ENG.). 22p. (J). 9.95 *(978-1-58117-281-2(8)*, Intervisual/Piggy Toes) Bendon, Inc.

Inkpen, Mick. Kipper's A to Z: An Alphabet Adventure. 2006. (Kipper Ser.). (Illus.). 54p. (gr. -1-2). 18.00 *(978-0-7569-6557-0(8))* Perfection Learning Corp.

Jackson, Brenda. Henrietta & the Pot-Bellied Pig. 2005. (J). 16.95 *(978-0-9773146-0-7(X))* Krisaran Publishing Co.

James, Andrea. Adventures at Ja-Mar Farms: Pup-Pup, Padluck & PIG Take a Walk in the Wet Woods. 1 vol. 2010. 48p. 24.95 *(978-1-4512-1005-7(1))* PublishAmerica, Inc.

James, Dalton. The Mudhogs. 2009. 30p. (J). pap. 13.95 *(978-1-4327-4560-8(3))* Outskirts Pr., Inc.

James, Larry W. Captain Petey: An Adventure at Sea. Ramos, Violet M., ed. James, Larry W. & Freshman, Floris R., illus. 2003. 28p. pap. 6.99 *(978-0-9742154-0-2(6))* Cross Pointe Printing.

James, Shilah & James, Michael. Little Land Adventures - Little Pig. Castles, Heather, illus. 2010. 24p. pap. *(978-1-926635-35-4(3))* Adlibbed, Ltd.

Jamieson, Victoria. Olympig! 2016. lib. bdg. 19.65 *(978-0-606-38844-3(3))* Turtleback.

Jeong, SoYun. Lulu the Shy Piglet. Orsolini, Laura, illus. rev. ed. 2014. (MySELF Bookshelf Ser.). (ENG.). 32p. (J). (gr. k-2). pap. 11.94 *(978-1-60357-654-3(1))*; lib. bdg. 25.27 *(978-1-59953-645-3(5))* Norwood Hse. Pr.

Jim Pig Is Mad: Short Vowel i: Level A. 6 vols. (Wright Skills Ser.). 12p. (gr. k-3). 17.95 *(978-0-322-03115-9(X))* Wright Group/McGraw-Hill.

Johns, Linda. The Three Shapely Pigs. 2004. (Shared Connections Ser.). (J). pap., instr.'s gde. ed. 27.00 *(978-1-4108-1614-6(1))* Benchmark Education Co.

—The Three Shapley Pigs. 2004. (Shared Connections Ser.). (J). pap. *(978-1-4108-1638-2(9))* Benchmark Education Co.

Johnson, Angela. Julius. Pilkey, Dav, illus. 2015. 32p. pap. 7.00 *(978-1-61003-548-4(8))* Center for the Collaborative Classroom.

Johnson, K. Ii. Pig Farm: Adventures of Sal & Snapper. 2011. 52p. pap. 31.99 *(978-1-4653-5058-9(6))* Xlibris Corp.

Johnson, Lindsay Lee. Ten Moonstruck Piglets. Cneut, Carll, illus. 2011. (ENG.). 32p. (J). (gr. -1-3). 16.99 *(978-0-618-86866-7(6)*, 100571, Clarion Bks.) HarperCollins Pubs.

Johnson, Maddie. How Tickles Saved Pickles: A True Story. Johnson, Maddie, photos by. 2018. (ENG., Illus.). 40p. (J). (gr. -1-3). 17.99 *(978-1-5344-3662-6(6)*, McElderry, Margaret K. Bks.) McElderry, Margaret K. Bks.

Johnson, Richard, illus. Three Little Pigs. (Flip-Up Fairy Tales Ser.). 24p. (J). 2007. (gr. -1-2). *(978-1-84643-087-9(9))* 2005. pap. *(978-1-904550-21-1(5))* Child's Play International Ltd.

Jones, Brandy. Petunia: The Plump Princess. 1 vol. 2010. 32p. 24.95 *(978-1-4489-4874-1(6))* PublishAmerica, Inc.

Josiah, Iris. Tiny Pig. 2012. (Illus.). 28p. (J). pap. *(978-0-9572728-1-1(2))* Tiny Island Pr.

Joyner, Andrew. Boris for the Win. 2013. (Boris Ser.: 3). lib. bdg. 14.75 *(978-0-606-31976-8(X))* Turtleback.

—Boris Gets a Lizard. 2013. (Boris Ser.: 2). lib. bdg. 14.75 *(978-0-606-31975-1(1))* Turtleback.

—Boris on the Move. 2013. (Boris Ser.: 1). lib. bdg. 14.75 *(978-0-606-31974-4(3))* Turtleback.

—Boris Sees the Light. 2013. (Boris Ser.: 4). lib. bdg. 14.75 *(978-0-606-32363-5(5))* Turtleback.

Jugran, Jan. Ibaby - Rub-a-Dub-Dub. Larranaga, Ana Martin, illus. 2007. (ENG.). 6p. (J). (gr. -1 — 1). 14.99 *(978-1-58476-555-4(0)*, IKIDS) Innovative Kids.

Kadohata, Cynthia. Saucy. Raskin, Marianna, illus. (ENG.). (J). (gr. 3-7). 2021. 320p. pap. 8.99 *(978-1-4424-1279-8(8))* 2020. 304p. 17.99 *(978-1-4424-1278-1(X)*, Atheneum/Caitlyn Dlouhy Books) Simon & Schuster Children's Publishing.

Kasza, Keiko. El Dia de Campo de Don Chancho. (Buenas Noches Ser.). (SPA., Illus.). (J). (gr. 1-3). 8.95 *(978-958-04-1426-1(2))* Norma S.A. COL. Dist: Lectorum Pubns., Inc., Distribuidora Norma, Inc.

—My Lucky Day. Kasza, Keiko, illus. (Illus.). 32p. (J). (gr. -1-3). 2005. pap. 8.99 *(978-0-14-240456-0(X)*, Puffin Books) 2003. 17.99 *(978-0-399-23874-1(3)*, G.P. Putnam's Sons Books for Young Readers) Penguin Young Readers Group.

—My Lucky Day. Kasza, Keiko, illus. 2005. (Illus.). (gr. -1-3). lib. bdg. 16.00 *(978-0-7569-5492-5(4))* Perfection Learning Corp.

—My Lucky Day. 2006. (J). (gr. k-3). 29.95 incl. audio compact disk *(978-0-8045-4136-7(1)*, SACD4136); incl. audio *(978-0-8045-6937-8(1)*, SAC6937) Spoken Arts, Inc.

Kaufmann, Nancy. Bye, Bye! Spetter, Jung-Hee, illus. 2004. (ENG.). 32p. (J). (gr. -1-1). 14.95 *(978-1-886910-95-9(2)*, Lemniscaat) Highlights Pr., c/o Highlights for Children, Inc.

Keiser, Paige. A Friend for Bently. Keiser, Paige, illus. 2019. (ENG., Illus.). 40p. (J). (gr. -1-3). 17.99 *(978-0-06-264332-2(0)*, HarperCollins) HarperCollins Pubs.

Kendall, Jodi. The Unlikely Story of a Pig in the City. Campion, Pascal, illus. (ENG.). (J). (gr. 3-7). 2018. 352p. pap. 9.99 *(978-0-06-248454-3(0))* 2017. 336p. 16.99 *(978-0-06-248453-6(2))* HarperCollins Pubs. (HarperCollins).

—The Unlikely Story of a Pig in the City. 2018. (J). lib. bdg. 17.20 *(978-0-606-41429-6(0))* Turtleback.

Kennemore, Tim. Alice's Birthday Pig. Spoor, Mike, illus. 2008. 54p. (J). (gr. 2-5). 12.00 *(978-0-8028-5335-6(8))* Eerdmans, William B. Publishing Co.

King-Smith, Dick. Lady Lollipop. Barton, Jill, illus. (ENG.). 128p. (J). (gr. 2-4). 2011. 18.69 *(978-0-7636-1269-6(3))* 2003. pap. 8.99 *(978-0-7636-2181-0(1))* Candlewick Pr.

Kinney, Jessica. The Pig Scramble. 1 vol. Brannen, Sarah S., illus. 2011. (ENG.). 36p. (J). 17.95 *(978-1-934031-61-2(5)*, 9b3aac0d-d540-4d58-830c-c0774aab40d2) Islandport Pr., Inc.

Kline, Trish & Donev, Mary. Coming Home: KA Reader 8. 2007. (Illus.). 32p. (J). per. 20.00 *(978-1-934307-01-4(7))* Ghost Hunter Productions.

Kneen, Maggie. The Christmas Surprise. Kneen, Maggie, illus. 2006. (Illus.). 18p. (J). (gr. k-4). reprint ed. 16.00 *(978-0-7567-9837-6(X))* DIANE Publishing Co.

Kneen, Maggie, illus. Some Pig! A Charlotte's Web Picture Book. 2006. (Charlotte's Web Ser.). 32p. (J). (gr. k-2). 17.89 *(978-0-06-078162-0(9))* HarperCollins Pubs.

Knight, Chris. Piggy's Party. 2011. (Illus.). 36p. (gr. 1-2). pap. 17.07 *(978-1-4520-9585-1(X))* AuthorHouse.

Koch, Claus. The Three Little Wolves & the Big Bad Boar. 2011. 68p. pap. 9.99 *(978-1-4520-5321-9(9))* AuthorHouse.

Koenig, Albert. Wood, Hay, & Pigs. Compton, Donna, illus. 2005. (J). 8.99 *(978-1-4183-0078-4(0))* Christ Inspired, Inc.

Kramer, Alan. The Three Little Pigs Wise up & the Princess Prince & the Vegetables. 2011. (Navigators Ser.). (J). pap. *(978-1-61672-962-2(7))* Benchmark Education Co.

Krensky, Stephen. The Three Little Pigs' Sledding Adventure. Shortley, Michele, illus. 2011. 28p. (J). pap. *(978-0-7680-3486-8(8))* SAE Intl.

Kuczenski, Tyler & Schumacher, Dan. Twelve Little Piggies. 2011. 28p. pap. 12.03 *(978-1-4567-5313-9(4))* AuthorHouse.

Kurtz, Chris. The Adventures of a South Pole Pig: A Novel of Snow & Courage. 2015. (ENG., Illus.). 288p. (J). (gr. 5-7).

P Q R

pap. 9.99 *(978-0-544-54070-5(0)*, 1608884, Clarion Bks.) HarperCollins Pubs.

La Rue, Coco. A New Pig in Town. May, Kyla, illus. 2013. 127p. (J). pap. *(978-0-545-46607-3(5))* Scholastic, Inc.

Ladybird Books Staff. Three Little Pigs. (First Fairy Tales Ser.: No. S852-2). (Illus.). (J). (gr. -1-2). pap. 3.95 *(978-0-7214-5059-9(8)*, Dutton Juvenile) Penguin Publishing Group.

Laird, Donivee Martin. The Magic Shark Learns to Cook. Johnson, Carol Ann, illus. 2004. 48p. (J). 9.95 *(978-1-57306-233-6(2))* Bess Pr., Inc.

Landolf, Diane Wright. Hog & Dog. Harris, Jennifer Beck, illus. 2005. (Step into Reading Ser.: Vol. 1). 32p. (J). (gr. -1-1). per. 4.99 *(978-0-375-83165-2(7)*, Random Hse. Bks. for Young Readers) Random Hse. Children's Bks.

Larson, D. J. Pigsley Brew. Larson, D. J., illus. 2003. (Illus.). 39p. (J). (gr. k-2). pap. 5.95 *(978-0-9728234-0-1(9))* Don't Look Publishing.

LaSala, Paige. Pig Kissing. Gullotti, Pat, illus. 2010. 24p. pap. 12.99 *(978-1-4520-2849-1(4))* AuthorHouse.

Latimer, Alex. Pig & Small. 1 vol. 2018. (ENG., Illus.). 32p. (J). (gr. -1-3). pap. 7.95 *(978-1-68263-036-5(6))* Peachtree Publishing Co. Inc.

Lawson, Barbara. Three Little Pigs Go to School. 2012. 28p. pap. 24.95 *(978-1-4626-8185-3(9))* America Star Bks.

Lee, George Douglas. Twyla the Truffle Pig. Lee, Brenda Donaloio, ed. Lee, George Douglas, illus. 2012. (Illus.). 34p. pap. 10.95 *(978-0-9848486-0-7(6))* Electric Theatre Radio Hour.

Lehrhaupt, Adam. Chicken in School. Kober, Shahar, illus. 2017. (ENG.). 40p. (J). (gr. -1-3). 17.99 *(978-0-06-236413-5(8)*, HarperCollins) HarperCollins Pubs.

—Chicken in Space. Kober, Shahar, illus. 2016. (ENG.). 40p. (J). (gr. -1-3). 17.99 *(978-0-06-236412-8(X)*, HarperCollins) HarperCollins Pubs.

Leonard, Barry, ed. The Three Little Pigs. 2003. (Illus.). 12p. (J). (gr. k-4). reprint ed. 17.00 *(978-0-7567-6860-7(8))* DIANE Publishing Co.

—Three Little Pigs. 2006. (Illus.). 61p. (J). (gr. k-4). reprint ed. 25.00 *(978-1-4223-5245-8(5))* DIANE Publishing Co.

Lester, Helen. Me First. Munsinger, Lynn, illus. 2013. (Laugh-Along Lessons Ser.). (ENG.). 32p. (J). (gr. -1-3). 8.99 *(978-0-544-00321-7(7)*, 1526363, Clarion Bks.) HarperCollins Pubs.

—Miss Nelson Is Missing! Munsinger, Lynn, illus. 2015. 32p. pap. 7.00 *(978-1-61003-507-1(0))* Center for the Collaborative Classroom.

Lindgren, Barbro. Benny's Had Enough! Dyssegaard, Elisabeth Kallick, tr. from SWE. Landstrom, Olof, illus. 2005. 28p. (J). (gr. -1-1). reprint ed. 6.95 *(978-91-29-66338-9(5))* R & S Bks. SWE. Dist: Macmillan.

Lindgren, Barbro & Lindgren, B. L. Oink, Oink Benny. Dyssegaard, Elisabeth Kallick, tr. from SWE. Landstrom, Olof, illus. 2008. 28p. (J). (gr. -1-1). 16.00 *(978-91-29-66855-1(7))* R & S Bks. SWE. Dist: Macmillan.

Liu, Eleanor. Lao Li & His Beancurd. 2011. 28p. pap. 21.99 *(978-1-4653-3712-2(1))* Xlibris Corp.

Liz, Pichon. Three Horrid Little Pigs. Liz, Pichon, illus. 2010. (ENG., Illus.). 32p. (J). pap. 7.95 *(978-1-58925-423-7(6))* Tiger Tales.

Lodge, Jo. Cosy Cuddlers: Pig. 2006. (ENG., Illus.). 8p. (J). (gr. -1-k). bds. 7.99 *(978-0-333-98752-0(7))* Macmillan Pubs., Ltd. GBR. Dist: Trafalgar Square Publishing.

Long, Ethan. Pig Has a Plan. (I Like to Read Ser.). (ENG.). (J). (gr. -1-3). 2017. 32p. 4.99 *(978-0-8234-3880-8(5))* 2013. 24p. pap. 7.99 *(978-0-8234-2911-0(3))* Holiday Hse., Inc.

Lowell, Susan & Luna Rising Editors. Los Tres Pequenos Jabalíes: The Three Little Javelinas. Harris, Jim, illus. 2004. (ENG.). 32p. (J). (gr. -1-3). 15.95 *(978-0-87358-661-0(1)*, NP611) Rowman & Littlefield Publishers, Inc.

Lyon, Tammie Speer, illus. This Little Piggy. gif. ed. 2006. 10p. (J). bds. 10.95 *(978-1-57791-212-5(8))* Brighter Minds Children's Publishing.

MacDonald, Alan. The Pig in a Wig. Hess, Paul, illus. 2003. 32p. (J). (gr. k-3). pap. 6.95 *(978-1-56145-299-6(8)*, Q32523) Peachtree Publishing Co. Inc.

MacDonald, Betty. Hello, Mrs. Piggle-Wiggle. Boiger, Alexandra, illus. 2007. (ENG.). 176p. (J). (gr. 3-7). pap. 7.99 *(978-0-06-440149-4(9)*, HarperCollins) HarperCollins Pubs.

—Hello, Mrs. Piggle Wiggle. Boiger, Alexandra, illus. 2007. (ENG.). 176p. (J). (gr. 3-7). 16.99 *(978-0-397-31715-8(8)*, HarperCollins) HarperCollins Pubs.

—Mrs. Piggle-Wiggle. Boiger, Alexandra, illus. rev. ed. 2007. (ENG.). 144p. (J). (gr. 3-7). 16.99 *(978-0-397-31712-7(3))*; pap. 8.99 *(978-0-06-440148-7(0))* HarperCollins Pubs. (HarperCollins).

MacDonald, Betty Bard. Happy Birthday, Mrs. Piggle-Wiggle. Boiger, Alexandra, illus. 2007. (Mrs. Piggle-Wiggle Ser.). 193p. (J). (gr. 3-7). lib. bdg. 16.89 *(978-0-06-072813-7(2))* HarperCollins Pubs.

—Mrs. Piggle-Wiggle's Magic. 2004. (Illus.). 144p. (J). (gr. 2-5). pap. 29.00 incl. audio *(978-1-4000-9001-3(6)*, Listening Library) Random Hse. Audio Publishing Group.

MacKoul, Eva. The Pig Who Didn't Want to Be Pink. 2013. (ENG.). 24p. pap. 12.45 *(978-1-4908-0071-4(9)*, WestBow Pr.) Author Solutions, LLC.

MacLean, Kerry Lee. Peaceful Piggy Meditation. MacLean, Kerry Lee, illus. 2004. (ENG., Illus.). 32p. (J). (gr. -1-3). 9.99 *(978-0-8075-6381-6(1)*, 807563811) Whitman, Albert & Co.

MacLean, Kerry Lee, creator. Pigs Ski over Colorado: The Top Ten Reasons Winter Is the Piggies Favorite Season. 2005. (J). per. 15.95 *(978-0-9652998-7-9(2))* On the Spot! Bks.

Maggiora, Linda Jean. The Three Little Pigs. 2012. 28p. (-18). pap. 11.00 *(978-1-4349-1288-6(4))* Dorrance Publishing Co., Inc.

Malepart, Celine, illus. When Pigs Fly: A Piggy Pop-up Book! 2008. (ENG.). 12p. 16.95 *(978-1-58117-671-1(6)*, Intervisual/Piggy Toes) Bendon, Inc.

Maloney, Brenna. Philomena's New Glasses. 2017. (Illus.). 40p. (J). (gr. -1-1). 17.99 *(978-0-425-28814-6(5)*, Viking Books for Young Readers) Penguin Young Readers Group.

Marko, Cyndi. This Little Piggy: An Owner's Manual. Marko, Cyndi, illus. 2017. (Pix Ser.). (ENG., Illus.). 64p. (J). (gr. 1-4). 14.99 *(978-1-4814-6826-8(X)*, Aladdin) Simon & Schuster Children's Publishing.

Marshall, James. Swine Lake. 2004. (Illus.). (J). (gr. k-5). spiral bd. *(978-0-616-01712-8(X))* Canadian National Institute for the Blind/Institut National Canadien pour les Aveugles.

—The Three Little Pigs. 2015. 32p. pap. 4.00 *(978-1-61003-557-6(7))* Center for the Collaborative Classroom.

McCarroll, Barbara. There's Always Two Sides to Every Story. 2005. 9.00 *(978-0-8059-9917-4(5))* Dorrance Publishing Co., Inc.

McCully, Emily Arnold. Pete Likes Bunny. 2016. (I Like to Read Ser.). (ENG., Illus.). 24p. (J). (gr. -1-3). 6.99 *(978-0-8234-3687-3(X))* Holiday Hse., Inc.

—Pete Won't Eat. 2014. (I Like to Read Ser.). (ENG., Illus.). 24p. (J). (gr. -1-3). pap. 7.99 *(978-0-8234-3183-0(5))* Holiday Hse., Inc.

McDonald, Lisa. The Adventures of Penelope the Tea Cup Pig. 2012. 36p. pap. 32.70 *(978-1-4771-3182-4(5))* Xlibris Corp.

Mcdoogle, Farrah. Olivia Says Good Night. 2016. (Olivia 8x8 Ser.). lib. bdg. 13.55 *(978-0-606-39244-0(0))* Turtleback.

McNaughton, Colin. Cyfres Meurig y Mochyn: M. W. S. G. Williams, Dylan, tr. 2005.Tr. of S. W. A. L. K. (WEL., Illus.). 32p. *(978-1-902416-62-5(7))* Cymdeithas Lyfrau Ceredigion.

—Gôl! Williams, Dylan, tr. McNaughton, Colin, illus. 2005.Tr. of Goal! (WEL., Illus.). 30p. *(978-0-948930-79-9(9))* Cymdeithas Lyfrau Ceredigion.

McNaughton, Colin, et al. Wps! 2005.Tr. of Oops! (WEL., Illus.). 28p. *(978-1-902416-29-8(5))* Cymdeithas Lyfrau Ceredigion.

McPhail, David. Baby Pig Pig Talks. McPhail, David, illus. 2014. (ENG., Illus.). 14p. (J). (— 1). bds. 6.95 *(978-1-58089-597-2(2))* Charlesbridge Publishing, Inc.

—Baby Pig Pig Walks. McPhail, David, illus. 2014. (ENG., Illus.). 14p. (J). (— 1). bds. 6.95 *(978-1-58089-596-5(4))* Charlesbridge Publishing, Inc.

—Big Pig & Little Pig. McPhail, David, illus. 2003. (Green Light Readers Ser.). (ENG., Illus.). 24p. (J). (gr. -1-3). pap. 4.99 *(978-0-15-204857-0(X)*, 1194667, Clarion Bks.) HarperCollins Pubs.

—Big Pig & Little Pig. 2003. (Green Light Readers Level 1 Ser.). (gr. k-3). lib. bdg. 13.50 *(978-0-613-63254-6(0))* Turtleback.

—Big Pig & Little Pig(Cerdo y Cerdito) 2009. (SPA & ENG., Illus.). 32p. (J). (gr. -1-1). 12.99 Houghton Mifflin Harcourt Trade & Reference Pubs.

—Big Pig & Little Pig/Cerdo y Cerdito: Bilingual English-Spanish. McPhail, David, illus. 2009. (Green Light Readers Ser.). (ENG., Illus.). 32p. (J). (gr. -1-3). pap. 4.99 *(978-0-15-206561-4(X)*, 1099026, Clarion Bks.) HarperCollins Pubs.

—Pig Pig Meets the Lion. McPhail, David, illus. 2012. (Illus.). pap. 15.95 *(978-1-60734-080-5(1))*; (ENG., 32p. (J). (gr. -1-3). 15.95 *(978-1-58089-358-9(9))* Charlesbridge Publishing, Inc.

—Pig Pig Returns. McPhail, David, illus. 2011. (ENG., Illus.). 32p. (J). (gr. -1-3). 15.95 *(978-1-58089-356-5(2))* Charlesbridge Publishing, Inc.

Meade, Rita. Edward Gets Messy. Stern, Olga, illus. 2016. (ENG.). 32p. (J). (gr. -1-3). 19.99 *(978-1-4814-3777-6(1)*, Simon & Schuster Bks. For Young Readers) Simon & Schuster Bks. For Young Readers.

Meadows, Michelle. Piggies in the Kitchen. Hoyt, Ard, illus. 2011. (ENG.). 32p. (J). (gr. -1-2). 14.99 *(978-1-4169-3787-6(0)*, Simon & Schuster Bks. For Young Readers) Simon & Schuster Bks. For Young Readers.

Meredith, Christopher. The King & Queen of Slop. 2013. 50p. 23.95 *(978-1-937912-89-5(2))* Cordon Pubns.

Merry, Margaret. The Wise Old Boar. 2009. 72p. pap. 21.50 *(978-1-60693-728-0(6)*, Strategic Bk. Publishing) Strategic Book Publishing & Rights Agency (SBPRA).

Messimer, Wanda Fay. Tiny Teacup & Pot Belly Pig Go to Africa to Meet the 'Great Lion' 2013. 24p. pap. 24.95 *(978-1-4626-8736-7(9))* America Star Bks.

The Midnight Pig, 6 vols., Pack. (Action Packs Ser.). 120p. (gr. 3-5). 44.00 *(978-0-7635-8399-6(5))* Rigby Education.

Miller, Carol. Maurice the Mole: Can You Guess Series. 2007. (ENG., Illus.). 24p. (J). lib. bdg. 18.95 *(978-0-9771641-3-4(6))* Defiance In Print.

Milne, Alan Alexander. In Which Piglet Meets a Heffalump. Shepard, Ernest H., illus. unabr. ed. (Winnie-the-Pooh Ser.). (J). incl. audio *(978-1-57375-014-1(X)*, 70124) Audioscope.

Milway, Alex. Pigsticks & Harold & the Incredible Journey. Milway, Alex, illus. 2015. (Candlewick Sparks Ser.). (ENG., Illus.). 84p. (J). (gr. k-4). pap. 6.99 *(978-0-7636-8105-0(9))* Candlewick Pr.

—Pigsticks & Harold Lost in Time! Milway, Alex, illus. 2017. (Pigsticks & Harold Ser.). (ENG., Illus.). 64p. (J). (gr. k-4). 12.99 *(978-0-7636-8186-9(5))* Candlewick Pr.

Mlawer, Teresa, tr. from ENG. Olivia Se Prepara para la Navidad. Falconer, Ian, illus. 2008.Tr. of Olivia Helps with Christmas. (SPA.). 58p. (J). (gr. k-1). 16.99 *(978-1-933032-42-9(1))* Lectorum Pubns., Inc.

Molly's Magic: Evaluation Guide. 2006. (J). *(978-1-55942-417-2(6))* Witcher Productions.

Montgomery, Lewis B. The Case of the Poisoned Pig (Book 2), No. 2. Wummer, Amy, illus. 2009. (Milo & Jazz Mysteries Ser.). 96p. (J). (gr. 2-6). pap. 6.99 *(978-1-57565-286-3(2)*, dccfda40-f72a-4587-96f6-a30894d647f4, Kane Press) Astra Publishing Hse.

Mr. Pig & Jumbo's Birthday Cake. 2004. (J). per. 15.99 *(978-0-9744205-7-8(3))* Golden Eagle Publishing Hse., Inc.

Mrs Molesworth & Molesworth. Mary Louisa S. The Thirteen Little Black Pigs & Other Stories. 2011. 66p. 16.95 *(978-1-4638-9845-8(2))*; pap. 8.95 *(978-1-4638-0052-9(5))* Rodgers, Alan Bks.

Mullarkey, Lisa. Freckles the Pig. Franco, Paula, illus. 2017. (Farmyard Friends Ser.). (ENG.). 32p. (J). (gr. -1-3). lib. bdg. 32.79 *(978-1-5321-4044-0(4)*, 25516, Calico Chapter Bks) Magic Wagon.

Munsch, Robert. Pigs. Martchenko, Michael, illus. (Classic Munsch Ser.). (J). (gr. -1-2). 2018. (ENG.). 32p. 19.95 *(978-1-77321-032-2(7))* 2018. 32p. pap. 7.95 *(978-1-77321-031-5(9))* 2014. (ENG.). 26p. bds. 7.99 *(978-1-55451-628-5(5)*, 9781554516285) Annick Pr., Ltd. CAN. Dist: Publishers Group West (PGW).

Muntean, Michaela. Do Not EVER Be a Babysitter! Lemaitre, Pascal, illus. 2020. (ENG.). 40p. (J). (gr. -1-3). 17.99 *(978-1-338-28390-7(1)*, Scholastic Pr.) Scholastic, Inc.

—Do Not Open This Book. Lemaitre, Pascal, illus. 2006. (ENG.). 40p. (J). (gr. -1-3). 17.99 *(978-0-439-69839-9(1)*, Scholastic Pr.) Scholastic, Inc.

Murray, Diana. Pizza Pig. 2019. (Step into Reading Ser.). (ENG.). 31p. (J). (gr. k-1). 14.96 *(978-0-87617-968-0(5))* Penworthy Co., LLC, The.

—Pizza Pig. 2018. (Step into Reading Ser.). (Illus.). 32p. (J). (gr. -1-1). pap. 5.99 *(978-1-5247-1334-8(1)*, Random Hse. Bks. for Young Readers) Random Hse. Children's Bks.

Nanette. Oinky the Yellow Pig. 2004. (Life on Granny's Farm Ser.). (J). 12.95 *(978-0-9741269-4-4(2))* St. Bernard Publishing, LLC.

Needham B.Ed, Louise. Flossie's Escape to Freedom. 2010. (Illus.). 44p. pap. 16.99 *(978-1-4490-9385-3(X))* AuthorHouse.

Nelid, Piper. Emilio & the Baby Pig. 1 vol., 1. 2015. (Rosen REAL Readers: STEM & STEAM Collection). (ENG.). 8p. (J). (gr. k-1). pap. 5.46 *(978-1-5081-1404-8(8)*, 1f0639a1-cde5-492e-a011-33dab066c02c, Rosen Classroom) Rosen Publishing Group, Inc., The.

Nero, Molly. Smarty Pig & the Test Taking Terror. Turchan, Monique, illus. 2012. 28p. pap. 12.95 *(978-1-61244-055-2(X))* Halo Publishing International.

Never Bring a Pigout Home. Date not set. 5.95 *(978-0-89868-355-4(6))* ARO Publishing Co.

Newman, Diana Marie. Gramps' Tales: Pig Ride. 2008. 14p. pap. 24.95 *(978-1-4241-9396-7(6))* America Star Bks.

—Gramps' Tales: Pig Ride, 1 vol. 2010. 16p. 24.95 *(978-1-4512-1479-6(0))* PublishAmerica, Inc.

Newth, Rebecca. Tinkum's Dog. Primm, Thomas, illus. 2005. 32p. (J). 15.00 *(978-0-9630310-7-5(4))* Will Hall Bks.

Nicholson, Melissa. Prissy & Pop Big Day Out. 2016. (ENG., Illus.). 32p. (J). (gr. -1-3). 17.99 *(978-0-06-243995-6(2)*, HarperCollins) HarperCollins Pubs.

Nicolle, Ethan. Kill the Devil. 2008. (ENG., Illus.). 120p. (YA). pap. 10.95 *(978-1-59362-099-8(3)*, 0f8a990a-8871-4328-bff9-80d1c3b0cf11) Slave Labor Bks.

Nilsen, Morten. Snyder: The Pig's Tale. Osenchakov, Yuri, illus. 2007. 116p. 24.95 *(978-0-9774906-0-8(2))* Counterbalance Bks.

Nordquist, Donna M. Petey the Pigasaurus. Fortune, Leslie, illus. 2011. 32p. pap. 24.95 *(978-1-4560-6051-0(1))* America Star Bks.

Norman, Kim. Puddle Pug. Yamaguchi, Keika, illus. 2018. 30p. (J). (— 1). bds. 7.95 *(978-1-4549-2715-0(1))* Sterling Publishing Co., Inc.

Norris II, Charles H. Fat Little Ugly Friend. 2008. 12p. per. 24.95 *(978-1-4241-9222-9(6))* America Star Bks.

North, Laura. The Big Bad Wolf & the Robot Pig. 2014. (Race Ahead with Reading Ser.). (ENG., Illus.). 32p. (J). (gr. 2-2). *(978-0-7787-1291-6(5))* Crabtree Publishing Co.

Norton Kreider, Barbara. Mr Squealy Goes to Town. Dimbylow, Jube, illus. 2013. 24p. pap. *(978-1-921883-41-5(3)*, MBS Pr.) Pick-a-Woo Woo Pubs.

—Mr Squealy Makes a Friend. Dimbylow, Jube, illus. 2013. 24p. pap. *(978-1-921883-52-1(9))* Pick-a-Woo Woo Pubs.

—Mr Squealy Meets Scarecrow. Dimbylow, Jube, illus. 2013. 24p. pap. *(978-1-921883-53-8(7))* Pick-a-Woo Woo Pubs.

Numeroff, Laura. Happy Valentine's Day, Mouse! Bond, Felicia, illus. 2019. (If You Give... Ser.). (ENG.). 24p. (J). (gr. -1 — 1). bds. 7.99 *(978-0-06-180432-8(0)*, HarperFestival) HarperCollins Pubs.

—If You Give a Pig a Party. Bond, Felicia, illus. 2005. (If You Give... Ser.). (ENG.). 32p. (J). (gr. -1-2). 19.99 *(978-0-06-028326-1(2))*; lib. bdg. 18.99 *(978-0-06-028327-8(0))* HarperCollins Pubs. (HarperCollins).

—Si le Haces una Fiesta a una Cerdita: If You Give a Pig a Party (Spanish Edition), 1 vol. Bond, Felicia, illus. 2006. (If You Give... Ser.).Tr. of If You Give a Pig a Party. (SPA.). 32p. (J). (gr. -1-3). 17.99 *(978-0-06-081532-5(9)*, HarperCollins) HarperCollins Pubs.

Numeroff, Laura Joffe. If You Give a Pig a Pancake. Bond, Felicia, illus. Date not set. (J). 6.99 *(978-0-694-01430-9(3))* HarperCollins Pubs.

—If You Give a Pig a Pancake Big Book. braille ed. 2004. (Illus.). (J). (gr. k-3). spiral bd. *(978-0-616-07243-1(0))*; spiral bd. *(978-0-616-07244-8(9))* Canadian National Institute for the Blind/Institut National Canadien pour les Aveugles.

—If You Give a Pig a Pumpkin: Book & Doll. Bond, Felicia, illus. Date not set. (J). 19.99 *(978-0-694-01432-3(X))* HarperCollins Pubs.

—Pig Stroller Songs. Bond, Felicia, illus. Date not set. (J). 10.99 *(978-0-694-01428-6(1))* HarperCollins Pubs.

Oddo, Jennifer M. Asim the Awesome Possum: Asim Gets His Awesome. Lamb, T. S., illus. 2012. 36p. 16.95 *(978-0-9855906-2-8(9))* Pie Plate Publishing Co.

Oldenburg, Richard. The Three Little Green Pigs, Llc: A Recycling Pig Tale. Samantha May Cerney, illus. 2013. 28p. 23.50 *(978-1-62516-753-8(9)*, Strategic Bk. Publishing) Strategic Book Publishing & Rights Agency (SBPRA).

—The Three Little Green Pigs, Llc: A Recycling Pig Tale. Cerney, Samantha May, illus. 2013. 28p. pap. 12.50 *(978-1-62516-649-4(4)*, Strategic Bk. Publishing) Strategic Book Publishing & Rights Agency (SBPRA).

Oliver, Ilanit. Olivia & the Best Teacher Ever. 2012. (Olivia 8x8 Ser.). lib. bdg. 13.55 *(978-0-606-26367-2(5))* Turtleback.

Once upon a Time Spanish Version-the Three Little Pigs. 2005. (J). *(978-1-57022-565-9(6))* ECS Learning Systems, Inc.

Ondrias, Rachel. There's a Pig in My Fridge. Scarborough, Casey, illus. 2006. (ENG.). 28p. (J). 16.95 *(978-1-933660-30-1(9)*, Tadpole Pr. 4 Kids) Mystic Harbor Pr., LLC.

Orihuela, Luz. Los Tres Cerditos - the Three Little Pigs. Sarfatti, Esther, tr. Rius, María, illus. 2006. (Bilingual Tales Ser.).Tr. of Three Little Pigs. (ENG & SPA.). 24p. (J). (gr. -1-3). pap. 3.99 *(978-0-439-77382-9(2)*, Scholastic en Espanol) Scholastic, Inc.

Oshiro, Kimberley. The Saga of Simon the Skinny Pig: Simon Saves the Day. Yee, Jeanne, illus. 2012. 38p. pap. 12.50 *(978-1-61170-089-3(2))* Robertson Publishing.

Oulton, Harry. Heather's Piglets. 2017. (Pig Called Heather Ser.: 3). (ENG., Illus.). 240p. (J). (gr. 4-7). pap. 8.99 *(978-1-84812-479-0(1))* Bonnier Publishing GBR. Dist: Independent Pubs. Group.

—The Return of a Pig Called Heather. 2017. (Pig Called Heather Ser.: 2). (ENG., Illus.). 192p. (J). (gr. 4-7). pap. 8.99 *(978-1-84812-473-8(2))* Bonnier Publishing GBR. Dist: Independent Pubs. Group.

Paine, Walter. Cousin John: The Story of a Boy & a Small Smart Pig. Dodson, Bert, illus. 2006. (ENG.). 96p. (J). (gr. 3-9). 17.95 *(978-1-59373-057-4(8))* Bunker Hill Publishing, Inc.

Palatini, Margie. Hogg, Hogg, & Hog. Palatini, Margie, illus. 2011. (ENG., Illus.). 32p. (J). (gr. -1-3). 15.99 *(978-1-4424-0322-2(5)*, Simon & Schuster Bks. For Young Readers) Simon & Schuster Bks. For Young Readers.

—Oink? Cole, Henry, illus. 2006. (ENG.). 40p. (J). (gr. -1-3). 19.99 *(978-0-689-86258-8(X)*, Simon & Schuster Bks. For Young Readers) Simon & Schuster Bks. For Young Readers.

—Under a Pig Tree: A History of the Noble Fruit (a Mixed-Up Book) Groenink, Chuck, illus. 2015. (ENG.). 40p. (J). (gr. -1-3). 16.95 *(978-1-4197-1488-7(0)*, 692301, Abrams Bks. for Young Readers) Abrams, Inc.

Pan, Hui-Mei. Piggy in My Pocket. 2004. (Illus.). 14p. (J). bds. 5.95 *(978-1-887734-96-7(1))* Star Bright Bks., Inc.

—Piggy in My Pocket: Spanish, 1 vol. 2004.Tr. of Piggy in My Pocket. (SPA., Illus.). 32p. (J). bds. 5.95 *(978-1-932065-04-6(0)*, 1-718-784-9112) Star Bright Bks., Inc.

—Piggy in My Pocket: Spanish/English, 1 vol. 2004. (ENG., Illus.). 32p. (J). bds. 5.95 *(978-1-932065-11-4(3))* Star Bright Bks., Inc.

Parkinson, Betsy. The Picky Eater. Clester, Shane, illus. 2018. (Little Boost Ser.). (ENG.). 32p. (J). (gr. -1-2). 14.95 *(978-1-5158-2943-0(X)*, 138476); lib. bdg. 23.99 *(978-1-5158-2942-3(1)*, 138475) Capstone. (Picture Window Bks.).

Parragon Staff, ed. Cerdito. 2010. pap. 4.95 *(978-1-4054-4915-1(2))* Parragon, Inc.

Pastis, Stephan. Beginning Pearls. 2013. lib. bdg. 20.85 *(978-0-606-31764-1(3))* Turtleback.

Paulson, Michael W. The Baker Street Bunch No. 1: A Double Mystery Book. l.t. ed. 2004. (Illus.). 154p. (J). per. *(978-0-9754241-0-0(6))* MiMar Publishing.

—The Baker Street Bunch & the Missing Pig Mystery. l.t. ed. 2004. (Illus.). 90p. (J). per. 3.95 *(978-0-9754241-1-7(4))* MiMar Publishing.

PC Treasures Staff, prod. The Three Little Pigs. 2007. (J). *(978-1-60072-016-1(1))* PC Treasures, Inc.

Penguin Books Staff, ed. The Three Little Pigs. (Fairy Tale Fun Ser.). (J). 3.95 *(978-0-7214-5431-3(3)*, Dutton Juvenile) Penguin Publishing Group.

Pennart, Geoffroy de. SOFIA LA VACA QUE AMABA LA MUSICA. 2005. (SPA.). 40p. (J). (gr. k-2). 22.95 *(978-84-8470-027-2(5))* Corimbo, Editorial S.L. ESP. Dist: Iaconi, Mariuccia Bk. Imports.

Peters, Rob. The Wolf & Pig Report. 2009. (ENG.). 60p. pap. 12.00 *(978-0-557-08112-7(2))* Lulu Pr., Inc.

Peterson, Mary & Rofé, Jennifer. Piggies in the Pumpkin Patch. Peterson, Mary, illus. 2010. (Illus.). 28p. (J). (gr. -1-2). pap. 7.99 *(978-1-57091-461-4(3))* Charlesbridge Publishing, Inc.

Petkovich, David. The Story of Pete the Pig: A Truly Twisted Tail. 2012. 52p. pap. 24.99 *(978-1-4817-0043-6(X))* AuthorHouse.

Petty, Colin, illus. The Three Little Pigs: A Tale about Working Hard. 2006. (J). 6.99 *(978-1-59939-016-1(7))* Cornerstone Pr.

Phelan, Connie. The Little Pink Pig That Was Different. 2009. 16p. pap. 8.95 *(978-1-4389-5180-5(9))* AuthorHouse.

Phelan, Matt. Pignic: A Springtime Book for Kids. Phelan, Matt, illus. 2018. (ENG., Illus.). 32p. (J). (gr. -1-3). 17.99 *(978-0-06-244339-7(9)*, Greenwillow Bks.) HarperCollins Pubs.

Pichon, Liz. The Three Horrid Little Pigs. Pichon, Liz, illus. 2008. (Illus.). 32p. (J). (gr. -1-2). 15.95 *(978-1-58925-077-2(X))* Tiger Tales.

Pig in a Blanket. 2004. (J). per. *(978-1-57657-517-8(9))* Paradise Pr., Inc.

Pinkowski, Vern V. A Twisted Pig's Tale. 2008. 144p. pap. 11.95 *(978-0-595-46595-8(1)*, iUniverse, Inc.) iUniverse, Inc.

Pinkowski, Vernon V. A Twisted Pig's Tale. 2008. 148p. 21.95 *(978-0-595-49022-6(0)*, iUniverse, Inc.) iUniverse, Inc.

Pittar, Gill. Milly, Molly & Betelgeuse (book W/dolls) 2006. 28p. pap. *(978-1-86972-095-7(4))* Milly Molly Bks.

—Milly, Molly & Oink. 28p. 2006. pap. *(978-1-86972-093-3(8))* 2004. (Illus.). *(978-1-86972-002-5(4))* Milly Molly Bks.

Plitt, Kay. Why Isn't Bobby Like Me, Mom? 2010. 32p. 14.75 *(978-1-4269-4038-5(6))* Trafford Publishing.

Pomerantz, Charlotte. The Piggy in the Puddle. Marshall, James, illus. 2018. (Classic Board Bks.). (ENG.). 32p. (J). (gr. -1-k). bds. 8.99 *(978-1-5344-0660-5(3)*, Little Simon) Little Simon.

Ponting, Susan. The Revenge of BB Wolf. 2011. 140p. (gr. -1). 28.98 *(978-1-4567-7528-5(6))*; (Illus.). pap. 17.23 *(978-1-4567-7011-2(X))* AuthorHouse.

Portis, Antoinette. Not a Stick. Portis, Antoinette, illus. 2007. (Not a Box Ser.). (ENG., Illus.). 32p. (J). (gr. -1-1). 15.99 *(978-0-06-112325-2(0)*, HarperCollins) HarperCollins Pubs.

Price, Mathew. Este Cerdito. (SPA.). pap. 3.95 *(978-950-07-2058-8(2))* Editorial Sudamericana S.A. ARG. Dist: Distribooks, Inc.

Priddy, Roger. Where Does Pig Live? A Barnyard Search-And-find Book. 2018. (Search & Find Ser.). (ENG., Illus.). 10p. (J). bds. 9.99 *(978-0-312-52545-3(1)*, 900180399) St. Martin's Pr.

Publications International Ltd. Staff, ed. Record Story Three Little Pigs. 2011. 18p. 17.98 *(978-1-4508-1911-4(7))* Phoenix International Publications, Inc.

Purcell, Susan. The Three Little Pigs, 1 vol. 2017. (Fairy-Tale Phonics Ser.). (ENG.). 24p. (J). (gr. 1-1). 26.27 *(978-1-5081-9379-1(7)*, 895101ac-e033-4385-82e6-eb9b17ce69c5); pap. 9.25 *(978-1-5081-9451-4(3)*, 0ef23af7-2a6b-45a3-85dd-9fda8b9e3233) Rosen Publishing Group, Inc., The. (Windmill Bks.).

Qualey, Marsha. Gracie Laroo at Pig Jubilee. Litten, Kristyna, illus. 2017. (Gracie Laroo Ser.). (ENG.). 40p. (J). (gr. k-2). lib.

bdg. 21.32 *(978-1-5158-1442-9(4)*, 135712, Picture Window Bks.) Capstone.
—Gracie Laroo Goes to School. Litten, Kristyna, illus. 2017. (Gracie Laroo Ser.). (ENG.). 40p. (J). (gr. k-2). lib. bdg. 21.32 *(978-1-5158-1440-5(8)*, 135710, Picture Window Bks.) Capstone.
—Gracie Laroo on the Big Screen. Litten, Kristyna, illus. 2017. (Gracie Laroo Ser.). (ENG.). 40p. (J). (gr. k-2). lib. bdg. 21.32 *(978-1-5158-1441-2(6)*, 135711, Picture Window Bks.) Capstone.
—Gracie Laroo Sets Sail. Litten, Kristyna, illus. 2017. (Gracie Laroo Ser.). (ENG.). 40p. (J). (gr. k-2). lib. bdg. 21.32 *(978-1-5158-1439-9(4)*, 135709, Picture Window Bks.) Capstone.
—The Marvelous, Amazing, Pig-Tastic Gracie Laroo! Litten, Kristyna & Litten, Kristyna, illus. 2018. (Gracie Laroo Ser.). (ENG.). 128p. (J). (gr. k-2). pap., pap. 5.95 *(978-1-5158-1458-0(0)*, 135717, Picture Window Bks.) Capstone.
R. Friend -Panic in the PigPen. 2007. (J). per. *(978-0-9743627-7-9(8))* Sunflower Seeds Pr.
Ransom, Jeanie Franz. Don't Squeal Unless It's a Big Deal: A Tale of Tattletales. Urbanovic, Jackie, illus. 2005. 32p. (J). (ENG.). 14.95 *(978-1-59147-239-1(3))*; (gr. -1-3). pap. 9.95 *(978-1-59147-240-7(7))* American Psychological Assn. (Magination Pr.).
Ray Charles Lockamy, Inez Eason. The Adventures of Tracks & Cookout. 2010. 40p. pap. *(978-1-4269-2159-9(4))* Trafford Publishing (UK) Ltd.
Ressy-Nieves, Cynthia Ann. Keek-A-Poo's Adventures. 2010. 48p. pap. 24.99 *(978-1-4535-1479-5(1))* Xlibris Corp.
RH Disney. The Three Little Pigs (Disney Classic) RH Disney, illus. 2004. (Little Golden Book Ser.). (ENG., Illus.). 24p. (J). (gr. -1-2). 5.99 *(978-0-7364-2312-0(5)*, Golden/Disney) Random Hse. Children's Bks.
Rhiger, Tenna. The Story about How the Spotted Wobblepig Got Its Spots. 2012. 40p. pap. *(978-1-84903-152-3(5))* Schiel & Denver Publishing Ltd.
Rigby Education Staff. Goodness Me, Mr. Magee! (Sails Literacy Ser.). (Illus.). 16p. (gr. 1-2). 27.00 *(978-0-7635-9904-1(2)*, 699042C99) Rigby Education.
—The Three Little Pigs. (Illus.). 16p. (J). pap. 30.00 *(978-0-7635-6442-1(7)*, 764427C99) Rigby Education.
Robe, Adam D. Robbie's Trail Through Adoption. Robe, Kim A., ed. Gavet, Nathalie, illus. 2010. 44p. pap. 23.99 *(978-1-935831-03-7(8))* Robe Communications, Inc.
—Robbie's Trail Through Adoption — Activity Book. Robe, Kim A., ed. Gavet, Nathalie, illus. 2010. 36p. pap. 16.99 *(978-1-935831-04-4(6))* Robe Communications, Inc.
—Robbie's Trail Through Adoption — Adult Guide. Robe, Kim A., ed. Gavet, Nathalie, illus. 2010. 28p. pap. 16.99 *(978-1-935831-05-1(4))* Robe Communications, Inc.
—Robbie's Trail Through Foster Care. Robe, Kim A., ed. Gavet, Nathalie, illus. 2010. 40p. pap. 23.99 *(978-1-935831-00-6(3))* Robe Communications, Inc.
—Robbie's Trail Through Foster Care — Activity Book. Robe, Kim A., ed. Gavet, Nathalie, illus. 2010. 36p. pap. 16.99 *(978-1-935831-01-3(1))* Robe Communications, Inc.
—Robbie's Trail Through Foster Care — Adult Guide. Robe, Kim A., ed. Gavet, Nathalie, illus. 2010. 28p. pap. 16.99 *(978-1-935831-02-0(X))* Robe Communications, Inc.
—Robbie's Trail Through Open Adoption. Robe, Kim A., ed. Gavet, Nathalie, illus. 2010. 44p. pap. 23.99 *(978-1-935831-06-8(2))* Robe Communications, Inc.
Robinson, Hilary. Three Pigs & a Gingerbread Man. Sanfilippo, Simona, illus. 2012. (ENG.). 32p. (J). *(978-0-7787-8026-7(0))*; pap. *(978-0-7787-8037-3(6))* Crabtree Publishing Co.
Robinson, Janie. Preston, the Not-So-Perfect-Pig. Snider, K. C., illus. 2009. 20p. pap. 10.95 *(978-1-935137-84-9(0))* Guardian Angel Publishing, Inc.
Rodda, Emily. Pigs Might Fly. 2019. (Illus.). 128p. 7.99 *(978-1-4607-5374-3(7)*, HarperCollins) HarperCollins Pubs.
Roots, Robert. Prepararse para el Lobo: Los secretos del exito a partir de Los Tres Cerditos. 2005. (SPA.). (YA). *(978-0-9715336-2-2(8))* Roots, Robert.
Rosen, Michael. Oww! Langley, Jonathan, illus. 2004. (ENG.). 32p. (J). (gr. k-2). pap. 9.99 *(978-0-00-712443-5(0)*, HarperCollins Children's Bks.) HarperCollins Pubs. Ltd. GBR. Dist: Independent Pubs. Group.
Rosenthal, Amy Krouse. Little Oink. Corace, Jen, illus. aut. ed. 2009. (ENG.). (J). 14.99 *(978-0-8118-8331-3(0))* Chronicle Bks. LLC.
—Little Oink: (Animal Books for Toddlers, Board Book for Toddlers) Corace, Jen, illus. 2017. (Little Bks.). (ENG.). 24p. (J). bds. 7.99 *(978-1-4521-5319-3(1))* Chronicle Bks. LLC.
Rosie's House, 6 Pack. (Literatura 2000 Ser.). (gr. 2-3). 33.00 *(978-0-7635-0237-9(5))* Rigby Education.
Rottenberg, David Ira & Rottenberg, David Ira. Gwendolyn Goes Hollywood. Anderson, Lesley, illus. 2011. 40p. (J). 16.99 *(978-0-910291-11-8(X))* Cedar Crest Bks.
Rowling, J. K. The Christmas Pig. Field, Jim, illus. 2021. (ENG.). 288p. (J). (gr. 3). 24.99 *(978-1-338-79023-8(4))* Scholastic, Inc.
Rusackas, Francesca. Daddy All Day Long. Burris, Priscilla, tr. Burris, Priscilla, illus. 2004. 32p. (J). (gr. -1-k). lib. bdg. 13.89 *(978-0-06-050285-0(1))* HarperCollins Pubs.
—I Love You All Day Long. Burris, Priscilla, illus. 2004. (ENG.). 32p. (J). (gr. -1-k). reprint ed. pap. 7.99 *(978-0-06-050278-2(9)*, HarperCollins) HarperCollins Pubs.
Rusu, Meredith. Learning to Share. 2018. (Peppa Pig 8x8 Bks). (ENG.). 24p. (J). (gr. -1-k). 13.89 *(978-1-64310-231-3(1))* Penworthy Co., LLC, The.
—Learning to Share. 2018. (Peppa Pig 8X8 Ser.). lib. bdg. 14.75 *(978-0-606-41179-0(8))* Turtleback.
—Peppa Goes Apple Picking. 2018. (Peppa Pig 8x8 Bks). (ENG.). 24p. (J). (gr. -1-1). 13.89 *(978-1-64310-540-6(X))* Penworthy Co., LLC, The.
—Peppa Goes Apple Picking (Peppa Pig), 1 vol. EOne, illus. 2018. (ENG.). 24p. (J). (gr. -1-k). pap. 4.99 *(978-1-338-32781-6(X))* Scholastic, Inc.
—Play Time for Peppa & George (Peppa Pig) EOne, illus. 2016. (ENG.). 32p. (J). (gr. -1-k). 8.99 *(978-1-338-03280-2(1))* Scholastic, Inc.
—The Pumpkin Contest (Peppa Pig: Level 1 Reader), 1 vol. EOne, illus. 2018. (Scholastic Reader, Level 1 Ser.). (ENG.). 32p. (J). (gr. -1-k). pap. 5.99 *(978-1-338-22881-6(1))* Scholastic, Inc.
Rylant, Cynthia. Poppleton. Teague, Mark, illus. 2015. 56p. pap. 4.00 *(978-1-61003-551-4(8))* Center for the Collaborative Classroom.
—Poppleton at Christmas: an Acorn Book (Poppleton #5) Teague, Mark, illus. 2022. (Poppleton Ser.: 5). (ENG.). 64p. (J). (gr. k-2). pap. 4.99 *(978-1-338-56677-2(6))* Scholastic, Inc.
—Poppleton in Fall: an Acorn Book (Poppleton #4), 5. Teague, Mark, illus. 2020. (Poppleton Ser.: 4). (ENG.). 64p. (J). (gr. k-2). pap. 4.99 *(978-1-338-56673-4(3))* Scholastic, Inc.
—Poppleton in Spring (Scholastic Reader, Level 3) Teague, Mark, illus. 2009. (Scholastic Reader, Level 3 Ser.). (ENG.). 48p. (J). (gr. -1-3). pap. 3.99 *(978-0-545-07867-2(9)*, Cartwheel Bks.) Scholastic, Inc.
—Poppleton in Winter. Teague, Mark, illus. 2008. 48p. (gr. -1-3). 14.00 *(978-0-7569-8910-1(8))* Perfection Learning Corp.
—Poppleton in Winter (Scholastic Reader, Level 3) Teague, Mark, illus. 2008. (Scholastic Reader, Level 3 Ser.). (ENG.). 48p. (J). (gr. -1-3). pap. 3.99 *(978-0-545-06823-9(1)*, Cartwheel Bks.) Scholastic, Inc.
—Poppleton Se Divierte. Teague, Mark, illus. 2006. (Poppleton Ser.). (SPA.). 48p. pap. 11.73 *(978-0-15-356487-1(3))* Harcourt Children's Bks.
Sally Spencer. Juanita's Flowers. Phil Brannan & Sunni Brannan, illus. 2009. 32p. pap. 14.49 *(978-1-4389-4841-6(7))* AuthorHouse.
Saltzberg, Barney. Cornelius P. Mud, Are You Ready for School? 2007. (Illus.). (J). *(978-1-4287-4764-7(8))* Candlewick Pr.
Sandu, Anca. Churchill's Tale of Tails, 1 vol. 2016. (ENG., Illus.). 32p. (J). (gr. -1-3). pap. 7.99 *(978-1-56145-782-3(5))* Peachtree Publishing Co. Inc.
Santillo, LuAnn. The Pig. Santillo, LuAnn, ed. 2003. (Half-Pint Kids Readers Ser.). (Illus.). 7p. (J). (gr. -1-1). pap. 1.00 *(978-1-59256-064-6(4))* Half-Pint Kids, Inc.
Sattler, Jennifer. Pig Kahuna Pirates! 2014. (Pig Kahuna Ser.). (ENG., Illus.). 32p. (J). E-Book 6.39 *(978-1-61963-203-5(9)*, Bloomsbury USA Childrens) Bloomsbury Publishing USA.
Scarry, Richard. Richard Scarry's Best Little Board Book Ever. Random House, illus. 2013. (ENG.). 24p. (J). (— 1). bds. 5.99 *(978-0-449-81901-2(9)*, Golden Bks.) Random Hse. Children's Bks.
—Richard Scarry's Postman Pig & His Busy Neighbors. 2015. lib. bdg. 14.75 *(978-0-606-36401-0(3))* Turtleback.
—Richard Scarry's the Night Before the Night Before Christmas! Scarry, Richard, illus. 2014. (ENG., Illus.). 48p. (J). (gr. -1-2). 17.99 *(978-0-385-38804-7(7)*, Golden Bks.) Random Hse. Children's Bks.
Schaefer, Elizabeth. Ballet Lesson. 2014. (Peppa Pig 8X8 Ser.). lib. bdg. 13.55 *(978-0-606-35866-8(8))* Turtleback.
—Ballet Lesson (Peppa Pig) 2018. (ENG.). 24p. (J). (gr. -1-k). pap. 4.99 *(978-1-338-32779-3(8))* Scholastic, Inc.
Scheunemann, Pam. Pig Pens. Nobens, C. A., illus. 2006. (Fact & Fiction Ser.). 24p. (J). pap. 48.42 *(978-1-59679-960-8(9))* ABDO Publishing Co.
Schindel, John. Busy Piggies. Holt, Steven, photos by. 2006. (Busy Book Ser.). (Illus.). 20p. (J). (gr. k — 1). 7.99 *(978-1-58246-169-4(4)*, Tricycle Pr.) Random Hse. Children's Bks.
Scholastic. Around the World with Peppa (Peppa Pig: Scholastic Reader, Level 1) EOne, illus. 2018. (Scholastic Reader, Level 1 Ser.). (ENG.). 32p. (J). (gr. -1-k). pap. 4.99 *(978-1-338-32773-1(9))* Scholastic, Inc.
—Bedtime for Peppa (Peppa Pig) EOne, illus. 2018. (ENG.). 24p. (J). (gr. -1-k). pap. 4.99 *(978-1-338-32774-8(7))* Scholastic, Inc.
—Class Trip (Peppa Pig) 2018. (ENG.). 24p. (J). (gr. -1-k). pap. 4.99 *(978-1-338-32775-5(5))* Scholastic, Inc.
—Dentist Trip (Peppa Pig), 1 vol. Scholastic, illus. 2015. (ENG.). 24p. (J). (gr. -1-k). pap. 4.99 *(978-0-545-89146-2(9))* Scholastic, Inc.
—Family Trip (Peppa Pig) EOne, illus. 2018. (ENG.). 24p. (J). (gr. -1-k). pap. 4.99 *(978-1-338-22875-5(7))* Scholastic, Inc.
—Fun at the Fair: a Sticker Storybook (Peppa Pig) EOne, illus. 2016.Tr. of (Peppa Pig). (ENG.). 24p. (J). (gr. -1-k). pap. 7.99 *(978-1-338-03281-9(X))* Scholastic, Inc.
—Fun with Friends (Peppa Pig) 2013. (ENG.). 16p. (J). (gr. -1-k). pap. 6.99 *(978-0-545-49861-6(9))* Scholastic, Inc.
—George Catches a Cold (Peppa Pig) EOne, illus. 2015. (Geronimo Stilton Cavemice Ser.). (ENG.). 24p. (J). (gr. 2-5). E-Book 7.99 *(978-1-338-05805-5(3))* Scholastic, Inc.
—Good Night, Peppa (Peppa Pig) 2015. (ENG., Illus.). 16p. (J). (gr. -1-k). bds. 7.99 *(978-0-545-88132-6(3))* Scholastic, Inc.
—My Daddy (Peppa Pig) EOne, illus. 2018. (ENG.). 16p. (J). (gr. -1-k). bds. 7.99 *(978-1-338-22878-6(1))* Scholastic, Inc.
—My Mommy (Peppa Pig) 2014. (ENG.). 16p. (J). (gr. -1-k). bds. 7.99 *(978-0-545-46804-6(3))* Scholastic, Inc.
—Peppa Goes Swimming (Peppa Pig) EOne, illus. 2018. (ENG.). 24p. (J). (gr. -1-k). pap. 5.99 *(978-1-338-32783-0(6))* Scholastic, Inc.
—Peppa Phonics Boxed Set (Peppa Pig), 1 vol. 2017. (ENG.). 16p. (J). (gr. -1-k). 12.99 *(978-1-338-13978-5(9))* Scholastic, Inc.
—Peppa's Chalk ABCs (Peppa Pig) 2015. (ENG.). 16p. (J). (gr. -1-1). bds. 10.99 *(978-0-545-82111-7(8))* Scholastic, Inc.
—Peppa's Christmas Wish (Peppa Pig) 2013. (ENG.). 24p. (J). (gr. -1-k). pap. 4.99 *(978-0-545-56511-0(1))* Scholastic, Inc.
—Peppa's Easter Egg Hunt (Peppa Pig) EOne, illus. 2018. (ENG.). 24p. (J). (gr. -1-k). pap. 4.99 *(978-1-338-32784-7(4))* Scholastic, Inc.
—Peppa's Halloween Party (Peppa Pig), 1 vol. EOne, illus. 2016. (ENG.). 24p. (J). (gr. -1-k). pap. 5.99 *(978-0-545-92543-3(6))* Scholastic, Inc.
—Peppa's Storytime Box (Peppa Pig), 1 vol. Scholastic, illus. 2016. (ENG.). 24p. (J). (gr. -1-k). pap., pap. 10.99 *(978-0-545-92544-0(4))* Scholastic, Inc.
—Peppa's Windy Fall Day (Peppa Pig) Scholastic, illus. 2018. (ENG.). 24p. (J). (gr. -1-k). pap. 4.99 *(978-1-338-32787-8(9))* Scholastic, Inc.
—The Story of Peppa Pig (Peppa Pig) (Follow Me Around... Ser.). (ENG.). 32p. (J). 2017. (gr. 3-4). E-Book 27.00 *(978-0-545-75743-0(6))* 2013. (gr. -1-k). 8.99 *(978-0-545-46805-3(1))* Scholastic, Inc.
Scholastic Editors. Bedtime for Peppa. 2015. (Peppa Pig 8X8 Ser.). (Illus.). (J). lib. bdg. 13.55 *(978-0-606-37768-3(9))* Turtleback.
—George Catches a Cold. 2017. (Peppa Pig 8X8 Ser.). (Illus.). (J). lib. bdg. 14.75 *(978-0-606-39735-3(3))* Turtleback.
Scholastic, Inc. Staff. Dentist Trip. 2015. (Peppa Pig 8X8 Ser.). (ENG.). 24p. (J). (gr. -1-k). lib. bdg. 14.75 *(978-0-606-38113-0(9))* Turtleback.
—Night Creatures: A Lift-the-Flap Book. EOne, illus. 2018. (ENG.). 14p. (J). (gr. -1-k). bds. 10.99 *(978-1-338-22879-3(X))* Scholastic, Inc.
—Peppa's Windy Fall Day. 2015. (Peppa Pig 8X8 Ser.). (Illus.). (J). lib. bdg. 13.55 *(978-0-606-37088-2(9))* Turtleback.
Scholastic, Inc. Staff, ed. Class Trip. 2013. (Peppa Pig 8X8 Ser.). lib. bdg. 13.55 *(978-0-606-32021-4(0))* Turtleback.
Scholastic, Inc. Staff & Ladybird Books Staff. Peppa's First Sleepover. 2014. (Peppa Pig 8X8 Ser.). lib. bdg. 13.55 *(978-0-606-36374-7(2))* Turtleback.
Schoolwide, compiled by. Elephant & Piggie: Favorite Characters & Series Grades K-1. 2015. pap. 39.96 *(978-1-62621-826-0(9))* Schoolwide, Inc.
Schwartz, Betty Ann & Seresin, Lynn. Run, Run Piglet: A Follow-Along Book. Ng, Neiko, illus. 2015. (Follow-Along Book Ser.). (ENG.). 10p. (J). (gr. -1 — 1). bds. 9.99 *(978-1-4521-2467-4(1))* Chronicle Bks. LLC.
Schwartz, Corey Rosen. The Three Ninja Pigs. Santat, Dan, illus. 2012. 40p. (J). (gr. k-3). 18.99 *(978-0-399-25514-4(1)*, G.P. Putnam's Sons Books for Young Readers) Penguin Young Readers Group.
Scieszka, Jon. The True Story of the 3 Little Pigs / la Verdadera Historiade Los TresCerditos. 2009. 64p. (J). (gr. k-3). pap. 8.99 *(978-0-14-241447-7(6)*, Puffin Books) Penguin Young Readers Group.
Sebring, Ruthie. Itty's Guinea Pig. 2009. 24p. pap. 24.95 *(978-1-61582-555-4(X))* America Star Bks.
Seibert, Patricia. The Three Little Pigs, Grades Pk - 3. 2005. (Keepsake Stories Ser.: 29).Tr. of Los Tres Cerditos. (ENG., Illus.). 32p. (gr. -1-3). pap. 3.99 *(978-0-7696-3818-8(X)*, 076963818X, Brighter Child) Carson-Dellosa Publishing, LLC.
Seltzer, Eric. Party Pigs! 2019. (Ready-To-Read Ser.). (ENG.). 32p. (J). (gr. k-1). 13.96 *(978-0-87617-998-7(7))* Penworthy Co., LLC, The.
—Party Pigs! Ready-To-Read Pre-Level 1. Disbury, Tom, illus. 2019. (Ready-To-Read Ser.). (ENG.). 32p. (J). (gr. -1-k). 17.99 *(978-1-5344-2879-9(8))*; pap. 4.99 *(978-1-5344-2878-2(X))* Simon Spotlight. (Simon Spotlight).
Sendak, Maurice. Bumble-Ardy. Sendak, Maurice, illus. 2011. (ENG., Illus.). 40p. (J). 17.95 *(978-0-06-205198-1(9)*, HarperCollins) HarperCollins Pubs.
Shaw, Natalie. A Guide to Being a Big Sister. 2014. (Olivia 8x8 Ser.). lib. bdg. 16.00 *(978-0-606-35761-6(0))* Turtleback.
—A Guide to Being a Friend. 2014. (Olivia 8x8 Ser.). lib. bdg. 16.00 *(978-0-606-36117-0(0))* Turtleback.
—I Can Do Anything! 2016. (Illus.). (J). *(978-1-5182-0411-1(2))* Simon & Schuster Children's Publishing.
—I Can Do Anything! 2016. (Olivia 8x8 Ser.). lib. bdg. 13.55 *(978-0-606-38242-7(9))* Turtleback.
—Olivia & the Perfect Valentine. 2013. (Olivia 8x8 Ser.). lib. bdg. 14.75 *(978-0-606-35200-0(7))* Turtleback.
Simmons, Jane. Beryl: a Pig's Tale. 2011. (ENG.). 224p. (J). (gr. 3-7). pap. 13.99 *(978-0-316-04413-4(X))* Little, Brown Bks. for Young Readers.
Simpson, Patrica Ann. Flick the little Runt. 2006. (J). lib. bdg. *(978-0-9779662-6-4(7))* Creative Bk. Pubs.
Sinha, Rhea. Latte's Vacation. Sinha, Rhea, illus. 2011. (Illus.). 20p. pap. 7.50 *(978-1-61170-045-9(0))* Robertson Publishing.
Sleator, William. Interstellar Pig. (Interstellar Pig Ser.: Bk. 1). 196p. (J). (gr. 4-6). pap. 4.99 *(978-0-8072-1381-0(0)*, Listening Library) Random Hse. Audio Publishing Group.
Smart Kidz, creator. This Little Piggy Went to Market. 2013. (Sing N Play Songs Ser.). (ENG., Illus.). (gr. -1). bds. 12.99 *(978-1-891100-09-3(2)*, Smart Kidz) Penton Overseas, Inc.
Smith, Dee. The Pigs of Pineapple Beach Anthology. 2009. (Illus.). 80p. pap. 15.00 *(978-1-59858-961-0(X))* Dog Ear Publishing, LLC.
Smith, Elwood. I'm Not a Pig in Underpants. Smith, Elwood, illus. 2013. (ENG., Illus.). 40p. (J). (gr. -1-k). 18.99 *(978-1-56846-229-5(8)*, 21615, Creative Editions) Creative Co., The.
Smith, Jeffrey B. Stubby. 2006. 15p. 8.28 *(978-1-4116-8215-3(7))* Lulu Pr., Inc.
Smith, John C. Popee the Purple Pig-a-Saurus. 2010. 40p. pap. 16.99 *(978-1-4490-9265-6(3))* AuthorHouse.
Smith, Lynda Faye. The Revenge of the Big Bad Wolf. 2012. pap. 9.95 *(978-0-7414-6529-0(9))* Infinity Publishing.
Snyder, Laurel. Baxter, the Pig Who Wanted to Be Kosher. 2010. (J). pap. 2.46 *(978-1-58246-373-5(5)*, Tricycle Pr.) Ten Speed Pr.
Solomon, Philippa. Settle down for Storytime. 2009. (Illus.). 64p. pap. 23.49 *(978-1-4389-6032-6(8))* AuthorHouse.
Sommer, Carl. Three Little Pigs. Budwine, Greg, illus. 2014. (J). pap. *(978-1-57537-968-5(6))* Advance Publishing, Inc.
—Three Little Pigs Read-Along. 2003. (Another Sommer-Time Story Ser.). (Illus.). 48p. (J). lib. bdg. 23.95 incl. audio *(978-1-57537-761-2(6))* Advance Publishing, Inc.
—Three Little Pigs(Los Tres Cerditos) Budwine, Greg & Vignolo, Enrique, illus. 2009. (Another Sommer-Time Story Bilingual Ser.). (SPA & ENG.). 48p. (J). lib. bdg. 16.95 *(978-1-57537-168-9(5))* Advance Publishing, Inc.
Soo, Kean, illus. The Great Desert Rally. 2015. (March Grand Prix Ser.). (ENG.). 48p. (J). (gr. 3-6). lib. bdg. 33.32 *(978-1-4342-9641-2(5)*, 126927, Capstone Young Readers) Capstone.
Spelman, Cornelia Maude. When I Feel Good about Myself. Parkinson, Kathy, illus. 2003. (Way I Feel Bks.). (ENG.). 24p. (J). (gr. -1-3). pap. 7.99 *(978-0-8075-8901-4(2)*, 807589012) Whitman, Albert & Co.
—When I Miss You. Parkinson, Kathy, illus. 2004. (Way I Feel Bks.). (ENG.). 24p. (J). (gr. -1-3). pap. 9.99 *(978-0-8075-8903-8(9)*, 807589039) Whitman, Albert & Co.
Sperling, Thomas, illus. The Three Little Pigs. 2005. (J). *(978-0-7664-1051-0(X))* Abrams, Inc.
Spinner, Cala. There You Are, Olivia! 2018. (Ready-To-Read Ser.). (ENG.). 32p. (J). (gr. -1-1). 13.89 *(978-1-64310-755-4(0))* Penworthy Co., LLC, The.
—There You Are, Olivia! 2017. (Illus.). (J). *(978-1-5182-5137-5(4)*, Simon Spotlight) Simon Spotlight.
Spratt, R. A. The Adventures of Nanny Piggins. Santat, Dan, illus. 2012. (Nanny Piggins Ser.: 1). (ENG.). 272p. (J). (gr. 3-7). pap. 8.99 *(978-0-316-06818-5(7))* Little, Brown Bks. for Young Readers.
—Nanny Piggins & the Wicked Plan. 2013. (Nanny Piggins Ser.: 2). (ENG.). 320p. (J). (gr. 3-7). pap. 17.99 *(978-0-316-19922-3(2))* Little, Brown Bks. for Young Readers.
Stanek, Linda. The Pig & Miss Prudence, 1 vol. Castillo, Lauren, illus. 2008. (ENG.). 32p. (J). (gr. -1-3). 15.95 *(978-1-59572-125-9(8))* Star Bright Bks., Inc.
Stanton, Elizabeth Rose. Peddles. Stanton, Elizabeth Rose, illus. 2016. (ENG., Illus.). 40p. (J). (gr. -1-3). 17.99 *(978-1-4814-1691-7(X)*, Simon & Schuster Bks. For Young Readers) Simon & Schuster Bks. For Young Readers.
Steele, K-Fai. A Normal Pig. Steele, K-Fai, illus. 2019. (ENG., Illus.). 40p. (J). (gr. -1-3). 17.99 *(978-0-06-274857-7(2)*, Balzer & Bray) HarperCollins Pubs.
Steers, Billy. Tractor Mac Farmers' Market. 2015. (Tractor Mac Ser.). (ENG., Illus.). 32p. (J). (gr. -1-k). 9.99 *(978-0-374-30107-1(7)*, 900138385, Farrar, Straus & Giroux (BYR)) Farrar, Straus & Giroux.
—Tractor Mac Farmers Market: Farmer's Market. Steers, Billy, illus. 2009. (ENG., Illus.). (J). 7.95 *(978-0-9826870-1-7(X))* Tractor Mac Inc.
—Tractor Mac Worth the Wait. 2017. (Tractor Mac Ser.). (ENG., Illus.). 32p. (J). 9.99 *(978-0-374-30115-6(8)*, 900138396, Farrar, Straus & Giroux (BYR)) Farrar, Straus & Giroux.
Steig, William. The Amazing Bone. Steig, William, illus. 2011. (ENG., Illus.). 32p. (J). (gr. k-3). pap. 8.99 *(978-0-312-56421-6(X)*, 900074774) Square Fish.
—Farmer Palmer's Wagon Ride. Steig, William, illus. 2014. (ENG., Illus.). 32p. (J). (gr. -1-3). 9.99 *(978-1-250-05791-4(4)*, 900139546) Square Fish.
Stein, Erin K. Peppa Pig: Family Fun Reusable Sticker Book. 2007. (Peppa Pig Ser.). 12p. (J). pap. 6.99 *(978-0-06-117373-8(8)*, Harper Entertainment) HarperCollins Pubs.
—Peppa Pig: Paint Book. 2007. (Peppa Pig Ser.). 32p. (J). pap. 4.99 *(978-0-06-117376-9(2)*, Harper Entertainment) HarperCollins Pubs.
Steps To Literacy Staff, compiled by. Mercy Watson Collection: Class Pack (4 Titles, 6 Each) 2010. (ENG., Illus.). (J). pap. 136.75 *(978-1-60923-560-4(6))* Steps To Literacy, LLC.
—Mercy Watson Collection: Variety Pack (4 Titles, 1 Each) 2010. (ENG., Illus.). (J). pap. 23.95 *(978-1-60923-559-8(2))* Steps To Literacy, LLC.
Steuerwald, Joy. The Peculiar Pig. Steuerwald, Joy, illus. 2019. (Illus.). 32p. (J). (-k). 17.99 *(978-0-399-54887-1(4)*, Nancy Paulsen Books) Penguin Young Readers Group.
Stolz, Mary. Emmett's Birthday Pig. 32p. (J). (gr. -1-2). Date not set. pap. 5.99 *(978-0-06-443633-5(0))* 2003. (Illus.). 16.89 *(978-0-06-028747-4(0))* HarperCollins Pubs.
Storad, Conrad J. Don't Ever Cross That Road! An Armadillo Story. Jensen, Nathaniel P., illus. 2006. (Sonoran Desert Tails Ser.). 32p. (J). (gr. k-4). 15.95 *(978-1-891795-08-4(2))* RGU Group, The.
Surplice, Holly. I Love You, Little One. Surplice, Holly, illus. 2019. (ENG., Illus.). 24p. (J). (-k). bds. 9.99 *(978-1-5362-0578-7(8))* Candlewick Pr.
Swartz, Patricia. Pig-A-Poo Moves to the Zoo. 2009. (Illus.). 28p. pap. 14.99 *(978-1-4490-4616-3(9))* AuthorHouse.
Tait, Elena. The Twisted Fairy Tale. 2009. 36p. pap. 16.99 *(978-1-4389-2774-9(6))* AuthorHouse.
Teague, Mark. Pigsty, 1 vol. Teague, Mark, illus. 2007. (ENG., Illus.). (J). (gr. -1-3). pap. 9.99 incl. audio compact disk *(978-0-545-00361-2(X))* Scholastic, Inc.
—The Three Little Pigs & the Somewhat Bad Wolf. Teague, Mark, illus. 2013. (ENG., Illus.). 48p. (J). (gr. -1-k). 18.99 *(978-0-439-91501-4(5)*, Orchard Bks.) Scholastic, Inc.
Ted in a Red Bed Kid Kit. 2004. (Kid Kits Ser.). (Illus.). 10p. (J). bds. 9.95 *(978-1-58086-404-6(X))* EDC Publishing.
Testa, Maggie. Olivia & Her Alien Brother. 2014. (Olivia 8x8 Ser.). lib. bdg. 13.55 *(978-0-606-35199-7(X))* Turtleback.
—Olivia & the Rain Dance. 2012. (Olivia Ready-To-Read Level 1 Ser.). lib. bdg. 13.55 *(978-0-606-23688-1(0))* Turtleback.
Thomas, Jan. Pumpkin Trouble. Thomas, Jan, illus. 2011. (ENG., Illus.). 40p. (J). (gr. -1-3). 9.99 *(978-0-06-169284-0(0)*, HarperCollins) HarperCollins Pubs.
Thompson, Kate. I'm Just a Little Pig. Reasoner, Charles E., illus. 2014. (ENG.). 12p. (gr. -1). *(978-1-78244-590-6(0))* Top That! Publishing PLC.
—I'm Just a Little Pig. Green, Barry, illus. 2017. (Googley-Eye Bks.). (ENG.). 12p. (J). (gr. -1-k). bds. 8.99 *(978-1-78445-871-3(6))* Top That! Publishing PLC GBR. Dist: Independent Pubs. Group.
Three Little Pigs. 2005. (J). bds. 3.99 *(978-1-933200-13-2(8))* Family Bks. at Home.
Three Little Pigs. 2004. (Treasure Tree Ser.). (Illus.). 32p. (J). *(978-0-7166-1602-3(5))* World Bk., Inc.
The Three Little Pigs. (Read-Along Ser.). (J). 7.99 incl. audio *(978-1-55723-015-7(3))* Walt Disney Records.
The Three Little Pigs: Lap Book. (Pebble Soup Explorations Ser.). 16p. (gr. -1-18). 21.00 *(978-0-7578-2111-0(1))* Rigby Education.
The Three Little Pigs: Small Book. (Pebble Soup Explorations Ser.). 16p. (gr. -1-18). 5.00 *(978-0-7578-2112-7(X))* Rigby Education.
Tiger Tales. Three Little Pigs. Jatkowska, Ag, illus. 2016. (My First Fairy Tales Ser.). (ENG.). 32p. (J). (gr. -1-2). pap. 8.99 *(978-1-58925-479-4(1))* Tiger Tales.
Tillworth, Mary, adapted by. Pua & Heihei. 2017. (Illus.). 21p. (J). *(978-1-5182-3745-4(2))* Random Hse., Inc.
Timm, Uwe. RENNSCHWEIN RUDI RÜSSEL. (GER.). pap. 16.95 *(978-3-423-70285-0(0))* Deutscher Taschenbuch Verlag GmbH & Co KG DEU. Dist: Distribooks, Inc.
Torgrimsen, Reidun. Timmy's Christmas, a Very Special Pig from Sugar Valley & His Best Friend. 2012. 30p. 24.95 *(978-1-62709-149-7(1))* America Star Bks.
Townsend, Amber C. Once upon a Time. 2007. (J). 7.95 *(978-0-9796978-6-9(7))* G Publishing LLC.
Los tres Cerditos: Lap Book. (Pebble Soup Exploraciones Ser.). (SPA.). 16p. (gr. -1-18). 21.00 *(978-0-7578-1674-1(6))* Rigby Education.

Trivizas, Eugene. The Three Little Wolves & the Big Bad Pig. 2004. (ENG., Illus.). 16p. (J). 24.95 (978-1-4052-0669-3(1)) Farshore GBR. Dist: Trafalgar Square Publishing.

—The Three Little Wolves & the Big Bad Pig: A Pop-up Storybook. Oxenbury, Helen, illus. 2006. 16p. (J). (gr. k-4). reprint ed. 27.00 (978-0-7567-9913-7(9)) DIANE Publishing Co.

—Los Tres Lobitos y el Cochino Feroz. Oxenbury, Helen, illus. 2003. (SPA.). 32p. (J). (gr. k-3). pap. 12.99 (978-980-257-246-5(2), EK1366) Ekare, Ediciones VEN. Dist: Lectorum Pubns., Inc., Kane Miller.

Les Trois Petits Cochons.Tr. of Three Little Pigs. (FRE.). 48p. (J). pap. 12.95 incl. audio compact disk (978-2-89558-053-9(7)) Coffragants CAN. Dist: Penton Overseas, Inc.

Les Trois Petits Cochons. (Musicontes Ser.).Tr. of Three Little Pigs. (FRE.). (J). 24.95 incl. audio (978-2-09-230469-3(0)) Nathan, Fernand FRA. Dist: Distribooks, Inc.

Tsutsumi, Robert Kondo and Dice. The Dam Keeper. 2017. (Dam Keeper Ser.: 1). (ENG., Illus.). 160p. (J). 25.99 (978-1-62672-426-6(1), 900156878, First Second Bks.) Roaring Brook Pr.

Tucker, Stephen. The Three Little Pigs, 2 vols. Sharratt, Nick, illus. 2016. (Lift-The-Flap Fairy Tales Ser.). (ENG.). 24p. (J). (gr. -1-k). bds. 11.99 (978-1-5098-1713-9(1)) Pan Macmillan GBR. Dist: Independent Pubs. Group.

Turner, Daniel. Cinnamon the Adventurous Guinea Pig Goes to Devil's Island. Skinner, Gayle, illus. 2013. (ENG.). 48p. (J). pap. 10.95 (978-1-4787-1753-9(X)) Outskirts Pr., Inc.

Two naughty Piglets. 2006. (J). per. 3.99 (978-1-934004-17-3(0)) Byeway Bks.

Twohy, Mike. Poindexter Makes a Friend. Twohy, Mike, illus. 2011. (ENG., Illus.). 32p. (J). (gr. -1-3). 15.99 (978-1-4424-0965-1(7), Simon & Schuster/Paula Wiseman Bks.) Simon & Schuster/Paula Wiseman Bks.

Tyler, Jenny. Big Pig on a Dig. Cartwright, Stephen, illus. 2004. (Easy Words to Read Ser.). (ENG.). 1p. (J). (gr. 1-18). pap. 6.99 (978-0-7460-3021-9(5)) EDC Publishing.

Usera, Abe. The Pigs & Friends. 2012. 52p. pap. 21.99 (978-1-4685-6152-4(9)) AuthorHouse.

van Genechten, Guido. Alex & the Tart. 2005. (Von Hamm Family Ser.). (Illus.). 32p. (J). (gr. -1-2). 6.95 (978-1-58925-393-3(0)) Tiger Tales.

Van Leeuwen, Jean. Amanda Pig & Her Big Brother Oliver. Schweninger, Ann, illus. (Oliver Pig Ser.). 56p. (J). (gr. k-2). pap. 3.99 (978-0-8072-1341-4(1), Listening Library) Random Hse. Audio Publishing Group.

—Amanda Pig & the Really Hot Day. Schweninger, Ann, illus. 2007. (Oliver & Amanda Ser.). (ENG.). 48p. (J). (gr. 1-3). pap. 4.99 (978-0-14-240775-2(5), Penguin Young Readers) Penguin Young Readers Group.

—Amanda Pig & the Really Hot Day. Schweninger, Ann, illus. 2007. (Oliver & Amanda Ser.). 47p. (J). (gr. -1-3). 11.65 (978-0-7569-8152-5(2)) Perfection Learning Corp.

—Amanda Pig & the Wiggly Tooth. Schweninger, Ann, illus. 2009. (Oliver & Amanda Ser.). (ENG.). 48p. (J). (gr. 1-3). mass mkt. 4.99 (978-0-14-241290-9(2), Penguin Young Readers) Penguin Young Readers Group.

—Amanda Pig, First Grader. Schweninger, Ann, illus. 2007. (Oliver & Amanda Ser.). 40p. (J). (978-1-4287-4781-4(8), Dial) Penguin Publishing Group.

—Amanda Pig, First Grader. Schweninger, Ann, illus. 2009. (Oliver & Amanda Ser.). (ENG.). 48p. (J). (gr. 1-3). mass mkt. 4.99 (978-0-14-241276-3(7), Penguin Young Readers) Penguin Young Readers Group.

—Tales of Oliver Pig. Schweninger, Ann, illus. (Oliver Pig Ser.). 64p. (J). (gr. k-2). pap. 3.99 (978-0-8072-1334-6(9), Listening Library) Random Hse. Audio Publishing Group.

Vasquez, Elisa Irene. My Little Piggy: A Bilingual English-Spanish Children's Book. 2010. 28p. 14.95 (978-1-4490-8716-6(7)) AuthorHouse.

Verville, Claudia. Piggy with the Curly Tail. 2013. 26p. pap. 14.50 (978-1-4817-1270-5(5)) AuthorHouse.

Vidal, Séverine. Mega Pig. Barroux, Stephane, illus. 2015. (Mega Hero Bks.). (ENG.). 28p. (J). (gr. k-2). 12.95 (978-1-77085-636-3(6), 11e8f369-8210-4994-bb03-4439833b7b6a); pap. 6.95 (978-1-77085-652-3(8), 100aae7c-4264-4068-8945-397c167fc0f1) Firefly Bks., Ltd.

Virjan, Emma J. What This Story Needs Is a Bang & a Clang. Virjan, Emma J., illus. 2017. (Pig in a Wig Book Ser.). (ENG., Illus.). 40p. (J). (gr. -1-3). 9.99 (978-0-06-241530-1(1), HarperCollins) HarperCollins Pubs.

—What This Story Needs Is a Vroom & a Zoom. Virjan, Emma J., illus. 2017. (Pig in a Wig Book Ser.). (ENG., Illus.). 40p. (J). (gr. -1-3). 9.99 (978-0-06-249431-3(7), HarperCollins) HarperCollins Pubs.

Vosloo, Isak. Kerneelsie Droom Groot. 2012. 32p. pap. 21.35 (978-1-4772-2329-1(0)) AuthorHouse.

Vosper Jr., William J. Martha the Pig. Jones, Sebastian, illus. 2004. (ENG.). 44p. pap. 17.99 (978-1-4134-3173-5(9)) Xlibris Corp.

Waddell, Martin. Captain Small Pig, 1 vol. Varley, Susan, illus. 2017. (ENG.). 32p. (J). (gr. -1-3). pap. 7.95 (978-1-56145-982-7(8)) Peachtree Publishing Co. Inc.

Walton, Rick. Pig Pigger Piggest. Holder, Jimmy, illus. 2003. (ENG.). 32p. (J). (gr. 1). reprint ed. pap. 6.99 (978-1-58685-318-1(X)) Gibbs Smith, Publisher.

Waterbury, Matthew. The Little Pig. Muro, Jenny, illus. 2013. 16p. pap. 24.95 (978-1-4512-2919-6(4)) America Star Bks.

Watt, Fiona. That's Not My Pig... Its Nose Is Too Fuzzy. Wells, Rachel, illus. 2014. (Usborne Touchy-Feely Board Bks.). (ENG.). 10p. (gr. -1). bds. 9.99 (978-0-7945-2666-5(7), Usborne) EDC Publishing.

Weeks, Sarah. I'm a Pig. Berry, Holly, illus. 2005. 32p. (J). (gr. -1-2). lib. bdg. 16.89 (978-0-06-074344-4(1), Geringer, Laura Book) HarperCollins Pubs.

Weinberg, Jennifer Liberts. This Little Piggy (Disney Junior: Minnie's Bow-Toons) RH Disney, illus. 2014. (Little Golden Book Ser.). (ENG.). 24p. (J). (-k). 4.99 (978-0-7364-3234-4(5), Golden/Disney) Random Hse. Children's Bks.

Weiss, Ellen & Friedman, Mel. Porky & Bess. Winborn, Marsha, illus. 2011. (Step into Reading Ser.). (ENG.). 48p. (J). (gr. 2-4). pap. 5.99 (978-0-375-86113-0(0), Random Hse. Bks. for Young Readers) Random Hse. Children's Bks.

Wesley, Valerie Wilson. Willimena & Mrs. Sweetly's Guinea Pig. 2005. (Illus.). (J). pap. (978-0-7868-1321-6(0)) Hyperion Bks. for Children.

Weston Woods Staff, creator. I Like Me! 2011. 29.95 (978-0-545-23373-6(9)); 18.95 (978-0-545-23376-7(3)); 38.75 (978-0-545-23378-1(X)) Weston Woods Studios, Inc.

—The Three Little Pigs. 2011. 18.95 (978-0-439-72901-7(7)); 38.75 (978-0-439-72902-4(5)) Weston Woods Studios, Inc.

—The True Story of the 3 Little Pigs. 2011. 38.75 (978-0-545-09460-3(7)) Weston Woods Studios, Inc.

Whatley, Bruce. Wait! No Paint! 2005. (ENG., Illus.). 32p. (J). (gr. -1-3). pap. 7.99 (978-0-06-443546-8(6), HarperCollins) HarperCollins Pubs.

Wheeler, Lisa. Invasion of the Pig Sisters: Ready-To-Read Level 3. Ansley, Frank, illus. 2006. (Fitch & Chip Ser.: 4). (ENG.). 48p. (J). (gr. 1-3). pap. 4.99 (978-0-689-84958-9(3), Simon Spotlight) Simon Spotlight.

—Invasion of the Pig Sisters: Ready-To-Read Level 3. Ansley, Frank, illus. 2006. (Fitch & Chip Ser.: 4). (ENG.). 48p. (J). (gr. 1-3). 16.99 (978-0-689-84953-4(2), Simon Spotlight) Simon Spotlight.

—New Pig in Town. Ansley, Frank, illus. 2005. 48p. (J). lib. bdg. 15.00 (978-1-59054-997-1(X)) Fitzgerald Bks.

—New Pig in Town: Ready-To-Read Level 3. Ansley, Frank, illus. 2003. (Fitch & Chip Ser.: 1). (ENG.). 48p. (J). (gr. 1-3). 16.99 (978-0-689-84950-3(8), Atheneum/Richard Jackson Bks.) Simon & Schuster Children's Publishing.

—New Pig in Town: Ready-To-Read Level 3. Ansley, Frank, illus. 2005. (Fitch & Chip Ser.: 1). (ENG.). 48p. (J). (gr. 1-3). pap. 3.99 (978-0-689-84955-8(9), Simon Spotlight) Simon Spotlight.

—When Pigs Fly. Ansley, Frank, illus. 2005. 48p. (J). lib. bdg. 15.00 (978-1-59054-996-4(1)) Fitzgerald Bks.

—When Pigs Fly. Ansley, Frank, illus. 2005. (Fitch & Chip Ser.). 48p. (gr. 1-3). 14.00 (978-0-7569-5472-7(X)) Perfection Learning Corp.

—When Pigs Fly: Ready-To-Read Level 3. Ansley, Frank, illus. 2003. (Fitch & Chip Ser.: 2). (ENG.). 48p. (J). (gr. 1-3). 16.99 (978-0-689-84951-0(6), Atheneum/Richard Jackson Bks.) Simon & Schuster Children's Publishing.

—When Pigs Fly: Ready-To-Read Level 3. Ansley, Frank, illus. 2005. (Fitch & Chip Ser.: 2). (ENG.). 48p. (J). (gr. 1-3). pap. 4.99 (978-0-689-84956-5(7), Simon Spotlight) Simon Spotlight.

—Who's Afraid of Granny Wolf? Ready-To-Read Level 3. Ansley, Frank, illus. 2004. (Fitch & Chip Ser.: 3). (ENG.). 48p. (J). (gr. 1-3). 16.99 (978-0-689-84952-7(4), Simon Spotlight) Simon Spotlight.

—Who's Afraid of Granny Wolf? Ready-To-Read Level 3. Ansley, Frank, illus. 2006. (Fitch & Chip Ser.: 3). (ENG.). 48p. (J). (gr. 1-3). pap. 4.99 (978-0-689-84957-2(5), Simon Spotlight) Simon Spotlight.

Wheiler, Robert. Wink's , Boo, & Who! 2012. 64p. pap. 13.49 (978-1-105-49858-9(1)) Lulu Pr., Inc.

White. Tela di Carlotta. pap. 13.95 (978-88-04-46241-5(8)) Mondadori ITA. Dist: Distribooks, Inc.

White, E. B. Charlotte's Web. Williams, Garth, illus. 2005. (Charming Classics). 192p. (J). pap. 7.99 (978-0-06-084594-0(5), HarperFestival) HarperCollins Pubs.

—Charlotte's Web. movie tie-in ed. 2006. (Charlotte's Web Ser.). (ENG., Illus.). 192p. (J). (gr. 4-7). per. 7.99 (978-0-06-112026-8(X)) HarperCollins Pubs.

—Charlotte's Web. Williams, Garth, illus. movie tie-in ed. 2006. (Charlotte's Web Ser.). (J). 192p. mass mkt. 7.99 (978-0-06-122874-2(5), Harper Trophy);Set. pap. 19.99 (978-0-06-121502-5(3)) HarperCollins Pubs.

—Charlotte's Web. Williams, Garth, illus. 2004. (CHI.). 158p. (YA). pap. (978-957-08-2568-8(5)) Linking Publishing Co., Ltd.

—Charlotte's Web. Williams, Garth, illus. 184p. (J). pap. 5.95 (978-0-8072-8305-9(3), Listening Library) Random Hse. Audio Publishing Group.

—Charlotte's Web. unabr. ed. 2004. 184p. (J). (gr. 3-7). pap. 36.00 incl. audio (978-0-8072-8304-2(5), YYA156SP, Listening Library) Random Hse. Audio Publishing Group.

—Charlotte's Web. 2012. (J). (gr. 3-6). 18.40 (978-0-8085-3772-4(5)) Turtleback.

—Wilbur's Adventure: A Charlotte's Web Picture Book. Kneen, Maggie, illus. 2008. (Charlotte's Web Ser.). 32p. (J). (gr. k-2). lib. bdg. 17.89 (978-0-06-078165-1(3)) HarperCollins Pubs.

White, E. B. & DiCamillo, Kate. Charlotte's Web: A Newbery Honor Award Winner. Williams, Garth, illus. 2012. (ENG.). (J). (gr. 3-7). 192p. 9.99 (978-0-06-112495-2(8)); 192p. 17.99 (978-0-06-026385-0(7)); 384p. pap. 8.99 (978-0-06-440055-8(7)) HarperCollins Pubs. (HarperCollins).

—Charlotte's Web Read-Aloud Edition: A Newbery Honor Award Winner. Williams, Garth, illus. 2006. (ENG.). 192p. (J). (gr. 3-7). 17.99 (978-0-06-088261-7(1), HarperCollins) HarperCollins Pubs.

Whitfield, Willie. Big Pigpen Willie's Inheritance. 2006. (Illus.). 40p. (J). (gr. -1-3). pap. 12.95 (978-1-56167-958-4(5)) American Literary Pr.

Wiesner, David. Los Tres Cerditos. 2003.Tr. of Three Little Pigs. (SPA.). 40p. (J). (gr. k-2). 21.99 (978-84-261-3291-8(X)) Juventud, Editorial ESP. Dist: Lectorum Pubns., Inc.

Wild, Margaret. This Little Piggy Went Dancing. Niland, Deborah, illus. 2014. (ENG.). 24p. (J). (-k). 15.99 (978-1-74331-511-8(2)) Allen & Unwin AUS. Dist: Independent Pubs. Group.

Wild, Margaret & Brooks, Ron. Old Pig. 2017. (ENG., Illus.). 32p. (J). (gr. -1-1). 17.99 (978-1-76029-389-5(X)) Allen & Unwin AUS. Dist: Independent Pubs. Group.

Wilhelm, Hans. Pigs in a Blanket (Board Books for Toddlers, Bedtime Stories, Goodnight Board Book) Salcedo, Erica, illus. 2019. (Pigs in A Ser.). (ENG.). 14p. (J). (gr. -1 — 1). bds. 9.99 (978-1-4521-6451-9(7)) Chronicle Bks. LLC.

Willems, Mo. A Big Guy Took My Ball!-An Elephant & Piggie Book. 2013. (Elephant & Piggie Book Ser.: 19). (ENG., Illus.). 64p. (J). (gr. 1-3). 10.99 (978-1-4231-7491-2(7), Hyperion Books for Children) Disney Publishing Worldwide.

—Can I Play Too? 2012. (Elephant & Piggie Bks.). (CHI & JPN.). (J). (gr. -1-3). pap. (978-986-189-329-7(6)) Grimm Cultural Ent., Co., Ltd.

—Can I Play Too?-An Elephant & Piggie Book. 2010. (Elephant & Piggie Book Ser.). (ENG., Illus.). 64p. (J). (gr. -1-k). 9.99 (978-1-4231-1991-3(6), Hyperion Books for Children) Disney Publishing Worldwide.

—¿Debo Compartir Mi Helado?-An Elephant & Piggie Book, Spanish Edition. 2015. (Elephant & Piggie Book Ser.). (SPA., Illus.). 64p. (J). (gr. -1-k). 10.99 (978-1-4847-2291-6(4), Hyperion Books for Children) Disney Publishing Worldwide.

—Elephant & Piggie: Are You Ready to Play Outside. 2015. (CHI.). (J). (978-7-5125-0740-1(2)) International Culture Publishing Corp.

—Elephant & Piggie: Happy Pig Day. 2015. (CHI.). (J). (978-7-5125-0741-8(0)) International Culture Publishing Corp.

—Elephant & Piggie: I Broke My Trunk. 2015. (CHI.). (J). (978-7-5125-0743-2(7)) International Culture Publishing Corp.

—Elephant & Piggie: I Love My New Toy. 2015. (CHI.). (J). (978-7-5125-0744-9(5)) International Culture Publishing Corp.

—Elephant & Piggie: Pigs Make Me Sneeze. 2015. (CHI.). (J). (978-7-5125-0742-5(9)) International Culture Publishing Corp.

—An Elephant & Piggie Biggie! 2017. (Elephant & Piggie Book Ser.). (ENG., Illus.). 320p. (J). (gr. 1-3). 16.99 (978-1-4847-9967-3(4), Hyperion Books for Children) Disney Publishing Worldwide.

—An Elephant & Piggie Biggie Volume 2! 2019. (Elephant & Piggie Book Ser.). (ENG., Illus.). 320p. (J). (gr. 1-3). 16.99 (978-1-368-04570-4(7), Hyperion Books for Children) Disney Publishing Worldwide.

—An Elephant & Piggie Biggie! Volume 3. 2020. (Elephant & Piggie Book Ser.). (ENG.). 320p. (J). (gr. 1-3). 16.99 (978-1-368-05715-8(2), Hyperion Books for Children) Disney Publishing Worldwide.

—An Elephant & Piggie Biggie! Volume 4. 2021. (Elephant & Piggie Book Ser.). (ENG.). 320p. (J). (gr. 1-3). 16.99 (978-1-368-07112-3(0), Hyperion Books for Children) Disney Publishing Worldwide.

—An Elephant & Piggie Biggie! Volume 5. 2022. (Elephant & Piggie Book Ser.). (ENG.). 320p. (J). (gr. 1-3). 16.99 (978-1-368-07224-3(0), Hyperion Books for Children) Disney Publishing Worldwide.

—Elephant & Piggie: the Complete Collection-An Elephant & Piggie Book. 2018. (Elephant & Piggie Book Ser.). (ENG., Illus.). 1600p. (J). (gr. 1-3). 150.00 (978-1-368-02131-9(X), Hyperion Books for Children) Disney Publishing Worldwide.

—Elephants Cannot Dance! 2012. (Elephant & Piggie Bks.). (CHI & ENG.). (J). pap. (978-986-189-325-9(3)) Grimm Cultural Ent., Co., Ltd.

—Elephants Cannot Dance! 2011. (ENG & KOR.). (J). (978-89-7184-930-9(4)) Pu-Reun-Sup Publishing Co., Ltd.

—Elephants Cannot Dance!-An Elephant & Piggie Book. 2009. (Elephant & Piggie Book Ser.: 9). (ENG., Illus.). 64p. (J). (gr. -1-k). 10.99 (978-1-4231-1410-9(8), Hyperion Books for Children) Disney Publishing Worldwide.

—¡Esperar No Es Fácil!-An Elephant & Piggie Book, Spanish Edition. 2017. (Elephant & Piggie Book Ser.). (ENG., Illus.). 64p. (J). (gr. 1-k). 10.99 (978-1-4847-8698-7(X), Hyperion Books for Children) Disney Publishing Worldwide.

—¡Estamos en un Libro!-An Elephant & Piggie Book, Spanish Edition. 2015. (Elephant & Piggie Book Ser.). (ENG., Illus.). 64p. (J). (gr. 1-3). 9.99 (978-1-4847-2288-6(4), Hyperion Books for Children) Disney Publishing Worldwide.

—Happy Pig Day!-An Elephant & Piggie Book. 2011. (Elephant & Piggie Book Ser.: 15). (ENG., Illus.). 64p. (J). (gr. -1-k). 9.99 (978-1-4231-4342-0(6), Hyperion Books for Children) Disney Publishing Worldwide.

—¡Hoy Volaré!-An Elephant & Piggie Book, Spanish Edition. 2015. (Elephant & Piggie Book Ser.). (ENG., Illus.). 64p. (J). (gr. 1-k). 9.99 (978-1-4847-2287-9(6), Hyperion Books for Children) Disney Publishing Worldwide.

—I Am Going!-An Elephant & Piggie Book. 2010. (Elephant & Piggie Book Ser.: 11). (ENG., Illus.). 64p. (J). (gr. -1-k). 9.99 (978-1-4231-1990-6(8), Hyperion Books for Children) Disney Publishing Worldwide.

—I Am Invited to a Party!-An Elephant & Piggie Book. rev. ed. 2007. (Elephant & Piggie Book Ser.). (ENG., Illus.). 64p. (J). (gr. -1-k). 9.99 (978-1-4231-0687-6(3), Hyperion Books for Children) Disney Publishing Worldwide.

—I Broke My Trunk!-An Elephant & Piggie Book. 2011. (Elephant & Piggie Book Ser.). (ENG., Illus.). 64p. (J). (gr. -1-k). 9.99 (978-1-4231-3309-4(9), Hyperion Books for Children) Disney Publishing Worldwide.

—I Love My New Toy!-An Elephant & Piggie Book. 2008. (Elephant & Piggie Book Ser.). (ENG., Illus.). 64p. (J). (gr. -1-k). 9.99 (978-1-4231-0961-7(9), Hyperion Books for Children) Disney Publishing Worldwide.

—I Really Like Slop!-An Elephant & Piggie Book. 2015. (Elephant & Piggie Book Ser.: 24). (ENG., Illus.). 64p. (J). (gr. 1-3). 10.99 (978-1-4847-2262-6(0), Hyperion Books for Children) Disney Publishing Worldwide.

—I Will Surprise My Friend!-An Elephant & Piggie Book. 2008. (Elephant & Piggie Book Ser.). (ENG., Illus.). 64p. (J). (gr. -1-k). 10.99 (978-1-4231-0962-4(7), Hyperion Books for Children) Disney Publishing Worldwide.

—I Will Take a Nap!-An Elephant & Piggie Book. 2015. (Elephant & Piggie Book Ser.: 23). (ENG., Illus.). 64p. (J). (gr. 1-3). 9.99 (978-1-4847-1630-4(2), Hyperion Books for Children) Disney Publishing Worldwide.

—I'm a Frog!-An Elephant & Piggie Book. 2013. (Elephant & Piggie Book Ser.: 20). (ENG., Illus.). 64p. (J). (gr. 1-3). 9.99 (978-1-4231-8305-1(3), Hyperion Books for Children) Disney Publishing Worldwide.

—Let's Go for a Drive!-An Elephant & Piggie Book. 2012. (Elephant & Piggie Book Ser.: 18). (ENG., Illus.). 64p. (J). (gr. -1-k). 9.99 (978-1-4231-6482-1(2), Hyperion Books for Children) Disney Publishing Worldwide.

—Listen to My Trumpet!-An Elephant & Piggie Book. 2012. (Elephant & Piggie Book Ser.: 17). (ENG., Illus.). 64p. (J). (gr. -1-k). 9.99 (978-1-4231-5404-4(5), Hyperion Books for Children) Disney Publishing Worldwide.

—My Friend Is Sad-An Elephant & Piggie Book. 2007. (Elephant & Piggie Book Ser.). (ENG., Illus.). 64p. (J). (gr. -1-k). 9.99 (978-1-4231-0297-7(5), Hyperion Books for Children) Disney Publishing Worldwide.

—Pigs Make Me Sneeze!-An Elephant & Piggie Book. 2009. (Elephant & Piggie Book Ser.: 10). (ENG., Illus.). 64p. (J). (gr. -1-k). 9.99 (978-1-4231-1411-6(6), Hyperion Books for Children) Disney Publishing Worldwide.

—Should I Share My Ice Cream?-An Elephant & Piggie Book. 2011. (Elephant & Piggie Book Ser.). (ENG., Illus.). 64p. (J). (gr. -1-k). 9.99 (978-1-4231-4343-7(4), Hyperion Books for Children) Disney Publishing Worldwide.

—Thank You Book, the-An Elephant & Piggie Book. 2016. (Elephant & Piggie Book Ser.: 25). (ENG., Illus.). 64p. (J). (gr. 1-3). 9.99 (978-1-4231-7828-6(9), Hyperion Books for Children) Disney Publishing Worldwide.

—There Is a Bird on Your Head!-An Elephant & Piggie Book. rev. ed. 2007. (Elephant & Piggie Book Ser.). (ENG., Illus.). 64p. (J). (gr. -1-k). 10.99 (978-1-4231-0686-9(5), Hyperion Books for Children) Disney Publishing Worldwide.

—¡Tienes un Pájaro en la Cabeza!-An Elephant & Piggie Book, Spanish Edition. 2017. (Elephant & Piggie Book Ser.). (SPA., Illus.). 64p. (J). (gr. 1-k). 10.99 (978-1-4847-8697-0(1), Hyperion Books for Children) Disney Publishing Worldwide.

—Today I Will Fly!-An Elephant & Piggie Book. 2007. (Elephant & Piggie Book Ser.). (ENG., Illus.). 64p. (J). (gr. -1-k). 9.99 (978-1-4231-0295-3(9), Hyperion Books for Children) Disney Publishing Worldwide.

—¡un Tipo Grande Se Llevó Mi Pelota!-An Elephant & Piggie Book, Spanish Edition. 2015. (Elephant & Piggie Book Ser.). (SPA., Illus.). 64p. (J). (gr. 1-k). 9.99 (978-1-4847-2285-5(X), Hyperion Books for Children) Disney Publishing Worldwide.

—Waiting Is Not Easy!-An Elephant & Piggie Book. 2014. (Elephant & Piggie Book Ser.). (ENG., Illus.). 64p. (J). (gr. 1-3). 10.99 (978-1-4231-9957-1(X), Hyperion Books for Children) Disney Publishing Worldwide.

—Watch Me Throw the Ball!-An Elephant & Piggie Book. 2009. (Elephant & Piggie Book Ser.: 8). (ENG., Illus.). 64p. (J). (gr. -1-k). 9.99 (978-1-4231-1348-5(9), Hyperion Books for Children) Disney Publishing Worldwide.

—We Are in a Book!-An Elephant & Piggie Book. 2010. (Elephant & Piggie Book Ser.). (ENG., Illus.). 64p. (J). (gr. -1-k). 9.99 (978-1-4231-3308-7(0), Hyperion Books for Children) Disney Publishing Worldwide.

Williams, Becky. Good Night Little Piggy. Howarth, Daniel, illus. 2007. (Night Light Book Ser.). 10p. (gr. -1-k). bds. (978-1-84666-129-7(3), Tide Mill Pr.) Top That! Publishing PLC.

Williams, Billie A. Fourteen Is Too Many: The Survivors. 2013. 24p. pap. 24.95 (978-1-63004-179-3(3)) America Star Bks.

Williams, Mark. Hooty & Pig: The Missing Christmas Pudding. Garrett, Keith, illus. 2013. 24p. pap. (978-1-78132-133-1(7)) SilverWood Bks.

Williams, Rose. Tres Porculi. L and L Enterprises, ed. Este, James, illus. 2006. (LAT.). spiral bd. 18.00 (978-0-9760046-5-3(8)) L & L Enterprises.

Williams, Rozanne. Pigs. 2017. (Learn-To-Read Ser.). (ENG., Illus.). (J). pap. 3.49 (978-1-68310-198-7(7)) Pacific Learning, Inc.

Wilson, Karma. Hogwash! McMullan, Jim, illus. 2011. (ENG.). 40p. (J). (gr. -1-3). 18.99 (978-0-316-98840-7(5)) Little, Brown Bks. for Young Readers.

Winter, Milo, illus. The Three Little Pigs - Shape Book. 2008. (Children's Die-Cut Shape Book Ser.). (ENG.). 16p. (J). (gr. -1-3). per. 10.95 (978-1-59583-265-8(3), 9781595832658, Green Tiger Pr.) Laughing Elephant.

Witkowski, Teri. Bunny & Piggy at the Beach. Ackley, Peggy Jo, illus. 2005. (J). (978-1-58485-961-1(X)) American Girl Publishing, Inc.

Wojtowycz, David. Let's Play, Dudley! Colors. 2003. (Dudley Ser.). (Illus.). (J). 3.95 (978-1-58925-667-5(0)) Tiger Tales.

Wolfe, Jane. Messy Pig. Benham, Tors, illus. 2013. 8p. (J). (gr. -1-k). bds. 6.99 (978-1-84322-777-9(0), Armadillo) Anness Publishing GBR. Dist: National Bk. Network.

Wood, Audrey. Piggy Pie Po. Wood, Audrey & Wood, Don, illus. (ENG.). 32p. (J). (gr. -1-3). 2018. pap. 9.99 (978-1-328-88612-5(3), 1698482) 2010. 17.99 (978-0-15-202494-9(8), 1192966) HarperCollins Pubs. (Clarion Bks.).

—Piggy Pie Po. 2018. lib. bdg. 18.40 (978-0-606-41002-1(3)) Turtleback.

Wood, Audrey & Wood, Don. Piggies Board Book. Wood, Don, illus. 2016. (ENG., Illus.). 30p. (J). (— 1). bds. 7.99 (978-0-544-79114-5(2), 1639281, Clarion Bks.) HarperCollins Pubs.

Yamaguchi, Kristi. Dream Big, Little Pig! Bowers, Tim, illus. 32p. (J). (gr. -1-3). 2022. 7.99 (978-1-7282-5259-9(8)) 2011. 16.99 (978-1-4022-5275-4(7)) Sourcebooks, Inc. (Sourcebooks Jabberwocky).

—It's a Big World, Little Pig! Bowers, Tim, illus. 32p. (J). (gr. -1-3). 2022. 7.99 (978-1-7282-5260-5(1)) 2012. 16.99 (978-1-4022-6644-7(8)) Sourcebooks, Inc. (Sourcebooks Jabberwocky).

Yonge, Charlotte M. The Stokesley Secret. 2005. 28.95 (978-1-4218-0319-7(4), 1st World Library - Literary Society) 1st World Publishing, Inc.

Young, Cynthia Anne. The Muddy Little Piggy's. 2011. 16p. pap. 24.95 (978-1-4560-8090-7(3)) America Star Bks.

Young, Polly G. Pokey Pig's Picnic. Raymond, Janet Y., illus. 2007. (J). pap. 15.00 (978-0-8059-7298-6(6)) Dorrance Publishing Co., Inc.

Zuill, Andrea & Zuill, Andrea. Business Pig. 2018. (Illus.). 32p. (J). (gr. -1-2). 16.95 (978-1-4549-2684-9(8)) Sterling Publishing Co., Inc.

PIGS—POETRY

Wohnoutka, Mike, illus. This Little Piggy. 2005. (J). (978-1-58987-106-9(5)) Kindermusik International.

PIKAS

Shaffer, Lindsay. Pikas. 2019. (Animals of the Mountains Ser.). (ENG., Illus.). 24p. (J). (gr. k-3). lib. bdg. 26.95 (978-1-64487-016-7(9), Blastoff! Readers) Bellwether Media.

PIKE, ZEBULON MONTGOMERY, 1779-1813

Calvert, Patricia. Zebulon Pike: Lost in the Rockies, 1 vol. 2006. (Great Explorations Ser.). (ENG.). 80p. (gr. 6-6). 36.93 (978-0-7614-1612-8(9), 4d70d369-f267-4e75-96e0-c7ced87675ca) Cavendish Square Publishing LLC.

Maynard, Charles W. Zebulon Pike: Soldier-Explorer of the American Southwest. 2009. (Famous Explorers of the American West Ser.). 24p. (gr. 3-4). 42.50 (978-1-61512-506-7(X), PowerKids Pr.) Rosen Publishing Group, Inc., The.

Sanford, William R. & Green, Carl R. Zebulon Pike: Courageous Rocky Mountain Explorer, 1 vol. 2013. (Courageous Heroes of the American West Ser.). (ENG., Illus.). 48p. (J). (gr. 5-7). lib. bdg. 25.27 *(978-0-7660-4012-0(7),* 05a2fcff-67b5-48be-a735-82bd326fcd47) Enslow Publishing, LLC.

Walsh, Steve. Zebulon Montgomery Pike: Explorer & Military Officer. 2011. (ENG & SPA., Illus.). 54p. (J). pap. 8.95 *(978-0-86541-123-4(9))* Filter Pr., LLC.

PILGRIM FATHERS

see Pilgrims (New Plymouth Colony)

PILGRIMS (NEW PLYMOUTH COLONY)

Arenstam, Peter, et al. MayFlower 1620: A New Look at a Pilgrim Voyage. 2004. (Illus.). 47p. (J). (gr. k-4). 18.00 *(978-0-7567-7967-2(7))* DIANE Publishing Co.

Bailey, Budd. Plymouth & the Settlement of New England, 1 vol. 2017. (Primary Sources of Colonial America Ser.). (ENG.). 64p. (gr. 6-6). 35.93 *(978-1-5026-3140-4(7),* ee943d94-d3c5-41c3-a484-dfbd813384cd); pap. 16.28 *(978-1-5026-3457-3(0),* 01ec0b91-6764-4305-ab12-d8280bde9a1b) Cavendish Square Publishing LLC.

Bartlett, Robert Merrill. The Story of Thanksgiving. Comport, Sally Wern, illus. rev. ed. 2004. 30p. (J). (gr. k-4). reprint ed. *(978-0-7567-7757-9(7))* DIANE Publishing Co.

—The Story of Thanksgiving. Comport, Sally Wern, illus. Date not set. 40p. (J). (gr. 2-5). 5.99 *(978-0-06-446238-9(2))* HarperCollins Pubs.

Benge, Janet & Benge, Geoff. Heroes of History - William Bradford: Plymouth's Rock. 2016. (ENG., Illus.). 200p. (YA). pap. 11.99 *(978-1-62486-092-8(3))* Emerald Bks.

Brindell Fradin, Dennis. The Mayflower Compact, 1 vol. 2007. (Turning Points in U. S. History Ser.). (ENG., Illus.). 48p. (gr. 4-4). lib. bdg. 34.07 *(978-0-7614-2125-2(4),* 047805e0-f50c-4cca-90d8-3562f332da95) Cavendish Square Publishing LLC.

Byers, Ann. Squanto, 1 vol. 2020. (Inside Guide: Famous Native Americans Ser.). (ENG.). 32p. (gr. 4-5). pap. 11.58 *(978-1-5026-5060-3(6),* ce942a61-8809-40a3-9ae2-0e11b981a031) Cavendish Square Publishing LLC.

Caswell, Max. My Journey Aboard the Mayflower, 1 vol. 2017. (My Place in History Ser.). (ENG.). 24p. (J). (gr. 2-3). pap. 9.15 *(978-1-5382-0217-3(4),* edf8b884-3702-4b22-9c1e-68fc6859bf6d) Stevens, Gareth Publishing LLLP.

—My Life in the Plymouth Colony, 1 vol. 2017. (My Place in History Ser.). 24p. (J). (gr. 2-3). (ENG.). pap. 9.15 *(978-1-5382-0305-7(7),* df02096f-11bd-46ba-b238-e6a666baecc2); pap. 48.90 *(978-1-5382-0306-4(5))* Stevens, Gareth Publishing LLLP.

Clark, Mary. Biographical Sketches of the Fathers of New England. 2003. 180p. 89.00 *(978-0-7950-4738-1(X))* New Library Press LLC.

Connors, Kathleen. The First Thanksgiving, 1 vol., Vol. 1. 2013. (What You Didn't Know about History Ser.). (ENG., Illus.). 24p. (J). (gr. 2-3). 25.27 *(978-1-4824-0581-1(4),* a32acce5-2977-40eb-a4fe-4662b029fe08); pap. 9.15 *(978-1-4824-0582-8(2),* 2da75e09-1664-42bc-8b67-0924117edce0) Stevens, Gareth Publishing LLLP.

Cook, Peter & Whelan, Kevin. You Wouldn't Want to Sail on the Mayflower! A Trip That Took Entirely Too Long. rev. ed. 2013. (ENG.). 32p. (J). 29.00 *(978-0-531-27107-0(2),* Watts, Franklin) Scholastic Library Publishing.

Crane, Carol. P Is for Pilgrim: A Thanksgiving Alphabet. Urban, Helle, illus. rev. ed. 2007. (ENG.). 40p. (J). (gr. 1-4). 7.95 *(978-1-58536-353-7(7),* 202306) Sleeping Bear Pr.

Davis, Kenneth C. Don't Know Much about the Pilgrims. Schindler, S. D., illus. 2006. (ENG.). 48p. (J). (gr. 1-4). pap. 8.99 *(978-0-06-446228-0(5),* HarperCollins) HarperCollins Pubs.

Dyan, Penelope. The Place of Tales — a Kid's Guide to Canterbury, Kent, England. Weigand, John, photos by. 2011. (Illus.). 40p. pap. 12.95 *(978-1-935630-66-1(0))* Bellissima Publishing, LLC.

Emminizer, Theresa. Aboard the Mayflower. 2019. (History on the High Seas Ser.). (ENG.). 24p. (gr. 2-3). 48.90 *(978-1-5382-3795-3(4))* Stevens, Gareth Publishing LLLP.

Englar, Mary. The Pilgrims & the First Thanksgiving, 1 vol. McDonnell, Peter, illus. 2006. (Graphic History Ser.). (ENG.). 32p. (J). (gr. 3-9). 8.10 *(978-0-7368-9656-6(2),* 93441); 31.32 *(978-0-7368-5492-4(4),* 90729) Capstone. (Capstone Pr.).

Fields, Terri. The First Thanksgiving. 2018. (Time to Discover Ser.). (ENG.). 16p. (gr. -1-2). lib. bdg. 28.50 *(978-1-64156-206-5(4),* 9781641562065) Rourke Educational Media.

Florence, Sarah. Pilgrim Foods & Recipes. 2009. (Reading Room Collection 2 Ser.). 24p. (gr. 3-4). 42.50 *(978-1-60851-983-5(X),* PowerKids Pr.) Rosen Publishing Group, Inc., The.

Griffis, William Elliot. Young People's History of the Pilgrims. 353p. reprint ed. 98.00 *(978-0-7222-6679-3(0))* Library Reprints, Inc.

Gunderson, Jessica. Life on the Mayflower, 1 vol. Dumm, Brian Caleb, illus. 2010. (Thanksgiving Ser.). (ENG.). 24p. (J). (gr. k-3). pap. 7.95 *(978-1-4048-6719-2(8),* 115518, Picture Window Bks.) Capstone.

—The Pilgrims' First Thanksgiving, 1 vol. Lucke, Deb, illus. 2010. (Thanksgiving Ser.). (ENG.). 24p. (J). (gr. k-3). pap. 8.95 *(978-1-4048-6720-8(1),* 115519, Picture Window Bks.) Capstone.

Harness, Cheryl. The Adventurous Life of Myles Standish: And the Amazing-but-True Survival Story of Plymouth Colony. (Cheryl Harness Histories Ser.). (Illus.). 144p. (J). (gr. 5-9). 2008. 9.95 *(978-1-4263-0284-8(3))* 2006. 16.95 *(978-0-7922-5918-3(1))* Disney Publishing Worldwide. (National Geographic Kids).

Harte, May. Thanksgiving. 2009. (My Library of Holidays Ser.). 24p. (gr. 1-1). 37.50 *(978-1-61514-697-0(0),* PowerKids Pr.) Rosen Publishing Group, Inc., The.

Holub, Joan. What Was the First Thanksgiving? 2013. (What Was... Ser.). lib. bdg. 16.00 *(978-0-606-31687-3(6))* Turtleback.

Honders, Christine. Mayflower Compact, 1 vol. 2016. (Documents of American Democracy Ser.). (ENG., Illus.). 32p. (J). (gr. 5-5). pap. 11.00 *(978-1-4994-2085-2(4),* 4d5a8336-b006-4995-923b-a2b9c7947e57, PowerKids Pr.) Rosen Publishing Group, Inc., The.

Isbell, Hannah. Squanto: Native American Translator & Guide, 1 vol. 2017. (Junior Biographies Ser.). (ENG.). 24p. (gr. 3-4). pap. 10.35 *(978-0-7660-9065-1(5),* bf71e6c5-83e5-46c8-af76-feebcd8d8af2) Enslow Publishing, LLC.

Jones, Emma. Recipes of the Pilgrims. (Cooking Your Way Through American History Ser.). (J). (gr. 3-3). 2017. pap. 63.60 *(978-1-5345-2097-4(X))* 2016. (ENG.). 24p. pap. 11.60 *(978-1-5345-2096-7(1),* 007ee261-d629-4474-a219-269f3fe78a21) 2016. (ENG.). 24p. lib. bdg. 28.88 *(978-1-5345-2098-1(8),* 5910fcfd-86e4-4882-8bdb-beafe6d4edd3) Greenhaven Publishing LLC. (KidHaven Publishing).

Kallio, Jamie. Mayflower Compact, 1 vol. 2013. (Foundations of Our Nation Ser.). (ENG.). 48p. (J). (gr. 4-8). lib. bdg. 35.64 *(978-1-61783-711-1(3),* 7820) ABDO Publishing Co.

Kessel, Joyce K. Squanto & the First Thanksgiving. Donze, Lisa, illus. rev. ed. 2003. (On My Own Holidays Ser.). (ENG.). 48p. (gr. 2-4). lib. bdg. 25.26 *(978-0-87614-941-6(7))* Lerner Publishing Group.

—Squanto & the First Thanksgiving, 2nd Edition. Donze, Lisa, illus. 2nd rev. ed. 2003. (On My Own Holidays Ser.). (ENG.). 48p. (J). (gr. 2-4). pap. 8.99 *(978-1-57505-585-5(6),* 7a820627-e0ae-495a-9499-accc5d2a0944, First Avenue Editions) Lerner Publishing Group.

—Squanto y el Primer Día de Accion de Gracias. Donze, Lisa, illus. 2007. (Yo Solo - Festividades (on My Own - Holidays) Ser.). 48p. (J). (gr. 4-7). per. 6.95 *(978-0-8225-7795-9(X))* Lerner Publishing Group.

—Squanto y el Primer Día de Acción de Gracias. Translations.com Staff, tr. from ENG. Donze, Lisa, illus. 2007. (Yo Solo - Festividades (on My Own - Holidays) Ser.). (SPA.). 48p. (gr. 2-4). lib. bdg. 25.26 *(978-0-8225-7792-8(5))* Lerner Publishing Group.

—Squanto Y el Primer Dia de Accion de Gracias; Squanto & the First Thanksgiving. 2008. pap. 40.95 *(978-0-8225-9678-3(4))* Lerner Publishing Group.

Lassieur, Allison. El Viaje del Mayflower. McDonnell, Peter, illus. 2006. (Historia Gráficas Ser.). (SPA.). 32p. (J). (gr. 3-9). 31.32 *(978-0-7368-6613-2(2),* 88094) Capstone.

Lusted, Marcia Amidon. The Mayflower Compact. 2019. (Shaping the United States of America Ser.). (ENG., Illus.). 24p. (J). (gr. 1-3). pap. 7.95 *(978-1-9771-1015-2(0),* 140958); lib. bdg. 25.99 *(978-1-9771-0916-3(0),* 140517) Capstone. (Pebble).

Lynch, P. J. The Boy Who Fell off the Mayflower, or John Howland's Good Fortune. Lynch, P. J., illus. (ENG., Illus.). 64p. (J). (gr. 2-5). 2018. 9.99 *(978-1-5362-0296-0(7))* 2015. 18.99 *(978-0-7636-6584-5(3))* Candlewick Pr.

Marsh, Carole. I'm Reading about the Pilgrims. 2016. (I'm Reading About Ser.). (ENG., Illus.). (J). lib. bdg. 24.99 *(978-0-635-12191-2(3))*; pap. 7.99 *(978-0-635-12192-9(1))* Gallopade International.

Metaxas, Eric. Squanto & the First Thanksgiving: The Legendary American Tale. Donato, Michael A., illus. 2004. 36p. (J). (gr. 3-8). reprint ed. 19.00 *(978-0-7567-7123-2(4))* DIANE Publishing Co.

National Geographic Learning. Reading Expeditions (Social Studies: Documents of Freedom): the Mayflower Compact. 2007. (ENG., Illus.). 32p. (J). pap. 18.95 *(978-0-7922-4553-7(9))* CENGAGE Learning.

Newman-D'Amico, Fran. The Story of the Pilgrims. 2005. (Dover American History Coloring Bks.). (ENG., Illus.). 30p. (J). (gr. -1-3). 3.99 *(978-0-486-44430-7(9),* 444309) Dover Pubns., Inc.

Osborne, Mary Pope & Boyce, Natalie Pope. Pilgrims: A Nonfiction Companion to Magic Tree House #27: Thanksgiving on Thursday. Murdocca, Sal, illus. 2005. (Magic Tree House (R) Fact Tracker Ser.: 13). 128p. (J). (gr. 2-5). 6.99 *(978-0-375-83219-2(X),* Random Hse. Bks. for Young Readers) Random Hse. Children's Bks.

Owens, L. L. Pilgrims in America. 2006. (Events in American History Ser.). (Illus.). 48p. (J). (gr. -1-1). lib. bdg. 31.36 *(978-1-60044-122-6(X))* Rourke Educational Media.

Philbrick, Nathaniel. The Mayflower & the Pilgrims' New World. 2009. (ENG.). 368p. (J). (gr. 5-18). 9.99 *(978-0-14-241458-3(1),* Puffin Books) Penguin Young Readers Group.

Plimoth Plantation, et al. Mayflower 1620: A New Look at a Pilgrim Voyage. 2007. (Illus.). 48p. (J). (gr. 3-7). per. 6.95 *(978-0-7922-6276-3(X),* National Geographic Kids) Disney Publishing Worldwide.

Poolos, J. The Mayflower, 1 vol. 2004. (Primary Sources in American History Ser.). (ENG., Illus.). 64p. (J). (gr. 5-8). lib. bdg. 37.13 *(978-0-8239-4514-6(6),* 305b2908-454e-4a89-977c-105c73594972, Rosen Reference) Rosen Publishing Group, Inc., The.

—The Mayflower: A Primary Source History of the Pilgrims' Journey to the New World. 2009. (Primary Sources in American History Ser.). (gr. 5-8). 58.50 *(978-1-60851-499-1(4))* Rosen Publishing Group, Inc., The.

Pumphrey, Margaret B. Stories of the Pilgrims. 2005. pap. 27.95 *(978-1-4179-1115-8(8))* Kessinger Publishing, LLC.

—Stories of the Pilgrims (Yesterday's Classics) 2006. (J). per. 10.95 *(978-1-59915-123-6(5))* Yesterday's Classics.

Rajczak, Michael. Life on the Mayflower, 1 vol., Vol. 1. 2013. (What You Didn't Know about History Ser.). (ENG.). 24p. (J). (gr. 2-3). 25.27 *(978-1-4824-0591-0(1),* 2e562962-9b3b-4209-98f1-f0e1f723e9f5) Stevens, Gareth Publishing LLLP.

Raum, Elizabeth. The Mayflower Compact, 1 vol. 2012. (Documenting U. S. History Ser.). (ENG.). 48p. (J). (gr. 3-6). lib. bdg. 33.32 *(978-1-4329-6750-5(9),* 119381, Heinemann) Capstone.

Riehecky, Janet & Williams, Gianna. La Colonia de Plymouth (the Settling of Plymouth), 1 vol. 2006. (Hitos de la Historia de Estados Unidos (Landmark Events in American History) Ser.). (SPA.). 48p. (gr. 5-8). pap. 12.70 *(978-0-8368-7471-6(4),* c4b0334d-2730-428d-b1e9-b4c540c786ce, Gareth Stevens Learning Library); (Illus.). lib. bdg. 29.67 *(978-0-8368-7464-8(1),* 08ac8c60-625b-40a5-bde2-463bc20e4058, Gareth Stevens Secondary Library) Stevens, Gareth Publishing LLLP.

Roop, Peter & Roop, Connie. Did Pilgrims Really Wear Black & White? And Other Questions about Colonial Times. 2007. (Illus.). 44p. (J). pap. *(978-0-439-02522-5(2))* Scholastic, Inc.

Santella, Andrew. Cornerstones of Freedom: the First Thanksgiving. 2003. (Cornerstones of Freedom Ser.). (ENG., Illus.). 48p. (YA). (gr. 4-7). 26.00 *(978-0-516-24204-0(0))* Scholastic Library Publishing.

Skaermas, Nancy J. The Story of Thanksgiving. 2011. (ENG., Illus.). 22p. (J). (gr. -1-1). bds. 7.99 *(978-0-8249-1883-5(5),* Ideals Pubns.) Worthy Publishing.

Smith, Andrea P. The First Thanksgiving. (Illus.). 24p. (J). 2012. 63.60 *(978-1-4488-5213-0(7))* 2011. (ENG., (gr. 2-3). pap. 11.60 *(978-1-4488-5212-3(9),* 29193eb1-58fc-449e-8ffd-c34f8ba58a56) 2011. (ENG., (gr. 2-3). lib. bdg. 28.93 *(978-1-4488-5187-4(4),* 558ed541-f06a-434a-870b-4905820ff6a9) Rosen Publishing Group, Inc., The. (PowerKids Pr.).

—The Journey of the Mayflower. (Illus.). 24p. (J). 2012. 63.60 *(978-1-4488-5211-6(0))* 2011. (ENG., (gr. 2-3). pap. 11.60 *(978-1-4488-5210-9(2),* ffb71748-c78c-4612-9f75-48faa5dd7d69) 2011. (ENG., (gr. 2-3). lib. bdg. 28.93 *(978-1-4488-5186-7(6),* aa04b287-2d9d-4f9d-b874-70411c20e5e6) Rosen Publishing Group, Inc., The. (PowerKids Pr.).

Son, John. If You Were a Kid on the Mayflower (If You Were a Kid) (Library Edition) Zanni, Roger, illus. 2018. (If You Were a Kid Ser.). (ENG.). 32p. (J). (gr. 2-4). lib. bdg. 26.00 *(978-0-531-23216-3(6),* Children's Pr.) Scholastic Library Publishing.

Stilwell, Norma Mintum. A Thought for Thanksgiving. Bingham, Pamela E., illus. 2011. 24p. pap. 14.95 *(978-1-936343-93-5(2))* Peppertree Pr., The.

Sullivan, Laura. Life As a Passenger on the Mayflower, 1 vol. 2016. (Life As... Ser.). (ENG., Illus.). 32p. (gr. 3-3). 30.21 *(978-1-5026-1789-7(7),* a10a046e-70bc-4514-9d97-a1c7631ba2da) Cavendish Square Publishing LLC.

Uhl, Xina M. & Poolos, Jamie. A Primary Source Investigation of the Mayflower, 1 vol. 2018. (Uncovering American History Ser.). (ENG.). 64p. (gr. 6-6). pap. 13.95 *(978-1-5081-8420-1(8),* 6638331e-e847-4929-9ddb-0edf86412945, Rosen Reference) Rosen Publishing Group, Inc., The.

Wagner, William Bradford (Leaders of the Colonial Era) 2010. (ENG.). 120p. (gr. 5-8). 35.00 *(978-1-60413-743-9(6),* P200195, Facts On File) Infobase Holdings, Inc.

Waters, Kate. Sarah Morton's Day: a Day in the Life of a Pilgrim Girl. Kendall, Russ, illus. 2008. (Scholastic Bookshelf Ser.). (ENG.). 32p. (J). (gr. -1-3). pap. 7.99 *(978-0-439-81220-7(8),* Scholastic Paperbacks) Scholastic, Inc.

Waxman, Laura Hamilton. Why Did the Pilgrims Come to the New World? & Other Questions about the Plymouth Colony. 2010. (Six Questions of American History Ser.). 48p. (J). pap. 9.95 *(978-0-7613-6123-7(5))*; pap. 56.72 *(978-0-7613-6951-6(1))* Lerner Publishing Group.

Whitcraft, Melissa. The Mayflower Compact. 2008. (Cornerstones of Freedom Ser.). (ENG., Illus.). 48p. (YA). (gr. 3-6). 18.69 *(978-0-516-24203-3(2))* Scholastic Library Publishing.

Whitehurst, Susan. The Mayflower. 2009. (Library of the Pilgrims Ser.). 24p. (gr. 3-4). 42.50 *(978-1-60853-914-7(8),* PowerKids Pr.) Rosen Publishing Group, Inc., The.

—The Pilgrims Before the Mayflower. 2009. (Library of the Pilgrims Ser.). 24p. (gr. 3-4). 42.50 *(978-1-60853-915-4(6),* PowerKids Pr.) Rosen Publishing Group, Inc., The.

—Plymouth Partnership: Pilgrims & Native Americans. 2009. (Library of the Pilgrims Ser.). 24p. (gr. 3-4). 42.50 *(978-1-60853-912-3(1),* PowerKids Pr.) Rosen Publishing Group, Inc., The.

—William Bradford & Plymouth: A Colony Grows. 2009. (Library of the Pilgrims Ser.). 24p. (gr. 3-4). 42.50 *(978-1-60853-916-1(4),* PowerKids Pr.) Rosen Publishing Group, Inc., The.

PILGRIMS (NEW PLYMOUTH COLONY)—FICTION

Bruchac, Joseph. Squanto's Journey: The Story of the First Thanksgiving. Shed, Greg, illus. 2007. (ENG.). 32p. (J). (gr. -1-3). pap. 7.99 *(978-0-15-206044-2(8),* 1198153, Clarion Bks.) HarperCollins Pubs.

—Squanto's Journey: The Story of the First Thanksgiving. 2014. 17.00 *(978-1-63419-743-4(7))* Perfection Learning Corp.

Burton, Jeffrey. The Itsy Bitsy Pilgrim. Rescek, Sanja, illus. 2016. (Itsy Bitsy Ser.). (ENG.). 16p. (J). (gr. -1 — 1). bds. 5.99 *(978-1-4814-6852-7(9),* Little Simon) Little Simon.

Dougherty, Brandi. The Littlest Pilgrim. Richards, Kirsten, illus. 2008. (Littlest Ser.). (ENG.). 32p. (J). (gr. -1-k). pap. 3.99 *(978-0-545-05372-3(2),* Cartwheel Bks.) Scholastic, Inc.

Greene, Rhonda Gowler. The Very First Thanksgiving Day. Gaber, Susan, illus. 2006. (ENG.). 32p. (J). (gr. -1-1). 7.99 *(978-1-4169-1916-2(3),* Atheneum Bks. for Young Readers) Simon & Schuster Children's Publishing.

Hillert, Margaret. Why We Have Thanksgiving. Marchesi, Stephen, illus. 2016. (BeginningtoRead Ser.). (ENG.). 32p. (J). (gr. 1-2). 22.60 *(978-1-59953-809-9(1))* Norwood Hse. Pr.

Klimo, Kate. Dash. 2014. (Dog Diaries: 5). lib. bdg. 18.40 *(978-0-606-36021-0(2))* Turtleback.

—Dog Diaries #5: Dash. Bk. 5. Jessell, Tim, illus. 2014. (Dog Diaries: 5). 160p. (J). (gr. 2-5). pap. 7.99 *(978-0-385-37338-8(4),* Random Hse. Bks. for Young Readers) Random Hse. Children's Bks.

Krulik, Nancy. Don't Be Such a Turkey! John and Wendy, illus. 2010. (Katie Kazoo, Switcheroo Ser.). 160p. (J). (gr. 2-4). pap. 6.99 *(978-0-448-45448-1(3),* Grosset & Dunlap) Penguin Young Readers Group.

Lawton, Wendy G. Almost Home: A Story Based on the Life of the Mayflower's Mary Chilton. 2003. (Daughters of the Faith Ser.). (ENG.). 160p. (YA). (gr. 3-3). pap. 8.99 *(978-0-8024-3637-5(4))* Moody Pubs.

Limbaugh, Rush. Rush Revere & the Brave Pilgrims: Time-Travel Adventures with Exceptional Americans. 2013. (Rush Revere Ser.: 1). (ENG., Illus.). 224p. 21.00 *(978-1-4767-5586-1(8),* Threshold Editions) Threshold Editions.

Osborne, Mary Pope, et al. Jueves de Acción de Gracias. Murdocca, Sal, illus. 2014. (SPA.). 88p. (J). (gr. 2-4). pap. 6.99 *(978-1-933032-94-8(4))* Lectorum Pubns., Inc.

Stanley, Diane. Thanksgiving on Plymouth Plantation. Berry, Holly, illus. 2004. (ENG.). 48p. (J). (gr. k-5). 17.99 *(978-0-06-027069-8(1),* HarperCollins) HarperCollins Pubs.

PILOTING (AERONAUTICS)

see Airplanes—Piloting

PILOTS, AIRPLANE

see Air Pilots

PILOTS AND PILOTAGE

see also Navigation

Gordon, Nick. Fighter Pilot. 2013. (Dangerous Jobs Ser.). (ENG., Illus.). 24p. (J). (gr. 3-7). lib. bdg. 26.95 *(978-1-60014-894-1(8),* Torque Bks.) Bellwether Media.

Hense, Mary & Stewart, Rhea A. How Fighter Pilots Use Math. 2009. (Math in the Real World Ser.). (ENG.). 32p. (gr. 4-6). 28.00 *(978-1-60413-605-0(7),* P466915, Chelsea Clubhse.) Infobase Holdings, Inc.

Loveless, Antony. Fighter Pilots. 2009. (World's Most Dangerous Jobs Ser.). (ENG., Illus.). 32p. (J). (gr. 3-6). pap. *(978-0-7787-5110-6(4),* 1302970); lib. bdg. *(978-0-7787-5096-3(5),* 1302970) Crabtree Publishing Co.

Loveless, Antony & Oxlade, Chris. Support Helicopter Pilots. 2012. (ENG.). 32p. (J). *(978-0-7787-5102-1(3))* Crabtree Publishing Co.

Smith, Sherri L. Who Were the Tuskegee Airmen? 2018. (Who Was... ? Ser.). lib. bdg. 16.00 *(978-0-606-41326-8(X))* Turtleback.

West, David. Fighter Pilots. 2008. 52p. (gr. 5-8). pap. 29.25 *(978-1-4358-3785-0(1))* Rosen Publishing Group, Inc., The.

Youngblood, Wayne. Mark Twain along the Mississippi, 1 vol. 2005. (In the Footsteps of American Heroes Ser.). (ENG., Illus.). 64p. (gr. 5-8). pap. 15.05 *(978-0-8368-6435-9(2),* fc650921-fafb-4dde-ae34-50f8069dd1ae); lib. bdg. 36.67 *(978-0-8368-6430-4(1),* 075f253e-b58f-4ce9-9e41-a0fcee83e823) Stevens, Gareth Publishing LLLP. (Gareth Stevens Secondary Library).

PINCKNEY, ELIZA LUCAS, 1723-1793

Krebs, Laurie. A Day in the Life of a Colonial Indigo Planter. (Library of Living & Working in Colonial Times Ser.). 24p. (gr. 3-3). 2009. 42.50 *(978-1-60853-732-7(3),* PowerKids Pr.) 2003. (ENG., Illus.). (J). lib. bdg. 26.27 *(978-0-8239-6229-7(6),* 4fbf7f8a-1b2e-4518-ba28-11908a0c5cf6) Rosen Publishing Group, Inc., The.

PINKERTON, ALLAN, 1819-1884

Moss, Marissa. The Eye That Never Sleeps: How Detective Pinkerton Saved President Lincoln. Holmes, Jeremy, illus. 2018. (ENG.). 48p. (J). (gr. 1-4). 17.99 *(978-1-4197-3064-1(9),* 1137601, Abrams Bks. for Young Readers) Abrams, Inc.

PINOCCHIO (FICTITIOUS CHARACTER)—FICTION

The Adventures of Pinocchio. 2011. 130p. pap. 9.99 *(978-1-61203-094-4(7))* Bottom of the Hill Publishing.

The Adventures of Pinocchio. (Twelve-Point Ser.). 2003. (J). lib. bdg. 25.00 *(978-1-58287-248-3(1))* 2004. 229p. 25.00 *(978-1-58287-732-7(7))* North Bks.

Las Aventuras de Pinocho. (SPA., Illus.). 160p. (YA). 14.95 *(978-84-7281-190-4(5),* AF1905) Auriga, Ediciones S.A. ESP. Dist: Continental Bk. Co., Inc.

Le Avventure di Pinocchio, Level B. (ITA.). (J). pap. 9.95 *(978-0-88436-050-6(4),* 55254) EMC/Paradigm Publishing.

Campillo, Carlo Collodi. Ilustrado por Susana. Las Aventuras de Pinocho. (Coleccion Cuentos Universales). (SPA.). (YA). (gr. 4-18). *(978-84-261-3145-4(X),* JV30301) Juventud, Editorial ESP. Dist: Lectorum Pubns., Inc.

Carsey, Alice, illus. Pinocchio. 2003. (Library of Tale Ser.). Tr. of Avventure di Pinocchio. (SPA.). 12p. (J). (gr. -1-7). pap. *(978-958-30-0986-0(5))* Panamericana Editorial.

—Pinocchio. 2005.Tr. of Avventure di Pinocchio. (ENG.). 136p. (J). (gr. 2-5). 19.95 *(978-1-933327-00-6(6))* Purple Bear Bks., Inc.

—Pinocchio, the Tale of a Puppet. 2011. 140p. pap. 12.99 *(978-1-61203-095-1(5))* Bottom of the Hill Publishing.

Carter, Scott William. Wooden Bones. (ENG., Illus.). 160p. (J). (gr. 3-7). 2013. pap. 6.99 *(978-1-4424-2752-5(3))* 2012. 15.99 *(978-1-4424-2751-8(5))* Simon & Schuster Bks. For Young Readers. (Simon & Schuster Bks. For Young Readers).

Cherubini, E. Pinocchio in Africa. 2007. pap. *(978-1-4065-1442-1(X))* Dodo Pr.

Collodi, C. The Adventures of Pinocchio. 2005. 216p. 27.95 *(978-1-4218-0608-2(8),* 1st World Library - Literary Society) 1st World Publishing, Inc.

—The Adventures of Pinocchio. Della Chiesa, Carol, tr. 2007. (ENG.). 160p. per. *(978-1-4065-1463-6(2))* Dodo Pr.

—The Adventures of Pinocchio. 2007. 108p. (gr. 4-7). per. 7.99 *(978-1-60459-012-8(2))* Wilder Pubns., Corp.

—Pinocchio: the Tale of a Puppet. Carsey, Alice, illus. 2007. (ENG.). 196p. per. *(978-1-4065-1462-9(4))* Dodo Pr.

Collodi, Carlo. The Adventures of Pinocchio. 2019.Tr. of Avventure Di Pinocchio. (ENG.). 220p. (YA). (gr. 7). 24.95 *(978-0-469-59358-9(X))*; pap. 14.95 *(978-0-469-59357-2(1))* Creative Media Partners, LLC. (Wentworth Pr.).

—The Adventures of Pinocchio. 2019.Tr. of Avventure Di Pinocchio. (ENG.). 262p. (YA). (gr. 7). pap. 18.99 *(978-1-6933-1615-9(3))* Independently Published.

—The Adventures of Pinocchio. 2014.Tr. of Avventure Di Pinocchio. (ENG.). 170p. (YA). (gr. 7). pap. 11.99 *(978-93-5223-173-7(2))* Maple Pr.

—Adventures of Pinocchio. 2009. (Oxford World's Classics Ser.). (ENG., Illus.). 256p. pap. 10.95 *(978-0-19-955398-3(X))* Oxford Univ. Pr., Inc.

—The Adventures of Pinocchio. Innocenti, Roberto, illus. rev. ed. 2004. 192p. (J). (gr. 2-5). 35.00 *(978-1-56846-190-8(9),* 22063) Creative Co., The.

—Le Avventure Di Pinocchio. 2019. (ITA.). (J). 438p. pap. 28.99 *(978-1-6933-1569-5(6))*; 442p. pap. 25.99 *(978-1-0706-3834-8(X))* Independently Published.

Fairy Tales - Pinocchio. 2005. (J). bds. *(978-1-4194-0101-5(7))* Paradise Pr., Inc.

Fairy Tales- Pinocchio. 2005. (J). bds. *(978-1-4194-0041-4(X))* Paradise Pr., Inc.

Fairy Tales s/s - Pinocchio. 2005. (J). bds. *(978-1-4194-0067-4(3))* Paradise Pr., Inc.

Kunhardt, Dorothy, ed. Pinocchio. (FRE.). 96p. (J). (gr. k-5). pap. 9.95 *(978-0-7859-8845-8(9))* French & European Pubns., Inc.

Leigh, Tom, illus. Pinocchio: A Tale of Honesty. 2006. (J). 6.99 *(978-1-59939-005-5(1))* Cornerstone Pr.

Leonard, Barry, ed. Pinocchio. 2003. (Illus.). 12p. (J). (gr. k-5). reprint ed. 17.00 *(978-0-7567-6862-1(4))* DIANE Publishing Co.

Linares, Jairo, illus. Pinocho. 2004. (Literatura Juvenil (Panamericana Editorial) Ser.).Tr. of Pinocchio. (SPA.). 283p. (J). (gr. 4-7). pap. *(978-958-30-0803-0(6),* PV30464) Centro de Informacion y Desarrollo de la Comunicacion y la Literatura MEX. Dist: Lectorum Pubns., Inc.

Morpurgo, Michael. Pinocchio: in His Own Words. Chichester Clark, Emma, illus. 2018. (ENG.). 272p. (J). 17.99 *(978-0-00-825769-9(8),* HarperCollins Children's Bks.) HarperCollins Pubs. Ltd. GBR. Dist: HarperCollins Pubs.

Murray, M. A., tr. Pinocchio, As First Translated into English by M a Murray & Illustrated by Charles Folkard. Folkard, Charles, illus. 2009. 280p. pap. 11.95 *(978-1-59915-177-9(4))* Yesterday's Classics.

Nickel. Pinocchio. Date not set. (J). 4.99 *(978-0-7214-5404-7(6))* Nickel Pr.

Parragon Staff. Pinocchio: The Magical Story. 2010. (Disney Padded Magical Storybks.). (Illus.). 32p. (J). (gr. -1-1). *(978-1-4075-8451-5(0))* Parragon, Inc.

Penri, Esyllt & Collodi, Carlo. Pinocchio. 2005. (WEL., Illus.). 40p. *(978-1-899877-05-8(3))* Y Ddraig Fach.

Pinocchio. (J). 22.95 *(978-0-88411-249-5(7))* Amereon Ltd.

Pinocchio. *(978-1-894998-20-8(0))* Lake, Jack Productions, Inc. CAN. Dist: Hushion Hse. Publishing, Ltd.

Pinocchio: A Classic Story about Honesty. 2003. (Illus.). 32p. per. 3.95 *(978-0-9747133-2-8(5),* Values to Live By Classic Stories) Thomas, Frederic Inc.

Pinocchio: The Human Body, Sea Life, The Bedroom. (FRE & ENG., Illus.). 24p. (J). (gr. -1-5). pap., stu. ed. 5.95 *(978-88-8148-243-6(6))* EMC/Paradigm Publishing.

Ruiz, Margarita, illus. Pinocho. (SPA & ENG.). 24p. (J). (gr. -1-5). pap. 5.95 incl. audio compact disk *(978-88-8148-253-5(3))* EMC/Paradigm Publishing.

Tyrrell, Melissa. Pinocchio. McMullen, Nigel, illus. 2005. (Fairytale Friends Ser.: Vol. 7). 12p. (J). (gr. -1-k). bds. 5.95 *(978-1-58117-151-8(X),* Intervisual/Piggy Toes) Bendon, Inc.

PIONEER LIFE

see Frontier and Pioneer Life

PIONEERS

see also Frontier and Pioneer Life

Allen, Nancy. Daniel Boone: Trailblazer, 1 vol. 2005. (ENG., Illus.). 32p. (J). (gr. k-3). 16.99 *(978-1-58980-212-4(8),* Pelican Publishing) Arcadia Publishing.

Améz, Lynda. My Wagon Train Adventure, 1 vol. 2015. (My Place in History Ser.). (ENG., Illus.). 24p. (J). (gr. 2-3). pap. 9.15 *(978-1-4824-4002-7(4),* 123566d3-91e8-4ad7-bc2b-ead566925690) Stevens, Gareth Publishing LLLP.

Améz, Lynda & Améz, Lynda. My Life As a Pioneer, 1 vol. 2015. (My Place in History Ser.). (ENG., Illus.). 24p. (J). (gr. 2-3). pap. 9.15 *(978-1-4824-3988-5(3),* 3d129dbf-065a-4a8c-b155-115028b734af) Stevens, Gareth Publishing LLLP.

Beckwith, Cheryl. William Bent: Frontiersman. 2011. (ENG & SPA., Illus.). 60p. (J). pap. 8.95 *(978-0-86541-117-3(4))* Filter Pr., LLC.

Benge, Janet & Benge, Geoff. Heroes of History - Davy Crockett: Ever Westward. 2011. (ENG.). 192p. (YA). pap. 11.99 *(978-1-932096-67-5(1))* Emerald Bks.

Benge, Janet & Geoff. Christian Heroes - Then & Now - Richard Wurmbrand: Love Your Enemies. 2017. 208p. (YA). pap. 11.99 *(978-1-57658-987-8(0))* YWAM Publishing.

Blair, Eric. Daniel Boone, 1 vol. Chambers-Goldberg, Micah, illus. 2011. (My First Classic Story Ser.). (ENG.). 32p. (J). (gr. k-3). lib. bdg. 23.32 *(978-1-4048-6578-5(0),* 114428, Picture Window Bks.) Capstone.

Bliss, John. Pioneers to the West, 1 vol. 2011. (Children's True Stories: Migration Ser.). (ENG.). 32p. (J). (gr. 3-5). pap. 8.29 *(978-1-4109-4082-7(9),* 114620, Raintree) Capstone.

Bornemann Spies, Karen. Buffalo Bill Cody: Legend of the Wild West, 1 vol. 2014. (Legendary American Biographies Ser.). (ENG.). 96p. (gr. 6-6). 29.60 *(978-0-7660-6450-8(6),* aa6858bf-b38b-4ffd-8af0-5e9f93e88d65); pap. 13.88 *(978-0-7660-6451-5(4),* b6001603-e87d-49d8-9217-04aaf37d967a) Enslow Publishing, LLC.

Brandt, Keith & Macken, JoAnn Early. Daniel Boone: Frontier Explorer. Lawn, John, illus. 2008. 55p. (J). pap. *(978-0-439-02020-6(4))* Scholastic, Inc.

Buffalo Bill Cody. 2010. (ENG., Illus.). 136p. (gr. 6-12). 35.00 *(978-1-60413-528-2(X),* P179304, Facts On File) Infobase Holdings, Inc.

Byers, Ann. Life As a Homesteader in the American West, 1 vol. 2016. (Life As... Ser.). (ENG., Illus.). 32p. (gr. 3-3). 30.21 *(978-1-5026-1787-3(0),* 84c36979-4d22-41c5-8662-4711540ae137) Cavendish Square Publishing LLC.

Cabose, Rachel Whitaker. Vision in the Storm. Mashburn, Marcus M., illus. 2018. 127p. (J). pap. *(978-0-8163-6421-3(4))* Pacific Pr. Publishing Assn.

Callery, Sean. The Dark History of America's Old West, 1 vol. 2011. (Dark Histories Ser.). (ENG.). 64p. (gr. 5-5). 35.50 *(978-1-60870-086-8(0),* ab883aea-2530-45bd-8ce6-bfe1e124ab05) Cavendish Square Publishing LLC.

Capek, Michael. Davy Crockett. 2017. (Illus.). 32p. (J). 25.70 *(978-1-61228-974-8(6))* Mitchell Lane Pubs.

Charles, Tami. Fearless Mary: Mary Fields, American Stagecoach Driver. Almon, Claire, illus. 2019. (ENG.). 32p. (J). (gr. -1-3). 17.99 *(978-0-8075-2305-6(4),* 807523054) Whitman, Albert & Co.

Chemerka, William. Davy Crockett from a to Z, 1 vol. 2013. (ABC Ser.). (ENG., Illus.). 32p. (J). (gr. k-3). 16.99 *(978-1-4556-1835-4(7),* Pelican Publishing) Arcadia Publishing.

Coddington, Andrew. Davy Crockett: Frontiersman, 1 vol. Lapegüe, Matías, illus. 2016. (American Legends & Folktales Ser.). (ENG.). 32p. (gr. 3-3). 30.21 *(978-1-5026-2193-1(2),* 9b7823f4-3a30-481b-a7ce-fac9d0a1a2a1) Cavendish Square Publishing LLC.

Demuth, Patricia Brennan. Who Was Laura Ingalls Wilder? 2013. (Who Was... ? Ser.). lib. bdg. 16.00 *(978-0-606-32134-1(9))* Turtleback.

Doeden, Matt. Oregon Trail: An Interactive History Adventure. 2013. (You Choose: History Ser.). (ENG., Illus.). 112p. (J). (gr. 3-7). 32.65 *(978-1-4765-0254-0(4),* 122324) Capstone.

—The Oregon Trail: An Interactive History Adventure. 2013. (You Choose: History Ser.). (ENG.). 112p. (J). (gr. 3-7). pap. 6.95 *(978-1-4765-3607-1(4),* 123611) Capstone.

Doherty, Kieran. Voyageurs, Lumberjacks & Farmers: Pioneers of the Midwest. 2003. (Shaping America Ser.: Vol. 5). (Illus.). 176p. (gr. 7-18). lib. bdg. 22.95 *(978-1-881508-54-0(4))* Oliver Pr., Inc.

Domnauer, Teresa. True Books: Life in the West. 2010. (True Book Ser.). (ENG.). 48p. (J). (gr. 2-5). 29.00 *(978-0-531-20583-9(5))* Scholastic Library Publishing.

Figley, Marty Rhodes. Who Was William Penn? And Other Questions about the Founding of Pennsylvania. 2012. (Six Questions of American History Ser.). (ENG.). 48p. (gr. 4-6). pap. 56.72 *(978-0-7613-9241-5(6))* Lerner Publishing Group.

Fleming, Candace. Presenting Buffalo Bill: The Man Who Invented the Wild West. 2016. (ENG., Illus.). 288p. (J). 19.99 *(978-1-59643-763-0(4),* 900080625) Roaring Brook Pr.

Ford, Anne. Davy Crockett. Vosburgh, Leonard, illus. 2011. 48p. 35.95 *(978-1-258-06913-1(X))* Literary Licensing, LLC.

Frachetti, Suzanne. Clara Brown: African-American Pioneer. 2011. (ENG & SPA., Illus.). 66p. (J). pap. 8.95 *(978-0-86541-124-1(7))* Filter Pr., LLC.

Freedman, Jeri. Life As a Pioneer on the Oregon Trail, 1 vol. 2015. (Life As... Ser.). (ENG., Illus.). 32p. (gr. 3-3). pap. 11.58 *(978-1-5026-1075-1(2),* f8b32e82-39dd-43e3-8323-f276e1cf91c9) Cavendish Square Publishing LLC.

Furstinger, Nancy. Davy Crockett. (Illus.). 24p. (J). 2018. pap. *(978-1-4896-9548-2(6),* AV2 by Weigl) 2003. lib. bdg. 24.45 *(978-1-59036-073-6(7))* Weigl Pubs., Inc.

Graham Gaines, Ann. Jim Bowie: Legendary Hero of the Alamo, 1 vol. 2014. (Legendary American Biographies Ser.). (ENG.). 96p. (gr. 6-6). 29.60 *(978-0-7660-6470-6(0),* 20886830-0978-4835-bd3b-f3448dd57751); pap. 13.88 *(978-0-7660-6471-3(9),* 4e35cfc2-f471-42df-88d1-e679e931f993) Enslow Publishing, LLC.

Gunderson, Jessica. Your Life As a Pioneer on the Oregon Trail. Dougherty, Rachel, illus. 2012. (Way It Was Ser.). (ENG.). 32p. (J). (gr. 2-5). pap. 8.95 *(978-1-4048-7250-9(7),* 118193, Picture Window Bks.) Capstone.

Haldy, Emma E. Davy Crockett. Bane, Jeff, illus. 2017. (My Early Library: My Itty-Bitty Bio Ser.). (ENG.). 24p. (J). (gr. k-1). lib. bdg. 30.64 *(978-1-63472-151-6(9),* 209176) Cherry Lake Publishing.

—Davy Crockett SP. Bane, Jeff, illus. 2018. (My Early Library: Mi Mini Biografía (My Itty-Bitty Bio) Ser.). (SPA.). 24p. (J). (gr. k-1). lib. bdg. 30.64 *(978-1-5341-2995-5(2),* 212028) Cherry Lake Publishing.

Hale, Nathan. Donner Dinner Party (Nathan Hale's Hazardous Tales #3) A Pioneer Tale. 2013. (Nathan Hale's Hazardous Tales Ser.). (ENG., Illus.). 128p. (J). (gr. 3-7). 14.99 *(978-1-4197-0856-5(2),* 1048001) Abrams, Inc.

Harkins, Susan Sales & Harkins, William H. The Donner Party. 2008. (What's So Great About... ? Ser.). (Illus.). 32p. (J). (gr. 2-4). lib. bdg. 25.70 *(978-1-58415-669-7(4))* Mitchell Lane Pubs.

Hay, John & Harwich, Mary Belle. Dancing Hands: Signs of Learning. Wapahi, Robert, illus. 2013. 78p. pap. 16.95 *(978-0-9888972-0-5(2))* Scotland Gate, Inc.

Hayhurst, Chris. John Sutter: California Pioneer / Pionero de California. 2009. (Famous People in American History/Grandes personajes en la historia de los Estados Unidos Ser.). (ENG & SPA.). 32p. (gr. 2-3). 47.90 *(978-1-61512-549-4(3),* Editorial Buenas Letras) Rosen Publishing Group, Inc., The.

—John Sutter: Pionero de California (John Sutter: California Pioneer) 2009. (Grandes personajes en la historia de los Estados Unidos (Famous People in American History) Ser.). (SPA.). 32p. (gr. 2-3). 47.90 *(978-1-61512-803-7(4),* Editorial Buenas Letras) Rosen Publishing Group, Inc., The.

Herman, Gail. Who Was Davy Crockett? 2013. (Who Was... ? Ser.). lib. bdg. 16.00 *(978-0-606-32133-4(0))* Turtleback.

Herman, Gail & Who HQ. Who Was Davy Crockett? Squier, Robert, illus. 2013. (Who Was? Ser.). (ENG.). 112p. (J). (gr. 3-7). 5.99 *(978-0-448-46704-7(6),* Penguin Workshop) Penguin Young Readers Group.

Isecke, Harriet. Stephen F. Austin: The Father of Texas, 1 vol. rev. ed. 2012. (Social Studies: Informational Text Ser.). (ENG.). 32p. (gr. 3-5). pap. 11.99 *(978-1-4333-5045-0(9))* Teacher Created Materials, Inc.

Jeffrey, Gary. The Oregon Trail, 1 vol. Poluzzi, Allesandro, illus. 2012. (Graphic History of the American West Ser.). (ENG.). 24p. (J). (gr. 3-3). pap. 9.15 *(978-1-4339-6745-0(6),* 6cef5d54-63c3-4008-83af-ec9d14b18589, Gareth Stevens Learning Library); lib. bdg. 26.60 *(978-1-4339-6743-6(X),* 0ad4de6b-3511-4850-a21f-171ad1720118) Stevens, Gareth Publishing LLLP.

Johnston, Marianne. Daniel Boone. 2009. (American Legends Ser.). 24p. (gr. 3-3). 42.50 *(978-1-61511-380-4(0),* PowerKids Pr.) Rosen Publishing Group, Inc., The.

Katirgis, Jane & Hayhurst, Chris. Meet John Sutter: California Gold Rush Pioneer, 1 vol. 2019. (Introducing Famous Americans Ser.). (ENG.). 32p. (gr. 3-4). pap. 11.53 *(978-1-9785-1142-2(6),* f7a55a55-7f7b-419c-9ced-c5f1585fc501) Enslow Publishing, LLC.

Kennedy, Emily. Daniel Boone & His Adventures, 1 vol. 2014. (American Legends & Folktales Ser.). (ENG., Illus.). 32p. (gr. 3-3). lib. bdg. 31.21 *(978-1-62712-280-1(X),* 4b4d32bf-716f-4e72-9cd0-7f03afc1a00b) Cavendish Square Publishing LLC.

Klepeis, Alicia Z. Buffalo Bill: Wild West Showman, 1 vol. William, Loma, illus. 2018. (American Legends & Folktales Ser.). (ENG.). 32p. (gr. 3-3). 30.21 *(978-1-5026-3678-2(6),* f84cb676-19ac-4d64-a22f-092a07c35f44) Cavendish Square Publishing LLC.

—Calamity Jane: Frontierswoman, 1 vol. Lapegüe, Matías, illus. 2016. (American Legends & Folktales Ser.). (ENG.). 32p. (gr. 3-3). pap. 11.58 *(978-1-5026-2200-6(9),* c37a9dbf-ec06-4c83-9eab-a41507a4d866); lib. bdg. 30.21 *(978-1-5026-2202-0(5),* be2713c3-ecd7-41e4-bc29-d72b9e97a177) Cavendish Square Publishing LLC.

Kundiger, Marion S. Izzie of Fergus Falls: A Minnesota Childhood in The 1880s. Kundiger, Marion S., illus. 2008. (ENG., Illus.). 56p. (J). 29.95 *(978-0-9659712-8-7(7))* Ravenstone Pr.

Landau, Elaine. The California Gold Rush: Would You Go for the Gold?, 1 vol. 2009. (What Would You Do? Ser.). (ENG., Illus.). 48p. (gr. 3-3). pap. 11.53 *(978-1-59845-193-1(6),* 2e64983a-5b64-44a6-b3ef-b5463dcc9b4c, Enslow Elementary) Enslow Publishing, LLC.

—The Gold Rush in California: Would You Catch Gold Fever?, 1 vol. 2014. (What Would You Do? Ser.). (ENG.). 48p. (gr. 3-4). 27.93 *(978-0-7660-6300-6(3),* 08e21d01-da92-4b3e-8582-4e751500f716); pap. 11.53 *(978-0-7660-6301-3(1),* e14f8cd9-1e01-446b-b9a5-c7ec50fce8ca, Enslow Elementary) Enslow Publishing, LLC.

Lappi, Megan. The Church: Pioneers of Canada. 2011. 24p. (YA). (gr. 2-4). *(978-1-77071-678-0(5));* pap. *(978-1-77071-682-7(3))* Weigl Educational Pubs. Ltd.

Leaf, Christina. Laura Ingalls Wilder. 2015. (Children's Storytellers Ser.). (ENG., Illus.). 24p. (J). (gr. 2-5). lib. bdg. 26.95 *(978-1-62617-269-2(2),* Blastoff! Readers) Bellwether Media.

Levy, Janey. William Penn: Shaping a Nation, 1 vol. (American History Milestones Ser.). 32p. (J). 2009. (ENG.). (gr. 5-5). lib. bdg. 28.93 *(978-1-4358-3016-5(4),* 24bd2188-de6c-4b3d-aa82-521f8e6f5069) 2009. (Illus.). 60.00 *(978-1-4358-0196-7(2),* 1291824) 2008. (ENG., Illus.). (gr. 5-5). pap. 10.00 *(978-1-4358-0195-0(4),* 513f85ca-cd43-44e9-a265-065502d0d251) Rosen Publishing Group, Inc., The. (PowerKids Pr.).

Lightfoot, D. J. Trail Fever: The Life of a Texas Cowboy. Bobbish, John, illus. exp. ed. 2003. 88p. (J). (gr. 3-18). pap. 12.95 *(978-0-9728768-0-3(4))* Seven Rivers Publishing.

Linde, Barbara M. The Price of a Pioneer Journey: Adding & Subtracting Two-Digit Dollar Amounts, 1 vol. 2010. (Math for the REAL World Ser.). (ENG.). 16p. (gr. 2-3). pap. 7.05 *(978-0-8239-8906-5(2),* ff1232da-ef8b-4cfe-850a-54a51b10a350, Rosen Classroom) Rosen Publishing Group, Inc., The.

Macy, Sue. Basketball Belles: How Stanford, Cal, & One Scrappy Player Put Womens Hoops on the Map. Collins, Matt, illus. 2019. 32p. (J). (gr. 1-4). pap. 7.99 *(978-0-8234-4175-4(X))* Holiday Hse., Inc.

Mara, Wil. Laura Ingalls Wilder. 2003. (Rookie Biographies Ser.). (ENG., Illus.). 32p. (J). (gr. 1-2). 20.50 *(978-0-516-22855-6(2),* Children's Pr.) Scholastic Library Publishing.

Maynard, Charles W. Jim Bridger: Frontiersman & Mountain Guide. 2009. (Famous Explorers of the American West Ser.). 24p. (gr. 3-4). 42.50 *(978-1-61512-502-9(7),* PowerKids Pr.) Rosen Publishing Group, Inc., The.

McCaslin, Nellie. Johnny Appleseed. 2003. (Players Press Nellie McCaslin Ser.). (Illus.). 16p. (J). (gr. 1-8). pap. 5.00 *(978-0-88734-447-3(X))* Players Pr., Inc.

Mead, James R., et al. Hunting & Trading in Kansas, 1859-1875. 2015. (J). *(978-1-929731-25-1(6))* Rowfant Pr.

Miller, Brandon Marie. Women of the Frontier: 16 Tales of Trailblazing Homesteaders, Entrepreneurs, & Rabble-Rousers. 2013. (Women of Action Ser.: 3). (ENG., Illus.). 256p. (J). (gr. 7). 19.95 *(978-1-883052-97-3(1))* Chicago Review Pr., Inc.

Morley, Jacqueline. You Wouldn't Want to... Be an American Pioneer! Antram, David, illus. rev. ed. 2012. (ENG.). 32p. (J). lib. bdg. 29.00 *(978-0-531-27500-9(0))* Scholastic Library Publishing.

Nichols, Kaitlyn. Davey Crockett. 2009. pap. 13.25 *(978-1-60559-057-8(6))* Hameray Publishing Group, Inc.

Oachs, Emily Rose. Death in the Donner Party: A Cause-And-Effect Investigation. 2016. (Cause-And-Effect Disasters Ser.). (ENG., Illus.). 40p. (J). (gr. 4-6). E-Book 46.65 *(978-1-5124-1126-3(4),* Lerner Pubns.) Lerner Publishing Group.

Peppas, Lynn. Why Charles Goodnight Matters to Texas, 1 vol. 2013. (Texas Perspectives Ser.). (ENG., Illus.). 32p. (J). (gr. 4-4). lib. bdg. 28.93 *(978-1-4777-0907-8(X),* 275a14bc-e2cc-4ff3-88dc-bff250ac8e56) Rosen Publishing Group, Inc., The.

—Why Martín de León Matters to Texas, 1 vol. 2013. (Texas Perspectives Ser.). (ENG., Illus.). 32p. (J). (gr. 4-4). lib. bdg. 28.93 *(978-1-4777-0916-0(9),* 137bd19a-875c-40dd-9aa4-4267a46f79a9) Rosen Publishing Group, Inc., The.

—Why Stephen F. Austin Matters to Texas, 1 vol. 2013. (Texas Perspectives Ser.). (ENG., Illus.). 32p. (J). (gr. 4-4). lib. bdg. 28.93 *(978-1-4777-0914-6(2),* b0ede1c3-3d3c-4048-8910-51b139ab69d1) Rosen Publishing Group, Inc., The.

Pioneer Spirit: The Westward Expansion, 12 vols. 2013. (Pioneer Spirit: the Westward Expansion Ser.). 24p. (J). (ENG.). (gr. 2-3). 157.62 *(978-1-4777-1145-3(7),* 2c6f42bd-d5a3-4258-b6d1-a93113f8492f); (gr. 3-6). pap. 297.00 *(978-1-4777-1248-1(8));* (gr. 3-6). pap. 49.50 *(978-1-4777-1247-4(X))* Rosen Publishing Group, Inc., The. (PowerKids Pr.).

Rajczak Nelson, Kristen. The Donner Party, 1 vol. 2015. (Doomed! Ser.). (ENG., Illus.). 32p. (J). (gr. 4-5). pap. 11.50 *(978-1-4824-2928-2(4),* b65c6e2c-00a0-43be-b0b6-56abfacb7c74) Stevens, Gareth Publishing LLLP.

—Laura Ingalls Wilder in Her Own Words, 1 vol. 2015. (Eyewitness to History Ser.). (ENG., Illus.). 32p. (J). (gr. 4-5). pap. 11.50 *(978-1-4824-4070-6(9),* 3dea84d2-3841-49e7-b25e-7baac428a4a5) Stevens, Gareth Publishing LLLP.

—Life on a Wagon Train, 1 vol. 2013. (What You Didn't Know about History Ser.). (ENG., Illus.). 24p. (J). (gr. 2-3). pap. 9.15 *(978-1-4339-8445-7(8),* 9b458fc3-3d4c-4a1d-a23f-1647e3661dab); lib. bdg. 25.27 *(978-1-4339-8444-0(X),* cd79e9b1-b73f-4f37-9a43-5ef18bc1fd78) Stevens, Gareth Publishing LLLP.

—20 Fun Facts about Pioneer Women, 1 vol. 2015. (Fun Fact File: Women in History Ser.). (ENG., Illus.). 32p. (J). (gr. 2-3). 27.93 *(978-1-4824-2806-3(7),* a193b127-d4d8-4801-84a3-e4a62a08cf9b) Stevens, Gareth Publishing LLLP.

Rau, Margaret. Belle of the West: The True Story of Belle Starr. 2004. (Women of the Frontier Ser.). (Illus.). 160p. (YA). (gr. 6-12). 23.95 *(978-1-883846-68-8(4),* First Biographies) Reynolds, Morgan Inc.

Revolutionary Discoveries of Scientific Pioneers, 16 vols. 2013. (Revolutionary Discoveries of Scientific Pioneers Ser.). (ENG.). 80p. (YA). (gr. 6-6). 307.28 *(978-1-4777-1818-6(4),* 44978647-d7c7-4a7d-ac59-5a2c32750025) Rosen Publishing Group, Inc., The.

Rice, Katelyn. Settling & Unsettling the West (America in The 1800s) rev. ed. 2017. (Social Studies: Informational Text Ser.). (ENG., Illus.). 32p. (gr. 4-8). pap. 11.99 *(978-1-4938-3797-7(4))* Teacher Created Materials, Inc.

Russell, Greta. Olive Boone: Frontier Woman. Hare, John, illus. 2014. (Notable Missourians Ser.). (ENG.). 48p. (J). lib. bdg. 24.00 *(978-1-61248-118-0(3))* Truman State Univ. Pr.

Sanford, William R. & Green, Carl R. Buffalo Bill Cody: Courageous Wild West Showman, 1 vol. 2013. (Courageous Heroes of the American West Ser.). (ENG., Illus.). 48p. (J). (gr. 5-7). 25.27 *(978-0-7660-4007-6(0),* acf6986c-0ec4-4e0c-8a8d-fd517137bc3d); pap. 11.53 *(978-1-4644-0090-2(3),* ca598850-b688-4425-8bbf-58bbc7301998) Enslow Publishing, LLC.

—Calamity Jane: Courageous Wild West Woman, 1 vol. 2013. (Courageous Heroes of the American West Ser.). (ENG., Illus.). 48p. (J). (gr. 5-7). 25.27 *(978-0-7660-4010-6(0),* 0ba4a326-e3fc-4036-9427-c886719c4386); pap. 11.53 *(978-1-4644-0093-3(8),* 3294d813-6625-4898-b0e3-ec98e86bcdec) Enslow Publishing, LLC.

—Daniel Boone: Courageous Frontiersman, 1 vol. 2013. (Courageous Heroes of the American West Ser.). (ENG., Illus.). 48p. (J). (gr. 5-7). 25.27 *(978-0-7660-4002-1(X),* e7ed4ece-6466-4883-85c1-b36dff28492c); pap. 11.53 *(978-1-4644-0085-8(7),* 7820d612-b137-454a-a658-ae080ae9c295) Enslow Publishing, LLC.

—Davy Crockett: Courageous Hero of the Alamo, 1 vol. 2013. (Courageous Heroes of the American West Ser.). (ENG., Illus.). 48p. (J). (gr. 5-7). 25.27 *(978-0-7660-4005-2(4),* 6a5cf7d7-f8de-4af4-b900-46401c5edaf1); pap. 11.53 *(978-1-4644-0086-5(5),* 5b090086-0a64-4b32-80db-f849a4ed5b0f) Enslow Publishing, LLC.

—Kit Carson: Courageous Mountain Man, 1 vol. 2013. (Courageous Heroes of the American West Ser.). (ENG., Illus.). 48p. (J). (gr. 5-7). 25.27 *(978-0-7660-4011-3(9),* 757f85d3-b04f-4e69-b4da-2cf66fb6c127); pap. 11.53 *(978-1-4644-0094-0(6),* c76bd838-258d-431a-a120-4cfb04bb164f) Enslow Publishing, LLC.

Sarantou, Katlin. James Bowie. Bane, Jeff, illus. 2019. (My Early Library: My Itty-Bitty Bio Ser.). (ENG.). 24p. (J). (gr. k-1). pap. 12.79 *(978-1-5341-4991-5(0),* 213271); lib. bdg. 30.64 *(978-1-5341-4705-8(5),* 213270) Cherry Lake Publishing.

Savage, Jeff. Pioneering Women: True Tales of the Wild West, 1 vol. 2012. (True Tales of the Wild West Ser.). (ENG., Illus.). 48p. (gr. 5-7). lib. bdg. 25.27 *(978-0-7660-4022-9(4),* ca454646-a36b-4509-8760-686725fe879c) Enslow Publishing, LLC.

Shoup, Kate. The Gold Rush, 1 vol. 2017. (Primary Sources of Westward Expansion Ser.). (ENG., Illus.). 64p. (gr. 6-6). 35.93 *(978-1-5026-2640-0(3),* d773888d-81ed-4297-9d1c-eb60d3a502f4) Cavendish Square Publishing LLC.

Smith, Andrea P. Daniel Boone. (Illus.). 24p. (J). 2012. 63.60 *(978-1-4488-5227-7(7))* 2011. (ENG., (gr. 2-3). pap. 11.60 *(978-1-4488-5226-0(9),* 3e6572b2-7fbe-448b-9b30-5f364d8f9ab8) 2011. (ENG., (gr. 2-3). lib. bdg. 28.93 *(978-1-4488-5194-2(7),* 6fedb0e8-f5a9-4101-8329-8e6fb1c21d30) Rosen Publishing Group, Inc., The. (PowerKids Pr.).

—Davy Crockett. (Illus.). 24p. (J). 2012. 63.60 *(978-1-4488-5223-9(4))* 2011. (ENG., (gr. 2-3). pap. 11.60 *(978-1-4488-5222-2(6),* f86cea71-ff29-4c80-9b17-a3d7ed457f3a) 2011. (ENG., (gr. 2-3). lib. bdg. 28.93 *(978-1-4488-5192-8(0),* bedb43e6-ebca-415a-b6a2-fe06de680194) Rosen Publishing Group, Inc., The. (PowerKids Pr.).

—Jim Bowie. (Illus.). 24p. (J). 2012. 63.60 *(978-1-4488-5231-4(5))* 2011. (ENG., (gr. 2-3). pap. 11.60 *(978-1-4488-5230-7(7),* 350e3856-77a0-4675-80e7-d692a70b936b) 2011. (ENG., (gr. 2-3). lib. bdg. 28.93 *(978-1-4488-5196-6(3),* 1d58db0c-2356-4f99-8a9c-b1fa3cc8f0f6) Rosen Publishing Group, Inc., The. (PowerKids Pr.).

Smith-Llera, Danielle. Stranded in the Sierra Nevada: The Story of the Donner Party. 2015. (Adventures on the American Frontier Ser.). (ENG., Illus.). 32p. (J). (gr. 3-6). pap. 7.95 *(978-1-4914-4912-7(8),* 128747, Capstone Pr.) Capstone.

Stefoff, Rebecca. Surviving the Oregon Trail: Stories in American History, 1 vol. 2012. (Stories in American History Ser.). (ENG., Illus.). 128p. (gr. 5-6). 35.93 *(978-0-7660-3955-1(2),* c1760ce8-dc06-4e25-9147-347b87cd367f); pap. 13.88 *(978-1-4644-0025-4(3),* c88db0fb-07e6-4a6c-9422-5bd8161ac3b2) Enslow Publishing, LLC.

Stuckey, Rachel. Go West with Famous Trailblazers. 2016. (ENG.). 32p. (J). *(978-0-7787-2324-0(0))* Crabtree Publishing Co.

Transgender Pioneers, 8 vols. 2016. (Transgender Pioneers Ser.). (ENG.). 112p. (gr. 7-7). 155.20 *(978-1-4777-8549-2(3),* 86b3bcaf-59b1-4416-86f5-cd9c2531f092, Rosen Young Adult) Rosen Publishing Group, Inc., The.

Uhl, Xina M. Settlers, Traders, & Trails. 2017. (Westward Expansion: America's Push to the Pacific Ser.). 48p. (J). (gr. 10-14). 84.30 *(978-1-5383-0017-6(6),* Britannica Educational Publishing) Rosen Publishing Group, Inc., The.

Wadsworth, Ginger. Survival in the Snow. Orback, Craig, illus. 2011. 48p. (J). pap. 6.95 *(978-0-7613-3941-0(8)*, First Avenue Editions) Lerner Publishing Group.

Warren, Andrea. The Boy Who Became Buffalo Bill: Growing up Billy Cody in Bleeding Kansas, 0 vols. 2015. (ENG., Illus.). 256p. (J). (gr. 4-9). 19.99 *(978-1-4778-2718-5(8)*, 9781477827185, Two Lions) Amazon Publishing.

PIONEERS—FICTION

Drummond, Ree. Stuck in the Mud. 2015. (I Can Read! Level 1 Ser.). (J). lib. bdg. 13.55 *(978-0-606-36469-0(2))* Turtleback.

Johnson, Mary L. Flinthills Frannie, 1 vol. 2009. 43p. pap. 24.95 *(978-1-61546-886-7(2))* America Star Bks.

Monroe, George. The Secret Cave on the Hill. 2012. 50p. pap. 21.99 *(978-1-4772-8840-5(6))* AuthorHouse.

Monson, Marianne. Pioneer Puzzle. 2010. (Illus.). 84p. (J). *(978-1-60641-669-3(3))* Deseret Bk. Co.

Parker, Amy Christine. Gated. 2014. (Gated Ser.). 368p. (YA). (gr. 9). pap. 9.99 *(978-0-449-81600-4(1)*, Ember) Random Hse. Children's Bks.

Santrey, Laurence & Macken, JoAnn Early. Davy Crockett: Young Pioneer. Livingston, Francis, illus. 2008. 55p. (J). pap. *(978-0-439-02048-0(4))* Scholastic, Inc.

Scott, Dan. The Secret of Fort Pioneer: A Bret King Mystery. Beeler, Joe, illus. 2011. 190p. 42.95 *(978-1-258-09951-0(9))* Literary Licensing, LLC.

Tarshis, Lauren. I Survived the Children's Blizzard, 1888 (I Survived #16) 2018. (I Survived Ser.: 16). (ENG.). 144p. (J). (gr. 2-5). pap. 4.99 *(978-0-545-91977-7(0)*, Scholastic Paperbacks) Scholastic, Inc.

—I Survived the Children's Blizzard, 1888 (I Survived #16) (Library Edition) 2018. (I Survived Ser.: 16). (ENG., Illus.). 144p. (J). (gr. 2-5). lib. bdg. 25.99 *(978-0-545-91978-4(9)*, Scholastic Paperbacks) Scholastic, Inc.

Webster, Raelyn & Rasmussen, Kenneth L. My Grandma Mary. Johnson, Kimberli Anne, illus. 2013. 38p. 22.95 *(978-1-940379-00-5(8))* Telling Family Tales.

PIPE FITTING—VOCATIONAL GUIDANCE

Payment, Simone. A Career as a Plumber, 1 vol. 2010. (Essential Careers Ser.). (ENG.). 80p. (YA). (gr. 6-6). lib. bdg. 37.47 *(978-1-4358-9473-0(1)*, b5090b56-9622-4089-b878-4b673c05f3d2) Rosen Publishing Group, Inc., The.

PIRATES

see also Privateering; United States—History—Tripolitan War, 1801-1805; Women Pirates

Abbott, Simon. 100 Questions about Pirates. 2018. (100 Questions Ser.). (ENG., Illus.). 48p. (J). 7.99 *(978-1-4413-2615-7(4)*, 9bfbafa0-85af-403f-b946-28315e34c903) Peter Pauper Pr. Inc.

AZ Books Staff. Secrets of Pirates. Naumovets, Elena, ed. 2012. (Mysteries of History Ser.). (ENG.). 18p. (J). (gr. 1-3). bds. 17.95 *(978-1-61889-089-4(1))* AZ Bks. LLC.

Barefoot Books, et al. Pirates Fun Activities. 2008. (ENG., Illus.). 16p. (J). pap. 4.99 *(978-1-84686-217-5(5))* Barefoot Bks., Inc.

Believe It Or Not, Ripley, compiled by. Ripley Twists: Pirates. 2015. (Twist Ser.: 14). (ENG., Illus.). 48p. (J). 12.95 *(978-1-60991-139-3(3))* Ripley Entertainment, Inc.

Believe It Or Not!, Ripleys, compiled by. Ripley Twists PB: Pirates. 2018. (Twist Ser.: 13). (ENG.). 48p. (J). pap. 7.99 *(978-1-60991-225-3(X))* Ripley Entertainment, Inc.

Bell, Robin. My Adventure with Pirates: Advanced My Adventure. 2009. (ENG.). 44p. (J). 8.99 *(978-1-59092-462-4(2))* Blue Forge Pr.

Biskup, Agnieszka. Captured by Pirates! An Isabel Soto History Adventure. Stewart, Roger, illus. 2012. (Graphic Expeditions Ser.). (ENG.). 32p. (gr. 3-4). pap. 47.70 *(978-1-4296-8471-2(2)*, Capstone Pr.) Capstone.

Bodden, Valerie. Pirates. 2017. (X-Books: Fighters Ser.). (ENG., Illus.). 32p. (J). (gr. 3-6). *(978-1-60818-814-7(0)*, 20375, Creative Education) Creative Co., The.

—X-Books: Pirates. 2017. (X-Bks.). (Illus.). 32p. (J). (gr. 3-7). pap. 9.99 *(978-1-62832-417-4(1)*, 20376, Creative Paperbacks) Creative Co., The.

Boshouwers, Suzan. Pirates. Hund, Marjolein, illus. 2012. (Want to Know Ser.). (ENG.). 30p. (J). (gr. k-2). 16.95 *(978-1-60537-135-1(1))* Clavis Publishing.

Brew, Jim. Pirates. 2012. (History's Greatest Warriors Ser.). (ENG., Illus.). 24p. (J). (gr. 3-7). lib. bdg. 26.95 *(978-1-60014-747-0(X)*, Torque Bks.) Bellwether Media.

Brown, Chris. Shiver Me Timbers: A Fun Book of Pirates, Sailors, & Other Sea-Farers. 2006. (ENG., Illus.). 32p. (J). (gr. 4-7). pap. 8.95 *(978-0-7145-3303-2(3))* Consortium Bk. Sales & Distribution.

Buckley, James, Jr. & Who HQ. Who Was Blackbeard? Qiu, Joseph J. M. , illus. 2015. (Who Was? Ser.). 112p. (J). (gr. 3-7). 6.99 *(978-0-448-48308-5(4)*, Penguin Workshop) Penguin Young Readers Group.

Buckley, James. Who Was Blackbeard? 2015. (Who Was... ? Ser.). lib. bdg. 16.00 *(978-0-606-37556-6(2))* Turtleback.

Bunting, Eve. P Is for Pirate: A Pirate Alphabet. Manders, John, illus. 2014. (ENG.). 40p. (J). (gr. 2-5). 16.95 *(978-1-58536-815-0(6)*, 203668) Sleeping Bear Pr.

Caldwell, Stella. Blackbeard's Pirateworld: Cut-Throats of the Caribbean. 2011. (Y Ser.). (ENG., Illus.). 80p. (J). (gr. 3-7). 19.95 *(978-1-84732-973-8(X))* Carlton Bks., Ltd. GBR. Dist: Two Rivers Distribution.

Callery, Sean. Treasure Hunt. 2011. (ENG.). 24p. (J). pap. *(978-0-7787-7874-5(6))*; (gr. 3-6). *(978-0-7787-7852-3(5))* Crabtree Publishing Co.

Caviezel, Giovanni. Pirates! Mesturini, C., illus. 2011. (Mini People Shape Bks.). 10p. (J). (gr. -1-1). bds. 5.99 *(978-0-7641-6441-5(4))* Sourcebooks, Inc.

Cawthorne, Nigel. Pirates: An Illustrated History. 2013. (Illus.). 144p. (J). *(978-1-4351-4657-0(3))* Metro Bks.

Claybourne, Anna. Pirate Secrets Revealed. 2010. (Extreme! Ser.). (ENG.). 32p. (gr. 3-4). pap. 47.70 *(978-1-4296-5024-3(9)*, Capstone Pr.) Capstone.

—Treasure Hunter's Handbook. 2011. (ENG.). 24p. (J). pap. *(978-0-7787-7866-0(5))*; (gr. 3-6). *(978-0-7787-7844-8(4))* Crabtree Publishing Co.

Clissold, Caroline. All about Pirates. 2007. (Trackers-Math Ser.). (gr. 2-5). pap. 5.00 *(978-1-59055-918-5(5))* Pacific Learning, Inc.

Cooke, Tim. Blackbeard: A Notorious Pirate in the Caribbean, 1 vol. 2015. (Wanted! Famous Outlaws Ser.). (ENG., Illus.). 48p. (J). (gr. 6-8). pap. 15.05 *(978-1-4824-4247-2(7)*, 8f808262-5a79-4559-b632-e546660fb970) Stevens, Gareth Publishing LLLP.

Davies, Kate & Stowell, Louie. Sticker Dressing Pirates. 2012. (Sticker Dressing Ser.). 24p. (J). pap. 8.99 *(978-0-7945-3165-2(2)*, Usborne) EDC Publishing.

Davis, Sarah K. Pirates. 2016. (Uncommon Women Ser.). (ENG., Illus.). 48p. (gr. 3-8). 27.99 *(978-1-62920-584-7(2))* Scobre Pr. Corp.

DeGagne, Mandie. Pirates. Dennis, Peter, illus. 2012. 31p. (J). *(978-1-58865-594-3(6))* Kidsbooks, LLC.

Design Eye Publishing Staff, et al. Amazing Automata — Pirates! 2013. (Dover Origami Papercraft Ser.). (ENG.). 24p. (J). (gr. 5). 14.99 *(978-0-486-49980-2(4)*, 499804) Dover Pubns., Inc.

DK. DKfindout! Pirates. 2017. (DK Findout! Ser.). (ENG., Illus.). 64p. (J). (gr. 1-4). pap. 10.99 *(978-1-4654-5752-3(6)*, DK Children) Dorling Kindersley Publishing, Inc.

Donaldson, Madeline. Pirates, Scoundrels, & Scallywags. 2015. (ShockZone (tm) — Villains Ser.). (ENG., Illus.). 32p. (J). (gr. 5-8). E-Book 46.65 *(978-1-4677-6005-8(6)*, 9781467760058, Lerner Digital) Lerner Publishing Group.

Drechsler, Lawrence. The Pirates. (Illus.). (Orig.). (J). (gr. 6-18). pap. *(978-0-935143-01-0(7))* Treadle Pr.

Elborough, Travis. Highwayman, Outlaws & Bandits of London. 2004. (... . of London Ser.). (ENG., Illus.). 96p. pap. 8.99 *(978-1-904153-13-9(5))* Watling St., Ltd. GBR. Dist: Trafalgar Square Publishing.

English, Alex. Pirates Don't Drive Diggers. Beedie, Duncan, illus. 2019. (Early Bird Readers — Orange (Early Bird Stories (tm)) Ser.). (ENG.). 32p. (J). (gr. k-3). 30.65 *(978-1-5415-4221-1(5)*, 9ac76b41-4605-4891-9cd5-ca610ae092db); pap. 9.99 *(978-1-5415-7414-4(1)*, 19707421-c580-497c-b567-bd6ce5f91e10) Lerner Publishing Group. (Lerner Pubns.).

Farndon, John. How to Live Like a Caribbean Pirate. Viana, Tatio, illus. 2016. (How to Live Like ... Ser.). (ENG.). 32p. (J). (gr. 3-6). 27.99 *(978-1-5124-0631-3(7)*, d8e6f336-30b3-42e7-a66a-805955e96d23, Hungry Tomato (r)) Lerner Publishing Group.

Feder, Joshua B. Pirates. 2003. (Illus.). 66p. (YA). (gr. 5-9). reprint ed. 22.00 *(978-0-7567-6684-9(2))* DIANE Publishing Co.

Fox, E. T. Pirates. 2017. (Illus.). 64p. (J). *(978-1-5182-2427-0(X))* Dorling Kindersley Publishing, Inc.

Gelletly, LeeAnne. Modern-Day Pirates. 2013. (J). *(978-1-61900-038-4(5))*; 34.95 *(978-1-61900-037-7(7))* Eldorado Ink.

Gilpin, Rebecca. Pirate Things to make & Do. 2005. 32p. (J). pap. 6.95 *(978-0-7945-1061-9(2)*, Usborne) EDC Publishing.

Gunderson, Jessica. Your Life as a Cabin Boy on a Pirate Ship. Burns, Mike, illus. 2012. (Way It Was Ser.). (ENG.). 32p. (J). (gr. 2-5). pap. 8.95 *(978-1-4048-7249-3(3)*, 118192, Picture Window Bks.) Capstone.

Hanel, Rachel. Pirates. 2007. (Fearsome Fighters Ser.). (ENG., Illus.). 48p. (J). (gr. 5-8). lib. bdg. 31.35 *(978-1-58341-537-5(8)*, 22147) Creative Co., The.

Harris, Nicholas. Let's Explore a Pirate Ship. Lee, Brian, illus. 2010. 36p. (J). 13.99 *(978-0-8437-1378-7(X))* Hammond World Atlas Corp.

Harrison, Paul. Pirates. (Up Close Ser.). 24p. (gr. 3-3). 2009. 47.90 *(978-1-60854-699-2(3))* 2007. (ENG., Illus.). (J). lib. bdg. 28.93 *(978-1-4042-4226-5(0)*, 66dedea1-491c-4300-aadb-1a60c35257ca) Rosen Publishing Group, Inc., The. (PowerKids Pr.).

Havercroft, Elizabeth. A Year on a Pirate Ship. 2008. (Time Goes By Ser.). (ENG.). (gr. k-3). pap. 39.62 *(978-0-7613-4716-3(X))*; (Illus.). 24p. lib. bdg. 22.60 *(978-1-58013-547-4(1))* Lerner Publishing Group.

Helbrough, Emma. A Day in the Life of a Pirate. 2009. (Day in the Life Ser.). 32p. (gr. 4-5). 47.90 *(978-1-61511-007-0(0)*, PowerKids Pr.) Rosen Publishing Group, Inc., The.

Hibbert, Clare. Real Pirates, 1 vol. James, John, illus. 2009. (Real Adventurers Ser.). (ENG.). 48p. (J). (gr. 3-3). 25.50 *(978-1-59270-018-9(7)*, 1f8913ca-45e0-44c6-a1ce-f080b521aeb2, Cavendish Square) Cavendish Square Publishing LLC.

Hunter, Nick. Pirate Treasure, 1 vol. 2013. (Treasure Hunters Ser.). (ENG., Illus.). 48p. (J). (gr. 5-8). lib. bdg. 32.65 *(978-1-4109-4953-0(2)*, 120945, Raintree) Capstone.

Jackman, Vernon. Bunnies & Butterflies in the Backyard & the Pirates Who Know Where They Live: Stories That Help Children Learn & Remember Their Address & Telephone Number. Theagene, Jeannisse, illus. l.t. ed. 2010. (ENG.). 32p. (J). pap. 6.99 *(978-0-9829371-1-2(3))* New Kid Safety.

Jenson-Elliott, Cindy & Sautter, Aaron. The Most Famous Pirates. 2013. (Illus.). 32p. (J). *(978-91-620-6520-1(3))* Capstone.

Kaplan, Arie. Swashbuckling Scoundrels: Pirates in Fact & Fiction. 2015. (ENG., Illus.). 72p. (YA). (gr. 5-12). lib. bdg. 33.32 *(978-1-4677-5252-7(5)*, 12a45b99-1878-4277-8f42-947d5bea1052); E-Book 50.65 *(978-1-4677-5253-4(3))* Lerner Publishing Group. (Twenty-First Century Bks.).

Keppeler, Jill. Pirate Legends, 1 vol. 2017. (Famous Legends Ser.). (ENG.). 32p. (J). (gr. 2-3). pap. 11.50 *(978-1-5382-0245-6(X)*, 3b6f6844-539a-445d-a4c4-3dfafbd9466d) Stevens, Gareth Publishing LLLP.

Keyworth, R. L. Do Pirates Like to Play Pattie Cake? A Pirate's Guide to Playing Nice. 2009. 40p. pap. 17.99 *(978-1-4389-4667-2(8))* AuthorHouse.

Krull, Kathleen. Lives of the Pirates: Swashbucklers, Scoundrels (Neighbors Beware!) Hewitt, Kathryn, illus. 2013. (Lives Of ... Ser.). (ENG.). 96p. (J). (gr. 5-7). pap. 8.99 *(978-0-544-10495-2(1)*, 1540801, Clarion Bks.) HarperCollins Pubs.

LaBaff, Stephanie. Draw Pirates in 4 Easy Steps: Then Write a Story, 1 vol. 2012. (Drawing in 4 Easy Steps Ser.). (ENG., Illus.). 48p. (gr. 3-3). 27.93 *(978-0-7660-3839-4(4)*, 72a65d75-aa6a-4408-bd7e-33c9e6627f57) Enslow Publishing, LLC.

Langley, Andrew. Pirates, 1 vol. 2014. (100 Facts You Should Know Ser.). (ENG., Illus.). 48p. (J). (gr. 4-5). lib. bdg. 33.60 *(978-1-4824-2181-1(X)*, d13c3b16-dd74-4d91-b0a8-2b74823f001f) Stevens, Gareth Publishing LLLP.

Leapfrog Learners - Pirates. (Awesome Adventures Ser.). 16p. (J). *(978-2-7643-0117-3(0))* Phidal Publishing, Inc./Editions Phidal, Inc.

Leblanc, Catherine. How to Pulverize Pirates. Garrigue, Roland, illus. 2013. (ENG.). 32p. (J). (gr. -1). 14.99 *(978-1-60887-192-6(4))* Insight Editions.

Leigh, Susannah. Puzzle Pirates. Haw, Brenda, illus. 2006. (Usborne Young Puzzles Ser.). 32p. (J). (gr. 1). lib. bdg. 14.99 *(978-1-58086-973-7(4)*, Usborne) EDC Publishing.

Lethbridge, Lucy. True Stories of Pirates. 2005. (True Adventure Stories Ser.). (Illus.). 144p. (J). pap. 4.99 *(978-0-7945-0875-3(8)*, Usborne) EDC Publishing.

Lewis, Jan, illus. Pirate Ship: Lift the Flaps to Follow the Clues & Discover the Fabulous Treasure. 2016. 10p. (J). (gr. -1-12). 7.99 *(978-1-86147-767-5(8)*, Armadillo) Anness Publishing GBR. Dist: National Bk. Network.

Lichtenheld, Tom. Everything I Know about Pirates. Lichtenheld, Tom, illus. 2003. (ENG., Illus.). 40p. (J). (gr. -1-3). pap. 8.99 *(978-0-689-86009-6(9)*, Simon & Schuster Bks. For Young Readers) Simon & Schuster Bks. For Young Readers.

Lincoln, Margarette. The Pirate's Handbook: How to Become a Rogue of the High Seas. (Illus.). (J). pap. 15.99 *(978-0-590-24558-6(9))* Scholastic, Inc.

Little & Large Sticker Activity Pirates. 2008. 24p. pap. *(978-1-84810-061-9(2))* Miles Kelly Publishing, Ltd.

Llimós, Anna & Llimós, Anna. Pirate Ship Adventure Crafts, 1 vol. 2010. (Fun Adventure Crafts Ser.). (ENG., Illus.). 32p. (gr. k-2). 26.60 *(978-0-7660-3728-1(2)*, c34e8dba-19cd-4345-bd93-d3945b0dc42c, Enslow Elementary) Enslow Publishing, LLC.

—Pirate Ship Adventure Crafts, 1 vol. 2010. (Fun Adventure Crafts Ser.). (ENG., Illus.). 32p. (gr. k-2). pap. 10.35 *(978-0-7660-3729-8(0)*, 5e6d7154-7660-4c99-bb59-10c660b0bff0, Enslow Elementary) Enslow Publishing, LLC.

Lloyd, Jones. 1001 Pirate Things to Spot. 2007. (ENG., Illus.). 32p. *(978-0-7460-7694-1(0)*, Usborne) EDC Publishing.

Lock, Deborah. Pirate Attack! 2017. (Illus.). 48p. (J). *(978-1-5379-5703-6(1))* Dorling Kindersley Publishing, Inc.

Loh-Hagan, Virginia. Pirates vs. Ninjas. 2019. (Battle Royale: Lethal Warriors Ser.). (ENG., Illus.). 32p. (J). (gr. 4-8). pap. 14.21 *(978-1-5341-5050-8(1)*, 213507); lib. bdg. 32.07 *(978-1-5341-4764-5(0)*, 213506) Cherry Lake Publishing. (45th Parallel Press).

Lombardo, Jennifer. Piracy: From the High Seas to the Digital Age, 1 vol. 2018. (World History Ser.). (ENG.). 104p. (gr. 7-7). lib. bdg. 41.53 *(978-1-5345-6382-7(2)*, 1d66689e-177b-47d4-ba39-535d5aa77164, Lucent Pr.) Greenhaven Publishing LLC.

Lubber, William. Pirateology: The Pirate Hunter's Companion. Steer, Dugald A., ed. 2006. (Ologies Ser.). (ENG., Illus.). 32p. (J). (gr. 3-7). 29.99 *(978-0-7636-3143-7(4))* Candlewick Pr.

Macdonald, Fiona. Nasty Pirates: You Wouldn't Want to Meet!, 1 vol. Antram, David, illus. 2010. (Top 10 Worst Ser.). (ENG.). 32p. (J). (gr. 3-5). pap. 11.50 *(978-1-4339-4086-6(8)*, 9708354b-7aa2-448b-83fa-b0d9d3c406d1); lib. bdg. 29.27 *(978-1-4339-4085-9(X)*, 7b0ad2ce-1090-497f-b5da-c392ab6df375) Stevens, Gareth Publishing LLLP. (Gareth Stevens Learning Library).

Macdonald, Fiona & Salariya, Daivid. Top 10 Worst Nasty Pirates: You Wouldn't Want to Meet! Antram, David, illus. 2013. 32p. (J). *(978-1-4351-5037-9(6))* Barnes & Noble, Inc.

Malam, John. Do You Want to Be a Pirate? 2015. (Do You Want to Be... Ser.). (Illus.). 32p. (gr. 3-6). 28.50 *(978-1-909645-36-3(2))* Book Hse. GBR. Dist: Black Rabbit Bks.

—You Wouldn't Want to... Be a Pirate's Prisoner! Antram, David, illus. rev. ed. 2012. (ENG.). 32p. (J). lib. bdg. 29.00 *(978-0-531-27502-3(7))* Scholastic Library Publishing.

Marley, David F. Daily Life of Pirates, 1 vol. 2012. (Greenwood Press Daily Life Through History Ser.). (ENG., Illus.). 312p. (C). 70.00 *(978-0-313-39563-5(2)*, 790751, Greenwood) Bloomsbury Publishing USA.

Mason, Paul. Pirate Adventures! 2011. (ENG.). 24p. (J). pap. *(978-0-7787-7878-3(9))*; (gr. 3-6). *(978-0-7787-7856-1(8))* Crabtree Publishing Co.

McCarthy, Tom. Pirates & Shipwrecks: True Stories. 2016. (Mystery & Mayhem Ser.). (ENG., Illus.). 128p. (J). (gr. 3-6). 19.95 *(978-1-61930-471-0(6)*, 106a9167-bf27-46d2-891a-440cbdec514f) Nomad Pr.

McDonald, Jake. The Pirate Colouring Book. McDonald, Jake, illus. 2015. (ENG., Illus.). 32p. (J). (gr. -1-3). pap. 7.99 *(978-1-78055-310-8(2))* O'Mara, Michael Bks., Ltd. GBR. Dist: Independent Pubs. Group.

McLeese, Don. Pirates. 2009. 32p. pap. 7.99 *(978-0-8249-1449-3(X)*, Ideals Pubns.) Worthy Publishing.

McNeil, Niki, et al. HOCPP 1139 Pirates. 2006. spiral bd. 19.00 *(978-1-60308-139-9(9))* In the Hands of a Child.

Meinking, Mary & Peschke, Marci. Kylie Jean Pirate Craft Queen, 1 vol. Mourning, Tuesday, illus. 2014. (Kylie Jean Craft Queen Ser.). (ENG.). 32p. (J). (gr. 1-3). lib. bdg. 27.32 *(978-1-4795-2192-0(2)*, 124030, Picture Window Bks.) Capstone.

Menges, Jeff A. Haunted Pirates Tattoos. 2004. (Dover Tattoos Ser.). (ENG., Illus.). 2p. (J). (gr. 1-4). pap. 3.50 *(978-0-486-43320-2(X)*, 43320X) Dover Pubns., Inc.

Miles, Liz. Meet the Pirates, 1 vol. 2014. (Encounters with the Past Ser.). (ENG.). 32p. (J). (gr. 3-4). 28.27 *(978-1-4824-0893-5(7)*, d44f17f2-ce31-4c8e-a8e0-5271e456158f) Stevens, Gareth Publishing LLLP.

Morris, Neil. Pirates. 2009. (Amazing History Ser.). (Illus.). 32p. (J). (gr. 4-7). pap. 7.95 *(978-1-59920-205-1(0))* Black Rabbit Bks.

Mould, Chris. The Great Flytrap Disaster. Mould, Chris, illus. 2019. (Pocket Pirates Ser.: 3). (ENG., Illus.). 144p. (J). (gr. 1-4). 17.99 *(978-1-4814-9121-1(0))*; pap. 6.99 *(978-1-4814-9120-4(2))* Simon & Schuster Children's Publishing. (Aladdin).

Nemmers, Tom. Pirates Scratch & Sketch: For Adventurous Artists & Explorers of All Ages. Zschock, Martha Day, illus. 2007. 64p. (J). 12.99 *(978-1-59359-871-6(8))* Peter Pauper Pr. Inc.

Nilsen, Anna. Pirates: All Aboard for Hours of Puzzling Fun! 2006. (Illus.). 32p. pap. *(978-1-921049-71-2(5))* Little Hare Bks. AUS. Dist: HarperCollins Pubs. Australia.

O'Donnell, Liam. Hop on the Pirate History Boat. 2017. (Pirates! Ser.). (ENG., Illus.). 32p. (J). (gr. 3-5). lib. bdg. 32.65 *(978-1-4109-8703-7(5)*, 135774, Raintree) Capstone.

Olson, Elsie. Pirates! Bold & Brutal Rebels. 2017. (History's Hotshots Ser.). (ENG., Illus.). 32p. (J). (gr. 3-6). lib. bdg. 32.79 *(978-1-5321-1273-7(4)*, 27597, Checkerboard Library) ABDO Publishing Co.

Pope, Miller. ABC-Pirate-Coloring Book. 2012. (ENG.). (J). pap. 5.99 *(978-1-4507-8603-4(0))* Independent Pub.

Price, Roger & Stern, Leonard. Pirates Mad Libs: World's Greatest Word Game. 2007. (Mad Libs Ser.). 48p. (J). (gr. 3-7). 5.99 *(978-0-8431-2313-5(3)*, Mad Libs) Penguin Young Readers Group.

Punter, R. Pirates. 2004. (Young Reading Ser.: Vol. 1). 48p. (J). (gr. 2-18). lib. bdg. 13.99 *(978-1-58086-608-8(5)*, Usborne) EDC Publishing.

Punter, Russell. Pirates Kid Kit. 2004. (Kid Kits Ser.). 48p. (J). 15.99 *(978-1-58086-732-0(4))*; 15.99 *(978-1-58086-735-1(9))* EDC Publishing. (Usborne).

Reid, Struan & Stowell, Louie. My First Pirate Book. Allen, Peter, illus. 2012. (My First Book Ser.). 16p. (J). ring bd. 6.99 *(978-0-7945-3228-4(4)*, Usborne) EDC Publishing.

Rice, Dona Herweck. Bad Guys & Gals on the High Seas, 1 vol. 2nd rev. ed. 2013. (TIME for KIDS(r): Informational Text Ser.). (ENG., Illus.). 64p. (J). (gr. 4-8). pap. 14.99 *(978-1-4333-4902-7(7))* Teacher Created Materials, Inc.

Riggs, Kate. Pirates. 2011. (Great Warriors Ser.). 24p. (J). (gr. k-2). 16.95 *(978-1-60818-002-8(6)*, Creative Education) Creative Co., The.

Robinson, Michelle. Happy Birthday to You, Pirate. Gausden, Vicki, illus. 2019. (ENG.). 32p. (J). pap. 6.99 *(978-0-00-824220-6(8)*, HarperCollins Children's Bks.) HarperCollins Pubs. Ltd. GBR. Dist: HarperCollins Pubs.

Robson, Kirsteen. Wipe-Clean Pirate Activities. 2015. (Wipe-Clean Bks.). (ENG.). 22p. (J). (gr. k-5). pap. 7.99 *(978-0-7945-3543-8(7)*, Usborne) EDC Publishing.

Ryland Peters and Small Staff, creator. Now I am a Pirate. 2008. (ENG., Illus.). 48p. *(978-1-84597-743-6(2))* Ryland Peters & Small.

Savery, Annabel. Pirates. 2012. (It's Amazing Ser.). (Illus.). 32p. (gr. 3-6). lib. bdg. 31.35 *(978-1-59920-690-5(0))* Black Rabbit Bks.

Shirley, Rebekah Joy. I Want to Be a Pirate, 1 vol. 2011. (Let's Play Dress Up Ser.). (ENG., Illus.). 24p. (J). (gr. 2-3). pap. 11.60 *(978-1-61533-393-6(2)*, e98abde6-c105-4496-bed0-335cb2661f6e, Windmill Bks.) Rosen Publishing Group, Inc., The.

Smith, Helen. Pirates, Swashbucklers & Buccaneers of London. 2004. (... . of London Ser.). (ENG., Illus.). 96p. pap. 8.99 *(978-1-904153-17-7(8))* Watling St., Ltd. GBR. Dist: Trafalgar Square Publishing.

Smith, Jeremy. Why Why Why... Did Pirates Bury Their Treasure? 2010. (Why Why Why Ser.). (Illus.). 32p. (J). (gr. 1-3). lib. bdg. 18.95 *(978-1-4222-1576-0(8))* Mason Crest.

Spence, David. Pirates. 2004. (Illus.). 32p. (J). (gr. 4-7). pap. 5.95 *(978-1-86007-001-3(9)*, TickTock Books) Octopus Publishing Group GBR. Dist: Independent Pubs. Group.

Spenceley, Angela, compiled by. Pirate Coloring & Sticker Book: Your Complete Guide to Famous Pirates. l.t. ed. 2006. (Illus.). 24p. (J). pap. 8.95 *(978-0-9702168-6-1(6))* Coconut Pr., LLC.

Steele, Philip. The Amazing History of Pirates: See What a Buccaneer's Life Was Really Like, with over 350 Exciting Pictures. 2016. (Illus.). 64p. (J). (gr. 3-7). 12.99 *(978-1-86147-711-8(2)*, Armadillo) Anness Publishing GBR. Dist: National Bk. Network.

Stefoff, Rebecca. Captain Kidd. 2015. (J). lib. bdg. *(978-1-62713-529-0(4))* 2014. (ENG.). 48p. (gr. 4-4). 33.07 *(978-1-5026-0205-3(9)*, 50a7e25c-f746-41b5-96c6-58937ec3879c) Cavendish Square Publishing LLC.

—Redbeard. 2015. (J). lib. bdg. *(978-1-62713-533-7(2))* 2014. (ENG.). 48p. (gr. 4-4). 33.07 *(978-1-5026-0199-5(0)*, e4b135dd-9834-4a92-bf28-59f105628332) Cavendish Square Publishing LLC.

Stewart, Alex. Pirates. 2013. (Greatest Warriors Ser.). 32p. (gr. 3-7). 28.50 *(978-1-78212-401-6(2))* Arcturus Publishing GBR. Dist: Black Rabbit Bks.

Stockton, Frank Richard. Buccaneers & Pirates of Our Coasts. 2008. 232p. 24.99 *(978-0-559-13822-5(9))* 2008. 228p. (gr. 4-7). 24.99 *(978-0-554-35563-4(9))* 2007. (ENG.). 206p. pap. 20.99 *(978-1-4346-0736-2(4))* Creative Media Partners, LLC.

—Buccaneers & Pirates of Our Coasts. 2007. (ENG., Illus.). 216p. (J). (gr. 4-7). per. *(978-1-4065-6187-6(8))* Dodo Pr.

—Buccaneers & Pirates of Our Coasts. Varian, George & Clinedinst, B. West, illus. 2008. 364p. (gr. 4-7). 46.95 *(978-1-4369-8234-4(0))*; pap. 31.95 *(978-1-4367-9391-9(2))* Kessinger Publishing, LLC.

—Buccaneers & Pirates of Our Coasts. 2013. (Notable American Authors Ser.). reprint ed. lthr. 79.00 *(978-0-7812-8936-8(X))* Reprint Services Corp.

—Buccaneers & Pirates of Our Coasts. 2005. pap. 30.95 *(978-1-885529-90-9(2))* Stevens Publishing.

—Buccaneers & Pirates of Our Coasts. 2005. 35.00 *(978-1-55742-497-6(7))*; pap. 15.95 *(978-1-55742-486-0(1))* Wildside Pr., LLC.

Storey, Rita. Pirates. 2013. (Have Fun with Arts & Crafts Ser.). 32p. (gr. 4-7). 31.35 *(978-1-59920-900-5(4))* Black Rabbit Bks.

Sullivan, Laura. Black Bart Roberts, 1 vol. 2014. (True-Life Pirates Ser.). (ENG.). 48p. (gr. 4-4). lib. bdg. 33.07 *(978-1-5026-0207-7(5)*, 01a2fd0b-19f9-48b7-836a-deaeffa57ba2) Cavendish Square Publishing LLC.

Sullivan, Laura L. Black Bart Roberts. 2015. (J). lib. bdg. *(978-1-62713-527-6(8))* Cavendish Square Publishing LLC.

—Blackbeard. 2015. (J). lib. bdg. *(978-1-62713-525-2(1))* Cavendish Square Publishing LLC.

—Sir Henry Morgan. 2015. (J). lib. bdg. *(978-1-62713-308-1(9))* Cavendish Square Publishing LLC.

Sutherland, Adam. The Fact or Fiction Behind Pirates, 1 vol. 2015. (Fact or Phony? Ser.). (ENG.). 96p. (J). (gr. 5-6). lib. bdg. 34.93 *(978-1-4824-4271-7(X)*, f0f7b124-3746-4a3a-9605-1d45541c1640) Stevens, Gareth Publishing LLLP.

Taplin, Sam. Pirates First Coloring Book. 2012. (First Sticker Coloring Bks). 16p. (J). pap. 6.99 *(978-0-7945-3260-4(8)*, Usborne) EDC Publishing.

Temple, Bob. The Golden Age of Pirates: An Interactive History Adventure. rev. ed. 2016. (You Choose: History Ser.). (ENG., Illus.). 112p. (J). (gr. 3-7). pap. 6.95 *(978-1-5157-4255-5(5)*, 134009, Capstone Pr.) Capstone.

Terp, Gail. Pirates. 2019. (History's Warriors Ser.). (ENG.). 32p. (J). (gr. 4-6). pap. 9.99 *(978-1-64466-043-0(1)*, 12761); (Illus.). lib. bdg. *(978-1-68072-852-1(0)*, 12760) Black Rabbit Bks. (Bolt).

True-Life Pirates, 12 vols. 2014. (True-Life Pirates Ser.). (ENG.). 48p. (J). (gr. 4-4). lib. bdg. 198.42 *(978-1-5026-0305-0(5)*, 3f643626-5e3e-40c4-95a2-62169079c472, Cavendish Square) Cavendish Square Publishing LLC.

Tucker, Rosalyn. Famous Pirates. 2015. (Pirates Ahoy! Ser.). (ENG., Illus.). 24p. (J). (gr. -1-2). lib. bdg. 27.32 *(978-1-4914-2111-6(8)*, 127596, Capstone Pr.) Capstone.

Usborne Books Staff, creator. Pirate Treasure Kid Kit. 2007. (Kid Kits Ser.). 32p. (J). (gr. 4-7). 19.99 *(978-1-60130-004-1(2)*, Usborne) EDC Publishing.

Valat, Pierre-Marie. Pirates. 2018. (My First Discoveries Ser.). (ENG., Illus.). 36p. (J). (gr. -1-3). spiral bd. 19.99 *(978-1-85103-469-7(2))* Moonlight Publishing, Ltd. GBR. Dist: Independent Pubs. Group.

Vonne, Mira. Gross Facts about Pirates. 2017. (Gross History Ser.). (ENG., Illus.). 32p. (J). (gr. 3-9). lib. bdg. 27.32 *(978-1-5157-4157-2(5)*, 133957, Capstone Pr.) Capstone.

Watt, Fiona. Pirate Sticker Book. Nichols, Paul, illus. 2011. (Sticker Activity Books Ser.). 24p. (J). pap. 8.99 *(978-0-7945-2915-4(1)*, Usborne) EDC Publishing.

Weintraub, Aileen. The Barbarossa Brothers: 16th-Century Pirates of the Barbary Coast. 2009. (Library of Pirates Ser.). 24p. (gr. 3-3). 42.50 *(978-1-60853-814-0(1)*, PowerKids Pr.) Rosen Publishing Group, Inc., The.

—Captain Kidd: 17th-Century Pirate of the Indian Ocean & African Coast. (Library of Pirates Ser.). 24p. (gr. 3-3). 2009. 42.50 *(978-1-60853-811-9(7)*, PowerKids Pr.) 2005. (ENG., Illus.). (YA). lib. bdg. 26.27 *(978-0-8239-5797-2(7)*, 9c5dfa96-1096-456b-a6f9-50a8f7c69632) Rosen Publishing Group, Inc., The.

—Henry Morgan: 17th-Century Buccaneer. 2009. (Library of Pirates Ser.). 24p. (gr. 3-3). 42.50 *(978-1-60853-812-6(5)*, PowerKids Pr.) Rosen Publishing Group, Inc., The.

—Jean Lafitte: Pirate Hero of the War Of 1812. 2009. (Library of Pirates Ser.). 24p. (gr. 3-3). 42.50 *(978-1-60853-813-3(3)*, PowerKids Pr.) Rosen Publishing Group, Inc., The.

—The Library of Pirates, 6 bks. Incl. Barbarossa Brothers: 16th-Century Pirates of the Barbary Coast. 2001. lib. bdg. 26.27 *(978-0-8239-5799-6(3)*, e8d1e5c3-d453-4177-a48a-9ec7fb9e5133); Captain Kidd: 17th-Century Pirate of the Indian Ocean & African Coast. 2005. lib. bdg. 26.27 *(978-0-8239-5797-2(7)*, 9c5dfa96-1096-456b-a6f9-50a8f7c69632); 24p. (YA). (gr. 3-4). (Illus.). 49.20 o.p. *(978-0-8239-7133-6(3)*, PowerKids Pr.) Rosen Publishing Group, Inc., The.

West, David. Lots of Things You Want to Know about Pirates. 2015. (Lots of Things You Want to Know About Ser.). (ENG.). 24p. (J). 28.50 *(978-1-62588-092-5(8)*, 19303, Smart Apple Media) Black Rabbit Bks.

White, Graham. A Maze Adventure: Search for Pirate Treasure. 2009. (Illus.). 32p. (J). (gr. 3-7). pap. 8.95 *(978-1-4263-0459-0(5)*, National Geographic Kids) Disney Publishing Worldwide.

Williams, Brian. Pirates. 2009. (History Explorers Ser.). (ENG.). 24p. (J). (gr. k-2). pap. 5.95 *(978-1-84696-211-0(0)*, TickTock Books) Octopus Publishing Group GBR. Dist: Independent Pubs. Group.

Wood, Alix. Pirates on the Map, 1 vol. 2014. (Fun with Map Skills Ser.). (ENG.). 32p. (J). (gr. 4-4). lib. bdg. 27.93 *(978-1-4777-6964-5(1)*, fec8c55f-d565-4b07-9de6-666ba09f7e0d, PowerKids Pr.) Rosen Publishing Group, Inc., The.

World Book, Inc. Staff, contrib. by. Pirates. 2019. (Illus.). 96p. (J). *(978-0-7166-3731-8(6))* World Bk., Inc.

Yancey, Diane. Piracy on the High Seas, 1 vol. 2012. (World History Ser.). (ENG., Illus.). 104p. (gr. 7-7). 41.53 *(978-1-4205-0679-2(X)*, 4da8dbe8-61ad-4dd3-b92a-20c3a90e6563, Lucent Pr.) Greenhaven Publishing LLC.

Zepke, Terrance. Pirates of the Carolinas for Kids. 2009. (Carolinas for Kids Ser.). (ENG.). 72p. (J). (gr. -1-12). pap. 12.95 *(978-1-56164-459-9(5))* Pineapple Pr., Inc.

PIRATES—FICTION

Abbott, Tony. The Race to Doobesh. 2005. (Secrets of Droon Ser.: No. 24). (Illus.). 127p. (J). lib. bdg. 15.38 *(978-1-4242-0311-6(2))* Fitzgerald Bks.

Adamson, Ged, illus. Meet the Mckaws. 2015. (ENG.). 32p. (J). (gr. -1-k). 16.95 *(978-1-62914-618-8(8)*, Sky Pony Pr.) Skyhorse Publishing Co., Inc.

Aguilar, Jose. Jovenes piratas/Youngs Pirates. 2008. 36p. *(978-84-934160-7-2(X))* Atalante.

Aikins, Dave. Haunted Houseboat. 2013. (SpongeBob Squarepants 8X8 Ser.). lib. bdg. 13.55 *(978-0-606-32220-1(5))* Turtleback.

Allabach, P. R. Dragon & Captain. Tumbloom, Lucas, illus. 2015. (ENG.). 32p. (J). (gr. k-2). 17.95 *(978-1-936261-33-8(2))* Flashlight Pr.

Anderson, Jon A. My T-Rex. 2010. 108p. 23.99 *(978-1-4520-0496-9(X))*; pap. 14.99 *(978-1-4520-0495-2(1))* AuthorHouse.

Anderson, Scoular. Pirate Treasure, 1 vol. Anderson, Scoular, illus. 2009. (Get Set Readers Ser.). (ENG., Illus.). 32p. (J). (gr. 1-1). lib. bdg. 27.27 *(978-1-60754-266-7(8)*, 55d0da16-5a6a-4a73-a7d5-8617c2a44137, Windmill Bks.) Rosen Publishing Group, Inc., The.

Andreae, Giles. Captain Flinn & the Pirate Dinosaurs. Ayto, Russell, illus. 2005. (Captain Flinn & the Pirate Dinosaurs Ser.). (ENG.). 32p. (J). (gr. -1-1). 19.99 *(978-1-4169-0713-8(0)*, McElderry, Margaret K. Bks.) McElderry, Margaret K. Bks.

—Captain Flinn & the Pirate Dinosaurs: Missing Treasure! Ayto, Russell, illus. 2008. (Captain Flinn & the Pirate Dinosaurs Ser.). (ENG.). 32p. (J). (gr. -1-3). 17.99 *(978-1-4169-6745-3(1)*, McElderry, Margaret K. Bks.) McElderry, Margaret K. Bks.

Applewood Books. Little Maid of New Orleans. 2011. (Little Maid Ser.). (ENG.). 236p. pap. 12.95 *(978-1-4290-9746-8(9))* Applewood Bks.

Arena, Felice & Kettle, Phil. Pirate Ship: By Felice Arena & Phil Kettle: Illustrated by Susy Boyer. Boyer, Susy, illus. 2004. (J). pap. *(978-1-59336-362-8(1))* Mondo Publishing.

Babbitt, Natalie. Jack Plank Tells Tales. Babbitt, Natalie, illus. 2011. (ENG.). 144p. (J). (gr. 3-7). pap. 6.99 *(978-0-545-00497-8(7))* Scholastic, Inc.

Bakewell, Lori. Savannah Adventure: Pirate's Treasure. 2007. 173p. (J). pap. 12.95 *(978-0-9799473-9-1(1))* Tailwind Press.

Ballantyne, R. The Coral Island. 2006. pap. 14.95 *(978-1-55742-666-6(X))* Wildside Pr., LLC.

Ballantyne, R. M. Blown to Bits; or, the Lonely Man of Rak. 2006. pap. *(978-1-4065-0515-3(3))* Dodo Pr.

Ballaz, Jesús, adapted by. Treasure Island, 1 vol. 2007. (Illustrated Classics Ser.). (ENG., Illus.). 40p. (gr. 3-5). lib. bdg. 28.67 *(978-0-8368-7665-9(2)*, b773f270-b217-4e0b-9a0d-18ca6eb20cb4, Gareth Stevens Learning Library) Stevens, Gareth Publishing LLLP.

Bardhan-Quallen, Sudipta. Pirate Princess. McElmurry, Jill, illus. 2012. (ENG.). 40p. (J). (gr. -1-3). 17.99 *(978-0-06-114242-0(5)*, HarperCollins) HarperCollins Pubs.

Barrie, J. M. Peter Pan. 2013. (Puffin Chalk Ser.). 224p. (J). (gr. 3-7). pap. 7.99 *(978-0-14-750865-2(7)*, Puffin Books) Penguin Young Readers Group.

Barrie, James Matthew. Peter Pan. 2013. (Vintage Children's Classics Ser.). (Illus.). 256p. (J). (gr. 4-7). pap. 10.99 *(978-0-09-957304-3(0))* Penguin Random Hse. GBR. Dist: Independent Pubs. Group.

—Peter Pan: The Story of Peter & Wendy [Photoplay Edition]. 2007. 244p. (gr. 4-7). 29.95 *(978-1-4344-8379-9(7))*; per. 17.95 *(978-1-4344-8378-2(9))* Wildside Pr., LLC.

Bass, Guy. The Pirate's Eye, 1 vol. Williamson, Pete, illus. 2013. (Stitch Head Ser.). (ENG.). 208p. (J). (gr. 3-6). 10.95 *(978-1-62370-008-9(6)*, 123265, Capstone Young Readers) Capstone.

Bateman, Teresa. Fluffy: Scourge of the Sea. Chesworth, Michael, illus. 2006. (ENG.). 32p. (J). (gr. -1-2). pap. 7.95 *(978-1-58089-152-3(7))* Charlesbridge Publishing, Inc.

Batson, Wayne Thomas. Isle of Fire, 1 vol. 2009. (ENG.). 352p. (J). pap. 9.99 *(978-1-4003-1512-3(3)*, Tommy Nelson) Nelson, Thomas Inc.

—Isle of Swords, 1 vol. 2008. (ENG.). 352p. (J). pap. 9.99 *(978-1-4003-1363-1(5)*, Tommy Nelson) Nelson, Thomas Inc.

Bauer, Christina. The Pirate Queen: A Timewalker Journey. 2005. 280p. (YA). 14.99 *(978-1-59092-224-8(7))* Blue Forge Pr.

Baxter, Nicola. The Great Pirate Adventure: Peek Inside the 3D Windows. Goulding, June, illus. 2012. 12p. (J). (gr. -1-12). 16.99 *(978-1-84322-966-7(8))* Anness Publishing GBR. Dist: National Bk. Network.

—The Perils of Pirates & Other Dastardly Deeds: A Compendium of Swashbuckling Pirate Adventure Stories. King, Colin, illus. 2012. 80p. (J). (gr. k-4). pap. 9.99 *(978-1-84322-802-8(5))* Anness Publishing GBR. Dist: National Bk. Network.

Bell, Hilari. Crown of Earth. Willis, Drew, illus. 2010. (Shield, Sword, & Crown Ser.: 3). (ENG.). 272p. (J). (gr. 3-7). pap. 5.99 *(978-1-4169-0599-8(5)*, Aladdin) Simon & Schuster Children's Publishing.

Bell, Rebecca. Capitano Ricco. Bell, Rebecca, illus. 2005. (Illus.). 36p. (J). 9.95 *(978-1-934138-06-9(1))* Bouncing Ball Bks., Inc.

Belle, Magnolia, adapted by. Pony Pirate Party! 2017. (Illus.). (J). *(978-1-5182-5214-3(1))* Little, Brown Bks. for Young Readers.

Bellville, Sharyn. The Pirate of Smith Point Beach. 2005. 85p. pap. 16.95 *(978-1-4137-8353-7(8))* PublishAmerica, Inc.

Bently, Peter. Captain Jack & the Pirates. Oxenbury, Helen, illus. 2016. (ENG.). 32p. (J). (-k). 18.99 *(978-0-525-42950-0(6)*, Dial Bks) Penguin Young Readers Group.

Benton, Lynne. Pirate Pete. Chapman, Neil, illus. 2008. (Tadpoles Ser.). (ENG.). 24p. (J). (gr. -1-3). pap. *(978-0-7787-3892-3(2))* Crabtree Publishing Co.

Berenstain, Mike. The Berenstain Bears Pirate Adventure. Berenstain, Mike, illus. 2016. (Berenstain Bears Ser.). (ENG., Illus.). 24p. (J). (gr. -1-3). pap. 4.99 *(978-0-06-235021-3(8)*, HarperFestival) HarperCollins Pubs.

Berger, Samantha. Pirate Potty. Cartwright, Amy, illus. 2010. (ENG.). 24p. (J). (gr. -1 — 1). pap. 6.99 *(978-0-545-17295-0(0)*, Cartwheel Bks.) Scholastic, Inc.

Bergeron, Alain M. & Sampar. Le Tresor des Tresors. 2004. (Boreal Maboul Ser.). (FRE., Illus.). 56p. (J). *(978-2-7646-0337-6(1)*, Spotlight Poets) Editions du Boreal, Les.

Big Idea, Inc. Staff. The Pirates Who Don't Do Anything: VBS Superkit. 2008. (J). 179.99 *(978-1-4003-1144-6(6))* Nelson, Thomas Inc.

Blain, Christophe. Los Hielos, Vol. 2. 2005. (Isaac el Pirata Ser.). (SPA., Illus.). 48p. (YA). (gr. 8-17). 19.95 *(978-1-59497-114-3(5))* Public Square Bks.

Bleu, Kennedy. Cotter Otter in Treasure Water. Goembel, Ponder, illus. 2014. (ENG.). 24p. (J). pap. 24.95 *(978-1-63004-814-3(3))* America Star Bks.

Bliven, Jeremy. Captain Stumpy the Pirate Cat. 2004. (ENG., Illus.). 44p. (J). pap. *(978-0-9713890-8-3(X))* Outer Banks Pr.

Bloomsbury USA. Lift-The-Flap Friends: Pirates. 2017. (ENG.). 14p. (J). bds. 9.99 *(978-1-68119-241-3(1)*, 900164373, Bloomsbury Activity Bks.) Bloomsbury Publishing USA.

Bondor-Stone, Annabeth & White, Connor. The Pirate Who's Afraid of Everything. Holden, Anthony, illus. 2015. (Shivers! Ser.: 1). (ENG.). 192p. (J). (gr. 3-7). 12.99 *(978-0-06-231387-4(8)*, HarperCollins) HarperCollins Pubs.

—The Pirate Who's Back in Bunny Slippers. Holden, Anthony, illus. 2016. (Shivers! Ser.: 2). (ENG.). 208p. (J). (gr. 3-7). 12.99 *(978-0-06-231389-8(4)*, HarperCollins) HarperCollins Pubs.

—Shivers!: the Pirate Book You've Been Looking For. Holden, Anthony, illus. 2018. (Shivers! Ser.: 3). (ENG.). 208p. (J). (gr. 3-7). 12.99 *(978-0-06-231391-1(6)*, HarperCollins) HarperCollins Pubs.

Bossley, Michele Martin. Bio-Pirate, 1 vol. 2008. (Orca Currents Ser.). (ENG.). (J). (gr. 4-7). 112p. 16.95 *(978-1-55143-895-5(X))*; 128p. pap. 9.95 *(978-1-55143-893-1(3))* Orca Bk. Pubs. USA.

Bradford, Chris. Bodyguard: Hijack (Book 3), Bk. 3. 2017. (Bodyguard Ser.: 3). (ENG.). 272p. (J). (gr. 5). pap. 8.99 *(978-1-5247-3701-6(1)*, Philomel Bks.) Penguin Young Readers Group.

—Bodyguard: Hostage (Book 2), Bk. 2. 2017. (Bodyguard Ser.: 2). (ENG.). 224p. (J). (gr. 5). pap. 8.99 *(978-1-5247-3699-6(6)*, Philomel Bks.) Penguin Young Readers Group.

—Bodyguard: Ransom (Book 4), Bk. 4. 2017. (Bodyguard Ser.: 4). (ENG.). 224p. (J). (gr. 5). pap. 9.99 *(978-1-5247-3703-0(8)*, Philomel Bks.) Penguin Young Readers Group.

Bradman, Tony. Polly & the Pirates (Reading Ladder Level 3) Davies, James, illus. 2nd ed. 2016. (Reading Ladder Level 3 Ser.). (ENG.). 48p. (gr. k-2). 4.99 *(978-1-4052-8249-9(5)*, Reading Ladder) Farshore GBR. Dist: HarperCollins Pubs.

Brady, Carolyn. The Adventures of Pelican Mcfeet: The Big Lumpy Green Monster. Phillips, Deborah, illus. 2008. 32p. pap. 16.95 *(978-1-4389-3539-3(0))* AuthorHouse.

Brallier, Max. Galactic Hot Dogs 3: Revenge of the Space Pirates. Maguire, Rachel & Kelley, Nichole, illus. 2017. (Galactic Hot Dogs Ser.: 3). (ENG.). 320p. (J). (gr. 3-7). 14.99 *(978-1-4814-2498-1(X)*, Aladdin) Simon & Schuster Children's Publishing.

Bramucci, Stephen. The Danger Gang & the Pirates of Borneo! Chung, Arree, illus. 2017. (ENG.). 384p. (J). 16.99 *(978-1-61963-692-7(1)*, 900145716, Bloomsbury USA Childrens) Bloomsbury Publishing USA.

Braswell, Liz. Straight on till Morning-A Twisted Tale. 2020. (Twisted Tale Ser.). (ENG.). 496p. (YA). (gr. 7-12). 17.99 *(978-1-4847-8130-2(9)*, Disney-Hyperion) Disney Publishing Worldwide.

Bray, Libba. Beauty Queens. 2012. (ENG.). 400p. (YA). (gr. 8). pap. 10.99 *(978-0-439-89598-9(7)*, Scholastic Paperbacks) Scholastic, Inc.

Brian, Kate, pseud. Confessions. 2007. (Private Ser.: No. 4). (ENG.). 240p. (YA). (gr. 9-12). pap. 9.99 *(978-1-4169-1876-9(0)*, Simon & Schuster Bks. For Young Readers) Simon & Schuster Bks. For Young Readers.

Brown, Barbara. The Adventures of Captain Crick, Super Hero. 2011. 28p. pap. 21.99 *(978-1-4568-5005-0(9))* Xlibris Corp.

Brown, Cathie. Today I am a Pirate. 2010. 24p. 11.49 *(978-1-4520-0461-7(7))* AuthorHouse.

Bruton, Georgia. Escape. 2012. 210p. pap. 11.95 *(978-1-938083-10-5(5))* Black Forge.

Bunting, Eve. Pirate Boy. Fortenberry, Julie, illus. 2012. (ENG.). 32p. (J). (gr. -1-3). pap. 8.99 *(978-0-8234-2546-4(0))* Holiday Hse., Inc.

—The Pirate Captain's Daughter. 2011. (Eve Bunting's Pirate Ser.). (ENG.). 208p. (J). (gr. 7-11). pap. 8.95 *(978-1-58536-525-8(4)*, 202318);1. lib. bdg. 15.95 *(978-1-58536-526-5(2)*, 202212) Sleeping Bear Pr.

—The Voyage of the Sea Wolf. 2012. (Eve Bunting's Pirate Ser.). (ENG.). 192p. (J). (gr. 7-11). pap. 8.95 *(978-1-58536-790-0(7)*, 202335); lib. bdg. 15.95 *(978-1-58536-789-4(3)*, 202334) Sleeping Bear Pr.

Burchett, Jan & Vogler, Sara. Skeleton Island. 2012. (ENG., Illus.). 128p. (J). (gr. 2-4). pap. 7.99 *(978-1-4440-0584-4(7)*, Orion Children's Bks.) Hachette Children's Group GBR. Dist: Hachette Bk. Group.

Burghard, Marie. Captain's Best Imbecile: A Young Pirate's Story. 2008. 184p. pap. 12.99 *(978-1-4357-3807-2(1))* Lulu Pr., Inc.

—Captain's Best Imbecile: A Young Pirate's Story: Collector's Edition. 2008. (ENG.). 184p. 29.99 *(978-1-4357-4521-6(3))* Lulu Pr., Inc.

Burnett, Melissa. Even Pirates Need Their Sleep. 2010. 32p. (J). pap. 15.00 *(978-1-4490-7092-2(2))* AuthorHouse.

Butterman, Stephen. Rootbeer Beard. 2012. 74p. pap. 8.95 *(978-1-61477-055-8(7))* Bellissima Publishing, LLC.

Cannon, Deborah. The Pirate Vortex: Elizabeth Latimer, Pirate Hunter. 2009. 260p. pap. 20.00 *(978-1-4269-0532-2(7))* Trafford Publishing.

Carlson, Caroline. The Buccaneers' Code. (Very Nearly Honorable League of Pirates Ser.: 3). (ENG.). 320p. (J). (gr. 3-7). 2016. pap. 7.99 *(978-0-06-219440-4(2))* 2015. 16.99 *(978-0-06-219439-8(9))* HarperCollins Pubs. (HarperCollins).

—Magic Marks the Spot. Phillips, Dave, illus. 2013. (ENG.). 368p. (J). pap. *(978-0-06-231467-3(X))* Harper & Row Ltd.

—Magic Marks the Spot. Phillips, Dave, illus. 2013. (Very Nearly Honorable League of Pirates Ser.: 1). (ENG.). 368p. (J). (gr. 3-7). 16.99 *(978-0-06-219434-3(8)*, HarperCollins) HarperCollins Pubs.

—The Terror of the Southlands. Phillips, Dave, illus. 2014. (ENG.). 336p. (J). pap. *(978-0-06-236178-3(3))* Harper & Row Ltd.

Carretero, Mónica. Pirate Handbook. Brokenbrow, Jon, tr. Carretero, Mónica, illus. 2011. (Handbooks Ser.). (ENG., Illus.). 32p. (J). (gr. k-3). 14.95 *(978-84-937814-8-4(7))* Cuento de Luz SL ESP. Dist: Publishers Group West (PGW).

Carris, Joan D. A Ghost of a Chance. 2003. (Legends of the Carolinas Ser.). 155p. (J). 8.95 *(978-1-928556-40-4(X))* Coastal Carolina Pr.

Castroman, Nicole. Blackhearts. 2016. (ENG., Illus.). 384p. (YA). (gr. 9). 17.99 *(978-1-4814-3269-6(9)*, Simon Pulse) Simon Pulse.

Charman, Katrina. Go, Go, Pirate Boat. Sharratt, Nick, illus. 2019. (New Nursery Rhymes Ser.). (ENG.). 24p. (J). bds. 8.99 *(978-1-5476-0319-0(4)*, 900211337, Bloomsbury Children's Bks.) Bloomsbury Publishing USA.

Child, Lauren. I Can Do Anything That's Everything All on My Own. 2008. (Charlie & Lola Ser.). (ENG., Illus.). 24p. (J). (gr. -1-k). mass mkt. 4.99 *(978-0-448-44792-6(4)*, Grosset & Dunlap) Penguin Young Readers Group.

—Ruby Redfort Take Your Last Breath. Child, Lauren, illus. (Ruby Redfort Ser.: 2). (ENG., Illus.). 432p. (J). (gr. 5-9). 2018. pap. 7.99 *(978-1-5362-0048-5(4))* 2013. 16.99 *(978-0-7636-5468-9(X))* Candlewick Pr.

Chin, Oliver. Baltazar & the Flying Pirates. Roth, Justin, illus. 2009. (ENG.). 36p. (J). (gr. -1-3). 15.95 *(978-1-59702-018-3(4))* Immedium.

Chizuru, Mio. The Pirate & the Princess Volume 1: the Timelight Stone: The Timelight Stone. 2007. 110p. (J). pap. 5.99 *(978-1-933164-43-4(3))* Seven Seas Entertainment, LLC.

—The Pirate & the Princess Volume 2: the Red Crystal: The Red Crystal. 2007. 110p. (J). pap. 5.99 *(978-1-933164-44-1(1))* Seven Seas Entertainment, LLC.

Cima, Alessandro V. Pirate Jack. 2007. 180p. pap. 11.95 *(978-1-615-14024-7(6))* Candlelight Stories, Inc.

Citak, Michael J. The Adventures of Leo- & the Treasure Cave. 2009. 51p. pap. 22.95 *(978-0-557-02994-5(5))* Lulu Pr., Inc.

Clark, Kent. Peter Powers & the Swashbuckling Sky Pirates! Bardin, Dave, illus. 2017. (Peter Powers Ser.: 6). (ENG.). 128p. (J). (gr. 1-5). pap. 9.99 *(978-0-316-43793-6(X))* Little, Brown Bks. for Young Readers.

Clark, Sherryl. The Littlest Pirate. Jellett, Tom, illus. 2019. (Puffin Nibbles Ser.). 80p. (J). (gr. k-2). pap. 9.99 *(978-0-14-131338-2(2)*, Puffin) Penguin Random Hse. AUS. Dist: Independent Pubs. Group.

Clibbon, Meg. Wicked Pirates. Clibbon, Lucy, illus. 2010. (My World Of... Ser.). (ENG.). 32p. (J). (gr. k-2). 21.19 *(978-1-84089-552-0(7))* Evans Brothers, Ltd. GBR. Dist: Children's Plus, Inc.

Coats, Lucy. Captain Beastlie's Pirate Party. Mould, Chris, illus. 2014. (ENG.). 32p. (J). (gr. -1-2). 15.99 *(978-0-7636-7399-4(4))* Candlewick Pr.

Cobb, Daryl K. Do Pirates Go to School. 2010. pap. 11.99 *(978-0-578-05535-0(X))* 10 To 2 Children's Bks.

Collard, Liz. The Secret of Pirate Taz. 2011. 28p. 13.54 *(978-1-4269-5268-5(6))* Trafford Publishing.

Collingwood, Harry. Across the Spanish Main. 204p. 2011. 26.95 *(978-1-4638-9643-0(3))* 2009. pap. 14.95 *(978-1-60664-390-7(8))* Rodgers, Alan Bks.

—The Cruise of The 'Esmeralda' 2009. 220p. pap. 15.95 *(978-1-60664-391-4(6))* Rodgers, Alan Bks.

—The Rover's Secret. 2011. 274p. 29.95 *(978-1-4638-9505-1(4))* Rodgers, Alan Bks.

—The Strange Adventures of Eric Blackburn. 2017. (ENG., Illus.). (J). 24.95 *(978-1-374-85314-0(3))*; pap. 14.95 *(978-1-374-85313-3(5))* Capital Communications, Inc.

—The Strange Adventures of Eric Blackburn. 2008. 164p. 25.95 *(978-1-60664-711-0(3))*; pap. 13.95 *(978-1-60664-210-8(3))* Rodgers, Alan Bks.

Collins, Tim. The Long-Lost Secret Diary of the World's Worst Pirate. Horne, Sarah, illus. 2018. (Long-Lost Secret Diary Ser.). (ENG.). 216p. (J). (gr. 4-5). lib. bdg. 28.50 *(978-1-63163-140-5(3)*, 1631631403, Jolly Fish Pr.) North Star Editions.

—World's Worst Pirate. Horne, Sarah, illus. 2017. (Long-Lost Secret Diary Ser.). (ENG.). 216p. (J). (gr. 4-5). pap. 9.99 *(978-1-63163-141-2(1)*, 1631631411, Jolly Fish Pr.) North Star Editions.

Cooper, Susan. The Word Pirates. Kellogg, Steven, illus. 2019. 40p. (J). (gr. -1-3). 18.99 *(978-0-8234-4359-8(0)*, Neal Porter Bks) Holiday Hse., Inc.

Cosson, M. J. The Pirate, Big Fist, & Me, 1 vol. Garvey, Brann, illus. 2006. (Vortex Bks.). (ENG.). 112p. (J). (gr. 5-9). 7.19 *(978-1-59889-279-6(7)*, 93373); 26.65 *(978-1-59889-068-6(9)*, 86536) Capstone. (Stone Arch Bks.).

Coughlin, Shirley. Toby & the Pirates. 2012. 58p. pap. 13.00 *(978-1-61204-745-4(9)*, Strategic Bk. Publishing) Strategic Book Publishing & Rights Agency (SBPRA).

Courtauld, Sarah. On a Pirate Ship. Davies, Benji, illus. 2007. (Picture Bks). 24p. (J). (gr. -1-3). 9.99 *(978-0-7945-1712-0(9)*, Usborne) EDC Publishing.

Cowell, Cressida. How to Be a Pirate. 2010. (ENG., Illus.). 240p. (J). *(978-0-340-99908-0(X)*, Hodder Children's Books) Hachette Children's Group GBR. Dist: Hachette Bk. Group.

—How to Train Your Dragon: How to Be a Pirate. 2010. (How to Train Your Dragon Ser.: 2). (ENG.). 240p. (J). (gr. 3-7). pap. 8.99 *(978-0-316-08528-1(6))* Little, Brown Bks. for Young Readers.

Cramer, Michelle Ann. The Chasers. 2006. (ENG.). 118p. pap. 9.74 *(978-1-84728-998-8(3))* Lulu Pr., Inc.

Crimi, Carolyn. Henry & the Buccaneer Bunnies. Manders, John, illus. 2009. (ENG.). 40p. (J). (gr. -1-3). pap. 8.99 *(978-0-7636-4540-3(0))* Candlewick Pr.

Croce, Pat & Slutsky, Adam. Plunder. 2015. (Plunder Ser.: 1). (ENG.). 336p. 31.95 *(978-1-68162-373-3(0))*; 338p. (J). pap. 16.95 *(978-1-63026-893-0(3))* Turner Publishing Co.

Crowe, Ellie & Fry, Juliet. HOKU the Stargazer: The Exciting Pirate Adventure! Petosa-Sigel, Kristi, illus. 2009. (ENG.). 28p. (J). *(978-1-59700-601-9(7))* Island Heritage Publishing.

Cullain, Adam, et al. The Pirates on Holiday. Van Wyk, Rupert, illus. 2014. (Race Ahead with Reading Ser.). (ENG.). 32p. (J). (gr. 2-2). *(978-0-7787-1311-1(3))* Crabtree Publishing Co.

Cullen, Sean. Hamish X Goes to Providence, Rhode Island. 2008. (ENG.). 336p. (J). *(978-0-670-06854-8(3))* Penguin Bks., Ltd.

Czajak, Paul. Monster Needs a Party. Grieb, Wendy, illus. 2015. (Monster & Me Ser.). (ENG.). 32p. (J). (-k). 16.95 *(978-1-938063-55-8(4)*, Mighty Media Kids) Mighty Media Pr.

Daffern, Brian. Prince Albert Bk. 3: The Realm Pirates. 2004. 192p. (YA). per. 13.95 *(978-0-9709104-7-9(9))* Hickory Tales Publishing.

Dale, Jay. Lazy Old Pirates. Diggory, Nick, illus. 2012. (Wonder Words Ser.). (ENG.). 16p. (J). (gr. k-2). pap. 36.94 *(978-1-4296-8931-1(5)*, 18361, Capstone Pr.) Capstone.

—Two Old Pirates. Diggory, Nick, illus. 2012. (Wonder Words Ser.). (ENG.). 16p. (J). (gr. k-2). pap. 36.94 *(978-1-4296-8929-8(3)*, 18360, Capstone Pr.) Capstone.

Dale, Jay & Scott, Kay. Lazy Old Pirates, 1 vol. Diggory, Nick, illus. 2012. (Wonder Words Ser.). (ENG.). 16p. (J). (gr. k-2). pap. 6.99 *(978-1-4296-8930-4(7)*, 119970, Capstone Pr.) Capstone.

—Two Old Pirates, 1 vol. Diggory, Nick, illus. 2012. (Wonder Words Ser.). (ENG.). 16p. (J). (gr. k-2). pap. 6.99 *(978-1-4296-8928-1(5)*, 119968, Capstone Pr.) Capstone.

Dale, Penny. Dinosaur Pirates! Dale, Penny, illus. 2017. (Dinosaurs on the Go Ser.). (ENG., Illus.). 32p. (J). (-k). 15.99 *(978-0-7636-9330-5(8))* Candlewick Pr.

Dalton, Annie. Making Waves (Mel Beeby, Agent Angel, Book 7), Book 7. 2010. (Mel Beeby, Agent Angel Ser.: 7). (ENG.).

208p. (gr. 4-7). pap. 9.99 *(978-0-00-720477-9(9),* HarperCollins Children's Bks.) HarperCollins Pubs. Ltd. GBR. Dist: HarperCollins Pubs.

Davidson, Susanna. Stories of Mermaids. 2009. (Young Reading 1 Ser.). 48p. (J). (gr. 2). 6.99 *(978-0-7945-2589-7(X),* Usborne) EDC Publishing.

Davies, Benji, illus. Bizzy Bear: Pirate Adventure. 2013. (Bizzy Bear Ser.). (ENG.). 8p. (J). (— 1). bds. 7.99 *(978-0-7636-6519-7(3))* Candlewick Pr.

Davis, Mike. Pirates, Bats, & Dragons. Simpson, William, illus. 2004. 174p. (J). 15.95 *(978-0-9747078-2-2(1))* Perceval Pr.

de la Cruz, Melissa. Rise of the Isle of the Lost-A Descendants Novel, Book 3: A Descendants Novel. 2018. (Descendants Ser.: 3). (ENG.). 304p. (J). (gr. 3-7). pap. 9.99 *(978-1-368-02831-8(4),* Disney-Hyperion) Disney Publishing Worldwide.

Dean, James, illus. Pete the Cat & the Treasure Map. 2017. (J). *(978-1-5182-3828-4(9))* HarperCollins Pubs. Ltd.

DeGorsky, Gregory J. The Christmas Pirate. DeGorsky, Jon, ed. 2007. (ENG., Illus.). 80p. (J). pap. 4.95 *(978-0-9678542-3-6(7))* Magnetic Image, Inc.

Delacre, Lulu. Rafi & Rosi Pirates, 1 vol. 2017. (Rafi & Rosi Ser.). (ENG., Illus.). 64p. (J). (gr. k-3). 16.95 *(978-0-89239-381-7(5),* leelowcbp, Children's Book Press) Lee & Low Bks., Inc.

—Rafi y Rosi ¡Piratas!, 1 vol. Delacre, Lulu, illus. 2017. (Rafi & Rosi Ser.). (SPA., Illus.). 64p. (J). (gr. k-3). 16.95 *(978-0-89239-428-9(5),* leelowcbp) Lee & Low Bks., Inc.

—Rafi y Rosi Piratas, 1 vol. 2017. (Rafi & Rosi Ser.). (SPA.). 64p. (J). (gr. k-3). pap. 11.95 *(978-0-89239-382-4(3),* leelowcbp) Lee & Low Bks., Inc.

Delaney, Rachelle. Guardians of Island X. 2. Guerlais, Gérald, illus. 2012. (Ship of Lost Souls Ser.). (ENG.). 224p. (J). (gr. 4-6). 22.44 *(978-0-448-45778-9(4),* Grosset & Dunlap) Penguin Publishing Group.

—The Hunt for the Panther, 3. Guerlais, Gérald, illus. 2013. (Ship of Lost Souls Ser.: 3). (ENG.). 224p. (J). (gr. 4-6). 22.44 *(978-0-448-45780-2(6))* Penguin Young Readers Group.

—The Ship of Lost Souls #1, 1. Guerlais, Gérald, illus. 2012. (Ship of Lost Souls Ser.). (ENG.). 256p. (J). (gr. 4-6). 22.44 *(978-0-448-45776-5(8),* Grosset & Dunlap) Penguin Publishing Group.

Delibero, Bob. Petrucchio. 2012. 234p. 24.95 *(978-1-4626-6155-8(6))* America Star Bks.

Demas, Corinne & Roehrig, Artemis. The Grumpy Pirate. Anstee, Ashlyn, illus. 2020. (ENG.). 40p. (J). (gr. -1-k). 17.99 *(978-1-338-22297-5(X),* Orchard Bks.) Scholastic, Inc.

Dennis, Peter & Rawson, Christopher. Treasure Island. 2004. (Young Reading Ser.). (Illus.). 64p. (J). (gr. 2-18). pap. 5.95 *(978-0-7945-0411-3(6),* Usborne) EDC Publishing.

Deutsch, Stacia, adapted by. The Pirate Fairy: The Chapter Book. 2014. 117p. *(978-0-316-33346-7(8))* Little Brown & Co.

Diamand, Emily. Raiders' Ransom. 2011. (Raiders' Ransom Ser.: 1). (ENG.). 368p. (J). (gr. 6-8). 22.44 *(978-0-545-14298-4(9))* Scholastic, Inc.

Dicamillo, Kate. Louise, the Adventures of a Chicken. Bliss, Harry, illus. 2009. (J). (gr. -1-2). 29.95 incl. audio compact disk *(978-1-4301-0688-3(3))* Live Oak Media.

Dickins, Rosie. Illustrated Pirate Stories IR. 2015. (Illustrated Stories Ser.). (ENG.). 269p. (J). (gr. k-5). 19.99 *(978-0-7945-3213-0(6),* Usborne) EDC Publishing.

Dietrich, Christopher & Character Building Studio (Firm) Staff. Pirate Tales. 2015. (Illus.). (J). *(978-1-4847-2335-7(X))* Disney Publishing Worldwide.

Disney Book Club Staff. Pirates of the Caribbean - On Stranger Tides: Six Sea Chanties - An Original Graphic Novel Anthology. 2011. (ENG.). 128p. (YA). (gr. 8-18). pap. 10.99 *(978-1-4231-3320-9(X))* Disney Pr.

Disney Enterprises (1996-) Staff, contrib. by. Pirates of the Caribbean Dead Mans Chest. 2006. (Illus.). 44p. incl. audio compact disk *(978-1-4054-7260-9(X))* Parragon Bk. Service Ltd.

Disney Press Staff, ed. Pirates of the Caribbean 3: Swann. 2007. (ENG.). 24p. (J). (gr. -1-2). pap. 3.99 *(978-1-4231-0375-2(0))* Disney Pr.

Disney Publishing Staff. Playing Pirates, 15 vols. 2003. (It's Fun to Learn Ser.). (Illus.). 32p. (J). (gr. -1-3). 3.99 *(978-1-57973-136-6(8))* Advance Pubs. LLC.

Disney Storybook Art Team. Jake & the Neverland Pirates: Playful Pirates: Play-A-Sound Book. Publications International Ltd. Staff, ed. 2013. (Play-A-Sound Ser.). (ENG.). 10p. (J). (gr. k-3). bds. *(978-1-4508-6772-6(3),* d1399e5b-b94b-4ab0-91ab-a035f527d2af) Phoenix International Publications, Inc.

Dixon, Franklin W. The Pirate Ghost. Gutierrez, Santy, illus. 2018. (Hardy Boys Clue Book Ser.: 7). (ENG.). 96p. (J). (gr. 1-4). 17.99 *(978-1-4814-8873-0(2));* pap. 5.99 *(978-1-4814-8872-3(4))* Simon & Schuster Children's Publishing. (Aladdin).

Dogiakis, Helen. Captain Terry the Pirate Cow's Adventure to Greece. 2012. 24p. pap. 17.99 *(978-1-4685-9403-4(6))* AuthorHouse.

—Captain Terry the Pirate Cow's Adventure to Italy. 2011. 32p. pap. 14.99 *(978-1-4567-3131-1(9))* AuthorHouse.

Donaldson, Julia. Charlie Cook's Favorite Book. Scheffler, Axel, illus. 2008. (ENG.). 32p. (J). (gr. -1-k). pap. 8.99 *(978-0-14-241138-4(8),* Puffin Books) Penguin Young Readers Group.

Dorison, Xavier. Lady Vivian Hastings. Saincantin, Jerome, tr. Lauffray, Mathieu, illus. 2011. (Long John Silver Ser.: 1). 56p. pap. 13.95 *(978-1-84918-062-7(8))* CineBook GBR. Dist: National Bk. Network.

—Neptune Vol. 2: Long John Silver. Lauffray, Mathieu, illus. 2011. (Long John Silver Ser.: 2). 56p. pap. 13.95 *(978-1-84918-072-6(5))* CineBook GBR. Dist: National Bk. Network.

Downey, Lisa & Fox, Kathleen. The Pirates of Plagiarism. Downey, Lisa, illus. 2010. (Illus.). 32p. (J). (gr. 1-4). lib. bdg. 17.95 *(978-1-60213-053-1(1),* Upstart Bks.) Highsmith Inc.

Duddle, Jonny. The Pirates Next Door. 2012. (ENG., Illus.). 44p. (J). (gr. -1-2). 17.99 *(978-0-7636-5842-7(1),* Templar) Candlewick Pr.

Duey, Kathleen. Time Soldiers - Patch. Epstein, Eugene, illus. Gould, Robert, photos by. 2005. (Time Soldiers Ser.: Bk. 3). (ENG.). 96p. (J). (gr. k-2). per. 5.95 *(978-1-929945-55-9(8))* Big Guy Bks., Inc.

Durango, Julia. Sea of the Dead. 2009. (ENG.). 144p. (J). (gr. 3-7). 16.99 *(978-1-4169-5778-2(2),* Simon & Schuster Bks. For Young Readers) Simon & Schuster Bks. For Young Readers.

Durbin, Amanda. Tree Houses & Treasures. 2013. 24p. pap. 24.95 *(978-1-63004-353-7(2))* America Star Bks.

Durrant, Geraldine. Pirate Gran. Forshall, Rose, illus. 2009. 32p. (J). 19.95 *(978-0-948065-96-5(6))* National Maritime Museum GBR. Dist: Independent Pubs. Group.

—Twinbane: an Appalling True History. 2010. 142p. pap. 16.95 *(978-1-4457-7998-0(6))* Lulu Pr., Inc.

Eagar, Lindsay. Race to the Bottom of the Sea. (ENG.). 432p. (J). (gr. 3-7). 2019. pap. 9.99 *(978-0-7636-9877-5(6))* 2017. 17.99 *(978-0-7636-7923-1(2))* Candlewick Pr.

Eames, Brian. The Dagger Quick. (Dagger Chronicles Ser.). (ENG.). (J). (gr. 3-7). 2013. Illus.). 352p. pap. 6.99 *(978-1-4424-8368-2(7))* 2011. 336p. 15.99 *(978-1-4424-2311-4(0))* Simon & Schuster/Paula Wiseman Bks. (Simon & Schuster/Paula Wiseman Bks.).

—The Dagger X. 2013. (Dagger Chronicles Ser.). (ENG.). 368p. (J). (gr. 3-7). 15.99 *(978-1-4424-6855-9(6),* Simon & Schuster Bks. For Young Readers) Simon & Schuster Bks. For Young Readers.

—The Dagger X. 2013. (Dagger Chronicles Ser.). (ENG., Illus.). 368p. (J). (gr. 3-7). pap. 6.99 *(978-1-4424-6856-6(4),* Simon & Schuster/Paula Wiseman Bks.) Simon & Schuster/Paula Wiseman Bks.

Easton, Tom. Pirates Can Be Honest, 1 vol., 1. 2015. (Pirate Pals Ser.). (ENG.). 32p. (J). (gr. 1-2). pap. 11.00 *(978-1-5081-9141-7(4),* 3fb6db26-0650-4bcf-b997-8e8f868a555e, Windmill Bks.) Rosen Publishing Group, Inc., The.

—Pirates Can Be Kind, 1 vol., 1. 2015. (Pirate Pals Ser.). (ENG.). 32p. (J). (gr. 1-2). pap. 11.00 *(978-1-5081-9145-2(X),* 5cbf1da5-5682-4587-b537-6466058a22b7, Windmill Bks.) Rosen Publishing Group, Inc., The.

—Pirates Can Be Polite, 1 vol., 1. 2015. (Pirate Pals Ser.). (ENG.). 32p. (J). (gr. 1-2). pap. 11.00 *(978-1-5081-9149-0(2),* c965e443-a12d-4da0-b039-90b7ec652f01, Windmill Bks.) Rosen Publishing Group, Inc., The.

—Pirates Can Pay Attention, 1 vol., 1. 2015. (Pirate Pals Ser.). (ENG.). 32p. (J). (gr. 1-2). pap. 11.00 *(978-1-5081-9152-0(2),* 2476b235-f7d5-4e67-b940-14e8d4cf90ba, Windmill Bks.) Rosen Publishing Group, Inc., The.

—Pirates Can Share, 1 vol., 1. 2015. (Pirate Pals Ser.). (ENG.). 32p. (J). (gr. 1-2). pap. 11.00 *(978-1-5081-9155-1(7),* 2d0334a5-b737-493e-b5fc-bfe6902603bf, Windmill Bks.) Rosen Publishing Group, Inc., The.

—Pirates Can Work Together, 1 vol., 1. 2015. (Pirate Pals Ser.). (ENG.). 32p. (J). (gr. 1-2). pap. 11.00 *(978-1-5081-9159-9(X),* 1452bada-a469-4883-8c3d-903008809d09, Windmill Bks.) Rosen Publishing Group, Inc., The.

Elfrig, Kate. I'll Be a Pirate: World of Discovery II. Graves, Dennis, illus. I.t. ed. 2006. (SPA & ENG.). 12p. (gr. k-2). pap. 7.95 *(978-1-57874-053-6(3),* Kaeden Bks.) Kaeden Corp.

Elkington, John. The Pirates of the Gayoso Bayou. 2012. 24p. pap. 15.99 *(978-1-4797-3940-0(5))* Xlibris Corp.

Enderle, Dotti. Book 13: Yo Ho No!, 1 vol. 2014. (Ghost Detectors Ser.). (ENG., Illus.). 80p. (J). (gr. 2-5). lib. bdg. 35.64 *(978-1-62402-001-8(1),* 8828, Calico Chapter Bks.) ABDO Publishing Co.

Eschler, Linda. The Strawberry Fairies & the Secret of Mystery Island. 2008. 57p. pap. 16.95 *(978-1-60610-960-1(X))* America Star Bks.

Evelyn Gill Hilton. Kidnapped by Pirates: Based on the true story of a fourteen year-old boy, Charles Tilton, who was kidnapped alone from an Amer. 2010. (ENG.). 124p. 21.95 *(978-1-4269-2018-9(0));* (gr. 1-2). pap. 11.95 *(978-1-4269-2017-2(2))* Trafford Publishing.

Fafoutakis, Anne. Enchanted Talisman & Other Stories for Children of All Ages. 2004. 132p. pap. 13.50 *(978-1-84426-296-0(0))* Upfront Publishing Ltd. GBR. Dist: Printondemand-worldwide.com.

Farren, Rick. Grandpa & the Pirate. 2003. (J). per. 9.95 *(978-0-9728716-4-8(0))* Journey Pubns., LLC.

—Grandpa & the Pirate. 2007. 49p. (J). per. 9.95 *(978-0-9794863-6-4(X))* Summerland Publishing.

Feldman, Thea. Backyard Pirates. Conger, Holli, illus. 2007. (Magnix Imagination Activity Bks.). 6p. bds. 5.99 *(978-1-932915-40-2(0))* Sandvik Innovations, LLC.

Ferrone, John M. Gus & the Pirate Treasure. Ferrone, John M., illus. Date not set. (Illus.). 36p. (J). (gr. -1-5). pap. 16.95 *(978-1-928811-01-5(9))* Story Stuff, Inc.

Ferry, Beth. Pirate's Perfect Pet. Myers, Matt, illus. 2016. (ENG.). 32p. (J). (gr. -1-3). 16.99 *(978-0-7636-7288-1(2))* Candlewick Pr.

Fitzgerald, Isaac. How to Be a Pirate. Barrager, Brigette, illus. 2020. (ENG.). 40p. (J). 17.99 *(978-1-68119-778-4(2),* 900186166, Bloomsbury Children's Bks.) Bloomsbury Publishing USA.

Flanagan, John. The Caldera. 2018. (Brotherband Chronicles Ser.: 7). (ENG.). 384p. (J). (gr. 5). 9.99 *(978-0-14-242729-3(2),* Puffin Books) Penguin Young Readers Group.

—The Ghostfaces. 2016. (Brotherband Chronicles Ser.: 6). (ENG.). 400p. (J). (gr. 5). 18.99 *(978-0-399-16357-9(3),* Philomel Bks.) Penguin Young Readers Group.

—The Hunters. 2014. (Brotherband Chronicles Ser.: 3). lib. bdg. 19.65 *(978-0-606-35708-1(4))* Turtleback.

—The Hunters: Brotherband Chronicles, Book 3. 2014. (Brotherband Chronicles Ser.: 3). (ENG.). 448p. (J). (gr. 5). pap. 9.99 *(978-0-14-242664-7(4),* Puffin Books) Penguin Young Readers Group.

—The Invaders. 2013. (Brotherband Chronicles Ser.: 2). lib. bdg. 19.65 *(978-0-606-26637-6(2))* Turtleback.

—The Invaders: Brotherband Chronicles, Book 2. 2013. (Brotherband Chronicles Ser.: 2). (ENG.). 448p. (J). (gr. 5). pap. 9.99 *(978-0-14-242663-0(6),* Puffin Books) Penguin Young Readers Group.

—Slaves of Socorro. 2015. (Brotherband Chronicles Ser.: 4). (ENG.). 496p. (J). (gr. 5). pap. 9.99 *(978-0-14-242726-2(8),* Puffin Books) Penguin Young Readers Group.

—Slaves of Socorro. 2015. (Brotherband Chronicles Ser.: 4). lib. bdg. 19.65 *(978-0-606-36771-4(3))* Turtleback.

Fleischman, Sid. The Ghost in the Noonday Sun. Sis, Peter, illus. 2007. (ENG.). 256p. (J). (gr. 3-7). per. 5.99 *(978-0-06-134502-9(4),* Greenwillow Bks.) HarperCollins Pubs.

—The Giant Rat of Sumatra: Or Pirates Galore. Hendrix, John, illus. 2006. (ENG.). 208p. (J). (gr. 5-9). reprint ed. pap. 7.99 *(978-0-06-074240-9(2),* Greenwillow Bks.) HarperCollins Pubs.

Fletcher, Corina. Playbook Pirates. Teckentrup, Britta, illus. 2013. (ENG.). 12p. (J). (gr. -1-2). 24.00 *(978-0-7636-6606-4(8))* Candlewick Pr.

Fliess, Sue. How to Be a Pirate. Dyson, Nikki, illus. 2014. (Little Golden Book Ser.). 24p. (J). (-k). 5.99 *(978-0-449-81309-6(6),* Golden Bks.) Random Hse. Children's Bks.

Foley, Lizzie K. & Foley, Elizabeth. Remarkable. 2013. (ENG.). 304p. (J). (gr. 4-6). 22.44 *(978-0-8037-3706-8(8),* Dial) Penguin Publishing Group.

Fontes, Justine & Fontes, Ron. Captured by Pirates: Book 1. Witt, David, illus. 2007. (Twisted Journeys (r) Ser.: 1). (ENG.). 112p. (J). (gr. 4-7). per. 12.99 *(978-0-8225-6202-3(2),* 510c53f7-4760-4666-ae3c-a9ec7a5e68f9, Graphic Universe™) Lerner Publishing Group.

Foster, Emily. The Drowning Eyes. 2016. (ENG.). 144p. pap. 13.99 *(978-0-7653-8768-4(9),* 900161511, Tor.com) Doherty, Tom Assocs., LLC.

Francis, Pauline, retold by. Treasure Island. 2010. (Essential Classics - Adventure Ser.). (Illus.). 48p. pap. *(978-0-237-54085-2(1))* Evans Brothers, Ltd.

Frank, Kevin. Scurvy Dogs. Frank, Kevin, illus. 2017. (ENG., Illus.). 96p. (J). pap. 5.99 *(978-1-61067-459-1(6))* Kane Miller.

Fravel, Gale. Fellsmere the Pirate, Chipley's Adventure. Fravel, Harold, illus. 2011. 28p. pap. 12.95 *(978-1-936343-79-9(7))* Peppertree Pr., The.

Freedman, Claire. Pirates Love Underpants. Cort, Ben, illus. 2013. (Underpants Bks.). (ENG.). 32p. (J). (gr. -1-2). 18.99 *(978-1-4424-8512-9(4),* Simon & Schuster/Paula Wiseman Bks.) Simon & Schuster/Paula Wiseman Bks.

Friesen, Ray. Pirate Penguin vs Ninja Chicken Volume 1: Troublems with Frenemies. 2011. (Pirate Penguin vs Ninja Chicken Ser.: 1). (Illus.). 96p. (J). (gr. 4-7). 9.95 *(978-1-60309-071-1(1),* 9781603090711) Top Shelf Productions.

Frisch, Aaron. Pirates at the Plate. Summers, Mark, illus. 2012. (ENG.). 32p. (J). (gr. 1-3). 17.99 *(978-1-56846-210-3(7),* 22024, Creative Editions) Creative Co., The.

Fry, Jason. The Jupiter Pirates #2: Curse of the Iris. 2016. (Jupiter Pirates Ser.: 2). (ENG.). 368p. (J). (gr. 3-7). pap. 6.99 *(978-0-06-223024-9(7),* HarperCollins) HarperCollins Pubs.

—The Jupiter Pirates: Hunt for the Hydra. 2014. (Jupiter Pirates Ser.: 1). (ENG.). 272p. (J). (gr. 3-7). pap. 6.99 *(978-0-06-223021-8(2),* HarperCollins) HarperCollins Pubs.

—Leia & the Great Island Escape. 2016. (Star Wars: Force Awakens 8X8 Ser.). (J). lib. bdg. 14.75 *(978-0-606-39934-0(8))* Turtleback.

Fuerst, Jeffrey B. & Benchmark Education Co., LLC. Robert Louis Stevenson's Treasure Island: My Sea Adventure Israel Hands. Hondru, Ovi, illus. 2014. (Text Connections Ser.). (J). (gr. 3). *(978-1-4509-9652-5(3))* Benchmark Education Co.

Gaiman, Neil. The Dangerous Alphabet. Grimly, Gris, illus. (ENG.). 32p. (J). (gr. -1-3). 2010. pap. 7.99 *(978-0-06-078335-8(4))* 2008. 17.99 *(978-0-06-078333-4(8))* HarperCollins Pubs. (HarperCollins).

Gamble, Adam & Jasper, Mark. Good Night Pirate Ship. Stevenson, Harvey, illus. 2015. (Good Night Our World Ser.). (ENG.). 26p. (J). (— 1). bds. 9.95 *(978-1-60219-217-1(0))* Good Night Bks.

Gates, Susan. Pirate!: Band 15/Emerald (Collins Big Cat), Bd. 15. McClellan, Maddy, illus. 2007. (Collins Big Cat Ser.). (ENG.). 48p. (J). (gr. 3-4). pap. 10.99 *(978-0-00-723095-2(8))* HarperCollins Pubs. Ltd. GBR. Dist: Independent Pubs. Group.

The Ghost Ship. 2013. (Illus.). (J). *(978-1-4351-4725-6(1))* Barnes & Noble, Inc.

Gilbert, Heather. Skyler the Pirate, 1 vol. 2009. 25p. pap. 24.95 *(978-1-60813-820-3(8))* America Star Bks.

Gilkerson, William. Pirate's Passage. 2014. (ENG., Illus.). 376p. (J). (gr. 4-7). pap. 16.95 *(978-1-61180-247-4(4),* Trumpeter) Shambhala Pubns., Inc.

Gilligan, Alison. Pirate Treasure of the Onyx Dragon. Utomo, Gabhor, illus. 2011. (ENG.). 144p. (J). (gr. 4-8). pap. 7.99 *(978-1-933390-99-4(9))* Chooseco LLC.

Gohmann, Johanna. A Bad Day at Pirate School. Innerebner, Jessika von, illus. 2017. (Pirate Kids Ser.). (ENG.). 32p. (J). (gr. -1-3). lib. bdg. 32.79 *(978-1-5321-3038-0(4),* 27040, Calico Chapter Bks) Magic Wagon.

—A Spooky Day at Sea. Innerebner, Jessika von, illus. 2017. (Pirate Kids Ser.). (ENG.). 32p. (J). (gr. -1-3). lib. bdg. 32.79 *(978-1-5321-3040-3(6),* 27042, Calico Chapter Bks) Magic Wagon.

—The Very Quiet Parrot. Innerebner, Jessika von, illus. 2017. (Pirate Kids Ser.). (ENG.). 32p. (J). (gr. -1-3). lib. bdg. 32.79 *(978-1-5321-3041-0(4),* 27043, Calico Chapter Bks) Magic Wagon.

Golden Books. Night of the Ghost Pirate (Paw Patrol) Lovett, Nate, illus. 2015. (ENG.). 64p. (J). (gr. -1-2). pap. 4.99 *(978-0-553-52390-4(2),* Golden Bks.) Random Hse. Children's Bks.

—Pirate Pups! (Paw Patrol) Petrossi, Fabrizio, illus. 2016. (Little Golden Book Ser.). (ENG.). 24p. (J). (gr. -1-k). 5.99 *(978-0-553-53888-5(8),* Golden Bks.) Random Hse. Children's Bks.

Golden, Christopher & Lebbon, Tim. The Sea Wolves Bk. 2, Bk. 2. Ruth, Greg, illus. 2012. (Secret Journeys of Jack London Ser.: 2). (ENG.). 400p. (YA). (gr. 8). 16.99 *(978-0-06-186320-2(3),* HarperTeen) HarperCollins Pubs.

Greene, Rhonda Gowler. No Pirates Allowed! Said Library Lou. Ajhar, Brian, illus. 2013. (ENG.). 40p. (J). (gr. 1-3). 15.95 *(978-1-58536-796-2(6),* 202364) Sleeping Bear Pr.

Guillain, Adam, et al. The Pirate Pie Ship. Van Wyk, Rupert, illus. 2014. (Race Ahead with Reading Ser.). (ENG.). 32p. (J). (gr. 2-2). *(978-0-7787-1309-8(1));* pap. *(978-0-7787-1368-5(7))* Crabtree Publishing Co.

Gurney, John Steven. The Bossy Pirate, 1 vol. 2018. (ENG., Illus.). 48p. (J). 16.99 *(978-0-7643-5625-4(9),* 9838) Schiffer Publishing, Ltd.

Halsey, Jacqueline & Muller, Carrie. The Terrible, Horrible, Smelly Pirate, 1 vol. Orchard, Eric, illus. 2008. (ENG.). 32p. (J). (gr. -1-k). pap. 11.95 *(978-1-55109-655-1(2),* bf2280e6-ca5d-4964-be00-1c8b95c6a4ac) Nimbus Publishing, Ltd. CAN. Dist: Baker & Taylor Publisher Services (BTPS).

Hamilton, Tisha. Piratas del Caribe. el viaje al fin del Mundo: Pirates of the Caribbean: at the World's End. 2007. (Illus.). 38p. (J). *(978-970-718-532-6(5),* Silver Dolphin en Español) Advanced Marketing, S. de R. L. de C. V.

Harley, Bill. Dirty Joe, the Pirate: A True Story. Davis, Jack E., illus. 2008. (ENG.). 32p. (J). (gr. k-3). 17.99 *(978-0-06-623780-0(7),* HarperCollins) HarperCollins Pubs.

Havercroft, Elizabeth. A Year on a Pirate Ship. 2009. (Time Goes By Ser.). (ENG., Illus.). 24p. (J). (gr. k-3). pap. 8.99 *(978-1-58013-799-7(7),* 0e71397e-7b0b-489e-80d4-2c57ef622365, First Avenue Editions) Lerner Publishing Group.

Hawes, Charles Boardman. The Dark Frigate. Chappell, Warren, illus. 2018. (ENG.). 240p. (gr. 3-7). pap. 7.99 *(978-0-486-82392-8(X),* 82392X) Dover Pubns., Inc.

—The Dark Frigate. 2005. pap. 27.95 *(978-1-4179-3209-2(0))* Kessinger Publishing, LLC.

Hawkins, Colin. Pirate Ship: A Pop-up Adventure. Hawkins, Colin et al, illus. 2006. 28p. (J). (gr. 4-8). reprint ed. 20.00 *(978-0-7567-9827-7(2))* DIANE Publishing Co.

Hawkins, Mia K. The Broken Guild of Twelve Pirates, 1 vol. 2009. 201p. pap. 24.95 *(978-1-61546-333-6(X))* PublishAmerica, Inc.

Hawley, Mabel C. Four Little Blossoms on Apple Tree Island. 2007. 80p. per. *(978-1-4068-1704-1(X))* Echo Library.

Head, Mat. Warduff & the Pelican Pirates. 2014. (ENG., Illus.). 32p. (J). (-k). pap. 9.99 *(978-1-84939-567-0(5))* Andersen Pr. GBR. Dist: Independent Pubs. Group.

Heilig, Heidi. The Girl from Everywhere. 2016. (ENG.). 464p. (YA). (gr. 8). 17.99 *(978-0-06-238075-3(3),* Greenwillow Bks.) HarperCollins Pubs.

Helquist, Brett. Roger: The Jolly Pirate. Helquist, Brett, illus. 2004. (ENG., Illus.). 40p. (J). (gr. -1-3). 16.99 *(978-0-06-623805-0(6))* HarperCollins Pubs.

—Roger, the Jolly Pirate. Helquist, Brett, illus. 2004. (Illus.). 40p. (J). (gr. -1-3). lib. bdg. 17.89 *(978-0-06-623806-7(4))* HarperCollins Pubs.

—Roger the Jolly Pirate. 2007. (ENG., Illus.). 40p. (J). (gr. -1-2). pap. 7.99 *(978-0-06-443851-3(1),* Balzer & Bray) HarperCollins Pubs.

Hemyng, Bracebridge. Jack Harkaway & His Son's Escape from the Brigands of Greece. 2004. reprint ed. pap. 1.99 *(978-1-4192-2705-9(X))* Kessinger Publishing, LLC.

Henry, James. The Cabinet of Curiosities. 2010. 240p. pap. 21.50 *(978-0-9559851-0-2(2))* Blue Cat GBR. Dist: Lulu Pr., Inc.

Heos, Bridget. Arrr, Mustache Baby! Ang, Joy, illus. 2019. (Mustache Baby Ser.). (ENG.). 40p. (J). (gr. -1-3). 17.99 *(978-1-328-50652-8(5),* 1718797, Clarion Bks.) HarperCollins Pubs.

Herwick Rice, Dona & Paris, Stephanie. Sal Fink, 1 vol. rev. ed. 2009. (Reader's Theater Ser.). (ENG.). 24p. (gr. 2-4). pap. 8.99 *(978-1-4333-0995-3(5))* Teacher Created Materials, Inc.

Higginson, Sheila Sweeny. Cubby's Mixed-Up Map. 2014. (Jake & the Never Land Pirates Ser.). (J). lib. bdg. 14.75 *(978-0-606-35262-8(7))* Turtleback.

Holden, Pam. Greedy Gus the Pirate, 1 vol. Whimp, Pauline, illus. 2009. (Red Rocket Readers Ser.). (ENG.). 18p. (gr. 2-2). pap. *(978-1-877363-74-0(X))* Flying Start Bks.

—Two Pirates, 1 vol. Whimp, Pauline, illus. 2009. (Red Rocket Readers Ser.). (ENG.). 23p. (gr. 2-2). pap. *(978-1-877363-71-9(5))* Flying Start Bks.

Hope, B. T. The Curse of the Bone Pirates: Nui Island Eco-Logical Adventures. 2008. 198p. (J). pap. 9.95 *(978-0-9817388-0-2(X))* Nui Media & Entertainment, LLC.

Hopkins, Douglas. Princess June & the Shadow Pirates, 1 vol. 2007. (ENG., Illus.). 32p. (J). (gr. -1-2). per. *(978-1-894294-88-1(2))* Breakwater Bks., Ltd.

Horn, Shannon. Pirates of the Mississippian: The Adventures of Jerry & Draco. 2012. 24p. pap. 17.99 *(978-1-4772-6991-6(6))* AuthorHouse.

Howard, Jenny. Bittersweet Voyage. 2012. 172p. pap. 12.95 *(978-1-4685-7573-6(2))* AuthorHouse.

Hritzay, Tami. The Hole in the Wall: J. B. & the Pirates. 2013. pap. 11.45 *(978-0-7414-8266-2(5))* Infinity Publishing.

Hunt, Elizabeth Singer. Secret Agent Jack Stalwart: Book 2: the Search for the Sunken Treasure: Australia. 2007. (Secret Agent Jack Stalwart Ser.: 2). (ENG., Illus.). 128p. (J). (gr. 1-4). per. 5.99 *(978-1-60286-002-5(5),* Running Pr. Kids) Running Pr.

Hunter, Derek. Brainwash Escape Victims, Vol. 2. 2006. (ENG., Illus.). 144p. (YA). pap. 12.95 *(978-1-59362-051-6(9),* 87d8783e-e029-478f-affe-985db42c2370) Slave Labor Bks.

Icanberry, Mark. A Pirate's Feast. 2011. (Illus.). 48p. 14.95 *(978-1-893327-08-5(6));* pap. 7.95 *(978-1-893327-09-2(4))* Ten Speed Pr. (Tricycle Pr.).

Jacques, Brian. The Angel's Command. 2005. (Castaways of the Flying Dutchman Ser.). (ENG., Illus.). 384p. (J). (gr. 3-7). 9.99 *(978-0-14-240285-6(0),* Firebird) Penguin Young Readers Group.

—The Angel's Command. 2003. (Castaways of the Flying Dutchman Ser.: No. 2). 1.00 *(978-1-4175-5393-8(6))* Recorded Bks., Inc.

—Mariel of Redwall. 2004. (Redwall Ser.). 1.00 *(978-1-4175-6449-1(0))* Recorded Bks., Inc.

James, Brian. Ahoy, Ghost Ship Ahead! #2. Zivoin, Jennifer, illus. 2007. (Pirate School Ser.: 2). 64p. (J). (gr. 1-3). pap. 4.99 *(978-0-448-44625-7(1),* Grosset & Dunlap) Penguin Young Readers Group.

James, Larry W. Captain Petey: An Adventure at Sea. Ramos, Violet M., ed. James, Larry W. & Freshman, Floris R., illus. 2003. 28p. pap. 6.99 *(978-0-9742154-0-2(6))* Cross Pointe Printing.

Jardine, Alan. Sloop John B: A Pirate's Tale. Pickering, Jimmy, illus. 2005. (ENG.). 32p. (J). (gr. 4-7). 17.95 *(978-1-59687-181-6(4))* IBks., Inc.

—Sloop John B: A Pirate's Tale. Pickering, Jimmy, illus. 2005. 32p. 17.95 *(978-0-689-03596-8(9))*, Milk & Cookies) ibooks, Inc.

—Sloop John B -A Pirate's Tale. Pickering, Jimmy, illus. 2016. (ENG.). 32p. (J). (gr. k-4). 32.00 *(978-1-59687-511-1(9))*, ipicturebooks) ibooks, Inc.

Jarman, Julia. Class Three at Sea. Chapman, Lynne, illus. 2008. (ENG.). 32p. (J). (gr. k-3). 16.95 *(978-0-8225-7617-4(1))*, Carolrhoda Bks.) Lerner Publishing Group.

Jeffrey, Rosemary. Allio, Are you Free. 2010. (ENG.). 176p. pap. 12.00 *(978-0-557-75342-0(2))* Lulu Pr., Inc.

Johnson, Myrna. Let's Take a Hike. 2013. (ENG., Illus.). 32p. (gr. -1-1). pap. 13.95 *(978-1-936205-79-0(3))*, P223206) Austin, Stephen F. State Univ. Pr.

Jones, Gareth P. Are You the Pirate Captain? Parsons, Garry, illus. 2016. (ENG.). 32p. (J). (gr. -1-3). 16.95 *(978-1-5124-0427-2(6))*, 2997a477-7620-4034-85ae-45644aa1f9e6). E-Book 27.99 *(978-1-5124-0446-3(2))* Lerner Publishing Group.

Jones, Rob Lloyd. See Inside Pirate Ships. Muhle, Jorg, illus. 2007. (See Inside Board Bks.). 15p. (J). (gr. -1-3). bds. 12.99 *(978-0-7945-1601-7(7))*, Usborne) EDC Publishing.

—The Story of Pirates. Dutrait, Vincent, illus. 2007. (Young Reading Series 3 Gift Bks). 63p. (J). (gr. 4-7). 8.99 *(978-0-7945-1618-5(1))*, Usborne) EDC Publishing.

Jones, T. Llew. Captain Morgan & the Pirate Treasure. 2015. (ENG.). 218p. (J). pap. 8.95 *(978-1-78562-068-3(1))* Gomer Pr. GBR. Dist: Casemate Pubs. & Bk. Distributors, LLC.

Jorgensen, Norman. Smuggler's Curse. 2017. 356p. (J). (gr. 4-7). 8.95 *(978-1-925164-19-0(5))* Fremantle Pr. AUS. Dist: Independent Pubs. Group.

Joyce, Melanie. What Pirates Really Do. Paterson, Alex, illus. 2016. (ENG.). 32p. (J). (gr. -1-3). 16.99 *(978-1-4998-0257-3(9))* Little Bee Books Inc.

Kann, Victoria. Pinkalicious & the Pirates. Kann, Victoria, illus. 2018. (I Can Read Level 1 Ser.). (ENG., Illus.). 32p. (J). (gr. -1-3). 16.99 *(978-0-06-256699-7(7))*; pap. 4.99 *(978-0-06-256698-0(9))* HarperCollins Pubs. (HarperCollins).

Kaserman, James & Kaserman, Sarah Jane. How the Pirates Saved Christmas. 2005. (Illus.). 64p. (J). per. 5.99 *(978-0-9674081-2-5(1))*, (239)939-4845) Pirate Publishing International.

Katar, Al. Captain Scratch: The Island of Simarj. 2008. 48p. pap. 21.99 *(978-1-4363-4188-2(4))* Xlibris Corp.

Keats, Israel. The Zephyr Conspiracy. 2017. (Level Up Ser.). (ENG.). 112p. (YA). (gr. 6-12). pap. 7.99 *(978-1-5124-5361-4(7))*, 7e569a6f-416c-40e8-8dfc-520ae09833c9); lib. bdg. 26.65 *(978-1-5124-3985-4(1))*, 07cc3b67-9541-407e-a23c-ab2e2516b1d9) Lerner Publishing Group. (Darby Creek).

Keene, Carolyn. Treasure Trouble. Pamintuan, Macky, illus. 2009. (Nancy Drew & the Clue Crew Ser.: 20). (ENG.). 112p. (J). (gr. 1-4). pap. 5.99 *(978-1-4169-7809-1(7))*, Aladdin) Simon & Schuster Children's Publishing.

Kehne, Carroll Harrison, Jr. & Kehne, Carroll Harrison. Buried Treasure, a Pirate's Tale, 1 vol. 2009. (ENG., Illus.). 34p. (J). (gr. 3-7). 12.95 *(978-0-87033-601-0(0))*, 3602, Cornell Maritime Pr./Tidewater Pubs.) Schiffer Publishing, Ltd.

Kennedy, Kim. Pirate Pete. Kennedy, Doug & Kennedy, Roy D., illus. 2010. (ENG.). 40p. (J). (gr. -1-3). pap. 8.95 *(978-0-8109-8923-8(9))* Abrams, Inc.

Kessler, Liz. Poppy the Pirate Dog & the Missing Treasure. Phillips, Mike, illus. (Candlewick Sparks Ser.). (ENG.). 64p. (J). (gr. k-4). 2016. pap. 5.99 *(978-0-7636-8772-4(3))* 2015. 14.99 *(978-0-7636-7497-7(4))* Candlewick Pr.

—Poppy the Pirate Dog's New Shipmate. Phillips, Mike, illus. (Candlewick Sparks Ser.). (ENG.). 64p. (J). (gr. k-4). 2015. pap. 4.99 *(978-0-7636-8031-2(1))* 2014. 14.99 *(978-0-7636-6751-1(X))* Candlewick Pr.

Kettle, Shey. Girl Pirates. Thomas, Meredith, illus. 2005. (Girlz Rock! Ser.). (J). pap. *(978-1-59336-701-5(5))* Mondo Publishing.

Kidd, Rob. Day of the Shadow. 4th ed. 2009. (Pirates of the Caribbean Ser.: No. 5). 256p. (YA). (gr. 5-18). pap. 6.99 *(978-1-4231-1041-5(2))* Disney Pr.

—Jack Sparrow: The Siren Song. Orpinas, Jean-Paul, illus. 2006. 122p. (J). lib. bdg. 16.00 *(978-1-4242-1571-3(4))* Fitzgerald Bks.

Kimmelman, Leslie. Trick ARRR Treat: A Pirate Halloween. Monlongo, Jorge, illus. (ENG.). 32p. (J). (gr. -1-3). 2017. pap. 7.99 *(978-0-8075-8066-0(X))*, 080758066X) 2015. 16.99 *(978-0-8075-8061-5(9))*, 807580619) Whitman, Albert & Co.

King, A. S. The Dust of 100 Dogs. 2017. 336p. (YA). (gr. 9). pap. 10.99 *(978-0-425-29057-6(3))*, Speak) Penguin Young Readers Group.

Kladstrup, Kristin. The Gingerbread Pirates. Tavares, Matt, illus. 2009. 32p. (J). (gr. -1-3). 16.99 *(978-0-7636-3223-6(6))* Candlewick Pr.

—The Gingerbread Pirates Gift Edition. Tavares, Matt, illus. gif. ed. 2012. (ENG.). 32p. (J). (gr. -1-3). 9.99 *(978-0-7636-6233-2(X))* Candlewick Pr.

Kleyn, Diana & Beeke, Joel R. How God Stopped the Pirates. rev. ed. 2008. (Building on the Rock Ser.). (ENG., Illus.). 176p. (J). pap. 8.99 *(978-1-85792-816-7(4))*, 9acf5c03-a0d7-4709-896b-6b203eab4004, CF4Kids) Christian Focus Pubns. GBR. Dist: Baker & Taylor Publisher Services (BTPS).

Kloepfer, John. The Zombie Chasers #6: Zombies of the Caribbean. DeGrand, David, illus. 2014. (Zombie Chasers Ser.: 6). (ENG.). 224p. (J). (gr. 3-7). 16.99 *(978-0-06-229024-3(X))*, HarperCollins) HarperCollins Pubs.

Knotoff, Karenann. The Island of Rouge. 2007. 96p. per. 19.95 *(978-1-4241-7575-8(5))* America Star Bks.

Konkle, Thomas. Red Skies. 2017. (Survive Ser.). (ENG.). 192p. (YA). (gr. 5-12). lib. bdg. 31.42 *(978-1-68076-733-9(X))*, 25400, Epic Escape) EPIC Pr.

Kremsner, Cynthia, illus. Swashbarklers of the Sea, 1 vol. 2019. (ENG.). 32p. (J). (gr. -1-3). 16.99 *(978-1-4556-2414-0(4))*, Pelican Publishing) Arcadia Publishing.

Kuhl, Debra. Black Bert the Pirate, 1 vol. 2009. 83p. pap. 19.95 *(978-1-60749-968-8(1))* America Star Bks.

La Rose, Melinda. Jake & the Neverland Pirates: X Marks the Croc! Batson, Alan, illus. 2014. (World of Reading Level Pre-1 (Leveled Readers) Ser.). (ENG.). 32p. (J). (gr. -1-2). lib. bdg. 31.36 *(978-1-61479-247-5(X))*, 1761) Spotlight.

—Surfin' Turf. 2019. (Illus.). 31p. (J). *(978-1-4242-5739-3(5))* Disney Publishing Worldwide.

La Rose, Melinda & Ward, Kelly. Treasure of the Tides. 2014. (Jake & the Never Land Pirates Ser.). (ENG., Illus.). 32p. (J). (gr. k-2). 16.19 *(978-1-4844-3449-9(8))* Disney Pr.

Lachmann, Carola. Gayo, a young pirate on a treasure Hunt. 2007. (ENG.). 68p. pap. 41.95 *(978-1-84753-250-3(0))* Lulu Pr., Inc.

Lake, Nick. Hostage Three. 2013. (ENG.). 320p. (gr. 7). E-Book 7.99 *(978-1-61963-149-6(0))*, Bloomsbury USA Childrens) Bloomsbury Publishing USA.

Lamphere-Slaughter, Sharyn. Droopy Drawers & the Peg Leg Pirate. 2009. 24p. pap. 12.99 *(978-1-4490-6055-8(2))* AuthorHouse.

LaReau, Kara. The Jolly Regina (the Unintentional Adventures of the Bland Sisters Book 1) Hill, Jen, illus. 2018. (Unintentional Adventures of the Bland Sisters Ser.). (ENG.). 184p. (J). (gr. 3-7). pap. 7.99 *(978-1-4197-2605-7(6))*, 1138303, Amulet Bks.) Abrams, Inc.

—Unintentional Adventures of the Bland Sisters: The Jolly Regina. Hill, Jen, illus. 2017. (ENG.). 176p. (J). (gr. 3-7). 14.95 *(978-1-4197-2136-6(4))*, 1138301, Amulet Bks.) Abrams, Inc.

Larose, Melinda. After a While, Crocodile. 2014. (Jake & the Never Land Pirates Ser.). (J). lib. bdg. 13.55 *(978-0-606-35267-3(8))* Turtleback.

—Treasure of the Tides. 2014. (Jake & the Never Land Pirates Ser.). (J). lib. bdg. 13.55 *(978-0-606-35269-7(4))* Turtleback.

LaRose, Melinda & Dubuc, Nicole. Jake & the Never Land Pirates: Surfin' Turf. Character Building Studio & Disney Storybook Art Team, illus. 2018. (World of Reading Level 1 Ser.). (ENG.). 32p. (J). (gr. -1-3). lib. bdg. 31.36 *(978-1-5321-4189-8(0))*, 31065) Spotlight.

Lasky, Kathryn. Pirate Bob. Clark, David, illus. alt. ed. 2008. (ENG.). 32p. (J). (gr. k-3). per. 8.95 *(978-1-57091-647-2(0))* Charlesbridge Publishing, Inc.

Laurence, Daniel. Captain & Matey Set Sail. Muñoz, Claudio, illus. 2003. (I Can Read Bks.). 64p. (gr. 1-3). 15.00 *(978-0-7569-1402-8(7))* Perfection Learning Corp.

Lawrence, Caroline. The Pirates of Pompeii. 2004. (Roman Mysteries Ser.). (Illus.). 159p. (J). (gr. 3-7). 13.65 *(978-0-7569-5938-8(1))* Perfection Learning Corp.

Lawrence, Iain. The Buccaneers. 2003. (High Seas Trilogy). (Illus.). 244p. (gr. 5-9). 16.50 *(978-0-7569-1454-7(X))* Perfection Learning Corp.

—The Buccaneers. 2003. (High Seas Trilogy Ser.). (ENG., Illus.). 256p. (J). (gr. 3-7). 8.99 *(978-0-440-41671-5(X))*, Yearling) Random Hse. Children's Bks.

Lawrenson, Judith. Petunia the Pirate of Port Royal Sound. 2007. (Illus.). (J). 14.95 *(978-0-9767278-0-4(3))* Mrs. L's Reading Room.

Le Gras, Gilbert. Joaquin & Olivier en Haute Mer! On the High Seas. 2009. 24p. pap. 8.20 *(978-1-4251-1980-5(8))* Trafford Publishing.

LeapFrog Staff. Pirates: The Treasure of Turtle Island. 2008. (J). 13.99 *(978-1-59319-927-2(9))* LeapFrog Enterprises, Inc.

Lee, Brian, illus. A Pirate Ship. 2005. (What's Inside? Ser.). *(978-0-7607-6809-9(9))* backpackbook.

Leigh, S. Uncle Pete's Pirate Adventure. rev. ed. 2004. (Young Puzzle Adventures Ser.). 32p. (J). (gr. 2-18). pap. 4.95 *(978-0-7945-0401-4(9))*; lib. bdg. 12.95 *(978-1-58086-545-6(3))* EDC Publishing.

Leigh, Susannah. Uncle Pete the Pirate. 2004. (Usborne Young Puzzle Adventures Ser.). (Illus.). 32p. (J). (gr. 2-18). pap. 4.95 *(978-0-7945-0400-7(0))*, Usborne) EDC Publishing.

—Uncle Pete's Pirate Adventure. Stowell, Louie, ed. Haw, Brenda & Dawes, Will, illus. rev. ed. 2007. (Young Puzzle Adventures Ser.). 32p. (J). (gr. -1-3). pap. 4.99 *(978-0-7945-1848-6(6))*, Usborne) EDC Publishing.

LernerClassroom Editors, ed. Twisted Journeys, Set 1. 2008. (Twisted Journeys (r) Ser.). (ENG.). (J). (gr. 4-7). pap. 271.89 *(978-1-58013-276-3(6))* Lerner Publishing Group.

Leung, Peyton. The Pirate Girl's Treasure: An Origami Adventure. Leung, Hilary, illus. 2012. (ENG.). 32p. (J). (gr. -1-3). 16.95 *(978-1-55453-660-3(X))* Kids Can Pr., Ltd. CAN. Dist: Hachette Bk. Group.

Levenseller, Tricia. Daughter of the Pirate King. 2018. (Daughter of the Pirate King Ser.: 1). (ENG.). 336p. (YA). pap. 10.99 *(978-1-250-14422-5(1))*, 900160921) Square Fish.

—Daughter of the Siren Queen. 2019. (Daughter of the Pirate King Ser.: 2). (ENG., Illus.). 368p. (YA). pap. 11.99 *(978-1-250-29460-9(6))*, 900160929) Square Fish.

Lewis, Michael. Cap'n Mcnasty's Pirate Guide, 1 vol. Jaskiel, Stan, illus. 2020. (ENG.). 32p. (J). (gr. 3-4). 16.99 *(978-1-4556-2525-3(6))*, Pelican Publishing) Arcadia Publishing.

—The Great Pirate Christmas Battle, 1 vol. Jaskiel, Stan, illus. 2014. (ENG.). 32p. (J). (gr. k-3). 16.99 *(978-1-4556-1934-4(5))*, Pelican Publishing) Arcadia Publishing.

—The Great Thanksgiving Food Fight, 1 vol. Jaskiel, Stan, illus. 2017. (ENG.). 32p. (J). (gr. -1-3). 16.99 *(978-1-4556-2285-6(0))*, Pelican Publishing) Arcadia Publishing.

Lindgren, Astrid. Ferien auf Saltkroken. pap. 19.95 *(978-3-423-70773-2(9))* Deutscher Taschenbuch Verlag GmbH & Co KG DEU. Dist: Distribooks, Inc.

Linklater, Eric. The Pirates in the Deep Green Sea. 2013. (ENG.). 314p. (YA). pap. *(978-1-4482-0582-0(4))*, 150371, Bloomsbury Reader) Bloomsbury Publishing Plc.

Lloyd, Hugh. Among the River Pirates. Fogel, Seymour, illus. 2011. 204p. 44.95 *(978-1-258-06703-8(X))* Literary Licensing, LLC.

Lock, Deborah. DK Readers L2: Pirate Attack! 2017. (DK Readers Level 2 Ser.). (ENG., Illus.). 48p. (J). (gr. k-2). pap. 3.99 *(978-1-4654-6473-6(5))*, DK Children) Dorling Kindersley Publishing, Inc.

Long, Melinda. How I Became a Pirate. Shannon, David, illus. 2003. (ENG.). 44p. (J). (gr. -1-3). 18.99 *(978-0-15-201848-1(4))*, 1191067, Clarion Bks.) HarperCollins Pubs.

—Pirates Don't Change Diapers. Shannon, David, illus. 2007. (ENG.). 44p. (J). (gr. -1-3). 19.99 *(978-0-15-205353-6(0))*, 1196124, Clarion Bks.) HarperCollins Pubs.

Lopez, Patricia A. Corky & Pirate Dan, 1 vol. 2009. 43p. pap. 24.95 *(978-1-61546-096-0(9))* PublishAmerica, Inc.

Lord, Kenniston. The Pirates of Peary Village. 2004. (ENG.). 180p. (J). pap. 9.18 *(978-1-4116-7893-4(1))* Lulu Pr., Inc.

The Lost Treasure of Skull Island. 2012. (Illus.). (J). *(978-1-4351-4328-9(0))* Barnes & Noble, Inc.

Lynes, William. Pirates, Scoundrels, & Kings. 2013. 450p. (gr. 10-12). 33.95 *(978-1-4759-6562-9(1))*; pap. 23.95 *(978-1-4759-6561-2(3))* iUniverse, Inc.

Lytle, Robert A. Pirate Party. Williams, Bill, illus. 2006. (Mackinac Passage Ser.). 258p. (J). (gr. 4-7). pap. 9.95 *(978-0-9749412-5-7(5))* EDCO Publishing, Inc.

MacKenzie, Ross. Zac & the Dream Stealers. 2013. 297p. (J). *(978-0-545-40107-4(0))*, Chicken Hse., The) Scholastic, Inc.

MacNeil, Stephen. Woolies & Worms. 2007. (ENG., Illus.). 192p. (J). (gr. 1-5). 16.95 *(978-0-8126-2751-0(2))* Cricket Bks.

Malcolm, Jahnna N. Pirate's Revenge. Comport, Sally Wern, illus. 2003. 77p. (J). *(978-1-931020-09-1(4))* HOP, LLC.

Manushkin, Fran. Pedro el Pirata. Trusted Translations, Trusted, tr. Lyon, Tammie, illus. 2018. (Pedro en Español Ser.). (SPA.). 32p. (J). (gr. k-2). lib. bdg. 21.32 *(978-1-5158-2514-2(0))*, 137573, Picture Window Bks.) Capstone.

—Pirate Pedro. Lyon, Tammie, illus. 2017. (Pedro Ser.). (ENG.). 32p. (J). (gr. k-2). lib. bdg. 21.32 *(978-1-5158-0872-5(6))*, 134403, Picture Window Bks.) Capstone.

Marillier, Juliet. Cybele's Secret. 2011. (Wildwood Dancing Ser.: 2). (ENG.). 448p. (YA). (gr. 7). pap. 9.99 *(978-0-553-49486-0(4))*, Knopf Bks. for Young Readers) Random Hse. Children's Bks.

Marks, Graham. Radio Radio. 224p. (YA). (gr. 7). 2007. pap. 11.95 *(978-0-7475-9087-3(7))* 2003. pap. 12.99 *(978-0-7475-5939-9(2))* Bloomsbury Publishing Plc GBR. Dist: Independent Pubs. Group.

Marsh, Carole. The Mystery of Blackbeard the Pirate. Marsh, Carole, photos by. 2009. (Real Kids, Real Places Ser.). (Illus.). 150p. (J). 18.99 *(978-0-635-06992-4(X))*, Marsh, Carole Mysteries) Gallopade International.

Masefield, John. Jim Davis. l.t. ed. 2007. (ENG.). 142p. pap. 19.99 *(978-1-4264-2384-0(5))* Creative Media Partners, LLC.

McClatchy, Lisa. Eloise's Pirate Adventure: Ready-To-Read Level 1. Lyon, Tammie, illus. (Eloise Ser.). (ENG.). 32p. (J). (gr. -1-1). 2017. 16.99 *(978-1-4814-9979-8(3))* 2007. pap. 4.99 *(978-1-4169-4979-4(8))* Simon Spotlight. (Simon Spotlight).

McCoy, Chris. Scurvy Goonda. 2011. (ENG.). 336p. (J). (gr. 6-8). lib. bdg. 22.44 *(978-0-375-95598-3(4))*, Knopf Bks. for Young Readers) Random Hse. Children's Bks.

McDonald, Megan. Judy Moody & Stink: la Loca, Loca Búsqueda Del Tesoro / JM & Stink: the Mad, Mad, Mad, Mad Treasure Hunt. 2011. (Judy Moody & Stink Ser.). (SPA., Illus.). 144p. (J). (gr. 2-5). pap. 14.95 *(978-1-61605-137-2(X))*, Alfaguara) Penguin Random House Grupo Editorial ESP. Dist: Penguin Random Hse. LLC.

—Judy Moody & Stink: the Mad, Mad, Mad, Mad Treasure Hunt. Reynolds, Peter H., illus. 2010. (Judy Moody & Stink Ser.: 2). (ENG.). 128p. (J). (gr. 1-4). pap. 7.99 *(978-0-7636-4351-5(3))* Candlewick Pr.

Mcdonald, Megan. The Mad, Mad, Mad, Mad Treasure Hunt. 2010. (Judy Moody & Stink Ser.: 2). lib. bdg. 18.40 *(978-0-606-01311-6(3))* Turtleback.

McKinley, Ryan. The Lost Crew. 2012. (ENG.). 144p. pap. 9.95 *(978-1-4327-9658-7(5))*; pap. 14.95 *(978-1-4327-9659-4(3))* Outskirts Pr., Inc.

—The Pirate Bride. 2010. 105p. 21.95 *(978-1-4327-5546-1(3))*; (Illus.). pap. 14.95 *(978-1-4327-5545-4(5))* Outskirts Pr., Inc.

McNee, Ian, illus. Treasure Island. 2006. 158p. (J). (gr. 5-9). per. 4.99 *(978-0-7945-1230-9(5))*, Usborne) EDC Publishing.

Meisel, Peter. Stinky Spike & the Royal Rescue. Meisel, Paul, illus. 2018. (Read & Bloom Ser.). (ENG.). 80p. (J). pap. 7.99 *(978-1-61963-886-0(X))*, 900150927, Bloomsbury Children's Bks.) Bloomsbury Publishing USA.

Meyer, Kai. Pirate Wars. Crawford, Elizabeth D., tr. 2008. (Wave Walkers Ser.: 3). (ENG.). 384p. (J). (gr. 5-9). pap. 8.99 *(978-1-4169-2477-7(9))*, McElderry, Margaret K. Bks.) McElderry, Margaret K. Bks.

Michaels, Craig. Blackbeard's Treasure. 2008. (J). *(978-0-936389-99-8(0))* Tudor Pubs., Inc.

Miles, Colin. Naughty Nicky & the Good Ship Oggy. Miles, Gail, illus. 2013. 24p. pap. *(978-1-909202-16-0(9))* Little Acorns Publishing.

Miller, Suzanne. Pirates! That Is Who We Be! 2010. 28p. pap. 13.50 *(978-1-4490-6362-7(4))* AuthorHouse.

Milway, Alex. Pigsticks & Harold & the Pirate Treasure. Milway, Alex, illus. (Candlewick Sparks Ser.). (ENG., Illus.). 64p. (J). (gr. k-4). 2018. pap. 6.99 *(978-0-7636-9960-4(8))* 2016. 12.99 *(978-0-7636-8157-9(1))* Candlewick Pr.

Miraucourt, Christophe. Pirate Treasure. 2015. (Race Further with Reading Ser.). (ENG., Illus.). 48p. (J). (gr. 3-3). *(978-0-7787-2031-7(4))* Crabtree Publishing Co.

—The Pirate's Daughter. 2015. (Race Further with Reading Ser.). (ENG., Illus.). 48p. (J). (gr. 3-3). *(978-0-7787-2088-1(8))* Crabtree Publishing Co.

Mizobuchi, Makoto. Pokémon Ranger & the Temple of the Sea. 2008. (Pokémon the Movie (manga) Ser.: 1). (ENG., Illus.). 192p. (J). (gr. 1). pap. 9.99 *(978-1-4215-2288-3(8))* Viz Media.

Mone, Gregory. Fish. 2010. (J). *(978-0-545-11631-2(7))*, Scholastic Pr.) Scholastic, Inc.

Morgan, Allen. Matthew & the Midnight Pirates, 1 vol. 2005. (First Flight Level 3 Ser.). (ENG., Illus.). 40p. (J). (gr. k-3). lib. bdg. 11.95 *(978-1-55041-902-3(1))*, c7047f02-b422-4280-915a-cf41b485ee54) Fitzhenry & Whiteside, Ltd. CAN. Dist: Firefly Bks., Ltd.

Morley, P. Kevin. The Stinky Pirate & the Princess. 2009. 36p. pap. 17.99 *(978-1-4490-4062-8(4))* AuthorHouse.

Morse, William A. Kurkle Kids: Pirate Lostman's Great Adventure. 2010. 44p. pap. 16.99 *(978-1-4490-6187-6(7))* AuthorHouse.

Moss, Tamara. Lintang & the Pirate Queen. 2019. (ENG.). 368p. (J). (gr. 5-7). 16.99 *(978-1-328-46030-1(4))*, 1712799, Clarion Bks.) HarperCollins Pubs.

Mould, Chris. The Great Cheese Robbery. Mould, Chris, illus. 2018. (Pocket Pirates Ser.: 1). (ENG., Illus.). 160p. (J). (gr. 1-4). 17.99 *(978-1-4814-9115-0(6))*; pap. 6.99 *(978-1-4814-9114-3(8))* Simon & Schuster Children's Publishing. (Aladdin).

—The Great Drain Escape. Mould, Chris, illus. 2018. (Pocket Pirates Ser.: 2). (ENG., Illus.). 144p. (J). (gr. 1-4). 17.99 *(978-1-4814-9118-1(0))*; pap. 6.99 *(978-1-4814-9117-4(2))* Simon & Schuster Children's Publishing. (Aladdin).

Moulder, Holly. Eyes of the Calusa. 2007. 111p. (J). pap. 8.95 *(978-0-9790405-0-4(7))* White Pelican Pr.

Murray, Pamela. Pirates of Texas. 2012. 28p. (-18). pap. 24.95 *(978-1-4626-9996-4(0))* America Star Bks.

Myers, Tim. Yao Bai & the Egg Pirates. Wong, Justin, illus. 2018. (J). *(978-1-5132-6102-7(9))* West Margin Pr.

Myers, Tim J. Yao Bai & the Egg Pirates. Pang, Bonnie, illus. 2019. (ENG.). 32p. (J). (gr. 1-4). 16.99 *(978-1-5132-6144-7(4))*, West Margin Pr.) West Margin Pr.

Myklusch, Matt. The Lost Prince. (Seaborne Ser.). (ENG.). 400p. (J). (gr. 3-6). 2017. pap. 9.99 *(978-1-5124-8175-4(0))*, e357d49a-1f6d-4710-86d4-0e1c1d4e4d77) 2015. E-Book 29.32 *(978-1-5124-0185-1(4))* Lerner Publishing Group. (Carolrhoda Bks.).

—Strangers in Atlantis. 2017. (Seaborne Ser.: 2). (ENG.). 280p. (J). (gr. 3-6). 18.99 *(978-1-5124-1375-5(5))*, e05ec5a2-2d78-405a-84fd-82f201d65d74); E-Book 29.32 *(978-1-5124-2691-5(1))* Lerner Publishing Group. (Carolrhoda Bks.).

Nannini, Randi. My Brother's A Pirate, 1 vol. Clark, Wendy, illus. 2010. 14p. pap. 24.95 *(978-1-4489-8576-0(5))* America Star Bks.

Nash, Scott. The High Skies Adventures of Blue Jay the Pirate. Nash, Scott, illus. 2012. (ENG., Illus.). 368p. (J). (gr. 4-7). 17.99 *(978-0-7636-3264-9(3))* Candlewick Pr.

Nash, Tim. The Club. 2009. 112p. pap. 12.49 *(978-1-4490-2087-3(9))* AuthorHouse.

Newland, Trevor. The Scallywag Solution, 1 vol. 2014. (ENG., Illus.). 64p. (J). (gr. k-7). 15.95 *(978-0-88962-990-5(0))*, 9780889629905) Mosaic Pr. CAN. Dist: Independent Pubs. Group.

Nicholls, Paul, illus. I Want to Be A... Pirate. 2014. (J). *(978-1-4351-5500-8(9))* Barnes & Noble, Inc.

Nix, Garth. Drowned Wednesday. 2006. (Keys to the Kingdom Ser.: No. 3). 389p. (gr. 4-7). 18.00 *(978-0-7569-6939-4(5))* Perfection Learning Corp.

Nolen, Jerdine. Block Party Surprise. Henninger, Michelle, illus. 2015. 41p. (J). *(978-1-4806-8574-1(7))* Harcourt.

Ocean, Davy. Long Fin Silver. Blecha, Aaron, illus. 2018. (Shark School Ser.: 9). (ENG.). 144p. (J). (gr. 1-4). 16.99 *(978-1-4814-6553-3(8))*; pap. 6.99 *(978-1-4814-6552-6(X))* Simon & Schuster Children's Publishing. (Aladdin).

Oda, Eiichiro. Recipe for Disaster. 2007. 90p. (J). pap. *(978-0-439-89722-8(X))* Scholastic, Inc.

O'Malley, Kevin & O'Brien, Patrick. Captain Raptor & the Space Pirates. O'Brien, Patrick, illus. 2007. (Captain Raptor Ser.). (ENG., Illus.). 32p. (J). (gr. k-3). 17.99 *(978-0-8027-9571-7(4))*, 900040057, Bloomsbury USA Childrens) Bloomsbury Publishing USA.

Oppel, Kenneth. Airborn: A Printz Honor Winner. (ENG., Illus.). (YA). (gr. 8-18). 2004. 368p. 18.99 *(978-0-06-053180-5(0))* 2005. 544p. reprint ed. pap. 11.99 *(978-0-06-053182-9(7))* HarperCollins Pubs. (HarperCollins).

—Skybreaker. (ENG., Illus.). 2007. 560p. (YA). (gr. 8). per. 11.99 *(978-0-06-053229-1(7))*, HarperCollins) 2005. 384p. (J). (gr. 6-10). 16.99 *(978-0-06-053227-7(0))* HarperCollins Pubs.

—Skybreaker. 2007. (Illus.). 544p. (YA). (gr. 8-12). lib. bdg. 20.85 *(978-1-4177-8130-0(0))* Turtleback.

Ornstein, Mike. Kindergarrrten Bus. Barry, Kevin M., illus. 2018. (ENG.). 32p. (J). (gr. -1 — 1). 16.99 *(978-1-58536-398-8(7))*, 204578) Sleeping Bear Pr.

Orsi, Tea. Tinker Bell & the Pirate Fairy. 2015. (Disney Fairies Graphic Novels Ser.: 16). (J). lib. bdg. 18.40 *(978-0-606-37294-7(6))* Turtleback.

Osborne, Mary Pope. Piratas Despues Del Mediodia. 2004. (Casa del Arbol Ser.: 4). (SPA.). (J). pap. 6.99 *(978-1-930332-52-2(1))* Lectorum Pubns., Inc.

Osteen, Victoria. Unexpected Treasures. Palmisciano, Diane, illus. 2009. (ENG.). 32p. (J). (gr. -1-3). 19.99 *(978-1-4169-5550-4(X))*, Little Simon Inspirations) Little Simon Inspirations.

Owen, Chris. Hairy Mole the Pirate 1. 2007. (Hairy Mole the Pirate Ser.). (ENG., Illus.). 82p. pap. *(978-1-84167-562-6(8))* Ransom Publishing Ltd.

Owen, Christopher. Hairy Mole's Adventures on the High Seas. Mostyn, David, illus. 2007. (Hairy Mole the Pirate Ser.). (ENG.). 80p. (J). per. *(978-1-84167-563-3(6))* Ransom Publishing Ltd.

Owens, Greg. Rupert the Wrong-Word Pirate. Beaky, Suzanne, illus. 2006. (J). *(978-1-58987-143-4(X))* Kindermusik International.

Oxley, Jennifer & Aronson, Billy. Peg + Cat: the Pirate Problem: a Level 2 Reader. 2017. (Peg + Cat Ser.). (ENG.). 48p. (J). (gr. k-3). 14.99 *(978-0-7636-9786-0(9))*, Candlewick Entertainment) Candlewick Pr.

P. I. Kids. Little Flashlight Box Jake & Nev- O/P. 2013. (ENG.). 8p. (J). (gr. k-4). pap. 10.99 *(978-1-4508-6836-5(3))*, 2baa77ff-d973-4d57-acdb-676cb1d56b2d) Phoenix International Publications, Inc.

Parker, Emma. The Lucky Pearl. 2010. (Illus.). 20p. pap. *(978-1-877561-18-4(5))* First Edition Ltd.

—One Leg Ned. 2010. (Illus.). pap. *(978-1-877561-12-2(6))* First Edition Ltd.

Parsley, Elise. If You Ever Want to Bring a Pirate to Meet Santa, Don't! 2018. (Magnolia Says DON'T! Ser.: 4). (ENG., Illus.). 40p. (J). (gr. -1-3). 17.99 *(978-0-316-46677-6(8))* Little, Brown Bks. for Young Readers.

Parus, M. V. The Adventures of Mamma Simone, Jodie & Zed: The Mystery of the Pirate's Lost Treasure. 2006. 115p. (YA). per. 12.95 *(978-1-58374-148-1(8))* Chicago Spectrum Pr.

Patterson, Rebecca. The Pirate House. 2013. (Illus.). (J). *(978-1-4351-4762-1(6))* Barnes & Noble, Inc.

Pearson, Maggie. The Pop Star Pirates. 2015. (Race Further with Reading Ser.). (ENG., Illus.). 48p. (J). (gr. 3-3). *(978-0-7787-2089-8(6))* Crabtree Publishing Co.

Pearson, Ridley. Peter & the Starcatchers-Peter & the Starcatchers, Book One. rev. ed. 2006. (Peter & the Starcatchers Ser.: 1). (ENG., Illus.). 480p. (J). (gr. 5-9). reprint ed. pap. 9.99 *(978-0-7868-4907-9(X),* Disney-Hyperion) Disney Publishing Worldwide.

Peck, Jan. Pirate Treasure Hunt!, 1 vol. Tans, Adrian, illus. 2008. (ENG.). 32p. (J). (gr. k-3). 16.99 *(978-1-58980-549-1(6),* Pelican Publishing) Arcadia Publishing.

Penn, Audrey. Blackbeard & the Gift of Silence. 2009. (ENG.). 350p. (J). (gr. 2-7). pap. 8.95 *(978-1-933718-32-3(3))* Tanglewood Pr.

—Blackbeard & the Sandstone Pillar: When Lightning Strikes. 2009. (ENG.). 350p. (J). (gr. 2-7). pap. 8.95 *(978-1-933718-31-6(5))* Tanglewood Pr.

Perkins, T. J. Wound Too Tight. 2006. (Illus.). 141p. (YA). 10.99 *(978-0-9777538-5-7(9))* GumShoe Press.

Perry, Fred. Gold Digger, Vol. 8. 2006. (ENG., Illus.). 200p. (YA). pap. 9.99 *(978-0-9768043-0-7(1),* 210010ca-d4ba-42be-a3d4-a0f61a74c84a) Antarctic Pr., Inc.

Peschke, Marci. Pirate Queen, 1 vol. Mourning, Tuesday, illus. 2013. (Kylie Jean Ser.). (ENG.). 112p. (J). (gr. 1-3). lib. bdg. 22.65 *(978-1-4048-7581-4(6),* 119873, Picture Window Bks.) Capstone.

Phillips, Dee. Pirate, 1 vol., Bk. 11. 2014. (Yesterday's Voices Ser.). (ENG.). 48p. (YA). (gr. 5-12). pap. 10.75 *(978-1-62250-913-3(7))* Saddleback Educational Publishing, Inc.

—Pirate: The Story of a Buccaneer. 2015. (Yesterday's Voices Ser.). (YA). lib. bdg. 19.60 *(978-0-606-36673-1(3))* Turtleback.

Platt, Richard. Pirate Diary: The Journal of Jake Carpenter. Riddell, Chris, illus. 2014. (ENG.). 128p. (J). (gr. 4-7). pap. 6.99 *(978-0-7636-7361-1(7))* Candlewick Pr.

Posner-Sanchez, Andrea. The Pirate Games (Disney Junior: Jake & the Neverland Pirates) RH Disney, illus. 2012. (Little Golden Book Ser.). (ENG.). 24p. (J). (-k). 4.99 *(978-0-7364-3028-9(8),* Golden/Disney) Random Hse. Children's Bks.

Powell, Huw. The Pirate King. 2017. (Spacejackers Ser.). (ENG.). 320p. (J). 16.99 *(978-1-68119-074-7(5),* 900163758, Bloomsbury USA Childrens) Bloomsbury Publishing USA.

Preller, James. A Pirate's Guide to First Grade. 2013. (J). lib. bdg. 18.40 *(978-0-606-31896-9(8))* Turtleback.

Pryor, Bonnie. Captain Hannah Pritchard: The Hunt for Pirate Gold, 1 vol. 2012. (Historical Fiction Adventures Ser.). (ENG., Illus.). 160p. (J). (gr. 3-5). pap. 13.88 *(978-1-59845-283-9(5),* 249245aa-07ef-41ea-a6ac-68d5be3db404); lib. bdg. 31.93 *(978-0-7660-3817-2(3),* d1bf7ad2-c916-402c-ba83-61c0f084aac6) Enslow Publishing, LLC.

—Hannah Pritchard: Pirate of the Revolution, 1 vol. 2008. (Historical Fiction Adventures Ser.). (ENG., Illus.). 160p. (J). (gr. 3-5). lib. bdg. 31.93 *(978-0-7660-2851-7(8),* 26121413-8628-47dc-9a2d-81661c6d5db1) Enslow Publishing, LLC.

—Pirate Hannah Pritchard: Captured!, 1 vol. 2010. (Historical Fiction Adventures Ser.). (ENG., Illus.). 160p. (J). (gr. 3-5). lib. bdg. 31.93 *(978-0-7660-3310-8(4),* 03ee45a8-be09-4257-aaca-0cd2071fb5cf) Enslow Publishing, LLC.

Publications International Ltd. Staff. Interactive Sound Pirates of the Caribbean 3. 2007. 24p. (J). 16.98 *(978-1-4127-8111-4(6))* Publications International, Ltd.

Publications International Ltd. Staff, ed. Look & Find Pirates of the Caribbean 3. 2007. 24p. (J). 7.10 *(978-1-4127-8019-3(5))* Publications International, Ltd.

—Pirate. 2008. (J). bds. 9.98 *(978-1-4127-9357-5(2))* Publications International, Ltd.

Punter, R. Pirate Adventures. 2009. (Kid Kits Ser.). 48p. (J). 16.99 *(978-1-60130-154-3(5))*; 16.99 *(978-1-60130-155-0(3))* EDC Publishing. (Usborne).

—Stories of Pirates. 2004. (Young Reading Ser.: Vol. 1). 48p. (J). (gr. 2-18). pap. 5.99 *(978-0-7945-0583-7(X))* EDC Publishing.

Punter, Russell. Percy & the Pirates. 2007. 48p. (J). 8.99 *(978-0-7945-1545-4(2),* Usborne) EDC Publishing.

—Pirate Adventures. Fox, Christyan, illus. 2007. (Usborne Young Reading: Series One Ser.). 48p. (J). (gr. 2). 13.99 *(978-1-58086-985-0(8))*; (gr. 4-7). pap. 5.99 *(978-0-7945-1447-1(2))* EDC Publishing. (Usborne).

—Pirate Stories for Little Children. 2015. (Stories for Little Children Gift Bks.). (ENG.). 176p. (J). 19.99 *(978-0-7945-2260-5(2),* Usborne) EDC Publishing.

Purtle, Louise. Potato Pie Pirate. Guiza, Victor, illus. 2009. 24p. (J). 15.99 *(978-0-9818145-0-6(6))* Biggaloo Bks.

Pyle, Howard. The Ruby of Kishmoor. 2004. reprint ed. pap. 1.99 *(978-1-4192-8126-6(7))*; pap. 15.95 *(978-1-4191-8126-9(2))* Kessinger Publishing, LLC.

—The Story of Jack Ballister's Fortunes: Being the Narrative of the Adventures of a Young Gentleman of Good Family, Who Was Kidnapped in the Year 1719 & Carried to the Plantations of the Continent of Virginia, Where He Fell in with That Famous Pirate Captain Edward Teach, or Blackbeard: of His Escape from the Pirates & the Rescue of a Young Lady from Out Their Hands. unabr. ed. 2012. (Illus.). 436p. 49.99 *(978-1-4622-8858-8(8))* Repressed Publishing LLC.

Pyle, Howard, illus. The Book of Pirates. 2020. (ENG.). 336p. (J). (gr. 3). pap. 39.95 *(978-0-486-84096-3(4),* 840964) Dover Pubns., Inc.

Quillen, Carl. Dragon Girl Myra. 2009. 53p. pap. 5.56 *(978-0-557-08268-1(4))* Lulu Pr., Inc.

Raine, Bonnie. Islands. MacMenamin, John, illus. 2003. 48p. (J). per. *(978-1-931456-74-6(7))* Athena Pr.

Ramos, Maria Cristina. Ruedamares Pirata de la Mar Bravia. (Torre de Papel Ser.). (SPA.). (J). (gr. 4-18). 8.95 *(978-958-04-3814-4(5))* Norma S.A. COL. Dist: Distribuidora Norma, Inc.

Reasoner, Charles. Inside Jolly Rodger's Pirate Ship. 2014. (Illus.). (J). *(978-1-4351-5466-7(5))* Barnes & Noble, Inc.

—Inside Jolly Roger's Pirate Ship. Reasoner, Charles, illus. 2007. (Story Book Ser.). (Illus.). 12p. (J). (gr. k). bds. *(978-1-84666-149-5(8),* Tide Mill Pr.) Top That! Publishing PLC.

Reeder, Marty. How to Become a Pirate Hunter. 2017. (ENG.). 200p. (YA). pap. 14.99 *(978-1-4621-1980-6(8),* Sweetwater Bks.) Cedar Fort, Inc./CFI Distribution.

Rees, Celia. Pirates! 2003. (Illus.). 368p. *(978-0-7475-5950-4(3))* Bloomsbury Publishing Plc GBR. Dist: Trafalgar Square Publishing.

Rees, Douglas. Uncle Pirate. Auth, Tony, illus. (ENG.). 112p. (J). (gr. 2-5). 2009. pap. 6.99 *(978-1-4169-4763-9(9))* 2008. 15.99 *(978-1-4169-4762-2(0))* McElderry, Margaret K. Bks. (McElderry, Margaret K. Bks.).

—Uncle Pirate to the Rescue. Auth, Tony, illus. 2010. (ENG.). 112p. (J). (gr. 2-5). pap. 6.99 *(978-1-4169-7505-2(5),* McElderry, Margaret K. Bks.) McElderry, Margaret K. Bks.

Rees, Lesley. How to Be a Pirate in 7 Days or Less. Lewis, Jan, illus. 2006. (How to be A Ser.). 32p. (J). (gr. k-3). 12.95 *(978-0-7534-6041-2(6),* Kingfisher) Roaring Brook Pr.

Regan, Dian Curtis. Space Boy & the Space Pirate. Neubecker, Robert, illus. 2016. (Space Boy Ser.). (ENG.). 40p. (J). (gr. -1-2). 16.95 *(978-1-59078-956-8(3),* Astra Young Readers) Astra Publishing Hse.

Remphry, Martin. Pirates Are Stealing Our Cows. Remphry, Martin, illus. 2014. (Race Ahead with Reading Ser.). (ENG., Illus.). 32p. (J). (gr. 2-2). *(978-0-7787-1330-2(X))* Crabtree Publishing Co.

RH Disney. Beware the Kakamora! (Disney Moana) RH Disney, illus. 2016. (Pictureback(R) Ser.). (ENG., Illus.). 24p. (J). (gr. -1-2). 4.99 *(978-0-7364-3601-4(4),* RH/Disney) Random Hse. Children's Bks.

—Peter Pan Step into Reading (Disney Peter Pan) RH Disney, illus. 2013. (Step into Reading Ser.). (ENG., Illus.). 32p. (J). (gr. -1-1). 5.99 *(978-0-7364-3114-9(4),* RH/Disney) Random Hse. Children's Bks.

Riddell, Andrew G. The Curse of Blackbeard's Ghost. 2010. 122p. (gr. 4-6). pap. 10.95 *(978-1-4502-6952-0(4))* iUniverse, Inc.

Rits, Susan Katherine. The Pirates of Bair Island. 2013. 234p. pap. 12.99 *(978-0-9894891-1-9(6))* Imprint.li.

Roberts, Scott A. The Rollicking Adventures of Tam O'Hare. 2007. (Illus.). 228p. (J). (gr. 4-7). per. 16.95 *(978-1-60037-289-6(9))* Morgan James Publishing.

Robinson, Michelle. Goodnight Pirate: The Perfect Bedtime Book! East, Nick, illus. 2015. (Goodnight Ser.). (ENG.). 32p. (J). (gr. -1 — 1). pap. 7.99 *(978-1-4380-0662-8(4))* Sourcebooks, Inc.

Rockwell, Carey. On the Trail of Space Pirates. Ley, Willy, ed. 2007. 140p. per. 11.95 *(978-1-60312-283-2(4))* Aegypan.

Roddy, Lee. Peril at Pirate's Point. 2006. (Ladd Family Adventure Ser.: Vol. 7). (Illus.). 153p. (J). (gr. 4-7). per. 7.99 *(978-0-88062-256-1(3))* Mott Media.

Roger, Moore & Ron, Kurtz. Arfie Plays Pirates. 2007. 40p. 17.95 *(978-0-9710343-5-8(4))* Photographs Naturally, Inc.

Rolt-Wheeler, Francis. Plotting in Pirate Seas. 2017. (ENG., Illus.). (J). 23.95 *(978-1-374-91224-3(7))* Capital Communications, Inc.

—Plotting in Pirate Seas. 2018. (ENG., Illus.). 142p. (J). 14.99 *(978-1-5154-2242-6(9))* Wilder Pubns., Corp.

Romeu, Emma. Gregorio y el Pirata. 2003.Tr. of Gregorio & the Pirate. (SPA., Illus.). 152p. (J). pap. 9.95 *(978-968-19-0553-8(9))* Santillana USA Publishing Co., Inc.

Root, Phyllis. Lilly & the Pirates. Shepperson, Rob, illus. 2013. (ENG.). 180p. (J). (gr. 3-7). pap. 8.95 *(978-1-62091-027-6(6),* Astra Young Readers) Astra Publishing Hse.

Rossell, Judith. Jack Jones & the Pirate Curse. 2006. 166p. *(978-1-921049-29-3(4))* Little Hare Bks. AUS. Dist: HarperCollins Pubs. Australia.

Rotstein, Adira. Little Jane & the Nameless Isle: A Little Jane Silver Adventure (Large Print 16pt) 2013. 324p. pap. *(978-1-4596-6322-0(5))* ReadHowYouWant.com, Ltd.

—Little Jane Silver: A Little Jane Silver Adventure. 2011. (Little Jane Silver Adventure Ser.: 1). (ENG., Illus.). 288p. (YA). (gr. 7). pap. 12.99 *(978-1-55488-878-8(6))* Dundurn Pr. CAN. Dist: Publishers Group West (PGW).

Rowland, Lucy. Pirate Pete & His Smelly Feet. Chambers, Mark, illus. 2017. (ENG.). 32p. (J). (gr. -1-1). 17.99 *(978-1-5098-1776-4(X),* Macmillan Children's Bks.) Pan Macmillan GBR. Dist: Independent Pubs. Group.

Roy, Oscar. I Was Captured by Pirates. 2013. 110p. pap. 11.00 *(978-1-62212-790-0(0),* Strategic Bk. Publishing) Strategic Book Publishing & Rights Agency (SBPRA).

Roy, Philip. Seas of South Africa. 2013. (ENG.). 250p. pap. 11.95 *(978-1-55380-247-1(0))* Ronsdale Pr. CAN. Dist: SPD-Small Pr. Distribution.

Ryan, Carrie & Davis, John Parke. City of Thirst. (Map to Everywhere Ser.: 2). (ENG., Illus.). (J). (gr. 3-7). 2016. 416p. pap. 19.99 *(978-0-316-24082-6(6))* 2015. 400p. 17.00 *(978-0-316-24084-0(2))* Little, Brown Bks. for Young Readers.

—Iron Tide Rising. 2018. (Map to Everywhere Ser.: 4). (ENG., Illus.). 352p. (J). (gr. 3-7). 17.99 *(978-0-316-24093-2(1))* Little, Brown Bks. for Young Readers.

—Shadows of the Lost Sun. 2017. (Map to Everywhere Ser.: 3). (ENG., Illus.). 368p. (J). (gr. 3-7). 35.99 *(978-0-316-24088-8(5))* Little, Brown Bks. for Young Readers.

Ryan, John. Captain Pugwash: A Pirate Story. (Illus.). 32p. (J). pap. 8.95 *(978-0-09-940874-1(0),* Arrow Bks., Ltd.) Penguin Random Hse. GBR. Dist: Trafalgar Square Publishing.

Sabatini, Rafael. The King's Messenger. 2004. reprint ed. pap. 1.99 *(978-1-4192-6824-3(4))* Kessinger Publishing, LLC.

Sabuda, Robert, illus. Peter Pan: Peter Pan. 2008. (ENG.). 16p. (J). 39.99 *(978-0-689-85364-7(5),* Little Simon) Little Simon.

Sagar, Marie. Pirate Hill. 2008. 17p. pap. 24.95 *(978-1-60610-705-8(4))* America Star Bks.

Sage, Angie. Skeleton Island. 2016. (Araminta Spookie Adventure Ser.: 2). (ENG., Illus.). 176p. (J). 16.99 *(978-1-61963-945-4(9),* 9781619639454, Bloomsbury USA Childrens) Bloomsbury Publishing USA.

Sams, Laura & Sams, Robert. A Pirate's Quest: For His Family Heirloom Peg Leg. Hertling, Heiner, illus. 2008. 48p. (J). 19.95 *(978-0-9770108-7-5(2))* Sams, II, Carl R. Photography, Inc.

Samuel, R. Skull & Bones: A Pirate's Odyssey. 2011. 192p. (gr. 1-2). 27.99 *(978-1-4634-0319-5(4))*; (gr. 10-12). pap. 18.49 *(978-1-4634-0320-1(8))* AuthorHouse.

Sander, Sonia. Scooby-Doo in Shiver Me Timbers, 1 vol. 2015. (Scooby-Doo! Ser.). (ENG., Illus.). 32p. (J). (gr. k-4). lib. bdg. 31.36 *(978-1-61479-408-0(1),* 19447, Picture Bk.) Spotlight.

Sava, Scott Christian. Gary the Pirate. 2008. (Illus.). 112p. 12.95 *(978-0-9789168-5-5(9))* Blue Dream Studios.

Savitsky, Steve, illus. Dora's Pirate Treasure Hunt. 2010. (Dora the Explorer Ser.). (ENG.). 12p. (J). (gr. -1-1). 6.99 *(978-1-4169-9927-0(2),* Simon Spotlight/Nickelodeon) Simon Spotlight/Nickelodeon.

Schaap, Annet. Of Salt & Shore. Watkinson, Laura, tr. from DUT. 2020. (ENG., Illus.). 352p. (J). (gr. 5). 16.99 *(978-1-62354-230-6(8))* Charlesbridge Publishing, Inc.

Schade, Susan. Riff Raff the Mouse Pirate. 2014. (I Can Read Level 2 Ser.). (ENG., Illus.). 24p. (J). (gr. -1-3). pap. 3.99 *(978-0-06-230507-7(7),* HarperCollins) HarperCollins Pubs.

Schaub, Michelle. The Lost Pirate. 2006. (Early Explorers Ser.). (J). pap. *(978-1-4108-6109-2(0))* Benchmark Education Co.

Schrowang, Irene. Sam & Joey's Pirate Ship Adventure. 2013. 16p. pap. 15.99 *(978-1-4817-0333-8(1))* AuthorHouse.

Schulz, Heidi. Hook's Revenge, Book 2: the Pirate Code. Hendrix, John, illus. 2016. (Hook's Revenge Ser.: 2). (ENG.). (J). (gr. 3-7). lib. bdg. 18.40 *(978-0-606-39169-6(X))* Turtleback.

Scieszka, Jon. El Pirata Barbanegra. Smith, Lane, illus. (SPA.). (J). (gr. 5-8). 7.95 *(978-958-04-3401-6(8),* NR8584) Norma S.A. COL. Dist: Lectorum Pubns., Inc., Distribuidora Norma, Inc.

Scollon, Bill. Beware the Kakamora! 2016. (Illus.). (J). *(978-1-5182-2416-4(4))* Random Hse., Inc.

Scollon, William. Jake & the Never Land Pirates: Pirate Campout. 2014. (World of Reading Ser.). (J). lib. bdg. 13.55 *(978-0-606-35266-6(X))* Turtleback.

Sconyers, Jennifer. The Map. 2010. 24p. pap. 12.99 *(978-1-4490-5731-2(4))* AuthorHouse.

Scott, Janine. The Noisy Parrot, 1 vol. Rigby, Deborah, illus. 2009. (Treasure Chest Readers Ser.). (ENG.). 24p. (J). (gr. 1-1). pap. 9.15 *(978-1-60754-680-1(9),* 2b2fd5e7-4c9c-454a-a346-2dda2788afe8); lib. bdg. 27.27 *(978-1-60754-679-5(5),* 8f7f1316-f8f0-4a48-be78-b1a3b98e3bb0) Rosen Publishing Group, Inc., The. (Windmill Bks.).

Seaworthy, Oscar. Port Side Pirates. 2008. (ENG., Illus.). 32p. (J). 9.99 *(978-1-84686-153-6(5))*; 6.99 *(978-1-84686-205-2(1))* Barefoot Bks., Inc.

—Port Side Pirates Puzzle. Harter, Debbie, illus. 2011. n/ap. (J). 14.99 *(978-1-84686-666-1(9))* Barefoot Bks., Inc.

Seuling, Barbara. Robert & the Happy Endings. Brewer, Paul, illus. 2007. (Robert Bks.). (ENG.). 160p. (J). (gr. 1-4). 16.95 *(978-0-8126-2748-0(2))* Cricket Bks.

Shadow, Jak. The Emerald Pirate. 2005. (F. E. A. R. Adventures S. Ser.). (ENG., Illus.). 110p. (J). 8.00 *(978-1-84046-690-4(1),* Wizard Books) Icon Bks., Ltd. GBR. Dist: Publishers Group Canada.

Sharp, Michael. Captain Tristan Am I. Van Tine, Laura, illus. 2009. 20p. (J). pap. *(978-1-897455-10-4(0))* Avatar Pubns., Inc.

Sheinkin, Steve. Abigail Adams, Pirate of the Caribbean. Swaab, Neil, illus. 2019. (Time Twisters Ser.). (ENG.). 176p. (J). pap. 6.99 *(978-1-250-20788-3(6),* 900201776) Roaring Brook Pr.

Shreve, Steve. Pirates: Or the Truth about Life on the High Seas. Shreve, Steve, illus. 2010. (Adventures of Charlie Ser.). (Illus.). 32p. pap. *(978-0-237-54286-3(2))* Evans Brothers, Ltd.

Shurtliff, Liesl. Time Castaways #1: the Mona Lisa Key. (Time Castaways Ser.: 1). (ENG.). (J). (gr. 3-7). 2019. 416p. pap. 6.99 *(978-0-06-256816-8(7))* 2018. 400p. 16.99 *(978-0-06-256813-7(2))* HarperCollins Pubs. (Tegen, Katherine Bks).

Simmons, Kristen. Pacifica. 2019. (ENG.). 384p. (YA). pap. 19.99 *(978-0-7653-3666-8(9),* 900121077, Tor Teen) Doherty, Tom Assocs., LLC.

Simon, Nadine. The Treasured Dream. 2009. 52p. pap. 9.95 *(978-1-60693-274-2(8),* Eloquent Bks.) Strategic Book Publishing & Rights Agency (SBPRA).

Simon Spotlight, creator. Dora & Diego's Adventures! 2007. (Dora the Explorer Ser.). (ENG., Illus.). 80p. (J). (gr. -1-2). 7.99 *(978-1-4169-3532-2(0),* Simon Spotlight/Nickelodeon) Simon Spotlight/Nickelodeon.

Simonson, Louise. Beauty & the Dreaded Sea Beast: A Graphic Novel. Frampton, Otis, illus. 2019. (Far Out Fairy Tales Ser.). (ENG.). 40p. (J). (gr. 3-6). pap. 5.95 *(978-1-4965-8442-7(2),* 140967); lib. bdg. 25.32 *(978-1-4965-8393-2(0),* 140684) Capstone. (Stone Arch Bks.).

Sís, Peter. Robinson. Sís, Peter, illus. 2017. (ENG.). 48p. (J). (gr. -1-3). 17.99 *(978-0-545-73166-9(6),* Scholastic Pr.) Scholastic, Inc.

Skrutskie, Emily. The Abyss Surrounds Us. 2016. (Abyss Ser.). (ENG., Illus.). 288p. (YA). (gr. 9-12). pap. 11.99 *(978-0-7387-4691-3(6),* 0738746916, Flux) North Star Editions.

—The Abyss Surrounds Us. 2016. lib. bdg. 23.30 *(978-0-606-38499-5(5))* Turtleback.

—The Edge of the Abyss. 2017. lib. bdg. 23.30 *(978-0-606-40232-3(2))* Turtleback.

Smith, Jeff & Robertson, Barny. Pirates of the 'I Don't Care'-Ibbean: A Kids' Musical about Storing up Treasures in Heaven. 2007. (ENG.). 104p. pap. 7.99 *(978-0-8341-7595-2(9),* 0834175959) Lillenas Publishing Co.

Sobel, June. Shiver Me Letters: A Pirate ABC. Cole, Henry, illus. (ENG.). 32p. (J). (gr. -1-3). 2009. pap. 8.99 *(978-0-15-206679-6(9),* 1199768) 2006. 17.99 *(978-0-15-216732-5(3),* 1201748) HarperCollins Pubs. (Clarion Bks.).

Soderberg, Erin. Puppy Pirates #1: Stowaway! 2015. (Puppy Pirates Ser.: 1). (Illus.). 96p. (J). (gr. 1-4). pap. 5.99 *(978-0-553-51167-3(X),* Random Hse. Bks. for Young Readers) Random Hse. Children's Bks.

—Puppy Pirates #2: X Marks the Spot. 2015. (Puppy Pirates Ser.: 2). (Illus.). 96p. (J). (gr. 1-4). 6.99 *(978-0-553-51170-3(X),* Random Hse. Bks. for Young Readers) Random Hse. Children's Bks.

—Puppy Pirates #4: Sea Sick. 2016. (Puppy Pirates Ser.: 4). (Illus.). 96p. (J). (gr. 1-4). 6.99 *(978-0-553-51176-5(9),* Random Hse. Bks. for Young Readers) Random Hse. Children's Bks.

—Puppy Pirates #5: Search for the Sea Monster. 2016. (Puppy Pirates Ser.: 5). (Illus.). 96p. (J). (gr. 1-4). 5.99 *(978-1-101-93776-1(9),* Random Hse. Bks. for Young Readers) Random Hse. Children's Bks.

—Puppy Pirates #6: Pug vs. Pug. 2017. (Puppy Pirates Ser.: 6). (Illus.). 96p. (J). (gr. 1-4). 5.99 *(978-1-5247-1410-9(0),* Random Hse. Bks. for Young Readers) Random Hse. Children's Bks.

—Puppy Pirates #7: Lost at Sea. 2019. (Puppy Pirates Ser.: 7). (Illus.). 96p. (J). (gr. 1-4). 5.99 *(978-0-525-57923-6(0),* Random Hse. Bks. for Young Readers) Random Hse. Children's Bks.

—Puppy Pirates Super Special #1: Ghost Ship. 2016. (Puppy Pirates Ser.: 1). (Illus.). 128p. (J). (gr. 1-4). 5.99 *(978-1-101-93773-0(4),* Random Hse. Bks. for Young Readers) Random Hse. Children's Bks.

—Puppy Pirates Super Special #2: Best in Class. 2017. (Puppy Pirates Ser.: 2). (Illus.). 128p. (J). (gr. 1-4). 5.99 *(978-1-5247-1328-7(7),* Random Hse. Bks. for Young Readers) Random Hse. Children's Bks.

—Puppy Pirates Super Special #3: Race to the North Pole. 2018. (Puppy Pirates Ser.: 3). (Illus.). 144p. (J). (gr. 1-4). 5.99 *(978-0-525-57920-5(6),* Random Hse. Bks. for Young Readers) Random Hse. Children's Bks.

Soderberg, Erin & Soderberg Downing, Erin. Puppy Pirates #6: Pug vs. Pug. 2017. (Puppy Pirates Ser.: 6). (ENG., Illus.). 96p. (J). (gr. 1-4). lib. bdg. 12.99 *(978-1-5247-1411-6(9),* Random Hse. Bks. for Young Readers) Random Hse. Children's Bks.

Somper, Justin. Dead Deep. 2009. pap. 1.00 *(978-1-4074-4559-5(6))* Recorded Bks., Inc.

—Demons of the Ocean. 2006. 1.00 *(978-1-4294-1974-1(1))* Recorded Bks., Inc.

—Demons of the Ocean. 2007. (Vampirates Ser.: 1). (Illus.). 330p. (J). 19.65 *(978-1-4177-8287-1(0))* Turtleback.

—Immortal War. 2013. (Vampirates Ser.: 6). (J). lib. bdg. 22.10 *(978-0-606-26696-3(8))* Turtleback.

—Vampirates: Demons of the Ocean. 2007. (Vampirates Ser.: 1). (ENG.). 352p. (J). (gr. 3-7). per. 18.99 *(978-0-316-01444-1(3))* Little, Brown Bks. for Young Readers.

—Vampirates: Black Heart. 2010. (Vampirates Ser.: 4). (ENG.). 512p. (J). (gr. 3-7). pap. 22.99 *(978-0-316-02088-6(5))* Little, Brown Bks. for Young Readers.

—Vampirates: Blood Captain. 2009. (Vampirates Ser.: 3). (ENG.). 592p. (J). (gr. 3-7). pap. 26.99 *(978-0-316-02086-2(9))* Little, Brown Bks. for Young Readers.

—Vampirates: Empire of Night. 2011. (Vampirates Ser.: 5). (ENG.). 512p. (J). (gr. 3-7). pap. 22.99 *(978-0-316-03323-7(5))* Little, Brown Bks. for Young Readers.

—Vampirates: Immortal War. 2013. (Vampirates Ser.: 6). (ENG.). 512p. (J). (gr. 3-7). pap. 23.99 *(978-0-316-03325-1(1))* Little, Brown Bks. for Young Readers.

—Vampirates: Tide of Terror. 2008. (Vampirates Ser.: 2). (ENG.). 480p. (J). (gr. 3-7). pap. 21.99 *(978-0-316-01445-8(1))* Little, Brown Bks. for Young Readers.

Southard, Patricia. Captain Andre's Adventure in the Sky. 2008. 27p. pap. 24.95 *(978-1-4241-8613-6(7))* America Star Bks.

Spangler, Brie, illus. We Both Read-The Mystery of Pirate's Point: Level 3. 2008. (We Both Read Ser.). 40p. (J). (gr. 1-5). per. 5.99 *(978-1-60115-010-3(5))* Treasure Bay, Inc.

Spendlove, Owen. Stanley Brambles & the Pirate's Treasure. 2007. 320p. per. 18.95 *(978-0-595-43792-4(3))* iUniverse, Inc.

Spires, Ashley. Small Saul. Spires, Ashley, illus. 2011. (ENG., Illus.). 32p. (J). (gr. -1-2). 16.95 *(978-1-55453-503-3(4))* Kids Can Pr., Ltd. CAN. Dist: Hachette Bk. Group.

Staley, Samuel. The Pirate of Panther Bay Classroom Guide. 2007. 75p. spiral bd. 15.00 *(978-0-9764684-2-4(5))* IZS, Inc.

Steele, Michael Anthony. Attack of the Zombie Mermaids: A 4D Book. Reeves, Pauline, illus. 2018. (Nearly Fearless Monkey Pirates Ser.). (ENG.). 48p. (J). (gr. k-2). lib. bdg. 23.99 *(978-1-5158-2677-4(5),* 137832, Picture Window Bks.) Capstone.

—Battle of the Pirate Bands: A 4D Book. Reeves, Pauline, illus. 2018. (Nearly Fearless Monkey Pirates Ser.). (ENG.). 48p. (J). (gr. k-2). pap. 7.95 *(978-1-5158-2687-3(2),* 137838); lib. bdg. 23.99 *(978-1-5158-2679-8(1),* 137834) Capstone. (Picture Window Bks.).

—Escape from Haunted Treasure Island: A 4D Book. Reeves, Pauline, illus. 2018. (Nearly Fearless Monkey Pirates Ser.). (ENG.). 48p. (J). (gr. k-2). lib. bdg. 23.99 *(978-1-5158-2678-1(3),* 137833, Picture Window Bks.) Capstone.

—Nearly Fearless Monkey Pirates. Reeves, Pauline, illus. 2018. (Nearly Fearless Monkey Pirates Ser.). (ENG.). 48p. (J). (gr. k-2). 95.96 *(978-1-5158-2697-2(X),* 27999, Picture Window Bks.) Capstone.

—Skeleton Crew Showdown. Jeralds, Scott, illus. 2017. (Scooby-Doo! Beginner Mysteries Ser.). (ENG.). 112p. (J). (gr. 1-3). lib. bdg. 22.65 *(978-1-4965-4769-9(1),* 135306, Stone Arch Bks.) Capstone.

Steele, Michael Anthony & Oda, Eiichiro. Shonen Jump's One Piece. 2007. 88p. (J). *(978-0-439-89720-4(3))* Scholastic, Inc.

Steinkraus, Kyla. Under the Sea. Brown, Alan, illus. 2016. (Paisley Atoms Ser.). (ENG.). 64p. (gr. 2-5). 28.50 *(978-1-68191-713-9(0),* 9781681917139) Rourke Educational Media.

Stevenson, R. L. Treasure Island. 2014. (ENG.). 186p. (J). (gr. 4-7). pap. 12.99 *(978-93-80005-46-1(6))* Maple Pr.

—Treasure Island N/R. abr. ed. 2018. (Palazzo Abridged Classics Ser.). (ENG., Illus.). 64p. (J). (gr. k-2). 16.99 *(978-1-78675-047-1(3))* Palazzo Editions, Ltd. GBR. Dist: Independent Pubs. Group.

Stevenson, Robert. Treasure Island. 2018. (ENG., Illus.). 210p. (J). (gr. 2-3). pap. 6.44 (978-1-61382-515-0(3)); (gr. 5). 12.99 (978-1-61382-514-3(5)) Simon & Brown.

Stevenson, Robert Louis. La Isla del Tesoro. (Coleccion Clasicos de la Juventud).Tr. of Treasure Island. (SPA., Illus.). 188p. (J). 12.95 (978-84-7189-017-7(8), ORT301) Ortells, Alfredo Editorial S.L. ESP. Dist: Continental Bk. Co., Inc.

—La Isla del Tesoro. (Coleccion Estrella).Tr. of Treasure Island. (SPA., Illus.). 64p. (J). 14.95 (978-950-11-0009-9(X), SGM009) Sigmar ARG. Dist: Continental Bk. Co., Inc.

—Secuestrado. 3rd ed. (Coleccion Clasicos en Accion).Tr. of Kidnapped. (SPA., Illus.). 80p. (YA). (gr. 5-8). 15.95 (978-84-241-5781-4(8), EV1487) Everest Editora ESP. Dist: Lectorum Pubns., Inc.

—Treasure Island, 1 vol. 2009. (Foundation Classics Ser.). (ENG., Illus.). 56p. (J). (gr. 5-5). lib. bdg. 32.60 (978-1-60754-543-9(8), 6b653e76-88e4-4e0d-8b9e-9c203184819d, Windmill Bks.) Rosen Publishing Group, Inc., The.

—Treasure Island. 2014. (Graphic Classics Ser.). (Illus.). 48p. (gr. 3-6). 37.10 (978-1-908973-91-7(9)) Book Hse. GBR. Dist: Black Rabbit Bks.

—Treasure Island. 2020. (ENG.). 184p. (J). (gr. 3-7). 19.95 (978-1-64799-711-3(9)) Bibliotech Pr.

—Treasure Island. (ENG.). (J). 2019. 182p. (gr. 5). pap. 22.96 (978-0-368-66429-8(5)) 2019. 182p. (gr. 5). pap. 18.80 (978-0-368-66427-4(9)) 2019. 236p. (gr. 5). 21.99 (978-0-368-45392-2(8)) 2019. 236p. (gr. 5). pap. 7.99 (978-0-368-45393-9(6)) 2019. (Illus.). 216p. (gr. 5). pap. 10.92 (978-1-388-01346-2(0)) 2017. (Illus.). pap. 9.99 (978-1-366-45332-7(8)) Blurb, Inc.

—Treasure Island. Lawrence, John, illus. 2009. (ENG.). 272p. (J). (gr. 4-7). 24.99 (978-0-7636-4445-1(5)) Candlewick Pr.

—Treasure Island. Blum, Alex A., illus. 2015. (Classics Illustrated Ser.: 21). 48p. pap. 9.95 (978-1-906814-47-2(3)) Classic Comic Store, Ltd. GBR. Dist: Casemate Pubs. & Bk. Distributors, LLC.

—Treasure Island. 2018. (ENG., Illus.). 100p. (J). (gr. 5). pap. 5.99 (978-1-9779-9826-2(7)) CreateSpace Independent Publishing Platform.

—Treasure Island. 2016. (ENG., Illus.). (J). pap. (978-3-7433-2049-9(5)) Creation Pubs.

—Treasure Island. (ENG.). (J). 2019. 310p. (gr. 5). 26.95 (978-0-353-94679-8(6), Wentworth Pr.) 2019. 318p. (gr. 5). 26.95 (978-0-469-32850-1(9), Wentworth Pr.) 2019. 318p. (gr. 5). 26.95 (978-0-469-75004-3(9), Wentworth Pr.) 2019. 318p. (gr. 5). pap. 16.95 (978-0-469-32849-5(5), Wentworth Pr.) 2019. 310p. (gr. 5). pap. 16.95 (978-0-353-94678-1(8), Wentworth Pr.) 2019. 318p. (gr. 5). pap. 16.95 (978-0-469-75003-6(0), Wentworth Pr.) 2018. 322p. (gr. 3-7). 26.95 (978-0-342-05400-8(7)) 2018. 370p. (gr. 5). 46.95 (978-0-343-84568-1(7)) 2018. 322p. (gr. 5). 44.95 (978-0-344-01421-5(5)) 2018. 298p. (gr. 5). 42.95 (978-0-344-31748-4(X)) 2018. 370p. (gr. 5). pap. 29.95 (978-0-343-84567-4(9)) 2018. 298p. (gr. 5). pap. 26.95 (978-0-344-31747-7(1)) 2018. 322p. (gr. 5). pap. 27.95 (978-0-344-01420-8(7)) 2018. (Illus.). 298p. (gr. 5). 25.95 (978-0-342-34871-8(X)) 2018. (Illus.). 370p. (gr. 5). 27.95 (978-0-341-88849-9(4)) 2018. (Illus.). 322p. (gr. 5). pap. 16.95 (978-0-342-05399-5(X)) 2018. (Illus.). 370p. (gr. 5). pap. 17.95 (978-0-341-88848-2(6)) 2017. (Illus.). pap. 15.95 (978-1-375-75765-2(2)) 2017. (Illus.). pap. 16.95 (978-1-375-59662-6(4)) 2017. (Illus.). pap. 17.95 (978-1-375-50488-1(6)) 2016. (Illus.). 26.95 (978-1-358-35578-3(9)) Creative Media Partners, LLC.

—Treasure Island. 2005. 116p. per. 5.95 (978-1-4209-2258-5(0)) Digireads.com Publishing.

—Treasure Island. (ENG.). (J). 2020. 184p. (gr. 3-7). pap. (978-1-77426-066-1(2)) 2018. 180p. (gr. 2-3). pap. (978-1-989201-18-3(0)) East India Publishing Co.

—Treasure Island. (ENG.). (J). 2019. 192p. (gr. 3-7). pap. 21.99 (978-1-7069-7099-6(4)) 2019. 376p. (gr. 3-7). pap. 14.99 (978-1-7023-4656-6(0)) 2019. 624p. (gr. 4-7). pap. 35.99 (978-1-6967-3078-5(3)) 2019. 212p. (gr. 4-7). pap. 16.99 (978-1-6963-6696-0(8)) 2019. 624p. (gr. 4-7). pap. 35.99 (978-1-6947-5622-0(X)) 2019. 216p. (gr. 4-7). pap. 14.10 (978-1-6929-7465-7(3)) 2019. 688p. (gr. 4-7). pap. 42.99 (978-1-6861-1129-7(0)) 2019. 350p. (gr. 4-7). pap. 19.99 (978-1-0898-7244-3(5)) 2019. 418p. (gr. 4-7). pap. 26.99 (978-1-0825-4210-7(5)) 2019. 350p. (gr. 4-7). pap. 19.99 (978-1-0830-0482-6(4)) 2019. 624p. (gr. 4-7). pap. 38.99 (978-1-0792-2768-0(7)) 2019. 376p. (gr. 4-7). pap. 19.99 (978-1-0794-8396-3(9)) 2019. 418p. (gr. 4-7). pap. 26.99 (978-1-0800-4196-1(6)) 2019. 390p. (gr. 4-7). pap. 22.99 (978-1-0807-2064-4(2)) 2019. 376p. (gr. 4-7). pap. 24.99 (978-1-0723-3269-5(8)) 2019. 420p. (gr. 4-7). pap. 24.99 (978-1-0711-1890-0(0)) 2019. 376p. (gr. 4-7). pap. 25.99 (978-1-0745-6431-5(6)) 2019. 376p. (gr. 4-7). pap. 24.99 (978-1-0705-2315-6(1)) 2019. 446p. (gr. 5). pap. 25.99 (978-1-0951-5195-2(9)) 2019. 624p. (gr. 5). pap. 35.99 (978-1-0968-5367-1(1)) 2019. 448p. (gr. 5). pap. 25.99 (978-1-0988-2953-7(0)) 2019. 260p. (gr. 5). pap. 13.99 (978-1-7968-9570-4(9)) 2018. (Illus.). 200p. (gr. 5). pap. 16.99 (978-1-7918-8128-3(9)) 2018. (Illus.). 464p. (gr. 5). pap. 29.90 (978-1-7915-8468-9(3)) 2018. (Illus.). 180p. (gr. 5). pap. 7.99 (978-1-7241-4680-9(7)) Independently Published.

—Treasure Island. 2020. (ENG.). 184p. (J). (gr. 3-7). 17.95 (978-1-64439-404-5(9)) IndoEuropeanPublishing.com.

—Treasure Island. 2004. reprint ed. pap. 1.99 (978-1-4192-9097-8(5)) Kessinger Publishing, LLC.

—Treasure Island. (Young Collector's Illustrated Classics Ser.). (Illus.). 192p. (J). (gr. 3-7). 9.95 (978-1-56156-456-9(7)) Kidsbooks, LLC.

—Treasure Island. Rhead, Louis, illus. 2015. (J). pap. (978-1-4677-7821-3(4), First Avenue Editions) Lerner Publishing Group.

—Treasure Island. 2017. (ENG., Illus.). (J). pap. 15.95 (978-1-387-04942-4(9)) Lulu Pr., Inc.

—Treasure Island. Gelev, Penko, illus. 2006. (Graphic Classics Ser.). (ENG.). 48p. (J). (gr. 5-8). 24.94 (978-0-7641-5976-3(3), B.E.S. Publishing) Peterson's.

—Treasure Island. 2014. (Word Cloud Classics Ser.). (ENG., Illus.). 208p. pap. 14.99 (978-1-62686-256-2(7), Canterbury Classics) Printers Row Publishing Group.

—Treasure Island. 2018. (Classics with Ruskin Ser.: Vol. 4). (ENG., Illus.). 274p. (J). (gr. 4-6). pap. (978-93-87693-88-3(0)) Speaking Tiger Publishing.

—Treasure Island. (ENG.). 2019. 224p. (YA). (gr. 7-12). (978-93-89440-47-8(5)) 2017. 238p. (J). (gr. 5). pap. (978-81-935458-8-1(5)) Sumaiyah Distributors Pvt Ltd.

—Treasure Island. 2018. (ENG., Illus.). 170p. (J). 19.99 (978-1-5154-2231-0(3)) Wilder Pubns., Corp.

—Treasure Island: With a Discussion of Courage. 2003. (Values in Action Illustrated Classics Ser.). (J). (978-1-59203-054-5(8)) Learning Challenge, Inc.

—Treasure Island: With Story of the Treasure of Normon Island. Date not set. (J). (gr. 5-6). reprint ed. lib. bdg. 22.95 (978-0-89190-236-2(8), American Reprint Co.) Amereon Ltd.

Stevenson, Robert Louis & Gaston, Charles Robert. Treasure Island. 2016. (ENG., Illus.). (J). 25.95 (978-1-358-93415-5(0)) Creative Media Partners, LLC.

Stevenson, Robert Louis & Vance, Hiram Albert. Treasure Island. 2016. (ENG., Illus.). (J). 25.95 (978-1-359-06744-9(2)); 25.95 (978-1-358-73513-4(1)) Creative Media Partners, LLC.

Stevenson, Robert Louis, et al. Treasure Island. 2016. (ENG., Illus.). (J). 26.95 (978-1-357-83050-2(5)) Creative Media Partners, LLC.

Stewart, Paul & Riddell, Chris. Edge Chronicles: the Curse of the Gloamglozer. 2009. (Edge Chronicles Ser.: 4). (ENG.). 384p. (J). (gr. 3-7). 10.99 (978-0-440-42099-6(7), Yearling) Random Hse. Children's Bks.

—Far-Flung Adventures: Fergus Crane. 2011. (Far-Flung Adventures Ser.). (ENG.). 240p. (J). (gr. 3-7). 7.99 (978-0-385-75112-4(5), Yearling) Random Hse. Children's Bks.

Stilton, Geronimo. Attack of the Bandit Cats (Geronimo Stilton #8) 2004. (Geronimo Stilton Ser.: 8). (ENG., Illus.). 128p. (J). (gr. 2-5). pap. 7.99 (978-0-439-55970-6(7), Scholastic Paperbacks) Scholastic, Inc.

—Geronimo Stilton Graphic Novels #3: The Coliseum Con, Vol. 3. 2009. (Geronimo Stilton Graphic Novels Ser.: 3). (ENG., Illus.). 56p. (J). (gr. 2-6). 9.99 (978-1-59707-172-7(2), 900063026, Papercutz) Mad Cave Studios.

—Geronimo Stilton Graphic Novels #6: Who Stole the Mona Lisa?, Vol. 6. 2010. (Geronimo Stilton Graphic Novels Ser.: 6). (ENG., Illus.). 56p. (J). (gr. 2-6). 9.99 (978-1-59707-221-2(4), 900070133, Papercutz) Mad Cave Studios.

—The Golden Statue Plot (Geronimo Stilton #55) 2018. (True Book (Relaunch) Ser.: 55). (ENG.). 128p. (J). (gr. 3-5). E-Book 31.00 (978-0-545-55681-1(3), Scholastic Paperbacks) Scholastic, Inc.

Stine, R. L. Creep from the Deep. 2008. (Goosebumps HorrorLand Ser.: No. 2). 137p. (gr. 4-7). 17.00 (978-0-7569-8815-9(2)) Perfection Learning Corp.

Stockton, Frank Richard. Buccaneers & Pirates of Our Coasts. 2006. 168p. (gr. 4-7). per. 13.95 (978-1-59818-872-1(0)); 25.95 (978-1-59818-255-2(2)) Aegypan.

—Kate Bonnet: The Romance of a Pirate's Daughter. reprint ed. pap. 28.00 (978-1-4047-8937-1(5)) Classic Textbooks.

—Kate Bonnet: The Romance of a Pirate's Daughter. 2007. 364p. (J). (gr. -1-7). 46.95 (978-0-548-02295-5(X)) Kessinger Publishing, LLC.

—Kate Bonnet: The Romance of a Pirate's Daughter. 2005. 29.95 (978-1-59818-254-5(4)) Wildside Pr., LLC.

Stowell, Louie. Wind-Up Pirate Ship. Fox, Christyan, illus. 2010. (Wind-up Bks). 13p. (J). bds. 29.99 (978-0-7945-2835-5(X), Usborne) EDC Publishing.

Strangway, Melissa. Finding Hope. 2012. 82p. pap. 11.65 (978-1-61933-676-6(6)) FastPrncil, Inc.

Stratemeyer, Edward. The Rover Boys on Treasure Isle. 2007. 268p. 27.95 (978-1-4218-4148-9(7)); per. 12.95 (978-1-4218-4246-2(7)) 1st World Publishing, Inc. (1st World Library - Literary Society).

Strong, Jeremy. The Indoor Pirates on Treasure Island. Sharratt, Nick, illus. (ENG.). 96p. (J). 7.95 (978-0-14-038637-0(8)) Penguin Bks., Ltd. GBR. Dist: Trafalgar Square Publishing.

Suen, Anastasia. The Pirate Map: A Robot & Rico Story. Laughead, Michael, illus. 2010. (Robot & Rico Ser.). (ENG.). 32p. (J). (gr. 1-2). pap. 6.25 (978-1-4342-2301-2(9), 103170, Stone Arch Bks.) Capstone.

Surget, Alain. Escape from Veracruz. 2015. (Jolly Roger Ser.). (Illus.). 96p. (gr. 3-6). 28.50 (978-1-909645-44-8(3)) Book Hse. GBR. Dist: Black Rabbit Bks.

—The Ghost Ship. 2015. (Jolly Roger Ser.). (Illus.). 96p. (gr. 3-6). 28.50 (978-1-909645-41-7(9)) Book Hse. GBR. Dist: Black Rabbit Bks.

—Shark Island. 2015. (Jolly Roger Ser.). (Illus.). 96p. (gr. 3-6). 28.50 (978-1-909645-42-4(7)) Book Hse. GBR. Dist: Black Rabbit Bks.

Surget, Alain & Yeardley, Glynne. Caesar, Who's He? Parme, Fabrice, illus. 2014. 95p. (J). (978-1-4351-5328-8(6)) Barnes & Noble, Inc.

Taplin, Sam. Noisy Pirates. Chambers, Mark, illus. 2014. (ENG.). (J). 19.99 (978-0-7945-2814-0(7), Usborne) EDC Publishing.

—The Usborne Official Pirate's Handbook. McNee, Ian, illus. 2007. (Usborne Official Handbooks Ser.). 80p. (J). (gr. -1-3). 12.99 (978-0-7945-1463-1(4), Usborne) EDC Publishing.

Taylor, Richard A. Ships of Children. 2nd rev. ed. 2006. (Illus.). 191p. (YA). lib. bdg. 37.95 (978-0-9764403-7-6(7)) Klare Taylor Pubs.

Teacher Created Resources Staff & Collins, Susan. A Guide for Using Time Soldiers in the Classroom. 2009. (ENG.). 48p. pap. 9.99 (978-1-4206-2003-0(7)) Teacher Created Resources, Inc.

Terry, Michael. Captain Wag & the Big Blue Whale. Terry, Michael, illus. 2008. (Captain Wag Ser.). (Illus.). 32p. (J). (gr. k-k). pap. 13.95 (978-0-7475-9254-9(3)) Bloomsbury Publishing Plc GBR. Dist: Independent Pubs. Group.

Thomas Nelson Publishing Staff. The Pirates Who Don't Do Anything - Veggietales Movie: Squawk-Along Songs & Games. 2008. (Adventures in Odyssey Activity Pack Ser.). 48p. (J). pap. 12.99 (978-1-4003-1235-1(3)) Nelson, Thomas Inc.

—The Pirates Who Don't Do Anything: A VeggieTales Movie: Cheesecurl Cave Snacks & Science. 2008. 48p. (J). pap. 12.99 (978-1-4003-1233-7(7)) Nelson, Thomas Inc.

—The Pirates Who Don't Do Anything: A VeggieTales Movie: Clapping Rocks Crafts. 2008. 48p. (J). pap. 12.99 (978-1-4003-1230-6(2)) Nelson, Thomas Inc.

—The Pirates Who Don't Do Anything: A VeggieTales Movie: Discovery Bay. 2008. 64p. (J). pap. 12.99 (978-1-4003-1234-4(5)) Nelson, Thomas Inc.

—The Pirates Who Don't Do Anything: A VeggieTales Movie: Elementary Director's Guide. 2008. 128p. (J). pap. 17.99 (978-1-4003-1226-9(4)) Nelson, Thomas Inc.

—The Pirates Who Don't Do Anything: A VeggieTales Movie: Preschool Director's Guide. 2008. 64p. (J). pap. 12.99 (978-1-4003-1231-3(0)) Nelson, Thomas Inc.

—The Pirates Who Don't Do Anything: A VeggieTales Movie: Rock Monster Science Lab. 2008. 48p. (J). pap. 12.99 (978-1-4003-1228-3(0)) Nelson, Thomas Inc.

—The Pirates Who Don't Do Anything: A VeggieTales Movie: Rowboat Bible Stories. 2008. 64p. (J). pap. 17.99 (978-1-4003-1232-0(9)) Nelson, Thomas Inc.

—The Pirates Who Don't Do Anything: A VeggieTales Movie: Spyglass Bible Theater Guide. 2008. 64p. (J). pap. 12.99 (978-1-4003-1227-6(2)) Nelson, Thomas Inc.

—The Pirates Who Don't Do Anything: A VeggieTales Movie: Whipcrack Island Games. 2008. 64p. (J). pap. 12.99 (978-1-4003-1229-0(9)) Nelson, Thomas Inc.

—The Pirates Who Don't Do Anything: A VeggieTales Movie: Yo-Ho-Ho Opening & Closing Show. 2008. 64p. (J). pap. 5.99 (978-1-4003-1236-8(1)) Nelson, Thomas Inc.

Thomson, Sarah L. Pirates, Ho!, 0 vols. Gilpin, Stephen, illus. 2012. (ENG.). 32p. (J). (gr. -1-3). pap. 7.99 (978-0-7614-6247-7(3), 9780761462477, Two Lions) Amazon Publishing.

Time, Nicholas O. Wrong Place, (Really) Wrong Time. 2016. (In Due Time Ser.: 3). (ENG., Illus.). 160p. (J). (gr. 3-7). pap. 6.99 (978-1-4814-7233-3(X), Simon Spotlight) Simon Spotlight.

Timothy E. Dillinger. The Pick Pocket Pirate: An Original Pirate Tale. 2009. 126p. (gr. 2-2). 21.99 (978-1-4389-4042-7(4)); pap. 15.99 (978-1-4389-4043-4(2)) AuthorHouse.

ToyBox Innovations, creator. The Curse of the Black Pearl. 2006. (Pirates of the Caribbean Ser.). (ENG., Illus.). 24p. (J). (gr. -1-3). pap. (978-0-7634-2176-2(6)) Walt Disney Records.

—Dead Man's Chest. 2006. (Pirates of the Caribbean Ser.). (ENG., Illus.). 24p. (J). (gr. -1-3). pap. (978-0-7634-2177-9(4)) Walt Disney Records.

Toybox Innovations, creator. Pirates of the Caribbean: the Complete Collection: The Curse of the Black Pearl/Dead Man's Chest/at World's End. 2007. (Disney's Read along Collection). (ENG., Illus.). (J). (gr. -1-3). pap. (978-0-7634-2194-6(4)) Walt Disney Records.

Toybox Innovations & Toybox Innovations, creators. At Worlds End. 2007. (Pirates of the Caribbean Ser.). (ENG., Illus.). (J). (gr. -1-3). pap. (978-0-7634-2186-1(3)) Walt Disney Records.

Trine, Greg. Pinkbeard's Revenge. Dormer, Frank W., illus. 2015. (Adventures of Jo Schmo Ser.: 4). (ENG.). 128p. (J). (gr. 1-4). pap. 7.99 (978-0-544-45601-3(7), 1599386, Clarion Bks.) HarperCollins Pubs.

Troupe, Thomas Kingsley. A Stegosaurus Would Not Make a Good Pirate. Calvert, Steph, illus. 2018. (Dinosaur Daydreams Ser.). (ENG.). 24p. (J). (gr. -1-2). lib. bdg. 27.99 (978-1-5158-2129-8(3), 136733, Picture Window Bks.) Capstone.

Tucker, Kathy. Do Pirates Take Baths? 2015. (Illus.). 27p. (J). (978-1-4896-3861-8(X)) Weigl Pubs., Inc.

Turkle, Brinton, illus. & text. Obadiah the Bold. Turkle, Brinton, text. 2018. (J). pap. (978-1-893103-73-3(0)) Beautiful Feet Bks.

Turnage, Sheila. The Law of Finders Keepers. 2019. (Mo & Dale Mysteries Ser.). 368p. (J). (gr. 5). 8.99 (978-0-14-242617-3(2), Puffin Books) Penguin Young Readers Group.

Underwood, Deborah. Pirate Mom. Gilpin, Stephen, illus. 2006. (Step into Reading Ser.: Vol. 3). 48p. (J). (gr. k-3). per. 5.99 (978-0-375-83323-6(4), Random Hse. Bks. for Young Readers) Random Hse. Children's Bks.

Usher, Sam. Sun. Usher, Sam, illus. 2018. (Seasons Quartet Ser.). (ENG., Illus.). 40p. (J). (gr. -1-2). 16.99 (978-0-7636-9949-9(7), Templar) Candlewick Pr.

Valor, De. Pirate Adventures of Sea Worthy: Featuring: the Treasure of Captain Blue Beard & the Return of Captain Blue Beard. 2013. 150p. (gr. 2-2). 20.35 (978-1-4669-7483-8(4)); pap. 10.35 (978-1-4269-9551-4(2)) Trafford Publishing.

VeggieTales, contrib. by. The Pirates Who Don't Do Anything. 2007. (VeggieTales (EMI-CMG Audio) Ser.). (J). (gr. -1-3). 12.99 (978-5-557-52681-4(1)) Big Idea Productions.

Vern, Jules. The Secret of the Island. Kingston, W. H. G., tr. 2008. 160p. 24.95 (978-1-60664-753-0(9)) Rodgers, Alan Bks.

Vogel-Placides, Joan Katherine. The Safe Place. Placides, Del S., illus. 2013. 58p. 13.99 (978-0-9888718-3-0(1)) DOMINIONHOUSE Publishing & Design.

Walker, Richard. The Barefoot Book of Pirates. Whelan, Olwyn, illus. (Barefoot Bks.). 64p. (J). 2008. 19.99 (978-1-84686-237-3(X)) 2004. (ENG.). (gr. 3-6). pap. 16.99 (978-1-84148-131-9(9)) Barefoot Bks., Inc.

Warner, Penny. The Mystery of the Pirate's Treasure. 2013. (Code Busters Club Ser.). (ENG.). 192p. (J). (gr. 4-7). 16.99 (978-1-60684-457-1(1), Darby Creek) Lerner Publishing Group.

Waters, Erica-Jane. Petticoat Pirates: The Mermaids of Starfish Reef. 2013. (ENG., Illus.). 96p. (J). (gr. 2-4). 7.99 (978-1-907411-96-0(8)) Little, Brown Book Group Ltd. GBR. Dist: Hachette Bk. Group.

Watt, Fiona. That's Not My Pirate. Wells, Rachel, illus. 2007. (Touchy-Feely Board Bks). 10p. (J). (gr. -1-k). bds. 8.99 (978-0-7945-1702-1(1), Usborne) EDC Publishing.

Weaver, Jack W. Cat & Dog Breath Meet the Last Pirates: How to Fly a Basset Hound. 2012. 164p. 24.95 (978-1-4626-6652-2(3)) America Star Bks.

Weisman, Greg. Traveler (World of Warcraft: Traveler, Book 1) Didier, Samwise, illus. 2016. (World of Warcraft: Traveler Ser.: 1). (ENG.). 384p. (J). (gr. 3-7). 14.99 (978-0-545-90667-8(9)) Scholastic, Inc.

—World of Warcraft: Traveler. 2016. (Illus.). 336p. (J). pap. (978-1-338-13301-1(2)) Scholastic, Inc.

West, Tracey. Pirates vs. Ninja. 2013. (Ninjago Readers Ser.: 6). lib. bdg. 13.55 (978-0-606-32026-9(1)) Turtleback.

Weston, Greg. Ocean View Terrace & the Blue Pirate Eater. 2008. 232p. pap. 14.95 (978-1-4092-0278-3(X)) Lulu Pr., Inc.

White, Wade Albert. The Adventurer's Guide to Treasure (and How to Steal It) 2019. (Adventurer's Guide Ser.: 3). (ENG., Illus.). 448p. (J). (gr. 3-7). 17.99 (978-0-316-51844-4(1)) Little, Brown Bks. for Young Readers.

Whybrow, Ian. Little Wolf, Terror of the Shivery Sea. Ross, Tony, illus. 2004. (Little Wolf Adventures Ser.). (ENG.). 144p. (J). (gr. 3-6). 14.95 (978-1-57505-629-6(1)) Lerner Publishing Group.

—Tim, Ted & the Pirates. Ayto, Russell, illus. (ENG.). 32p. (J). 2014. 17.99 (978-0-00-755930-5(5), HarperCollins Children's Bks.) 2nd ed. 2008. pap. 9.95 (978-0-00-713124-2(0)) HarperCollins Pubs. Ltd. GBR. Dist: HarperCollins Pubs., Independent Pubs. Group.

Wigington, Patti. Pirate's Alphabet. Umscheid, Kit, illus. 2007. (ENG.). 32p. (J). (gr. -1-3). lib. bdg. 15.95 (978-0-9766805-8-1(0)) Keene Publishing.

Wilhelm, Doug. Curse of the Pirate Mist. Semionov, Vladimir, illus. 2011. (ENG.). 144p. (J). (gr. 4-8). pap. 7.99 (978-1-937133-02-3(8)) Chooseco LLC.

Williams, Rozanne Lanczak. Captain Jack's Journal. Grayson, Rick, illus. 2006. (Learn to Write Ser.). 16p. (J). (gr. k-2). pap. 2.99 (978-1-59198-303-3(7), 6197) Creative Teaching Pr., Inc.

—Captain Jack's Journal. Maio, Barbara, ed. Grayson, Rick, illus. 2006. (J). per. 8.99 (978-1-59198-361-3(4)) Creative Teaching Pr., Inc.

Winbolt-Lewis, Martin. The Soggy Saga of Samuel Sprat. Mason, Abi, illus. 2013. 24p. pap. (978-1-78222-152-4(2)) Paragon Publishing, Rothersthorpe.

Winfield, A. C. The Star Pirate. 2013. (Illus.). 184p. pap. (978-1-909202-11-5(8)) Little Acorns Publishing.

Wininger, Stephen T. The Adventure of Pirate Pete Moss. 2004. (J). pap. (978-1-59196-466-7(0)) Instant Pub.

Winstanley, Nicola. The Pirate's Bed. James, Matt, illus. 2015. 32p. (J). (gr. -1-2). 17.99 (978-1-77049-616-3(5), Tundra Bks.) Tundra Bks. CAN. Dist: Penguin Random Hse. LLC.

Winters, Kari-Lynn. Good Pirate. Griffiths, Dean, illus. 2016. (ENG.). 32p. (J). (gr. k-3). 17.95 (978-1-927485-80-4(0)) Pajama Pr. CAN. Dist: Publishers Group West (PGW).

Wolfe, Lena. The Princess Bride: a Counting Story. Robinson, Bill, illus. 2020. (ENG.). 20p. (J). (gr. -1 — 1). bds. 8.99 (978-0-316-49770-1(3)) Little, Brown Bks. for Young Readers.

Wolfram, Amy & Sanchez, Ricardo. Party, Party & Silicon Valley Cyborg. Corona, Jorge & Bates, Ben, illus. 2019. (DC Teen Titans Go! Ser.). (ENG.). 32p. (J). (gr. 2-6). lib. bdg. 21.93 (978-1-4965-7995-9(X), 139826, Stone Arch Bks.) Capstone.

Wood, Francis. The SnowPeople. Larsen, Dan, illus. 2003. 96p. (YA). per. 14.95 (978-0-9746372-0-4(3)) Tip-Of-The-Moon Publishing Co.

Wood, James Playsted. The Queen's Most Honorable Pirate. Fisher, Leonard Everett, illus. 2011. 192p. 42.95 (978-1-258-09722-6(2)) Literary Licensing, LLC.

Wood, Jane R. Adventures on Amelia Island: A Pirate, a Princess, & Buried Treasure. Blacker, Elizabeth A., illus. Wood, Jane R., photos by. 2007. (ENG.). 132p. (J). (gr. 3-8). pap. 8.99 (978-0-9792304-0-0(3)) Florida Kids Pr., Inc.

Wronski, Gareth. Holly Farb & the Princess of the Galaxy. (ENG.). 320p. (J). (gr. 3-7). 2018. pap. 7.99 (978-1-4814-7178-7(3)) 2017. (Illus.). 16.99 (978-1-4814-7177-0(5)) Simon & Schuster Children's Publishing. (Aladdin).

Yolen, Jane. The Ballad of the Pirate Queens. 2004. (J). (gr. k-3). spiral bd. (978-0-616-01821-7(5)) Canadian National Institute for the Blind/Institut National Canadien pour les Aveugles.

Young, Jessica. All Paws on Deck: a Branches Book (Haggis & Tank Unleashed #1) Burks, James, illus. 2016. (Haggis & Tank Unleashed Ser.: 1). (ENG.). 80p. (J). (gr. k-2). pap. 5.99 (978-0-545-81886-5(9)) Scholastic, Inc.

Zellerhoff, Christi. Princesses Can Be Pirates Too! Davis, Amy, illus. 2012. 38p. 17.99 (978-1-935961-68-0(3)); pap. 8.99 (978-1-935961-95-6(0)) Booktrope. (Booktrope Editions).

Ziegler-Sullivan, Ursula. Pirate Pups! Petrossi, Fabrizio, illus. 2016. (J). (978-1-4806-9717-1(6), Golden Bks.) Random Hse. Children's Bks.

Zullo, Allan. Kid Pirates: Their Battles, Shipwrecks, & Narrow Escapes. 2007. 147p. (J). pap. (978-0-439-91813-8(8)) Scholastic, Inc.

PITTSBURGH PIRATES (BASEBALL TEAM)

Frager, Ray. Pittsburgh Pirates, 1 vol. 2015. (Inside MLB Ser.). (ENG., Illus.). 48p. (J). (gr. 3-6). lib. bdg. 34.21 (978-1-62403-481-7(0), 17125, SportsZone) ABDO Publishing Co.

Goodman, Michael E. The Story of the Pittsburgh Pirates. 2007. (Baseball, the Great American Game Ser.). (Illus.). 48p. (YA). (gr. 4-7). lib. bdg. 32.80 (978-1-58341-498-9(3)) Creative Co., The.

LeBoutillier, Nate. The Story of the Pittsburgh Pirates. 2011. (Illus.). 48p. (J). 35.65 (978-1-60818-052-3(2), Creative Education) Creative Co., The.

Marsh, Carole. Roberto Clemente: Baseball Hero & Humanitarian: Baseball Hero & Humanitarian. 2003. 12p. (gr. k-4). 2.95 (978-0-635-02140-3(4)) Gallopade International.

Stewart, Mark. The Pittsburgh Pirates. 2012. (Team Spirit Ser.). 48p. (J). (gr. 3-6). lib. bdg. 29.27 (978-1-59953-493-0(2)) Norwood Hse. Pr.

Wesley, Caroline. Pittsburgh Pirates. 2018. (MLB's Greatest Teams Ser.). (ENG., Illus.). 32p. (J). (gr. 2-5). lib. bdg. 34.21 (978-1-5321-1813-5(9), 30672, Big Buddy Bks.) ABDO Publishing Co.

Winter, Jonah. Roberto Clemente: Pride of the Pittsburgh Pirates. ón, Raúl, illus. 2008. (ENG.). 40p. (J). (gr. -1-3). 8.99 (978-1-4169-5082-0(6), Atheneum Bks. for Young Readers) Simon & Schuster Children's Publishing.

—Roberto Clemente: Pride of the Pittsburgh Pirates. ón, Raúl, illus. 2005. (ENG.). 40p. (J). (gr. -1-3). 19.99 (978-0-689-85643-3(1)) Simon & Schuster, Inc.

PIUS V, SAINT, POPE, 1566-1572

Daughters of St. Paul Staff. No Place for Defeat. Date not set. (Encounter Ser.). 96p. (J). (gr. 3-9). pap. 2.00 (978-0-8198-5100-0(0)) Pauline Bks. & Media.

PIUS XII, POPE, 1876-1958

Marchione, Margherita. Pope Pius XII: Bilingual Coloring Book. Elliott, John, illus. 2004. (SPA & ENG.). 32p. 1.00 *(978-0-8091-6721-0(2),* 6721-2) Paulist Pr.

PIZARRO, FRANCISCO, APPROXIMATELY 1475-1541

Baicker, Karen. Conquistador: Francisco Pizarro Ravages the Inca Empire. 2011. (J). pap. *(978-0-545-32940-8(X))* Scholastic, Inc.

DiConsiglio, John. Francisco Pizarro: Destroyer of the Inca Empire. 2008. (Wicked History Ser.). (ENG., Illus.). 128p. (J). 31.00 *(978-0-531-18551-3(6),* Watts, Franklin) Scholastic Library Publishing.

Hoogenboom, Lynn. Francisco Pizarro. 2009. (Primary Source Library of Famous Explorers Ser.). 24p. (gr. 4-4). 42.50 *(978-1-60854-121-8(5),* PowerKids Pr.) Rosen Publishing Group, Inc., The.

—Francisco Pizarro: A Primary Source Biography, 1 vol. 2005. (Primary Source Library of Famous Explorers Ser.). (ENG., Illus.). 24p. (YA). (gr. 4-4). lib. bdg. 26.27 *(978-1-4042-3038-5(6),* 95430adb-f0c1-40d6-92c8-2deb73222514) Rosen Publishing Group, Inc., The.

Meltzer, Milton. Francisco Pizarro: The Conquest of Peru, 1 vol. 2006. (Great Explorations Ser.). (ENG.). 80p. (gr. 6-6). 36.93 *(978-0-7614-1607-4(2),* d34a59b9-c1ee-4d6b-92b8-645c03990423) Cavendish Square Publishing LLC.

O'Brien, Cynthia. Explore with Francisco Pizarro. 2015. (Travel with the Great Explorers Ser.). (ENG., Illus.). 32p. (J). (gr. 4-5). *(978-0-7787-1700-3(3))* Crabtree Publishing Co.

Ramen, Fred. Francisco Pizarro: The Exploration of Peru & the Conquest of the Inca. (Library of Explorers & Exploration Ser.). 112p. (gr. 5-8). 2009. 66.50 *(978-1-60853-603-0(3))* 2003. (ENG., Illus.). lib. bdg. 39.80 *(978-0-8239-3618-2(X),* 454f043b-0827-483f-87cc-4bcb424cb0fe) Rosen Publishing Group, Inc., The. (Rosen Reference).

Sonneborn, Liz. Pizarro: Conqueror of the Mighty Incas, 1 vol. 2009. (Great Explorers of the World Ser.). (ENG., Illus.). 112p. (gr. 6-7). 35.93 *(978-1-59845-128-3(6),* ce5cbabd-8cf7-41e3-9f9d-207cc7f6e5da) Enslow Publishing, LLC.

Zronik, John Paul & Zronik, John. Francisco Pizarro: Journeys Through Peru & South America, 1 vol. 2005. (In the Footsteps of Explorers Ser.). (ENG., Illus.). 32p. (J). (gr. -1-9). pap. *(978-0-7787-2447-6(6))* Crabtree Publishing Co.

PLACE NAMES

see Names, Geographical

PLAGUE

see also Black Death

Andrews, Lawrence. The Plague. 2015. (J). lib. bdg. *(978-1-62713-377-7(1))* 2014. (ENG.). 64p. (YA). (gr. 8-8). 35.93 *(978-1-5026-0087-5(0),* 5dbd2d57-35b7-4190-bc52-92aefffb61c4) Cavendish Square Publishing LLC.

Elliott, Lynne. Medieval Medicine & the Plague, 1 vol. 2005. (Medieval World Ser.). (ENG., Illus.). 32p. (J). (gr. 5-9). pap. *(978-0-7787-1390-6(3))* Crabtree Publishing Co.

Griffin, Mary. The Black Death, 1 vol. 2019. (Look at World History Ser.). (ENG.). 32p. (gr. 2-2). pap. 11.50 *(978-1-5382-4126-4(9),* 454dff46-657e-463c-a748-97a8a83b9825) Stevens, Gareth Publishing LLLP.

Hamen, Susan E. The 12 Worst Health Disasters of All Time. 2019. (All-Time Worst Disasters Ser.). (ENG., Illus.). 32p. (J). (gr. 3-6). 14.25 *(978-1-63235-602-4(3),* 13919); 32.80 *(978-1-63235-537-9(X),* 13911) Bookstaves, LLC. (12-Story Library).

Hardman, Lizabeth. Plague, 1 vol. 2009. (Diseases & Disorders Ser.). (ENG.). 104p. (gr. 7-7). 41.53 *(978-1-4205-0145-2(3),* 04f16a49-2709-45a0-b82a-1c9483ccb49a, Lucent Pr.) Greenhaven Publishing LLC.

Jarrow, Gail. Bubonic Panic: When Plague Invaded America. 2016. (Deadly Diseases Ser.). (ENG., Illus.). 200p. (J). (gr. 5-12). 22.99 *(978-1-62091-738-1(6),* 1405837, Calkins Creek) Highlights Pr., c/o Highlights for Children, Inc.

Koch, Falynn. Science Comics: Plagues: The Microscopic Battlefield. 2017. (Science Comics Ser.). (ENG., Illus.). 128p. (J). pap. 12.99 *(978-1-62672-752-6(X),* 900172681, First Second Bks.) Roaring Brook Pr.

Leone, Bruno. Disease in History. 2016. (ENG.). 104p. (J). (gr. 5-12). 38.60 *(978-1-60152-960-2(0))* ReferencePoint Pr., Inc.

Levy, Janey. Plaga: la Peste Negra (Plague: the Black Death), 1 vol. Sarfatti, Esther, tr. 2015. (Desastres (Doomed) Ser.). (SPA., Illus.). 32p. (J). (gr. 4-5). lib. bdg. 28.27 *(978-1-4824-3248-0(X),* 69106c09-1ca7-48a8-b418-b03572d64109) Stevens, Gareth Publishing LLLP.

Macdonald, Fiona. The Plague & Medicine in the Middle Ages, 1 vol. 2005. (World Almanac(r) Library of the Middle Ages Ser.). (ENG., Illus.). 48p. (gr. 5-8). pap. 15.05 *(978-0-8368-5907-2(3),* 25481dcd-08c1-4109-b4a2-a3dc84c670aa, Gareth Stevens Secondary Library) Stevens, Gareth Publishing LLLP.

Narayan, Natasha. Black Death & Other Putrid Plagues of London. 2004. (.... of London Ser.). (Illus.). 96p. 8.99 *(978-1-904153-01-6(1))* Watling St., Ltd. GBR. Dist: Independent Pubs. Group.

Orme, David. Plagues. 2010. (Fact to Fiction Grafx Ser.). (Illus.). 36p. (J). lib. bdg. 16.95 *(978-1-60686-472-2(6))* Perfection Learning Corp.

Peppas, Lynn. Plague! 2013. (ENG.). 48p. (J). *(978-0-7787-1102-5(1));* (Illus.). pap. *(978-0-7787-1122-3(6))* Crabtree Publishing Co.

Person, Stephen. Bubonic Plague: The Black Death! (Nightmare Plagues Ser.). 32p. (gr. 4-9). 2016. (ENG., Illus.). (J). pap. 7.99 *(978-1-944998-69-1(1))* 2010. (YA). lib. bdg. 28.50 *(978-1-936088-03-4(7))* Bearport Publishing Co., Inc.

Peters, Stephanie True. The Black Death, 1 vol. 2005. (Epidemic! Ser.). (ENG.). 80p. (gr. 6-6). 35.50 *(978-0-7614-1633-3(1),* aadc8c05-66c0-4cfd-a59a-e690189c10b2) Cavendish Square Publishing LLC.

Throp, Claire. The Horror of the Bubonic Plague. 2017. (Deadly History Ser.). (ENG., Illus.). 48p. (J). (gr. 3-6). lib. bdg. 35.99 *(978-1-4846-4167-5(1),* 136217, Heinemann) Capstone.

Walker, Richard. KFK Epidemics & Plagues. 2007. (Kingfisher Knowledge Ser.). 8.95 *(978-0-7534-6181-5(1),* Kingfisher) Roaring Brook Pr.

Whiting, Jim. Bubonic Plague. 2006. (Natural Disasters Ser.). (Illus.). 32p. (J). (gr. 1-4). lib. bdg. 25.70 *(978-1-58415-494-5(2))* Mitchell Lane Pubs.

PLAGUE—FICTION

Barker, M. A. R. Lords of Tsamra 2003. (Illus.). 296p. (YA). per. 19.95 *(978-0-9725880-1-0(9),* 2) Zottola Publishing, Inc.

Brandes, Nadine. Fawkes: A Novel, 1 vol. 2018. (ENG.). 448p. (YA). 16.99 *(978-0-7852-1714-5(2))* Nelson, Thomas Inc.

Collins, Suzanne. Gregor & the Curse of the Warmbloods. 2006. (Underland Chronicles: Bk. 3). 358p. (gr. 4-7). 17.00 *(978-0-7569-6766-6(X))* Perfection Learning Corp.

—Gregor & the Curse of the Warmbloods (the Underland Chronicles #3) 2013. (Underland Chronicles Ser.: 3). (ENG.). 368p. (J). (gr. 4-7). pap. 7.99 *(978-0-439-65624-5(9),* Scholastic Paperbacks) Scholastic, Inc.

Cullen, Lyn. I Am Rembrandt's Daughter. 2011. 8.88 *(978-0-7848-3491-6(1),* Everbind) Marco Bk. Co.

Dixon, Heather. Illusionarium. 2015. (ENG.). 368p. (YA). (gr. 8). 17.99 *(978-0-06-200105-4(1),* Greenwillow Bks.) HarperCollins Pubs.

Furlong, C. T. Killer Genes. 2012. (Arctic6 Adventure Ser.). 192p. (YA). (gr. 4-6). pap. 45.54 *(978-0-7613-9209-5(2))* Lerner Publishing Group.

Furlong, Carol T. Killer Genes. 2012. (Arctic6 Adventure Ser.). 192p. (YA). (gr. 4-6). pap. 7.99 *(978-0-9562315-7-4(8))* Lerner Publishing Group.

Grant, Michael. Plague. (Gone Ser.: 4). (ENG.). (YA). (gr. 8). 2014. 528p. pap. 12.99 *(978-0-06-144914-7(8))* 2011. 512p. 17.99 *(978-0-06-144912-3(1))* HarperCollins Pubs. (Tegen, Katherine Bks).

Gray, Claudia. Defy the Worlds. 2019. (Defy the Stars Ser.: 2). (ENG.). 496p. (YA). (gr. 9-17). pap. 12.99 *(978-0-316-39407-9(6))* Little, Brown Bks. for Young Readers.

Kaufman, Amie. Illuminae. 2017. lib. bdg. 24.50 *(978-0-606-39847-3(3))* Turtleback.

Keeling, Annie E. Andrew Golding A Tale of the Great Plague. 2004. reprint ed. pap. 15.95 *(978-1-4191-0694-1(5));* pap. 1.99 *(978-1-4192-0694-8(X))* Kessinger Publishing, LLC.

Lu, Marie. Champion. 2014. (Legend Ser.: 3). lib. bdg. 20.85 *(978-0-606-36605-2(9))* Turtleback.

—Champion: A Legend Novel. (Legend Ser.: 3). (ENG.). (YA). (gr. 7). 2014. 416p. pap. 12.99 *(978-0-14-751228-4(X),* Speak) 2013. (Illus.). 384p. 19.99 *(978-0-399-25677-6(6),* G.P. Putnam's Sons Books for Young Readers) Penguin Young Readers Group.

—Legend. aut. ltd. collector's ed. 2013. (Legend Trilogy: Bk. 1). (Illus.). 306p. (YA). mass mkt. 100.00 net. *(978-1-934267-38-7(4))* Gauntlet, Inc.

—Legend. 2011. (Legend Trilogy: Bk. 1). (ENG.). (YA). (gr. 8-12). 54.99 *(978-1-61657-044-6(X),* Penguin AudioBooks) Penguin Publishing Group.

—Legend. (Legend Ser.: 1). (ENG.). (YA). (gr. 7). 2013. 352p. pap. 12.99 *(978-0-14-242207-6(X),* Speak) 2011. 320p. 19.99 *(978-0-399-25675-2(X),* G.P. Putnam's Sons Books for Young Readers) Penguin Young Readers Group.

—Legend. l.t. ed. 2012. (Legend Trilogy: Bk. 1). (ENG.). 394p. (J). (gr. 7-12). 23.99 *(978-1-4104-4606-0(9))* Thorndike Pr.

—Legend. (Legend Graphic Novels Ser.: 1). 2015. lib. bdg. 26.95 *(978-0-606-38424-7(3))* 2013. lib. bdg. 20.85 *(978-0-606-31701-6(5))* Turtleback.

—Legend: the Graphic Novel. 2015. (Legend Ser.: 1). (ENG., Illus.). 160p. (YA). (gr. 7). pap. 15.99 *(978-0-399-17189-5(4),* G.P. Putnam's Sons Books for Young Readers) Penguin Young Readers Group.

Marriott, Zoë. Darkness Hidden: the Name of the Blade, Book Two. 2015. (Name of the Blade Ser.: 2). (ENG.). 352p. (YA). (gr. 7). 16.99 *(978-0-7636-6958-4(X))* Candlewick Pr.

O'Hearn, Kate. Origins of Olympus. 2014. (Pegasus Ser.: 4). (ENG., Illus.). 432p. (J). (gr. 3-7). 19.99 *(978-1-4424-9715-3(7),* Simon & Schuster/Paula Wiseman Bks.) Simon & Schuster/Paula Wiseman Bks.

—Origins of Olympus. 2015. (Pegasus Ser.: 4). lib. bdg. 19.65 *(978-0-606-38366-0(2))* Turtleback.

Orme, David. Plagues. 2010. (Fact to Fiction Grafx Ser.). (Illus.). 36p. (J). pap. 7.45 *(978-0-7891-7997-5(0))* Perfection Learning Corp.

Owen, Margaret. The Merciful Crow. 2019. (Merciful Crow Ser.: 1). (ENG., Illus.). 384p. (YA). 18.99 *(978-1-250-19192-2(0),* 900192893, Holt, Henry & Co. Bks. For Young Readers) Holt, Henry & Co.

—The Merciful Crow. 2020. (Merciful Crow Ser.: 1). (ENG.). 400p. (YA). pap. 10.99 *(978-1-250-25094-0(3),* 900192894) Square Fish.

Revis, Beth. Give the Dark My Love. 2019. (ENG.). 384p. (YA). (gr. 7). pap. 10.99 *(978-1-59514-718-9(7),* Razorbill) Penguin Young Readers Group.

Russell, Christopher. Hunted. 2007. (J). (gr. 5-9). 254p. 15.99 *(978-0-06-084119-5(2));* 272p. lib. bdg. 16.89 *(978-0-06-084120-1(6),* Greenwillow Bks.) HarperCollins Pubs.

Scarrow, Alex. Plague Land. 2017. (Plague Land Ser.: 1). (ENG.). 384p. (YA). (gr. 8-12). pap. 10.99 *(978-1-4926-5210-6(5))* Sourcebooks, Inc.

—Plague Land: Reborn. 2018. (Plague Land Ser.: 2). (ENG.). 416p. (YA). (gr. 8-12). pap. 10.99 *(978-1-4926-6023-1(X))* Sourcebooks, Inc.

Suvada, Emily. This Mortal Coil. (Mortal Coil Ser.). (ENG.). (YA). (gr. 9). 2018. 448p. pap. 12.99 *(978-1-4814-9634-6(4))* 2017. (Illus.). 432p. 19.99 *(978-1-4814-9633-9(6))* Simon Pulse. (Simon Pulse).

Taranta, Mary. Shimmer & Burn. 2018. (ENG.). 352p. (YA). (gr. 9). pap. 11.99 *(978-1-4814-7200-5(3),* McElderry, Margaret K. Bks.) McElderry, Margaret K. Bks.

—Splendor & Spark. (ENG.). 336p. (YA). (gr. 9). 2019. pap. 12.99 *(978-1-4814-7203-6(8))* 2018. (Illus.). 18.99 *(978-1-4814-7202-9(X))* McElderry, Margaret K. Bks. (McElderry, Margaret K. Bks.).

Zarcinas, Scott. The Golden Chalice: A Pilgrim's Chronicle. 2013. 200p. pap. *(978-0-9875975-9-5(0))* DoctorZed Publishing.

—The Golden Chalice: A Pilgrim's Chronicle (Large Print 16pt) l.t. ed. 2013. 284p. (YA). pap. *(978-1-4596-7063-1(9))* ReadHowYouWant.com, Ltd.

PLANE CRASHES

see Aircraft Accidents

PLANE GEOMETRY

see Geometry

PLANE TRIGONOMETRY

see Trigonometry

PLANETS

see also Life on Other Planets; Solar System; Stars
also names of planets, e.g. Venus (Planet)

Aguilar, David A. Seven Wonders of the Solar System. 2017. (Smithsonian Ser.). (Illus.). 80p. (J). (gr. 5). 18.99 *(978-0-451-47685-2(9),* Viking Books for Young Readers) Penguin Young Readers Group.

—13 Planets: The Latest View of the Solar System. 2011. (Illus.). 64p. (J). (gr. 3-7). 16.95 *(978-1-4263-0770-6(5),* National Geographic Kids) Disney Publishing Worldwide.

Anderson, Michael. The Nature of Planets, Dwarf Planets, & Space Objects, 1 vol. 2011. (Solar System Ser.). (ENG., Illus.). 96p. (J). (gr. 8-8). lib. bdg. 35.29 *(978-1-61530-517-9(3),* 58422bec-8a3c-42ac-8ffa-a5a83dda5ab4) Rosen Publishing Group, Inc., The.

Applesauce, Press. Discovering Planets & Moons: The Ultimate Guide to the Most Fascinating Features of Our Solar System (Features Glow in Dark Book Cov. 2018. (Discovering Ser.). (ENG., Illus.). 96p. (J). 19.95 *(978-1-60433-800-3(8),* Applesauce Pr.) Cider Mill Pr. Bk. Pubs., LLC.

Arlon, Penelope & Gordon-Harris, Tory. Planets. 2012. (J). lib. bdg. *(978-0-531-22957-6(2))* Scholastic, Inc.

Arnold, Quinn M. Earth. 2018. (Illus.). 24p. (J). *(978-1-56660-965-4(8),* Creative Education) Creative Co., The.

Ashby, Ruth. The Outer Planets. 2003. (New Solar System Ser.). (J). lib. bdg. 28.50 *(978-1-58340-290-0(X))* Black Rabbit Bks.

Askew, Amanda. Complete Guides Space. 2012. (ENG.). 144p. (J). *(978-1-4351-4409-5(0))* Barnes & Noble, Inc.

Aspen-Baxter, Linda & Kissock, Heather. Los Planetas, with Code. 2012. (Mirando Al Cielo Ser.). (SPA., Illus.). 24p. (J). (gr. k-2). lib. bdg. 27.13 *(978-1-61913-215-3(X),* AV2 by Weigl) Weigl Pubs., Inc.

Baines, Becky. Explore My World Planets. 2016. (Explore My World Ser.). (Illus.). 32p. (J). (gr. -1-k). pap. 4.99 *(978-1-4263-2322-5(0),* National Geographic Kids) Disney Publishing Worldwide.

Basher, Simon & Gilpin, Dan. Basher Science: Planet Earth: What Planet Are You On? Basher, Simon, illus. 2010. (Basher Science Ser.). (ENG., Illus.). 128p. (J). (gr. 5-9). pap. 9.99 *(978-0-7534-6412-0(8),* 900066946, Kingfisher) Roaring Brook Pr.

Bauer, Jeff. The Planets. 2007. (Illus.). 16p. (J). 3.95 *(978-0-545-00733-7(X))* Scholastic, Inc.

Bell, Trudy E. The Inner Planets. 2003. (New Solar System Ser.). (J). lib. bdg. 28.50 *(978-1-58340-288-7(8))* Black Rabbit Bks.

Berkes, Marianne. Going Around the Sun: Some Planetary Fun, 1 vol. Mason, Janeen, illus. 2012. (ENG.). 32p. (J). (gr. k-4). 16.95 *(978-1-58469-099-3(2));* pap. 8.95 *(978-1-58469-100-6(X))* Sourcebooks, Inc. (Dawn Pubns.).

Bing & Bong's Tiny Planets. (Bing & Bong's Tiny Planets Ser.). (Illus.). 12p. (J). pap. *(978-1-84222-875-3(7))* Carlton Bks., Ltd.

Birch, Robin. Dwarf Planets. 2nd rev. ed. 2009. (New Solar System Ser.). (ENG.). 32p. (gr. 3-6). 23.00 *(978-1-60413-216-8(7),* P166424, Facts On File) Infobase Holdings, Inc.

Blevins, Wiley. Planets, 6 vols., Set. 2004. (Phonics Readers Books 37-72 Ser.). (ENG.). 8p. (gr. k-1). pap. 35.70 *(978-0-7368-4066-8(4))* Capstone.

Bloom, J. P. Planets, 8 vols. 2015. (Planets Ser.: 8). (ENG.). 24p. (J). (gr. -1-2). lib. bdg. 262.32 *(978-1-62970-714-3(7),* 17227, Abdo Kids) ABDO Publishing Co.

—Planets, 8 vols. 2017. (Planets Ser.). (ENG.). 24p. (J). (gr. -1-2). pap., pap., pap. 63.60 *(978-1-4966-1288-5(4),* 26361, Capstone Classroom) Capstone.

Bowman, Donna H. What Is the Moon Made Of? And Other Questions Kids Have about Space, 1 vol. Lubach, Peter, illus. 2010. (Kids' Questions Ser.). (ENG.). 24p. (J). (gr. k-2). pap. 7.49 *(978-1-4048-6726-0(0),* 115554, Picture Window Bks.) Capstone.

Branley, Franklyn M. The Planets in Our Solar System. O'Malley, Kevin, illus. 2015. (Let's-Read-And-Find-Out Science 2 Ser.). (ENG.). 32p. (J). (gr. -1-3). pap. 6.99 *(978-0-06-238194-1(6),* HarperCollins) HarperCollins Pubs.

Brasch, Pamela. J Is for Jupiter: A-Z of People, Places & Things in Jupiter, Florida. Kindt, Kathleen G., illus. 2011. 52p. (J). pap. 19.95 *(978-0-9846071-7-4(X))* Middle River Pr.

Carlson-Berne, Emma. Totally Wacky Facts about Planets & Stars. 2015. (Mind Benders Ser.). (ENG., Illus.). 112p. (J). (gr. 3-6). lib. bdg. 23.99 *(978-1-4914-6523-3(9),* 129022, Capstone Pr.) Capstone.

Carlson-Berne, Emma, et al. Planets. 2015. (Planets Ser.). (ENG.). 32p. (J). (gr. 2-4). 277.20 *(978-1-4914-6957-6(9),* 22985) Capstone.

Carney, Elizabeth. National Geographic Readers: Planets. 2012. (Readers Ser.). (ENG., Illus.). 32p. (J). (gr. 1-3). lib. bdg. 14.90 *(978-1-4263-1037-9(4),* National Geographic Children's Bks.) Disney Publishing Worldwide.

—Planets. 2012. (Readers Ser.). (Illus.). 32p. (J). (gr. 1-3). pap. 5.99 *(978-1-4263-1036-2(6),* National Geographic Kids) Disney Publishing Worldwide.

—Planets (1 Hardcover/1 CD) 2017. (National Geographic Kids Ser.). (ENG.). (J). 29.95 *(978-1-4301-2677-5(9))* Live Oak Media.

—Planets (1 Paperback/1 CD) 2017. (National Geographic Kids Ser.). (ENG.). (J). pap. 19.95 *(978-1-4301-2676-8(0))* Live Oak Media.

—Planets (4 Paperbacks/1 CD), 4 vols. 2017. (National Geographic Kids Ser.). (ENG.). (J). pap. 31.95 *(978-1-4301-2678-2(7))* Live Oak Media.

Carson, Mary Kay & Carson, Mary K. Extreme Planets Q & A. 2008. (Illus.). 48p. (J). (gr. k-4). 17.99 *(978-0-06-089975-2(1))* HarperCollins Pubs.

Channing, Margot. Stars & Planets. 2014. (Closer Look At... Ser.). (Illus.). 32p. (gr. 3-6). 31.35 *(978-1-905087-08-2(X),* 1374553) Book Hse. GBR. Dist: Black Rabbit Bks.

Chiger, Arielle & Elkin, Matthew. 20 Fun Facts about Gas Giants, 1 vol. 2014. (Fun Fact File: Space! Ser.). (ENG.). 32p. (J). (gr. 2-3). 27.93 *(978-1-4824-1001-3(X),* 7ae9a641-b1d0-422a-9dfe-2c66f19a7594); pap. 11.50 *(978-1-4824-1002-0(8),* ed9d7e5f-5dcd-478b-80bf-bb18a853525b) Stevens, Gareth Publishing LLLP.

Clissold, Caroline. Out of This World. 2007. (Trackers-Math Ser.). (gr. 2-5). pap. 5.00 *(978-1-59055-917-8(7))* Pacific Learning, Inc.

Cole, Joanna. Lost in the Solar System. Degen, Bruce, illus. 2010. (Magic School Bus Ser.). (ENG.). (J). (gr. 2-5). audio compact disk 18.99 *(978-0-545-22337-9(7))* Scholastic, Inc.

Crabtree Editors & Donaldson, Chelsea. The Planets. 2012. (Journey Through Space Ser.). (ENG., Illus.). 24p. (J). (gr. 3-6). lib. bdg. *(978-0-7787-5307-0(7),* 1331626) Crabtree Publishing Co.

Culp, Jennifer. How We Find Other Earths: Technology & Strategies to Detect Planets Similar to Ours, 1 vol., 1. 2015. (Search for Other Earths Ser.). (ENG., Illus.). 112p. (J). (gr. 7-7). 38.80 *(978-1-4994-6292-0(1),* 420a1f57-be56-415d-81f2-9f198fab51ac, Rosen Young Adult) Rosen Publishing Group, Inc., The.

Dalmatian Press Staff. My Race into Space! 2008. (ENG.). 9p. bds. 4.95 *(978-1-58117-717-6(8),* Intervisual/Piggy Toes) Bendon, Inc.

The Deep Blue Planet, 5 bks., Set. Incl. Along the Coasts. Massa, Renato. Davenport, Neil F., tr. (YA). 1998. lib. bdg. 28.54 *(978-0-8172-4654-9(1));* Back to the Sea. Massa, Renato. Davenport, Neil F., tr. (YA). 1998. lib. bdg. 28.54 *(978-0-8172-4653-2(3));* Coral Reef. Massa, Renato. Serio, Linda, tr. (YA). 1997. lib. bdg. 28.54 *(978-0-8172-4652-5(5));* Ocean Environments. Voglino, Alex & Massa, Renato. Davenport, Neil F., tr. (YA). 1998. lib. bdg. 28.54 *(978-0-8172-4651-8(7));* Oceans & Seas. Voglino, Alex. (J). 1997. lib. bdg. 28.54 *(978-0-8172-4650-1(9));* 56p. (gr. 6-12). (Illus.). Set lib. bdg. 142.70 *(978-0-8172-4655-6(X))* Heinemann-Raintree.

Dickmann, Nancy. Planets, 1 vol. 2018. (Space Facts & Figures Ser.). (ENG.). 32p. (gr. 2-3). 28.93 *(978-1-5081-9518-4(8),* ed4995c0-62c3-4451-8bf6-213313076b96, Windmill Bks.) Rosen Publishing Group, Inc., The.

DiSiena, Laura Lyn & Eliot, Hannah. Saturn Could Sail: And Other Fun Facts. Oswald, Pete & Spurgeon, Aaron, illus. 2014. (Did You Know? Ser.). (ENG.). 32p. (J). (gr. -1-3). 17.99 *(978-1-4814-1429-6(1));* pap. 7.99 *(978-1-4814-1428-9(3))* Little Simon. (Little Simon).

DK. Geography: a Visual Encyclopedia. 2013. (DK Children's Visual Encyclopedias Ser.). (ENG.). 304p. (J). (gr. 3-7). pap. 19.99 *(978-1-4654-0885-3(1),* DK Children) Dorling Kindersley Publishing, Inc.

—My Best Pop-Up Space Book. 2015. (Noisy Pop-Up Bks.). (ENG., Illus.). 18p. (J). (-k). bds. 15.99 *(978-1-4654-3914-7(5),* DK Children) Dorling Kindersley Publishing, Inc.

Donaldson, Chelsea. The Planets, 1 vol. 2012. (ENG., Illus.). 24p. (J). pap. *(978-0-7787-5312-4(3),* 1331626) Crabtree Publishing Co.

Evert, Laura. Planets, Moons, & Stars. Garrow, Linda, illus. 2003. (Take along Guides). (ENG.). 48p. (J). (gr. 2-5). pap. 7.95 *(978-1-55971-842-4(0))* Cooper Square Publishing Llc.

Extreme Planet [Capstone Sole Source]. 2010. (Extreme Planet Ser.). 24p. lib. bdg. 143.94 *(978-1-4296-5857-7(6),* Capstone Pr.) Capstone.

Farndon, John. The Awesome Book of Planets & Their Moons: Awesome. Thompson, Ian, illus. 2014. (ENG.). 32p. (J). (gr. 3-7). 7.99 *(978-1-4867-0342-5(9))* Flowerpot Children's Pr. Inc. CAN. Dist: Cardinal Pubs. Group.

Faust, Daniel R. After Earth: Living on a Different Planet, 1 vol. 2007. (Jr. Graphic Environmental Dangers Ser.). (ENG., Illus.). 24p. (gr. 4-4). pap. 10.60 *(978-1-4042-4596-9(0),* 28de1bbc-0b6a-429c-8d79-07461d445bfb, PowerKids Pr.) Rosen Publishing Group, Inc., The.

—Más Allá de la Tierra: Vivir en Otro Planeta, 1 vol. 2009. (Historietas Juveniles: Peligros Del Medioambiente (Jr. Graphic Environmental Dangers) Ser.). (SPA., Illus.). 24p. (gr. 4-4). pap. 10.60 *(978-1-4358-8472-4(8),* 7b74d532-cf15-43b9-bf13-828cca7b1dea); (YA). lib. bdg. 28.93 *(978-1-4358-8471-7(X),* 564ad328-dade-409e-b98f-5396878a160c) Rosen Publishing Group, Inc., The.

Finton, Nancy. Explore the Solar System! 2010. (Illus.). 29p. (J). *(978-0-545-28884-2(3))* Scholastic, Inc.

Galat, Joan Marie. Dot to Dot in the Sky: Stories of the Planets, 1 vol. Bennett, Lorna, illus. 2003. (Dot to Dot in the Sky Ser.: 0). (ENG.). 64p. (J). (gr. 6-8). pap. 12.95 *(978-1-55285-392-4(6),* 92a3548d-a226-43b7-b584-596f3d3b1e35) Whitecap Bks., Ltd. CAN. Dist: Firefly Bks., Ltd.

Galvin, Laura Gates. I Love My Planet Earth. 2010. (ENG.). 16p. (J). (gr. -1). 5.95 *(978-1-60727-140-6(0))* Soundprints.

Gendell, Megan & Sweitzer, James. Spinning 'round the Sun: Everything You Wanted to Know about the Solar System & Everything in It. 2008. (Illus.). 32p. (J). pap. *(978-0-545-04459-2(6))* Scholastic, Inc.

Gibbons, Gail. The Planets (Fourth Edition) 4th rev. ed. 2018. (ENG.). 32p. (J). (gr. -1-3). 7.99 *(978-0-8234-3967-6(4));* (Illus.). 17.95 *(978-0-8234-3966-9(6))* Holiday Hse., Inc.

Gillespie, Katie. Planets. 2018. (Illus.). 24p. (J). *(978-1-4896-5677-3(4),* AV2 by Weigl) Weigl Pubs., Inc.

Gitlin, Marty. The Cassini Mission. 2018. lib. bdg. 29.95 *(978-1-68020-170-3(0))* Mitchell Lane Pubs.

Goldstein, Margaret J. The Sun. 2003. (Our Universe Ser.). (ENG., Illus.). 32p. (gr. 2-4). lib. bdg. 22.60 *(978-0-8225-4647-4(7))* Lerner Publishing Group.

Graham, Ian. Planets Far from Earth. 2015. (Space Ser.). (Illus.). 24p. (gr. 3-6). lib. bdg. 28.50 *(978-1-62588-211-0(4))* Black Rabbit Bks.

—Planets near Earth. 2015. (Space Ser.). (Illus.). 24p. (gr. 3-6). lib. bdg. 28.50 *(978-1-62588-212-7(2))* Black Rabbit Bks.

Grant, Donald & Delafosse, Claude. In the Sky. Grant, Donald, illus. 2013. (ENG., Illus.). 36p. (J). (gr. -1-k). spiral bd. 19.99 *(978-1-85103-419-2(6))* Moonlight Publishing, Ltd. GBR. Dist: Independent Pubs. Group.

Group/McGraw-Hill, Wright. Earth & Physical Science: Our Solar System, 6 vols. (Book2WebTM Ser.). (gr. 4-8). 36.50 *(978-0-322-04427-2(8))* Wright Group/McGraw-Hill.

Halpern, Paul. Faraway Worlds: Planets Beyond Our Solar System. Cook, Lynette R., illus. 2004. 32p. (J). (gr. 2-5). pap. 7.99 *(978-1-57091-617-5(9))* Charlesbridge Publishing, Inc.

Hamilton, John. New Horizons: Exploring Jupiter, Pluto, & Beyond. 2017. (Xtreme Spacecraft Ser.). (ENG., Illus.). 32p. (J). (gr. 3-9). lib. bdg. 32.79 *(978-1-5321-1010-8(3)*, 25596, Abdo & Daughters) ABDO Publishing Co.

Hand, Carol. Is There Life Out There? The Likelihood of Alien Life & What It Would Look Like, 1 vol., 1. 2015. (Search for Other Earths Ser.). (ENG., Illus.). 112p. (J). (gr. 7-7). 38.80 *(978-1-4994-6294-4(8)*, accb05cb-b4fc-43b6-9fd4-dff3ddfb8939, Rosen Young Adult) Rosen Publishing Group, Inc., The.

Hantula, Richard & Asimov, Isaac. Marte (Mars), 1 vol. 2003. (Isaac Asimov's Biblioteca Del Universo Del Siglo XXI (Isaac Asimov's 21st Century Library of the Universe) Ser.).Tr. of Mars: Our Mysterious Neighbor. (SPA., Illus.). 32p. (gr. 3-5). lib. bdg. 28.67 *(978-0-8368-3856-5(4)*, e4c4282c-98b2-4093-a7fb-af1ed9e982f0, Gareth Stevens Learning Library) Stevens, Gareth Publishing LLLP.

—Plutón y Caronte (Pluto & Charon), 1 vol. 2003. (Isaac Asimov's Biblioteca Del Universo Del Siglo XXI (Isaac Asimov's 21st Century Library of the Universe) Ser.). (SPA., Illus.). 32p. (gr. 3-5). lib. bdg. 28.67 *(978-0-8368-3859-6(9)*, 3ae2196b-697f-47c9-b87e-33d46b0492ac, Gareth Stevens Learning Library) Stevens, Gareth Publishing LLLP.

Harman, Alice. Planets, 1 vol., 1. 2015. (Fact Finders: Space Ser.). (ENG., Illus.). 24p. (J). (gr. 2-2). pap. 9.25 *(978-1-5081-9133-9(6)*, 1b6bc0e0-f267-457f-8e9e-da57821281fb, Windmill Bks.) Rosen Publishing Group, Inc., The.

Hartson, Tamara. Planets, 1 vol. 2018. (Mega Machines Ser.). (ENG., Illus.). 64p. (J). pap. 6.99 *(978-1-926700-88-5(0)*, 9d23404f-6062-4abf-bf4b-368c290af7e8) Blue Bike Bks. CAN. Dist: Lone Pine Publishing USA.

Hawksett, David. Beyond the Asteroid Belt: Can You Explore the Outer Planets?, 1 vol. 2017. (Be a Space Scientist! Ser.). (ENG.). 48p. (J). (gr. 5-5). pap. 12.75 *(978-1-5383-2290-1(0)*, 8dc9b7fa-23d8-49de-9027-b9b4e81a054f); (Illus.). 31.93 *(978-1-5383-2197-3(1)*, 29627733-8fd8-442f-80bd-21b045f73ded) Rosen Publishing Group, Inc., The. (PowerKids Pr.).

—Earth's Nearest Neighbors: Can You Explore the Inner Planets?, 1 vol. 2017. (Be a Space Scientist! Ser.). (ENG.). 48p. (J). (gr. 5-5). pap. 12.75 *(978-1-5383-2292-5(7)*, 59354c16-92a0-43d1-b473-ac466ffd66f2); (Illus.). 31.93 *(978-1-5383-2199-7(8)*, 7f11b839-9099-44dd-b787-edaa2968a566) Rosen Publishing Group, Inc., The. (PowerKids Pr.).

Hirsch, Rebecca E. Planets in Action (an Augmented Reality Experience) 2020. (Space in Action: Augmented Reality (Alternator Books (r)) Ser.). (ENG., Illus.). 32p. (J). (gr. 3-6). 31.99 *(978-1-5415-7878-4(3)*, ef4d75cc-e332-4a14-8ef4-1e3fb085f32c, Lerner Pubns.) Lerner Publishing Group.

Hirschmann, Kris. Space & the Planets. Bollinger, Peter, illus. 2003. (Magic School Bus Science Fact Finder Ser.). (ENG.). 96p. (J). (gr. 3-6). 16.19 *(978-0-439-38175-8(4))* Scholastic, Inc.

Hilton, Lisa. Gravity, Orbiting Objects, & Planetary Motion, 1 vol. 2016. (Space Systems Ser.). (ENG., Illus.). 112p. (J). (gr. 8-8). 44.50 *(978-1-5026-2287-7(4)*, 9146c42b-baf6-483f-9283-948d39cac69f) Cavendish Square Publishing LLC.

Hoffmann, Sara. The Little Book of Space. 2005. (Little Bks.). (ENG., Illus.). 24p. (J). (gr. -1-2). 9.95 *(978-1-58728-485-4(5))* Cooper Square Publishing Llc.

Hollar, Sherman. The Outer Planets: Jupiter, Saturn, Uranus, & Neptune, 1 vol. 2011. (Solar System Ser.). (ENG.). 96p. (J). (gr. 8-8). lib. bdg. 35.29 *(978-1-61530-518-6(1)*, 56cb4bec-e6a0-4243-a33e-f2baf30a1596) Rosen Publishing Group, Inc., The.

Holt, Rinehart and Winston Staff. Holt Science & Technology Chapter 21: Earth Science: The Family of Planets. 5th ed. 2004. (Illus.). pap. 12.86 *(978-0-03-030346-3(X))* Holt McDougal.

Hopping, Lorraine Jean. Space Rocks: The Story of Planetary Geologist Adriana Ocampo. 2006. (ENG., Illus.). 128p. (gr. 7-9). per. 19.95 *(978-0-309-09555-6(7)*, Joseph Henry Pr.) National Academies Pr.

Jankéliowitch, Anne. Barefoot Books Solar System. Buxton, Annabelle, illus. 2019. (ENG.). 52p. (J). (gr. 3-7). 19.99 *(978-1-78285-823-2(7))* Barefoot Bks., Inc.

Jemison, Mae & Rau, Dana Meachen. Discovering New Planets. 2013. (True Book™—Dr. Mae Jemison & 100 Year Starship™ Ser.). (ENG., Illus.). 48p. (J). lib. bdg. 29.00 *(978-0-531-25503-2(4))* Scholastic Library Publishing.

—Discovering New Planets (a True Book: Dr. Mae Jemison & 100 Year Starship) 2013. (True Book (Relaunch) Ser.). (ENG., Illus.). 48p. (J). (gr. 3-5). pap. 6.95 *(978-0-531-24063-2(0)*, Children's Pr.) Scholastic Library Publishing.

Kazunas, Ariel. Saturn. 2011. (21st Century Junior Library: Solar System Ser.). (ENG., Illus.). 24p. (gr. 2-5). lib. bdg. 29.21 *(978-1-61080-087-7(7)*, 201084) Cherry Lake Publishing.

Kenah, Katharine. Fantastic Planet. 2005. (Extreme Readers Level 2 - Emerging Reader Ser.). (ENG., Illus.). 32p. (gr. k-3). 16.19 *(978-0-7696-3186-8(X))* School Specialty, Incorporated.

Kenney, Karen Latchana. Breakthroughs in Planet & Comet Research. 2019. (Space Exploration (Alternator Books (r)) Ser.). (ENG., Illus.). 32p. (J). (gr. 3-6). 29.32 *(978-1-5415-3870-2(6)*, fee970a7-9c67-48b0-a7b4-dc837a3f8879, Lerner Pubns.) Lerner Publishing Group.

—Exoplanets: Worlds Beyond Our Solar System. 2017. (ENG., Illus.). 88p. (YA). (gr. 6-12). 35.99 *(978-1-5124-0086-1(6)*, 86a5be55-95a7-4036-921b-3b9c217a1cdc); E-Book 54.65 *(978-1-5124-3909-0(6)*, 9781512439090); E-Book 9.99 *(978-1-5124-3908-3(8)*, 9781512439083); E-Book 54.65 *(978-1-5124-2849-0(3))* Lerner Publishing Group. (Twenty-First Century Bks.).

Kerrod, Robin. Jupiter. 2005. (Planet Library). (Illus.). 32p. (gr. 3-8). lib. bdg. 21.27 *(978-0-8225-3907-0(1))* Lerner Publishing Group.

—Mercury & Venus. 2005. (Planet Library). (Illus.). 32p. (gr. 3-8). 21.27 *(978-0-8225-3904-9(7))* Lerner Publishing Group.

—Planet Earth. 2005. (Planet Library). (Illus.). 32p. (gr. 3-8). lib. bdg. 21.27 *(978-0-8225-3902-5(0))* Lerner Publishing Group.

—Saturn. 2005. (Planet Library). (Illus.). 32p. (gr. 3-8). lib. bdg. 21.27 *(978-0-8225-3909-4(8))* Lerner Publishing Group.

—Uranus, Neptune, & Pluto. 2005. (Planet Library). (Illus.). 32p. (J). (gr. 3-8). lib. bdg. 21.27 *(978-0-8225-3908-7(X))* Lerner Publishing Group.

Kissock, Heather. Planets. 2011. (J). *(978-1-61690-958-1(7))*; *(978-1-61690-604-7(9))* Weigl Pubs., Inc.

Kops, Deborah. Exploring Exoplanets. 2011. (Searchlight Books Whats Amazing about Space Ser.). (ENG., Illus.). (gr. 3-5). pap. 51.01 *(978-0-7613-8415-1(4))* Lerner Publishing Group.

Kortenkamp, Steve. The Dwarf Planets, 1 vol. 2010. (Solar System & Beyond Ser.). (ENG., Illus.). 32p. (J). (gr. 3-6). pap. 8.10 *(978-1-4296-6242-0(5)*, 115394, Capstone Pr.) Capstone.

—The Planets of Our Solar System. 2010. (Solar System & Beyond Ser.). (ENG.). 32p. (J). (gr. 3-4). pap. 48.60 *(978-1-4296-6410-3(X)*, 16156, Capstone Pr.); lib. bdg. 27.99 *(978-1-4296-5396-1(5)*, 113819); (Illus.). pap. 8.10 *(978-1-4296-6241-3(7)*, 115393) Capstone.

Kukla, Lauren. Planets. 2016. (Exploring Our Universe Ser.). (ENG., Illus.). 32p. (J). (gr. 3-6). lib. bdg. 32.79 *(978-1-68078-406-0(4)*, 23671, Checkerboard Library) ABDO Publishing Co.

La Bella, Laura. The Goldilocks Zone: Conditions Necessary for Extraterrestrial Life, 1 vol., 1. 2015. (Search for Other Earths Ser.). (ENG., Illus.). 112p. (J). (gr. 7-7). 38.80 *(978-1-4994-6298-2(0)*, c9973932-942a-47f7-bbe6-8aede45759f5, Rosen Young Adult) Rosen Publishing Group, Inc., The.

Labrecque, Ellen. Earth & Other Planets. 2019. (Our Place in the Universe Ser.). (ENG., Illus.). 24p. (J). (gr. 1-3). 25.99 *(978-1-9771-0848-7(2)*, 140466, Pebble) Capstone.

Lancaster, Juliana. PBIS- Planetary Forecaster. 2005. pap. 8.00 *(978-1-58591-567-5(X))* It's About Time, Herff Jones Education Div.

Leigh, Autumn. A Trip Through Our Solar System. (Reading Room Collection 1 Ser.). 16p. (gr. 2-3). 2009. 37.50 *(978-1-60851-940-8(6))* 2005. (ENG., Illus.). (J). lib. bdg. 22.27 *(978-1-4042-3345-4(8)*, 2f245f59-80a4-4f91-bc4b-eb088fbe60b6) Rosen Publishing Group, Inc., The. (PowerKids Pr.).

Levy, Janey. Viaje Al Centro de la Tierra (a Trip to the Center of the Earth), 1 vol. 2014. (Maravillosos Viajes a Través de la Ciencia (Fantastic Science Journeys) Ser.). (SPA., Illus.). 32p. (J). (gr. 2-3). 26.93 *(978-1-4824-2025-8(2)*, 36ba9118-db68-4855-901a-a95e98d92399) Stevens, Gareth Publishing LLLP.

L'Hommedieu, Arthur John. Our Solar System. 2018. (Information Bks.). (Illus.). 36p. (J). *(978-1-84643-594-2(3))* Child's Play International Ltd.

Llimós, Anna & Llimós, Anna. Space Adventure Crafts, 1 vol. 2010. (Fun Adventure Crafts Ser.). (ENG., Illus.). 32p. (gr. k-2). 26.60 *(978-0-7660-3732-8(0)*, 774d4439-51b5-4f80-bd8c-51aclade1ce2f, Enslow Elementary) Enslow Publishing, LLC.

—Space Adventure Crafts, 1 vol. 2010. (Fun Adventure Crafts Ser.). (ENG., Illus.). 32p. (gr. k-2). pap. 10.35 *(978-0-7660-3733-5(9)*, b19ca19c-8762-40d6-be0e-32d4c79ec7bb, Enslow Elementary) Enslow Publishing, LLC.

Loewen, Nancy. Amazing Science - Planets, 9 vols., Set. Yesh, Jeffrey, illus. Incl. Nearest to the Sun: The Planet Mercury. lib. bdg. 27.32 *(978-1-4048-3954-0(2)*, 94526); Our Home Planet: Earth. lib. bdg. 27.32 *(978-1-4048-3951-9(8)*, 94520); (J). (gr. k-4). (Amazing Science: Planets Ser.). (ENG., Illus.). 24p. 2008. 81.96 o.p. *(978-1-4048-4360-8(4)*, 166794, Picture Window Bks.) Capstone.

London, Jude. Powering Our Planet, 1 vol. 2013. (Rosen Readers Ser.). (ENG.). 24p. (J). (gr. 2-2). pap. 8.25 *(978-1-4777-2286-2(6)*, 764ab32e-19cb-464f-bb07-a96f3f649873); pap. 49.50 *(978-1-4777-2287-9(4))* Rosen Publishing Group, Inc., The. (Rosen Classroom).

Mader, Jan. How Do Planets Move?, 1 vol. 2018. (How Does It Move? Forces & Motion Ser.). (ENG.). 32p. (gr. 3-3). 30.21 *(978-1-5026-3767-3(7)*, 75620337-0d92-4d79-8e5c-22fd9d7cb0ba) Cavendish Square Publishing LLC.

The Magic School Bus: Lost in the Solar System. 2011. (J). audio compact disk 9.99 *(978-0-545-22880-0(8))* Scholastic, Inc.

Mapua, Jeff. What Is a Planet?, 1 vol. 2014. (Let's Find Out! Space Science Ser.). 32p. (J). (ENG.). (gr. 2-3). 26.06 *(978-1-62275-456-4(5)*, cf67ae54-8667-4c4a-839d-77292efaf39a); (ENG.). (gr. 2-3). pap. 13.90 *(978-1-62275-458-8(1)*, 8d140452-1aad-428d-9aa9-fcdfc424123a); (gr. 3-6). pap. 77.40 *(978-1-62275-459-5(X))* Rosen Publishing Group, Inc., The.

Martin, Justin McCory. Planets. 2010. (Illus.). 16p. (J). pap. *(978-0-545-13738-6(1))* Scholastic, Inc.

Mason Crest. Giant Planets, Vol. 7. 2016. (Solar System Ser.: Vol. 7). (ENG., Illus.). 48p. (J). (gr. 5-8). 20.95 *(978-1-4222-3551-5(3))* Mason Crest.

—Near Planets, Vol. 7. 2016. (Solar System Ser.: Vol. 7). (ENG.). 48p. (J). (gr. 5-8). 20.95 *(978-1-4222-3552-2(1))* Mason Crest.

Massey Steve. Space Stars & Planets. 2009. (Young Reed Ser.). 1p. (J). 14.95 *(978-1-921073-06-9(3))* New Holland Pubs. Pty, Ltd. AUS. Dist: Tuttle Publishing.

Mazurkiewicz, Jessica, et al. Skyscapes. 2012. (Adult Coloring Books: Nature Ser.). (ENG.). 64p. (J). (gr. 3). pap. 5.99 *(978-0-486-48834-9(9)*, 488349) Dover Pubns., Inc.

McGranaghan, John. Meet the Planets, 1 vol. Allen Klein, Laurie, illus. 2011. (ENG.). 32p. (J). (gr. k-5). 16.95 *(978-1-60718-123-1(1))* Arbordale Publishing.

—Meet the Planets, 1 vol. Klein, Laurie Allen, illus. 2011. (ENG.). 32p. (J). (gr. 2-3). pap. 10.95 *(978-1-60718-869-8(4)*, 5e404ef3-2e85-459a-8a0e-313c78697a63) Arbordale Publishing.

—Meet the Planets, 1 vol. Allen Klein, Laurie, illus. 2011. (SPA.). 32p. (J). (gr. 2-3). pap. 11.95 *(978-1-62855-411-3(8)*, 9eb8a5f1-e6ae-4452-a965-6f7128491aa7) Arbordale Publishing.

Meachen Rau, Dana & Picture Window Books Staff. Giran en el Espacio: Un Libro Sobre Los Planetas. Robledo, Sol, tr. Shea, Denise, illus. 2007. (Ciencia Asombrosa: Exploremos el Espacio Ser.). (SPA.). 24p. (J). (gr. k-4). 27.32 *(978-1-4048-3231-2(9)*, 93780, Picture Window Bks.) Capstone.

Mi Planeta, 6 Packs. (Chiquilibros Ser.). (SPA.). (gr. k-1). 23.00 *(978-0-7635-8620-1(X))* Rigby Education.

Miller, Derek. Investigating Space Through Modeling, 1 vol. 2019. (Science Investigators Ser.). (ENG.). 48p. (gr. 5-5). pap. 13.93 *(978-1-5026-5252-2(8)*, 9340a597-bebf-49fd-a1ea-f28470fde29f) Cavendish Square Publishing LLC.

Miller, Ron. Seven Wonders of the Gas Giants & Their Moons. 2011. (Seven Wonders Ser.). (ENG.). 80p. (gr. 5-8). lib. bdg. 33.26 *(978-0-7613-5449-9(2))* Lerner Publishing Group.

—Seven Wonders of the Rocky Planets & Their Moons. 2011. (Seven Wonders Ser.). (ENG.). 80p. (gr. 5-8). lib. bdg. 33.26 *(978-0-7613-5448-2(4))* Lerner Publishing Group.

—Uranus & Neptune. 2003. (Worlds Beyond Ser.). (Illus.). 80p. (gr. 7-18). lib. bdg. 27.93 *(978-0-7613-2357-0(0)*, Twenty-First Century Bks.) Lerner Publishing Group.

Moore Niver, Heather. 20 Fun Facts about Rocky Planets, 1 vol. 2014. (Fun Fact File: Space! Ser.). (ENG.). 32p. (J). (gr. 2-3). 27.93 *(978-1-4824-1008-2(7)*, 603d641b-2835-4241-aa32-8c2465202a07); pap. 11.50 *(978-1-4824-1009-9(5)*, ad98232a-be03-45fa-8f88-b90f4cee65d8) Stevens, Gareth Publishing LLLP.

Moving & Shaking: Individual Title Six-Packs. (Bookweb Ser.). 32p. (gr. 4-18). 34.00 *(978-0-7635-3743-2(8))* Rigby Education.

Nicolson, Cynthia. Discover the Planets. Slavin, Bill, illus. 2005. 32p. (J). lib. bdg. 15.38 *(978-1-4242-1194-4(8))* Fitzgerald Bks.

Nussbaum, Ben. All about Planets: Stitch Explores the Solar System. 2005. (All about Ser.). (ENG., Illus.). 40p. (J). (gr. -1-3). 12.99 *(978-1-59069-452-7(X)*, 1A703) Studio Mouse LLC.

Objects in Space, 12 vols. 2014. (Objects in Space Ser.). (ENG.). 32p. (J). (gr. 4-4). 167.58 *(978-1-4777-5728-4(7)*, dbd41978-3ff8-4d75-b3e8-6721b05d2b5b, PowerKids Pr.) Rosen Publishing Group, Inc., The.

Olien, Rebecca. Exploring the Planets in Our Solar System. (Objects in the Sky Ser.). 24p. (gr. 3-3). 2009. 42.50 *(978-1-60851-141-9(3))* 2007. (ENG., Illus.). (J). lib. bdg. 26.27 *(978-1-4042-3467-3(5)*, a3e1acfe-1a80-4987-9269-aac56a1fa428) Rosen Publishing Group, Inc., The. (PowerKids Pr.).

Our Solar System. (Jump Ser.). 36p. (J). (gr. 2-7). pap. *(978-1-882210-23-7(9))* Action Publishing, Inc.

Owen, Ruth. Objects in Space, 1 vol. 2015. (Objects in Space Ser.). (ENG.). 32p. (J). pap. 60.00 *(978-1-4994-0318-3(6)*, PowerKids Pr.) Rosen Publishing Group, Inc., The.

Oxlade, Chris. Space Watch: The Sun. 2010. (Eye on Space Ser.). 24p. (J). pap. 8.25 *(978-1-61532-548-1(4)*, PowerKids Pr.); (ENG.). (gr. 1-1). lib. bdg. 26.27 *(978-1-61532-542-9(5)*, 4848f06e-f9c4-4190-bd81-e353245e193e) Rosen Publishing Group, Inc., The.

Parker, Steve. Probes to the Planets. West, David, illus. 2015. (Story of Space Ser.). (ENG.). 32p. (J). (gr. 3-6). 31.35 *(978-1-62588-077-2(4))* Black Rabbit Bks.

Peters, Elisa. The Planets, 1 vol. 2012. (PowerKids Readers: the Universe Ser.). (ENG., Illus.). 24p. (J). (gr. k-k). pap. 9.25 *(978-1-4488-7468-2(8)*, 61ef777b-7c63-4423-b844-ff3e09940789); lib. bdg. 26.27 *(978-1-4488-7389-0(4)*, 6a069236-6acb-4c72-87f4-a82cd76b7241) Rosen Publishing Group, Inc., The. (PowerKids Pr.).

—The Planets: Los Planetas, 1 vol. 2012. (PowerKids Readers: el Universo / the Universe Ser.). (SPA & ENG., Illus.). 24p. (J). (gr. k-k). lib. bdg. 26.27 *(978-1-4488-7825-3(X)*, 4be1d7d2-c7de-47a4-a856-e6dda99b01a8, PowerKids Pr.) Rosen Publishing Group, Inc., The.

Petrikowski, Nicki Peter. Critical Perspectives on the Viability of Human Life on Other Planets, 1 vol. 2016. (Analyzing the Issues Ser.). (ENG.). 208p. (gr. 8-8). 50.93 *(978-0-7660-7674-7(1)*, 963ad279-23df-4f9d-b8fa-584403eefd5b) Enslow Publishing, LLC.

Planetary Exploration, 18 vols. 2016. (Planetary Exploration Ser.). (ENG.). 00032p. (J). (gr. 2-3). 234.54 *(978-1-5081-0288-5(0)*, c1b4c9e3-94eb-4c40-bcf6-6174b45f2852, Britannica Educational Publishing) Rosen Publishing Group, Inc., The.

Los Planetas, 6 vols., Vol. 2. (Explorers. Exploradores Nonfiction Sets Ser.). (SPA.). 32p. (gr. 3-6). 44.95 *(978-0-7699-0642-3(7))* Shortland Pubns. (U. S. A.) Inc.

Planetas y Satelites. (SPA.). (J). 10.00 *(978-84-342-1468-2(7))* Parramon Ediciones S.A. ESP. Dist: Distribuidora Norma, Inc.

Planets: Level L, 6 vols. (Wonder Worldtm Ser.). 16p. 34.95 *(978-0-7802-2020-1(X))* Wright Group/McGraw-Hill.

The Planets: Level P, 6 vols., Vol. 2. (Explorers Ser.). 32p. (gr. 3-6). 44.95 *(978-0-7699-0606-5(0))* Shortland Pubns. (U. S. A.) Inc.

Portman, Michael. Could We Live on Other Planets?, 1 vol. 2013. (Space Mysteries Ser.). 32p. (J). (gr. 2-3). (ENG.). 29.27 *(978-1-4339-9213-1(2)*, bbad8ea4-3f7b-46e8-b98c-271ade45be96); (ENG.). pap. 11.50 *(978-1-4339-9214-8(0)*, a6397b46-8a17-4864-a1b7-007917983e7c); pap. 63.00 *(978-1-4339-9215-5(9))* Stevens, Gareth Publishing LLLP.

—Why Isn't Pluto a Planet?, 1 vol. 2013. (Space Mysteries Ser.). (ENG., Illus.). 32p. (J). (gr. 2-3). 29.27 *(978-1-4339-8282-8(X)*, d87fa3cf-0460-4f48-9030-04a7ff8c251c); pap. 11.50 *(978-1-4339-8283-5(8)*, 564528c8-0dcf-46f0-8f22-31854a810c6b) Stevens, Gareth Publishing LLLP. (Gareth Stevens Learning Library).

Prendergast, Gabrielle. If Pluto Was a Pea. Gerlings, Rebecca, illus. 2019. (ENG.). 40p. (J). (gr. -1-3). 17.99 *(978-1-5344-0435-9(X)*, McElderry, Margaret K. Bks.) McElderry, Margaret K. Bks.

PRESS, Celebration. The Case of the Missing Planet. 2003. (ENG.). (J). (gr. 2-5). pap., stu. ed. 34.95 *(978-0-673-62845-9(0)*, Celebration Pr.) Savvas Learning Co.

Price, Jane. Underworld: Exploring the Secret World Beneath Your Feet. 0 vols. Hancock, James Gulliver, illus. 2014. (ENG.). 96p. (J). (gr. 3-7). 18.95 *(978-1-894786-89-8(0))* Kids Can Pr., Ltd. CAN. Dist: Hachette Bk. Group.

Priddy, Roger. Smart Kids Space: With More Than 30 Stickers. 2018. (Smart Kids Ser.). (ENG., Illus.). 24p. (J). pap. 5.99 *(978-0-312-52289-6(4)*, 900175811) St. Martin's Pr.

Pulliam, Christine & Daniels, Patricia. Space Encyclopedia: A Tour of Our Solar System & Beyond. Aguilar, David A., illus. 2013. 191p. (J). *(978-1-4263-1629-6(1))* National Geographic Society.

Rabe, Tish. Planet Name Game. 2015. (Step into Reading Level 2 Ser.). lib. bdg. 13.55 *(978-0-606-37271-8(7))* Turtleback.

Rathburn, Betsy. Planets. 2018. (Space Science Ser.). (ENG., Illus.). 24p. (J). (gr. 3-7). lib. bdg. 26.95 *(978-1-62617-861-8(5)*, Torque Bks.) Bellwether Media.

Red Bird Press Staff, creator. Planets. 2005. (Glow in the Dark Ser.). (Illus.). 19p. (J). (gr. -1 — 1). *(978-1-902626-73-4(7))* Red Bird Publishing.

Reilly, Carmel. The Planets, 1 vol. 2012. (Sky Watching Ser.). (ENG.). 32p. (gr. 5-5). 31.21 *(978-1-60870-582-5(X)*, 91a02b3f-17c0-4980-bc15-659c3f60a3d1) Cavendish Square Publishing LLC.

Reyes, Sonja. How Do Planets Move? What Will Happen?, 1 vol. 2017. (Computer Science for the Real World Ser.). (ENG.). 16p. (gr. 2-3). pap. *(978-1-5383-5234-2(6)*, 7d3dd3b8-f52c-45cf-858a-da71edb69505, Rosen Classroom) Rosen Publishing Group, Inc., The.

Riggs, Kate. Planets. 2015. (Across the Universe Ser.). (ENG.). 24p. (J). (gr. 1-4). pap. 9.99 *(978-1-62832-084-8(2)*, 21125, Creative Paperbacks); *(978-1-60818-484-2(6)*, 21124, Creative Education) Creative Co., The.

Ring, Susan & Roumanis, Alexis. Dwarf Planets. 2016. (Illus.). 24p. (J). *(978-1-5105-0968-9(2))* SmartBook Media, Inc.

Roumanis, Alexis. Dwarf Planets. 2015. (J). *(978-1-4896-3312-5(X))* Weigl Pubs., Inc.

Royston, Angela. What Do You Know about Plants?, 1 vol. 2017. (Test Your Science Skills Ser.). (ENG.). 32p. (J). (gr. 5-5). 29.27 *(978-1-5383-2215-4(3)*, c69ad355-f6fb-495e-b85f-1845ce703cb4); pap. 12.75 *(978-1-5383-2310-6(9)*, 6e1fb312-b197-4846-b66f-8b844c5e0a8a) Rosen Publishing Group, Inc., The. (PowerKids Pr.).

Roza, Greg. Pluto, 1 vol. 2010. (Our Solar System Ser.). (ENG.). 24p. (J). (gr. k-2). pap. 9.15 *(978-1-4339-3837-5(5)*, f8359e61-e868-46b1-a1b1-6567ba7099d7); (Illus.). lib. bdg. 25.27 *(978-1-4339-3836-8(7)*, 65b7f419-4308-4e88-a895-ff6fb3180f2a) Stevens, Gareth Publishing LLLP.

Rustad, Martha E. H. Los Planetas/the Planets. 2012. (En el Espacio/Out in Space Ser.). (MUL.). 24p. (J). (gr. -1-2). pap. 5.95 *(978-1-4296-8554-2(9)*, 118526) Capstone.

—Los Planetas. 2012. (En el Espacio/Out in Space Ser.).Tr. of Planets. (MUL.). 24p. (gr. k-1). pap. 35.70 *(978-1-4296-8555-9(7))* Capstone.

—The Planets: Revised Edition. rev. ed. 2008. (Out in Space Ser.). (ENG., Illus.). 24p. (J). (gr. -1-2). pap. 6.29 *(978-1-4296-2814-3(6)*, 95332, Pebble) Capstone.

—The Planets [Scholastic]. 2009. (Out in Space Ser.). 24p. (gr. k-1). pap. 2.50 *(978-1-4296-4050-3(2)*, Pebble) Capstone.

Ryback, Carol. The Planets, 1 vol. 2005. (In the Sky Ser.). (ENG., Illus.). 24p. (J). (gr. 2-4). pap. 9.15 *(978-0-8368-6349-9(6)*, b506d231-3b5d-45e9-b7a7-45c0c2bdac92); lib. bdg. 24.67 *(978-0-8368-6344-4(5)*, f4630638-7d9c-44be-b55a-717544b4ec4b) Stevens, Gareth Publishing LLLP. (Weekly Reader Leveled Readers).

Salas, Laura Purdie. Eight Great Planets! A Song about the Planets, 1 vol. De Giorgi, Sergio, illus. 2010. (Science Songs Ser.). (ENG.). 24p. (J). (gr. 1-3). lib. bdg. 27.32 *(978-1-4048-5765-0(6)*, 102502, Picture Window Bks.) Capstone.

Sian revision Planets&stars. 2004. (J). *(978-1-59242-057-5(5))* Delta Education, LLC.

Simon, Seymour. Exoplanets. 2018. (ENG., Illus.). 40p. (J). (gr. 1-5). 17.99 *(978-0-06-247058-4(2))*; pap. 7.99 *(978-0-06-247057-7(4))* HarperCollins Pubs. (HarperCollins).

—Planets. 2006. (Illus.). 24p. (J). *(978-0-439-77702-5(X))* Scholastic, Inc.

Sommer, Nathan. Pluto & the Dwarf Planets. 2019. (Space Science Ser.). (ENG., Illus.). 24p. (J). (gr. 3-7). lib. bdg. 26.95 *(978-1-62617-977-6(8)*, Torque Bks.) Bellwether Media.

Space!, 12 vols., Set. Incl. Asteroids, Meteors, & Comets. Sherman, Josepha. lib. bdg. 35.50 *(978-0-7614-4252-3(9)*, cc1d488f-8aac-4101-980d-527efb6bf637); Dwarf Planet Pluto. Lew, Kristi. lib. bdg. 35.50 *(978-0-7614-4243-1(X)*, 3544f434-d28b-4cfd-aa14-ab88baf177c2); Earth & the Moon. Hicks, Terry Allan. lib. bdg. 35.50 *(978-0-7614-4254-7(5)*, b684035f-a814-47fc-8233-c422509a6af0); Jupiter. Capaccio, George. lib. bdg. 35.50 *(978-0-7614-4244-8(8)*, dd5e55e2-59d4-4cc4-8de3-4f316daa9ec8); Mars. Capaccio, George. lib. bdg. 35.50 *(978-0-7614-4247-9(2)*, 67891272-d4ac-40cc-af7f-6b78d9b98751); Mercury. Colligan, L. H. lib. bdg. 35.50 *(978-0-7614-4239-4(1)*, 6e76b094-35fa-4eb1-8b7a-515ba181678e); Neptune. Sherman, Josepha. lib. bdg. 35.50 *(978-0-7614-4246-2(4)*, d91b43d2-82d9-4db3-a383-ed6a607b5085); Saturn. Hicks, Terry Allan. lib. bdg. 35.50 *(978-0-7614-4249-3(9)*, d15e59fc-e270-4f69-8034-b5bdf0be87f1); Stars. Mack, Gail. lib. bdg. 35.50 *(978-0-7614-4250-9(2),* ad10bcef-0904-4021-bccd-059791a73db8); Sun. Capaccio, George. lib. bdg. 35.50 *(978-0-7614-4242-4(1),* 54a401fd-eeaa-45a0-b8fa-49625e4a1261); Uranus. Sherman, Josepha. lib. bdg. 35.50 *(978-0-7614-4248-6(0),* 70c8f133-407c-4c01-a3ba-2773ba84606a); Venus. Bjorklund, Ruth. lib. bdg. 35.50 *(978-0-7614-4251-6(0),* 4bbc101c-81b3-4b74-b831-547ef5dc9c4b); 64p. (gr. 5-5). 2010. (Space! Ser.). 2009. Set lib. bdg. 393.48 o.p. *(978-0-7614-4237-0(5),* Cavendish Square) Cavendish Square Publishing LLC.

Sparrow, Giles. Earth & the Inner Planets. 2011. (Exploring Space: Space Travel Guides). 32p. (gr. 3-6). 31.35 *(978-1-59920-663-9(3))* Black Rabbit Bks.

—The Outer Planets. 2011. (Exploring Space: Space Travel Guides). 32p. (gr. 3-6). lib. bdg. 31.35 *(978-1-59920-664-6(1))* Black Rabbit Bks.

—Planets & Moons, 1 vol. 2006. (Secrets of the Universe Ser.). (ENG., Illus.). 48p. (gr. 6-8). pap. 15.05 *(978-0-8368-7285-9(1),* 7792af19-1ce3-499b-afe2-1672a07fa1e6); lib. bdg. 33.67 *(978-0-8368-7278-1(9),* 44bac476-1097-4830-904e-8fe2cda5fec4) Stevens, Gareth Publishing LLLP. (Gareth Stevens Secondary Library).

Storad, Conrad J. Our Sun Brings Life. 2011. (My Science Library). (ENG., Illus.). 24p. (gr. k-1). pap. 9.95 *(978-1-61741-925-6(7),* 9781617419256) Rourke Educational Media.

Stott, Carole. Mission: Space: Explore the Galaxy. 2016. (Illus.). 128p. (J). *(978-1-4654-5376-1(8))* Dorling Kindersley Publishing, Inc.

Sutter, Debra, et al. Moons of Jupiter. Klofkorn, Lisa, illus. Hoyt, Richard & Bergman Publishing Co. Staff, photos by. 2003. (Great Explorations in Math & Science Ser.). 116p. (J). pap., tchr. ed. 16.00 *(978-0-924886-87-4(0),* GEMS) Univ. of California, Berkeley, Lawrence Hall of Science.

Swatling, Todd. What Happens to Space Probes?, 1 vol. 2018. (Space Mysteries Ser.). (ENG.). 32p. (gr. 2-3). 29.27 *(978-1-5382-1959-1(X),* 41b9eae3-a043-4dcc-95fc-2b04d56f53fc) Stevens, Gareth Publishing LLLP.

Terp, Gail. La Búsqueda de Nuevos Planetas. 2018. (Descubrimiento Del Espacio Profundo Ser.). (SPA.). 32p. (J). (gr. 4-6). lib. bdg. *(978-1-68072-973-3(X),* 12456, Bolt) Black Rabbit Bks.

—Earth & Other Inner Planets. 2018. (Deep Space Discovery Ser.). (ENG.). 32p. (gr. 2-7). 9.95 *(978-1-68072-713-5(3));* (J). (gr. 4-6). pap. 9.99 *(978-1-64466-266-3(3),* 12317); (Illus.). (J). (gr. 4-6). lib. bdg. *(978-1-68072-419-6(3),* 12316) Black Rabbit Bks. (Bolt).

—Plutón y Otros Planetas Enanos. 2018. (Descubrimiento Del Espacio Profundo Ser.). (SPA., Illus.). 32p. (J). (gr. 4-6). lib. bdg. *(978-1-68072-971-9(3),* 12450, Bolt) Black Rabbit Bks.

—Saturn & Other Outer Planets. 2018. (Deep Space Discovery Ser.). (ENG.). 32p. (gr. 2-7). 9.95 *(978-1-68072-716-6(8));* (J). (gr. 4-6). pap. 9.99 *(978-1-64466-269-4(8),* 12329); (Illus.). (J). (gr. 4-6). lib. bdg. *(978-1-68072-422-6(3),* 12328) Black Rabbit Bks. (Bolt).

—Saturno y Otros Planetas Exteriores. 2018. (Descubrimiento Del Espacio Profundo Ser.). (SPA., Illus.). 32p. (J). (gr. 4-6). lib. bdg. *(978-1-68072-972-6(1),* 12453, Bolt) Black Rabbit Bks.

—The Search for New Planets. 2018. (Deep Space Discovery Ser.). (ENG.). 32p. (gr. 2-7). 9.95 *(978-1-68072-717-3(6));* (J). (gr. 4-6). pap. 9.99 *(978-1-64466-270-0(1),* 12333); (Illus.). (J). (gr. 4-6). lib. bdg. *(978-1-68072-423-3(1),* 12332) Black Rabbit Bks. (Bolt).

Time for Kids Editors. Time for Kids - Planets! 2005. (Time for Kids Ser.). (ENG., Illus.). 32p. (J). 14.99 *(978-0-06-078203-0(X))* HarperCollins Pubs.

Watt, E. Planeta Tierra: Ciencia y Experimentos. (SPA.). (J). pap. *(978-950-724-135-2(3))* Lumen.

Waxman, Laura Hamilton. Crayola (r) Out-Of-This-World Space Colors. 2020. (ENG., Illus.). 32p. (J). (gr. k-3). 27.99 *(978-1-5415-7755-8(8),* ee61cd0b-4d4b-4980-823f-e2875b2aa3ea, Lerner Pubns.) Lerner Publishing Group.

Wells, Robert E. What's So Special about Planet Earth? 2012. (J). *(978-1-61913-154-5(4))* Weigl Pubs., Inc.

Wilkins, Mary-Jane. The Inner Planets. 2017. (Our Solar System Ser.). (ENG., Illus.). 24p. (J). (gr. 2-4). 28.50 *(978-1-78121-366-7(6),* 16654) Brown Bear Bks.

—The Outer Planets. 2017. (Our Solar System Ser.). (ENG., Illus.). 24p. (J). (gr. 2-4). 28.50 *(978-1-78121-367-4(4),* 16656) Brown Bear Bks.

Willett, Edward. Space Q&a. 2014. (Science Discovery Ser.). (ENG., Illus.). 48p. (J). (gr. 4-7). lib. bdg. 28.55 *(978-1-4896-0692-1(0),* AV2 by Weigl) Weigl Pubs., Inc.

Williams, Dave. Destination: Space. 2019. (Dr. Dave Astronaut Ser.). (ENG.). 52p. (J). (gr. 4-6). 22.96 *(978-1-64310-805-6(0))* Penworthy Co., LLC, The.

Williams, Dave & Cunti, Loredana. Destination: Space. 2018. (Dr. Dave - Astronaut Ser.). (Illus.). 52p. (J). (gr. 4-7). pap. 12.95 *(978-1-77321-057-5(2))* Annick Pr., Ltd. CAN. Dist: Publishers Group West (PGW).

Wood, Matthew Brenden. Planetary Science: Explore New Frontiers. Carbaugh, Samuel, illus. 2017. (Inquire & Investigate Ser.). (ENG.). 128p. (J). (gr. 7-9). 22.95 *(978-1-61930-567-0(4),* 3f0c280f-7c1a-45b1-9ed3-d288037cb3b9); pap. 17.95 *(978-1-61930-571-7(2),* 42affcf1-61b1-43f4-955e-d02fa7b29d04) Nomad Pr.

World Book, Inc. Staff, contrib. by. Alien Planets. 2010. (Illus.). 64p. (J). *(978-0-7166-9551-6(0))* World Bk., Inc.

—A Place in Space. 2017. (J). *(978-0-7166-7950-9(7))* World Bk., Inc.

Yakola, Carrie C. Clayton & the Planets. 2009. 32p. pap. 15.99 *(978-1-4343-5275-0(7))* AuthorHouse.

Young-Brown, Fiona. The Universe to Scale: Similarities & Differences in Objects in Our Solar System, 1 vol. 2016. (Space Systems Ser.). (ENG., Illus.). 112p. (YA). (gr. 8-8). 44.50 *(978-1-5026-2289-1(0),* ece1adab-8861-44af-99d0-697a79ce0e77) Cavendish Square Publishing LLC.

PLANETS, LIFE ON OTHER

see Life on Other Planets

PLANNED PARENTHOOD

see Birth Control

PLANNING, CITY

see City Planning

PLANNING, ECONOMIC

see Economic Policy; Social Policy

see names of countries, states, etc. with the subdivision Economic Policy, e.g. United States—Economic Policy

PLANNING, NATIONAL

see Economic Policy; Social Policy

see names of countries with the subdivision Economic Policy, Social Policy; e.g. United States—Economic Policy; United States—Social policy

PLANS

see Architectural Drawing; Geometrical Drawing; Map Drawing; Maps; Mechanical Drawing

PLANT ANATOMY

Aloian, Molly. Plants Are Alive! 2012. (ENG., Illus.). 24p. (J). *(978-0-7787-4219-7(9));* pap. *(978-0-7787-4224-1(5))* Crabtree Publishing Co.

—What Are Bulbs & Roots? 2012. (ENG., Illus.). 24p. (J). *(978-0-7787-4220-3(2));* pap. *(978-0-7787-4225-8(3))* Crabtree Publishing Co.

—What Are Seeds? 2012. (ENG., Illus.). 24p. (J). *(978-0-7787-4221-0(0));* pap. *(978-0-7787-4226-5(1))* Crabtree Publishing Co.

—What Are Stems? 2012. (ENG., Illus.). 24p. (J). *(978-0-7787-4222-7(9));* pap. *(978-0-7787-4227-2(X))* Crabtree Publishing Co.

Batchelor, Jacob. Flowers, Leaves & Other Plant Parts (a True Book: Incredible Plants!) (Library Edition) 2019. (True Book (Relaunch) Ser.). (ENG.). 48p. (J). (gr. 3-5). lib. bdg. 31.00 *(978-0-531-23463-1(0),* Children's Pr.) Scholastic Library Publishing.

Bodach, Vijaya K. Roots [Scholastic]. 2010. (Plant Parts Ser.). 24p. pap. 0.52 *(978-1-4296-5059-5(1),* Capstone Pr.) Capstone.

Dickmann, Nancy. Plant Structures, 1 vol. 2015. (Earth Figured Out Ser.). (ENG., Illus.). 32p. (gr. 4-4). pap. 11.58 *(978-1-5026-0874-1(X),* f18107b4-8a43-41fe-9a08-303eddb7a829) Cavendish Square Publishing LLC.

Griffin, Maeve. Plant Parts: Roots, Stems, & Leaves, 1 vol. 2008. (Real Life Readers Ser.). (ENG.). 16p. (gr. 2-3). pap. 7.05 *(978-1-4358-0037-3(0),* 0485eceb-1d58-43ff-9f48-030ec4d78b79, Rosen Classroom) Rosen Publishing Group, Inc., The.

Hill, Christina. Inside a Plant, 1 vol. rev. ed. 2014. (Science: Informational Text Ser.). (ENG., Illus.). 24p. (gr. 1-2). pap. 9.99 *(978-1-4807-4560-5(X))* Teacher Created Materials, Inc.

Hollar, Sherman. A Closer Look at Plant Classifications, Parts, & Uses, 1 vol. 2011. (Introduction to Biology Ser.). (ENG.). 88p. (J). (gr. 8-8). lib. bdg. 35.29 *(978-1-61530-529-2(7),* a0004127-2b10-4774-8d53-5700d0f9b227) Rosen Publishing Group, Inc., The.

Johnson, Rebecca L. Powerful Plant Cells. 2008. pap. 52.95 *(978-0-8225-9383-6(1))* Lerner Publishing Group.

—Powerful Plant Cells. Desrocher, Jack & Fairman, Jennifer, illus. 2007. (Microquests Ser.). (ENG.). 48p. (gr. 3-5). lib. bdg. 29.27 *(978-0-8225-7141-4(2),* Millbrook Pr.) Lerner Publishing Group.

Konicek-Moran, Richard & Konicek-Moran, Kathleen. From Flower to Fruit. 2017. (ENG., Illus.). 30p. (J). (gr. k-2). pap. 13.99 *(978-1-941316-34-4(4),* P527719) National Science Teachers Assn.

LernerClassroom Editors. First Step Nonfiction-Parts of Plants. 2009. pap., tchr. ed. 7.95 *(978-0-8225-1798-6(1))* Lerner Publishing Group.

Midthun, Joseph. Plant Structure & Classification. 2014. (Illus.). 32p. (J). *(978-0-7166-2823-1(6))* World Bk., Inc.

Plant Anatomy, 6 vols. 2015. (Plant Anatomy Ser.: 6). (ENG.). 24p. (J). (gr. -1-2). lib. bdg. 196.74 *(978-1-68080-134-7(1),* 19359, Abdo Kids) ABDO Publishing Co.

Plant Parts [Scholastic]. 2010. (Plant Parts Ser.). pap. 2.08 *(978-1-4296-5061-8(3),* Capstone Pr.) Capstone.

Rake, Jody S. Roots, Bulbs, & Bacteria: Growths of the Underground. 2015. (Underground Safari Ser.). (ENG., Illus.). 24p. (J). (gr. 1-3). lib. bdg. 27.99 *(978-1-4914-5062-8(2),* 128773, Capstone Pr.) Capstone.

Ripley, Mark. Picking Fruit, 1 vol. 2017. (Plants in My World Ser.). (ENG., Illus.). 24p. (J). (gr. 1-1). pap. 9.25 *(978-1-5081-6163-9(1),* 9cd7bfe8-5f39-4a77-a671-69ffe9201257, PowerKids Pr.) Rosen Publishing Group, Inc., The.

Rissman, Rebecca. Plants: Real Size Science. 2013. (Real Size Science Ser.). (ENG.). 24p. (J). (gr. -1-1). pap. 6.95 *(978-1-4329-7887-7(X),* 122827, Heinemann) Capstone.

Spilsbury, Louise. What Is the Structure of a Plant?, 1 vol., 1. 2013. (Let's Find Out! Life Science Ser.). (ENG.). 32p. (gr. 2-3). 27.04 *(978-1-62275-251-5(1),* 2299c029-3add-4fad-8887-91d73a57d1e3) Rosen Publishing Group, Inc., The.

Sterling, Kristin. Exploring Flowers. 2011. (First Step Nonfiction — Let's Look at Plants Ser.). (gr. k-2). (ENG., Illus.). 24p. (J). pap. 6.99 *(978-0-7613-7832-7(4),* d52a2f38-31fb-4d7f-af65-352c5e0c3602); pap. 33.92 *(978-0-7613-8614-8(9));* (ENG.). 24p. lib. bdg. 23.93 *(978-0-7613-5779-7(3))* Lerner Publishing Group.

—Exploring Leaves. 2011. (First Step Nonfiction / Let's Look at Plants Ser.). pap. 33.92 *(978-0-7613-8615-5(7));* lib. bdg. 21.27 *(978-0-7613-5780-3(7))* Lerner Publishing Group.

—Exploring Roots. 2011. (First Step Nonfiction — Let's Look at Plants Ser.). (gr. k-2). (ENG., Illus.). 24p. (J). pap. 6.99 *(978-0-7613-7834-1(0),* 56b38d1c-32aa-4c0c-91e0-e90c88fe8809); pap. 33.92 *(978-0-7613-8616-2(5));* (Illus.). 23p. lib. bdg. 21.27 *(978-0-7613-5781-0(5))* Lerner Publishing Group.

—Exploring Seeds. 2011. (First Step Nonfiction — Let's Look at Plants Ser.). (gr. k-2). (ENG., Illus.). 24p. (J). pap. 6.99 *(978-0-7613-7835-8(9),* 47f5a4eb-c679-44f6-b0fe-186f47e0b906); pap. 33.92 *(978-0-7613-8617-9(3));* lib. bdg. 21.27 *(978-0-7613-5782-7(3))* Lerner Publishing Group.

—Exploring Stems. 2011. (First Step Nonfiction — Let's Look at Plants Ser.). (gr. k-2). (ENG., Illus.). 24p. (J). pap. 6.99 *(978-0-7613-7836-5(7),* 0767f0f1-1255-403f-8e3c-5508970a5ca5); pap. 33.92 *(978-0-7613-8618-6(1));* (ENG.). 24p. lib. bdg. 23.93 *(978-0-7613-5783-4(1))* Lerner Publishing Group.

Throp, Claire. All about Flowers. rev. ed. 2016. (All about Plants Ser.). (ENG.). 24p. (J). (gr. -1-1). pap. 5.99 *(978-1-4846-3846-0(8),* 134787, Heinemann) Capstone.

—All about Leaves. rev. ed. 2016. (All about Plants Ser.). (ENG.). 24p. (J). (gr. -1-1). pap. 5.99 *(978-1-4846-3847-7(6),* 134788, Heinemann) Capstone.

—All about Roots, 1 vol. (All about Plants Ser.). (ENG.). 24p. (J). (gr. -1-1). 2014. 25.32 *(978-1-4846-0508-0(X),* 126624) 2016. pap. 5.99 *(978-1-4846-3848-4(4),* 134789) Capstone. (Heinemann).

—All about Seeds. rev. ed. 2016. (All about Plants Ser.). (ENG.). 24p. (J). (gr. -1-1). pap. 5.99 *(978-1-4846-3849-1(2),* 134790, Heinemann) Capstone.

—All about Stems, 1 vol. (All about Plants Ser.). (ENG.). 24p. (J). (gr. -1-1). 2014. 25.32 *(978-1-4846-0510-3(1),* 126626) 2016. pap. 5.99 *(978-1-4846-3850-7(6),* 134791) Capstone. (Heinemann).

Weiss, Ellen. Scholastic News Nonfiction Readers: from Bulb to Daffodil. 2007. (Scholastic News Nonfiction Readers Ser.). (ENG., Illus.). 24p. (J). (gr. 1-2). 22.00 *(978-0-531-18534-6(6))* Scholastic Library Publishing.

PLANT DISEASES

Halfmann, Janet. Plant Tricksters. 2003. (Watts Library). (Illus.). 64p. (J). 25.50 *(978-0-531-12278-5(6),* Watts, Franklin) Scholastic Library Publishing.

Lay, Richard & Zarrinnaal, Laura Nienhaus. A Green Kid's Guide to Preventing Plant Diseases, 1 vol. 2013. (Green Kid's Guide to Gardening! Ser.). (ENG.). 24p. (J). (gr. -1-4). 31.36 *(978-1-61641-946-2(6),* 9343, Looking Glass Library) Magic Wagon.

Stewart, Melissa & Young, Allen. No Monkeys, No Chocolate. Wong, Nicole, illus. 32p. (J). (gr. k-3). 2018. pap. 7.99 *(978-1-58089-288-9(4))* 2013. 16.95 *(978-1-58089-287-2(6))* Charlesbridge Publishing, Inc.

Wright, Russell G. Blight! Investigations in Plant Diseases. (Event-Based Science Ser.). 32p. (gr. 5-9). pap., tchr.'s training gde. ed. 25.95 incl. VHS *(978-0-7690-0022-0(3))* Seymour, Dale Pubns.

PLANT DISTRIBUTION

Dodson Wade, Mary. Plants Live Everywhere!, 1 vol. 2009. (I Like Plants! Ser.). (ENG., Illus.). 24p. (gr. k-2). pap. 10.35 *(978-0-7660-3615-4(4),* c5cf50a1-a050-40a7-9dbd-9702a7e3888c, Enslow Elementary); lib. bdg. 25.27 *(978-0-7660-3155-5(1),* 5fbc518b-9742-4b3d-99a5-334558034bf9) Enslow Publishing, LLC.

Rector, Rebecca Kraft. Where Plants Grow, 1 vol. 2018. (Let's Find Out! Plants Ser.). (ENG.). 32p. (gr. 2-3). lib. bdg. 26.06 *(978-1-5383-0205-7(5),* ff4975b3-4c01-4654-9743-b2a37da06067, Britannica Educational Publishing) Rosen Publishing Group, Inc., The.

PLANT ECOLOGY

Anderson, Michael. A Closer Look at Plant Reproduction, Growth, & Ecology, 1 vol. 2011. (Introduction to Biology Ser.). (ENG.). 88p. (J). (gr. 8-8). lib. bdg. 35.29 *(978-1-61530-530-8(0),* 43fceb89-a7ef-4218-9607-fafad592de56) Rosen Publishing Group, Inc., The.

Bodden, Valerie. Critical Plant Life. 2010. (Earth Issues Ser.). 48p. (YA). (gr. 5-18). 23.95 *(978-1-58341-984-7(5),* Creative Education) Creative Co., The.

Boothroyd, Jennifer. Plants & the Environment. 2008. pap. 34.95 *(978-0-8225-9358-4(0))* Lerner Publishing Group.

Cohn, Scotti. Animal Partners, 1 vol. Bersani, Shennen, illus. 2015. (ENG.). 32p. (J). (gr. 2-5). 17.95 *(978-1-62855-448-9(7))* Arbordale Publishing.

Exploring the Native Plant World Grades 3-4: Survival. 2004. 74p. (J). pap. 14.95 *(978-1-57168-835-4(8),* Eakin Pr.) Eakin Pr.

Gibson, J. Phil & Gibson, Terri R. Plant Ecology. 2006. (Green World Ser.). (ENG., Illus.). 189p. (gr. 6-12). lib. bdg. 37.50 *(978-0-7910-8566-0(X),* P114299, Facts On File) Infobase Holdings, Inc.

Gould, Margee. Prickly Plants, 1 vol. 2011. (Strangest Plants on Earth Ser.). (ENG., Illus.). 24p. (J). (gr. 2-3). lib. bdg. 26.27 *(978-1-4488-4991-8(8),* 4cc76903-d6d3-435f-b1b9-37fe0c437c1f) Rosen Publishing Group, Inc., The.

Hwang, Jay. Amazing Animals: Strange Animal Partnerships: Multiplying Fractions (Grade 4) 2017. (Mathematics in the Real World Ser.). (ENG., Illus.). 32p. (gr. 4-5). pap. 11.99 *(978-1-4258-5555-0(5))* Teacher Created Materials, Inc.

Jang, Ki-hwa & Kim, In-sook. Good Friends: Symbiotic Relationships. Cowley, Joy, ed. Oh, Seung-min, illus. 2015. (Science Storybooks Ser.). (ENG.). 32p. (gr. k-3). 7.99 *(978-1-925246-72-8(8));* 26.65 *(978-1-925246-20-9(5))* ChoiceMaker Pty. Ltd., The AUS. (Big and SMALL). Dist: Lerner Publishing Group.

Jenkins, Steve & Page, Robin. How to Clean a Hippopotamus: A Look at Unusual Animal Partnerships. 2013. lib. bdg. 18.40 *(978-0-606-31663-7(9))* Turtleback.

Kalman, Bobbie. Hogares de los Seres Vivos. 2008.Tr. of. Living Things Need Water. (SPA.). 24p. (J). pap. *(978-0-7787-8687-0(0))* Crabtree Publishing Co.

—Symbiosis: How Different Animals Relate. 2016. (Big Science Ideas Ser.). (ENG., Illus.). 32p. (J). (gr. 3-6). lib. bdg. *(978-0-7787-2785-9(8))* Crabtree Publishing Co.

Kim, In-Sook. Good Friends: Animal Mutualism. Oh, Seung-min, illus. 2015. (Science Storybooks Ser.). (ENG.). 32p. (J). (gr. k-4). 27.99 *(978-1-925233-58-2(8),* c65f5211-174f-4f26-a7ae-9f98b8cf17f4, Big and SMALL) ChoiceMaker Pty. Ltd., The AUS. Dist: Lerner Publishing Group.

Kurzius, Alexa. Plants & Ecosystems (a True Book: Incredible Plants!) (Library Edition) 2019. (True Book (Relaunch) Ser.). (ENG., Illus.). 48p. (J). (gr. 3-5). lib. bdg. 31.00 *(978-0-531-23464-8(9),* Children's Pr.) Scholastic Library Publishing.

Lady Bird Johnson Wildflower Center Staff, Lady Bird Johnson, compiled by. Exploring the Native Plant World Grades 1-2: Changes. 2004. 62p. (J). pap. *(978-1-57168-827-9(7),* Eakin Pr.) Eakin Pr.

—Exploring the Native Plant World Pre-K-K: Patterns & Shapes. 2004. 44p. (J). pap. 14.95 *(978-1-57168-680-0(0),* Eakin Pr.) Eakin Pr.

Lawrence, Ellen. Prickly Plants: Stuck! 2012. (Science Slam: Plant-Ology Ser.). 24p. (J). (gr. -1-3). lib. bdg. 26.99 *(978-1-61772-588-3(9))* Bearport Publishing Co., Inc.

Owen, Ruth. How Do Plants Defend Themselves?, 1 vol. 2014. (World of Plants Ser.). (ENG.). 32p. (J). (gr. 2-3). lib. bdg. 27.93 *(978-1-4777-7157-0(3),* 91beb2cf-5345-4e20-9a42-8c8eb91c0a93, PowerKids Pr.) Rosen Publishing Group, Inc., The.

Pryor, Kimberley Jane. Mimicry & Relationships, 1 vol. 2010. (Animal Attack & Defense Ser.). (ENG.). 32p. (gr. 3-3). 31.21 *(978-0-7614-4421-3(1),* ec5fd99a-863c-4588-a09c-4570ea57432c) Cavendish Square Publishing LLC.

Rector, Rebecca Kraft. Where Plants Grow, 1 vol. 2018. (Let's Find Out! Plants Ser.). (ENG.). 32p. (gr. 2-3). lib. bdg. 26.06 *(978-1-5383-0205-7(5),* ff4975b3-4c01-4654-9743-b2a37da06067, Britannica Educational Publishing) Rosen Publishing Group, Inc., The.

Rhodes, Mary Jo & Hall, David. Partners in the Sea. Hall, David, photos by. 2006. (Undersea Encounters Ser.). (ENG., Illus.). 48p. (J). (gr. 3-7). per. 6.95 *(978-0-516-25492-0(8),* Children's Pr.) Scholastic Library Publishing.

Russell, Margaret. Exploring the Native Plant World: A Life Science Curriculum, 5th-6th Grade: Adaptations in the Native Plant World. Thompson, Maria, illus. 2004. 63p. (J). (gr. 5-6). per. 14.95 *(978-1-57168-851-4(X),* Eakin Pr.) Eakin Pr.

Rustad, Martha E. H. Ants & Aphids Work Together. 2011. (Animals Working Together Ser.). (ENG.). 24p. (gr. k-1). pap. 41.70 *(978-1-4296-6366-3(9),* Capstone Pr.) Capstone.

—Clown Fish & Sea Anemones Work Together. 2010. (Animals Working Together Ser.). (ENG.). 24p. (J). (gr. k-1). pap. 43.74 *(978-1-4296-6367-0(7),* 16120); (Illus.). (gr. -1-2). pap. 7.29 *(978-1-4296-6198-0(4),* 115351) Capstone. (Capstone Pr.).

—Zebras & Oxpeckers Work Together. 2011. (Animals Working Together Ser.). (ENG.). 24p. (gr. k-1). pap. 41.70 *(978-1-4296-6369-4(3),* Capstone Pr.) Capstone.

Silverstein, Alvin, et al. Symbiosis. rev. ed. 2007. (Science Concepts, Second Ser.). (Illus.). 96p. (YA). (gr. 5-9). lib. bdg. 31.93 *(978-0-8225-6799-8(7))* Lerner Publishing Group.

Walker, Kate. Plants, 1 vol. 2012. (Investigating Earth Ser.). (ENG.). 32p. (gr. 2-2). 31.21 *(978-1-60870-559-7(5),* 0cd5658d-156c-46b0-9145-50eeac9b11ad) Cavendish Square Publishing LLC.

World Book, Inc. Staff, contrib. by. Animals Depending on Other Animals. 2018. (Illus.). 48p. (J). *(978-0-7166-2729-6(9))* World Bk., Inc.

Zayarny, Jack. Symbiosis. (Illus.). 24p. (J). 2017. *(978-1-5105-0944-3(5))* 2016. *(978-1-5105-0942-9(9))* SmartBook Media, Inc.

PLANT PHYSIOLOGY

see also Growth (Plants)

Amstutz, Lisa J. Which Seed Is This? 2012. (Nature Starts Ser.). (ENG.). 32p. (gr. 1-2). pap. 47.70 *(978-1-4296-8297-8(3),* Capstone Pr.) Capstone.

Beth, Georgia & Fielder, Heidi. Growing Plants in Space. rev. ed. 2019. (Smithsonian: Informational Text Ser.). (ENG., Illus.). 32p. (J). (gr. 2-3). pap. 10.99 *(978-1-4938-6670-0(2))* Teacher Created Materials, Inc.

Griffin, Maeve. Plant Parts: Roots, Stems, & Leaves, 1 vol. 2008. (Real Life Readers Ser.). (ENG.). 16p. (gr. 2-3). pap. 7.05 *(978-1-4358-0037-3(0),* 0485eceb-1d58-43ff-9f48-030ec4d78b79, Rosen Classroom) Rosen Publishing Group, Inc., The.

Holt, Rinehart and Winston Staff. Holt Science & Technology Chapter 13: Life Science: Plant Processes. 5th ed. 2004. (Illus.). pap. 12.86 *(978-0-03-030217-6(X))* Holt McDougal.

Jordan, Helene J. How a Seed Grows. Krupinski, Loretta, illus. 2015. (Let's-Read-And-Find-Out Science 1 Ser.). (ENG.). 32p. (J). (gr. -1-3). pap. 8.99 *(978-0-06-238188-0(1),* HarperCollins) HarperCollins Pubs.

Julivert, Maria Angels. La Vida de Las Plantas. (SPA.). 288p. (J). 10.00 *(978-84-342-1465-1(2))* Parramon Ediciones S.A. ESP. Dist: Distribuidora Norma, Inc.

Kalman, Bobbie & Sjonger, Rebecca. Las Plantas de Distintos Habitats. 2006. (Cambios Que Suceden en la Naturaleza Ser.). (SPA., Illus.). 32p. (J). (gr. 3-7). pap. *(978-0-7787-8391-6(X));* lib. bdg. *(978-0-7787-8377-0(4))* Crabtree Publishing Co.

Machajewski, Sarah. How Plants Communicate, 1 vol. 2018. (Let's Find Out! Plants Ser.). (ENG.). 32p. (gr. 2-3). lib. bdg. 26.06 *(978-1-5383-0185-2(7),* 890637fd-8389-4d23-9e75-fd6c11dd9667, Britannica Educational Publishing) Rosen Publishing Group, Inc., The.

Oxlade, Edwin. Plant Physiology: The structure of plants Explained. 2007. Orig. Title: Understanding Plant Physiology. (ENG., Illus.). 156p. (C). *(978-1-84285-048-0(2))* GLMP Ltd.

Royston, Angela. Flowers. (Illus.). 32p. (YA). (gr. 2-18). lib. bdg. 27.10 *(978-1-932333-39-8(8))* Chrysalis Education.

Somervill, Barbara A. Plant Cells & Life Processes, 1 vol. 2010. (Investigating Cells Ser.). (ENG.). 48p. (J). (gr. 3-6). 35.99 *(978-1-4329-3878-9(9),* 112794, Heinemann) Capstone.

Troupe, Thomas Kingsley. Do Plants Have Heads? Learning about Plant Parts with the Garbage Gang. Toye, Derek, illus. 2015. (Garbage Gang's Super Science Questions Ser.). (ENG.). 24p. (J). (gr. k-2). lib. bdg. 27.32 *(978-1-4795-7059-1(1),* 128894, Picture Window Bks.) Capstone.

PLANT PROPAGATION

see also Seeds

Colby, Jennifer. Growing New Plants. 2014. (21st Century Junior Library: Plants Ser.). (ENG., Illus.). 24p. (J). (gr. 2-5). 29.21 *(978-1-63188-036-0(5),* 205551) Cherry Lake Publishing.

PLANT STRUCTURE

see Plant Anatomy

PLANTATION LIFE

Bober, Natalie S. Thomas Jefferson: Draftsman of a Nation. 2008. (ENG., Illus.). 376p. per. 16.95 *(978-0-8139-2732-9(3),* P144204) University of Virginia Pr.

Broida, Marian. Projects about Plantation Life, 1 vol. Prato, Rodica, illus. 2005. (Hands-On History Ser.). (ENG.). 48p. (J). (gr. 3-3). lib. bdg. 34.07 *(978-0-7614-1605-0(6),* 4e83b963-f952-4a94-950a-7c4889c7bf22) Cavendish Square Publishing LLC.

Dickmann, Nancy. Watch It Grow, 1 vol., Set. Incl. Apple's Life. (Illus.). pap. 6.29 *(978-1-4329-4150-5(X),* 113276); Dog's Life. pap. 6.29 *(978-1-4329-4232-8(8),* 113372); Sunflower's Life. (Illus.). pap. 6.29 *(978-1-4329-4153-6(4),* 113279); (J). (gr. -1-1). (Watch It Grow Ser.). (ENG.). 24p. 2010. pap., pap., pap. 31.45 o.p. *(978-1-4329-4154-3(2),* 15102, Heinemann) Capstone.

Draper, Allison Stark. What People Wore on Southern Plantations. 2009. (Clothing, Costumes, & Uniforms Throughout American History Ser.). 24p. (gr. 3-3). 42.50 *(978-1-61511-882-3(9),* PowerKids Pr.) Rosen Publishing Group, Inc., The.

Erickson, Paul. Daily Life on a Southern Plantation. Gabbey, Terry, illus. Slingsby, Miki, photos by. 2006. 48p. (J). (gr. 2-5). reprint ed. pap. 8.00 *(978-1-4223-5727-9(9))* DIANE Publishing Co.

Gullo, Jim. A Travel Guide to the Plantation South. 2005. (Travel Guide To Ser.). (ENG., Illus.). 112p. (J). (gr. 5-8). lib. bdg. 30.85 *(978-1-59018-360-1(6),* Lucent Bks.) Cengage Gale.

Hill, George. The Fall of Irish Chiefs & Clans & the Plantation of Ulster: Including the Names of Irish Catholics, & Protestant Settlers. 2004. Orig. Title: An Historical Account of the Plantation in Ulster at the Commencement of the 17th Century. (Illus.). 276p. lib. bdg. 39.00 *(978-0-940134-42-3(X))* Irish Genealogical Foundation.

Krebs, Laurie. A Day in the Life of a Colonial Indigo Planter. (Library of Living & Working in Colonial Times Ser.). 24p. (gr. 3-3). 2009. 42.50 *(978-1-60853-732-7(3),* PowerKids Pr.) 2003. (ENG., Illus.). (J). lib. bdg. 26.27 *(978-0-8239-6229-7(6),* 4fbf7f8a-1b2e-4518-ba28-11908a0c5cf6) Rosen Publishing Group, Inc., The.

Levy, Debbie. Slaves on a Southern Plantation. 2004. (Daily Life Ser.). (ENG., Illus.). 48p. (J). 27.50 *(978-0-7377-1827-0(7),* Greenhaven Pr., Inc.) Cengage Gale.

Rikson, Paule. Daily Life on a Southern Plantation 1853. 2004. (Illus.). 48p. (J). (gr. 4-8). reprint ed. 17.00 *(978-0-7567-7709-8(7))* DIANE Publishing Co.

PLANTING

see Agriculture; Gardening; Landscape Gardening; Tree Planting

PLANTS

see also Desert Plants; Endangered Plants; Flower Gardening; Flowers; Forage Plants; Forest Plants; Freshwater Plants; Gardening; Marine Plants; Shrubs also names of plants (e.g. Mosses, etc.)

Aitken, Stephen. Plants & Insects, 1 vol. 2013. (Climate Crisis Ser.). (ENG.). 64p. (gr. 5-5). 34.07 *(978-1-60870-462-0(9),* 138091a1-296c-41f3-ac88-1749ea08b7ca); pap. 16.28 *(978-1-62712-042-5(4),* 843683d0-84be-4ef0-81f8-710ee6b15b5a) Cavendish Square Publishing LLC.

Akeroyd, John. Plant: An Eyewitness 3-D Book. 2004. (Illus.). 52p. (gr. 4-8). reprint ed. 17.00 *(978-0-7567-7415-8(2))* DIANE Publishing Co.

Aldrich, William & Williamson, Don. Annuals for Illinois, 1 vol. rev. ed. 2004. (ENG., Illus.). 296p. (gr. 4). pap. 18.95 *(978-1-55105-380-6(2),* 2a4d8832-4a36-4c1d-b331-b8e59f56161b) Lone Pine Publishing USA.

—Perennials for Illinois, 1 vol. rev. ed. 2003. (ENG., Illus.). 344p. (gr. 4). pap. 19.95 *(978-1-55105-378-3(0),* 184de316-2406-4736-b46a-96ad8b7084b4) Lone Pine Publishing USA.

All about Plants, 6 vols., Pack. (gr. k-1). 23.00 *(978-0-7635-8839-7(3))* Rigby Education.

Allan, John. Plants. 2019. (Amazing Life Cycles Ser.). (ENG., Illus.). 32p. (J). (gr. 1-3). lib. bdg. 29.32 *(978-1-912108-05-3(4),* 51c6323c-829b-4714-9c8b-8b87485e4cc5, Hungry Tomato (r)) Lerner Publishing Group.

Allyn, Daisy. Seeds & Plants, 1 vol. 2012. (InfoMax Readers Ser.). (ENG., Illus.). 16p. (J). (gr. k-k). pap. 7.00 *(978-1-4488-8932-7(4),* 2876ca2a-4ec7-453a-91e9-5b812c8eda1a, Rosen Classroom) Rosen Publishing Group, Inc., The.

Aloian, Molly. Plants Are Alive! 2012. (ENG., Illus.). 24p. (J). *(978-0-7787-4219-7(9));* pap. *(978-0-7787-4224-1(5))* Crabtree Publishing Co.

Amstutz, L. J. Investigating Plant Life Cycles. 2015. (Searchlight Books (tm) — What Are Earth's Cycles? Ser.). (ENG., Illus.). 40p. (J). (gr. 3-5). 30.65 *(978-1-4677-8056-8(1),* 57264c51-bc9a-4cd8-b97c-7ee01ac20abe, Lerner Pubns.) Lerner Publishing Group.

An, Vickie. Plant Invaders. rev. ed. 2018. (Smithsonian: Informational Text Ser.). (ENG., Illus.). 32p. (J). (gr. 4-8). pap. 11.99 *(978-1-4938-6719-6(9))* Teacher Created Materials, Inc.

Andersen, Jill. Plants Need Light, 1 vol. 2016. (Rosen REAL Readers: STEM & STEAM Collection). (ENG.). 8p. (gr. k-1). pap. 5.46 *(978-1-5081-2386-6(1),* d6604804-4507-4839-a131-4294e3f4b2a0, Rosen Classroom) Rosen Publishing Group, Inc., The.

Anderson, Michael. A Closer Look at Plant Reproduction, Growth, & Ecology, 1 vol. 2011. (Introduction to Biology Ser.). (ENG.). 88p. (J). (gr. 8-8). lib. bdg. 35.29 *(978-1-61530-530-8(0),* 43fceb89-a7ef-4218-9607-fafad592de56) Rosen Publishing Group, Inc., The.

Apple Tree. 2003. stu. ed. 36.95 *(978-0-8136-9258-6(X))* Modern Curriculum Pr.

Bailey, Diane. Pollination Problems: The Battle to Save Bees & Other Vital Animals. 2017. (Illus.). 64p. (J). *(978-1-4222-3876-9(8))* Mason Crest.

Baker, Wendy & Haslam, Andrew. Plants. (Make It Work! (Eureka!) Ser.). (Illus.). (J). (FRE.). pap. 9.99 *(978-0-590-24331-5(4));* pap. 15.95 *(978-0-590-74523-9(9))* Scholastic, Inc.

Ballard, Carol. Plant Variation & Classification, 1 vol. 2009. (Living Processes Ser.). (ENG., Illus.). 48p. (gr. 5-5). (J). pap. 12.75 *(978-1-61532-346-3(5),* 567f996d-5f20-4a17-8e68-7f71e647ba6b); (YA). lib. bdg. 34.47 *(978-1-61532-345-6(7),* 2f1cb5f8-a0ce-4fff-b2f9-2a3042dc2522) Rosen Publishing Group, Inc., The. (Rosen Reference).

Bang, Molly & Chisholm, Penny. Ocean Sunlight: How Tiny Plants Feed the Seas. Bang, Molly, illus. 2012. (ENG., Illus.). 48p. (J). (gr. -1-3). 19.99 *(978-0-545-27322-0(6),* Blue Sky Pr., The) Scholastic, Inc.

Barlowe, Dot. Grand Canyon Plants & Animals. 2010. (Dover Nature Coloring Book Ser.). (ENG., Illus.). 32p. (gr. 3-8). pap. 4.99 *(978-0-486-47294-2(9),* 472949) Dover Pubns., Inc.

Barnham, Kay & Frost, Maddie. The Amazing Life Cycle of Plants. 2018. (ENG., Illus.). 32p. (J). (gr. k-3). 14.99 *(978-1-4380-5043-0(7))* Sourcebooks, Inc.

Bartholomew, Linda & Bartholomew, Al. The Rain Forest Book for Kids. Bartholomew, Linda & Bartholomew, Al, photos by. 2005. (Illus.). 32p. (J). 9.00 *(978-0-9764802-0-4(4))* Solutions for Human Services, LLC.

Bateman, Donna M. Deep in the Swamp. Lies, Brian, illus. 2007. 32p. (J). (gr. -1-3). 16.95 *(978-1-57091-596-3(2));* (ENG.). pap. 7.95 *(978-1-57091-597-0(0))* Charlesbridge Publishing, Inc.

Bath, Louella. Plants That Mimic, 1 vol. 2016. (Plant Defenses Ser.). (ENG.). 24p. (J). (gr. 3-3). pap. 9.25 *(978-1-4994-2151-4(6),* 3073bb00-d0fb-4825-b69c-fd86b82eca9e, PowerKids Pr.) Rosen Publishing Group, Inc., The.

Battista, Brianna. Why Do Pitcher Plants Eat Bugs? And Other Odd Plant Adaptations, 1 vol. 2018. (Odd Adaptations Ser.). (ENG.). 32p. (gr. 3-4). 28.27 *(978-1-5382-2031-3(8),* 7170a027-e7ca-4a1b-a79d-fb91a8cff1a7) Stevens, Gareth Publishing LLLP.

Bayden, Maya. What Is Chemical Energy?, 1 vol. 2017. (Let's Find Out! Forms of Energy Ser.). (ENG., Illus.). 32p. (J). (gr. 2-3). pap. 13.90 *(978-1-68048-693-3(4),* 51c976cf-83f2-4d1a-8c13-51fcf1a9017c, Britannica Educational Publishing) Rosen Publishing Group, Inc., The.

Benbow, Ann & Mably, Colin. Lively Plant Science Projects, 1 vol. 2009. (Real Life Science Experiments Ser.). (ENG., Illus.). 48p. (gr. 3-3). lib. bdg. 27.93 *(978-0-7660-3146-3(2),* 10ba494d-e5a1-4107-b9ee-b45352db7d44) Enslow Publishing, LLC.

Benchmark Education Company, compiled by. Amazing Plants & Plantas Asombrosas. 2005. (J). 62.00 net. *(978-1-4108-4495-8(1))* Benchmark Education Co.

Benchmark Education Company, LLC Staff, compiled by. Plants: Theme Set. 2006. (J). spiral bd. 195.00 *(978-1-4108-7107-7(X))* Benchmark Education Co.

—Plants & Animal Life: Theme Set. 2006. (J). 178.00 *(978-1-4108-7083-4(9))* Benchmark Education Co.

—Plants & Animals: Theme Set. 2006. (J). 173.00 *(978-1-4108-7137-4(1));* spiral bd. 174.00 *(978-1-4108-7063-6(4))* Benchmark Education Co.

Bennett, Doraine. Coastal Plain. 2009. (J). *(978-1-935077-51-0(1));* pap. *(978-1-935077-52-7(X))* State Standards Publishing, LLC.

Beullens-Maoui, Nathalie, ed. Plants: Armenian, 01 vols., 1. 2016. (Our Wonderful World Ser.). (ENG & SPA.). 8p. (J). pap. 9.35 *(978-1-5081-1212-9(6),* Rosen Classroom) Rosen Publishing Group, Inc., The.

—Plants: Cantonese, 01 vols., 1. 2016. (Our Wonderful World Ser.). (ENG & SPA.). 8p. (J). pap. 9.35 *(978-1-5081-1224-2(X),* Rosen Classroom) Rosen Publishing Group, Inc., The.

—Plants: Filipino, 01 vols., 1. 2016. (Our Wonderful World Ser.). (ENG & SPA.). 8p. (J). pap. 9.35 *(978-1-5081-1218-1(5),* Rosen Classroom) Rosen Publishing Group, Inc., The.

—Plants: Hmong Green, 01 vols., 1. 2016. (Our Wonderful World Ser.). (ENG & SPA.). 8p. (J). pap. 9.35 *(978-1-5081-1230-3(4),* Rosen Classroom) Rosen Publishing Group, Inc., The.

—Plants: Hmong White, 01 vols., 1. 2016. (Our Wonderful World Ser.). (ENG & SPA.). 8p. (J). pap. 9.35 *(978-1-5081-1236-5(3),* Rosen Classroom) Rosen Publishing Group, Inc., The.

—Plants: Korean, 01 vols., 1. 2016. (Our Wonderful World Ser.). (ENG & SPA.). 8p. (J). pap. 9.35 *(978-1-5081-1242-6(8),* Rosen Classroom) Rosen Publishing Group, Inc., The.

—Plants: Russian, 01 vols., 1. 2016. (Our Wonderful World Ser.). (ENG & SPA.). 8p. (J). pap. 9.35 *(978-1-5081-1248-8(7),* Rosen Classroom) Rosen Publishing Group, Inc., The.

—Plants: Spanish, 01 vols., 1. 2016. (Our Wonderful World Ser.). (ENG & SPA.). 8p. (J). pap. 9.35 *(978-1-5081-1254-9(1),* Rosen Classroom) Rosen Publishing Group, Inc., The.

—Plants: Vietnamese, 01 vols., 1. 2016. (Our Wonderful World Ser.). (ENG & SPA.). 8p. (J). pap. 9.35 *(978-1-5081-1260-0(6),* Rosen Classroom) Rosen Publishing Group, Inc., The.

Bishop, Celeste. ¿Por Qué Las Plantas Tienen Raíces? / Why Do Plants Have Roots?, 1 vol., 1. 2015. (Partes de la Planta / Plant Parts Ser.). (ENG & SPA., Illus.). 24p. (J). (gr. 1-1). 25.27 *(978-1-5081-4742-8(6),* 2e452fd1-a274-4896-b638-fe2d5f08cc94, PowerKids Pr.) Rosen Publishing Group, Inc., The.

—¿Por Qué Las Plantas Tienen Semillas? / Why Do Plants Have Seeds?, 1 vol., 1. 2015. (Partes de la Planta / Plant Parts Ser.). (ENG & SPA., Illus.). 24p. (J). (gr. 1-1). 25.27 *(978-1-5081-4732-9(9),* d861f168-84d1-4b2b-8132-424f3c292c9f, PowerKids Pr.) Rosen Publishing Group, Inc., The.

—¿Por Qué Las Plantas Tienen Tallos? / Why Do Plants Have Stems?, 1 vol., 1. 2015. (Partes de la Planta / Plant Parts Ser.). (ENG & SPA., Illus.). 24p. (J). (gr. 1-1). 25.27 *(978-1-5081-4731-2(0),* 809157d3-4d20-47e8-8f3b-db2aa8132cea, PowerKids Pr.) Rosen Publishing Group, Inc., The.

—Why Do Plants Have Roots?, 1 vol., 1. 2015. (Plant Parts Ser.). (ENG., Illus.). 24p. (J). (gr. 1-1). pap. 9.25 *(978-1-5081-4225-6(4),* 33292852-f434-4ec9-ae37-d2b1c568b672, PowerKids Pr.) Rosen Publishing Group, Inc., The.

—Why Do Plants Have Seeds?, 1 vol., 1. 2015. (Plant Parts Ser.). (ENG., Illus.). 24p. (J). (gr. 1-1). pap. 9.25 *(978-1-5081-4229-4(7),* c1e04ee5-1e8c-429c-99c6-96a5ec588e84, PowerKids Pr.) Rosen Publishing Group, Inc., The.

—Why Do Plants Have Stems?, 1 vol., 1. 2015. (Plant Parts Ser.). (ENG., Illus.). 24p. (J). (gr. 1-1). 25.27 *(978-1-4994-1851-4(5),* ca831fb1-f880-45cc-93e1-5a8a4f1e1f44, PowerKids Pr.) Rosen Publishing Group, Inc., The.

Blackaby, Susan. Plant Packages: A Book about Seeds, 1 vol. Delage, Charlene, illus. 2003. (Growing Things Ser.). (ENG.). 24p. (J). (gr. -1-2). per. 8.95 *(978-1-4048-0384-8(X),* 92535, Picture Window Bks.) Capstone.

Blashfield, Jean F. Plant Life, 1 vol. 2007. (Gareth Stevens Vital Science Library: Life Science Ser.). (ENG.). 48p. (gr. 5-8). pap. 15.05 *(978-0-8368-8451-7(5),* c0aa5ac1-5a87-4603-a2b5-766ecc8507dc); (Illus.). lib. bdg. 29.67 *(978-0-8368-8442-5(6),* 9d8d4a48-efe0-4d88-bc07-1fd7c449f563) Stevens, Gareth Publishing LLLP. (Gareth Stevens Secondary Library).

Blevins, Wiley. Ninja Plants: Survival & Adaptation in the Plant World. 2017. (ENG., Illus.). 96p. (YA). (gr. 6-12). 35.99 *(978-1-5124-1013-6(6),* 36cd1eb2-1a97-4d06-914e-902f1763a9b1); E-Book 54.65 *(978-1-5124-3915-1(0),* 9781512439151); E-Book 54.65 *(978-1-5124-2853-7(1));* E-Book 9.99 *(978-1-5124-3914-4(2),* 9781512439144) Lerner Publishing Group. (Twenty-First Century Bks.).

Bocknek, Jonathan. Plants. 2007. (Life Science (Weigl Hardcover) Ser.). (Illus.). 32p. (J). (gr. 4-7). lib. bdg. 26.00 *(978-1-59036-717-9(0));* per. 9.95 *(978-1-59036-718-6(9))* Weigl Pubs., Inc.

Bodach, Vijaya Khisty. Stems. rev. ed. 2016. (Plant Parts Ser.). (ENG.). 24p. (J). (gr. -1-2). pap. 7.29 *(978-1-5157-4247-0(4),* 134005, Capstone Pr.) Capstone.

Boothroyd, Jennifer. Self-Pollination. 2015. (First Step Nonfiction - Pollination Ser.). (ENG., Illus.). 24p. (gr. k-2). 39.99 *(978-1-4677-8908-0(9),* Lerner Digital) Lerner Publishing Group.

Born, Alan & Rylands, Warren. Plants. 2019. (Illus.). 24p. (J). *(978-1-4896-8003-7(9),* AV2 by Weigl) Weigl Pubs., Inc.

Bow, James. Wetlands Inside Out. 2014. (Ecosystems Inside Out Ser.). (ENG., Illus.). 32p. (J). (gr. 4-5). *(978-0-7787-0641-0(9))* Crabtree Publishing Co.

Braun, Eric. Corpse Flower vs. Venus Flytrap. 2018. (Versus! Ser.). (ENG.). 24p. (J). (gr. 4-6). pap. 9.99 *(978-1-64466-330-1(9),* 12155); lib. bdg. *(978-1-68072-347-2(2),* 12154) Black Rabbit Bks. (Hi Jinx).

Brooks, Marigold. Let's Plant a Tree, 1 vol. 2017. (Plants in My World Ser.). (ENG.). 24p. (gr. 1-1). pap. 9.25 *(978-1-5383-2120-1(3),* dda8b4b5-e70a-4072-a8f4-9bdeefaf86b9, PowerKids Pr.) Rosen Publishing Group, Inc., The.

Brown Bear Books. Plants & Microorganisms. 2011. (Introducing Biology Ser.). (ENG.). 64p. (J). (gr. 8-11). lib. bdg. 39.95 *(978-1-936333-02-8(3),* 16513) Brown Bear Bks.

Brown, Carron. Secrets of the Rain Forest. 2015. (ENG., Illus.). 36p. (J). 12.99 *(978-1-61067-325-9(5))* Kane Miller.

Bryan, Lynn. Where Do Plants Grow? 2004. (ENG., Illus.). 8p. (J). (gr. k-k). pap. 7.56 *(978-0-7652-5145-9(0),* Celebration Pr.) Savvas Learning Co.

Brynie, Faith Hickman. What Helps Plants Grow? The Nitrogen Cycle Case. 2003. (J). *(978-1-58417-151-5(0))* Lake Street Pubs.

Buchanan, Shelly. Plant Reproduction. 2015. (Science: Informational Text Ser.). (ENG., Illus.). 32p. (J). (gr. 3-5). pap. 11.99 *(978-1-4807-4676-3(2))* Teacher Created Materials, Inc.

Bullard, Lisa. Crayola (r) Tundra Colors. 2020. (Crayola (r) Colorful Biomes Ser.). (ENG., Illus.). 32p. (J). (gr. k-3). 29.32 *(978-1-5415-7753-4(1),* 741fc6f4-1a78-483d-b4bc-e783e1ee3fe9, Lerner Pubns.) Lerner Publishing Group.

Burnie, David. DK Eyewitness Books: Plant: Discover the Fascinating World of Plants. 2011. (DK Eyewitness Ser.). (ENG.). 72p. (J). (gr. 3-7). 16.99 *(978-0-7566-6035-2(1),* DK Children) Dorling Kindersley Publishing, Inc.

Burton, Margie, et al. Plants & Las Plantas: 6 English, 6 Spanish Adaptations. 2011. (J). spiral bd. 75.00 net. *(978-1-4108-5638-8(0))* Benchmark Education Co.

Butt, Kyle. God Made Plants. 2007. (ENG., Illus.). (J). 3.00 *(978-0-932859-85-3(2))* Apologetics Pr., Inc.

Butterfield, Moira & Jacobs, Pat. Plants, 1 vol. 2015. (Know It All! Ser.). (ENG., Illus.). 32p. (gr. 5-5). pap. 11.58 *(978-1-5026-0894-9(4),* c9afe3af-b9ec-483d-afb8-c163555572ce) Cavendish Square Publishing LLC.

Cameron, Ken. La genética de las Plantas. Hanner, Albert & Hortens, Mike, illus. 2011. (SPA.). 32p. (J). pap. 49.00 net. *(978-1-4108-2341-0(5),* A23415) Benchmark Education Co.

Canavan, Thomas. Do Plants Really Eat Insects? Questions & Answers about the Science of Plants. 2013. (Science F. A. Q. Ser.). (Illus.). 32p. (gr. 3-6). 31.35 *(978-1-78212-392-7(X))* Arcturus Publishing GBR. Dist: Black Rabbit Bks.

Capon, Brian. Plant Survival: Adapting to a Hostile World. 2009. (ENG., Illus.). 144p. pap. 19.99 *(978-0-88192-287-5(0),* 682287) Timber Pr., Inc.

Carle, Eric. The Tiny Seed/Ready-To-Read Level 2. Carle, Eric, illus. 2015. (World of Eric Carle Ser.). (ENG., Illus.). 32p. (J). (gr. k-2). pap. 4.99 *(978-1-4814-3575-8(2),* Simon Spotlight) Simon Spotlight.

Carr, Aaron. Plants. (World Languages Ser.). 2017. (ENG.). 24p. (J). (gr. -1-1). lib. bdg. 35.70 *(978-1-4896-6620-8(6),* AV2 by Weigl) 2013. lib. bdg. 20.00 *(978-1-62127-492-6(6))* Weigl Pubs., Inc.

Carr, Joaquin. Habitats of South America: Text Pairs. 2008. (Bridges/Navigators Ser.). (J). (gr. 3). 81.00 *(978-1-4108-8361-2(2))* Benchmark Education Co.

Cavell-Clarke, Steffi. Plant Parts, 1 vol. 2016. (Closer Look at Living Things Ser.). (ENG.). 24p. (J). (gr. 2-2). pap. 9.25 *(978-1-5345-2069-1(4),* 0985a12a-d462-467d-ae3e-c5ebdb7c436b); lib. bdg. 26.23 *(978-1-5345-2070-7(8),* edf139c9-014c-4d31-9b5e-0e89667c2cca) Greenhaven Publishing LLC. (KidHaven Publishing).

Charman, Andrew. I Wonder Why Leaves Change Color: And Other Questions about Plants. 2012. (I Wonder Why Ser.). (ENG., Illus.). (J). (gr. k-3). pap. 6.99 *(978-0-7534-6697-1(X),* 900076411, Kingfisher) Roaring Brook Pr.

Cheshire, Gerald. Living World. 2013. (World of Wonder Ser.). (ENG., Illus.). 32p. (gr. 1-3). lib. bdg. 31.35 *(978-1-908973-99-3(4))* Book Hse. GBR. Dist: Black Rabbit Bks.

Clasky, Leonard. My Little Plant: If... Then, 1 vol. 2017. (Computer Science for the Real World Ser.). (ENG.). 8p. (gr. k-1). pap. *(978-1-5383-5104-8(8),* cf2e1d4f-5cd4-4c7f-961a-ee0599cbfb8a, Rosen Classroom) Rosen Publishing Group, Inc., The.

Claybourne, Anna. Killer Plants & Other Green Gunk. 2014. (Disgusting & Dreadful Science Ser.). (ENG., Illus.). 32p. (J). (gr. 3-3). *(978-0-7787-1400-2(4))* Crabtree Publishing Co.

Colby, Jennifer. Growing New Plants. 2014. (21st Century Junior Library: Plants Ser.). (ENG., Illus.). 24p. (J). (gr. 2-5). 29.21 *(978-1-63188-036-0(5),* 205551) Cherry Lake Publishing.

—Plants Need Sunlight. 2014. (21st Century Junior Library: Plants Ser.). (ENG., Illus.). 24p. (J). (gr. 2-5). 29.21 *(978-1-63188-038-4(1),* 205559) Cherry Lake Publishing.

—Poison Ivy Makes Me Itch. 2015. (Tell Me Why Library). (ENG., Illus.). 24p. (J). (gr. 2-5). 29.21 *(978-1-63362-615-7(6),* 206644) Cherry Lake Publishing.

—What Is a Plant? 2014. (21st Century Junior Library: Plants Ser.). (ENG., Illus.). 24p. (J). (gr. 2-5). 29.21 *(978-1-63188-042-1(X),* 205575) Cherry Lake Publishing.

Cole, Tayler. Corpse Flowers Smell Nasty!, 1 vol. 2016. (World's Weirdest Plants Ser.). (ENG., Illus.). 24p. (J). (gr. 2-3). pap. 9.15 *(978-1-4824-5607-3(9),* 1e8ccd0a-ff90-4a05-aeef-672fdc0d42b0) Stevens, Gareth Publishing LLLP.

Collier, Elise. What Grows in an Orchard?, 1 vol. 2017. (Plants in My World Ser.). (ENG.). 24p. (gr. 1-1). pap. 9.25 *(978-1-5081-6159-2(3),* 5a7b56a0-533e-4b3e-b7c3-2ba49e426f4f, PowerKids Pr.) Rosen Publishing Group, Inc., The.

Colson, Mary. GMOs, 1 vol. 2016. (Cutting-Edge Technology Ser.). (ENG.). 48p. (YA). (gr. 6-8). lib. bdg. 33.60 *(978-1-4824-5157-3(3),* 6bc9bfb6-7191-49ff-b679-80e50ffa0200) Stevens, Gareth Publishing LLLP.

Colvin, L. Living World Encyclopedia. 2009. pap. 14.99 *(978-0-7945-2784-6(1))* EDC Publishing.

Connolly, Randy, et al. Poison Ivy, Pets & People: Scratching the Poison Ivy, Oak & Sumac Itch. 2005. (10thingstoknow about ... Ser.). (Illus.). 104p. pap. 9.95 *(978-0-9722400-1-7(2))* 2Lakes Publishing.

Cook, Trevor. Experiments with Plants & Other Living Things, 1 vol. 2009. (Science Lab Ser.). (ENG.). 32p. (J). (gr. 4-4). lib. bdg. 30.27 *(978-1-4358-2806-3(2),* 12dab627-f167-4724-9575-ff54721c5842, PowerKids Pr.) Rosen Publishing Group, Inc., The.

Crane, Cody. What's That Plant? (a True Book: Incredible Plants!) (Library Edition) 2019. (True Book (Relaunch) Ser.). (ENG., Illus.). 48p. (J). (gr. 3-5). lib. bdg. 31.00 *(978-0-531-23467-9(3),* Children's Pr.) Scholastic Library Publishing.

De la Bédoyère, Camilla. Plants. 2013. (Illus.). 40p. (J). *(978-1-4351-5095-9(3))* Barnes & Noble, Inc.

Delafosse, Claude & Broutin, Christian. Let's Look at the Jungle. Broutin, Christian, illus. 2012. (ENG., Illus.). 38p. (J). (gr. k-3). spiral bd. 11.99 *(978-1-85103-332-4(7))* Moonlight Publishing, Ltd. GBR. Dist: Independent Pubs. Group.

Delta Education. Sci Res Bk Foss Grade 1 Next Gen Ea. 2015. (Illus.). 244p. (J). lib. bdg. *(978-1-62571-445-9(9))* Delta Education, LLC.

—Sci Res Bk Foss Grade 2 Next Gen Ea. 2014. (Illus.). 251p. (J). lib. bdg. *(978-1-62571-446-6(7))* Delta Education, LLC.

Los Desiertos. (Coleccion Planeta Vivo).Tr. of Deserts. (SPA.). (J). (gr. 5-8). 12.00 *(978-84-342-1947-2(6))* Parramon Ediciones S.A. ESP. Dist: Distribuidora Norma, Inc.

Devera, Czeena. In My Backyard. 2019. (I Can See Ser.). (ENG.). 16p. (J). (gr. -1-2). pap. 11.36 *(978-1-5341-3917-6(6),* 212501, Cherry Blossom Press) Cherry Lake Publishing.

DK. Trees, Leaves, Flowers & Seeds: A Visual Encyclopedia of the Plant Kingdom. 2019. (DK Our World in Pictures Ser.). (ENG., Illus.). 192p. (J). (gr. 4-7). 22.99 *(978-1-4654-8242-6(3),* DK Children) Dorling Kindersley Publishing, Inc.

Dodson Wade, Mary. Plants Grow!, 1 vol. 2009. (I Like Plants! Ser.). (ENG., Illus.). 24p. (gr. k-2). pap. 10.35 *(978-0-7660-3612-3(X),* e6a0ee27-d5ad-4193-bd6c-142675436642, Enslow Elementary) Enslow Publishing, LLC.

—Seeds Sprout!, 1 vol. 2009. (I Like Plants! Ser.). (ENG., Illus.). 24p. (gr. k-2). pap. 10.35 *(978-0-7660-3614-7(6),* c671c95c-4b63-406e-85f0-5fc891a28b1c, Enslow Elementary) Enslow Publishing, LLC.

—Trees, Weeds, & Vegetables: So Many Kinds of Plants!, 1 vol. 2009. (I Like Plants! Ser.). (ENG., Illus.). 24p. (gr. k-2). pap. 10.35 *(978-0-7660-3616-1(2),* 55096451-35fa-4b72-9bcc-fc1f3b1e5528, Enslow Elementary); lib. bdg. 25.27 *(978-0-7660-3156-2(X),* 8be6b907-f0ce-463c-84d7-094c9a833193) Enslow Publishing, LLC.

Dorion, Christiane. How Plants & Trees Work: A Hands-On Guide to the Natural World. Young, Beverley, illus. 2017. (Explore the Earth Ser.). (ENG.). 18p. (J). (gr. 2-5). 19.99 *(978-0-7636-9298-8(0),* Templar) Candlewick Pr.

Duke, Shirley. Perennial Plants & Annual Plants Explained, 1 vol. 2016. (Distinctions in Nature Ser.). (ENG., Illus.). 32p. (gr. 3-3). 30.21 *(978-1-5026-1742-2(0),* ef2bd1fc-1e22-4321-8a74-c351bd08c1a5) Cavendish Square Publishing LLC.

Duling, Kaitlyn. A Plant That Eats Spiders & Other Cool Green-And-Growing Facts. 2019. (Mind-Blowing Science Facts Ser.). (ENG., Illus.). 32p. (J). (gr. 4-6). lib. bdg. 28.65 *(978-1-5435-5771-8(6),* 139727) Capstone.

DuneCraft & Soffer, Ruth. DuneCraft Weird & Wacky Plantlife. 2015. (Dover Nature Coloring Book Ser.). (ENG., Illus.). 32p.

(J). (gr. 3-5). pap. 3.99 (978-0-486-79386-3(9), 793869) Dover Pubns., Inc.

Editorial Staff, Gareth. Things at the Park, 1 vol. 2006. (Things in My World Ser.). (ENG., Illus.). 16p. (gr. k-1). pap. 6.30 (978-0-8368-6816-6(1), c39592ac-5429-40dd-b892-06768d2098f4, Weekly Reader Leveled Readers) Stevens, Gareth Publishing LLLP.

—Things at the Park / Las Cosas Del Parque, 1 vol. 2006. (Things in My World / Las Cosas de Mi Mundo Ser.). (ENG & SPA., Illus.). 16p. (gr. k-1). pap. 6.30 (978-0-8368-7228-6(2), e8e86d10-fdc4-4678-8d5f-f5fe7200cdaf, Weekly Reader Leveled Readers) Stevens, Gareth Publishing LLLP.

Edom, Helen. Science with Plants. Abel, Simone, illus. rev. ed. 2007. (Science Activities Ser.). 24p. (J). (gr. 3-7). pap. 5.99 (978-0-7945-1485-3(5), Usborne) EDC Publishing.

Edwards, Nicola. Flowers, 1 vol. 2007. (See How Plants Grow Ser.). (ENG., Illus.). 24p. (J). (gr. 2-2). lib. bdg. 26.27 (978-1-4042-3699-8(6), df9d6b4e-be0e-438a-ad8d-fd084915a46b) Rosen Publishing Group, Inc., The.

Encyclopaedia Britannica, Inc. Staff. Britannica Illustrated Science Library Series (18 Title Series), 18 vols. 2010. 599.00 (978-1-61535-423-8(9)) Encyclopaedia Britannica, Inc.

Encyclopaedia Britannica, Inc. Staff, compiled by. Britannica Illustrated Science Library: Plants, 16 vols. 2008. (Illus.). (J). 29.95 (978-1-59339-394-6(6)) Encyclopaedia Britannica, Inc.

—My First Britannica: Plants. 2008. (gr. 7-12). (978-1-59339-410-3(1)) Encyclopaedia Britannica, Inc.

Encyclopedia Britannica Staff, creator. Plants, Algae, & Fungi. 2011. (Britannica Illustrated Science Library Ser.). 104p. (J). 37.44 (978-1-61535-461-0(1)) Encyclopaedia Britannica, Inc.

Engebretson, Don & Williamson, Don. Annuals for Minnesota & Wisconsin, 1 vol., Vol. 1. rev. ed. 2004. (ENG., Illus.). 296p. (gr. 4). pap. 19.95 (978-1-55105-381-3(0), e87bccb6-6d65-4f00-8534-88f1b9b7cfff) Lone Pine Publishing USA.

Farndon, John. Flowers. 2005. 24p. (J). (gr. 2-4). pap. 22.45 (978-1-4103-0517-6(1), Blackbirch Pr., Inc.) Cengage Gale.

Felix, Rebecca. What Happens to Plants in Summer? 2014. (21st Century Basic Skills Library: Let's Look at Summer Ser.). (ENG., Illus.). 24p. (J). (gr. k-3). 26.35 (978-1-63137-603-0(9), 205195) Cherry Lake Publishing.

—What Happens to Plants in Winter? 2014. (21st Century Basic Skills Library: Let's Look at Winter Ser.). (ENG., Illus.). 24p. (J). (gr. k-3). 26.35 (978-1-63137-608-5(X), 205215) Cherry Lake Publishing.

Ferrie, Chris. 8 Little Planets. Doyle, Lizzy, illus. 2018. 18p. (J). (gr. -1-k). bds. 10.99 (978-1-4926-7124-4(X)) Sourcebooks, Inc.

Fleisher, Paul. Forest Food Webs in Action. 2013. (Searchlight Books (tm) — What Is a Food Web? Ser.). (ENG., Illus.). 40p. (J). (gr. 3-5). pap. 9.99 (978-1-4677-1553-9(0), 295e0025-bd15-44ff-b5d6-a2db5b9d0066) Lerner Publishing Group.

—Grassland Food Webs in Action. 2013. (Searchlight Books (tm) — What Is a Food Web? Ser.). (ENG., Illus.). 40p. (J). (gr. 3-5). pap. 9.99 (978-1-4677-1554-6(9), 77dfc86f-5e84-4030-9009-bffa92fa930a); lib. bdg. 30.65 (978-1-4677-1293-4(0), 0aed10a8-abe3-4830-9b4f-aeb50c8a2ee2, Lerner Pubns.) Lerner Publishing Group.

Forshaw, Nick. Plants! Exley, William, illus. 2019. (Explorer Ser.). (ENG.). 38p. (J). 14.95 (978-0-9955770-8-4(0)) What on Earth Bks GBR. Dist: Ingram Publisher Services.

Fortuna, Lois. Growing Plants, 1 vol. 2015. (We Can Do It! Ser.). (ENG., Illus.). 24p. (J). (gr. k-k). pap. 9.15 (978-1-4824-3803-1(8), 4e567fe7-6576-4457-a9a4-1d7ae1ebed3d) Stevens, Gareth Publishing LLLP.

La Fresa. (Coleccion Ciclos Vitales). (SPA., Illus.). (J). (gr. 3-5). pap. (978-84-236-2653-3(9), ED4700) Edebé ESP. Dist: Lectorum Pubns., Inc.

Fuhr, Ute. Let's Look at the Rainforest. Sautai, Raoul, illus. 2012. (ENG.). 38p. (J). (gr. 1-4). spiral bd. 11.99 (978-1-85103-360-7(2)) Moonlight Publishing, Ltd. GBR. Dist: Independent Pubs. Group.

Gaertner, Meg. Spring Plants. 2020. (Spring Is Here Ser.). (ENG., Illus.). 16p. (J). (gr. k-1). 25.64 (978-1-64493-023-6(4), 1644930234, Focus Readers) North Star Editions.

Gagliano, Eugene. V Is for Venus Flytrap: A Plant Alphabet. Traynor, Elizabeth, illus. 2009. (Science Alphabet Ser.). (ENG.). 40p. (J). (gr. 1-4). 17.95 (978-1-58536-350-6(2), 202137) Sleeping Bear Pr.

Gaines, Alison. Invasive Plants & Birds, 1 vol. 2016. (Invasive Species Ser.). (ENG., Illus.). 48p. (gr. 4-4). 33.07 (978-1-5026-1834-4(6), 255b9437-e088-4187-a2db-8ae2fa06ab7f) Cavendish Square Publishing LLC.

Gallagher, Belinda. British Garden Life Handbook. Kelly, Richard, ed. 2017. (ENG., Illus.). 224p. (J). pap. 14.99 (978-1-78209-128-8(9)) Miles Kelly Publishing, Ltd. GBR. Dist: Parkwest Pubns., Inc.

Ganeri, Anita. All Kinds of Plants Blue Band. 2016. (Cambridge Reading Adventures Ser.). (ENG., Illus.). 16p. pap. 7.95 (978-1-316-60579-0(5)) Cambridge Univ. Pr.

Garassino, Alessandro. Las Plantas. (SPA.). 40p. (YA). (gr. 5-8). 10.36 (978-84-207-5190-0(1)) Grupo Anaya, S.A. ESP. Dist: Lectorum Pubns., Inc.

Gardner, Robert. Experimenting with Plants Science Projects, 1 vol. 2013. (Exploring Hands-On Science Projects Ser.). (ENG.). 128p. (gr. 5-6). 30.60 (978-0-7660-4144-8(1), c42715f4-3e95-49a8-9360-3b5be576efef); pap. 13.88 (978-1-4644-0220-3(5), 2de183d7-e580-454f-bdda-37f7eb465c5f) Enslow Publishing, LLC.

Gardner, Robert & Perry, Phyllis J. Ace Your Plant Science Project: Great Science Fair Ideas, 1 vol. 2009. (Ace Your Biology Science Project Ser.). (ENG., Illus.). 104p. (gr. 5-6). lib. bdg. 35.93 (978-0-7660-3221-7(3), b42cfa45-7169-46fe-afd0-d0d729d41ab9) Enslow Publishing, LLC.

Gibbons, Gail. From Seed to Plant. Gibbons, Gail, illus. 2012. (Illus.). audio compact disk 18.95 (978-1-4301-1079-8(1)) Live Oak Media.

Gibbs, Maddie. Types of Plants, 1 vol. 2018. (Let's Find Out! Plants Ser.). (ENG.). 32p. (gr. 2-3). lib. bdg. 26.06 (978-1-5383-0201-9(2), 86778697-96e8-4031-b91b-23d25cde721f, Britannica Educational Publishing) Rosen Publishing Group, Inc., The.

Gleisner, Jenna Lee. Plants in Winter. 2018. (Welcoming the Seasons Ser.). (ENG.). 24p. (J). (gr. -1-2). lib. bdg. 32.79 (978-1-5038-2388-4(1), 212231) Child's World, Inc, The.

—What Blossoms in Spring? 2014. (21st Century Basic Skills Library: Let's Look at Spring Ser.). (ENG.). 24p. (J). (gr. k-3). pap. 12.79 (978-1-62431-686-9(7), 203149); (Illus.). 26.35 (978-1-62431-659-3(X), 203148) Cherry Lake Publishing.

Gleisner, Jenna Lee & Willis, John. Plants. 2018. (J). (978-1-4896-9580-2(X), AV2 by Weigl) Weigl Pubs., Inc.

Goldsworthy, Kaite. Producers. 2016. (Illus.). 24p. (J). (978-1-4896-5779-4(7)) 2011. (J). (gr. 4-6). pap. 12.95 (978-1-61690-716-7(9), AV2 by Weigl) 2011. (Illus.). 24p. (YA). (gr. 2-5). 27.13 (978-1-61690-710-5(X)) Weigl Pubs., Inc.

Goodman, Emily. Plant Secrets. Tildes, Phyllis Limbacher, illus. 2009. (ENG.). 40p. (J). (gr. -1-3). pap. 7.95 (978-1-58089-205-6(1)) Charlesbridge Publishing, Inc.

Grack, Rachel. Bulb to Tulip. 2020. (Beginning to End Ser.). (ENG.). 24p. (J). (gr. k-3). lib. bdg. 26.95 (978-1-64487-137-9(8), Blastoff! Readers) Bellwether Media.

Gray, Judy Silverstein. How Plants Reproduce, 1 vol. 2018. (Let's Find Out! Plants Ser.). (ENG.). 32p. (gr. 2-3). lib. bdg. 26.06 (978-1-5383-0193-7(8), 20ba2732-5b4a-4baf-a351-85f9695c4515, Britannica Educational Publishing) Rosen Publishing Group, Inc., The.

Gray, Leon. Plant Classification, 1 vol. 2013. (Life Science Stories Ser.). (ENG., Illus.). 32p. (J). (gr. 3-4). pap. 11.50 (978-1-4339-8720-5(1), c98003aa-e88d-4e99-9ed3-719429c471e2); lib. bdg. 29.27 (978-1-4339-8719-9(8), e91faacb-3ea7-44cf-a827-0819be47bdaf) Stevens, Gareth Publishing LLLP.

Gray, Rita. Flowers Are Calling. Pak, Kenard, illus. 2015. (ENG.). 32p. (J). (gr. -1-3). 17.99 (978-0-544-34012-1(4), 1584710, Clarion Bks.) HarperCollins Pubs.

Gray, Susan H. Junior Scientists: Experiment with Plants. 2010. (Explorer Junior Library: Science Explorer Junior Ser.). (ENG., Illus.). 32p. (gr. 3-6). lib. bdg. 32.07 (978-1-60279-839-7(7), 200544) Cherry Lake Publishing.

—Plants. 2009. (Explorer Library: Science Explorer Ser.). (ENG., Illus.). 32p. (gr. 4-8). lib. bdg. 32.07 (978-1-60279-522-8(3), 200286) Cherry Lake Publishing.

Green, Jen. Projects with Plants, 1 vol. 2014. (Make & Learn Ser.). (ENG., Illus.). 32p. (J). (gr. 4-4). 29.27 (978-1-4777-7161-7(1), bebb6453-94d0-4741-b280-30dccd89109c, PowerKids Pr.) Rosen Publishing Group, Inc., The.

A Green Kid's Guide to Gardening!, 5 vols. 2013. (Green Kid's Guide to Gardening! Ser.: 6). (ENG.). 24p. (J). (gr. -1-4). lib. bdg. 156.80 (978-1-61641-942-4(3), 9335, Looking Glass Library) Magic Wagon.

Gregoire, Maryellen. We All Need Plants, 1 vol. 2011. (Wonder Readers Early Level Ser.). (ENG.). 16p. (gr. -1-1). (J). pap. 6.25 (978-1-4296-7878-0(X), 118210); pap. 35.94 (978-1-4296-8200-8(0)) Capstone. (Capstone Pr.).

Gregory, Josh. Why We Need Plants (a True Book: Incredible Plants!) (Library Edition) 2019. (True Book (Relaunch) Ser.). (ENG., Illus.). 48p. (J). (gr. 3-5). lib. bdg. 31.00 (978-0-531-23466-2(5), Children's Pr.) Scholastic Library Publishing.

Griffiths, Rachel. Why Do Leaves Change Colour? Level 3 Factbook. 2010. (Cambridge Young Readers Ser.). (ENG., Illus.). 16p. pap. 6.00 (978-0-521-13715-7(2)) Cambridge Univ. Pr.

Group/McGraw-Hill, Wright. Donde Viven Algunos Animales, 6 vols. (First Explorers. Primeros Exploradores Nonfiction Sets Ser.). (SPA.). (gr. 1-2). 29.95 (978-0-7699-1472-5(1)) Shortland Pubns. (U. S. A.) Inc.

—El Mundo de Las Plantas, 6 vols. (First Explorers. Primeros Exploradores Nonfiction Sets Ser.). (SPA.). (gr. 1-2). 29.95 (978-0-7699-1474-9(8)) Shortland Pubns. (U. S. A.) Inc.

Grunbaum, Mara. Plant Life Cycles (a True Book: Incredible Plants!) (Library Edition) 2019. (True Book (Relaunch) Ser.). (ENG., Illus.). 48p. (J). (gr. 3-5). lib. bdg. 31.00 (978-0-531-23465-5(7), Children's Pr.) Scholastic Library Publishing.

Hainnu, Rebecca & Ziegler, Anna. A Walk on the Tundra, 1 vol. Leng, Qin, illus. 2018. (ENG.). 40p. (J). (gr. 1-3). 12.95 (978-1-77227-185-0(3)) Inhabit Media Inc. CAN. Dist: Consortium Bk. Sales & Distribution.

Hamalainen, Karina. Crazy Plants (a True Book: Incredible Plants!) (Library Edition) 2019. (True Book (Relaunch) Ser.). (ENG.). 48p. (J). (gr. 3-5). lib. bdg. 31.00 (978-0-531-23462-4(2), Children's Pr.) Scholastic Library Publishing.

Harkrader, Lisa. Unusual Plants. 2016. (Spring Forward Ser.). (J). (gr. 1). (978-1-4900-2243-7(0)) Benchmark Education Co.

Heddle, Becca. Plants, Pollen & Pollinators: Band 13/Topaz (Collins Big Cat) 2016. (Collins Big Cat Ser.). (ENG., Illus.). 32p. (J). (gr. 2-3). pap. 10.95 (978-0-00-816385-3(5)) HarperCollins Pubs. Ltd. GBR. Dist: Independent Pubs. Group.

Hedegaard, Lise. Plants in Disguise: Features of Creatures in Flowers & Foliage. Schmid, Debi, illus. 2017. (J). 15.00 (978-0-87842-673-7(6)) Mountain Pr. Publishing Co., Inc.

Heller, Ruth. The Reason for a Flower. (FRE.). (J). 6.99 (978-0-590-71999-5(8)) Scholastic, Inc.

Heos, Bridget. Just Like Us! Plants. Clark, David, illus. (Just Like Us! Ser.). (ENG.). 32p. (J). (gr. -1-3). 2019. pap. 7.99 (978-0-358-00388-5(1), 1736320) 2018. 14.99 (978-0-544-57094-8(4), 1612571) HarperCollins Pubs. (Clarion Bks.).

Hewitt, Sally. Amazing Plants. 2007. (Amazing Science Ser.). (ENG.). 32p. (J). pap. (978-0-7787-3628-8(8)) Crabtree Publishing Co.

—Plants. (Illus.). 32p. (YA). (gr. 2-18). lib. bdg. 27.10 (978-1-932333-30-5(4)) Chrysalis Education.

Higgins, Nadia. Experiment with a Plant's Living Environment. 2015. (Lightning Bolt Books (r) — Plant Experiments Ser.). (ENG., Illus.). 32p. (J). (gr. 1-3). pap. 9.99 (978-1-4677-6072-0(2), 3ec044bf-02b8-4c15-b52e-4bbc28d6a3ab) Lerner Publishing Group.

Hileman, Jane. The Life of a Dandelion. 2016. (1G Our Natural World Ser.). (ENG., Illus.). 20p. (J). pap. 8.00 (978-1-63437-411-8(8)) American Reading Co.

Hill, Christina. Inside a Plant, 1 vol. rev. ed. 2014. (Science: Informational Text Ser.). (ENG., Illus.). 24p. (gr. 1-2). lib. bdg. 22.96 (978-1-4938-1147-2(9)); pap. 9.99 (978-1-4807-4560-5(X)) Teacher Created Materials, Inc.

—What Makes a Plant?, 1 vol. rev. ed. 2014. (Science: Informational Text Ser.). (ENG., Illus.). 24p. (gr. 1-2). pap. 9.99 (978-1-4807-4559-9(6)) Teacher Created Materials, Inc.

Hirsch, Rebecca. The Life Cycles of Plants. 2011. (Explorer Library: Language Arts Explorer Ser.). (ENG.). 32p. (gr. 4-8). pap. 14.21 (978-1-61080-293-2(4), 201215) Cherry Lake Publishing.

—Science Lab: the Life Cycles of Plants. 2011. (Explorer Library: Language Arts Explorer Ser.). (ENG., Illus.). 32p. (gr. 4-8). lib. bdg. 32.07 (978-1-61080-204-8(7), 201184) Cherry Lake Publishing.

Hirsch, Rebecca E. Plants Can't Sit Still. Posada, Mia, illus. 2016. (ENG.). 32p. (J). (gr. k-4). 19.99 (978-1-4677-8031-5(6), dde7e872-4ac4-4bf5-9e8d-9f22718c1f02); E-Book 30.65 (978-1-5124-1109-6(4)) Lerner Publishing Group. (Millbrook Pr.).

Hirschmann, Kris. Real Life Zombies. 2013. (Illus.). 32p. (J). (978-0-545-53563-2(8)) Scholastic, Inc.

Hodge, Judith. Plants We Use: Set Of 6. 2010. (Navigators Ser.). (J). 48.00 net. (978-1-4108-0435-8(6)) Benchmark Education Co.

—Plants We Use & Las plantas que Usamos: 6 English, 6 Spanish Adaptations. 2011. (ENG & SPA.). (J). 97.00 net. (978-1-4108-5708-8(5)) Benchmark Education Co.

Hoff, Mary. Pollination. 2003. (World of Wonder Ser.). (Illus.). 32p. (J). lib. bdg. (978-1-58341-270-1(0), Creative Education) Creative Co., The.

Hoffman, Mary Ann. Plant Experiments: What Affects Plant Growth?, 1 vol. (Look at Life Science Ser.). (ENG.). 24p. (gr. 3-3). 2009. (J). lib. bdg. 26.27 (978-1-4358-2971-8(9), 0fc7de98-ee46-4903-add8-a5679043538c, PowerKids Pr.) 2008. pap. 8.25 (978-1-4358-0131-8(8), 026b8619-2305-4a84-9a05-a9a9a786bbf3, Rosen Classroom) Rosen Publishing Group, Inc., The.

Hoffmann, Sara E. Kinds of Flowers. 2012. (First Step Nonfiction — Kinds of Plants Ser.). (ENG., Illus.). 8p. (J). (gr. k-2). pap. 5.99 (978-1-4677-0500-4(4), b7c8e392-b36f-4b32-ae0f-19349a80960b) Lerner Publishing Group.

Hollar, Sherman. A Closer Look at Plant Classifications, Parts, & Uses, 1 vol. 2011. (Introduction to Biology Ser.). (ENG.). 88p. (J). (gr. 8-8). lib. bdg. 35.29 (978-1-61530-529-2(7), a0004127-2b10-4774-8d53-5700d0f9b227) Rosen Publishing Group, Inc., The.

Holmes, Porter. Plants in My Pond, 1 vol. 2017. (Plants in My World Ser.). (ENG.). 24p. (gr. 1-1). pap. 9.25 (978-1-5383-2124-9(6), 2da6da22-0043-4d10-aa96-e0c79925c52b, PowerKids Pr.) Rosen Publishing Group, Inc., The.

Holt, Rinehart and Winston Staff. Holt Science & Technology Chapter 12: Life Science: Introduction to Plants. 5th ed. 2004. (Illus.). pap. 12.86 (978-0-03-030216-9(1)) Holt McDougal.

Hotchkins, Dewayne. The Biggest Tomato, 1 vol. 2016. (Rosen REAL Readers: STEM & STEAM Collection). (ENG.). 12p. (gr. 1-2). pap. 6.33 (978-1-5081-2673-7(9), a0483dc6-bec7-4fb3-b2a4-1e39b92fa98f, Rosen Classroom) Rosen Publishing Group, Inc., The.

Huntington, Harriet E. Forest Giants: The Story of the California Redwoods. 2011. 52p. 36.95 (978-1-258-02773-5(9)) Literary Licensing, LLC.

Iasevoli, Brenda, told to. Plants! 2006. (Time for Kids Science Scoops Ser.). (ENG., Illus.). 32p. (J). (gr. 1-3). 14.99 (978-0-06-078219-1(6)) HarperCollins Pubs.

Jacobs, Pat. Why Do Plants Have Flowers? And Other Questions about Evolution & Classification, 1 vol. 2016. (Wildlife Wonders Ser.). (ENG.). 32p. (J). (gr. 3-3). 27.93 (978-1-4994-3273-2(9), dc2895ff-a191-4c7e-a2c8-1886213cfd3f, PowerKids Pr.) Rosen Publishing Group, Inc., The.

James, Wayan. Food for Plants, 1 vol. 2016. (Rosen REAL Readers: STEM & STEAM Collection). (ENG.). 8p. (gr. k-1). pap. 5.46 (978-1-5081-2377-4(2), aef0935c-00bd-43d2-a50c-6b72da13c114, Rosen Classroom) Rosen Publishing Group, Inc., The.

Jennings, Dorothy. Our Flower Garden, 1 vol. 2017. (Plants in My World Ser.). (ENG.). 24p. (gr. 1-1). pap. 9.25 (978-1-5383-2117-1(3), d4b71621-c084-4ed4-8980-23b7fa1a0fc8, PowerKids Pr.) Rosen Publishing Group, Inc., The.

Jennings, Rosemary. I Can Grow Plants!, 1 vol. 2012. (InfoMax Readers Ser.). (ENG., Illus.). 24p. (J). (gr. 1-1). pap. 8.25 (978-1-4488-8989-1(8), 5676dc9e-3401-4296-a74e-cb487b442d97, Rosen Classroom) Rosen Publishing Group, Inc., The.

Johnson, Terry. Growing New Plants. 2008. (21st Century Junior Library: Plants Ser.). (ENG., Illus.). 24p. (gr. 2-5). lib. bdg. 29.21 (978-1-60279-279-1(8), 200183) Cherry Lake Publishing.

Kallio, Jamie. 12 Things to Know about Invasive Species. 2015. (Today's News Ser.). (ENG., Illus.). 32p. (J). (gr. 3-6). 32.80 (978-1-63235-030-5(0), 11608, 12-Story Library) Bookstaves, LLC.

Kalman, Bobbie. The ABCs of Plants, 1 vol. 2007. (ABCs of the Natural World Ser.). (ENG., Illus.). 32p. (J). (gr. 1-4). pap. (978-0-7787-3433-8(1)) Crabtree Publishing Co.

—Los Animales Crecen y Cambian. 2008.Tr. of Plants are Living Things. (SPA.). 24p. (J). pap. (978-0-7787-8686-3(2)) Crabtree Publishing Co.

—¿Cómo Se Mueve? 2009. (SPA.). 24p. (J). (978-0-7787-8704-4(4)); pap. (978-0-7787-8743-3(5)) Crabtree Publishing Co.

—How Do Plants Help Us? 2011. (ENG.). 16p. (J). pap. (978-0-7787-9586-5(1)); lib. bdg. (978-0-7787-9561-2(6)) Crabtree Publishing Co.

—How Does It Move? 2008. (Looking at Nature Ser.). (ENG., Illus.). 24p. (J). (gr. -1-2). pap. (978-0-7787-3342-3(4)); lib. bdg. (978-0-7787-3322-5(X)) Crabtree Publishing Co.

—Plants Are Living Things, 1 vol. 2007. (Introducing Living Things Ser.). (ENG., Illus.). 24p. (J). (gr. 1-4). pap. (978-0-7787-3257-0(6)) Crabtree Publishing Co.

—?Que Son Las Plantas? 2005. (Ciencia de los Seres Vivos Ser.). (SPA., Illus.). 32p. (J). (gr. 3-4). lib. bdg. (978-0-7787-8759-4(1)) Crabtree Publishing Co.

—¿Qué Son Las Plantas? 2005. (Ciencia de los Seres Vivos Ser.). (SPA., Illus.). 32p. (J). (gr. 7-12). pap. (978-0-7787-8805-8(9)) Crabtree Publishing Co.

Kalman, Bobbie & Sjonger, Rebecca. Plants in Different Habitats, 1 vol. 2006. (Nature's Changes Ser.). (ENG., Illus.). 32p. (J). (gr. 4-7). pap. (978-0-7787-2316-5(X)) Crabtree Publishing Co.

Kavanagh, James & Waterford Press Staff. My First Arctic: Nature Activity Book. Leung, Raymond, illus. 2011. (Nature Activity Book Ser.). (ENG.). 32p. (J). (gr. -1-8). pap., act. bk. ed. 6.95 (978-1-58355-586-6(2)) Waterford Pr., Inc.

Kenah, Katharine. Weird & Wacky Plants, Level 3. 2005. (Extreme Readers Level 3 - Confident Reader Ser.). (ENG., Illus.). 32p. (gr. k-3). 16.19 (978-0-7696-3184-4(3)) School Specialty, Incorporated.

Kim, Cecil. One Little Bean: Observation - Life Cycle. Dattola, Chiara, illus. 2015. (Step up — Creative Thinking Ser.). (ENG.). 32p. (J). (gr. -1-2). 27.99 (978-1-925186-40-6(7), cae3efbf-9a34-4817-b745-df19be9c2a4d, Big and SMALL) ChoiceMaker Pty. Ltd., The AUS. Dist: Lerner Publishing Group.

Kinsner, Kathy. Amazing Plants. 2004. (Shared Connections Ser.). (J). pap. (978-1-4108-1647-4(8)); instr.'s gde. ed. 27.00 (978-1-4108-1623-8(0)) Benchmark Education Co.

Knapke, Debra & Beck, Alison. Annuals for Ohio, 1 vol. rev. ed. 2003. (ENG., Illus.). 296p. (gr. 4). pap. 18.95 (978-1-55105-388-2(8), 61740626-ed86-4765-a0a5-f9b3d6a8c458) Lone Pine Publishing USA.

—Perennials for Ohio, 1 vol. rev. ed. 2003. (ENG., Illus.). 352p. (gr. 4). pap. 19.95 (978-1-55105-386-8(1), ff61de41-d64d-4aba-a4a1-15daf8afd5b7) Lone Pine Publishing USA.

Kochanoff, Peggy. Be a City Nature Detective: Solving the Mysteries of How Plants & Animals Survive in the Urban Jungle, 1 vol. 2018. (Be a Nature Detective Ser.). (ENG., Illus.). 56p. (J). (gr. 1-3). pap. 14.95 (978-1-77108-572-4(X), 3a4ae7f0-44fa-4d06-a3d6-cf305e5aaeb4) Nimbus Publishing, Ltd. CAN. Dist: Baker & Taylor Publisher Services (BTPS).

Krezel, Cindy. 101 Kid-Friendly Plants: Fun Plants & Family Garden Projects. 2008. (ENG., Illus.). 160p. (J). (gr. 1-7). pap. 19.95 (978-1-883052-54-6(8)) Chicago Review Pr., Inc.

Kuskowski, Alex. Hanging Gardens: A Kid's Guide to Gardening. 2015. (Super Simple Gardening Ser.). (ENG.). 32p. (J). (gr. k-4). 34.21 (978-1-62403-523-4(X), 17329, Super SandCastle) ABDO Publishing Co.

Lawrence, Ellen. Freaky Plant Facts: Extreme Greens. 2012. (Science Slam: Plant-Ology Ser.). 24p. (J). (gr. -1-3). lib. bdg. 26.99 (978-1-61772-591-3(9)) Bearport Publishing Co., Inc.

—How Plants Clean the Air. 2014. (Science Slam: Plant-Ology Ser.). (ENG.). 24p. (J). (gr. -1-3). lib. bdg. 26.99 (978-1-62724-305-6(4)) Bearport Publishing Co., Inc.

—Plants. 2016. (FUN-Damental Experiments Ser.). (ENG., Illus.). 24p. (J). (gr. -1-3). 26.99 (978-1-943553-17-4(3)) Bearport Publishing Co., Inc.

—Why Do Most Plants Need Soil? 2015. (Down & Dirty Ser.). (ENG., Illus.). 24p. (J). (gr. -1-3). lib. bdg. 26.99 (978-1-62724-837-2(4)) Bearport Publishing Co., Inc.

Lay, Richard & Zarrinnaal, Laura Nienhaus. A Green Kid's Guide to Watering Plants, 1 vol. 2013. (Green Kid's Guide to Gardening! Ser.). (ENG.). 24p. (J). (gr. -1-4). 31.36 (978-1-61641-948-6(2), 9347, Looking Glass Library) Magic Wagon.

Leedy, Loreen & Schuerger, Andrew. Amazing Plant Powers: How Plants Fly, Fight, Hide, Hunt, & Change the World. 32p. (J). (gr. -1-3). 2018. pap. 8.99 (978-0-8234-4047-4(8)) 2015. (ENG., Illus.). 17.95 (978-0-8234-2256-2(9)) Holiday Hse., Inc.

Legg, Gerald & Weston, Steve. The World of Plant Life. 2012. (ENG., Illus.). 48p. (J). 15.00 (978-1-899762-75-0(2)) Award Pubns. Ltd. GBR. Dist: Parkwest Pubns., Inc.

LernerClassroom Editors. Plant Life Cycles. 2009. (Illus.). pap. 7.95 (978-0-8225-4786-0(4)) Lerner Publishing Group.

Levine, Shar. Plants: Flowering Plants, Ferns, Mosses, & Other Plants. 2010. (Class of Their Own Ser.). (ENG., Illus.). 48p. (J). (gr. 5-8). pap. (978-0-7787-5390-2(5)); lib. bdg. (978-0-7787-5376-6(X)) Crabtree Publishing Co.

Levy, Janey. Dragon Arum Smells Awful!, 1 vol. 2019. (World's Weirdest Plants Ser.). (ENG.). 24p. (J). (gr. 2-3). pap. 9.15 (978-1-5382-4638-2(4), 6a78eea0-7bd4-4bb8-b760-55e8f7553cda) Stevens, Gareth Publishing LLLP.

—Dragon's Blood Trees Bleed!, 1 vol. 2019. (World's Weirdest Plants Ser.). (ENG.). 24p. (gr. 2-3). pap. 9.15 (978-1-5382-4642-9(2), 398ba70c-1f9a-47ca-ad6b-f6aad17e6efd) Stevens, Gareth Publishing LLLP.

—Freaky Stories about Plants, 1 vol. 2016. (Freaky True Science Ser.). (ENG., Illus.). 32p. (J). (gr. 4-5). pap. 11.50 (978-1-4824-4831-3(9), a100f90b-2264-4c93-abd2-198bf7d8ebcb) Stevens, Gareth Publishing LLLP.

—How Invasive Species Take Over, 1 vol. 2019. (Top Secret Life of Plants Ser.). (ENG.). 24p. (gr. 2-3). pap. 9.15 (978-1-5382-3375-7(4), a7fabffd-b7c2-4644-9083-8e943771783c) Stevens, Gareth Publishing LLLP.

—Life in a Rain Forest Ecosystem, 1 vol. (Science Scope Ser.). (ENG.). 32p. (J). (gr. 5-5). 2009. lib. bdg. 28.93 (978-1-4358-2997-8(2), f33ed6b8-b3a2-42dd-b3d2-3a0d5760c8d0) 2008. (Illus.). pap. 10.00 (978-1-4358-0189-9(X), 11d1d291-344f-42ed-a4a3-e1069c36a10a) Rosen Publishing Group, Inc., The. (PowerKids Pr.).

—Plants That Grow Without Soil, 1 vol. 2019. (Top Secret Life of Plants Ser.). (ENG.). 24p. (gr. 2-3). pap. 9.15 (978-1-5382-3395-5(9),

7f84120f-66a8-4ea1-9538-2fa31dbdeb79) Stevens, Gareth Publishing LLLP.

Lilly, Melinda. Make It Grow. Thompson, Scott M., illus. 2003. (Rourke Discovery Library). 24p. (J). 22.79 (978-1-58952-637-2(6)) Rourke Educational Media.

Linde, Barbara M. Pitcher Plants Eat Meat!, 1 vol. 2016. (World's Weirdest Plants Ser.). (ENG.). 24p. (J). (gr. 2-3). pap. 9.15 (978-1-4824-5632-5(X), fba71078-96c1-48bf-8156-04f4476370ad) Stevens, Gareth Publishing LLLP.

Lindeen, Mary. Animals Help Plants. 2018. (BeginningtoRead Ser.). (ENG.). 32p. (J). (gr. -1-2). lib. bdg. 22.60 (978-1-59953-902-7(0)); (gr. k-2). pap. 13.26 (978-1-68404-149-7(X)) Norwood Hse. Pr.

—What Plants Need. 2018. (BeginningtoRead Ser.). (ENG.). 32p. (J). (gr. -1-2). lib. bdg. 22.60 (978-1-59953-898-3(9)); (gr. k-2). pap. 13.26 (978-1-68404-145-9(7)) Norwood Hse. Pr.

Lindström, Karin. Tiny Life on Plants. (Rookie Read-About Science Ser.). (ENG., Illus.). 32p. (J). (gr. 1-2). 2006. per. 4.95 (978-0-516-25478-4(2)) 2005. lib. bdg. 20.50 (978-0-516-25297-1(6)) Scholastic Library Publishing. (Children's Pr.).

Littlefield, Angie & Littlefield, Jennifer. The 10 Deadliest Plants. 2007. (J). 14.99 (978-1-55448-511-6(8)) Scholastic Library Publishing.

Llewellyn, Claire. How Plants Grow. 2006. (I Know That, Growth & Change Set Ser.). (Illus.). 24p. (J). lib. bdg. 24.25 (978-1-59771-021-3(0)) Sea-To-Sea Pubns.

—The Life of Plants. 2007. (Understanding Plants/Watts Ser.). (Illus.). 30p. (YA). (gr. 2-5). lib. bdg. 28.50 (978-1-59920-033-0(3)) Black Rabbit Bks.

—Plants of the World. 2007. (Understanding Plants/Watts Ser.). (Illus.). 30p. (YA). (gr. 2-5). lib. bdg. 28.50 (978-1-59920-032-3(5)) Black Rabbit Bks.

Loewer, Peter. The Moonflower, 1 vol. Loewer, Jean, illus. rev. ed. 2019. 32p. (J). (gr. -1-3). pap. 7.95 (978-1-68263-101-0(X)) Peachtree Publishing Co. Inc.

Lomberg, Michelle. Plant Cells. 2016. (Illus.). 32p. (J). (978-1-5105-1188-0(1)) SmartBook Media, Inc.

Long, Erin. Plants & Their Environments, 1 vol. 2016. (Spotlight on Ecology & Life Science Ser.). (ENG.). 24p. (J). (gr. 4-6). pap. 11.00 (978-1-4994-2587-1(2), 5ebe792f-5595-4d5e-bad1-f7599fe1eb64, PowerKids Pr.) Rosen Publishing Group, Inc., The.

Loukopoulos, Beatrice. Plants That Are Huge, 1 vol. 2018. (Peculiar Plants of the World Ser.). (ENG.). 24p. (J). (gr. 3-3). 25.27 (978-1-5383-4488-0(2), d45b6a79-3267-4829-929b-17aecb345656, PowerKids Pr.) Rosen Publishing Group, Inc., The.

Lundgren, Julie K. Plant Adaptations. 2011. (My Science Library). (ENG., Illus.). 24p. (gr. 1-2). pap. 9.95 (978-1-61741-937-9(0), 9781617419379) Rourke Educational Media.

—Plant Life Cycles. 2011. (My Science Library). (ENG., Illus.). 24p. (gr. 1-2). pap. 9.95 (978-1-61741-936-2(2), 9781617419362) Rourke Educational Media.

—Seeds, Bees, & Pollen. 2011. (My Science Library). (ENG., Illus.). 24p. (gr. 2-3). pap. 9.95 (978-1-61741-950-8(8), 9781617419508) Rourke Educational Media.

Lynch, Wayne. The Arctic. Lynch, Wayne, photos by. 2007. (Our Wild World Ser.). (ENG., Illus.). 64p. (J). (gr. 3-7). pap. 8.95 (978-1-55971-961-2(3)) Cooper Square Publishing Llc.

Lynette, Rachel. Plants, 1 vol. 2012. (Science Behind Ser.). (ENG., Illus.). 32p. (J). (gr. 2-4). pap. 8.29 (978-1-4109-4495-5(6), 117688, Raintree) Capstone.

MacAulay, Kelley. How Do Plants Survive? 2013. (ENG., Illus.). 24p. (J). (978-0-7787-1285-5(0)); pap. (978-0-7787-0003-6(8)) Crabtree Publishing Co.

Macceca, Michael L. The World of Plants, 1 vol. rev. ed. 2007. (Science: Informational Text Ser.). (ENG.). 32p. (gr. 3-6). pap. 12.99 (978-0-7439-0589-3(X)) Teacher Created Materials, Inc.

MacDonald, Margaret. Spring Plants. 2011. (Learn-Abouts Ser.). (Illus.). 16p. (J). pap. 7.95 (978-1-59920-651-6(X)) Black Rabbit Bks.

Machajewski, Sarah. How Plants Communicate, 1 vol. 2018. (Let's Find Out! Plants Ser.). (ENG.). 32p. (gr. 2-3). lib. bdg. 26.06 (978-1-5383-0185-2(7), 890637fd-8389-4d23-9e75-fd6c11dd9667, Britannica Educational Publishing) Rosen Publishing Group, Inc., The.

—How Plants Protect Themselves, 1 vol. 2019. (Top Secret Life of Plants Ser.). (ENG.). 24p. (gr. 2-3). pap. 9.15 (978-1-5382-3379-5(7), 695e94ab-82d1-43ef-8875-0539d0282cda) Stevens, Gareth Publishing LLLP.

—We Need Plants, 1 vol. 2015. (Creatures We Can't Live Without Ser.). (ENG.). 24p. (J). (gr. 3-4). 25.27 (978-1-4994-1042-6(5), 0eb10005-cf9e-4528-b777-89c8cccd059a, PowerKids Pr.) Rosen Publishing Group, Inc., The.

Mack, Molly. Plants That Move, 1 vol. 2016. (Plant Defenses Ser.). (ENG.). 24p. (J). (gr. 3-3). pap. 9.25 (978-1-4994-2147-7(8), a709dc90-6526-4181-a395-438b40055bd7, PowerKids Pr.) Rosen Publishing Group, Inc., The.

Madgwick, Wendy. Animals & Plants: 10 Easy-to-Follow Experiments for Learning Fun - Find Out about Nature & How Things Live! 2014. (Illus.). 270p. (J). (gr. -1-12). 8.99 (978-1-86147-349-3(4), Armadillo) Anness Publishing GBR. Dist: National Bk. Network.

Maloof, Torrey. Photosynthesis, 1 vol. 2015. (Science: Informational Text Ser.). (ENG., Illus.). 32p. (gr. 3-4). pap. 11.99 (978-1-4807-4640-4(1)) Teacher Created Materials, Inc.

Mann, Rachel. Plants Grow from Seeds, 6 vols., Set. 2003. (Phonics Readers 1-36 Ser.). (ENG.). 8p. (gr. k-1). pap. 29.70 (978-0-7368-3207-6(6)) Capstone.

El Manzano. (Coleccion Ciclos Vitales). (SPA., Illus.). (J). (gr. 3-5). pap. 7.96 (978-84-236-2659-5(8), ED4704) Edebé ESP. Dist: Lectorum Pubns., Inc.

La Mariposa y la Oruga. (Coleccion Ciclos Vitales). (SPA., Illus.). (J). (gr. 3-5). pap. 7.96 (978-84-236-2663-2(6), ED4702) Edebé ESP. Dist: Lectorum Pubns., Inc.

La Mariquita. (Coleccion Ciclos Vitales). (SPA., Illus.). (J). (gr. 3-5). pap. 7.96 (978-84-236-2661-8(X), ED4701) Edebé ESP. Dist: Lectorum Pubns., Inc.

Marshall Cavendish Corporation Staff, contrib. by. Wildlife & Plants, 20 Vols., Set. 3rd ed. 2007. (Illus.). 1280p. (J). (gr. 4-8). lib. bdg. 514.21 (978-0-7614-7693-1(8), Cavendish Square) Cavendish Square Publishing LLC.

Matheson, Christie. Plant the Tiny Seed. 2017. (ENG., Illus.). 40p. (J). (gr. -1-3). 18.99 (978-0-06-239339-5(1), Greenwillow Bks.) HarperCollins Pubs.

McClanahan, Ben. We Need Plankton. 2019. (Animal Files Ser.). (ENG., Illus.). 32p. (J). (gr. 3-5). pap. 9.95 (978-1-64185-370-5(0), 1641853700); lib. bdg. 31.35 (978-1-64185-312-5(3), 1641853123) North Star Editions. (Focus Readers).

McEvoy, Paul. Plants. (Make it Work Ser.). (J). 42p. (gr. 4-8). pap. (978-1-882210-41-1(7)); (Illus.). 32p. (gr. 2-7). pap. 4.95 (978-1-882210-31-2(X)) Action Publishing, Inc.

McGinlay, Richard. My First Encyclopedia of British Wildlife: Mammals, Birds, Fish, Bugs, Flowers, Trees. 2020. (ENG., Illus.). 24p. (J). (gr. -1-12). pap. 7.99 (978-1-86147-849-8(6), Armadillo) Anness Publishing GBR. Dist: National Bk. Network.

—My First Encyclopedia of the Rainforest: A Great Big Book of Amazing Animals & Plants. 2018. (Illus.). 24p. (J). (gr. -1-12). pap. 7.99 (978-1-86147-848-1(8), Armadillo) Anness Publishing GBR. Dist: National Bk. Network.

McGowan, Timothy. Plants Around the World, 1 vol. 2012. (InfoMax Readers Ser.). (ENG., Illus.). 24p. (J). (gr. 1-1). pap. 8.25 (978-1-4488-9016-3(0), b97a721b-1c74-477b-b71e-d51fbee6f121, Rosen Classroom) Rosen Publishing Group, Inc., The.

McGraw-Hill, Wright. Amazing Plants, 6 vols. (Comprehension Strand Ser.). (gr. 4-8). 54.00 (978-0-322-06030-2(3)) Wright Group/McGraw-Hill.

Meachen Rau, Dana. Las Plantas / Plants, 1 vol. 2010. (Los Ciclos de la Naturaleza / Nature's Cycles Ser.). (ENG & SPA.). 32p. (gr. 1-2). lib. bdg. 25.50 (978-0-7614-4790-0(3), af024ce9-decb-486a-9611-df4e150437dc) Cavendish Square Publishing LLC.

—Plants, 1 vol. 2010. (Nature's Cycles Ser.). (ENG.). 32p. (gr. 1-2). 25.50 (978-0-7614-4097-0(6), db00efba-461a-4a43-86fb-99db11bd8002) Cavendish Square Publishing LLC.

Midthun, Joseph. Plant Structure & Classification. 2014. (Illus.). 32p. (J). (978-0-7166-2823-1(6)) World Bk., Inc.

Mikoley, Kate. How Plants Survive Wildfires, 1 vol. 2019. (Top Secret Life of Plants Ser.). (ENG.). 24p. (gr. 2-3). pap. 9.15 (978-1-5382-3387-0(8), 4cc221da-4915-4f03-a772-b41484ec0bb3) Stevens, Gareth Publishing LLLP.

—What Are Plants?, 1 vol. 2019. (Look at Life Science Ser.). (ENG.). 32p. (gr. 2-2). pap. 11.50 (978-1-5382-4859-1(X), b42f4988-4a2a-49db-9372-2f3df3bf6418) Stevens, Gareth Publishing LLLP.

Milet Publishing Staff. My First Bilingual Book - Plants, 1 vol. 2014. (My First Bilingual Book Ser.). (ENG., Illus.). 20p. (J). (— 1). bds. 7.99 (978-1-84059-885-8(9)); bds. 8.99 (978-1-84059-874-2(3)); bds. 7.99 (978-1-84059-883-4(2)); bds. 8.99 (978-1-84059-876-6(X)); bds. 8.99 (978-1-84059-879-7(4)); bds. 7.99 (978-1-84059-887-2(5)) Milet Publishing.

—My First Bilingual Book - Plants (English-Farsi), 1 vol. 2014. (My First Bilingual Book Ser.). (ENG., Illus.). 20p. (J). (— 1). bds. 7.99 (978-1-84059-877-3(8)) Milet Publishing.

—My First Bilingual Book - Plants (English-Korean), 1 vol. 2014. (My First Bilingual Book Ser.). (ENG., Illus.). 20p. (J). (— 1). bds. 7.99 (978-1-84059-881-0(6)) Milet Publishing.

—Plants - My First Bilingual Book, 1 vol. 2014. (My First Bilingual Book Ser.). (ENG., Illus.). 20p. (J). (— 1). bds. 7.99 (978-1-84059-889-6(1)); bds. 8.99 (978-1-84059-884-1(0)); bds. 7.99 (978-1-84059-886-5(7)); bds. 7.99 (978-1-84059-888-9(3)); bds. 7.99 (978-1-84059-880-3(8)); bds. 7.99 (978-1-84059-882-7(4)); bds. 7.99 (978-1-84059-875-9(1)); bds. 8.99 (978-1-84059-878-0(6)) Milet Publishing.

Mills, Nathan & Abbott, Henry. How Plants Live & Grow, 1 vol. 2012. (Rosen Readers Ser.). (ENG., Illus.). 24p. (J). (gr. 1-1). pap. 8.25 (978-1-4488-8770-5(4), a768a005-06c8-4b26-be71-44f2887d1e8a, Rosen Classroom) Rosen Publishing Group, Inc., The.

Mills, Nathan & Herman, Alley. Plants Live Everywhere, 1 vol. 2012. (Rosen Readers Ser.). (ENG., Illus.). 24p. (J). (gr. 1-1). pap. 8.25 (978-1-4488-8797-2(6), 4a08fad2-8458-474e-877a-0f42fcda11ca, Rosen Classroom) Rosen Publishing Group, Inc., The.

Mills, Nathan & Lewis, Charlotte. Plant Parts, 1 vol. 2012. (Rosen Readers Ser.). (ENG., Illus.). 16p. (J). (gr. k-k). pap. 7.00 (978-1-4488-8725-5(9), 95e328ce-500e-4ade-afad-d3040bde258b, Rosen Classroom) Rosen Publishing Group, Inc., The.

Mis, Melody S. Exploring Canyons. 2009. (Geography Zone: Landforms Ser.). 24p. (gr. 2-3). 42.50 (978-1-61512-692-7(9)); (ENG.). (J). lib. bdg. 26.27 (978-1-4358-2716-5(3), 95c1f95e-58b4-48ce-ac80-4a4c1b3e96ab); (ENG., Illus.). (J). pap. 9.25 (978-1-4358-3114-8(4), 9f39dda8-9801-4629-8ebb-664ae9800f83) Rosen Publishing Group, Inc., The. (PowerKids Pr.).

Misztal, Yvonne. How Bugs & Plants Live Together. 2013. (InfoMax Readers Ser.). (ENG.). 24p. (J). (gr. 2-3). pap. 49.50 (978-1-4777-2447-7(8)); (Illus.). pap. 8.25 (978-1-4777-2446-0(X), d06eb8b4-2143-4879-bde3-853a008b5d11) Rosen Publishing Group, Inc., The. (Rosen Classroom).

Mitchell, Melanie. Flowers. 2004. (First Step Nonfiction — Parts of Plants Ser.). (ENG., Illus.). 8p. (J). (gr. k-2). pap. 5.99 (978-0-8225-3917-9(9), 197be7fc-74f8-44ee-9d28-3b9466588954) Lerner Publishing Group.

Monster Plants. 2004. (I-Quest Ser.). (Illus.). 48p. (J). per. (978-1-84510-192-3(8)) Top That! Publishing PLC.

Mooney, Carla. Sunscreen for Plants. 2009. (Great Idea Ser.). (Illus.). 48p. (J). (gr. 4-6). lib. bdg. 26.60 (978-1-59953-344-5(8)) Norwood Hse. Pr.

Morgan, Sally. Collins Big Cat Phonics for Letters & Sounds - Living Fossils: Band 07/Turquoise, Bd. 7. Kundu, Kunal, illus. 2018. (Collins Big Cat Phonics Ser.). (ENG.). 24p. (J). (gr. 1-2). pap. 9.99 (978-0-00-825180-2(0)) HarperCollins Pubs. Ltd. GBR. Dist: Independent Pubs. Group.

—How We Use Plants for Making Everyday Things, 1 vol. 2008. (How We Use Plants Ser.). (ENG.). 32p. (gr. 3-3). pap. 10.60 (978-1-4358-2614-4(0), c1bf9749-4b67-4333-a28a-6c968f75040a, Rosen Classroom) Rosen Publishing Group, Inc., The.

—How We Use Plants to Make Everyday Things, 1 vol. 2008. (How We Use Plants Ser.). (ENG., Illus.). 32p. (gr. 3-3). lib. bdg. 30.27 (978-1-4042-4424-5(7), 930ddae6-ded3-4237-8643-367c6b673643, PowerKids Pr.) Rosen Publishing Group, Inc., The.

—The Plant Cycle, 1 vol. 2008. (Nature's Cycles Ser.). (ENG.). 32p. (J). (gr. 5-5). lib. bdg. 30.27 (978-1-4358-2867-4(4), dfdf9750-a048-4b66-b154-56d918e4be8a, PowerKids Pr.) Rosen Publishing Group, Inc., The.

—Plant Life Cycles. 2011. (Earth Cycles Ser.). 32p. (YA). (gr. 3-6). lib. bdg. 28.50 (978-1-59920-524-3(6)) Black Rabbit Bks.

Morley, Margaret W. Little Wanderers. 2009. (Illus.). 116p. pap. 8.95 (978-1-59915-317-9(3)) Yesterday's Classics.

Mulder, Michelle. Going Wild: Helping Nature Thrive in Cities, 1 vol. 2018. (Orca Footprints Ser.: 12). (ENG., Illus.). 48p. (J). (gr. 4-7). 19.95 (978-1-4598-1287-1(5)) Orca Bk. Pubs. USA.

Mullins, Matt. Think Like a Scientist in the Backyard. 2011. (Explorer Junior Library: Science Explorer Junior Ser.). (ENG., Illus.). 32p. (gr. 4-8). lib. bdg. 32.07 (978-1-61080-167-6(9), 201104) Cherry Lake Publishing.

—Think Like a Scientist in the Garden. 2011. (Explorer Junior Library: Science Explorer Junior Ser.). (ENG., Illus.). 32p. (gr. 4-8). lib. bdg. 32.07 (978-1-61080-166-9(0), 201102) Cherry Lake Publishing.

National Geographic Learning. Reading Expeditions (Science: Life Science): Classification Clues. 2007. (Nonfiction Reading & Writing Workshops Ser.). (ENG., Illus.). 32p. (J). pap. 18.95 (978-0-7922-4576-6(8)) CENGAGE Learning.

—Windows on Literacy Step up (Science: Plants Around Us): Plants in the Park. 2007. (ENG., Illus.). 8p. (J). pap. 9.95 (978-0-7922-8463-5(1)) CENGAGE Learning.

Nelson, Robin. Apple Trees. 2009. (First Step Nonfiction - Plant Life Cycles Ser.). (ENG.). 24p. (gr. k-2). 23.93 (978-0-7613-4071-3(8), Lerner Pubns.) Lerner Publishing Group.

El Nido del Pajaro. (Coleccion Ciclos Vitales). (SPA., Illus.). (J). (gr. 3-5). pap. 7.96 (978-84-236-2651-9(2), ED4699) Edebé ESP. Dist: Lectorum Pubns., Inc.

Nsrc. Science & Technology for Children Books: Experiments with Plants. 2004. (Illus.). 64p. (J). (978-1-933008-08-0(3)) Smithsonian Science Education Ctr. (SSEC).

Nunn, Daniel. Food, 1 vol. 2012. (Why Living Things Need Ser.). (ENG.). 24p. (gr. -1-1). pap. 6.29 (978-1-4329-5920-3(4), 117622, Heinemann) Capstone.

Los Oceanos.Tr. of Oceans. (SPA.). (J). (gr. 5-8). 12.00 (978-84-342-1949-6(2)) Parramon Ediciones S.A. ESP. Dist: Distribuidora Norma, Inc.

O'Gorman, Neil. Plants & Their Environments, 1 vol. 2008. (Real Life Readers Ser.). (ENG.). 16p. (gr. 2-3). pap. 7.05 (978-1-4358-0067-0(2), ba207a28-f723-4ea3-8065-e768d2bb41b1, Rosen Classroom) Rosen Publishing Group, Inc., The.

Ohanesian, Diane C. Seeds & Plants: Grades 2 & 3. (Illus.). (J). pap., wbk. ed. 4.99 (978-0-88743-961-2(6)) School Zone Publishing Co.

Olson, Nathan. Plant Patterns. rev. ed. 2016. (Finding Patterns Ser.). (ENG.). 32p. (J). (gr. -1-2). pap. 8.10 (978-1-5157-3510-6(9), 133495, Capstone Pr.) Capstone.

Orme, Helen. Seeds, Bulbs, Plants & Flowers. 2010. (Science Everywhere! Ser.). 24p. 24.25 (978-1-84898-291-8(7)) Black Rabbit Bks.

Owen, Ruth. How Do Plants Make Their Own Food?, 1 vol. 2014. (World of Plants Ser.). (ENG.). 32p. (J). (gr. 2-3). lib. bdg. 27.93 (978-1-4777-7149-5(2), 527d63d7-921d-4279-bba1-81f8705751f0, PowerKids Pr.) Rosen Publishing Group, Inc., The.

—Roots, Stems, Leaves, & Flowers: Let's Investigate Plant Parts. 2017. (Get Started with STEM Ser.). (ENG., Illus.). 32p. (J). (gr. k-3). 9.99 (978-1-78856-121-1(X), 9bba5e23-c785-4711-90b5-d0dca2f738f1) Ruby Tuesday Books Limited GBR. Dist: Lerner Publishing Group.

—Science & Craft Projects with Plants & Seeds, 1 vol. 2013. (Get Crafty Outdoors Ser.). (ENG., Illus.). 32p. (J). (gr. 2-3). 30.27 (978-1-4777-0247-5(4), 7d5a3b0c-ada1-4af8-a0f7-023eb105439d); pap. 12.75 (978-1-4777-0257-4(1), 145185e6-8bb6-44f9-9b9f-db3c07dde47a) Rosen Publishing Group, Inc., The. (PowerKids Pr.).

—What Do Roots, Stems, Leaves, & Flowers Do?, 1 vol. 2014. (World of Plants Ser.). (ENG.). 32p. (J). (gr. 2-3). lib. bdg. 27.93 (978-1-4777-7137-2(9), 73734378-9cc3-4b7c-a6fc-63aba6a08bcd, PowerKids Pr.) Rosen Publishing Group, Inc., The.

Paderewski, Elliot. Plants, Animals, & People Live Together, 1 vol. 2016. (Rosen REAL Readers: STEM & STEAM Collection). (ENG.). 8p. (gr. k-1). pap. 5.46 (978-1-5081-2398-9(5), 7f6f209f-1afa-4ade-bac2-5dc8331a411f, Rosen Classroom) Rosen Publishing Group, Inc., The.

El Paisaje. (Coleccion Planeta Vivo).Tr. of Topography. (SPA.). (YA). (gr. 5-8). 10.36 (978-84-342-1948-9(4)) Parramon Ediciones S.A. ESP. Dist: Lectorum Pubns., Inc.

Parker, Steve. Survival & Change. (Life Processes Ser.). 32p. pap. 7.50 (978-1-4034-4076-1(X)) Heinemann-Raintree.

Parsons, Alexandra & Barnes, Jon. Plants. (Make It Work! Ser.). (Illus.). 48p. (J). pap. 7.95 (978-0-590-24403-9(5)) Scholastic, Inc.

Pascoe, Elaine. The Ecosystem of a Milkweed Patch. 2009. (Library of Small Ecosystems Ser.). 24p. (gr. 3-4). 47.90 (978-1-60853-854-6(0), PowerKids Pr.) Rosen Publishing Group, Inc., The.

—Plant Clones. 2003. (Illus.). 48p. (J). 27.45 (978-1-56711-444-7(X), Blackbirch Pr., Inc.) Cengage Gale.

La Patata. (Coleccion Ciclos Vitales). (SPA., Illus.). pap. 7.96 (978-84-236-2657-1(1), ED4698) Edebé ESP. Dist: Lectorum Pubns., Inc.

Pearson, Scott. Kudzu. 2016. (Invasive Species Takeover Ser.). (ENG.). 32p. (J). (gr. 4-6). pap. 9.99 (978-1-64466-146-8(2), 10286); (Illus.). 31.35 (978-1-68072-015-0(5), 10285) Black Rabbit Bks. (Bolt).

Penguin Books Staff, ed. Plants. (Learners Ser.). (Illus.). 48p. (J). 3.50 (978-0-7214-1709-7(4), Dutton Juvenile) Penguin Publishing Group.

Perish, Patrick. Disgusting Plants. 2014. (Totally Disgusting Ser.). (ENG., Illus.). 24p. (J). (gr. 3-7). 26.95 (978-1-62617-132-9(7), Epic Bks.) Bellwether Media.

Petersen, Christine. Plants Need Sunlight. 2008. (21st Century Junior Library: Plants Ser.). (ENG., Illus.). 24p. (gr. 2-5). lib. bdg. 29.21 (978-1-60279-273-9(9), 200178) Cherry Lake Publishing.

Peterson, Cris. Seed, Soil, Sun: Earth's Recipe for Food. Lundquist, David R., photos by. 2012. (ENG., Illus.). 32p. (J). (gr. k-3). pap. 8.99 (978-1-59078-947-6(4), Astra Young Readers) Astra Publishing Hse.

Phillips, Dee. Find It in the Park, 1 vol. 2005. (Can You Find It? Ser.). (ENG., Illus.). 24p. (gr. 1-3). lib. bdg. 25.67 (978-0-8368-6301-7(1), d6bcf569-3b67-42ef-9b9e-5b3d2ef82333, Gareth Stevens Learning Library) Stevens, Gareth Publishing LLLP.

Plant Defenses, 12 vols. 2016. (Plant Defenses Ser.). 24p. (gr. 3-3). (ENG.). 151.62 (978-1-4994-1917-7(1), 219fdd46-1a6e-4fbc-9508-31cc5fb198ac); pap. 49.50 (978-1-4994-2454-6(X)) Rosen Publishing Group, Inc., The. (PowerKids Pr.).

The Plant Kingdom: Level Q, 6 vols., Vol. 2. (Explorers Ser.). 32p. (gr. 3-6). 44.95 (978-0-7699-0605-8(2)) Shortland Pubns. (U. S. A.) Inc.

Plants & Seeds, 6 vols. (Sunshinetm Science Ser.). 24p. (gr. 1-2). 31.50 (978-0-7802-0291-7(0)) Wright Group/McGraw-Hill.

Plants in My World, 12 vols. 2017. (Plants in My World Ser.). 24p. (ENG.). (gr. 1-1). 151.62 (978-1-5081-6185-1(2), dce922dd-9fcc-4246-82c7-9955922b335d); (gr. 4-6). pap. 49.50 (978-1-5081-6187-5(9)) Rosen Publishing Group, Inc., The. (PowerKids Pr.).

Puri, Devi. Plants That Hide, 1 vol. 2016. (Plant Defenses Ser.). (ENG., Illus.). 24p. (J). (gr. 3-3). pap. 9.25 (978-1-4994-2143-9(5), c29eca3a-34ae-48eb-a043-27f0f60a5c87, PowerKids Pr.) Rosen Publishing Group, Inc., The.

—Seeds, Bulbs, & Sprouts, 1 vol. 2015. (Garden Squad! Ser.). (ENG., Illus.). 24p. (J). (gr. 3-4). pap. 9.25 (978-1-4994-0977-2(X), 911b40a8-7696-4945-94b5-7db88d9964fc, PowerKids Pr.) Rosen Publishing Group, Inc., The.

Questions about Plants. 2003. 62p. pap. (978-7-80051-848-5(5)) Dolphin Books, China.

Raintree. Itip 2004 Sprouts Pkg (29 Titl. 2004. pap. (978-1-4109-1565-8(4)) Harcourt Schl. Pubs.

Rappoport, Bernice. Habitats of Africa: Text Pairs. 2008. (Bridges/Navigators Ser.). (J). (gr. 3). 81.00 (978-1-4108-8359-9(0)) Benchmark Education Co.

Rattini, Kristin Baird. National Geographic Readers: Seed to Plant. 2014. (Readers Ser.). (Illus.). 32p. (J). (gr. -1-k). pap. 5.99 (978-1-4263-1470-4(1), National Geographic Kids) Disney Publishing Worldwide.

Reader dsm-3 classroom plants Ea. 2004. (J). (978-1-59242-521-1(6)) Delta Education, LLC.

Reader dsm-3 plant&animal population Ea. 2004. (J). (978-1-59242-524-2(0)) Delta Education, LLC.

Readman, Jo & Roberts, Ley Honor. The World Came to My Place Today. 2003. (ENG., Illus.). 32p. 19.99 (978-1-903919-01-9(0), Eden Project Children's) Random House Children's Books GBR. Dist: Trafalgar Square Publishing.

Relf, Patricia. Magic School Plants Seeds. 2014. 14.00 (978-1-63419-672-7(4)) Perfection Learning Corp.

Reyes, Gabrielle & Ruelos, Joanne. Odd Animal Helpers. 2011. (Scholastic Reader, Level 3 Ser.). (ENG.). 32p. (J). (gr. 1-3). pap. 3.99 (978-0-545-33147-0(1), Scholastic Paperbacks) Scholastic, Inc.

Rice, Dona Herweck. Buen Trabajo. 2nd rev. ed. 2016. (TIME for KIDS(r): Informational Text Ser.). (SPA., Illus.). 12p. (gr. -1-k). 7.99 (978-1-4938-3020-6(1)) Teacher Created Materials, Inc.

—Good Work. 2nd rev. ed. 2015. (TIME for KIDS(r): Informational Text Ser.). (ENG., Illus.). 12p. (gr. -1-k). 7.99 (978-1-4938-2139-6(3)) Teacher Created Materials, Inc.

—Pollination, 1 vol. rev. ed. 2014. (Science: Informational Text Ser.). (ENG.). 32p. (gr. 2-3). pap. 10.99 (978-1-4807-4598-8(7)) Teacher Created Materials, Inc.

Rigby Education Staff. Bugs on the Menu. (Sails Literacy Ser.). (Illus.). 16p. (gr. 2-3). 27.00 (978-0-7635-9954-6(9), 699549C99) Rigby Education.

Riggs, Kate. A Seed Needs Sun. Dogi, Fiammetta, illus. 2014. 14p. (J). (gr. -1-k). bds. 9.99 (978-1-56846-254-7(9), 21594, Creative Editions) Creative Co., The.

Riggs, Sandy. Habitats of Australia: Text Pairs. 2008. (Bridges/Navigators Ser.). (J). (gr. 3). 94.00 (978-1-4108-8360-5(4)) Benchmark Education Co.

Riley, Peter. Ways into Science: All about Plants. 2016. (Ways into Science Ser.). (ENG., Illus.). 32p. (J). (gr. k-2). pap. 11.99 (978-1-4451-3470-3(5), Franklin Watts) Hachette Children's Group GBR. Dist: Hachette Bk. Group.

Rissman, Rebecca. Plants: Real Size Science. 2013. (Real Size Science Ser.). (ENG.). 24p. (J). (gr. -1-1). pap. 6.95 (978-1-4329-7887-7(X), 122827, Heinemann) Capstone.

Rivera, Andrea. Plants. 2016. (Our Renewable Earth Ser.). (ENG., Illus.). 24p. (J). (gr. -1-2). lib. bdg. 31.36 (978-1-68079-939-2(8), 24182, Abdo Zoom-Launch) ABDO Publishing Co.

Rivera, Sheila. Wetland. 2005. (First Step Nonfiction Ser.). (Illus.). 23p. (J). (gr. 3-7). lib. bdg. 18.60 (978-0-8225-2598-1(4), Lerner Pubns.) Lerner Publishing Group.

Robinson, Fay. Plants in Different Habitats. 2016. (Spring Forward Ser.). (J). (gr. 2). (978-1-4900-9480-9(6)) Benchmark Education Co.

Romero, Libby. Characteristics of Plants. 2006. (J). pap. (978-1-4108-6480-2(4)) Benchmark Education Co.

—Discover Plants. 2006. (J). pap. (978-1-4108-6483-3(9)) Benchmark Education Co.

Root, Phyllis. Plant a Pocket of Prairie. Bowen, Betsy, illus. 2014. (ENG.). 40p. 17.95 (978-0-8166-7980-5(0)) Univ. of Minnesota Pr.

Rosenberg, Pam. What Is a Plant? 2008. (21st Century Junior Library: Plants Ser.). (ENG., Illus.). 24p. (gr. 2-5). lib. bdg.

29.21 (978-1-60279-272-2(0), 200177) Cherry Lake Publishing.
Ross, Michael Elsohn. Plantology: 30 Activities & Observations for Exploring the World of Plants. 2010. (Young Naturalists Ser.: 5). (ENG., Illus.). 144p. (J). (gr. 2). pap. 15.99 (978-1-61373-737-8(8)) Chicago Review Pr., Inc.
Rushworth, Gary. What Makes a Plant a Plant? Set Of 6. 2011. (Navigators Ser.). (J). pap. 48.00 net. (978-1-4108-6229-7(1)) Benchmark Education Co.
—What Makes a Plant a Plant: Text Pairs. 2008. (Bridges/Navigators Ser.). (J). (gr. 4). 89.00 (978-1-4108-8400-8(7)) Benchmark Education Co.
Rustad, Martha E. H. Do Trees Get Hungry? Noticing Plant & Animal Traits. Moran, Mike, illus. 2015. (Cloverleaf Books (tm) — Nature's Patterns Ser.). (ENG.). 24p. (J). (gr. k-2). pap. 8.99 (978-1-4677-8605-8(5), 6ea3f1a2-52ad-48c7-aaf9-12413f464108); lib. bdg. 25.32 (978-1-4677-8559-4(8), e8fac711-bc92-49fc-a0b8-45ed7bda81f4) Lerner Publishing Group. (Millbrook Pr.).
—Plants in Spring, 1 vol. 2012. (All about Spring Ser.). (ENG.). 24p. (J). (gr. -1-2). pap. 7.29 (978-1-4296-9362-2(2), 120386); (gr. -1-2). lib. bdg. 27.32 (978-1-4296-8656-3(1), 118993); (gr. k-1). pap. 43.74 (978-1-4296-9363-9(0), 18576) Capstone. (Capstone Pr.).
Saavedra, Eusebio. The Tree & Annly el Árbol y Annly. Rowley, Jillian, illus. 2011. 8p. (J). 7.00 (978-0-9742432-9-0(9)) Flying Scroll Publishing, LLC.
Samson, Tess. They Grow Plants. 2010. (Sight Word Readers Ser.). (J). 3.49 (978-1-60719-616-7(6)) Newmark Learning LLC.
Sanchez, Anita. Leaflets Three, Let It Be! The Story of Poison Ivy. Brickman, Robin, illus. 2015. (ENG.). 32p. (J). (gr. -1-3). 16.95 (978-1-62091-445-8(X), Astra Young Readers) Astra Publishing Hse.
Schaefer, Lola M. Pick, Pull, Snap! Where Once a Flower Bloomed. 2003. (ENG., Illus.). 32p. (J). (gr. k-5). 17.99 (978-0-688-17834-5(0), Greenwillow Bks.) HarperCollins Pubs.
School Zone Publishing Company Staff. Seeds & Plants. (Illus.). (J). 19.99 incl. audio compact disk (978-0-88743-922-3(5)) School Zone Publishing Co.
Schuh, Mari. Carrots Grow Underground, 1 vol. 2010. (How Fruits & Vegetables Grow Ser.). (ENG., Illus.). 24p. (J). (gr. -1-2). pap. 6.29 (978-1-4296-6185-0(2), 115333, Pebble) Capstone.
—Lettuce Grows on the Ground. 2010. (How Fruits & Vegetables Grow Ser.). (ENG.). 24p. (J). (gr. k-1). pap. 37.74 (978-1-4296-6356-4(1), 16109, Pebble) Capstone.
Science & Technology for Children Books, Experiments with Plants Set, 8 vols. 2004. (Illus.). 64p. (J). (978-1-933008-20-2(2)) Smithsonian Science Education Ctr. (SSEC).
Science Stories Foss Spanish New Plants EA CR05. 2005. (J). (978-1-59242-583-9(6)) Delta Education, LLC.
Scott, Janine. Growing a Plant. 2011. (Early Connections Ser.). (J). (978-1-61672-230-2(4)) Benchmark Education Co.
Selwyn, Josephine. What Do Plants Need? 2012. (Level A Ser.). (ENG., Illus.). 16p. (J). (gr. k-2). pap. 7.95 (978-1-927136-06-9(3), 19420) RiverStream Publishing.
Shea, Therese M. Watch Peas Grow / ¡Mira Cómo Crecen Los Guisantes!, 1 vol. 2011. (Watch Plants Grow! / ¡Mira Cómo Crecen Las Plantas! Ser.). (SPA & ENG., Illus.). 24p. (J). (gr. k-k). 25.27 (978-1-4339-4837-4(0), 5c397763-f36b-47bd-9bca-3e4a8ecfa2ed) Stevens, Gareth Publishing LLLP.
Sian Flowering Plants. 2004. (J). (978-1-59242-030-8(3)) Delta Education, LLC.
Slade, Suzanne. What Do You Know about Plant Life? (20 Questions: Science Ser.). 24p. (gr. 2-3). 2009. 42.50 (978-1-60854-965-8(8), PowerKids Pr.) 2007. (ENG., Illus.). (J). lib. bdg. 26.27 (978-1-4042-4200-5(7), 0c1afb3a-3b53-428a-862b-2e46410d3352) Rosen Publishing Group, Inc., The.
Slingerland, Janet. The Secret Lives of Plants! Kemarskaya, Oksana, illus. 2012. (Adventures in Science Ser.). (ENG.). 32p. (gr. 3-4). pap. 47.70 (978-1-4296-8467-5(4), Capstone Pr.); (J). pap. 8.10 (978-1-4296-7989-3(1), 118321) Capstone.
Small, Cathleen. How Plants Grow, 1 vol. 2018. (Let's Find Out! Plants Ser.). (ENG.). 32p. (gr. 2-3). lib. bdg. 26.06 (978-1-5383-0189-0(X), 2a47c799-66fb-4884-96d3-3bdad2c827af, Britannica Educational Publishing) Rosen Publishing Group, Inc., The.
Smith, Jodene Lynn & Garbani, Tony. Oats, Peas, Beans, & Barley Grow. 2010. (Early Literacy Ser.). (ENG., Illus.). 16p. (gr. k-1). 19.99 (978-1-4333-1490-2(8)); 6.99 (978-1-4333-1489-6(4)) Teacher Created Materials, Inc.
Smith, Jodene Lynn & Reid, Stephanie. Las Plantas. rev. ed. 2010. (Early Literacy Ser.). (SPA., Illus.). 16p. (gr. -1-1). 19.99 (978-1-4333-2121-4(1)) Teacher Created Materials, Inc.
—Plantas. rev. ed 2010. (Early Literacy Ser.).Tr. of Plants. (SPA., Illus.). 16p. (gr. -1-1). 6.99 (978-1-4333-2120-7(3)) Teacher Created Materials, Inc.
—Plants, 1 vol. rev. ed. 2010. (Early Literacy Ser.). (ENG., Illus.). 16p. (gr. -1-1). 6.99 (978-1-4333-1485-8(1)); 19.99 (978-1-4333-1486-5(X)) Teacher Created Materials, Inc.
Smith, Jodene Lynn & Rice, Dona. Si Fuera un Árbol. rev. ed. 2010. (Early Literacy Ser.). (SPA., Illus.). 16p. (gr. k-1). 6.99 (978-1-4333-2101-6(7)) Teacher Created Materials, Inc.
Smith, Jodene Lynn & Rice, Dona Herweck. Si Fuera un Arbol. rev. ed. 2010. (Early Literacy Ser.).Tr. of If I Were a Tree. (SPA., Illus.). 16p. (gr. k-1). 19.99 (978-1-4333-2102-3(5)) Teacher Created Materials, Inc.
Sohn, Emily. New Plants. 2019. (IScience Ser.). (ENG., Illus.). 24p. (J). (gr. k-2). pap. 13.26 (978-1-68404-361-3(1)) Norwood Hse. Pr.
Sol90 Editorial Staff. A Visual Guide to Plants, Algae, & Fungi, 1 vol. 2018. (Visual Exploration of Science Ser.). (ENG.). 104p. (gr. 8-8). 38.80 (978-1-5081-8239-9(6), 8a277e6a-12a0-4d2e-97fe-c93ec951ab7e, Rosen Young Adult) Rosen Publishing Group, Inc., The.
Souza, Dorothy M. Plant Invaders. 2003. (Watts Library). (Illus.). 64p. (J). 25.50 (978-0-531-12211-2(5), Watts, Franklin) Scholastic Library Publishing.
Spalding, Maddie. Plants in Summer. 2018. (Welcoming the Seasons Ser.). (ENG.). 24p. (J). (gr. -1-2). lib. bdg. 32.79 (978-1-5038-2381-5(4), 212224) Child's World, Inc, The.
Spalding, Maddie & Willis, John. Plants. 2018. (Illus.). 24p. (J). (978-1-4896-9681-6(4), AV2 by Weigl) Weigl Pubs., Inc.
Spilsbury, Louise. Creeping Killers: Extreme Plants, 1 vol. 2014. (Extreme Biology Ser.). (ENG., Illus.). 48p. (J). (gr. 4-4). lib. bdg. 33.60 (978-1-4824-2234-4(4), 6be5d85a-1c1d-4b52-9d83-2a367eaff655) Stevens, Gareth Publishing LLLP.
—Superstar Plants, 1 vol. 2014. (Nature's Got Talent Ser.). (ENG.). 32p. (J). (gr. 3-3). lib. bdg. 27.93 (978-1-4777-7072-6(0), 6f4d1788-3ded-4c97-bf70-8bb49011c53e, PowerKids Pr.) Rosen Publishing Group, Inc., The.
Spilsbury, Louise & Spilsbury, Richard. Killer Plants. 2017. (Engineered by Nature Ser.). (ENG., Illus.). 32p. (J). (gr. 3-8). lib. bdg. 27.95 (978-1-62617-590-7(X), Pilot Bks.) Bellwether Media.
Staff, Gareth Editorial Staff. Things at the Park, 1 vol. 2006. (Things in My World Ser.). (ENG., Illus.). 16p. (gr. k-1). lib. bdg. 21.67 (978-0-8368-6809-8(9), 99d3a442-747e-409f-b906-be1797eae969, Weekly Reader Leveled Readers) Stevens, Gareth Publishing LLLP.
—Things at the Park / Las Cosas Del Parque, 1 vol. 2006. (Things in My World / Las Cosas de Mi Mundo Ser.). (ENG & SPA., Illus.). 16p. (gr. k-1). lib. bdg. 21.67 (978-0-8368-7221-7(5), 75ebe2b3-9403-460e-a47a-692f4ba1fd9d, Weekly Reader Leveled Readers) Stevens, Gareth Publishing LLLP.
Stefoff, Rebecca. The Flowering Plant Division, 1 vol. 2007. (Family Trees Ser.). (ENG., Illus.). 96p. (gr. 6-6). lib. bdg. 36.93 (978-0-7614-1817-7(2), 09339412-3f95-42db-bcb8-bfe5885f0328) Cavendish Square Publishing LLC.
Stewart, Melissa. How Does a Seed Sprout? And Other Questions about Plants. Schwartz, Carol, illus. 2014. (Good Question! Ser.). (ENG.). 32p. (J). (gr. 1). pap. 6.95 (978-1-4549-0671-1(5)) Sterling Publishing Co., Inc.
—A Seed Is the Start. 2018. (Illus.). 32p. (J). (gr. 1-3). 17.99 (978-1-4263-2977-7(6)); (ENG.). lib. bdg. 27.90 (978-1-4263-2978-4(4)) Disney Publishing Worldwide. (National Geographic Kids).
Stierle, Cynthia. Let It Grow: A Frozen Guide to Gardening. 2019. (ENG., Illus.). 32p. (J). (gr. 2-5). 27.99 (978-1-5415-3913-6(3), Lerner Pubns.) Lerner Publishing Group.
Stockland, Patricia M. Look at an Ash Tree. 2012. (First Step Nonfiction — Look at Trees Ser.). (ENG., Illus.). 8p. (J). (gr. k-2). pap. 5.99 (978-1-4677-0526-4(8), 24e2903f-2b20-47f1-8632-d765d43933bc) Lerner Publishing Group.
Stone, Lynn. Stems. 2007. (ENG., Illus.). 24p. (gr. 2-3). per. 8.95 (978-1-60044-696-2(5)) Rourke Educational Media.
Stradling, Jan. Plants all Around: Level H, 6 vols. (First Explorers Ser.). 24p. (gr. 1-2). 29.95 (978-0-7699-1450-3(0)) Shortland Pubns. (U. S. A.) Inc.
Sullivan, Laura. Flowering & Nonflowering Plants Explained, 1 vol. 2016. (Distinctions in Nature Ser.). (ENG.). 32p. (gr. 3-3). pap. 11.58 (978-1-5026-2177-1(0), 148eced9-76bd-4240-b6f2-982d8157fade); lib. bdg. 30.21 (978-1-5026-2179-5(7), a65c38db-aa04-473f-9141-40f57629fcf0) Cavendish Square Publishing LLC.
Sundance/Newbridge LLC Staff. Where Plants Live. 2004. (Reading PowerWorks Ser.). (gr. 1-3). 37.50 (978-0-7608-7799-9(8)); pap. 6.10 (978-0-7608-7800-2(5)) Sundance/Newbridge Educational Publishing.
Swain, Cynthia. A Plant Has Parts. 2006. (Early Explorers Ser.). (J). pap. (978-1-4108-6024-8(8)) Benchmark Education Co.
Taylor, Barbara. Inside Plants, 1 vol. 2011. (Invisible Worlds Ser.). (ENG.). 48p. (gr. 4-4). 31.21 (978-0-7614-4189-2(1), 48f69d59-04c2-43dc-9d61-db480390a09d) Cavendish Square Publishing LLC.
Taylor-Butler, Christine. Experiments with Plants. 2011. (True Bk Ser.). (Illus.). 48p. (J). (ENG.). pap. 6.95 (978-0-531-26647-2(8)); lib. bdg. 29.00 (978-0-531-26347-1(9)) Scholastic Library Publishing. (Children's Pr.).
Tell Me Why, Tell Me How, 12 vols., Group 3. Incl. How Do Caterpillars Become Butterflies? Bailer, Darice. 32.64 (978-0-7614-3987-5(0), dac13246-c0ec-4976-8304-e12a8660a29c); How Do Mountains Form? Hicks, Terry Allan. 32.64 (978-0-7614-3992-9(7), a8f8a923-b56f-4c40-8251-d52754e27fdd); Why Do Bears Hibernate? Bailer, Darice. 32.64 (978-0-7614-3990-5(0), 9842ecfd-f64-47d1-88b4-b94c49faa2e6); Why Do Volcanoes Erupt? Mara, Wil. 32.64 (978-0-7614-3989-9(7), 98188da6-bd9e-42b7-9d2c-b6a3f1b18060); Why Does It Rain? Mara, Wil. 32.64 (978-0-7614-3991-2(9), c05579b7-5861-4743-92a1-872870ab1603); Why Does the Sun Set? Hicks, Terry Allan. 32.64 (978-0-7614-3993-6(5), dbac377f-8741-4b5f-b064-c5ae72121529); 32p. (gr. 3-3). (Tell Me Why, Tell Me How Ser.). (ENG.). 2010. Set lib. bdg. 195.84 (978-0-7614-3986-8(2), 137b0a86-f4ea-4e63-b639-2128877586fd, Cavendish Square) Cavendish Square Publishing LLC.
Thrarp, Claire. All about Plants. rev. ed. 2016. (All about Plants Ser.). (ENG.). 24p. (J). (gr. -1-1). pap., pap., pap. 29.95 (978-1-4846-3861-3(1), 26139, Heinemann) Capstone.
Tidey, John & Tidey, Jackie. Plants, 1 vol. 2008. (China: Land, Life, & Culture Ser.). (ENG.). 32p. (gr. 5-5). lib. bdg. 21.27 (978-0-7614-3159-6(4), ac65e368-66d6-4477-991c-4c706aab3646) Cavendish Square Publishing LLC.
Time For Kids, Editors. Time for Kids: Plants! 2006. (Time for Kids Ser.). (ENG., Illus.). 32p. (J). (gr. 1-3). pap. 3.99 (978-0-06-078218-4(8)) HarperCollins Pubs.
Top That Publishing Staff, ed. Monster Plants. 2004. 48p. (J). pap. (978-1-84510-193-0(6)) Top That! Publishing PLC.
Tower, Eric J. The Unofficial Guide to Growing Plants in Minecraft, 1 vol. 2018. (STEM Projects in Minecraft(r) Ser.). (ENG.). 24p. (gr. 3-3). pap. 9.25 (978-1-5383-4244-2(8), a91b0fb6-8893-4c2d-ad4c-f5fb34544d4a, PowerKids Pr.) Rosen Publishing Group, Inc., The.
Twist, Clint. A Little Book of Slime: Everything That Oozes, from Killer Slime to Living Mold. 2012. (ENG., Illus.). 80p. (J). (gr. 4-18). 9.95 (978-1-77085-006-4(6), a2c264b0-6815-4f17-bb6d-05b45e45c159) Firefly Bks., Ltd.
Urquhart, Mercedes Kristina. Botanical Illustration (Grade 3) rev. ed. 2018. (Smithsonian: Informational Text Ser.). (ENG., Illus.). 32p. (J). (gr. 3-4). pap. 11.99 (978-1-4938-6683-0(4)) Teacher Created Materials, Inc.
Van Manen, Dave. Plants of the Pueblo Mountain Park. 2005. (Illus.). 120p. per. 19.95 (978-0-9743791-7-3(4)) Medici Publishing, Inc.
Van Tol, Alex. Aliens among Us: Invasive Animals & Plants in British Columbia, 1 vol. Deas, Mike, illus. 2015. (ENG.). 144p. (J). pap. 14.95 (978-0-7726-6853-0(1), 3c93c366-fe45-4839-b5e9-f4cf4cc8a30e) Royal British Columbia Museum CAN. Dist: Independent Pubs. Group.
Veitch, Catherine. Learning about Plants, 1 vol. 2013. (Natural World Ser.). (ENG., Illus.). 24p. (J). (gr. -1-1). pap. 6.95 (978-1-4109-5406-0(4), 123357, Raintree) Capstone.
Wadsworth, Pamela. Golwg Gyntaf Ar Bethau Byw. Owen, Ken & Owen, Siân, illus. 2005. (WEL.). 24p. pap. (978-1-85596-250-7(0)) Dref Wen.
—Golwg Gyntaf Ar Wahanol Blanhigion AC Anifeiliaid. 2005. (WEL., Illus.). 24p. pap. (978-1-85596-254-5(3)) Dref Wen.
—Gwahanol Blanhigion AC Anifeiliaid. Owen, Ken & Owen, Siân, illus. 2005. (WEL.). 24p. pap. (978-1-85596-223-1(3)) Dref Wen.
—Rhagor Am Bethau Byw Ar Waith. 2005. (WEL., Illus.). 24p. pap. (978-1-85596-234-7(9)) Dref Wen.
—Rhagor Am Wahanol Blanhigion Ac Anifeiliaid. 2005. (WEL., Illus.). 24p. pap. (978-1-85596-224-8(1)) Dref Wen.
Walker, Colin. Plants Grow Almost Anywhere. Simons, Sally, illus. 2012. (Concept Science: Plants Ser.). (ENG.). 16p. (J). (gr. k-3). pap. 8.50 (978-0-8136-7331-8(3)) Modern Curriculum Pr.
Walker, Colin, et al. Las Differentes Cosas Que Vienende las Plantas. (Coleccion Conceptos de Ciencia en Big Books). (SPA.). (J). (gr. k-3). 12.00 (978-0-8136-6753-9(4)) Modern Curriculum Pr.
Walker, Kate. Plants, 1 vol. 2012. (Investigating Earth Ser.). (ENG.). 32p. (gr. 2-2). 31.21 (978-1-60870-559-7(5), 0cd5658d-156c-46b0-9145-50eeac9b11ad) Cavendish Square Publishing LLC.
Wallace, Marianne D. America's Seashores: Guide to Plants & Animals. 2005. (America's Ecosystems Ser.). (ENG., Illus.). 48p. (J). (gr. 3-7). pap. 11.95 (978-1-55591-483-7(7), 1250708) Fulcrum Publishing.
Wanjie, Anne, ed. The Basics of Plant Structures, 1 vol. 2013. (Core Concepts Ser.). (ENG., Illus.). 96p. (YA). (gr. 7-7). lib. bdg. 39.77 (978-1-4777-0553-7(8), 9807c5d6-5f28-4f05-afc3-fa80f4d738ee) Rosen Publishing Group, Inc., The.
Ward, Jennifer. What Will Grow? Ghahremani, Susie, illus. 2017. (ENG.). 40p. (J). 17.99 (978-1-68119-030-3(3), 900156309, Bloomsbury USA Childrens) Bloomsbury Publishing USA.
Warren, Howard. The Life Cycle of Plants: Set Of 6. 2010. (Navigators Ser.). (J). pap. 44.00 net. (978-1-4108-6224-2(0)) Benchmark Education Co.
—The Life Cycle of Plants: Text Pairs. 2008. (Bridges/Navigators Ser.). (J). (gr. 3). 89.00 (978-1-4108-8363-6(9)) Benchmark Education Co.
Watts, Barrie. Bean. 2004. (Watch It Grow Ser.). (J). (gr. k-3). lib. bdg. 27.10 (978-1-58340-503-1(8)) Black Rabbit Bks.
—El Hámster. (Coleccion Ciclos Vitales). (SPA., Illus.). 32p. (J). (gr. 3-5). (978-84-236-2665-6(2), ED4704) Edebé ESP. Dist: Lectorum Pubns., Inc.
Weakland, Mark. Yogi Bear's Guide to Plants. Cornia, Christian, illus. 2015. (Yogi Bear's Guide to the Great Outdoors Ser.). (ENG.). 32p. (J). (gr. k-2). lib. bdg. 28.65 (978-1-4914-6547-9(6), 129037) Capstone.
Whited, Zillah. Flower Fables. 2011. 28p. pap. 35.95 (978-1-258-02350-8(4)) Literary Licensing, LLC.
Williams, Kathryn. National Geographic Readers: Plants (Level 1 Coreader) 2017. (Readers Ser.). (Illus.). 48p. (J). (gr. -1-k). pap. 4.99 (978-1-4263-2694-3(7), National Geographic Kids) Disney Publishing Worldwide.
Wiseman, Blaine. The Midwest. 2014. (Illus.). 32p. (J). (978-1-4896-1226-7(2)) Weigl Pubs., Inc.
—The Northeast. 2014. (Illus.). 32p. (J). (978-1-4896-1230-4(0)) Weigl Pubs., Inc.
—The Southeast. 2014. (Illus.). 32p. (J). (978-1-4896-1234-2(3)) Weigl Pubs., Inc.
—The Southwest. 2014. (Illus.). 32p. (J). (978-1-4896-1238-0(6)) Weigl Pubs., Inc.
—The West. 2014. (Illus.). 32p. (J). (978-1-4896-1242-7(4)) Weigl Pubs., Inc.
World Book, Inc. Staff, contrib. by. Encyclopedia of Plants. 2013. (J). (978-0-7166-7522-8(6)) World Bk., Inc.
—Learning about Plants. 2011. (J). (978-0-7166-0230-9(X)) World Bk., Inc.
—Plants Around the World. 2010. (J). (978-0-7166-7742-0(3)) World Bk., Inc.
—Resources & Cumulative Index. 2005. (World Book's Science & Nature Guides Ser.). 80p. (J). (978-0-7166-4216-9(6)) World Bk., Inc.
The World of Plants, 12 vols. 2014. (World of Plants Ser.). (ENG.). 32p. (J). (gr. 2-3). 167.58 (978-1-4777-7093-1(3), 5ae51f02-4e91-4a2b-83bf-44488873f961, PowerKids Pr.) Rosen Publishing Group, Inc., The.
World's Weirdest Plants. 2016. (World's Weirdest Plants Ser.). 00024p. (J). pap. 48.90 (978-1-4824-5837-4(3)) Stevens, Gareth Publishing LLLP.
York, M. J. Plants in Spring. 2017. (Welcoming the Seasons Ser.). (ENG.). 24p. (J). (gr. -1-2). lib. bdg. 32.79 (978-1-5038-1654-1(0), 211507) Child's World, Inc, The.
York, M. J. & Willis, John. Plants. 2018. (Illus.). 24p. (J). pap. (978-1-4896-9670-0(9), AV2 by Weigl) Weigl Pubs., Inc.
Zorzi, Gina & Sánchez, Lucía M. Desiertos: This Is a Desert. 2012. (2G Ecosistemas Ser.). (SPA.). 36p. (J). (gr. k-2). pap. 9.60 (978-1-61541-424-6(X)) American Reading Co.
Zuchora-Walske, Christine. That Bull Is Seeing Red! Science's Biggest Mistakes about Animals & Plants. 2014. (Science Gets It Wrong Ser.). (ENG., Illus.). 32p. (J). (gr. 4-6). pap. 7.99 (978-1-4677-4550-5(2), b697ac4c-95fd-40bf-a1f3-bfa785aaf674) Lerner Publishing Group.

PLANTS—ANATOMY
see Plant Anatomy

PLANTS, CULTIVATED
see also Plants, Edible
Beth, Georgia & Fielder, Heidi. Growing Plants in Space. rev. ed. 2019. (Smithsonian: Informational Text Ser.). (ENG., Illus.). 32p. (J). (gr. 2-3). pap. 10.99 (978-1-4938-6670-0(2)) Teacher Created Materials, Inc.

PLANTS—DISEASES
see Plant Diseases

PLANTS—ECOLOGY
see Plant Ecology

PLANTS, EDIBLE
Amstutz, Lisa J. Edible Gardening: Growing Your Own Vegetables, Fruits, & More. 2016. (Gardening Guides). (ENG., Illus.). 32p. (J). (gr. 3-9). lib. bdg. 28.65 (978-1-4914-8235-3(4), 130701, Capstone Pr.) Capstone.
Bae, Yea Jee. The Importance of Plants to Life on Earth, 1 vol. 2018. (Let's Find Out! Plants Ser.). (ENG.). 32p. (gr. 2-3). lib. bdg. 26.06 (978-1-5383-0197-5(0), d09f418b-fbdd-489d-af1e-a81a201a8493, Britannica Educational Publishing) Rosen Publishing Group, Inc., The.
Colby, Jennifer. Plants We Eat. 2014. (21st Century Junior Library: Plants Ser.). (ENG., Illus.). 24p. (J). (gr. 2-5). 29.21 (978-1-63188-039-1(X), 205563) Cherry Lake Publishing.
—Plants We Wear. 2014. (21st Century Junior Library: Plants Ser.). (ENG., Illus.). 24p. (J). (gr. 2-5). 29.21 (978-1-63188-040-7(3), 205567) Cherry Lake Publishing.
Dodson Wade, Mary. People Need Plants!, 1 vol. 2009. (I Like Plants! Ser.). (ENG., Illus.). 24p. (J). (gr. k-2). pap. 10.35 (978-0-7660-3613-0(8), e15d2df6-0c0a-42c3-8cd5-895a33be673b, Enslow Elementary); lib. bdg. 25.27 (978-0-7660-3153-1(5), a0111120-7ad8-4b5c-a9a5-879e2fb6abe6) Enslow Publishing, LLC.
Domnauer, Teresa & Kenah, Katharine. Incredible Edibles. 2006. (Extreme Readers: Level 3 Ser.). (Illus.). 32p. (gr. 1-2). 13.95 (978-0-7569-6851-9(8)) Perfection Learning Corp.
Encyclopaedia Britannica, Inc. Staff, compiled by. Food Plants. 2003. (Illus.). 64p. 14.95 (978-1-59339-044-0(0)) Encyclopaedia Britannica, Inc.
Encyclopaedia Britannica Publishers, Inc. Staff. Food Plants. 2003. (Illus.). 64p. 14.95 (978-1-59339-013-6(0)) Encyclopaedia Britannica, Inc.
Feldman, Sarah. Incredible, Edible Plants. 2011. (Early Connections Ser.). (J). (978-1-61672-664-5(4)) Benchmark Education Co.
—Incredible, Edible Plants: Set Of 6. 2011. (Early Connections Ser.). (J). pap. 39.00 net. (978-1-4108-1541-5(2)) Benchmark Education Co.
Hollar, Sherman. A Closer Look at Plant Classifications, Parts, & Uses, 1 vol. 2011. (Introduction to Biology Ser.). (ENG.). 88p. (J). (gr. 8-8). lib. bdg. 35.29 (978-1-61530-529-2(7), a0004127-2b10-4774-8d53-5700d0f9b227) Rosen Publishing Group, Inc., The.
Lundgren, Julie K. Plants As Food, Fuel, & Medicine. 2012. (My Science Library). (ENG.). 24p. (gr. 4-5). pap. 8.95 (978-1-61810-235-5(4), 9781618102355) Rourke Educational Media.
Morgan, Sally. How We Use Plants: For Food, 1 vol. 2008. (How We Use Plants Ser.). (ENG.). 32p. (gr. 3-3). pap. 10.60 (978-1-4358-2611-3(6), ac04d363-5bbe-4d21-b82d-6904ef1d71cc, Rosen Classroom); (Illus.). (J). lib. bdg. 30.27 (978-1-4042-4421-4(2), 885e65f7-2ad2-4ca9-bc95-14d456063985, PowerKids Pr.) Rosen Publishing Group, Inc., The.
Rockwell, Lizzy. Plants Feed Me. 2015. (ENG., Illus.). 32p. (J). (gr. -1-k). 8.99 (978-0-8234-3307-0(2)) Holiday Hse., Inc.
Sweet, Muriel. Common Edible & Useful Plants of the West. rev. ed. 2003. (Illus.). 64p. (J). pap. 7.95 (978-0-87961-046-3(8)) Naturegraph Pubs., Inc.

PLANTS, EXTINCT
see Plants, Fossil

PLANTS—FICTION
Anchin, Lisa. The Little Green Girl. Anchin, Lisa, illus. 2019. (Illus.). 40p. (J). (-k). 17.99 (978-0-7352-3073-6(0), Dial Bks) Penguin Young Readers Group.
Anderson, AnnMarie. Attack of the Plants. 2019. (Branches Early Ch Bks). (ENG., Illus.). 96p. (J). (gr. 2-4). 15.96 (978-1-64310-823-0(9)) Penworthy Co., LLC, The.
—The Attack of the Plants (the Magic School Bus Rides Again #5) 2018. (Magic School Bus Rides Again Ser.: 5). (ENG., Illus.). 96p. (J). (gr. 1-3). pap. 5.99 (978-1-338-29079-0(7)) Scholastic, Inc.
Anthony, Joseph. The Dandelion Seed's Big Dream. Arbo, Cris, illus. 2014. 32p. (J). (gr. k-4). 16.99 (978-1-58469-496-0(3)); pap. 8.99 (978-1-58469-497-7(1)) Sourcebooks, Inc. (Dawn Pubns.).
Archambault, Marc. Teevert the Little Green Leaf. 2010. 31p. 18.98 (978-0-557-17967-1(X)) Lulu Pr., Inc.
Bardsley-Sirois, Lois. Katherine's Winter Garden. 2012. 24p. pap. 12.99 (978-1-4525-6269-8(5)) Balboa Pr.
Barkow, Henriette. The Giant Turnip. Johnson, Richard, illus. 2004. 32p. (J). (POL & ENG.). pap. (978-1-85269-743-3(1)); (ENG & BEN.). pap. (978-1-85269-734-1(2)); (ENG & POR.). pap. (978-1-85269-744-0(X)); (ENG & PAN.). pap. (978-1-85269-742-6(3)); (ENG & URD.). pap. (978-1-85269-750-1(4)) Mantra Lingua.
Barton, Tamra Clum. The Adventures of Lucky the Leaf. 2007. 32p. per. 18.65 (978-1-4257-3026-0(4)) Xlibris Corp.
Belew, Elizabeth A. There's Always a Place for Mr. Plant. 2010. 24p. 11.32 (978-1-4520-8656-9(7)) AuthorHouse.
Bennett, Marilyn J. The Poinsettia Adventure. 2010. 60p. pap. 21.99 (978-1-4490-7108-0(2)) AuthorHouse.
Blevins, Wiley. The Princess & the Poison Pea. Cox, Steve, illus. 2017. (Scary Tales Retold Ser.). (ENG.). 24p. (J). (gr. k-3). pap. 6.99 (978-1-63440-170-8(0), 1e625a92-dd6c-461f-855c-8bc07f2d6894); lib. bdg. 27.99 (978-1-63440-166-1(2), 986a4545-bd42-4178-9a49-2644d76af4f0) Red Chair Pr.
Brenner, Barbara & Sweet, Melissa. The Plant That Kept on Growing. 2015. (ENG., Illus.). 34p. (J). pap. 11.95 (978-1-899694-59-4(5), ipicturebooks) ibooks, Inc.

Bryan, Marcia. Dandy Lion: The Adventure Begins. 2006. (Illus.). 40p. (J). (gr. -1-5). 18.95 (978-1-57736-376-7(0)) Providence Hse Pubs.

Burton-Hupp, Lynne. Venus the Very Proper Fly Trap. 2009. 28p. pap. 24.95 (978-1-60563-993-2(1)) America Star Bks.

Canetti, Yanitzia. ABC's of Plants. 2010. (ENG.). 40p. (J). pap. 8.99 (978-1-59835-118-7(4), BrickHouse Education) Cambridge BrickHouse, Inc.

—Abecedario de Plantas. 2010. (SPA.). 40p. (J). pap. 8.99 (978-1-59835-119-4(2), BrickHouse Education) Cambridge BrickHouse, Inc.

Capeci, Anne. Little Lab or Horrors. 2003. (Dexter's Laboratory Science Log Ser.: Vol. 4). (Illus.). 78p. (J). (978-0-439-47242-5(3)) Scholastic, Inc.

Carbone, Courtney. Flower Power! (DC Super Friends) Schoening, Dan, illus. 2014. (Little Golden Book Ser.). (ENG.). 24p. (J). (-k). 4.99 (978-0-385-37396-8(1), Golden Bks.) Random Hse. Children's Bks.

Carle, Eric. The Tiny Seed: With Seeded Paper to Grow Your Own Flowers! Carle, Eric, illus. 2009. (World of Eric Carle Ser.). (ENG., Illus.). 36p. (J). (gr. -1-3). 8.99 (978-1-4169-7917-3(4), Little Simon) Little Simon.

Castrillon, Melissa. The Balcony. Castrillon, Melissa, illus. 2019. (ENG., Illus.). 48p. (J). (gr. -1-3). 18.99 (978-1-5344-0588-2(7), Simon & Schuster/Paula Wiseman Bks.) Simon & Schuster/Paula Wiseman Bks.

Clark, Danell. Daisy. Irwin, April, illus. 2008. 23p. pap. 11.95 (978-1-59858-642-8(4)) Dog Ear Publishing, LLC.

Coates, Theresa. Imaginary Time of Life. 2007. 102p. pap. 10.95 (978-0-7414-4067-9(9)) Infinity Publishing.

Cordone Warner, Debra. Buddy & A Walk in the Woods. 2010. 38p. pap. 18.99 (978-0-557-60690-0(X)) Lulu Pr., Inc.

Curious George Plants a Seed (Reader Level 1) 2007. (Curious George TV Ser.). (ENG., Illus.). 24p. (J). (gr. -1-3). 4.99 (978-0-618-77710-5(5), 448949, Clarion Bks.) HarperCollins Pubs.

Dompierre, Judith E. Wow, What's That? 2012. 48p. pap. 24.95 (978-1-4626-9332-0(6)) America Star Bks.

DuTemple, Leslie A. One Little Balsam Fir: A Northwoods Counting Book. Robinson, Susan, illus. 2006. 32p. (J). per. (978-1-892384-37-9(X)) Avery Color Studios, Inc.

Edwards, Tanille & Edwards, Latoya. Jordan & Justine's Weekend Adventures Pts. 1-2: Plants. 2007. (SPA.). 32p. (J). (gr. k-3). 12.95 (978-0-9787302-3-9(2)) Fire Flies Entertainment, LLC.

Ehlert, Lois. Leaf Man. 2005. (ENG., Illus.). 40p. (J). (gr. -1-3). 19.99 (978-0-15-205304-8(2), 1195981, Clarion Bks.) HarperCollins Pubs.

Eisele, Barbara. Miss Thistle & Friends. 2009. 48p. pap. 12.99 (978-1-4490-2007-1(0)) AuthorHouse.

Ering, Timothy Basil. The Story of Frog Belly Rat Bone. Ering, Timothy Basil, illus. 2013. (ENG., Illus.). 48p. (J). (gr. -1-3). 18.99 (978-0-7636-6661-3(0)) Candlewick Pr.

Everett, Clare. Henrietta - a Rabbit's Tale of Summer Time Fun. 2012. 116p. pap. (978-1-84914-296-0(3)) CompletelyNovel.com.

Falwell, Cathryn. Mystery Vine. Falwell, Cathryn, illus. 2009. (Illus.). 32p. (J). lib. bdg. 17.89 (978-0-06-177197-2(X), Greenwillow Bks.) HarperCollins Pubs.

Fleischman, Paul. Weslandia. braille ed. 2004. (Illus.). (J). (gr. k-3). spiral bd. (978-0-616-01641-1(7)) Canadian National Institute for the Blind/Institut National Canadien pour les Aveugles.

—Weslandia. Hawkes, Kevin, illus. 2006. (gr. -1-3). 17.00 (978-0-7569-6566-2(7)) Perfection Learning Corp.

Frommer, Julia. Happiness Is Yours. 2007. 24p. 13.95 (978-1-4303-1176-8(2)) Lulu Pr., Inc.

Gibbs, Lynne. Time to Share: A Story of Sharing, 1 vol. Mitchell, Missy, illus. 2009. (Let's Grow Together Ser.). (ENG.). 32p. (J). (gr. k-1). lib. bdg. 27.27 (978-1-60754-757-0(0), a262b884-7f2d-4103-aad4-a1ff78ae63e4, Windmill Bks.) Rosen Publishing Group, Inc., The.

Giff, Patricia Reilly. The Garden Monster. Palmisciano, Diane, illus. 2013. (J). (978-0-545-24460-2(9), Orchard Bks.) Scholastic, Inc.

Glennon, Michelle. My Big Green Teacher: Taking the Green Road. Glennon, Michelle, illus. 2008. (Illus.). 32p. (J). 19.95 (978-0-9796625-7-7(5)) GDG Publishing.

Gordon, Michele Lynne. The Springing Singing Sprout: Little Tales of a Little Sprout. 2008. 54p. pap. 19.95 (978-1-4241-8942-7(X)) America Star Bks.

Grandma Carol's Plant: Individual Title Six-Packs. (gr. k-1). 23.00 (978-0-7635-9039-0(8)) Rigby Education.

Griffiths, Neil. Who'd Be a Fly? Nash, Doug, illus. 2015. (ENG.). 24p. (J). pap. 9.99 (978-0-9545353-5-3(9), Red Robin Bks.) Corner To Learn Ltd. GBR. Dist: Parkwest Pubns., Inc.

Hapka, Catherine, pseud. Plants vs. Zombies. 2014. (I Can Read! Level 2 Ser.). (J). lib. bdg. 13.55 (978-0-606-35477-6(8)) Turtleback.

Harris, Joel Chandler. Nights with Uncle Remus. 2008. 288p. 29.95 (978-1-60664-915-2(9)) Aegypan.

Hausman, Sid. Cactus Critter Bash. Hausman, Sid, illus. 2006. (ENG., Illus.). 32p. (J). 21.95 (978-1-929115-15-0(6)) Azro Pr., Inc.

Heidari, Mahdi. Little Red Fire. Taylor, Adam, illus. 2012. 40p. (J). pap. 12.99 (978-0-9838321-8-8(3)) Higher Ground Pr.

Hofmeister, Alan, et al. The Seed. (Reading for All Learners Ser.). (Illus.). (J). pap. (978-1-56861-112-9(9)) Swift Learning Resources.

Hood, Susan. Rooting for You. Cordell, Matthew, illus. 2014. (ENG.). 32p. (J). (gr. -1-k). 16.99 (978-1-4231-5230-9(1)) Disney Pr.

Hughes, Mónica. The Big Turnip: Band 00/Lilac (Collins Big Cat) Williams, Lisa, illus. 2006. (Collins Big Cat Ser.). (ENG.). 32p. (J). (gr. -1-k). pap. 7.99 (978-0-00-718644-0(4)) HarperCollins Pubs. Ltd. GBR. Dist: Independent Pubs. Group.

Hulin, Pamela. Down under in Australia. Mendoza, Carlos, illus. 2007. 20p. per. 24.95 (978-1-4241-8929-8(2)) America Star Bks.

Hunt, Connie. Planting Love: A Tale of Love & Growing. 2012. 48p. 18.10 (978-1-4669-0965-6(X)); pap. 8.10 (978-1-4669-0967-0(6)) Trafford Publishing.

Ioan, Elwyn. Ici'r Ddôl A'r Corrach Coch. 2005. (WEL., Illus.). 36p. pap. (978-0-86243-428-1(9)) Y Lolfa.

James, Lauren & Kisloski, Carolyn. Planting Seeds. Grott, Isabella, illus. 2017. (Seasons Around Me Ser.). (ENG.). 24p. (gr. -1-2). pap. 9.95 (978-1-68342-789-6(0), 9781683427896) Rourke Educational Media.

Jarrell, Pamela R. Planting a Seed. Meler, Kerry L., illus. l.t. ed. 2006. 12p. (J). (gr. -1-k). pap. 10.95 (978-1-57332-350-5(0), HighReach Learning, Incorporated) Carson-Dellosa Publishing, LLC.

Jenson-Elliott, Cindy. Weeds Find a Way. Fisher, Carolyn, illus. 2014. (ENG.). 40p. (J). (gr. -1-3). 17.99 (978-1-4424-1260-6(7)) Simon & Schuster Children's Publishing.

Johnson, Richard, illus. The Giant Turnip. 2004. (J). 24p. (978-1-85269-745-7(8)); 24p. (978-1-85269-746-4(6)); 24p. (978-1-85269-747-1(4)); 24p. (978-1-85269-748-8(2)); 24p. (978-1-85269-749-5(0)); 24p. (978-1-85269-789-1(X)); 24p. (978-1-85269-733-4(4)); 24p. (978-1-85269-735-8(0)); 24p. (978-1-85269-736-5(9)); 24p. (978-1-85269-739-6(3)); 24p. (978-1-85269-740-2(7)); 24p. (978-1-85269-741-9(5)); (ENG & RUS.). 32p. pap. (978-1-85269-788-4(1)); 2nd ed. (PER.). 24p. (978-1-85269-737-2(7)) Mantra Lingua.

Juslin, Lee. Nurse Frosty Saves the Day. 2009. 35p. pap. 22.00 (978-0-557-09486-8(0)) Lulu Pr., Inc.

Kaplan, Madeline. Planet Earth Gets Well. 2008. (ENG.). 24p. pap. 9.99 (978-1-4196-8986-4(X)) CreateSpace Independent Publishing Platform.

Kiernan, Tim. Liams Luck & Finnegans Fortune. 2009. (ENG.). 144p. pap. 10.95 (978-1-933916-43-4(6), Ferne Pr.) Nelson Publishing & Marketing.

Kim, Cecil. One Little Bean: Observation - Life Cycle. Cowley, Joy, ed. Dattola, Chiara, illus. 2015. (Step up - Creative Thinking Ser.). (ENG.). 32p. (gr. -1-2). 26.65 (978-1-925246-38-4(8)); 7.99 (978-1-925246-64-3(7)); 26.65 (978-1-925246-12-4(4)) ChoiceMaker Pty. Ltd., The AUS. (Big and SMALL). Dist: Lerner Publishing Group.

Kitami, Yoko. Cactus. 2005. (Los Especiales de A la Orilla del Viento Ser.).Tr. of Cactus. (SPA., Illus.). 36p. (J). (gr. 2-4). (978-968-16-7386-4(7), FC15223) Fondo de Cultura Economica.

Korngold, Jamie. Sadie's Snowy Tu B'Shevat. Fortenberry, Julie, illus. 2017. (ENG.). 32p. (J). (gr. -1-1). 17.99 (978-1-5124-2677-9(6), cc2842f7-c68a-4c05-8326-0b0af8b8de00, Kar-Ben Publishing) Lerner Publishing Group.

Krauss, Ruth. The Carrot Seed: 75th Anniversary. Johnson, Crockett, illus. 60th anniv. ed. 2020. (ENG.). 32p. (J). (gr. -1-3). pap. 7.99 (978-0-06-443210-8(6), HarperCollins) HarperCollins Pubs.

Larsen, Kirsten. Lily's Pesky Plant. Clarke, Judith Holmes & Disney Storybook Artists Staff, illus. 2006. (Disney Fairies Chapters Ser.). (ENG.). 110p. (J). (gr. 1-4). 18.69 (978-0-7364-2374-8(5)) Random Hse. Bks. for Young Readers.

The Laughing Lavender Field. 2005. (J). 5.00 (978-0-9765731-0-4(5)) DTJ, LLC.

Leszczynski, Diana. Fern Verdant & the Silver Rose. 2009. (Playaway Children Ser.). (J). 59.99 (978-1-4332-7708-5(5)) Findaway World, LLC.

Loos, Jody C. Alex the Alien: Bubble Magic. 2013. 24p. pap. 14.95 (978-1-4787-0322-8(9)) Outskirts Pr., Inc.

Lotfy, Evelyn. Ms. Plant & Friends. 2011. (ENG.). 24p. (gr. -1). pap. 14.98 (978-1-4567-5448-8(3)) AuthorHouse.

Lucas, Nancy T. Peppy's Coral Kingdom. 2008. (ENG.). 24p. pap. 12.99 (978-1-4196-9046-4(9)) CreateSpace Independent Publishing Platform.

Lucas, Ronne Kay. How the Cactus Got Its Thorns. 2013. 20p. pap. 24.95 (978-1-4626-8915-6(9)) America Star Bks.

Luke, Melinda. The Green Dog. Manning, Jane K., illus. 2006. (Science Solves It Ser.). 32p. (J). pap. 7.99 (978-0-15-356581-6(0)) Houghton Mifflin Harcourt School Pubs.

MacLachlan, Patricia. Prairie Days. Archer, Micha, illus. 2020. (ENG.). 40p. (J). (gr. -1-3). 17.99 (978-1-4424-4191-0(7), McElderry, Margaret K. Bks.) McElderry, Margaret K. Bks.

Magers, Ramona Hirsch. Walter's Discovery. Hirsch, Charmaine, illus. 2008. 26p. pap. 24.95 (978-1-60563-623-8(1)) America Star Bks.

Martin, Dawn L. Freeze Dance: A Story of the Dancing Cactus. 2011. 36p. pap. (978-1-4269-8196-8(1)) Trafford Publishing (UK) Ltd.

May, Eleanor. Let's Go, Snow! Temperature Measurement. Pillo, Cary, illus. 2017. (Math Matters (r) Ser.). (ENG.). 32p. (J). (gr. k-3). E-Book 23.99 (978-1-57565-808-7(9)) Astra Publishing Hse.

McArthur, Nancy. The Mystery of the Plant That Ate Dirty Socks. 2004. 162p. pap. 11.95 (978-0-595-33693-7(0), Backinprint.com) iUniverse, Inc.

—The Plant That Ate Dirty Socks. (Plant That Ate Dirty Socks Ser.: Bk. 1). 119p. (J). (gr. k-3). pap. 4.50 (978-0-8072-1494-7(9), Listening Library) Random Hse. Audio Publishing Group.

McQuinn, Anna. A Leo le Gusta Bebelandia. Hearson, Ruth, illus. 2015. (Leo Can! Ser.). (SPA.). 24p. (J). (— 1). lib. bdg. 9.95 (978-1-58089-704-4(5)) Charlesbridge Publishing, Inc.

Meddaugh, Susan. Just Teenie. 2006. (ENG., Illus.). 32p. (J). (gr. -1-3). 16.00 (978-0-618-68565-3(0), 591422, Clarion Bks.) HarperCollins Pubs.

Merchant, Richard. The Anise Seed. 2013. 24p. pap. 24.95 (978-1-63004-371-1(0)) America Star Bks.

Metzger, Steve. The Biggest Leaf Pile. Dubin, Jill, illus. 2003. (J). (978-0-439-55657-6(0)) Scholastic, Inc.

—We're Going on a Leaf Hunt. Sakamoto, Miki, illus. (J). 2008. (ENG.). 32p. (gr. -1-3). pap. 7.99 (978-0-439-87377-2(0), Cartwheel Bks.) 2005. pap. (978-0-439-77361-4(X)) Scholastic, Inc.

Minger, Janet. How Do Strawberries & Green Beans Sleep at Night? 2011. 28p. pap. 13.54 (978-1-4567-2239-5(5)) AuthorHouse.

Morgan, Ruth. Jess & the Bean Root. Vagnozzi, Barbara, illus. 2005. (ENG.). 24p. (J). lib. bdg. 23.65 (978-1-59646-732-3(0)) Dingles & Co.

Nolen, Jerdine. Plantzilla Goes to Camp. Catrow, David, illus. 2006. (ENG.). 32p. (J). (gr. k-3). 19.99 (978-0-689-86803-0(0), Simon & Schuster/Paula Wiseman Bks.) Simon & Schuster/Paula Wiseman Bks.

Nolen, Jerdine & Kelher, Brian. Plantzilla. Catrow, David, illus. 2005. (ENG.). 32p. (J). (gr. -1-3). reprint ed. pap. 7.99 (978-0-15-205392-5(1), 1196232, Clarion Bks.) HarperCollins Pubs.

O'Connor, Jane. Poison Ivy Expert. Glasser, Robin Preiss & Enik, Ted, illus. 2008. (Fancy Nancy - I Can Read! Ser.). 32p. (J). lib. bdg. 13.55 (978-1-4364-5050-8(0)) Turtleback.

Oliver, Jane. The Birthday Surprise, 1 vol. Raga, Silvia, illus. 2009. (Get Ready Readers Ser.). (ENG.). 32p. (J). (gr. k-k). lib. bdg. 27.27 (978-1-60754-257-5(9), 8b234709-44a4-424b-806d-18a05a759930, Windmill Bks.) Rosen Publishing Group, Inc., The.

Ozgur, Lynne Emily. Darryl & the Mountain. Abay, Ismail, illus. 2009. (ENG.). 32p. (J). (gr. 2-4). 9.95 (978-1-59784-138-2(2), Tughra Bks.) Blue Dome, Inc.

Pacheco, Maria & Garcia-Martinez, Julia. The Hamburger Tree. Hergenroeder, Ernie, illus. 2006. 24p. (J). (978-0-9776835-0-5(8)) Run With Me Publishing.

Park, Linda Sue. Wing & Claw #1: Forest of Wonders. Madsen, Jim, illus. 2016. (Wing & Claw Ser.: 1). (ENG.). 352p. (J). (gr. 3-7). 16.99 (978-0-06-232738-3(0), HarperCollins) HarperCollins Pubs.

Parker, Emma. Chuck the Chilli. 2010. (Illus.). pap. (978-1-877547-92-8(1)) First Edition Ltd.

Pier, Daniel Wayne. Ferrous the Venus Fly Trap Meets the Cactus. 2008. 36p. pap. 24.95 (978-1-60441-645-9(9)) PublishAmerica, Inc.

Pike, Aprilynne. Hechizos. 2012.Tr. of Spells. (UND & SPA.). 352p. (YA). pap. 18.95 (978-84-96886-27-8(1)) Ediciones Urano S. A. ESP. Dist: Spanish Pubs., LLC.

—Spells. 2011. (Wings Ser.: 2). (ENG.). 384p. (YA). (gr. 8). pap. 9.99 (978-0-06-166808-1(7), HarperTeen) HarperCollins Pubs.

—Spells, 7 vols. 2010. (YA). 78.75 (978-1-4407-8375-3(6)) Recorded Bks., Inc.

—Wings. 2011. (Wings Ser.: 1). (ENG.). 320p. (YA). (gr. 8). pap. 9.99 (978-0-06-166805-0(2), HarperTeen) HarperCollins Pubs.

Pittar, Gill. Milly, Molly & Jimmy's Seeds. 2004. (Illus.). 28p. (978-1-86972-000-1(8)) Milly Molly Bks.

Pizzoli, Greg. The Watermelon Seed. Pizzoli, Greg, illus. 2013. (ENG., Illus.). 40p. (J). (gr. -1-k). 18.99 (978-1-4231-7101-0(2)) Little, Brown Bks. for Young Readers.

Prignano, Barbara. How Bunnies Got Their Cottontails. 2009. (Illus.). 20p. pap. 11.95 (978-1-60860-675-7(9), Eloquent Bks.) Strategic Book Publishing & Rights Agency (SBPRA).

Prose, Francine. Rhino, Rhino, Sweet Potato. Armstrong, Matthew S., illus. 2009. 32p. (J). (gr. -1-1). lib. bdg. 18.89 (978-0-06-008079-2(5)) HarperCollins Pubs.

Pugliano-Martin, Carol. The Great Big Giant Turnip: Set Of 6. 2010. (Early Connections Ser.). (J). pap. 39.00 net. (978-1-4108-1553-8(6)) Benchmark Education Co.

Rere The Storyteller. I Am a Wish. 2013. 36p. 25.99 (978-1-4808-0090-8(2)) Archway Publishing.

Rey, H. A. Curious George Plants a Seed/Jorge el Curioso Siembra una Semilla: Bilingual English-Spanish. 2007. (Curious George TV Ser.). (ENG., Illus.). 24p. (J). (gr. -1-3). mass mkt. 5.99 (978-0-618-89688-2(0), 498198, Clarion Bks.) HarperCollins Pubs.

Rey, H. A. & Rey, Margret. The H. A. Rey Treasury of Stories. 2015. (Dover Children's Classics Ser.). (ENG., Illus.). 112p. (J). (gr. 2-4). pap. 14.99 (978-0-486-78468-7(1), 784681) Dover Pubns., Inc.

Robinson, Bonita. The Little Seed That Could. 2011. 24p. pap. 24.95 (978-1-4626-4234-2(9)) America Star Bks.

Rochelin, Ghyslaine. The Coconut Tree. Bertoni, Oliver, illus. 2010. (HAT.). 32p. (J). pap. 14.95 (978-1-60195-319-3(4)) International Step by Step Assn.

Root, Phyllis. One North Star: A Counting Book. Prange, Beckie & Bowen, Betsy, illus. 2016. (ENG.). 36p. 16.95 (978-0-8166-5063-7(2)) Univ. of Minnesota Pr.

Rovetch, L. Bob. TLC Grow with Me! McLeod, Chum, illus. 2005. (J). (978-1-58987-114-4(6)) Kindermusik International.

Santos, Penelope. A Seed's Story, 1 vol. 2015. (Rosen REAL Readers: STEM & STEAM Collection). (ENG.). 8p. (gr. k-1). pap. 5.46 (978-1-4994-9569-0(2), f3dcc44a-3f3f-481d-b496-45f54991dfbb, Rosen Classroom) Rosen Publishing Group, Inc., The.

Shivers, Juliette. Brenda Doesn't Like Broccoli. 2004.Tr. of Brenda no le Gusta Bróculi. (Illus.). 25p. (J). 6.50 (978-0-9769379-0-6(5)) Ingram's Nutrition Consultations.

Simonson, Louise. Harley Quinn's Crazy Creeper Caper. Vecchio, Luciano, illus. 2017. (Batman & Robin Adventures Ser.). (ENG.). 88p. (J). (gr. 2-6). lib. bdg. 26.65 (978-1-4965-5347-8(0), 136289, Stone Arch Bks.) Capstone.

Sommer, Cindy. Salvando Las Flores de Camelia, 1 vol. Allen Klein, Laurie, illus. 2016. (SPA.). 32p. (J). (gr. k-1). pap. 11.95 (978-1-62855-872-2(5), 5ad6fc34-bb4d-46a9-94a6-a2ee62c8206b) Arbordale Publishing.

Spalding, Esta. Knock about with the Fitzgerald-Trouts. Smith, Sydney, illus. 2017. (ENG.). 320p. (J). (gr. 3-7). 16.99 (978-0-316-29860-5(3)) Little, Brown Bks. for Young Readers.

Splawn, "E". Planting Fruitful Seeds. 2011. 32p. pap. 12.77 (978-1-4567-3896-9(8)) AuthorHouse.

Swain, Cynthia. Sorting at the Nature Center. 2006. (Early Explorers Ser.). (J). pap. (978-1-4108-6039-2(6)) Benchmark Education Co.

Swanson, Tina M. Silly Sierra & the Mysterious Mushroom. 2011. 28p. pap. 13.99 (978-1-4634-3594-3(0)) AuthorHouse.

Switzer, Vern. Lucy the Cantaloupe. Connally, Perry L., Sr., illus. 2005. 32p. (J). 15.95 (978-0-9753542-1-6(3)) Rural Farm Productions.

—Puffy the Watermelon. Listokin, David & Connally, Perry L., Sr., illus. 2004. 24p. (J). 15.95 (978-0-9753542-0-9(5)) Rural Farm Productions.

The Story Pirates & West, Jacqueline. The Story Pirates Present. Aly, Hatem, illus. 2019. (Story Pirates Ser.: 2). 288p. (J). (gr. 3-7). 13.99 (978-1-63565-091-4(7), 9781635650914, Random Hse. Bks. for Young Readers) Random Hse. Children's Bks.

Thompson, Holly. The Wakame Gatherers. Wilds, Kazumi, illus. 2007. (Wakame Gatherers Ser.). 32p. (J). (gr. -1-3). 16.95 (978-1-885008-33-6(3), Shen's Bks.) Lee & Low Bks., Inc.

Tobin, Paul. Lawnmageddon #1. Chan, Ron & Rainwater, Matthew J., illus. 2016. (Plants vs. Zombies Ser.). (ENG.). 28p. (J). (gr. 3-7). lib. bdg. 31.36 (978-1-61479-540-7(1), 21447, Graphic Novels) Spotlight.

—Lawnmageddon #2. Chan, Ron & Rainwater, Matthew J., illus. 2016. (Plants vs. Zombies Ser.). (ENG.). 28p. (J). (gr. 3-7). lib. bdg. 31.36 (978-1-61479-541-4(X), 21448, Graphic Novels) Spotlight.

—Lawnmageddon #3. Chan, Ron & Rainwater, Matthew J., illus. 2016. (Plants vs. Zombies Ser.). (ENG.). 28p. (J). (gr. 3-7). lib. bdg. 31.36 (978-1-61479-542-1(8), 21449, Graphic Novels) Spotlight.

—Plants vs. Zombies: War & Peas, Vol .11. Churilla, Brian et al, illus. 2018. 88p. (J). (gr. 3-7). 10.99 (978-1-5067-0677-1(0), Dark Horse Books) Dark Horse Comics.

—Plants vs. Zombies: Garden Warfare Volume 2. Lattie, Tim, illus. 2018. 88p. (J). (gr. 3-7). 10.99 (978-1-5067-0548-4(0), Dark Horse Books) Dark Horse Comics.

—Plants vs. Zombies Volume 13: Snow Thanks. Farris, Cat, illus. 2019. 88p. (J). (gr. 3-7). 10.99 (978-1-5067-0839-3(0), Dark Horse Books) Dark Horse Comics.

—Plants vs. Zombies Volume 8: Lawn of Doom. Chan, Ron, illus. 2017. 80p. (J). (gr. 2-5). 10.99 (978-1-5067-0204-9(X), Dark Horse Books) Dark Horse Comics.

—Plants vs. Zombies Volume 9: the Greatest Show Unearthed. Chabot, Jacob & Rainwater, Matt J., illus. 2018. 80p. (J). (gr. 3-7). 10.99 (978-1-5067-0298-8(8), Dark Horse Books) Dark Horse Comics.

Tolstoy, Aleksei. The Gigantic Turnip. Sharkey, Niamh, illus. 2005. (ENG.). 40p. (J). (gr. -1-2). pap. 9.99 (978-1-905236-58-9(1)) Barefoot Bks., Inc.

Vagnozzi, Barbara, illus. Jack & the Beanstalk. 2005. (Flip-Up Fairy Tales Ser.). 24p. (J). pap. (978-1-904550-20-4(7)) Child's Play International Ltd.

Walker, Richard. Jack & the Beanstalk. 2009. (ENG., Illus.). (J). 16.99 (978-1-84686-297-7(3)) Barefoot Bks., Inc.

—Juan y Los Frijoles Magico. Sharkey, Niamh, illus. 2008. 40p. (J). (gr. -1-2). pap. 10.99 (978-1-84686-216-8(7)) Barefoot Bks., Inc.

Weisenfluh, Craig. ABC's in the Trees, a LittleWeeds Adventure: A book for Little Ones. 2007. (Illus.). (J). 11.95 (978-0-9746782-1-4(X)) B'Squeak Productions.

Wheeler, Eliza. Miss Maple's Seeds. Wheeler, Eliza, illus. (Illus.). (J). 2017. 40p. (-k). pap. 8.99 (978-0-425-28889-4(7), Puffin Books) 2013. 32p. (gr. -1-k). 17.99 (978-0-399-25792-6(6), Nancy Paulsen Books) Penguin Young Readers Group.

—Miss Maple's Seeds. 2017. lib. bdg. 19.65 (978-0-606-40087-9(7)) Turtleback.

Williams, Dawn. Very Little Venus & the Very Friendly Fly. Chou, Joey, illus. 2007. 48p. (J). 15.00 (978-0-9770783-2-5(9)) SunriseHouse Pubs.

Wolchansky, Molly Kay. The Cactus & the Balloon. 2009. 24p. pap. 12.99 (978-1-4490-1037-9(7)) AuthorHouse.

Woodbridge, Nancy Garfield. A Bouquet of Fairy Tales. 2012. 108p. pap. 15.99 (978-1-4771-4492-3(7)) Xlibris Corp.

Zhang, Gracey. Lala's Words. Zhang, Gracey, illus. 2021. (ENG., Illus.). 48p. (J). (gr. -1-3). 18.99 (978-1-338-64823-2(3), Orchard Bks.) Scholastic, Inc.

PLANTS, FOSSIL

Aspen-Baxter, Linda. Plants. 2004. (Prehistoric Life Ser.). (Illus.). 32p. (J). lib. bdg. 26.00 (978-1-59036-114-6(8)) Weigl Pubs., Inc.

Aspen-Baxter, Linda & Lomberg, Michelle. Planets. 2004. (Prehistoric Life Ser.). (Illus.). 24p. (J). (gr. -1-3). pap. 9.95 (978-1-59036-174-0(1)) Weigl Pubs., Inc.

Connors, Kathleen. Petrified Forests, 1 vol. 2012. (Fossilized! Ser.). (ENG., Illus.). 24p. (J). (gr. 2-3). pap. 9.15 (978-1-4339-6422-0(8), 3e9525dd-2397-45c3-9121-12a7caede176); lib. bdg. 25.27 (978-1-4339-6420-6(1), fcf837aa-9432-4e66-8aa4-6a67b2c17dfe) Stevens, Gareth Publishing LLLP.

Hyde, Natalie. Plant Fossils. 2013. (ENG., Illus.). 32p. (J). (978-0-7787-1264-0(8)); pap. (978-0-7787-1268-8(0)) Crabtree Publishing Co.

Matthews, Rupert. 100 Facts Prehistoric Life. Kelly, Richard, ed. 2017. 48p. (J). pap. 9.95 (978-1-78209-385-5(0)) Miles Kelly Publishing, Ltd. GBR. Dist: Parkwest Pubns., Inc.

PLANTS—GROWTH

see Growth (Plants)

PLANTS, MEDICINAL

see Botany, Medical

PLANTS—PROPAGATION

see Plant Propagation

PLANTS—STRUCTURE

see Plant Anatomy

PLANTS, USEFUL

see Botany, Economic; Plants, Edible

PLASTIC MATERIALS

see Plastics

PLASTICS

see also Synthetic Products

Blaxland, Wendy. Helmets, 1 vol. 2010. (How Are They Made? Ser.). (ENG., Illus.). 32p. (gr. 4-4). lib. bdg. 21.27 (978-0-7614-4755-9(5), ae6d9dcc-5a31-4433-ba4f-003f5d14d277) Cavendish Square Publishing LLC.

Blevins, Wiley. The Not-So-Right Day. Kreloff, Elliot, illus. (Basic Concepts Ser.). (ENG.). 24p. (J). (gr. -1 — 1). 2018. pap. 6.99 (978-1-63440-418-1(1), 8453da2e-8fc6-4e7b-b073-fc950f93c2c8) 2016. lib. bdg. 14.99 (978-1-63440-083-1(6), 5550f1e4-ab94-4bff-a266-6f2209a71aaf) Red Chair Pr. (Rocking Chair Kids).

Colich, Abby. Plastic, 1 vol. 2013. (Exploring Materials Ser.). (ENG.). 24p. (J). (gr. -1-1). pap. 6.95 (978-1-4329-8025-2(4), 123181, Heinemann) Capstone.

Goodstein, Madeline. Plastics & Polymers Science Fair Projects, Using the Scientific Method, 1 vol. rev. exp. ed. 2010. (Chemistry Science Projects Using the Scientific Method Ser.). (ENG., Illus.). 160p. (gr. 5-6). 38.60 (978-0-7660-3412-9(7), f3dfba6c-ef48-41a9-ab5d-d360bd356248) Enslow Publishing, LLC.

Graham, Ian. You Wouldn't Want to Live Without Plastic! 2015. (You Wouldn't Want to Live Without Ser.). lib. bdg. 20.80 *(978-0-606-37472-9(8))* Turtleback.

Jennings, Terry. Plastic. 2006. (Illus.). 32p. (YA). (gr. 1-18). lib. bdg. 27.10 *(978-1-932333-03-9(7))* Chrysalis Education.

Kachur, Matthew. A Miracle Material & un material Milagroso: 6 English, 6 Spanish Adaptations. 2011. (ENG & SPA.). (J). 97.00 net. *(978-1-4108-5717-0(4))* Benchmark Education Co.

Langley, Andrew. Plastic. 2008. (Everyday Materials Ser.). (ENG., Illus.). 24p. (J). (gr. k-3). pap. *(978-0-7787-4136-7(2))* Crabtree Publishing Co.

Lepetit, Angie. Trash Magic: A Book about Recycling a Plastic Bottle, 1 vol. 2013. (Earth Matters Ser.). (ENG.). 32p. (J). (gr. -1-2). pap. 8.10 *(978-1-62065-743-0(0)*, 121727); (gr. -1-2). lib. bdg. 27.99 *(978-1-62065-049-3(5)*, 120744); (gr. 1-2). pap. 48.60 *(978-1-62065-744-7(9)*, 19325, Capstone Pr.) Capstone.

Llewellyn, Claire. Plastic. 2005. (I Know That! Ser.). (Illus.). 24p. (J). (gr. 1-3). lib. bdg. 22.80 *(978-1-932889-53-6(1))* Sea-To-Sea Pubns.

Lombardo, Jennifer. Should Plastic Bags Be Banned?, 1 vol. 2019. (Points of View Ser.). (ENG.). 24p. (gr. 3-3). lib. bdg. 26.23 *(978-1-5345-3194-9(7)*, 81c015e3-499e-42eb-873a-acb5ed6fd790, KidHaven Publishing) Greenhaven Publishing LLC.

Macken, JoAnn Early. Take a Closer Look at Plastic. 2016. (Core Content Science — Take a Closer Look Ser.). (ENG., Illus.). 40p. (J). (gr. 2-4). lib. bdg. 26.65 *(978-1-63440-050-3(X)*, c1b35a51-c21c-4fc0-b92b-0e7d2726c6b3) Red Chair Pr.

Malue, Jenna. Recycling Plastic: Understand Place Value, 1 vol. 2014. (Math Masters: Number & Operations in Base Ten Ser.). (ENG., Illus.). 24p. (J). (gr. 2-2). 25.27 *(978-1-4777-6427-5(5)*, 6cacfd0c-4026-462f-acd8-f3d5ad0a19dc); pap. 8.25 *(978-1-4777-4651-6(X)*, c66434b2-cbd6-4407-aef6-31e2ef3b6079) Rosen Publishing Group, Inc., The. (Rosen Classroom).

Manchester, Meta. Oops! It's Plastic!, 1 vol. 2019. (Accidental Scientific Discoveries That Changed the World Ser.). (ENG.). 32p. (gr. 3-4). pap. 11.50 *(978-1-5382-3994-0(9)*, e5685627-53ad-4e38-b7e2-205b2cd1e470) Stevens, Gareth Publishing LLLP.

Meachen Rau, Dana. Plastic, 1 vol. 2012. (Use It! Reuse It! Ser.). (ENG.). 24p. (gr. 3-3). 25.50 *(978-1-60870-518-4(8)*, 375f26ec-d144-4cff-bf1d-260ee00fc530) Cavendish Square Publishing LLC.

Mitchell, Melanie S. Plastic. 2003. (First Step Nonfiction - Materials Ser.). (ENG., Illus.). 24p. (gr. k-2). lib. bdg. 23.93 *(978-0-8225-4620-7(5))* Lerner Publishing Group.

Morris, Neil. Plastics. 2010. (Materials That Matter Ser.). (ENG.). 32p. (J). (gr. 4-6). lib. bdg. 28.50 *(978-1-60753-068-8(6)*, 14867) Amicus.

Newman, Patricia. Plastic, Ahoy! Investigating the Great Pacific Garbage Patch. Crawley, Annie, illus. 2014. (ENG.). 48p. (J). (gr. 3-6). lib. bdg. 30.65 *(978-1-4677-1283-5(3)*, 79120d0d-5b42-47f6-80e4-e7af8c1d8d00, Millbrook Pr.) Lerner Publishing Group.

Oxlade, Chris. Global Warming. 2012. (Mapping Global Issues Ser.). 48p. (J). (gr. 7-9). lib. bdg. 34.25 *(978-1-59920-508-3(4))* Black Rabbit Bks.

Rae, Alison. Oil, Plastics, & Power. 2010. (Development Without Damage Ser.). (YA). (gr. 5-9). 34.25 *(978-1-59920-251-8(4))* Black Rabbit Bks.

Ridley, Sarah. A Plastic Toy, 1 vol. 2006. (How It's Made Ser.). (ENG., Illus.). 32p. (gr. 2-4). lib. bdg. 28.67 *(978-0-8368-6704-6(1)*, 797fdafb-6b96-46ad-8d20-35d61e7a7ad2, Gareth Stevens Learning Library) Stevens, Gareth Publishing LLLP.

Ritchie, Scot. Join the No-Plastic Challenge! A First Book of Reducing Waste. Ritchie, Scot, illus. 2019. (Exploring Our Community Ser.). (ENG., Illus.). 32p. (J). (gr. -1-2). 16.99 *(978-1-5253-0240-4(X))* Kids Can Pr., Ltd. CAN. Dist: Hachette Bk. Group.

Rivera, Andrea. Plastic. 2017. (Materials Ser.). (ENG., Illus.). 24p. (J). (gr. -1-2). lib. bdg. 31.36 *(978-1-5321-2033-6(8)*, 25302, Abdo Zoom-Launch) ABDO Publishing Co.

Royston, Angela. Plastic: Let's Look at the Frisbee. 2005. (J). *(978-1-4109-1820-8(3))*; (ENG.). 24p. pap. *(978-1-4109-1829-1(7))* Steck-Vaughn.

Shores, Lori. Cómo Hacer Slime. 2010. (Divertirse con la Ciencia/Hands-On Science Fun Ser.).Tr. of How to Make Slime. (MUL.). 24p. (J). (gr. -1-2). lib. bdg. 27.32 *(978-1-4296-6106-5(2)*, 115129) Capstone.

—How to Make Slime: A 4D Book. rev. ed. 2018. (Hands-On Science Fun Ser.). (ENG., Illus.). 24p. (J). (gr. -1-2). lib. bdg. 29.32 *(978-1-5435-0942-7(8)*, 137649, Capstone Pr.) Capstone.

Smith-Llera, Danielle. You Are Eating Plastic Every Day: What's in Our Food? 2019. (Informed! Ser.). (ENG., Illus.). 64p. (J). (gr. 5-9). 37.32 *(978-0-7565-6174-1(4)*, 140657); pap. 8.95 *(978-0-7565-6229-8(5)*, 140930) Capstone. (Compass Point Bks.).

Sterngass, Jon & Katchur, Matt. Plastics, 1 vol. 2005. (Great Inventions Ser.). (ENG., Illus.). 48p. (gr. 5-8). lib. bdg. 33.67 *(978-0-8368-5878-5(6)*, 04947a13-7daa-4be0-a97d-580bec7fd030, Gareth Stevens Secondary Library) Stevens, Gareth Publishing LLLP.

Walker, Kate. Plastic Bottles & Bags, 1 vol. Vanzet, Gaston, illus. 2011. (Recycling Ser.). (ENG.). 32p. (J). (gr. 1-1). 31.21 *(978-1-60870-133-9(6)*, f86dcce6-61ab-46d8-9160-42ace951affc) Cavendish Square Publishing LLC.

Wallace, Holly. Plastic. 2007. (How We Use Materials/Watts Ser.). (Illus.). 30p. (J). (gr. 4-7). lib. bdg. 28.50 *(978-1-59920-005-7(8))* Black Rabbit Bks.

PLATYPUS

Antill, Sara. Platypus, 1 vol. 2010. (Unusual Animals Ser.). (ENG., Illus.). 24p. (J). (gr. 2-3). pap. 9.15 *(978-1-60754-997-0(2)*, d24aa32e-3b4a-4af5-9ee7-4168786187a1); lib. bdg. 27.27 *(978-1-60754-991-8(3)*, 38e1b2bd-d5fb-4c82-8bcc-d9e906416ff5) Rosen Publishing Group, Inc., The. (Windmill Bks.).

Borgert-Spaniol, Megan. Platypuses. 2015. (Animal Safari Ser.). (ENG., Illus.). 24p. (J). (gr. k-3). lib. bdg. 26.95 *(978-1-62617-212-8(9)*, Blastoff! Readers) Bellwether Media.

Caper, William. Platypus: A Century-Long Mystery. 2008. (Uncommon Animals Ser.). (Illus.). 32p. (YA). (gr. 2-5). lib. bdg. 28.50 *(978-1-59716-735-2(5)*, 1284359) Bearport Publishing Co., Inc.

Clarke, Ginjer L. Platypus! Mirocha, Paul, illus. 2004. (Step into Reading Ser.). (ENG.). 32p. (J). (gr. -1-1). pap. 5.99 *(978-0-375-82417-3(0)*, Random Hse. Bks. for Young Readers) Random Hse. Children's Bks.

Collard, Sneed B., III & Collard, Sneed B. A Platypus, Probably. Plant, Andrew, illus. 2005. 32p. (J). (gr. k-3). per. 7.95 *(978-1-57091-584-0(9))* Charlesbridge Publishing, Inc.

Leaf, Christina. Platypus. 2014. (Extremely Weird Animals Ser.). (ENG., Illus.). 24p. (J). (gr. 3-8). lib. bdg. 27.95 *(978-1-62617-076-6(2)*, Pilot Bks.) Bellwether Media.

Lunis, Natalie. Electric Animals. 2011. (Animals with Super Powers Ser.). 24p. (YA). (gr. 2-5). lib. bdg. 26.99 *(978-1-61772-121-2(2))* Bearport Publishing Co., Inc.

Meister, Cari. Do You Really Want to Meet a Platypus? Fabbri, Daniele, illus. 2014. (Do You Really Want to Meet ... ? Ser.). (ENG.). 24p. (J). (gr. 1-4). lib. bdg. 27.10 *(978-1-60753-460-0(6)*, 15898) Amicus.

Rudolph, Jessica. Platypus. 2017. (Weirder & Cuter Ser.). (ENG.). 24p. (J). (gr. -1-3). 17.95 *(978-1-68402-264-9(9))* Bearport Publishing Co., Inc.

PLAY

see also Amusements; Games; Recreation; Sports

Ajmera, Maya & Ivanko, John D. Come Out & Play: A Global Journey. 2020. 32p. (J). (gr. -1-3). 16.99 *(978-1-62354-163-7(8))* Charlesbridge Publishing, Inc.

Alizadeh, Kip. Quiet! Alizadeh, Kip, illus. 2017. (Child's Play Library). (ENG., Illus.). 32p. (J). *(978-1-84643-887-5(X))* Child's Play International Ltd.

Allan, Delores. Magical Moments with Roy & Toni: Fun at the Fair. 2011. 28p. pap. 13.59 *(978-1-4634-1546-4(X))* AuthorHouse.

Armstrong, Linda. Game On! Screen-Free Fun for Children Two & Up. 2018. (ENG., Illus.). 168p. pap. 19.95 *(978-1-60554-548-6(1))* Redleaf Pr.

Atlantic, Leonard. We Play with Pets!, 1 vol. 2017. (Ways to Play Ser.). (ENG.). 24p. (gr. k-k). pap. 9.15 *(978-1-4824-6357-6(1)*, 83478db0-a5a7-425e-843d-7596e30c5cfd) Stevens, Gareth Publishing LLLP.

Baker, Sue & Stockham, Jessica. Sleep Tight! Stockham, Jess, illus. 2006. (Blanket Babies Ser.). (ENG.). 12p. (J). (gr. -1-k). bds. *(978-1-904550-90-7(8))* Child's Play International Ltd.

The Bees & the Bear: Individual Title Six-Packs. (Story Steps Ser.). (gr. k-2). 32.00 *(978-0-7635-9806-8(2))* Rigby Education.

Benchmark Education Co., LLC. Play, Play, Play All Day Big Book. 2014. (Shared Reading Foundations Ser.). (J). (gr. -1). *(978-1-4509-9434-7(2))* Benchmark Education Co.

Bidder, Jane. Inventions We Use for Play, 1 vol. 2006. (Everyday Inventions Ser.). (ENG., Illus.). 32p. (gr. 2-4). lib. bdg. 28.67 *(978-0-8368-6900-2(1)*, b2a5ce2c-f124-406f-a42a-d74d2a0455df, Gareth Stevens Learning Library) Stevens, Gareth Publishing LLLP.

Cartwright, Mary. Splish, Splash, Splosh Bath Bk. Wells, Rachel, illus. 2007. 8p. (J). 14.99 *(978-0-7945-1619-2(X)*, Usborne) EDC Publishing.

Carver, Patty, et al. The Amazing Adventures of Peter Rabbit: An Interactive Musical Based on the Story by Beatrix Potter. 2013. 43p. *(978-0-87602-395-2(2))* Family Plays.

Chohan, Satinder, et al. Migration Plays: Four Large Cast Ensemble Stories for Teenagers. Kennedy, Fin, ed. 2019. (ENG.). 136p. pap. *(978-1-350-09041-5(7)*, 415900, Methuen Drama) Bloomsbury Publishing Plc.

Colich, Abby. A Babysitter's Guide to Keeping the Kids Entertained. 2017. (Go-To Guides). (ENG., Illus.). 32p. (J). (gr. 3-9). lib. bdg. 28.65 *(978-1-5157-3664-6(4)*, 133649, Capstone Pr.) Capstone.

Conner, Bobbi. Unplugged Play: No Batteries. No Plugs. Pure Fun. 2007. (ENG., Illus.). 516p. (J). (gr. -1-5). pap. 16.95 *(978-0-7611-4390-1(4)*, 14390) Workman Publishing Co., Inc.

Connors, Kathleen. We Play House!, 1 vol. 2018. (Ways to Play Ser.). (ENG.). 24p. (J). (gr. k-k). lib. bdg. 24.27 *(978-1-5382-2880-7(7)*, 772a5420-75bf-4614-b203-086ae0367f8c) Stevens, Gareth Publishing LLLP.

—We Play Kitchen!, 1 vol. 2018. (Ways to Play Ser.). (ENG.). 24p. (gr. k-k). 24.27 *(978-1-5382-2881-4(5)*, cae721c7-7b67-41e9-ab6e-af1d5615aa79) Stevens, Gareth Publishing LLLP.

—We Play Outside!, 1 vol. 2018. (Ways to Play Ser.). (ENG.). 24p. (gr. k-k). lib. bdg. 24.27 *(978-1-5382-2882-1(3)*, d1efff10-e58a-4a4e-b9fd-37faceba41b2) Stevens, Gareth Publishing LLLP.

—We Play Superheroes!, 1 vol. 2018. (Ways to Play Ser.). (ENG.). 24p. (gr. k-k). lib. bdg. 24.27 *(978-1-5382-2884-5(X)*, ad10dae0-b6e6-4706-ae9b-9a3affc33ad4) Stevens, Gareth Publishing LLLP.

D'Andrea, Deborah & Borlasca, Hector. Pretend & Play Kitty: With Real Crown You Can Wear! 2004. 10p. (J). (gr. -1-18). bds. *(978-1-57151-735-7(9))* Playhouse Publishing.

Desalle, Nicole. Safe at Play. 2011. pap. 39.95 *(978-0-7664-3752-4(3))* Abrams & Co. Pubs., Inc.

Dewberry, Melba. Rainy Day Fun, 1 vol. 2016. (We Love Spring! Ser.). (ENG., Illus.). 24p. (J). (gr. k-k). pap. 9.15 *(978-1-4824-5503-8(X)*, 5dca9e0d-6e29-4ce6-9d57-0f08da5f65cc) Stevens, Gareth Publishing LLLP.

Dixon, Dallas L. Little Boys Run. Little Boys Play. Williams, Nancy E., ed. Cappoen, Jennifer Tipton, illus. 2013. 44p. (J). pap. 12.98 *(978-1-938526-40-4(6))* Laurus Co., Inc., The.

Editorial Staff, Gareth. Things I Play With, 1 vol. 2007. (Things in My World Ser.). (ENG., Illus.). 16p. (gr. k-1). pap. 6.30 *(978-0-8368-6818-0(8)*, f49a7141-e4e2-4f56-bb6e-4968e525115f, Weekly Reader Leveled Readers) Stevens, Gareth Publishing LLLP.

—Things I Play with / Las Cosas con Las Que Juego, 1 vol. 2006. (Things in My World / Las Cosas de Mi Mundo Ser.). (ENG & SPA.). 16p. (gr. k-1). pap. 6.30 *(978-0-8368-7230-9(4)*, cc9d8dce-82a6-4daa-b9ca-40de87dc1d82, Weekly Reader Leveled Readers) Stevens, Gareth Publishing LLLP.

English, Alex. Mine, Mine, Mine Said the Porcupine. Levey, Emma, illus. 2019. (Early Bird Readers — Blue (Early Bird Stories (tm)) Ser.). (ENG.). 32p. (J). (gr. -1-2). 30.65 *(978-1-5415-4173-3(1)*, b037c99e-c022-438e-9914-09036213cf0c, Lerner Pubns.) Lerner Publishing Group.

Gaertner, Meg. People in Spring. 2020. (Spring Is Here Ser.). (ENG., Illus.). 16p. (J). (gr. k-1). pap. 7.95 *(978-1-64493-100-4(1)*, 1644931001); lib. bdg. 25.64 *(978-1-64493-021-2(8)*, 1644930218) North Star Editions. (Focus Readers).

Harbison, Lawrence, ed. 5-Minute Plays for Teens. 2017. (Applause Acting Ser.). 272p. pap. 16.99 *(978-1-4950-6925-3(7)*, 1495069257, Applause Theatre & Cinema) Leonard, Hal Corp.

Higgins, Melissa. Let's Play! Awesome Activities Every Babysitter Needs to Know, 1 vol. 2014. (Babysitter's Backpack Ser.). (ENG., Illus.). 32p. (J). (gr. 3-9). lib. bdg. 28.65 *(978-1-4914-0763-9(8)*, 125995) Capstone.

Hirose, George, photos by. I Catch My Moment: Art & Writing by Children on the Life of Play. 2008. (ENG., Illus.). 56p. (J). (gr. -1-3). pap. 10.00 *(978-1-929299-06-5(0))* Touchstone Ctr. Pubns.

Holden, Pam. Toys That Can Go, 1 vol. 2009. (Red Rocket Readers Ser.). (ENG., Illus.). 16p. (gr. -1-1). pap. *(978-1-877435-93-5(7))* Flying Start Bks.

Jordan, Pat. Plays from Around the World: Every Teacher's Friend Classroom Plays. Alliger, Richard, illus. 2010. (ENG.). 128p. (J). spiral bd. 25.00 *(978-0-88734-975-1(7))* Players Pr., Inc.

Kelly, Sheila M. & Rotner, Shelley. School Days. Rotner, Shelley, photos by. 2020. (ENG., Illus.). 32p. (J). (gr. -1-2). 26.65 *(978-1-5415-5776-5(X)*, 02383e8d-5fe8-4935-9616-e5b47e2a2329, Millbrook Pr.) Lerner Publishing Group.

Kingsland, Robin. Porky Pies: Wolves, Squeals & Dodgy Deals: A Play with Songs for School Performances. 2012. *(978-0-88734-076-5(8))* Players Pr., Inc.

Kramer, Daniel Elihu. Coyote Tales. 2008. (ENG.). 52p. per. 6.50 *(978-0-87440-297-1(2))* Baker's Plays.

Kulsa, Wha. Childs Play: Positive Affirmations for Children to Sing & Dramatize. Gardner, Stephen, illus. Date not set. 30p. (J). (gr. 1-7). pap. *(978-1-886942-08-0(0))* White Lion Pr.

Lindeen, Mary. Playing Together. 2015. (Beginning-To-Read Ser.). (ENG., Illus.). 32p. (J). (gr. k-2). pap. 13.26 *(978-1-60357-762-5(9))* Norwood Hse. Pr.

Lindeen, Mary & Peggy, Nille. Playing Together. 2015. (BeginningtoRead Ser.). (ENG., Illus.). 32p. (J). (gr. k-2). lib. bdg. 22.60 *(978-1-59953-702-3(8))* Norwood Hse. Pr.

Lobdell-Bulson, Jodi. The Toddler Room: Free Play. 2013. 16p. pap. 7.95 *(978-1-4582-1256-6(4)*, Abbott Pr.) Author Solutions, LLC.

MacDonald, John. Child's Play in Poetry. 2013. 60p. pap. 11.99 *(978-1-62839-169-5(3))* Salem Author Services.

MacDonald, Margaret. What Things Did Your Parents Play With? 2012. (Level E Ser.). (ENG., Illus.). 16p. (J). (gr. k-2). pap. 7.95 *(978-1-927136-41-6(5)*, 19427) RiverStream Publishing.

Marsico, Katie. Play Fair! 2012. (21st Century Basic Skills Library: Kids Can Make Manners Count Ser.). (ENG.). 24p. (gr. k-3). pap. 12.79 *(978-1-61080-612-1(3)*, 202222); (Illus.). 26.35 *(978-1-61080-438-7(4)*, 202048) Cherry Lake Publishing.

Massie, Elizabeth. Playing Fair. 2016. (Spring Forward Ser.). (J). (gr. 1). *(978-1-4900-9378-9(8))* Benchmark Education Co.

McLeod, Len & Martens, Elisabeth. The Faery Flag of Dunvegan. 2012. (ENG., Illus.). 38p. 17.00 *(978-1-84426-877-1(2)*, Fastprint Publishing) Upfront Publishing Ltd. GBR. Dist: Printondemand-worldwide.com.

McMurchy-Barber, Gina. When Children Play: The Story of Right to Play, 1 vol. 2013. (Ripple Effects Ser.). (ENG.). 56p. (YA). (gr. 5-10). 19.95 *(978-1-55455-154-5(4)*, 254c4623-4fbf-4088-9811-ad6bc7ec8564) Trifolium Bks., Inc. CAN. Dist: Firefly Bks., Ltd.

Meiners, Cheri J. I Play: A Board Book about Discovery & Cooperation. Weber, Penny, illus. 2018. (Learning about Me & You Ser.). (ENG.). 26p. (J). (-k). bds. 9.99 *(978-1-63198-220-0(6)*, 82200) Free Spirit Publishing Inc.

—Join in & Play. Johnson, Meredith, illus. 2003. (Learning to Get Along(r) Ser.). (ENG.). 40p. (J). (gr. -1-3). pap. 11.99 *(978-1-57542-152-0(6)*, 839) Free Spirit Publishing Inc.

—Join in & Play / Participa y Juega. Johnson, Meredith, illus. 2019. (Learning to Get Along(r) Ser.). (ENG.). 48p. (J). pap. 12.99 *(978-1-63198-440-2(3)*, 84402) Free Spirit Publishing Inc.

Michaels, Chris. Playtime at Home. 2010. (Sight Word Readers Ser.). (J). 3.49 *(978-1-60719-624-2(7))* Newmark Learning LLC.

Miller, Amanda. This Is the Way We Play. 2009. (Scholastic News Nonfiction Readers: Kids Like Me Ser.). (ENG.). 24p. (J). (gr. k-3). lib. bdg. 21.19 *(978-0-531-21342-1(0))*; (gr. 1-2). pap. 6.95 *(978-0-531-21442-8(7)*, Children's Pr.) Scholastic Library Publishing.

Moerbeek, Kees, illus. & des. Space. Moerbeek, Kees, des. 2008. (Roly Poly Box Bks.). 24p. (J). (gr. -1-1). spiral bd. *(978-1-84643-246-0(4))* Child's Play International Ltd.

Mortensen, Lori. Manners Matter on the Playground. Hunt, Lisa, illus. (First Graphics: Manners Matter Ser.). (ENG.). 24p. (gr. 1-2). 2011. pap. 35.70 *(978-1-4296-6395-3(2))* 2010. (J). lib. bdg. 24.65 *(978-1-4296-5332-9(9)*, 113760) Capstone.

Nelson, Robin. Playing Safely. 2006. (Pull Ahead Books — Health Ser.). (ENG., Illus.). 32p. (J). (gr. k-3). pap. 7.99 *(978-0-8225-2770-1(7)*, 283fd47c-7885-4707-8005-05d030a0341f) Lerner Publishing Group.

Oppenheim, Joanne F. & Oppenheim, Stephanie. A Leer y Jugar! con Bebés y Niños Pequeños. Auclair, Joan, illus. 2006.Tr. of Read It! Play It! with Babies & Toddlers. (SPA.). 102p. pap. 10.00 *(978-0-9721050-5-7(0))* Oppenheim Toy Portfolio, Inc.

—Read It! Play It! with Babies & Toddlers. 2006. (Illus.). pap. 10.00 *(978-0-9721050-4-0(2))* Oppenheim Toy Portfolio, Inc.

Petty, Kate. Playtime. 2006. (World Show-And-Tell Ser.). (ENG., Illus.). 32p. (J). (gr. -1-1). 14.95 *(978-1-58728-549-3(5))*; pap. 8.95 *(978-1-58728-546-2(0))* Cooper Square Publishing Llc.

Publications International Ltd. Staff, ed. Sesame Play a Sound Stero. 2011. 24p. (J). 9.39 net. *(978-1-4508-1704-2(1)*, 1450817041) Phoenix International Publications, Inc.

Redmond, Diane. The Odyssey. Smith, Barry, illus. 2012. 48p. *(978-0-88734-067-3(9))* Players Pr., Inc.

Rice, Dona Herweck. I Can, 1 vol. 2nd rev. ed. 2014. (TIME for KIDS(r): Informational Text Ser.). (ENG., Illus.). 12p. (J). (gr. k-1). lib. bdg. 15.96 *(978-1-4807-1008-5(3))* Teacher Created Materials, Inc.

Rissman, Rebecca. Play, 1 vol. 2013. (Say What You See Ser.). (ENG., Illus.). 24p. (J). (gr. -1-1). 23.32 *(978-1-4109-5049-9(2)*, 121275, Raintree) Capstone.

—Playing with Friends: Comparing Past & Present, 1 vol. 2014. (Comparing Past & Present Ser.). (ENG., Illus.). 24p. (J). (gr. -1-1). lib. bdg. 25.32 *(978-1-4329-8993-4(6)*, 124790, Heinemann) Capstone.

The Roach Approach, Don't Miss the Boat! Coloring & Activity Book. 2003. (J). 5.99 *(978-0-9742997-3-0(1))* Wacky World Studios LLC.

Rosen, Michael J. & Kaboom! Staff. Let's Build a Playground. Kelson, Ellen & Cecil, Jennifer, illus. 2013. (ENG.). 32p. (J). (gr. 1-4). 15.99 *(978-0-7636-5532-7(5))* Candlewick Pr.

Schumacher, Bev, creator. Play Action. 2005.Tr. of Juego en Accion. (Illus.). 20p. (J). lib. bdg. 9.95 *(978-0-9768706-1-6(4))* Learning Props.

Scott, Steph & Akers, Katie. Rainy Day Kids Adventure Book: Outdoor Games & Activities for the Wind, Rain & Snow. 2017. (ENG., Illus.). 160p. (gr. k-4). pap. 12.95 *(978-1-84994-438-0(5)*, Batsford) Pavilion Bks. GBR. Dist: Penguin Random Hse. LLC.

Senker, Cath. Exercise & Play, 1 vol. 2007. (Healthy Choices Ser.). (ENG., Illus.). 24p. (J). (gr. 1-2). lib. bdg. 26.27 *(978-1-4042-4305-7(4)*, 311ab516-b2a5-4f67-8124-5eac72dbcc0a, PowerKids Pr.) Rosen Publishing Group, Inc., The.

Staff, Gareth Editorial Staff. Things I Play With, 1 vol. 2006. (Things in My World Ser.). (ENG., Illus.). 16p. (gr. k-1). lib. bdg. 21.67 *(978-0-8368-6811-1(0)*, 1d12b862-901a-4f65-85bc-83a71490106d, Weekly Reader Leveled Readers) Stevens, Gareth Publishing LLLP.

—Things I Play with / Las Cosas con Las Que Juego, 1 vol. 2006. (Things in My World / Las Cosas de Mi Mundo Ser.). (ENG & SPA., Illus.). 16p. (gr. k-1). lib. bdg. 21.67 *(978-0-8368-7223-1(1)*, 3cf90720-9500-4bef-80ff-dff9e4345b79, Weekly Reader Leveled Readers) Stevens, Gareth Publishing LLLP.

Studio Mouse, creator. Let's Play: Nursery Rhymes for Playing & Learning. 2005. (Read-Aloud Book Ser.). (ENG., Illus.). 36p. (J). 7.95 *(978-1-59249-535-1(4)*, 1D205) Soundprints.

Thalhamer, Ellen Viola. I'm a Daddy: I Love to Pretend! 2010. 36p. pap. 16.49 *(978-1-4490-7489-0(8))* AuthorHouse.

The Toddler Room: Free Play. 2013. 16p. pap. 7.95 *(978-1-4582-1259-7(9)*, Abbott Pr.) Author Solutions, LLC.

Tuxworth, Nicola. Messy. 2016. (Illus.). 20p. (J). (gr. -1-k). bds. 6.99 *(978-1-86147-690-6(6)*, Armadillo) Anness Publishing GBR. Dist: National Bk. Network.

Umansky, Kaye. The Emperor's New Clothes. Crossland, Caroline, illus. 2012. *(978-0-88734-074-1(1))* Players Pr., Inc.

—Noah's Ark. Richardson-Jones, Tessa, illus. 2012. *(978-0-88734-071-0(7))* Players Pr., Inc.

—Sleeping Beauty. Crossland, Caroline, illus. 2012. *(978-0-88734-070-3(9))* Players Pr., Inc.

Verdick, Elizabeth & Lisovskis, Marjorie. Play: A Board Book about Playtime. 2014. (Happy Healthy Baby(r) Ser.). (ENG., Illus.). 24p. (J). (— 1). bds. 7.99 *(978-1-57542-426-2(6))* Free Spirit Publishing Inc.

—Play / Jugar: A Board Book about Playtime/un Libro de Carton Sobre Actividades y Diversiones. 2019. (Happy Healthy Baby(r) Ser.). (ENG., Illus.). 24p. (J). (— 1). bds. 7.99 *(978-1-63198-446-4(2)*, 84464) Free Spirit Publishing Inc.

Ways to Play. 2017. (Ways to Play Ser.). 24p. (gr. k-k). pap. 48.90 *(978-1-5382-0230-2(1))*; (ENG.). lib. bdg. 145.62 *(978-1-5382-0229-6(8)*, 517762a3-2828-4157-8e1e-52909e195951) Stevens, Gareth Publishing LLLP.

Woehlke, Joshua. Shakespeare's Painless Romeo & Juliet. 2008. 64p. pap. 12.50 *(978-0-557-02661-6(X))* Lulu Pr., Inc.

Wood, David. The Christmas Story. 2012. *(978-0-88734-069-7(5))* Players Pr., Inc.

Woodruff, Elvira. The Christmas Doll (Full) 2014. 110p. (J). pap. 9.95 *(978-1-58342-870-2(4))* Dramatic Publishing Co.

PLAY—FICTION

Abbott, Jacob. Rollo at Play. 2009. 148p. pap. 8.95 *(978-1-59915-343-8(2))* Yesterday's Classics.

—Rollo at Work. 2009. 124p. 23.95 *(978-1-60664-636-6(2))*; pap. 10.95 *(978-1-60664-261-0(8))* Rodgers, Alan Bks.

Adams, Colleen. Jugando en la nieve (Playing in the Snow) 2007. (Lecturas del barrio (Neighborhood Readers) Ser.). (SPA.). 8p. 29.95 *(978-1-4042-7064-0(7)*, Rosen Classroom) Rosen Publishing Group, Inc., The.

—Playing in the Snow. (Neighborhood Readers Ser.). (ENG.). 8p. 2007. 29.95 *(978-1-4042-7059-6(0))* 2006. pap. 5.15 *(978-1-4042-5657-6(1)*, 4320a7bb-8d68-4736-8d92-88b1d246c4d7) Rosen Publishing Group, Inc., The. (Rosen Classroom).

Adams, Jennifer. Animal Babies Like to Play. Lundquist, Mary, illus. 2019. (ENG.). 32p. (J). (gr. -1-3). 17.99 *(978-0-06-239447-7(9)*, Balzer & Bray) HarperCollins Pubs.

Adams, Tonya. Sam the Walrus: A Grumpy Day to Play. Johnson, Amber W., illus. 2008. 28p. pap. 24.95 *(978-1-60672-861-1(X))* America Star Bks.

Aiken, David & Zora. Busy Bodies: Play Like the Animals, 1 vol. 2011. (ENG., Illus.). 32p. (J). 14.99 *(978-0-7643-3832-8(3)*, 4277, Schiffer Publishing Ltd) Schiffer Publishing, Ltd.

Albee, Sarah. Clever Trevor. Billin-Frye, Paige, illus. 2003. (Science Solves It! Ser.). (ENG.). 32p. (J). (gr. 1-3). pap. 5.99 *(978-1-57565-123-1(8)*, 9560d511-25ca-4b6e-bd24-1a8756121141, Kane Press) Astra Publishing Hse.

—Fun in the Sun. Williams, Sue, illus. 2006. (Step-By-Step Readers Ser.). (J). pap. *(978-1-59939-058-1(2)*, Reader's Digest Young Families, Inc.) Studio Fun International.

Alborough, Jez. Play. Alborough, Jez, illus. 2018. (ENG., Illus.). 32p. (J). (— 1). 15.99 *(978-0-7636-9599-6(8))* Candlewick Pr.

Allen, J. J. Hello Kitty's Fun Friend Day! 2003. (Illus.). 32p. (J). pap. *(978-0-439-44917-5(0))* Scholastic, Inc.

Amatangelo, Sergio Lino. Forever Four, Finally Five. 2008. (Illus.). 32p. (J). pap. 8.00 *(978-0-8059-7680-9(9))* Dorrance Publishing Co., Inc.

Amato, Gaetano. Upside Right: A Children's Guide to Movement. 2010. (J). 19.95 *(978-0-615-38545-7(1))* Amato, G. J.

Anderson, Lynne. Charlie's Championships: Set Of 6. 2010. (Early Connections Ser.). (J). pap. 37.00 net. *(978-1-4108-1370-1(3))* Benchmark Education Co.

Anderson, Peggy Perry. Joe on the Go. 2012. (Green Light Readers Level 1 Ser.: 1). lib. bdg. 13.55 *(978-0-606-24018-5(7))* Turtleback.

Arena, Felice & Kettle, Phil. Olympics. Cox, David, illus. 2004. (J). pap. *(978-1-59336-374-1(5))* Mondo Publishing.

—Pirate Ship: By Felice Arena & Phil Kettle: Illustrated by Susy Boyer. Boyer, Susy, illus. 2004. (J). pap. *(978-1-59336-362-8(1))* Mondo Publishing.

—Secret Agent Heroes. Vane, Mitch, illus. 2004. (J). pap. *(978-1-59336-355-0(9))* Mondo Publishing.

Asani, Samantha. Everyone Is Special: A Lesson in Teamwork. 2012. 28p. pap. 19.99 *(978-1-4685-5320-8(8))* AuthorHouse.

Ashbe, Jeanne. Eso No Se Hace! 2003. (SPA.). 32p. *(978-84-95150-35-6(2))* Corimbo, Editorial S.L.

At Play. 2003. (J). per. *(978-1-57657-963-3(8))* Paradise Pr., Inc.

Bader, Bonnie. Go to Bed, Blue. Robertson, Michael, illus. 2014. (Penguin Young Readers, Level 1 Ser.). 32p. (J). (gr. k-1). pap. 5.99 *(978-0-448-48219-4(3)*, Penguin Young Readers) Penguin Young Readers Group.

—Play with Blue. Robertson, Michael, illus. 2013. (Penguin Young Readers, Level 1 Ser.). 32p. (J). (gr. k-1). mass mkt. 4.99 *(978-0-448-46254-7(0)*, Penguin Young Readers) Penguin Young Readers Group.

Baker, Karle Wilson. The Garden of the Plynck (Illustrated Ed. 2006. (Illus.). pap. *(978-1-4065-0482-8(3))* Dodo Pr.

The Ball: KinderReaders Individual Title Six-Packs. (Kinderstarters Ser.). 8p. (gr. -1-1). 21.00 *(978-0-7635-8645-4(5))* Rigby Education.

Balouch, Kristen. The Little Little Girl with the Big Big Voice. Balouch, Kristen, illus. 2011. (ENG., Illus.). 32p. (J). (gr. -1-k). 14.99 *(978-1-4424-0808-1(1)*, Little Simon) Little Simon.

Barchers, Suzanne I. Rose & Dad, 1 vol. rev. ed. 2011. (Phonics Ser.). (ENG.). 16p. (gr. k-2). 6.99 *(978-1-4333-2912-8(3))* Teacher Created Materials, Inc.

Barnett, Penny. Matilda & Puppy's Beach Adventure. 2012. 24p. pap. 15.99 *(978-1-4797-1106-2(3))* Xlibris Corp.

Barton, Chris. Shark vs. Train. Lichtenheld, Tom, illus. 2010. (ENG.). 40p. (J). (gr. -1-3). 18.99 *(978-0-316-00762-7(5))* Little, Brown Bks. for Young Readers.

Batchelor, Louise. Whoops! (Illus.). 21p. *(978-1-84089-079-2(7)*, 26143) Zero to Ten, Ltd.

Baumgarten, Josephine & Baumgarten, Michael. My Baby Monsters & I went to the Park. 2005. 32p. pap. 14.99 *(978-1-4116-6348-0(9))* Lulu Pr., Inc.

Beckford, Avril. I Love You 65 Bulldozers. 2009. 36p. pap. 15.49 *(978-1-4389-4048-9(3))* AuthorHouse.

Bedford, David. Big Bears Can! Hansen, Gaby, illus. 2007. (Storytime Board Bks.). 16p. (J). (gr. -1-k). bds. 6.95 *(978-1-58925-826-6(6))* Tiger Tales.

Bennett, Bonnie. Meet Cinnamon Bear. 2009. 48p. pap. 16.95 *(978-1-60749-496-6(5))* America Star Bks.

Bianchi, John. We Can Play. 2012. (1-3Y Bird, Bunny & Bear Ser.). (ENG., Illus.). 16p. (J). pap. 9.60 *(978-1-63437-486-6(X))* American Reading Co.

Bittle Jr., Paul. Me too, Little Puppies, Me Too, 1 vol. 2010. 16p. pap. 24.95 *(978-1-61582-922-4(9))* PublishAmerica, Inc.

Black, Robyn Hood. Sir Mike. Murphy, David, illus. 2006. (Rookie Reader Skill Set Ser.). (ENG.). 32p. (J). (gr. k-2). per. 4.95 *(978-0-516-25020-5(5)*, Children's Pr.) Scholastic Library Publishing.

Blackaby, Susan. El Lugar de Luis, 1 vol. Ruíz, Carlos & Ruíz, Carlos, trs. Gallagher-Cole, Mernie, illus. 2006. (Read-It! Readers en Español: Story Collection).Tr. of Place for Mike. (SPA.). 24p. (J). (gr. -1-3). 22.65 *(978-1-4048-1688-6(7)*, 90854, Picture Window Bks.) Capstone.

Blackmon, Rodney Allan. A Kitten Named Buddy: Buddy Stays Clean. 2013. 20p. pap. 24.95 *(978-1-62709-675-1(2))* America Star Bks.

Bledsoe, Josh. Hammer & Nails. Warrick, Jessica, illus. 2016. (ENG.). 32p. (J). (gr. k-2). 17.95 *(978-1-936261-36-9(7))* Flashlight Pr.

Blevins-Counts, Charlotte. A Pot Full of Te. 2009. 24p. pap. 12.95 *(978-1-59858-962-7(8))* Dog Ear Publishing, LLC.

Bloom, Suzanne. A Mighty Fine Time Machine. 2014. (ENG., Illus.). 32p. (J). (gr. -1-3). pap. 6.95 *(978-1-62091-605-6(3)*, Astra Young Readers) Astra Publishing Hse.

—What about Bear? 2012. (Goose & Bear Stories Ser.). (ENG., Illus.). 32p. (J). (gr. -1 — 1). pap. 9.99 *(978-1-59078-913-1(X)*, Astra Young Readers) Astra Publishing Hse.

Bogart, Mike. Ice Warriors, 1 vol. 2010. 72p. pap. 19.95 *(978-1-4489-3885-8(6))* America Star Bks.

Boland, Janice. Zippers. Pfeiffer, Judith, illus. 2003. (Books for Young Learners). (ENG.). 8p. (J). pap. 15.00 *(978-1-57274-700-5(5)*, BB2220, Bks. for Young Learners) Owen, Richard C. Pubs., Inc.

Bolton, Robin. Sunny Goes Out to Play. 2011. 28p. pap. 12.03 *(978-1-4634-2530-2(9))* AuthorHouse.

BooydeGraaff, Wendy. Salad Pie. Langdo, Bryan, illus. 2016. (ENG.). 44p. (J). (gr. k-7). 17.99 *(978-0-9913866-4-2(7))* Ripple Grove Pr.

Boukov, Lubima. The Magic Swing, 1 vol. 2009. 15p. pap. 24.95 *(978-1-60749-612-0(7))* America Star Bks.

Brabham, Barbara. Donkey Tales — Color with Paco! [English/Spanish Versions]. 2006. (J). 2.95 *(978-1-882185-86-3(2))* Cornerstone Publishing, Inc.

Brimner, Larry Dane. Summer Fun. Tripp, Christine, illus. 2003. (Rookie Choices Ser.). (ENG.). 32p. (J). (gr. 1-2). 20.50 *(978-0-516-22548-7(0)*, Children's Pr.) Scholastic Library Publishing.

Britton, Faith. If You'D Only Believe. 2009. 24p. pap. 12.99 *(978-1-4490-1741-5(X))* AuthorHouse.

Brooks, Yvonne & Grant, Steven. Meet the Goat Kids. l.t. ed. 2006. (Illus.). 32p. (J). 14.95 *(978-0-9791021-0-3(3)*, 978-0-9791021-0-3) Lotus Pond Media.

Brown, Jo. Hoppity Skip Little Chick. 2005. (Illus.). 32p. (J). 15.95 *(978-1-58925-045-1(1))* Tiger Tales.

Browne, Anthony. Things I Like. 2014. 24p. pap. 7.00 *(978-1-61003-372-5(8))* Center for the Collaborative Classroom.

Brunel, Aude. Let's Go to Work. Mancek, Marjan, illus. 2007. 32p. (J). (POL & ENG.). pap. 16.95 *(978-1-60195-101-4(9))*; (ARA & ENG.). pap. 16.95 *(978-1-60195-089-5(6))* International Step by Step Assn.

Bug, Judy. A Day to Play, 1 vol. 2010. 26p. 24.95 *(978-1-4489-4007-3(9))* PublishAmerica, Inc.

Bunting, Philip. Sandcastle. 2019. (ENG., Illus.). 32p. (J). (gr. -1-1). 16.99 *(978-1-76029-538-7(8))* Allen & Unwin AUS. Dist: Independent Pubs. Group.

Byrd, Lee Merrill. Birdie's Beauty Parlor: El Salón de Belleza de Birdy. Delgado, Francisco, illus. 2018. (SPA & ENG.). (J). *(978-1-947627-02-4(3)*, Cinco Puntos Press) Lee & Low Bks., Inc.

—Birdie's Beauty Parlor / el Salón de Belleza de Birdie, 1 vol. Delgado, Francisco, illus. 2020. (ENG.). 32p. (J). (gr. -1-2). 18.95 *(978-1-947627-28-4(7)*, 23353382, Cinco Puntos Press) Lee & Low Bks., Inc.

Byrne, Marlene. Follow the Leader. Graber, Jesse, illus. 2009. (ENG.). 39p. (J). 14.99 *(978-0-9777135-1-6(2))* Good Stories Publishing.

Campbell, Susan. Little Jimmy: The Itty Bitty Fifty Foot Tall Giraffe. 2011. 24p. pap. 24.95 *(978-1-4626-2929-9(6))* America Star Bks.

Candlewick Press. Peppa Pig & the Year of Family Fun. 2016. (Peppa Pig Ser.). (ENG., Illus.). 10p. (J). (gr. -1-2). 17.99 *(978-0-7636-8739-7(1)*, Candlewick Entertainment) Candlewick Pr.

Cano, Felipe. Bonjour Camille. Aguilar, Laia, illus. 2014. (ENG.). 32p. (J). (gr. 1-4). 12.99 *(978-1-4521-2407-0(8))* Chronicle Bks. LLC.

Capucilli, Alyssa Satin. Biscuit & the Little Pup. Schories, Pat, illus. 2007. (My First I Can Read Ser.). (ENG.). 32p. (J). (gr. -1 — 1). 16.99 *(978-0-06-074170-9(8))*; pap. 4.99 *(978-0-06-074172-3(4))* HarperCollins Pubs. (HarperCollins).

—Biscuit's Big Field Schories, Pat, illus. 2008. (Biscuit Ser.). (ENG.). 32p. (J). pap. 3.99 *(978-0-06-112844-8(9)*, HarperFestival) HarperCollins Pubs.

—Biscuit's Pet & Play Christmas: A Touch & Feel Book: a Christmas Holiday Book for Kids. Schories, Pat & Young, Mary O'Keefe, illus. 2006. (Biscuit Ser.). (ENG.). 12p. (J). (gr. -1 — 1). bds. 9.99 *(978-0-06-009470-6(2)*, HarperFestival) HarperCollins Pubs.

—Katy Duck Makes a Friend: Ready-To-Read Level 1. Cole, Henry, illus. 2012. (Katy Duck Ser.). (ENG.). 24p. (J). (gr. -1-1). 16.99 *(978-1-4424-1977-3(6))*; pap. 4.99 *(978-1-4424-1976-6(8))* Simon Spotlight. (Simon Spotlight).

—Ralph & the Rocket Ship: Ready-To-Read Level 1. Cole, Henry, illus. 2016. (Ready-To-Read Ser.). (ENG.). 24p. (J). (gr. -1-1). pap. 4.99 *(978-1-4814-5866-5(3)*, Simon Spotlight) Simon Spotlight.

Carey, Catherine Elaine. The Colorful & Playful Animal Friends, 1 vol. 2009. 73p. pap. 16.95 *(978-1-60749-480-5(9))* PublishAmerica, Inc.

Carpenter, Cindy. The Little Inchworm. 2008. 16p. per. 24.95 *(978-1-4241-9681-4(7))* America Star Bks.

Carter, Candace. Sid's Surprise. Kim, Joung Un, illus. 2005. (Green Light Readers Level 1 Ser.). (gr. -1-3). 13.95 *(978-0-7569-5242-6(5))* Perfection Learning Corp.

Carter, David A. Bugs at the Beach: Ready-To-Read Level 1. Carter, David A., illus. 2016. (David Carter's Bugs Ser.). (ENG., Illus.). 24p. (J). (gr. -1-1). pap. 4.99 *(978-1-4814-4050-9(0)*, Simon Spotlight) Simon Spotlight.

—Busy Bug Builds a Fort: Ready-To-Read Level 1. Carter, David A., illus. 2016. (David Carter's Bugs Ser.). (ENG., Illus.). 24p. (J). (gr. -1-1). pap. 3.99 *(978-1-4814-4047-9(0)*, Simon Spotlight) Simon Spotlight.

Carver, David. Leafy Leafs Where Is Lester?, 1 vol. Carver, Erin, illus. 2009. 34p. pap. 19.95 *(978-1-4489-2203-1(8))* PublishAmerica, Inc.

Chichester Clark, Emma. I'll Show You, Blue Kangaroo! (Blue Kangaroo) Chichester Clark, Emma, illus. 2019. (Blue Kangaroo Ser.). (ENG., Illus.). 32p. (J). pap. 6.99 *(978-0-00-826627-1(1)*, HarperCollins Children's Bks.) HarperCollins Pubs. Ltd. GBR. Dist: HarperCollins Pubs.

Child, Lauren. Slightly Invisible. Child, Lauren, illus. 2011. (Charlie & Lola Ser.). (ENG., Illus.). 40p. (J). (gr. -1-2). 16.99 *(978-0-7636-5347-7(0))* Candlewick Pr.

Christelow, Eileen. Five Little Monkeys Play Hide & Seek. Christelow, Eileen, illus. 2010. (Five Little Monkeys Story Ser.). (ENG., Illus.). 40p. (J). (gr. -1-3). pap. 9.99 *(978-0-547-33787-6(6)*, 1418278, Clarion Bks.) HarperCollins Pubs.

Christopher, Kathleen. Janie's First Day of School. 2012. 32p. pap. 24.95 *(978-1-62709-914-1(X))* America Star Bks.

Chronicle Books & ImageBooks. Little Dolphin: Finger Puppet Book: (Finger Puppet Book for Toddlers & Babies, Baby Books for First Year, Animal Finger Puppets) 2012. (Little Finger Puppet Board Bks.: FING). (ENG., Illus.). 12p. (J). (gr. -1 — 1). bds. 7.99 *(978-1-4521-0816-2(1))* Chronicle Bks. LLC.

—Little Shark: Finger Puppet Book: (Puppet Book for Baby, Little Toy Board Book, Baby Shark) 2013. (Little Finger Puppet Board Bks.). (ENG., Illus.). 12p. (J). (gr. -1 — 1). 7.99 *(978-1-4521-1251-0(7))* Chronicle Bks. LLC.

Chung, Arree. Ninja! Chung, Arree, illus. 2014. (Ninja! Ser.: 1). (ENG., Illus.). 40p. (J). (gr. -1-2). 18.99 *(978-0-8050-9911-9(5)*, 900125303, Holt, Henry & Co. Bks. For Young Readers) Holt, Henry & Co.

Clish, Marian L. I Wonder What a Fish Would Wish For? Swaim, Mike, illus. 2009. 29p. pap. 24.95 *(978-1-60836-289-9(2))* America Star Bks.

Come Out to Play. (J). 7.95 *(978-0-8126-0082-7(7))* Open Court Publishing Co.

Cook, Gary. The Best Saturday Ever! Sward, Adam, illus. 2013. (Robbie's Big Adventures Ser.). (ENG.). 40p. (J). (gr. k-3). 15.95 *(978-1-938063-25-1(2)*, Mighty Media Kids) Mighty Media Pr.

Cordell, Matthew. King Alice. 2018. (ENG., Illus.). 40p. (J). 17.99 *(978-1-250-04749-6(8)*, 900132178) Feiwel & Friends.

Cordwell, Mary Hebert. The Dirty-Foot Fairy. 2010. 28p. 13.99 *(978-1-4490-9153-8(9))* AuthorHouse.

Cossi, Olga. Playing Your Heart Out. 2013. 138p. pap. 9.95 *(978-1-938083-21-1(0))* Black Forge.

Coulton, Mia. Danny & Abby Play Tag. Coulton, Mia, photos by. 2004. (ENG., Illus.). pap. 5.35 *(978-0-9746475-3-1(5))* Maryruth Bks., Inc.

Courtin, Thierry. L imagier de T Choupi. 19.95 *(978-2-09-202283-2(0))* Nathan, Fernand FRA. Dist: Distribooks, Inc.

Cousineau-Peiffer, Trisha. Have You Ever Heard of a Rainbow Farm. Everett-Hawkes, Bonnie, illus. 2006. 32p. (J). 12.95 *(978-0-9792084-1-6(6))* Dream Ridge Pr.

—Have You Ever Heard of a Rainbow Farm: The Missing Color Kittens. Everett-Hawkes, Bonnie, illus. 2007. 48p. (J). per. 15.95 *(978-0-9792084-2-3(4))* Dream Ridge Pr.

Cousins, Lucy. I Am Little Fish! a Finger Puppet Book. Cousins, Lucy, illus. 2018. (Little Fish Ser.). (ENG., Illus.). 16p. (J). (— 1). bds. 12.99 *(978-1-5362-0023-2(9))* Candlewick Pr.

—Where Is Maisy? A Maisy Lift-The-Flap Book. Cousins, Lucy, illus. 2010. (Maisy Ser.). (ENG., Illus.). 14p. (J). (gr. k-k). bds. 6.99 *(978-0-7636-4673-8(3))* Candlewick Pr.

Covell, David. Run Wild. 2018. (Illus.). 40p. (J). (-k). 18.99 *(978-0-670-01411-8(7)*, Viking Books for Young Readers) Penguin Young Readers Group.

Cowell, Cressida. That Rabbit Belongs to Emily Brown. Layton, Neal, illus. 2007. (ENG.). 40p. (gr. -1-3). 16.99 *(978-1-4231-0645-6(8))* Hyperion Pr.

Coyle, Carmela Lavigna. Do Princesses Have Best Friends Forever? Gordon, Mike & Gordon, Carl, illus. 2010. (ENG.). 32p. (J). E-Book *(978-1-58979-543-3(1))* Taylor Trade Publishing.

—Do Princesses Have Best Friends Forever? Gordon, Carl & Gordon, Mike, illus. 2010. (Do Princesses Ser.). (ENG.). 32p. (J). (gr. -1-3). 15.95 *(978-1-58979-542-6(3))* Taylor Trade Publishing.

—Do Princesses Scrape Their Knees? 2006. (Do Princesses Ser.). (ENG., Illus.). 32p. (J). (gr. -1-2). 15.95 *(978-0-87358-909-3(2))* Cooper Square Publishing Llc.

Crane, Noelle L. The Clever Pug. Crane, Noelle L., illus. 2013. (Illus.). 66p. pap. 9.99 *(978-0-9846119-8-0(3))* Pluriverse Publishing.

Crews, Donald. Cloudy Day Sunny Day. Crews, Donald, illus. 2003. (Green Light Readers Level 1 Ser.). (ENG., Illus.). 24p. (J). (gr. -1-3). pap. 4.99 *(978-0-15-204850-1(2)*, 1194645, Clarion Bks.) HarperCollins Pubs.

—Cloudy Day Sunny Day. 2003. (Green Light Readers Level 1 Ser.). (gr. -1-2). 13.50 *(978-0-613-62277-6(4))* Turtleback.

Cronick, Mitch. In the Garden. 2005. (Big Cat Ser.). (gr. k-2). pap. 6.50 *(978-1-60457-007-6(5))* Pacific Learning, Inc.

Curry, Don L. Fall Leaves. Jasinski, Aaron, illus. 2004. (Rookie Readers Ser.). 23p. (J). 19.50 *(978-0-516-25904-8(0)*, Children's Pr.) Scholastic Library Publishing.

Dadoo Stops Playing. . . 2003. (J). per. 5.50 *(978-0-9742714-0-8(3))* I C Creative, Inc.

Dagostino, Argus. Belcher Bomb. 2008. 53p. pap. 16.95 *(978-1-60441-596-4(7))* America Star Bks.

Dahl, Michael. Little Dinos Don't Push, 1 vol. Record, Adam, illus. 2013. (Little Dinos Ser.). (ENG.). 20p. (J). (gr. -1-k). bds. 7.99 *(978-1-4048-7534-0(4)*, 119831, Picture Window Bks.) Capstone.

—Me & My Cat. Persico, Zoe, illus. 2016. (Me & My Pet Ser.). (ENG.). 24p. (J). (gr. -1-k). lib. bdg. 23.32 *(978-1-5158-0239-6(6)*, 132471, Picture Window Bks.) Capstone.

—Me & My Dog. Persico, Zoe, illus. 2016. (Me & My Pet Ser.). (ENG.). 24p. (J). (gr. -1-k). 6.95 *(978-1-62370-793-4(5)*, 133227, Capstone Young Readers) Capstone.

—Playdate for Panda. Vidal, Oriol, illus. 2016. (Hello Genius Ser.). (ENG.). 20p. (J). (gr. -1 — 1). bds. 7.99 *(978-1-4795-8741-4(9)*, 131130, Picture Window Bks.) Capstone.

Darling, Helen. Hide-n-seek Monday. Glickstein, Jennifer, ed. Sona and Jacob, illus. 2007. (J). 10.00 *(978-0-9797674-0-1(7))* My Darling-Tots Pubns.

Davies, Benji, illus. Bizzy Bear: Let's Go & Play. 2011. (Bizzy Bear Ser.). (ENG.). 8p. (J). (gr. k — 1). bds. 7.99 *(978-0-7636-5880-9(4))* Candlewick Pr.

Davis, Jacky. The Amazing Adventures of Bumblebee Boy. Soman, David, illus. 2011. (Ladybug Girl Ser.). 40p. (J). (gr. -1-k). 17.99 *(978-0-8037-3418-0(2)*, Dial Bks) Penguin Young Readers Group.

—I Love You, Bingo. 2015. (Penguin Young Readers Level 2 Ser.). lib. bdg. 13.55 *(978-0-606-37578-8(3))* Turtleback.

—Ladybug Girl. Soman, David, illus. 2008. (Ladybug Girl Ser.). 40p. (J). (gr. -1-k). 18.99 *(978-0-8037-3195-0(7)*, Dial Bks) Penguin Young Readers Group.

—Ladybug Girl & Bumblebee Boy. Soman, David, illus. 2009. (Ladybug Girl Ser.). 40p. (J). (gr. -1-k). 17.99 *(978-0-8037-3339-8(9)*, Dial Bks) Penguin Young Readers Group.

—Ladybug Girl & Her Papa. Soman, David, illus. 2017. (Ladybug Girl Ser.). 14p. (J). (— 1). bds. 6.99 *(978-0-8037-4035-8(2)*, Dial Bks) Penguin Young Readers Group.

—Ladybug Girl & the Best Ever Playdate. Soman, David, illus. 2015. (Ladybug Girl Ser.). 40p. (J). (gr. -1-k). 17.99 *(978-0-8037-4030-3(1)*, Dial Bks) Penguin Young Readers Group.

—Ladybug Girl & the Bug Squad. Soman, David, illus. 2011. (Ladybug Girl Ser.). 40p. (J). (gr. -1-k). 17.99 *(978-0-8037-3419-7(0)*, Dial Bks) Penguin Young Readers Group.

—Ladybug Girl Loves... Soman, David, illus. 2010. (Ladybug Girl Ser.). 12p. (J). (gr. -1 — 1). bds. 6.99 *(978-0-448-45374-3(6)*, Grosset & Dunlap) Penguin Young Readers Group.

—Ladybug Girl Plays. Soman, David, illus. 2013. (Ladybug Girl Ser.). (ENG.). 14p. (J). (gr. -1 — 1). bds. 5.99 *(978-0-8037-3892-8(7)*, Dial Bks) Penguin Young Readers Group.

—Ladybug Girl: the Super Fun Edition. Soman, David, illus. 2015. (Ladybug Girl Ser.). 40p. (J). (-k). 18.99 *(978-1-101-99433-7(9)*, Dial Bks) Penguin Young Readers Group.

—Who Can Play? Soman, David, illus. 2013. (Ladybug Girl Ser.). 32p. (J). (gr. k-1). pap. 4.99 *(978-0-448-46501-2(9)*, Penguin Young Readers) Penguin Young Readers Group.

Daywalt, Drew. This Is MY Fort! (Monkey & Cake) Tallec, Olivier, illus. 2019. (Monkey & Cake Ser.: 2). (ENG.). 56p. (J). (gr. -1-3). 9.99 *(978-1-338-14390-4(5)*, Orchard Bks.) Scholastic, Inc.

De Sena, Joseph. Little Sammy Sunshine & the Frightful Forest. 2008. 64p. pap. 27.95 *(978-1-4327-3119-9(X))* Outskirts Pr., Inc.

Dean, James & Dean, Kimberly. Pete the Cat: Robo-Pete. Dean, James, illus. 2015. (Pete the Cat Ser.). (ENG., Illus.). 24p. (J). (gr. -1-3). pap. 5.99 *(978-0-06-230427-8(5)*, HarperFestival) HarperCollins Pubs.

Delval, Marie-Hélène. Lili et Mistigri jouent a Cache. (FRE.). pap. 14.95 *(978-2-227-75602-1(0))* Bayard Editions FRA. Dist: Distribooks, Inc.

Denos, Julia. Swatch: the Girl Who Loved Color. Denos, Julia, illus. 2016. (ENG., Illus.). 40p. (J). (gr. -1-3). 18.99 *(978-0-06-236638-2(6)*, Balzer & Bray) HarperCollins Pubs.

Derby, Sally. Mi Escalera (Spanish Edition), 1 vol. 2005. (SPA., Illus.). 32p. (J). (gr. k-2). pap. 12.95 *(978-1-880000-75-5(X)*, leelowbooks) Lee & Low Bks., Inc.

—My Steps, 1 vol. Burrowes, Adjoa J., illus. 2005. (ENG.). 32p. (J). (gr. k-2). pap. 11.95 *(978-1-880000-84-7(9)*, leelowbooks) Lee & Low Bks., Inc.

Derrick, David G., Jr. Play with Your Food. 2014. (ENG., Illus.). 40p. (J). (gr. -1-3). 15.95 *(978-1-59702-102-9(4))* Immedium.

Dewdney, Anna. Llama Llama Zippity-Zoom. 2012. (Llama Llama Ser.). 14p. (J). (gr. -1 — 1). bds. 7.99 *(978-0-670-01328-9(5)*, Viking Books for Young Readers) Penguin Young Readers Group.

—Nelly Gnu & Daddy Too. (Illus.). (J). 2017. 36p. (-k). bds. 9.99 *(978-0-425-28977-8(X))* 2014. 32p. (gr. -1-k). 17.99 *(978-0-670-01227-5(0))* Penguin Young Readers Group. (Viking Books for Young Readers).

Dicamillo, Kate. La La La: A Story of Hope. Kim, Jaime, illus. 2017. (ENG.). 72p. (J). (gr. -1-3). 17.99 *(978-0-7636-5833-5(2))* Candlewick Pr.

Disney Princess Staff, adapted by. Princess Enchanted Palace: Storybook & Play Castle. 2010. (Playbox Ser.). (ENG., Illus.). 32p. (J). (gr. -1-2). bds. 19.99 *(978-0-7944-2035-2(4))* Reader's Digest Assn., Inc., The.

DK. Bedtime Peekaboo! Touch-And-Feel & Lift-the-Flap. 2006. (Peekaboo! Ser.). (ENG., Illus.). 12p. (J). (gr. -1-k). bds. 7.99 *(978-0-7566-1622-9(0)*, DK Children) Dorling Kindersley Publishing, Inc.

Doerrfeld, Cori. Maggie & Wendel: Imagine Everything! Doerrfeld, Cori, illus. 2016. (ENG., Illus.). 48p. (J). (gr. -1-3). 19.99 *(978-1-4814-3974-9(X)*, Simon & Schuster Bks. For Young Readers) Simon & Schuster Bks. For Young Readers.

Dufresne, Michèle. Bella & Rosie Play Hide & Seek: Bella & Rosie Yellow Set. 2003. (Bella & Rosie Set 1 Ser.). (J). pap. 7.67 *(978-1-932570-11-3(X))* Pioneer Valley Bks.

—Gilbert in the Snow. 2005. (Gilbert the Pig Chapter Ser.). (J). pap. 7.67 *(978-1-58453-297-2(1))* Pioneer Valley Bks.

—Spaceboy Plays Hide & Seek: SPaceboy Set 1. 2003. (Spaceboy Set 1 Ser.). (ENG.). (J). pap. 7.33 *(978-1-932570-05-2(5))* Pioneer Valley Bks.

Dwyer, Kevin & Dwyer, Shawnae. The Blue Baboon. Harman, Micah, illus. 2007. 40p. per. 13.95 *(978-1-59800-247-8(3))* Outskirts Pr., Inc.

Earley, Catherine. Outside Fun, 1. Earley, Catherine, ed. Art&Script, illus. 2005. 12p. (J). 6.95 *(978-0-9769589-1-8(0))* Naynay Bks.

Eaton, Deborah J. My Wild Woolly. Karas, G. Brian, illus. 2005. (Green Light Readers Level 2 Ser.). (gr. k-2). 13.95 *(978-0-7569-5445-1(2))* Perfection Learning Corp.

Edwards, Jean Pearce. Little Jean's War. 2008. (Illus.). 208p. pap. 14.49 *(978-1-4343-9133-9(7))* AuthorHouse.

Elk, Ronit. A Surprise at Dancing Fields. 2009. 76p. pap. 10.49 *(978-1-4490-2064-4(X))* AuthorHouse.

Ellery, Amanda. If I Had a Dragon. Ellery, Tom, illus. 2006. (ENG.). 40p. (J). (gr. -1-3). 19.99 *(978-1-4169-0924-8(9)*, Simon & Schuster Bks. For Young Readers) Simon & Schuster Bks. For Young Readers.

Elya, Susan Middleton. Maya Papaya & Amigos Play Dress-Up. Mola, Maria, illus. 2018. 32p. (J). (gr. -1-2). lib. bdg. 16.99 *(978-1-58089-803-4(3))* Charlesbridge Publishing, Inc.

Farley, Brianne. Secret Tree Fort. Farley, Brianne, illus. 2016. (ENG., Illus.). 32p. (J). (gr. -1-3). 16.99 *(978-0-7636-6297-4(6))* Candlewick Pr.

Farrow, Nancy L. Lucas & Leroy, 1 vol. Schoonmaker, Christina, illus. 2009. 32p. pap. 24.95 *(978-1-60836-232-5(9))* America Star Bks.

Feather, Tami Flaming. A Wondrous World of Home. Porter, Tammy, illus. 2012. 24p. pap. 24.95 *(978-1-4626-4544-2(5))* America Star Bks.

Fenske, Jonathan. Let's Play, Crabby!: an Acorn Book (a Crabby Book #2) Fenske, Jonathan, illus. 2019. (Crabby Book Ser.: 2). (ENG., Illus.). 48p. (J). (gr. -1-1). pap. 4.99 *(978-1-338-28155-2(0))* Scholastic, Inc.

Fenwick, Margaret. Stella's Hair. 2009. 36p. pap. 14.75 *(978-1-60693-857-7(6)*, Eloquent Bks.) Strategic Book Publishing & Rights Agency (SBPRA).

Fergus, Maureen. Buddy & Earl, 1 vol. Sookocheff, Carey, illus. (Buddy & Earl Ser.: 1). (ENG.). 32p. (J). (gr. k-2). 2018. pap. 7.95 *(978-1-77306-119-1(4))* 2015. 16.95 *(978-1-55498-712-2(1))* Groundwood Bks. CAN. Dist: Publishers Group West (PGW).

Ferreri, Della Ross. Star of the Show. Weinstock, Tony, illus. 2009. (ENG.). 36p. (J). (gr. -1-3). 15.95 *(978-1-934860-03-8(4))* Shenanigan Bks.

Ficocelli, Elizabeth. Kid Tea. Dibley, Glin, illus. 2009. 32p. (J). (gr. -1). bds. 7.99 *(978-0-7614-5533-2(7))* Marshall Cavendish Corp.

Fine, Anne. Jamie & Angus Together. Dale, Penny, illus. 2007. (Jamie & Angus Ser.). (ENG.). 112p. (J). (gr. -1-1). 15.99 *(978-0-7636-3374-5(7))* Candlewick Pr.

Fleming, David. Charlie Blue Berry Fipple Berry. 2012. 88p. 19.95 *(978-1-4759-1945-5(X))*; pap. 9.95 *(978-1-4759-1944-8(1))* iUniverse, Inc.

Flett, Julie. We All Play. Flett, Julie, illus. 2021. (Illus.). 40p. (J). (gr. -1-2). 17.95 *(978-1-77164-607-9(1)*, Greystone Kids) Greystone Books Ltd. CAN. Dist: Publishers Group West (PGW).

Flying Frog Pub, creator. ABC Fun with Elmo & Friends. 2011. (Sesame Street (Publications International) Ser.). (ENG., Illus.). 14p. (J). (gr. -1). bds. 3.99 *(978-1-60745-030-6(5))* Flying Frog Publishing.

—Big & Small Fun with Elmo & Friends. 2011. (ENG., Illus.). 14p. (gr. -1-k). bds. 3.99 *(978-1-60745-033-7(X))* Flying Frog Publishing.

Franklin, Teil L. Ameelia's Adventures: Ameelia's First Play. 2010. 32p. pap. 16.49 *(978-1-4520-3613-7(6))* AuthorHouse.

Friedman, Becky. Daniel Learns to Share. 2016. (Simon & Schuster Ready-To-Read Level 1 Ser.). lib. bdg. 13.55 *(978-0-606-39754-4(X))* Turtleback.

Fruchter, Jason, illus. Daniel Goes to the Playground. 2015. (Daniel Tiger's Neighborhood Ser.). (ENG.). 24p. (J). (gr. -1-2). pap. 3.99 *(978-1-4814-5198-7(7)*, Simon Spotlight) Simon Spotlight.

—Daniel Learns to Share: Ready-To-Read Pre-Level 1. 2016. (Daniel Tiger's Neighborhood Ser.). (ENG.). 32p. (J). (gr. -1-k). pap. 4.99 *(978-1-4814-6751-3(4)*, Simon Spotlight) Simon Spotlight.

—Daniel Plays at School: Ready-To-Read Pre-Level 1. 2016. (Daniel Tiger's Neighborhood Ser.). (ENG.). 32p. (J). (gr. -1-k). pap. 4.99 *(978-1-4814-6102-3(8)*, Simon Spotlight) Simon Spotlight.

Fucile, Tony. Let's Do Nothing! Fucile, Tony, illus. 2012. (ENG., Illus.). 40p. (J). (gr. -1-3). pap. 8.99 *(978-0-7636-5269-2(5))* Candlewick Pr.

Fudge, Keith. The Rainy Day Discovery. 2006. (J). per. 11.95 *(978-1-889743-37-0(2))* Robbie Dean Pr.

Fujikawa, Gyo. Oh, What a Busy Day. 2010. (Illus.). 72p. (J). (gr. -1-2). 12.95 *(978-1-4027-6819-4(2))* Sterling Publishing Co., Inc.

Fuller, Bob, illus. The Costume Trunk. 2011. (J). *(978-1-936169-01-6(0))* Paddywhack Lane LLC.

Galvin, Laura Gates. Baby Lamb Finds a Friend. 2008. (Smithsonian Baby Animals Ser.). (ENG., Illus.). 16p. (gr. -1-k). 13.95 *(978-1-59249-790-4(X))* Soundprints.

—Baby Pig Time to Play. 2008. (ENG., Illus.). 16p. (J). (gr. -1-k). 6.95 *(978-1-59249-787-4(X))* Soundprints.

—Baby Polar Bear Learns to Swim. 2008. (ENG., Illus.). 16p. (J). (gr. -1-k). 6.95 *(978-1-59249-785-0(3))* Soundprints.

—Black Bear Cub at Sweet Berry Trail. 2008. (ENG., Illus.). 32p. (J). (gr. k-2). 9.95 *(978-1-59249-779-9(9))* Soundprints.

—Black Bear Cub at Sweet Berry Trail. Nelson, Will, illus. 2008. (ENG.). 32p. (J). (gr. k-2). 6.95 *(978-1-59249-775-1(6))*; pap. 8.95 *(978-1-59249-777-5(2))*; 19.95 *(978-1-59249-776-8(4))*; 16.95 *(978-1-59249-773-7(X))*; pap. 6.95 *(978-1-59249-774-4(8))* Soundprints.

Galvin, Laura Gates & Odierno, Lisa. Puppy Explores. 2008. (ENG.). 16p. (J). (gr. -1-k). 6.95 *(978-1-59249-863-5(9))* Soundprints.

Gasior, Julie. Samy the Star. 2008. 46p. 27.95 *(978-0-615-18884-3(2))* Gasior, Julie.

Gates, Josephine Scribner. The live dolls' play Days. Keep, Virginia, illus. 2007. 110p. (J). lib. bdg. 59.00 *(978-1-60304-008-2(0))* Dollworks.

—The Story of Live Dolls: Being an Account of How, on a Certain June Morning. unabr. ed. 2012. (Illus.). 104p. 39.99 *(978-1-4622-8158-9(3))* Repressed Publishing LLC.

Gauch, Patricia Lee. Christina Katerina & the Box. Burns, Doris, illus. 2012. (ENG.). 48p. (J). (gr. -1-3). 9.99 *(978-1-59078-915-5(6)*, Astra Young Readers) Astra Publishing Hse.

Gay, Marie-Louise. Stella, Queen of the Snow. 2004. (J). (gr. -1-1). spiral bd. *(978-0-616-08493-9(5))* Canadian National Institute for the Blind/Institut National Canadien pour les Aveugles.

—Stella, Reine des Neiges. 2004.Tr. of Stella, Queen of the Snow. (FRE., Illus.). (J). (gr. k-3). spiral bd. *(978-0-616-14596-8(9))* Canadian National Institute for the Blind/Institut National Canadien pour les Aveugles.

Gay, Marie-Louise, illus. Stella, Queen of the Snow. braille ed. 2004. (J). (gr. -1-1). spiral bd. *(978-0-616-08492-2(7))* Canadian National Institute for the Blind/Institut National Canadien pour les Aveugles.

Gehl, Laura. Except When They Don't. Heinsz, Joshua, illus. 2019. (ENG.). 32p. (J). (gr. -1-3). 16.99 *(978-1-4998-0804-9(6))* Little Bee Books Inc.

Giggle & grow with Plush. 2007. bds. 15.95 *(978-1-58117-644-5(9)*, Intervisual/Piggy Toes) Bendon, Inc.

Gigi, Jessy. The Sky Ride of Jimmy & Friends. 2011. 20p. pap. 24.95 *(978-1-4626-2723-3(4))* America Star Bks.

Gillis, Jennifer B. What Do You Say? 2006. (Reader's Clubhouse Level 2 Reader Ser.). (Illus.). 24p. (J). (gr. k-1). pap. 3.99 *(978-0-7641-3298-8(9))* Sourcebooks, Inc.

Gordon, David. Extremely Cute Animals Operating Heavy Machinery. Gordon, David, illus. 2016. (ENG., Illus.). 48p. (J). (gr. -1-3). 17.99 *(978-1-4169-2441-8(8)*, Simon & Schuster Bks. For Young Readers) Simon & Schuster Bks. For Young Readers.

Gosier, Phil. Snow Beast Comes to Play. Gosier, Phil, illus. 2017. (ENG., Illus.). 32p. (J). 17.99 *(978-1-62672-519-5(5)*, 9781626725195) Roaring Brook Pr.

Graham, Tamara. Little Miss Litterbug. 2008. 24p. pap. 12.99 *(978-1-4389-2519-6(0))* AuthorHouse.

Grandma Sue. Bubba the Bear. 2010. 12p. pap. 8.49 *(978-1-4490-1813-9(0))* AuthorHouse.

Green, Corey. Managing Stan: Buckley School Books #1. 2007. (ENG.). 162p. (J). 16.95 *(978-1-934437-01-8(8))*; pap. 7.99 *(978-1-934437-02-5(6))* Abligio Bks.

Gritton, Steve. ... & Then I... 2007. (Illus.). (J). 17.95 *(978-0-9795361-1-3(1))* Bad Frog Art/SMG Bks.

Groves. Mud Cake, Bk. 3A. Date not set. (Illus.). 16p. (J). pap. 129.15 *(978-0-582-18794-8(X))* Addison-Wesley Longman, Ltd. GBR. Dist: Trans-Atlantic Pubns., Inc.

Gudeon, Adam. Me & Meow. Gudeon, Adam, illus. 2011. (ENG., Illus.). 32p. (J). (gr. -1-k). 12.99 *(978-0-06-199821-8(4)*, HarperCollins) HarperCollins Pubs.

Guerin, F. A. The Witch at NO46: Verbrola. 2011. (Illus.). 140p. pap. 14.69 *(978-1-4567-7118-8(3))* AuthorHouse.

Gutierrez, Akemi. The Mummy & Other Adventures of Sam & Alice. 2005. (ENG., Illus.). 64p. (J). (gr. -1-3). 16.00 *(978-0-618-50761-0(2)*, 560974, Clarion Bks.) HarperCollins Pubs.

Gutman, Dan. My Weird School #5: Miss Small Is off the Wall! Paillot, Jim, illus. 2005. (My Weird School Ser.: 5). (ENG.). 112p. (J). (gr. 1-5). pap. 4.99 *(978-0-06-074518-9(5)*, HarperCollins) HarperCollins Pubs.

Guy, Ginger Foglesong. Bravo! 2010. (ENG., Illus.). 32p. (J). (gr. -1-k). 17.99 *(978-0-06-173180-8(3)*, Greenwillow Bks.) HarperCollins Pubs.

H & T Imaginations Unlimited, Inc. Sand Castles with Professor Woodpecker. 2009. 12p. pap. 8.49 *(978-1-4389-7262-6(8))* AuthorHouse.

Haesche, Richard, Sr. A Dog Named Wishbone. 2007. 155p. (J). 6.75 *(978-0-9798536-2-3(1))* Kreative X-Pressions Pubns.

Haladay, Max. Max Gets Mad. 1 vol. 2006. (Neighborhood Readers Ser.). (ENG.). 8p. (gr. 1-2). pap. 5.15 *(978-1-4042-6811-1(1)*, 937b21d8-5e4c-4b3c-8801-b2ad27c26bb7, Rosen Classroom) Rosen Publishing Group, Inc., The.

Hall, Bureda Ann Greathouse. Stories of My Little Blue Monkey. 2007. (Illus.). 32p. (J). pap. 15.00 *(978-0-8059-7397-6(4))* Dorrance Publishing Co., Inc.

Hannigan, Katherine. Dirt + Water = Mud. Hannigan, Katherine, illus. 2016. (ENG., Illus.). 40p. (J). (gr. -1-3). 17.99 *(978-0-06-234517-2(6)*, Greenwillow Bks.) HarperCollins Pubs.

Hapka, Cathy, pseud. Pretend & Play Kitty: With Real Crown You Can Wear! Borlasca, Hector, illus. 2004. (Role Play Ser.). 10p. (J). (gr. -1-18). bds. 6.99 *(978-1-57151-742-5(1))* Playhouse Publishing.

Harper, Charise Mericle. Mae & June & the Wonder Wheel. Spires, Ashley, illus. 2018. (ENG.). 128p. (J). (gr. 1-4). pap. 7.99 *(978-1-328-90012-8(6)*, 1700041, Clarion Bks.) HarperCollins Pubs.

—Mae & June & the Wonder Wheel. 2018. lib. bdg. 17.20 *(978-0-606-40999-5(8))* Turtleback.

Harris, Angela. Night Light. 2008. 28p. pap. 12.95 *(978-1-4389-1971-3(9))* AuthorHouse.

Harris, Donna. Lucie & the Garden Fairies. 2008. (Illus.). 40p. pap. 18.49 *(978-1-4389-1312-4(5))* AuthorHouse.

Hart, Caryl. Let's Go to Playgroup. Tobia, Lauren, illus. 2017. (ENG.). 32p. (J). 11.99 *(978-1-61067-581-9(9))* Kane Miller.

Havill, Juanita. Jamaica's Find Book & Cd. O'Brien, Anne Sibley, illus. 2009. (ENG.). 32p. (J). (gr. -1-3). audio compact disk 10.99 *(978-0-547-11961-8(5)*, 1047233, Clarion Bks.) HarperCollins Pubs.

HB Staff. Where Babies Play. 97th ed. 2003. (First-Place Reading Ser.). (gr. 1-18). pap. 16.50 *(978-0-15-308136-1(8))* Harcourt Schl. Pubs.

Heape, David. R. That's What Friends Do. l.t. ed. 2006. (ENG., Illus.). 28p. per. 9.95 *(978-1-4327-0177-2(0))* Outskirts Pr., Inc.

Heiman, Laura. My Favorite Michael. Keen, Sophie, illus. 2009. (J). (gr. -1-2). 32p. 15.95 *(978-1-58925-086-4(9))*; 24p. pap. 7.95 *(978-1-58925-419-0(8))* Tiger Tales.

Helou, Sandra & Chown, Xanna Eve. Grover on the Case: Follow the Reader Level 1. 2008. (Sesame Street Ser.). (ENG.). 24p. (J). 24.99 *(978-1-4169-5852-9(5)*, Simon Scribbles) Simon Scribbles.

Hilb, Nora, illus. Itsy Bitsy Spider. 2012. (Classic Books with Holes Board Book Ser.). (J). 14p. spiral bd. *(978-1-84643-509-6(9))*; 16p. pap. *(978-1-84643-498-3(X))* Child's Play International Ltd.

Hill, Eric. Spot Goes to the Park. Hill, Eric, illus. 2005. (Spot Ser.). (ENG., Illus.). 24p. (J). (gr. -1 — 1). bds. 9.99 *(978-0-399-24363-9(1)*, Warne) Penguin Young Readers Group.

Hill, Ros. Unexpected Tails. 2010. (ENG.). 32p. (J). (gr. -1-3). pap. 15.95 *(978-1-59687-861-7(4)*, Milk & Cookies) ibooks, Inc.

Hillert, Margaret. Birthday Car. 2016. (Beginning-To-Read Ser.). (ENG., Illus.). 32p. (J). (gr. k-2). pap. 13.26 *(978-1-60357-936-0(2))* Norwood Hse. Pr.

—Play Ball. Kemarskaya, Oksana, illus. 2016. (BeginningtoRead Ser.). (ENG.). 32p. (J). (gr. k-2). 22.60 *(978-1-59953-819-8(9))* Norwood Hse. Pr.

—Where Is Dear Dragon? Schimmell, David, illus. 2012. (BeginningtoRead Ser.). 32p. (J). (-2). lib. bdg. 22.60 *(978-1-59953-546-3(7))* Norwood Hse. Pr.

Hills, Tad & Hills, Tad. Rocket's Very Fine Day. 2019. (Step into Reading Ser.). (Illus.). 32p. (J). (gr. -1-1). pap. 5.99 *(978-0-525-64494-1(6)*, Schwartz & Wade Bks.) Random Hse. Children's Bks.

Hilton, Jennifer & McCurry, Kristen. Clap, Sing, Dance! A Book about Praising God. Rimmington, Natasha, illus. 2017. (Frolic First Faith Ser.). 22p. (J). 6.99 *(978-1-5064-1783-7(3)*, Sparkhouse Family) 1517 Media.

Hoban, Russell. How Tom Beat Captain Najork & His Hired Sportsmen. Blake, Quentin, illus. 2006. (ENG.). 32p. (J). (gr. k-4). pap. 7.95 *(978-1-56792-322-3(4))* Godine, David R. Pub.

Hochman, Marisa. A Walk in Pirate's Cove, 1 vol. 2012. (ENG., Illus.). 32p. (J). *(978-0-9865679-0-2(6))* Fitzhenry & Whiteside, Ltd.

Hofmeister, Alan, et al. Fun with the Sheet. (Reading for All Learners Ser.). (Illus.). (J). pap. *(978-1-56861-115-0(3))* Swift Learning Resources.

—In the Mud. (Reading for All Learners Ser.). (Illus.). (J). pap. *(978-1-56861-127-3(7))* Swift Learning Resources.

—Will We Win? (Reading for All Learners Ser.). (Illus.). (J). pap. *(978-1-56861-110-5(2))* Swift Learning Resources.

Holden, Pam. Hunting for Treasure, 1 vol. Whimp, Pauline, illus. 2009. (Red Rocket Readers Ser.). (ENG.). 17p. (gr. 2-2). pap. *(978-1-877363-65-8(0)*, Red Rocket Readers) Flying Start Bks.

—Too Big & Heavy, 1 vol. Hatam, Samer, illus. 2009. (Red Rocket Readers Ser.). (ENG.). 22p. (gr. 2-2). pap. *(978-1-877363-70-2(7))* Flying Start Bks.

Hollon, Frank Turner, et al. Glitter Girl & the Crazy Cheese. Dulemba, Elizabeth O., illus. 2006. (ENG.). 32p. (J). (gr. -1-3). *(978-1-59692-137-5(4))* MacAdam/Cage Publishing, Inc.

Holub, Joan. Dig, Scoop, Ka-Boom! Gordon, David, illus. 2013. (Step into Reading Ser.). 24p. (J). (gr. -1-1). pap. 5.99 *(978-0-375-86910-5(7)*, Random Hse. Bks. for Young Readers) Random Hse. Children's Bks.

—Itty Bitty Kitty & the Rainy Play Day. Burks, James, illus. 2016. (ENG.). 32p. (J). (gr. -1-3). 17.99 *(978-0-06-232220-3(6)*, HarperCollins) HarperCollins Pubs.

Hooks, Gwendolyn. Block Party, 1 vol. Ng-Benitez, Shirley, illus. 2017. (Confetti Kids Ser.: 3). (ENG.). 32p. (J). (gr. 1-5). 14.95 *(978-1-62014-341-4(0)*, leelowbooks) Lee & Low Bks., Inc.

—Music Time, 1 vol., Vol. 1. Ng-Benitez, Shirley, illus. 2017. (Confetti Kids Ser.: 4). (ENG.). 32p. (J). (gr. k-2). 14.95 *(978-1-62014-343-8(7)*, leelowbooks) Lee & Low Bks., Inc.

Hooper, Jaci. Gary: #Exodus 20. 2013. 32p. pap. 16.95 *(978-1-4908-1120-8(6)*, WestBow Pr.) Author Solutions, LLC.

Hope, Laura Lee. Freddie & Flossie. Pyle, Chuck, illus. 2006. (Bobbsey Twins Ser.). 32p. (J). (gr. -1-2). 22.78 *(978-1-59961-095-5(7))* Spotlight.

—Freddie & Flossie & Snap: Ready-To-Read Pre-Level 1. Pyle, Chuck, illus. 2005. (Bobbsey Twins Ser.). (ENG.). 32p. (J). (gr. -1-k). pap. 13.99 *(978-1-4169-0267-6(8)*, Simon Spotlight) Simon Spotlight.

Howard-Parham, Pam. Playing on the Playground. Crowell, Knox, illus. l.t. ed. 2005. (HRL Big Book Ser.). (J). (gr. k-18). pap. 10.95 *(978-1-57332-335-2(7))*; pap. 10.95 *(978-1-57332-336-9(5))* Carson-Dellosa Publishing, LLC. (HighReach Learning, Incorporated).

—Spending Time Outdoors. Teeple, Jackie, illus. l.t. ed. 2005. (HRL Little Book Ser.). (J). (gr. k-18). pap. 10.95 *(978-1-57332-334-5(9))*; pap. 10.95 *(978-1-57332-333-8(0))* Carson-Dellosa Publishing, LLC. (HighReach Learning, Incorporated).

Huber, Mike. Bree Finds a Friend. Cowman, Joseph, illus. 2014. (ENG.). 32p. (gr. -1). 15.95 *(978-1-60554-211-9(3))* Redleaf Pr.

—Rita & the Firefighters. Cowman, Joseph, illus. 2014. (ENG.). 32p. (gr. -1-k). 15.95 *(978-1-60554-208-9(3))* Redleaf Pr.

Hudson, Katy. A Loud Winter's Nap. Hudson, Katy, illus. 2017. (ENG., Illus.). 32p. (J). (gr. -1-1). 15.95 *(978-1-62370-869-6(9)*, 135087, Capstone Young Readers) Capstone.

Hudson, Wade. Places I Love to Go. 2008. (Illus.). 24p. (J). (gr. -1-3). 3.99 *(978-0-60349-008-5(6)*, Marimba Bks.) Just Us Bks., Inc.

Hulst, W. G. van de & Hulst, Willem G. van de, illus. The Rockity Rowboat. 2014. (J). *(978-1-928136-18-7(4))* Inheritance Pubns.

Hunter, Sally. Humphrey's Playtime. 2013. (Illus.). (J). *(978-1-4351-4766-9(9))* Barnes & Noble, Inc.

Hupf, Zetta & Hupf, Mitchell. Henry Goes to the Park, 1 vol. Hupf, Zetta, illus. 2009. (Illus.). 33p. pap. 24.95 *(978-1-61546-279-7(1))* America Star Bks.

Hutton, John. Blocks: Baby Unplugged. Hutton, John, ed. Kang, Andrea, illus. 2013. (Baby Unplugged Ser.). (ENG.). 14p. (J). (— 1). bds. 7.99 *(978-1-936669-13-4(7))* Blue Manatee Press.

I DOUBLE Dare You. 2008. (Illus.). 36p. (J). *(978-0-9792686-5-6(6))* Lehman Publishing.

I Love to Play. 2003. (J). per. *(978-1-57657-962-6(X))* Paradise Pr., Inc.

I Want to Go to . . . the All-American Soap Box Derby Race. 2003. (Illus.). 40p. (J). per. 9.99 *(978-0-9742667-0-1(1))* Creative Image Pubs.

Intrater, Roberta Grobel. Peek-a-Boo, You! Intrater, Roberta Grobel, photos by. 2nd rev. l.t. ed. 2005. (Illus.). 14p. (J). 14.99 *(978-0-9764985-0-6(2))* 1212 Pr.

Isaacs, Latricia. Mason & Lilly Visit Grandpa. 2011. 16p. 8.32 *(978-1-4567-2788-8(5))* AuthorHouse.

Isabel, Delgado Maria. Chave's Memories / Los Recuerdos de Chave. Yvonne, Symank, illus. 2008. 32p. (J). pap. 7.95 *(978-1-55885-244-0(1)*, Piñata Books) Arte Publico Pr.

It's a Bit Tricky: Individual Title Six-Packs. (gr. k-1). 23.00 *(978-0-7635-9022-2(3))* Rigby Education.

Iwamura, Kazuo. Hooray for Snow! 2009. (ENG., Illus.). 24p. (J). (gr. -1-2). 17.95 *(978-0-7358-2219-1(0))* North-South Bks., Inc.

Jackson, Richard. This Beautiful Day. Lee, Suzy., illus. 2017. (ENG.). 40p. (J). (gr. -1-3). 15.99 *(978-1-4814-4139-1(6)*, Atheneum/Caitlyn Dlouhy Books) Simon & Schuster Children's Publishing.

Jakubowski, Michele. Outside Surprise. Waters, Erica-Jane, illus. 2015. (Perfectly Poppy Ser.). (ENG.). 32p. (J). (gr. k-2). 22.65 *(978-1-4795-5802-5(8)*, 126832, Picture Window Bks.) Capstone.

—Snowy Blast. Waters, Erica-Jane, illus. 2014. (Perfectly Poppy Ser.). (ENG.). 32p. (J). (gr. k-2). lib. bdg. 22.65 *(978-1-4795-2283-5(X)*, 124318, Picture Window Bks.) Capstone.

James, Thomas & Thomas, James. What Will I Play While You Are Away? 2010. 28p. pap. 16.09 *(978-1-4269-2924-3(2))* Trafford Publishing.

Jarrell, Pamela R. Who Is in the Backyard? Crowell, Knox, illus. l.t. ed. 2004. (HRL Board Book Ser.). 8p. (J). (gr. -1). pap. 10.95 *(978-1-57332-281-2(4)*, HighReach Learning, Incorporated) Carson-Dellosa Publishing, LLC.

Jeffries, Alison. Sam & the Bag. Andreasen, Dan, illus. 2004. (Green Light Readers Level 1 Ser.). (gr. -1-1). 13.95 *(978-0-7569-4331-8(0))* Perfection Learning Corp.

Jenson-Elliott, Cindy. Dig In! Peterson, Mary, illus. 2016. (ENG.). 40p. (J). (gr. -1-3). 18.99 *(978-1-4424-1261-3(5)*, Beach Lane Bks.) Beach Lane Bks.

Jobes, Cecily. Playtime, 1 vol. 2016. (It's Time Ser.). (ENG.). 24p. (gr. 1-1). pap. 9.25 *(978-1-4994-2284-9(9)*, 113b0c3e-ceb4-4b49-9c12-535f1dbec912, PowerKids Pr.) Rosen Publishing Group, Inc., The.

John, Jory. The Couch Potato. Oswald, Pete, illus. 2020. (Food Group Ser.). (ENG.). 40p. (J). (gr. -1-3). 18.99 *(978-0-06-295453-4(9)*, HarperCollins) HarperCollins Pubs.

John, Jory & Arthur, Jeremy. The Couch Potato. Oswald, Pete, illus. 2020. (ENG.). (J). 41.95 *(978-1-952183-55-3(3))* Library Ideas, LLC.

Johnson, Jim. One Shoe on & One Shoe Off. Ciesinska, Izabela, illus. 2009. (ENG.). 24p. pap. 15.99 *(978-1-4415-5560-1(9))* Xlibris Corp.

Johnson, Linda Louisa. Needle in a Haystack. 2003. 78p. (YA). pap. 10.95 *(978-0-7414-1541-7(0))* Infinity Publishing.

Jolin, Dominique. Toupie Veut Jouer. braille ed. 2004. (FRE.). (J). (gr. 1). spiral bd., bds. *(978-0-616-07270-7(8))* Canadian National Institute for the Blind/Institut National Canadien pour les Aveugles.

Judybee. The Zoo Crew Play Ball. LittlePinkPebble, illus. 2011. 40p. pap. *(978-1-78092-000-9(8))* MX Publishing, Ltd.

Kahler, Alex R. Playing Wicked. Whitehouse, Ben, illus. 2020. (ENG.). 32p. (J). (gr. -1-3). 16.99 *(978-0-8075-8739-3(7)*, 807587397) Whitman, Albert & Co.

Kalar, Bonnie. Ann Paints & Plays. Spreen, Kathe, illus. Date not set. 12p. (J). (gr. -1-2). pap. *(978-1-891619-40-3(3))* Corona Pr.

Kane, Kim. The Crazy Friend. 2018. (Ginger Green, Playdate Queen Ser.). (ENG., Illus.). 64p. (J). (gr. 1-3). pap. 5.95 *(978-1-5158-1953-0(1)*, 136636, Picture Window Bks.) Capstone.

—The Crazy Friend. Davis, Jon, illus. 2017. (Ginger Green, Playdate Queen Ser.). (ENG.). 64p. (J). (gr. 1-3). lib. bdg. 23.32 *(978-1-5158-1947-9(7)*, 136630, Picture Window Bks.) Capstone.

—The Fancy Friend. 2018. (Ginger Green, Playdate Queen Ser.). (ENG., Illus.). 64p. (J). (gr. 1-3). pap. 5.95 *(978-1-5158-1954-7(X)*, 136637, Picture Window Bks.) Capstone.

—The Fancy Friend. Davis, Jon, illus. 2017. (Ginger Green, Playdate Queen Ser.). (ENG.). 64p. (J). (gr. 1-3). lib. bdg. 23.32 *(978-1-5158-1948-6(5)*, 136631, Picture Window Bks.) Capstone.

—The New Friend. 2018. (Ginger Green, Playdate Queen Ser.). (ENG., Illus.). 64p. (J). (gr. 1-3). pap. 5.95 *(978-1-5158-1952-3(3)*, 136635, Picture Window Bks.) Capstone.

—The New Friend. Davis, Jon, illus. 2017. (Ginger Green, Playdate Queen Ser.). (ENG.). 64p. (J). (gr. 1-3). lib. bdg. 23.32 *(978-1-5158-1946-2(9)*, 136629, Picture Window Bks.) Capstone.

—The Next Door Friend. 2018. (Ginger Green, Playdate Queen Ser.). (ENG., Illus.). 64p. (J). (gr. 1-3). pap. 5.95 *(978-1-5158-2011-6(4)*, 136658, Picture Window Bks.) Capstone.

—The Next Door Friend. Davis, Jon, illus. 2017. (Ginger Green, Playdate Queen Ser.). (ENG.). 64p. (J). (gr. 1-3). lib. bdg. 23.32 *(978-1-5158-1949-3(3)*, 136632, Picture Window Bks.) Capstone.

—The Only Friend. Davis, Jon, illus. 2018. (Ginger Green, Playdate Queen Ser.). (ENG.). 64p. (J). (gr. 1-3). pap. 5.95 *(978-1-5158-2012-3(2)*, 136659, Picture Window Bks.) Capstone.

Kane, Kim & Davis, Jon. Ginger Green, Playdate Queen, 6 vols. 2018. (Ginger Green, Playdate Queen Ser.). (ENG.). 64p. (J). (gr. 1-3). pap., pap., pap. 35.70 *(978-1-5158-2049-9(1)*, 27367, Picture Window Bks.) Capstone.

Kathleen, Jo Ann. Buddy Can't Tie Shoes. l.t. ed. 2006. (ENG., Illus.). 28p. per. 9.95 *(978-1-4327-0238-0(6))* Outskirts Pr., Inc.

Katz, Danny. Little Lunch Four. Vane, Mitch, illus. 2005. (Little Lunch Ser.). 64p. (J). pap. *(978-1-876372-84-2(2)*, Black Dog Books) Walker Bks. Australia Pty. Ltd.

Katz, Karen. ¡Cu-Cú, Bebé! (Peek-A-Baby) Katz, Karen, illus. 2009. (SPA., Illus.). 14p. (J). (gr. -1 — 1). bds. 7.99 *(978-1-4169-7938-8(7)*, Libros Para Ninos) Libros Para Ninos.

—Peek-A-Baby: A Lift-The-Flap Book/Lap Edition. Katz, Karen, illus. 2010. (ENG., Illus.). 14p. (J). (gr. -1 — 1). 11.99 *(978-1-4424-0790-9(5)*, Little Simon) Little Simon.

Kawai, Ritsuko. Hamtaro. Kawai, Ritsuko, illus. 2003. (ENG., Illus.). 16p. (J). pap. 7.95 *(978-1-56931-815-7(8))* Viz Media.

—Hamtaro, Vol. 1. Kawai, Ritsuko, illus. 2003. (ENG., Illus.). 16p. (J). pap. 7.95 *(978-1-56931-814-0(X))* Viz Media.

Kearney, Rena. Mimi Fairy's Purple Hair. 2009. 32p. pap. 15.99 *(978-1-4490-1554-1(9))* AuthorHouse.

Keats Curtis, Jennifer. Baby Owl's Rescue, 1 vol. Jacques, Laura, illus. 2009. (ENG.). 32p. (J). (gr. -1-3). 16.95 *(978-1-934359-95-2(5)*, 9781934359952) Arbordale Publishing.

Keats, Ezra Jack. Regards to the Man in the Moon. 2009. 40p. (J). (gr. -1-2). 17.99 *(978-0-670-01137-7(1)*, Viking Books for Young Readers) Penguin Young Readers Group.

Kettle, Shey. Girl Pirates. Thomas, Meredith, illus. 2005. (Girlz Rock! Ser.). (J). pap. *(978-1-59336-701-5(5))* Mondo Publishing.

Kirwan-Mason, Sandra. My Doll, Dollie. 2005. (ENG.). 28p. per. 18.00 *(978-1-4208-3481-9(9))* AuthorHouse.

Kitzing, Constanze V. Can't Catch Me! Kitzing, Constanze V., illus. 2019. (ENG., Illus.). 32p. (J). (gr. -1 — 1). pap. *(978-1-78285-403-6(7))* Barefoot Bks., Ltd.

Koppens, Judith. The Seesaw. van Lindenhuizen, Eline, illus. 2013. (Animal Square Ser.). (ENG.). 32p. (J). (gr. -1-k). 14.95 *(978-1-60537-152-8(1))* Clavis Publishing.

Krebs, Patricia, illus. On Your Mark, Get Set, Go! 2009. 32p. (J). 16.95 *(978-0-9796380-1-5(1))* Three Wishes Publishing Co.

Krutop, Lee, creator. Go Out to Play. 2008. (Illus.). 10p. (J). (gr. -1-1). bds. *(978-1-74178-572-2(3))* Brimax Books Ltd.

Kuhlman, Evan. Hank's Big Day: The Story of a Bug. Groenink, Chuck, illus. 2016. 40p. (J). (gr. -1-2). 17.99 *(978-0-553-51150-5(5)*, Schwartz & Wade Bks.) Random Hse. Children's Bks.

Kula, Cheryl. Play Day with Daddy. Trolenberg, Karl, illus. 2013. 20p. pap. 6.95 *(978-1-4575-2336-6(1))* Dog Ear Publishing, LLC.

Ladd, Debbie. Puddles. Morejon, Tom, illus. 2006. 32p. (J). pap. 8.95 *(978-0-9727615-4-3(3))* Deb on Air Bks.

Landolf, Diane Wright. Hog & Dog. Harris, Jennifer Beck, illus. 2005. (Step into Reading Ser.: Vol. 1). 32p. (J). (gr. -1-1). per. 4.99 *(978-0-375-83165-2(7)*, Random Hse. Bks. for Young Readers) Random Hse. Children's Bks.

Leah. The Alligator Named Ally, 1 vol. 2009. 20p. pap. 24.95 *(978-1-60749-726-4(3))* America Star Bks.

Lee, Suzy. Mirror. 2010. (ENG., Illus.). 48p. (gr. -1). 15.95 *(978-1-934734-39-1(X))* Seven Footer Pr.

Lehman, Barbara. Rainstorm. 2007. (ENG., Illus.). 32p. (J). (gr. -1-3). 17.99 *(978-0-618-75639-1(6)*, 519814, Clarion Bks.) HarperCollins Pubs.

Lenart, Claudia, illus. Seasons of Joy: Every Day Is for Outdoor Play. 2017. 27p. (J). pap. *(978-1-61599-317-8(7))* Loving Healing Pr., Inc.

Leonard, Marcia. Saltar, Brincar, Correr; Hop, Skip, Run. 2008. pap. 34.95 *(978-0-8225-9497-0(8))* Lerner Publishing Group.

Letourneau, Marie. Argyle Fox. 2017. (ENG., Illus.). 32p. (J). (gr. -1-3). 17.99 *(978-1-939100-09-2(7))* Tanglewood Pr.

Let's Play at the Playground. 2013. (Illus.). 38p. 19.95 *(978-0-9885741-1-3(X))* Community Voice Media, LLC.

Let's Pretend: Individual Title Six-Packs. (gr. -1-2). 23.00 *(978-0-7635-9001-7(0))* Rigby Education.

Levy, Janey. Play Ball!, 1 vol. 2006. (Neighborhood Readers Ser.). (ENG.). 8p. (gr. k-1). pap. 5.15 *(978-1-4042-5659-0(8),* 709d2fcb-1a3a-4e01-bf93-a457749fe8c2, Rosen Classroom) Rosen Publishing Group, Inc., The.

Lewis, Edwina. Who Plays? Parker, Ant, illus. 2003. (Who... Ser.). 16p. (J). *(978-1-85602-469-3(5),* Pavilion Children's Books) Pavilion Bks.

Lin, Grace. Ling & Ting: Together in All Weather. 2016. (ENG.). 48p. (J). (gr. 1-4). pap. 4.99 *(978-0-316-33548-5(7))* Little, Brown Bks. for Young Readers.

Little Blue Kite & Friends Activity Book. 2005. (YA). per. *(978-1-59872-122-5(4))* Instant Pub.

Litwin, Eric. The Nuts: Bedtime at the Nut House. Magoon, Scott, illus. 2014. (ENG.). 32p. (J). (gr. -1-3). 18.99 *(978-0-316-32244-7(X))* Little, Brown Bks. for Young Readers.

—The Nuts: Sing & Dance in Your Polka-Dot Pants. Magoon, Scott, illus. 2015. (ENG.). 32p. (J). (gr. -1-3). 18.99 *(978-0-316-32250-8(4))* Little, Brown Bks. for Young Readers.

Lombardi, Charles. A Friend up in the Clouds. 2010. (ENG.). 24p. pap. 15.99 *(978-1-4500-4075-4(6))* Xlibris Corp.

Long, Ethan. Clara & Clem Take a Ride. 2012. (Penguin Young Readers: Level 1 Ser.). lib. bdg. 13.55 *(978-0-606-26639-0(9))* Turtleback.

Loti, Pierre. The Story of a Child. 2004. reprint ed. pap. 20.95 *(978-1-4191-8367-6(2))* Kessinger Publishing, LLC.

—The Story of A Child. 2004. reprint ed. pap. 1.99 *(978-1-4192-8367-3(7))* Kessinger Publishing, LLC.

Love, Pamela. Dos Pies Suben, Dos Pies Bajan. Chapman, Lynne, illus. 2005. (Rookie Reader Español Ser.). (SPA & ESP.). 31p. (J). (gr. k-2). per. 4.95 *(978-0-516-25532-3(0),* Children's Pr.) Scholastic Library Publishing.

Lovell, Patty. Have Fun, Molly Lou Melon. Catrow, David, illus. 2012. (ENG.). 32p. (J). (gr. k-3). 18.99 *(978-0-399-25406-2(4),* G.P. Putnam's Sons Books for Young Readers) Penguin Young Readers Group.

Lowery, Marie Hayes. Beau & Friends. 2012. 20p. pap. 17.99 *(978-1-4817-0106-8(1))* AuthorHouse.

Lundquist, Mary. Cat & Bunny. 2015. (ENG., Illus.). 32p. (J). (gr. -1-3). 17.99 *(978-0-06-228780-9(X),* Balzer & Bray) HarperCollins Pubs.

Lynn, Cheryl. Kayla's Day at the Park. 2008. 16p. pap. 24.95 *(978-1-60813-169-3(6))* America Star Bks.

Lynn, Sarah. 1-2-3 Va-Va-Vroom! A Counting Book, 0 vols. Griffo, Daniel, illus. 2012. (ENG.). 32p. (J). (gr. -1-1). 16.99 *(978-0-7614-6162-3(0),* 9780761461623, Two Lions) Amazon Publishing.

Maccarone, Grace. The Gingerbread Family: A Scratch-And-Sniff Book. Gardner, Louise, illus. 2010. (ENG.). 14p. (J). (gr. -1-k). bds. 8.99 *(978-1-4424-0678-0(X),* Little Simon) Little Simon.

Maddox, Jake. Striker Assist, 1 vol. Tiffany, Sean, illus. 2012. (Jake Maddox Sports Stories Ser.). (ENG.). 72p. (J). (gr. 3-6). pap. 5.95 *(978-1-4342-4208-2(0),* 120267, Stone Arch Bks.) Capstone.

Mahoney, Daniel J., illus. I See a Monster. 2008. (ENG.). 12p. (J). bds. 5.95 *(978-1-58117-729-9(1),* Intervisual/Piggy Toes) Bendon, Inc.

Mahoney, Jean. Swan Lake Ballet Theatre. Seddon, Viola Anne, illus. 2009. (ENG.). 16p. (J). (gr. 1-4). 24.99 *(978-0-7636-4396-6(3))* Candlewick Pr.

Maisner, Heather & Stephenson, Kristina. It's My Turn! 2005. (First-Time Stories Ser.). (ENG., Illus.). 24p. (J). (gr. -1-1). pap. 16.19 *(978-0-7534-5740-5(7),* 9780753457405) Kingfisher Publications, plc GBR. Dist: Children's Plus, Inc.

Maldonado, Luis, illus. Friends Having Fun. Maldonado, Luis, . 2007. 48p. (J). 3.95 *(978-0-9790699-1-8(2))* Empty Harbor Productions, LLC.

Mallat, Kathy. Just Ducky. 2004. (Illus.). 24p. (J). (gr. -1-1). 16.85 *(978-0-8027-8825-2(4))* Walker & Co.

Man-Kong, Mary. My Visit to the Doctor. Riley, Kellee, illus. 2017. (J). *(978-1-5182-2648-9(5))* Random Hse., Inc.

Manushkin, Fran. Pedro el Pirata: Trusted Translations, Trusted, tr. Lyon, Tammie, illus. 2018. (Pedro en Español Ser.). (SPA.). 32p. (J). (gr. k-2). lib. bdg. 21.32 *(978-1-5158-2514-2(0),* 137573, Picture Window Bks.) Capstone.

—Pirate Pedro. Lyon, Tammie, illus. 2017. (Pedro Ser.). (ENG.). 32p. (J). (gr. k-2). lib. bdg. 21.32 *(978-1-5158-0872-5(6),* 134403, Picture Window Bks.) Capstone.

Marconi, Martina. Birthday Wishes, 1 vol. 2010. 20p. pap. 24.95 *(978-1-4489-6067-5(3))* PublishAmerica, Inc.

Martin, David. Peep & Ducky. Walker, David M., illus. (Peep & Ducky Ser.). (ENG.). (J). (— 1). 2015. 24p. bds. 6.99 *(978-0-7636-7243-0(2))* 2013. 32p. 14.99 *(978-0-7636-5039-1(0))* Candlewick Pr.

—Three Little Bears Play All Day: Brand New Readers. Gutierrez, Akemi, illus. 2010. (Brand New Readers Ser.). (ENG.). 48p. (J). (gr. -1-3). pap. 6.99 *(978-0-7636-4230-3(4))* Candlewick Pr.

Matchett, Gillian. The Adventures of Weston Super Cat with Activities. 2009. (Illus.). 92p. pap. 30.49 *(978-1-4389-2241-6(8))* AuthorHouse.

Matsutani, Miyoko. Peek-A-Boo. Segawa, Yasuo, illus. 2006. 20p. (J). (gr. -1). 10.95 *(978-1-74126-047-2(7))* R.I.C. Pubns. AUS. Dist: SCB Distributors.

May, Sophie. Dotty Dimple at Play. 2018. (ENG., Illus.). 80p. (YA). (gr. 7-12). pap. *(978-93-5297-346-0(1))* Alpha Editions.

—Dotty Dimple at Play. 2004. reprint ed. pap. 15.95 *(978-1-4191-1661-2(4))*; pap. 1.99 *(978-1-4192-1661-9(9))* Kessinger Publishing, LLC.

Mayer, Mercer. The Bravest Knight. 2007. (Illus.). 32p. (J). (gr. -1-3). 17.99 *(978-0-8037-3206-3(6),* Dial Bks) Penguin Young Readers Group.

McBratney, Sam. A Surprise for the Nutbrown Hares. Jeram, Anita, illus. 2009. (J). *(978-0-7636-4903-6(1))* Candlewick Pr.

McClatchy, Lisa. Eloise's Pirate Adventure: Ready-To-Read Level 1. Lyon, Tammie, illus. 2017. (Eloise Ser.). (ENG.). 32p. (J). (gr. -1-1). 16.99 *(978-1-4814-9979-8(3),* Simon Spotlight) Simon Spotlight.

McClure, Brian D. The Bubble. 2006. (Illus.). 64p. (J). 14.95 *(978-1-933426-05-1(5))* Universal Flag Publishing.

McClure, Leigh. Donna Plays Double Dutch: Working at the Same Time, 1 vol. 2017. (Computer Science for the Real World Ser.). (ENG.). 12p. (gr. 1-2). pap. *(978-1-5383-5174-1(9),* a1ff68b0-32f0-4e97-bccd-ef5fb8c67d78, Rosen Classroom) Rosen Publishing Group, Inc., The.

McClure, Nikki. In. 2015. (ENG., Illus.). 36p. (J). (gr. -1-k). 16.95 *(978-1-4197-1486-3(4),* 1090001) Abrams, Inc.

McCully, Emily Arnold. 3, 2, 1, Go! 2015. (I Like to Read Ser.). (ENG., Illus.). 24p. (J). (gr. -1-3). 7.99 *(978-0-8234-3314-8(5))*; 14.95 *(978-0-8234-3288-2(2))* Holiday Hse., Inc.

McDonald, Kirsten. The Big Rain, 1 vol. Meza, Erika, illus. 2015. (Carlos & Carmen Ser.). (ENG.). 32p. (J). (gr. k-3). 32.79 *(978-1-62402-137-4(9),* 19071, Calico Chapter Bks) Magic Wagon.

McDonald, Megan. Judy Moody & the NOT Bummer Summer. Reynolds, Peter H., illus. 2018. (Judy Moody Ser.: 10). (ENG.). 208p. (J). (gr. 1-4). pap. 5.99 *(978-1-5362-0084-3(0))* Candlewick Pr.

Mcdonald, Megan. Judy Moody & the Not Bummer Summer. 2012. (Judy Moody Ser.: 10). lib. bdg. 16.00 *(978-0-606-23800-7(X))* Turtleback.

McGougan, Kathy. Buddy Plays Ball. 2007. (J). pap. 5.00 *(978-0-9799980-4-1(2))* Buddy Bks. Publishing.

McKay, Sindy. We Both Read - Little Chipper. Hanson, Sydney, illus. 2017. (ENG.). 41p. (J). 9.95 *(978-1-60115-295-4(7))* Treasure Bay, Inc.

—We Both Read-Jack & the Toddler. Zivoin, Jennifer, illus. 2011. (ENG.). 44p. (J). 9.95 *(978-1-60115-249-7(3))*; pap. 5.99 *(978-1-60115-250-3(7))* Treasure Bay, Inc.

McLerran, Alice. Roxaboxen. Cooney, Barbara, illus. 2004. (ENG.). 32p. (J). (gr. -1-3). pap. 9.99 *(978-0-06-052633-7(5),* HarperCollins) HarperCollins Pubs.

McMahon, Kara. Playdates Are Not Scary! Ready-To-Read Level 1. McClellan, Maddy, illus. 2015. (Friday the Scaredy Cat Ser.). (ENG.). 24p. (J). (gr. -1-1). pap. 4.99 *(978-1-4814-3591-8(4),* Simon Spotlight) Simon Spotlight.

McOmber, Rachel B., ed. McOmber Phonics Storybooks: A Nifty Ball of String. rev. ed. (Illus.). (J). *(978-0-944991-50-3(5))* Swift Learning Resources.

McPhail, David. Olivia Loves Owl. 2016. (ENG., Illus.). 20p. (J). (gr. -1 — 1). bds. 8.95 *(978-1-4197-2127-4(5),* 1128510, Abrams Appleseed) Abrams, Inc.

McQuinn, Anna. A Leo le Gusta Bebelandia. Hearson, Ruth, illus. 2015. (Leo Can! Ser.). (SPA.). 24p. (J). (— 1). lib. bdg. 9.95 *(978-1-58089-704-4(5))* Charlesbridge Publishing, Inc.

—Leo Loves Baby Time. Hearson, Ruth, illus. 2014. (Leo Can! Ser.). (ENG.). 24p. (J). (— 1). lib. bdg. 9.95 *(978-1-58089-665-8(0))* Charlesbridge Publishing, Inc.

Meachen Rau, Dana. ¡a Rodar! (Rolling), 1 vol. 2008. (En Movimiento (on the Move) Ser.). (SPA., Illus.). 32p. (gr. k-1). lib. bdg. 25.50 *(978-0-7614-2419-2(9),* 9332c010-8b6a-4b38-970a-84a3088edc44) Cavendish Square Publishing LLC.

—¡a Trepar! (Climbing), 1 vol. 2008. (En Movimiento (on the Move) Ser.). (SPA., Illus.). 32p. (gr. k-1). lib. bdg. 25.50 *(978-0-7614-2424-6(5),* 57c869a9-5085-43c9-9d4e-1fdb1a2e78cd) Cavendish Square Publishing LLC.

Meddaugh, Susan. Toy Trouble. 2010. (Martha Speaks Ser.). (ENG., Illus.). 24p. (J). (gr. -1-3). pap. 3.99 *(978-0-547-21078-0(7))* Houghton Mifflin Harcourt Publishing Co.

Meisel, Paul. See Me Play. 2019. (I Like to Read Ser.). (Illus.). 32p. (J). (gr. -1-3). 15.99 *(978-0-8234-3832-7(5))* Holiday Hse., Inc.

Merberg, Julie. I'm So Not Wearing a Dress! Kemble, Mai, illus. 2010. (ENG.). 32p. (J). 11.99 *(978-1-935703-05-1(6))* Downtown Bookworks.

Merry, Margaret. The Adventures of Princess the Pony. 2009. 64p. pap. 19.50 *(978-1-60860-936-9(7),* Eloquent Bks.) Strategic Book Publishing & Rights Agency (SBPRA).

Metz, Teresa L. Friends for Phoebe. 2009. (ENG.). 43p. pap. 24.40 *(978-0-557-16884-2(8))* Lulu Pr., Inc.

Metzger, Steve. Five Little Bunnies Hopping on a Hill. 2006. (J). *(978-0-439-80382-3(9))* Scholastic, Inc.

Meyer, Ken, Jr., illus. Lucky Lionel. 2009. (J). *(978-1-60108-020-2(4))* Red Cygnet Pr.

Meyers, Susan. This Is the Way a Baby Rides. Nakata, Hiroe, illus. 2005. (ENG.). 40p. (J). (gr. -1-1). 15.95 *(978-0-8109-5763-3(9),* Abrams Bks. for Young Readers) Abrams, Inc.

Milbourne, Anna. The Snowy Day. Temporin, Elena, illus. 2007. (J). *(978-0-439-88988-9(X))* Scholastic, Inc.

Miller, Paula K. Amy, Louise & Me. 2008. 24p. pap. 24.95 *(978-1-4241-9757-6(0))* America Star Bks.

Mlawer, Teresa. If I Had a Dragon/Si Yo Tuviera un Dragon. Ellery, Tom & Ellery, Amanda, illus. 2006. (ENG & SPA.). (J). (gr. -1-3). per. 3.99 *(978-1-933032-17-7(0))*; 32p. (gr. 5-6). 12.99 *(978-1-933032-16-0(2))* Lectorum Pubns., Inc.

Moradian, Afsaneh. Jamie Is Jamie: A Book about Being Yourself & Playing Your Way. Bogade, Maria, illus. 2018. (Jamie Is Jamie Ser.). (ENG.). 32p. (J). (gr. -1-3). 15.99 *(978-1-63198-139-5(0),* 81395) Free Spirit Publishing Inc.

Morgante, Roxanne & Callies, Pat. Justin & Travis: Games They Play, 1 vol. 2010. 62p. pap. 19.95 *(978-1-4489-4458-3(9))* PublishAmerica, Inc.

Munsch, Robert. Playhouse. Martchenko, Michael, illus. 2022. (ENG.). 32p. (J). (gr. -1-3). pap. 7.99 *(978-0-439-98959-6(0))* Scholastic Canada, Ltd. CAN. Dist: Publishers Group West (PGW).

Murguia, Bethanie. Princess! Fairy! Ballerina! Murguia, Bethanie, illus. 2016. (ENG., Illus.). 40p. (J). (gr. -1-k). 17.99 *(978-0-545-73240-6(9))* Scholastic, Inc.

Murphy, Jill. All for One. 2004. (Illus.). (J). (gr. -1-2). spiral bd. *(978-0-616-14592-0(6))*; spiral bd. *(978-0-616-14591-3(8))* Canadian National Institute for the Blind/Institut National Canadien pour les Aveugles.

Murphy, Stuart J. Freda Says Please. Jones, Tim, illus. 2013. (I See I Learn Ser.: 15). 32p. (J). (-k). pap. 6.95 *(978-1-58089-475-3(5))* Charlesbridge Publishing, Inc.

—Happy, Healthy Ajay! 2012. (I See I Learn Ser.: 12). (ENG., Illus.). 32p. (J). (-k). pap. 7.99 *(978-1-58089-471-5(2))* Charlesbridge Publishing, Inc.

—Percy Plays It Safe. 2010. (I See I Learn Ser.: 4). (Illus.). 32p. (J). (gr. -1-k). 14.95 *(978-1-58089-452-4(6))* Charlesbridge Publishing, Inc.

Murray, Kirsty. Puddle Hunters. Blair, Karen, illus. 2019. (ENG.). 32p. (J). (gr. -1-1). 16.99 *(978-1-76029-674-2(0))* Allen & Unwin AUS. Dist: Independent Pubs. Group.

Nelid, Piper. The Turkey Day Play, 1 vol., 1. 2015. (Rosen REAL Readers: STEM & STEAM Collection). (ENG.). 8p. (J). (gr. k-1). pap. 5.46 *(978-1-5081-1492-5(7),* ba7c9e34-b12b-49eb-bc68-96ce99f10d3e, Rosen Classroom) Rosen Publishing Group, Inc., The.

Nolan, Allia Zobel. God's Winter Wonderland. Mitchell, Melanie, illus. 2006. 10p. (J). bds. 8.99 *(978-0-8254-5526-1(X))* Kregel Pubns.

Nolen, Gale. Johnny, My Favorite Mouse. Cain, Doreyl Ammons, illus. 2007. 32p. (J). per. 18.95 *(978-0-9753023-7-8(X))* Ammons Communications, Ltd.

Nora Juega Todo el Dia: Nora Plays All Day. 2005. (Take-Home Bks.). (SPA.). (YA). (gr. -1-3). 15.75 *(978-0-8215-1204-3(8))* Sadlier, William H. Inc.

Nora Juega Todo el Dia/Nora Plays All Day. 2005. (Libros en Espanol Para Ninos Ser.). (SPA.). (YA). (gr. -1-1). 11.97 *(978-0-8215-0994-4(2))* Sadlier, William H. Inc.

Nora Plays All Day: Take-Home Book. 2005. (Emergent Library: Vol. 2). (YA). (gr. -1-1). 12.60 *(978-0-8215-7259-7(8))* Sadlier, William H. Inc.

Norman, Kim. Come Next Season. Miyares, Daniel, illus. 2019. (ENG.). 40p. (J). 17.99 *(978-0-374-30598-7(6),* 900173047, Farrar, Straus & Giroux (BYR)) Farrar, Straus & Giroux.

November, Deborah, et al. Let's Visit Sesame Street. Mathieu, Joe, illus. 2010. (ENG.). 24p. (J). bds. 14.99 *(978-0-7944-2101-4(6))* Reader's Digest Assn., Inc., The.

Nugent, Penn. Come down & Play. 2004. (Illus.). 40p. (J). 7.95 *(978-1-880849-90-3(9))* Chapel Hill Press, Inc.

O'Connor, Jane. Fancy Nancy - There's No Day Like a Snow Day. 2012. (Fancy Nancy Picture Bks.). (J). lib. bdg. 14.75 *(978-0-606-26857-8(X))* Turtleback.

Odierno, Lisa. Bunny Hide-and-Seek. 2009. (Smithsonian Baby Animals Ser.). (ENG., Illus.). 16p. (J). (gr. -1-k). 6.95 *(978-1-60727-092-8(7))* Soundprints.

—Kitten & Her Sister. 2009. (ENG.). 16p. (J). 6.95 *(978-1-60727-000-3(5))* Soundprints.

Odierno, Lisa & Soundprints Staff. Bunny Hide-and-Seek. 2009. (Smithsonian Baby Animals Ser.). (ENG., Illus.). 16p. (J). (gr. -1-k). 6.95 *(978-1-60727-105-5(2))* Soundprints.

O'Keefe, Lauren. Raindrop Flies a Kite. 2012. 16p. pap. 12.68 *(978-1-4669-7000-7(6))* Trafford Publishing.

Olsen, Leigh & S. I. International. What Do You Say? A Book about Manners. 2009. (Playskool Ser.). (ENG.). 16p. (J). (gr. -1). pap. 6.99 *(978-1-4169-8518-1(2),* Simon Spotlight) Simon Spotlight.

Oram, Hiawyn. Snowboy & the Last Tree Standing. Sif, Birgitta, illus. 2018. (ENG.). 32p. (J). (gr. -1-2). 16.99 *(978-0-7636-9572-9(6))* Candlewick Pr.

Ostow, Micol. GoldenGirl. 2009. (Bradford Ser.). (ENG.). 224p. (YA). (gr. 9-18). pap. 9.99 *(978-1-4169-6118-5(6),* Simon Pulse) Simon Pulse.

Pace, Anne Marie. Vampirina in the Snow-A Vampirina Ballerina Book. 2018. (Vampirina Ser.: 4). (ENG., Illus.). 40p. (J). (gr. -1-k). 17.99 *(978-1-368-02318-4(5),* Disney-Hyperion) Disney Publishing Worldwide.

Pagratis, Maggie & Pagratis, Illustrator Liliane, MaggieGrenier. Go Away Booboo! 2005. 29p. (J). 11.88 *(978-1-4116-3689-7(9))* Lulu Pr., Inc.

Parent, Nancy, adapted by. Chez Nancy. 2018. (Illus.). 32p. (J). *(978-1-5444-0825-5(0))* Harper & Row Ltd.

Parker, David. We Can All Play. Lucas, Margeaux, illus. 2007. (J). *(978-0-545-00390-2(3))* Scholastic, Inc.

Parnell, Declan. Playground Fun, 1 vol., 1. 2015. (Rosen REAL Readers: STEM & STEAM Collection). (ENG.). 12p. (J). (gr. 1-2). pap. 6.33 *(978-1-5081-1557-1(5),* 9f258ef7-c8c9-496b-ad08-7861860efe72, Rosen Classroom) Rosen Publishing Group, Inc., The.

Parragon Staff, ed. Cerdito. 2010. pap. 4.95 *(978-1-4054-4915-1(2))* Parragon, Inc.

—Corderito. 2010. pap. 5.95 *(978-1-4054-4914-4(4))* Parragon, Inc.

Parton, Paula. I Always Wondered. Parton, Paula, illus. 2009. (Illus.). 44p. pap. 11.95 *(978-1-935118-48-0(X))* Bellissima Publishing, LLC.

Patricelli, Leslie. Higher! Higher! Patricelli, Leslie, illus. 2010. (Leslie Patricelli Board Bks.). (ENG., Illus.). 30p. (J). (-k). bds. 7.99 *(978-0-7636-4433-8(1))* Candlewick Pr.

Paula Yoo. Want to Play? (Confetti Kids), 1 vol. 2016. (Confetti Kids Ser.: 2). (ENG., Illus.). 32p. (J). (gr. k-2). 14.95 *(978-1-62014-250-9(3),* leelowbooks) Lee & Low Bks., Inc.

Paulhus, Jonathan. Chester, the Light Golden Retriever. 2013. 36p. pap. 24.95 *(978-1-63004-640-8(X))* America Star Bks.

Pendergrass, Daphne. Daniel Plays at School. 2016. (Daniel Tiger's Neighborhood Ready-To-Read Ser.). lib. bdg. 13.55 *(978-0-606-38991-4(1))* Turtleback.

Perez, Irene. Rain or Shine. 2008. 16p. pap. 12.50 *(978-1-4389-0873-1(3))* AuthorHouse.

Peters, Lou. The Owl & the Turtle. 2010. 32p. pap. 15.95 *(978-0-557-51727-5(3))* Lulu Pr., Inc.

Peto, Judith E. & Talwar, Robert B. Jenny & Benny: Friends 2005. (Illus.). 28p. (J). (gr. -1-3). 16.95 *(978-0-9767511-0-6(0))* Lasting Bks. Publishing Co.

Petty, Dev. There's Nothing to Do! Boldt, Mike, illus. 2019. 32p. (J). (gr. -1-2). pap. 8.99 *(978-0-593-11897-9(9),* Dragonfly Bks.) Random Hse. Children's Bks.

Phelan, Matt. Pignic: A Springtime Book for Kids. Phelan, Matt, illus. 2018. (ENG., Illus.). 32p. (J). (gr. -1-3). 17.99 *(978-0-06-244339-7(9),* Greenwillow Bks.) HarperCollins Pubs.

Phillips, Dee. What Can I Be? 2010. (Look at Me! Ser.). (ENG.). 5p. (J). (gr. -1-k). bds. 6.95 *(978-1-84696-199-1(8),* TickTock Books) Octopus Publishing Group GBR. Dist: Independent Pubs. Group.

—Who Can I Be? 2010. (Look at Me! Ser.). (ENG.). 5p. (J). (gr. -1-k). bds. 6.95 *(978-1-84696-200-4(5),* TickTock Books) Octopus Publishing Group GBR. Dist: Independent Pubs. Group.

Phillips, Dee & Ticktock Media, Ltd. Staff. What Do Kangaroos Do? 2009. (What Do Animals Do? Ser.). (ENG.). 5p. (J). (gr. k — 1). bds. 4.95 *(978-1-84696-959-1(X),* TickTock Books) Octopus Publishing Group GBR. Dist: Independent Pubs. Group.

—What Do Monkeys Do? 2009. (What Do Animals Do? Ser.). (ENG.). 5p. (J). (gr. k — 1). bds. 4.95 *(978-1-84696-960-7(3),* TickTock Books) Octopus Publishing Group GBR. Dist: Independent Pubs. Group.

—What Do Rabbits Do? 2009. (What Do Animals Do? Ser.). (ENG.). 5p. (J). (gr. k — 1). bds. 4.95 *(978-1-84696-961-4(1),* TickTock Books) Octopus Publishing Group GBR. Dist: Independent Pubs. Group.

Phuong, Thai My, illus. Mario & the Aliens (SC) 2019. (ENG.). 40p. (J). pap. 9.99 *(978-1-64124-040-6(7),* 0406) Fox Chapel Publishing Co., Inc.

Piantedosi, John J. The Cat That Purred. Maglio-Macullar, Andrea, illus. 2014. (ENG.). (J). pap. 11.95 *(978-1-56548-540-2(8))* New City Press of the Focolare.

Piggy Toes Press, creator. Color Party! 2007. (ENG., Illus.). 12p. (gr. -1-k). bds. 7.99 *(978-1-58117-585-1(X),* Intervisual/Piggy Toes) Bendon, Inc.

—Giggle & Grow Baby's Body! 2007. (ENG., Illus.). 14p. (gr. -1-k). bds. 7.99 *(978-1-58117-586-8(8),* Intervisual/Piggy Toes) Bendon, Inc.

Piggy Toes Press Staff, creator. Little Feet Like: A Tiny Tootsie Touch & Feel Book. 2008. (ENG., Illus.). 12p. (gr. -1-k). 9.95 *(978-1-58117-692-6(9),* Intervisual/Piggy Toes) Bendon, Inc.

Pitt, Marilyn & Hileman, Jane. My Babies. 2010. pap. 39.62 *(978-1-61541-066-8(X))* American Reading Co.

—Pretty Cat. 2010. pap. 39.62 *(978-1-61541-068-2(6))* American Reading Co.

The Playful Kitten. 2003. (J). per. *(978-1-57657-888-9(7))* Paradise Pr., Inc.

Ponko, Cindy A. Busy Busy Days. 2006. (Illus.). (J). *(978-0-9768230-1-8(2))* Some Kids I Know.

Ponti, Claude. Chick & Chickie in Play All Day! 2013. (Toon Books Level 1 Ser.). lib. bdg. 14.75 *(978-0-606-31595-1(0))* Turtleback.

—Chick & Chickie Play All Day! Toon Books Level 1. Ponti, Claude, illus. 2012. (ENG., Illus.). 36p. (J). (gr. -1-3). 12.95 *(978-1-935179-14-6(4),* TOON Books) Astra Publishing Hse.

Poole, Catherine Cheyenne. Batboy's Crazy Day. Murphy, Fredrick, illus. 2008. 24p. pap. 8.95 *(978-1-935105-18-3(3))* Avid Readers Publishing Group.

Portis, Antoinette. Not a Stick. Portis, Antoinette, illus. 2007. (Not a Box Ser.). (ENG., Illus.). 32p. (J). (gr. -1-1). 15.99 *(978-0-06-112325-2(0),* HarperCollins) HarperCollins Pubs.

Pousette, Kelly, illus. Do Not Rake Your Garden in a Party Dress. 2020. (ENG.). 32p. (J). (gr. k-2). 16.95 *(978-1-944903-85-5(2),* Cameron Kids) Cameron + Co.

Preston, Helen M. Gra Gra's Stories. 2012. 72p. pap. 28.99 *(978-1-4772-9783-4(9))* AuthorHouse.

Puck. Bookstore Babies. Lemay, Violet, illus. 2019. 22p. (J). bds. 7.95 *(978-1-947458-50-5(7),* 805850) Duo Pr. LLC.

Rabe, Tish. On the First Day of Summer Vacation. Jennings, Sarah, illus. 2019. (ENG.). 32p. (J). (gr. -1-3). 9.99 *(978-0-06-266852-3(8),* HarperCollins) HarperCollins Pubs.

Rabouin, Rochelle. Shapes Friends. 2009. (ENG.). 52p. 24.99 *(978-1-4363-8329-5(3))*; pap. 15.99 *(978-1-4363-8328-8(5))* Xlibris Corp.

Raden, Tammy. Priscilla Play. 2010. (ENG.). 28p. pap. 12.49 *(978-1-4520-0808-0(6))* AuthorHouse.

Rand, Edward A. The Knights of the White Shield; or, up-the-Ladder Club Series, Round One Play. 2007. 120p. per. *(978-1-4068-3739-1(3))* Echo Library.

Rao, Lisa. Playtime in Trucktown. Shannon, David et al, illus. 2008. (Jon Scieszka's Trucktown Ser.). (ENG.). 24p. (J). (gr. -1-1). 5.99 *(978-1-4169-4197-2(5),* Simon Scribbles) Simon Scribbles.

Raudenbush, Amy. Lucy More Needs Less. 2006. 48p. (J). pap. 13.99 *(978-1-4116-6120-2(6))* Lulu Pr., Inc.

Rayner, Shoo, illus. & concept. Cat & Dog Play Hide & Seek: Band 02A/Red a (Collins Big Cat) Rayner, Shoo, concept. 2006. (Collins Big Cat Ser.). (ENG.). 16p. (J). (gr. -1-k). pap. 7.99 *(978-0-00-718660-0(6))* HarperCollins Pubs. Ltd. GBR. Dist: Independent Pubs. Group.

Rea, Ba. Monarch! Come Play with Me. Rea, Ba, illus. 2006. (Illus.). 32p. (J). per. 10.95 *(978-0-9657472-5-7(5))* Bas Relief, LLC.

Reasoner, Charles. No Peeking! 2003. (ENG., Illus.). 14p. bds. 4.99 *(978-0-8431-0227-7(6),* Price Stern Sloan) Penguin Publishing Group.

Reed, Jennifer. That's Not Fair! DuFalla, Anita, illus. 2012. (Little Birdie Bks.). (ENG.). 24p. (gr. 1-2). lib. bdg. 29.93 *(978-1-61810-176-1(5),* 9781618101761) Rourke Educational Media.

Reidy, Jean. Too Princessy! Leloup, Geneviève, illus. 2013. (Too! Bks.). (ENG.). 26p. (J). (gr. -1 — 1). bds. 7.99 *(978-1-59990-955-4(3),* 9781599909554, Bloomsbury USA Childrens) Bloomsbury Publishing USA.

Reilly, Carmel. The Boy at the Park. Reynolds, Pat, illus. 2009. 24p. pap. 10.67 *(978-1-4190-5517-1(8))* Rigby Education.

Rex, Michael. Eat Pete. Rex, Michael, illus. 2018. (Illus.). 32p. (J). (-k). 17.99 *(978-1-5247-3880-8(8),* Nancy Paulsen Books) Penguin Young Readers Group.

Rey, H. A. Curious George Hide-And-Seek Tabbed Board Book. 2008. (Curious George Ser.). (ENG., Illus.). 10p. (J). (gr. -1 — 1). bds. 6.99 *(978-0-618-89199-3(4),* 569446, Clarion Bks.) HarperCollins Pubs.

Rice, Dona. What Kind of Weather? 2009. (Early Literacy Ser.). (ENG., Illus.). 16p. (gr. k-1). 19.99 *(978-1-4333-1459-9(2))* Teacher Created Materials, Inc.

Richmond, Lori. Bunny's Staycation (Mama's Business Trip) 2018. (ENG., Illus.). 32p. (J). (gr. -1-k). 17.99 *(978-0-545-92589-1(4),* Scholastic Pr.) Scholastic, Inc.

Riley, Kellee, illus. Tolee's Rhyme Time. 2009. (Ni Hao, Kai-Lan Ser.). (ENG.). 24p. (J). pap. 3.99 *(978-1-4169-9024-6(0),* Simon Spotlight/Nickelodeon) Simon Spotlight/Nickelodeon.

Rinne, Teresa & Dillon, Preston. Snail Tails: Let's Play Ball! 2009. 40p. pap. 16.99 *(978-1-4389-7076-9(5))* AuthorHouse.

Rippin, Sally. The Crazy Cousins. Spartels, Stephanie, illus. 2012. (Hey Jack! Ser.). (ENG.). 42p. (J). *(978-1-61067-135-4(X))* Kane Miller.
Rocklin, Joanne. Good Guys, Bad Guys. Carpenter, Nancy, illus. 2020. (ENG.). 32p. (J). (gr. -1-3). 16.99 *(978-1-4197-3417-5(2))*, 1138401, Abrams Bks. for Young Readers) Abrams, Inc.
Rodriguez, Paul. Let's All Play! Character Education/ Anti-Bullying. Rodriguez, Paul, illus. 2003. (Illus.). 32p. (J). lib. bdg. 15.99 *(978-0-9744770-0-8(1))* Rodro.
Romano, Melissa. Mama, Lions Don't Listen. 2008. 24p. pap. 11.99 *(978-1-4343-9907-6(9))* AuthorHouse.
Rose, C. T. Don't Play with the Craft, 1 vol. 2009. 82p. pap. 19.95 *(978-1-61582-871-5(0))* America Star Bks.
Rosen, Robert. Our Snowy Day. Curzon, Brett, illus. 2017. (Seasons Around Me Ser.). (ENG.). 24p. (gr. -1-2). pap. 9.95 *(978-1-68342-797-1(1))*, 9781683427971) Rourke Educational Media.
Ross, Theodore J. Lucy Wants to Play. 2003. (Illus.). 16p. (J). 3.99 *(978-1-59384-029-7(2))* Parklane Publishing.
Rubiano, Brittany. Frozen: Anna Loves Elsa. 2015. (ENG., Illus.). 14p. (J). (gr. -1-k). bds. 9.99 *(978-1-4847-2470-5(4))*, Disney Press Books) Disney Publishing Worldwide.
Ruiz, Jackson. It's Cool in the Furnace: The first graphic novel by Jackson Ruiz. 2010. 32p. pap. 16.99 *(978-1-4520-2634-3(3))* AuthorHouse.
Rusu, Meredith. Play Time for Peppa & George (Peppa Pig) EOne, illus. 2016. (ENG.). 32p. (J). (gr. -1-k). 8.99 *(978-1-338-03280-2(1))* Scholastic, Inc.
Rylant, Cynthia. Annie & Snowball & the Magical House: Ready-To-Read Level 2. Stevenson, Suçie & Stevenson, Suçie, illus. (Annie & Snowball Ser.: 7). (ENG.). 40p. (J). (gr. k-2). 2011. pap. 4.99 *(978-1-4169-3949-8(0))* 2010. 17.99 *(978-1-4169-3945-0(8))* Simon Spotlight. (Simon Spotlight).
—The Brownie & Pearl Collection: Brownie & Pearl Step Out; Brownie & Pearl Get Dolled up; Brownie & Pearl Grab a Bite; Brownie & Pearl See the Sights; Brownie & Pearl Go for a Spin; Brownie & Pearl Hit the Hay. Biggs, Brian, illus. 2016. (Brownie & Pearl Ser.). (ENG.). 144p. (J). (gr. -1-k). 12.99 *(978-1-4814-8653-8(5))*, Simon Spotlight) Simon Spotlight.
—Brownie & Pearl Get Dolled Up. Biggs, Brian, illus. 2010. (Brownie & Pearl Ser.). (ENG.). 24p. (J). (gr. -1-3). 15.99 *(978-1-4169-8631-7(6))*, Beach Lane Bks.) Beach Lane Bks.
—Brownie & Pearl Get Dolled Up: Ready-To-Read Pre-Level 1. Biggs, Brian, illus. 2014. (Brownie & Pearl Ser.). (ENG.). 24p. (J). (gr. -1-k). 17.99 *(978-1-4424-9568-5(5))*; pap. 4.99 *(978-1-4424-9567-8(7))* Simon Spotlight. (Simon Spotlight).
Sandall, Ellie. Everybunny Dance! Sandall, Ellie, illus. 2017. (ENG., Illus.). 32p. (J). (gr. -1-3). 17.99 *(978-1-4814-9822-7(3))*, McElderry, Margaret K. Bks.) McElderry, Margaret K. Bks.
Sanders, Rob. Ball & Balloon. Yoon, Helen, illus. 2019. (ENG.). 40p. (J). (gr. -1-3). 17.99 *(978-1-5344-2562-0(4))*, McElderry, Margaret K. Bks.) McElderry, Margaret K. Bks.
—Rodzilla. Santat, Dan, illus. 2017. (ENG.). 48p. (J). (gr. -1-3). 17.99 *(978-1-4814-5779-8(9))*, McElderry, Margaret K. Bks.) McElderry, Margaret K. Bks.
Sansone, V. K. A Daunting Quest for Quincy & Quigley. 2008. (ENG.). 32p. pap. 8.98 *(978-0-557-03594-6(5))* Lulu Pr., Inc.
Santillo, LuAnn. Mike. Santillo, LuAnn, ed. 2003. (Half-Pint Kids Readers Ser.). (Illus.). 7p. (J). (gr. -1-1). pap. 1.00 *(978-1-59256-100-1(4))* Half-Pint Kids, Inc.
Santirso, Liliana. Me Gusta Jugar Con los Libros. Gomez, Patricio & Villagomez, Raul, illus. (SPA.). (J). (gr. k-1). pap. *(978-968-6465-48-8(0))* Casa de Estudios de Literatura y Talleres Artisticos Amaquemecan A.C. MEX. Dist: Lectorum Pubns., Inc.
Santos de las Heras, José María. Cachicos. 2007. 176p. pap. 20.95 *(978-1-84799-885-9(2))* Lulu Pr., Inc.
Sarah, Linda. Big Friends. Davies, Benji, illus. 2016. (ENG.). 32p. (J). 19.99 *(978-1-62779-330-8(5))*, 900146698, Holt, Henry & Co. Bks. For Young Readers) Holt, Henry & Co.
Sattler, Jennifer. Dollop & Mrs. Fabulous. 2019. (ENG., Illus.). 32p. (J). (gr. -1-2). lib. bdg. 20.99 *(978-0-399-55336-3(3))*, Knopf Bks. for Young Readers) Random Hse. Children's Bks.
—Pig Kahuna Pirates! 2014. (Pig Kahuna Ser.). (ENG., Illus.). 32p. (J). E-Book 6.39 *(978-1-61963-203-5(9))*, Bloomsbury USA Childrens) Bloomsbury Publishing USA.
Sauer, Tammi. Truck, Truck, Goose! Waring, Zoe, illus. 2017. (ENG.). 40p. (J). (gr. -1 — 1). 14.99 *(978-0-06-242153-1(0))*, HarperCollins) HarperCollins Pubs.
Saunders, Brianna. The Magic Marble. 2013. 32p. pap. 24.95 *(978-1-63004-598-2(5))* America Star Bks.
Scheffler, Axel, illus. Pip & Posy: the New Friend. 2017. (Pip & Posy Ser.). (ENG.). 32p. (J). (-k). 12.99 *(978-0-7636-9339-8(1))* Candlewick Pr.
Schertle, Alice. The Adventures of Old Bo Bear. Parkins, David, illus. 2005. (J). 16.95 *(978-978-081-183-9(4))* Chronicle Bks. LLC.
Schneider, Josh. Ultrabot's First Playdate. Schneider, Josh, illus. 2019. (ENG., Illus.). 32p. (J). (gr. -1-3). 17.99 *(978-1-328-49013-1(0))*, 1716817, Clarion Bks.) HarperCollins Pubs.
Schoenherr, Ian. Cat & Mouse. Schoenherr, Ian, illus. 2008. (Illus.). 40p. (J). (gr. -1). lib. bdg. 17.89 *(978-0-06-136314-6(6))*, Greenwillow Bks.) HarperCollins Pubs.
Schwartz, Joanne. Pinny in Summer, 1 vol. Malenfant, Isabelle, illus. 2016. (ENG.). 32p. (J). (gr. -1-2). 16.95 *(978-1-55498-782-5(2))* Groundwood Bks. CAN. Dist: Publishers Group West (PGW).
Sconyers, Jennifer. The Map. 2010. 24p. pap. 12.99 *(978-1-4490-5731-2(4))* AuthorHouse.
Scott, Lucy. Busy Busy! Scott, Lucy, illus. 2016. (ENG., Illus.). 32p. (J). (gr. -1-k). 15.99 *(978-1-939547-25-5(3))*, dc92e402-14ce-417a-b081-11729ad5bd4d) Creston Bks.
Scotton, Rob. Splat the Cat & the Snowy Day Surprise. 2014. (Splat the Cat Ser.). (ENG., Illus.). 16p. (J). (gr. -1-3). pap. 7.99 *(978-0-06-197864-7(7))*, HarperFestival) HarperCollins Pubs.
Shepherd, Donna J. OUCH! Sunburn. Collier, Kevin Scott, illus. 2007. 27p. (J). E-Book 9.95 incl. cd-rom *(978-1-933090-60-3(X))* Guardian Angel Publishing, Inc.
Shields, Gillian. Library Lily. Chessa, Francesca, illus. 2011. (ENG.). 26p. (YA). 16.00 *(978-0-8028-5401-8(X))* Eerdmans, William B. Publishing Co.
Short, Carol. Todd's Nine Lives. 2009. 28p. pap. 12.49 *(978-1-4389-3893-6(4))* AuthorHouse.
Siewert, Pauline, illus. Look What I Can Do!, 1 vol. 2009. (Watch This! Ser.). (ENG.). 32p. (J). (gr. k-k). 27.27 *(978-1-60754-452-4(0))*, acb23e7d-13c5-4276-84d7-12d1112d97cd); pap. 11.55 *(978-1-60754-453-1(9))*, f334c715-d8d4-4c33-83aa-f82398bc05fb) Rosen Publishing Group, Inc., The. (Windmill Bks.).
—Look What I Can Make!, 1 vol. 2009. (Watch This! Ser.). (ENG.). 32p. (J). (gr. k-k). 27.27 *(978-1-60754-446-3(6))*, a06f717f-42cf-4140-95e1-261031ac5105); pap. 11.55 *(978-1-60754-447-0(4))*, 44af912d-1d2e-43ea-96c8-260566aae781) Rosen Publishing Group, Inc., The. (Windmill Bks.).
—Look What I Can Play!, 1 vol. 2009. (Watch This! Ser.). (ENG.). 32p. (J). (gr. k-k). 27.27 *(978-1-60754-458-6(X))*, fff6835c-a8c5-42e7-a381-10f778f733bc); pap. 11.55 *(978-1-60754-586-6(1))*, 9f392d93-3a40-429b-8db6-d4c5152d052f) Rosen Publishing Group, Inc., The. (Windmill Bks.).
—See What I Can Do!, 1 vol. 2009. (Watch This! Ser.). (ENG.). 32p. (J). (gr. k-k). 27.27 *(978-1-60754-455-5(5))*, d905df3e-46de-4b90-8471-059243550147); pap. 11.55 *(978-1-60754-456-2(3))*, 730e0ae6-c331-4287-92d4-cd76323a35cd) Rosen Publishing Group, Inc., The. (Windmill Bks.).
—See What I Can Make!, 1 vol. 2009. (Watch This! Ser.). (ENG.). 32p. (J). (gr. k-k). 27.27 *(978-1-60754-449-4(0))*, 6e938a32-e4a4-4678-ad78-2004ce05e66a); pap. 11.55 *(978-1-60754-450-0(4))*, d1f6b53e-1449-43b7-918d-ebd2618c7241) Rosen Publishing Group, Inc., The. (Windmill Bks.).
—See What I Can Play!, 1 vol. 2009. (Watch This! Ser.). (ENG.). 32p. (J). (gr. k-k). 27.27 *(978-1-60754-461-6(X))*, 7eebd41e-1543-41ca-b5d0-a8c48d9caab3); pap. 11.55 *(978-1-60754-462-3(8))*, 6a6756ad-8c81-4aac-be3e-2f2d761721aa) Rosen Publishing Group, Inc., The. (Windmill Bks.).
Siewart, Pauline. Look What I Can Play! 2009. (YA). pap. 10.55 *(978-1-60754-586-4(5))* Windmill Bks.
Silver, Skye. Baby Play / Jugando con Bebé. 2019. (ENG., Illus.). 16p. (J). (gr. -1-k). bds. 7.99 *(978-1-78285-736-5(2))* Barefoot Bks., Inc.
Singer, Marilyn. Tallulah's Ice Skates: A Winter & Holiday Book for Kids. Boiger, Alexandra, illus. 2018. (Tallulah Ser.). (ENG.). 48p. (J). (gr. -1-3). 17.99 *(978-0-544-59692-4(7))*, 1615570, Clarion Bks.) HarperCollins Pubs.
Smith, Joy V. Why Won't Anyone Play with Me? 2007. 20p. per. 24.95 *(978-1-4241-8634-1(X))* America Star Bks.
Smith, Kathy Jo. Come Play with Me. 2009. 26p. (J). pap. 17.95 *(978-1-4327-3464-0(4))* Outskirts Pr., Inc.
Smith, Michael. My Ducky Buddy. Oliva, Octavio, illus. 2011. 23p. (J). *(978-0-9821675-4-0(7))* East West Discovery Pr.
—My Ducky Buddy. Oliva, Octavio, illus. 2015. (ARA & ENG.). 23p. (J). *(978-0-9913454-3-4(6))* East West Discovery Pr.
Smith, Michael & Wang, Emily. My Ducky Buddy. Oliva, Octavio, illus. 2011. (CHI & ENG.). 23p. (J). *(978-0-9821675-7-1(1))* East West Discovery Pr.
Smith, Mildred M. Louie the Blue Frog. 2012. 24p. pap. 24.95 *(978-1-62709-122-0(X))* America Star Bks.
Snyder, Betsy, illus. I Can Play. 2015. (I Can Interactive Board Bks.). (ENG.). 14p. (J). (gr. -1 — 1). bds. 8.99 *(978-1-4521-2905-1(3))* Chronicle Bks. LLC.
Soman, David & Davis, Jacky. Who Can Play? 2013. (Penguin Young Readers: Level 1 Ser.). lib. bdg. 13.55 *(978-0-606-32148-8(9))* Turtleback.
Spalding, Andrea. Dance Baby Dance, 1 vol. 2009. (ENG., Illus.). 24p. (J). (gr. -1 — 1). bds. 9.95 *(978-1-55469-079-4(X))* Orca Bk. Pubs. USA.
Spence, Ann. Elmo's Play Day. 2003. (Play-A-Sound Ser.). (ENG., Illus.). 6p. (J). bds. 6.10 net. *(978-0-7853-8441-0(3))*, bf44e002-35f9-4261-a92b-a83ebb9e048b) Phoenix International Publications, Inc.
Spinelli, Jerry. Hokey Pokey. 2013. 282p. (J). pap. *(978-0-375-83201-7(7))*, Knopf Bks. for Young Readers) Random Hse. Children's Bks.
Spurr, Elizabeth. In the Rain, 1 vol. Oliphant, Manelle, illus. 2018. (In the Weather Ser.). (ENG.). 22p. (J). (gr. -1 — 1). bds. 7.99 *(978-1-56145-853-0(8))* Peachtree Publishing Co. Inc.
Stanisha, Terésa (Tracey). Especially for Rachel - Butterflies Abound. 2009. 84p. pap. 16.97 *(978-0-557-04450-4(2))* Lulu Pr., Inc.
Steig, William. Pedro Es una Pizza. (Buenas Noches Ser.). (SPA., Illus.). (J). (gr. -1-5). 7.95 *(978-958-04-6034-3(5))* Norma S.A. COL. Dist: Lectorum Pubns., Inc., Distribuidora Norma, Inc.
—Pete's a Pizza. 2004. (Illus.). 32p. (J). (gr. -1-2). 28.95 incl. audio compact disk *(978-1-59112-740-6(8))* Live Oak Media.
Sterer, Gideon. From Ed's to Ned's. Cummins, Lucy Ruth, illus. 2020. (ENG.). 48p. (J). (gr. -1-2). 20.99 *(978-0-525-64807-9(0))*, Knopf Bks. for Young Readers) Random Hse. Children's Bks.
Steve Cormey. The Brothers Foot: A Hare Raising Story. Ronda Eden, illus. 2009. 56p. pap. 21.99 *(978-1-4389-4269-8(9))* AuthorHouse.
Stevenson-Spurgon, Barbara J. Have You Ever Made Mud Pies on a Hot Summer Day? This is a Bitty Book. Ruffin, Aurzella, illus. 2006. 36p. (J). (gr. -1-4). per. 19.95 *(978-1-60002-234-0(0))*, 4073) Mountain Valley Publishing, LLC.
Still, Cynthia W. Gypsy Travels the World. 2012. 48p. pap. 21.99 *(978-1-4685-5839-5(0))* AuthorHouse.
Stinson, Aimee. The Championship Game, 1 vol. 2009. 52p. pap. 16.95 *(978-1-60813-645-2(0))* PublishAmerica, Inc.
Strom, Maria Diaz. Joe Arco Iris y Yo, 1 vol. Strom, Maria Diaz, illus. 2008.Tr. of Rainbow Joe & Me. (SPA., Illus.). 32p. (J). (gr. -1-3). pap. 12.95 *(978-1-60060-278-8(9))*, leelowbooks) Lee & Low Bks., Inc.
Suen, Anastasia. The Pirate Map: A Robot & Rico Story. Laughead, Michael, illus. 2010. (Robot & Rico Ser.). (ENG.). 32p. (J). (gr. 1-2). pap. 6.25 *(978-1-4342-2301-2(9))*, 103170, Stone Arch Bks.) Capstone.
—We're Going on a Dinosaur Dig. Myer, Ed, illus. 2012. (Little Birdie Bks.). (ENG.). 24p. (gr. k-1). pap. 9.95 *(978-1-61810-299-7(0))*, 9781618102997) Rourke Educational Media.
Sullivan, Deirdre. Ming Goes to School. Löfdahl, Maja, illus. 2016. (ENG.). 32p. (J). (gr. -1-k). 16.99 *(978-1-5107-0050-5(1))*, Sky Pony Pr.) Skyhorse Publishing Co., Inc.
Swanson Sateren, Shelley. Max & Zoe at School, 1 vol. Sullivan, Mary, illus. 2013. (Max & Zoe Ser.). (ENG.). 32p. (J). (gr. k-2). pap. 5.19 *(978-1-4048-8059-7(3))*, 121735, Picture Window Bks.) Capstone.
Tankard, Jeremy. Sleepy Bird. Tankard, Jeremy, illus. 2018. (ENG., Illus.). 32p. (J). (gr. -1-k). 16.99 *(978-1-338-15785-7(X))*, Scholastic Pr.) Scholastic, Inc.
Taylor, Sean. I Am Actually a Penguin. Matyjaszek, Kasia, illus. 2018. (ENG.). 32p. (J). (-k). 16.99 *(978-1-5362-0278-6(9))*, Templar) Candlewick Pr.
Templar Books. I Thought I Saw a Dinosaur! Nichols, Lydia, illus. 2018. (I Thought I Saw Ser.). (ENG.). 10p. (J). (— 1). bds. 8.99 *(978-0-7636-9945-1(4))*, Templar) Candlewick Pr.
—I Thought I Saw a Lion! Nichols, Lydia, illus. 2018. (I Thought I Saw Ser.). (ENG.). 10p. (J). (— 1). bds. 8.99 *(978-0-7636-9946-8(2))*, Templar) Candlewick Pr.
Thomas, Jan. Here Comes the Big, Mean Dust Bunny! Thomas, Jan, illus. 2009. (ENG., Illus.). 40p. (J). (gr. -1-3). 17.99 *(978-1-4169-9150-2(6))*, Beach Lane Bks.) Beach Lane Bks.
Thomas, Janet. Can I Play? Bartlett, Alison, illus. 2005. 32p. (J). 8.99 *(978-1-4052-0597-9(0))* Farshore GBR. Dist: Trafalgar Square Publishing.
Thomas, Shelley Moore. No, No, Kitten! Nichols, Lori, illus. 2015. (ENG.). 40p. (J). (gr. -1-2). 16.95 *(978-1-62091-631-5(2))*, Astra Young Readers) Astra Publishing Hse.
Thompson, Elissa. Tryin' Ryan. 2006. (J). 15.00 *(978-0-9787341-0-7(6))* Aidan's Butterfly Pubns.
Thompson, Lauren. Little Quack's Hide & Seek. Anderson, Derek, illus. 2007. (Classic Board Bks.). (ENG.). 34p. (J). (gr. -1-k). bds. 8.99 *(978-1-4169-0325-3(9))*, Little Simon) Little Simon.
—Little Quack's New Friend. Anderson, Derek, illus. 2008. (Classic Board Bks.). (ENG.). 34p. (J). (gr. -1-1). bds. 8.99 *(978-1-4169-4923-7(2))*, Little Simon) Little Simon.
—Little Quack's New Friend. Anderson, Derek, illus. 2006. (ENG.). 32p. (J). (gr. -1-3). 19.99 *(978-0-689-86893-1(6))*, Simon & Schuster Bks. For Young Readers) Simon & Schuster Bks. For Young Readers.
Thorpe, Kiki. Dónde Está Boots? - Cuento para Levantar la Tapita. Savitsky, Steven, illus. 2005. (Dora the Explorer Ser.).Tr. of Where Is Boots? - A Lift-the-Flap Story. (SPA.). 16p. (J). pap. 5.99 *(978-1-4169-0621-6(5))*, Libros Para Ninos) Libros Para Ninos.
Thrasher, Grady. Tim & Sally's Beach Adventure. Rabon, Elaine Hearn, illus. 2008. (ENG.). 48p. (J). (gr. -1-3). 18.95 *(978-1-58818-161-9(8))* Hill Street Pr., LLC.
Tidhar, Lavie. Central Station, 1 vol. unabr. ed. 2017. (ENG.). 9.99 *(978-1-5436-2453-3(7))*, 9781543624533, Audible Studios on Brilliance Audio) Brilliance Publishing, Inc.
Toki, Sela Tuita. Pati Loves to Walk Barefoot to School. 2009. 44p. pap. 24.95 *(978-1-60749-433-1(7))* America Star Bks.
Top That. Press Out & Play Magic Castle. 2008. *(978-1-84666-600-1(7))* Top That! Publishing PLC.
Tougas, Chris. Dojo Daycare. 2014. (Dojo Ser.: 1). (ENG., Illus.). 32p. (J). (gr. -1-3). 16.95 *(978-1-77147-057-5(7))*, Owlkids) Owlkids Bks. Inc. CAN. Dist: Publishers Group West (PGW).
Tsiang, Sarah. Sugar & Snails. Wimmer, Sonja, illus. 2018. (J). pap. *(978-1-77321-004-9(1))* Annick Pr., Ltd.
Tullet, Hervé. Let's Play! (Interactive Books for Kids, Preschool Colors Book, Books for Toddlers) 2016. (ENG., Illus.). 68p. (J). (gr. -1-k). 15.99 *(978-1-4521-5477-0(5))* Chronicle Bks. LLC.
Turner, Dannie E. You Don't Know Beans: the Great Frog Adventure. 2008. 28p. pap. 24.95 *(978-1-60474-711-9(0))* America Star Bks.
Twin Sister Produtions. Sesame Street What Did Elmo Say? 2008. (ENG.). 20p. (J). (gr. -1-3). 9.99 *(978-1-59069-657-6(3))* Studio Mouse LLC.
Twin Sister Produtions & Galvin, Laura Gates. Sesame Street What Did Elmo Say? 2010. (J). (gr. k-2). 14.99 *(978-1-59922-633-0(2))* Twin Sisters IP, LLC.
Twin Sister Produtions Staff & Galvin, Laura Gates. Sesame Street What Did Elmo Say? 2010. (J). (gr. k-2). 14.99 *(978-1-59922-524-1(7))* Twin Sisters IP, LLC.
Ulbrich, Jasper. The Little Owl. 2009. (Illus.). 32p. pap. 16.50 *(978-1-60860-047-2(5))*, Eloquent Bks.) Strategic Book Publishing & Rights Agency (SBPRA).
Valentino, Carla. When Can We Run, Play & Dance Again? An Enchanting Story about Family, Learning & Imagination. 2011. 32p. (gr. 2-4). pap. 17.95 *(978-1-4567-5495-2(5))* AuthorHouse.
Van Camp, Katie. Harry & Horsie. Agnew, Lincoln, illus. 2009. (Harry & Horsie Adventures Ser.: 1). (ENG.). 32p. (J). (gr. -1-1). 16.99 *(978-0-06-175598-9(2))*, Balzer & Bray) HarperCollins Pubs.
Veil, Kamey. Sun & Moon Play Hide & Seek: A Children's Story. 2012. 24p. (-18). pap. 24.95 *(978-1-4626-9401-3(2))* America Star Bks.
Veissid, Jacqueline. Ruby's Sword. Zakimi, Paola, illus. 2019. (ENG.). 40p. (J). (gr. -1-k). 16.99 *(978-1-4521-6391-8(X))* Chronicle Bks. LLC.
Viau, Nancy. First Snow. Shipman, Talitha, illus. 2018. (ENG.). 32p. (J). (gr. -1-3). 16.99 *(978-0-8075-2440-4(9))*, 807524409) Whitman, Albert & Co.
Villarrubias, Pía. ¿A QUÉ JUEGAN NICO Y MAX? (SPA.). 36p. 11.95 *(978-84-207-1250-5(7))* Grupo Anaya, S.A. ESP. Dist: Distribooks, Inc.
—Juguemos a Volar! (SPA.). 36p. 11.95 *(978-84-207-1255-0(8))* Grupo Anaya, S.A. ESP. Dist: Distribooks, Inc.
—LINA TAMBIÉN JUEGA. (SPA.). 36p. 11.95 *(978-84-207-1251-2(5))* Grupo Anaya, S.A. ESP. Dist: Distribooks, Inc.
Voght, Victor A. Fun with Huff & Puff, 1 vol. 2009. 15p. pap. 24.95 *(978-1-60749-853-7(7))* America Star Bks.
Voigtsberger, Sandra A. Jack's Pockets. 2008. 17p. pap. 24.95 *(978-1-60563-546-0(4))* America Star Bks.
Waddell, Martin. You & Me, Little Bear. 2004. (Illus.). (J). (gr. -1-2). spiral bd. *(978-0-616-01803-3(7))*; spiral bd. *(978-0-616-01802-6(9))* Canadian National Institute for the Blind/Institut National Canadien pour les Aveugles.
Wales, Sid. Freddie & Mee. Bryant, Kerry, illus. 2013. 28p. pap. *(978-1-78222-097-8(6))* Paragon Publishing, Rothersthorpe.
Walters, Abby. What Is Sam Making? Grott, Isabella, illus. 2017. (Play Time Ser.). (ENG.). 24p. (gr. -1-2). 28.50 *(978-1-68342-746-9(7))*, 9781683427469); pap. 9.95 *(978-1-68342-798-8(X))*, 9781683427988) Rourke Educational Media.
Ward, M. The Evergreens Get Wet: The Evergreens. 2009. (Illus.). 28p. pap. 12.49 *(978-1-4389-8960-0(1))* AuthorHouse.
Watts, Jan. CAKE! A comedy script for young People. 2010. 55p. pap. 21.95 *(978-1-4452-4587-4(6))* Lulu Pr., Inc.
Weatherall, Barry. Jay & the Worm Save the Day. 2005. 40p. 14.28 *(978-1-4116-4717-6(3))* Lulu Pr., Inc.
Weiner, Brahm. Toad Catchers' Creek. Weintraub, Claudia & Frederick, Robin, eds. Cannon, Martin, illus. 2005. 40p. (J). lib. bdg. 17.99 *(978-1-932949-58-2(5))* Illusion Factory, The.
Weiss, Ellen. Playtime for Twins. Williams, Sam, illus. 2012. (ENG.). 30p. (J). (gr. -1 — 1). bds. 7.99 *(978-1-4424-3027-3(3))*, Little Simon) Little Simon.
Wells, Rosemary. Max & Ruby Play School. 2003. (All Aboard Reading Ser.). (gr. -1-2). lib. bdg. 13.55 *(978-0-613-64064-0(0))* Turtleback.
—Max & Ruby's Preschool Pranks. 2016. (Max & Ruby Ser.). (Illus.). 40p. (J). (-k). 17.99 *(978-0-670-78462-2(1))*, Viking Books for Young Readers) Penguin Young Readers Group.
Wenger, Brahm. Dewey Doo-It at the Jingle Jangle Jamboree: A Musical Storybook Inspired by Arnold Schwarzenegger to Benefit Inner-City Games. 2006. (ENG.). 32p. (J). (gr. -1-3). 18.95 *(978-0-9745143-4-5(9))* RandallFraser Publishing.
Weston Woods Staff, creator. Pete's a Pizza. 2011. 29.95 *(978-0-439-74519-2(5))* Weston Woods Studios, Inc.
—A Weeekend with Wendell. 2004. 29.95 *(978-1-55592-129-3(9))*; (J). 18.95 *(978-1-55592-116-3(7))* Weston Woods Studios, Inc.
—A Weekend with Wendell. 2004. (J). 38.75 *(978-1-55592-647-2(9))* Weston Woods Studios, Inc.
What Shall We Play. 2004. (J). per. *(978-1-57657-459-1(8))* Paradise Pr., Inc.
Wheeler, Lisa. Invasion of the Pig Sisters: Ready-To-Read Level 3. Ansley, Frank, illus. 2006. (Fitch & Chip Ser.: 4). (ENG.). 48p. (J). (gr. 1-3). 16.99 *(978-0-689-84953-4(2))*, Simon Spotlight) Simon Spotlight.
White, Naja Plays Hide-Go-Seek, 1 vol. Hyatt, Sean, illus. 2010. 28p. pap. 24.95 *(978-1-4489-8842-6(X))* America Star Bks.
White, Ramy Allison. Sunny Boy & His Playmates. 2006. pap. *(978-1-4068-3390-4(8))* Echo Library.
Wilkenstanley, Ellen. Berryville Bully. 2011. 24p. pap. 11.50 *(978-1-61204-527-6(8))*, Strategic Bk. Publishing) Strategic Book Publishing & Rights Agency (SBPRA).
Willems, Mo. Are You Ready to Play Outside?-An Elephant & Piggie Book. 2008. (Elephant & Piggie Book Ser.: 7). (ENG., Illus.). 64p. (J). (gr. -1-k). 9.99 *(978-1-4231-1347-8(0))*, Hyperion Books for Children) Disney Publishing Worldwide.
—A Big Guy Took My Ball!-An Elephant & Piggie Book. 2013. (Elephant & Piggie Book Ser.: 19). (ENG., Illus.). 64p. (J). (gr. 1-3). 10.99 *(978-1-4231-7491-2(7))*, Hyperion Books for Children) Disney Publishing Worldwide.
—Can I Play Too? 2012. (Elephant & Piggie Bks.). (CHI & JPN.). (J). (gr. -1-3). pap. *(978-986-189-329-7(6))* Grimm Cultural Ent., Co., Ltd.
—Can I Play Too?-An Elephant & Piggie Book. 2010. (Elephant & Piggie Book Ser.). (ENG., Illus.). 64p. (J). (gr. -1-k). 9.99 *(978-1-4231-1991-3(6))*, Hyperion Books for Children) Disney Publishing Worldwide.
—An Elephant & Piggie Biggie! 2017. (Elephant & Piggie Book Ser.). (ENG., Illus.). 320p. (J). (gr. 1-3). 16.99 *(978-1-4847-9967-3(4))*, Hyperion Books for Children) Disney Publishing Worldwide.
—An Elephant & Piggie Biggie Volume 2! 2019. (Elephant & Piggie Book Ser.). (ENG., Illus.). 320p. (J). (gr. 1-3). 16.99 *(978-1-368-04570-4(7))*, Hyperion Books for Children) Disney Publishing Worldwide.
—An Elephant & Piggie Biggie! Volume 3. 2020. (Elephant & Piggie Book Ser.). (ENG.). 320p. (J). (gr. 1-3). 16.99 *(978-1-368-05715-8(2))*, Hyperion Books for Children) Disney Publishing Worldwide.
—An Elephant & Piggie Biggie! Volume 4. 2021. (Elephant & Piggie Book Ser.). (ENG.). 320p. (J). (gr. 1-3). 16.99 *(978-1-368-07112-3(0))*, Hyperion Books for Children) Disney Publishing Worldwide.
—An Elephant & Piggie Biggie! Volume 5. 2022. (Elephant & Piggie Book Ser.). (ENG.). 320p. (J). (gr. 1-3). 16.99 *(978-1-368-07224-3(0))*, Hyperion Books for Children) Disney Publishing Worldwide.
—¡un Tipo Grande Se Llevó Mi Pelota!-An Elephant & Piggie Book, Spanish Edition. 2015. (Elephant & Piggie Book Ser.). (SPA., Illus.). 64p. (J). (gr. 1-k). 9.99 *(978-1-4847-2285-5(X))*, Hyperion Books for Children) Disney Publishing Worldwide.
William H. Sadlier Staff. Nora Plays All Day. 2005. (Emergent Library: Vol. 2). (gr. -1-1). 24.00 net. *(978-0-8215-8929-8(6))* Sadlier, William H. Inc.
Williams, Rozanne. How to Make a Mudpie. 2017. (Learn-To-Read Ser.). (ENG., Illus.). (J). pap. 3.49 *(978-1-68310-195-6(2))* Pacific Learning, Inc.
Wineinger, Cheryiann. Corgy & His Friends: A Trip to the Unknown. 2011. 24p. pap. 12.79 *(978-1-4520-0349-8(1))* AuthorHouse.
Witek, Jo. In My Room: A Book of Creativity & Imagination. 2017. (Growing Hearts Ser.). (ENG., Illus.). 32p. (J). (gr. -1 — 1). 16.95 *(978-1-4197-2644-6(7))*, 1196601) Abrams, Inc.
Wojtowycz, David. Let's Play, Dudley! Colors. 2003. (Dudley Ser.). (Illus.). (J). 3.95 *(978-1-58925-667-5(0))* Tiger Tales.
Won, Brian. Hooray for Today! 2016. (ENG., Illus.). 40p. (J). (gr. -1-3). 16.99 *(978-0-544-74803-3(4))*, 1633259, Clarion Bks.) HarperCollins Pubs.
Woodcock, Fiona. Hello. Woodcock, Fiona, illus. 2019. (ENG., Illus.). 40p. (J). (gr. -1-3). 17.99 *(978-0-06-264456-5(4))*, Greenwillow Bks.) HarperCollins Pubs.
Woolf, Julia. Duck & Penguin Are NOT Friends, 1 vol. 2019. (ENG., Illus.). 32p. (J). (gr. -1-3). 16.95 *(978-1-68263-132-4(X))* Peachtree Publishing Co. Inc.

Yacoubou, Jeanne. Wanna Play? Coloring-Story Book. Stebakova, Elena, illus. 2005. 16p. (J). *(978-0-9788737-5-2(0))* Alaafia Kids Co.

Ying, Jonathan. Not Quite Black & White Board Book. Ying, Victoria, illus. 2017. (ENG.). 28p. (J). (gr. -1 — 1). bds. 7.99 *(978-0-06-238067-8(2)*, HarperFestival) HarperCollins Pubs.

Yolen, Jane. How Do Dinosaurs Play with Their Friends? Teague, Mark, illus. 2006. (ENG.). 6p. (J). (gr. -1-k). bds. 7.99 *(978-0-439-85654-6(X)*, Blue Sky Pr., The) Scholastic, Inc.

—What to Do with a Box. Sheban, Chris, illus. (ENG.). (J). 2018. 14p. (gr. -1-1). bds. 8.99 *(978-1-56846-320-9(0)*, 19702) 2016. 32p. (gr. 1-3). 18.99 *(978-1-56846-289-9(1)*, 19704) Creative Co., The. (Creative Editions).

—What to Do with a String. Payne, C. F., illus. 2019. 32p. (J). (gr. 1-3). 18.99 *(978-1-56846-322-3(7)*, 18910, Creative Editions) Creative Co., The.

Yorinks, Arthur. Flappy & Scrappy. 2010. (I Can Read Level 2 Ser.). (ENG., Illus.). 48p. (J). (gr. k-3). pap. 4.99 *(978-0-06-205913-0(0)*, HarperCollins) HarperCollins Pubs.

Young, Cybèle. A Few Blocks, 1 vol. 2011. (ENG., Illus.). 48p. (J). (gr. -1-2). 18.95 *(978-0-88899-995-5(X))* Groundwood Bks. CAN. Dist: Publishers Group West (PGW).

Young, Jessica. All Paws on Deck: a Branches Book (Haggis & Tank Unleashed #1) Burks, James, illus. 2016. (Haggis & Tank Unleashed Ser.: 1). (ENG.). 80p. (J). (gr. k-2). pap. 5.99 *(978-0-545-81886-5(9))* Scholastic, Inc.

Young, T. M. Playing Church. Washington, Victoria, ed. Cromwell, Danielle, illus. 2012. 32p. pap. 24.95 *(978-1-4626-7883-9(1))* America Star Bks.

Zanotti, Carolina. Mario & the Aliens. Phuong, Thai My, illus. 2019. (ENG.). 40p. (J). 14.99 *(978-1-64124-027-7(X)*, 0277) Fox Chapel Publishing Co., Inc.

Zepeda, Gwendolyn. Level up / Paso de Nivel. Baeza Ventura, Gabriela, tr. from ENG. Torrecilla, Pablo, illus. 2012. (SPA & ENG.). (J). (gr. 5-9). 16.95 *(978-1-55885-747-6(8)*, Piñata Books) Arte Publico Pr.

123 Sesame Street, ed. When Zoe Grows Up. 2009. (ENG.). 20p. 9.99 *(978-1-59069-820-4(7))* Studio Mouse LLC.

PLAY CENTERS

see Playgrounds

PLAY DIRECTION (THEATER)

see Theater—Production and Direction

PLAY PRODUCTION

see Theater—Production and Direction

PLAY WRITING

see Drama—Technique

PLAYGROUNDS

Atkins, Jill. Ned in Bed & Fun at the Park. Wray, Jordan, illus. 2019. (Early Bird Readers — Pink (Early Bird Stories (tm)) Ser.). (ENG.). 32p. (J). (gr. -1-2). 30.65 *(978-1-5415-4160-3(X)*, a5dc0e4e-497c-49a5-b9e5-493d626ea377, Lerner Pubns.) Lerner Publishing Group.

Bloom, Paul. Rules on the Playground, 1 vol. 2015. (School Rules Ser.). (ENG.). 24p. (gr. k-k). pap. 9.15 *(978-1-4824-2657-1(9)*, f73415d2-d125-4479-8de4-77e20c898c1d) Stevens, Gareth Publishing LLLP.

Devera, Czeena. Lend a Hand on the Playground. 2019. (Helping Out Ser.). (ENG., Illus.). 16p. (J). (gr. -1-2). pap. 11.36 *(978-1-5341-4978-6(3)*, 213223, Cherry Blossom Press) Cherry Lake Publishing.

Enz, Tammy. Hidden Worlds, 4 vols., Set. Incl. Behind the Racks: Exploring the Secrets of a Shopping Mall. lib. bdg. 27.32 *(978-1-4296-3386-4(7)*, 95892); Beyond the Bars: Exploring the Secrets of a Police Station. lib. bdg. 27.32 *(978-1-4296-3377-2(8)*, 95884); (J). (gr. 3-9). (Hidden Worlds Ser.). (ENG.). 32p. 2010. 81.96 o.p. *(978-1-4296-3777-0(3)*, 168679, Capstone Pr.) Capstone.

Finn, Carrie. Manners on the Playground. Lensch, Chris, illus. (Way to Be!: Manners Ser.). 24p. (gr. -1-2). 2009. pap. 2.76 *(978-1-4048-6053-7(3))* 2009. pap. 0.63 *(978-1-4048-5995-1(0))* 2007. (ENG.). (J). per. 7.95 *(978-1-4048-3559-7(8)*, 93929) Capstone. (Picture Window Bks.).

Heos, Bridget. Be Safe on the Playground. Baroncelli, Silvia, illus. 2015. (Be Safe! Ser.). 24p. (J). 25.65 *(978-1-60753-446-4(0))* Amicus Learning.

Hicks, Dwayne. Rules in the Playground, 1 vol. 2019. (Rules at School Ser.). (ENG.). 24p. (gr. 1-1). 25.27 *(978-1-5383-4438-5(6)*, 161b2236-b6f0-43c2-8735-412b2fb209ee, PowerKids Pr.) Rosen Publishing Group, Inc., The.

Hidden Worlds [Capstone Sole Source]. 2010. (Hidden Worlds Ser.). 32p. lib. bdg. 101.28 *(978-1-4296-5865-2(7)*, Capstone Pr.) Capstone.

James, Dawn L. Playground Math, 1 vol. 2014. (Math Around Us Ser.). (ENG.). 24p. (gr. 1-1). lib. bdg. 25.93 *(978-1-5026-0152-0(4)*, 8e636f14-b735-45f5-8dce-9219195bf939) Cavendish Square Publishing LLC.

Knowlton, MaryLee. Safety at the Playground. Andersen, Gregg, photos by. 2008. (Staying Safe Ser.). (ENG., Illus.). 32p. (J). (gr. -1-3). lib. bdg. *(978-0-7787-4318-7(7))* Crabtree Publishing Co.

Knowlton, MaryLee & Dowdy, Penny. Safety at the Playground, 1 vol. Andersen, Gregg, photos by. 2008. (Staying Safe Ser.). (ENG., Illus.). 32p. (J). (gr. -1-3). pap. *(978-0-7787-4323-1(3))* Crabtree Publishing Co.

Laks Gorman, Jacqueline. The Playground, 1 vol. 2004. (I Like to Visit Ser.). (ENG.). 24p. (gr. k-2). pap. 9.15 *(978-0-8368-4461-0(0)*, 53a6b701-39ba-4480-839f-fe1f2d3a4456); (Illus.). lib. bdg. 24.67 *(978-0-8368-4454-2(8)*, 5fe73166-c998-4dc0-8736-dda65b20bbb0) Stevens, Gareth Publishing LLLP. (Weekly Reader Leveled Readers).

—The Playground / el Parque, 1 vol. 2004. (I Like to Visit / Me Gusta Visitar Ser.). (Illus.). 24p. (gr. k-2). (ENG & SPA.). pap. 9.15 *(978-0-8368-4605-8(2)*, e88b3f05-bf56-4c66-82ef-683c241275c9); (SPA & ENG., lib. bdg. 24.67 *(978-0-8368-4598-3(6)*, 73c99212-fc4d-4e63-837f-4217008e847f) Stevens, Gareth Publishing LLLP. (Weekly Reader Leveled Readers).

Mara, Wil. What Should I Do? on the Playground. 2011. (Community Connections: What Should I Do? Ser.). (ENG., Illus.). 24p. (gr. 2-5). lib. bdg. 29.21 *(978-1-61080-054-9(0)*, 201050) Cherry Lake Publishing.

Mattern, Joanne. Playgrounds & Adventure Parks. 2018. (Kids' Day Out Ser.). (ENG., Illus.). 32p. (J). (gr. 2-4). lib. bdg. 25.32 *(978-1-63440-389-4(4)*, dc3e6006-9656-41f5-a05b-0ae561040326) Red Chair Pr.

Mortensen, Lori. Manners Matter on the Playground. Hunt, Lisa, illus. (First Graphics: Manners Matter Ser.). (ENG.). 24p. (gr. 1-2). 2011. pap. 35.70 *(978-1-4296-6395-3(2))* 2010. (J). lib. bdg. 24.65 *(978-1-4296-5332-9(9)*, 113760) Capstone.

Myers, Edward. Let's Build a Playground. 2012. (ENG., Illus.). 48p. (J). (gr. 2-3). pap. 11.00 net. *(978-0-7652-0882-8(2)*, Modern Curriculum Pr.) Savvas Learning Co.

The Playground: Individual Title Two-Packs. (Chiquilibros Ser.). (gr. -1-1). 12.00 *(978-0-7635-8528-0(9))* Rigby Education.

Raatma, Lucia. Staying Safe on the Playground. 2011. (Staying Safe Ser.). (ENG.). 24p. (J). (gr. 1-2). pap. 43.74 *(978-1-4296-7198-9(X)*, 16766); pap. 7.29 *(978-1-4296-7197-2(1)*, 116817) Capstone. (Capstone Pr.).

Randolph, Joanne. The Slide at School, 1 vol. 2015. (Rosen REAL Readers: STEM & STEAM Collection). (ENG.). 8p. (gr. k-1). pap. 5.46 *(978-1-4994-9733-5(4)*, 858aa500-b16a-47c2-8595-b10ee4290dff, Rosen Classroom) Rosen Publishing Group, Inc., The.

Rosen, Michael J. & Kaboom! Staff. Let's Build a Playground. Kelson, Ellen & Cecil, Jennifer, illus. 2013. (ENG.). 32p. (J). (gr. 1-4). 15.99 *(978-0-7636-5532-7(5))* Candlewick Pr.

Sandler, Michael. Stupendous Sports Stadiums. 2011. (So Big Compared to What? Ser.). 24p. (YA). (gr. 1-4). lib. bdg. 26.99 *(978-1-61772-302-5(9))* Bearport Publishing Co., Inc.

Thomas, Mark. Maracaná: El estadio de fútbol más grande del mundo (the Maracaná: World's Largest Soccer Stadium) 2009. (Estructuras extraordinarias (Record-Breaking Structures) Ser.). (SPA.). 24p. (gr. 1-2). 42.50 *(978-1-61512-315-5(6)*, Editorial Buenas Letras) Rosen Publishing Group, Inc., The.

What Happens When You Recycle? Individual Title Six-Packs. (Discovery World Ser.). 16p. (gr. 1-2). 28.00 *(978-0-7635-8464-1(9))* Rigby Education.

PLAYGROUNDS—FICTION

Benenfeld, Rikki. Let's Go to the Park. 2015. (ENG., Illus.). 36p. (J). 11.99 *(978-1-929628-82-7(X))* Hachai Publishing.

Bond, Roland. Harvey Plumstead & the Dinnertime Dog. 2012. (Illus.). 96p. (gr. 4-18). pap. 13.66 *(978-1-4772-4317-6(8))* AuthorHouse.

Bonnell, Kris. Too Big to Play. 2006. (J). pap. 5.95 *(978-1-933727-35-6(7))* Reading Reading Bks., LLC.

BooydeGraaff, Wendy. Salad Pie. Langdo, Bryan, illus. 2016. (ENG.). 44p. (J). (gr. k-7). 17.99 *(978-0-9913866-4-2(7))* Ripple Grove Pr.

Brown, Cornelia. Constance the Little Angel Wants Curls. 2009. 28p. pap. 15.99 *(978-1-4490-3962-2(6))* AuthorHouse.

Clanchy, Kate. Our Cat Henry Comes to the Swings. Bird, Jemima, illus. 2007. 32p. (J). (gr. -1-1). 16.00 *(978-1-56148-563-5(2)*, Good Bks.) Skyhorse Publishing Co., Inc.

Copeland, Cynthia L. What Are You Waiting For? Gordon, Mike, illus. 2003. (Silly Millies Ser.: 1). 32p. lib. bdg. 17.90 *(978-0-7613-2804-9(1)*, Millbrook Pr.) Lerner Publishing Group.

Copeland, Cynthia L. & Gordon, Mike. What Are You Waiting For? 2003. (Silly Millies Ser.: Vol.1). (Illus.). 32p. (J). (gr. -1-1). pap. 4.99 *(978-0-7613-1828-6(3))* Lerner Publishing Group.

Coppock, Phil & Bower's 2008-2009 4th Grade Class. Rubber Tuesday. 2010. 70p. pap. 12.95 *(978-1-4327-5751-9(2))* Outskirts Pr., Inc.

Dean, James. Construction Destruction. 2015. (Pete the Cat (HarperCollins) Ser.). (J). lib. bdg. 14.75 *(978-0-606-36489-8(7))* Turtleback.

Dean, James & Dean, Kimberly. Pete the Cat: Construction Destruction: Includes over 30 Stickers! Dean, James, illus. 2015. (Pete the Cat Ser.). (ENG., Illus.). 24p. (J). (gr. -1-3). pap. 5.99 *(978-0-06-219861-7(0)*, HarperFestival) HarperCollins Pubs.

dePaola, Tomie. When Andy Met Sandy. dePaola, Tomie, illus. (Andy & Sandy Book Ser.). (ENG., Illus.). 32p. (J). (gr. -1-3). 2018. 5.99 *(978-1-5344-1372-6(3))* 2016. 8.99 *(978-1-4814-4155-1(8))* Simon & Schuster Bks. For Young Readers. (Simon & Schuster Bks. For Young Readers).

Evans, Nate. Bang! Boom! Roar! a Busy Crew of Dinosaurs. 2012. (ENG., Illus.). 40p. (J). (gr. -1-2). 15.99 *(978-0-06-087960-0(2)*, HarperCollins) HarperCollins Pubs.

Evans, Nate & Brown, Stephanie Gwyn. Dinosaur ABC. Santoro, Christopher, illus. 2011. (J). lib. bdg. 16.89 *(978-0-06-087962-4(9))* HarperCollins Pubs.

Feldman, Thea. Fun Around the Town. 2006. 3p. 5.99 *(978-1-932915-34-1(6))* Sandvik Publishing.

Harrar, Frank W. Wee Dragonslayers. Galan-Robles, Francisco, illus. 2008. 45p. pap. 24.95 *(978-1-60610-851-2(4))* America Star Bks.

Harris, Meena. Kamala & Maya's Big Idea. González, Ana Ramírez, illus. 2020. (ENG.). 32p. (J). (gr. -1-3). 18.99 *(978-0-06-293740-7(5)*, Balzer & Bray) HarperCollins Pubs.

Hillert, Margaret. Juega, Juega, Juega, Querido Dragón/Play, Play, Play, Dear Dragon. del Risco, Eida, tr. Schimmell, David, illus. 2010. (BeginningtoRead Ser.). 32p. (J). (-2). pap. 11.94 *(978-1-60357-551-5(0))* Norwood Hse. Pr.

—Play, Play, Play Dear Dragon. Schimmell, David, illus. 2009. (BeginningtoRead Ser.). 32p. (J). (gr. k-2). lib. bdg. 22.60 *(978-1-59953-294-3(8))* Norwood Hse. Pr.

—Play, Play, Play, Dear Dragon (Juega, Juega, Juega, Querido Dragon) Del Risco, Eida, tr. Schimmell, David, illus. 2010. (BeginningtoRead Ser.). (SPA & ENG.). 32p. (J). (gr. k-2). lib. bdg. 22.60 *(978-1-59953-363-6(4))* Norwood Hse. Pr.

Howard-Parham, Pam. Playing on the Playground. Crowell, Knox, illus. l.t. ed. 2005. (HRL Little Book Ser.). (J). (gr. k-18). pap. 10.95 *(978-1-57332-336-9(5))*; pap. 10.95 *(978-1-57332-335-2(7))* Carson-Dellosa Publishing, LLC. (HighReach Learning, Incorporated).

Kaputa, Christine C. Jungle Gym Me & Him! 2008. 24p. pap. 10.95 *(978-1-59858-781-4(1))* Dog Ear Publishing, LLC.

Kemp, Hill & Kemp, Siena. Lucky Penny. 2007. 88p. pap. 6.95 *(978-1-933090-87-0(1))* Guardian Angel Publishing, Inc.

Klein, Adria F. Sophie Screwdriver, 1 vol. Rowland, Andrew, illus. 2011. (Tool School Ser.). (ENG.). 32p. (J). (gr. 1-2). pap. 6.25 *(978-1-4342-3386-8(3)*, 116393); lib. bdg. 22.65 *(978-1-4342-3044-7(9)*, 114622) Capstone. (Stone Arch Bks.).

Kyung, Hyewon. Bigger Than You. 2018. (ENG., Illus.). 32p. (J). (gr. -1-3). 17.99 *(978-0-06-268312-0(8)*, Greenwillow Bks.) HarperCollins Pubs.

Leman, Nora. The Alpha Building Crew. Hartmann, April, illus. 2005. (J). *(978-1-58987-110-6(3))* Kindermusik International.

Lewis, Joan Lane. See with Me. Hough, Hannah Bliss, illus. 2011. 32p. pap. 24.95 *(978-1-4626-2347-1(6))* America Star Bks.

Luna, James. Growing up on the Playground / Nuestro Patio de Recreo. Barela-Di Bisceglie, Monica, illus. 2018. (ENG & SPA.). 32p. (J). (gr. -1-3). 17.95 *(978-1-55885-871-8(7)*, Piñata Books) Arte Publico Pr.

Merz, Jennifer. Playground Day. 2007. 32p. 16.00 *(978-978-061-896-4(1)*, Clarion Bks.) HarperCollins Pubs.

Parnell, Declan. Playground Fun, 1 vol., 1. 2015. (Rosen REAL Readers: STEM & STEAM Collection). (ENG.). 12p. (J). (gr. 1-2). pap. 6.33 *(978-1-5081-1557-1(5)*, 9f258ef7-c8c9-496b-ad08-7861860efe72, Rosen Classroom) Rosen Publishing Group, Inc., The.

Preller, James. Everybody Needs a Buddy. 2019. (Big Idea Gang Ser.). (ENG., Illus.). 96p. (J). (gr. 1-4). pap. 6.99 *(978-1-328-97340-5(9)*, 1708135, Clarion Bks.) HarperCollins Pubs.

Queen Latifah. Queen of the Scene. Morrison, Frank, illus. 2006. 32p. (J). (gr. -1-3). 17.89 incl. audio compact disk *(978-0-06-077857-6(1)*, Geringer, Laura Book) HarperCollins Pubs.

Sandra De Mos. Cleo's Playground Adventure. 2009. 40p. pap. 16.99 *(978-1-4389-2049-8(0))* AuthorHouse.

Sattler, Jennifer. Jungle Gym. Sattler, Jennifer, illus. 2018. (ENG., Illus.). 22p. (J). (gr. -1-k). bds. 7.99 *(978-1-58536-390-2(1)*, 204398) Sleeping Bear Pr.

Schorr, Titus. A Playground Adventure, 1 vol., 1. 2015. (Rosen REAL Readers: STEM & STEAM Collection). (ENG.). 8p. (J). (gr. k-1). pap. 5.46 *(978-1-5081-1469-7(2)*, 5f0d89f0-73f5-4a37-9fc9-f78c7ee54d3d, Rosen Classroom) Rosen Publishing Group, Inc., The.

Shaw, Mary. Brady Brady & the Cleanup Hitters. Temple, Chuck, illus. 2008. 32p. (J). pap. *(978-1-897169-11-7(6))* Brady Brady, Inc.

Shofner, Melissa Raé. Good Manners at the Playground, 1 vol. 2017. (Manners Matter Ser.). (ENG.). 24p. (gr. 1-1). 25.27 *(978-1-5081-5729-8(4)*, 38ee01ac-b6f5-4c76-9b5f-c136d5205eae, PowerKids Pr.) Rosen Publishing Group, Inc., The.

Stefanescu, Estera. Megan's Great Day. 2009. 20p. pap. 15.99 *(978-1-4389-6318-1(1))* AuthorHouse.

PLAYHOUSES

see Theaters

PLAYING CARDS

see Cards

PLAYS

Abley, Sean. Tortoise vs. Hare 2: This Time It's Personal! 2017. 31p. pap. *(978-1-68069-970-8(9))* Playscripts, Inc.

Adam & Eve Playbook. 2006. (J). *(978-0-9792640-2-3(2))* GSP Players, LLC.

Adam & Eve Workbook. 2006. (J). *(978-0-9792640-1-6(4))* GSP Players, LLC.

Adams, Jennifer. Pride & Prejudice Playset, 1 vol. Oliver, Alison, illus. 2013. (ENG.). 22p. (J). (gr. k-1). bds. 19.99 *(978-1-4236-3515-4(9))* Gibbs Smith, Publisher.

Adams, Karin. Lights! Curtains! Cows!, 1 vol. 2009. (Lorimer Streetlights Ser.). (ENG.). 132p. (J). (gr. 2-4). 8.95 *(978-1-55277-426-7(0)*, 426) James Lorimer & Co. Ltd., Pubs. CAN. Dist: Formac Lorimer Bks. Ltd.

Agbaje, Salihah. Mouth Almighty a Play. Akhtar, Waheed, illus. 2012. 144p. pap. *(978-0-9565861-0-0(4))* Spoken World Productions.

Agboluaje, Oladipo, et al. Class Acts: New Plays for Children to Act. 2010. (Oberon Plays for Young People Ser.). (ENG.). 92p. (J). pap. 14.95 *(978-1-84002-933-8(1)*, 900241496) Oberon Bks., Ltd. GBR. Dist: Macmillan.

Alcott, Louisa. Comic Tragedies. 2009. 324p. 25.99 *(978-1-103-79747-9(6))*; pap. 19.99 *(978-1-103-79738-7(7))* Creative Media Partners, LLC.

—Comic Tragedies. 2010. 82p. pap. 19.83 *(978-1-151-98760-0(3))* 2009. 88p. pap. 14.14 *(978-1-151-52805-6(6))* General Bks. LLC.

—Comic Tragedies. 2008. 324p. pap. *(978-1-4097-0064-7(X))* Read Bks.

—Comic Tragedies. 2013. 110p. pap. 3.99 *(978-1-61720-909-3(0))* Wilder Pubns., Corp.

—Comic Tragedies: Written by Jo & Meg & Acted by the Little Women. 2010. 320p. 36.76 *(978-1-163-54988-9(6))* 2010. 320p. pap. 24.76 *(978-1-163-28090-4(9))* 2007. (ENG.). 318p. 45.95 *(978-0-548-24869-0(9))* 2007. (ENG.). 320p. per. 30.95 *(978-1-4326-5113-8(7))* Kessinger Publishing, LLC.

—Comic Tragedies/ Written by Jo & Meg & Acted by the Little Women. 2012. 334p. (-18). pap. *(978-1-4076-6141-4(8))* HardPr.

Alcott, Louisa & Meg, Meg. Comic Tragedies/ Written by Jo & Meg & Acted by the Little Women. 2010. (ENG.). 328p. pap. 31.75 *(978-1-177-42111-9(9))* Creative Media Partners, LLC.

Alcott, Louisa & Pratt, Anna Bronson Alcott. Comic Tragedies. 2010. 326p. pap. 30.75 *(978-1-177-67911-4(6))* Creative Media Partners, LLC.

Alexander, Sue & Huffman, Thomas. Small Plays for Special Days. 2003. (ENG., Illus.). 64p. (J). (gr. -1-3). pap. 6.95 *(978-0-618-37834-0(0)*, 100322, Clarion Bks.) HarperCollins Pubs.

Alfreda. Taestella A Black Cinderella Folder Leaf Edition. 2007. (YA). 3.25 *(978-1-56820-442-0(6)*, folder leaf) Story Time Stories That Rhyme.

Allen, Laurie. Middle School Mania: Comedy Duos for Guy / Girl, 8 bklts. 2003. (YA). pap. 19.95 *(978-1-932404-53-1(8)*, 915) Brooklyn Pubs.

—Thirty-Three Short Comedy Plays for Teens: Plays for Small Casts. 2011. (ENG.). 208p. (J). pap. 17.95 *(978-1-56608-181-8(5))* Meriwether Publishing, Ltd.

Andersen, Hans Christian. The Little Mermaid. 2005. (Oberon Modern Plays Ser.). (ENG.). 64p. (gr. 3-7). per. 14.95 *(978-1-84002-487-6(9)*, 900242834) Oberon Bks., Ltd. GBR. Dist: Macmillan.

Anderson, Wes. Fantastic Mr. Fox: The Making of the Motion Picture. 2009. (ENG., Illus.). 192p. 35.00 *(978-0-8478-3354-2(2))* Rizzoli International Pubns., Inc.

Angels, Company of. Theatre Cafe: Plays One. 2009. (Oberon Modern Playwrights Ser.). (ENG.). 156p. (J). pap. 17.95 *(978-1-84002-893-5(9)*, 900241462) Oberon Bks., Ltd. GBR. Dist: Macmillan.

Armstrong, James. The New Mrs. Jones: A One-Act Comedy Play. 2003. (YA). pap. 4.50 *(978-1-932404-62-3(7)*, 760) Brooklyn Pubs.

Asher, Sandra Fenichel. Blackbirds & Dragons, Mermaids & Mice. 2003. (Illus.). 150p. (YA). pap. 9.95 *(978-1-58342-174-1(2)*, BB1) Dramatic Publishing Co.

Aston, Neil, contrib. by. Bailed Up. 22p. pap. *(978-1-875739-29-5(7))* Wizard Bks.

Atkinson, Lawrence. Great Ideas. 2003. (YA). 8.00 *(978-0-9679552-3-0(8))* Mushroom Cloud Pr. of Orlando.

Averill, Ric. The Pied Piper of Hamelin (musical) 2014. 58p. (J). pap. 9.95 *(978-1-58342-898-6(4))* Dramatic Publishing Co.

Avi, et al. Acting Out. 2010. (ENG.). 192p. (J). (gr. 3-7). pap. 6.99 *(978-1-4169-3849-1(4)*, Atheneum Bks. for Young Readers) Simon & Schuster Children's Publishing.

Baker, Thomas. The Fine Lady's Airs. 2006. pap. *(978-1-4065-0502-3(1))* Dodo Pr.

Balkin, Alfred & Grimm, Jacob. The Musicians of Bremen: A Not-So-Grimm Modern Musical Fairy Tale. 2013. 62p. *(978-0-87602-428-7(2))* Family Plays.

Baptist, Leona. Daniel Boone. (Illus.). (YA). (gr. 6-12). 6.00 *(978-0-87602-118-7(6))* Family Plays.

Barchers, Suzanne I. War Stories for Readers Theatre: World War II. 2010. (Readers Theatre Ser.). (ENG.). 232p. E-Book 45.00 *(978-1-59884-676-8(0)*, F2883E); pap. 45.00 *(978-1-59158-750-7(6)*, 900316575) ABC-CLIO, LLC. (Libraries Unlimited).

Barchers, Suzanne I. & Ruscoe, Michael. Against All Odds: Readers Theatre for Grades 3-8, 1 vol. 2008. (Readers Theatre Ser.). (ENG.). 264p. pap. 45.00 *(978-1-59158-677-7(1)*, 900308608, Libraries Unlimited) ABC-CLIO, LLC.

Barrie, J.m. & Hollindale, Peter. Peter Pan & Other Plays: The Admirable Crichton; Peter Pan; When Wendy Grew up; What Every Woman Knows; Mary Rose. 2008. (Oxford World's Classics Ser.). (ENG.). 384p. pap. 14.95 *(978-0-19-953783-9(6))* Oxford Univ. Pr., Inc.

Bartlett, Lynne, et al, adapted by. H. M. S. Pinafore: Or the Lass That Loved a Sailor. 2012. (ENG.). 64p. pap. 8.95 *(978-1-58342-727-9(9))* Dramatic Publishing Co.

Bawden, Nina. Carrie's War. 2007. (Oberon Modern Plays Ser.). (ENG.). 148p. per. 16.95 *(978-1-84002-720-4(7)*, 900241308) Oberon Bks., Ltd. GBR. Dist: Macmillan.

Benchmark Education Company, LLC Staff. Reader's Theater for Fluency & Comprehension Handbook. 2004. (Reader's Theater Ser.). pap., instr.'s hndbk. ed. 10.00 *(978-1-4108-1320-6(7))* Benchmark Education Co.

Bennett, Doraine. Readers Theatre for Global Explorers, 1 vol. 2010. (Readers Theatre Ser.). (ENG.). 208p. pap. 45.00 *(978-1-59884-515-0(2)*, 900316600, Libraries Unlimited) ABC-CLIO, LLC.

Bergman, Steven. Critic's Carnival: A Ten-Minute Dramatic Monologue. 2003. 12p. (YA). pap. 4.50 *(978-1-932404-26-5(0)*, 279) Brooklyn Pubs.

Bernardi, Philip & Havens, Diane. Twice upon a Time. 2003. (Theater for Young Audiences Ser.). (Illus.). 24p. (J). (gr. k-6). pap. 6.00 *(978-0-88734-425-1(9))* Players Pr., Inc.

Beth, Georgia. The Swimming Hole (Science) rev. ed. 2015. (Reader's Theater Ser.). (ENG., Illus.). 24p. (gr. 3-4). pap. 8.99 *(978-1-4938-1515-9(6))* Teacher Created Materials, Inc.

Bible Drama: 136 Stories to Be Read or Acted as Plays. 2004. pap. 29.95 *(978-1-879415-41-6(0)*, Bearly Cooking) Mountain n' Air Bks.

Bland, Janice. Allie's Class. 2010. (YA). pap. 12.00 *(978-0-88734-984-3(6))* Players Pr., Inc.

Blane, Francisco. The Little Girl with Curl. Kelley, Gerald, illus. 2009. (Reader's Theater Nursery Rhymes & Songs Set B Ser.). 48p. (J). pap. *(978-1-60859-157-2(3))* Benchmark Education Co.

—Little Jack Horner Eats Pie. Price, Nick, illus. 2009. (Reader's Theater Nursery Rhymes & Songs Set B Ser.). 48p. (J). pap. *(978-1-60859-158-9(1))* Benchmark Education Co.

—One Raining, Pouring Morning. 2008. (Reader's Theater Nursery Rhymes & Songs Ser.). (Illus.). 48p. (J). (gr. k-1). pap. *(978-1-60437-977-8(4))* Benchmark Education Co.

—Tim Rows a Boat Gently down the Stream. 2008. (Reader's Theater Nursery Rhymes & Songs Ser.). (Illus.). 48p. (J). (gr. k-1). pap. *(978-1-60437-980-8(4))* Benchmark Education Co.

Blum, Renon. California Wax Museum. 2003. (Ideal for Teens Ser.). 16p. (J). (gr. 4-8). pap. 5.00 *(978-0-88734-518-0(2))* Players Pr., Inc.

Bogard, Jerrod. Jack & the Soy Beanstalk. 2010. (ENG.). 47p. (J). pap. 8.95 *(978-0-87440-659-7(5))* Baker's Plays.

Bradley, Jeffery & Miller, Britt Ekland. Positive African American Plays for Children Book 2: Building High Self Esteem & Confidence Through Plays. 2005. 128p. (J). per. 19.95 *(978-1-884163-92-0(0)*, Juba Bks.) NetNia Publishing Co.

Breslin, Theresa, et al. Divided City: The Play. 2013. (Critical Scripts Ser.). (ENG., Illus.). 162p. (J). pap. *(978-1-4081-8157-7(6)*, 226166, Methuen Drama) Bloomsbury Publishing Plc.

Brooks, Laurie. Franklin's Apprentice. 2006. 48p. pap. 9.00 *(978-0-8222-2069-5(5))* Dramatists Play Service, Inc.

Brown, Susan Taylor. Enrique Esparza & the Battle of the Alamo. Reeves, Jeni, illus. 2010. (History Speaks: Picture Books Plus Reader's Theater Ser.). (ENG.). 48p. (gr. 2-4). pap. 9.95 *(978-0-7613-3942-7(6))* Lerner Publishing Group.

Bruchac, Joseph. Pushing up the Sky. Flavin, Teresa, illus. 2015. 96p. pap. 10.00 *(978-1-61003-552-1(6))* Center for the Collaborative Classroom.

—Pushing up the Sky: Seven Native American Plays for Children. Flavin, Teresa, illus. 2019. (ENG.). 96p. (J). (gr. 2-5). pap. 9.99 *(978-1-9848-1483-8(4)*, Puffin Books) Penguin Young Readers Group.

Buchanan, Matt. Ernie's Place: A Play for Young Audiences. 2006. 36p. (YA). pap. 5.95 *(978-1-60003-200-4(1)*, 618) Brooklyn Pubs.
—Prince Ugly: One Act Youth Play. rev. ed. 2005. 40p. (YA). pap. 5.95 *(978-1-60003-169-4(2)*, 613) Brooklyn Pubs.
—Sleeping Walter: One Act Youth Play. rev. ed. 2005. 32p. (YA). pap. 5.95 *(978-1-60003-170-0(6)*, 614) Brooklyn Pubs.
Burian, Peter. Euripides: Helen. 2007. (Aris & Phillips Classical Texts). (ENG.). 292p. (C). 118.90 *(978-0-85668-650-4(6)*, 9780856686504); pap. 38.50 *(978-0-85668-651-1(4)*, 9780856686511) Liverpool Univ. Pr. GBR. Dist: Oxford Univ. Pr., Inc.
Bushore-Fallis, Martha. Book of Lyrics: Freedom Found, the Musical Drama. 2013. 106p. 44.95 *(978-1-4582-1195-8(9)*, Abbott Pr.) Author Solutions, LLC.
Butler, Dori; Flounders. The Winter Weather Machine. Flounders, Anne, ed. 2004. (Reader's Theater Content-Area Concepts Ser.). (ENG.). (J). (gr. 1-2). 5.00 net. *(978-1-4108-2293-2(1)*, A22931) Benchmark Education Co.
Cain, Candice. The Tortoise & the Hare. 2010. (ENG.). 23p. pap. 4.50 *(978-0-87440-739-6(7))* Baker's Plays.
Carr, Diane. River Dragon Activity Book: Just Add Kids. 2003. (J). 15.00 *(978-1-59094-051-8(2)*, Jawbreakers for Kids) Jawbone Publishing Corp.
Carriere, Jean-claude. The Little Black Book. 2003. (ENG.). 86p. pap. 18.95 *(978-0-9542330-7-5(7))* Aurora Metro Pubns. Ltd. GBR. Dist: Publishers Group West (PGW).
Carter, Pip. Double Dare. (Illus.). 128p. (J). (gr. 4-6). *(978-1-875739-48-6(3))* Wizard Bks.
—The Little People. (Illus.). 112p. (J). (gr. 3-5). *(978-1-875739-70-7(X))* Wizard Bks.
Carter, Richard. A Community Shakespeare Company Edition of the TWO GENTLEMEN of VERONA. 2007. 80p. (J). per. 10.95 *(978-0-595-45825-7(4))* iUniverse, Inc.
Cerio, Johnathan. The Cathedral. 2003. (YA). 7.99 *(978-0-9679552-8-5(9))* Mushroom Cloud Pr. of Orlando.
Chanko, Pamela. 25 Fun Phonics Plays for Beginning Readers. 2009. (ENG.). 64p. (gr. k-2). pap. 11.99 *(978-0-545-10339-8(8)*, Teaching Resources) Scholastic, Inc.
Charles, Nancy Linehan. Romeo & Juliet or the Old You-Know-I-Really-Love-You-but-My-Father-Really-Hates-You Blues. 2004. 72p. (YA). pap. 4.50 *(978-1-58342-236-6(6)*, R74) Dramatic Publishing Co.
Charles, Nancy Linehan, adapted by. A Midsummer Night's Dream or the Night They Missed the Forest for the Trees. (Illus.). 78p. (YA). 6.25 *(978-1-58342-092-8(4)*, MD1) Dramatic Publishing Co.
Chesterton, G. K. Magic: A Fantastic Comedy in Three Acts. 2007. 64p. per. 11.99 *(978-1-59547-789-7(6))* NuVision Pubns., LLC.
Children's Theatre Company, Children's Theatre. Igniting Wonder: Plays for Preschoolers. Brosius, Peter & Adams, Elissa, eds. 2013. (ENG., Illus.). 152p. pap. 15.95 *(978-0-8166-8114-3(7))* Univ. of Minnesota Pr.
Child's Play. Getting Ready. Cocoretto, illus. 2017. (Tactile Bks.). (ENG.). 12p. (J). *(978-1-84643-886-8(1))* Child's Play International Ltd.
Chorpenning, Charlotte B. The Indian Captive. (Illus.). (YA). (gr. 6-12). 6.00 *(978-0-87602-139-2(9))* Family Plays.
Christiansen, Diane. Scenes for Teens, by Teens: A collection by Diane Christiansen. 2010. 76p. pap. 10.95 *(978-1-4502-1878-8(4))* iUniverse, Inc.
Christopher, Garrett. Good Masters! Sweet Ladies! A Study Guide. Friedland, Joyce & Kessler, Rikki, eds. 2008. (Novel-Ties Ser.). (Illus.). 41p. pap. 16.95 *(978-0-7675-4257-9(6))* Learning Links Inc.
Clark, Ouida Ouijella. He Planned to Be A Leader: First Drama of Children of the 21st Century. 2006. pap. 25.00 *(978-0-9777289-4-7(3))* Clark Productions Ltd. Inc.
Coble, Eric. Cinderella Confidential. 2004. 48p. (YA). pap. 6.50 *(978-1-58342-201-4(3)*, CB5) Dramatic Publishing Co.
—Pecos Bill & the Ghost Stampede. 2003. (Illus.). 48p. (YA). pap. 6.50 *(978-1-58342-202-1(1)*, PA3) Dramatic Publishing Co.
Coble, Eric, adapted by. The Giver. 2010. (ENG.). 64p. pap. 7.50 *(978-1-58342-662-3(0))* Dramatic Publishing Co.
Coburn, Ann. Alex & the Warrior. 2005. (Oberon Modern Plays Ser.). (ENG., Illus.). 78p. per. 14.95 *(978-1-84002-502-6(6)*, 900242847) Oberon Bks., Ltd. GBR. Dist: Macmillan.
—Alex & the Winter Star. 2009. (Oberon Plays for Young People Ser.). (ENG.). 76p. (J). pap. 14.95 *(978-1-84002-849-2(1)*, 900241420) Oberon Bks., Ltd. GBR. Dist: Macmillan.
Cohen, Frumi. The Magic Flute RELOADED: (play Script) 2006. (YA). pap. 7.00 *(978-0-87602-415-7(0))* Family Plays.
—Try a Little Shakespeare. 2003. (J). pap. 10.00 *(978-0-88734-519-7(0))* Players Pr., Inc.
Coleman, Wim & Perrin, Pat. Follow the Drinking Gourd: Come along the Underground Railroad. Martin, Courtney, illus. 2014. (Setting the Stage for Fluency Ser.). (ENG.). 40p. (J). (gr. 3-5). pap. 8.99 *(978-1-939656-10-0(9)*, 2dbc45f4-2459-4293-be7d-bc52ffe6979a) Red Chair Pr.
—My Sprig of Lilac: Remembering Abraham Lincoln. Catalano, Dominic, illus. 2014. (Setting the Stage for Fluency Ser.). (ENG.). 40p. (J). (gr. 3-5). lib. bdg. 27.99 *(978-1-939656-54-4(0)*, 78b9ba65-5925-4841-bb70-72e4bd84d172) Red Chair Pr.
—Sequoyah & His Talking Leaves: A Play about the Cherokee Syllabary. Feeney, Siri Weber, illus. 2014. (Setting the Stage for Fluency Ser.). (ENG.). 40p. (J). (gr. 3-5). pap. 8.99 *(978-1-939656-35-3(4)*, f083207b-3e57-4a1a-8709-a9f06e5430b5) Red Chair Pr.
—Steam! Taming the River Monster. Todd, Sue, illus. 2015. (Setting the Stage for Fluency Ser.). (ENG.). 40p. (J). (gr. 3-5). lib. bdg. 27.99 *(978-1-939656-74-2(5)*, 4f21153c-357c-438f-b602-7c15f64909de) Red Chair Pr.
Collette, Paul & Wright, Robert. Huddles: Playscript. 2003. (Musicals for Young Audiences Ser.). 28p. (Orig.). (YA). (gr. 3-12). pap. 7.00 *(978-0-88734-512-8(3))* Players Pr., Inc.
Collodi, Carlo. Pinocchio. 2005. (Oberon Modern Plays Ser.). Tr. of Avventure Di Pinocchio. (ENG.). 120p. per. 14.95 *(978-1-84002-529-3(8)*, 900242872) Oberon Bks., Ltd. GBR. Dist: Macmillan.
Cook, Christopher. Washington Irving's the Legend of Sleepy Hollow. 2008. 158p. 23.00 *(978-1-4259-3427-9(7))* AuthorHouse.
—Washington Irving's The Legend of Sleepy Hollow: A Play in Two Acts. 2008. 158p. pap. 12.00 *(978-1-4259-3428-6(5))* AuthorHouse.
Cooper, John. Putting on Your Pantos. 2012. (ENG., Illus.). 96p. 17.00 *(978-1-78035-412-5(6)*, Fastprint Publishing) Upfront Publishing Ltd. GBR. Dist: Printondemand-worldwide.com.
Cosgrove, Stephen & Higgins, Kitty. The el juicio del pastelero & Tasty Tort Trial. 2005. spiral bd. 76.00 *(978-1-4108-5793-4(X))* Benchmark Education Co.
—Semillas de Estrellamelón Star-Melon Seeds. 2005. spiral bd. 76.00 *(978-1-4108-5791-0(3))* Benchmark Education Co.
Cosgrove, Stephen; Hirschfeld. Star-Melon Seeds. Hirschfeld, Pam, ed. 2004. (Reader's Theater Content-Area Concepts Ser.). (ENG.). (J). (gr. 3-4). 5.00 net. *(978-1-4108-1139-4(5))* Benchmark Education Co.
Craddock, Chris. Naked at School: Three Plays for Teens. 2005. (Prairie Plays Ser.). (ENG., Illus.). 162p. pap. 12.95 *(978-1-896300-46-7(4))* NeWest Pubs., Ltd. CAN. Dist: Strauss Consultants.
Crawley, Brian; Flounders. Halloween Math. Flounders, Anne, ed. 2004. (Reader's Theater Content-Area Concepts Ser.). (ENG., Illus.). (J). (gr. 2). 5.00 net. *(978-1-4108-2300-7(8)*, A23008) Benchmark Education Co.
Croft, Steven. Othello. Beal, Duncan & Jurksaitis, Dinah, eds. 2004. (Nelson Thornes Shakespeare Ser.). (ENG., Illus.). 208p. (YA). pap. 14.95 *(978-0-7487-8601-5(5))* Nelson Thornes Ltd. GBR. Dist: Trans-Atlantic Pubns., Inc.
Crouch, Tim. I, Cinna (the Poet) 2012. (Oberon Plays for Young People Ser.). (ENG., Illus.). 164p. pap. *(978-1-84943-403-4(4)*, 513584) Oberon Bks., Ltd.
—I, Shakespeare. 2011. (Oberon Modern Plays Ser.). (ENG.). 96p. pap. *(978-1-84943-126-2(4)*, 513350) Oberon Bks., Ltd.
Crozier, Eric. Let's Make an Opera! - an Entertainment for Young People in Three Acts. 2008. 100p. pap. 26.45 *(978-1-4437-0249-2(8))* Audubon Pr. & Christian Bk. Service.
Cruz Gonzalez, Jose. Thaddeus & Tila (A Crane & Frog Tale) 2006. pap. 6.50 *(978-1-58342-352-3(4))* Dramatic Publishing Co.
Cudney, Chriss. The Brothers Are Here! Preschool Years. 2011. 60p. 24.99 *(978-1-4628-5275-8(0))*; pap. 15.99 *(978-1-4628-5274-1(2))* Xlibris Corp.
Dabrowski, Kristen. My First Scene Book: 51 One-Minute Scenes about Etiquette. 2009. (My First Acting Ser.). 288p. (J). (gr. k-4). pap. *(978-1-57525-603-0(7))* Smith & Kraus Pubs., Inc.
Dahl, Roald. The BFG. Walmsley, Jane, illus. 2008. 119p. 16.00 *(978-0-7569-8346-8(0))* Perfection Learning Corp.
—The BFG: a Set of Plays: A Set of Plays. 2007. (ENG., Illus.). 128p. (J). (gr. 3-7). 6.99 *(978-0-14-240792-9(5)*, Puffin Books) Penguin Young Readers Group.
—Charlie & the Chocolate Factory: a Play. 2007. (ENG., Illus.). 96p. (J). (gr. 3-7). 6.99 *(978-0-14-240790-5(9)*, Puffin Books) Penguin Young Readers Group.
—James & the Giant Peach: a Play. 2007. (ENG., Illus.). 96p. (J). (gr. 3-7). 6.99 *(978-0-14-240791-2(7)*, Puffin Books) Penguin Young Readers Group.
Dahl, Roald & Wood, David. The BFG. 2010. (ENG., Illus.). 46p. pap. *(978-0-573-05094-7(5)*, French, Samuel , Ltd.) Concord Theatricals.
—The Twits: Stage Adaptation. 2015. (ENG.). 45p. pap. *(978-0-573-05125-8(9)*, French, Samuel , Ltd.) Concord Theatricals.
Davis, Buddy, et al. Buddy Davis' Cool Critters of the Ice Age. 2015. (ENG., Illus.). 60p. (J). 13.99 *(978-0-89051-858-8(0)*, Master Books) New Leaf Publishing Group.
De Maupassant, Guy. The Necklace. Kelley, Gary, illus. 2004. (ENG.). 48p. (J). (gr. 4-7). 19.95 *(978-1-56846-193-9(3)*, 22067) Creative Co., The.
DeFerie, Steph. After the Rain King. 2003. 101p. *(978-0-87440-197-4(6))* Baker's Plays.
Deferie, Steph. Ghost Rider: The Final Journey on the Underground Railroad. 2008. (ENG.). 60p. mass mkt. 6.50 *(978-0-87440-181-3(X))* Baker's Plays.
Desmarattes, J. Lyonel. Lakòl Medam Yo. 2004. Orig. Title: L' Ecole des Femmes. (CRP.). 80p. (YA). per. 15.00 *(978-1-58432-170-5(9))* Educa Vision Inc.
Desmon, Jeremy. Cyrano de BurgerShack: A Pop Musical. 2014. 90p. (J). pap. 9.99 *(978-1-62384-479-0(7))* Playscripts, Inc.
Diaz, Enrique Perez. Letters from Alain. 2008. (ENG., Illus.). 130p. pap. 16.95 *(978-0-9551566-4-9(5))* Theatre Communications Group, Inc.
Dirksing, Donna. First Stage: A Collection of Musical Plays for Children's First Performances Arranged with Orff Instruments for Grades 1-3. 2006. 24.95 *(978-0-89328-020-8(8))* Heritage Music Pr.
Donaldson, Julia. Bombs & Blackberries: A World War Two Play. Dupasquier, Philippe, illus. (ENG.). 48p. (YA). *(978-0-7502-4124-3(1)*, Wayland) Hachette Children's Group.
Doolittle, Joyce, ed. Playhouse: Six Fantasy Plays for Children, 1 vol. 2003. (Drama Ser.). (ENG., Illus.). 208p. (J). (gr. 6-12). pap. 9.95 *(978-0-88995-028-3(8))* Red Deer Pr. CAN. Dist: Ingram Publisher Services.
Doyle, Alfreda C. Alfreda's Reader's Theatre: Comedy Club. Date not set. (Illus.). (J). spiral bd. 8.95 *(978-1-56820-362-1(4))* Story Time Stories That Rhyme.
—Alfreda's Reader's Theatre: Dialogues. Date not set. (Illus.). (J). spiral bd. 10.95 *(978-1-56820-361-4(6))* Story Time Stories That Rhyme.
—Alfreda's Reader's Theatre: Public Transportation. Date not set. (Illus.). (J). spiral bd. 8.95 *(978-1-56820-360-7(8))* Story Time Stories That Rhyme.
—The Missing Sugar Beet. Date not set. (Illus.). (J). (gr. 5-8). spiral bd. 8.95 *(978-1-56820-355-3(1))* Story Time Stories That Rhyme.
Duffield, Neil. Plays for Youth Theatres & Large Casts. 2010. (ENG., Illus.). 240p. (J). pap. 28.95 *(978-1-906582-06-7(8))* Aurora Metro Pubns. Ltd. GBR. Dist: Publishers Group West (PGW).
Dugan, Michael. Life's a Riot! 21p. (J). (gr. 4-6). pap. *(978-1-875739-30-1(0))* Wizard Bks.
Dyer, Kevin. Monster under the Bed: A Play for Children. 2010. (ENG., Illus.). 90p. (J). pap. 20.95 *(978-1-906582-07-4(6))* Aurora Metro Pubns. Ltd. GBR. Dist: Publishers Group West (PGW).
El-Bushra, Suhayla, et al. National Theatre Connections 2017: Three; #YOLO; Fomo; Status Update; Musical Differences; Extremism; the School Film; Zero for the Young Dudes!; the Snow Dragons; the Monstrum. 2017. (Plays for Young People Ser.). (ENG.). 680p. (C). pap. *(978-1-350-03359-7(6)*, 354788, Methuen Drama) Bloomsbury Publishing Plc.
Elish, Dan, et al. 13: The Complete Book & Lyrics of the Broadway Musical the Applause Libretto Library. 2011. (Applause Libretto Library). (ENG.). 104p. pap. 16.99 *(978-1-55783-777-6(5)*, 1557837775, Applause Theatre & Cinema) Leonard, Hal Corp.
Elzbieta. Mimi's Scary Theater: A Play in Nine Scenes for Seven Characters & an Egg. Elzbieta & Hawcock, David, illus. 2004. 20p. (J). (gr. -1-3). reprint ed. 15.00 *(978-0-7567-8299-3(6))* DIANE Publishing Co.
Evans, Olive. Secrets of the Forest: Playscript. 2003. (Theater for Young Audiences Ser.). 44p. (J). (gr. 3-12). reprint ed. pap. 6.00 *(978-0-88734-502-9(6))* Players Pr., Inc.
Ewald, Thomas. Christian Reader's Theater. Flint, Russ, illus. 2005. 64p. (J). per. 8.99 *(978-1-59441-077-2(1)*, CD-204004) Carson-Dellosa Publishing, LLC.
Falconer, Ian. Teatro Olivia: Swan Lake; Romeo & Juliet; Turandot. Falconer, Ian, illus. 2004. (Olivia Ser.). (Illus.). 10p. (J). 19.95 *(978-0-689-87816-9(8))* Simon & Schuster, Inc.
Fenichel Asher, Sandra. Too Many Frogs! 2007. pap. 6.95 *(978-1-58342-404-9(0))* Dramatic Publishing Co.
Figley, Marty Rhodes. John Greenwood's Journey to Bunker Hill. Orback, Craig, illus. 2010. (History Speaks: Picture Books Plus Reader's Theater Ser.). (ENG.). 48p. (gr. 2-4). pap. 9.95 *(978-0-7613-6134-3(0))* Lerner Publishing Group.
—President Lincoln, Willie Kettles, & the Telegraph Machine. Riley, David, illus. 2010. (History Speaks: Picture Books Plus Reader's Theater Ser.). (ENG.). 48p. (gr. 2-4). pap. 9.95 *(978-0-7613-6131-2(6))* Lerner Publishing Group.
Flagg, Phyllis. Five Fun Plays for Christian Kids: Including Two Christmas Plays. 2012. 64p. pap. 13.95 *(978-1-4497-3151-9(1)*, WestBow Pr.) Author Solutions, LLC.
Fleischman, Paul. Zap: A Play. 2005. (ENG.). 96p. (YA). (gr. 9-18). 16.99 *(978-0-7636-2774-4(7))* Candlewick Pr.
—Zap: A Play. 2003. 160p. (YA). (gr. 7-11). 16.95 *(978-0-8126-2687-2(7))* Cricket Bks.
—Zap: A Play. Revised Edition. 2015. (ENG.). 96p. (YA). (gr. 9). pap. 7.99 *(978-0-7636-8013-8(3))* Candlewick Pr.
Flounders, Anne, ed. The Pattern Hike, 6 vols. DuFalla, Anita; Flounders, illus. 2004. (Reader's Theater Content-Area Concepts Ser.). (ENG.). (J). (gr. 1). 5.00 net. *(978-1-4108-2290-1(7)*, A22907) Benchmark Education Co.
Fogg, Scott. Power Skits for Youth & Young Adults: 25 Faith-Awakening, Disciple-Making Drama Presentations. 2006. 175p. pap. *(978-0-8280-1883-8(9))* Review & Herald Publishing Assn.
Foon, Dennis. Kindness. 2010. (ENG.). 64p. pap. 14.95 *(978-0-88754-857-4(1))* Playwrights Canada Pr. CAN. Dist: Consortium Bk. Sales & Distribution.
Foster, Norm. Dear Santa. 2017. (ENG.). 84p. pap. 13.00 *(978-0-88754-695-2(1))* Playwrights Canada Pr. CAN. Dist: Consortium Bk. Sales & Distribution.
France, Anatole. The Man Who Married a Dumb Wife. Landes, William-Alan, ed. 2003. 28p. (YA). (gr. 8-12). pap. 7.00 *(978-0-88734-850-1(5))* Players Pr., Inc.
Francis, Claudette. Jesus Is Risen: An Easter Play for Children. 2009. (ENG.). 52p. pap. 11.99 *(978-1-4389-8103-1(1))* AuthorHouse.
Frankie Dolan, Ragtime Orphan. 2nd ed. 2006. (YA). pap. *(978-1-932663-13-6(4))* History Compass, LLC.
Frazier, Bessie. Decisions: A Teenage Play. 2009. 64p. pap. 10.49 *(978-1-4490-4014-7(4))* AuthorHouse.
Fredericks, Anthony D. African Legends, Myths, & Folktales for Readers Theatre, 1 vol. 2008. (ENG., Illus.). 192p. pap. 45.00 *(978-1-59158-633-3(X)*, 900308605, Libraries Unlimited) ABC-CLIO, LLC.
Friedman, Rosalind. Hannukah Holiday. Friedman, Rosalind, 2008. (ENG.). 16p. mass mkt. 5.50 *(978-0-87440-303-9(0))* Baker's Plays.
Fuerst, Jeffrey B. Baa Baa Black Sheep Sells Her Wool. 2008. (Reader's Theater Nursery Rhymes & Songs Ser.). (Illus.). 48p. (J). (gr. k-1). pap. *(978-1-60437-965-5(0))* Benchmark Education Co.
—Bear Goes over the Mountain. 2008. (Reader's Theater Nursery Rhymes & Songs Ser.). (Illus.). 48p. (J). (gr. k-1). pap. *(978-1-60437-972-3(3))* Benchmark Education Co.
—Bingo, Come Home! Greenhead, Bill, illus. 2009. (Reader's Theater Nursery Rhymes & Songs Set B Ser.). 48p. (J). pap. *(978-1-60859-151-0(4))* Benchmark Education Co.
—Chuck, Woodchuck, Chuck! Greenhead, Bill, illus. 2009. (Reader's Theater Nursery Rhymes & Songs Set B Ser.). 48p. (J). pap. *(978-1-60859-152-7(2))* Benchmark Education Co.
—Hickory Dickory Dock; or, Go, Mouse, Go! 2008. (Reader's Theater Nursery Rhymes & Songs Ser.). (Illus.). 48p. (J). (gr. k-1). pap. *(978-1-60437-960-0(X))* Benchmark Education Co.
—Hot Cross Buns for Everyone. Abbott, Jason, illus. 2009. (Reader's Theater Nursery Rhymes & Songs Set B Ser.). 48p. (J). pap. *(978-1-60859-153-4(0))* Benchmark Education Co.
—Hunting We Will Go. 2008. (Reader's Theater Nursery Rhymes & Songs Ser.). (Illus.). 48p. (J). (gr. k-1). pap. *(978-1-60437-974-7(X))* Benchmark Education Co.
—Itsy Bitsy Spider Climbs Again. 2008. (Reader's Theater Nursery Rhymes & Songs Ser.). (Illus.). 48p. (J). (gr. k-1). pap. *(978-1-60437-968-6(5))* Benchmark Education Co.
—Jack B. Nimble Jumps. Colby, Garry, illus. 2009. (Reader's Theater Nursery Rhymes & Songs Set B Ser.). 48p. (J). pap. *(978-1-60859-154-1(9))* Benchmark Education Co.
—Lazy Mary Gets Up. Kelley, Gerald, illus. 2009. (Reader's Theater Nursery Rhymes & Songs Set B Ser.). 48p. (J). pap. *(978-1-60859-156-5(5))* Benchmark Education Co.
—Lunch with Little Miss Muffet. 2008. (Reader's Theater Nursery Rhymes & Songs Ser.). (Illus.). 48p. (J). (gr. k-1). pap. *(978-1-60437-961-7(8))* Benchmark Education Co.
—Miss Mary Mack & the Jumping Elephants. Workman, Terry, illus. 2009. (Reader's Theater Nursery Rhymes & Songs Set B Ser.). 48p. (J). pap. *(978-1-60859-161-9(1))* Benchmark Education Co.
—The Old Gray Mare IS What She Used to Be. Currant, Gary, illus. 2009. (Reader's Theater Nursery Rhymes & Songs Set B Ser.). 48p. (J). pap. *(978-1-60859-162-6(X))* Benchmark Education Co.
—Old MacDonald. Greenhead, Bill, illus. 2010. (Rising Readers Ser.). (J). 3.49 *(978-1-60719-694-5(8))* Newmark Learning LLC.
—Old MacDonald's Noisy Farm. 2008. (Reader's Theater Nursery Rhymes & Songs Ser.). (Illus.). (J). (gr. k-1). pap. 35.00 *(978-1-60437-967-9(7))* Benchmark Education Co.
—Party Time with Old King Cole. 2008. (Reader's Theater Nursery Rhymes & Songs Ser.). (Illus.). 48p. (J). (gr. k-1). pap. *(978-1-60437-962-4(6))* Benchmark Education Co.
—Peter Pumpkin Eater Loses His Appetite. Greenhead, Bill, illus. 2009. (Reader's Theater Nursery Rhymes & Songs Set B Ser.). 48p. (J). pap. *(978-1-60859-164-0(6))* Benchmark Education Co.
—Pies for Simple Simon. Ledger, Bill, illus. 2009. (Reader's Theater Nursery Rhymes & Songs Set B Ser.). 48p. (J). pap. *(978-1-60859-165-7(4))* Benchmark Education Co.
—Run, Three Blind Mice! Walker, Sholto, illus. 2009. (Reader's Theater Nursery Rhymes & Songs Set B Ser.). 48p. (J). pap. *(978-1-60859-168-8(9))* Benchmark Education Co.
—Sing a Song of Sixpence, the King's Special Pie. 2008. (Reader's Theater Nursery Rhymes & Songs Ser.). (Illus.). 48p. (J). (gr. k-1). pap. *(978-1-60437-979-2(0))* Benchmark Education Co.
—Wishing on a Bright Star. 2008. (Reader's Theater Nursery Rhymes & Songs Ser.). (Illus.). 48p. (J). (gr. k-1). pap. *(978-1-60437-971-6(5))* Benchmark Education Co.
—The Woman Who Lived in a Shoe. Greenhead, Bill, illus. 2009. (Reader's Theater Nursery Rhymes & Songs Set B Ser.). 48p. (J). pap. *(978-1-60859-172-5(7))* Benchmark Education Co.
Fuerst, Jeffrey B.; DuFalla. How the Hubba-Dubbas Saved Lake Ni-Ni. DuFalla, Anita, illus. 2004. (Reader's Theater Content-Area Concepts Ser.). (ENG.). (J). (gr. 1-2). 5.00 net. *(978-1-4108-2292-5(3)*, A22925) Benchmark Education Co.
Gabridge, Pat. Den of Iniquity: A Ten-Minute Comedy Duet. 2003. 16p. (YA). pap. 4.50 *(978-1-932404-19-7(8)*, 155A) Brooklyn Pubs.
—Flying the Friendly Skies: A Ten-Minute Dramatic Duet. 2003. 16p. (YA). pap. 4.50 *(978-1-932404-20-3(1)*, 156A) Brooklyn Pubs.
—The Invisible Husband: A Ten-Minute Dramatic Duet. 2003. 16p. (YA). pap. 4.50 *(978-1-931805-99-5(7)*, 151A) Brooklyn Pubs.
—It's a Girl! A Ten-Minute Comedy Duet. 2003. (YA). pap. 4.50 *(978-1-931805-95-7(4)*, 147A) Brooklyn Pubs.
—Measuring Matthew: A Ten-Minute Comedy Duet. 2003. (YA). pap. 4.50 *(978-1-931805-92-6(X)*, 144A) Brooklyn Pubs.
—Phoenix Funeral Draft 3: A Ten-Minute Comedy Duet. 2003. 16p. (YA). pap. 4.50 *(978-1-931805-98-8(9)*, 150A) Brooklyn Pubs.
Gabridge, Patrick. The Sky Is Falling: A One-Act Comedy Play. 2003. (YA). pap. 4.50 *(978-1-932404-58-6(9)*, 756) Brooklyn Pubs.
Giannakeff, Dianne D., adapted by. The Young Actor's Bible: Stories from the Bible. 2004. (J). spiral bd. 39.95 *(978-0-9762297-0-4(6))* Lucia Pubs.
Gill, Jim. A Soup Opera. Moose, David, illus. 2009. (ENG.). 32p. (J). lib. bdg. *(978-0-9815721-0-9(3))* Gill, Jim Music.
Gingerich, Neeltje. Mini-Musicals for Christmas. 2011. 32p. (J). pap. 7.00 *(978-0-88734-998-0(6))* Players Pr., Inc.
Glavich, Mary Kathleen. Gospel Theater for the Whole Community: 92 Plays for Education & Worship. 2006. 215p. per. 29.95 *(978-1-58595-563-3(9))* Twenty-Third Pubns./Bayard.
Glennon, William. The Trial of the Arkansas Bear. 2003. 52p. (YA). pap. 6.25 *(978-1-58342-158-1(0)*, TE5) Dramatic Publishing Co.
Goldberg, Moses. Sleeping Beauty (Dornroschen) (Play Script) 2006. (J). pap. 6.00 *(978-0-87602-416-4(9))* Family Plays.
Golden, Joseph. Johnny Moonbeam & the Silver Arrow: An Adventure for Young People in Narration & Mime. 2011. 42p. 35.95 *(978-1-258-09981-7(0))* Literary Licensing, LLC.
Goldenthal, Jolene. The Beautiful Truth: A One-Act Comedy Play. 2003. (YA). pap. 4.50 *(978-1-932404-64-7(3)*, 762) Brooklyn Pubs.
Goode, Jeff. PRINCESS GRAY & the BLACK & WHITE KNIGHT. 2008. 39p. per. *(978-0-87440-281-0(6))* Baker's Plays.
—Rumpelstiltskin. 2009. (ENG.). 48p. mass mkt. 9.95 *(978-0-87440-314-5(6))* Baker's Plays.
Goodwin, Debbie Salter. Quick Start Drama for Kids: No Rehearsal Bible Skits for Classroom or Performance. 2005. (ENG.). 40p. pap. 19.99 *(978-0-8341-7410-8(3)*, MP-858) Lillenas Publishing Co.
Gorky, Maxim. The Lower Depths. Landes, William-Alan, ed. Covan, Jennie, tr. from RUS. unabr. ed. 2003. (Players Press Classic Plays Ser.). 64p. (YA). (gr. 4-12). pap. 7.50 *(978-0-88734-815-0(7))* Players Pr., Inc.
Gourlay, Catherine. Family Matters: Plays about Family Changes. 2010. (Get into Character Ser.). (ENG., Illus.). 32p. (J). (gr. 3-6). pap. *(978-0-7787-7375-7(2))*; lib. bdg. *(978-0-7787-7361-0(2))* Crabtree Publishing Co.
—Flashpoints! Plays about Controlling Anger, 1 vol. 2010. (Get into Character Ser.). (ENG., Illus.). 32p. (J). (gr. 3-6). pap. *(978-0-7787-7376-4(0))*; lib. bdg. *(978-0-7787-7362-7(0))* Crabtree Publishing Co.
—Friend or Foe? Plays about Bullying. 2010. (Get into Character Ser.). (ENG., Illus.). 32p. (J). (gr. 3-6). pap. *(978-0-7787-7377-1(9))*; lib. bdg. *(978-0-7787-7363-4(9))* Crabtree Publishing Co.
—The Invisible Me: Plays about Self-Image, 1 vol. 2010. (Get into Character Ser.). (ENG., Illus.). 32p. (J). (gr. 3-6). pap. *(978-0-7787-7379-5(5))*; lib. bdg. *(978-0-7787-7365-8(5))* Crabtree Publishing Co.
—What's the Difference? Plays about Tolerance. 2010. (Get into Character Ser.). (ENG., Illus.). 32p. (J). (gr. 3-6). pap. *(978-0-7787-7378-8(7))*; lib. bdg. *(978-0-7787-7364-1(7))* Crabtree Publishing Co.
—Where Do I Belong? Plays about Fitting In. 2010. (Get into Character Ser.). (ENG., Illus.). 32p. (J). (gr. 3-6). pap.

(978-0-7787-7380-1(9)); lib. bdg. (978-0-7787-7366-5(3)) Crabtree Publishing Co.
Graham, Joseph. Who's Gonna Save Me? It's Time to Tell Your Secrets. 2005. 126p. (YA). pap. 14.00 (978-0-9767778-0-9(0), 704-724-1683) Alpha & Omega Publishing.
Gravois, Michael. Aesop's Fable-Ous Barnyard Bash. 2014. 63p. (J). pap. 9.95 (978-1-58342-975-4(1)) Dramatic Publishing Co.
Gray, Keith & Miller, Carl. Ostrich Boys: Improving Standards in English Through Drama at Key Stage 3 & GCSE. Bunyan, Paul & Moore, Ruth, eds. 2011. (Critical Scripts Ser.). (ENG., Illus.). 112p. pap. (978-1-4081-3082-7(3), 16858, Methuen Drama) Bloomsbury Publishing Plc.
Greenidge, Kirsten. Familiar. 2004. (YA). pap. 6.50 (978-1-58342-175-8(0), F79) Dramatic Publishing Co.
Gregg, Stephen. S. P. A. R. a play / 2003. 26p. (YA). pap. 4.25 (978-1-58342-157-4(2), SH5) Dramatic Publishing Co.
Greig, Noel, adapted by. The Tin Soldier: And Other Plays for Children. 2011. (ENG., Illus.). 112p. (J). (gr. 1). pap. 22.95 (978-1-906582-19-7(X)) Aurora Metro Pubns. Ltd. GBR. Dist: Publishers Group West (PGW).
Group/McGraw-Hill, Wright. Queen of the Trail Play 8: Decodable Plays, 6 vols. (Fast Track Reading Ser.). 24p. (gr. 4-8). 40.95 (978-0-322-05999-3(2)) Wright Group/McGraw-Hill.
—Saws Don't Pounce Play 9: Decodable Plays, 6 vols. (Fast Track Reading Ser.). 24p. (gr. 4-8). 40.95 (978-0-322-06001-2(X)) Wright Group/McGraw-Hill.
Groves. Six Silly Plays. Date not set. (Illus.). 58p. pap. 65.00 (978-0-582-24379-8(3)) Addison-Wesley Longman, Ltd. GBR. Dist: Trans-Atlantic Pubns., Inc.
Grudzina, Rebecca. A Baby Bumblebee for Mommy. Boyer, Lyn, illus. 2009. (Reader's Theater Nursery Rhymes & Songs Set B Ser.). 48p. (J). pap. (978-1-60859-149-7(2)) Benchmark Education Co.
—Pease Porridge, Please! Harrington, David, illus. 2009. (Reader's Theater Nursery Rhymes & Songs Set B Ser.). 48p. (J). pap. (978-1-60859-163-3(8)) Benchmark Education Co.
—Red Roses, Blue Violets, And...? Ledger, Bill, illus. 2009. (Reader's Theater Nursery Rhymes & Songs Set B Ser.). 48p. (J). pap. (978-1-60859-167-1(0)) Benchmark Education Co.
Guderjahn, Ernie L. A Children's Trilogy: Ali's Flying Rug, the Shadow Workers, & the Magic Cricket (Playscript) 2003. (Theater for Young Audiences Ser.). 32p. (Orig.). (J). (gr. 3-18). pap. 6.00 (978-0-88734-504-3(2)) Players Pr., Inc.
Haddon, Mark & Stephens, Simon. The Curious Incident of the Dog in the Night-Time: The Play. 2013. (Critical Scripts Ser.). (ENG., Illus.). 160p. (J). pap. (978-1-4081-8521-6(0), 233870, Methuen Drama) Bloomsbury Publishing Plc.
Haehnel, Alan. The Blender: A One-Act Dark Comedy Play. 2003. (YA). pap. 4.50 (978-1-932404-57-9(0), 755) Brooklyn Pubs.
—The Twisting-Turning Death Machine: Ten-Minute Comedy Duet. 2003. (YA). pap. 9.00 (978-1-932404-02-9(3), 139A) Brooklyn Pubs.
—What the Doctor Ordered: Ten-Minute Comedy Duet. 2003. (YA). pap. 9.00 (978-1-932404-00-5(7), 137A) Brooklyn Pubs.
Halligan, Terry. Funny Skits & Sketches. Behr, Joyce, illus. unabr. ed. 2003. 128p. (YA). (gr. 4-12). pap. 15.00 (978-0-88734-688-0(X)) Players Pr., Inc.
Harder, Eleanor. What'd Ya Do Today, Billy Joe? 2003. 40p. (YA). pap. 4.50 (978-1-58342-188-8(2), W98) Dramatic Publishing Co.
Harris, Brooke. Baby Gets a Cake. Beckstrand, Jared, illus. 2009. (Reader's Theater Nursery Rhymes & Songs Set B Ser.). 48p. (J). pap. (978-1-60859-150-3(6)) Benchmark Education Co.
—Brother John, Wake Up! 2008. (Reader's Theater Nursery Rhymes & Songs Ser.). (Illus.). 48p. (J). (gr. k-1). pap. (978-1-60437-973-0(1)) Benchmark Education Co.
—Jack & Jill Play on the Hill. 2008. (Reader's Theater Nursery Rhymes & Songs Ser.). (Illus.). 48p. (J). (gr. k-1). pap. (978-1-60437-964-8(2)) Benchmark Education Co.
—Little Boy Blue, Where are You? 2008. (Reader's Theater Nursery Rhymes & Songs Ser.). (Illus.). 48p. (J). (gr. k-1). pap. (978-1-60437-976-1(6)) Benchmark Education Co.
—London Bridge Has Fallen Down. Boyer, Lyn, illus. 2009. (Reader's Theater Nursery Rhymes & Songs Set B Ser.). 48p. (J). pap. (978-1-60859-159-6(X)) Benchmark Education Co.
—Mary's Garden: How Does it Grow? Xin, Xiao, illus. 2009. (Reader's Theater Nursery Rhymes & Songs Set B Ser.). 48p. (J). pap. (978-1-60859-160-2(3)) Benchmark Education Co.
—The Purple Cow. Hohnstadt, Cedric, illus. 2009. (Reader's Theater Nursery Rhymes & Songs Set B Ser.). 48p. (J). pap. (978-1-60859-166-4(2)) Benchmark Education Co.
—This Little Pig, That Little Pig. 2008. (Reader's Theater Nursery Rhymes & Songs Ser.). (Illus.). 48p. (J). (gr. k-1). pap. (978-1-60437-969-3(3)) Benchmark Education Co.
—The Twinkling Stars. Harrington, David, illus. 2009. (Reader's Theater Nursery Rhymes & Songs Set B Ser.). 48p. (J). pap. (978-1-60859-170-1(0)) Benchmark Education Co.
—Where Has My Little Dog Gone? 2008. (Reader's Theater Nursery Rhymes & Songs Ser.). (Illus.). 48p. (J). (gr. k-1). pap. (978-1-60437-975-4(8)) Benchmark Education Co.
—Working on the Railroad. 2008. (Reader's Theater Nursery Rhymes & Songs Ser.). (Illus.). 48p. (J). (gr. k-1). pap. (978-1-60437-981-5(2)) Benchmark Education Co.
Harris, Valerie. The Saga of Henry Box Brown: A Play for Black History Month. 2004. (Illus.). 35p. spiral bd. 12.95 (978-0-9772126-0-6(2)) BPT Media.
Harrison, Jordan & Gray, Richard. Hans Christian Anderson's the Flea & the Professor. 2012. (ENG.). (J). pap. 8.95 (978-0-573-70095-8(8), French, Samuel, Inc.) Concord Theatricals.
Haupt, Wolfgang & Bland, Janice. Tales of the Little Hedgehogs: Fairy Plays. Mouraviova, Yulia, illus. 2009. (J). (978-0-88734-978-2(1)) Players Pr., Inc.
Hendrickson, Clyde. The Altos: A Clyde Hendrickson Joint. 2003. (YA). 7.99 (978-0-9679552-7-8(0)) Mushroom Cloud Pr. of Orlando.
—Special Places. 2003. (AFR.). 20p. (YA). 8.50 (978-0-9679552-5-4(4)) Mushroom Cloud Pr. of Orlando.
—Squirrel. 2003. (YA). 11.00 (978-0-9679552-6-1(2)) Mushroom Cloud Pr. of Orlando.
Henry, Lenworth. Gilbert the Mighty Hurricane: A Jamaican Experience. 2010. 48p. pap. 9.95 (978-0-595-48923-7(0)) iUniverse, Inc.
Herweck, Diana. The Indestructible Pele (Science) rev. ed. 2015. (Reader's Theater Ser.). (ENG., Illus.). 24p. (J). (gr. 3-4). pap. 8.99 (978-1-4938-1516-6(4)) Teacher Created Materials, Inc.
Heslep, William. Tower of London. 2003. 23p. (J). pap. 6.00 (978-0-88734-418-3(6)) Players Pr., Inc.
Hezlep, William. Bigfoot! 2004. (Travelers Ser.). 24p. (J). (gr. 3-6). pap. 5.00 (978-0-88734-485-5(2)) Players Pr., Inc.
—Bog Bodies. 2004. (Travelers Ser.). 20p. (J). pap. 5.00 (978-0-88734-467-1(4)) Players Pr., Inc.
—Cayman Duppy: Playscript. 2003. (Illus.). 16p. (J). (gr. 5-18). pap. 5.00 (978-0-88734-403-9(8)) Players Pr., Inc.
—Curse of the Tomb Raiders. 2005. (Travelers Ser.). 32p. (J). pap. 6.00 (978-0-88734-565-4(4)) Players Pr., Inc.
—How Come Christmas? 2003. (Theater for Young Audiences Ser.). 18p. (J). pap. 5.00 (978-0-88734-424-4(0)) Players Pr., Inc.
—Kokopelli's Cave. 2003. (Travelers Ser.). 24p. (J). (gr. k-6). pap. 5.00 (978-0-88734-466-4(6)) Players Pr., Inc.
—Merlin's Cave. 2003. (Theater for Young Audiences Ser.). 55p. (Orig.). (J). (gr. k-12). pap. 6.00 (978-0-88734-420-6(8)) Players Pr., Inc.
—Nessie: Playscript. 2003. 24p. (J). (gr. 3-12). reprint ed. pap. 6.00 (978-0-88734-401-5(1)) Players Pr., Inc.
—Pharaoh's Dagger: Playscript. 2003. (Illus.). 70p. (Orig.). (J). (gr. 3-12). reprint ed. pap. 6.00 (978-0-88734-404-6(6)) Players Pr., Inc.
—Shipwrecked. Landes, William Alan, ed. unabr. ed. 2003. (Ideal for Teens Ser.). 21p. (J). (gr. 3-8). pap. 5.00 (978-0-88734-484-8(4)) Players Pr., Inc.
—Time Travelers, 16 vols. 2006. (Travelers Ser.). 36p. (J). (gr. 3-6). pap. 6.00 (978-0-88734-573-9(5)) Players Pr., Inc.
—Treasure of the Mayans. 2003. 28p. (Orig.). (J). (gr. 3-8). pap. 6.00 (978-0-88734-405-3(4)) Players Pr., Inc.
Higgins, Frank. The Slave Dancer's Choice. 2003. (Illus.). 40p. (YA). pap. 6.50 (978-1-58342-166-6(1), SH6) Dramatic Publishing Co.
Higgins, Kitty. The Three Sisters. Flounders, Anne; Higgins, ed. 2004. (Reader's Theater Content-Area Concepts Ser.). (ENG., Illus.). (J). (gr. 4-5). 5.00 net. (978-1-4108-2312-0(1), A23121) Benchmark Education Co.
Higgins, Kitty; Flounders. Above the Clouds. Flounders, Anne, ed. 2004. (Reader's Theater Content-Area Concepts Ser.). (ENG.). (J). (gr. 4-5). 5.00 net. (978-1-4108-2309-0(1), A23091) Benchmark Education Co.
—As the Crow Flies. Flounders, Anne, ed. 2004. (Reader's Theater Content-Area Concepts Ser.). (ENG., Illus.). (J). (gr. 3-5). 5.00 net. (978-1-4108-2304-5(0), A23040) Benchmark Education Co.
Higgins, Kitty; Leon. Great Beasts of the Great Plains. Leon, Karen, illus. 2004. (Reader's Theater Content-Area Concepts Ser.). (ENG.). (J). (gr. 4-5). 5.00 net. (978-1-4108-2311-3(3), A23113) Benchmark Education Co.
Hilderbrandt, Sandra June. Wilbur's Great Adventure. Merrell, Vernon R., illus. 2011. 32p. (J). 19.95 (978-1-59649-587-6(1)) Whispering Pine Pr. International, Inc.
Hodge, Bill. Cyril: Tales of a Teenage Cyrano. 31p. (YA). (gr. 7-12). pap. 4.00 (978-1-57514-153-4(1), 1160) Encore Performance Publishing.
Hoover, Nicolas. The Red Merit Badge of Courage. 2010. (ENG.). 23p. pap. 4.50 (978-0-87440-392-3(8)) Baker's Plays.
House, Behrman. Extraordinary Jews. 2005. (ENG., Illus.). 1p. per. 19.95 (978-0-86705-051-6(9), 8a9197e9-686b-451a-b9bd-f41d66afb726) Behrman Hse., Inc.
Howard, Annabelle; DuFalla. Alex in Numberland. DuFalla, Anita, illus. 2004. (Reader's Theater Content-Area Concepts Ser.). (ENG.). (J). (gr. 3-4). 5.00 net. (978-1-4108-2303-8(2), A23032) Benchmark Education Co.
Howard, Annabelle; Flounders. Battle for the Ballot. Flounders, Anne, ed. 2004. (Reader's Theater Content-Area Concepts Ser.). (ENG., Illus.). (J). (gr. 3-5). 5.00 net. (978-1-4108-2305-2(9), A23059) Benchmark Education Co.
Howard, Jane R. Maria's Loom: An Original Fairy Tale with Music (play Script) 2007. (ENG.). 48p. (J). pap. 7.00 (978-0-87602-417-1(7)) Family Plays.
Hutchins, Laurence. I'm the King of the Castle. 2005. (Oberon Plays for Young People Ser.). (ENG., Illus.). 108p. per. 16.95 (978-1-84002-486-9(0), 900242833) Oberon Bks., Ltd. GBR. Dist: Macmillan.
Hutt, Rosamunde, ed. Theatre Centre - Plays for Young People Vol. 1: Celebrating 50 Years of Theatre Centre. 2003. (ENG., Illus.). 300p. pap. 28.95 (978-0-9542330-5-1(0)) Aurora Metro Pubns. Ltd. GBR. Dist: Publishers Group West (PGW).
Ibsen, Henrik. A Doll's House - Literary Touchstone Edition. 2005. 88p. (YA). per. 3.99 (978-1-58049-598-1(2), PWH5982) Prestwick Hse., Inc.
In the Mind of the Beholder: A Ten-Minute Dramatic Duet. 2003. (YA). pap. 4.50 (978-1-932404-22-7(8), 158A) Brooklyn Pubs.
Janet & Donald Play 7: Decodable Plays, 6 vols. (Fast Track Reading Ser.). 24p. (gr. 4-8). 40.95 (978-0-322-05998-6(4)) Wright Group/McGraw-Hill.
Jasspon, Ethel Reed. Ritual & Dramatized Folkways. 2006. (Illus.). pap. 24.95 (978-1-4286-6016-8(X)) Kessinger Publishing, LLC.
Jeffries, Katherine. Tim's Head, Shoulders, Knees, & Toes. Price, Nick, illus. 2009. (Reader's Theater Nursery Rhymes & Songs Set B Ser.). 48p. (J). pap. (978-1-60859-169-5(7)) Benchmark Education Co.
Jenkins, Diana R. All Year Long! Funny Readers Theatre for Life's Special Times, 1 vol. 2007. (ENG., Illus.). 264p. per. 40.00 (978-1-59158-436-0(1), 900303907, Libraries Unlimited) ABC-CLIO, LLC.
—Just Deal with It! Funny Readers Theatre for Life's Not-So-Funny Moments, 1 vol. 2004. (Readers Theatre Ser.). (ENG., Illus.). 256p. pap. 37.00 (978-1-59158-043-0(9), 900301583, Libraries Unlimited) ABC-CLIO, LLC.
—Spotlight on Saints! A Year of Funny Readers Theater for Today's Catholic Kids. Richards, Virginia Helen, illus. 2009. 180p. (J). (gr. 4-7). pap. 18.95 (978-0-8198-7119-0(2)) Pauline Bks. & Media.
—STALKER MOM & OTHER PLAYS. 2009. (ENG.). 60p. mass mkt. 5.50 (978-0-87440-220-9(4)) Baker's Plays.
Jennings, Coleman A. & Berghammer, Gretta, eds. Theatre for Youth II: More Plays with Mature Themes. 2016. (ENG.). 488p. pap. 34.95 (978-1-4773-1004-5(5)) Univ. of Texas Pr.
Johnson, Judith. Scary Play. 2007. (Collins National Theatre Plays Ser.). (ENG.). 320p. (YA). (gr. 7-10). pap. 13.99 (978-0-00-725489-7(X)) HarperCollins Pubs. Ltd. GBR. Dist: Independent Pubs. Group.
Jonas, J. J. Conflagration: A Ten-Minute Dramatic Duet. 2003. 20p. pap. 4.50 (978-1-932404-17-3(1), 153A) Brooklyn Pubs.
—Last of the Lotto Laity: A Ten-Minute Comedy Monologue. 2003. 16p. (YA). pap. 4.50 (978-1-932404-29-6(5), 282) Brooklyn Pubs.
—Revenge of the Coach's Daughter: A Ten-Minute Comedy Monologue. 2003. 12p. (YA). pap. 4.50 (978-1-932404-28-9(7), 281) Brooklyn Pubs.
—Running on Empty: A Ten-Minute Dramatic Monologue. 2003. 16p. (YA). pap. 4.50 (978-1-932404-27-2(9), 280) Brooklyn Pubs.
—Twitcher: A Ten-Minute Dramatic Duet. 2003. (YA). pap. 4.50 (978-1-931805-93-3(8), 145A) Brooklyn Pubs.
Jordan, Pat. Adventures of King Arthur: From the Every Teacher's Friend Classroom Plays Series. 2010. 20p. (J). pap. 5.00 (978-0-88734-986-7(2)) Players Pr., Inc.
—Alice in Wonderland: From the Every Teacher's Friend Classroom Plays Series. 2010. 20p. (YA). pap. 5.00 (978-0-88734-987-4(0)) Players Pr., Inc.
—Classic Literature for Teens: Every Teachers Friend Classroom Plays. Aliger, Richard, illus. 2007. 118p. pap. 25.00 (978-0-88734-692-7(8)) Players Pr., Inc.
—Little Women, or the March Girls of New England: From the Every Teacher's Friend Classroom Plays Series. 2010. 20p. (YA). pap. 5.00 (978-0-88734-989-8(7)) Players Pr., Inc.
—Mini-Myths: Eleven Short Plays & Mimes of Favorite Greek & Roman Myths. 2010. 72p. pap. 8.00 (978-0-88734-993-5(5)) Players Pr., Inc.
—Mini-Myths for Pre-Teens & Teens Vol. 2: Every Teacher's Friend Classroom Plays. Aliger, Richard, illus. 2008. (Every Teacher's Friend Classroom Plays Ser.: Vol. 2). 122p. pap. 25.00 (978-0-88734-964-5(1)) Players Pr., Inc.
—Mother Goose Plays: From Every Teacher's Friend Classroom Plays Vol. 4: Mother Goose Plays. 2011. 36p. (J). pap. 5.00 (978-0-88734-065-9(2)) Players Pr., Inc.
—Oliver Twist: From the Every Teacher's Friend Classroom Plays Series. 2010. 20p. (YA). pap. 5.00 (978-0-88734-990-4(0)) Players Pr., Inc.
—The Secret Garden: From the Every Teacher's Friend Classroom Plays Series. 2010. 20p. (YA). pap. 5.00 (978-0-88734-988-1(9)) Players Pr., Inc.
Juwell, et al. The Ab-Solute Truth. 2006. (Platinum Teen Ser.: Vol. 2). 111p. (J). (gr. 5-11). per. 6.99 (978-0-9729325-4-7(2)) Preciousstymes Entertainment, LLC.
Karczewski, Deborah. Cheerleader Meets the Goth: A Ten-Minute Comedy Monologue. 2003. 16p. (YA). pap. 4.50 (978-1-932404-25-8(2), 278) Brooklyn Pubs.
Katz, Leon. Fables: A Collection for Youth. 2006. 68p. (YA). pap. 5.95 (978-1-60003-199-1(4), 617) Brooklyn Pubs.
Kaye, Leon. Cooking on the Street: A Comedy Monologue. 2003. (YA). pap. 4.50 (978-1-932404-33-3(3), 286) Brooklyn Pubs.
—Eat a Can: A Comedy Skit, 3 Booklets. 2003. (YA). pap. 9.00 (978-1-932404-36-4(8), 324) Brooklyn Pubs.
Keene, Daniel. Terminus & Other Plays. 2003. (Modern Drama Ser.). (ENG.). 280p. pap. (978-1-876857-18-9(8)) Salt Publishing.
Kehret, Peg. Tell It Like It is: Fifty Monologs for Talented Teens, 1 vol. 2007. (ENG.). 118p. per. 15.95 (978-1-56608-144-3(0)) Meriwether Publishing, Ltd.
Kelso, Brendan. Shakespeare's a Midsummer Night's Dream for Kids: 3 Short Melodramatic Plays for 3 Group Sizes. Lopez, Shana, illus. 2008. (ENG.). 54p. pap. 9.99 (978-1-4196-8552-1(X)) CreateSpace Independent Publishing Platform.
Kemp, Robert. The Other Dear Charmer. 2006. 80p. (YA). (gr. 6-12). pap. 6.00 (978-0-88734-566-1(2)) Players Pr., Inc.
Kherouf, Allel. I Want to Fly: A Play for Children in Four Parts. 2012. (ENG.). 201p. pap. 12.95 (978-1-4327-8007-4(7)) Outskirts Pr., Inc.
Kingsland, Robin. Porky Pies. unabr. ed. 2003. (Plays & Play Collections). (Illus.). 64p. (J). (gr. 1-6). reprint ed. pap. 15.00 (978-0-7136-5370-0(1), A&C Black) Bloomsbury Publishing Plc GBR. Dist: Players Pr., Inc.
Kipling, Rudyard. The Jungle Book, Bk. 1. 2012. (ENG., Illus.). 88p. (J). (gr. k). pap. 20.95 (978-1-906582-26-5(2)) Aurora Metro Pubns. Ltd. GBR. Dist: Publishers Group West (PGW).
Kirkeby, Jennifer. Dot & Tot of Merryland - 2004. 80p. (J). pap. 7.50 (978-1-58342-237-3(4), D04) Dramatic Publishing Co.
—Harriet & Walt. 2010. (ENG.). 57p. pap. 7.00 (978-0-87440-234-6(4)) Baker's Plays.
Korty, Carol. Plays from African Folktales. Landes, William-Alan, ed. unabr. ed. 2003. (International Black Plays & Folk Tales Ser.). (Illus.). 98p. (J). (gr. 3-12). pap. 17.00 (978-0-88734-659-0(6)) Players Pr., Inc.
—Silly Soup. Landes, William-Alan, ed. Colombo, David, illus. Helms, Tina, photos by. 2003. (Plays & Play Collections). 128p. (Orig.). (J). (gr. k-6). pap. 17.00 (978-0-88734-679-8(0)) Players Pr., Inc.
Kramer, Alan. Bajo el mar con Jacques Cousteau & under the Sea with Jacques Cousteau. 2005. spiral bd. 76.00 (978-1-4108-5789-7(1)) Benchmark Education Co.
—Escape de la extinción & Path from Extinction. 2005. spiral bd. 76.00 (978-1-4108-5794-1(8)) Benchmark Education Co.
Krensky, Stephen. Lizzie Newton & the San Francisco Earthquake. Tugeau, Jeremy, illus. 2010. (History Speaks: Picture Books Plus Reader's Theater Ser.). (ENG.). 48p. (gr. 2-4). pap. 9.95 (978-0-7613-3944-1(2)) Lerner Publishing Group.
Kroll, Virginia L. The Christmas Cow. 2003. 55p. (Orig.). (J). (gr. 1-6). pap. 5.00 (978-0-88734-481-7(X)) Players Pr., Inc.
Kropp, Paul & Jamison, Lori. HIP Readers' Theater Plays. (978-1-897039-40-3(9)) High Interest Publishing (HIP).
Kruh, David. Top of the World, Ma! A Ten-Minute Comedy Duet. 2003. 12p. (YA). pap. 4.50 (978-1-932404-16-6(3), 152A) Brooklyn Pubs.
Lamedman, Debbie. Twenty 10-Minute Plays For Teens By Teens, Vol. 3. 2007. 176p. 14.95 (978-1-57525-456-2(5)) Smith & Kraus Pubs., Inc.
Landes, William-Alan. Aladdin n' His Magic Lamp. rev. ed. 2003. (Wondrawhopper Ser.). 51p. (J). (gr. 3-12). pap. 6.00 (978-0-88734-102-1(0)) Players Pr., Inc.
—Alice n' Wonderland. 2003. (Wondrawhopper Ser.). 32p. (Orig.). (YA). (gr. 3-18). pap. 6.00 (978-0-88734-112-0(8)) Players Pr., Inc.
—Jack 'n the Beanstalk: Playscript. rev. ed. 2003. (Wondrawhopper Ser.). 40p. (J). (gr. 3-12). pap. 6.00 (978-0-88734-101-4(2)) Players Pr., Inc.
—Peter 'n the Wolf: Acting Edition. rev. ed. 2003. (Wondrawhopper Ser.). 36p. (J). (gr. 3-12). pap. 6.00 (978-0-88734-106-9(3)) Players Pr., Inc.
—Rapunzel 'n the Witch. rev. ed. 2003. (Wondrawhopper Ser.). 48p. (J). (gr. 3-12). pap. 6.00 (978-0-88734-107-6(1)) Players Pr., Inc.
—Rhyme Tyme: Playscript. rev. ed. 2003. (Wondrawhopper Ser.). 40p. (J). (gr. 3-12). pap. 6.00 (978-0-88734-108-3(X)) Players Pr., Inc.
—Rumpelstiltskin. 2011. (Wondrawhopper Ser.). (J). (978-0-88734-117-5(9)) Players Pr., Inc.
—Rumpelstiltskin: Playscript. rev. ed. 2003. (Wondrawhopper Ser.). 52p. (J). (gr. 3-12). pap. 6.00 (978-0-88734-104-5(7)) Players Pr., Inc.
Landes, William-Alan & Lasky, Mark A. Grandpa's Bedtime Story. rev. ed. 2003. (Theater for Young Audiences Ser.). 36p. (YA). (gr. 3-12). pap. 6.00 (978-0-88734-505-0(0)) Players Pr., Inc.
Landes, William-Alan & Standish, Marilyn. The Wizard of Oz. rev. ed. 2003. (Wondrawhopper Ser.). 40p. (J). (gr. 3-12). pap. 6.00 (978-0-88734-105-2(5)) Players Pr., Inc.
Landry, Deb. Sticks Stones & Stumped the Play & Teacher's Guide. 2008. (Illus.). 40p. pap. 29.95 (978-0-9773738-2-6(7)) Bryson Taylor Publishing.
Lawall, Gilbert & Kindel, Gerde. The Phaedra of Seneca. 2nd ed. 2007. (ENG., Illus.). 238p. (J). (gr. 9-12). pap. 39.00 (978-0-86516-016-3(3)) Bolchazy-Carducci Pubs.
Leaf, Claudia. Radical Will. unabr. ed. 2003. (Shakespeare Ser.). 28p. (YA). (gr. 6-12). pap. 6.00 (978-0-85343-614-0(2)) Miller, J. Garnet Ltd. GBR. Dist: Empire Publishing Service.
Leese, Joan, et al. Three Plays for Women. 2003. (Full-Length Plays Ser.). 44p. (YA). (gr. 8-12). pap. 6.00 (978-0-88734-932-4(3)) Players Pr., Inc.
LeMaster, David. Sir Saddlesore & the Dragon: One-Act Children's Comedy Play. rev. ed. 2005. 12p. (YA). pap. 4.95 (978-1-60003-094-9(7), 783) Brooklyn Pubs.
LeMaster, David J. Homeland Insecurity: A Comedy Skit, 4 Booklets. 2003. (YA). pap. 4.50 (978-1-932404-38-8(4), 322) Brooklyn Pubs.
—Paper, Rock, Scissors, Bomb! A Ten-Minute Comedy Duet. 2003. 16p. (YA). pap. 4.50 (978-1-932404-18-0(X), 154A) Brooklyn Pubs.
—Shakespeare, Horny Toads & Banana Peels: Ten-Minute Comedy Duet. 2003. (YA). pap. 9.00 (978-1-932404-04-3(X), 141A) Brooklyn Pubs.
Levine, Karen. Hana's Suitcase on Stage, 1 vol. 2006. (Holocaust Remembrance Series for Young Readers Ser.: 7). (ENG., Illus.). 172p. (J). (gr. 3-12). pap. 18.95 (978-1-897187-05-0(X)) Second Story Pr. CAN. Dist: Orca Bk. Pubs. USA.
Liebenow, Todd, et al. Beyond Words 2. 2003. (Illus.). 56p. (YA). 20.00 (978-1-58302-228-3(7)) Creative Ministry Solutions.
Lieberman, Paulette (Peshe Razel) Fein. Jewish Plays for Children: For successful educational fun & fundraising Purposes. 2008. 236p. pap. 18.95 (978-0-595-52944-5(5)) iUniverse, Inc.
Lodato, Victor & Pen, Polly. Arlington. 2015. 49p. (978-0-8222-3165-3(4)) Dramatists Play Service, Inc.
Mabian, Mercy. The Little Crying Hearts: A Play. 2009. 116p. pap. 13.99 (978-1-4389-5035-8(7)) AuthorHouse.
MacDonald, Margaret Read. The Skit Book: 101 Skits from Kids. Scull, Marie-Louise, illus. 2006. (ENG.). 160p. (J). (gr. -1-12). per. 17.95 (978-0-87483-785-8(5)) August Hse. Pubs., Inc.
MacDougal, P. Paullette. Waiting for MacArthur. 2003. (Illus.). 58p. (YA). (gr. 10). pap. 6.50 (978-1-58342-183-3(1), W97) Dramatic Publishing Co.
Mahfouz, Sabrina, et al. National Theatre Connections 2014: Plays for Young People: Same; Horizon; the Wardrobe; Heritage; a Letter to Lacey; a Shop Selling Speech; Angels; Hearts; Pronoun; Tomorrow. Banks, Anthony, ed. 2014. (Plays for Young People Ser.). (ENG.). 728p. pap. (978-1-4725-7143-4(6), 256783, Methuen Drama) Bloomsbury Publishing Plc.
Mamet, Clara & Quaid, Jack. Solvit Kids. 2012. (ENG.). 41p. (J). pap. 8.95 (978-0-573-70087-3(7), French, Samuel, Inc.) Concord Theatricals.
Mankowski, Sarah. Fallout: An original Screenplay. 2004. (YA). spiral bd. 10.95 (978-0-9745268-6-7(X)) WordThunder Pubns.
Manning, Mick & Brita, Granström. Mi Primer Libro de Teatro. Granström, Brita, illus.Tr. of Drama School. (SPA.). (J). (gr. 3-5). 15.16 (978-84-241-7922-9(6)) Everest Editora ESP. Dist: Lectorum Pubns., Inc.
Mapleson, Peter & Mapleson, Robyn. Bill the Bunyip. (J). (gr. 3-6). pap. (978-1-875739-82-0(3)) Wizard Bks.
Marlin, Therese. Cindyrella. 2006. (ENG.). 32p. pap. 5.50 (978-0-87440-254-4(9), 1726-B) Baker's Plays.
Martin, Judith. Out of the Bag: The Paper Bag Players Book of Plays. Chwast, Seymour, illus. 2005. 48p. (J). (gr. k-4). reprint ed. pap. 14.00 (978-0-7567-8530-7(8)) DIANE Publishing Co.
Maxwell, Glyn. Merlin & the Woods of Time. 2011. (Oberon Modern Plays Ser.). (ENG.). 96p. (J). (gr. k). pap. (978-1-84943-224-5(4), 513500) Oberon Bks., Ltd.
Maxwell-Snyder, Hope. Lullaby for George. 2005. (J). 9.95 (978-0-9753285-4-5(9)) H.B.P., Inc.

May, Bob. Snowmen, elves & Nutcrackers. 2008. (ENG.). 144p. mass mkt. 6.00 *(978-0-87440-306-0(5))* Baker's Plays.
Mayer, Mindy & Mayer, Allie. Sheltered Friends. 2008. mass mkt. 6.50 *(978-0-87440-248-3(4))* Baker's Plays.
McBride-Smith, Barbara. Tell It Together: Foolproof Scripts for Story Theatre. 2005. (ENG.). 192p. (gr. 3-6). 24.95 *(978-0-87483-655-4(7))*; pap. 17.95 *(978-0-87483-650-9(6))* August Hse. Pubs., Inc.
McCaslin, Nellie. Angel of the Battlefield. 2003. (Players Press Nellie McCaslin Ser.). (Illus.). 20p. (YA). (gr. 4-12). pap. 5.00 *(978-0-88734-430-5(5))* Players Pr., Inc.
—The Bailiff's Wonderful Coat. 2003. (Players Press Nellie McCaslin Ser.). 55p. (J). (gr. 1-6). pap. 5.00 *(978-0-88734-453-4(4))* Players Pr., Inc.
—Bluebonnets. 2003. (Players Press Nellie McCaslin Ser.). 18p. (YA). (gr. 4-12). pap. 5.00 *(978-0-88734-439-8(9))* Players Pr., Inc.
—Brave New Banner. 2003. (Players Press Nellie McCaslin Ser.). (Illus.). 20p. (YA). (gr. 6-12). pap. 5.00 *(978-0-88734-436-7(4))* Players Pr., Inc.
—Broken Rehearsal. 2006. 16p. (gr. 6-12). pap. 6.00 *(978-0-88734-580-7(8))* Players Pr., Inc.
—Cold Face - Warm Heart. 2003. 20p. (J). (gr. k-6). pap. 5.00 *(978-0-88734-440-4(2))* Players Pr., Inc.
—The Legend of Minna Lamourrie. 2003. (Players Press Nellie McCaslin Ser.). (Illus.). 20p. (J). (gr. k-6). pap. 5.00 *(978-0-88734-438-1(0))* Players Pr., Inc.
—Legends in Action: Ten Plays of Ten Lands. 2003. (Plays & Play Collections). (Illus.). xii, 142p. (J). pap. 20.00 *(978-0-88734-633-0(2))* Players Pr., Inc.
—Paul Bunyan: Lumberjack. 2003. (Players Press Nellie McCaslin Ser.). 55p. (Orig.). (J). (gr. 1-6). pap. 5.00 *(978-0-88734-477-0(1))* Players Pr., Inc.
—A Straight Shooter (Playscript) 2003. (Players Press Nellie McCaslin Ser.). 16p. (YA). (gr. 6-12). pap. 5.00 *(978-0-88734-429-9(1))* Players Pr., Inc.
—Three Meals a Day. 2003. 55p. (J). (gr. 1-7). pap. 5.00 *(978-0-88734-445-9(3))* Players Pr., Inc.
—Too Many Cooks. 2003. (Players Press Nellie McCaslin Ser.). (Illus.). 20p. (J). pap. 5.00 *(978-0-88734-434-3(8))* Players Pr., Inc.
McCullough, L. E. Classroom Plays for Social Studies America in the 1800s, 4 vols. Mason, Mark, illus. 2003. 48p. (J). per. 7.99 *(978-1-56472-242-3(2))* Edupress, Inc.
—Classroom Plays for Social Studies American Biographies, 4. Mason, Mark, illus. 2003. 48p. (J). per. 7.99 *(978-1-56472-243-0(0))* Edupress, Inc.
—Classroom Plays for Social Studies Ancient Civilizations, 4 vols. Mason, Mark, illus. 2003. 48p. (J). per. 7.99 *(978-1-56472-240-9(6))* Edupress, Inc.
—Classroom Plays for Social Studies Early America, 4 vols. Mason, Mark, illus. 2003. 48p. (J). per. 7.99 *(978-1-56472-241-6(4))* Edupress, Inc.
McDonald, Trevy. Time Will Tell. 2nd ed. 2017. (ENG., Illus.). 390p. *(978-0-9670712-2-0(4))* zReyomi Publishing.
McGregor, Rex. Girls on the Brink: Seven Female-Forward Plays for Young Adults. 2016. (ENG.). 72p. pap. 7.95 *(978-1-62088-584-0(0))* YouthPlays.
McKinnon, Robert Scott. The Tooth Fairy Came to Gopher Gulch. 2010. 64p. (J). 3.00 *(978-0-9651943-4-1(5))* McKinnon, Robert Scott.
McLaren, Maria. Seven with One Blow. 2003. (Theater for Young Audiences Ser.). 24p. (J). (gr. 1-6). pap. 6.00 *(978-0-88734-517-3(4))* Players Pr., Inc.
Mead, Maggie. Suffrage Sisters: The Fight for Liberty. Feeney, Siri Weber, illus. 2015. (Setting the Stage for Fluency Ser.). (ENG.). 40p. (J). (gr. 3-5). lib. bdg. 27.99 *(978-1-939656-68-1(0)*, cba2213e-f392-453b-a774-0004d9f7cb99) Red Chair Pr.
Meadows, Kelly. Dumping Ground: A Ten-Minute Comedy Duet. 2003. (YA). pap. 4.50 *(978-1-931805-94-0(6)*, 146A) Brooklyn Pubs.
—A Ghost of a Chance: A One-Act Comedy Play. 2003. (YA). pap. 4.50 *(978-1-932404-59-3(7)*, 757) Brooklyn Pubs.
—Not Ready! A Ten-Minute Comedy Monologue. 2003. 12p. (YA). pap. 4.50 *(978-1-932404-31-9(7)*, 284) Brooklyn Pubs.
—Teen Comedy Playlets: A Collection of Six Skits: Third Time's a Charm, 8 Booklets. 2003. (YA). pap. 19.95 *(978-1-932404-49-4(X)*, 911) Brooklyn Pubs.
—Ten Easy Steps to Humiliation: A Ten-Minute Comedy Duet. 2003. (YA). pap. 4.50 *(978-1-931805-96-4(2)*, 148A) Brooklyn Pubs.
Meighan, Julie. Drama Start Two Drama Activities & Plays for Children. 2012. 92p. pap. *(978-0-9568966-1-2(8))* JemBks.
—Stage Start 20 Plays for Children. 2013. 76p. pap. *(978-0-9568966-2-9(6))* JemBks.
Mercati, Cindy. Faces of Freedom. 2003. 48p. (YA). pap. 6.50 *(978-1-58342-199-4(8)*, F81) Dramatic Publishing Co.
Middleton, Alasdair. The Enchanted Pig. 2007. (Oberon Plays for Young People Ser.). (ENG.). 80p. per. 14.95 *(978-1-84002-717-4(7)*, 900241305) Oberon Bks., Ltd. GBR. Dist: Macmillan.
Mihalko, Ross & Swift, Donna. Ant & the Grasshopper (Play) 2013. (ENG.). pap. 8.95 *(978-0-573-70111-5(3)*, French, Samuel , Inc.) Concord Theatricals.
—Beanstalk! the Play! 2012. (ENG.). 32p. (J). pap. 8.95 *(978-0-573-70113-9(X)*, French, Samuel , Inc.) Concord Theatricals.
Mini Plays & Folktale Plays that Build Reading Skills. 2005. (J). pap. *(978-1-60015-036-4(5))* Steps To Literacy, LLC.
Molnar, Ferenc. Liliom. 2003. 68p. (YA). (gr. 4-12). pap. 7.50 *(978-0-88734-798-6(3))* Players Pr., Inc.
Morgan, Robert F. The Partners: A Three Act Play. 2007. 20p. (J). (gr. 6). pap. 25.00 *(978-1-885679-05-5(X))* Morgan Foundation Pubs.: International Published Innovations.
Morreale, Vin, Jr. The Day the Woods Were One. 2003. (Theater for Young Audiences Ser.). 20p. (Orig.). (J). (gr. 3-18). pap. 6.00 *(978-0-88734-507-4(7))* Players Pr., Inc.
—Nicky's Secret. 2003. 48p. (YA). pap. 6.50 *(978-1-58342-186-4(6)*, N53) Dramatic Publishing Co.
Morris, Kathleen. Lost & Found - a Children's Christmas Play. 2013. 32p. pap. *(978-1-927828-25-0(2))* Rouge Publishing.
Morss, Ben. Cinderella's Mice. Morss, Ben, . 2009. 48p. (J). mass mkt. 7.00 *(978-0-87440-216-2(6))* Baker's Plays.
Morton, Carlos. The Drop-Out. Landes, William-Alan, ed. 2003. (Players Press Carlos Morton Collection). 55p. (Orig.). (YA). (gr. 6-12). pap. 5.00 *(978-0-88734-443-5(7))* Players Pr., Inc.
—Drug-O. Landes, William-Alan, ed. 2003. (Carlos Morton Collection). 55p. (Orig.). (YA). (gr. 6-12). pap. 6.00 *(978-0-88734-444-2(5))* Players Pr., Inc.
—Los Fatherless. Landes, William-Alan, ed. 2003. (Players Press Carlos Morton Collection). 55p. (YA). (gr. 6-12). pap. 5.00 *(978-0-88734-376-6(7))* Players Pr., Inc.
Mowery, Milo. El Zorrito. 2014. (SPA & ENG.). 64p. (J). pap. 9.95 *(978-1-58342-992-1(1))* Dramatic Publishing Co.
Muir, Kerry. Three New Plays for Young Actors: From the Young Actor's Studio. 2004. (Limelight Ser.). (ENG., Illus.). 218p. (Orig.). pap. 19.99 *(978-0-87910-957-8(2)*, 0879109572, Limelight Editions) Leonard, Hal Corp.
Muschell, David. The Invisible Princess: A Full-Length Comedy-Dramatic Play. 2003. (YA). pap. 5.00 *(978-1-932404-67-8(8)*, 609) Brooklyn Pubs.
Nehls, David & Kelso, Betsy. The Great American Trailer Park Christmas Musical. 2014. 62p. pap. 10.00 *(978-0-8222-3104-2(2))* Dramatists Play Service, Inc.
Neipris, Janet. Jeremy & the Thinking Machine: A Musical for Young Audiences. 2004. 26p. (YA). pap. *(978-0-573-05139-5(9)*, French, Samuel , Inc.) Concord Theatricals.
Nesbit, E. Beautiful Stories from Shakespeare (Yesterday's Classics) 2006. (J). per. 11.95 *(978-1-59915-029-1(8))* Yesterday's Classics.
Nield, Maureen. How Different from Us. 2003. 28p. (YA). (gr. 4-12). pap. 5.00 *(978-0-88734-767-2(3))* Players Pr., Inc.
Nimmo, Paul. Will Shakespeare Save Us! Will Shakespeare Save the King! 2003. (Shakespeare Ser.). 58p. (J). (gr. k-8). pap. 12.00 *(978-0-88734-658-3(8))* Players Pr., Inc.
Nolan, Ernie. Snow White & the Seven Dwarfs as Performed by Professor TJ Barker's Troupe of Theatricals. 2011. (Illus.). 78p. pap. 7.50 *(978-1-58342-713-2(9))* Dramatic Publishing Co.
Norden, Barbara. Meteorite. 2004. (Oberon Modern Plays Ser.). (ENG.). 64p. pap. 14.95 *(978-1-84002-401-2(1)*, 900242770) Oberon Bks., Ltd. GBR. Dist: Macmillan.
Novel Units. Much Ado about Nothing Novel Units Teacher Guide. 2019. (ENG.). (YA). pap. 12.99 *(978-1-56137-925-5(5)*, Novel Units, Inc.) Classroom Library Co.
Nyberg, Judy. Just Pretend. 2007. pap. 12.95 *(978-1-59647-259-4(6))* Good Year Bks.
Nyman, Debbie & Wortzman, Ricki. The 10 Best Plays. 2008. 14.99 *(978-1-55448-503-1(7))* Scholastic Library Publishing.
Oglesby, Tamsin. The Mouse & His Child. 2012. (Oberon Plays for Young People Ser.). (ENG.). 90p. pap. *(978-1-84943-465-2(4)*, 513701) Oberon Bks., Ltd.
Orr, Wendy. Nim's Island. 2008. lib. bdg. 17.20 *(978-1-4178-1829-7(8))* Turtleback.
Osment, Philip. Plays for Young People. 2006. (Oberon Modern Playwrights Ser.). (ENG.). 218p. per. 26.95 *(978-1-84002-272-8(8)*, 900242684) Oberon Bks., Ltd. GBR. Dist: Macmillan.
Owen, Gary. Mrs Reynolds & the Ruffian. 2011. (Oberon Modern Plays Ser.). (ENG.). 136p. (gr. 7). pap. 14.95 *(978-1-84943-065-4(9)*, 900241612) Oberon Bks., Ltd. GBR. Dist: Macmillan.
Pagnol, Marcel. Manon des Sources, Level C. (FRE.). (YA). (gr. 7-12). 9.95 *(978-0-8219-1865-4(6)*, 40341) EMC/Paradigm Publishing.
Palacios, John, illus. Readers' Theater: Scripts for Young Readers: How the Tiger Got Its Stripes. 2009. 16p. (J). pap. 16.95 *(978-1-60184-162-9(0))* Primary Concepts, Inc.
Palacious, John, illus. Readers' Theater Paul Bunyan: Scripts for Young Readers. 2009. 16p. (J). pap. *(978-1-60184-144-5(2))* Primary Concepts, Inc.
Perkins, David & Dooley, Caroline. The Selfish Giant: A Children's Musical. 2003. (ENG.). xv, 28p. (J). pap. *(978-0-573-08123-1(9)*, French, Samuel , Inc.) Concord Theatricals.
Peter, David, et al. Cyrano de Bergerac: A Heroic Comedy in Five Acts. (Classics Illustrated Ser.). (Illus.). 52p. (YA). pap. 4.95 *(978-1-57209-019-4(7))* Classics International Entertainment, Inc.
Peters, Andrew & Peters, Polly. Dragon Chaser. (ENG., Illus.). 64p. 19.99 *(978-0-7502-3457-3(1))* Hodder & Stoughton GBR. Dist: Trafalgar Square Publishing.
Pettus, Tiffany. The Sweetness of Christmas: The Candy Cane Story. 2009. 54p. pap. 19.95 *(978-1-4327-4964-4(1))* Outskirts Pr., Inc.
Phillips, Louis. Late Night in the Rain Forest. Strozier, M. Stefan & Torke, Kyle, eds. 2009. 122p. pap. 17.99 *(978-1-935444-99-2(9))* World Audience Pubs.
Polsky, Milton, et al. Houdini - The King of Escapes: Playscript. 2003. (Musicals Ser.). 32p. (Orig.). (J). (gr. 3-12). pap. 8.00 *(978-0-88734-510-4(7))* Players Pr., Inc.
Pop-Out Play-Pak: Bats. Orig. Title: Child's Play. (Illus.). 14p. (J). (gr. -1-4). reprint ed. *(978-1-881469-81-0(6))* Safari, Ltd.
Pop-Out Play-Pak: Butterfly. Orig. Title: Child's Play. (Illus.). 14p. (J). (gr. -1-4). reprint ed. *(978-1-881469-78-0(6))* Safari, Ltd.
Pop-Out Play-Pak: Frogs. Orig. Title: Child's Play. (Illus.). 14p. (J). (gr. -1-4). reprint ed. *(978-1-881469-82-7(4))* Safari, Ltd.
Pop-Out Play-Pak: Spider. Orig. Title: Child's Play. (Illus.). 14p. (J). (gr. -1-4). reprint ed. *(978-1-881469-79-7(4))* Safari, Ltd.
Pop-Out Play-Pak: Time Tunnel. Orig. Title: Child's Play. (Illus.). 24p. (J). (gr. -1-4). *(978-1-881469-76-6(X))* Safari, Ltd.
Porter, Steven. The Prairie Man. 2003. 62p. (YA). pap. 6.00 *(978-0-9625372-0-2(9))* Phantom Pubns., Inc.
Porter Zasada, Marc. Alice Through the Looking Glass - a Children's Play. 2011. 62p. pap. 19.95 *(978-0-557-74883-9(6))* Lulu Pr., Inc.
Post, Sam. Responsibility: A Comedy Skit, 3 Booklets. 2003. (YA). pap. 9.00 *(978-1-932404-40-1(6)*, 326) Brooklyn Pubs.
Potter, Beatrix. Two Beatrix Potter Plays. 2010. (Oberon Modern Plays Ser.). (ENG.). 96p. pap. 14.95 *(978-1-84002-519-4(0)*, 900242863) Oberon Bks., Ltd. GBR. Dist: Macmillan.
Pratchett, Terry & Holmes, Matthew. Collins Musicals - Terry Pratchett's the Amazing Maurice & His Educated Rodents, 1 vol. 2011. (and C Black Musicals Ser.). (ENG.). 76p. (J). (gr. 4). pap. 47.95 incl. audio compact disk *(978-1-4081-4563-0(4))* HarperCollins Pubs. Ltd. GBR. Dist: Independent Pubs. Group.
Pratt, Anna Bronson Alcott. Comic Tragedies. 2010. 332p. pap. 31.75 *(978-1-144-42717-5(7))* Creative Media Partners, LLC.
Pugliano-Martin, Carol; Flounders. Milton the Mole. Flounders, Anne, ed. 2004. (Reader's Theater Content-Area Concepts Ser.). (ENG.). (J). (gr. 1). 22.00 *(978-1-4108-2295-6(8)*, A22958) Benchmark Education Co.
Pullman, Philip. The Firework Maker's Daughter. 2011. (Oberon Modern Plays Ser.). (ENG.). 64p. (gr. 2). pap. 14.95 *(978-1-84943-069-2(1)*, 900241615) Oberon Bks., Ltd. GBR. Dist: Macmillan.
—The Scarecrow & His Servant. 2009. (Oberon Modern Plays Ser.). (ENG.). 96p. (J). pap. 14.95 *(978-1-84002-899-7(8)*, 900241467) Oberon Bks., Ltd. GBR. Dist: Macmillan.
Pyle, Howard. The Wonder Clock. 2009. (Illus.). 440p. pap. 15.95 *(978-1-59915-339-1(4))* Yesterday's Classics.
Quinn, Stephanie. Little Stars Creative Drama for Preschoolers. 2008. 100p. per. 19.95 *(978-0-9773099-5-5(9))* Quinn Entertainment.
Rabushka, Jerry. The Casket & the Casserole: A Ten-Minute Comedy Duet. 2003. 16p. (YA). pap. 4.50 *(978-1-932404-23-4(6)*, 159A) Brooklyn Pubs.
—The Frying Pan: A Dramatic Skit, 4 Booklets. 2003. (YA). pap. 4.50 *(978-1-932404-37-1(6)*, 323) Brooklyn Pubs.
—On Location: A Ten-Minute Comedy Duet. 2003. 16p. (YA). pap. 4.50 *(978-1-931805-97-1(0)*, 149A) Brooklyn Pubs.
—Saucy Mamasita: A Dramatic Monologue. 2003. (YA). pap. 4.50 *(978-1-932404-30-2(9)*, 283) Brooklyn Pubs.
—White Elephant: Comedy Monologue. 2003. (YA). pap. 4.50 *(978-1-932404-08-1(2)*, 276) Brooklyn Pubs.
Rajagopal, P. & Pullens, Evelien. Aiyappan & the Magic Horse. 2005. (Illus.). 70p. *(978-81-8146-153-7(3))* Tulika Pubs.
Ramirez, Frank. The Bee Attitudes: And 5 More Extraordinary Plays for Ordinary Days. 2007. 84p. (J). pap. 12.95 *(978-0-7880-2435-1(3))* CSS Publishing Co.
Ransome, Arthur. Swallows & Amazons. 2012. (ENG.). 120p. pap. 24.95 *(978-1-84842-237-7(7))* Hern, Nick Bks., Ltd. GBR. Dist: Consortium Bk. Sales & Distribution.
Rapier, Darren. The Little Mermaid. 2008. (ENG.). 68p. pap. 16.95 *(978-0-9556798-1-0(8))* Tualen GBR. Dist: Lulu Pr., Inc.
Raspanti, Celeste. The Terezin Promise. 2004. 40p. (YA). pap. 4.50 *(978-1-58342-200-7(5)*, TF7) Dramatic Publishing Co.
Ravenhill, Mark. Plays for Young People: Citizenship; Scenes from Family Life; Totally over You. 2010. (Play Anthologies Ser.). (ENG., Illus.). 176p. pap. 24.95 *(978-1-4081-2861-9(6)*, 900070275, Methuen Drama) Bloomsbury Publishing Plc GBR. Dist: Macmillan.
Rechenspiele. (Duden-Schuelerhilfen Ser.). (GER.). 79p. (J). (gr. 4-5). *(978-3-411-02611-1(1))* Bibliographisches Institut & F. A. Brockhaus AG DEU. Dist: International Bk. Import Service, Inc.
Rector, Rebecca Kraft. Drama. 2016. (Essential Literary Genres Ser.). (ENG., Illus.). 112p. (J). (gr. 6-12). lib. bdg. 41.36 *(978-1-68078-378-0(5)*, 23521, Essential Library) ABDO Publishing Co.
Redmond, Diane. Odyssey, Vol. 4. unabr. ed. 2003. (Curtain Up Ser.: Vol. 4). (Illus.). 48p. (J). (gr. 1-4). pap. 15.00 *(978-0-7136-4628-3(4)*, A&C Black) Bloomsbury Publishing Plc GBR. Dist: Players Pr., Inc.
Reese, Kevin M., adapted by. Chicken Little Henny Penny (Non-Musical Version) 2004. (J). *(978-1-932240-60-3(8))* KMR Scripts.
—The Pied Piper (Non-Musical Version) 2004. (J). 4.00 net. *(978-1-932240-62-7(4))* KMR Scripts.
—The True Story of the Tortoise & the Hare (Non-Musical Version) 2005. (J). 4.00 net. *(978-1-932240-64-1(0))* KMR Scripts.
Reese, Kevin M., adapted by. Chicken Little Henny Penny. Reese, Kevin M., . 2004. (J). 4.00 *(978-1-932240-59-7(4))* KMR Scripts.
—The Pied Piper. Reese, Kevin M., . 2004. (J). 4.00 net. *(978-1-932240-61-0(6))* KMR Scripts.
—The True Story of the Tortoise & the Hare. Reese, Kevin M., . 2005. (J). 4.00 net. *(978-1-932240-63-4(2))* KMR Scripts.
Rickards, Lynne. Four Clever Brothers 1 Pathfinders. Bernstein, Galia, illus. 2017. (Cambridge Reading Adventures Ser.). (ENG.). 24p. pap. 7.35 *(978-1-108-41081-6(2))* Cambridge Univ. Pr.
Riosley, Lane. The Attack of the Crab Nebula. (Lucky Hightops & the Cosmic Cat Patrol Ser.: No. 2). (Illus.). (J). (gr. 2-8). pap. 4.00 *(978-1-57514-268-5(6)*, 1027) Encore Performance Publishing.
—Captives of the Dog Star. (Lucky Hightops & the Cosmic Cat Patrol Ser.: No. 1). (Illus.). (J). (gr. 2-8). pap. 4.00 *(978-1-57514-267-8(8)*, 1026) Encore Performance Publishing.
—Polaris, the Robot King. (Lucky Hightops & the Cosmic Cat Patrol Ser.: No. 3). (Illus.). (J). (gr. 2-8). pap. 4.00 *(978-1-57514-269-2(4)*, 1028) Encore Performance Publishing.
—Revenge of the Dog Robber. (Lucky Hightops & the Cosmic Cat Patrol Ser.: No. 4). (Illus.). (J). (gr. 2-8). pap. 4.00 *(978-1-57514-270-8(8)*, 1116) Encore Performance Publishing.
Rizzo, Joe. On the Same Frequency: A One-Act Comedy Play. 2003. (YA). pap. 4.50 *(978-1-932404-63-0(5)*, 761) Brooklyn Pubs.
Robinette, Joseph & Tierney, Thomas. The Fabulous Fable Factory. 2004. 56p. (YA). pap. 6.50 *(978-1-58342-216-8(1)*, F82) Dramatic Publishing Co.
Robinette, Joseph. Dorothy Meets Alice or the Wizard of Wonderland. 2004. 48p. (YA). pap. 6.50 *(978-1-58342-221-2(8)*, D82) Dramatic Publishing Co.
Romer, Marcus & Hinton, S. E. Rumble Fish. 2003. (Illus.). 62p. pap. 6.25 *(978-1-58342-154-3(8)*, R69) Dramatic Publishing Co.
Rooyackers, Paul, et al. 101 Dialogues, Sketches & Skits: Instant Theatre for Teens & Tweens. 2014. (SmartFun Activity Bks.). (ENG., Illus.). 144p. (J). (gr. 1). pap. 17.99 *(978-0-89793-677-4(9)*, Hunter Hse.) Turner Publishing Co.
Rosenberg, Joe, ed. Aplauso! Hispanic Children's Theater. 2nd ed. 2003. (Latin-American Play Anthologies Ser.). (Illus.). 274p. (YA). (gr. 4-10). pap. 10.00 *(978-1-55885-127-6(5)*, Piñata Books) Arte Publico Pr.
Ross, Kathryn & Pruitt, Kimberly. Artic Skits. Utley, David, illus. 2006. 88p. (J). per. 24.95 *(978-0-9725803-9-7(5))* Children's Publishing.
Ruditis, Paul. The Devil's in the Diva: The Four Dorothys; Everyone's a Critic. 2010. (Drama! Ser.). (ENG.). 496p. (YA). (gr. 7). pap. 9.99 *(978-1-4424-1444-0(8)*, Simon Pulse) Simon Pulse.
—Everyone's a Critic. 2007. (Drama! Ser.). (ENG.). 256p. (YA). (gr. 7-12). pap. 12.99 *(978-1-4169-3392-2(1)*, Simon Pulse) Simon Pulse.
—The Four Dorothys. 2007. (Drama! Ser.: No. 1). (ENG., Illus.). 288p. (YA). (gr. 7-12). pap. 11.99 *(978-1-4169-3391-5(3)*, Simon Pulse) Simon Pulse.
Rumble, P. Barry. Full Moon. 2003. (One Act Plays Ser.). 14p. (J). pap. 5.00 *(978-0-88734-422-0(4))* Players Pr., Inc.
Russell, Willy. Our Day Out: Improving Standards in English Through Drama at Key Stage 3 & GCSE. Gunton, Mark, ed. 2011. (Critical Scripts Ser.). (ENG., Illus.). 160p. pap. *(978-1-4081-3485-6(3)*, 17252, Methuen Drama) Bloomsbury Publishing Plc.
Ryan, Tammy. The Music Lesson. 2003. 72p. (YA). pap. 6.50 *(978-1-58342-207-6(2)*, MD8) Dramatic Publishing Co.
Sabato, George F. The New Improved Santa. Landes, William-Alan, ed. 2003. (Theater for Young Audiences Ser.). 55p. (Orig.). (J). (gr. k-7). pap. 5.00 *(978-0-88734-457-2(7))* Players Pr., Inc.
Sanders, D. J. Metatheatre: A Ten-Minute Comedy Duet. 2003. (YA). pap. 4.50 *(978-1-932404-43-2(0)*, 131A) Brooklyn Pubs.
Schlitz, Laura Amy. A Drowned Maiden's Hair: A Melodrama. 2006. (ENG., Illus.). 400p. (J). (gr. 5-9). 16.99 *(978-0-7636-2930-4(8))* Candlewick Pr.
—Good Masters! Sweet Ladies! Voices from a Medieval Village. Byrd, Robert, illus. (ENG.). 96p. (J). (gr. 5-9). 2011. pap. 7.99 *(978-0-7636-5094-0(3))* 2008. pap. 12.99 *(978-0-7636-4332-4(7))* Candlewick Pr.
Schnitzler, Arthur. Anatol. Landes, William-Alan, ed. unabr. ed. 2003. (Players Press Classic Plays Ser.). (Illus.). 68p. (J). (gr. 4-6). pap. 7.50 *(978-0-88734-817-4(3))* Players Pr., Inc.
Schnupp, Al. Censored. 2003. (Full-Length Plays Ser.). 76p. (YA). (gr. 8-12). pap. 15.00 *(978-0-88734-868-6(8))* Players Pr., Inc.
Schoenfeld, Jeff. Information: A Ten-Minute Comedy Duet. 2003. 16p. (YA). pap. 4.50 *(978-1-932404-24-1(4)*, 160A) Brooklyn Pubs.
Schreibspiele. (Duden-Schuelerhilfen Ser.). (GER.). 79p. (J). (gr. 3-4). *(978-3-411-02612-8(X))* Bibliographisches Institut & F. A. Brockhaus AG DEU. Dist: International Bk. Import Service, Inc.
Schroeder-Arce, Roxanne. Mariachi Girl. 2014. 53p. (J). pap. 9.50 *(978-1-58342-932-7(8))* Dramatic Publishing Co.
Shakespeare, William. As You Like It. 2008. (Easy Reading Shakespeare Ser.). (ENG., Illus.). 72p. pap., act. bk. ed. 10.95 *(978-1-55576-329-9(4)*, EDSC301B) EDCON Publishing Group.
—Julius Caesar. abr. ed. 2011. (Go Shakespeare - Set 1 Ser.). (ENG.). (YA). (gr. 9-12). 49.93 *(978-1-61641-423-8(5)*, Abdo & Daughters) ABDO Publishing Co.
—Macbeth. Cheung, Charly, illus. 2013. (William Shakespeare Ser.). (ENG.). 64p. pap. 7.95 *(978-1-906230-47-0(1))* Real Reads Ltd. GBR. Dist: Casemate Pubs. & Bk. Distributors, LLC.
—The Merchant of Venice. abr. ed. 2011. (Go Shakespeare - Set 1 Ser.). (ENG.). (YA). (gr. 9-12). 49.93 *(978-1-61641-426-9(X)*, Abdo & Daughters) ABDO Publishing Co.
—A Midsummer Night's Dream. Cheung, Charly, illus. 2013. (William Shakespeare Ser.). (ENG.). 64p. pap. 7.95 *(978-1-906230-44-9(7))* Real Reads Ltd. GBR. Dist: Casemate Pubs. & Bk. Distributors, LLC.
—Pyramus & Thisbe: A Dramatization Arranged from Shakespeare's A Midsummer Night's Dream. Landes, William-Alan, ed. rev. ed. 2003. (One Act Plays Ser.). 55p. (Orig.). (J). (gr. 4-12). pap. 5.00 *(978-0-88734-103-8(9))* Players Pr., Inc.
—Romeo & Juliet. Cheung, Charly, illus. 2013. (William Shakespeare Ser.). (ENG.). 64p. pap. 7.95 *(978-1-906230-45-6(5))* Real Reads Ltd. GBR. Dist: Casemate Pubs. & Bk. Distributors, LLC.
—The Tempest. 2008. (Shakespeare Ser.: Level 2). (Illus.). 72p. pap., act. bk. ed. 10.95 *(978-1-55576-327-5(8)*, EDSC-201B) EDCON Publishing Group.
—The Tempest. Cheung, Charly, illus. 2014. (William Shakespeare Ser.). (ENG.). 64p. pap. 7.95 *(978-1-906230-46-3(3))* Real Reads Ltd. GBR. Dist: Casemate Pubs. & Bk. Distributors, LLC.
—Twelfth Night: Classicscript. Landes, William-Alan, ed. abr. ed. 2003. (Shakespeare Ser.: Vol. 3). 68p. (J). (gr. 4-12). pap. 7.00 *(978-0-88734-530-2(1))* Players Pr., Inc.
—The Two Gentlemen of Verona. 2008. (Easy Reading Shakespeare Ser.). (ENG., Illus.). 72p. pap., act. bk. ed. 10.95 *(978-1-55576-350-3(2)*, EDSC-305B) EDCON Publishing Group.
Shapiro, Gordon & Crafts, Gregory. Super Sidekick: The Musical. 2012. (ENG.). 55p. (J). pap. 8.95 *(978-0-573-70096-5(6)*, French, Samuel , Inc.) Concord Theatricals.
Shaw, George Bernard. Annajanska. Landes, William-Alan, ed. 2003. (George Bernard Shaw Collection). 20p. (YA). (gr. 6-12). 8.00 *(978-0-88734-863-1(7))* Players Pr., Inc.
—The Dark Lady of the Sonnets. abr. ed. 2005. (Stratford Festival Ser.). (gr. 9-12). *(978-0-660-17979-7(2))* Canadian Broadcasting Corp./Societe Radio-Canada.
—The Inca of Perusalem. Landes, William-Alan, ed. 2003. (Players Press G. B. Shaw Collection). 28p. (YA). (gr. 4-12). 8.00 *(978-0-88734-864-8(5))* Players Pr., Inc.
—O'Flaherty V. C. Landes, William-Alan, ed. 2003. (George Bernard Shaw Collection). 28p. (YA). (gr. 6-12). pap. 8.00 *(978-0-88734-350-6(3))* Players Pr., Inc.
Shepard, Aaron. Folktales on Stage: Children's Plays for Readers Theater, with 16 Reader's Theatre Play Scripts from World Folk & Fairy Tales & Legends, Including Asian, African, Middle Eastern, & Native American. 2004. 180p. pap. 10.00 *(978-0-938497-20-2(0))* Shepard Pubns.
Shepherd, C. A., et al. The Sly Fox (Playscript) 2003. (Musicals for Young Audiences Ser.). 32p. (Orig.). (YA). (gr. 3-12). pap. 8.00 *(978-0-88734-503-6(4))* Players Pr., Inc.

Shockey, Marilyn. What's a Wolf to Do? (Musical) 42p. (YA). pap. 7.50 *(978-1-58342-182-6(3),* WD7) Dramatic Publishing Co.

Shucart, Deborah. ABC Scripts. 2010. 120p. 21.49 *(978-1-4520-0407-5(2));* pap. 10.99 *(978-1-4520-0406-8(4))* AuthorHouse.

Siddons, Annie. Rapunzel. 2006. (Oberon Modern Plays Ser.). (ENG.). 72p. pap. 15.95 *(978-1-84002-698-6(7),* 900241290) Oberon Bks., Ltd. GBR. Dist: Macmillan.

Simandan, Voicu Mihnea. The Ironman. A Play. 2009. (ENG.). 32p. pap. 15.10 *(978-0-557-06395-6(7))* Lulu Pr., Inc.

Simonson, Louise & Mason, Jane. Junior High Drama, 4 vols. Cho, Sumin, illus. 2018. (Junior High Drama Ser.). (ENG.). 64p. (J). (gr. 3-6). 106.60 *(978-1-4965-4754-5(3),* 26528); pap., pap., pap. 27.80 *(978-1-4965-7419-0(2),* 28679) Capstone. (Stone Arch Bks.).

SINGH, H. Happy peace Day. 2008. 52p. per. 15.95 *(978-1-4357-0773-3(7))* Lulu Pr., Inc.

Smith, Carrie. Humpty Dumpty's Fall. 2008. (Reader's Theater Nursery Rhymes & Songs Ser.). (Illus.). 48p. (J). (gr. k-1). pap. *(978-1-60437-958-7(8))* Benchmark Education Co.

—The Jumping Monkeys. Harpster, Steve, illus. 2009. (Reader's Theater Nursery Rhymes & Songs Set B Ser.). 48p. (J). pap. *(978-1-60859-155-8(7))* Benchmark Education Co.

—Mary Has a Little Lamb. 2008. (Reader's Theater Nursery Rhymes & Songs Ser.). (Illus.). 48p. (J). (gr. k-1). pap. *(978-1-60437-978-5(2))* Benchmark Education Co.

—One Silly Hey Diddle Day. 2008. (Reader's Theater Nursery Rhymes & Songs Ser.). (Illus.). 48p. (J). (gr. k-1). pap. *(978-1-60437-963-1(4))* Benchmark Education Co.

—Where Are Bo Peep's Sheep? Abbott, Jason, illus. 2009. (Reader's Theater Nursery Rhymes & Songs Set B Ser.). 48p. (J). pap. *(978-1-60859-171-8(9))* Benchmark Education Co.

Snyder, Geraldine Ann. Johnny Appleseed: Musical. 2003. (Illus.). 41p. (YA). pap. 6.95 *(978-1-58342-127-7(0),* J04) Dramatic Publishing Co.

Soto, Gary. Novio Boy: A Play. 2006. 78p. (gr. 7-12). 17.00 *(978-0-7569-6684-3(1))* Perfection Learning Corp.

SparkNotes. King Lear (No Fear Shakespeare) 2003. (No Fear Shakespeare Ser.: 6). (Illus.). 320p. pap. 7.99 *(978-1-58663-853-5(X),* Spark Notes) Sterling Publishing Co., Inc.

—Macbeth (No Fear Shakespeare) 2003. (No Fear Shakespeare Ser.: 1). (Illus.). 240p. pap. 7.99 *(978-1-58663-846-7(7),* Spark Notes) Sterling Publishing Co., Inc.

—Much Ado about Nothing (No Fear Shakespeare) 2004. (No Fear Shakespeare Ser.: 11). (Illus.). 256p. per. 6.95 *(978-1-4114-0101-3(8),* Spark Notes) Sterling Publishing Co., Inc.

—The Tempest (No Fear Shakespeare) 2003. (No Fear Shakespeare Ser.: 5). (Illus.). 224p. pap. 6.99 *(978-1-58663-849-8(1),* Spark Notes) Sterling Publishing Co., Inc.

Spiers, Julia, illus. Fairy Tale Play: A Pop-Up Storytelling Book. 2019. (ENG.). 8p. (J). (gr. 1-4). 19.99 *(978-1-78627-428-1(0),* King, Laurence Publishing) Orion Publishing Group, Ltd. GBR. Dist: Hachette Bk. Group.

Sr. Hariette. Princess Frisky. 2008. 28p. pap. 13.99 *(978-1-4389-0466-5(5))* AuthorHouse.

Stevenson, Augusta. Children's Classics in Dramatic Form, Book Two. 2017. (ENG., Illus.). (J). pap. *(978-0-649-48533-8(5))* Trieste Publishing Pty Ltd.

Stevenson, Robert Louis. Treasure Island. 2003. (More for Teens Ser.). 64p. (Orig.). (YA). (gr. 6-12). pap. 6.00 *(978-0-88734-412-1(7))* Players Pr., Inc.

Stewart, Kelly, ed. Readers' Theater: Scripts for Young Readers. Palacios, John, illus. 2009. 16p. (J). pap. 16.95 *(978-1-60184-154-4(X));* pap. 16.95 *(978-1-60184-146-9(9));* pap. 16.95 *(978-1-60184-148-3(5));* pap. 16.95 *(978-1-60184-150-6(7));* pap. 16.95 *(978-1-60184-152-0(3));* pap. 16.95 *(978-1-60184-160-5(4));* pap. 16.95 *(978-1-60184-166-7(3))* Primary Concepts, Inc.

—Readers' Theater: Scripts for Young Readers: the Monkey & the Crocodile. Palacios, John, illus. 2009. 16p. (J). pap. 16.95 *(978-1-60184-164-3(7))* Primary Concepts, Inc.

—Readers' Theater: Scripts for Young Readers: the Peach Boy. Palacios, John, illus. 2009. 16p. (J). pap. 16.95 *(978-1-60184-156-8(6))* Primary Concepts, Inc.

—Readers' Theater: Scripts for Young Readers: the Spear Throwing Contest. Palacios, John, illus. 2009. 16p. (J). pap. 16.95 *(978-1-60184-158-2(2))* Primary Concepts, Inc.

Stewart, Kelly, retold by. Readers' Theater Stone Soup: Scripts for Young Readers. 2008. (Illus.). 16p. (J). 12.95 *(978-1-60184-121-6(3))* Primary Concepts, Inc.

—Readers' Theater the Magic Porridge Pot: Scripts for Young Readers: the Magic Porridge Pot. 2008. (Illus.). 16p. (J). 12.95 *(978-1-60184-117-9(5))* Primary Concepts, Inc.

—Readers' Theater the Mitten: Scripts for Young Readers: the Mitten. 2008. (Illus.). 16p. (J). 12.95 *(978-1-60184-123-0(X))* Primary Concepts, Inc.

—Readers' Theater the Princess & the Pea: Scripts for Young Readers: the Princess & the Pea. 2008. (Illus.). 16p. (J). 12.95 *(978-1-60184-115-5(9))* Primary Concepts, Inc.

Stickland, Eugene. Two Plays: Sitting on Paradise & a Guide to Mourning. 2003. (Plays & Play Collections). 168p. (YA). (gr. 6-12). pap. 15.00 *(978-0-88734-931-7(5))* Players Pr., Inc.

Strand, John. The Diaries. 2004. 104p. (J). pap. 6.50 *(978-1-58342-232-8(3),* D83) Dramatic Publishing Co.

Sturkie, Joan & Cassady, Marsh. Acting It Out - Junior. 2003. (Plays & Play Collections). 249p. (YA). (gr. 6-8). pap. 22.00 *(978-0-89390-240-7(3))* Resource Pubns., Inc.

Sugarek, Trisha. The Exciting Exploits of an Effervescent Elf. 2009. (ENG.). 58p. mass mkt. 9.95 *(978-0-87440-217-9(4))* Baker's Plays.

Surface, Mary Hall. Spirit Shall Fly: (play Script) 2007. (YA). 7.00 *(978-0-87602-418-8(5))* Family Plays.

Swajeski, Donna M. One Magic Kiss: Snow White & the Seven Dwarfs. 2014. 72p. (J). pap. 9.50 *(978-1-58342-948-8(4))* Dramatic Publishing Co.

—The Revolution Machine: Playscript. rev. ed. 2003. (Musicals Ser.). 55p. (Orig.). (J). (gr. 3-12). pap. 8.00 *(978-0-88734-511-1(5))* Players Pr., Inc.

Taylor, Ali. Cotton Wool. 2009. (ENG.). 80p. (J). pap. 18.95 *(978-1-85459-536-2(9))* Hern, Nick Bks., Ltd. GBR. Dist: Consortium Bk. Sales & Distribution.

Thistle, Louise. Little Red Snares the Wolf. (J). pap. 4.25 *(978-1-58342-036-2(3),* L49) Dramatic Publishing Co.

Thurston, Cheryl M. A Frog King's Daughter Is Nothing to Sneeze At: Playscript. 2003. (Musicals for Young Audiences Ser.). 32p. (Orig.). (YA). (gr. k-12). pap. 10.00 *(978-0-88734-513-5(1))* Players Pr., Inc.

Top Cat: Individual Title Six-Packs. (Story Steps Ser.). (gr. k-2). 32.00 *(978-0-7635-9851-8(8))* Rigby Education.

ToyBox Innovations, creator. Disney's Cinderella Read-along. 2006. (Disney's Read Along Ser.). (Illus.). 24p. (J). pap. *(978-0-7634-2171-7(5))* Walt Disney Records.

Treasure, Kevin A. Decisions Determine Destiny: Stories & Scenarios. 2010. 128p. pap. 13.99 *(978-1-4520-3102-6(9))* AuthorHouse.

Twead, Victoria. Morgan & the Martians. 2012. 60p. pap. *(978-1-78176-111-3(6))* FeedARead.com.

Umansky, Kaye. Cinderella. Crossland, Caroline, illus. 2012. 48p. *(978-0-88734-072-7(5))* Players Pr., Inc.

—Emperor's New Clothes. 2003. (Curtain Up Ser.: Vol. 6). (Illus.). 48p. (J). (gr. 1-4). pap. *(978-0-7136-4624-5(1),* A&C Black) Bloomsbury Publishing Plc.

—Sleeping Beauty. 2003. (Plays & Play Collections). (Illus.). 48p. (J). pap. 15.00 *(978-0-7136-5371-7(X),* A&C Black) Bloomsbury Publishing Plc GBR. Dist: Players Pr., Inc.

Varod, Gil, et al. Oedipus for Kids. 2009. (ENG.). 88p. pap. 9.95 *(978-0-573-66358-1(0),* French, Samuel , Inc.) Concord Theatricals.

Verrier, Steven. Don't Needle Me: A Ten-Minute Comedy Duet. 2003. 16p. (YA). pap. 4.50 *(978-1-932404-21-0(X),* 157A) Brooklyn Pubs.

—Golf Doctor: A Ten-Minute Comedy Duet. 2003. 16p. (YA). pap. 4.50 *(978-1-932404-41-8(4),* 108) Brooklyn Pubs.

Walker, Geof. William Shakespeare's 'A Midsummer Night's Dream' - a playscript for younger Students. 2006. 49p. pap. 19.45 *(978-1-4116-4407-6(7))* Lulu Pr., Inc.

Walker, George F. Moss Park & Tough! The Bobby & Tina Plays. 2015. (ENG.). 192p. pap. 19.95 *(978-0-88922-954-9(6))* Talonbooks, Ltd. CAN. Dist: Consortium Bk. Sales & Distribution.

Walter, Kristin. The Elves & the Shoemaker. 2010. (ENG.). 47p. (J). pap. 8.95 *(978-0-87440-730-3(3))* Baker's Plays.

—Hansel & Gretel. 2010. (ENG.). 59p. pap. 7.00 *(978-0-87440-269-8(7))* Baker's Plays.

—Last of the Dragons: Based on the sotry by Edith Nesbit. 2011. (ENG.). 41p. (J). pap. 8.95 *(978-0-87440-258-2(1))* Baker's Plays.

Washington Sr., Von H. The Journey Begins: Seven Stops to Freedom & Contact in Harmonia. 2009. 108p. 20.95 *(978-0-595-51190-7(2));* pap. 10.95 *(978-0-595-50468-8(X))* iUniverse, Inc.

Way, Charles. The Classic Fairytales. 2003. (ENG., Illus.). 204p. pap. 20.50 *(978-0-9542330-0-6(X))* Aurora Metro Pubns. Ltd. GBR. Dist: Publishers Group West (PGW).

—New Plays for Young People. 2014. (ENG., Illus.). 224p. pap. 24.95 *(978-1-906582-51-7(3))* Aurora Metro Pubns. Ltd. GBR. Dist: Publishers Group West (PGW).

—A Spell of Cold Weather. 2004. (ENG.). 96p. (gr. 1-7). pap. 18.95 *(978-0-9542330-8-2(5))* Aurora Metro Pubns. Ltd. GBR. Dist: Publishers Group West (PGW).

Way, Charles, adapted by. Classic Fairytales 2: Retold for the Stage. 2008. (ENG., Illus.). 250p. pap. 20.99 *(978-0-9551566-7-0(X))* Aurora Metro Pubns. Ltd. GBR. Dist: Publishers Group West (PGW).

Welch, Fay. The Magic Swap Shop. rev. ed. 2003. 48p. (YA). (gr. 3-12). pap. 6.00 *(978-0-88734-509-8(3))* Players Pr., Inc.

Westley, Joan. Readers' Theater the Emperor's New Clothes: Scripts for Young Readers. 2008. (Illus.). 32p. (J). 12.95 net. *(978-1-60184-125-4(6))* Primary Concepts, Inc.

Westley, Joan, retold by. Readers' Theater the Ugly Duckling: Scripts for Young Readers: the Ugly Duckling. 2008. (Illus.). 16p. (J). 12.95 *(978-1-60184-119-3(1))* Primary Concepts, Inc.

Wheeler, Jacque & Hartsfield, Mariella G. Tall Betsy & the Crackerbarrel Tales. 2003. 32p. (YA). (gr. k-12). pap. 6.00 *(978-0-88734-265-3(5))* Players Pr., Inc.

Wilde, Oscar. Oscar Wilde: Three Plays for Children. 2008. (Oberon Modern Playwrights Ser.). (ENG.). 128p. (J). pap. 18.95 *(978-1-84002-816-4(5),* 900241388) Oberon Bks., Ltd. GBR. Dist: Macmillan.

Williams, David L. The Bully. 2014. 53p. pap. 9.95 *(978-1-58342-906-8(9))* Dramatic Publishing Co.

Williams, Guy. Billy Budd. 2003. (More for Teens Ser.). 32p. (Orig.). (YA). (gr. 6-12). pap. 5.00 *(978-0-88734-415-2(1))* Players Pr., Inc.

—David & Goliath. 2003. (Players Press Classicscripts Ser.). (Illus.). 20p. (Orig.). (J). (gr. 3-18). pap. 6.00 *(978-0-88734-411-4(9))* Players Pr., Inc.

—Nicholas Nickleby: Playscript. 2003. (Ideal for Teens Ser.). 36p. (YA). (gr. 6-12). pap. 6.00 *(978-0-88734-515-9(8))* Players Pr., Inc.

Wilson, Jacqueline. Beauty & the Beast. Kavanagh, Peter, illus. 2012. *(978-0-88734-073-4(3))* Players Pr., Inc.

Wim, Coleman. Classroom Plays by Wim Coleman. 2012. 48p. (J). pap. 12.95 *(978-1-935178-26-2(1),* ChironBooks) Coleman/Perrin.

Winther, Barbara. India, Burma/Thailand, Vietnam. 2004. (Plays from Asian Tales Ser.: No. 1). 52p. (YA). (gr. 3-12). pap. 10.00 *(978-0-88734-486-2(0))* Players Pr., Inc.

—India, Indonesia/Malaysia, China. 2004. (Plays from Asian Tales Ser.: No. 2). 60p. (YA). (gr. 3-12). pap. 10.00 *(978-0-88734-487-9(9))* Players Pr., Inc.

—Japan & Korea. 2004. (Plays from Asian Tales Ser.: No. 3). 56p. (J). pap. 10.00 *(978-0-88734-488-6(7))* Players Pr., Inc.

Wistrand, Carolyn Nur. Beauty in Black Performance: Plays for African American Youth. 2006. (Illus.). (YA). 151p. *(978-1-59221-379-5(0));* (ENG., 158p. pap. *(978-1-59221-380-1(4))* Africa World Pr.

Wolak, Camilla H. Squire Gullible & the Dragon. rev. ed. 2003. (Theater for Young Audiences Ser.). 40p. (YA). (gr. 3-12). pap. 6.00 *(978-0-88734-508-1(5))* Players Pr., Inc.

Wood, David. The Twits. 62p. (YA). (gr. 6). pap. 6.25 *(978-1-58342-172-7(6),* TD6) Dramatic Publishing Co.

Wood, David & Dahl, Roald. Danny the Champion of the World. 2006. (ENG.). 70p. pap. *(978-0-573-15016-6(8),* French, Samuel , Inc.) Concord Theatricals.

Wood, Nick. Warrior Square. 2004. (ENG.). 64p. (gr. 5-17). pap. 18.95 *(978-0-9546912-0-2(2))* Aurora Metro Pubns. Ltd. GBR. Dist: Publishers Group West (PGW).

Wordwindow, illus. Shakespeare for Children Picture Book. 2007. 32p. (J). 14.95 *(978-0-9774484-8-7(7))* Wordwindow LLC.

Woyiwada, Allison. The Little Fir Tree: A Musical for Primary Children Based on a Story by Hans Christian Andersen. 2003. (Musicals for Young Audiences Ser.). 16p. (J). (gr. k-6). pap. 5.00 *(978-0-88734-428-2(3))* Players Pr., Inc.

Wright, Roosevelt, Jr. Deacon Willie's Last Will & Testament. 2004. (YA). *(978-0-943751-36-8(5))* Free Pr. Pubs.

—For Such a Time As This. 2004. (YA). 5.00 *(978-0-943751-31-3(4))* Free Pr. Pubs.

Wright, Roosevelt, Sr. The Prodigals. 2004. (YA). *(978-0-943751-35-1(7))* Free Pr. Pubs.

Wright, Roosevelt, Jr. Shoe Shine. 2004. (YA). 8.00 *(978-0-943751-38-2(1))* Free Pr. Pubs.

Wright, Roosevelt, Jr. & Wright, Roosevelt. Honey Babe's Treasure: A Black Heritage Drama in Two Acts. 2003. 24p. 6.00 *(978-0-943751-22-1(5))* Free Pr. Pubs.

Yee, Lauren D. How to Be the Perfect Parent: A Comedy Monologue. 2003. (YA). pap. 4.50 *(978-1-932404-35-7(X),* 288) Brooklyn Pubs.

—My Mother's Touch: A Dramatic Monologue. 2003. (YA). pap. 4.50 *(978-1-932404-34-0(1),* 287) Brooklyn Pubs.

Zacarias, Karen. Chasing George Washington: A White House Adventure. 2013. 59p. (J). pap. 9.95 *(978-1-58342-828-3(3))* Dramatic Publishing Co.

Zacarias, Karen. Einstein Is a Dummy. 2013. 80p. (J). pap. *(978-1-58342-825-2(9))* Dramatic Publishing Co.

Zacarias, Karen. Einstein Is a Dummy (small-Cast Musical) 2013. 62p. (J). pap. 9.95 *(978-1-58342-826-9(7))* Dramatic Publishing Co.

Zacarias, Karen. Looking for Roberto Clemente. 2013. (Illus.). 72p. (J). pap. *(978-1-58342-827-6(5))* Dramatic Publishing Co.

Zeder, Suzan. Wiley & the Hairy Man (musical) 2014. 69p. pap. 9.95 *(978-1-58342-916-7(6))* Dramatic Publishing Co.

Zindel, Paul. The Effect of Gamma Rays on Man-In-the-Moon Marigolds. 2005. (ENG.). 112p. (YA). (gr. 8-18). pap. 10.99 *(978-0-06-075738-0(8),* HarperTeen) HarperCollins Pubs.

Zuber, Diane. The Broken Doll A Musical Play for Christmas. 2006. (J). 29.95 *(978-0-9785551-0-8(4))* Zuber Publishing.

PLAYS—FICTION

Bryant, Annie. Out of Bounds. 2005. (Beacon Street Girls Ser.: No. 4). 255p. (J). 7.99 *(978-0-9746587-9-7(0),* Beacon Street Girls) B*tween Productions, Inc.

Butler, Dori Hillestad. The Ghost Backstage #3. Damant, Aurore, illus. 2014. (Haunted Library: 3). 128p. (J). (gr. 1-3). 6.99 *(978-0-448-46246-2(X),* Grosset & Dunlap) Penguin Young Readers Group.

Child, Lauren. I Can't Stop Hiccuping! 2010. (Charlie & Lola Ser.). lib. bdg. 13.55 *(978-0-606-10629-0(4))* Turtleback.

Christopher, Lawrence. The Tickle Fingers: Where Is Pinky? Christopher, Lawrence, illus. 2006. (ENG., Illus.). 24p. (J). (gr. -1-18). 9.95 *(978-0-9712278-3-5(7))* MF Unlimited.

Chronicle Books & ImageBooks. Little Horse: Finger Puppet Book: (Finger Puppet Book for Toddlers & Babies, Baby Books for First Year, Animal Finger Puppets) 2013. (Little Finger Puppet Board Bks.). (ENG., Illus.). 12p. (J). (gr. -1 — 1). 7.99 *(978-1-4521-1249-7(5))* Chronicle Bks. LLC.

Cook, Gina J. Just a Little Lion: A Little Cheetah Learns the Truth about Little Lions As We Learn the Truth about Little Lies. 2012. 38p. pap. 13.95 *(978-1-4497-6352-7(9),* WestBow Pr.) Author Solutions, LLC.

Doti, James. Jimmy Finds His Voice. Mertins, Lisa, illus. 2013. (J). 14.95 *(978-1-935204-47-3(5))* Salem Author Services.

Engelbreit, Mary. Queen of the Class. Engelbreit, Mary, illus. 2007. (Illus.). 24p. (J). 16.00 *(978-1-4223-6705-6(3))* DIANE Publishing Co.

Ficocelli, Elizabeth. Kid Tea, 0 vols. Dibley, Glin, illus. 2013. (ENG.). 36p. (J). (gr. -1-1). pap. 9.99 *(978-1-4778-4738-1(3),* 9781477847381, Two Lions) Amazon Publishing.

Gilman, Phoebe. Jillian Jiggs & the Secret Surprise. 2004. (J). (gr. -1-2). spiral bd. *(978-0-616-01655-8(7))* Canadian National Institute for the Blind/Institut National Canadien pour les Aveugles.

Graves, Damien. The Deadly Catch. 2006. (Midnight Library: 8). (ENG., Illus.). 170p. (J). (gr. 6-8). 18.69 *(978-0-439-89395-4(X))* Scholastic, Inc.

Hairston, Kennard Lee. Rosie Bear Plays Baseball. 2009. 48p. pap. 19.49 *(978-1-4389-7343-2(8))* AuthorHouse.

Harper, Charise Mericle. Just Grace, Star on Stage. 2014. (Just Grace Ser.: 9). (ENG., Illus.). 208p. (J). (gr. 1-4). pap. 7.99 *(978-0-544-22533-6(3),* 1563387, Clarion Bks.) HarperCollins Pubs.

Holmes, Sara. Operation Yes. 2009. 234p. (J). pap. *(978-0-545-20418-7(6))* Scholastic, Inc.

Hutchins, Hazel. Robyn's Monster Play, 1 vol. Cathcart, Yvonne, illus. 2008. (Formac First Novels Ser.). (ENG.). 64p. (J). (gr. 2-5). 5.95 *(978-0-88780-748-0(8),* 748); 14.95 *(978-0-88780-750-3(X),* 750) Formac Publishing Co., Ltd. CAN. Dist: Formac Lorimer Bks. Ltd.

Koch, Joann. Annie's World. 2009. 20p. (J). pap. 9.95 *(978-1-4327-4063-4(6))* Outskirts Pr., Inc.

Korda, Lerryn. It's Vacation Time: Playtime with Little Nye. Korda, Lerryn, illus. 2010. (Playtime with Little Nye Ser.). (ENG., Illus.). 26p. (J). (— 1). 8.99 *(978-0-7636-4813-8(2))* Candlewick Pr.

Kristina Takes the Stage. 2008. (Illus.). 56p. (J). mass mkt. 10.95 *(978-0-9792361-3-6(4))* Inspire U., LLC.

Little Engine - Playing Together. 2005. (J). bds. *(978-1-4194-0022-3(3))* Paradise Pr., Inc.

Mason, Jane B. & Hines-Stephens, Sarah. Let Sleeping Dogs Spy. Phillips, Craig, illus. 2012. 91p. (J). pap. *(978-0-545-37470-5(7))* Scholastic, Inc.

Reed-Guldin, Emily. Sarah & Sammi's Playhouse: Mermaid Adventure. 2009. 36p. pap. 16.99 *(978-1-4389-9342-3(0))* AuthorHouse.

—Sarah & Sammi's Playhouse Bedroom. 2009. 32p. pap. 14.49 *(978-1-4389-5881-1(1))* AuthorHouse.

Renna, G. M. Meticulous Nicholas Goes to Camp. 2009. 64p. pap. 10.49 *(978-1-4490-2784-1(9))* AuthorHouse.

Routley, Becky. Moon Golf. 2009. (Illus.). 28p. pap. 12.49 *(978-1-4490-4713-9(0))* AuthorHouse.

Rud, Jeff. Crossover, 1 vol. 2008. (Orca Sports Ser.). (ENG.). 176p. (J). (gr. 4-7). pap. 9.95 *(978-1-55143-981-5(6))* Orca Bk. Pubs. USA.

Schmidt, Gary D. The Wednesday Wars. 2008. *(978-0-545-10562-0(5))* Scholastic, Inc.

—The Wednesday Wars. 2009. lib. bdg. 18.40 *(978-0-606-10573-6(5))* Turtleback.

—The Wednesday Wars: A Newbery Honor Award Winner. (ENG.). (J). (gr. 5-7). 2009. 288p. pap. 9.99 *(978-0-547-23760-2(X),* 1083872) 2007. 272p. 18.99 *(978-0-618-72483-3(4),* 100515) HarperCollins Pubs. (Clarion Bks.).

The School Play: Individual Title Six-Packs. (gr. -1-2). 27.00 *(978-0-7635-9473-2(3))* Rigby Education.

Su, Lucy. Play Hide & Seek. Su, Lucy, illus. 2003. (Kitten & Baby Kitten Ser.). (Illus.). 42p. (J). pap. *(978-1-85602-538-6(1),* Pavilion Children's Books) Pavilion Bks.

Ventura, Marne. Jittery Jake Conquers Stage Fright. Trinidad, Leo, illus. 2016. (Worry Warriors Ser.). (ENG.). 96p. (J). (gr. 2-4). lib. bdg. 25.99 *(978-1-4965-3612-9(6),* 132818, Stone Arch Bks.) Capstone.

Walters, Celeste. Treading the Boards. 2007. (ENG.). 208p. *(978-1-921049-80-4(4))* Little Hare Bks. AUS. Dist: HarperCollins Pubs. Australia.

Wheeler, Lisa. Invasion of the Pig Sisters: Ready-To-Read Level 3. Ansley, Frank, illus. 2006. (Fitch & Chip Ser.: 4). (ENG.). 48p. (J). (gr. 1-3). pap. 4.99 *(978-0-689-84958-9(3),* Simon Spotlight) Simon Spotlight.

Winkler, Henry & Oliver, Lin. Bookmarks Are People Too! 2014. (Here's Hank Ser.: 1). lib. bdg. 16.00 *(978-0-606-34142-4(0))* Turtleback.

—Bookmarks Are People Too! #1, No. 1. Garrett, Scott, illus. 2014. (Here's Hank Ser.: 1). (ENG.). 128p. (J). (gr. 1-3). 6.99 *(978-0-448-47997-2(4),* Penguin Workshop) Penguin Young Readers Group.

PLAYS, CHRISTMAS

see Christmas Plays

PLAYS FOR CHILDREN

see Plays

PLAYWRIGHTS

see Dramatists

PLAYWRITING

see Drama—Technique

PLESKIT (FICTITIOUS CHARACTER)—FICTION

Coville, Bruce. I Lost My Grandfather's Brain. unabr. ed. 2004. (I Was a Sixth Grade Alien Ser.: Vol. 3). 160p. (J). (gr. 3-6). pap. 29.00 incl. audio *(978-0-8072-8385-1(1),* YA180SP, Listening Library) Random Hse. Audio Publishing Group.

—I Was a Sixth Grade Alien. (I Was a Sixth Grade Alien Ser.: Vol. 1). 170p. (J). (gr. 4-6). pap. 3.99 *(978-0-8072-8202-1(2));* 2004. (gr. 3-6). pap. 29.00 incl. audio *(978-0-8072-8201-4(4),* S YA 138 SP) Random Hse. Audio Publishing Group. (Listening Library).

PLOT-YOUR-OWN STORIES

Here are entered works of fiction in which the reader chooses from a number of possible options for developing the story.

Baxendale, Trevor & BBC. Doctor Who: Choose the Future: Terror Moon. 2016. (ENG.). 208p. (J). pap. 9.99 *(978-1-4059-2651-5(1),* 8d68da6f-aacb-4610-84c3-1e50439fc6c3) Penguin Bks., Ltd. GBR. Dist: Diamond Comic Distributors, Inc.

Becket, Jim. Inca Gold: Choose Your Own Adventure #20. Nugent, Suzanne, illus. 2007. (ENG.). 144p. (J). (gr. 4-8). per. 7.99 *(978-1-933390-20-8(4),* CHCL20) Chooseco LLC.

Blade, Adam. Beast Quest: Master Your Destiny 1: the Dark Cauldron. 2014. (Beast Quest Ser.). (ENG., Illus.). 112p. (J). (gr. 2-4). pap. 5.99 *(978-1-4083-0943-8(2),* Orchard Bks.) Hachette Children's Group GBR. Dist: Hachette Bk. Group.

—Beast Quest: Master Your Destiny 2: the Dagger of Doom. 2014. (Beast Quest Ser.). (ENG., Illus.). 128p. (J). (gr. 2-4). 5.99 *(978-1-4083-1406-7(1),* Orchard Bks.) Hachette Children's Group GBR. Dist: Hachette Bk. Group.

—Beast Quest: Master Your Destiny 3: the Pirate's Curse. 2016. (Beast Quest Ser.). (ENG., Illus.). 144p. (J). (gr. 2-4). pap. 5.99 *(978-1-4083-1840-9(7),* Orchard Bks.) Hachette Children's Group GBR. Dist: Hachette Bk. Group.

Blashfield, Jean F. Realm of the Enchanter. 2007. (Paths of Doom Ser.). (Illus.). 127p. (J). per. 4.99 *(978-1-931567-73-2(5))* Margaret Weis Productions, Ltd.

Borgenicht, David & Khan, Hena. Amazon: You Decide How to Survive! 2015. (Worst-Case Scenario Ultimate Adventure Ser.). (ENG., Illus.). 204p. (J). (gr. 3-8). 47.10 *(978-1-59920-980-7(2),* 19400, Smart Apple Media) Black Rabbit Bks.

Borgenicht, David & Lurie, Alexander. Deadly Seas: You Decide How to Survive! 2015. (WorstCase Scenario Ultimate Adventure Ser.). (ENG., Illus.). 204p. (gr. 3-8). 47.10 *(978-1-59920-981-4(0))* Black Rabbit Bks.

Bosch, Pseudonymous. Write This Book: A Do-It-Yourself Mystery. (Secret Ser.). (ENG., Illus.). (J). (gr. 3-7). 2014. 304p. pap. 8.99 *(978-0-316-20780-5(2))* 2013. 288p. 16.99 *(978-0-316-20781-2(0))* Little, Brown Bks. for Young Readers.

Braun, Eric. Goldilocks & the Three Bears: An Interactive Fairy Tale Adventure. López, Alex, illus. 2015. (You Choose: Fractured Fairy Tales Ser.). (ENG.). 112p. (J). (gr. 3-7). lib. bdg. 32.65 *(978-1-4914-5855-6(0),* 128818, Capstone Pr.) Capstone.

—Little Red Riding Hood: An Interactive Fairy Tale Adventure. Epelbaum, Mariano, illus. 2015. (You Choose: Fractured Fairy Tales Ser.). (ENG.). 112p. (J). (gr. 3-7). pap. 6.95 *(978-1-4914-5929-4(8),* 128849, Capstone Pr.) Capstone.

—Rumpelstiltskin: An Interactive Fairy Tale Adventure. Brown, Alan, illus. 2017. (You Choose: Fractured Fairy Tales Ser.). (ENG.). 112p. (J). (gr. 3-7). pap. 6.95 *(978-1-5157-8777-8(X),* 136328); lib. bdg. 32.65 *(978-1-5157-8775-4(3),* 136326) Capstone. (Capstone Pr.).

Braun, Eric & Gunderson, Jessica. Cinderella: An Interactive Fairy Tale Adventure. Lopez, Ayesha, illus. 2015. (You Choose: Fractured Fairy Tales Ser.). (ENG.). 112p. (J). (gr. 3-7). lib. bdg. 32.65 *(978-1-4914-5854-9(2),* 128817, Capstone Pr.) Capstone.

Brezenoff, Steve. The Library Shelves: An Interactive Mystery Adventure. Calo, Marcos, illus. 2019. (You Choose Stories: Field Trip Mysteries Ser.). (ENG.). 112p. (J). (gr. 3-7). lib. bdg. 32.65 (978-1-4965-4860-3(4), 135459, Stone Arch Bks.) Capstone.

—The Messed-Up Museum: An Interactive Mystery Adventure. Calo, Marcos, illus. 2019. (You Choose Stories: Field Trip Mysteries Ser.). (ENG.). 112p. (J). (gr. 3-7). lib. bdg. 32.65 (978-1-4965-4859-7(0), 135458, Stone Arch Bks.) Capstone.

Brezenoff, Steven. The Missing Bully: An Interactive Mystery Adventure. Calo, Marcos, illus. 2017. (You Choose Stories: Field Trip Mysteries Ser.). (ENG.). 112p. (J). (gr. 3-7). lib. bdg. 32.65 (978-1-4965-2642-7(2), 131205, Stone Arch Bks.) Capstone.

Bright, J. E. Seed Bank Heist. Beavers, Ethen, illus. 2015. (You Choose Stories: Batman Ser.). (ENG.). 112p. (J). (gr. 2-6). pap. 6.95 (978-1-4342-9709-9(8), 127029, Stone Arch Bks.) Capstone.

Brooks, Minnie. Carl, Colonel of the Carrot Colony. 2012. 40p. pap. 24.99 (978-1-62230-714-2(3)) Salem Author Services.

Burgan, Michael. World War II Pilots: An Interactive History Adventure. 2013. (You Choose: World War II Ser.). (ENG.). 112p. (J). (gr. 3-4). pap. 41.70 (978-1-62065-719-5(8), 19311, Capstone Pr.) Capstone.

Clark, Bridie. Maybe Tonight? 2013. (Snap Decision Ser.: 1). (ENG.). 224p. (YA). (gr. 7). pap. 18.99 (978-1-59643-816-3(9), 900087053) Roaring Brook Pr.

—You Only Live Once: Every Decision You Make Has Consequences. 2014. (Snap Decision Ser.: 2). (ENG.). 224p. (YA). (gr. 7). pap. 16.99 (978-1-59643-817-0(7), 900087054) Roaring Brook Pr.

David, Juliet. The Christmas Story, 1 vol. Parry, Jo, illus. 2009. (Candle Read & Play Ser.). 12p. (J). bds., bds. 11.99 (978-0-8254-7400-2(0), Candle Bks.) Lion Hudson PLC GBR. Dist: Kregel Pubns.

DeHoratius, Ed. The Journey of Odysseus. Delandro Hardison, Brian, illus. 2009. (Follow Your Fates Ser.). (ENG.). 116p. (J). pap. 12.00 (978-0-86516-710-0(9)) Bolchazy-Carducci Pubs.

—Wrath of Achilles. 2009. (ENG.). 62p. pap. 12.00 (978-0-86516-708-7(7)) Bolchazy-Carducci Pubs.

Dever, Joe. Caverns of Kalte. 2007. (ENG., Illus.). 320p. (YA). pap. 14.95 (978-1-906103-20-0(8)) Mongoose Publishing GBR. Dist: Diamond Bk. Distributors.

Doeden, Matt. At Battle in World War II: An Interactive Battlefield Adventure. 2015. (You Choose: Battlefields Ser.). (ENG., Illus.). 112p. (J). (gr. 3-7). lib. bdg. 32.65 (978-1-4914-2152-9(5), 127633, Capstone Pr.) Capstone.

—At the Battle of Antietam: An Interactive Battlefield Adventure. 2018. (You Choose: American Battles Ser.). (ENG., Illus.). 112p. (J). (gr. 3-7). lib. bdg. 32.65 (978-1-5435-0288-6(1), 137158, Capstone Pr.) Capstone.

—Beauty & the Beast: An Interactive Fairy Tale Adventure. Miramon, Sabrina, illus. 2018. (You Choose: Fractured Fairy Tales Ser.). (ENG.). 112p. (J). (gr. 3-7). lib. bdg. 32.65 (978-1-5435-3007-0(9), 138604, Capstone Pr.) Capstone.

—Can You Survive a Global Blackout? An Interactive Doomsday Adventure. Nathan, James, illus. 2015. (You Choose: Doomsday Ser.). (ENG.). 112p. (J). (gr. 3-7). lib. bdg. 32.65 (978-1-4914-5850-1(X), 128813, Capstone Pr.) Capstone.

—Can You Survive an Aritificial Intelligence Uprising? An Interactive Doomsday Adventure. Fisher-Johnson, Paul, illus. 2016. (You Choose: Doomsday Ser.). (ENG.). 112p. (J). (gr. 3-7). lib. bdg. 32.65 (978-1-4914-8107-3(2), 130598, Capstone Pr.) Capstone.

—Can You Survive an Asteroid Strike? An Interactive Doomsday Adventure. Davidson, Paul, illus. 2016. (You Choose: Doomsday Ser.). (ENG.). 112p. (J). (gr. 3-7). lib. bdg. 32.65 (978-1-4914-8109-7(9), 130600, Capstone Pr.) Capstone.

—The Civil War [Scholastic]: An Interactive History Adventure. 2010. (You Choose: History Ser.). 112p. pap. 0.90 (978-1-4296-5977-2(7), Capstone Pr.) Capstone.

—Hansel & Gretel: An Interactive Fairy Tale Adventure. Miramon, Sabrina, illus. 2017. (You Choose: Fractured Fairy Tales Ser.). (ENG.). 112p. (J). (gr. 3-7). pap. 6.95 (978-1-5157-6952-1(6), 135424); lib. bdg. 32.65 (978-1-5157-6944-6(5), 135418) Capstone. (Capstone Pr.).

—The Queen Mary: A Chilling Interactive Adventure. 2016. (You Choose: Haunted Places Ser.). (ENG., Illus.). 112p. (J). (gr. 3-7). lib. bdg. 32.65 (978-1-5157-2578-7(2), 132921, Capstone Pr.) Capstone.

Doyle, Bill & Borgenicht, David. Everest: You Decide How to Survive! 2015. (Worst-Case Scenario Ultimate Adventure Ser.). (ENG., Illus.). 204p. (J). (gr. 3-8). 47.10 (978-1-59920-978-4(0), 19401, Smart Apple Media) Black Rabbit Bks.

Dragonology: Pocket Adventures, 4 vols. 2007. (Illus.). (J). (978-0-7636-3697-5(5)); (978-0-7636-3696-8(7)); (978-0-7636-3699-9(1)); (978-0-7636-3698-2(3)) Candlewick Pr.

Enderle, Dotti. Beyond the Grave: An Up2U Mystery Adventure, 1 vol. Uhles, Mary, illus. 2013. (Up2U Adventures Ser.). (ENG.). 80p. (J). (gr. 2-5). 35.64 (978-1-61641-964-6(4), 15211, Calico Chapter Bks.) ABDO Publishing Co.

—Clawed! An Up2U Horror Adventure, 1 vol. To, Vivienne, illus. 2013. (Up2U Adventures Ser.). (ENG.). 80p. (J). (gr. 2-5). lib. bdg. 35.64 (978-1-61641-965-3(2), 15213, Calico Chapter Bks.) ABDO Publishing Co.

Ernst, Kathleen. Gunpowder & Tea Cakes: My Journey with Felicity. 2017. 185p. (J). (978-1-5182-4407-0(6), American Girl) American Girl Publishing, Inc.

Fabregat, Antonio-Manuel. Los Cuentos de Mi Escuela. (SPA.). 128p. (J). (gr. 4-6). (978-84-216-1185-2(2), BU3866) Bruño, Editorial ESP. Dist: Lectorum Pubns., Inc.

Falligant, Erin. Prints in the Sand. 2017. 183p. (J). (978-1-5182-5318-8(0), American Girl) American Girl Publishing, Inc.

Fields, Jan. Ghost Light Burning: An Up2U Mystery Adventure, 1 vol. Fabbretti, Valerio, illus. 2015. (Up2U Adventures Ser.). (ENG.). 80p. (J). (gr. 2-5). 35.64 (978-1-62402-092-6(5), 17353, Calico Chapter Bks.) ABDO Publishing Co.

—Really New School: An Up2U Action Adventure, 1 vol. To, Vivienne, illus. 2013. (Up2U Adventures Ser.). (ENG.). 80p. (J). (gr. 2-5). lib. bdg. 35.64 (978-1-61641-969-1(5), 15221, Calico Chapter Bks.) ABDO Publishing Co.

Fison, Julie. The Call of the Wild. 2015. (ENG.). 288p. (J). pap. (978-1-61067-388-4(3)) Kane Miller.

Fontes, Justine & Fontes, Ron. The Fifth Musketeer. Meconis, Dylan, illus. 2012. (Twisted Journeys Ser.: 19). (ENG.). 112p. (J). (gr. 4-7). lib. bdg. 27.93 (978-0-7613-4594-7(9), Graphic Universe™) Lerner Publishing Group.

Gilligan, Alison. Pirate Treasure of the Onyx Dragon. Utomo, Gabhor, illus. 2011. (ENG.). 144p. (J). (gr. 4-8). pap. 7.99 (978-1-933390-99-4(9)) Chooseco LLC.

—Search for the Black Rhino. Semionov, Vladimir, illus. 2011. (ENG.). 144p. (J). (gr. 4-8). pap. 7.99 (978-1-937133-01-6(X)) Chooseco LLC.

Gilligan, Shannon. The Case of the Silk King. Pornkerd, Vorrarit et al, illus. 2006. (ENG.). 144p. (J). (gr. 4-8). per. 7.99 (978-1-933390-14-7(X), CHCL14) Chooseco LLC.

—The Case of the Silk King. 2005. 116p. (J). pap. (978-0-7608-9702-7(6)) Sundance/Newbridge Educational Publishing.

—Choose Your Own Adventure: The Case of the Silk King. 2007. 144p. (J). pap. (978-1-74169-069-9(2)) Chooseco LLC.

—Cup of Death. Nugent, Suzanne, illus. 2007. (ENG.). 144p. (J). (gr. 4-8). per. 7.99 (978-1-933390-70-3(0)) Chooseco LLC.

—Ghost Island. Newton, Keith, illus. 2008. (ENG.). 80p. (J). (gr. 3-3). pap. 8.99 (978-1-933390-57-4(3)) Chooseco LLC.

—The Lake Monster Mystery. Newton, Keith, illus. 2009. (ENG.). 80p. (J). (gr. 2-2). pap. 8.99 (978-1-933390-60-4(3)) Chooseco LLC.

—Princess Island. Arroyo, Fian, illus. 2015. (ENG.). 96p. (J). (gr. 2-2). pap. 7.99 (978-1-937133-50-4(8)) Chooseco LLC.

—Struggle down Under. Semionov, Vladimir, illus. 2007. (ENG.). 144p. (J). (gr. 4-8). pap. 7.99 (978-1-933390-21-5(2)) Chooseco LLC.

Goodhart, Pippa & Sharratt, Nick. You Choose! (ENG., Illus.). 32p. (J). 19.99 (978-0-385-60176-4(X), Doubleday Children's) Random House Children's Books GBR. Dist: Trafalgar Square Publishing.

Gunderson, Jessica. Olympians vs. Titans: An Interactive Mythological Adventure. Arcabascio, Carolyn, illus. 2017. (You Choose: Ancient Greek Myths Ser.). (ENG.). 112p. (J). (gr. 3-7). lib. bdg. 32.65 (978-1-5157-4820-5(0), 134436, Capstone Pr.) Capstone.

—Sleeping Beauty: An Interactive Fairy Tale Adventure. Epelbaum, Mariano, illus. 2018. (You Choose: Fractured Fairy Tales Ser.). (ENG.). 112p. (J). (gr. 3-7). lib. bdg. 32.65 (978-1-5435-3006-3(0), 138603, Capstone Pr.) Capstone.

—Snow White & the Seven Dwarfs: An Interactive Fairy Tale Adventure. Miramon, Sabrina, illus. 2017. (You Choose: Fractured Fairy Tales Ser.). (ENG.). 112p. (J). (gr. 3-7). pap. 6.95 (978-1-5157-6951-4(8), 135423); lib. bdg. 32.65 (978-1-5157-6943-9(7), 135417) Capstone. (Capstone Pr.).

Gunderson, Jessica, et al. You Choose: Fractured Fairy Tales. 2015. (You Choose: Fractured Fairy Tales Ser.). (ENG.). 112p. (gr. 3-4). 127.96 (978-1-4914-6969-9(2), Capstone Pr.) Capstone.

Hoena, B. A. Can You Survive an Alien Invasion? An Interactive Doomsday Adventure. Fisher-Johnson, Paul, illus. 2015. (You Choose: Doomsday Ser.). (ENG.). 112p. (J). (gr. 3-7). lib. bdg. 32.65 (978-1-4914-5853-2(4), 128816, Capstone Pr.) Capstone.

—Jack & the Beanstalk: An Interactive Fairy Tale Adventure. Tayal, Amit, illus. 2015. (You Choose: Fractured Fairy Tales Ser.). (ENG.). 112p. (J). (gr. 3-7). pap. 6.95 (978-1-4914-5930-0(1), 128850, Capstone Pr.) Capstone.

Hoena, Blake. Can You Survive a Supervolcano Eruption? An Interactive Doomsday Adventure. Vanzo, Filippo, illus. 2016. (You Choose: Doomsday Ser.). (ENG.). 112p. (J). (gr. 3-7). lib. bdg. 32.65 (978-1-4914-8108-0(0), 130599, Capstone Pr.) Capstone.

—Could You Escape a Deserted Island? An Interactive Survival Adventure. 2019. (You Choose: Can You Escape? Ser.). (ENG., Illus.). 112p. (J). (gr. 3-7). pap. 6.95 (978-1-5435-7560-6(9), 141092); lib. bdg. 32.65 (978-1-5435-7395-4(9), 140691) Capstone.

—Fighting for Independence: An Interactive American Revolution Adventure. 2018. (You Choose: Founding the United States Ser.). (ENG., Illus.). 112p. (J). (gr. 3-7). lib. bdg. 32.65 (978-1-5435-1540-4(1), 137908, Capstone Pr.) Capstone.

—Jason, the Argonauts, & the Golden Fleece: An Interactive Mythological Adventure. Nathan, James, illus. 2016. (You Choose: Ancient Greek Myths Ser.). (ENG.). 112p. (J). (gr. 3-7). lib. bdg. 32.65 (978-1-4914-8113-4(7), 130604, Capstone Pr.) Capstone.

—The Quest of Theseus: An Interactive Mythological Adventure. Arcabascio, Carolyn, illus. 2017. (You Choose: Ancient Greek Myths Ser.). (ENG.). 112p. (J). (gr. 3-7). pap. 6.95 (978-1-5157-4826-7(X), 134441, Capstone Pr.) Capstone.

—The Quest of Theseus: An Interactive Mytholoical Adventure. Arcabascio, Carolyn, illus. 2017. (You Choose: Ancient Greek Myths Ser.). (ENG.). 112p. (J). (gr. 3-7). lib. bdg. 32.65 (978-1-5157-4821-2(9), 134437, Capstone Pr.) Capstone.

—The Trojan War: An Interactive Mythological Adventure. Takvorian, Nadine, illus. 2017. (You Choose: Ancient Greek Myths Ser.). (ENG.). 112p. (J). (gr. 3-7). lib. bdg. 32.65 (978-1-5157-4822-9(7), 134438, Capstone Pr.) Capstone.

Iparraguirre, Sylvia., et al. Terminemos el Cuento. 2003. (SPA., Illus.). 128p. (YA). (gr. 9-12). 9.95 (978-84-204-4965-4(2)) Ediciones Alfaguara ESP. Dist: Santillana USA Publishing Co., Inc.

Jackson, Sharinese. Choices: Upper Elementary. Nyamor, Eric, illus. 2010. 112p. pap. 12.95 (978-0-9840660-3-2(9)) Second Time Media & Communications.

Jackson, Steve. The Citadel of Chaos. 2003. 208p. pap. (978-0-7434-7510-5(0)) ibooks, Inc.

Jackson, Steve & Livingstone, Ian. The Worlock of Firetop Mountain. 2003. 192p. pap. 6.99 (978-0-7434-7511-2(9)) ibooks, Inc.

Jakubowski, Michele. Rapunzel: An Interactive Fairy Tale Adventure. Frenna, Federica, illus. 2017. (You Choose: Fractured Fairy Tales Ser.). (ENG.). 112p. (J). (gr. 3-7). pap. 6.95 (978-1-5157-8778-5(8), 136329); lib. bdg. 32.65 (978-1-5157-8776-1(1), 136327) Capstone. (Capstone Pr.).

Jimenez, Adan & Tsang, Evonne. Hero City: Book 22, No. 22. Torres, German, illus. 2012. (Twisted Journeys (r) Ser.: 22). (ENG.). 112p. (J). (gr. 4-7). lib. bdg. 27.99 (978-0-7613-4595-4(7), 225fd18d-e103-4487-b37d-92ca793121df, Graphic Universe™) Lerner Publishing Group.

Johnson, Alaya Dawn. Detective Frankenstein. Ota, Yuko, illus. 2011. (Twisted Journeys Ser.: 17). (ENG.). 112p. (J). (gr. 4-7). pap. 45.32 (978-0-7613-7613-2(5), Graphic Universe™) Lerner Publishing Group.

Korté, Steve. Myth Monster Mayhem. Lozano, Omar, illus. 2019. (You Choose Stories: Wonder Woman Ser.). (ENG.). 112p. (J). (gr. 2-6). pap. 6.95 (978-1-4965-8439-7(2), 140964); lib. bdg. 32.65 (978-1-4965-8349-9(3), 140643) Capstone. (Stone Arch Bks.).

—Superman Day Disaster. Brizuela, Dario, illus. 2018. (You Choose Stories: Superman Ser.). (ENG.). 112p. (J). (gr. 2-6). lib. bdg. 32.65 (978-1-4965-5824-4(3), 136912, Stone Arch Bks.) Capstone.

Landon, Lucinda. Meg Mackintosh & the April Fools' Day Mystery: A Solve-It-Yourself Mystery. 2018. (Meg Mackintosh Mystery Ser.). (ENG., Illus.). 48p. (J). (gr. 2-4). pap. 6.95 (978-1-888695-15-1(3)) Secret Passage Pr.

Lassieur, Allison. At Battle in World War I: An Interactive Battlefield Adventure. 2015. (You Choose: Battlefields Ser.). (ENG., Illus.). 112p. (J). (gr. 3-7). lib. bdg. 32.65 (978-1-4914-2151-2(7), 127632, Capstone Pr.) Capstone.

—The Attack on Pearl Harbor [Scholastic]: An Interactive History Adventure. 2009. (You Choose: History Ser.). 112p. (gr. 3-4). pap. 0.86 (978-1-4296-4046-6(4), Capstone Pr.) Capstone.

Lay, Kathryn. The Substitutes: An Up2U Action Adventure, 1 vol. Calo, Marcos, illus. 2015. (Up2U Adventures Ser.). (ENG.). 80p. (J). (gr. 2-5). 35.64 (978-1-62402-095-7(X), 17359, Calico Chapter Bks.) ABDO Publishing Co.

Leibold, Jay. Secret of the Ninja. Nugent, Suzanne, illus. 2006. (ENG.). 144p. (J). (gr. 4-8). per. 7.99 (978-1-933390-16-1(6)) Chooseco LLC.

—Surf Monkeys. Utomo, Gabhor, illus. 2017. (ENG.). 144p. (J). (gr. 4-8). pap. 6.99 (978-1-937133-24-5(9)) Chooseco LLC.

Livingstone, Ian. Deathtrap Dungeon. 2003. 224p. pap. 6.99 (978-0-7434-7967-7(X)) ibooks, Inc.

Magaziner, Lauren. Case Closed #1: Mystery in the Mansion. (Case Closed Ser.: 1). (ENG.). 400p. (J). (gr. 3-7). 2019. pap. 7.99 (978-0-06-267628-3(8)) 2018. (Illus.). 16.99 (978-0-06-267627-6(X)) HarperCollins Pubs. (Tegen, Katherine Bks).

Manning, Matthew K. Apokolips Invasion. Brizuela, Dario, illus. 2018. (You Choose Stories: Superman Ser.). (ENG.). 112p. (J). (gr. 2-6). lib. bdg. 32.65 (978-1-4965-5825-1(1), 136913, Stone Arch Bks.) Capstone.

—The League of Laughs. Doescher, Erik, illus. 2018. (You Choose Stories: Justice League Ser.). (ENG.). 112p. (J). (gr. 2-6). pap. 6.95 (978-1-4965-6556-3(8), 138569, Stone Arch Bks.) Capstone.

—The Mystery of the Mayhem Mansion. Neely, Scott, illus. 2016. (You Choose Stories: Scooby-Doo Ser.). (ENG.). 112p. (J). (gr. 2-6). lib. bdg. 32.65 (978-1-4965-2661-8(9), 131220, Stone Arch Bks.) Capstone.

—The Ultimate Weapon. Doescher, Erik, illus. 2018. (You Choose Stories: Justice League Ser.). (ENG.). 112p. (J). (gr. 2-6). pap. 6.95 (978-1-4965-6557-0(6), 138570, Stone Arch Bks.) Capstone.

Manuro. Hocus & Pocus: the Legend of Grimm's Woods: The Comic Book You Can Play. Gorobei, illus. 2018. (Comic Quests Ser.: 1). 152p. (J). (gr. 3-7). pap. 9.99 (978-1-68369-057-3(5)) Quirk Bks.

Matthews, T. J. The Canoeing Safari. Rheburg, Judy, illus. 2004. (J). (978-0-938978-35-0(7)) Wycliffe Bible Translators.

Mayhall, Robin. The Quest for Dragon Mountain. Martinez, Alitha, illus. 16th rev. ed. 2010. (Twisted Journeys (r) Ser.: 16). (ENG.). (J). (gr. 4-7). pap. 45.32 (978-0-7613-6999-8(6)) Lerner Publishing Group.

McMurtry, Ken. Zombie Penpal. Louie, Wes, illus. 2010. (ENG.). 144p. (J). (gr. 4-8). pap. 7.99 (978-1-933390-34-5(4)) Chooseco LLC.

Miller, Connie Colwell. You Can Follow the Rules: Cheat or Play Fair? Assanelli, Victoria, illus. 2019. (Making Good Choices Ser.). (ENG.). 24p. (J). (gr. 1-3). pap. 9.99 (978-1-68152-476-4(7), 11062) Amicus.

Montgomery, Anson. Dragon Day. Newton, Keith, illus. 2010. (ENG.). 80p. (J). (gr. 2-2). pap. 7.99 (978-1-933390-61-1(1)) Chooseco LLC.

—Escape from the Haunted Warehouse. Newton, Keith, illus. 2015. (ENG.). 144p. (J). (gr. 4-8). pap. 7.99 (978-1-937133-47-4(8)) Chooseco LLC.

—Moon Quest. Semionov, Vladimir, illus. 2008. (ENG.). 144p. (J). (gr. 4-8). pap. 7.99 (978-1-933390-26-0(3)) Chooseco LLC.

—Search for the Dragon Queen. Newton, Keith, illus. 2010. (ENG.). 80p. (J). (gr. 2-2). pap. 7.99 (978-1-933390-56-7(5)) Chooseco LLC.

—Your Grandparents Are Zombies! Newton, Keith, illus. 2010. (ENG.). 80p. (J). (gr. 2-2). pap. 7.99 (978-1-933390-90-1(5)) Chooseco LLC.

Montgomery, R. A. The Abominable Snowman: (Choose Your Own Adventure #1) Peguy, Laurence, illus. 2006. (ENG.). 144p. (J). (gr. 4-8). per. 7.99 (978-1-933390-01-7(8), CHCL01) Chooseco LLC.

—Always Picked Last. Newton, Keith, illus. 2009. 64p. (J). (gr. 2). pap. 7.99 (978-1-933390-38-3(7)) Chooseco LLC.

—Behind the Wheel. Sundaravej, Sittisan, illus. 2010. (ENG.). 144p. (J). (gr. 4-8). pap. 7.99 (978-1-933390-35-2(2)) Chooseco LLC.

—Beyond Escape. 2005. (Choose Your Own Adventure Ser.). (Illus.). 118p. (gr. 4-8). pap. 5.50 (978-0-7608-9703-4(4)) Sundance/Newbridge Educational Publishing.

—Beyond Escape! Millet, Jason, illus. 2006. (ENG.). 144p. (J). (gr. 4-8). per. 7.99 (978-1-933390-15-4(8), CHCL15) Chooseco LLC.

—Blood on the Handle. Michel, Jean, illus. 2010. (ENG.). 144p. (J). (gr. 4-8). pap. 7.99 (978-1-933390-33-8(6)) Chooseco LLC.

—The Brilliant Dr. Wogan. 2005. (Choose Your Own Adventure Ser.). (Illus.). 112p. (J). (gr. 4-8). pap. 5.50 (978-0-7608-9705-8(0)) Sundance/Newbridge Educational Publishing.

—The Brilliant Dr. Wogan. Trod, Mariano et al, illus. 2006. (ENG.). 144p. (J). (gr. 4-8). per. 7.99 (978-1-933390-17-8(4), CHC:17) Chooseco LLC.

—Chinese Dragons. Semionov, Vladimir, illus. 2009. (ENG.). 144p. (J). (gr. 4-8). pap. 7.99 (978-1-933390-30-7(1)) Chooseco LLC.

—Choose Your Own Adventure: 4-Book Boxed Set #1. 2006.Tr. of (the Abominable Snowman, Journey under the Sea, Space & Beyond, the Lost Jewels of Nabooti). (ENG., Illus.). 576p. (J). (gr. 2-9). pap. 25.99 (978-1-933390-94-9(8)) Chooseco LLC.

—Choose Your Own Adventure: 6- Book Boxed Set #1. 2011.Tr. of (the Abominable Snowman, Journey under the Sea, Space & Beyond, the Lost Jewels of Nabooti, Mystery of the Maya, House of Danger). (ENG., Illus.). 864p. (J). pap. 35.99 (978-1-933390-91-8(3), CHCL91) Chooseco LLC.

—Choose Your Own Adventure 4-Book Boxed Set: Lost on the Amazon , Prisoner of the Ant People, Trouble on Planet Earth, War with the Evil Power Master. 2011.Tr. of #3. (ENG., Illus.). 576p. (J). pap. 22.99 (978-1-933390-96-3(4)) Chooseco LLC.

—Choose Your Own Adventure 4-Book Boxed Set: Mystery of the Maya, House of Danger, Race Forever, Escape. 2006.Tr. of #2. (ENG., Illus.). 576p. (J). pap. 25.99 (978-1-933390-95-6(6)) Chooseco LLC.

—Choose Your Own Adventure 6-Book Boxed Set: Race Forever; Escape, Lost on the Amazon; Prisoner of the Ant People; Trouble on Planet Earth; War with the Evil Power Master. 2011.Tr. of #2. (ENG., Illus.). 864p. (J). pap. 33.99 (978-1-933390-92-5(1), CHCL92) Chooseco LLC.

—Escape. Millet, Jason & Sundaravej, Sittisan, illus. 2006. (ENG.). 144p. (J). (gr. 4-8). per. 7.99 (978-1-933390-08-6(5), CHCL08) Chooseco LLC.

—Fire! Newton, Keith, illus. 2015. (ENG.). 80p. (Orig.). (J). (gr. 3-3). pap. 7.99 (978-1-937133-49-8(4)) Chooseco LLC.

—Forecast from Stonehenge. Semionov, Vladimir, illus. 2007. (ENG.). 144p. (J). (gr. 4-8). pap. 7.99 (978-1-933390-19-2(0)) Chooseco LLC.

—The Haunted House. Newton, Keith, illus. 2007. (ENG.). 80p. (J). (gr. 2-2). pap. 7.99 (978-1-933390-51-2(4)) Chooseco LLC.

—House of Danger. 2005. (Choose Your Own Adventure Ser.). (Illus.). 108p. (gr. 4-8). pap. 5.50 (978-0-7608-9694-5(1)) Sundance/Newbridge Educational Publishing.

—House of Danger. Sundaravej, Sittisan, illus. 2006. (ENG.). 144p. (J). (gr. 4-8). per. 7.99 (978-1-933390-06-2(9), CHCL06) Chooseco LLC.

—Indian Trail. Millet, Jason, illus. 2007. (ENG.). 80p. (J). (gr. 2-2). pap. 7.99 (978-1-933390-53-6(0)) Chooseco LLC.

—Island of Time. Louie, Wes & Cannella, Marco, illus. 2009. (ENG.). 144p. (J). (gr. 4-8). pap. 6.99 (978-1-933390-28-4(X)) Chooseco LLC.

—Journey under the Sea. Sundaravej, Sittisan, illus. 2006. (ENG.). 144p. (J). (gr. 4-8). per. 7.99 (978-1-933390-02-4(6), CHCL02) Chooseco LLC.

—Journey under the Sea. 2006. (Choose Your Own Adventure Ser.: 2). 17.20 (978-1-4177-6410-5(4)) Turtleback.

—Lost Dog! Newton, Keith, illus. 2010. (ENG.). 80p. (J). (gr. 2-2). pap. 7.99 (978-1-933390-00-0(X)) Chooseco LLC.

—The Lost Jewels of Nabooti. Kommaneeroj, T. et al, illus. 2006. (ENG.). 144p. (J). (gr. 4-8). per. 7.99 (978-1-933390-04-8(2), CHCL04) Chooseco LLC.

—Lost on the Amazon. 2007. 144p. (J). pap. (978-1-86504-931-1(X)) Chooseco LLC.

—Lost on the Amazon. Millet, Jason, illus. 2006. (ENG.). 144p. (J). (gr. 4-8). per. 6.99 (978-1-933390-09-3(3), CHCL09) Chooseco LLC.

—Lost on the Amazon. 2005. (Choose Your Own Adventure Ser.). (Illus.). 114p. (gr. 4-8). pap. 5.50 (978-0-7608-9697-6(6)) Sundance/Newbridge Educational Publishing.

—Monsters of the Deep. Newton, Keith, illus. 2010. (ENG.). 80p. (J). (gr. 3-3). pap. 7.99 (978-1-933390-37-6(9)) Chooseco LLC.

—Mystery of the Maya. Pornkerd, Vorrarit et al, illus. 2006. (ENG.). 144p. (J). (gr. 4-8). per. 6.99 (978-1-933390-05-5(0), CHCL05) Chooseco LLC.

—Owl Tree. Utomo, Gabhor, illus. 2009. (ENG.). 80p. (Orig.). (J). (gr. 3-3). pap. 7.99 (978-1-933390-80-2(8)) Chooseco LLC.

—Prisoner of the Ant People. 2007. 144p. (J). pap. (978-1-86504-932-8(8)) Chooseco LLC.

—Prisoner of the Ant People. Millet, Jason, illus. 2006. (ENG.). 144p. (J). (gr. 4-8). per. 7.99 (978-1-933390-10-9(7), CHCL10) Chooseco LLC.

—Prisoner of the Ant People. 2005. (Illus.). 115p. (J). pap. (978-0-7608-9698-3(4)) Sundance/Newbridge Educational Publishing.

—Project UFO. Semionov, Vladimir & Cannella, Marco, illus. 2008. (ENG.). 144p. (J). (gr. 4-8). pap. 7.99 (978-1-933390-27-7(1)) Chooseco LLC.

—Race Forever. 2005. (Illus.). 122p. (J). (978-0-7608-9695-2(X)) Sundance/Newbridge Educational Publishing.

—Race Forever. Sundaravej, Sittisan, illus. 2006. (ENG.). 144p. (J). (gr. 4-8). per. 7.99 (978-1-933390-07-9(7), CHCL07) Chooseco LLC.

—Return to Atlantis. 2005. (Choose Your Own Adventure Ser.). (Illus.). 119p. (gr. 4-8). pap. 5.50 (978-0-7608-9706-5(9)) Sundance/Newbridge Educational Publishing.

—Return to Atlantis. Sundaravej, Sittisan & Thongmoon, Kriangsak, illus. 2006. (ENG.). 144p. (J). (gr. 4-8). per. 7.99 (978-1-933390-18-5(2), CHCL18) Chooseco LLC.

—Return to Haunted House. Newton, Keith, illus. 2010. (ENG.). 80p. (J). (gr. 2-2). pap. 7.99 (978-1-933390-40-6(9)) Chooseco LLC.

—Sand Castle. Newton, Keith, illus. 2009. (ENG.). 80p. (J). (gr. 3-3). pap. 8.99 (978-1-933390-59-8(X)) Chooseco LLC.

—Silver Wings. Semionov, Vladimir, illus. 2007. (ENG.). 144p. (J). (gr. 4-8). pap. 7.99 *(978-1-933390-23-9(9))* Chooseco LLC.
—Smoke Jumpers. Peguy, Laurence, illus. 2009. (ENG.). 144p. (J). (gr. 4-8). pap. 7.99 *(978-1-933390-29-1(8))* Chooseco LLC.
—Space & Beyond. Pornkerd, Vorrarit et al, illus. 2006. (ENG.). 144p. (J). (gr. 4-8). pap. 7.99 *(978-1-933390-03-1(4),* CHCL03) Chooseco LLC.
—Space Pup. Newton, Keith, illus. 2014. (ENG.). 80p. (J). (gr. 2-2). pap. 8.99 *(978-1-937133-43-6(5))* Chooseco LLC.
—Tattoo of Death. Cannella, Marco, illus. 2007. (ENG.). 144p. (J). (gr. 4-8). pap. 7.99 *(978-1-933390-22-2(0))* Chooseco LLC.
—Track Star! Louie, Wes, illus. 2009. (ENG.). 144p. (J). (gr. 4-8). pap. 7.99 *(978-1-933390-31-4(X))* Chooseco LLC.
—The Trail of Lost Time. Semionov, Vladimir, illus. 2011. (ENG.). 144p. (J). (gr. 4-8). mass mkt. 7.99 *(978-1-937133-03-0(6))* Chooseco LLC.
—Trouble on Planet Earth. 2007. 144p. (J). pap. *(978-1-86504-933-5(6))* Chooseco LLC.
—Trouble on Planet Earth. Trod, Mariano et al, illus. 2006. (ENG.). 144p. (J). (gr. 4-8). per. 6.99 *(978-1-933390-11-6(5),* CHCL11) Chooseco LLC.
—Trouble on Planet Earth. 2005. (Illus.). 113p. (J). pap. *(978-0-7608-9699-0(2))* Sundance/Newbridge Educational Publishing.
—War with the Evil Power Master. 2005. (Illus.). 123p. (J). pap. *(978-0-7608-9700-3(X))* Sundance/Newbridge Educational Publishing.
—War with the Evil Power Master. Millet, Jason, illus. 2006. (ENG.). 144p. (J). (gr. 4-8). per. 7.99 *(978-1-933390-12-3(3),* CHCL12) Chooseco LLC.
—Your Purrr-Fect Birthday. Newton, Keith, illus. 2008. (ENG.). 64p. (J). (gr. 3-3). per. 8.99 *(978-1-933390-55-0(7))* Chooseco LLC.
—Your Very Own Robot: (Choose Your Own Adventure - Dragonlark) Newton, Keith, illus. 2007. (ENG.). 80p. (J). (gr. 2-2). pap. 8.99 *(978-1-933390-52-9(2))* Chooseco LLC.
—Your Very Own Robot Goes Cuckoo-Bananas! Newton, Keith, illus. 2010. (ENG.). 80p. (J). (gr. 2-2). pap. 7.99 *(978-1-933390-39-0(5))* Chooseco LLC.
Montgomery, R. A. & Gilligan, Shannon. Gus vs. the Robot King. Newton, Keith, illus. 2014. (ENG.). 80p. (J). (gr. 3-3). pap. 7.99 *(978-1-937133-44-3(3))* Chooseco LLC.
Montgomery, Ramsey. U.N. Adventure: Mission to Molowa. Louie, Wes, illus. 2009. (ENG.). 144p. (J). (gr. 4-8). pap. 7.99 *(978-1-933390-32-1(8))* Chooseco LLC.
Mullarkey, John & Mullarkey, Lisa. Johnstown Flood: An Up2U Historical Fiction Adventure, 1 vol. Martin, Dana, illus. 2013. (Up2U Adventures Ser.). (ENG.). 80p. (J). (gr. 2-5). lib. bdg. 35.64 *(978-1-61641-967-7(9),* 15217, Calico Chapter Bks.) ABDO Publishing Co.
Packard, Edward. Return to the Cave of Time. Willis, Drew, illus. 2012. (U-Ventures Ser.). (ENG.). 160p. (Orig.). (J). (gr. 3-7). pap. 5.99 *(978-1-4424-3427-1(9))* Simon & Schuster, Inc.
—Through the Black Hole. Willis, Drew, illus. 2012. (U-Ventures Ser.). (ENG.). 160p. (J). (gr. 3-7). pap. 6.99 *(978-1-4424-3426-4(0))* Simon & Schuster, Inc.
Pomaska, Anna. Scruffy & Muffin in the Land of Enchantment: A Dot-to-Dot Storybook. 2004. (Dover Kids Activity Books: Fantasy Ser.). (ENG., Illus.). 32p. (J). (gr. -1-2). pap. 3.95 *(978-0-486-43566-4(0),* 435660) Dover Pubns., Inc.
Raum, Elizabeth. The Aztec Empire: An Interactive History Adventure. 2012. (You Choose: Historical Eras Ser.). (ENG.). 112p. (J). (gr. 3-4). pap. 42.70 *(978-1-4296-9475-9(0),* 18650, Capstone Pr.) Capstone.
—Christmas Crossroads. 2015. 133p. (J). *(978-1-62856-046-6(0),* Bloomsbury Visual Arts) BJU Pr.
—Crossroads among the Gentiles. 2018. (Illus.). xii, 128p. (J). pap. *(978-1-62856-490-7(3))* BJU Pr.
—Crossroads in Galilee. 2016. (Illus.). xii, 139p. (J). *(978-1-62856-239-2(0))* BJU Pr.
Ray, Cindy & Kids Write On, creators. The Stapler Caper: You Write the Story. 2008. (ENG., Illus.). 28p. (J). 16.95 *(978-0-615-23574-5(3))* Kids Write On, LLC.
Riley, James. Pick the Plot. (Story Thieves Ser.: 4). (ENG.). (J). (gr. 3-7). 2018. 400p. pap. 9.99 *(978-1-4814-6129-0(X))* 2017. (Illus.). 384p. 17.99 *(978-1-4814-6128-3(1))* Simon & Schuster Children's Publishing. (Aladdin).
Ruckdeschel, Liz & James, Sara. What If ... All Your Friends Turned on You. 2009. (What If... Ser.). (ENG.). 320p. (YA). (gr. 7-12). 26.19 *(978-0-385-73818-7(8),* Delacorte Pr.) Random Hse. Children's Bks.
Sazaklis, John. Clayface Returns. Beavers, Ethen, illus. 2016. (You Choose Stories: Batman Ser.). (ENG.). 112p. (J). (gr. 2-6). lib. bdg. 32.65 *(978-1-4965-3089-9(6),* 131974, Stone Arch Bks.) Capstone.
—The Lazarus Plan. Beavers, Ethen, illus. 2016. (You Choose Stories: Batman Ser.). (ENG.). 112p. (J). (gr. 2-6). lib. bdg. 32.65 *(978-1-4965-3088-2(8),* 131973, Stone Arch Bks.) Capstone.
—The Mystery of the Maze Monster, 1 vol. Neely, Scott, illus. 2014. (You Choose Stories: Scooby-Doo Ser.). (ENG.). 112p. (J). (gr. 2-6). pap. 6.95 *(978-1-4342-7928-6(6),* 124639, Stone Arch Bks.) Capstone.
—Super-Villain Smackdown! Beavers, Ethen, illus. 2015. (You Choose Stories: Batman Ser.). (ENG.). 112p. (J). (gr. 2-6). lib. bdg. 32.65 *(978-1-4965-0528-6(X),* 128600, Stone Arch Bks.) Capstone.
Schweizer, Chris. Tricky Coyote Tales. Thomas, Chad, illus. 2011. (Tricky Journeys Ser.: 1). (ENG.). (J). (gr. 2-4). pap. 39.62 *(978-0-7613-8625-4(4))* Lerner Publishing Group.
—Tricky Coyote Tales: Book 1, No. 1. Thomas, Chad Allen, illus. 2011. (Tricky Journeys (tm) Ser.: 1). (ENG.). 64p. (J). (gr. 2-4). pap. 7.99 *(978-0-7613-7859-4(6),* 513902bc-847d-4785-a0b6-e28bea2dd54c, Graphic Universe™) Lerner Publishing Group.
—Tricky Fox Tales. Paroline, Shelli & Paroline, Michelle, illus. 2011. (Tricky Journeys Ser.: 3). (ENG.). (J). (gr. 2-4). pap. 39.62 *(978-0-7613-8627-8(0))* Lerner Publishing Group.
—Tricky Monkey Tales. Thomas, Chad, illus. 2011. (Tricky Journeys Ser.: 6). (ENG.). (J). (gr. 2-4). pap. 39.62 *(978-0-7613-8630-8(0))* Lerner Publishing Group.
—Tricky Rabbit Tales. Giallongo, Zack, illus. 2011. (Tricky Journeys Ser.: 2). (ENG.). (J). (gr. 2-4). pap. 39.62 *(978-0-7613-8626-1(2))* Lerner Publishing Group.
—Tricky Raven Tales. Witt, David, illus. 2011. (Tricky Journeys Ser.: 4). (ENG.). (J). pap. 39.62 *(978-0-7613-8628-5(9))* Lerner Publishing Group.
—Tricky Spider Tales. Huddleston, Courtney, illus. 2011. (Tricky Journeys Ser.: 5). (ENG.). (J). (gr. 2-4). pap. 39.62 *(978-0-7613-8629-2(7))* Lerner Publishing Group.
Shiga, Jason. Meanwhile: Pick Any Path. 3,856 Story Possibilities. 2010. (ENG., Illus.). 80p. (J). (gr. 3-9). 17.99 *(978-0-8109-8423-3(7),* 665501, Amulet Bks.) Abrams, Inc.
Shuky. Knights Club: the Bands of Bravery: The Comic Book You Can Play. Waltch & Novy, illus. 2018. (Comic Quests Ser.: 2). 184p. (J). (gr. 3-7). pap. 9.99 *(978-1-68369-055-9(9))* Quirk Bks.
Simpson, C. E. Eighth Grade Witch. Utomo, Gabhor, illus. 2014. (ENG.). 144p. (J). (gr. 4-8). mass mkt. 6.99 *(978-1-937133-45-0(1))* Chooseco LLC.
Soria, Gabe. Excellent Ernesto Cousins 3/Wrestlevania: A Play-Your-Way Adventure. Hale, Kendall, illus. 2019. (Midnight Arcade Ser.: 2). 288p. (J). (gr. 5). pap. 8.99 *(978-0-593-09366-5(6),* Penguin Workshop) Penguin Young Readers Group.
Steele, Michael Anthony. The Case of the Fright Flight. Neely, Scott, illus. 2016. (You Choose Stories: Scooby-Doo Ser.). (ENG.). 112p. (J). (gr. 2-6). lib. bdg. 32.65 *(978-1-4965-2662-5(7),* 131221, Stone Arch Bks.) Capstone.
—Metallo Attacks! Brizuela, Dario, illus. 2018. (You Choose Stories: Superman Ser.). (ENG.). 112p. (J). (gr. 2-6). lib. bdg. 32.65 *(978-1-4965-5826-8(X),* 136914, Stone Arch Bks.) Capstone.
—Movie Magic Madness. Lozano, Omar, illus. 2019. (You Choose Stories: Wonder Woman Ser.). (ENG.). 112p. (J). (gr. 2-6). pap. 6.95 *(978-1-4965-8440-3(6),* 140965); lib. bdg. 32.65 *(978-1-4965-8350-5(7),* 140644) Capstone. (Stone Arch Bks.).
Stephens, Sarah Hines. Metropolis Mayhem. Brizuela, Dario, illus. 2018. (You Choose Stories: Superman Ser.). (ENG.). 112p. (J). (gr. 2-6). lib. bdg. 32.65 *(978-1-4965-5827-5(8),* 136915, Stone Arch Bks.) Capstone.
Stine, R. L. Slappy's Tales of Horror. 2015. (Goosebumps Graphix Ser.). lib. bdg. 24.50 *(978-0-606-37761-4(1))* Turtleback.
Storrie, Paul D., et al. Twisted Journeys(r): Spring 2012 New Releases. 2012. (Twisted Journeys Ser.). (Illus.). 112p. (J). (gr. 4-7). lib. bdg. 55.86 *(978-0-7613-8910-1(5),* Graphic Universe™) Lerner Publishing Group.
Suen, Anastasia. A Great Idea? An Up2U Character Education Adventure, 1 vol. Dippold, Jane, illus. 2013. (Up2U Adventures Ser.). (ENG.). 80p. (J). (gr. 2-5). 35.64 *(978-1-62402-093-3(3),* 17355, Calico Chapter Bks.) ABDO Publishing Co.
—New Girl: An Up2U Character Education Adventure, 1 vol. Dippold, Jane, illus. 2013. (Up2U Adventures Ser.). (ENG.). 80p. (J). (gr. 2-5). lib. bdg. 35.64 *(978-1-61641-968-4(7),* 15219, Calico Chapter Bks.) ABDO Publishing Co.
Sutton, Laurie S. Cosmic Conquest. Doescher, Erik, illus. 2018. (You Choose Stories: Justice League Ser.). (ENG.). 112p. (J). (gr. 2-6). pap. 6.95 *(978-1-4965-6559-4(2),* 138572); lib. bdg. 32.65 *(978-1-4965-6555-6(X),* 138568) Capstone. (Stone Arch Bks.).
—The Crystal Quest. Lozano, Omar, illus. 2019. (You Choose Stories: Wonder Woman Ser.). (ENG.). 112p. (J). (gr. 2-6). pap. 6.95 *(978-1-4965-8441-0(4),* 140966); lib. bdg. 32.65 *(978-1-4965-8351-2(5),* 140645) Capstone. (Stone Arch Bks.).
—The Fright at Zombie Farm. Neely, Scott, illus. 2015. (You Choose Stories: Scooby-Doo Ser.). (ENG.). 112p. (J). (gr. 2-6). lib. bdg. 32.65 *(978-1-4342-9713-6(6),* 127039, Stone Arch Bks.) Capstone.
—The Ghost of the Bermuda Triangle, 1 vol. Neely, Scott, illus. 2014. (You Choose Stories: Scooby-Doo Ser.). (ENG.). 112p. (J). (gr. 2-6). 32.65 *(978-1-4342-9126-4(X),* 125571, Stone Arch Bks.) Capstone.
—The Heart of Hades. Lozano, Omar, illus. 2019. (You Choose Stories: Wonder Woman Ser.). (ENG.). 112p. (J). (gr. 2-6). pap. 6.95 *(978-1-4965-8438-0(4),* 140963); lib. bdg. 32.65 *(978-1-4965-8348-2(5),* 140642) Capstone. (Stone Arch Bks.).
—The House on Spooky Street. Neely, Scott, illus. 2015. (You Choose Stories: Scooby-Doo Ser.). (ENG.). 112p. (J). (gr. 2-6). lib. bdg. 32.65 *(978-1-4342-9714-3(4),* 127040, Stone Arch Bks.) Capstone.
—The Joker's Dozen. Beavers, Ethen, illus. 2015. (You Choose Stories: Batman Ser.). (ENG.). 112p. (J). (gr. 2-6). lib. bdg. 32.65 *(978-1-4342-9707-5(1),* 127026, Stone Arch Bks.) Capstone.
—The Mystery of the Aztec Tomb, 1 vol. Neely, Scott, illus. 2014. (You Choose Stories: Scooby-Doo Ser.). (ENG.). 112p. (J). (gr. 2-6). 32.65 *(978-1-4342-9127-1(8),* 125572, Stone Arch Bks.) Capstone.
—The Portal of Doom. Doescher, Erik, illus. 2018. (You Choose Stories: Justice League Ser.). (ENG.). 112p. (J). (gr. 2-6). pap. 6.95 *(978-1-4965-6558-7(4),* 138571, Stone Arch Bks.) Capstone.
—The Secret of the Flying Saucer. Neely, Scott, illus. 2015. (You Choose Stories: Scooby-Doo Ser.). (ENG.). 112p. (J). (gr. 2-6). lib. bdg. 32.65 *(978-1-4965-0478-4(X),* 128504, Stone Arch Bks.) Capstone.
—The Secret of the Sea Creature, 1 vol. Neely, Scott, illus. 2014. (You Choose Stories: Scooby-Doo Ser.). (ENG.). 112p. (J). (gr. 2-6). pap. 6.95 *(978-1-4342-7925-5(1),* 124637, Stone Arch Bks.) Capstone.
—The Terrible Trio. Beavers, Ethen, illus. 2015. (You Choose Stories: Batman Ser.). (ENG.). 112p. (J). (gr. 2-6). lib. bdg. 32.65 *(978-1-4965-0529-3(8),* 128601, Stone Arch Bks.) Capstone.
Terman, D. By Balloon to the Sahara. Millet, Jason, illus. 2015. (ENG.). 144p. (J). (gr. 4-8). pap. 7.99 *(978-1-937133-48-1(6))* Chooseco LLC.
Turner, Tracey. Lost in the Crater of Fear. 2016. (ENG., Illus.). 128p. (J). *(978-0-7787-2353-0(4))* Crabtree Publishing Co.
—Lost in the Desert of Dread. 2014. (LOST: Can You Survive? Ser.). (ENG., Illus.). 128p. (J). (gr. 6-6). *(978-0-7787-0725-7(3))* Crabtree Publishing Co.
—Lost in the Jungle of Doom. 2014. (LOST: Can You Survive? Ser.). (ENG., Illus.). 128p. (J). (gr. 6-6). *(978-0-7787-0727-1(X))* Crabtree Publishing Co.
—Lost in the Mountains of Death. 2014. (LOST: Can You Survive? Ser.). (ENG., Illus.). 128p. (J). (gr. 6-6). *(978-0-7787-0729-5(6))* Crabtree Publishing Co.
—Lost in the Sea of Despair. 2014. (LOST: Can You Survive? Ser.). (ENG., Illus.). 128p. (J). (gr. 6-6). *(978-0-7787-0731-8(8))* Crabtree Publishing Co.
—Lost in the Swamp of Terror. 2016. (ENG., Illus.). 128p. (J). *(978-0-7787-2354-7(2))* Crabtree Publishing Co.
Wallace, Jim. Search for the Mountain Gorillas. Nugent, Suzanne & Donploypetch, Jintanan, illus. 2008. (ENG.). 144p. (J). (gr. 4-8). pap. 7.99 *(978-1-933390-25-3(5))* Chooseco LLC.
—Terror on the Titanic. Sundaravej, Sittisan, illus. 2007. (ENG.). 144p. (J). (gr. 4-8). pap. 7.99 *(978-1-933390-24-6(7))* Chooseco LLC.
Wallace, Rich. Backcourt Battle: An Up2U Character Education Adventure. King, Chris, illus. 2017. (Up2U Adventures Set 3 Ser.). (ENG.). 80p. (J). (gr. 2-5). lib. bdg. 35.64 *(978-1-5321-3028-1(7),* 25504, Calico Chapter Bks.) ABDO Publishing Co.
—Double-Crossed at Cactus Flats: An Up2 U Western Adventure, 1 vol. Mitchell, Hazel, illus. 2013. (Up2U Adventures Ser.). (ENG.). 80p. (J). (gr. 2-5). lib. bdg. 35.64 *(978-1-61641-966-0(0),* 15215, Calico Chapter Bks.) ABDO Publishing Co.
—The Room of Woe: An Up2U Horror Adventure, 1 vol. Emroca Flores, Jose, illus. 2015. (Up2U Adventures Ser.). (ENG.). 80p. (J). (gr. 2-5). 35.64 *(978-1-62402-094-0(1),* 17357, Calico Chapter Bks.) ABDO Publishing Co.
Weetman, Nova. A Hot Cold Summer: Choose Your Own Ever After. 2016. (ENG.). 256p. (J). pap. 5.99 *(978-1-61067-354-9(9))* Kane Miller.
Welshman, Kate. Make up or Break Up. 2015. (Choose Your Own Ever After Ser.). (ENG.). 277p. (J). *(978-1-61067-447-8(2))* Kane Miller.
—Make up or Break Up: Choose Your Own Ever After. 2016. (ENG.). 256p. (J). pap. 5.99 *(978-1-61067-387-7(5))* Kane Miller.
Wiley, Jesse. The Oregon Trail: Danger at the Haunted Gate. 2018. (Oregon Trail Ser.: 2). (ENG., Illus.). 160p. (J). (gr. 1-5). 14.99 *(978-1-328-55001-9(X),* 1724255, Clarion Bks.) HarperCollins Pubs.
—The Oregon Trail: Danger at the Haunted Gate. 2018. (Oregon Trail Ser.: 2). (ENG., Illus.). 160p. (J). (gr. 1-5). pap. 7.99 *(978-1-328-54997-6(6),* 1724097, Clarion Bks.) HarperCollins Pubs.
—The Oregon Trail: the Race to Chimney Rock. 2018. (Oregon Trail Ser.: 1). (ENG., Illus.). 160p. (J). (gr. 1-5). pap. 7.99 *(978-1-328-54996-9(8),* 1724095, Clarion Bks.) HarperCollins Pubs.
—The Oregon Trail: the Road to Oregon City. 2018. (Oregon Trail Ser.: 4). (ENG., Illus.). 176p. (J). (gr. 1-5). pap. 7.99 *(978-1-328-54999-0(2),* 1724101, Clarion Bks.) HarperCollins Pubs.
—The Oregon Trail: the Search for Snake River. 2018. (Oregon Trail Ser.: 3). (ENG., Illus.). 160p. (J). (gr. 1-5). pap. 7.99 *(978-1-328-54998-3(4),* 1724099, Clarion Bks.) HarperCollins Pubs.
—The Oregon Trail: the Search for Snake River. 2018. (Oregon Trail Ser.: 3). (ENG., Illus.). 160p. (J). (gr. 1-5). 14.99 *(978-1-328-55002-6(8),* 1724257, Clarion Bks.) HarperCollins Pubs.
—The Oregon Trail: the Wagon Train Trek. 2019. (Oregon Trail Ser.). (ENG., Illus.). 176p. (J). (gr. 1-5). 14.99 *(978-1-328-62714-8(4),* 1734407); pap. 7.99 *(978-1-328-62715-5(2),* 1734409) HarperCollins Pubs. (Clarion Bks.).
Wilhelm, Doug. Curse of the Pirate Mist. Semionov, Vladimir, illus. 2011. (ENG.). 144p. (J). (gr. 4-8). pap. 7.99 *(978-1-937133-02-3(8))* Chooseco LLC.
Windover, Liz. Blood Island. Utomo, Gabhor, illus. 2014. (ENG.). 144p. (J). (gr. 4-8). mass mkt. 6.99 *(978-1-937133-46-7(X))* Chooseco LLC.
Young, J. E. Horror in Space. Huddleston, Courtney, illus. 2011. (Twisted Journeys Ser.: 18). (ENG.). 112p. (J). (gr. 4-7). pap. 45.32 *(978-0-7613-7614-9(3),* Graphic Universe™) Lerner Publishing Group.
Zuckerman, Lilla & Zuckerman, Nora. Beauty Queen Blowout: Miss Adventure #2. 2003. (ENG.). 240p. pap. 15.99 *(978-0-7432-3846-5(X),* Touchstone) Touchstone.

PLUMBING

Freedman, Jeri. Plumber, 1 vol. 2015. (Careers in Construction Ser.). (ENG., Illus.). 112p. (YA). (gr. 7-7). lib. bdg. 44.50 *(978-1-5026-0982-3(7),* 1434de1c-88a6-492a-bb9e-940dc7b3d037) Cavendish Square Publishing LLC.
Given-Wilson, Rachel & Payment, Simone. Your Future As a Plumber, 1 vol. 2019. (High-Demand Careers Ser.). (ENG.). 80p. (gr. 7-7). pap. 16.30 *(978-1-5081-8788-2(6),* 8c7200d0-81d4-4243-adb3-d24ea5cd3935) Rosen Publishing Group, Inc., The.
Isle, Mick. Everything You Need to Know about Food Poisoning. 2009. (Need to Know Library). 64p. (gr. 5-5). 58.50 *(978-1-60854-069-3(3))* Rosen Publishing Group, Inc., The.
Kamberg, Mary-Lane. A Career As a Plumber, Pipefitter, or Steamfitter, 1 vol. 2018. (Jobs for Rebuilding America Ser.). (ENG., Illus.). 80p. (J). (gr. 6-6). 38.80 *(978-1-5081-7991-7(3),* 3974f796-b274-4764-9c50-512421c0f794) Rosen Publishing Group, Inc., The.
Mara, Wil. Be a Plumber. 2019. (21st Century Skills Library: Guide to the Trades Ser.). (ENG., Illus.). 32p. (J). (gr. 4-7). pap. 14.21 *(978-1-5341-5105-5(2),* 213727); lib. bdg. 32.07 *(978-1-5341-4819-2(1),* 213726) Cherry Lake Publishing.
Meister, Cari. Plumbers. 2014. (Illus.). 24p. (J). lib. bdg. 25.65 *(978-1-62031-095-3(3),* Bullfrog Bks.) Jump! Inc.
Moening, Kate. Plumbers. 2019. (Community Helpers Ser.). (ENG., Illus.). 24p. (J). (gr. k-3). lib. bdg. 26.95 *(978-1-62617-904-2(2),* Blastoff! Readers) Bellwether Media.
Morkes, Andrew. Plumber, Vol. 10. 2018. (Careers in the Building Trades: a Growing Demand Ser.). 80p. (J). (gr. 7). lib. bdg. 33.27 *(978-1-4222-4118-9(1))* Mason Crest.
Payment, Simone. A Career as a Plumber, 1 vol. 2010. (Essential Careers Ser.). (ENG.). 80p. (YA). (gr. 6-6). lib. bdg. 37.47 *(978-1-4358-9473-0(1),* b5090b56-9622-4089-b878-4b673c05f3d2) Rosen Publishing Group, Inc., The.
Plumbing, Heating, Air Conditioning & Refrigeration Student Activity. 2004. (YA). cd-rom *(978-1-57078-954-0(1),* CEV60033) C E V Multimedia, Ltd.
Rose, Simon. Plumber. 2014. (Illus.). 24p. (J). *(978-1-4896-2994-4(7))* Weigl Pubs., Inc.

PLUMBING—FICTION

Candlewick Press. FETCH! with Ruff Ruffman: Doggie Duties. WGBH, illus. 2014. (Fetch! with Ruff Ruffman Ser.). (ENG.). 48p. (J). (gr. 1-4). pap. 5.99 *(978-0-7636-6815-0(X),* Candlewick Entertainment) Candlewick Pr.
Curious George Plumber's Helper. 2010. (Curious George Ser.). (ENG., Illus.). 24p. (J). (gr. -1-3). pap. 4.99 *(978-0-547-23589-9(5),* 1083294, Clarion Bks.) HarperCollins Pubs.
Klise, Kate. Regarding the Sink: Where, Oh Where, Did Waters Go? Klise, Kate & Klise, M. Sarah, illus. 2006. (Regarding the Fountain Ser.: Bk. 2). (ENG.). 144p. (J). (gr. 2-4). 21.19 *(978-0-15-205019-1(1))* Harcourt Children's Bks.

PLUMBING—VOCATIONAL GUIDANCE

Gregory, Josh. Plumber. 2011. (21st Century Skills Library: Cool Careers Ser.). (ENG., Illus.). 32p. (gr. 4-8). lib. bdg. 32.07 *(978-1-60279-984-4(9),* 200974) Cherry Lake Publishing.
Lüsted, Marcia Amidon. Working As a Plumber in Your Community, 1 vol. 2015. (Careers in Your Community Ser.). (ENG.). 80p. (YA). (gr. 7-8). 37.47 *(978-1-4994-6119-0(4),* 67f3a090-c3cd-4d56-86ed-3d9970b4a4c9, Rosen Young Adult) Rosen Publishing Group, Inc., The.
Worthington, Niles. A Plumber's Job, 1 vol. 2015. (Community Workers Ser.). (ENG., Illus.). 24p. (gr. 1-1). pap. 9.23 *(978-1-5026-0433-0(7),* b9a211da-a54d-4137-8735-bb3bbe801832) Cavendish Square Publishing LLC.

PLUTO (DWARF PLANET)

Adamson, Thomas K. Pluto [Scholastic]: A Dwarf Planet. 2010. (Exploring the Galaxy Ser.). (ENG.). 24p. pap. 0.49 *(978-1-4296-5817-1(7),* Capstone Pr.) Capstone.
Carson, Mary Kay. Mission to Pluto: The First Visit to an Ice Dwarf & the Kuiper Belt. 2017. (Scientists in the Field Ser.). (ENG., Illus.). 80p. (J). (gr. 5-7). 18.99 *(978-0-544-41671-0(6),* 1594758, Clarion Bks.) HarperCollins Pubs.
Glaser, Chaya & Sawyer, J. Clark. Pluto: Not a Planet. 2015. (Out of This World Ser.). (ENG.). 24p. (J). (gr. -1-3). lib. bdg. 26.99 *(978-1-62724-571-5(5))* Bearport Publishing Co., Inc.
Goldstein, Margaret. Pluto. 2009. pap. 6.95 *(978-0-8225-4766-2(X))* Lerner Publishing Group.
Goldstein, Margaret J. Pluto. 2003. (Our Universe Ser.). (ENG., Illus.). 32p. (gr. 2-4). lib. bdg. 22.60 *(978-0-8225-4656-6(6))* Lerner Publishing Group.
Hantula, Richard & Asimov, Isaac. Plutón y Caronte (Pluto & Charon), 1 vol. 2003. (Isaac Asimov's Biblioteca Del Universo Del Siglo XXI (Isaac Asimov's 21st Century Library of the Universe) Ser.). (SPA., Illus.). 32p. (gr. 3-5). lib. bdg. 28.67 *(978-0-8368-3859-6(9),* 3ae2196b-697f-47c9-b87e-33d46b0492ac, Gareth Stevens Learning Library) Stevens, Gareth Publishing LLLP.
Hayhurst, Chris. Pluto. 2009. (Library of Planets Ser.). 48p. (gr. 5-8). 55.90 *(978-1-60853-820-1(6),* Rosen Reference) Rosen Publishing Group, Inc., The.
—Pluto & Other Dwarf Planets, 1 vol. 2007. (Library of Planets (Second Edition) Ser.). (ENG.). 48p. (J). (gr. 5-5). 34.47 *(978-1-4042-1965-6(X),* e03a38db-d01e-432b-aa11-bebb0bcb1a82) Rosen Publishing Group, Inc., The.
Jefferis, David. Ice Dwarfs: Pluto & Beyond. 2008. (Exploring Our Solar System Ser.). (ENG., Illus.). 32p. (J). (gr. 3-7). pap. *(978-0-7787-3752-0(7))* Crabtree Publishing Co.
Kaspar, Anna. A Look at Pluto & Other Dwarf Planets. 2009. (Astronomy Now! Ser.). 24p. (gr. 2-3). 42.50 *(978-1-61511-472-6(6),* PowerKids Pr.) Rosen Publishing Group, Inc., The.
Korba, Joanna & Benchmark Education Co., LLC. Pluto, the Planet That Was. 2014. (Text Connections Ser.). (J). (gr. 3). *(978-1-4509-9662-4(0))* Benchmark Education Co.
Kruesi, Liz. Voyage to Pluto. 2018. (Destination Space Ser.). (ENG., Illus.). 48p. (J). (gr. 5-6). pap. 11.95 *(978-1-63517-572-1(0),* 1635175720); lib. bdg. 34.21 *(978-1-63517-500-4(3),* 1635175003) North Star Editions. (Focus Readers).
—Voyage to Pluto. 2018. (Illus.). 48p. (J). pap. *(978-1-4896-9801-8(9),* AV2 by Weigl) Weigl Pubs., Inc.
Lawrence, Riley. Exploring Pluto & Other Dwarf Planets. 2017. (Journey Through Our Solar System Ser.). 24p. (gr. 1-2). 49.50 *(978-1-5345-2252-7(2),* KidHaven Publishing); (ENG.). pap. 9.25 *(978-1-5345-2290-9(5),* 9802c36f-29ee-4218-8bdb-347d6e558b51); (ENG.). lib. bdg. 26.23 *(978-1-5345-2280-0(8),* 2621fda4-f1dd-4c96-bd66-7050b54e38f7) Greenhaven Publishing LLC.
Lew, Kristi. The Dwarf Planet Pluto, 1 vol. 2010. (Space! Ser.). (ENG.). 64p. (gr. 5-5). lib. bdg. 35.50 *(978-0-7614-4243-1(X),* 3544f434-d28b-4cfd-aa14-ab88baf177c2) Cavendish Square Publishing LLC.
McGinty, Alice B. The Girl Who Named Pluto: The Story of Venetia Burney. Haidle, Elizabeth, illus. 2019. 40p. (J). (gr. -1-3). 18.99 *(978-1-5247-6831-7(6),* Schwartz & Wade Bks.) Random Hse. Children's Bks.
Miller, Ron. Mercury & Pluto. 2003. (Worlds Beyond Ser.). (Illus.). 80p. (J). (gr. 7-18). lib. bdg. 27.93 *(978-0-7613-2361-7(9),* Twenty-First Century Bks.) Lerner Publishing Group.
Owen, Ruth. Pluto & Other Dwarf Planets, 1 vol. 2013. (Explore Outer Space Ser.). (ENG.). 32p. (J). (gr. 2-3). 29.93 *(978-1-61533-730-9(X),* e47a158f-c9aa-415e-aaad-d41b5a83e0f8); pap. 11.00 *(978-1-61533-777-4(6),* 701c14f2-440a-4355-b51a-4a896876032d) Rosen Publishing Group, Inc., The. (Windmill Bks.).

—Pluto & Other Dwarf Planets. 2013. (Explore Outer Space Ser.). 32p. (J). (gr. 3-6). pap. 60.00 *(978-1-61533-778-1(4))* Windmill Bks.
Oxlade, Chris. Jupiter, Neptune, & Other Outer Planets, 1 vol. 2007. (Earth & Space Ser.). (ENG., Illus.). 48p. (YA). (gr. 6-6). lib. bdg. 34.47 *(978-1-4042-3736-0(4),* 24557517-dcfe-4798-aa18-f3a4a8c9c1d5) Rosen Publishing Group, Inc., The.
Portman, Michael. Why Isn't Pluto a Planet?, 1 vol. 2013. (Space Mysteries Ser.). (ENG., Illus.). 32p. (J). (gr. 2-3). 29.27 *(978-1-4339-8282-8(X),* d87fa3cf-0460-4f48-9030-04a7ff8c251c); pap. 11.50 *(978-1-4339-8283-5(8),* 564528c8-0dcf-46f0-8f22-31854a810c6b) Stevens, Gareth Publishing LLLP. (Gareth Stevens Learning Library).
Prendergast, Gabrielle. If Pluto Was a Pea. Gerlings, Rebecca, illus. 2019. (ENG.). 40p. (J). (gr. -1-3). 17.99 *(978-1-5344-0435-9(X),* McElderry, Margaret K. Bks.) McElderry, Margaret K. Bks.
Ring, Susan. Pluto. (Exploring Planets Ser.). (J). 2004. pap. 8.95 *(978-1-59036-228-0(4))* 2003. (Illus.). 24p. lib. bdg. 24.45 *(978-1-59036-101-6(6))* Weigl Pubs., Inc.
Roland, James. Pluto: A Space Discovery Guide. 2017. (Space Discovery Guides). (ENG., Illus.). 48p. (J). (gr. 4-6). 31.99 *(978-1-5124-2587-1(7),* 44dc1493-f977-4681-91f4-7cea63a3e628); E-Book 47.99 *(978-1-5124-3813-0(8),* 9781512438130); E-Book 47.99 *(978-1-5124-2796-7(9));* E-Book 4.99 *(978-1-5124-3812-3(X),* 9781512438123) Lerner Publishing Group. (Lerner Pubns.).
Rusch, Elizabeth & Francis, Guy. The Planet Hunter: The Story Behind What Happened to Pluto. 2007. (ENG., Illus.). 32p. (J). (gr. -1-3). 15.95 *(978-0-87358-926-0(2))* Cooper Square Publishing Llc.
Sawyer, J. Clark. PlutÓN: No Es un Planeta. 2015. (Fuera de Este Mundo Ser.). (SPA., Illus.). 24p. (J). (gr. -1-3). lib. bdg. 26.99 *(978-1-62724-595-1(2))* Bearport Publishing Co., Inc.
Sommer, Nathan. Pluto & the Dwarf Planets. 2019. (Space Science Ser.). (ENG., Illus.). 24p. (J). (gr. 3-8). lib. bdg. 26.95 *(978-1-62617-977-6(8),* Torque Bks.) Bellwether Media.
Sparrow, Giles. Destination Uranus, Neptune, & Pluto, 1 vol. 2009. (Destination Solar System Ser.). (ENG., Illus.). 32p. (J). (gr. 3-4). 28.93 *(978-1-4358-3446-0(1),* 05e1d277-a173-4544-8294-068018bd164f); pap. 11.00 *(978-1-4358-3463-7(1),* da375e81-83d8-47ac-b022-097405e0edbb) Rosen Publishing Group, Inc., The. (PowerKids Pr.).
Stefoff, Rebecca. Pluto, 1 vol. 2003. (Blastoff! Ser.). (ENG., Illus.). 64p. (gr. 5-5). 34.07 *(978-0-7614-1404-9(5),* 80d30cc6-5cec-4486-a869-031def38d906) Cavendish Square Publishing LLC.
Stewart, Kellie. Journey to Pluto & Other Dwarf Planets, 1 vol. 2014. (Spotlight on Space Science Ser.). (ENG.). 32p. (J). (gr. 5-5). pap. 12.75 *(978-1-4994-0375-6(5),* 7d7dd6e5-1cc1-4b9a-bd43-74681ac973e0, PowerKids Pr.) Rosen Publishing Group, Inc., The.
Taylor-Butler, Christine. Pluto: Dwarf Planet. 2007. (Scholastic News Nonfiction Readers Ser.). (ENG., Illus.). 24p. (J). (gr. 1-2). 22.00 *(978-0-531-14751-1(7))* Scholastic Library Publishing.
—Pluto: Dwarf Planet (Scholastic News Nonfiction Readers: Space Science) 2008. (Scholastic News Nonfiction Readers Ser.). (ENG., Illus.). 24p. (J). (gr. 1-2). pap. 6.95 *(978-0-531-14766-5(5),* Children's Pr.) Scholastic Library Publishing.
Terp, Gail. Pluto & Other Dwarf Planets. 2018. (Deep Space Discovery Ser.). (ENG.). 32p. (gr. 2-7). 9.95 *(978-1-68072-715-9(X));* (J). (gr. 4-6). pap. 9.99 *(978-1-64466-268-7(X),* 12325); (Illus.). (J). (gr. 4-6). lib. bdg. *(978-1-68072-421-9(5),* 12324) Black Rabbit Bks. (Bolt).
—Plutón y Otros Planetas Enanos. 2018. (Descubrimiento Del Espacio Profundo Ser.). (SPA., Illus.). 32p. (J). (gr. 4-6). lib. bdg. *(978-1-68072-971-9(3),* 12450, Bolt) Black Rabbit Bks.
Vogt, Gregory. The Dwarf Planet Pluto. 2009. (Early Bird Astronomy Ser.). (ENG.). 48p. (gr. 2-5). lib. bdg. 26.60 *(978-0-7613-4157-4(9))* Lerner Publishing Group.
—Pluto: A Dwarf Planet. 2009. (Early Bird Astronomy Ser.). (ENG., Illus.). 48p. (gr. 2-5). pap. 8.95 *(978-0-7613-4988-4(X),* Lerner Pubns.) Lerner Publishing Group.
Weitekamp, Margaret. Pluto's Secret: an Icy World's Tale of Discovery: An Icy World's Tale of Discovery. Kidd, Diane, illus. 2013. (ENG.). 40p. (J). (gr. k-4). 16.95 *(978-1-4197-0423-9(0),* 1005001, Abrams Bks. for Young Readers) Abrams, Inc.
Weitekamp, Margaret & DeVorkin, David. Pluto's Secret: An Icy World's Tale of Discovery. Kidd, Diane, illus. 2015. (ENG.). 40p. (J). (gr. 1-4). pap. 9.95 *(978-1-4197-1526-6(7),* 1005003) Abrams, Inc.
Weitekamp, Margaret & Devorkin, David. Pluto's Secret: An Icy World's Tale of Discovery. 2015. (J). lib. bdg. 20.80 *(978-0-606-37376-0(4))* Turtleback.
World Book, Inc. Staff, contrib. by. Neptune & Pluto. 2006. (World Book's Solar System & Space Exploration Library). (Illus.). 63p. (J). *(978-0-7166-9507-3(3))* World Bk., Inc.
—Neptune & the Distant Dwarf Planets. 2nd ed. 2006. (World Book's Solar System & Space Exploration Library). (Illus.). 64p. (J). *(978-0-7166-9518-9(9))* World Bk., Inc.

PLUTO (FICTITIOUS CHARACTER)—FICTION

Disney Staff. The Story of Pluto the Pup. 2004. (Illus.). 96p. (J). 35.00 incl. audio compact disk *(978-1-55709-356-1(3))* Applewood Bks.

PLUTO (PLANET)

see Pluto (Dwarf Planet)

PLYMOUTH (MASS.)—HISTORY

Cipriano, Jeri. Three Historical Communities of North America: Text Pairs. 2008. (Bridges/Navigators Ser.). (J). (gr. 3). 89.00 *(978-1-4108-8375-9(2))* Benchmark Education Co.
Wagner, William Bradford (Leaders of the Colonial Era) 2010. (ENG.). 120p. (gr. 5-8). 35.00 *(978-1-60413-743-9(6),* P200195, Facts On File) Infobase Holdings, Inc.

POCAHONTAS, -1617

Adams, Colleen. Pocahontas. 2009. (Reading Room Collection 1 Ser.). 16p. (gr. 2-3). 37.50 *(978-1-60851-949-1(X),* PowerKids Pr.) Rosen Publishing Group, Inc., The.
—Pocahontas: The Life of an Indian Princess, 1 vol. 2005. (Reading Room Collection 1 Ser.). (ENG., Illus.). 16p. (J). (gr. 2-3). lib. bdg. 22.27 *(978-1-4042-3348-5(2),* 9742d742-8b33-4c42-acaf-7741d03ed4f6) Rosen Publishing Group, Inc., The.
—The True Story of Pocahontas. (What Really Happened? Ser.). 24p. (gr. 2-3). 2009. 42.50 *(978-1-60854-765-4(5),* PowerKids Pr.) 2008. (ENG., Illus.). (J). lib. bdg. 26.27 *(978-1-4042-4475-7(1),* f0084636-13eb-497c-aee5-c454b0859aa2) Rosen Publishing Group, Inc., The.
Becker, Sandra. Pocahontas. (Illus.). 24p. (J). 2018. pap. *(978-1-4896-9563-5(X),* AV2 by Weigl) 2003. lib. bdg. 24.45 *(978-1-59036-074-3(5))* Weigl Pubs., Inc.
Benjamin, Andrew. Pocahontas: & Her Incredible Journey, 1 vol. 2014. (American Legends & Folktales Ser.). (ENG., Illus.). 32p. (gr. 3-3). lib. bdg. 31.21 *(978-1-62712-292-4(3),* 1fd542a3-1afc-4997-b539-ce92d7df1a51) Cavendish Square Publishing LLC.
Brimner, Larry Dane. Pocahontas: Bridging Two Worlds, 1 vol. 2009. (American Heroes Ser.). (ENG.). 48p. (gr. 3-3). lib. bdg. 32.64 *(978-0-7614-3065-0(2),* c65e5cb1-d030-467f-884c-63fc62bac5d7) Cavendish Square Publishing LLC.
Bruchac, Joseph. Pocahontas. 2005. (ENG., Illus.). 192p. (YA). (gr. 7-12). pap. 7.99 *(978-0-15-205465-6(0),* 1196444, Clarion Bks.) HarperCollins Pubs.
—Pocahontas. 2005. (Illus.). 173p. (gr. 7). 15.95 *(978-0-7569-5604-2(8))* Perfection Learning Corp.
Edison, Erin. Pocahontas, 1 vol. 2013. (Great Women in History Ser.). (ENG.). 24p. (J). (gr. -1-2). lib. bdg. 24.65 *(978-1-62065-074-5(6),* 120776) Capstone.
Fritz, Jean. The Double Life of Pocahontas. l.t. ed. 2003. (Children's Large Print Ser.). 24.95 *(978-1-58118-109-8(4))* LRS.
Harkins, Susan Sales & Harkins, William H. Pochantas. 2008. (What's So Great About...? Ser.). (Illus.). 32p. (J). (gr. 2-4). lib. bdg. 25.70 *(978-1-58415-682-6(1))* Mitchell Lane Pubs.
Kirkman, Marissa. The Life & Times of Pocahontas & the First Colonies. 2016. (Life & Times Ser.). (ENG., Illus.). 24p. (J). (gr. 1-3). lib. bdg. 27.99 *(978-1-5157-2477-3(8),* 132849, Capstone Pr.) Capstone.
Ledgerwood, Maja. Pocahontas: Princess of Faith & Courage. 2008. (Illus.). 48p. pap. 17.99 *(978-1-4343-4394-9(4))* AuthorHouse.
Nagle, Jeanne. Pocahontas: Facilitating Exchange Between the Powhatan & the Jamestown Settlers, 1 vol. 2017. (Women Who Changed History Ser.). (ENG., Illus.). 48p. (J). (gr. 6-7). pap. 15.05 *(978-1-68048-653-7(5),* f27feb14-1c67-4feb-a53f-db24e1cfb8b5, Britannica Educational Publishing) Rosen Publishing Group, Inc., The.
Nettleton, Pamela Hill. Pocahontas: Peacemaker & Friend to the Colonists. Yesh, Jeff, illus. 2003. (Biographies Ser.). (ENG.). 24p. (J). (gr. k-3). 27.32 *(978-1-4048-0187-5(1),* 90433, Picture Window Bks.) Capstone.
Patterson, Marie. Pocahontas, 1 vol. rev. ed. 2004. (Social Studies: Informational Text Ser.). (ENG.). 24p. (J). (gr. 4-8). pap. 10.99 *(978-0-7439-8745-5(4))* Teacher Created Materials, Inc.
Polette, Nancy. Pocahontas. 2003. (Rookie Biographies Ser.). (ENG., Illus.). 32p. (J). (gr. 1-2). 20.50 *(978-0-516-22859-4(5),* Children's Pr.) Scholastic Library Publishing.
—Rookie Biographies: Pocahontas. 2003. (Rookie Biographies Ser.). (ENG.). 32p. (J). (gr. 1-2). pap. 4.95 *(978-0-516-27782-0(0),* Children's Pr.) Scholastic Library Publishing.
Schwartz, Heather E. Pocahontas: Her Life & Legend. rev. ed. 2016. (Social Studies: Informational Text Ser.). (ENG., Illus.). 32p. (gr. 4-8). pap. 11.99 *(978-1-4938-3072-5(4))* Teacher Created Materials, Inc.
Sita, Lisa. Pocahontas: The Powhatan Culture & the Jamestown Colony. (Library of American Lives & Times Ser.). 112p. (gr. 5-5). 2009. 69.20 *(978-1-60853-500-2(2))* 2004. (ENG., Illus.). (J). lib. bdg. 38.27 *(978-1-4042-2653-1(2),* 0630cc02-b680-457c-b3b0-922753babdca) Rosen Publishing Group, Inc., The.
Sjonger, Rebecca & Kalman, Bobbie. Life of the Powhatan, 1 vol. 2004. (Native Nations of North America Ser.). (ENG., Illus.). 32p. (J). (gr. 2-5). pap. *(978-0-7787-0472-0(6));* (gr. 5). lib. bdg. *(978-0-7787-0380-8(0))* Crabtree Publishing Co.
Strand, Jennifer. Pocahontas. 2017. (Native American Leaders Ser.). (ENG., Illus.). 24p. (J). (gr. -1-2). lib. bdg. 31.36 *(978-1-5321-2024-4(9),* 25312, Abdo Zoom-Launch) ABDO Publishing Co.
Sullivan, Laura L. Pocahontas, 1 vol. 2020. (Inside Guide: Famous Native Americans Ser.). (ENG.). 32p. (gr. 4-5). pap. 11.58 *(978-1-5026-5124-2(6),* a8740c85-5a2a-4b28-abd2-27d4158dc690) Cavendish Square Publishing LLC.
Weinberger, Kimberly. Let's Read About — Pocahontas. Marchesi, Stephen, illus. 2003. (Scholastic First Biographies Ser.). (J). pap. *(978-0-439-56148-8(5))* Scholastic, Inc.

POCAHONTAS, -1617—FICTION

Kudlinski, Kathleen V. My Lady Pocahontas, 0 vols. unabr. ed. 2013. (ENG.). 288p. (J). (gr. 4-8). pap. 9.99 *(978-1-4778-1711-7(5),* 9781477817117, Skyscape) Amazon Publishing.
Lawton, Wendy G. The Captive Princess: A Story Based on the Life of Young Pocahontas. 2008. (Daughters of the Faith Ser.). (ENG.). 144p. (gr. 3-3). per. 8.99 *(978-0-8024-7640-1(6))* Moody Pubs.
LeSourd, Nancy. Adventures in Jamestown, 1 vol. 2008. (Liberty Letters Ser.). (ENG., Illus.). 240p. (J). pap. 7.99 *(978-0-310-71392-0(7))* Zonderkidz.
Marsh, Carole. Pocahontas. (Read-Along Ser.). (J). 7.99 incl. audio *(978-1-55723-739-2(5))* Walt Disney Records.
Smith, Andrea P. Pocahontas & John Smith. (Illus.). 24p. (J). 2012. 63.60 *(978-1-4488-5219-2(6))* 2011. (ENG., (gr. 2-3). pap. 11.60 *(978-1-4488-5218-5(8),* b60ab931-cd98-4c6a-8e80-ee5088d5964a) 2011. (ENG., (gr. 2-3). lib. bdg. 28.93 *(978-1-4488-5190-4(4),* 7856ab38-7648-4ab9-abab-e8472a2624c3) Rosen Publishing Group, Inc., The. (PowerKids Pr.).
Steinkraus, Kyla. Pastries with Pocahontas. Wood, Katie, illus. 2017. (Time Hop Sweets Shop Ser.). (ENG.). 32p. (gr. 1-3). 24.22 *(978-1-68342-330-0(5),* 9781683423300) Rourke Educational Media.
Walt Disney Company Staff. Pocahontas. 2005. (WEL., Illus.). 24p. *(978-1-899877-04-1(5))* Y Ddraig Fach.

POE, EDGAR ALLAN, 1809-1849

Amper, Susan. Bloom's How to Write about Edgar Allan Poe. 2008. (Bloom's How to Write about Literature Ser.). (ENG.). 232p. (gr. 9-12). 45.00 *(978-0-7910-9488-4(X),* P142847, Facts On File) Infobase Holdings, Inc.
Binns, Tristan Boyer. Edgar Allan Poe: Master of Suspense. 2005. (Great Life Stories Ser.). (ENG., Illus.). 128p. (J). (gr. 6-8). lib. bdg. 30.50 *(978-0-531-16751-9(8),* Watts, Franklin) Scholastic Library Publishing.
Burlingame, Jeff. Edgar Allan Poe: Deep into That Darkness Peering, 1 vol. 2008. (Americans: the Spirit of a Nation Ser.). (ENG., Illus.). 128p. (gr. 5-6). lib. bdg. 35.93 *(978-0-7660-3020-6(2),* 3c672f43-22b2-44b4-9055-f3fff1034fc4) Enslow Publishing, LLC.
Frisch, Aaron. Edgar Allan Poe. 2005. (Voices in Poetry Ser.). (Illus.). 48p. (J). (gr. 5-9). lib. bdg. 21.95 *(978-1-58341-344-9(8),* Creative Education) Creative Co., The.
—Edgar Allan Poe. Kelley, Gary, illus. 2014. (Voices in Poetry Ser.). (ENG.). 48p. (J). (gr. 5-8). lib. bdg. 35.65 *(978-1-60818-324-1(6),* 21446, Creative Education) Creative Co., The.
—Edgar Allan Poe. 2014. (Voices in Poetry Ser.). (ENG.). 48p. (J). (gr. 5-8). pap. 12.00 *(978-1-62832-052-7(4),* 21447, Creative Paperbacks) Creative Co., The.
Gigliotti, Jim. Who Was Edgar Allan Poe? Foley, Tim, illus. 2015. (Who Was-? Chapters Ser.). (ENG.). 112p. (J). (gr. 3-6). 18.69 *(978-1-4844-6178-5(9),* Penguin Workshop) Penguin Young Readers Group.
Mcarthur, Debra. Reading & Interpreting the Works of Edgar Allan Poe, 1 vol. 2015. (Lit Crit Guides). (ENG., Illus.). 160p. (gr. 8-8). lib. bdg. 41.60 *(978-0-7660-7342-5(4),* 733f64e4-075a-4b2e-ab24-f4902a461c6b) Enslow Publishing, LLC.
Meltzer, Milton. Edgar Allan Poe: A Biography. 2003. (Literary Greats Ser.). (ENG., Illus.). 144p. (gr. 7-12). lib. bdg. 33.26 *(978-0-7613-2910-7(2),* Twenty-First Century Bks.) Lerner Publishing Group.
Ray, Caitlin. Revenge, 1 vol. 2015. (Essential Literary Themes Ser.). (ENG., Illus.). 112p. (YA). (gr. 6-12). 41.36 *(978-1-62403-808-2(5),* 17814, Essential Library) ABDO Publishing Co.
Schoell, William. Mystery & Terror: The Story of Edgar Allan Poe. 2004. (Illus.). 128p. (YA). (gr. 6-12). 23.95 *(978-1-931798-39-6(7))* Reynolds, Morgan Inc.
Streissguth, Thomas. Edgar Allan Poe. 2005. (Biography Ser.). (Illus.). 112p. (J). (gr. 6-12). lib. bdg. 27.93 *(978-0-8225-4991-8(3))* Lerner Publishing Group.
Streissguth, Tom. Edgar Allan Poe. 2007. (Just the Facts Biographies Ser.). (ENG., Illus.). 112p. (gr. 5-12). lib. bdg. 27.93 *(978-0-8225-6800-1(4),* Lerner Pubns.) Lerner Publishing Group.
Wallace, Elise. The Prehistoric Masters of Literature Volume 1: Discover Literary History with a Prehistoric Twist! Isik, Semur, illus. 2018. (Jurassic Classics Ser.). (ENG.). 32p. (J). (gr. 4-7). lib. bdg. 26.65 *(978-1-942875-55-0(X),* 5dd27ad0-30fb-4ce7-a68e-d1ced05396be, Walter Foster Jr) Quarto Publishing Group USA.
—The Prehistoric Masters of Literature Volume 2: Discover Literary History with a Prehistoric Twist! Isik, Semur, illus. 2018. (Jurassic Classics Ser.). (ENG.). 32p. (J). (gr. 4-7). lib. bdg. 26.65 *(978-1-942875-56-7(8),* 83333adc-1433-4bd6-b1f8-7de331dd16e6, Walter Foster Jr) Quarto Publishing Group USA.
Whiting, Jim. Edgar Allan Poe. 2005. (Classic Storytellers Ser.). (Illus.). 48p. (J). (gr. 4-8). lib. bdg. 29.95 *(978-1-58415-373-3(3))* Mitchell Lane Pubs.

POE, EDGAR ALLAN, 1809-1849—FICTION

Amato, Mary. Open Mic Night at Westminster Cemetery. 2018. (ENG.). 272p. (YA). (gr. 8-12). 18.99 *(978-1-5124-6531-0(3),* db1e3ad9-57c6-4b00-9794-37cdeb14b0e3, Carolrhoda Lab™) Lerner Publishing Group.
Avi. The Man Who Was Poe. 2013. (ENG.). 224p. (J). (gr. 6-8). 21.19 *(978-0-545-50523-9(2))* Scholastic, Inc.
Bowen, Carl. The Murders in the Rue Morgue, 1 vol. Dimaya, Emerson, illus. 2013. (Edgar Allan Poe Graphic Novels Ser.). (ENG.). 72p. (J). (gr. 5-9). 28.65 *(978-1-4342-3033-1(3),* 114578); pap. 6.10 *(978-1-4342-4259-4(5),* 120321) Capstone. (Stone Arch Bks.).
Creagh, Kelly. Enshadowed: A Nevermore Book. (ENG., Illus.). (YA). (gr. 7). 2013. 464p. pap. 9.99 *(978-1-4424-0206-5(7))* 2012. 448p. 17.99 *(978-1-4424-0204-1(0),* Atheneum Bks. for Young Readers) Simon & Schuster Children's Publishing.
—Nevermore. 2011. (ENG., Illus.). 576p. (YA). (gr. 9). pap. 16.99 *(978-1-4424-0201-0(6),* Atheneum Bks. for Young Readers) Simon & Schuster Children's Publishing.
Dunn, Joeming. Cask of Amontillado, 1 vol. 2014. (Graphic Horror Ser.). (ENG.). 32p. (J). (gr. 5-8). lib. bdg. 32.79 *(978-1-62402-015-5(1),* 9100, Graphic Planet - Fiction) Magic Wagon.
—Raven, 1 vol. 2014. (Graphic Horror Ser.). (ENG.). 32p. (J). (gr. 5-8). lib. bdg. 32.79 *(978-1-62402-017-9(8),* 9104, Graphic Planet - Fiction) Magic Wagon.
Fields, Jan. A Novel Nightmare: The Purloined Story, 1 vol. Altmann, Scott, illus. 2013. (Adventures in Extreme Reading Ser.). (ENG.). 112p. (J). (gr. 2-5). 38.50 *(978-1-61641-924-0(5),* 68, Calico Chapter Bks.) ABDO Publishing Co.
Gustafson, Scott. Eddie: The Lost Youth of Edgar Allan Poe. Gustafson, Scott, illus. 2012. (ENG., Illus.). 208p. (J). (gr. 3-7). pap. 6.99 *(978-1-4169-9765-8(2),* Simon & Schuster Bks. For Young Readers) Simon & Schuster Bks. For Young Readers.
—Eddie: The Lost Youth of Edgar Allan Poe. Gustafson, Scott, illus. 2011. (ENG., Illus.). 208p. (J). (gr. 3-7). 15.99 *(978-1-4169-9764-1(4))* Simon & Schuster, Inc.
Harper, Benjamin. The Tell-Tale Heart, 1 vol. Calero, Dennis, illus. 2013. (Edgar Allan Poe Graphic Novels Ser.). (ENG.). 72p. (J). (gr. 5-9). lib. bdg. 27.99 *(978-1-4342-3023-2(6),* 114516, Stone Arch Bks.) Capstone.
Hinds, Gareth. Poe: Stories & Poems: A Graphic Novel Adaptation by Gareth Hinds. Hinds, Gareth, illus. 2017. (ENG., Illus.). 120p. (J). (gr. 7). 22.99 *(978-0-7636-8112-8(1))* Candlewick Pr.
—Poe: Stories & Poems: A Graphic Novel Adaptation by Gareth Hinds. 2017. (ENG., Illus.). 120p. (J). (gr. 7). pap. 14.99 *(978-0-7636-9509-5(2))* Candlewick Pr.
Kirov, Erica. Magickeepers: The Eternal Hourglass. Fortune, Eric, illus. 2010. 256p. (J). (gr. 4-7). pap. 10.99 *(978-1-4022-3855-0(X))* Sourcebooks, Inc.
Manning, Matthew K. The Fall of the House of Usher, 1 vol. Jimenez, Jim, illus. 2013. (Edgar Allan Poe Graphic Novels Ser.). (ENG.). 72p. (J). (gr. 5-9). pap. 6.10 *(978-1-4342-4258-7(7),* 120320, Stone Arch Bks.) Capstone.
McAlpine, Gordon. The Tell-Tale Start. Zuppardi, Sam, illus. 2013. (Misadventures of Edgar & Allan Poe Ser.: 1). 208p. (J). (gr. 3-7). pap. 7.99 *(978-0-14-242346-2(7),* Puffin Books) Penguin Young Readers Group.
Novel Units. Edgar Allan Poe: A Collection of Stories Novel Units Student Packet. 2019. (ENG.). (YA). pap. 13.99 *(978-1-58130-510-4(9),* Novel Units, Inc.) Classroom Library Co.
Poe, Edgar Allan. Edgar Allan Poe's Tales of Death & Dementia. Grimly, Gris, illus. 2009. (ENG.). 144p. (J). (gr. 6-9). 22.99 *(978-1-4169-5025-7(7),* Atheneum Bks. for Young Readers) Simon & Schuster Children's Publishing.
Tulien, Sean. The Pit & the Pendulum, 1 vol. Fabul, J. C., illus. 2013. (Edgar Allan Poe Graphic Novels Ser.). (ENG.). 72p. (J). (gr. 5-9). pap. 6.10 *(978-1-4342-4260-0(9),* 120322); lib. bdg. 27.99 *(978-1-4342-4024-8(X),* 118405) Capstone. (Stone Arch Bks.).

POETICS

Here are entered works on the art and technique of poetry. Works on the appreciation and philosophy of poetry are entered under Poetry.

see also Rhythm; Versification

Anderson, Jennifer Joline. Poetry. 2016. (Essential Literary Genres Ser.). (ENG., Illus.). 112p. (J). (gr. 6-12). lib. bdg. 41.36 *(978-1-68078-382-7(3),* 23529, Essential Library) ABDO Publishing Co.
Bodden, Valerie. Picturing Words in a Poem. 2016. (Write Me a Poem Ser.). (ENG., Illus.). 24p. (J). (gr. 1-4). *(978-1-60818-621-1(0),* 20550, Creative Education) Creative Co., The.
Early Macken, JoAnn. Read, Recite, & Write Narrative Poems. 2014. (Poet's Workshop Ser.). (ENG., Illus.). 32p. (J). (gr. 4-4). *(978-0-7787-0410-2(6))* Crabtree Publishing Co.
Fandel, Jennifer. Metaphors, Similes, & Other Word Pictures. 2005. (Understanding Poetry Ser.). (Illus.). 48p. (YA). (gr. 4-7). lib. bdg. 21.95 *(978-1-58341-340-1(5))* Creative Co., The.
—Puns, Allusions, & Other Word Secrets. 2005. (Understanding Poetry Ser.). (Illus.). 48p. (YA). (gr. 4-7). lib. bdg. 21.95 *(978-1-58341-341-8(3))* Creative Co., The.
—Rhyme, Meter, & Other Word Music. 2005. (Understanding Poetry Ser.). (Illus.). 48p. (YA). (gr. 4-7). lib. bdg. 21.95 *(978-1-58341-342-5(1))* Creative Co., The.
Herrera, Juan Felipe. Jabberwalking. Herrera, Juan Felipe, illus. 2018. (ENG., Illus.). 144p. (J). (gr. 5). 22.99 *(978-1-5362-0140-5(5));* pap. 14.99 *(978-0-7636-9264-3(6))* Candlewick Pr.
Lázaro León, Georgina & Genovés, Graciela. Jorge Luis Borges. Genovés, Graciela, illus. 2009. (Cuando los Grandes Eran Pequenos Ser.). (SPA., Illus.). 32p. (J). (gr. 4-6). 14.99 *(978-1-933032-40-5(5))* Lectorum Pubns., Inc.
Lesynski, Loris. I Did It Because... How a Poem Happens. Martchenko, Michael, illus. 3rd ed. 2006. (ENG.). 64p. (J). (gr. 2-5). pap. 9.95 *(978-1-55451-017-7(1),* 9781554510177) Annick Pr., Ltd. CAN. Dist: Publishers Group West (PGW).
Lombardo, Mary A. Poetry & Pop-Ups: An Art-Enhanced Approach to Writing Poetry, 1 vol. 2003. (ENG., Illus.). 96p. (gr. 4-6). pap. 15.95 *(978-1-58683-082-3(1),* 900303811, Linworth Publishing, Inc.) ABC-CLIO, LLC.
Lyon, George Ella. Where I'm From. 2004. (Writers & Young Writers Ser.: 2). 98p. pap. 13.95 *(978-1-888842-18-0(0))* Absey & Co.
Prelutsky, Jack. Pizza, Pigs, & Poetry: How to Write a Poem. 2008. (ENG.). 208p. (J). (gr. 2-5). pap. 7.99 *(978-0-06-143448-8(5),* Greenwillow Bks.) HarperCollins Pubs.
Rogers, Fred. A Beautiful Day in the Neighborhood: The Poetry of Mister Rogers. Flowers, Luke, illus. 2019. (Mister Rogers Poetry Bks.: 1). 144p. (J). (gr. 1-3). 19.99 *(978-1-68369-113-6(X))* Quirk Bks.
Roza, Greg. Patterns in Poetry: Recognizing & Analyzing Poetic Form & Meter, 1 vol. (Math for the REAL World Ser.). 32p. 2010. (ENG.). (gr. 5-6). pap. 10.00 *(978-1-4042-5146-5(4),* 958f6876-3fb5-411e-84ee-dd3bd321fd6c) 2009. (gr. 4-5). 47.90 *(978-1-60851-415-1(3))* 2004. (ENG., Illus.). (J). (gr. 5-6). lib. bdg. 28.93 *(978-1-4042-2941-9(8),* 8a7f09a5-770d-46ee-9aec-22a7ac2b168e) Rosen Publishing Group, Inc., The. (PowerKids Pr.).
Walsh, Brendan, et al. Opinions about Three Victorian Era Poets: Christina Rossetti, Robert Louis Stevenson, Emily Dickinson. 2014. (Text Connections Ser.). (J). (gr. 3). *(978-1-4509-9657-0(4))* Benchmark Education Co.

POETRY

see also Ballads; Free Verse; Hymns; Love Poetry; Nature—Poetry

also American Poetry; English Poetry, etc.; and general subjects, names of historical events, places and famous persons with the subdivision Poetry, e.g. Animals—poetry

La Abajita que Habla (the Talking Bumblebee) 2003. (J). *(978-1-56870-477-7(1))* Hewell Publishing.
ABC Memory Verses. 2003. 32p. (J). per. 9.99 *(978-0-88724-137-6(9))* Carson-Dellosa Publishing, LLC.
Abell, Angel Morgan. The Alphabliss of Miss: Poems & Pictures. 2005. (Illus.). 54p. (J). 30.00 *(978-1-885679-20-8(3))* Morgan Foundation Pubs.: International Published Innovations.
Abodehman, Ahmed. El Cinturón. Lovillo, Pilar Ortiz, tr. Sanchez, Andres & Tagle, illus. 2006. (la Orilla del Viento Ser.). (SPA.). 121p. (J). per. 8.50 *(978-968-16-6670-5(4))* Fondo de Cultura Economica USA.
Acheson, Alison. The Cul-De-Sac Kids, 1 vol. Vol. Gutiérrez, Elisa, illus. 2012. (ENG.). 72p. (J). (gr. 1-3). pap. 8.95

PQR

(978-1-896580-99-9(8)) Tradewind Bks. CAN. Dist: Orca Bk. Pubs. USA.

Ada, Alma Flor. Pio Peep! 2006. (ENG., Illus.). 64p. (J). (gr. -1-1). audio compact disk 16.99 *(978-0-06-111666-7(1)*, HarperFestival) HarperCollins Pubs.

Adam, Ryan. New Orleans Mother Goose, 1 vol. Gentry, Marita, illus. 2014. (Mother Goose Ser.). (ENG.). 40p. (J). 17.99 *(978-1-4556-1953-5(1)*, Pelican Publishing) Arcadia Publishing.

Adams, Shireen, illus. Colours of Islam. 2013. (ENG.). 40p. (J). (gr. k-2). 22.95 *(978-0-86037-591-3(9))* Kube Publishing Ltd. GBR. Dist: Consortium Bk. Sales & Distribution.

Adedjouma, Davida. The Palm of My Heart: Poetry by African American Children, 1 vol. Christie, R. Gregory, illus. 2013. (ENG.). 32p. (J). (gr. 1-6). pap. 10.95 *(978-1-880000-76-2(8)*, 85317516-6487-400d-9d23-ac907fc2a2eb) Lee & Low Bks., Inc.

Adlerman, Danny. Africa Calling, Nighttime Falling, 1 vol. Adlerman, Kim, illus. 2018. (Amazing Ser.). (ENG.). 40p. (J). (gr. 2-12). pap. 12.95 *(978-1-62014-805-1(6)*, leelowbooks) Lee & Low Bks., Inc.

Ageledis, Ida. First Foil Poetry Seasons, 2 vols. Berg, Michelle, illus. 2005. (First Foil Poetry Haikus Ser.). 10p. (J). 6.95 *(978-1-58117-188-4(9)*, Intervisual/Piggy Toes) Bendon, Inc.

Alarcón, Francisco X. Angels Ride Bikes & Other Fall Poems: Los Angeles Andan Bicicletas y Otros Poemas de Otoño, 1 vol. Gonzalez, Maya Christina, illus. 2013. (Cycle of Seasons Ser.). (ENG.). 32p. (J). (gr. 2-6). per. 11.95 *(978-0-89239-198-1(7)*, leelowcbp) Lee & Low Bks., Inc.

—Animal Poems of the Iguazú: Animalario del Iguazú. Gonzalez, Maya Christina, illus. 2008. (SPA & ENG.). 32p. (J). (gr. k). 16.95 *(978-0-89239-225-4(8))* Lee & Low Bks., Inc.

—Family Poems for Every Day of the Week: Poemas Familiares para Cada día de la Semana, 1 vol. Gonzalez, Maya Christina, illus. 2017. (SPA.). 40p. (J). (gr. 1-7). 20.95 *(978-0-89239-275-9(4)*, leelowcbp) Lee & Low Bks., Inc.

—From the Bellybutton of the Moon & Other Summer Poems: Del Ombligo de la Luna y Otros Poemas de Verano, 1 vol. Gonzalez, Maya Christina, illus. 2013. (Cycle of Seasons Ser.). (ENG.). 32p. (J). (gr. 2-6). per. 11.95 *(978-0-89239-201-8(0)*, leelowcbp) Lee & Low Bks., Inc.

—Iguanas in the Snow & Other Winter Poems: Iguanas en la Nieve y Otros Poemas de Invierno, 1 vol. Gonzalez, Maya Christina, illus. (Cycle of Seasons Ser.).Tr. of Iguanas in the Snow & Other Winter Poems. (ENG.). 32p. (J). 2013. (gr. 2-6). per. 10.95 *(978-0-89239-202-5(9)*, leelowcbp) 2004. (gr. 1-18). 16.95 *(978-0-89239-168-4(5))* Lee & Low Bks., Inc.

—Poems to Dream Together/poemas para Sonar Juntos: Poemas para Sonar Juntos. 2005. (ENG., Illus.). 32p. (J). (gr. 2-5). 16.95 *(978-1-58430-233-9(X))* Lee & Low Bks., Inc.

Alarcón, Francisco X., et al. Border Voices: The San Diego Celebration of Poetry & Music: the 10th Annual Anthology of Poetry. 2003. (ENG.). per. 12.95 *(978-0-9719906-1-6(1))* Webb, Jack.

Alberti, Rafael. RAFAEL ALBERTI PARA NIÑOS. (SPA., Illus.). 164p. (J). (gr. 4-6). 20.76 *(978-84-305-9290-6(3)*, SU0175) Susaeta Ediciones, S.A. ESP. Dist: Lectorum Pubns., Inc.

Alderson, Sue Ann. Eco-Diary of Kiran Singer, 1 vol. Ballance, Millie, illus. 2007. (ENG.). 88p. (J). (gr. 4-7). 15.95 *(978-1-896580-47-0(5))* Tradewind Bks. CAN. Dist: Orca Bk. Pubs. USA.

Alexander, Elizabeth & Nelson, Marilyn. Miss Crandall's School for Young Ladies & Little Misses of Color. Cooper, Floyd, illus. 2007. (ENG.). 48p. (J). (gr. 1-4). 17.95 *(978-1-59078-456-3(1)*, Wordsong) Highlights Pr., c/o Highlights for Children, Inc.

Alexander-Heaton, Susanne & Gabriell, Chantal T. The ABC Field Guide to Faeries: Inspiring Reminders of Respect for Ourselves, Each Other & the Environment. 2nd ed. 2009. *(978-0-9813048-0-9(X))* Alexander-Heaton, Susanne.

Alexander, Kwame, et al. Out of Wonder: Poems Celebrating Poets. Holmes, Ekua, illus. 2017. (ENG.). 56p. (J). (gr. 3-7). 18.99 *(978-0-7636-8094-7(X))* Candlewick Pr.

Alexander, Martha, illus. & selected by. Poems & Prayers for the Very Young. Alexander, Martha, selected by. 32p. (J). Random Hse. Children's Bks.

Allan, Shaun. Zits'n'bits. 2011. (ENG.). 54p. pap. 6.50 *(978-1-4716-1244-2(9))* Lulu Pr., Inc.

Allison, Hugh A. Intrigue of Love. 2012. 108p. (gr. -1). pap. 19.40 *(978-1-4343-9444-6(1))* AuthorHouse.

Alston, Stanley E. Faith, Love & Life. Sharps, Angelique, ed. Alston, Sheila Y., photos by. (Illus.). 48p. (YA). (gr. 4-18). pap. 12.95 *(978-0-9719897-0-2(2))* Magnatic Music.

Altein, Chani. The Aleph Bias Ship on the Aleph Bias Trip. Rosenfeld, D. L., ed. Becker, Baruch, illus. 2009. (ENG.). 30p. (J). 11.99 *(978-1-929628-25-4(0))* Hachai Publishing.

—Oif der Aleph Bais Shif. Brod, Chani, tr. from ENG. Becker, Baruch, illus. 2014.Tr. of Aleph Bais Trip on the Aleph Bais Ship. (YID.). 32p. (J). 1.99 *(978-1-929628-77-3(3))* Hachai Publishing.

Anderson, Allan W. SONGS from the MIFFLINGER SEA & a little cove of NONSENSE. 2009. (ENG.). 68p. pap. 24.99 *(978-1-4363-9076-7(1))* Xlibris Corp.

Anderson, Laurie Halse. Shout. 2019. (ENG.). 304p. (YA). (gr. 9). 18.99 *(978-0-670-01210-7(6)*, Viking Books for Young Readers) Penguin Young Readers Group.

Anderson, Lillian. My Sandwich. Uhlig, Elizabeth, illus. 2012. 32p. (J). pap. 12.95 *(978-0-9834030-3-6(1))* Marble Hse. Editions.

Andreacchi, Grace. Little Poems for Children. 2010. (Illus.). 64p. pap. 26.95 *(978-1-4457-6338-5(9))* Lulu Pr., Inc.

Andreae, Giles. Cock-A-doodle-doo! Barnyard Hullabaloo. Wojtowycz, David, illus. 2004. (ENG.). 32p. (J). (gr. -1-2). reprint ed. pap. 9.99 *(978-1-58925-387-2(6))* Tiger Tales.

Andricain, Sergio. Arco Iris de Poesia: Poemmas de las Americas y Espana. Cuellar, Olga, illus. 2008. (SPA.). 40p. (J). (gr. -1-3). 15.99 *(978-1-930332-59-1(9))* Lectorum Pubns., Inc.

Angelou, Maya, et al. Life Doesn't Frighten Me (Twenty-Fifth Anniversary Edition) 25th ed. 2018. (ENG., Illus.). 40p. (J). (gr. -1-17). 19.95 *(978-1-4197-2748-1(6)*, 1198401) Abrams, Inc.

Anholt, Laurence. Royal Rap: Band 08/Purple (Collins Big Cat) Morentorn, Alice, illus. 2015. (Collins Big Cat Ser.). (ENG.). 24p. (J). (gr. 2-2). pap. 8.99 *(978-0-00-759113-8(6))* HarperCollins Pubs. Ltd. GBR. Dist: Independent Pubs. Group.

Anon. A Collection of Animal Poems for Children. 2012. 26p. pap. 8.45 *(978-1-4474-5458-8(8))* Palmer Pr., The.

Anonymous. The Child's Book of Poetry a Selection of Poems, Ballads & Hymns. 2011. (Illus.). 238p. pap. 26.75 *(978-1-241-56870-2(7)*, British Library, Historical Print Editions) Creative Media Partners, LLC.

—Required Poems for Reading & Memorizing: Third & Fourth Grades, Prescribed by State Courses of Study. l.t. ed. 2007. (ENG.). 168p. pap. 19.99 *(978-1-4264-3925-4(3))* Creative Media Partners, LLC.

Antunes, Ana Claudia. The Sea Sons. 2009. 53p. pap. 9.99 *(978-1-4357-2479-2(8))* Lulu Pr., Inc.

Antwine, Tajiye Lavonne. Changing the World 1 Poem @ a Time. 2012. 42p. pap. 9.95 *(978-0-9834275-1-3(8))* Blacktastic.net.

Appelt, Kathi. Just People & Paper - Pen - Poem: A Young Writer's Way to Begin. Appelt, Kenneth, photos by. 2004. (Writers & Young Writers Ser.: Vol. 1). (Illus.). 91p. (YA). pap. 11.95 *(978-1-888842-07-4(5)*, 1020) Absey & Co.

Applewood Books. Wonderful Willie! What He & Tommy Did to Spain. 2013. (Applewood Bks.). (ENG., Illus.). 52p. (gr. 4-8). pap. 24.95 *(978-1-4290-9806-9(6))* Applewood Bks.

Archer, Peggy. From Dawn to Dreams: Poems for Busy Babies. Wakiyama, Hanako, illus. 2007. (ENG.). 32p. (J). (gr. k-k). 15.99 *(978-0-7636-2467-5(5))* Candlewick Pr.

Argueta, Jorge. Arroz con Leche / Rice Pudding: Un Poema para Cocinar / a Cooking Poem, 1 vol. Amado, Elisa, tr. Vilela, Fernando, illus. 2016. (Bilingual Cooking Poems Ser.). (SPA.). 32p. (J). (gr. -1-2). 8.95 *(978-1-55498-887-7(X))* Groundwood Bks. CAN. Dist: Publishers Group West (PGW).

—Guacamole: A Cooking Poem / Guacamole: un Poema para Cocinar. 2016. (ENG & SPA.). lib. bdg. 19.60 *(978-0-606-38493-3(6))* Turtleback.

—Guacamole: Un Poema para Cocinar / a Cooking Poem, 1 vol. Amado, Elisa, tr. Sada, Margarita, illus. 2016. (Bilingual Cooking Poems Ser.). (SPA.). 32p. (J). (gr. -1-2). pap. 10.99 *(978-1-55498-888-4(8))* Groundwood Bks. CAN. Dist: Publishers Group West (PGW).

—Movie in My Pillow/una Pelicula en Mi Al, 1 vol., Vol. 1. 2013.Tr. of Movie in My Pillow. (ENG., Illus.). 32p. (J). (gr. 2-6). pap. 11.95 *(978-0-89239-219-3(3)*, leelowcbp) Lee & Low Bks., Inc.

—Somos Como Las Nubes / We Are Like the Clouds, 1 vol. Amado, Elisa, tr. Ruano, Alfonso, illus. 2016. (ENG.). 36p. (J). (gr. 2-7). 19.99 *(978-1-55498-849-5(7))* Groundwood Bks. CAN. Dist: Publishers Group West (PGW).

—Sopa de Frijoles / Bean Soup: Un Poema para Cocinar / a Cooking Poem, 1 vol. Yockteng, Rafael, illus. 2017. (Bilingual Cooking Poems Ser.: 2). (SPA.). 32p. (J). (gr. -1-2). 9.99 *(978-1-77306-002-6(3))* Groundwood Bks. CAN. Dist: Publishers Group West (PGW).

—Tamalitos: Un Poema para Cocinar / a Cooking Poem, 1 vol. Amado, Elisa, tr. Domi, illus. 2017. (Bilingual Cooking Poems Ser.: 3). (ENG.). 32p. (J). (gr. k-2). 8.95 *(978-1-77306-091-0(0))* Groundwood Bks. CAN. Dist: Publishers Group West (PGW).

Armstrong, Charles. Laugh & Pray Today. 2013. 58p. 21.99 *(978-1-62839-199-2(5))*; pap. 12.99 *(978-1-62839-156-5(1))* Salem Author Services.

Arneson, Guy. Kiddy Ditties. 2009. 32p. pap. 14.50 *(978-1-4389-8137-6(6))*; 36p. pap. 16.99 *(978-1-4389-8165-9(1))*; 28p. pap. 14.50 *(978-1-4389-8126-0(0))*; 40p. pap. 18.49 *(978-1-4389-8127-7(9))*; 32p. pap. 14.50 *(978-1-4389-6783-7(7))* AuthorHouse.

Arnold, Daniela. Daniela's Big Book of Poppin' Poetry. Guillory, Mike, illus. 2017. (J). *(978-1-942945-55-0(8))* Night Heron Media.

Asher, Melissa. Magical, Mystical, Majestic. 2009. 88p. pap. 19.95 *(978-1-4489-8991-1(4))* America Star Bks.

Asher, Sandra Fenichel. Somebody Catch My Homework. 2004. (YA). pap. 4.50 *(978-1-58342-171-0(8)*, SH8) Dramatic Publishing Co.

Atkins, Jeannine. Borrowed Names: Poems about Laura Ingalls Wilder, Madam C. J. Walker, Marie Curie, & Their Daughters. 2010. (ENG., Illus.). 224p. (J). (gr. 7-12). 29.99 *(978-0-8050-8934-9(9)*, 900055287, Holt, Henry & Co. Bks. For Young Readers) Holt, Henry & Co.

—Borrowed Names: Poems about Laura Ingalls Wilder, Madam C. J. Walker, Marie Curie, & Their Daughters. 2018. (ENG.). 224p. (YA). pap. 9.99 *(978-1-250-18340-8(5)*, 900190820) Square Fish.

Atwood, Megan. Connor & Clara Build a Concrete Poem. Butler, Reginald, illus. 2011. (Poetry Builders Ser.). 32p. (J). (gr. 2-4). lib. bdg. 25.27 *(978-1-59953-434-3(7))* Norwood Hse. Pr.

Audet, Martine. Que Ferais-Je du Jour? Sylvestre, Daniel, tr. 2003. (New Poetry Ser.). (FRE.). 36p. (J). (gr. 7). pap. *(978-2-89021-621-1(7))* Diffusion du livre Mirabel (DLM).

Austin, Norma J. Baby's Bedtime Poems: Sleepy Time Rhymes. 2010. 48p. pap. 8.95 *(978-1-4401-9403-0(3))* iUniverse, Inc.

Avery, Carrie L. A String of Pearls. 2003. 68p. (YA). pap. 9.95 *(978-0-7414-1540-0(2))* Infinity Publishing.

Ayers, Linda. There's Something in My Sandwich. Hunt, Jane, illus. 50p. (J). 2006. 13.95 *(978-0-9760505-7-5(9))* 2005. per. 6.95 *(978-0-9760505-5-1(2))* Blue Thistle Pr.

AZ Books, creator. Being a Princess. 2013. (Jingle-Jangle Ser.). (ENG., Illus.). 10p. (J). (gr. -1-k). bds. 9.95 *(978-1-61889-236-2(3))* AZ Bks. LLC.

—Come & Play. 2013. (Everyday Rhymes Ser.). (ENG., Illus.). 14p. (J). (gr. -1-k). bds. 15.95 *(978-1-61889-225-6(8))* AZ Bks. LLC.

—Do Like Me. 2013. (Jingle-Jangle Ser.). (ENG., Illus.). 10p. (J). (gr. -1-k). bds. 9.95 *(978-1-61889-238-6(X))* AZ Bks. LLC.

—It's Playtime. 2013. (Jingle-Jangle Ser.). (ENG., Illus.). 10p. (J). (-k). bds. 9.95 *(978-1-61889-237-9(1))* AZ Bks. LLC.

—My Favorite Toy. 2013. (Everyday Rhymes Ser.). (ENG., Illus.). 14p. (J). (gr. -1-k). bds. 15.95 *(978-1-61889-227-0(4))* AZ Bks. LLC.

—What I Say. 2013. (Everyday Rhymes Ser.). (ENG., Illus.). 14p. (J). (gr. -1-k). bds. 15.95 *(978-1-61889-228-7(2))* AZ Bks. LLC.

AZ Books Staff. Animal Wonder. 2013. (Everyday Rhymes Ser.). (ENG., Illus.). 14p. (J). (gr. -1-k). bds. 15.95 *(978-1-61889-226-3(6))* AZ Bks. LLC.

—Animals on the Go. 2013. (Jingle-Jangle Ser.). (ENG., Illus.). 10p. (J). (gr. -1-k). bds. 9.95 *(978-1-61889-239-3(8))* AZ Bks. LLC.

B. A. O'Reilly. You've Got a Friend in Me. 2012. 52p. pap. 17.50 *(978-1-61897-713-7(X)*, Strategic Bk. Publishing) Strategic Book Publishing & Rights Agency (SBPRA).

Bagert, Brod. Shout!: Little Poems That Roar. Yoshikawa, Sachiko, illus. 2007. 32p. (J). (gr. -1-3). 17.99 *(978-0-8037-2972-8(3)*, Dial Bks) Penguin Young Readers Group.

Bagert, Brod, ed. Poetry for Young People: Edgar Allan Poe. Cobleigh, Carolynn, illus. (Poetry for Young People Ser.: 3). 48p. (J). (gr. 3). 2014. 14.95 *(978-1-4549-1348-1(7))* 2008. (ENG.). pap. 8.99 *(978-1-4027-5472-2(8))* Sterling Publishing Co., Inc.

Bain, A. Watson, compiled by. A Poetry Book for Children. 2012. (ENG., Illus.). 122p. pap. 39.99 *(978-1-107-66147-9(1))* Cambridge Univ. Pr.

Baker, Jaime. Bedtime Baby, 1 vol. Noble, Roger, illus. 2010. 16p. pap. 24.95 *(978-1-4489-6234-1(X))* PublishAmerica, Inc.

Baker, Kenneth, ed. Children's English History in Verse. Stower, Adam, illus. 2007. 289p. pap. 20.00 *(978-1-4223-9012-2(8))* DIANE Publishing Co.

Bannatyne, Lesley. Witches' Night Before Halloween, 1 vol. Tans, Adrian, illus. 2007. (ENG.). 32p. (J). (gr. k-3). 19.99 *(978-1-58980-485-2(6)*, Pelican Publishing) Arcadia Publishing.

Bar-el, Dan. Pussycat, Pussycat, Where Have You Been? Mate, Rae, illus. 2011. (ENG.). 32p. (J). (gr. -1-3). 16.95 *(978-1-897476-46-8(9))* Simply Read Bks. CAN. Dist: Ingram Publisher Services.

Bardsley, Jacqueline. Dandelion Days. 2011. 28p. pap. 15.99 *(978-1-4568-2219-4(5))* Xlibris Corp.

Barker, Cicely Mary. A Flower Fairies Treasury. 2007. 14.99 *(978-0-7232-5973-2(9))* Penguin Publishing Group.

Barker, Geoff. What Is a Poem?, 1 vol., 1. 2013. (Britannica Common Core Library). (ENG., Illus.). 32p. (J). (gr. 2-3). 27.04 *(978-1-62275-220-1(1)*, 594045f6-0db2-406e-b2a9-57d857863c8c) Rosen Publishing Group, Inc., The.

Barnett, Mac. Guess Again! Rex, Adam, illus. 2009. (ENG.). 32p. (J). (gr. -1-3). 19.99 *(978-1-4169-5566-5(6)*, Simon & Schuster Bks. For Young Readers) Simon & Schuster Bks. For Young Readers.

Bartlett, Irene. The New Testament: Bible Poems for Children. 2007. (Illus.). 96p. per. *(978-1-84748-207-5(4))* Athena Pr.

Barton, Matthew. The Winding Road: A Child's Treasury of Poems, Verses, & Prayers, 24 vols. 2004. 224p. pap. 19.95 *(978-1-903458-47-1(1))* Hawthorn Pr. GBR. Dist: Independent Pubs. Group.

Bauer, Marion Dane. Halloween Forest. Shelley, John, illus. 2018. 32p. (J). (gr. -1-3). pap. 7.99 *(978-0-8234-4038-2(9))* Holiday Hse., Inc.

Baugh, Helen. Collins Big Cat Phonics for Letters & Sounds - a Bee on a Lark: Band 02B/Red B, Bd. 2B. Green, Keri, illus. 2018. (Collins Big Cat Phonics Ser.). (ENG.). 16p. (J). pap. 6.99 *(978-0-00-825148-2(7))* HarperCollins Pubs. Ltd. GBR. Dist: Independent Pubs. Group.

Baxter, Nicola. Childrens's Book of Classic Poems & Rhymes. 2013. (Illus.). 240p. (J). (gr. 3-7). pap. 14.99 *(978-1-84322-920-9(X))* Anness Publishing GBR. Dist: National Bk. Network.

—Classic Poetry for Children. Shuttleworth, Cathie, illus. 2013. (ENG.). 80p. (J). (gr. k-4). pap. 9.99 *(978-1-84322-820-2(3))* Anness Publishing GBR. Dist: National Bk. Network.

—The Ultimate Treasury of Stories & Rhymes: A Collection of 215 Tales & Poems. 2013. (Illus.). 576p. (J). (gr. -1-3). 16.99 *(978-1-84322-886-8(6)*, Armadillo) Anness Publishing GBR. Dist: National Bk. Network.

Baxter, Nicola, ed. Christmas Lullabies for Children. Finn, Rebecca, illus. 2014. (ENG.). 12p. (J). (gr. k-5). bds. 14.99 incl. audio compact disk *(978-1-84322-931-5(5)*, Armadillo) Anness Publishing GBR. Dist: National Bk. Network.

Beal, Jane. Magical poems for Girls. 2009. 76p. pap. 9.99 *(978-0-557-09280-2(9))* Lulu Pr., Inc.

Beaton, Clare & Kletter, Dana. Mrs. Moon: Lullabies for Bedtime. 2007. (ENG., Illus.). 48p. (J). 19.99 *(978-1-84686-067-6(9))* Barefoot Bks., Inc.

Becker, Joseph. Annabelle & Aiden in the Story of Life. Becker, Joseph, illus. 2016. (Illus.). 20p. pap. 9.95 *(978-0-9978066-0-1(5))* Imaginarium Pr.

The Beginning of Love. 2005. per. 12.00 net. *(978-0-9720046-2-6(9))* Bluestone Bks.

Belgrove, Teresa. A Collection of Children's Poems, Verses & Rhymes for All Ages. 2007. (Illus.). 216p. per. 20.78 *(978-1-4251-0945-5(4))* Trafford Publishing.

Bell, Marvin. A Primer about the Flag. Raschka, Chris, illus. 2011. (ENG.). 32p. (J). (gr. -1-3). 15.99 *(978-0-7636-4991-3(0))* Candlewick Pr.

Benjamin, Lisa & Benchmark Education Co. Staff. The Story of Casey at the Bat. 2014. (Text Connections Ser.). (J). (gr. 5). *(978-1-4900-1365-7(2))* Benchmark Education Co.

A Benji's Pup Set, 6 vols. 32p. (gr. 1-3). 37.50 *(978-0-322-00338-5(5))*; 31.50 incl. 5.25 hd *(978-0-7802-8045-8(8))* Wright Group/McGraw-Hill.

Bennett Hopkins, Lee. Amazing Faces. Soentpiet, Chris, illus. 2011. (ENG.). 40p. (J). (gr. 1-18). 18.95 *(978-1-60060-334-1(3))* Lee & Low Bks., Inc.

—Amazing Places. Soentpiet, Chris & Hale, Christy, illus. 2015. (ENG.). 40p. (J). 18.95 *(978-1-60060-653-3(9))* Lee & Low Bks., Inc.

Benson, Catherine. It Must Have Been a Sunday, 1 vol. 2005. (ENG.). 32p. pap. *(978-1-902382-79-1(X))* Smith/Doorstop Books.

Bernier-Grand, Carmen T. César: ¡Sí, Se Puede! Yes, We Can!, 0 vols. Diaz, David, illus. 2012. (ENG.). 49p. (J). (gr. 3-6). pap. 7.99 *(978-0-7614-5833-3(6)*, 9780761458333, Two Lions) Amazon Publishing.

Berry, James. A Nest Full of Stars. Bryan, Ashley, illus. 2004. 104p. (J). (gr. 2-18). 16.89 *(978-0-06-052748-8(X))* HarperCollins Pubs.

Bhikha, Zain. Allah Made Everything: The Song Book. Momin, Azra, illus. 2019. (Song Book Ser.: 1). 30p. (J). 11.95 *(978-0-86037-770-2(9))* Kube Publishing Ltd. GBR. Dist: Consortium Bk. Sales & Distribution.

Bills, Taylor, illus. Twas the Night before Christmas. 2009. 24p. 12.95 *(978-0-9776845-4-0(7))* 3D Alley, Inc.

bint Mahmood, Ayesha. Thank You o Allah! 2016. (ENG., Illus.). 24p. (J). (gr. -1-k). 8.95 *(978-0-86037-335-3(5))* Kube Publishing Ltd. GBR. Dist: Consortium Bk. Sales & Distribution.

Birchall, Lorrie L. The Purple Glurple. 2012. 76p. pap. 12.95 *(978-0-9857816-0-6(2))* Birchall Publishing.

Bishop, Rudine Sims. Bishop Daniel A. Payne: Great Black Leader. 2009. (Poetry from the Masters Ser.). 88p. (YA). (gr. 4-18). pap. 9.95 *(978-1-933491-13-4(2))* Just Us Bks., Inc.

Bits & Pieces: The Poems of Melvin E. Giles, 1 vol. 2004. (Illus.). 235p. per. 14.50 *(978-0-9656364-1-4(0))* Oakdale Pr.

Blanco, Alberto. Tambien Los Insectos Son Perfectos. Radaviciute, Diana, illus. 2005.Tr. of Insects Are Perfect, Too. (SPA.). (J). (gr. k-2). pap. 10.95 *(978-968-494-054-3(8))* Centro de Informacion y Desarrollo de la Comunicacion y la Literatura MEX. Dist: Iaconi, Mariuccia Bk. Imports.

Blane, Francisco. Looking for the Muffin Man. 2008. (Reader's Theater Nursery Rhymes & Songs Ser.). (Illus.). 48p. (J). (gr. k-1). pap. *(978-1-60437-966-2(9))* Benchmark Education Co.

Blatz-Harvey, Elizabeth. The Windows of My World. Blatz-Harvey, Elizabeth, illus. 2011. (Illus.). 32p. *(978-0-9868730-3-4(9))* Cheaper Cheeper Copy.

Bloom, Valerie. Hot Like Fire. Lush, Debbie, illus. 2009. (J). (gr. 4-7). pap. 11.95 *(978-0-7475-9973-9(4))* Bloomsbury Publishing Plc GBR. Dist: Independent Pubs. Group.

—Let Me Touch the Sky: Selected Poems for Children. 2003. (Illus.). 90p. (J). 19.99 *(978-0-333-78067-1(1))* Macmillan Pubs., Ltd. GBR. Dist: Trafalgar Square Publishing.

—Mighty Mountains, Swirling Seas: Band 11/Lime. Cimatoribus, Alessandra, illus. 2015. (Collins Big Cat Ser.). (ENG.). 32p. (J). (gr. 2-2). pap. 7.95 *(978-0-00-759126-8(8))* HarperCollins Pubs. Ltd. GBR. Dist: Independent Pubs. Group.

Bloomquist, Stephen, ed. The Sun with Loving Light: A Reader for Young Children - Stories, Songs, Poems & Verses, 1 vol. Dalton, Pamela, illus. 2nd ed. 2021. Orig. Title: Der Sonne Licht. (ENG.). 110p. (J). (gr. k-5). reprint ed. 21.00 *(978-1-936367-63-4(7))* Waldorf Publications.

Blue Set. (Dias y Dias de Poesia Ser.). (SPA.). (gr. -1-6). 293.52 *(978-1-56334-270-7(7)*, DI8630) CENGAGE Learning.

Bodden, Valerie. Finding the Rhyme in a Poem. 2016. (Write Me a Poem Ser.). (ENG.). 24p. (J). (gr. 1-4). pap. 9.99 *(978-1-62832-252-1(7)*, 20545, Creative Paperbacks) Creative Co., The.

—Picturing Words in a Poem. 2016. (Write Me a Poem Ser.). (ENG.). 24p. (J). (gr. 1-4). pap. 9.99 *(978-1-62832-253-8(5)*, 20548, Creative Paperbacks); (Illus.). *(978-1-60818-621-1(0)*, 20550, Creative Education) Creative Co., The.

—Poking Fun in a Poem. 2016. (Write Me a Poem Ser.). (ENG.). 24p. (J). (gr. 1-4). pap. 9.99 *(978-1-62832-254-5(3)*, 20551, Creative Paperbacks); (Illus.). *(978-1-60818-622-8(9)*, 20553, Creative Education) Creative Co., The.

—Who Is a Poet? 2016. (Write Me a Poem Ser.). (ENG., Illus.). 24p. (J). (gr. 1-4). *(978-1-60818-623-5(7)*, 20556, Creative Education) Creative Co., The.

—Write Me a Poem: Finding the Rhyme in a Poem. 2016. (Write Me a Poem Ser.). (ENG., Illus.). 24p. (J). (gr. 1-4). *(978-1-60818-620-4(2)*, 20547, Creative Education) Creative Co., The.

Bogdan, Diane. Twigs Is a Poet. 2010. 108p. pap. 10.95 *(978-1-4502-1971-6(3))* iUniverse, Inc.

Bolding, Clarissa. Life Is A Song Worth Singing. 2005. 88p. per. 12.00 *(978-0-9762924-7-0(5))* InnerCircle Publishing.

Bolin, Frances Schoonmaker, ed. Poetry for Young People: Emily Dickinson. Chung, Chi, illus. (Poetry for Young People Ser.: 2). 48p. (J). (gr. 3). 2014. (ENG.). 14.95 *(978-1-4549-1346-7(0))* 2008. pap. 8.99 *(978-1-4027-5473-9(6))* Sterling Publishing Co., Inc.

Bollen, Christine. Three Munch-y Cherries. 2007. (J). per. 11.99 *(978-1-59879-376-5(4))* Lifevest Publishing, Inc.

Bolocan, D. Stephie learns about Animals. 2010. 54p. pap. 10.50 *(978-1-4457-7447-3(X))* Lulu Pr., Inc.

Bond, Felicia. Tumble Bumble. braille ed. 2004. (Illus.). (J). (gr. 1). spiral bd., bds. *(978-0-616-03081-3(9))* Canadian National Institute for the Blind/Institut National Canadien pour les Aveugles.

Borisov, Vadim & Borisova, Alina. Krylataia Mechta. 2012. (RUS., Illus.). 39p. pap. 24.55 *(978-1-4678-8959-9(8))* AuthorHouse.

Bouchard, David. Nokum: Ma Voix et Mon Coeur, 1 vol. Sapp, Allen, illus. 2006. (FRE.). 32p. (J). (gr. 1-2). 24.95 *(978-0-88995-383-3(X)*, 2fc19e06-9804-4135-8c14-365f131b05d4) Red Deer Pr. CAN. Dist: Firefly Bks., Ltd.

—Voices from the Wild: An Animal Sensagoria, 1 vol. Parker, Ron, illus. 2014. (ENG.). 72p. (J). (gr. 5-8). 24.95 *(978-1-55455-295-5(8)*, 47cab0a1-9388-454d-9fac-bbc7eb6f774b) Trifolium Bks., Inc. CAN. Dist: Firefly Bks., Ltd.

Boulden, Lowell E. Why Not Me? 2008. 40p. pap. 20.99 *(978-1-4389-1505-0(5))* AuthorHouse.

Bowcut~, ~Jan. Seasons of Poetry: A Guide for Young Writers Grades 3-6. 2012. 40p. pap. 20.99 *(978-1-4772-3708-3(9))* AuthorHouse.

BOWE, Andi. Alphabet book 1: a to z in song & Verse. 2008. (ENG.). 49p. pap. 28.50 *(978-0-557-04239-5(9))* Lulu Pr., Inc.

—Alphabet book 2: a to z in song & Verse. 2008. (ENG.). 44p. pap. 27.95 *(978-0-557-02784-2(5))* Lulu Pr., Inc.

Bower, Gary. The Garden Where I Grow: And Other Poems for Cultivating a Happy Family. Bower, Jan, illus. 2012. (Bright Future Bks.). (ENG.). 32p. (J). 11.99 *(978-0-9845236-2-7(6))* Storybook Meadow Publishing.

Bowyer, Mary. Tony Turtle & Friends. 2004. 56p. (J). pap. 9.95 *(978-0-595-32152-0(6))* iUniverse, Inc.

The check digit for ISBN-10 appears in parentheses after the full ISBN-13

Boychuk, Carol. The Tiny World: Poems by Carol Boychuk. 2010. (Illus.). 24p. 14.95 *(978-1-4269-3186-4(7))* Trafford Publishing.
Boynton, Sandra. Snuggle Puppy! A Love Song. (ENG., Illus.). 144p. 101.70 *(978-0-7611-4101-3(4),* 24101) Workman Publishing Co., Inc.
—Snuggle Puppy Valentine Ed 12-Copy Prepack. gif. ed. (ENG., Illus.). 1p. (J). bds. 83.40 *(978-0-7611-3455-8(7),* 23455) Workman Publishing Co., Inc.
Bradbury, Ken & Crowe, Robert L. Wait ... Don't Leave Yet. Crowe, Robert L., ed. 2003. (YA). ring bd. 10.00 *(978-0-9707173-7-5(7))* Consortium Publishing Co.
Bradford, Imani. People Can't Save You. 2004. (J). pap. 7.00 *(978-0-9671796-0-5(2))* Segue Pubs.
Breckon, Brett, illus. Dragon Days. 2004. (ENG.). 82p. 17.95 *(978-1-84323-301-5(0))* Beekman Bks., Inc.
Brenna, Beverley. The Bug House Family Restaurant, 1 vol. Mongeau, Marc, illus. 2014. (ENG.). 64p. (J). (gr. 1-3). pap. 12.95 *(978-1-926890-01-2(9))* Tradewind Bks. CAN. Dist: Orca Bk. Pubs. USA.
Brennan, Michael. The Imageless World. 2004. (ENG., Illus.). 108p. pap. 14.99 *(978-1-84471-005-8(X))* Salt Publishing GBR. Dist: SPD-Small Pr. Distribution.
Brewin, Barbara. Treasure Box of Children's Poetry: A magical world for Children. 2009. (Illus.). 56p. pap. 23.99 *(978-1-4389-5592-6(8))* AuthorHouse.
Bride of the Wolf (UNCUT EDITION), 5 vols., Vol. 2. anniv. ed. 2012. (ENG., Illus.). 162p. (YA). per. 11.99 *(978-0-9769819-4-7(7),* M.S.C. Bks.) Mustard Seed Comics.
Brilis, Michael Nicholas. Joy & Tears in Life: Perspectives of a Greek Immigrant. 2004. (GRE.). 49p. pap. 24.95 *(978-0-9753454-0-5(0),* CQ-003) ComQwest, LLC.
Brock, Justin. Have You Seen My Pencil? Poems & Musings. Wright, Christopher, illus. 2007. (J). pap. *(978-0-9796210-0-0(3))* OPUS II Bks.
Brockett, Keith. The Nutcracker's Night Before Christmas. Cowman, Joseph, illus. 2015. (ENG.). 32p. (J). (gr. 1-3). 17.99 *(978-1-58536-889-1(X),* 203954) Sleeping Bear Pr.
Brockway, Margaret. David, the Son of Jesse. 2011. 20p. (gr. 1-2). pap. 10.03 *(978-1-4567-4915-6(3))* AuthorHouse.
Brookman, Darin. Where Sagebrush Grows. 2004. per. 20.00 *(978-0-9749518-0-5(3))* Pair'a Spurs Pr.
Brooks, Gwendolyn. Bronzeville Boys & Girls. Ringgold, Faith, illus. 2007. 48p. (J). (gr. 2-5). 18.89 *(978-0-06-029506-6(6))* HarperCollins Pubs.
—Bronzeville Boys & Girls. 2015. (J). lib. bdg. 17.20 *(978-0-606-36468-3(4))* Turtleback.
Brown, Calef. The Ghostly Carousel: Delightfully Frightful Poems. Brown, Calef, illus. 2018. (ENG., Illus.). 32p. (J). (gr. 1-4). 17.99 *(978-1-5124-2661-8(X),* deb83a4a-c795-4b2f-9da6-d2ff1c54ed94, Carolrhoda Bks.) Lerner Publishing Group.
Brown, Daniel. Gerard Manley Hopkins. 2004. (Writers & Their Work Ser.). (ENG., Illus.). 128p. pap. 44.99 *(978-0-7463-0975-9(9),* 9780746309759) Liverpool Univ. Pr. GBR. Dist: Oxford Univ. Pr., Inc.
Brown, Margaret Wise. The Fathers Are Coming Home. Savage, Stephen, illus. 2010. (ENG.). 32p. (J). (gr. -1-k). 19.99 *(978-0-689-83345-8(8),* McElderry, Margaret K. Bks.) McElderry, Margaret K. Bks.
—Where Have You Been? Dillon, Leo and Diane, illus. 2004. (ENG.). 32p. (J). (gr. -1-1). lib. bdg. 16.89 *(978-0-06-028379-7(3),* HarperCollins) HarperCollins Pubs.
Brown, Skila. Slickety Quick: Poems about Sharks. Kolar, Bob, illus. 2016. (ENG.). 32p. (J). (gr. 1-4). 17.99 *(978-0-7636-6543-2(6))* Candlewick Pr.
Brown, Suzanne. The Night Before Christmas in Ski Country. Schlingman, Dana, illus. 2013. 32p. (J). 17.95 *(978-1-56579-658-4(6),* Westcliffe Pubs.) Bower Hse.
Browning, Robert. The Pied Piper of Hamelin, Illustrated by Hope Dunlap. Dunlap, Hope, illus. 2008. 52p. pap. 12.95 *(978-1-59915-265-3(7))* Yesterday's Classics.
Brunette, Steffan. Cough, Achoo, & Roar! 2013. 16p. pap. 7.99 *(978-1-4624-0632-6(7),* Inspiring Voices) Author Solutions, LLC.
Bruno, Elsa Knight. Punctuation Celebration. Whitehead, Jenny, illus. 2012. (ENG.). 32p. (J). (gr. 1-4). pap. 9.99 *(978-1-250-00335-5(0),* 900079869) Square Fish.
Brush & Paint. 2003. (Gateways to the Sun Ser.). 32p. (J). (gr. 1-2). pap. 11.95 *(978-1-58105-575-7(7))* Santillana USA Publishing Co., Inc.
Bryan, Ashley. Ashley Bryan's Puppets: Making Something from Everything. Bryan, Ashley, illus. 2014. (ENG., Illus.). 80p. (J). (gr. -1). 19.99 *(978-1-4424-8728-4(3),* Atheneum Bks. for Young Readers) Simon & Schuster Children's Publishing.
Bryce, Clara. Just My Imagination: Children's Poems. 2010. 44p. pap. 16.99 *(978-1-4490-6615-4(1))* AuthorHouse.
Bryer, Tom. Fun Poems for Kids. Bryer, Tom, illus. 2012. (Illus.). 26p. *(978-1-908341-74-7(2))* Paragon Publishing, Rothersthorpe.
Bulion, Leslie. At the Sea Floor Café: Odd Ocean Critter Poems, 1 vol. Evans, Leslie, illus. 2016. 48p. (J). (gr. 3-7). pap. 7.99 *(978-1-56145-920-9(8))* Peachtree Publishing Co. Inc.
Bunnaby Bunny (G) Toddler Reader. 2006. (Illus.). 20p. (J). bds. *(978-0-9712816-3-9(7))* Third Week Bks.
Burroughs, William S. Live Performance, Vol. 1. Hoffman, Kathelin, ed. Phillips, Zelmer, illus. (C). 12.95 incl. audio *(978-0-929856-00-1(7))* Caravan of Dreams Productions.
Buscher, Nancy Tancey. Kaleidoscope of Children's Poems. 2009. 28p. pap. 12.95 *(978-1-936051-53-3(2))* Peppertree Pr., The.
Bush Rage: Collected Verse. 2nd ed. 2005. *(978-0-9765948-0-2(3))* Diomo Square Bks.
Butler, Rosemary. My Merry Menagerie: Lighthearted Verses & Drawings. Butler, Rosemary, illus. 2013. (Illus.). 144p. 19.99 *(978-1-883378-22-6(2))* Sun on Earth Bks.
Byrd, Bill Scott. The Story of Rap & Tap. Ayzenberg, Nina, illus. 2006. 9.95 *(978-0-9776805-0-4(9))* Byrd, Fay T.
Cabrera, Jane. Twinkle, Twinkle, Little Star. 2019. (Jane Cabrera's Story Time Ser.). (ENG.). (J). 32p. (-k). 18.99 *(978-0-8234-4469-4(4));* 24p. (gr. -1 — 1). bds. 7.99 *(978-0-8234-4468-7(6))* Holiday Hse., Inc.
Cabreros, Beryl. Melting Pot of Children's Poetry, 1 vol. 2010. 77p. pap. 19.95 *(978-1-4489-5765-1(6))* America Star Bks.
Cain, Vernice. The Little Green Tree. 2012. 24p. (-18). pap. 17.99 *(978-1-4685-9446-1(X))* AuthorHouse.
Calderon, Marcela, illus. Poems by the Sea, 1 vol. 2017. (Poems Just for Me Ser.). (ENG.). 32p. (gr. 3-3). 28.93 *(978-1-4994-8388-8(0),* 29a507a6-cb1d-43d1-930a-4e763d6f0632, Windmill Bks.) Rosen Publishing Group, Inc., The.
A Camel Called Bump-Along, 6 vols., Set B. 32p. (gr. 1-3). 31.50 *(978-0-7802-8049-6(0))* Wright Group/McGraw-Hill.
Canetti, Yanitzia. Canciones para Dormir a Las Munecas: Dulce Compania. 2010. (SPA.). 32p. (J). pap. 6.99 *(978-1-59835-256-6(3),* BrickHouse Education) Cambridge BrickHouse, Inc.
—Canciones para dormir a los Peluches. 2010. (SPA.). 32p. (J). pap. *(978-1-59835-258-0(X),* BrickHouse Education) Cambridge BrickHouse, Inc.
—I'm Proud to Be Me! 2010. (Illus.). 32p. (J). pap. 9.99 *(978-1-59835-286-3(5),* BrickHouse Education) Cambridge BrickHouse, Inc.
—Imagina un mundo Mejor. 2010. (SPA., Illus.). 32p. (J). pap. *(978-1-59835-283-2(0),* BrickHouse Education) Cambridge BrickHouse, Inc.
—Soy Original, ¡genial! 2010. (SPA.). (J). pap. *(978-1-59835-285-6(7))* Cambridge BrickHouse, Inc.
Cannon, Nick. Neon Aliens Ate My Homework & Other Poems. 2015. (Illus.). 142p. (J). *(978-0-545-80178-2(8))* Scholastic, Inc.
Canton, William. Invisible Playmate A Story of the Unseen. 2006. pap. 19.95 *(978-1-4286-3869-3(5))* Kessinger Publishing, LLC.
Capstone Press. The Poet's Toolbox: Set of 4, 4 vols. (Poet's Toolbox Ser.). (ENG., Illus.). 32p. (C). (gr. 3-5). 90.40 *(978-0-7565-0713-8(8),* Compass Point Bks.) Capstone.
Carangelo, Audrey. On the Street: Poems about Paintings. 2006. (Illus.). 8p. (J). *(978-0-439-73410-3(X))* Scholastic, Inc.
Carle, Eric. Eric Carle's Dragons, Dragons. 2004. (ENG., Illus.). 68p. (J). (gr. 1-4). pap. 12.99 *(978-0-14-240103-3(X))* Penguin Young Readers Group.
Carlson, Lori Marie. Cool Salsa: Bilingual Poems on Growing up Latino in the United States. 2013. (SPA & ENG.). (J). lib. bdg. 22.10 *(978-0-606-28551-3(2))* Turtleback.
Carlson, Lori Marie, ed. Cool Salsa: Bilingual Poems on Growing up Latino in the United States. 2013. (SPA., Illus.). 160p. (J). (gr. 4-7). pap. 10.99 *(978-1-250-01678-2(9),* 900087092) Square Fish.
Carney, Audrey McDonald. It's Me Mommy, I've Been Sent from Heaven Above. 2011. 28p. pap. 24.95 *(978-1-4560-4372-6(3))* America Star Bks.
Carney, Larry, adapted by. Three Billy Goats Gruff. 2009. (ENG., Illus.). 24p. (J). 6.95 *(978-1-60072-114-4(1))* PC Treasures, Inc.
Carol Joan Campbell. Verses from A Garden, & Other Nature Things. 2006. (ENG.). 44p. pap. 17.99 *(978-1-4257-2004-9(8))* Xlibris Corp.
Carr, Holly, illus. What Is Pink? 2003. 24p. (J). (gr. -1-1). *(978-0-921156-92-5(8))* Plumleaf Press.
Carroll, Lewis, pseud. The Nonsense Verse of Lewis Caroll. Hussey, Lorna, illus. 2004. 32p. (J). (gr. 4). pap. 12.99 *(978-0-7475-5019-8(0))* Bloomsbury Publishing Plc GBR. Dist: Independent Pubs. Group.
Carroll, Yvonne. A Child's Treasury of Irish Stories & Poems. Waters, Fiona, ed. 2004. (ENG., Illus.). 194p. (J). 32.95 *(978-0-7171-3795-4(3))* Gill Bks. IRL. Dist: Casemate Pubs. & Bk. Distributors, LLC.
Carter, Cheri. The Misfitz: A Book of Poems. 2011. 108p. (gr. -1). 21.23 *(978-1-4567-5890-5(X));* pap. 12.84 *(978-1-4567-5891-2(8))* AuthorHouse.
Carter, James. Around the World: Band 03/Yellow (Collins Big Cat) 2007. (Collins Big Cat Ser.). (ENG.). 24p. (J). (gr. k-1). pap. 7.99 *(978-0-00-718658-7(4))* HarperCollins Pubs. Ltd. GBR. Dist: Independent Pubs. Group.
Carter, K. D. Vacation into Nonsense. 2009. 60p. pap. 16.95 *(978-1-4489-2590-2(8))* America Star Bks.
Carthew, Mark. Flabbergaster, 1 vol. rev. ed. 2013. (Literary Text Ser.). (ENG., Illus.). 28p. (gr. 2-3). pap. 10.99 *(978-1-4333-5603-2(1))* Teacher Created Materials, Inc.
—Speak Up!, 1 vol. rev. ed. 2013. (Literary Text Ser.). (ENG., Illus.). 20p. (gr. 1-2). (J). lib. bdg. 15.96 *(978-1-4807-1152-5(7));* 7.99 *(978-1-4333-5496-0(9))* Teacher Created Materials, Inc.
—Vroom! Vroom! Poems about Things with Wheels, 1 vol. rev. ed. 2013. (Literary Text Ser.). (ENG., Illus.). 24p. (gr. 2-3). pap. 8.99 *(978-1-4333-5521-9(3))* Teacher Created Materials, Inc.
Casey, Barbara. Slightest in the House. 2003. 100p. pap. 12.95 *(978-1-932162-23-3(2))* Benoy Publishing.
Casey, Dawn. A Lullaby for Little One. Fuge, Charles, illus. 2017. (ENG.). 20p. (J). (-k). bds. 9.99 *(978-0-7636-8661-1(1))* Candlewick Pr.
Cashman, Seamus. Something Beginning with P: New Poems from Irish Poets. Askin, Corrina & Clarke, Alan, illus. 2004. (ENG.). 160p. *(978-0-86278-868-1(4))* O'Brien Pr., Ltd., The.
Caswell, Deanna. Guess Who, Haiku. Shea, Bob, illus. 2016. (Guess Who Haiku Ser.). (ENG.). 24p. (J). (gr. -1-k). 14.95 *(978-1-4197-1889-2(4),* 1127501, Abrams Appleseed) Abrams, Inc.
Catalano, Tom. Rhymes for Teens: Poems Older Students Can Enjoy. Romango, Jim, illus. 2004. 80p. (YA). per. 9.95 *(978-1-882646-48-7(7))* Wordsmith Bks.
Celebrate Freedom: Songs, Symbols, & Sayings of the United States. 2003. (Scott Foresman Social Study Ser.). (Illus.). 32p. (gr. k-2). pap. *(978-0-328-03672-1(2));* 48p. (gr. 3-6). *(978-0-328-03674-5(9))* Addison-Wesley Educational Pubs., Inc. (Scott Foresman).
Center for Learning Network Staff. Paradise Lost: Curriculum Unit. 2003. (Novel Ser.). 100p. (YA). tchr. ed., spiral bd. 19.95 *(978-1-56077-732-8(X))* Center for Learning, The.
Cephas, Shelley A. Animal Tales: Poetry for Children & the Child at Heart. 2013. 70p. pap. 12.47 *(978-1-61704-171-6(8))* River Styx Publishing Co.
Champagne, Elena. Where Do Raindrops Go? Sarna, Billy, illus. l.t. ed. 2006. 24p. (J). (gr. -1-3). per. 10.99 *(978-1-59879-233-1(4))* Lifevest Publishing, Inc.
Champlin, DeeAnn. Eddie E & the Eggs. Champlin, DeeAnn, illus. Date not set. (Little Lyrics Short Vowel Collection: Vol. 2). (Illus.). (J). (gr. k-2). pap. 12.00 *(978-1-893429-26-0(1))* Little Lyrics Pubns.
Chandler, Tom. Sad Jazz. 2003. 80p. 18.00 *(978-0-9726869-0-7(8))* Table Rock Bks.
Charles, Veronika. Fairy Tales in the Classroom: Teaching Students to Create Stories with Meaning Through Traditional Tales, 1 vol. 2009. (ENG., Illus.). 256p. pap. 34.95 *(978-1-55455-020-3(3),* e401cfa7-e81a-4845-bde0-e781f50717a3) Trifolium Bks., Inc. CAN. Dist: Firefly Bks., Ltd.
Cheng, Ainsley. Being Just Me, Myself, & I! 2006. (J). pap. 16.00 *(978-0-8059-7189-7(0))* Dorrance Publishing Co., Inc.
Chiasson, Herménégilde. L' Oiseau Tatoué. Lafrance, David, illus. 2004. (Poetry Ser.). (FRE.). 36p. (J). (gr. 7). pap. *(978-2-89021-675-4(6))* Diffusion du livre Mirabel (DLM).
A Chicago Winds Set, 6 vols. 32p. (gr. 1-3). 26.50 *(978-0-7802-8047-2(4))* Wright Group/McGraw-Hill.
Child, Lydia Maria. Bitty Bear's Sleigh Ride. Ackley, Peggy Jo, illus. 2006. (J). *(978-1-59369-157-8(2))* American Girl Publishing, Inc.
Chronicle Books Staff. Nick Jr. Nursery Rhyme Time: A Touch-and-See Activity Book. (J). 15.95 *(978-0-8118-4726-1(8))* Chronicle Bks. LLC.
Cinar, Lisa. Paulina P. 2009. (ENG., Illus.). 32p. (J). (gr. -1-3). 16.95 *(978-1-897476-09-3(4))* Simply Read Bks. CAN. Dist: Ingram Publisher Services.
Cirillo, Todd, et al. Roxy: The Girl in the Platform Shoes, with the Black Dress On. 2003. (Illus.). 94p. per. 12.95 *(978-0-9722958-0-2(1))* Crow, R.L. Pubns.
Claiborn, Trevor M. Li'l Missy & Antman: Colors. 2012. 28p. pap. 19.99 *(978-1-4772-0983-7(2))* AuthorHouse.
Clark, Ann Nolan. In My Mother's House. Herrera, Velino, illus. 2004. 56p. (J). (gr. k-3). reprint ed. pap. 14.00 *(978-0-7567-7104-1(8))* DIANE Publishing Co.
Class Pack. (Cuentacuentos Ser.). (SPA.). (gr. k-18). 813.22 *(978-1-56334-799-3(7))* CENGAGE Learning.
Clay Lamberton Elementary School Students. Who Let the Cougars Out? 2006. (ENG., Illus.). 209p. per. *(978-1-59146-095-4(6),* Crystal Dreams Publishing) Multi-Media Pubns., Inc.
Cleary, Brian P. I Saw an Invisible Lion Today: Quatrains. Watson, Richard, illus. 2016. (Poetry Adventures Ser.). (ENG.). 32p. (J). (gr. 2-5). E-Book 39.99 *(978-1-4677-9732-0(4),* Millbrook Pr.) Lerner Publishing Group.
—Peanut Butter & Jellyfishes: A Very Silly Alphabet Book. Snyder, Betsy E., illus. 2007. (ENG.). 32p. (J). (gr. -1-2). 15.95 *(978-0-8225-6188-0(3),* Millbrook Pr.) Lerner Publishing Group.
—Underneath My Bed: List Poems. Watson, Richard, illus. 2016. (Poetry Adventures Ser.). (ENG.). 32p. (J). (gr. 2-5). E-Book 39.99 *(978-1-5124-1112-6(4),* Millbrook Pr.) Lerner Publishing Group.
Clemens, Edgar T. Trail Back: Epic Verse & Poems of The 1800s. 2003. (Illus.). 96p. pap. 11.95 *(978-0-9718677-1-0(2))* Infusionmedia Publishing.
Coach B. God's Animal Tales. 2008. 36p. pap. 16.99 *(978-1-4389-3047-3(X))* AuthorHouse.
Cobb, Soozi Bruun. Skis for Feet. 2011. (ENG.). 34p. 19.99 *(978-0-557-26740-8(4))* Lulu Pr., Inc.
Cohn, Jessica. Poems about Choices, 1 vol. 2014. (Experiencing Poetry Ser.). (ENG., Illus.). 64p. (J). (gr. 6-11). lib. bdg. 38.65 *(978-1-4329-9560-7(X),* 124869, Heinemann) Capstone.
Collins, Katrina. The voice from our Souls. 2009. 41p. pap. 10.02 *(978-0-557-20475-5(5))* Lulu Pr., Inc.
Collins-Philippe, Jane. Sail Away with Me. Beingessner, Laura, illus. 2010. 32p. (J). (gr. -1-2). 15.95 *(978-0-88776-842-2(3),* Tundra Bks.) Tundra Bks. CAN. Dist: Penguin Random Hse. LLC.
Conway, Kathleen E. Journey to the Stars: A Child's Dream. 2008. 72p. pap. 10.49 *(978-1-4343-8627-4(9))* AuthorHouse.
Cookson, Paul. Unzip Your Lips. (ENG., Illus.). 144p. (J). pap. 9.99 *(978-0-330-37062-2(6))* Pan Macmillan GBR. Dist: Trafalgar Square Publishing.
Coolidge, Susan. Verses. 2007. (ENG.). 124p. per. *(978-1-4065-1526-8(4))* Dodo Pr.
Coombs, Kate. Breathe & Be: A Book of Mindfulness Poems. 2017. (ENG., Illus.). 32p. (J). 17.95 *(978-1-62203-937-1(8),* 900220831) Sounds True, Inc.
—Monster School: (Poetry Rhyming Books for Children, Poems about Kids, Spooky Books) Gatlin, Lee, illus. 2018. (ENG.). 40p. (J). (gr. k-3). 16.99 *(978-1-4521-2938-9(X))* Chronicle Bks. LLC.
Cope, Steven R. Crow 2. Baumgardner, Julie, illus. 2012. 158p. pap. 16.00 *(978-1-936138-49-4(2))* Wind Pubns.
Corchin, D. J. Band Nerds: Poetry from the 13th Chair Trombone Player. Dougherty, Dan, illus. 2020. (Band Nerds Ser.). 144p. (YA). (gr. 7-12). pap. 12.99 *(978-1-7282-1982-0(5))* Sourcebooks, Inc.
Corr, Christopher, illus. Heaven in a Poem: An Anthology of Poems. 48p. 19.99 *(978-0-7459-4259-9(8),* Lion Books) Lion Hudson PLC GBR. Dist: Trafalgar Square Publishing.
Craig, Sienna R. A Sacred Geography: Sonnets of the Himalaya & Tibet. Heebner, Mary D., illus. 100th collector's ed. 2005. 24p. bds. 85.00 *(978-0-9766811-0-6(2))* Simplemente Maria Pr.
Crebbin, June, et al. We See a Cloud: Band 11/Lime (Collins Big Cat) Wren, Jenny, illus. 2015. (Collins Big Cat Ser.). (ENG.). 32p. (J). (gr. 2-2). pap. 9.95 *(978-0-00-759125-1(X))* HarperCollins Pubs. Ltd. GBR. Dist: Independent Pubs. Group.
Cribbs, Randy, narrated by. Tales from the Oldest City: Selected Readings Vol 1. 2005. (YA). cd-rom 8.95 *(978-0-9725796-3-6(X))* River Pr.
Cricket Magazine Group, Cricket Magazine. Ladybug, Ladybug: And Other Favorite Poems. 2007. (ENG., Illus.). 40p. (J). (gr. k-k). 17.95 *(978-0-8126-7936-6(9))* Cricket Bks.
Crozier, Lorna. Lots of Kisses, 1 vol. 2014. (ENG., Illus.). 24p. (J). (gr. -1 — 1). bds. 9.95 *(978-1-4598-0745-7(6))* Orca Bk. Pubs. USA.
Crystian, Carol Payne. Jas & Poetic Lucy. Crystian, Carol Payne, illus. l.t. ed. 2006. (Illus.). 21p. (J). (gr. -1-3). per. 10.99 *(978-1-59879-154-9(0))* Lifevest Publishing, Inc.
Culver, Kathy. Things I See When I Open My Eyes. Hauck, Christie, illus. 2007. 32p. per. 13.95 *(978-1-59858-306-9(9))* Dog Ear Publishing, LLC.
Cummings, Priscilla. Beddy Bye in the Bay, 1 vol. 2010. (ENG., Illus.). 32p. (J). 14.99 *(978-0-7643-3450-4(6),* 3780) Schiffer Publishing, Ltd.
Cushion, Hazel. Triplet Tales. Platt, Brian, illus. 2006. 32p. pap. *(978-0-9547092-1-1(7))* Accent Pr. Ltd.
Cushman, Doug. Pigmares: Porcine Poems of the Silver Screen. 2012. 44p. 12.95 *(978-1-60734-457-5(2));* (YA). pap. 12.95 *(978-1-58089-402-9(X))* Charlesbridge Publishing, Inc.
—Pigmares: Porcine Poems of the Silver Screen. Cushman, Doug, illus. 2012. (ENG., Illus.). 44p. (J). (gr. 2-5). 12.95 *(978-1-58089-401-2(1))* Charlesbridge Publishing, Inc.
Dafydd, Myrddin ap, ed. Llyfrau Lloerig: Chwarae Plant. Morris, Siôn, illus. 2005. (WEL.). 68p. pap. *(978-0-86381-431-0(X))* Gwasg Carreg Gwalch.
—Llyfrau Lloerig: Mul Bach Ar Gefn Ei Geffyl. Morris, Siôn, illus. 2005. (WEL.). 76p. pap. *(978-0-86381-314-6(3))* Gwasg Carreg Gwalch.
Dafydd, Myrddin ap & Gwalch, Gwasg Carreg. Mae Modfedd Yn Llawer Mewn Trwyn. 2005. (Barddoniaeth Poetry Ser.). (WEL., Illus.). 117p. pap. *(978-0-86381-857-8(9))* Gwasg Carreg Gwalch.
Dahl, Roald. Reekin Rhymes: Revolting Rhymes in Scots. Fitt, Matthew, tr. Blake, Quentin, illus. 2018. (SCO.). 52p. (J). (gr. 4-7). pap. 13.99 *(978-1-78530-183-4(7))* Black and White Publishing Ltd. GBR. Dist: Independent Pubs. Group.
Dailey, Victoria, afterword by. Let's Play. 2009. (ENG., Illus.). 50p. 75.00 *(978-0-9819597-0-2(9))* Bk. Club of California, The.
Dakos, Kalli. A Funeral in the Bathroom: And Other School Poems. Beech, Mark, illus. 2017. (ENG.). 48p. (J). (gr. -1-3). pap. 7.99 *(978-0-8075-2676-7(2),* 807526762) Whitman, Albert & Co.
Dallas SCORES Students. Learning Kicks! a Dallas Scores Anthology. 2006. 148p. per. 15.95 *(978-0-9779530-9-7(2))* Pen & Publish, LLC.
Dance me a Poem. 2005. (YA). per. 15.00 *(978-1-59872-089-1(9))* Instant Pub.
Daniel, Claire & Benchmark Education Co. Staff. The True Story of Paul Revere's Ride. 2014. (Text Connections Ser.). (J). (gr. 6). *(978-1-4900-1523-1(X))* Benchmark Education Co.
Daniels, Nicole M. Potpourri in the Wind: Nursery Rhymes from One Kid to Another. 2005. (Illus.). 64p. (J). pap. 19.95 *(978-0-9771447-8-5(X))* Twinkle Twinkle Little Bks.
Dannenbring, Cheryl & Hess, Anna. Beaver, Bear, & Snowshoe Hare: Mammal poems. 2009. (Illus.). 32p. (J). (gr. 1-2). pap. 9.95 *(978-0-9819307-1-8(9))* Raven Productions, Inc.
—Beaver, Bear, & Snowshoe Hare: Mammal Poems. 2009. (Illus.). 32p. (gr. 1-2). 18.95 *(978-0-9819307-0-1(0))* Raven Productions, Inc.
d'Aquino, Alfonso. Fauna Mayor. Riglietti, Serena, illus. 2005. (SPA.). (J). (gr. k-2). pap. 10.95 *(978-968-494-100-7(5))* Centro de Informacion y Desarrollo de la Comunicacion y la Literatura MEX. Dist: Iaconi, Mariuccia Bk. Imports.
Darkhor, P. H. Silent Being. 2010. 36p. pap. 15.49 *(978-1-4520-2998-6(9))* AuthorHouse.
David C. Cook Publishing Company Staff. Nursery Rhymes. 2003. (My Jesus Pocket Bks.). (Illus.). 32p. (J). pap., pap. 8.90 *(978-1-55513-102-9(6),* 1555131026) Cook, David C.
David, Carole. Averses et Réglisses Noires. Athanassiadis, Kiki, illus. 2004. (Poetry Ser.). (FRE.). 36p. (J). (gr. 7). pap. *(978-2-89021-674-7(8))* Diffusion du livre Mirabel (DLM).
David Cook Publishers, creator. God Is My Song. 2008. (Land of Milk & Honey Ser.). (Illus.). 32p. (J). (gr. -1-k). bds. 9.99 *(978-1-4347-9944-9(1))* Cook, David C.
Davidson, Arden. Playing Hopscotch on a Rubber Roof. 2006. 56p. pap. 16.95 *(978-1-4241-1170-1(6))* America Star Bks.
Davidson, Margot, creator. Stories with a View. 2004. (J). pap. 21.50 *(978-0-9766386-1-2(4))* Hillside Education.
Davis, Crystal. School Rhymes. 2011. 70p. pap. 10.00 *(978-1-4568-7578-7(7))* Xlibris Corp.
Davis, Will. Simply for Kids. 2012. 48p. (gr. 2-2). pap. 11.50 *(978-1-4634-3048-1(5))* AuthorHouse.
DAVIS**DECEASED**, David. The Twelve Days of Christmas — In Texas, That Is, 1 vol. 2011. (ENG., Illus.). 32p. (gr. k-3). 16.99 *(978-1-58980-924-6(6),* Pelican Publishing) Arcadia Publishing.
A Day for JJ & Me Set B, 6 vols. 32p. (gr. 1-3). 31.50 *(978-0-7802-8050-2(4))* Wright Group/McGraw-Hill.
Day, Lucille. Chain Letter. Dworkin, Doug, illus. 2005. 32p. (J). (gr. 3-7). 14.95 *(978-1-59714-011-9(2))* Heyday.
de la Mare, Walter. Rhymes & Verses: Collected Poems for Young People. Blaisdell, Elinore, illus. 2005. 351p. (J). (gr. 4-8). reprint ed. 19.00 *(978-0-7567-8944-2(3))* DIANE Publishing Co.
De Vos, Philip. Carnival of the Animals. Grobler, Piet, illus. 32p. (J). *(978-0-7981-3823-9(8))* Human & Rousseau.
Deltoro, Antonio. La Plaza. Ochoa, Francisco, illus. 2004.Tr. of Plaza. (SPA.). (J). (gr. k-2). pap. 11.99 *(978-968-494-045-1(9))* Centro de Informacion y Desarrollo de la Comunicacion y la Literatura MEX. Dist: Lectorum Pubns., Inc.
Demery, Ramona. Hey, Little Bird: Verses for Children. 2012. 48p. (gr. 10-12). pap. 9.95 *(978-1-4759-2766-5(5))* iUniverse, Inc.
Derby, Sally. A New School Year: Stories in Six Voices. Song, Mika, illus. 2017. 48p. (J). (gr. k-4). lib. bdg. 16.99 *(978-1-58089-730-3(4))* Charlesbridge Publishing, Inc.
Desautels, Denise. La Marathonienne. Chronopoulos, Maria, illus. 2004. (Poetry Ser.). (FRE.). 36p. (J). (gr. 7). pap. *(978-2-89021-673-0(X))* Diffusion du livre Mirabel (DLM).
Di Bella, Brenda. I'm up to Big Things. 2010. 14.95 *(978-0-615-38253-1(3))* Di Bella, Brenda.
Diane Bogdan. Twigs Is a Poet! 2009. 104p. pap. 9.95 *(978-1-4401-6202-2(6))* iUniverse, Inc.
Dias y Dias de Poesia. (Dias y Dias de Poesia Ser.). (SPA.). (gr. -1-6). 388.10 *(978-1-56334-279-0(0),* CO9637); 632.60 *(978-1-56334-280-6(4),* CO9638); suppl. ed. 207.23 *(978-1-56334-269-1(3),* PO9639) CENGAGE Learning.
Dickinson, Emily. Poetry for Kids: Emily Dickinson. Snively, Susan, ed. Davenier, Christine, illus. 2016. (Poetry for Kids Ser.). (ENG.). 48p. (J). (gr. 3-7). 17.95 *(978-1-63322-117-8(2),* 223805, Moondance) Quarto Publishing Group USA.

Diehn, Andi. Explore Poetry! With 25 Great Projects. Stone, Bryan, illus. 2015. (Explore Your World Ser.). (ENG.). 96p. (J). (gr. 1-5). 19.95 *(978-1-61930-279-2(9),* 638b125b-17a6-4e15-b179-9722a3dbfeba) Nomad Pr.

Dieter, Debra. Lightning & Mikey. 2012. 16p. (-18). pap. 15.99 *(978-1-4772-8405-6(2))* AuthorHouse.

DKSmith. My Inner Child. 2006. 57p. pap. 16.95 *(978-1-4241-0689-9(3))* America Star Bks.

Dockrill, Laura. My Mum's Growing Down. Tazzyman, David, illus. 2017. (ENG.). 160p. (J). pap. 9.95 *(978-0-571-33506-0(3),* Faber & Faber Children's Bks.) Faber & Faber, Inc.

Dodds, John Thomas. A Sneaky Twitch of an Itch. 2010. 44p. pap. 19.95 *(978-0-557-44341-3(5))* Lulu Pr., Inc.

Donaldson, Julia. Wriggle & Roar. Sharratt, Nick, illus. 2015. (ENG.). 32p. (J). (gr. -1-1). pap. 14.99 *(978-1-4472-7665-4(5),* 900326056, Macmillan Children's Bks.) Pan Macmillan GBR. Dist: Macmillan.

Dotlich, Rebecca Kai. In the Spin of Things: Poetry of Motion. Dugan, Karen, illus. 2010. (ENG.). 32p. (J). (gr. k-2). pap. 11.95 *(978-1-59078-828-8(1),* Wordsong) Highlights Pr., c/o Highlights for Children, Inc.

—When Riddles Come Rumbling: Poems to Ponder. Dugan, Karen, illus. 2013. (ENG.). 32p. (J). (gr. 1-4). pap. 7.95 *(978-1-62091-031-3(4),* Wordsong) Highlights Pr., c/o Highlights for Children, Inc.

Drake, Michael. The Growing Books: My Inside Is Outside. 2009. 68p. pap. 25.49 *(978-1-4389-6337-2(8));* (Illus.). 60p. pap. 23.99 *(978-1-4389-6336-5(X))* AuthorHouse.

Dranoel, Elttem. Elttem Dranoel: Judgement Day. 2003. 110p. (YA). pap. 11.95 *(978-0-595-26320-2(8),* Writers Club Pr.) iUniverse, Inc.

Dressler, Craig. Kids' Bible Poems. 2006. (J). per. 4.99 *(978-0-9679062-7-0(X))* Dressler, Craig.

Duggan, Laurie. Mangroves. 2003. 186p. (J). pap. *(978-0-7022-3351-7(X))* Univ. of Queensland Pr.

Dyan, Penelope. A Book for Girls about Being a Girl. 2006. (J). per. 7.95 *(978-0-9771916-9-7(9))* Bellissima Publishing, LLC.

—Flying High in the Sky — -for Boys Only. Weigand, John D., photos by. 2009. (Illus.). 42p. pap. 13.95 *(978-1-935118-66-4(8))* Bellissima Publishing, LLC.

—For Boys Only! No Girls Allowed! 2005. (Illus.). 80p. (J). per. 7.95 *(978-0-9768417-1-5(1))* Bellissima Publishing, LLC.

—For the Matterhorn's Face, Zermatt Is the Place, a Kid's Guide to Zermatt, Switzerland. Weigand, John D., photos by. 2010. (Illus.). 50p. pap. 11.95 *(978-1-935630-04-3(0))* Bellissima Publishing, LLC.

—Hair We Are! Dyan, Penelope, illus. 2009. (Illus.). 44p. pap. 11.95 *(978-1-935118-61-9(7))* Bellissima Publishing, LLC.

—I Am a Monster! Dyan, Penelope, illus. 2010. (Illus.). 34p. pap. 11.95 *(978-1-935630-24-1(5))* Bellissima Publishing, LLC.

—I Am Eight! Dyan, Penelope, illus. 2010. (Illus.). 34p. pap. 11.95 *(978-1-935630-17-3(2))* Bellissima Publishing, LLC.

—Just Look Out the Window! Dyan, Penelope, illus. 2010. (Illus.). 34p. pap. 11.95 *(978-1-935630-25-8(3))* Bellissima Publishing, LLC.

—Life in the Pits. Dyan, Penelope, illus. 2010. (Illus.). 34p. pap. 11.95 *(978-1-935630-18-0(0))* Bellissima Publishing, LLC.

—A Nose by Any Other Name Is Still a Nose! Dyan, Penelope, illus. 2009. (Illus.). 44p. pap. 11.95 *(978-1-935118-62-6(5))* Bellissima Publishing, LLC.

—Over the Edge, a Kid's Guide to Niagara Falls, Ontario, Canad. Weigand, John D., photos by. 2010. (Illus.). 48p. pap. 11.95 *(978-1-935630-07-4(5))* Bellissima Publishing, LLC.

—Pink Patti Pinkerton. Dyan, Penelope, illus. 2009. (Illus.). 44p. pap. 11.95 *(978-1-935118-63-3(3))* Bellissima Publishing, LLC.

—Spend a Day in Old Pompeii, a Kid's Travel Guide to Ancient Pompeii, Italy. Weigand, John D., photos by. 2010. (Illus.). 50p. pap. 11.95 *(978-1-935630-01-2(6))* Bellissima Publishing, LLC.

—Sticks — -Because Sticks Are Also People. Dyan, Penelope, illus. 2008. (Illus.). 52p. pap. 11.95 *(978-1-935118-07-7(2))* Bellissima Publishing, LLC.

—There Are Bees in My Trees! Dyan, Penelope, illus. 2009. (Illus.). 44p. pap. 11.95 *(978-1-935118-59-6(5))* Bellissima Publishing, LLC.

—There's a Chicken in My Kitchen! Dyan, Penelope, illus. 2009. (Illus.). 44p. pap. 11.95 *(978-1-935118-60-2(9))* Bellissima Publishing, LLC.

—There's a Racoon in My House! Dyan, Penelope, illus. 2009. (Illus.). 44p. pap. 11.95 *(978-1-935118-58-9(7))* Bellissima Publishing, LLC.

—There's an Alligator in My Closet! Dyan, Penelope, illus. 2009. (Illus.). 44p. pap. 11.95 *(978-1-935118-64-0(1))* Bellissima Publishing, LLC.

—This Means War! for Boys Only. Dyan, Penelope, illus. 2009. (Illus.). 44p. pap. 11.95 *(978-1-935118-65-7(X))* Bellissima Publishing, LLC.

—When in Rome, a Kid's Guide to Rome. Weigand, John, photos by. 2010. (Illus.). 50p. pap. 11.95 *(978-1-935630-00-5(8))* Bellissima Publishing, LLC.

—Who's the Fairest of Them All? Dyan, Penelope, illus. 2010. (Illus.). 34p. pap. 11.95 *(978-1-935630-20-3(2))* Bellissima Publishing, LLC.

Ebia, Iris. When the Wind Blows What Is That Noise? 2010. 28p. pap. 12.88 *(978-1-4490-2939-5(6))* AuthorHouse.

Eckles, Alice. My Life as a Flower Chapters 1&2: Color, Fragrance. 2004. 66p. 6.85 *(978-0-9742516-2-2(3))* Minimal Pr., The.

Edgar, M. G. A Treasury of Poems for Children. Pogány, Willy, illus. 2010. (Dover Children's Classics Ser.). (ENG.). 272p. (J). (gr. -1-3). pap. 9.99 *(978-0-486-47376-5(7),* 473767) Dover Pubns., Inc.

Editors of Studio Fun International. My First Mother Goose Nursery Rhymes. McCue, Lisa, illus. 2018. (ENG.). 20p. (J). (gr. -1 — 1). bds. 8.99 *(978-0-7944-4163-0(7),* Studio Fun International) Printers Row Publishing Group.

Eleven. Spirit Comes to Earth: Renewing Your Heart's Mission. Eleven, illus. 2005. (Illus.). 128p. (YA). per. 13.95 *(978-0-9743540-0-2(7),* By title) Peace Love Karma Publishing.

Eliot, T. S. Mungojerrie & Rumpelteazer. Robins, Arthur, illus. 2018. (Old Possum Picture Bks.). (ENG.). 32p. (J). pap. 9.95 *(978-0-571-32486-6(X),* Faber & Faber Children's Bks.) Faber & Faber, Inc.

Elliott, David. In the Wild. Meade, Holly, illus. 2013. (ENG.). 32p. (J). (gr. -1-3). pap. 7.99 *(978-0-7636-6337-7(9))* Candlewick Pr.

Elliott, Zetta. Bird, 1 vol. 2017. (ENG.). 48p. (J). (gr. 3-8). pap. 12.95 *(978-1-62014-348-3(8),* leelowbooks) Lee & Low Bks., Inc.

Engelbreit, Mary. Mary Engelbreit's Mother Goose: One Hundred Best-Loved Verses. Engelbreit, Mary, illus. 2005. (ENG., Illus.). 128p. (J). (gr. -1-k). 19.99 *(978-0-06-008171-3(6),* HarperCollins) HarperCollins Pubs.

Engle, Janice. Rainbows Stories & Poetry for Children. 2004. (ENG.). 102p. (J). pap. 15.08 *(978-1-4116-8612-0(8))* Lulu Pr., Inc.

Engle, Margarita. Hurricane Dancers: The First Caribbean Pirate Shipwreck. 2011. (ENG.). 160p. (YA). (gr. 7-12). 30.99 *(978-0-8050-9240-0(4),* 900066644, Holt, Henry & Co. Bks. For Young Readers) Holt, Henry & Co.

—The Lightning Dreamer. 2015. lib. bdg. 18.40 *(978-0-606-37463-7(9))* Turtleback.

—The Lightning Dreamer: Cuba's Greatest Abolitionist. 2015. (ENG.). 192p. (YA). (gr. 7). pap. 7.99 *(978-0-544-54112-2(X),* 1608874, Clarion Bks.) HarperCollins Pubs.

—Miguel y Su Valiente Caballero: El Joven Cervantes Sueña a Don Quijote, 1 vol. ón, Raúl, illus. 2018. 32p. (J). (gr. 3-7). 18.95 *(978-1-68263-019-8(6))* Peachtree Publishing Co. Inc.

—Miguel's Brave Knight: Young Cervantes & His Dream of Don Quixote, 1 vol. ón, Raúl, illus. 2017. 32p. (J). (gr. 3-7). 17.99 *(978-1-56145-856-1(2))* Peachtree Publishing Co. Inc.

—The Surrender Tree: Poems of Cuba's Struggle for Freedom. 2010. (YA). lib. bdg. 22.10 *(978-0-606-10545-3(X))* Turtleback.

—The Surrender Tree / el árbol de la Rendición: Poems of Cuba's Struggle for Freedom/ Poemas de la Lucha de Cuba Por Su Libertad (Bilingual) 2010. (ENG.). 384p. (YA). (gr. 7-12). pap. 11.99 *(978-0-312-60871-2(3),* 900065171) Square Fish.

Engler, Jerry. Highly Embellished Truth & Some Poetry Just Folks Three. 2008. 232p. pap. 14.95 *(978-0-9771255-2-4(1))* 6-mile Roots.

Ernst, Carol. Messages to the Heart. 2nd ed. 2003. spiral bd. 9.95 net. *(978-0-9668868-3-2(6))* Leadership Horizons, LLC.

Espinosa Guerra, Julio. La Poesia Del Siglo XX en Chile. 2006. (SPA.). 506p. E-Book 36.99 *(978-84-7522-788-7(0))* Visor Libros ESP. Dist: AIMS International Bks., Inc.

Estrada, Xinia M. Pluma en Silencio. 2004. (SPA.). 54p. (YA). per. 10.95 *(978-0-9746855-5-7(0))* Refined Savage Editions / Ediciones El Salvaje Refinado, The.

Evans, Olive. The Thrift Store Bears. Woolley, Patricia, illus. 2004. (ENG.). 41p. (J). 18.97 *(978-0-9748954-0-6(7))* Teddy Traveler Co.

Everett, Melissa. The Owl & the Kitty Cat. Kummer, Mark, illus. 2013. (ENG.). 20p. (J). (gr. -1-3). 8.99 *(978-1-77093-535-8(5))* Flowerpot Children's Pr. Inc. CAN. Dist: Cardinal Pubs. Group.

Ewing, Juliana Horatia. Verses for Children & Songs for Music. 2007. (Illus.). 136p. per. *(978-1-4065-2521-2(9))* Dodo Pr.

Ewing, Thor, ed. 50 Classic Poems Every Boy Should Know. 2015. (ENG., Illus.). 144p. (J). pap. *(978-1-910075-03-6(5))* Welkin Bks.

Factor, June, ed. All Right, Vegemite. 2017. (Far Out! Ser.). (ENG.). 112p. (J). (gr. k-2). pap. 8.99 *(978-1-925386-07-3(4),* Brolly Bks.) Borghesi & Adam Pubs. Pty Ltd AUS. Dist: Independent Pubs. Group.

—Far Out, Brussel Sprout. 2017. (Far Out! Ser.). (ENG.). 112p. (J). (gr. k-2). pap. 8.99 *(978-1-925386-06-6(6),* Brolly Bks.) Borghesi & Adam Pubs. Pty Ltd AUS. Dist: Independent Pubs. Group.

Fajardo, Alexis E. Kid Beowulf: the Blood-Bound Oath. 2016. (Kid Beowulf Ser.: 1). (ENG., Illus.). 240p. (J). pap. 12.99 *(978-1-4494-7589-5(2))* Andrews McMeel Publishing.

Fandel, Jennifer. Keats, Shakespeare, & Other Wordsmiths. 2005. (Understanding Poetry Ser.). (Illus.). 48p. (YA). (gr. 4-7). lib. bdg. 21.95 *(978-1-58341-343-2(X))* Creative Co., The.

Fandel, Jennifer & Miller, Connie. Thorns, Horns, & Crescent Moons: Reading & Writing Nature Poems, 1 vol. Burkes-Larrañaga, Dustin et al, illus. 2014. (Poet in You Ser.). (ENG.). 32p. (J). (gr. 2-4). lib. bdg. 27.99 *(978-1-4795-2197-5(3),* 124033, Picture Window Bks.) Capstone.

Fandel, Jennifer, et al. Trust, Truth, & Ridiculous Goofs: Reading & Writing Friendship Poems, 1 vol. Smith, Simon et al, illus. 2014. (Poet in You Ser.). (ENG.). 32p. (J). (gr. 2-4). lib. bdg. 27.99 *(978-1-4795-2199-9(X),* 124035, Picture Window Bks.) Capstone.

Farjeon, Eleanor & Harvey, Anne. Blackbird Has Spoken: Selected Poems for Children. 2003. (ENG.). 112p. (J). 16.95 *(978-0-333-74133-7(1))* Macmillan Pubs., Ltd. GBR. Dist: Trafalgar Square Publishing.

Farnsworth, Scott & Hoyt, Peggy R. Like a Library Burning. 2008. 144p. pap. 19.95 *(978-0-9719177-7-4(9))* Legacy Planning Partners, LLC.

Farrell, Eric L. & Holmes, Will, Jr. Seeking Solace: In a Time of Distress. 2003. (Illus.). 128p. 19.95 *(978-1-931855-33-4(1),* 1-800-Bookway) Emaculate Publishing.

Farrey-Latz, Benjamin. I Can Learn Social Skills! Poems about Getting along, Being a Good Friend, & Growing Up. 2018. (ENG., Illus.). 64p. (J). (gr. k-4). pap. 11.99 *(978-1-63198-280-4(X),* 82804) Free Spirit Publishing Inc.

Faulks, Rebecca Rachel. The Curtains Ate My Grandma. 2010. (Illus.). 40p. pap. 16.99 *(978-1-4490-7454-8(5))* AuthorHouse.

Fawcett, Gay, et al. Rhythm & Rhyme Literacy Time Level K. rev. ed. 2015. (Rhythm & Rhyme: Literacy Time Ser.). (ENG., Illus.). 144p. (gr. k-k). pap. 24.99 *(978-1-4258-1336-9(4))* Shell Educational Publishing.

Field, Eugene. Dibdin's Ghost. 2013. (Notable American Authors Ser.). 425p. reprint ed. lthr. 79.00 *(978-0-7812-2649-3(X))* Reprint Services Corp.

—Love Songs of Childhood. 2006. 124p. per. 16.99 *(978-1-4255-0825-8(1))* Michigan Publishing.

—The Love Songs of Childhood. 2013. (Notable American Authors Ser.). 425p. reprint ed. lthr. 79.00 *(978-0-7812-2645-5(7))* Reprint Services Corp.

—Lullaby Land: Songs of Childhood. Robinson, Charles, illus. 2006. 236p. per. 20.99 *(978-1-4255-1951-3(2))* Michigan Publishing.

—Lullaby Land: Songs of Childhood. 2013. (Notable American Authors Ser.). 231p. reprint ed. lthr. 79.00 *(978-0-7812-2646-2(5))* Reprint Services Corp.

—Second Book of Verse. 2013. (Notable American Authors Ser.). 260p. reprint ed. lthr. 79.00 *(978-0-7812-2644-8(9))* Reprint Services Corp.

—Songs & Other Verse. 2007. 140p. per. *(978-1-4065-2394-2(1))* Dodo Pr.

—The Sugar-Plum Tree & Other Verses: Includes a Read-and-Listen. Peat, Fern Bisel, illus. 2010. (Dover Read & Listen Ser.). (ENG.). 80p. (J). (gr. 1-5). pap. 14.99 *(978-0-486-47675-9(8))* Dover Pubns., Inc.

—With Trumpet & Drum. 2006. 140p. per. 16.99 *(978-1-4255-1004-6(3))* Michigan Publishing.

Fields, Terri. After the Death of Anna Gonzales. 2018. (ENG.). 112p. (YA). pap. 18.99 *(978-1-250-18945-5(4),* 900192245) Square Fish.

Figueroa, Ephraim. The Prince of Belverdere & Other Poems. 2003. 11.95 *(978-0-9745799-0-0(4))* Tabor Pr.

Fitch, Janet. White Olander. 2010. mass mkt. 10.99 *(978-0-316-01757-2(4))* Little Brown & Co.

Fitch, Sheree. Mabel Murple (pb), 1 vol. Smith, Sydney, illus. 2011. (ENG.). 24p. (J). (gr. 1-3). pap. 13.95 *(978-1-55109-859-3(8),* bd59a94b-f60c-406f-80e5-c51013270273) Nimbus Publishing, Ltd. CAN. Dist: Baker & Taylor Publisher Services (BTPS).

—Night Sky Wheel Ride, 1 vol. Yayo, illus. 2013. (ENG.). 32p. (J). (gr. -1-k). 16.95 *(978-1-896580-67-8(X))* Tradewind Bks. CAN. Dist: Orca Bk. Pubs. USA.

—Sleeping Dragons All Around Pb, 1 vol. Nidenoff, Michele, illus. 2010. (ENG.). 32p. (J). (gr. 1-3). pap. 12.95 *(978-1-55109-772-5(9),* 8ef729bf-f6ba-4f61-a9d4-c32e68cca838) Nimbus Publishing, Ltd. CAN. Dist: Baker & Taylor Publisher Services (BTPS).

—There Were Monkeys in My Kitchen (pb), 1 vol. Smith, Sydney, illus. 2nd ed. 2013. (ENG.). 32p. (J). (gr. k-2). pap. 12.95 *(978-1-55109-994-1(2),* ec9cb7f4-3849-4804-9153-183955421a24) Nimbus Publishing, Ltd. CAN. Dist: Baker & Taylor Publisher Services (BTPS).

Fitch, Sheree & Fitzpatrick, Deanne. Singily Skipping Along, 1 vol. 2013. (ENG., Illus.). 32p. (J). (gr. 1-3). 19.95 *(978-1-77108-091-0(4),* 39455853-d71f-488a-81eb-6e794be24106) Nimbus Publishing, Ltd. CAN. Dist: Baker & Taylor Publisher Services (BTPS).

Fitzgerald, Joanne. Yum! Yum!!, 1 vol. 2009. (ENG.). 32p. (J). (gr. -1-k). bds. 9.95 *(978-1-55455-137-8(4),* d662387f-8226-432d-87b5-6a3297ceb613) Fitzhenry & Whiteside, Ltd. CAN. Dist: Firefly Bks., Ltd.

Fitzmaurice, Gabriel. G. F. Woz Ere. MacDonald, Stella, illus. 2009. (ENG.). 96p. (J). pap. 12.95 *(978-1-85635-622-0(1))* Mercier Pr., Ltd., The IRL. Dist: Dufour Editions, Inc.

—I'm Proud to Be Me: Poems for Children & Their Parents. Phelan, Nicky, illus. 2005. (ENG.). 96p. (J). pap. 12.95 *(978-1-85635-474-5(1))* Mercier Pr., Ltd., The IRL. Dist: Dufour Editions, Inc.

Fitzmaurice, Gabriel & Macdonald, Stella. Splat: And Other Great Poems. Phelan, Nicky, illus. 2012. (ENG.). 96p. (J). pap. 13.95 *(978-1-85635-953-5(0))* Mercier Pr., Ltd., The IRL. Dist: Dufour Editions, Inc.

Flavin, Dick. Red Sox Rhymes: Verses & Curses. 2015. (ENG.). 224p. 19.99 *(978-0-06-239152-0(6),* Morrow, William & Co.) HarperCollins Pubs.

Fleischman, Paul. Joyful Noise: A Newbery Award Winner. Beddows, Eric, illus. rev. ed. 2019. (ENG.). 64p. (J). (gr. 3-7). pap. 6.99 *(978-0-06-446093-4(2),* HarperCollins) HarperCollins Pubs.

—Joyful Noise: Poems for Two Voices. 2005. (J). (gr. 3-6). 16.00 *(978-0-8335-8555-4(X))* Turtleback.

Fletcher, Ralph. A Writing Kind of Day: Poems for Young Poets. 2005. (ENG., Illus.). 32p. (J). (gr. 3-7). pap. 9.99 *(978-1-59078-353-5(0),* Wordsong) Highlights Pr., c/o Highlights for Children, Inc.

Fletter, Sharon Sofia. My Guardian Angel. Fletter, Sharon Sofia, illus. Lt. ed. 2007.Tr. of Mi Angel Guardian, il Mio Angelo, Meu Anjo Da Guarda, Mein Schutzengel, Mon Ange Guardian. (SPA, ITA, POR, GER & FRE., Illus.). 44p. (J). per. 17.95 *(978-0-9793113-0-7(6))* SoulSong Publishing.

FLH Students & Lutz, Suzanne. Many Voices: Where Dreams Take Flight III. 2008. 149p. pap. 14.95 *(978-0-7414-4569-8(7))* Infinity Publishing.

Flint, Norman. Rag & Bone: Visit London. 2010. 28p. pap. 12.49 *(978-1-4520-4093-6(1))* AuthorHouse.

Flor Ada, Alma & Campoy, F. Isabel. Chuchurumbe. (Literature Collection of Puertas Al Sol Ser.). (SPA.). 32p. (J). (gr. k-6). pap. 12.95 *(978-1-59437-709-9(X))* Santillana USA Publishing Co., Inc.

—Dreaming Fish. (Literature Collection of Gateways to the Sun Ser.). 32p. (J). (gr. k-6). pap. 12.95 *(978-1-59437-712-9(X))* Santillana USA Publishing Co., Inc.

—Flying Dragon. (Literature Collection of Gateways to the Sun Ser.). 32p. (J). (gr. k-6). pap. 12.95 *(978-1-59437-721-1(9))* Santillana USA Publishing Co., Inc.

—Laughing Crocodiles. (Literature Collection of Gateways to the Sun Ser.). 32p. (J). (gr. k-6). pap. 12.95 *(978-1-59437-715-0(4))* Santillana USA Publishing Co., Inc.

—Mambrú. (Literature Collection of Puertas Al Sol Ser.). (SPA.). 32p. (J). (gr. k-6). pap. 12.95 *(978-1-59437-706-8(5))* Santillana USA Publishing Co., Inc.

—Pimpón. (Literature Collection of Puertas Al Sol Ser.). (SPA.). 32p. (J). (gr. k-6). pap. 12.95 *(978-1-59437-700-6(6))* Santillana USA Publishing Co., Inc.

Florian, Douglas. Bing Bang Boing. 2007. (ENG., Illus.). 144p. (J). (gr. 1-4). pap. 8.00 *(978-0-15-205860-9(5),* 1197601, Clarion Bks.) HarperCollins Pubs.

—Comets, Stars, the Moon, & Mars: Space Poems & Paintings. Florian, Douglas, illus. 2007. (ENG., Illus.). 56p. (J). (gr. -1-3). 19.99 *(978-0-15-205372-7(7),* 1196175, Clarion Bks.) HarperCollins Pubs.

—Dinothesaurus: Prehistoric Poems & Paintings. Florian, Douglas, illus. 2009. (ENG., Illus.). 56p. (J). (gr. 1-5). 19.99 *(978-1-4169-7978-4(6),* Beach Lane Bks.) Beach Lane Bks.

—Friends & Foes: Poems about Us All. Florian, Douglas, illus. 2018. (ENG., Illus.). 48p. (J). (gr. -1-5). 18.99 *(978-1-4424-8795-6(X),* Beach Lane Bks.) Beach Lane Bks.

—Lizards, Frogs, & Polliwogs. Florian, Douglas, illus. 2005. (ENG., Illus.). 48p. (J). (gr. 1-4). reprint ed. pap. 8.99 *(978-0-15-205248-5(8),* 1195812, Clarion Bks.) HarperCollins Pubs.

—Shiver Me Timbers! Pirate Poems & Paintings. Neubecker, Robert, illus. 2012. (ENG.). 32p. (J). (gr. 1-5). 19.99 *(978-1-4424-1321-4(2),* Beach Lane Bks.) Beach Lane Bks.

—UnBEElievables: Honeybee Poems & Paintings. Florian, Douglas, illus. 2012. (ENG., Illus.). 32p. (J). (gr. k-3). 18.99 *(978-1-4424-2652-8(7),* Beach Lane Bks.) Beach Lane Bks.

Folami Abiade. In Daddy's Arms I Am Tall: African Americans Celebrating Fathers, 1 vol. 2013. (ENG., Illus.). 32p. (J). (gr. 1-6). pap. 10.95 *(978-1-58430-016-8(7),* leelowbooks) Lee & Low Bks., Inc.

Fondo de Cultura Económica (Mexico) Staff, creator. Despertar del Jaguar, Vol. 2. 2003. (Vida Y Palabra de Los Indios de America Ser.). (SPA., Illus.). 229p. (J). 20.99 *(978-968-16-6593-7(7))* Fondo de Cultura Economica USA.

Forler, Nan. Winterberries & Apple Blossoms: Reflections & Flavors of a Mennonite Year. Snyder, Peter Etril, illus. 2011. 40p. (J). (gr. k-4). 22.95 *(978-1-77049-254-7(2),* Tundra Bks.) Tundra Bks. CAN. Dist: Penguin Random Hse. LLC.

Forman, Ruth. Young Cornrows Callin Out the Moon. Bayoc, Cbabi, illus. 2007. (ENG.). 24p. (J). (gr. -1-3). lib. bdg. 16.95 *(978-0-89239-218-6(5))* Lee & Low Bks., Inc.

Forrest, George. Echoes with a Western Air. 2007. 192p. (YA). per. 16.95 *(978-0-595-45286-6(8))* iUniverse, Inc.

Fort, Gary W. Mom, I Love Spaghetti. Schultz, Michael, illus. 2011. 86p. pap. 24.00 *(978-1-60911-562-3(7),* Eloquent Bks.) Strategic Book Publishing & Rights Agency (SBPRA).

Foster, John, ed. Ridiculous Rhymes. 2011. (ENG., Illus.). 96p. (gr. k-4). pap. 5.99 *(978-0-00-711212-8(2),* HarperCollins Children's Bks.) HarperCollins Pubs. Ltd. GBR. Dist: HarperCollins Pubs.

Foster, John, selected by. A Century of Children's Poems. 2011. (ENG., Illus.). 160p. pap. 7.99 *(978-0-00-714001-5(0),* HarperCollins Children's Bks.) HarperCollins Pubs. Ltd. GBR. Dist: HarperCollins Pubs.

—Dead Funny. 2011. (ENG., Illus.). 96p. (gr. k-4). pap. 5.99 *(978-0-00-711213-5(0),* HarperCollins Children's Bks.) HarperCollins Pubs. Ltd. GBR. Dist: HarperCollins Pubs.

—Teasing Tongue-Twisters. 2011. (ENG., Illus.). 96p. pap. 5.99 *(978-0-00-711214-2(9),* HarperCollins Children's Bks.) HarperCollins Pubs. Ltd. GBR. Dist: HarperCollins Pubs.

Foston, Rebera E. Beyond a Reasonable Doubt. 2003. 96p. (YA). pap. *(978-1-930362-04-8(8))* Foston Adolescent Workshop, Inc.

—A New Day. 2003. 96p. (YA). pap. *(978-1-930362-03-1(X))* Foston Adolescent Workshop, Inc.

—No Cross, No Crown. 2003. 96p. (YA). per. *(978-1-930362-08-6(0))* Foston Adolescent Workshop, Inc.

—No Forwarding Address. 2003. 96p. (YA). per. *(978-1-930362-09-3(9))* Foston Adolescent Workshop, Inc.

—Pictures of the Wedding. 2003. 96p. (YA). per. *(978-1-930362-11-6(0))* Foston Adolescent Workshop, Inc.

—Sweet Memories. 2003. 96p. (YA). per. *(978-1-930362-12-3(9))* Foston Adolescent Workshop, Inc.

—When You Have Been Alone. 2003. 96p. (YA). per. *(978-1-930362-14-7(5))* Foston Adolescent Workshop, Inc.

—While You Were Gone. 2003. 96p. (YA). per. *(978-1-930362-15-4(3))* Foston Adolescent Workshop, Inc.

Foxworthy, Jeff. Silly Street. Björkman, Steve, illus. 2009. 32p. (J). (ENG.). (gr. -1-2). 17.99 *(978-0-06-171918-9(8));* (gr. k-2). lib. bdg. 18.89 *(978-0-06-171919-6(6))* HarperCollins Pubs.

—Silly Street: Selected Poems. Bjorkman, Steve, illus. 2010. (I Can Read Level 2 Ser.). (ENG.). 32p. (J). (gr. k-3). pap. 4.99 *(978-0-06-176528-5(7),* HarperCollins) HarperCollins Pubs.

Frampton, David. Mr. Ferlinghetti's Poem. Frampton, David, illus. 2006. (Illus.). 32p. (J). (gr. k-4). 18.00 *(978-0-8028-5290-8(4),* Eerdmans Bks For Young Readers) Eerdmans, William B. Publishing Co.

Franco, Betsy. Bees, Snails, & Peacock Tails: Patterns & Shapes ... Naturally. Jenkins, Steve, illus. 2008. (ENG.). 40p. (J). (gr. -1-3). 19.99 *(978-1-4169-0386-4(0),* McElderry, Margaret K. Bks.) McElderry, Margaret K. Bks.

—Messing Around on the Monkey Bars: And Other School Poems for Two Voices. Hartland, Jessie, illus. 2009. (ENG.). 48p. (J). (gr. 3-7). 18.99 *(978-0-7636-3174-1(4))* Candlewick Pr.

—A Spectacular Selection of Sea Critters: Concrete Poems. Wertz, Michael, illus. 2015. (ENG.). 32p. (J). (gr. 2-5). E-Book 30.65 *(978-1-4677-8849-6(X),* Millbrook Pr.) Lerner Publishing Group.

Franco, Betsy, ed. Falling Hard: 100 Love Poems by Teenagers. 2010. (ENG., Illus.). 160p. (YA). (gr. 9). pap. 6.99 *(978-0-7636-4839-8(6))* Candlewick Pr.

Frank, John. Lend a Hand: Poems about Giving, 1 vol. Ladd, London, illus. (ENG.). 32p. (J). 2019. (gr. 1-5). pap. 11.95 *(978-1-62014-829-7(3),* leelowbooks) 2014. 17.95 *(978-1-60060-970-1(8))* Lee & Low Bks., Inc.

Franskevich, Ala, compiled by. Underwater World. 2013. (Everyday Rhymes Ser.). (ENG., Illus.). 14p. (J). (-k). bds. 15.95 *(978-1-61889-229-4(0))* AZ Bks. LLC.

Freeman, Ken. I Hope You Know: A Message from Dad. 2012. 32p. pap. 19.99 *(978-1-4685-7466-1(3))* AuthorHouse.

Frodsham, Ken. The Mobile Phone of Jeremy Bone. 2014. (ENG., Illus.). 118p. pap. 14.95 *(978-1-4918-7950-4(5),* ccd1116e-7ccc-4130-862c-c81bb3f3b5d9) AuthorHouse.

Froh, Joanne. Imagine This! Plagens, Frances, illus. 2006. 32p. (J). 19.95 *(978-0-9777640-0-6(1))* Joanne Frances Pr.

Frost, Helen. Among a Thousand Fireflies. Lieder, Rick, illus. 2016. (ENG.). 32p. (J). (gr. -1-2). 15.99 *(978-0-7636-7642-1(X))* Candlewick Pr.

—Among a Thousand Fireflies. Lieder, Rick, illus. 2019. (ENG.). 32p. (J). (gr. -1-2). 7.99 *(978-1-5362-0562-6(1))* Candlewick Pr.

Frost, Robert. The Cow in Apple Time. Yeagle, Dean, illus. 2005. 32p. (J). 15.95 *(978-0-9758970-1-0(2))* Beekman & Hathaway.

—Poetry for Kids: Robert Frost. Parini, Jay, ed. Paraskevas, Michael, illus. 2017. (Poetry for Kids Ser.). (ENG.). 48p. (J). (gr. 3-8). 17.95 *(978-1-63322-220-5(9)*, 224898, Moondance) Quarto Publishing Group USA.

Fuat Bilkan, Ali. Tales from Rumi: Mathnawi Selections for Young Readerws. 2008. (Illus.). 160p. (J). (gr. 7-17). 12.95 *(978-1-59784-124-5(2)*, Tughra Bks.) Blue Dome, Inc.

Fuerst, Jeffrey B. Peter Piper Picks & Pickles Peppers. 2008. (Reader's Theater Nursery Rhymes & Songs Ser.). (Illus.). 48p. (J). (gr. k-1). pap. *(978-1-60437-970-9(7))* Benchmark Education Co.

Fuertes, Gloria. Diccionario Estrafalario. 2003. (SPA.). 168p. *(978-84-305-8462-8(5)*, SU3166) Susaeta Ediciones, S.A. ESP. Dist: Lectorum Pubns., Inc.

—4 Poemas de Gloria Fuertes y Una Calabaza Vestida de Luna. Aguilar, Jose, illus. 2007. (SPA.). 36p. (J). *(978-84-934160-9-6(6))* Atalante.

Fugate, Alonzo. Pumpkin Guts. 2008. (ENG.). 96p. pap. 13.93 *(978-0-557-01914-4(1))* Lulu Pr., Inc.

Fuller, T. Nat. Creature vs. Teacher. Meyer, Alex Eben, illus. 2018. (ENG.). 16p. (J). (gr. -1 — 1). bds. 7.99 *(978-1-4197-3155-6(6)*, 1186810, Abrams Appleseed) Abrams, Inc.

Furlong, Frank. Before We Were. 2011. 24p. pap. 10.95 *(978-1-4575-0269-9(0))* Dog Ear Publishing, LLC.

Furlong, Frank, illus. Not Yet: Poems for Kids Five & Up. 2011. 24p. pap. 14.95 *(978-1-4575-0467-9(7))* Dog Ear Publishing, LLC.

Fuschia. China Doll's Charm. 2012. 28p. pap. 16.95 *(978-1-4525-4674-2(6))* Balboa Pr.

Fusek Peters, Andrew, compiled by. Poems about Earth. 2007. (Elements in Poetry Ser.). (Illus.). 30p. (J). *(978-0-237-52887-4(8))* Evans Brothers, Ltd.

Fusek Peters, Andrew & Peters, Polly. Poems with Attitude. 2003. (ENG.). 96p. pap. *(978-0-7502-4189-2(6)*, Wayland) Hachette Children's Group.

Fyleman, Rose & Philip, Neil. Mary Middling & Other Silly Folk: Nursery Rhymes & Nonsense Poems. Bandlow, Katja, illus. 2004. (ENG.). 32p. (J). (gr. -1-3). tchr. ed. 16.00 *(978-0-618-38141-8(4)*, 100334, Clarion Bks.) HarperCollins Pubs.

Gagliano, Eugene. My Teacher Dances on the Desk. Mai-Wyss, Tatjana, illus. 2009. (ENG.). 48p. (J). (gr. 1-4). pap. 6.95 *(978-1-58536-446-6(0)*, 202171) Sleeping Bear Pr.

Galdone, Paul. Three Little Kittens. Galdone, Paul, illus. 2013. (Paul Galdone Nursery Classic Ser.). (ENG., Illus.). 32p. (J). (gr. -1-3). pap. 26.99 *(978-0-547-99480-2(X)*, 1525235, Clarion Bks.) HarperCollins Pubs.

Galdone, Paul & Lear, Edward. The Owl & the Pussycat. Galdone, Paul, illus. 2015. (Paul Galdone Nursery Classic Ser.). (ENG., Illus.). 40p. (J). (gr. -1-3). 8.99 *(978-0-544-39295-3(7)*, 1593570, Clarion Bks.) HarperCollins Pubs.

Gallegos, Michael. Mommy Do You Love Me? 2013. 20p. pap. 24.95 *(978-1-62709-265-4(X))* America Star Bks.

Ganeri, Anita. I Can Write Poems, 1 vol. 2013. (I Can Write Ser.). (ENG., Illus.). 32p. (gr. 1-3). pap. 8.29 *(978-1-4329-6943-1(9)*, 119869, Heinemann) Capstone.

García Lorca, Federico. Canciones (1921-1924) (SPA.). 96p. (J). 13.25 *(978-84-206-6106-3(6)*, AZ6106) Alianza Editorial, S. A. ESP. Dist: Continental Bk. Co., Inc.

—Canciones y Poemas para Ninos. (Coleccion Poemas Juvenil). (SPA., Illus.). 96p. (J). 9.50 *(978-84-335-8401-4(4)*, DD4014) Labor, Editorial S. A. ESP. Dist: Continental Bk. Co., Inc.

—Canciones y Poemas para Ninos. (SPA., Illus.). 64p. (J). (gr. 4-6). pap. 6.95 net. *(978-1-887578-59-2(5)*, SO0128) SpanPress, Inc.

—FEDERICO GARCÍA LORCA PARA NIÑOS. (Coleccion Grandes Autores para Ninos). (SPA., Illus.). 154p. (J). (gr. 4-6). 20.76 *(978-84-305-9302-6(0)*, SU4866) Susaeta Ediciones, S.A. ESP. Dist: Lectorum Pubns., Inc.

García Lorca, Federico. & Aguilar, José. 4 Poemas de Lorca y un Viaje a Nueva York. 2008. (SPA., Illus.). 36p. *(978-84-934160-3-4(7))* Atalante.

García Ordaz, Daniel. You Know What I'm Sayin'? Poetry Drama. 2nd rev. ed. 2006. (ENG & SPA.). 80p. (YA). per. 10.00 *(978-0-9789954-1-6(4))* El Zarape Pr.

Garfield, Cari. After All, I'm Just a Ball: Children's Poetry Guessing Book. 2005. 32p. pap. 18.00 *(978-1-4208-2492-6(9))* AuthorHouse.

Garrison, Tommy. Imagination Celebration. 2009. 50p. pap. 10.00 *(978-0-557-07835-6(0))* Lulu Pr., Inc.

Gasca, Theresa & Juarez, Amanda. Mere Words Can Only Say... 2003. 162p. (YA). pap. 14.95 *(978-0-595-27669-1(5))* iUniverse, Inc.

Gatell, Angelina. Mis Primeras Lecturas Poeticas. (SPA.). 256p. (J). (gr. 5-8). *(978-84-7175-180-5(1)*, EN1279) Twenty-Nine Ediciones ESP. Dist: Lectorum Pubns., Inc.

Gauthier, Glenn G. The A to Z Book. Gauthier, Glenn G., illus. 2006. (Illus.). 32p. (J). 16.95 *(978-1-887542-42-5(6))* Bk. Pubs. Network.

Gbala, Deswin R. Rock University: A Collection of Short Stories & Poems. Gbala, Deswin R., illus. Date not set. (Illus.). 51p. (Orig.). (J). (gr. 3-10). pap. 8.50 *(978-0-9650629-2-3(9))* Coulee Region Pubns., Inc.

Gedichte Analysieren. (Duden Abiturhilfen Ser.). (GER.). 112p. (YA). (gr. 12-13). *(978-3-411-70141-4(2))* Bibliographisches Institut & F. A. Brockhaus AG DEU. Dist: International Bk. Import Service, Inc.

George, Elizabeth. A Little Girl after God's Own Heart: Learning God's Ways in My Early Days. 2006. (ENG., Illus.). 32p. (J). (gr. k-2). 16.99 *(978-0-7369-1545-8(1)*, 6915451) Harvest Hse. Pubs.

George, Jim & George, Elizabeth. Through the Bible One Rhyme at a Time. 2017. (ENG., Illus.). 48p. (J). (gr. -1-2). 14.99 *(978-0-7369-2748-2(4)*, 6927482) Harvest Hse. Pubs.

George, Kristine O'Connell. Emma Dilemma: Big Sister Poems. Carpenter, Nancy, illus. 2011. (ENG.). 48p. (J). (gr. 1-4). 17.99 *(978-0-618-42842-7(9)*, 100346, Clarion Bks.) HarperCollins Pubs.

—The Great Frog Race: And Other Poems. Kiesler, Kate, illus. 2005. (ENG.). 48p. (J). (gr. -1-3). reprint ed. 7.99 *(978-0-618-60478-4(2)*, 100436, Clarion Bks.) HarperCollins Pubs.

—Old Elm Speaks: Tree Poems. Kiesler, Kate, illus. 2007. (ENG.). 48p. (J). (gr. -1-3). 7.99 *(978-0-618-75242-3(0)*, 100524, Clarion Bks.) HarperCollins Pubs.

Ghigna, Charles. Animal Tracks: Wild Poems to Read Aloud. Speirs, John, illus. 2004. (ENG.). 36p. (J). (gr. -1-1). 14.95 *(978-0-8109-4841-9(9))* Abrams, Inc.

—Little Seeds [Scholastic]. AG Jatkowska, illus. 2012. (My Little Planet Ser.). (ENG.). 24p. (gr. -1 — 1). pap. 0.50 *(978-1-4795-1671-1(6)*, Picture Window Bks.) Capstone.

Giles, W. Marie. Open Your Mind, Open Your Heart: A Collection of Words of Wisdom, Heartfelt Thoughts, & Original Poetry. 2003. 112p. per. 19.95 *(978-0-9728944-0-1(3))* Giles, Willie M.

Gillespie, Esther A. & Clark, Thomas Curtis, eds. A Child's Thought of God: Religious Poems for Children. 2006. (ENG.). 136p. per. 20.95 *(978-1-4286-2999-8(8))* Kessinger Publishing, LLC.

Gillooly, Eileen, ed. Poetry for Young People: Rudyard Kipling. Spector, Joel & Sharpe, Jim, illus. 2010. (Poetry for Young People Ser.: 8). (ENG.). 48p. (J). (gr. 3). pap. 6.95 *(978-1-4027-7293-1(9))* Sterling Publishing Co., Inc.

Gilmartin, Erin. Stretched into Shadow with No End: A Collection of Poems, 1 book. 2004. (Illus.). 88p. (YA). pap. 11.95 *(978-0-9702497-0-8(5)*, Meister-Home Pr.) Meister-Home, Inc.

Giovanni, Nikki. I Am Loved. Bryan, Ashley, illus. 2018. (ENG.). 32p. (J). (gr. -1-3). 18.99 *(978-1-5344-0492-2(9)*, Atheneum/Caitlyn Dlouhy Books) Simon & Schuster Children's Publishing.

Gittens, Sandra L. Hooray! We're Making Memories Today! PA Illustrator, illus. 2011. 48p. pap. 24.95 *(978-1-4560-0914-4(1))* America Star Bks.

Givens, Florence Rosie. A Little More Cream Please Poem Collection by Florence Rosie Givens. 2003. (Illus.). 232p. per. 12.95 *(978-0-9705819-3-8(9))* FloBound Poems Publications.

Godden, Rumer. Cockcrow to Starlight: A Day Full of Poetry. Kneen, Maggie, illus. 2003. (ENG.). 144p. (J). pap. 13.99 *(978-0-330-34302-2(5)*, Pan) Pan Macmillan GBR. Dist: Trafalgar Square Publishing.

Godula, Ellen Kjelgaard & Godula, Brian. Queen Mab, Musical Verses Volume 3. 2007. (J). audio compact disk 16.99 *(978-0-9764109-3-5(1))* Pillar Rock Publishing.

Goel, Samir. My Favorite Children's Poems. 2009. 28p. pap. 12.49 *(978-1-4389-7306-7(3))* AuthorHouse.

Gonsalves, Gloria D. Diamonds Forever: Never Let Your Inner Child Stop from Glittering. 2008. (ENG., Illus.). 100p. pap. 31.99 *(978-1-4389-0428-3(2))* AuthorHouse.

Gonzalez, Ray. El Conejito Claudio (G) Para Bebés de 1 a 3 Años. Giannini, Claudia, tr. 2006. (SPA., Illus.). 20p. (J). bds. *(978-0-9712816-4-6(5))* Third Week Bks.

Goodridge, Walt F. J. Lyrics for Living Vol. 2: Just Because I Am. Owens-Waters, Zelda, ed. 2003. 64p. (C). 10.00 *(978-0-9629202-5-7(8)*, LL002) Passion Profit Co., The/NicheMarket.

Gooseberry, Philbert & Cluett, Matthew. Philbert Gooseberry's Book of Preposterous Poems. 2016. (ENG.). 92p. (J). pap. 10.95 *(978-1-78554-168-1(4)*, d068c4c1-935f-4659-9056-7300055651d5) Austin Macauley Pubs. Ltd. GBR. Dist: Baker & Taylor Publisher Services (BTPS).

Gorey, Edward & Lear, Edward, illus. Jumblies. 2010. 48p. 14.95 *(978-0-7649-5426-9(1))* Pomegranate Communications, Inc.

Granados, Antonio. Poemas de Juguete 1. 2003. (SPA., Illus.). 191p. 8.95 *(978-968-19-0627-6(6))* Aguilar, Altea, Taurus, Alfaguara, S.A. de C.V MEX. Dist: Santillana USA Publishing Co., Inc.

—Versos de Dulce y de Sal. (SPA.). 166p. (J). pap. 13.95 *(978-968-7205-28-1(8)*, AIM288) Amaquemecan, Editorial MEX. Dist: Continental Bk. Co., Inc.

Grandits, John. Blue Lipstick: Concrete Poems. 2007. (ENG., Illus.). 48p. (J). (gr. 5-7). 7.99 *(978-0-618-85132-4(1)*, 100566, Clarion Bks.) HarperCollins Pubs.

—Technically, It's Not My Fault: Concrete Poems. 2005. (Illus.). 40p. (gr. 4-8). 17.00 *(978-0-7569-5513-7(0))* Perfection Learning Corp.

Grant, Shauntay. Up Home, 1 vol. Tooke, Susan, illus. 2011. (ENG.). 32p. (J). (gr. -1-k). pap. 12.95 *(978-1-55109-911-8(0)*, e6c30a43-fc9e-4141-9a69-a0c7bd350230) Nimbus Publishing, Ltd. CAN. Dist: Baker & Taylor Publisher Services (BTPS).

Graves, Robert. Ann at Highwood Hall. Ardizzone, Edward, illus. 2017. 56p. (J). (gr. k-4). 16.95 *(978-1-60980-743-6(X)*, Triangle Square) Seven Stories Pr.

Green, Paula. Flamingo Bendalingo: Poems from the Zoo. Hight, Michael, illus. 2006. (ENG.). 100p. (gr. 4-7). 24.95 *(978-1-86940-353-9(3))* Auckland Univ. Pr. NZL. Dist: Independent Pubs. Group.

—A Treasury of NZ Poems for Children. Cooper, Jenny, illus. 2017. (ENG.). 288p. (J). (gr. k-2). 39.95 *(978-0-14-377219-4(8))* Penguin Group New Zealand, Ltd. NZL. Dist: Independent Pubs. Group.

Green Set. (Dias y Dias de Poesia Ser.). (SPA.). (gr. -1-6). 207.23 *(978-1-56334-273-8(1)*, DI8633); 293.52 *(978-1-56334-274-5(X)*, DI8634) CENGAGE Learning.

Greenberg, Jan, ed. Side by Side: New Poems Inspired by Art from Around the World. 2008. (ENG., Illus.). 80p. (J). (gr. 2-7). 21.95 *(978-0-8109-9471-3(2)*, 6152-03, Abrams Bks. for Young Readers) Abrams, Inc.

Greene, Leslie. Papa & Breannah Bear on a Treasure Hunt. 2008. 31p. pap. 24.95 *(978-1-60563-985-7(0))* America Star Bks.

Greenfield Educational Center Staff. Words Through Poetry, Level 2. 2005. (CHI., Illus.). 31p. (J). pap. 7.99 *(978-962-563-029-8(5))*; pap., wbk. ed. 4.99 *(978-962-563-030-4(9))* Greenfield Enterprises, Ltd. HKG. Dist: Cheng & Tsui Co.

Greenfield, Eloise. Brothers & Sisters. 2009. (Illus.). 32p. (J). 18.89 *(978-0-06-056285-4(4))* HarperCollins Pubs.

—Brothers & Sisters: Family Poems. Gilchrist, Jan Spivey, illus. 2008. (ENG.). 32p. (J). (gr. -1-3). 17.99 *(978-0-06-056284-7(6)*, HarperCollins) HarperCollins Pubs.

—The Friendly Four. Gilchrist, Jan Spivey, illus. 2006. (ENG.). 48p. (J). (gr. -1-3). 17.99 *(978-0-06-000759-1(1)*, HarperCollins) HarperCollins Pubs.

Griffin Llanas, Sheila. Modern American Poetry: Echoes & Shadows, 1 vol. 2010. (Poetry Rocks! Ser.). (ENG., Illus.). 160p. (gr. 9-10). lib. bdg. 38.60 *(978-0-7660-3275-0(2)*, b5616fb7-10cf-488c-8636-66893c6aae1b) Enslow Publishing, LLC.

Grimes, Nikki. Thanks a Million. Cabrera, Cozbi A., illus. 2006. 32p. (J). (gr. k-3). 17.99 *(978-0-688-17292-3(X))*; (ENG.). 17.89 *(978-0-688-17293-0(8)*, Greenwillow Bks.) HarperCollins Pubs.

—When Daddy Prays. Ladwig, Tim, illus. 2004. 32p. (J). (ENG.). pap. 8.00 *(978-0-8028-5266-3(1))*; 16.00 *(978-0-8028-5152-9(5))* Eerdmans, William B. Publishing Co.

Gs Troop 1358. A Thanksgiving Poem. 2011. 24p. pap. 9.99 *(978-1-4575-0749-6(8))* Dog Ear Publishing, LLC.

Guillén, Nicolás. Por el Mar de las Antillas Anda un Barco de Papel. 3rd ed. 2003. (Rosa y Manzana Ser.). (SPA., Illus.). 44p. *(978-84-85334-32-2(9)*, LG1397) Lóguez Ediciones ESP. Dist: Lectorum Pubns., Inc.

Guilmette, Patty. Finding Kyle Some Style, 1 vol. Whitman, Diana McManus, illus. 2009. 32p. pap. 24.95 *(978-1-60703-962-4(1))* America Star Bks.

Hablandole A Tu Corazon. 2005. (SPA.). (YA). 11.99 *(978-0-9765663-1-1(1))* Guevara, Alexis S.

Hall, Jennifer. Winston Rabbit & other Poems. 2010. (ENG., Illus.). 48p. pap. *(978-1-84748-735-3(1))* Athena Pr.

Hamburger, Maria. The Story of Aum. 2006. (J). *(978-0-9759226-1-3(0))* BrainFriendly Learning.

Hamilton, Carol. I'm Not from Neptune. 2003. 117p. (YA). (gr. 4-5). pap. 9.99 *(978-0-88092-537-2(X))* Royal Fireworks Publishing Co.

Hansen, Nichole. When I Was a Grown-Up. Hansen, Tevin, illus. 2015. (ENG.). 28p. (YA). pap. 9.49 *(978-1-941429-13-6(0))* Handersen Publishing.

Hanson, Sharon. The 10 Best Love Poems. 2008. 14.99 *(978-1-55448-543-7(6))* Scholastic Library Publishing.

Hardy, Ed & Young, Jim. Pollywogs & Other Friends. Motley, Chris and Jim Young, illus. 2007. 28p. per. 24.95 *(978-1-4137-2834-7(0))* America Star Bks.

Harris, Elle. Lullaby World. 2013. 26p. pap. 13.95 *(978-1-4908-1456-8(6)*, WestBow Pr.) Author Solutions, LLC.

Harrison, David L. Crawly School for Bugs: Poems to Drive You Buggy. Bayless, Julie, illus. 2018. 32p. (J). (gr. k-4). 17.95 *(978-1-62979-204-0(7)*, Wordsong) Highlights Pr., c/o Highlights for Children, Inc.

Harter, Penny. The Beastie Book: An Alphabestiary. Miller, Alexandra, illus. 2009. (ENG.). 56p. (J). 21.95 *(978-1-934860-05-2(0))* Shenanigan Bks.

Hattrup, Cheryl. The Little Woman Handbook. 2008. 25p. pap. 11.95 *(978-1-4327-1636-3(0))* Outskirts Pr., Inc.

Headstream, John H. Bright Stories & Little Literature for Children. 2007. pap. 10.00 *(978-0-8059-7028-9(2))* Dorrance Publishing Co., Inc.

Heard, Georgia, ed. Falling down the Page: A Book of List Poems. 2011. (ENG.). 48p. (J). (gr. 3-7). pap. 10.99 *(978-1-59643-666-4(2)*, 900070070) Square Fish.

Hearn, Emily. Batchawana Silly Stuff. Valleau, Gailon, illus. 2011. *(978-1-897475-70-6(5))* Hidden Brook Pr.

Heart of the Moment. 2005. (YA). per. *(978-1-59872-142-3(9))* Instant Pub.

Heidbreder, Robert. A Sea-Wishing Day. Denton, Kady MacDonald, illus. 2007. 32p. (J). (gr. -1-3). 15.95 *(978-1-55337-707-8(9))* Kids Can Pr., Ltd. CAN. Dist: Hachette Bk. Group.

—See Saw Saskatchewan. Ritchie, Scot, illus. 2005. 32p. (J). (gr. -1-4). 7.95 *(978-1-55337-968-3(3))* Kids Can Pr., Ltd. CAN. Dist: Hachette Bk. Group.

—Shake-Awakes, 1 vol. Mongeau, Marc, illus. 2012. (ENG.). 40p. (J). (gr. 1-3). 18.95 *(978-1-896580-71-5(8))* Tradewind Bks. CAN. Dist: Orca Bk. Pubs. USA.

Heiman, Diane & Suneby, Liz. That's a Mitzvah. Molk, Laurel, illus. 2014. (ENG.). 24p. (J). bds. 10.99 *(978-1-58023-804-5(1)*, 111caa34-316a-4f5f-8071-8473379a8103, Jewish Lights Publishing) LongHill Partners, Inc.

Hemphill, Stephanie. Your Own, Sylvia: A Verse Portrait of Sylvia. 2011. 9.84 *(978-0-7848-3501-2(2)*, Everbind) Marco Bk. Co.

—Your Own, Sylvia: A Verse Portrait of Sylvia Plath. 2008. (ENG.). 272p. (YA). (gr. 7). pap. 7.99 *(978-0-440-23968-0(0)*, Knopf Bks. for Young Readers) Random Hse. Children's Bks.

Hempstead, Jim. Come, Journey to Bethlehem. 2012. 34p. pap. 14.95 *(978-1-105-90106-5(8))* Lulu Pr., Inc.

Henchey, Agnes Braceland. This 'N' That. 2012. 84p. pap. 41.99 *(978-1-4691-3124-5(2))* Xlibris Corp.

Henderson, Scott. I Want to Be a Pig. 2013. 116p. 24.95 *(978-1-62646-415-5(4))* Booklocker.com, Inc.

Henderson, Stewart. All Things Weird & Wonderful. Baines, Nigel, illus. 2004. (ENG.). 96p. (J). (gr. 2-4). pap. 8.99 *(978-0-7459-4898-0(7)*, b68d3fd0-b9bd-4481-9e59-aa9b0ca70d4e, Lion Books) Lion Hudson PLC GBR. Dist: Baker & Taylor Publisher Services (BTPS).

Henry, Lori. Silent Screams: Into & Out of Bulimia Through Poetry. 3rd ed. 2014. (ENG., Illus.). 150p. (J). pap. *(978-0-9918659-3-2(6))* Dancing Traveller Media.

Heppermann, Christine. Poisoned Apples: Poems for You, My Pretty. 2014. (ENG.). 128p. (YA). (gr. 8). 18.99 *(978-0-06-228957-5(8)*, Greenwillow Bks.) HarperCollins Pubs.

Herford, Oliver. The Peter Pan Alphabet. Herford, Oliver, illus. 2015. (ENG., Illus.). 62p. pap. 5.99 *(978-1-61242-874-1(6)*, Serenity Pubs.) Arc Manor.

Hernández, José. Poemas Clasicos Para Jovenes. 2018.Tr. of Childrens Poetry. (SPA.). 152p. (YA). (gr. 7-12). pap. 6.95 *(978-968-403-854-7(2))* Selector, S.A. de C.V. MEX. Dist: Spanish Pubs., LLC.

Heymann, Irene Rommel. Fanciful Tales & Poems: For Grandchildren of Any Age. Heyman, Frank J., ed. Bessey, Vance, illus. 2012. 102p. (-18). pap. 14.95 *(978-1-934949-63-4(9))* Just Write Bks.

Higgins, Nadia. Henry & Hala Build a Haiku. Dumm, Brian, illus. 2011. (Poetry Builders Ser.). 32p. (J). (gr. 2-4). lib. bdg. 25.27 *(978-1-59953-435-0(5))* Norwood Hse. Pr.

High School, West Scranton & Mazzino, Christopher. Four Years to Life. 2004. 339p. (YA). 33.95 *(978-0-595-66333-0(8))* iUniverse, Inc.

Hillert, Margaret. Come Play with Me. 2016. (BeginningtoRead Ser.). (ENG., Illus.). 32p. (J). (-2). 22.60 *(978-1-59953-814-3(8))* Norwood Hse. Pr.

Hinckley, Betts. Adventure's of Charlie Girl. 2012. 44p. pap. 21.99 *(978-1-4691-4364-4(X))* Xlibris Corp.

Hines, Anna Grossnickle. Winter Lights: A Season in Poems & Quilts. Hines, Anna Grossnickle, illus. 2005. (Illus.). 32p. (J). lib. bdg. 17.89 *(978-0-06-000818-5(0))* HarperCollins Pubs.

Hirschfield, Beth. What's Eating You, Girls 'n Boysenberries? Veno, Joe, illus. 2009. 32p. (J). 16.95 *(978-0-9818126-3-2(5))* Ampersand, Inc.

Hoberman, Mary Ann. The Llama Who Had No Pajama: 100 Favorite Poems. Fraser, Betty, illus. 2006. (ENG.). 68p. (J). (gr. 1-4). pap. 8.99 *(978-0-15-205571-4(1)*, 1196756, Clarion Bks.) HarperCollins Pubs.

—My Song Is Beautiful: Poems & Pictures in Many Voices. 2009. (Illus.). 32p. pap. 6.99 *(978-0-316-06835-2(7))* Little, Brown Bks. for Young Readers.

—You Read to Me, I'll Read to You: Very Short Fairy Tales to Read Together. 2012. (J). lib. bdg. 17.20 *(978-0-606-26685-7(2))* Turtleback.

Hoena, Blake, et al. Tickles, Pickles, & Floofing Persnickles: Reading & Writing Nonsense Poems, 1 vol. Smith, Simon et al, illus. 2014. (Poet in You Ser.). (ENG.). 32p. (J). (gr. 2-4). lib. bdg. 27.99 *(978-1-4795-2198-2(1)*, 124034, Picture Window Bks.) Capstone.

Hogg, James. The Magical Mermaids. Atkins, Alison, illus. 2007. (Sparkling Jigsaw Book Ser.). 10p. (J). (gr. k-3). *(978-1-84666-373-4(3)*, Tide Mill Pr.) Top That! Publishing PLC.

Hoguet, Susan Ramsay. Maine ABC. 2013. (ENG.). 32p. (J). (gr. -1-k). 14.99 *(978-1-60893-182-8(X))* Down East Bks.

Holbrook, Sara E. Zombies! Evacuate the School! Sandstrom, Karen, illus. 2014. (ENG.). 56p. (J). (gr. 4-7). pap. 7.99 *(978-1-62979-110-4(5)*, Wordsong) Highlights Pr., c/o Highlights for Children, Inc.

Hollins, Paula. Christopher Makes Words! A Personalized World of Words Based on the Letters in the Name Christopher, with Humorous Poems & Colorful Illustrations. 2013. (Illus.). 42p. pap. 9.25 *(978-0-9897278-5-3(8))* PHD Ink.

—Isabella Makes Words! A Personalized World of Words Based on the Letters in the Name Isabella, with Humorous Poems & Colorful Illustrations. 2013. 36p. pap. 9.25 *(978-1-941104-00-2(2))* PHD Ink.

—Isabelle Makes Words! A Personalized World of Words Based on the Letters in the Name Isabelle, with Humorous Poems & Colorful Illustrations. 2013. 36p. pap. 9.25 *(978-1-941104-01-9(0))* PHD Ink.

—Katherine Makes Words! A Personalized World of Words Based on the Letters in the Name Katherine, with Humorous Poems & Colorful Illustrations. 2013. 38p. pap. 9.25 *(978-0-9897278-7-7(4))* PHD Ink.

—Michael Makes Words! A Personalized World of Words Based on the Letters in the Name Michael, with Humorous Poems & Colorful Illustrations. 2013. (Illus.). 38p. pap. 9.25 *(978-0-9897278-6-0(6))* PHD Ink.

—Sophie Makes Words! A Personalized World of Words Based on the Letters in the Name Sophie, with Humorous Poems & Colorful Illustrations. 2013. 30p. pap. 9.25 *(978-0-9897278-4-6(X))* PHD Ink.

Hollowell, Lorraine L. The Oatmeal Bath: And Other Poems That Make Kids Laugh. 2013. 112p. (gr. 2-4). pap. 12.06 *(978-1-4669-7926-0(7))* Trafford Publishing.

—Outside Is Where I'd Rather Be: And Other Poems for Kids Like Me. 2013. 84p. (gr. 2-4). pap. 9.10 *(978-1-4669-9012-8(0))* Trafford Publishing.

Holt, Lindsey Leann. The Green Jellybean: A Book of Children's Poems, 1 vol. 2010. 72p. pap. 19.95 *(978-1-4489-8559-3(5))* America Star Bks.

Homer. The Odyssey. Fagles, Robert, tr. 2006. (Illus.). 560p. (gr. 12-18). 18.00 *(978-0-14-303995-2(4)*, Penguin Classics) Penguin Publishing Group.

Homewood, Terry Stewart. From Then until Now. 2011. 116p. (gr. -1). 23.89 *(978-1-4634-2397-1(7))*; pap. 12.01 *(978-1-4634-2396-4(9))* AuthorHouse.

Hood, Karen Jean Matsko. Tanka Thoughts: A Collection of Poetry, bk. 11. Whispering Pine Press International, ed. Artistic Design Service Staff, illus. 2014. (Hood Poetry Ser.). 224p. pap. 19.95 *(978-1-930948-52-5(2)*, 1-930948-52-2) Whispering Pine Pr. International, Inc.

—Under the Lilacs: A Collection of Children's Poetry, Vol. 1. Whispering Pine Press International, ed. Artistic Design Service Staff, illus. 2014. (Hood Children's Poetry Book Ser.). 160p. (J). 29.95 *(978-1-930948-51-8(4)*, 1-930948-51-4) Whispering Pine Pr. International, Inc.

Hopkins, Lee. Amazing Faces, 1 vol. Soentpiet, Chris, illus. 2015. (Amazing Ser.). (ENG.). 40p. (J). (gr. 1-8). 12.95 *(978-1-62014-223-3(6)*, leelowbooks) Lee & Low Bks., Inc.

Hopkins, Lee Bennett. All the World's a Stage. Billout, Guy, illus. 2013. (ENG.). 40p. (J). (gr. 3-6). 19.99 *(978-1-56846-218-9(2)*, 21613, Creative Editions) Creative Co., The.

—Alphathoughts. Baggetta, Maria, illus. 2015. (ENG.). 32p. (J). (gr. k-2). 6.95 *(978-1-62091-792-3(0)*, Wordsong) Highlights Pr., c/o Highlights for Children, Inc.

—Been to Yesterdays: Poems of a Life. Rendeiro, Charlene, illus. 2007. 64p. (gr. 3-7). 21.45 *(978-0-7569-7966-9(8))* Perfection Learning Corp.

—A Bunch of Punctuation. Bloch, Serge, illus. 2018. (ENG.). 32p. (J). (gr. 3-7). 17.95 *(978-1-59078-994-0(6)*, Wordsong) Highlights Pr., c/o Highlights for Children, Inc.

—Got Geography! Stanton, Philip, illus. 2006. (ENG.). 32p. (J). (gr. k-5). 16.99 *(978-0-06-055601-3(3)*, Greenwillow Bks.) HarperCollins Pubs.

—Hamsters, Shells, & Spelling Bees: School Poems. Yoshikawa, Sachiko, illus. 2008. (I Can Read Bks.). 48p. (J). (gr. -1-3). lib. bdg. 17.89 *(978-0-06-074113-6(9))* HarperCollins Pubs.

—School People. Shi, Ellen, illus. 2018. (ENG.). 32p. (J). (gr. k-3). 17.99 *(978-1-62979-703-8(0)*, Wordsong) Highlights Pr., c/o Highlights for Children, Inc.

—Worlds of Poetry, 9 bks. 2005. (Poetry Ser.). (gr. k-3). 270.00 *(978-0-8215-0539-7(4))* Sadlier, William H. Inc.

P
Q
R

Hopkins, Lee Bennett, ed. I Remember: Poems & Pictures of Heritage, 1 vol. 2019. (ENG., Illus.). 56p. (J). (gr. 3-12). 21.95 (978-1-62014-311-7(9), leelowbooks) Lee & Low Bks., Inc.

Hopkins, Lee Bennett & Alcorn, Stephen. Little Bill: Extra Thankful Thanksgiving. 2004. (Illus.). (J). pap. 3.99 (978-0-439-35244-4(4), Orchard Bks.) Scholastic, Inc.

Hopwood, Mererid, et al. Byd Llawn Hud. Glynn, Chris, illus. 2005. (WEL.). 32p. pap. 4.99 (978-1-84323-342-8(8)); pap. 12.99 (978-1-84323-343-5(6)) Gomer Pr. GBR. Dist: Gomer Pr.

Horton, Joan. I Brought My Rat for Show-And-Tell: And Other Funny School Poems. 2004. (Penguin Young Readers, Level 3 Ser.). (Illus.). 48p. (J). (gr. 1-3). mass mkt. 4.99 (978-0-448-43364-6(8), Penguin Young Readers) Penguin Young Readers Group.

Hosein, Alana. My Little One & Me. 2010. (ENG.). 26p. pap. 15.99 (978-1-4535-4679-6(0)) Xlibris Corp.

Hosford, Kate. Feeding the Flying Fanellis: And Other Poems from a Circus Chef. Kawa, Cosei, illus. 2015. (ENG.). 32p. (J). (gr. 1-3). E-Book 27.99 (978-1-4677-7511-3(8), Carolrhoda Bks.) Lerner Publishing Group.

Hotaling, Gwenn. A Child's Book of Seasons. 2003. (Illus.). 64p. 19.95 (978-0-9728838-0-1(0)) Little Bird Publishing.

Hovey, Kate. Voices of the Trojan War. Gore, Leonid, illus. 2012. (ENG.). 128p. (J). (gr. 3-7). pap. 7.99 (978-1-4424-8880-9(8), McElderry, Margaret K. Bks.) McElderry, Margaret K. Bks.

Howard, Cheryl L. It's Turtle Time. Kapart, illus. 2011. 28p. pap. 24.95 (978-1-4560-6676-5(5)) America Star Bks.

Howitt, Mary. The Spider & the Fly: 10th Anniversary Edition. DiTerlizzi, Tony, illus. 2012. (ENG.). 40p. (J). (gr. 1-4). 19.99 (978-1-4424-5454-5(7), Simon & Schuster Bks. For Young Readers) Simon & Schuster Bks. For Young Readers.

Hudson, Cheryl Willis. Many Colors of Mother Goose. 2004. (Illus.). 32p. (J). (gr. -1-3). pap. 7.95 (978-0-940975-91-0(2), Sankofa Bks.) Just Us Bks., Inc.

Hudson, Wade. Poetry from the Masters: The Pioneers. Hudson, Stephen J., illus. 2003. (Poetry from the Masters Ser.). (ENG.). 88p. (J). pap. 9.95 (978-0-940975-96-5(3), Sankofa Bks.) Just Us Bks., Inc.

Hughes, Langston. I, Too, Am America. Collier, Bryan, illus. 2012. (ENG.). 40p. (J). (gr. -1-3). 19.99 (978-1-4424-2008-3(1), Simon & Schuster Bks. For Young Readers) Simon & Schuster Bks. For Young Readers.

—That Is My Dream! A Picture Book of Langston Hughes's Dream Variation. Miyares, Daniel, illus. 2017. 32p. (J). (gr. -1-3). 18.99 (978-0-399-55017-1(8), Schwartz & Wade Bks.) Random Hse. Children's Bks.

Hughes, Shirley. Out & about: a First Book of Poems. Hughes, Shirley, illus. 2015. (ENG., Illus.). 56p. (J). (-k). 18.99 (978-0-7636-7644-5(6)) Candlewick Pr.

Hullinger, C. D. Mother Goose Rhymes (Las Rimas de Mama Oca), Grades PK - 3. 2007. (Keepsake Stories Ser.: 23). (ENG., Illus.). 32p. (gr. -1-3). pap. 3.99 (978-0-7696-5416-4(9), 0769654169, Brighter Child) Carson-Dellosa Publishing, LLC.

Hulme, Joy N. & Guthrie, Donna. How to Write, Recite, & Delight in All Kinds of Poetry. 2003. (Single Titles Ser.: Vol. 8). 96p. (J). (gr. 3-6). pap. 9.95 (978-0-7613-1831-6(3)) Lerner Publishing Group.

Hutchins, Hazel J. A Second Is a Hiccup: A Child's Book of Time. Denton, Kady MacDonald, illus. 2004. (ENG.). 32p. (J). (978-0-439-97400-4(3), North Winds Pr) Scholastic Canada, Ltd.

If You're Happy & You Know It & Other Favorites. 2005. (Meet Mother Goose Ser.). (ENG., Illus.). 36p. (J). 10.95 (978-1-59069-211-0(X), MD1108) Studio Mouse LLC.

Intermediate School, Parkview, compiled by. School Memories. 2006. per. 19.95 (978-0-9768391-3-2(X)) Pen & Publish, LLC.

Irish, Janice. The Gift of Words: A Resource for Parents & Educators. 2011. 92p. pap. 9.99 (978-1-4567-1969-2(6)) AuthorHouse.

Isaac, Denise. Agape to You. 2003. (YA). per. 12.99 (978-1-59352-038-0(7)) Christian Services Publishing.

Iyengar, Malathi Michelle. Tan to Tamarind: Poems about the Color Brown. Akib, Jamel, illus. 2013. (ENG.). 32p. (J). (gr. k). 16.95 (978-0-89239-227-8(4)) Lee & Low Bks., Inc.

—Tan to Tamarind: Poems about the Color Brown, 1 vol. Akib, Jamel, illus. 2017. (ENG.). 32p. (J). (gr. 1-6). pap. 10.95 (978-0-89239-412-8(9), leelowcbp, Children's Book Press) Lee & Low Bks., Inc.

Jackie, Nana. Nana Jackie Presents Sage Garden Poetry. 2010. (ENG.). 42p. pap. 21.99 (978-1-4500-6481-1(7)) Xlibris Corp.

Jackson, Anna. Catullus for Children. 2004. (ENG.). 64p. pap. 12.95 (978-1-86940-308-9(8)) Auckland Univ. Pr. NZL. Dist: Independent Pubs. Group.

Jackson, Demond, Sr. The Turnaround Book of Poetry: Complete Series. 2004. (YA). per. 20.00 (978-0-9753028-6-6(8), TA-04) Turnaround Bk. Publishing Corp.

Jager, Phyllis. Introducing Myself. Jager, Korin Elizabeth, illus. 2005. (J). 9.95 (978-1-59571-080-2(9)) Word Association Pubs.

James, Corinne M. A Zoo Party. 2008. 24p. pap. 11.49 (978-1-4389-1828-0(3)) AuthorHouse.

James, Simon, illus. & compiled by. Days Like This: A Collection of Small Poems. James, Simon, compiled by. 2005. (ENG.). 48p. (J). (gr. 1-4). reprint ed. pap. 8.99 (978-0-7636-2314-2(8)) Candlewick Pr.

Janeczko, Paul B. The Death of the Hat: a Brief History of Poetry in 50 Objects. Raschka, Chris, illus. (ENG.). 80p. (J). (gr. 3-7). 2018. pap. 9.99 (978-0-7636-9968-0(3)) 2015. 17.99 (978-0-7636-6963-8(6)) Candlewick Pr.

—Firefly July: a Year of Very Short Poems. Sweet, Melissa, illus. 2018. (ENG.). 48p. (J). (gr. -1-3). pap. 8.99 (978-0-7636-9971-0(3)) Candlewick Pr.

—A Foot in the Mouth: Poems to Speak, Sing, & Shout. Raschka, Chris, illus. 2012. (ENG.). 64p. (J). (gr. 3-7). pap. 9.99 (978-0-7636-6083-3(3)) Candlewick Pr.

—Poetry from a to Z: A Guide for Young Writers. Bobak, Cathy, illus. 2012. (ENG.). 144p. (J). (gr. 4-7). pap. 8.99 (978-1-4424-6061-4(X), Simon & Schuster Bks. For Young Readers) Simon & Schuster Bks. For Young Readers.

—Requiem: Poems of the Terezin Ghetto. 2011. (ENG., Illus.). 112p. (YA). (gr. 9). 16.99 (978-0-7636-4727-8(6)) Candlewick Pr.

—Worlds Afire. 2007. (ENG., Illus.). 112p. (YA). (gr. 7-18). per. 8.99 (978-0-7636-3400-1(X)) Candlewick Pr.

Jargowsky, Doris E. Captain Mcgee & the East Point Lighthouse. 2010. (ENG.). 26p. pap. 15.99 (978-1-4500-7275-5(5)) Xlibris Corp.

Jeffs, Stephanie. Come into the Ark with Noah. Reynolds, Annette, ed. Saunderson, Chris, illus. 2007. (Action Rhymes Ser.). (ENG.). 16p. (J). (gr. -1-2). pap. 4.99 (978-0-9789056-6-8(0)) New Day Publishing, Inc.

—Follow the Star with the Wise Men. Reynolds, Annette, ed. Saunderson, Chris, illus. 2007. (Action Rhymes Ser.). (ENG.). 16p. (J). (gr. -1-3). per. 4.99 (978-0-9789056-3-7(6)) New Day Publishing, Inc.

—March Round the Walls with Joshua. Reynolds, Annette, ed. Saunderson, Chris, illus. 2007. (Action Rhymes Ser.). (ENG.). 16p. (J). (gr. -1-2). pap. 4.99 (978-0-9789056-7-5(9)) New Day Publishing, Inc.

Jenkins, Mike. Poems for Underage Thinkers. 2004. (ENG., Illus.). 48p. pap. 12.95 (978-1-84323-359-6(2)) Beekman Bks., Inc.

Jenkins-Tate, Nesha L. The 10 Love Poems to Empower Young Souls: A Gift Book to Encourage Young People You Love. 2004. 56p. (YA). per. 21.00 (978-0-9753245-0-9(0), BBR) BBR: Books for Brilliance & Resilience.

Jiang, Emily. Summoning the Phoenix: Poems & Prose about Chinese Musical Instruments, 1 vol. Chu, April, illus. 2014. (ENG.). 32p. (J). (gr. 3-6). 19.95 (978-1-885008-50-3(3), leelowshens) Lee & Low Bks., Inc.

Jilson, Emily. The Five Little Mice: A Collection of Children's Poems. 2010. 24p. pap. 13.99 (978-1-4490-9739-4(1)) AuthorHouse.

Jiménez, Juan Ramón. Canta Pajaro Lejano. 14th ed. (SPA., Illus.). 128p. (J). (gr. 4-6). 14.95 (978-84-239-8892-1(9), EC2591) Espasa Calpe, S.A. ESP. Dist: Lectorum Pubns., Inc., Distribooks, Inc.

John Blake. Pound a Poem. 2010. (ENG., Illus.). 288p. 16.95 (978-1-84454-833-0(3)) Blake, John Publishing, Ltd. GBR. Dist: Independent Pubs. Group.

John Blake Publishing Staff. Pound a Poem: The Winning Entries from the National Schools Poetry Competition. Sayers, Myrna, illus. 2007. (ENG.). 256p. 19.95 (978-1-84454-436-3(2)) Blake, John Publishing, Ltd. GBR. Dist: Independent Pubs. Group.

John, Rebecca Mary. The Musings of a Young Girl. 2012. 48p. pap. 21.99 (978-1-4772-9280-8(2)) AuthorHouse.

Johnson, Celia, ed. 100 Great Poems for Girls. 2011. (ENG.). 208p. (J). pap., pap. 13.00 (978-0-446-56384-0(6)) Grand Central Publishing.

Johnson-Hall, Wanda. You Can Be: Yes! He Can! 2005. 16p. (YA). 10.00 (978-1-59633-000-9(7)) Goose Creek Pubs., Inc.

Johnston, Gail. Whispers in the Mist. 2010. 144p. pap. 11.70 (978-1-4520-9673-5(2)) AuthorHouse.

Jones, Susan Smith & Warren, Dianne. Vegetable Soup - The Fruit Bowl. Lindman, Amy Sorvaag, illus. rev. ed. 2006. 64p. (J). (gr. -1-3). per. 14.95 (978-0-9652736-0-2(1)) Oasis Pubns.

Jones, V. C. When You're Sick. 2010. 16p. 8.49 (978-1-4490-8265-9(3)) AuthorHouse.

José, González Torices. Poemas para la paz. 2004. (SPA., Illus.). 68p. (J). (gr. 2-3). 14.99 (978-84-241-8726-2(1)) Everest Editora ESP. Dist: Lectorum Pubns., Inc.

Joyner, A. Bernard. Out of the Mouths of Babes! A Book of Childrenrsquo;s Poetry. 2007. (ENG.). 68p. per. 16.95 (978-1-4241-6643-5(8)) PublishAmerica, Inc.

Judd, Lissa Elaine. A Slightly Larger Book of Kick-Arse Poetry. 2013. 90p. pap. (978-0-473-26612-7(1)) Idea Factory, The.

—A Small Book of Kick-Arse Poetry. 2012. 62p. pap. (978-0-473-22562-9(X)) Idea Factory, The.

Kahla, Robert. Mr. X from Planet X: And Other Animules. (Animules Ser.). (Illus.). 64p. (J). pap. 8.95 (978-1-882820-00-9(2)) kahla, bob.

Kalantary, Tanya. So Can You! 2010. 34p. pap. 14.50 (978-1-60911-928-7(2), Eloquent Bks.) Strategic Book Publishing & Rights Agency (SBPRA).

Kamerling, Yvonne. TLC for Teenagers & their Parents: Inspirational Quotes, Poetry, Touching Stories. 2004. 122p. (YA). 22.95 (978-0-595-66340-8(0)) iUniverse, Inc.

Kammeraad, Kevin & Kammeraad, Stephanie. A Curious Glimpse of Michigan. Kammeraad, Kevin & Hipp, Ryan, illus. 2004. 32p. (J). (gr. 3-7). 19.95 (978-0-9712692-9-3(7)) EDCO Publishing, Inc.

Kanaan. Literati: A Revolution of Living. 2003. 230p. (YA). pap. 18.95 (978-0-595-30381-6(1)) iUniverse, Inc.

Kasper, Catherine. Field Stone: Poems. 2005. 57p. per. 14.00 (978-0-9764726-0-5(0), 1A) Winnow Pr.

Kass, Ed. D. Playground Time: A Skip-Counting Rhyme. 2010. 32p. pap. 13.49 (978-1-4490-6795-3(6)) AuthorHouse.

Katz, Alan. Oops! Koren, Edward, illus. 2008. (ENG.). 176p. (J). (gr. 2-5). 19.99 (978-1-4169-0204-1(X), McElderry, Margaret K. Bks.) McElderry, Margaret K. Bks.

Katz, Susan. Oh, Theodore! 2007. (ENG., Illus.). 48p. (J). (gr. -1-3). 16.00 (978-0-618-70222-0(9), 100491, Clarion Bks.) HarperCollins Pubs.

Kauenhofen, Jessica. My First A B C Book. Kauenhofen, Jessica, illus. 2007. (Little Jewel Book Ser.). (Illus.). 24p. (J). (gr. 2). pap. 2.70 (978-0-7399-2385-6(4)) Rod & Staff Pubs., Inc.

Kaufman, Caroline. Light Filters In: Poems. 2018. (ENG., Illus.). 224p. (YA). (gr. 8). 14.99 (978-0-06-284468-2(7), HarperCollins) HarperCollins Pubs.

—When the World Didn't End: Poems. Bryksenkova, Yelena, illus. 2019. (ENG.). 192p. (YA). (gr. 8). 16.99 (978-0-06-291038-7(8), HarperCollins) HarperCollins Pubs.

Kay, Francesca. One Busy Book. Glynn, Chris, illus. 2004. (ENG.). 32p. pap. 12.95 (978-1-84323-344-2(4)) Beekman Bks., Inc.

Keane, Sarah. My Foot Fell Asleep, 1 vol. rev. ed. 2013. (Literary Text Ser.). (ENG., Illus.). 28p. (gr. 2-3). pap. 9.99 (978-1-4333-5567-7(1)) Teacher Created Materials, Inc.

Kearney, Meg. The Secret of Me. 2005. (Karen & Michael Braziller Bks.). (ENG.). 128p. (YA). (gr. 7). 17.95 (978-0-89255-322-8(7)) Persea Bks., Inc.

Keaton, Bobby J. The Closet Monster. 2011. 48p. pap. 19.26 (978-1-4567-3087-1(8)) AuthorHouse.

Keats, John. A Song about Myself. Raschka, Chris, illus. 2017. (ENG.). 40p. (J). (gr. 1-4). 17.99 (978-0-7636-5090-2(0)) Candlewick Pr.

Keller-Miller, LeAnn Marie, illus. When I Grow Up: An A-Z Poem Book for Children & Their Dreams. 2005. (978-0-9711480-4-8(X)) ICanPublish.

Kelman, Louise & Kelman, Suzanne. Big Purple Undies. Dowling, Jane, ed. Baker, Penny, illus. 2004. 64p. (J). pap. (978-0-9580869-6-7(6)) Inhoa Publishing.

Kennedy, Caroline. A Family of Poems: My Favorite Poetry for Children. Muth, Jon J., illus. 2005. (ENG.). 144p. (J). (gr. 5-9). 21.99 (978-0-7868-5111-9(2)) Little, Brown Bks. for Young Readers.

—Poems to Share. Muth, Jon J., illus. 2008. 32p. 17.99 (978-1-4231-1658-5(5)) Hyperion Pr.

Kennedy, X. J. City Kids: Street & Skyscraper Rhymes, 1 vol. Béha, Phillippe, illus. 2010. (ENG.). 86p. (J). (gr. 1-3). 17.95 (978-1-896580-44-9(0)) Tradewind Bks. CAN. Dist: Orca Bk. Pubs. USA.

Key, Prinzeono. All Children. 2006. (ENG.). 61p. pap. 7.32 (978-0-615-13786-5(5)) Key, Veverly & Prinzwono.

Kids: Sagebrush Prairie. 2004. (J). 1.00 (978-1-888631-34-0(1)) Project WET Foundation.

Kim, Aerim. A Tiny Bud. Kim, Lindsey, illus. 2008. 80p. (J). 29.95 (978-0-9789624-0-1(0)) Blue Lotus Wave.

Kim, Isabel Joy & Prasad, Siona. Tangled in Beauty: Contemplative Nature Poems. Kim, Isabel Joy, illus. 2013. (Illus.). 74p. pap. 7.99 (978-0-9912472-0-2(5)) Philokalos Pr.

Kimble, George J. Poetry for the Road, 1. annot. ed. 2005. (Illus.). 157p. per. 15.00 (978-0-9767024-0-5(1)) Kimble, George J.

King, Michael Riano, Jr. Let's Learn Together. 2007. (J). 8.00 (978-0-8059-7295-5(1)) Dorrance Publishing Co., Inc.

Klanot, Khaya Dawn. Just Hanging Out, a Collection of Poems for Kids. Pimot, Karen Hutchins, illus. 2008. 48p. pap. 16.95 (978-0-9814894-5-2(1)) Peppertree Pr., The.

Klein, A. M. Doctor Dwarf & Other Poems for Children. Date not set. (Illus.). 32p. 12.95 (978-0-919627-41-3(2)); pap. 6.95 (978-0-919627-43-7(9)) Quarry Pr. CAN. Dist: LPC/InBook.

Knight, Nelson & Knight, Suzanne. The ABCs of Southern Virginia University. 2013. (J). 14.95 (978-1-62086-063-2(5)) Amplify Publishing Group.

Kochner, Donna Rose Porta. Through the Night. Cote, Nacy, illus. 2012. (ENG.). 24p. pap. 10.95 (978-1-4497-6999-4(3), WestBow Pr.) Author Solutions, LLC.

Koertge, Ronald. The Brimstone Journals. 2004. (ENG., Illus.). 128p. (YA). (gr. 9-18). pap. 7.99 (978-0-7636-1742-4(3)) Candlewick Pr.

Korhel, Erik. My Tooth Fell in My Soup: And Other Poems. Baker, Celia M., illus. 2009. 26p. (J). 14.95 (978-1-935359-02-9(9)) Bk. Pubs. Network.

Korr, David. I Think That It Is Wonderful (Sesame Street) Delaney, A., illus. 2018. (Little Golden Book Ser.). 24p. (J). (-k). 4.99 (978-1-5247-6826-3(X), Golden Bks.) Random Hse. Children's Bks.

Kovner, Vladimir, tr. from ENG. Prilaskaite L'va: Amerikanskiye i Angliiskiye Stikhi Dlya Detei. Braslavskii, Felix, illus. 2010. (RUS.). 110p. (J). pap. (978-1-934881-43-9(0), M-Graphics) M-Graphics Publishing.

Koziara, Colleen. Thirteen Silver Moons. Koziara, Colleen, illus. 2004. (Illus.). (J). per. (978-0-9763205-0-0(9)) Mystical Willow Productions.

Kram, T. Gooey Desserts & Messy Shirts Poetry F. 2007. 125p. pap. 19.95 (978-1-4241-6072-3(3)) America Star Bks.

Krensky, Stephen, et al. Arturo y el Concurso de Poesia. 2004.Tr. of Arthur & the Poetry Contest. (SPA., Illus.). (J). pap. 4.95 (978-1-930332-61-4(0)) Lectorum Pubns., Inc.

Kroelinger, Melanie. Ocean: A Lullaby Book. 2013. 20p. pap. 17.99 (978-1-4817-0817-3(1)) AuthorHouse.

Kubler, Annie, illus. Pussy Cat, Pussy Cat. 2010. (Baby Board Bks.). 12p. (J). bds. (978-1-84643-340-5(1)) Child's Play International Ltd.

Kumuhana High, Kukulu. The Hala Grove of Wakiu, Vol. II. 2005. (YA). per. 19.95 (978-1-59571-047-5(7)) Word Association Pubs.

Kurkela, Robert W. Lilies on the Moon. Kurkela, Cassidy S., illus. 2005. 32p. (J). 16.95 (978-0-9760220-0-8(1)) Kidzpoetz Publishing.

Laisney, Sarah. Ice Flowers & Pomegranates, 1 vol. 2010. 98p. pap. 19.95 (978-1-4489-4900-7(9)) America Star Bks.

Lalli, Judy. I Like Being Me: Poems about Kindness, Friendship, & Making Good Choices. rev. ed. 2016. (ENG., Illus.). 64p. (J). (gr. -1-2). pap. 11.99 (978-1-63198-092-3(0)) Free Spirit Publishing Inc.

Lambert, Kelly. Sounds of a Coo. 2012. (ENG.). 45p. (J). pap. 23.95 (978-1-4327-8303-7(3)); pap. 32.95 (978-1-4327-8316-7(5)) Outskirts Pr., Inc.

Land, Autumn. The Monarch & the Monarch. 2009. 112p. pap. 11.99 (978-1-60647-428-0(6)) Salem Author Services.

Landry, Leo. Home Run, Touchdown, Basket, Goal! Sports Poems for Little Athletes. Landry, Leo, illus. 2019. (ENG., Illus.). 32p. (J). 17.99 (978-1-62779-349-0(6), 900147060, Holt, Henry & Co. Bks. For Young Readers) Holt, Henry & Co.

Lane, Diane Luby & Get Lit Players, the. Get Lit Rising: Words Ignite. Claim Your Poem. Claim Your Life. 2016. (ENG., Illus.). 272p. (YA). (gr. 7). 21.99 (978-1-58270-576-7(3)) Simon Pulse/Beyond Words.

Lane, Leena. Climb up the Tree with Zacchaeus. Reynolds, Annette, ed. Saunderson, Chris, illus. 2007. (Action Rhymes Ser.). (ENG.). 16p. (J). (gr. -1-2). pap. 4.99 (978-0-9789056-2-0(8)) New Day Publishing, Inc.

Lang, Tiffany. Mango Leaves Strings in Your Teeth. 2003. (J). per. (978-1-59196-409-4(1)) Instant Pub.

Language Through Poetry (Gr. PreK-5) 2003. (J). (978-1-58232-119-6(1)) ECS Learning Systems, Inc.

Lanksy, Bruce. Rolling in the Aisles: A Collection of Laugh-Out-Loud Poems. Carpenter, Stephen, illus. 2004. 116p. (J). (978-0-88166-473-7(1)) Meadowbrook Pr.

Lansana, Quraysh Ali & Lightfoot, Toni Asante. The Sixth Wave. 2008. 88p. (YA). (gr. 4-18). pap. 9.95 (978-1-933491-14-1(0)) Just Us Bks., Inc.

Lansky, Bruce. My Teacher's in Detention: Kids' Favorite Funny School Poems. Carpenter, Stephen, illus. 2006. (Giggle Poetry Ser.). (ENG.). 80p. (J). (gr. 1-7). per. 8.99 (978-0-689-05245-3(6), Running Pr.) Running Pr.

Lansky, Bruce, ed. Dinner with Dracula. Gordon, Mike & Gordon, Carl, illus. 2006. 32p. (J). (978-0-88166-512-3(6)) Meadowbrook Pr.

Larkin, Shabazz. A Moose Boosh: A Few Choice Words About Food. Larkin, Shabazz, illus. 2nd ed. 2014. (ENG., Illus.). 96p. (J). (gr. 4-7). 18.95 (978-0-9836615-5-9(3)) READERS to EATERS.

Larsen, Alison. What Makes You Smile? Larsen, Alison, illus. 2006. (Illus.). 23p. (J). (gr. -1-3). per. 13.95 (978-1-60002-094-0(1)) Mountain Valley Publishing, LLC.

Lassiter, Gianna Bari. Rosy Proses: Whimsical Verses & Sanity Journal for Big People Who Have Little People in Their Lives. gif. ed. 2005. (Illus.). 40p. (YA). spiral bd. 10.00 (978-0-9773324-0-3(3)) MentorSource, LLC.

Latham, Irene & Waters, Charles. Can I Touch Your Hair? Poems of Race, Mistakes, & Friendship. Alko, Selina & Qualls, Sean, illus. 2018. (ENG.). 40p. (J). (gr. 3-6). 17.99 (978-1-5124-0442-5(X), ea8fdcca-1845-47b4-b2b5-64a86f1ee9b0, Carolrhoda Bks.) Lerner Publishing Group.

Law, Felicia. Family. Knight, Paula, illus. 2015. (Patchwork Ser.). (ENG.). 24p. (J). (gr. k-3). pap. 11.94 (978-1-60357-801-1(3)) Norwood Hse. Pr.

Lawson, JonArno. Black Stars in a White Night Sky. Tjia, Sherwin, illus. 2006. (ENG.). 80p. (978-1-897141-07-6(6)) Pedlar Pr.

—Down in the Bottom of the Bottom of the Box. 2012. (ENG., Illus.). 80p. (J). pap. 16.95 (978-0-88984-354-7(6)) Porcupine's Quill, Inc. CAN. Dist: Univ. of Toronto Pr.

—The Man in the Moon-Fixer's Mask. Tjia, Sherwin, illus. 2004. (ENG.). 88p. (J). (gr. 3-7). (978-0-9732140-9-3(0)) Pedlar Pr.

—A Voweller's Bestiary: From Aardvark to Guineafowl. 2008. (ENG., Illus.). 96p. (J). (gr. 4-7). pap. 14.95 (978-0-88984-300-4(7)) Porcupine's Quill, Inc. CAN. Dist: Univ. of Toronto Pr.

Layne, Steven. The Principal's Night Before Christmas, 1 vol. Rice, James, illus. 2004. (Night Before Christmas Ser.). (ENG.). 32p. (J). (gr. k-3). 16.99 (978-1-58980-252-0(7), Pelican Publishing) Arcadia Publishing.

Le, Le Pham. From Where the Wind Blows. Arbuthnot, Nancy, tr. 2003.Tr. of Gio Thoi Phuong Nao. (VIE.). per. 12.00 (978-0-9746300-0-7(4)) Vietnamese International Poetry Society.

Lear, Edward. Nonsense Drolleries: The Owl & the Pussy-Cat, the Duck & the Kangaroo. Foster, William, illus. 2007. 32p. pap. 10.95 (978-1-60355-050-5(X)) Juniper Grove.

—The Owl & the Pussycat. Mortimer, Anne, illus. 2006. (ENG.). 32p. (J). (gr. -1-4). 17.99 (978-0-06-027228-9(7), Tegen, Katherine Bks) HarperCollins Pubs.

Lear, Edward & Campbell, Lori M. The Complete Nonsense Books of Edward Lear. 2008. (Illus.). xxxiii, 409p. pap. (978-1-4351-0325-2(4)) Barnes & Noble Bks.-Imports.

Learn along with Lily. 2008. (Illus.). 32p. (J). 15.95 (978-0-9799677-0-2(8)) Raindrop Bks.

Lebachen, Medyhne. Hilhairyass Poems: By a Six Year Old Adult. Payne, Mark, illus. 2012. 76p. (YA). (978-0-9872816-4-7(X)) Heart Space Pubns.

Lee, Dennis. Alligator Pie Brd Bk. Nichols, Sandy, illus. 2014. (ENG.). 13p. (J). bds. 10.50 (978-1-4434-1161-5(2), HarperCollins) HarperCollins Pubs.

—Alligator Pie Classic Edition. Newfeld, Frank, illus. 2012. (ENG.). 64p. (J). 15.99 (978-1-4434-1151-6(5), HarperCollins) HarperCollins Pubs.

—The Cat & the Wizard. 2004. (Illus.). (J). (gr. k-3). spiral bd. (978-0-616-11115-4(0)); spiral bd. (978-0-616-11116-1(9)) Canadian National Institute for the Blind/Institut National Canadien pour les Aveugles.

—The Dreadful Doings of Jelly Belly. Hilb, Nora, illus. rev. ed. 2009. (ENG.). 16p. (J). (gr. k-k). bds. (978-1-55263-767-8(0)) Me to We.

—Good Night, Good Night. Leng, Qin, illus. 2018. (ENG.). 26p. (J). (gr. -1-k). bds. 10.50 (978-1-4434-1165-3(5), HarperCollins) HarperCollins Pubs.

—The Kitty Ran up the Tree. Hilb, Nora, illus. rev. ed. 2009. (ENG.). 16p. (J). (gr. k-k). bds. (978-1-55263-813-2(8)) Me to We.

—Silverly/Good Night, Good Night. Hilb, Nora, illus. rev. ed. 2008. (ENG.). 16p. (J). (gr. k-k). bds. (978-1-55263-769-2(7)) Me to We.

—Skyscraper. Hilb, Nora, illus. rev. ed. 2009. (ENG.). 16p. (J). (gr. k-k). bds. (978-1-55263-811-8(1)) Me to We.

—Willoughby Wallaby Woo. Hilb, Nora, illus. rev. ed. 2008. (ENG.). 16p. (J). (gr. k-k). bds. (978-1-55263-676-3(3)) Me to We.

Lee, Patty. Wild Animals: What Is That I Ask? Lee, Jack, illus. 2013. 30p. pap. 14.00 (978-1-4349-3518-2(3), RoseDog Bks.) Dorrance Publishing Co., Inc.

Lee, Patty & Lee, Jack. Biblical: Who Is That I Ask? a Children's Poetry Book. 2013. 28p. pap. 19.99 (978-1-4817-1096-1(6)) AuthorHouse.

Lehman, David, ed. Great American Prose Poems: From Poe to the Present. 2003. (ENG.). 352p. pap. 18.00 (978-0-7432-4350-6(1), Scribner) Scribner.

Leppanen, Debbie. Trick-Or-Treat: A Happy Haunter's Halloween. Carpenter, Tad, illus. 2013. (ENG.). 40p. (J). (gr. k-3). 16.99 (978-1-4424-3398-4(1)) Simon & Schuster Children's Publishing.

Lesynski, Loris. Cabbagehead. 2003. (ENG., Illus.). 32p. (J). (gr. k-3). 18.95 (978-1-55037-805-4(8), 9781550378054) Annick Pr., Ltd. CAN. Dist: Publishers Group West (PGW).

—Cabbagehead. Martchenko, Michael, illus. 2003. (ENG.). 32p. (J). (gr. k-3). pap. 6.95 (978-1-55037-804-7(X), 9781550378047) Annick Pr., Ltd. CAN. Dist: Publishers Group West (PGW).

—Crazy about Basketball! Rasmussen, Gerry, illus. 2013. (Crazy about Sports Ser.). (ENG.). 32p. (J). (gr. 3-5). 22.95 (978-1-55451-541-7(6), 9781554515417); pap. 12.95 (978-1-55451-540-0(8), 9781554515400) Annick Pr., Ltd. CAN. Dist: Publishers Group West (PGW).

—Crazy about Soccer. Rasmussen, Gerry, illus. 2012. (Crazy about Sports Ser.). (ENG.). 48p. (J). (gr. 2-5). pap. 12.95 (978-1-55451-421-2(5), 9781554514212); 2nd ed. 22.95 (978-1-55451-422-9(3), 9781554514229) Annick Pr., Ltd. CAN. Dist: Publishers Group West (PGW).

—Shoe Shakes. Martchenko, Michael, illus. 2007. (ENG.). 32p. (J). (gr. -1-k). pap. 9.95 (978-1-55451-105-1(4),

9781554511051) Annick Pr., Ltd. CAN. Dist: Publishers Group West (PGW).
Levine, Diana. The Dancing Waves. 2007. 68p. per. 10.00 *(978-1-4257-5337-5(X))* Xlibris Corp.
Lewis, Anthony, illus. Humpty Dumpty: American Sign Language. 2013. (Hands-On Songs Ser.). (ENG.). 12p. (J). bds. *(978-1-84643-627-7(3))* Child's Play International Ltd.
Lewis, J. Patrick. Blackbeard the Pirate King. 2006. (Illus.). 32p. (J). (gr. 3-7). 16.95 *(978-0-7922-5585-7(2)*, National Geographic Children's Bks.) Disney Publishing Worldwide.
—Face Bug. Murphy, Kelly, illus. Siskind, Fred, photos by. 2013. (ENG.). 36p. (J). (gr. 1-4). 16.95 *(978-1-59078-925-4(3)*, Wordsong) Highlights Pr., c/o Highlights for Children, Inc.
—Freedom Like Sunlight. Thompson, John, illus. 2014. (ENG.). 40p. (J). (gr. 5-8). pap. 9.99 *(978-0-89812-973-1(7)*, 22682, Creative Paperbacks) Creative Co., The.
—God Made the Skunk: And Other Animal Poems. King, Jerry, illus. 2005. 60p. (J). 14.95 *(978-0-9722820-1-7(7))* Doggerel Daze.
—The House. Innocenti, Roberto, illus. 2010. (ENG.). 64p. (J). (gr. 2-5). 25.00 *(978-1-56846-201-1(8)*, 22065, Creative Editions) Creative Co., The.
—Keep a Pocket in Your Poem: Classic Poems & Playful Parodies. Wright, Johanna, illus. 2017. (ENG.). 32p. (J). (gr. k-4). 17.99 *(978-1-59078-921-6(0)*, Wordsong) Highlights Pr., c/o Highlights for Children, Inc.
—Let's Celebrate Halloween (Rookie Poetry: Holidays & Celebrations) 2018. (Rookie Poetry Ser.). (ENG., Illus.). 24p. (J). (gr. 1-2). pap. 5.95 *(978-0-531-22680-3(8)*, Children's Pr.) Scholastic Library Publishing.
—Let's Celebrate Thanksgiving (Rookie Poetry: Holidays & Celebrations) 2018. (Rookie Poetry Ser.). (ENG., Illus.). 24p. (J). (gr. 1-2). pap. 5.95 *(978-0-531-22693-3(X)*, Children's Pr.) Scholastic Library Publishing.
—Self-Portrait with Seven Fingers. Chagall, Marc., illus. 2010. (ENG.). 40p. (J). (gr. 5-8). 18.99 *(978-1-56846-211-0(5)*, 22060, Creative Editions) Creative Co., The.
—Underwear Salesman: Underwear Salesman. 2009. (ENG., Illus.). 64p. (J). (gr. 2-5). 19.99 *(978-0-689-85325-8(4)*, Atheneum Bks. for Young Readers) Simon & Schuster Children's Publishing.
—World Rat Day: Poems about Real Holidays You've Never Heard Of. Raff, Anna, illus. 2013. (ENG.). 40p. (J). (gr. k-3). 17.99 *(978-0-7636-5402-3(7))* Candlewick Pr.
Lewis, J. Patrick & Thompson, John. Freedom Like Sunlight. 2005. (Illus.). pap. 7.95 *(978-0-89812-382-1(8))* Creative Co., The.
Lewis, J. Patrick & Yolen, Jane. Self-Portrait with Seven Fingers: the Life of Marc Chagall in Verse. 2014. (ENG.). 40p. (J). (gr. 5-8). pap. 12.00 *(978-0-89812-974-8(5)*, 22061, Creative Paperbacks) Creative Co., The.
Lewis, Ophelia S. My Dear Liberia: Recollections, Poetic Memoirs from My Heart. 2004. (YA). per. 9.95 *(978-0-9753609-0-3(6))* Village Tales Publishing.
Lewis, Richard. Cave: An Evocation of the Beginnings of Art. Crawford, Elizabeth, illus. Hirose, George, photos by. 2003. (ENG.). 56p. pap. 14.00 *(978-1-929299-03-4(6))* Touchstone Ctr. Pubns.
—Play, Said the Earth to Air. Neilson, Heidi, illus. 2013. (ENG.). 44p. (J). (gr. -1). pap. 12.00 *(978-1-929299-12-6(5))* Touchstone Ctr. Pubns.
—A Tree Lives. Baen, Noah, illus. 2006. (ENG.). 48p. per. 12.00 *(978-1-929299-04-1(4))* Touchstone Ctr. Pubns.
Lewis, Sian. Dim Mwnci'n y Dosbarth. Glynn, Chris, illus. 2005. (WEL.). 64p. pap. 4.99 *(978-1-84323-427-2(0))* Gomer Pr. GBR. Dist: Gomer Pr.
Liddle-Pirouet, Leasal. I Love You More Than Ice Cream Dipped in Sprinkles. 2010. 28p. pap. 14.95 *(978-1-4251-7577-1(5))* Trafford Publishing.
Linda (Mimi') Wise. Come Grow with Me: Inspirational Poems for Children. 2009. 28p. pap. 12.49 *(978-1-4389-2754-1(1))* AuthorHouse.
Little, Jean. Hey World, Here I Am! Truesdell, Sue, illus. 2015. 96p. pap. 6.00 *(978-1-61003-607-8(7))* Center for the Collaborative Classroom.
Littlewood, Graham. Restless Owl & Other Stories. Preston, Carole, illus. 2010. (ENG.). 56p. pap. *(978-1-84748-778-0(5))* Athena Pr.
Lloyd, Sophie. Behind Brown Eyes. 2012. (Illus.). 44p. pap. *(978-0-9568247-5-2(7))* Cloister Hse. Pr., The.
Lofficier, Randy. If Your Possum Go Daylight. OKeefe, Raven, illus. 2009. (ENG.). 60p. (J). pap. 12.95 *(978-1-934543-78-8(0))* HollywoodComics.com, LLC.
Long, Sylvia, illus. Sylvia Long's Big Book for Small Children. 2018. (Family Treasure Nature Encylopedias Ser.). (ENG.). 112p. (J). (gr. -1 — 1). 22.99 *(978-0-8118-3441-4(7))* Chronicle Bks. LLC.
Longfellow, Henry. Paul Revere's Ride: The Landlord's Tale. Santore, Charles, illus. 2005. 28p. (J). (gr. 4-8). reprint ed. 17.00 *(978-0-7567-9202-2(9))* DIANE Publishing Co.
—Paul Revere's Ride: The Landlord's Tale. Santore, Charles, illus. 2003. 40p. (J). lib. bdg. 17.89 *(978-0-06-623747-3(5))* HarperCollins Pubs.
—Song of Hiawatha. 2003. 252p. pap. 14.95 *(978-1-59224-329-7(0))* Wildside Pr., LLC.
Longfellow, Henry Wadsworth. Evangeline, 1 vol. 3rd ed. 2013. (ENG., Illus.). 77p. pap. 9.95 *(978-1-77108-097-2(3)*, 8b2f979c-4bd6-434e-a2db-aceeb19e0588) Nimbus Publishing, Ltd. CAN. Dist: Baker & Taylor Publisher Services (BTPS).
—Paul Revere's Ride. Vachula, Monica, illus. 2011. (ENG.). 32p. (J). (gr. 4-7). pap. 11.95 *(978-1-59078-869-1(9)*, Astra Young Readers) Astra Publishing Hse.
—Paul Revere's Ride. 2014. (Charles Santore Children's Classics Ser.). (ENG., Illus.). 36p. (J). 19.95 *(978-1-60433-493-7(2)*, Applesauce Pr.) Cider Mill Pr. Bk. Pubs., LLC.
—Paul Revere's Ride. 2011. (ENG., Illus.). 32p. (gr. 3-6). 26.19 *(978-1-56397-799-2(0))* Highlights Pr., c/o Highlights for Children, Inc.
Lorenz, Colton. I Am a New York City. 2008. 180p. pap. 16.95 *(978-0-595-51062-7(0))* iUniverse, Inc.
Loski, Krystie C. Ode to Me & My Day. 2011. 24p. pap. 24.95 *(978-1-4626-0668-9(7))* America Star Bks.
Lottridge, Celia Barker. Mother Goose, 1 vol. 2009. (ENG., Illus.). 64p. (J). (gr. -1 — 1). bds. 9.95 *(978-0-88899-933-7(X))* Groundwood Bks. CAN. Dist: Publishers Group West (PGW).
Low, Elizabeth Cothen. Big Book of Seasons, Holidays, & Weather: Rhymes, Fingerplays, & Songs for Children, 1 vol. 2011. (ENG., Illus.). 168p. pap. 45.00 *(978-1-59884-623-2(X)*, 826740, Libraries Unlimited) Bloomsbury Publishing USA.
Lucas, Scott. Lies Nostalgia & Cow Gas. 2008. 192p. pap. 14.95 *(978-0-615-16630-8(X))* Feather River Publishing.
Ludwig VanDerwater, Amy. Dreaming of You. DeWitt, Aaron, illus. 2018. (ENG.). 32p. (J). (gr. -1-k). 17.95 *(978-1-62979-212-5(8)*, Astra Young Readers) Astra Publishing Hse.
—Read! Read! Read! O'Rourke, Ryan, illus. 2017. (ENG.). 32p. (J). (gr. k-4). 17.99 *(978-1-59078-975-9(X)*, Wordsong) Highlights Pr., c/o Highlights for Children, Inc.
Luján, Jorge. Colors! / Colores!, 1 vol. Simon, John & Parfitt, Rebecca, trs. Grobler, Piet, illus. 2008.Tr. of Colors! (ENG.). 36p. (J). (gr. -1-1). 18.95 *(978-0-88899-863-7(5))* Groundwood Bks. CAN. Dist: Publishers Group West (PGW).
—Numeralia, 1 vol. Ouriou, Susan, tr. Isol, illus. 2014. (ENG.). 32p. (J). (gr. -1-1). 18.95 *(978-1-55498-444-2(0))* Groundwood Bks. CAN. Dist: Publishers Group West (PGW).
—Rooster / Gallo, 1 vol. Amado, Elisa, tr. Monroy, Manuel, illus. 2016. (ENG.). 24p. (J). (gr. -1). 8.95 *(978-1-55498-936-2(1))* Groundwood Bks. CAN. Dist: Publishers Group West (PGW).
LuzMarie. Suicidal Beauty, 1 vol. 2010. 88p. pap. 19.95 *(978-1-4489-4950-2(5))* America Star Bks.
Lynch, Ryan. Just a Pup: And Other Poems for Children. 2007. 216p. per. 24.95 *(978-1-4241-5640-5(8))* America Star Bks.
Lynette, Shannon. A Place with No Name. 2003. 120p. (YA). pap. 14.95 *(978-0-7414-1534-9(8))* Infinity Publishing.
Lyons, John. Dancing in the Rain: Poems for Young People, 1 vol. 2016. (ENG., Illus.). 64p. (J). (gr. 4-7). pap. 17.95 *(978-1-84523-301-3(8))* Peepal Tree Pr., Ltd. GBR. Dist: Independent Pubs. Group.
Mac, Gi Gi. Poetry Stories for the Rug Rat the Ankle Biter & the Bun in the Oven. 2013. 24p. pap. *(978-1-4602-0945-5(1))* FriesenPress.
MacCormick SEcure Center, Residents. Another Sad Inning: Incarcerated Youth Reveal Their Trials, Tribulations & Loves. MacCormick Secure Center, Residents, illus. 2003. 90p. (YA). per. 17.00 *(978-0-9740184-1-6(4)*, MAC-2) Durland Alternatives Library.
MacDonald, John. Child's Play in Poetry. 2013. 60p. pap. 11.99 *(978-1-62839-169-5(3))* Salem Author Services.
MacGregor, Kim. Button, Buckle, Tie. Snider, Sharon & Reny, Todd, trs. 2004. (Illus.). 24p. *(978-0-9731301-4-0(8))*; pap. *(978-0-9731301-3-3(X))* Beautiful Beginnings Youth, Inc.
—Yummy Yummy Nummy Nummy, Should I Put This in My Tummy? Ioannou, Gregory Phillip, ed. Snider, Sharon & Reny, Todd, illus. 2004. 24p. *(978-0-9731301-0-2(5))* Beautiful Beginnings Youth, Inc.
Machado, Antonio. Yo Voy Sonando Caminos. (Coleccion Poemas Juvenil). (SPA., Illus.). 96p. (J). 9.50 *(978-84-335-8423-6(5)*, DD4236) Labor, Editorial S. A. ESP. Dist: Continental Bk. Co., Inc.
Macken, JoAnn Early. Read, Recite, & Write Cinquains. 2015. (Poet's Workshop Ser.). (ENG., Illus.). 32p. (J). (gr. 4-4). *(978-0-7787-1962-5(6))* Crabtree Publishing Co.
—Read, Recite, & Write Concrete Poems. 2015. (Poet's Workshop Ser.). (ENG., Illus.). 32p. (J). (gr. 4-4). *(978-0-7787-1963-2(4))* Crabtree Publishing Co.
—Read, Recite, & Write List Poems. 2015. (Poet's Workshop Ser.). (ENG., Illus.). 32p. (J). (gr. 4-4). *(978-0-7787-1965-6(0))* Crabtree Publishing Co.
MacLachlan, Patricia & Charest, Emily MacLachlan. Cat Talk. Moser, Barry, illus. 2013. (ENG.). 32p. (J). (gr. -1-3). lib. bdg. 18.89 *(978-0-06-027979-0(6)*, Tegen, Katherine Bks) HarperCollins Pubs.
MacMillan, Lesley. Draw Me a Picture. 2006. (Illus.). 37p. (J). per. 12.90 *(978-1-59879-301-7(2))* Lifevest Publishing, Inc.
Make a Joyful Sound. 2003. (J). 13.95 *(978-0-590-28205-5(0))* Scholastic, Inc.
Malenfant, Paul Chanel. Si Tu Allais Quelque Part. 2003. (New Poetry Ser.). (FRE.). 36p. (J). (gr. 7). pap. *(978-2-89021-622-8(5))* Diffusion du livre Mirabel (DLM).
Manley, Molly. On a Vineyard Veranda. Marshall, Janet, illus. 2007. (ENG.). 24p. (J). (gr. k-3). 12.95 *(978-1-933212-46-3(2)*, Commonwealth Editions) Applewood Bks.
Mannis, Celeste Davidson. One Leaf Rides the Wind. Hartung, Susan Kathleen, illus. 2005. (gr. -1-3). 17.00 *(978-0-7569-5213-6(1))* Perfection Learning Corp.
Marcamo, Thais. Vivencias & Despertar. Vilma Muises, ed. 2004. (SPA., Illus.). 96p. (YA). pap. 15.00 *(978-1-931481-34-2(2))* LiArt-Literature & Art.
Margaret Scollan. The Gods of Rome: Dei Romae. 2009. 20p. pap. 15.00 *(978-1-4269-1871-1(2))* Trafford Publishing.
Mari?!?, ?Uro. How Children Grow. 2013. (Illus.). 86p. pap. 13.66 *(978-1-4817-7605-9(3))* AuthorHouse.
Marjorie, as told by. A Flower Unfolds: Inspirational Teachings in Verse from Kwan Yin, Bodhisattva of Mercy & Compassion. I.t. ed. 2003. (Illus.). 52p. 12.95 *(978-0-9745712-0-1(2))* Sun Sprite Publishing.
Mark, Jan. A Jetblack Sunrise: Poems about War & Conflict. 2005. (ENG., Illus.). (J). 16.99 *(978-0-7502-4293-6(0))* Hodder & Stoughton GBR. Dist: Trafalgar Square Publishing.
Marrero, Rafelito. Amar sin decir Nada. 1000th I.t. ed. 2003. 137p. per. 14.95 net. *(978-0-9747569-0-5(3))* Marrero, Rafael.
Marston, J. D., photos by. The Poems for Pequenines (Poemas Para Pequenines) 2004. (Baby Einstein Ser.). (SPA., Illus.). 12p. (J). bds. *(978-970-718-159-5(1)*, Silver Dolphin en Español) Advanced Marketing, S. de R. L. de C. V.
Martin, Bill, Jr., ed. The Bill Martin Jr Big Book of Poetry. 2008. (ENG., Illus.). 176p. (J). (gr. -1-3). 24.99 *(978-1-4169-3971-9(7)*, Simon & Schuster Bks. For Young Readers) Simon & Schuster Bks. For Young Readers.
Martin, Tamara. Little Robin Redbreast: An Illustrated Poem. I.t. ed. 2014. (Illus.). 24p. (J). 14.95 *(978-1-935656-07-4(4)*, Little Red Acorns) Little Red Tree Publishing LLC.
Mataya, Marybeth. Luke & Leo Build a Limerick. Richard, Ilene, illus. 2011. (Poetry Builders Ser.). 32p. (J). (gr. 2-4). lib. bdg. 25.27 *(978-1-59953-436-7(3))* Norwood Hse. Pr.
Matthews, Jennifer V. For A Ghetto Child: An Anthology of Poems & Art. 2010. 40p. pap. 16.99 *(978-1-4259-1752-4(6))* AuthorHouse.
Maude, Tony. Without Surprise. Monica, Brufton, illus. 2013. 60p. pap. *(978-2-917183-29-8(2))* Nigeria Baptist Convention, Pubns. Dept.
Maxey, Ann. Country Style Oklahoma. 2005. (Illus.). 71p. (YA). per. 15.95 *(978-0-9771939-1-2(8)*, 0001) New World Publishing.
Mays, Charli. A Lifetime from Before, 1 vol. 2009. (ENG.). 103p. pap. 19.95 *(978-1-61546-102-8(7))* America Star Bks.
McClarrin Vaupel, Lynn. The Queen of Hearts. 2007. 9.00 *(978-0-8059-8378-4(3))* Dorrance Publishing Co., Inc.
McClellan, Cheryl. Bunny Flu Flu Gets Well. 2004. (J). per. 7.99 *(978-0-9719241-9-2(8))* Chosen Word Publishing.
McDevitt, Brian. Ode to General George Washington. 2003. 20p. (YA). 6.00 *(978-1-888032-14-7(6))* Library Sales of N.J.
McDonald, J. Donnelly. I Gazed in Amazement: (Ordinary Creatures Do Extraordinary Things) 2008. 40p. pap. 16.99 *(978-1-4343-9211-4(2))* AuthorHouse.
McDougal-Littell Publishing Staff. Literature Connections English: Dogsong. 2004. (McDougal Littell Literature Connections Ser.). (ENG.). 224p. (gr. 6-8). 16.90 *(978-0-395-77527-1(2)*, 2-80096) Great Source Education Group, Inc.
McDougall, Carol & LaRamee-Jones, Shanda. Baby Play, 1 vol. 2012. (Baby Steps Ser.). (ENG., Illus.). 12p. (J). (gr. -1 — 1). bds. 8.95 *(978-1-55109-902-6(0)*, 532766b9-46b0-411a-81ec-abd8f836ae71) Nimbus Publishing, Ltd. CAN. Dist: Baker & Taylor Publisher Services (BTPS).
McGougan, Kathy. NO, Buddy! 2007. (J). pap. 5.00 *(978-0-9799980-6-5(9))* Buddy Bks. Publishing.
McGough, Roger. Wicked Poems. Layton, Neal, illus. 2004. 208p. (gr. 2-4). pap. 15.00 *(978-0-7475-6195-8(8))* Bloomsbury Publishing Plc GBR. Dist: Independent Pubs. Group.
McGrath, Noelle. The Dupes & How Not to Be Them: A Primer on the Perils of Political Correctness. 2010. 76p. pap. 76.00 *(978-1-4520-1221-6(0))* AuthorHouse.
McHenry, Eric. Mommy Daddy Evan Sage, 1 vol. Garland, Nicholas, illus. 2011. (ENG.). 72p. (J). 18.00 *(978-1-904130-45-1(3))* Waywiser Pr., The GBR. Dist: SPD-Small Pr. Distribution.
Mckenzie, Natalie. The Children of New York City: Straight from the Heart 2009. 2009. (ENG.). 64p. pap. 14.99 *(978-1-4269-1300-6(1))* Trafford Publishing.
McKeown, Theresa. The ABCs of Being Me. 2007. (J). 17.00 *(978-0-8059-7235-1(8))* Dorrance Publishing Co., Inc.
McMachan, Susan K. The Forest of the Leprechauns. Skiadas, Melissa & Skiadas, Stephanie, illus. 2008. 36p. pap. 15.95 *(978-1-4389-1325-4(7))* AuthorHouse.
McMahon, Jeff & Warrick, Jessica. Running to the Sun: Another Collection of Rhymes Without Reason. 2015. (ENG., Illus.). 192p. (J). 19.98 *(978-0-9890270-1-4(5))* Leisure Time Pr.
McMahon, Michael. Space Ace, 1 vol. rev. ed. 2013. (Literary Text Ser.). (ENG., Illus.). 32p. (J). (gr. 3-4). pap. 11.99 *(978-1-4333-5638-4(4))* Teacher Created Materials, Inc.
McNabb, Vincent. The Children's Hour of Heaven on Earth. Symington, Lindsay, illus. 2007. 48p. per. 21.95 *(978-0-9782985-2-4(7))* Catholic Authors Pr.
Me, Myself, & I! Take-Home Book. 2005. (Lee Bennett Hopkins Worlds of Poetry Classroom Library). (YA). (gr. k-3). 13.50 *(978-0-8215-0565-6(3))* Sadlier, William H. Inc.
Mehan, Matthew. Mr. Mehan's Mildly Amusing Mythical Mammals. Folley, John, illus. 2018. (ENG.). 140p. (J). (gr. 3-7). 24.95 *(978-1-5051-1249-8(4)*, 2756) TAN Bks.
Meinke, Peter & Meinke, Jeanne, illus. The Elf Poem, or, Nine Not Very Golden Rules for Children Who Like to Write Poetry. 2015. 104p. (J). pap. *(978-1-59732-129-7(X))* Univ. of Tampa Pr.
Meister, Cari. Pony Poems for Little Pony Lovers. Rhys, Sara, illus. 2019. (ENG.). 40p. (J). (gr. -1-3). 17.99 *(978-1-4814-9814-2(2)*, Beach Lane Bks.) Beach Lane Bks.
Memoirs on Love & Life: A Poetic Expression, 4. 2003. (YA). per. 13.00 *(978-0-9742010-0-9(6))* California Is Me.
Mena Ccc-Slp, Gretchen. I Won't Bite. 2009. 16p. pap. 10.49 *(978-1-4389-6449-2(8))* AuthorHouse.
Mercer, Gerald. What's Going on at the Time Tonight?, 1 vol. DeWolf, Holly, illus. 2013. (ENG.). 32p. (J). (gr. k-3). 19.95 *(978-1-77108-004-0(3)*, fc4a4075-f281-4c80-8dce-12da8fa7d061) Nimbus Publishing, Ltd. CAN. Dist: Baker & Taylor Publisher Services (BTPS).
Merrill, Karen Grill. Rhyme Time. 2007. 48p. per. 10.00 *(978-1-4257-4947-7(X))* Xlibris Corp.
Michelson, Richard. Animals Anonymous. Fischer, Scott M., illus. 2008. (ENG.). 96p. (YA). (gr. 9-18). 14.99 *(978-1-4169-1424-2(2)*, Simon & Schuster Bks. For Young Readers) Simon & Schuster Bks. For Young Readers.
Middleton, Peter. Aftermath. 2003. (Modern Poets Ser.). (ENG.). 188p. pap. *(978-1-876857-63-9(3))* Salt Publishing.
Mike. Lemon Drop Rain: Poems & Drawings by Mr. Mike. Mike, illus. I.t. ed. 2003. (ENG., Illus.). 180p. (J). pap. 14.95 *(978-0-9658365-6-2(8))* Beetle Bug Bks.
Miller, Ann. Proverbs, Prayers, Poems for Children & Teens. 2005. (J). lib. bdg. 14.95 *(978-0-9748165-1-7(5))* Jaylil Publishing Co.
Miller, Susan. Cowboy Nativity: A Narrative Poem. 2016. (ENG., Illus.). (J). (gr. 2-5). pap. 9.95 *(978-1-61984-492-6(3)*, Gatekeeper Pr.) Gatekeeper Pr.
Millman, Selena. Ever Notice. 2006. (Illus.). (J). 11.18 *(978-1-4243-2354-8(1))* Independent Publisher Services.
Mills, Lois. Saddles & Sails. 2005. reprint ed. pap. 15.95 *(978-1-4191-0458-9(6))* Kessinger Publishing, LLC.
Milne, A. A. When We Were Very Young Deluxe Edition. deluxe ed. 2009. (Winnie-The-Pooh Ser.). (ENG., Illus.). 112p. (J). (gr. 3-7). 19.99 *(978-0-525-47930-7(9)*, Dutton Books for Young Readers) Penguin Young Readers Group.
Milstein, Larry. Spring's Bright Colors. 2007. (Illus.). 24p. (J). 15.99 *(978-0-9798421-0-8(7))* Wonderful Publishing.
Minden, Cecilia & Roth, Kate. How to Write a Poem. 2011. (Explorer Junior Library: How to Write Ser.). (ENG., Illus.). 24p. (gr. 1-4). lib. bdg. 29.21 *(978-1-60279-995-0(4)*, 200990) Cherry Lake Publishing.
—Writing a Poem. 2019. (Write It Right Ser.). (ENG., Illus.). 24p. (J). (gr. 1-4). pap. 12.79 *(978-1-5341-3941-1(9)*, 212593); lib. bdg. 30.64 *(978-1-5341-4285-5(1)*, 212592) Cherry Lake Publishing.
Minter, Peter. Blue Grass. 2006. (ENG.). 128p. per. *(978-1-84471-246-5(X))* Salt Publishing.
Miracles Can Happen. 2003. 96p. (YA). per. *(978-1-930362-07-9(2))* Foston Adolescent Workshop, Inc.
Mistral, Gabriela. Poesia Infantil. (Coleccion Poemas Juvenil). (SPA.). (gr. 2-4). pap. 9.50 *(978-956-13-1083-4(X)*, AB0120) Bello, Andres CHL. Dist: Continental Bk. Co., Inc.
Mitchell, Katherine. Another Day & Lots to Do. 2012. 16p. pap. 15.99 *(978-1-4772-0541-9(1))* AuthorHouse.
Mitchell, Stephen. The Wishing Bone, & Other Poems. Pohrt, Tom, illus. 2003. (ENG.). 56p. (J). (gr. k-12). 16.99 *(978-0-7636-1118-7(2))* Candlewick Pr.
Mohanraj, Amirthi. The Poet's Journey. 2008. 30p. 16.95 *(978-0-615-18889-8(3))* Serendib Pr.
Mondragon, Philip. Going Beyond. 2009. 120p. pap. 12.95 *(978-0-595-53051-9(6))* iUniverse, Inc.
Montale, Eugenio. Selected Poems. Young, David et al, trs. 2004. (ENG.). 164p. pap. 19.95 *(978-0-932440-98-3(3))* Oberlin College Pr.
Moolenaar Bernier, Ashley-Ruth. Sand, Sea & Poetry. Fundora, Yolanda V., illus. 2014. (J). pap. *(978-1-934370-35-3(5))* Editorial Campana.
Moore, Clement C. The Night Before Christmas: Peek Inside the 3D Windows. Alderson, Lisa, illus. 2013. (ENG.). 12p. (J). (gr. -1-3). 16.99 *(978-1-84322-923-0(4)*, Armadillo) Anness Publishing GBR. Dist: National Bk. Network.
—Twas the Night Before Christmas. Sita, Sofia, illus. 2016. (ENG.). 32p. (J). (gr. -1-2). pap. 9.99 *(978-1-5324-0083-4(7))* Xist Publishing.
Moore, Clement Clarke. Twas the Night Before Christmas. Goodell, Jon, illus. 2013. (ENG.). 26p. (J). bds. 9.99 *(978-1-4494-3557-8(2))* Andrews McMeel Publishing.
Moore, Lilian. Mural on Second Avenue & Other City Poems. Karas, Roma, illus. 2013. (ENG.). 32p. (J). (gr. k-4). pap. 8.99 *(978-0-7636-6349-0(2))* Candlewick Pr.
Moore, Mel. Way Cool Book of Poetry. 2006. (Illus.). 21p. (J). per. *(978-0-9775919-0-9(5))* Carpe Diem Publishing.
Moore, Natalia, illus. Animal Poems, 1 vol. 2017. (Poems Just for Me Ser.). (ENG.). 32p. (gr. 3-3). pap. 11.00 *(978-1-4994-8389-5(9)*, 5b28ac0c-948b-4ff0-84ea-faa180528525, Windmill Bks.) Rosen Publishing Group, Inc., The.
Moore, Shelbie. Words Scribbled in My Notebook. 2008. 100p. pap. 9.99 *(978-0-9814650-4-3(8))* G Publishing LLC.
Mora, Pat. Confeti: Poemas para Ninos (Spanish), 1 vol. 2006. (SPA., Illus.). 32p. (J). (gr. k-4). pap. 12.95 *(978-1-58430-270-4(4)*, leelowbooks) Lee & Low Bks., Inc.
—Confetti: Poems for Children, 1 vol. 2006. (ENG., Illus.). 32p. (J). (gr. k-4). pap. 11.95 *(978-1-880000-85-4(7)*, leelowbooks) Lee & Low Bks., Inc.
—The Desert is My Mother/El Desierto Es Mi Madre: CD & Book Set. Lechon, Daniel, illus. 2008. 32p. (J). pap. 18.95 *(978-0-9815686-2-1(9))* Lorito Bks., Inc.
—Join Hands! The Ways We Celebrate Life. 2008. (Illus.). 32p. (J). (gr. -1-3). 15.95 *(978-1-58089-202-5(7))* Charlesbridge Publishing, Inc.
—Yum! Mmmm! Que Rico! America's Sproutings, 1 vol. López, Rafael, illus. 2007. 32p. (J). (gr. -1-3). lib. bdg. 16.95 *(978-1-58430-271-1(2))* Lee & Low Bks., Inc.
—Yum! ¡MmMm! ¡Qué Rico!, 1 vol. 2016. (ENG., Illus.). 32p. (J). (gr. k-6). pap. 11.95 *(978-1-60060-892-6(2)*, leelowbooks) Lee & Low Bks., Inc.
—Yum! Que Rico! Brotes de Las Americans. Lopez, Rafael, illus. 2009. (SPA.). 32p. (J). 17.95 *(978-1-60060-430-0(7))* Lee & Low Bks., Inc.
Mora, Pat & López, Rafael. Yum! Mmmm! Que Rico! America's Sproutings. Mora, Pat & López, Rafael, illus. 2008. (SPA & ENG., Illus.). (J). (gr. k-6). 7.95 *(978-1-60060-267-2(3))* Lee & Low Bks., Inc.
Mora, Pat, et al. Yum! Que Rico! Brotes de Las Americans: Spanish, 1 vol. Lopez, Rafael, illus. 2007.Tr. of Yum! ¡MmMm! ¡Qué rico! America's Sproutings. (SPA.). 32p. (J). (gr. k-6). pap. 12.95 *(978-1-60060-268-9(1)*, leelowbooks) Lee & Low Bks., Inc.
More, Francisco J., Sr. Carousel de Fantasias, 1. 2000th I.t. ed. 2003. (SPA., Illus.). 26p. (J). lib. bdg. 4.95 *(978-0-9747851-0-3(5))* More, Francisco J.
Morellon, Judi. Vamos a Leer. Mercado, Mary M., tr. from ENG. Teis, Kyra, illus.Tr. of Read to Me. (SPA.). 12p. (J). 2005. bds. 6.95 *(978-1-59572-015-3(4))* 2004. 6.95 *(978-1-932065-50-3(4))* Star Bright Bks., Inc.
Morenz, Justin, creator. Cardlings. 2004. (Illus.). 30p. (YA). 10.95 *(978-0-9760108-0-7(1))* Cardlings.
Morgenstern, Constance. Waking Day. 2006. (Picture Book Ser.). (ENG., Illus.). 32p. (J). (gr. k-2). 17.95 *(978-1-55971-919-3(2))* Cooper Square Publishing Llc.
Mornard, Germaine & Farish, Catherine. La Fille Orange. 2003. (New Poetry Ser.). (FRE., Illus.). 36p. (J). (gr. 7). pap. *(978-2-89021-623-5(3))* Diffusion du livre Mirabel (DLM).
Morpurgo, Michael & Morpurgo, Clare. Where My Wellies Take Me. Lomenech Gill, Olivia, illus. 2013. (ENG.). 110p. (J). (gr. 1-4). 29.99 *(978-0-7636-6629-3(7)*, Templar) Candlewick Pr.
Morris, Jackie. The Barefoot Book of Classic Poems. 2006. (Illus.). 128p. (J). (gr. 3-6). 19.99 *(978-1-905236-56-5(5))* Barefoot Bks., Inc.
Morris, Jackie, illus. The Barefoot Book of Classic Poems. 2018. (ENG.). 128p. (J). (gr. 3-7). 19.99 *(978-1-78285-427-2(4))* Barefoot Bks., Inc.
Morrison, Lillian. Guess Again! Riddle Poems. Hale, Christy, illus. 2006. (ENG.). 48p. (J). (gr. 1-4). 16.95 *(978-0-87483-730-8(8))* August Hse. Pubs., Inc.
Mortensen, Lyn. My Favorite Flower is the Daisy... & other Silly Poems. Mortensen, Lyn, illus. 2005. (Illus.). 48p. (J). per. *(978-0-9767570-0-9(1))* Wild daisy art.
Morton, Jim. Let's Make Memories ... 2004. 100p. per. 9.00 net. *(978-0-9763253-0-7(6)*, 004) Windchimes Publishing.
Moses, Brian, ed. Performance Poems. Pascoe, Jed, illus. 2013. (ENG.). 80p. pap. 16.50 *(978-1-85741-087-7(4))* Southgate Pubs. GBR. Dist: Parkwest Pubns., Inc.
Mozz. In Search of the Holey Whale: The Top Secret Riddles & Left-Handed Scribbles of Mozz. Mozz, illus. 2008. (Illus.).

176p. (J). (gr. 3-6). lib. bdg. 17.95 *(978-0-9726130-3-3(X))* Goofy Guru Publishing.

Muldrow, Diane. We Planted a Tree. Staake, Bob, illus. 2016. 40p. (J). (gr. -1-2). 8.99 *(978-0-553-53903-5(5)*, Dragonfly Bks.) Random Hse. Children's Bks.

Munro, David. Lyrical Poetry for Boys & Girls 1891. 2006. 156p. per. *(978-1-4067-1339-8(2)*, Hesperides Pr.) Read Bks.

Murdock Elementary Student Council. Gallop to Glory: Mustangs Write Like the Wind: Volume 2. 2008. pap. 14.95 *(978-0-7414-4779-1(7))* Infinity Publishing.

Murphy, Charles R. The Waking Hour: A Collection of Illustrated Verse. 2010. 32p. 24.95 *(978-0-9845798-0-8(X))* True North Studio.

Murray, Barbara. The Seasons of Life. Corbin, Marissa, illus. 2013. 36p. 19.95 *(978-0-9885370-8-8(7))* RIVERRUN BOOKSTORE INC.

Murray, P. D. Cat & Caboodle. 2008. 82p. pap. 9.50 *(978-0-615-20153-5(9))* Oh My Stars Publishing.

Musmanno, Albert J. Little Poems about Big Ideas in Science. 2012. 198p. pap. 23.95 *(978-1-4759-3988-0(4))* iUniverse, Inc.

Mussari, Mark. Poetry, 1 vol. 2012. (Craft of Writing Ser.). (ENG.). 96p. (YA). (gr. 7-7). 36.93 *(978-1-60870-500-9(5)*, faf1b72a-cbdc-4ea1-9b68-fdbdcc1e1b66) Cavendish Square Publishing LLC.

My Voice Matters. 2004. (J). 5.00 *(978-0-9664455-6-5(2))* Rhode Island State Council, International Reading Assn.

Myers, Walter Dean. Jazz. Myers, Christopher, illus. 2008. (ENG.). 48p. (J). (gr. 3-7). pap. 12.99 *(978-0-8234-2173-2(2))* Holiday Hse., Inc.

Myrddin ap Dafydd. Briwsion Yn y Clustiau: Cyfrol O Farddoniaeth I Blant. 2005. (WEL., Illus.). 76p. pap. *(978-0-86381-300-9(3))* Gwasg Carreg Gwalch.

Myrddin ap Dafydd & Morris, Siôn. Armadilo Ar Fy Mhen. 2005. (WEL., Illus.). 64p. pap. *(978-0-86381-625-3(8))* Gwasg Carreg Gwalch.

—Sach Gysgu Yn Llawn O Greision. 2005. (WEL., Illus.). 80p. pap. *(978-0-86381-626-0(6))* Gwasg Carreg Gwalch.

—Tabledi-Gwneud-'Chi-Wenu: Dôs Arbennig O Farddoniaeth Loerig Am Salwch AC Afiechydon. 2005. (WEL., Illus.). 72p. pap. *(978-0-86381-678-9(9))* Gwasg Carreg Gwalch.

Myrddin ap Dafydd, et al. Caneuon y Coridorau: Barddoniaeth Ar Gyfer Pobl Ifanc. 2005. (WEL., Illus.). 84p. pap. *(978-0-86381-970-4(2))* Gwasg Carreg Gwalch.

Nathan, Jeff. Calling All Animals: The First Book of PunOETRY. Ball, Liz, illus. 2003. 96p. per. 9.95 *(978-0-9702730-1-7(0))* Chucklebks. Publishing.

Neal, Kathleen A. The Sun Begins Its Daily Flight. 2013. 32p. pap. 24.95 *(978-1-63004-158-8(0))* America Star Bks.

Nelson, Alexis Andria. Sing Mommie Sing: Lullabies from the Heart. 2010. 36p. 21.99 *(978-1-4490-9405-8(8))* AuthorHouse.

Nesbitt, Kenn. One Minute till Bedtime: 60-Second Poems to Send You off to Sleep. Niemann, Christoph, illus. 2016. (ENG.). 176p. (J). (gr. -1-3). 19.99 *(978-0-316-34121-9(5))* Little, Brown Bks. for Young Readers.

—Revenge of the Lunch Ladies: The Hilarious Book of School Poetry. Gordon, Mike & Gordon, Carl, illus. 2007. 80p. *(978-0-88166-527-7(4))* Meadowbrook Pr.

—When the Teacher Isn't Looking: And Other Funny School Poems. Gordon, Mike, illus. 2005. 80p. (J). *(978-0-88166-489-8(8))* Meadowbrook Pr.

—When the Teacher Isn't Looking: And Other Funny School Poems. Gordon, Mike, illus. 2010. (Giggle Poetry Ser.). (ENG.). 80p. (J). (gr. k-7). per. 9.99 *(978-0-684-03128-6(0)*, Running Pr.) Running Pr.

New, William. Dream Helmet. Bevis, Vivian, illus. 2005. (ENG.). 32p. (J). 11.95 *(978-1-55380-021-7(4))* Ronsdale Pr. CAN. Dist: Literary Pr. Group of Canada.

—Llamas in the Laundry. Bevis, Vivian, illus. 2005. (ENG.). 32p. (J). 12.95 *(978-0-921870-97-5(3))* Ronsdale Pr. CAN. Dist: Literary Pr. Group of Canada.

—The Year I Was Grounded, 1 vol. 2009. (ENG., Illus.). 64p. (YA). (gr. 8-12). pap. 12.95 *(978-1-896580-35-7(1))* Tradewind Bks. CAN. Dist: Orca Bk. Pubs. USA.

Newbold, Dale L. Funny Facts & Fun Facts! 2006. 20.00 *(978-0-8059-9019-5(4))* Dorrance Publishing Co., Inc.

Newell, Peter. The Slant Book. 2007. (Illus.). 52p. per. *(978-1-4065-3053-7(0))* Dodo Pr.

Nicholls, Judith. The Sun in Me: Poems about the Planet. Krommes, Beth, illus. 2008. 40p. (J). (gr. -1). pap. 12.99 *(978-1-84686-161-1(6))* Barefoot Bks., Inc.

Nicholls, Judith, ed. The Sun in Me: Poems about the Planet. Krommes, Beth, illus. 2003. 40p. (J). pap. 16.99 *(978-1-84148-058-9(4))* Barefoot Bks., Inc.

Nickerson, Karen. Phoenix & Drake Explore Canada. 2018. (ENG., Illus.). 24p. (J). pap. 13.07 *(978-0-9959829-4-9(5))* Blurb, Inc.

Nicolson, Paula. The Love Book Healing Poems for Broken Hearts. (Illus.). 40p. (J). 9.95 *(978-1-880976-18-0(8))* Brookshire Pubns., Inc.

Nield, Sue. Raps & Rhymes about Primary School Times: A Children's Poetry Anthology. 2012. 112p. (gr. 4-6). pap. 14.95 *(978-1-4678-8893-6(1))* AuthorHouse.

—Raps & Rhymes about Tudor Times: A Poetic Interpretation of History. 2012. (Illus.). 56p. pap. 11.95 *(978-1-4678-8001-5(9))* AuthorHouse.

Nino, Jairo Anibal. Los Papeles de Miguela. Rincon, Fernando, illus. 2003. (Literatura Juvenil (Panamericana Editorial) Ser.). (SPA.). 78p. (J). (gr. -1-7). pap. *(978-958-30-0336-3(0)*, PV30462) Centro de Informacion y Desarrollo de la Comunicacion y la Literatura MEX. Dist: Lectorum Pubns., Inc.

Niqo, Jairo Anmbal. Preguntario. Gonzalez, Henry, illus. 2007. (Literatura Juvenil (Panamericana Editorial) Ser.). (SPA.). 188p. (gr. 5-7). pap. 18.99 *(978-958-30-0497-1(9)*, PV30461) Panamericana Editorial COL. Dist: Lectorum Pubns., Inc.

Nishat-Botero, Hannah. Hannah Banana's Book of Poems. 2012. (Illus.). 48p. pap. 18.31 *(978-1-4567-9693-8(3))* AuthorHouse.

Nnamoko, Johanan U. The Greatest Mom, 1 vol. 2009. 25p. pap. 24.95 *(978-1-61546-678-8(9))* PublishAmerica, Inc.

Noda, Takayo. Dear World. 2005. (Illus.). 32p. (J). (gr. k-3). reprint ed. pap. 7.99 *(978-0-14-240280-1(X)*, Puffin Books) Penguin Young Readers Group.

Noyes, Alfred. The Highwayman. Keeping, Charles, illus. 2015. 32p. pap. 12.95 *(978-0-19-279442-0(6))* Oxford Univ. Pr., Inc.

—The Highwayman. Riswold, Gilbert, illus. 2003. (ENG.). 31p. (gr. 6-6). cd-rom 147.47 net. *(978-0-13-036517-0(3)*, Prentice Hall) Savvas Learning Co.

Nuno, Fran & Nuño, Fran. Postromario. 2013. (SPA.). 54p. (gr. 2-4). pap. 9.99 *(978-84-15207-62-7(X))* Almadraba Infantil y Juvenil ESP. Dist: Lectorum Pubns., Inc.

Nuttall, Neil & Hawkins, Andy, eds. Second Thoughts. Fell, Jenny, illus. 2004. (ENG.). 64p. pap. 14.95 *(978-1-84323-046-5(1))* Beekman Bks., Inc.

Nye, Naomi Shihab. Honeybee: Poems & Short Prose. 2008. (ENG.). 176p. (J). (gr. 5-9). 16.99 *(978-0-06-085390-7(5)*, Greenwillow Bks.) HarperCollins Pubs.

—Time You Let Me In: 25 Poets Under 25. 2010. (ENG.). 256p. (YA). (gr. 8-18). 17.99 *(978-0-06-189637-8(3)*, Greenwillow Bks.) HarperCollins Pubs.

—Voices in the Air: Poems for Listeners. 2018. (ENG., Illus.). 208p. (YA). (gr. 8). 17.99 *(978-0-06-269184-2(8)*, Greenwillow Bks.) HarperCollins Pubs.

—19 Varieties of Gazelle: Poems of the Middle East. 2005. (ENG.). 160p. (YA). (gr. 5). reprint ed. pap. 8.99 *(978-0-06-050404-5(8)*, Greenwillow Bks.) HarperCollins Pubs.

Ode, Eric. Sea Star Wishes. Brooks, Erik, illus. 2018. 32p. (J). (gr. -1-3). pap. 10.99 *(978-1-63217-154-2(6)*, Little Bigfoot) Sasquatch Bks.

—Tall Tales of the Wild West: A Humorous Collection of Cowboy Poems & Songs. Crane, Ben, illus. 2007. 32p. *(978-0-88166-524-6(X))* Meadowbrook Pr.

Of Love Expressed. 2005. per. 8.50 *(978-0-9770594-2-3(1))* Grimes, Richard.

Olowoyeye, Ola. Rhythm & Motion. 2010. 28p. pap. 12.49 *(978-1-4520-2584-1(3))* AuthorHouse.

The Open Door. 2004. per. *(978-0-9747704-0-6(X))* Writers in the Schools (WITS).

Opie, Ian, ed. My Very First Mother Goose. Wells, Rosemary, illus. 2004. 107p. (J). reprint ed. 17.00 *(978-0-7567-8384-6(4))* DIANE Publishing Co.

Orme, Nicholas. Fleas, Flies, & Friars: Children's Poetry from the Middle Ages. 2012. (ENG., Illus.). 120p. (gr. 17). 125.00 *(978-0-8014-5102-7(7)*, 978-0-8014-5102-7); pap. 22.95 *(978-0-8014-7775-1(1)*, 978-0-8014-7775-1) Cornell Univ. Pr.

Ortegon, Sharon A. You. 2013. 40p. pap. 19.57 *(978-1-4669-9981-7(0))* Trafford Publishing.

Ostashevsky, Eugene, tr. The Fire Horse: Children's Poems by Vladimir Mayakovsky, Osip Mandelstam & Daniil Kharms. 2017. (Illus.). 48p. (J). (gr. 1-3). 16.95 *(978-1-68137-092-7(1)*, NYR Children's Collection) New York Review of Bks., Inc., The.

Osundare, Niyi. Early Birds: Poems for Junior Secondary Schools. 2004. (Illus.). 100p. pap. *(978-978-029-530-1(5))* Spectrum Bks., Ltd. NGA. Dist: Michigan State Univ. Pr.

Overton, Hollie. Baby Doll. 2018. (ENG., Illus.). 400p. mass mkt. 7.99 *(978-0-316-52710-1(6))* Orbit.

Pace, Yolantha. Wing-Plucked Butterfly: A Survivor Speaks One Woman's War on Hate Crimes Against Women & Children. 2004. 146p. per. 15.00 *(978-0-9747017-8-3(5))* Neshee Pubn.

Pacheva, Svetla & Cholakova, Maiia. Kushtichka S Gatanki. 2008. (Illus.). 17p. *(978-954-443-730-5(4))* Balgarski pisatel, Izdatelstvo.

Page, P. K. A Brazilian Alphabet for the Younger Reader. 2005. (ENG., Illus.). 64p. (J). (gr. -1-1). pap. 16.95 *(978-0-88984-265-6(5))* Porcupine's Quill, Inc. CAN. Dist: Univ. of Toronto Pr.

—Jake, the Baker, Makes a Cake. 2008. (ENG., Illus.). 40p. pap. 19.95 *(978-0-88982-245-0(X))* Oolichan Bks. CAN. Dist: Univ. of Toronto Pr.

Pahn, Latosha. Come go on a Read along Ride with Me: Read along Ride. 2008. 68p. pap. 9.95 *(978-1-4184-4896-7(6))* AuthorHouse.

Park, Linda Sue. The One Thing You'd Save. Sae-Heng, Robert, illus. 2021. (ENG.). 72p. (J). (gr. 3-7). 16.99 *(978-1-328-51513-1(3)*, 1719818, Clarion Bks.) HarperCollins Pubs.

—Tap Dancing on the Roof: Sijo (Poems) Banyai, Istvan, illus. 2015. (ENG.). 48p. (J). (gr. -1-3). 7.99 *(978-0-544-55551-8(1)*, 1610458, Clarion Bks.) HarperCollins Pubs.

Parower, Alec. So I Wrote It Down. 2008. 84p. pap. 11.95 *(978-0-595-51259-1(3))* iUniverse, Inc.

Parveen, Tahmina. Realistic Rhymes. 2004. 92p. pap. *(978-1-84401-287-9(5))* Athena Pr.

Paschen, Elise. Poetry Speaks to Children. 2005. (Poetry Speaks Experience Ser.: 0). (ENG., Illus.). 112p. (gr. k-3). 19.95 *(978-1-4022-0329-9(2)*, Sourcebooks MediaFusion) Sourcebooks, Inc.

—Poetry Speaks Who I Am: Poems of Discovery, Inspiration, Independence, & Everything Else. Raccah, Dominique, ed. 2010. (Poetry Speaks Experience Ser.: 0). 176p. (J). (gr. 7-12). 19.99 *(978-1-4022-1074-7(4)*, Sourcebooks Jabberwocky) Sourcebooks, Inc.

Patten, Brian & Assorted Staff. The Puffin Book of Utterly Brilliant Poetry. Patten, Brian, ed. (Illus.). 144p. (J). pap. 15.00 *(978-0-14-038421-5(9))* Penguin Bks., Ltd. GBR. Dist: Trafalgar Square Publishing.

Paul, Julia Marian. Song of the Teapot: Poems about Little Babies, Little Jerry, Little Susie, & Other Things. 2007. (ENG.). 60p. per. 16.95 *(978-1-4241-4299-6(7))* PublishAmerica, Inc.

Paz Lozano, Octavio. La Rama. Kitora, Tetsuo, illus. 2005.Tr. of Branch. (SPA.). (J). (gr. k-2). pap. 10.95 *(978-968-494-046-8(7))* Centro de Informacion y Desarrollo de la Comunicacion y la Literatura MEX. Dist: Iaconi, Mariuccia Bk. Imports.

Pearl, Beverly. Little Cat Snowshoes. 2010. (ENG.). 56p. pap. 22.30 *(978-0-557-24481-2(1))* Lulu Pr., Inc.

Pearson, Susan. Grimericks. 0 vols. Grimly, Gris, illus. 2013. (ENG.). 32p. (J). (gr. 1-4). pap. 9.99 *(978-0-7614-5444-1(6)*, 9780761454441, Two Lions) Amazon Publishing.

—Who Swallowed Harold? And Other Poems about Pets, 1 vol. Slonim, David, illus. 2005. (ENG.). 32p. (J). (gr. k-4). 16.95 *(978-0-7614-5193-8(5))* Marshall Cavendish Corp.

Pedigo, Kim Tran. Having Fun with Kandai the Elephant. Pedigo, Kim Tran, illus. 2012. (Illus.). 36p. pap. 12.95 *(978-1-61244-105-4(X))* Halo Publishing International.

Perkins, Jill E. Cherubs Chatter: A Collection of Original Songs & Poems. 2004. (Illus.). 88p. (J). per. 7.95 *(978-0-9749862-2-7(4))* Theragogy.com.

Perkins, Useni Eugene. Hey Black Child. Collier, Bryan, illus. (ENG.). (J). (gr. -1 — 1). 2019. 22p. bds. 7.99 *(978-0-316-36029-6(5))* 2017. 40p. 18.99 *(978-0-316-36030-2(9))* Little, Brown Bks. for Young Readers.

Perry, Robert. My Vancouver Sketchbook. Guzek, Greta, illus. unabr. ed. 2010. (ENG.). 32p. (J). pap. 9.95 *(978-0-88971-248-5(4)*, 1dfb37bc-2d9f-4b8a-ba0f-89a7befea260) Nightwood Editions CAN. Dist: Harbour Publishing Co., Ltd.

Peters, Lisa Westberg. Earthshake: Poems from the Ground Up. Felstead, Cathie, illus. 2003. (ENG.). 32p. (J). (gr. k-5). 17.99 *(978-0-06-029265-2(2)*, Greenwillow Bks.) HarperCollins Pubs.

—Volcano Wakes Up! 2016. (J). lib. bdg. 19.65 *(978-0-606-38430-8(8))* Turtleback.

Petway, Jessie. A Child's Book of Poetry. 2007. per. 12.00 *(978-0-9791154-5-5(0)*, MSP) Yetto Publishing Co.

Phelps Williams, Janice, illus. Still Her Spirit Sings: One Dog's Love, Lessons, Life & Legacy. 2010. 32p. (J). (gr. k-2). 16.95 *(978-0-9760220-1-5(X))* Kidzpoetz Publishing.

Phethean, Ellen. Wall, 1 vol. 2014. (ENG.). 152p. pap. 18.00 *(978-0-9551061-6-3(8))* Smokestack Bks. GBR. Dist: Dufour Editions, Inc.

Phillips, Dee. Samurai, 1 vol., Bk. 7. 2014. (Yesterday's Voices Ser.). (ENG.). 48p. (YA). (gr. 5-12). pap. 10.75 *(978-1-62250-909-6(9))* Saddleback Educational Publishing, Inc.

Phinn, Gervase. What I Like! Poems for the Very Young. Eccles, Jane, illus. 2004. (Poetry Ser.). 32p. (J). (gr. 2-3). pap. *(978-1-904550-12-9(6))* Child's Play International Ltd.

Pickard, Ben & Pickard, Carolyn. A Fish! Don't You Wish. 2003. 265p. 29.95 *(978-0-595-65747-6(8))*; pap. 19.95 *(978-0-595-28229-6(6))* iUniverse, Inc.

Pierre, Manes. Spinning the Globe. 2008. 132p. 23.95 *(978-0-595-49576-4(1))*; pap. 13.95 *(978-0-595-49925-0(2))* iUniverse, Inc.

Pirie, Mark. Gallery: A Selection. 2003. (Modern Poets Ser.). (ENG.). 116p. pap. *(978-1-876857-24-0(2))* Salt Publishing.

Pittman, Rickey. Scottish Alphabet, 1 vol. McLennan, Connie, illus. 2008. (ABC Ser.). (ENG.). 32p. (J). (gr. 1-3). 16.99 *(978-1-58980-596-5(8)*, Pelican Publishing) Arcadia Publishing.

Plaza, José María & María, Plaza José. Alibaru: La Ronda de las Estaciones. (SPA.). 120p. *(978-84-392-8119-1(6))* Gaviota Ediciones ESP. Dist: Lectorum Pubns., Inc.

—Pajarulí: Poemas para Seguir Andando. Villamuza, Noemi, illus. (SPA.). (J). *(978-84-392-8120-7(X)*, EV0782) Gaviota Ediciones ESP. Dist: Lectorum Pubns., Inc.

—Tungaira: Mis Primeras Poesías. Lucini, Carmen, illus. (SPA.). 96p. (J). 8.99 *(978-84-392-8115-3(3)*, EV4870) Gaviota Ediciones ESP. Dist: Lectorum Pubns., Inc.

Plourd, Brenden. My New Brother. 2011. 20p. pap. 24.95 *(978-1-4489-6811-4(9))* America Star Bks.

Pockell, Leslie, ed. 100 Great Poems for Boys. 2011. (ENG.). 256p. (J). pap., pap. 16.99 *(978-0-446-56382-6(X))* Grand Central Publishing.

Poe, Edgar. The Raven: Includes Sound! 2011. (ENG.). 48p. 8.95 *(978-0-7624-4282-9(4))* Running Pr.

Poemas y Cantares de America y el Mundo. (SPA.). (YA). (gr. 5-8). pap. *(978-956-13-1606-5(4)*, AB2725) Bello, Andres CHL. Dist: Lectorum Pubns., Inc.

Poems & Rhymes (Gr. 1-2) 2003. (J). *(978-1-58232-070-0(5))* ECS Learning Systems, Inc.

Poems Just for Me, 8 vols. 2017. (Poems Just for Me Ser.). 32p. (ENG.). (gr. 3-3). 115.72 *(978-1-4994-8273-7(6)*, c21c3700-fa03-4de9-ba37-0e6dde30ddd3); (gr. 7-8). pap. 40.00 *(978-1-4994-8407-6(0))* Rosen Publishing Group, Inc., The. (Windmill Bks.).

Poesia Una Al Dia. (SPA.). 32p. (J). (gr. 3-5). 15.95 *(978-84-204-4334-8(4))* Santillana USA Publishing Co., Inc.

Poetry & Rhymes. Date not set. 256p. (J). 5.98 *(978-0-7525-7690-9(9))* Parragon, Inc.

Poetry Power ESL: Complete Set. 2003. (SPA., Illus.). 225.50 *(978-0-8136-0715-3(9))* Modern Curriculum Pr.

Poetry Tapes & Small Books. (Dias y Dias de Poesia Ser.). (SPA.). (gr. -1-6). 182.43 *(978-1-56334-281-3(2))* CENGAGE Learning.

Poetry Works! Complete Set. 2003. (SPA., Illus.). (J). (gr. -1-k). 183.95 *(978-0-8136-0719-1(1))* Modern Curriculum Pr.

Polisar, Barry Louis. Something Fishy. Clark, David, illus. 2013. (ENG.). 32p. (J). (gr. k-6). 14.95 *(978-0-938663-53-9(4)*, 929e0758-82fc-4faa-a666-61ba235fb1b4) Rainbow Morning Music Alternatives.

Polk, James G. Gift of Love, Vol. 2. Rudkin, Shawn, ed. Rudkin, Tracy, illus. (YA). *(978-0-9727753-1-1(5))* New Wave Bks. & CD.

Popper, Garry. Big World. Johnson, Andi, illus. 2004. 36p. (gr. -1-7). 4.00 *(978-1-84161-052-8(6))* Ravette Publishing, Ltd. GBR. Dist: Parkwest Pubns., Inc.

Pottle, Robert. I'm Allergic to School: Funny Poems & Songs about School. Gordon, Mike & Gordon, Carl, illus. 2007. 32p. *(978-0-88166-522-2(3))* Meadowbrook Pr.

—Maine: A Wicked Good Book of Verse: the Way Wildlife Should Be. Hardwick, Holly, illus. 2005. 64p. (J). per. 8.95 *(978-0-9709569-3-4(2))* Blue Lobster Pr.

—Moxie Day the Prankster: Another Laugh & Learn Book of Poetry. Jonathan Siruno, illus. 2004. 64p. (J). per. 8.95 *(978-0-9709569-2-7(4)*, MDTP) Blue Lobster Pr.

—Poems with Moxie: Funny Poems & Funny Songs. 2008. (Illus.). 96p. (J). per. 9.95 *(978-0-9709569-4-1(0))* Blue Lobster Pr.

Potts, William. Under My Pillow. 2010. 38p. pap. 17.50 *(978-0-557-51217-1(4))* Lulu Pr., Inc.

Powell, Amy. Me. 2006. (Illus.). 21p. (J). (gr. -1-3). per. 15.00 *(978-0-9773608-3-3(0))* Shiny Red Ball Publishing.

Powers, Lillian. Girl Child: (The Transition - in Poetic Form) 2004. 64p. (YA). per. 9.95 *(978-0-9761523-2-3(0))* Mama Incense Publishing.

Prelutsky, Jack. Awful Ogre Running Wild. Zelinsky, Paul O., illus. 2008. 40p. (J). (gr. -1-3). lib. bdg. 18.89 *(978-0-06-623867-8(6)*, Greenwillow Bks.) HarperCollins Pubs.

—Behold the Bold Umbrellaphant: And Other Poems. Berger, Carin, illus. 2006. (ENG.). 40p. (J). (gr. -1-4). 17.99 *(978-0-06-054317-4(5)*, Greenwillow Bks.) HarperCollins Pubs.

—It's Raining Pigs & Noodles. Stevenson, James, illus. 2012. (ENG.). 160p. (J). (gr. k-5). reprint ed. pap. 10.99 *(978-0-06-076390-9(6)*, Greenwillow Bks.) HarperCollins Pubs.

—It's Snowing! It's Snowing! Winter Poems. Abolafia, Yossi, illus. 2006. (I Can Read Bks.). 48p. (J). (gr. -1-3). lib. bdg. 16.89 *(978-0-06-053716-6(7))* HarperCollins Pubs.

—It's Thanksgiving! Hafner, Marylin, illus. 2008. (I Can Read Level 3 Ser.). (ENG.). 48p. (J). (gr. k-3). pap. 4.99 *(978-0-06-053711-1(6)*, HarperCollins) HarperCollins Pubs.

—It's Valentine's Day. Hafner, Marylin, illus. 2013. (I Can Read Level 3 Ser.). (ENG.). 48p. (J). (gr. -1-3). pap. 4.99 *(978-0-06-053714-2(0)*, Greenwillow Bks.) HarperCollins Pubs.

—Me I Am! Davenier, Christine, illus. 2007. (ENG.). 32p. (J). (gr. -1-1). 19.99 *(978-0-374-34902-8(9)*, 900021998, Farrar, Straus & Giroux (BYR)) Farrar, Straus & Giroux.

—My Dog May Be a Genius. 2008. (ENG., Illus.). 160p. (J). (gr. k-5). 18.99 *(978-0-06-623862-3(5)*, Greenwillow Bks.) HarperCollins Pubs.

—My Parents Think I'm Sleeping. Abolafia, Yossi, illus. (I Can Read Level 3 Ser.). 48p. (J). (gr. k-3). 2008. (ENG.). pap. 5.99 *(978-0-06-053722-7(1)*, HarperCollins) 2007. lib. bdg. 16.89 *(978-0-06-053721-0(3))* HarperCollins Pubs.

—Scranimals. Sis, Peter, illus. 2006. (ENG.). 48p. (J). (gr. -1-3). reprint ed. pap. 8.99 *(978-0-06-075368-9(4)*, Greenwillow Bks.) HarperCollins Pubs.

—Something Big Has Been Here. Stevenson, James, illus. 2010. (ENG.). 160p. (J). (gr. k-5). pap. 10.99 *(978-0-06-185775-1(0)*, Greenwillow Bks.) HarperCollins Pubs.

—Stardines Swim High Across the Sky & Other Poems. 2013. (ENG., Illus.). 40p. (J). (gr. -1-3). 17.99 *(978-0-06-201464-1(1)*, Greenwillow Bks.) HarperCollins Pubs.

—There's No Place Like School. 2010. (ENG., Illus.). 32p. (J). (gr. k-5). 16.99 *(978-0-06-082338-2(0)*, Greenwillow Bks.) HarperCollins Pubs.

—What a Day It Was at School! Cushman, Doug, illus. 2009. (ENG.). 40p. (J). (gr. k-5). pap. 7.99 *(978-0-06-082337-5(2)*, Greenwillow Bks.) HarperCollins Pubs.

Prendergast, R. L. Baby, Please Go to Sleep. Maciborski, Charmaine, illus. 2013. 16p. (J). pap. *(978-0-9784548-4-5(7))* Dekko Publishing.

Prescott, Brian. Chloe Saves Christmas. 2013. 24p. pap. *(978-1-909192-45-4(7))* Beaten Track Publishing.

—Chloe the Campervan Goes on Holiday. 2013. 28p. pap. *(978-1-909192-40-9(6))* Beaten Track Publishing.

Price, Aleksandra. What Do You See? Poems for Young Children. 2008. 16p. pap. 12.95 *(978-1-59858-811-8(7))* Dog Ear Publishing, LLC.

Price, Erika. The Turnaround: Book of Poetry. 2004. (YA). per. 7.00 *(978-0-9753028-0-4(9))* Turnaround Bk. Publishing Corp.

Price, Erika, contrib. by. The Turnaround: Book of Poetry. 2004. (YA). per. 7.00 *(978-0-9753028-2-8(5))*; per. 7.00 *(978-0-9753028-1-1(7))* Turnaround Bk. Publishing Corp.

Price, Margaret Evans, ed. & illus. Mother Goose: Book of Rhymes. Price, Margaret Evans, illus. 2007. (Children's Die-Cut Shape Book Ser.). (ENG.). 16p. (J). (gr. 4-7). 10.95 *(978-1-59583-134-7(7)*, 9781595831347, Green Tiger Pr.) Laughing Elephant.

Pritchard, Mary. Mrs P's Poems. Gasking, Terry, ed. 2013. 52p. pap. *(978-1-907953-58-3(2))* TwigBooks.

Professor Bubbledunk. Stories from the Mugglewhuft. 2013. 36p. pap. 15.50 *(978-1-4669-6044-2(2))* Trafford Publishing.

Proudfit, Benjamin. Writing Poems, 1 vol. 2014. (Write Right! Ser.). (ENG., Illus.). 24p. (J). (gr. 2-3). 25.27 *(978-1-4824-1124-9(5)*, 75e500db-096e-4b04-8960-0dc16415c945) Stevens, Gareth Publishing LLLP.

Pruitt, Christine Lee. I'm Alright Day & Night! 2012. 16p. pap. 12.68 *(978-1-4669-6065-7(5))* Trafford Publishing.

Pujari, M. Nathalie. 20 Umbrellas. Sananmuang, Chatree, illus. 2007. (J). *(978-0-9715865-0-5(0))* Abuzz Bks.

Pyle, Howard. The Wonder Clock Or, Four & Twenty Marvelous Tales. 2012. (Dover Children's Classics Ser.). (ENG., Illus.). 319p. (J). (gr. 3-8). per. 12.95 *(978-0-486-21446-7(X)*, 21446X) Dover Pubns., Inc.

Pynn Taylor, Susan. The Colours of My Home: A Portrait of Newfoundland & Labrador, 1 vol. 2007. (ENG., Illus.). 32p. (J). (gr. -1-2). pap. *(978-1-897174-06-7(3))* Breakwater Bks., Ltd.

—A Puppy Story, 1 vol. Keating, Nancy, illus. 2007. (ENG.). 32p. (J). (gr. -1-3). pap. *(978-1-897174-18-0(7))* Breakwater Bks., Ltd.

Quattlebaum, Mary. Family Reunion. Shine, Andrea, illus. 2004. 32p. (J). 16.00 *(978-0-8028-5237-3(8))* Eerdmans, William B. Publishing Co.

Quiñones, Magaly. Quiero una Noche Azul. 2007. 64p. 14.95 *(978-0-8477-0732-4(6))* Univ. of Puerto Rico Pr.

Quintavalle, Paola. Crescendo. 2019. (Illus.). 104p. (J). 19.95 *(978-1-59270-255-8(4))* Enchanted Lion Bks., LLC.

Quintero, Aramis. Todo el Cielo un Juguete Poemas para Ninos. 2003. (J). *(978-956-240-374-0(2))* Arrayán Editores S.A.

Rabisa, Tabitha. I Dream of Angels... yet I Live with Demons. 2008. 76p. pap. 10.95 *(978-0-595-52719-9(1))* iUniverse, Inc.

Raczka, Bob. Wet Cement: A Mix of Concrete Poems. 2016. (ENG.). 48p. (J). 18.99 *(978-1-62672-236-1(6)*, 900146234) Roaring Brook Pr.

Radunsky, Vladimir & Raschka, Chris. Alphabetabum: An Album of Rare Photographs & Medium Verses. 2014. (Illus.). 80p. (J). (gr. -1-3). 19.95 *(978-1-59017-817-1(3)*, NYR Children's Collection) New York Review of Bks., Inc., The.

Randall, Alex. Rhyming Book. 2010. (ENG.). 32p. pap. 15.00 *(978-0-557-66356-9(3))* Lulu Pr., Inc.

Raphael, Solli. Limelight. 2019. (ENG.). 128p. (J). pap. 14.99 *(978-1-4494-9936-5(8))* Andrews McMeel Publishing.

Raschka, Chris, illus. A Kick in the Head: An Everyday Guide to Poetic Forms. 2009. (ENG.). 64p. (J). (gr. 3-7). pap. 9.99 (978-0-7636-4132-0(4)) Candlewick Pr.

Rasmussen, Halfdan, et al. A Little Bitty Man & Other Poems for the Very Young. Hawkes, Kevin, illus. 2011. (ENG.). 32p. (J). (gr. -1-2). 15.99 (978-0-7636-2379-1(2)) Candlewick Pr.

Ravishankar, Anushka. Catch That Crocodile! Biswas, Pulak, illus. collector's ed. 2007. 40p. (J). (gr. -1-2). 25.00 (978-81-86211-94-6(2)) Tara Publishing IND. Dist: Consortium Bk. Sales & Distribution.

Rebelo, Gabriel Bastos. Let's Go To... Work!: the Let's Go! Children's Book Series. 2004. (Illus.). 54p. pap. (978-1-84401-197-1(6)) Athena Pr.

Reddin, Brian. What Do Rabbits Think? And Other Fun Poems for Kids. Fox, Woody, illus. 2006. (ENG.). 64p. (J). pap. 17.95 (978-1-85635-517-9(9)) Mercier Pr., Ltd., The IRL. Dist: Dufour Editions, Inc.

Reflections of a Fool. 2004. (Illus.). 115p. (YA). per. 14.95 (978-1-931084-33-8(5)) Balloon Magic.

Resnicoff, Stan. Tom, the Talking Toilet. 2012. (ENG.). (J). pap. (978-1-4675-1536-8(1)) Independent Pub.

Rex, Adam. Frankenstein Takes the Cake. 2012. lib. bdg. 18.40 (978-0-606-26615-4(1)) Turtleback.

Rex, Adam & Malk, Steven. Frankenstein Makes a Sandwich. 2011. (ENG., Illus.). 40p. (J). (gr. 1-4). pap. 7.99 (978-0-547-57683-1(8), 1458444, Clarion Bks.) HarperCollins Pubs.

Rexroad, Danese. Naked Baby. 2012. 20p. pap. 12.70 (978-1-4669-5409-0(4)) Trafford Publishing.

Reynolds, Jason. For Every One. 2018. (ENG., Illus.). 112p. (YA). (gr. 7). 15.99 (978-1-4814-8624-8(1), Atheneum/Caitlyn Dlouhy Books) Simon & Schuster Children's Publishing.

Reynolds, Jason & Griffin, Jason. My Name Is Jason. Mine Too: Our Story. Our Way. 2011. (ENG.). (YA). 13.08 (978-0-7848-3419-0(9), Everbind) Marco Bk. Co.

Reynolds, Lauren F. Deep Sea Poetry: For Children. 2012. (Illus.). 28p. pap. 19.99 (978-1-4772-8019-5(7)) AuthorHouse.

RH Disney. Mother Goose (Disney Classic) RH Disney, illus. 2004. (Little Golden Book Ser.). (ENG., Illus.). 24p. (J). (gr. -1-2). 5.99 (978-0-7364-2310-6(9), Golden/Disney) Random Hse. Children's Bks.

Rhodes, Sam. Native American Rhymes: The People of the Far North, 9 vols. Howard, Kimberley, ed. Haas, Deborah, illus. 2003. 92p. (J). (gr. 3-5). mass mkt. 7.50 (978-0-9743214-0-0(0)) Rhodes Educational Pubns.

Richardson, Bill. The Alphabet Thief, 1 vol. Bikadoroff, Roxanna, illus. 2017. (ENG.). 40p. (J). (gr. k-4). 16.95 (978-1-55498-877-8(2)) Groundwood Bks. CAN. Dist: Publishers Group West (PGW).

Richardson, Sandra Lee. The Backyard Series: Volume One, 1 vol. 2009. 37p. pap. 24.95 (978-1-60836-945-4(5)) America Star Bks.

Richmond, Marianne. The Gift of an Angel Vol. 1: For Parents Welcoming a New Child. l.t. ed. 2003. (ENG., Illus.). 40p. (YA). 15.95 (978-0-9741465-2-2(8), Marianne Richmond Studios, Inc.) Sourcebooks, Inc.

Rickards, Lynne. You & Me 2 Wayfarers. Brecon, Connah & Painter, Andrew, illus. 2017. (Cambridge Reading Adventures Ser.). (ENG.). 24p. pap. 7.35 (978-1-108-41083-0(9)) Cambridge Univ. Pr.

Riddle, Peter H. No Room: A Read-Aloud Story of Christmas. Hustins, Shelley, illus. 2009. 40p. (J). pap. (978-1-926585-43-7(7), CCB Publishing) CCB Publishing.

Riehle, Mary Ann McCabe. The Little Kids' Table. Uhles, Mary Reaves, illus. 2015. (ENG.). 32p. (J). (gr. k-3). 16.99 (978-1-58536-913-3(6), 203952) Sleeping Bear Pr.

Ritter-Henley, Sharlene. 123 Count Drive Nursery Rhyme, 1 vol. 2010. 20p. pap. 24.95 (978-1-4489-8141-0(7)) PublishAmerica, Inc.

Roberts, Emrys. Pwdin Semolina: Cerddi Cynganeddol I Blant. 2005. (WEL.). 80p. pap. (978-0-86381-402-0(6)) Gwasg Carreg Gwalch.

Robinson, Gary. Native American Night Before Christmas. Hummingbird, Jesse T., illus. 2007. (ENG.). 40p. (J). (978-1-57416-093-2(1)) Clear Light Pubs.

Roche, Patricia Jo. I Am More Than a Name. 2009. 187p. pap. 24.95 (978-1-60703-520-6(0)) America Star Bks.

Rodda, Geri. Lyme in Rhyme. 2005. (J). 7.50 (978-0-9793602-1-3(8)) Pumpkin Hill Productions.

Rodriguez, Luis J. Counting Time Like People Count Stars: Poems by the Girls of Our Little Roses, San Pedro Sula, Honduras. Reece, Spencer, ed. 2017. (ENG., Illus.). 120p. pap. 19.95 (978-1-882688-55-5(4)) Tia Chucha Pr.

Rogé. Haiti My Country, 1 vol. 2014. (ENG., Illus.). 44p. (J). (gr. 5-8). pap. 14.95 (978-1-927083-23-9(0), 3791d6ea-4b4f-4b05-9d0e-28038870cee4) Fifth Hse. Pubs. CAN. Dist: Firefly Bks., Ltd.

Rogé, illus. Mingan: My Village, 1 vol. 2014. (ENG.). 42p. (J). (gr. 4-6). pap. 14.95 (978-1-927083-24-6(9), 7f88a446-7544-4c83-b5b0-b52e3e6c7da6) Fifth Hse. Pubs. CAN. Dist: Firefly Bks., Ltd.

Rojas, Emilio. Poemas de Amor de un Adolescente. 2003. (SPA.). 66p. (YA). 9.95 (978-968-5432-09-2(0)) EDITER'S Publishing Hse. MEX. Dist: EDITER'S Publishing Hse.

Rolando Elementary School. Children's Words of Wonder: A Poetry Anthology. 2008. 133p. pap. 13.95 (978-0-7414-4828-6(9)) Infinity Publishing.

Rondeno, Lisa. Fly, Boys & Girls Fly! 2012. 24p. pap. 17.99 (978-1-4772-5259-8(2)) AuthorHouse.

Rose, Dilys. When I Wear My Leopard Hat: Poems for Young Children. Allan, Gill, illus. 40p. pap. 6.95 (978-1-899827-70-1(6)) Scottish Children's Pr. GBR. Dist: Gatewood Pr.

Rose, Elizabeth. Daft Doggerels. 2013. 38p. pap. 12.99 (978-0-9851157-1-5(8)) Quillrunner Publishing LLC.

—Dotty Ditties. 2013. 36p. pap. 12.99 (978-0-9851157-2-2(6)) Quillrunner Publishing LLC.

Rosen, Michael. Centrally Heated Knickers. 2018. (Illus.). 160p. (J). (gr. 4-6). pap. 12.99 (978-0-14-138896-0(X)) Penguin Bks., Ltd. GBR. Dist: Independent Pubs. Group.

—A Great Big Cuddle: Poems for the Very Young. Riddell, Chris, illus. 2015. (ENG.). 80p. (J). (gr. -1-2). 19.99 (978-0-7636-8116-6(4)) Candlewick Pr.

—Nonsense. Mackie, Clare, illus. 2003. (ENG.). 48p. pap. (978-0-7500-2671-0(5), Wayland) Hachette Children's Group.

—Something's Drastic: Band 12/Copper (Collins Big Cat) Archbold, Tim, illus. 2007. (Collins Big Cat Ser.). (ENG.). 32p. (J). (gr. 2-4). pap. 10.99 (978-0-00-723077-8(X)) HarperCollins Pubs. Ltd. GBR. Dist: Independent Pubs. Group.

—What Is Poetry?: the Essential Guide to Reading & Writing Poems. Calder, Jill, illus. 2019. (ENG.). 208p. (J). (gr. 3-7). 15.99 (978-1-5362-0159-8(6)); pap. 8.99 (978-1-5362-0158-1(8)) Candlewick Pr.

—You Wait till I'm Older Than You! 2016. (Puffin Poetry Ser.). (Illus.). 128p. (J). (gr. 4-6). pap. 11.99 (978-0-14-137421-5(7)) Penguin Bks., Ltd. GBR. Dist: Independent Pubs. Group.

Rosen, Michael J. The Horse's Haiku. Fellows, Stan, illus. 2018. 48p. (J). (gr. 1-4). 17.99 (978-0-7636-8916-2(5)) Candlewick Pr.

Rosenberg, Liz. I Just Hope It's Lethal: Poems of Sadness, Madness, & Joy. 2005. (ENG.). 208p. (YA). (gr. 7-12). pap. 13.95 (978-0-618-56452-1(7), 460920, Clarion Bks.) HarperCollins Pubs.

Rosenblatt, Danielle. The Ant in the Cellar. Kirk, Jacqueline, illus. 2008. 127p. per. 19.95 (978-0-9788985-3-3(2)) W & B Pubs.

Rosenstock, Gabriel. I Met a Man from Artikelly: Verse for the Young & Young at Heart. Staunton, Mathew, illus. 2013. 96p. pap. (978-1-78201-032-6(7)) Evertype.

Ross, H. K., ed. & intro. Great American Story Poems. Ross, H. K., intro. 160p. (YA). (gr. 5-12). lib. bdg. 13.95 (978-0-87460-363-7(3)) Lion Bks.

Ross, Mandy. Wake up, Sleepy Head! Early Morning Poems. Kolanovic, Dubravka, illus. 2004. (Poems for the Young Ser.). 32p. (J). (gr. 2-3). pap. (978-1-904550-33-4(9)) Child's Play International Ltd.

Rowan, Charles A. I Like to Love. 2012. 28p. pap. 24.95 (978-1-4626-8110-5(7)) America Star Bks.

Roy, Brenda & Lantis, Lora. Night Noise. 2010. 40p. pap. 16.99 (978-1-4490-5426-7(9)) AuthorHouse.

Roza, Greg. Patterns in Poetry: Recognizing & Analyzing Poetic Form & Meter, 1 vol. (Math for the REAL World Ser.). 32p. 2010. (ENG.). (gr. 5-6). pap. 10.00 (978-1-4042-5146-5(4), 958f6876-3fb5-411e-84ee-dd3bd321fd6c) 2009. (gr. 4-5). 47.90 (978-1-60851-415-1(3)) 2004. (ENG., Illus.). (J). (gr. 5-6). lib. bdg. 28.93 (978-1-4042-2941-9(8), 8a7f09a5-770d-46ee-9aec-22a7ac2b168e) Rosen Publishing Group, Inc., The. (PowerKids Pr.).

Rubenz, Sima. Bringing up Parents: A Biography in Verse. 2011. 98p. 38.95 (978-1-258-08664-0(6)) Literary Licensing, LLC.

Ruddell, Deborah. A Whiff of Pine, a Hint of Skunk: A Forest of Poems. Rankin, Joan, illus. 2009. (ENG.). 40p. (J). (gr. -1-3). 18.99 (978-1-4169-4211-5(4), McElderry, Margaret K. Bks.) McElderry, Margaret K. Bks.

Russo, Joseph Anthony. For My Love Endures Forever: Poetry & Prose. 2013. 64p. (gr. -1). 20.43 (978-1-4669-9578-9(5)); pap. 10.43 (978-1-4669-9579-6(3)) Trafford Publishing.

Ryan, Christopher. The Moon & the Mouse. Tillson, Linda L., illus. 2011. 32p. pap. 24.95 (978-1-4626-1586-5(4)) America Star Bks.

Ryan, Ruth. In the Swamp, Oh Yeah, in the Swamp. Seahorse, Risa, illus. 2012. 54p. pap. (978-1-55483-922-3(X)) Insomniac Pr.

Rylant, Cynthia. Baby Face: A Book of Love for Baby. Goode, Diane, illus. 2008. (ENG.). 40p. (J). (gr. -1-3). 17.99 (978-1-4169-4909-1(7), Simon & Schuster/Paula Wiseman Bks.) Simon & Schuster/Paula Wiseman Bks.

S., LaTisha & Lee, Mykle. One Giant Leap: Love Poems. Blob, Anjali & Beverly-Patterson, Sylvia Dianne, eds. 2003. 72p. (YA). per. 8.95 (978-0-9744929-0-2(6)) Leeway Pubs.

Sack, Nancy. Puppies & Poems. Fuchs, Kaitlyn, illus. 2012. (ENG.). 32p. (J). 19.95 (978-1-4327-8470-6(6)) Outskirts Pr., Inc.

Salas, Laura Purdie. And Then There Were Eight: Poems about Space. rev. ed. 2016. (Poetry Ser.). (ENG.). 32p. (J). (gr. -1-2). pap. 8.10 (978-1-5157-6153-2(3), 135040, Capstone Pr.) Capstone.

—Bookspeak! Poems about Books. Bisaillon, Josée, illus. 2011. (ENG.). 32p. (J). (gr. -1-3). 17.99 (978-0-547-22300-1(5), 1061778, Clarion Bks.) HarperCollins Pubs.

—Catch Your Breath: Writing Poignant Poetry. 2015. (Writer's Notebook Ser.). (ENG., Illus.). 64p. (J). (gr. 4-8). lib. bdg. 35.32 (978-1-4914-5990-4(5), 128918) Capstone.

Sánchez Beras, César. Sapito Azul. Díaz, Raquel, illus. 2004. (SPA.). 32p. (J). (978-1-58018-056-6(6)) Cambridge BrickHouse, Inc.

Sandburg, Carl. Poetry for Kids: Carl Sandburg. Benzel, Kathryn, ed. Crawford, Robert, illus. 2017. (Poetry for Kids Ser.). (ENG.). 48p. (J). (gr. 3-8). 17.95 (978-1-63322-151-2(2), 224355, Moondance) Quarto Publishing Group USA.

Santana, Sr. Sabina Stella. Happy Ending Children's Stories, & More: Poems, Tongue-Twisters, Proverbs, & Brain-Teasers. 2008. 64p. pap. 13.50 (978-1-4303-1344-1(7)) Lulu Pr., Inc.

Santore, Charles. Night Before Christmas Board Book: The Classic Edition (the New York Times Bestseller) 2013. (Classic Edition Ser.). (ENG., Illus.). 24p. (J). (gr. -1). bds. 8.95 (978-1-60433-438-8(X), Applesauce Pr.) Cider Mill Pr. Bk. Pubs., LLC.

Sarkisov, Anton G. Curse of the Gemini. 2009. 102p. pap. 15.99 (978-1-4415-9560-7(0)) Xlibris Corp.

Sarreshtedari, Mehdi, narrated by. Hasht Ketab/ Sohrab Sepehri: Eight Books, 1DVD. 2005. (YA). 42.99 (978-1-933429-00-7(3)) Ketabe Gooya Publishing LLC.

Sattgast, L. J. The Rhyme Bible Storybook, 1 vol. Cleyet-Merle, Laurence, illus. 2012. (ENG.). 344p. (J). 22.99 (978-0-310-72602-9(6)) Zonderkidz.

Saunders, Tom. I Want to Go to the Moon. Nugent, Cynthia, illus. 2012. 32p. (J). (gr. -1-2). 16.95 (978-1-897476-56-7(6)) Simply Read Bks. CAN. Dist: Ingram Publisher Services.

Savino, Bob. Black Butterfly: Poems for a Muse. 2009. 72p. pap. 11.95 (978-1-59858-820-0(6)) Dog Ear Publishing, LLC.

Sayre, April Pulley. Go, Go, Grapes! A Fruit Chant. Sayre, April Pulley, photos by. 2012. (ENG., Illus.). 32p. (J). (gr. -1-3). 18.99 (978-1-4424-3390-8(6), Beach Lane Bks.) Beach Lane Bks.

Schaffer, Angel Boi. Blessed Child. 2004. (YA). per. 29.99 (978-0-9755352-0-2(X)) Angel's Boy Enterprises.

Schaub, Michelle. Fresh-Picked Poetry: A Day at the Farmers' Market. Huntington, Amy, illus. 2017. 32p. (J). (gr. -1-3). lib. bdg. 16.99 (978-1-58089-547-7(6)) Charlesbridge Publishing, Inc.

Schertle, Alice. Button Up! Wrinkled Rhymes. Mathers, Petra, illus. 2013. (ENG.). 40p. (J). (gr. -1-3). pap. 7.99 (978-0-544-02269-0(6), 1528491, Clarion Bks.) HarperCollins Pubs.

—A Lucky Thing: Poems & Paintings. Minor, Wendell, illus. 2006. 28p. (J). (gr. 4-8). reprint ed. 17.00 (978-1-4223-5417-9(2)) DIANE Publishing Co.

Schiffner, Frederick A. My Back Yard: Poems to Read to Your Children. Guenther, Kim, illus. 2004. 32p. (J). 14.95 (978-0-9765782-0-8(4)) Schiffner, Frederick A.

Schkade, Jonathan. Icky, Sticky, Hairy Scary Bible Stories: 60 Poems for Kids. Mourning, Tuesday, illus. 2010. 125p. (J). pap. 14.99 (978-0-7586-2671-4(1)) Concordia Publishing Hse.

Schmidt, Amy. Back to Dog-Gone School. Schmidt, Ron, illus. 2016. (Step into Reading Ser.). (ENG.). 32p. (J). (gr. -1-1). 5.99 (978-1-101-93511-8(1), Random Hse. Bks. for Young Readers) Random Hse. Children's Bks.

Schmidt, Gary D., ed. Poetry for Young People: Robert Frost. Sorensen, Henri, illus. 2008. (Poetry for Young People Ser.: 1). 48p. (J). (gr. 3). pap. 8.99 (978-1-4027-5475-3(2)) Sterling Publishing Co., Inc.

Scholastic. Twinkle, Twinkle Time for Bed (Rookie Toddler) 2009. (Rookie Toddler Ser.). (ENG.). 14p. (J). (gr. -1 — 1). bds. 6.95 (978-0-531-24544-6(6), Children's Pr.) Scholastic Library Publishing.

Schoonmaker, Frances, ed. Poetry for Young People: Henry Wadsworth Longfellow. Wallace, Chad, illus. 2010. (Poetry for Young People Ser.: 6). (ENG.). 48p. (J). (gr. 3). pap. 7.95 (978-1-4027-7292-4(0)) Sterling Publishing Co., Inc.

Schutz, Samantha. I Don't Want to Be Crazy. 2019. (ENG.). 288p. (J). (gr. 7-7). pap. 9.99 (978-1-338-33749-5(1)) Scholastic, Inc.

Scillian, Devin. Missile Toe: A Very Confused Christmas. Kelley, Marty, illus. 2017. (ENG.). 32p. (J). (gr. k-3). 16.99 (978-1-58536-371-1(5), 204328) Sleeping Bear Pr.

Searles, H. Louise. Sit Down little Sister & Let me Talk to You Vol. 1: The Voices of the Sparkletts. 84p. (Orig.). (J). pap. (978-0-9706187-0-2(0)) As Sparkle Speaks & Informs/ASSI.

Senchyne, Jonathan & Sikorskyj, Jerod, eds. Living Forge. 2003. (YA). per. 10.00 (978-1-932583-05-2(X)) Bates Jackson Engraving Co., Inc.

Seuss. Seuss-Isms! A Guide to Life for Those Just Starting Out... & Those Already on Their Way. 2018. (ENG.). 64p. (J). (gr. 2-12). 17.99 (978-0-525-58065-2(4), Random Hse. Bks. for Young Readers) Random Hse. Children's Bks.

—Seuss-Isms! a Guide to Life for Those Just Starting Out... & Those Already on Their Way. 2015. (Illus.). 64p. (J). (gr. 2-12). 10.99 (978-0-553-50841-3(5), Random Hse. Bks. for Young Readers) Random Hse. Children's Bks.

Shapiro, Phylis Stacey. Open Your Eyes. 2009. 40p. pap. 21.99 (978-1-4363-9029-3(X)) Xlibris Corp.

Shay, Cynthia K. 32 Libritos de Rimas: 32 Spanish Rhyming Flip Books. 2nd ed. 2008. (ENG., Illus.). 48p. (Orig.). (J). (gr. -1-2). pap. 9.95 (978-1-893447-01-1(4), Bilingual Language Materials) MAAT Resources, Inc.

Sheene, Chris. Painted Footsteps: A Creative Collection of Poetry. 2011. 152p. (gr. 4-6). 22.23 (978-1-4634-2459-6(0)); pap. 11.70 (978-1-4634-2460-2(4)) AuthorHouse.

Sherrard, Valerie. There's a Cow under My Bed, 1 vol. Jardine, David, illus. 2008. (ENG.). 32p. (J). (gr. 1-8). (978-1-897174-34-0(9)) Breakwater Bks., Ltd.

Shiner, Jack. Raking Leaves: Poems. 2004. 148p. (YA). per. 14.95 (978-0-922224-12-8(9)) Tonepoet Publishing.

Shiplett, Danaye. Paint My World with Colors. 2009. (ENG.). 36p. pap. 19.80 (978-0-557-06342-0(6)) Lulu Pr., Inc.

Shore, Diane Z. & Alexander, Jessica. This Is the Dream. Ransome, James, illus. 2005. (ENG.). 40p. (J). (gr. k-5). 16.99 (978-0-06-055519-1(X), Amistad) HarperCollins Pubs.

Shoulders, Michael. D Is for Dump Truck: A Construction Alphabet. Culotta, Kent, illus. 2019. (ENG.). 22p. (J). (gr. k-3). bds. 7.99 (978-1-5341-1035-9(6), 204721) Sleeping Bear Pr.

Showell, Isaiah, Sr. Faith Found New, 1. Nichols, Clayton, illus. 2004. 82p. (YA). per. 15.00 incl. audio compact disk (978-0-9754489-0-8(0)) Divine Intertwine Publishing.

Shurin, Masha. A Great Time: Children's Poems in Russian & English. Morris, Brian, ed. Barton, Alica, tr. Ginukov, Valentin, illus. 2007. (RUS & ENG.). 32p. (J). 19.95 (978-0-9792583-2-9(4)) White Stag Pr.

Shuttleworth, Cathie, illus. The Children's Treasury of Classic Poetry. 176p. (J). pap. (978-1-84322-143-2(8)) Bookmart Ltd.

Shuttleworth, Cathy, illus. Classic Poems for Children: Classic Verse from the Great Poets, Including Lewis Carroll, John Keats & Walt Whitman. 2011. (ENG.). 192p. (J). (gr. -1-12). 9.99 (978-1-84322-788-5(6)) Anness Publishing GBR. Dist: National Bk. Network.

Sidman, Joyce. Butterfly Eyes & Other Secrets of the Meadow. Krommes, Beth, illus. 2006. (ENG.). 48p. (J). (gr. 3-7). 17.99 (978-0-618-56313-5(X), 595784, Clarion Bks.) HarperCollins Pubs.

—Swirl by Swirl: Spirals in Nature. Krommes, Beth, illus. 2011. (ENG.). 40p. (J). (gr. -1-3). 19.99 (978-0-547-31583-6(X), 1415339, Clarion Bks.) HarperCollins Pubs.

—This Is Just to Say: Poems of Apology & Forgiveness. Zagarenski, Pamela, illus. 2007. (ENG.). 48p. (J). (gr. 5-7). 17.99 (978-0-618-61680-0(2), 546941, Clarion Bks.) HarperCollins Pubs.

—What the Heart Knows: Chants, Charms, & Blessings. Zagarenski, Pamela, illus. 2013. (ENG.). 80p. (YA). (gr. 7). 17.99 (978-0-544-10616-1(4), 1540739, Clarion Bks.) HarperCollins Pubs.

Siebert, Diane. Heartland. Minor, Wendell, illus. 2015. (ENG.). 32p. (J). (gr. -1-3). 17.95 (978-1-56792-535-7(9)) Godine, David R. Pub.

—Spring, Summer, Autumn, Winter. Burckhardt, Marc, illus. 2005. (J). (978-1-59336-299-7(4)); pap. (978-1-59336-300-0(1)) Mondo Publishing.

Silvano, Wendi. What Does the Wind Say? Delehanty, Joan M., illus. 2006. (ENG.). 32p. (J). (gr. -1-k). 15.95 (978-1-55971-954-4(0)) Cooper Square Publishing Llc.

Silverstein, Shel. Cayendo Hacia Arriba. 2011.Tr. of Falling Up. (SPA.). 178p. (J). 16.99 (978-1-933032-80-1(4)) Lectorum Pubns., Inc.

—A Light in the Attic. Silverstein, Shel, illus. 2005. (ENG., Illus.). 176p. (J). (gr. -1-3). 19.99 (978-0-06-025673-9(7), HarperCollins) HarperCollins Pubs.

Simmons, Kenneth. Mr Ken's Rhymes. 2007. 184p. per. 15.95 (978-0-595-44328-4(1)) iUniverse, Inc.

Simmons, Sukether Williams. Deep in My Soul Poems by Sukether Simmons. 2003. pap. 10.00 (978-0-9678182-1-4(4)) Shrewsbury Publishing.

Simms, B. D. A Place in My Heart. 2003. 38p. (YA). pap. 10.95 (978-0-7414-1681-0(6)) Infinity Publishing.

Simon, Margaret Gibson. Bayou Song. Cantrell, Anna, illus. Cancienne, Henry, photos by. 2018. (J). (978-1-946160-23-2(7)) Univ. of Louisiana at Lafayette Pr.

Simpson, Patricia Ann. The Twinkle Collection. 2006. 19.95 (978-0-9779662-4-0(0)) Creative Bk. Pubs.

Sin I Si Tou. A Child's Creation: Stories & Poems. 2012. (Illus.). 124p. pap. 41.19 (978-1-4678-7811-1(1)) AuthorHouse.

Singer, Marilyn. Echo Echo: Reverso Poems about Greek Myths. Masse, Josée, illus. 2016. 32p. (J). (gr. 1-4). 17.99 (978-0-8037-3992-5(3), Dial Bks) Penguin Young Readers Group.

—A Full Moon Is Rising. 2013. 31.95 (978-1-4301-1441-3(X)) Live Oak Media.

—A Full Moon Is Rising. Cairns, Julia, illus. 2011. (ENG.). 48p. (J). (gr. 1-18). 19.95 (978-1-60060-364-8(5)) Lee & Low Bks., Inc.

—Have You Heard about Lady Bird? Poems about Our First Ladies. Carpenter, Nancy, illus. 2018. (ENG.). 56p. (J). (gr. -1-3). 17.99 (978-1-4847-2660-0(X)) Disney Pr.

—A Stick Is an Excellent Thing: Poems Celebrating Outdoor Play. Pham, LeUyen, illus. 2012. (ENG.). 40p. (J). (gr. -1-3). 18.99 (978-0-547-12493-3(7), 1047756, Clarion Bks.) HarperCollins Pubs.

Singer, Marilyn & Cairns, Julia. A Full Moon Is Rising, 1 vol. 2011. (ENG.). 48p. (J). (gr. 1-8). pap. 12.95 (978-1-62014-196-0(5), leelowbooks) Lee & Low Bks., Inc.

Singh, Belveen. A Kaleidoscopic Life: Poems for the Childrens Heart. 2012. 52p. pap. 37.37 (978-1-4797-4534-0(0)) Xlibris Corp.

Singing Horse. 2003. (Gateways to the Sun Ser.). 32p. (J). (gr. 2-3). lib. bdg. 9.95 (978-1-58105-579-5(X)) Santillana USA Publishing Co., Inc.

Skinner, Ada & Wickes, Frances. A Child's Own Book of Verse, Book One (Yesterday's Classics) Petersham, Maud & Petersham, Miska, illus. 2006. (J). pap. 8.95 (978-1-59915-051-2(4)) Yesterday's Classics.

—A Child's Own Book of Verse, Book Three (Yesterday's Classics) Petersham, Maud & Petersham, Miska, illus. 2006. (J). pap. 8.95 (978-1-59915-053-6(0)) Yesterday's Classics.

—A Child's Own Book of Verse, Book Two (Yesterday's Classics) Petersham, Maud & Petersham, Miska, illus. 2006. (J). pap. 8.95 (978-1-59915-052-9(2)) Yesterday's Classics.

Sleith III, Eric. You & Me = We. 2009. 52p. pap. 8.99 (978-0-557-20616-2(2)) Lulu Pr., Inc.

Smith, Catherine. On My Knees. 2012. 32p. pap. 13.95 (978-1-4497-6143-1(7), WestBow Pr.) Author Solutions, LLC.

Smith, Ernest Lynnwood. Raw Poetry & Prose in Transition. 2005. 50p. 25.00 (978-0-9729154-2-7(7)) Smith, Ernest.

—The Road to Oneness. 2003. 56p. 25.00 (978-0-9729154-1-0(9)) Smith, Ernest.

Smith Meyer, Ruth. Tyson's Sad Bad Day. 2009. 30p. pap. (978-1-926676-43-2(2)) Word Alive Pr.

Smith, Michael. Relativity. Oliva, Octavio, illus. 2011. 30p. (J). (978-0-9799339-8-1(6)) East West Discovery Pr.

Smith, Michael & Oliva, Octavio. Relativity: Relatividad. Oliva, Octavio, illus. 2011. (SPA & ENG., Illus.). (J). (978-0-9832278-3-0(7)) East West Discovery Pr.

Smith, Simon. Reverdy Road. 2003. (Modern Poets Ser.). (ENG.). 252p. pap. (978-1-84471-027-0(0)) Salt Publishing.

Smith, Vivian. Along the Line. 2006. (ENG.). 132p. per. (978-1-84471-066-9(1)) Salt Publishing.

Sneed, Nancy Glascock. Grains of Sand: Beach Poems. 2013. 60p. pap. 23.95 (978-1-4497-9576-4(5), WestBow Pr.) Author Solutions, LLC.

Snyder, Betsy E. Haiku Baby. Snyder, Betsy E., illus. 2008. (Illus.). 14p. (J). (gr. k — 1). bds. 6.99 (978-0-375-84395-2(7), Random Hse. Bks. for Young Readers) Random Hse. Children's Bks.

Snyder, Edward B., et al. Through Tiger's Eyes. 2008. 24p. 24.00 (978-0-615-18259-9(3)) Cyber Tiger Pr.

Snyder, Max. The King with No Kingdom. Snyder, Max & Snyder, Ili, illus. 2013. 42p. 18.99 (978-0-9911512-9-5(1)) Mindstir Media.

So, Meilo, illus. Read a Rhyme, Write a Rhyme. 2009. (ENG.). 32p. (J). (gr. 1-4). pap. 8.99 (978-0-385-73727-2(0), Dragonfly Bks.) Random Hse. Children's Bks.

Sones, S. Stop Pretending: What Happened When My Sister Went Crazy. 2004. (YA). 15.65 (978-0-7569-4250-2(0)) Perfection Learning Corp.

Sorrentino, Dawn. Look at Me. 2012. 20p. pap. 10.49 (978-1-4678-6813-6(2)) AuthorHouse.

Soto, Gary. Neighborhood Odes. Diaz, David, illus. 2005. (ENG.). 80p. (J). (gr. 3-7). pap. 7.99 (978-0-15-205364-2(6), 1196154, Clarion Bks.) HarperCollins Pubs.

—Partly Cloudy: Poems of Love & Longing. 2009. (ENG., Illus.). 112p. (J). (gr. 7-12). 21.19 (978-0-15-206301-6(3)) Harcourt Children's Bks.

—Partly Cloudy: Poems of Love & Longing. 2012. (ENG., Illus.). 112p. (YA). (gr. 7). pap. 9.99 (978-0-547-57737-1(0), 1458546, Clarion Bks.) HarperCollins Pubs.

Soundprints Staff. If You're Happy & You Know It & Other Favorites. 2005. (Meet Mother Goose Ser.). (ENG., Illus.). 36p. (J). 14.95 (978-1-59069-213-4(6), MPD1108) Studio Mouse LLC.

—Little Miss Muffet & Other Favorites. 2005. (Meet Mother Goose Ser.). (Illus.). 36p. (J). 10.95 (978-1-59069-215-8(2)); bds. 14.95 incl. audio compact disk (978-1-59069-217-2(9)) Studio Mouse LLC.

Southwick Elementary Students. Soaring on the Wings of Eagles. 2008. 200p. per. 14.95 *(978-0-9800429-3-1(3))* Pen & Publish, LLC.

Soy de dos lugares: Poesia Juvenil: 6 Small Books. (Saludos Ser.: Vol. 2). (SPA.). (gr. 3-5). 31.00 *(978-0-7635-1767-0(4))* Rigby Education.

Soy de dos lugares: Poesia Juvenil: Big Book. (Saludos Ser.: Vol. 2). (SPA.). (gr. 3-5). 31.00 *(978-0-7635-3162-1(6))* Rigby Education.

Spanish Poetry Packs: Combo Pack. (SPA.). (gr. k-2). 61.62 *(978-1-56334-415-2(7))* CENGAGE Learning.

Spanish Poetry Packs: Jumbo Pack. (SPA.). (gr. k-2). 332.75 *(978-1-56334-414-5(9))* CENGAGE Learning.

Sparkle Little One! 2004. (Illus.). 28p. (J). 6.95 *(978-0-9746779-0-3(6))* Children of Color/The Indra Collection.

Sparshott, Francis. The Naming of the Beasts, 1 vol. 2003. (ENG., Illus.). 80p. pap. *(978-0-88753-055-5(9))* Black Moss Pr. CAN. Dist: LitDistCo.

Spensley, Joe. Home Thoughts from A Broader Perspective. 2005. 96p. (YA). per. 12.00 *(978-1-932496-26-0(2))* Penman Publishing, Inc.

Spicer, Maggee & Thompson, Richard. We'll All Go Exploring, 1 vol. LaFave, Kim, illus. 2003. (ENG.). 32p. (J). (gr. -1-k). 5.95 *(978-1-55041-732-6(0),* b1486790-a190-4d29-8f5d-05ff2b1c7934) Fitzhenry & Whiteside, Ltd. CAN. Dist: Firefly Bks., Ltd.

A Spicy-Herby Day, 6 vols.; set. 32p. (gr. 1-3). 26.50 *(978-0-7802-8044-1(X))* Wright Group/McGraw-Hill.

St. Pierre, Todd-Michael. A Woolly Mammoth on Amelia Street: Read Aloud Poems4Kids (and Grownups Too!) Douglas, Keith Cartoon Man, illus. 2003. 164p. (J). mass mkt. 15.95 *(978-0-9742602-0-4(7))* Prytania Pr.

Stedman, Edmund Clarence. Rip Van Winkle & His Wonderful Nap. 2011. 18p. pap. 11.99 *(978-1-4181-8988-4(X))* Michigan Publishing.

Steig, Jeanne. Alpha Beta Chowder. Steig, William, illus. 2016. (ENG.). 48p. (J). (gr. -1-3). 17.99 *(978-1-4814-4060-8(8),* Atheneum/Caitlyn Dlouhy Books) Simon & Schuster Children's Publishing.

Steinberg, D. J. First Grade, Here I Come! Bishop, Tracy, illus. 2016. (Here I Come! Ser.). 32p. (J). (gr. -1-1). pap. 5.99 *(978-0-448-48920-9(1),* Grosset & Dunlap) Penguin Young Readers Group.

—Grasshopper Pie & Other Poems. Sinnott, Adrian, illus. 2004. (Penguin Young Readers, Level 3 Ser.). 48p. (J). (gr. 1-3). pap. 4.99 *(978-0-448-43347-9(8),* Penguin Young Readers) Penguin Young Readers Group.

Stephens, Chris S. Rapping on the Window. Carpenter, Suzanne, illus. 2004. (ENG.). 48p. pap. 12.95 *(978-1-84323-360-2(6))* Beekman Bks., Inc.

Steps To Literacy Staff, compiled by. Bruce Lansky School Poems Collection of 2 Titles: Pro534. 2005. (ENG., Illus.). (J). pap. 29.95 *(978-1-59564-874-7(7))* Steps To Literacy, LLC.

Stevenson, Robert Louis. Block City. Kirk, Daniel, illus. 2005. (ENG.). 32p. (J). (gr. -1-3). 19.99 *(978-0-689-86964-8(9),* Simon & Schuster Bks. For Young Readers) Simon & Schuster Bks. For Young Readers.

—A Child's Garden of Verses: A Collection of Scriptures, Prayers & Poems. l.t. ed. 2005. 64p. pap. *(978-1-84637-255-1(0))* Echo Library.

—A Child's Garden of Verses: A Collection of Scriptures, Prayers & Poems. Fujikawa, Gyo, illus. 2007. 104p. (J). (gr. -1-2). 12.95 *(978-1-4027-5062-5(5))* Sterling Publishing Co., Inc.

—My Shadow. Sanchez, Sara, illus. 2016. (ENG.). 32p. (J). (gr. -1-k). 16.99 *(978-1-63450-178-1(0),* Sky Pony Pr.) Skyhorse Publishing Co., Inc.

—Poetry For Young People: Robert Louis Stevenson. 2003. cd-rom 19.00 *(978-0-931968-62-4(3))* Seltzer Bks.

—The Swing. Morstad, Julie, illus. 2012. 16p. (J). 8.95 *(978-1-897476-48-2(5))* Simply Read Bks. CAN. Dist: Ingram Publisher Services.

Stewart, Es. Who Made the Moon, Mummy? 2013. 24p. pap. 11.95 *(978-1-61897-799-1(7),* Strategic Bk. Publishing) Strategic Book Publishing & Rights Agency (SBPRA).

Storad, Conrad J. Don't Ever Cross That Road! An Armadillo Story. Jensen, Nathaniel P., illus. 2006. (Sonoran Desert Tails Ser.). 32p. (J). (gr. k-4). 15.95 *(978-1-891795-08-4(2))* RGU Group, The.

—Lizards for Lunch: A Roadrunner's Tale. 2009. (Sonoran Desert Tails Ser.). (Illus.). 32p. (J). (gr. k-4). 6.95 *(978-1-891795-00-8(7))* RGU Group, The.

Stroud, Bettye. The World's Wide Open. Cummings, Pat, illus. 2016. (J). *(978-0-689-84026-5(8))* Simon & Schuster Bks. For Young Readers.

Students of Fletcher Hills Elementary School. Many Voices: Where Dreams Take Flight II. 2007. 131p. pap. 13.95 *(978-0-7414-3748-8(1))* Infinity Publishing.

Stutman, Suzanne. If Your Nose Was Polka Dot Blue, What Would You Do? 2013. (ENG.). 185p. pap. 15.95 *(978-0-9648261-8-2(6),* b45a0827-813c-4a2d-a3d7-b10328254808) Medical Manor Bks.

Suarez, Nora & Gertz, Mercedes, concepts. When Words Dream, Cuando las Palabras Sueñan: Children's Poetry, Poesía Infantil. 1000th ed. 2006. (ENG & SPA., Illus.). 36p. lib. bdg. 25.95 *(978-0-9789544-0-6(8))* Hundred Ways LLC, A.

Sullivan, E. J. The Tennessee Night Before Christmas. Eldredge, Larry, illus. 2005. (Night Before Christmas Ser.). (J). (gr. -1-3). 12.95 *(978-1-58173-395-2(X))* Sweetwater Pr.

Sullivan, Ellen. The North Carolina Night Before Christmas. Eldredge, Ernie, illus. 2006. (J). *(978-1-60261-163-4(7))* Sweetwater Pr.

Sullivan, Ellen & Moore, Clement C. The Virginia Night Before Christmas. Franks, C. J., illus. 2005. (J). *(978-1-58173-392-1(5))* Sweetwater Pr.

Sullivan, Lisa, compiled by. Happy Days. 2013. (Jingle-Jangle Ser.). (ENG., Illus.). 10p. (J). (-k). bds. 9.95 *(978-1-61889-240-9(1))* AZ Bks. LLC.

Suresh, Shreyas. Joy! a Book of Poems. 2010. (ENG., Illus.). 62p. pap. 6.99 *(978-0-557-71631-9(4))* Lulu Pr., Inc.

Swarmer, Kristina, illus. Festival Poems, 1 vol. 2017. (Poems Just for Me Ser.). (ENG.). 32p. (gr. 3-3). 28.93 *(978-1-4994-8386-4(4),* 9085f1c8-7338-490a-a4f1-8cd6ffb64900, Windmill Bks.) Rosen Publishing Group, Inc., The.

Sycolin Creek Elementary School (Leesburg, Va.) Staff, contrib. by. Greatest Homework Excuse Book Ever. 2009. (Illus.). 25p. *(978-0-545-21329-5(0))* Scholastic, Inc.

Tagore, Rabindranath. Crescent Moon - Child Poems. 2007. 128p. per. 11.45 *(978-1-59462-738-5(X),* Bk. Jungle) Standard Publications, Inc.

The Talking Bumblebee. 2003. (J). *(978-1-56870-476-0(3))* Hewell Publishing.

Tall Tales, 9 vols., Set. 2004. (Tall Tales Ser.). (ENG., Illus.). 32p. (gr. 3-5). 54.64 *(978-0-7565-0712-1(X),* Compass Point Bks.) Capstone.

Tamblyn, Amber. Free Stallion: Poems. 2011. (ENG.). 96p. (YA). (gr. 8). pap. 6.99 *(978-1-4424-3087-7(7),* Simon & Schuster Bks. For Young Readers) Simon & Schuster Bks. For Young Readers.

Taplin, Sam. Christmas Poems. Luraschi, Anna, illus. 2006. (Christmas Poems Ser.). 95p. (J). 12.99 *(978-0-7945-1471-6(5),* Usborne) EDC Publishing.

—The Usborne Book of Poems for Little Children. Furukawa, Masumi, illus. 2007. 47p. (J). 11.99 *(978-0-7945-1426-6(X),* Usborne) EDC Publishing.

Taplin, Sam, compiled by. Poems for Young Children. 2005. (Poems for Young Children Ser.). 96p. (J). 14.95 *(978-0-7945-0924-8(X),* Usborne) EDC Publishing.

Tavakkoli, Aryan. Abc Animals Are My Friends. 2012. 60p. pap. 31.99 *(978-1-4691-3263-1(X))* Xlibris Corp.

Tavares, Gary Gene. Inspirational & Educational Poems. 2007. 60p. per. 9.95 *(978-0-595-45911-7(0))* iUniverse, Inc.

Taylor, Darlene. Thank You Notes from Grandma. 2013. 24p. pap. *(978-1-4602-0948-6(6))* FriesenPress.

Taylor, Michelle A. If Bees Rode Shiny Bicycles. 2003. (Illus.). 152p. (J). pap. *(978-0-7022-3382-1(X))* Univ. of Queensland Pr.

Teacher's Selection: Anthology of Eighth Grade Poetry. 2005. 158p. (YA). 16.95 *(978-1-883931-57-5(6))* Anthology of Poetry, Inc.

Temple, John. Collected Poems. 2003. (Salt Modern Poets). (ENG.). 196p. pap. *(978-1-876857-56-1(0))* Salt Publishing.

Thaxter, Celia. Poems for Children, by Celia Thaxter; with Illustrations by Miss a G Plympton. 2006. 164p. per. 18.99 *(978-1-4255-1219-4(4))* Michigan Publishing.

Thomas-Bakker, Oslyn. Poetry for Children. 2007. pap. 9.00 *(978-0-8059-8527-6(1))* Dorrance Publishing Co., Inc.

Thomas, Joyce Carol. The Blacker the Berry: A Coretta Scott King Award Winner. Cooper, Floyd, illus. 2008. (ENG.). 32p. (J). (gr. -1-3). 17.99 *(978-0-06-025375-2(4),* Amistad) HarperCollins Pubs.

Thomas, Mark Lawton. My Lemonade Stand Can't Stand Me. Hoke, Jeenhyun, illus. 114p. 2013. pap. 9.99 *(978-1-935711-23-0(7))* 2012. (ENG.). (J). pap. 9.99 *(978-1-935711-22-3(9))* Peak City Publishing, LLC.

Thomas, Patricia. Nature's Paintbox: A Seasonal Gallery of Art & Verse. Orback, Craig, illus. 2007. (Millbrook Picture Books Ser.). (ENG.). 32p. (J). (gr. 2-4). lib. bdg. 16.95 *(978-0-8225-6807-0(1),* Millbrook Pr.) Lerner Publishing Group.

Thompson, David. Poems & Illustrations for Preschool Children. 2013. 40p. pap. 19.57 *(978-1-4669-7886-7(4))* Trafford Publishing.

Thornton, Geoffrey. The Illustrated Wynken, Blynken, & Nod. 2007. (Illus.). 28p. per. 19.95 *(978-1-59858-373-1(5))* Dog Ear Publishing, LLC.

Thouw, Jennifer. Under the Rainbow. 2010. 136p. pap. 71.99 *(978-1-4535-0341-6(2))* Xlibris Corp.

Thunder from the Earth, 6, Pack. (Greetings Ser.: Vol. 2). (gr. 3-5). 31.00 *(978-0-7635-2062-5(4))* Rigby Education.

Tize W. Clark. Twin Poems. 2012. (ENG.). per. 24.95 *(978-0-9766770-1-7(6))* BAU Publishing Group.

To Light A Match. 2004. (Illus.). 88p. (YA). spiral bd. 11.95 *(978-1-931084-37-6(8));* per. 11.95 *(978-1-931084-10-9(6))* Balloon Magic.

Toland, Mischa P., creator. She Ain't Angry for Nothin' Intervention & Behavior Modification Curriculum. 2008. (ENG.). 160p. (YA). per. 30.00 *(978-0-9754191-3-0(0))* Morals & Values Pr.

Tolkien, Michael G. R. Wish. 2010. (Illus.). 132p. pap. 38.49 *(978-1-4490-9652-6(2))* AuthorHouse.

Tracy, Kathleen. The Life & Times of Homer. 2004. (Biography from Ancient Civilizations Ser.). (Illus.). 48p. (J). (gr. 4-8). lib. bdg. 29.95 *(978-1-58415-260-6(5))* Mitchell Lane Pubs.

Trainer, Maria T. Kids Are Gifts from Heaven, 1 vol. 2009. 108p. pap. 19.95 *(978-1-4489-8381-0(9))* America Star Bks.

Trueit, Trudi Strain. What Is Poetry? 2014. (Name That Text Type! Ser.). (ENG., Illus.). 32p. (J). (gr. 2-4). lib. bdg. 26.65 *(978-1-4677-3667-1(8),* e49046e2-685f-4305-84a6-a34759e06415, Lerner Pubns.) Lerner Publishing Group.

Truswell, P. Diane. Star Climber. 2008. 36p. pap. 21.99 *(978-1-4363-2546-2(3))* Xlibris Corp.

Tuggle, Le Ann S. Let's Go Fishing. 2006. (Illus.). 32p. (J). (gr. -1). 16.95 *(978-0-9770912-7-0(9),* Blue Marble Bks.) Sphinx Publishing.

Tully, Sandra M. Cherry Pie Charlie & More Poems for Children. Sadowski, Jeff, illus. 2007. (J). 15.00 *(978-1-933556-86-4(2))* Publishers' Graphics, L.L.C.

Turner, Queen of England Patrenia. Queen Patreniaila - A Canadian Story Poem. Turner, Keeng of England Troyius, ed. 2015. (Illus.). pap. *(978-0-578-18000-7(6))* Royalty Patrenia Turner Publications.

Tuttle, Justin J. If My Toes Could Talk. 2009. (Illus.). 20p. pap. 12.99 *(978-1-4389-3953-7(1))* AuthorHouse.

Tuwim, Julian. Locomotive. 2017. (Illus.). 48p. (J). (gr. -1-5). 16.95 *(978-0-500-65097-4(7),* 565097) Thames & Hudson.

Twain, Mark, pseud. tr. Slovenly Peter. Kredel, Fritz, illus. 2013. (Calla Editions Ser.). (ENG.). 48p. (gr. 5). 20.00 *(978-1-60660-048-1(6),* 600486) Dover Pubns., Inc.

Tyler, Michael. The Skin You Live In. Csicsko, David Lee, illus. 2005. (ENG.). 32p. (J). (gr. k-2). 15.95 *(978-0-9759580-0-1(3))* Chicago Children's Museum.

Tyson, Ian. La Primera: The Story of Wild Mustangs. Halvorson, Adeline, illus. 2009. 32p. (J). (gr. 2-4). 20.95 *(978-0-88776-863-7(6),* Tundra Bks.) Tundra Bks. CAN. Dist: Penguin Random Hse. LLC.

Uhlig, Elizabeth. Children Just Like You. Uhlig, Elizabeth, illus. 2007. (Illus.). (J). pap. 12.95 *(978-0-9786745-6-4(1))* Marble Hse. Editions.

Updike, John. A Child's Calendar, 4 bks. Hyman, Trina Schart, illus. 2004. (J). (gr. k-4). pap. 37.95 incl. audio *(978-1-59112-473-3(5))* Live Oak Media.

The Valentine Poem Book. 10p. (J). bds. *(978-2-89393-865-3(5))* Phidal Publishing, Inc./Editions Phidal, Inc.

Van Camp, Richard. We Sang You Home, 1 vol. Flett, Julie, illus. 2016. (ENG.). 24p. (J). (gr. -1 — 1). bds. 10.95 *(978-1-4598-1178-2(X))* Orca Bk. Pubs. USA.

—Welcome Song for Baby / ni Nikamon 'Tawâw Nipepîmis', 1 vol. Collins, Mary Cardinal, tr. 2018. (7 Generations Ser.). Orig. Title: Welcome Song for Baby. (CRE & ENG., Illus.). 24p. (J). (gr. -1-k). 6.95 *(978-1-4598-2010-4(X))* Orca Bk. Pubs. USA.

Van De Luecht, Susan. Children's Poetry - Dreams & Visons. 2005. 58p. (J). pap. 20.73 *(978-1-4116-6469-2(8))* Lulu Pr., Inc.

VanAllen, Cindy. Animal ABC's: A little book to make you glad, Hot off the press, from Nana¿s Pad. 2008. 32p. pap. 24.95 *(978-1-60703-255-7(4))* America Star Bks.

Vance, Rodney. De'Monte Love. 2007. (Illus.). (J). per. 17.99 *(978-1-933156-15-6(5),* Visikid Bks.) GSVQ Publishing.

VanDerwater, Amy Ludwig. With My Hands: Poems about Making Things. Fancher, Lou & Johnson, Steve, illus. 2018. (ENG.). 32p. (J). (gr. -1-3). 17.99 *(978-0-544-31340-8(2),* 1581615, Clarion Bks.) HarperCollins Pubs.

VanHecke, Susan. Under the Freedom Tree. Ladd, London, illus. 2019. 32p. (J). (gr. 1-4). pap. 7.99 *(978-1-58089-551-4(4))* Charlesbridge Publishing, Inc.

VanTine, Karl. Sweet Dreams: A Lullaby. 2012. 16p. pap. 17.99 *(978-1-4685-6477-8(3))* AuthorHouse.

Varikyan, Arpine & Wallace, Dejuanna. From the Inside Out. 2004. (ENG.). 80p. (YA). per. *(978-0-595-33149-9(1))* iUniverse, Inc.

Vaughan, Tom. A Few Leaves: Children's Poems & Pictures from Terezin & Osvtim. 2008. (ENG.). 104p. per. 34.99 *(978-1-4257-0692-0(4))* Xlibris Corp.

VeJauan, Sherea. Realistically Speaking: Speaking What's Real... Keeping What's Holy. 2003. 85p. (YA). per. 14.99 *(978-0-9727874-0-6(2))* Realistically Speaking Publishing Co.

VERSE! Poetry for Young Children: Lessons for 4 to 6 Year-olds. 2006. spiral bd. *(978-0-9727635-9-2(7))* Univ. of Arizona, Poetry Ctr., Arizona Board of Regents.

Vestergaard, Hope. Digger, Dozer, Dumper. Slonim, David, illus. (ENG.). (J). 2018. 32p. (gr. -1-3). 5.99 *(978-0-7636-9969-7(1))* 2016. 30p. (-k). bds. 7.99 *(978-0-7636-8893-6(2))* Candlewick Pr.

—Digger, Dozer, Dumper. 2018. lib. bdg. 14.75 *(978-0-606-40901-8(7))* Turtleback.

Vigil, Florida. A Child's Imagination: Childhood Poems. 2012. 36p. 24.95 *(978-1-4575-1255-1(6));* pap. 16.95 *(978-1-4575-1430-2(3))* Dog Ear Publishing, LLC.

von Rosenberg, Byron. O Christmas Treed. 2006. 30p. (J). 10.95 *(978-0-9759858-5-4(X))* Red Mountain Creations.

Wahid, Kelli. As Children Grow: Poetry for Children. 2011. 86p. pap. 19.95 *(978-1-4560-6692-5(7))* America Star Bks.

Walker, Alice. There Is a Flower at the Tip of My Nose Smelling Me. Vitale, Stefano, illus. 2006. (ENG.). 32p. (J). (gr. -1-3). 17.99 *(978-0-06-057080-4(6),* HarperCollins) HarperCollins Pubs.

Walker, Kennesha M. A Word in Due Season. 2003. 47p. (YA). pap. 9.95 *(978-0-7414-1555-4(0))* Infinity Publishing.

Walker, Sally M. Earth Verse: Haiku from the Ground Up. Grill, William, illus. 2018. (ENG.). 48p. (J). (gr. 2-4). 17.99 *(978-0-7636-7512-7(1))* Candlewick Pr.

Walking: Individual Title Six-Packs. (Literatura 2000 Ser.). (gr. 2-3). 33.00 *(978-0-7635-0215-7(4))* Rigby Education.

Walsh, Russ. Snack Attack & Other Poems for Developing Fluency in Beginning Readers. 2011. pap. 10.95 *(978-0-7414-6431-6(4))* Infinity Publishing.

Ward, Jean Elizabeth. Rabbits Too. 2008. 114p. pap. 18.99 *(978-1-4357-3329-9(0))* Lulu Pr., Inc.

Ward, Jean Elizabeth, Poet Laureate. A BARBARA ANNE BUSHY TALE: Book I. 2008. 101p. pap. 18.99 *(978-1-4357-3223-0(5))* Lulu Pr., Inc.

—A BARBARA ANNE BUSHY TALE Book III. 2008. 148p. pap. 22.50 *(978-1-4357-3216-2(2))* Lulu Pr., Inc.

Warrick, Natalie. A Mighty Warrior Is the Ant. 2013. 52p. pap. 9.99 *(978-0-9886315-7-1(1))* CHB Media.

Washington, Joy Louise. The Gingerbread House. 2009. 12p. pap. 8.99 *(978-1-4389-2805-0(X))* AuthorHouse.

Washington, Peter, ed. Eat, Drink, & Be Merry: Poems about Food & Drink. 2003. (Everyman's Library Pocket Poets Ser.). (ENG.). 256p. 14.95 *(978-1-4000-4023-0(X),* Everyman's Library) Knopf Doubleday Publishing Group.

Waters, Fiona. Fire & Stone, Wind & Tide: Poems About the Elements. Corfield, Robin Bell, illus. 2006. 43p. (gr. 4-8). reprint ed. 24.00 *(978-1-4223-5595-4(0))* DIANE Publishing Co.

Watkins, Bessie. Presidents in Profile: Three Views of One Face. 2003. (Illus.). 60p. (J). per. 11.95 *(978-0-9728674-1-2(4))* Dr Monica Y Jackson Education & Design Services.

Watson Bain, E., ed. A Poetry Book for Boys & Girls. 2014. (ENG.). 196p. pap. 16.99 *(978-1-107-44062-3(9))* Cambridge Univ. Pr.

Webb, Sarah. A Sailor Went to Sea, Sea, Sea: Favourite Rhymes from an Irish Childhood. McCarthy, Steve, illus. 2017. (ENG.). 64p. (J). 27.00 *(978-0-84717-794-0(8))* O'Brien Pr., Ltd., The IRL. Dist: Casemate Pubs. & Bk. Distributors, LLC.

Webster, Keith. Why Can't My Turtle Be a Ninja? 2006. 160p. per. 12.95 *(978-1-59858-193-5(7))* Dog Ear Publishing, LLC.

Weil, Jennifer. Marvin's Lump. 2006. (J). 15.95 *(978-1-889743-47-9(X))* Robbie Dean Pr.

Weinert, Stella, compiled by. Come on Clouds, Fly Away! 2013. 64p. pap. *(978-1-926635-80-4(9))* Adlibbed, Ltd.

Weitl, Joe. My Book of Poems to Enjoy: Volume 1, 1 vol. 2009. 92p. pap. 16.95 *(978-1-61582-540-0(1))* PublishAmerica, Inc.

Wells, Philip. The Alien Guide from Inner Space: And Other Poems. 2013. (ENG.). 80p. pap. *(978-1-84471-816-0(6))* Salt Publishing.

West, Lorraine, illus. I Like You but I Love Me. 2006. 36p. (J). pap. 12.95 *(978-0-9768674-1-8(9))* Hip Hop Schl. Hse.

Wethington, Constance. Mystic Imaginations. 2008. 137p. pap. 24.95 *(978-1-60563-807-2(2))* America Star Bks.

Whamsby, Dawud. A Picnic of Poems: In Allah's Green Garden. 2011. (ENG., Illus.). 44p. (J). (gr. k). 22.95 *(978-0-86037-444-2(0))* Kube Publishing Ltd. GBR. Dist: Consortium Bk. Sales & Distribution.

Wheeler, David & Twigg, Natalie. My Pirate Grandad. 2013. (Illus.). 26p. pap. *(978-0-9573384-5-6(7))* Red Axe Bks.

Wheeler, Tonika Yvonne. Damaged Goods. Attaway, Anelda, ed. Edwards, Cedric, illus. 2013. 100p. pap. 13.99 *(978-0-9892656-0-7(9))* Jazzy Kitty Pubns.

White, Eleanor Dantzler. Sincere Sentiments. 2003. 180p. (YA). per. *(978-0-9679516-2-1(3))* Full Effect Gospel Ministries, Inc.

Whitman, Walt. Nothing but Miracles. 2003. (ENG., Illus.). 32p. (J). (gr. -1-3). 15.95 *(978-0-7922-6143-8(7),* National Geographic Children's Bks.) National Geographic Society.

Whittingham, Brian. Septimus Pitt & the Grumbleoids, 22 vols. Sinclair, Mandy, illus. 2007. (ENG.). 46p. (J). 17.95 *(978-1-905222-81-0(5),* 6ad3493d-bd75-480a-84c9-23c996ad6c41) Luath Pr. Ltd. GBR. Dist: Midpoint Trade Bks., Inc.

Whittington, Phillip. What a Hullabaloo! 2009. 56p. pap. 10.49 *(978-1-4389-9219-8(X))* AuthorHouse.

Whyman, Jennifer E., text. Heavenly Blessings: Baby's Book of Bible Blessing/Baby's Book of Bible Promises. 2008. (Land of Milk & Honey Ser.). (Illus.). 32p. (J). (gr. -1-k). bds. 9.99 *(978-1-4347-9945-6(X))* Cook, David C.

Wilson, Gabriella S. Anything on Earth Poems: Children's Poetry. l.t. ed. 2005. (Illus.). 34p. (J). per. 9.99 *(978-1-59879-083-2(8))* Lifevest Publishing, Inc.

Willey, Sarah Jo. Lullaby for Birds. 2012. 24p. pap. 17.99 *(978-1-4772-8134-5(7))* AuthorHouse.

Williams, Adele Knight. What's in a Smile. 2010. 28p. pap. 16.95 *(978-1-4490-5638-4(5))* AuthorHouse.

Williams, Julie. Escaping Tornado Season: A Story in Poems. 2004. 272p. (J). 16.89 *(978-0-06-008640-4(8),* HarperTeen) HarperCollins Pubs.

Williams, Laura M. Why Was Jesus Born. 2013. 18p. pap. 9.99 *(978-1-62839-346-0(7))* Salem Author Services.

Williams, Lyndsay. NonSense! It's Banana Cheese! 2007. (ENG.). 84p. per. 19.95 *(978-1-4241-6736-4(1))* America Star Bks.

Williams, Vera B. Amber Was Brave, Essie Was Smart. Williams, Vera B., illus. 2004. (Illus.). 17.00 *(978-0-7569-3181-0(9))* Perfection Learning Corp.

Williamson, Greg. The Hole Story of Kirby the Sneak & Arlo the True, 1 vol. Bowes, Brian, illus. 2015. (ENG.). 128p. pap. 15.00 *(978-1-904130-83-3(6))* Waywiser Pr., The GBR. Dist: SPD-Small Pr. Distribution.

Wilmot, Rod. The Meal of Magic Cards, 1 vol. 2003. (ENG., Illus.). 41p. pap. *(978-0-88753-010-4(9))* Black Moss Pr. CAN. Dist: LitDistCo.

Wilson, Adele Tolley. Plum Gum & Other Chunk Poems: Teacher Tested Kid Approved Poems for Building Fluency Through Phonics. 2004. 112p. 11.95 *(978-1-4140-5443-8(2))* AuthorHouse.

Wilson, Karma. Bear Hugs: Romantically Ridiculous Animal Rhymes. Watts, Suzanne, illus. 2007. (ENG.). 32p. (J). (gr. -1-3). 7.99 *(978-1-4169-4958-9(5),* McElderry, Margaret K. Bks.) McElderry, Margaret K. Bks.

Wilson, Murray. Goofus & Other Silly Poems, 1 vol. Morrison, Tyler, illus. 2010. 28p. pap. 24.95 *(978-1-4489-6288-4(9))* PublishAmerica, Inc.

Wilson, Vicky, ed. Touch Wood. 2012. (Illus.). 68p. pap. *(978-1-904662-16-7(1))* Categorical Bks.

Winborne, Stephanie. A Peace of Heaven on Earth. 2009. 70p. pap. 15.99 *(978-1-4500-1586-8(7))* Xlibris Corp.

Wing, Natasha. The Night Before Father's Day. Wummer, Amy, illus. 2012. (Night Before Ser.). 32p. (J). (gr. -1-k). pap. 5.99 *(978-0-448-45871-7(3),* Grosset & Dunlap) Penguin Young Readers Group.

—The Night Before Father's Day. 2012. (Night Before Ser.). lib. bdg. 14.75 *(978-0-606-26073-2(0))* Turtleback.

—The Night Before Mother's Day. Wummer, Amy, illus. 2010. (Night Before Ser.). 32p. (J). (gr. -1-k). 4.99 *(978-0-448-45213-5(8),* Grosset & Dunlap) Penguin Young Readers Group.

—The Night Before New Year's. Wummer, Amy, illus. 2009. (Night Before Ser.). (ENG.). 32p. (J). (gr. -1-k). pap. 5.99 *(978-0-448-45212-8(X),* Grosset & Dunlap) Penguin Young Readers Group.

Winners: Poems & Stories, 2003 Spring Writing Contest. 2003. (J). 5.00 *(978-0-9702646-2-6(3));* (YA). 5.00 *(978-0-9702646-3-3(1))* New Sweden Pr.

Winters, Kari-Lynn & Sherritt-Fleming, Lori. Hungry for Math: Poems to Munch On, 1 vol. Collins, Peggy, illus. 2014. (ENG.). 32p. (J). (gr. 1-4). 18.95 *(978-1-55455-307-5(5),* aac6e31d-b110-4a20-92b4-40aa93d7223b) Fitzhenry & Whiteside, Ltd. CAN. Dist: Firefly Bks., Ltd.

—Hungry for Science: Poems to Crunch On, 1 vol. Collins, Peggy, illus. 2018. (ENG.). 32p. (J). (gr. k-3). 18.95 *(978-1-55455-396-9(2),* 50a381d4-f6e4-47a0-ad42-a243e4fd7137) Fitzhenry & Whiteside, Ltd. CAN. Dist: Firefly Bks., Ltd.

Winters, Kay. Did You See What I Saw? Weston, Martha, illus. 2015. 32p. pap. 7.00 *(978-1-61003-529-3(1))* Center for the Collaborative Classroom.

—Voices of Ancient Egypt. 2009. (Illus.). 32p. (J). (gr. 3-7). 6.95 *(978-1-4263-0400-2(5),* National Geographic Kids) Disney Publishing Worldwide.

Wissinger, Tamera Will. There Was an Old Lady Who Gobbled a Skink. Bermejo, Ana, illus. 2016. (ENG.). 36p. (J). (gr. -1-k). 16.99 *(978-1-63220-428-8(2),* Sky Pony Pr.) Skyhorse Publishing Co., Inc.

Witmer, Edith. Dancing Buttercups: Poems for Little Children. 2003. (Illus.). 83p. (gr. -1-7). 4.95 *(978-0-7399-2303-0(X),* 2183) Rod & Staff Pubs., Inc.

Wodehouse, Pelham Grenville. William Tell Told Again - Illustrated in Color. Philip Dadd, illus. 2009. 76p. pap. 14.95 *(978-1-60386-208-0(0),* Watchmaker Publishing) Wexford College Pr.

Wolff, Pat. Noah's Faith: A Children's Poem. 2007. (Illus.). (J). bds. 10.99 *(978-0-9788324-2-1(6))* Playing Pig Pr.

Wondrous Tales of Wicked Winston. (illus.). pap. *(978-0-920236-18-5(9))* Annick Pr., Ltd.

Wong, Janet S. Twist: Yoga Poems. Paschkis, Julie, illus. 2007. (ENG.). 40p. (J). (gr. 2-5). 19.99 *(978-0-689-87394-2(8),* McElderry, Margaret K. Bks.) McElderry, Margaret K. Bks.

Wood, Robert Williams. How to Tell the Birds from the Flowers. 2011. 54p. 16.99 *(978-1-61720-185-1(5));* pap. 6.99 *(978-1-61720-186-8(3))* Wilder Pubns., Corp.

Woodbury, Karl. England Is Truly a Magical Place. 2008. (Illus.). 96p. per. *(978-1-84748-191-7(4))* Athena Pr.

Woodson, Jacqueline. Brown Girl Dreaming. l.t. ed. (ENG.). 2018. (J). pap. 15.99 *(978-1-4328-5042-5(3))* 2017. 412p. 24.95 *(978-1-4328-4315-1(X))* Cengage Gale.

—Brown Girl Dreaming. (ENG., Illus.). (J). (gr. 5). 2016. 368p. pap. 10.99 *(978-0-14-751582-7(3),* Puffin Books) 2014. 352p. 18.99 *(978-0-399-25251-8(7),* Nancy Paulsen Books) Penguin Young Readers Group.

—Brown Girl Dreaming. 2016. (ENG., Illus.). 368p. (J). (gr. 5). 22.10 *(978-0-606-39310-2(2))* Turtleback.

Woolf-Wade, Sarah J. Nightsong. 2003. (Illus.). 114p. (YA). per. 12.00 *(978-1-930648-45-6(6),* 207-832-6665) Goose River Pr.

Wooten, Terry. When the Bear Came Back: The Whole Story. Lechler, Louan, illus. 2006. (J). per. 9.49 *(978-1-893972-27-8(5))* Wordsmith Pr.

Word, Sharon. The Word Is Alphabet Poems. 2011. 33p. (J). 13.99 *(978-1-935906-29-2(1))* Intermedia Publishing Group.

Wright, Alice & Bridges, LaVon. Alaska Animals We Love You: Chants & Poems for Children. 2005. (J). 16.95 *(978-1-59433-028-5(X),* Publishing Consultants) Publication Consultants.

Xinran, Xinran, et al. Motherbridge of Love. Masse, Josée, illus. 2007. (ENG.). 32p. (J). (gr. -1-5). 16.99 *(978-1-84686-047-8(4))* Barefoot Bks., Inc.

Yardman, Barbara M. Crawl, Fly or Run Book. 2009. 60p. pap. 23.99 *(978-1-4389-0872-4(5))* AuthorHouse.

Yeats, W. B. The Moon Spun Round: W. B. Yeats for Children. Doody, Noreen, ed. Macdonald, Shona Shirley, illus. 2016. (ENG.). 64p. 30.00 *(978-1-84717-738-4(7))* O'Brien Pr., Ltd., The IRL. Dist: Casemate Pubs. & Bk. Distributors, LLC.

Yolen, Jane. The Alligator's Smile: And Other Poems. Stemple, Jason, photos by. 2016. (ENG., Illus.). 32p. (J). (gr. 3-6). 19.99 *(978-1-4677-5575-7(3),* 128e7ad1-4c39-4355-a7ed-70e6e7ba7e2b); E-Book 30.65 *(978-1-5124-1110-2(8))* Lerner Publishing Group. (Millbrook Pr.).

—An Egret's Day. Stemple, Jason, photos by. 2010. (ENG., Illus.). 32p. (J). (gr. 4-7). 17.95 *(978-1-59078-650-5(5),* Wordsong) Highlights Pr., c/o Highlights for Children, Inc.

—Snow, Snow: Winter Poems for Children. Stemple, Jason, photos by. 2005. (ENG., Illus.). 32p. (J). (gr. 4-7). pap. 12.95 *(978-1-59078-346-7(8),* Astra Young Readers) Astra Publishing Hse.

—Thunder Underground. Masse, Josée, illus. 2017. (ENG.). 32p. (J). (gr. k-4). 17.99 *(978-1-59078-936-0(9),* Wordsong) Highlights Pr., c/o Highlights for Children, Inc.

—Water Music: Poems for Children. Stemple, Jason, photos by. 2003. (ENG., Illus.). 40p. (J). (gr. 4-7). pap. 9.99 *(978-1-59078-251-4(8),* Wordsong) Highlights Pr., c/o Highlights for Children, Inc.

Yolen, Jane & Dotlich, Rebecca Kai. Grumbles from the Forest: Fairy-Tale Voices with a Twist. Mahurin, Matt, illus. 2013. (ENG.). 40p. (J). (gr. 2-5). 16.99 *(978-1-59078-867-7(2),* Wordsong) Highlights Pr., c/o Highlights for Children, Inc.

Young, Wanda. Joyous Poems for Children. 2007. (YA). per. *(978-1-933594-66-8(7))* FBC Pubns. & Printing.

Yungul, Elizabeth. I'm Looking from My Window — I'm Looking from My Room. 2009. 48p. pap. 17.49 *(978-1-4343-7160-7(3))* AuthorHouse.

Zager, Jack. Where Do the Tigers Go? A Collection of Children's Poetry. 2004. (Illus.). 32p. (J). lib. bdg. 9.95 *(978-1-930580-57-2(6),* Luminary Media Group) Pine Orchard, Inc.

Zavyalov, Diana. The Little Humpy: Derivative Translation from Russian Fairy Tale by Ershov. 2012. 56p. pap. 24.20 *(978-1-4669-6955-1(5))* Trafford Publishing.

Zephaniah, Benjamin. Talking Turkeys. (ENG., Illus.). 96p. (J). 9.95 *(978-0-14-036330-2(0))* Penguin Bks., Ltd. GBR. Dist: Trafalgar Square Publishing.

—Wicked World! 2022. (ENG., Illus.). 96p. (J). (gr. 3-6). pap. 9.99 *(978-0-14-130683-4(1),* Puffin) Penguin Bks., Ltd. GBR. Dist: Independent Pubs. Group.

Zeringue, Dona. I Am I. Zeringue, Dona, illus. (Illus.). 32p. (Orig.). (YA). (gr. 6-12). pap. 7.50 *(978-1-882913-02-2(7))* Thornton Publishing.

Zimmerman, Mary Joyce. Good Morning Baby! Hartzler, Maria, illus. 2013. 48p. (J). pap. *(978-0-7399-2458-7(3))* Rod & Staff Pubs., Inc.

Zobel-Nolan, Allia. Smelly Feet Sandwich: And Other Silly Poems. Leake, Kate, illus. 2008. 22p. (J). (gr. -1-2). 7.95 *(978-1-58925-836-5(3))* Tiger Tales.

100 Verses about Laura Ingalls Wilder. 2005. (YA). 9.99 *(978-0-9765951-0-6(9))* Little Hse. Site Tours LLC.

POETRY—COLLECTIONS

see also American Poetry—Collections; English Poetry—Collections

Adedjouma, Davida. The Palm of My Heart: Poetry by African American Children, 1 vol. Christie, R. Gregory, illus. 2013. (ENG.). 32p. (J). (gr. 1-6). pap. 10.95 *(978-1-880000-76-2(8),* 85317516-6487-400d-9d23-ac907fc2a2eb) Lee & Low Bks., Inc.

Akister, Finola, et al, selected by. Sea Poems & Space Poems. 2008. (Illus.). 32p. (J). pap. 10.95 *(978-1-59646-611-1(1))* Dingles & Co.

—Sports Poems & Mouse Poems. 2008. (Illus.). 32p. (J). pap. 10.95 *(978-1-59646-619-7(7))* Dingles & Co.

Akister, Finola, et al. Sea Poems & Space Poems. 2008. (Illus.). 32p. (J). lib. bdg. 23.65 *(978-1-59646-610-4(3))* Dingles & Co.

—Sports Poems & Mouse Poems. 2008. (Illus.). 32p. (J). lib. bdg. 23.65 *(978-1-59646-618-0(9))* Dingles & Co.

Andrew, Moira, et al, selected by. Night Poems & Ghost Poems. 2008. (Illus.). 32p. (J). pap. 10.95 *(978-1-59646-623-4(5))* Dingles & Co.

Andrew, Moira, et al. Night Poems & Ghost Poems. 2008. (Illus.). 32p. (J). lib. bdg. 23.65 *(978-1-59646-622-7(7))* Dingles & Co.

Andrews, David, et al, selected by. Water Poems & Bug Poems. 2008. (Illus.). 32p. (J). pap. 10.95 *(978-1-59646-603-6(0))* Dingles & Co.

Andrews, David, et al. Water Poems & Bug Poems. 2008. (Illus.). 32p. (J). lib. bdg. 23.65 *(978-1-59646-602-9(2))* Dingles & Co.

Barbour, Karen, illus. Wonderful Words: Poems about Reading, Writing, Speaking, & Listening. 2004. (ENG.). 32p. (J). (gr. 1-6). 19.99 *(978-0-689-83588-9(4),* Simon & Schuster Bks. For Young Readers) Simon & Schuster Bks. For Young Readers.

Bennett, Rowena, et al, selected by. Monkey Poems & Seed Poems. 2008. (Illus.). 32p. (J). pap. 10.95 *(978-1-59646-613-5(8))* Dingles & Co.

Bennett, Rowena, et al. Monkey Poems & Seed Poems. 2008. (Illus.). 32p. (J). lib. bdg. 23.65 *(978-1-59646-612-8(X))* Dingles & Co.

Bevan, Clare, et al, selected by. Clothes Poems & Weather Poems. 2008. (Illus.). (J). 32p. pap. 10.95 *(978-1-59646-585-5(9));* 24p. lib. bdg. 23.65 *(978-1-59646-584-8(0))* Dingles & Co.

—Party Poems & Out & about Poems. 2008. (Illus.). 24p. (J). pap. 10.95 *(978-1-59646-583-1(2))* Dingles & Co.

Bevan, Clare, et al. Party Poems & Out & about Poems. 2008. (Illus.). 24p. (J). lib. bdg. 23.65 *(978-1-59646-582-4(4))* Dingles & Co.

Boldes, Gary. Thoughts of a Sailor. 2003. 58p. pap. 7.00 *(978-1-4116-0425-4(3))* Lulu Pr., Inc.

Bradman, Tony, et al, selected by. Castle Poems & Dragon Poems. 2008. (Illus.). 32p. (J). pap. 10.95 *(978-1-59646-615-9(4))* Dingles & Co.

—Machine Poems & Music Poems. 2008. (Illus.). 32p. (J). pap. 10.95 *(978-1-59646-601-2(4))* Dingles & Co.

—Pirate Poems & Monster Poems. 2008. (Illus.). 32p. (J). pap. 10.95 *(978-1-59646-621-0(9))* Dingles & Co.

Bradman, Tony, et al. Castle Poems & Dragon Poems. 2008. (Illus.). 32p. (J). lib. bdg. 23.65 *(978-1-59646-614-2(6))* Dingles & Co.

—Machine Poems & Music Poems. 2008. (Illus.). 32p. (J). lib. bdg. 23.65 *(978-1-59646-600-5(6))* Dingles & Co.

—Pirate Poems & Monster Poems. 2008. (Illus.). 32p. (J). lib. bdg. 23.50 *(978-1-59646-620-3(0))* Dingles & Co.

Brooks, Marie, et al, selected by. Pet Poems & Special Day Poems. 2008. (Illus.). 32p. (J). pap. 10.95 *(978-1-59646-599-2(9))* Dingles & Co.

Clark, Lucinda. View from the Middle of the Road: Where the Greenest Grass Grows, 3 vols., volume I. Brenda, Baratto, ed. Audrey, Crosby, illus. 2004. 55p. per. 9.00 *(978-0-9727703-1-6(3),* 706 855-6173) P.R.A. Publishing.

Cookson, Paul, et al, selected by. Body Poems & Movement Poems. 2008. (Illus.). 32p. (J). pap. 10.95 *(978-1-59646-589-3(1))* Dingles & Co.

Cooling, Wendy, ed. Come to the Great World: Poems from Around the Globe. Moxley, Sheila, tr. Moxley, Sheila, illus. 2004. (ENG.). 48p. (J). (gr. k-3). tchr. ed. 17.95 *(978-0-8234-1822-0(7))* Holiday Hse., Inc.

Corbett, Pie, et al, selected by. Color Poems & Sounds Poems. 2008. (Illus.). 32p. (J). pap. 10.95 *(978-1-59646-591-6(3))* Dingles & Co.

Corbett, Pie, et al. Color Poems & Sounds Poems. 2008. (Illus.). 32p. (J). lib. bdg. 23.65 *(978-1-59646-590-9(5))* Dingles & Co.

Cordova, Soledad. Poemas de Perros y Gatos. Graullera, Fabiola, illus. 2003. (SPA.). 21p. (J). (gr. 3-5). pap. 7.95 *(978-968-19-0987-1(9))* Santillana USA Publishing Co., Inc.

Coville, Bruce. The Unicorn Treasury: Stories, Poems, & Unicorn Lore. 2004. (ENG., Illus.). 224p. (J). (gr. 3-7). pap. 7.99 *(978-0-15-205216-4(X),* 1195730, Clarion Bks.) HarperCollins Pubs.

Cowling, Sue, et al, selected by. Giant Poems & Wizzard Poems. 2008. (Illus.). 32p. (J). pap. 10.95 *(978-1-59646-607-4(3))* Dingles & Co.

Cruz-Contarini, Rafael & Rafael, Cruz-Contarini. Zaranda. (SPA., Illus.). 84p. (J). 7.50 *(978-84-241-3367-2(6))* Everest Editora ESP. Dist: Lectorum Pubns., Inc.

Daly, Catherine. DaDaDa. 2003. (Modern Poets Ser.). (ENG.). 224p. pap. *(978-1-876857-95-0(1))* Salt Publishing.

Daniels, John. Love & Pain. 2004. 70p. (YA). mass mkt. 14.95 *(978-0-9755489-0-5(5))* New Birth Publishing.

Dawson, Mary, et al, selected by. Snow Poems & Star Poems. 2008. (Illus.). 32p. (J). pap. 10.95 *(978-1-59646-617-3(0))* Dingles & Co.

Dawson, Mary, et al. Snow Poems & Star Poems. 2008. (Illus.). 32p. (J). lib. bdg. 23.65 *(978-1-59646-616-6(2))* Dingles & Co.

Douthwaite, Gina, et al, selected by. Farm Poems & Seasons Poems. 2008. (Illus.). 32p. (J). pap. 10.95 *(978-1-59646-597-8(2))* Dingles & Co.

Douthwaite, Gina, et al. Farm Poems & Seasons Poems. 2008. (Illus.). 32p. (J). lib. bdg. 23.65 *(978-1-59646-596-1(4))* Dingles & Co.

Eulalie. Buds, Blossoms, & Leaves: Eulalie's Collected Poems. 2003. 200p. lib. bdg. 25.00 *(978-0-9708005-3-4(3))* Singing Tree Pr.

Factor. Language Works Jelly Plate. 16p. (J). *(978-0-8136-3520-0(9))* Modern Curriculum Pr.

Fairfield Middle School. Poetry 2006 by 6th Grade Students of Fairfield Middle School. 2006. 120p. per. 14.95 *(978-1-59540-886-0(X))* 1st World Publishing, Inc.

Favorite Poems, 20 vols. 2014. (Favorite Poems Ser.). (ENG.). 40p. (J). (gr. 2-3). lib. bdg. 336.00 *(978-1-4824-2169-9(0),* 4f9d271e-f36a-43c0-92de-7c901da05baa) Stevens, Gareth Publishing LLLP.

Field, Eugene. A Little Book of Western Verse. 2017. (ENG., Illus.). (J). 23.95 *(978-1-374-86636-2(9));* pap. 13.95 *(978-1-374-86635-5(0))* Capital Communications, Inc.

—A Little Book of Western Verse. (ENG., Illus.). (J). 2017. pap. 14.95 *(978-1-376-04231-3(2))* 2016. 24.95 *(978-1-358-07868-2(8))* Creative Media Partners, LLC.

—A Little Book of Western Verse. 2013. (Notable American Authors Ser.). 202p. reprint ed. lthr. 79.00 *(978-0-7812-2642-4(2))* Reprint Services Corp.

—A Little Book of Western Verse. 2017. (ENG., Illus.). (J). pap. *(978-0-649-04391-0(X)); pap. (978-0-649-29346-9(0))* Trieste Publishing Pty Ltd.

Finney, Eric, et al, selected by. Shopping Poems & Food Poems. 2008. (Illus.). 32p. (J). pap. 10.95 *(978-1-59646-595-4(6))* Dingles & Co.

Finney, Eric, et al. Shopping Poems & Food Poems. 2008. (Illus.). 32p. (J). lib. bdg. 23.65 *(978-1-59646-594-7(8))* Dingles & Co.

Flowers, Audrey X. Rhymes of the Times II. (Orig.). (J). reprint ed. pap. 10.00 *(978-1-56411-146-3(6))* UBUS Communications Systems.

FMS Students. Poetry by 6th Grade Students of FMS. 2005. 21.95 *(978-1-59540-968-3(8));* 13.95 *(978-1-59540-962-1(9))* 1st World Publishing, Inc. (1st World Publishing).

Foster, John, et al, selected by. Transportation Poems & Senses Poems. 2008. (Illus.). 32p. (J). pap. 10.95 *(978-1-59646-605-0(7))* Dingles & Co.

Foster, John & Mellor, Robin. Alphabet Poems & Number Poems. 2008. (Illus.). 32p. (J). lib. bdg. 23.65 *(978-1-59646-592-3(1))* Dingles & Co.

Foster, John & Mellor, Robin, selected by. Alphabet Poems & Number Poems. 2008. (Illus.). 32p. (J). pap. 10.95 *(978-1-59646-593-0(X))* Dingles & Co.

Foster, John & Williams, Brenda. Animal Poems & Family Poems. 2008. (Illus.). 24p. (J). lib. bdg. 23.65 *(978-1-59646-586-2(7))* Dingles & Co.

Foster, John & Williams, Brenda, selected by. Animal Poems & Family Poems. 2008. (Illus.). 32p. (J). pap. 10.95 *(978-1-59646-587-9(5))* Dingles & Co.

Foster, John, et al. Body Poems & Movement Poems. 2008. (Illus.). 32p. (J). lib. bdg. 23.65 *(978-1-59646-588-6(3))* Dingles & Co.

—Transportation Poems & Senses Poems. 2008. (Illus.). 32p. (J). lib. bdg. 23.65 *(978-1-59646-604-3(9))* Dingles & Co.

Fuchs, A. P. The Hand I've Been Dealt: A Collection of Poetry & Song Streams of Thought & Reflection. 2003. 110p. (YA). 22.95 *(978-0-595-66096-4(7));* pap. 12.95 *(978-0-595-29976-8(8))* iUniverse, Inc.

Fuertes, Gloria. Poesias, Rimas y Disparates: Pienso Mesa y Digo Silla. 2003. (SPA.). 128p. *(978-84-305-8535-9(4),* SU4859) Susaeta Ediciones, S.A. ESP. Dist: Lectorum Pubns., Inc.

Fujikawa, Gyo, illus. A Child's Book of Poems. 2007. 128p. (J). (gr. -1-2). 14.99 *(978-1-4027-5061-8(7))* Sterling Publishing Co., Inc.

Greenfield, Eloise. In the Land of Words: New & Selected Poems. Gilchrist, Jan Spivey, illus. 2016. (ENG.). 48p. (J). (gr. -1-3). pap. 7.99 *(978-0-06-443692-2(6),* HarperCollins) HarperCollins Pubs.

Haan, Wanda. The Macaroon Moon: A Book of Poems & Rhymes for Children. Christensen, Donald, illus. 2004. 32p. (J). 17.95 *(978-0-913337-51-6(X))* Southfarm Pr.

Hairston, Angelica. Did Noah Have Whales on the Ark? Ferguson, Tamara, illus. l.t. ed. 2004. 44p. (J). *(978-0-9716136-1-4(3))* Broadcast Quality Productions, Inc.

Hale, Christy, tr. & illus. It Rained All Day That Night: Autograph Album Verses & Inscriptions. Hale, Christy, illus. 2005. (ENG.). 80p. (J). (gr. 3-7). pap. 9.95 *(978-0-87483-726-1(X))* August Hse. Pubs., Inc.

Hopkins, Lee Bennett. Halloween Howls: Holiday Poetry. Schuett, Stacey, illus. 2005. (I Can Read Bks.). 32p. (J). (gr. k-3). 15.99 *(978-0-06-008060-0(4));* lib. bdg. 16.89 *(978-0-06-008061-7(2))* HarperCollins Pubs.

I Am of Two Places: Children's Poetry, Vol. 2. (Greetings Ser.: Vol. 2). 24p. (gr. 3-5). 31.00 *(978-0-7635-3163-8(4))* Rigby Education.

I Am of Two Places: Children's Poetry: 6 Small Books. (Greetings Ser.: Vol. 2). 24p. (gr. 3-5). 31.00 *(978-0-7635-1762-5(3))* Rigby Education.

Idaho Writers League Coeur d'Alene Chapter. Kaleidoscope: A Collection of Tantalizing Tales. 2003. (Illus.). (YA). (gr. 6-18). pap. 15.00 *(978-0-9740481-0-9(0))* Children's Village Foundation, Inc.

Jauregui, Patricia. Sentimientos. Jauregui, Reginald, ed. Pineda, Jesus, illus. l.t. ed. 2004. (SPA.). 39p. (YA). pap. 19.95 *(978-1-931481-41-0(5))* LiArt-Literature & Art.

Johanson, Paula. World Poetry: Evidence of Life, 1 vol. 2010. (Poetry Rocks! Ser.). (ENG., Illus.). 160p. (gr. 9-10). 38.60 *(978-0-7660-3280-4(9),* 0b3813ef-84c2-47e4-922a-a7b20f32c49c); pap. 13.88 *(978-1-59845-382-9(3),* 3f29468d-7e9d-4e72-923c-d7bd664a1d5f) Enslow Publishing, LLC.

Johnson, Angela. In Daddy's Arms, I Am Tall. 2004. (Illus.). (J). (gr. k-3). spiral bd. *(978-0-616-03094-3(0))* Canadian National Institute for the Blind/Institut National Canadien pour les Aveugles.

Kantor, Stuart. Call Me Collective. 2003. 365p. (YA). pap. 24.95 *(978-0-595-27982-1(1))* iUniverse, Inc.

Kassandra, ed. V antologia nuevo Milenio: Narración (Cuentos) y Poesía. Ramirez, Antonio & Morrissey, Kay, photos by. l.t. ed. 2004. (SPA., Illus.). 100p. (YA). pap. 12.00 *(978-1-931481-86-1(5))* LiArt-Literature & Art.

Katsuura, Jaden. Glimpses. 2004. 276p. (YA). pap. 20.95 *(978-0-595-30896-5(1))* iUniverse, Inc.

Kenward, Jean, et al, selected by. Egg Poems & Fox Poems. 2008. (Illus.). 32p. (J). pap. 10.95 *(978-1-59646-609-8(X))* Dingles & Co.

Kenward, Jean, et al. Egg Poems & Fox Poems. 2008. (Illus.). 32p. (J). lib. bdg. 23.65 *(978-1-59646-608-1(1))* Dingles & Co.

Lansky, Bruce, ed. Miles of Smiles: A Collection of Laugh-Out-Loud Poems. Carpenter, Stephen, illus. 2013. (Giggle Poetry Ser.). (ENG.). 132p. (J). (gr. 1-7). pap. 9.99 *(978-0-689-03461-9(X),* Running Pr.) Running Pr.

Larcom, March. Date not set. (Illus.). 32p. (J). (gr. -1-3). 14.99 *(978-0-06-024307-4(4));* lib. bdg. 15.89 *(978-0-06-024308-1(2))* HarperCollins Pubs.

Maddox, Nellie Hazel. Grandmother Nellie's Poems, Vol. I. 2004. (Illus.). 200p. per. 24.95 *(978-0-9755255-0-0(6))* Fletcher, C J Publishing LLC.

Mandel, Ruth. How to Tell Your Children about the Holocaust. 2003. (ENG., Illus.). 1p. (J). pap. 22.95 *(978-1-894692-06-9(3),* Virago Press) McGilligan Bks., Inc. CAN. Dist: Univ. of Toronto Pr.

Mannari, Kaitlyn, et al. Out of Order. 2003. 186p. (YA). pap. 16.95 *(978-0-595-30045-7(6))* iUniverse, Inc.

Mao, Xian. Children's Version of 60 Classical Chinese Poems. 2012. 68p. pap. 28.99 *(978-1-4685-5904-0(4))* AuthorHouse.

Mboya, Sharif. Heart Fealt Doses of Reality. Mboya, Sharif, illus. 2004. (Illus.). 148p. (YA). per. 14.99 *(978-0-9754024-5-0(5))* Doses of Reality, Inc.

McCollough, Aaron. Double Venus. 2003. (Modern Poets Ser.). (ENG.). 108p. pap. *(978-1-84471-003-4(3))* Salt Publishing.

McKenzie, Richard. Poems from the Playground & Other Places. Gervasi, Christine, illus. 2004. (J). 12.00 *(978-0-9725901-0-5(2))* Lekha Pubs., LLC.

Moore, Ralph. Thoughts of Roses: A Collection of Poems by Ralph S. Moore 2003. (Illus.). 72p. 19.95 *(978-0-9741193-1-1(8))* Roland & Eleanor Bergthold.

Morrison, Lillian. I Scream, You Scream: A Feast of Food Rhymes. Dunaway, Nancy, illus. 2005. (Story Cove Ser.). (ENG.). 96p. (J). (gr. -1-3). 12.95 *(978-0-87483-495-6(3))* August Hse. Pubs., Inc.

Mozz. The Pearls of Wisdumb: The Electric Light Verse & Shocking Scribbles of Mozz. 2003. (ENG., Illus.). 176p. (J). lib. bdg. 17.95 *(978-0-9726130-0-2(5))* Goofy Guru Publishing.

Nuestro Mundo en la Poesia: Complete Set. 2003. (SPA., Illus.). (J). 225.50 *(978-0-8136-0705-4(1))* Modern Curriculum Pr.

Protopopescu, Orel O. A Thousand Peaks: Poems from China. Liu, SiYu, tr. from CHI. Liu, SiYu, illus. 2003. (CHI & ENG.). 52p. (gr. 7-18). 19.95 *(978-1-881896-24-1(2),* THPE) Pacific View Pr.

Replogle, Steve & Carlsen, Wendy Vergoz, eds. From a Kid's Life: A Collection of Poetry by Bromwell Students. 2004. 160p. (J). per. 10.00 *(978-0-9753345-0-8(6))* Bromwell Bks.

Rette's Last Stand: Poems by Everette Maddox. 2004. (YA). pap. 15.00 *(978-0-9746444-0-0(4))* Tensaw Pr., Inc., The.

Robbins, Michelle. Leaving the Scars Behind. 2004. 114p. (YA). pap. 12.95 *(978-0-595-31257-3(8))* iUniverse, Inc.

Rodgers, Denise. Great Lakes Rhythmn & Rhyme 2003. (Illus.). 64p. (J). per. 9.95 *(978-0-938682-80-6(6))* River Road Pubns., Inc.

Shane, Bill. Hey Batter Batter: A Collection of Baseball Poems for Kids. 2003. (Illus.). 88p. (J). (gr. k-9). pap. 7.95 *(978-1-931643-20-7(2))* Seven Locks Pr.

Shapiro, Karen Jo. Because I Could Not Stop My Bike. Faulkner, Matt, illus. 2005. (ENG.). 32p. (J). (gr. 2-5). pap. 7.95 *(978-1-58089-105-9(5))* Charlesbridge Publishing, Inc.

Shea, Pegi Deitz, ed. African American Picture-Poetry Collection for Children. Date not set. (Illus.). (J). 17.95 *(978-0-8050-7377-5(9),* Holt, Henry & Co. Bks. For Young Readers) Holt, Henry & Co.

Siegen-Smith, Nikki. Welcome to the World: A Celebration of Birth & Babies from Many Cultures. 2005. (ENG., Illus.). 48p. (J). 18.99 *(978-1-84148-890-5(9))* Barefoot Bks., Inc.

Stepping Stones of Life, 1 vol. 2003. (Illus.). 110p. pap. 19.95 *(978-0-9743964-0-8(0))* Roseann Miller & Linda Stephens-Hooe.

Stutman, Suzanne. All the Power Rests with You. 2005. (ENG.). 188p. pap. 12.95 *(978-0-9648261-7-5(8),* 88bc57e2-584b-481f-8bef-c70f73c8ca35) Medical Manor Bks.

Tarazona, Oscar, illus. Volando con Alas Propias. l.t. ed. 2004. (SPA.). 116p. (YA). pap. 12.00 *(978-1-931481-88-5(1))* LiArt-Literature & Art.

Thomas, Tamara. ABC Poem Book. Thomas, Tamara, illus. 2004. (Illus.). (YA). (gr. 1-6). pap. *(978-1-930200-28-9(5))* Martell Publishing Co.

To Whom It May Concern. 2006. (YA). per. 16.95 *(978-0-9661256-8-9(1))* Youth Communication - New York Center.

Washington Elementary School. Principal Dusanek. 2006. 15.95 *(978-1-59540-981-2(5),* 1st World Publishing) 1st World Publishing, Inc.

Whitman, Walt. When I Heard the Learn'd Astronomer. Long, Loren, illus. 2004. (ENG.). 32p. (J). (gr. k-4). 19.99 *(978-0-689-86397-4(7),* Simon & Schuster Bks. For Young Readers) Simon & Schuster Bks. For Young Readers.

Woods, Gemal. From the Limbs of My Poetree: Selected Poems by Omekongo Dibinga, 1 disc. 2004. (ENG, FRE & SWA., Illus.). 183p. per. 24.95 incl. DVD *(978-0-9760056-0-5(3))* Free Your Mind Publishing.

Yolen, Jane. Color Me a Rhyme: Nature Poems for Young People. Stemple, Jason, photos by. 2003. (ENG., Illus.). 32p. (J). (gr. -1-1). pap. 7.95 *(978-1-59078-172-2(4),* Wordsong) Highlights Pr., c/o Highlights for Children, Inc.

POETRY—FICTION

Amato, Mary. Edgar Allan's Official Crime Investigation Notebook. 2010. (ENG.). 176p. (J). (gr. 4-6). 21.19 *(978-0-8234-2271-5(2))* Holiday Hse., Inc.

—Open Mic Night at Westminster Cemetery. 2018. (ENG.). 272p. (YA). (gr. 8-12). 18.99 *(978-1-5124-6531-0(3),* db1e3ad9-57c6-4b00-9794-37cdeb14b0e3, Carolrhoda Lab™) Lerner Publishing Group.

Archer, Micha. Daniel Finds a Poem. Archer, Micha, illus. 2016. (Illus.). 32p. (J). (gr. k-3). 18.99 *(978-0-399-16913-7(X),* Nancy Paulsen Books) Penguin Young Readers Group.

—Daniel's Good Day. Archer, Micha, illus. 2019. (Illus.). 32p. (J). (-k). 18.99 *(978-0-399-54672-3(3),* Nancy Paulsen Books) Penguin Young Readers Group.

Bennett, Jill. Grandad's Tree: Poems about Families. Cairns, Julia, illus. 2003. 32p. (J). 16.99 *(978-1-84148-541-6(1))* Barefoot Bks., Inc.

Bledsoe, Michele & Bledsoe, Richard. The Secret Kingdom. 2013. 36p. 20.95 *(978-1-4787-0362-4(8))* Outskirts Pr., Inc.

Bryant, Jen. Call Me Marianne. Johnson, David, illus. 2006. 32p. (J). (gr. 1-4). 16.00 *(978-0-8028-5242-7(4),* Eerdmans Bks For Young Readers) Eerdmans, William B. Publishing Co.

Calhoun, Dia. Eva of the Farm. Slater, Kate, illus. 2012. (ENG.). 256p. (J). (gr. 4-7). 16.99 *(978-1-4424-1700-7(5),* Atheneum Bks. for Young Readers) Simon & Schuster Children's Publishing.

Cartaya, Pablo. The Epic Fail of Arturo Zamora. (ENG.). (J). (gr. 5). 2018. 272p. 8.99 *(978-1-101-99725-3(7),* Puffin Books) 2017. 256p. 17.99 *(978-1-101-99723-9(0),* Viking Books for Young Readers) Penguin Young Readers Group.

PQR

Cassidy, Sara. Skylark. 1 vol. 2014. (Orca Soundings Ser.). (ENG.). 136p. (YA). (gr. 8-12). pap. 9.95 *(978-1-4598-0590-3(9))* Orca Bk. Pubs. USA.

Cazet, Denys, reader. Minnie & Moo: Will You Be My Valentine? 2004. (Read-Alongs for Beginning Readers Ser.). (Illus.). (J). (gr. -1-3). 25.95 incl. audio *(978-1-59112-892-2(7))*; pap. 29.95 incl. audio *(978-1-59112-893-9(5))*; pap. 31.95 incl. audio compact disk *(978-1-59112-897-7(8))* Live Oak Media.

Cline-Ransome, Lesa. Finding Langston. (Finding Langston Trilogy Ser.). 112p. (J). (gr. 3-7). 2020. pap. 7.99 *(978-0-8234-4582-0(8))* 2018. 16.99 *(978-0-8234-3960-7(7))* Holiday Hse., Inc.

Cofer, Judith Ortiz. The Poet Upstairs. Ortiz, Oscar, illus. 2012. (J). (gr. 5-9). 16.95 *(978-1-55885-704-9(4)*, Piñata Books) Arte Publico Pr.

—La Poeta Del Piso de Arriba. Baeza Ventura, Gabriela, tr. from ENG. Ortiz, Oscar, illus. 2014. (SPA.). (J). 17.95 *(978-1-55885-788-9(5)*, Piñata Books) Arte Publico Pr.

Creech, Sharon. Hate That Cat: A Novel. (ENG.). (J). (gr. 3-7). 2010. 176p. pap. 7.99 *(978-0-06-143094-7(3))* 2008. 160p. 16.99 *(978-0-06-143092-3(7))* HarperCollins Pubs. (HarperCollins).

—Love That Dog. 2008.Tr. of Mwen Renmen Chen Sa A. (J). (gr. 3-6). lib. bdg. 17.20 *(978-0-613-61715-4(0))* Turtleback.

—Love That Dog: A Novel. 2008. (ENG.). 128p. (J). (gr. 3-7). pap. 9.99 *(978-0-06-440959-9(7)*, HarperCollins) HarperCollins Pubs.

Davies, Jacqueline. The Candy Smash. 2022. (Lemonade War Ser.: 4). (ENG., Illus.). 240p. (J). (gr. 3-7). pap. 9.99 *(978-0-544-22500-8(7)*, 1563385, Clarion Bks.) HarperCollins Pubs.

Dean, Carolee. Comfort. 2004. (ENG.). 256p. (YA). (gr. 7-18). pap. 14.95 *(978-0-618-43912-6(9)*, 410118, Clarion Bks.) HarperCollins Pubs.

Dotlich, Rebecca Kai. Bella & Bean. Leijten, Aileen, illus. 2009. (ENG.). 40p. (J). (gr. -1-3). 19.99 *(978-0-689-85616-7(4)*, Atheneum Bks. for Young Readers) Simon & Schuster Children's Publishing.

Factor, June, ed. Real Keen, Baked Bean. 2017. (Far Out! Ser.). (ENG.). 104p. (J). (gr. -1-k). pap. 8.99 *(978-1-925386-09-7(0)*, Brolly Bks.) Borghesi & Adam Pubs. Pty Ltd AUS. Dist: Independent Pubs. Group.

—Unreal, Banana Peel. 2017. (Far Out! Ser.). (ENG.). 112p. (J). (gr. -1-k). pap. 8.99 *(978-1-925386-08-0(2)*, Brolly Bks.) Borghesi & Adam Pubs. Pty Ltd AUS. Dist: Independent Pubs. Group.

Fajardo, Alexis E. Kid Beowulf. 2016. (Illus.). xvi, 223p. (J). lib. bdg. 22.10 *(978-0-606-38999-0(7))* Turtleback.

Fitzmaurice, Kathryn. Destiny, Rewritten. 2015. (ENG.). 368p. (J). (gr. 3-7). pap. 6.99 *(978-0-06-162503-9(5)*, Tegen, Katherine Bks) HarperCollins Pubs.

Flores-Scott, Patrick. Jumped In. 2014. (ENG., Illus.). 304p. (YA). (gr. 7). pap. 15.99 *(978-1-250-05398-5(6)*, 900137223) Square Fish.

Gilman, Grace. Dixie & the Best Day Ever. 2014. (I Can Read Level 1 Ser.). (ENG., Illus.). 32p. (J). (gr. -1-3). pap. 4.99 *(978-0-06-208659-4(6)*, HarperCollins) HarperCollins Pubs.

Gooney Bird Is So Absurd. 2013. (Gooney Bird Greene Ser.: 4). (ENG., Illus.). 112p. (J). (gr. 1-4). pap. 7.99 *(978-0-547-87559-0(2)*, 1505831, Clarion Bks.) HarperCollins Pubs.

Grimes, Nikki. Bronx Masquerade. 2017. (ENG.). 192p. (YA). (gr. 7). pap. 10.99 *(978-0-425-28976-1(1)*, Speak) Penguin Young Readers Group.

—Bronx Masquerade. 2003. (gr. 7-12). lib. bdg. 17.20 *(978-0-613-81701-1(X))* Turtleback.

—Poems in the Attic. 1 vol. Zunon, Elizabeth, illus. 2015. (ENG.). 48p. (J). (gr. 1-6). 21.95 *(978-1-62014-027-7(6)*, leelowbooks) Lee & Low Bks., Inc.

—Rich: a Dyamonde Daniel Book. Christie, R. Gregory, illus. 2009. (Dyamonde Daniel Book Ser.: 2). (ENG.). 112p. (J). (gr. 2-4). 13.99 *(978-0-399-25176-4(6)*, G.P. Putnam's Sons Books for Young Readers) Penguin Young Readers Group.

Grover, Lorie Ann. Hit. 1 vol. 2015. (ENG.). 224p. (YA). pap. 8.99 *(978-0-310-72938-9(6))* Blink.

Gutman, Dan. Ms. Coco Is Loco! Paillot, Jim, illus. 2007. (My Weird School Ser.: 16). (J). 14.75 *(978-1-4177-7428-9(2))* Turtleback.

Harris, Teresa E. Gabriela. 1. 2018. (American Girl Contemporary Ser.). (ENG.). 196p. (J). (gr. 3-5). 18.36 *(978-1-64310-560-4(4))* Penworthy Co., LLC, The.

Herrera, Robin. Hope Is a Ferris Wheel. 2014. (ENG., Illus.). 272p. (YA). (gr. 3-7). 16.95 *(978-1-4197-1039-1(7)*, 1071501, Amulet Bks.) Abrams, Inc.

Holabird, Katharine & Craig, Helen, creators. Angelina & the Tummy Butterflies. 2013. (Angelina Ballerina Ser.). (ENG., Illus.). 24p. (J). (gr. -1-1). 17.44 *(978-0-448-46281-3(8))* Penguin Young Readers Group.

Holub, Joan & Williams, Suzanne. Calliope the Muse. 2016. (Goddess Girls Ser.: 20). (ENG., Illus.). 256p. (J). (gr. 3-7). pap. 8.99 *(978-1-4814-5004-1(2)*, Aladdin) Simon & Schuster Children's Publishing.

—Calliope the Muse. 2016. (Goddess Girls Ser.: 20). lib. bdg. 18.40 *(978-0-606-38972-3(5))* Turtleback.

Johnson, Peter. The Life & Times of Benny Alvarez. 2014. (ENG.). 224p. (J). (gr. 3-7). 16.99 *(978-0-06-221596-3(5)*, HarperCollins) HarperCollins Pubs.

Kephart, Beth. Undercover. 2009. (ENG.). 304p. (YA). (gr. 8). pap. 8.99 *(978-0-06-123895-6(3)*, HarperTeen) HarperCollins Pubs.

Koertge, Ron. Shakespeare Makes the Playoffs. (ENG., Illus.). 176p. (YA). (gr. 7). 2012. pap. 7.99 *(978-0-7636-5852-6(9))* 2010. 15.99 *(978-0-7636-4435-2(8))* Candlewick Pr.

Koertge, Ronald. Shakespeare Bats Cleanup. 2006. 116p. (gr. 7-12). 16.00 *(978-0-7569-6571-6(3))* Perfection Learning Corp.

Mangum, Kay Lynn. When the Bough Breaks. 2007. 352p. (YA). pap. 15.95 *(978-1-59038-748-1(1))* Deseret Bk. Co.

Manushkin, Fran. It Doesn't Need to Rhyme, Katie: Writing a Poem with Katie Woo. 1 vol. Lyon, Tammie, illus. 2013. (Katie Woo: Star Writer Ser.). (ENG.). 32p. (J). (gr. k-2). pap. 6.95 *(978-1-4795-1923-1(5)*, 123630); lib. bdg. 21.32 *(978-1-4048-8128-0(X)*, 121935) Capstone. (Picture Window Bks.).

McNamara, Margaret. A Poem in Your Pocket (Mr. Tiffin's Classroom Series) Karas, G. Brian, illus. 2015. (Mr. Tiffin's Classroom Ser.). 40p. (J). (gr. -1-3). 17.99 *(978-0-307-97947-6(4)*, Schwartz & Wade Bks.) Random Hse. Children's Bks.

Murphy, Sally. Pearl Verses the World. Potter, Heather, illus. 2011. (ENG.). 80p. (J). (gr. 3-7). 14.99 *(978-0-7636-4821-3(3))* Candlewick Pr.

Nikki, Grimes. Bronx Masquerade. 2014. (ENG.). 176p. (YA). 11.24 *(978-1-63245-077-7(1))* Lectorum Pubns., Inc.

O'Connor, Jane. Fancy Nancy: Poet Extraordinaire! Glasser, Robin Preiss, illus. 2010. (Fancy Nancy Ser.). (ENG.). 32p. (J). (gr. -1-2). 12.99 *(978-0-06-189643-9(8)*, HarperCollins) HarperCollins Pubs.

Pearson, Susan. Slugs in Love. 0 vols. O'Malley, Kevin, illus. 2012. (ENG.). 34p. (J). (gr. -1-3). pap. 7.99 *(978-0-7614-6248-4(1)*, 9780761462484, Two Lions) Amazon Publishing.

Schroeder, Lisa. Falling for You. 2013. (ENG., Illus.). 384p. (YA). (gr. 9). pap. 9.99 *(978-1-4424-4400-3(2)*, Simon Pulse) Simon Pulse.

Scieszka, Jon. Science Verse. Smith, Lane, illus. 2004. 40p. (J). (gr. 2-5). 18.99 *(978-0-670-91057-1(0)*, Viking Books for Young Readers) Penguin Young Readers Group.

Sharon, Creech. Love That Dog. 2014. (ENG.). 112p. (J). (gr. 7-9). 10.24 *(978-1-63245-159-0(X))* Lectorum Pubns., Inc.

Spinelli, Eileen. Another Day As Emily. Lew-Vriethoff, Joanne, illus. 2015. 240p. (J). (gr. 3-7). 8.99 *(978-0-449-80989-1(7)*, Yearling) Random Hse. Children's Bks.

Stavans, Ilan. Golemito. Villegas, Teresa, illus. 2013. (ENG.). 32p. (J). 16.95 *(978-1-58838-292-4(3)*, 8804, NewSouth Bks.) NewSouth, Inc.

Stone, Tamara Ireland. Every Last Word. 2017. (ENG.). (YA). (gr. 7-12). lib. bdg. 20.85 *(978-0-606-39885-5(6))* Turtleback.

Vere, Ed. How to Be a Lion. 2018. (ENG., Illus.). 32p. (J). (gr. -1-2). 18.99 *(978-0-525-57805-5(6)*, Doubleday Bks. for Young Readers) Random Hse. Children's Bks.

Wagstaff, Janiel M. Stella: Poet Extraordinaire. 2018. (ENG.). 32p. (gr. k-3). pap. 7.99 *(978-1-339-26478-4(8))* Scholastic, Inc.

Weiss, Ellen & Friedman, Mel. Porky & Bess. Winborn, Marsha, illus. 2011. (Step into Reading Ser.). (ENG.). 48p. (J). (gr. 2-4). pap. 5.99 *(978-0-375-86113-0(0)*, Random Hse. Bks. for Young Readers) Random Hse. Children's Bks.

Whybrow, Ian. Little Wolf's Handy Book of Poems. Ross, Tony, illus. 2005. (Little Wolf Adventures Ser.). 80p. (gr. 3-6). pap., lib. bdg. 14.95 *(978-0-87614-927-0(1))* Lerner Publishing Group.

Wigden, Susan. Silly Rhymes for Fun Times. Columbin, Corey, illus. 2011. 20p. pap. 11.95 *(978-1-60888-107-9(5))* Nimble Bks. LLC.

Yeh, Kat. The Way to Bea. 2018. (ENG.). 368p. (J). (gr. 3-7). pap. 7.99 *(978-0-316-23669-0(1))* Little, Brown Bks. for Young Readers.

POETRY—HISTORY AND CRITICISM

Bodden, Valerie. Concrete Poetry. 2009. (Poetry Basics Ser.). (Illus.). 32p. (J). 19.95 *(978-1-58341-775-1(3)*, 1300261, Creative Education) Creative Co., The.

—Haikus. 2009. (Poetry Basics Ser.). (Illus.). 32p. 19.95 *(978-1-58341-776-8(1)*, 1300262, Creative Education) Creative Co., The.

Buckwalter, Stephanie. Death Poetry: Death, Be Not Proud. 1 vol. 2014. (Pure Poetry Ser.). (ENG.). 128p. (gr. 9-10). lib. bdg. 35.93 *(978-0-7660-4257-5(X)*, 5aa15619-24ab-41a1-9b0e-b82df41cdfd3) Enslow Publishing, LLC.

Griffin Llanas, Sheila. Beauty Poetry: She Walks in Beauty. 1 vol. 2014. (Pure Poetry Ser.). (ENG.). 128p. (gr. 9-10). lib. bdg. 35.93 *(978-0-7660-4243-8(X)*, da4c6f15-1f7c-45c7-b172-7e25d3d9365b) Enslow Publishing, LLC.

—Modern American Poetry: Echoes & Shadows. 1 vol. 2010. (Poetry Rocks! Ser.). (ENG., Illus.). 160p. (gr. 9-10). pap. 13.88 *(978-1-59845-379-9(3)*, df03772e-75fb-490a-a8a4-9b211c562cd6) Enslow Publishing, LLC.

Johanson, Paula. Love Poetry: How Do I Love Thee?. 1 vol. 2014. (Pure Poetry Ser.). (ENG.). 128p. (gr. 9-10). lib. bdg. 35.93 *(978-0-7660-4284-1(7)*, defa762f-abae-4185-af83-fb63b144b297) Enslow Publishing, LLC.

—World Poetry: Evidence of Life. 1 vol. 2010. (Poetry Rocks! Ser.). (ENG., Illus.). 160p. (gr. 9-10). 38.60 *(978-0-7660-3280-4(9)*, 0b3813ef-84c2-47e4-922a-a7b20f32c49c); pap. 13.88 *(978-1-59845-382-9(3)*, 3f29468d-7e9d-4e72-923c-d7bd664a1d5f) Enslow Publishing, LLC.

Moore Niver, Heather. Poems. 1 vol. 2018. (Let's Learn about Literature Ser.). (ENG.). 24p. (gr. 1-2). 24.27 *(978-0-7660-9755-1(2)*, fa8385da-0ee8-4d41-bf07-cb004e31e304) Enslow Publishing, LLC.

POETRY—PHILOSOPHY

see Poetry

POETRY—SELECTIONS

see Poetry—Collections

POETRY—TECHNIQUE

see Poetics

POETRY FOR CHILDREN

see Nursery Rhymes; Poetry

POETRY OF LOVE

see Love Poetry

POETRY OF NATURE

see Nature—Poetry

POETS

see also Dramatists

Anne, Fine. An Interview with Anne Fine. (ENG., Illus.). 96p. (YA). pap. 5.50 *(978-1-4052-0053-0(7))* Farshore GBR. Dist: Trafalgar Square Publishing.

Ashby, Ruth. Caedmon's Song. Slavin, Bill, illus. 2006. (ENG.). 32p. (J). (gr. k). 16.00 *(978-0-8028-5241-0(6)*, Eerdmans Bks For Young Readers) Eerdmans, William B. Publishing Co.

Berne, Jennifer. On Wings of Words: The Extraordinary Life of Emily Dickinson (Emily Dickinson for Kids, Biography of Female Poet for Kids) Stadtlander, Becca, illus. 2020. (ENG.). 52p. (J). (gr. k-3). 18.99 *(978-1-4521-4297-5(1))* Chronicle Bks. LLC.

Berry, S. L. E. E. Cummings. 2014. (Voices in Poetry Ser.). (ENG.). 48p. (J). (gr. 5-8). *(978-1-60818-325-8(4)*, 21442, Creative Education); pap. 12.00 *(978-1-62832-053-4(2)*, 21443, Creative Paperbacks) Creative Co., The.

Berry, S. L. & Dickinson, Emily. Emily Dickinson. 2014. (Illus.). 47p. (J). *(978-1-60818-326-5(2)*, Creative Education) Creative Co., The.

Bodden, Valerie. Who Is a Poet? 2016. (Write Me a Poem Ser.). (ENG.). 24p. (J). (gr. 1-4). pap. 9.99 *(978-1-62832-255-2(1)*, 20554, Creative Paperbacks) Creative Co., The.

Bowman, Chris. Nikki Grimes. 2017. (Children's Storytellers Ser.). (ENG., Illus.). 24p. (J). (gr. 2-5). lib. bdg. 26.95 *(978-1-62617-650-8(7)*, Blastoff! Readers) Bellwether Media.

Brown, Monica. Pablo Neruda: Poet of the People. Paschkis, Julie, illus. 2011. (ENG.). 32p. (J). (gr. 1-4). 18.99 *(978-0-8050-9198-4(X)*, 900065887, Holt, Henry & Co. Bks. For Young Readers) Holt, Henry & Co.

Bryant, Jen. A River of Words: The Story of William Carlos Williams. Sweet, Melissa, illus. 2008. (ENG.). 34p. (J). (gr. 4-7). 17.50 *(978-0-8028-5302-8(1)*, Eerdmans Bks For Young Readers) Eerdmans, William B. Publishing Co.

Buckwalter, Stephanie. Early American Poetry: Beauty in Words. 1 vol. 2010. (Poetry Rocks! Ser.). (ENG., Illus.). 160p. (gr. 9-10). pap. 13.88 *(978-1-59845-378-2(5)*, 763f289b-6aa1-41fe-89a3-9ff36ed3c2cc); lib. bdg. 38.60 *(978-0-7660-3277-4(9)*, dcdcb0b7-cb7e-45f0-a9f4-484b0d349c13) Enslow Publishing, LLC.

Burgess, Matthew. Enormous Smallness: A Story of E. E. Cummings. Di Giacomo, Kris, illus. 2015. 64p. (J). (gr. -1-3). 17.95 *(978-1-59270-171-1(X))* Enchanted Lion Bks., LLC.

Burleigh, Robert. O Captain, My Captain: Walt Whitman, Abraham Lincoln, & the Civil War. Hundley, Sterling, illus. 2019. (ENG.). 64p. (J). (gr. 5-17). 19.99 *(978-1-4197-3358-1(3)*, 1120101, Abrams Bks. for Young Readers) Abrams, Inc.

Burnett, Alan & Burnett, Allan. Robert Burns & All That. Anderson, Scoular, illus. 2016. (and All That Ser.). 112p. (gr. 4-8). pap. 7.95 *(978-1-78027-391-4(6))* Birlinn, Ltd. GBR. Dist: Casemate Pubs. & Bk. Distributors, LLC.

Carey Rohan, Rebecca. Langston Hughes: Poet. 1 vol. 2016. (Artists of the Harlem Renaissance Ser.). (ENG.). 128p. (YA). (gr. 9-9). lib. bdg. 47.36 *(978-1-5026-1064-5(7)*, 4b3113c7-d634-4c78-936b-ba94b919b293) Cavendish Square Publishing LLC.

Carradice, Phil. A Child's Dylan Thomas. 2014. (ENG., Illus.). 32p. (gr. 4-6). pap. 13.99 *(978-1-84851-749-3(1))* Gomer Pr. GBR. Dist: Independent Pubs. Group, Casemate Pubs. & Bk. Distributors, LLC.

Center for Learning Network Staff. I Know Why the Caged Bird Sings: Curriculum Unit. 2005. (Novel Ser.). 75p. (YA). tchr. ed., spiral bd. 19.95 *(978-1-56077-787-8(7))* Center for Learning, The.

Cheng, Andrea. Etched in Clay: The Life of Dave, Enslaved Potter & Poet. 1 vol. Cheng, Andrea, illus. (ENG., Illus.). (J). 2018. 160p. (gr. 4-12). pap. 13.95 *(978-1-62014-807-5(2)*, leelowbooks) 2013. 146p. 17.95 *(978-1-60060-451-5(X))* Lee & Low Bks., Inc.

Clinton, Catherine. Phillis's Big Test. Qualls, Sean, illus. 2008. (ENG.). 32p. (J). (gr. -1-3). 16.00 *(978-0-618-73739-0(1)*, 596218, Clarion Bks.) HarperCollins Pubs.

Cody, Sherwin. Four American Poets. 2009. 198p. pap. 14.14 *(978-0-217-47860-1(3))* General Bks. LLC.

Collard, Sneed B., III. Phillis Wheatley. 1 vol. 2010. (American Heroes Ser.). (ENG., Illus.). 48p. (gr. 3-3). 32.64 *(978-0-7614-4057-4(7)*, b5aabf94-bd02-4815-9f30-a3d8be34143b) Cavendish Square Publishing LLC.

Davis, Rebecca Henry. Fanny Crosby: Queen of Gospel Songs. 2003. (Illus.). 107p. (J). 6.49 *(978-1-57924-970-0(1))* BJU Pr.

Demi. Rumi: Persian Poet, Whirling Dervish. 0 vols. Demi, illus. 2012. (ENG.). 40p. (J). (gr. 4-6). 19.99 *(978-0-7614-5527-1(2)*, 9780761455271, Two Lions) Amazon Publishing.

Dennis, John. Heroes of Literature: English Poets, a B. 2006. pap. 34.95 *(978-1-4254-9436-0(6))* Kessinger Publishing, LLC.

Derby, Sally. Jump Back, Paul: The Life & Poems of Paul Laurence Dunbar. Qualls, Sean, illus. 2015. (ENG.). 128p. (J). (gr. 4-7). 18.99 *(978-0-7636-6070-3(1))* Candlewick Pr.

Doak, Robin S. Phillis Wheatley: The Inspiring Life Story of the American Poet. 2016. (Inspiring Stories Ser.). (ENG., Illus.). 112p. (J). (gr. 5-7). lib. bdg. 38.65 *(978-0-7565-5166-7(8)*, 128794, Compass Point Bks.) Capstone.

Duncan, Alice Faye. A Song for Gwendolyn Brooks. Gordon, Xia, illus. 2019. (People Who Shaped Our World Ser.: 3). (ENG.). 48p. (J). (gr. k). 17.99 *(978-1-4549-3088-4(8))* Sterling Publishing Co., Inc.

Etinde-Crompton, Charlotte & Crompton, Samuel Willard. Countee Cullen: Poet of the Harlem Renaissance. 1 vol. 2019. (Celebrating Black Artists Ser.). (ENG.). 104p. (gr. 7-7). 38.93 *(978-1-9785-0355-7(5)*, f137ac76-65d3-46ed-abaa-1d6fd8ff2aeb) Enslow Publishing, LLC.

—Langston Hughes: Jazz Poet of the Harlem Renaissance. 1 vol. 2019. (Celebrating Black Artists Ser.). (ENG.). 104p. (gr. 7-7). 38.93 *(978-1-9785-0358-8(X)*, 7f9222cf-248f-4522-910a-2c66af2795d9) Enslow Publishing, LLC.

Flor Ada, Alma & Campoy, F. Isabel, contrib. by. Paths. (Literature Collection of Gateways to the Sun Ser.). 48p. (J). (gr. k-6). pap. 16.95 *(978-1-59437-722-8(7))* Santillana USA Publishing Co., Inc.

Gigliotti, Jim. Who Was Edgar Allan Poe? Foley, Tim, illus. 2015. (Who Was-? Chapters Ser.). (ENG.). 112p. (J). (gr. 3-6). 18.69 *(978-1-4844-6178-5(9)*, Penguin Workshop) Penguin Young Readers Group.

Glaser, Linda. Emma's Poem: The Voice of the Statue of Liberty. Nivola, Claire A., illus. 2010. (ENG.). 32p. (J). (gr. -1-3). 17.99 *(978-0-547-17184-5(6)*, 1054295, Clarion Bks.) HarperCollins Pubs.

Goddu, Krystyna Poray. A Girl Called Vincent: The Life of Poet Edna St. Vincent Millay. 2018. (ENG.). 224p. (J). (gr. 4). pap. 12.99 *(978-0-912777-85-6(0))* Chicago Review Pr., Inc.

Griffin Llanas, Sheila. Contemporary American Poetry: Not the End, but the Beginning. 1 vol. 2010. (Poetry Rocks! Ser.). (ENG., Illus.). 160p. (gr. 9-10). 38.60 *(978-0-7660-3279-8(5)*, d66715e8-7538-415b-baff-bb6f848cd6bb) Enslow Publishing, LLC.

—Modern American Poetry: Echoes & Shadows. 1 vol. 2010. (Poetry Rocks! Ser.). (ENG., Illus.). 160p. (gr. 9-10). lib. bdg. 38.60 *(978-0-7660-3275-0(2)*, b5616fb7-10cf-488c-8636-66893c6aae1b) Enslow Publishing, LLC.

Hegedus, Bethany. Rise! From Caged Bird to Poet of the People, Maya Angelou. 1 vol. Engel, Tonya, illus. 2019. (ENG.). 48p. (J). (gr. 2-8). 21.95 *(978-1-62014-587-6(1)*, leelowbooks) Lee & Low Bks., Inc.

Herrera, Juan Felipe. Imagine. Castillo, Lauren, illus. 2018. (ENG.). 32p. (J). (gr. k-4). 17.99 *(978-0-7636-9052-6(X))* Candlewick Pr.

—Upside down Boy/el Nino de Cabeza. 1 vol. 2013.Tr. of Nino de Cabeza. (ENG., Illus.). 32p. (J). (gr. 1-5). per. 11.95 *(978-0-89239-217-9(7)*, leelowcbp, Children's Book Press) Lee & Low Bks., Inc.

Hill, Laban Carrick. Dave the Potter: Artist, Poet, Slave. 2012. (CHI, ENG & JPN., Illus.). 42p. (J). *(978-4-89572-839-3(0))* Mitsumura Kyouiku Tosho Co., Ltd.

—Dave the Potter (Caldecott Honor Book) Artist, Poet, Slave. Collier, Bryan, illus. 2010. (ENG.). 40p. (J). (gr. -1-3). 19.99 *(978-0-316-10731-0(X))* Little, Brown Bks. for Young Readers.

Hill, Laban Carrik. Dave the Potter: Artist, Poet, Slave. 2011. (J). *(978-1-4618-1706-2(4))* Recorded Bks., Inc.

Hoehne, Marcia. Anne Bradstreet: America's Puritan Poet. 2007. 203p. pap. *(978-1-888105-75-9(5))* Avisson Pr., Inc.

Houle, Michelle M. Modern British Poetry: the World Is Never the Same. 1 vol. 2010. (Poetry Rocks! Ser.). (ENG., Illus.). 160p. (gr. 9-10). pap. 13.88 *(978-1-59845-381-2(5)*, 74db4771-a860-4006-834b-cc297bdddb1b) Enslow Publishing, LLC.

Jarnow, Jesse. Phillis Wheatley. 1 vol. 2003. (Primary Sources of Famous People in American History Ser.). (ENG., Illus.). 32p. (J). (gr. 3-4). lib. bdg. 29.13 *(978-0-8239-4119-3(1)*, e4040339-04fc-4aa7-8995-5cc37f904356, Rosen Reference) Rosen Publishing Group, Inc., The.

—Phillis Wheatley: African American Poet / Poeta Afroamericana. 2009. (Famous People in American History/Grandes personajes en la historia de los Estados Unidos Ser.). (ENG & SPA.). 32p. (gr. 2-3). 47.90 *(978-1-61512-554-8(X)*, Editorial Buenas Letras) Rosen Publishing Group, Inc., The.

—Phillis Wheatley: Poeta afroamericana (Phillis Wheatley: African American Poet) 2009. (Grandes personajes en la historia de los Estados Unidos (Famous People in American History) Ser.). (SPA.). 32p. (gr. 2-3). 47.90 *(978-1-61512-807-5(7)*, Editorial Buenas Letras) Rosen Publishing Group, Inc., The.

Jarnow, Jesse & Moriarty, J. T. Phillis Wheatley. 1 vol. 2003. (Primary Sources of Famous People in American History Ser.). (ENG., Illus.). 32p. (J). (gr. 3-4). pap. 10.00 *(978-0-8239-4191-9(4)*, 6948aa9e-1aea-4182-8015-183b51df0027) Rosen Publishing Group, Inc., The.

Johanson, Paula. Early British Poetry: Words That Burn. 1 vol. 2010. (Poetry Rocks! Ser.). (ENG., Illus.). 160p. (gr. 9-10). pap. 13.88 *(978-1-59845-383-6(1)*, a31eb492-d683-4c3b-b694-d3b24277444a); lib. bdg. 38.60 *(978-0-7660-3276-7(0)*, d2077f63-ee5b-4936-8d0f-ef74cb56b4e9) Enslow Publishing, LLC.

—World Poetry: Evidence of Life. 1 vol. 2010. (Poetry Rocks! Ser.). (ENG., Illus.). 160p. (gr. 9-10). pap. 13.88 *(978-1-59845-382-9(3)*, 3f29468d-7e9d-4e72-923c-d7bd664a1d5f) Enslow Publishing, LLC.

Jones, Veda Boyd. Jazz Age Poet: A Story about Langston Hughes. Kiwak, Barbara, illus. 2005. (Creative Minds Biographies Ser.). (ENG.). 64p. (gr. 4-8). lib. bdg. 22.60 *(978-1-57505-757-6(3)*, Carolrhoda Bks.) Lerner Publishing Group.

Kent, Jacqueline C. Phillis Wheatley. 2003. (Women of the Revolution Ser.). (J). pap. *(978-1-58417-089-1(1))*; lib. bdg. *(978-1-58417-026-6(3))* Lake Street Pubs.

Kerley, Barbara. Walt Whitman: Words for America. 1 vol. Selznick, Brian, illus. 2004. (ENG.). 56p. (gr. 2-5). 19.99 *(978-0-439-35791-3(8)*, Scholastic Pr.) Scholastic, Inc.

Kirkpatrick, Patricia. John Keats. Delessert, Etienne, illus. 2005. (Voices in Poetry Ser.). 43p. (J). (gr. 5-9). 21.95 *(978-1-58341-345-6(6)*, Creative Education) Creative Co., The.

Lasky, Kathryn. A Voice of Her Own: Candlewick Biographies: The Story of Phillis Wheatley, Slave Poet. Lee, Paul, illus. 2012. (Candlewick Biographies Ser.). (ENG.). 48p. (J). (gr. 3-7). 14.99 *(978-0-7636-6427-5(8))*; pap. 6.99 *(978-0-7636-6091-8(4))* Candlewick Pr.

Leon, Georgina Lazaro. Conoce a Gabriela Mistral: Get to Know Gabriela Mistral. Palacios, Sara Helena, illus. 2014. (Personajes Del Mundo Hispnico Ser.). (ENG & SPA.). 32p. (J). (gr. -1-3). 15.95 *(978-1-61435-351-5(4)*, Alfaguara) Santillana USA Publishing Co., Inc.

Loewen, Nancy. Walt Whitman. Day, Rob, illus. 2014. (Voices in Poetry Ser.). (ENG.). 48p. (J). (gr. 5-8). 35.65 *(978-1-60818-329-6(7)*, 21458, Creative Education) Creative Co., The.

Lukes, Bonnie L. Henry Wadsworth Longfellow: America's Beloved Poet. 2nd rev. exp. ed. 2004. (World Writers Ser.). (Illus.). 144p. (YA). (gr. 6-12). 23.95 *(978-1-931798-07-5(9))* Reynolds, Morgan Inc.

Marsh, Carole. Phillis Wheatley. 2003. 12p. (gr. k-4). 2.95 *(978-0-635-02371-1(7))* Gallopade International.

Mattern, Joanne. Geoffrey Chaucer: Medieval Writer. 1 vol. rev. ed. 2012. (Social Studies: Informational Text Ser.). (ENG.). 32p. (gr. 4-8). pap. 11.99 *(978-1-4333-5006-1(8))* Teacher Created Materials, Inc.

McLeese, Don. Phillis Wheatley. 2004. (Heroes of the American Revolution Ser.). (Illus.). 32p. (J). (gr. -1 — 1). pap. 5.95 *(978-1-59515-320-3(9))* Rourke Educational Media.

McLendon, Jacquelyn. Phillis Wheatley: A Revolutionary Poet. 2009. (Library of American Lives & Times Ser.). 112p. (gr. 5-5). 69.20 *(978-1-60853-499-9(5))* Rosen Publishing Group, Inc., The.

Meltzer, Milton. Emily Dickinson: A Biography. 2006. (Literary Greats Ser.). (ENG.). 128p. (gr. 7-12). lib. bdg. 33.26 *(978-0-7613-2949-7(8)*, Millbrook Pr.) Lerner Publishing Group.

Moriarty, J. T. Phillis Wheatley: African American Poet. 2009. (Primary Sources of Famous People in American History Ser.). 32p. (gr. 2-3). 47.90 *(978-1-60851-717-6(9))* Rosen Publishing Group, Inc., The.

—Phillis Wheatley: African American Poet = Poeta Afroamericana, 1 vol. 2003. (Famous People in American History / Grandes Personajes en la Historia de Los Estados Unidos Ser.). (ENG & SPA., Illus.). 32p. (J). (gr. 3-4). lib. bdg. 29.13 *(978-0-8239-4167-4(1)*, d6c50ca0-35d0-44e5-b6e3-2c186c5b8a60, Editorial Buenas Letras) Rosen Publishing Group, Inc., The.

Nagle, Jeanne & Schull, Jodie A. Pablo Neruda: Nobel Prize-Winning Poet, 1 vol. 2015. (Influential Latinos Ser.). (ENG., Illus.). 128p. (gr. 7-8). lib. bdg. 38.93 *(978-0-7660-7314-2(9)*, 0cbb6f43-d3ae-4804-8529-01fb511b129a) Enslow Publishing, LLC.

Neis, Therese. Extraordinary African-American Poets, 1 vol. 2012. (African-American Collective Biographies Ser.). (ENG.). 112p. (gr. 5-6). 35.93 *(978-1-59845-139-9(1)*, fd8fd55a-379e-452e-b5a2-23100b743777) Enslow Publishing, LLC.

Poets & Playwrights, 5 vols., Set. Incl. Carl Sandburg. Murcia, Rebecca Thatcher. lib. bdg. 37.10 *(978-1-58415-430-3(6))*; Emily Dickinson. Griskey, Michele. lib. bdg. 37.10 *(978-1-58415-429-7(2))*; Langston Hughes. Gibson, Karen Bush. lib. bdg. 37.10 *(978-1-58415-431-0(4))*; Tennessee Williams. Tracy, Kathleen. lib. bdg. 37.10 *(978-1-58415-427-3(6))*; William Shakespeare. Whiting, Jim. lib. bdg. 37.10 *(978-1-58415-426-6(8))*; (Illus.). 112p. (J). (gr. 3-7). 2007. 2007. Set lib. bdg. 185.50 *(978-1-58415-284-2(2))* Mitchell Lane Pubs.

Reef, Catherine. E. E. Cummings: A Poet's Life. 2006. (ENG., Illus.). 160p. (YA). (gr. 7-9). 21.00 *(978-0-618-56849-9(2)*, 100411, Clarion Bks.) HarperCollins Pubs.

—The Life of Paul Laurence Dunbar: Portrait of a Poet, 1 vol. 2014. (Legendary African Americans Ser.). (ENG., Illus.). 96p. (gr. 6-7). (J). pap. 13.88 *(978-0-7660-6153-8(1)*, ff7daa50-878c-4d39-b6da-a9bbda840938); 31.61 *(978-0-7660-6152-1(3)*, e6b3ee09-17ce-430d-b9bd-48353b4a0300) Enslow Publishing, LLC.

—Poetry Came in Search of Me: The Story of Pablo Neruda. 2012. (World Writers Ser.). (gr. 7-12). 28.95 *(978-1-59935-170-4(6))* Reynolds, Morgan Inc.

Rhynes, Martha E. Gwendolyn Brooks: Poet from Chicago. 2004. (World Writers Ser.). (Illus.). 112p. (YA). (gr. 6-12). 23.95 *(978-1-931798-05-1(2))* Reynolds, Morgan Inc.

Rhys, Ann Gruffydd & Bryntirion, Gwasg. Nansi Dolwar. 2005. (WEL., Illus.). 32p. pap. *(978-1-85049-212-2(3))* Bryntirion Pr.

Robertson, David A. The Poet: Pauline Johnson. Henderson, Scott B., illus. 2014. (Tales from Big Spirit Ser.: 5). (ENG.). 30p. (J). (gr. 4-6). pap. *(978-1-55379-481-3(8)*, ab04cc8e-58f6-479c-9f04-879c4a722ff3, HighWater Pr.) Portage & Main Pr.

Roza, Greg. Guide My Pen: The Poems of Phillis Wheatley. 2009. (Great Moments in American History Ser.). 32p. (gr. 3-3). 47.90 *(978-1-61513-133-4(7))* Rosen Publishing Group, Inc., The.

Santillian, Beatriz & Randall, Bernard. Solon: Athenian Statesman & Poet, 1 vol. 2017. (Leaders of the Ancient World Ser.). (ENG., Illus.). 112p. (J). (gr. 6-6). 38.80 *(978-1-5081-7493-6(8)*, 9e229bc7-da52-47ff-8710-b22f9277c86a, Rosen Young Adult) Rosen Publishing Group, Inc., The.

Simons, Lisa M. Bolt. Nikki Grimes. Byers, Michael, illus. 2017. (Your Favorite Authors Ser.). (ENG.). 24p. (J). (gr. 1-3). lib. bdg. 27.99 *(978-1-5157-3559-5(1)*, 133572, Capstone Pr.) Capstone.

Slade, Suzanne. Exquisite: The Poetry & Life of Gwendolyn Brooks. Cabrera, Cozbi A., illus. 2020. (ENG.). 48p. (J). (gr. 1-4). 18.99 *(978-1-4197-3411-3(3)*, 1180701) Abrams, Inc.

Smith, Emily R. & Conklin, Wendy. Phillis Wheatley. 2020. (Social Studies: Informational Text Ser.). (SPA., Illus.). 32p. (J). (gr. 3-5). pap. 11.99 *(978-0-7439-1362-1(0))* Teacher Created Materials, Inc.

Stewart, Gail B. Maya Angelou, 1 vol. 2009. (People in the News Ser.). (ENG., Illus.). 104p. (gr. 7-7). lib. bdg. 41.03 *(978-1-4205-0092-9(9)*, 5f651b45-e104-47a3-ac40-23df64948fc3, Lucent Pr.) Greenhaven Publishing LLC.

Strong, Amy. Lee Bennett Hopkins: A Children's Poet. 2003. (Great Life Stories: Writers & Poets Ser.). (ENG., Illus.). 112p. (J). 30.50 *(978-0-531-12315-7(4)*, Watts, Franklin) Scholastic Library Publishing.

Taylor, Charlotte. Phillis Wheatley: Colonial African-American Poet, 1 vol. 2015. (Exceptional African Americans Ser.). (ENG.). 24p. (gr. 3-3). pap. 10.35 *(978-0-7660-7324-1(6)*, 3d1fd880-69e9-423d-8fdc-5ac2f8f06497) Enslow Publishing, LLC.

Thomas, Dylan. A Child's Christmas in Wales. Raskin, Ellen, illus. 2003. (New Directions Paperbook Ser.: Vol. 972). (ENG.). 32p. reprint ed. pap. 8.00 *(978-0-8112-1560-2(1))* New Directions Publishing Corp.

Tracy, Kathleen. The Life & Times of Homer. 2004. (Biography from Ancient Civilizations Ser.). (Illus.). 48p. (J). (gr. 4-8). lib. bdg. 29.95 *(978-1-58415-260-6(5))* Mitchell Lane Pubs.

Wallace, Maurice O. Langston Hughes: The Harlem Renaissance, 1 vol. 2008. (Writers & Their Works). (ENG., Illus.). 144p. (YA). (gr. 7-7). lib. bdg. 45.50 *(978-0-7614-2591-5(8)*, ec06498b-e4bb-4abd-b507-d0949568fddc) Cavendish Square Publishing LLC.

Watson-Doost, Valeria. Phillis Wheatley. 2008. (ENG.). 35p. pap. 21.50 *(978-0-557-03153-5(2))* Lulu Pr., Inc.

Weidenbach, Kristin. Meet... Banjo Paterson. Gulliver Hancock, James, illus. 2016. 36p. (J). (gr. k-2). 15.99 *(978-0-85798-009-0(2))* Random Hse. Australia AUS. Dist: Independent Pubs. Group.

POETS—FICTION

Byars, Betsy. Keeper of the Doves. 2004. (Illus.). 128p. (J). (gr. 3-7). reprint ed. 7.99 *(978-0-14-240063-0(7)*, Puffin Books) Penguin Young Readers Group.

Dana, Barbara. Emily Dickinson: Fictionalized Biography. Date not set. (J). (gr. 3-7). mass mkt. 4.99 *(978-0-06-440843-1(4))* HarperCollins Pubs.

Figley, Marty Rhodes. Emily & Carlo. Stock, Catherine, illus. 2012. 32p. (J). (gr. k-3). 15.95 *(978-1-58089-274-2(4))* Charlesbridge Publishing, Inc.

Furnari, Eva. Fuzz Mcflops. Entrekin, Alison, tr. 2015. (ENG., Illus.). 56p. (J). (gr. k-3). pap. 12.95 *(978-1-78269-075-7(1)*, Pushkin Press) Steerforth Pr.

Giardino, Alexandria. Ode to an Onion: Pablo Neruda & His Muse. Sala, Felicita, illus. 2018. (ENG.). 40p. (J). (gr. -1-3). 19.99 *(978-1-944903-34-3(8)*, 1320401, Cameron Kids) Cameron + Co.

Hawes, Louise. The Language of Stars. 2016. (ENG., Illus.). 368p. (YA). (gr. 7). 17.99 *(978-1-4814-6241-9(5)*, McElderry, Margaret K. Bks.) McElderry, Margaret K. Bks.

Herrera, Juan Felipe. SkateFate. 2015. (ENG.). 128p. (YA). (gr. 8). pap. 9.99 *(978-0-06-143289-7(X)*, HarperTeen) HarperCollins Pubs.

MacColl, Michaela. Nobody's Secret. 2014. (ENG.). 256p. (YA). (gr. 7-17). pap. 9.99 *(978-1-4521-2854-2(5))* Chronicle Bks. LLC.

MacDonald, George. Home Again. 2017. (ENG., Illus.). (J). pap. 13.95 *(978-1-374-90785-0(5))* Capital Communications, Inc.

—Home Again. 2009. 124p. 22.95 *(978-1-60664-613-7(3))*; pap. 10.95 *(978-1-60664-351-8(7))* Rodgers, Alan Bks.

MacLachlan, Patricia. Fly Away. 2014. (ENG., Illus.). 128p. (J). (gr. 2). 15.99 *(978-1-4424-6008-9(3)*, McElderry, Margaret K. Bks.) McElderry, Margaret K. Bks.

Moody Publishing Staff & Lawton, Wendy G. Freedom's Pen: A Story Based on the Life of Freed Slave & Author Phillis Wheatley 2009. (Daughters of the Faith Ser.). (ENG.). 144p. (gr. 3-3). pap. 8.99 *(978-0-8024-7639-5(2))* Moody Pubs.

Moulton, Mark Kimball. The Visit. Winget, Susan, tr. Winget, Susan, illus. 2003. (ENG.). 56p. (J). 14.95 *(978-0-8249-5859-6(4)*, Ideals Pubns.) Worthy Publishing.

—The Visit: The Origin of the Night Before Christmas (hc), 1 vol. Winget, Susan, illus. 2013. (ENG.). 56p. (gr. 3-6). 16.99 *(978-0-7643-4575-3(3)*, 4985) Schiffer Publishing, Ltd.

—The Visit: The Origin of the Night Before Christmas (pb), 1 vol. Winget, Susan, illus. 2019. (ENG.). 52p. (gr. 3-6). pap. 9.99 *(978-0-7643-5703-9(4)*, 16397) Schiffer Publishing, Ltd.

Muten, Burleigh. Miss Emily. Phelan, Matt, illus. 2014. (ENG.). 144p. (J). (gr. 2-5). 15.99 *(978-0-7636-5734-5(4))* Candlewick Pr.

Myers, Tim. Basho & the River Stones, 0 vols. Han, Oki S., illus. 2013. (ENG.). 34p. (J). (gr. 1-3). pap. 9.99 *(978-1-4778-1682-0(8)*, 9781477816820, Two Lions) Amazon Publishing.

Nilsen, Morten. Snyder: The Pig's Tale. Osenchakov, Yuri, illus. 2007. 116p. 24.95 *(978-0-9774906-0-8(2))* Counterbalance Bks.

Peck, Steven L. The Rifts of Rime (Quickened Chronicles) 2012. pap. 14.99 *(978-1-59955-967-4(6))* Cedar Fort, Inc./CFI Distribution.

The Poet's Basket. 2006. (J). 10.00 *(978-0-9769827-0-8(6))* Wren Song Pr.

Rinaldi, Ann. Hang a Thousand Trees with Ribbons: The Story of Phillis Wheatley. 2005. (Great Episodes Ser.). (ENG.). 352p. (YA). (gr. 7-8). pap. 10.99 *(978-0-15-205393-2(X)*, 1196235, Clarion Bks.) HarperCollins Pubs.

—Hang a Thousand Trees with Ribbons: The Story of Phillis Wheatley. 2005. (Great Episodes Ser.). 336p. (gr. 5-9). 18.00 *(978-0-7569-5018-7(X))* Perfection Learning Corp.

Ryan, Pam Muñoz. The Dreamer, 1 vol. Sís, Peter & Sís, Peter, illus. 2012. (ENG.). 384p. (gr. 4-9). pap. 12.99 *(978-0-439-26998-8(9)*, Scholastic Paperbacks) Scholastic, Inc.

—The Dreamer, 1 vol. Sís, Peter, illus. 2010. (ENG.). 384p. (J). (gr. 4-9). 21.99 *(978-0-439-26970-4(9)*, Scholastic Pr.) Scholastic, Inc.

—The Dreamer. 2012. lib. bdg. 19.65 *(978-0-606-23940-0(5))* Turtleback.

Sharp, Margery. The Rescuers. Williams, Garth, illus. 2016. (ENG.). 160p. (J). (gr. 4-7). pap. 11.99 *(978-1-68137-007-1(7)*, NYRB Kids) New York Review of Bks., Inc., The.

Williams-Garcia, Rita. One Crazy Summer. 2009. (KOR.). 272p. (J). pap. *(978-89-7199-494-8(0))* Dolbegae Publishing Co.

—One Crazy Summer. 2011. (ENG.). 240p. (J). (gr. 3-7). pap. 9.99 *(978-0-06-076090-8(7)*, Quill Tree Bks.) HarperCollins Pubs.

—One Crazy Summer. (J). 2011. 1.25 *(978-1-4498-2201-9(0))* 2010. 69.75 *(978-1-4498-2197-5(9))* 2010. 67.75 *(978-1-4498-2199-9(5))* Recorded Bks., Inc.

—One Crazy Summer. 2011. (J). lib. bdg. 17.20 *(978-0-606-23555-6(8))* Turtleback.

—One Crazy Summer: A Newbery Honor Award Winner. 2010. (ENG.). 224p. (J). (gr. 3-7). 18.99 *(978-0-06-076088-5(5))*; lib. bdg. 16.89 *(978-0-06-076089-2(3))* HarperCollins Pubs. (Quill Tree Bks.).

POISONOUS PLANTS

Bradley, Timothy J. Terror in the Tropics, 1 vol. 2nd rev. ed. 2013. (TIME for KIDS(r): Informational Text Ser.). (ENG., Illus.). 64p. (J). (gr. 4-8). lib. bdg. 31.96 *(978-1-4333-7421-0(8))* Teacher Created Materials, Inc.

Claybourne, Anna. 100 Deadliest Things on the Planet. 2012. (100 Most... Ser.). lib. bdg. 18.40 *(978-0-606-26744-1(1))* Turtleback.

Gould, Margee. Poisonous Plants, 1 vol. 2011. (Strangest Plants on Earth Ser.). (ENG., Illus.). 24p. (J). (gr. 2-3). lib. bdg. 26.27 *(978-1-4488-4989-5(6)*, a4d7e42e-a9d0-41d3-9fd4-2e04d2968bc8) Rosen Publishing Group, Inc., The.

Hicks, Dwayne. Plants That Poison, 1 vol. 2016. (Plant Defenses Ser.). (ENG., Illus.). 24p. (J). (gr. 3-3). pap. 9.25 *(978-1-4994-2155-2(9)*, 75c0720f-ef0b-4f28-9791-59fb8566bf6c, PowerKids Pr.) Rosen Publishing Group, Inc., The.

Hirsch, Rebecca E. When Plants Attack: Strange & Terrifying Plants. 2019. (ENG., Illus.). 48p. (J). (gr. 4-8). 31.99 *(978-1-5415-2670-9(8)*, 6cb5bfff-4e48-4fb2-ad56-59233b4193e9, Millbrook Pr.) Lerner Publishing Group.

Lawler, Janet. Scary Plants! 2017. (Smithsonian Ser.). (Illus.). 48p. (J). (gr. 1-3). pap. 3.99 *(978-0-451-53371-5(2)*, Penguin Young Readers) Penguin Young Readers Group.

Lawrence, Ellen. Poison Petals: Don't Eat! 2012. (Science Slam: Plant-Ology Ser.). 24p. (J). (gr. -1-3). lib. bdg. 26.99 *(978-1-61772-590-6(0))* Bearport Publishing Co., Inc.

Levy, Janey. Poisonous Plants, 1 vol. 2019. (Mother Nature Is Trying to Kill Me! Ser.). (ENG.). 24p. (gr. 2-3). pap. 9.15 *(978-1-5382-3974-2(4)*, 79ab7d03-4398-4c39-8ee4-dbb59a9dd782) Stevens, Gareth Publishing LLLP.

Loukopoulos, Beatrice. Plants That Are Poisonous, 1 vol. 2018. (Peculiar Plants of the World Ser.). (ENG.). 24p. (J). (gr. 3-3). 25.27 *(978-1-5383-4489-7(0)*, 20a7adf9-c1ca-4d3e-9326-aa8bf674323a, PowerKids Pr.) Rosen Publishing Group, Inc., The.

Miller, Connie Colwell. The Deadliest Plants on Earth. 2010. (World's Deadliest Ser.). (ENG.). 32p. (J). (gr. 3-9). lib. bdg. 27.32 *(978-1-4296-3933-0(4)*, 102543, Capstone Pr.) Capstone.

Sanchez, Anita. Itch! Everything You Didn't Want to Know about What Makes You Scratch. Ford, Gilbert, illus. 2018. (ENG.). 80p. (J). (gr. 3-7). 17.99 *(978-0-544-81101-0(1)*, 1641759, Clarion Bks.) HarperCollins Pubs.

Spilsbury, Louise. Creeping Killers: Extreme Plants, 1 vol. 2014. (Extreme Biology Ser.). (ENG., Illus.). 48p. (J). (gr. 4-4). lib. bdg. 33.60 *(978-1-4824-2234-4(4)*, 6be5d85a-1c1d-4b52-9d83-2a367eaff655) Stevens, Gareth Publishing LLLP.

POISONS

Albee, Sarah. Poison: Deadly Deeds, Perilous Professions, & Murderous Medicines. 2017. (Illus.). 192p. (J). (gr. 3-7). pap. 17.99 *(978-1-101-93223-0(6)*, Crown Books For Young Readers) Random Hse. Children's Bks.

Bellisario, Gina. Poison Alert! My Tips to Avoid Danger Zones at Home. Conger, Holli, illus. 2014. (Cloverleaf Books (tm) — My Healthy Habits Ser.). (ENG.). 24p. (J). (gr. k-2). lib. bdg. 25.32 *(978-1-4677-1353-5(8)*, c6cc7171-b1b0-4520-a1a6-61681468ee68, Millbrook Pr.) Lerner Publishing Group.

Hodge, Susie. Toxic! [Scholastic]: Killer Cures & Other Poisonings. 2011. (Extreme! Ser.). 32p. pap. 1.00 *(978-1-4296-6488-2(6)*, Capstone Pr.) Capstone.

Jackson, Tom. Snake Bite. 2008. (ENG., Illus.). 32p. (J). (gr. 5-9). lib. bdg. *(978-0-7787-3772-8(1))* Crabtree Publishing Co.

Jakubiak, David J. Protecting Our Planet: What Can We Do about Toxins in the Environment? (Illus.). 24p. 2012. (J). 49.50 *(978-1-4488-5122-5(X)*, PowerKids Pr.) 2011. (ENG., (J). (gr. 2-3). pap. 9.25 *(978-1-4488-5121-8(1)*, 2ddc6fca-8ea9-4369-bf16-fdcd2521e68c, PowerKids Pr.) 2011. (ENG., (YA). (gr. 2-3). lib. bdg. 26.27 *(978-1-4488-4987-1(X)*, cad654b2-9427-4f55-a4fc-92a390da2b1d) Rosen Publishing Group, Inc., The.

Lloyd Kyi, Tanya. 50 Poisonous Questions: A Book with Bite. Kinnaird, Ross, illus. 2011. (50 Questions Ser.). (ENG.). 112p. (J). (gr. 4-7). 21.95 *(978-1-55451-281-2(6)*, 9781554512812) Annick Pr., Ltd. CAN. Dist: Publishers Group West (PGW).

Loh-Hagan, Virginia. Venom. 2016. (Wild Wicked Wonderful Ser.). (ENG., Illus.). 32p. (J). (gr. 4-8). 32.07 *(978-1-63470-507-3(6)*, 207759) Cherry Lake Publishing.

Manley, Claudia B. Crack & Your Circulatory System: The Incredibly Disgusting Story. 2009. (Incredibly Disgusting Drugs Ser.). 48p. (gr. 5-8). 53.00 *(978-1-61513-494-6(8)*, Rosen Reference) Rosen Publishing Group, Inc., The.

Marlowe, Christie. Protecting Your Body: Germs, Super Bugs, Poison & Deadly Diseases. Stephens, Ronald, ed. 2014. (Safety First Ser.: 11). 48p. (J). (gr. 5-18). 20.95 *(978-1-4222-3051-0(1))* Mason Crest.

Meister, Cari. Venomous Animals. Fretland VanVoorst, Jenny, ed. 2016. (Back off! Animal Defenses). (Illus.). 24p. (J). (gr. 2-5). lib. bdg. *(978-1-62031-313-8(8)*, Pogo) Jump! Inc.

Prokos, Anna. 24/7: Science Behind the Scenes: Forensic Files: Killer Wallpaper. Prokos, Anna, illus. 2007. (24/7: Science Behind the Scenes Ser.). (ENG., Illus.). 640p. (YA). (gr. 9-12). 29.00 *(978-0-531-12061-3(9)*, Watts, Franklin) Scholastic Library Publishing.

Roza, Greg. Sting! The Scorpion & Other Animals That Sting, 1 vol. 2011. (Armed & Dangerous Ser.). (ENG., Illus.). 24p. (J). (gr. 2-3). 26.27 *(978-1-4488-2548-6(2)*, 9e9b4535-819e-480c-a0ed-dd6cb5799b2c); pap. 9.25 *(978-1-4488-2680-3(2)*, 286ac118-1094-450e-a17c-2cc64979c994, PowerKids Pr.) Rosen Publishing Group, Inc., The.

Shackleton, Caroline. Poison: Medicine, Murder, & Mystery High Intermediate Book with Online Access, 1 vol. 2014. (ENG., Illus.). 28p. (J). pap., E-Book 9.50 *(978-1-107-62260-9(3))* Cambridge Univ. Pr.

Singer, Marilyn. Venom. 2014. (ENG., Illus.). 96p. (YA). (gr. 5-12). pap. 12.99 *(978-1-4677-4909-1(5)*, 341736da-49b2-47d5-ad2f-c860dcb8dcd1, Millbrook Pr.) Lerner Publishing Group.

Spilsbury, Louise. Harmful Substances, 1 vol. 2011. (Healthy & Happy Ser.). (ENG., Illus.). 32p. (J). (gr. 2-2). lib. bdg. 30.27 *(978-1-4488-5276-5(5)*, a57554fb-5993-4b27-9375-6c619669210b) Rosen Publishing Group, Inc., The.

POKEMON (FICTITIOUS CHARACTERS)—FICTION

Barbo, Maria S. Go, Popplio! 2018. (Scholastic Readers Ser.). (ENG.). 32p. (J). (gr. -1-k). 13.89 *(978-1-64310-232-0(X))* Penworthy Co., LLC, The.

—The Rescue Mission. 2016. (Pokemon Reader Ser.: 1). lib. bdg. 13.55 *(978-0-606-39736-0(1))* Turtleback.

—The Rescue Mission (Pokémon Kalos: Scholastic Reader, Level 2) 2016. (Scholastic Reader, Level 2 Ser.: 1). (ENG.). 32p. (J). (gr. -1-3). pap. 5.99 *(978-1-338-11290-0(2))* Scholastic, Inc.

—Team Rocket to the Rescue. 2016. (Pokemon Reader Ser.: 2). lib. bdg. 13.55 *(978-0-606-39725-4(6))* Turtleback.

—Ultimate Sketch Challenge. Scholastic, Inc. Staff, illus. 2nd ed. 2018. (ENG.). 64p. (J). (gr. -1-3). 12.99 *(978-1-338-23756-6(X))* Scholastic, Inc.

—Welcome to Alola! (Pokémon Alola: Scholastic Reader, Level 2) 2017. (Scholastic Reader, Level 2 Ser.). (ENG.). 32p. (J). (gr. -1-3). pap. 5.99 *(978-1-338-14864-0(8))* Scholastic, Inc.

Chlebowski, Rachel. Ash & Pikachu: Alola Region/Team Rocket: Alola Region (Pokémon) Random House, illus. 2017. (Pictureback(R) Ser.). (ENG.). 32p. (J). (gr. -1-2). pap. 5.99 *(978-1-5247-7008-2(6)*, Random Hse. Bks. for Young Readers) Random Hse. Children's Bks.

—Famous Friends & Foes (Pokémon) Random House, illus. 2017. (Pictureback(R) Ser.). 32p. (J). (gr. -1-2). pap. 5.99 *(978-1-5247-7010-5(8)*, Random Hse. Bks. for Young Readers) Random Hse. Children's Bks.

Dewin, Howard & Dewin, Howie. The Four-Star Challenge (Pokémon: Chapter Book) 2017. (Pokémon Chapter Bks.). (ENG.). 96p. (J). (gr. 2-5). pap. 4.99 *(978-1-338-17573-8(4))* Scholastic, Inc.

Harukaze, Santa. Pokémon Pocket Comics: Black & White. 2013. (Pokémon Pocket Comics Ser.: 1). (ENG., Illus.). 320p. (J). pap. 9.99 *(978-1-4215-5910-0(2))* Viz Media.

—Pokémon Pocket Comics Box Set: Black & White / Legendary Pokemon, Vols. 1 & 2 2016. (Pokémon Pocket Comics Box Set Ser.: 1). (ENG., Illus.). 576p. (J). pap. 16.99 *(978-1-4215-8964-0(8))* Viz Media.

—Pokémon X * y Pocket Comics. 2016. (Pokémon Pocket Comics Ser.: 3). (ENG., Illus.). 240p. (J). pap. 10.99 *(978-1-4215-8693-9(2))* Viz Media.

Hijioka, Makoto. Pokémon: Giratina & the Sky Warrior! 2009. (Pokémon the Movie (manga) Ser.: 1). (ENG., Illus.). 192p. (J). pap. 9.99 *(978-1-4215-2701-7(4))* Viz Media.

Ihara, Shigekatsu. Pokémon Diamond & Pearl Adventure!, Vol. 1. 2008. (ENG., Illus.). 188p. (J). (gr. k). pap. 9.99 *(978-1-4215-2286-9(1))* Viz Media.

—Pokémon Diamond & Pearl Adventure!, Vol. 2. 2008. (ENG., Illus.). 192p. (J). (gr. 1). pap. 9.99 *(978-1-4215-2287-6(X))* Viz Media.

—Pokémon Diamond & Pearl Adventure!, Vol. 3. 2009. (ENG., Illus.). 192p. (J). pap. 9.99 *(978-1-4215-2574-7(7))* Viz Media.

—Pokémon Diamond & Pearl Adventure!, Vol. 4, Vol. 4. 2009. (ENG., Illus.). 200p. (J). pap. 9.99 *(978-1-4215-2674-4(3))* Viz Media.

—Pokémon Diamond & Pearl Adventure!, Vol. 6. 2010. (ENG., Illus.). 192p. (J). pap. 9.99 *(978-1-4215-3170-0(4))* Viz Media.

—Pokémon Diamond & Pearl Adventure!, Vol. 7. 2010. (ENG., Illus.). 192p. (J). pap. 9.99 *(978-1-4215-3491-6(6))* Viz Media.

—Pokémon Diamond & Pearl Adventure!, Vol. 8 Vol. 8. 2010. (ENG., Illus.). 192p. (J). pap. 9.99 *(978-1-4215-3671-2(4))* Viz Media.

Inoue, Momota. Pokémon the Movie: Kyurem vs. the Sword of Justice. 2013. (Pokémon the Movie (manga) Ser.: 15). (ENG.). 192p. (J). pap. 9.99 *(978-1-4215-5690-1(1))* Viz Media.

—Pokémon the Movie: White — Victini & Zekrom. movie tie-in ed. 2012. (Pokémon the Movie (manga) Ser.: 1). (ENG.). 192p. (J). pap. 9.99 *(978-1-4215-4954-5(9))* Viz Media.

—Pokémon: the Movie: Zoroark: Master of Illusions. 2011. (Pokémon the Movie (manga) Ser.: 1). (ENG.). 192p. (J). pap. 9.99 *(978-1-4215-4221-8(8))* Viz Media.

Johnson, Jennifer & Heller, S. E. Psyduck Ducks Out (Pokémon: Chapter Book) 2017. (Pokémon Chapter Bks.: 15). (ENG.). 96p. (J). (gr. 2-5). pap. 4.99 *(978-1-338-17596-7(3))* Scholastic, Inc.

Johnson, Jennifer & Johnson, Jennifer L. Secrets of the GS Ball (Pokémon Classic Chapter Book #16) 2018. (Pokémon Chapter Bks.: 16). (ENG.). 96p. (J). (gr. 2-5). pap. 4.99 *(978-1-338-28412-6(6))* Scholastic, Inc.

Kamimura, Gin. Pokemon the Movie: Hoopa & the Clash of Ages. 2016. (Pokémon the Movie (manga) Ser.: 1). (ENG., Illus.). 192p. (J). pap. 9.99 *(978-1-4215-8782-0(3))* Viz Media.

Kawamoto, Kemon. Pokémon the Movie: Volcanion & the Mechanical Marvel. 2017. (Pokémon the Movie (manga) Ser.). (ENG., Illus.). 200p. (J). pap. 9.99 *(978-1-4215-9419-4(6))* Viz Media.

Kitamura, Kenji. Pokémon the Movie: Diancie & the Cocoon of Destruction. 2015. (Pokémon the Movie (manga) Ser.: 17). (ENG., Illus.). 200p. (J). pap. 9.99 *(978-1-4215-8051-7(9))* Viz Media.

Kudo, Maki. The Pokémon Cookbook: Easy & Fun Recipes. 2016. (Pokémon Cookbook Ser.: 1). (ENG., Illus.). 80p. 14.99 *(978-1-4215-8989-3(3))* Viz Media.

Kusaka, Hidenori. Pokemon Adventures. 2015. (Pokemon Adventures Ser.: 29). lib. bdg. 20.85 *(978-0-606-37897-0(9))*; lib. bdg. 20.85 *(978-0-606-37244-2(X))* Turtleback.

—Pokémon Adventures: Black 2 & White 2, Vol. 1. Yamamoto, Satoshi, illus. 2017. (Pokémon Adventures: Black 2 & White 2 Ser.: 1). (ENG.). 200p. (J). pap. 9.99 *(978-1-4215-8437-9(9))* Viz Media.

—Pokémon Adventures: Black 2 & White 2, Vol. 2. Yamamoto, Satoshi, illus. 2018. (Pokémon Adventures: Black 2 & White 2 Ser.: 2). (ENG.). 208p. (J). pap. 9.99 *(978-1-4215-8438-6(7))* Viz Media.

—Pokémon Adventures: Black & White, Vol. 1 Vol. 1. 2013. (Pokémon Adventures: Black & White Ser.: 1). (ENG., Illus.). 104p. (J). pap. 9.99 *(978-1-4215-5898-1(X))* Viz Media.

—Pokémon Adventures: Black & White, Vol. 2. 2013. (Pokémon Adventures: Black & White Ser.: 2). (ENG., Illus.). 208p. (J). pap. 9.99 *(978-1-4215-5899-8(8))* Viz Media.

—Pokémon Adventures: Black & White, Vol. 3 Vol. 3. 2014. (Pokémon Adventures: Black & White Ser.: 3). (ENG., Illus.). 208p. (J). pap. 9.99 *(978-1-4215-6178-3(6))* Viz Media.

—Pokémon Adventures: Black & White, Vol. 4. 2014. (Pokémon Adventures: Black & White Ser.: 4). (ENG., Illus.). 200p. (J). pap. 9.99 *(978-1-4215-6180-6(8))* Viz Media.

—Pokémon Adventures: Black & White, Vol. 5. 2014. (Pokémon Adventures: Black & White Ser.: 5). (ENG., Illus.). 208p. (J). pap. 9.99 *(978-1-4215-6181-3(6))* Viz Media.

—Pokémon Adventures: Black & White, Vol. 6. 2015. (Pokémon Adventures: Black & White Ser.: 6). (ENG., Illus.). 216p. (J). pap. 9.99 *(978-1-4215-7181-2(1))* Viz Media.

—Pokémon Adventures: Black & White, Vol. 7. 2015. (Pokémon Adventures: Black & White Ser.: 7). (ENG., Illus.). 216p. (J). pap. 9.99 *(978-1-4215-7836-1(0))* Viz Media.

—Pokémon Adventures: Black & White, Vol. 9 Vol. 9. 2015. (Pokémon Adventures: Black & White Ser.: 9). (ENG., Illus.). 192p. (J). pap. 9.99 *(978-1-4215-7961-0(8))* Viz Media.

—Pokémon Adventures Diamond & Pearl / Platinum Box Set: Includes Volumes 1-11. Yamamoto, Satoshi, illus. 2014. (Pokémon Manga Box Sets Ser.). (ENG.). 2304p. (J). pap. 89.99 *(978-1-4215-7777-7(1))* Viz Media.

—Pokémon Adventures: Diamond & Pearl/Platinum, Vol. 1 Vol. 1, 1. 2011. (Pokémon Adventures: Diamond & Pearl/Platinum Ser.: 1). (ENG., Illus.). 208p. (J). (gr. 4-6). pap. 9.99 *(978-1-4215-3816-7(4))* Viz Media.

—Pokémon Adventures: Diamond & Pearl/Platinum, Vol. 10. 2014. (Pokémon Adventures: Diamond & Pearl/Platinum Ser.: 10). (ENG., Illus.). 192p. (J). pap. 9.99 *(978-1-4215-5406-8(2))* Viz Media.

—Pokémon Adventures: Diamond & Pearl/Platinum, Vol. 11 Vol. 11. 2014. (Pokémon Adventures: Diamond & Pearl/Platinum Ser.: 11). (ENG., Illus.). 224p. (J). pap. 9.99 *(978-1-4215-6179-0(4))* Viz Media.

—Pokémon Adventures: Diamond & Pearl/Platinum, Vol. 2 Vol. 2, 2. 2011. (Pokémon Adventures: Diamond & Pearl/Platinum Ser.: 2). (ENG., Illus.). 216p. (J). (gr. 4-6). pap. 9.99 *(978-1-4215-3817-4(2))* Viz Media.

—Pokémon Adventures: Diamond & Pearl/Platinum, Vol. 3 Vol. 3. 2011. (Pokémon Adventures: Diamond & Pearl/Platinum Ser.: 3). (ENG., Illus.). 208p. (J). pap. 9.99 *(978-1-4215-3818-1(0))* Viz Media.

—Pokémon Adventures: Diamond & Pearl/Platinum, Vol. 4. 2012. (Pokémon Adventures: Diamond & Pearl/Platinum Ser.: 4). (ENG., Illus.). 208p. (J). pap. 9.99 *(978-1-4215-3912-6(8))* Viz Media.

—Pokémon Adventures: Diamond & Pearl/Platinum, Vol. 5 Vol. 5. 2012. (Pokémon Adventures: Diamond & Pearl/Platinum Ser.: 5). (ENG., Illus.). 208p. (J). pap. 9.99 *(978-1-4215-3913-3(6))* Viz Media.

—Pokémon Adventures: Diamond & Pearl/Platinum, Vol. 6, Vol. 6. 2012. (Pokémon Adventures: Diamond & Pearl/Platinum Ser.: 6). (ENG., Illus.). 216p. (J). pap. 9.99 *(978-1-4215-3914-0(4))* Viz Media.

—Pokémon Adventures: Diamond & Pearl/Platinum, Vol. 7, Vol. 7. 2013. (Pokémon Adventures: Diamond & Pearl/Platinum Ser.: 7). (ENG., Illus.). 208p. (J). pap. 9.99 *(978-1-4215-4247-8(1))* Viz Media.

—Pokémon Adventures: Diamond & Pearl/Platinum, Vol. 8. 2013. (Pokémon Adventures: Diamond & Pearl/Platinum Ser.: 8). (ENG., Illus.). 192p. (J). pap. 9.99 *(978-1-4215-5404-4(6))* Viz Media.

—Pokémon Adventures: Diamond & Pearl/Platinum, Vol. 9 Vol. 9. 2013. (Pokémon Adventures: Diamond & Pearl/Platinum Ser.: 9). (ENG., Illus.). 192p. (J). pap. 9.99 *(978-1-4215-5405-1(4))* Viz Media.

—Pokémon Adventures (Emerald), Vol. 26. 2015. (Pokémon Adventures Ser.: 26). (ENG., Illus.). 208p. (J). pap. 9.99 *(978-1-4215-3560-9(2))* Viz Media.

—Pokémon Adventures (Emerald), Vol. 27. 2015. (Pokémon Adventures Ser.: 27). (ENG., Illus.). 208p. (J). pap. 9.99 *(978-1-4215-3561-6(0))* Viz Media.

—Pokémon Adventures (Emerald), Vol. 28. 2015. (Pokémon Adventures Ser.: 28). (ENG., Illus.). 208p. (J). pap. 9.99 *(978-1-4215-3562-3(9))* Viz Media.

—Pokémon Adventures (Emerald), Vol. 29. 2015. (Pokémon Adventures Ser.: 29). (ENG., Illus.). 224p. (J). pap. 9.99 *(978-1-4215-3563-0(7))* Viz Media.

—Pokémon Adventures FireRed & LeafGreen / Emerald Box Set: Includes Vols. 23-29. Yamamoto, Satoshi, illus. 2015. (Pokémon Manga Box Sets Ser.). (ENG.). 1576p. (J). pap. 54.99 *(978-1-4215-8278-8(3))* Viz Media.

—Pokémon Adventures Gold & Silver Box Set (Set Includes Vols. 8-14) Yamamoto, Satoshi & MATO, illus. 2012. (Pokémon Manga Box Sets Ser.: 2). (ENG.). 1552p. (J). pap. 54.99 *(978-1-4215-5007-7(5))* Viz Media.

—Pokémon Adventures (Gold & Silver), Vol. 10. 2010. (Pokémon Adventures Ser.: 10). (ENG., Illus.). 200p. (J). pap. 9.99 *(978-1-4215-3063-5(5))* Viz Media.

—Pokémon Adventures (Gold & Silver), Vol. 11. 2011. (Pokémon Adventures Ser.: 11). (ENG., Illus.). 208p. (J). pap. 9.99 *(978-1-4215-3545-6(9))* Viz Media.

—Pokémon Adventures (Gold & Silver), Vol. 12. 2011. (Pokémon Adventures Ser.: 12). (ENG., Illus.). 208p. (J). pap. 9.99 *(978-1-4215-3546-3(7))* Viz Media.

—Pokémon Adventures (Gold & Silver), Vol. 13. 2011. (Pokémon Adventures Ser.: 13). (ENG., Illus.). 208p. (J). pap. 9.99 *(978-1-4215-3547-0(5))* Viz Media.

—Pokémon Adventures (Gold & Silver), Vol. 14. 2011. (Pokémon Adventures Ser.: 14). (ENG., Illus.). 272p. (J). pap. 9.99 *(978-1-4215-3548-7(3))* Viz Media.

—Pokémon Adventures (Gold & Silver), Vol. 8. 2010. (Pokémon Adventures Ser.: 8). (ENG., Illus.). 232p. (J). pap. 9.99 *(978-1-4215-3061-1(9))* Viz Media.

—Pokémon Adventures (Gold & Silver), Vol. 9. 2010. (Pokémon Adventures Ser.: 9). (ENG., Illus.). 224p. (J). pap. 9.99 *(978-1-4215-3062-8(7))* Viz Media.

—Pokémon Adventures: HeartGold & SoulSilver, Vol. 1. 2013. (Pokémon Adventures: HeartGold & SoulSilver Ser.: 1). (ENG., Illus.). 208p. (J). pap. 9.99 *(978-1-4215-5900-1(5))* Viz Media.

—Pokémon Adventures: HeartGold & SoulSilver, Vol. 2. 2013. (Pokémon Adventures: HeartGold & SoulSilver Ser.: 2). (ENG., Illus.). 272p. (J). pap. 9.99 *(978-1-4215-5901-8(3))* Viz Media.

—Pokémon Adventures Red & Blue Box Set (Set Includes Vols. 1-7) Mato, illus. 2012. (Pokémon Manga Box Sets Ser.: 1). (ENG.). 1504p. (J). pap. 54.99 *(978-1-4215-5006-0(7))* Viz Media.

—Pokémon Adventures (Red & Blue), Vol. 1. 2nd ed. 2009. (Pokémon Adventures Ser.: 1). (ENG., Illus.). 200p. (J). pap. 9.99 *(978-1-4215-3054-3(6))* Viz Media.

—Pokémon Adventures (Red & Blue), Vol. 2. 2nd ed. 2009. (Pokémon Adventures Ser.: 2). (ENG., Illus.). 200p. (J). pap. 9.99 *(978-1-4215-3055-0(4))* Viz Media.

—Pokémon Adventures (Red & Blue), Vol. 3. 2nd ed. 2009. (Pokémon Adventures Ser.: 3). (ENG., Illus.). 240p. (J). pap. 9.99 *(978-1-4215-3056-7(2))* Viz Media.

—Pokémon Adventures (Red & Blue), Vol. 4. 2nd ed. 2009. (Pokémon Adventures Ser.: 4). (ENG., Illus.). 216p. (J). pap. 9.99 *(978-1-4215-3057-4(0))* Viz Media.

—Pokémon Adventures (Red & Blue), Vol. 5. 2nd ed. 2010. (Pokémon Adventures Ser.: 5). (ENG., Illus.). 216p. (J). pap. 9.99 *(978-1-4215-3058-1(9))* Viz Media.

—Pokémon Adventures (Red & Blue), Vol. 6. 2nd ed. 2010. (Pokémon Adventures Ser.: 6). (ENG., Illus.). 208p. (J). pap. 9.99 *(978-1-4215-3059-8(7))* Viz Media.

—Pokémon Adventures (Red & Blue), Vol. 7. 2nd ed. 2010. (Pokémon Adventures Ser.: 7). (ENG., Illus.). 224p. (J). pap. 9.99 *(978-1-4215-3060-4(0))* Viz Media.

—Pokémon Adventures Ruby & Sapphire Box Set: Includes Volumes 15-22. Yamamoto, Satoshi, illus. 2014. (Pokémon Manga Box Sets Ser.). (ENG.). 1576p. (J). pap. 59.99 *(978-1-4215-7776-0(3))* Viz Media.

—Pokémon Adventures (Ruby & Sapphire), Vol. 15. 2013. (Pokémon Adventures Ser.: 15). (ENG., Illus.). 144p. (J). pap. 9.99 *(978-1-4215-3549-4(1))* Viz Media.

—Pokémon Adventures (Ruby & Sapphire), Vol. 16. 2013. (Pokémon Adventures Ser.: 16). (ENG., Illus.). 208p. (J). pap. 9.99 *(978-1-4215-3550-0(5))* Viz Media.

—Pokémon Adventures (Ruby & Sapphire), Vol. 17. 2013. (Pokémon Adventures Ser.: 17). (ENG., Illus.). 208p. (J). pap. 9.99 *(978-1-4215-3551-7(3))* Viz Media.

—Pokémon Adventures (Ruby & Sapphire), Vol. 18. 2013. (Pokémon Adventures Ser.: 18). (ENG., Illus.). 192p. (J). pap. 9.99 *(978-1-4215-3552-4(1))* Viz Media.

—Pokémon Adventures (Ruby & Sapphire), Vol. 19. 2013. (Pokémon Adventures Ser.: 19). (ENG., Illus.). 192p. (J). pap. 9.99 *(978-1-4215-3553-1(X))* Viz Media.

—Pokémon Adventures (Ruby & Sapphire), Vol. 20. 2014. (Pokémon Adventures Ser.: 20). (ENG., Illus.). 208p. (J). pap. 9.99 *(978-1-4215-3554-8(8))* Viz Media.

—Pokémon Adventures (Ruby & Sapphire), Vol. 21. 2014. (Pokémon Adventures Ser.: 21). (ENG., Illus.). 208p. (J). pap. 9.99 *(978-1-4215-3555-5(6))* Viz Media.

—Pokémon Adventures (Ruby & Sapphire), Vol. 22. 2014. (Pokémon Adventures Ser.: 22). (ENG., Illus.). 184p. (J). pap. 9.99 *(978-1-4215-3556-2(4))* Viz Media.

—Pokémon Black & White, Vol. 7. Yamamoto, Satoshi, illus. 2012. (Pokemon: Black & White Ser.). (ENG.). 96p. (J). (gr. 3-6). 17.44 *(978-1-4215-4282-9(X))* Viz Media.

—Pokémon Omega Ruby & Alpha Sapphire, Vol. 1, Vol. 1. Yamamoto, Satoshi, illus. 2016. (Pokémon Omega Ruby & Alpha Sapphire Ser.: 1). (ENG.). 96p. (J). pap. 4.99 *(978-1-4215-9070-7(0))* Viz Media.

—Pokémon Omega Ruby & Alpha Sapphire, Vol. 2, Vol. 2. Yamamoto, Satoshi, illus. 2016. (Pokémon Omega Ruby & Alpha Sapphire Ser.: 2). (ENG.). 112p. (J). pap. 4.99 *(978-1-4215-9016-5(6))* Viz Media.

—Pokémon Omega Ruby & Alpha Sapphire, Vol. 3, Vol. 3. Yamamoto, Satoshi, illus. 2017. (Pokémon Omega Ruby & Alpha Sapphire Ser.: 3). (ENG.). 96p. (J). pap. 4.99 *(978-1-4215-9156-8(1))* Viz Media.

—Pokémon Omega Ruby & Alpha Sapphire, Vol. 4, Vol. 4. Yamamoto, Satoshi, illus. 2017. (Pokémon Omega Ruby & Alpha Sapphire Ser.: 4). (ENG.). 96p. (J). pap. 4.99 *(978-1-4215-9223-7(1))* Viz Media.

—Pokémon Omega Ruby & Alpha Sapphire, Vol. 6. Yamamoto, Satoshi, illus. 2018. (Pokémon Omega Ruby & Alpha Sapphire Ser.: 6). (ENG.). 120p. (J). pap. 4.99 *(978-1-4215-9738-6(1))* Viz Media.

—Pokémon: Sun & Moon, Vol. 1. Yamamoto, Satoshi, illus. 2018. (Pokémon: Sun & Moon Ser.: 1). (ENG.). 80p. (J). pap. 4.99 *(978-1-9747-0075-2(5))* Viz Media.

—Pokémon: Sun & Moon, Vol. 2. Yamamoto, Satoshi, illus. 2018. (Pokémon: Sun & Moon Ser.: 2). (ENG.). 120p. (J). pap. 4.99 *(978-1-9747-0130-8(1))* Viz Media.

—Pokemon Xy, Vol. 11. 2017. (Pokemon X Y Ser.: 11). lib. bdg. 14.75 *(978-0-606-40299-6(3))* Turtleback.

—Pokémon X*y, Vol. 1, Vol. 1. Yamamoto, Satoshi, illus. 2014. (Pokémon X*y Ser.: 1). (ENG.). 96p. (J). pap. 4.99 *(978-1-4215-7980-1(4))* Viz Media.

—Pokémon X*y, Vol. 10. Yamamoto, Satoshi, illus. 2017. (Pokémon X*y Ser.: 10). (ENG.). 112p. (J). pap. 4.99 *(978-1-4215-9164-3(2))* Viz Media.

—Pokémon X*y, Vol. 11. Yamamoto, Satoshi, illus. 2017. (Pokémon X*y Ser.: 11). (ENG.). 96p. (J). pap. 4.99 *(978-1-4215-9066-0(2))* Viz Media.

—Pokémon X*y, Vol. 2, Vol. 2. Yamamoto, Satoshi, illus. 2015. (Pokémon X*y Ser.: 2). (ENG.). 112p. (J). pap. 4.99 *(978-1-4215-7834-7(4))* Viz Media.

—Pokémon X*y, Vol. 5, Vol. 5. Yamamoto, Satoshi, illus. 2015. (Pokémon X*y Ser.: 5). (ENG.). 96p. (J). pap. 4.99 *(978-1-4215-8250-4(3))* Viz Media.

—Pokémon X*y, Vol. 6. Yamamoto, Satoshi, illus. 2016. (Pokémon X*y Ser.: 6). (ENG.). 96p. (J). pap. 4.99 *(978-1-4215-8335-8(6))* Viz Media.

—Pokémon X*y, Vol. 7. Yamamoto, Satoshi, illus. 2016. (Pokémon X*y Ser.: 7). (ENG.). 96p. (J). pap. 4.99 *(978-1-4215-8777-6(7))* Viz Media.

—Pokémon X*y, Vol. 8, Vol. 8. Yamamoto, Satoshi, illus. 2016. (Pokémon X*y Ser.: 8). (ENG.). 96p. (J). pap. 4.99 *(978-1-4215-8779-0(3))* Viz Media.

—Pokémon X*y, Vol. 9. Yamamoto, Satoshi, illus. 2017. (Pokémon X*y Ser.: 9). (ENG.). 96p. (J). pap. 4.99 *(978-1-4215-9155-1(3))* Viz Media.

Lane, Jeanette. The Great Pancake Race. 2018. (Scholastic Readers Ser.). (ENG.). 32p. (J). (gr. -1-k). 13.89 *(978-1-64310-233-7(8))* Penworthy Co., LLC, The.

—The Great Pancake Race. 2018. (Pokemon Reader Ser.). lib. bdg. 14.75 *(978-0-606-41177-6(1))* Turtleback.

Mayer, Helena. The Lost Riolu: Pokémon Academy. 2009. (Pokémon Ser.). (Illus.). 62p. (J). pap. *(978-0-545-20050-9(4))* Scholastic, Inc.

Mizobuchi, Makoto. The Complete Pokémon Pocket Guide, Vol. 1. 2017. (Complete Pokémon Pocket Guide Ser.: 1). (ENG.). 256p. (J). pap. 10.99 *(978-1-4215-9543-6(5))* Viz Media.

—The Complete Pokémon Pocket Guide, Vol. 2. 2017. (Complete Pokémon Pocket Guide Ser.: 2). (ENG.). 256p. (J). pap. 10.99 *(978-1-4215-9544-3(3))* Viz Media.

—Pokémon: Arceus & the Jewel of Life. 2011. (Pokémon the Movie (manga) Ser.: 1). (ENG., Illus.). 200p. (J). pap. 9.99 *(978-1-4215-3802-0(4))* Viz Media.

—Pokémon Ranger & the Temple of the Sea. 2008. (Pokémon the Movie (manga) Ser.: 1). (ENG., Illus.). 192p. (J). (gr. 1). pap. 9.99 *(978-1-4215-2288-3(8))* Viz Media.

Moore, Ken A. Ghost Island & the Mystery of Charmander: An Unofficial Adventure for Pokémon GO Fans. 2016. (ENG.). 236p. (J). (gr. 2-7). pap. 9.99 *(978-1-5107-2296-5(3)*, Sky Pony Pr.) Skyhorse Publishing Co., Inc.

Pikachu, Press. Pokemon Mini-Sticker Book: White Edition. 2012. (ENG.). 80p. (J). (gr. -1). 4.99 *(978-1-60438-163-4(9))* Pokemon, USA, Inc.

Pikachu Press, . Catch Oshawott! a Pokémon Look & Listen Set Set. 2012. (Pokemon Pikachu Press Ser.). (ENG.). 32p. (J). (gr. 3-6). 12.99 *(978-1-60438-158-0(2))* Pokemon, USA, Inc.

—Catch Snivy! a Pokémon Look & Listen Set. 2012. (Pokemon Pikachu Press Ser.). (ENG.). 32p. (J). (gr. 3-6). 12.99 *(978-1-60438-157-3(4))* Pokemon, USA, Inc.

—Catch Tepig! a Pokémon Look & Listen Set Set. 2012. (Pokemon Pikachu Press Ser.). (ENG.). 32p. (J). (gr. 3-6). 12.99 *(978-1-60438-159-7(0))* Pokemon, USA, Inc.

—Pokémon Find 'Em All: Welcome to Unova! 2012. (Pokemon Pikachu Press Ser.). (ENG.). 42p. (J). (gr. 3-6). 9.99 *(978-1-60438-161-0(2))* Pokemon, USA, Inc.

Pokemon 1: Advanced Box Set [2 Discs / Subtitles / Box Set]. 2005. 39.98 incl. DVD *(978-1-4215-0214-4(3))* Viz Media.

Polan, Alex. Catching the Jigglypuff Thief. 2016. (Unofficial Adventures for Pokemon GO Players Ser.: 1). lib. bdg. 18.40 *(978-0-606-39657-8(8))* Turtleback.

—Chasing Butterfree. 2016. (Unofficial Adventures for Pokemon GO Players Ser.: 3). lib. bdg. 18.40 *(978-0-606-39655-4(1))* Turtleback.

—Cracking the Magikarp Code. 2016. (Unofficial Adventures for Pokemon GO Players Ser.: 4). lib. bdg. 18.40 *(978-0-606-39656-1(X))* Turtleback.

—Following Meowth's Footprints. 2016. (Unofficial Adventures for Pokemon GO Players Ser.: 2). lib. bdg. 18.40 *(978-0-606-39658-5(6))* Turtleback.

Press, Pikachu. Catch Pikachu! DELUXE Look & Listen Set. 2012. (ENG.). 48p. (J). 16.99 *(978-1-60438-171-9(X))* Pokemon, USA, Inc.

—Guide to Pokemon Legends. 2012. (ENG.). 32p. (J). 17.99 *(978-1-60438-175-7(2))* Pokemon, USA, Inc.

—Super Pokemon Pop-Up: Black Kyurem. 2013. (ENG.). 5p. (J). (gr. 3-6). 9.99 *(978-1-60438-179-5(5))* Pokemon, USA, Inc.

—Super Pokemon Pop-Up: White Kyurem. 2013. (ENG.). 5p. (J). (gr. 3-6). 9.99 *(978-1-60438-180-1(9))* Pokemon, USA, Inc.

Random House. Pokémon Storybook Treasury (Pokémon) Random House, illus. 2018. (ENG., Illus.). 96p. (J). (gr. -1-2). 9.99 *(978-1-5247-7259-8(3)*, Random Hse. Bks. for Young Readers) Random Hse. Children's Bks.

Sander, Sonia. Play Ball, Pikachu! (Pokémon Alola Reader), 1 vol. 2018. (ENG.). 32p. (J). (gr. -1-3). pap. 5.99 *(978-1-338-23752-8(7))* Scholastic, Inc.

Scholastic. Kalos Region Handbook (Pokémon) 2014. (Pokémon Chapter Bks.). (ENG.). 272p. (J). (gr. 2-5). pap. 8.99 *(978-0-545-64602-4(2))* Scholastic, Inc.

Scholastic & Scholastic. Pokémon: Kalos Essential Activity Book (Pokémon) An Epic Kingdom of Fantasy Adventure. 2015. (ENG.). 80p. (J). (gr. 2-5). pap. 12.99 *(978-0-545-92749-9(8))* Scholastic, Inc.

Scholastic Editors. Classic Collector's Handbook: An Official Guide to the First 151 Pokemon. 2016. lib. bdg. 19.65 *(978-0-606-39550-2(4))* Turtleback.

Sweeny, Sheila. Scyther, Heart of a Champion (Pokémon: Chapter Book) 2017. (Pokémon Chapter Bks.). (ENG.). 96p. (J). (gr. 2-5). pap. 4.99 *(978-1-338-17579-0(3))* Scholastic, Inc.

Takamisaki, Ryo. Pokémon: the Rise of Darkrai. 2008. (Pokémon the Movie (manga) Ser.: 1). (ENG., Illus.). 192p. (J). (gr. 1). pap. 9.99 *(978-1-4215-2289-0(8))* Viz Media.

Viz_Unknown. Pokémon Seek & Find: Hoenn. 2018. (Pokémon Seek & Find Ser.). (ENG.). 32p. (J). 9.99 *(978-1-4215-9812-3(4))* Viz Media.

—Pokémon Seek & Find: Johto. 2018. (Pokémon Seek & Find Ser.). (ENG.). 32p. (J). 9.99 *(978-1-4215-9811-6(6))* Viz Media.

—Pokémon Seek & Find: Kanto. 2018. (Pokémon Seek & Find Ser.). (ENG.). 32p. (J). 9.99 *(978-1-4215-9810-9(8))* Viz Media.

—Pokémon Seek & Find: Legendary Pokémon. 2018. (Pokémon Seek & Find Ser.). (ENG.). 32p. (J). 9.99 *(978-1-4215-9814-7(0))* Viz Media.

—Pokémon Seek & Find: Pikachu. 2018. (Pokémon Seek & Find Ser.). (ENG.). 32p. (J). 9.99 *(978-1-4215-9813-0(2))* Viz Media.

West, Tracey. Ash Ketchum, Pokémon Detective (Pokémon Classic Chapter Book #10) 2018. (Pokémon Chapter Bks.: 10). (ENG.). 96p. (J). (gr. 2-5). pap. 4.99 *(978-1-338-28403-4(7))* Scholastic, Inc.

—The Haunted Gym. 2003. (Pokemon Readers Ser.: No. 3). (ENG.). 32p. (J). pap. 3.99 *(978-0-439-42988-7(9))* Scholastic, Inc.

—Journey to the Orange Islands (Pokémon: Chapter Book) 2017. (Pokémon Chapter Bks.). (ENG.). 96p. (J). (gr. 2-5). pap. 4.99 *(978-1-338-17565-3(3))* Scholastic, Inc.

—Race to Danger (Pokémon: Chapter Book) 2017. (Pokémon Chapter Bks.). (ENG.). 96p. (J). (gr. 2-5). pap. 4.99 *(978-1-338-17585-1(8))* Scholastic, Inc.

—Secret of the Pink Pokémon (Pokémon: Chapter Book) 2017. (Pokémon Chapter Bks.). (ENG.). 96p. (J). (gr. 2-5). pap. 4.99 *(978-1-338-17567-7(X))* Scholastic, Inc.

—Talent Showdown (Pokémon: Chapter Book) 2017. (Pokémon Chapter Bks.). (ENG.). 96p. (J). (gr. 2-5). pap. 4.99 *(978-1-338-17591-2(2))* Scholastic, Inc.

West, Tracey, adapted by. Bagon Can Fly! 2005. (Illus.). 45p. *(978-0-439-72184-4(9))* Scholastic, Inc.

—Phantom Unmasked. 2006. (Illus.). 62p. (J). pap. *(978-0-439-80000-6(5))* Scholastic, Inc.

—Pokémon: I Feel Skitty. 2005. 45p. *(978-0-439-80940-5(1))* Scholastic, Inc.

Whitehill, Simcha. Official Guide to Legendary & Mythical Pokemon. 2016. lib. bdg. 18.40 *(978-0-606-39551-9(2))* Turtleback.

Yabuno, Ten'ya, creator. Pokémon Horizon: Sun & Moon, Vol. 1. 2018. (Pokémon Horizon: Sun & Moon Ser.: 1). (ENG., Illus.). 192p. (J). pap. 9.99 *(978-1-9747-0058-5(5))* Viz Media.

Yamamoto, Satoshi. Pokémon Adventures (FireRed & LeafGreen), Vol. 24. 2014. (Pokémon Adventures Ser.: 24). (ENG., Illus.). 216p. (J). pap. 9.99 *(978-1-4215-3558-6(0))* Viz Media.

—Pokémon Adventures (FireRed & LeafGreen), Vol. 25. 2014. (Pokémon Adventures Ser.: 25). (ENG., Illus.). 272p. (J). pap. 9.99 *(978-1-4215-3559-3(9))* Viz Media.

POKEMON (GAME)

Aihara, Kazunori, illus. Let's Find Pokémon! Special Complete Edition (2nd Edition) 2017. (Let's Find Pokémon! Special Complete Edition (2nd Edition) Ser.). (ENG.). 88p. (J). 16.99 *(978-1-4215-9579-5(6))* Viz Media.

Barbo, Maria S. Team Rocket to the Rescue! (Pokémon Kalos: Scholastic Reader, Level 2) 2016. (Scholastic Reader, Level 2 Ser.). (ENG.). 32p. (J). (gr. -1-3). pap. 3.99 *(978-1-338-11795-0(5))* Scholastic, Inc.

Green, Sara. Pokemon. 2017. (Brands We Know Ser.). (ENG., Illus.). 24p. (J). (gr. 3-8). lib. bdg. 27.95 *(978-1-62617-655-3(8)*, Pilot Bks.) Bellwether Media.

Hartley, Ned. The Ultimate Trainer's Guide: Pokémon (Independent & Unofficial) 2019. (Y Ser.). (ENG., Illus.). 64p. (J). (gr. 1-3). pap. 9.95 *(978-1-78739-289-2(9))* Carlton Bks., Ltd. GBR. Dist: Two Rivers Distribution.

Harukaze, Santa. Pokémon Pocket Comics: Legendary Pokemon. 2015. (Pokémon Pocket Comics Ser.: 2). (ENG., Illus.). 256p. (J). pap. 9.99 *(978-1-4215-8128-6(0))* Viz Media.

Noll, Katherine & West, Tracey. Pokémon: Kanto Handbook. 2005. (Illus.). 80p. (J). *(978-0-439-74146-0(7))* Scholastic, Inc.

Polinsky, Paige V. Pokémon Designer: Satoshi Tajiri. 2017. (Toy Trailblazers Set 2 Ser.). (ENG., Illus.). 32p. (J). (gr. 3-6). lib. bdg. 32.79 *(978-1-5321-1097-9(9)*, 25770, Checkerboard Library) ABDO Publishing Co.

Prima Games Staff. Pokemon Activity Book. 2009. 80p. pap. 12.99 *(978-0-7615-6164-4(1)*, Prima Games) Random Hse. Information Group.

Scholastic. Alola Region Handbook (Pokémon) 2017. (ENG., Illus.). 192p. (J). (gr. 2-5). pap. 9.99 *(978-1-338-14862-6(1))* Scholastic, Inc.

Scholastic Editors. Pokemon Deluxe Essential Handbook. 2015. lib. bdg. 23.30 *(978-0-606-37083-7(8))* Turtleback.

Silverman, Buffy. The World of Pokémon. 2018. (Searchlight Books (tm) — the World of Gaming Ser.). (ENG., Illus.). 32p. (J). (gr. 3-5). pap. 9.99 *(978-1-5415-1199-6(9)*, c16b86b0-b603-4b4f-bcb4-29b07c7f9d1d) Lerner Publishing Group.

Watson, Silje, et al. Classic Collector's Handbook: an Official Guide to the First 151 Pokémon (Pokémon) 2016.Tr. of (Pokémon). (ENG., Illus.). 128p. (J). (gr. k-6). pap. 8.99 *(978-1-338-15823-6(6))* Scholastic, Inc.

West, Tracey & Nolls, Katherine. Official Pokémon Pokédex. 2006. (Illus.). 111p. (J). *(978-0-439-85586-0(1))* Scholastic, Inc.

Whitehill, Simcha. Now You See It! Watch Pokémon Evolve — Right Before Your Eyes! 2012. (Illus.). 63p. (J). pap. *(978-0-545-45356-1(9))* Scholastic, Inc.

POLAND

Ainsley, Dominic J. Poland, Vol. 16. 2018. (European Countries Today Ser.). (Illus.). 96p. (J). (gr. 7). lib. bdg. 34.60 *(978-1-4222-3989-6(6))* Mason Crest.

Anderson, Dale. Polish Americans, 1 vol. 2006. (World Almanac(r) Library of American Immigration Ser.). (ENG., Illus.). 48p. (gr. 5-8). pap. 15.05 *(978-0-8368-7330-6(0)*, 054bfccb-8f9e-435c-abec-2ea4ff185456); lib. bdg. 33.67 *(978-0-8368-7317-7(3)*, 2426dbf8-898d-490d-aed2-d3c12b595460) Stevens, Gareth Publishing LLLP. (Gareth Stevens Secondary Library).

Andronik, Catherine M. Copernicus: Founder of Modern Astronomy, 1 vol. 2009. (Great Minds of Science Ser.). (ENG., Illus.). 128p. (gr. 5-6). lib. bdg. 35.93 *(978-0-7660-3013-8(X)*, b3478fbe-6f61-44ec-9b62-deddb6bd1675) Enslow Publishing, LLC.

—Copernicus: Genius of Modern Astronomy, 1 vol. 2014. (Genius Scientists & Their Genius Ideas Ser.). (ENG.). 96p. (gr. 5-5). 29.60 *(978-0-7660-6550-5(2)*, bfe05577-815c-48ba-8497-7a409113bb20); pap. 13.88 *(978-0-7660-6551-2(0)*, 320bbef2-c240-4e3a-91ef-c288f4003a3b) Enslow Publishing, LLC.

Barghoorn, Linda. Cultural Traditions in Poland. 2017. (Cultural Traditions in My World Ser.). (Illus.). 32p. (J). (gr. 2-3). *(978-0-7787-8098-4(8))* Crabtree Publishing Co.

Brandman, Bronia & Bierman, Carol. The Girl Who Survived: A True Story of the Holocaust. 2010. 91p. (J). pap. *(978-0-545-17574-6(7))* Scholastic, Inc.

Brooks, Susie. Let's Visit Poland, 1 vol. 2009. (Around the World Ser.). (ENG., Illus.). 32p. (J). (gr. 2-3). pap. 11.00 *(978-1-4358-8614-8(3)*, 7e0b4c24-c931-430d-8e52-cc3bbd29f5d1); lib. bdg. 28.93 *(978-1-4358-3030-1(X)*, 633ffa51-fb1c-4c3f-9d0e-1e74279248c7) Rosen Publishing Group, Inc., The. (PowerKids Pr.).

Cregan, Elizabeth R. C. Marie Curie: Pioneering Physicist, 1 vol. rev. ed. 2007. (Science: Informational Text Ser.). (ENG., Illus.). 32p. (gr. 3-6). pap. 12.99 *(978-0-7439-0570-1(9))* Teacher Created Materials, Inc.

Docalavich, Heather & Indovino, Shaina C. Poland. Bruton, John, ed. 2012. (Major European Union Nations Ser.). 64p. (J). (gr. 7). 22.95 *(978-1-4222-2254-6(3))* Mason Crest.

Docalavich, Heather & Indovino, Shaina Carmel. Poland. 2012. (J). pap. *(978-1-4222-2285-0(3))* Mason Crest.

Edison, Erin. Marie Curie, 1 vol. 2014. (Great Women in History Ser.). (ENG., Illus.). 24p. (J). (gr. -1-2). lib. bdg. 24.65 *(978-1-4765-4216-4(3)*, 124314, Pebble) Capstone.

Fisher, Teresa. Poland. 2010. (Illus.). 32p. (J). *(978-1-84234-548-1(6))* Cherrytree Bks.

Goldish, Meish. Poland. 2016. (Countries We Come From Ser.). (ENG., Illus.). 32p. (J). (gr. -1-3). 28.50 *(978-1-944998-30-1(6))* Bearport Publishing Co., Inc.

Hardyman, Robyn. Pierre & Marie Curie. 2014. (Dynamic Duos of Science Ser.). 48p. (YA). (gr. 5-8). pap. 84.30 *(978-1-4824-1287-1(X))* Stevens, Gareth Publishing LLLP.

Heale, Jay & Grajnert, Paul. Poland, 1 vol. 2nd rev. ed. 2005. (Cultures of the World (Second Edition)(r) Ser.). (ENG., Illus.). 144p. (gr. 5-5). 49.79 *(978-0-7614-1847-4(4)*, a83d02fc-6954-4025-9f08-a98f94b3d161) Cavendish Square Publishing LLC.

Landau, Abraham, et al. Branded on My Arm & in My Soul: A Holocaust Memoir. 2011. (Illus.). 144p. 50.00 *(978-0-932027-20-7(2))* Spinner Pubns., Inc.

—Branded on My Arm & in My Soul: The Holocaust Memoir of Abraham Landau. 2011. (Illus.). 144p. pap. 25.00 *(978-0-932027-19-1(9))* Spinner Pubns., Inc.

Laub, Frima. Between the Shadows. Laub, Frima & Uhlig, Elizabeth, illus. 2009. 81p. (J). pap. 12.95 *(978-0-9815345-2-7(X))* Marble Hse. Editions.

Leyson, Leon. The Boy on the Wooden Box: How the Impossible Became Possible ... on Schindler's List. (ENG., Illus.). (J). (gr. 4-9). 2015. 256p. pap. 9.99 *(978-1-4424-9782-5(3))* 2013. 240p. 19.99 *(978-1-4424-9781-8(5))* Simon & Schuster Children's Publishing. (Atheneum Bks. for Young Readers).

—The Boy on the Wooden Box: How the Impossible Became Possible ... on Schindler's List. 2015. lib. bdg. 19.65 *(978-0-606-36097-5(2))* Turtleback.

Lin, Yoming S. The Curies & Radioactivity, 1 vol. 2011. (Eureka! Ser.). (ENG., Illus.). 24p. (YA). (gr. 2-3). lib. bdg. 26.27 *(978-1-4488-5033-4(9)*, d43d97f6-388e-4142-b041-debbe22dca81) Rosen Publishing Group, Inc., The.

Lobel, Anita. No Pretty Pictures: A Child of War. 2008. (J). (gr. 5-8). lib. bdg. 18.40 *(978-0-613-28590-2(5))* Turtleback.

Loh-Hagan, Virginia. Marie Curie. Bane, Jeff, illus. 2018. (Mi Mini Biografía (My Itty-Bitty Bio): My Early Library). (ENG.). 24p. (J). (gr. k-1). pap. 12.79 *(978-1-5341-0814-1(9)*, 210620); lib. bdg. 30.64 *(978-1-5341-0715-1(0)*, 210619) Cherry Lake Publishing.

Mattern, Joanne. Poland, 1 vol. 2019. (Exploring World Cultures (First Edition) Ser.). (ENG.). 32p. (gr. 3-3). pap. 12.16 *(978-1-5026-5156-3(4)*, 337f5366-df15-4621-8655-76d73735711e) Cavendish Square Publishing LLC.

McCollum, Sean. Poland. 2009. pap. 52.95 *(978-0-7613-4732-3(1))*; (ENG., Illus.). 48p. (J). (gr. 2-4). 29.32 *(978-1-58013-597-9(8)*, a21d02d9-6cf1-4dcc-8456-328c622d7cd2, Lerner Pubns.) Lerner Publishing Group.

Mis, Melody S. How to Draw Poland's Sights & Symbols. 2009. (Kid's Guide to Drawing the Countries of the World Ser.). 48p. (gr. 4-4). 53.00 *(978-1-61511-122-0(0)*, PowerKids Pr.) Rosen Publishing Group, Inc., The.

Murray, Julie. Poland. 2017. (Explore the Countries Set 4 Ser.). (ENG., Illus.). 40p. (J). (gr. 2-5). lib. bdg. 35.64 *(978-1-5321-1051-1(0)*, 25678, Big Buddy Bks.) ABDO Publishing Co.

Opdyke, Irene Gut. In My Hands: Memories of a Holocaust Rescuer. 2016. (ENG., Illus.). 288p. (YA). (gr. 9). pap. 10.99 *(978-0-553-53884-7(5)*, Ember) Random Hse. Children's Bks.

Pavlovic, Zoran. Poland. 2008. (Modern World Nations Ser.). (ENG., Illus.). 128p. (gr. 6-12). 35.00 *(978-0-7910-9674-1(2)*, P150771, Facts On File) Infobase Holdings, Inc.

Pohl, Kathleen. Descubramos Polonia (Looking at Poland), 1 vol. 2008. (Descubramos Países Del Mundo (Looking at Countries) Ser.). (SPA., Illus.). 32p. (gr. 2-4). (J). lib. bdg. 28.67 *(978-0-8368-9068-6(X)*, cf4088f8-8b08-44f2-8617-cdc15b30b7aa); pap. 11.50 *(978-0-8368-9069-3(8)*, c221d178-427f-4ebe-b660-6baac6cbd414, Gareth Stevens Learning Library) Stevens, Gareth Publishing LLLP.

—Looking at Poland, 1 vol. 2008. (Looking at Countries Ser.). (ENG.). 32p. (gr. 2-4). (J). lib. bdg. 28.67 *(978-0-8368-9066-2(3)*, 23d59d8a-abff-4c6e-9dfa-7556d395972f); pap. 11.50 *(978-0-8368-9067-9(1)*, 621b3043-e1b5-4186-a839-e4cbbdad18ac) Stevens, Gareth Publishing LLLP. (Gareth Stevens Learning Library).

Poynter, Margaret. Marie Curie: Genius Researcher of Radioactivity, 1 vol. 2014. (Genius Scientists & Their Genius Ideas Ser.). (ENG.). 96p. (gr. 5-5). 29.60 *(978-0-7660-6580-2(4)*, a3db81f8-40fd-46cc-b837-a7bb5153a8e2); pap. 13.88 *(978-0-7660-6581-9(2)*, 8f2d2bac-c943-4272-a43c-f9ec89b6545d) Enslow Publishing, LLC.

Ricciuti, Edward R. Poland, 1 vol. 2004. (Discovering Cultures Ser.). (ENG., Illus.). 48p. (gr. 3-4). lib. bdg. 31.21 *(978-0-7614-1724-8(9)*, 1c982a06-f6ae-4af4-9520-4cbd55a5bab7) Cavendish Square Publishing LLC.

Roberto, Brother. Music for Millions: A Story of Ignace Paderewski. Jagodits, Carolyn Lee, illus. 2011. 94p. 38.95 *(978-1-258-09336-5(7))* Literary Licensing, LLC.

Sheen, Barbara. Foods of Poland, 1 vol. 2011. (Taste of Culture Ser.). (ENG.). 64p. (gr. 3-6). lib. bdg. 36.83 *(978-0-7377-5951-8(8)*, 93d398e3-c840-4e97-9a31-0efec3ba7fc9, KidHaven Publishing) Greenhaven Publishing LLC.

Simmons, Walter. Poland. 2012. (Exploring Countries Ser.). (ENG., Illus.). 32p. (J). (gr. 3-7). lib. bdg. 27.95 *(978-1-60014-732-6(1)*, Pilot Bks.) Bellwether Media.

Simons, Lisa M. Bolt. Marie Curie: Physicist & Chemist. 2018. (STEM Scientists & Inventors Ser.). (ENG., Illus.). 24p. (J). (gr. 1-3). lib. bdg. 27.99 *(978-1-5435-0643-3(7)*, 137406, Capstone Pr.) Capstone.

Thomson, Ruth. Poland, 1 vol. 2011. (Countries Ser.). (ENG., Illus.). 24p. (J). (gr. 2-2). lib. bdg. 26.27 *(978-1-4488-3277-4(2)*, 9c9e6b45-8545-4c19-bc0d-488f655b0a25) Rosen Publishing Group, Inc., The.

Vaughan, Marcia & Mazellan, Ron. Irena's Jars of Secrets, 1 vol. 2011. (ENG.). 40p. (J). (gr. 2-7). pap. 10.95 *(978-1-62014-252-3(X)*, leelowbooks) Lee & Low Bks., Inc.

Wallace, Susan Helen. Saint John Paul II: Be Not Afraid. Craig, Charles, illus. 2011. (Encounter the Saints Ser.). 128p. (J). (gr. 3-7). pap. 8.95 *(978-0-8198-1178-3(5))* Pauline Bks. & Media.

Wilson, Rosie. Discover Poland. 2010. (Illus.). 32p. (J). 63.60 *(978-1-61532-295-4(7)*, 1307265); (ENG., (gr. 4-4). pap. 11.60 *(978-1-61532-294-7(9)*, d9d7e1d9-9942-4ec8-83f7-942237e7937f) Rosen Publishing Group, Inc., The. (PowerKids Pr.).

Wilson, Rosie & Ward, Chris. Discover Poland, 1 vol. 2010. (Discover Countries Ser.). (ENG., Illus.). 32p. (J). (gr. 4-4). 30.27 *(978-1-61532-288-6(4)*, 1e1cdf9a-eee0-4090-9af9-622bf1d25add) Rosen Publishing Group, Inc., The.

Zuchora-Walske, Christine. Poland, 1 vol. 2013. (Countries of the World Set 2 Ser.). (ENG.). 144p. (YA). (gr. 6-12). lib. bdg. 42.79 *(978-1-61783-634-3(6)*, 4892, Essential Library) ABDO Publishing Co.

Zuehlke, Jeffrey. Poland in Pictures. 2006. (Visual Geography Series, Second Ser.). (ENG., Illus.). 80p. (gr. 5-12). 31.93 *(978-0-8225-2676-6(X))* Lerner Publishing Group.

POLAND—FICTION

Aaron, Chester. Gideon. 2009. (ENG., Illus.). 190p. (YA). pap. 12.99 *(978-1-934841-62-4(5)*, Zumaya Thresholds) Zumaya Pubns. LLC.

Balazy, Elizabeth M. Prince to the Rescue. 2008. 48p. pap. 24.95 *(978-1-60474-812-3(5))* America Star Bks.

Boyne, John. The Boy in the Striped Pajamas. 2023. (ENG.). lib. bdg. 24.99 Cengage Gale.

—The Boy in the Striped Pajamas. 2006. (ENG.). 224p. (YA). (gr. 7). 17.99 *(978-0-385-75106-3(0))* Fickling, David Bks. GBR. Dist: Penguin Random Hse. LLC.

—The Boy in the Striped Pajamas. 2011. 10.54 *(978-0-7848-3514-2(4)*, Everbind) Marco Bk. Co.

—The Boy in the Striped Pajamas. 2008. 215p. (gr. 7-12). 20.00 *(978-0-7569-8943-9(4))* Perfection Learning Corp.

—The Boy in the Striped Pajamas. 2007. (ENG.). 224p. (YA). (gr. 7-18). pap. 12.99 *(978-0-385-75153-7(2)*, Ember) Random Hse. Children's Bks.

—The Boy in the Striped Pajamas. rev. l.t. ed. 2007. (Thorndike Literacy Bridge Ser.). (ENG.). 247p. (YA). (gr. 7-12). 23.95 *(978-0-7862-9425-1(6))* Thorndike Pr.

—The Boy in the Striped Pajamas. 2007. 215p. (YA). (gr. 7-12). 20.85 *(978-1-4178-1823-5(9))* Turtleback.

—The Boy in the Striped Pajamas (Movie Tie-In Edition) movie tie-in ed. 2008. (ENG.). 240p. (YA). (gr. 7). pap. 12.99 *(978-0-385-75189-6(3))* Fickling, David Bks. GBR. Dist: Penguin Random Hse. LLC.

Cerrito, Angela. The Safest Lie. 2018. 192p. (J). (gr. 3-7). pap. 7.99 *(978-0-8234-4046-7(X))* Holiday Hse., Inc.

Ciddor, Anna. The Family with Two Front Doors. 2018. (ENG., Illus.). 208p. (J). (gr. 3-6). 12.99 *(978-1-5415-0011-2(3)*, cde459b6-6cee-4eae-8964-4b6e58cdfefc); pap. 6.99 *(978-1-5415-0012-9(1)*, 7bf0f625-be94-4f2c-aa3e-8be52aaf66e4) Lerner Publishing Group. (Kar-Ben Publishing).

Draus, Naudia Burtwell. My Grandma Wears A Number: How One Girl Survived World War Ii. 2011. 40p. (gr. 4-6). pap. 19.57 *(978-1-4269-3351-6(7))* Trafford Publishing.

Frankel, Valerie Estelle. Chelm for the Holidays. Wimmer, Sonja, illus. 2019. (ENG.). 72p. (J). (gr. 3-9). pap. 8.99 *(978-1-5415-5462-7(0)*, afdf6bb4-341d-400d-b5f2-173f45c6a355, Kar-Ben Publishing) Lerner Publishing Group.

Glaser, Linda. Way Too Many Latkes: A Hanukkah in Chelm. Zolotic, Aleksandar, illus. 2017. (ENG.). 32p. (J). (gr. -1-2). 17.99 *(978-1-5124-2092-0(1)*, 6f2e3963-2317-45ae-963d-a2da005bd7eb, Kar-Ben Publishing) Lerner Publishing Group.

Gleitzman, Morris. Once. 2005. 160p. (J). pap. *(978-0-14-330195-0(0)*, Puffin) Penguin Publishing Group.

—Once. 2013. (Once Ser.: 1). (ENG.). 192p. (YA). (gr. 7). pap. 10.99 *(978-0-312-65304-0(2)*, 900069444) Square Fish.

—Then. 2013. (Once Ser.: 2). (ENG.). 224p. (YA). (gr. 7). pap. 11.99 *(978-1-250-00341-6(5)*, 900079882) Square Fish.

—Then. 2013. (YA). lib. bdg. 20.85 *(978-0-606-31904-1(2))* Turtleback.

Got, Eli & Gold, D., illus. The Cryptic Script. 2018. 74p. (J). *(978-1-68091-257-9(7))* Kinder Shpiel USA, Inc.

Hemingway, Mike. The Legend of Vysallimore. 2010. 72p. pap. 28.00 *(978-1-4520-5648-7(X))* AuthorHouse.

Jane, Yolen. The Devil's Arithmetic. 2014. (ENG.). 176p. (J). 11.24 *(978-1-63245-218-4(9))* Lectorum Pubns., Inc.

Kacer, Kathy. The Diary of Laura's Twin, 1 vol. 2008. (Holocaust Remembrance Series for Young Readers Ser.: 9). (ENG., Illus.). 202p. (J). (gr. 4-8). pap. 14.95 *(978-1-897187-39-5(4))* Second Story Pr. CAN. Dist: Orca Bk. Pubs. USA.

—The Sound of Freedom. 2018. (Heroes Quartet Ser.: 1). (ENG.). 256p. (J). (gr. 4-7). pap. 9.95 *(978-1-55451-969-9(1))* Annick Pr., Ltd. CAN. Dist: Publishers Group West (PGW).

Kimmel, Eric A. Right Side up: Adventures in Chelm. Brown, Steve, illus. 2019. (ENG.). 96p. (J). 17.95 *(978-1-68115-548-7(6)*, c295129e-51ee-4ea9-98d4-29044d1bf1e4, Apples & Honey Pr.) Behrman Hse., Inc.

Lehman, Theodore H. Defying Odds. 2014. (YA). pap. *(978-1-935604-63-1(5))* Gaon Bks.

Lewis, J. Patrick. The Wren & the Sparrow. Nayberg, Yevgenia, illus. 2015. (ENG.). 32p. (J). (gr. 3-6). E-Book 27.99 *(978-1-4677-6210-6(5)*, Kar-Ben Publishing) Lerner Publishing Group.

Moskowitz-Sweet, Gloria & Smith, Hope Anita. It Rained Warm Bread: Moishe Moskowitz's Story of Hope. Lyon, Lea, illus. 2019. (ENG.). 160p. (J). 16.99 *(978-1-250-16572-5(5)*, 900187113, Holt, Henry & Co. Bks. For Young Readers) Holt, Henry & Co.

Nielsen, Jennifer A. Resistance (Scholastic Gold) 2018. (ENG.). 400p. (J). (gr. 3-7). 17.99 *(978-1-338-14847-3(8)*, Scholastic Pr.) Scholastic, Inc.

Palmer, Tom. The Real Thing, Bk. 3. 3rd ed. 2009. (Football Academy Ser.). (Illus.). 176p. (J). (gr. 2-4). pap. 10.99 *(978-0-14-132469-2(4))* Penguin Bks., Ltd. GBR. Dist: Independent Pubs. Group.

Platt, Randall. The Girl Who Wouldn't Die. 2017. (ENG.). 368p. (J). (gr. 8-8). 16.99 *(978-1-5107-0809-9(X)*, Sky Pony Pr.) Skyhorse Publishing Co., Inc.

Pressler, Mirjam. Malka. Murdoch, Brian, tr. 2005. 280p. (YA). (gr. 7-12). 13.65 *(978-0-7569-5217-4(4))* Perfection Learning Corp.

Pryor, Bonnie. Simon's Escape: A Story of the Holocaust, 1 vol. 2011. (Historical Fiction Adventures Ser.). (ENG., Illus.). 160p. (J). (gr. 3-5). 31.93 *(978-0-7660-3388-7(0)*, 77eae799-a832-47e4-96ef-4e05fa560d75); pap. 13.88 *(978-1-59845-216-7(9)*, 5304890e-e1fa-4a41-9faf-e8971ad9e71f) Enslow Publishing, LLC.

Romero, R. M. The Dollmaker of Krakow. 2017. (ENG.). 336p. (J). (gr. 3-7). lib. bdg. 19.99 *(978-1-5247-1540-3(9)*, Delacorte Bks. for Young Readers) Random Hse. Children's Bks.

Rosner, Mina. I Am a Witness. (Illus.). 112p. (YA). (gr. 3-18). pap. *(978-0-920534-92-2(9))* Hyperion Pr., Ltd.

Roy, Jennifer. Yellow Star, 0 vols. 2014. (ENG.). 256p. (J). (gr. 4-6). pap. 9.99 *(978-0-7614-6310-8(0)*, 9780761463108, Two Lions) Amazon Publishing.

Sasso, Sandy Eisenberg. Butterflies under Our Hats. Rothenberg, Joani Keller, illus. 2014. (ENG.). 32p. (J). (gr. k-5). pap. 15.99 *(978-1-61261-583-7(X)*, 5837) Paraclete Pr., Inc.

Savit, Gavriel. Anna & the Swallow Man. 2016. (CHI.). 272p. (YA). (gr. 7). pap. *(978-957-33-3251-0(5))* Crown Publishing Co., Ltd.

—Anna & the Swallow Man. 2017. (ENG.). 256p. (YA). (gr. 7). pap. 9.99 *(978-0-553-52208-2(6)*, Ember) Random Hse. Children's Bks.

—Anna & the Swallow Man. 2017. lib. bdg. 20.85 *(978-0-606-39876-3(7))* Turtleback.

Sax, Aline. The War Within These Walls. 2013. (ENG., Illus.). 176p. (YA). 17.00 *(978-0-8028-5428-5(1)*, Eerdmans Bks For Young Readers) Eerdmans, William B. Publishing Co.

Stuchner, Joan Betty. Can Hens Give Milk?, 1 vol. Weissmann, Joe, illus. 2013. (ENG.). 32p. (J). (gr. -1-k). 9.95 *(978-1-4598-0427-2(9))* Orca Bk. Pubs. USA.

Surber, Mary Brigid. The Last Stork Summer. 2015. (ENG., Illus.). 128p. (J). (gr. -1-12). pap. 13.95 *(978-1-78279-934-4(6)*, Top Hat Bks.) Hunt, John Publishing Ltd. GBR. Dist: National Bk. Network.

Tak, Bibi Dumon. Soldier Bear. Philip Hopman, illus. 2011. (ENG.). 158p. (J). 13.00 *(978-0-8028-5375-2(7)*, Eerdmans Bks For Young Readers) Eerdmans, William B. Publishing Co.

Tarshis, Lauren. I Survived the Nazi Invasion 1944. 2014. (I Survived Ser.: No. 9). lib. bdg. 14.75 *(978-0-606-35397-7(6))* Turtleback.

—I Survived the Nazi Invasion, 1944 (I Survived #9) 2014. (I Survived Ser.: 9). (ENG., Illus.). 112p. (J). (gr. 3-7). pap. 5.99 *(978-0-545-45938-9(9))* Scholastic, Inc.

Upjohn, Rebecca. The Secret of Village Fool, 1 vol. Benoit, Renné, illus. 2012. (ENG.). 32p. (J). (gr. 2-4). lib. bdg. 18.95 *(978-1-926920-75-7(9))* Second Story Pr. CAN. Dist: Orca Bk. Pubs. USA.

Wulf, Linda Press. The Night of the Burning. 2007. 224p. pap. *(978-0-7475-9051-4(6))* Bloomsbury Publishing Plc.

Yolen, Jane. The Devil's Arithmetic (Puffin Modern Classics) 2004. (Puffin Modern Classics Ser.). (ENG.). 208p. (J). (gr. 5-5). pap. 8.99 *(978-0-14-240109-5(9)*, Puffin Books) Penguin Young Readers Group.

POLAR EXPEDITIONS

see Antarctica; Arctic Regions; North Pole; Polar Regions; South Pole

POLAR REGIONS

see also Antarctica; Arctic Regions; North Pole; South Pole

Allgor, Marie. Endangered Animals of Antarctica & the Arctic, 1 vol. 2011. (Save Earth's Animals! Ser.). (ENG., Illus.). 24p. (J). (gr. 2-3). pap. 9.25 *(978-1-4488-2652-0(7)*, b8c4e7ba-ef01-4d97-90ff-1348aa6c8284); lib. bdg. 26.27 *(978-1-4488-2534-9(2)*, 3f0a08e6-91a1-4a34-b6dc-328679992ce2) Rosen Publishing Group, Inc., The. (PowerKids Pr.).

—Endangered Tundra Animals, 1 vol. 2012. (Save Earth's Animals! Ser.). (ENG., Illus.). 24p. (J). (gr. 2-3). pap. 9.25 *(978-1-4488-7494-1(7)*, 2bf75c81-2a1b-40d2-9752-1df0a540f6e0); lib. bdg. 26.27 *(978-1-4488-7421-7(1)*, ddae7440-71ec-44fd-8b02-0b69d2b99bfb) Rosen Publishing Group, Inc., The. (PowerKids Pr.).

Amstutz, Lisa J. Polar Animal Adaptations. 2011. (Amazing Animal Adaptations Ser.). (ENG.). 32p. (J). (gr. 1-2). pap. 49.60 *(978-1-4296-7039-5(8)*, 16662, Capstone Pr.) Capstone.

—Show Me Polar Animals: My First Picture Encyclopedia, 1 vol. 2013. (My First Picture Encyclopedias Ser.). (ENG.). 32p. (J). (gr. -1-2). pap. 8.10 *(978-1-4765-3791-7(7))* Capstone.

Anderson, Harry S. Exploring the Polar Regions. 2nd rev. ed. 2009. (Discovery & Exploration Ser.). (ENG., Illus.). 120p. (gr. 5-8). 35.00 *(978-1-60413-190-1(X)*, P174271, Facts On File) Infobase Holdings, Inc.

Andrews Henningfeld, Diane, ed. The North & South Poles, 1 vol. 2009. (Opposing Viewpoints Ser.). (ENG., Illus.). 224p. (gr. 10-12). pap. 34.80 *(978-0-7377-4535-1(5)*, 74eb206d-8cde-4f4d-917f-950ea477b92f); lib. bdg. 50.43 *(978-0-7377-4534-4(7)*, 02432482-4db4-46fa-aa32-09b261ac3886) Greenhaven Publishing LLC. (Greenhaven Publishing).

Apte, Sunita. Polar Regions: Surviving in Antarctica. 2005. (X-treme Places Ser.). (Illus.). 32p. (YA). (gr. 2-5). lib. bdg. 25.27 *(978-1-59716-088-9(1))* Bearport Publishing Co., Inc.

Arctic & Antarctic Habitats. 2013. (Discovery Education: Habitats Ser.). 32p. (J). (gr. 3-6). pap. 60.00 *(978-1-4777-1482-9(0)*, PowerKids Pr.) Rosen Publishing Group, Inc., The.

AZ Books Staff. Polar Animals. Gorojan, Elena, ed. 2012. (My First Library). (ENG.). 12p. (J). (-k). bds. 8.95 *(978-1-61889-122-8(7))* AZ Bks. LLC.

Bailey, Diane. Polar Exploration: Courage & Controversy. 2017. (Exploring the Polar Regions Today Ser.: Vol. 8). (ENG., Illus.). 64p. (J). (gr. 7-12). 23.95 *(978-1-4222-3870-7(9))* Mason Crest.

Benduhn, Tea. Living in Polar Regions, 1 vol. 2007. (Life on the Edge Ser.). (ENG.). 24p. (gr. 2-4). pap. 9.15 *(978-0-8368-8348-0(9)*, f6a78355-a834-401d-9589-3931f462d0aa); (Illus.). lib. bdg. 24.67 *(978-0-8368-8343-5(8)*, c9a8930b-dec2-4db8-ac00-f9c294df0f52) Stevens, Gareth Publishing LLLP. (Weekly Reader Leveled Readers).

—La Vida en Las Regiones Polares (Living in Polar Regions), 1 vol. 2007. (Vida Al límite (Life on the Edge) Ser.). (SPA., Illus.). 24p. (gr. 2-4). lib. bdg. 24.67 *(978-0-8368-8353-4(5)*, 4d8bde61-7af0-43e7-bfb8-ed4aeb42f423, Weekly Reader Leveled Readers) Stevens, Gareth Publishing LLLP.

Bennett, Elizabeth. Polar Opposites. 2014. (Illus.). (J). pap. *(978-0-545-61303-3(5))* Scholastic, Inc.

Berger, Melvin & Berger, Gilda. Polar Animals in Danger. 2006. (Scholastic Reader Ser.). (Illus.). (J). *(978-0-439-81535-2(5))* Scholastic, Inc.

Britton, Arthur K. Life at a Polar Research Station, 1 vol. 2013. (Extreme Jobs in Extreme Places Ser.). (ENG., Illus.). 32p. (J). (gr. 3-4). pap. 11.50 *(978-1-4339-8483-9(0)*, 064a0bd4-e9e5-44ff-8bcc-dc0c35ec13ec); lib. bdg. 29.27 *(978-1-4339-8482-2(2)*, fc7c6c94-19c6-45a1-be98-c589bb32321b) Stevens, Gareth Publishing LLLP.

Burgan, Michael. Climate Change & the Polar Regions. 2017. (Exploring the Polar Regions Today Ser.: Vol. 8). (ENG., Illus.). 64p. (J). (gr. 7-12). 23.95 *(978-1-4222-3868-4(7))* Mason Crest.

—Polar Politics: Earth's Next Battlegrounds? 2017. (Exploring the Polar Regions Today Ser.: Vol. 8). (ENG., Illus.). 64p. (J). (gr. 7-12). 23.95 *(978-1-4222-3871-4(7))* Mason Crest.

Cooper, Wade. Polar Animals (Scholastic Reader, Level 1) 2009. (Scholastic Reader, Level 1 Ser.). (ENG.). 32p. (J). (gr. -1-3). pap. 3.99 *(978-0-545-05766-0(3)*, Cartwheel Bks.) Scholastic, Inc.

Dinmont, Kerry. It's a Snowy Owl! 2018. (Bumba Books (r) — Polar Animals Ser.). (ENG., Illus.). 24p. (J). (gr. -1-1). pap. 8.99 *(978-1-5415-2697-6(X)*, 12d23341-f85c-464f-99bc-61b5bc5608a0) Lerner Publishing Group.

DK. Ice: Chilling Stories from a Disappearing World. 2019. (ENG., Illus.). 160p. (J). (gr. 4-7). 19.99 *(978-1-4654-8170-2(2)*, DK Children) Dorling Kindersley Publishing, Inc.

Dowswell, Paul. True Polar Adventures. Woodcock, John, illus. 2004. (True Adventure Stories Ser.). 144p. (J). pap. 4.95 *(978-0-7945-0404-5(3)*, Usborne) EDC Publishing.

Gardeski, Christina Mia. All about the North & South Poles. 2017. (Habitats Ser.). (ENG., Illus.). 24p. (J). (gr. -1-2). pap. 6.95 *(978-1-5157-7647-5(6)*, 135931, Pebble) Capstone.

Gifford, Clive. In Focus: Polar Lands. 2017. (In Focus Ser.). (ENG.). 64p. (J). 17.99 *(978-0-7534-7351-1(8)*, 900175024, Kingfisher) Roaring Brook Pr.

Goodman, Susan E. Life on the Ice. Doolittle, Michael J., illus. Doolittle, Michael J., photos by. 2006. 32p. (J). 22.60 *(978-0-7613-2775-2(4)*, Millbrook Pr.) Lerner Publishing Group.

Gordon, Anne. Animals of the Ice & Snow. 2007. (Literacy 2000 Ser.). (Illus.). 24p. (J). (gr. 4-7). pap. *(978-0-7327-0888-7(5)*, Rigby) Pearson Education Australia.

Gray, Leon. Polar Lands. 2015. (Amazing Biomes Ser.). (ENG., Illus.). 32p. (J). (gr. 3-6). 31.35 *(978-1-78121-245-5(7)*, 16391) Brown Bear Bks.

Green, Jen. Deserts & Polar Regions Around the World, 1 vol. 2009. (Geography Now! Ser.). (ENG.). 32p. (gr. 5-5). (YA). lib. bdg. 30.27 *(978-1-4358-2874-2(7)*, c2db17f1-0b8d-441a-b7b9-2c0c006b4299); (Illus.). (J). pap. 11.00 *(978-1-4358-2960-2(3)*, 31885e9d-5401-4b64-ad17-b43b1d8946f8, PowerKids Pr.) Rosen Publishing Group, Inc., The.

Hall, Katharine. Osos Polares y Pingüinos: Un Libro de Comparaci�n y Contraste (Spanish Edition) 2014.Tr. of Polar Bears & Penguins: a Compare & Contrast Book. (SPA., Illus.). 32p. (J). (gr. 2-3). pap. 11.95 *(978-1-62855-227-0(1)*, 93935288-1716-4142-a470-72278f59bb8c) Arbordale Publishing.

—Polar Bears & Penguins: a Compare & Contrast Book, 1 vol. 2014. (Compare & Contrast Ser.). (ENG., Illus.). 32p. (J). (gr. -1-3). 17.95 *(978-1-62855-209-6(3))* Arbordale Publishing.

Heos, Bridget. Do You Really Want a Hamster? Longhi, Katya, illus. 2013. (Do You Really Want a Pet? Ser.). (ENG.). 24p. (J). (gr. 1-4). 27.10 *(978-1-60753-206-4(9)*, 16248) Amicus.

Hodge, Deborah. Who Lives Here? Polar Animals. Stephens, Pat, illus. 2008. (Who Lives Here? Ser.). (ENG.). 24p. (J). (gr. -1-2). pap. 5.99 *(978-1-55453-044-1(X))* Kids Can Pr., Ltd. CAN. Dist: Hachette Bk. Group.

Holland, Simon. First Animal Encyclopedia Polar Animals. 2015. (First Animal Encyclopedia Ser.). (ENG., Illus.). 64p. (J). (gr. -1-3). 13.99 *(978-1-4729-1344-9(2)*, 900152994, A&C Black Childrens & Educational) Bloomsbury Publishing Plc GBR. Dist: Macmillan.

Hollar, Sherman. Investigating Earth's Polar Biomes, 1 vol. 2011. (Introduction to Earth Science Ser.). (ENG.). 88p. (J). (gr. 8-8). lib. bdg. 35.29 *(978-1-61530-501-8(7)*, a075e7ed-3709-4fe0-a16d-f34f9e9f1465) Rosen Publishing Group, Inc., The.

Hynes, Margaret. Polar Lands. 2014. 56p. pap. 8.00 *(978-1-61003-361-9(2))* Center for the Collaborative Classroom.

Isn't It Cool? Individual Title Six-Packs. (Action Packs Ser.). 128p. (gr. 3-5). 44.00 *(978-0-7635-3307-6(6))* Rigby Education.

Jacobs, Pat. I Wonder Why Penguins Can't Fly. 2014. 32p. pap. 7.00 *(978-1-61003-350-3(7))* Center for the Collaborative Classroom.

—I Wonder Why Penguins Can't Fly: And Other Questions about Polar Lands. 2011. (I Wonder Why Ser.). (ENG., Illus.). 32p. (J). (gr. k-3). pap. 6.99 *(978-0-7534-6530-1(2)*, 900070299, Kingfisher) Roaring Brook Pr.

Jaycox, Jaclyn. Snowy Owls Are Awesome. 2019. (Polar Animals Ser.). (ENG., Illus.). 32p. (J). (gr. -1-2). pap. 7.95 *(978-1-9771-1001-5(0)*, 140944, Pebble) Capstone.

Johnson, Allen L. Kayaking Around Iceland: Adventures with Grandchildren. 2003. (Illus.). 196p. 15.00 *(978-1-880675-07-6(2))* Creative Enterprises.

Kalman, Bobbie & Aloian, Molly. Les Océans Polaires. 2009. (FRE., Illus.). 32p. (J). pap. 9.95 *(978-2-89579-248-2(8))* Bayard Canada Livres CAN. Dist: Crabtree Publishing Co.

Katirgis, Jane. Baby Snow Animals, 1 vol. 2010. (All about Baby Animals Ser.). (ENG., Illus.). 24p. (-1). pap. 10.35 *(978-1-59845-160-3(X),* dbdf7c35-9323-401a-9564-2537392978f3); (gr. -1-1). lib. bdg. 25.27 *(978-0-7660-3797-7(5),* d03aa03a-4a44-4e75-bd06-48fab892010a) Enslow Publishing, LLC. (Enslow Publishing).

Kerr, James. Polar Regions. rev. ed. 2016. (Earth's Final Frontiers Ser.). (ENG.). 48p. (J). (gr. 6-9). pap. 8.99 *(978-1-4846-3698-5(8),* 134110, Heinemann) Capstone.

Latta, Sara L. Polar Scientists: Studying the Antarctic, 1 vol. 2015. (Extreme Science Careers Ser.). (ENG., Illus.). 128p. (gr. 7-7). 38.93 *(978-0-7660-6966-4(4),* 6d3e77f8-911a-4630-9914-94b78d91c8d7) Enslow Publishing, LLC.

Mack, Lorrie & Dorling Kindersley Publishing Staff. Arctic & Antarctic. 2006. (DK Eye Wonder Ser.). (ENG., Illus.). 48p. (J). (gr. 3-6). 22.44 *(978-0-7566-1980-0(7))* Dorling Kindersley Publishing, Inc.

Mason, Paul. Polar Regions. 2004. (Geography Fact Files Ser.). (J). lib. bdg. 28.50 *(978-1-58340-428-7(7))* Black Rabbit Bks.

McAllan, Kate. Arctic & Antarctic Habitats, 1 vol. 2013. (Discovery Education: Habitats Ser.). (ENG.). 32p. (J). (gr. 4-5). 28.93 *(978-1-4777-1323-5(9),* b698b149-2871-426b-91f1-646e3bb68886); pap. 11.00 *(978-1-4777-1481-2(2),* 0f11baf2-7a1f-465c-b25d-1ebd93b4e015) Rosen Publishing Group, Inc., The. (PowerKids Pr.).

McNeil, Niki, et al. Polar Habitats. 2007. (In the Hands of a Child: Custom Designed Project Pack Ser.). (Illus.). 51p. spiral bd. 22.50 *(978-1-60308-119-1(4))* In the Hands of a Child.

Murphy, Patricia J. Why Are the North & South Poles So Cold? (Library of Why Ser.). 24p. (gr. 3-4). 2009. 42.50 *(978-1-60853-962-8(8))* 2003. (ENG., Illus.). (J). lib. bdg. 26.27 *(978-0-8239-6233-4(4),* d9826596-b4ad-449d-b219-fabbe0e8d853) Rosen Publishing Group, Inc., The. (PowerKids Pr.).

Nichols, Catherine. Polar Adventures. 2003. (True Tales Ser.). (ENG., Illus.). 48p. (J). 22.50 *(978-0-516-22920-1(6),* Children's Pr.) Scholastic Library Publishing.

NorthWord Books for Young Readers Editors, contrib. by. Polar Babies. 2003. (Animal Babies Ser.). (ENG., Illus.). 22p. (J). (gr. -1 — 1). bds. 5.95 *(978-1-55971-875-2(7))* Cooper Square Publishing Llc.

Parker, Steve & Kelly, Miles. Polar Lands. Kelly, Richard, ed. 2017. (Illus.). 480p. (J). pap. 9.95 *(978-1-84810-236-1(4))* Miles Kelly Publishing, Ltd. GBR. Dist: Parkwest Pubns., Inc.

Peters, Katie. Polar Animals. 2019. (Let's Look at Animal Habitats (Pull Ahead Readers — Nonfiction) Ser.). (ENG., Illus.). 16p. (J). (gr. -1-1). pap. 8.99 *(978-1-5415-7313-0(7),* a270efed-7333-49d9-8919-ba90d3da13d7, Lerner Pubns.) Lerner Publishing Group.

Pyers, Greg. Biodiversity of Polar Regions, 1 vol. 2011. (Biodiversity Ser.). (ENG.). 32p. (gr. 4-4). 31.21 *(978-1-60870-072-1(0),* 41f2a9a6-5c45-430e-bd96-332dd9ecd761) Cavendish Square Publishing LLC.

Rissman, Rebecca. Living & Nonliving in the Polar Regions, 1 vol. 2013. (Is It Living or Nonliving? Ser.). (ENG.). 24p. (J). (gr. k-2). pap. 6.95 *(978-1-4109-5390-2(4),* 123330, Raintree) Capstone.

Rodríguez, Ana María & Rodríguez, Ana María. Polar Bears, Penguins, & Other Mysterious Animals of the Extreme Cold, 1 vol. 2012. (Extreme Animals in Extreme Environments Ser.). (ENG., Illus.). 48p. (gr. 5-7). 27.93 *(978-0-7660-3695-6(2),* f606a367-8d8d-424b-ad32-4e6960a8d4c7) Enslow Publishing, LLC.

Rose, Simon. Polar Ice Caps. 2014. (Illus.). 32p. (J). *(978-1-62127-486-5(1))* Weigl Pubs., Inc.

—Polar Regions. 2017. (J). *(978-1-5105-2173-5(9))* SmartBook Media, Inc.

Sill, Cathryn. About Habitats: Polar Regions, 1 vol. Sill, John, illus. 2015. (About Habitats Ser.: 7). 48p. (J). (gr. -1-2). 16.95 *(978-1-56145-832-5(5))* Peachtree Publishing Co. Inc.

Snowden, Maxine. Polar Explorers for Kids: Historic Expeditions to the Arctic & Antarctic with 21 Activities. 2003. (For Kids Ser.: 5). (ENG.). 160p. (J). (gr. 4). pap. 19.99 *(978-1-55652-500-1(1))* Chicago Review Pr., Inc.

Soll, Karen. Coldest Places on the Planet. 2016. (Extreme Earth Ser.). (ENG., Illus.). 24p. (J). (gr. -1-2). lib. bdg. 27.32 *(978-1-4914-8340-4(7),* 130810, Capstone Pr.) Capstone.

Spilbury, Louise. Polar Regions. 2015. (Research on the Edge Ser.). (ENG., Illus.). 32p. (J). (gr. 3-8). 31.35 *(978-1-62588-159-5(2),* 19354, Smart Apple Media) Black Rabbit Bks.

Spilsbury, Louise. How to Survive in the Arctic & Antarctica, 1 vol. 2012. (Tough Guides). (ENG., Illus.). 32p. (J). (gr. 4-5). pap. 11.00 *(978-1-4488-7931-1(0),* 0129535c-14f4-473c-96bc-b28f0785be89); lib. bdg. 28.93 *(978-1-4488-7866-6(7),* 28868d93-7882-4c13-a732-09956e89d72a) Rosen Publishing Group, Inc., The. (PowerKids Pr.).

St. John, Sally. Polar Regions. 2010. (Illus.). 16p. *(978-0-545-24809-9(4))* Scholastic, Inc.

Taylor, Barbara. Polar Habitats, 1 vol. 2006. (Exploring Habitats Ser.). (ENG., Illus.). 36p. (gr. 4-6). lib. bdg. 28.67 *(978-0-8368-7256-9(8),* 8e6a0166-bc9f-4a6d-90a5-058ca654ef4d, Gareth Stevens Learning Library) Stevens, Gareth Publishing LLLP.

Townsend, Emily Rose. Polar Animals, 4 bks. Incl. Seals. (ENG., Illus.). 24p. (gr. k-1). 2004. 21.32 *(978-0-7368-2359-3(X),* Pebble); (Polar Animals Ser.). (ENG.). Illus.). 24p. 2004. Set lib. bdg. 87.96 o.p. *(978-0-7368-2532-0(0),* Pebble) Capstone.

Wade, Rosalyn. Polar Worlds. 2011. (Insiders Ser.). (ENG.). 64p. (J). (gr. 3-7). 19.99 *(978-1-4424-3275-8(6),* Simon & Schuster Bks. For Young Readers) Simon & Schuster Bks. For Young Readers.

Waldron, Melanie. Polar Regions, 1 vol. 2012. (Habitat Survival Ser.). (ENG.). 32p. (J). (gr. 2-4). pap. 8.29 *(978-1-4109-4608-9(8),* 119112, Raintree) Capstone.

West, David. Polar Animals. 2015. (Safari Sam's Wild Animals Ser.). (ENG.). 24p. (J). (gr. k-3). 28.50 *(978-1-62588-074-1(X),* 19366, Smart Apple Media) Black Rabbit Bks.

—Ten of the Best Adventures in Frozen Landscapes. 2015. (Ten of the Best: Stories of Exploration & Adventure Ser.). (ENG., Illus.). 24p. (J). (gr. 3-4). *(978-0-7787-1834-5(4))* Crabtree Publishing Co.

Williams, Lily. If Polar Bears Disappeared. Williams, Lily, illus. 2018. (If Animals Disappeared Ser.). (ENG., Illus.). 40p. (J). 18.99 *(978-1-250-14319-8(5),* 900180475) Roaring Brook Pr.

Woods, Michael & Woods, Mary B. Seven Natural Wonders of the Arctic, Antarctica, & the Oceans. 2009. (Seven Wonders Ser.). (ENG., Illus.). 80p. (gr. 5-8). 33.26 *(978-0-8225-9075-0(1))* Lerner Publishing Group.

World Book, Inc. Staff, contrib. by. Icy Worlds. 2011. (J). *(978-0-7166-1788-4(9))* World Bk., Inc.

—Oceans, Islands, & Polar Regions. 2008. (J). *(978-0-7166-1402-9(2))* World Bk., Inc.

POLAR REGIONS—FICTION

Ballantyne, R. M. The World of Ice. 2006. (Illus.). pap. *(978-1-4065-0533-7(1))* Dodo Pr.

Bastedo, Jamie. On Thin Ice, 1 vol. 2006. (ENG.). 176p. (YA). (gr. 7-9). pap. 13.95 *(978-0-88995-337-6(6),* ddb2db2a-f434-441f-b269-869287edad3c) Red Deer Pr. CAN. Dist: Firefly Bks., Ltd.

Bergen, Lara. The Polar Bears' Home: A Story about Global Warming. Nguyen, Vincent, illus. 2008. (Little Green Bks.). (ENG.). 24p. (J). (gr. -1-1). pap. 4.99 *(978-1-4169-6787-3(7),* Little Simon) Little Simon.

Bhasin, Kamla. Malu Bhalu. 2022. (ENG., Illus.). 32p. (J). (gr. -1-k). pap. 11.99 ***(978-81-86896-01-3(5))*** Tulika Pubs. IND. Dist: Independent Pubs. Group.

Brooks, Erik. Polar Opposites. 0 vols. Brooks, Erik, illus. 2012. (ENG., Illus.). 32p. (J). (gr. k-3). 16.99 *(978-0-7614-5685-8(6),* 9780761456858, Two Lions) Amazon Publishing.

Czerneda, Julie E., ed. Polaris: A Celebration of Polar Science, 1 vol. Normand, Jean-Pierre, illus. 2007. (Wonder Zone Ser.). (ENG.). 174p. (YA). (gr. 5-8). per. 6.95 *(978-0-88995-372-7(4),* 63753e61-0c66-46f2-9525-7e3b0b04cfb2) Red Deer Pr. CAN. Dist: Firefly Bks., Ltd.

Freedman, Claire. Where Snowflakes Fall. Macnaughton, Tina, illus. 2012. 24p. (J). *(978-1-4351-4321-0(3))* Barnes & Noble, Inc.

Gevry, Claudine, illus. One Little Penguin & His Friends: A Pushing, Turning, Counting Book. 2012. (ENG.). 10p. (J). bds. *(978-1-84956-027-6(7))* Top That! Publishing PLC.

Grau, Sheila. Polar Distress: Dr. Critchlore's School for Minions #3. Sutphin, Joe, illus. 2017. (Dr. Critchlore's School for Minions Ser.). (ENG.). 288p. (J). (gr. 3-7). 14.95 *(978-1-4197-2294-3(8),* 1132101) Abrams, Inc.

Heinz, Brian J. Nanuk, Lord of the Ice. Manchess, Gregory, illus. 2005. (J). *(978-0-936335-13-1(0));* pap. *(978-0-936335-14-8(9))* Ballyhoo BookWorks, Inc.

Lumry, Amanda & Hurwitz, Laura. Polar Bear Puzzle. 2007. (Adventures of Riley Ser.). (Illus.). (J). (gr. -1-3). 33p. 15.95 *(978-1-60040-004-9(3));* 36p. 18.95 *(978-1-60040-005-6(1))* Eaglemont Pr.

Rockhill, Dennis. Sueno Polar. 2008. 32p. 16.95 *(978-1-932746-76-1(5))* Sacred Garden Fellowship.

White, Andrea. Surviving Antarctica: Reality TV 2083. 2005. 336p. (J). (gr. 7-18). 16.99 *(978-0-06-055454-5(1),* HarperCollins) HarperCollins Pubs.

Willis, Jeanne. Poles Apart. Jarvis, illus. 2016. (ENG.). 32p. (J). (gr. -1-2). 15.99 *(978-0-7636-8944-5(0))* Candlewick Pr.

POLARITY

see also Good and Evil

Allen-Fletcher, Carly. Animal Antipodes. 2019. (ENG., Illus.). 32p. (J). (gr. 2-3). 17.99 *(978-1-939547-49-1(0),* b132424b-9bee-4352-895c-6cacb525ef53) Creston Bks.

Bennett, Elizabeth. Polar Opposites. 2014. (Illus.). (J). pap. *(978-0-545-61303-3(5))* Scholastic, Inc.

Blackstone, Stella. You & Me. Manna, Giovanni, illus. 2009. (ENG.). 32p. (J). 14.99 *(978-1-84686-336-3(8))* Barefoot Bks., Inc.

Christopher, Jennifer R. What If a Fork Was a Spoon. Christopher, Marie & Christopher, Jennifer, illus. 2006. (ENG.). 29p. (J). (gr. -1-3). per. 19.99 *(978-1-4257-0847-4(1))* Xlibris Corp.

Coat, Janik. Hippopposites. 2012. (Grammar Zoo Book Ser.). (ENG., Illus.). 36p. (J). (gr. -1 — 1). bds. 15.95 *(978-1-4197-0151-1(7),* 1007901, Abrams Appleseed) Abrams, Inc.

Coulton, Mia. Danny & Bee's Book of Opposites. Coulton, Mia, photos by. 2006. (ENG., Illus.). pap. 5.35 *(978-1-933624-02-0(7))* Maryruth Bks., Inc.

Davis, Caroline. First Opposites. 2012. (Illus.). 10p. (J). (gr. -1-1). bds. 7.99 *(978-1-84322-844-8(0),* Armadillo) Anness Publishing GBR. Dist: National Bk. Network.

Del Moral, S., tr. Contrarios. 2006. (Disney Learning (Silver Dolphin en Espanol) Ser.). (Illus.). 22p. (J). (gr. -1). *(978-970-718-428-2(0),* Silver Dolphin en Español) Advanced Marketing, S. de R. L. de C. V.

Dicmas, Courtney. Opposites. Dicmas, Courtney, illus. 2017. (Wild! Concepts Ser.: 4). (Illus.). 14p. (J). spiral bd. *(978-1-84643-997-1(3))* Child's Play International Ltd.

Dodd, Emma. Opposites. 2017. (Illus.). 12p. (J). (gr. -1-12). bds. 9.99 *(978-1-86147-843-6(7),* Armadillo) Anness Publishing GBR. Dist: National Bk. Network.

Emberley, Rebecca. My Opposites (Mis Opuestos) braille ed. 2004. (SPA, ENG & FRE.). (J). (gr. 1). spiral bd., bds. *(978-0-616-07271-4(6))* Canadian National Institute for the Blind/Institut National Canadien pour les Aveugles.

Erickson, Sharon. The Opposites. Ready, D. M., illus. 2008. 24p. pap. 24.95 *(978-1-60672-551-1(3))* America Star Bks.

Eszterhas, Suzi. Panda Opposites. 2019. (ENG., Illus.). 24p. (J). (gr. -1-1). bds. 9.95 *(978-1-77147-330-9(4))* Owlkids Bks. Inc. CAN. Dist: Publishers Group West (PGW).

Evanson, Ashley. London: A Book of Opposites. Evanson, Ashley, illus. 2015. (Hello, World Ser.). (Illus.). 16p. (J). (— 1). bds. 7.99 *(978-0-448-48916-2(3),* Penguin Workshop) Penguin Young Readers Group.

Fisher, Valorie. Everything I Need to Know Before I'm Five. Fisher, Valorie, illus. 2011. (Illus.). 40p. (J). (gr. k-k). 17.99 *(978-0-375-86865-8(8),* Schwartz & Wade Bks.) Random Hse. Children's Bks.

Friedland, Katy & Shoemaker, Marla K. Art Museum Opposites. 2010. (Illus.). *(978-0-87633-222-1(X))* Philadelphia Museum of Art.

—Art Museum Opposites. 2010. (ENG., Illus.). 44p. (J). (gr. -1-3). 16.95 *(978-1-4399-0523-4(1))* Temple Univ. Pr.

Galvin, Laura Gates. Quack's Opposites. 2006. (Peep & the Big Wide World Ser.). (ENG., Illus.). 24p. (J). (gr. -1-2). 15.99 *(978-1-59249-520-7(6),* 1C302) Soundprints.

Gordon, Sharon. Arriba, Abajo (up, Down), 1 vol. 2008. (Exactamente lo Opuesto (Just the Opposite) Ser.). (SPA., Illus.). 24p. (gr. k-1). lib. bdg. 25.50 *(978-0-7614-2369-0(9),* a449db45-1be9-45a5-95c3-95ecfacce9ba) Cavendish Square Publishing LLC.

—Duro, Blando / Hard, Soft, 1 vol. 2008. (Exactamente lo Opuesto / Just the Opposite Ser.). (ENG & SPA., Illus.). 24p. (gr. k-1). lib. bdg. 25.50 *(978-0-7614-2448-2(2),* e7a0b9fe-3b20-4d53-8a86-dbe4029fea9e) Cavendish Square Publishing LLC.

—Duro, Blando (Hard, Soft), 1 vol. 2008. (Exactamente lo Opuesto (Just the Opposite) Ser.). (SPA., Illus.). 24p. (gr. k-1). lib. bdg. 25.50 *(978-0-7614-2368-3(0),* ee981e10-202d-411b-bd7e-97638fc06451) Cavendish Square Publishing LLC.

—Exactamente lo Opuesto, 6 bks., Set. Incl. Arriba, Abajo (up, Down) lib. bdg. 25.50 *(978-0-7614-2369-0(9),* a449db45-1be9-45a5-95c3-95ecfacce9ba); Duro, Blando (Hard, Soft) lib. bdg. 25.50 *(978-0-7614-2368-3(0),* ee981e10-202d-411b-bd7e-97638fc06451); Grande, Pequeno (Big, Small) lib. bdg. 25.50 *(978-0-7614-2364-5(8),* 18668f7b-abaa-4ab5-abc8-170939c31ba0); Mojado, Seco (Wet, Dry) lib. bdg. 25.50 *(978-0-7614-2370-6(2),* 627444d3-31b6-4961-936c-7f75ceaae11d); Rapido, Lento (Fast, Slow) lib. bdg. 25.50 *(978-0-7614-2367-6(2),* 8e3a2a49-9830-474b-97b7-88c66e82fba2); Sucio, Limpio (Dirty, Clean) lib. bdg. 25.50 *(978-0-7614-2365-2(6),* eb087f62-1791-4696-9d4f-739faa124c48); (Illus.). 24p. (gr. k-1). 2008. (Bookworms — Spanish Editions: Exactamente lo Opuesto Ser.). (SPA.). 2006. lib. bdg. *(978-0-7614-2363-8(X),* Cavendish Square) Cavendish Square Publishing LLC.

—Fast, Slow, 1 vol. (Just the Opposite Ser.). (ENG.). 24p. (gr. k-1). 2008. pap. 9.23 *(978-0-7614-3281-4(7),* f218e495-952f-454b-bcd1-27ce65deb44a) 2003. (Illus.). lib. bdg. 25.50 *(978-0-7614-1570-1(X),* 26f23ffd-f5e2-4020-8fcb-f4b5419afa79, Cavendish Square) Cavendish Square Publishing LLC.

—Grande, Pequeno (Big, Small), 1 vol. 2008. (Exactamente lo Opuesto (Just the Opposite) Ser.). (SPA., Illus.). 24p. (gr. k-1). lib. bdg. 25.50 *(978-0-7614-2364-5(8),* 18668f7b-abaa-4ab5-abc8-170939c31ba0) Cavendish Square Publishing LLC.

—Hard, Soft, 1 vol. (Just the Opposite Ser.). (ENG.). 24p. (gr. k-1). 2008. pap. 9.23 *(978-0-7614-3282-1(5),* 95986292-9ea2-4c60-bb28-0e5fb90be301) 2003. (Illus.). lib. bdg. 25.50 *(978-0-7614-1571-8(8),* 855fec19-0da3-4bad-93bd-7d336d70124b, Cavendish Square) Cavendish Square Publishing LLC.

—Just the Opposite (Exactamente lo Opuesto), 6 bks., Set. Incl. Arriba, Abajo / up, Down. lib. bdg. 25.50 *(978-0-7614-2449-9(0),* 9075ad88-93a7-4103-b890-72201cb69161); Duro, Blando / Hard, Soft. lib. bdg. 25.50 *(978-0-7614-2448-2(2),* e7a0b9fe-3b20-4d53-8a86-dbe4029fea9e); Grande, Pequeno / Big, Small. lib. bdg. 25.50 *(978-0-7614-2445-1(8),* c7e50626-85f5-4c65-948e-adb87f3dfcc2); Mojado, Seco / Wet, Dry. lib. bdg. 25.50 *(978-0-7614-2450-5(4),* 7dce8a20-236b-4a2f-8c91-c1712ceda405); Rapido, Lento / Fast, Slow. lib. bdg. 25.50 *(978-0-7614-2447-5(4),* c9a1db90-b7b1-4bb7-8403-86a7dd0b0861); Sucio, Limpio / Dirty, Clean. lib. bdg. 25.50 *(978-0-7614-2446-8(6),* 19c2fad5-e8a7-44c5-98f5-b9843f68b624); (Illus.). 24p. (gr. k-1). 2008. (Bookworms — Bilingual Editions: Just the Opposite/Exactamente lo Opuesto Ser.). (SPA.). 2006. lib. bdg. *(978-0-7614-2443-7(1),* Cavendish Square) Cavendish Square Publishing LLC.

—Mojado, Seco / Wet, Dry, 1 vol. 2008. (Exactamente lo Opuesto / Just the Opposite Ser.). (ENG & SPA., Illus.). 24p. (gr. k-1). lib. bdg. 25.50 *(978-0-7614-2450-5(4),* 7dce8a20-236b-4a2f-8c91-c1712ceda405) Cavendish Square Publishing LLC.

—Mojado, Seco (Wet, Dry), 1 vol. 2008. (Exactamente lo Opuesto (Just the Opposite) Ser.). (SPA., Illus.). 24p. (gr. k-1). lib. bdg. 25.50 *(978-0-7614-2370-6(2),* 627444d3-31b6-4961-936c-7f75ceaae11d) Cavendish Square Publishing LLC.

—Rapido, Lento / Fast, Slow, 1 vol. 2008. (Exactamente lo Opuesto / Just the Opposite Ser.). (ENG & SPA., Illus.). 24p. (gr. k-1). lib. bdg. 25.50 *(978-0-7614-2447-5(4),* c9a1db90-b7b1-4bb7-8403-86a7dd0b0861) Cavendish Square Publishing LLC.

—Rapido, Lento (Fast, Slow), 1 vol. 2008. (Exactamente lo Opuesto (Just the Opposite) Ser.). (SPA., Illus.). 24p. (gr. k-1). lib. bdg. 25.50 *(978-0-7614-2367-6(2),* 8e3a2a49-9830-474b-97b7-88c66e82fba2) Cavendish Square Publishing LLC.

—Sucio, Limpio (Dirty, Clean), 1 vol. 2008. (Exactamente lo Opuesto (Just the Opposite) Ser.). (SPA., Illus.). 24p. (gr. k-1). lib. bdg. 25.50 *(978-0-7614-2365-2(6),* eb087f62-1791-4696-9d4f-739faa124c48) Cavendish Square Publishing LLC.

—Wet, Dry, 1 vol. (Just the Opposite Ser.). (ENG.). 24p. (gr. k-1). 2008. pap. 9.23 *(978-0-7614-3285-2(X),* f621d150-b5a8-4e40-bb36-2b8da27f7231) 2003. (Illus.). lib. bdg. 25.50 *(978-0-7614-1572-5(6),* c9d48325-609d-4791-a2bb-34f6f7950bce, Cavendish Square) Cavendish Square Publishing LLC.

Gunzi, Christiane. Opposites. Murrell, Deborah, ed. 2nd rev. ed. 2015. (ENG., Illus.). 34p. (J). bds. 7.99 *(978-1-906572-21-1(6))* Award Pubns. Ltd. GBR. Dist: Parkwest Pubns., Inc.

Heath, Beverly C. Opposites. Floyd, John, Jr., illus. 2006. 8p. (J). (gr. -1). bds. 5.95 *(978-0-9752860-3-6(X))* OurRainbow Pr., LLC.

Hitchen, Danielle. Let There Be Light: An Opposites Primer. 2018. (Baby Believer Ser.). (ENG., Illus.). 20p. (J). (— 1). bds. 12.99 *(978-0-7369-7236-9(6),* 6972369) Harvest Hse. Pubs.

Holland, Gini. I Know Opposites, 8 vols., Set. Incl. Alive & Not Alive. lib. bdg. 21.67 *(978-0-8368-8293-3(8),* c21adca9-87f4-4870-8dfe-3912dbf78aa2); Hot & Cold. lib. bdg. 21.67 *(978-0-8368-8294-0(6),* 79ca3edb-a8dc-4b48-ac23-8acb4fc55dde); Light & Heavy. lib. bdg. 21.67 *(978-0-8368-8295-7(4),* dc8e6bda-1299-4499-af24-7e18bbd09502); Soft & Hard. lib. bdg. 21.67 *(978-0-8368-8296-4(2),* 09da00ae-05fe-483b-b859-eec519b91511); (gr. k-2). (I Know Opposites Ser.). (ENG.). 16p. 2007. Set lib. bdg. 86.01 *(978-0-8368-8292-6(X),* 6ec48cea-46b0-40f4-ae3d-727797f9dd36, Weekly Reader Leveled Readers) Stevens, Gareth Publishing LLLP.

Honsek, Larissa. Opposites. 2019. (ENG., Illus.). 20p. (J). (gr. -1-k). bds. 9.99 *(978-1-64170-143-3(9),* 550143) Familius LLC.

Hood, Susan. Double Take! a New Look at Opposites. Fleck, Jay, illus. 2017. (ENG.). 32p. (J). (gr. -1-2). 18.99 *(978-0-7636-7291-1(2))* Candlewick Pr.

Hughes, Tom. Tight & Loose, 1 vol. 2016. (All about Opposites Ser.). (ENG., Illus.). 24p. (gr. k-1). pap. 10.35 *(978-0-7660-8116-1(8),* 7f258722-5854-4fa3-9a20-7d895836c511) Enslow Publishing, LLC.

Jeffries, Joyce. Big & Small, 1 vol. 2013. (Dinosaur School Ser.). (ENG., Illus.). 24p. (J). (gr. k-k). pap. 9.15 *(978-1-4339-8084-8(3),* 9275d23c-ca29-426b-813b-13b52b4563b5); lib. bdg. 25.27 *(978-1-4339-8083-1(5),* c3bde0ec-060d-4464-934b-5ce83129e8bb) Stevens, Gareth Publishing LLLP.

—Heavy & Light, 1 vol. 2013. (Dinosaur School Ser.). (ENG., Illus.). 24p. (gr. k-k). 25.27 *(978-1-4339-8087-9(8),* 1f9d2c59-08ed-48da-9978-ee55e27c4205); pap. 9.15 *(978-1-4339-8088-6(6),* 1d755ca5-8145-47eb-8203-b7aff10753d9) Stevens, Gareth Publishing LLLP.

—Hot & Cold, 1 vol. 2013. (Dinosaur School Ser.). (ENG., Illus.). 24p. (gr. k-k). 25.27 *(978-1-4339-8091-6(6),* cde8c1de-3f5d-455d-a83c-f440d5db0e9f); pap. 9.15 *(978-1-4339-8092-3(4),* b0f170e3-8102-4b67-8c01-bb732bce44d6) Stevens, Gareth Publishing LLLP.

—Long & Short, 1 vol. 2013. (Dinosaur School Ser.). (ENG., Illus.). 24p. (gr. k-k). 25.27 *(978-1-4339-8095-4(9),* 356f2a75-b6db-4c49-8409-ae2a2632b448); pap. 9.15 *(978-1-4339-8096-1(7),* 2b5c1f5f-24bc-45f7-b42a-9320efd5935e) Stevens, Gareth Publishing LLLP.

Jopp, Kelsey. Happy & Sad. 2019. (Opposites Ser.). (ENG., Illus.). 16p. (J). (gr. k-1). 25.64 *(978-1-64185-346-0(8),* 1641853468, Focus Readers) North Star Editions.

—Near & Far. 2019. (Opposites Ser.). (ENG., Illus.). 16p. (J). (gr. k-1). 25.64 *(978-1-64185-350-7(6),* 1641853506, Focus Readers) North Star Editions.

Jordan, Apple. Heavy / Light, 1 vol. 2nd rev. ed. 2012. (Opposites Ser.). (ENG.). 16p. (gr. k-1). 24.07 *(978-1-60870-408-8(4),* 061610bb-3971-4197-9552-f0f7fcf38fae) Cavendish Square Publishing LLC.

—Hot / Cold, 1 vol. 2nd rev. ed. 2012. (Opposites Ser.). (ENG., Illus.). 16p. (J). (gr. k-1). 24.07 *(978-1-60870-409-5(2),* 1f87f308-e1e4-428f-9019-bd0162e0dec4) Cavendish Square Publishing LLC.

Kalman, Bobbie. Is It the Same or Different?, 1 vol. 2007. (Looking at Nature Ser.). (ENG., Illus.). 24p. (J). (gr. -1-2). pap. *(978-0-7787-3337-9(8))* Crabtree Publishing Co.

—What Are Opposites in Nature? 2010. (Looking at Nature Ser.). (ENG.). 24p. (J). (gr. -1-2). lib. bdg. *(978-0-7787-3326-3(2))* Crabtree Publishing Co.

Katirgis, Jane. Back & Front, 1 vol. 2011. (All about Opposites Ser.). (ENG., Illus.). 24p. (gr. -1-1). pap. 10.35 *(978-1-59845-259-4(2),* ccb80e3c-3534-4d01-8037-21eed8834307); lib. bdg. 25.27 *(978-0-7660-3916-2(1),* 06389617-d898-4746-a520-2811e2d27cf3) Enslow Publishing, LLC. (Enslow Publishing).

—Big & Little, 1 vol. 2011. (All about Opposites Ser.). (ENG., Illus.). 24p. (gr. -1-1). pap. 10.35 *(978-1-59845-263-1(0),* 39add510-cb02-4eb7-a1d5-df937438332f); lib. bdg. 25.27 *(978-0-7660-3911-7(0),* 4d9ae2c1-22fc-4afb-b9ea-fc4c97749968) Enslow Publishing, LLC. (Enslow Publishing).

—Day & Night, 1 vol. 2011. (All about Opposites Ser.). (ENG., Illus.). 24p. (gr. -1-1). (J). lib. bdg. 25.27 *(978-0-7660-3915-5(3),* 485378d7-4d0d-477e-9ae7-f50d300be7c8); pap. 10.35 *(978-1-59845-262-4(2),* 41142589-e229-47b1-8f2d-4e5d40470dad) Enslow Publishing, LLC. (Enslow Publishing).

—Over & Under, 1 vol. 2011. (All about Opposites Ser.). (ENG., Illus.). 24p. (gr. -1-1). pap. 10.35 *(978-1-59845-260-0(6),* 89ce72c4-d57d-4db1-a38d-22ebb6b1d7d2); lib. bdg. 25.27 *(978-0-7660-3914-8(5),* 4231853a-1991-4520-ad05-26d624c5f85d) Enslow Publishing, LLC. (Enslow Publishing).

—Tall & Short, 1 vol. 2011. (All about Opposites Ser.). (ENG., Illus.). 24p. (gr. -1-1). pap. 10.35 *(978-1-59845-261-7(4),* 391f7971-182c-4e4d-8ea7-45616864c273); lib. bdg. 25.27 *(978-0-7660-3912-4(9),* 0254e529-15b8-4887-9e30-094a65b0f303) Enslow Publishing, LLC. (Enslow Publishing).

—Up & Down, 1 vol. 2011. (All about Opposites Ser.). (ENG., Illus.). 24p. (gr. -1-1). pap. 10.35 *(978-1-59845-258-7(4),* 9b6ef717-bdc4-406f-af78-51a42e64ce90); lib. bdg. 25.27 *(978-0-7660-3913-1(7),* e6174b0e-e323-4f82-a84b-b36009fc8899) Enslow Publishing, LLC. (Enslow Publishing).

Knight, Margy Burns, et al. Who Belongs Here? (Teachers Guide) 2nd ed. 2005. (ENG., Illus.). 40p. (gr. 3-8). pap., tchr. ed., tchr.'s training gde. ed. 9.95 *(978-0-88448-111-9(5))* Tilbury Hse. Pubs.

PQR

Lluch, Alex A. I Like to Learn Opposites: Amazing Bugs. 2011. 32p. (J). (gr. -1-k). bds. 4.95 *(978-1-934386-03-3(0))* WS Publishing.

Max and Sid, illus. Learning. 2016. (What Can You Spot? Ser.). (ENG.). 18p. (J). (gr. -1 — 1). bds. 7.99 *(978-1-4998-0270-2(6))* Little Bee Books Inc.

McDonald, Jill. Opposites: A Play-with-Me BK. 2007. (ENG.). 10p. bds. 6.95 *(978-1-58117-605-6(8)*, Intervisual/Piggy Toes) Bendon, Inc.

McDonnell, Rory. In or Out?, 1 vol. 2019. (All about Opposites Ser.). (ENG.). 24p. (gr. k-k). pap. 9.15 *(978-1-5382-3726-7(1)*, aab60d62-bcf5-4582-b0cd-4f955300d036) Stevens, Gareth Publishing LLLP.

—Near or Far? 2019. (All about Opposites Ser.). (ENG.). 24p. (gr. k-k). 48.90 *(978-1-5382-3731-1(8))* Stevens, Gareth Publishing LLLP.

—Up or Down?, 1 vol. 2019. (All about Opposites Ser.). (ENG.). 24p. (gr. k-k). 24.27 *(978-1-5382-3736-6(9)*, ccf7ee8d-a6d9-497b-909d-97dbc1554093) Stevens, Gareth Publishing LLLP.

McKee, David. Elmer's Opposites. McKee, David, illus. 2012. (ENG., Illus.). 10p. (J). (gr. -1-2). bds. 7.95 *(978-0-7613-8998-9(9)*, b80b42ba-5cb6-4102-983d-a4df6a6e5723) Lerner Publishing Group.

Murray, Julie. Big & Small. 2018. (Opposites Ser.). (ENG., Illus.). 24p. (J). (gr. -1-2). lib. bdg. 31.36 *(978-1-5321-8177-1(9)*, 29827, Abdo Kids) ABDO Publishing Co.

—Fast & Slow. 2018. (Opposites Ser.). (ENG., Illus.). 24p. (J). (gr. -1-2). lib. bdg. 31.36 *(978-1-5321-8178-8(7)*, 29829, Abdo Kids) ABDO Publishing Co.

—Hard & Soft. 2018. (Opposites Ser.). (ENG., Illus.). 24p. (J). (gr. -1-2). lib. bdg. 31.36 *(978-1-5321-8179-5(5)*, 29831, Abdo Kids) ABDO Publishing Co.

—Long & Short. 2018. (Opposites Ser.). (ENG., Illus.). 24p. (J). (gr. -1-2). lib. bdg. 31.36 *(978-1-5321-8182-5(5)*, 29837, Abdo Kids) ABDO Publishing Co.

National Wildlife Federation. My First Book of Animal Opposites (National Wildlife Federation) 2016. (Illus.). 22p. (J). (— 1). bds. 6.95 *(978-1-62354-062-3(3))* Charlesbridge Publishing, Inc.

National Wildlife Federation Staff & Bové, Jennifer. Animal Opposites. 2017. (Ranger Rick: Animal Fun for Young Children Ser.). (Illus.). 32p. (J). (gr. -1-1). pap. 5.99 *(978-1-63076-292-6(X))* Muddy Boots Pr.

Nestling, Rose. Babies Love Opposites. Cottage Door Press, ed. Hogan, Martina, illus. 2015. (Babies Love Ser.). (ENG.). 12p. (J). (gr. -1 — 1). bds. 7.99 *(978-1-68052-028-6(8)*, 1000291) Cottage Door Pr.

Page, Liza & Innovative Kids Staff. Opposites. Larrañaga, Ana Martin, illus. 2008. (ENG.). 12p. (J). (gr. -1 — 1). bds. 5.99 *(978-1-58476-654-4(9))* Innovative Kids.

Patricelli, Leslie. Baby Happy Baby Sad/Bebè Feliz Bebè Triste. Patricelli, Leslie, illus. 2018. (Leslie Patricelli Board Bks.). (Illus.). 24p. (J). (— 1). bds. 8.99 *(978-1-5362-0348-6(3))* Candlewick Pr.

—Grande Pequeño. Rozarena, P., tr. Patricelli, Leslie, illus. 2003. (SPA., Illus.). 25p. (J). (gr. -1-k). bds. 7.95 *(978-970-29-0988-0(0))* Santillana USA Publishing Co., Inc.

—No No Yes Yes. Patricelli, Leslie, illus. 2008. (Leslie Patricelli Board Bks.). (ENG., Illus.). 24p. (J). (— 1). bds. 8.99 *(978-0-7636-3244-1(9))* Candlewick Pr.

—No No Yes Yes/No No Sí Sí. Patricelli, Leslie, illus. 2018. (Leslie Patricelli Board Bks.). (Illus.). 24p. (J). (— 1). bds. 8.99 *(978-1-5362-0349-3(1))* Candlewick Pr.

PatrickGeorge. Contrarios. 2012. (SPA.). 26p. (J). (gr. -1-1). pap. 19.99 *(978-84-261-3885-9(3))* Juventud, Editorial ESP. Dist: Lectorum Pubns., Inc.

Priddy Books Staff. First Concepts: Opposite. 2003. (Illus.). (J). bds. 8.95 *(978-0-312-49231-1(6)*, Priddy Bks.) St. Martin's Pr.

Priddy, Roger. My Fun School Bus Lift-The-flap. 2018. (My Fun Flap Bks.). (ENG., Illus.). 10p. (J). bds. 10.99 *(978-0-312-52649-8(0)*, 900185562) St. Martin's Pr.

Reich, Kass. Up Hamster, down Hamster, 1 vol. 2015. (ENG., Illus.). 24p. (J). (gr. -1 — 1). bds. 9.95 *(978-1-4598-1013-6(9))* Orca Bk. Pubs. USA.

Rossiter, Brienna. Fast & Slow. 2019. (Opposites Ser.). (ENG., Illus.). 16p. (J). (gr. k-1). 25.64 *(978-1-64185-345-3(X)*, 164185345X, Focus Readers) North Star Editions.

—High & Low. 2019. (Opposites Ser.). (ENG., Illus.). 16p. (J). (gr. k-1). 25.64 *(978-1-64185-347-7(6)*, 1641853476, Focus Readers) North Star Editions.

—More & Less. 2019. (Opposites Ser.). (ENG., Illus.). 16p. (J). (gr. k-1). 25.64 *(978-1-64185-349-1(2)*, 1641853492, Focus Readers) North Star Editions.

—Tall & Short. 2019. (Opposites Ser.). (ENG., Illus.). 16p. (J). (gr. k-1). 25.64 *(978-1-64185-351-4(4)*, 1641853514, Focus Readers) North Star Editions.

—Wet & Dry. 2019. (Opposites Ser.). (ENG., Illus.). 16p. (J). (gr. k-1). 25.64 *(978-1-64185-352-1(2)*, 1641853522, Focus Readers) North Star Editions.

Saunders, Katie, illus. Let's Learn Opposites. 2013. 10p. (J). *(978-1-4351-4940-3(8))* Barnes & Noble, Inc.

Savary, Fabien & Vadeboncoeur, Isabelle. Caillou: Los Contrarios. Tipeo, illus. 2004. (Caillou Ser.).Tr. of What's the Difference? (SPA.). 12p. (J). (gr. -1 — 1). bds. 4.95 *(978-1-58728-348-2(4))* Cooper Square Publishing Llc.

Saviola, Ava. Dinosaur Opposites, 1 vol. 2012. (Dinosaur School Ser.). (ENG., Illus.). 24p. (J). (gr. k-k). pap. 9.15 *(978-1-4339-7144-0(5)*, 2354eb32-89b8-485d-a8ac-edfd89a2be2b); lib. bdg. 25.27 *(978-1-4339-7143-3(7)*, 5ad9a397-c5ac-435c-863b-870bec3d0c36) Stevens, Gareth Publishing LLLP.

Schiller, Pamela Byrne. Sing a Song of Opposites. Bartkowiak, Richele, photos by. 2014. (Illus.). 24p. (J). *(978-1-60128-859-2(X))* Frog Street Pr.

Sheldon, Kaylene Kauwila. I Know Ka'a'awa. 2008.Tr. of Ike Au la Ka'a'awa. (ENG & HAW., Illus.). 17p. (J). lib. bdg. *(978-0-9773495-6-2(X))* Na Kamalei Koolauloa Early Education Program.

Shulman, Mark. Big Bagel, Little Bagel. Milne, Bill, photos by. 2006. (Illus.). 10p. (J). (gr. k-4). reprint ed. 6.00 *(978-1-4223-5709-5(0))* DIANE Publishing Co.

Silver Dolphin en Español Editors. Disney Tesoro de libros de Calcomanías: Disney Sticker Book Treasury, Spanish-Language Edition. 2007. (Illus.). 48p. (J). *(978-970-718-447-3(7)*, Silver Dolphin en Español) Advanced Marketing, S. de R. L. de C. V.

Singh, Lee. The Greatest Opposites Book on Earth. Frost, Tom, illus. 2017. (ENG.). 16p. (J). (gr. -1-2). bds. 18.99 *(978-0-7636-9554-5(8)*, Big Picture Press) Candlewick Pr.

Smith, Sian. Hard & Soft, 1 vol. 2014. (Opposites Ser.). (ENG.). 24p. (J). (gr. -1-1). pap. 5.99 *(978-1-4846-0333-8(8)*, 126423, Heinemann) Capstone.

—Hot & Cold, 1 vol. 2014. (Opposites Ser.). (ENG.). 24p. (J). (gr. -1-1). pap. 5.99 *(978-1-4846-0334-5(6)*, 126422, Heinemann) Capstone.

—Old & New, 1 vol. 2014. (Opposites Ser.). (ENG.). 24p. (J). (gr. -1-1). pap. 5.99 *(978-1-4846-0335-2(4)*, 126424, Heinemann) Capstone.

—Opposites, 1 vol. 2014. (Opposites Ser.). (ENG.). 24p. (J). (gr. -1-1). pap., pap., pap. 35.94 *(978-1-4846-0338-3(9)*, 21695, Heinemann) Capstone.

—Opposites Big Book, 1 vol. 2014. (Opposites Ser.). (ENG., Illus.). 24p. (J). (gr. -1-1). 26.00 *(978-1-4846-0339-0(7)*, 195266, Heinemann) Capstone.

—Wet & Dry, 1 vol. 2014. (Opposites Ser.). (ENG.). 24p. (J). (gr. -1-1). pap. 5.99 *(978-1-4846-0337-6(0)*, 126426, Heinemann) Capstone.

Teckentrup, Britta, illus. My Book of Opposites. 2014. (J). *(978-1-4351-5678-4(1))* Barnes & Noble, Inc.

The Trustees of the British Museum, illus. Opposites: Early Learning at the Museum. 2018. (Early Learning at the Museum Ser.). (ENG.). 20p. (J). (— 1). bds. 7.99 *(978-1-5362-0270-0(3))* Candlewick Pr.

WrightGroup/McGraw-Hill. Dlm Early Childhood Express: Sing a Song of Opposites Little Book English. 2014. (Illus.). 24p. (J). pap. *(978-0-07-572407-0(3))* Frog Street Pr.

Yates, Gene. The Dragon Opposites Book. 2005. (Illus.). 14p. (J). *(978-1-58865-283-6(1))* Kidsbooks, LLC.

Yates, Gene, illus. The Dragon Opposites Book. 2006. (J). *(978-1-58865-362-8(5))* Kidsbooks, LLC.

Zubek, Adeline. Fast or Slow?, 1 vol. 2019. (All about Opposites Ser.). (ENG.). 24p. (gr. k-k). 24.27 *(978-1-5382-3716-8(4)*, 60fb01b2-8fb8-4e67-96a0-20fcc3052a0f) Stevens, Gareth Publishing LLLP.

—Front or Back?, 1 vol. 2019. (All about Opposites Ser.). (ENG.). 24p. (gr. k-k). 24.27 *(978-1-5382-3720-5(2)*, 51b658b4-75d7-4fad-bf16-9ee1c130c2f9) Stevens, Gareth Publishing LLLP.

—Heavy or Light?, 1 vol. 2019. (All about Opposites Ser.). (ENG.). 24p. (gr. k-k). pap. 9.15 *(978-1-5382-3722-9(9)*, fca8bd9d-12b6-45f2-a6b9-c5b4f6aa23e9) Stevens, Gareth Publishing LLLP.

POLARITY—FICTION

Arena, Jennifer. Marta! Big & Small. 2016. (ENG., Illus.). 32p. (J). 18.99 *(978-1-62672-243-9(9)*, 900146476) Roaring Brook Pr.

Austin, Ruth. Hide Seek Stinky Sweet: a Little Book of Opposites: Board Book. 2018. (ENG., Illus.). (gr. -1-k). bds. 12.95 *(978-1-946873-08-8(X))* Compendium, Inc., Publishing & Communications.

Coward, Fiona. Swing High, Swing Low. Manna, Giovanni, illus. 2005. (ENG.). 32p. (J). 16.99 *(978-1-84148-170-8(X))* Barefoot Bks., Inc.

Disney. Big Bear, Little Bear. 2012. (Disney Princess Step into Reading Ser.). lib. bdg. 13.55 *(978-0-606-26391-7(8))* Turtleback.

Duskey Rinker, Sherri & Long, Ethan. Crane Truck's Opposites: Goodnight, Goodnight, Construction Site (Educational Construction Truck Book for Preschoolers, Vehicle & Truck Themed Board Book for 5 to 6 Year Olds, Opposite Book) 2019. (Goodnight, Goodnight Construction Site Ser.). (ENG., Illus.). 20p. (J). (gr. -1 — 1). bds. 6.99 *(978-1-4521-5317-9(5))* Chronicle Bks. LLC.

Fernandez, Rajiv. Baby to Big. 2017. (ENG., Illus.). 32p. (J). (— 1). 6.99 *(978-1-57687-826-2(0)*, powerHouse Bks.) powerHse. Bks.

Hamlyn, Charlotte Rose. Opposite Land. 2017. 144p. (J). (gr. 2-4). pap. 13.99 *(978-0-14-378081-6(6))* Random Hse. Australia AUS. Dist: Independent Pubs. Group.

Henderson, Robert. I See, I See. 2019. (ENG., Illus.). 48p. (J). (gr. -1-k). 17.99 *(978-1-4521-8334-3(1))* Chronicle Bks. LLC.

Idle, Molly. Flora & the Ostrich: An Opposites Book by Molly Idle (Flora & Flamingo Board Books, Picture Books for Toddlers, Baby Books with Animals) 2017. (Flora & Friends Ser.). (ENG., Illus.). 20p. (J). (gr. -1 — 1). bds. 9.99 *(978-1-4521-4658-4(6))* Chronicle Bks. LLC.

Jordan, Apple. Fast Kart, Slow Kart. 2013. (Step into Reading - Level 1 Ser.). lib. bdg. 13.55 *(978-0-606-26980-3(0))* Turtleback.

Lagonegro, Melissa. Big Friend, Little Friend. 2010. (Disney Princess Step into Reading Ser.). lib. bdg. 13.55 *(978-0-606-07043-0(5))* Turtleback.

Makso, Malisa. Inside & Outside. 2010.Tr. of Anndan ak Deyò. (HAT., Illus.). 8p. (J). 4.50 *(978-1-58432-829-2(0))* Educa Vision Inc.

Running Press Staff. Opposites. 2004. (Sticker Math Ser.). (ENG.). 1p. (J). pap., act. bk. ed. 4.95 *(978-0-7945-0042-9(0)*, Usborne) EDC Publishing.

Scholastic, Inc. Staff. Opposites. 2015. (Rookie Toddler(r) Ser.). (ENG.). 12p. (J). bds. 6.95 *(978-0-531-20569-3(X))* Scholastic Library Publishing.

Schwartz, Betty & Seresin, Lynn. Puppies, Puppies, Everywhere! A Back-And-Forth Opposites Book. Powell, Luciana Navarro, illus. 2015. (J). *(978-1-62370-236-6(4)*, Capstone Young Readers) Capstone.

Seuss. The Foot Book. abr. ed. 2016. (Big Bright & Early Board Book Ser.). (ENG., Illus.). 24p. (J). (gr. -1 — 1). bds. 6.99 *(978-0-553-53630-0(3)*, Random Hse. Bks. for Young Readers) Random Hse. Children's Bks.

Webster, Christy. Big Fish, Little Fish (Disney/Pixar Finding Dory) The Disney Storybook Art Team, illus. 2016. (Step into Reading Ser.). (ENG.). 24p. (J). (gr. -1-1). E-Book *(978-0-7364-3705-9(3)*, RH/Disney) Random Hse. Children's Bks.

Williams, Brenda. Outdoor Opposites. Oldfield, Rachel, illus. 2015. (Barefoot Singalongs Ser.). (ENG.). 32p. (J). (gr. -1-2). pap. 10.99 *(978-1-78285-095-3(3))* Barefoot Bks., Inc.

POLICE

see also Criminal Investigation; Detectives; Secret Service

Adamson, Heather. A Day in the Life of a Police Officer, 1 vol. 2003. (Community Helpers at Work Ser.). (ENG., Illus.). 24p. (J). (gr. 1-3). 25.99 *(978-0-7368-2285-5(2)*, 89393) Capstone.

Aleo, Cyndy, ed. Critical Perspectives on Effective Policing & Police Brutality, 1 vol. 2017. (Analyzing the Issues Ser.). (ENG.). 232p. (gr. 8-8). 50.93 *(978-0-7660-9170-2(8)*, 56057bdf-634b-41c0-9481-99ea263b0300) Enslow Publishing, LLC.

Ames, Michelle. Police Officers in Our Community. 2009. (Illus.). 24p. (J). 49.50 *(978-1-4358-2464-5(4)*, 1300573); (ENG., (gr. 1-1). pap. 9.25 *(978-1-4358-2453-9(9)*, 6e51018c-8b0a-4fbb-a2c0-5d52ebf35425); (ENG., (gr. 1-1). lib. bdg. 26.27 *(978-1-4042-8057-1(X)*, c321816b-c9de-46d1-bbb6-732d3b969610) Rosen Publishing Group, Inc., The. (PowerKids Pr.).

Anderson, Sheila. Police Station. 2008. pap. 22.95 *(978-0-8225-9373-7(4))*; (ENG., Illus.). 8p. (J). pap. 5.99 *(978-0-8225-8842-9(0)*, c9605fe8-5239-4b77-8437-735ad3183db2) Lerner Publishing Group.

Arnold, Tedd. Fly Guy Presents: Police Officers (Scholastic Reader, Level 2) Arnold, Tedd, illus. 2018. (Scholastic Reader, Level 2 Ser.: 11). (ENG., Illus.). 32p. (J). (gr. k-2). pap. 4.99 *(978-1-338-21717-9(8))* Scholastic, Inc.

Arnold, Tedd, illus. Police Officers. 2018. (J). *(978-1-5444-0550-6(2))* Scholastic, Inc.

Aronin, Miriam. Highway Patrol Officers. 2016. (Police: Search & Rescue! Ser.). (ENG., Illus.). 32p. (J). (gr. 2-7). 28.50 *(978-1-943553-14-3(9))* Bearport Publishing Co., Inc.

Aronson, Marc. Master of Deceit: J. Edgar Hoover & America in the Age of Lies. (ENG.). 240p. (gr. 9). 2019. (J). pap. 14.99 *(978-1-5362-0630-2(X))* 2012. (Illus.). (YA). 25.99 *(978-0-7636-5025-4(0))* Candlewick Pr.

Askew, Amanda & Crowson, Andrew. Police Officer. 2012. (ENG., Illus.). 24p. (J). (gr. 1-3). pap. 7.95 *(978-1-926853-49-9(0))* Saunders Bk. Co. CAN. Dist: RiverStream Publishing.

Bell, Samantha. Police Officer. Bane, Jeff, illus. 2017. (My Early Library: My Friendly Neighborhood Ser.). (ENG.). 24p. (J). (gr. k-1). lib. bdg. 30.64 *(978-1-63472-826-3(2)*, 209730) Cherry Lake Publishing.

Bellisario, Gina. Police Officers in My Community. Atkinson, Cale, illus. 2018. (Meet a Community Helper (Early Bird Stories (tm)) Ser.). (ENG.). 24p. (J). (gr. k-2). 29.32 *(978-1-5415-2020-2(3)*, f186daa0-e543-4a23-9836-3b79730c5345, Lerner Pubns.) Lerner Publishing Group.

Bernhardt, Carolyn. Sound. 2018. (Science Starters Ser.). (ENG., Illus.). 24p. (J). (gr. k-3). pap. 7.99 *(978-1-61891-467-5(7)*, 12120, Blastoff! Readers) Bellwether Media.

Blake, Kevin. City Cops. 2016. (Police: Search & Rescue! Ser.). (ENG., Illus.). 32p. (J). (gr. 2-7). 28.50 *(978-1-943553-11-2(4))* Bearport Publishing Co., Inc.

Bourgeois, Paulette. Police Officers. LaFave, Kim, illus. 2004. (Kids Can Read Level 3 Ser.). (ENG.). 32p. (J). (gr. k-3). 16.19 *(978-1-55337-742-9(7))* Kids Can Pr., Ltd. CAN. Dist: Children's Plus, Inc.

Bowman, Chris. Police Officer. 2014. (Dangerous Jobs Ser.). (ENG., Illus.). 24p. (J). (gr. 3-7). lib. bdg. 26.95 *(978-1-62617-112-1(2)*, Torque Bks.) Bellwether Media.

Capici, Gaetano. What Do They Do? Police Officers. 2010. (Community Connections: What Do They Do? Ser.). (ENG., Illus.). 24p. (gr. 2-5). lib. bdg. 29.21 *(978-1-60279-803-8(6)*, 200496) Cherry Lake Publishing.

Carr, Aaron. The Police Station. 2013. 24p. pap. 12.95 *(978-1-62127-347-9(4))* Weigl Pubs., Inc.

Charles, Audrey. I Can Be a Police Officer, 1 vol. 2017. (I Can Be Anything! Ser.). (ENG.). 24p. (gr. k-k). pap. 9.15 *(978-1-4824-6325-5(3)*, ec1274e8-c704-42bd-bbcc-0274de04a816) Stevens, Gareth Publishing LLLP.

Christopher, Nick. Que Hacen Los Policias? / What Do Police Officers Do?, 1 vol. 2015. (Ayudantes de la Comunidad / Helping the Community Ser.). (ENG & SPA.). 24p. (J). (gr. 1-1). 25.27 *(978-1-4994-0615-3(0)*, ec9c8710-31fc-4a11-a22a-61e10094b88a, PowerKids Pr.) Rosen Publishing Group, Inc., The.

—What Do Police Officers Do?, 1 vol. 2015. (Helping the Community Ser.). (ENG., Illus.). 24p. (J). (gr. 1-1). pap. 9.25 *(978-1-4994-0656-6(8)*, dae6e81b-7fac-4702-af7c-733c13663421, PowerKids Pr.) Rosen Publishing Group, Inc., The.

Christy, Lee Louis. I Go to Work as a Police Officer. 2003. (I Go to Work As Ser.). (Illus.). (J). *(978-1-58417-040-2(9))*; pap. *(978-1-58417-103-4(0))* Lake Street Pubs.

Clark, Katie. Police Horses. 2013. (We Work! Animals with Jobs Ser.). (Illus.). 24p. (J). (gr. -1-3). lib. bdg. 25.65 *(978-1-61772-896-9(9))* Bearport Publishing Co., Inc.

Coan, Sharon. Trabajadores Que Me Cuidan. 2nd rev. ed. 2016. (TIME for KIDS(r): Informational Text Ser.). (SPA., Illus.). 12p. (gr. -1-k). 7.99 *(978-1-4938-3028-2(7))* Teacher Created Materials, Inc.

Coldwell, Lamar. Shaniqua's Mom Is a Policewoman, 1 vol. 2016. (Rosen REAL Readers: Social Studies Nonfiction / Fiction: Myself, My Community, My World Ser.). (ENG.). 12p. (gr. k-1). pap. 6.33 *(978-1-5081-2314-9(4)*, d7baf3b6-ec63-44af-8096-e75448469f42, Rosen Classroom) Rosen Publishing Group, Inc., The.

Crabtree, Marc. Meet My Neighbor, the Police Officer. 2012. (ENG., Illus.). 24p. (J). *(978-0-7787-4561-7(9))*; pap. *(978-0-7787-4566-2(X))* Crabtree Publishing Co.

Doering Tourville, Amanda. A Visit to the Police Station. Thompson, Jeffrey, illus. 2011. (First Graphics: My Community Ser.). (ENG.). 24p. (gr. 1-2). pap. 35.70 *(978-1-4296-6402-8(9))* Capstone.

Dudley, William. Do Police Abuse Their Powers? 2016. (ENG.). 80p. (J). (gr. 5-12). lib. bdg. *(978-1-68282-072-8(6))* ReferencePoint Pr., Inc.

Enz, Tammy. Beyond the Bars: Exploring the Secrets of a Police Station. 2010. (Hidden Worlds Ser.). (ENG.). 32p. (J). (gr. 3-9). lib. bdg. 27.32 *(978-1-4296-3377-2(8)*, 95884, Capstone Pr.) Capstone.

—Hidden Worlds, 4 vols., Set. Incl. Behind the Racks: Exploring the Secrets of a Shopping Mall. lib. bdg. 27.32 *(978-1-4296-3386-4(7)*, 95892); Beyond the Bars: Exploring the Secrets of a Police Station. lib. bdg. 27.32 *(978-1-4296-3377-2(8)*, 95884); (J). (gr. 3-9). (Hidden Worlds Ser.). (ENG.). 32p. 2010. 81.96 o.p. *(978-1-4296-3777-0(3)*, 168679, Capstone Pr.) Capstone.

Espejo, Roman, ed. Community Policing, 1 vol. 2014. (Opposing Viewpoints Ser.). (ENG., 216p. (gr. 10-12). Illus.). pap. 34.80 *(978-0-7377-6952-4(1)*, 3ddc0763-fe68-4dc6-8a15-db074e25edb5); lib. bdg. 50.43 *(978-0-7377-6951-7(3)*, ec6e39ab-893c-4ba4-a0a8-cbd3cc63ecc0) Greenhaven Publishing LLC. (Greenhaven Publishing).

Evans, Colin. New York Police Department. 2011. (ENG., Illus.). 120p. (gr. 6-12). 35.00 *(978-1-60413-614-2(6)*, P189867, Facts On File) Infobase Holdings, Inc.

Extreme Law Enforcement, 12 vols. 2013. (Extreme Law Enforcement Ser.). (ENG.). 112p. (YA). (gr. 7-7). 238.62 *(978-1-4777-1720-2(X)*, 6c7112c5-b94f-4227-9ba9-cada235b2f0b) Rosen Publishing Group, Inc., The.

Fitzgerald, Lee. Mounted & Canine Police, 1 vol., 1. 2015. (Careers for Heroes Ser.). (ENG., Illus.). 24p. (J). (gr. 3-4). pap. 9.25 *(978-1-5081-4384-0(6)*, 900ded64-f60d-42b7-8383-ca3c94fcd2cf, PowerKids Pr.) Rosen Publishing Group, Inc., The.

Fitzgerald, Sheila, ed. Police Brutality, 1 vol. 2006. (Opposing Viewpoints Ser.). (ENG., Illus.). 184p. (gr. 10-12). pap. 34.80 *(978-0-7377-3359-4(4)*, bf568233-9741-4276-b9fc-8534b6a0d15e, Greenhaven Publishing) Greenhaven Publishing LLC.

Forest, Anne. SWAT Teams, 1 vol., 1. 2015. (Careers for Heroes Ser.). (ENG., Illus.). 24p. (J). (gr. 3-4). pap. 9.25 *(978-1-5081-4398-7(6)*, 0f746c96-4e35-4cf7-b1e8-46cd95edcd3c, PowerKids Pr.) Rosen Publishing Group, Inc., The.

Forrest, Glen C. Police Technology: 21st Century Crime Fighting Tools, 1 vol. 2016. (Law Enforcement & Intelligence Gathering Ser.). (ENG., Illus.). 104p. (J). (gr. 8-8). lib. bdg. 37.82 *(978-1-5081-0379-0(8)*, 3b8600ff-e9be-4298-a2e2-bb1f8a47c3d5) Rosen Publishing Group, Inc., The.

Freeman, Marcia S. Police Cars [Scholastic]. 2009. (Community Vehicles Ser.). 24p. (gr. k-1). pap. 0.36 *(978-1-4296-4244-6(0)*, Pebble) Capstone.

Gaertner, Meg. Police Officers. 2018. (Community Workers Ser.). (ENG., Illus.). 24p. (J). (gr. 1-1). pap. 8.95 *(978-1-63517-809-8(6)*, 1635178096) North Star Editions.

—Police Officers. 2018. (Community Workers Ser.). (ENG., Illus.). 24p. (J). (gr. k-3). lib. bdg. 31.36 *(978-1-5321-6014-1(3)*, 28660, Pop! Cody Koala) Pop!

Garner, Gerald W. News Media Relations for Law Enforcement Leaders. 2nd ed. 2018. 230p. pap. 34.95 *(978-0-398-09243-6(5))* Thomas, Charles C. Pub., Ltd.

Gersh, Camilla. Emergency Rescue. 2016. (Illus.). 64p. (J). *(978-1-4806-9867-3(9))* Dorling Kindersley Publishing, Inc.

Gilpin, Dan & Brush, Jim. Police Units. 2011. (Action Force Ser.). (ENG.). 32p. (YA). (gr. 4-7). pap. 28.50 *(978-1-59771-293-4(0))* Sea-To-Sea Pubns.

Givén-Wilson, Rachel & Watson, Stephanie. Your Future As a Police Officer, 1 vol. 2019. (High-Demand Careers Ser.). (ENG., Illus.). 80p. (J). (gr. 7-7). 37.47 *(978-1-5081-8792-9(4)*, 052105ef-761b-434e-9219-6599ee8da09c) Rosen Publishing Group, Inc., The.

Goldish, Meish. Sheriffs & Deputies. 2016. (Police: Search & Rescue! Ser.). (ENG., Illus.). 32p. (J). (gr. 2-7). 28.50 *(978-1-943553-16-7(5))* Bearport Publishing Co., Inc.

—State Troopers. 2016. (Police: Search & Rescue! Ser.). (ENG., Illus.). 32p. (J). (gr. 2-7). 28.50 *(978-1-943553-15-0(7))* Bearport Publishing Co., Inc.

Gonzalez, Lissette. Police in Action. (Dangerous Jobs Ser.). 24p. (gr. 2-3). 2009. 42.50 *(978-1-61512-134-2(X)*, PowerKids Pr.) 2007. (ENG., Illus.). (J). lib. bdg. 26.27 *(978-1-4042-3778-0(X)*, f2dd4d0-f602-472e-99c1-b433cedd7bfa) Rosen Publishing Group, Inc., The.

Grayson, Robert. SWAT Teams: The Missions, 1 vol. 2013. (American Special Ops Ser.). (ENG.). 48p. (J). (gr. 5-9). 32.65 *(978-1-4765-0112-3(2)*, 122177) Capstone.

Herweck, Diana. All in a Day's Work: Police Officer, 1 vol. 2nd rev. ed. 2013. (TIME for KIDS(r): Informational Text Ser.). (ENG., Illus.). 64p. (J). (gr. 4-8). lib. bdg. 31.96 *(978-1-4333-7428-9(5))* Teacher Created Materials, Inc.

—All in a Day's Work - Police Officer, 1 vol. 2nd rev. ed. 2013. (TIME for KIDS(r): Informational Text Ser.). (ENG., Illus.). 64p. (J). (gr. 4-8). pap. 14.99 *(978-1-4333-4905-8(1))* Teacher Created Materials, Inc.

Hidden Worlds [Capstone Sole Source]. 2010. (Hidden Worlds Ser.). 32p. lib. bdg. 101.28 *(978-1-4296-5865-2(7)*, Capstone Pr.) Capstone.

Huffman, Mindy. I Want to Be a Police Officer! Roles in My Community, 1 vol. 2018. (Civics for the Real World Ser.). (ENG.). 8p. (gr. k-1). pap. *(978-1-5383-6349-2(6)*, 4409222c-69ec-45ce-8897-aff82415fe8a, Rosen Classroom) Rosen Publishing Group, Inc., The.

Hynes, Patricia. Cyber Cop. 2007. (21st Century Skills Library: Cool Science Careers Ser.). (ENG., Illus.). 32p. (gr. 4-8). lib. bdg. 32.07 *(978-1-60279-056-8(6)*, 200013) Cherry Lake Publishing.

Jeffries, Joyce. Meet the Policeman, 1 vol. 2012. (People Around Town Ser.). (Illus.). 24p. (J). (gr. k-k). (ENG.). (J). 25.27 *(978-1-4339-7336-9(7)*, 137a25c0-3912-47c9-bb9c-84bd19e2823d); (ENG., (J). pap. 9.15 *(978-1-4339-7337-6(5)*, 0fc267ea-6669-46f6-9ef8-4d9bac8787dc); 69.20 *(978-1-4339-8062-6(2))* Stevens, Gareth Publishing LLLP.

—Meet the Policeman / Te Presento a Los Policias, 1 vol. 2012. (People Around Town / Gente de Mi Ciudad Ser.). (SPA & ENG., Illus.). 24p. (J). (gr. k-k). 25.27 *(978-1-4339-7390-1(1)*, 22100ae0-d28d-49b1-8511-8bfb4aabc355) Stevens, Gareth Publishing LLLP.

Kalman, Bobbie. Emergency Workers Are on Their Way! 2004. (My Community & Its Helpers Ser.). (ENG., Illus.). 32p.

pap. *(978-0-7787-2122-2(1))*; lib. bdg. *(978-0-7787-2094-2(2))* Crabtree Publishing Co.

Katz, Samuel M. Global Counterstrike: International Counterterrorism. 2005. (Terrorist Dossiers Ser.). (Illus.). 72p. (J). (gr. 6-12). 26.60 *(978-0-8225-1566-1(0))* Lerner Publishing Group.

—U. S. Counterstrike: American Counterterrorism. 2005. (Terrorist Dossiers Ser.). (Illus.). 72p. (J). (gr. 6-12). 26.60 *(978-0-8225-1569-2(5))* Lerner Publishing Group.

Keogh, Josie. A Trip to the Police Station, 1 vol. 2012. (PowerKids Readers: My Community Ser.). (ENG., Illus.). 24p. (J). (gr. k-k). pap. 9.25 *(978-1-4488-7484-2(X)*, 98d4cac2-6a8d-44b5-878c-5b38bf37693d); lib. bdg. 26.27 *(978-1-4488-7405-7(X)*, 737e8393-4638-435f-b3f8-e2e89b8647db) Rosen Publishing Group, Inc., The. (PowerKids Pr.).

Keogh, Josie & Alamán, Eduardo. A Trip to the Police Station: De Visita en la Estación de Policía, 1 vol. 2012. (PowerKids Readers: Mi Comunidad / My Community Ser.). (SPA & ENG., Illus.). 24p. (J). (gr. k-k). lib. bdg. 26.27 *(978-1-4488-7829-1(2)*, 89371271-c388-4675-8a2c-850b4c27c730, PowerKids Pr.) Rosen Publishing Group, Inc., The.

Kerrigan, Michael. Police Crime Prevention. 2004. (Rescue & Prevention Ser.). (Illus.). 96p. (J). (gr. 6-18). lib. bdg. 22.95 *(978-1-59084-406-9(8))* Mason Crest.

—Stopping Crime: The Police. 2017. (Illus.). 80p. (J). *(978-1-4222-3771-7(0))* Mason Crest.

Kirby, Lisa. The Life of a Cop. 2017. (Text Connections Guided Close Reading Ser.). (J). (gr. 2). *(978-1-4900-1849-2(2))* Benchmark Education Co.

Laks Gorman, Jacqueline. Police Officers, 1 vol. 2010. (People in My Community (Second Edition) Ser.). (ENG., Illus.). 24p. (gr. k-2). 25.27 *(978-1-4339-3350-9(0)*, 5ac21996-3d00-48ba-a5f4-79634e190ea6); pap. 9.15 *(978-1-4339-3351-6(9)*, cb580bad-1d18-42b1-8380-9f0ff8e7a313) Stevens, Gareth Publishing LLLP.

—Police Officers / Policías, 1 vol. 2010. (People in My Community / Mi Comunidad Ser.). (SPA & ENG., Illus.). 24p. (gr. k-2). pap. 9.15 *(978-1-4339-3769-9(7)*, 1c7c1d4d-bf2c-4f74-8982-decb89af60cd) Stevens, Gareth Publishing LLLP.

Larson, Kirsten W. SWAT Teams. 2016. (Protecting Our People Ser.). (ENG., Illus.). 32p. (J). (gr. 2-5). lib. bdg. 20.95 *(978-1-60753-985-8(3)*, 15776) Amicus.

Leaf, Christina. Police Officers. 2018. (Community Helpers Ser.). (ENG., Illus.). 24p. (J). (gr. k-3). pap. 7.99 *(978-1-61891-309-8(3)*, 12095, Blastoff! Readers) Bellwether Media.

Less, Emma. Police Officers. 2018. (Real-Life Superheroes Ser.). (ENG.). 16p. (J). (gr. k-2). pap. 7.99 *(978-1-68152-280-7(2)*, 14920) Amicus.

Liebman, Dan. Je Veux Etre Policier. Lior, Tsipora, tr. 2006. (Je Veux Etre Ser.). (FRE., Illus.). 24p. (J). (gr. -1-2). pap. 5.95 *(978-1-55407-109-8(7)*, 9829fe94-3e6f-48ba-9388-f162dd8ef6c5) Firefly Bks., Ltd.

Liebman, Dan & Liebman, Dan. I Want to Be a Police Officer. 2nd rev. ed. 2018. (I Want to Be Ser.). (ENG., Illus.). 24p. (J). (gr. -1-2). pap. 3.99 *(978-0-2281-0101-7(8)*, 84794909-8072-4665-a6f0-56b03a42da1a) Firefly Bks., Ltd.

Lindeen, Mary. A Visit to the Police Station. 2018. (BeginningtoRead Ser.). (ENG.). 32p. (J). (gr. -1-2). lib. bdg. 22.60 *(978-1-59953-911-9(X))*; (gr. k-2). pap. 13.26 *(978-1-68404-167-1(8))* Norwood Hse. Pr.

Loveless, Antony. Bodyguards. 2009. (World's Most Dangerous Jobs Ser.). (ENG., Illus.). 32p. (J). (gr. 3-6). pap. *(978-0-7787-5108-3(2))*; lib. bdg. *(978-0-7787-5094-9(9))* Crabtree Publishing Co.

Loveless, Antony & Tisdale, Rachel. Police Officers. 2012. (The World's Most Dangerous Jobs Ser.). (ENG.). 32p. (J). pap. *(978-0-7787-5115-1(5))*; lib. bdg. *(978-0-7787-5101-4(5))* Crabtree Publishing Co.

Mara, Wil. Cyber Cop. 2015. (21st Century Skills Library: Cool STEAM Careers Ser.). (ENG., Illus.). 32p. (J). (gr. 4-7). 32.07 *(978-1-63362-557-0(5)*, 206412) Cherry Lake Publishing.

Márquez, Herón. George W. Bush. 2005. (Just the Facts Biographies Ser.). (ENG., Illus.). 112p. (gr. 5-12). lib. bdg. 27.93 *(978-0-8225-2647-6(6)*, Lerner Pubns.) Lerner Publishing Group.

Mattern, Joanne. Mounted Police. 2009. (Working Together Ser.). 24p. (gr. 1-2). 42.50 *(978-1-60854-831-6(7)*, PowerKids Pr.) Rosen Publishing Group, Inc., The.

—Policía Montada, 1 vol. 2003. (Trabajo en Grupo (Working Together) Ser.). (SPA., Illus.). 24p. (J). (gr. 1-2). lib. bdg. 26.27 *(978-0-8239-6843-5(X)*, c226fe34-072f-4314-b2b3-faf39c5f3672) Rosen Publishing Group, Inc., The.

—Policía montada (Mounted Police) 2009. (Trabajo en grupo (Working Together) Ser.). (SPA.). 24p. (gr. 1-2). 42.50 *(978-1-60854-578-0(4)*, Editorial Buenas Letras) Rosen Publishing Group, Inc., The.

Matthews, Kendall J. Mommy I Want to Be a Cop. 2006. 48p. pap. 16.00 *(978-1-4184-6422-6(8))* AuthorHouse.

Mauro, Paul & Melton, H. Keith. Crime Scene & Surveillance Photography. 2004. (Detective Academy Ser.). (Illus.). 48p. (J). *(978-0-439-57182-1(0))* Scholastic, Inc.

McDougal, Anna. Police Officers Help Out! Roles in My Community, 1 vol. 2018. (Civics for the Real World Ser.). (ENG.). 8p. (gr. k-1). pap. *(978-1-5383-6352-2(6)*, da8bc3a0-eaf8-449e-b7e4-234e58ce35e9, Rosen Classroom) Rosen Publishing Group, Inc., The.

McGuire, Leslie. Big Mike's Police Car. Mathieu, Joe, illus. 2003. (Please Read to Me Ser.). (ENG.). 24p. (J). (gr. -1-3). 16.19 *(978-0-375-82334-3(4))* Random House Publishing Group.

Meachen Rau, Dana. Una Oficial de la Policía (Police Officer), 1 vol. 2009. (Trabajos en Pueblos y Ciudades (Jobs in Town) Ser.). (SPA., Illus.). 24p. (gr. k-1). lib. bdg. 25.50 *(978-0-7614-2786-5(4)*, 21f61cbe-c6ba-43fd-8543-07c8ae0c8acc) Cavendish Square Publishing LLC.

Meachen Rau, Dana & Vargus, Nanci Reginelli. Police Officer, 1 vol. 2008. (Jobs in Town Ser.). (ENG., Illus.). 24p. (gr. k-1). lib. bdg. 25.50 *(978-0-7614-2618-9(3)*, cdb8220e-dea8-4f92-ae49-c0fb219df403, Cavendish Square) Cavendish Square Publishing LLC.

Meister, Cari. Police Officers. 2013. (ENG., Illus.). 24p. (J). lib. bdg. 25.65 *(978-1-62031-078-6(3))* Jump! Inc.

Meter, Larry A. Van. Miranda V. Arizona. McNeese, Tim, ed. 2006. (ENG., Illus.). 112p. (gr. 5-9). 32.95 *(978-0-7910-9259-0(3)*, P114592, Facts On File) Infobase Holdings, Inc.

Meyer, Jared. Homeland Security Officers. (Extreme Careers Ser.). 64p. (gr. 5-5). 2009. 58.50 *(978-1-61512-398-8(9)*, Rosen Reference) 2007. (ENG., Illus.). (J). lib. bdg. 37.13 *(978-1-4042-0945-9(X)*, 03f95474-3eae-4225-b097-7fb2f15f714d) Rosen Publishing Group, Inc., The.

Michele, Tracey. What Do Police Officers Do? 2011. (Learn-Abouts Ser.). (Illus.). 16p. (J). pap. 7.95 *(978-1-59920-624-0(2))* Black Rabbit Bks.

Miller, Connie Colwell. I'll Be a Police Officer. Baroncelli, Silvia, illus. 2018. (When I Grow Up Ser.). (ENG.). 24p. (J). (gr. 1-4). pap. 8.99 *(978-1-68152-318-7(3)*, 15059); *(978-1-68151-398-0(6)*, 15053) Amicus.

Miller, Derek L. A Day with a Police Officer. 2019. (J). pap. *(978-1-5026-5317-8(6))* Musa Publishing.

Monnig, Alex. SWAT Team Members in Action. 2017. (Dangerous Jobs in Action Ser.). (ENG.). 32p. (J). (gr. 3-6). lib. bdg. 35.64 *(978-1-5038-1634-3(6)*, 211150) Child's World, Inc, The.

Murley, Leon. Working the Case: Law Enforcement, Police Work, & Police Organizations, 1 vol. 2016. (Law Enforcement & Intelligence Gathering Ser.). (ENG., Illus.). 96p. (J). (gr. 8-8). lib. bdg. 37.82 *(978-1-5081-0380-6(1)*, 1addad64-fe5b-47a1-8942-6d3b5ed23bdc, Britannica Educational Publishing) Rosen Publishing Group, Inc., The.

Murphy, Patricia J. The Police Station: A 4D Book. rev. ed. 2018. (Visit To... Ser.). (ENG., Illus.). 24p. (J). (gr. -1-2). lib. bdg. 29.32 *(978-1-5435-0831-4(6)*, 137594, Capstone Pr.) Capstone.

Murray, Aaron R. Police Officers Help Us, 1 vol. 2012. (All about Community Helpers Ser.). (ENG., Illus.). 24p. (gr. -1-1). 25.27 *(978-0-7660-4048-9(8)*, b818f777-e172-416f-b475-75c2eb56810f, Enslow Publishing) Enslow Publishing, LLC.

Murray, Julie. Park Rangers. 2018. (My Community: Jobs Ser.). (ENG., Illus.). 24p. (J). (gr. -1-2). lib. bdg. 31.36 *(978-1-5321-0789-4(7)*, 28139, Abdo Kids) ABDO Publishing Co.

—Police Officers, 1 vol. 2015. (My Community: Jobs Ser.). (ENG., Illus.). 24p. (J). (gr. -1-2). 31.36 *(978-1-62970-916-1(6)*, 18290, Abdo Kids) ABDO Publishing Co.

—The Police Station, 1 vol. 2016. (My Community: Places Ser.). (ENG., Illus.). 24p. (J). (gr. -1-2). lib. bdg. 31.36 *(978-1-68080-538-3(X)*, 21356, Abdo Kids) ABDO Publishing Co.

Nakaya, Andrea. Thinking Critically: Police Powers. 2017. (Thinking Critically Ser.). (ENG., Illus.). 80p. (YA). (gr. 5-12). *(978-1-68282-269-2(9))* ReferencePoint Pr., Inc.

Noll, Elizabeth. Coding in Transportation. 2018. (Coding Is Everywhere Ser.). (ENG., Illus.). 24p. (J). (gr. k-3). pap. 7.99 *(978-1-61891-479-8(0)*, 12132, Blastoff! Readers) Bellwether Media.

—Police Robots. 2017. (World of Robots Ser.). (ENG., Illus.). 32p. (J). (gr. 3-8). lib. bdg. 27.95 *(978-1-62617-691-1(4)*, Blastoff! Discovery) Bellwether Media.

Oachs, Emily Rose. Police Cars. 2017. (Mighty Machines in Action Ser.). (ENG., Illus.). 24p. (J). (gr. k-3). lib. bdg. 26.95 *(978-1-62617-607-2(8)*, Blastoff! Readers) Bellwether Media.

O'Brian, Virginia. A Police Officer's Job, 1 vol. 2014. (Community Workers Ser.). (ENG.). 24p. (gr. 1-1). lib. bdg. 25.93 *(978-1-62712-361-7(X)*, 12b7d590-974e-4249-8bea-c38b13943c25) Cavendish Square Publishing LLC.

Orr, Tamra B. USMC Special Reaction Teams, 1 vol. 2008. (Inside Special Operations Ser.). (ENG., Illus.). 64p. (gr. 6-6). pap. 12.95 *(978-1-4358-5130-6(7)*, a38b48b0-f178-4f01-848c-75afaebc9cce, Rosen Classroom) Rosen Publishing Group, Inc., The.

Owen, Ann. Keeping You Safe: A Book about Police Officers, 1 vol. Thomas, Eric, illus. 2003. (Community Workers Ser.). (ENG.). 24p. (J). (gr. -1-3). per. 8.95 *(978-1-4048-0483-8(8)*, 92520, Picture Window Bks.) Capstone.

Parkes, Elle. Hooray for Police Officers! 2016. (Bumba Books (r) — Hooray for Community Helpers! Ser.). (ENG., Illus.). 24p. (J). (gr. -1-1). lib. bdg. 26.65 *(978-1-5124-1440-0(9)*, f537231e-806b-4175-ba65-6d109e30715b, Lerner Pubns.) Lerner Publishing Group.

—¡Que Vivan Los Oficiales de Policía! (Hooray for Police Officers!) 2017. (Bumba Books (r) en Español — ¡Que Vivan Los Ayudantes Comunitarios! (Hooray for Community Helpers!) Ser.). (SPA., Illus.). 24p. (J). (gr. -1-1). 26.65 *(978-1-5124-4135-2(X)*, 68d60f39-91ba-4ee4-a4ab-734601889e6b, Ediciones Lerner) Lerner Publishing Group.

Pender, Lionel. To Serve & Protect: The History of Policing, 1 vol. 2016. (Law Enforcement & Intelligence Gathering Ser.). (ENG., Illus.). 96p. (J). (gr. 8-8). lib. bdg. 37.82 *(978-1-5081-0381-3(X)*, 577c43a0-4ac9-4820-b5be-3ffe11fdb161, Britannica Educational Publishing) Rosen Publishing Group, Inc., The.

Perish, Patrick. SWAT Team Member. 2015. (Dangerous Jobs Ser.). (ENG., Illus.). 24p. (J). (gr. 3-7). lib. bdg. 26.95 *(978-1-62617-198-5(X)*, Torque Bks.) Bellwether Media.

Perritano, John. SWAT Team, Vol. 12. 2015. (On a Mission Ser.). 48p. (J). (gr. 5). lib. bdg. 20.95 *(978-1-4222-3402-0(9))* Mason Crest.

Petersen, Justin. Bomb Disposal Units: Disarming Deadly Explosives. 2016. (Emergency! Ser.). (ENG., Illus.). 32p. (J). (gr. 3-9). lib. bdg. 28.65 *(978-1-4914-8028-1(9)*, 130530, Capstone Pr.) Capstone.

Pina, Andrew. A Career As a Border Patrol Agent, 1 vol. 2015. (Federal Forces: Careers As Federal Agents Ser.). (ENG., Illus.). 32p. (J). (gr. 4-5). 27.93 *(978-1-4994-1109-6(X)*, e0081f68-6e1b-4763-aea1-edd80b9246ba, PowerKids Pr.) Rosen Publishing Group, Inc., The.

Police Work. 2005. (Book Treks Ser.). (J). (gr. 3-18). stu. ed. 34.95 *(978-0-673-62839-8(6))* Celebration Pr.

Randolph, Joanne. Police Cars, 1 vol. 2008. (To the Rescue! Ser.). (ENG., Illus.). 24p. (J). (gr. 1-1). lib. bdg. 26.27 *(978-1-4042-4153-4(1)*, 2151a274-04d3-4d7f-9256-082389f7a226, PowerKids Pr.) Rosen Publishing Group, Inc., The.

Reeves, Diane Lindsey. Law & Public Safety. 2017. (Bright Futures Press: World of Work Ser.). (ENG., Illus.). 32p. (J). (gr. 4-7). lib. bdg. 32.07 *(978-1-63472-626-9(X)*, 209538) Cherry Lake Publishing.

Ricciuti, Edward R. Que Hay Dentro de la Estacion de Policía? / What's Inside a Police Station?, 1 vol. 2008. (Qué Hay Dentro? / What's Inside? Ser.). (ENG & SPA., Illus.). 32p. (gr. 1-2). lib. bdg. 25.50 *(978-0-7614-2476-5(8)*, 4a53371a-ee94-4d46-ba27-081398a23d19) Cavendish Square Publishing LLC.

—Que Hay Dentro de la Estacion de Policía? (What's Inside a Police Station?), 1 vol. 2008. (Qué Hay Dentro? (What's Inside?) Ser.). (SPA., Illus.). 32p. (gr. 1-2). lib. bdg. 25.50 *(978-0-7614-2398-0(2)*, 21309504-d750-45f7-84d8-3c143e4148dc) Cavendish Square Publishing LLC.

—What's Inside a Police Car?, 1 vol. 2005. (What's Inside? Ser.). (ENG., Illus.). 32p. (gr. 1-2). lib. bdg. 25.50 *(978-0-7614-1565-7(3)*, fd7a978c-3a5b-4493-8a89-62a8375ce42c, Cavendish Square) Cavendish Square Publishing LLC.

—What's Inside a Police Station?, 1 vol. 2005. (What's Inside? Ser.). (ENG., Illus.). 32p. (gr. 1-2). lib. bdg. 25.50 *(978-0-7614-1566-4(1)*, 255d1509-163e-433d-a43b-56cb96605299) Cavendish Square Publishing LLC.

—What's Inside a Police Station, 1 vol. 2008. (What's Inside? Ser.). (ENG., Illus.). 32p. (gr. 1-2). pap. 9.23 *(978-0-7614-3349-1(X)*, acab09c2-4bc4-43c8-83b5-4a964cc25d5e) Cavendish Square Publishing LLC.

Rivera, Sheila. Police Officer. 2005. (First Step Nonfiction — Work People Do Ser.). (ENG., Illus.). 8p. (J). (gr. k-2). pap. 5.99 *(978-0-8225-5359-5(7)*, d17a7d75-390c-4a1d-a052-41f682e8e374) Lerner Publishing Group.

Rockwell, Anne. At the Police Station. 2005. *(978-0-06-056230-4(7))*; *(978-0-06-056231-1(5))* HarperCollins Canada, Ltd.

Rogers, Kate. Police Officers on the Job. (Jobs in Our Community Ser.). 24p. (J). (gr. 1-1). 2017. pap. 49.50 *(978-1-5345-2154-4(2))* 2016. (ENG.). 26.23 *(978-1-5345-2155-1(0)*, 1f422e6b-79ab-4ff6-9c83-c65403c839d9) 2016. (ENG.). pap. 9.25 *(978-1-5345-2153-7(4)*, a4c9517b-5db5-4265-a9c4-6759b6a05417) Greenhaven Publishing LLC. (KidHaven Publishing).

—Police Officers on the Job. 2017. (Jobs in Our Community Ser.). (ENG.). 8p. (J). (gr. -1-1). 19.05 *(978-1-5311-8631-9(9))* Perfection Learning Corp.

Sanna, Ellyn. Homeland Security Officer. Riggs, Ernestine G. & Gholar, Cheryl, eds. 2013. (Careers with Character Ser.: 18). 96p. (J). (gr. 7-18). 22.95 *(978-1-4222-2757-2(X))* Mason Crest.

Santillo, LuAnn. The Cop. Santillo, LuAnn, ed. 2003. (Half-Pint Kids Readers Ser.). (Illus.). 7p. (J). (gr. -1-1). pap. 1.00 *(978-1-59256-122-3(5))* Half-Pint Kids, Inc.

Schauer, Pete, ed. Police Training & Excessive Force, 1 vol. 2017. (Current Controversies Ser.). (ENG.). 176p. (YA). (gr. 10-12). 48.03 *(978-1-5345-0237-6(8)*, 591c39af-a987-4f03-b6fa-fd0f2b8da4cb) Greenhaven Publishing LLC.

Schuh, Mari. All about Police Officers. 2020. (Sesame Street (r) Loves Community Helpers Ser.). (ENG., Illus.). 32p. (J). (gr. -1-2). 29.32 *(978-1-5415-8998-8(X)*, 6e6d78e4-e263-4605-b975-0ed8c6b379c8, Lerner Pubns.) Lerner Publishing Group.

Settle, Melissa A. Police Then & Now , 1 vol. rev. ed. 2006. (Social Studies: Informational Text Ser.). (ENG., Illus.). 32p. (gr. 2-3). pap. 11.99 *(978-0-7439-9372-2(1))* Teacher Created Materials, Inc.

Shepherd, Jodie. A Day with Police Officers. 2012. (Rookie Read-About Community Ser.). (ENG., Illus.). 32p. (J). pap. 5.95 *(978-0-531-29255-6(X))*; lib. bdg. 23.00 *(978-0-531-28955-6(9))* Scholastic Library Publishing.

Siemens, Jared. Police Officers. 2015. (Illus.). 24p. (J). *(978-1-4896-3653-9(6))* Weigl Pubs., Inc.

Spaight, Anne J. Carros de Policía en Acción (Police Cars on the Go) 2017. (Bumba Books (r) en Español — Máquinas en Acción (Machines That Go) Ser.). (SPA., Illus.). 24p. (J). (gr. -1-1). 26.65 *(978-1-5124-2880-3(9)*, da1bb92e-ee4c-49fa-b7ca-126fc3c8f9ed, Ediciones Lerner) Lerner Publishing Group.

—Police Cars on the Go. 2016. (Bumba Books (r) — Machines That Go Ser.). (ENG., Illus.). 24p. (J). (gr. -1-1). lib. bdg. 26.65 *(978-1-5124-1449-3(2)*, aba76b9c-1316-4aa4-856e-1f0f8c933d81, Lerner Pubns.) Lerner Publishing Group.

Steffens, Bradley. Threats to Civil Liberties: Policing. 2018. (Threats to Civil Liberties Ser.). (ENG.). 80p. (YA). (gr. 6-12). 39.93 *(978-1-68282-449-8(7))* ReferencePoint Pr., Inc.

Torr, James D. Responding to Attack: Firefighters & Police. 2003. (Lucent Library of Homeland Security). (Illus.). 112p. (J). 30.85 *(978-1-59018-375-5(4)*, Lucent Bks.) Cengage Gale.

Waxman, Laura Hamilton. Police Officer Tools. 2019. (Bumba Books (r) — Community Helpers Tools of the Trade Ser.). (ENG., Illus.). 24p. (J). (gr. -1-1). 26.65 *(978-1-5415-5557-0(0)*, 92b0ff4d-fc26-404e-b65d-42ba85890f7f, Lerner Pubns.) Lerner Publishing Group.

White, Nancy. Police Officers to the Rescue. 2011. (Work of Heroes: First Responders in Action Ser.). 32p. (YA). (gr. 1-4). lib. bdg. 28.50 *(978-1-61772-283-7(9))* Bearport Publishing Co., Inc.

Wood, Alix. Killer Evidence: Be a Police Detective. 2017. (Crime Solvers Ser.). 48p. (gr. 6-6). pap. 84.30 *(978-1-5382-0620-1(X))* Stevens, Gareth Publishing LLLP.

Yomtov, Nel. Peacekeeping. 2016. (Military Missions Ser.). (ENG., Illus.). 24p. (J). (gr. 3-7). 26.95 *(978-1-62617-436-8(9)*, Epic Bks.) Bellwether Media.

Zemlicka, Shannon & Knudsen, Shannon. Police Officers. 2005. (Pull Ahead Bks.). (Illus.). 32p. (J). lib. bdg. 22.60 *(978-0-8225-1693-4(4))* Lerner Publishing Group.

POLICE—FICTION

Acosta, Daniel. Iron River, 1 vol. 2018. (ENG.). 224p. (YA). (gr. 9-12). 19.95 *(978-1-941026-93-9(1)*, 23353382); pap. 13.95 *(978-1-941026-94-6(X)*, 23353382) Lee & Low Bks., Inc. (Cinco Puntos Press).

Balasubramanian, Lalitha. The Twins at the Ancient Villa, 1 vol. 2009. 48p. pap. 16.95 *(978-1-61582-601-8(7))* America Star Bks.

Barnett, Mac. Brixton Brothers Mysterious Case of Cases: The Case of the Case of Mistaken Identity; the Ghostwriter Secret; It Happened on a Train; Danger Goes Berserk. Rex, Adam & Myers, Matt, illus. 2013. (Brixton Brothers Ser.). (ENG.). 1024p. (J). (gr. 3-7). pap. 33.99 *(978-1-4424-9818-1(8)*, Simon & Schuster Bks. For Young Readers) Simon & Schuster Bks. For Young Readers.

—The Case of the Case of Mistaken Identity. Rex, Adam, illus. (Brixton Brothers Ser.: 1). (ENG.). (J). (gr. 3-7). 2010. 208p. pap. 7.99 *(978-1-4169-7816-9(X))* 2009. 192p. 15.99 *(978-1-4169-7815-2(1))* Simon & Schuster Bks. For Young Readers. (Simon & Schuster Bks. For Young Readers).

Bayle, B. J. Shadow Riders. 2010. (ENG.). 256p. (YA). (gr. 7). pap. 10.99 *(978-1-55488-724-8(0))* Dundurn Pr. CAN. Dist: Publishers Group West (PGW).

Beaumier, Randy P. Snapshot Billy: I Remember. 2012. 36p. pap. 24.95 *(978-1-4626-1787-6(5))* America Star Bks.

Becker, Jason Earl. Hero Corps: The Rookie. Moutafis, Greg, illus. 2005. (YA). per. 7.95 *(978-0-9765125-0-9(5))* Baby Shark Productions.

Blair, Candice. Rosie's Pink House, 1 vol. Cato, Andrea, illus. 2010. 18p. 24.95 *(978-1-4489-4619-8(0))* America Star Bks.

Bustani, Juma. Adventure in Nairobi. 2005. (Illus.). 72p. pap. *(978-9966-46-842-0(0))* Heinemann Kenya, Limited (East African Educational Publishers Ltd E.A.E.P.) KEN. Dist: Michigan State Univ. Pr.

Carbone, Courtney. The Safety First! EOne, illus. 2018. (Scholastic Reader, Level 1 Ser.). (ENG.). 32p. (J). (gr. -1-k). pap. 4.99 *(978-1-338-22882-3(X))* Scholastic, Inc.

—The Safety First! (Peppa Pig: Level 1 Reader) EOne, illus. 2015. (ENG.). 32p. (J). (gr. -1-k). E-Book 8.99 *(978-1-338-29114-8(9))* Scholastic, Inc.

Clark, Marshunna & Jones, Patrick. Duty or Desire. 2016. (Unbarred Ser.). (ENG.). 112p. (YA). (gr. 6-12). pap. 7.99 *(978-1-5124-0089-2(0)*, 7e7f910c-b924-41c6-8a5b-472ea3801b0f); E-Book 42.65 *(978-1-5124-0090-8(4))* Lerner Publishing Group. (Darby Creek).

Clasicos Policiales. (Clasicos Juveniles Coleccion). (SPA.). (YA). (gr. 5-8). pap. *(978-950-11-1284-9(5)*, SG4722) Sigmar ARG. Dist: Lectorum Pubns., Inc.

Cohen, Alana. Heroes! (LEGO City: Lift-The-Flap Board Book) White, David & White, Dave, illus. 2011. (LEGO City Ser.). (ENG.). 16p. (J). (gr. -1-k). bds. 9.99 *(978-0-545-27439-5(7))* Scholastic, Inc.

Coles, Jay. Tyler Johnson Was Here. 2019. (ENG.). 304p. (YA). (gr. 9-17). pap. 10.99 *(978-0-316-47218-0(2))* Little, Brown Bks. for Young Readers.

Conn, Maria. At the Police Station with Dear Dragon, 10 vols. 2019. (Dear Dragon Developing Readers Ser.). (ENG., Illus.). 24p. (J). (gr. k-k). 23.94 *(978-1-68450-988-1(2))* Norwood Hse. Pr.

Cook, Jacqueline. The Little Bear Who Worried Too Much: Suzie Bear Goes to London. 2011. 34p. (gr. 1-4). pap. 13.50 *(978-1-60976-875-1(2)*, Eloquent Bks.) Strategic Book Publishing & Rights Agency (SBPRA).

Deen, Natasha. Burned, 1 vol. 2015. (Orca Soundings Ser.: 1). (ENG.). 168p. (YA). (gr. 8-12). pap. 9.95 *(978-1-4598-0726-6(X))* Orca Bk. Pubs. USA.

Delgado, Linda D. The Visitors. 2006. 169p. (J). per. *(978-0-9767861-1-5(7))* Muslim Writers Publishing.

Dembar Greene, Jacqueline. Speak up, Tommy! Melmon, Deborah, illus. 2012. (ENG.). 32p. (J). (gr. -1-3). lib. bdg. 7.99 *(978-0-7613-7497-8(3)*, b2cb5815-831a-4c38-bdc1-077c718db263, Kar-Ben Publishing) Lerner Publishing Group.

Driscoll, Laura. I Want to Be a Police Officer. Echeverri, Catalina, illus. 2018. (I Can Read Level 1 Ser.). (ENG.). 32p. (J). (gr. -1-3). 16.99 *(978-0-06-243245-2(1))*; pap. 5.99 *(978-0-06-243243-8(5))* HarperCollins Pubs. (HarperCollins).

Dunn, Jancee. I'm Afraid Your Teddy Is in Trouble Today. Nash, Scott, illus. 2017. (ENG.). 40p. (J). (gr. -1-2). 15.99 *(978-0-7636-7537-0(7))* Candlewick Pr.

Echols, Jennifer. Going Too Far. 2009. (ENG.). 256p. (YA). pap. 16.99 *(978-1-4165-7173-5(6)*, MTV Bks.) MTV Books.

Ennis, Tom R. The Stranger & the Three Little Children. 2009. 32p. pap. 13.75 *(978-1-60860-509-5(4)*, Strategic Bk. Publishing) Strategic Book Publishing & Rights Agency (SBPRA).

Felsen, Henry Gregor. Rag Top. Felsen, Holly, illus. 2013. 212p. pap. 15.00 *(978-1-62272-001-9(6))* Felsen Ink.

Flores, Catty, illus. Les Misérables. adapted ed. 2014. (ENG.). 64p. pap. 7.95 *(978-1-906230-79-1(X))* Real Reads Ltd. GBR. Dist: Casemate Pubs. & Bk. Distributors, LLC.

Gianferrari, Maria. Officer Katz & Houndini: A Tale of Two Tails. Chatzikonstantinou, Danny, illus. 2016. (ENG.). 32p. (J). (gr. -1-2). 17.99 *(978-1-4814-2265-9(0)*, Aladdin) Simon & Schuster Children's Publishing.

Giuliani, Alfred. Zootopia. Wu, Vivien, illus. 2016. (J). *(978-1-4806-9720-1(6)*, Golden Bks.) Random Hse. Children's Bks.

Gosling, Sharon. The Diamond Thief. 2014. (Diamond Thief Ser.). (ENG.). 336p. (J). (gr. 9-12). 16.95 *(978-1-63079-002-8(8)*, 126763, Switch Pr.) Capstone.

—The Ruby Airship. 2015. (Diamond Thief Ser.). (ENG.). 496p. (YA). (gr. 9-12). 16.95 *(978-1-63079-004-2(4)*, 126924, Switch Pr.) Capstone.

Grant, Myrna. Ivan & the Daring Escape. rev. ed. 2006. (Flamingo Fiction 9-13s Ser.). (ENG., Illus.). 144p. (J). (gr. 4-7). per. 6.99 *(978-1-84550-132-7(2)*, 6a061cd0-b8f2-4a06-bb6c-179f7a430555) Christian Focus Pubns. GBR. Dist: Baker & Taylor Publisher Services (BTPS).

Greene, Janice & Thomas, Terri. Read My Lips, 1 vol. unabr. ed. 2010. (Q Reads Ser.). (ENG.). 32p. (YA). (gr. 9-12). pap. 8.50 *(978-1-61651-216-3(4))* Saddleback Educational Publishing, Inc.

Gundel, Jean. The Mystery Key at Camp Green Meadow. Robertson, R. H., illus. 2011. (J). pap. 14.95 *(978-1-59571-730-6(7))* Word Association Pubs.

Hamilton, Kersten. Police Officers on Patrol. Alley, R. W., illus. 2009. 32p. (J). (gr. -1-k). 17.99 *(978-0-670-06315-4(0)*, Viking Books for Young Readers) Penguin Young Readers Group.

Harber, Chris. Simon the Policeman on Safari - Claude the Camel. Harber, Hulya, illus. 2013. 24p. pap. *(978-0-7552-1552-2(4)*, Bright Pen) Authors OnLine, Ltd.

—Simon the Policeman on the Number Planet. Harber, Hulya, illus. 2013. 28p. pap. *(978-0-7552-1560-7(5)*, Bright Pen) Authors OnLine, Ltd.

Harrison, Michael. Cop's Night Before Christmas, 1 vol. Miles, David, illus. 2010. (Night Before Christmas Ser.). (ENG.). 32p. (J). (gr. k-3). 16.99 *(978-1-58980-800-3(2)*, Pelican Publishing) Arcadia Publishing.

Hinkes, Enid. Police Cat. 2015. (Illus.). 32p. (J). *(978-1-4896-3873-1(3))* Weigl Pubs., Inc.

Hubbard, L. Ron, contrib. by. Common Core Literature Guide: Dead Men Kill: Literature Guide for Teachers & Librarians Based on Common Core ELA Standards for Classrooms 6-9. 2013. (Stories from the Golden Age Ser.). (ENG.). 35p. (gr. 6-9). pap., tchr. ed. 14.95 *(978-1-61986-218-0(2))* Galaxy Pr., LLC.

Hutton, Sam. Countdown (Special Agents, Book 3). Book 3. 2011. (Special Agents Ser.: 3). (ENG.). 224p. pap. 9.99 *(978-0-00-714843-1(7)*, HarperCollins Children's Bks.) HarperCollins Pubs. Ltd. GBR. Dist: HarperCollins Pubs.

—Deep End (Special Agents) 2010. (Special Agents Ser.). (ENG.). 240p. (gr. 5-7). pap. 9.99 *(978-0-00-714842-4(9)*, HarperCollins Children's Bks.) HarperCollins Pubs. Ltd. GBR. Dist: HarperCollins Pubs.

—Final Shot (Special Agents, Book 2), Book 2. 2010. (Special Agents Ser.: 2). (ENG.). 224p. (J). (gr. 5-7). pap. 9.99 *(978-0-00-714844-8(5)*, HarperCollins Children's Bks.) HarperCollins Pubs. Ltd. GBR. Dist: HarperCollins Pubs.

Johnson, Gerald J. J. Officer Buck MacDuck. Miltenberger, Dave & Jeri, illus. 2013. 24p. pap. 24.95 *(978-1-62709-429-0(6))* America Star Bks.

Johnson, Virginia. Officer Rick & the Raccoon — a True Story. 2011. 24p. pap. 11.50 *(978-1-60976-114-1(6)*, Eloquent Bks.) Strategic Book Publishing & Rights Agency (SBPRA).

King, Trey. Detective Chase McCain: Save That Cargo! 2013. (LEGO City 8X8 Ser.). lib. bdg. 13.55 *(978-0-606-32393-2(7))* Turtleback.

Krosoczka, Jarrett J. Platypus Police Squad: the Frog Who Croaked. Krosoczka, Jarrett J., illus. 2013. (Platypus Police Squad Ser.: 1). (ENG., Illus.). 240p. (J). (gr. 3-7). 13.99 *(978-0-06-207164-4(5)*, Walden Pond Pr.) HarperCollins Pubs.

Kudina Steinberg, Ganna V. The Princess Conspiracy: an Inspector Poopchyk Mystery. 2009. 143p. 30.00 *(978-0-557-08936-9(0))* Lulu Pr., Inc.

Lennon, Thomas. Ronan Boyle & the Bridge of Riddles (Ronan Boyle #1) Hendrix, John, illus. (Ronan Boyle Ser.). (ENG.). (J). (gr. 5-9). 2020. 336p. pap. 8.99 *(978-1-4197-4093-0(8)*, 1266903) 2019. 304p. 17.99 *(978-1-4197-3491-5(1)*, 1266901) Abrams, Inc. (Amulet Bks.).

—Ronan Boyle & the Bridge of Riddles (Ronan Boyle #1) 2019. (ENG., Illus.). 304p. (J). pap. *(978-1-4197-3905-7(0)*, Amulet Bks.) Abrams, Inc.

Lenski, Lois. Policeman Small. 2006. (Lois Lenski Bks.). (Illus.). 32p. (J). (— 1). 6.99 *(978-0-375-83569-8(5)*, Random Hse. Bks. for Young Readers) Random Hse. Children's Bks.

Loughead, Deb. Caught in the Act, 1 vol. 2013. (Orca Currents Ser.). (ENG.). 128p. (J). (gr. 4-7). pap. 9.95 *(978-1-4598-0496-8(1))* Orca Bk. Pubs. USA.

Lyga, Barry. Game: The Sequel to "I Hunt Killers" 2014. (I Hunt Killers Ser.: 2). (ENG.). 544p. (YA). (gr. 10-17). pap. 11.99 *(978-0-316-12585-7(7))* Little, Brown Bks. for Young Readers.

MacAndrewRichard. The Black Pearls Starter/Beginner. 2008. (Cambridge English Readers Ser.). (ENG.). 32p. pap. 14.75 *(978-0-521-73289-5(1))* Cambridge Univ. Pr.

Maddox, Jake. Free Climb, 1 vol. Tiffany, Sean, illus. 2008. (Jake Maddox Sports Stories Ser.). (ENG.). 72p. (J). (gr. 3-6). pap. 5.95 *(978-1-4342-0880-4(X)*, 95237, Stone Arch Bks.) Capstone.

Magill, Sharon L. Chloe Madison & the Beach Heists. 2009. 60p. pap. 10.49 *(978-1-4389-4191-2(9))* AuthorHouse.

Marano, John. Kody the Kid Cop: And the Case of the Missing Cat. 2012. 20p. pap. 17.99 *(978-1-4685-9555-0(5))* AuthorHouse.

Marsh, Carole. The Adventure Diaries of the Perils of Pauline, the Police Officer!, 2 vols. 2003. 48p. (J). (gr. 1-4). pap. 5.95 *(978-0-635-01144-2(1))* Gallopade International.

McCann, David. Garda Gaby: The Danger of Playing Truant. Brundige, Britt, ed. Bauknecht, Julie, illus. Lt. ed. 2003. 14p. (J). (gr. k-5). spiral bd. 5.99 *(978-1-929063-92-5(X)*, 324) Moons & Stars Publishing For Children.

Mccarthy, Rebecca L. Save This Christmas! 2012. (LEGO City 8X8 Ser.). lib. bdg. 13.55 *(978-0-606-26767-0(0))* Turtleback.

McGovan, Michael. The Bobby Dazzlers. 2011. (Illus.). 28p. pap. 14.11 *(978-1-4567-8862-9(0))* AuthorHouse.

Meadows, Michelle. Traffic Pups. Andreasen, Dan, illus. 2011. (ENG.). 32p. (J). (gr. -1-3). 15.99 *(978-1-4169-2485-2(X)*, Simon & Schuster Bks. For Young Readers) Simon & Schuster Bks. For Young Readers.

Meddaugh, Susan. Detective Dog. 2013. (Martha Speaks Ser.). (ENG., Illus.). 96p. (J). (gr. 1-4). pap. 5.99 *(978-0-547-77512-8(1))* Houghton Mifflin Harcourt Publishing Co.

—Martha Speaks: Detective Dog (Chapter Book) 2013. (Martha Speaks Ser.). (ENG., Illus.). 96p. (J). (gr. 1-4). 14.99 *(978-0-547-86021-3(8))* Houghton Mifflin Harcourt Publishing Co.

Myers, Walter Dean & Workman, Ross. Kick. 2012. (ENG.). 224p. (YA). (gr. 9). pap. 10.99 *(978-0-06-200491-8(3)*, HarperTeen) HarperCollins Pubs.

Nelson, James Gary. Smileytooth & the Plaque Attack. Bumstead, Debbie, illus. 2008. 20p. pap. 10.95 *(978-1-935137-48-1(4))* Guardian Angel Publishing, Inc.

Newberry, Geoffrey C. The Cape Don Adventure. 2011. 48p. pap. 6.99 *(978-1-61667-262-1(5))* Raider Publishing International.

O'Brien, Jack. Silver Chief's Revenge. Wiese, Kurt, illus. 2011. 222p. 44.95 *(978-1-258-09709-7(5))* Literary Licensing, LLC.

Patterson, James. Ali Cross: the Secret Detective. 2022. (Ali Cross Ser.: 3). (ENG.). 272p. (J). (gr. 5-9). 16.99 *(978-0-316-40991-9(X)*, Jimmy Patterson) Little Brown & Co.

Paulsen, Gary. The Glass Cafe or, the Stripper & the State: How My Mother Started a War with the System That Made Us Kind of Rich & a Little Bit Famous. 2004. 99p. (J). 13.65 *(978-0-7569-3105-6(3))* Perfection Learning Corp.

Pierce, Tamora. Bloodhound: The Legend of Beka Cooper #2. 2010. (Beka Cooper Ser.: 2). (ENG., Illus.). 576p. (YA). (gr. 7-11). pap. 11.99 *(978-0-375-83817-0(1)*, Ember) Random Hse. Children's Bks.

—Mastiff: The Legend of Beka Cooper #3. 2012. (Beka Cooper Ser.: 3). (ENG.). 608p. (YA). (gr. 7-11). pap. 11.99 *(978-0-375-83818-7(X)*, Ember) Random Hse. Children's Bks.

—Terrier: The Legend of Beka Cooper #1. 2007. (Beka Cooper Ser.: 1). (ENG., Illus.). 608p. (YA). (gr. 7-11). pap. 11.99 *(978-0-375-83816-3(3)*, Ember) Random Hse. Children's Bks.

Pilkey, Dav. Dog Man, 1. 2016. (Dog Man Ser.). (ENG.). 240p. (gr. 1-4). 31.19 *(978-1-4844-9091-4(6)*, Graphix) Scholastic, Inc.

—Dog Man: A Graphic Novel. Pilkey, Dav, illus. 2016. (Dog Man Ser.: 1). (ENG., Illus.). 240p. (J). (gr. 2). 9.99 *(978-0-545-58160-8(5)*, Graphix) Scholastic, Inc.

—Dog Man - A Tale of Two Kitties: Creator of Captain Underpants. Pilkey, Dav, illus. 2017. (Dog Man Ser.: 3). (ENG., Illus.). 256p. (J). (gr. 2-5). 9.99 *(978-0-545-93521-0(0)*, Graphix) Scholastic, Inc.

—Dog Man: a Graphic Novel (Dog Man #1): from the Creator of Captain Underpants (Library Edition) Pilkey, Dav, illus. 2019. (Dog Man Ser.: 1). (ENG., Illus.). 240p. (J). (gr. 2-2). 24.99 *(978-1-338-61194-6(1)*, Graphix) Scholastic, Inc.

—Dog Man & Cat Kid: Creator of Captain Underpants, Vol. 4. Pilkey, Dav, illus. 2017. (Dog Man Ser.: 4). (ENG., Illus.). 256p. (J). (gr. 2). 9.99 *(978-0-545-93518-0(0)*, Graphix) Scholastic, Inc.

—Dog Man & Cat Kid: a Graphic Novel (Dog Man #4): from the Creator of Captain Underpants (Library Edition) Pilkey, Dav, illus. 2017. (Dog Man Ser.: 4). (ENG., Illus.). 256p. (J). (gr. 2). lib. bdg. 16.99 *(978-1-338-23037-6(9)*, Graphix) Scholastic, Inc.

—Dog Man: Fetch-22: a Graphic Novel (Dog Man #8): from the Creator of Captain Underpants. Pilkey, Dav, illus. 2019. (Dog Man Ser.: 8). (ENG., Illus.). 240p. (J). (gr. 2). 12.99 *(978-1-338-32321-4(0)*, Graphix) Scholastic, Inc.

—Dog Man: the Epic Collection: from the Creator of Captain Underpants (Dog Man #1-3 Box Set), 1 vol., Vol. 1. Pilkey, Dav, illus. 2017. (Dog Man Ser.). (ENG., Illus.). 720p. (J). (gr. 2-2). 29.97 *(978-1-338-23064-2(6)*, Graphix) Scholastic, Inc.

—Dog Man Unleashed. 2016. (Dog Man Ser.: 2). (ENG.). (J). (gr. 2). lib. bdg. 20.85 *(978-0-606-39709-4(4))*; 240p. 20.85 *(978-0-606-39115-3(0))* Turtleback.

—Dog Man: Unleashed: Creator of Captain Underpants, Vol. 2. Pilkey, Dav, illus. 2016. (Dog Man Ser.: 2). (ENG., Illus.). 224p. (J). (gr. 2-7). 9.99 *(978-0-545-93520-3(2)*, Graphix) Scholastic, Inc.

—Dog Man Unleashed: a Graphic Novel (Dog Man #2): from the Creator of Captain Underpants (Library Edition) Pilkey, Dav, illus. 2019. (Dog Man Ser.: 2). (ENG., Illus.). 224p. (J). (gr. 2-2). 24.99 *(978-1-338-61198-4(4)*, Graphix) Scholastic, Inc.

—A Tale of Two Kitties. 2017. (Dog Man Ser.: 3). lib. bdg. 20.85 *(978-0-606-40547-8(X))* Turtleback.

Poe. Breve Ant de Ctos Policiales. (SPA.). pap. 11.95 *(978-950-07-1006-0(4))* Editorial Sudamericana S.A. ARG. Dist: Distribooks, Inc.

Reynolds, Jason & Brendan Kiely. All American Boys. 2017. (ENG.). (YA). lib. bdg. 20.85 *(978-0-606-39493-2(1))* Turtleback.

Reynolds, Jason & Kiely, Brendan. All American Boys. 2015. (ENG., Illus.). 320p. (YA). (gr. 7). 19.99 *(978-1-4814-6333-1(0)*, Atheneum/Caitlyn Dlouhy Books) Simon & Schuster Children's Publishing.

Ripley, Esther. Heroes to the Rescue. 2016. (DK Reader Level 2 Ser.). lib. bdg. 13.55 *(978-0-606-38711-8(0))* Turtleback.

Rossell, Judith. Inspector Stilton & the Missing Jewels. Rossell, Judith, illus. 2005. (ENG., Illus.). 32p. pap. *(978-1-921049-09-5(X))* Little Hare Bks. AUS. Dist: HarperCollins Pubs. Australia.

Sander, Sonia. Calling All Cars! 2010. (LEGO City Adventures Scholastic Readers Level 1 Ser.: 3). lib. bdg. 13.55 *(978-0-606-07120-8(2))* Turtleback.

—LEGO City Reader Collection: LEGO City Emergency. 2012. (Illus.). 127p. (J). *(978-1-4351-3985-5(2))* Scholastic, Inc.

Santillo, LuAnn. Jim & the Thug. Santillo, LuAnn, ed. 2003. (Half-Pint Kids Readers Ser.). (Illus.). 7p. (J). (gr. -1-1). pap. 1.00 *(978-1-59256-078-3(4))* Half-Pint Kids, Inc.

Scarry, Richard. Richard Scarry's a Day at the Police Station. Scarry, Richard, illus. 2004. (Look-Look Ser.). (Illus.). 24p. (J). (gr. -1-2). pap. 5.99 *(978-0-375-82822-5(2)*, Golden Bks.) Random Hse. Children's Bks.

Sonberg, Caryn. Six Dogs & a Police Officer. Dorenkamp, Michelle, illus. 2006. 31p. pap. 8.40 *(978-1-55501-776-7(2))* Ballard & Tighe Pubs.

Steele, Michael Anthony. Catch That Crook! Wang, Sean, illus. 2012. 23p. (J). *(978-1-4242-5333-3(0))* Scholastic, Inc.

—Catch That Crook! 2012. (LEGO City 8X8 Ser.). (Illus.). 23p. (J). lib. bdg. 13.55 *(978-0-606-23960-8(X))* Turtleback.

—LEGO City: Catch That Crook! 2012. (LEGO City Ser.). (ENG., Illus.). 24p. (J). (gr. -1-k). pap. 3.99 *(978-0-545-36991-6(6))* Scholastic, Inc.

Steve Van Der Merwe. Policeman Bobby & Stinky. 2009. (Illus.). 24p. pap. 12.99 *(978-1-4389-6935-0(X))* AuthorHouse.

Stewart, Bob. Baily Bumble Bee. Gorum, Jerry, illus. 2009. (ENG.). 32p. pap. 14.49 *(978-1-4389-7254-1(7))* AuthorHouse.

Stone, Nic. Dear Martin. (ENG.). (gr. 9). 2018. 240p. (YA). pap. 10.99 *(978-1-101-93952-9(4)*, Ember) 2017. 224p. (YA). 18.99 *(978-1-101-93949-9(4)*, Crown Books For Young Readers)1. 2018. 240p. 28.69 *(978-1-5364-4655-5(6)*, Ember) Random Hse. Children's Bks.

—Dear Martin. 2018. lib. bdg. 20.85 *(978-0-606-41555-2(6))* Turtleback.

Swartout, Jenny. The Little One Behind the Badge. 2017. (ENG., Illus.). (J). (gr. -1-3). pap. 7.99 *(978-1-935666-95-0(9))* Nodin Pr.

Tharp, Tim. Mojo. 2014. (ENG.). 288p. (YA). (gr. 7). pap. 8.99 *(978-0-375-86402-5(4)*, Ember) Random Hse. Children's Bks.

Thompson, Kate. The New Policeman. 2005. (Illus.). 416p. (J). *(978-0-370-32878-2(7)*, Bodley Head Childrens) Random House Children's Books.

Thoughts Staff. Police Stories: the fight Call. 2005. 16p. 8.99 *(978-1-4116-2267-8(7))* Lulu Pr., Inc.

Timothy Nixon. Henry to the Rescue. 2009. (Illus.). 24p. pap. 12.99 *(978-1-4389-4960-4(X))* AuthorHouse.

Turnbull, Ann. Deep Water. 3rd ed. 2013. 102p. pap. *(978-1-78132-160-7(4))* SilverWood Bks.

Van Der Merwe, Steve. Policeman Bobby. 2008. 68p. pap. 11.99 *(978-1-4389-1899-0(2))* AuthorHouse.

A Visit to the Police Station. 2003. (J). per. *(978-1-57657-901-5(8))* Paradise Pr., Inc.

White, Kiersten. Paranormalcy. 2011. (Paranormalcy Ser.: 1). (ENG.). 368p. (YA). (gr. 8). pap. 9.99 *(978-0-06-198585-0(6)*, HarperTeen) HarperCollins Pubs.

Wiess, Laura. Leftovers. 2008. (ENG.). 256p. (YA). (gr. 9-18). pap. 14.99 *(978-1-4165-4662-7(6)*, MTV Bks.) MTV Books.

POLICE—VOCATIONAL GUIDANCE

Boothroyd, Jennifer. How to Be a Zootopia Police Officer: Grit with Judy Hopps. 2019. (Disney Great Character Guides). (ENG., Illus.). 32p. (J). (gr. 1-4). 27.99 *(978-1-5415-3898-6(6)*, Lerner Pubns.) Lerner Publishing Group.

Brezina, Corona. Careers in the Homicide Unit, 1 vol. 2013. (Extreme Law Enforcement Ser.). (ENG., Illus.). 112p. (J). (gr. 7-7). 39.77 *(978-1-4777-1710-3(2)*, b5edb15e-5226-4bb9-88e2-d145843307ee) Rosen Publishing Group, Inc., The.

Christy, Lee Louis. I Go to Work as a Police Officer. 2003. (I Go to Work As Ser.). (Illus.). (J). *(978-1-58417-040-2(9))*; pap. *(978-1-58417-103-4(0))* Lake Street Pubs.

Harmon, Daniel E. Working As a Law Enforcement Officer in Your Community, 1 vol. 2015. (Careers in Your Community Ser.). (ENG., Illus.). 80p. (J). (gr. 7-8). 37.47 *(978-1-4994-6115-2(1)*, 9d3b3cbf-9eaf-465d-b807-9ddd762c9e6c, Rosen Young Adult) Rosen Publishing Group, Inc., The.

Lewis, Daniel. Public Safety & Law, Vol. 10. 2018. (Careers in Demand for High School Graduates Ser.). 112p. (J). (gr. 7). 34.60 *(978-1-4222-4141-7(6))* Mason Crest.

Suen, Anastasia. Careers with Swat Teams, 1 vol. 2013. (Extreme Law Enforcement Ser.). (ENG., Illus.). 112p. (J). (gr. 7-7). 39.77 *(978-1-4777-1708-0(0)*, 802afed7-68bb-403d-a035-4bd24e0413dc) Rosen Publishing Group, Inc., The.

Uschan, Michael V. Careers in Law Enforcement. 2017. (ENG., Illus.). 80p. (J). (gr. 5-12). *(978-1-68282-106-0(4))* ReferencePoint Pr., Inc.

Watson, Stephanie. A Career as a Police Officer, 1 vol. 2010. (Essential Careers Ser.). (ENG.). 80p. (YA). (gr. 6-6). lib. bdg. 37.47 *(978-1-4358-9469-3(3)*, b7a8281b-d194-4a9e-93b1-8b74823c0e47) Rosen Publishing Group, Inc., The.

Woog, Adam. Careers in State, County, & City Police Forces, 1 vol. 2014. (Law & Order Jobs Ser.). (ENG., Illus.). 96p. (gr. 6-6). 42.63 *(978-1-62712-425-6(X)*, 45f3ce27-625b-479a-879e-4babb914c919) Cavendish Square Publishing LLC.

POLICE DOGS

Albright, Rosie. Police Dogs, 1 vol. 2012. (Animal Detectives Ser.). (ENG., Illus.). 24p. (J). (gr. 1-1). pap. 9.25 *(978-1-4488-6254-2(X)*, 4f18f263-97b5-4b9a-8ed8-a952af92cd34); lib. bdg. 26.27 *(978-1-4488-6148-4(9)*, 6a592a97-deea-44a9-98a3-d72bb700c923) Rosen Publishing Group, Inc., The. (PowerKids Pr.).

—Police Dogs: Perros Policías, 1 vol. Alamán, Eduardo, tr. 2012. (Animal Detectives / Detectives Del Reino Animal Ser.). (SPA & ENG.). 24p. (gr. 1-1). lib. bdg. 26.27 *(978-1-4488-6714-1(2)*, 002ec9a0-7c9d-43db-a387-33b7031af2e9) Rosen Publishing Group, Inc., The.

Anderson, Bendix. Security Dogs. 2005. (Dog Heroes Ser.). (Illus.). 32p. (J). lib. bdg. 28.50 *(978-1-59716-015-5(6))* Bearport Publishing Co., Inc.

Bluemel Oldfield, Dawn. Police Dogs. 2014. (Bow Wow! Dog Helpers Ser.). 24p. (J). (gr. -1-3). lib. bdg. 26.99 *(978-1-62724-120-5(5))* Bearport Publishing Co., Inc.

Boothroyd, Jennifer. Hero Law Enforcement Dogs. 2017. (Lightning Bolt Books (r) — Hero Dogs Ser.). (ENG., Illus.). 32p. (J). (gr. 1-3). 29.32 *(978-1-5124-2542-0(7)*, f4620bbc-5d3f-4ca0-93c9-c1baf1947ae5); E-Book 42.65 *(978-1-5124-3644-0(5)*, 9781512436440); E-Book 42.65 *(978-1-5124-2800-1(0))*; E-Book 4.99 *(978-1-5124-3645-7(3)*, 9781512436457) Lerner Publishing Group. (Lerner Pubns.).

Bozzo, Linda. Police Dog Heroes, 1 vol. 2010. (Amazing Working Dogs with American Humane Ser.). (ENG., Illus.). 48p. (J). (gr. 3-3). 27.93 *(978-0-7660-3197-5(7)*, 6a6f5778-996a-4cb9-a680-0636d1c64d62) Enslow Publishing, LLC.

Burling, Alexis. Animal Crime Fighters, 1 vol. 2018. (Animals at Work Ser.). (ENG.). 32p. (gr. 3-3). 26.93 *(978-0-7660-9615-8(7)*, aa27a2a3-8dfa-4ef5-80cd-1e3f90a6d6dd) Enslow Publishing, LLC.

Gagne, Tammy. Police Dogs, 1 vol. 2013. (Dogs on the Job Ser.). (ENG.). 32p. (J). (gr. 3-9). 28.65 *(978-1-4765-0129-1(7)*, 122206, Capstone Pr.) Capstone.

Goldish, Meish. Bomb-Sniffing Dogs. 2012. (Dog Heroes Ser.). 32p. (J). (gr. 2-7). lib. bdg. 28.50 *(978-1-61772-455-8(6))* Bearport Publishing Co., Inc.

Green, Sara. Police Dogs. 2013. (Dogs to the Rescue! Ser.). (ENG., Illus.). 24p. (J). (gr. 3-8). lib. bdg. 27.95 *(978-1-60014-957-3(X)*, Pilot Bks.) Bellwether Media.

Hoffman, Mary Ann. Police Dogs, 1 vol. 2011. (Working Dogs Ser.). (ENG., Illus.). 24p. (J). (gr. 2-3). lib. bdg. 25.27 *(978-1-4339-4659-2(9)*, 8abbb261-9548-4353-ac3e-5cc2fe61c11c) Stevens, Gareth Publishing LLLP.

Kids, National Geographic. Doggy Defenders: Tiger the Police Dog. 2019. (Doggy Defenders Ser.). (Illus.). 48p. (J). (gr. -1-k). 9.99 *(978-1-4263-3297-5(1)*, National Geographic Kids) Disney Publishing Worldwide.

Mezzanotte, Jim. Police, 1 vol. 2011. (Working Animals Ser.). (ENG.). 64p. (gr. 5-5). 31.21 *(978-1-60870-166-7(2)*, a8196bcc-b54c-489c-b5e2-3d9dfe94873c) Cavendish Square Publishing LLC.

Miller, Marie-Therese. Police Dogs. 2007. (Dog Tales: True Stories about Amazing Dogs Ser.). (ENG., Illus.). 80p. (gr. 4-6). lib. bdg. 28.00 *(978-0-7910-9036-7(1)*, P159777, Facts On File) Infobase Holdings, Inc.

Murray, Julie. Crime-Fighting Animals. 2019. (Working Animals Ser.). (ENG., Illus.). 24p. (J). (gr. k-4). lib. bdg. 31.36 *(978-1-5321-2731-1(6)*, 31669, Abdo Zoom-Dash) ABDO Publishing Co.

Raum, Elizabeth. K-9 Police Dogs. 2013. (Animals with Jobs Ser.). (ENG.). 32p. (J). (gr. 2-5). 28.50 *(978-1-60753-377-1(4)*, 16290) Amicus.

Ruffin, Frances E. Police Dogs. 2005. (Dog Heroes Ser.). (Illus.). 32p. (J). lib. bdg. 28.50 *(978-1-59716-014-8(8))* Bearport Publishing Co., Inc.

Schuh, Mari. K-9 Police Dogs, 1 vol. 2010. (Working Dogs Ser.). (ENG.). 24p. (J). (gr. -1-2). 27.32 *(978-1-4296-4470-9(2)*, 102942, Capstone Pr.) Capstone.

Terrell, Brandon. Police Dogs on the Job. 2017. (Helping Dogs Ser.). (ENG.). 24p. (J). (gr. 2-5). lib. bdg. 32.79 *(978-1-5038-1614-5(1)*, 211173) Child's World, Inc, The.

Troup, Roxanne. Detection Dogs on the Job. 2017. (Helping Dogs Ser.). (ENG.). 24p. (J). (gr. 2-5). lib. bdg. 32.79 *(978-1-5038-1611-4(7)*, 211170) Child's World, Inc, The.

POLIO

see Poliomyelitis

POLIOMYELITIS

Ayarbe, Heidi. Life with Spina Bifida. 2018. (Everyday Heroes Ser.). (ENG.). 24p. (J). (gr. 3-6). lib. bdg. 32.79 *(978-1-5038-2516-1(7)*, 212343, MOMENTUM) Child's World, Inc, The.

Colson, Mary. Fighting Polio. 2014. (Tiny Battlefields Ser.). (Illus.). 48p. (J). (gr. 6-8). pap. 84.30 *(978-1-4824-1313-7(2))* Stevens, Gareth Publishing LLLP.

Grayson-Jones, Timothy. Polio. 2015. (J). lib. bdg. *(978-1-62713-379-1(8))* 2014. (ENG.). 64p. (YA). (gr. 8-8). 35.93 *(978-1-5026-0088-2(9)*, 81a50388-a122-4dd8-a36e-77e11c35341b) Cavendish Square Publishing LLC.

Hantula, Richard. Jonas Salk, 1 vol. 2004. (Trailblazers of the Modern World Ser.). (ENG., Illus.). 48p. (J). (gr. 5-8). lib. bdg. 33.67 *(978-0-8368-5100-7(5)*, 91b76e1b-e792-41ca-b702-2c41f73c8f78, Gareth Stevens Secondary Library) Stevens, Gareth Publishing LLLP.

Hecht, Alan. Polio. 2003. (Deadly Diseases & Epidemics Ser.). (ENG., Illus.). 112p. (gr. 9-13). 34.95 *(978-0-7910-7462-6(5)*, P113849, Facts On File) Infobase Holdings, Inc.

Jd, Duchess Harris & Hudak, Heather C. The Discovery of the Polio Vaccine. 2018. (Perspectives on American Progress Ser.). (ENG., Illus.). 48p. (J). (gr. 4-8). lib. bdg. 35.64 *(978-1-5321-1488-5(5)*, 29108) ABDO Publishing Co.

McLeese, Don. Jonas Salk. 2005. (Rourke Discovery Library). (Illus.). 24p. (J). (gr. 2-5). lib. bdg. *(978-1-59515-436-1(1))* Rourke Educational Media.

Peters, Stephanie True. The Battle Against Polio, 1 vol. 2005. (Epidemic! Ser.). (ENG., Illus.). 80p. (J). (gr. 6-6). lib. bdg. 35.50 *(978-0-7614-1635-7(8)*, 3f7b37a7-3e0a-4d03-a83a-7b8cb853a38b) Cavendish Square Publishing LLC.

Rooney, Anne. Jonas Salk & the First Polio Vaccine. 2012. (Miracle Makers Ser.). (ENG.). 48p. (YA). (gr. 5-8). 27.95 *(978-1-4488-6034-0(2)*, Rosen Reference) Rosen Publishing Group, Inc., The.

POLISH AMERICANS

Anderson, Dale. Polish Americans, 1 vol. 2006. (World Almanac(r) Library of American Immigration Ser.). (ENG., Illus.). 48p. (gr. 5-8). pap. 15.05 *(978-0-8368-7330-6(0)*, 054bfccb-8f9e-435c-abec-2ea4ff185456); lib. bdg. 33.67 *(978-0-8368-7317-7(3)*, 2426dbf8-898d-490d-aed2-d3c12b595460) Stevens, Gareth Publishing LLLP. (Gareth Stevens Secondary Library).

Greene, Meg. Polish Americans. 2003. (Immigrants in America Ser.). (ENG., Illus.). 112p. (J). 30.85 *(978-1-59018-516-2(1)*, Lucent Bks.) Cengage Gale.

Moreno, Barry. The Polish Americans. (Major American Immigration Ser.). (YA). 2010. (Illus.). 64p. (gr. 9-12). 22.95 *(978-1-4222-0616-4(5))* 2007. pap. 9.95 *(978-1-4222-0683-6(1))* Mason Crest.

Nickles, Greg. The Poles: We Came to North America. 2006. (Illus.). 32p. (J). (gr. 4-8). reprint ed. 19.00 *(978-0-7567-9907-6(4))* DIANE Publishing Co.

Wales, Dirk. Twice a Hero: Polish American Heroes of the American Revolutuion. Peterson, Lynn Ihsen, illus. 2007. 31p. (J). (gr. 4-9). 18.95 incl. audio compact disk *(978-0-9632459-4-6(5))* Great Plains Pr.

POLISH AMERICANS—FICTION

Cushman, Karen. Rodzina. 2020.Tr. of Rodzina. (ENG.). 240p. (J). (gr. 3-7). pap. 7.99 *(978-0-358-09751-8(7)*, 1747610, Clarion Bks.) HarperCollins Pubs.

Estes, Eleanor. The Hundred Dresses. Slobodkin, Louis, illus. anniv. ed. 2004. (ENG.). 96p. (J). (gr. 1-4). 17.99 *(978-0-15-205170-9(8)*, 1195595); pap. 8.99 *(978-0-15-205260-7(7)*, 1195848) HarperCollins Pubs. (Clarion Bks.).

Faigen, Anne G. New World Waiting. 2006. iii, 188p. (J). pap. *(978-0-9744715-5-6(0))* Local History Co., The.

Harlow, Joan Hiatt. Breaker Boy. 2017. (ENG., Illus.). 288p. (J). (gr. 3-7). 16.99 *(978-1-4814-6537-3(6)*, McElderry, Margaret K. Bks.) McElderry, Margaret K. Bks.

Leighton, Maxinne Rhea. An Ellis Island Christmas. Nolan, Dennis, illus. 2018. 32p. (J). (gr. k-3). pap. 7.99 *(978-0-451-48133-7(X)*, Puffin Books) Penguin Young Readers Group.

Pellowski, Anne & Sharpe, Roseanne. First Farm in the Valley: Anna's Story. 2008. (ENG., Illus.). 183p. (J). (gr. 3-9). pap. 12.95 *(978-1-932350-24-1(1))* Ignatius Pr.

—Stairstep Farm: Anna Rose's Story. 2011. (Latsch Valley Farm Ser.). (ENG., Illus.). 182p. (J). (gr. 3-4). pap. 12.95 *(978-1-932350-40-1(3))* Ignatius Pr.

Swigut, Bernadetta. First Star: Vigilja- First Star. 2006. (J). 16.99 *(978-0-9790026-0-1(5))* Steinschneider, Bernadetta.

POLISH LANGUAGE

Kudela, Katy R. My First Book of Polish Words. Translations.com Staff, tr. 2011. (Bilingual Picture Dictionaries Ser.). (MUL.). 32p. (gr. 1-2). pap. 47.70 *(978-1-4296-6168-3(2),* Capstone Pr.) Capstone.

Milet Publishing Staff. Animals, 60 vols. 2011. (My First Bilingual Book Ser.). (ENG & POR., Illus.). 24p. (J). (gr. k — 1). bds. 8.99 *(978-1-84059-616-8(3))* Milet Publishing.

—Bilingual Visual Dictionary. 2011. (Milet Multimedia Ser.). (ENG, POL & POR., Illus.). 1p. (J). (gr. k-2). cd-rom 19.95 *(978-1-84059-588-8(4))* Milet Publishing.

—Fruit - My First Bilingual Book, 1 vol. 2011. (My First Bilingual Book Ser.). (ENG & POR., Illus.). 24p. (J). (gr. k — 1). bds. 7.99 *(978-1-84059-632-8(5))* Milet Publishing.

—Home (English-Polish), 1 vol. 2011. (My First Bilingual Book Ser.). (ENG & POR., Illus.). 24p. (J). (gr. k — 1). bds. 8.99 *(978-1-84059-648-9(1))* Milet Publishing.

—Music, 1 vol. 2012. (My First Bilingual Book Ser.). (ENG & POR., Illus.). 24p. (J). (gr. k — 1). bds. 8.99 *(978-1-84059-724-0(0))* Milet Publishing.

—My Bilingual Book-Hearing (English-Polish), 1 vol. 2014. (My Bilingual Book Ser.). (ENG & POR., Illus.). 24p. (J). (gr. -1-k). 9.95 *(978-1-84059-780-6(1))* Milet Publishing.

—My Bilingual Book-Sight (English-Polish), 1 vol. 2014. (My Bilingual Book Ser.). (ENG & POR., Illus.). 24p. (J). (gr. -1-k). 9.95 *(978-1-84059-796-7(8))* Milet Publishing.

—My Bilingual Book-Smell (English-Polish), 1 vol. 2014. (My Bilingual Book Ser.). (ENG & POR., Illus.). 24p. (J). (gr. -1-k). 9.95 *(978-1-84059-812-4(3))* Milet Publishing.

—My Bilingual Book-Taste (English-Polish), 1 vol. 2014. (My Bilingual Book Ser.). (ENG & POR., Illus.). 24p. (J). (gr. -1-k). 9.95 *(978-1-84059-828-5(X))* Milet Publishing.

—My First Bilingual Book - Jobs, 1 vol. 2012. (My First Bilingual Book Ser.). (ENG & POR., Illus.). 24p. (J). (gr. k — 1). bds. 7.99 *(978-1-84059-708-0(9))* Milet Publishing.

—My First Bilingual Book-Opposites (English-Polish), 1 vol. 2012. (My First Bilingual Book Ser.). (ENG & POR., Illus.). 24p. (J). (gr. k — 1). bds. 7.99 *(978-1-84059-741-7(0))* Milet Publishing.

—My First Bilingual Book-Sports (English-Polish), 1 vol. 2012. (My First Bilingual Book Ser.). (ENG & POR., Illus.). 24p. (J). (gr. k — 1). bds. 7.99 *(978-1-84059-756-1(9))* Milet Publishing.

Nunn, Daniel. Colors in Polish: Kolory, 1 vol. 2012. (World Languages - Colors Ser.). (POL.). 24p. (gr. 1-3). (J). lib. bdg. 25.32 *(978-1-4329-6654-6(5),* 119267); pap. 6.29 *(978-1-4329-6661-4(8),* 119273) Capstone. (Heinemann).

—Families in Polish: Rodziny. 2013. (World Languages - Families Ser.). (POL., Illus.). 24p. (J). (gr. 1-3). pap. 6.29 *(978-1-4329-7182-3(4),* 121195); lib. bdg. 25.32 *(978-1-4329-7175-5(1),* 121189) Capstone. (Heinemann).

—Numbers in Polish: Liczby. 2012. (World Languages - Numbers Ser.). (POL.). 24p. (gr. 1-3). (J). lib. bdg. 25.32 *(978-1-4329-6675-1(8),* 119295); pap. 6.29 *(978-1-4329-6682-9(0),* 119301) Capstone. (Heinemann).

The Rosetta Stone Language Library: Polish Level 1. 2005. (J). (gr. 1-18). cd-rom 209.00 *(978-1-58022-035-4(5))* Rosetta Stone Ltd.

POLISH LANGUAGE—DICTIONARIES—ENGLISH

Hippocrene Books Staff, creator. Hippocrene Polish Children's Dictionary: English-Polish/Polish-English. 2006. (ENG & POL., Illus.). 108p. (J). (gr. 3-7). pap. 14.95 *(978-0-7818-1127-9(9))* Hippocrene Bks., Inc.

Milet Publishing Staff. Milet Bilingual Visual Dictionary, 1 vol. 2012. (Milet Bilingual Visual Dictionary Ser.). (ENG & POR., Illus.). 148p. (J). (gr. k-2). 34.95 *(978-1-84059-692-2(9))* Milet Publishing.

—Vegetables, 1 vol. 2011. (My First Bilingual Book Ser.). (ENG & POR., Illus.). 24p. (J). (gr. k — 1). bds. 7.99 *(978-1-84059-664-9(3))* Milet Publishing.

Turhan, Sedat. New Bilingual Visual Dictionary (English-Polish), 1 vol. 2nd ed. 2017. (New Bilingual Visual Dictionary Ser.). (ENG., Illus.). 148p. (J). (gr. k-2). 19.95 *(978-1-78508-889-6(0))* Milet Publishing.

Turhan, Sedat & Hagin, Sally. Milet Picture Dictionary, 1 vol. 2005. (Milet Picture Dictionary Ser.). (ENG., Illus.). 48p. (J). (gr. -1-3). 14.95 *(978-1-84059-466-9(7))* Milet Publishing.

POLITENESS

see Courtesy; Etiquette

POLITICAL CORRUPTION

Brezina, Corona. America's Political Scandals in the Late 1800s: Boss Tweed & Tammany Hall. 2009. (America's Industrial Society in the 19th Century Ser.). 32p. (gr. 4-4). 47.90 *(978-1-61511-336-1(3))* Rosen Publishing Group, Inc., The.

Doeden, Matt. Whistle-Blowers: Exposing Crime & Corruption. 2015. (ENG., Illus.). 96p. (YA). (gr. 6-12). lib. bdg. 33.32 *(978-1-4677-4209-2(0),* 9445ce2b-8c56-4f2f-b4d7-0b512bf7098d); E-Book 50.65 *(978-1-4677-6312-7(8))* Lerner Publishing Group. (Twenty-First Century Bks.).

Espejo, Roman, ed. Voter Fraud, 1 vol. 2010. (At Issue Ser.). (ENG., Illus.). 112p. (gr. 10-12). 41.03 *(978-0-7377-4693-8(9),* f5d2dd87-a570-4beb-9806-479d9f7fad71, Greenhaven Publishing) Greenhaven Publishing LLC.

Gay, Oonagh & Leopold, Patricia, eds. Conduct Unbecoming? The Regulation of Parliamentary Behaviour. Gay, Oonagh & Leopold, Patricia, trs. 2004. vi, 378p. 39.95 *(978-1-84275-055-1(0))* Politico's Publishing Ltd. GBR. Dist: Consortium Bk. Sales & Distribution.

Lansford, Tom. Corruption & Transparency, Vol. 8. Lansford, Tom, ed. 2016. (Foundations of Democracy Ser.). (Illus.). 64p. (J). (gr. 7). 23.95 *(978-1-4222-3627-7(7))* Mason Crest.

Lucas, Eileen, ed. Political Corruption, 1 vol. 2018. (At Issue Ser.). (ENG.). 128p. (gr. 10-12). lib. bdg. 41.03 *(978-1-5345-0380-9(3),* c8d69661-a5b6-41e9-af7e-abae5fd2c763, Greenhaven Publishing) Greenhaven Publishing LLC.

Machajewski, Sarah. Political Corruption & the Abuse of Power, 1 vol. 2018. (Hot Topics Ser.). (ENG.). 104p. (gr. 7-7). 41.03 *(978-1-5345-6341-4(5),* 0349d882-e971-4062-99ed-2e7fac42ecdf, Lucent Pr.) Greenhaven Publishing LLC.

Miller, Debra A. Political Corruption, 1 vol. 2007. (Hot Topics Ser.). (ENG., Illus.). 112p. (gr. 7-7). lib. bdg. 41.03 *(978-1-59018-982-5(5),* a376933a-5e2f-4065-b5ea-526c456915b6, Lucent Pr.) Greenhaven Publishing LLC.

Scherer, Randy, ed. Political Scandals, 1 vol. 2007. (At Issue Ser.). (ENG., Illus.). 112p. (gr. 10-12). pap. 28.80 *(978-0-7377-3764-6(6),* ab028217-28d0-4c5f-96fc-26ccb7840e8b, Greenhaven Publishing) Greenhaven Publishing LLC.

Shoup, Kate. Corruption in Politics, 1 vol. 2019. (Dilemmas in Democracy Ser.). (ENG.). 80p. (gr. 7-7). lib. bdg. 37.36 *(978-1-5026-4501-2(7),* 15f8fe0d-f44f-421c-9db2-1a8912c9505c) Cavendish Square Publishing LLC.

Young, Mitchell, ed. Political Corruption, 1 vol. 2009. (Issues on Trial Ser.). (ENG., Illus.). 184p. (gr. 10-12). 49.93 *(978-0-7377-3981-7(9),* 992f2306-6eaa-4bab-b25a-3f46a6f2f408, Greenhaven Publishing) Greenhaven Publishing LLC.

POLITICAL CORRUPTION—FICTION

Emerson, Scott. The Case of the Cat with the Missing Ear: From the Notebooks of Edward R. Smithfield D. V. M. Mullett, Viv, illus. 2011. (Adventures of Samuel Blackthorne Ser.: 1). (ENG.). 240p. (J). (gr. 3-7). pap. 11.99 *(978-0-689-87615-8(7),* Simon & Schuster Bks. For Young Readers) Simon & Schuster Bks. For Young Readers.

Jones, Frewin. The Faerie Path #3: the Seventh Daughter. 2009. (Faerie Path Ser.: 3). (ENG.). 352p. (YA). (gr. 8). pap. 9.99 *(978-0-06-087110-9(5),* HarperTeen) HarperCollins Pubs.

Mulligan, Andy. Trash. 2011. (ENG., Illus.). 240p. (YA). (gr. 7-12). pap. 11.99 *(978-0-385-75216-9(4),* Ember) Random Hse. Children's Bks.

Schraff, Anne. Time of Courage, 1 vol. unabr. ed. 2010. (Urban Underground Ser.). (ENG.). 197p. (YA). (gr. 9-12). pap. 11.95 *(978-1-61651-270-5(9))* Saddleback Educational Publishing, Inc.

Skarmeta, Antonio. The Composition, 1 vol. Ruano, Alfonso, illus. 2003. (ENG.). 36p. (J). (gr. 3-3). pap. 8.95 *(978-0-88899-550-6(4))* Groundwood Bks. CAN. Dist: Publishers Group West (PGW).

Sleator, William. Test. 2010. (ENG.). 320p. (YA). (gr. 7-11). pap. 7.95 *(978-0-8109-8989-4(1),* 620703, Amulet Bks.) Abrams, Inc.

Stone, Peter. The Perfect Candidate. 2019. (ENG.). 384p. (YA). (gr. 7). pap. 12.99 *(978-1-5344-2218-6(8))* Simon & Schuster, Inc.

POLITICAL CRIMES AND OFFENSES

see also Anarchism; Assassination; Bombings; Concentration Camps; Terrorism

Archer, Jules. Treason in America: Disloyalty Versus Dissent. 2016. (Jules Archer History for Young Readers Ser.). (ENG.). 208p. (J). (gr. 6-6). 16.99 *(978-1-63450-628-1(6),* Sky Pony Pr.) Skyhorse Publishing Co., Inc.

Katz, Samuel M. Raging Within: Ideological Terrorism. 2003. (Terrorist Dossiers Ser.). (Illus.). 72p. (J). (gr. 6-12). 26.60 *(978-0-8225-4032-8(0))* Lerner Publishing Group.

Shea, Nicole. Poaching & Illegal Trade. 2013. (Animal 911: Environmental Threats Ser.). 48p. (J). (gr. 3-5). pap. 84.30 *(978-1-4339-9720-4(7));* (ENG., Illus.). (gr. 4-4). lib. bdg. 34.61 *(978-1-4339-9718-1(5),* 976303fe-d4be-4535-91b8-d8c9c251a1ab) Stevens, Gareth Publishing LLLP.

Zeinert, Karen. McCarthyism & the Communist Scare in United States History, 1 vol. 2014. (In United States History Ser.). (ENG.). 96p. (gr. 5-5). pap. 13.88 *(978-0-7660-6346-4(1),* 4c26452c-05a6-48ab-91dc-21b46a12e8e8) Enslow Publishing, LLC.

POLITICAL CRIMES AND OFFENSES—FICTION

Dowd, Siobhan. Bog Child. 2010. (ENG.). 336p. (YA). (gr. 7). pap. 10.99 *(978-0-375-84135-4(0))* Fickling, David Bks. GBR. Dist: Penguin Random Hse. LLC.

POLITICAL ECONOMY

see Economics

POLITICAL PARTIES

see also Politics, Practical; Right and Left (Political Science)

also names of parties, e.g. Democratic Party

Berlatsky, Noah, ed. Does the U. S. Two-Party System Still Work?, 1 vol. 2010. (At Issue Ser.). (ENG., Illus.). 104p. (gr. 10-12). 41.03 *(978-0-7377-4644-0(0),* 3aab93c9-d62f-48a9-8d1f-5e0ccadeed47, Greenhaven Publishing) Greenhaven Publishing LLC.

Bjornlund, Lydia. Modern Political Parties, 1 vol. 2016. (American Citizenship Ser.). (ENG., Illus.). 48p. (J). (gr. 4-8). lib. bdg. 35.64 *(978-1-68078-242-4(8),* 22085) ABDO Publishing Co.

Braun, Eric. Protest Movements: Then & Now. 2018. (America: 50 Years of Change Ser.). (ENG., Illus.). 64p. (J). (gr. 5-9). lib. bdg. 34.65 *(978-1-5435-0385-2(3),* 137210, Capstone Pr.) Capstone.

Burgan, Michael & Hoena, Blake A. Political Parties, 1 vol. Barnett, Charles et al, illus. 2008. (Cartoon Nation Ser.). (ENG.). 32p. (J). (gr. 3-9). lib. bdg. 31.32 *(978-1-4296-1334-7(3),* 94607, Capstone Pr.) Capstone.

Finne, Stephanie. How Political Parties Work, 1 vol. 2015. (How the US Government Works). (ENG.). 48p. (J). (gr. 4-8). lib. bdg. 35.64 *(978-1-62403-634-7(1),* 17043) ABDO Publishing Co.

Horn, Geoffrey M. Political Parties, Interest Groups, & the Media, 1 vol. 2003. (World Almanac(r) Library of American Government Ser.). (ENG., Illus.). 48p. (gr. 5-8). pap. 15.05 *(978-0-8368-5483-1(7),* 97efc7c4-510b-4e32-8f0f-c646243b1f7f, Gareth Stevens Secondary Library) Stevens, Gareth Publishing LLLP.

Jeffries, Joyce. What Are Political Parties?, 1 vol. 2018. (What's the Issue? Ser.). (ENG.). 24p. (gr. 3-3). pap. 9.25 *(978-1-5345-2813-0(X),* 837788f3-1e0f-4232-8855-d098cabff33c, KidHaven Publishing) Greenhaven Publishing LLC.

Kawa, Katie. What Are Protests?, 1 vol. 2018. (What's the Issue? Ser.). (ENG.). 24p. (gr. 3-3). pap. 9.25 *(978-1-5345-2809-3(1),* 05a49487-06e5-4678-ab77-fe7ce59ec6d7, KidHaven Publishing) Greenhaven Publishing LLC.

Krasner, Barbara, ed. The Two-Party System in the United States, 1 vol. 2018. (Current Controversies Ser.). (ENG.). 200p. (gr. 10-12). 48.03 *(978-1-5345-0389-2(7),* 6d742bf6-bee8-46f7-a2db-d0437d161e62) Greenhaven Publishing LLC.

Landau, Elaine. Friendly Foes: A Look at Political Parties. 2003. (How Government Works). (ENG., Illus.). 56p. (gr. 4-8). lib. bdg. 25.26 *(978-0-8225-1349-0(8))* Lerner Publishing Group.

Leavitt, Amie Jane. A History of the Republican Party. 2012. (J). lib. bdg. 29.95 *(978-1-61228-261-9(X))* Mitchell Lane Pubs.

McCabe, Matthew. 12 Things to Know about Political Parties. 2015. (Today's News Ser.). (ENG.). 32p. (J). (gr. 3-6). 32.80 *(978-1-63235-031-2(9),* 11609, 12-Story Library) Bookstaves, LLC.

McPherson, Stephanie Sammartino. Political Parties: From Nominations to Victory Celebrations. 2015. (Inside Elections Ser.). (ENG., Illus.). 64p. (J). (gr. 6-8). 26.65 *(978-1-4677-7910-4(5),* 267c9873-a98c-4879-8c21-97514d4a402a, Lerner Pubns.) Lerner Publishing Group.

Payan, Gregory. The Federalists & Anti-Federalists: How & Why Political Parties Were Formed in Young America. (Life in the New American Nation Ser.). 32p. (gr. 4-4). 2009. 47.90 *(978-1-61514-283-5(5))* 2003. (ENG., Illus.). lib. bdg. 29.13 *(978-0-8239-4038-7(1),* e78e0c7c-0271-49cd-b08c-5a56d241777c, Rosen Reference) Rosen Publishing Group, Inc., The.

Porterfield, Jason. Problems & Progress in American Politics: The Growth of the Democratic Party in the Late 1800s. 2009. (America's Industrial Society in the 19th Century Ser.). 32p. (gr. 4-4). 47.90 *(978-1-61511-339-2(8))* Rosen Publishing Group, Inc., The.

Sanders, Rob. Peaceful Fights for Equal Rights. Schorr, Jared Andrew, illus. 2018. (ENG.). 48p. (J). (gr. -1-3). 17.99 *(978-1-5344-2943-7(3),* Simon & Schuster Bks. For Young Readers) Simon & Schuster Bks. For Young Readers.

Skahill, Carolyn M. The Socialist Party: Eugene V. Debs & the Radical Politics of the American Working Class. 2009. (Progressive Movement 1900-1920: Efforts to Reform America's New Industrial Society Ser.). 32p. (gr. 3-4). 47.90 *(978-1-60854-174-4(6))* Rosen Publishing Group, Inc., The.

Sommers, Michael. Ehud Olmert: Prime Minister of Israel. 2009. (Newsmakers Ser.). 112p. (gr. 9-10). 63.90 *(978-1-60851-131-0(6))* Rosen Publishing Group, Inc., The.

Topinka, Joseph Baar. Just Judy: A Citizen & Leader for Illinois. 2017. (ENG.). (J). pap. 16.95 *(978-0-9983282-2-5(7))* Hilton Publishing Co.

Wesgate, Kathryn. The History of Political Parties, 1 vol. 2020. (Look at U. S. Elections Ser.). (ENG.). 32p. (gr. 2-2). pap. 11.50 *(978-1-5382-5946-7(X),* daf288df-329d-4058-84e9-8b29fff35b9e) Stevens, Gareth Publishing LLLP.

Zilber, Jeremy. Why Mommy Is a Democrat. Firsova, Yuliya, illus. 2005. 28p. (J). pap. 8.00 *(978-0-9786688-0-8(4))* Zilber, Jeremy.

POLITICAL SCIENCE

see also Anarchism; Aristocracy (Social Class); Church and State; Citizenship; Civil Rights; Civil Service; Communism; Constitutional Law; Democracy; Government, Resistance to; Kings, Queens, Rulers, etc.; Law; Liberty; Local Government; Municipal Government; Political Parties; Power (Social Sciences); Public Administration; Revolutions; Right and Left (Political Science); Socialism; State Governments; Suffrage; World Politics

Aldritt, Jeremy. Thomas Paine & the Power of Common Sense, 1 vol. 2015. (Spotlight on American History Ser.). (ENG., Illus.). 24p. (J). (gr. 4-6). pap. 11.00 *(978-1-4994-1765-4(9),* 6d93e3a5-db18-41c4-af43-5de9b1569455, PowerKids Pr.) Rosen Publishing Group, Inc., The.

Allen, Mitchell. Our Bill of Rights: Sharing & Reusing, 1 vol. 2017. (Computer Kids: Powered by Computational Thinking Ser.). (ENG.). 24p. (J). (gr. 3-4). 25.27 *(978-1-5383-2422-6(9),* 888aba33-f967-4752-8dc6-60235df686d4, PowerKids Pr.); pap. *(978-1-5081-3769-6(2),* ecf6de88-24f7-4d8c-be1c-bd47c0bdb6a1, Rosen Classroom) Rosen Publishing Group, Inc., The.

Analyzing the Issues: Set 4, 12 vols. 2017. (Analyzing the Issues Ser.). (ENG.). (J). (gr. 8-8). lib. bdg. 305.58 *(978-0-7660-9171-9(6),* 23d4b126-e807-4d52-8b10-14f8398669d1) Enslow Publishing, LLC.

Anderson, Wayne. The ETA: Spain's Basque Terrorists. 2009. (Inside the World's Most Infamous Terrorist Organizations Ser.). 64p. (gr. 5-5). 58.50 *(978-1-61513-578-3(2))* Rosen Publishing Group, Inc., The.

Army JROTC: Leadership Education & Training, Cadet Reference. 2nd ed. 2003. (Illus.). vi, 56p. (J). *(978-0-536-74189-9(1),* Dept. of the Army) United States Government Printing Office.

Baden-Powell, Robert. Scouting for Boys. 2013. pap. 16.99 *(978-1-4621-1233-3(1),* Horizon Pubs.) Cedar Fort, Inc./CFI Distribution.

Be a Community Leader, 12 vols. 2014. (Be a Community Leader Ser.). (ENG.). 32p. (J). (gr. 5-5). 167.58 *(978-1-4777-6654-5(5),* 310d814e-df73-4774-8983-3b8f582e0b15, PowerKids Pr.) Rosen Publishing Group, Inc., The.

Beasley, Ava. My Point of View: Civic Virtues, 1 vol. 2018. (Civics for the Real World Ser.). (ENG.). 16p. (gr. 2-3). pap. *(978-1-5383-6496-3(4),* 7b3f8d8e-554c-442b-937b-425176c8d0d7, Rosen Classroom) Rosen Publishing Group, Inc., The.

Beckett, Leslie. What's Activism?, 1 vol. 2019. (What's the Issue? Ser.). (ENG.). 24p. (gr. 3-3). 26.23 *(978-1-5345-6741-2(0),* b5b57cb3-f0d8-46d8-825a-749a0a34871b, KidHaven Publishing) Greenhaven Publishing LLC.

Bedesky, Baron & Bedesky, Baron. What Is a Government? 2008. (Your Guide to Government Ser.). (ENG., Illus.). 32p. (J). (gr. k-5). pap. *(978-0-7787-4333-0(0))* Crabtree Publishing Co.

Benchmark Education Company, LLC Staff, compiled by. Power, Authority, & Governance. 2005. spiral bd. 50.00 *(978-1-4108-4501-6(X));* spiral bd. 145.00 *(978-1-4108-5419-3(1))* Benchmark Education Co.

Bernay, Emma, et al. Kids' Guide to Government. 2018. (Kids' Guide to Government Ser.). (ENG.). 32p. (J). (gr. 3-6). 119.96 *(978-1-5435-0336-4(5),* 27624, Capstone Pr.) Capstone.

Board, Tempra. Who Are Libertarians & What Do They Believe In?, 1 vol. 2019. (Politics Today Ser.). (ENG.). 64p. (gr. 7-7). pap. 16.28 *(978-1-5026-4524-1(6),* cac30a3c-bfd1-4f2e-99f8-cfeb7ac25bb4) Cavendish Square Publishing LLC.

Bonwill, Ann. We Have a Government (Rookie Read-About Civics) (Library Edition) 2019. (Rookie Read-About Civics Ser.). (ENG., Illus.). 32p. (J). (gr. 1-2). lib. bdg. 25.00 *(978-0-531-12916-6(0),* Children's Pr.) Scholastic Library Publishing.

Brexel, Bernadette. The Populist Party: A Voice for the Farmers in an Industrial Society. 2009. (America's Industrial Society in the 19th Century Ser.). 32p. (gr. 4-4). 47.90 *(978-1-61511-344-6(4))* Rosen Publishing Group, Inc., The.

Brezina, Corona. Jean-Jacques Rousseau & the Social Contract. 2016. (J). lib. bdg. *(978-1-5081-0227-4(9))* Rosen Publishing Group, Inc., The.

Burgan, Michael. The Branches of U. S. Government. 2011. (Cornerstones of Freedom, Third Ser.). (Illus.). 64p. (J). lib. bdg. 30.00 *(978-0-531-25028-0(8),* Children's Pr.) Scholastic Library Publishing.

Byers, Ann. Lebanon's Hezbollah. 2009. (Inside the World's Most Infamous Terrorist Organizations Ser.). 64p. (gr. 5-5). 58.50 *(978-1-61513-576-9(6))* Rosen Publishing Group, Inc., The.

Careers in Focus: Politics. 2nd rev. ed. 2011. (ENG., Illus.). 194p. (gr. 6-12). 32.95 *(978-0-8160-8035-9(6),* P189791, Ferguson Publishing Company) Infobase Holdings, Inc.

Cassutto, George. Civics Student Activity Book: Student Activities Book. 2003. (Illus.). stu. ed., ring bd., wbk. ed. *(978-1-931680-36-3(1),* Expert Systems for Teachers) Teaching Point, Inc.

Citizens & Their Governments (Set), 10 vols. 2010. (21st Century Skills Library: Citizens & Their Governments Ser.). (ENG.). 32p. (gr. 4-8). 320.70 *(978-1-60279-108-4(2),* 200001) Cherry Lake Publishing.

Cómo Ponerse en Contacto con un Oficial Electo, 1 vol. 2014. (Sé un líder de la Comunidad (Be a Community Leader) Ser.). (SPA., Illus.). 32p. (J). (gr. 5-5). lib. bdg. 27.93 *(978-1-4777-6909-6(9),* 711b9307-270f-48b6-9125-6d07a75a7103, PowerKids Pr.) Rosen Publishing Group, Inc., The.

Connolly, Sean. Monarchy. 2012. (Systems of Government Ser.). (ENG., Illus.). 48p. (J). (gr. 6-9). lib. bdg. 37.10 *(978-1-59920-805-3(9),* 17437, Smart Apple Media) Black Rabbit Bks.

—Political Messages & Propaganda. 2010. (J). 34.25 *(978-1-59920-349-2(9))* Black Rabbit Bks.

Conway, Sommer. The Journey of a Law: Understanding Government, 1 vol. 2018. (Civics for the Real World Ser.). (ENG.). 16p. (gr. 2-3). pap. *(978-1-5383-6530-4(8),* 2d08692a-0478-44cf-8789-038a59957df1, Rosen Classroom) Rosen Publishing Group, Inc., The.

Cooke, Tim. Politics & Democracy, 1 vol. 2017. (What's the Big Idea? a History of the Ideas That Shape Our World Ser.). (ENG.). 48p. (gr. 6-6). lib. bdg. 33.07 *(978-1-5026-2814-5(7),* 1e7d6a51-4577-4627-8cab-4b0116787aef) Cavendish Square Publishing LLC.

Csedrik, Alex. Thomas Hobbes & Leviathan. 2016. (J). lib. bdg. *(978-1-68048-550-9(4))* Windmill Bks.

De Capua, Sarah. True Books: Being a Governor. 2004. (True Bks.). (ENG.). 48p. 25.00 *(978-0-516-22797-9(1),* Watts, Franklin) Scholastic Library Publishing.

Doyle, Eamon, ed. Public Outrage & Protest, 1 vol. 2019. (At Issue Ser.). (ENG.). 128p. (gr. 10-12). pap. 28.80 *(978-1-5345-0528-5(8),* 137a2541-acf0-4e6f-98e0-e581ec82f404) Greenhaven Publishing LLC.

Ebner, Aviva. Physical Science Experiments. 2011. (ENG., Illus.). 156p. (gr. 5-8). 35.00 *(978-1-60413-855-9(6),* P189925, Facts On File) Infobase Holdings, Inc.

Ellis, Roman. Our Town Park: Taking Civic Action, 1 vol. 2018. (Civics for the Real World Ser.). (ENG.). 12p. (gr. 1-2). pap. *(978-1-5383-6475-8(1),* 2d6b7828-2be0-48f4-90dc-20cdc7fdc52b, Rosen Classroom) Rosen Publishing Group, Inc., The.

Fitzpatrick, Anne. Dictatorship. 2016. (Odysseys in Government Ser.). (ENG., Illus.). 80p. (J). (gr. 7-10). pap. 14.99 *(978-1-62832-321-4(3),* 20674, Creative Paperbacks) Creative Co., The.

Ford, Jeanne Marie. Respecting Opposing Viewpoints, 1 vol. 2017. (Civic Values Ser.). (ENG.). 32p. (gr. 3-3). pap. 11.58 *(978-1-5026-2936-4(4),* 2d51c185-7d2b-41d9-a1fb-1fbb0c26baa7) Cavendish Square Publishing LLC.

Freeman, Martha. If You're Going to a March. Kim, Violet, illus. 2018. (ENG.). 32p. (J). (gr. k). 16.95 *(978-1-4549-2993-2(6))* Sterling Publishing Co., Inc.

Fridell, Ron. Dictatorship, 1 vol. 2008. (Political Systems of the World Ser.). (ENG., Illus.). 160p. (YA). (gr. 8-8). lib. bdg. 45.50 *(978-0-7614-2627-1(2),* f99ef2bb-450f-4015-90b5-bc127562f308) Cavendish Square Publishing LLC.

Galè. Junior Worldmark Encyclopedia of the Nations, 10 vols. 6th ed. 2012. (Junior Worldmark Encyclopedia of the Nations Ser.). (ENG., Illus.). 3266p. lib. bdg. 995.00 *(978-1-4144-6313-1(8),* UXL) Cengage Gale.

Gelletly, LeeAnne. Monarchy. Colton, Timothy J., ed. 2012. (Major Forms of World Government Ser.). (Illus.). 64p. (J). (gr. 5). 22.95 *(978-1-4222-2141-9(5))* Mason Crest.

—Oligarchy. Colton, Timothy J., ed. 2012. (Major Forms of World Government Ser.). (Illus.). 64p. (J). (gr. 5). 22.95 *(978-1-4222-2142-6(3))* Mason Crest.

Gillespie, Larry. The Evolution of Government, Vol. 8. 2018. (Systems of Government Ser.). (Illus.). 96p. (J). (gr. 7). 34.60 *(978-1-4222-4018-2(5))* Mason Crest.

—Monarchy: Sovereignty of a King or Queen, Vol. 8. 2018. (Systems of Government Ser.). (Illus.). 96p. (J). (gr. 7). 34.60 *(978-1-4222-4020-5(7))* Mason Crest.

—Oligarchy: Power of the Wealthy Elite, Vol. 8. 2018. (Systems of Government Ser.). (Illus.). 96p. (J). (gr. 7). 34.60 *(978-1-4222-4021-2(5))* Mason Crest.

Grant, Moyra. Government & Politics. 2005. (ENG., Illus.). 232p. (C). pap. 47.50 *(978-0-7487-9032-6(2))* Nelson Thornes Ltd. GBR. Dist: Trans-Atlantic Pubns., Inc.

Hall, Kevin. Montesquieu & the Spirit of Laws. 2016. (J). lib. bdg. *(978-1-68048-546-2(6))* Rosen Publishing Group, Inc., The.

Harcourt School Publishers Staff. Our Government, No. 2. 2nd ed. 2003. (Illus.). pap. 139.70 *(978-0-15-337566-8(3))* Harcourt Schl. Pubs.

Harkrader, Lisa. Government & You. 2016. (Spring Forward Ser.). (J). (gr. 2). *(978-1-4900-9425-0(3))* Benchmark Education Co.

Harris, Nancy. What's Government? rev. ed. 2016. (First Guide to Government Ser.). (ENG.). 32p. (J). (gr. 1-3). pap. 8.29 *(978-1-4846-3688-6(0)*, 134100, Heinemann) Capstone.

Harris, Nathaniel. Monarchy, 1 vol. 2005. (Systems of Government Ser.). (ENG., Illus.). 48p. (gr. 6-8). pap. 15.05 *(978-0-8368-5890-7(5)*, aba184b4-0f0c-4a4d-a2e7-43048b05690c); lib. bdg. 33.67 *(978-0-8368-5885-3(9)*, 7462c000-22a0-4fa0-aeef-8b76b5901fc3) Stevens, Gareth Publishing LLLP. (Gareth Stevens Secondary Library).

Hawker, Louise, ed. Colonialism in Chinua Achebe's Things Fall Apart, 1 vol. 2010. (Social Issues in Literature Ser.). (ENG., Illus.). 168p. (gr. 10-12). lib. bdg. 48.03 *(978-0-7377-4650-1(5)*, dc68b1be-2d2e-4765-92d5-afa15d16d746, Greenhaven Publishing) Greenhaven Publishing LLC.

—Colonialism in Chinua Achebe's Things Fall Apart, 1 vol. 2010. (Social Issues in Literature Ser.). (ENG., Illus.). 168p. (gr. 10-12). pap. 33.00 *(978-0-7377-4651-8(3)*, 4a6dc33c-b842-4b0b-a326-d6ed6a68a1fd, Greenhaven Publishing) Greenhaven Publishing LLC.

Hobbes, Emma. Thomas More & Utopia. 2016. (J). lib. bdg. *(978-1-68048-551-6(2))* Rosen Publishing Group, Inc., The.

Holt, Rinehart and Winston Staff. American Civics: Answer Key for Guided Reading Strategies. 5th ed. 2004. pap. 8.00 *(978-0-03-038723-4(X))* Holt McDougal.

—American Civics: Chapter Tutorials for Students. 5th ed. 2004. pap. 26.60 *(978-0-03-038719-7(1))* Holt McDougal.

—American Civics: Guided Reading Strategies. 5th ed. 2004. pap. 25.80 *(978-0-03-038716-6(7))* Holt McDougal.

Hosein, Ann. Political Science: The Study of Nations, Government, & Governing, 1 vol., 1. 2015. (Britannica Guide to the Social Sciences Ser.). (ENG., Illus.). 192p. (J). (gr. 10-10). 37.82 *(978-1-62275-546-2(4)*, 5b05d70c-34cb-4c24-9675-f948617aecbe, Britannica Educational Publishing) Rosen Publishing Group, Inc., The.

How to Contact an Elected Official, 1 vol. 2014. (Be a Community Leader Ser.). (ENG.). 32p. (J). (gr. 5-5). lib. bdg. 27.93 *(978-1-4777-6689-7(8)*, 096fb5da-0710-4444-b19c-34a0ada7a0ec, PowerKids Pr.) Rosen Publishing Group, Inc., The.

Huffman, Mindy. Listening to Both Sides: Civic Virtues, 1 vol. 2018. (Civics for the Real World Ser.). (ENG.). 12p. (gr. 1-2). pap. *(978-1-5383-6406-2(9)*, 58381544-024b-4f15-ae55-407eb412022e, Rosen Classroom) Rosen Publishing Group, Inc., The.

Hurt, Avery Elizabeth. Thomas Paine's Common Sense, 1 vol. 2018. (America's Most Important Documents: Inquiry into Historical Sources Ser.). (ENG.). 64p. (gr. 6-6). lib. bdg. 37.36 *(978-1-5026-3601-0(8)*, c05511b4-ee61-48f5-bf4c-393681f4ec9d) Cavendish Square Publishing LLC.

Kenney, Karen. Civic Responsibilities. 2014. (U. S. Government & Civics Ser.). (ENG.). 24p. (J). (gr. 3-5). 19.75 *(978-1-5311-7665-5(8))* Perfection Learning Corp.

Laks Gorman, Jacqueline. Know Your Government, 12 vols., Set. Incl. Governor. lib. bdg. 24.67 *(978-1-4339-0091-4(2)*, 4d9474d2-1d82-4063-b5e1-ddf85e520bfa); Judge. lib. bdg. 24.67 *(978-1-4339-0092-1(0)*, 47543302-1c8a-4a6e-b628-f83895760594); Mayor. lib. bdg. 24.67 *(978-1-4339-0093-8(9)*, 7f0bba5b-a99d-43e1-9352-93e7e14fd7b6); Member of Congress. lib. bdg. 24.67 *(978-1-4339-0094-5(7)*, 2ff26ad8-8cbd-4683-b732-3009679d7942); President. lib. bdg. 24.67 *(978-1-4339-0095-2(5)*, d05ecc19-fc9f-4b56-8a4b-d3d369cd2647); Vice President. lib. bdg. 24.67 *(978-1-4339-0096-9(3)*, af6c4021-b770-4c03-bd5f-1423e73340a6); (J). (gr. 3-3). (Know Your Government Ser.). (ENG.). 24p. 2009. Set lib. bdg. 148.02 *(978-1-4339-0097-6(1)*, da7e447f-db69-4157-ac39-f1afb9f3d5bd, Weekly Reader Leveled Readers) Stevens, Gareth Publishing LLLP.

LernerClassroom Editors. First Step Nonfiction-Government Teaching Guide. 2009. pap. 7.95 *(978-0-8225-6884-1(5))* Lerner Publishing Group.

Let's Find Out! Government, 32 vols. 2015. (Let's Find Out! Government Ser.). (ENG.). 32p. (J). (gr. 2-3). 416.96 *(978-1-68048-197-6(5)*, 708c44d9-847b-4003-9e5a-854cf9803ccd, Britannica Educational Publishing) Rosen Publishing Group, Inc., The.

A Look at Your Government. 2017. (Look at Your Government Ser.). 32p. (gr. 2-2). pap. 63.00 *(978-1-4824-6289-0(3))*; (ENG.). lib. bdg. 169.62 *(978-1-4824-6287-6(7)*, 2fb11fda-b5ce-427d-9ac3-aff642356cde) Stevens, Gareth Publishing LLLP.

Lord, Jonathan. John Locke & the Second Treatise of Civil Government. 2016. (J). lib. bdg. *(978-1-68048-548-6(2))* Rosen Publishing Group, Inc., The.

Luthringer, Chelsea. So What Is Citizenship Anyway? 2009. (Student's Guide to American Civics Ser.). 48p. (gr. 5-8). 53.00 *(978-1-61511-238-8(3)*, Rosen Reference) Rosen Publishing Group, Inc., The.

MacDonald, Fiona & Weaver, Clare. Human Rights. 2003. (World Issues Ser.). (Illus.). 57p. (J). (gr. 5-18). lib. bdg. 29.95 *(978-1-931983-82-2(8))* Chrysalis Education.

Machajewski, Sarah. What Are State & Local Governments?, 4 vols. 2015. (Let's Find Out! Government Ser.). (ENG.). 32p. (J). (gr. 2-3). 52.12 *(978-1-62275-988-0(5)*, 92b98fd9-9785-41ca-8636-b0c735405eb1, Britannica Educational Publishing) Rosen Publishing Group, Inc., The.

Mara, Wil. Politics & the Media. 2018. (21st Century Skills Library: Global Citizens: Modern Media Ser.). (ENG., Illus.). 32p. (J). (gr. 4-7). lib. bdg. 32.07 *(978-1-5341-2929-0(4)*, 211760) Cherry Lake Publishing.

Marsh, Carole. Pass the Test! Civics & Economics. (Virginia Experience! Ser.). lab manual ed. 195.00 incl. cd-rom *(978-0-635-01593-8(5)*, 15935); cd-rom 395.00 *(978-0-635-01594-5(3)*, 15943); 2004. cd-rom 24.95 *(978-0-635-01592-1(7)*, 15927) Gallopade International.

—Political Parties & Elections - Common Core Lessons & Activities. 2015. (Common Core Ser.). (ENG.). (J). pap. 4.99 *(978-0-635-11987-2(0))* Gallopade International.

—Washington Government Projects: 30 Cool, Activities, Crafts, Experiments & More for Kids to Do to Learn about Your State! 2003. (Washington Experience Ser.). 32p. (gr. k-5). pap. 5.95 *(978-0-635-01966-0(3)*, Marsh, Carole Bks.) Gallopade International.

—West Virginia Government Projects: 30 Cool, Activities, Crafts, Experiments & More for Kids to Do to Learn about Your State! 2003. (West Virginia Experience Ser.). 32p. (gr. k-5). pap. 5.95 *(978-0-635-01967-7(1)*, Marsh, Carole Bks.) Gallopade International.

—Wisconsin Government Projects: 30 Cool, Activities, Crafts, Experiments & More for Kids to Do to Learn about Your State! 2003. (Wisconsin Experience Ser.). 32p. (gr. k-5). pap. 5.95 *(978-0-635-01968-4(X)*, Marsh, Carole Bks.) Gallopade International.

—Wyoming Government Projects: 30 Cool, Activities, Crafts, Experiments & More for Kids to Do to Learn about Your State! 2003. (Wyoming Experience Ser.). 32p. (gr. k-5). pap. 5.95 *(978-0-635-01969-1(8)*, Marsh, Carole Bks.) Gallopade International.

Martin, Bobi. Let's Find Out! Government Set. 2015. (Let's Find Out! Government Ser.). (ENG.). 32p. (J). (gr. 2-3). pap., pap., pap. 103.20 *(978-1-68048-149-5(5)*, Britannica Educational Publishing) Rosen Publishing Group, Inc., The.

Martinez, Manuel. I Meet the Mayor! Understanding Government, 1 vol. 2018. (Civics for the Real World Ser.). (ENG.). 12p. (gr. 1-2). pap. *(978-1-5383-6421-5(2)*, a6c7cc17-8c3f-438d-a2dc-c97325b81a3e, Rosen Classroom) Rosen Publishing Group, Inc., The.

Mason, Helen. Be an Active Citizen at Your School. 2016. (Citizenship in Action Ser.). (ENG., Illus.). 24p. (J). (gr. 1-3). *(978-0-7787-2600-5(2))*; pap. *(978-0-7787-2606-7(1))* Crabtree Publishing Co.

—Be an Active Citizen at Your School. 2016. (Citizenship in Action Ser.). (ENG.). 24p. (J). (gr. 1-3). 18.75 *(978-1-5311-8587-9(8))* Perfection Learning Corp.

—Be an Active Citizen in Your Community. 2016. (Citizenship in Action Ser.). (ENG., Illus.). 24p. (J). (gr. 1-3). *(978-0-7787-2601-2(0))* Crabtree Publishing Co.

—Be an Active Citizen in Your Community. 2016. (Citizenship in Action Ser.). (ENG.). 24p. (J). (gr. 1-3). 18.75 *(978-1-5311-8586-2(X))* Perfection Learning Corp.

Masters, Nancy Robinson. Airplanes. 2008. (21st Century Skills Library: Global Products Ser.). (ENG., Illus.). 32p. (gr. 4-8). lib. bdg. 32.07 *(978-1-60279-119-0(8)*, 200091) Cherry Lake Publishing.

McGraw Hill. Civics Today: Citizenship, Economics, & You, Interactive Tutor Self-Assessment. 4th ed. 2007. (Civics Today: Citzshp Econ You Ser.). (ENG.). (gr. 6-10). cd-rom 120.64 *(978-0-07-879108-6(1)*, 0078791081) McGraw-Hill Education.

—Civics Today: Citizenship, Economics, & You, Reading Essentials & Note-Taking Guide Workbook. 4th ed. 2007. (Civics Today: Citzshp Econ You Ser.). (ENG., Illus.). 272p. (gr. 6-10). per., wbk. ed. 6.60 *(978-0-07-877672-4(4)*, 0078776724) McGraw-Hill Education.

Meredith, Susan Markowitz. Government for All. 2016. (Spring Forward Ser.). (J). (gr. 2). *(978-1-4900-9448-9(2))* Benchmark Education Co.

Micronations: Invent Your Own Country & Culture with 25 Projects. 2014. (Build It Yourself Ser.). (ENG., Illus.). 128p. (J). (gr. 3-7). 21.95 *(978-1-61930-218-1(7)*, 4abb41ae-a126-4e65-8b4e-fa03e4c4412d) Nomad Pr.

Miller, Debra A., ed. Politics & Religion, 1 vol. 2013. (Current Controversies Ser.). (ENG., Illus.). 176p. (gr. 10-12). pap. 33.00 *(978-0-7377-6885-5(1)*, 5671de04-0cf1-4249-ae64-b066e9737323); lib. bdg. 48.03 *(978-0-7377-6884-8(3)*, e709936c-99a7-4e35-8b25-c0217e0e4be3) Greenhaven Publishing LLC. (Greenhaven Publishing).

Miller, Reagan, et al. Government in the Ancient World, 1 vol. Crabtree Publishing Co. Staff, ed. 2011. (Life in the Ancient World Ser.: No. 3). (ENG., Illus.). 32p. (J). (gr. 5-8). pap. *(978-0-7787-1741-6(0))* Crabtree Publishing Co.

Morris, Neil. Modern World Leaders. 2003. (History Makers (Chrysalis) Ser.). (Illus.). 48p. (J). (gr. 5-18). lib. bdg. 29.95 *(978-1-932333-79-4(7))* Chrysalis Education.

My Government. 2015. (My Government Ser.). (ENG.). 32p. (J). (gr. 4-4). pap., pap., pap. 63.48 *(978-1-5026-0694-5(1))*; lib. bdg. 181.26 *(978-1-5026-0358-6(6)*, 7dd05061-39f0-440c-8adf-a42225a4b065) Cavendish Square Publishing LLC. (Cavendish Square).

My Government (Group 2) (My Government Ser.). (ENG.). (J). 2018. pap. 84.64 *(978-1-5026-3376-7(0))* 2017. (gr. 3-3). lib. bdg. 241.68 *(978-1-5026-3223-4(3)*, e23dc240-f60f-4fa9-a982-2b9e684a2512) Cavendish Square Publishing LLC.

Nagelhout, Ryan. Thomas Paine's Common Sense, 1 vol. 2013. (Documents That Shaped America Ser.). (ENG.). 32p. (J). (gr. 4-5). 29.27 *(978-1-4339-9013-7(X)*, 6422b8d2-5c0a-49a8-abeb-412a02746314); pap. 11.50 *(978-1-4339-9014-4(8)*, cbade4d6-c6c0-4be1-8220-bf76bf726e50) Stevens, Gareth Publishing LLLP.

National Geographic Learning. Reading Expeditions (Social Studies: Kids Make a Difference): Kids Are Citizens. 2007. (ENG., Illus.). 32p. (J). pap. 18.95 *(978-0-7922-8683-7(9))* CENGAGE Learning.

Ogden, Charlie. Government & Democracy. 2017. (Our Values - Level 3 Ser.). (Illus.). 32p. (J). (gr. 5-6). *(978-0-7787-3266-2(5))* Crabtree Publishing Co.

Okonowski, Anne. Who Are Nationalists & What Do They Believe In?, 1 vol. 2019. (Politics Today Ser.). (ENG.). 64p. (gr. 7-7). pap. 16.28 *(978-1-5026-4515-9(7)*, d4ae12cf-a292-4ade-aaa4-4e110dd0f2a0) Cavendish Square Publishing LLC.

Othello: Activity Pack. 2003. 156p. (YA). pap. *(978-1-58049-631-5(8)*, PA6318) Prestwick Hse., Inc.

Pace, Marisa. I Learn about How Laws Are Made: Understanding Government, 1 vol. 2018. (Civics for the Real World Ser.). (ENG.). 16p. (gr. 2-3). pap. *(978-1-5081-3943-0(1)*, 90eacd68-6eaf-40c2-8d64-76a54c340aad, Rosen Classroom) Rosen Publishing Group, Inc., The.

—Listening to Others: Civic Virtues, 1 vol. 2018. (Civics for the Real World Ser.). (ENG.). 8p. (gr. k-1). pap. *(978-1-5383-6340-9(2)*, 1786f8a0-39b8-4e34-8814-e79f770eea0d, Rosen Classroom) Rosen Publishing Group, Inc., The.

Paine, Thomas. Common Sense & Other Works. 2019. (J). *(978-1-5415-4132-0(4)*, First Avenue Editions) Lerner Publishing Group.

Perkins, Anne. Trailblazers in Politics, 1 vol. 2014. (Original Thinkers Ser.). (ENG.). 136p. (J). (gr. 10-10). 44.13 *(978-1-4777-8144-9(7)*, 0a1208f6-b1e5-4601-b5f8-153924d3d07b, Rosen Young Adult) Rosen Publishing Group, Inc., The.

Perl, Lila. Theocracy, 1 vol. 2008. (Political Systems of the World Ser.). (ENG., Illus.). 160p. (YA). (gr. 8-8). lib. bdg. 45.50 *(978-0-7614-2631-8(0)*, c616a9e7-7eb1-4d11-bcc2-73bc986b1871) Cavendish Square Publishing LLC.

Phillips, Miriam. I Write Letters to Local Leaders: Taking Civic Action, 1 vol. 2018. (Civics for the Real World Ser.). (ENG.). 12p. (gr. 1-2). pap. *(978-1-5383-6478-9(6)*, 1a9c9af8-c973-4db4-ae62-ad9e7ac0f437, Rosen Classroom) Rosen Publishing Group, Inc., The.

Political & Economic Systems, 28 vols. 2014. (Political & Economic Systems Ser.). (ENG.). (YA). (gr. 10-10). 192 - 312p. 666.26 *(978-1-62275-760-2(2)*, 2776d6c3-460a-403c-bff5-ea6aac814f6c); 312p. 333.13 *(978-1-62275-365-9(8)*, 1ce72c83-3fc2-4d25-ab13-cd54a52b3126) Rosen Publishing Group, Inc., The.

Porterfield, Jason. Julian Assange & Wikileaks, 1 vol. 2012. (Internet Biographies Ser.). (ENG., Illus.). 128p. (J). (gr. 7-7). lib. bdg. 39.80 *(978-1-4488-6915-2(3)*, 4d649a04-2071-4483-bd02-3061d607f39d) Rosen Publishing Group, Inc., The.

Prentice-Hall Staff. When Legend. 2nd ed. (J). stu. ed. *(978-0-13-717281-8(8))* Prentice Hall (Schl. Div.).

Raatma, Lucia. Citizenship. 2009. (21st Century Junior Library: Character Education Ser.). (ENG., Illus.). 24p. (gr. 2-5). lib. bdg. 29.21 *(978-1-60279-324-8(7)*, 200220) Cherry Lake Publishing.

Redfern, Nicholas. Top Secret Government Archives: Missing Files & Conspiracy Paper Trails, 1 vol. 2014. (Conspiracies & Cover-Ups Ser.). (ENG.). 221p. (YA). (gr. 8-8). 41.47 *(978-1-4777-8153-1(6)*, ee5edaf8-8489-46f4-8c81-44f735bfa0f6, Rosen Young Adult) Rosen Publishing Group, Inc., The.

Rees, Peter. Shockwave: Liberty. 2007. (Shockwave: the Human Experience Ser.). (ENG., Illus.). 36p. (J). (gr. 3-5). 25.00 *(978-0-531-17760-0(2)*, Children's Pr.) Scholastic Library Publishing.

Reyes, Sonja. What Is a Jury? Understanding Government, 1 vol. 2018. (Civics for the Real World Ser.). (ENG.). 16p. (gr. 2-3). pap. *(978-1-5383-6536-6(7)*, 50078350-06b3-4349-8cff-5ba22a0eba8a, Rosen Classroom) Rosen Publishing Group, Inc., The.

Rodger, Ellen. How Does the Canadian Government Work? 2013. (ENG.). 32p. (J). *(978-0-7787-0903-9(5))*; pap. *(978-0-7787-0908-4(6))* Crabtree Publishing Co.

Russell, Danica & Russell, Jason. A Little Radical: The ABCs of Activism. Russell, Danica, illus. 2017. (ENG., Illus.). 60p. (J). 20.00 *(978-0-692-82451-1(0))* Broomstick Engine LLC.

Santos, Rita. Zoom in on Making Decisions As a Group, 1 vol. 2018. (Zoom in on Civic Virtues Ser.). (ENG.). 24p. (gr. 2-2). 25.60 *(978-0-7660-9775-9(7)*, 3fb67cf1-598a-49d6-b6d8-55262d920388) Enslow Publishing, LLC.

Santos, Rita, ed. The Deep State, 1 vol. 2018. (At Issue Ser.). (ENG.). 128p. (gr. 10-12). pap. 28.80 *(978-1-5345-0320-5(X)*, 39371ff8-108e-4ffb-8028-6eed7195ab3f, Greenhaven Publishing) Greenhaven Publishing LLC.

Saxena, Shalini, ed. Dictatorship, Fascism, & Totalitarianism, 1 vol. 2014. (Political & Economic Systems Ser.). (ENG.). 192p. (YA). (gr. 10-10). 47.59 *(978-1-62275-350-5(X)*, 453bdf07-61a4-41c0-8e04-5f8bc94f07ed) Rosen Publishing Group, Inc., The.

Silva, Sadie. What Does the Mayor Do? Understanding Government, 1 vol. 2018. (Civics for the Real World Ser.). (ENG.). 12p. (gr. 1-2). pap. *(978-1-5383-6424-6(7)*, e16c6063-6035-47cf-b78c-6bf056a512f7, Rosen Classroom) Rosen Publishing Group, Inc., The.

Steele, Philip. Epic!: Empires. 2019. (Epic! Ser.). (ENG., Illus.). 32p. (J). (gr. 5-7). pap. 11.99 *(978-0-7502-9732-5(8)*, Wayland) Hachette Children's Group GBR. Dist: Hachette Bk. Group.

Stefoff, Rebecca. Monarchy, 1 vol. 2008. (Political Systems of the World Ser.). (ENG., Illus.). 160p. (YA). (gr. 8-8). lib. bdg. 45.50 *(978-0-7614-2630-1(2)*, 4a59bcca-88a5-4935-bbc4-4a29f2d8318f) Cavendish Square Publishing LLC.

Strand, Jennifer. Legendary Leaders, 6 vols. 2016. (Legendary Leaders Ser.). (ENG.). 24p. (J). (gr. -1-2). 299.64 *(978-1-68079-401-4(9)*, 23022, Abdo Zoom-Launch) ABDO Publishing Co.

Systems of Government, 4 vols. 2005. (Systems of Government Ser.). (ENG.). 48p. (gr. 6-8). lib. bdg. 67.34 *(978-0-8368-5881-5(6)*, b68b7357-0752-407c-b45a-5f9887296beb, Gareth Stevens Secondary Library) Stevens, Gareth Publishing LLLP.

Tears of a Tiger: Activity Pack. 2003. 165p. (YA). pap. *(978-1-58049-629-2(6)*, PA6296) Prestwick Hse., Inc.

Thomas Paine's Common Sense. 2013. (Documents That Shaped America Ser.). 32p. (J). (gr. 4-6). pap. 63.00 *(978-1-4339-9015-1(6))* Stevens, Gareth Publishing LLLP.

Turner, Joshua. How Rules & Laws Change Society, 1 vol. 2018. (Civic Virtue: Let's Work Together Ser.). (ENG.). 24p. (gr. 3-3). 25.27 *(978-1-5081-6675-7(7)*, 2cf1cd33-43e8-455e-bdd0-f4ba09cd7d6f, PowerKids Pr.) Rosen Publishing Group, Inc., The.

—How to Identify Core Civic Virtues, 1 vol. 2018. (Civic Virtue: Let's Work Together Ser.). (ENG.). 24p. (gr. 3-3). 25.27 *(978-1-5081-6679-5(X)*, 0f0adba9-2e4f-4dea-abf0-24b994aed622, PowerKids Pr.) Rosen Publishing Group, Inc., The.

—How to Make Decisions As a Group, 1 vol. 2018. (Civic Virtue: Let's Work Together Ser.). (ENG.). 24p. (gr. 3-3). 25.27 *(978-1-5081-6683-2(8)*, fdcb68eb-7d6f-487c-815e-a32239a22313, PowerKids Pr.) Rosen Publishing Group, Inc., The.

—How to Promote the Common Good, 1 vol. 2018. (Civic Virtue: Let's Work Together Ser.). (ENG.). 24p. (J). (gr. 3-3). 25.27 *(978-1-5081-6686-3(2)*, bc9a5c61-104f-42bb-be26-44ea63a683a2, PowerKids Pr.) Rosen Publishing Group, Inc., The.

—How to Take Informed Action, 1 vol. 2018. (Civic Virtue: Let's Work Together Ser.). (ENG.). 24p. (gr. 3-3). 25.27 *(978-1-5081-6690-0(0)*, 88c4f836-3c58-46eb-8987-c86a7a7e578e, PowerKids Pr.) Rosen Publishing Group, Inc., The.

—What Is Respect?, 1 vol. 2019. (Principles of Democracy Ser.). (ENG.). 24p. (gr. 3-3). pap. 9.25 *(978-1-5383-4284-8(7)*, 20666ec8-59f9-499e-bf7e-2878366d6340, PowerKids Pr.) Rosen Publishing Group, Inc., The.

Turning Points in History, 8 vols., Set. Incl. Britannica Guide to Explorers & Explorations That Changed the Modern World. Pletcher, Kenneth. 352p. lib. bdg. 48.59 *(978-1-61530-028-0(7)*, 79cb531e-1d74-4c92-b4ad-ad724030f85f); Britannica Guide to Inventions That Changed the Modern World. Curley, Robert, ed. 392p. lib. bdg. 48.59 *(978-1-61530-020-4(1)*, bba4d0b9-7e2d-4177-831f-805bf7bf43f6); (YA). (gr. 10-10). (Turning Points in History Ser.). (ENG., Illus.). 392p. 2010. Set lib. bdg. 194.36 *(978-1-61530-034-1(1)*, 268cedcd-6aa1-4252-b38b-d7180145ee35) Rosen Publishing Group, Inc., The.

Uschan, Michael V. Careers If You Like Government & Politics. 2016. (ENG.). 80p. (J). (gr. 5-12). lib. bdg. *(978-1-68282-000-1(9))* ReferencePoint Pr., Inc.

Waxman, Laura Hamilton. An Uncommon Revolutionary: A Story about Thomas Paine. Orback, Craig, illus. 2003. (Creative Minds Biography Ser.). (J). pap. 5.95 *(978-1-57505-608-1(9)*, Carolrhoda Bks.) Lerner Publishing Group.

Weiss, Nancy E. Asking Questions about Political Campaigns. 2015. (21st Century Skills Library: Asking Questions about Media Ser.). (ENG., Illus.). 32p. (J). (gr. 4-8). 32.07 *(978-1-63362-490-0(0)*, 206868) Cherry Lake Publishing.

Wells, Naomi. What Happens at City Hall? Understanding Government, 1 vol. 2018. (Civics for the Real World Ser.). (ENG.). 12p. (gr. 1-2). pap. *(978-1-5383-6436-9(0)*, b0ad6c44-b46b-46d0-af86-a58ab6783925, Rosen Classroom) Rosen Publishing Group, Inc., The.

Williams, Jane A. A Bluestocking Guide - Political Philosophies: Companion Workbook to Richard J. Maybury's Are You Liberal? Conservative? or Confused? Daniels, Kathryn, ed. 2004. (Bluestocking Guide Ser.). (ENG.). 63p. (YA). pap. 12.95 *(978-0-942617-47-4(9))* Bluestocking Pr.

Young-Brown, Fiona. Edward Snowden: NSA Contractor & Whistle-Blower, 1 vol. 2018. (Hero or Villain? Claims & Counterclaims Ser.). (ENG.). 112p. (YA). (gr. 8-8). 45.93 *(978-1-5026-3538-9(0)*, 25ebc332-8bb7-4e49-ae70-a79c2bfb5760) Cavendish Square Publishing LLC.

Zschock, Martha Day. Hello Congress! 2013. (Hello! Ser.). (ENG., Illus.). 16p. (J). (gr. -1-k). bds. 9.95 *(978-1-933212-06-7(3)*, Commonwealth Editions) Applewood Bks.

POLITICIANS

see also Legislators; Presidents; Statesmen

Acker, Kerry. Gerhard Schroeder. 2003. (Major World Leaders Ser.). (ENG., Illus.). 112p. (gr. 6-12). 30.00 *(978-0-7910-7652-1(0)*, P113945, Facts On File) Infobase Holdings, Inc.

Alembi, Ezekiel. Jaramogi Oginga Odinga: People's Revolutionary. 2004. (Lion Books). (Illus.). x, 78p. (J). *(978-9966-951-24-3(5))* Sasa Sema Publications Ltd.

Aretha, David. Mitt Romney. 2012. (Illus.). 112p. (J). *(978-1-59935-344-9(X))* Reynolds, Morgan Inc.

—No Compromise: The Story of Harvey Milk. 2009. (Civil Rights Leaders Ser.). 100p. (YA). (gr. 5-9). lib. bdg. 28.95 *(978-1-59935-129-2(3))* Reynolds, Morgan Inc.

Barile, Mary Collins. J. Milton Turner; an American Hero. Guest, Peggy, illus. 2013. 52p. 24.95 *(978-0-9889643-0-3(9))* MathisJones Communications, LLC.

Barton, Chris. The Amazing Age of John Roy Lynch. Tate, Don, illus. 2015. (ENG.). 50p. (J). 17.00 *(978-0-8028-5379-0(X)*, Eerdmans Bks For Young Readers) Eerdmans, William B. Publishing Co.

Brezina, Corona. America's Political Scandals in the Late 1800s: Boss Tweed & Tammany Hall. 2009. (America's Industrial Society in the 19th Century Ser.). 32p. (gr. 4-4). 47.90 *(978-1-61511-336-1(3))* Rosen Publishing Group, Inc., The.

Buttigieg, Chasten. I Have Something to Tell You — For Young Adults: A Memoir. 2023. (ENG., Illus.). 224p. (YA). (gr. 7). 18.99 *(978-1-6659-0437-7(2)*, Atheneum Bks. for Young Readers) Simon & Schuster Children's Publishing.

Conley, Kate. Our Elected Leaders, 1 vol. 2016. (American Citizenship Ser.). (ENG., Illus.). 48p. (J). (gr. 4-8). lib. bdg. 35.64 *(978-1-68078-243-1(6)*, 22087) ABDO Publishing Co.

Coy, Cissie. Dennis Chávez: The First Hispanic US Senator / Dennis Chávez: el Primer Senador Hispano de Los Estados Unidos. 2017. (SPA & ENG., Illus.). 64p. (J). (gr. 4-8). pap. 9.95 *(978-1-55885-852-7(0)*, Piñata Books) Arte Publico Pr.

Cullerton Johnson, Jen. Seeds of Change: Wangari's Gift to the World, 1 vol. Sadler, Sonia Lynn, illus. 2013. (ENG.). 32p. (J). (gr. 1-6). 19.95 *(978-1-60060-367-9(X)*, leelowbooks) Lee & Low Bks., Inc.

Demi. Confucius: The Heart of China, 1 vol. 2018. (ENG., Illus.). 48p. (J). (gr. 3-12). 21.00 *(978-1-62014-193-9(0)*, leelowshens) Lee & Low Bks., Inc.

Doeden, Matt. Muhammad Ali: The Greatest. 2017. (Gateway Biographies Ser.). (ENG.). 48p. (J). (gr. 4-8). 12.99

(978-1-5124-4433-9(2)); 39.99 (978-1-5124-4434-6(0)); (Illus.). 31.99 (978-1-5124-4431-5(6), 27b6c0da-f8b0-485e-bf6f-de2be80949a9); (Illus.). E-Book 47.99 (978-1-5124-4432-2(4)) Lerner Publishing Group. (Lerner Pubns.).

Donohue, Caitlin. She Represents: 44 Women Who Are Changing Politics ... & the World. 2020. (ENG., Illus.). 216p. (YA). (gr. 8-12). pap. 16.99 (978-1-5415-7901-9(1), 211f4145-8df6-4719-b92d-3cba3a65ff9b, Zest Bks.) Lerner Publishing Group.

Ellis, Carol. African American Activists. 2012. (J). pap. (978-1-4222-2384-0(1)) Mason Crest.

—African American Activists. Hill, Marc Lamont, ed. 2012. (Major Black Contributions from Emancipation to Civil Rights Ser.). 64p. (J). (gr. 5). 22.95 (978-1-4222-2371-0(X)) Mason Crest.

Faulkner, Nicholas, ed. Top 101 Reformers, Revolutionaries, Activists, & Change Agents, 1 vol. 2016. (People You Should Know Ser.). (ENG.). 184p. (J). (gr. 8-8). lib. bdg. 38.84 (978-1-68048-509-7(1), 749d7355-96be-4e83-8f64-e594d02e586a) Rosen Publishing Group, Inc., The.

Favor, Lesli J. Eva Perón, 1 vol. 2011. (Leading Women Ser.). (ENG.). 96p. (YA). (gr. 7-7). 42.64 (978-0-7614-4962-1(0), 45b3cf21-59b9-44ad-a63a-82c2334b62f3) Cavendish Square Publishing LLC.

Frier, Raphaële. Malala: Activist for Girls' Education. Fronty, Aurélia, illus. 2017. 45p. (J). (978-1-63289-592-9(7)) Charlesbridge Publishing, Inc.

—Malala: Activist for Girls' Education. Fronty, Aurélia, illus. 2023. (ENG.). 48p. (J). (gr. 1-4). pap. 8.99 (978-1-58089-517-0(4)) Charlesbridge Publishing, Inc.

Ganeri, Anita. The Top Ten Leaders That Changed the World. 2009. (J). 60.00 (978-1-4358-9166-1(X), PowerKids Pr.); (ENG., Illus.). 32p. (J). (gr. 4-5). pap. 11.00 (978-1-4358-9165-4(1), 3b811668-8509-412a-9644-35bfef082751, PowerKids Pr.); (ENG., Illus.). 32p. (YA). (gr. 4-5). 30.27 (978-1-4358-9164-7(3), 2ce1f0bb-e00f-44c3-8ff3-31056aced95f) Rosen Publishing Group, Inc., The.

Grant, R. G. Superstars of History: The Good, the Bad, & the Brainy. Basher, Simon, illus. 2014. (ENG.). 96p. (J). (gr. 3-7). pap. 7.99 (978-0-545-68024-0(7), Scholastic Paperbacks) Scholastic, Inc.

Greenhaven Press Staff, ed. Mitt Romney. 2012. (People in the News Ser.). (ENG., Illus.). 128p. (gr. 7-10). lib. bdg. 33.95 (978-1-4205-0877-2(6), Lucent Bks.) Cengage Gale.

Grinapol, Corinne. Harvey Milk: Pioneering Gay Politician, 1 vol. 2014. (Remarkable LGBTQ Lives Ser.). (ENG., Illus.). 112p. (J). (gr. 7-7). 38.80 (978-1-4777-7399-9(3), baf68c2c-f448-4cc9-9914-b6fc012920ba, Rosen Young Adult) Rosen Publishing Group, Inc., The.

Hart, Joyce. Kim Jong Il: Leader of North Korea. 2009. (Newsmakers Ser.). 112p. (gr. 9-10). 63.90 (978-1-60851-133-4(2)) Rosen Publishing Group, Inc., The.

Hollander, Barbara Gottfried. Harvey Milk: The First Openly Gay Elected Official in the United States. 2017. (Spotlight on Civic Courage: Heroes of Conscience Ser.). 48p. (J). (gr. 10-15). 70.50 (978-1-5383-8093-2(5)); (ENG.). (gr. 6-6). pap. 12.75 (978-1-5383-8092-5(7), 82e9e281-3c17-4b47-ab96-0eb334981d4b) Rosen Publishing Group, Inc., The. (Rosen Young Adult).

Hughes, Chris. The Constitutional Convention. 2005. (People at the Center of Ser.). (Illus.). 48p. (J). (gr. -1-7). lib. bdg. 24.95 (978-1-56711-918-3(2), Blackbirch Pr., Inc.) Cengage Gale.

Kulling, Monica. Eliza Hamilton: Founding Mother. Fabbretti, Valerio, illus. 2018. (Step into Reading Ser.). 48p. (J). (gr. k-3). pap. 4.99 (978-1-5247-7232-1(1), Random Hse. Bks. for Young Readers) Random Hse. Children's Bks.

Leslie, Jay. Who Did It First? 50 Politicians, Activists, & Entrepreneurs Who Revolutionized the World. Hart, Alex, ed. Myers, Nneka, illus. 2020. (Who Did It First? Ser.: 2). (ENG.). 128p. (J). 18.99 (978-1-250-21172-9(7), 900203647, Holt, Henry & Co. Bks. For Young Readers) Holt, Henry & Co.

Linde, Barbara M. African Americans in Political Office: From the Civil War to the White House, 1 vol. 2017. (Lucent Library of Black History Ser.). (ENG.). 104p. (gr. 7-7). lib. bdg. 41.03 (978-1-5345-6075-8(0), a3fefef9-8027-49ac-a2a6-56a6f037d1c7, Lucent Pr.) Greenhaven Publishing LLC.

Macken, Ultan. The Story of Daniel O'Connell. 2009. (Irish Heroes for Children Ser.). (ENG., Illus.). 128p. (J). 17.95 (978-1-85635-596-4(9)) Mercier Pr., Ltd., The IRL. Dist: Dufour Editions, Inc.

Main, Mary & Thomason, Cathy. African-Americans in Law & Politics. 2012. (J). pap. (978-1-4222-2391-8(4)) Mason Crest.

—African-Americans in Law & Politics. Hill, Marc Lamont, ed. 2012. (Major Black Contributions from Emancipation to Civil Rights Ser.). 64p. (J). (gr. 5). 22.95 (978-1-4222-2378-9(7)) Mason Crest.

Malaspina, Ann. Nelson Mandela: Fighting to Dismantle Apartheid, 1 vol. 2017. (Rebels with a Cause Ser.). (ENG.). 128p. (YA). (gr. 8-8). lib. bdg. 38.93 (978-0-7660-8517-6(1), 0b4489f0-6cb5-4f8d-9265-b48760337c0e) Enslow Publishing, LLC.

Mapua, Jeff. Hillary Clinton, 1 vol. 2014. (Britannica Beginner Bios Ser.). (ENG., Illus.). 32p. (J). (gr. 2-3). 26.06 (978-1-62275-689-6(4), c6a1ac5c-edfc-4d9f-8b71-fe87854a49f1, Britannica Educational Publishing) Rosen Publishing Group, Inc., The.

Marsh, Carole. John Kerry: Successful Senator & 2004 Presidential Candidate. 2004. (J). 24p. pap. 5.95 (978-0-635-02537-1(X)); 24.95 (978-0-635-02542-5(6)) Gallopade International.

—Samuel Adams. 2003. 12p. (gr. k-4). 2.95 (978-0-635-02367-4(9)) Gallopade International.

McCabe, Matthew. 12 Political Leaders Who Changed the World. 2016. (Change Makers Ser.). (ENG., Illus.). 32p. (J). (gr. 3-6). 32.80 (978-1-63235-148-7(X), 11938, 12-Story Library) Bookstaves, LLC.

McCartin, Brian. Thomas Paine: Common Sense, & Revolutionary Pamphleteering. 2009. (Library of American Lives & Times Ser.). 112p. (gr. 5-5). 69.20 (978-1-60853-509-5(6)) Rosen Publishing Group, Inc., The.

McElroy, Lisa Tucker. Alberto Gonzales: Attorney General. 2006. (Gateway Biographies Ser.). (Illus.). 48p. (J). (gr. 4-8). lib. bdg. 23.93 (978-0-8225-3418-1(5)) Lerner Publishing Group.

Miller, Debra A., ed. Women in Politics, 1 vol. 2012. (Current Controversies Ser.). (ENG.). 168p. (gr. 10-12). pap. 33.00 (978-0-7377-6250-1(0), 0d6dc3f5-914a-46b7-b56b-495cf13532e8); lib. bdg. 48.03 (978-0-7377-6249-5(7), bfff8edf-097c-45bb-9133-1ebe9a2a4a7b) Greenhaven Publishing LLC. (Greenhaven Publishing).

Mis, Melody S. Meet Al Sharpton. (Civil Rights Leaders Ser.). 24p. (gr. 2-3). 2009. 42.50 (978-1-61511-850-2(0), PowerKids Pr.) 2007. (ENG., Illus.). (YA). lib. bdg. 26.27 (978-1-4042-4213-5(9), 98a6ed84-b3cf-4724-8502-4b7661d70999) Rosen Publishing Group, Inc., The.

Moritz, Rachel. Julian Assange: Founder of WikiLeaks. 2017. (Newsmakers Set 2 Ser.). (ENG., Illus.). 48p. (J). (gr. 4-8). lib. bdg. 35.64 (978-1-5321-1179-2(7), 25934) ABDO Publishing Co.

Ni Dheirg, Iosold. The Story of Michael Collins. 2009. (Irish Heroes for Children Ser.). (ENG.). 123p. (J). 17.95 (978-1-85635-595-7(0)) Mercier Pr., Ltd., The IRL. Dist: Dufour Editions, Inc.

Nichols, Susan. Famous Immigrant Politicians, 1 vol. 2017. (Making America Great: Immigrant Success Stories Ser.). (ENG.). 112p. (gr. 7-7). 38.93 (978-0-7660-9242-6(9), ee579d74-0ecd-42ba-8a74-c5ee8cdf1b9e); pap. 20.95 (978-0-7660-9588-5(6), a5050563-b210-405d-b14e-a8d3cc810d73) Enslow Publishing, LLC.

Paulus, Rajdeep. The Most Influential Women in Politics, 1 vol. 2018. (Breaking the Glass Ceiling: the Most Influential Women Ser.). (ENG.). 112p. (gr. 8-8). 40.13 (978-1-5081-7968-9(9), 84b1d5fc-6861-43a5-9eed-63eddbecb077) Rosen Publishing Group, Inc., The.

Perkins, Anne. Trailblazers in Politics, 1 vol. 2014. (Original Thinkers Ser.). (ENG.). 136p. (J). (gr. 10-10). 44.13 (978-1-4777-8144-9(7), 0a1208f6-b1e5-4601-b5f8-153924d3d07b, Rosen Young Adult) Rosen Publishing Group, Inc., The.

Rajczak Nelson, Kristen. Who Do People Vote For?, 1 vol. 2018. (Why Voting Matters Ser.). (ENG.). 24p. (gr. 2-2). 25.27 (978-1-5383-3019-7(9), 543efb7e-cae9-4e3c-b868-497234cdac7f, PowerKids Pr.) Rosen Publishing Group, Inc., The.

Rebels with a Cause: Set 1, 16 vols. 2017. (Rebels with a Cause Ser.). (ENG.). 128p. (gr. 8-8). lib. bdg. 311.44 (978-0-7660-8574-9(0), 2bde8acc-8828-4a99-ace5-fc3cf7f721ad9) Enslow Publishing, LLC.

Sakany, Lois. Progressive Leaders: The Platforms & Policies of America's Reform Politicians. (Progressive Movement 1900-1920: Efforts to Reform America's New Industrial Society Ser.). 32p. (gr. 3-4). 2009. 47.90 (978-1-60854-168-3(1)) 2006. (ENG., Illus.). (YA). lib. bdg. 30.47 (978-1-4042-0193-4(9), 440d7278-674c-4b79-8c8c-36efba421ac9) Rosen Publishing Group, Inc., The.

Sanders, Rob. Pride: the Story of Harvey Milk & the Rainbow Flag. Salerno, Steven, illus. 2018. (ENG.). 48p. (J). (gr. k-3). 18.99 (978-0-399-55531-2(5), Random Hse. Bks. for Young Readers) Random Hse. Children's Bks.

Sanna, Ellyn. Politician. 2004. (Careers with Character Ser.). (Illus.). 96p. (YA). (gr. 7-18). lib. bdg. 22.95 (978-1-59084-320-8(7)) Mason Crest.

Schlesinger, Arthur M., ed. Recep Tayyip Erdogan. 2005. (Major World Leaders Ser.). (ENG., Illus.). 144p. (gr. 6-12). 30.00 (978-0-7910-8263-8(6), P114247, Facts On File) Infobase Holdings, Inc.

Small, Cathleen. Chelsea Manning: Intelligence Analyst, 1 vol. 2018. (Hero or Villain? Claims & Counterclaims Ser.). (ENG.). 112p. (YA). (gr. 8-8). lib. bdg. 45.93 (978-1-5026-3535-8(6), 4ec726a6-867b-419e-8e9f-3bea2012cdb3) Cavendish Square Publishing LLC.

Southwell, David. Unsolved Political Mysteries. 2009. (Mysteries & Conspiracies Ser.). 80p. (gr. 10-10). 61.20 (978-1-61514-747-2(0)) Rosen Publishing Group, Inc., The.

Southwell, David & Twist, Sean. Unsolved Political Mysteries, 1 vol. 2007. (Mysteries & Conspiracies Ser.). (ENG., Illus.). 80p. (YA). (gr. 10-10). lib. bdg. 38.47 (978-1-4042-1083-7(0), 22459ed0-c097-42d8-b4df-4471a5b1fe0b) Rosen Publishing Group, Inc., The.

Sturgis, James. Adam Beck, 1 vol. 2003. (Canadians Ser.). (ENG., Illus.). 64p. (J). (gr. 5-8). pap. 6.95 (978-1-55041-828-6(9), 4fa64a35-435a-418d-83aa-1446b547a2f6) Trifolium Bks., Inc. CAN. Dist: Firefly Bks., Ltd.

Sutherland, Adam. Political Leaders, 1 vol. 2012. (Black History Makers Ser.). (ENG., Illus.). 24p. (J). (gr. 4-4). pap. 9.25 (978-1-4488-7056-1(9), 90401ddd-546c-4862-99c1-7cfbf2dece50); lib. bdg. 26.27 (978-1-4488-6639-7(1), ffa2e0af-f5fb-44fc-a2b6-f4bd02d26a81) Rosen Publishing Group, Inc., The. (PowerKids Pr.).

Sutoski, Jennifer. Stephen Harper. 2015. (Canadian Biographies Ser.). (ENG., Illus.). 24p. (J). (gr. -1-2). lib. bdg. 27.32 (978-1-4914-7833-2(0), 130182, Capstone Pr.) Capstone.

Tukan, Jaytoe Anthony, Sr. John Reid Edwards: The People's Senator. 2003. per. 19.95 (978-0-9665909-4-4(5)) Kalawantis Publishing Services, Inc.

Winter, Jeanette. Wangari's Trees of Peace: A True Story from Africa. Winter, Jeanette, illus. (ENG., Illus.). 32p. (J). (gr. -1-3). 2018. pap. 8.99 (978-1-328-86921-0(0), 1696685) 2008. 17.99 (978-0-15-206545-4(8), 1199505) HarperCollins Pubs. (Clarion Bks.).

Worth, Richard. Pervez Musharraf. 2nd rev. ed. 2007. (Modern World Leaders Ser.). (ENG., Illus.). 104p. (gr. 7-12). lib. bdg. 30.00 (978-0-7910-9264-4(X), P124699, Facts On File) Infobase Holdings, Inc.

Wright, David K. The Life of Paul Robeson: Actor, Singer, Political Activist, 1 vol. 2014. (Legendary African Americans Ser.). (ENG.). 96p. (gr. 6-7). 31.61 (978-0-7660-6157-6(4), 6f8e9895-253b-47ce-b998-cc41b66e00f4) Enslow Publishing, LLC.

Wyborny, Sheila. Kim Jong Il, 1 vol. 2009. (People in the News Ser.). (ENG., Illus.). 104p. (gr. 7-7). lib. bdg. 41.03 (978-1-4205-0091-2(0), bce6fd4e-5a78-42b1-8c19-1ce498c0d927, Lucent Pr.) Greenhaven Publishing LLC.

Yasuda, Anita. Political Leaders. 2010. (Illus.). 48p. (978-1-55388-691-4(7)); pap. (978-1-55388-696-9(8)) Weigl Educational Pubs. Ltd.

POLITICIANS—FICTION

Calloway, Cassidy. Secrets of a First Daughter. 2010. (ENG.). 208p. (YA). (gr. 8-18). pap. 8.99 (978-0-06-172442-8(4), HarperTeen) HarperCollins Pubs.

Fine, Sarah. Beneath the Shine. 2017. (ENG.). 304p. (YA). (gr. 10-13). pap. 9.99 (978-1-4778-2327-9(1), 9781477823279, Skyscape) Amazon Publishing.

Grainger, A. J. Captive. 2016. (ENG.). 272p. (YA). (gr. 7). pap. 11.99 (978-1-4814-2904-7(3)) Simon & Schuster Children's Publishing.

Lavonne, Victoria. Twas the Night at the Capitol: A Narrative Featuring the First African American Family. 2012. 28p. pap. 24.95 (978-1-4626-9799-1(2)) America Star Bks.

MacLean, Roddy. An Creanaiche (the Sufferer), 1 vol. 2021. (Lasag Ser.). (ENG.). 90p. (YA). pap. 14.99 (978-1-910124-78-9(8)) Sandstone Pr. Ltd. GBR. Dist: Casemate Pubs. & Bk. Distributors, LLC.

Mcdonald, Megan. Stink. 2013. (Stink Ser.: 1). lib. bdg. 14.75 (978-0-606-31587-6(X)) Turtleback.

Tashjian, Janet. Larry & the Meaning of Life. 2014. (Larry Ser.: 3). (ENG., Illus.). 240p. (YA). (gr. 7-12). pap. 15.99 (978-1-250-05035-9(9), 900133985) Square Fish.

Wilson, Mark A. The Old Man's Secret Friend, 1 vol. 2009. 19p. pap. 19.95 (978-1-61582-315-4(8)) PublishAmerica, Inc.

POLITICS, PRACTICAL

see also Elections; Lobbying; Television in Politics

Banigan, Melissa. Developing a Strategy for a Political Campaign, 1 vol. 2019. (Be the Change! Political Participation in Your Community Ser.). (ENG.). 64p. (gr. 7-7). pap. 13.95 (978-1-7253-4074-9(7), 971277c5-4cd4-4f87-8719-7e40caa5fdb1) Rosen Publishing Group, Inc., The.

Beyer, Mark. The Election of 1800: Congress Helps Settle a Three-Way Vote, 1 vol. 2003. (Primary Sources of Life in the New American Nation Ser.). (ENG., Illus.). 32p. (gr. 4-5). pap. 10.00 (978-0-8239-4255-8(4), fe1b84cf-fcb7-471d-8dbe-062a4f707a3d) Rosen Publishing Group, Inc., The.

—The Election Of 1800: Congress Helps Settle a Three-Way Vote. 2009. (Life in the New American Nation Ser.). 32p. (gr. 4-4). 47.90 (978-1-61514-282-8(7)) Rosen Publishing Group, Inc., The.

Christelow, Eileen. Vote! Christelow, Eileen, illus. 2004. (Illus.). 48p. (J). (gr. 1-5). 47.60 (978-0-618-51723-7(5), Clarion Bks.) HarperCollins Pubs.

Donovan, Sandy. Running for Office: A Look at Political Campaigns. 2003. (How Government Works). (ENG., Illus.). 56p. (gr. 4-8). lib. bdg. 25.26 (978-0-8225-4700-6(7)) Lerner Publishing Group.

Kowalski, Kathiann M. Campaign Politics: What's Fair, What's Foul? 2005. (Pro/Con Ser.). (Illus.). 144p. (gr. 6-12). lib. bdg. 25.26 (978-0-8225-2630-8(1)) Lerner Publishing Group.

McGowen, Tom. The 1968 Democratic Convention. 2003. (Cornerstones of Freedom Ser.). (ENG., Illus.). 48p. (YA). (gr. 4-7). 26.00 (978-0-516-24220-0(2)) Scholastic Library Publishing.

Penguin Young Readers. The Little Book of Little Activists. 2017. (Illus.). 48p. (J). (gr. k-4). 10.99 (978-0-451-47854-2(1), Viking Books for Young Readers) Penguin Young Readers Group.

Shetterly, Robert. Americans Who Tell the Truth. 2008. (Illus.). 46p. (gr. 4-6). 18.00 (978-0-7569-8912-5(4)) Perfection Learning Corp.

World Leaders Set, vols. 8, vol. 8. Incl. Adolf Hitler & Nazi Germany. Rice, Earle. (Illus.). 176p. (J). (gr. 3-7). 2006. lib. bdg. 28.95 (978-1-931798-78-5(8)); Alexander the Great: Conqueror of the Known World. Nardo, Don. (Illus.). 100p. (J). 2009. 28.95 (978-1-59935-126-1(9)); Che Guevara: In Search of Revolution. Miller, Calvin Craig. (Illus.). 192p. (J). (gr. 6-12). 2006. lib. bdg. 26.95 (978-1-931798-93-8(1)); Cleopatra: Ruler of Egypt. (Illus.). 176p. (gr. 6-12). 2007. lib. bdg. 27.95 (978-1-59935-035-6(1)); Empire in the East: The Story of Genghis Khan. Rice, Earle, Jr. (Illus.). 160p. (J). (gr. 3-7). 2005. 28.95 (978-1-931798-62-4(1)); Fidel Castro & the Cuban Revolution. Naden, Corinne J. & Blue, Rose. (Illus.). 144p. (J). (gr. 3-7). 2006. lib. bdg. 27.95 (978-1-59935-029-5(7)); Fighting Wars, Planning for Peace: The Story of George C. Marshall. Gimpel, Lee. (Illus.). 176p. (J). (gr. 6-12). 2005. lib. bdg. 26.95 (978-1-931798-66-2(4)); Hugo Chavez: Leader of Venezuela. (Illus.). 128p. 2007. lib. bdg. 27.95 (978-1-59935-068-4(8)); Joseph Stalin & the Soviet Union. (Illus.). 208p. (J). (gr. 6-12). 2006. lib. bdg. 26.95 (978-1-931798-94-5(X)); Mao Zedong & the Chinese Revolution. Naden, Corinne J. 144p. (YA). (gr. 6-9). 2008. lib. bdg. 28.95 (978-1-59935-100-1(5)); Velvet Revolution: Vaclav Havel & the Fall of Communism. Duberstein, John. (Illus.). 160p. (gr. 6-12). 2006. lib. bdg. 28.95 (978-1-931798-85-3(0)); Woodrow Wilson & the Progressive Era. Lukes, Bonnie L. (Illus.). 192p. (J). (gr. 6-10). 2006. lib. bdg. 26.95 (978-1-931798-79-2(6)); 2009. Set lib. bdg. 247.60 (978-1-59935-013-4(0)) Reynolds, Morgan Inc.

POLITICS, PRACTICAL—FICTION

Alberto, Daisy. Pete for President! Sims, Blanche, illus. 2004. (Social Studies Connects Ser.). 32p. (J). (gr. 1-3). pap. 5.99 (978-1-57565-142-2(4), b2d5eed8-13d1-4a23-936c-a290da5684c3, Kane Press) Astra Publishing Hse.

Baratz-Logsted, Lauren. Red Girl, Blue Boy: An If Only Novel. 2015. (If Only... Ser.). (ENG.). 304p. (YA). (gr. 7). pap. 9.99 (978-1-61963-685-9(9), 900145469, Bloomsbury USA Childrens) Bloomsbury Publishing USA.

Barnes, Peter W. & Barnes, Cheryl Shaw. Woodrow for President: A Tail of Voting, Campaigns, & Elections. 2012. (ENG.). 32p. (J). (gr. k-3). 18.99 (978-1-59698-786-9(3)) Regnery Publishing.

Barshaw, Ruth McNally. The Ellie Mcdoodle Diaries: Ellie for President. 2014. (Ellie Mcdoodle Ser.). (ENG., Illus.). 176p. (YA). (gr. 3-6). 13.99 (978-1-61963-061-1(3), 900118520, Bloomsbury USA Childrens) Bloomsbury Publishing USA.

Bateman, Anya. The Makeover of James Orville Wickenbee. 2007. 262p. (J). pap. (978-1-59038-707-8(4)) Deseret Bk. Co.

Benton, Jim. The Frandidate. Benton, Jim, illus. 2009. (Franny K. Stein, Mad Scientist Ser.: 7). (ENG., Illus.). 112p. (J). (gr. 2-5). pap. 6.99 (978-1-4169-0234-8(1), Simon & Schuster Bks. For Young Readers) Simon & Schuster Bks. For Young Readers.

—The Frandidate. Benton, Jim, illus. 2011. (Franny K. Stein, Mad Scientist Ser.). (ENG., Illus.). 128p. (J). (gr. 2-6). 31.36 (978-1-59961-823-4(0), 7833, Chapter Bks.) Spotlight.

Bransford, Nathan. Jacob Wonderbar for President of the Universe, 2 vols., 2. 2013. (Jacob Wonderbar Ser.: 2). (ENG.). 224p. (J). (gr. 4-6). 22.44 (978-0-8037-3538-5(3), Dial) Penguin Publishing Group.

Bruel, Nick. Bad Kitty for President. 2012. (Bad Kitty Chapter Bks.). (J). lib. bdg. 17.20 (978-0-606-26568-3(6)) Turtleback.

—Bad Kitty for President (paperback Black-And-white Edition) 2012. (Bad Kitty Ser.). (ENG., Illus.). 160p. (J). (gr. 2-5). pap. 6.99 (978-1-250-01016-2(0), 900084753) Square Fish.

Calonita, Jen. Belles. 2012. (Belles Ser.: 1). (ENG.). 384p. (YA). (gr. 7-17). pap. 19.99 (978-0-316-09112-1(X), Poppy) Little, Brown Bks. for Young Readers.

Collard, Sneed B., III. The Governor's Dog Is Missing. 2011. (Slate Stephens Mysteries Ser.). 176p. (J). (gr. 4-6). 16.00 (978-0-9844460-1-8(X)) Bucking Horse Bks.

Cronin, Doreen. Duck for President. Lewin, Betsy, illus. 2004. (Click Clack Book Ser.). (ENG.). 32p. (J). (gr. -1-3). 19.99 (978-0-689-86377-6(2), Atheneum Bks. for Young Readers) Simon & Schuster Children's Publishing.

—Duck for President. Lewin, Betsy, illus. 2006. (Doreen Cronin: Click-Clack & More Ser.). (ENG.). 32p. (J). (gr. k-5). lib. bdg. 31.36 (978-1-59961-091-7(4), 5419, Picture Bk.) Spotlight.

—Pato para Presidente. Lewin, Betsy, illus. 2008.Tr. of Duck for President. (SPA.). (J). (gr. k-2). pap. 7.99 (978-1-930332-74-4(2), LC32509) Lectorum Pubns., Inc.

Czajak, Paul. Monster Needs Your Vote. Grieb, Wendy, illus. 2015. (Monster & Me Ser.). (ENG.). 32p. (J). (gr. -1-3). 16.95 (978-1-938063-63-3(5), Mighty Media Kids) Mighty Media Pr.

Doctorow, Cory. Homeland. 2014. (Little Brother Ser.: 2). (ENG.). 448p. (YA). (gr. 8). pap. 19.99 (978-0-7653-3370-4(8), 900086721, Tor Teen) Doherty, Tom Assocs., LLC.

—Homeland. 2014. (YA). lib. bdg. 24.50 (978-0-606-38513-8(4)) Turtleback.

Feiffer, Kate. President Pennybaker. Goode, Diane, illus. 2008. (ENG.). 32p. (J). (gr. -1-3). 16.99 (978-1-4169-1354-2(8)) Simon & Schuster, Inc.

—President Pennybaker. Goode, Diane, illus. 2012. (ENG.). 32p. (J). (gr. -1-3). 7.99 (978-1-4169-1355-9(6), Simon & Schuster/Paula Wiseman Bks.) Simon & Schuster/Paula Wiseman Bks.

FitzGerald, Dawn. Soccer Chick Rules. 2007. (ENG.). 160p. (J). (gr. 5-9). per. 16.99 (978-0-312-37662-8(6), 900048593) Square Fish.

Freeman, Martha. Fourth-Grade Weirdo. 2004. (Illus.). 147p. (gr. 4-7). 15.50 (978-0-7569-4117-8(2)) Perfection Learning Corp.

Giunta, Brian. The Seven Presidents. Chapin, Patrick O., illus. I.t. ed. 2003. 24p. (J). 8.95 (978-1-58597-172-5(3)) Leathers Publishing.

Gutman, Dan. The Kid Who Ran for President. 2012. (gr. 3-6). 17.20 (978-0-613-03562-0(3)) Turtleback.

Hale, Bruce. The Possum Always Rings Twice. Hale, Bruce, illus. 2007. (Chet Gecko Ser.: 11). (ENG., Illus.). 128p. (J). (gr. 3-7). pap. 7.99 (978-0-15-205233-1(X), 1195769, Clarion Bks.) HarperCollins Pubs.

Hall, Kirsten. Vote for Me: All about Civics. Luedecke, Bev, illus. 2003. (Beastieville Ser.). 32p. (J). 19.50 (978-0-516-22897-6(8), Children's Pr.) Scholastic Library Publishing.

Hall, Teri. The Line. 2011. 224p. (J). (gr. 7-12). 21.19 (978-0-8037-3466-1(2)) Penguin Young Readers Group.

Holm, Jennifer L. & Holm, Matthew. Babymouse #16: Babymouse for President. Holm, Jennifer L. & Holm, Matthew, illus. 2012. (Babymouse Ser.: 16). (ENG., Illus.). 96p. (J). (gr. 2-5). pap. 7.99 (978-0-375-86780-4(5)) Penguin Random Hse. LLC.

Kirby, Stan. Captain Awesome for President. O'Connor, George, illus. 2018. (Captain Awesome Ser.: 20). (ENG.). 128p. (J). (gr. k-4). 17.99 (978-1-5344-2084-7(3)); pap. 5.99 (978-1-5344-2083-0(5)) Little Simon. (Little Simon).

Levithan, David. Wide Awake. 2008. (ENG.). 240p. (YA). (gr. 9). pap. 11.99 (978-0-375-83467-7(2), Knopf Bks. for Young Readers) Random Hse. Children's Bks.

Lieb, Josh. I Am a Genius of Unspeakable Evil & I Want to Be Your Class President. 2010. (J). (ENG.). 272p. (gr. 7-12). 24.94 (978-1-59514-240-5(1)); 304p. (gr. 5-7). 9.99 (978-1-59514-354-9(8)) Penguin Young Readers Group. (Razorbill).

Lupica, Mike. Hero. 2011. (ENG.). 304p. (J). (gr. 5-18). 8.99 (978-0-14-241960-1(5), Puffin Books) Penguin Young Readers Group.

Lyons, Kelly Starling. Class Act #2. Brantley-Newton, Vanessa, illus. 2017. (Jada Jones Ser.: 2). 96p. (J). (gr. 1-3). (ENG.). 6.99 (978-0-451-53427-9(1)); lib. bdg. 15.99 (978-0-451-53428-6(X)) Penguin Young Readers Group. (Penguin Workshop).

Meek, Nora. Sniffing for Democracy. 2004. (J). per. (978-0-9753852-0-3(8)) PM, INK.

Monroe, Ella. Truth or Dare: A Capital Girls Novel. 2013. (Capital Girls Ser.: 3). (ENG.). 304p. (YA). (gr. 8). pap. 20.99 (978-0-312-62304-3(6), 900076855, St. Martin's Griffin) St. Martin's Pr.

Moolenschot, Catherine. A Rough Road. 2008. (ENG.). 142p. pap. 17.96 (978-1-4092-4153-9(X)) Lulu Pr., Inc.

Morgenroth, Kate. Jude. 2006. (ENG., Illus.). 288p. (YA). (gr. 7-12). reprint ed. mass mkt. 8.99 (978-1-4169-1267-5(3), Simon Pulse) Simon Pulse.

Ogden, Charles. Hot Air. Carton, Rick, illus. 2008. (Edgar & Ellen Nodyssey Ser.: 1). (ENG.). 192p. (J). (gr. 3-7). 9.99

(978-1-4169-5465-1(1), Aladdin) Simon & Schuster Children's Publishing.

Parish, Herman. Amelia Bedelia's First Vote. Avril, Lynne, illus. 2012. (Amelia Bedelia Ser.). (ENG.). 32p. (J). (gr. -1-3). 16.99 (978-0-06-209405-6(X), Greenwillow Bks.) HarperCollins Pubs.

Paulsen, Gary. Vote. 2014. (Liar Liar Ser.). (ENG.). 144p. (J). (gr. 4-7). pap. 7.99 (978-0-385-74229-0(0), Yearling) Random Hse. Children's Bks.

Pollock, Hal. Monster for President. Parisi, Anthony, illus. 2008. 28p. 14.95 (978-0-9816554-1-3(6)) Esquire Publishing, Inc.

Press, J. Double Trouble #2, 2. Kline, Michael, illus. 2013. (Doodles of Sam Dibble Ser.: 2). (ENG.). 128p. (J). (gr. 1-3). 17.44 (978-0-448-46108-3(0)) Penguin Young Readers Group.

Salvatierra, Dante. The Latchkey Kids & the Escape from California. 2008. 260p. pap. 14.50 (978-1-4357-0876-1(8)) Lulu Pr., Inc.

Sommer, Carl. Mayor for a Day. 2003. (Another Sommer-Time Story Ser.). (Illus.). 48p. (J). (gr. 1-4). 16.95 incl. audio (978-1-57537-562-5(1)) Advance Publishing, Inc.

—Mayor for a Day. Westbrook, Dick, illus. 2003. (Another Sommer-Time Story Ser.). (ENG.). 48p. (J). (gr. k-4). lib. bdg. 23.95 incl. audio compact disk (978-1-57537-713-1(6)); (gr. 1-4). 16.95 incl. audio compact disk (978-1-57537-513-7(3)) Advance Publishing, Inc.

Sotomayor, Sonia. Just Help! How to Build a Better World. Dominguez, Angela, illus. 2022. 32p. (J). (gr. -1-3). 17.99 (978-0-593-20626-3(6), Philomel Bks.) Penguin Young Readers Group.

Tashjian, Janet. Vote for Larry. 2008. (Larry Ser.: 2). (ENG.). 256p. (YA). (gr. 7-12). pap. 14.99 (978-0-312-38446-3(7), 900053432) Square Fish.

Truss, Jan. A Very Small Rebellion, 1 vol. 2005. (ENG.). 160p. (J). (gr. 4-7). pap. 7.95 (978-1-55041-930-6(7), 9a078287-72ad-4fc2-8b4a-61f5c2c54d2b) Trifolium Bks., Inc. CAN. Dist: Firefly Bks., Ltd.

Weissman, Elissa Brent. Standing for Socks. 2010. (ENG., Illus.). 224p. (J). (gr. 3-7). pap. 6.99 (978-1-4169-9777-1(6), Atheneum Bks. for Young Readers) Simon & Schuster Children's Publishing.

—Standing for Socks. Sonkin, Jessica, illus. 2009. (ENG.). 224p. (J). (gr. 3-7). 15.99 (978-1-4169-4801-8(5), Atheneum Bks. for Young Readers) Simon & Schuster Children's Publishing.

Wells, Rosemary. Otto Runs for President. Wells, Rosemary, illus. 2011. (Illus.). (J). (gr. -1-4). 29.95 (978-0-545-10690-0(7)) Weston Woods Studios, Inc.

Weston Woods Staff, creator. Duck for President. 2004. 29.95 (978-0-7882-0540-8(4)) Weston Woods Studios, Inc.

—Otto Runs for President. 2011. 18.95 (978-0-545-31400-8(3)); 38.75 (978-0-545-31401-5(1)) Weston Woods Studios, Inc.

POLK, JAMES K. (JAMES KNOX), 1795-1849

Bailey, Diane & Nash, Philip. James K. Polk: The 11th President. 2016. (First Look at America's Presidents Ser.). (ENG., Illus.). 24p. (J). (gr. -1-3). 26.99 (978-1-944102-66-1(3)) Bearport Publishing Co., Inc.

Behrman, Carol H. James K. Polk. 2005. (Presidential Leaders Ser.). (ENG., Illus.). 112p. (gr. 6-12). lib. bdg. 29.27 (978-0-8225-1396-4(X)) Lerner Publishing Group.

Mis, Melody S. How to Draw the Life & Times of James K. Polk. (Kid's Guide to Drawing the Presidents of the United States of America Ser.). 32p. (gr. 4-4). 2009. 50.50 (978-1-61511-147-3(6), PowerKids Pr.) 2005. (ENG.). (YA). 30.27 (978-1-4042-2988-4(4), 32d91457-792d-434a-b46f-3f83ffa4adcb) Rosen Publishing Group, Inc., The.

Rumsch, BreAnn. James K. Polk, 1 vol. 2016. (United States Presidents *2017 Ser.). (ENG., Illus.). 40p. (J). (gr. 2-5). lib. bdg. 35.64 (978-1-68078-113-7(8), 21843, Big Buddy Bks.) ABDO Publishing Co.

Venezia, Mike. James K. Polk: Eleventh President, 1845-1849. Venezia, Mike, illus. 2005. (Getting to Know the U. S. Presidents Ser.). (ENG., Illus.). 32p. (J). (gr. 3-4). 28.00 (978-0-516-22616-3(9), Children's Pr.) Scholastic Library Publishing.

POLLUTION

Here are entered works on the condition resulting from the action of environmental contaminants.

see also Air—Pollution; Hazardous Wastes; Refuse and Refuse Disposal; Water—Pollution

Addison, D. R. Garbage Trucks at Work, 1 vol. 2009. (Big Trucks Ser.). (ENG., Illus.). 24p. (J). (gr. 1-1). pap. 9.25 (978-1-4358-3085-1(7), d1ce0bbc-57ef-4a37-a3c0-a07da30b143f, PowerKids Pr.) Rosen Publishing Group, Inc., The.

Bellamy, Rufus. Waste & Pollution. 2010. (Sustaining Our Environment Ser.). 48p. (J). 35.65 (978-1-60753-139-5(9)) Amicus Learning.

Bily, Cynthia A., ed. Pollution, 1 vol. 2010. (Issues That Concern You Ser.). (ENG., Illus.). 120p. (gr. 7-10). 43.63 (978-0-7377-4746-1(3), 4214f148-57f8-42da-b5c9-9b29f61b11c0, Greenhaven Publishing) Greenhaven Publishing LLC.

Boothroyd, Jennifer. Fight Pollution, Big Bird! 2020. (Go Green with Sesame Street (r) Ser.). (ENG., Illus.). 32p. (J). (gr. -1-2). lib. bdg. 27.99 (978-1-5415-7261-4(0), e06b2088-3be9-4a0e-a49a-62c2a1387e39, Lerner Pubns.) Lerner Publishing Group.

Bullard, Lisa. Go Green by Fighting Pollution. Thomas, John Wes, illus. 2018. (Go Green (Early Bird Stories (tm)) Ser.). (ENG.). 24p. (J). (gr. k-2). pap. 9.99 (978-1-5415-2713-3(5), fdcb0da1-827f-4bfb-86de-391d8431aed1); lib. bdg. 29.32 (978-1-5415-2016-5(5), 11b5a4bf-0c6d-4762-8e86-e91e08afd2b1, Lerner Pubns.) Lerner Publishing Group.

—Power up to Fight Pollution. Thomas, Wes, illus. 2011. (Planet Protectors Ser.). pap. 39.62 (978-0-7613-8655-1(6), Millbrook Pr.) Lerner Publishing Group.

—Power up to Fight Pollution. Thomas, John Wes, illus. 2011. (Cloverleaf Books (tm) — Planet Protectors Ser.). (ENG.). 24p. (J). (gr. k-2). pap. 8.99 (978-0-7613-8515-8(0), fa0ddafd-a49c-41bb-b3ba-ed63fbef8b79, Millbrook Pr.) Lerner Publishing Group.

Burton, Margie, et al. Are We Hurting the Earth? 2011. (Early Connections Ser.). (J). (978-1-61672-480-1(3)) Benchmark Education Co.

Carmichael, L. E. How Can We Reduce Agricultural Pollution? 2016. (Searchlight Books (tm) — What Can We Do about Pollution? Ser.). (ENG., Illus.). 40p. (J). (gr. 3-5). lib. bdg. 30.65 (978-1-4677-9514-2(3), c26d0447-7a3c-4e07-ac36-362010f6bcaf, Lerner Pubns.) Lerner Publishing Group.

Crelin, Bob. There Once Was a Sky Full of Stars. Ziner, Amie, illus. 2005. 36p. pap. 12.95 (978-1-931559-04-1(X)) Sky Publishing.

Dickmann, Nancy. Burning Out: Energy from Fossil Fuels. 2016. (Next Generation Energy Ser.). (ENG., Illus.). 32p. (J). (gr. 5-8). (978-0-7787-2372-1(0)) Crabtree Publishing Co.

Dorion, Christiane. Earth's Garbage Crisis, 1 vol. 2007. (What If We Do Nothing? Ser.). (ENG., Illus.). 48p. (J). (gr. 5-8). pap. 15.05 (978-0-8368-8153-0(2), d45608f7-1f16-4d4f-ac3f-e9beea4635e9); lib. bdg. 33.67 (978-0-8368-7753-3(5), 5f0a2111-63ef-4c86-b249-7f8445a04dce, Gareth Stevens Secondary Library) Stevens, Gareth Publishing LLLP.

—Pollution, 1 vol. 2009. (What If We Do Nothing? Ser.). (ENG.). 48p. (YA). (gr. 4-7). lib. bdg. 33.67 (978-1-4339-1984-8(2), fc18992a-f909-49b2-b880-a17457bf3014) Stevens, Gareth Publishing LLLP.

Dudley Gold, Susan. Clean Air & Clean Water Acts, 1 vol. 2012. (Landmark Legislation Ser.). (ENG., Illus.). 128p. (J). (gr. 8-8). 42.64 (978-1-60870-484-2(X), 84312260-e63e-4eb7-9a9d-c66ffc8fba43) Cavendish Square Publishing LLC.

Eagen, Rachel. Environmental Chemistry. 2011. (Chemtastrophe! Ser.). (ENG.). 32p. (J). (gr. 5-8). pap. (978-0-7787-5302-5(6)); lib. bdg. (978-0-7787-5285-1(2)) Crabtree Publishing Co.

Flynn, Sarah Wassner. This Book Stinks! Gross Garbage, Rotten Rubbish, & the Science of Trash. 2017. 128p. (J). (gr. 3-7). pap. 14.99 (978-1-4263-2730-8(7), National Geographic Kids) Disney Publishing Worldwide.

Friedman, Lauri S., ed. Pollution, 1 vol. 2007. (Writing the Critical Essay: an Opposing Viewpoints Guide Ser.). (ENG., Illus.). 136p. (J). (gr. 7-12). lib. bdg. 39.93 (978-0-7377-3198-9(2), 2d0a2d8f-f675-4f3a-8255-3225e1753b26, Greenhaven Publishing) Greenhaven Publishing LLC.

Galat, Joan Marie. Dark Matters: Nature's Reaction to Light Pollution, 1 vol. 2017. (ENG., Illus.). 72p. (J). (gr. 3-4). 19.95 (978-0-88995-515-8(8), 52502136-8966-4fb5-ab02-e478b9dfb46d) Trifolium Bks., Inc. CAN. Dist: Firefly Bks., Ltd.

Goldstein, Margaret J. Garbage in Space: A Space Discovery Guide. 2017. (Space Discovery Guides). (ENG., Illus.). 48p. (J). (gr. 4-6). E-Book 4.99 (978-1-5124-3806-2(5), 9781512438062); E-Book 47.99 (978-1-5124-3807-9(3), 9781512438079); E-Book 47.99 (978-1-5124-2798-1(5)) Lerner Publishing Group. (Lerner Pubns.).

Greeley, August. Poisoned Planet: Pollution in our World, 1 vol. 2008. (Planet Earth Ser.). (ENG.). 24p. (gr. 5-8). pap. 8.25 (978-1-4358-2675-5(2), 05cbe768-efd2-4153-ad8d-d4f9dedca6ad, Rosen Classroom) Rosen Publishing Group, Inc., The.

Green, Robert. Pollution. 2008. (21st Century Skills Library: Global Perspectives Ser.). (ENG., Illus.). 32p. (gr. 4-8). lib. bdg. 32.07 (978-1-60279-130-5(9), 200105) Cherry Lake Publishing.

Greenan, Amy. Constructing Towns & Cities, 1 vol. 2018. (Impacting Earth: How People Change the Land Ser.). (ENG.). 24p. (gr. 2-2). pap. 9.25 (978-1-5383-4185-8(9), d35ba34b-13a9-4090-9b8b-4845127646dd, PowerKids Pr.) Rosen Publishing Group, Inc., The.

Griffin Burns, Loree. Tracking Trash: Flotsam, Jetsam, & the Science of Ocean Motion. 2010. (Scientists in the Field Ser.). (ENG., Illus.). 64p. (J). (gr. 5-7). pap. 10.99 (978-0-547-32860-7(5), 1416942, Clarion Bks.) HarperCollins Pubs.

Hand, Carol. Dead Zones: Why Earth's Waters Are Losing Oxygen. 2016. (ENG., Illus.). 80p. (YA). (gr. 6-12). E-Book 53.32 (978-1-4677-9575-3(5), Twenty-First Century Bks.) Lerner Publishing Group.

Hansen, Amy. Fossil Fuels: Buried in the Earth, 1 vol. 2010. (Powering Our World Ser.). 24p. (J). (ENG.). (gr. 3-3). pap. 9.25 (978-1-4358-9738-0(2), edd5c2c1-666e-4dfd-9ad3-fdf870546c7b); (Illus.). 49.50 (978-1-4358-9739-7(0), 1307107) Rosen Publishing Group, Inc., The. (PowerKids Pr.).

Hansen, Amy S. Fossil Fuels: Buried in the Earth. 2010. (Powering Our World Ser.). 24p. (J). (gr. 2-5). E-Book 42.50 (978-1-4488-0195-4(8)); (ENG., Illus.). (gr. 3-3). lib. bdg. 26.27 (978-1-4358-9325-2(5), dcce9aba-c7e0-4028-96b8-7ceddd84c184, PowerKids Pr.) Rosen Publishing Group, Inc., The.

Hay, Jeff, ed. Pollution, 1 vol. 2008. (Issues on Trial Ser.). (ENG., Illus.). 176p. (J). (gr. 10-12). 49.93 (978-0-7377-4181-0(3), 223368c0-b7ef-4117-b2db-43b45437872b, Greenhaven Publishing) Greenhaven Publishing LLC.

Head, Honor. Poisoned Oceans, 1 vol. 2018. (Totally Toxic Ser.). (ENG.). 48p. (gr. 4-5). pap. 15.05 (978-1-5382-3494-5(7), b5c78486-9c4b-4b67-8c9b-c5cfa11ff3f5) Stevens, Gareth Publishing LLLP.

—Poisoned Wetlands, 1 vol. 2018. (Totally Toxic Ser.). (ENG.). 48p. (gr. 4-5). pap. 15.05 (978-1-5382-3497-6(1), ef1b4358-f6f7-4965-9c34-7d4a5c530517) Stevens, Gareth Publishing LLLP.

Holt, Rinehart and Winston Staff. Decisions for Health Blue, Chptr. 21: Health & Environment. 4th ed. 2004. pap. 11.20 (978-0-03-068057-1(3)) Holt McDougal.

Howell, Izzi. Pollution Eco Facts. 2019. (Eco Facts Ser.). (ENG., Illus.). 32p. (J). (gr. 5-5). pap. (978-0-7787-6365-9(X), b66c65b3-f1e3-4702-918c-77e5985cdb5c); lib. bdg. (978-0-7787-6355-0(2), b7282a0d-58a9-411e-b324-0d77ac238493) Crabtree Publishing Co.

Iyer, Rani. Endangered Energy: Investigating the Scarcity of Fossil Fuels. 2015. (Endangered Earth Ser.). (ENG., Illus.). 32p. (J). (gr. 3-6). lib. bdg. 27.99 (978-1-4914-2037-9(5), 127515, Capstone Pr.) Capstone.

Jakab, Cheryl. Greenhouse Gases, 1 vol. Morden, Richard & Lauricella, Domenic, illus. 2011. (Environment in Focus Ser.). (ENG.). 32p. (gr. 4-4). 31.21 (978-1-60870-091-2(7), b3d0f4f2-4ea8-46e4-b42a-2912c8838bcf) Cavendish Square Publishing LLC.

—Pollution, 1 vol. Lauricella, Domenic, illus. 2011. (Environment in Focus Ser.). (ENG.). 32p. (gr. 4-4). 31.21 (978-1-60870-089-9(5), 760b19db-3f1b-4eb1-8384-48d300c0ea21) Cavendish Square Publishing LLC.

Jakubiak, David J. Protecting Our Planet: What Can We Do about Oil Spills & Ocean Pollution? (Illus.). 24p. (J). 2012. 49.50 (978-1-4488-5113-3(0)) 2011. (ENG., (gr. 2-3). pap. 9.25 (978-1-4488-5112-6(2), e582d72d-2ae2-40b9-a71c-d78af4772444) Rosen Publishing Group, Inc., The. (PowerKids Pr.).

Jones, Keisha. Halting Pollution, 1 vol. 2016. (Global Guardians Ser.). (ENG.). 24p. (J). (gr. 3-3). pap. 9.25 (978-1-4994-2756-1(5), 24284a20-72e7-47fc-a755-b5e1f6ed8652, PowerKids Pr.) Rosen Publishing Group, Inc., The.

Kortemeier, Todd. Finding an Energy Solution. 2017. (Science Frontiers Ser.). (ENG., Illus.). 32p. (J). (gr. 3-6). pap. 9.95 (978-1-63235-395-5(4), 11880, 12-Story Library) Bookstaves, LLC.

—Finding an Energy Solution. 2017. (Illus.). 32p. (J). (978-1-62143-519-8(9)) Pr. Room Editions LLC.

Lawrence, Ellen. Garbage Galore. 2014. (Science Slam: Green World, Clean World Ser.). 24p. (J). (gr. -1-3). lib. bdg. 26.99 (978-1-62724-102-1(7)) Bearport Publishing Co., Inc.

Leaney, Cindy. Pollution. 2008. (Contemporary Issues Companion Ser.). 240p. (gr. 10-12). 36.20 (978-0-7377-3950-3(9)); pap. 24.95 (978-0-7377-3951-0(7)) Cengage Gale. (Greenhaven Pr., Inc.).

Levete, Sarah. Destroying the Oceans. 2010. (Protecting Our Planet Ser.). (ENG., Illus.). 32p. (J). (gr. 3-6). (978-0-7787-5211-0(9)); pap. (978-0-7787-5228-8(3)) Crabtree Publishing Co.

Linde, Barbara M. Pollution, 1 vol. 2013. (Habitat Havoc Ser.). (ENG.). 32p. (gr. 3-4). pap. 11.50 (978-1-4339-9857-7(2), 6495b7ce-24a8-436d-92ca-f52d0b1649c4); (Illus.). (J). lib. bdg. 29.27 (978-1-4339-9926-0(9), dff8dedc-c8ee-4740-93c0-a6e20833174d) Stevens, Gareth Publishing LLLP.

Llewellyn, Claire. Let's Recycle. 2005. (Illus.). 32p. (YA). (gr. 1-18). lib. bdg. 27.10 (978-1-932333-22-0(3)) Chrysalis Education.

—Protect Natural Habitats. 2005. (Illus.). 32p. (YA). (gr. 1-18). lib. bdg. 27.10 (978-1-932333-20-6(7)) Chrysalis Education.

Mara, Wil & Bredeson, Carmen. The Chernobyl Disaster: Legacy & Impact on the Future of Nuclear Energy, 1 vol. 2011. (Perspectives On Ser.). (ENG.). 112p. (YA). (gr. 8-8). 42.64 (978-0-7614-4984-3(1), 06c8c4c1-aad7-47bd-8039-4f9679c22535) Cavendish Square Publishing LLC.

McKenzie, Precious. Cleaning up the Earth. 2011. (Green Earth Science Discovery Library). (ENG., Illus.). 24p. (gr. k-2). pap. 9.95 (978-1-61741-970-6(2), 9781617419706) Rourke Educational Media.

Mileham, Rebecca. Global Pollution. 2013. (21st Century Science Ser.). (ENG.). 64p. (J). (gr. 4-7). pap. 7.95 (978-1-84898-193-5(7), TickTock Books) Octopus Publishing Group GBR. Dist: Independent Pubs. Group.

Morrison, Yvonne. Earth Partners: Saving the Planet. 2007. (Shockwave Science Ser.). (Illus.). 36p. (J). (gr. 4-6). pap. 6.95 (978-0-531-15489-2(0), Children's Pr.) Scholastic Library Publishing.

—Shockwave Science: Earth Partners. 2007. (Shockwave: History & Politics Ser.). (ENG., Illus.). 36p. (J). (gr. 4-6). lib. bdg. 25.00 (978-0-531-17753-2(X), Children's Pr.) Scholastic Library Publishing.

National Geographic Learning. World Windows 3 (Science): Taking Care of Earth: Content Literacy, Nonfiction Reading, Language & Literacy. 2011. (World Windows Ser.). (ENG., Illus.). 16p. (J). stu. ed. 10.95 (978-1-133-56615-1(4)) Cengage Heinle.

National Marine Fisheries Service (U.S.), ed. Understanding Marine Debris: Games & Activities for Kids of All Ages. 2009. (ENG., Illus.). 22p. 2.50 (978-0-16-083974-0(2), 003-017-00558-5, National Marine Fisheries Service) United States Government Printing Office.

Orme, Helen. Pollution. 2008. (Earth in Danger Ser.). (Illus.). 32p. (YA). (gr. 3-6). lib. bdg. 25.27 (978-1-59716-724-6(X), 1284354) Bearport Publishing Co., Inc.

Owen, Ruth. Let's Investigate Plastic Pollution: On Land & in the Oceans. 2018. (Get Started with STEM Ser.). (ENG., Illus.). 32p. (J). (gr. k-3). 9.99 (978-1-78856-124-2(4), 09d5f135-6f43-49c0-bc1b-6c8285134b6b) Ruby Tuesday Books Limited GBR. Dist: Lerner Publishing Group.

Parker, Russ. Pollution Crisis, 1 vol. 2009. (Planet in Crisis Ser.). (ENG.). 32p. (gr. 5-5). (J). pap. 11.00 (978-1-4358-0682-5(4), ba22af9b-ec42-4136-910b-414626d4145e); (YA). lib. bdg. 30.47 (978-1-4358-5252-5(4), 0ac48b14-5400-4179-b2f6-d70bc09f567c) Rosen Publishing Group, Inc., The. (Rosen Reference).

Patent, Dorothy Hinshaw. Call of the Osprey. Muñoz, William, illus. 2015. (Scientists in the Field Ser.). (ENG.). 80p. (J). (gr. 5-7). 18.99 (978-0-544-23268-6(2), 1564093, Clarion Bks.) HarperCollins Pubs.

Paul, Miranda. One Plastic Bag: Isatou Ceesay & the Recycling Women of the Gambia. Zunon, Elizabeth, illus. 2015. (ENG.). 32p. (J). (gr. k-3). lib. bdg. 19.99 (978-1-4677-1608-6(1), 3ec140d3-02bb-43c0-9289-c7820c301191, Millbrook Pr.) Lerner Publishing Group.

Petersen, Christine. Controlling Earth's Pollutants, 1 vol. 2011. (Environment at Risk Ser.). (ENG.). 112p. (YA). (gr. 7-7). 42.64 (978-0-7614-4005-5(4), 47ba427e-3740-418d-adde-5bd9c766bbc3) Cavendish Square Publishing LLC.

Pollution: Level H, 6 vols. (Wonder Worldtm Ser.). 16p. 29.95 (978-0-7802-1233-6(9)) Wright Group/McGraw-Hill.

Rake, Jody S. Endangered Oceans: Investigating Oceans in Crisis. 2015. (Endangered Earth Ser.). (ENG., Illus.). 32p. (J). (gr. 3-6). lib. bdg. 27.99 (978-1-4914-2038-6(3), 127516, Capstone Pr.) Capstone.

Rice, Dona Herweck. Too Much Trash!, 1 vol. rev. ed. 2014. (Science: Informational Text Ser.). (ENG., Illus.). 24p. (gr. -1-1). pap. 9.99 (978-1-4807-4534-6(0)) Teacher Created Materials, Inc.

Silverstein, Alvin & Silverstein, Virginia. Smog, Oil Spills, Sewage, & More: The Yucky Pollution Book, 1 vol. 2010. (Yucky Science Ser.). (ENG., Illus.). 48p. (gr. 5-7). 27.93 (978-0-7660-3313-9(9), 46eb430a-86e9-4831-ad51-01e078ad60aa) Enslow Publishing, LLC.

Slade, Suzanne. What Can We Do about Pollution?, 1 vol. 2009. (Protecting Our Planet Ser.). (ENG., Illus.). 24p. (gr. 2-3). (J). pap. 9.25 (978-1-4358-2485-0(7), 7dda323a-0218-4623-9cc6-d62319809437, PowerKids Pr.); (YA). lib. bdg. 26.27 (978-1-4042-8083-0(9), ddb5e678-c0c6-4c70-b1c8-ed714e13819c) Rosen Publishing Group, Inc., The.

Smith-Llera, Danielle. Trash Vortex: How Plastic Pollution Is Choking the World's Oceans. 2018. (Captured Science History Ser.). (ENG., Illus.). 64p. (J). (gr. 5-9). lib. bdg. 35.32 (978-0-7565-5745-4(3), 137541, Compass Point Bks.) Capstone.

Solway, Andrew. Secrets of Pollution & Conservation, 1 vol. 2011. (Science Secrets Ser.). (ENG.). 32p. (gr. 4-4). 31.21 (978-1-60870-140-7(9), 61813dcf-3c41-42ce-bd73-949e3dc3501a) Cavendish Square Publishing LLC.

Spilsbury, Louise. Waste & Recycling Challenges. 2009. (Illus.). 48p. (J). 70.50 (978-1-4358-5487-1(X), Rosen Reference); (ENG., (gr. 5-5). pap. 12.75 (978-1-4358-5486-4(1), 25f3ffa9-c7f9-4330-bcde-21e0c9967f81, Rosen Reference); (ENG., (gr. 5-5). lib. bdg. 34.47 (978-1-4358-5355-3(5), 7e370fac-d619-48e6-8ec4-957f881bfe7b) Rosen Publishing Group, Inc., The.

Spilsbury, Richard & Spilsbury, Louise. Pollution, 1 vol. 2018. (Flowchart Smart Ser.). (ENG.). 48p. (gr. 4-5). pap. 15.05 (978-1-5382-3491-4(2), 063b1090-88df-4999-9d97-5d07bd315fb9) Stevens, Gareth Publishing LLLP.

Watson, Stephanie, ed. Critical Perspectives on Pollution. (Scientific American Critical Anthologies on Environment & Climate Ser.). 224p. (gr. 9-9). 2009. 63.90 (978-1-60853-069-4(8)) 2006. (ENG., Illus.). (J). 42.47 (978-1-4042-0690-8(6), 7ca37693-6ed9-4696-a88c-231a8a5be298) Rosen Publishing Group, Inc., The.

West, David & Parker, Steve. Ecological Disasters. 2011. (ENG., Illus.). 32p. (J). pap. (978-0-7787-7578-2(X)); lib. bdg. (978-0-7787-7573-7(9)) Crabtree Publishing Co.

World Book, Inc. Staff, contrib. by. Pollution. 2008. (J). (978-0-7166-1406-7(5)) World Bk., Inc.

Young, Karen Romano. Space Junk: The Dangers of Polluting Earth's Orbit. 2016. (ENG., Illus.). 64p. (YA). (gr. 6-12). 33.32 (978-1-4677-5600-6(8), d84a65bb-18e5-40f4-aea0-55c7f2de372e); E-Book 50.65 (978-1-4677-8806-9(6)) Lerner Publishing Group. (Twenty-First Century Bks.).

POLLUTION—FICTION

Atwell, Debby. River. 2004. (ENG., Illus.). 32p. (J). (gr. -1-3). reprint ed. pap. 6.95 (978-0-618-43952-2(8), 490912, Clarion Bks.) HarperCollins Pubs.

Beauregard, Lynda. The Yucky Duck Rescue No. 8: A Mystery about Pollution. Torres, German, illus. 2013. (Summer Camp Science Mysteries Ser.: 8). (ENG.). 48p. (J). (gr. 3-6). pap. 6.95 (978-1-4677-0736-7(8), 88b5c33c-0762-4d74-855a-0c8aece40cae, Graphic Universe™) Lerner Publishing Group.

Bernay, Emma & Berne, Emma Carlson. Oil-Soaked Wings. Madrid, Erwin, illus. 2019. (Seaside Sanctuary Ser.). (ENG.). 112p. (J). (gr. 3-7). lib. bdg. 25.99 (978-1-4965-7861-7(9), 139400, Stone Arch Bks.) Capstone.

Bottoms, Bud. Davey & the GOM Giant Oil Monster. 2008. (Illus.). 39p. (J). (gr. -1-5). per. 14.95 (978-0-9795444-1-5(6)) Summerland Publishing.

Bradman, Tony. The Ugly Duckling Returns, 1 vol. Warburton, Sarah, illus. 2014. (After Happily Ever After Ser.). (ENG.). 56p. (J). (gr. 3-6). lib. bdg. 25.99 (978-1-4342-7953-8(7), 124702, Stone Arch Bks.) Capstone.

Cornfield, Lynda Ellis. Rocks for Clean Oceans. 2009. 28p. pap. 13.99 (978-1-4389-8417-9(0)) AuthorHouse.

dePaola, Tomie. Michael Bird-Boy. dePaola, Tomie, illus. 2015. (ENG., Illus.). 32p. (J). (gr. -1-3). 16.99 (978-1-4814-4333-3(X), Simon & Schuster Bks. For Young Readers) Simon & Schuster Bks. For Young Readers.

Diesen, Deborah. The Pout-Pout Fish Cleans up the Ocean. Hanna, Dan, illus. 2019. (Pout-Pout Fish Adventure Ser.: 4). (ENG.). 32p. (J). 18.99 (978-0-374-30934-3(5), 900189997, Farrar, Straus & Giroux (BYR)) Farrar, Straus & Giroux.

Douglas, Babette. Kiss a Me to the Rescue. Rockwell, Barry, illus. 2006. (Kiss a Me Teacher Creature Stories Ser.). (J). (gr. -1-3). 9.99 (978-1-890343-11-8(0)) Kiss A Me Productions, Inc.

Flounders, Anne, ed. Return to Earth. Wolk-Stanley, Jessica; Flounders, illus. 2004. (Reader's Theater Content-Area Concepts Ser.). (ENG.). (J). (gr. 3-5). 5.00 net. (978-1-4108-2306-9(7), A23067) Benchmark Education Co.

Foreman, Michael. One World. 2012. (ENG., Illus.). 32p. (J). (gr. -1-k). pap. 12.99 (978-1-84939-304-1(4)) Andersen Pr. GBR. Dist: Independent Pubs. Group.

Galliez, Roxane Marie. The Earth Has Caught Cold. Lhomme, Sandrine, illus. 2009. 24p. (J). (gr. -1-3). 9.99 (978-0-8416-7140-9(0)) Hammond World Atlas Corp.

Grabenstein, Chris. Riley Mack Stirs up More Trouble. 2013. (Riley Mack Ser.: 2). (ENG.). 336p. (J). (gr. 3-7). 16.99 (978-0-06-202622-4(4)) HarperCollins Pubs.

Gratz, Alan. Something Rotten, 1. 2007. (Horatio Wilkes Mystery Ser.). (ENG.). 208p. (J). (gr. 7-12). 21.19 (978-0-8037-3216-2(3)) Penguin Young Readers Group.

Gratz, Alan M. Something Rotten. 2009. 224p. (YA). (gr. 7-18). 8.99 (978-0-14-241297-8(X), Speak) Penguin Young Readers Group.

Inches, Alison. I Can Save the Ocean! The Little Green Monster Cleans up the Beach. Garofoli, Viviana, illus. 2010.

(Little Green Bks.). (ENG.). 24p. (J). (gr. -1-1). 9.99 *(978-1-4169-9514-2(5),* Little Simon) Little Simon.

Keene, Carolyn. Green with Envy: Book Two in the Eco Mystery Trilogy, 40. 2010. (Nancy Drew (All New) Girl Detective Ser.: 40). (ENG.). 160p. (J). (gr. 3-7). pap. 7.99 *(978-1-4169-7842-8(9),* Aladdin) Simon & Schuster Children's Publishing.

—Seeing Green: Book Three in the Eco Mystery Trilogy, 41. 2010. (Nancy Drew (All New) Girl Detective Ser.: 41). (ENG.). 160p. (J). (gr. 3-7). pap. 6.99 *(978-1-4169-7845-9(3),* Aladdin) Simon & Schuster Children's Publishing.

King, Amy Sarig. Me & Marvin Gardens (Scholastic Gold) 2019. (ENG.). 272p. (J). (gr. 3-7). pap. 8.99 *(978-0-545-87076-4(3))* Scholastic, Inc.

Liberto, Lorenzo. Save the Planet / Salva el Planeta. Gomez, Rocio, tr. Torres, Irving, illus. 2005. (Matt the Rat Ser. / La Serie de Ratón Mateo). (ENG & SPA.). 32p. (J). lib. bdg. 20.00 *(978-0-9743668-5-2(4))* Harvest Sun Pr., LLC.

Manos, John. Samantha Saves the Stream. 2006. (Early Explorers Ser.). (J). pap. *(978-1-4108-6125-2(2))* Benchmark Education Co.

McMillan, Dawn. Seagull Sid: And the Naughty Things His Seagulls Did! Kinnaird, Ross, illus. 2019. (ENG.). 32p. (gr. 1-5). pap. 8.99 *(978-0-486-83247-0(3),* 832473) Dover Pubns., Inc.

Nelson, Bruce M. The Magician's Hat. 2006. 127p. pap. 19.95 *(978-1-4241-2301-8(1))* America Star Bks.

Newton, R. H. Oceannis. 2010. pap. 16.95 *(978-0-7414-5911-4(6))* Infinity Publishing.

Oe, Patricia Daly. Where Are My Stripes? Oe, Patricia Daly, illus. 2007. (R. I. C. Story Chest Ser.). (Illus.). 20p. (J). (gr. -1-k). 11.95 incl. audio compact disk *(978-1-74126-438-8(3))* R.I.C. Pubns. AUS. Dist: SCB Distributors.

Pelletier, Maryse. La Chasse au Plomb. Grimard, Gabrielle, illus. 2004. (Roman Jeunesse Ser.). (FRE.). 96p. (J). (gr. 4-7). pap. *(978-2-89021-692-1(6))* Diffusion du livre Mirabel (DLM).

Pon, Cindy. Ruse. 2019. (ENG., Illus.). 304p. (YA). (gr. 9). 18.99 *(978-1-5344-1992-6(6),* Simon Pulse) Simon Pulse.

—Want. (ENG.). (YA). (gr. 9). 2019. 352p. pap. 12.99 *(978-1-4814-8923-2(2))* 2017. (Illus.). 336p. 19.99 *(978-1-4814-8922-5(4))* Simon Pulse. (Simon Pulse).

Poon, Janice. Claire & the Water Wish. Poon, Janice, illus. 2009. (Illus.). 120p. (J). (gr. 2-5). 7.95 *(978-1-55453-382-4(1));* (gr. 3-6). 22.44 *(978-1-55453-381-7(3))* Kids Can Pr., Ltd. CAN. Dist: Hachette Bk. Group, Children's Plus, Inc.

Reynolds, Paul A. Sydney & Simon: Go Green! Reynolds, Peter H., illus. 2015. (Sydney & Simon Ser.: 2). 48p. (J). (gr. 1-4). lib. bdg. 12.95 *(978-1-58089-677-1(4))* Charlesbridge Publishing, Inc.

Santore, Charles, illus. William the Curious: Knight of the Water Lilies. 2012. (J). *(978-1-60464-034-2(0))* Appleseed Pr. Bk. Pub. LLC.

Scraper, Katherine. Save the Fairy Penguins. 2005. (J). pap. *(978-1-4108-4214-5(2))* Benchmark Education Co.

Seuss. El lórax (the Lorax Spanish Edition) 2019. (Classic Seuss Ser.). (SPA.). 72p. (J). (gr. 1-4). 16.99 *(978-0-525-70731-8(X));* lib. bdg. 19.99 *(978-0-525-70732-5(8))* Random Hse. Children's Bks. (Random Hse. Bks. for Young Readers).

Spratt, Niall & Meehan, Patrick. The Shamrogues: First Challenge. 2013. (ENG.). 224p. (J). pap. 12.95 *(978-1-871305-57-9(8))* Orpen Pr. IRL. Dist: Dufour Editions, Inc.

Suneby, Elizabeth. Iqbal & His Ingenious Idea: How a Science Project Helps One Family & the Planet. Green, Rebecca, illus. 2018. (CitizenKid Ser.). (ENG.). 32p. (J). (gr. 3-7). 18.99 *(978-1-77138-720-0(3))* Kids Can Pr., Ltd. CAN. Dist: Hachette Bk. Group.

Thaler, Mike. Earth Day from the Black Lagoon. Lee, Jared D., illus. 2013. 64p. (J). *(978-0-545-47669-0(0))* Scholastic, Inc.

—Earth Day from the Black Lagoon. Lee, Jared, illus. 2016. (Black Lagoon Adventures Set 4 Ser.). (ENG.). 64p. (J). (gr. 2-6). lib. bdg. 31.36 *(978-1-61479-603-9(3),* 24336, Chapter Bks.) Spotlight.

Van Allsburg, Chris. Just a Dream. Van Allsburg, Chris, illus. 2014. (Illus.). 48p. pap. 9.00 *(978-1-61003-182-0(2))* Center for the Collaborative Classroom.

—Just a Dream. Van Allsburg, Chris, illus. 2011. (ENG., Illus.). 48p. (J). (gr. -1-3). pap. 9.99 *(978-0-547-52026-1(3),* 1445465, Clarion Bks.) HarperCollins Pubs.

—Just a Dream 25th Anniversary Edition. Van Allsburg, Chris, illus. 2015. (ENG., Illus.). 48p. (J). (gr. -1-3). 18.99 *(978-0-544-42283-4(X),* 1595321, Clarion Bks.) HarperCollins Pubs.

Wildsmith, Brian. Professor Noah's Spaceship, 1 vol. 2008. (ENG., Illus.). 32p. (J). 16.95 *(978-1-59572-124-2(X))* Star Bright Bks., Inc.

Yellowknife, Jessica. Spring Break Adventure. 2011. 84p. pap. 11.11 *(978-1-4269-6952-2(X))* Trafford Publishing.

POLLUTION OF AIR

see Air—Pollution

POLLUTION OF WATER

see Water—Pollution

POLO, MARCO, 1254-1323?

Bailey, Gerry & Foster, Karen. Marco Polo's Silk Purse, 1 vol. Radford, Karen & Noyes, Leighton, illus. 2008. (Stories of Great People Ser.). (ENG.). 40p. (J). (gr. 3-8). pap. *(978-0-7787-3710-0(1));* lib. bdg. *(978-0-7787-3688-2(1))* Crabtree Publishing Co.

Boyd, David. Marco Polo & the Roc. Ng, Drew, illus. 2007. 48p. (J). lib. bdg. 23.08 *(978-1-4242-1621-5(4))* Fitzgerald Bks.

Childress, Diana. Marco Polo's Journey to China. 2007. (Pivotal Moments in History Ser.). (ENG.). 160p. (gr. 9-12). lib. bdg. 38.60 *(978-0-8225-5903-0(X))* Lerner Publishing Group.

Cooke, Tim. Explore with Marco Polo. 2014. (Travel with the Great Explorers Ser.). (ENG., Illus.). 32p. (J). (gr. 4-5). *(978-0-7787-1428-6(4))* Crabtree Publishing Co.

Crompton, Samuel Willard. Marco Polo: Epic Traveler Throughout Asia. 2017. (Spotlight on Explorers & Colonization Ser.). (Illus.). 48p. (J). (gr. 10-11). 70.50 *(978-1-5081-7504-9(7),* Rosen Young Adult) Rosen Publishing Group, Inc., The.

Feinstein, Stephen. Marco Polo: Amazing Adventures in China, 1 vol. 2009. (Great Explorers of the World Ser.). (ENG.). 112p. (gr. 6-7). pap. 13.88 *(978-0-7660-5430-1(6),* 4d94171e-7792-48db-9a83-fa0fb79bcacf); (Illus.). lib. bdg. 35.93 *(978-1-59845-103-0(0),* d387f151-8d23-47c6-a78f-fcb3f955c476) Enslow Publishing, LLC.

Hain-Jun, Yue & Soldevilla, Juan Manuel. Marco Polo: La Ruta de las Maravillas. 2006.Tr. of Marco Polo & the Route of Wonders. (SPA.). (J). (gr. 6-8). 9.60 *(978-84-316-7173-0(4),* W32814) Vicens-Vives, Editorial, S.A. ESP. Dist: Lectorum Pubns., Inc.

Holub, Joan. Who Was Marco Polo? O'brien, John, illus. 2007. (Who Was... ? Ser.). 105p. (gr. 4-7). 15.00 *(978-0-7569-8165-5(4))* Perfection Learning Corp.

Holub, Joan & Who HQ. ¿Quién Fue Marco Polo? O'Brien, John, illus. 2012. (¿Quién Fue? Ser.). 112p. (J). (gr. 3-7). pap. 6.99 *(978-0-448-46174-8(9),* Penguin Workshop) Penguin Young Readers Group.

—Who Was Marco Polo? O'Brien, John, illus. 2007. (Who Was? Ser.). 112p. (J). (gr. 3-7). pap. 5.99 *(978-0-448-44540-3(9),* Penguin Workshop) Penguin Young Readers Group.

Macdonald, Fiona. The Story of Marco Polo. Mark Bergin, illus. 2017. (Explorers Ser.). 32p. (J). (gr. 3-6). 31.35 *(978-1-910706-91-6(4))* Book Hse. GBR. Dist: Black Rabbit Bks.

Marsh, Carole. Marco Polo. 2004. 12p. (gr. k-4). 2.95 *(978-0-635-02376-6(8))* Gallopade International.

McCarty, Nick. Marco Polo: El Joven Que Viajo Por el Mundo Medieval. 2007. (World History Biographies Ser.). (Illus.). 64p. (J). (gr. 3-7). *(978-84-372-2470-1(5))* Altea, Ediciones, S.A. - Grupo Santillana.

—World History Biographies: Marco Polo: The Boy Who Traveled the Medieval World. 2008. (National Geographic World History Biographies Ser.). (Illus.). 64p. (J). (gr. 3-7). pap. 6.95 *(978-1-4263-0296-1(7),* National Geographic Kids) Disney Publishing Worldwide.

—World History Biographies: Marco Polo: The Boy Who Traveled the Medieval World. 2006. (National Geographic World History Biographies Ser.). (ENG., Illus.). 64p. (J). (gr. 3-7). 17.95 *(978-0-7922-5893-3(2),* National Geographic Children's Bks.) National Geographic Society.

Morley, Jacqueline. You Wouldn't Want to Explore with Marco Polo! A Really Long Trip You'd Rather Not Take. Antram, David, illus. 2009. (You Wouldn't Want to Ser.). (ENG.). 32p. (J). (gr. 3-12). 29.00 *(978-0-531-21327-8(7))* Scholastic Library Publishing.

Otfinoski, Steven. Marco Polo: To China & Back, 1 vol. 2003. (Great Explorations Ser.). (ENG., Illus.). 80p. (gr. 6-6). 36.93 *(978-0-7614-1480-3(0),* bc412359-15d9-4a18-998c-a1ba06a718b2) Cavendish Square Publishing LLC.

Riddle, John. Marco Polo. 2004. (Great Names Ser.). (Illus.). 32p. (J). (gr. 3-18). lib. bdg. 19.95 *(978-1-59084-136-5(0))* Mason Crest.

—Marco Polo: 13th Century Italian Trader. 2013. (People of Importance Ser.: 21). (Illus.). 32p. (J). (gr. 4-18). 19.95 *(978-1-4222-2850-0(9))* Mason Crest.

Rosen, Michael J. The Million Stories of Marco Polo. 2016. (Illus.). 32p. (J). (gr. 5-8). 18.99 *(978-1-56846-290-5(5),* 20818, Creative Editions) Creative Co., The.

Smalley, Roger. The Adventures of Marco Polo, 1 vol. Bascle, Brian, illus. 2005. (Graphic History Ser.). (ENG.). 32p. (J). (gr. 3-9). per. 8.10 *(978-0-7368-5240-1(9),* 86986, Capstone Pr.) Capstone.

—Las Aventuras de Marco Polo. Bascle, Brian, illus. 2006. (Historia Gráficas Ser.). (SPA.). 32p. (J). (gr. 3-9). 31.32 *(978-0-7368-6054-3(1),* 90133) Capstone.

Strand, Jennifer. Marco Polo. 2016. (Pioneering Explorers Ser.). (ENG.). 24p. (J). (gr. -1-2). 49.94 *(978-1-68079-413-7(2),* 23034, Abdo Zoom-Launch) ABDO Publishing Co.

Tabilio, Marco. Marco Polo: Dangers & Visions. Tabilio, Marco, illus. 2017. (ENG., Illus.). 208p. (YA). (gr. 9-12). 29.32 *(978-1-5124-1182-9(5),* c306a5aa-a0b3-46a7-b100-1aee4dbcff34, Graphic Universe™) Lerner Publishing Group.

Zannos, Susan. The Life & Times of Marco Polo. 2004. (Biography from Ancient Civilizations Ser.). (Illus.). 48p. (J). (gr. 4-8). lib. bdg. 29.95 *(978-1-58415-264-4(8))* Mitchell Lane Pubs.

Zelenyj, Alexander. Marco Polo: Overland to China, 1 vol. 2005. (In the Footsteps of Explorers Ser.). (ENG., Illus.). 32p. (J). (gr. 4-5). pap. *(978-0-7787-2453-7(0))* Crabtree Publishing Co.

POLO, MARCO, 1254-1323?—FICTION

Armstrong, Alan W. Looking for Marco Polo. Jessell, Tim, illus. 2011. (ENG.). 304p. (J). (gr. 4-6). lib. bdg. 21.19 *(978-0-375-93321-9(2),* Yearling) Random Hse. Children's Bks.

Johnson, Vargie. Marco Polo the Adventurer: What Made Them Famous? 2006. 156p. (J). per. 15.00 *(978-1-931195-98-0(6))* KiwE Publishing, Ltd.

Maisner, Heather. Diary of a Princess: A Tale from Marco Polo's Travels. Moxley, Sheila, illus. 2006. 26p. (gr. k-4). reprint ed. pap. 8.00 *(978-1-4223-5302-8(8))* DIANE Publishing Co.

Scieszka, Jon. Marco? Polo!, 16. McCauley, Adam, illus. 2006. (Time Warp Trio Ser.: 16). (ENG.). 80p. (J). (gr. 2-4). 17.44 *(978-0-670-06104-4(2))* Penguin Young Readers Group.

—Marco? Polo! McCauley, Adam, illus. 2008. (Time Warp Trio Ser.: No. 16). 90p. (J). (gr. 4-6). 12.65 *(978-0-7569-8923-1(X))* Perfection Learning Corp.

—Marco? Polo! #16, No. 16. McCauley, Adam, illus. 2008. (Time Warp Trio Ser.: 16). 96p. (J). (gr. 2-4). 5.99 *(978-0-14-241177-3(9),* Puffin Books) Penguin Young Readers Group.

Sylvester, Kevin. Neil Flambé & the Marco Polo Murders. Sylvester, Kevin, illus. 2014. (Neil Flambe Capers Ser.: 1). (ENG., Illus.). 320p. (J). (gr. 3-7). pap. 8.99 *(978-1-4424-4605-2(6),* Simon & Schuster Bks. For Young Readers) Simon & Schuster Bks. For Young Readers.

Tabilio, Marco. Marco Polo: Dangers & Visions. Tabilio, Marco, illus. 2017. (ENG., Illus.). 208p. (YA). (gr. 9-12). pap. 11.99 *(978-1-5124-3069-1(2),* 275e57e8-881a-4e55-8d5f-f96fde9d19bf, Graphic Universe™) Lerner Publishing Group.

POLTERGEISTS

see Ghosts

POLYMERS

see also Plastics

Goodstein, Madeline. Plastics & Polymers Science Fair Projects, Using the Scientific Method, 1 vol. rev. exp. ed. 2010. (Chemistry Science Projects Using the Scientific Method Ser.). (ENG., Illus.). 160p. (gr. 5-6). 38.60 *(978-0-7660-3412-9(7),* f3dfba6c-ef48-41a9-ab5d-d360bd356248) Enslow Publishing, LLC.

Small, Cathleen. Fab Lab Creating with Vinyl Cutters, 1 vol. 2016. (Getting Creative with Fab Lab Ser.). (ENG.). 64p. (J). (gr. 6-6). 36.13 *(978-1-5081-7350-2(8),* e849f08c-76ad-4558-a5ef-9a99fbad08d7) Rosen Publishing Group, Inc., The.

POLYNESIA

Montgomery, Sy. The Octopus Scientists. Ellenbogen, Keith, illus. 2015. (Scientists in the Field Ser.). (ENG.). 80p. (J). (gr. 5-7). 18.99 *(978-0-544-23270-9(4),* 1564095, Clarion Bks.) HarperCollins Pubs.

Webster, Christine. Polynesians. 2003. (Indigenous Peoples Ser.). (J). pap. 9.95 *(978-1-59036-158-0(X));* (Illus.). 32p. lib. bdg. 26.00 *(978-1-59036-123-8(7))* Weigl Pubs., Inc.

World Book, Inc. Staff, contrib. by. The Polynesians. 2009. (J). *(978-0-7166-2140-9(1))* World Bk., Inc.

POLYNESIA—FICTION

Disney Books. Moana ReadAlong Storybook & CD. 2016. (Read-Along Storybook & CD Ser.). (ENG., Illus.). 32p. (J). (gr. 1-3). pap. 6.99 *(978-1-4847-4361-4(X),* Disney Press Books) Disney Publishing Worldwide.

O'Neill, Katrina. The Red Rain of Easter Island. 2007. (Illus.). 52p. (J). pap. *(978-1-4207-0723-6(X))* Sundance/Newbridge Educational Publishing.

Owen, Rena. Moana: Read-Along Storybook & CD. 2016. (Illus.). (J). *(978-1-5182-2280-1(3))* Disney Publishing Worldwide.

Sperry, Armstrong. Call It Courage. 2008. (ENG.). 128p. (YA). (gr. 7). mass mkt. 6.99 *(978-1-4169-5368-5(X),* Simon Pulse) Simon Pulse.

POMPEII (EXTINCT CITY)

Ball, Karen. Pompeii. Cerisier, Emmanuel, illus. 2006. (Usborne Young Reading Ser.). 64p. (J). (gr. 3-7). 8.99 *(978-0-7945-1270-5(4),* Usborne) EDC Publishing.

Collins, Terry. Escape from Pompeii: An Isabel Soto Archaeology Adventure. 2010. (Graphic Expeditions Ser.). (ENG., Illus.). 32p. (J). (gr. 3-4). pap. 48.60 *(978-1-4296-5714-3(6),* 15497, Capstone Pr.) Capstone.

Conklin, Wendy. You Are There! Pompeii 79. 2nd rev. ed. 2017. (TIME(r): Informational Text Ser.). (ENG., Illus.). 32p. (gr. 6-8). pap. 13.99 *(978-1-4938-3615-4(3))* Teacher Created Materials, Inc.

—You Are There! Pompeii 79. 2017. (Time for Kids Nonfiction Readers Ser.). lib. bdg. 19.65 *(978-0-606-40293-4(4))* Turtleback.

Deem, James M. Bodies from the Ash: Life & Death in Ancient Pompeii. 2017. (ENG., Illus.). 64p. (J). (gr. 5-7). pap. 9.99 *(978-1-328-74083-0(8),* 1677116, Clarion Bks.) HarperCollins Pubs.

Dunn, Mary. My Adventure at Pompeii. 2006. 44p. (J). 8.99 *(978-1-59092-411-2(8))* Blue Forge Pr.

Gimpel, Diane Marczely. Pompeii, 1 vol. 2014. (Digging up the Past Ser.). (ENG.). 112p. (YA). (gr. 6-12). lib. bdg. 41.36 *(978-1-62403-236-3(2),* 1304, Essential Library) ABDO Publishing Co.

Johnson, Robin. Pompeii. 2012. (ENG., Illus.). 48p. (J). *(978-0-7787-7927-8(0));* pap. *(978-0-7787-7936-0(X))* Crabtree Publishing Co.

Kaplan, Sarah Pitt. Pompeii: City of Ashes. 2005. (High Interest Bks.). (ENG., Illus.). 48p. (J). (gr. 3-7). per. 6.95 *(978-0-516-25091-5(4),* Children's Pr.) Scholastic Library Publishing.

Levy, Janey. The City of Pompeii, 1 vol. 2015. (Doomed! Ser.). (ENG., Illus.). 32p. (J). (gr. 4-5). pap. 11.50 *(978-1-4824-2924-4(1),* 7ccf4d46-c6cc-4dd1-b1ba-24064f046aa3) Stevens, Gareth Publishing LLLP.

Lindeen, Mary. Ashes to Ashes: Uncovering Pompeii. 2008. (Illus.). 36p. (J). pap. *(978-0-531-15544-8(7))* Children's Pr., Ltd.

—Shockwave: Ashes to Ashes. 2007. (Shockwave: People & Communities Ser.). (ENG., Illus.). 36p. (J). (gr. 3-5). 25.00 *(978-0-531-17745-7(9),* Children's Pr.) Scholastic Library Publishing.

Malam, John. Live in Pompeii! A Volcanic Eruption You'd Rather Avoid. Antram, David, illus. 2008. (You Wouldn't Want to Ser.). (ENG.). 32p. (J). (gr. 2-5). 29.00 *(978-0-531-18748-7(9));* pap. 9.95 *(978-0-531-16900-1(6),* Watts, Franklin) Scholastic Library Publishing.

Oachs, Emily Rose. Pompeii. 2019. (Digging up the Past Ser.). (ENG., Illus.). 24p. (J). (gr. 3-7). lib. bdg. 26.95 *(978-1-64487-069-3(X),* Torque Bks.) Bellwether Media.

O'Connor, Jim. What Was Pompeii? 2014. (What Was... Ser.). lib. bdg. 16.00 *(978-0-606-34155-4(2))* Turtleback.

O'Connor, Jim & Who HQ. What Was Pompeii? Hinderliter, John, illus. 2014. (What Was? Ser.). 112p. (J). (gr. 3-7). 6.99 *(978-0-448-47907-1(9),* Penguin Workshop) Penguin Young Readers Group.

Osborne, Mary Pope & Boyce, Natalie Pope. Ancient Rome & Pompeii: A Nonfiction Companion to Magic Tree House #13: Vacation under the Volcano. Murdocca, Sal, illus. 2006. (Magic Tree House (R) Fact Tracker Ser.: 14). 128p. (J). (gr. 2-5). 6.99 *(978-0-375-83220-8(3),* Random Hse. Bks. for Young Readers) Random Hse. Children's Bks.

Roberts, Russell. Mt. Vesuvius & the Destruction of Pompei, A. D. 79. 2005. (Natural Disasters Ser.). (Illus.). 32p. (J). (gr. 1-4). lib. bdg. 25.70 *(978-1-58415-419-8(5))* Mitchell Lane Pubs.

Samuel, Charlie. Solving the Mysteries of Pompeii, 1 vol. 2009. (Digging into History Ser.). (ENG.). 32p. (gr. 3-3). lib. bdg. 32.64 *(978-0-7614-3105-3(5),* 21049f22-8522-4083-9fdc-a84a8f306340) Cavendish Square Publishing LLC.

Samuels, Charlie. What Happened to Pompeii?, 1 vol. 2017. (Mysteries in History: Solving the Mysteries of the Past Ser.). (ENG.). 48p. (gr. 5-5). lib. bdg. 33.07 *(978-1-5026-2802-2(3),* a490bd70-a5b1-409e-9260-8f1a105d02ad) Cavendish Square Publishing LLC.

Sonneborn, Liz. Pompeii. 2008. (Unearthing Ancient Worlds Ser.). (ENG., Illus.). 80p. (J). (gr. 5-8). lib. bdg. 30.60 *(978-0-8225-7505-4(1))* Lerner Publishing Group.

Waxman, Laura Hamilton. Mysteries of Pompeii. 2017. (Ancient Mysteries (Alternator Books (r)) Ser.). (ENG., Illus.). 32p. (J). (gr. 3-6). 29.32 *(978-1-5124-4017-1(5),* 98785757-b2c3-4e2d-80d7-229f550db457, Lerner Pubns.) Lerner Publishing Group.

Weakland, Mark. Scooby-Doo! & the Buried City of Pompeii: The Ghastly Guide. Cornia, Christian, illus. 2018. (Unearthing Ancient Civilizations with Scooby-Doo! Ser.). (ENG.). 32p. (J). (gr. 3-6). lib. bdg. 27.99 *(978-1-5157-7512-6(7),* 135892, Capstone Pr.) Capstone.

POMPEII (EXTINCT CITY)—FICTION

Collins, Terry. Escape from Pompeii: An Isabel Soto Archaeology Adventure, 1 vol. Martin, Cynthia, illus. 2010. (Graphic Expeditions Ser.). (ENG.). 32p. (J). (gr. 3-9). pap. 8.10 *(978-1-4296-5634-4(4),* 114125); lib. bdg. 31.32 *(978-1-4296-4771-7(X),* 103300) Capstone. (Capstone Pr.).

Gutman, Dan. Flashback Four #3: the Pompeii Disaster. (Flashback Four Ser.: 3). (ENG.). (J). (gr. 3-7). 2019. 272p. pap. 7.99 *(978-0-06-237445-5(1))* 2018. 256p. 16.99 *(978-0-06-237444-8(3))* HarperCollins Pubs. (HarperCollins).

Osborne, Mary Pope. Vacation under the Volcano. unabr. ed. 2004. (Magic Tree House Ser.: No. 13). 74p. (J). (gr. k-3). pap. 17.00 incl. audio *(978-0-8072-0782-6(9),* LFTR 241 SP, Listening Library) Random Hse. Audio Publishing Group.

Peacock, L. A. Panic in Pompeii. Hale, Nathan, illus. 2011. 92p. (J). pap. *(978-0-545-34062-5(4))* Scholastic, Inc.

Tarshis, Lauren. I Survived the Destruction of Pompeii, AD 79. Dawson, Scott, illus. 2014. 95p. (J). *(978-0-545-77568-7(X),* Scholastic Pr.) Scholastic, Inc.

—I Survived the Destruction of Pompeii, AD 79 (I Survived #10) 2014. (I Survived Ser.: 10). (ENG., Illus.). 112p. (J). (gr. 2-5). pap. 5.99 *(978-0-545-45939-6(7))* Scholastic, Inc.

PONCE DE LEON, JUAN, 1460?-1521

Donohue, Moira Rose. Juan Ponce de León. 2013. (Illus.). 24p. (J). *(978-1-938813-06-1(5))* State Standards Publishing, LLC.

Eagen, Rachel. Ponce de Leon: Exploring Florida & Puerto Rico, 1 vol. 2005. (In the Footsteps of Explorers Ser.). (ENG., Illus.). 32p. (J). (gr. 4-5). pap. *(978-0-7787-2448-3(4))* Crabtree Publishing Co.

Greenberger, Robert. Juan Ponce de Leon: The Exploration of Florida & the Search for the Fountain of Youth. rev. ed. (Library of Explorers & Explorationtm Ser.). (Illus.). 112p. (YA). (gr. 5-8). lib. bdg. 31.95 *(978-1-4042-0635-9(3),* Rosen Reference) Rosen Publishing Group, Inc., The.

Hoogenboom, Lynn. Juan Ponce de Leon. 2009. (Primary Source Library of Famous Explorers Ser.). 24p. (gr. 4-4). 42.50 *(978-1-60854-128-7(2),* PowerKids Pr.) Rosen Publishing Group, Inc., The.

—Juan Ponce de Leon: A Primary Source Biography, 1 vol. 2005. (Primary Source Library of Famous Explorers Ser.). (ENG., Illus.). 24p. (YA). (gr. 4-4). lib. bdg. 26.27 *(978-1-4042-3040-8(8),* 6954b8cb-fefa-417b-bed2-d9851cc67eab) Rosen Publishing Group, Inc., The.

O'Brien, Cynthia. Explore with Ponce de León. 2014. (Travel with the Great Explorers Ser.). (ENG., Illus.). 32p. (J). (gr. 4-5). *(978-0-7787-1429-3(2))* Crabtree Publishing Co.

Otfinoski, Steven. Juan Ponce de León: Discoverer of Florida, 1 vol. 2006. (Great Explorations Ser.). (ENG.). 80p. (gr. 6-6). 36.93 *(978-0-7614-1610-4(2),* d48d0e75-fb3a-47b2-8f29-f852efe45614) Cavendish Square Publishing LLC.

Pelleschi, Andrea. Juan Ponce de Leon, 1 vol. 2013. (Jr. Graphic Famous Explorers Ser.). (ENG., Illus.). 24p. (J). (gr. 2-3). pap. 11.60 *(978-1-4777-0131-7(1),* f6946dde-86cf-4540-899d-5cf107a78138); lib. bdg. 28.93 *(978-1-4777-0073-0(0),* 43e92445-d896-4a81-9b3f-e4a887366395) Rosen Publishing Group, Inc., The. (PowerKids Pr.).

Shafer, Susan. Ponce de Leon & the Fountain of Youth. 2005. (J). pap. *(978-1-4108-4231-2(2))* Benchmark Education Co.

Sutcliffe, Jane. Juan Ponce de Leon. 2005. (History Maker Bios Ser.). (Illus.). 48p. (J). (gr. 3-7). lib. bdg. 26.60 *(978-0-8225-2944-6(0),* Lerner Pubns.) Lerner Publishing Group.

Wallus Sammons, Sandra. Ponce de Leon & the Discovery of Florida. 2013. (ENG., Illus.). 72p. (J). (gr. -1-12). pap. 9.95 *(978-1-56164-593-0(1))* Pineapple Pr., Inc.

POND ECOLOGY

see Freshwater Biology

PONIES

see also Horses

Andrekson, Judy. Little Squire: The Jumping Pony. Parkins, David, illus. 2007. (True Horse Stories Ser.: 5). 80p. (J). (gr. 4-7). pap. 7.99 *(978-0-88776-770-8(2),* Tundra Bks.) Tundra Bks. CAN. Dist: Penguin Random Hse. LLC.

Aspen-Baxter, Linda & Kissock, Heather. Ponies. 2012. (SPA.). (J). *(978-1-61913-191-0(9))* Weigl Pubs., Inc.

Aspley, Brenda. I Love Ponies. McNicolas, Shelagh, illus. 2013. 20p. (J). (gr. -1-k). 7.99 *(978-1-84322-565-2(4),* Armadillo) Anness Publishing GBR. Dist: National Bk. Network.

Boone, Mary. Care for a Wild Chincoteague Pony. 2008. (How to Convince Your Parents You Can ... Ser.). (Illus.). 32p. (YA). (gr. 1-4). lib. bdg. 25.70 *(978-1-58415-663-5(5))* Mitchell Lane Pubs.

Crabtree, Marc & Kalman, Bobbie. Les Poneys. 2012. (FRE., Illus.). 32p. (J). pap. 9.95 *(978-2-89579-439-4(1))* Bayard Canada CAN. Dist: Crabtree Publishing Co.

Curry, Marion. Horse & Pony Basics, 1 vol. 2006. (Horses & Ponies Ser.). (ENG., Illus.). 32p. (gr. 3-5). lib. bdg. 25.67 *(978-0-8368-6831-9(5),* cd523aa4-2845-4958-a143-b72c350cec85, Gareth Stevens Learning Library) Stevens, Gareth Publishing LLLP.

—Horse & Pony Care, 1 vol. 2006. (Horses & Ponies Ser.). (ENG., Illus.). 32p. (gr. 3-5). lib. bdg. 25.67 *(978-0-8368-6833-3(1),* ef407a2c-d6fb-424b-826c-7a727c6fdc02, Gareth Stevens Learning Library) Stevens, Gareth Publishing LLLP.

De La Bédoyère, Camilla. Horses & Ponies, 1 vol. 2015. (100 Facts You Should Know Ser.). (ENG., Illus.). 48p. (J). (gr. 4-5). pap. 15.05 *(978-1-4824-3199-5(8),* e241bf26-922d-49d1-90ae-762ecc616c08) Stevens, Gareth Publishing LLLP.

Dickins, Rosie & Pratt, Leonie. Horse & Pony Treasury. Sims, Lesley, ed. Young, Norman & Ablett, Barry, illus. 2006. (Horse & Pony Treasury Ser.). 93p. (J). 19.99 *(978-0-7945-1431-0(6),* Usborne) EDC Publishing.

DK. Touch & Feel: Ponies. 2013. (Touch & Feel Ser.). (ENG.). 12p. (J). (gr. -1 — 1). bds. 6.99 *(978-1-4654-0919-5(X),* DK Children) Dorling Kindersley Publishing, Inc.

—Ultimate Sticker Book: Horses & Ponies: More Than 250 Reusable Stickers. 2017. (Ultimate Sticker Book Ser.). (ENG.). 32p. (J). (gr. k-2). pap. 6.99 *(978-1-4654-5692-2(9),* DK Children) Dorling Kindersley Publishing, Inc.

Draper, Judith & Roberts, Matthew. My First Horse & Pony Book: From Breeds & Bridles to Jodhpurs & Jumping. 2005. (My First Horse & Pony Ser.). (ENG., Illus.). 48p. (J). (gr. k-3). 11.99 *(978-0-7534-5878-5(0),* 900052701, Kingfisher) Roaring Brook Pr.

Evans, Shira. National Geographic Readers: Trot, Pony! 2016. (Readers Ser.). (Illus.). 24p. (J). (gr. -1-k). pap. 4.99 *(978-1-4263-2413-0(8),* National Geographic Kids) Disney Publishing Worldwide.

Gates, Josephine Scribner. The land of Delight: Child life on a Pony Farm. 2007. (Illus.). 116p. (J). lib. bdg. 59.00 *(978-1-60304-022-8(6))* Dollworks.

Green, Sara. The Shetland Pony. 2011. (Horse Breed Roundup Ser.). (ENG., Illus.). 24p. (J). (gr. 3-8). lib. bdg. 27.95 *(978-1-60014-658-9(9),* Pilot Bks.) Bellwether Media.

Gunzi, Christiane. Little Ponies: A Feels Real Book to Touch & Share. 2015. (ENG., Illus.). 8p. (J). bds. 9.99 *(978-1-909763-10-4(1))* Award Pubns. Ltd. GBR. Dist: Parkwest Pubns., Inc.

Harvey, G. & Dickens, R. Riding & Pony Care. 2004. (Complete Book of Riding & Pony Care Ser.). (Illus.). 144p. (J). (gr. 3-18). lib. bdg. 23.95 *(978-1-58086-422-0(8))* EDC Publishing.

Head, Honor. Horses & Ponies. 2007. (QEB Know Your Pet Ser.). (Illus.). 32p. (J). lib. bdg. 19.95 *(978-1-59566-219-4(7))* QEB Publishing Inc.

Henry, Lynn. Think Like a Pony: Foundation Book. 2008. (Think Like a Pony Ser.). (ENG., Illus.). 80p. (J). (gr. 3-18). pap. 16.95 *(978-1-905693-09-2(5))* Quiller Publishing, Ltd. GBR. Dist: Independent Pubs. Group.

—Think Like a Pony on the Ground, 3 vols. 2008. (Think Like a Pony Ser.). (ENG., Illus.). 112p. (J). (gr. 3-18). pap., wbk. ed. 16.95 *(978-1-905693-10-8(9))* Quiller Publishing, Ltd. GBR. Dist: Independent Pubs. Group.

Hudak, Heather C. Ponies. 2006. (Farm Animals Ser.). (Illus.). 24p. (J). (gr. 3-7). lib. bdg. 24.45 *(978-1-59036-426-0(0));* per. 8.95 *(978-1-59036-433-8(3))* Weigl Pubs., Inc.

Jacobs, Pat. Pony Pals. 2018. (Pet Pals Ser.). (Illus.). 32p. (J). (gr. 3-3). pap. *(978-0-7787-5734-4(X))* Crabtree Publishing Co.

Kaster, Pam. Molly the Pony: A True Story. 2008. (ENG., Illus.). 36p. (gr. 3-7). 17.95 *(978-0-8071-3320-0(5),* 1403) Louisiana State Univ. Pr.

—Molly the Pony: A True Story. 2012. (My Readers: Level 3 Ser.). (J). lib. bdg. 13.55 *(978-0-606-26125-8(7))* Turtleback.

Kelly, Miles. Horses & Ponies. Kelly, Richard, ed. 2nd ed. 2017. 480p. (J). pap. 9.95 *(978-1-78617-013-2(2))* Miles Kelly Publishing, Ltd. GBR. Dist: Parkwest Pubns., Inc.

Khan, Sarah. Little Book of Horses & Ponies. Lambert, Stephen, illus. 2010. (Miniature Editions Ser.). 64p. (YA). (gr. 3-18). 6.99 *(978-0-7945-2791-4(4),* Usborne) EDC Publishing.

Kissock, Heather & Aspen-Baxter, Linda. Ponies. 2011. (J). *(978-1-61690-929-1(3)); (978-1-61690-575-0(1))* Weigl Pubs., Inc.

Krementz, Jill. A Very Young Rider. Krementz, Jill, photos by. 2006. (Illus.). 124p. (gr. 4-7). 24.95 *(978-0-9755516-2-2(0))* DreamHse. Publishing Inc.

Landau, Elaine. Shetland Ponies Are My Favorite! 2012. (My Favorite Horses Ser.). (ENG.). 24p. (gr. 3-5). lib. bdg. 22.60 *(978-0-7613-6534-1(6),* Lerner Pubns.) Lerner Publishing Group.

Lange, Nikki Bataille. My Little Pony: A Very Minty Christmas. LoRaso, Carlo, illus. gif. ed. 2005. 22p. (J). (gr. -1-1). bds. 13.99 *(978-1-57791-191-3(1))* Brighter Minds Children's Publishing.

MacAulay, Kelley & Kalman, Bobbie. Ponies, 1 vol. Crabtree, Marc, illus. Crabtree, Marc, photos by. 2004. (Pet Care Ser.). (ENG.). 32p. (J). pap. *(978-0-7787-1790-4(9))* Crabtree Publishing Co.

Marsh, Laura. National Geographic Readers - Ponies. 2011. (Readers Ser.). (Illus.). 32p. (J). (gr. 1-3). pap. 5.99 *(978-1-4263-0849-9(3),* National Geographic Kids) Disney Publishing Worldwide.

—National Geographic Readers: Ponies. 2011. (Readers Ser.). (ENG., Illus.). 32p. (J). (gr. 1-3). lib. bdg. 14.90 *(978-1-4263-0850-5(7),* National Geographic Kids) Disney Publishing Worldwide.

—Ponies (1 Hardcover/1 CD) 2016. (National Geographic Readers: Pre-Reader Ser.). (ENG.). (J). *(978-1-4301-2105-3(X))* Live Oak Media.

—Ponies (1 Paperback/1 CD) 2016. (National Geographic Readers: Pre-Reader Ser.). (ENG.). (J). pap. *(978-1-4301-2104-6(1))* Live Oak Media.

Mason, Theodore. The South Pole Ponies. 2007. 232p. (gr. 7). per. 18.00 *(978-1-59048-251-3(4))* Long Riders' Guild Pr., The.

Milbourne, Anna. Horses & Ponies. Gaudenzi, Giacinto & Haggerty, Tim, illus. 2006. (Beginners Nature: Level 1 Ser.). 32p. (J). (gr. k-2). 4.99 *(978-0-7945-1397-9(2),* Usborne) EDC Publishing.

National Geographic. National Geographic Readers: Favorite Animals Collection. 2013. (Readers Ser.). (Illus.). 128p. (J). (gr. -1-k). pap. 7.99 *(978-1-4263-1333-2(0),* National Geographic Kids) Disney Publishing Worldwide.

National Geographic Kids. National Geographic Kids Ponies & Horses Sticker Activity Book: Over 1,000 Stickers! 2015. (NG Sticker Activity Bks.). 56p. (J). (gr. -1-k). pap., act. bk. ed. 6.99 *(978-1-4263-1902-0(9),* National Geographic Kids) Disney Publishing Worldwide.

Needham, Kate. Pony Guide. 2006. (Illus.). 31p. (J). *(978-0-439-78703-1(3))* Scholastic, Inc.

Needham, Louise. An Adventure with Katy the Pony. 2009. (Illus.). 36p. pap. 15.49 *(978-1-4490-3972-1(3))* AuthorHouse.

Parise-Peterson, Amanda. Shetland Ponies. 2018. (Horse Breeds Ser.). (ENG.). 32p. (J). (gr. 3-9). pap. 7.95 *(978-1-5435-0040-0(4),* 137001); lib. bdg. 28.65 *(978-1-5435-0034-9(X),* 136987) Capstone. (Capstone Pr.).

Patchett, Fiona. Ponies (First Sticker Book) Finn, Rebecca, illus. 2011. (First Sticker Book Ser.). 24p. (J). pap. 6.99 *(978-0-7945-2921-5(6),* Usborne) EDC Publishing.

Pickeral, Tamsin. The Encyclopedia of Horses & Ponies. 2003. 384p. (YA). pap. 19.95 *(978-0-7525-8277-1(1))* Parragon, Inc.

Pollack, Pam & Belviso, Meg. Ponies, Vol. 2. Bonforte, Lisa, illus. 2003. (Penguin Young Readers, Level 2 Ser.: Vol. 2). 48p. (J). (gr. 1-2). mass mkt. 5.99 *(978-0-448-42524-5(6),* Penguin Young Readers) Penguin Young Readers Group.

Ponies at Play. 12p. (J). *(978-2-7643-0191-3(X))* Phidal Publishing, Inc./Editions Phidal, Inc.

Pony Club. 2012. (Illus.). 120p. (J). *(978-1-4351-4412-5(0))* Barnes & Noble, Inc.

Reid, Struan. Dictionary of horses & ponies - internet Linked. Khan, Aziz, illus. rev. ed. 2004. 128p. (J). pap. 14.95 *(978-0-7945-0843-2(X),* Usborne) EDC Publishing.

Roberts, Angela. Ponies! 2017. (Step into Reading Ser.). (Illus.). 32p. (J). (gr. -1-1). pap. 5.99 *(978-1-5247-1440-6(2),* Random Hse. Bks. for Young Readers) Random Hse. Children's Bks.

Siemens, Jared. Ponies. 2017. (Illus.). 24p. (J). *(978-1-5105-0623-7(3))* SmartBook Media, Inc.

Silverman, Buffy. Can You Tell a Horse from a Pony? 2012. (Animal Look-Alikes Ser.). 32p. (gr. k-2). pap. 45.32 *(978-0-7613-9256-9(4))* Lerner Publishing Group.

Smith, L. The Usborne Book of Horses & Ponies. rev. ed. 2004. (Young Nature Ser.). (Illus.). 32p. (Orig.). (J). pap. 6.95 *(978-0-7945-0850-0(2),* Usborne) EDC Publishing.

Szymanski, Lois. Chincoteague Pony Identification Cards, 1 vol. 2013. (ENG., Illus.). 75p. pap. 19.99 *(978-0-7643-4453-4(6),* 9780764344534) Schiffer Publishing, Ltd.

Titmus, Dawn. Horses & Ponies, 1 vol. 2018. (Cool Pets for Kids Ser.). (ENG.). 32p. (J). (gr. 3-3). 27.93 *(978-1-5383-3797-4(5),* 9c1ed5cc-33d8-4ac3-b50f-e3ea900249b5, PowerKids Pr.) Rosen Publishing Group, Inc., The.

Turnbull, Stephanie. Ponies. 2015. (My Favorite Horses Ser.). (ENG.). 24p. (J). (gr. 2-5). 28.50 *(978-1-62588-181-6(9),* 17308) Black Rabbit Bks.

—Ponies. 2015. (ENG., Illus.). 24p. (J). pap. 8.95 *(978-1-77092-227-3(X))* RiverStream Publishing.

Walker, Kathryn. See How Horses & Ponies Grow, 1 vol. 2009. (See How They Grow Ser.). (ENG.). 24p. (J). (gr. 2-2). lib. bdg. 26.27 *(978-1-4358-2832-2(1),* 03d7e79f-2828-4a53-930c-468247261106); (Illus.). pap. 9.25 *(978-1-4358-2881-0(X),* 171b123e-2d21-4319-b622-88b0e613f62e) Rosen Publishing Group, Inc., The. (PowerKids Pr.).

Walter Foster Jr. Creative Team. Horses & Ponies Drawing & Activity Book: Learn to Draw 17 Different Breeds. 2018. (Drawing & Activity Ser.). (ENG.). 64p. (J). (gr. 1-3). spiral bd. 12.95 *(978-1-63322-664-7(6),* 305671, Walter Foster Jr) Quarto Publishing Group USA.

Watt, Fiona. Little Sticker Dolly Dressing Ponies. 2018. (Little Sticker Dolly Dressing Ser.). (ENG.). 24p. (J). pap. 8.99 *(978-0-7945-4212-2(3),* Usborne) EDC Publishing.

Watts, Ana Dearborn & Dearborn, Dorothy. The Pony Princess. Taylor, Carol, illus. 2008. (ENG.). 32p. pap. 6.00 *(978-1-896543-32-1(4))* DreamCatcher Publishing CAN. Dist: Univ. of Toronto Pr.

PONIES—FICTION

Abdo Publishing, et al. My Little Pony: Friendship Is Magic, 8 vols. Breckel, Heather et al, illus. 2015. (My Little Pony: Friendship Is Magic Ser.: Vol. 8). (ENG.). 24p. (J). (gr. 2-5). 250.88 *(978-1-61479-375-5(1),* 18206, Graphic Novels) Spotlight.

Alexander, Louise. Happy Haunting. 2016. (My Little Pony 8X8 Picture Bks.). (J). lib. bdg. 13.55 *(978-0-606-38324-0(7))* Turtleback.

—The Reason for the Season. 2015. (My Little Pony 8X8 Picture Bks.). (J). lib. bdg. 13.55 *(978-0-606-37511-5(2))* Turtleback.

—School Spirit! 2015. (My Little Pony 8X8 Picture Bks.). (J). lib. bdg. 13.55 *(978-0-606-37225-1(3))* Turtleback.

Alexander, Samantha. Rachel, Vol. 6. 6th ed. (ENG.). 128p. mass mkt. 6.99 *(978-0-330-36841-4(9),* Pan) Pan Macmillan GBR. Dist: Trafalgar Square Publishing.

Anderson, C. W. Blaze Finds Forgotten Roads. Anderson, C. W., illus. 2018. (Billy & Blaze Ser.). (ENG., Illus.). 48p. (J). (gr. k-3). pap. 9.99 *(978-1-5344-1367-2(7),* Aladdin) Simon & Schuster Children's Publishing.

Anderson, Ted & Cook, Katie. My Little Pony: Equestria Girls. 2016. lib. bdg. 30.60 *(978-0-606-37807-9(3))* Turtleback.

—My Little Pony: Friendship Is Magic Volume 17. Sherron, Kate & Price, Andy, illus. 2019. (My Little Pony Ser.: 17). 144p. (J). (gr. 4-7). pap. 19.99 *(978-1-68405-526-5(1))* Idea & Design Works, LLC.

Anderson, Ted & Whitley, Jeremy. My Little Pony: Friendship Is Magic Volume 16. Kuusisto, Toni et al, illus. 2019. (My Little Pony Ser.: 16). 120p. (J). (gr. 4-7). pap. 17.99 *(978-1-68405-428-2(1))* Idea & Design Works, LLC.

—My Little Pony: Friendship Is Magic Volume 6. Garbowska, Agnes et al, illus. 2015. (My Little Pony Ser.: 6). 104p. (J). (gr. 4-7). pap. 17.99 *(978-1-63140-203-6(X),* 9781631402036) Idea & Design Works, LLC.

Angleberger, Tom. Crankee Doodle. Bell, Cece, illus. 2018. (ENG.). 32p. (J). (gr. -1-3). pap. 7.99 *(978-1-328-86928-9(8),* 1696689, Clarion Bks.) HarperCollins Pubs.

Ann, Sharrie. Granddaughter & King Green Warts. 2008. 24p. pap. 12.99 *(978-1-4343-9470-5(0))* AuthorHouse.

Asquith, Ros. Trixie & the Dream Pony of Doom. 2010. (ENG., Illus.). 208p. (gr. 3-6). pap. 9.99 *(978-0-00-722358-9(7),* HarperCollins Children's Bks.) HarperCollins Pubs. Ltd. GBR. Dist: HarperCollins Pubs.

Baglio, Ben M. Searching for Sunshine. Beckett, Andrew & Aubrey, Meg Kelleher, illus. 2005. 158p. (J). *(978-0-439-79249-3(5))* Scholastic, Inc.

Bak, Jenny. Color & Poster Book. Middleton, Gayle & Edwards, Ken, illus. 2006. (My Little Pony Ser.). 32p. (J). (gr. -1-1). 3.99 *(978-0-06-079470-5(4),* HarperFestival) HarperCollins Pubs.

Baker, Nancy Scott. Peggy Sue at the Pony Barn. Reese, Shelbye J., illus. 2009. (ENG.). 24p. pap. 15.99 *(978-1-4415-6593-8(0))* Xlibris Corp.

Barkhouse, Joyce & Barkhouse, Janet. Pit Pony: The Picture Book. Smith, Sydney, illus. 2012. (ENG.). 32p. (J). (gr. -1-2). 14.95 *(978-1-4595-0143-0(8),* 0143) Formac Publishing Co., Ltd. CAN. Dist: Formac Lorimer Bks. Ltd.

Bates, M. The Perfect Pony. 2004. (Sandy Lane Stables Ser.). (ENG.). 118p. (J). pap. 4.99 *(978-0-7945-0505-9(8))* EDC Publishing.

Batts, Laura. Love Your Pony, Love Your Planet: All about Pony Poo & Other Helpful Things We Can Do! 2013. (ENG., Illus.). 16.95 *(978-1-62086-303-9(0))* Amplify Publishing Group.

Baxter, Nicola. My Book of Magical Pony Tales: 12 Beautifully Illustrated Stories. Shuttleworth, Cathie, illus. 2013. (ENG.). 80p. (J). (gr. -1-12). pap. 9.99 *(978-1-84322-965-0(X))* Anness Publishing GBR. Dist: National Bk. Network.

Beaton, Kate. The Princess & the Pony. Beaton, Kate, illus. 2015. (ENG., Illus.). 40p. (J). (gr. -1-3). 17.99 *(978-0-545-63708-4(2))* Scholastic, Inc.

Belle, Magnolia. My Little Pony: Power Ponies to the Rescue! 2015. (Passport to Reading Level 1 Ser.). (J). lib. bdg. 13.55 *(978-0-606-37224-4(5))* Turtleback.

—Pinkie Pie Keeps a Secret. 2016. (Passport to Reading Level 1 Ser.). (Illus.). 32p. (J). lib. bdg. 14.75 *(978-0-606-38323-3(9))* Turtleback.

—We Are Family. 2017. (Illus.). 32p. (J). *(978-1-5182-4449-0(1))* Little Brown & Co.

—We Are Family. 2017. (My Little Pony Leveled Readers Ser.). (ENG., Illus.). 32p. (J). (gr. -1-3). lib. bdg. 31.36 *(978-1-5321-4098-3(3),* 26971) Spotlight.

Belle, Magnolia, adapted by. Pony Pirate Party! 2017. (Illus.). (J). *(978-1-5182-5214-3(1))* Little, Brown Bks. for Young Readers.

Belle, Magnolia & Berrow, Gillian M. Pinkie Pie Keeps a Secret. 2017. (My Little Pony Leveled Readers Ser.). (ENG., Illus.). 32p. (J). (gr. -1-3). lib. bdg. 31.36 *(978-1-5321-4095-2(9),* 26968) Spotlight.

Beloat, Betty. The Winged Pony. Schwartz, Wendy, illus. 2005. 32p. (J). (gr. k-5). pap. 5.99 *(978-0-9701008-8-7(4))* Bicast, Inc.

Benjamin, Ruth. My Little Pony: A Secret Gift. Middleton, Gayle, illus. 2006. 24p. (J). lib. bdg. 15.00 *(978-1-4242-1536-2(6))* Fitzgerald Bks.

—A Secret Gift/el Regalo Secreto. Abboud, Adela, tr. from ENG. Middleton, Gayle, illus. 2006. (I Can Read Bks.). (SPA & ENG.). 24p. (J). (gr. k-3). per. 3.99 *(978-0-06-112391-7(9),* Rayo) HarperCollins Pubs.

Bentley, Sue. Circus Surprise #7. Swan, Angela, illus. 2014. (Magic Ponies Ser.: 7). (ENG.). 128p. (J). (gr. 1-3). 6.99 *(978-0-448-46734-4(8),* Grosset & Dunlap) Penguin Young Readers Group.

—A New Beginning #1, No. 1. Swan, Angela, illus. 2009. (Magic Puppy Ser.: 1). (ENG.). 128p. (J). (gr. 1-3). pap. 6.99 *(978-0-448-45044-5(5),* Grosset & Dunlap) Penguin Young Readers Group.

—A New Friend. 2013. (Magic Ponies Ser.: 1). lib. bdg. 16.00 *(978-0-606-29584-0(4))* Turtleback.

—A New Friend #1, 1. Swan, Angela, illus. 2013. (Magic Ponies Ser.: 1). (ENG.). 128p. (J). (gr. 1-3). 6.99 *(978-0-448-46205-9(2),* Grosset & Dunlap) Penguin Young Readers Group.

—Pony Camp. 2014. (Magic Ponies Ser.: 8). lib. bdg. 16.00 *(978-0-606-34139-4(0))* Turtleback.

—Pony Camp #8. Swan, Angela, illus. 2014. (Magic Ponies Ser.: 8). (ENG.). 128p. (J). (gr. 1-3). 6.99 *(978-0-448-46787-0(9),* Grosset & Dunlap) Penguin Young Readers Group.

—Riding Rescue #6. Swan, Angela, illus. 2013. (Magic Ponies Ser.: 6). (ENG.). 128p. (J). (gr. 1-3). 6.99 *(978-0-448-46735-1(6),* Grosset & Dunlap) Penguin Young Readers Group.

—Show-Jumping Dreams. 2013. (Magic Ponies Ser.: 4). lib. bdg. 14.75 *(978-0-606-31679-8(5))* Turtleback.

—Show-Jumping Dreams #4. Swan, Angela, illus. 2013. (Magic Ponies Ser.: 4). (ENG.). 128p. (J). (gr. 1-3). pap. 5.99 *(978-0-448-46208-0(7),* Grosset & Dunlap) Penguin Young Readers Group.

—A Special Wish. 2013. (Magic Ponies Ser.: 2). lib. bdg. 14.75 *(978-0-606-29758-5(8))* Turtleback.

—A Special Wish #2, No. 2. Swan, Angela, illus. 2013. (Magic Ponies Ser.: 2). (ENG.). 128p. (J). (gr. 1-3). pap. 6.99 *(978-0-448-46206-6(0),* Grosset & Dunlap) Penguin Young Readers Group.

—A Twinkle of Hooves #3. Swan, Angela, illus. 2013. (Magic Ponies Ser.: 3). (ENG.). 128p. (J). (gr. 1-3). pap. 5.99 *(978-0-448-46207-3(9),* Grosset & Dunlap) Penguin Young Readers Group.

—Winter Wonderland. 2013. (Magic Ponies Ser.: 5). lib. bdg. 16.00 *(978-0-606-32118-1(7))* Turtleback.

—Winter Wonderland #5. Swan, Angela, illus. 2013. (Magic Ponies Ser.: 5). (ENG.). 128p. (J). (gr. 1-3). 6.99 *(978-0-448-46786-3(0),* Grosset & Dunlap) Penguin Young Readers Group.

Berenstain, Jan & Berenstain, Mike. The Berenstain Bears & the Shaggy Little Pony. Berenstain, Jan & Berenstain, Mike, illus. 2011. (I Can Read Level 1 Ser.). (ENG., Illus.). 32p. (J). (gr. k-3). 16.99 *(978-0-06-168972-7(6));* pap. 4.99 *(978-0-06-057419-2(4))* HarperCollins Pubs. (HarperCollins).

Berrow, G. M. Discord & the Ponyville Players Dramarama. 2015. (My Little Pony Chapter Bks.). (J). lib. bdg. 16.00 *(978-0-606-37226-8(1))* Turtleback.

—Fluttershy & the Fine Furry Friends Fair. 2015. (My Little Pony Chapter Bks.). (J). lib. bdg. 16.00 *(978-0-606-35942-9(7))* Turtleback.

—Lyra & Bon Bon & the Mares from S. M. I. L. E. 2016. (My Little Pony Chapter Bks.). (J). lib. bdg. 16.00 *(978-0-606-38301-1(8))* Turtleback.

—Pinkie Pie Keeps a Secret. 2016. (Illus.). 32p. (J). *(978-1-5182-1664-0(1))* Little Brown & Co.

—Rainbow Dash & the Daring Do Double Dare. 2014. (My Little Pony Chapter Bks.). (J). lib. bdg. 16.00 *(978-0-606-34089-2(0))* Turtleback.

—Rarity & the Curious Case of Charity. 2014. (My Little Pony Chapter Bks.). (J). lib. bdg. 16.00 *(978-0-606-35300-7(3))* Turtleback.

—The Trouble with Trixie. 2017. (My Little Pony Chapter Bks.). (Illus.). 116p. (J). lib. bdg. 16.00 *(978-0-606-39477-2(X))* Turtleback.

—Twilight Sparkle & the Crystal Heart Spell. 2013. (My Little Pony Chapter Bks.). (J). lib. bdg. 16.00 *(978-0-606-31733-7(3))* Turtleback.

Betancourt, Jeanne. Pony Mysteries #1: Penny & Pepper (Scholastic Reader, Level 3) Riley, Kellee, illus. 2011. (Scholastic Reader, Level 3 Ser.). (ENG.). 48p. (J). (gr. 1-3). pap. 3.99 *(978-0-545-11508-7(6),* Cartwheel Bks.) Scholastic, Inc.

Bhakta, Sanjini. The Chocolate Pony. 2010. 28p. pap. 12.99 *(978-1-4490-9761-5(8))* AuthorHouse.

Blabey, Aaron. Thelma the Unicorn. 2017. (ENG., Illus.). 28p. (J). (gr. -1-k). 14.99 *(978-1-338-15842-7(2),* Scholastic Pr.) Scholastic, Inc.

Blacker, Terence. Racing Manhattan. 2018. (ENG.). 352p. (J). (gr. 7). 17.99 *(978-0-7636-9273-5(5))* Candlewick Pr.

Blyton, Enid. Pretty Star the Pony: And Other Stories. 2013. (ENG., Illus.). 192p. (J). 9.95 *(978-1-84135-459-0(7))* Award Pubns. Ltd. GBR. Dist: Parkwest Pubns., Inc.

Braddock, Pauline. Humbug. 2010. 108p. pap. 8.48 *(978-1-4452-9227-4(0))* Lulu Pr., Inc.

Brooks, Heather. Running Horse Ridge #2: Hercules: a Matter of Trust. 2nd ed. 2009. (Running Horse Ridge Ser.: 2). (ENG.). 224p. (J). (gr. 5-18). pap. 6.99 *(978-0-06-142981-1(3),* HarperCollins) HarperCollins Pubs.

Brown, Kathryn. Adventures at Aaron Loch Farm. 2009. (ENG.). 50p. pap. 23.50 *(978-1-4092-6961-8(2))* Lulu Pr., Inc.

Burgess, Pauline. Pony Palace Camp. Harbinson, Karen, illus. 2014. (Pony Friends Forever Ser.). (ENG.). 96p. (J). pap. 12.00 *(978-0-85640-923-3(5))* Blackstaff Pr., Ltd. GBR. Dist: Casemate Pubs. & Bk. Distributors, LLC.

—Pony Surprise. 2015. (Pony Friends Forever Ser.). (ENG., Illus.). 93p. (J). pap. 12.00 *(978-0-85640-936-3(7))* Blackstaff Pr., Ltd. GBR. Dist: Casemate Pubs. & Bk. Distributors, LLC.

Cabrera, Aleix. Princess Suque's Pony, 1 vol. Bonilla, Rocío, illus. 2017. (Little Princesses Ser.). (ENG.). 32p. (J). (gr. 1-2). 28.93 *(978-1-5081-9401-9(7),* f44ec0c4-9196-4a07-8a80-067799ab665e); pap. 11.00 *(978-1-5081-9461-3(0),* 85966d3b-ac9d-43dc-9d87-1eb232aba5d2) Rosen Publishing Group, Inc., The. (Windmill Bks.).

Carithers, Rochelle. The Purple with Pink Polka Dot Ponies. Weber, Caressa, illus. 2010. 102p. pap. 7.95 *(978-1-936107-31-5(7))* Salem Author Services.

Carlson, Nolan. Lame Eagle & Wind Chaser. 2005. (YA). per. *(978-0-9772745-1-2(9))* Mennonite Pr. Inc.

Causton, Linda. Lester's Rainy Lake Pony. l.t. ed. 2004. (Illus.). 32p. (J). 12.00 *(978-1-930374-09-6(7))* DeForest Pr.

Chapman, Linda. Flying High. Hull, Biz & Farley, Andrew, illus. 2004. (My Secret Unicorn Ser.). 118p. (J). *(978-0-439-65273-5(1))* Scholastic, Inc.

—Starlight Surprise, Vol. 4. 4th ed. 2003. (ENG., Illus.). 144p. pap. *(978-0-14-131344-3(7),* Puffin) Penguin Bks., Ltd.

—Starlight Surprise. Hull, Biz, illus. 2003. (My Secret Unicorn Ser.). 130p. (J). *(978-0-439-65275-9(8))* Scholastic, Inc.

—Twilight Magic. Kronheimer, Ann, illus. 2008. 149p. (J). pap. *(978-0-545-03160-8(5))* Scholastic, Inc.

Chapman, Marian. The Purple Pony. 2004. 56p. pap. 20.99 *(978-1-4134-2363-1(9))* Xlibris Corp.

Chase, Diana. Daisy Street. Bradley, Vanessa, illus. 2005. 128p. (Orig.). (J). pap. 13.50 *(978-1-920731-11-3(3))* Fremantle Pr. AUS. Dist: Independent Pubs. Group.

Chasing Gold. 2014. (Marguerite Henry's Ponies of Chincoteague Ser.: 3). (ENG., Illus.). 192p. (J). (gr. 3-7). pap. 7.99 *(978-1-4814-0342-9(7),* Aladdin) Simon & Schuster Children's Publishing.

Chester, Laura. Marvel the Marvelous. Lippincott, Gary A., illus. 2008. (ENG.). 176p. (J). 18.95 *(978-1-59543-841-6(6))* Willow Creek Pr., Inc.

Clover, Peter. Rescue Riders: Ghost Pony. l.t. ed. 2007. 92p. per. *(978-1-905665-28-0(8))* Pollinger In Print.

—Rescue Riders: Race Against Time. l.t. ed. 2007. 88p. per. *(978-1-905665-29-7(6))* Pollinger In Print.

—Sheltie & the Stray. 2005. (Illus.). 91p. (J). *(978-0-439-68890-1(6))* Scholastic, Inc.

—Sheltie in Trouble. 2005. 89p. (J). *(978-0-439-68889-5(2))* Scholastic, Inc.

Cochrane, Ian. Shian & the Corryvreckan. 2013. (Illus.). 96p. pap. *(978-1-909465-09-1(7))* Cloister Hse. Pr., The.

Cook, Katie. My Little Pony: Friendship Is Magic. Price, Andy et al, illus. 2015. (My Little Pony: Friendship Is Magic Ser.). (ENG.). 24p. (J). (gr. 2-5). lib. bdg. 31.36 *(978-1-61479-376-2(X),* 18207, Graphic Novels) Spotlight.

—My Little Pony: Friendship Is Magic. Breckel, Heather et al, illus. 2015. (My Little Pony: Friendship Is Magic Ser.). (ENG.). 24p. (J). (gr. 2-5). lib. bdg. 31.36 *(978-1-61479-377-9(8),* 18208);3. lib. bdg. 31.36 *(978-1-61479-378-6(6),* 18209) Spotlight. (Graphic Novels).

—My Little Pony: Friendship Is Magic, 4. Price, Andy et al, illus. 2015. (My Little Pony: Friendship Is Magic Ser.). (ENG.). 24p. (J). (gr. 2-5). lib. bdg. 31.36 *(978-1-61479-379-3(4),* 18210, Graphic Novels) Spotlight.

—My Little Pony: Friendship Is Magic Volume 1, Vol. 1. Price, Andy, illus. 2014. (My Little Pony Ser.: 1). 104p. (J). (gr. 4-7). pap. 17.99 *(978-1-61377-605-6(5),* 9781613776056) Idea & Design Works, LLC.

Cook, Katie & Nuhfer, Heather. My Little Pony: Friendship Is Magic. Uyetake, Neil & Breckel, Heather, illus. 2015. (My Little Pony: Friendship Is Magic Ser.). (ENG.). 24p. (J). (gr. 2-5). lib. bdg. 31.36 *(978-1-61479-380-9(8),* 18211, Graphic Novels) Spotlight.

—My Little Pony: Friendship Is Magic. Mebberson, Amy & Uyetake, Neil, illus. 2015. (My Little Pony: Friendship Is Magic Ser.). (ENG.). 24p. (J). (gr. 2-5). lib. bdg. 31.36 *(978-1-61479-383-0(2),* 18214, Graphic Novels) Spotlight.

—My Little Pony: Friendship Is Magic. Mebberson, Amy et al, illus. 2015. (My Little Pony: Friendship Is Magic Ser.). (ENG.). 24p. (J). (gr. 2-5). lib. bdg. 31.36 *(978-1-61479-382-3(4),* 18213);6. lib. bdg. 31.36 *(978-1-61479-381-6(6),* 18212) Spotlight. (Graphic Novels).
Costain, Meredith. Pony School Showdown. McDonald, Danielle, illus. 2016. (Ella Diaries Ser.). (ENG.). 143p. (J). *(978-1-61067-568-0(1))* Kane Miller.
—Pony School Showdown: The Ella Diaries. McDonald, Danielle, illus. 2017. 144p. (J). pap. 5.99 *(978-1-61067-524-6(X))* Kane Miller.
Crawford, Hannah. The Fight for Light by Hannah Crawford. 2012. (ENG., Illus.). 86p. pap. 8.50 *(978-1-78035-335-7(9),* Fastprint Publishing) Upfront Publishing Ltd. GBR. Dist: Printondemand-worldwide.com.
—The Fight with Darkness. 2013. (ENG., Illus.). 79p. pap. 8.49 *(978-1-78035-586-3(6),* Fastprint Publishing) Upfront Publishing Ltd. GBR. Dist: Printondemand-worldwide.com.
Dahl, Michael. Pony Brushes His Teeth. 1 vol. Vidal, Oriol, illus. 2010. (Hello Genius Ser.). (ENG.). 20p. (J). (gr. -1 — 1). bds. 7.99 *(978-1-4048-5727-8(3),* 102304, Picture Window Bks.) Capstone.
David, Erica. The Big Pony Race. Fruchter, Jason, illus. 2006. 27p. (J). *(978-0-7172-9869-3(8))* Scholastic, Inc.
Davidson, Susanna. Princess Polly & the Pony. Hill, Dave, illus. 2007. (First Reading Level 4 Ser.). 48p. (J). 8.99 *(978-0-7945-1756-4(0),* Usborne) EDC Publishing.
—Stories of Magic Ponies. Costa, Jana, illus. 2007. (Young Reading Series 1 Gift Bks). 48p. (J). 8.99 *(978-0-7945-1790-8(0),* Usborne) EDC Publishing.
Davis, David Denton. Polly's Promise: A Story about Thriving Rather Than Simply Surviving... Turning Apparent Disability into Gifted Ability. 2013. 80p. pap. 21.95 *(978-1-4787-0275-7(3))* Outskirts Pr., Inc.
Dawson, JoAnn S. Lady's Big Surprise. 2004. 288p. pap. 8.95 *(978-0-9746561-6-8(X));* (Illus.). 15.95 *(978-0-9746561-5-1(1))* FT Richards Publishing.
—Star of Wonder. 2005. (Illus.). 268p. pap. 8.95 *(978-0-9746561-4-4(3))* FT Richards Publishing.
De Campi, Alex, et al. My Little Pony: Friends Forever Omnibus, Vol. 1, Vol. 1. 2016. (MLP FF Omnibus Ser.: 1). (Illus.). 292p. (J). (gr. 4-7). pap. 24.99 *(978-1-63140-771-0(6),* 9781631407710) Idea & Design Works, LLC.
Doty, Jean Slaughter. Can I Get There by Candlelight? 2012. (ENG.). 128p. (YA). (gr. 7). pap. 7.99 *(978-1-4424-8608-9(2),* Simon & Schuster Bks. For Young Readers) Simon & Schuster Bks. For Young Readers.
—The Valley of the Ponies. 2012. (ENG.). 96p. (YA). (gr. 7-7). pap. 6.99 *(978-1-4424-8607-2(4),* Simon & Schuster Bks. For Young Readers) Simon & Schuster Bks. For Young Readers.
—Winter Pony. Sanderson, Ruth, illus. 2008. (Stepping Stones Chapter Book: Fiction Ser.). (ENG.). 128p. (J). (gr. 2-4). lib. bdg. 16.19 *(978-0-375-94710-0(8))* Random House Publishing Group.
Doucet, Patricia. The Adventures of Blackie & Brownie. 2012. 26p. pap. 19.99 *(978-1-62230-887-3(5))* Salem Author Services.
Dowling, Iris Gray. A Pony for My Birthday. Bouthyette, Valerie, illus. 2012. 36p. pap. 10.99 *(978-1-937129-50-7(0))* Faithful Life Pubs.
Dream Pony (revised) 2017. (Sandy Lane Stables Ser.). (ENG.). (J). pap. 5.99 *(978-0-7945-3624-4(7),* Usborne) EDC Publishing.
Earhart, Kristin. Finding Luck. Geddes, Serena, illus. 2016. (Marguerite Henry's Misty Inn Ser.: 4). (ENG.). 128p. (J). (gr. 2-5). pap. 6.99 *(978-1-4814-1422-7(4),* Aladdin) Simon & Schuster Children's Publishing.
—Roscoe & the Pony Parade. Gurney, John, illus. 2008. (Little Apple Ser.). 88p. (J). *(978-0-545-08094-1(0))* Scholastic, Inc.
Edmonds, Lin. Jaden & the Terrible Terrible Toad. 2011. 36p. pap. 15.14 *(978-1-4634-1112-1(X))* AuthorHouse.
—Patric the Pony & the Golden Salamander. Connors, Mary, illus. 2009. (ENG.). 32p. pap. 13.99 *(978-1-4389-8021-8(3))* AuthorHouse.
Elliott, Rebecca. Eva & the Lost Pony, 8. 2019. (Branches Early Ch Bks). (ENG.). 72p. (J). (gr. 2-3). 15.36 *(978-0-87617-986-4(3))* Penworthy Co., LLC, The.
—Eva & the Lost Pony. 2018. (Owl Diaries — Branches Ser.: 8). lib. bdg. 14.75 *(978-0-606-41142-4(9))* Turtleback.
—Eva & the Lost Pony: a Branches Book (Owl Diaries #8) Elliott, Rebecca, illus. 2018. (Owl Diaries: 8). (ENG., Illus.). 80p. (J). (gr. k-2). pap. 4.99 *(978-1-338-16303-2(5))* Scholastic, Inc.
—Eva & the Lost Pony: a Branches Book (Owl Diaries #8) (Library Edition), Vol. 8. Elliott, Rebecca, illus. 2018. (Owl Diaries: 8). (ENG., Illus.). 80p. (J). (gr. k-2). lib. bdg. 24.99 *(978-1-338-16304-9(3))* Scholastic, Inc.
Eveleigh, Victoria. Katy's Pony Surprise, Bk. 3. 2012. (ENG., Illus.). 128p. (J). (gr. 2-4). 7.99 *(978-1-4440-0553-0(7),* Orion Children's Bks.) Hachette Children's Group GBR. Dist: Hachette Bk. Group.
Feaster, Raven Joye Raye. Merrileggs of Macon County. 2011. 72p. (gr. -1). pap. 10.75 *(978-1-4567-6971-0(5))* AuthorHouse.
Fidler, Kathleen. Haki the Shetland Pony. 28 vols. 3rd rev. ed. 2018. (Illus.). 144p. (J). pap. 9.95 *(978-1-78250-493-1(1),* Kelpies) Floris Bks. GBR. Dist: Consortium Bk. Sales & Distribution.
Fisher, Marilyn Anne. Pony Tales. 2005. (Illus.). 75p. (J). per. 20.00 *(978-1-890306-90-8(8))* Warwick Hse. Publishing.
Flaxenwick, Dim. Dobbin, Our Favourite Pony: Dobbin & the Little Red Squirrel. 2012. 44p. pap. 20.72 *(978-1-4669-2179-5(X))* Trafford Publishing.
Foltz, Joanna "Gwen". The Owl Tree. 2011. 28p. pap. 13.59 *(978-1-4634-1199-2(5))* AuthorHouse.
Fox, Jennifer. We Like Spike! 2015. (Passport to Reading Level 1 Ser.). (J). lib. bdg. 13.55 *(978-0-606-37512-2(0))* Turtleback.
Francis, Anwen. Siani Shetland. 2008. (ENG., Illus.). 84p. (J). pap. 9.95 *(978-1-905762-62-0(3))* Parthian Bks. GBR. Dist: Independent Pubs. Group.
Garis, Howard R. The Curlytops & Their Pets. 2009. 120p. 22.95 *(978-1-60664-609-0(5));* pap. 10.95 *(978-1-60664-341-9(X))* Rodgers, Alan Bks.
—The Curlytops at Uncle Frank's Ranch; or, Little Folks on Ponyback. 2007. 160p. per. *(978-1-4065-2763-6(7))* Dodo Pr.
Gaydos, Nora. Phonics Comics: Pony Tales - Level 1. Hamilton, Pamela, illus. 2007. (ENG.). 24p. (J). (gr. 1-17). per. 3.99 *(978-1-58476-553-0(4))* Innovative Kids.
Gleadhill, Christa J. Here Comes Lucky! 2011. 16p. pap. 9.99 *(978-1-257-03275-4(5))* Lulu Pr., Inc.
Gorman, Patrick. Alicia & Policia, 1 vol. Gorman, Kyrsten, illus. 2010. 24p. 24.95 *(978-1-4489-6425-3(3))* PublishAmerica, Inc.
Green, D. L. Sparkling Jewel: a Branches Book (Silver Pony Ranch #1) Wallis, Emily, illus. 2015. (Silver Pony Ranch Ser.: 1). (ENG.). 96p. (J). (gr. 1-3). pap. 5.99 *(978-0-545-79765-8(9))* Scholastic, Inc.
Gregg, Stacy. Comet & the Champion's Cup (Pony Club Secrets, Book 5), Book 5. 2020. (Pony Club Secrets Ser.: 5). (ENG., Illus.). 256p. (J). pap. 6.99 *(978-0-00-727030-9(5),* HarperCollins Children's Bks.) HarperCollins Pubs. Ltd. GBR. Dist: HarperCollins Pubs.
—Issie & the Christmas Pony: Christmas Special (Pony Club Secrets) 2017. (Pony Club Secrets Ser.). (ENG.). 176p. (J). 6.99 *(978-0-00-825118-5(5),* HarperCollins Children's Bks.) HarperCollins Pubs. Ltd. GBR. Dist: HarperCollins Pubs.
—Stardust & the Daredevil Ponies, Book 4. 2020. (Pony Club Secrets Ser.: 4). (ENG., Illus.). 256p. (J). pap. 6.99 *(978-0-00-724516-1(5),* HarperCollins Children's Bks.) HarperCollins Pubs. Ltd. GBR. Dist: HarperCollins Pubs.
—The Thunderbolt Pony. 2018. (ENG.). 256p. (J). 6.99 *(978-0-00-825700-2(0),* HarperCollins Children's Bks.) HarperCollins Pubs. Ltd. GBR. Dist: HarperCollins Pubs.
Griffiths, Gary Wayne. Hawaiian Ponies: A Mystery in Paradise, 1 vol. 2010. 48p. pap. 16.95 *(978-1-4489-4793-5(6))* America Star Bks.
Grimes, Terri & Timmons, Jasmine. A Pony Named Penny. 2007. 16p. 11.95 *(978-0-615-15990-4(7))* Dm Productions.
Grovet, Heather. Blondie's Big Ride. 2008. (Illus.). 95p. (J). pap. 5.97 *(978-0-8163-2225-1(2))* Pacific Pr. Publishing Assn.
—A Friend for Zipper. 2008. (J). pap. 5.97 *(978-0-8163-2226-8(0))* Pacific Pr. Publishing Assn.
—Super Star Problems. 2008. (J). pap. 5.97 *(978-0-8163-2255-8(4))* Pacific Pr. Publishing Assn.
Haas, Jessie. Birthday Pony. Apple, Margot, illus. 2004. 80p. (J). (gr. 2-18). 15.99 *(978-0-06-057359-1(7))* HarperCollins Pubs.
Haberler, Julia. Carnival Pony. 2008. (ENG.). 46p. pap. 18.95 *(978-0-557-03179-5(6))* Lulu Pr., Inc.
Hagman, Harvey. Majesty from Assateague, 1 vol. 2009. (ENG., Illus.). 80p. (J). pap. 8.95 *(978-0-87033-552-5(9),* 3670, Cornell Maritime Pr./Tidewater Pubs.) Schiffer Publishing, Ltd.
Hapka, Catherine, pseud. Back in the Saddle. 2016. (Marguerite Henry's Ponies of Chincoteague Ser.: 7). (ENG., Illus.). 192p. (J). (gr. 3-7). pap. 7.99 *(978-1-4814-5993-8(7),* Aladdin) Simon & Schuster Children's Publishing.
—Back in the Saddle. 2016. (Marguerite Henry's Ponies of Chincoteague Ser.: 7). (ENG., Illus.). 192p. (J). (gr. 3-7). 17.99 *(978-1-4814-5994-5(5),* Simon & Schuster/Paula Wiseman Bks.) Simon & Schuster/Paula Wiseman Bks.
—Blue Ribbon Summer. 2014. (Marguerite Henry's Ponies of Chincoteague Ser.: 2). (ENG., Illus.). 208p. (J). (gr. 3-7). pap. 7.99 *(978-1-4814-0339-9(7),* Aladdin) Simon & Schuster Children's Publishing.
—The Camping Trip. 2014. (Pony Scouts: I Can Read! Ser.). (J). lib. bdg. 13.55 *(978-0-606-35069-3(1))* Turtleback.
—Marguerite Henry's Ponies of Chincoteague Complete Collection (Boxed Set) Maddie's Dream; Blue Ribbon Summer; Chasing Gold; Moonlight Mile; a Winning Gift; True Riders; Back in the Saddle; the Road Home. 2017. (Marguerite Henry's Ponies of Chincoteague Ser.). (ENG., Illus.). 1584p. (J). (gr. 3-7). pap. 59.99 *(978-1-5344-1429-7(0),* Aladdin) Simon & Schuster Children's Publishing.
—Moonlight Mile. 2015. (Marguerite Henry's Ponies of Chincoteague Ser.: 4). (ENG., Illus.). 192p. (J). (gr. 3-7). pap. 7.99 *(978-1-4814-0345-0(1),* Aladdin) Simon & Schuster Children's Publishing.
—Pony Scouts: At the Show. Kennedy, Anne, illus. 2011. (I Can Read Level 2 Ser.). (ENG.). 32p. (J). (gr. -1-3). pap. 4.99 *(978-0-06-125544-1(0),* HarperCollins) HarperCollins Pubs.
—Pony Scouts: Back in the Saddle. 2011. (I Can Read Level 2 Ser.). (ENG., Illus.). 32p. (J). (gr. k-3). pap. 4.99 *(978-0-06-125541-0(6),* HarperCollins) HarperCollins Pubs.
—Pony Scouts: Runaway Ponies! Kennedy, Anne, illus. 2012. (I Can Read Level 2 Ser.). (ENG.). 32p. (J). (gr. -1-3). 16.99 *(978-0-06-208669-3(3),* HarperCollins) HarperCollins Pubs.
—Pony Scouts: The Camping Trip. 2014. (I Can Read Level 2 Ser.). (ENG., Illus.). 32p. (J). (gr. -1-3). 16.99 *(978-0-06-208665-5(0));* pap. 5.99 *(978-0-06-208663-1(4))* HarperCollins Pubs. (HarperCollins).
—Pony Scouts: The New Pony. 2013. (I Can Read Level 2 Ser.). (ENG., Illus.). 32p. (J). (gr. -1-3). 16.99 *(978-0-06-208674-7(X),* HarperCollins) HarperCollins Pubs.
—Pony Scouts: The Trail Ride. 2012. (I Can Read Level 2 Ser.). (ENG., Illus.). 32p. (J). (gr. -1-3). pap. 5.99 *(978-0-06-208670-9(7),* HarperCollins) HarperCollins Pubs.
—Pony Scouts: Pony Crazy. Kennedy, Anne, illus. 2009. (I Can Read Level 2 Ser.). (ENG.). 32p. (J). (gr. -1-3). 16.99 *(978-0-06-125533-5(5),* HarperCollins) HarperCollins Pubs.
—Pony Scouts: Pony Party. Kennedy, Anne, illus. 2013. (I Can Read Level 2 Ser.). (ENG.). 32p. (J). (gr. -1-3). pap. 4.99 *(978-0-06-208679-2(0),* HarperCollins) HarperCollins Pubs.
—Pony Scouts: Runaway Ponies! Kennedy, Anne, illus. 2012. (I Can Read Level 2 Ser.). (ENG.). 32p. (J). (gr. -1-3). pap. 5.99 *(978-0-06-208667-9(7),* HarperCollins) HarperCollins Pubs.
—Pony Scouts: the Trail Ride. Kennedy, Anne, illus. 2012. (I Can Read Level 2 Ser.). (ENG.). 32p. (J). (gr. -1-3). 16.99 *(978-0-06-208671-6(5),* HarperCollins) HarperCollins Pubs.
—The Road Home. 2017. (Marguerite Henry's Ponies of Chincoteague Ser.: 8). (ENG., Illus.). 192p. (J). (gr. 3-7). pap. 7.99 *(978-1-4814-5996-9(1),* Simon & Schuster/Paula Wiseman Bks.) Simon & Schuster/Paula Wiseman Bks.
—True Riders. 2015. (Marguerite Henry's Ponies of Chincoteague Ser.: 6). (ENG., Illus.). 192p. (J). (gr. 3-7). 17.99 *(978-1-4814-3972-5(3),* Aladdin) Simon & Schuster Children's Publishing.
—A Winning Gift. 2015. (Marguerite Henry's Ponies of Chincoteague Ser.: 5). (ENG., Illus.). 192p. (J). (gr. 3-7). pap. 7.99 *(978-1-4814-3968-8(5),* Aladdin) Simon & Schuster Children's Publishing.
—A Winning Gift. 2015. (Ponies of Chincoteague Ser.: 5). lib. bdg. 17.20 *(978-0-606-37135-3(4))* Turtleback.
Harlow, Joan Hiatt. Secret of the Night Ponies. 2010. (ENG.). 352p. (J). (gr. 3-7). pap. 7.99 *(978-1-4169-0784-8(X),* McElderry, Margaret K. Bks.) McElderry, Margaret K. Bks.
—Secret of the Night Ponies. 2009. (ENG.). 336p. (J). (gr. 3-7). 16.99 *(978-1-4169-0783-1(1))* Simon & Schuster, Inc.
HarperCollins Publishers Ltd. Staff. A My Little Pony. 2003. 115.84 *(978-0-06-056197-0(1))* HarperCollins Pubs.
Harrison, Paula. The Sea Pony. Williams, Sophy, illus. 2018. (Secret Rescuers Ser.: 6). (ENG.). 128p. (J). (gr. 2-5). 16.99 *(978-1-4814-7623-2(8));* pap. 6.99 *(978-1-4814-7622-5(X))* Simon & Schuster Children's Publishing. (Aladdin).
Henry, Marguerite. Misty of Chincoteague. 2011. (CHI.). 165p. (J). (gr. 3-7). pap. *(978-7-5434-8018-6(2))* Hebei Jiaoyu Chubanshe.
—Misty of Chincoteague. Dennis, Wesley, illus. 2007. 173p. (gr. 3-7). 17.00 *(978-0-7569-8227-0(8))* Perfection Learning Corp.
—Misty of Chincoteague. Dennis, Wesley, illus. 60th ed. 2006. (ENG.). 176p. (J). (gr. 3-7). pap. 7.99 *(978-1-4169-2783-9(2),* Aladdin) Simon & Schuster Children's Publishing.
—Sea Star: Orphan of Chincoteague. Dennis, Wesley, illus. 2007. (ENG.). 176p. (J). (gr. 3-7). pap. 7.99 *(978-1-4169-2784-6(0),* Aladdin) Simon & Schuster Children's Publishing.
—Stormy, Misty's Foal. Dennis, Wesley, illus. (ENG.). (J). (gr. 3-7). 2015. 256p. 21.99 *(978-1-4814-2561-2(7))* 2007. 224p. pap. 7.99 *(978-1-4169-2788-4(3))* Simon & Schuster Children's Publishing. (Aladdin).
Herman, R. A. Pal Saves the Day. Ogden, Betina, illus. 2004. (Pal the Pony Ser.). 32p. (J). pap. *(978-0-439-64985-8(4));* pap. *(978-0-439-57746-5(2))* Scholastic, Inc.
Hesse, Laura. The Great Pumpkin Ride. 2004. ix, 133p. (J). *(978-0-9734013-1-8(1))* Running L. Productions.
Hilburn, L. M. Little Princesses to the Rescue. 2008. 24p. pap. 24.95 *(978-1-60672-783-6(4))* America Star Bks.
Hope, Lee Laura. Bunny Brown & His Sister Sue & Their Shetland Pony. 2007. 172p. 41.99 *(978-1-4280-7508-5(9));* per. 35.99 *(978-1-4280-7514-6(3))* IndyPublish.com.
Hughes, Emily C. Ponies Love Pets! 2017. (My Little Pony Leveled Readers Ser.). (ENG.). 32p. (J). (gr. -1-3). lib. bdg. 31.36 *(978-1-5321-4096-9(7),* 26969) Spotlight.
—Ponies Love Pets! 2014. (Passport to Reading Level 1 Ser.). (J). lib. bdg. 13.55 *(978-0-606-35298-7(8))* Turtleback.
Jaegly, Peggy. Sweetheart's Gift: A Healing Chincoteague Pony Story. 2011. 28p. pap. 14.95 *(978-1-4575-0287-3(9))* Dog Ear Publishing, LLC.
Jakobs, D. Holly, Jolly Harmony. 2013. (Passport to Reading Level 2 Ser.). (J). lib. bdg. 14.75 *(978-0-606-32276-8(0))* Turtleback.
—Tricks & Treats. 2014. (My Little Pony 8X8 Picture Bks.). (J). lib. bdg. 16.00 *(978-0-606-35302-1(X))* Turtleback.
Jakobs, D. & Williams, Merriwether. Holly, Jolly Harmony. 2017. (My Little Pony Leveled Readers Ser.). (ENG.). 32p. (J). (gr. -1-3). lib. bdg. 31.36 *(978-1-5321-4092-1(4),* 26965) Spotlight.
James, Scilla. Ponies at Owls' Wood. 2013. 112p. pap. *(978-0-9568148-2-1(4))* Swift Publishing.
Jeffers, Susan. Jingle Bells: A Christmas Holiday Book for Kids. Jeffers, Susan, illus. 2017. (ENG., Illus.). 40p. (J). (gr. -1-3). 17.99 *(978-0-06-236020-5(5),* HarperCollins) HarperCollins Pubs.
—My Pony. Jeffers, Susan, illus. 2008. (ENG., Illus.). 32p. (J). (gr. -1-k). 8.99 *(978-1-4231-1295-2(4))* Little, Brown Bks. for Young Readers.
Johnson, Gwen & Johnson, Carl. The Treasure of Diamond's Shoal. Lt. ed. 2007. (ENG., Illus.). 24p. (J). 8.95 *(978-0-9795860-0-2(3))* Fish Tales Publishing.
Johnston, Gail. The Shaggy Pony & the Spotted Pup. 2010. 24p. 11.32 *(978-1-4520-9653-7(8))* AuthorHouse.
Kaster, Pam. Molly the Pony: A True Story. 2012. (My Readers Ser.). (ENG., Illus.). 48p. (J). (gr. 1-3). pap. 4.99 *(978-0-312-61121-7(8),* 900065490) Square Fish.
Katschke, Judy. Home at Last. Geddes, Serena, illus. 2018. (Marguerite Henry's Misty Inn Ser.: 8). (ENG.). 144p. (J). (gr. 2-5). 17.99 *(978-1-4814-6995-1(9));* pap. 6.99 *(978-1-4814-6994-4(0))* Simon & Schuster Children's Publishing. (Aladdin).
—Teacher's Pet. Geddes, Serena, illus. 2017. (Marguerite Henry's Misty Inn Ser.: 7). (ENG.). 128p. (J). (gr. 2-5). pap. 5.99 *(978-1-4814-6991-3(6),* Aladdin) Simon & Schuster Children's Publishing.
Keene, Carolyn. Pony Problems. Pamintuan, Macky, illus. 3rd ed. 2006. (Nancy Drew & the Clue Crew Ser.: 3). (ENG.). 96p. (J). (gr. 1-4). pap. 5.99 *(978-1-4169-1815-8(9),* Aladdin) Simon & Schuster Children's Publishing.
Kelly, Lynda. Magazine-Page Pony. 2013. 190p. pap. *(978-1-903053-37-9(4))* Kelly Pubns.
—The Most Horrible Pony! 2013. 202p. pap. *(978-1-903053-36-2(6))* Kelly Pubns.
Kelly, Miles. Horse & Pony Stories. Kelly, Richard, ed. 2017. (Illus.). 512p. (J). pap. 23.95 *(978-1-78617-077-4(9))* Miles Kelly Publishing, Ltd. GBR. Dist: Parkwest Pubns., Inc.
Kelly, Theresa. Tony the Pony. Sampson, Jody, illus. Lt. ed. 2003. 12p. (J). 5.95 *(978-1-59466-003-0(4))* Port Town Publishing.
—Tony the Pony: Bugs Are Not Bad. Sampson, Jody, illus. 2005. (J). per. 7.95 *(978-1-59466-030-6(1))* Port Town Publishing.
Kimpton, Diana. Pony-Crazed Princess: Princess Ellie's Mystery. Finlay, Lizzie, illus. 3rd rev. ed. 2006. (ENG.). 96p. (gr. 1-4). pap. 3.99 *(978-0-7868-4872-0(3))* Hyperion Pr.
—Pony-Crazed Princess Super Special: Princess Ellie's Summer Vacation. Finlay, Lizzie, illus. 2007. (ENG.). 144p. (gr. 1-4). pap. 4.99 *(978-1-4231-0616-6(4))* Hyperion Pr.
—Princess Ellie Solves a Mystery. Finlay, Lizzie, illus. 8th rev. ed. 2007. (ENG.). 96p. (gr. 1-4). pap. 3.99 *(978-1-4231-0901-3(5))* Hyperion Pr.
—Princess Ellie to the Rescue. Finlay, Lizzie, illus. 2006. (ENG.). 96p. (gr. 1-4). pap. 3.99 *(978-0-7868-4870-6(7))* Hyperion Pr.
—Princess Ellie's Moonlight Mystery. 2015. (Pony-Crazed Princess Ser.). (ENG.). 96p. (J). (gr. k-5). pap. 4.99 *(978-0-7945-3431-8(7),* Usborne) EDC Publishing.
—Princess Ellie's Royal Jamboree No. 11. Finlay, Lizzie, illus. 11th ed. 2008. (ENG.). 96p. (gr. 1-4). pap. 3.99 *(978-1-4231-1531-1(7))* Hyperion Pr.
—Princess Ellie's Secret No. 2. Finlay, Lizzie, illus. 2nd rev. ed. 2006. (ENG.). 96p. (gr. 1-4). pap. 3.99 *(978-0-7868-4871-3(5))* Hyperion Pr.
—Princess Ellie's Snowy Ride. Finlay, Lizzie, illus. 2007. (Pony-Crazed Princess Ser.). 90p. (J). 11.65 *(978-0-7569-8352-9(5))* Perfection Learning Corp.
—Princess Ellie's Snowy Ride No. 9. Finlay, Lizzie, illus. 9th rev. ed. 2007. (ENG.). 96p. (gr. 1-4). pap. 3.99 *(978-1-4231-0902-0(3))* Hyperion Pr.
—Princess Ellie's Treasure Hunt No. 10. Finlay, Lizzie, illus. 10th ed. 2008. (ENG.). 96p. (gr. -1-3). pap. 3.99 *(978-1-4231-1414-7(0))* Hyperion Pr.
—A Surprise for Princess Ellie. 2015. (Pony-Crazed Princess Ser.). (ENG.). 96p. (J). (gr. k-5). pap. 4.99 *(978-0-7945-3432-5(5),* Usborne) EDC Publishing.
—A Surprise for Princess Ellie. Finlay, Lizzie, illus. 6th rev. ed. 2006. (ENG.). 96p. (gr. 1-4). pap. 3.99 *(978-0-7868-4875-1(8))* Hyperion Pr.
Klein-Carroll, Theodora. Tippy & the Runaway Cloud. 2013. 28p. pap. 16.95 *(978-1-4525-7390-8(5),* Balboa Pr.) Author Solutions, LLC.
Knight, Barbara. The Cowboys with penny the mustang Pony. 2006. (Penny the Mustang Pony Ser.). (Illus.). 16p. (J). 14.95 net. *(978-0-9766270-1-2(9))* Mustang BKS.
—The Rescue, with Penny the Mustang Pony. 2005. (Penny the Mustang Pony Ser.). *(978-0-9766270-0-5(0))* Mustang BKS.
Knight, Barbara Maxine. The Storm. 2007. (Penny the Mustang Pony Ser.). (Illus.). 32p. (J). 14.95 *(978-0-9766270-2-9(7))* Mustang BKS.
Kuc, Jessica. Mawby the Christmas Pony. 2011. 36p. pap. 15.14 *(978-1-4634-2521-0(X))* AuthorHouse.
Lawrence, Iain. The Winter Pony. 2012. (ENG., Illus.). 256p. (J). (gr. 4-6). lib. bdg. 21.19 *(978-0-385-90394-3(4))* Random Hse. Bks. for Young Readers.
—The Winter Pony. 2012. (Illus.). 256p. (J). (gr. 4-7). 7.99 *(978-0-440-23972-7(9),* Yearling) Random Hse. Children's Bks.
Lawson, Dorie McCullough. Tex: A Book for Little Dreamers. 2011. (ENG., Illus.). 44p. (J). (gr. -1-k). 15.95 *(978-1-57076-501-8(4))* Trafalgar Square Bks.
Lee, Barbara R. Pookey the Pony. 2004. 35p. pap. 24.95 *(978-1-4137-3396-9(4))* PublishAmerica, Inc.
Leigh, S. Runaway Pony. 2004. (Sandy Lane Stables Ser.). (J). (ENG.). 118p. pap. 4.95 *(978-0-7945-0507-3(4));* 100p. lib. bdg. 12.95 *(978-1-58086-575-3(5))* EDC Publishing.
Lester, Alison. Noni the Pony. Lester, Alison, illus. 2012. (Noni the Pony Ser.). (ENG., Illus.). 32p. (J). (gr. -1-k). 18.99 *(978-1-4424-5959-5(X),* Beach Lane Bks.) Beach Lane Bks.
—Noni the Pony. Lester, Alison, illus. 2019. (Noni the Pony Ser.). (ENG., Illus.). 28p. (J). (gr. -1-k). bds. 7.99 *(978-1-5344-5355-5(5),* Little Simon) Little Simon.
—Noni the Pony Goes to the Beach. Lester, Alison, illus. 2015. (Noni the Pony Ser.). (ENG., Illus.). 32p. (J). (gr. -1-3). 17.99 *(978-1-4814-4625-9(8),* Beach Lane Bks.) Beach Lane Bks.
—The Snow Pony. 2006. (ENG., Illus.). 208p. (J). (gr. 5-7). pap. 12.95 *(978-0-618-77125-7(5),* 489867, Clarion Bks.) HarperCollins Pubs.
Lindsay, Elizabeth. Annie Saves the Day. Eastwood, John, illus. 2003. 92p. (J). *(978-0-439-44651-8(1))* Scholastic, Inc.
—Unicorn Dreams (Book 1) 2011. (Silverlake Fairy School Ser.). 96p. (J). pap. 4.99 *(978-0-7945-3062-4(1),* Usborne) EDC Publishing.
London, Olivia. Meet the Ponies of Ponyville. 2017. (My Little Pony Leveled Readers Ser.). (ENG., Illus.). 32p. (J). (gr. -1-3). lib. bdg. 31.36 *(978-1-5321-4093-8(2),* 26966) Spotlight.
—Meet the Ponies of Ponyville. 2013. (Passport to Reading Level 1 Ser.). (J). lib. bdg. 14.75 *(978-0-606-31732-0(5))* Turtleback.
—Welcome to Equestria! 2013. (My Little Pony 8X8 Picture Bks.). (J). lib. bdg. 13.55 *(978-0-606-31731-3(7))* Turtleback.
—Welcome to Rainbow Falls! 2014. (My Little Pony 8X8 Picture Bks.). (J). lib. bdg. 14.75 *(978-0-606-35297-0(X))* Turtleback.
—Welcome to the Crystal Empire! 2013. (My Little Pony 8X8 Picture Bks.). (J). lib. bdg. 14.75 *(978-0-606-32275-1(2))* Turtleback.
—Welcome to the Everfree Forest! 2014. (My Little Pony 8X8 Picture Bks.). (J). lib. bdg. 13.55 *(978-0-606-35940-5(0))* Turtleback.
Mackall, Dandi Daley. A Perfect Pony, 1 vol. Wolf, Claudia, illus. 2011. (I Can Read! / a Horse Named Bob Ser.). (ENG.). 32p. (J). pap. 4.99 *(978-0-310-71783-6(3))* Zonderkidz.
Manning, Matthew K. Revenge of the One-Trick Pony. Ellis, Joey, illus. 2018. (Xander & the Rainbow-Barfing Unicorns Ser.). (ENG.). 128p. (J). (gr. 3-5). lib. bdg. 22.65 *(978-1-4965-5712-4(3),* 136701, Stone Arch Bks.) Capstone.
Mattern, Joanne & Toohey, Cathy. My Little Pony Phonics Fun/[stories by Joanne Mattern]; [phonics Scope & Sequence by Cathy Toohey; Pictures by Carlo Lo Rosa ... [et Al.], 12 vols. Lo Raso, Carlo et al, illus. 2008. (J). *(978-0-06-123176-6(2)); (978-0-06-123184-1(3)); (978-0-06-123183-4(5)); (978-0-06-123182-7(7)); (978-0-06-123181-0(9)); (978-0-06-123180-3(0)); (978-0-06-123179-7(7)); (978-0-06-123178-0(9)); (978-0-06-123175-9(4)); (978-0-06-123174-2(6)); (978-0-06-123173-5(8)); (978-0-06-123171-1(1))* HarperCollins Pubs. (Harper Trophy).
Matty & the Problem Ponies. 2006. (J). *(978-1-933343-18-1(4))* Stabenfeldt Inc.
May, Tallulah. Pinkie Pie Big Baking Bonanza! Persico, Zoe, illus. 2018. (J). *(978-1-5444-0210-9(4),* Golden Bks.) Random Hse. Children's Bks.
—Rainbow Dash: Reading Rainboom! Persico, Zoe, illus. 2018. (J). *(978-1-5444-0924-5(9),* Golden Bks.) Random Hse. Children's Bks.

May, Tallulah, adapted by. Crystal Heart Kisses. 2016. (Illus.). (J). *(978-1-5182-3830-7(0))* Little, Brown Bks. for Young Readers.

McCarthy, Meghan. My Little Pony: Twilight's Kingdom. 2017. (MLP Episode Adaptations Ser.). (Illus.). 144p. (J). (gr. 1-3). pap. 7.99 *(978-1-68405-064-2(2))* Idea & Design Works, LLC.

McCarthy, Meghan & Hsiao, Rita. My Little Pony: the Movie Adaptation. 2017. (MLP the Movie Ser.). (Illus.). 148p. (J). (gr. 4-7). pap. 7.99 *(978-1-68405-116-8(9))* Idea & Design Works, LLC.

McCarthy, Meghan & Larson, Mitch. My Little Pony: When Cutie Calls. 2014. (MLP Episode Adaptations Ser.: 1). (Illus.). 128p. (J). (gr. 1-3). pap. 7.99 *(978-1-61377-830-2(9))*, 9781613778302) Idea & Design Works, LLC.

McKain, Kelly. Megan & Mischief. 2008. (Pony Camp Diaries: Vol. 1). 96p. (J). (gr. 3-5). 3.99 *(978-1-56148-646-5(9))*, Good Bks.) Skyhorse Publishing Co., Inc.

—Poppy & Prince. 2008. (Pony Camp Diaries: Vol. 2). 96p. (J). (gr. 3-5). 3.99 *(978-1-56148-647-2(7))*, Good Bks.) Skyhorse Publishing Co., Inc.

Meadows, Daisy. Penny the Pony Fairy. 2008. (Rainbow Magic — the Pet Fairies Ser.). lib. bdg. 14.75 *(978-1-4178-3008-4(5))* Turtleback.

Melchionno, Marion. Patty & the Little Ponies That Could: Hunt for the Collar of Sparkle. 2013. 28p. pap. 24.95 *(978-1-4626-9973-5(1))* America Star Bks.

—Patty & the Little Pony That Could. 2012. 44p. 24.95 *(978-1-4626-9475-4(6))*; pap. 24.95 *(978-1-4626-7552-4(2))* America Star Bks.

Milbourne, Anna. Little Pony. Roberti, Alessandra, illus. 2009. (Picture Bks). 24p. (J). (gr. -1). 9.99 *(978-0-7945-2198-1(3))*, Usborne) EDC Publishing.

Miller, Debra J. The Pony Tale: The Story from Timberlin. 2005. 4.00 *(978-0-9776014-1-7(2))* Miller, Debra Juanita.

Miller, Lorna. Jumper the Pony: Thomas Learns a Lesson. 2008. 32p. per. 24.95 *(978-1-4241-9578-7(0))* America Star Bks.

Mills, Enos A. Cricket, A Mountain Pony, 1 vol. l.t. ed. 2006. (Illus.). 67p. 9.95 *(978-1-928878-37-7(7))* Temporal Mechanical Pr.

Muschinske, Victoria. Honey Pie Pony's Book: A Fun with Fillies Adventure. 2005. (Illus.). 39p. *(978-0-439-70471-7(5))* Scholastic, Inc.

My Little Pony. 2003. (J). 144.80 *(978-0-06-056336-3(2))*; (Illus.). 115.84 *(978-0-06-056195-6(5))* HarperCollins Pubs.

My Little Pony, 6 vols. 2015. (My Little Pony Ser.: Vol. 6). (ENG.). 24p. (J). (gr. 1-8). 188.16 *(978-1-61479-330-4(1))*, 17152, Graphic Novels) Spotlight.

Myers, Linda. Stoney the Pony's Most Inspiring Year: Teaching Children about Addiction Through Metaphor. 2012. 36p. pap. 16.99 *(978-1-4624-0311-0(5))*, Inspiring Voices) Author Solutions, LLC.

Nanette. Pancake the Purple Pony. 2004. (Life on Granny's Farm Ser.). (J). 12.95 *(978-0-9741269-8-2(5))* St. Bernard Publishing, LLC.

Natsukawa, Maiko. Rachel, Grace, & Pony Club. 2013. 32p. pap. 13.95 *(978-1-4525-7543-8(6))*, Balboa Pr.) Author Solutions, LLC.

Nault, Susan. Mr Scruffpot's Pony. Nault, S. &R, illus. 2013. 30p. pap. *(978-0-9870744-1-6(5))* Kingdom Pr.

Newbery, L. El Poni de Mermelada. (Raton de Biblioteca Coleccion). (SPA.). 80p. (J). (gr. 3). 7.95 *(978-84-88061-68-3(4))* Serres, Ediciones, S. L. ESP. Dist: Lectorum Pubns., Inc.

Nicholas, Soraya. Gymkhana Hijinks. 2017. (Starlight Stables Ser.: 2). 192p. (J). (gr. 2-4). 8.99 *(978-0-14-330863-8(7))* Random Hse. Australia AUS. Dist: Independent Pubs. Group.

O'Donnell, Liam. Daisy on the Farm. 2005. (ENG., Illus.). 32p. (J). (gr. -1-2). 9.95 *(978-1-59249-452-1(8))*, 1B037) Soundprints.

—Daisy on the Farm. Hatala, Dan, illus. 2005. (Pet Tales Ser.). (ENG.). 32p. (J). (gr. -1-2). 2.95 *(978-1-59249-451-4(X))*, 1B036) Soundprints.

—Daisy the Farm Pony. Hatala, Dan, illus. 2005. (Pet Tales Ser.). (ENG.). 32p. (J). (gr. -1 — 1). 4.95 *(978-1-59249-450-7(1))*, 1B035) Soundprints.

Oliver, Charles Folkes. Little Willy & the Party Animals. 2011. (Illus.). 20p. (gr. -1). pap. 14.99 *(978-1-4567-5138-8(7))* AuthorHouse.

Olson, John J. Wild Child & Annie. 2010. (ENG.). 44p. pap. 26.49 *(978-0-557-32534-4(X))* Lulu Pr., Inc.

Ongman, Gudrun. Sleep Pony Dreams. l.t. ed. 2006. (Illus.). 32p. (J). pap. 16.95 *(978-0-9677204-2-5(7))* Mindcastle Bks., Inc.

Orr, Wendy. Stolen! - A Pony Called Pebbles. 2012. (Rainbow Street Shelter Ser.: 5). (J). lib. bdg. 16.00 *(978-0-606-26719-9(0))* Turtleback.

Parker, Vic, ed. The Goblin Pony & Other Stories, 1 vol. 2015. (Scary Fairy Tales Ser.). (ENG.). 40p. (J). (gr. 3-4). pap. 15.05 *(978-1-4824-3077-6(0))*, b9a75ebd-0171-4623-b3dd-058c40ab0bab) Stevens, Gareth Publishing LLLP.

Pearce, Arline June. Sunrise the Barnegat Pony. Pearce, Arline June, illus. 2011. (ENG., Illus.). 26p. pap. 15.99 *(978-1-4628-8601-2(9))* Xlibris Corp.

Pegg, Laura Wittman. The Patch Quilt Pony. 2006. 17.00 *(978-0-8059-7346-4(X))* Dorrance Publishing Co., Inc.

Pelizzari, Nora. Crystal Princess: The Runaway Rainbow. 2006. (My Little Pony Ser.). (Illus.). 12p. (J). (gr. -1-1). 6.99 *(978-0-06-111692-6(0))*, HarperFestival) HarperCollins Pubs.

Pennell, Kathleen. The Phantom Stallion. Pennell, Lauren, illus. 2003. (Pony Investigators Ser.: Vol. 4). 118p. (J). (gr. 3-7). pap. 5.95 *(978-1-930353-73-2(1))* Masthof Pr.

—The Secret Passage: Pony Investigators Series #5. 2005. (Pony Investigators Ser.: 5). (Illus.). 108p. (J). pap. 5.95 *(978-1-932864-42-7(3))* Masthof Pr.

Perfect Pony (revised) 2017. (Sandy Lane Stables Ser.). (ENG.). (J). pap. 5.99 *(978-0-7945-3623-7(9))*, Usborne) EDC Publishing.

Pony Girls, 4 vols. 2015. (Pony Girls Ser.: 4). (ENG.). 112p. (J). (gr. 1-4). lib. bdg. 154.00 *(978-1-62402-126-8(3))*, 19373, Calico Chapter Bks.) ABDO Publishing Co.

Prentice-Hall Staff. The Red Pony. 2nd ed. (J). stu. ed. *(978-0-13-717133-0(1))* Prentice Hall (Schl. Div.).

Price, Cheryl A. Follow the Sun. 2010. (Calico Pony Ser.: Bk. 1). 48p. (J). pap. 17.49 *(978-1-4490-7217-9(8))* AuthorHouse.

Randolph, Joanne. The Pony Ride, 1 vol. 2015. (Rosen REAL Readers: STEM & STEAM Collection). (ENG.). 8p. (gr. k-1). pap. 5.46 *(978-1-4994-9617-8(6))*, ecb4c49e-2b80-433f-9518-bc98b10876be, Rosen Classroom) Rosen Publishing Group, Inc., The.

Renne. The Ice Horse, 34 vols. 2003. (ENG., Illus.). 32p. (J). 17.95 *(978-0-86315-384-6(4))* Floris Bks. GBR. Dist: SteinerBooks, Inc.

Ricchiazzi, Lisa Gail. The Adventures of Fella & Dawn: Help One Another. 2012. (ENG.). 24p. pap. 13.77 *(978-1-4669-7170-7(3))* Trafford Publishing.

—Fella Finds a Friend: (You Are Never Alone) 2012. (ENG.). 24p. (J). pap. 14.93 *(978-1-4669-2985-2(5))* Trafford Publishing.

Rice, Christina, et al. My Little Pony: Friendship Is Magic Volume 10, Vol. 10. Garbowska, Agnes & Hickey, Brenda, illus. 2016. (My Little Pony Ser.: 10). 124p. (J). (gr. 4-7). pap. 19.99 *(978-1-63140-688-1(4))*, 9781631406881) Idea & Design Works, LLC.

Riddle, Peter H. The Painted Ponies of Partequineus & the Summer of the Kittens: Two Novels for Young Readers. 2009. (Illus.). 260p. (J). pap. *(978-1-926585-19-2(4))*, CCB Publishing) CCB Publishing.

Rigo, Laura. Little Pony. 2011. (Look at Me Bks.). (Illus.). 10p. (J). (gr. -1). bds. 8.99 *(978-0-7641-6448-4(1))* Sourcebooks, Inc.

Rippin, Sally. The Bumpy Ride: Hey Jack! 2014. (ENG., Illus.). 48p. (J). pap. 4.99 *(978-1-61067-187-3(2))* Kane Miller.

Rising, Janet. Runaway Rescue. 2010. (Pony Whisperer Ser.: Bk. 3). (ENG.). 256p. (J). pap. *(978-0-340-98843-5(6))*, Hodder Children's Books) Hachette Children's Group GBR. Dist: Hachette Bk. Group.

—Team Challenge. 2010. (Pony Whisperer Ser.: Bk. 2). (ENG.). 256p. (J). pap. *(978-0-340-98842-8(8))*, Hodder Children's Books) Hachette Children's Group GBR. Dist: Hachette Bk. Group.

—The Word on the Yard. 2010. (Pony Whisperer Ser.: Bk. 1). (ENG.). 256p. (J). pap. *(978-0-340-98841-1(X))*, Hodder Children's Books) Hachette Children's Group GBR. Dist: Hachette Bk. Group.

—The Word on the Yard, 1. 2010. (Pony Whisperer Ser.: 1). (ENG.). 208p. (J). (gr. 4-7). pap. 9.99 *(978-1-4022-3952-6(1))* Sourcebooks, Inc.

Rosen, Lucy. My Little Pony: Meet Princess Twilight Sparkle. 2014. (Passport to Reading Level 1 Ser.). (J). lib. bdg. 13.55 *(978-0-606-35939-9(7))* Turtleback.

Roy, Ron. Calendar Mysteries #7: July Jitters. Gurney, John Steven, illus. 2012. (Calendar Mysteries Ser.: 7). 80p. (J). (gr. 1-4). 7.99 *(978-0-375-86882-5(8))*, Random Hse. Bks. for Young Readers) Random Hse. Children's Bks.

—July Jitters. 2012. (Calendar Mysteries Ser.: 7). lib. bdg. 14.75 *(978-0-606-26402-0(7))* Turtleback.

Runaway Pony (revised) 2017. (Sandy Lane Stables Ser.). (ENG.). (J). pap. 5.99 *(978-0-7945-3622-0(0))*, Usborne) EDC Publishing.

Ryder, Chloe. Princess Ponies 1: a Magical Friend. 2014. (Princess Ponies Ser.). (ENG., Illus.). 128p. (J). (gr. 1-3). pap. 5.99 *(978-1-61963-165-6(2))*, 900123295, Bloomsbury USA Childrens) Bloomsbury Publishing USA.

—Princess Ponies 10: the Pumpkin Ghost. 2019. (Princess Ponies Ser.). (ENG., Illus.). 128p. (J). pap. 5.99 *(978-1-5476-0166-0(3))*, 900201119, Bloomsbury Children's Bks.) Bloomsbury Publishing USA.

—Princess Ponies 12: an Enchanted Heart. 2019. (Princess Ponies Ser.). (ENG., Illus.). 128p. (J). pap. 5.99 *(978-1-5476-0190-5(6))*, 900203169, Bloomsbury Children's Bks.) Bloomsbury Publishing USA.

—Princess Ponies 2: a Dream Come True. 2014. (Princess Ponies Ser.). (ENG., Illus.). 128p. (J). (gr. 1-3). pap. 6.99 *(978-1-61963-167-0(9))*, 900123305, Bloomsbury USA Childrens) Bloomsbury Publishing USA.

—Princess Ponies 3: the Special Secret. 2014. (Princess Ponies Ser.). (ENG., Illus.). 128p. (J). (gr. 2-4). pap. 6.99 *(978-1-61963-237-0(3))*, 900128207, Bloomsbury USA Childrens) Bloomsbury Publishing USA.

—Princess Ponies 4: a Unicorn Adventure! 2014. (Princess Ponies Ser.). (ENG., Illus.). 128p. (J). (gr. 2-4). pap. 6.99 *(978-1-61963-294-3(2))*, 900132055, Bloomsbury USA Childrens) Bloomsbury Publishing USA.

—Princess Ponies 5: an Amazing Rescue. 2015. (Princess Ponies Ser.). (ENG., Illus.). 128p. (J). (gr. 2-4). pap. 6.99 *(978-1-61963-403-9(1))*, 900135708, Bloomsbury USA Childrens) Bloomsbury Publishing USA.

—Princess Ponies 6: Best Friends Forever! 2015. (Princess Ponies Ser.). (ENG., Illus.). 128p. (J). (gr. 2-4). pap. 5.99 *(978-1-61963-405-3(8))*, 900135710, Bloomsbury USA Childrens) Bloomsbury Publishing USA.

—Princess Ponies 7: a Special Surprise. 2015. (Princess Ponies Ser.). (ENG., Illus.). 128p. (J). (gr. 2-4). pap. 5.99 *(978-1-61963-565-4(8))*, 900140702, Bloomsbury USA Childrens) Bloomsbury Publishing USA.

—Princess Ponies 8: a Singing Star. 2015. (Princess Ponies Ser.). (ENG., Illus.). 128p. (J). (gr. 2-4). pap. 5.99 *(978-1-61963-567-8(4))*, 900140704, Bloomsbury USA Childrens) Bloomsbury Publishing USA.

—Princess Ponies 9: the Lucky Horseshoe. 2019. (Princess Ponies Ser.). (ENG., Illus.). 128p. (J). pap. 5.99 *(978-1-5476-0164-6(7))*, 900201120, Bloomsbury Children's Bks.) Bloomsbury Publishing USA.

Sanderson, Whitney. Darcy. 2013. (Horse Diaries: 10). lib. bdg. 18.40 *(978-0-606-27001-4(9))* Turtleback.

—Horse Diaries #10: Darcy. Sanderson, Ruth, illus. 2013. (Horse Diaries: 10). 160p. (J). (gr. 3-7). 7.99 *(978-0-307-97635-2(1))*, Random Hse. Bks. for Young Readers) Random Hse. Children's Bks.

—Horse Diaries #15: Lily. Sanderson, Ruth, illus. 2018. (Horse Diaries: 15). 160p. (J). (gr. 3-7). pap. 7.99 *(978-1-5247-6654-2(2))*, Random Hse. Bks. for Young Readers) Random Hse. Children's Bks.

Sargent, Dave & Sargent, Pat. Sweetpea: (Purple Corn Welsh) Be Happy, 30 vols., Vol. 58. Lenoir, Jane, illus. 2003. (Saddle up Ser.: Vol. 58). 42p. (J). pap. 10.95 *(978-1-56763-816-5(3))*; lib. bdg. 23.60 *(978-1-56763-815-8(5))* Ozark Publishing.

Scott, Lisa Ann. All That Glitters. Burns, Heather, illus. 2017. 117p. (J). pap. *(978-1-338-13559-6(7))* Scholastic, Inc.

—Dreams That Sparkle, 4. Burns, Heather, illus. 2017. (Enchanted Pony Academy Ser.). (ENG.). 128p. (J). (gr. 1-4). 17.44 *(978-1-5364-0219-3(2))* Scholastic, Inc.

—Dreams That Sparkle (Enchanted Pony Academy #4) 2017. (Enchanted Pony Academy Ser.: 4). (ENG., Illus.). 128p. (J). (gr. 2-5). pap. 4.99 *(978-0-545-90897-9(3))*, Scholastic Paperbacks) Scholastic, Inc.

—Let It Glow, 3. Burns, Heather, illus. 2017. (Enchanted Pony Academy Ser.). (ENG.). 128p. (J). (gr. 1-4). 17.44 *(978-1-5364-0218-6(4))* Scholastic, Inc.

Seeley, Bonnie L. Chincoteague Daisy Chain. Lidard, Kelly & Seeley, Douglas A., illus. 2003. 32p. (J). bds. 12.95 *(978-0-9728380-0-9(7))* Seelcraft Publishing.

Shepherd, Jodie. Merry Christmas, Rarity! Fletcher, Lyn, illus. 2006. (My Little Pony Ser.). 32p. (J). (gr. -1-1). pap., act. bk. ed. 3.99 *(978-0-06-079472-9(0))*, HarperFestival) HarperCollins Pubs.

Shire, Poppy. Magic Pony Carousel #1: Sparkle the Circus Pony. Berg, Ron, illus. 2007. (Magic Pony Carousel Ser.: 1). (ENG.). 96p. (J). (gr. 2-5). pap. 3.99 *(978-0-06-083779-2(9))*, HarperCollins) HarperCollins Pubs.

—Magic Pony Carousel #3: Star the Western Pony. Berg, Ron, illus. 2007. (Magic Pony Carousel Ser.: 3). (ENG.). 96p. (J). (gr. 2-5). pap. 3.99 *(978-0-06-083785-3(3))*, HarperCollins) HarperCollins Pubs.

—Magic Pony Carousel #4: Jewel the Midnight Pony. Berg, Ron, illus. 2008. (Magic Pony Carousel Ser.: 4). (ENG.). 96p. (J). (gr. 2-5). pap. 4.99 *(978-0-06-083788-4(8))*, HarperCollins) HarperCollins Pubs.

—Magic Pony Carousel #5: Flame the Desert Pony. Berg, Ron, illus. 2008. (Magic Pony Carousel Ser.: 5). (ENG.). 96p. (J). (gr. 2-5). pap. 3.99 *(978-0-06-083794-5(2))*, HarperCollins) HarperCollins Pubs.

Shirt, Virginia. Angels of Clover Farm. Lane, Rob, ed. 2012. 132p. pap. *(978-1-78176-546-3(4))* FeedARead.com.

Silver Dolphin en Español Editors. Mi Pequeno Pony Dibuja con los Ponys. 2006. (Illus.). 22p. (J). (gr. -1). bds. *(978-970-718-361-2(6))*, Silver Dolphin en Español) Advanced Marketing, S. de R. L. de C. V.

—Mi Pequeno Pony Figuras Magicas: Las Maravillosas Estaciones. 2006. (Illus.). 8p. (J). (gr. -1). bds. *(978-970-718-359-9(4))*, Silver Dolphin en Español) Advanced Marketing, S. de R. L. de C. V.

Simon-Kerr, Julia. Princess Party Paint Book. Edwards, Ken, illus. 2005. (My Little Pony Ser.). 32p. (J). 3.99 *(978-0-06-074699-5(8))*, HarperFestival) HarperCollins Pubs.

Simone, Yve. Little Valentine. 2013. 72p. pap. 28.99 *(978-1-4817-0496-0(6))* AuthorHouse.

Slaughter Doty, Jean. Summer Pony. Sanderson, Ruth, illus. 2008. (Stepping Stone Book(TM) Ser.). (ENG.). 144p. (J). (gr. 1-4). pap. 6.99 *(978-0-375-84709-7(X))*, Random Hse. Bks. for Young Readers) Random Hse. Children's Bks.

—Winter Pony. Sanderson, Ruth, illus. 2008. (Stepping Stone Book(TM) Ser.). (ENG.). 144p. (J). (gr. 1-4). 4.99 *(978-0-375-84710-3(3))*, Random Hse. Bks. for Young Readers) Random Hse. Children's Bks.

Slinkard, Doreen. Wicky Wacky Farm Stories: Peppi Goes to China. 2012. 44p. pap. 14.97 *(978-1-60976-309-1(2))*, Strategic Bk. Publishing) Strategic Book Publishing & Rights Agency (SBPRA).

Small, Lily. Paige the Pony: Fairy Animals of Misty Wood. 2017. (Fairy Animals of Misty Wood Ser.: 10). (ENG., Illus.). 144p. (J). pap. 6.99 *(978-1-250-12700-6(9))*, 900175306, Holt, Henry & Co. Bks. For Young Readers) Holt, Henry & Co.

—Poppy the Pony: Fairy Animals of Misty Wood. 2016. (Fairy Animals of Misty Wood Ser.: 5). (ENG., Illus.). 144p. (J). pap. 6.99 *(978-1-62779-734-4(3))*, 900158787, Holt, Henry & Co. Bks. For Young Readers) Holt, Henry & Co.

Smith, Donna Campbell. An Independent Spirit: The Tale of Betsy Dowdy & Black Bess. 2006. (Illus.). 182p. (J). per. 11.95 *(978-0-9779889-0-7(2))* Faithful Publishing.

Spinner, Stephanie. Paddywack. Howarth, Daniel, illus. 2010. (Step into Reading Ser.). 48p. (J). (gr. k-3). pap. 4.99 *(978-0-375-86186-4(6))*, Random Hse. Bks. for Young Readers) Random Hse. Children's Bks.

Stamm, Linda J. Lilly & Zander: A Children's Story about Equine-Assisted Activities. Whitaker, Suzanne, illus. 2014. (J). pap. *(978-1-938313-03-5(8))* Graphite Pr.

Steveson, Nanci Turner. Lizzie Flying Solo. 2019. (ENG.). 336p. (J). (gr. 3-7). 16.99 *(978-0-06-267318-3(1))*, HarperCollins) HarperCollins Pubs.

Szymanski, Lois K. A Pony in Need. 2008. (Charming Ponies Ser.). 80p. (J). (gr. 2-5). 4.99 *(978-0-06-128873-9(X))*, HarperFestival) HarperCollins Pubs.

Thompson, Chad. Yankee Doodle. 2011. (Early Literacy Ser.). (ENG.). 16p. (gr. k-1). 19.99 *(978-1-4333-2365-2(6))*; 6.99 *(978-1-4333-2364-5(8))* Teacher Created Materials, Inc.

Tirey, Rodney. Copperhoso Saves the Sarge's Saddle! Tirey, Rodney, illus. 2007. (Illus.). 32p. (J). 16.95 *(978-0-9789591-0-4(8))* MirthMarks Publishing.

Trimmer, Christian. Snow Pony & the Seven Miniature Ponies. Sima, Jessie, illus. 2018. (ENG.). 48p. (J). (gr. -1-3). 17.99 *(978-1-4814-6268-6(7))*, Simon & Schuster Bks. For Young Readers) Simon & Schuster Bks. For Young Readers.

Tull, Linda Handy. Fofo's Journey. 2012. 40p. pap. 24.95 *(978-1-4626-7275-2(2))* America Star Bks.

Tutu el Caballito Volador. 2004. (SPA.). (J). per. *(978-0-9744408-6-6(8))* Editorial Busqueda.

Vanderlaan, Karen. Special Friends. 2008. 28p. pap. 24.95 *(978-1-60813-353-6(2))* America Star Bks.

Watt, Fiona. That's Not My Pony... Its Mane Is Too Fluffy. Wells, Rachel, illus. 2007. (Usborne Touchy-Feely Board Bks.). 10p. (J). (gr. -1-k). bds. 7.99 *(978-0-7945-1630-7(0))*, Usborne) EDC Publishing.

Webster, Frank V. Jack of the Pony Express. 2005. 26.95 *(978-1-4218-1036-2(0))*; 172p. pap. 11.95 *(978-1-4218-1136-9(7))* 1st World Publishing, Inc. (1st World Library - Literary Society).

Wedekind, Annie. Little Prince: The Story of a Shetland Pony. 2009. (Breyer Horse Collection: 2). (ENG.). 128p. (J). (gr. 4-7). pap. 12.99 *(978-0-312-59918-8(8))*, 900063864) Feiwel & Friends.

Whitley, Jeremy. My Little Pony: Legends of Magic, Vol. 2. Fleecs, Tony, illus. 2018. (MLP Legends of Magic Ser.: 2). 144p. (J). (gr. 4-7). pap. 19.99 *(978-1-68405-158-8(4))* Idea & Design Works, LLC.

Whitley, Jeremy & Rice, Christina. My Little Pony: Friends Forever Omnibus, Vol. 2, Vol. 2. Garbowska, Agnes et al, illus. 2017. (MLP FF Omnibus Ser.: 2). 296p. (J). (gr. 4-7). pap. 24.99 *(978-1-63140-882-3(8))*, 9781631408823) Idea & Design Works, LLC.

—My Little Pony: Friends Forever Omnibus, Vol. 3, Vol. 3. Fleecs, Tony et al, illus. 2018. (MLP FF Omnibus Ser.: 3). 320p. (J). (gr. 4-7). pap. 24.99 *(978-1-68405-050-5(2))* Idea & Design Works, LLC.

Wilson, Kelly. Cameo, the Street Pony. 2018. (Showtym Adventures Ser.: 2). (Illus.). 176p. (J). (gr. 2-4). 9.99 *(978-0-14-377220-0(1))* Penguin Group New Zealand, Ltd. NZL. Dist: Independent Pubs. Group.

—Casper, the Spirited Arabian. 2019. (Showtym Adventures Ser.: 3). (Illus.). 176p. (J). (gr. 2-4). 10.99 *(978-0-14-377224-8(4))* Penguin Group New Zealand, Ltd. NZL. Dist: Independent Pubs. Group.

—Chessy, the Welsh Pony. 2019. (Showtym Adventures Ser.: 4). (Illus.). 176p. (J). (gr. 2-4). 10.99 *(978-0-14-377262-0(7))* Penguin Group New Zealand, Ltd. NZL. Dist: Independent Pubs. Group.

—Koolio: The Problem Pony. 2020. (Showtym Adventures Ser.: 5). (Illus.). 176p. (J). (gr. 2-4). 10.99 *(978-0-14-377226-2(0))* Penguin Group New Zealand, Ltd. NZL. Dist: Independent Pubs. Group.

Wilson, Kelly B. Dandy, the Mountain Pony. 2018. (Showtym Adventures Ser.: 1). (Illus.). 160p. (J). (gr. 2-4). 9.99 *(978-0-14-377149-4(3))* Penguin Group New Zealand, Ltd. NZL. Dist: Independent Pubs. Group.

Wright, Tish. The Boy & the Blue Painted Pony. 2012. 94p. (gr. -1). pap. 13.95 *(978-1-4685-6606-2(7))* AuthorHouse.

Zimet, Sara Goodman. Hannah & the Perfect Picture Pony: A Story of the Great Depression. Fuller, Sandy Ferguson, illus. 2005. 24p. (J). lib. bdg. 16.95 *(978-0-9645159-2-5(X))* Discovery Pr. Pubns., Inc.

PONY EXPRESS

Bougie, Matt. Life As a Pony Express Rider in the Wild West, 1 vol. 2017. (Life As... Ser.). (ENG.). 32p. (gr. 3-3). pap. 11.58 *(978-1-5026-3047-6(8))*, 28e222f3-7275-4195-8fcd-3769a491db99) Cavendish Square Publishing LLC.

Brill, Marlene Targ. Bronco Charlie & the Pony Express. Orback, Craig, illus. 2004. (On My Own History Ser.). (ENG.). 48p. (gr. 2-4). (J). pap. 8.99 *(978-1-57505-618-0(6))*, b654f654-7cd7-4cb8-bb97-9329189d66f0, First Avenue Editions); lib. bdg. 25.26 *(978-1-57505-587-9(2))* Lerner Publishing Group.

—Bronco Charlie y el Pony Express. Orback, Craig, illus. 2005. (Yo Solo Historia Ser.). (SPA.). 46p. (J). (gr. 2-5). per. 6.95 *(978-0-8225-3093-0(7))* Lerner Publishing Group.

—Bronco Charlie Y el Pony Express; Bronco Charlie & the Pony Express. 2008. pap. 40.95 *(978-0-8225-3866-0(0))* Lerner Publishing Group.

Dolan, Edward F., Jr. & Dolan, Edward F. The Pony Express, 1 vol. 2003. (Kaleidoscope: American History Ser.). (ENG., Illus.). 48p. (gr. 4-4). 32.64 *(978-0-7614-1458-2(4))*, 313b616a-7b69-406c-b1b1-b20943b229d7) Cavendish Square Publishing LLC.

Dunn, Joeming W. The Pony Express, 1 vol. Martin, Cynthia, illus. 2008. (Graphic History Ser.). (ENG.). 32p. (J). (gr. 3-8). 32.79 *(978-1-60270-184-7(9))*, 9060, Graphic Planet - Fiction) Magic Wagon.

Jeffrey, Gary. The Pony Express, 1 vol. Riley, Terry, illus. 2012. (Graphic History of the American West Ser.). (ENG.). 24p. (J). (gr. 3-3). pap. 9.15 *(978-1-4339-6749-8(9))*, 48a12229-d95d-4464-944d-8821c5729f53, Gareth Stevens Learning Library); lib. bdg. 26.60 *(978-1-4339-6747-4(2))*, fbe13987-bdb7-456a-ab4a-454d8ec20547) Stevens, Gareth Publishing LLLP.

Leigh, Autumn. Making History: A Horse Sock Puppet, 1 vol. 2005. (Content-Area Literacy Collections). (ENG.). 24p. (gr. 3-4). pap. 8.85 *(978-1-4042-5588-3(5))*, bc8e3750-8487-4eb2-8d5d-fd9af12da011) Rosen Publishing Group, Inc., The.

Mattern, Joanne. The Pony Express. 2017. 25.70 *(978-1-61228-964-9(9))* Mitchell Lane Pubs.

Micklos, John, Jr. Bold Riders: The Story of the Pony Express. 2015. (Adventures on the American Frontier Ser.). (ENG., Illus.). 32p. (J). (gr. 3-6). pap. 7.95 *(978-1-4914-4910-3(1))*, 128745, Capstone Pr.) Capstone.

Ongman, Gudrun. Sleep Pony Dreams. l.t. ed. 2006. (Illus.). 32p. (J). pap. 16.95 *(978-0-9677204-2-5(7))* Mindcastle Bks., Inc.

Payment, Simone. The Pony Express, 1 vol. 2004. (Primary Sources in American History Ser.). (ENG., Illus.). 64p. (J). (gr. 5-8). lib. bdg. 37.13 *(978-1-4042-0181-1(5))*, fa6e2996-1591-480a-8b4f-102f7f3ba513) Rosen Publishing Group, Inc., The.

—The Pony Express: A Primary Source History of the Race to Bring Mail to the American West. 2009. (Primary Sources in American History Ser.). 64p. (gr. 5-8). 58.50 *(978-1-60851-502-8(8))* Rosen Publishing Group, Inc., The.

Quiri, Patricia R. The Groundbreaking Pony Express. 2017. (Landmarks in U. S. History Ser.). (ENG., Illus.). 32p. (J). (gr. 3-6). lib. bdg. 27.99 *(978-1-5157-7115-9(6))*, 135516, Capstone Pr.) Capstone.

Ratliff, Thomas. You Wouldn't Want to Be a Pony Express Rider! A Dusty, Thankless Job You'd Rather Not Do. Bergin, Mark, illus. 2012. (ENG.). 32p. (J). lib. bdg. 29.00 *(978-0-531-20872-4(9))* Scholastic Library Publishing.

Rau, Margaret. The Mail Must Go Through: The Story of the Pony Express. 2005. (America's Moving Frontier Ser.). (Illus.). 176p. (J). (gr. 3-7). lib. bdg. 26.95 *(978-1-931798-63-1(X))* Reynolds, Morgan Inc.

Rea, Amy C. The Pony Express. 2016. (Wild West Ser.). (ENG., Illus.). 48p. (J). (gr. 4-8). lib. bdg. 35.64 *(978-1-68078-259-2(2))*, 22119) ABDO Publishing Co.

Riddle, John. The Pony Express. 2004. (History of the Old West Ser.). (Illus.). 64p. (YA). (gr. 5-18). lib. bdg. 19.95 *(978-1-59084-061-0(5))* Mason Crest.

Savage, Jeff. Daring Pony Express Riders: True Tales of the Wild West, 1 vol. 2012. (True Tales of the Wild West Ser.). (ENG., Illus.). 48p. (gr. 5-7). pap. 11.53 *(978-1-4644-0031-5(8))*, ca5e0880-db02-4c69-884a-4fd104eb36de); lib. bdg. 25.27

P
Q
R

(978-0-7660-4023-6(2), e694efd9-a05f-4e1f-bda0-8f114b3b5b2f) Enslow Publishing, LLC.

Steele, William O. We Were There with the Pony Express. 2007. 125p. (J). pap. 13.95 *(978-0-9779000-3-9(7))* American Home-School Publishing, LLC.

PONY EXPRESS—FICTION

Bailer, Darice. The Pony Express. Antonishak, Tom, illus. 3rd ed. 2003. (Soundprints' Read-and-Discover Ser.). (ENG.). 48p. (J). (gr. -1-3). pap. 3.95 *(978-1-59249-019-6(0),* S2008) Soundprints.

Brill, Marlene Targ. The Rough-Riding Adventure of Bronco Charlie, Pony Express Rider. 2010. pap. 51.02 *(978-0-7613-6920-2(1))* Lerner Publishing Group.

Chellis, Marie. The Hayburner, 1 vol. 2010. 60p. pap. 19.95 *(978-1-4512-9053-0(5))* America Star Bks.

Rose, Caroline Starr. Ride on, Will Cody! A Legend of the Pony Express. Lillington, Joe, illus. 2017. (ENG.). 32p. (J). (gr. -1-3). 16.99 *(978-0-8075-7068-5(0),* 807570680) Whitman, Albert & Co.

Schnetzler, Pattie L. Fast 'n Snappy. Manning, Jane K., tr. Manning, Jane K., illus. 2004. (Carolrhoda Picture Books Ser.). 32p. (J). (gr. k-3). 16.95 *(978-1-57505-539-8(2))* Lerner Publishing Group.

Wilson, Diane Lee. Black Storm Comin' 2006. (ENG.). 240p. (J). (gr. 5-9). pap. 8.99 *(978-0-689-87138-2(4),* McElderry, Margaret K. Bks.) McElderry, Margaret K. Bks.

—Black Storm Comin' 2006. (Illus.). 291p. (gr. 5-9). 17.00 *(978-0-7569-6908-0(5))* Perfection Learning Corp.

POODLES

Bayliss, Rebecca. Poodle. 2017. (Dog Lover's Guides: Vol. 18). (ENG., Illus.). 128p. (J). (gr. 3-7). 26.95 *(978-1-4222-3859-2(8))* Mason Crest.

Berry, Breanna. Poodles. 2015. (Awesome Dogs Ser.). (ENG., Illus.). 24p. (J). (gr. k-3). lib. bdg. 26.95 *(978-1-62617-243-2(9),* Blastoff! Readers) Bellwether Media.

Bodden, Valerie. Poodles. 2014. (Fetch! Ser.). (ENG., 24p. (J). (gr. 1-4). Illus.). pap. 7.99 *(978-0-89812-942-7(7),* 21516, Creative Paperbacks); 25.65 *(978-1-60818-363-0(7),* 21515, Creative Education) Creative Co., The.

Bozzo, Linda. I Like Poodles!, 1 vol. 2012. (Discover Dogs with the American Canine Association Ser.). (ENG., Illus.). 24p. (gr. k-2). pap. 10.35 *(978-1-4644-0118-3(7),* 5bfa7287-d5e4-4542-83a3-0087646d5ff1, Enslow Elementary) Enslow Publishing, LLC.

Fitzpatrick, Anne. Poodles. 2003. (Dog Breeds Ser.). 24p. (J). lib. bdg. 21.35 *(978-1-58340-314-3(0))* Black Rabbit Bks.

Johnson, Jinny. Poodle. 2013. (My Favorite Dogs Ser.). 24p. (gr. k-3). 28.50 *(978-1-59920-845-9(8))* Black Rabbit Bks.

Kalman, Bobbie. Les Caniches. 2011. (FRE., Illus.). 32p. (J). pap. 9.95 *(978-2-89579-392-2(1))* Bayard Canada CAN. Dist: Crabtree Publishing Co.

MacAulay, Kelley & Kalman, Bobbie. Los Caniches o Poodles. 2007. (Cuidado de las Mascotas Ser.). (SPA & ENG., Illus.). 32p. (J). (gr. -1-4). lib. bdg. *(978-0-7787-8461-6(4))* Crabtree Publishing Co.

—Los Caniches o Poodles. Crabtree, Marc, photos by. rev. ed. 2007. (Cuidado de las Mascotas Ser.). (SPA & ENG., Illus.). 32p. (J). (gr. -1-4). pap. *(978-0-7787-8483-8(5))* Crabtree Publishing Co.

—Poodles. Crabtree, Marc, photos by. 2006. (Pet Care Ser.). (ENG., Illus.). 32p. (J). (gr. -1-4). lib. bdg. *(978-0-7787-1763-8(1),* 1259506) Crabtree Publishing Co.

Noll, Elizabeth. Poodles. 2017. (Doggie Data Ser.). (ENG., Illus.). 32p. (J). (gr. 4-6). lib. bdg. *(978-1-68072-154-6(2),* 10492, Bolt) Black Rabbit Bks.

Rustad, Martha E. H. Poodles. 2017. (Favorite Dog Breeds Ser.). (ENG., Illus.). 24p. (J). (gr. 1-4). 20.95 *(978-1-68151-129-0(0),* 14672) Amicus.

Rustad, Martha E.H. Poodles. 2018. (Favorite Dog Breeds Ser.). (ENG., Illus.). 24p. (J). (gr. 1-4). pap. 8.99 *(978-1-68152-160-2(1),* 14791) Amicus.

Schuh, Mari. Poodles. 2008. (Dog Breeds Ser.). (ENG., Illus.). 24p. (J). (gr. 2-5). lib. bdg. 26.95 *(978-1-60014-220-8(6))* Bellwether Media.

POOH (FICTITIOUS CHARACTER)—FICTION

see Winnie-the-Pooh (Fictitious Character)—Fiction

POPES

Abdo Publishing. Pope John Paul II, 1 vol. 2015. (Essential Lives Set 9 Ser.). (ENG.). 112p. (YA). (gr. 6-12). 41.36 *(978-1-62403-895-2(6),* 17822, Essential Library) ABDO Publishing Co.

Cooke, Tim. Pope Francis, 1 vol. 2018. (Meet the Greats Ser.). (ENG.). 48p. (gr. 5-5). lib. bdg. 34.93 *(978-1-5382-2575-2(1),* f5ea815f-a49b-4505-80fe-ccd93c8e4d30) Stevens, Gareth Publishing LLLP.

Costello, Hugh. Pope John Paul II: Pontiff, 1 vol. 2016. (History Makers Ser.). (ENG.). 144p. (YA). (gr. 9-9). 47.36 *(978-1-5026-2451-2(6),* 81852971-0a97-4ae2-b86f-99b3767925a4) Cavendish Square Publishing LLC.

Daughters of St. Paul Staff. No Place for Defeat. Date not set. (Encounter Ser.). 96p. (J). (gr. 3-9). pap. 2.00 *(978-0-8198-5100-0(0))* Pauline Bks. & Media.

Furgang, Kathy. Pope Francis: Priest of the People, 1 vol. 2017. (Junior Biographies Ser.). (ENG.). 24p. (gr. 3-4). pap. 10.35 *(978-0-7660-9049-1(3),* b5d5d0d3-ca41-4ca9-88d0-c78325e119f5) Enslow Publishing, LLC.

Garza, Fabiola. The Story of Saint John Paul II: A Boy Who Became Pope. Garza, Fabiola, illus. 2014. (Illus.). (J). 15.95 *(978-0-8198-9013-9(8))* Pauline Bks. & Media.

Gormley, Beatrice. Pope Francis: The People's Pope. 2017. (Real-Life Story Ser.). (ENG., Illus.). 272p. (J). (gr. 3-7). 17.99 *(978-1-4814-8141-0(X),* Aladdin) Simon & Schuster Children's Publishing.

Green, John. Popes Coloring Book. 2015. (Dover Religious Coloring Book Ser.). (ENG.). 32p. (gr. 3). pap. 3.99 *(978-0-486-79236-1(6),* 792366) Dover Pubns., Inc.

Hansen, Grace. Pope Francis: Religious Leader, 1 vol. 2015. (History Maker Biographies (Abdo Kids Jumbo) Ser.). (ENG., Illus.). 24p. (J). (gr. -1-2). lib. bdg. 32.79 *(978-1-62970-705-1(8),* 17017, Abdo Kids) ABDO Publishing Co.

—Pope Francis: Religious Leader. 2017. (History Maker Biographies Ser.). (ENG.). 24p. (J). (gr. -1-2). pap. 7.95 *(978-1-4966-1228-1(0),* 134992, Capstone Classroom) Capstone.

Hoffman, Mary Hramiec. Lolek the Boy Who Became Pope John Paul II. Hoffman, Mary Hramiec, illus. 2008. (Illus.). 56p. (J). 18.95 *(978-0-9746901-1-7(2))* Hramiec Hoffman Publishing.

Jopp, Kelsey. Pope Francis: Leader of the Catholic Church: Leader of the Catholic Church. 2019. (World Leaders Set 2 Ser.). (ENG., Illus.). 48p. (J). (gr. 5-6). pap. 11.95 *(978-1-64185-422-1(7),* 1641854227); lib. bdg. 34.21 *(978-1-64185-364-4(6),* 1641853646) North Star Editions. (Focus Readers).

Kramer, Barbara. National Geographic Readers: Pope Francis. 2015. (Readers Bios Ser.). 32p. (J). (gr. -1-k). pap. 4.99 *(978-1-4263-2253-2(4),* National Geographic Kids) Disney Publishing Worldwide.

Lanser, Amanda. Pope Francis: Spiritual Leader & Voice of the Poor, 1 vol. 2013. (Essential Lives Set 8 Ser.). (ENG.). 112p. (YA). (gr. 6-12). lib. bdg. 41.36 *(978-1-61783-704-3(0),* 6759, Essential Library) ABDO Publishing Co.

Mohan, Claire Jordan. Joseph from Germany: The Life of Pope Benedict XVI for Children. Craig, Charlie, illus. 2007. 38p. (J). 8.95 *(978-0-8198-3988-6(4))* Pauline Bks. & Media.

Monge, Marlyn & Wolfe, Jaymie Stuart. Jorge de Argentina: Historia Del Papa Francisco para Ninos. 2013. (Illus.). 64p. (J). pap. 8.95 *(978-0-8198-4007-3(6))* Pauline Bks. & Media.

—Jorge from Argentina: The Story of Pope Francis for Children. Kizlauskas, Diana, illus. 2013. 64p. (J). pap. 8.95 *(978-0-8198-4006-6(8))* Pauline Bks. & Media.

Morini, Manuel & Segesso, Ignacio. Pope Francis. 2017. (Graphic Lives Ser.). (ENG., Illus.). 80p. (J). (gr. 3-9). lib. bdg. 32.65 *(978-1-5157-9162-1(9),* 136604, Capstone Pr.) Capstone.

Otheguy, Emma. Papa Francisco: Creador de Puentes. Dominguez, Oliver, illus. 2018. (SPA.). 32p. (J). 17.99 *(978-1-5476-0013-7(6),* 900194853, Bloomsbury Children's Bks.) Bloomsbury Publishing USA.

—Pope Francis: Builder of Bridges. Dominguez, Oliver, illus. 2018. (ENG.). 48p. (J). 17.99 *(978-1-68119-560-5(7),* 900177833, Bloomsbury Children's Bks.) Bloomsbury Publishing USA.

Pagotto, Toni. Pope John Paul II. Toppi, Sergio, illus. 2006. (Comic Book Ser.). 64p. (J). pap. 7.95 *(978-0-8198-5957-0(5))* Pauline Bks. & Media.

Perego, Jeanne, et al. Max & Benedict: A Bird's Eye View of the Pope's Daily Life. Casagrande, Donata Dal Molin, illus. 2009. (ENG.). 52p. (J). (gr. -1-3). 17.95 *(978-1-58617-407-1(X))* Ignatius Pr.

Sheen, Barbara. Pope Benedict XVI, 1 vol. 2008. (People in the News Ser.). (ENG., Illus.). 104p. (gr. 7-7). lib. bdg. 41.03 *(978-1-4205-0093-6(7),* 9831e1cf-8282-4b38-9853-68d2d90f1564, Lucent Pr.) Greenhaven Publishing LLC.

Spinner, Stephanie & Who HQ. Who Is Pope Francis? Putra, Dede, illus. 2017. (Who Was? Ser.). 112p. (J). (gr. 3-7). 5.99 *(978-0-451-53336-4(4),* Penguin Workshop) Penguin Young Readers Group.

Stanley, George E. Pope John Paul II: Young Man of the Church. 2005. (Childhood of World Figures Ser.). (ENG.). 176p. (J). (gr. 3-7). pap. 9.99 *(978-1-4169-1282-8(7),* Aladdin) Simon & Schuster Children's Publishing.

Wallace, Susan Helen. Saint John Paul II: Be Not Afraid. Craig, Charles, illus. 2011. (Encounter the Saints Ser.). 128p. (J). (gr. 3-7). pap. 8.95 *(978-0-8198-1178-3(5))* Pauline Bks. & Media.

Watson, Stephanie. Pope Francis: First Pope from the Americas. (Gateway Biographies Ser.). (ENG., Illus.). 48p. (J). (gr. 4-8). 2013. lib. bdg. 31.99 *(978-1-4677-2176-9(X),* 413cf2ec-9b9f-4d01-87c4-982a3004898a, Lerner Pubns.) 2015. E-Book 46.65 *(978-1-4677-5977-9(5),* 9781467759779, Lerner Digital) Lerner Publishing Group.

Wheeler, Jill C. Pope John Paul II. 2003. (Breaking Barriers Ser.). (Illus.). 64p. (gr. 3-8). lib. bdg. 27.07 *(978-1-57765-740-8(3),* Abdo & Daughters) ABDO Publishing Co.

Wilson, M. Leonora. Karol from Poland: The Life of Pope John Paul II for Children. Koch, Carla, illus. rev. ed. 2006. 38p. (J). pap. 7.95 *(978-0-8198-4209-1(5))* Pauline Bks. & Media.

Winkler, Jude. Pope Francis: Man of Peace. 2014. (ENG., Illus.). 32p. (J). 2.95 *(978-1-941243-19-0(3),* 534) Catholic Bk. Publishing Corp.

Woll, Kris. Pope Francis: Catholic Spiritual Leader, 1 vol. 2015. (Newsmakers Ser.). (ENG., Illus.). 48p. (J). (gr. 4-8). lib. bdg. 35.64 *(978-1-62403-644-6(9),* 17187) ABDO Publishing Co.

Worth, Richard. Pope Francis: The People's Pope, 1 vol. 2015. (Influential Latinos Ser.). (ENG., Illus.). 128p. (gr. 7-8). 38.93 *(978-0-7660-7328-9(9),* 8c3478f2-aa7a-4674-9515-7755363d7641) Enslow Publishing, LLC.

POPPINS, MARY (FICTITIOUS CHARACTER)—FICTION

Druvert, Hélène. Mary Poppins up, up & Away. 2017. (ENG., Illus.). 36p. (J). (gr. k-4). 24.95 *(978-0-500-65104-9(3),* 565104) Thames & Hudson.

Travers, P. L. Mary Poppins. (Mary Poppins Ser.: No. 1). 202p. (J). (gr. 3-5). pap. 6.00 *(978-0-8072-1536-4(8),* Listening Library) Random Hse. Audio Publishing Group.

—Mary Poppins & Mary Poppins Comes Back. 2007. (Mary Poppins Ser.: No 1 and 2). (ENG., Illus.). 368p. (J). (gr. 5-7). 19.99 *(978-0-15-205922-4(9),* 1197779, Clarion Bks.) HarperCollins Pubs.

—Mary Poppins in the Kitchen: A Cookery Book with a Story. Shepard, Mary, illus. 2006. (Mary Poppins Ser.: No. 6). (ENG.). 88p. (J). (gr. 5-7). 16.99 *(978-0-15-206080-0(4),* 1198263, Clarion Bks.) HarperCollins Pubs.

—Mary Poppins in the Park. Shepard, Mary, illus. 2015. (Mary Poppins Ser.). (ENG.). 272p. (J). (gr. 5-7). pap. 7.99 *(978-0-544-51384-6(3),* 1605889, Clarion Bks.) HarperCollins Pubs.

—Mary Poppins Opens the Door. Shepard, Mary, illus. 2015. (Mary Poppins Ser.). (ENG.). 256p. (J). (gr. 5-7). pap. 7.99 *(978-0-544-43958-0(9),* 1596852, Clarion Bks.) HarperCollins Pubs.

—Mary Poppins: the Illustrated Gift Edition. Sardà, Júlia, illus. 2018. (Mary Poppins Ser.). (ENG.). 248p. (J). (gr. 5-7). 24.99 *(978-1-328-49884-7(0),* 1717674, Clarion Bks.) HarperCollins Pubs.

Travers, P. L. & Shepard, Mary. Mary Poppins Abc. Shepard, Mary, illus. 2018. (Mary Poppins Ser.). (ENG., Illus.). 26p. (J). (— 1). bds. 8.99 *(978-1-328-91118-6(7),* 1702057, Clarion Bks.) HarperCollins Pubs.

POPULAR GOVERNMENT

see Democracy

POPULAR MUSIC

Abdo, Kenny. Khalid. 2018. (Star Biographies Ser.). (ENG.). 24p. (J). (gr. 2-8). lib. bdg. 31.36 *(978-1-5321-2545-4(3),* 30099, Abdo Zoom-Fly) ABDO Publishing Co.

Anniss, Matt. The History of Modern Music. 2015. (Music Scene Ser.). (J). lib. bdg. 37.10 *(978-1-59920-910-4(1))* Black Rabbit Bks.

—Start a Band! 2013. (Find Your Talent Ser.). (Illus.). 32p. (J). (gr. 5-8). 28.50 *(978-1-84858-571-3(3))* Arcturus Publishing GBR. Dist: Black Rabbit Bks.

—The Story of Pop Music. 2013. (Pop Histories Ser.). 32p. (gr. 4-7). 31.35 *(978-1-59920-970-8(5))* Black Rabbit Bks.

Anniss, Matthew. Create Your Own Music. 2016. (Media Genius Ser.). (ENG., Illus.). 48p. (J). (gr. 5-8). lib. bdg. 35.99 *(978-1-4109-8112-7(6),* 131006, Raintree) Capstone.

Barden, Christine H., et al. Music for Little Mozarts — Little Mozarts Go to Hollywood, Bk 3-4: 10 Favorites from TV, Movies & Radio. 2008. (Music for Little Mozarts Ser.: Bk 3-4). (ENG.). 24p. (J). pap. 7.95 *(978-0-7390-5014-9(1))* Alfred Music.

Bednar, Chuck. American Idol Profiles Index: Top Finalists from Each Season (82 Contestants) 2009. (Dream Big: American Idol Superstars Ser.). 64p. (YA). (gr. 5-18). pap. 9.95 *(978-1-4222-1593-7(8))* Mason Crest.

—Insights into American Idol. 2009. (Dream Big: American Idol Superstars Ser.). 64p. (YA). (gr. 5-18). pap. 9.95 *(978-1-4222-1600-2(4));* lib. bdg. 22.95 *(978-1-4222-1514-2(8))* Mason Crest.

Carr, Aaron. Pop. 2015. (J). *(978-1-4896-3585-3(8))* Weigl Pubs., Inc.

Cohn, Jessica. The Electronic Music Scene: The Stars, the Fans, the Music, 1 vol. 2009. (Music Scene Ser.). (ENG., Illus.). 48p. (J). (gr. 5-7). lib. bdg. 27.93 *(978-0-7660-3398-6(8),* 8f5a3464-dbb2-44dc-afe4-7cae7957ea60) Enslow Publishing, LLC.

Daily, Lisa. Pop Music. 2019. (Music Scene Ser.). (ENG.). 80p. (J). (gr. 6-12). 41.27 *(978-1-68282-641-6(4))* ReferencePoint Pr., Inc.

Garofoli Zamora, Wendy. Hip-Hop History [Scholastic]. 2010. (Hip-Hop World Ser.). 48p. pap. 1.00 *(978-1-4296-5979-6(3))* Capstone.

Gilpin, Daniel. Start Your Own Band, 1 vol. 2013. (Quick Expert's Guide Ser.). 64p. (J). (gr. 5-5). (ENG.). 37.12 *(978-1-4777-2827-7(9),* 3a3cc7f4-f01f-43c5-a089-65b99fbebf64); (ENG.). pap. 13.95 *(978-1-4777-2829-1(5),* 43b91aa0-5b82-4b4e-9bcb-c8608df6941b); pap. 77.70 *(978-1-4777-2830-7(9))* Rosen Publishing Group, Inc., The. (Rosen Reference).

Hal Leonard Corp. Staff, creator. Disney Movie Hits for Tenor Sax: Play along with a Full Symphony Orchestra! 2003. (ENG.). 20p. pap. 14.99 *(978-0-634-04383-3(8),* 00841686) Leonard, Hal Corp.

Hapka, Catherine, pseud. Blast from the Past. 2004. (Star Power Ser.: 5). (ENG.). 160p. (J). (gr. 4-8). pap. 8.99 *(978-0-689-86791-0(3),* Simon & Schuster/Paula Wiseman Bks.) Simon & Schuster/Paula Wiseman Bks.

Hegel, Claudette. African-American Musicians. 2012. (J). pap. *(978-1-4222-2387-1(6))* Mason Crest.

—African-American Musicians. Hill, Marc Lamont, ed. 2012. (Major Black Contributions from Emancipation to Civil Rights Ser.). 64p. (J). (gr. 5). 22.95 *(978-1-4222-2374-1(4))* Mason Crest.

Horning, Nicole. Pop Music: Chart-Toppers Throughout History, 1 vol. 2018. (Music Library). (ENG.). 104p. (gr. 7-7). pap. 20.99 *(978-1-5345-6539-5(6),* f686327e-2462-4514-a49d-a3e29a51b857, Lucent Pr.) Greenhaven Publishing LLC.

Hubbard, Ben. History of Pop. 2009. (Crabtree Contact Ser.). (ENG., Illus.). 32p. (J). (gr. 6-8). pap. *(978-0-7787-3843-5(4),* 1294276); lib. bdg. *(978-0-7787-3822-0(1),* 1294276) Crabtree Publishing Co.

Jones, Edward Huws, ed. Unbeaten Tracks for Trumpet. 2003. (Faber Edition: Unbeaten Tracks Ser.). (ENG.). 32p. (gr. 4-7). pap. 13.99 *(978-0-571-52005-3(7))* Faber & Faber, Ltd. GBR. Dist: Alfred Publishing Co., Inc.

Kallen, Stuart A. The History of American Pop, 1 vol. 2012. (Music Library). (ENG., Illus.). 136p. (gr. 7-10). lib. bdg. 41.03 *(978-1-4205-0672-3(2),* 52f04563-53a7-42aa-a896-c22a84914530, Lucent Pr.) Greenhaven Publishing LLC.

—K-Pop: Korea's Musical Explosion. 2014. (ENG., Illus.). 64p. (YA). (gr. 6-12). lib. bdg. 33.32 *(978-1-4677-2042-7(9),* e792689b-ac3e-4e00-99f3-ac7e6feeb14a, Twenty-First Century Bks.) Lerner Publishing Group.

Kaplan, Arie. American Pop: Hit Makers, Superstars, & Dance Revolutionaries. 2012. (American Music Milestones Ser.). (ENG., Illus.). 64p. (J). (gr. 5-12). lib. bdg. 30.65 *(978-0-7613-4504-6(3),* 342882fa-0554-4fce-b27a-ba6e82bdfdfc, Twenty-First Century Bks.) Lerner Publishing Group.

Klepeis, Alicia Z. Music Trivia: What You Never Knew about Rock Stars, Recording Studios, & Smash-Hit Songs. 2018. (Not Your Ordinary Trivia Ser.). (ENG., Illus.). 32p. (J). (gr. 3-9). lib. bdg. 28.65 *(978-1-5435-2529-8(6),* 138026, Capstone Pr.) Capstone.

Lajiness, Katie. Charlie Puth. 2018. (Big Buddy Pop Biographies Ser.). (ENG.). 32p. (J). (gr. 2-5). lib. bdg. 34.21 *(978-1-5321-1802-9(3),* 30650, Big Buddy Bks.) ABDO Publishing Co.

Latham, Donna. Music: Investigate the Evolution of American Sound. Stone, Bryan, illus. 2013. (Inquire & Investigate Ser.). (ENG.). 128p. (J). (gr. 6-10). 21.95 *(978-1-61930-199-3(7),* c8e0a689-8a68-4956-b22f-6fb881594f5b); pap. 16.95 *(978-1-61930-203-7(9),* 4b42538f-feca-4fe2-be1f-72c891415544) Nomad Pr.

Lindeen, Mary. Cool Latin Music: Create & Appreciate What Makes Music Great! 2008. (Cool Music Ser.). (ENG., Illus.). 32p. (J). (gr. 3-6). 34.21 *(978-1-59928-972-4(5),* 368, Checkerboard Library) ABDO Publishing Co.

MacKay, Jennifer. The Art of Songwriting, 1 vol. 2013. (Music Library). (ENG., Illus.). 112p. (gr. 7-10). lib. bdg. 41.03 *(978-1-4205-0943-4(8),* 206205f0-abb2-4af0-8932-066ea2907ac8, Lucent Pr.) Greenhaven Publishing LLC.

Manuel, Peter & Neely, Daniel. The Reggae Scene: The Stars, the Fans, the Music, 1 vol. 2009. (Music Scene Ser.). (ENG., Illus.). 48p. (J). (gr. 5-7). lib. bdg. 27.93 *(978-0-7660-3400-6(3),* d1d54f93-b640-419a-bfa4-6e09256d9afe) Enslow Publishing, LLC.

McAneney, Caitie. Gareth's Guide to Becoming a Pop Star. 2017. (Gareth Guides to an Extraordinary Life Ser.). 32p. (gr. 4-5). pap. 63.00 *(978-1-5382-0335-4(9))* Stevens, Gareth Publishing LLLP.

Pina, Andrew. The Story of African American Music, 1 vol. 2017. (Lucent Library of Black History Ser.). (ENG.). 104p. (gr. 7-7). 41.03 *(978-1-5345-6073-4(4),* 1b9809ee-96f3-4059-9f43-10147a4bdf4b, Lucent Pr.) Greenhaven Publishing LLC.

Raffi. Everything Grows. 2004. (ENG., Illus.). 32p. (J). (gr. -1-2). 15.95 *(978-1-57940-097-2(3))* Rounder Bks.

Rauf, Don & Vescia, Monique. Pop Musician. 2008. (Virtual Apprentice Ser.). (Illus.). 64p. (gr. 4-9). per. 9.95 *(978-0-8160-7552-2(2),* Checkmark Bks.) Infobase Holdings, Inc.

Regan, Lisa. Pop Star, 1 vol. 2012. (Stage School Ser.). (ENG., Illus.). 32p. (J). (gr. 2-3). pap. 11.00 *(978-1-4488-8155-0(2),* 0c8114ad-77a0-43a4-841a-a56de596fc0c, Windmill Bks.) Rosen Publishing Group, Inc., The.

Rice, Dona Herweck. Communicate! Pop Song Lyrics (Level 3) 2017. (TIME for KIDS(r): Informational Text Ser.). (ENG., Illus.). 32p. (J). (gr. 3-4). pap. 12.99 *(978-1-4258-4973-3(3))* Teacher Created Materials, Inc.

Robertson, Robbie, et al. Legends, Icons & Rebels: Music That Changed the World. 2016. (Illus.). 128p. (J). (gr. 4-7). pap. 18.99 *(978-1-101-91868-5(3),* Tundra Bks.) Tundra Bks. CAN. Dist: Penguin Random Hse. LLC.

Salazar, Sam. One Direction, 1 vol. 2013. (Rising Stars Ser.). 32p. (J). (ENG.). (gr. 1-1). 27.93 *(978-1-4339-8985-8(9),* c06fcd84-9ebd-48f8-8cbe-a54b786c18af); (ENG.). (gr. 1-1). pap. 11.50 *(978-1-4339-8986-5(7),* a8a18fd2-6d58-4cf1-878d-93b9ce9f83d4); (gr. 3-6). pap. 63.00 *(978-1-4339-8987-2(5))* Stevens, Gareth Publishing LLLP.

Schweitzer, Karen. Making the Band. 2010. (Major Competitive Reality Shows Ser.). 48p. (YA). (gr. 7-18). lib. bdg. 19.95 *(978-1-4222-1674-3(8))* Mason Crest.

StarNews Media, compiled by. Stars of K-Pop: Boys Edition. 2014. (Illus.). 188p. (J). pap. 24.95 *(978-1-935690-49-8(3))* Watermark Publishing, LLC.

—Stars of K-Pop: Girls Edition. 2014. (Illus.). 192p. (J). pap. 24.95 *(978-1-935690-48-1(5))* Watermark Publishing, LLC.

Stewart, Mark. Music Legends, 1 vol. 2009. (Ultimate 10: Entertainment Ser.). (ENG.). 48p. (gr. 3-3). (J). pap. 11.50 *(978-1-4339-2213-8(4),* 5545e1c1-8bf0-4979-828b-2c94ed101110); (YA). lib. bdg. 33.67 *(978-0-8368-9165-2(1),* 5f494f81-e911-4c16-8b2a-fb4ea4d5c341) Stevens, Gareth Publishing LLLP.

Trier, George. Music of Heartohopia. 2003. (Illus.). 240p. (YA). (gr. 2-18). per. 19.95 *(978-0-9725184-0-6(1))* Heartohopia Pr.

Triumph Books Staff. One Direction: What Makes You Beautiful. 2012. (ENG.). 112p. (J). (gr. 5). pap. 12.95 *(978-1-60078-777-5(0))* Triumph Bks.

Tsoukanelis, Erika Alexia. The Latin Music Scene: The Stars, the Fans, the Music, 1 vol. 2009. (Music Scene Ser.). (ENG., Illus.). 48p. (J). (gr. 5-7). lib. bdg. 27.93 *(978-0-7660-3399-3(6),* 3bfc1b40-1da7-4db3-bd34-f01fdae5b201) Enslow Publishing, LLC.

Weston Woods Staff, creator. The Star Spangled Banner. 2004. 38.75 *(978-1-55592-644-1(4))* Weston Woods Studios, Inc.

Woog, Adam. The History of Gospel Music, 1 vol. 2014. (Music Library). (ENG., Illus.). 136p. (gr. 7-10). lib. bdg. 41.03 *(978-1-4205-0945-8(4),* 8751f184-f116-455c-bf56-5a8bb4494010, Lucent Pr.) Greenhaven Publishing LLC.

POPULAR MUSIC—BIOGRAPHY

Dougherty, Terri. Justin Timberlake, 1 vol. 2008. (People in the News Ser.). (ENG., Illus.). 104p. (gr. 7-7). lib. bdg. 41.03 *(978-1-4205-0056-1(2),* 39716d2c-3241-4d87-8d41-751f6be1be9d, Lucent Pr.) Greenhaven Publishing LLC.

Orgill, Roxane. Shout, Sister, Shout! Ten Girl Singers Who Shaped a Century. 2007. (ENG.). 160p. (YA). (gr. 7). pap. 12.95 *(978-1-4169-6391-2(X),* McElderry, Margaret K. Bks.) McElderry, Margaret K. Bks.

POPULAR MUSIC—FICTION

Calonita, Jen. VIP: Battle of the Bands. 2017. (VIP Ser.: 2). (ENG.). 320p. (J). (gr. 3-7). pap. 17.99 *(978-0-316-25978-1(0))* Little, Brown Bks. for Young Readers.

Davis, Lisa Selin. Lost Stars. 2017. (ENG.). 288p. (YA). (gr. 9). pap. 9.99 *(978-1-328-78731-6(1),* 1684477, Clarion Bks.) HarperCollins Pubs.

Gadsby, Maggie. Owl Be Home for Christmas. 2012. (J). 14.95 *(978-1-62086-064-9(3))* Amplify Publishing Group.

Geiger, A. V. Tell Me No Lies. 2018. (Follow Me Back Ser.: 2). 336p. (YA). (gr. 8-12). pap. 10.99 *(978-1-4926-4825-3(6))* Sourcebooks, Inc.

Goo, Maurene. Somewhere Only We Know. 2019. (ENG.). 336p. (YA). 17.99 *(978-0-374-31057-8(2),* 900193167, Farrar, Straus & Giroux (BYR)) Farrar, Straus & Giroux.

—Somewhere Only We Know. 2020. (ENG.). 336p. (YA). pap. 10.99 *(978-1-250-25078-0(1),* 900193168) Square Fish.

Hapka, Catherine, pseud. Over the Top. 2005. (Star Power Ser.: 7). (ENG.). 144p. (J). (gr. 4-8). pap. 8.99 *(978-0-689-87669-1(6),* Simon & Schuster/Paula Wiseman Bks.) Simon & Schuster/Paula Wiseman Bks.

Philbin, Joanna. The Daughters Take the Stage. 2011. (Daughters Ser.: 3). (ENG.). 304p. (YA). (gr. 7-17). pap. 16.99 *(978-0-316-04908-5(5),* Poppy) Little, Brown Bks. for Young Readers.

Shaw, Deirdre. Fair Play. 2005. (American Dreams Ser.: 5). (ENG.). 176p. (YA). mass mkt. 5.99 *(978-0-689-87850-3(8))* Pocket Books.
Shine, Joe. Bobby Sky: Boy Band or Die. 2019. 288p. (YA). (gr. 9). 10.99 *(978-1-61695-851-0(0),* Soho Teen) Soho Pr., Inc.
Stout, Katie M. Hello, I Love You. 2015. (ENG.). 304p. (YA). pap. *(978-1-250-08195-7(5),* St. Martin's Griffin) St. Martin's Pr.

POPULARITY

Espejo, Roman. Celebrity Culture. 2010. (Opposing Viewpoints Ser.). 177p. pap. 29.45 *(978-0-7377-5214-4(9),* Greenhaven Pr., Inc.) Cengage Gale.
Espejo, Roman, ed. Celebrity Culture, 1 vol. 2010. (Opposing Viewpoints Ser.). (ENG.). 192p. (gr. 10-12). 50.43 *(978-0-7377-5213-7(0),* 332a8c37-bb4f-4e16-a25f-c9fd44b6fcf4, Greenhaven Publishing) Greenhaven Publishing LLC.
Van Wagenen, Maya. Popular: A Memoir. 2015. lib. bdg. 22.10 *(978-0-606-36796-7(9))* Turtleback.

POPULARITY—FICTION

Allen, Crystal. The Laura Line. 2016. (ENG.). 352p. (J). (gr. 3-7). pap. 6.99 *(978-0-06-249021-6(4),* Balzer & Bray) HarperCollins Pubs.
Anderson, Jodi Lynn. Loser/Queen. Lee, Brittney, illus. 2010. (ENG.). 272p. (YA). (gr. 7-18). pap. 9.99 *(978-1-4169-9646-0(X),* Simon & Schuster Bks. For Young Readers) Simon & Schuster Bks. For Young Readers.
Applegate, Katherine. Never Walk in Shoes That Talk. Biggs, Brian, illus. 2009. (Roscoe Riley Rules Ser.: 6). (ENG.). 96p. (J). (gr. 1-5). pap. 4.99 *(978-0-06-114891-0(1))* HarperCollins Pubs.
—Never Walk in Shoes That Talk. 2009. (Roscoe Riley Rules Ser.: 06). lib. bdg. 14.75 *(978-0-606-05019-7(1))* Turtleback.
—Roscoe Riley Rules #6: Never Walk in Shoes That Talk. Biggs, Brian, illus. 2009. (Roscoe Riley Rules Ser.: 6). (ENG.). 96p. (J). (gr. 1-5). 14.99 *(978-0-06-114892-7(X),* HarperCollins) HarperCollins Pubs.
Atkinson, Elizabeth. From Alice to Zen & Everyone in Between. 2008. (Exceptional Reading & Language Arts Titles for Intermediate Grades Ser.). 247p. (YA). (gr. 4-7). 16.95 *(978-0-8225-7271-8(0))* Lerner Publishing Group.
Babich, Elaine. You Never Called Me Princess. 2012. 210p. pap. 14.00 *(978-1-105-70209-9(X))* Lulu.com GBR. Dist: Lulu Pr., Inc.
Backes, M. Molly. The Princesses of Iowa. (ENG.). 464p. (YA). (gr. 9). 2014. pap. 9.99 *(978-0-7636-7161-7(4))* 2012. (Illus.). 16.99 *(978-0-7636-5312-5(8))* Candlewick Pr.
Badger, Meredith. Fairy School Dropout Undercover. 2011. (Fairy School Ser.: 2). (ENG., Illus.). 160p. (J). (gr. 2-4). pap. 15.99 *(978-0-312-61951-0(0),* 900065967) Square Fish.
Bailey, Em. Shift. 2016. (ENG.). 320p. (YA). (gr. 9). pap. 18.99 *(978-1-76012-698-8(5))* Hardie Grant Children's Publishing AUS. Dist: Independent Pubs. Group.
Barcellona, Kelley Powell. The Hive. 2009. 92p. 14.95 *(978-0-9824095-1-0(6))* Pegasus Bks. for Children.
Baskin, Nora Raleigh. Runt. (ENG., Illus.). 208p. (J). (gr. 3-7). 2014. pap. 7.99 *(978-1-4424-5808-6(9))* 2013. 15.99 *(978-1-4424-5807-9(0))* Simon & Schuster Bks. For Young Readers. (Simon & Schuster Bks. For Young Readers).
Bateman, Anya. The Makeover of James Orville Wickenbee. 2007. 262p. (J). pap. *(978-1-59038-707-8(4))* Deseret Bk. Co.
Birchall, Katy. The It Girl. 2016. (It Girl Ser.: 1). (ENG., Illus.). 352p. (J). (gr. 4-8). 16.99 *(978-1-4814-6362-1(4),* Aladdin) Simon & Schuster Children's Publishing.
—The It Girl in Rome. (It Girl Ser.: 3). (ENG.). (J). (gr. 4-8). 2019. 336p. pap. 8.99 *(978-1-4814-6367-6(5))* 2018. (Illus.). 320p. 16.99 *(978-1-4814-6368-3(3))* Simon & Schuster Children's Publishing. (Aladdin).
Bodi, Sari. The Ghost in Allie's Pool. 2007. 192p. (J). (gr. 5-18). pap. 8.95 *(978-0-9768126-6-1(5))* Brown Barn Bks.
Boyce, Frank Cottrell. Desirable. 2012. (Stoke Books Titles Ser.). 64p. (J). (gr. 5-8). pap. 45.32 *(978-0-7613-9216-3(5))* Stoke Bks.
Breen, Steve. Violet the Pilot. 2008. (Illus.). 40p. (J). (gr. -1-3). 17.99 *(978-0-8037-3125-7(6),* Dial Bks) Penguin Young Readers Group.
Brian, Kate, pseud. Ambition. 2008. (Private Ser.: No. 7). (ENG.). 288p. (YA). (gr. 9-18). pap. 12.99 *(978-1-4169-5882-6(7),* Simon & Schuster Bks. For Young Readers) Simon & Schuster Bks. For Young Readers.
—Invitation Only. 2009. (Private Ser.: No. 2). (ENG.). 272p. (YA). pap. 9.99 *(978-1-4169-9947-8(7),* Simon & Schuster Bks. For Young Readers) Simon & Schuster Bks. For Young Readers.
Brown, Teri. Read My Lips. 2008. (ENG.). 256p. (YA). (gr. 9-12). pap. 8.99 *(978-1-4169-5868-0(1),* Simon Pulse) Simon Pulse.
Cabot, Meg. How to Be Popular. 2008. (ENG.). 320p. (YA). (gr. 8-12). pap. 8.99 *(978-0-06-088014-9(7),* HarperTeen) HarperCollins Pubs.
—How to Be Popular: When You're a Social Reject Like Me, Steph L. 2006. (ENG.). 304p. (YA). (gr. 7-12). 16.99 *(978-0-06-088012-5(0),* HarperTeen) HarperCollins Pubs.
Calame, Don. Beat the Band. 2011. (ENG., Illus.). 400p. (YA). (gr. 9). pap. 11.99 *(978-0-7636-5663-8(1))* Candlewick Pr.
Chamberlain, Adrian. FaceSpace, 1 vol. 2013. (Orca Currents Ser.). (ENG., Illus.). 128p. (J). (gr. 4-7). pap. 9.95 *(978-1-4598-0150-9(4))* Orca Bk. Pubs. USA.
Choldenko, Gennifer. If a Tree Falls at Lunch Period. 2007. (ENG., Illus.). 224p. (YA). (gr. 9-12). 18.69 *(978-0-15-205753-4(6))* Harcourt Children's Bks.
—If a Tree Falls at Lunch Period. 2009. (ENG., Illus.). 224p. (J). (gr. 5-7). pap. 7.99 *(978-0-15-206644-4(6),* 1099003, Clarion Bks.) HarperCollins Pubs.
Christopher, Matt. QB Blitz. 2011. (ENG.). 144p. (J). (gr. 3-7). pap. 10.99 *(978-0-316-17682-8(6))* Little, Brown Bks. for Young Readers.
Cook, Julia. Cliques Just Don't Make Cents, Volume 1. DuFalla, Anita, illus. 2012. (Building Relationships Ser.). (ENG.). 31p. (J). (gr. k-6). pap. 11.95 *(978-1-934490-39-6(3))* Boys Town Pr.
Cooper, Gael. My Name Is Kermeena Kermudgeon. 2009. 28p. pap. 12.49 *(978-1-4490-2932-6(9))* AuthorHouse.
Cotterill, Colin. Average Alan. 2013. 150p. pap. *(978-616-7503-18-9(4))* Asia Document Bureau, Ltd.
Cronn-Mills, Kirstin. Beautiful Music for Ugly Children. 2012. (ENG.). 288p. (YA). (gr. 9-12). pap. 14.99 *(978-0-7387-3251-0(6),* 0738732516, Flux) North Star Editions.
Cusick, John M. Girl Parts. 2010. (ENG., Illus.). 240p. (YA). (gr. 9-18). 16.99 *(978-0-7636-4930-2(9))* Candlewick Pr.
de la Cruz, Melissa. The Ashley Project. 2014. (Ashley Project Ser.: 1). (ENG., Illus.). 288p. (J). (gr. 4-8). pap. 6.99 *(978-1-4424-9033-8(0),* Aladdin) Simon & Schuster Children's Publishing.
De la Cruz, Melissa. Jealous? 2008. (Ashleys Ser.: Bk. 2). (ENG.). 256p. (YA). (gr. 4-8). pap. 9.99 *(978-1-4169-3407-3(3),* Simon & Schuster Bks. For Young Readers) Simon & Schuster Bks. For Young Readers.
de la Cruz, Melissa. Popularity Takeover. 2015. (Ashley Project Ser.: 4). (ENG., Illus.). 272p. (J). (gr. 4-8). 17.99 *(978-1-4814-0974-2(3),* Aladdin) Simon & Schuster Children's Publishing.
—Social Order. 2014. (Ashley Project Ser.: 2). (ENG., Illus.). 288p. (J). (gr. 4-8). 16.99 *(978-1-4814-0667-3(1),* Simon & Schuster/Paula Wiseman Bks.) Simon & Schuster/Paula Wiseman Bks.
Dean, Carolee. Forget Me Not. (ENG.). (YA). (gr. 9). 2013. 400p. pap. 11.99 *(978-1-4424-3255-0(1))* 2012. 384p. 16.99 *(978-1-4424-3254-3(3))* Simon Pulse. (Simon Pulse).
Dowell, Frances O'Roark. The Sound of Your Voice, Only Really Far Away. (Secret Language of Girls Trilogy Ser.). (ENG., Illus.). (J). (gr. 5-9). 2014. 256p. pap. 7.99 *(978-1-4424-3290-1(X),* Atheneum Bks. for Young Readers) 2013. 240p. 16.99 *(978-1-4424-3289-5(6))* Simon & Schuster Children's Publishing.
Echols, Jennifer. Perfect Couple. 2015. (Superlatives Ser.). (ENG., Illus.). 336p. (YA). (gr. 9). pap. 12.99 *(978-1-4424-7448-2(3),* Simon Pulse) Simon Pulse.
Faris, Stephanie. 25 Roses. 2015. (Mix Ser.). (ENG., Illus.). 224p. (J). (gr. 4-8). pap. 7.99 *(978-1-4814-2420-2(3),* Aladdin) Simon & Schuster Children's Publishing.
Flinn, Alex. Mirrored. 2015. (Kendra Chronicles Ser.: 3). (ENG.). 384p. (YA). (gr. 8). 17.99 *(978-0-06-213451-6(5),* HarperTeen) HarperCollins Pubs.
Frost, Helen. Diamond Willow. 2011. (ENG.). 144p. (J). (gr. 5-9). pap. 8.99 *(978-0-312-60383-0(5),* 900076343) Square Fish.
Gadot, Eran. Supernatural Hero. 2019. (ENG., Illus.). 176p. (J). (gr. 3-6). pap. 7.99 *(978-1-58270-688-7(3),* Beyond Words) Simon & Schuster.
Garfinkle, D. L. Stuck in the 70's. 2007. 182p. (YA). *(978-1-4287-4661-9(7))* Penguin Publishing Group.
Gephart, Donna. How to Survive Middle School. 2011. (ENG.). 256p. (J). (gr. 3-7). 8.99 *(978-0-375-85411-8(8),* Yearling) Random Hse. Children's Bks.
Geragotelis, Brittany. What the Spell. (Life's a Witch Ser.). (ENG., Illus.). (YA). (gr. 9). 2014. 352p. pap. 9.99 *(978-1-4424-6707-1(X))* 2013. 336p. 16.99 *(978-1-4424-6815-3(7))* Simon & Schuster Bks. For Young Readers. (Simon & Schuster Bks. For Young Readers).
Giles, Gail. Shattering Glass. 2004. 215p. (J). (gr. 7-18). pap. 37.00 incl. audio *(978-1-4000-9013-6(X),* Listening Library) Random Hse. Audio Publishing Group.
Gonzalez, Gabriela & Triana, Gaby. Backstage Pass. 2004. (Illus.). 224p. (J). (gr. 7-18). lib. bdg. 16.89 *(978-0-06-056018-8(5))* HarperCollins Pubs.
Goo, Maurene. Since You Asked... 2013. (YA). 262p. pap. *(978-0-545-44822-2(0))*; (ENG.). 272p. (gr. 7). 17.99 *(978-0-545-44821-5(2))* Scholastic, Inc. (Scholastic Pr.).
Gorman, Carol. A Midsummer Night's Dork. 2004. (ENG.). 224p. (J). 15.99 *(978-0-06-050718-3(7))* HarperCollins Pubs.
Gownley, Jimmy. True Things (Adults Don't Want Kids to Know) Gownley, Jimmy, illus. 2010. (Amelia Rules! Ser.). (ENG., Illus.). 176p. (J). (gr. 2-7). 19.99 *(978-1-4169-8611-9(1))*; pap. 12.99 *(978-1-4169-8609-6(X))* Simon & Schuster Children's Publishing. (Atheneum Bks. for Young Readers).
—The Tweenage Guide to Not Being Unpopular. Gownley, Jimmy, illus. 2010. (Amelia Rules! Ser.). (ENG., Illus.). 192p. (J). (gr. 2-7). pap. 12.99 *(978-1-4169-8608-9(1),* Atheneum Bks. for Young Readers) Simon & Schuster Children's Publishing.
Grab, Daphne. Halftime. 2010. (J). *(978-0-385-90693-7(5))*; *(978-0-385-73783-8(1))* Random House Publishing Group. (Delacorte Pr).
Green, Jessica. Diary of a Would-Be Princess: The Journal of Jillian Jones, 5b. 2007. (Illus.). 236p. (J). (gr. 4-7). 15.95 *(978-1-58089-166-0(7))* Charlesbridge Publishing, Inc.
Halpern, Julie. Into the Wild Nerd Yonder. 2011. (ENG.). 272p. (YA). (gr. 8-12). 17.99 *(978-0-312-65307-1(7),* 900069445) Square Fish.
Hapka, Catherine, pseud. Friends 4 Ever? 2008. (High School Musical Stories from East High Ser.). 124p. (J). (gr. 3-7). 12.65 *(978-0-7569-8820-3(9))* Perfection Learning Corp.
Harrison, Emma. Toe the Line: A Rival High Novel. 2008. (YA). *(978-1-4114-0526-4(9),* Spark Publishing Group) Sterling Publishing Co., Inc.
Harrison, Lisi. P. S. I Loathe You. 2008. (Clique Novels Ser.). 208p. 20.00 *(978-1-60686-338-1(X))* Perfection Learning Corp.
—Sealed with a Diss. 2008. (Clique Novels Ser.). 248p. 20.00 *(978-1-60686-345-9(2))* Perfection Learning Corp.
Harvey, Sarah N. Shattered, 1 vol. 2011. (Orca Soundings Ser.). (ENG.). 128p. (YA). (gr. 8-12). pap. 9.95 *(978-1-55469-845-5(6))*; lib. bdg. 16.95 *(978-1-55469-846-2(4))* Orca Bk. Pubs. USA.
Haston, Meg. How to Rock Best Friends & Frenemies. 2013. (How to Rock Ser.: 2). (ENG.). 352p. (J). (gr. 3-7). pap. 18.99 *(978-0-316-06827-7(6),* Poppy) Little, Brown Bks. for Young Readers.
—How to Rock Braces & Glasses. (How to Rock Ser.: 1). (ENG.). (J). (gr. 3-7). 2012. 352p. pap. 18.99 *(978-0-316-06824-6(1))* 2011. 336p. 16.99 *(978-0-316-06825-3(X))* Little, Brown Bks. for Young Readers. (Poppy).
Holder, Amy. The Lipstick Laws. 2011. (ENG.). 240p. (YA). (gr. 7-18). pap. 13.99 *(978-0-547-36306-6(0),* 1421941, Clarion Bks.) HarperCollins Pubs.
Holm, Jennifer L. Miss Communication. Holm, Matthew, illus. 2018. (Babymouse Tales from the Locker Ser.: 2). (ENG.). 208p. (J). (gr. 3-7). 13.99 *(978-0-399-55441-4(6),* Random Hse. Bks. for Young Readers) Random Hse. Children's Bks.
Holm, Jennifer L. & Holm, Matthew. Squish #2: Brave New Pond. Holm, Jennifer L. & Holm, Matthew, illus. 2011. (Squish Ser.: 2). (Illus.). 96p. (J). (gr. 3-7). (ENG.). 12.99 *(978-0-375-93784-2(6))*; pap. 6.99 *(978-0-375-84390-7(6))* Penguin Random Hse. LLC.
Horowitz, Lena. Dancing with Molly. 2016. (ENG.). 272p. (YA). (gr. 9). pap. 11.99 *(978-1-4814-1551-4(4),* Simon Pulse) Simon Pulse.
Hurley, Tonya. Ghostgirl. 2010. (Ghostgirl Ser.: 1). (ENG., Illus.). 336p. (YA). (gr. 7-17). pap. 17.99 *(978-0-316-03635-1(8))* Little, Brown Bks. for Young Readers.
Ignatow, Amy. The Popularity Papers: Book Five: the Awesomely Awful Melodies of Lydia Goldblatt & Julie Graham-Chang, Bk. 5. 2014. (Popularity Papers). (ENG., Illus.). 208p. (J). (gr. 3-7). pap. 9.95 *(978-1-4197-1308-8(6),* 1046603, Amulet Bks.) Abrams, Inc.
—The Popularity Papers: Book Four: the Rocky Road Trip of Lydia Goldblatt & Julie Graham-Chang. 2012. (ENG., Illus.). 208p. (J). (gr. 4-8). 16.95 *(978-1-4197-0182-5(7),* 1003701, Amulet Bks.) Abrams, Inc.
—The Popularity Papers: Research for the Social Improvement & General Betterment of Lydia Goldblatt & Julie Graham-Chang. 2011. (Popularity Papers). (ENG., Illus.). 208p. (J). (gr. 3-7). pap. 10.99 *(978-0-8109-9723-3(1),* 675503, Amulet Bks.) Abrams, Inc.
—The Popularity Papers Bk. 2: Book Two: the Long-Distance Dispatch Between Lydia Goldblatt & Julie Graham-Chang. 2012. (Popularity Papers). (ENG., Illus.). 208p. (J). (gr. 3-7). pap. 9.95 *(978-1-4197-0183-2(5),* 675603, Amulet Bks.) Abrams, Inc.
—The Popularity Papers: Book Three: Words of (Questionable) Wisdom from Lydia Goldblatt & Julie Graham-Chang. 2013. (ENG., Illus.). 208p. (J). (gr. 3-7). pap. 10.99 *(978-1-4197-0535-9(0),* 1003603, Amulet Bks.) Abrams, Inc.
—The Popularity Papers: Book Two: The Long-Distance Dispatch Between Lydia Goldblatt & Julie Graham-Chang. 2011. (ENG., Illus.). 208p. (J). (gr. 4-8). 16.95 *(978-0-8109-9724-0(X),* 675601, Amulet Bks.) Abrams, Inc.
Jaden, Denise. Never Enough. 2012. (ENG.). 400p. (YA). (gr. 9). pap. 9.99 *(978-1-4424-2907-9(0),* Simon Pulse) Simon Pulse.
Jerry, Spinelli. Stargirl. 2014. (ENG.). 208p. (YA). 11.24 *(978-1-63245-152-1(2))* Lectorum Pubns., Inc.
John, Jory. The Cool Bean. Oswald, Pete, illus. 2019. (Food Group Ser.). (ENG.). 40p. (J). (gr. -1-3). 18.99 *(978-0-06-295452-7(0),* HarperCollins) HarperCollins Pubs.
Juby, Susan. Getting the Girl: A Guide to Private Investigation, Surveillance, & Co Okery. 2010. (ENG.). 352p. (YA). (gr. 8). pap. 8.99 *(978-0-06-076528-6(3),* HarperTeen) HarperCollins Pubs.
Kaplan, Isabel. Hancock Park. 2010. (ENG.). 272p. (YA). (gr. 9). pap. 8.99 *(978-0-06-137370-1(2),* HarperTeen) HarperCollins Pubs.
Karre, Elizabeth. All You Are. 2014. (Gift Ser.). (ENG.). 120p. (YA). (gr. 6-12). pap. 7.95 *(978-1-4677-4477-5(8),* eb718cc1-6713-4a48-b567-548e6a7ebfcf, Darby Creek) Lerner Publishing Group.
Kats, Jewel. Miss Popular Steals the Show: Girls in Wheelchairs Rule! Stenton, Murray, illus. 2014. 37p. (J). pap. 14.95 *(978-1-61599-236-2(7))* Loving Healing Pr., Inc.
Keating, Jess. How to Outrun a Crocodile When Your Shoes Are Untied. 2014. (My Life Is a Zoo Ser.: 1). 288p. (J). (gr. 4-7). pap. 11.99 *(978-1-4022-9755-7(6),* 9781402297557) Sourcebooks, Inc.
—How to Outswim a Shark Without a Snorkel. 2015. (My Life Is a Zoo Ser.: 2). 304p. (J). (gr. 4-7). pap. 11.99 *(978-1-4022-9758-8(0),* 9781402297588) Sourcebooks, Inc.
Kerr, M. E., pseud. If I Love You, Am I Trapped Forever?, 0 vols. 2012. (ENG.). 192p. (YA). (gr. 7-12). pap. 9.99 *(978-0-7614-5839-5(5),* 9780761458395, Skyscape) Amazon Publishing.
Kittle, Katrina. Reasons to Be Happy. 2011. 288p. (J). (gr. 6-8). pap. 10.99 *(978-1-4022-6020-9(2))* Sourcebooks, Inc.
Kowitt, Holly. The Principal's Underwear Is Missing. Kowitt, Holly, illus. 2018. (ENG., Illus.). 224p. (J). pap. 16.99 *(978-1-250-15862-8(1),* 900185519) Square Fish.
—The Principal's Underwear Is Missing. 2018. (J). lib. bdg. 18.40 *(978-0-606-41102-8(X))* Turtleback.
Kowitt, Holly, illus. The Loser List. 2011. 213p. (J). pap. *(978-0-545-32900-2(0),* Scholastic Pr.) Scholastic, Inc.
—Revenge of the Loser. 2012. 233p. (J). *(978-0-545-42611-4(1),* Scholastic Pr.) Scholastic, Inc.
Kramer, Stacy & Thomas, Valerie. Karma Bites. 2010. (ENG.). 348p. (J). (gr. 5-7). pap. 18.99 *(978-0-547-36301-1(X),* 1422027, Clarion Bks.) HarperCollins Pubs.
Lean, Sarah. Hero. 2015. (ENG.). 208p. (J). (gr. 3-7). 17.99 *(978-0-06-212238-4(X),* Tegen, Katherine Bks) HarperCollins Pubs.
Leveen, Tom. Random. 2014. (ENG., Illus.). 224p. (YA). (gr. 9). 17.99 *(978-1-4424-9956-0(7),* Simon Pulse) Simon Pulse.
Levine, Gail Carson. The Wish. 2005. (ENG.). 256p. (J). (gr. 3-7). pap. 6.99 *(978-0-06-075911-7(9),* HarperCollins) HarperCollins Pubs.
—The Wish. 2004. 197p. (gr. 3-7). 16.00 *(978-0-7569-4272-4(1))* Perfection Learning Corp.
Lubar, David. My Rotten Life. 2009. (Nathan Abercrombie, Accidental Zombie Ser.: 1). (ENG., Illus.). 160p. (J). (gr. 3-7). pap. 13.99 *(978-0-7653-1634-9(X),* 900038898, Starscape) Doherty, Tom Assocs., LLC.
Ludwig, Trudy. The Invisible Boy. Barton, Patrice, illus. 2013. (ENG.). 40p. (J). (gr. 1-4). 18.99 *(978-1-58246-450-3(2),* Knopf Bks. for Young Readers) Random Hse. Children's Bks.
Lundin, Britta. Ship It. 2018. *(978-1-368-01698-8(7))* Disney Publishing Worldwide.
Maciejewski, Mark. Electric Boogerloo: I Am Fartacus. 2018. (Max Ser.). (ENG.). 352p. (J). (gr. 4-8). 17.99 *(978-1-4814-6423-9(X))*; (Illus.). pap. 7.99 *(978-1-4814-6422-2(1))* Simon & Schuster Children's Publishing. (Aladdin).
—I Am Fartacus. 2017. (Max Ser.). (ENG., Illus.). 336p. (J). (gr. 4-8). pap. 8.99 *(978-1-4814-6419-2(1),* Simon & Schuster/Paula Wiseman Bks.) Simon & Schuster/Paula Wiseman Bks.
Mackall, Dandi Daley. A Horse's Best Friend. 2018. (Winnie the Early Years Ser.: 2). (ENG., Illus.). 112p. (J). pap. 6.99 *(978-1-4964-3284-1(3),* 20_31613, Tyndale Kids) Tyndale Hse. Pubs.
Maizel, Rebecca. Between Us & the Moon. 2015. (ENG.). 384p. (YA). (gr. 9). 17.99 *(978-0-06-232761-1(5),* HarperTeen) HarperCollins Pubs.
McCafferty, Megan. Jessica Darling's It List: The (Totally Not) Guaranteed Guide to Popularity, Prettiness & Perfection. 2014. (Jessica Darling's It List Ser.: 1). (ENG.). 240p. (J). (gr. 3-7). pap. 14.99 *(978-0-316-24498-5(8),* Poppy) Little, Brown Bks. for Young Readers.
—Jessica Darling's It List 2: The (Totally Not) Guaranteed Guide to Friends, Foes & Faux Friends. 2015. (Jessica Darling's It List Ser.: 2). (ENG.). 208p. (J). (gr. 3-7). pap. 12.99 *(978-0-316-24503-6(8),* Poppy) Little, Brown Bks. for Young Readers.
—Jessica Darling's It List 3: The (Totally Not) Guaranteed Guide to Stressing, Obsessing & Second-Guessing. 2015. (Jessica Darling's It List Ser.: 3). (ENG.). 224p. (J). (gr. 3-7). 30.99 *(978-0-316-33324-5(7),* Poppy) Little, Brown Bks. for Young Readers.
McNish, Cliff. Angel. 2008. (Exceptional Reading & Language Arts Titles for Intermediate Grades Ser.). 311p. (YA). (gr. 8-12). 16.95 *(978-0-8225-8900-6(1))* Lerner Publishing Group.
Mechling, Lauren, et al. The Rise & Fall of a 10th Grade Social Climber. 2005. (ENG.). 304p. (YA). (gr. 7). pap. 16.99 *(978-0-618-55519-2(6),* 491380, Clarion Bks.) HarperCollins Pubs.
Mitchell, Todd. The Secret to Lying. (ENG., Illus.). 336p. (YA). (gr. 9). 2011. pap. 7.99 *(978-0-7636-5620-1(8))* 2010. 17.99 *(978-0-7636-4084-2(0))* Candlewick Pr.
Morgan, Melissa J. Freaky Tuesday #17, 17 vols. 2007. (Camp Confidential Ser.: 17). 160p. (J). (gr. 3-7). pap. 4.99 *(978-0-448-44651-6(0),* Grosset & Dunlap) Penguin Young Readers Group.
Morris, Taylor. Blowout, 1. Higgins, Anne Keenan, illus. 2011. (Hello, Gorgeous! Ser.: 1). (ENG.). 224p. (J). (gr. 6-8). 18.69 *(978-0-448-45526-6(9),* Grosset & Dunlap) Penguin Publishing Group.
Myracle, Lauren. Rhymes with Witches. (ENG.). (YA). (gr. 8-17). 2006. 272p. pap. 7.95 *(978-0-8109-9215-3(9))* 2005. 224p. 16.95 *(978-0-8109-5859-3(7),* Amulet Bks.) Abrams, Inc.
Night, P. J. Don't Drink the Punch! 2012. (Creepover Ser.: 11). lib. bdg. 16.00 *(978-0-606-26901-8(0))* Turtleback.
Nigro, D. M. The Wolfman, the Shrink & the Eighth-Grade Election. 2006. 116p. (J). pap. 13.50 *(978-1-931201-66-7(8))* Twilight Times Bks.
Noel, Alyson. Forever Summer. 2011. (ENG.). 464p. (YA). (gr. 8-12). pap. 29.99 *(978-0-312-60439-4(4),* 900076464, St. Martin's Griffin) St. Martin's Pr.
Nunn, Malla. When the Ground Is Hard. 2019. (ENG.). 272p. (YA). (gr. 7). 17.99 *(978-0-525-51557-9(7),* G.P. Putnam's Sons Books for Young Readers) Penguin Young Readers Group.
Oakes, Colleen. Blood of Wonderland. 2017. (Queen of Hearts Ser.: 2). (ENG.). (YA). (gr. 8). 352p. pap. 9.99 *(978-0-06-240977-5(8))*; 336p. 17.99 *(978-0-06-240976-8(X))* HarperCollins Pubs. (HarperTeen).
O'Connor, Barbara. Fame & Glory in Freedom, Georgia. 2008. (ENG.). 112p. (J). (gr. 2-4). pap. 8.99 *(978-0-374-40018-7(0),* 900050869) Square Fish.
Oliver, Lauren. Before I Fall. (ENG.). (YA). (gr. 9). 2021. 544p. pap. 11.99 *(978-0-06-172681-1(8))* 2010. 480p. 17.99 *(978-0-06-172680-4(X))* HarperCollins Pubs. (HarperCollins).
—Before I Fall. 2010. 368p. pap. *(978-0-340-98090-3(7),* Hodder Paperbacks) Hodder & Stoughton.
—Before I Fall. 2016. (YA). lib. bdg. 22.10 *(978-0-606-23576-1(0))* Turtleback.
Oliver, Lin. Double-Crossed #3. 2013. (Almost Identical Ser.: 3). 224p. (J). (gr. 3-7). pap. 7.99 *(978-0-448-45193-0(X),* Grosset & Dunlap) Penguin Young Readers Group.
—Double-Crossed #3 (HC). 3. 2013. (Almost Identical Ser.). (ENG.). 224p. (J). (gr. 4-6). 22.44 *(978-0-448-46161-8(7))* Penguin Young Readers Group.
Palmer, Robin. Geek Charming. 2009. 368p. (YA). (gr. 7-12). 9.99 *(978-0-14-241122-3(1),* Speak) Penguin Young Readers Group.
Patterson, James & Papademetriou, Lisa. Middle School: Big Fat Liar. Swaab, Neil, illus. 2014. (Middle School Ser.: 3). (ENG.). 304p. (J). (gr. 3-7). 13.99 *(978-0-316-32203-4(2),* Jimmy Patterson) Little Brown & Co.
—Middle School: My Brother Is a Big, Fat Liar. Swaab, Neil, illus. 2013. (Middle School Ser.: 3). (ENG.). 304p. (J). (gr. 3-7). 33.99 *(978-0-316-20754-6(3),* Jimmy Patterson) Little Brown & Co.
Perez, Marlene. The Comeback. 2009. (ENG.). 208p. (J). (gr. 7). pap. 8.99 *(978-0-545-08807-7(0))* Scholastic, Inc.
Piner, Huston. My Life As a Myth. 2017. (ENG., Illus.). (YA). pap. 11.99 *(978-1-947139-73-2(8))* NineStar Pr.
Plank, Alex & Plank, Lisa. How Bad Could It Be? 2007. (ENG.). 64p. per. 19.95 *(978-1-4241-6217-8(3))* America Star Bks.
Plata, Sebastian J. Freak 'N' Gorgeous. 2018. (ENG.). 288p. (YA). (gr. 8-12). 16.99 *(978-1-5107-3210-0(1),* Sky Pony Pr.) Skyhorse Publishing Co., Inc.
Polacco, Patricia. Bully. Polacco, Patricia, illus. 2012. (ENG., Illus.). 48p. (J). (gr. 2-5). 18.99 *(978-0-399-25704-9(7),* G.P. Putnam's Sons Books for Young Readers) Penguin Young Readers Group.
Pons, Lele & de la Cruz, Melissa. Surviving High School: A Novel. 2017. (ENG.). 272p. (gr. 8). pap. 16.00 *(978-1-5011-2054-1(9),* Gallery Bks.) Gallery Bks.
Prostko, Andrea. Strike One! 2010. 220p. pap. 13.95 *(978-1-60911-546-3(5),* Eloquent Bks.) Strategic Book Publishing & Rights Agency (SBPRA).
Raskin, Joyce. My Misadventures As a Teenage Rock Star. Chu, Carol, illus. 2011. (ENG.). 112p. (YA). (gr. 7-18). pap. 8.99 *(978-0-547-39311-7(3),* 1426898, Clarion Bks.) HarperCollins Pubs.

Robberecht, Thierry. Superhero School. Goossens, Philippe, illus. 2012. (ENG.). 30p. (J). (gr. -1-k). 16.95 *(978-1-60537-140-5(8))* Clavis Publishing.

Robbins, Jacqui. Two of a Kind. Phelan, Matt, illus. 2009. (ENG.). 32p. (J). (gr. -1-2). 19.99 *(978-1-4169-2437-1(X),* Atheneum Bks. for Young Readers) Simon & Schuster Children's Publishing.

Rodkey, Geoff. The Tapper Twins Go Viral. 2017. (Tapper Twins Ser.: 4). (ENG., Illus.). 256p. (J). (gr. 3-7). 13.99 *(978-0-316-29784-4(4))* Little, Brown Bks. for Young Readers.

—The Tapper Twins Go Viral. 2018. (Tapper Twins Ser.: 4). (J). lib. bdg. 17.20 *(978-0-606-40992-6(0))* Turtleback.

Rudetsky, Seth. My Awesome/Awful Popularity Plan. 2013. 224p. (YA). (gr. 7). pap. 8.99 *(978-0-375-89997-3(9),* Ember) Random Hse. Children's Bks.

Rue, Ginger. Hard Rock. 2017. (Tig Ripley Ser.). (ENG.). 368p. (YA). (gr. 4-7). 16.99 *(978-1-58536-947-8(0),* 204223) Sleeping Bear Pr.

—Rock 'n' Roll Rebel. 2016. (Tig Ripley Ser.). (ENG.). 349p. (J). (gr. 4-7). 16.99 *(978-1-58536-945-4(4),* 204106) Sleeping Bear Pr.

Russell, Rachel Renee. Dork Diaries: Tales from a Not-So-Fabulous Life. 2009. (Illus.). 282p. (J). *(978-0-85707-475-1(X),* Simon & Schuster/Paula Wiseman Bks.) Simon & Schuster/Paula Wiseman Bks.

Russell, Rachel Renée. Dork Diaries 1: Tales from a Not-So-Fabulous Life. Russell, Rachel Renée, illus. 2009. (Dork Diaries: 1). (ENG., Illus.). 352p. (J). (gr. 4-8). 14.99 *(978-1-4169-8006-3(7),* Aladdin) Simon & Schuster Children's Publishing.

—Dork Diaries 11: Tales from a Not-So-Friendly Frenemy. Russell, Rachel Renée, illus. 2016. (Dork Diaries: 11). (ENG., Illus.). 288p. (J). (gr. 4-8). 13.99 *(978-1-4814-7920-2(2),* Aladdin) Simon & Schuster Children's Publishing.

—Dork Diaries 2: Tales from a Not-So-Popular Party Girl. Russell, Rachel Renée, illus. 2010. (Dork Diaries: 2). (ENG., Illus.). 288p. (J). (gr. 4-8). 14.99 *(978-1-4169-8008-7(3),* Aladdin) Simon & Schuster Children's Publishing.

—Dork Diaries 3: Tales from a Not-So-Talented Pop Star. Russell, Rachel Renée, illus. 2011. (Dork Diaries: 3). (ENG., Illus.). 336p. (J). (gr. 4-8). 14.99 *(978-1-4424-1190-6(2),* Aladdin) Simon & Schuster Children's Publishing.

—Dork Diaries 4: Tales from a Not-So-Graceful Ice Princess. Russell, Rachel Renée, illus. 2012. (Dork Diaries: 4). (ENG., Illus.). 368p. (J). (gr. 4-8). 14.99 *(978-1-4424-1192-0(9),* Aladdin) Simon & Schuster Children's Publishing.

—Dork Diaries 5: Tales from a Not-So-Smart Miss Know-It-All. Russell, Rachel Renée, illus. 2012. (Dork Diaries: 5). (ENG., Illus.). 368p. (J). (gr. 4-8). 14.99 *(978-1-4424-4961-9(6),* Aladdin) Simon & Schuster Children's Publishing.

—Dork Diaries Boxed Set (Books 1-3) Set: Dork Diaries; Dork Diaries 2; Dork Diaries 3, Set. Russell, Rachel Renée, illus. 2011. (Dork Diaries: Nos. 1-3). (ENG., Illus.). 928p. (J). (gr. 4-8). 41.99 *(978-1-4424-2662-7(4),* Aladdin) Simon & Schuster Children's Publishing.

—Tales from a Not-So-Fabulous Life. 2009. (Dork Diaries: 1). lib. bdg. 25.75 *(978-0-606-32419-9(4))* Turtleback.

—Tales from a Not-So-Popular Party Girl. 2010. (Dork Diaries: 2). lib. bdg. 25.75 *(978-0-606-32420-5(8))* Turtleback.

Russell, Rachel Renée, et al. Tales from a Not-So-Friendly Frenemy. 2016. (Illus.). 243p. (J). *(978-1-5182-1819-4(9),* Aladdin) Simon & Schuster Children's Publishing.

—Tales from a Not-So-Popular Party Girl. 2010. (ENG.). pap. *(978-1-4424-4042-5(2),* Aladdin Paperbacks) Simon & Schuster Children's Publishing.

Schechter, Lynn R. My Big Fat Secret: How Jenna Takes Control of Her Emotions & Eating. Chin, Jason, illus. 2009. 64p. (J). (gr. 3-7). 14.95 *(978-1-4338-0540-0(5))*; pap. 9.95 *(978-1-4338-0541-7(3))* American Psychological Assn. (Magination Pr.).

Schraff, Anne. To Be Somebody. 2008. (Passages Ser.). 120p. (J). (gr. 4-6). lib. bdg. 13.95 *(978-0-7569-8390-1(8))* Perfection Learning Corp.

Schreiber, Ellen. Magic of the Moonlight, 2. 2012. (Full Moon Ser.: 2). (ENG.). 256p. (YA). (gr. 8-12). pap. 9.99 *(978-0-06-198656-7(9),* Tegen, Katherine Bks) HarperCollins Pubs.

—Once in a Full Moon. 2011. (Full Moon Ser.: 1). (ENG.). 320p. (YA). (gr. 8). pap. 9.99 *(978-0-06-198652-9(6),* Tegen, Katherine Bks) HarperCollins Pubs.

Scott, Kieran. I Was a Non-Blonde Cheerleader. 2007. (ENG.). 272p. (YA). (gr. 7-18). 8.99 *(978-0-14-240910-7(3),* Speak) Penguin Young Readers Group.

Sedita, Francesco. Miss Popularity. 2007. 120p. (J). pap. *(978-0-545-00828-0(X))* Scholastic, Inc.

Segal, Zoe. Confessions of a Tenth-Grade Social Climber. 2005. 290p. (YA). *(978-0-618-44981-1(7))* Houghton Mifflin Harcourt Publishing Co.

Shannon, David. A Bad Case of Stripes. 2015. 32p. pap. 7.00 *(978-1-61003-539-2(9))* Center for the Collaborative Classroom.

—A Bad Case of Stripes. 2004. (Scholastic Bookshelf Ser.). (Illus.). (gr. -1-3). 17.00 *(978-0-7569-3183-4(5))* Perfection Learning Corp.

—A Bad Case of Stripes. 2007. (ENG.). (J). (gr. -1-3). 18.95 *(978-0-439-02328-3(9))* Scholastic, Inc.

—A Bad Case of Stripes, 1 vol. Shannon, David, illus. 2006. (ENG., Illus.). 32p. (J). (gr. -1-3). pap. 10.99 incl. audio compact disk *(978-0-439-92494-8(4))* Scholastic, Inc.

Shepard, Sara. Ali's Pretty Little Lies. 2013. (Pretty Little Liars Ser.). (YA). lib. bdg. 20.85 *(978-0-606-35048-8(9))* Turtleback.

—Pretty Little Liars: Ali's Pretty Little Lies. 2013. (Pretty Little Liars Companion Novel Ser.). (ENG.). (YA). (gr. 9). 320p. pap. 10.99 *(978-0-06-223337-0(8))*; 304p. 17.99 *(978-0-06-223336-3(X))* HarperCollins Pubs. (HarperTeen).

Shreve, Susan Richards. Kiss Me Tomorrow. 2006. 220p. (J). *(978-1-4156-5592-4(8),* Levine, Arthur A. Bks.) Scholastic, Inc.

Simon, Coco. Alexis Cool As a Cupcake. 2013. (Cupcake Diaries: 8). (ENG., Illus.). 160p. (J). (gr. 3-7). 17.99 *(978-1-4424-8569-3(8),* Simon Spotlight) Simon Spotlight.

—Alexis Cool as a Cupcake. 2012. (Cupcake Diaries: 8). lib. bdg. 16.00 *(978-0-606-26334-4(9))* Turtleback.

—Katie Starting from Scratch. 2014. (Cupcake Diaries: 21). (ENG., Illus.). 160p. (J). (gr. 3-7). pap. 7.99 *(978-1-4814-0471-6(7),* Simon Spotlight) Simon Spotlight.

—Mia in the Mix. (Cupcake Diaries: 2). (ENG.). 160p. (J). (gr. 3-7). 2013. Illus.). 17.99 *(978-1-4424-7491-8(2))* 2011. pap. 7.99 *(978-1-4424-2277-3(7))* Simon Spotlight. (Simon Spotlight).

Smith, Bryan. Is There an App for That? Wish, Katia, illus. 2015. (ENG.). 31p. (J). (gr. k-6). pap. 10.95 *(978-1-934490-74-7(1))* Boys Town Pr.

Sones, Sonya. What My Girlfriend Doesn't Know. 2011. 9.68 *(978-0-7848-3389-6(3),* Everbind) Marco Bk. Co.

—What My Girlfriend Doesn't Know. 2013. (ENG., Illus.). 320p. (YA). (gr. 7). pap. 12.99 *(978-1-4424-9384-1(4),* Simon & Schuster Bks. For Young Readers) Simon & Schuster Bks. For Young Readers.

Spinelli, Jerry. Stargirl. 2003. (EMC Masterpiece Series Access Editions). xiv, 199p. (YA). 12.99 *(978-0-8219-2504-1(0),* 35378) EMC/Paradigm Publishing.

—Stargirl. unabr. ed. 2004. 192p. (J). (gr. 7-18). pap. 40.00 incl. audio *(978-0-8072-0855-7(8),* LYA 323 SP, Listening Library) Random Hse. Audio Publishing Group.

—Stargirl. 2004. (Stargirl Ser.: 1). (ENG.). 208p. (YA). (gr. 7). mass mkt. 9.99 *(978-0-440-41677-7(9),* Laurel Leaf) Random Hse. Children's Bks.

St. Claire, Roxanne. They All Fall Down. 2016. (ENG.). 352p. (YA). (gr. 7). pap. 10.99 *(978-0-385-74272-6(X),* Ember) Random Hse. Children's Bks.

Standish, Burt L. Frank Merriwell's Fame. Rudman, Jack, ed. 2003. (Frank Merriwell Ser.). 29.95 *(978-0-8373-9336-0(1))*; pap. 9.95 *(978-0-8373-9036-9(2))* Merriwell, Frank Inc.

Staniszewski, Anna. Dirt Diary. 2014. (Dirt Diary Ser.: 1). 256p. (J). (gr. 5-9). pap. 11.99 *(978-1-4022-8636-0(8),* 9781402286360) Sourcebooks, Inc.

—The Gossip File. 2015. (Dirt Diary Ser.: 3). 224p. (J). (gr. 5-9). pap. 9.99 *(978-1-4926-0463-1(1),* 9781492604631) Sourcebooks, Inc.

Summers, Courtney. What Goes Around. 2013. (ENG.). 480p. (YA). (gr. 9-12). pap. 29.99 *(978-1-250-03844-9(8),* 900122299, St. Martin's Griffin) St. Martin's Pr.

Toliver, Wendy. The Secret Life of a Teenage Siren. 2012. (Romantic Comedies Ser.). (ENG.). 304p. (YA). (gr. 7). pap. 14.99 *(978-1-4424-7494-9(7),* Simon Pulse) Simon Pulse.

Tracy, Kristen. Project (un)Popular Book #1. 2017. (Project (un)Popular Ser.: 1). (ENG.). 336p. (J). (gr. 5). 8.99 *(978-0-553-51051-5(7),* Yearling) Random Hse. Children's Bks.

—Project (un)Popular Book #2: Totally Crushed. 2017. (Project (un)Popular Ser.: 2). (ENG.). 224p. (J). (gr. 5). 16.99 *(978-0-553-51052-2(5),* Delacorte Bks. for Young Readers) Random Hse. Children's Bks.

—Totally Crushed. 2017. 211p. (J). *(978-0-553-51053-9(3),* Delacorte Pr) Random House Publishing Group.

Trueit, Trudi. The Sister Solution. 2015. (Mix Ser.). (ENG., Illus.). 240p. (J). (gr. 4-8). pap. 7.99 *(978-1-4814-3239-9(7),* Aladdin) Simon & Schuster Children's Publishing.

—Stealing Popular. 2012. (Mix Ser.). (ENG.). 240p. (J). (gr. 4-8). pap. 6.99 *(978-1-4424-4154-5(2),* Aladdin) Simon & Schuster Children's Publishing.

Vail, Rachel. Lucky. 2009. (Avery Sisters Trilogy Ser.: 1). (ENG.). 256p. (YA). (gr. 8). pap. 9.99 *(978-0-06-089045-2(2),* HarperTeen) HarperCollins Pubs.

—Unfriended. 2015. 304p. (J). (gr. 5). 8.99 *(978-0-14-751154-6(2),* Puffin Books) Penguin Young Readers Group.

Van Dolzer, Krista. Don't Vote for Me. 2016. (ENG.). 240p. (J). (gr. 5-8). pap. 10.99 *(978-1-4926-3184-2(1),* 9781492631842) Sourcebooks, Inc.

Vrettos, Adrienne Maria. The Exile of Gigi Lane. 2011. (ENG.). 368p. (YA). (gr. 7). pap. 8.99 *(978-1-4424-2121-9(5),* McElderry, Margaret K. Bks.) McElderry, Margaret K. Bks.

Walde, Christine. The Candy Darlings. 2006. (ENG.). 310p. (YA). (gr. 9-12). per. 18.95 *(978-0-618-58969-2(4),* 497559, Clarion Bks.) HarperCollins Pubs.

Weatherly, L. A. Them. 2013. (ENG.). 80p. (YA). (gr. 6-12). pap. 6.95 *(978-1-78112-185-6(0))*; lib. bdg. 22.60 *(978-1-78112-184-9(2))* Lerner Publishing Group.

Weber, Lori. Yellow Mini, 1 vol. 2011. (ENG.). 243p. (YA). (gr. 7-9). pap. 9.95 *(978-1-55455-199-6(4),* 41752833-3e0a-484f-9722-80b0cdf3f540) Fitzhenry & Whiteside, Ltd. CAN. Dist: Firefly Bks., Ltd.

Whitaker, Alecia. The Queen of Kentucky. 2013. (ENG.). 384p. (J). (gr. 7-17). pap. 19.99 *(978-0-316-12494-2(X),* Poppy) Little, Brown Bks. for Young Readers.

Williams, Erika. Through the Shattered Glass, 1 vol. 2010. 62p. pap. 19.95 *(978-1-4489-5149-9(6))* America Star Bks.

Willner-Pardo, Gina. The Hard Kind of Promise. 2011. (ENG.). 204p. (J). (gr. 5-7). pap. 12.99 *(978-0-547-55017-6(0),* 1450220, Clarion Bks.) HarperCollins Pubs.

Wong, Janet S. Me & Rolly Maloo. Buttler, Elizabeth, illus. 2014. 240p. (J). (gr. 2-5). pap. 7.95 *(978-1-58089-159-2(4))* Charlesbridge Publishing, Inc.

Wright, Lanikka. The Fab Four 2: Eva's Obsession. 2012. (ENG.). 244p. pap. 13.95 *(978-1-4327-9846-8(4))* Outskirts Pr., Inc.

Yee, Lisa. Warp Speed. 2011. (ENG.). 320p. (J). (gr. 4-7). 16.99 *(978-0-545-12276-4(7),* Levine, Arthur A. Bks.) Scholastic, Inc.

Yoo, David. The Detention Club. 2012. (ENG.). 304p. (J). (gr. 5). pap. 6.99 *(978-0-06-178380-7(3),* Balzer & Bray) HarperCollins Pubs.

Zadoff, Allen. Food, Girls, & Other Things I Can't Have. 2011. (ENG., Illus.). 320p. (gr. 9). pap. 9.99 *(978-1-60684-151-8(3),* Carolrhoda Lab™) Lerner Publishing Group.

Ziegler, Jennifer. How Not to Be Popular. 2010. 352p. (YA). (gr. 7). mass mkt. 8.99 *(978-0-440-24024-2(7),* Delacorte Bks. for Young Readers) Random Hse. Children's Bks.

POPULATION

see also Birth Control; Migration, Internal

also names of countries, cities, etc. with the subdivision Population, e.g. United States—Population

Amidon Lusted, Marcia, ed. Climate Change & Population Displacement, 1 vol. 2019. (Global Viewpoints Ser.). (ENG.). 200p. (gr. 10-12). 47.83 *(978-1-5345-0554-4(7),* 49850032-01b5-4880-ad91-1a34dab9d097) Greenhaven Publishing LLC.

Anderson, Joanna. The Many People of America, 1 vol. 2012. (I'm an American Citizen Ser.). (ENG., Illus.). 24p. (J). (gr. 1-2). 26.27 *(978-1-4488-8591-6(4),* d0f7d528-ba0f-4f24-85e6-957351610874, PowerKids Pr.) Rosen Publishing Group, Inc., The.

Anniss, Matt. Planet under Pressure: Too Many People on Earth?, 1 vol. 2013. (Ask the Experts Ser.). (ENG., Illus.). 48p. (gr. 6-8). 34.60 *(978-1-4339-8643-7(4),* ba9a4679-8fc9-481e-89d7-dcd3e08b8840); pap. 15.05 *(978-1-4339-8644-4(2),* 104d6700-c607-4c06-a7c3-f24abfa7f72b) Stevens, Gareth Publishing LLLP. (Gareth Stevens Secondary Library).

Bellamy, Rufus. Population Growth. 2010. (Sustaining Our Environment Ser.). 48p. (J). 35.65 *(978-1-60753-137-1(2))* Amicus Learning.

Bodden, Valerie. The Threat of Overpopulation. 2010. (Earth Issues Ser.). 48p. (YA). (gr. 5-18). 23.95 *(978-1-58341-983-0(7),* Creative Education) Creative Co., The.

Einspruch, Andrew. Overpopulation, 1 vol. 2012. (Discovery Education: the Environment Ser.). (ENG., Illus.). 32p. (J). (gr. 4-5). pap. 11.00 *(978-1-4488-7978-6(7),* 96782d30-8dcd-46aa-8b6f-a7f6bf15b6c5); lib. bdg. 28.93 *(978-1-4488-7890-1(X),* 124e4a1f-b06e-4ac7-8f2a-cba091997bd0) Rosen Publishing Group, Inc., The. (PowerKids Pr.).

Gitlin, Martin, ed. America's Changing Demographics, 1 vol. 2019. (Opposing Viewpoints Ser.). (ENG.). 200p. (gr. 10-12). pap. 34.80 *(978-1-5345-0600-8(4),* 68fdb3d2-266c-43be-a4b6-f3ea01aa2bb1) Greenhaven Publishing LLC.

Gordon, Sharon. At Home in the City, 1 vol. 2007. (At Home Ser.). (ENG.). 32p. (gr. k-2). pap. 9.23 *(978-0-7614-3306-4(6),* 7b58ea65-4129-4e6e-bb81-e1f8353abe5f) Cavendish Square Publishing LLC.

Green, Robert. Overpopulation. 2008. (21st Century Skills Library: Global Perspectives Ser.). (ENG., Illus.). 32p. (gr. 4-8). lib. bdg. 32.07 *(978-1-60279-127-5(9),* 200102) Cherry Lake Publishing.

Hardyman, Robyn. The Race to Control the Population, 1 vol. 2014. (World in Crisis Ser.). (ENG.). 48p. (YA). (gr. 5-5). 33.47 *(978-1-4777-7850-0(0),* 1e60792e-15ec-44e2-bd27-d58d90e3b54f, Rosen Reference) Rosen Publishing Group, Inc., The.

Haugen, David M. & Musser, Susan, eds. The Millennial Generation, 1 vol. 2012. (Opposing Viewpoints Ser.). (ENG., Illus.). 216p. (gr. 10-12). pap. 34.80 *(978-0-7377-6327-0(2),* b112c8dc-9cb2-48f8-9c88-6d6cc693e634); lib. bdg. 50.43 *(978-0-7377-6326-3(4),* 87215dc6-fe20-42a0-a98a-dee82786f067) Greenhaven Publishing LLC. (Greenhaven Publishing).

—Population, 1 vol. 2011. (Opposing Viewpoints Ser.). (ENG., Illus.). 232p. (gr. 10-12). 50.43 *(978-0-7377-5755-2(8),* 4e623f3d-fba9-49d0-b88c-27cdcf80334c); pap. 34.80 *(978-0-7377-5756-9(6),* 97610eee-edde-4257-b638-325899a61c70) Greenhaven Publishing LLC. (Greenhaven Publishing).

Howell, Izzi. Overpopulation Eco Facts. 2019. (Eco Facts Ser.). (ENG., Illus.). 32p. (J). (gr. 5-5). pap. *(978-0-7787-6364-2(1),* ffc58a90-70ee-4810-a161-44be1609ee42); lib. bdg. *(978-0-7787-6354-3(4),* d973c060-2479-4a87-be26-a432d7654a1c) Crabtree Publishing Co.

—Population & Settlement Geo Facts. 2018. (Geo Facts Ser.). (Illus.). 32p. (J). (gr. 5-5). *(978-0-7787-4385-9(3))* Crabtree Publishing Co.

Hyde, Natalie. Population Patterns: What Factors Determine the Location & Growth of Human Settlements?, 1 vol. 2010. (Investigating Human Migration & Settlement Ser.). (ENG., Illus.). 48p. (J). (gr. 5-8). *(978-0-7787-5182-3(1))*; pap. *(978-0-7787-5197-7(X))* Crabtree Publishing Co.

Kalman, Bobbie. What Is a Biome? 2008. (ENG.). 32p. (J). *(978-0-7787-7640-6(9))* Crabtree Publishing Co.

Kirk, Ellen. Human Footprint: Everything You Will Eat, Use, Wear, Buy, & Throw Out in Your Lifetime. 2011. (Illus.). 32p. (J). (gr. 3-7). pap. 6.95 *(978-1-4263-0767-6(5),* National Geographic Kids) Disney Publishing Worldwide.

Mason, Paul. Earthquakes. 2012. (Disaster Watch! Ser.). 32p. (gr. 4-6). lib. bdg. 28.50 *(978-1-59920-423-9(1))* Black Rabbit Bks.

McDougal, Anna. The Population of Chicago: Analyzing Data, 1 vol. 2017. (Computer Kids: Powered by Computational Thinking Ser.). (ENG.). 24p. (J). (gr. 4-5). 25.27 *(978-1-5383-2434-9(2),* 4e20239d-f6c2-4980-8e35-e68804b5c8ec, PowerKids Pr.); pap. *(978-1-5081-3766-5(8),* ae995c46-9df5-44a2-b756-872831054c20, Rosen Classroom) Rosen Publishing Group, Inc., The.

Newton, David E. Overpopulation: 7 Billion People & Counting, 1 vol. 2015. (End of Life As We Know It Ser.). (ENG., Illus.). 160p. (gr. 7-8). 38.93 *(978-0-7660-7312-8(2),* 170d0cfe-f830-40ed-bff2-2bdb49f1e696) Enslow Publishing, LLC.

Obadina, Tunde. Population & Overcrowding. Ojakorotu, Victor & Rotberg, Robert I., eds. 2013. (Africa: Progress & Problems Ser.: 13). (Illus.). 112p. (J). (gr. 7-18). 24.95 *(978-1-4222-2945-3(9))* Mason Crest.

Smith, David J. If: A Mind-Bending New Way of Looking at Big Ideas & Numbers. Adams, Steve, illus. 2014. (ENG.). 40p. (J). (gr. 3-7). 19.99 *(978-1-894786-34-8(3))* Kids Can Pr., Ltd. CAN. Dist: Hachette Bk. Group.

—If the World Were a Village - Second Edition: A Book about the World's People. Armstrong, Shelagh, illus. (CitizenKid Ser.). (ENG.). 32p. (J). (gr. 3-7). 2020. pap. 10.99 *(978-1-55337-732-0(X))* 2nd ed. 2011. 18.99 *(978-1-55453-595-8(6))* Kids Can Pr., Ltd. CAN. Dist: Hachette Bk. Group.

Sterling, Kristin. Living in Urban Communities. 2008. pap. 34.95 *(978-0-8225-9480-2(3))* Lerner Publishing Group.

Stewart, Gail B. Population. 2011. (J). *(978-1-60217-033-9(9))* Erickson Pr.

—Ripped from the Headlines: Population. 2008. (J). *(978-1-60217-026-1(6))* Erickson Pr.

POPULATION, FOREIGN

see Emigration and Immigration

POPULIST PARTY

Brexel, Bernadette. The Populist Party: A Voice for the Farmers in an Industrial Society. 2009. (America's Industrial Society in the 19th Century Ser.). 32p. (gr. 4-4). 47.90 *(978-1-61511-344-6(4))* Rosen Publishing Group, Inc., The.

—The Populist Party: A Voice for the Farmers in the Industrialized Society, 1 vol. 2003. (Primary Sources of America's Industrial Society in the 19th Century Ser.). (ENG., Illus.). 32p. (gr. 4-5). pap. 10.00 *(978-0-8239-4284-8(8),* 9512a6c0-88be-4c92-b6cc-31c3d0a8a398); lib. bdg. 29.13 *(978-0-8239-4029-5(2),* e5331fa0-9bce-418d-bb2d-dabead132b0b, Rosen Reference) Rosen Publishing Group, Inc., The.

PORCELAIN

Loman & Petula Eng, Loman &. Collecting American Belleek, 1 vol. 2003. (ENG., Illus.). 160p. 39.95 *(978-0-7643-1860-3(8),* 2218) Schiffer Publishing, Ltd.

PORCUPINES

Abrams, Taharra. Growing up Porcupine!, 1 vol. 2013. (Rosen Readers Ser.). (ENG.). 24p. (J). (gr. 3-3). pap. 8.25 *(978-1-4777-2455-2(9),* bb1471c7-fa82-44a0-952d-54ae7c80195d); pap. 49.50 *(978-1-4777-2456-9(7))* Rosen Publishing Group, Inc., The. (Rosen Classroom).

Avery, Sebastian. Porcupines, 1 vol. 2016. (Creatures of the Forest Habitat Ser.). (ENG.). 24p. (J). (gr. 3-3). pap. 9.25 *(978-1-4994-2757-8(3),* a96dee79-f875-465f-8435-c396b0e64d78, PowerKids Pr.) Rosen Publishing Group, Inc., The.

Bergeron, Alain M. & Quintin, Michel. Do You Know Porcupines?, 1 vol. Sampar, illus. 2013. (Do You Know? Ser.). (ENG.). 64p. (J). (gr. 2-4). pap. 9.95 *(978-1-55455-321-1(0),* e5bf74ff-2e52-4213-845e-c991ad31f0f7) Trifolium Bks., Inc. CAN. Dist: Firefly Bks., Ltd.

Colby, Jennifer. Porcupine Quills to Needles. 2019. (21st Century Junior Library: Tech from Nature Ser.). (ENG.). 24p. (J). (gr. 2-5). pap. 12.79 *(978-1-5341-3952-7(4),* 212637); (Illus.). lib. bdg. 30.64 *(978-1-5341-4296-1(7),* 212636) Cherry Lake Publishing.

Dunn, Mary R. Porcupines. 2011. (Nocturnal Animals Ser.). (ENG.). 24p. (gr. k-1). pap. 41.70 *(978-1-4296-6362-5(6),* Capstone Pr.) Capstone.

Early Macken, JoAnn. Porcupines, 1 vol. (Animals That Live in the Forest (First Edition) Ser.). (ENG., 24p. (gr. 1-1). 2004. Illus.). pap. 9.15 *(978-0-8368-4492-4(0),* caf8c627-6b64-4b68-ba0e-a44f39758ed8, Weekly Reader Leveled Readers) 2004. (Illus.). lib. bdg. 25.27 *(978-0-8368-4485-6(8),* c3010b5d-25ab-47a4-b77f-97f54fc1c970) 2nd rev. ed. 2009. (J). pap. 9.15 *(978-1-4339-2483-5(8),* 6803dcc2-c97b-467e-b5b5-690b803fa9dd) 2nd rev. ed. 2009. (J). lib. bdg. 25.27 *(978-1-4339-2407-1(2),* 38a7ad76-368e-4d17-bf6a-9e1058b7b690) Stevens, Gareth Publishing LLLP.

—Porcupines / Puercoespines, 1 vol. 2nd rev. ed. 2009. (Animals That Live in the Forest / Animales Del Bosque Ser.). 24p. (J). (gr. 1-1). (SPA & ENG.). pap. 9.15 *(978-1-4339-2490-3(0),* 8b74ea23-521a-47da-a9ae-ef29935d7996); (ENG & SPA.). lib. bdg. 25.27 *(978-1-4339-2439-2(0),* 5e1f8b22-6b6d-45de-a7c7-b1d1acce335e) Stevens, Gareth Publishing LLLP. (Weekly Reader Leveled Readers).

Green, Emily. Porcupines. 2011. (Backyard Wildlife Ser.). (ENG., Illus.). 24p. (J). (gr. k-3). lib. bdg. 26.95 *(978-1-60014-562-9(0),* Blastoff! Readers) Bellwether Media.

—Porcupines. 2011. (Backyard Wildlife Ser.). 24p. (J). (gr. k-1). lib. bdg. 22.00 *(978-0-531-20488-7(X),* Children's Pr.) Scholastic Library Publishing.

Green, Jen. Porcupines. 2008. (Illus.). 52p. (J). *(978-0-7172-6278-6(2))* Grolier, Ltd.

James, Lincoln. A Prickle of Porcupines, 1 vol. 2013. (Animal Groups Ser.). (ENG., Illus.). 24p. (gr. 1-2). 25.27 *(978-1-4339-8219-4(6),* a84328bb-62bc-4643-bbb7-8cc2e51a4c82); pap. 9.15 *(978-1-4339-8220-0(X),* 1fcb9ab9-f3f6-4069-9de1-e3c8c3e65b58) Stevens, Gareth Publishing LLLP.

—A Prickle of Porcupines / una Manada de Puercoespines, 1 vol. 2013. (Animal Groups / Grupos de Animales Ser.). (ENG & SPA., Illus.). 24p. (gr. 1-2). 25.27 *(978-1-4339-8812-7(7),* 0e9ab318-c703-440a-8be1-4da66cec725b) Stevens, Gareth Publishing LLLP.

Jango-Cohen, Judith. Porcupines, 1 vol. 2007. (Animals, Animals Ser.). (ENG., Illus.). 48p. (gr. 5-5). lib. bdg. 32.64 *(978-0-7614-1868-9(7),* c8a0c10c-4617-4391-afc7-d4d0915b074e) Cavendish Square Publishing LLC.

Lang, Aubrey. Baby Porcupine, 1 vol. Lynch, Wayne, photos by. 2005. (Nature Babies Ser.). (ENG., Illus.). 36p. (J). (gr. k-3). 16.95 *(978-1-55041-560-5(3),* ca98cd6c-8a88-4f13-8a03-01feca1d3f8f); pap. 7.95 *(978-1-55041-562-9(X),* 75589ef0-15ed-42d5-95e4-b0f98b0fa0ba) Trifolium Bks., Inc. CAN. Dist: Firefly Bks., Ltd.

Leaf, Christina. Porcupines. 2015. (North American Animals Ser.). (ENG., Illus.). 24p. (J). (gr. k-3). lib. bdg. 26.95 *(978-1-62617-262-3(5),* Blastoff! Readers) Bellwether Media.

Markle, Sandra. Los Puercoespines (Porcupines) 2009. (SPA.). pap. 46.95 *(978-0-7613-4720-0(8))* Lerner Publishing Group.

—Porcupines. 2008. (Animal Prey Ser.). (Illus.). 39p. (J). (gr. 3-7). per. 7.95 *(978-0-8225-6442-3(4),* First Avenue Editions); pap. 46.95 *(978-0-8225-9322-5(X))* Lerner Publishing Group.

—Los Puercoespines (Porcupines) 2008. 40p. (J). pap. 7.95 *(978-0-7613-3900-7(0),* Ediciones Lerner) Lerner Publishing Group.

Mattern, Joanne. Porcupines & Hedgehogs. 2018. (Core Content Science — Animal Look-Alikes Ser.). (ENG., Illus.). 32p. (J). (gr. 2-4). lib. bdg. 23.99 *(978-1-63440-213-2(8),* 552593fa-9dbb-44e7-a46b-17922771e9bb) Red Chair Pr.

Nichols, Catherine. Prickly Porcupines. 2008. (Gross-Out Defenses Ser.). (Illus.). 24p. (J). (gr. k-3). lib. bdg. 26.99 *(978-1-59716-721-5(5),* 1284311) Bearport Publishing Co., Inc.

Rockwood, Leigh. Tell Me the Difference Between a Porcupine & a Hedgehog, 1 vol. 2013. (How Are They Different? Ser.). (ENG., Illus.). 24p. (J). (gr. 2-3). pap. 9.25 *(978-1-4488-9732-2(7),* 85c67ac9-d7f3-4aa8-a391-0e6be399efec); lib. bdg. 26.27 *(978-1-4488-9637-0(1),* fbf05031-2e82-47c2-ae1e-714617aba224) Rosen Publishing Group, Inc., The. (PowerKids Pr.).

Rouche, Jeffrey. Porcupines in the Wild. 2013. (InfoMax Readers Ser.). (ENG.). 24p. (J). (gr. 3-4). pap. 49.50 *(978-1-4777-2470-5(2));* (Illus.). pap. 8.25 *(978-1-4777-2469-9(9),* 9ae06563-b2d0-43cc-967b-71c3d158a492) Rosen Publishing Group, Inc., The. (Rosen Classroom).

Schuh, Mari. Porcupines. 2016. (My First Animal Library). (Illus.). 24p. (J). (gr. k-2). lib. bdg. 25.65 *(978-1-62031-290-2(5),* Bullfrog Bks.) Jump! Inc.

Sherman, Jill. Los Puercoespines. 2018. (Animales Norteamericanos Ser.). (SPA.). 24p. (J). (gr. 1-4). lib. bdg. *(978-1-68151-624-0(1),* 15232) Amicus.

—Porcupines. 2018. (North American Animals Ser.). (ENG.). 24p. (J). (gr. 1-4). pap. 8.99 *(978-1-68152-338-5(8),* 15123); lib. bdg. *(978-1-68151-418-5(4),* 15115) Amicus.

Webster, Christine. Porcupines. 2009. (Backyard Animals Ser.). (Illus.). 24p. (J). (gr. 3-5). pap. 8.95 *(978-1-60596-079-1(9));* lib. bdg. 24.45 *(978-1-60596-078-4(0))* Weigl Pubs., Inc.

Yoon, Salina. Duck, Duck, Porcupine! 2017. (J). lib. bdg. 16.00 *(978-0-606-40593-5(3))* Turtleback.

PORCUPINES—FICTION

Archer, Dosh. The Case of Piggy's Bank (Detective Paw of the Law: Time to Read, Level 3) Archer, Dosh, illus. 2018. (Time to Read Ser.: 1). (ENG., Illus.). 48p. (J). (gr. k-2). 12.99 *(978-0-8075-1557-0(4),* 807515574) Whitman, Albert & Co.

—The Case of the Icky Ice Cream (Detective Paw of the Law: Time to Read, Level 3) Archer, Dosh, illus. 2020. (Time to Read Ser.). (ENG., Illus.). 48p. (J). (gr. k-2). 12.99 *(978-0-8075-1571-6(X),* 080751571X) Whitman, Albert & Co.

Avi. Poppy & Ereth. Floca, Brian, illus. 2020. (Poppy Ser.: 7). (ENG.). 240p. (J). (gr. 3-7). pap. 7.99 *(978-0-06-111971-2(7),* HarperCollins) HarperCollins Pubs.

—Poppy & Rye. Floca, Brian, illus. 2020. (Poppy Ser.: 4). (ENG.). 240p. (J). (gr. 3-7). pap. 9.99 *(978-0-380-79717-2(8),* HarperCollins) HarperCollins Pubs.

—Poppy & Rye. Floca, Brian, illus. 2006. (Poppy Stories Ser.: 3). 182p. (J). (gr. 3-7). lib. bdg. 17.20 *(978-0-613-17447-3(X))* Turtleback.

Bentley, Dawn. The Prickly Porcupine. Stover, Beth, illus. 2003. (Soundprints' Read-and-Discover Ser.). (ENG.). 32p. (J). (gr. -1-3). 12.95 *(978-1-59249-014-1(X),* PS2065); pap. 3.95 *(978-1-59249-013-4(1),* S2015) Soundprints.

Blabey, Aaron, illus. I Need a Hug. 2018. (ENG.). 32p. (J). (gr. -1-k). 14.99 *(978-1-338-29710-2(4),* Scholastic Pr.) Scholastic, Inc.

Brown, Derrick. Valentine the Porcupine Dances Funny. Lewis, Jenn, illus. 2011. (ENG.). 44p. 20.00 *(978-1-935904-18-2(3),* Write Fuzzy) Write Bloody Publishing.

Burach, Ross. Pine & Boof: The Lucky Leaf. 2017. (ENG., Illus.). 40p. (J). (gr. -1-3). 17.99 *(978-0-06-241850-0(5),* HarperCollins) HarperCollins Pubs.

Burgess, Thornton W. The Adventures of Prickly Porky. 2007. 140p. (gr. 4-7). per. 11.95 *(978-1-60312-048-7(3));* 24.95 *(978-1-60312-953-4(7))* Aegypan.

—The Adventures of Prickly Porky. 2011. 138p. 25.95 *(978-1-4638-9572-3(0))* Rodgers, Alan Bks.

Cakal, Kimberly. Today I Hugged a Porcupine. 2007. 20p. per. 24.95 *(978-1-4241-8561-0(0))* America Star Bks.

Chaconas, Dori. The Babysitters. McCue, Lisa, illus. 2014. (Cork & Fuzz Ser.: 6). 32p. (J). (gr. 1-3). pap. 4.99 *(978-0-448-48050-3(6),* Penguin Young Readers) Penguin Young Readers Group.

Covey, Sean. Just the Way I Am: Habit 1. Curtis, Stacy, illus. 2018. (7 Habits of Happy Kids Ser.: 1). (ENG.). 32p. (J). (gr. -1-1). 6.99 *(978-1-5344-1577-5(7),* Simon & Schuster Bks. For Young Readers) Simon & Schuster Bks. For Young Readers.

—Just the Way I Am: Habit 1 (Ready-To-Read Level 2) Curtis, Stacy, illus. 2019. (7 Habits of Happy Kids Ser.: 1). (ENG.). 32p. (J). (gr. k-2). 17.99 *(978-1-5344-4445-4(9));* pap. 4.99 *(978-1-5344-4444-7(0))* Simon Spotlight. (Simon Spotlight).

Crenshaw, Glenda. Friends of the Enchanted Forest: How they Save Christmas. 2011. 28p. pap. 15.47 *(978-1-4520-0512-6(5))* AuthorHouse.

Day, Ralph M. Peter Porcupine One Quill. 2010. 40p. 19.95 *(978-1-4269-3747-7(4))* Trafford Publishing.

deRubertis, Barbara. Polly Porcupine's Painting Prize. Alley, R. W., illus. 2011. (Animal Antics A to Z Ser.). 32p. (J). pap. 45.32 *(978-0-7613-7662-0(3));* lib. bdg. 22.60 *(978-1-57565-337-2(0))* Astra Publishing Hse.

deRubertis, Barbara & DeRubertis, Barbara. Polly Porcupine's Painting Prizes. Alley, R. W., illus. 2012. (Animal Antics A to Z Ser.). 32p. (J). (gr. 2 — 1). cd-rom 7.95 *(978-1-57565-409-6(1))* Astra Publishing Hse.

Dillemuth, Julie. Camilla, Cartographer. Wood, Laura, illus. 2019. (ENG.). 32p. (J). *(978-1-4338-3033-4(7),* Magination Pr.) American Psychological Assn.

Hetzer, Michael. A Hug for Percy Porcupine. Clayton, Kim, illus. 2005. 32p. (J). (gr. k-2). 2nd collector's ed. 18.95 *(978-0-9728222-4-4(0))* 3rd ed. 18.95 *(978-0-9728222-3-7(2))* Webster Henrietta Publishing.

Isern, Susanna. The Magic Ball of Wool. Brokenbrow, Jon, tr. Hilb, Nora, illus. (ENG.). 32p. (J). 2019. (gr. -1-k). 11.95 *(978-84-16733-66-8(X))* 2013. (gr. k-3). 16.95 *(978-84-15619-89-5(8))* Cuento de Luz SL ESP. Dist: Publishers Group West (PGW).

Isop, Laurie. How Do You Hug a Porcupine? Millward, Gwen, illus. 2011. (ENG.). 32p. (J). (gr. -1-1). 18.99 *(978-1-4424-1291-0(7),* Simon & Schuster Bks. For Young Readers) Simon & Schuster Bks. For Young Readers.

Kantner, Seth. Pup & Pokey. Hill, Beth, illus. 2014. (ENG.). 48p. pap. 15.95 *(978-1-60223-241-9(5))* Univ. of Alaska Pr.

Koehn, Wendel. Love Problematic: And Other Stories. 2012. 24p. pap. 14.93 *(978-1-4669-1851-1(9))* Trafford Publishing.

Lasher, Shelby. Spiky the Grumpy Porcupine. 2012. 28p. pap. 24.95 *(978-1-4626-7844-0(0))* America Star Bks.

Lester, Helen. A Porcupine Named Fluffy. Munsinger, Lynn, illus. 2013. (Laugh-Along Lessons Ser.). (ENG.). 32p. (J). (gr. -1-3). 8.99 *(978-0-544-00319-4(5),* 1526352, Clarion Bks.) HarperCollins Pubs.

Michie, Brandon J. Caleb the Porcupine: Animal Lessons. 2011. 16p. pap. 10.75 *(978-1-4634-3015-3(9))* AuthorHouse.

Morgan, Mary. Pip Sits. 2017. (I Like to Read Ser.). (ENG.). 24p. (J). (gr. -1-3). 7.99 *(978-0-8234-3778-8(7));* (Illus.). 14.95 *(978-0-8234-3676-7(4))* Holiday Hse., Inc.

Mortensen, Lori, retold by. How Porcupine Got Quills. 2016. (Spring Forward Ser.). (J). (gr. 2). *(978-1-4900-9465-6(2))* Benchmark Education Co.

Nelson, Scott. Patch the Porcupine & the Bike Shop Job. Nelson, Scott, illus. 2004. (Illus.). 28p. (J). 14.95 *(978-0-9745715-3-9(9))* KRBY Creations, LLC.

Oramas, Jennifer. Peter's Purpose. Huseman, Ryan, illus. 2012. 34p. 24.95 *(978-1-4626-6585-3(3))* America Star Bks.

Prasadam-Halls, Smriti. You Make Me Happy. 2019. (ENG., Illus.). 32p. (J). 17.99 *(978-1-68119-849-1(5),* 900189373, Bloomsbury Children's Bks.) Bloomsbury Publishing USA.

Raines, Jennifer. Laughs for Porcupine, 1 vol. 2009. 18p. pap. 24.95 *(978-1-60836-784-9(3))* America Star Bks.

Ratzlaff, Aaron J. Quills. 2011. (ENG.). 40p. (J). pap. 13.99 *(978-0-8361-9509-5(4))* Herald Pr.

Renauld, Laura. Porcupine's Pie. Poh, Jennie, illus. 2018. (Woodland Friends Ser.). 32p. (J). 16.99 *(978-1-5064-3180-2(1),* Beaming Books) 1517 Media.

Rosenthal, Betsy R. Porcupine's Picnic: Who Eats What? Capizzi, Giusi, illus. 2017. (ENG.). 32p. (J). (gr. -1-2). 19.99 *(978-1-4677-9519-7(4),* 35b32061-ef3d-44ab-b216-87a602614795); E-Book 30.65 *(978-1-5124-2840-7(X))* Lerner Publishing Group. (Millbrook Pr.).

Saéz Castán, Javier. Los Tres Erizos. 2005. (SPA.). (J). (gr. k-1). pap. 6.95 *(978-980-257-297-7(7))* Ekare, Ediciones VEN. Dist: Iaconi, Mariuccia Bk. Imports.

Sargent, Dave & Sargent, Pat. Peggy Porcupine: Don't Wander Off, 15 vols., Vol. 13. Huff, Jeane, illus. 2nd rev. ed. 2003. (Animal Pride Ser.: 13). 42p. (J). (AFA.). pap. 10.95 *(978-1-56763-784-7(1));* lib. bdg. 20.95 *(978-1-56763-783-0(3))* Ozark Publishing.

Schmid, Paul. Hugs from Pearl. Schmid, Paul, illus. 2011. (ENG., Illus.). 40p. (J). (gr. -1-2). 14.99 *(978-0-06-180434-2(7),* HarperCollins) HarperCollins Pubs.

—Perfectly Percy. Schmid, Paul, illus. 2013. (ENG., Illus.). 40p. (J). (gr. -1-3). 17.99 *(978-0-06-180436-6(3),* HarperCollins) HarperCollins Pubs.

Skilbeck, Carol. Adventures of Melonhead. 2011. 56p. 24.99 *(978-1-4568-7464-3(0));* pap. 15.99 *(978-1-4568-7463-6(2))* Xlibris Corp.

Smith, Ivy. Stickers VIP. 2011. (Illus.). 30p. (J). 19.95 *(978-0-9635757-9-1(1))* Red Tail Publishing.

—Stickers VIP. Maney, Melissa, illus. 2011. (ENG.). 30p. (J). pap. 11.99 *(978-0-9847756-0-6(9))* Red Tail Publishing.

Soundprints. Prickly Porcupine: Wilderness Adventures. 2012. (ENG.). 48p. (J). pap. 3.95 *(978-1-60727-870-2(7))* Soundprints.

Tireman, Loyd. Quills. Douglass, Ralph, illus. 2015. (Mesaland Ser.). (ENG.). 48p. (J). 12.95 *(978-0-8263-5609-3(5),* P476037) Univ. of New Mexico Pr.

Underwood, Deborah K. A Balloon for Isabel. Rankin, Laura, illus. 2010. (ENG.). 32p. (J). (gr. -1-2). 16.99 *(978-0-06-177967-9(3),* Greenwillow Bks.) HarperCollins Pubs.

Wilson, George H. The Path of the Little Porcupine. 2010. (Illus.). 50p. (J). 15.00 *(978-0-9778477-2-3(1))* A Story Plus Children Bks.

Yoon, Salina. Duck, Duck, Porcupine! 2017. (Duck, Duck, Porcupine Book Ser.: 1). (ENG., Illus.). 64p. (J). pap. 6.99 *(978-1-61963-724-5(3),* 900146367, Bloomsbury USA Childrens) Bloomsbury Publishing USA.

—My Kite Is Stuck! & Other Stories. (Duck, Duck, Porcupine Book Ser.: 2). (ENG., Illus.). 64p. (J). 2020. pap. 6.99 *(978-1-61963-890-7(8),* 900150918, Bloomsbury Children's Bks.) 2017. 9.99 *(978-1-61963-887-7(8),* 900150931, Bloomsbury USA Childrens) Bloomsbury Publishing USA.

—My Kite Is Stuck! & Other Stories. 2019. (J). lib. bdg. 16.00 *(978-0-606-41071-7(6))* Turtleback.

—That's My Book! & Other Stories. 2017. (Duck, Duck, Porcupine Book Ser.: 3). (ENG., Illus.). 64p. (J). 9.99 *(978-1-61963-891-4(6),* 900150940, Bloomsbury USA Childrens) Bloomsbury Publishing USA.

Zenz, Aaron, illus. Porcupine Valentine. 2016. (J). *(978-0-545-90155-0(3))* Scholastic, Inc.

PORNOGRAPHY

Hurt, Avery Elizabeth. Everything You Need to Know about Sextortion, 1 vol. 2017. (Need to Know Library). (ENG., Illus.). 64p. (J). (gr. 5-6). pap. 13.95 *(978-1-5081-7406-6(7),* 64e12a49-b530-489d-85fd-88acf923c4c2, Rosen Young Adult) Rosen Publishing Group, Inc., The.

Wilcox, Christine. How Is Online Pornography Affecting Society? 2015. (ENG., Illus.). 96p. (J). lib. bdg. *(978-1-60152-882-7(5))* ReferencePoint Pr., Inc.

PORNOGRAPHY—FICTION

Connis, Dave. The Temptation of Adam: A Novel. 2017. (ENG.). 352p. (gr. 9-13). 16.99 *(978-1-5107-0730-6(1),* Sky Pony Pr.) Skyhorse Publishing Co., Inc.

PORPOISES

Avery, Sebastian. Porpoises, 1 vol., 1. 2015. (Ocean Friends Ser.). (ENG., Illus.). 24p. (J). (gr. 1-1). pap. 9.25 *(978-1-5081-4176-1(2),* 73dbc1bf-aa3e-4077-b9fd-7b4ed67e3558, PowerKids Pr.) Rosen Publishing Group, Inc., The.

Brust, Beth Wagner. Dolphins. rev. ed. 2003. (Illus.). 24p. 10.95 *(978-1-888153-94-1(6),* Zoo Bks.) National Wildlife Federation.

Morgan, Sally. Dolphins & Porpoises: Animal Lives Series. 2008. 32p. (J). lib. bdg. 18.95 *(978-1-59566-537-9(4))* QEB Publishing Inc.

Orr, Tamra. Porpoise or Dolphin. 2019. (21st Century Junior Library: Which Is Which? Ser.). (ENG., Illus.). 24p. (J). (gr. 2-5). pap. 12.79 *(978-1-5341-5022-5(6),* 213395); lib. bdg. 30.64 *(978-1-5341-4736-2(5),* 213394) Cherry Lake Publishing.

Ryndak, Rob. Dolphin or Porpoise?, 1 vol. 2015. (Animal Look-Alikes Ser.). (ENG., Illus.). 24p. (J). (gr. 1-2). pap. 9.15 *(978-1-4824-2712-7(5),* eb8eee1e-0711-40e7-8f11-daa92699bb98) Stevens, Gareth Publishing LLLP.

Shepherd, Jodie. Porpoises (Nature's Children) (Library Edition) 2018. (Nature's Children, Fourth Ser.). (ENG., Illus.). 48p. (J). (gr. 3-5). lib. bdg. 30.00 *(978-0-531-23482-2(7),* Children's Pr.) Scholastic Library Publishing.

Silverman, Buffy. Can You Tell a Dolphin from a Porpoise? 2011. (Lightning Bolt Books (r) — Animal Look-Alikes Ser.). (ENG., Illus.). 32p. (J). (gr. 1-3). pap. 9.99 *(978-0-7613-7848-8(0),* ed05e190-e973-413d-bb81-49725286323a) Lerner Publishing Group.

—Can You Tell A Dolphin from A Porpoise? 2011. (Animal Look-Alikes Ser.). pap. 45.32 *(978-0-7613-8385-7(9))* Lerner Publishing Group.

Terp, Gail. Is It a Dolphin or a Porpoise? 2019. (Can You Tell the Difference? Ser.). (ENG.). 24p. (J). (gr. 2-4). pap. 8.99 *(978-1-64466-054-6(7),* 12909); (Illus.). (gr. 4-6). lib. bdg. *(978-1-68072-899-6(7),* 12908) Black Rabbit Bks. (Hi Jinx).

Worth, Bonnie. A Whale of a Tale! All about Porpoises, Dolphins, & Whales. Ruiz, Aristides, illus. 2006. (Cat in the Hat's Learning Library). (ENG.). 48p. (J). (gr. -1-3). 9.99 *(978-0-375-82279-7(8),* Random Hse. Bks. for Young Readers) Random Hse. Children's Bks.

PORPOISES—FICTION

Edgemon, Darcie. Seamore, the Very Forgetful Porpoise. Seibold, J. Otto, illus. 2008. 48p. (J). (gr. -1-3). lib. bdg. 17.89 *(978-0-06-085076-0(0))* HarperCollins Pubs.

Manzel, Michael, illus. Moby's Tale. 2004. 248p. (YA). pap. 19.95 *(978-0-9746345-0-0(6))* River of Life Publishing.

Moore, Debbie. Penelope, the Peculiar Purple Porpoise. 2011. 48p. pap. 24.95 *(978-1-4560-6577-5(7))* America Star Bks.

Nikolet, C. T. From Bullies to Friends. Howe, Cindy T., illus. 2008. 25p. pap. 24.95 *(978-1-60610-121-6(8))* America Star Bks.

PORTRAIT PAINTING

see also Crayon Drawing; Pastel Drawing

Frisch-Schmoll, Joy. Portraits. 2013. (Brushes with Greatness Ser.). (ENG.). 48p. (J). (gr. 5-9). pap. 12.00 *(978-0-89812-765-2(3),* 21946, Creative Paperbacks) Creative Co., The.

Gittings, Clare. What Are You Looking At? Band 15/Emerald. 2007. (Collins Big Cat Ser.). (ENG., Illus.). 48p. (J). (gr. 3-4). pap. 11.99 *(978-0-00-723091-4(5))* HarperCollins Pubs. Ltd. GBR. Dist: Independent Pubs. Group.

Medina, Mariana & Mcintosh Wooten, Sara. Frida Kahlo: Self-Portrait Artist, 1 vol. 2015. (Influential Latinos Ser.). (ENG., Illus.). 128p. (gr. 7-7). 38.93 *(978-0-7660-6997-8(4),* 07bd4b04-4536-45a2-b6f1-5574150be40a) Enslow Publishing, LLC.

PORTRAITS

see also Cartoons and Comics

Handler, Daniel. Girls Standing on the Lawn. Kalman, Maira, illus. 2014. (ENG.). 64p. (gr. 5-17). 14.95 *(978-0-87070-908-1(9))* Museum of Modern Art.

Lach, Will. Master-Pieces: Flip & Flop 10 Great Works of Art. 2016. (ENG., Illus.). 28p. (J). (-3). 15.95 *(978-0-7892-1274-0(9),* 791274, Abbeville Kids) Abbeville Pr., Inc.

Lozano Carbayo, Pilar. Retratos. (Coleccion Mundo Maravilloso).Tr. of Portraits. (SPA.). 226p. (J). (gr. 3-5). *(978-84-348-4448-3(6))* SM Ediciones.

Nardo, Don. Edward S. Curtis Chronicles Native Nations. 2017. (Defining Images Ser.). (ENG.). 112p. (J). (gr. 6-12). 59.93 *(978-1-68078-800-6(0),* 26201, Essential Library) ABDO Publishing Co.

PORTS

see Harbors

PORTSMOUTH (N.H.)—HISTORY

Holbrook, Flannery B. A Great Day in Portsmouth. 2013. 54p. 18.99 *(978-1-939739-13-1(6))* RIVERRUN BOOKSTORE INC.

PORTUGAL

Ainsley, Dominic J. Portugal, Vol. 16. 2018. (European Countries Today Ser.). (Illus.). 96p. (J). (gr. 7). lib. bdg. 34.60 *(978-1-4222-3990-2(X))* Mason Crest.

Blauer, Ettagale & Lauré, Jason. Portugal (Enchantment of the World) (Library Edition) 2019. (Enchantment of the World, Second Ser.). (ENG., Illus.). 144p. (J). (gr. 5-9). lib. bdg. 40.00 *(978-0-531-12699-8(4),* Children's Pr.) Scholastic Library Publishing.

Etingoff, Kim. Portugal. 2007. (European Union Ser.). (Illus.). 88p. (YA). (gr. 3-7). lib. bdg. 21.95 *(978-1-4222-0059-9(0))* Mason Crest.

Etingoff, Kim & Indovino, Shaina C. Portugal. Bruton, John, ed. 2012. (Major European Union Nations Ser.). (Illus.). 64p. (J). (gr. 7). 22.95 *(978-1-4222-2255-3(1))* Mason Crest.

Fischer, David. Cristiano Ronaldo: International Soccer Star, 1 vol. 2018. (Influential Lives Ser.). (ENG.). 128p. (gr. 7-7). 40.27 *(978-0-7660-9205-1(4),* 7bee6757-e708-4971-b86e-4126e204bff4) Enslow Publishing, LLC.

Heale, Jay & Koh, Angeline. Portugal, 1 vol. 2nd rev. ed. 2006. (Cultures of the World (Second Edition)(r) Ser.). (ENG., Illus.). 144p. (gr. 5-5). lib. bdg. 49.79 *(978-0-7614-2053-8(3),* 929308a1-b9ae-4981-ad6c-9c5f9b301711) Cavendish Square Publishing LLC.

Hoogenboom, Lynn. Amerigo Vespucci. 2009. (Primary Source Library of Famous Explorers Ser.). 24p. (gr. 4-4). 42.50 *(978-1-60854-118-6(5),* PowerKids Pr.) Rosen Publishing Group, Inc., The.

Hurwicz, Claude. Henry the Navigator. 2009. (Primary Source Library of Famous Explorers Ser.). 24p. (gr. 4-4). 42.50 *(978-1-60854-124-9(X),* PowerKids Pr.) Rosen Publishing Group, Inc., The.

Landau, Jennifer. Vasco Da Gama, 1 vol. 2016. (Spotlight on Explorers & Colonization Ser.). (ENG., Illus.). 48p. (J). (gr. 6-6). pap. 12.75 *(978-1-4777-8825-7(5),* 0dcfd2c6-469b-4658-ac93-d3ade34a11ee) Rosen Publishing Group, Inc., The.

Logothetis, Paul. Cristiano Ronaldo: International Soccer Star. 2015. (Playmakers Ser.). (ENG., Illus.). 32p. (J). (gr. 2-5). 32.79 *(978-1-62403-841-9(7),* 18052, SportsZone) ABDO Publishing Co.

Mis, Melody S. How to Draw Portugal's Sights & Symbols. 2009. (Kid's Guide to Drawing the Countries of the World Ser.). 48p. (gr. 4-4). 53.00 *(978-1-61511-123-7(9),* PowerKids Pr.) Rosen Publishing Group, Inc., The.

Rose, Elizabeth. A Primary Source Guide to Portugal. (Countries of the World). 24p. (gr. 2-3). 2009. 42.50 *(978-1-61512-043-7(2))* 2003. (ENG., Illus.). (J). lib. bdg. 26.27 *(978-0-8239-6733-9(6),* 4a18a7b4-9ecc-47dc-b8e5-32912a5e297b) Rosen Publishing Group, Inc., The. (PowerKids Pr.).

Strand, Jennifer. Ferdinand Magellan. 2016. (Pioneering Explorers Ser.). (ENG., Illus.). 24p. (J). (gr. -1-2). 49.94 *(978-1-68079-409-0(4),* 23030, Abdo Zoom-Launch) ABDO Publishing Co.

Torres, John A. Cristiano Ronaldo: Champion Soccer Star, 1 vol. 2017. (Sports Star Champions Ser.). (ENG.). 48p. (gr. 5-6). lib. bdg. 29.60 *(978-0-7660-8688-3(7),* e8c03239-ad53-44e6-8c61-64774db5f07a) Enslow Publishing, LLC.

—Soccer Star Cristiano Ronaldo, 1 vol. 2014. (Goal! Latin Stars of Soccer Ser.). (ENG.). 48p. (gr. 4-6). 30.60 *(978-1-62285-222-2(2),* c2c70be1-411e-4860-821e-483cf75a58fb) Enslow Publishing, LLC.

PORTUGAL—FICTION

Beck, Barbara. Bill Every Cloud Has a Silver Lining. 2012. 108p. pap. 19.95 *(978-1-4626-9718-2(6))* America Star Bks.

Dixon, Franklin. The Secret of the Soldier's Gold. 2005. (Hardy Boys II Ser.: No. 182). 147p. (J). lib. bdg. 15.00 *(978-1-59054-852-3(3))* Fitzgerald Bks.

Kelahan, Renee. Agua, the Mysterious Portuguese Water Dog. 2009. 108p. 20.95 *(978-1-4401-5443-0(0));* pap. 10.95 *(978-1-4401-5442-3(2))* iUniverse, Inc.

Lerasle, Magdeleine. Songs from a Journey with a Parrot: Lullabies & Nursery Rhymes from Portugal & Brazil. Fronty, Aurélia, illus. 2013. (POR & ENG.). 52p. (J). (gr. -1-k). 16.95 *(978-2-923163-99-4(0))* La Montagne Secrete CAN. Dist: Independent Pubs. Group.

Oldfield, Matt & Oldfield, Tom. Figo. 2018. (Football Heroes - International Editions Ser.). (ENG., Illus.). 176p. (J). (gr. 4-7). pap. 9.99 *(978-1-78606-923-8(7))* Blake, John Publishing, Ltd. GBR. Dist: Independent Pubs. Group.

—Ronaldo. 2018. (Football Heroes - International Editions Ser.). (ENG., Illus.). 176p. (J). (gr. 4-7). pap. 9.99 *(978-1-78606-937-5(7))* Blake, John Publishing, Ltd. GBR. Dist: Independent Pubs. Group.

Saramago, José. The Lizard. Caistor, Nick & Caistor, Lucia, trs. Borges, J, illus. 2019. (ENG.). 24p. (J). (gr. 1-4). 17.95 *(978-1-60980-933-1(5),* Triangle Square) Seven Stories Pr.

PORTUGAL—HISTORY

Birdoff, Ariel Factor. Portugal. 2019. (Countries We Come From Ser.). (ENG., Illus.). 32p. (J). (gr. k-3). 19.95 *(978-1-64280-194-1(1))* Bearport Publishing Co., Inc.

Carvalho, Sérgio Luís de. A Children's History of Portugal. Lima, Inês, tr. Salvador, António, illus. 2017. (Non-Series Titles from Tagus Press Ser.). (ENG.). 52p. (J). (gr. 3-6). 20.00 *(978-1-933227-79-5(6))* Tagus Pr.

Draper, Allison Stark. Vasco da Gama: The Portuguese Quest for a Sea Route from Europe to India. rev. ed. (Library of Explorers & Explorationtm Ser.). (Illus.). 112p. (YA). (gr. 5-8). lib. bdg. 31.95 *(978-1-4042-0637-3(X),* Rosen Reference) Rosen Publishing Group, Inc., The.

Dyan, Penelope. Color Your Life! a Kid's Guide to Lisbon, Portugal. Weigand, John D., photos by. 2012. (Illus.). 34p. pap. 11.95 *(978-1-61477-030-5(1))* Bellissima Publishing, LLC.

Gould, Jane H. Ferdinand Magellan, 1 vol. 2013. (Jr. Graphic Famous Explorers Ser.). (ENG., Illus.). 24p. (J). (gr. 2-3). pap. 11.60 *(978-1-4777-0123-2(0),* e3cb2c07-ada3-43c9-aede-62dac39b22fe); lib. bdg. 28.93 *(978-1-4777-0069-3(2),* 3784f612-3280-40e5-9727-85860ff7d0c1) Rosen Publishing Group, Inc., The. (PowerKids Pr.).

Heale, Jay, et al. Portugal, 1 vol. 3rd rev. ed. 2016. (Cultures of the World (Third Edition)(r) Ser.). (ENG., Illus.). 144p. (gr. 5-5). 48.79 *(978-1-5026-1693-7(9),* 27fde1b3-d3b1-4cd3-b42b-c0767566630ef) Cavendish Square Publishing LLC.

Klepeis, Alicia Z. Portugal, 1 vol. 2017. (Exploring World Cultures (First Edition) Ser.). (ENG.). 32p. (gr. 3-3). pap. 12.16 *(978-1-5026-3023-0(0),* 555701b4-3430-4c3f-94e2-c79bf72bc288) Cavendish Square Publishing LLC.

Macdonald, Fiona. The Story of Magellan. Mark Bergin, illus. 2017. (Explorers Ser.). 32p. (gr. 3-6). 31.35 *(978-1-910706-90-9(6))* Book Hse. GBR. Dist: Black Rabbit Bks.

Ray, Michael, ed. Portugal & Spain, 4 vols. 2013. (Britannica Guide to Countries of the European Union Ser.). (ENG.). 344p. (YA). (gr. 10-10). 113.18 *(978-1-61530-994-8(2),* bae25e48-a1c3-4d1d-b9c1-1c01ab935d54); 56.59 *(978-1-61530-967-2(5),* 974873cf-0eec-4910-a3e1-d4fc24fec110) Rosen Publishing Group, Inc., The.

Schuetz, Kari. Portugal. 2012. (Exploring Countries Ser.). (ENG., Illus.). 32p. (J). (gr. 3-7). lib. bdg. 27.95 *(978-1-60014-733-3(X),* Blastoff! Readers) Bellwether Media.

Sebastian, Emily. The Colonial & Postcolonial Experience in Latin America & the Caribbean, 1 vol. 2016. (Colonial & Postcolonial Experience Ser.). (ENG., Illus.). 256p. (J). (gr. 10-10). 55.59 *(978-1-5081-0439-1(5),* 6083d7af-3889-4012-9b3a-9c8057fca86a) Rosen Publishing Group, Inc., The.

PORTUGUESE—UNITED STATES—FICTION

Lang, Andrew, ed. & compiled by. The Orange Fairy Book. Lang, Andrew, compiled by. 2011. 234p. 27.95 *(978-1-4638-9520-4(8))* Rodgers, Alan Bks.

PORTUGUESE LANGUAGE

Da Guia, Higina. Pajamas O Pijam. 2008. 32p. pap. 18.95 *(978-1-4327-2055-1(4))* Outskirts Pr., Inc.

Kudela, Katy R. My First Book of Portuguese Words, 1 vol. Translations.com Staff, tr. 2010. (Bilingual Picture Dictionaries Ser.). (MUL.). 32p. (J). (gr. -1-2). lib. bdg. 27.99 *(978-1-4296-5965-9(3),* 114592); (Illus.). pap. 8.10 *(978-1-4296-6169-0(0),* 115318) Capstone. (Capstone Pr.).

PQR

—My First Book of Portuguese Words. Translations.com, tr. 2010. (Bilingual Picture Dictionaries Ser.). (MUL.). 32p. (J). (gr. 1-2). pap. 48.60 *(978-1-4296-6170-6(4)*, 16052, Capstone Pr.) Capstone.

Martin, A - Weissmann. Diccionario Portugues - Español. (SPA.). 524p. (J). 29.95 *(978-84-261-2888-1(2))* Juventud, Editorial ESP. Dist: AIMS International Bks., Inc.

Milet Publishing. My First Bilingual Book-Vegetables (English-Portuguese), 1 vol. 2011. (My First Bilingual Book Ser.). (ENG., Illus.). 24p. (J). (gr. k — 1). bds. 7.99 *(978-1-84059-665-6(1))* Milet Publishing.

Milet Publishing Staff. Animals, 60 vols. 2011. (My First Bilingual Book Ser.). (ENG., Illus.). 24p. (J). (gr. k — 1). bds. 8.99 *(978-1-84059-617-5(1))* Milet Publishing.

—Bilingual Visual Dictionary. 2011. (Milet Multimedia Ser.). (ENG & POR., Illus.). 1p. (J). (gr. k-2). cd-rom 19.95 *(978-1-84059-589-5(2))* Milet Publishing.

—Home (English-Portuguese), 60 vols. 2011. (My First Bilingual Book Ser.). (ENG., Illus.). 24p. (J). (gr. k — 1). bds. 8.99 *(978-1-84059-649-6(X))* Milet Publishing.

—Jobs Empregos, 1 vol. 2012. (My First Bilingual Book Ser.). (ENG., Illus.). 24p. (J). (gr. k — 1). bds. 7.99 *(978-1-84059-709-7(7))* Milet Publishing.

—Milet Bilingual Visual Dictionary (English-Portuguese), 1 vol. 2012. (Milet Bilingual Visual Dictionary Ser.). (ENG., Illus.). 148p. (J). (gr. k-2). 34.95 *(978-1-84059-693-9(7))* Milet Publishing.

—Music - My First Bilingual Book, 1 vol. 2012. (My First Bilingual Book Ser.). (ENG., Illus.). 24p. (J). (gr. k — 1). bds. 7.99 *(978-1-84059-725-7(9))* Milet Publishing.

—My Bilingual Book-Hearing (English-Portuguese), 1 vol. 2014. (My Bilingual Book Ser.). (ENG & POR., Illus.). 24p. (J). (gr. -1-k). 9.95 *(978-1-84059-781-3(X))* Milet Publishing.

—My Bilingual Book-Sight (English-Portuguese), 1 vol. 2014. (My Bilingual Book Ser.). (ENG & POR., Illus.). 24p. (J). (gr. -1-k). 9.95 *(978-1-84059-797-4(6))* Milet Publishing.

—My Bilingual Book-Taste (English-Portuguese), 1 vol. 2014. (My Bilingual Book Ser.). (ENG & POR., Illus.). 24p. (J). (gr. -1-k). 9.95 *(978-1-84059-829-2(8))* Milet Publishing.

—My Bilingual Book-Touch (English-Portuguese), 1 vol. 2014. (My Bilingual Book Ser.). (ENG & POR., Illus.). 24p. (J). (gr. -1-k). 9.95 *(978-1-84059-845-2(X))* Milet Publishing.

—My First Bilingual Book - Colors, 60 vols. 2011. (My First Bilingual Book Ser.). (ENG.). 24p. (J). (gr. k — 1). bds. 8.99 *(978-1-84059-602-1(3))* Milet Publishing.

—My First Bilingual Book - Fruit, 1 vol. 2011. (My First Bilingual Book Ser.). (ENG., Illus.). 24p. (J). (gr. k — 1). bds. 8.99 *(978-1-84059-633-5(3))* Milet Publishing.

—My First Bilingual Book-Opposites, 1 vol. 2012. (My First Bilingual Book Ser.). (ENG., Illus.). 24p. (J). (gr. k — 1). bds. 7.99 *(978-1-84059-740-0(2))* Milet Publishing.

—Smell O olfato, 1 vol. 2014. (My Bilingual Book Ser.). (ENG & POR., Illus.). 24p. (J). (gr. -1-k). 9.95 *(978-1-84059-813-1(1))* Milet Publishing.

—Sports, 1 vol. 2012. (My First Bilingual Book Ser.). (ENG., Illus.). 24p. (J). (gr. k — 1). bds. 7.99 *(978-1-84059-757-8(7))* Milet Publishing.

Monckeberg, Paulina. Pascualina 2006 Portuguese. 2005. (Pascualina Family of Products Ser.). (ENG.). 272p. (J). spiral bd. 16.99 *(978-956-8222-29-1(4))* Pascualina Producciones S.A.

The Rosetta Stone Language Library: Portugese Level 2. 2005. (J). (gr. 1-18). cd-rom 239.00 *(978-1-883972-67-7(1))* Rosetta Stone Ltd.

POSSUM

see Opossums

POST-IMPRESSIONISM (ART)

Sabbeth, Carol. Van Gogh & the Post-Impressionists for Kids: Their Lives & Ideas, 21 Activities. 2011. (For Kids Ser.: 34). (ENG., Illus.). 144p. (J). (gr. 4-18). pap. 19.99 *(978-1-56976-275-2(9))* Chicago Review Pr., Inc.

Spence, David. Gauguin. 2010. (Great Artists & Their World Ser.). (Illus.). 48p. (YA). 32.80 *(978-1-84898-316-8(6))* Black Rabbit Bks.

—Picasso. 2010. (Great Artists & Their World Ser.). 48p. 32.80 *(978-1-84898-315-1(8))* Black Rabbit Bks.

POST OFFICE

see Postal Service

POSTAGE STAMPS

Esten, Sidney R. Bird Stamps of All Countries, with a Natural History of Each Bird. Cox, William Drought, ed. 2011. 62p. 36.95 *(978-1-258-07239-1(4))* Literary Licensing, LLC.

Fandel, Jennifer. The Postage Stamp. 2007. (What in the World? Ser.). (Illus.). 48p. (J). (gr. 4-7). lib. bdg. 32.80 *(978-1-58341-554-2(8)*, Creative Education) Creative Co., The.

Smith, Ben. Why Do We Celebrate? 2012. (Level D Ser.). (ENG., Illus.). 16p. (J). (gr. k-2). pap. 7.95 *(978-1-927136-31-7(8)*, 19461) RiverStream Publishing.

POSTAL SERVICE

see also Pony Express

Armentrout, David & Armentrout, Patricia. The Post Office: Our Community. 2008. (Illus.). 24p. (J). lib. bdg. 22.79 *(978-1-60472-340-3(8))* Rourke Educational Media.

At the Post Office, 6, Packs. (gr. -1-2). 27.00 *(978-0-7635-9437-4(7))* Rigby Education.

Bellamy, Adam. This Is My Post Office, 1 vol. 2016. (All about My World Ser.). (ENG., Illus.). 24p. (gr. k-1). pap. 10.35 *(978-0-7660-8102-4(8)*, aae5398f-fa39-4df4-9a39-b475bb82c106) Enslow Publishing, LLC.

Berger, Melvin. Where Does the Mail Go? (Discovery Readers Ser.). (ENG.). 48p. (J). pap. 3.95 *(978-0-8249-5313-3(4)*, Ideals Pubns.) Worthy Publishing.

Bourgeois, Paulette. Postal Workers. LaFave, Kim, illus. 2005. (Kids Can Read Ser.). (ENG.). 32p. (J). (gr. 1-3). 3.95 *(978-1-55337-747-4(8))* Kids Can Pr., Ltd. CAN. Dist: Hachette Bk. Group.

Brill, Marlene Targ. Bronco Charlie & the Pony Express. Orback, Craig, illus. 2004. (On My Own History Ser.). (ENG.). 48p. (gr. 2-4). (J). pap. 8.99 *(978-1-57505-618-0(6)*, b654f654-7cd7-4cb8-bb97-9329189d66f0, First Avenue Editions); lib. bdg. 25.26 *(978-1-57505-587-9(2))* Lerner Publishing Group.

—Bronco Charlie y el Pony Express. Orback, Craig, illus. 2005. (Yo Solo Historia Ser.). (SPA.). 46p. (J). (gr. 2-5). per. 6.95 *(978-0-8225-3093-0(7))* Lerner Publishing Group.

—Bronco Charlie Y el Pony Express; Bronco Charlie & the Pony Express. 2008. pap. 40.95 *(978-0-8225-3866-0(0))* Lerner Publishing Group.

Butz, Christopher. Follow That Letter: From the Post Office to Our Mailbox. 2003. (From Here to There Ser.). (J). *(978-1-58417-198-0(7))*; pap. *(978-1-58417-199-7(5))* Lake Street Pubs.

—I Go to Work as a Letter Carrier. 2003. (I Go to Work As Ser.). (Illus.). (J). pap. *(978-1-58417-104-1(9))*; lib. bdg. *(978-1-58417-041-9(7))* Lake Street Pubs.

Capici, Gaetano. How Did That Get to My House? Mail. 2009. (Community Connections: How Did That Get to My House? Ser.). (ENG.). 24p. (gr. 2-5). lib. bdg. 29.21 *(978-1-60279-478-8(2)*, 200249) Cherry Lake Publishing.

Chiu, David. Choosing a Career in the Post Office. 2009. (World of Work Ser.). 64p. (gr. 5-5). 58.50 *(978-1-60854-339-7(0))* Rosen Publishing Group, Inc., The.

Christopher, Nick. What Do Mail Carriers Do?, 1 vol. 2015. (Helping the Community Ser.). (ENG., Illus.). 24p. (J). (gr. 1-1). pap. 9.25 *(978-1-4994-0650-4(9)*, 59f5aca0-08c1-4a45-b1ba-dc5cea248765, PowerKids Pr.) Rosen Publishing Group, Inc., The.

Colby, Jennifer. Post Office. 2016. (21st Century Junior Library: Explore a Workplace Ser.). (ENG., Illus.). 24p. (J). (gr. 2-5). 29.21 *(978-1-63471-076-3(2)*, 208383) Cherry Lake Publishing.

Davis, Mackey Cathy. Postal Workers Then & Now, 1 vol. rev. ed. 2006. (Social Studies: Informational Text Ser.). (ENG.). 32p. (gr. 2-3). pap. 11.99 *(978-0-7439-9381-4(0))* Teacher Created Materials, Inc.

Devera, Czeena. Mail Carrier. Bane, Jeff, illus. 2018. (Mi Mini Biografía (My Itty-Bitty Bio): My Early Library). (ENG.). 24p. (J). (gr. k-1). pap. 12.79 *(978-1-5341-0816-5(5)*, 210628); lib. bdg. 30.64 *(978-1-5341-0717-5(7)*, 210627) Cherry Lake Publishing.

Dolan, Edward F., Jr. & Dolan, Edward F. The Pony Express, 1 vol. 2003. (Kaleidoscope: American History Ser.). (ENG., Illus.). 48p. (gr. 4-4). 32.64 *(978-0-7614-1458-2(4)*, 313b616a-7b69-406c-b1b1-b20943b229d7) Cavendish Square Publishing LLC.

Dunn, Joeming W. The Pony Express, 1 vol. Martin, Cynthia, illus. 2008. (Graphic History Ser.). (ENG.). 32p. (J). (gr. 3-8). 32.79 *(978-1-60270-184-7(9)*, 9060, Graphic Planet - Fiction) Magic Wagon.

Early Macken, JoAnn. Mail Carriers, 1 vol. 2010. (People in My Community (Second Edition) Ser.). (ENG., Illus.). 24p. (gr. k-2). pap. 9.15 *(978-1-4339-3345-5(4)*, a15a20a5-f602-4614-96dd-7cbd8ed78626) Stevens, Gareth Publishing LLLP.

—Mail Carriers / Carteros, 1 vol. 2010. (People in My Community / Mi Comunidad Ser.). (SPA & ENG., Illus.). 24p. (gr. k-2). pap. 9.15 *(978-1-4339-3763-7(8)*, 9e6c44c4-7613-4698-a386-a15aa3d4fa78) Stevens, Gareth Publishing LLLP.

Fandel, Jennifer. The Postage Stamp. 2007. (What in the World? Ser.). (Illus.). 48p. (J). (gr. 4-7). lib. bdg. 32.80 *(978-1-58341-554-2(8)*, Creative Education) Creative Co., The.

Jeffrey, Gary. The Pony Express, 1 vol. Riley, Terry, illus. 2012. (Graphic History of the American West Ser.). (ENG.). 24p. (J). (gr. 3-3). pap. 9.15 *(978-1-4339-6749-8(9)*, 48a12229-d95d-4464-944d-8821c5729f53, Gareth Stevens Learning Library); lib. bdg. 26.60 *(978-1-4339-6747-4(2)*, fbe13987-bdb7-456a-ab4a-454d8ec20547) Stevens, Gareth Publishing LLLP.

Kawa, Katie. My First Trip to the Post Office, 1 vol. Livingston, Jessica, illus. 2012. (My First Adventures Ser.). (ENG.). 24p. (J). (gr. k-k). 25.27 *(978-1-4339-6253-0(5)*, d65e9219-7cfc-4404-a688-bf8abfcf5e12); pap. 9.15 *(978-1-4339-6255-4(1)*, 096f2820-90b6-46c4-a667-1c4362e41d6a) Stevens, Gareth Publishing LLLP.

—My First Trip to the Post Office / Mi Primera Visita Al Correo, 1 vol. Livingston, Jessica, illus. 2012. (My First Adventures / Mis Primeras Aventuras Ser.). (ENG & SPA.). 24p. (J). (gr. k-k). lib. bdg. 25.27 *(978-1-4339-6633-0(6)*, d0a73918-5b9b-4d63-869f-bb86c97b58d5) Stevens, Gareth Publishing LLLP.

Kenan, Tessa. Hooray for Mail Carriers! 2017. (Bumba Books (r) — Hooray for Community Helpers! Ser.). (ENG., Illus.). 24p. (J). (gr. -1-1). pap. 8.99 *(978-1-5124-5554-0(7)*, 13c0278b-a139-4fae-b338-3f49bb61f49b); lib. bdg. 26.65 *(978-1-5124-3354-8(3)*, c478f5bd-69d7-4d91-9a6c-9367ec14c583, Lerner Pubns.) Lerner Publishing Group.

—¡Que Vivan Los Carteros! (Hooray for Mail Carriers!) 2018. (Bumba Books (r) en Español — ¡Que Vivan Los Ayudantes Comunitarios! (Hooray for Community Helpers!) Ser.). (SPA., Illus.). 24p. (J). (gr. -1-1). lib. bdg. 26.65 *(978-1-5124-9754-0(1)*, b73496a0-36c5-4b00-8f41-83bb2498390a, Ediciones Lerner) Lerner Publishing Group.

Keogh, Josie. A Trip to the Post Office, 1 vol. 2012. (PowerKids Readers: My Community Ser.). (ENG., Illus.). 24p. (J). (gr. k-k). pap. 9.25 *(978-1-4488-7483-5(1)*, b54299ec-c962-4eaf-9ed4-47f2cebedbaf); lib. bdg. 26.27 *(978-1-4488-7404-0(1)*, 5a33cffa-8915-4fe4-ae37-51a1e978b790) Rosen Publishing Group, Inc., The.

Keogh, Josie & Alamán, Eduardo. A Trip to the Post Office: De Visita en el Correo, 1 vol. 2012. (PowerKids Readers: Mi Comunidad / My Community Ser.). (SPA & ENG., Illus.). 24p. (J). (gr. k-k). lib. bdg. 26.27 *(978-1-4488-7828-4(4)*, 314e6ad8-e91a-4426-b124-0a86af9bf7be, PowerKids Pr.) Rosen Publishing Group, Inc., The.

Knudsen, Shannon. Postal Workers. 2005. (Pull Ahead Books: Community Helpers Ser.). (ENG., Illus.). 32p. (gr. k-3). lib. bdg. 22.60 *(978-0-8225-2846-3(0))* Lerner Publishing Group.

Kreisman, Rachelle. Places We Go: A Kids' Guide to Community Sites. Haggerty, Tim, illus. 2015. (Start Smart (tm) — Community Ser.). (ENG.). 32p. (J). (gr. 1-3). E-Book 39.99 *(978-1-937529-36-9(3))* Red Chair Pr.

Leaf, Christina. Mail Carriers. 2018. (Community Helpers Ser.). (ENG., Illus.). 24p. (J). (gr. k-3). pap. 7.99 *(978-1-61891-308-1(5)*, 12094, Blastoff! Readers) Bellwether Media.

Leigh, Autumn. Making History: A Horse Sock Puppet, 1 vol. 2005. (Content-Area Literacy Collections). (ENG.). 24p. (gr. 3-4). pap. 8.85 *(978-1-4042-5588-3(5)*, bc8e3750-8487-4eb2-8d5d-fd9af12da011) Rosen Publishing Group, Inc., The.

Linde, Barbara M. Working at the Post Office: Learning to Subtract 2 Three-Digit Numbers Without Renaming, 1 vol. 2010. (Math for the REAL World Ser.). (ENG.). 16p. (gr. 2-3). pap. 7.05 *(978-0-8239-8855-6(4)*, 8f15937e-ed02-4e87-821d-42417fa601dd, Rosen Classroom) Rosen Publishing Group, Inc., The.

Marsico, Katie. Working at the Post Office. 2009. (21st Century Junior Library: Careers Ser.). (ENG., Illus.). 24p. (gr. 2-5). lib. bdg. 29.21 *(978-1-60279-512-9(6)*, 200280) Cherry Lake Publishing.

Meachen Rau, Dana. Un Cartero (Mail Carrier), 1 vol. 2009. (Trabajos en Pueblos y Ciudades (Jobs in Town) Ser.). (SPA., Illus.). 24p. (gr. k-1). lib. bdg. 25.50 *(978-0-7614-2785-8(6)*, 5bbe1ef7-1cb9-494f-9798-dad73e9a73e9) Cavendish Square Publishing LLC.

—Mail Carrier, 1 vol. 2008. (Jobs in Town Ser.). (ENG., Illus.). 24p. (gr. k-1). lib. bdg. 25.50 *(978-0-7614-2620-2(5)*, 2e12060d-0fc2-4d32-b5d5-49264fd65210) Cavendish Square Publishing LLC.

Meyer, Koston. Where Does the Mail Go?, 1 vol. 2012. (Everyday Mysteries Ser.). (ENG., Illus.). 24p. (J). (gr. 2-2). pap. 9.15 *(978-1-4339-6331-5(0)*, ec1b9a0b-e544-447c-882a-437796524bc9); lib. bdg. 25.27 *(978-1-4339-6329-2(9)*, 33b340d8-6b88-4902-930a-947d9c83ab35) Stevens, Gareth Publishing LLLP.

Micklos, John, Jr. Bold Riders: The Story of the Pony Express. 2015. (Adventures on the American Frontier Ser.). (ENG., Illus.). 32p. (J). (gr. 3-6). pap. 7.95 *(978-1-4914-4910-3(1)*, 128745, Capstone Pr.) Capstone.

Murray, Julie. The Post Office. 2016. (My Community: Places Ser.). (ENG., Illus.). 24p. (J). (gr. -1-2). lib. bdg. 31.36 *(978-1-68080-539-0(8)*, 21358, Abdo Kids) ABDO Publishing Co.

Owen, Ann & National Geographic Learning Staff. Delivering Your Mail: A Book about Mail Carriers. Thomas, Eric, illus. 2003. (Community Workers Ser.). (ENG.). 24p. (J). (gr. -1-3). per. 8.95 *(978-1-4048-0485-2(4)*, 92624, Picture Window Bks.) Capstone.

Patrick, Roman. Spanish Words at the Post Office, 1 vol., Vol. 1. 2013. (Learn My Language! Spanish Ser.). (ENG., Illus.). 24p. (J). (gr. 1-2). 25.27 *(978-1-4824-0350-3(1)*, 9b8b1ff8-487b-4887-8194-78f13114b7ae) Stevens, Gareth Publishing LLLP.

Payment, Simone. The Pony Express, 1 vol. 2004. (Primary Sources in American History Ser.). (ENG., Illus.). 64p. (J). (gr. 5-8). lib. bdg. 37.13 *(978-1-4042-0181-1(5)*, fa6e2996-1591-480a-8b4f-102f7f3ba513) Rosen Publishing Group, Inc., The.

—The Pony Express: A Primary Source History of the Race to Bring Mail to the American West. 2009. (Primary Sources in American History Ser.). 64p. (gr. 5-8). 58.50 *(978-1-60851-502-8(8))* Rosen Publishing Group, Inc., The.

Quiri, Patricia R. The Groundbreaking Pony Express. 2017. (Landmarks in U. S. History Ser.). (ENG., Illus.). 32p. (J). (gr. 3-6). lib. bdg. 27.99 *(978-1-5157-7115-9(6)*, 135516, Capstone Pr.) Capstone.

Ratliff, Thomas. You Wouldn't Want to Be a Pony Express Rider! A Dusty, Thankless Job You'd Rather Not Do. Bergin, Mark, illus. 2012. (ENG.). 32p. (J). lib. bdg. 29.00 *(978-0-531-20872-4(9))* Scholastic Library Publishing.

Rice, Dona. La Historia Del Correo: Datos. rev. ed. 2019. (Mathematics in the Real World Ser.). (SPA., Illus.). 24p. (J). (gr. 1-2). pap. 9.99 *(978-1-4258-2850-9(7))* Teacher Created Materials, Inc.

Rice, Dona Herweck. The History of Mail. 2018. (Mathematics in the Real World Ser.). (ENG., Illus.). 24p. (J). (gr. 1-2). pap. 9.99 *(978-1-4258-5688-5(8))* Teacher Created Materials, Inc.

Riddle, John. The Pony Express. 2004. (History of the Old West Ser.). (Illus.). 64p. (YA). (gr. 5-18). lib. bdg. 19.95 *(978-1-59084-061-0(5))* Mason Crest.

Rivera, Sheila. Postal Carrier. 2005. (First Step Nonfiction — Work People Do Ser.). (ENG., Illus.). 8p. (J). (gr. k-2). pap. 5.99 *(978-0-8225-5360-1(0)*, 09f992a8-1fef-4e54-9450-2a21e3a123aa) Lerner Publishing Group.

Rosario, Miguel T. A Mail Carrier's Job, 1 vol. 2014. (Community Workers Ser.). (ENG.). 24p. (gr. 1-1). pap. 9.23 *(978-1-62712-351-8(2)*, bb2cae82-7a1e-433c-8d7e-c459a9a8de25) Cavendish Square Publishing LLC.

Santillo, LuAnn. The Mailman. Santillo, LuAnn, ed. 2003. (Half-Pint Kids Readers Ser.). (Illus.). 7p. (J). (gr. -1-1). pap. *(978-1-59256-125-4(X))* Half-Pint Kids, Inc.

Savage, Jeff. Daring Pony Express Riders: True Tales of the Wild West, 1 vol. 2012. (True Tales of the Wild West Ser.). (ENG., Illus.). 48p. (gr. 5-7). pap. 11.53 *(978-1-4644-0031-5(8)*, ca5e0880-db02-4c69-884a-4fd104eb36de); lib. bdg. 25.27 *(978-0-7660-4023-6(2)*, e694efd9-a05f-4e1f-bda0-8f114b3b5b2f) Enslow Publishing, LLC.

Schaefer, Lola M. Letter to a Friend. 2011. (Early Connections Ser.). (J). *(978-1-61672-639-3(3))* Benchmark Education Co.

Schuh, Mari. All about Mail Carriers. 2020. (Sesame Street (r) Loves Community Helpers Ser.). (ENG., Illus.). 32p. (J). (gr. -1-2). 29.32 *(978-1-5415-8999-5(8)*, 93fcfe53-f898-429b-b7a1-2b5d7905bb8c, Lerner Pubns.) Lerner Publishing Group.

Shepherd, Jodie. A Day with Mail Carriers. 2012. (ENG., Illus.). 32p. (J). lib. bdg. 23.00 *(978-0-531-28953-2(2))* Scholastic Library Publishing.

Stokes, Betty Southard. Postcards from George, 1763-1781: George Rogers Clark Writes Home to Virginia from the Kentucky Wilderness. Cable, Annette, illus. 2010. (J). *(978-1-935497-12-7(X))* Butler Bks.

Uphall, Margaret. The U. S. Postal Service: The History of America's Mail System, 1 vol. 2017. (Landmarks of Democracy: American Institutions Ser.). (ENG.). 24p. (J). (gr. 3-3). pap. 9.25 *(978-1-5081-6105-9(4)*, 770973fd-9259-48bf-a2fb-abb5b6d6049b, PowerKids Pr.) Rosen Publishing Group, Inc., The.

POSTAL SERVICE—FICTION

Arnau, Marta, illus. El cartero de los Suenos. 2004. (Cuentos con miga Ser.). 69p. pap. 12.95 *(978-84-931888-2-5(4))* Editorial Brief ESP. Dist: Independent Pubs. Group.

Bailer, Darice. The Pony Express. Antonishak, Tom, illus. 3rd ed. 2003. (Soundprints' Read-and-Discover Ser.). (ENG.). 48p. (J). (gr. -1-3). pap. 3.95 *(978-1-59249-019-6(0)*, S2008) Soundprints.

Banks, Steven. Special Delivery. DePorter, Vince, illus. 2005. (Ready-to-Read Ser.). 32p. (J). lib. bdg. 15.00 *(978-1-59054-986-5(4))* Fitzgerald Bks.

Bell, P. G. The Train to Impossible Places: a Cursed Delivery. 2019. (Train to Impossible Places Ser.: 1). (ENG.). 400p. (J). pap. 7.99 *(978-1-250-21142-2(5)*, 900192256) Square Fish.

Berger, Samantha. Snail Mail. Patton, Julia, illus. 2018. (ENG.). 32p. (J). (gr. -1-3). 17.99 *(978-0-7624-6251-3(5)*, Running Pr. Kids) Running Pr.

Blackstone, Stella. Bear at Work. Harter, Debbie, illus. (ENG & SPA.). 24p. (J). (gr. -1-k). 2011. pap. 6.99 *(978-1-84686-554-1(9))* 2008. pap. 8.99 *(978-1-84686-110-9(1))* Barefoot Bks., Inc.

—Bear at Work (Oso en el Trabajo) 2012. (ENG & SPA., Illus.). 24p. (J). pap. 7.99 *(978-1-84686-769-9(X))* Barefoot Bks., Inc.

—L'Ours au Travail. 2012.Tr. of Bear at Work. (FRE & ENG.). (J). 6.99 *(978-1-84686-770-5(3))* Barefoot Bks., Inc.

Bourgeois, Paulette. Postal Workers. LaFave, Kim, illus. 2005. 32p. (J). lib. bdg. 15.38 *(978-1-4242-1192-0(1))* Fitzgerald Bks.

Clanton, Ben. It Came in the Mail. Clanton, Ben, illus. (ENG., Illus.). 40p. (J). (gr. -1-3). 2019. 8.99 *(978-1-5344-5321-0(0))* 2016. 18.99 *(978-1-4814-0360-3(5))* Simon & Schuster Bks. For Young Readers. (Simon & Schuster Bks. For Young Readers).

Clayton, Lisa. Melvin the Mailman. Clayton, Sean & Spears, Ashley, illus. 2005. 8p. (J). 3.49 *(978-0-9773723-0-0(8))* Trent's Prints.

Cunliffe, John. Paints Ceiling. (Postman Pat Ser.: No. 7). (ENG., Illus.). 32p. (J). pap. 8.99 *(978-0-340-70407-3(1))* Hodder & Stoughton GBR. Dist: Trafalgar Square Publishing.

—Postman Pat & Frog Pie Dinner. (ENG., Illus.). 20p. (J). *(978-0-340-71435-5(2))* Hodder & Stoughton.

—Postman Pat & the Big Surprise. (Postman Pat Ser.: No. 9). (ENG., Illus.). 32p. (J). pap. *(978-0-340-70409-7(8))* Hodder & Stoughton.

—Postman Pat & the Hole in the Road. (ENG., Illus.). 32p. (J). pap. *(978-0-340-70384-7(9))* Hodder & Stoughton.

—Postman Pat & the Mystery Tour. (Postman Pat Ser.: Bk. 13). (ENG., Illus.). 32p. (J). pap. 8.99 *(978-0-340-71333-4(X))* Hodder & Stoughton GBR. Dist: Trafalgar Square Publishing.

—Postman Pat & the Robot. (ENG., Illus.). 32p. (J). *(978-0-340-67814-5(3))* Hodder & Stoughton.

—Postman Pat & the Sheep of Many Colours. (ENG., Illus.). (J). mass mkt. 7.99 *(978-0-340-73715-6(8))* Hodder & Stoughton GBR. Dist: Trafalgar Square Publishing.

—Postman Pat Follows a Trail. (ENG., Illus.). 32p. (J). pap. 8.99 *(978-0-340-70387-8(3))* Hodder & Stoughton GBR. Dist: Trafalgar Square Publishing.

—Postman Pat Has the Best Village. (Postman Pat Ser.: No. 6). (ENG., Illus.). 32p. (J). pap. 8.99 *(978-0-340-70388-5(1))* Hodder & Stoughton GBR. Dist: Trafalgar Square Publishing.

—Postman Pat in a Muddle. (Postman Pat Ser.: No. 3). (ENG., Illus.). 32p. (J). pap. 8.99 *(978-0-340-70385-4(7))* Hodder & Stoughton GBR. Dist: Trafalgar Square Publishing.

—Postman Pat Misses the Show. (Postman Pat Ser.: No. 4). (ENG., Illus.). 32p. (J). pap. 8.99 *(978-0-340-70386-1(5))* Hodder & Stoughton GBR. Dist: Trafalgar Square Publishing.

—Postman Pat Takes Flight. (ENG., Illus.). 32p. (J). *(978-0-340-67815-2(1))* Hodder & Stoughton.

—The Robot. (Postman Pat Ser.: Bk. 10). (ENG., Illus.). (J). pap. 8.99 *(978-0-340-70915-3(4))* Hodder & Stoughton GBR. Dist: Trafalgar Square Publishing.

Dubuc, Marianne. Mr. Postmouse's Rounds. Dubuc, Marianne, illus. 2015. (ENG., Illus.). 24p. (J). (gr. -1-2). 17.95 *(978-1-77138-572-5(3))* Kids Can Pr., Ltd. CAN. Dist: Hachette Bk. Group.

Greene, Rhonda Gowler. Mail Monkeys. Bender, Robert, illus. 2006. (J). pap. *(978-1-58669-217-9(8))* Childcraft Education Corp.

Herron, Edward A. The Return of the Alaskan: Mailboat in the Outpost. Langley, Gene, illus. 2011. 190p. 42.95 *(978-1-258-09093-7(7))* Literary Licensing, LLC.

Horning, Sandra. The Giant Hug. Gorbachev, Valeri, illus. 2008. (ENG.). 40p. (J). (gr. -1-2). pap. 8.99 *(978-0-553-11262-7(7)*, Dragonfly Bks.) Random Hse. Children's Bks.

Klise, Kate. The Phantom of the Post Office. Klise, M. Sarah, illus. 2013. (43 Old Cemetery Road Ser.: 4). (ENG.). 160p. (J). (gr. 3-7). pap. 7.99 *(978-0-544-02281-2(5)*, 1528502, Clarion Bks.) HarperCollins Pubs.

—The Phantom of the Post Office. 2013. (43 Old Cemetery Road Ser.: 4). lib. bdg. 17.20 *(978-0-606-31668-2(X))* Turtleback.

Leigh, Autumn. Door to Door, 1 vol. 2006. (Neighborhood Readers Ser.). (ENG.). 12p. (gr. k-1). pap. 5.90 *(978-1-4042-6469-4(8)*, 7e49d46b-15f2-4557-936d-1c3e673e7a0b, Rosen Classroom) Rosen Publishing Group, Inc., The.

Manos, John. The Mail Comes to Main Street. 2006. (Early Explorers Ser.). (J). pap. *(978-1-4108-6118-4(X))* Benchmark Education Co.

Mcadams, Kate. Flynn the Post Office Mouse. 2010. 28p. pap. 12.49 *(978-1-4520-0816-5(7))* AuthorHouse.

MJ Illustrations (Group) Staff, contrib. by. The Pups Save Friendship Day! 2016. (Illus.). (J). *(978-1-5182-2299-3(4)*, Golden Bks.) Random Hse., Inc.

Murray, Eva. Island Birthday, 1 vol. Hogan, Jamie, illus. 2015. (ENG.). 32p. (J). (gr. 1-7). 16.95 *(978-0-88448-425-7(4)*, 884425) Tilbury Hse. Pubs.

Rogers, Jacqueline. Jack Jones off to the Post Office. 2012. 20p. pap. 13.77 *(978-1-4669-0808-6(4))* Trafford Publishing.
Tunnell, Michael O. Mailing May. Rand, Ted, illus. 2015. 32p. pap. 7.00 *(978-1-61003-610-8(7))* Center for the Collaborative Classroom.
A Visit to the Post Office. 2003. (J). per. *(978-1-57657-902-2(6))* Paradise Pr., Inc.

POSTERS

see also Signs and Signboards

Donahue, Peter. Farm & Zoo. 2010. (Dover Animal Coloring Bks.). (ENG., Illus.). 48p. (J). (gr. 3-5). pap. 4.99 *(978-0-486-47947-7(1),* 479471) Dover Pubns., Inc.
Gottesman, Eric. Color Your Own Patriotic Posters. 2003. (Dover Art Masterpieces to Color Ser.). (ENG., Illus.). 32p. (J). (gr. 3-8). pap. 5.99 *(978-0-486-42650-1(5),* 426505) Dover Pubns., Inc.
Noble, Marty. Color Your Own Classic Movie Posters. 2006. (Dover Art Masterpieces to Color Ser.). (ENG., Illus.). 32p. (gr. 6-8). pap. 4.99 *(978-0-486-44812-1(6),* 448126) Dover Pubns., Inc.
Roytman, Arkady. Fairy Princess. 2010. (Dover Fantasy Coloring Bks.). (ENG., Illus.). 48p. (J). (gr. 3-5). pap. 4.99 *(978-0-486-47943-9(9),* 479439) Dover Pubns., Inc.
—Knights & Dragons. 2010. (Dover Fantasy Coloring Bks.). (ENG., Illus.). 48p. (J). (gr. 3-5). pap. 4.99 *(978-0-486-47942-2(0),* 479420) Dover Pubns., Inc.
Sovak, Jan. Build a Giant Poster Coloring Book — Under the Sea. 2013. (Dover Sea Life Coloring Bks.). (ENG., Illus.). 48p. (J). (gr. 2-6). pap. 4.99 *(978-0-486-49139-4(0),* 491390) Dover Pubns., Inc.
Zourelias, Diana. Build a Giant Poster Coloring Book — United States Map. 2013. (Dover Kids Coloring Bks.). (ENG., Illus.). 48p. (J). (gr. 3-5). pap. 4.99 *(978-0-486-49152-3(8),* 491528) Dover Pubns., Inc.

POSTIMPRESSIONISM (ART)

see Post-Impressionism (Art)

POTTER, BEATRIX, 1866-1943

Fabiny, Sarah. Who Was Beatrix Potter? Lacey, Mike, illus. 2015. 105p. (J). *(978-1-4806-8934-3(3),* Grosset & Dunlap) Penguin Publishing Group.
Fabiny, Sarah & Who HQ. Who Was Beatrix Potter? Lacey, Mike, illus. 2015. (Who Was? Ser.). 112p. (J). (gr. 3-7). 5.99 *(978-0-448-48305-4(X),* Penguin Workshop) Penguin Young Readers Group.
Hopkinson, Deborah. Beatrix Potter & the Unfortunate Tale of a Borrowed Guinea Pig. Voake, Charlotte, illus. 2016. (ENG.). 44p. (J). (gr. -1-3). 17.99 *(978-0-385-37325-8(2),* Schwartz & Wade Bks.) Random Hse. Children's Bks.
Hurtig, Jennifer. The Animal World of Beatrix Potter. 2016. (J). *(978-1-5105-1951-0(3))* SmartBook Media, Inc.
—Beatrix Potter. 2008. (My Favorite Writer Ser.). (Illus.). 32p. (YA). (gr. 5-18). pap. 9.95 *(978-1-59036-923-4(8));* lib. bdg. 26.00 *(978-1-59036-922-7(X))* Weigl Pubs., Inc.
Yuan, Margaret Speaker. Beatrix Potter. 2005. (Who Wrote That? Ser.). (ENG., Illus.). 112p. (gr. 6-12). lib. bdg. 35.00 *(978-0-7910-8655-1(0),* P114366, Facts On File) Infobase Holdings, Inc.

POTTER, HARRY (FICTITIOUS CHARACTER)

Bankston, John. Daniel Radcliffe. l.t. ed. 2003. (Blue Banner Biography Ser.). (Illus.). 32p. (J). (gr. 3-8). lib. bdg. 25.70 *(978-1-58415-250-7(8))* Mitchell Lane Pubs.
Bucholz, Dinah. The Unofficial Harry Potter Cookbook: From Cauldron Cakes to Knickerbocker Glory — More Than 150 Magical Recipes for Wizards & Non-Wizards Alike. 2010. (Unofficial Cookbook Ser.). (ENG., Illus.). 256p. 19.95 *(978-1-4405-0325-2(7))* Adams Media Corp.
Burton, Bonnie. J. K. Rowling's Wizarding World: Movie Magic Volume Three: Amazing Artifacts. 2017. (J. K. Rowling's Wizarding World Ser.). (ENG., Illus.). 96p. (J). (gr. 5). 29.99 *(978-0-7636-9584-2(X))* Candlewick Pr.
Davis, Graeme. The Unauthorized Harry Potter Quiz Book: 165 Questions Ranging from the Sorcerer's Stone to the Deathly Hallows. 2008. 76p. pap. 15.38 *(978-1-934840-44-3(0))* Nimble Bks. LLC.
Farrow, Joanna. The Official Harry Potter Baking Book: 40+ Recipes Inspired by the Films. 2021. (ENG., Illus.). 128p. (J). (gr. 5-5). 19.99 *(978-1-338-28526-0(2))* Scholastic, Inc.
Farrow, Joanna. The Official Harry Potter Cookbook: 40+ Recipes Inspired by the Films. 2023. (ENG.). 128p. (J). (gr. 3). 19.99 ***(978-1-338-89307-6(6))*** Scholastic, Inc.
Gaines, Ann Graham. J. K. Rowling. 2004. (Blue Banner Biography Ser.). (Illus.). 32p. (J). (gr. 3-8). lib. bdg. 25.70 *(978-1-58415-325-2(3))* Mitchell Lane Pubs.
Hallett, Cynthia & Huey, Peggy. J. K. Rowling, 1 vol. 2012. (New Casebooks Ser.: 20). (ENG., Illus.). 224p. (C). 95.00 *(978-0-230-00849-6(6),* 900264231); pap. 30.95 *(978-0-230-00850-2(X),* 900260558) Palgrave Macmillan Ltd. GBR. (Red Globe Pr.). Dist: Macmillan.
Harrington, Jamie. The Unofficial Guide to Crafting the World of Harry Potter: 30 Magical Crafts for Witches & Wizards — From Pencil Wands to House Colors Tie-Dye Shirts. 2016. (ENG., Illus.). 192p. pap. 17.99 *(978-1-4405-9504-2(6))* Adams Media Corp.
Hill, Mary. J. K. Rowling. 2003. (Welcome Books: Real People Ser.). (ENG., Illus.). 24p. (J). (gr. k-3). 17.44 *(978-0-516-25866-9(4))* Scholastic Library Publishing.
Insight Editions. Harry Potter: Magical Film Projections: Patronus Charm. 2017. (Harry Potter Ser.). (ENG., Illus.). 16p. (J). (gr. 2-5). 16.99 *(978-0-7636-9586-6(6))* Candlewick Pr.
Magic Eye, Inc. Staff. Harry Potter Magic Eye Book: 3D Magical Creatures, Beasts & Beings. 2010. (ENG., Illus.). 32p. (J). 16.99 *(978-0-7407-9770-5(0))* Andrews McMeel Publishing.
—Harry Potter Magic Eye Book: 3D Magical Moments. 2011. (ENG.). 32p. 16.99 *(978-1-4494-0141-2(4))* Andrews McMeel Publishing.
The Magical Worlds of Harry Potter Spellbinding Map & Book of Secrets. 2004. (Illus.). 32p. (J). 8.99 *(978-0-9708442-2-4(0))* Lumina Pr. LLC.
Moore, P.D. About Harry Potter: What Every Kid Should Know... Moore, Rema Harracksingh- & Delande, J., eds. 2003. (Illus.). 170p. (YA). pap. *(978-0-9543596-3-8(1))* Lux-Verbi Bks.
Peterson-Hilleque, Victoria. J. K. Rowling: Extraordinary Author, 1 vol. 2010. (Essential Lives Set 5 Ser.). (ENG.). 112p. (YA). (gr. 6-12). lib. bdg. 41.36 *(978-1-61613-517-1(4),* 6717, Essential Library) ABDO Publishing Co.
Pezzi, Bryan. J. K. Rowling. (J). 2012. 28.55 *(978-1-61913-057-9(2))* 2012. pap. 13.95 *(978-1-61913-596-3(5))* 2005. (Illus.). 32p. (gr. 5-7). lib. bdg. 26.00 *(978-1-59036-287-7(X))* Weigl Pubs., Inc.
Price, Joan. J. K. Rowling, 1 vol. 2004. (Trailblazers of the Modern World Ser.). (ENG., Illus.). 48p. (gr. 5-8). pap. 15.05 *(978-0-8368-5268-4(0),* 70983876-d844-4b12-aa22-60b340b12030); lib. bdg. 33.67 *(978-0-8368-5499-2(3),* 685e19f2-3ac5-4998-bd5f-d3b6e0426510) Stevens, Gareth Publishing LLLP. (Gareth Stevens Secondary Library).
Pyne, Erin A. A Fandom of Magical Proportions: S: an Unauthorized History of the Harry Potter Phenomenon. 2007. (Illus.). 84p. (J). per. 8.36 *(978-0-9788138-8-8(X))* Nimble Bks. LLC.
Rowling, J. K. Harry Potter & the Chamber of Secrets, Bk. 2. Kay, Jim, illus. 2016. (Harry Potter Ser.: 2). (ENG.). 272p. (J). (gr. 3). 39.99 *(978-0-545-79132-8(4),* Levine, Arthur A. Bks.) Scholastic, Inc.
—Harry Potter & the Goblet of Fire. Kay, Jim, illus. 2019. (Harry Potter Ser.: 4). (ENG.). 464p. (J). (gr. 3). 47.99 *(978-0-545-79142-7(1),* Levine, Arthur A. Bks.) Scholastic, Inc.
Scholastic, Inc. Staff, contrib. by. The World of Harry Potter: Harry Potter Poster Book. 2011. (Illus.). 125p. (J). pap. *(978-0-545-31482-4(8))* Scholastic, Inc.
Senker, Cath. J. K. Rowling: Creator of Harry Potter, 1 vol. 2011. (Famous Lives Ser.). (ENG., Illus.). 32p. (YA). (gr. 3-4). lib. bdg. 30.27 *(978-1-4488-3288-0(8),* 898cfb36-976b-437d-a19a-adc2303d6b29) Rosen Publishing Group, Inc., The.
Sexton, Colleen. J. K. Rowling. 2008. pap. 52.95 *(978-1-57505-984-6(3))* Lerner Publishing Group.
Sexton, Colleen A. J. K. Rowling. 2007. (Biography Ser.). (Illus.). 112p. (J). (gr. -1). lib. bdg. 30.60 *(978-0-8225-7949-6(9))* Lerner Publishing Group.
—J.K. Rowling. 2006. (Just the Facts Biographies Ser.). (Illus.). 112p. (J). 27.93 *(978-0-8225-3423-5(1),* Lerner Pubns.) Lerner Publishing Group.
Shapiro, Marc. J. K. Rowling: the Wizard Behind Harry Potter: The Wizard Behind Harry Potter. 4th ed. 2007. (ENG., Illus.). 288p. pap. 20.99 *(978-0-312-37697-0(9),* 900049029, St. Martin's Griffin) St. Martin's Pr.

POTTER, HARRY (FICTITIOUS CHARACTER)—FICTION

Davis, Graeme. Re-Read Harry Potter & the Chamber of Secrets Today! an Unauthorized Guide. 2008. 112p. pap. 15.49 *(978-1-934840-72-6(6))* Nimble Bks. LLC.
Frankel, Valerie. Henry Potty & the Pet Rock: An Unauthorized Harry Potter Parody. 2006. 112p. (J). pap. *(978-1-59594-088-9(X),* Wingspan Pr.) WingSpan Publishing.
K., J. Harry Potter e Il Prigioniero Di Azkaban. (Harry Potter Ser.: Year 3). (ITA.). pap. 32.95 *(978-88-7782-852-1(8))* Salani ITA. Dist: Distribooks, Inc.
—Harry Potter e la Pietra Filosofale. (Harry Potter Ser.: Year 1). (ITA., Illus.). 293p. pap. 32.95 *(978-88-7782-702-9(5))* Salani ITA. Dist: Distribooks, Inc.
Novel Units. Harry Potter & the Prisoner of Azkaban Novel Units Student Packet. 2019. (Harry Potter Ser.: Year 3). (ENG.). (J). pap., stu. ed. 13.99 *(978-1-58130-657-6(1),* Novel Units, Inc.) Classroom Library Co.
—Harry Potter & the Prisoner of Azkaban Novel Units Teacher Guide. 2019. (Harry Potter Ser.: Year 3). (ENG.). (J). pap., tchr. ed. 12.99 *(978-1-58130-656-9(3),* Novel Units, Inc.) Classroom Library Co.
Rowling, J. K. Hare Pota Me Te Whatu Manapou [Harry Potter & the Philosopher's Stone]. Blake, Leon Heketu, tr. 2021. (Kotahi Rau Pukapuka Ser.: 1). 328p. pap. 24.99 *(978-1-86940-914-2(0))* Auckland Univ. Pr. NZL. Dist: Independent Pubs. Group.
—Harrius Potter et Philosophi Lapis: (Harry Potter & the Philosopher's Stone) 2003. (Harry Potter Ser.).Tr. of Harry Potter & the Philosopher's Stone. (LAT., Illus.). 256p. (YA). (gr. 7). 29.99 *(978-1-58234-825-4(1),* 900020066, Bloomsbury USA Childrens) Bloomsbury Publishing USA.
—Harry Potter à l'École des Sorciers. Menard, Jean-François, tr. from ENG. 2007. (Harry Potter Ser.: Year 1).Tr. of Harry Potter & the Sorcerer's Stone. 311p. (J). per. 14.95 *(978-2-07-061236-9(8))* Gallimard, Editions FRA. Dist: Distribooks, Inc.
—Harry Potter & the Chamber of Secrets. 2009. 9.64 *(978-0-7848-1444-4(9),* Everbind) Marco Bk. Co.
—Harry Potter & the Chamber of Secrets. unabr. ed. 2004. (Harry Potter Ser.: Year 2). 352p. (J). (gr. 3-18). pap. 46.00 incl. audio *(978-0-8072-8207-6(3),* S YA 137 SP, Listening Library) Random Hse. Audio Publishing Group.
—Harry Potter & the Chamber of Secrets. (Harry Potter Ser.: 2). (J). 2006. 1.25 *(978-1-4193-8079-2(6))* 2003. 78.75 *(978-1-4025-6698-1(0))* Recorded Bks., Inc.
—Harry Potter & the Chamber of Secrets. (Harry Potter Ser.: Year 2). (RUS., Illus.). 28.95 *(978-5-8451-0947-7(7))* Rosmen-Izdat RUS. Dist: Distribooks, Inc.
—Harry Potter & the Chamber of Secrets, Bk. 2. Selznick, Brian & GrandPré, Mary, illus. 2018. (Harry Potter Ser.: 2). (ENG.). 368p. (J). (gr. 3). pap. 12.99 *(978-1-338-29915-1(8),* Levine, Arthur A. Bks.) Scholastic, Inc.
—Harry Potter & the Chamber of Secrets. l.t. ed. 2003. (Harry Potter Ser.: Year 2). (ENG.). 466p. pap. 13.95 *(978-1-59413-001-4(9))* Thorndike Pr.
—Harry Potter & the Chamber of Secrets (Latin) Harrius Potter et Camera Secretorum. Needham, Peter, tr. 2016. (Harry Potter Ser.). (LAT.). 288p. 29.99 *(978-1-4088-6911-6(X),* 900210040, Bloomsbury Children's Bks.) Bloomsbury Publishing USA.
—Harry Potter & the Deathly Hallows. (Illus.). 2008. 832p. pap. *(978-0-7475-9586-1(0))* 2007. (ENG., 608p. *(978-0-7475-9106-1(7))* Bloomsbury Publishing Plc.
—Harry Potter & the Deathly Hallows. Menard, Jean-François, tr. 2017. (FRE.). 896p. (J). (gr. 4-10). pap. *(978-2-07-058523-6(9))* Gallimard, Editions.
—Harry Potter & the Deathly Hallows. braille ed. 2007. (Harry Potter Ser.: Year 7). (J). (gr. 4-7). 34.99 *(978-0-939173-57-0(3))* National Braille Pr.
—Harry Potter & the Deathly Hallows. 2010. 25.00 *(978-1-60686-882-9(9))* Perfection Learning Corp.
—Harry Potter & the Deathly Hallows, 17 vols. 2007. (Harry Potter Ser.: 7). (YA). 129.79 *(978-1-4281-6654-7(8));* 131.75 *(978-1-4281-6652-3(1))* Recorded Bks., Inc.
—Harry Potter & the Deathly Hallows, Bk. 7. Selznick, Brian & GrandPré, Mary, illus. 2018. (Harry Potter Ser.: 7). (ENG.). 784p. (J). (gr. 3). pap. 16.99 *(978-1-338-29920-5(4),* Levine, Arthur A. Bks.) Scholastic, Inc.
—Harry Potter & the Deathly Hallows, 7 vols., Bk. 7. GrandPré, Mary, illus. 2007. (Harry Potter Ser.: 7). (ENG.). 784p. (J). (gr. 3-9). 37.99 *(978-0-545-01022-1(5),* Levine, Arthur A. Bks.) Scholastic, Inc.
—Harry Potter & the Deathly Hallows. l.t. ed. 2009. (ENG.). 970p. pap. 14.95 *(978-1-59413-355-8(7),* Large Print Pr.) 2007. (Harry Potter Ser.: Year 7). (Illus.). 969p. (J). (gr. 4-7). 34.95 *(978-0-7862-9665-1(8))* Thorndike Pr.
—Harry Potter & the Deathly Hallows. (Harry Potter (Kazu Kibuishi Illustrations) Ser.: 7). 2013. lib. bdg. 29.40 *(978-0-606-32351-2(1))* 2009. lib. bdg. 26.95 *(978-0-606-00420-6(3))* Turtleback.
—Harry Potter & the Deathly Hallows. Bar-hillel, Gili, tr. from ENG. 2007. (Harry Potter Ser.: Year 7). (HEB., Illus.). 568p. (J). (gr. 4-7). pap. *(978-965-482-635-8(6))* Yediot Aharonot Bks., Miscal.
—Harry Potter & the Goblet of Fire. 2009. 10.24 *(978-0-7848-1587-8(9),* Everbind) Marco Bk. Co.
—Harry Potter & the Goblet of Fire. (Harry Potter Ser.: 4). (J). 2006. 1.25 *(978-1-4193-8531-5(3))* 2003. 101.75 *(978-1-4025-6702-5(2))* Recorded Bks., Inc.
—Harry Potter & the Goblet of Fire, Bk. 4. Selznick, Brian & GrandPré, Mary, illus. 2018. (Harry Potter Ser.: 4). (ENG.). 768p. (J). (gr. 3). pap. 14.99 *(978-1-338-29917-5(4),* Levine, Arthur A. Bks.) Scholastic, Inc.
—Harry Potter & the Goblet of Fire. GrandPré, Mary, illus. l.t. ed. 2003. (Harry Potter Ser.: Vol. 4). (ENG.). 936p. pap. 11.66 *(978-1-59413-003-8(5))* Thorndike Pr.
—Harry Potter & the Half-Blood Prince. 2005. audio compact disk *(978-0-7475-8258-8(0))* Bloomsbury Publishing Plc.
—Harry Potter & the Half-Blood Prince, 9 vols. braille ed. 2005. (Harry Potter Ser.: Year 6). (J). (gr. 4-8). 29.99 *(978-0-939173-39-6(5),* HALF) National Braille Pr.
—Harry Potter & the Half-Blood Prince. GrandPré, Mary, illus. 2006. (Harry Potter Ser.: Year 6). 652p. (gr. 4-8). 23.00 *(978-0-7569-6765-9(1))* Perfection Learning Corp.
—Harry Potter & the Half-Blood Prince. (Harry Potter Ser.: 6). (J). 2007. 1.25 *(978-1-4193-5430-4(2))* 2006. 110.75 *(978-1-4193-5436-6(1))* 2006. 193.75 *(978-1-4193-5432-8(9))* 2005. 113.75 *(978-1-4193-5434-2(5))* Recorded Bks., Inc.
—Harry Potter & the Half-Blood Prince, Bk. 6. Selznick, Brian & GrandPré, Mary, illus. 2018. (Harry Potter Ser.: 6). (ENG.). 688p. (J). (gr. 3). pap. 14.99 *(978-1-338-29919-9(0),* Levine, Arthur A. Bks.) Scholastic, Inc.
—Harry Potter & the Half-Blood Prince, Bk. 6. GrandPré, Mary, illus. 2005. (Harry Potter Ser.: 6). (ENG.). 672p. (J). (gr. 3-8). 32.99 *(978-0-439-78454-2(9),* Levine, Arthur A. Bks.) Scholastic, Inc.
—Harry Potter & the Half-Blood Prince. l.t. ed. (Illus.). (J). (gr. 4-7). 2007. (ENG.). 832p. per. 14.95 *(978-1-59413-221-6(6))* 2005. (Harry Potter Ser.: Year 6). 831p. 29.95 *(978-0-7862-7745-2(9))* Thorndike Pr. (Large Print Pr.).
—Harry Potter & the Half-Blood Prince. 2013. (Harry Potter (Kazu Kibuishi Illustrations) Ser.: 6). lib. bdg. 26.95 *(978-0-606-32350-5(3))* Turtleback.
—Harry Potter & the Half Blood Prince - Chinese Language. 2005. (Harry Potter Ser.: Year 6). (CHI.). 496p. (YA). (gr. 4-8). pap. 28.95 *(978-7-02-005323-0(8),* HAP06) People's Literature Publishing Hse. CHN. Dist: Chinasprout, Inc.
—Harry Potter & the Order of the Phoenix. 768p. (J). (gr. 6-10). pap. *(978-0-7475-6107-1(9))* Bloomsbury Publishing Plc.
—Harry Potter & the Order of the Phoenix. 2008. *(978-977-14-2697-4(4))* Nahdat Misr Bkshop for Printing and Pubs.
—Harry Potter & the Order of the Phoenix, 13 vols. braille ed. 2003. (Harry Potter Ser.: Year 5). (YA). 29.99 *(978-0-939173-38-9(7))* National Braille Pr.
—Harry Potter & the Order of the Phoenix. 2003. (Harry Potter Ser.: Year 5). (CHI.). 575p. (YA). pap. 26.95 *(978-7-02-004327-9(5),* HAP05) People's Literature Publishing Hse. CHN. Dist: Chinasprout, Inc.
—Harry Potter & the Order of the Phoenix. 2004. (Harry Potter Ser.). 870p. (gr. 4-6). 16.49 *(978-0-7569-4163-5(6))* Perfection Learning Corp.
—Harry Potter & the Order of the Phoenix. 2003. (ENG.). 768p. *(978-1-55192-570-7(2))* Raincoast Bk. Distribution.
—Harry Potter & the Order of the Phoenix. 2004. (JPN.). (J). (gr. 6-10). *(978-4-915512-51-3(7))* Sayzansha.
—Harry Potter & the Order of the Phoenix, Bk. 5. Selznick, Brian & GrandPré, Mary, illus. 2018. (Harry Potter Ser.: 5). (ENG.). 912p. (J). (gr. 3). pap. 14.99 *(978-1-338-29918-2(2),* Levine, Arthur A. Bks.) Scholastic, Inc.
—Harry Potter & the Order of the Phoenix, Bk. 5. GrandPré, Mary, illus. 2003. (Harry Potter Ser.: 5). (ENG.). 896p. (gr. 3-7). 32.99 *(978-0-439-35806-4(X),* Levine, Arthur A. Bks.) Scholastic, Inc.
—Harry Potter & the Order of the Phoenix. l.t. ed. 2003. (Harry Potter Ser.: Year 5). 1093p. 29.95 *(978-0-7862-5778-2(4),* Large Print Pr.) Thorndike Pr.
—Harry Potter & the Order of the Phoenix. GrandPré, Mary, illus. l.t. ed. 2003. (Thorndike Young Adult Ser.). (ENG.). 1232p. (J). (gr. 4-7). per. 14.95 *(978-1-59413-112-7(0),* Large Print Pr.) Thorndike Pr.
—Harry Potter & the Order of the Phoenix. 2004. (Harry Potter Ser.: 5). lib. bdg. 24.50 *(978-0-613-99916-8(9))* Turtleback.
—Harry Potter & the Philosopher's Stane: Harry Potter & the Philosopher's Stone in Scots. Fitt, Matthew, tr. 2018. (SCO.). 320p. (J). (gr. 4-6). pap. 14.95 *(978-1-78530-154-4(3))* Black and White Publishing Ltd. GBR. Dist: Independent Pubs. Group.
—Harry Potter & the Philosopher's Stone. 2014. (ENG., Illus.). 352p. *(978-1-4088-5589-8(5))* Bloomsbury Publishing Plc.
—Harry Potter & the Philosopher's Stone (Irish) 2015. (ENG.). 272p. (J). *(978-1-4088-6619-1(6),* 283017, Bloomsbury Children's Bks.) Bloomsbury Publishing Plc.
—Harry Potter & the Philosopher's Stone (Latin) Harrius Potter et Philosophi Lapis (Latin) Needham, Peter, tr. 2015. (LAT.). 256p. (J). *(978-1-4088-6618-4(8),* 283019, Bloomsbury Children's Bks.) Bloomsbury Publishing Plc.
—Harry Potter & the Prisoner of Azkaban. 2009. 9.64 *(978-0-7848-1542-7(9),* Everbind) Marco Bk. Co.
—Harry Potter & the Prisoner of Azkaban. 2005. (Harry Potter Ser.: Year 3). (CHI.). 260p. (YA). pap. 16.95 *(978-7-02-003345-4(8),* HAP03) People's Literature Publishing Hse. CHN. Dist: Chinasprout, Inc.
—Harry Potter & the Prisoner of Azkaban, 10 vols. 2003. (Harry Potter Ser.: 3). (J). 84.75 *(978-1-4025-6700-1(6))* Recorded Bks., Inc.
—Harry Potter & the Prisoner of Azkaban, Bk. 3. Selznick, Brian & GrandPré, Mary, illus. 2018. (Harry Potter Ser.: 3). (ENG.). 464p. (J). (gr. 3). pap. 12.99 *(978-1-338-29916-8(6),* Levine, Arthur A. Bks.) Scholastic, Inc.
—Harry Potter & the Prisoner of Azkaban. l.t. ed. 2003. (Harry Potter Ser.: Year 3). (ENG.). 592p. pap. 13.95 *(978-1-59413-002-1(7),* Large Print Pr.) Thorndike Pr.
—Harry Potter & the Prisoner of Azkaban. 2013. (Harry Potter (Kazu Kibuishi Illustrations) Ser.: 3). lib. bdg. 24.50 *(978-0-606-32347-5(3))* Turtleback.
—Harry Potter & the Sorcerer's Stone. 2014. (ENG.). lthr. 79.00 *(978-1-62715-772-8(7))* Leatherbound Bestsellers.
—Harry Potter & the Sorcerer's Stone. 2009. 8.44 *(978-0-7848-2438-2(X));* 10.84 *(978-0-7848-1357-7(4))* Marco Bk. Co. (Everbind).
—Harry Potter & the Sorcerer's Stone. 2003. (Harry Potter Ser.: Year 1). (CHI.). 191p. (YA). pap. 14.95 *(978-7-02-003343-0(1),* HAP01) People's Literature Publishing Hse. CHN. Dist: Chinasprout, Inc.
—Harry Potter & the Sorcerer's Stone. (Harry Potter Ser.: 1). (J). 2004. 1.25 *(978-1-4025-6757-5(X))* 2003. 80.75 *(978-1-4025-6696-7(4))* Recorded Bks., Inc.
—Harry Potter & the Sorcerer's Stone, Bk. 1. Selznick, Brian & GrandPré, Mary, illus. 2018. (Harry Potter Ser.: 1). (ENG.). 336p. (J). (gr. 3). pap. 12.99 *(978-1-338-29914-4(X),* Levine, Arthur A. Bks.) Scholastic, Inc.
—Harry Potter & the Sorcerer's Stone, Bk. 1. Kay, Jim, illus. 2015. (Harry Potter Ser.: 1). (ENG.). 256p. (J). (gr. 3). 39.99 *(978-0-545-79035-2(2),* Levine, Arthur A. Bks.) Scholastic, Inc.
—Harry Potter & the Sorcerer's Stone. 2013. (Harry Potter (Kazu Kibuishi Illustrations) Ser.: 1). lib. bdg. 24.50 *(978-0-606-32345-1(7))* Turtleback.
—Harry Potter Coffret: Harry Potter à l'École des Sorciers; Harry Potter et la Chambre des Secrets; Harry Potter et le Prisonnier d'Azkaban. (Harry Potter Ser.: Years 1-3).Tr. of Harry Potter Boxed Set: Harry Potter & the Chamber of Secrets; Harry Potter & the Sorcerer's Stone; Harry Potter & the Prisoner of Azkaban. pap. 69.95 *(978-2-07-054972-6(0))* Gallimard, Editions FRA. Dist: Distribooks, Inc.
—Harry Potter e a Camara Secreta. (Harry Potter Ser.: Year 2).Tr. of Harry Potter & the Chamber of Secrets. (POR.). pap. 28.95 *(978-85-325-1166-9(X))* Rocco, Editora, Ltda BRA. Dist: Distribooks, Inc.
—Harry Potter e a Pedra Filosofal. (Harry Potter Ser.: Year 1).Tr. of Harry Potter & the Philosopher's Stone. (POR.). pap. 28.95 *(978-85-325-1101-0(5))* Rocco, Editora, Ltda BRA. Dist: Distribooks, Inc.
—Harry Potter e a Prisioneiro de Azkaban. (Harry Potter Ser.: Year 3).Tr. of Harry Potter & the Prisoner of Azkaban. (POR.). pap. 29.95 *(978-85-325-1206-2(2))* Rocco, Editora, Ltda BRA. Dist: Distribooks, Inc.
—Harry Potter e la Camera Dei Segreti. (Harry Potter Ser.: Year 2). (ITA.). pap. 32.95 *(978-88-7782-703-6(3))* Salani ITA. Dist: Distribooks, Inc.
—Harry Potter e o Cálice de Fogo. (Harry Potter Ser.: Year 4).Tr. of Harry Potter & the Goblet of Fire. (POR.). pap. 38.95 *(978-85-325-1252-9(6))* Rocco, Editora, Ltda BRA. Dist: Distribooks, Inc.
—Harry Potter et la Coupe de Feu. (Harry Potter Ser.: Year 4).Tr. of Harry Potter & the Goblet of Fire. (FRE., Illus.). 766p. pap. 19.95 *(978-2-07-054351-9(X))* Gallimard, Editions FRA. Dist: Distribooks, Inc.
—Harry Potter I Czara Ognia. (Harry Potter Ser.: Year 4). pap. 29.95 *(978-83-7278-021-8(8))* Media Rodzina POL. Dist: Distribooks, Inc.
—Harry Potter I Kamie D. (Harry Potter Ser.: Year 1). pap. 18.95 *(978-83-7278-000-3(5))* Media Rodzina POL. Dist: Distribooks, Inc.
—Harry Potter I Komnata Tajem. (Harry Potter Ser.: Year 1). pap. 18.95 *(978-83-7278-007-2(2))* Media Rodzina POL. Dist: Distribooks, Inc.
—Harry Potter I wi Zied Azkab. (Harry Potter Ser.: Year 3). pap. 29.95 *(978-83-7278-014-0(5))* Media Rodzina POL. Dist: Distribooks, Inc.
—Harry Potter Signature Hardback Boxed Set X 7, 7 vols., Set. 2011. (ENG.). 7p. *(978-1-4088-2594-5(5))* Bloomsbury Publishing Plc.
—Harry Potter Y la Orden del Fenix. 2004. (Harry Potter Ser.: Year 5).Tr. of Harry Potter & the Order of the Phoenix. (SPA.). 893p. (YA). 23.99 *(978-84-7888-901-3(9))* Emece Editores ESP. Dist: Lectorum Pubns., Inc.
—Harry Potter Y la Orden del Fenix. Ortega, Gemma Rovira, tr. from ENG. 2004. (Harry Potter Ser.: Year 5).Tr. of Harry Potter & the Order of the Phoenix. (SPA.). 893p. (YA). pap. 17.99 *(978-84-7888-884-9(5))* Emece Editores ESP. Dist: Lectorum Pubns., Inc.
—Harry Potter Y la Orden del Fenix. 2004. (Harry Potter Ser.: Year 5).Tr. of Harry Potter & the Order of the Phoenix. 1000p. 69.95 *(978-0-320-04850-0(0))* French & European Pubns., Inc.
Rowling, J. K. & Xocuasvili, Cico. Hari Poteri Da Sikvdilis Sacukrebi. 2008. (GEO.). 636p. (J). *(978-9941-403-14-9(7))* Georgian Biographic Ctr., Ltd.
Rowling, J.k. Harry Potter y el cáliz de fuego (Harry Potter 4) 2004. (Harry Potter Ser.: Year 4). (SPA., Illus.). 240p. (YA). 19.95 *(978-84-7888-645-6(1),* SAL30169) Emece Editores ESP. Dist: Lectorum Pubns., Inc.
—Harry Potter y el prisionero de Azkaban (Harry Potter 3) 2004. (Harry Potter Ser.: Year 3). (SPA., Illus.). 360p. (gr. 3-18). 17.95 *(978-84-7888-519-0(6),* SAL1889) Emece Editores ESP. Dist: Lectorum Pubns., Inc.
—Harry Potter y la cámara secreta (Harry Potter 2) 2004. (Harry Potter Ser.: Year 2). (SPA., Illus.). 288p. (YA). (gr. 3-18). 15.95 *(978-84-7888-495-7(5),* SAL4595) Emece Editores ESP. Dist: Lectorum Pubns., Inc.
—Harry Potter y la piedra filosofal (Harry Potter 1) 2004. (Harry Potter Ser.: Year 1). (SPA., Illus.). 256p. (YA). (gr. 7-18).

15.95 (978-84-7888-445-2(9), SAL2819) Emece Editores ESP. Dist: Lectorum Pubns., Inc.

Scholastic, Inc. Staff. Hidden Hogwarts: Scratch Magic. Warner Bros. & Bull, Carolyn, illus. 2018. (Harry Potter Ser.). (ENG.). 64p. (J). (gr. 2-2). 12.99 (978-1-338-24610-0(0)) Scholastic, Inc.

Warner Bros. Consumer Products Inc., . Harry Potter Poster Collection: The Definitive Movie Posters. 2012. (Insights Poster Collections). (ENG., Illus.). 40p. (gr. 2). pap. 24.99 (978-1-60887-113-1(4)) Insight Editions.

—Harry Potter Poster Collection: The Quintessential Images. 2012. (Insights Poster Collections). (ENG., Illus.). 40p. (gr. 2). pap. 24.99 (978-1-60887-142-1(8)) Insight Editions.

Wizard Academies I: The Heart of Darkness. 2006. 658p. pap. 24.96 (978-1-4116-7787-6(0)) Lulu Pr., Inc.

Zimmerman, W. Frederick. Unauthorized Harry Potter & the Alchemist's Cell News: Half-Blood Prince Analysis & Speculation. 2006. 160p. per. 14.94 (978-0-9777424-7-9(4)) Nimble Bks. LLC.

—Unauthorized Harry Potter & the Chariots of Light News: Half-Blood Prince Analysis & Speculation. 2006. 160p. per. 14.94 (978-0-9777424-8-6(2)) Nimble Bks. LLC.

POTTERS

Cheng, Andrea. Etched in Clay: The Life of Dave, Enslaved Potter & Poet, 1 vol. Cheng, Andrea, illus. 2018. (ENG., Illus.). 160p. (J). (gr. 4-12). pap. 13.95 (978-1-62014-807-5(2), leelowbooks) Lee & Low Bks., Inc.

Hill, Laban Carrick. Dave the Potter: Artist, Poet, Slave. 2012. (CHI, ENG & JPN., Illus.). 42p. (J). (978-4-89572-839-3(0)) Mitsumura Kyouiku Tosho Co., Ltd.

—Dave the Potter (Caldecott Honor Book) Artist, Poet, Slave. Collier, Bryan, illus. 2010. (ENG.). 40p. (J). (gr. -1-3). 19.99 (978-0-316-10731-0(X)) Little, Brown Bks. for Young Readers.

Hill, Laban Carrik. Dave the Potter: Artist, Poet, Slave. 2011. (J). (978-1-4618-1706-2(4)) Recorded Bks., Inc.

POTTERS—FICTION

Holliday, Bobby. A Lump of Clay. Price, Rebecca, illus. 2010. 28p. (J). 18.99 (978-0-9829082-1-1(0)) Lady Hawk Pr.

POTTERY

see also Porcelain

Andrews-Goebel, Nancy. La Vasija Que Juan Fabrico (Spanish Edition), 1 vol. 2004. (SPA., Illus.). 32p. (J). (gr. 1-6). pap. 12.95 (978-1-58430-230-8(5), leelowbooks) Lee & Low Bks., Inc.

Clough, Peter. Clay in the Classroom. 2005. (Illus.). 111p. reprint ed. pap. 22.00 (978-0-7567-9594-3(X)) DIANE Publishing Co.

Johnson, Donald-Brian, et al. Ceramic Arts Studio: The Legacy of Betty Harrington, 1 vol. 2003. (ENG., Illus.). 264p. (gr. 10-13). 59.95 (978-0-7643-1826-9(8), 2213) Schiffer Publishing, Ltd.

Kassinger, Ruth. Ceramics: From Magic Pots to Man-Made Bones. 2003. (Material World Ser.). (Illus.). 80p. (gr. 6-8). lib. bdg. 25.90 (978-0-7613-2108-8(X), Twenty-First Century Bks.) Lerner Publishing Group.

Kenney, Karen Latchana. Super Simple Clay Projects: Fun & Easy-to-Make Crafts for Kids, 1 vol. 2009. (Super Simple Crafts Ser.). (ENG., Illus.). 32p. (J). (gr. -1-4). 34.21 (978-1-60453-623-2(3), 13928, Super SandCastle) ABDO Publishing Co.

Nancy Andrews-Goebel. The Pot That Juan Built (Pura Belpre Honor Book Illustrator (Awards)) 2013. (ENG., Illus.). 32p. (J). (gr. 1-18). 17.95 (978-1-58430-038-0(8)) Lee & Low Bks., Inc.

Quan, Adalucia. The Magic of Clay. 2003. (Illus.). 29p. (J). 18.95 (978-0-9742956-0-2(4)) Cholita Prints & Pub. Co.

Spilsbury, Richard. Decorated Pottery, 1 vol. 2008. (Stories in Art Ser.). (ENG., Illus.). 32p. (J). (gr. 4-4). lib. bdg. 30.27 (978-1-4042-4437-5(9), 763b7a85-5df8-4b86-916a-2f64a7de9936, PowerKids Pr.) Rosen Publishing Group, Inc., The.

Staff, Gareth Editorial Staff. Clay, 1 vol. 2003. (Let's Create! Ser.). (ENG., Illus.). 32p. (gr. 2-4). lib. bdg. 28.67 (978-0-8368-3746-9(0), 8df06667-54be-484b-a38c-95e4d88a6189, Gareth Stevens Learning Library) Stevens, Gareth Publishing LLLP.

Stephens, Pam. Dropping in on ... Puffer Learns about Ceramics. 2013. (ENG., Illus.). 32p. (J). 15.95 (978-1-56290-707-5(7)) Crystal Productions.

POTTERY—FICTION

Alexander, Lloyd. The Black Cauldron. 2nd rev. ed. 2006. (Chronicles of Prydain Ser.: 2). (ENG., Illus.). 208p. (J). (gr. 3-7). pap. 7.99 (978-0-8050-8049-0(X), 900038436) Square Fish.

Brandeis, Madeline. The Little Mexican Donkey Boy. 2011. 226p. 44.95 (978-1-258-09794-3(X)) Literary Licensing, LLC.

Camila & Clay-Old-Woman, 6 pack. (Greetings Ser.: Vol. 1). (gr. 3-5). 31.00 (978-0-7635-1745-8(3)) Rigby Education.

Carter, Aubrey Smith. The Enchanted Lizard: La Lagartijita Mágica. Nelson, Esther Whitt, ed. Branton, Molly, illus. 2006. (ENG & SPA.). 96p. (J). 18.95 (978-1-893271-38-8(2), Maverick Bks.) Trinity Univ. Pr.

de la Ramée, Louise & Ouida. Bimbi. 2007. 152p. per. 13.95 (978-1-60312-344-0(X)); 24.95 (978-1-60312-682-3(1)) Aegypan.

A First Clay Gathering (Review Multiple Meanings), Level C. 2003. ("Plaid" Phonics & Stories Libraries). 43.50 (978-0-8136-9234-0(2)) Modern Curriculum Pr.

Krug, R. Lyding. The Treasure of Ferson Creek. 2006. 133p. (YA). pap. 9.95 (978-1-4116-3683-5(X)) Lulu Pr., Inc.

Novel Units. A Single Shard Novel Units Student Packet. 2019. (ENG.). (J). (gr. 5-6). pap., stu. ed. 13.99 (978-1-58130-771-9(3), Novel Units, Inc.) Classroom Library Co.

Park, Linda Sue. A Single Shard. unabr. ed. 2004. (Middle Grade Cassette Librariestm Ser.). (J). (gr. 5-9). pap. 36.00 incl. audio (978-0-8072-1760-3(3), S YA 349 SP, Listening Library) Random Hse. Audio Publishing Group.

—A Single Shard. 2011. (gr. 5-8). lib. bdg. 18.40 (978-0-613-57327-6(7)) Turtleback.

—A Single Shard: A Newbery Award Winner. 2011. (ENG.). 176p. (J). (gr. 5-7). pap. 10.99 (978-0-547-53426-8(4), 1447661, Clarion Bks.) HarperCollins Pubs.

Romero-Anderson, Emerita. Milagro of the Spanish Bean Pot. Pijoan, Randall, illus. 2011. (ENG.). 128p. (J). (gr. 4-6). 18.95 (978-0-89672-681-9(9), P200877) Texas Tech Univ. Pr.

Stephens, Dawn. The Little Pot. 2009. (Illus.). (J). (gr. -1-3). 17.95 (978-1-933982-11-3(X), bPlus Bks.) Bumble Bee Publishing.

POTTINGER, ROSE RITA (FICTITIOUS CHARACTER)—FICTION

Bellairs, John. The House with a Clock in Its Walls. Gorey, Edward, illus. 2004. (Lewis Barnavelt Ser.: Bk. 1). (ENG.). 192p. (J). (gr. 3-7). pap. 7.99 (978-0-14-240257-3(5), Puffin Books) Penguin Young Readers Group.

—The House with a Clock in Its Walls. Gorey, Edward, illus. 2004. (John Bellairs Mysteries Ser.). 179p. (J). (gr. 3-7). 13.65 (978-0-7569-5257-0(3)) Perfection Learning Corp.

—The House with a Clock in Its Walls. (Lewis Barnavelt Ser.: Bk. 1). 179p. (J). (gr. 4-6). pap. 4.50 (978-0-8072-1423-7(X), Listening Library) Random Hse. Audio Publishing Group.

—The House with a Clock in Its Walls. 2004. 17.20 (978-1-4176-3513-9(4)) Turtleback.

POULTRY

see also names of domesticated birds, e.g. Ducks; Geese; Turkeys, etc.

Harmon, Daniel E. Poultry: From the Farm to Your Table, 1 vol. 2012. (Truth about the Food Supply Ser.). (ENG., Illus.). 48p. (J). (gr. 5-5). lib. bdg. 34.47 (978-1-4488-6798-1(3), 1c69d8b1-df89-40bb-9f03-b568711894de, Rosen Reference) Rosen Publishing Group, Inc., The.

Markovics, Pearl. In the Henhouse. 2019. (Farm Charm Ser.). (ENG.). 16p. (J). (gr. -1-1). 6.99 (978-1-64280-376-1(6)) Bearport Publishing Co., Inc.

Mercer, Abbie. Chickens on a Farm, 1 vol. 2009. (Barnyard Animals Ser.). (ENG., Illus.). 24p. (J). (gr. 1-1). lib. bdg. 26.27 (978-1-4358-3840-6(8), cf51b745-86f7-4bb4-90b7-cf4cfe1f6038, PowerKids Pr.) Rosen Publishing Group, Inc., The.

Miller, Debra A., ed. Factory Farming, 1 vol. 2013. (Current Controversies Ser.). (ENG., Illus.). 152p. (gr. 10-12). pap. 33.00 (978-0-7377-6873-2(8), 8d80092b-c366-489c-be35-4b2986de1970); lib. bdg. 48.03 (978-0-7377-6872-5(X), d8d83683-124a-4f40-8a60-e13cd147c851) Greenhaven Publishing LLC. (Greenhaven Publishing).

Page, Robin. A Chicken Followed Me Home! Questions & Answers about a Familiar Fowl. Page, Robin, illus. 2015. (ENG., Illus.). 40p. (J). (gr. k-5). 17.99 (978-1-4814-1028-1(8), Beach Lane Bks.) Beach Lane Bks.

Quinton, Sasha. Peck-A -peck: A Phonics Reader. 2009. (Illus.). pap. (978-1-936199-08-2(4)) Book Shop, Ltd., The.

Soudée, Guirec. The Hen Who Sailed Around the World: A True Story. 2018. (ENG., Illus.). 40p. (J). (gr. -1-3). 17.99 (978-0-316-44884-0(2)) Little, Brown Bks. for Young Readers.

Stone, Tanya Lee. Chickens. 2003. (Wild Wild World Ser.). 24p. (YA). 24.94 (978-1-56711-812-4(7), Blackbirch Pr., Inc.) Cengage Gale.

Walker, Sylvia & Coloring Books Staff. Easter Egg Hunt Coloring Book. 2012. (Dover Holiday Coloring Book Ser.). (ENG., Illus.). 32p. (J). (gr. -1-3). pap. 3.99 (978-0-486-48521-8(8), 485218) Dover Pubns., Inc.

POULTRY—FICTION

Aimé, Elizabeth Mary & Aimé, Elizabeth Mary. A Peaceful Home for Red Rock Hen. Aimé, Victor Leo, illus. 2012. (ENG.). 30p. pap. 19.99 (978-1-4772-1340-7(6)) AuthorHouse.

Allen, Christina. A Micro-Chip on my Shoulder: A True Story of a Little Poult. 2010. 28p. pap. 13.99 (978-1-4490-6681-9(X)) AuthorHouse.

Davis, Peg. After the Storm: A Napoleon & Marigold Adventure. 2009. 40p. pap. 16.50 (978-1-60860-222-3(2), Eloquent Bks.) Strategic Book Publishing & Rights Agency (SBPRA).

Galdone, Paul. The Little Red Hen. Galdone, Paul, illus. 2011. (Paul Galdone Nursery Classic Ser.). (ENG., Illus.). 48p. (J). (gr. -1-3). 9.99 (978-0-547-37018-7(0), 1423281, Clarion Bks.) HarperCollins Pubs.

Hayes, Beverly. Charlie Chicken Hawk, 1 vol. Ashcraft Jr, D. C., illus. 2009. 20p. pap. 24.95 (978-1-60836-673-6(1)) America Star Bks.

Jones, Christianne C. The Little Red Hen, 1 vol. Magnuson, Natalie, illus. 2011. (My First Classic Story Ser.). (ENG.). 32p. (J). (gr. k-3). pap. 7.10 (978-1-4048-7356-8(2), 118572, Picture Window Bks.) Capstone.

Josiah, Iris. Tiny Hen. 2012. (Illus.). 28p. (J). pap. (978-0-9572728-3-5(9)) Tiny Island Pr.

Julian, Russell. Happy Cockerel. 2005. (Farm Board Book Ser.). (ENG., Illus.). 12p. (J). bds. 9.99 (978-1-4052-1030-0(3)) Farshore GBR. Dist: Trafalgar Square Publishing.

Page, P. K. The Old Woman & the Hen. 2008. (ENG., Illus.). 32p. (J). pap. 10.95 (978-0-88984-309-7(0)) Porcupine's Quill, Inc. CAN. Dist: Univ. of Toronto Pr.

Plitt, Kay. Why Isn't Bobby Like Me, Mom? 2010. 32p. 14.75 (978-1-4269-4038-5(6)) Trafford Publishing.

Simon, Francesca. Higgledy Piggledy the Hen Who Loved to Dance. Moseng, Elisabeth, illus. 2016. (ENG.). 32p. (J). 17.99 (978-0-00-813946-9(6), HarperCollins Children's Bks.) HarperCollins Pubs. Ltd. GBR. Dist: HarperCollins Pubs.

Stoeke, Janet Morgan. The Loopy Coop Hens. Stoeke, Janet Morgan, illus. 2013. (Loopy Coop Hens Ser.). (Illus.). 32p. (J). (gr. 1-2). mass mkt. 4.99 (978-0-448-46272-1(9), Penguin Young Readers) Penguin Young Readers Group.

Swanberg, Arvon & Spicer, Carolyn. The Big, Blue, Overstuffed Chair. 2013. 46p. pap. 17.99 (978-1-4808-0432-6(0)) Archway Publishing.

Ungermann Marshall, Yana. Gilda Gets Wise. Ungermann Marshall, Yana, illus. 2008. (Illus.). 34p. (J). pap. (978-0-9670982-6-5(2)) Yana's Kitchen.

Wiggin, Kate Douglas. The Diary of a Goose Girl. 2007. 108p. per. 9.95 (978-1-60312-330-3(X)); 22.95 (978-1-60312-748-6(8)) Aegypan.

POVERTY

see also Homelessness

see also names of countries with the subdivision Economic Conditions and Social Conditions e.g. United States—Economic Conditions; United States—Social Conditions

Black, Donnette. Madam C. J. Walker's Road to Success. 2010. 36p. pap. 17.50 (978-1-4520-2443-1(X)) AuthorHouse.

Bojang, Ali Brownlie. Aid & Development. 2009. (J). 32.80 (978-1-59920-099-6(6)) Black Rabbit Bks.

Green, Robert. Poverty. 2008. (21st Century Skills Library: Global Perspectives Ser.). (ENG., Illus.). 32p. (gr. 4-8). lib. bdg. 32.07 (978-1-60279-126-8(0), 200106) Cherry Lake Publishing.

Heitkamp, Kristina Lyn, ed. Learned Helplessness, Welfare, & the Poverty Cycle, 1 vol. 2018. (Current Controversies Ser.). (ENG.). 176p. (gr. 10-12). 48.03 (978-1-5345-0388-5(9), aa5eed77-34c7-42a4-99bd-8f85ad49ce98) Greenhaven Publishing LLC.

Hopkinson, Deborah. Shutting Out the Sky: Life in the Tenements of New York, 1880-1924 (Scholastic Focus) 2003. (ENG., Illus.). 144p. (J). (gr. 4-7). 19.99 (978-0-439-37590-0(8)) Scholastic, Inc.

Information Plus Homeless in America November 2005. 2005. 49.00 (978-1-4144-0418-9(2)) Cengage Gale.

Kalman, Bobbie. ¿Qué Necesito? 2010. (SPA.). 16p. (J). pap. (978-0-7787-8587-3(4)); lib. bdg. (978-0-7787-8561-3(0)) Crabtree Publishing Co.

—What Do I Need? 2010. (My World Ser.). (ENG., Illus.). 16p. (J). (gr. k-2). (978-0-7787-9436-3(9)); pap. (978-0-7787-9480-6(6)) Crabtree Publishing Co.

Laine, Carolee. The War on Poverty. 2016. (Special Reports Set 2 Ser.). (ENG., Illus.). 112p. (J). (gr. 6-12). lib. bdg. 41.36 (978-1-68078-399-5(8), 23563, Essential Library) ABDO Publishing Co.

Marsico, Katie. The Salvation Army. 2014. (Community Connections: How Do They Help? Ser.). (ENG., Illus.). 24p. (J). (gr. 2-5). 29.21 (978-1-63188-029-2(2), 205523) Cherry Lake Publishing.

McCoy, Erin L. & Axelrod-Contrada, Joan. Poverty: Public Crisis or Private Struggle?, 1 vol. 2018. (Today's Debates Ser.). (ENG.). 144p. (gr. 7-7). lib. bdg. 47.36 (978-1-5026-4260-8(3), fda21703-2033-4963-84df-7fbf24e81d9a) Cavendish Square Publishing LLC.

Merino, Noël, ed. Poverty & Homelessness, 1 vol. 2014. (Current Controversies Ser.). (ENG., Illus.). 216p. (gr. 10-12). pap. 33.00 (978-0-7377-6887-9(8), cdb638c5-90f3-4fd3-9812-57a43bdae045, Greenhaven Publishing) Greenhaven Publishing LLC.

—Poverty & Homelessness, 1 vol. 2014. (Current Controversies Ser.). (ENG., Illus.). 216p. (gr. 10-12). lib. bdg. 48.03 (978-0-7377-6886-2(X), 9e061163-a37e-4270-80f2-430bcda8e2e2, Greenhaven Publishing) Greenhaven Publishing LLC.

Moore, Elizabeth. Wants or Needs, 1 vol. 2011. (Wonder Readers Early Level Ser.). (ENG.). 16p. (gr. -1-1). (J). pap. 6.25 (978-1-4296-7876-6(3), 118208); pap. 35.94 (978-1-4296-8197-1(7)) Capstone. (Capstone Pr.).

Muñoz, Mercedes, ed. Is Poverty a Serious Threat?, 1 vol. 2006. (At Issue Ser.). (ENG.). 120p. (gr. 10-12). pap. 28.80 (978-0-7377-2726-5(8), 67bbbcf5-3d1f-4c5e-8ce4-b93dccad5032, Greenhaven Publishing) Greenhaven Publishing LLC.

—Is Poverty a Serious Threat?, 1 vol. 2006. (At Issue Ser.). (ENG., Illus.). 120p. (gr. 10-12). lib. bdg. 41.03 (978-0-7377-2725-8(X), 79768d3e-67a1-442d-b77a-875a58a10170, Greenhaven Publishing) Greenhaven Publishing LLC.

Saul, Laya. Ways to Help Disadvantaged Youth: A Guide to Giving Back. 2010. (How to Help Ser.). (Illus.). 48p. (J). (gr. 4-8). lib. bdg. 29.95 (978-1-58415-918-6(9)) Mitchell Lane Pubs.

Senker, Cath. Poverty, 1 vol. 2007. (What If We Do Nothing? Ser.). (ENG., Illus.). 48p. (gr. 5-8). lib. bdg. 33.67 (978-0-8368-7757-1(8), e07c7ef9-859b-486a-aefd-60c5242134af, Gareth Stevens Secondary Library) Stevens, Gareth Publishing LLLP.

Sharif, Meghan. Poverty & Economic Inequality, 1 vol. 2018. (Hot Topics Ser.). (ENG.). 104p. (gr. 7-7). 41.03 (978-1-5345-6353-7(9), 135c7192-f87b-4bd2-9ada-9a45bbbfa28f, Lucent Pr.) Greenhaven Publishing LLC.

Steinman, Karen. Critical World Issues: Poverty, Vol. 16. 2016. (Critical World Issues Ser.: Vol. 16). (ENG., Illus.). 112p. (J). (gr. 7-12). 25.95 (978-1-4222-3658-1(7)) Mason Crest.

Turner, Amanda. Helping Those in Poverty. 2019. (Careers Making a Difference Ser.). 80p. (J). (gr. 12). lib. bdg. 34.60 (978-1-4222-4261-2(7)) Mason Crest.

Wilson, Mike, ed. Poverty, 1 vol. 2009. (Introducing Issues with Opposing Viewpoints Ser.). (ENG.). 152p. (gr. 7-10). 38.43 (978-0-7377-4340-1(9), a11077a4-595e-497a-9934-3eba44a3a7f1, Greenhaven Publishing) Greenhaven Publishing LLC.

POVERTY—FICTION

Alexander, James W. Good - Better - Best: Classic Treatment of a Christian's Duty to the Poor. 2009. 224p. pap. 17.00 (978-1-59925-143-1(4)) Solid Ground Christian Bks.

Alger Jr. Horatio Staff. Herbert Carter's Legacy. rev. ed. 2006. 264p. 28.95 (978-1-4218-1756-9(X)); pap. 13.95 (978-1-4218-1856-6(6)) 1st World Publishing, Inc. (1st World Library - Literary Society).

Ardizzone, Edward. Sarah & Simon & No Red Paint. Ardizzone, Edward, illus. 2011. (ENG., Illus.). 48p. (J). 17.95 (978-1-56792-410-7(7)) Godine, David R. Pub.

Armstrong, William H. Sounder. l.t. ed. 2005. 111p. (YA). pap. 10.95 (978-0-7862-7915-6(X)) Thorndike Pr.

—Sounder: A Newbery Award Winner. Barkley, James, illus. 2019. (ENG.). 128p. (J). (gr. 3-7). reprint ed. pap. 9.99 (978-0-06-440020-6(4), HarperCollins) HarperCollins Pubs.

Bayard, Louis. Lucky Strikes. 2016. (ENG., Illus.). 320p. (YA). 29.99 (978-1-62779-390-2(9), 900148815, Holt, Henry & Co. Bks. For Young Readers) Holt, Henry & Co.

—Lucky Strikes. 2017. (YA). lib. bdg. 20.85 (978-0-606-39951-7(8)) Turtleback.

Bennion, Jay B. From Here to There. 2013. 136p. pap. 9.99 (978-0-9826175-0-2(X)) Pearl Publishing, LLC.

Bertrand, Diane Gonzales. El Momento de Trino. Sanmiguel, Rosario, tr. from ENG. 2006. (SPA.). 181p. (J). (gr. 3-7). per. 9.95 (978-1-55885-473-4(8), Piñata Books) Arte Publico Pr.

Blackwood, Gary. Curiosity. 2015. 336p. (J). (gr. 4-7). 8.99 (978-0-14-242448-3(X), Puffin Books) Penguin Young Readers Group.

Boelts, Maribeth. Those Shoes. Jones, Noah Z., illus. 2009. (ENG.). 40p. (J). (gr. k-3). pap. 8.99 (978-0-7636-4284-6(3)) Candlewick Pr.

—Those Shoes. Jones, Noah, illus. 2007. (J). (978-1-4287-6554-2(9)) Candlewick Pr.

—Those Shoes. 2014. 17.00 (978-1-63419-735-9(6)) Perfection Learning Corp.

Booth, Coe. Tyrell. 2011. 9.04 (978-0-7848-3385-8(0), Everbind) Marco Bk. Co.

Brandt, Lois. La Nevera de Maddi. Vogel, Vin, illus. 2018. (SPA.). 32p. (J). (gr. k-2). 16.95 (978-1-936261-97-0(9)) Flashlight Pr.

Brenner, Summer. Ivy, Homeless in San Francisco. Bowes, Brian, illus. 2nd ed. 2011. (Reach & Teach Ser.). (ENG.). 176p. (YA). (gr. 4-7). pap. 15.00 (978-1-60486-317-8(X)) PM Pr.

Campbell, Marcy. Adrian Simcox Does NOT Have a Horse. Luyken, Corinna, illus. 2018. 40p. (J). (-k). 18.99 (978-0-7352-3037-8(4), Dial Bks) Penguin Young Readers Group.

Casanova, Mary. Ice-Out. 2016. (ENG., Illus.). 264p. (YA). 16.95 (978-0-8166-9417-4(6)) Univ. of Minnesota Pr.

Chinn, Karen. Sam & the Lucky Money, 1 vol. Hu, Ying-Hwa & Van Wright, Cornelius, illus. 2013. (ENG.). 32p. (J). (gr. k-3). reprint ed. pap. 11.95 (978-1-880000-53-3(9), leelowbooks) Lee & Low Bks., Inc.

Condé, Maryse. Reves Amers. pap. 17.95 (978-2-7470-0350-6(7)) Bayard Editions FRA. Dist: Distribooks, Inc.

Cory, Kim Delmar. Tending Ben's Garden. 2009. 121p. (J). pap. (978-0-88092-778-9(X)) Royal Fireworks Publishing Co.

Cruz, Marie Miranda. Everlasting Nora. 2018. 287p. (YA). (978-1-250-31468-0(2), Starscape) Doherty, Tom Assocs., LLC.

Cullen, Lyn. I Am Rembrandt's Daughter. 2011. 8.88 (978-0-7848-3491-6(1), Everbind) Marco Bk. Co.

Cummins, Maria S. The Lamplighter. 2011. 308p. pap. 16.99 (978-1-61203-228-3(1)) Bottom of the Hill Publishing.

Curtis, Christopher Paul. The Mighty Miss Malone. 320p. (J). (gr. 4-7). 2013. pap. 8.99 (978-0-440-42214-3(0), Yearling) 2012. 15.99 (978-0-385-73491-2(3), Lamb, Wendy Bks.) Random Hse. Children's Bks.

—The Mighty Miss Malone. 2013. lib. bdg. 18.40 (978-0-606-27007-6(8)) Turtleback.

Cushman, Karen. Alchemy & Meggy Swann. 2020. (ENG.). 192p. (J). (gr. 3-7). pap. 7.99 (978-0-358-09749-5(5), 1747606, Clarion Bks.) HarperCollins Pubs.

Dallas, Sandra. Someplace to Call Home. (ENG., Illus.). 240p. (J). (gr. 3-6). 2020. pap. 9.99 (978-1-58536-415-2(0), 204766) 2019. 15.95 (978-1-58536-414-5(2), 204752) Sleeping Bear Pr.

De Los Santos, Elizabeth G. The Secret House. 2011. 18p. pap. 16.95 (978-1-4626-4409-4(0)) America Star Bks.

Dembkoski, Kacey. Believe. 2004. 60p. (YA). pap. 8.95 (978-0-595-30549-0(0)) iUniverse, Inc.

Desai, Anita. The Village by the Sea. 2019. (ENG.). 276p. (J). (gr. 4-7). pap. 12.99 (978-1-68137-351-5(3), NYRB Kids) New York Review of Bks., Inc., The.

Deuker, Carl. Runner. 2007. (ENG.). 224p. (YA). (gr. 7-12). pap. 15.99 (978-0-618-73505-1(4), 410112, Clarion Bks.) HarperCollins Pubs.

Dunagan, Ted M. A Yellow Watermelon. 2014. (ENG.). 240p. (J). pap. 17.95 (978-1-58838-301-3(6), 8630, NewSouth Bks.) NewSouth, Inc.

Elliott, Ruth & Elliott, David. The Richest Kid in the Poor House. Elliott, Ruth, illus. 2008. (Illus.). (J). pap. (978-0-9795017-4-6(1)) Edu Designs.

Ellis, Deborah. No Ordinary Day, 1 vol. 2011. (ENG.). (J). 144p. (gr. 3-7). 16.95 (978-1-55498-134-2(4)); 160p. (gr. 4-7). pap. 9.95 (978-1-55498-108-3(5)) Groundwood Bks. CAN. Dist: Publishers Group West (PGW).

Falk, Karen. Tacianna & the Endless Ball of String. 2006. 83p. pap. 19.95 (978-1-4241-3287-4(8)) PublishAmerica, Inc.

Fine, Edith. Armando & the Blue Tarp School, 1 vol. 2007. (ENG., Illus.). 32p. (J). (gr. -1-3). lib. bdg. 17.95 (978-1-58430-278-0(X)) Lee & Low Bks., Inc.

Fine, Edith Hope & Pinkerton Josephson, Judith. Armando y la Escuela de Lona Azul: Armando & the Blue Tarp School, 1 vol. Sosa, Hernán, illus. 2014.Tr. of Armando & the Blue Tarp School. (SPA.). 32p. (J). (gr. 3-5). pap. 12.95 (978-1-60060-449-2(8), leelowbooks) Lee & Low Bks., Inc.

Foreman, Michael. El Jardin del Nino: Una Historia de Esperanza. Diego, Rapi & Flores, Martha, illus. 2009. (SPA.). 30p. (J). (gr. 1-3). 14.99 (978-1-933032-56-6(1)) Lectorum Pubns., Inc.

Godby, Ron. The King of Imperial Hill. 2006. 76p. pap. 16.95 (978-1-4241-1061-2(0)) PublishAmerica, Inc.

Goyer, Deb. The Raggedy Beggar. Johnson, Lauren, illus. 2008. 19p. pap. 24.95 (978-1-60703-698-2(3)) America Star Bks.

Harlow, Joan Hiatt. Firestorm! (ENG.). 336p. (J). (gr. 3-7). 2011. pap. 8.99 (978-1-4169-8486-3(0)) 2010. (Illus.). 16.99 (978-1-4169-8485-6(2)) McElderry, Margaret K. Bks. (McElderry, Margaret K. Bks.).

Hartnett, Sonya. Thursday's Child. 2019. (ENG.). 272p. (J). (gr. 9). pap. 7.99 (978-1-5362-0643-2(1)) Candlewick Pr.

Hebert, Marie-Francine. This Side of the Sky, 1 vol. Ouriou, Susan, tr. 2006. (ENG.). 112p. (YA). (gr. 9-18). per. 6.95 (978-0-88995-369-7(4), 6769f377-a38f-45b0-b953-5cf946544e52) Trifolium Bks., Inc. CAN. Dist: Firefly Bks., Ltd.

Helget, Nicole. The End of the Wild. 2018. (ENG., Illus.). 288p. (J). (gr. 3-7). pap. 7.99 (978-0-316-24513-5(5)) Little, Brown Bks. for Young Readers.

Hobbs, Valerie. Maggie & Oliver or a Bone of One's Own. Thermes, Jennifer, illus. 2013. (ENG.). 208p. (J). (gr. 8-12). pap. 21.19 (978-1-250-01672-0(X), 9781250016720) Square Fish.

Horvath, Polly. Very Rich. 2018. 304p. (J). (gr. 3-7). 17.99 (978-0-8234-4028-3(1), Margaret Ferguson Books) Holiday Hse., Inc.
Hubbard, Suzanna. The Lady Who Lived in a Car. 2004. (Illus.). 32p. (J). (978-1-84458-046-0(6), Pavilion Children's Books) Pavilion Bks.
Hudson, Bonnie Rose. The Hidden Village. 2017. (J). (978-1-62856-311-5(7)) BJU Pr.
Hulst, W. G. van de & Hulst, Willem G. van de, illus. The Search for Christmas. 2014. (J). (978-1-928136-12-5(5)) Inheritance Pubns.
Jarman, Benjamin. Tony's Last Touchdown, 1 vol. 2012. (Champion Sports Story Ser.). (ENG.). 104p. (J). (gr. 3-5). 30.60 (978-0-7660-3885-1(8), 88dd6ebb-4e5a-4e51-a3e0-3bbed8fd734f); pap. 13.88 (978-1-4644-0004-9(0), f04c313c-3386-4d8c-802d-e318174c0684) Enslow Publishing, LLC.
Jesperson, Per. Wonder & Magic: The David Tales. 2003. 50p. pap. (978-1-84401-017-2(1)) Athena Pr.
Kehret, Peg. Dangerous Deception. 2015. 208p. (J). (gr. 5). 7.99 (978-0-14-751175-1(5), Puffin Books) Penguin Young Readers Group.
Lachenmeyer, Nathaniel. Broken Beaks. Ingpen, Robert R., illus. 2005. 32p. (J). 15.95 (978-0-85572-335-4(1)) Warwick Publishing CAN. Dist: Two Rivers Distribution.
Lehrer, Ruth. Being Fishkill. 2017. (ENG.). 320p. (YA). (gr. 9). 17.99 (978-0-7636-8442-6(2)) Candlewick Pr.
Lipp, Frederick. Running Shoes. Gaillard, Jason, illus. 2008. 32p. (J). (gr. 2-5). pap. 7.95 (978-1-58089-176-9(4)) Charlesbridge Publishing, Inc.
Lupita Manana. 3rd ed. (J). pap., stu. ed. (978-0-13-772500-7(0)) Prentice Hall (Schl. Div.).
Madden, Kerry. Gentle's Holler. 2007. (Maggie Valley Ser.). 237p. (gr. 4-7). 17.00 (978-0-7569-8090-0(9)) Perfection Learning Corp.
Mancil, Arlene. The Angel Explains Christmas Blessings. McKinnon, Joy, illus. 2008. 16p. pap. 24.95 (978-1-60813-297-3(8)) America Star Bks.
Massachusetts Sabbath School Society Staff. Winnie Malone Written for the Mass S S Society, & Approved by the Committee of Publication. 2006. 144p. per. 18.99 (978-1-4255-1163-0(5)) Michigan Publishing.
McKissack, Patricia C. What Is Given from the Heart. Harrison, April, illus. 2019. 40p. (J). (gr. -1-3). 17.99 (978-0-375-83615-2(2), Schwartz & Wade Bks.) Random Hse. Children's Bks.
Morgan, Nicola. Fleshmarket. 2003. (ENG.). 272p. (J). (gr. 7-17). pap. 9.99 (978-0-340-85557-7(6)) Hachette Children's Group GBR. Dist: Hachette Bk. Group.
Morpurgo, Michael. Private Peaceful. 2006. 18.00 (978-0-7569-6630-0(2)) Perfection Learning Corp.
—Private Peaceful. 2006. (YA). 1.25 (978-1-4193-2976-0(6)) Recorded Bks., Inc.
—Private Peaceful. 2006. (ENG., Illus.). 224p. (J). (gr. 7-12). per. 8.99 (978-0-439-63653-7(1), Scholastic Paperbacks) Scholastic, Inc.
Mulligan, Andy. Trash. 2011. (ENG., Illus.). 240p. (YA). (gr. 7-12). pap. 11.99 (978-0-385-75216-9(4), Ember) Random Hse. Children's Bks.
Nargi, Lela. A Heart Just Like My Mother's. Cis, Valeria, illus. 2018. (ENG.). 32p. (J). (gr. -1-2). pap. 7.99 (978-1-5124-2099-9(9), 862306a5-0512-4e3c-b235-a7651e28407a, Kar-Ben Publishing) Lerner Publishing Group.
Nesbit, E. The Story of the Treasure Seekers. 2009. 128p. (gr. 4-7). pap. 5.50 (978-1-60459-695-3(3)) Wilder Pubns., Corp.
—The Story of the Treasure Seekers: Being the Adventures of the Bastable Children in Search of A Fortune. 2006. 132p. (gr. 4-7). per. 10.95 (978-1-59818-963-6(8)); 24.95 (978-1-59818-172-2(6)) Aegypan.
Noble, Trinka Hakes. The Orange Shoes. Ettinger, Doris, illus. rev. ed. 2007. (ENG.). 40p. (J). (gr. 1-4). 16.95 (978-1-58536-277-6(8), 202088) Sleeping Bear Pr.
—Rettie & the Ragamuffin Parade: A Thanksgiving Story. Gardner, David C., illus. 2017. (Tales of Young Americans Ser.). (ENG.). 32p. (J). (gr. 1-4). 17.95 (978-1-58536-960-7(8), 204322) Sleeping Bear Pr.
Optic, Oliver, pseud. Poor & Proud; or, the Fortunes of Katy Redburn a Story for Young Folks by Oliver Optic [Pseud]. 2006. 280p. (gr. 4-7). per. 23.99 (978-1-4255-2551-4(2)) Michigan Publishing.
Platt, Randall. Liberty's Christmas. 2012. (ENG.). 200p. (YA). (gr. 7-12). 19.95 (978-0-89672-766-3(1), P208775) Texas Tech Univ. Pr.
Qamar, Amjed. Beneath My Mother's Feet. (ENG.). 208p. (YA). (gr. 7). 2011. pap. 12.99 (978-1-4424-1451-8(0)) 2008. 16.99 (978-1-4169-4728-8(0)) Simon & Schuster Children's Publishing. (Atheneum Bks. for Young Readers).
Reynolds Naylor, Phyllis. I Like Him, He Likes Her: Alice Alone; Simply Alice; Patiently Alice. 2010. (Alice Ser.). (ENG.). 640p. (J). (gr. 7). pap. 12.99 (978-1-4424-0978-1(9), Atheneum Bks. for Young Readers) Simon & Schuster Children's Publishing.
Richardson, Bill. The Promise Basket, 1 vol. Kolesar, Slavka, illus. 2019. (ENG.). 32p. (J). (gr. k-3). 17.95 (978-1-77306-089-7(9)) Groundwood Bks. CAN. Dist: Publishers Group West (PGW).
Rothshank, Brooke, illus. Cups Held Out. 2006. 40p. (J). (gr. -1-3). per. 12.99 (978-0-8361-9316-9(4)) Herald Pr.
Schraff, Anne. The One for Me, 1 vol. 2013. (Urban Underground Ser.). (ENG.). 199p. (YA). (gr. 9-12). pap. 11.95 (978-1-62250-042-0(3)) Saddleback Educational Publishing, Inc.
—Second Chances, 1 vol. 2013. (Urban Underground Ser.). (ENG.). 192p. (YA). (gr. 9-12). pap. 11.95 (978-1-62250-044-4(X)) Saddleback Educational Publishing, Inc.
Sidney, Margaret. Five Little Peppers & How They Grew. 2017. (ENG., Illus.). (J). 24.95 (978-1-374-93472-6(0)); pap. 14.95 (978-1-374-93471-9(2)) Capital Communications, Inc.
—Five Little Peppers & How They Grew. 2006. (Dover Children's Classics Ser.). (ENG., Illus.). 224p. (J). (gr. 3-5). per. 9.95 (978-0-486-45267-8(0), 452670) Dover Pubns., Inc.
Smith, Joye. What Does It Mean to Be Poor? 2005. (Illus.). 30p. (J). 8.99 (978-1-56309-880-2(6)) Woman's Missionary Union.
Snicket, Lemony, pseud. Una Funesta Finestra. pap. 21.95 (978-88-7782-953-5(2)) Salani ITA. Dist: Distribooks, Inc.
Stellings, Caroline. The Contest, 1 vol. 2009. (ENG.). 160p. (J). (gr. 4-7). pap. 9.95 (978-0-9779183-5-5(1), 7th Generation) BPC.
Strasser, Todd. If I Grow Up. (ENG.). 240p. (YA). (gr. 7). 2010. pap. 10.99 (978-1-4169-9443-5(2)) 2009. 17.99 (978-1-4169-2523-1(6)) Simon & Schuster Bks. For Young Readers. (Simon & Schuster Bks. For Young Readers).
Stretton, Hesba. Cassy. Hymper, W. & Stacey, W. S., illus. 2006. (Golden Inheritance Ser.: Vol. 9). 117p. (J). pap. (978-0-921100-94-2(9)) Inheritance Pubns.
—Jessica's First Prayer. Doe, Charles J., ed. 2008. (ENG., Illus.). 54p. (YA). pap. 7.95 (978-0-9817505-2-1(4)) Curiosmith.
—Jessica's First Prayer. 2004. reprint ed. pap. 1.99 (978-1-4192-2751-6(3)); pap. 15.95 (978-1-4191-2751-9(9)) Kessinger Publishing, LLC.
—Jessica's First Prayer. 2006. 84p. pap. 9.95 (978-1-59462-373-8(2), 409, Bk. Jungle) Standard Publications, Inc.
—Lost Gip. 2003. (Golden Inheritance Ser.: Vol. 7). (Illus.). 121p. (J). (978-0-921100-93-5(0)) Inheritance Pubns.
Torres, Jennifer. The Fresh New Face of Griselda. 2019. (ENG., Illus.). 256p. (J). (gr. 3-7). 31.99 (978-0-316-45260-1(2)) Little, Brown Bks. for Young Readers.
Turk, Cheri. The Stone Between Kings. Turk, Cheri, illus. 2012. (Illus.). 36p. pap. 12.99 (978-0-9860024-0-3(2)) Specialty Greetings.
Walters, Eric. Hope Springs. Fernandes, Eugenie, illus. 2014. 32p. (J). (gr. 1-4). 17.99 (978-1-77049-530-2(4), Tundra Bks.) Tundra Bks. CAN. Dist: Penguin Random Hse. LLC.
Wenxuan, Cao. Bronze & Sunflower. So, Meilo, illus. 2019. (ENG.). 400p. (J). (gr. 4-7). pap. 9.99 (978-1-5362-0637-1(7)) Candlewick Pr.
—Bronze & Sunflower. Wang, Helen, tr. So, Meilo, illus. 2017. (ENG.). 400p. (J). (gr. 4-7). 17.99 (978-0-7636-8816-5(9)) Candlewick Pr.
Wessel-Estes, Pam. A Quilt & a Home. 2012. 36p. pap. 14.95 (978-1-4575-1489-0(3)); 24.95 (978-1-4575-1490-6(7)) Dog Ear Publishing, LLC.
Williams, Emma. The Story of Hurry. Quraishi, Ibrahim, illus. 2014. 36p. (J). (gr. -1-2). 16.95 (978-1-60980-589-0(5), Triangle Square) Seven Stories Pr.

POWELL, JOHN WESLEY, 1834-1902

Curtis, Suzanne. John Wesley Powell: American Hero. 2013. (ENG & SPA., Illus.). 78p. (J). pap. 8.95 (978-0-86541-178-4(6)) Filter Pr., LLC.
Maynard, Charles W. John Wesley Powell: Soldier, Scientist, & Explorer. 2009. (Famous Explorers of the American West Ser.). 24p. (gr. 3-4). 42.50 (978-1-61512-505-0(1), PowerKids Pr.) Rosen Publishing Group, Inc., The.
Ross, Michael Elsohn. Exploring the Earth with John Wesley Powell. Smith, Wendy, illus. 2005. (Naturalist's Apprentice Biographies Ser.). 48p. (gr. 3-6). lib. bdg. 19.93 (978-1-57505-254-0(7)) Lerner Publishing Group.
Souza, D. M. John Wesley Powell. 2004. (Watts Library). (ENG., Illus.). 64p. (J). (gr. 5-7). pap. 8.95 (978-0-531-16653-6(8), Watts, Franklin) Scholastic Library Publishing.
Waldman, Stuart. The Last River: John Wesley Powell & the Colorado River Exploring Expedition. Manchess, Gregory, illus. 2015. (ENG.). 48p. (J). (gr. 4-8). pap. 12.95 (978-1-931414-58-6(0), 801deecd-d05d-466d-9a20-9b35acbd1225) Mikaya Pr.

POWER (MECHANICS)

see also Electric Power; Force and Energy; Machinery; Water Power

Alpert, Barbara. How to Make a Pom-Pom Flyer: A 4D Book. 2019. (Hands-On Science Fun Ser.). (ENG., Illus.). 24p. (J). (gr. -1-2). lib. bdg. 29.32 (978-1-9771-0224-9(7), 139237, Capstone Pr.) Capstone.
Bishop, Amanda. Energy Conservation, 1 vol. 2009. (Saving Our World Ser.). (ENG.). 32p. (gr. 4-4). lib. bdg. 31.21 (978-0-7614-3224-1(8), ef0d4ce0-c74e-4134-a440-54eb70a8532c) Cavendish Square Publishing LLC.
Braun, Eric. Lance Dragon Defends His Castle with Simple Machines, 1 vol. Briglia, Anthony, illus. 2012. (In the Science Lab Ser.). (ENG.). 24p. (J). (gr. k-3). pap. 9.95 (978-1-4048-7708-5(8), 120444, Picture Window Bks.) Capstone.
Carlson Berne, Emma. Speeding! Mechanical Energy, 1 vol. 2013. (Energy Everywhere Ser.). (ENG., Illus.). 24p. (J). (gr. 2-3). 26.27 (978-1-4488-9651-6(7), 35f8944f-e054-4e0b-b6ef-5d20aead914e); pap. 9.25 (978-1-4488-9760-5(2), 6a727174-7ef7-46c7-938e-23e73d45abc3) Rosen Publishing Group, Inc., The. (PowerKids Pr.).
Claybourne, Anna. Electric Shocks & Other Energy Evils. 2013. (ENG., Illus.). 32p. (J). (978-0-7787-0926-8(4)); pap. (978-0-7787-0953-4(1)) Crabtree Publishing Co.
Farndon, John. Energy, 1 vol. 2003. (Science Experiments Ser.). (ENG.). 32p. (gr. 4-4). 32.64 (978-0-7614-1469-8(X), 8a510038-4e8e-40ee-8e67-99d49abcd187) Cavendish Square Publishing LLC.
Gardner, Robert. Energy: Green Science Projects about Solar, Wind, & Water Power, 1 vol. 2011. (Team Green Science Projects Ser.). (ENG., Illus.). 128p. (gr. 5-6). lib. bdg. 35.93 (978-0-7660-3643-7(X), 7bbbfa62-fcc7-4ac6-af68-c2aa75b8ac5e) Enslow Publishing, LLC.
Greenberger, Robert. How Do We Know the Nature of Energy. (Great Scientific Questions & the Scientists Who Answered Them Ser.). 112p. (gr. 7-12). 2009. 63.90 (978-1-61513-201-0(5)) 2004. (ENG., Illus.). (J). lib. bdg. 39.80 (978-1-4042-0076-0(2), 0f343935-a40f-41ff-b54b-8c387d900053) Rosen Publishing Group, Inc., The.
Heitkamp, Kristina Lyn. What Is Mechanical Energy?, 1 vol. 2017. (Let's Find Out! Forms of Energy Ser.). (ENG., Illus.). 32p. (J). (gr. 2-3). pap. 13.90 (978-1-68048-709-1(4), 7b2d27c2-a1a2-4635-9725-3d836422c8e9, Britannica Educational Publishing) Rosen Publishing Group, Inc., The.
Herweck, Don. All about Energy, 1 vol. rev. ed. 2007. (Science: Informational Text Ser.). (ENG.). 32p. (gr. 3-6). pap. 12.99 (978-0-7439-0571-8(7)) Teacher Created Materials, Inc.
Higgins, Melissa. Energy. 2019. (Little Physicist Ser.). (ENG., Illus.). 32p. (J). (gr. 1-3). pap. 6.95 (978-1-9771-1063-3(0), 141137); lib. bdg. 28.65 (978-1-9771-0960-6(8), 140551) Capstone. (Pebble).
Hyde, Natalie. Pushing & Pulling. 2014. (Motion Close-Up Ser.). (ENG., Illus.). 24p. (J). (-1). (978-0-7787-0529-1(3)) Crabtree Publishing Co.
Jennings, Terry. Forces. 2009. (Science Alive Ser.). (ENG., Illus.). 32p. (J). pap. (978-1-897563-54-0(X)) Saunders Bk. Co.
Jennings, Terry J. Forces. 2009. (J). 28.50 (978-1-59920-269-3(7)) Black Rabbit Bks.
Johanson, Paula. What Is Energy?, 1 vol. 2014. (Let's Find Out! Physical Science Ser.). (ENG.). 32p. (J). (gr. 2-3). 26.06 (978-1-62275-492-2(1), 33356fbb-7633-4ed2-808b-cdd6701955dd) Rosen Publishing Group, Inc., The.
National Geographic Learning. Reading Expeditions (Science: Physical Science): Introduction to Energy. 2007. (Nonfiction Reading & Writing Workshops Ser.). (ENG., Illus.). 32p. (J). pap. 18.95 (978-0-7922-4580-3(6)) CENGAGE Learning.
Nixon, Jonathan. Energy Engineering & Powering the Future. 2016. (Engineering in Action Ser.). (ENG., Illus.). 32p. (J). (gr. 5-9). (978-0-7787-7539-3(9)) Crabtree Publishing Co.
Petersen, Kristen. Understanding Kinetic Energy. 2015. (J). lib. bdg. (978-1-62713-435-4(2)) Cavendish Square Publishing LLC.
Plummer, Todd. I've Discovered Energy!, 1 vol. 2009. (Eureka! Ser.). (ENG.). 32p. (gr. 4-4). lib. bdg. 31.21 (978-0-7614-3202-9(7), 25358759-a218-48c2-9cbd-71f075c4fd90) Cavendish Square Publishing LLC.
Rau, Dana Meachen. Levers & Pulleys. 2009. (Explorer Library: Science Explorer Ser.). (ENG., Illus.). 32p. (gr. 4-8). lib. bdg. 32.07 (978-1-60279-537-2(1), 200282) Cherry Lake Publishing.
Stoyles, Pennie & Pentland, Peter. Everyday Technology, 1 vol. 2012. (Energy in Action Ser.). (ENG.). 32p. (gr. 6-6). 31.21 (978-1-60870-567-2(6), 86fb157f-53e4-4bf8-b1dc-fb1bdeed770a) Cavendish Square Publishing LLC.
Walker, Sally M. & Feldmann, Roseann. Palancas. King, Andy, photos by. 2009. (Libros de Fisica para Madrugadores Ser.). (SPA., Illus.). 47p. (J). (gr. 3-7). pap. 11.95 (978-0-8225-2973-6(4)) Lerner Publishing Group.
West, Herbert. Forms of Energy, 1 vol. (Amazing Science Ser.). (ENG., 24p. (gr. 3-3). 2009. Illus.). (J). lib. bdg. 26.27 (978-1-4358-2975-6(1), 8570a3ba-b202-4b32-8328-887565a77f22, PowerKids Pr.) 2008. pap. 8.25 (978-1-4358-0123-3(7), f4e7db09-96a0-4f31-a25a-fdbb23c23572, Rosen Classroom) Rosen Publishing Group, Inc., The.

POWER (SOCIAL SCIENCES)

Lankford, Ronald D., Jr., ed. Are America's Wealthy Too Powerful?, 1 vol. 2010. (At Issue Ser.). (ENG.). 112p. (gr. 10-12). 41.03 (978-0-7377-5087-4(1), 924e6a5c-2a36-4487-b8ed-9893e22dc4c3); pap. 28.80 (978-0-7377-5088-1(X), 8a835fae-2adf-4940-8c1b-8b259dda60ae) Greenhaven Publishing LLC. (Greenhaven Publishing).
Wiener, Gary, ed. Privilege in America, 1 vol. 2019. (Opposing Viewpoints Ser.). (ENG.). 200p. (gr. 10-12). pap. 34.80 (978-1-5345-0602-2(0), d970db98-a64c-43db-a0a7-defe6b30442c) Greenhaven Publishing LLC.
Wilkerson, Isabel. Caste (Adapted for Young Adults) 2022. (ENG.). 352p. (YA). (gr. 7). 18.99 (978-0-593-42794-1(7)); lib. bdg. 21.99 (978-0-593-42795-8(5)) Random Hse. Children's Bks. (Delacorte Pr.).
Wilkerson, Isabel, contrib. by. Caste (Adapted for Young Adults) 2023. (ENG.). 352p. (YA). (gr. 7). pap. 12.99 **(978-0-593-42797-2(1)**, Ember) Random Hse. Children's Bks.

POWER BOATS

see Motorboats

POWER RESOURCES

see also Electric Power; Fuel; Solar Energy; Water Power

Aitken, Stephen, illus. How to Cure Earth's Fever. 2011. (J). (978-1-61641-674-4(2)) Magic Wagon.
Alkire, Jessie. Natural Gas Energy: Putting Gas to Work. 2018. (Earth's Energy Innovations Ser.). (ENG., Illus.). 24p. (J). (gr. k-4). lib. bdg. 32.79 (978-1-5321-1572-1(5), 28998, Super SandCastle) ABDO Publishing Co.
—Natural Gas Energy Projects: Easy Energy Activities for Future Engineers! 2018. (Earth's Energy Experiments Ser.). (ENG., Illus.). 32p. (J). (gr. k-4). lib. bdg. 34.21 (978-1-5321-1563-9(6), 28980, Super SandCastle) ABDO Publishing Co.
Aloian, Molly. Green Energy. 2013. (ENG., Illus.). 24p. (J). (978-0-7787-0265-8(0)); pap. (978-0-7787-0284-9(7)) Crabtree Publishing Co.
Bailey, Diane. Hydropower. 2014. (Harnessing Energy Ser.). (ENG.). 48p. (J). (gr. 5-8). pap. 12.00 (978-0-89812-996-0(6), 21353, Creative Paperbacks) Creative Co., The.
—Natural Gas Power. 2014. (Harnessing Energy Ser.). (ENG.). 48p. (J). (gr. 5-8). pap. 12.00 (978-0-89812-995-3(8), 21356, Creative Paperbacks) Creative Co., The.
Bailey, Gerry. Out of Energy, 1 vol. 2011. (Planet SOS Ser.). (ENG., Illus.). 48p. (J). (gr. 4-5). pap. 15.05 (978-1-4339-4979-1(2), ca3aae56-c396-4b06-abe1-98ea9e16d790); lib. bdg. 34.60 (978-1-4339-4978-4(4), f084b4fd-2536-4f54-8523-1986dc22daf0) Stevens, Gareth Publishing LLLP. (Gareth Stevens Learning Library).
Bard, Mariel. Geothermal Energy: Harnessing the Power of Earth's Heat, 1 vol. 2017. (Powered up! a STEM Approach to Energy Sources Ser.). (ENG.). 24p. (J). (gr. 3-3). pap. 9.25 (978-1-5383-2851-4(8), c80a5c3a-a2bb-4e8c-b867-43d08313b3a0, PowerKids Pr.) Rosen Publishing Group, Inc., The.
Barker, Geoff. How Renewable Energy Works, 1 vol. 2013. (EcoWorks Ser.). 32p. (J). (gr. 3-4). (ENG.). pap. 11.50 (978-1-4339-9569-9(7), 67c1c161-0574-4af8-855a-94b4192334de); pap. 63.00 (978-1-4339-9570-5(0)); (ENG., Illus.). lib. bdg. 29.27 (978-1-4339-9568-2(9), abe542d1-95fb-42fc-afe8-4c3df8d5899b) Stevens, Gareth Publishing LLLP.
Barnham, Kay. Save Energy. 2007. (Environment Action Ser.). (ENG.). 32p. (J). (gr. 3-7). pap. (978-0-7787-3670-7(9)) Crabtree Publishing Co.
Bayden, Maya. What Is Chemical Energy?, 1 vol. 2017. (Let's Find Out! Forms of Energy Ser.). (ENG., Illus.). 32p. (J). (gr. 2-3). pap. 13.90 (978-1-68048-693-3(4), 51c976cf-83f2-4d1a-8c13-51fcf1a9017c, Britannica Educational Publishing) Rosen Publishing Group, Inc., The.
Benchmark Education Company, LLC Staff. Energy Resources Around the World Teacher's Guide. 2004. (978-1-4108-2587-2(6)) Benchmark Education Co.
Benduhn, Tea. Energy for Today, 8 vols., Set. Incl. Ethanol & Other New Fuels. lib. bdg. 24.67 (978-0-8368-9260-4(7), 864984a0-bbfe-44da-a754-9dfcd168eed6); Nuclear Power. lib. bdg. 24.67 (978-0-8368-9262-8(3), 75a03bf9-9898-4309-8a58-3c22a49f5885); Oil, Gas, & Coal. lib. bdg. 24.67 (978-0-8368-9261-1(5), 2f03570a-dc2b-40bb-85ab-7bfd48783f3b); Solar Power. lib. bdg. 24.67 (978-0-8368-9263-5(1), 00ea634b-05b8-49a6-a454-a6097b38e363); Water Power. lib. bdg. 24.67 (978-0-8368-9264-2(X), 31418883-593d-4e1b-8b3f-326adad1666d); (J). (gr. 3-3). (Energy for Today Ser.). (ENG.). 24p. 2008. Set lib. bdg. 98.68 (978-0-8368-9318-2(2), 6e476b70-42b0-4230-8711-093c5c8665e2, Weekly Reader Leveled Readers) Stevens, Gareth Publishing LLLP.
—Etanol y Otros Combustibles Nuevos (Ethanol & Other New Fuels), 1 vol. 2008. (Energía para el Presente (Energy for Today) Ser.). (SPA.). 24p. (gr. 3-3). (J). lib. bdg. 24.67 (978-0-8368-9266-6(6), a1d5a969-5b9b-48e7-96b1-a6e1ebbe7abc); pap. 9.15 (978-0-8368-9365-6(4), f0e752a7-8dde-4f80-b78d-42f27b3f95a1) Stevens, Gareth Publishing LLLP. (Weekly Reader Leveled Readers).
—Ethanol & Other New Fuels, 1 vol. 2008. (Energy for Today Ser.). (ENG.). 24p. (gr. 3-3). (J). lib. bdg. 24.67 (978-0-8368-9260-4(7), 864984a0-bbfe-44da-a754-9dfcd168eed6); pap. 9.15 (978-0-8368-9359-5(X), 6b6eba5d-72bd-45c4-8ff9-f3accce9c18c) Stevens, Gareth Publishing LLLP. (Weekly Reader Leveled Readers).
—Petróleo, Gas y Carbón (Oil, Gas, & Coal), 1 vol. 2008. (Energía para el Presente (Energy for Today) Ser.). (SPA.). 24p. (gr. 3-3). (J). lib. bdg. 24.67 (978-0-8368-9267-3(4), c1ae05a3-f486-4854-912a-1cad33c1762c); pap. 9.15 (978-0-8368-9366-3(2), a8e99776-3372-46b6-b2d0-edc38b4920f5) Stevens, Gareth Publishing LLLP. (Weekly Reader Leveled Readers).
—Solar Power, 1 vol. 2008. (Energy for Today Ser.). (ENG.). 24p. (gr. 3-3). (J). lib. bdg. 24.67 (978-0-8368-9263-5(1), 00ea634b-05b8-49a6-a454-a6097b38e363); pap. 9.15 (978-0-8368-9362-5(X), 52b8eae1-7221-4d42-8de3-13e122439133) Stevens, Gareth Publishing LLLP. (Weekly Reader Leveled Readers).
Beres, Samantha. Energy Resources Around the World: Set Of 6. 2011. (Navigators Ser.). (J). pap. 50.00 net. (978-1-4108-2572-8(8)) Benchmark Education Co.
—Energy Resources Around the World & Recursos energéticos alrededor del Mundo: 6 English, 6 Spanish Adaptations. 2011. (ENG & SPA.). (J). 101.00 net. (978-1-4108-5738-5(7)) Benchmark Education Co.
Bickerstaff, Linda. Oil Power of the Future: New Ways of Turning Petroleum into Energy. 2009. (Library of Future Energy Ser.). 64p. (gr. 5-5). 58.50 (978-1-60853-628-3(9)) Rosen Publishing Group, Inc., The.
Bishop, Amanda. Energy Conservation, 1 vol. 2009. (Saving Our World Ser.). (ENG.). 32p. (gr. 4-4). lib. bdg. 31.21 (978-0-7614-3224-1(8), ef0d4ce0-c74e-4134-a440-54eb70a8532c) Cavendish Square Publishing LLC.
Bjorklund, Ruth. The Pros & Cons of Algae Biofuel, 1 vol. 2015. (Economics of Energy Ser.). (ENG.). 80p. (YA). (gr. 7-7). 37.36 (978-1-5026-0954-0(1), 4a7971c7-3820-44db-81ea-4dc2f05dab16) Cavendish Square Publishing LLC.
Bow, James. Energy from Earth's Core: Geothermal Energy. 2015. (Next Generation Energy Ser.). (ENG., Illus.). 32p. (J). (gr. 5-5). (978-0-7787-1979-3(0)) Crabtree Publishing Co.
—Energy from the Sun: Solar Power. 2015. (Next Generation Energy Ser.). (ENG., Illus.). 32p. (J). (gr. 5-5). (978-0-7787-1982-3(0)) Crabtree Publishing Co.
Bowden, Rob. Energy Sources: The Impact of Science & Technology, 1 vol. 2009. (Pros & Cons Ser.). (ENG.). 64p. (YA). (gr. 5-8). lib. bdg. 37.67 (978-1-4339-1987-9(7), c7e1e19f-fd2e-4217-a717-d0a976696695) Stevens, Gareth Publishing LLLP.
Brearley, Laurie. Solar Power: Capturing the Sun's Energy (a True Book: Alternative Energy) 2018. (True Book (Relaunch) Ser.). (ENG., Illus.). 48p. (J). (gr. 3-5). pap. 7.95 (978-0-531-23943-8(8), Children's Pr.) Scholastic Library Publishing.
—Solar Power: Capturing the Sun's Energy (a True Book: Alternative Energy) (Library Edition) 2018. (True Book (Relaunch) Ser.). (ENG., Illus.). 48p. (J). (gr. 3-5). lib. bdg. 31.00 (978-0-531-23686-4(2), Children's Pr.) Scholastic Library Publishing.
Brennan, Linda Crotta. Geothermal Power. 2013. (Explorer Library: Language Arts Explorer Ser.). (ENG.). 32p. (gr. 4-8). pap. 14.21 (978-1-61080-919-1(X), 202557); (Illus.). 32.07 (978-1-61080-894-1(0), 202555); (Illus.). E-Book 49.21 (978-1-61080-969-6(6), 202558) Cherry Lake Publishing.
Brezina, Corona. Jobs in Sustainable Energy. 2010. (Green Careers Ser.). 80p. (YA). (gr. 7-12). E-Book 61.20 (978-1-4488-0136-7(2)); (ENG., Illus.). (gr. 6-6). lib. bdg. 38.47 (978-1-4358-3569-6(7), 848f836d-2c52-4bf5-b300-bbad9698cb46) Rosen Publishing Group, Inc., The.

Brown Bear Books. Power & Energy. 2012. (Invention & Technology Ser.). (ENG.). 64p. (J). (gr. 8-11). lib. bdg. 39.95 (978-1-936333-39-4(2), 16525) Brown Bear Bks.

Bryan, Bethany. How Electricity Changed the World, 1 vol. 2018. (Inventions That Changed the World Ser.). (ENG.). 64p. (J). (gr. 5-5). pap. 16.28 (978-1-5026-4104-5(6), a357ea00-9502-4859-b96e-f7a3b0c768c4) Cavendish Square Publishing LLC.

Burgan, Michael. Energy, Vol. 10. 2016. (Stem in Current Events Ser.). (Illus.). 64p. (J). (gr. 7). 23.95 (978-1-4222-3589-8(0)) Mason Crest.

Carr, Aaron. Oil Security. 2018. (J). (978-1-5105-2229-9(8)) SmartBook Media, Inc.

Cartlidge, Cherese. Alternative Energy. (J). 2011. (978-1-60217-029-2(0)) 2008. (978-1-60217-022-3(3)) Erickson Pr.

Centore, Michael. Renewable Energy, Vol. 12. 2015. (North American Natural Resources Ser.). (Illus.). 64p. (J). (gr. 7). 23.95 (978-1-4222-3387-0(1)) Mason Crest.

Chambers, Catherine. Energy in Crisis. 2010. (Protecting Our Planet Ser.). (ENG., Illus.). 32p. (J). (gr. 3-6). (978-0-7787-5212-7(7)); pap. (978-0-7787-5229-5(1)) Crabtree Publishing Co.

Cunningham, Anne C. Critical Perspectives on Fossil Fuels vs. Renewable Energy, 1 vol. 2016. (Analyzing the Issues Ser.). (ENG.). 208p. (gr. 8-8). lib. bdg. 50.93 (978-0-7660-8131-4(1), 94479f9f-1b34-4ee3-965a-9948e468eeb1) Enslow Publishing, LLC.

De la Garza, Amanda, ed. Biomass: Energy from Plants & Animals, 1 vol. 2006. (Fueling the Future Ser.). (ENG., Illus.). 112p. (gr. 10-12). lib. bdg. 46.23 (978-0-7377-3586-4(4), 6164039c-b3a3-459e-b5b1-2f2b8c4ce3d8, Greenhaven Publishing) Greenhaven Publishing LLC.

Dickmann, Nancy. Energy from Nuclear Fission: Splitting the Atom. 2015. (Next Generation Energy Ser.). (ENG., Illus.). 32p. (J). (gr. 5-5). (978-0-7787-1981-6(2)) Crabtree Publishing Co.

—Harnessing Geothermal Energy, 1 vol. 2016. (Future of Power Ser.). (ENG., Illus.). 32p. (J). (gr. 4-5). pap. 11.00 (978-1-4994-3211-4(9), dcd36dc6-fffb-4619-a7d7-e1f62aec43e3, PowerKids Pr.) Rosen Publishing Group, Inc., The.

—Harnessing Hydroelectric Energy, 1 vol. 2016. (Future of Power Ser.). (ENG.). 32p. (J). (gr. 4-5). pap. 11.00 (978-1-4994-3212-1(7), b5b5b52f-3d8e-4a5a-b6a6-5b1195d3400c, PowerKids Pr.) Rosen Publishing Group, Inc., The.

—Using Renewable Energy. 2018. (Putting the Planet First Ser.). (Illus.). 32p. (J). (gr. 4-4). (978-0-7787-5032-1(9)) Crabtree Publishing Co.

Diehn, Andi. Energy. Li, Hui, illus. 2018. (Picture Book Science Ser.). (ENG.). 32p. (J). (gr. k-3). 19.95 (978-1-61930-639-4(5), 4226f10c-b2e6-4c06-abf6-1c0183c553dc) Nomad Pr.

Doeden, Matt. Finding Out about Wind Energy. 2014. (Searchlight Books (tm) — What Are Energy Sources? Ser.). (ENG., Illus.). 40p. (J). (gr. 3-5). pap. 9.99 (978-1-4677-4558-1(8), 49dcd6db-b31c-4dc5-b0b4-bbd59237d414) Lerner Publishing Group.

Draper, Allison Stark. Hydropower of the Future: New Ways of Turning Water into Energy. 2009. (Library of Future Energy Ser.). 64p. (gr. 5-5). 58.50 (978-1-60853-626-9(2)) Rosen Publishing Group, Inc., The.

Drummond, Alan. Energy Island: How One Community Harnessed the Wind & Changed Their World. 2015. (J). lib. bdg. 18.40 (978-0-606-37353-1(5)) Turtleback.

Drummond, Allan. Energy Island: How One Community Harnessed the Wind & Changed Their World. Drummond, Allan, illus. 2011. (Green Power Ser.). (ENG., Illus.). 40p. (J). (gr. 1-5). 19.99 (978-0-374-32184-0(1), 900065067, Farrar, Straus & Giroux (BYR)) Farrar, Straus & Giroux.

Eboch, M. M. The 12 Biggest Breakthroughs in Energy Technology. 2014. (ENG.). 32p. (J). 32.80 (978-1-63235-013-8(0), 12-Story Library) Bookstaves, LLC.

The Economics of Energy, 12 vols. 2014. (Economics of Energy Ser.). (ENG.). 80p. (YA). (gr. 7-7). 224.16 (978-1-62713-132-2(9), 09602b32-4c8a-4e14-98b1-79a567b2233f, Cavendish Square) Cavendish Square Publishing LLC.

Einspruch, Andrew. What Is Energy?, 1 vol., 1. 2014. (Discovery Education: How It Works). (ENG.). 32p. (gr. 4-5). 28.93 (978-1-4777-6321-6(X), 634d0cd1-b7c9-46ae-a2d4-a5264bfa9154, PowerKids Pr.) Rosen Publishing Group, Inc., The.

Enz, Tammy. Harness It: Invent New Ways to Harness Energy & Nature. 2012. (Invent It Ser.). (ENG.). 32p. (gr. 3-4). pap. 47.70 (978-1-4296-8456-9(9), Capstone Pr.); (J). pap. 8.10 (978-1-4296-7982-4(4), 118314) Capstone.

Farrell, Courtney. Save the Planet: Using Alternative Energies. 2010. (Explorer Library: Language Arts Explorer Ser.). (ENG.). 32p. (gr. 4-8). pap. 14.21 (978-1-60279-672-0(6), 200919) Cherry Lake Publishing.

—Save the Planet: Using Alternative Energies. 2010. (Explorer Library: Language Arts Explorer Ser.). (ENG., Illus.). 32p. (gr. 4-8). lib. bdg. 32.07 (978-1-60279-663-8(7), 200356) Cherry Lake Publishing.

Faulkner, Nicholas & Johanson, Paula. Nonrenewable Resources & You, 1 vol. 2018. (How Our Choices Impact Earth Ser.). (ENG.). 64p. (gr. 6-6). 36.13 (978-1-5081-8150-7(0), f428a863-b2c1-4734-b905-b4459b1453a2, Rosen Reference) Rosen Publishing Group, Inc., The.

Faust, Daniel R. Energy Crisis: The Future of Fossil Fuels, 1 vol. 2007. (Jr. Graphic Environmental Dangers Ser.). (ENG., Illus.). 24p. (gr. 4-4). (J). lib. bdg. 28.93 (978-1-4042-4231-9(7), efd1c6ec-b591-4b55-a0d5-a7ca0761f88f); pap. 10.60 (978-1-4042-4598-3(7), 77a33dff-9955-4124-b054-8e07a8e5610f) Rosen Publishing Group, Inc., The.

Faust, Daniel R. & Obregón, José María. Crisis Energética: El Futuro de Los Combustibles Fósiles, 1 vol. 2009. (Historietas Juveniles: Peligros Del Medioambiente (Jr. Graphic Environmental Dangers) Ser.). (SPA., Illus.). 24p. (gr. 4-4). pap. 10.60 (978-1-4358-8466-3(3), 40072f0a-23f3-4d06-b984-3d919e93fab1); (YA). lib. bdg. 28.93 (978-1-4358-8465-6(5), 4a340f1d-cead-4747-9af7-1b2a30eaf61c) Rosen Publishing Group, Inc., The.

Flath, Camden. Careers in Green Energy: Fueling the World with Renewable Resources. 2010. (New Careers for the 21st Century Ser.). 64p. (YA). (gr. 7-18). lib. bdg. 22.95 (978-1-4222-1812-9(0)) Mason Crest.

Fridell, Ron. Earth-Friendly Energy. 2008. (Saving Our Living Earth Ser.). 72p. (YA). (gr. 4-7). lib. bdg. 30.60 (978-0-8225-7563-4(9)) Lerner Publishing Group.

The Future of Power, 12 vols. 2016. (Future of Power Ser.). (ENG.). 00032p. (J). (gr. 4-5). 167.58 (978-1-4994-3187-2(2), b7969f44-98cb-4954-a371-db919b3efc89, PowerKids Pr.) Rosen Publishing Group, Inc., The.

Gerdes, Louise I., ed. Wave & Tidal Power, 1 vol. 2010. (At Issue Ser.). (ENG.). 120p. (gr. 10-12). 41.03 (978-0-7377-4900-7(8), 24e3fa32-8c53-41f5-8754-40044c0ff2a4, Greenhaven Publishing) Greenhaven Publishing LLC.

Gibbons, Gail. Clean Energy. 2014. (J). (978-0-8234-3068-0(5)) Holiday Hse., Inc.

Gillett, Jack & Gillett, Meg. Energy-Resource Maps, 1 vol. 2012. (Maps of the Environmental World Ser.). (ENG., Illus.). 32p. (J). (gr. 5-5). 30.27 (978-1-4488-8614-2(7), 48bc3b16-ac65-46b5-aaa5-35d3e26b33f7); pap. 11.60 (978-1-4488-8621-0(X), 44fa476c-f05a-4139-9419-2dc5140d5975) Rosen Publishing Group, Inc., The. (PowerKids Pr.).

Gish, Melissa. Energy. 2005. (My First Look at Science Ser.). (Illus.). 24p. (J). (gr. k-3). lib. bdg. 15.95 (978-1-58341-372-2(3), Creative Education) Creative Co., The.

Goodman, Polly. Energy Today & Tomorrow, 1 vol. 2011. (Earth Alert! Ser.). (ENG.). 32p. (YA). (gr. 3-4). lib. bdg. 29.27 (978-1-4339-6002-4(8), f430d1b0-d362-479c-bea8-e3b7587488e9) Stevens, Gareth Publishing LLLP.

Gordon, Sherri Mabry. Green & Clean Energy: What You Can Do, 1 vol. 2010. (Green Issues in Focus Ser.). (ENG., Illus.). 128p. (gr. 6-7). lib. bdg. 35.93 (978-0-7660-3348-1(1), c094651a-f5e1-4fdf-a161-0b458439d606) Enslow Publishing, LLC.

Gosman, Gillian. Earth-Friendly Energy, 1 vol. 2011. (How to Be Earth Friendly Ser.). (ENG., Illus.). 32p. (gr. 3-4). (J). pap. 11.00 (978-1-4488-2763-3(9), 29a930f7-7d9f-4bc9-8461-597b0f9b5f24, PowerKids Pr.); (YA). lib. bdg. 28.93 (978-1-4488-2587-5(3), 19bb172b-ac83-4c7a-9b70-1f02375fe079) Rosen Publishing Group, Inc., The.

Green, Jen. Energy for the Future. 2006. (Illus.). 32p. (YA). (gr. 4-18). lib. bdg. 27.10 (978-1-59389-119-0(9)) Chrysalis Education.

—Using Energy Wisely, 1 vol. 2011. (Sherlock Bones Looks at the Environment Ser.). (ENG., Illus.). 32p. (YA). (gr. 5-5). lib. bdg. 29.93 (978-1-61533-346-2(0), a6f795e3-883e-4978-a7d4-5a50c47cbc0a, Windmill Bks.) Rosen Publishing Group, Inc., The.

Green, Robert. How Renewable Energy Is Changing Society. 2015. (ENG., Illus.). 80p. (J). lib. bdg. (978-1-60152-904-6(X)) ReferencePoint Pr., Inc.

Gregory, Joy. Energy. 2017. (978-1-5105-1931-2(9)) SmartBook Media, Inc.

Gunderson, Jessica. The Energy Dilemma. 2010. (Earth Issues Ser.). 48p. (YA). (gr. 5-18). 23.95 (978-1-58341-980-9(2), Creative Education) Creative Co., The.

Hall, Linley Erin, ed. Critical Perspectives on Energy & Power. 2009. (Scientific American Critical Anthologies on Environment & Climate Ser.). 208p. (gr. 9-9). 63.90 (978-1-60853-065-6(5)) Rosen Publishing Group, Inc., The.

Hand, Carol. The Great Hope for an Energy Alternative: Laser-Powered Fusion Energy, 1 vol. 2010. (In the News Ser.). (ENG.). 64p. (YA). (gr. 6-6). pap. 13.95 (978-1-4488-1682-8(3), 5988e8f6-11d3-467d-b066-6ee585513c31); lib. bdg. 37.13 (978-1-4358-9450-1(2), f7d454c3-c008-4b2c-a91c-cc86710f8898) Rosen Publishing Group, Inc., The.

Haugen, David M. & Musser, Susan, eds. Renewable Energy, 1 vol. 2012. (Opposing Viewpoints Ser.). (ENG., Illus.). 256p. (gr. 10-12). pap. 34.80 (978-0-7377-6140-5(7), 5e7e8cc6-2163-48af-afe6-f8a5ac22c063); lib. bdg. 50.43 (978-0-7377-6139-9(3), 901a548c-5495-49f5-9e18-d8d9f7ff53f7) Greenhaven Publishing LLC. (Greenhaven Publishing).

Hawbaker, Emily. Energy Lab for Kids: 40 Exciting Experiments to Explore, Create, Harness, & Unleash Energy, Volume 11. 2017. (Lab for Kids Ser.: 11). (ENG., Illus.). 144p. (J). (gr. 5-9). pap. 22.99 (978-1-63159-250-8(5), 223698, Quarry Bks.) Quarto Publishing Group USA.

Heinrichs, Ann. Sustaining Earth's Energy Resources, 1 vol. 2011. (Environment at Risk Ser.). (ENG.). 112p. (YA). (gr. 7-7). 42.64 (978-0-7614-4007-9(0), 91ead577-e9d7-4a26-b43b-cd10a492902b) Cavendish Square Publishing LLC.

Herweck, Don. All about Energy, 1 vol. rev. ed. 2007. (Science: Informational Text Ser.). (ENG.). 32p. (gr. 3-6). pap. 12.99 (978-0-7439-0571-8(7)) Teacher Created Materials, Inc.

Hewitt, Sally. Using Energy. 2008. (Green Team Ser.). (ENG., Illus.). 32p. (J). (gr. 3-7). pap. (978-0-7787-4103-9(6), 1286252); lib. bdg. (978-0-7787-4096-4(X), 1286252) Crabtree Publishing Co.

Hicks, Dwayne. Solving the Energy Crisis, 1 vol. 2016. (Global Guardians Ser.). (ENG.). 24p. (J). (gr. 3-3). pap. 9.25 (978-1-4994-2752-3(2), fd8bd52f-5880-4ac8-8daf-a79fecc9cb43, PowerKids Pr.) Rosen Publishing Group, Inc., The.

Higgins, Melissa. Energy. 2019. (Little Physicist Ser.). (ENG., Illus.). 32p. (J). (gr. 1-3). pap. 6.95 (978-1-9771-1063-3(0), 141137); lib. bdg. 28.65 (978-1-9771-0960-6(8), 140551) Capstone. (Pebble).

Holt, Rinehart and Winston Staff. Environmental Science Chptr. 17: Nonrenewable Energy. 4th ed. Date not set. pap. 11.20 (978-0-03-068078-6(6)) Holt McDougal.

—Holt Science & Technology Chapter 5: Earth Science: Energy Resources. 5th ed. 2004. (Illus.). pap. 12.86 (978-0-03-030286-2(2)) Holt McDougal.

Howell, Izzi. Energy Eco Facts. 2019. (Eco Facts Ser.). (ENG., Illus.). 32p. (J). (gr. 5-5). pap. (978-0-7787-6362-8(5), 0039eab2-ce12-43e0-bb93-23b6f0d810f9); lib. bdg. (978-0-7787-6346-8(3), 4d1e2ec4-014b-47bb-9f0f-2a497d2d4856) Crabtree Publishing Co.

Hunter, Nick. Energy for Everyone? the Business of Energy, 1 vol. 2012. (Big-Buck Business Ser.). (ENG., Illus.). 48p. (J). (gr. 6-6). 34.60 (978-1-4339-7751-0(6), c838accc-d019-461e-997a-4f0c9194f90e); pap. 15.05 (978-1-4339-7752-7(4), bc001b91-93c6-4104-8427-3e363f5a8842) Stevens, Gareth Publishing LLLP. (Gareth Stevens Secondary Library).

—Science vs. the Energy Crisis, 1 vol. 2013. (Science Fights Back Ser.). (ENG., Illus.). 48p. (gr. 4-5). 34.60 (978-1-4339-8695-6(7), 3a11a179-8409-4ff1-a01f-d33347aff0c0); pap. 15.05 (978-1-4339-8696-3(5), f2be7ecc-5636-4107-82b7-228068a69dbe) Stevens, Gareth Publishing LLLP. (Gareth Stevens Learning Library).

Hunter, Rebecca. Energy Supply. 2012. (Eco Alert! Ser.). (ENG., Illus.). 32p. (gr. 4-6). lib. bdg. 28.50 (978-1-59771-296-5(5)) Sea-To-Sea Pubns.

Ivanovich, Nikolai. Sources of Energy, 1 vol. 2013. (InfoMax Readers Ser.). (ENG.). 24p. (J). (gr. 3-3). pap. 8.25 (978-1-4777-2643-3(8), 2bee3b57-abf7-4609-83e3-fcf5f85bec01); pap. 49.50 (978-1-4777-2644-0(6)) Rosen Publishing Group, Inc., The. (Rosen Classroom).

James, Alice. See Inside Energy IR. 2018. (See Inside Board Bks.). (ENG.). 16p. 14.99 (978-0-7945-4131-6(3), Usborne) EDC Publishing.

Jefferis, David. Green Power: Eco-Energy Without Pollution. 2006. (Science Frontiers Ser.). (ENG., Illus.). 32p. (J). (gr. 4-7). lib. bdg. (978-0-7787-2857-3(9), 1253435) Crabtree Publishing Co.

Johanson, Paula. What Is Energy?, 1 vol. 2014. (Let's Find Out! Physical Science Ser.). (ENG.). 32p. (J). (gr. 2-3). 26.06 (978-1-62275-492-2(1), 33356fbb-7633-4ed2-808b-cdd6701955dd) Rosen Publishing Group, Inc., The.

Jones, Susan. Solar Power of the Future: New Ways of Turning Sunlight into Energy. 2009. (Library of Future Energy Ser.). 64p. (gr. 5-5). 58.50 (978-1-60853-629-0(7)) Rosen Publishing Group, Inc., The.

Kallen, Stuart A. Cutting Edge Energy Technology. 2016. (ENG., Illus.). 80p. (J). (gr. 5-12). (978-1-68282-038-4(6)) ReferencePoint Pr., Inc.

Katschke, Judy. Monster Power: Exploring Renewable Energy: a Branches Book (the Magic School Bus Rides Again) Artful Doodlers Ltd., illus. 2017. (Magic School Bus Rides Again Ser.: 2). (ENG.). 96p. (J). (gr. 1-3). pap. 5.99 (978-1-338-19444-9(5)) Scholastic, Inc.

Kenney, Karen Latchana. Energy. 2010. (Everyday Science Ser.). (ENG.). 24p. (J). (gr. k-2). lib. bdg. 25.65 (978-1-60753-018-3(X), 17134) Amicus.

—Energy Investigations. 2017. (Key Questions in Physical Science (Alternator Books (r)) Ser.). (ENG., Illus.). 32p. (J). (gr. 3-6). 29.32 (978-1-5124-4003-4(5), 3474451b-a346-4366-9111-ff41cef7335f, Lerner Pubns.) Lerner Publishing Group.

Killian, Maryellen. Energy for Earth. 2013. (InfoMax Readers Ser.). (ENG.). 24p. (J). (gr. 2-3). pap. 49.50 (978-1-4777-2435-4(4)); (Illus.). pap. 8.25 (978-1-4777-2434-7(6), 2dc4e581-12d6-4361-a0d1-2da53eaf3a05) Rosen Publishing Group, Inc., The. (Rosen Classroom).

Knight M J. Why Should I Switch off the Light? 2009. (One Small Step Ser.). (ENG., Illus.). 32p. (J). (gr. -1-3). pap. (978-1-897563-48-9(5)) Saunders Bk. Co.

Kopp, Megan. Energy from Wind: Wind Farming. 2015. (Next Generation Energy Ser.). (ENG., Illus.). 32p. (J). (gr. 5-5). (978-0-7787-1983-0(9)) Crabtree Publishing Co.

—Top Secret Science in Energy. 2019. (Top Secret Science Ser.). (Illus.). 48p. (J). (gr. 5-5). (978-0-7787-5993-5(8)); pap. (978-0-7787-5999-7(7)) Crabtree Publishing Co.

Kowalski, Kathiann M. Alternative Energy Sources, 1 vol. 2011. (Controversy! Ser.). (ENG.). 112p. (YA). (gr. 8-8). 39.79 (978-0-7614-4899-0(3), a99006f3-2233-44ed-80ac-8f52a3fb4bc5) Cavendish Square Publishing LLC.

Kravetz, Jonathan. Learning about Energy with Graphic Organizers. (Graphic Organizers in Science Ser.). 24p. (gr. 3-4). 2009. 42.50 (978-1-61513-030-6(6), PowerKids Pr.) 2006. (ENG., Illus.). (YA). lib. bdg. 26.27 (978-1-4042-3409-3(8), a0288516-b9f5-4b12-88f8-1c961b17ec81) Rosen Publishing Group, Inc., The.

Labrecque, Ellen. Renewable Energy. 2017. (21st Century Skills Library: Global Citizens: Environmentalism Ser.). (ENG., Illus.). 32p. (J). (gr. 4-7). lib. bdg. 32.07 (978-1-63472-867-6(X), 209894) Cherry Lake Publishing.

Lachner, Elizabeth. Hydroelectricity, 1 vol. 2018. (Exploring Energy Technology Ser.). (ENG.). 48p. (gr. 6-6). pap. 15.05 (978-1-5081-0618-0(5), dad045eb-aeea-4e08-976a-16a463afc2c1, Britannica Educational Publishing) Rosen Publishing Group, Inc., The.

Laidlaw, Jill. Cities. 2010. (Sustaining Our Environment Ser.). 48p. (J). lib. bdg. 35.65 (978-1-60753-135-7(6)) Amicus Learning.

—Energy. 2010. (Sustaining Our Environment Ser.). 48p. (J). 35.65 (978-1-60753-136-4(4)) Amicus Learning.

Laidlaw, Jill A. Cities. 2012. (What's in My Food Ser.). 32p. (gr. 1-4). lib. bdg. 27.10 (978-1-59920-421-5(5)) Black Rabbit Bks.

—Energy. 2012. (What's in My Food Ser.). 32p. (gr. 1-4). lib. bdg. 27.10 (978-1-59920-422-2(3)) Black Rabbit Bks.

Landau, Elaine. The History of Energy. 2005. (Major Inventions Through History Ser.). (ENG., Illus.). 56p. (gr. 5-8). lib. bdg. 26.60 (978-0-8225-3806-6(7), Twenty-First Century Bks.) Lerner Publishing Group.

Lawrence, Ellen. Poop Power. 2017. (Scoop on Poop Ser.). (ENG., Illus.). 24p. (J). (gr. -1-3). lib. bdg. 26.99 (978-1-68402-246-5(0)) Bearport Publishing Co., Inc.

Leardi, Jeanette. Making Cities Green. 2009. (Going Green Ser.). (Illus.). 32p. (YA). (gr. 3-6). lib. bdg. 28.50 (978-1-59716-961-5(7)) Bearport Publishing Co., Inc.

Let's Find Out! Forms of Energy, 12 vols. 2017. (Let's Find Out! Forms of Energy Ser.). 32p. (ENG.). (gr. 2-3). 156.36 (978-1-5081-0533-6(2), 4479bcf4-9182-4619-8d73-cc6c1e327384); (gr. 6-8). pap. 77.40 (978-1-5081-0535-0(9)) Rosen Publishing Group, Inc., The. (Britannica Educational Publishing).

Llewellyn, Claire. Save Energy. 2005. (Illus.). 32p. (YA). (gr. 1-18). lib. bdg. 27.10 (978-1-932333-23-7(1)) Chrysalis Education.

MacDonald, Margaret. Who Can Save Power? 2012. (Level B Ser.). (ENG., Illus.). 16p. (J). (gr. k-2). pap. 7.95 (978-1-927136-14-0(8), 19448) RiverStream Publishing.

Manolis, Kay. Energy. 2007. (First Science Ser.). (ENG., Illus.). 24p. (J). (gr. 2-5). lib. bdg. 26.95 (978-1-60014-096-9(3)) Bellwether Media.

—Energy. (Blastoff! Readers Ser.). 24p. (J). 2011. (Illus.). (gr. 2). pap. 5.95 (978-0-531-28453-7(0)) 2007. (ENG.). (gr. k-2). 20.00 (978-0-531-14724-5(X)) Scholastic Library Publishing. (Children's Pr.).

Marcovitz, Hal. Can Renewable Energy Replace Fossil Fuels? 2010. (In Controversy Ser.). (Illus.). 96p. (J). (gr. 7-12). 41.27 (978-1-60152-113-2(8), 1316134) ReferencePoint Pr., Inc.

Mason, Helen. Energy Entrepreneurs. 2018. (Science & Technology Start-Up Stars Ser.). (ENG., Illus.). 32p. (J). (gr. 5-5). (978-0-7787-4411-5(6)) Crabtree Publishing Co.

Mason, Paul. How Big Is Your Energy Footprint?, 1 vol. 2010. (Environmental Footprints Ser.). (ENG.). 32p. (gr. 4-4). 31.21 (978-0-7614-4411-4(4), 0333b885-5461-4a1e-8b6e-7bd14f13e3d8) Cavendish Square Publishing LLC.

Massie, Elizabeth. Nonrenewable & Renewable Energy Resources. 2016. (Spring Forward Ser.). (J). (gr. 2). (978-1-4900-9468-7(7)) Benchmark Education Co.

McKinney, Barbara Shaw. Pass the Energy, Please! Wallace, Chad, illus. 2004. (Sharing Nature with Children Book Ser.). 32p. (YA). (gr. 1-8). pap. 16.95 (978-1-58469-001-6(1)) Take Heart Pubns.

McLeish, Ewan. Challenges to Our Energy Supply. 2009. (J). 70.50 (978-1-4358-5491-8(8), Rosen Reference); (ENG.). 48p. (YA). (gr. 5-5). pap. 12.75 (978-1-4358-5490-1(X), 9dfc846f-c2f9-49e7-b0c3-d9934e37a98c, Rosen Reference); (ENG., Illus.). 48p. (J). (gr. 5-5). lib. bdg. 34.47 (978-1-4358-5357-7(1), 034516aa-7c89-4c30-915f-892353166af5) Rosen Publishing Group, Inc., The.

Miller, Debra A. Energy Production & Alternative Energy, 1 vol. 2010. (Confronting Global Warming Ser.). (ENG.). 136p. (gr. 10-12). lib. bdg. 45.93 (978-0-7377-5106-2(1), 35b728ef-53e8-4cd5-8510-c2632f544c6a, Greenhaven Publishing) Greenhaven Publishing LLC.

Miller, Debra A., ed. Gasoline, 1 vol. 2012. (Current Controversies Ser.). (ENG.). 184p. (gr. 10-12). lib. bdg. 48.03 (978-0-7377-6227-3(6), 52ed72f7-b878-434f-817c-7f69e4efb7a0, Greenhaven Publishing) Greenhaven Publishing LLC.

—Oil, 1 vol. 2010. (Current Controversies Ser.). (ENG.). 224p. (gr. 10-12). 48.03 (978-0-7377-4919-9(9), e47eee70-e221-4fe1-ac26-45cd578a4ab2); pap. 33.00 (978-0-7377-4920-5(2), 9d85d746-7b75-44bb-a07c-f1c81193fa5c) Greenhaven Publishing LLC. (Greenhaven Publishing).

mooney, carla. What Is the Future of Hydrogen Power? 2012. (Illus.). 80p. (YA). lib. bdg. (978-1-60152-274-0(6)) ReferencePoint Pr., Inc.

Morkes, Andrew. Renewable Energy Workers. 2019. (Cool Careers in Science Ser.). 96p. (J). (gr. 12). lib. bdg. 34.60 (978-1-4222-4301-5(X)) Mason Crest.

Morris, Neil. The Energy Mix. 2010. (J). 34.25 (978-1-59920-338-6(3)) Black Rabbit Bks.

—Geothermal Power. 2007. (Energy Sources Ser.). (Illus.). 32p. (YA). (gr. 4-7). lib. bdg. 28.50 (978-1-58340-906-0(8)) Black Rabbit Bks.

Mulder, Michelle. Brilliant! Shining a Light on Sustainable Energy, 1 vol. (Orca Footprints Ser.: 3). (ENG., Illus.). 48p. (J). (gr. 4-7). 2016. pap. 14.95 (978-1-4598-1214-7(X)) 2013. 19.95 (978-1-4598-0221-6(7)) Orca Bk. Pubs. USA.

Murray, Laura K. Ocean Energy. 2016. (Alternative Energy Ser.). (ENG., Illus.). 48p. (J). (gr. 4-8). lib. bdg. 35.64 (978-1-68078-458-9(7), 23853) ABDO Publishing Co.

Muschal, Frank. Bio-Fuels. 2007. (21st Century Skills Library: Power Up! Ser.). (ENG., Illus.). 32p. (gr. 4-8). lib. bdg. 32.07 (978-1-60279-045-2(0), 200051) Cherry Lake Publishing.

Nakaya, Andrea C. Energy Alternatives. 2007. (Compact Research Ser.). (Illus.). 112p. (YA). (gr. 7-12). lib. bdg. 43.93 (978-1-60152-017-3(4)) ReferencePoint Pr., Inc.

Nardo, Don. Careers in Renewable Energy. 2018. (ENG.). 80p. (YA). (gr. 5-12). (978-1-68282-315-6(6)) ReferencePoint Pr., Inc.

Newell, Ella. Energy, 1 vol. 2013. (Physical Science Ser.). 48p. (J). (gr. 4-5). (ENG.). pap. 15.05 (978-1-4339-9509-5(3), ecd4736a-d1f0-4176-90ef-751c6b41176e); pap. 84.30 (978-1-4339-9510-1(7)); (ENG., Illus.). lib. bdg. 34.61 (978-1-4339-9508-8(5), 1402bcc0-c9b9-416e-8a2b-9711f8cc6233) Stevens, Gareth Publishing LLLP.

Nixon, Jonathan. Energy Engineering & Powering the Future. 2016. (Engineering in Action Ser.). (ENG., Illus.). 32p. (J). (gr. 5-9). (978-0-7787-7539-3(9)) Crabtree Publishing Co.

Olson, Elsie. Oil Energy. 2018. (Earth's Energy Resources Ser.). (ENG., Illus.). 24p. (J). (gr. -1-3). lib. bdg. 29.93 (978-1-5321-1555-4(5), 28964, SandCastle) ABDO Publishing Co.

O'Neal, Claire. How to Use Wind Power to Light & Heat Your Home. 2009. (Tell Your Parents Ser.). (Illus.). 48p. (J). (gr. 4-7). lib. bdg. 29.95 (978-1-58415-762-5(3)) Mitchell Lane Pubs.

Orme, Helen. Energy for the Future. 2008. (Earth in Danger Ser.). (Illus.). 32p. (YA). (gr. 3-6). lib. bdg. 25.27 (978-1-59716-727-7(4), 1284324) Bearport Publishing Co., Inc.

Orr, Tamra B. Geothermal Energy. 2007. (21st Century Skills Library: Power Up! Ser.). (ENG., Illus.). 32p. (gr. 4-8). lib. bdg. 32.07 (978-1-60279-044-5(2), 200053) Cherry Lake Publishing.

Owen, Ruth. Energy from Inside Our Planet: Geothermal Power, 1 vol. 2013. (Power: Yesterday, Today, Tomorrow Ser.). (ENG., Illus.). 32p. (J). (gr. 4-5). 28.93 (978-1-4777-0268-0(7), 6b8e2cd0-431e-48ed-a6e1-4b1faf467834); pap. 12.75 (978-1-4777-0275-8(X), 30b9c170-6010-4d6f-8f9e-f89841760d9d) Rosen Publishing Group, Inc., The. (PowerKids Pr.).

—Energy from Plants & Trash: Biofuels & Biomass Power, 1 vol. 2013. (Power: Yesterday, Today, Tomorrow Ser.). (ENG., Illus.). 32p. (J). (gr. 4-5). 28.93 (978-1-4777-0267-3(9), 37b7263b-224e-44b9-88f7-de8a583a9f66); pap. 12.75 (978-1-4777-0273-4(3), 37c807cc-afef-413a-ad9b-6591b2128446) Rosen Publishing Group, Inc., The. (PowerKids Pr.).

Oxlade, Chris & Jennings, Terry. Energy. 2009. (Science Alive Ser.). (ENG., Illus.). 32p. (J). pap. (978-1-897563-53-3(1)) Saunders Bk. Co.

Oxlade, Chris & Jennings, Terry J. Energy. 2009. (J). 28.50 (978-1-59920-273-0(5)) Black Rabbit Bks.

Paleja, Shaker. Power Up! A Visual Exploration of Energy. Glenda, Tse, illus. 2015. (ENG.). 56p. (J). (gr. 4-7). pap. 12.95 (978-1-55451-726-8(5), 9781554517268) Annick Pr., Ltd. CAN. Dist: Publishers Group West (PGW).

Parker, Russ. Energy Supplies in Crisis, 1 vol. 2009. (Planet in Crisis Ser.). (ENG.). 32p. (gr. 5-5). (YA). lib. bdg. 30.47 (978-1-4358-5251-8(6), 5f5d54dc-07d6-4853-acc4-55fd26a34f65); (Illus.). (J). pap. 11.00 (978-1-4358-0681-8(6), 202d423e-7f6b-44fd-8d7e-bd68474e68c8) Rosen Publishing Group, Inc., The. (Rosen Reference).

Parker, Steve. Energy & Power. 2010. (How It Works Ser.). 40p. (J). (gr. 3-18). lib. bdg. 19.95 (978-1-4222-1794-8(9)) Mason Crest.

Parker, Vic. Let's Think about Sustainable Energy, 1 vol. 2014. (Let's Think About Ser.). (ENG., Illus.). 48p. (J). (gr. 3-6). pap. 8.99 (978-1-4846-0297-3(8), 126389, Heinemann) Capstone.

Parks, Peggy J. Coal Power. 2010. (Compact Research Ser.). 96p. (YA). (gr. 7-12). 41.27 (978-1-60152-107-1(3)) ReferencePoint Pr., Inc.

Passero, Barbara. Energy Alternatives. 2006. (Opposing Viewpoints Ser.). (ENG., Illus.). 238p. (J). (gr. 3-7). 27.50 (978-0-7377-3351-8(9)); pap. 39.70 (978-0-7377-3350-1(0)) Cengage Gale. (Greenhaven Pr., Inc.).

Peppas, Lynn. Ocean, Tidal & Wave Energy: Power from the Sea, 1 vol. 2008. (Energy Revolution Ser.). (ENG., Illus.). 32p. (J). (gr. 3-8). pap. (978-0-7787-2933-4(8)); lib. bdg. (978-0-7787-2919-8(2)) Crabtree Publishing Co.

Pettiford, Rebecca. Energy. 2018. (Science Starters Ser.). (ENG., Illus.). 24p. (J). (gr. k-3). lib. bdg. 26.95 (978-1-62617-806-9(2), Blastoff! Readers) Bellwether Media.

Pipe, Jim. Oil. 2010. (J). 28.50 (978-1-59604-211-7(7)) Black Rabbit Bks.

Povey, Karen D. Energy Alternatives, 1 vol. 2007. (Hot Topics Ser.). (ENG., Illus.). 112p. (gr. 7-7). lib. bdg. 41.03 (978-1-59018-980-1(9), cc059952-0a3e-4a5c-87bd-070e22e1edf3, Lucent Pr.) Greenhaven Publishing LLC.

The Race to Find Energy, 1 vol. 2014. (World in Crisis Ser.). (ENG., Illus.). 48p. (J). (gr. 5-5). 33.47 (978-1-4777-7842-5(X), 8ab250db-c8bb-4a7c-a0e4-a0de29548528) Rosen Publishing Group, Inc., The.

Redmond, Jim. Oil Makes Gasoline Power. 2003. (From Resource to Energy Source Ser.). (J). (978-1-58417-292-5(4)); pap. (978-1-58417-293-2(2)) Lake Street Pubs.

Riddle, John. Coal Power of the Future: New Ways of Turning Coal into Energy. 2009. (Library of Future Energy Ser.). 64p. (gr. 5-5). 58.50 (978-1-60853-624-5(6)) Rosen Publishing Group, Inc., The.

Rigsby, Mike. Doable Renewables: 16 Alternative Energy Projects for Young Scientists. 2010. (ENG., Illus.). 224p. (J). (gr. 4-18). pap. 16.95 (978-1-56976-343-8(7)) Chicago Review Pr., Inc.

Rodger, Ellen. Is There a Future for Fossil Fuels?, 1 vol. 2010. (ENG., Illus.). 32p. (J). pap. (978-0-7787-2937-2(0)); lib. bdg. (978-0-7787-2923-5(0)) Crabtree Publishing Co.

Rusch, Elizabeth. The Next Wave: The Quest to Harness the Power of the Oceans. 2014. (Scientists in the Field Ser.). (ENG., Illus.). 80p. (J). (gr. 5-7). 18.99 (978-0-544-09999-9(0), 1539199, Clarion Bks.) HarperCollins Pubs.

Saunders, Nigel. Geothermal Energy, 1 vol. 2007. (Energy for the Future & Global Warming Ser.). (ENG.). 32p. (gr. 3-3). pap. 12.70 (978-0-8368-8409-8(4), 906f2cf7-1b02-4364-a72b-39c8184347a4); (Illus.). lib. bdg. 29.67 (978-0-8368-8400-5(0), 6169338a-728e-4025-b46b-58364b039626) Stevens, Gareth Publishing LLLP.

Savage, Lorraine, ed. Geothermal Power, 1 vol. 2006. (Fueling the Future Ser.). (ENG., Illus.). 128p. (gr. 10-12). lib. bdg. 39.83 (978-0-7377-3579-6(1), 52957e58-cddb-4ef8-bede-04514d1b1491, Greenhaven Publishing) Greenhaven Publishing LLC.

Saving the Planet Through Green Energy, 12 vols. 2016. (Saving the Planet Through Green Energy Ser.). (ENG.). 24p. (J). (gr. 3-3). lib. bdg. 145.62 (978-0-7660-8402-5(7), bd40c534-d5fa-4166-a52d-8dbf8161a02f) Enslow Publishing, LLC.

Science & Voege, Debra. Energy Today, 8 vols., Set. 2010. (Energy Today Ser.). (gr. 4-6). 240.00 (978-1-60413-964-8(1), Chelsea Clubhse.) Infobase Holdings, Inc.

Sechrist, Darren. Powerful Planet: Can Earth's Renewable Energy Save Our Future? 2009. (Current Science Ser.). (ENG.). 48p. (J). (gr. 4-6). pap. 8.95 (978-1-4339-2245-9(2), Gareth Stevens Learning Library) Stevens, Gareth Publishing LLLP.

—Powerful Planet: Can Earth's Renewable Energy Save Our Future?, 1 vol. 2009. (Current Science Ser.). (ENG.). 48p. (YA). (gr. 4-6). lib. bdg. 33.67 (978-1-4339-2241-1(X), efab3d28-a852-4223-80de-15b613b97e2d) Stevens, Gareth Publishing LLLP.

Shoals, James. The Danger of Greenhouse Gases. 2019. (Illus.). 48p. (J). (978-1-4222-4353-4(2)) Mason Crest.

—Preserving Energy. 2019. (Illus.). 48p. (J). (978-1-4222-4360-2(5)) Mason Crest.

Silverman, Buffy. Energy All Around. 2012. (My Science Library). (ENG.). 24p. (gr. 3-4). pap. 8.95 (978-1-61810-228-7(1), 9781618102287) Rourke Educational Media.

Silverstein, Alvin, et al. Energy. 2008. (Science Concepts Ser.). (YA). (gr. 5-9). lib. bdg. 31.93 (978-0-8225-8655-5(X)) Twenty First Century Bks.

Slade, Suzanne. What Can We Do about the Energy Crisis?, 1 vol. 2009. (Protecting Our Planet Ser.). (ENG., Illus.). 24p. (gr. 2-3). (J). pap. 9.25 (978-1-4358-2481-2(4), 47e911b6-2fb0-4128-957e-d6a576f2490e, PowerKids Pr.); (YA). lib. bdg. 26.27 (978-1-4042-8081-6(2), eb97979c-9a59-45a4-a320-169f276ebc80) Rosen Publishing Group, Inc., The.

Small, Cathleen. Wind, Waves, & the Sun: The Rise of Alternative Energy, 1 vol. 2017. (History of Conservation: Preserving Our Planet Ser.). (ENG.). 112p. (YA). (gr. 9-9). 44.50 (978-1-5026-3132-9(6), 0d3c8f5a-bddc-46ef-bb72-efb8f17f82e7) Cavendish Square Publishing LLC.

Smith, A. G. Green Power: Earth-Friendly Energy Through the Ages. 2010. (Dover Nature Coloring Book Ser.). (ENG., Illus.). 32p. (J). (gr. 3-8). pap. 3.99 (978-0-486-47447-2(X)) Dover Pubns., Inc.

Smith, Eileen M. ElectriCity Beyond the Curve of Deregulation: Neighborhood Energy Watch Groups & the Ethos of Commerce. 2003. per. (978-0-9741412-9-9(1)) Ethos Of Commerce Pubs., Ltd.

Sneideman, Joshua & Twamley, Erin. Renewable Energy: Discover the Fuel of the Future. Brinesh, Heather Jane, illus. 2016. (Build It Yourself Ser.). (ENG.). 128p. (J). (gr. 3-7). 22.95 (978-1-61930-356-0(6), 0a982676-d101-4a2c-b796-0e2e5a66665d) Nomad Pr.

Sobey, Ed. Solar Cell & Renewable Energy Experiments, 1 vol. 2011. (Cool Science Projects with Technology Ser.). (ENG., Illus.). 128p. (gr. 5-6). lib. bdg. 35.93 (978-0-7660-3305-4(8), d441f769-82b6-493f-8db7-6ede76d6ecad) Enslow Publishing, LLC.

Sobha, Geeta. Green Technology: Earth-Friendly Innovations, 1 vol. 2007. (In the News Ser.). (ENG., Illus.). 64p. (YA). (gr. 6-6). lib. bdg. 37.13 (978-1-4042-1914-4(5), cdb65425-01f2-4ef2-8139-bb82aaace90a) Rosen Publishing Group, Inc., The.

—Green Technology: Earth-friendly Innovations. 2009. (In the News Ser.). 64p. (gr. 6-6). 58.50 (978-1-61513-467-0(0)) Rosen Publishing Group, Inc., The.

Solway, Andrew. Exploring Energy, 1 vol. 2007. (Exploring Physical Science Ser.). (ENG., Illus.). 48p. (YA). (gr. 6-6). lib. bdg. 34.47 (978-1-4042-3748-3(8), f1f7e682-f8df-409f-9f3b-c97a094af617) Rosen Publishing Group, Inc., The.

—From Crashing Waves to Music Download: An Energy Journey Through the World of Sound. 2015. (Energy Journeys Ser.). (ENG., Illus.). 48p. (J). (gr. 3-6). 35.99 (978-1-4846-0883-8(6), 127967, Heinemann) Capstone.

—From Sunlight to Blockbuster Movies: An Energy Journey Through the World of Light. 2015. (Energy Journeys Ser.). (ENG., Illus.). 48p. (J). (gr. 3-6). 35.99 (978-1-4846-0882-1(8), 127966, Heinemann) Capstone.

Solway, Andrew & Graham, Ian. Energy Journeys. 2015. (Energy Journeys Ser.). (ENG.). 48p. (J). (gr. 3-6). 143.96 (978-1-4846-0886-9(0), 22351, Heinemann) Capstone.

Spilsbury, Richard. The Debate about Energy Resources, 1 vol. 2010. (Ethical Debates Ser.). (ENG.). 48p. (YA). (gr. 6-6). lib. bdg. 34.47 (978-1-4358-9651-2(3), 91aabda2-08da-4ce5-98b6-6ee6c66670fa, Rosen Reference) Rosen Publishing Group, Inc., The.

Steele, Philip. Saving Water & Energy. 2009. (Now We Know About... Ser.). (ENG., Illus.). 24p. (J). (gr. k-3). pap. (978-0-7787-4740-6(9)); lib. bdg. (978-0-7787-4723-9(9)) Crabtree Publishing Co.

Stewart, Audrey. Our Natural Resources, 1 vol. 2013. (InfoMax Readers Ser.). (ENG.). 24p. (J). (gr. 2-2). pap. 8.25 (978-1-4777-2356-2(0), e71e7dff-7c69-4d50-b7c2-4187f305ba5c); pap. 49.50 (978-1-4777-2357-9(9)) Rosen Publishing Group, Inc., The. (Rosen Classroom).

Stoyles, Pennie & Pentland, Peter. Power & Fuel, 1 vol. Porcellato, Nives, illus. 2012. (Energy in Action Ser.). (ENG.). 32p. (gr. 6-6). 31.21 (978-1-60870-569-6(2), cbcb48e7-f221-420f-b97b-53fd11b5d4c5) Cavendish Square Publishing LLC.

Stuckey, Rachel. Energy from Living Things: Biomass Energy. 2015. (Next Generation Energy Ser.). (ENG., Illus.). 32p. (J). (gr. 5-5). (978-0-7787-1980-9(4)) Crabtree Publishing Co.

Syrewicz, Connor. Energizing Energy Markets: Clean Coal, Shale, Oil, Wind, & Solar. 2013. (Earning $50,000 - $100,000 with a High School Diploma or Less Ser.: 14). 64p. (J). (gr. 7-18). 22.95 (978-1-4222-2894-4(0)) Mason Crest.

Tell Your Parents, 5 vols., Set. Incl. All about Electrice & Hybrid Cars. Bearce, Stephanie. (Illus.). 48p. lib. bdg. 25.70 (978-1-58415-763-2(1)); Green Changes You Can Make Around the House. Smalley, Carol. (Illus.). 48p. lib. bdg. 29.95 (978-1-58415-764-9(X)); How to Harness Solar Power for Your Home. Bearce, Stephanie. (Illus.). 48p. lib. bdg. 29.95 (978-1-58415-761-8(5)); How to Use Wind Power to Light & Heat Your Home. O'Neal, Claire. (Illus.). 48p. lib. bdg. 29.95 (978-1-58415-762-5(3)); How You Can Use Waste Energy to Heat & Light Your Home. Brager, Bruce L. 29.95 (978-1-58415-765-6(8)); (J). (gr. 4-7). 2009. 2009. Set lib. bdg. 149.75 (978-1-58415-766-3(6)) Mitchell Lane Pubs.

Thaddeus, Eva. Powering the Future: New Energy Technologies. 2010. (Barbara Guth Worlds of Wonder Science Series for Young Readers Ser.). (ENG., Illus.). 131p. (J). (gr. 4-18). 34.95 (978-0-8263-4901-9(3), P174722) Univ. of New Mexico Pr.

Thomas, Isabel. The Pros & Cons of Biomass Power, 1 vol. 2007. (Energy Debate Ser.). (ENG., Illus.). 48p. (YA). (gr. 6-6). lib. bdg. 34.47 (978-1-4042-3742-1(9), 793959c3-c66b-44dd-a522-2d1d419fdb02) Rosen Publishing Group, Inc., The.

Tiner, John Hudson. Coal Makes Electric Power. 2003. (From Resource to Energy Source Ser.). (J). (978-1-58417-294-9(0)); (978-1-58417-295-6(9)) Lake Street Pubs.

Top That Publishing Staff, ed. Lets Learn about Energy. 2004. (Fun Kits Ser.). (Illus.). 48p. (J). (978-1-904748-98-4(8)) Top That! Publishing PLC.

VanCleave, Janice. Janice VanCleave's Energy for Every Kid: Easy Activities That Make Learning Science Fun. 2005. (Science for Every Kid Ser.: 15). (ENG., Illus.). 240p. (gr. 3-7). pap. 14.95 (978-0-471-33099-8(X)) Wiley, John & Sons, Inc.

Washburne, Sophie. Alternative Energy Sources: The End of Fossil Fuels?, 1 vol. 2018. (Hot Topics Ser.). (ENG.). 104p. (gr. 7-7). pap. 20.99 (978-1-5345-6508-1(6), f730bdff-4303-4a41-8b2e-0829dd673c00, Lucent Pr.) Greenhaven Publishing LLC.

Way, Steve & Bailey, Gerry. Energy, 1 vol. 2008. (Simply Science Ser.). (ENG., Illus.). 32p. (J). (gr. 3-5). lib. bdg. 28.67 (978-0-8368-9227-7(5), eab5f34d-a594-450f-812b-719386ef65f1) Stevens, Gareth Publishing LLLP.

Whitehouse, Patty. Energia Por Dondequiera / Energy Everywhere. 2006. (Construction Forces Discovery Library). (Illus.). 24p. (J). (gr. k-2). lib. bdg. 22.79 (978-1-60044-274-2(9)) Rourke Educational Media.

—Energy Everywhere. 2006. (Construction Forces Discovery Library). (Illus.). 24p. (J). (gr. k-2). lib. bdg. 22.79 (978-1-60044-189-9(0)) Rourke Educational Media.

Whittaker, Helen & Lewis, Helen. Energy: Information & Projects to Reduce Your Environmental Footprint, 1 vol. Porcellato, Nives, illus. 2012. (Living Green Ser.). (ENG.). 32p. (gr. 4-4). 31.21 (978-1-60870-573-3(0), 15567a1e-4f6c-404e-807d-c408a043c9db) Cavendish Square Publishing LLC.

Winnick, Nick. Green Energy. 2016. (Illus.). 32p. (J). (978-1-5105-2219-0(0)) SmartBook Media, Inc.

—Green Power. 2010. (Being Green Ser.). (Illus.). 32p. (YA). (gr. 3-6). lib. bdg. 27.13 (978-1-61690-097-7(0)); (J). (gr. 4-6). pap. 12.95 (978-1-61690-098-4(9)) Weigl Pubs., Inc.

Woll, Kris. Wind Energy. 2016. (Alternative Energy Ser.). (ENG., Illus.). 48p. (J). (gr. 4-8). lib. bdg. 35.64 (978-1-68078-460-2(9), 23857) ABDO Publishing Co.

World Book, Inc. Staff, contrib. by. Zac Newton Investigates Extraordinary Electricity. 2018. (J). (978-0-7166-4058-5(9)) World Bk., Inc.

Zuchora-Walske, Christine. Energy in the Real World. 2013. (Science in the Real World Ser.). (ENG.). 48p. (J). (gr. 4-8). pap. 18.50 (978-1-61783-789-0(X), 14613) ABDO Publishing Co.

POWER SUPPLY

see Power Resources

POWER TRANSMISSION, ELECTRIC

see Electric Lines

PRACTICAL POLITICS

see Politics, Practical

PRAIRIE DOGS

Bailer, Darice. Prairie Dogs, 1 vol. 2012. (Animals, Animals Ser.). (ENG., Illus.). 48p. (gr. 5-5). 32.64 (978-0-7614-4876-1(4), 2bc3a686-a08b-4490-a684-8d926c8c8164) Cavendish Square Publishing LLC.

Borgert-Spaniol, Megan. Prairie Dogs. 2016. (North American Animals Ser.). (ENG., Illus.). 24p. (J). (gr. k-3). 26.95 (978-1-62617-402-3(4), Blastoff! Readers) Bellwether Media.

Emminizer, Theresa. What If Prairie Dogs Disappeared?, 1 vol. 2019. (Life Without Animals Ser.). (ENG.). 24p. (gr. 1-2). 24.27 (978-1-5382-3820-2(9), 89e7f0aa-c96a-403a-90ec-f6decdee8c35) Stevens, Gareth Publishing LLLP.

Forest, Christopher. Prairie Dog Burrows. 2018. (Animal Engineers Ser.). (ENG., Illus.). 32p. (J). (gr. 2-3). pap. 9.95 (978-1-63517-963-7(7), 1635179637); lib. bdg. 31.35 (978-1-63517-862-3(2), 1635178622) North Star Editions. (Focus Readers).

—Prairie Dog Burrows. 2018. (Illus.). 32p. (J). (978-1-4896-9757-8(8), AV2 by Weigl) Weigl Pubs., Inc.

George, Lynn. Prairie Dogs: Tunnel Diggers, 1 vol. 2010. (Animal Architects Ser.). (ENG.). 24p. (J). (gr. 2-3). pap. 9.25 (978-1-4488-1351-3(4), 3a556566-d1f7-44d1-ae58-88ac7acecbaf); lib. bdg. 26.27 (978-1-4488-0695-9(X), 7e0dd2a5-2757-445c-b136-b469e53f3abd) Rosen Publishing Group, Inc., The. (PowerKids Pr.).

Gish, Melissa. Prairie Dogs. 2017. (Living Wild Ser.). (ENG., Illus.). 48p. (J). (gr. 4-7). (978-1-60818-833-8(7), 20204, Creative Education) Creative Co., The.

Grucella, A. J. Prairie Dogs in Danger. 2013. (Animals at Risk Ser.). 24p. (J). (gr. 2-5). pap. 48.90 (978-1-4339-9166-0(7)); (ENG., Illus.). lib. bdg. 25.27 (978-1-4339-9164-6(0), 011f74be-f999-4baa-a4dd-7d8a81d8b200) Stevens, Gareth Publishing LLLP.

Jackson, Tom. Prairie Dogs. 2008. (Nature's Children Ser.). (Illus.). 52p. (J). (978-0-7172-6242-7(1)) Grolier, Ltd.

Johnson, Jinny. Prairie Dog. 2014. (North American Mammals Ser.). (ENG.). 24p. (J). (gr. 1-4). 28.50 (978-1-62588-034-5(0), 17373) Black Rabbit Bks.

—Prairie Dog. 2014. (North American Mammals Ser.). (ENG., Illus.). 24p. (J). (gr. -1-4). pap. 8.95 (978-1-77092-170-2(2)) Saunders Bk. Co. CAN. Dist: RiverStream Publishing.

Kalman, Bobbie. An Animal Community. 2010. (My World Ser.). (ENG., Illus.). 24p. (J). (gr. k-2). (978-0-7787-9446-2(6)); pap. (978-0-7787-9490-5(3)) Crabtree Publishing Co.

Kopp, Megan. Prairie Dogs. 2011. (J). (gr. 2-4). pap. 12.95 (978-1-61690-630-6(8), AV2 by Weigl); (Illus.). 24p. 27.13 (978-1-61690-624-5(3)) Weigl Pubs., Inc.

Magby, Meryl. Prairie Dogs, 1 vol. 2012. (American Animals Ser.). (ENG., Illus.). 24p. (J). (gr. 2-3). pap. 9.25 (978-1-4488-6323-5(6), 8759cdd0-6fa2-4f60-bbe2-8a723c4768c8, PowerKids Pr.); lib. bdg. 26.27 (978-1-4488-6182-8(9), 5dd70642-7c84-46ea-94c0-b83e623aca98) Rosen Publishing Group, Inc., The.

Markle, Sandra. Los Perritos de Las Praders (Prairie Dogs) 2009. (SPA.). pap. 46.95 (978-0-7613-4718-7(6)) Lerner Publishing Group.

—Los Perritos de Las Praderas. Translations.com Staff, tr. from ENG. 2008. (Animales Presa (Animal Prey) Ser.). (SPA.). 40p. (gr. 3-6). 25.26 (978-0-7613-3896-3(9)) Lerner Publishing Group.

—Los perritos de las praderas (Prairie Dogs) 2008. 40p. (J). pap. 7.95 (978-0-7613-3901-4(9), Ediciones Lerner) Lerner Publishing Group.

—Prairie Dogs. 2008. pap. 46.95 (978-0-8225-9323-2(8)) 2008. (ENG., Illus.). 40p. (gr. 3-6). per. 7.95 (978-0-8225-6441-6(6), First Avenue Editions) 2007. (ENG., Illus.). 40p. (J). (gr. 3-6). lib. bdg. 25.32 (978-0-8225-6438-6(6), 18f6fc3b-4d9f-49bd-8ab7-c717ea5b04b1, Lerner Pubns.) Lerner Publishing Group.

Redmond, Shirley Raye. Lewis & Clark: A Prairie Dog for the President. Manders, John, illus. 2003. (Step into Reading Ser.). 48p. 14.00 (978-0-7569-1697-8(6)) Perfection Learning Corp.

Schuetz, Kristin. Prairie Dogs. 2014. (Backyard Wildlife Ser.). (ENG.). 24p. (J). (gr. k-3). lib. bdg. 26.95 (978-1-60014-971-9(5), Blastoff! Readers) Bellwether Media.

Schuh, Mari. Perritos de Las Praderas. Aparicio Publishing LLC, Aparicio Publishing, tr. 2020. (Animals en Espanol Ser.).Tr. of Prairie Dogs. (SPA., Illus.). 32p. (J). (gr. 1-3). lib. bdg. 31.32 (978-1-9771-2552-1(2), 200629, Pebble) Capstone.

—Prairie Dogs. 2019. (Spot Backyard Animals Ser.). (ENG.). 16p. (J). (gr. -1-2). lib. bdg. (978-1-68151-545-8(8), 14507) Amicus.

—Prairie Dogs. 2020. (Animals Ser.). (ENG., Illus.). 32p. (J). (gr. 1-3). pap. 6.95 (978-1-9771-1798-4(8), 142159); lib. bdg. 31.32 (978-1-9771-1345-0(1), 141466) Capstone. (Pebble).

Smalls, June. We Need Prairie Dogs. 2019. (Animal Files Ser.). (ENG., Illus.). 32p. (J). (gr. 3-5). 31.35 (978-1-64185-313-2(1), 1641853131, Focus Readers) North Star Editions.

Zuchora-Walske, Christine. Peeking Prairie Dogs. 2003. (Pull Ahead Bks.). (Illus.). 32p. (J). (gr. k-2). pap. 5.95 (978-0-8225-3622-2(6)) Lerner Publishing Group.

PRAIRIE DOGS—FICTION

Baum, L. Frank & Montileaux, Donald F. The Enchanted Buffalo. 2010. (Prairie Tales Ser.). (ENG., Illus.). 40p. (gr. 2-5). 14.95 (978-0-9822749-3-4(9), P240878, South Dakota State Historical Society Pr.) South Dakota Historical Society Pr.

Brix, Liz. Josephine Prairie Dog. 2009. 28p. pap. 12.70 (978-1-4389-4448-7(9)) AuthorHouse.

Crummel, Susan Stevens. The Great Fuzz Frenzy. Stevens, Janet, illus. 2017. (ENG.). 56p. (J). (gr. -1-3). pap. 7.99 (978-0-544-94391-9(0), 1659042, Clarion Bks.) HarperCollins Pubs.

Marable, Justin. Noco. 2010. (ENG., Illus.). 50p. pap. 12.95 (978-0-9831104-0-8(9)) Marable, Justin.

Meyer, Deanna. Buffalo on the Ridge. 2010. pap. 12.95 (978-0-7414-6103-2(X)) Infinity Publishing.

Murray, Caryn Eve. Philomena's Homecoming: The (mostly) true story of a New York prairie dog's search for a Family. 2010. 48p. pap. 8.95 (978-1-4502-2769-8(4)) iUniverse, Inc.

Rheaume, Sherry D. Lulu the Prairie Dog. 2011. 16p. pap. 24.95 (978-1-4626-3987-8(9)) America Star Bks.

Stevens, Janet & Crummel, Susan Stevens. The Great Fuzz Frenzy. unabr. ed. 2006. (J). (gr. k-3). 27.99 incl. audio (978-0-8045-6940-8(1), SAC6941) Spoken Arts, Inc.

—The Great Fuzz Frenzy. 2017. (ENG.). (J). (gr. -1-3). lib. bdg. 18.40 (978-0-606-39816-9(3)) Turtleback.

PRAIRIES

AZ Books Staff. In the Prairie & Desert. Efimova, Tatiana & Goncharik, Irina, eds. 2012. (Animal Sounds Ser.). (ENG.). 14p. (J). (gr. -1-k). bds. 7.95 (978-1-61889-128-0(6)) AZ Bks. LLC.

Dayton, Connor. Prairie Animals. 2009. (American Habitats Ser.). 24p. (gr. 2-3). 42.50 (978-1-61511-357-6(6), PowerKids Pr.); (ENG.). (YA). lib. bdg. 26.27 (978-1-4358-2767-7(8), 5f1bcde7-5374-4c07-a026-d711c75ed4ac); (ENG., Illus.). (J). pap. 9.25 (978-1-4358-3196-4(9), e70558dd-685c-4034-b686-cded4685bed8, PowerKids Pr.) Rosen Publishing Group, Inc., The.

Endres, Hollie. Prairies. 2011. (Blastoff! Readers Ser.). 24p. (J). pap. 5.95 (978-0-531-26034-0(8), Children's Pr.) Scholastic Library Publishing.

Fredericks, Anthony D. P Is for Prairie Dog: A Prairie Alphabet. Bowles, Doug, illus. 2011. (Science Alphabet Ser.). (ENG.). 32p. (J). (gr. 1-4). 16.95 (978-1-58536-508-1(4), 202201) Sleeping Bear Pr.

Frisch, Aaron. Prairies. 2008. (Our World Ser.). (Illus.). 24p. (J). (gr. -1-3). lib. bdg. 24.25 (978-1-58341-572-6(6), Creative Education) Creative Co., The.

Heos, Bridget. Do You Really Want to Visit a Prairie? Fabbri, Daniele, illus. 2014. (Do You Really Want to Visit Earth's Biomes? Ser.). (ENG.). 24p. (J). (gr. 1-4). lib. bdg. 27.10 (978-1-60753-452-5(5), 15886) Amicus.

Lemke, Donald B. The Schoolchildren's Blizzard. 2007. (Disasters in History Ser.). (ENG., Illus.). 32p. (J). (gr. 3-9). 31.32 (978-1-4296-0157-3(4), 94140, Capstone Pr.) Capstone.

Levy, Janey. What Lives on a Prairie? 2009. (Reading Room Collection 2 Ser.). 24p. (gr. 3-4). 42.50 (978-1-60852-001-5(3), PowerKids Pr.) Rosen Publishing Group, Inc., The.

Lion, David C. La Vida en la Pradera. 2008. (SPA., Illus.). 24p. (J). 22.00 (978-0-531-20722-2(6), Children's Pr.) Scholastic Library Publishing.

McGehee, Claudia. A Tallgrass Prairie Alphabet. 2004. (Bur Oak Book Ser.). (ENG., Illus.). 32p. (J). 17.95 (978-0-87745-897-5(9)) Univ. of Iowa Pr.

Munson Scullin, Wendy. Young Person's Guide to the Prairie. 2006. (Illus.). 160p. (YA). per. 11.95 (978-0-9770764-0-6(7)) South River Pr.

Pettiford, Rebecca. Prairie Food Chains. 2016. (Who Eats What?). (Illus.). 24p. (J). (gr. 2-5). lib. bdg. 25.65 (978-1-62031-303-9(0), Pogo) Jump! Inc.

Tarbox, A. D. A Paire Food Chain. 2008. (Nature's Bounty Ser.). (ENG., Illus.). 48p. (J). (gr. 5-8). 22.95 (978-1-58341-600-6(5), 23012, Creative Education) Creative Co., The.

PRAYER

see also Prayers

Al-Ghazali. Al-Ghazali: The Mysteries of Prayer for Children. 2018. (Illus.). 312p. (J). *(978-1-941610-38-1(2))* Fons Vitae of Kentucky, Inc.

Baden, Robert. Psalms for Kids. 2004. 64p. (J). 7.49 *(978-0-570-07141-9(0))* Concordia Publishing Hse.

Bagley, Val Chadwick & Beckstrand, Tamara, trs. My Little Book about Prayer. Bagley, Val Chadwick, illus. 2004. (Illus.). (J). bds. 10.95 *(978-1-59156-096-8(9))* Covenant Communications, Inc.

Batterson, Mark. Big Dreams & Powerful Prayers Illustrated Bible: 30 Inspiring Stories from the Old & New Testament, 1 vol. Aranda, Omar, illus. 2020. (ENG.). 224p. (J). 18.99 *(978-0-310-74682-9(5))* Zonderkidz.

Becky, Terri And Melissa. Garden Prayer for Little Farmers: Seeds of Evangelism Series (Book 1) 2013. 36p. pap. 15.49 *(978-1-4669-8787-6(1))* Trafford Publishing.

Bible Visuals International Staff, compiled by. Prayer: New Testament Volume 09. 2006. (Illus.). (J). pap. *(978-1-932381-39-9(2)*, 1009) Bible Visuals International, Inc.

Billingsley, Mary. The Life of Jesus. 2010. (ENG., Illus.). 56p. (J). 20.00 *(978-0-8028-5362-2(5)*, Eerdmans Bks For Young Readers) Eerdmans, William B. Publishing Co.

Burrin, Angela M. Jesus Speaks to Me on My First Holy Communion. Lo Cascio, Maria Cristina, illus. 2009. 39p. (J). (gr. 1-5). 12.95 *(978-1-59325-149-9(1))* Word Among Us Pr.

Butcher, Sam, illus. Precious Moments: Storybook Bible & Girl Prayer Pal Set. 2003. 14.60 *(978-0-7180-0569-6(4))* Nelson, Thomas Inc.

Carr, Josie. IGod: Prayers & Promises to Connect to You with Him. 2008. 86p. (YA). pap. 4.99 *(978-1-57794-885-8(8))* Harrison House Pubs.

Cavanaugh, Karen. The Rosary for Children. 2003. (ENG., Illus.). 32p. (gr. -1-3). pap. 3.95 *(978-0-88271-456-1(2)*, RG10350) Regina Pr., Malhame & Co.

Center for Learning Staff. Prayer & Worship. 2007. (Religion Ser.). 138p. (YA). spiral bd. 18.95 *(978-1-56077-785-4(0))* Center for Learning, The.

Christensen, Catherine. I Can Pray Every Day. Eggbert, Corey, illus. 2015. (J). 14.99 *(978-1-4621-1646-1(9)*, Horizon Pubs.) Cedar Fort, Inc./CFI Distribution.

Concordia Publishing House. Portals of Prayer for Kids: 365 Daily Devotions. 2017. (ENG.). (J). 16.99 *(978-0-7586-5776-3(5))* Concordia Publishing Hse.

Cook, LaVelle. Little Jimmie & the Lord's Prayer. 2005. (J). 14.95 *(978-1-882185-45-0(5))* Cornerstone Publishing, Inc.

Crockett, Chelsea. Above All Else: 60 Devotions for Young Women, 1 vol. 2019. (ENG.). 208p. (YA). 15.99 *(978-0-310-76726-8(1))* Zondervan.

Cursha Pierce-Lunderman. God's Going Too! His Promises for Kids During Deployments. 2009. 20p. pap. 13.00 *(978-1-4389-1612-5(4))* AuthorHouse.

Daily Whispers of Wisdom for Girls Journal. 2014. (ENG.). 384p. (J). pap. 14.99 *(978-1-62836-945-8(0)*, Barbour Bks.) Barbour Publishing, Inc.

Daniel, Mikhal. Children's Picture Prayer Book: Sh'ma, V'ahavta & Shemoneh Esrei. 2009. (ENG.). 56p. pap. 29.80 *(978-0-557-05763-4(9))* Lulu Pr., Inc.

—Children's Prayer Book: A Messianic Siddur. 2009. 58p. pap. 15.32 *(978-0-557-05875-4(9))* Lulu Pr., Inc.

Darens, Cat. My Morning Angel. Oliver, Julia, illus. 2010. 18p. (J). (gr. -1-k). 7.95 *(978-0-8091-6753-1(0)*, Ambassador Bks.) Paulist Pr.

David C Cook. Baby's Bedtime Prayer Book, Bk. 4. 2007. (Land of Milk & Honey Ser.). (ENG.). 16p. (J). (gr. 1-3). bds. 6.99 *(978-0-7814-4527-6(2)*, 105358) Cook, David C.

David C. Cook Publishing Company Staff. Land of Milk & Honey, Bk. 3. 2007. (LMH Ser.). 16p. (J). (gr. 1-3). 6.99 *(978-0-7814-4526-9(4))* Cook, David C.

David, Juliet. Candle Prayers for Toddlers & Candle Bible for Toddlers, 2 vols. Prole, Helen, illus. 2009. (Candle Bible for Toddlers Ser.). 528p. (J). 24.99 *(978-0-8254-7380-7(2)*, Candle Bks.) Lion Hudson PLC GBR. Dist: Kregel Pubns.

DeVries, Mike & Murphy, Troy. Exodus: The Sacred Journey. 2003. (No Limits Ser.). (ENG.). 112p. (gr. 3-7). per. 12.99 *(978-0-8341-5005-8(0)*, 083-415-0050) Beacon Hill Pr. of Kansas City.

DeWitt, Becky. Destiny's Closet: Circle of Friends. 2010. 68p. pap. 17.99 *(978-1-4520-8364-3(9))* AuthorHouse.

DiCianni, Ron. Praying with the Presidents: One Nation's Legacy of Prayer. 2004. 48p. (J). (gr. k-3). 10.99 *(978-1-59185-408-1(3)*, Charisma Kids) Charisma Media.

Donaghy, Thomas J. Joyful Prayers (St. Joseph Tab Book) 2009. (ENG., Illus.). 12p. (J). bds. 7.95 *(978-0-89942-663-1(8)*, 856/22) Catholic Bk. Publishing Corp.

D'Oyen, Fatima & Kidwai, Abdur Raheem, compiled by. What Should We Say? 2016. (ENG., Illus.). 36p. (J). (gr. 2-7). 9.95 *(978-0-86037-267-7(7))* Kube Publishing Ltd. GBR. Dist: Consortium Bk. Sales & Distribution.

Eddie Ree Stolinski, Ree Stolinski & Stolinski, Eddie Ree. The Prayer Closet. 2010. (Illus.). 28p. (J). 14.93 *(978-1-4269-2995-3(1))* Trafford Publishing.

Edwards, Fran. The Lord's Prayer. 2013. 28p. pap. 11.95 *(978-1-61244-120-7(3))* Halo Publishing International.

Elkins, Stephen. First Steps in Prayer. Colton, Ellie, illus. 2006. (First Steps Ser.). 32p. (J). 9.99 *(978-0-8054-2663-2(9))* B&H Publishing Group.

—Tell Me about Prayer. 2014. (Train 'Em Up Ser.). (ENG.). 24p. (J). pap. 4.99 *(978-1-4143-9680-4(5)*, 4608670) Tyndale Hse. Pubs.

Fischer, Jean. I Prayed for You, 1 vol. 2018. (ENG., Illus.). 32p. (J). 16.99 *(978-1-4003-1281-8(7)*, Tommy Nelson) Nelson, Thomas Inc.

Flamini, Lorella, illus. Thank You Dear God! Prayers for Little Ones. 2006. 40p. (J). (gr. -1-k). bds. 11.95 *(978-0-8198-7417-7(5))* Pauline Bks. & Media.

Flowerpot Press Staff. A Child's Book of Prayers: Good Night, Dear God. 2013. (ENG., Illus.). 20p. (J). 8.99 *(978-1-77093-636-2(X))* Flowerpot Children's Pr. Inc. CAN. Dist: Cardinal Pubs. Group.

Gamber, Jenifer & Seamans, Timothy J. S. Common Prayer for Children & Families. Jones, Perry Hodgkins, illus. 2020. (ENG.). 136p. (J). (gr. 3-7). pap. 17.95 *(978-1-64065-264-4(7)*, fe68aecd-2f4e-4651-b5c8-d428feb7b20d) Church Publishing, Inc.

Ghani, Aisha. I Can Pray Anywhere! 2010. (ENG., Illus.). 15p. (J). (gr. -1-k). bds. 9.95 *(978-0-86037-339-1(8))* Kube Publishing Ltd. GBR. Dist: Consortium Bk. Sales & Distribution.

Gibson, Roxie. Talking with God. Gibson, Jim, illus. 2007. (ENG.). 24p. (J). (gr. -1-3). 7.99 *(978-1-933725-75-8(3))* Premium Pr. America.

Gold, August. Does God Hear My Prayer? Waller, Diane Hardy, photos by. 2005. (ENG., Illus.). 32p. (J). pap. 8.99 *(978-1-59473-102-0(0)*, d5782d0a-b2cb-4f47-96fc-23e42ba4e9f4, Skylight Paths Publishing) LongHill Partners, Inc.

Goldsmith, Joel S. Class Lessons with Joel Goldsmith. 2008. 116p. pap. *(978-0-9793119-3-2(4))* Editorial Benei Noaj.

Grace, Will. Thank You Prayer. Geist, Ken, ed. Watanabe, Kaori, illus. 2006. (My First Taggies Book Ser.). (ENG.). 8p. (J). (gr. k — 1). 12.99 *(978-0-439-87564-6(1)*, Cartwheel Bks.) Scholastic, Inc.

Grandma's Prayer. 2006. (J). 8.00 *(978-0-9774822-1-4(9))* Crosam Pr.

Groth, Jeanette L. Prayer: Learning How to Talk to God. rev. ed. 2003. (Illus.). 24p. (J). 6.49 *(978-0-570-07188-4(7))* Concordia Publishing Hse.

Grube, Edward C. Teens Pray: Conversations with God. 2003. 96p. (YA). 10.49 *(978-0-7586-0035-6(6))* Concordia Publishing Hse.

Gruen, K. W. Teaching the Message of the Lord's Prayer. 2013. (Illus.). 36p. pap. 16.99 *(978-1-4497-8146-0(2)*, WestBow Pr.) Author Solutions, LLC.

Hahn, Samuel J. Stories Told under the Sycamore Tree: Bible Plant Object Lessons. Patton, Scott, tr. Patton, Scott, illus. 2003. 191p. (J). pap. 19.95 *(978-0-7880-1972-2(4))* CSS Publishing Co.

Hartley, Bob. Childrens Adoration Prayer Book. Clonts, E. M. M., illus. 2012. 114p. pap. 24.95 *(978-0-615-58840-7(9))* Deeper Waters.

Harvest House Publishers. One-Minute Prayers for Boys. 2018. (One-Minute Prayers Ser.). (ENG.). 160p. (J). (gr. 2-7). pap. 9.99 *(978-0-7369-7345-8(1)*, 6973458) Harvest Hse. Pubs.

—One-Minute Prayers for Girls. 2018. (One-Minute Prayers Ser.). (ENG.). 160p. (J). (gr. 2-7). pap. 9.99 *(978-0-7369-7346-5(X)*, 6973465) Harvest Hse. Pubs.

Hilton, Jennifer & McCurry, Kristen. Pray to God: A Book about Prayer. 2016. (Frolic First Faith Ser.). (Illus.). 22p. (J). (gr. -1 — 1). bds. 6.99 *(978-1-5064-1046-3(4)*, Sparkhouse Family) 1517 Media.

Hilton, Jennifer Sue & McCurry, Kristen. Ora a Dios. Garton, Michael, illus. 2016. (SPA.). (J). *(978-1-5064-2093-6(1))* 1517 Media.

Hoopes, Scott. Joseph's First Prayer. 2017. (ENG.). (J). bds. 12.99 *(978-1-4621-2033-8(4))* Cedar Fort, Inc./CFI Distribution.

Hydeck, Michelle A. R. Wings Up: All with a Little Help from Our Angels. 2012. 40p. pap. 12.95 *(978-1-4525-5595-9(8))* Balboa Pr.

I Can Pray! 2006. (Faith Discovery Ser.). (Illus.). 24p. (J). bds. 6.99 *(978-0-7847-1398-3(7)*, 04058) Standard Publishing.

Jahsmann, Allan Hart & Simon, Martin P. Little Visits with God. White, Deborah, illus. 4th ed. 2006. (Little Visits Ser.). 413p. (J). (gr. 5-7). per. 13.49 *(978-0-7586-0847-5(0))* Concordia Publishing Hse.

Jelenek, Frank X. Journey to the Heart: Centering Prayer for Children. Boyajian, Ann, illus. 2007. (ENG.). 32p. (J). (gr. -1-3). pap. 18.99 *(978-1-55725-482-5(6)*, 4826) Paraclete Pr., Inc.

Johnson, Kevin. Pray: Talk to the King of the Universe, 1 vol. 2007. (Deeper Ser.). (ENG., Illus.). 112p. (gr. 13). pap. 7.99 *(978-0-310-27492-6(3))* Zondervan.

Keefer, Mikal & Harrington, David. Friends with God Devotions for Kids: 54 Delightfully Fun Ways to Grow Closer to Jesus, Family, & Friends. 2017. (ENG., Illus.). 224p. (J). 16.99 *(978-1-4707-4862-3(2))* Group Publishing, Inc.

Kendrick, Stephen, et al. PrayerWorks: Prayer Strategy & Training for Kids. Manuzak, Lisa, illus. 2015. (ENG.). 128p. (J). (gr. 3-6). 12.99 *(978-1-4336-8869-0(7)*, 005765908, B&H Kids) B&H Publishing Group.

—This Means War: A Strategic Prayer Journal. 2015. (ENG.). 224p. (J). (gr. 8-12). pap. 12.99 *(978-1-4336-8870-6(0)*, 005765911, B&H Kids) B&H Publishing Group.

Kennedy, Pamela & Brady, Anne Kennedy. Very Veggie Bedtime Prayers. Reed, Lisa, illus. 2018. (VeggieTales Ser.). (ENG.). 26p. (J). (gr. -1-k). bds. 11.99 *(978-0-8249-1670-1(0))* Worthy Publishing.

The Kids Prayed & God Arrived. 2004. (YA). *(978-1-59581-083-0(8))* Brentwood Communications Group.

Kirgiss, Crystal & Lyon, Christopher. A Teenager's Daily Prayer Book. Publications International Ltd. Staff, ed. 2005. (Illus.). 384p. 10.98 *(978-0-7853-4909-9(X)*, 3337100) Publications International, Ltd.

Lafferty, Jill C. Devociones para Niños Chispita. Grosshauser, Peter, illus. 2016. (SPA.). (J). *(978-1-5064-2101-8(6))* 1517 Media.

Le Feyer, Diane. My Little Prayers, 1 vol. 2016. (ENG., Illus.). 96p. (J). 6.99 *(978-0-7180-4019-2(8)*, Tommy Nelson) Nelson, Thomas Inc.

Lee, Stephi. Where Do My Prayers Go? Zareba, Lukasz, illus. 2013. (ENG.). 32p. (J). 14.95 *(978-0-578-11938-0(2))* Stephi /Lee.

Legacy. 7.50 *(978-0-8054-5927-2(8))* B&H Publishing Group.

Lemon, Willie Sells. Prayer Changes Things. 2011. 24p. (gr. -1). 17.50 *(978-1-4567-3829-7(1))* AuthorHouse.

Lewis, Jan, illus. First Prayers for Little Ones: Prayers for Every Day, Special Occasions & the Family. 2016. 48p. (J). (gr. -1-12). 9.99 *(978-1-86147-716-3(3)*, Armadillo) Anness Publishing GBR. Dist: National Bk. Network.

The Lord's Prayer: Prayer Cards. 2004. *(978-0-8294-1406-6(1))* Loyola Pr.

Lounsbury, Pete. Jesus & the Blind Man. 2007. (J). per. 12.95 *(978-1-59879-408-3(6))* Lifevest Publishing, Inc.

Lovasik, Lawrence G. A Child's Prayer Treasury (Puzzle Book) St. Joseph Puzzle Book: Book Contains 5 Exciting Jigsaw Puzzles. 2004. (ENG., Illus.). 12p. bds. 9.95 *(978-0-89942-719-5(7)*, 973/97) Catholic Bk. Publishing Corp.

MacArthur, John. My Faith & Prayer Journal. 2004. 64p. (J). pap. 4.99 *(978-1-4003-0441-7(5))* Nelson, Thomas Inc.

MacBeth, Sybil. Praying in Color. 2009. (ENG., Illus.). 40p. (J). (gr. 1-5). pap. 17.99 *(978-1-55725-595-2(4))* Paraclete Pr., Inc.

MacKenzie, Catherine. Helen Roseveare: What's in the Parcel? rev. ed. 2012. (Little Lights Ser.). (ENG.). 24p. (J). 7.99 *(978-1-84550-383-3(X)*, a968cdf5-b466-4c2a-886f-66cec838ae8d) Christian Focus Pubns. GBR. Dist: Baker & Taylor Publisher Services (BTPS).

Make Believe Ideas. God Bless the Moon. Machell, Dawn, illus. 2018. (ENG.). 24p. (J). (gr. -1 — 1). bds. 8.99 *(978-1-78692-906-8(6))* Make Believe Ideas GBR. Dist: Scholastic, Inc.

Marietta, C. S. I Like to Talk with God. (ENG., Illus.). 26p. (J). 2018. 19.95 *(978-1-948282-46-8(1))* 2017. pap. 9.95 *(978-1-947825-15-4(1))* Yorkshire Publishing Group.

May the Faith Be with You: 180 Devotions That Are Out of This World, 1 vol. 2015. (ENG.). 192p. (J). 9.99 *(978-0-310-75345-2(7))* Zonderkidz.

McIntosh, Kenneth R. Following Aslan: A Book of Devotions for Children Based on the Chronicles of Narnia by C. S. Lewis. 2006. (ENG.). 124p. (J). pap. 11.95 *(978-1-933630-02-1(7)*, Anamchara Bks.) Harding Hse. Publishing Sebice Inc.

Meyer, Naama, illus. Siddurchik: Prayer Book for Young Children. 2006. 32p. 12.95 *(978-965-229-328-2(8))* Gefen Publishing Hse., Ltd ISR. Dist: Gefen Bks.

Miller, Ann. Proverbs, Prayers, Poems for Children & Teens. 2005. (J). lib. bdg. 14.95 *(978-0-9748165-1-7(5))* Jaylil Publishing Co.

Mills, Charles. Eye of the Crocodile: And Other Bite-Sized Devotions for Juniors. 2019. (J). *(978-0-8163-6562-3(8))* Pacific Pr. Publishing Assn.

Mitzo Thompson, Kim, et al. Good Night, God: Bedtime Prayers for Little Ones. 2018. (ENG.). 8p. (J). bds. 4.99 *(978-1-68322-583-6(X)*, Shiloh Kidz) Barbour Publishing, Inc.

Montgomery Gibson, Jane. Maker of Prayer. Montgomery Gibson, Jane, illus. 2005. (Illus.). (YA). bds. 8.99 *(978-1-4183-0047-0(0))* Christ Inspired, Inc.

Mordi, Nicku. Know Before You Grow. 2012. 18p. pap. 9.99 *(978-1-61996-394-8(9))* Salem Author Services.

My Rosary. 2006.Tr. of Il Mio Rosario. (Illus.). 32p. pap. 3.95 *(978-0-8189-1235-1(9)*, St. Pauls) St Pauls/Alba Hse. Pubs.

Nalls, Charles. Prayer: A field Guide. 2008. 84p. pap. 10.95 *(978-0-595-49142-1(1))* iUniverse, Inc.

Odendahl, Jodi. Praying Hands. 2013. 20p. pap. 12.45 *(978-1-4497-9596-2(X)*, WestBow Pr.) Author Solutions, LLC.

Ogunkoya, Olukayode. Godly Children, Praying Children. 2012. 52p. pap. 23.99 *(978-1-61379-470-8(3))* Salem Author Services.

Omartian, Stormie. I Talk to God about How I Feel: Learning to Pray, Knowing He Cares. 2010. (Power of a Praying Kid Ser.). (ENG., Illus.). 32p. (J). (-k). 15.99 *(978-0-7369-2685-0(2)*, 6926850) Harvest Hse. Pubs.

—The Power of a Praying Kid. 2015. (Power of a Praying Kid Ser.). (ENG.). 112p. (J). (gr. 1-6). pap. 12.99 *(978-0-7369-6603-0(X)*, 6966030) Harvest Hse. Pubs.

—What Happens When I Talk to God? The Power of Prayer for Boys & Girls. 2007. (Power of a Praying Kid Ser.). (ENG., Illus.). 32p. (J). (gr. -1-2). 15.99 *(978-0-7369-1676-9(8)*, 6916768) Harvest Hse. Pubs.

Paiva, Johannah Gilman, ed. A Child's Book of Prayers: Please. 2013. (ENG., Illus.). 20p. (J). 8.99 *(978-1-77093-637-9(8))* Flowerpot Children's Pr. Inc. CAN. Dist: Cardinal Pubs. Group.

—A Child's Book of Prayers: Thank You. 2013. (ENG., Illus.). 20p. (J). 8.99 *(978-1-77093-638-6(6))* Flowerpot Children's Pr. Inc. CAN. Dist: Cardinal Pubs. Group.

Parr, Susan Sherwood. Christopher's Adventures: A Prayer on Angel Wings. Paraschiv, Doina, illus. 2004. (ENG.). 16p. 10.95 *(978-0-9728590-3-5(9)*, Kid-E Bks.) Word Productions.

—30 Days Out of Depression. 2004. (ENG., Illus.). 58p. 3.95 *(978-0-9728590-5-9(5))* Word Productions.

Perkins, Nicole. I Believe God Will: Book of Devotion & Prayer for Children. Perkins, Nicole & Frisk, Maria, illus. 2008. 32p. (J). 7.00 *(978-0-9755566-1-0(4))* Azreal Publishing Co.

Pharr, Nancy Elizabeth. When Should I Pray? Rose, Heidi, illus. 2003. 40p. (J). pap. 8.95 *(978-0-8198-8304-9(2)*, 332-412) Pauline Bks. & Media.

Pohl, Mayumi Ishimoto. Morning Prayer. 2012. (ENG.). 23p. (J). pap. 8.95 *(978-1-4327-7153-9(1))* Outskirts Pr., Inc.

Porsenna, Sandy. My first prayer Book. 2010. 34p. pap. 20.00 *(978-0-557-46986-4(4))* Lulu Pr., Inc.

Prayer For Peace. 2004. 1.75 *(978-0-8294-1073-0(2))* Loyola Pr.

The Prayer Jesus Gave Us. (Two Great Ways to Share God's Love Ser.). 16p. (gr. -1-k). 15.00 *(978-0-570-00315-1(6))* Concordia Publishing Hse.

Praying with the Church Fathers. 2008. (Illus.). 30p. (J). pap. 15.00 *(978-0-9800065-3-7(8))* ACTS Pr.

Redden, Vicki, et al. God's Amazing Creation. 2005. (Review Kids Ser.). 375p. (J). *(978-0-8280-1871-5(5))* Review & Herald Publishing Assn.

Reeves, Eira. Oraciones a la Hora de Dormir (Prayers at Bedtime) (SPA.). (J). 1.89 *(978-0-7899-0478-2(0)*, 498665) Editorial Unilit.

Remond-Dalyac, Emmanuelle. Good Night: A Toddler's Bedtime Prayer. Dieterle, Nathatlie, illus. 2017. (ENG.). (J). bds. 7.99 *(978-1-5064-2497-2(X)*, Sparkhouse Family) 1517 Media.

Roddy, Lauren S. My Scriptural Rosary. Darrenkamp, Julia Mary, illus. rev. ed. 2006. (J). 4.95 *(978-0-8198-4845-1(X))* Pauline Bks. & Media.

The Rosary: Prayer Cards. 2004. *(978-0-8294-1403-5(7))* Loyola Pr.

Rose-Heim, Donna. Dream Walking for Kids: 21 Prayer Activities for Children & Adults. 2011. 64p. (gr. -1). pap. 12.95 *(978-1-4634-4204-0(1))* AuthorHouse.

Rossner, Marianne. You Are with Me: Prayers for Every Part of the Day. Antoni, Birgit, illus. 2017. (ENG.). (J). bds. 7.99 *(978-1-5064-2498-9(8)*, Sparkhouse Family) 1517 Media.

Rowland, Wil. Wise & Silly. 2011. (Illus.). (J). *(978-1-56722-857-1(7))* Word Aflame Pr.

Rubin, Scott & Oestreicher, Mark. My Future, 1 vol. 2008. (Middle School Survival Ser.). (ENG., Illus.). 208p. (YA). pap. 9.99 *(978-0-310-27884-9(8))* Zondervan.

Sawyer, Judith L. This Is How I Pray. Sawyer, Judith L., illus. 2008. (Illus.). 24p. (J). pap. *(978-1-926585-11-6(9)*, CCB Publishing) CCB Publishing.

Saxon, Terrill. Now I Lay Me down to Sleep. 2006. (Baby Blessings Ser.). (Illus.). 12p. bds. 11.99 *(978-0-7847-1241-2(7)*, 04053) Standard Publishing.

Scarfi, Margaret Rose. I Pray the Rosary! Richards, Virginia Helen & Dick, Regina Frances, illus. 2005. 47p. (J). (gr. -1-3). pap. 4.95 *(978-0-8198-3689-2(3)*, 332-141) Pauline Bks. & Media.

Schmitt, Betsy & Veerman, David R. 365 Trivia Twist Devotions: An Almanac of Fun Facts & Spiritual Truth for Every Day of the Year. 2005. (ENG., Illus.). 384p. (J). (gr. 4-8). per. 16.99 *(978-0-7847-1737-0(0)*, 23350, B&H Kids) B&H Publishing Group.

Schultz, Karl A. St. Joseph Guide to Lectio Divina. 2009. (ENG.). 192p. pap. 11.00 *(978-0-89942-677-8(8)*, 657/04) Catholic Bk. Publishing Corp.

Setzer, Lee Ann. Tiny Talks #6: I will Trust in Heavenly Father & His Son, Jesus Christ-Their Promises are Sure, Vol. 6. 2005. (J). pap. 7.99 *(978-1-55517-889-5(8))* Cedar Fort, Inc./CFI Distribution.

Shaw, S. B. Children's Edition of Touching Incidents. 2005. pap. 15.95 *(978-1-59605-735-7(1)*, Cosimo Classics) Cosimo, Inc.

Silverman, Morris & Silverman, Hillel. Prayer Book for Summer Camps. (J). (gr. 3-12). 8.95 *(978-0-87677-060-3(X))*; pap. 6.95 *(978-0-87677-061-0(8))* Prayer Bk. Pr., Inc.

Simon, Mary Manz. Little Visits for Toddlers. Munger, Nancy, illus. 3rd ed. 2006. (Little Visits Ser.). Orig. Title: Little Visits 1-2-3. 275p. (J). (gr. -1-3). per. 13.49 *(978-0-7586-0845-1(4))* Concordia Publishing Hse.

—Little Visits with Jesus. Warren, Beverly, illus. 4th ed. 2006. (Little Visits Ser.). 266p. (J). (gr. -1-3). per. 13.49 *(978-0-7586-0846-8(2))* Concordia Publishing Hse.

Skevington, Andrea. Prayers & Verses Through the Bible. Skevington, Andrea, illus. 2016. (ENG., Illus.). 128p. (J). 11.99 *(978-0-7459-7663-1(8)*, e46af608-57f8-4973-9fe4-f2bc1437c776, Lion Books) Lion Hudson PLC GBR. Dist: Baker & Taylor Publisher Services (BTPS).

Small Offerings. 2005. 48p. 15.99 *(978-1-4003-0563-6(2))* Nelson, Thomas Inc.

Spraggett, Daphne. Window on the World: Prayer Atlas for All. 2006. (ENG., Illus.). 221p. pap. 19.99 *(978-1-932805-91-8(5))* Authentic Media GBR. Dist: Send The Light Distribution LLC.

Stanley, Charles. Every Day with Jesus: 365 Devotions for Kids, 1 vol. 2018. (ENG.). 400p. (J). 17.99 *(978-0-7180-9854-4(4)*, Tommy Nelson) Nelson, Thomas Inc.

Stortz, Diane. Say & Pray Devotions, 1 vol. 2016. (ENG.). 40p. (J). bds. 9.99 *(978-0-7180-8691-6(0)*, Tommy Nelson) Nelson, Thomas Inc.

Stortz, Diane & Holder, Jennifer. I Can Pray! Nobens, C. A., illus. 2014. (Faith That Sticks Bks.). (ENG.). 24p. (J). pap. 3.99 *(978-1-4964-0085-7(2)*, 4611760, Faith that Sticks) Tyndale Hse. Pubs.

Tataryn, Myroslaw. How to Pray with Icons: An Introduction for Children. 2003. (Illus.). 32p. *(978-2-89088-348-2(5))* Novalis Publishing.

Tetz, RosAnne C., told to. God's Big Idea. 2003. 377p. (J). 13.99 *(978-0-8280-1762-6(X))* Review & Herald Publishing Assn.

Tewkesbury, Alexa. Pens Special Edition: Prayer. 2017. (Pens Ser.). (ENG., Illus.). 32p. (J). pap. 4.99 *(978-1-78259-675-2(5)*, 96f6beb5-5790-4722-8ab1-fac559ea804d) Crusade for World Revival GBR. Dist: Baker & Taylor Publisher Services (BTPS).

Thank You God 2001. 2004. (My First Prayers Ser.). 10p. (J). bds. 3.99 *(978-1-85854-405-2(X))* Brimax Books Ltd. GBR. Dist: Byeway Bks.

Thomas Nelson Publishing Staff. My Pretty Pink Prayer Purse. 2014. (ENG.). 20p. (J). 9.99 *(978-0-529-12409-8(2))* Nelson, Thomas Inc.

Tortorella, Jackie. Our Father: Living the Lord's Prayer, 1 vol. 2009. (ENG.). 49p. pap. 16.95 *(978-1-61582-040-5(X))* America Star Bks.

Twenty-Third Publications, creator. Celebrating Eucharist: A Mass Book for Children. 2012. (ENG., Illus.). 34p. pap. 5.95 *(978-1-58595-855-9(7))* Twenty-Third Pubns./Bayard.

Veritas. Children's Everyday Prayerbook: For four to seven year Olds. 2008. (ENG., Illus.). 32p. (J). pap. 10.95 *(978-1-84730-098-0(7))* Veritas Pubns. IRL. Dist: Casemate Pubs. & Bk. Distributors, LLC.

Wangerin, Walter, Jr., et al. Little Ones Talk with God: A Book of Prayers. Rama, Sue, illus. 2006. 56p. 7.49 *(978-0-7586-1132-1(3))* Concordia Publishing Hse.

Williford, Barbara. A Child's Prayer. 2007. (J). 7.95 *(978-0-9796978-7-6(5))* G Publishing LLC.

WorthyKids. My First Book of Prayers. Flint, Gillian, illus. 2018. (ENG.). 20p. (J). (gr. -1-k). bds. 6.99 *(978-0-8249-1683-1(2))* Worthy Publishing.

York Lumbard, Alexis. Everyone Prays: Celebrating Faith Around the World. Sadeghian, Alireza, illus. 2014. 28p. (J). (gr. -1-3). 17.95 *(978-1-937786-19-9(6)*, Wisdom Tales) World Wisdom, Inc.

Zonderkidz. Bedtime Collection: 20 Favorite Bible Stories & Prayers, 1 vol. 2018. (Beginner's Bible Ser.). (ENG., Illus.). 128p. (J). 13.99 *(978-0-310-76328-4(2))* Zonderkidz.

PRAYERS

see also Prayer

Abraham, Ken. Jesus Loves Me Bible Storybook & Devotional Combo. 2003. (Illus.). 672p. (J). 24.99 *(978-1-4003-0185-0(8))* Nelson, Thomas Inc.

Adams, Carol J. God Listens to Your Care: Prayers for All the Animals of the World. 2006. (God Listens Ser.). (Illus.). 48p. (J). (gr. 3-7). per. 8.00 *(978-0-8298-1666-2(6))* Pilgrim Pr., The/United Church Pr.

—God Listens to Your Love: Prayers for Living with Animal Friends. 2005. (God Listens Ser.). 48p. (J). (gr. -1-3). per.

8.00 *(978-0-8298-1665-5(8))* Pilgrim Pr., The/United Church Pr.

—God Listens When You're Afraid: Prayers for When Animals Scare You. 2006. (God Listens Ser.). 48p. (J). (gr. -1). per. *(978-0-8298-1741-6(7))* Pilgrim Pr., The/United Church Pr.

Aiken, Nick, compiled by. Prayers for Teenagers. 2003. 112p. 10.00 *(978-0-281-05543-2(2))* SPCK Publishing GBR. Dist: Pilgrim Pr., The/United Church Pr.

Allsopp, Sophie, illus. Thank You, God! A Year of Blessings & Prayers for Little Ones. 2009. (ENG.). 16p. (J). (gr. -1-3). 12.99 *(978-1-4169-4754-7(X),* Little Simon Inspirations) Little Simon Inspirations.

El Alvidadizo David (Bramble Forgets) (Granja Oso de Miel Ser.). (SPA., Illus.). (J). bds. 4.99 *(978-0-7899-0610-6(4),* 495052) Editorial Unilit.

Anonymous. Twenty-Four Hours a Day for Teens: Daily Meditations. 2004. (Hazelden Meditations Ser.). (ENG.). 416p. pap. 18.95 *(978-1-59285-078-5(2),* Z2095) Hazelden.

Arterburn, Stephen & Florea, Jesse. The One Year Every Day Devotions: Devotions to Help You Stand Strong. 2008. (ENG.). 384p. (J). pap. 17.99 *(978-1-4143-1814-1(6),* 4600676, Tyndale Kids) Tyndale Hse. Pubs.

Arthur, Kay & Arndt, Janna. Lord Teach Me to Pray for Kids. 2006. (Discover-4-Yourself for Kids Ser.). 176p. (J). pap. 9.99 *(978-1-888655-30-8(5))* Precept.

Award Publications Staff. My First Book of Prayers. 2012. (ENG., Illus.). 32p. (J). 8.50 *(978-1-84135-875-8(4))* Award Pubns. Ltd. GBR. Dist: Parkwest Pubns., Inc.

Award Publications Staff & Award, Anna. A Child's Book of Prayers & Graces. 2012. (ENG., Illus.). 36p. (J). 9.95 *(978-1-84135-599-3(2))* Award Pubns. Ltd. GBR. Dist: Parkwest Pubns., Inc.

Barnhill, Carla. The One Year Devotions for Preschoolers 2. Kucharik, Elena, illus. 2010. (Little Blessings Ser.). (ENG.). 384p. (J). 17.99 *(978-1-4143-3445-5(1),* 4602435, Tyndale Kids) Tyndale Hse. Pubs.

Bauer, Judith. Catholic Baby's First Prayers. 2013. (ENG.). 20p. (gr. -1-k). bds. 16.95 *(978-0-88271-715-9(4),* RG10411) Regina Pr., Malhame & Co.

Bernard, M. My First Mass Book. Date not set. (J). (gr. -1-3). pap. 1.95 *(978-0-88271-165-2(2))* Regina Pr., Malhame & Co.

Bowman, Crystal. The One Year Devotions for Preschoolers. Kucharik, Elena, illus. 2004. (Little Blessings Ser.). (ENG.). 384p. (J). 15.99 *(978-0-8423-8940-2(7),* 6089407, Tyndale Kids) Tyndale Hse. Pubs.

Box, Su. My Rainbow Book of Bedtime Prayers, 1 vol. Brown, Jo, illus. 2009. 16p. (J). bds. 9.99 *(978-0-8254-7917-5(7),* Lion Children's) Lion Hudson PLC GBR. Dist: Kregel Pubns.

—My Rainbow Book of Everyday Prayers, 1 vol. Brown, Jo, illus. 2009. 16p. (J). bds. 9.99 *(978-0-8254-7918-2(5),* Lion Children's) Lion Hudson PLC GBR. Dist: Kregel Pubns.

Boyd, Annalisa. Special Agents of Christ: A Prayer Book for Young Orthodox Saints. 2012. (ENG., Illus.). 96p. (J). pap. 10.95 *(978-1-936270-55-2(2))* Ancient Faith Publishing.

Brewer, Dottie A. Praying 101 for Kids & Teens. 2004. (Illus.). 68p. (J). per. 4.95 *(978-0-9707945-2-9(5))* Billion $ Baby Pubns.

Brichto, Mira Pollak. The God Around Us Vol. 2: The Valley of Blessings. Alko, Selina, illus. 2004. 32p. (gr. -1-3). 13.95 *(978-0-8074-0738-7(0),* 101074) URJ Pr.

Brown, Monica & Musgrave, Hilary. Be Still & know... God Is Here: Be Still. 2011. (J). pap. *(978-0-9750732-8-5(1))* Emmaus Productions.

Brown, Rev. Joe. God's Gift, G G Brown: A True Story. 2012. 36p. pap. 24.95 *(978-1-4626-8165-5(4))* America Star Bks.

Burrin, Angela M. A Family Journey with Jesus through Lent: Prayers & Activities for Each Day. 2004. (J). pap. 13.95 *(978-1-59325-050-8(9))* Word Among Us Pr.

Bus, Sabrina. Hail Mary. 2nd ed. 2006. (Illus.). 12p. (J). (gr. -1). bds. 8.00 *(978-0-8028-5312-7(9),* Eerdmans Bks For Young Readers) Eerdmans, William B. Publishing Co.

Butcher, Sam, illus. Precious Moments: Angel Kisses & Snuggle Time Prayers with Dolly. 2003. 8.40 *(978-0-7180-0575-7(9))* Nelson, Thomas Inc.

—Precious Moments: Angel Kisses & Snuggle Time Prayers with Teddy Bear. 2003. 8.40 *(978-0-7180-0567-2(8))* Nelson, Thomas Inc.

Campbell, Herman. A Child's Prayer from the Heart. 2011. 24p. pap. 14.93 *(978-1-4269-5589-1(8))* Trafford Publishing.

Cannizzo, Karen, ed. Mass Prayers: For Young Catholics. 2006. (Illus.). 31p. (J). (gr. -1-2). per. 2.25 *(978-1-933178-40-0(X))* Pflaum Publishing Group.

Carr, Jacqueline. Tiny Tot Prayers: Baby's First Prayers. 2010. 24p. pap. 11.49 *(978-1-4520-2186-7(4))* AuthorHouse.

Casse-Dasilva, Christel. Little Prayers for the Children. 2012. (Illus.). 24p. pap. *(978-1-908341-96-9(3))* Paragon Publishing, Rothersthorpe.

Catholic Book Publishing Corp. Thank You Prayers (Rattle Book) 2008. (ENG., Illus.). 14p. (gr. -1-k). bds. 7.95 *(978-0-89942-722-5(7),* 981/22) Catholic Bk. Publishing Corp.

Cavanaugh, Karen. The Illustrated Rosary for Children. 2003. (ENG., Illus.). 32p. 5.95 *(978-0-88271-215-4(2),* RG14500) Regina Pr., Malhame & Co.

—My First Prayer Book. 2005. (ENG., Illus.). 32p. 6.95 *(978-0-88271-216-1(0),* RG14510) Regina Pr., Malhame & Co.

Chand, Candy. The Twelve Prayers of Christmas. 2009. (ENG., Illus.). 32p. (J). (gr. -1-2). 16.99 *(978-0-06-077636-7(6),* HarperCollins) HarperCollins Pubs.

Children's Bible Hour Staff. Tesoros Para Niños, Tomo 2: 365 Historias Devocionales Para Ninos y jovenes, 1 vol., 2. 2005.Tr. of Keys for Kids. (SPA.). 368p. (J). pap. 12.99 *(978-0-8254-1113-7(0),* Editorial Portavoz) Kregel Pubns.

Church, Caroline Jayne & Page, Josephine. Thank You Prayer. Church, Caroline Jayne, illus. 2005. (ENG., Illus.). 24p. (J). (gr. -1-k). 8.99 *(978-0-439-68099-8(9),* Cartwheel Bks.) Scholastic, Inc.

Collins, Rachel. Soul Sprouts. 2010. (ENG.). 41p. pap. 18.21 *(978-0-557-35421-4(8))* Lulu Pr., Inc.

Concordia Publishing House, creator. Happy Birthday: God's Blessings to You! 2007. (Illus.). 22p. (J). (gr. -1-k). bds. 6.49 *(978-0-7586-1331-8(8))* Concordia Publishing Hse.

Concordia Publishing House Staff, contrib. by. A Child's Garden of Prayer. 2005. (Illus.). 80p. 7.95 *(978-0-7586-0785-0(7))* Concordia Publishing Hse.

Cook, Cheryl. Kids Prayer Time Series: Lord, Teach me how to pray, Lord, Teach me how to walk by faith, Lord, Teach me how to love others, Lord, Teach me how to take care of the Temple. 2006. (J). 10.99 *(978-0-9746361-5-3(0))* Heavenly C. Publishing.

Cotner, June. House Blessings: Prayers, Poems, & Toasts Celebrating Home & Family. 2005. (ENG., Illus.). 164p. (gr. 8-17). 16.95 *(978-0-9748486-0-0(3))* Chronicle Bks. LLC.

Dalmatian Press Staff. God Bless Me. (Timeless Treasures Ser.). (ENG.). 28p. (J). bds. 7.99 *(978-1-4037-0856-4(8),* Spirit Pr.) Bendon, Inc.

—My First Prayers: Happy Tale Storybook. 2005. (ENG.). 24p. (J). 2.99 *(978-1-4037-1271-4(9),* Spirit Pr.) Bendon, Inc.

Darcy-Bérubé, Françoise & Berube, John Paul. Growing up a Friend of Jesus: A Guide to Discipleship for Children. 2003. (Illus.). 128p. *(978-2-89507-041-2(5))* Novalis Publishing.

Darens, Cat. My Bedtime Angel. Oliver, Julia, illus. 2010. 18p. (J). (gr. -1-k). 7.95 *(978-0-8091-6745-6(X),* Ambassador Bks.) Paulist Pr.

Dateno, Maria Grace. I Pray the Stations of the Cross. Richards, Virginia Helen, illus. 2006. (J). 4.50 *(978-0-8198-3691-5(5))* Pauline Bks. & Media.

David C. Cook Publishing Company Staff. Twenty-Third Psalm, 10 vols. 2003. (Jesus Pocket Bks.). (Illus.). 32p. (J). pap., pap. 8.90 *(978-1-55513-134-0(4),* 1555131344) Cook, David C.

David, Juliet. Candle Day by Day Bible & Prayers Gift Set, 1 vol. Heyes, Jane, illus. 2017. (ENG.). 560p. (J). bds. 27.99 *(978-1-78128-346-2(X),* 76336733-3d2e-47ce-a160-826eb15c3fc9, Candle Bks.) Lion Hudson PLC GBR. Dist: Baker & Taylor Publisher Services (BTPS).

DaySpring Greeting Card Staff & Jensen, Bonnie Rickner. Really Woolly Bedtime Prayers, 1 vol. 2009. (Really Woolly Ser.). (ENG., Illus.). 40p. (J). bds. 9.99 *(978-1-4003-1539-0(5),* Tommy Nelson) Nelson, Thomas Inc.

Dearborn, Sabrina. The Barefoot Book of Blessings: From Many Faiths & Cultures. Whelan, Olwyn, illus. 2007. (ENG.). 40p. (J). (gr. -1-3). 18.99 *(978-1-84686-069-0(5))* Barefoot Bks., Inc.

Deffenbaugh, David & McFarland, Bill. Strength for the Journey: A daily devotional Guide. Waldroop, Wista, ed. 2007. 388p. per. 15.99 *(978-0-9766703-5-3(6))* Little Acorn LLC.

Derico, Laura. Prayers for a Child's Day. Allen, Joy, illus. 2003. 32p. (J). 7.99 *(978-0-7847-1273-3(5),* 04033) Standard Publishing.

Dobell, Steve. A Child's Book of Prayer. 2012. (Illus.). 64p. (J). (gr. 2-7). 9.99 *(978-1-84322-867-7(X))* Anness Publishing GBR. Dist: National Bk. Network.

Doxey, Heidi. Tiny Talks, Vol. 14. 2013. pap. 8.99 *(978-1-4621-1357-6(5),* Horizon Pubs.) Cedar Fort, Inc./CFI Distribution.

D'Oyen, Fatima. Islamic Manners Activity Book. Zulkifli, Azhari, illus. 2012. (ENG.). 64p. (J). (gr. -1-2). pap., act. bk. ed. 5.95 *(978-0-86037-463-3(7))* Kube Publishing Ltd. GBR. Dist: Consortium Bk. Sales & Distribution.

Egbert, Elaine. Nature in a Nutshell. 2003. (Review Kids Ser.). 384p. (J). 13.99 *(978-0-8280-1669-8(0))* Review & Herald Publishing Assn.

Elkins, Stephen. The Bible Prayer Collection: 30 Life Changing Prayers from the Bible for Children. Colton, Ellie, illus. 2003. 64p. (J). (gr. k-3). 9.99 incl. audio compact disk *(978-0-8054-2758-5(9))* B&H Publishing Group.

—Special Times Bible Prayers for Toddlers. Reagan, Susan Joy, illus. 2004. (Special Times Ser.). 32p. (J). (gr. -1-18). 9.97 *(978-0-8054-2660-1(4))* B&H Publishing Group.

—Special Times Bible Promises for Toddlers. Reagan, Susan Joy, illus. 2005. (Special Times Ser.). 32p. (J). (gr. -1-18). 9.97 *(978-0-8054-2678-6(7))* B&H Publishing Group.

—Stories That End with a Prayer. Menck, Kevin, illus. 32p. (J). (gr. k-8). 12.98 *(978-1-56919-003-6(8))* Wonder Workshop.

Ellis, Gwen. Our Daily Bread: Prayers, Graces, & Slices of Scripture. 2006. (ENG., Illus.). 10p. (J). (gr. -1-k). bds. 10.99 *(978-0-7847-1852-0(0),* B&H Kids) B&H Publishing Group.

Esquinaldo, Virginia, illus. My Book of Prayers. 2006. 48p. (J). 3.95 *(978-0-8198-4843-7(3))* Pauline Bks. & Media.

Everyday Prayers for Sleepyheads. 2003. (J). *(978-0-7648-0995-8(4))* Liguori Pubns.

Ficocelli, Elizabeth. Child's Guide to the Rosary. Blake, Anne Catharine, illus. 2009. (ENG.). 32p. (J). 10.95 *(978-0-8091-6736-4(0))* Paulist Pr.

Field, Rachel. Prayer for a Child. Jones, Elizabeth Orton, illus. 2005. (ENG.). 32p. (J). (gr. -1-k). bds. 7.99 *(978-0-689-87886-2(9),* Little Simon) Little Simon.

—Prayer for a Child: Diamond Anniversary Edition. Jones, Elizabeth Orton, illus. 100th anniv. ed. 2004. (ENG.). 32p. (J). (gr. -1-3). 15.99 *(978-0-689-87356-0(5),* Simon & Schuster Bks. For Young Readers) Simon & Schuster Bks. For Young Readers.

—Prayer for a Child: Lap Edition. Jones, Elizabeth Orton, illus. 2013. (ENG.). 32p. (J). (gr. -1-2). bds. 12.99 *(978-1-4424-7659-2(1),* Little Simon) Little Simon.

Fincher, Kathy. A Catholic Baby's First Prayer Book. 2006. (ENG., Illus.). 16p. (gr. -1-k). bds. 10.95 *(978-0-88271-706-7(5),* RG13001) Regina Pr., Malhame & Co.

Flanagan, Anne. Come to Jesus: A Kids' Book for Eucharistic Adoration. Cleary, Janice, illus. 2006. (J). 4.50 *(978-0-8198-1577-4(2))* Pauline Bks. & Media.

Flowerpot Press. Good Morning, Dear God. 2013. (ENG., Illus.). 20p. (J). 8.99 *(978-1-77093-635-5(1))* Flowerpot Children's Pr. Inc. CAN. Dist: Cardinal Pubs. Group.

Forte, Bruno & Tarzia, Antonio. My Prayers: To God with Love & Joy. 2003. (Illus.). 65p. (J). pap. 6.95 *(978-0-8198-4831-4(X),* 332-222) Pauline Bks. & Media.

Friedl, Natalie. Help Me Pray Today. 2008. (Illus.). 32p. (J). *(978-0-9797429-1-0(9))* Halo Publishing International.

Friedrich, Eliza. Play Pray & Hooray. 2004. 128p. 10.99 *(978-0-7586-0117-9(4))* Concordia Publishing Hse.

Frotuna, Stan, told to. U Got 2 Pray. 2004. (Illus.). 255p. (YA). per. 9.95 *(978-1-931709-96-5(3))* Our Sunday Visitor, Publishing Div.

Fryar, Jane L. & Varvaris, Cathy. Jesus, Can I Talk with You? A Prayer Journal for Kids. 2003. 32p. (J). pap. 2.99 *(978-0-9718985-2-3(9))* C T A, Inc.

Garneau, Jean-Yves. Bedtime Prayers. 2004. (ENG., Illus.). 104p. pap. 6.95 *(978-0-8146-2890-4(7))* Liturgical Pr.

Geisler, Ruth. It's a Great, Awful, In-Between Day: Devotions for Young Readers. 2003. (Illus.). 112p. (J). (gr. 1-4). 10.99 *(978-0-7586-0124-7(7))* Concordia Publishing Hse.

Goble, Paul. Song of Creation. 2004. (ENG., Illus.). 32p. (J). 17.00 *(978-0-8028-5271-7(8))* Eerdmans, William B. Publishing Co.

God Made 2001. 2004. (My First Prayers Ser.). 10p. (J). bds. 3.99 *(978-1-85854-399-4(1))* Brimax Books Ltd. GBR. Dist: Byeway Bks.

God's Awesome Promises. Date not set. (YA). pap. 7.95 *(978-0-937347-71-3(X))* C&D International.

Gomez, Elena, illus. A World of Prayers. 2006. (ENG.). 32p. (J). (gr. k). 16.00 *(978-0-8028-5265-4(8),* Eerdmans Bks For Young Readers) Eerdmans, William B. Publishing Co.

Grand, Dee Ann. A Child's First Prayers. 2003. 24p. (J). bds. 12.99 *(978-0-8254-5504-9(9))* Kregel Pubns.

Hail Mary: Prayer Cards. 2004. *(978-0-8294-1405-9(3))* Loyola Pr.

Hall, Hannah. God Bless Our Bedtime Prayers, 1 vol. Whitlow, Steve, illus. 2018. (God Bless Book Ser.). (ENG.). 20p. (J). bds. 9.99 *(978-0-7180-9639-7(8),* Tommy Nelson) Nelson, Thomas Inc.

Hamdani, Ibrahim. Salah: The Prescribed Daily Prayers. 2003. 32p. (YA). *(978-0-9769245-5-5(2))* Islamic Ctr. of Sacramento, The.

Hare, Eric B. Skyscrapers: 365 Stories That Build You up: Daily Devotions for Juniors. 2009. (J). *(978-0-8280-2466-2(9))* Review & Herald Publishing Assn.

Henriques, S. M. My Little Book of Prayer. 2004. 160p. (gr. -1-3). pap. 6.95 *(978-1-58334-034-9(3),* F/S) Worthy Publishing.

Herrera, Erik, et al. Acquire the Fire: 40 Teen Devotionals, Vol. 1. Mauss, Doug, ed. 2006. (Teen Mania Ser.). (Illus.). 100p. (J). (gr. 4-7). per. 5.99 *(978-0-7814-4352-4(0),* 0781443520) Cook, David C.

Hess, Ingrid. Sleep in Peace. 2007. (ENG., Illus.). 40p. (J). (gr. 3-7). per. 12.99 *(978-0-8361-9381-7(4))* Herald Pr.

—Walk in Peace. 2009. (ENG.). 44p. (J). (gr. -1-k). pap. 13.99 *(978-0-8361-9469-2(1))* Herald Pr.

Hill, Karen. All God's Creatures. Johnson, Steve & Fancher, Lou, illus. 2005. (ENG.). 14p. (J). (gr. -1 — 1). 9.99 *(978-0-689-87819-0(2),* Little Simon) Little Simon.

Hite, LaDonna J. I Love to Pray. 2007. 24p. per. 14.45 *(978-0-9765898-9-1(3))* FAITHTOGO.

Hoagland, Victor. My Mass Book. 2008. (ENG., Illus.). 32p. (gr. -1-3). pap. 2.95 *(978-0-88271-542-1(9),* RG10356) Regina Pr., Malhame & Co.

Hodgson, Joan. Our Father. Ripper, Peter, illus. 2003. 24p. (gr. k-7). 5.95 *(978-0-85487-040-0(7))* White Eagle Publishing Trust GBR. Dist: DeVorss & Co.

Holl, Kristi. What's a Girl to Do? Finding Faith in Everyday Life, 1 vol. 2007. (Faithgirlz Ser.). (ENG.). 192p. (J). (gr. 3-7). pap. 9.99 *(978-0-310-71348-7(X))* Zonderkidz.

The Holy Sacrifice of the Mass. (J). 7.00 *(978-1-931555-29-6(X))* Our Lady of Victory Schl.

Hopkins, Lee Bennett & Moore, Gigi. Hear My Prayer, 1 vol. 2011. (ENG., Illus.). 32p. (J). (gr. -1-2). 12.99 *(978-0-310-71811-6(2))* Zonderkidz.

Horwitz, Brad, ed. & tr. With All Your Heart (A Weekday Prayer Book) Horwitz, Brad, tr. (ENG.). 80p. (J). 14.95 *(978-1-58013-144-5(1),* Kar-Ben Publishing) Lerner Publishing Group.

Hudson, Cheryl Willis. Come by Here Lord: Everyday Prayers for Children. 2004. (Illus.). 32p. (J). (gr. 2). 10.95 *(978-0-940975-92-7(0),* Sankofa Bks.) Just Us Bks., Inc.

Hudson, Lauriece. Prayers for the Smallest Hands. 2008. (Illus.). 24p. (J). (gr. -1-3). 6.95 *(978-1-60349-003-0(5),* Marimba Bks.) Just Us Bks., Inc.

Ippolito, Eva Marie. Hear, O Lord. Ippolito, Eva Marie, ed. l.t. ed. 2009. (Illus.). 72p. (YA). (gr. 7-12). pap. 13.69 *(978-1-4389-2422-9(4))* AuthorHouse.

Jeep, Elizabeth McMahon. Blessings & Prayers through the Year: A Resource for School & Parish. 2004. (J). 49.95 incl. audio compact disk *(978-1-56854-369-7(7),* CLASS) Liturgy Training Pubns.

—Children's Daily Prayer 2005 - 2006. 2005. (J). pap. 16.00 *(978-1-56854-538-7(X),* CDP06) Liturgy Training Pubns.

John Paul II, Pope, pseud. My Dear Young Friends: Pope John Paul II Speaks to Youth on Life, Love, & Courage. Vitek, John, ed. 2003. (Illus.). 144p. (YA). pap. 9.95 *(978-0-88489-748-4(6))* Saint Mary's Press of Minnesota.

Johnson, Lois Walfrid. Burnt Cookies. 2006. 96p. (J). pap. 6.99 *(978-0-7847-1510-9(6),* 42180) Standard Publishing.

Jones, Susan. Guided by His Light: A Child's Bedtime Prayer Book. Siewert, Pauline, illus. 2017. (ENG.). 64p. (J). (gr. k). 9.99 *(978-1-68099-282-3(1),* Good Bks.) Skyhorse Publishing Co., Inc.

Knox, Lorna Ann. I Came from Joy: Spiritual Affirmations & Activities for Children. 2nd rev. ed. 2004. (ENG., Illus.). 172p. (gr. k-7). pap. 19.95 *(978-1-56589-146-3(5))* Crystal Clarity Pubs.

Kowalski, Gary. Earth Day: An Alphabet Book. Baviera, Rocco, illus. 2009. (ENG.). 32p. (J). (gr. -1-4). 12.00 *(978-1-55896-542-3(4),* 1297770, Skinner Hse. Bks.) Unitarian Universalist Assn.

Larkin, Jean, ed. Prayers & Guidelines for Young Catholics. 2003. (Illus.). 28p. pap. 1.95 *(978-0-89837-231-1(3),* 4658) Pflaum Publishing Group.

Larsen, Carolyn. Prayers for Little Boys. Turk, Caron, illus. 2008. (Prayers For... Ser.). 131p. (J). (gr. -1-3). *(978-1-86920-527-0(8))* Christian Art Pubs.

—Prayers for Little Girls. Turk, Caron, illus. 2008. (Prayers For... Ser.). 131p. (J). (gr. -1-3). *(978-1-86920-526-3(X))* Christian Art Pubs.

Lee, Helen. Where in the World? Stories from Everywhere: Daily Devotions for Juniors. 2006. 373p. (J). *(978-0-8280-1874-6(X))* Review & Herald Publishing Assn.

Levivier, Juliette. Prayers Around the Crib. Gravier, Anne, illus. 2012. (ENG.). 48p. (J). (gr. -1-3). 9.99 *(978-1-58617-773-7(7))* Ignatius Pr.

Lewis, Jan. Baby's First Book of Prayers. 2013. (Illus.). 24p. (J). (gr. -1-12). bds. 6.99 *(978-1-86147-340-0(0),* Armadillo) Anness Publishing GBR. Dist: National Bk. Network.

Little Folded Hands: Prayers for Childre. 2005. pap. 8.95 *(978-1-59605-640-4(1),* Cosimo Classics) Cosimo, Inc.

Little Treasury Sac Heart. 15p. pap. *(978-0-8198-4461-3(6),* 332-164) Pauline Bks. & Media.

Living Out Christ's Love Prayer Journals, 12 vols. 2005. (YA). 9.95 *(978-0-9772313-2-4(1))* The 101 Group, Inc.

Living the Good News Staff. Kids in Common: A Children's Book of Common Prayer. 2004. (Illus.). 32p. (J). 4.95 *(978-1-931960-29-8(1),* Living the Good News) Church Publishing, Inc.

Lonsdale, Mary, illus. My Prayers for Everyday. 2004. 10p. (J). bds. 7.99 *(978-1-85854-438-0(6))* Brimax Books Ltd. GBR. Dist: Byeway Bks.

The Lord's Prayer: Forgive Us. 2003. (Illus.). 50p. (J). pap. 6.00 *(978-1-58572-052-1(6))* Ambassador Pubns.

Lords Prayer for Children. 2006. 10p. (YA). bds. 11.99 *(978-0-7847-1772-1(9),* 04724) Standard Publishing.

Lubomirski, H. S. H. Prince Alexi. Thank You for My Dreams: Bedtime Prayers of Gratitude. 2019. (ENG., Illus.). 96p. 16.99 *(978-1-4494-9742-2(X))* Andrews McMeel Publishing.

Lucado, Max. Lucado Treasury of Bedtime Prayers, 1 vol. 2015. (ENG., Illus.). 160p. (J). 19.99 *(978-0-7180-1631-9(9),* Tommy Nelson) Nelson, Thomas Inc.

Lyttle, Marcy. Catching Fireflies: Family Night Devotional Fun. Irwin, Kendra, illus. 2007. 273p. 18.99 *(978-1-932307-77-1(X),* Ambassador International) Emerald Hse. Group, Inc.

Make Believe Ideas, Ltd. Build Your Own Prayers: Magnetic Prayer Book. 2007. (Illus.). 14p. (J). (gr. k-3). 12.95 *(978-1-59145-554-7(5))* Nelson, Thomas Inc.

Manhardt, Laurie Watson. Friends of God: Catholic Bible Study for Children. Co, Aileen & Dayton, Melissa, illus. 2006. (Come & See Kids Ser.). 124p. (J). (gr. -1-2). per. 9.95 *(978-1-931018-41-8(3))* Emmaus Road Publishing.

Martin, Carolyn. Book of Childhood Prayers. (ENG., Illus.). 63p. (J). *(978-0-340-56763-0(5))* Hodder & Stoughton.

Mass, Wendy. Autumn: Poems, Songs, Prayers. 2004. (Weather Windows Ser.). 4.99 *(978-0-570-07168-6(2))* Concordia Publishing Hse.

Medina, Sarah. A Day to Remember. Brecknell, Annie, illus. 48p. pap. 8.99 *(978-0-7459-4770-9(0),* Lion Books) Lion Hudson PLC GBR. Dist: Trafalgar Square Publishing.

Mercer, Gabrielle. Prayers for Boys. Ede, Lara, illus. 2012. (ENG.). 22p. (J). (— 1). bds. 6.99 *(978-1-78065-845-2(1))* Make Believe Ideas GBR. Dist: Scholastic, Inc.

—Prayers for Girls. Ede, Lara, illus. 2012. (ENG.). 22p. (J). (— 1). bds. 6.99 *(978-1-78065-745-5(5))* Make Believe Ideas GBR. Dist: Scholastic, Inc.

Miller, Woody, illus. Teflat Haderech: The Traveler's Prayer. 2012. (ENG.). 32p. (J). 17.95 *(978-0-939144-69-3(7))* EKS Publishing Co.

—Teflat Haderech: The Traveler's Pryaer. 2012. (ENG.). 32p. (J). pap. 11.95 *(978-0-939144-68-6(9))* EKS Publishing Co.

Morneau, Robert F., ed. Children's Book of Classic Catholic Prayers. 2008. (ENG., Illus.). 32p. (J). (gr. -1-5). pap. 6.95 *(978-0-8091-6666-4(6),* 6666-6) Paulist Pr.

Mundy, Michaelene. A Book of Prayers for All Your Cares. Alley, R. W., illus. 2004. (J). per. 7.95 *(978-0-87029-382-5(6))* Abbey Pr.

Muñiz, Emme. Lord Help Me: Inspiring Prayers for Every Day. Figueroa, Brenda, illus. 2020. (ENG.). 40p. (J). (gr. -1-2). 18.99 *(978-0-593-12008-8(6));* lib. bdg. 21.99 *(978-0-593-12009-5(4))* Random Hse. Children's Bks. (Crown Books For Young Readers).

My Little Book of Prayers. 2008. (Deluxe Charm Book Ser.). 12p. *(978-1-4075-3329-2(0))* Parragon, Inc.

Myers, Walter Dean. The Gifts We Bring. Date not set. 96p. (J). (gr. 3-7). 5. 14.99 *(978-0-06-027809-0(9))*No. 6. 14.99 *(978-0-06-027810-6(2))* HarperCollins Pubs.

Nelson, Thomas. Precious Moments: God Watches over Me, 1 vol. 2015. (Precious Moments Ser.). (ENG., Illus.). 32p. (J). bds. 9.99 *(978-0-7180-1108-6(2),* Tommy Nelson) Nelson, Thomas Inc.

Oberthür, Rainer. Our Father. Nascimbeni, Barbara, illus. 2016. (ENG.). 58p. (J). 16.00 *(978-0-8028-5468-1(0),* Eerdmans Bks For Young Readers) Eerdmans, William B. Publishing Co.

O'Loughlin, Declan & McKenna, Donna, eds. Fone a Friend: A Prayer Book by Children for Children. 2010. (ENG.). 47p. (J). pap. 12.95 *(978-1-84730-197-0(5))* Veritas Pubns. IRL. Dist: Casemate Pubs. & Bk. Distributors, LLC.

Omartian, Stormie. The Prayer That Makes God Smile. 2009. (Power of a Praying Kid Ser.). (ENG., Illus.). 32p. (J). (gr. k-2). 14.99 *(978-0-7369-2314-9(4),* 6923149) Harvest Hse. Pubs.

P, I. Kids. PT 6x6 My Little Treasury First P- O/P. 2014. (ENG., Illus.). 160p. (J). *(978-1-4508-7299-7(9),* 1450872999) Publications International, Ltd.

Paltro, Piera. Learning My Prayers, 8 bks. Daughters of St. Paul Staff, tr. Curti, Anna M., illus. Incl. Angel of God. 16p. (gr. k-3). 1981. pap. 2.95 *(978-0-8198-0739-7(7),* CH0031P); Eternal Rest: A Prayer for People Who Have Died. 15p. (gr. k-3). 1992. pap. 2.50 *(978-0-8198-2332-8(5));* Glory to the Father. 21p. (gr. -1-18). 1987. pap. 2.50 *(978-0-8198-3043-2(7),* CH0227); Hail, Holy Queen. 15p. (gr. k-3). 1992. pap. 2.50 *(978-0-8198-3365-5(7));* Hail Mary. 22p. (gr. k-3). 1992. pap. 2.50 *(978-0-8198-3316-7(9));* I Believe: The Profession of Faith or Creed. 29p. (gr. k-3). 1992. pap. 2.50 *(978-0-8198-3664-9(8));* My Mass. 32p. (gr. k-3). 1992. pap. 2.50 *(978-0-8198-4765-2(8));* Our Father. 23p. (gr. -1-1). 1991. pap. 2.95 *(978-0-8198-5416-2(6),* CH0416P); (J). (Illus.). Set pap. 18.80 *(978-0-8198-4483-5(7))* Pauline Bks. & Media.

Peralas, Jorge. Oracional Bilingue Para Ninos: A Children's Prayerbook in Spanish-English. Domeier, Renee & Grisewood, Therese U., eds. 2012. (ENG., Illus.). 96p. (gr. 3-7). pap. 9.95 *(978-0-8146-2459-3(6))* Liturgical Pr.

Peterson, Mary Joseph. Holy Mass in My Pocket. 2008. (Illus.). 32p. (J). 1.95 *(978-0-8198-3392-1(4))* Pauline Bks. & Media.

—Rosary in My Pocket. 2008. (Illus.). 32p. (J). 1.95 *(978-0-8198-6485-7(4))* Pauline Bks. & Media.

Peterson, Mary Joseph, illus. Basic Prayers in My Pocket. 2009. 32p. (J). pap. 1.95 *(978-0-8198-1173-8(4))* Pauline Bks. & Media.

Philip, Neil. In the House of Happiness: A Book of Prayer & Praise. Brent, Isabelle, illus. 2003. (ENG.). 64p. (YA). (gr. 7). tchr. ed. 17.00 *(978-0-618-23481-3(0),* 111178, Clarion Bks.) HarperCollins Pubs.

Piper, Sophie. An Arkful of Animal Prayers, 1 vol. Macnaughton, Tina, illus. 2009. 64p. (J). 9.95 *(978-0-8254-7840-6/5)*, Lion Children's) Lion Hudson PLC GBR. Dist: Kregel Pubns.

—The Lion Book of Prayers to Read & Know, 1 vol. Lewis, Anthony, illus. 2010. (ENG.). 96p. (J). 12.99 *(978-0-8254-7898-7/7)*, Lion Children's) Lion Hudson PLC GBR. Dist: Kregel Pubns.

—My Baptism Book. Kolanovic, Dubravka, illus. 2007. (ENG.). 64p. (J). (gr. -1-1). 14.99 *(978-1-55725-535-8/0)*, 5358) Paraclete Pr., Inc.

—Prayers for Each & Every Day. Wilson, Anne, illus. 2008. (ENG.). 64p. (J). (gr. -1-2). 14.95 *(978-1-55725-622-5/5)* Paraclete Pr., Inc.

—Thinking of Heaven: Prayers for Sad Goodbyes, 1 vol. Hudson, Annabel, illus. 2009. 48p. (J). 7.95 *(978-0-8254-7856-7/1)*, Lion Children's) Lion Hudson PLC GBR. Dist: Kregel Pubns.

Poser, Cynthia M. Hotline to Heaven. 2012. pap. 8.95 *(978-0-7414-7624-1/X)* Infinity Publishing.

—Hotline to Heaven - Color. 2012. pap. 11.95 *(978-0-7414-7625-8/8)* Infinity Publishing.

Prayers for Sleepyheads, Set. 2003. (J). pap. 10.95 net. *(978-0-7648-0994-1/6)* Liguori Pubns.

Prayers of Jesus for Children. (J). *(978-0-88271-162-1/8)* Regina Pr., Malhame & Co.

Prayers That Avail Much for Teens. (YA). 14.99 *(978-0-89274-902-7/4)* Harrison House Pubs.

Promiseland. 2008. (J). per. 8.00 *(978-0-9664736-0-5/4)* Grace Walk Resources, LLC.

Publications International Ltd. Staff, ed. My Little Prayer Book. 2010. 384p. 10.98 *(978-1-60553-972-0/4)* Publications International, Ltd.

Randazzo, Dottie. Praying 101 for Kids & Teens. 2007. (ENG.). 101p. pap. 10.95 *(978-0-615-14725-3/9)* Creative Dreaming Ltd.

Reehorst, Jane. Guided Meditations for Children. 2015. 312p. pap. 38.00 *(978-1-4982-3293-7/0)*, Wipf and Stock) Wipf & Stock Pubs.

Reeves, Eira. El Padre Nuestro (The Lord's Prayer) (SPA.). (J). 1.89 *(978-0-7899-0480-5/2)*, 498667) Editorial Unilit.

Roche, Maïte. My First Bedtime Prayers. 2011. (ENG., Illus.). 14p. (J). (gr. -1-k). bds. 8.99 *(978-1-58617-503-0/3)* Ignatius Pr.

Rock, Lois. Al Final del Dia. Rawlings, Louise, illus. (Coleccion Luz de Noche). (SPA.). (J). (gr. k-3). *(978-84-236-5039-2/1)* Edebé ESP. Dist: Lectorum Pubns., Inc.

—A Gift for Baby's Christening, 1 vol. Rescek, Sanja, illus. 2014. (ENG.). 48p. (J). (— 1). 7.99 *(978-0-7459-6490-4/7)*, 57dc4a6c-0fd3-48a6-bad6-1f19af0ba00c, Lion Children's) Lion Hudson PLC GBR. Dist: Baker & Taylor Publisher Services (BTPS).

—The Lion Book of Prayers to Keep for Ever. Allsopp, Sophie, illus. 2016. (ENG.). 64p. (J). (gr. 2-4). 10.99 *(978-0-7459-7641-9/7)*, 7b71f7cc-80b1-42ba-a6ae-2329a9d44460, Lion Children's) Lion Hudson PLC GBR. Dist: Baker & Taylor Publisher Services (BTPS).

—Todos los Dias Contigo. Rawlings, Louise, illus. (Coleccion Luz de Noche). (SPA.). (J). (gr. k-3). *(978-84-236-4916-7/4)* Edebé ESP. Dist: Lectorum Pubns., Inc.

Rylant, Cynthia. Give Me Grace: Give Me Grace. 2005. (ENG., Illus.). 32p. (J). (gr. -1-k). bds. 8.99 *(978-0-689-87885-5/0)*, Little Simon) Little Simon.

Sabado, Joe, illus. Mommy Teach Us to Pray. Fujii, Jason, photos by. Lt. ed. 2006. 31p. (J). 15.95 *(978-1-59879-122-8/2)* Lifevest Publishing, Inc.

Sanders, Angela. 100 Days: The Glory Experiment. 2018. 224p. (J). pap. *(978-1-4627-9942-8/6)* Lifeway Christian Resources.

Savary, Louis M. Rosary for Children. Date not set. (J). (gr. -1-3). pap. 1.25 *(978-0-88271-158-4/X)* Regina Pr., Malhame & Co.

—Way of the Cross. Date not set. (J). (gr. -1-3). pap. 1.95 *(978-0-88271-160-7/1)* Regina Pr., Malhame & Co.

Sheeran, Beth. A Child's Book of Prayer. 2005. (ENG.). 90p. pap. 14.00 *(978-0-7343-0615-9/6)*, Penguin Global) Penguin Publishing Group.

Shenton, Tim. Readings from James: Trials + Faith + Riches + Prayer. 2005. (Daily Readings From Ser.). (Illus.). 68p. (J). pap. 6.50 *(978-1-903087-61-9/9)* DayOne Pubns. GBR. Dist: Send The Light Distribution LLC.

Sherman, Karin Holsinger. Candle Walk: A Bedtime Prayer to God. 2019. (ENG., Illus.). 40p. (J). (gr. -1-6). 19.95 *(978-1-64065-132-6/2)*, ddfb7d77-b548-4844-80df-cc6639f6a910) Church Publishing, Inc.

Simon, Mary Manz. My First Read & Learn Book of Prayers. Duendes Del Sur, illus. 2007. (ENG.). 38p. (J). (gr. -1-k). bds. 9.99 *(978-0-439-90632-6/6)* Scholastic, Inc.

Spafford, Suzy, illus. My Little Book of Prayers. gif. ed. 2005. 32p. 9.99 *(978-0-7369-1495-6/1)* Harvest Hse. Pubs.

SPCK. I Can Join in Common Worship: A Children's Communion Book. 2003. (Illus.). 24p. 5.00 *(978-0-281-05568-5/8)* SPCK Publishing GBR. Dist: Pilgrim Pr., The/United Church Pr.

St. John, Patricia. Talking & Listening to God. 2004. (ENG., Illus.). 128p. (J). pap. 6.99 *(978-1-85792-840-2/7)*, Christian Focus) Christian Focus Pubns. GBR. Dist: Send The Light Distribution LLC.

Stephanie Longfoot Staff. God Bless 2001. 2004. (My First Prayers Ser.). 10p. (J). bds. 3.99 *(978-1-85854-403-8/3)* Brimax Books Ltd. GBR. Dist: Byeway Bks.

Stipp, Launa N. The Gift of Prayer. 2009. (ENG.). 26p. pap. 15.99 *(978-1-4415-6840-3/9)* Xlibris Corp.

Strauss, Ed. Devotions to Make You Smarter, 1 vol. 2007. (2:52 Ser.). (ENG., Illus.). 192p. (J). (gr. 3-7). pap. 9.99 *(978-0-310-71312-8/9)* Zonderkidz.

—Devotions to Take You Deeper, 1 vol. 2007. (2:52 Ser.). (ENG.). 192p. (J). (gr. 4-7). pap. 9.99 *(978-0-310-71313-5/7)* Zonderkidz.

Strong, Cynda. Where Do Angels Sleep? Denos, Julia, illus. 2007. 24p. (J). (gr. -1-3). 14.99 *(978-0-7586-1298-4/2)* Concordia Publishing Hse.

Stuckey, Denise. Jesus, I Feel Close to You. Saroff, Phyllis, illus. 2005. 32p. (J). 10.95 *(978-0-8091-6718-0/2)*, 6718-2) Paulist Pr.

Suzanne, Rentz. Daughters of Heaven Devotional. 2004. pap. 12.99 *(978-1-57794-560-4/3)* Harrison House Pubs.

Swamp, Jake. Giving Thanks: A Native American Good Morning Message. braille ed. 2004. (Illus.). (J). (gr. k-3). spiral bd. *(978-0-616-03096-7/7)* Canadian National Institute for the Blind/Institut National Canadien pour les Aveugles.

Swarner, Kristina, illus. The Bedtime Sh'ma: A Good Night Book. 2007. (ENG & HEB.). 40p. (J). 17.95 *(978-0-939144-55-6/7)*; pap. 11.95 *(978-0-939144-54-9/9)* EKS Publishing Co.

—The BEDTIME SH'MA, Book & CD Set. 2007. (ENG & HEB.). 40p. (J). 24.95 incl. audio compact disk *(978-0-939144-58-7/1)* EKS Publishing Co.

—Modeh Ani: A Good Morning Book. 2010. (HEB & ENG.). 32p. (J). 17.95 *(978-0-939144-64-8/6)*; pap. 11.95 *(978-0-939144-63-1/8)* EKS Publishing Co.

Talaro, Theresa. Mommy Teach Us to Pray. Lt. ed. 2006. (Illus.). 31p. (J). (gr. -1-5). per. 12.95 *(978-1-59879-121-1/4)* Lifevest Publishing, Inc.

—A Mother's Prayer: A Life Changing Prayer for Children. Castulo Aten, Vicky Talaro & Ikaia Aten, Dayle Marc, illus. French, Peter, photos by. 2007. 44p. (J). 23.99 *(978-1-59879-335-2/7)*, Lifevest) Lifevest Publishing, Inc.

Taylor, Caroline. All Things Bright & Beautiful. Longfoot, Stephanie, illus. 2004. (My First Prayers Ser.). 10p. (J). bds. 3.99 *(978-1-85854-238-6/3)* Brimax Books Ltd. GBR. Dist: Byeway Bks.

—All Things Wise & Wonderful. Longfoot, Stephanie, illus. 2004. (My First Prayers Ser.). 10p. (J). bds. 3.99 *(978-1-85854-239-3/1)* Brimax Books Ltd. GBR. Dist: Byeway Bks.

The Prayer Children. Whispers in God's Ears. 2003. (Illus.). 82p. (J). per. 12.95 *(978-0-87029-377-1/X)* Abbey Pr.

Thomas, Scott. Prayers & Pledges. 2010. 24p. pap. 12.99 *(978-0-9824931-9-9/3)* Faithful Life Pubs.

Trumpet Of God Ministries. E I I Children's Prayers from the Heart. 2012. (Illus.). 28p. pap. 13.99 *(978-1-4497-5478-5/3)*, WestBow Pr.) Author Solutions, LLC.

Tucker, Terra. Daughter of the King: Daughter of the King: Book with Audio CD. Marsee, Kimberly, illus. 2007. 48p. (J). 19.95 *(978-0-9794578-0-7/7)* Tucker, Terra.

Veritas. Children's Everyday Prayer Book. 2008. (ENG., Illus.). 32p. (J). pap. 9.95 *(978-1-84730-060-7/X)* Veritas Pubns. IRL. Dist: Casemate Pubs. & Bk. Distributors, LLC.

Walsh, Sheila. Sweet Dreams Princess: God's Little Princess Bedtime Bible Stories, Devotions, & Prayers, 1 vol. 2008. (ENG.). 336p. (J). 17.99 *(978-1-4003-1297-9/3)*, Tommy Nelson) Nelson, Thomas Inc.

Waltersdorff, Christy J. 25 Days to Jesus. Miller, Mitchell, illus. 2018. (J). *(978-0-87178-258-8/8)* Brethren Pr.

Watson, Carol. 365 Children's Prayers: Prayers Old & New for Today & Every Day. 2016. (ENG.). 160p. (J). 14.99 *(978-1-4347-1017-8/3)* Cook, David C.

Watson Manhardt, Laurie. In the Beginning: Catholic Bible Study for Children. Aileen Co & Dayton, Melissa, illus. 2008. (Come & See Kids Ser.). 108p. (J). (gr. -1-2). per. 9.95 *(978-1-931018-42-5/1)* Emmaus Road Publishing.

Wells, Aurora. Prayers That Bring Deliverance for Teens. 2013. 92p. pap. 10.99 *(978-1-62419-669-0/1)* Salem Author Services.

Weston Woods Staff, creator. Giving Thanks. 2011. 38.75 *(978-0-439-72676-4/X)*; 18.95 *(978-0-439-72673-3/5)*; 29.95 *(978-0-439-73469-1/X)* Weston Woods Studios, Inc.

Wigger, J. Bradley. Thank You, God. Jago, illus. 2014. (ENG.). 26p. (J). 16.00 *(978-0-8028-5424-7/9)*, Eerdmans Bks For Young Readers) Eerdmans, William B. Publishing Co.

Wikler, Madeline & Groner, Judyth. Thank You, God! A Jewish Child's Book of Prayers. Haas, Shelly O., illus. 2003. (ENG.). 32p. (J). (gr. -1-2). pap. 8.99 *(978-1-58013-101-8/8)*, 503b5039-5df0-4281-b204-5a29b180a432, Kar-Ben Publishing) Lerner Publishing Group.

Wiley, Patricia Ann, creator. Time to Change: A Daily Devotional. 2nd ed. 2004. Orig. Title: It's Time to Change. (YA). per. 10.00 *(978-0-9760734-0-6/4)* Pouring the Oil: Poetic Praise Pubns.

Wilkinson, Bruce & Suggs, Robb. The Prayer of Jabez for Young Hearts. Martinez, Sergio, illus. 2004. 32p. (J). (gr. -1-3). 15.99 *(978-0-8499-7932-3/3)* Nelson, Thomas Inc.

Will, Julianne, ed. Catholic Prayer Book for Children. 2004. (J). pap. 3.95 *(978-1-59276-047-3/3)*; per. 10.95 *(978-1-59276-046-6/5)* Our Sunday Visitor, Publishing Div.

William H. Sadlier, Inc Staff, contrib. by. We Believe & Pray: Prayers & Practices for Young Catholics. 2008. 64p. (J). pap. *(978-0-8215-5700-6/9)* Sadlier, William H. Inc.

Wright, Sally Ann. A Child's Book of Prayers. Ayres, Honor, illus. 2009. 96p. (J). (gr. -1). 10.99 *(978-0-7586-1662-3/7)* Concordia Publishing Hse.

Yaconelli, Mark. Wonder, Fear, & Longing: A Book of Prayers, 1 vol. 2009. (ENG.). 176p. (YA). pap. 9.99 *(978-0-310-28360-7/4)* Zondervan.

Young, Jeanna. Princess Prayers, 1 vol. Aranda, Omar, illus. 2017. (Princess Parables Ser.). (ENG.). 30p. (J). bds. 9.99 *(978-0-310-75869-3/6)* Zonderkidz.

Young, Sarah. Jesus Calling Little Book of Prayers, 1 vol. Farias, Carolina, illus. 2018. (Jesus Calling(r) Ser.). (ENG.). 26p. (J). bds. 8.99 *(978-0-7180-9753-0/X)*, Tommy Nelson) Nelson, Thomas Inc.

Ytreeide, Arnold. Tabitha's Travels: A Family Story for Advent, 1 vol. 2010. (Illus.). 160p. (J). (gr. 7-18). pap. 16.99 *(978-0-8254-4172-1/2)* Kregel Pubns.

PRAYING MANTIS

Bergeron, Alain M. & Quintin, Michel. Do You Know Praying Mantises?, 1 vol. Sampar, illus. 2014. (Do You Know? Ser.). (ENG.). 64p. (J). (gr. 2-4). pap. 9.95 *(978-1-55455-337-2/7)*, 0b2cf7c3-8016-4fb5-8674-c46a23ac2fb3) Trifolium Bks., Inc. CAN. Dist: Firefly Bks., Ltd.

Borgert-Spaniol, Megan. Praying Mantises. 2016. (Creepy Crawlies Ser.). (ENG., Illus.). 24p. (J). (gr. k-3). lib. bdg. 26.95 *(978-1-62617-300-2/1)*, Blastoff! Readers) Bellwether Media.

Goldish, Meish. Deadly Praying Mantises. 2008. (No Backbone! Ser.). (Illus.). 24p. (J). (gr. k-3). lib. bdg. 26.99 *(978-1-59716-582-2/4)* Bearport Publishing Co., Inc.

Hesper, Sam. Praying Mantises, 1 vol. 2014. (Animal Cannibals Ser.). (ENG.). 24p. (J). (gr. 2-3). lib. bdg. 25.27 *(978-1-4777-5771-0/6)*, 8fdfa3fc-6cfa-4688-88fe-30eb8e04a2d5, PowerKids Pr.) Rosen Publishing Group, Inc., The.

Hipp, Andrew. The Life Cycle of a Praying Mantis. 2009. (Life Cycles Library). 24p. (gr. 3-4). 42.50 *(978-1-60853-993-2/8)*, PowerKids Pr.) Rosen Publishing Group, Inc., The.

Hudak, Heather C. Praying Mantises. 2008. (World of Wonder Ser.). (Illus.). 24p. (J). (gr. k-3). pap. 8.95 *(978-1-59036-873-2/8)*; lib. bdg. 24.45 *(978-1-59036-872-5/X)* Weigl Pubs., Inc.

Klepeis, Alicia Z. Praying Mantis vs. Giant Hornet: Battle of the Powerful Predators. 2016. (Bug Wars Ser.). (ENG., Illus.). 32p. (J). (gr. 3-9). lib. bdg. 28.65 *(978-1-4914-8067-0/X)*, 130571, Capstone Pr.) Capstone.

Macheske, Felicia. Lanky Legs: Praying Mantis. 2016. (Guess What Ser.). (ENG., Illus.). 24p. (J). (gr. k-2). 30.64 *(978-1-63470-720-6/6)*, 207591) Cherry Lake Publishing.

Markle, Sandra. Praying Mantises. 2008. pap. 52.95 *(978-1-58013-285-5/5)* Lerner Publishing Group.

—Praying Mantises: Hungry Insect Heroes. 2008. (Insect World Ser.). (ENG., Illus.). 48p. (gr. 4-8). lib. bdg. 27.93 *(978-0-8225-7300-5/8)*, Lerner Pubns.) Lerner Publishing Group.

Meisel, Paul. My Awesome Summer by P. Mantis. 2017. (Nature Diary Ser.: 1). (ENG., Illus.). 40p. (J). (gr. -1-3). 16.99 *(978-0-8234-3671-2/3)* Holiday Hse., Inc.

Orr, Tamra B. Praying Mantis. 2015. (21st Century Junior Library: Creepy Crawly Critters Ser.). (ENG., Illus.). 24p. (J). (gr. k-3). 29.21 *(978-1-63362-593-8/1)*, 206556) Cherry Lake Publishing.

Roza, Greg. Mysterious Mantises. 2011. (World of Bugs Ser.). (Illus.). 24p. (J). (gr. k-2). 69.20 *(978-1-4339-6143-4/1)*; (ENG., (J). pap. 9.15 *(978-1-4339-4604-2/1)*, 8dfab79e-8afc-4911-ab2c-9d82aa9500a9); (ENG., (J). lib. bdg. 25.27 *(978-1-4339-4603-5/3)*, a4bf859b-7d04-47cc-a691-10afced5239c) Stevens, Gareth Publishing LLLP.

Sexton, Colleen. Praying Mantises. 2007. (World of Insects Ser.). (ENG., Illus.). 24p. (J). (gr. k-3). lib. bdg. 26.95 *(978-1-60014-053-2/X)* Bellwether Media.

PREACHERS

see Clergy

PRECIOUS METALS

see also Gold; Silver

McDonnell, Julia. How Precious Metals Form, 1 vol. 2016. (From the Earth: How Resources Are Made Ser.). (ENG., Illus.). 32p. (J). (gr. 3-4). pap. 11.50 *(978-1-4824-4727-9/4)*, 19178746-c5de-4e77-9270-e3045d306209) Stevens, Gareth Publishing LLLP.

PRECIOUS STONES

Here are entered mineralogical and technological works on potential and actual engraved stones and jewels. Antiquarian or artistic works on engraved stones and jewels are entered under Gems.

see also Gems

also names of precious stones, e.g. Diamonds

Cole, Tayler. Aquamarine, 1 vol. 2015. (Gems: Nature's Jewels Ser.). (ENG., Illus.). 24p. (J). (gr. 2-3). 25.27 *(978-1-4824-2862-9/8)*, f80756a5-0092-4132-9e99-3d95592818a5); pap. 9.15 *(978-1-4824-2860-5/1)*, 862ace3a-978e-4f8d-9189-0fa8117a6fb7) Stevens, Gareth Publishing LLLP.

Dayton, Connor. Gemstones. (Rocks & Minerals Ser.). 24p. (gr. 2-3). 2009. 42.50 *(978-1-60852-500-3/7)*, PowerKids Pr.) 2007. (ENG., Illus.). (YA). lib. bdg. 26.27 *(978-1-4042-3686-8/4)*, c20b98f2-57c6-4139-9647-fa661c9e94e6) Rosen Publishing Group, Inc., The.

Edwards, Ron & Dickie, Lisa. Diamonds & Gemstones. 2004. (Rocks, Minerals, & Resources Ser.). (ENG., Illus.). 32p. (J). pap. *(978-0-7787-1446-0/2)* Crabtree Publishing Co.

Ethan, Eric. Turquoise, 1 vol. 2011. (Gems: Nature's Jewels Ser.). (ENG., Illus.). 24p. (J). (gr. 2-3). pap. 9.15 *(978-1-4339-4712-4/9)*, fe8f150c-dc6a-4737-bac8-2a26291be1af); lib. bdg. 25.27 *(978-1-4339-4711-7/0)*, b2d63051-318b-487e-8bd0-8ed25b94f109) Stevens, Gareth Publishing LLLP. (Gareth Stevens Learning Library).

Hansen, Grace. Gems, 1 vol. 2015. (Geology Rocks! (Abdo Kids Jumbo) Ser.). (ENG., Illus.). 24p. (J). (gr. -1-2). 32.79 *(978-1-62970-906-2/9)*, 18270, Abdo Kids) ABDO Publishing Co.

Hayes, Amy. Garnets, 1 vol. 2015. (Gems: Nature's Jewels Ser.). (ENG., Illus.). 24p. (J). (gr. 2-3). pap. 9.15 *(978-1-4824-2864-3/4)*, 1cba79b6-24b8-4778-b2ac-dbbf4c0b1b0f) Stevens, Gareth Publishing LLLP.

Hoffman, Steven M. Gems, Crystals, & Precious Rocks, 1 vol. 2011. (Rock It! Ser.). (ENG., Illus.). 24p. (J). (gr. 3-4). 26.27 *(978-1-4488-2561-5/X)*, 9e2ff842-5c1e-4746-87f2-1cb7578744bb); pap. 9.25 *(978-1-4488-2708-4/6)*, 9f7c8e76-73c9-4aa3-979b-14d43e44a896) Rosen Publishing Group, Inc., The. (PowerKids Pr.).

Keppeler, Jill. How Gems Are Formed, 1 vol. 2016. (From the Earth: How Resources Are Made Ser.). (ENG., Illus.). 32p. (J). (gr. 3-4). pap. 11.50 *(978-1-4824-4709-5/6)*, ea6d1e4d-41db-4685-bdfe-9a1e507c78e2) Stevens, Gareth Publishing LLLP.

Mahoney, Emily. Amethysts, 1 vol. 2015. (Gems: Nature's Jewels Ser.). (ENG., Illus.). 24p. (J). (gr. 2-3). pap. 9.15 *(978-1-4824-2856-8/3)*, a7f97dc8-8a9f-4610-94b2-617ec0d19199) Stevens, Gareth Publishing LLLP.

McAneney, Caitie. Topaz, 1 vol. 2015. (Gems: Nature's Jewels Ser.). (ENG., Illus.). 24p. (J). (gr. 2-3). pap. 9.15 *(978-1-4824-2872-8/5)*, 74cac7dc-bfd0-44ad-a5d5-d71c10422598) Stevens, Gareth Publishing LLLP.

Perish, Patrick. Gemstones. 2019. (Rocks & Minerals Ser.). (ENG., Illus.). 32p. (J). (gr. 3-8). lib. bdg. 27.95 *(978-1-64487-074-7/6)*, Blastoff! Discovery) Bellwether Media.

Rajczak, Michael. Amber, 1 vol. 2015. (Gems: Nature's Jewels Ser.). (ENG., Illus.). 24p. (J). (gr. 2-3). 25.27 *(978-1-4824-2854-4/7)*, 808864d9-76e1-417b-a996-de7b7c3e4a31) Stevens, Gareth Publishing LLLP.

Rivera, Andrea. Gems. 2017. (Rocks & Minerals (Launch!) Ser.). (ENG., Illus.). 24p. (J). (gr. -1-2). lib. bdg. 31.36 *(978-1-5321-2044-2/3)*, 25338, Abdo Zoom-Launch) ABDO Publishing Co.

Salzano, Tammi J. Rocks, Minerals, & Gemstones. Jankowski, Daniel, illus. 2009. 24p. (J). pap. *(978-0-545-19868-4/2)* Scholastic, Inc.

Squire, Ann O. Gemstones. 2012. (True Book Ser.). (ENG.). 48p. (J). pap. 6.95 *(978-0-531-26251-1/0)*; lib. bdg. 29.00 *(978-0-531-26143-9/3)* Scholastic Library Publishing.

Symes, R. F. & Harding, Robert. Crystal & Gem. Eyewitness Books. Keates, Colin, photos by. 2004. (Illus.). 63p. (J). (gr. 4-8). reprint ed. 19.00 *(978-0-7567-7687-9/2)* DIANE Publishing Co.

Trueit, Trudi Strain. Rocks, Gems, & Minerals. 2003. (Watts Library). (ENG.). 64p. (gr. 5-7). pap. 8.95 *(978-0-531-16241-5/9)*, Watts, Franklin) Scholastic Library Publishing.

Ward, Charlotte, ed. Gem Care. Ward, Fred, photos by. 2nd ed. 2003. (Fred Ward Gem Book Ser.). (Illus.). 32p. pap. 9.95 *(978-1-887651-07-3/1)* Gem Bk. Pubs.

PREGNANCY

see also Childbirth

Akin, Jessica. Pregnancy & Parenting: The Ultimate Teen Guide. (It Happened to Me Ser.: 48). (Illus.). 226p. (J). (gr. -1-12). 2017. pap. 32.00 *(978-0-8108-9545-4/5)* 2016. 59.00 *(978-1-4422-4302-6/3)* Rowman & Littlefield Publishers, Inc.

Amos, Janine. Is Helen Pregnant. 2003. (Body Matters Ser.: 1). (ENG., Illus.). 32p. (YA). 19.99 *(978-0-84234-107-0/3)* Evans Brothers, Ltd. GBR. Dist: Independent Pubs. Group.

Banigan, Melissa. Coping with Teen Pregnancy, 1 vol. 2018. (Coping Ser.). (ENG.). 112p. (gr. 7-7). pap. 19.24 *(978-1-5081-8324-2/4)*, f29cb6b3-7df7-40f1-9e7a-103e1bad70bf) Rosen Publishing Group, Inc., The.

Campbell, Carol P. & Orr, Tamra. Frequently Asked Questions about Teen Pregnancy, 1 vol. 2011. (FAQ: Teen Life Ser.). (ENG.). 64p. (J). (gr. 5-6). lib. bdg. 37.13 *(978-1-4488-4627-6/7)*, 9a2b4b13-04ad-47a8-ba3e-25c407cf0820) Rosen Publishing Group, Inc., The.

Colby, Jennifer. I Have a Belly Button. 2015. (Tell Me Why Library). (ENG., Illus.). 24p. (J). (gr. 2-5). 29.21 *(978-1-63362-612-6/1)*, 206632) Cherry Lake Publishing.

Cooper, Robbi, creator. Help! We're Having a Baby: Solicited Advice from Family & Friends. 2004. 70p. ring bd. 35.00 *(978-0-9749643-0-0/1)* Cooper, Robbi.

Gordon, Elaine R. Mommy, Did I Grow in Your Tummy? Where Some Babies Come From. Clo, Kathy, illus. Date not set. 28p. (Orig.). (J). (gr. -1-4). pap. 9.95 *(978-0-9634561-0-6/5)* EM Greenberg Pr., Inc.

Hall, Margaret. Penguins & Their Chicks: A 4D Book. rev. ed. 2018. (Animal Offspring Ser.). (ENG., Illus.). 24p. (J). (gr. -1-2). pap. 6.95 *(978-1-5435-0837-6/5)*, 137600, Capstone Pr.) Capstone.

Hammerslough, Jane. Everything You Need to Know about Teen Motherhood. 2009. (Need to Know Library). 64p. (gr. 5-5). 58.50 *(978-1-60854-090-7/1)* Rosen Publishing Group, Inc., The.

Having a Healthy Baby - Planning Your Pregnancy. 2004. (YA). pap. 4.00 net. *(978-1-930996-55-7/1)* Planned Parenthood Federation of America, Inc.

Jamiolkowski, Raymond M. A Baby Doesn't Make the Man: Alternative Sources of Power & Manhood for Young Men. 2009. (Teen Pregnancy Prevention Library). 64p. (gr. 5-5). 58.50 *(978-1-60854-244-4/0)* Rosen Publishing Group, Inc., The.

Juettner, Bonnie. Abortion. 2007. (Ripped from the Headlines Ser.). (YA). (gr. 7-12). 23.95 *(978-1-60217-020-9/7)* Erickson Pr.

Kamberg, Mary-Lane. Teen Pregnancy & Motherhood, 1 vol. 2012. (Young Woman's Guide to Contemporary Issues Ser.). (ENG., Illus.). 112p. (YA). (gr. 8-9). lib. bdg. 39.80 *(978-1-4488-8397-4/0)*, de728837-cdb4-417e-832c-48df6c059baf) Rosen Publishing Group, Inc., The.

Koya, Lena & Kamberg, Mary-Lane. Teen Pregnancy & What Comes Next, 1 vol. 2017. (Women in the World Ser.). (ENG.). 112p. (J). (gr. 6-6). 38.80 *(978-1-5081-7722-7/8)*, 827b8adc-abcb-4dfd-9242-6087e380ed8d) Rosen Publishing Group, Inc., The.

Krueger, Lisa, ed. Teen Pregnancy & Parenting, 1 vol. 2010. (Current Controversies Ser.). (ENG.). 184p. (gr. 10-12). 48.03 *(978-0-7377-4923-6/7)*, 36060e2a-f79b-4808-8f6a-2b78ba2d24ec); pap. 33.00 *(978-0-7377-4924-3/5)*, 854ee047-98b8-498e-8cde-a8df636255d7) Greenhaven Publishing LLC. (Greenhaven Publishing).

Lange, Donna. Contraception & Pregnancy. Forman, Sara & McDonnell, Mary Ann, eds. 2013. (Young Adult's Guide to the Science of Health Ser.). (Illus.). 128p. (J). (gr. 7-18). pap. 14.95 *(978-1-4222-3005-3/8)* Mason Crest.

—Contraception & Pregnancy. McDonnell, Mary Ann & Forman, Sara, eds. 2013. (Young Adult's Guide to the Science of Health Ser.: 15). (Illus.). 128p. (J). (gr. 7-18). 24.95 *(978-1-4222-2805-0/3)* Mason Crest.

Mahoney, Emily & MacKay, Jennifer. Dealing with Teen Pregnancy, 1 vol. 2016. (Hot Topics Ser.). (ENG.). 112p. (YA). (gr. 7-7). lib. bdg. 41.03 *(978-1-5345-6019-2/X)*, dfbc257c-9458-48a1-a86a-2e2782833de9, Lucent Pr.) Greenhaven Publishing LLC.

Marti, Meritxell. Grow, Baby, Grow! Watch Baby Grow Month by Month! Salomo, Xavier, illus. 2019. (ENG.). 18p. (J). (gr. k-2). 24.99 *(978-1-64170-100-6/5)*, 550100) Familius LLC.

McDowell, JOsh & Stewart, Ed. Struggling with Unplanned Pregnancy. rev. ed. 2009. (Project 17:17 Ser.). (ENG.). 64p. (J). mass mkt. 4.99 *(978-1-84550-440-3/2)*, f9026558-4072-4e2f-b868-d8ef05782e89) Christian Focus Pubns. GBR. Dist: Baker & Taylor Publisher Services (BTPS).

McDowell, Pamela. Teen Pregnancy, 1 vol. 2010. (ENG.). 48p. (J). pap. *(978-0-7787-2139-0/6)*; lib. bdg. *(978-0-7787-2132-1/9)* Crabtree Publishing Co.

Meister, Deborah. What Catholics Teens Should Know If Pregnant & Panicked. Larkin, Jean K., ed. 2004. (What Catholic Teens Should Know Ser.). (Illus.). 8p. (YA). 7.95 *(978-0-89837-237-3(2)*, 440710) Pflaum Publishing Group.

Murkoff, Heidi. What to Expect When Mommy's Having a Baby. Rader, Laura, illus. 2004. (ENG.). 24p. (J). (gr. -1-3). pap. 3.99 *(978-0-06-053802-6(3)*, HarperFestival) HarperCollins Pubs.

Nykiel, Connie. After the Loss of Your Baby: For Teen Mothers. 2004. (ENG.). 24p. (Orig.). (YA). pap. 3.50 *(978-1-56123-156-0(8)*, ALBC) Centering Corp.

Parker, Gary E. Life Before Birth: A Christian Family Book. 2nd ed. 2003. 85p. (J). (gr. 5-7). 12.99 *(978-0-89051-164-0(0)*, LIBEBI, Master Books) New Leaf Publishing Group.

parks, peggy j. Teenage Sex & Pregnancy. 2011. (Compact Research Ser.). 96p. (YA). (gr. 7-12). lib. bdg. 43.93 *(978-1-60152-168-2(5))* ReferencePoint Pr., Inc.

Paul, Miranda. Nine Months: Before a Baby Is Born. Chin, Jason, illus. 2019. 32p. (J). (gr. -1-3). 18.99 *(978-0-8234-4161-7(X)*, Neal Porter Bks) Holiday Hse., Inc.

Piehl, Norah, ed. Teenage Pregnancy, 1 vol. 2009. (Social Issues Firsthand Ser.). (ENG., Illus.). 112p. (gr. 10-12). lib. bdg. 39.93 *(978-0-7377-4254-1(2)*, 4e9620c7-54c2-489d-9abe-2663a984a38f, Greenhaven Publishing) Greenhaven Publishing LLC.

Rigby Education Staff. Carrying Babies. (Sails Literacy Ser.). (Illus.). 16p. (gr. 1-2). 27.00 *(978-0-7635-9886-0(0)*, 698860C99) Rigby Education.

Rodriguez, Gaby. The Pregnancy Project: A Memoir. 2013. (ENG., Illus.). 240p. (YA). (gr. 9). pap. 12.99 *(978-1-4424-4623-6(4)*, Simon & Schuster Bks. For Young Readers) Simon & Schuster Bks. For Young Readers.

Silverberg, Cory. ¿Cómo Se Hace un Bebé? Spanish Language Edition. Smyth, Fiona, illus. 2017. 36p. (J). (gr. -1-2). 11.95 *(978-1-60980-769-6(3)*, Siete Cuentos Editorial) Seven Stories Pr.

—What Makes a Baby. Smyth, Fiona, illus. 2013. 36p. (J). (gr. -1-2). 18.95 *(978-1-60980-485-5(6)*, Triangle Square) Seven Stories Pr.

Simons, Rae. Teen Parents. 2010. (Changing Face of Modern Families Ser.). (Illus.). 64p. (YA). (gr. 5-18). lib. bdg. 22.95 *(978-1-4222-1491-6(5))* Mason Crest.

Stroble, Chris. There IS Hope after a Teen Pregnancy: A Collection of Inspiring Mother-Daughter Success Stories plus the Handbook for Teen Moms Anonymous. 2006. pap. 14.95 *(978-1-933559-00-1(4))* Wellness pH Productions.

Surprise in Mommy's Tummy. Date not set. (J). (gr. -1-3). 5.50 *(978-0-89259-115-2(3))* American Trust Pubns.

Thiel, Kristin. Dealing with Teen Pregnancy, 1 vol. 2019. (Helping Yourself, Helping Others Ser.). (ENG.). 112p. (gr. 7-7). pap. 20.99 *(978-1-5026-4635-4(8)*, 40935b11-ee92-4455-99ff-286df23110db) Cavendish Square Publishing LLC.

Waters, Sophie. The Female Reproductive System. (Girls' Health Ser.). 48p. (gr. 5-6). 2009. 53.00 *(978-1-61512-732-0(1)*, Rosen Reference) 2007. (ENG., Illus.). (YA). lib. bdg. 34.47 *(978-1-4042-1950-2(1)*, bec46854-9404-4f1e-8bfa-6cfa840272ea) Rosen Publishing Group, Inc., The.

Williams, Heidi, ed. Teen Pregnancy, 1 vol. 2009. (Issues That Concern You Ser.). (ENG., Illus.). 144p. (gr. 7-10). 43.63 *(978-0-7377-4498-9(7)*, ee468f84-382b-4745-a8f1-ea677dee1107, Greenhaven Publishing) Greenhaven Publishing LLC.

Wright, Sally Ann. Where Do Babies Come From? Ayres, Honor, illus. 2007. 29p. (J). 9.95 *(978-0-8198-8311-7(5))* Pauline Bks. & Media.

PREGNANCY—FICTION

Adams, Lenora. Baby Girl. 2007. (ENG.). 240p. (YA). (gr. 9). pap. 6.99 *(978-1-4169-2512-5(0)*, Simon Pulse) Simon Pulse.

Atkins, Jill. Cry, Baby. 2004. (Shades Ser.). 62p. (J). pap. *(978-0-237-52810-2(X))* Evans Brothers, Ltd.

Baer, Marianna. The Inconceivable Life of Quinn. 2017. (ENG.). 384p. (YA). (gr. 8-17). 18.95 *(978-1-4197-2302-5(2)*, 1158201) Abrams, Inc.

Baratz-Logsted, Lauren. Angel's Choice. 2006. (ENG.). 256p. (YA). (gr. 9-12). pap. 6.99 *(978-1-4169-2524-8(4)*, Simon Pulse) Simon Pulse.

Barrow, Rebecca. You Don't Know Me but I Know You. 2017. (ENG.). 336p. (YA). (gr. 9). 17.99 *(978-0-06-249419-1(8)*, HarperTeen) HarperCollins Pubs.

Bennett, James W. & Bennett, James. Faith Wish. 2003. (ENG.). 160p. (J). (gr. 7-18). tchr. ed. 16.95 *(978-0-8234-1778-0(6))* Holiday Hse., Inc.

Berk, Sheryl & Berk, Carrie. Baby Cakes. 2014. (Cupcake Club Ser.: 5). 160p. (J). (gr. 3-7). pap. 12.99 *(978-1-4022-8330-7(X))* Sourcebooks, Inc.

Blackall, Sophie. The Baby Tree. Blackall, Sophie, illus. 2014. (Illus.). 40p. (J). (gr. k-3). 18.99 *(978-0-399-25718-6(7)*, Nancy Paulsen Books) Penguin Young Readers Group.

Brassill, Amber M. My Greatest Mistake, 1 vol. 2010. 236p. pap. 24.95 *(978-1-4489-9143-3(9))* America Star Bks.

Buckley, Kate. Choices: A Novel. 2009. 208p. (J). pap. 14.95 *(978-1-935359-12-8(6))* Bk. Pubs. Network.

Burnett, Frances. The Head of the House of Coombe. 2008. 252p. 29.95 *(978-1-60664-769-1(5))*; pap. 15.95 *(978-1-60664-142-2(5))* Aegypan.

Butler, Dori Hillestad. Alexandra Hopewell, Labor Coach. 2005. 136p. (J). (gr. 3-6). 15.99 *(978-0-8075-0242-6(1))* Whitman, Albert & Co.

Caletti, Deb. The Six Rules of Maybe. 2011. (ENG.). 352p. (YA). (gr. 7). pap. 12.99 *(978-1-4169-7971-5(9)*, Simon Pulse) Simon Pulse.

Calkin, Abigail B. The Carolyne Letters: A Story of Birth, Abortion & Adoption. 2013. (ENG., Illus.). 230p. (YA). (gr. 9-12). pap. 14.95 *(978-1-938301-15-5(3)*, 559115) Familius LLC.

Castellarin, Loretta & Roberts, Ken. Degrassi Junior High: Spike, 1 vol. 2006. (Degrassi Junior High Ser.). (ENG.). 184p. (YA). (gr. 5-10). 7.95 *(978-1-55028-925-1(X)*, 925) James Lorimer & Co. Ltd., Pubs. CAN. Dist: Formac Lorimer Bks. Ltd.

Choyce, Lesley. Reacción, 1 vol. 2012. (Spanish Soundings Ser.). (SPA.). 112p. (YA). (gr. 8-12). pap. 9.95 *(978-1-4598-0308-4(6))* Orca Bk. Pubs. USA.

Clarke, Kathryn. The Breakable Vow. 2004. 480p. (YA). (gr. 7-18). 16.89 *(978-0-06-051822-6(7))* HarperCollins Pubs.

Clarke, Kathryn Ann. The Breakable Vow. 2004. (ENG.). 480p. (YA). (gr. 8-18). pap. 8.99 *(978-0-06-051821-9(9)*, HarperTeen) HarperCollins Pubs.

Coll, Ivar Da. Carlos. Coll, Ivar Da, illus. 2003. (SPA., Illus.). 52p. (J). (gr. k-3). pap. 9.95 *(978-958-8061-64-1(4))* Santillana USA Publishing Co., Inc.

Cook, Makayla. Voice of the Unborn. 2010. 142p. pap. 16.99 *(978-1-60957-924-1(0))* Salem Author Services.

Creech, Sharon. Heartbeat. 2012. (ENG.). 208p. (J). (gr. 3-7). pap. 7.99 *(978-0-06-054024-1(9)*, HarperCollins) HarperCollins Pubs.

de Gramont, Nina. Every Little Thing in the World. 2011. (ENG., Illus.). 288p. (YA). (gr. 9). pap. 8.99 *(978-1-4169-8015-5(6)*, Atheneum Bks. for Young Readers) Simon & Schuster Children's Publishing.

Dessen, Sarah. Someone Like You. 2011. 10.36 *(978-0-7848-3539-5(X)*, Everbind) Marco Bk. Co.

—Someone Like You. 2004. (ENG.). 304p. (YA). (gr. 7-7). 10.99 *(978-0-14-240177-4(3)*, Speak) Penguin Young Readers Group.

—Someone Like You. 2004. 281p. (YA). (gr. 7). 16.65 *(978-0-7569-4967-9(X))* Perfection Learning Corp.

—Someone Like You. 2004. 281p. (gr. 7). lib. bdg. 22.10 *(978-1-4176-2674-8(7))* Turtleback.

Draper, Sharon M. November Blues. 2011. 9.00 *(978-0-7848-3495-4(4)*, Everbind) Marco Bk. Co.

—November Blues. (Jericho Trilogy Ser.: 2). (ENG., Illus.). (YA). (gr. 7). 2017. 336p. pap. 11.99 *(978-1-4814-9031-3(1)*, Atheneum/Caitlyn Dlouhy Books) 2007. 320p. 19.99 *(978-1-4169-0698-8(3)*, Atheneum Bks. for Young Readers) Simon & Schuster Children's Publishing.

Evans, Mari. I'm Late: The Story of Laneese & Moonlight & Alisha Who Didn't Have Anyone of Her Own. 2006. (Illus.). 86p. (J). (gr. 7-18). 14.95 *(978-1-933491-00-4(0))* Just Us Bks., Inc.

Fearnley, Jan. A Special Something. 2004. (ENG., Illus.). 32p. pap. 7.95 *(978-0-7497-4639-1(4))* Farshore GBR. Dist: Trafalgar Square Publishing.

Feiffer, Kate. The Wild, Wild Inside: A View from Mommy's Tummy! Huliska-Beith, Laura, illus. 2010. (ENG.). 32p. (J). (gr. -1-3). 15.99 *(978-1-4169-4099-9(5)*, Simon & Schuster/Paula Wiseman Bks.) Simon & Schuster/Paula Wiseman Bks.

Furniss, Clare. How Not to Disappear. 2017. (ENG., Illus.). 448p. (YA). (gr. 7). 17.99 *(978-1-4814-2102-7(6)*, McElderry, Margaret K. Bks.) McElderry, Margaret K. Bks.

Gilmore, Jennifer. If Only. 2018. (ENG.). 288p. (YA). (gr. 9). 17.99 *(978-0-06-239363-0(4)*, HarperTeen) HarperCollins Pubs.

Hart, Karen. Butterflies in May: A Novel. 2006. (ENG.). 201p. (J). (gr. 8-12). pap. 16.95 *(978-1-890862-44-2(4)*, 2e7458cc-00f9-441e-9366-0d7e24a44851) Bancroft Pr.

Harvey, Sarah N. The Lit Report, 1 vol. 2008. (ENG.). 208p. (YA). (gr. 8-12). pap. 12.95 *(978-1-55143-905-1(0))* Orca Bk. Pubs. USA.

Hearn, Julie. The Minister's Daughter. 2006. (ENG.). 272p. (YA). (gr. 7-12). pap. 7.99 *(978-0-689-87691-2(2)*, Atheneum Bks. for Young Readers) Simon & Schuster Children's Publishing.

Heppermann, Christine. Ask Me How I Got Here. 2016. (ENG.). 240p. (YA). (gr. 9). 17.99 *(978-0-06-238795-0(2)*, Greenwillow Bks.) HarperCollins Pubs.

Hoole, Elissa Janine. The Memory Jar. 2016. (ENG.). 336p. (YA). (gr. 9-12). pap. 11.99 *(978-0-7387-4731-6(9)*, 0738747319, Flux) North Star Editions.

Hooper, Mary. Newes from the Dead. 2010. (ENG., Illus.). 272p. (YA). (gr. 9-13). pap. 17.99 *(978-0-312-60864-4(0)*, 900065166) Square Fish.

Hopkins, Ellen. Crank. (Crank Trilogy Ser.). (ENG.). (YA). (gr. 9). 2013. Illus.). 576p. pap. 14.99 *(978-1-4424-7181-8(6))* 2010. 544p. 24.99 *(978-1-4169-9513-5(7))* McElderry, Margaret K. Bks. (McElderry, Margaret K. Bks.).

—Crank. 2013. lib. bdg. 24.50 *(978-0-606-35118-8(3))* Turtleback.

Hornby, Nick. Slam. 2009. (JPN.). 444p. (YA). *(978-4-8340-2418-0(0))* Fukuinkan Shoten.

—Slam. (ENG.). 320p. (gr. 12). 2009. 17.00 *(978-1-59448-471-1(6))* 2008. 15.00 *(978-1-59448-345-5(0))* Penguin Publishing Group. (Riverhead Bks.).

Jarwin. Love in the Springtime. 2012. 224p. 24.95 *(978-1-4626-6818-2(6))* America Star Bks.

Johnson, Angela. The First Part Last. 2003. (ENG., Illus.). 144p. (YA). (gr. 7-18). 17.99 *(978-0-689-84922-0(2)*, Simon & Schuster Bks. For Young Readers) Simon & Schuster Bks. For Young Readers.

—The First Part Last. 2005. (ENG.). 144p. (YA). (gr. 7). reprint ed. pap. 7.99 *(978-0-689-84923-7(0)*, Simon Pulse) Simon Pulse.

—The First Part Last. l.t. ed. 2005. 241p. pap. 10.95 *(978-0-7862-7379-9(8)*, Large Print Pr.) Thorndike Pr.

Kelly, Mij. The Bump. Allan, Nicholas, illus. 2012. (ENG.). 32p. (J). *(978-1-58925-107-6(5))* Tiger Tales.

Kemmerer, Brigid. Call It What You Want. 2019. (ENG.). 384p. (YA). 18.99 *(978-1-68119-809-5(6)*, 900187438, Bloomsbury Young Adult) Bloomsbury Publishing USA.

Kephart, Beth. Small Damages. 2013. (Illus.). 304p. (YA). (gr. 9). pap. 8.99 *(978-0-14-242641-8(5)*, Speak) Penguin Young Readers Group.

Kern, Peggy. The Test. 2011. (Bluford Ser.: 18). 139p. (YA). (gr. k-12). pap. 4.95 *(978-1-59194-234-4(9))* Townsend Pr.

Larsen, Elizabeth. Kendra's Decision. 2013. 48p. pap. 16.95 *(978-1-63000-662-4(9))* America Star Bks.

Leavitt, Caroline. Girls in Trouble: A Novel. 2005. (ENG.). 368p. pap. 22.99 *(978-0-312-33973-9(9)*, 900028982, St. Martin's Griffin) St. Martin's Pr.

Lee, Shelley R. Before I Knew You. Lee, Shelley R., ed. Lehman, Denise, illus. 2006. (J). lib. bdg. 20.00 *(978-0-9786757-0-7(3))* Lee, Shelley.

Leicht, Martin & Neal, Isla. Mothership. 2012. (Ever-Expanding Universe Ser.: 1). (ENG., Illus.). 320p. (YA). (gr. 9). 16.99 *(978-1-4424-2960-4(7)*, Simon & Schuster Bks. For Young Readers) Simon & Schuster Bks. For Young Readers.

Lewis, Ali. Timber Creek Station. (ENG., Illus.). 240p. (YA). (gr. 6-12). 2018. pap. 9.99 *(978-1-5415-1485-0(8)*, 47e70c69-8468-4ffd-8046-f0b9cfc5bca9) 2016. E-Book 27.99 *(978-1-4677-8816-8(3))* Lerner Publishing Group. (Carolrhoda Lab™).

Liebert, Emily. Those Secrets We Keep. 2015. 336p. (gr. 12). pap. 16.00 *(978-0-451-47187-1(3)*, Berkley) Penguin Publishing Group.

Lloyd, Sam. What's in Your Tummy Mummy? 2007. (ENG., Illus.). 24p. (J). (gr. -1-k). pap. 13.95 *(978-1-84365-091-1(6)*, Pavilion Children's Books) Pavilion Bks. GBR. Dist: HarperCollins Pubs.

Loeffelholz, Sarah, illus. Can You Just Imagine. 2007. 40p. (J). 14.95 *(978-0-9786850-1-0(6))* Overdue Bks.

Look, Lenore. Alvin Ho: Allergic to Babies, Burglars, & Other Bumps in the Night. Pham, LeUyen, illus. 2014. (Alvin Ho Ser.: 5). 192p. (J). (gr. 1-4). 7.99 *(978-0-385-38600-5(1)*, Yearling) Random Hse. Children's Bks.

Lowe, Natasha. Lucy Castor Finds Her Sparkle. 2018. (ENG., Illus.). 240p. (J). (gr. 3-7). 16.99 *(978-1-5344-0196-9(2)*, Simon & Schuster/Paula Wiseman Bks.) Simon & Schuster/Paula Wiseman Bks.

Mac, Carrie. The Way Back, 1 vol. 2014. (Orca Soundings Ser.). (ENG.). 168p. (YA). (gr. 8-12). pap. 9.95 *(978-1-4598-0715-0(4))* Orca Bk. Pubs. USA.

Mackall, Dandi Daley. There's a Baby in There!, 0 vols. Whitt, Carlynn, illus. 2012. (ENG.). 32p. (J). (gr. -1-k). 16.99 *(978-0-7614-6191-3(4)*, 9780761461913, Two Lions) Amazon Publishing.

Madonia, Kristen-Paige. Fingerprints of You. (ENG., Illus.). 272p. (YA). (gr. 9). 2013. pap. 9.99 *(978-1-4424-2921-5(6))* 2012. 16.99 *(978-1-4424-2920-8(8))* Simon & Schuster Bks. For Young Readers. (Simon & Schuster Bks. For Young Readers).

Maggi, Nicole. What They Don't Know. 2018. 368p. (YA). (gr. 8-12). pap. 10.99 *(978-1-4926-7265-4(3))* Sourcebooks, Inc.

Martinez, Jessica. The Space Between Us. (ENG., (YA). (gr. 9). 2013. Illus.). 416p. pap. 9.99 *(978-1-4424-2056-4(1))* 2012. 400p. 16.99 *(978-1-4424-2055-7(3))* Simon Pulse. (Simon Pulse).

Mather, Janice Lynn. Learning to Breathe. 2018. (ENG., Illus.). 336p. (YA). (gr. 9). 19.99 *(978-1-5344-0601-8(8)*, Simon & Schuster Bks. For Young Readers) Simon & Schuster Bks. For Young Readers.

McCafferty, Megan. Bumped. 2012. (Bumped Ser.: 1). (ENG.). 352p. (YA). (gr. 9). pap. 9.99 *(978-0-06-196275-2(9)*, Balzer & Bray) HarperCollins Pubs.

—Thumped. 2013. (Bumped Ser.: 2). (ENG.). 304p. (YA). (gr. 8). pap. 8.99 *(978-0-06-196277-6(5)*, Balzer & Bray) HarperCollins Pubs.

Mceldowney, Connie. Josiah's Journey. 2009. 34p. pap. 12.99 *(978-1-4490-0489-7(X))* AuthorHouse.

Millward, Carol. Star in the Middle. 2009. 304p. (YA). (gr. 9-12). 16.95 *(978-1-934813-13-3(3))* Westside Bks.

Nolan, Han. Pregnant Pause. 2012. (ENG.). 352p. (YA). (gr. 9). pap. 8.99 *(978-0-547-85414-4(5)*, 1501157, Clarion Bks.) HarperCollins Pubs.

Orante, Ann-Jeanette P. Best Sisters for Life... 2007. (ENG., Illus.). 36p. (J). per. 11.95 *(978-1-59800-972-9(9))* Outskirts Pr., Inc.

Paratore, Coleen Murtagh. Willa by Heart. 2008. (Wedding Planner's Daughter Ser.). (ENG.). 240p. (J). (gr. 3-7). 15.99 *(978-1-4169-4076-0(6)*, Simon & Schuster Bks. For Young Readers) Simon & Schuster Bks. For Young Readers.

—Willa by Heart. 2009. (Wedding Planner's Daughter Ser.). (ENG.). 240p. (J). (gr. 4-8). pap. 6.99 *(978-1-4169-7470-3(9)*, Aladdin) Simon & Schuster Children's Publishing.

Poston, Karen. A Baby for Mabel & Frederick. 2005. 20p. (J). 11.28 *(978-1-4116-6024-3(2))* Lulu Pr., Inc.

Pratt, Non. Trouble. 2015. (ENG., Illus.). 400p. (YA). (gr. 9). pap. 10.99 *(978-1-4424-9773-4(1)*, Simon & Schuster, Inc.

Quintero, Isabel. Gabi, a Girl in Pieces, 1 vol. 2014. (ENG.). 208p. (YA). (gr. 9-12). pap. 16.95 *(978-1-935955-95-5(0)*, 23353382, Cinco Puntos Press) Lee & Low Bks., Inc.

Reynolds, Jason. Lu. 2019. (Track Ser.: 4). (ENG.). 240p. (J). (gr. 5). pap. 7.99 *(978-1-4814-5025-6(5)*, Atheneum Bks. for Young Readers) Simon & Schuster Children's Publishing.

Ritchie, Kate. I Just Couldn't Wait to Meet You. Somerville, Hannah, illus. 2015. 32p. (J). (-k). 22.99 *(978-0-85798-970-3(7))* Random Hse. Australia AUS. Dist: Independent Pubs. Group.

Romero, Bernardita. Mummy, What's in Your Tummy? Romero, Bernardita, illus. 2020. (ENG., Illus.). 20p. (J). (gr. -1-k). bds. 8.99 *(978-1-78285-976-5(4))* Barefoot Bks., Inc.

Royal, Stephen. The Journey Inside the Womb. 2012. (Illus.). 16p. pap. 18.30 *(978-1-4772-2604-9(4))* AuthorHouse.

Ryan, Darlene. Saving Grace, 1 vol. 2006. (Orca Soundings Ser.). (ENG.). 112p. (YA). (gr. 8-12). per. 9.95 *(978-1-55143-508-4(X))* Orca Bk. Pubs. USA.

Rylant, Cynthia. A Kindness. Date not set. (Sky Bks.). 104p. pap. 54.75 *(978-0-582-08106-2(8))* Addison-Wesley Longman, Ltd. GBR. Dist: Trans-Atlantic Pubns., Inc.

Sauer, Tammi. Dear Jack. 2004. 164p. (YA). mass mkt. 6.99 *(978-0-9753367-0-0(3))* Onstage Publishing, LLC.

Scheerger, Sarah Lynn. The Opposite of Love. 2014. (ENG.). 272p. (YA). (gr. 8-12). 16.99 *(978-0-8075-6132-4(0)*, 807561320) Whitman, Albert & Co. 53.32

Simon, Charnan. Plan B. 2015. (Surviving Southside Ser.). (ENG.). 104p. (YA). (gr. 6-12). E-Book 53.32 *(978-1-4677-6009-6(9)*, 9781467760096, Lerner Digital) Lerner Publishing Group.

Snelson, Brian & Sellars, Rodney. Shaturanga: The Story of Onus. 2003. 244p. pap. 16.95 *(978-0-595-29569-2(X))* iUniverse, Inc.

Sutton, Michelle. It's Not about Him. 2012. (Second Glances Ser.). (ENG.). 228p. pap. 12.99 *(978-0-9838836-0-9(2))* Sword of the Spirit Publishing.

Sweeney, Joyce. Waiting for June, 0 vols. 2012. (ENG.). 158p. (YA). (gr. 7-12). pap. 7.99 *(978-0-7614-5329-1(6)*, 9780761453291, Skyscape) Amazon Publishing.

Thomas-Roots, Pamela. FACTS & MEMOIRS of BABY DIARY: A Diary to Record & Save Valuable Information on Facts & Memoirs of Your Pregnancy & Baby from Birth to Age 18. 2010. 48p. pap. 9.99 *(978-0-557-03410-9(8))* Lulu Pr., Inc.

Touchell, Dianne. A Small Madness, 1 vol. 2016. (ENG.). 192p. (YA). (gr. 9). 16.95 *(978-1-55498-837-2(3))* Groundwood Bks. CAN. Dist: Publishers Group West (PGW).

Velasquez, Gloria. Teen Angel. 2003. (Roosevelt High School Ser.). 160p. (J). pap. 9.95 *(978-1-55885-391-1(X)*, Piñata Books) Arte Publico Pr.

Waters, Tawni. The Long Ride Home. 2017. (ENG.). 240p. (YA). (gr. 8-12). pap. 10.99 *(978-1-4926-4543-6(5))* Sourcebooks, Inc.

Watts, Irene N. When the Bough Breaks. 2007. 152p. (YA). (gr. 7-7). pap. 9.95 *(978-0-88776-821-7(0)*, Tundra Bks.) Tundra Bks. CAN. Dist: Penguin Random Hse. LLC.

Welford, Sue. Nowhere to Run. l.t. ed. 2006. 180p. per. *(978-1-905665-15-0(6))* Pollinger In Print.

Werlin, Nancy. Impossible. 2011. 11.04 *(978-0-7848-3488-6(1)*, Everbind) Marco Bk. Co.

Whelan, Gloria. Chu Ju's House. 2005. (ENG.). 240p. (J). (gr. 5). reprint ed. pap. 7.99 *(978-0-06-050726-8(8)*, HarperCollins) HarperCollins Pubs.

Winkler, Henry & Oliver, Lin. Who Ordered This Baby? Definitely Not Me! 2007. (Hank Zipzer Ser.: No. 13). (Illus.). 152p. (gr. 4-7). 15.00 *(978-0-7569-8163-1(8))* Perfection Learning Corp.

Woodson, Jacqueline. The Dear One. 2010. (ENG.). 176p. (YA). (gr. 7-18). 8.99 *(978-0-14-241705-8(X)*, Puffin Books) Penguin Young Readers Group.

—Pecan Pie Baby. Blackall, Sophie, illus. (ENG.). 32p. (J). (gr. k-3). 2013. 8.99 *(978-0-14-751128-7(3)*, Puffin Books) 2010. 17.99 *(978-0-399-23987-8(1)*, G.P. Putnam's Sons Books for Young Readers) Penguin Young Readers Group.

Writing Club, Dancing Pencils, compiled by. Budding Words: An Anthology. 2007. 60p. pap. *(978-1-86900-871-0(5))* UmSinsi Pr. ZAF. Dist: Michigan State Univ. Pr.

Zarr, Sara. How to Save a Life. 2012. (ENG.). 368p. (YA). (gr. 7-17). pap. 18.99 *(978-0-316-03605-4(6))* Little, Brown Bks. for Young Readers.

PREHISTORIC ANIMALS

see Fossils

PREHISTORIC HUMANS

see Prehistoric Peoples

PREHISTORIC PEOPLES

Brooks, Philip. The Story of Prehistoric Peoples, 1 vol. 2011. (Journey Through History Ser.). (ENG., Illus.). 64p. (J). (gr. 5-6). lib. bdg. 37.13 *(978-1-4488-4790-7(7)*, 5a6288ee-ffe7-48b2-8df8-d4c5a1ac0e31, Rosen Reference) Rosen Publishing Group, Inc., The.

Brooks, Susie. Prehistoric People, 1 vol. 2009. (Flashback History Ser.). (ENG., Illus.). 48p. (gr. 4-4). (J). pap. 12.75 *(978-1-4358-5505-2(1)*, 6ea561d4-45dc-4518-9b4a-ba1859764298, PowerKids Pr.); (YA). 32.93 *(978-1-4358-5504-5(3)*, c90486d4-efdd-4587-8d54-bca29cf56570) Rosen Publishing Group, Inc., The.

Brown, Robin C. The Crafts of Florida's First People. 2003. (ENG., Illus.). 66p. (J). (gr. -1-12). pap. 14.95 *(978-1-56164-282-3(7))* Pineapple Pr., Inc.

Chandler, Fiona. Prehistoric World. 2004. (World History Ser.). (SPA., Illus.). 96p. (J). (gr. 3-18). lib. bdg. 27.95 *(978-1-58086-270-7(5))* EDC Publishing.

Clodd, Edward. Fetish Worship & Idolatry. 2006. pap. 9.95 *(978-1-4286-7861-3(1))* Kessinger Publishing, LLC.

—Myths about the Earth & Man. 2006. pap. 9.95 *(978-1-4286-7865-1(4))* Kessinger Publishing, LLC.

Cole, Joanna. The Human Body. 2014. (Magic School Bus Presents Ser.). lib. bdg. 17.20 *(978-0-606-35815-6(3))* Turtleback.

Croy, Anita. Exploring the Past, 1 vol. 2011. (Invisible Worlds Ser.). (ENG.). 48p. (gr. 4-4). 31.21 *(978-0-7614-4194-6(8)*, 47904848-fa3e-4923-b390-4e80134b4ade) Cavendish Square Publishing LLC.

Deem, James M. Bodies from the Bog. 2003. (ENG., Illus.). 48p. (J). (gr. 5-7). pap. 9.99 *(978-0-618-35402-3(6)*, 484404, Clarion Bks.) HarperCollins Pubs.

Facchini, Fiorenzo. A Day with Homo Sapiens: Life 15,000 Years Ago. 2003. (Early Humans Ser.). (Illus.). 48p. (gr. 6-18). lib. bdg. 23.90 *(978-0-7613-2768-4(1)*, Twenty-First Century Bks.) Lerner Publishing Group.

—A Day with Neanderthal Man: Life 70,000 Years Ago. Baldanzi, Alessandro, illus. 2003. (Early Humans Ser.). 48p. (gr. 6-18). lib. bdg. 23.90 *(978-0-7613-2767-7(3)*, Twenty-First Century Bks.) Lerner Publishing Group.

Forbes, Claire. Ancient Peoples. 2004. (Discovery Guides Ser.). (ENG., Illus.). 32p. (J). (gr. 2-5). pap. 6.95 *(978-1-58728-217-1(8)*, Two-Can Publishing) T&N Children's Publishing.

Gray, Susan H. Scholastic News Nonfiction Readers: Prehistoric World, 6 bks., Set. Incl. Dinosaur Armor. 22.00 *(978-0-531-17481-4(6))*; Dinosaur Dig! 22.00 *(978-0-531-17482-1(4))*; Dinosaur Eggs. 22.00 *(978-0-531-17483-8(2))*; Dinosaur Teeth. 22.00 *(978-0-531-17484-5(0))*; Dinosaur Tracks. 22.00 *(978-0-531-17485-2(9))*; (Illus.). 24p. (J). (gr. 1-2). 2007. 114.00 o.p. *(978-0-531-12605-9(6)*, Children's Pr.) Scholastic Library Publishing.

Green, Dan. The Magic School Bus Presents: the Human Body: a Nonfiction Companion to the Original Magic School Bus Series. Bracken, Carolyn, illus. 2014. (Magic School Bus Presents Ser.). (ENG.). 32p. (J). (gr. 1-3). pap. 7.99 *(978-0-545-68364-7(5))* Scholastic, Inc.

Heitkamp, Kristina Lyn. The Rift Valley & the Archaeological Evidence of the First Humans, 1 vol. 2016. (First Humans & Early Civilizations Ser.). (ENG., Illus.). 64p. (J). (gr. 6-6). pap. 13.95 *(978-1-4994-6318-7(9)*, e0dcd735-919b-4479-b819-257db2d78f47) Rosen Publishing Group, Inc., The.

Howell, Izzi. Fact Cat: History: Early Britons: Stone Age to Iron Age. 2017. (Fact Cat: History: Early Britons Ser.). (ENG., Illus.). 24p. (J). (gr. k-2). pap. 9.99 *(978-0-7502-9938-1(X)*, Wayland) Hachette Children's Group GBR. Dist: Hachette Bk. Group.

Hynes, Margaret. My Best Book of Early People. White, Mike, illus. (Best Book Of Ser.). (ENG.). 32p. (J). 2019. pap. 7.99 *(978-0-7534-7499-0(9)*, 900198577) 2003. tchr. ed. 12.99 *(978-0-7534-5577-7(3)*, 900052548) Roaring Brook Pr. (Kingfisher).

Joseph, Frank. Archaeological Discoveries of Ancient America, 1 vol., 1. 2013. (Discovering Ancient America Ser.). (ENG.). 296p. (YA). (gr. 8-8). 42.41 *(978-1-4777-2809-3(0)*,

259f79bb-b6a2-438a-addb-0efcd7460002) Rosen Publishing Group, Inc., The.

Lanser, Amanda. Ötzi the Iceman, 1 vol. 2014. (Digging up the Past Ser.). (ENG., Illus.). 112p. (YA). (gr. 6-12). lib. bdg. 41.36 (978-1-62403-235-6(4), 1302, Essential Library) ABDO Publishing Co.

Matthews, Rupert. 100 Facts Prehistoric Life. Kelly, Richard, ed. 2017. 48p. (J). pap. 9.95 (978-1-78209-385-5(0)) Miles Kelly Publishing, Ltd. GBR. Dist: Parkwest Pubns., Inc.

Morris, Neil. Everyday Life in Prehistory. 2005. (Uncovering History Ser.). (Illus.). 46p. (J). (gr. 6-9). lib. bdg. 29.95 (978-1-58340-709-7(X)) Black Rabbit Bks.

—Everyday Life in Prehistory. 2008. (Uncovering History Ser.). (ENG., Illus.). 48p. (J). (gr. 2-7). 19.95 (978-88-89272-59-6(7)) McRae Bks. Srl ITA. Dist: Independent Pubs. Group.

Newland, Sonya. Explore!: Stone, Bronze & Iron Ages. 2017. (Explore! Ser.). (ENG., Illus.). 32p. (J). (gr. 4-6). pap. 12.99 (978-0-7502-9736-3(0), Wayland) Hachette Children's Group GBR. Dist: Hachette Bk. Group.

Oachs, Emily Rose. The Cave of Altamira. 2019. (Digging up the Past Ser.). (ENG., Illus.). 24p. (J). (gr. 3-7). lib. bdg. 26.95 (978-1-64487-066-2(5), Torque Bks.) Bellwether Media.

Pacchini, Fiorenzo. A Day with Homo Habilis: Life 2,000,000 Years Ago. 2003. (Early Humans Ser.). (Illus.). 48p. (gr. 6-18). lib. bdg. 23.90 (978-0-7613-2765-3(7), Twenty-First Century Bks.) Lerner Publishing Group.

Passport to the Past, 10 vols., Set. Incl. Ancient Egypt. Steele, Philip. (J). lib. bdg. 37.13 (978-1-4358-5173-3(0), 13e74bd3-12d1-4211-a7ef-78d319e0d2d1); Ancient Greece. Tames, Richard. (J). lib. bdg. 37.13 (978-1-4358-5175-7(7), e38936c0-d500-4f08-9969-96bff2856d39); Ancient India. Ali, Daud. (YA). lib. bdg. 37.13 (978-1-4358-5169-6(2), bead4ed8-34e3-4eed-8010-8a3985dd1e24); Aztec & Maya Worlds. MacDonald, Fiona. (J). lib. bdg. 37.13 (978-1-4358-5170-2(6), 2a9cf459-f86d-4f32-8df2-cb55b7465b45); Roman Empire. Steele, Philip. (J). lib. bdg. 37.13 (978-1-4358-5176-4(5), 63416eb8-27c2-444f-adeb-aa359b405bde); World of North American Indians. Stotter, Mike. (YA). lib. bdg. 37.13 (978-1-4358-5171-9(4), 70b09dda-e5e6-4175-ace1-e3b9fe1299ff); (Illus.). 64p. (gr. 5-6). 2009. (Passport to the Past Ser.). (ENG.). 2008. Set lib. bdg. 185.65 (978-1-4358-5215-0(X), 3a50e030-1c48-4cb7-9b59-6ac059890295) Rosen Publishing Group, Inc., The.

Pearce, Q. L. Stonehenge, 1 vol. 2009. (Mysterious Encounters Ser.). (ENG., Illus.). 48p. (gr. 4-8). 33.58 (978-0-7377-4572-6(X), 62ebb5de-63ca-47ec-b702-cfa256dc4bae, KidHaven Publishing) Greenhaven Publishing LLC.

Prehistoric People. 2019. (J). (978-0-7166-3767-7(7)) World Bk., Inc.

Riggs, Kate. Easter Island. 2009. (Places of Old Ser.). 24p. (J). (gr. 1-5). lib. bdg. 24.25 (978-1-58341-710-2(9), Creative Education) Creative Co., The.

Rubalcaba, Jill & Robertshaw, Peter. Every Bone Tells a Story: Hominin Discoveries, Deductions, & Debates. 2010. (Illus.). 192p. (J). (gr. 5-8). 18.95 (978-1-58089-164-6(0)) Charlesbridge Publishing, Inc.

Schomp, Virginia. Prehistoric World, 10 vols., Group 3. Incl. Ceratosaurus & Other Horned Meat-Eaters. lib. bdg. 32.64 (978-0-7614-2009-5(6), 84dfb728-212f-4237-b1d0-f505569c2b38); Iguanodon & Other Spiky-Thumbed Plant-Eaters. lib. bdg. 32.64 (978-0-7614-2005-7(3), f2ecee9c-8a01-4084-a81e-6c4fe6d3b578); Ornithomimus & Other Speedy Ostrich Dinosaurs. lib. bdg. 32.64 (978-0-7614-2006-4(1), 8b6734b2-23ec-4e6a-bbb3-2f84ec213eba); Plateosaurus & Other Early Long-Necked Plant-Eaters. lib. bdg. 32.64 (978-0-7614-2008-8(8), 443e6cd1-2536-4105-b43e-1abc0159c2d4); Therizinosaurus & Other Colossal-Clawed Plant-Eaters. lib. bdg. 32.64 (978-0-7614-2007-1(X), c721dc20-3d20-4f3a-887f-559a55f44d2f); (Illus.). 32p. (gr. 3-3). (Prehistoric World Ser.). (ENG.). 2007. 163.20 (978-0-7614-2004-0(5), cb018868-fa0a-4a29-a058-cd9241bd329c, Cavendish Square) Cavendish Square Publishing LLC.

Wood, Robert Muir. Discovering Prehistory. 2012. (Illus.). 48p. (J). 15.00 (978-1-899762-87-3(6)) Award Pubns. Ltd. GBR. Dist: Parkwest Pubns., Inc.

PREHISTORIC PEOPLES—FICTION

Angeletti, Roberta. The Cave Painter of Lascaux. 2004. (Illus.). 32p. (J). 16.95 (978-1-56290-323-7(3)) Crystal Productions.

Brett, Jan. The First Dog. Brett, Jan, illus. 2015. (ENG., Illus.). 32p. (J). (gr. -1-k). 17.99 (978-0-399-17270-0(X), G.P. Putnam's Sons Books for Young Readers) Penguin Young Readers Group.

Brooks, Mel & Reiner, Carl. The 2000 Year Old Man Goes to School. Bennett, James, illus. 2006. 32p. (J). (gr. 4-8). reprint ed. 18.00 (978-1-4223-5622-7(1)) DIANE Publishing Co.

—The 2000 Year Old Man Goes to School. Bennett, James, illus. 2005. (ENG.). 40p. (J). (gr. -1-3). 17.99 (978-0-06-076676-4(X)) HarperCollins Pubs.

Christopher, John. In the Beginning. 2015. (ENG., Illus.). 288p. (J). (gr. 5-9). pap. 7.99 (978-1-4814-2003-7(8), Aladdin) Simon & Schuster Children's Publishing.

Clark, Patricia Nikolina. In the Shadow of the Mammoth. LeTourneau, Anthony Alex, illus. (J). 2005. 14.99 (978-0-9674602-8-4(X)) 2003. 190p. pap. 6.99 (978-0-9674602-4-6(7)) Blue Marlin Pubns.

Dolenz, Micky. Gakky Two-Feet. Clark, David, illus. 2006. (J). (978-1-4156-8089-6(2), Putnam Juvenile) Penguin Publishing Group.

Donaldson, Julia. Cave Baby, 3. Gravett, Emily, illus. 2nd ed. 2011. (ENG.). 32p. (J). (gr. -1-k). 14.99 (978-0-330-52276-2(0), 900326070, Macmillan Children's Bks.) Pan Macmillan GBR. Dist: Macmillan.

Doyle, Arthur Conan. The Lost World, 1 vol. 2009. (Real Reads Ser.). (ENG., Illus.). 64p. (J). (gr. 5-5). pap. 14.55 (978-1-60754-395-4(8), 49a60ade-2b66-439a-88f7-600b078eef55); lib. bdg. 33.93 (978-1-60754-394-7(X), 222eeae2-6661-460a-8103-8cfc7225ef8f) Rosen Publishing Group, Inc., The. (Windmill Bks.).

Fidler, Kathleen. The Boy with the Bronze Axe, 56 vols. 3rd rev. ed. (ENG., Illus.). 176p. 11.95 (978-0-86315-488-1(3)) Floris Bks. GBR. Dist: SteinerBooks, Inc.

Fox Mazer, Norma. Saturday, the Twelfth of October. 2015. (ENG.). 274p. (J). (gr. 3). pap. 13.95 (978-1-939601-31-5(2)) Ig Publishing, Inc.

Fragoso. Paleo Pals: Jimmy & the Carrot Rocket Ship. 2012. (ENG., Illus.). 80p. (gr. -1-2). pap. 19.95 (978-1-936608-88-1(X)) Victory Belt Publishing.

Fraser, Ian. Life with Mammoth, 0 vols. Fraser, Mary Ann, illus. (Ogg & Bob Ser.: 2). (ENG.). 64p. (J). 2013. (gr. k-3). pap. 9.99 (978-1-4778-1615-8(1), 9781477816158) 2012. (gr. 1-3). 14.99 (978-0-7614-5722-0(4), 9780761457220) Amazon Publishing. (Two Lions).

—Meet Mammoth, 0 vols. Fraser, Mary Ann, illus. 2013. (Ogg & Bob Ser.: 1). (ENG.). 64p. (J). (gr. 1-3). pap. 9.99 (978-1-4778-1617-2(8), 9781477816172, Two Lions) Amazon Publishing.

Freedman, Claire. Dinosaurs Love Underpants. Cort, Ben, illus. 2009. (Underpants Bks.). (ENG.). 32p. (J). (gr. -1-2). 18.99 (978-1-4169-8938-7(2), Aladdin) Simon & Schuster Children's Publishing.

Gerstein, Mordicai. The First Drawing. 2013. (ENG., Illus.). 40p. (J). (gr. -1-3). 18.99 (978-0-316-20478-1(1)) Little, Brown Bks. for Young Readers.

Grant, John. Littlenose Collection: the Explorer. Collins, Ross, illus. 2014. (ENG.). 336p. (J). pap. 8.99 (978-1-4711-2135-7(6), Simon & Schuster Children's) Simon & Schuster, Ltd. GBR. Dist: Simon & Schuster, Inc.

—Littlenose Collection: the Magician. Collins, Ross, illus. 2014. (ENG.). 352p. (J). pap. 8.99 (978-1-4711-2137-1(2), Simon & Schuster Children's) Simon & Schuster, Ltd. GBR. Dist: Simon & Schuster, Inc.

—Littlenose the Magician. Collins, Ross, illus. 2009. (ENG.). 112p. (J). (gr. k-12). pap. 5.99 (978-1-84738-201-6(0), Simon & Schuster Children's) Simon & Schuster, Ltd. GBR. Dist: Simon & Schuster, Inc.

Greenburg, J. C. Andrew Lost #12: in the Ice Age. Gerardi, Jan, illus. 2005. (Andrew Lost Ser.: 12). 96p. (J). (gr. 1-4). 4.99 (978-0-375-82952-9(0), Random Hse. Bks. for Young Readers) Random Hse. Children's Bks.

Grimaldi, Flora. Welcome to the Tribe! Book 1. Bannister, illus. 2013. (Tib & Tumtum Ser.). (ENG.). (J). (gr. 2-5). 1. 48p. E-Book 39.99 (978-1-4677-1656-7(1))No. 1. 56p. pap. 7.99 (978-1-4677-1522-5(0), 10d07610-403e-4447-a929-861b45bbb066)No. 1. 48p. lib. bdg. 26.65 (978-1-4677-1297-2(3), 6ec46086-0841-458b-91d0-59b495738f64) Lerner Publishing Group. (Graphic Universe™).

Layton, Neal. The Mammoth Academy. Layton, Neal, illus. 2010. (ENG., Illus.). 176p. (J). (gr. 4-6). 21.19 (978-0-312-60882-8(9)) Square Fish.

Lowry, Lois. The Windeby Puzzle: History & Story. 2023. (ENG., Illus.). 224p. (J). (gr. 5). 19.99 (978-0-358-67250-0(3), Clarion Bks.) HarperCollins Pubs.

McDonnell, Patrick. Tek: The Modern Cave Boy. 2016. (ENG., Illus.). 40p. (J). (gr. -1-3). 15.99 (978-0-316-33805-9(2)) Little, Brown Bks. for Young Readers.

Montgomery, R. A. The Trail of Lost Time. Semionov, Vladimir, illus. 2011. (ENG.). 144p. (J). (gr. 4-8). mass mkt. 7.99 (978-1-937133-03-0(6)) Chooseco LLC.

Osborne, Mary Pope. Un Tigre Dientes de Sable en el Ocaso. 2004. (Casa del Arbol Ser.: 7).Tr. of Sunset of the Sabretooth. (SPA., Illus.). (J). pap. 6.99 (978-1-930332-68-3(8)) Lectorum Pubns., Inc.

Paver, Michelle. Chronicles of Ancient Darkness #1: Wolf Brother. Taylor, Geoff, illus. 2006. (Chronicles of Ancient Darkness Ser.: 1). (ENG.). 320p. (J). (gr. 5-9). reprint ed. per. 9.99 (978-0-06-072827-4(2), Tegen, Katherine Bks) HarperCollins Pubs.

—Chronicles of Ancient Darkness #2: Spirit Walker, 2. Taylor, Geoff, illus. 2007. (Chronicles of Ancient Darkness Ser.: 2). (ENG.). 384p. (J). (gr. 5-8). pap. 7.99 (978-0-06-072830-4(2), Tegen, Katherine Bks) HarperCollins Pubs.

—Chronicles of Ancient Darkness #3: Soul Eater. Taylor, Geoff, illus. 2008. (Chronicles of Ancient Darkness Ser.: 3). (ENG.). 352p. (J). (gr. 5). pap. 7.99 (978-0-06-072833-5(7), Tegen, Katherine Bks) HarperCollins Pubs.

—Chronicles of Ancient Darkness #4: Outcast, 4. Taylor, Geoff, illus. 2009. (Chronicles of Ancient Darkness Ser.: 4). (ENG.). 352p. (J). (gr. 5-8). pap. 6.99 (978-0-06-072836-6(1), Tegen, Katherine Bks) HarperCollins Pubs.

—Chronicles of Ancient Darkness #5: Oath Breaker. Taylor, Geoff, illus. (Chronicles of Ancient Darkness Ser.: 5). (ENG.). (J). (gr. 5-18). 2009. 304p. 16.99 (978-0-06-072837-3(X))5. 2010. 320p. pap. 7.99 (978-0-06-072839-7(6)) HarperCollins Pubs. (Tegen, Katherine Bks).

—Chronicles of Ancient Darkness #6: Ghost Hunter, 6. Taylor, Geoff, illus. 2011. (Chronicles of Ancient Darkness Ser.: 6). (ENG.). 304p. (J). (gr. 5-8). pap. 7.99 (978-0-06-072842-7(6), Tegen, Katherine Bks) HarperCollins Pubs.

—Gods & Warriors. 2013. (Gods & Warriors Ser.: 1). (ENG.). 336p. (J). (gr. 5). pap. 8.99 (978-0-14-242284-7(3), Puffin Books) Penguin Young Readers Group.

—HERMANO LOBO: CRÓNICAS DE LA PREHISTORIA I. 2005. (SPA., Illus.). 222p. 17.25 (978-84-7888-933-4(7)) Emece Editores ESP. Dist: Ediciones Universal.

—Soul Eater. 2007. (Chronicles of Ancient Darkness: No. 3). (Illus.). 323p. (J). (gr. 5-9). 16.99 (978-0-06-072831-1(0), Tegen, Katherine Bks) HarperCollins Pubs.

—Wolf Brother, 6 vols. 2005. (Chronicles of Ancient Darkness Ser.: 1). (J). 89.75 (978-1-4193-3811-3(0)); 76.75 (978-1-4193-2628-8(7)); 91.75 (978-1-4193-3809-0(9)); 73.75 (978-1-4193-2630-1(9)) Recorded Bks., Inc.

Popescu, Petru. Footprints in Time. 2008. 256p. (J). (gr. 5). lib. bdg. 17.89 (978-0-06-088400-0(2), Geringer, Laura Book) HarperCollins Pubs.

Preston-Gannon, Frann. Dave's Cave. Preston-Gannon, Frann, illus. 2018. (ENG., Illus.). 32p. (J). (gr. -1-2). 15.99 (978-0-7636-9628-3(5)) Candlewick Pr.

Reynolds, Aaron. Caveboy Dave: More Scrawny Than Brawny. McAndrew, Phil, illus. 2016. (Caveboy Dave Ser.: 1). 256p. (J). (gr. 3-7). bds. 13.99 (978-0-14-751658-9(7), Viking Books for Young Readers) Penguin Young Readers Group.

Richardson, Faith. The Peacock's Stone. 2003. 192p. (J). 21.95 (978-0-9744989-0-4(4)); (Illus.). pap. 12.95 (978-0-9744989-1-1(2)) Fox Song Bks.

Rolli. Kabungo, 1 vol. Pavlović, Milan, illus. 2016. (ENG.). 176p. (J). (gr. 2-5). 14.95 (978-1-55498-804-4(7)) Groundwood Bks. CAN. Dist: Publishers Group West (PGW).

Scieszka, Jon. Your Mother Was a Neanderthal. Smith, Lane, illus. 2006. (Time Warp Trio Ser.: No. 4). 78p. (gr. 4-7). 15.00 (978-0-7569-6782-6(1)) Perfection Learning Corp.

—Your Mother Was a Neanderthal. Smith, Lane, illus. 2004. (Time Warp Trio Ser.: 4). 78p. (J). 16.00 (978-1-4176-3603-7(3)) Turtleback.

—Your Mother Was a Neanderthal #4. Smith, Lane, illus. 2004. (Time Warp Trio Ser.: 4). 80p. (J). (gr. 2-4). pap. 5.99 (978-0-14-240048-7(3), Puffin Books) Penguin Young Readers Group.

Shickman, Allan Richard. Dael & the Painted People. 2011. (Zan-Gah Ser.). 155p. (YA). pap. 9.95 (978-0-9790357-6-0(7)) Earthshaker Bks.

—Zan-Gah: A Prehistoric Adventure. 2007. 160p. (J). (gr. 4-7). per. 9.95 (978-0-9790357-0-8(8)) Earthshaker Bks.

—Zan-Gah & the Beautiful Country. 2009. 151p. pap. 9.95 (978-0-9790357-1-5(6)) Earthshaker Bks.

Stilton, Gerónimo. Get the Scoop, Geronimo! 2015. (Geronimo Stilton Cavemice Ser.: 9). 128p. (J). lib. bdg. 17.20 (978-0-606-37779-9(4)) Turtleback.

—Help, I'm in Hot Lava! 2013. (Geronimo Stilton Cavemice Ser.: 3). lib. bdg. 17.20 (978-0-606-32407-6(0)) Turtleback.

—The Stone of Fire. 2013. (Geronimo Stilton Cavemice Ser.: 1). lib. bdg. 18.40 (978-0-606-31526-5(8)) Turtleback.

Stilton, Geronimo. The Stone of Fire (Geronimo Stilton Cavemice #1) 2004. (Geronimo Stilton Ser.: 1). (ENG.). 128p. (J). (gr. 2-5). E-Book 7.99 (978-0-545-52048-5(7), Scholastic Paperbacks) Scholastic, Inc.

Stilton, Gerónimo & Heim, Julia. My Autosaurus Will Win! Facciotto, Giuseppe et al, illus. 2016. 113p. (J). (978-1-5182-0304-6(3)) Scholastic, Inc.

Storm, Zed. Will Solvit & the Cannibal Cavemen. 2010. (Will Solvit Ser.: Bk. 5). (Illus.). 128p. (J). (gr. 1-7). pap. (978-1-4075-8983-1(0)) Parragon, Inc.

Talbott, Hudson. From Wolf to Woof: The Story of Dogs. Talbott, Hudson, illus. 2016. (Illus.). 40p. (J). (gr. k-3). 16.99 (978-0-399-25404-8(8), Nancy Paulsen Books) Penguin Young Readers Group.

Turnbull, Ann & Giblin, James Cross. Maroo of the Winter Caves: A Winter & Holiday Book for Kids. 20th anniv. ed. 2004. (ENG., Illus.). 144p. (J). (gr. 3-7). pap. 7.99 (978-0-618-44299-7(5), 100368, Clarion Bks.) HarperCollins Pubs.

Ward, David. Archipelago, 1 vol. 2008. (ENG.). 176p. (YA). (gr. 7-12). pap. 6.95 (978-0-88995-400-7(3), cc069aac-4386-4e25-8415-a5f97ad33438) Trifolium Bks., Inc. CAN. Dist: Firefly Bks., Ltd.

Williams, Susan. Wind Rider. 2006. 309p. (J). (gr. 5-9). 16.99 (978-0-06-087236-6(5)) HarperCollins Pubs.

Winterhager, Randerath -. Vuela, Yoa, vuela! 2012. (SPA.). 32p. (J). (gr. 2-3). pap. 19.99 (978-84-261-3918-4(3)) Juventud, Editorial ESP. Dist: Lectorum Pubns., Inc.

Zeltser, David. Blast from the North. 2016. (Lug Ser.: 2). (ENG., Illus.). 160p. (J). (gr. 3-6). E-Book 23.99 (978-1-5124-0890-4(5), Carolrhoda Bks.) Lerner Publishing Group.

PREHISTORY

see Archaeology; Prehistoric Peoples; Stone Age

PREJUDICES

see also Antisemitism

Acks, Alex. The Bubble of Confirmation Bias, 1 vol. 2018. (Critical Thinking about Digital Media Ser.). (ENG.). 80p. (gr. 7-7). 37.60 (978-1-9785-0471-4(3), c3e82a2f-8005-4533-b0f4-c4ef4d8a965b) Enslow Publishing, LLC.

Adams, Christine. God Made Us One by One: How to See Prejudice & Celebrate Differences. Alley, R. W., illus. 2008. (J). mass mkt. 7.95 (978-0-87029-418-1(0)) Abbey Pr.

Aikins, Anne Marie. Racism: Deal with It Before It Gets under Your Skin, 1 vol. Murray, Steven, illus. 2010. (Lorimer Deal with It Ser.). (ENG.). 32p. (J). (gr. 4-9). 24.95 (978-1-55277-495-3(3), 6fce289c-0693-4839-abea-6c8584332140) James Lorimer & Co. Ltd., Pubs. CAN. Dist: Lerner Publishing Group.

Chambers, Catherine. How to Handle Discrimination & Prejudice. 2014. (Under Pressure Ser.). 48p. (gr. 4-7). 37.10 (978-1-59920-827-5(X)) Black Rabbit Bks.

Cunningham, Anne C., ed. Environmental Racism & Classism, 1 vol. 2016. (At Issue Ser.). (ENG.). 160p. (J). (gr. 10-12). pap. 28.80 (978-1-5345-0040-2(5), 4f9a596d-7f09-446d-b3ff-f8a5dd5ed776); lib. bdg. 41.03 (978-1-5345-0016-7(2), 0be850a1-cd82-451e-9893-84154bbe5763) Greenhaven Publishing LLC. (Greenhaven Publishing).

Davidson, Tish. Prejudice. (Life Balance Ser.). (ENG.). 80p. 2004. (YA). (gr. 5-8). pap. 6.95 (978-0-531-15572-1(2)) 2003. (Illus.). (J). 20.50 (978-0-531-12252-5(2)) Scholastic Library Publishing. (Watts, Franklin).

Ford, Jeanne Marie. Challenging Stereotypes & Prejudices, 1 vol. 2017. (Active Citizenship Today Ser.). (ENG.). 32p. (gr. 3-3). pap. 11.58 (978-1-5026-2916-6(X), fbb62af8-e662-4ac3-87ed-4874cfbcf064) Cavendish Square Publishing LLC.

Gay, Kathlyn. Cultural Diversity: Conflicts & Challenges. 2003. (It Happened to Me Ser.: 6). (ENG., Illus.). 144p. pap. 55.00 (978-0-8108-4805-4(8)) Scarecrow Pr., Inc.

Hanes, Richard Clay, et al. Prejudice in the Modern World. 2007. (J). (978-1-4144-0206-2(6)); (978-1-4144-0205-5(8)) Cengage Gale.

—Prejudice Throughout History Reference Library 4 Vol Set, 5 vols. rev. ed. 2007. (Prejudice in the Modern World Reference Library). (ENG., Illus.). 230p. (J). 454.00 (978-1-4144-0203-1(1), UXL) Cengage Gale.

Harrison, Geoffrey C. & Scott, Thomas F. The Fight for Freedom. Stewart, Mark & Kennedy, Mike, eds. 2014. (Great Debates Ser.). (ENG.). 48p. (J). (gr. 5-8). lib. bdg. 29.27 (978-1-59953-588-3(2)) Norwood Hse. Pr.

Henneberg, Susan, ed. Race in America, 1 vol. 2016. (Opposing Viewpoints Ser.). (ENG.). 208p. (YA). (gr. 10-12). pap. 34.80 (978-1-5345-0028-0(6), aeeebecc-869f-4874-95a1-ff12564b3ed1); lib. bdg. 50.43 (978-1-5345-0022-8(7), 5aced661-562f-43e5-8463-2e697dd7f025) Greenhaven Publishing LLC. (Greenhaven Publishing).

Hill, Z. B. Gallup Guides for Youth Facing Persistent Prejudice. 2012. (Gallup Guides for Youth Facing Persistent Prejudice Ser.). 64p. (J). (gr. 7-8). 22.95 (978-1-4222-2463-2(5)) Mason Crest.

Kendi, Ibram X. & Stone, Nic. How to Be a (Young) Antiracist. 2023. 208p. (YA). (gr. 7). (ENG.). pap. 14.99 **(978-0-593-46161-7(4))**; (Illus.). 19.99 (978-0-593-46160-0(6)) Penguin Young Readers Group. (Kokila).

Kyi, Tanya Lloyd. This Is Your Brain on Stereotypes: How Science Is Tackling Unconscious Bias. Shannon, Drew, illus. 2020. (ENG.). 88p. (J). (gr. 6-9). 18.99 (978-1-5253-0016-5(4)) Kids Can Pr., Ltd. CAN. Dist: Hachette Bk. Group.

McCage, Crystal, ed. Prejudice, 1 vol. 2009. (Issues That Concern You Ser.). (ENG., Illus.). 112p. (gr. 7-10). lib. bdg. 43.63 (978-0-7377-4349-4(2), d447bc16-0825-49f1-b7b9-c4ed022423d7, Greenhaven Publishing) Greenhaven Publishing LLC.

McIntosh, Kenneth & Walker, Ida. Youth with Cultural/Language Differences: Interpreting an Alien World. 2009. (Helping Youth with Mental, Physical, & Social Challenges Ser.). (Illus.). 128p. (YA). (gr. 7-18). lib. bdg. 24.95 (978-1-4222-0141-1(4)) Mason Crest.

Palmer, Bill. Gallup Guides for Youth Facing Persistent Prejudice. 2012. (Gallup Guides for Youth Facing Persistent Prejudice Ser.). 64p. (J). (gr. 7-8). 22.95 (978-1-4222-2466-3(X)) Mason Crest.

Patrick, Denise Lewis. A Lesson for Martin Luther King Jr: Ready-To-Read Level 2. Pate, Rodney S., illus. 2003. (Ready-To-Read Childhood of Famous Americans Ser.). (ENG.). 32p. (J). (gr. k-2). pap. 4.99 (978-0-689-85397-5(1), Simon Spotlight) Simon Spotlight.

Reynolds, Jason & Kendi, Ibram X. Stamped: Racism, Antiracism, & You: A Remix of the National Book Award-Winning Stamped from the Beginning. 2020. (ENG.). 320p. (YA). (gr. 7-17). 18.99 (978-0-316-45369-1(2)) Little, Brown Bks. for Young Readers.

Rodger, Marguerite & Rodger, Jessie. Racism & Prejudice. 2010. (Straight Talk about... Ser.). (ENG.). 48p. (J). (gr. 7-10). lib. bdg. (978-0-7787-2129-1(9)) Crabtree Publishing Co.

Sanna, Ellyn. Gallup Guides for Youth Facing Persistent Prejudice Muslims. 2012. (Gallup Guides for Youth Facing Persistent Prejudice Ser.). 64p. (J). (gr. 7-8). 22.95 (978-1-4222-2468-7(6)) Mason Crest.

—People with Mental & Physical Challenges. 2012. (Gallup Guides for Youth Facing Persistent Prejudice Ser.). (Illus.). 64p. (J). (gr. 7-8). 22.95 (978-1-4222-2470-0(8)) Mason Crest.

Scheunemann, Pam. Tolerance. 2003. (United We Stand Ser.). (Illus.). 24p. (J). (gr. k-3). lib. bdg. 24.21 (978-1-57765-881-8(7), SandCastle) ABDO Publishing Co.

Seba, Jaime. Gallup Guides for Youth Facing Persistent Prejudice: Blacks. 2012. (Gallup Guides for Youth Facing Persistent Prejudice Ser.). 64p. (J). (gr. 7-8). 22.95 (978-1-4222-2464-9(3)) Mason Crest.

Steele, Philip. Race & Crime. 2016. (Behind the News Ser.). (Illus.). 48p. (J). (gr. 6-9). (978-0-7787-2588-6(X)) Crabtree Publishing Co.

Thomson Gale Staff. Prejudice in the Modern World. Hanes, Sharon M., ed. rev. ed. 2007. (Prejudice in the Modern World Reference Library). (ENG., Illus.). 256p. (J). 129.00 (978-1-4144-0208-6(2), UXL) Cengage Gale.

—Prejudice in the Modern World - Almanac, 2 vols. Hanes, Richard C. et al, eds. rev. ed. 2007. (Prejudice in the Modern World Reference Library). (ENG.). 462p. (YA). 233.00 (978-1-4144-0204-8(X), UXL) Cengage Gale.

Thomson Gale Staff & Hermsen, Sarah. Prejudice in the Modern World: Biographies. Hanes, Richard C. & Rudd, Kelly, eds. rev. ed. 2007. (Prejudice in the Modern World Reference Library). (ENG., Illus.). 288p. (J). 129.00 (978-1-4144-0207-9(4), UXL) Cengage Gale.

—Prejudice in the Modern World: Cumulative Index. rev. ed. 2007. (Prejudice in the Modern World Reference Library). (ENG.). 34p. (YA). 5.00 (978-1-4144-0209-3(0), UXL) Cengage Gale.

Wallace, Elise. Unsung Heroes: Pioneers in Science. rev. ed. 2018. (TIME(r): Informational Text Ser.). (ENG.). 48p. (J). (gr. 6-8). pap. 13.99 (978-1-4258-5001-2(4)) Teacher Created Materials, Inc.

Webber, Diane & Mandel, Laurie. Totally Tolerant: Spotting & Stopping Prejudice. 2008. (Scholastic Choices Ser.). (ENG., Illus.). 112p. (J). (gr. 7-12). 27.00 (978-0-531-13867-0(4), Children's Pr.) Scholastic Library Publishing.

Wright, John D. Race & Crime. 2004. (Crime & Detection Ser.). (Illus.). 96p. (YA). (gr. 7-18). lib. bdg. 22.95 (978-1-59084-378-9(9)) Mason Crest.

PREJUDICES—FICTION

Ahmed, Samira. Internment. (ENG.). 400p. (YA). (gr. 7-17). 2020. pap. 11.99 (978-0-316-52270-0(8)) 2019. 17.99 (978-0-316-52269-4(4)) Little, Brown Bks. for Young Readers.

Ainslie, Claire. Detained. 2019. (Al High Ser.). (ENG.). 104p. (YA). (gr. 6-12). 26.65 (978-1-5415-5692-8(5), acbab631-3222-4307-b9a4-4c6567198253, Darby Creek) Lerner Publishing Group.

Alexander, Jill S. The Sweetheart of Prosper County. 2010. (ENG.). 240p. (YA). (gr. 7-12). pap. 18.99 (978-0-312-54857-5(5), 900055795) Square Fish.

Alexander, Kwame. The Door of No Return. l.t. ed. 2023. (ENG.). (J). lib. bdg. 22.99 Cengage Gale.

—The Door of No Return. 2022. (ENG., Illus.). 432p. (J). (gr. 5-17). 17.99 (978-0-316-44186-5(4)) Little, Brown Bks. for Young Readers.

Ali, S. K. Love from a to Z. 2019. (ENG., Illus.). 352p. (YA). (gr. 9). 19.99 (978-1-5344-4272-6(3), Salaam Reads) Simon & Schuster Bks. For Young Readers.

Allison, Teresa J. Bobble Stories: The Oddbobble's Visit. Allison, Charles T., illus. 2013. 48p. pap. 12.99 (978-0-9887612-0-9(3)) Tawnsy Publishing.

Armistead, John. The $66 Summer: A Novel of the Segregated South. 2nd ed. 2006. (Milkweed Prize for Children's Literature Ser.). (ENG., Illus.). 240p. (J). (gr. 3-8). reprint ed. per. 8.00 (978-1-57131-663-9(9)) Milkweed Editions.

Austin, Cassie Rita. Peppermint. Austin, Cassie Rita, illus. 2011. (Illus.). 53p. 15.95 (978-0-9846151-1-7(3)) Paintbrush Tales Publishing, LLC.

Bacon, Lee. The Last Human. 2019. (Last Human Ser.). (ENG., Illus.). 288p. (YA). (gr. 3-7). 16.99 (978-1-4197-3691-9(4), 1266301, Amulet Bks.) Abrams, Inc.

Bailey, Loren. Star-Crossed. 2019. (Al High Ser.). (ENG.). 112p. (YA). (gr. 6-12). 26.65 (978-1-5415-5690-4(9), ab0a6a2b-9bef-4d5f-af0d-d1d05a0fe21c); pap. 7.99 (978-1-5415-7293-5(9), d1461ebf-f2cb-4661-bde4-629992a9e777) Lerner Publishing Group. (Darby Creek).

Banks, Jacqueline Turner. A Day for Vincent Chin & Me. 2005. (ENG.). 128p. (J). (gr. 5-7). pap. 11.95 (978-0-618-54879-8(3), 481194, Clarion Bks.) HarperCollins Pubs.

Baskin, Nora Raleigh. My Bat Mitzvah. 2008. (ENG.). 144p. (J). (gr. 6-8). 18.69 (978-1-4169-3558-2(4)) Simon & Schuster, Inc.

—The Truth about My Bat Mitzvah. 2009. (Mix Ser.). (ENG.). 144p. (J). (gr. 4-8). pap. 7.99 (978-1-4169-7469-7(5), Aladdin) Simon & Schuster Children's Publishing.

Bell, Anthea. Frog in Love. Velthuijs, Max, illus. 2015. (J). (978-1-4351-5750-7(8)) Barnes & Noble, Inc.

Beus, Bryan. Westly: A Spider's Tale. Beus, Bryan, illus. 2015. (ENG., Illus.). 176p. (J). (gr. 4-6). 15.99 (978-1-62972-068-5(2), 5136479, Shadow Mountain) Shadow Mountain Publishing.

Bilé, Serge & Bernabé, Joby. Tiwa et la Pierre Miroir. Yapo Yapo, Martial, illus. 2017. (FRE.). 34p. (978-2-916868-43-1(7)) Cercle éditions.

Blackman, Malorie. Black & White. 2007. (ENG.). 512p. (YA). (gr. 9-12). pap. 13.99 (978-1-4169-0017-7(9), Simon & Schuster Bks. For Young Readers) Simon & Schuster Bks. For Young Readers.

Blume, Judy. Iggie's House. 2014. (ENG., Illus.). (J). (gr. 3-7). 160p. 18.99 (978-1-4814-1410-4(0)); 176p. pap. 7.99 (978-1-4814-1104-2(7)) Simon & Schuster Children's Publishing. (Atheneum Bks. for Young Readers).

Boedoe, Geefwee. Arrowville. Boedoe, Geefwee, illus. 2004. (Illus.). 40p. (J). (gr. -1-2). 16.89 (978-0-06-055599-3(8), Geringer, Laura Book) HarperCollins Pubs.

Bradbury, Bianca. Flight into Spring. 2005. (ENG.). 190p. (gr. 7). per. 11.95 (978-1-932350-01-2(2)) Ignatius Pr.

Bradley, John Ed. Call Me by My Name. (ENG.). (YA). (gr. 7). 2015. 288p. pap. 12.99 (978-1-4424-9794-8(7)) 2014. (Illus.). 272p. 17.99 (978-1-4424-9793-1(9), Atheneum Bks. for Young Readers) Simon & Schuster Children's Publishing.

Brown, Celease N. & Mubarak, Enoch. The Color Orange. 2004. (Illus.). 32p. (978-1-55306-742-9(8), Guardian Bks.) Essence Publishing.

Calhoun, Dia. Avielle of Rhia, 1 vol. 2006. (ENG.). 400p. (J). (gr. 6). 16.99 (978-0-7614-5320-8(2)) Marshall Cavendish Corp.

Celano, Marianne, et al. Something Happened in Our Town: A Child's Story about Racial Injustice. Zivoin, Jennifer, illus. 2018. (ENG.). 40p. (J). (978-1-4338-2854-6(5), Magination Pr.) American Psychological Assn.

Charles, Tami. All Because You Matter (an All Because You Matter Book) Collier, Bryan, illus. 2020. (ENG.). 40p. (J). (gr. -1-3). 17.99 (978-1-338-57485-2(X), Orchard Bks.) Scholastic, Inc.

Chen, Justina. Nothing but the Truth (and a Few White Lies) 2007. (Justina Chen Novel Ser.). (ENG.). 256p. (J). (gr. 7-17). per. 15.99 (978-0-316-01131-0(2)) Little, Brown Bks. for Young Readers.

Chotjewitz, David & Orgel, Doris. Daniel, Half Human: And the Good Nazi. 2004. 298p. (J). (978-3-551-58045-0(6)) Carlsen Verlag DEU. Dist: Distribooks, Inc.

Clements, Andrew. The Jacket. 2014. (ENG.). 96p. (J). (gr. 3-7). 10.24 (978-1-63245-301-3(0)) Lectorum Pubns., Inc.

—The Jacket. Henderson, McDavid, illus. 2003. (ENG.). 96p. (J). (gr. 3-7). pap. 6.99 (978-0-689-86010-2(2), Atheneum Bks. for Young Readers) Simon & Schuster Children's Publishing.

Clifton Wisler, G. All for Texas. 2004. 140p. (J). lib. bdg. 16.92 (978-1-4242-0767-1(3)) Fitzgerald Bks.

Coats, J. Anderson. The Wicked & the Just. 2013. (ENG.). 352p. (YA). (gr. 7). pap. 9.99 (978-0-544-02221-8(1), 1528479, Clarion Bks.) HarperCollins Pubs.

Cocca-Leffler, Maryann. The Belonging Tree. Lombardi, Kristine A., illus. 2020. (ENG.). 40p. (J). 18.99 (978-1-250-30513-8(6), 900197497, Holt, Henry & Co. Bks. For Young Readers) Holt, Henry & Co.

Cohen, Miriam. Layla's Head Scarf, 1 vol. Himler, Ronald, illus. 2009. (ENG.). 32p. (J). (gr. -1-3). 15.95 (978-1-59572-177-8(0)); pap. 5.95 (978-1-59572-178-5(9)) Star Bright Bks., Inc.

Curtis, Christopher Paul. The Watsons Go to Birmingham — 1963. 2013. (ENG., Illus.). 224p. (J). (gr. 3-7). 8.99 (978-0-385-38294-6(4), Yearling) Random Hse. Children's Bks.

—The Watsons Go to Birmingham 1963. 210p. (YA). (gr. 5-18). pap. 5.50 (978-0-8072-8336-3(3)); 2004. (J). (gr. 4-18). pap. 38.00 incl. audio (978-0-8072-8335-6(5), YA166SP) Random Hse. Audio Publishing Group. (Listening Library).

Curtis, Christopher Paul & Vega, Eida de la. Los Watson Van a Birmingham - 1963. 2016. (SPA.). 200p. (J). (gr. 5-12). pap. 12.99 (978-1-63245-640-3(0)) Lectorum Pubns., Inc.

Cutler, Jane. Susie Q Fights Back. 2018. (ENG.). 112p. (J). (gr. 3-7). pap. 6.99 (978-0-8234-3993-5(3)) Holiday Hse., Inc.

Daniels Taylor, Annette. Dreams on Fire, 1 vol. 2018. (YA Verse Ser.). (ENG.). 200p. (YA). (gr. 3-4). 25.80 (978-1-5383-8248-6(2), f03a2e4c-471d-4267-a7eb-63cc319d6d8b); pap. 16.35 (978-1-5383-8247-9(4), 6a2e7dfe-d621-4d97-b5c1-8a8c3540fe56) Enslow Publishing, LLC.

Dembar Greene, Jacqueline. Walk till You Disappear. Sawyer, Odessa, illus. 2019. (ENG.). 208p. (J). (gr. 3-7). 12.99 (978-1-5415-5722-2(0), bff435b6-3586-44fc-908e-e4371282a43d, Kar-Ben Publishing) Lerner Publishing Group.

Draper, Sharon M. Stella by Starlight. (ENG., Illus.). (J). (gr. 4-8). 2016. 352p. pap. 9.99 (978-1-4424-9498-5(0)) 2015. 336p. 19.99 (978-1-4424-9497-8(2), Atheneum Bks. for Young Readers) Simon & Schuster Children's Publishing.

—Stella by Starlight. 2016. lib. bdg. 18.40 (978-0-606-38255-7(0)) Turtleback.

Dunagan, Ted M. A Yellow Watermelon. 2014. (ENG.). 240p. (J). pap. 17.95 (978-1-58838-301-3(6), 8630, NewSouth Bks.) NewSouth, Inc.

Echeverria-Bis, Olivia. The EGGbees. Echeverria Gyorkos, Charmaine, illus. 2009. (ENG & SPA.). 32p. (J). (gr. -1-3). 16.95 (978-1-55885-529-8(7), Piñata Books) Arte Publico Pr.

Ecton, Anne Massey. Passing Through Camelot. 2006. (J). (978-0-88092-620-1(1)) Royal Fireworks Publishing Co.

Eugenio, Johnny. Lil Jordan's 9 Holes of Fear. 2009. 48p. (J). 11.95 (978-1-60747-706-8(8)) Phoenix Bks., Inc.

Eversole, Robyn. East Dragon, West Dragon. Campbell, Scott, illus. 2012. (ENG.). 40p. (J). (gr. -1-2). 19.99 (978-0-689-85828-4(0), Atheneum Bks. for Young Readers) Simon & Schuster Children's Publishing.

Ferrari, G. m. Lake, Sky, Dragonfly. 2009. 44p. pap. 16.99 (978-1-4490-2895-4(0)) AuthorHouse.

Fine, Sarah. Of Metal & Wishes. 2015. (ENG., Illus.). 352p. (YA). (gr. 9). pap. 11.99 (978-1-4424-8359-0(8), McElderry, Margaret K. Bks.) McElderry, Margaret K. Bks.

Finger, Mary E. Charlotte Bakeman Has Her Say. Batti, Kimberly Rose, illus. 2007. 96p. (J). 16.00 (978-0-9746911-2-1(7)) Little Pear Pr.

Fletcher, Susan. Walk Across the Sea. 2003. (ENG., Illus.). 224p. (J). (gr. 4-8). pap. 11.95 (978-0-689-85707-2(1), Atheneum Bks. for Young Readers) Simon & Schuster Children's Publishing.

Flood, C. J. Infinite Sky. (ENG., Illus.). 256p. (YA). (gr. 7). 2015. pap. 10.99 (978-1-4814-0659-8(0)) 2014. 17.99 (978-1-4814-0658-1(2), Atheneum Bks. for Young Readers) Simon & Schuster Children's Publishing.

Frazier, Sundee T. The Other Half of My Heart. 2011. 304p. (J). (gr. 3-7). 8.99 (978-0-440-24006-8(9), Yearling) Random Hse. Children's Bks.

Frazier, Sundee Tucker. The Other Half of My Heart. 2011. (ENG.). 304p. (J). (gr. 4-6). lib. bdg. 21.19 (978-0-385-90446-9(0), Delacorte Pr.) Random Hse. Children's Bks.

Gantos, Jack. Desire Lines. 2006. (ENG.). 144p. (YA). (gr. 7-12). reprint ed. pap. 16.99 (978-0-374-41703-1(2), 900037941, Farrar, Straus & Giroux (BYR)) Farrar, Straus & Giroux.

Garcia, Maria. Las Aventuras de Connie y Diego. 2004. (ENG & SPA., Illus.). (J). (gr. k-3). spiral bd. (978-0-616-14605-7(1)) Canadian National Institute for the Blind/Institut National Canadien pour les Aveugles.

Gilliland, Raquel Vasquez. Sia Martinez & the Moonlit Beginning of Everything. 2020. (ENG., Illus.). 432p. (YA). (gr. 7). 19.99 (978-1-5344-4863-6(2), Simon Pulse) Simon Pulse.

Gilmore, Rachna. A Group of One, 1 vol. 2005. (ENG.). 184p. (YA). (gr. 6-11). pap. 12.95 (978-1-55041-925-2(0), e4efbebf-1b4d-45dd-b868-3ff0947c418d) Trifolium Bks., Inc. CAN. Dist: Firefly Bks., Ltd.

Going, K. L. The Liberation of Gabriel King. 2007. (ENG.). 160p. (J). (gr. 3-7). 7.99 (978-0-14-240766-0(6), Puffin Books) Penguin Young Readers Group.

—The Liberation of Gabriel King. 2007. 151p. (gr. 3-7). 17.00 (978-0-7569-7762-7(2)) Perfection Learning Corp.

Green, Poppy. A New Friend. Bell, Jennifer A., illus. 2015. (Adventures of Sophie Mouse Ser.: 1). (ENG.). 128p. (J). (gr. k-4). pap. 6.99 (978-1-4814-2832-3(2), Little Simon) Little Simon.

Greene, Bette. The Drowning of Stephan Jones. 2012. 220p. pap. 9.99 (978-0-9834681-3-4(3)) Greene & Sandell.

—Summer of My German Soldier (Puffin Modern Classics) 2006. (Puffin Modern Classics Ser.). (ENG.). 240p. (J). (gr. 5-18). 8.99 (978-0-14-240651-9(1), Puffin Books) Penguin Young Readers Group.

Harper Bowron, Leah. Colorblind: A Novel. 2017. (ENG.). 184p. (YA). pap. 16.95 (978-1-943006-08-3(3)) SparkPr. (a Bks.parks Imprint).

Harrison, Lisi. Monster High. 2011. (Monster High Ser.: 1). (YA). lib. bdg. 19.65 (978-0-606-23459-7(4)) Turtleback.

Hays, Barrett K. Odelette. 2011. 20p. (gr. 1-2). pap. 10,03 (978-1-4567-2690-4(0)) AuthorHouse.

Hesse, Karen. Witness. 2004. 168p. (J). (gr. 5-9). pap. 29.00 incl. audio (978-0-8072-2094-8(9), Listening Library) Random Hse. Audio Publishing Group.

—Witness (Scholastic Gold) (ENG.). (J). (gr. 4-7). 2019. 192p. pap. 7.99 (978-1-338-35967-1(3)) 2003. (Illus.). 176p. pap. 7.99 (978-0-439-27200-1(9), Scholastic Paperbacks) Scholastic, Inc.

Hobbs, Valerie. Minnie Mcclary Speaks Her Mind. 2013. (ENG.). 240p. (J). (gr. 4-8). pap. 17.99 (978-1-250-03408-3(6), 900120578) Square Fish.

Hoffman, Alice. Incantation. rev. ed. 2007. (ENG., Illus.). 192p. (YA). (gr. 7-17). per. 12.99 (978-0-316-15428-4(8)) Little, Brown Bks. for Young Readers.

Hoffman, Emily Allen. A Friend of the Enemy. 2003. 108p. (J). pap. 7.95 (978-1-57249-312-4(7), White Mane Kids) White Mane Publishing Co., Inc.

Holt, K. A. Brains for Lunch: A Zombie Novel in Haiku?! Wilson, Gahan, illus. 2010. (ENG.). 96p. (J). (gr. 4-9). 22.99 (978-1-59643-629-9(8), 900068270) Roaring Brook Pr.

Hopkins, Ellen. People Kill People. (ENG.). (YA). (gr. 9). 2019. 464p. pap. 13.99 (978-1-4814-4294-7(5)) 2018. (Illus.). 448p. 19.99 (978-1-4814-4293-0(7)) McElderry, Margaret K. Bks. (McElderry, Margaret K. Bks.).

Houston, Julian. New Boy. 2008. (ENG.). 288p. (YA). (gr. 7-12). pap. 7.99 (978-0-618-88405-6(X), 488284, Clarion Bks.) HarperCollins Pubs.

—New Boy. 2007. 282p. (gr. 7-12). 18.00 (978-0-7569-8139-6(5)) Perfection Learning Corp.

Hughes, Dean. Four-Four-Two. 2016. (ENG., Illus.). 272p. (YA). (gr. 7). 18.99 (978-1-4814-6252-5(0), Atheneum Bks. for Young Readers) Simon & Schuster Children's Publishing.

Hughes, Shirley. The Christmas Eve Ghost. Hughes, Shirley, illus. 2010. (ENG., Illus.). 32p. (J). (gr. -1-3). 15.99 (978-0-7636-4472-7(2)) Candlewick Pr.

Hurwin, Davida Wills. Freaks & Revelations. 2012. (ENG.). 240p. (YA). (gr. 10-17). pap. 14.99 (978-0-316-04997-9(2)) Little, Brown Bks. for Young Readers.

Ikeda, Daisaku. Over the Deep Blue Sea. McCraughrean, Geraldine, tr. from JPN. Wildsmith, Brian, illus. 2013. 6.95 (978-1-935523-59-8(7)) World Tribune Pr.

Ioannides, Mara W. Cohen. A Shout in the Sunshine. 2007. (ENG.). 120p. (gr. 5). per. 14.95 (978-0-8276-0838-2(1)) Jewish Pubn. Society.

Ish-Kishor, Sulamith. A Boy of Old Prague. Shahn, Ben, illus. 2008. (Dover Children's Classics Ser.). (ENG.). 96p. (J). (gr. 4-6). pap. 3.99 (978-0-486-46766-5(X), 46766X) Dover Pubns., Inc.

James, Brian. The Heights. 2009. (ENG.). 272p. (YA). (gr. 7-12). 22.44 (978-0-312-60736-4(9)) Square Fish.

Jeter, Derek. Fair Ball. (Jeter Publishing Ser.). (ENG.). (J). (gr. 3-7). 2018. 192p. pap. 7.99 (978-1-4814-9149-5(0)) 2017. (Illus.). 176p. 17.99 (978-1-4814-9148-8(2)) Simon & Schuster/Paula Wiseman Bks. (Simon & Schuster/Paula Wiseman Bks.).

Johnson, Joanne. Pen Pals. 2011. 52p. pap. 16.95 (978-1-4560-6853-0(9)) America Star Bks.

Jones, Patrick. Heart or Mind. 2016. (Unbarred Ser.). (ENG.). 120p. (YA). (gr. 6-12). E-Book 42.65 (978-1-5124-0092-2(0), Darby Creek) Lerner Publishing Group.

Jordan, Sherryl. The Raging Quiet. 2018. (ENG.). 272p. (YA). (gr. 9-7). pap. 17.99 (978-1-5344-4119-4(0), Simon Pulse) Simon Pulse.

—The Raging Quiet. l.t. ed. 2005. 416p. 22.95 (978-0-7862-7313-3(5), Large Print Pr.) Thorndike Pr.

Jungle Crossing. 2011. (ENG.). 228p. (J). (gr. 5-7). pap. 13.99 (978-0-547-55009-1(X), 1450218, Clarion Bks.) HarperCollins Pubs.

Keene, Carolyn. Identity Theft: Book Two in the Identity Mystery Trilogy. 34th ed. 2009. (Nancy Drew (All New) Girl Detective Ser.: 34). (ENG.). 176p. (J). (gr. 3-7). pap. 6.99 (978-1-4169-6831-3(8), Aladdin) Simon & Schuster Children's Publishing.

Kendi, Ibram X. Antiracist Baby Board Book. Lukashevsky, Ashley, illus. 2020. 24p. (J). (— 1). bds. 8.99 (978-0-593-11041-6(2), Kokila) Penguin Young Readers Group.

—Antiracist Baby Picture Book. Lukashevsky, Ashley, illus. 2020. (ENG.). 32p. (J). (— 1). 8.99 (978-0-593-11050-8(1), Kokila) Penguin Young Readers Group.

—Goodnight Racism. Bayoc, Cbabi, illus. 2022. 32p. (J). (gr. -1-2). 18.99 (978-0-593-11051-5(X), Kokila) Penguin Young Readers Group.

Kerr, M. E., pseud. Someone Like Summer. 2007. (gr. 7-12). 272p. (J). lib. bdg. 17.89 (978-0-06-114100-3(3)); 208p. (YA). 16.99 (978-0-06-114099-0(6)) HarperCollins Pubs. (HarperTeen).

King, A. S. Ask the Passengers. 2013. (ENG.). 336p. (YA). (gr. 10-17). pap. 18.99 (978-0-316-19467-9(0)) Little, Brown Bks. for Young Readers.

—Dig. 2019. (ENG.). 400p. (YA). (gr. 9). 17.99 (978-1-101-99491-7(6), Dutton Books for Young Readers) Penguin Young Readers Group.

King-Smith, Dick. Dinosaur Trouble: A Picture Book. Bruel, Nick, illus. 2012. (ENG.). 128p. (J). (gr. 2-5). pap. 16.99 (978-1-59643-935-1(1), 900122930) Roaring Brook Pr.

Konigsburg, E. L. T-Backs, T-Shirts, Coat, & Suit. 2008. (ENG.). 192p. (J). (gr. 4-8). pap. 7.99 (978-1-4169-5877-2(0), Atheneum Bks. for Young Readers) Simon & Schuster Children's Publishing.

Lambert, Noelle. Can I Play Too? 2009. (ENG., Illus.). 24p. (J). pap. 18.95 (978-1-85390-944-3(0)) Veritas Pubns. IRL. Dist: Casemate Pubs. & Bk. Distributors, LLC.

Lawlor, Laurie. Wind on the River. 2004. 156p. (J). lib. bdg. 16.92 (978-1-4242-0771-8(1)) Fitzgerald Bks.

Leblanc, Louise. Leo's Midnight Rescue. Prud'homme, Jules, illus. 2004. 62p. (J). lib. bdg. 12.00 (978-1-4242-1217-0(0)) Fitzgerald Bks.

—Leo's Midnight Rescue, 1 vol. Cummins, Sarah, tr. Prud'homme, Jules, illus. 2004. (Formac First Novels Ser.: 53). (ENG.). 64p. (J). (gr. 2-5). 4.95 (978-0-88780-640-7(6), 640); 14.95 (978-0-88780-641-4(4), 641) Formac Publishing Co., Ltd. CAN. Dist: Formac Lorimer Bks. Ltd.

Les Becquets, Diane. The Stones of Mourning Creek, 0 vols. 2012. (ENG.). 320p. (YA). (gr. 7-12). reprint ed. pap. 9.99 (978-0-7614-5238-6(9), 9780761452386, Skyscape) Amazon Publishing.

Levine, Kristin. The Best Bad Luck I Ever Had. 2010. 288p. (J). (gr. 5-18). 8.99 (978-0-14-241648-8(7), Puffin Books) Penguin Young Readers Group.

Levithan, David. Wide Awake. 2008. (ENG.). 240p. (YA). (gr. 9). pap. 11.99 (978-0-375-83467-7(2), Knopf Bks. for Young Readers) Random Hse. Children's Bks.

Loney, Andrea J. Bunnybear. 2018. (2019 Av2 Fiction Ser.). (ENG.). 32p. (J). (gr. -1-3). lib. bdg. 34.28 (978-1-4896-8251-2(1), AV2 by Weigl) Weigl Pubs., Inc.

Lucado, Max. Best of All. Martinez, Sergio, illus. 2003. (Max Lucado's Wemmicks Ser.: 4). (ENG.). 32p. (J). 16.99 (978-1-58134-501-8(1)) Crossway.

Lupica, Mike. Point Guard. 2017. (Home Team Ser.). (ENG., Illus.). 272p. (J). (gr. 3-7). 19.99 (978-1-4814-1003-8(2), Simon & Schuster Bks. For Young Readers) Simon & Schuster Bks. For Young Readers.

—Point Guard. 2018. (Home Team Ser.). (ENG.). 288p. (J). (gr. 3-7). pap. 8.99 (978-1-4814-1005-2(9), Simon & Schuster Bks. For Young Readers) Simon & Schuster Bks. For Young Readers.

—Point Guard. 2018. (Home Team Ser.). lib. bdg. 18.40 (978-0-606-40839-4(8)) Turtleback.

Maddox, Jake. Soccer Stand-Off. 2016. (Jake Maddox JV Ser.). (ENG., Illus.). 96p. (J). (gr. 4-6). lib. bdg. 26.65 (978-1-4965-3983-0(4), 133206, Stone Arch Bks.) Capstone.

Malley, Gemma. The Returners. 2010. (Declaration Ser.). (ENG.). 256p. (YA). (gr. 7-18). 16.99 (978-1-59990-443-6(8), 900063947, Bloomsbury USA Childrens) Bloomsbury Publishing USA.

Marsden, Carolyn. The Gold-Threaded Dress. 2006. (ENG.). 80p. (J). (gr. 2-4). reprint ed. per. 7.99 (978-0-7636-2993-9(6)) Candlewick Pr.

—The Gold-Threaded Dress. 2006. 73p. (gr. 2-4). 17.00 (978-0-7569-6574-7(8)) Perfection Learning Corp.

Martin, Ann M. Here Today. 2005. 308p. (gr. 5-9). 18.00 (978-0-7569-5104-7(6)) Perfection Learning Corp.

Mason, Jo-Anne. Paddy, the Goat That Saved Rainbow Island. 2003. 48p. (gr. -1-3). 13.95 (978-0-333-97062-1(4)) Macmillan Caribbean GBR. Dist: Interlink Publishing Group, Inc.

Mawhinney, Lynnette. Lulu the One & Only. Poh, Jennie, illus. 2020. 32p. (J). (978-1-4338-3159-1(7), Magination Pr.) American Psychological Assn.

McAllister, Margaret. The Octave of Angels. 2004. 128p. (J). pap. 8.00 (978-0-8028-5240-3(8)) Eerdmans, William B. Publishing Co.

McClintock, Norah. Trial by Fire, 1 vol. 2016. (Riley Donovan Ser.: 1). (ENG.). 240p. (YA). (gr. 8-12). pap. 10.95 (978-1-4598-0936-9(X)) Orca Bk. Pubs. USA.

McIntyre, Sarah. The New Neighbors. 2019. (ENG., Illus.). 32p. (J). (gr. -1-2). 17.99 (978-1-5247-8996-1(8), Penguin Workshop) Penguin Young Readers Group.

Meminger, Neesha. Shine, Coconut Moon. 2010. (ENG.). 256p. (YA). (gr. 9). pap. 11.99 (978-1-4424-0305-5(5), McElderry, Margaret K. Bks.) McElderry, Margaret K. Bks.

Mendelsohn, Martha. Bromley Girls. 2015. (ENG.). 192p. (YA). pap. 14.95 (978-0-89672-922-3(2)) Texas Tech Univ. Pr.

Mendez, Matt. Barely Missing Everything. (ENG.). 320p. (YA). (gr. 9). 2020. pap. 11.99 (978-1-5344-0446-5(5)) 2019. (Illus.). 18.99 (978-1-5344-0445-8(7)) Simon & Schuster Children's Publishing.

Miklowitz, Gloria D. Secrets in the House of Delgado. 2004. (ENG.). 192p. (J). (gr. 4-18). pap. 8.00 (978-0-8028-5210-6(6)) Eerdmans, William B. Publishing Co.

Miller, William. Joe Louis, My Champion, 1 vol. Pate, Rodney S., illus. 2004. (ENG.). 32p. (J). (gr. 1-5). pap. 11.95 (978-1-60060-426-3(9), leelowbooks); 16.95 (978-1-58430-161-5(9)) Lee & Low Bks., Inc.

Mobin-Uddin, Asma. My Name Is Bilal. Kiwak, Barbara, illus. 2005. (ENG.). 32p. (J). (gr. 1-4). 17.99 (978-1-59078-175-3(9), Astra Young Readers) Astra Publishing Hse.

Mochizuki, Ken. Baseball Saved Us, 1 vol. Lee, Dom, illus. 2018. (ENG.). 32p. (J). (gr. k-3). pap. 10.95 (978-1-880000-19-9(9), leelowbooks) Lee & Low Bks., Inc.

—Baseball Saved Us. Lee, Dom, illus. (Picture Book Readalong Ser.). pap. 39.95 incl. audio compact disk (978-1-59112-917-2(6)); 2004. (J). (gr. -1-2). 25.95 incl. audio (978-1-59112-456-6(5)) Live Oak Media.

Moore, Stephanie Perry. True Friends, 1. 2005. (Carmen Browne Ser.: 1). (ENG.). 128p. (YA). (gr. 4-6). pap. 6.99 (978-0-8024-8172-6(8)) Moody Pubs.

Myers, Walter Dean. Down to the Last Out: the Journal of Biddy Owens, the Negro Leagues, Birmingham, Alabama 1948. 2013. (ENG.). 144p. (J). (gr. 3-7). pap. 6.99 (978-0-545-53050-7(4), Scholastic Paperbacks) Scholastic, Inc.

—Juba! A Novel. 2016. (ENG., Illus.). 208p. (YA). (gr. 8). pap. 10.99 (978-0-06-211273-6(2), Quill Tree Bks.) HarperCollins Pubs.

—Slam! 2008. (Point Signature Ser.). 266p. (gr. 7-12). lib. bdg. 19.65 (978-0-613-12111-8(2)) Turtleback.

Napoli, Donna Jo. Alligator Bayou. 288p. (YA). (gr. 7). 2010. pap. 8.99 (978-0-553-49417-4(1)) 2009. (ENG.). lib. bdg. 24.94 (978-0-385-90891-7(1)) Random Hse. Children's Bks. (Lamb, Wendy Bks.).

Neale, Cynthia. Hope in New York City: The Continuing Story of the Irish Dresser. 2008. (ENG.). 176p. (J). pap. 7.95 (978-1-57249-387-2(9), White Mane Kids) White Mane Publishing Co., Inc.

Novel Units. Summer of My German Soldier Novel Units Teacher Guide. 2019. (ENG.). (YA). pap. 12.99 (978-1-56137-113-6(0), Novel Units, Inc.) Classroom Library Co.

Oh, Ellen. Finding Junie Kim. 2021. (ENG.). 368p. (J). (gr. 3-7). 16.99 (978-0-06-298798-3(4), HarperCollins) HarperCollins Pubs.

Olivas, Daniel. Benjamin & the Word: Benjamín y la Palabra. Baeza Ventura, Gabriela, tr. Dyen, Don, illus. 2011. 32p. (J). pap. 7.95 (978-1-55885-687-5(0), Piñata Books) Arte Publico Pr.

—Benjamin & Word Benjamin Y la Palabra. (SPA & ENG., Illus.). 32p. 15.95 (978-1-55885-413-0(4), Piñata Books) Arte Publico Pr.

Olsen, Sylvia. Middle Row, 1 vol. 2008. (Orca Soundings Ser.). (ENG.). 136p. (YA). (gr. 8-12). pap. 9.95 (978-1-55143-899-3(2)) Orca Bk. Pubs. USA.

Otey Little, Mimi. Yoshiko & the Foreigner. Otey Little, Mimi, illus. 2004. (Illus.). 31p. (J). (gr. 4-8). reprint ed. 16.00 (978-0-7567-7510-0(8)) DIANE Publishing Co.

Park, Linda Sue. Project Mulberry. 2022. (ENG.). 272p. (J). (gr. 3-7). pap. 7.99 (978-0-544-93521-1(7), 1658126, Clarion Bks.) HarperCollins Pubs.

—Project Mulberry. 2007. 225p. (gr. 4-7). 17.00 (978-0-7569-7921-8(8)) Perfection Learning Corp.

Parker, Robert. Edenville Owls. 2008. 194p. (gr. 4-6). 18.00 (978-0-7569-8920-0(5)) Perfection Learning Corp.

Paul, Curtis Christopher. The Watsons Go to Birmingham 1963. 2014. (ENG.). 224p. (J). (gr. 12-12). 11.24 (978-1-63245-108-8(5)) Lectorum Pubns., Inc.

Pearsall, Shelley. Jump into the Sky. 2013. 352p. (J). (gr. 4-7). pap. 8.99 (978-0-440-42140-5(3), Yearling) Random Hse. Children's Bks.

Platt, Randall. Incommunicado. 2017. (ENG.). 352p. (J). (gr. 5-8). pap. 9.99 (978-1-5107-0991-1(6), Sky Pony Pr.) Skyhorse Publishing Co., Inc.

Plum-Ucci, Carol. What Happened to Lani Garver. 2004. (ENG.). 336p. (YA). (gr. 9). reprint ed. pap. 18.99 (978-0-15-205088-7(4), 1195362, Clarion Bks.) HarperCollins Pubs.

Porter, Pamela. The Crazy Man. 2013. 164p. pap. (978-1-4596-6446-3(9)) ReadHowYouWant.com, Ltd.

Porter, Sarah. Tentacle & Wing. 2017. (ENG.). 272p. (J). (gr. 5-7). 16.99 (978-1-328-70733-8(4), 1672696, Clarion Bks.) HarperCollins Pubs.

Raschke, Erik. The Book of Samuel: A Novel. 2009. (ENG.). 256p. (YA). (gr. 4-7). pap. 19.99 (978-0-312-37969-8(2), 900050340, St. Martin's Griffin) St. Martin's Pr.

Reece, Colleen L. Last Page in the Diary. 2011. 94p. pap. 8.95 (978-1-61633-179-5(8)) Guardian Angel Publishing, Inc.

Reed, Vernon. Children of the Hollow. 2006. (ENG.). 188p. per. 24.95 *(978-1-4241-3668-1(7))* PublishAmerica, Inc.

Reynolds Naylor, Phyllis. Alice on the Outside. 2012. (Alice Ser.: 11). (ENG., Illus.). 208p. (J). (gr. 5-9). pap. 7.99 *(978-1-4424-3495-0(3))*, Atheneum Bks. for Young Readers) Simon & Schuster Children's Publishing.

—A Shiloh Christmas. 2015. (Shiloh Quartet Ser.). (ENG., Illus.). 256p. (J). (gr. 3-7). 17.99 *(978-1-4814-4151-3(5))* Simon & Schuster Children's Publishing.

Richardson, Faith. The Peacock's Stone. 2003. 192p. (J). 21.95 *(978-0-9744989-0-4(4))*; (Illus.). pap. 12.95 *(978-0-9744989-1-1(2))* Fox Song Bks.

Rinaldi, Ann. The Education of Mary: A Little Miss of Color, 1832. 2005. 176p. (J). pap. *(978-0-7868-1377-3(6))* Hyperion Pr.

Robinson, Sharon. The Hero Two Doors down: Based on the True Story of Friendship Between a Boy & a Baseball Legend. 2017. (ENG.). 208p. (J). (gr. 4-7). pap. 7.99 *(978-0-545-80452-3(3))*, Scholastic Paperbacks) Scholastic, Inc.

Ross, Jeff. Up North, 1 vol. 2017. (Orca Soundings Ser.). (ENG.). 144p. (YA). (gr. 8-12). pap. 9.95 *(978-1-4598-1456-1(8))* Orca Bk. Pubs. USA.

Ross, Susan. Kiki & Jacques: A Refugee Story. 2019. (ENG.). 144p. (J). (gr. 3-7). pap. 7.99 *(978-0-8234-4180-8(6))* Holiday Hse., Inc.

Russ, Tim & Roskilly, Jedda. Bugsters! 2008. (Illus.). 32p. (J). 16.95 *(978-0-9795131-7-6(0))* Woods N' Water Pr., Inc.

Schraff, Anne. Freedom Knows No Color. 2008. (Passages to History Ser.). 118p. (J). lib. bdg. 13.95 *(978-0-7569-8392-5(4))*; (YA). (gr. 7-12). pap. 8.50 *(978-0-7891-7567-0(3))* Perfection Learning Corp.

—The Hyena Laughs at Night. 2008. (Passages 2000 Ser.). 111p. lib. bdg. 13.95 *(978-0-7569-8407-6(6))* Perfection Learning Corp.

—Leap of Faith, 1 vol. unabr. ed. 2011. (Urban Underground Ser.). (ENG.). 201p. (YA). (gr. 9-12). pap. 11.95 *(978-1-61651-588-1(0))* Saddleback Educational Publishing, Inc.

Schronk, Julie. The Grass Grows Green. 2007. 208p. per. 24.95 *(978-1-60441-057-0(4))* America Star Bks.

Scoppettone, Sandra. Happy Endings Are All Alike. 2014. (ENG., Illus.). 184p. (gr. 6). pap. 12.95 *(978-1-939601-04-9(5))* Ig Publishing, Inc.

Self, Jeffery. A Very, Very Bad Thing. 2017. (ENG.). 240p. (YA). (gr. 9). 17.99 *(978-1-338-11840-7(4))*, PUSH) Scholastic, Inc.

Siddoway, Richard M. The Cottage Park Puzzle. 2015. 200p. (YA). pap. 14.99 *(978-1-4621-1562-4(4))* Cedar Fort, Inc./CFI Distribution.

Speare, Elizabeth George. The Witch of Blackbird Pond. 2011. (ENG.). 272p. (J). (gr. 5-7). pap. 8.99 *(978-0-547-55029-9(4))*, 1450238, Clarion Bks.) HarperCollins Pubs.

St. James, James. Freak Show. 2008. (ENG.). 304p. (YA). (gr. 9-18). 8.99 *(978-0-14-241231-2(7))*, Puffin Books) Penguin Young Readers Group.

Stiver, Joan. The Door in the Floor: An Underground Railroad Adventure. 2008. 48p. pap. 4.99 *(978-1-4343-2953-0(4))* AuthorHouse.

Stone, Nic. Clean Getaway. (ENG., Illus.). 240p. (J). (gr. 3-7). 2021. 7.99 *(978-1-9848-9300-0(9))*, Yearling) 2020. 16.99 *(978-1-9848-9297-3(5))*, Crown Books For Young Readers) Random Hse. Children's Bks.

Suen, Anastasia. Girls Can, Too! A Tolerence Story, 1 vol. Ebbeler, Jeff, illus. 2008. (Main Street School~ Kids with Character Ser.). (ENG.). 32p. (J). (gr. k-4). 32.79 *(978-1-60270-271-4(3))*, 11277, Looking Glass Library) Magic Wagon.

Sullivan, Jacqueline Levering. Annie's War. 2007. (Illus.). 183p. (J). (gr. 3-7). 15.00 *(978-0-8028-5325-7(0))*, Eerdmans Bks For Young Readers) Eerdmans, William B. Publishing Co.

Sumrow, Melanie. The Inside Battle. 2020. (ENG.). 336p. (J). (gr. 6). 16.99 *(978-1-4998-0917-6(4))*, Yellow Jacket) Bonnier Publishing USA.

Taylor, Mildred D. The Friendship. 2014. (ENG.). 56p. (J). (gr. 3-7). 11.24 *(978-1-63245-342-6(8))* Lectorum Pubns., Inc.

—Roll of Thunder, Hear My Cry. 2004. 276p. (gr. 4-8). reprint ed. pap. 10.00 *(978-0-7567-7955-9(3))* DIANE Publishing Co.

—Roll of Thunder, Hear My Cry: 40th Anniversary Special Edition. 40th anniv. ed. 2016. (ENG., Illus.). 304p. (J). (gr. 3-7). 19.99 *(978-1-101-99388-0(X))*, Dial Bks) Penguin Young Readers Group.

Taylor, Theodore. The Cay. 2003. (ENG.). 160p. (J). (gr. 5-7). mass mkt. 7.99 *(978-0-440-22912-4(X))*, Laurel Leaf) Random Hse. Children's Bks.

Taylor, Theodore & Taylor, Theodore. The Cay. 2003. (gr. 5-8). lib. bdg. 17.20 *(978-0-613-72282-7(5))* Turtleback.

Tuttle, Todd. Spot. Tuttle, Todd, illus. 2007. (Illus.). 20p. (J). 19.95 *(978-1-889829-16-6(1))* Window Bks.

Uchida, Yoshiko. Samurai of Gold Hill. Forberg, Ati, illus. 2005. 119p. (J). (gr. 2). per. 8.95 *(978-1-59714-015-7(5))* Heyday.

Ulick, Michael Ackerman. Romeo the Rhino's Rocky Romance: A Cautionary Tale about Differences. Guy, Will, illus. 32p. (J). 15.95 *(978-0-9679813-0-7(1))* Footprints Pr.

Vaughn, Carrie. Voices of Dragons. 2011. (ENG.). 336p. (YA). (gr. 8). pap. 9.99 *(978-0-06-154790-4(5))*, HarperTeen) HarperCollins Pubs.

Velthuijs, Max. Frog & the Stranger. 2014. (ENG., Illus.). 32p. (J). (-k). pap. 12.95 *(978-1-78344-143-3(7))* Andersen Pr. GBR. Dist: Independent Pubs. Group.

Venkatraman, Padma. Climbing the Stairs. 2008. (ENG.). 256p. (YA). (gr. 7-18). 26.19 *(978-0-399-24746-0(7))* Penguin Young Readers Group.

Vernick, Shirley Reva. The Blood Lie. (ENG.). 144p. (YA). (gr. 9-12). 2015. pap. 16.95 *(978-1-941026-09-0(5))*, 23353382) 2011. 15.95 *(978-1-933693-84-2(3))*, 23353382) Lee & Low Bks., Inc. (Cinco Puntos Press).

Villareal, Ray. Alamo Wars. 2008. 187p. (J). (gr. 6-18). pap. 10.95 *(978-1-55885-513-7(0))*, Piñata Books) Arte Publico Pr.

Volponi, Paul. Response. 2010. 176p. (YA). (gr. 7-18). 6.99 *(978-0-14-241603-7(7))*, Speak) Penguin Young Readers Group.

Waters, Daniel. Kiss of Life. 2009. (Generation Dead Ser.: Bk. 2). (ENG.). 432p. (J). (gr. 7-12). 22.44 *(978-1-4231-0924-2(4))* Hyperion Bks. for Children.

Wein, Elizabeth. The Pearl Thief. (ENG.). (YA). (gr. 7-12). 2018. 352p. pap. 10.99 *(978-1-4847-2370-8(8))* 2017. 336p. 18.99 *(978-1-4847-1716-5(3))* Hyperion Bks. for Children.

—The Pearl Thief. 2018. (YA). lib. bdg. 20.85 *(978-0-606-40964-3(5))* Turtleback.

Whelan, Gloria. In Andal's House. Hall, Amanda, illus. 2013. (Tales of the World Ser.). (ENG.). 40p. (J). (gr. 2-5). 17.95 *(978-1-58536-603-3(X))*, 202358) Sleeping Bear Pr.

Wildsmith, Brian. The Little Wood Duck, 1 vol. Wildsmith, Brian, illus. (ENG., Illus.). 32p. (J). 2007. (gr. -1-3). 16.95 *(978-1-59572-042-9(1))* 2006. pap. 6.95 *(978-1-59572-049-8(9))* Star Bright Bks., Inc.

Williams, Alicia D. Genesis Begins Again. 2019. (ENG., Illus.). 384p. (J). (gr. 4-8). 17.99 *(978-1-4814-6580-9(5))*, Atheneum/Caitlyn Dlouhy Books) Simon & Schuster Children's Publishing.

Wilson, Diane Lee. Tracks. (ENG., (J). (gr. 5-9). 2013. Illus.). 304p. pap. 6.99 *(978-1-4424-2014-4(6))* 2012. 288p. 16.99 *(978-1-4424-2013-7(8))* McElderry, Margaret K. Bks. (McElderry, Margaret K. Bks.).

Woods, Brenda. The Unsung Hero of Birdsong, USA. 2019. 208p. (J). (gr. 5). 16.99 *(978-1-5247-3709-2(7))*, Nancy Paulsen Books) Penguin Young Readers Group.

Woodson, Jacqueline. Feathers. 2007. (ENG.). 128p. (J). (gr. 5-7). 17.99 *(978-0-399-23989-2(8))*, G.P. Putnam's Sons Books for Young Readers) Penguin Young Readers Group.

Yep, Laurence. The Traitor. 2004. (Golden Mountain Chronicles). 310p. (J). (gr. 5). 14.65 *(978-0-7569-3457-6(5))* Perfection Learning Corp.

Yoon, David. Frankly in Love. (ENG.). (YA). (gr. 9). 2020. 448p. pap. 12.99 *(978-1-9848-1222-3(X))*, Penguin Books) 2019. 432p. 18.99 *(978-1-9848-1220-9(3))*, G.P. Putnam's Sons Books for Young Readers) Penguin Young Readers Group.

Zimmerman, Diana S. Kandide & the Secret of the Mists, Bk. 1. Gadd, Maxine, illus. 2008. (Calabiyau Chronicles Ser.). 290p. (J). (gr. 4-7). pap. 9.99 *(978-0-9794328-2-8(0))* Noesis Publishing.

PRESCHOOL EDUCATION

see Nursery Schools

PRESENTS

see Gifts

PRESERVATION OF FOOD

see Food—Preservation

PRESERVATION OF FORESTS

see Forests and Forestry

PRESERVATION OF NATURAL RESOURCES

see Conservation of Natural Resources

PRESERVATION OF NATURAL SCENERY

see Natural Monuments

PRESERVATION OF WILDLIFE

see Wildlife Conservation

PRESERVING

see Canning and Preserving

PRESIDENTS

Abrams, Dennis. Viktor Yushchenko. 2007. (Modern World Leaders Ser.). (ENG., Illus.). 120p. (gr. 7-12). lib. bdg. 30.00 *(978-0-7910-9266-8(6))*, P114597, Facts On File) Infobase Holdings, Inc.

Alagna, Magdalena. Anwar Sadat, 1 vol. 2003. (Middle East Leaders Ser.). (ENG., Illus.). 112p. (J). (gr. 5-8). lib. bdg. 39.80 *(978-0-8239-4464-4(6))*, 4c4dbcaf-7d24-4dbf-98ac-1bb5a29fa445, Rosen Reference) Rosen Publishing Group, Inc., The.

Albee, Sarah. George Washington: The First President. Ko, Chin, illus. 2017. 32p. (J). *(978-1-5182-5283-9(4))* HarperCollins Pubs.

Allen, John. Idi Amin. 2003. (History's Villains Ser.). (Illus.). 112p. (J). 28.70 *(978-1-56711-759-2(7))*, Blackbirch Pr., Inc.) Cengage Gale.

Anderson, Dale. Saddam Hussein. 2004. (A&E Biography Ser.). (Illus.). 112p. (J). 29.27 *(978-0-8225-5005-1(9))*, Lerner Pubns.) Lerner Publishing Group.

Antonio Lopez de Santa Anna. 2010. (ENG., Illus.). 104p. (gr. 6-12). 35.00 *(978-1-60413-734-7(7))*, P179359, Facts On File) Infobase Holdings, Inc.

Baptiste, Tracey. Nelson Mandela: Nobel Peace Prize-Winning Champion for Hope & Harmony, 4 vols. 2015. (Britannica Beginner Bios Ser.). (ENG.). 32p. (J). (gr. 2-3). 52.12 *(978-1-62275-943-9(5))*, a2f77d99-a713-4e04-9c46-41666fe29d1e, Britannica Educational Publishing) Rosen Publishing Group, Inc., The.

—Nelson Mandela: Nobel Peace Prize-Winning Warrior for Hope & Harmony, 1 vol. 2015. (Britannica Beginner Bios Ser.). (ENG., Illus.). 32p. (J). (gr. 2-3). 26.06 *(978-1-62275-941-5(9))*, 9c880c74-7f67-442d-b141-497ece6499c4, Britannica Educational Publishing) Rosen Publishing Group, Inc., The.

Barter, James. Idi Amin. 2004. (Heroes & Villains Ser.). (ENG., Illus.). 112p. (J). (gr. 7-10). 32.10 *(978-1-59018-553-7(6))*, Lucent Bks.) Cengage Gale.

Baxter, Kathleen & McConnell, Robert L., contrib. by. Assassination & Its Aftermath: How a Photograph Reassured a Shocked Nation, 1 vol. 2013. (Captured History Ser.). (ENG., Illus.). 64p. (J). (gr. 5-9). 35.32 *(978-0-7565-4692-2(3))*, Compass Point Bks.) Capstone.

Belviso, Meg & Pollack, Pam. Who Is Nelson Mandela? 2014. (Who Was... ? Ser.). lib. bdg. 16.00 *(978-0-606-34158-5(7))* Turtleback.

Boomhower, Ray E. Mr. President: A Life of Benjamin Harrison. 2018. (J). *(978-0-87195-427-5(3))* Indiana Historical Society.

Boothroyd, Jennifer. Nelson Mandela: A Life of Persistence. (Pull Ahead Books — Biographies Ser.). (ENG., Illus.). 32p. (gr. k-3). 2007. (J). pap. 7.99 *(978-0-8225-6434-8(3))*, 4ba9e03a-1644-4461-a60e-7c4961301a45) 2006. lib. bdg. 22.60 *(978-0-8225-6385-3(1))*, Lerner Pubns.) Lerner Publishing Group.

Brexel, Bernadette. Yasser Arafat. 2009. (Middle East Leaders Ser.). 112p. (gr. 5-8). 66.50 *(978-1-61514-649-9(0))*, Rosen Reference) Rosen Publishing Group, Inc., The.

Brill, Marlene Targ. Barack Obama: President for a New Era. rev. ed. 2009. (Gateway Biographies Ser.). (ENG.). 48p. (gr. 4-8). 26.60 *(978-1-57505-950-1(9))* Lerner Publishing Group.

Burch, Joann J. Jefferson Davis: Soldier & President of the Confederacy, 1 vol. 2014. (Legendary American Biographies Ser.). (ENG.). 96p. (gr. 6-6). pap. 13.88 *(978-0-7660-6466-9(2))*, 6e28cb08-5155-4f1c-8bb7-3d1cb3483692) Enslow Publishing, LLC.

Cefery, Holly. Yasser Arafat, 1 vol. 2003. (Middle East Leaders Ser.). (ENG., Illus.). 112p. (J). (gr. 5-8). lib. bdg. 39.80 *(978-0-8239-4469-9(7))*, b6f139c6-f41f-49bf-a31a-60d4f1b04fbc, Rosen Reference) Rosen Publishing Group, Inc., The.

Childress, Diana. Omar Al-Bashir's Sudan. 2009. (Dictatorships Ser.). (ENG., Illus.). 160p. (J). (gr. 9-12). 38.60 *(978-0-8225-9096-5(4))*, 1299570) Lerner Publishing Group.

Collin, Grace. Man of Destiny: The Life of Leopold Sedar Senghor. Bostic, Alex, illus. 2006. 32p. (J). lib. bdg. 16.95 *(978-1-886366-15-2(2))* Sights Productions.

Cox, Vicki. Oscar Arias Sanchez. 2007. (Modern Peacemakers Ser.). (ENG., Illus.). 118p. (gr. 9-12). lib. bdg. 30.00 *(978-0-7910-8999-6(1))*, P114506, Facts On File) Infobase Holdings, Inc.

Dakers, Diane. Nelson Mandela: South Africa's Anti-Apartheid Revolutionary. 2014. (Crabtree Groundbreaker Biographies Ser.). (ENG., Illus.). 112p. (J). (gr. 6-6). *(978-0-7787-1241-1(9))* Crabtree Publishing Co.

Day, Meredith, ed. Lyndon B. Johnson, 1 vol. 2016. (Pivotal Presidents: Profiles in Leadership Ser.). (ENG., Illus.). 80p. (gr. 8-8). lib. bdg. 36.47 *(978-1-68048-527-1(X))*, 5e555973-7621-4474-aec5-45e2fe88a7dc) Rosen Publishing Group, Inc., The.

Dodson Wade, Mary. Presidents' Day, 1 vol. 2016. (Story of Our Holidays Ser.). (ENG., Illus.). 32p. (gr. 3-3). pap. 11.52 *(978-0-7660-8345-5(4))*, 062ea253-ce24-487f-a0a8-1def4836fc84) Enslow Publishing, LLC.

Doeden, Matt. Nelson Mandela: World Leader for Human Rights. 2014. (Gateway Biographies Ser.). (ENG., Illus.). 48p. (J). (gr. 4-8). lib. bdg. 31.99 *(978-1-4677-5197-1(9))*, d0f1c40a-f447-4632-a27b-fd7328cbc513, Lerner Pubns.) Lerner Publishing Group.

Dougherty, Steve. Idi Amin. 2010. (Wicked History Ser.). 128p. (J). (gr. 6-12). pap. 5.95 *(978-0-531-22354-3(X))*; (ENG., Illus.). (gr. 7-12). 18.69 *(978-0-531-20754-3(4))* Scholastic Library Publishing. (Watts, Franklin).

Finlayson, Reggie. Nelson Mandela. pap. 9.95 *(978-0-8225-5743-2(6))* Lerner Publishing Group.

Friedman, Lita. Mary Robinson: Fighter for Human Rights. 2004. (Avisson Young Adult Ser.). (Illus.). 142p. (YA). pap. 19.95 *(978-1-888105-65-0(8))* Avisson Pr., Inc.

Giraldo, Paola. Gamal Abdel Nasser -el faraón Rojo. 2005. (SPA.). 112p. (YA). *(978-958-30-1689-9(6))* Panamericana Editorial.

Gormley, Beatrice. Nelson Mandela: South African Revolutionary. 2015. (Real-Life Story Ser.). (ENG., Illus.). 256p. (J). (gr. 3-7). 17.99 *(978-1-4814-2059-4(3))*, Aladdin) Simon & Schuster Children's Publishing.

Graham Gaines Rodriguez, Ann. Nelson Mandela & the End of Apartheid, 1 vol. 2015. (People & Events That Changed the World Ser.). (ENG., Illus.). 128p. (J). (gr. 7-8). 38.93 *(978-0-7660-7300-5(9))*, a27ea591-870c-45ea-8587-10e2d5002b79) Enslow Publishing, LLC.

Gunderson, Megan M. James Buchanan, 1 vol. 2016. (United States Presidents *2017 Ser.). (ENG., Illus.). 40p. (J). (gr. 2-5). lib. bdg. 35.64 *(978-1-68078-084-0(0))*, 21785, Big Buddy Bks.) ABDO Publishing Co.

Haldy, Emma E. George Washington. Bane, Jeff, illus. 2017. (My Early Library: My Itty-Bitty Bio Ser.). (ENG.). 24p. (J). (gr. k-1). lib. bdg. 30.64 *(978-1-63472-152-3(7))*, 209180) Cherry Lake Publishing.

—Jimmy Carter. Bane, Jeff, illus. 2016. (My Early Library: My Itty-Bitty Bio Ser.). (ENG.). 24p. (J). (gr. k-1). 30.64 *(978-1-63471-014-5(2))*, 208006) Cherry Lake Publishing.

Harmon, Daniel E. Pervez Musharraf: President of Pakistan, 1 vol. 2007. (Newsmakers Ser.). (ENG., Illus.). 112p. (YA). (gr. 9-10). lib. bdg. 39.80 *(978-1-4042-1905-2(6))*, 2b59f01f-5a05-4609-971b-4dbb22d8f3e5) Rosen Publishing Group, Inc., The.

HARMON, Daniel E. Pervez Musharraf: President of Pakistan. 2009. (Newsmakers Ser.). 112p. (gr. 9-10). 63.90 *(978-1-60851-135-8(9))* Rosen Publishing Group, Inc., The.

Harris, Duchess & Lusted, Marcia Amidon. Russian Hacking in American Elections. 2018. (Special Reports). (ENG., Illus.). 112p. (J). (gr. 6-12). lib. bdg. 41.36 *(978-1-5321-1682-7(9))*, 30616, Essential Library) ABDO Publishing Co.

Headlam, George. Yasir Arafat. 2004. (A&E Biography Ser.). (Illus.). 112p. (J). 29.27 *(978-0-8225-5004-4(0))*, Lerner Pubns.) Lerner Publishing Group.

Henry, Mike. Christmas with the Presidents: Holiday Lessons for Today's Kids from America's Leaders. 2017. (Illus.). 188p. 79.00 *(978-1-4758-3782-7(8))* Rowman & Littlefield Publishers, Inc.

Holland, Gini & O'Hern, Kerri. Nelson Mandela, 1 vol. (Biografías Gráficas (Graphic Biographies) Ser.). (Illus.). 32p. (gr. 3-3). 2007. (SPA.). pap. 11.50 *(978-0-8368-7888-2(4))*, c0856dc9-2ca1-4644-99c6-dd783962ddac) 2007. (SPA., lib. bdg. 29.67 *(978-0-8368-7881-3(7))*, b3c04f14-f5db-498a-8d90-9e9bb7ba5e50) 2005. (ENG., pap. 11.50 *(978-0-8368-6249-2(X))*, 187ebf93-9b41-4f9e-8153-9c4bdab7a428) Stevens, Gareth Publishing LLLP.

Hollingsworth, Tamara. Nelson Mandela: Leading the Way, 1 vol. 2nd rev. ed. 2013. (TIME for KIDS(r): Informational Text Ser.). (ENG., Illus.). 48p. (J). (gr. 4-5). lib. bdg. 29.96 *(978-1-4807-1116-7(0))* Teacher Created Materials, Inc.

Johnson, Kristin F. Ho Chi Minh: North Vietnamese President, 1 vol. 2011. (Essential Lives Set 7 Ser.). (ENG., Illus.). 112p. (YA). (gr. 6-12). lib. bdg. 41.36 *(978-1-61783-006-8(2))*, 6751, Essential Library) ABDO Publishing Co.

Josephson, Judith P. Nelson Mandela. 2009. (History Maker Biographies Ser.). (ENG.). 48p. (gr. 3-6). 27.93 *(978-1-58013-703-4(2))*, Lerner Pubns.) Lerner Publishing Group.

Katirgis, Jane & Egan, Tracie. Meet George Washington: America's First President, 1 vol. 2019. (Introducing Famous Americans Ser.). (ENG.). 32p. (gr. 3-4). pap. 11.53 *(978-1-9785-1122-4(1))*, 4e427baa-29bf-4aa7-9083-aa9e57796dac) Enslow Publishing, LLC.

Kawa, Katie. 20 Fun Facts about George Washington. 2017. (Fun Fact File: Founding Fathers Ser.). 32p. (gr. 2-3). pap. 63.00 *(978-1-5382-0272-2(7))* Stevens, Gareth Publishing LLLP.

Keller, Bill. Tree Shaker: The Life of Nelson Mandela. 2013. (New York Times Ser.). (ENG., Illus.). 128p. (J). (gr. 5-9). pap. 14.99 *(978-1-59643-533-9(X))*, 900061088) Square Fish.

Kraft, Betsy Harvey. Theodore Roosevelt: Champion of the American Spirit. 2003. (ENG., Illus.). 192p. (J). (gr. 5-7). tchr. ed. 19.00 *(978-0-618-14264-4(9))*, 111112, Clarion Bks.) HarperCollins Pubs.

Kramer, Ann. World History Biographies: Mandela: The Hero Who Led His Nation to Freedom. 2008. (National Geographic World History Biographies Ser.). (Illus.). 64p. (J). (gr. 3-7). pap. 7.99 *(978-1-4263-0173-5(1))*, National Geographic Kids) Disney Publishing Worldwide.

Krull, Kathleen. Lives of the Presidents: Fame, Shame (and What the Neighbors Thought) Hewitt, Kathryn, illus. 2011. (Lives Of ... Ser.). (ENG.). 104p. (J). (gr. 5-7). 21.00 *(978-0-547-49809-6(8))*, 1442014, Clarion Bks.) HarperCollins Pubs.

Kukla, Amy & Kukla, Jon. Thomas Jefferson: Life, Liberty, & the Pursuit of Happiness, 1 vol. 2004. (Library of American Lives & Times Ser.). (ENG., Illus.). 112p. (YA). (gr. 5-5). lib. bdg. 38.27 *(978-1-4042-2655-5(9))*, dc1c3fb6-97ec-4a36-b098-de511a783f4d, PowerKids Pr.) Rosen Publishing Group, Inc., The.

Landau, Elaine. Warren G. Harding. 2005. (Presidential Leaders Ser.). (Illus.). 120p. (J). 29.27 *(978-0-8225-0850-2(8))*, Lerner Pubns.) Lerner Publishing Group.

Lewison, Wendy Cheyette. P Is for President. Fabbretti, Valerio, illus. 2016. 32p. (J). (-k). pap. 4.99 *(978-1-101-99611-9(0))*, Grosset & Dunlap) Penguin Young Readers Group.

Liebman, Dan. I Want to Be President. 2009. (I Want to Be Ser.). (ENG., Illus.). 24p. (J). (gr. -1-2). 16.19 *(978-1-55407-562-1(9))*, cb95673d-e9d3-436c-8b37-61d5b91436db); pap. 3.99 *(978-1-55407-563-8(7))*, 744b5193-9d08-442b-a5d3-4b3c75d6e2a8) Firefly Bks., Ltd.

—Quiero Ser Presidente. 2009. (Quiero Ser.). (SPA., Illus.). 24p. (J). (gr. -1-2). pap. 5.99 *(978-1-55407-565-2(3))*, 98a169f8-0492-4c6a-869d-160f38a861a5) Firefly Bks., Ltd.

Magoon, Kekla. Nelson Mandela: A Leader for Freedom, 1 vol. 2008. (Essential Lives Set 2 Ser.). (ENG., Illus.). 112p. (YA). (gr. 6-12). lib. bdg. 41.36 *(978-1-60453-038-4(3))*, 6657, Essential Library) ABDO Publishing Co.

Marabini, Sergio. Juan D. Perón. 2004. (Protagonistas Ser.). (SPA.). (YA). *(978-987-1129-46-1(7))* Grupo Visor E.A.S.A.

Marsh, Carole. Jefferson Davis, Civil War Hero. 2004. 12p. (gr. k-4). 2.95 *(978-0-635-02366-7(0))* Gallopade International.

—Jimmy Carter. 2003. 12p. (gr. k-4). 2.95 *(978-0-635-02126-7(9))* Gallopade International.

McCollum, Sean. Deadly Despot: Idi Amin Rains Terror on Uganda. 2011. (J). pap. *(978-0-545-32936-1(1))* Scholastic, Inc.

Meyer, Susan. Nelson Mandela: South African President & Anti-Apartheid Activist. 2017. (Spotlight on Civic Courage: Heroes of Conscience Ser.). 48p. (J). (gr. 10-15). 70.50 *(978-1-5383-8089-5(7))*; (ENG.). (gr. 6). pap. 12.75 *(978-1-5383-8088-8(9))*, d7b4d779-7010-4b28-9fdf-11e0b9b95b88) Rosen Publishing Group, Inc., The. (Rosen Young Adult).

Nelson, Kadir. Nelson Mandela. Nelson, Kadir, illus. (ENG., Illus.). 40p. (J). (gr. -1-3). 2019. pap. 9.99 *(978-0-06-178377-7(3))* 2013. 17.99 *(978-0-06-178374-6(9))* 2013. lib. bdg. 18.89 *(978-0-06-178376-0(5))* HarperCollins Pubs. (Tegen, Katherine Bks).

—Nelson Mandela. 2014. (SPA.). (J). (gr. 2-4). 21.99 *(978-84-261-4069-2(6))* Juventud, Editorial ESP. Dist: Lectorum Pubns., Inc.

Nichols, Susan. Vladimir Putin: Russian Prime Minister & President, 1 vol. 2018. (Influential Lives Ser.). (ENG.). 128p. (gr. 7-7). 40.27 *(978-0-7660-9204-4(6))*, b5217e73-6c68-4675-a98f-f5e80d656f48) Enslow Publishing, LLC.

Piven, Hanoch, illus. What Presidents Are Made Of. 2004. (ENG.). 40p. (J). (gr. 1-5). 19.99 *(978-0-689-86880-1(4))*, Atheneum Bks. for Young Readers) Simon & Schuster Children's Publishing.

Rajczak Nelson, Kristen. Nelson Mandela, 1 vol. 2015. (Heroes of Black History Ser.). (ENG., Illus.). 32p. (J). (gr. 3-4). pap. 11.50 *(978-1-4824-2908-4(X))*, b39b2d5c-3cb7-42ed-81f5-4043e85c1433) Stevens, Gareth Publishing LLLP.

Rausch, Monica. Thomas Jefferson, 1 vol. 2007. (Great Americans Ser.). (ENG., Illus.). 24p. (gr. 2-4). pap. 9.15 *(978-0-8368-7691-8(1))*, d67c8373-d0d8-4d03-83af-e3d6765ca2f2); lib. bdg. 24.67 *(978-0-8368-7684-0(9))*, ff86d974-794f-4499-8286-be4c3be4e118) Stevens, Gareth Publishing LLLP. (Weekly Reader Leveled Readers).

Rice, Dona Herweck. Mountain of Presidents (Foundations) 2nd rev. ed. 2015. (TIME for KIDS(r): Informational Text Ser.). (ENG., Illus.). 12p. (gr. -1-k). 7.99 *(978-1-4938-2057-3(5))* Teacher Created Materials, Inc.

Riggs, Kate. The Release of Nelson Mandela. 2009. (Days of Change Ser.). (ENG., Illus.). 48p. (J). (gr. 5-8). 22.95 *(978-1-58341-736-2(2))*, 22145) Creative Co., The.

Rose, Simon. Nelson Mandela. 2010. (Remarkable People Ser.). (Illus.). 24p. (J). (gr. 3-5). lib. bdg. 25.70 *(978-1-61690-172-1(1))*; (gr. 4-6). pap. 11.95 *(978-1-61690-173-8(X))* Weigl Pubs., Inc.

Rosenberg, Aaron. Gamal-Abdel Nasser, 1 vol. 2003. (Middle East Leaders Ser.). (ENG., Illus.). 112p. (gr. 5-8). lib. bdg. 39.80 *(978-0-8239-4466-8(2))*, e97de3b2-5409-442f-b308-d166d5a5fdc5, Rosen Reference) Rosen Publishing Group, Inc., The.

—Vladimir Putin: President of Russia. (Newsmakers Ser.). 112p. (gr. 9-10). 2009. 63.90 *(978-1-60851-136-5(7))* 2007. (ENG., Illus.). (YA). lib. bdg. 39.80 *(978-1-4042-1903-8(X))*,

90db8c7b-879e-4e9c-8022-de6cf561dabe) Rosen Publishing Group, Inc., The.

Rowell, Rebecca. Emmanuel Macron: President of France. 2018. (World Leaders Ser.). (ENG., Illus.). 48p. (J). (gr. 5-6). pap. 11.95 *(978-1-63517-620-9(4)*, 1635176204); lib. bdg. 34.21 *(978-1-63517-548-6(8)*, 1635175488) North Star Editions. (Focus Readers).

Rumsch, BreAnn. Abraham Lincoln, 1 vol. 2016. (United States Presidents *2017 Ser.). (ENG., Illus.). 40p. (J). (gr. 2-5). 35.64 *(978-1-68078-106-9(5)*, 21829, Big Buddy Bks.) ABDO Publishing Co.

Schroeder, Alan. Abe Lincoln: His Wit & Wisdom from A-Z. O'Brien, John, illus. 2016. (ENG.). 32p. (J). (gr. 1-4). 7.99 *(978-0-8234-3575-3(X))* Holiday Hse., Inc.

Senker, Cath. Nelson Mandela. 2015. (Against the Odds Biographies Ser.). (ENG., Illus.). 48p. (J). (gr. 3-6). 35.99 *(978-1-4846-2465-4(3)*, 129623, Heinemann) Capstone.

Sheafer, Silvia Anne. Roh Moo Hyun. 2008. (Modern World Leaders Ser.). (ENG., Illus.). 136p. (gr. 7-12). 30.00 *(978-0-7910-9760-1(9)*, P159141, Facts On File) Infobase Holdings, Inc.

Shields, Charles J. Saddam Hussein. 2nd rev. ed. 2005. (Major World Leaders Ser.). (ENG., Illus.). 112p. (gr. 6-12). 30.00 *(978-0-7910-8576-9(7)*, P114308, Facts On File) Infobase Holdings, Inc.

Shone, Rob. Nelson Mandela: The Life of an African Statesman. 2009. (Graphic Nonfiction Biographies Ser.). (ENG.). 48p. (YA). (gr. 4-5). 58.50 *(978-1-61513-023-8(3)*, Rosen Reference) Rosen Publishing Group, Inc., The.

—Nelson Mandela: The Life of an African Statesman, 1 vol. Reed, Neil, illus. 2006. (Graphic Nonfiction Biographies Ser.). (ENG.). 48p. (gr. 4-5). (J). lib. bdg. 37.13 *(978-1-4042-0860-5(7)*, 7a196e9f-b30e-495d-9ddc-967f20e6af60); pap. 14.05 *(978-1-4042-0923-7(9)*, 6dc1dd53-2e23-47a5-933c-762eb0508d10) Rosen Publishing Group, Inc., The.

Stamper, G. C. Nelson Mandela. 2005. (Illus.). 32p. (J). pap. *(978-0-7367-2922-2(4))* Zaner-Bloser, Inc.

Strand, Jennifer. Nelson Mandela. 2016. (Legendary Leaders Ser.). (ENG.). 24p. (J). (gr. -1-2). 49.94 *(978-1-68079-407-6(8)*, 23028, Abdo Zoom-Launch) ABDO Publishing Co.

Trussell-Cullen, Alan. Nelson Mandela. 2009. pap. 13.25 *(978-1-60559-067-7(3))* Hameray Publishing Group, Inc.

Turner, Myra Faye. People That Changed the Course of History: The Story of Nelson Mandela 100 Years after His Birth. 2017. (J). *(978-1-62023-450-1(5))* Atlantic Publishing Group, Inc.

—People Who Changed the Course of History: The Story of Nelson Mandela 100 Years after His Birth. 2018. (ENG.). 238p. (YA). pap. 19.95 *(978-1-62023-446-4(7)*, 0df6c692-20ee-481c-b071-04ecc3e6f8e5) Atlantic Publishing Group, Inc.

Venezia, Mike. John F. Kennedy: Thirty-Fifth President 1961-1963. 32. Venezia, Mike, illus. 2007. (Getting to Know the U. S. Presidents Ser.). (ENG., Illus.). 32p. (J). (gr. 3-6). 22.44 *(978-0-516-22639-2(8))* Scholastic Library Publishing.

—Lyndon B. Johnson: Thirty-Sixth President, 1963-1969. Venezia, Mike, illus. 2007. (Getting to Know the U. S. Presidents Ser.). (Illus.). 32p. (J). (gr. 3-4). 28.00 *(978-0-516-22640-8(1)*, Children's Pr.) Scholastic Library Publishing.

—Richard M. Nixon: Thirty-Seventh President, 1969-1974. Venezia, Mike, illus. 2007. (Getting to Know the U. S. Presidents Ser.). (Illus.). 32p. (J). (gr. 3-4). 28.00 *(978-0-516-22641-5(X)*, Children's Pr.) Scholastic Library Publishing.

Wheeler, Jill C. Saddam Hussein. 2004. (War in Iraq Ser.). 48p. (gr. 4-8). lib. bdg. 27.07 *(978-1-59197-499-4(2)*, Abdo & Daughters) ABDO Publishing Co.

Wingate, Brian. Saddam Hussein. 2009. (Middle East Leaders Ser.). 112p. (gr. 5-8). 66.50 *(978-1-61514-648-2(2)*, Rosen Reference) Rosen Publishing Group, Inc., The.

—Saddam Hussein: The Rise & Fall of a Dictator, 1 vol. 2003. (Middle East Leaders Ser.). (ENG., Illus.). 112p. (J). (gr. 5-8). lib. bdg. 39.80 *(978-0-8239-4468-2(9)*, 68b0eda3-efe6-4bf3-9363-2402c836c45b, Rosen Reference) Rosen Publishing Group, Inc., The.

Witte, Sam. Gamal Abdel Nasser. 2009. (Middle East Leaders Ser.). 112p. (gr. 5-8). 66.50 *(978-1-61514-646-8(6)*, Rosen Reference) Rosen Publishing Group, Inc., The.

Wolny, Philip. Hamid Karzai: President of Afghanistan. (Newsmakers Ser.). 112p. (gr. 9-10). 2009. 63.90 *(978-1-60851-132-7(4))* 2007. (ENG., Illus.). (YA). lib. bdg. 39.80 *(978-1-4042-1902-1(1)*, a6ec2242-dea3-4ec5-b35a-516a0b8a7953) Rosen Publishing Group, Inc., The.

Wyborny, Sheila & Wagner, Viqi. Muammar Qaddafi, 1 vol. 2012. (People in the News Ser.). (ENG., Illus.). 112p. (J). (gr. 7-7). lib. bdg. 41.03 *(978-1-4205-0759-1(1)*, cb70e344-b10d-481a-91cc-7f9634a31010, Lucent Pr.) Greenhaven Publishing LLC.

Yoshimi, Kusaba, ed. The World's Poorest President Speaks Out. Wong, Andrew, tr. Gaku, Nakagawa, illus. 2020. 40p. (J). 16.95 *(978-1-59270-289-3(9))* Enchanted Lion Bks., LLC.

Zahler, Kathy A. The Assads' Syria. 2009. (Dictatorships Ser.). (ENG.). 160p. (gr. 9-12). 38.60 *(978-0-8225-9095-8(6))* Lerner Publishing Group.

PRESIDENTS—UNITED STATES

Abbey, Jed. The Life of George Washington, 1 vol. 2012. (InfoMax Readers Ser.). (ENG., Illus.). 24p. (J). (gr. 1-1). pap. 8.25 *(978-1-4488-8986-0(3)*, 7d07b071-19ae-41e8-9060-ff114c5e7394, Rosen Classroom) Rosen Publishing Group, Inc., The.

ABDO Publishing Company Staff & Hansen, Grace. United States President Biographies, 9 vols. 2014. (United States President Biographies (Abdo Kids Jumbo) Ser.: 6). (ENG.). 24p. (J). (gr. -1-2). lib. bdg. 262.32 *(978-1-62970-084-7(3)*, 1715, Abdo Kids) ABDO Publishing Co.

Abnett, Dan. Abraham Lincoln & the Civil War. (Jr. Graphic Biographies Ser.). (ENG.). 24p. (gr. 2-3). 2009. (J). 47.90 *(978-1-61513-807-4(2)*, PowerKids Pr.) 2006. (Illus.). (J). lib. bdg. 28.93 *(978-1-4042-3392-8(X)*, 92e3c8e5-f3e2-4a55-954a-8ef3b235e069) 2006. (Illus.). pap. 10.60 *(978-1-4042-2145-1(X)*, 0586a643-99bf-4e0d-bd7a-2e7c219dab67, PowerKids Pr.) Rosen Publishing Group, Inc., The.

—Abraham Lincoln y la Guerra Civil, 1 vol. 2009. (Historietas Juveniles: Biografías (Jr. Graphic Biographies) Ser.). (SPA., Illus.). 24p. (gr. 2-3). (J). 28.93 *(978-1-4358-8561-5(9)*, 7466c29f-c43f-4229-a2b0-ce29cbcf5047); pap. 10.60 *(978-1-4358-3316-6(3)*, 6881a164-d615-429e-aaaf-9ff20b30d04e) Rosen Publishing Group, Inc., The.

—George Washington & the American Revolution. (Jr. Graphic Biographies Ser.). (ENG.). 24p. (gr. 2-3). 2009. (J). 47.90 *(978-1-61513-813-5(7)*, PowerKids Pr.) 2006. (Illus.). (J). lib. bdg. 28.93 *(978-1-4042-3395-9(4)*, f5ebb962-806c-4e30-beef-2ed75efa306a) 2006. (Illus.). pap. 10.60 *(978-1-4042-2148-2(4)*, 27420dd3-e201-4cdf-8332-ff4d4b4b3df1, PowerKids Pr.) Rosen Publishing Group, Inc., The.

—George Washington y la Guerra de Independencia, 1 vol. 2009. (Historietas Juveniles: Biografías (Jr. Graphic Biographies) Ser.). (SPA., Illus.). 24p. (gr. 2-3). pap. 10.60 *(978-1-4358-3322-7(8)*, a38fe106-c9b7-4c5c-9508-fd86a6c2150a); (YA). 28.93 *(978-1-4358-8564-6(3)*, 97102909-4df6-44a2-b6ce-f4870ffe0e02) Rosen Publishing Group, Inc., The.

Aboff, Marcie. A Day for Presidents. 2016. (Spring Forward Ser.). (J). (gr. 1). *(978-1-4900-9374-1(5))* Benchmark Education Co.

Abraham, Philip. How to Draw the Life & Times of George Washington. (Kid's Guide to Drawing the Presidents of the United States of America Ser.). 32p. (gr. 4-4). 2009. 50.50 *(978-1-61511-140-4(9)*, PowerKids Pr.) 2005. (ENG., Illus.). (YA). 30.27 *(978-1-4042-2978-5(7)*, 01f6367d-53e7-4aef-af91-e848c1d203e7) Rosen Publishing Group, Inc., The.

Abraham, Philip & Turner, Cherie. How to Draw the Life & Times of George Washington, 1 vol. 2004. (Extreme Careers Ser.). (ENG.). 64p. (YA). (gr. 5-5). lib. bdg. 37.13 *(978-1-4042-0364-8(8)*, 2d865cf3-8843-4031-8a7f-f27328c5456a, PowerKids Pr.) Rosen Publishing Group, Inc., The.

Adams, Simon. Presidents of the United States. 2004. (ENG., Illus.). 96p. (J). (gr. 3-6). pap. 9.95 *(978-1-58728-092-4(2)*, Two-Can Publishing) T&N Children's Publishing.

Adelson, Bruce. Benjamin Harrison. 2006. (Presidential Leaders Ser.). (Illus.). 112p. (J). (gr. 3-7). lib. bdg. 29.27 *(978-0-8225-1497-8(4)*, Lerner Pubns.) Lerner Publishing Group.

Adler, David A. Colonel Theodore Roosevelt. 2014. (ENG., Illus.). 144p. (J). (gr. 5). 22.99 *(978-0-8234-2950-9(4))* Holiday Hse., Inc.

—A Parade for George Washington. O'Brien, John, illus. 2020. 32p. (J). (gr. -1-3). 17.99 *(978-0-8234-4252-2(7))* Holiday Hse., Inc.

—A Picture Book of George Washington. Wallner, John & Wallner, Alexandra, illus. 2018. (Picture Book Biography Ser.). 32p. (J). (gr. -1-3). pap. 7.99 *(978-0-8234-4059-7(1))* Holiday Hse., Inc.

—A Picture Book of John F. Kennedy. Casilla, Robert, illus. 2018. (Picture Book Biography Ser.). (ENG.). 32p. (J). (gr. -1-3). 7.99 *(978-0-8234-4048-1(6))* Holiday Hse., Inc.

—A Picture Book of Thomas Jefferson. Wallner, John & Wallner, Alexandra, illus. 2018. (Picture Book Biography Ser.). (ENG.). 32p. (J). (gr. -1-3). 7.99 *(978-0-8234-4049-8(4))* Holiday Hse., Inc.

Albee, Sarah. George Washington: The First President. Ko, Chin, illus. 2017. (I Can Read Level 2 Ser.). (ENG.). 32p. (J). (gr. -1-3). pap. 4.99 *(978-0-06-243266-7(4)*, HarperCollins) HarperCollins Pubs.

—George Washington: the First President. Ko, Chin, illus. 2017. (I Can Read Level 2 Ser.). (ENG.). 32p. (J). (gr. -1-3). 16.99 *(978-0-06-243267-4(2)*, HarperCollins) HarperCollins Pubs.

Allen, John. The Trump Presidency. 2020. (ENG.). 80p. (J). (gr. 6-12). 41.27 *(978-1-68282-759-8(3))* ReferencePoint Pr., Inc.

Allen, Susan. The Remarkable Ronald Reagan: Cowboy & Commander in Chief. Harrington, Leslie, illus. 2013. (ENG.). 36p. (J). (gr. 1). 16.99 *(978-1-62157-038-7(X))* Regnery Publishing.

Allen, Thomas B. George Washington, Spymaster: How the Americans Outspied the British & Won the Revolutionary War. 2007. (Illus.). 192p. (J). (gr. 5-9). per. 7.95 *(978-1-4263-0041-7(7)*, National Geographic Kids) Disney Publishing Worldwide.

Aller, Susan Bivin. Ulysses S. Grant. 2006. (History Maker Bios Ser.). (Illus.). 48p. (J). (gr. 3-7). lib. bdg. 26.60 *(978-0-8225-2438-0(4)*, Lerner Pubns.) Lerner Publishing Group.

Alphin, Elaine Marie & Alphin, Arthur B. Dwight D. Eisenhower. 2005. (History Maker Bios Ser.). (Illus.). 48p. (J). (gr. 3-5). lib. bdg. 26.60 *(978-0-8225-1544-9(X))* Lerner Publishing Group.

Alter, Judy & Messersmith, Patrick. Mirabeau B. Lamar: Second President of Texas. 2005. (Stars of Texas Ser.: 2). (ENG., Illus.). 72p. (J). (gr. 4-7). 17.95 *(978-1-880510-97-1(9)*, P067769) State Hse. Pr.

Amédékanya, Ben-Kofi. Pillars of Pride. 2011. 32p. pap. 15.99 *(978-1-4567-3458-9(X))* AuthorHouse.

American Presidents in World History. [5 Volumes], 5 vols., Vol. 1. 2003. (ENG., Illus.). 144p. (C). (gr. 6-8). 254.00 *(978-0-313-32564-9(2)*, 900297228, Bloomsbury Academic) Bloomsbury Publishing Plc GBR. Dist: Macmillan.

Amidon Lusted, Marcia, ed. Executive Orders, 1 vol. 2018. (Current Controversies Ser.). (ENG.). 200p. (gr. 10-12). 48.03 *(978-1-5345-0304-5(8)*, b11d55d7-0db0-4dc2-b66f-64cb8c2a9bda) Greenhaven Publishing LLC.

Anderson, Catherine Corley. John F. Kennedy. 2004. (Presidential Leaders Ser.). (ENG., Illus.). 112p. (gr. 6-12). 29.27 *(978-0-8225-0812-0(5)*, Lerner Pubns.) Lerner Publishing Group.

Anderson, Michael, contrib. by. Abraham Lincoln, 1 vol. 2012. (Pivotal Presidents: Profiles in Leadership Ser.). (ENG., Illus.). 80p. (gr. 8-8). (J). lib. bdg. 36.47 *(978-1-61530-942-9(X)*, 3e79c9e2-6cf7-49e1-8a7e-6f531fd252d5); (YA). 72.94 *(978-1-61530-953-5(5)*, fe64ec48-46cf-4b6d-afb3-c461b9174bea) Rosen Publishing Group, Inc., The.

—Ronald Reagan, 4 vols. 2012. (Pivotal Presidents: Profiles in Leadership Ser.). (ENG., Illus.). 80p. (YA). (gr. 8-8). 72.94 *(978-1-61530-958-0(6)*, dd617cf5-f55d-4034-bafa-3b0e589d19a9); lib. bdg. 36.47 *(978-1-61530-944-3(6)*, 698e3007-eb10-440b-80f9-551da23be232) Rosen Publishing Group, Inc., The.

—Thomas Jefferson, 1 vol. 2012. (Pivotal Presidents: Profiles in Leadership Ser.). (ENG.). 80p. (YA). (gr. 8-8). lib. bdg. 36.47 *(978-1-61530-940-5(3)*, 6d704455-cf16-4556-9645-37410ab7e520); (Illus.). 72.94 *(978-1-61530-959-7(4)*, a3e4e882-20c6-4ce3-9198-2e9402760d1f) Rosen Publishing Group, Inc., The.

Anderson, Sheila. Jimmy Carter. 2008. pap. 40.95 *(978-0-8225-9472-7(2))* Lerner Publishing Group.

—Jimmy Carter: A Life of Friendship. 2008. (Pull Ahead Books-Biographies Ser.). (ENG., Illus.). 32p. (gr. k-3). lib. bdg. 22.60 *(978-0-8225-8585-5(5)*, Lerner Pubns.) Lerner Publishing Group.

Andronik, Catherine M. & Kenney, Karen Latchana. Abraham Lincoln's Presidency. 2016. (Presidential Powerhouses Ser.). (ENG., Illus.). 104p. (YA). (gr. 6-12). 35.99 *(978-1-4677-7925-8(3)*, 9e967ebf-e20b-4c3c-82d8-9a5d2ae0b0db); E-Book 54.65 *(978-1-4677-8547-1(4))* Lerner Publishing Group. (Lerner Pubns.).

Appleby, Alex. I Can Be the President, 1 vol. 2014. (When I Grow Up Ser.). (ENG.). 24p. (J). (gr. k-k). 24.27 *(978-1-4824-1030-3(3)*, 5728fbf3-4e38-429f-a6bd-fc7807dd5a85) Stevens, Gareth Publishing LLLP.

—Puedo Ser Presidente / I Can Be the President, 1 vol. 2014. (Cuando Sea Grande / When I Grow Up Ser.). (SPA & ENG.). 24p. (J). (gr. k-k). 24.27 *(978-1-4824-0867-6(8)*, 4af76403-0e0b-48ae-bbb9-b4e58771e109) Stevens, Gareth Publishing LLLP.

Aretha, David A. Jefferson Davis. 2009. (ENG., Illus.). 144p. (gr. 6-12). 35.00 *(978-1-60413-297-7(3)*, P163832, Facts On File) Infobase Holdings, Inc.

Armentrout, David & Armentrout, Patricia. The Emancipation Proclamation. 2005. (Documents that Shaped the Nation Ser.). (Illus.). 48p. (J). (gr. 4-6). 20.95 *(978-1-59515-233-6(4))* Rourke Educational Media.

Aronin, Miriam. Dwight D. Eisenhower. 2016. (First Look at America's Presidents Ser.). (ENG., Illus.). 24p. (J). (gr. -1-3). 26.99 *(978-1-943553-31-0(9))* Bearport Publishing Co., Inc.

—Woodrow Wilson. 2016. (First Look at America's Presidents Ser.). (ENG., Illus.). 24p. (J). (gr. -1-3). 26.99 *(978-1-943553-30-3(0))* Bearport Publishing Co., Inc.

Aronson, Billy. Abraham Lincoln, 1 vol. 2009. (Presidents & Their Times Ser.). (ENG.). 96p. (gr. 6-6). lib. bdg. 36.93 *(978-0-7614-2839-8(9)*, a404bef1-3923-404a-bd06-75978e2cbebe) Cavendish Square Publishing LLC.

—Richard M. Nixon, 1 vol. 2008. (Presidents & Their Times Ser.). (ENG., Illus.). 96p. (gr. 6-6). lib. bdg. 36.93 *(978-0-7614-2428-4(8)*, 7d1fb918-7384-47cb-80e3-91d437f81f88) Cavendish Square Publishing LLC.

—Ulysses S. Grant, 1 vol. 2008. (Presidents & Their Times Ser.). (ENG., Illus.). 96p. (gr. 6-6). lib. bdg. 36.93 *(978-0-7614-2430-7(X)*, 0d48df73-e370-4f52-aced-ea6cd56d6e16) Cavendish Square Publishing LLC.

Ashby, Ruth. James & Dolley Madison, 1 vol. 2005. (Presidents & First Ladies Ser.). (ENG., Illus.). 48p. (gr. 5-8). lib. bdg. 33.67 *(978-0-8368-5757-3(7)*, 479a0864-fbda-4f8c-9f0a-e044e1df8fb2, Gareth Stevens Secondary Library) Stevens, Gareth Publishing LLLP.

—John & Abigail Adams, 1 vol. 2004. (Presidents & First Ladies Ser.). (ENG., Illus.). 48p. (gr. 5-8). lib. bdg. 33.67 *(978-0-8368-5755-9(0)*, 21feeb52-5560-4f47-8b3a-496dbf55c165, World Almanac Library) Stevens, Gareth Publishing LLLP.

—Woodrow & Edith Wilson, 1 vol. 2004. (Presidents & First Ladies Ser.). (ENG., Illus.). 48p. (gr. 5-8). lib. bdg. 33.67 *(978-0-8368-5759-7(3)*, 08a66539-4499-45c2-9cb6-cafc5a450a33, World Almanac Library) Stevens, Gareth Publishing LLLP.

Ashley, Susan. The White House, 1 vol. 2004. (Places in American History Ser.). (ENG., Illus.). 24p. (gr. 2-4). pap. 9.15 *(978-0-8368-4152-7(2)*, 4ea8d8d2-7318-48aa-ad29-d3c09860beea); lib. bdg. 24.67 *(978-0-8368-4145-9(X)*, 97d0acb8-2dc2-49e9-92b3-e0d3d1e66f35) Stevens, Gareth Publishing LLLP. (Weekly Reader Leveled Readers).

Autrey, Jacquelyn & Yeager, Alice. U.S. Presidents & Their Animal Friends. Passarella, Jennie, illus. 2004. 32p. (J). *(978-1-59421-005-1(5))* Seacoast Publishing, Inc.

B. Yes I Can for Kids. 2009. 36p. pap. 17.95 *(978-1-4490-1585-5(9))* AuthorHouse.

Bader, Bonnie. My Little Golden Book about Abraham Lincoln. Garofoli, Viviana, illus. 2016. (Little Golden Book Ser.). 24p. (J). (gr. -1-3). 5.99 *(978-1-101-93971-0(0)*, Golden Bks.) Random Hse. Children's Bks.

Bailey, Diane & Nash, Philip. James K. Polk: The 11th President. 2016. (First Look at America's Presidents Ser.). (ENG., Illus.). 24p. (J). (gr. -1-3). 26.99 *(978-1-944102-66-1(3))* Bearport Publishing Co., Inc.

—John Quincy Adams: The 6th President. 2016. (First Look at America's Presidents Ser.). (ENG., Illus.). 24p. (J). (gr. -1-3). 26.99 *(978-1-944102-65-4(5))* Bearport Publishing Co., Inc.

—William Mckinley, the 25th President. 2016. (First Look at America's Presidents Ser.). (ENG., Illus.). 24p. (J). (gr. -1-3). 26.99 *(978-1-944102-68-5(X))* Bearport Publishing Co., Inc.

Baldwin, James. Four Great Americans. 2006. pap. *(978-1-4065-0509-2(9))* Dodo Pr.

—Four Great Americans: Washington Franklin Webster Lincoln: a Book for Young Americans. 2017. (ENG., Illus.). (J). (gr. 3-7). 23.95 *(978-1-374-89694-9(2))*; pap. 13.95 *(978-1-374-89693-2(4))* Capital Communications, Inc.

—Four Great Americans: Washington, Franklin, Webster, Lincoln. a Book for Young Americans. 2017. (ENG., Illus.). (J). (gr. 3-7). pap. *(978-0-649-58735-3(9))* Trieste Publishing Pty Ltd.

Barber, James. Presidents. 2017. (Eyewitness Bks.). lib. bdg. 20.85 *(978-0-606-39897-8(X))* Turtleback.

Barfell, Judy. Learn & Sign Funtime: The United States Presidents. 2005. (J). per. 29.90 *(978-0-9753717-4-9(6))* Learn & Sign Funtime Bks.

Barnes, Peter W. President Adams' Alligator: And Other White House Pets. Barnes, Cheryl Shaw, illus. 2003. 32p. (J). 16.95 *(978-1-893622-13-5(4)*, VSP Bks.) Vacation Spot Publishing.

Barnes, Peter W. & Barnes, Cheryl Shaw, illus. President Adams' Alligator: And Other White House Pets. 2013. (ENG.). 40p. (J). (gr. k-5). 16.95 *(978-1-62157-035-6(5)*, Little Patriot Pr.) Regnery Publishing.

Barretta, Gene. Lincoln & Kennedy: A Pair to Compare. Barretta, Gene, illus. 2016. (ENG., Illus.). 40p. (J). 18.99 *(978-0-8050-9945-4(X)*, 900127126, Holt, Henry & Co. Bks. For Young Readers) Holt, Henry & Co.

Bartlett, Melissa. Meet President Obama, 1 vol. 2012. (InfoMax Readers Ser.). (ENG., Illus.). 24p. (J). (gr. 1-1). pap. 8.25 *(978-1-4488-9058-3(6)*, 3b21bce9-0ef2-415b-963c-861164ba3644, Rosen Classroom) Rosen Publishing Group, Inc., The.

Barton Billman, Hilary. How to Draw the Life & Times of William Henry Harrison. 2009. (Kid's Guide to Drawing the Presidents of the United States of America Ser.). 32p. (gr. 4-4). 50.50 *(978-1-61511-164-0(6)*, PowerKids Pr.) Rosen Publishing Group, Inc., The.

Behnke, Alison. Millard Fillmore. 2005. (Presidential Leaders Ser.). (Illus.). 112p. (J). (gr. 3-7). lib. bdg. 29.27 *(978-0-8225-1495-4(8)*, Lerner Pubns.) Lerner Publishing Group.

Behrman, Carol H. Andrew Jackson. 2004. (History Maker Biographies Ser.). (ENG., Illus.). 48p. (gr. 3-6). 27.93 *(978-0-8225-1543-2(1))* Lerner Publishing Group.

—James K. Polk. 2005. (Presidential Leaders Ser.). (ENG., Illus.). 112p. (gr. 6-12). lib. bdg. 29.27 *(978-0-8225-1396-4(X))* Lerner Publishing Group.

—John Adams. 2004. (Presidential Leaders Ser.). (Illus.). 112p. (J). 29.27 *(978-0-8225-0820-5(6)*, Lerner Pubns.) Lerner Publishing Group.

Benge, Janet & Benge, Geoff. Heroes of History - Ronald Reagan: Destiny at His Side. 2010. (ENG.). 224p. (YA). pap. 11.99 *(978-1-932096-65-1(5))* Emerald Bks.

—Heroes of History - Theodore Roosevelt: An American Original. 2004. (ENG., Illus.). 224p. (YA). pap. 11.99 *(978-1-932096-10-1(8))* Emerald Bks.

Benjamin, Jenny. Barack Obama. 2019. (Influential People Ser.). (ENG., Illus.). 32p. (J). (gr. 4-6). pap. 7.95 *(978-1-5435-6040-4(7)*, 140086); lib. bdg. 28.65 *(978-1-5435-5795-4(3)*, 139751) Capstone.

Bennett, Doraine. Jimmy Carter: Georgia, My State Biographies. l.t. ed. 2008. (ENG., Illus.). 24p. (J). (gr. k-2). 22.60 *(978-1-935077-00-8(7))*; pap. 22.60 *(978-1-935077-07-7(4))* State Standards Publishing, LLC.

—Thomas Jefferson. 2012. (Illus.). 24p. (J). *(978-1-935884-39-2(5))*; pap. *(978-1-935884-48-4(4))* State Standards Publishing, LLC.

Benoit, Peter. Abraham Lincoln. (Cornerstones of Freedom, Third Ser.). (J). 2012. (ENG.). 64p. (gr. 4-6). lib. bdg. 24.94 *(978-0-531-25025-9(3))* 2011. (Illus.). 48p. pap. 6.95 *(978-0-531-26621-2(4))* Scholastic Library Publishing. (Children's Pr.).

Benson, Michael. William H. Taft. 2004. (Presidential Leaders Ser.). (ENG., Illus.). 112p. (gr. 6-12). 29.27 *(978-0-8225-0849-6(4)*, Lerner Pubns.) Lerner Publishing Group.

Berenger, Al. Pocket Bios: Abraham Lincoln. Berenger, Al, illus. 2018. (Pocket Bios Ser.). (ENG., Illus.). 32p. (J). 14.99 *(978-1-250-16611-1(X)*, 900187188) Roaring Brook Pr.

Berlatsky, Noah, ed. Presidential Powers, 1 vol. 2010. (Opposing Viewpoints Ser.). (ENG.). 240p. (gr. 10-12). 50.43 *(978-0-7377-4982-3(2)*, 285674de-1b70-4b52-96aa-20bc2bea0435); pap. 34.80 *(978-0-7377-4983-0(0)*, ec7968ef-eaf6-4045-a5d7-dd9e0bf6eda7) Greenhaven Publishing LLC. (Greenhaven Publishing).

Bertsch, Michael L. Leaning Forward. rev. ed. 2010. (ENG.). 277p. (C). 125.99 *(978-0-7575-8105-2(6)*, P695129) Kendall Hunt Publishing Co.

Best, B. J. Abraham Lincoln, the Emancipation Proclamation, & the 13th Amendment, 1 vol. 2015. (Primary Sources of the Abolitionist Movement Ser.). (ENG., Illus.). 64p. (gr. 6-6). lib. bdg. 35.93 *(978-1-5026-0530-6(9)*, 5c51cbc4-3e82-49b1-ae18-5508c4cc5f81) Cavendish Square Publishing LLC.

Billman, Hilary Barton. How to Draw the Life & Times of William Henry Harrison, 1 vol. 2005. (Kid's Guide to Drawing the Presidents of the United States of America Ser.). (ENG., Illus.). 32p. (YA). (gr. 4-4). 30.27 *(978-1-4042-2986-0(8)*, b3bae0ab-9985-4ec7-8881-88ef937142a5) Rosen Publishing Group, Inc., The.

Biskup, Agnieszka. George Washington: The Rise of America's First President, 1 vol. Mallea, Cristian & Mallea, Cristian, illus. 2012. (American Graphic Ser.). (ENG.). 32p. (J). (gr. 3-9). lib. bdg. 31.32 *(978-1-4296-8621-1(9)*, 118642) Capstone.

Blake, Kevin. Harry S. Truman: The 33rd President. 2016. (First Look at America's Presidents Ser.). (ENG., Illus.). 24p. (J). (gr. -1-3). 26.99 *(978-1-943553-29-7(7))* Bearport Publishing Co., Inc.

—Lyndon B. Johnson. 2016. (First Look at America's Presidents Ser.). (ENG., Illus.). 24p. (J). (gr. -1-3). 26.99 *(978-1-943553-32-7(7))* Bearport Publishing Co., Inc.

Bober, Natalie S. Thomas Jefferson: Draftsman of a Nation. 2008. (ENG., Illus.). 376p. per. 16.95 *(978-0-8139-2732-9(3)*, P144204) University of Virginia Pr.

Bolden, Tonya. Emancipation Proclamation: Lincoln & the Dawn of Liberty. 2013. (ENG., Illus.). 128p. (J). (gr. 5-9). 24.95 *(978-1-4197-0390-4(0)*, 672401, Abrams Bks. for Young Readers) Abrams, Inc.

Boshier, Rosa. Ronald Reagan: 40th US President, 1 vol. 2013. (Essential Lives Set 8 Ser.). (ENG.). 112p. (YA). (gr. 6-12). lib. bdg. 41.36 *(978-1-61783-895-8(0)*, 6767, Essential Library) ABDO Publishing Co.

Bow, James. What Is the Executive Branch? 2013. (ENG.). 32p. (J). (978-0-7787-0902-2(7)); pap. (978-0-7787-0907-7(8)) Crabtree Publishing Co.

—What Is the Executive Branch. 2013. (Your Guide to Government Ser.). (ENG.). 32p. (J). (gr. 3-6). 19.75 (978-1-68065-726-5(7)) Perfection Learning Corp.

Brandt, Keith & Macken, JoAnn Early. Abraham Lincoln: Road to the White House. Lawn, John, illus. 2007. 53p. (J). (978-0-439-88005-3(X)) Scholastic, Inc.

Brennan, Linda Crotta. Franklin D. Roosevelt's Presidency. 2016. (Presidential Powerhouses Ser.). (ENG., Illus.). 104p. (YA). (gr. 6-12). 35.99 (978-1-4677-7928-9(8), ab64e692-1d98-4b8b-ae25-219dbb29d6c0); E-Book 54.65 (978-1-4677-8549-5(0)) Lerner Publishing Group. (Lerner Pubns.).

Britton, Tamara L. Barack Obama, 1 vol. 2016. (United States Presidents *2017 Ser.). (ENG., Illus.). 40p. (J). (gr. 2-5). lib. bdg. 35.64 (978-1-68078-111-3(1), 21839, Big Buddy Bks.) ABDO Publishing Co.

—Dwight D. Eisenhower, 1 vol. 2016. (United States Presidents *2017 Ser.). (ENG., Illus.). 40p. (J). (gr. 2-5). lib. bdg. 35.64 (978-1-68078-091-8(3), 21799, Big Buddy Bks.) ABDO Publishing Co.

—George Washington, 1 vol. (United States Presidents *2017 Ser.). (ENG., Illus.). 40p. (J). 2016. (gr. 2-5). lib. bdg. 35.64 (978-1-68078-122-9(7), 21861, Big Buddy Bks.) 2009. (gr. 3-6). 34.21 (978-1-60453-479-5(6), 15121, Checkerboard Library) ABDO Publishing Co.

Brown, Jonatha A. John F. Kennedy, 1 vol. 2005. (People We Should Know Ser.). (ENG., Illus.). 24p. (gr. 2-4). lib. bdg. 24.67 (978-0-8368-4747-5(4), d187ed88-dbf8-4aa8-9c08-c0def88c1eff, Weekly Reader Leveled Readers) Stevens, Gareth Publishing LLLP.

Buller, Jon, et al. Smart about the Presidents. Weber, Jill, illus. 2004. (Smart about History Ser.). 64p. (J). (gr. k-4). mass mkt. 7.99 (978-0-448-43372-1(9), Grosset & Dunlap) Penguin Young Readers Group.

Burgan, Michael. Barack Obama. rev. ed. 2016. (Front-Page Lives Ser.). (ENG.). 112p. (J). (gr. 6-9). pap. 11.99 (978-1-4846-3813-2(1), 134676, Heinemann) Capstone.

—George W. Bush, 1 vol. 2012. (Presidents & Their Times Ser.). (ENG., Illus.). 96p. (gr. 6-6). 36.93 (978-1-60870-184-1(0), d293d34a-0f32-4c99-8601-47e769e581b8) Cavendish Square Publishing LLC.

—James Buchanan, 1 vol. 2011. (Presidents & Their Times Ser.). (ENG.). 96p. (gr. 6-6). 36.93 (978-0-7614-4810-5(1), d50287da-903e-4eee-ba4d-c7d01410e0fc) Cavendish Square Publishing LLC.

—Ronald Reagan. 2011. 128p. pap. 14.99 (978-0-7566-7739-8(4)); (ENG., Illus.). (J). (gr. 5-8). 18.69 (978-0-7566-7075-7(6)) Dorling Kindersley Publishing, Inc.

Burgan, Michael & Who HQ. Who Was Theodore Roosevelt? Hoare, Jerry, illus. 2014. (Who Was? Ser.). 112p. (J). (gr. 3-7). 5.99 (978-0-448-47945-3(1), Penguin Workshop) Penguin Young Readers Group.

Burke, Melissa Blackwell & Sharp, Katie John. Presidents: Profiles in Courage of the Men Who Have Led Our Nation. 2007. (Illus.). 32p. 10.98 (978-1-4127-1335-1(8)) Publications International, Ltd.

Burleigh, Robert. O Captain, My Captain: Walt Whitman, Abraham Lincoln, & the Civil War. Hundley, Sterling, illus. 2019. (ENG.). 64p. (J). (gr. 5-17). 19.99 (978-1-4197-3358-1(3), 1120101, Abrams Bks. for Young Readers) Abrams, Inc.

Burnett, Iris & Greager, Clay. So You Think You Can Be President? 200 Questions to Determine If You Are Right (or Left) Enough to Be the Next Commander-In-Chief. 2008. (ENG.). 240p. pap. 12.95 (978-1-60239-202-1(1)) Skyhorse Publishing Co., Inc.

Burns, Ken. Grover Cleveland, Again! A Treasury of American Presidents. Kelley, Gerald, illus. 2016. (ENG.). 96p. (J). (gr. 5-12). 25.00 (978-0-385-39209-9(5), Knopf Bks. for Young Readers) Random Hse. Children's Bks.

Byers, Ann. The Emancipation Proclamation, 1 vol. 2018. (America's Most Important Documents: Inquiry into Historical Sources Ser.). (ENG.). 64p. (J). (gr. 6-6). lib. bdg. 37.36 (978-1-5026-3598-3(4), 7f22fdda-24b7-47c9-8648-ab69c99a32a1) Cavendish Square Publishing LLC.

Cane, Ella. The U. S. Presidency. 2014. (Our Government Ser.). (ENG., Illus.). 24p. (J). (gr. 1-3). pap. 6.95 (978-1-4765-5144-9(8), 124463); lib. bdg. 27.99 (978-1-4765-4200-3(7), 124304) Capstone.

Canetti, Yanitzia. Yo También Puedo Ser Presidente. 2009. (SPA.). 32p. (J). (gr. k-3). pap. 7.99 (978-1-59835-100-2(1)) Cambridge BrickHouse, Inc.

Canetti, Yanitzia & Keating, Alison. I Can Be President, Too! 2009. (J). (978-1-59835-101-9(X), CBH Bks.) Cambridge BrickHouse, Inc.

Caplan, Jeremy. Franklin D Roosevelt A Leader in Troubled Times. 2006. 44p. (J). lib. bdg. 15.00 (978-1-4242-0848-7(3)) Fitzgerald Bks.

Carser, A. R. Donald Trump: 45th US President. 2016. (Essential Lives Set 10 Ser.). (ENG., Illus.). 112p. (J). (gr. 6-12). lib. bdg. 41.36 (978-1-68078-366-7(1), 23222, Essential Library) ABDO Publishing Co.

Casciato, Daniel. Expansion & Reform: (Early 1800s-1861) 2007. (Presidents of the United States Ser.). (Illus.). 48p. (J). (gr. 4-7). lib. bdg. 29.05 (978-1-59036-741-4(3)) Weigl Pubs., Inc.

—Expansion & Reform: Early 1800s-1861. 2007. (Presidents of the United States Ser.). (Illus.). 48p. (J). (gr. 4-7). per. 11.95 (978-1-59036-742-1(1)) Weigl Pubs., Inc.

Cella, Clara. Presidents' Day, 1 vol. 2012. (Let's Celebrate Ser.). (ENG., Illus.). 24p. (J). (gr. -1-2). lib. bdg. 27.32 (978-1-4296-8734-8(7), 119527, Capstone Pr.) Capstone.

Chandra, Deborah & Comora, Madeleine. George Washington's Teeth. Cole, Brock, illus. 2007. (ENG.). 40p. (J). (gr. -1-3). pap. 8.99 (978-0-312-37604-8(9), 900048324) Square Fish.

Childress, Diana. George H. W. Bush. 2007. (Presidential Leaders Ser.). (Illus.). 112p. (J). (gr. 3-7). lib. bdg. 29.27 (978-0-8225-1510-4(5), Lerner Pubns.) Lerner Publishing Group.

Clark, Willow. The True Story of the Emancipation Proclamation, 1 vol. 2013. (What Really Happened? Ser.). (ENG., Illus.). 24p. (J). (gr. 2-3). 26.27 (978-1-4488-9695-0(9), ed9c49fd-1083-41ae-b071-1a993beabfb5); pap. 9.25 (978-1-4488-9848-0(X), f7848aa6-8a09-463b-b38a-5f880afeb521) Rosen Publishing Group, Inc., The. (PowerKids Pr.).

Coddington, Andrew. Thomas Jefferson: Architect of the Declaration of Independence, 1 vol. 2016. (Great American Thinkers Ser.). (ENG., Illus.). 128p. (YA). (gr. 9-9). 47.36 (978-1-5026-1924-2(5), 75a7aea4-6e46-499f-8c25-a7a46fbc5d49) Cavendish Square Publishing LLC.

Colbert, David. Abraham Lincoln. 2009. (10 Days Ser.). (ENG.). 160p. (J). (gr. 3-9). pap. 8.99 (978-1-4169-6807-8(5), Aladdin) Simon & Schuster Children's Publishing.

Colbert, Nancy A. Great Society: The Story of Lyndon Baines Johnson. 2004. (Notable Americans Ser.). (Illus.). 144p. (YA). (gr. 6-12). 23.95 (978-1-883846-84-8(6), First Biographies) Reynolds, Morgan Inc.

Collard, Sneed B., III. Abraham Lincoln: A Courageous Leader, 1 vol. 2007. (American Heroes Ser.). (ENG., Illus.). 48p. (gr. 3-3). lib. bdg. 32.64 (978-0-7614-2162-7(9), a82c585e-4cbb-4af2-9285-a34c366a5da6) Cavendish Square Publishing LLC.

—George Washington, 1 vol. 2010. (American Heroes Ser.). (ENG.). 48p. (gr. 3-3). 32.64 (978-0-7614-4060-4(7), 2757fb59-5b7f-48ba-b248-ebe59643b8d1) Cavendish Square Publishing LLC.

—John Adams: Our Second President, 1 vol. 2007. (American Heroes Ser.). (ENG., Illus.). 48p. (gr. 3-3). 32.64 (978-0-7614-2159-7(9), 5302f21c-d1f8-4327-9f07-352329765f38) Cavendish Square Publishing LLC.

—Thomas Jefferson: Let Freedom Ring!, 1 vol. 2009. (American Heroes Ser.). (ENG.). 48p. (gr. 3-3). lib. bdg. 32.64 (978-0-7614-3067-4(9), 8eac1ebf-a575-4a39-a66b-9e82fcc32ff5) Cavendish Square Publishing LLC.

Conklin, Wendy. Civil War Leaders, 1 vol. rev. ed. 2005. (Social Studies: Informational Text Ser.). (ENG.). 24p. (gr. 4-8). pap. 10.99 (978-0-7439-8917-6(1)) Teacher Created Materials, Inc.

Connors, Kathleen. What Does the President Do?, 1 vol. 2017. (Look at Your Government Ser.). (ENG., Illus.). 32p. (J). (gr. 2-2). pap. 11.50 (978-1-4824-6051-3(3), 75a95ae0-8116-460e-b43d-f8c17d0cc01d) Stevens, Gareth Publishing LLLP.

—What's It Like to Be the President?, 1 vol. 2014. (White House Insiders Ser.). (ENG.). 24p. (J). (gr. 2-3). 24.27 (978-1-4824-1095-2(8), 5ae68ffb-4850-4d18-ab22-6c764445d3d6) Stevens, Gareth Publishing LLLP.

—What's It Like to Be the President's Pet?, 1 vol. 2014. (White House Insiders Ser.). (ENG.). 24p. (J). (gr. 2-3). 24.27 (978-1-4824-1105-8(9), 943bbde3-9474-462b-b23a-078c1452866c) Stevens, Gareth Publishing LLLP.

—What's It Like to Live in the White House?, 1 vol. 2014. (White House Insiders Ser.). (ENG.). 24p. (J). (gr. 2-3). 24.27 (978-1-4824-1110-2(5), 0e5887f2-5ddf-45cd-8ed2-be6de588169d) Stevens, Gareth Publishing LLLP.

Corey, Shana. Barack Obama: Out of Many, One. 2009. (Step into Reading Ser.). (Illus.). 48p. (J). (gr. k-3). pap. 4.99 (978-0-375-86339-4(7), Random Hse. Bks. for Young Readers) Random Hse. Children's Bks.

—A Time to Act: John F. Kennedy's Big Speech. Christie, R. Gregory, illus. 2017. (ENG.). 56p. (J). (gr. 3). 18.95 (978-0-7358-4275-5(2)) North-South Bks., Inc.

Cosson, Jody. Civil War & Reconstruction: 1850-1877. 2007. (Presidents of the United States Ser.). (Illus.). (J). (gr. 4-7). 47p. lib. bdg. 29.05 (978-1-59036-743-8(X)); 48p. per. 10.95 (978-1-59036-744-5(8)) Weigl Pubs., Inc.

Crabtree Staff & Aloian, Molly. George Washington: Hero of the American Revolution. 2012. (ENG., Illus.). 48p. (J). pap. (978-0-7787-0810-0(1)) Crabtree Publishing Co.

Criscione, Rachel. How to Draw the Life & Times of Chester A. Arthur, 1 vol. 2005. (Kid's Guide to Drawing the Presidents of the United States of America Ser.). (ENG.). 32p. (YA). (gr. 4-4). 30.27 (978-1-4042-2998-3(1), d04bb148-f896-4c5d-9a8d-c2d0bea4bf5b) Rosen Publishing Group, Inc., The.

Criscon, R. D. How to Draw the Life & Times of Chester A. Arthur. 2009. (Kid's Guide to Drawing the Presidents of the United States of America Ser.). 32p. (gr. 4-4). 50.50 (978-1-61511-135-0(2), PowerKids Pr.) Rosen Publishing Group, Inc., The.

Cronkite, Walter, frwd. Great American Presidents. (Illus.). (gr. 4-8). pap. (978-0-7910-8048-1(X), Facts On File) Infobase Holdings, Inc.

Daly, Ruth. John Adams. 2015. (Padres Fundadores Ser.). (SPA.). (J). (gr. -1-3). lib. bdg. 27.13 (978-1-4896-2799-5(5), AV2 by Weigl) Weigl Pubs., Inc.

Darby, Jean. Dwight D. Eisenhower. 2004. (Presidential Leaders Ser.). (Illus.). 112p. (J). (gr. 6-12). lib. bdg. 29.27 (978-0-8225-0813-7(3)) Lerner Publishing Group.

Dash, Meredith. Presidents' Day, 1 vol. 2014. (National Holidays Ser.). (ENG., Illus.). 24p. (J). (gr. -1-2). lib. bdg. 32.79 (978-1-62970-046-5(0), 1535, Abdo Kids) ABDO Publishing Co.

D'Aulaire, Ingri & D'Aulaire, Edgar Parin. Abraham Lincoln. 2008. (Illus.). (978-1-893103-27-6(7)); pap. (978-1-893103-26-9(9)) Beautiful Feet Bks.

D'Aulaire, Ingri & D'Aulaire, Edgar Parin, illus. Abraham Lincoln. 75th ed. 2015. (J). (978-1-893103-60-3(9)) Beautiful Feet Bks.

Davis, Gibbs. First Kids. Comport, Sally Wern, illus. 2009. (Step into Reading: Step 4 Ser.). (ENG.). 48p. (J). (gr. 1-3). lib. bdg. 16.19 (978-0-375-92218-3(0)) Random House Publishing Group.

Davis, Kenneth C. Don't Know Much about the Presidents. Martin, Pedro, illus. rev. ed. 2009. (ENG.). 64p. (J). (gr. k-4). pap. 7.99 (978-0-06-171823-6(8), HarperCollins) HarperCollins Pubs.

—In the Shadow of Liberty: The Hidden History of Slavery, Four Presidents, & Five Black Lives. 2019. (ENG., Illus.). 304p. (J). pap. 12.99 (978-1-250-14411-9(6), 900180617) Square Fish.

—The Presidents. Martin, Pedro, illus. 2003. (Don't Know Much About Ser.). (ENG.). 64p. (J). (gr. 1-4). reprint ed. pap. 6.99 (978-0-06-446231-0(5)) HarperCollins Pubs.

Dayton, Connor. Presidents' Day, 1 vol. 2012. (American Holidays Ser.). (ENG., Illus.). 24p. (J). (gr. 1-1). pap. 9.25 (978-1-4488-6242-9(6), 2561629b-cfaa-442a-80cd-8c3650d2d59c); lib. bdg. 26.27 (978-1-4488-6142-2(X), 82401d5e-c56c-405b-9b30-4fdbd5f9a52d) Rosen Publishing Group, Inc., The. (PowerKids Pr.).

—Presidents' Day: Día de Los Presidentes, 1 vol. Alamán, Eduardo, tr. 2012. (American Holidays / Celebraciones en Los Estados Unidos Ser.). (SPA & ENG., Illus.). 24p. (J). (gr. 1-1). lib. bdg. 26.27 (978-1-4488-6708-0(8), 01d0d499-6abc-47ba-97b2-c55aa0a5fcdf, PowerKids Pr.) Rosen Publishing Group, Inc., The.

Dean, Sheri. Presidents' Day, 1 vol. (Our Country's Holidays (Second Edition) Ser.). (ENG.). 24p. (gr. k-2). 2010. (J). pap. 9.15 (978-1-4339-3924-2(X), 097b69ed-a8b0-4354-9bbd-6e507a371c12) 2010. (J). lib. bdg. 25.27 (978-1-4339-3923-5(1), b71048f6-12e1-4340-b743-6c8b96cb56e3) 2006. (Illus.). pap. 9.15 (978-0-8368-6515-8(4), a373ec74-336e-49ac-9c56-6c78673d92b5, Weekly Reader Leveled Readers) 2005. (Illus.). lib. bdg. 24.67 (978-0-8368-6508-0(1), d6994cbb-bbd2-4f33-9fb2-913147a5eba5) Stevens, Gareth Publishing LLLP.

DeMauro, Lisa & Time for Kids Editors. Theodore Roosevelt: The Adventurous President. 2005. (Time for Kids Ser.). (ENG., Illus.). 48p. (J). (gr. 2-4). 15.99 (978-0-06-057606-6(5)); pap. 3.99 (978-0-06-057604-2(9)) HarperCollins Pubs.

Demi. President Lincoln: From Log Cabin to White House. 2016. (Illus.). 32p. (J). (gr. k-3). 16.95 (978-1-937786-50-2(1), Wisdom Tales) World Wisdom, Inc.

Denenberg, Barry. Lincoln Shot: A President's Life Remembered. Bing, Christopher, illus. 2011. (ENG.). 96p. (J). (gr. 5-9). pap. 14.99 (978-0-312-60442-4(4), 900076473) Square Fish.

Devera, Czeena. Lyndon B. Johnson. Bane, Jeff, illus. 2017. (My Early Library: My Itty-Bitty Bio Ser.). (ENG.). 24p. (J). (gr. k-1). 30.64 (978-1-63472-817-1(3), 209694) Cherry Lake Publishing.

DiCianni, Ron. Praying with the Presidents: One Nation's Legacy of Prayer. 2004. 48p. (J). (gr. k-3). 10.99 (978-1-59185-408-1(3), Charisma Kids) Charisma Media.

DiConsiglio, John. Encyclopedia of Presidents: Franklin Pierce. 2004. (Encyclopedia of Presidents Ser.). (ENG., Illus.). 112p. (YA). (gr. 5-9). 34.00 (978-0-516-24235-4(0)) Scholastic Library Publishing.

Diemer, Lauren & Cuthbert, Megan. Abraham Lincoln. 2014. (Illus.). 24p. (J). (978-1-62127-308-0(3)) Weigl Pubs., Inc.

Doak, Robin S. Barack Obama. 2013. (True Book(tm), A — Biographies Ser.). (ENG., Illus.). 48p. (J). lib. bdg. 31.00 (978-0-531-21904-1(6)); pap. 6.95 (978-0-531-23875-2(X)) Scholastic Library Publishing.

Dodson Wade, Mary. Amazing President Theodore Roosevelt, 1 vol. 2009. (Amazing Americans Ser.). (ENG., Illus.). 24p. (gr. k-2). pap. 10.35 (978-0-7660-5979-5(0), af962ef4-87ed-43ee-a462-c18d93131367, Enslow Elementary); lib. bdg. 25.27 (978-0-7660-3284-2(1), f3d5441f-19f5-4a3c-86f8-68b088cac5ca) Enslow Publishing, LLC.

Dolan, Edward F. George Washington, 1 vol. 2008. (Presidents & Their Times Ser.). (ENG., Illus.). 96p. (gr. 6-6). lib. bdg. 36.93 (978-0-7614-2427-7(X), cd0e6306-5e7f-48f3-821e-9706b4b1c5a7) Cavendish Square Publishing LLC.

Dommermuth-Costa, Carol. Woodrow Wilson. 2003. (Presidential Leaders Ser.). (Illus.). 112p. (J). 29.27 (978-0-8225-0094-0(9), Lerner Pubns.) Lerner Publishing Group.

Donaldson, Madeline. Richard Nixon. 2009. pap. 52.95 (978-0-7613-4956-3(1)) 2008. (ENG.). 48p. (gr. 3-6). 27.93 (978-0-8225-8896-2(X), Lerner Pubns.) Lerner Publishing Group.

Dooling, Sandra. James Madison, 1 vol. 2012. (Jr. Graphic Founding Fathers Ser.). (ENG., Illus.). 24p. (J). (gr. 2-3). pap. 11.60 (978-1-4488-7992-2(2), f4d38373-b864-4032-9f27-d95f85561fd1); lib. bdg. 28.93 (978-1-4488-7898-7(5), b0da6c67-4e46-4e62-98f3-3e24bfa5e3b4) Rosen Publishing Group, Inc., The. (PowerKids Pr.).

Douglas, Lloyd G. The White House. 2003. (Welcome Bks.). (ENG., Illus.). 24p. (J). (gr. -1-2). pap. 4.95 (978-0-516-27878-0(9), Children's Pr.) Scholastic Library Publishing.

Dover Publications Inc. Staff, ed. Abraham Lincoln, Kit. 2008. (ENG.). 96p. (J). (gr. 1). 19.99 (978-0-486-46720-7(1)) Dover Pubns., Inc.

Drevitch, Gary. Presidents FYI. 2008. (Illus.). 80p. (J). (gr. 3-7). 16.99 (978-0-06-089992-9(1)); (ENG., pap. 7.99 (978-0-06-089991-2(3), Collins) HarperCollins Pubs.

Driscoll, Laura. Presidential Pets. Slade, Christian, illus. 2009. (ENG.). 64p. (J). (gr. 1-3). 17.44 (978-0-448-45250-0(2), Grosset & Dunlap) Penguin Publishing Group.

Dudley Gold, Susan. Lyndon B. Johnson, 1 vol. 2009. (Presidents & Their Times Ser.). (ENG.). 96p. (gr. 6-6). lib. bdg. 36.93 (978-0-7614-2837-4(2), b7365e2b-017f-4a6b-b790-7837fd51eb6c) Cavendish Square Publishing LLC.

Duignan, Brian & DeCarlo, Carolyn, eds. The Executive Branch: Carrying Out & Enforcing Laws, 1 vol. 2018. (Checks & Balances in the U. S. Government Ser.). (ENG.). 128p. (gr. 10-10). 39.00 (978-1-5383-0164-7(4), 1b0fb071-6f66-47ac-9a9b-1d06e5b0b739, Britannica Educational Publishing) Rosen Publishing Group, Inc., The.

Duling, Kaitlyn. George Washington, 1 vol. 2017. (Great Military Leaders Ser.). (ENG.). 128p. (YA). (gr. 9-9). 47.36 (978-1-5026-2784-1(1), bff19b63-d71d-426b-a194-d1610cdd3180) Cavendish Square Publishing LLC.

DuMont, Brianna. Weird but True! U. S. Presidents. 2017. (Weird but True Ser.). (Illus.). 192p. (J). (gr. 3-7). pap. 12.99 (978-1-4263-2796-4(X), National Geographic Kids) Disney Publishing Worldwide.

—Weird but True Know-It-All: U. S. Presidents. 2017. (Weird but True Ser.). (ENG., Illus.). 192p. (J). (gr. 3-7). lib. bdg. 22.90 (978-1-4263-2797-1(8), National Geographic Kids) Disney Publishing Worldwide.

Dyan, Penelope. This Is the House George Built! a Kid's Guide to Mount Vernon. Weigand, John D., photos by. 2009. (Illus.). 44p. pap. 11.95 (978-1-935118-83-1(8)) Bellissima Publishing, LLC.

Edge, Laura Bufano. William Mckinley. 2007. (Presidential Leaders Ser.). (Illus.). 112p. (J). (gr. 3-7). lib. bdg. 29.27 (978-0-8225-1508-1(3), Twenty-First Century Bks.) Lerner Publishing Group.

Edison, Erin. Abraham Lincoln, 1 vol. 2012. (Presidential Biographies Ser.). (ENG., Illus.). 24p. (J). (gr. -1-2). lib. bdg. 27.32 (978-1-4296-8735-5(5), 119528, Capstone Pr.) Capstone.

—Franklin D. Roosevelt, 1 vol. (Presidential Biographies Ser.). (ENG.). 24p. (J). (gr. -1-2). 2014. pap. 6.29 (978-1-4765-9630-3(1), 125426, Pebble) 2012. (Illus.). lib. bdg. 27.32 (978-1-4296-8736-2(3), 119529, Capstone Pr.) Capstone.

—George Washington, 1 vol. 2012. (Presidential Biographies Ser.). (ENG., Illus.). 24p. (J). (gr. -1-2). lib. bdg. 27.32 (978-1-4296-8737-9(1), 119530, Capstone Pr.) Capstone.

—John F. Kennedy, 1 vol. (Presidential Biographies Ser.). (ENG.). 24p. (J). (gr. -1-2). 2014. pap. 6.29 (978-1-4765-9632-7(8), 125428, Pebble) 2012. lib. bdg. 27.32 (978-1-4296-8738-6(X), 119531, Capstone Pr.) Capstone.

Edwards, Roberta. Barack Obama: Presidente de Estados Unidos. Call, Ken, illus. 2009.Tr. of Barack Obama: United States President. (SPA.). 64p. (J). (gr. 2-5). pap. 9.99 (978-1-63113-956-7(8), Loqueleo) Santillana USA Publishing Co., Inc.

—Who Was George Washington? 2009. (Who Was... ? Ser.). lib. bdg. 16.00 (978-0-606-04042-6(0)) Turtleback.

Edwards, Roberta & Who HQ. Who Is Barack Obama? O'Brien, John, illus. 2009. (Who Was? Ser.). 112p. (J). (gr. 3-7). pap. 5.99 (978-0-448-45330-9(4), Penguin Workshop) Penguin Young Readers Group.

—Who Was George Washington? Kelley, True, illus. 2009. (Who Was? Ser.). 112p. (J). (gr. 3-7). pap. 5.99 (978-0-448-44892-3(0), Penguin Workshop) Penguin Young Readers Group.

Egan, Tracie. George Washington: Padre de la Patria, 1 vol. 2003. (Grandes Personajes en la Historia de Los Estados Unidos (Famous People in American History) Ser.). (SPA.). 32p. (gr. 3-4). pap. 10.00 (978-0-8239-4229-9(5), b074e87f-15d9-4a7a-bf4f-9c638418e7b2, Rosen Classroom); (Illus.). lib. bdg. 29.13 (978-0-8239-4135-3(3), f48d0b7b-f6de-4849-8a09-87ae1b9d2aa7, Editorial Buenas Letras) Rosen Publishing Group, Inc., The.

—George Washington: Padre de la patria (George Washington: Father of the American Nation) 2009. (Grandes personajes en la historia de los Estados Unidos (Famous People in American History) Ser.). (SPA.). 32p. (gr. 2-3). 47.90 (978-1-61512-800-6(X), Editorial Buenas Letras) Rosen Publishing Group, Inc., The.

—George Washington: The Father of the American Nation. 2009. (Primary Sources of Famous People in American History Ser.). 32p. (gr. 2-3). 47.90 (978-1-60851-683-4(0)) Rosen Publishing Group, Inc., The.

—The President & the Executive Branch. (Primary Source Library of American Citizenship Ser.). 32p. (gr. 5-5). 2009. 47.90 (978-1-61511-229-6(4)) 2003. (ENG., Illus.). lib. bdg. 29.13 (978-0-8239-4477-4(8), 826a953c-71e4-40ff-a4f6-4cebcbef54a2) Rosen Publishing Group, Inc., The. (Rosen Reference).

Eldridge, Alison & Eldridge, Stephen. The White House: An American Symbol, 1 vol. 2012. (All about American Symbols Ser.). (ENG.). 24p. (gr. -1-1). 25.27 (978-0-7660-4062-5(3), 79e314ad-ddb0-4055-8358-566f1484a2f2); (Illus.). pap. 10.35 (978-1-4644-0050-6(4), d4022209-cb74-403a-9b14-a017d8525bb8) Enslow Publishing, LLC. (Enslow Publishing).

Elish, Dan. Franklin Delano Roosevelt, 1 vol. 2009. (Presidents & Their Times Ser.). (ENG.). 96p. (gr. 6-6). lib. bdg. 36.93 (978-0-7614-2841-1(0), 871c231b-419f-45ad-9a9f-f5b6ca2d4cf1) Cavendish Square Publishing LLC.

—James Madison, 1 vol. 2008. (Presidents & Their Times Ser.). (ENG., Illus.). 96p. (gr. 6-6). lib. bdg. 36.93 (978-0-7614-2432-1(6), fa0cbdb0-9a1c-489c-b7b7-cf602998b5fc) Cavendish Square Publishing LLC.

—John Quincy Adams, 1 vol. 2012. (Presidents & Their Times Ser.). (ENG.). 96p. (gr. 6-6). 36.93 (978-1-60870-182-7(4), e7b0cd96-616c-4dbd-b651-d700e8973432) Cavendish Square Publishing LLC.

—Theodore Roosevelt, 1 vol. 2008. (Presidents & Their Times Ser.). (ENG., Illus.). 96p. (gr. 6-6). lib. bdg. 36.93 (978-0-7614-2429-1(6), e53764ff-c12a-46d7-9a3e-003c63dc9c9d) Cavendish Square Publishing LLC.

Elston, Heidi. Calvin Coolidge, 1 vol. 2016. (United States Presidents *2017 Ser.). (ENG., Illus.). 40p. (J). (gr. 2-5). 35.64 (978-1-68078-090-1(5), 21797, Big Buddy Bks.) ABDO Publishing Co.

—Chester Arthur, 1 vol. 2016. (United States Presidents *2017 Ser.). (ENG.). 40p. (J). (gr. 2-5). 35.64 (978-1-68078-083-3(2), 21783, Big Buddy Bks.) ABDO Publishing Co.

—George H. W. Bush, 1 vol. 2016. (United States Presidents *2017 Ser.). (ENG., Illus.). 40p. (J). (gr. 2-5). lib. bdg. 35.64 (978-1-68078-085-7(9), 21787, Big Buddy Bks.) ABDO Publishing Co.

—Harry S. Truman, 1 vol. 2016. (United States Presidents *2017 Ser.). (ENG., Illus.). 40p. (J). (gr. 2-5). 35.64 (978-1-68078-119-9(7), 21855, Big Buddy Bks.) ABDO Publishing Co.

—Jimmy Carter, 1 vol. 2016. (United States Presidents *2017 Ser.). (ENG., Illus.). 40p. (J). (gr. 2-5). lib. bdg. 35.64 (978-1-68078-087-1(5), 21791, Big Buddy Bks.) ABDO Publishing Co.

—John Adams, 1 vol. 2016. (United States Presidents *2017 Ser.). (ENG., Illus.). 40p. (J). (gr. 2-5). lib. bdg. 35.64 *(978-1-68078-081-9(6)*, 21779, Big Buddy Bks.) ABDO Publishing Co.

—John Quincy Adams, 1 vol. 2016. (United States Presidents *2017 Ser.). (ENG., Illus.). 40p. (J). (gr. 2-5). lib. bdg. 35.64 *(978-1-68078-082-6(4)*, 21781, Big Buddy Bks.) ABDO Publishing Co.

—Millard Fillmore, 1 vol. 2016. (United States Presidents *2017 Ser.). (ENG., Illus.). 40p. (J). (gr. 2-5). lib. bdg. 35.64 *(978-1-68078-092-5(1)*, 21801, Big Buddy Bks.) ABDO Publishing Co.

—William H. Harrison. 2016. (United States Presidents *2017 Ser.). (ENG., Illus.). 40p. (J). (gr. 2-5). 52.79 *(978-1-68077-518-1(9)*, 22409); lib. bdg. 35.64 *(978-1-68078-098-7(0)*, 21813) ABDO Publishing Co. (Big Buddy Bks.).

The Emancipation Proclamation & the End of Slavery in America, 1 vol. 2014. (Celebration of the Civil Rights Movement Ser.). (ENG., Illus.). 80p. (J). (gr. 6-6). 37.47 *(978-1-4777-7749-7(0)*, 20d82c0d-2d59-4140-9fc1-adf790e79e4c) Rosen Publishing Group, Inc., The.

Encyclopaedia Britannica, ed. The American Presidency. 2009. (Illus.). 144p. (YA). (gr. 7-12). 29.95 *(978-1-59339-843-9(3))* Encyclopaedia Britannica, Inc.

Englar, Mary. An Illustrated Timeline of U. S. Presidents, 1 vol. Epstein, Len, illus. 2012. (Visual Timelines in History Ser.). (ENG.). 32p. (J). (gr. 2-4). pap. 7.49 *(978-1-4048-7254-7(X)*, 118199); lib. bdg. 29.32 *(978-1-4048-7161-8(6)*, 117156) Capstone. (Picture Window Bks.).

Epstein, Len. Presidents Facts & Fun Activity Book. 2012. (Dover Kids Activity Books: U. S. A. Ser.). (ENG.). 48p. (J). (gr. 3-5). pap. 4.99 *(978-0-486-48277-4(4)*, 482774) Dover Pubns., Inc.

Etingoff, Kim. Harry Truman: From Farmer to President. 2012. (J). pap. *(978-1-4222-2485-4(6))*; 64p. (gr. 7-8). 22.95 *(978-1-4222-2482-3(1))* Mason Crest.

Falk, Laine. Meet President Barack Obama. 2009. (Scholastic News Nonfiction Readers Ser.). (ENG., Illus.). 24p. (J). (gr. k-3). 21.19 *(978-0-531-23403-7(7)*, Children's Pr.) Scholastic Library Publishing.

—Meet President John McCain. 2009. (J). *(978-0-531-23650-5(1))* Children's Pr., Ltd.

Famous Americans, Vol. 3. 2005. (First Biographies Ser.). (YA). (gr. k-3). 118.80 *(978-0-7368-4197-9(0)*, Pebble) Capstone.

Feinstein, Stephen & Taylor, Charlotte. Barack Obama: First African-American President, 1 vol. 2015. (Exceptional African Americans Ser.). (ENG.). 24p. (gr. 3-4). pap. 10.35 *(978-0-7660-7122-3(7)*, 6d9583a1-f228-4f6b-a009-bf3345f11287); (Illus.). 24.27 *(978-0-7660-7124-7(3)*, 30bf2328-d3e3-4cc0-a789-bb42085be796) Enslow Publishing, LLC.

Feldman, Ruth Tenzer. Chester A. Arthur. 2006. (Presidential Leaders Ser.). (Illus.). 111p. (J). (gr. 3-7). lib. bdg. 29.27 *(978-0-8225-1512-8(1)*, Twenty-First Century Bks.) Lerner Publishing Group.

Ferry, Joseph. Thomas Jefferson. 2004. (Childhood of the Presidents Ser.). (Illus.). 48p. (J). (gr. 4-18). lib. bdg. 17.95 *(978-1-59084-271-3(5))* Mason Crest.

Foley, Tim. American Presidents Sticker Book. 2011. (Dover Sticker Bks.). (ENG., Illus.). 4p. (J). (gr. 1-5). 6.99 *(978-0-486-47879-1(3)*, 478793) Dover Pubns., Inc.

Ford, Carin T. The Emancipation Proclamation, Lincoln, & Slavery Through Primary Sources, 1 vol. 2013. (Civil War Through Primary Sources Ser.). (ENG.). 48p. (gr. 4-6). pap. 11.53 *(978-1-4644-0187-9(X)*, 39a9f8dc-63ab-4b9b-94df-bb3af9d021ae); (Illus.). (J). lib. bdg. 27.93 *(978-0-7660-4129-5(8)*, b2263e7e-8ce7-4531-a353-b06b36d2fe69) Enslow Publishing, LLC.

Frith, Margaret & Who HQ. Who Was Franklin Roosevelt? O'Brien, John, illus. 2010. (Who Was? Ser.). 112p. (J). (gr. 3-7). pap. 5.99 *(978-0-448-45346-0(0)*, Penguin Workshop) Penguin Young Readers Group.

Fry, Sonali. Let's Read About — George W. Bush. Heyer, Carol, illus. 2003. (Scholastic First Biographies Ser.). (J). pap. *(978-0-439-45953-2(2))* Scholastic, Inc.

Fuqua, Nell & Jankowki, Dan. U. S. Presidents: Feats & Foul-Ups. Saunders, Zina, illus. 2003. 48p. (J). pap. *(978-0-439-54081-0(X))* Lemondrop Pr.

Furgang, Kathy. The Declaration of Independence & Thomas Jefferson of Virginia. 2009. (Framers of the Declaration of Independence Ser.). 24p. (gr. 3-3). 42.50 *(978-1-61512-633-0(3)*, PowerKids Pr.) Rosen Publishing Group, Inc., The.

Gaff, Jackie. George Washington: The Life of an American Patriot, 1 vol. 2005. (Graphic Nonfiction Biographies Ser.). (ENG., Illus.). 48p. (YA). (gr. 4-6). lib. bdg. 37.13 *(978-1-4042-0236-8(6)*, 6309c903-837f-4795-a83c-03b9fb9476ef) Rosen Publishing Group, Inc., The.

Gaines, Ann. Woodrow Wilson. 2003. (Great American Presidents Ser.). (ENG., Illus.). 100p. (gr. 5-8). 30.00 *(978-0-7910-7597-5(4)*, P113900, Facts On File) Infobase Holdings, Inc.

Gedacht, Daniel C. George Washington: Leader of a New Nation. (Library of American Lives & Times Ser.). 112p. (gr. 5-5). 2009. 69.20 *(978-1-60853-484-5(7))* 2003. (ENG., Illus.). (J). lib. bdg. 38.27 *(978-0-8239-6622-6(4)*, cc7bd966-2ad0-441a-b726-1adbbf4f7df3) Rosen Publishing Group, Inc., The.

Geller, Kevin. Harry S. Truman, 1 vol. 2017. (Pivotal Presidents: Profiles in Leadership Ser.). (ENG., Illus.). 80p. (J). (gr. 8-8). lib. bdg. 36.47 *(978-1-68048-633-9(0)*, 6fbd2e3d-226b-4f14-9f06-044fc28f431d, Britannica Educational Publishing) Rosen Publishing Group, Inc., The.

Gherman, Beverly. First Son & President: A Story about John Quincy Adams. Bird, Matthew, illus. 2005. (Creative Minds Biographies Ser.). (ENG.). 64p. (gr. 4-8). lib. bdg. 22.60 *(978-1-57505-756-9(5)*, Carolrhoda Bks.) Lerner Publishing Group.

Gigliotti, Jim. Ronald Reagan, the 40th President. 2016. (First Look at America's Presidents Ser.). (ENG., Illus.). 24p. (J). (gr. -1-3). 26.99 *(978-1-944102-69-2(8))* Bearport Publishing Co., Inc.

Gilpin, Caroline Crosson. National Geographic Readers: Abraham Lincoln. 2012. (Readers Bios Ser.). 32p. (J). (gr. 1-3). pap. 4.99 *(978-1-4263-1085-0(4)*, National Geographic Kids); (ENG.). lib. bdg. 14.90 *(978-1-4263-1086-7(2)*, National Geographic Children's Bks.) Disney Publishing Worldwide.

—National Geographic Readers: Barack Obama. 2014. (Readers Bios Ser.). 32p. (J). (gr. 1-3). pap. 4.99 *(978-1-4263-1759-0(X)*, National Geographic Kids) Disney Publishing Worldwide.

—National Geographic Readers: George Washington. 2014. (Readers Bios Ser.). (Illus.). 32p. (J). (gr. 1-3). pap. 4.99 *(978-1-4263-1468-1(X)*, National Geographic Kids) Disney Publishing Worldwide.

Giovanni, Nikki. Lincoln & Douglass: An American Friendship. Collier, Bryan, illus. 2013. (ENG.). 40p. (J). (gr. 2-6). 10.99 *(978-1-250-01869-4(2)*, 900087706) Square Fish.

—Lincoln & Douglass: An American Friendship. Collier, Bryan, illus. 2011. (J). (gr. -1-3). 29.95 *(978-0-545-13457-6(9))* Weston Woods Studios, Inc.

Gitlin, Martin. The Great Depression & World War II: 1929-1945. 2007. (Presidents of the United States Ser.). (Illus.). 48p. (J). (gr. 4-7). lib. bdg. 29.05 *(978-1-59036-749-0(9))*; per. 10.95 *(978-1-59036-750-6(2))* Weigl Pubs., Inc.

—Post-War United States: 1945-Early 1970s. 2007. (Presidents of the United States Ser.). (Illus.). 48p. (J). (gr. 4-7). lib. bdg. 29.05 *(978-1-59036-751-3(0))*; per. 10.95 *(978-1-59036-752-0(9))* Weigl Pubs., Inc.

Goddu, Krystyna Poray. George Washington's Presidency. 2016. (Presidential Powerhouses Ser.). (ENG., Illus.). 104p. (YA). (gr. 6-12). 35.99 *(978-1-4677-7924-1(5)*, 5ef17340-8503-4d31-9be2-86617a0a3921); E-Book 54.65 *(978-1-4677-8598-3(9))* Lerner Publishing Group. (Lerner Pubns.).

Goldsmith, Howard. John F. Kennedy & the Stormy Sea. Benoit, Renné, illus. 2006. 32p. (J). lib. bdg. 15.00 *(978-1-4242-0958-3(7))* Fitzgerald Bks.

Goodman, Susan E. See How They Run: Campaign Dreams, Election Schemes, & the Race to the White House. Smith, Elwood, illus. 2nd rev. ed. 2012. (ENG.). 96p. (J). (gr. 3-12). pap. 12.99 *(978-1-59990-897-7(2)*, 900083806, Bloomsbury USA Childrens) Bloomsbury Publishing USA.

Gormley, Beatrice. Barack Obama: Our Forty-Fourth President. 2015. (Real-Life Story Ser.). (ENG., Illus.). 272p. (J). (gr. 3-7). 17.99 *(978-1-4814-4648-8(7)*, Aladdin) Simon & Schuster Children's Publishing.

—George W. Bush: Our Forty-Third President. 2015. (Real-Life Story Ser.). (ENG., Illus.). 256p. (J). (gr. 3-7). 17.99 *(978-1-4814-4645-7(2)*, Aladdin) Simon & Schuster Children's Publishing.

—President George W. Bush: Our Forty-Third President. 2005. (ENG., Illus.). 208p. (J). (gr. 4-9). pap. 10.99 *(978-0-689-87834-3(6)*, Simon & Schuster/Paula Wiseman Bks.) Simon & Schuster/Paula Wiseman Bks.

Gosman, Gillian. Abraham Lincoln, 1 vol. 2011. (Life Stories Ser.). (Illus.). 24p. (J). (gr. 3-3). (ENG.). pap. 9.25 *(978-1-4488-2753-4(1)*, c38f1529-a0ed-443e-bf35-44e20428e06e, PowerKids Pr.); (ENG., lib. bdg. 26.27 *(978-1-4488-2582-0(2)*, 07f83246-a876-470e-b803-905a492eb466, PowerKids Pr.); (SPA & ENG., lib. bdg. 26.27 *(978-1-4488-3216-3(0)*, 9ff069b3-954b-4d8d-8616-3464ce80badb) Rosen Publishing Group, Inc., The.

—Franklin D. Roosevelt, 1 vol. 2011. (Life Stories Ser.). (ENG., Illus.). 24p. (J). (gr. 3-3). pap. 9.25 *(978-1-4488-3182-1(2)*, 4c99ad0e-7380-4e41-8192-3dcff322e2bf, PowerKids Pr.); lib. bdg. 26.27 *(978-1-4488-3222-4(5)*, 96acf089-22e2-4d2e-a6e6-8a4da767b5e9); lib. bdg. 26.27 *(978-1-4488-3179-1(2)*, 3f0b1701-e059-4701-bc74-6783a09d3a80, PowerKids Pr.) Rosen Publishing Group, Inc., The.

—George Washington, 1 vol. 2011. (Life Stories Ser.). (Illus.). 24p. (J). (gr. 3-3). (ENG.). pap. 9.25 *(978-1-4488-2751-0(5)*, 6b3ec24a-8848-4d8d-b62d-34dc2df64d9c, PowerKids Pr.); (SPA & ENG., lib. bdg. 26.27 *(978-1-4488-3215-6(2)*, 58af38af-7a01-4498-8784-0f44b808ec4b); (ENG., lib. bdg. 26.27 *(978-1-4488-2581-3(4)*, 44b4d329-a6e9-4b5e-88ff-2844598ba48b, PowerKids Pr.) Rosen Publishing Group, Inc., The.

—Thomas Jefferson, 1 vol. 2011. (Life Stories Ser.). (Illus.). 24p. (J). (gr. 3-3). (ENG.). pap. 9.25 *(978-1-4488-3180-7(6)*, aa940604-afba-402c-9f00-9fa5315e3895, PowerKids Pr.); (SPA & ENG., lib. bdg. 26.27 *(978-1-4488-3221-7(7)*, e5e60a96-36ef-45db-b4dc-d760cd59aa5a); (ENG., lib. bdg. 26.27 *(978-1-4488-3178-4(4)*, 6e7e2cdf-68fc-42f2-98e4-ec91f3c5b148, PowerKids Pr.) Rosen Publishing Group, Inc., The.

Gottfried, Ted. Millard Fillmore, 1 vol. 2008. (Presidents & Their Times Ser.). (ENG., Illus.). 96p. (gr. 6-6). lib. bdg. 36.93 *(978-0-7614-2431-4(8)*, a45fa7df-8893-4ace-9783-fbc698df63d9) Cavendish Square Publishing LLC.

Gould, Sloane. I Want to Be the President! Understanding Government, 1 vol. 2018. (Civics for the Real World Ser.). (ENG.). 16p. (gr. 2-3). pap. *(978-1-5383-6522-9(7)*, 410c087e-0fba-464a-ae52-bbc9a7daff44, Rosen Classroom) Rosen Publishing Group, Inc., The.

Greene, Meg. William H. Harrison. 2007. (Presidential Leaders Ser.). (Illus.). 112p. (J). (gr. 3-7). lib. bdg. 29.27 *(978-0-8225-1511-1(3)*, Twenty-First Century Bks.) Lerner Publishing Group.

Gregory, Josh. Abraham Lincoln: The 16th President. 2015. (First Look at America's Presidents Ser.). (ENG.). 24p. (J). (gr. -1-3). lib. bdg. 26.99 *(978-1-62724-554-8(5))* Bearport Publishing Co., Inc.

—Andrew Jackson: The 7th President. 2015. (First Look at America's Presidents Ser.). (ENG.). 24p. (J). (gr. -1-3). lib. bdg. 26.99 *(978-1-62724-556-2(1))* Bearport Publishing Co., Inc.

—Bill Clinton. 2014. (ENG.). 64p. (J). pap. 8.95 *(978-0-531-25825-5(4))* Scholastic Library Publishing.

—Franklin D. Roosevelt: The 32nd President. 2015. (First Look at America's Presidents Ser.). (ENG.). 24p. (J). (gr. -1-3). lib. bdg. 26.99 *(978-1-62724-555-5(3))* Bearport Publishing Co., Inc.

—George Washington: The 1st President. 2015. (First Look at America's Presidents Ser.). (ENG.). 24p. (J). (gr. -1-3). lib. bdg. 26.99 *(978-1-62724-552-4(9))* Bearport Publishing Co., Inc.

—Theodore Roosevelt: The 26th President. 2015. (First Look at America's Presidents Ser.). (ENG.). 24p. (J). (gr. -1-3). lib. bdg. 26.99 *(978-1-62724-557-9(X))* Bearport Publishing Co., Inc.

—Thomas Jefferson: The 3rd President. 2015. (First Look at America's Presidents Ser.). (ENG.). 24p. (J). (gr. -1-3). lib. bdg. 26.99 *(978-1-62724-553-1(7))* Bearport Publishing Co., Inc.

Gregory, Josh & Bose, Meenekshi. James Madison: The 4th President. 2015. (First Look at America's Presidents Ser.). (ENG.). 24p. (J). (gr. -1-3). lib. bdg. 26.99 *(978-1-62724-559-3(6))* Bearport Publishing Co., Inc.

—John Adams: The 2nd President. 2015. (First Look at America's Presidents Ser.). (ENG.). 24p. (J). (gr. -1-3). lib. bdg. 26.99 *(978-1-62724-558-6(8))* Bearport Publishing Co., Inc.

Gross, M. J. How to Draw the Life & Times of William Jefferson Clinton. 2009. (Kid's Guide to Drawing the Presidents of the United States of America Ser.). 32p. (gr. 4-4). 50.50 *(978-1-61511-166-4(2)*, PowerKids Pr.) Rosen Publishing Group, Inc., The.

Gross, Miriam. How to Draw the Life & Times of James Monroe. 2009. (Kid's Guide to Drawing the Presidents of the United States of America Ser.). 32p. (gr. 4-4). 50.50 *(978-1-61511-149-7(2)*, PowerKids Pr.) Rosen Publishing Group, Inc., The.

—John Adams: Patriot, Diplomat, & Statesman, 1 vol. 2004. (Library of American Lives & Times Ser.). (ENG., Illus.). 112p. (J). (gr. 5-5). lib. bdg. 38.27 *(978-1-4042-2649-4(4)*, a175961f-8801-4ce3-a07a-580cc696f4d5) Rosen Publishing Group, Inc., The.

Gross, Miriam J. How to Draw the Life & Times of William Jefferson Clinton, 1 vol. 2005. (Kid's Guide to Drawing the Presidents of the United States of America Ser.). (ENG., Illus.). 32p. (YA). (gr. 4-4). 30.27 *(978-1-4042-3018-7(1)*, 9ef53009-8f18-4d1c-9340-4ea065708d69) Rosen Publishing Group, Inc., The.

Gunderson, Jessica. The Election Of 1860: A Nation Divides on the Eve of War. 2016. (Presidential Politics Ser.). (ENG., Illus.). 48p. (J). (gr. 3-6). lib. bdg. 29.99 *(978-1-4914-8240-7(0)*, 130711) Capstone.

Gunderson, Megan M. Andrew Jackson, 1 vol. 2016. (United States Presidents *2017 Ser.). (ENG., Illus.). 40p. (J). (gr. 2-5). 35.64 *(978-1-68078-101-4(4)*, 21819, Big Buddy Bks.) ABDO Publishing Co.

—Andrew Johnson, 1 vol. 2016. (United States Presidents *2017 Ser.). (ENG., Illus.). 40p. (J). (gr. 2-5). 35.64 *(978-1-68078-103-8(0)*, 21823, Big Buddy Bks.) ABDO Publishing Co.

—Benjamin Harrison, 1 vol. 2016. (United States Presidents *2017 Ser.). (ENG., Illus.). 40p. (J). (gr. 2-5). 35.64 *(978-1-68078-097-0(2)*, 21811, Big Buddy Bks.) ABDO Publishing Co.

—Franklin D. Roosevelt, 1 vol. 2016. (United States Presidents *2017 Ser.). (ENG., Illus.). 40p. (J). (gr. 2-5). lib. bdg. 35.64 *(978-1-68078-115-1(4)*, 21847, Big Buddy Bks.) ABDO Publishing Co.

—Gerald Ford, 1 vol. 2016. (United States Presidents *2017 Ser.). (ENG., Illus.). 40p. (J). (gr. 2-5). lib. bdg. 35.64 *(978-1-68078-093-2(X)*, 21803, Big Buddy Bks.) ABDO Publishing Co.

—James A. Garfield, 1 vol. 2016. (United States Presidents *2017 Ser.). (ENG., Illus.). 40p. (J). (gr. 2-5). 35.64 *(978-1-68078-094-9(8)*, 21805, Big Buddy Bks.) ABDO Publishing Co.

—James Madison, 1 vol. 2016. (United States Presidents *2017 Ser.). (ENG., Illus.). 40p. (J). (gr. 2-5). lib. bdg. 35.64 *(978-1-68078-107-6(3)*, 21831, Big Buddy Bks.) ABDO Publishing Co.

—James Monroe, 1 vol. 2016. (United States Presidents *2017 Ser.). (ENG., Illus.). 40p. (J). (gr. 2-5). lib. bdg. 35.64 *(978-1-68078-109-0(X)*, 21835, Big Buddy Bks.) ABDO Publishing Co.

—John F. Kennedy, 1 vol. 2016. (United States Presidents *2017 Ser.). (ENG., Illus.). 40p. (J). (gr. 2-5). lib. bdg. 35.64 *(978-1-68078-105-2(7)*, 21827, Big Buddy Bks.) ABDO Publishing Co.

—John Tyler, 1 vol. 2016. (United States Presidents *2017 Ser.). (ENG., Illus.). 40p. (J). (gr. 2-5). lib. bdg. 35.64 *(978-1-68078-120-5(0)*, 21857, Big Buddy Bks.) ABDO Publishing Co.

—Lyndon B. Johnson, 1 vol. 2016. (United States Presidents *2017 Ser.). (ENG., Illus.). 40p. (J). (gr. 2-5). lib. bdg. 35.64 *(978-1-68078-104-5(9)*, 21825, Big Buddy Bks.) ABDO Publishing Co.

—William Mckinley, 1 vol. 2016. (United States Presidents *2017 Ser.). (ENG., Illus.). 40p. (J). (gr. 2-5). lib. bdg. 35.64 *(978-1-68078-108-3(1)*, 21833, Big Buddy Bks.) ABDO Publishing Co.

Hajeski, Nancy J. The Big Book of Presidents: From George Washington to Joseph R. Biden. 2015. (ENG., Illus.). 144p. (J). (gr. 3-7). 19.95 *(978-1-62914-644-7(7)*, Sky Pony Pr.) Skyhorse Publishing Co., Inc.

Haldy, Emma E. Abraham Lincoln. Bane, Jeff, illus. 2016. (My Early Library: My Itty-Bitty Bio Ser.). (ENG.). 24p. (J). (gr. k-1). 30.64 *(978-1-63470-476-2(2)*, 207635) Cherry Lake Publishing.

—Abraham Lincoln SP. Bane, Jeff, illus. 2018. (My Early Library: Mi Mini Biografía (My Itty-Bitty Bio) Ser.). (SPA.). 24p. (J). (gr. k-1). lib. bdg. 30.64 *(978-1-5341-2993-1(6)*, 212020) Cherry Lake Publishing.

—George Washington SP. Bane, Jeff, illus. 2018. (My Early Library: Mi Mini Biografía (My Itty-Bitty Bio) Ser.). (SPA.). 24p. (J). (gr. k-1). lib. bdg. 30.64 *(978-1-5341-2996-2(0)*, 212032) Cherry Lake Publishing.

Hale, Sarah Elder, ed. Abraham Lincoln: Defender of the Union. 2005. (ENG., Illus.). 48p. (J). (gr. 3-9). 17.95 *(978-0-8126-7902-1(4))* Cobblestone Pr.

—Jefferson Davis & the Confederacy. 2005. (ENG., Illus.). 48p. (J). (gr. 3-9). 17.95 *(978-0-8126-7908-3(3))* Cobblestone Pr.

—Ulysses S. Grant: Confident Leader & Hero. 2005. (ENG., Illus.). 48p. (J). (gr. 3-9). 17.95 *(978-0-8126-7906-9(7))* Cobblestone Pr.

Hall, Brianna. Freedom from Slavery: Causes & Effects of the Emancipation Proclamation, 1 vol. 2014. (Cause & Effect Ser.). (ENG., Illus.). 32p. (J). (gr. 3-6). lib. bdg. 27.99 *(978-1-4765-3930-0(8)*, 123928) Capstone.

Hally, Ashleigh. Abraham Lincoln. 2012. (Illus.). 24p. (J). *(978-1-935884-41-5(7))*; pap. *(978-1-935884-50-7(6))* State Standards Publishing, LLC.

Hamilton, Lynn. Presidents' Day. 2015. (Illus.). 24p. (J). *(978-1-5105-0116-4(9))* SmartBook Media, Inc.

—Presidents' Day. 2010. (American Celebrations Ser.). (Illus.). 24p. (J). (gr. 3-5). pap. 11.95 *(978-1-60596-931-2(1))*; lib. bdg. 18.99 *(978-1-60596-773-8(4))* Weigl Pubs., Inc.

Hammond World Atlas Corporation Staff. Presidents: An Illustrated History of America's Leaders. 2009. 144p. (J). (gr. 4-7). 19.99 *(978-0-8437-1848-5(X))* Hammond World Atlas Corp.

Hansen, Grace. Abraham Lincoln, 1 vol. 2014. (United States President Biographies (Abdo Kids Jumbo) Ser.). (ENG.). 24p. (J). (gr. -1-2). lib. bdg. 32.79 *(978-1-62970-085-4(1)*, 1716, Abdo Kids) ABDO Publishing Co.

—Barack Obama, 1 vol. 2014. (United States President Biographies (Abdo Kids Jumbo) Ser.). (ENG.). 24p. (J). (gr. -1-2). lib. bdg. 32.79 *(978-1-62970-086-1(X)*, 1717, Abdo Kids) ABDO Publishing Co.

—Barack Obama. 2015. (Biografías de Los Presidentes de Los Estados Unidos Ser.). (SPA., Illus.). 24p. (J). (gr. -1-2). pap. 7.95 *(978-1-4966-0403-3(2)*, 130251, Capstone Classroom) Capstone.

—Bill Clinton, 1 vol. 2014. (United States President Biographies (Abdo Kids Jumbo) Ser.). (ENG.). 24p. (J). (gr. -1-2). lib. bdg. 32.79 *(978-1-62970-087-8(8)*, 1718, Abdo Kids) ABDO Publishing Co.

—Donald Trump. 2016. (United States President Biographies Ser.). (ENG., Illus.). 24p. (J). (gr. -1-2). lib. bdg. 32.79 *(978-1-68080-939-8(3)*, 23361, Abdo Kids) ABDO Publishing Co.

—Franklin Delano Roosevelt, 1 vol. 2014. (United States President Biographies (Abdo Kids Jumbo) Ser.). (ENG.). 24p. (J). (gr. -1-2). lib. bdg. 32.79 *(978-1-62970-088-5(6)*, 1719, Abdo Kids) ABDO Publishing Co.

—George Washington, 1 vol. 2014. (United States President Biographies (Abdo Kids Jumbo) Ser.). (ENG.). 24p. (J). (gr. -1-2). lib. bdg. 32.79 *(978-1-62970-089-2(4)*, 1720, Abdo Kids) ABDO Publishing Co.

—John F. Kennedy, 1 vol. 2014. (United States President Biographies (Abdo Kids Jumbo) Ser.). (ENG.). 24p. (J). (gr. -1-2). lib. bdg. 32.79 *(978-1-62970-090-8(8)*, 1721, Abdo Kids) ABDO Publishing Co.

Harmon, Daniel E. Andrew Jackson. 2004. (Childhoods of the Presidents Ser.). (Illus.). 48p. (J). (gr. 4-18). lib. bdg. 17.95 *(978-1-59084-274-4(X))* Mason Crest.

—Woodrow Wilson. 2004. (Childhoods of the Presidents Ser.). (Illus.). 48p. (J). (gr. 4-18). lib. bdg. 17.95 *(978-1-59084-277-5(4))* Mason Crest.

Harness, Cheryl. Abe Lincoln Goes to Washington: 1837-1865. 2nd ed. 2008. (Illus.). 48p. (J). (gr. 3-7). pap. 7.95 *(978-1-4263-0436-1(6)*, National Geographic Children's Bks.) Disney Publishing Worldwide.

—The Remarkable Rough-Riding Life of Theodore Roosevelt & the Rise of Empire America: Wild America Gets a Protector; Panama's Canal; the Big Stick & the Bull Moose; Kids, Pets, & Spitballs in the White House; & Much, Much More. 2007. (Cheryl Harness Histories Ser.). (Illus.). 144p. (J). (gr. 3-7). 16.95 *(978-1-4263-0008-0(5)*, National Geographic Children's Bks.) Disney Publishing Worldwide.

—Thomas Jefferson. 2007. (Illus.). 48p. (J). (gr. 3-7). per. 7.95 *(978-1-4263-0043-1(3)*, National Geographic Children's Bks.) Disney Publishing Worldwide.

—Young Abe Lincoln: The Frontier Days: 1809-1837. 2nd ed. 2008. (Illus.). 32p. (J). (gr. 3-7). pap. 7.95 *(978-1-4263-0437-8(4)*, National Geographic Children's Bks.) Disney Publishing Worldwide.

Harris, Laurie Lanzen. Presidents of the Uited States. 3rd ed. 2009. (J). lib. bdg. 55.00 *(978-1-931360-45-6(6))* Favorable Impressions.

Harris, Nancy. Mount Rushmore. rev. ed. 2016. (Patriotic Symbols Ser.). (ENG.). 24p. (J). (gr. -1-1). pap. 6.29 *(978-1-4846-3588-9(4)*, 133656, Heinemann) Capstone.

Hassellus, Michelle M. Lyndon B. Johnson, 1 vol. 2014. (Presidential Biographies Ser.). (ENG.). 24p. (J). (gr. -1-2). lib. bdg. 27.32 *(978-1-4765-9611-2(5)*, 125417, Capstone Pr.) Capstone.

—Richard M. Nixon, 1 vol. 2014. (Presidential Biographies Ser.). (ENG.). 24p. (J). (gr. -1-2). lib. bdg. 27.32 *(978-1-4765-9612-9(3)*, 125418, Capstone Pr.) Capstone.

Havelin, Kate. Andrew Johnson. 2005. (Presidential Leaders Ser.). (Illus.). 112p. (J). (gr. 6-12). lib. bdg. 29.27 *(978-0-8225-1000-0(6))* Lerner Publishing Group.

—John Tyler. 2005. (Presidential Leaders Ser.). (Illus.). 112p. (J). (gr. 3-7). lib. bdg. 29.27 *(978-0-8225-1395-7(1))* Lerner Publishing Group.

—Ulysses S. Grant. 2004. (Presidential Leaders Ser.). (Illus.). 112p. (J). 29.27 *(978-0-8225-0814-4(1)*, Lerner Pubns.) Lerner Publishing Group.

Heiligman, Deborah. High Hopes (Direct Mail Edition) A Photobiography of John F. Kennedy. 2003. (Photobiographies Ser.). (ENG., Illus.). 64p. (J). (gr. 5-9). 17.95 *(978-0-7922-6141-4(0))* National Geographic Society.

Henry, Mike. Tell Me about the Presidents: Lessons for Today's Kids from America's Leaders. 2015. (Illus.). 128p. 61.00 *(978-1-4758-1703-4(7))* Rowman & Littlefield Publishers, Inc.

Herweck, Dona. George Washington, 1 vol. 2nd rev. ed. 2013. (TIME for KIDS(r): Informational Text Ser.). (ENG., Illus.). 28p. (J). (gr. 2-3). lib. bdg. 23.96 *(978-1-4807-1061-0(X))* Teacher Created Materials, Inc.

Hess, Debra. The White House, 1 vol. 2008. (Symbols of America Ser.). (ENG.). 40p. (gr. 3-3). pap. 9.23 *(978-0-7614-3394-1(5)*, 78d1cc54-bf2e-4dee-85fe-37161aa93683) Cavendish Square Publishing LLC.

Hicks, Kelli L., ed. Complete History of Our Presidents Encyclopedia, 14 vols., Set. 2014. (ENG., Illus.). 896p. (gr. 3-8). lib. bdg. 570.00 *(978-1-60694-293-2(X))* Rourke Educational Media.

P
Q
R

Hicks, Kelli L. & Weber, Michael. Rourke's Complete History of Our Presidents Encyclopedia, 14 vols. 2009. (Illus.). (J). (978-1-60694-304-5(9)); (978-1-60694-305-2(7)); (978-1-60694-307-6(3)); (978-1-60694-303-8(0)); (978-1-60694-302-1(2)); (978-1-60694-301-4(4)); (978-1-60694-300-7(6)); (978-1-60694-299-4(9)); (978-1-60694-306-9(5)); (978-1-60694-294-9(8)); (978-1-60694-295-6(6)); (978-1-60694-296-3(4)); (978-1-60694-297-0(2)); (978-1-60694-298-7(0)) Rourke Educational Media.

Hinman, Bonnie. Donald Trump: 45th President of the United States. 2017. (Newsmakers Set 2 Ser.). (ENG., Illus.). 48p. (J). (gr. 4-8). lib. bdg. 35.64 (978-1-5321-1185-3(1), 25946) ABDO Publishing Co.

—Donald Trump: 45th President of the United States. 2017. (Newsmakers Set 2 Ser.). (ENG., Illus.). 48p. (J). (gr. 4-8). 55.65 (978-1-68078-970-6(8), 26371) ABDO Publishing Co.

—The Executive Branch. 2011. (My Guide to the Constitution Ser.). 48p. (J). (gr. 3-6). pap. 16.50 (978-1-61228-185-8(0)); (Illus.). lib. bdg. 29.95 (978-1-58415-943-8(X)) Mitchell Lane Pubs.

Hinman, Bonnie & Benchmark Education Co. Staff. Opinions about Presidential Speeches. 2014. (Text Connections Ser.). (J). (gr. 5). (978-1-4900-1368-8(7)) Benchmark Education Co.

Hollar, Sherman, contrib. by. Andrew Jackson, 1 vol. 2012. (Pivotal Presidents: Profiles in Leadership Ser.). (ENG., Illus.). 80p. (gr. 8-8). (J). lib. bdg. 36.47 (978-1-61530-941-2(1), 737af3a6-c513-49f6-acf9-24697e25672b); (YA). 72.94 (978-1-61530-954-2(3), 02050021-ca99-4165-b09b-f75bed6bd80e) Rosen Publishing Group, Inc., The.

—Barack Obama, 1 vol. 2012. (Pivotal Presidents: Profiles in Leadership Ser.). (ENG.). 80p. (gr. 8-8). (J). lib. bdg. 36.47 (978-1-61530-945-0(4), 89b6f3bd-1123-481f-8f7c-3208d4fdadaa); (Illus.). (YA). 72.94 (978-1-61530-955-9(1), 302b40ce-9005-4894-bfe5-8b13bde0bbc1) Rosen Publishing Group, Inc., The.

—George Washington, 1 vol. 2012. (Pivotal Presidents: Profiles in Leadership Ser.). (ENG., Illus.). 80p. (gr. 8-8). (J). lib. bdg. 36.47 (978-1-61530-939-9(X), 5406dae3-454b-476c-bd1c-9cfe62bfa85b); (YA). 72.94 (978-1-61530-956-6(X), 6d4e4612-5ccc-4364-9d13-da5d6b06182c) Rosen Publishing Group, Inc., The.

—John F. Kennedy, 1 vol. 2012. (Pivotal Presidents: Profiles in Leadership Ser.). (ENG.). 80p. (YA). (gr. 8-8). lib. bdg. 36.47 (978-1-61530-943-6(8), 1599df6c-2c8d-4a10-a865-042c024199ca); (Illus.). 72.94 (978-1-61530-957-3(8), 7f6f0469-f9a4-415a-abc3-9184509f4c6b) Rosen Publishing Group, Inc., The.

Hollihan, Kerrie Logan. Theodore Roosevelt for Kids: His Life & Times, 21 Activities. 2010. (For Kids Ser.: 33). (ENG., Illus.). 144p. (J). (gr. 4-18). pap. 16.95 (978-1-55652-955-9(4), 1311179) Chicago Review Pr., Inc.

Holub, Joan. This Little President: A Presidential Primer. Roode, Daniel, illus. 2016. (This Little Ser.). (ENG.). 26p. (J). (gr. -1-k). bds. 7.99 (978-1-4814-5850-4(7), Little Simon) Little Simon.

Hopkinson, Deborah. John Adams Speaks for Freedom: Ready-To-Read Level 3. Orback, Craig, illus. 2005. (Ready-To-Read Stories of Famous Americans Ser.). (ENG.). 32p. (J). (gr. 1-3). pap. 4.99 (978-0-689-86907-5(X), Simon Spotlight) Simon Spotlight.

Hoppe, Ludwig Augustin. Die Epiklesis Der Griechischen Und Orientalischen Liturgieen Und Der Römische Consekrationskanon (German Edition) 2010. 350p. pap. 32.75 (978-1-142-96440-5(X)) Creative Media Partners, LLC.

Horn, Geoffrey M. The Presidency, 1 vol. 2003. (World Almanac(r) Library of American Government Ser.). (ENG., Illus.). 48p. (gr. 5-8). lib. bdg. 33.67 (978-0-8368-5458-9(6), 20237a60-d17b-4dc3-b116-a4b89a0da031, Gareth Stevens Secondary Library) Stevens, Gareth Publishing LLLP.

Houran, Lori Haskins. My Little Golden Book about George Washington. Garofoli, Viviana, illus. 2016. (Little Golden Book Ser.). 24p. (J). (gr. -1-3). 5.99 (978-1-101-93969-7(9), Golden Bks.) Random Hse. Children's Bks.

Huddle, Lorena. Woodrow Wilson, 1 vol. 2017. (Pivotal Presidents: Profiles in Leadership Ser.). (ENG., Illus.). 80p. (J). (gr. 8-8). lib. bdg. 36.47 (978-1-68048-635-3(7), e35b543f-74c9-482f-8d07-267b266ea228, Britannica Educational Publishing) Rosen Publishing Group, Inc., The.

Isecke, Harriet. Lyndon B. Johnson: A Texan in the White House, 1 vol. rev. ed. 2012. (Social Studies: Informational Text Ser.). (ENG.). 32p. (gr. 3-5). pap. 11.99 (978-1-4333-5052-8(1)) Teacher Created Materials, Inc.

—Lyndon B. Johnson: Un Texano en la Casa Blanca / Lyndon B. Johnson - A Texan in the White House. 2013. (Primary Source Readers Ser.). (SPA.). lib. bdg. 19.65 (978-0-606-31873-0(9)) Turtleback.

Jakubiak, David J. What Does the President Do?, 1 vol. 2010. (How Our Government Works). 24p. (J). (gr. 3-3). (ENG.). pap. 9.25 (978-1-4358-9810-3(9), 6a746901-36f3-476f-89ee-0b42cd5eb478, PowerKids Pr.); lib. bdg., E-Book 42.50 (978-1-4488-0020-9(X)); (ENG., Illus.). lib. bdg. 26.27 (978-1-4358-9357-3(3), 2da102a5-9dda-4280-99bb-0230c16564fe, PowerKids Pr.) Rosen Publishing Group, Inc., The.

January, Brendan. Cornerstones of Freedom: Air Force One. (Cornerstones of Freedom Ser.). (ENG.). 48p. 2008. (J). pap. 5.95 (978-0-531-20826-7(5), Children's Pr.) 2004. (Illus.). (YA). (gr. 4-7). 26.00 (978-0-516-24236-1(9)) Scholastic Library Publishing.

Jeffrey, Gary. Abraham Lincoln: The Life of America's Sixteenth President. 2009. (Graphic Nonfiction Biographies Ser.). (ENG.). 48p. (YA). (gr. 4-5). 58.50 (978-1-61513-011-5(X), Rosen Reference) Rosen Publishing Group, Inc., The.

—Thomas Jefferson & the Declaration of Independence, 1 vol. 2011. (Graphic Heroes of the American Revolution Ser.). (ENG., Illus.). 24p. (J). (gr. 3-3). 26.60 (978-1-4339-6025-3(7), b3ad44c5-2d19-400f-8ba3-6b2e6bef69a2); pap. 9.15 (978-1-4339-6026-0(5), 6bfbc259-f45e-48b1-85a7-4b2b3c1cce56, Gareth Stevens Learning Library) Stevens, Gareth Publishing LLLP.

Jennett, Pamela & Marchant, Sherry. Electing Our President: The Process to Elect the Nation's Leader. Jennett, Pamela, ed. Hillam, Corbin & Grayson, Rick, illus. 2004. 48p. pap. 8.99 (978-0-88160-379-8(1), LW-436) Creative Teaching Pr., Inc.

Jennings, Ken. U. S. Presidents. Lowery, Mike, illus. 2014. (Ken Jennings' Junior Genius Guides). (ENG.). 160p. (J). (gr. 3-5). pap. 9.99 (978-1-4424-7332-4(0), Little Simon) Little Simon.

Johansen, H. L. How to Draw the Life & Times of Calvin Coolidge. 2009. (Kid's Guide to Drawing the Presidents of the United States of America Ser.). 32p. (gr. 4-4). 50.50 (978-1-61511-134-3(4), PowerKids Pr.) Rosen Publishing Group, Inc., The.

Johansen, Heidi Leigh. How to Draw the Life & Times of Calvin Coolidge, 1 vol. 2005. (Kid's Guide to Drawing the Presidents of the United States of America Ser.). (ENG., Illus.). 32p. (YA). (gr. 4-4). 30.27 (978-1-4042-3006-4(8), 2eb0637a-9df3-435f-8d77-c6f6900f75b1) Rosen Publishing Group, Inc., The.

Johnson, Robin. Why Mirabeau Lamar Matters to Texas, 1 vol. 2013. (Texas Perspectives Ser.). (ENG., Illus.). 32p. (J). (gr. 4-4). lib. bdg. 28.93 (978-1-4777-0915-3(0), 9a524f75-7fb1-4734-83db-fd638a6e26be) Rosen Publishing Group, Inc., The.

Jones, Veda Boyd. John F. Kennedy. 2006. (Rookie Biographies Ser.). (ENG., Illus.). 32p. (J). (gr. 1-2). pap. 4.95 (978-0-516-29797-2(X), Children's Pr.) Scholastic Library Publishing.

Junyk, Myra. The 10 Greatest Presidents. 2007. (J). 14.99 (978-1-55448-457-7(X)) Scholastic Library Publishing.

Jurmain, Suzanne Tripp. George Did It. Day, Larry, illus. 2007. (gr. -1-3). 17.00 (978-0-7569-8161-7(1)) Perfection Learning Corp.

Kalman, Maira. Looking at Lincoln. Kalman, Maira, illus. 2017. (ENG., Illus.). 48p. (J). (gr. k-3). pap. 8.99 (978-0-14-751798-2(2), Puffin Books) Penguin Young Readers Group.

Kanefield, Teri. Abraham Lincoln: The Making of America #3. (Making of America Ser.). (ENG.). (J). (gr. 5-9). 2019. 256p. pap. 7.99 (978-1-4197-3625-4(6), 1198003) 2018. (Illus.). 240p. 16.99 (978-1-4197-3159-4(9), 1198001, Abrams Bks. for Young Readers) Abrams, Inc.

—Andrew Jackson: The Making of America #2. 2019. (ENG., Illus.). 256p. (J). (gr. 5-9). pap. 7.99 (978-1-4197-3421-2(0), 1197903, Abrams Bks. for Young Readers) Abrams, Inc.

Katirgis, Jane. Celebrating President Barack Obama in Pictures, 1 vol. 2009. (Obama Family Photo Album Ser.). (ENG., Illus.). 32p. (gr. 3-3). lib. bdg. 26.60 (978-0-7660-3651-2(0), 652e8ba5-dae8-470c-b17d-906ca29eb724) Enslow Publishing, LLC.

Katz, Vladimir. A Timeline of the Life of George Washington. (Timelines of American History Ser.). 32p. (gr. 4-4). 2009. 47.90 (978-1-60854-388-5(9)) 2004. (ENG., Illus.). lib. bdg. 29.13 (978-0-8239-4538-2(3), 2fa8f672-9994-452f-b005-cfc1b954837f) Rosen Publishing Group, Inc., The. (Rosen Reference).

Kawa, Katie. Barack Obama: First African American President, 1 vol. 2012. (Beginning Biographies Ser.). (ENG., Illus.). 24p. (J). (gr. 1-2). 26.27 (978-1-4488-8595-4(7), cf17b6d8-b99a-452b-8894-50f2af33c147, PowerKids Pr.) Rosen Publishing Group, Inc., The.

—Before John F. Kennedy Was President, 1 vol. 2017. (Before They Were President Ser.). (ENG.). 24p. (J). (gr. 2-3). pap. 9.15 (978-1-5382-1072-7(X), b9174323-4f41-4e85-b4bd-5757181b3fb4) Stevens, Gareth Publishing LLLP.

—The Most Powerful Presidential Words, 1 vol. 2019. (Words That Shaped America Ser.). (ENG.). 32p. (gr. 4-5). pap. 11.50 (978-1-5382-4795-2(X), a7a51070-e634-4726-b426-d350f2e5ccce) Stevens, Gareth Publishing LLLP.

Keating, Frank. Abraham. Wimmer, Mike, illus. 2017. (Mount Rushmore Presidential Ser.). (ENG.). 32p. (J). (gr. 1-4). 17.99 (978-1-4424-9319-3(4), Simon & Schuster/Paula Wiseman Bks.) Simon & Schuster/Paula Wiseman Bks.

—George: George Washington, Our Founding Father. Wimmer, Mike, illus. 2012. (Mount Rushmore Presidential Ser.). (ENG.). 32p. (J). (gr. 1-4). 17.99 (978-1-4169-5482-8(1), Simon & Schuster/Paula Wiseman Bks.) Simon & Schuster/Paula Wiseman Bks.

—Theodore. Wimmer, Mike, illus. 2006. (Mount Rushmore Presidential Ser.). (ENG.). 32p. (J). (gr. 1-4). 19.99 (978-0-689-86532-9(5), Simon & Schuster/Paula Wiseman Bks.) Simon & Schuster/Paula Wiseman Bks.

Keenan, Sheila. John F. Kennedy the Brave. Ko, Chin, illus. 2017. 25p. (J). (978-1-5182-4585-5(4)) Harper & Row Ltd.

Kelley, K. C. Grover Cleveland: The 22nd & 24th President. 2016. (First Look at America's Presidents Ser.). (ENG., Illus.). 24p. (J). (gr. -1-3). 26.99 (978-1-944102-67-8(1)) Bearport Publishing Co., Inc.

—James Monroe: The 5th President. 2016. (First Look at America's Presidents Ser.). (ENG., Illus.). 24p. (J). (gr. -1-3). 26.99 (978-1-944102-64-7(7)) Bearport Publishing Co., Inc.

Kenison, Misti. Where's Your Hat, Abe Lincoln? 2017. (Young Historians Ser.: 0). (Illus.). 28p. (J). (gr. -1-k). bds. 9.99 (978-1-4926-5250-2(4)) Sourcebooks, Inc.

Kennedy, Marge. Pets at the White House. 2009. (Scholastic News Nonfiction Readers Ser.). (Illus.). 24p. (J). (gr. 1-2). 22.00 (978-0-531-21096-3(0)) Scholastic Library Publishing.

—Scholastic News Nonfiction Readers: Let's Visit the White House, 6 vols., Set. Incl. Having Fun at the White House. Kennedy, Marge M. (Illus.). (gr. 1-2). 22.00 (978-0-531-21095-6(2)); Pets at the White House. (Illus.). (gr. 1-2). 22.00 (978-0-531-21096-3(0)); See Inside the White House. (Illus.). (gr. 1-2). 22.00 (978-0-531-21097-0(9)); Story of the White House. Kennedy, Marge M. (Illus.). (gr. 1-2). 22.00 (978-0-531-21094-9(4)); Time to Eat at the White House. (gr. k-3). 21.19 (978-0-531-21098-7(7), Children's Pr.); Who Works at the White House? (Illus.). (gr. 1-2). 22.00 (978-0-531-21099-4(5)); 24p. (J). 2009. Set lib. bdg. 132.00 (978-0-531-27902-1(2), Children's Pr.) Scholastic Library Publishing.

—Who Works at the White House? 2009. (Scholastic News Nonfiction Readers Ser.). (Illus.). 24p. (J). (gr. 1-2). 22.00 (978-0-531-21099-4(5)) Scholastic Library Publishing.

Kennedy, Marge M. & Kennedy, Marge. Having Fun at the White House. 2009. (Scholastic News Nonfiction Readers Ser.). (Illus.). 24p. (J). (gr. 1-2). 22.00 (978-0-531-21095-6(2)) Scholastic Library Publishing.

—The Story of the White House. 2009. (Scholastic News Nonfiction Readers Ser.). (Illus.). 24p. (J). (gr. 1-2). 22.00 (978-0-531-21094-9(4)) Scholastic Library Publishing.

Kent, Deborah. Franklin Delano Roosevelt: Nothing to Fear! 2006. (Defining Moments Ser.). (Illus.). 32p. (YA). (gr. 2-5). lib. bdg. 28.50 (978-1-59716-272-2(8)) Bearport Publishing Co., Inc.

—James A. Garfield. 2004. (Encyclopedia of Presidents Ser.). (ENG., Illus.). 112p. (YA). (gr. 5-9). 34.00 (978-0-516-22886-0(2)) Scholastic Library Publishing.

Keppeler, Jill. 20 Fun Facts about Thomas Jefferson. 2017. (Fun Fact File: Founding Fathers Ser.). 32p. (J). (gr. 2-3). pap. 63.00 (978-1-5382-0274-6(3)) Stevens, Gareth Publishing LLLP.

Kerley, Barbara. What to Do about Alice? 2011. (J). (gr. 2-5). 18.95 (978-0-545-29821-6(0)) Weston Woods Studios, Inc.

King, David C. Have Fun with the Presidents: Activities, Projects, & Fascinating Facts. 2007. (ENG., Illus.). 128p. (J). (gr. 3-9). pap. 14.95 (978-0-471-67905-9(4), Jossey-Bass) Wiley, John & Sons, Inc.

—Herbert Hoover, 1 vol. 2010. (Presidents & Their Times Ser.). (ENG.). 96p. (gr. 6-6). 36.93 (978-0-7614-3626-3(X), 615aec33-0c81-4349-9feb-512d0ea69ed3) Cavendish Square Publishing LLC.

King, Wilma. Children of the Emancipation. 2005. (Picture the American Past Ser.). (Illus.). 48p. (J). (gr. 2-5). 22.60 (978-1-57505-396-7(9)) Lerner Publishing Group.

Kirkman, Marissa. The Life & Times of Abraham Lincoln & the U. S. Civil War. 2016. (Life & Times Ser.). (ENG., Illus.). 24p. (J). (gr. 1-3). lib. bdg. 27.99 (978-1-5157-2474-2(3), 132846, Capstone Pr.) Capstone.

—The Life & Times of George Washington & the American Revolution. 2016. (Life & Times Ser.). (ENG., Illus.). 24p. (J). (gr. 1-3). lib. bdg. 27.99 (978-1-5157-2476-6(X), 132848, Capstone Pr.) Capstone.

Kishel, Ann-Marie. Thomas Jefferson: A Life of Patriotism. 2006. (Pull Ahead Books — Biographies Ser.). (ENG., Illus.). 32p. (J). (gr. k-3). lib. bdg. 22.65 (978-0-8225-3480-8(0), 7e675b82-3fea-41a6-889e-074788415669, Lerner Pubns.) Lerner Publishing Group.

—Thomas Jefferson: Una Vida de Patriotismo. Translations.com Staff, tr. 2006. (Libros para Avanzar-Biografias (Pull Ahead Books-Biographies) Ser.). (ENG & SPA., Illus.). 32p. (gr. k-3). lib. bdg. 22.60 (978-0-8225-6238-2(3), Ediciones Lerner) Lerner Publishing Group.

Kissock, Heather. White House. 2017. (Illus.). 24p. (J). (978-1-5105-0611-4(X)) SmartBook Media, Inc.

Kit, Oscar. A Timeline of the Life of Thomas Jefferson. (Timelines of American History Ser.). 32p. (gr. 4-4). 2009. 47.90 (978-1-60854-389-2(7)) 2004. (ENG., Illus.). lib. bdg. 29.13 (978-0-8239-4539-9(1), 47a2bcaf-4d4e-4142-9348-ee6f4d4c961c) Rosen Publishing Group, Inc., The. (Rosen Reference).

Klein, Adria F. Barack Obama. 2009. pap. 13.25 (978-1-60559-055-4(X)) Hameray Publishing Group, Inc.

Klepeis, Alicia Z. Understanding the Impeachment Process, 1 vol. 2017. (What's up with Your Government? Ser.). (ENG.). 32p. (J). (gr. 4-5). pap. 11.00 (978-1-5383-2326-7(5), cb388572-a972-413d-ab8d-571c59cde45a); (Illus.). 27.93 (978-1-5383-2230-7(7), ac74e5e2-57d0-449f-bdcd-a6e1ea3e3b35) Rosen Publishing Group, Inc., The. (PowerKids Pr.).

Knudsen, Shannon. When Were the First Slaves Set Free During the Civil War? And Other Questions about the Emancipation Proclamation. 2010. (Six Questions of American History Ser.). (ENG.). (gr. 4-6). pap. 56.72 (978-0-7613-6948-6(1)); (Illus.). 48p. (J). pap. 11.99 (978-0-7613-6121-3(9), 439921d9-9f33-4651-8e71-fe9a4cd4c225) Lerner Publishing Group.

Kops, Deborah. Encyclopedia of Presidents: Zachary Taylor. 2004. (Encyclopedia of Presidents Ser.). (ENG., Illus.). 112p. (YA). (gr. 5-9). 34.00 (978-0-516-23442-7(0)) Scholastic Library Publishing.

Koutras Bozonelis, Helen. 200 Years with Abraham Lincoln: One Man's Life & Legacy, 1 vol. 2008. (Prime (Middle/Senior) Ser.). (ENG., Illus.). 64p. (gr. 5-6). lib. bdg. 31.93 (978-0-7660-3266-8(3), 89afca66-0494-4089-b103-803fdf0a9798) Enslow Publishing, LLC.

Kozleski, Lisa. James Madison. 2004. (Childhoods of the Presidents Ser.). (Illus.). 48p. (J). (gr. 4-18). lib. bdg. 17.95 (978-1-59084-269-0(3)) Mason Crest.

Krasner, Barbara. Exploring the Executive Branch. 2019. (Searchlight Books (tm) — Getting into Government Ser.). (ENG., Illus.). 32p. (J). (gr. 3-5). pap. 9.99 (978-1-5415-7478-6(8), 157e6fd0-330c-4ceb-aec9-73a20feec9a4); lib. bdg. 30.65 (978-1-5415-5589-1(9), 3ace73bf-22e1-4519-bb0c-9001a6ca34cc) Lerner Publishing Group. (Lerner Pubns.).

Krensky, Stephen. George Washington's First Victory: Ready-To-Read Level 2. Hearn, Diane Dawson, illus. 2005. (Ready-To-Read Childhood of Famous Americans Ser.). (ENG.). 32p. (J). (gr. k-2). pap. 4.99 (978-0-689-85942-7(2), Simon Spotlight) Simon Spotlight.

Krull, Kathleen. A Boy Named FDR: How Franklin D. Roosevelt Grew up to Change America. Johnson, Steve & Fancher, Lou, illus. 2016. 48p. (J). (gr. 1-4). 7.99 (978-1-101-93251-3(1), Dragonfly Bks.) Random Hse. Children's Bks.

—The Brothers Kennedy: John, Robert, Edward. Bates, Amy June, illus. 2010. (ENG.). 40p. (J). (gr. -1-3). 16.99 (978-1-4169-9158-8(1), Simon & Schuster Bks. For Young Readers) Simon & Schuster Bks. For Young Readers.

Krull, Kathleen & Brewer, Paul. Lincoln Tells a Joke: How Laughter Saved the President (and the Country) Innerst, Stacy, illus. 2010. (ENG.). 40p. (J). (gr. 1-4). 17.99 (978-0-15-206639-0(X), 1199695, Clarion Bks.) HarperCollins Pubs.

Kukla, Amy. Thomas Jefferson: Life, Liberty, & the Pursuit of Happiness. 2009. (Library of American Lives & Times Ser.). 112p. (gr. 5-5). 69.20 (978-1-60853-508-8(8)) Rosen Publishing Group, Inc., The.

Kukla, Amy & Kukla, Jon. Thomas Jefferson: Life, Liberty, & the Pursuit of Happiness, 1 vol. 2004. (Library of American Lives & Times Ser.). (ENG., Illus.). 112p. (YA). (gr. 5-5). lib. bdg. 38.27 (978-1-4042-2655-5(9), dc1c3fb6-97ec-4a36-b098-de511a783f4d, PowerKids Pr.) Rosen Publishing Group, Inc., The.

Laks Gorman, Jacqueline. President, 1 vol. 2009. (Know Your Government Ser.). (ENG.). 24p. (gr. 3-3). (J). lib. bdg. 24.67 (978-1-4339-0095-2(5), d05ecc19-fc9f-4b56-8a4b-d3d369cd2647); pap. 9.15 (978-1-4339-0123-2(4), a99a3eaa-61e0-43e4-a2f9-ddc9e17d2631) Stevens, Gareth Publishing LLLP. (Weekly Reader Leveled Readers).

—Presidente (President), 1 vol. 2009. (Conoce Tu Gobierno (Know Your Government) Ser.). (SPA., Illus.). 24p. (J). (gr. 3-3). pap. 9.15 (978-1-4339-0130-0(7), f87c49a4-e42d-40d3-92ec-9a45591298ff); lib. bdg. 24.67 (978-1-4339-0102-7(1), e1be5049-46ae-4e25-a5bd-ec2fbf9246d1) Stevens, Gareth Publishing LLLP. (Weekly Reader Leveled Readers).

Landau, Elaine. The Emancipation Proclamation: Would You Do What Lincoln Did?, 1 vol. 2008. (What Would You Do? Ser.). (ENG., Illus.). 48p. (gr. 3-3). (J). lib. bdg. 27.93 (978-0-7660-2899-9(2), 39c1ee83-f4bc-4608-8499-383b6829d109); pap. 11.53 (978-1-59845-194-8(4), ecefcba4-d07c-4bb8-83db-4ac89f6f1c78) Enslow Publishing, LLC. (Enslow Elementary).

—Lincoln's Emancipation Proclamation: Would You Sign the Great Document?, 1 vol. 2014. (What Would You Do? Ser.). (ENG.). 48p. (gr. 3-4). (J). 27.93 (978-0-7660-6290-0(2), 37f0154d-481d-46d8-bc19-2898c06edb7a); pap. 11.53 (978-0-7660-6291-7(0), a46b69f5-a3d3-442c-86d5-136b35468973, Enslow Elementary) Enslow Publishing, LLC.

—The President, Vice President, & Cabinet: A Look at the Executive Branch. 2012. (Searchlight Books How Does Government Work Ser.). (ENG., Illus.). 40p. (gr. 3-5). pap. 51.01 (978-0-7613-9234-7(3)); (J). pap. 9.99 (978-0-7613-8563-9(0), a4d67bce-5304-4e5b-8d0a-58dd34fef595) Lerner Publishing Group.

—Warren G. Harding. 2005. (Presidential Leaders Ser.). (Illus.). 120p. (J). 29.27 (978-0-8225-0850-2(8), Lerner Pubns.) Lerner Publishing Group.

Lassieur, Allison. The Real John Adams: The Truth Behind the Legend. 2019. (Real Revolutionaries Ser.). (ENG., Illus.). 64p. (J). (gr. 5-9). lib. bdg. 34.65 (978-0-7565-6251-9(1), 141184, Compass Point Bks.) Capstone.

Lazo, Caroline Evensen. Franklin Pierce. 2007. (Presidential Leaders Ser.). (Illus.). 112p. (J). (gr. 3-7). lib. bdg. 29.27 (978-0-8225-1492-3(3), Twenty-First Century Bks.) Lerner Publishing Group.

—Harry S. Truman. 2003. (Presidential Biography Ser.). (Illus.). 112p. (J). (gr. 6-12). lib. bdg. 29.27 (978-0-8225-0096-4(5)) Lerner Publishing Group.

Leavitt, Amie. Understanding the Line of Succession, 1 vol. 2017. (What's up with Your Government? Ser.). (ENG., Illus.). 32p. (J). (gr. 4-5). 27.93 (978-1-5383-2232-1(3), 16972d6b-673f-4848-8ae0-60b4fc3dbabf); pap. 11.00 (978-1-5383-2328-1(1), c4792241-8036-47f7-8940-12be9211d929) Rosen Publishing Group, Inc., The. (PowerKids Pr.).

Lee, Sally. George W. Bush, 1 vol. (Presidential Biographies Ser.). (ENG.). 24p. (J). (gr. -1-2). 2014. pap. 6.29 (978-1-4765-9628-0(X), 125423, Pebble) 2012. (Illus.). lib. bdg. 27.32 (978-1-4296-8586-3(7), 118593, Capstone Pr.) Capstone.

—William Jefferson Clinton, 1 vol. (Presidential Biographies Ser.). (ENG.). 24p. (J). (gr. -1-2). 2014. pap. 6.29 (978-1-4765-9627-3(1), 125424, Pebble) 2012. (Illus.). lib. bdg. 27.32 (978-1-4296-8585-6(9), 118592, Capstone Pr.) Capstone.

Lee, T. S. The Lincoln Story: The Boy Who Embraced a Nation. 4th ed. 2010. (Great Heroes Ser.). 184p. (J). pap. 14.95 (978-0-9819542-3-3(5)) DASANBOOKS.

—The Obama Story: The Boy with the Biggest Dream! Shin, Janet Jaywan, tr. from KOR. 2009. 207p. (J). (gr. 6-18). pap. 14.95 (978-0-9819542-0-2(0)) DASANBOOKS.

Leidtke, Leila. If I Were President. 2012. 32p. pap. 16.50 (978-1-4685-5093-1(4)) AuthorHouse.

Leighton, Marian. George Washington. Salvador, Martin, illus. 2005. (Heroes of America Ser.). 239p. (gr. 3-8). lib. bdg. 27.07 (978-1-59679-262-3(0), Abdo & Daughters) ABDO Publishing Co.

Lemay, Violet, illus. The Obamas: A Lift-The-Flap Book. 2019. 22p. (J). (gr. -1-k). bds. 9.95 (978-1-947458-82-6(5), 805882) Duo Pr. LLC.

LeVert, Suzanne. The President, 1 vol. 2003. (Kaleidoscope: Government Ser.). (ENG., Illus.). 48p. (gr. 4-4). 32.64 (978-0-7614-1454-4(1), 14b6243c-5233-4d0c-a812-b6720137a07f) Cavendish Square Publishing LLC.

Levine, Michelle & Waxman, Laura Hamilton. Franklin D. Roosevelt. 2005. (History Maker Bios Ser.). (Illus.). 48p. (J). (gr. 3-5). 26.60 (978-0-8225-1545-6(8)) Lerner Publishing Group.

Levy, Debbie. James Monroe. 2005. (Presidential Leaders Ser.). (Illus.). 112p. (J). 29.27 (978-0-8225-0824-3(9), Lerner Pubns.) Lerner Publishing Group.

—John Quincy Adams. 2004. (Presidential Leaders Ser.). (Illus.). 112p. (J). (gr. 3-7). lib. bdg. 29.27 (978-0-8225-0825-0(7)) Lerner Publishing Group.

—Lyndon B. Johnson. 2003. (Presidential Leaders Ser.). (Illus.). 112p. (J). 29.27 (978-0-8225-0097-1(3), Lerner Pubns.) Lerner Publishing Group.

—Rutherford B. Hayes. 2006. (Presidential Leaders Ser.). (Illus.). 112p. (J). (gr. 3-7). lib. bdg. 29.27 (978-0-8225-1493-0(1), Lerner Pubns.) Lerner Publishing Group.

Levy, Janey. Before George Washington Was President, 1 vol. 2018. (Before They Were President Ser.). (ENG.). 24p. (gr. 2-3). lib. bdg. 24.27 *(978-1-5382-2912-5(9),* 2e7aa5d5-9059-4ab8-9cc2-c0e16b0731d5) Stevens, Gareth Publishing LLLP.

—20 Fun Facts about the Presidency, 1 vol. 2013. (Fun Fact File: U. S. History! Ser.). 32p. (J). (ENG.). (gr. 2-3). 27.93 *(978-1-4339-9188-2(8),* ea29d269-1aa0-4e22-8780-bd2eec29f2f1); (ENG.). (gr. 2-3). pap. 11.50 *(978-1-4339-9189-9(6),* 78afe067-ebea-4cd6-bd32-b93f4b281f57); (gr. 3-6). pap. 63.00 *(978-1-4339-9190-5(X))* Stevens, Gareth Publishing LLLP.

Lewis K., Parker. How to Draw the Life & Times of Richard M. Nixon, 1 vol. 2005. (Kid's Guide to Drawing the Presidents of the United States of America Ser.). (ENG., Illus.). 32p. (YA). (gr. 4-4). 30.27 *(978-1-4042-3013-2(0),* 1f1b6ca4-e13a-40d6-9ca7-bc451b930ad4) Rosen Publishing Group, Inc., The.

Linde, Barbara. The History of Presidents' Day, 1 vol. 2019. (History of Our Holidays Ser.). (ENG.). 24p. (gr. 1-2). pap. 9.15 *(978-1-5382-3866-0(7),* dea2952b-388d-429d-8fd4-1f023ef8964a) Stevens, Gareth Publishing LLLP.

Lukes, Bonnie L. John Adams: Public Servant. 2004. (Notable Americans Ser.). (Illus.). 128p. (J). (gr. 6-12). 23.95 *(978-1-883846-80-0(3),* First Biographies) Reynolds, Morgan Inc.

—Woodrow Wilson & the Progressive Era. 2006. (World Leaders Ser.). (Illus.). 192p. (J). (gr. 6-10). lib. bdg. 26.95 *(978-1-931798-79-2(6))* Reynolds, Morgan Inc.

Lusted, Marcia Amidon. Revolution & the New Nation: 1750-Early 1800s. 2007. (Presidents of the United States Ser.). (Illus.). 48p. (J). (gr. 4-7). lib. bdg. 29.05 *(978-1-59036-739-1(1));* per. 10.95 *(978-1-59036-740-7(5))* Weigl Pubs., Inc.

Lynch, Seth. The Emancipation Proclamation, 1 vol. 2018. (Look at U. S. History Ser.). (ENG.). 32p. (J). (gr. 2-2). 28.27 *(978-1-5382-2119-8(5),* 6585d053-970a-4d85-9432-f4efcb166780) Stevens, Gareth Publishing LLLP.

Lynne, Douglas. Contemporary United States: 1968 to the Present. 2007. (Presidents of the United States Ser.). (Illus.). 48p. (J). (gr. 4-7). lib. bdg. 29.05 *(978-1-59036-753-7(7));* per. 10.95 *(978-1-59036-754-4(5))* Weigl Pubs., Inc.

Machajewski, Sarah. Standing in the President's Shoes, 1 vol. 2015. (My Government Ser.). (ENG., Illus.). 32p. (gr. 4-4). pap. 11.58 *(978-1-5026-0460-6(4),* 16b31938-b529-49a8-ad33-17d1d618c0ad) Cavendish Square Publishing LLC.

Magoon, Kekla. Abraham Lincoln, 1 vol. 2007. (Essential Lives Set 1 Ser.). (ENG., Illus.). 112p. (gr. 6-12). lib. bdg. 41.36 *(978-1-59928-839-0(7),* 6631, Essential Library) ABDO Publishing Co.

Maloof, Torrey. Abraham Lincoln: Addressing a Nation. rev. ed. 2017. (Social Studies: Informational Text Ser.). (ENG., Illus.). 32p. (gr. 4-8). pap. 11.99 *(978-1-4938-3805-9(9))* Teacher Created Materials, Inc.

—George Washington & the Men Who Shaped America. rev. ed. 2016. (Social Studies: Informational Text Ser.). (ENG., Illus.). 32p. (gr. 4-8). pap. 11.99 *(978-1-4938-3081-7(3))* Teacher Created Materials, Inc.

—James Madison & the Making of the United States. rev. ed. 2017. (Social Studies: Informational Text Ser.). (ENG., Illus.). 32p. (gr. 4-8). pap. 11.99 *(978-1-4938-3795-3(8))* Teacher Created Materials, Inc.

—Thomas Jefferson & the Empire of Liberty. rev. ed. 2017. (Social Studies: Informational Text Ser.). (ENG., Illus.). 32p. (gr. 4-8). pap. 11.99 *(978-1-4938-3792-2(3))* Teacher Created Materials, Inc.

Mapua, Jeff. Bill & Hillary Clinton, 1 vol. 2014. (Making a Difference: Leaders Who Are Changing the World Ser.). 48p. (YA). (gr. 5-5). (ENG.). 28.41 *(978-1-62275-425-0(5),* e10cbf68-8220-4825-b884-6f256183833c); (ENG.). pap. 15.05 *(978-1-62275-427-4(1),* 09ac0fd0-2ff9-48a5-ad53-c10d0c1c31c3); pap. 84.30 *(978-1-62275-428-1(X))* Rosen Publishing Group, Inc., The.

Mara, Wil. Abraham Lincoln. 2014. (Rookie Biographies(r) Ser.). (ENG.). 32p. (J). lib. bdg. 23.00 *(978-0-531-21058-1(8))* Scholastic Library Publishing.

—Dwight Eisenhower, 1 vol. 2011. (Presidents & Their Times Ser.). (ENG.). 96p. (gr. 6-6). 36.93 *(978-0-7614-4812-9(8),* fbe0cc09-90ad-4c1b-8501-498b0c193ab9) Cavendish Square Publishing LLC.

—Gerald Ford, 1 vol. 2010. (Presidents & Their Times Ser.). (ENG.). 96p. (gr. 6-6). 36.93 *(978-0-7614-3629-4(4),* 40f28fc5-cbd7-405e-8248-dcf8c10a7788) Cavendish Square Publishing LLC.

—Harry Truman, 1 vol. 2012. (Presidents & Their Times Ser.). (ENG., Illus.). 96p. (gr. 6-6). 36.93 *(978-1-60870-185-8(9),* 1e388eab-e112-43b3-81e4-33d929da8328) Cavendish Square Publishing LLC.

—James Garfield, 1 vol. 2012. (Presidents & Their Times Ser.). (ENG.). 96p. (gr. 6-6). 36.93 *(978-1-60870-183-4(2),* b6c2533b-d1a1-4e87-9ecd-733fe6496115) Cavendish Square Publishing LLC.

—John Adams, 1 vol. 2009. (Presidents & Their Times Ser.). (ENG.). 96p. (gr. 6-6). lib. bdg. 36.93 *(978-0-7614-2840-4(2),* 3b9f9669-22b1-48e0-814f-6ca137b38924) Cavendish Square Publishing LLC.

—John F. Kennedy, 1 vol. 2010. (Presidents & Their Times Ser.). (ENG.). 96p. (gr. 6-6). 36.93 *(978-0-7614-3628-7(6),* 467bf370-4420-4ea1-848f-38b72f6db0e4) Cavendish Square Publishing LLC.

—Rookie Biographies: Franklin D. Roosevelt. 2004. (Rookie Biographies Ser.). (ENG., Illus.). 32p. (J). 20.50 *(978-0-516-21844-1(1),* Children's Pr.) Scholastic Library Publishing.

—Rookie Biographies: George W. Bush. 2003. (Rookie Biographies Ser.). (ENG.). 32p. (J). (gr. 1-2). pap. 4.95 *(978-0-516-27838-4(X),* Children's Pr.) Scholastic Library Publishing.

—Theodore Roosevelt. 2007. (Rookie Biographies Ser.). (Illus.). 32p. (J). (gr. 1-2). pap. 4.95 *(978-0-516-27304-4(3),* Children's Pr.) Scholastic Library Publishing.

Marcovitz, Hal. Barack. 2007. (Obamas Ser.). (Illus.). 64p. (YA). (gr. 3-6). pap. 9.95 *(978-1-4222-1484-8(2));* (gr. 4-7). lib. bdg. 19.95 *(978-1-4222-1477-0(X))* Mason Crest.

—Bill Clinton. 2004. (Childhoods of the Presidents Ser.). (Illus.). 48p. (J). (gr. 4-18). lib. bdg. 17.95 *(978-1-59084-273-7(1))* Mason Crest.

—James Monroe. 2004. (Childhoods of the Presidents Ser.). (Illus.). 48p. (J). (gr. 4-18). lib. bdg. 17.95 *(978-1-59084-283-6(9))* Mason Crest.

—John Adams. 2004. (Childhoods of the Presidents Ser.). (Illus.). 48p. (J). (gr. 4-18). lib. bdg. 17.95 *(978-1-59084-268-3(5))* Mason Crest.

—John F. Kennedy. 2004. (Childhood of the Presidents Ser.). (Illus.). 48p. (J). (gr. 4-18). lib. bdg. 17.95 *(978-1-59084-272-0(3))* Mason Crest.

—The Obama Family Tree. 2007. (Obamas Ser.). (Illus.). 64p. (YA). (gr. 3-6). pap. 9.95 *(978-1-4222-1488-6(5));* (gr. 4-7). lib. bdg. 19.95 *(978-1-4222-1481-7(8))* Mason Crest.

—Obama Mania. 2007. (Obamas Ser.). (Illus.). 64p. (YA). (gr. 3-6). pap. 9.95 *(978-1-4222-1489-3(3));* (gr. 4-7). lib. bdg. 19.95 *(978-1-4222-1482-4(6))* Mason Crest.

—Theodore Roosevelt. 2004. (Childhood of the Presidents Ser.). (Illus.). 48p. (J). (gr. 4-18). lib. bdg. 17.95 *(978-1-59084-278-2(2))* Mason Crest.

—The White House: The Home of the U. S. President. Moreno, Barry, ed. 2014. (Patriotic Symbols of America Ser.: 20). 48p. (J). (gr. 4-18). lib. bdg. 20.95 *(978-1-4222-3134-0(8))* Mason Crest.

Margaret, Amy. Franklin D. Roosevelt Library & Museum. 2009. (Presidential Libraries Ser.). 24p. (gr. 3-3). 42.50 *(978-1-60851-483-0(8),* PowerKids Pr.) Rosen Publishing Group, Inc., The.

—George Bush Presidential Library. 2009. (Presidential Libraries Ser.). 24p. (gr. 3-3). 42.50 *(978-1-60851-484-7(6),* PowerKids Pr.) Rosen Publishing Group, Inc., The.

—Gerald R. Ford Library & Museum. 2009. (Presidential Libraries Ser.). 24p. (gr. 3-3). 42.50 *(978-1-60851-485-4(4),* PowerKids Pr.) Rosen Publishing Group, Inc., The.

—Ronald Reagan Presidential Library. (Presidential Libraries Ser.). 24p. (gr. 3-3). 2009. 42.50 *(978-1-60851-488-5(9))* 2003. (ENG., Illus.). (J). lib. bdg. 26.27 *(978-0-8239-6272-3(5),* 82b1aa28-ee96-4b10-920c-2b991a063138) Rosen Publishing Group, Inc., The. (PowerKids Pr.).

Markel, Rita J. Grover Cleveland. 2006. (Presidential Leaders Ser.). (Illus.). 112p. (J). (gr. 3-7). lib. bdg. 29.27 *(978-0-8225-1494-7(X),* Lerner Pubns.) Lerner Publishing Group.

Markovics, Joyce. White & Majestic: What Am I? 2018. (American Place Puzzlers Ser.). (ENG.). 24p. (J). (gr. -1-3). E-Book 41.36 *(978-1-68402-543-5(5))* Bearport Publishing Co., Inc.

Markovics, Joyce L. White & Majestic: What Am I? 2018. (American Place Puzzlers Ser.). (ENG.). 24p. (J). (gr. -1-3). lib. bdg. 26.99 *(978-1-68402-485-8(4))* Bearport Publishing Co., Inc.

Marquez, Heron. George W. Bush. 2005. (Presidential Leaders Ser.). (Illus.). 112p. (J). (gr. 6-12). lib. bdg. 29.27 *(978-0-8225-1507-4(5),* Lerner Pubns.) Lerner Publishing Group.

—Richard M. Nixon. 2003. (Presidential Leaders Ser.). (Illus.). 112p. (J). 29.27 *(978-0-8225-0098-8(1),* Lerner Pubns.) Lerner Publishing Group.

Marrin, Albert. FDR & the American Crisis. (Illus.). 336p. (YA). (gr. 7). 2016. pap. 15.99 *(978-0-385-75362-3(4),* Ember) 2015. 24.99 *(978-0-385-75359-3(4),* Knopf Bks. for Young Readers) Random Hse. Children's Bks.

Marsh, Carole. Andrew Jackson. 2003. 12p. (gr. k-4). 2.95 *(978-0-635-02360-5(1))* Gallopade International.

—Barack Obama: Biography FunBook. 2009. (J). (gr. 2-9). pap. 3.99 *(978-0-635-07053-1(7))* Gallopade International.

—Barack Obama - America's 44th President. 2009. (Here & Now Ser.). 40p. (J). (gr. 2-9). 29.99 *(978-0-635-06983-2(0))* Gallopade International.

—Barack Obama Presidential Coloring Book! 2008. (Here & Now Ser.). (J). 5.99 *(978-0-635-07050-0(2))* Gallopade International.

—I'm Reading about Donald Trump: America's 45th President. 2017. (I'm Reading About Ser.). (ENG., Illus.). (J). pap. 7.99 *(978-0-635-12564-4(1));* lib. bdg. 24.99 *(978-0-635-12565-1(X))* Gallopade International.

—John Adams. 2003. 12p. (gr. k-4). 2.95 *(978-0-635-02357-5(1))* Gallopade International.

—John F. Kennedy. 2003. 12p. (gr. k-4). 2.95 *(978-0-635-02127-4(7))* Gallopade International.

—The Obama Family - Life in the White House: President Barack Obama, First Lady Michelle Obama, First Children Malia & Sasha. 2008. (Here & Now Ser.). 32p. (J). (gr. 2-9). pap. 8.99 *(978-0-635-07051-7(0))* Gallopade International.

—Theodore Roosevelt. 2004. 12p. (gr. k-4). 2.95 *(978-0-635-02362-9(8))* Gallopade International.

Marsico, Katie. Andrew Jackson, 1 vol. 2011. (Presidents & Their Times Ser.). (ENG.). 96p. (gr. 6-6). 36.93 *(978-0-7614-4813-6(6),* fd698aa9-6430-4c86-ad70-db96aebfbad4) Cavendish Square Publishing LLC.

—Ronald Reagan, 1 vol. 2011. (Presidents & Their Times Ser.). (ENG.). 96p. (gr. 6-6). 36.93 *(978-0-7614-4814-3(4),* a120eb10-6f7c-4e8f-ab7d-8a44a1d07704) Cavendish Square Publishing LLC.

—Woodrow Wilson, 1 vol. 2011. (Presidents & Their Times Ser.). (ENG.). 96p. (gr. 6-6). 36.93 *(978-0-7614-4815-0(2),* 03eb9ec5-0cf2-4556-9379-b3d42426852e) Cavendish Square Publishing LLC.

Mattern, David B. James Madison: Patriot, Politician, & President, 1 vol. 2004. (Library of American Lives & Times Ser.). (ENG., Illus.). 112p. (gr. 5-5). lib. bdg. 38.27 *(978-1-4042-2648-7(6),* 897734e1-fb85-40c8-bb97-6177b50e76ca) Rosen Publishing Group, Inc., The.

Mattern, Joanne. Air Force One: The President's Plane. 2014. (Rookie Read-About(r) American Symbols Ser.). (ENG.). 32p. (J). pap. 5.95 *(978-0-531-21841-9(4));* lib. bdg. *(978-0-531-21568-5(7))* Scholastic Library Publishing.

—Barack Obama. 2013. (Rookie Biographies(r) Ser.). (ENG.). 32p. (J). pap. 5.95 *(978-0-531-24701-3(5));* lib. bdg. 23.00 *(978-0-531-24735-8(X))* Scholastic Library Publishing.

—President Donald Trump. 2017. (Rookie Biographies(tm) Ser.). (ENG., Illus.). 32p. (J). lib. bdg. 25.00 *(978-0-531-23226-2(3),* Children's Pr.) Scholastic Library Publishing.

—Rookie Biographies: President Donald Trump. 2017. (Rookie Biographies Ser.). (ENG., Illus.). 32p. (J). pap. 5.95 *(978-0-531-23860-8(1),* Children's Pr.) Scholastic Library Publishing.

—A True Book: President Donald Trump. 2017. (True Book(tm), A — Biographies Ser.). (ENG., Illus.). 48p. (J). 31.00 *(978-0-531-22718-3(9));* pap. 7.95 *(978-0-531-23014-5(7))* Scholastic Library Publishing. (Children's Pr.).

Matthas, Seth. A President's Job: Understanding Government, 1 vol. 2018. (Civics for the Real World Ser.). (ENG.). 16p. (gr. 2-3). pap. *(978-1-5383-6525-0(1),* 64426e68-237c-4f60-8923-f1a8bca7a650, Rosen Classroom) Rosen Publishing Group, Inc., The.

McAuliffe, Bill. The Presidential Cabinet. 2016. (By the People Ser.). (ENG., Illus.). 48p. (J). (gr. 4-7). pap. 12.00 *(978-1-62832-269-9(1),* 20570, Creative Paperbacks) Creative Co., The.

—The U. S. Presidency. 2016. (By the People Ser.). (ENG., Illus.). 48p. (J). (gr. 4-7). pap. 12.00 *(978-1-62832-272-9(1),* 20576, Creative Paperbacks) Creative Co., The.

—The U.S. Presidency. 2016. (By the People Ser.). (ENG., Illus.). 48p. (J). (gr. 4-7). 39.95 *(978-1-60818-676-1(8),* 20578, Creative Education) Creative Co., The.

Mcdonough, Yona Zeldis. Quien Fue John F. Kennedy? (Who Was John F. Kennedy?) 2018. (Who Was... ? Ser.). lib. bdg. 20.85 *(978-0-606-41276-6(X))* Turtleback.

McDowell, Pamela. James Madison. 2015. (Padres Fundadores Ser.). (SPA.). (J). lib. bdg. 27.13 *(978-1-4896-2796-4(0),* AV2 by Weigl) Weigl Pubs., Inc.

McLeese, Don. Thomas Jefferson. 2005. (Heroes of the American Revolution Ser.). (Illus.). 32p. (gr. 2-5). 19.95 *(978-1-59515-217-6(2))* Rourke Educational Media.

McPherson, Stephanie. My Dear Husband: Important Letters of Abigail Adams. 2009. (Great Moments in American History Ser.). 32p. (gr. 3-3). 47.90 *(978-1-61513-134-1(5))* Rosen Publishing Group, Inc., The.

McPherson, Stephanie Sammartino. Bill Clinton. 2009. pap. 52.95 *(978-0-7613-4960-0(X))* 2008. (ENG.). 48p. (gr. 3-6). 27.93 *(978-0-8225-7986-1(3),* Lerner Pubns.) Lerner Publishing Group.

—Theodore Roosevelt. 2005. (Presidential Leaders Ser.). (Illus.). 112p. (J). 29.27 *(978-0-8225-0999-8(7),* Lerner Pubns.) Lerner Publishing Group.

Mead, Wendy. William H. Taft, 1 vol. 2012. (Presidents & Their Times Ser.). (ENG.). 96p. (gr. 6-6). 36.93 *(978-1-60870-186-5(7),* c3f6f76c-90ed-45ce-9fab-680c514e816d) Cavendish Square Publishing LLC.

Meltzer, Brad. I Am Abraham Lincoln. Eliopoulos, Christopher, illus. 2014. (Ordinary People Change the World Ser.). 40p. (J). (gr. k-4). 15.99 *(978-0-8037-4083-9(2),* Dial Bks) Penguin Young Readers Group.

—I Am George Washington. Eliopoulos, Christopher, illus. 2016. (Ordinary People Change the World Ser.). 40p. (J). (gr. k-4). 15.99 *(978-0-525-42848-0(8),* Dial Bks) Penguin Young Readers Group.

Metzger, Steve & Kronheimer, Ann. Lincoln & Grace: Why Abraham Lincoln Grew a Beard: Why Abraham Lincoln Grew a Beard. 2013. (ENG.). 40p. (J). (gr. 2-5). pap. 6.99 *(978-0-545-48432-9(4))* Scholastic, Inc.

Mikoley, Kate. George Washington Wasn't the First President: Exposing Myths about US Presidents. 2019. (Exposed! More Myths about American History Ser.). (ENG.). 32p. (gr. 2-3). 63.00 *(978-1-5382-3751-9(2))* Stevens, Gareth Publishing LLLP.

Miller, Amanda. What Does the President Do? 2009. (Scholastic News Nonfiction Readers Ser.). (Illus.). 24p. (J). (gr. 1-2). 22.00 *(978-0-531-21088-8(X))* Scholastic Library Publishing.

Miller, Brandon Marie. George Washington for Kids: His Life & Times with 21 Activities. 2007. (For Kids Ser.: 22). (ENG., Illus.). 144p. (J). (gr. 4-7). pap. 18.99 *(978-1-55652-655-8(5))* Chicago Review Pr., Inc.

—Thomas Jefferson for Kids: His Life & Times with 21 Activities. 2011. (For Kids Ser.: 37). (ENG., Illus.). 144p. (J). (gr. 4). pap. 16.95 *(978-1-56976-348-3(8))* Chicago Review Pr., Inc.

Miller, Derek. Executive Orders, 1 vol. 2018. (How Government Works). (ENG.). 64p. (J). (gr. 5-5). pap. 16.28 *(978-1-5026-4059-8(7),* 7f7ef42d-e930-48b0-8cd1-6a14bf040f1e) Cavendish Square Publishing LLC.

Mills, Nathan & Kawa, Katie. Barack Obama: First African American President, 1 vol. 2012. (Rosen Readers Ser.). (ENG., Illus.). 24p. (J). (gr. 1-2). pap. 8.25 *(978-1-4488-8845-0(X),* ea0c8872-d080-4456-9eee-8359b89c1646, Rosen Classroom) Rosen Publishing Group, Inc., The.

Mis, M. S. How to Draw the Life & Times of Franklin Delano Roosevelt. 2009. (Kid's Guide to Drawing the Presidents of the United States of America Ser.). 32p. (gr. 4-4). 50.50 *(978-1-61511-136-7(0),* PowerKids Pr.) Rosen Publishing Group, Inc., The.

—How to Draw the Life & Times of Lyndon B. Johnson. 2009. (Kid's Guide to Drawing the Presidents of the United States of America Ser.). 32p. (gr. 4-4). 50.50 *(978-1-61511-154-1(9),* PowerKids Pr.) Rosen Publishing Group, Inc., The.

—How to Draw the Life & Times of Ronald Reagan. 2009. (Kid's Guide to Drawing the Presidents of the United States of America Ser.). 32p. (gr. 4-4). 50.50 *(978-1-61511-158-9(1),* PowerKids Pr.) Rosen Publishing Group, Inc., The.

—How to Draw the Life & Times of Woodrow Wilson. 2009. (Kid's Guide to Drawing the Presidents of the United States of America Ser.). 32p. (gr. 4-4). 50.50 *(978-1-61511-168-8(9),* PowerKids Pr.) Rosen Publishing Group, Inc., The.

Mis, Melody S. How to Draw the Life & Times of Andrew Jackson. (Kid's Guide to Drawing the Presidents of the United States of America Ser.). 32p. (gr. 4-4). 2009. 50.50 *(978-1-61511-131-2(X),* PowerKids Pr.) 2005. (ENG.). (YA). 30.27 *(978-1-4042-2984-6(1),* 9f2575b6-163f-468c-b48f-ad0b5dd3d467) Rosen Publishing Group, Inc., The.

—How to Draw the Life & Times of Benjamin Harrison. (Kid's Guide to Drawing the Presidents of the United States of America Ser.). 32p. (gr. 4-4). 2009. 50.50 *(978-1-61511-133-6(6),* PowerKids Pr.) 2005. (ENG., Illus.). (YA). 30.27 *(978-1-4042-3000-2(9),* ad12cfdf-aefb-413c-99ac-784bab7a44ac) Rosen Publishing Group, Inc., The.

—How to Draw the Life & Times of Franklin Delano Roosevelt, 1 vol. 2005. (Kid's Guide to Drawing the Presidents of the United States of America Ser.). (ENG., Illus.). 32p. (YA). (gr. 4-4). 30.27 *(978-1-4042-3008-8(4),* 4a6b2a2d-17e9-42d2-bd59-e1e04aa5593e) Rosen Publishing Group, Inc., The.

—How to Draw the Life & Times of James Buchanan. (Kid's Guide to Drawing the Presidents of the United States of America Ser.). 32p. (gr. 4-4). 2009. 50.50 *(978-1-61511-146-6(8),* PowerKids Pr.) 2005. (ENG.). (YA). 30.27 *(978-1-4042-2992-1(2),* b45eb2a1-8dd1-46a2-882d-b7a427fdd9a3) Rosen Publishing Group, Inc., The.

—How to Draw the Life & Times of James K. Polk. (Kid's Guide to Drawing the Presidents of the United States of America Ser.). 32p. (gr. 4-4). 2009. 50.50 *(978-1-61511-147-3(6),* PowerKids Pr.) 2005. (ENG.). (YA). 30.27 *(978-1-4042-2988-4(4),* 32d91457-792d-434a-b46f-3f83ffa4adcb) Rosen Publishing Group, Inc., The.

—How to Draw the Life & Times of Lyndon B. Johnson, 1 vol. 2005. (Kid's Guide to Drawing the Presidents of the United States of America Ser.). (ENG., Illus.). 32p. (YA). (gr. 4-4). 30.27 *(978-1-4042-3012-5(2),* d67b7c7f-fbff-4357-a198-f971f81927bc) Rosen Publishing Group, Inc., The.

—How to Draw the Life & Times of Ronald Reagan, 1 vol. 2005. (Kid's Guide to Drawing the Presidents of the United States of America Ser.). (ENG., Illus.). 32p. (YA). (gr. 4-4). 30.27 *(978-1-4042-3016-3(5),* 7e454ea0-edb8-4ce5-a3a4-8ec6be2e3e2c) Rosen Publishing Group, Inc., The.

—How to Draw the Life & Times of Rutherford B. Hayes. (Kid's Guide to Drawing the Presidents of the United States of America Ser.). 32p. (gr. 4-4). 2009. 50.50 *(978-1-61511-159-6(X),* PowerKids Pr.) 2005. (ENG., Illus.). (J). 30.27 *(978-1-4042-2996-9(5),* 61a26fdb-fef6-496d-87f0-9bc8963fc562) Rosen Publishing Group, Inc., The.

—How to Draw the Life & Times of Thomas Jefferson. 2009. (Kid's Guide to Drawing the Presidents of the United States of America Ser.). 32p. (gr. 4-4). 50.50 *(978-1-61511-161-9(1),* PowerKids Pr.) Rosen Publishing Group, Inc., The.

—How to Draw the Life & Times of Woodrow Wilson, 1 vol. 2005. (Kid's Guide to Drawing the Presidents of the United States of America Ser.). (ENG., Illus.). 32p. (YA). (gr. 4-4). 30.27 *(978-1-4042-3004-0(1),* 242bf2d5-bd7f-402d-87e1-47edfe543e9b) Rosen Publishing Group, Inc., The.

Moberg, Julia. Presidential Pets: The Weird, Wacky, Little, Big, Scary, Strange Animals That Have Lived in the White House. 2012. 96p. pap. 14.95 *(978-1-60734-471-1(8))* Charlesbridge Publishing, Inc.

—Presidential Pets: the Weird, Wacky, Little, Big, Scary, Strange Animals That Have Lived in the White House. Jeff Albrecht Studios, Jeff Albrecht, illus. 2016. 96p. (J). (gr. 3-7). pap. 9.95 *(978-1-62354-086-9(0))* Charlesbridge Publishing, Inc.

Modifica, Lisa. A Timeline of the White House. (Timelines of American History Ser.). 32p. (gr. 4-4). 2009. 47.90 *(978-1-60854-393-9(5))* 2004. (ENG., Illus.). lib. bdg. 29.13 *(978-0-8239-4543-6(X),* d525a8ac-c718-47fa-8248-0b89d5f2071f) Rosen Publishing Group, Inc., The. (Rosen Reference).

Mooney, Carla. George Washington: 25 Great Projects You Can Build Yourself. Carbaugh, Samuel, illus. 2010. (Build It Yourself Ser.). (ENG.). 128p. (J). (gr. 3-7). 21.95 *(978-1-934670-64-4(2),* 14bb8ad7-0628-4a6b-8e67-672face52822) Nomad Pr.

Morlock, Rachael. Barack Obama: A Life of Leadership, 1 vol. annot. ed. 2019. (People in the News Ser.). (ENG.). 104p. (gr. 7-7). pap. 20.99 *(978-1-5345-6840-2(9),* 1dbae1b7-6a06-489e-8227-e56a3ac990bb); lib. bdg. 41.03 *(978-1-5345-6841-9(7),* ca00a648-b9d2-4f3f-ae82-795d317aa70f) Greenhaven Publishing LLC. (Lucent Pr.).

Morlock, Theresa. Before Abraham Lincoln Was President, 1 vol. 2017. (Before They Were President Ser.). (ENG.). 24p. (J). (gr. 2-3). pap. 9.15 *(978-1-5382-1056-7(8),* 8cbab250-9a8d-4368-9727-89120df16c3b) Stevens, Gareth Publishing LLLP.

Morris, Deborah & Morris, Larry. American History: Presidents: Grade 4-5. Carlson, Andy, illus. 2005. (Skill Builders (Rainbow Bridge Publishing) Ser.). 80p. per. 3.99 *(978-1-59441-267-7(7),* RB-904000) Carson-Dellosa Publishing, LLC.

Mulhall, Jill K. James Madison, 1 vol. rev. ed. 2005. (Social Studies: Informational Text Ser.). (ENG.). 24p. (gr. 4-8). pap. 10.99 *(978-0-7439-8908-4(2))* Teacher Created Materials, Inc.

—Thomas Jefferson, 1 vol. rev. ed. 2004. (Social Studies: Informational Text Ser.). (ENG.). 24p. (gr. 4-8). pap. 10.99 *(978-0-7439-8747-9(0))* Teacher Created Materials, Inc.

Murphy, Frank. George Washington & the General's Dog. Walz, Richard, illus. 2015. 48p. pap. 5.00 *(978-1-61003-605-4(0))* Center for the Collaborative Classroom.

—George Washington & the General's Dog. 2003. (J). 1.25 *(978-1-4025-4103-2(1))* Recorded Bks., Inc.

—Thomas Jefferson's Feast. Walz, Richard, illus. 2004. (Step into Reading Ser.). 48p. 14.00 *(978-0-7569-3235-0(1))* Perfection Learning Corp.

Murray, Julie. President. 2017. (My Government Ser.). (ENG., Illus.). 24p. (J). (gr. -1-2). lib. bdg. 31.36 *(978-1-5321-0399-5(9),* 26525, Abdo Kids) ABDO Publishing Co.

Naden, Corinne J. & Blue, Rose. James Monroe, 1 vol. 2009. (Presidents & Their Times Ser.). (ENG.). 96p. (gr. 6-6). lib. bdg. 36.93 *(978-0-7614-2838-1(0),* e4f2cacd-fce0-428c-9759-526bc3220fdb) Cavendish Square Publishing LLC.

Nagelhout, Ryan. Before Donald Trump Was President, 1 vol. 2017. (Before They Were President Ser.). (ENG.). 24p. (J). (gr. 2-3). pap. 9.15 *(978-1-5382-1064-2(9),* 3e0a1dcc-caeb-4c75-a338-e2a712d99cd5); lib. bdg. 24.27 *(978-1-5382-1066-6(5),* 7d4d45f5-1c41-432c-a773-1fda7f91527c) Stevens, Gareth Publishing LLLP.

—20 Fun Facts about the White House, 1 vol. 2013. (Fun Fact File: U. S. History! Ser.). (ENG.). 32p. (J). (gr. 2-3). pap. 11.50 *(978-1-4339-9204-9(3),* 1bf1c4bf-cd86-47c6-b2ab-6fa6c844db87) Stevens, Gareth Publishing LLLP.

Nagle, Jeanne. How George Washington Fought the Revolutionary War, 1 vol. 2017. (Presidents at War Ser.). (ENG.). 128p. (gr. 8-8). lib. bdg. 38.93 *(978-0-7660-8523-7(6),* 525f9128-4e87-4008-8471-cda23af7b720) Enslow Publishing, LLC.

N.C.B.L.A. Our White House: Looking In, Looking Out. 2010. (ENG., Illus.). 256p. (J). (gr. 5). pap. 16.99 *(978-0-7636-4609-7(1))* Candlewick Pr.

Nelson, Maria. The Life of Abraham Lincoln, 1 vol. 2012. (Famous Lives Ser.). (ENG., Illus.). 24p. (J). (gr. 1-2). pap. 9.15 *(978-1-4339-6343-8(4),* 35b633d2-3bab-4aff-b2f9-48b3fbaf0130); lib. bdg. 25.27 *(978-1-4339-6341-4(8),* 2e73a321-4531-40ed-b3a9-a2ce545666ac) Stevens, Gareth Publishing LLLP.

—The Life of Abraham Lincoln / la Vida de Abraham Lincoln, 1 vol. 2012. (Famous Lives / Vidas Extraordinarias Ser.). (ENG & SPA., Illus.). 24p. (J). (gr. 1-2). 25.27 *(978-1-4339-6651-4(4),* f9d4d72c-d9cb-4703-8cc6-fafb97e5a16e) Stevens, Gareth Publishing LLLP.

—The Life of George Washington, 1 vol. 2012. (Famous Lives Ser.). (ENG.). 24p. (J). (gr. 1-2). pap. 9.15 *(978-1-4339-6351-3(5),* 04b50bd1-3b14-4e89-9569-56cc24340b3d) Stevens, Gareth Publishing LLLP.

—The Life of George Washington / la Vida de George Washington, 1 vol. 2012. (Famous Lives / Vidas Extraordinarias Ser.). (ENG & SPA., Illus.). 24p. (J). (gr. 1-2). 25.27 *(978-1-4339-6655-2(7),* f4783f2b-ef40-42a4-bf3c-4941cf9ca8de) Stevens, Gareth Publishing LLLP.

Nelson, Robin. George Washington: A Life of Leadership. 2006. (Pull Ahead Bks.). (Illus.). 32p. (J). (gr. 3-7). lib. bdg. 22.60 *(978-0-8225-3474-7(6),* Lerner Pubns.) Lerner Publishing Group.

—George Washington: Una Vida de Liderazgo. 2006. (Libros para Avanzar Ser.). (ENG & SPA., Illus.). 32p. (J). (gr. 3-7). lib. bdg. 22.60 *(978-0-8225-6235-1(9),* Ediciones Lerner) Lerner Publishing Group.

—George Washington: Una vida de liderazgo (A Life of Leadership) 2006. (Libros para Avanzar-Biografías (Pull Ahead Books-Biographies Ser.). (Illus.). 32p. (J). (gr. -1-3). per. 6.95 *(978-0-8225-6555-0(2),* Ediciones Lerner) Lerner Publishing Group.

Nicolay, Helen. The Boys' Life of Abraham Lincoln. 2007. 136p. per. *(978-1-4065-4046-8(3))* Dodo Pr.

—The Boys Life of Abraham Lincoln. 2004. 192p. per. 15.95 *(978-1-59540-991-1(2),* 1st World Library - Literary Society) 1st World Publishing, Inc.

Norwich, Grace. I Am George Washington (I Am #5) 2012. (I Am Ser.: 5). (ENG.). 128p. (J). (gr. 3-5). pap. 5.99 *(978-0-545-48435-0(9))* Scholastic, Inc.

Oachs, Emily Rose. Thomas Jefferson's Presidency. 2016. (Presidential Powerhouses Ser.). (ENG., Illus.). 104p. (YA). (gr. 6-12). 35.99 *(978-1-4677-7923-4(7),* f04c63b9-b37c-4da8-81b6-da668eacffa, Lerner Pubns.) Lerner Publishing Group.

Obama, Barack. Our Enduring Spirit: President Barack Obama's First Words to America. Ruth, Greg, illus. 2009. 48p. (J). lib. bdg. 18.89 *(978-0-06-183456-1(4))* HarperCollins Pubs.

O'Connor, Jane. If the Walls Could Talk: Family Life at the White House. Hovland, Gary, illus. 2004. (ENG.). 48p. (J). (gr. 1-4). 19.99 *(978-0-689-86863-4(4),* Simon & Schuster/Paula Wiseman Bks.) Simon & Schuster/Paula Wiseman Bks.

Olesen, Andrew. George Washington: The First President of the United States, 1 vol. 2015. (Spotlight on American History Ser.). (ENG., Illus.). 24p. (J). (gr. 4-6). pap. 11.00 *(978-1-4994-1751-7(9),* 4fbc47f3-6d10-49d7-bbac-8141eaab4641, PowerKids Pr.) Rosen Publishing Group, Inc., The.

Olson, Nathan. John F. Kennedy: American Visionary, 1 vol. Bascle, Brian, illus. 2007. (Graphic Biographies Ser.). (ENG.). 32p. (J). (gr. 3-9). per. 8.10 *(978-0-7368-7904-0(8),* 93901) Capstone.

O'Neal, Claire. What's So Great about Barack Obama. 2009. (What's So Great About... ? Ser.). 32p. (J). (gr. 2-4). lib. bdg. 25.70 *(978-1-58415-830-1(1))* Mitchell Lane Pubs.

Oney, Yannick. Abe Lincoln: President for the People. 2005. (World Discovery History Readers Ser.). (Illus.). 32p. (J). pap. *(978-0-439-66556-8(6))* Scholastic, Inc.

Orr, Tamra. Ronald Reagan. 2004. (Childhoods of the Presidents Ser.). (Illus.). 48p. (J). (gr. 4-18). lib. bdg. 17.95 *(978-1-59084-280-5(4))* Mason Crest.

Osborne, Mary Pope & Boyce, Natalie Pope. Abraham Lincoln: A Nonfiction Companion to Magic Tree House Merlin Mission #19: Abe Lincoln at Last. Murdocca, Sal, illus. 2011. (Magic Tree House (R) Fact Tracker Ser.: 25). 128p. (J). (gr. 2-5). 6.99 *(978-0-375-87024-8(5),* Random Hse. Bks. for Young Readers) Random Hse. Children's Bks.

Otfinoski, Steven. Calvin Coolidge, 1 vol. 2009. (Presidents & Their Times Ser.). (ENG.). 96p. (gr. 6-6). lib. bdg. 36.93 *(978-0-7614-2836-7(4),* cb4552eb-4174-4f33-af09-b9be6fa8978e) Cavendish Square Publishing LLC.

—Chester Arthur, 1 vol. 2010. (Presidents & Their Times Ser.). (ENG.). 96p. (gr. 6-6). 36.93 *(978-0-7614-3625-6(1),* 9a6cdf39-a798-4217-a1e7-87fe1f5d246a) Cavendish Square Publishing LLC.

—Grover Cleveland, 1 vol. 2011. (Presidents & Their Times Ser.). (ENG.). 96p. (gr. 6-6). 36.93 *(978-0-7614-4811-2(X),* 5b89a4d8-b2d1-48b8-b613-51b12e079d94) Cavendish Square Publishing LLC.

—Rutherford B. Hayes. 2004. (Encyclopedia of Presidents Ser.). (ENG., Illus.). 112p. (J). (gr. 5-9). 34.00 *(978-0-516-22866-2(8))* Scholastic Library Publishing.

—Zachary Taylor, 1 vol. 2012. (Presidents & Their Times Ser.). (ENG., Illus.). 96p. (gr. 6-6). 36.93 *(978-1-60870-187-2(5),* 593983e0-e8e3-4513-8e82-b2c01b38c1ca) Cavendish Square Publishing LLC.

Our Presidents & First Ladies of the White House. 119.40 *(978-0-8249-6046-9(7),* Ideals Pubns.) Worthy Publishing.

Owen, John. #Presidents: Follow the Leaders. 2015. (Illus.). 115p. (J). pap. *(978-0-545-85127-5(0))* Scholastic, Inc.

Pace, Betty. Abraham Lincoln. Walker, Bobbie H., illus. 2008. 32p. pap. 12.99 *(978-1-4343-7969-5(8))* AuthorHouse.

Pagel-Hogan, Elizabeth. So You Want to Be President of the United States. 2019. (Being in Government Ser.). (ENG., Illus.). 32p. (J). (gr. 3-6). pap. 7.95 *(978-1-5435-7530-9(7),* 141061); lib. bdg. 27.99 *(978-1-5435-7194-3(8),* 140439) Capstone.

Palmer, Erin. U. S. Presidents. 2017. (Weird, True Facts Ser.). (ENG.). 32p. (gr. 4-8). 32.79 *(978-1-68342-367-6(4),* 9781683423676) Rourke Educational Media.

Panchyk, Richard. Franklin Delano Roosevelt for Kids: His Life & Times with 21 Activities. 2007. (For Kids Ser.: 24). (ENG., Illus.). 160p. (J). (gr. 4-8). pap. 14.95 *(978-1-55652-657-2(1))* Chicago Review Pr., Inc.

Parachini, Jodie. The Complete Guide to U.S. Presidents. 2015. (Illus.). 144p. (J). *(978-1-4351-6169-6(6))* Barnes & Noble, Inc.

Parker, Christi E. Abraham Lincoln, 1 vol. rev. ed. 2005. (Social Studies: Informational Text Ser.). (ENG.). 24p. (gr. 4-8). pap. 10.99 *(978-0-7439-8916-9(3))* Teacher Created Materials, Inc.

—George Washington, 1 vol. rev. ed. 2004. (Social Studies: Informational Text Ser.). (ENG.). 24p. (gr. 4-8). pap. 10.99 *(978-0-7439-8749-3(7))* Teacher Created Materials, Inc.

Parker, Lewis. How to Draw the Life & Times of George H. W. Bush. 2009. (Kid's Guide to Drawing the Presidents of the United States of America Ser.). 32p. (gr. 4-4). 50.50 *(978-1-61511-138-1(7),* PowerKids Pr.) Rosen Publishing Group, Inc., The.

—How to Draw the Life & Times of Harry S. Truman. 2009. (Kid's Guide to Drawing the Presidents of the United States of America Ser.). 32p. (gr. 4-4). 50.50 *(978-1-61511-143-5(3),* PowerKids Pr.) Rosen Publishing Group, Inc., The.

—How to Draw the Life & Times of James A. Garfield. 2009. (Kid's Guide to Drawing the Presidents of the United States of America Ser.). 32p. (gr. 4-4). 50.50 *(978-1-61511-145-9(X),* PowerKids Pr.) Rosen Publishing Group, Inc., The.

—How to Draw the Life & Times of Richard M. Nixon. 2009. (Kid's Guide to Drawing the Presidents of the United States of America Ser.). 32p. (gr. 4-4). 50.50 *(978-1-61511-157-2(3),* PowerKids Pr.) Rosen Publishing Group, Inc., The.

—How to Draw the Life & Times of Warren G. Harding. 2009. (Kid's Guide to Drawing the Presidents of the United States of America Ser.). 32p. (gr. 4-4). 50.50 *(978-1-61511-163-3(8),* PowerKids Pr.) Rosen Publishing Group, Inc., The.

—How to Draw the Life & Times of William Mckinley. 2009. (Kid's Guide to Drawing the Presidents of the United States of America Ser.). 32p. (gr. 4-4). 50.50 *(978-1-61511-167-1(0),* PowerKids Pr.) Rosen Publishing Group, Inc., The.

Parker, Lewis K. How to Draw the Life & Times of George H. W. Bush, 1 vol. 2005. (Kid's Guide to Drawing the Presidents of the United States of America Ser.). (ENG., Illus.). 32p. (J). (gr. 4-4). 30.27 *(978-1-4042-3017-0(3),* 18065570-1076-47f0-a3c3-e3149a8b9b0e) Rosen Publishing Group, Inc., The.

—How to Draw the Life & Times of Harry S. Truman, 1 vol. 2005. (Kid's Guide to Drawing the Presidents of the United States of America Ser.). (ENG., Illus.). 32p. (YA). (gr. 4-4). lib. bdg. 30.27 *(978-1-4042-3009-5(2),* 5bcc9da0-a969-4832-8968-c374049d2fcc) Rosen Publishing Group, Inc., The.

—How to Draw the Life & Times of James A. Garfield, 1 vol. 2005. (Kid's Guide to Drawing the Presidents of the United States of America Ser.). (ENG.). 32p. (YA). (gr. 4-4). 30.27 *(978-1-4042-2997-6(3),* 99a9c8f7-1b1e-4782-bb8c-49e4b3385b08) Rosen Publishing Group, Inc., The.

—How to Draw the Life & Times of Warren G. Harding, 1 vol. 2005. (Kid's Guide to Drawing the Presidents of the United States of America Ser.). (ENG., Illus.). 32p. (J). (gr. 4-4). 30.27 *(978-1-4042-3005-7(X),* 93d17962-c3ed-458f-bfc7-756e3e6d030d) Rosen Publishing Group, Inc., The.

—How to Draw the Life & Times of William McKinley, 1 vol. 2005. (Kid's Guide to Drawing the Presidents of the United States of America Ser.). (ENG., Illus.). 32p. (YA). (gr. 4-4). 30.27 *(978-1-4042-3001-9(7),* 4b41591a-019f-47db-a80e-4e2ffb0aff5b) Rosen Publishing Group, Inc., The.

Pascal, Janet B. & Who HQ. Who Was Abraham Lincoln? O'Brien, John, illus. 2008. (Who Was? Ser.). 112p. (J). (gr. 3-7). pap. 5.99 *(978-0-448-44886-2(6),* Penguin Workshop) Penguin Young Readers Group.

Patrick, Bethanne Kelly. Ulysses S. Grant. 2004. (Childhoods of the Presidents Ser.). (Illus.). 48p. (J). (gr. 4-18). lib. bdg. 17.95 *(978-1-59084-276-8(6))* Mason Crest.

Peacock, L. A. The Truth (and Myths) about the Presidents. Wigsby, Nick, illus. 2014. 94p. (J). pap. *(978-0-545-56848-7(X))* Scholastic, Inc.

Peckham, Howard Henry. William Henry Harrison, Young Tippecanoe: Childhood of Famous Americans Series. Laune, Paul, illus. 2011. 190p. 42.95 *(978-1-258-07766-2(3))* Literary Licensing, LLC.

Pelleschi, Andrea. George Washington, 1 vol. 2012. (Jr. Graphic Founding Fathers Ser.). (ENG., Illus.). 24p. (J). (gr. 2-3). pap. 11.60 *(978-1-4488-7991-5(4),* af978e28-1877-4c21-8638-55bad2dc85c0); lib. bdg. 28.93 *(978-1-4488-7897-0(7),* bc4d46dd-3b20-4d80-b64a-a9f9f821ad5d) Rosen Publishing Group, Inc., The. (PowerKids Pr.).

—Thomas Jefferson, 1 vol. 2012. (Jr. Graphic Founding Fathers Ser.). (ENG., Illus.). 24p. (J). (gr. 2-3). pap. 11.60 *(978-1-4488-7994-6(9),* c5665c08-ef12-44d8-9855-490e1be876af); lib. bdg. 28.93 *(978-1-4488-7900-7(0),* abe1e8b1-36a7-402f-9565-b3e200393a16) Rosen Publishing Group, Inc., The. (PowerKids Pr.).

Peppas, Lynn. Presidents' Day. 2009. (Celebrations in My World Ser.). (ENG., Illus.). 32p. (J). (gr. k-2). pap. *(978-0-7787-4774-1(3));* (gr. 1-3). *(978-0-7787-4756-7(5))* Crabtree Publishing Co.

—Why Anson Jones Matters to Texas, 1 vol. 2013. (Texas Perspectives Ser.). (ENG., Illus.). 32p. (J). (gr. 4-4). lib. bdg. 28.93 *(978-1-4777-0911-5(8),* 92d13227-1293-4a6c-9ba9-4e668df35827) Rosen Publishing Group, Inc., The.

Perl, Erica S. Truth or Lie: Presidents! Slack, Michael, illus. 2019. (Step into Reading Ser.). (ENG.). 48p. (J). (gr. k-3). pap. 4.99 *(978-1-9848-9391-8(2),* Random Hse. Bks. for Young Readers) Random Hse. Children's Bks.

Petty, Kate. Abraham Lincoln: The Life of America's Sixteenth President, 1 vol. 2005. (Graphic Nonfiction Biographies Ser.). (ENG., Illus.). 48p. (YA). (gr. 4-6). lib. bdg. 37.13 *(978-1-4042-0237-5(4),* 54d2fdab-786d-46f7-b0aa-86fcc4d88aac) Rosen Publishing Group, Inc., The.

Phillips, Ellen Blue. Abraham Lincoln: From Pioneer to President. 2007. (Sterling Biographies Ser.). (ENG., Illus.). 124p. (J). (gr. 6-8). 18.69 *(978-1-4027-4745-8(4))* Sterling Publishing Co., Inc.

Pingry, Patricia A. Meet Thomas Jefferson. Johnson, Meredith, ed. Johnson, Meredith, illus. 2003. 32p. (J). 9.95 *(978-0-8249-5459-8(9),* Ideals Pubns.) Worthy Publishing.

—The Story of Ronald Reagan. Mahan, Ben, illus. 2006. (ENG.). 26p. (J). (gr. -1-k). bds. 7.69 *(978-0-8249-6621-8(X),* Ideals Pubns.) Worthy Publishing.

Piven, Hanoch. What Presidents are Made Of. 2012. lib. bdg. 18.40 *(978-0-606-23670-6(8))* Turtleback.

Piven, Hanoch, illus. What Presidents Are Made Of. (ENG.). 40p. (J). (gr. 1-5). 2012. 7.99 *(978-1-4424-4433-1(9))* 2004. 19.99 *(978-0-689-86880-1(4))* Simon & Schuster Children's Publishing. (Atheneum Bks. for Young Readers).

Pivotal Presidents: Profiles in Leadership: Set 2, 8 vols. 2016. (Pivotal Presidents: Profiles in Leadership Ser.). (ENG.). 80p. (gr. 8-8). 145.88 *(978-1-5081-0225-0(2),* f126922e-ac47-4bcf-90f7-f98f43ef05d2, Britannica Educational Publishing) Rosen Publishing Group, Inc., The.

Pivotal Presidents: Profiles in Leadership: Set 3, 8 vols. 2017. (Pivotal Presidents: Profiles in Leadership Ser.). (ENG.). 80p. (gr. 8-8). 145.88 *(978-1-5081-0540-4(5),* 9e68a46e-cd2a-4b67-aaee-624beb486edf, Britannica Educational Publishing) Rosen Publishing Group, Inc., The.

Plaut, Michael. How to Draw the Life & Times of Gerald R. Ford. 2009. (Kid's Guide to Drawing the Presidents of the United States of America Ser.). 32p. (gr. 4-4). 50.50 *(978-1-61511-141-1(7),* PowerKids Pr.) Rosen Publishing Group, Inc., The.

Plaut, Michael F. How to Draw the Life & Times of Gerald R. Ford, 1 vol. 2005. (Kid's Guide to Drawing the Presidents of the United States of America Ser.). (ENG., Illus.). 32p. (YA). (gr. 4-4). lib. bdg. 30.27 *(978-1-4042-3014-9(9),* 6737fce3-fd98-4920-acf1-608e7689388b) Rosen Publishing Group, Inc., The.

Porterfield, Jason. How Lyndon B. Johnson Fought the Vietnam War, 1 vol. 2017. (Presidents at War Ser.). (ENG.). 128p. (gr. 8-8). lib. bdg. 38.93 *(978-0-7660-8531-2(7),* d7431810-368e-46b2-bba1-293a64dd0532) Enslow Publishing, LLC.

—What Is the Executive Branch?, 1 vol. 2015. (Let's Find Out! Government Ser.). (ENG., Illus.). 32p. (J). (gr. 2-3). 26.06 *(978-1-62275-922-4(2),* c33ba41a-8b0d-4501-ac15-0d5474ace423, Britannica Educational Publishing) Rosen Publishing Group, Inc., The.

Powell, Walter. How to Draw the Life & Times of Andrew Johnson. 2009. (Kid's Guide to Drawing the Presidents of the United States of America Ser.). 32p. (gr. 4-4). 50.50 *(978-1-61511-132-9(8),* PowerKids Pr.) Rosen Publishing Group, Inc., The.

Prentzas, G. S. The Emancipation Proclamation. 2011. (Cornerstones of Freedom, Third Ser.). (Illus.). 64p. (J). (ENG.). pap. 8.95 *(978-0-531-26557-4(9));* lib. bdg. 30.00 *(978-0-531-25032-7(6))* Scholastic Library Publishing. (Children's Pr.).

Presidents. Date not set. (Mini Question & Answers America Ser.). 32p. (J). 3.98 *(978-0-7525-9874-1(0))* Parragon, Inc.

Presidents: U.S. Presidents: Feats & Foul-Ups. 2005. (Illus.). 32p. (J). pap. *(978-0-439-78476-4(X))* Scholastic, Inc.

Presidents & Their Times - Group 2, 12 vols., Set. Incl. Abraham Lincoln. Aronson, Billy. lib. bdg. 36.93 *(978-0-7614-2839-8(9),* a404bef1-3923-404a-bd06-75978e2cbebe); Calvin Coolidge. Otfinoski, Steven. lib. bdg. 36.93 *(978-0-7614-2836-7(4),* cb4552eb-4174-4f33-af09-b9be6fa8978e); Franklin Delano Roosevelt. Elish, Dan. lib. bdg. 36.93 *(978-0-7614-2841-1(0),* 871c231b-419f-45ad-9a9f-f5b6ca2d4cf1); James Monroe. Naden, Corinne J. & Blue, Rose. lib. bdg. 36.93 *(978-0-7614-2838-1(0),* e4f2cacd-fce0-428c-9759-526bc3220fdb); John Adams. Mara, Wil. lib. bdg. 36.93 *(978-0-7614-2840-4(2),* 3b9f9669-22b1-48e0-814f-6ca137b38924); Lyndon B. Johnson. Dudley Gold, Susan. lib. bdg. 36.93 *(978-0-7614-2837-4(2),* b7365e2b-017f-4a6b-b790-7837fd51eb6c); (gr. 6-6). (Presidents & Their Times Ser.). (ENG.). 96p. 2009. Set lib. bdg. 221.58 *(978-0-7614-2834-3(8),* fa3b4d1e-260d-4133-adb2-97a95bb9f762, Cavendish Square) Cavendish Square Publishing LLC.

Presidents At War, 14 vols. 2017. (Presidents at War Ser.). (ENG.). 128p. (gr. 8-8). lib. bdg. 272.51 *(978-0-7660-8596-1(1),* ca66d6bc-f948-4ffc-8388-0168d724d00d) Enslow Publishing, LLC.

Price, Sean. U. S. Presidents: Truth & Rumors. Doty, Eldon, illus. 2010. (Truth & Rumors Ser.). (ENG.). 32p. (J). (gr. 3-9). lib. bdg. 30.65 *(978-1-4296-3952-1(0),* 102562, Capstone Pr.) Capstone.

Raatma, Lucia. Profiles of the Presidents, 42 bks. Incl. John F. Kennedy. (ENG., Illus.). 64p. (gr. 5-6). 2002. lib. bdg. 29.32 *(978-0-7565-0205-8(5),* Compass Point Bks.); (Profiles of the Presidents Ser.). (ENG.). Illus.). 64p. 2003. Set lib. bdg. 1169.61 o.p. *(978-0-7565-0408-3(2),* Compass Point Bks.) Capstone.

Rajczak, Michael. Becoming President, 1 vol. 2015. (Who's Your Candidate? Choosing Government Leaders Ser.). (ENG., Illus.). 32p. (J). (gr. 3-4). pap. 11.50 *(978-1-4824-4039-3(3),* bcb12e6d-e565-4fa1-9a06-5f2e58218a21) Stevens, Gareth Publishing LLLP.

—Before Andrew Jackson Was President, 1 vol. 2017. (Before They Were President Ser.). (ENG.). 24p. (J). (gr. 2-3). pap. 9.15 *(978-1-5382-1060-4(6),* b174df3e-496d-4bd7-8722-4404184e127b) Stevens, Gareth Publishing LLLP.

—Before Franklin D. Roosevelt Was President, 1 vol. 2018. (Before They Were President Ser.). (ENG.). 24p. (gr. 2-3). lib. bdg. 24.27 *(978-1-5382-2910-1(2),* 82caad16-4ada-44e5-a486-f28154c27b4a) Stevens, Gareth Publishing LLLP.

—Before Thomas Jefferson Was President, 1 vol. 2018. (Before They Were President Ser.). (ENG.). 24p. (gr. 2-3). lib. bdg. 24.27 *(978-1-5382-2913-2(7),* 099a0c98-7425-4e15-86c0-b759e6216a9b) Stevens, Gareth Publishing LLLP.

—Meet the President, 1 vol. 2012. (Guide to Your Government Ser.). (ENG., Illus.). 32p. (J). (gr. 4-5). 29.27 *(978-1-4339-7256-0(5),* 36217204-3942-4c93-aab1-175b9ff09371); pap. 11.50 *(978-1-4339-7257-7(3),* 341b264a-faa9-4f5f-9eec-dd9e4b513cdb) Stevens, Gareth Publishing LLLP. (Gareth Stevens Learning Library).

Rajczak Nelson, Kristen. Jefferson Davis: Leader of the Confederacy, 1 vol. 2018. (Junior Biographies Ser.). (ENG.). 24p. (gr. 3-4). 24.27 *(978-1-9785-0203-1(6),* 66549cc9-3003-4fbb-98d8-fdcc793ef11e) Enslow Publishing, LLC.

Rand, Casey. George Washington, 1 vol. Oxford Designers and Illustrators, illus. 2012. (American Biographies Ser.). (ENG.). 48p. (J). (gr. 4-6). lib. bdg. 35.32 *(978-1-4329-6452-8(6),* 119051, Heinemann) Capstone.

Randolph, Ryan P. How to Draw the Life & Times of Andrew Johnson, 1 vol. 2005. (Kid's Guide to Drawing the Presidents of the United States of America Ser.). (ENG.). 32p. (YA). (gr. 4-4). 30.27 *(978-1-4042-2994-5(9),* cbd7b5dc-17ac-4aa1-a539-24dd3ee629b1) Rosen Publishing Group, Inc., The.

—How to Draw the Life & Times of Dwight D. Eisenhower, 1 vol. 2005. (Kid's Guide to Drawing the Presidents of the United States of America Ser.). (ENG., Illus.). 32p. (YA). (gr. 4-4). 30.27 *(978-1-4042-3010-1(6),* 8daeeea5-d8e1-4b83-86cc-6dfc3bfd8600) Rosen Publishing Group, Inc., The.

—How to Draw the Life & Times of John Adams. (Kid's Guide to Drawing the Presidents of the United States of America Ser.). 32p. (gr. 4-4). 2009. 50.50 *(978-1-61511-150-3(6),* PowerKids Pr.) 2005. (ENG.). (YA). 30.27 *(978-1-4042-2979-2(5),* adf79ff2-54f4-4baf-94b4-5cf75f1b411a) Rosen Publishing Group, Inc., The.

—How to Draw the Life & Times of Millard Fillmore. (Kid's Guide to Drawing the Presidents of the United States of America Ser.). 32p. (gr. 4-4). 2009. 50.50 *(978-1-61511-156-5(5),* PowerKids Pr.) 2005. (ENG.). (YA). 30.27 *(978-1-4042-2990-7(6),* 4f00ebb9-df25-4abf-a13a-cb9d8a6d969b) Rosen Publishing Group, Inc., The.

—How to Draw the Life & Times of William Howard Taft, 1 vol. 2005. (Kid's Guide to Drawing the Presidents of the United States of America Ser.). (ENG., Illus.). 32p. (YA). (gr. 4-4). 30.27 *(978-1-4042-3003-3(3),* 04d8ccfb-589a-48c8-833e-ad21ebc569b3) Rosen Publishing Group, Inc., The.

Ransom, Candice. George Washington. 2018. (Founding Fathers Ser.). (ENG., Illus.). 24p. (J). (gr. 1-1). pap. 8.95 *(978-1-63517-817-3(7),* 1635178177) North Star Editions.

—George Washington. 2018. (Founding Fathers Ser.). (ENG., Illus.). 24p. (J). (gr. k-3). lib. bdg. 31.36 *(978-1-5321-6022-6(4),* 28676, Pop! Cody Koala) Pop!

—James Madison. 2018. (Founding Fathers Ser.). (ENG., Illus.). 24p. (J). (gr. 1-1). pap. 8.95 *(978-1-63517-816-6(9),* 1635178169) North Star Editions.

—James Madison. 2018. (Founding Fathers Ser.). (ENG., Illus.). 24p. (J). (gr. k-3). lib. bdg. 31.36 *(978-1-5321-6021-9(6),* 28674, Pop! Cody Koala) Pop!

—Thomas Jefferson. 2018. (Founding Fathers Ser.). (ENG., Illus.). 24p. (J). (gr. 1-1). pap. 8.95 *(978-1-63517-815-9(0),* 1635178150) North Star Editions.

—Thomas Jefferson. 2018. (Founding Fathers Ser.). (ENG., Illus.). 24p. (J). (gr. k-3). lib. bdg. 31.36 *(978-1-5321-6020-2(8),* 28672, Pop! Cody Koala) Pop!

Rappaport, Doreen. Abe's Honest Words. Nelson, Kadir, illus. 2009. (J). (gr. 2-4). 27.95 incl. audio *(978-0-8045-6984-2(3))* Spoken Arts, Inc.

—Abe's Honest Words: The Life of Abraham Lincoln. Nelson, Kadir, illus. (Big Words Book Ser.: 5). (ENG.). 48p. (J). (gr. -1-3). 2016. pap. 8.99 *(978-1-4847-4958-6(8))* 2008. 16.99 *(978-1-4231-0408-7(0))* Little, Brown Bks. for Young Readers.

—Jack's Path of Courage: The Life of John F. Kennedy. Tavares, Matt, illus. (Big Words Book Ser.: 6). (ENG.). 48p. (J). (gr. 1-3). 2016. pap. 8.99 *(978-1-4847-4961-6(8))* 2010. 17.99 *(978-1-4231-2272-2(0))* Little, Brown Bks. for Young Readers.

Rauf, Don. Washington's Farewell Address, 1 vol. 2016. (Let's Find Out! Primary Sources Ser.). (ENG., Illus.). 32p. (J). (gr. 2-3). lib. bdg. 26.06 *(978-1-5081-0407-0(7),* 8aea0638-2193-4c99-bb41-0151eb8a6b8a) Rosen Publishing Group, Inc., The.

Raum, Elizabeth. Abraham Lincoln, 1 vol. Oxford Designers and Illustrators, illus. 2012. (American Biographies Ser.). (ENG.). 48p. (gr. 4-6). pap. 9.95 (978-1-4329-6464-1(X), 119063); (J). lib. bdg. 35.32 (978-1-4329-6453-5(4), 119052) Capstone. (Heinemann).

Rausch, Monica. Andrew Jackson, 1 vol. 2007. (Grandes Personajes (Great Americans) Ser.). 24p. (gr. 2-4). (SPA.). pap. 9.15 (978-0-8368-7989-6(9), 17f7e0be-a6fd-4de2-9b75-31ac3cf2329f, Weekly Reader Leveled Readers); (ENG., Illus.). pap. 9.15 (978-0-8368-7690-1(3), 510d4909-8d8c-45d2-9052-f8bee0eadc45, Weekly Reader Leveled Readers); (SPA., Illus.). lib. bdg. 24.67 (978-0-8368-7982-7(1), 3ffc0869-c621-4fff-a0e9-6226247195e8); (ENG., Illus.). lib. bdg. 24.67 (978-0-8368-7683-3(0), 254c7830-155a-43c0-bdc8-699aafed0d92, Weekly Reader Leveled Readers) Stevens, Gareth Publishing LLLP.

—Thomas Jefferson, 1 vol. 2007. (Grandes Personajes (Great Americans) Ser.). (SPA., Illus.). 24p. (gr. 2-4). lib. bdg. 24.67 (978-0-8368-7983-4(X), ed472768-1ea2-495d-b495-d8cd58814b41) Stevens, Gareth Publishing LLLP.

Reed, Ellis M. John Adams. 2018. (Founding Fathers Ser.). (ENG., Illus.). 24p. (J). (gr. 1-1). pap. 8.95 (978-1-63517-812-8(6), 1635178126) North Star Editions.

—John Adams. 2018. (Founding Fathers Ser.). (ENG., Illus.). 24p. (J). (gr. k-3). lib. bdg. 31.36 (978-1-5321-6017-2(8), 28666, Pop! Cody Koala) Pop!

Reeves, Diane Lindsey & White, Kelly. Choose a Career Adventure at the White House. 2016. (Bright Futures Press: Choose a Career Adventure Ser.). (ENG., Illus.). 32p. (J). (gr. 4-6). 32.07 (978-1-63471-916-2(6), 208985) Cherry Lake Publishing.

Regan, Michael. George Washington & the American Presidency. 2017. (Foundations of Our Nation Ser.). (ENG., Illus.). 32p. (J). (gr. 3-5). pap. 9.95 (978-1-63517-313-0(2), 1635173132); lib. bdg. 31.35 (978-1-63517-248-5(9), 1635172489) North Star Editions. (Focus Readers).

Rice, Earle, Jr. How Franklin D. Roosevelt Fought World War II, 1 vol. 2017. (Presidents at War Ser.). (ENG.). 128p. (gr. 8-8). lib. bdg. 38.93 (978-0-7660-8527-5(9), 90068e3a-c02b-490c-960b-c2d1bf00735c) Enslow Publishing, LLC.

—Ulysses S. Grant: Defender of the Union. 2005. (Civil War Leaders Ser.). (Illus.). 176p. (J). (gr. 6-12). 28.95 (978-1-931798-48-8(6)) Reynolds, Morgan Inc.

Rice, Dona Herweck. Jimmy Carter: For the People. rev. ed. 2016. (Social Studies: Informational Text Ser.). (ENG., Illus.). 32p. (gr. 2-4). pap. 10.99 (978-1-4938-2561-5(5)) Teacher Created Materials, Inc.

—Teedie: The Boy Who Would Be President. rev. ed. 2015. (Reader's Theater Ser.). (ENG., Illus.). 24p. (gr. 1-3). pap. 8.99 (978-1-4938-1513-5(X)) Teacher Created Materials, Inc.

Rivera, Sheila. Abraham Lincoln: Una Vida de Respeto. 2006. (Libros para Avanzar Ser.). (ENG & SPA., Illus.). 32p. (J). (gr. 3-7). lib. bdg. 22.60 (978-0-8225-6236-8(7)) Lerner Publishing Group.

Robb, Don. Hail to the Chief: The American Presidency. Witschonke, Alan, illus. rev. ed. 2010. 32p. (J). (gr. 1-4). 17.95 (978-1-58089-285-8(X)); pap. 7.95 (978-1-58089-286-5(8)) Charlesbridge Publishing, Inc.

Roberts, Jeremy. Franklin D. Roosevelt. 2003. (Presidential Leaders Ser.). (Illus.). 112p. (J). (gr. 6-12). lib. bdg. 29.27 (978-0-8225-0095-7(7)) Lerner Publishing Group.

—James Madison. 2004. (Presidential Leaders Ser.). (Illus.). 112p. (J). (gr. 6-12). lib. bdg. 29.27 (978-0-8225-0823-6(0)) Lerner Publishing Group.

Robinson, Peg. Andrew Jackson: Populist President, 1 vol. 2018. (Hero or Villain? Claims & Counterclaims Ser.). (ENG.). 112p. (YA). (gr. 8-8). 45.93 (978-1-5026-3526-6(7), b86265d9-7922-4379-8388-727033706c5d) Cavendish Square Publishing LLC.

Robinson, Tom. Barack Obama: 44th U. S. President. 2009. (J). lib. bdg. 32.79 (978-1-60453-528-0(8)); (ENG., Illus.). 112p. (YA). (gr. 6-12). lib. bdg. 41.36 (978-1-60453-527-3(X), 6683) ABDO Publishing Co. (Essential Library).

—The Development of the Industrial United States: 1870-1900. 2007. (Presidents of the United States Ser.). (Illus.). 48p. (J). (gr. 4-7). lib. bdg. 29.05 (978-1-59036-745-2(6)) Weigl Pubs., Inc.

—Development of the Industrial United States: 1870-1900. 2007. (Presidents of the United States Ser.). (Illus.). 48p. (J). (gr. 4-7). per. 10.95 (978-1-59036-746-9(4)) Weigl Pubs., Inc.

Rockwell, Anne. Big George: How a Shy Boy Became President Washington. Phelan, Matt, illus. 2015. (ENG.). 48p. (J). (gr. 1-4). pap. 8.99 (978-0-544-58246-0(2), 1613675, Clarion Bks.) HarperCollins Pubs.

Roleff, Tamara L., ed. What Limits Should Be Placed on Presidential Powers?, 1 vol. 2006. (At Issue Ser.). (ENG., Illus.). 120p. (gr. 10-12). 41.03 (978-0-7377-3629-8(1), f17c8318-70e5-49b3-a281-12ae7e5cebb5); pap. 28.80 (978-0-7377-3630-4(5), ef4f3d1a-807f-4349-a77b-01e3b5cf1ebb) Greenhaven Publishing LLC. (Greenhaven Publishing).

Roome, Hugh. Franklin D. Roosevelt: American Hero (Rookie Biographies) 2017. (Rookie Biographies Ser.). (ENG., Illus.). 32p. (J). (gr. 1-2). pap. 5.95 (978-0-531-23863-9(6), Children's Pr.) Scholastic Library Publishing.

—Franklin D. Roosevelt: American Hero (Rookie Biographies) (Library Edition) 2017. (Rookie Biographies Ser.). (ENG., Illus.). 32p. (J). (gr. 1-2). lib. bdg. 25.00 (978-0-531-23229-3(8), Children's Pr.) Scholastic Library Publishing.

Rose, Simon. The Office of the President. 2014. (J). (978-1-4896-1950-1(X)) Weigl Pubs., Inc.

—Office of the President. 2016. (J). (978-1-5105-2247-3(6)) SmartBook Media, Inc.

Rowell, Rebecca. John F. Kennedy's Presidency. 2016. (Presidential Powerhouses Ser.). (ENG., Illus.). 104p. (YA). (gr. 6-12). E-Book 54.65 (978-1-4677-8600-3(4), Lerner Pubns.) Lerner Publishing Group.

Roxburgh, Ellis. Thomas Jefferson vs. John Adams: Founding Fathers & Political Rivals, 1 vol. 2015. (History's Greatest Rivals Ser.). (ENG., Illus.). 48p. (J). (gr. 6-8). pap. 15.05 (978-1-4824-4239-7(6), 349f4b41-e98f-45d4-8ece-ef7a1fda66f9) Stevens, Gareth Publishing LLLP.

Ruffin, Frances E. How to Draw the Life & Times of Theodore Roosevelt. 2009. (Kid's Guide to Drawing the Presidents of the United States of America Ser.). 32p. (gr. 4-4). 50.50 (978-1-61511-160-2(3), PowerKids Pr.) Rosen Publishing Group, Inc., The.

Rumsch, BreAnn. Bill Clinton, 1 vol. 2016. (United States Presidents *2017 Ser.). (ENG., Illus.). 40p. (J). (gr. 2-5). lib. bdg. 35.64 (978-1-68078-089-5(1), 21795, Big Buddy Bks.) ABDO Publishing Co.

—Franklin Pierce, 1 vol. 2016. (United States Presidents *2017 Ser.). (ENG., Illus.). 40p. (J). (gr. 2-5). 35.64 (978-1-68078-112-0(X), 21841, Big Buddy Bks.) ABDO Publishing Co.

—George W. Bush, 1 vol. 2016. (United States Presidents *2017 Ser.). (ENG., Illus.). 40p. (J). (gr. 2-5). lib. bdg. 35.64 (978-1-68078-086-4(7), 21789, Big Buddy Bks.) ABDO Publishing Co.

—Grover Cleveland, 1 vol. 2016. (United States Presidents *2017 Ser.). (ENG., Illus.). 40p. (J). (gr. 2-5). 35.64 (978-1-68078-088-8(3), 21793, Big Buddy Bks.) ABDO Publishing Co.

—Herbert Hoover, 1 vol. 2016. (United States Presidents *2017 Ser.). (ENG., Illus.). 40p. (J). (gr. 2-5). lib. bdg. 35.64 (978-1-68078-100-7(6), 21817, Big Buddy Bks.) ABDO Publishing Co.

—James K. Polk, 1 vol. 2016. (United States Presidents *2017 Ser.). (ENG., Illus.). 40p. (J). (gr. 2-5). lib. bdg. 35.64 (978-1-68078-113-7(8), 21843, Big Buddy Bks.) ABDO Publishing Co.

—Martin Van Buren, 1 vol. 2016. (United States Presidents *2017 Ser.). (ENG., Illus.). 40p. (J). (gr. 2-5). lib. bdg. 35.64 (978-1-68078-121-2(9), 21859, Big Buddy Bks.) ABDO Publishing Co.

—Rutherford B. Hayes, 1 vol. 2016. (United States Presidents *2017 Ser.). (ENG., Illus.). 40p. (J). (gr. 2-5). lib. bdg. 35.64 (978-1-68078-099-4(9), 21815, Big Buddy Bks.) ABDO Publishing Co.

Ruth, Amy. Herbert Hoover. 2004. (Presidential Leaders Ser.). (Illus.). 112p. (J). (gr. 6-12). lib. bdg. 29.27 (978-0-8225-0821-2(4)) Lerner Publishing Group.

Saddleback Educational Publishing Staff, ed. Abraham Lincoln, 1 vol. unabr. ed. 2007. (Graphic Biographies Ser.). (ENG., Illus.). 25p. (YA). (gr. 4-12). per. 9.75 (978-1-59905-211-3(3)) Saddleback Educational Publishing, Inc.

—Franklin Roosevelt, 1 vol. unabr. ed. 2007. (Graphic Biographies Ser.). (ENG., Illus.). 25p. (YA). (gr. 4-12). pap. 9.75 (978-1-59905-222-9(9)) Saddleback Educational Publishing, Inc.

—George Washington, 1 vol. unabr. ed. 2007. (Graphic Biographies Ser.). (ENG., Illus.). 25p. (YA). (gr. 4-12). pap. 9.75 (978-1-59905-223-6(7)) Saddleback Educational Publishing, Inc.

—Thomas Jefferson, 1 vol. unabr. ed. 2007. (Graphic Biographies Ser.). (ENG., Illus.). 25p. (YA). (gr. 4-12). pap. 9.75 (978-1-59905-229-8(6)) Saddleback Educational Publishing, Inc.

Saffer, Barbara. Harry S. Truman. 2004. (Childhoods of the Presidents Ser.). (Illus.). 48p. (J). (gr. 4-18). lib. bdg. 17.95 (978-1-59084-282-9(0)) Mason Crest.

Santella, Andrew. Air Force One. 2003. (Illus.). 48p. (gr. 4-18). (J). pap. 8.95 (978-0-7613-1926-9(3)); (Women at War Ser.: up). lib. bdg. 24.90 (978-0-7613-2617-5(0)) Lerner Publishing Group. (Millbrook Pr.).

Santow, Dan. Encyclopedia of Presidents: Millard Fillmore. 2004. (Encyclopedia of Presidents Ser.). (ENG., Illus.). 112p. (YA). (gr. 5-9). 34.00 (978-0-516-22888-4(9)) Scholastic Library Publishing.

Sarantou, Katlin. George H. W. Bush. Bane, Jeff, illus. 2019. (My Early Library: My Itty-Bitty Bio Ser.). (ENG.). 24p. (J). (gr. k-1). pap. 12.79 (978-1-5341-4992-2(9), 213275); lib. bdg. 30.64 (978-1-5341-4706-5(3), 213274) Cherry Lake Publishing.

Scarbrough, Mary Hertz. Presidential Politics by the Numbers. 2016. (Presidential Politics Ser.). (ENG., Illus.). 48p. (J). (gr. 3-6). lib. bdg. 29.99 (978-1-4914-8238-4(9), 130709) Capstone.

Schanzer, Rosalyn. George vs. George. 2007. (ENG.). 64p. (J). (gr. 4-7). 17.75 (978-1-5311-7657-0(7)) Perfection Learning Corp.

—George vs. George: The American Revolution As Seen from Both Sides. 2007. (Illus.). 64p. (J). (gr. 3-7). per. 6.95 (978-1-4263-0042-4(5), National Geographic Kids) Disney Publishing Worldwide.

—George vs. George: The Revolutionary War As Seen by Both Sides. 2004. (Illus.). 64p. (J). (gr. 3-7). 16.95 (978-0-7922-7349-3(4), National Geographic Children's Bks.) Disney Publishing Worldwide.

Schmidt, Roderic. How to Draw the Life & Times of Abraham Lincoln. (Kid's Guide to Drawing the Presidents of the United States of America Ser.). 32p. (gr. 4-4). 2009. 50.50 (978-1-61511-130-5(1), PowerKids Pr.) 2005. (ENG.). (YA). 30.27 (978-1-4042-2993-8(0), e616c85a-5859-425f-a597-fb99df3a7e08) Rosen Publishing Group, Inc., The.

—How to Draw the Life & Times of George W. Bush. 2009. (Kid's Guide to Drawing the Presidents of the United States of America Ser.). 32p. (gr. 4-4). 50.50 (978-1-61511-139-8(5), PowerKids Pr.) Rosen Publishing Group, Inc., The.

—How to Draw the Life & Times of James Madison. (Kid's Guide to Drawing the Presidents of the United States of America Ser.). 32p. (gr. 4-4). 2009. 50.50 (978-1-61511-148-0(4), PowerKids Pr.) 2005. (ENG.). (YA). 30.27 (978-1-4042-2981-5(7), 36be9f8b-f29f-4ed2-8bcd-cc4e76561da3) Rosen Publishing Group, Inc., The.

—How to Draw the Life & Times of Martin Van Buren. (Kid's Guide to Drawing the Presidents of the United States of America Ser.). 32p. (gr. 4-4). 2009. 50.50 (978-1-61511-155-8(7), PowerKids Pr.) 2005. (ENG.). (YA). 30.27 (978-1-4042-2985-3(X), e46db694-b581-44ce-a01a-f83a179c8a2c) Rosen Publishing Group, Inc., The.

—How to Draw the Life & Times of Zachary Taylor. (Kid's Guide to Drawing the Presidents of the United States of America Ser.). 32p. (gr. 4-4). 2009. 50.50 (978-1-61511-169-5(7), PowerKids Pr.) 2005. (ENG.). (YA). 30.27 (978-1-4042-2989-1(2), 6b491a5a-bc35-437b-8c04-cf49a647ecd2) Rosen Publishing Group, Inc., The.

Schroeder, Alan. Abe Lincoln: His Wit & Wisdom from A to Z. O'brien, John, illus. 2015. (ENG.). 32p. (J). (gr. 1-4). 17.95 (978-0-8234-2420-7(0)) Holiday Hse., Inc.

Schubert, Barbara. George Washington. 2009. pap. 13.25 (978-1-60559-060-8(6)) Hameray Publishing Group, Inc.

Schuh, Mari. The White House. 2018. (Symbols of American Freedom Ser.). (ENG., Illus.). 24p. (J). (gr. k-3). pap. 7.99 (978-1-61891-476-7(6), 12129); lib. bdg. 26.95 (978-1-62617-890-8(9)) Bellwether Media. (Blastoff! Readers).

Schuh, Mari C. The U. S. Presidency, 1 vol. 2012. (U. S. Government Ser.). (ENG.). 24p. (J). (gr. -1-2). lib. bdg. 27.32 (978-1-4296-7566-6(7), 117162, Capstone Pr.) Capstone.

Seeley, M. H. Before John Adams Was President, 1 vol. 2017. (Before They Were President Ser.). (ENG.). 24p. (J). (gr. 2-3). pap. 9.15 (978-1-5382-1067-3(3), 38a269f1-5c05-430a-a43d-63d1c0e88e10) Stevens, Gareth Publishing LLLP.

Seidman, David. Jimmy Carter: Peacemaker & President. 2004. (Great Life Stories Ser.). (ENG., Illus.). 127p. (J). 30.50 (978-0-531-12374-4(X), Watts, Franklin) Scholastic Library Publishing.

Shea, John M. Thomas Jefferson in His Own Words, 1 vol., Vol. 1. 2014. (Eyewitness to History Ser.). (ENG.). 32p. (J). (gr. 4-5). 29.27 (978-1-4339-9873-7(4), 83721893-7690-4eb5-8f24-0b77d0692070); pap. 11.50 (978-1-4339-9933-8(1), f9f6647c-6c19-4b67-a2a0-1619deb0ac5d) Stevens, Gareth Publishing LLLP.

Shea, Therese M. Before Ronald Reagan Was President, 1 vol. 2018. (Before They Were President Ser.). (ENG.). 24p. (gr. 2-3). lib. bdg. 24.27 (978-1-5382-2911-8(0), dc9577f9-9282-4610-8848-188518851e6d) Stevens, Gareth Publishing LLLP.

—Before Teddy Roosevelt Was President, 1 vol. 2017. (Before They Were President Ser.). (ENG.). 24p. (J). (gr. 2-3). pap. 9.15 (978-1-5382-1076-5(2), 53e6b187-3b7b-49f4-a3b2-937901cef493) Stevens, Gareth Publishing LLLP.

Shepherd, Jodie. Barack Obama: Groundbreaking President. 2016. (Rookie Biographies(tm) Ser.). (ENG., Illus.). 32p. (J). lib. bdg. 25.00 (978-0-531-21681-1(0), Children's Pr.) Scholastic Library Publishing.

—Presidents of the United States of America. 2015. (Illus.). 50p. (J). (978-1-4351-6156-6(4)) Barnes & Noble, Inc.

Sherman, Jill. Donald Trump: Outspoken Personality & President. 2017. (Gateway Biographies Ser.). (ENG., Illus.). 48p. (J). (gr. 4-8). lib. bdg. 31.99 (978-1-5124-2596-3(6), 73ddd6e7-9543-41d2-9c95-2b6efefcc36c, Lerner Pubns.) Lerner Publishing Group.

Sherman, Patrice. George W. Bush: Texan Governor & U. S. President, 1 vol. rev. ed. 2012. (Social Studies: Informational Text Ser.). (ENG.). 32p. (gr. 3-5). pap. 11.99 (978-1-4333-5054-2(8)) Teacher Created Materials, Inc.

—What It's Like to Be President Barack Obama? Vega, Eida de la, tr. 2009. (What It's Like to Be/Que se Siente al Ser Ser.). (SPA & ENG., Illus.). 32p. (J). (gr. -1-2). 25.70 (978-1-58415-843-1(3)) Mitchell Lane Pubs.

Silate, Jennifer. The White House. (Primary Sources of American Symbols Ser.). 24p. (gr. 3-3). 2009. 42.50 (978-1-60851-512-7(5), PowerKids Pr.) 2005. (ENG., Illus.). (J). lib. bdg. 26.27 (978-1-4042-2695-1(8), 5e07579f-ac16-4a0d-acb7-e7a6cbae7d70) Rosen Publishing Group, Inc., The.

Singer, Allison & DK. DK Readers L2: What Is the President's Job? 2017. (DK Readers Level 2 Ser.). (ENG., Illus.). 48p. (J). (gr. k-2). pap. 4.99 (978-1-4654-5748-6(8), DK Children) Dorling Kindersley Publishing, Inc.

Smith, Adam I. P. Abraham Lincoln: President, 1 vol. 2016. (History Makers Ser.). (ENG., Illus.). 144p. (J). (gr. 9-9). 47.36 (978-1-5026-1912-9(1), a00797b5-af27-4994-925c-24cf2ac38b7d) Cavendish Square Publishing LLC.

Smith-Llera, Danielle. The Real James Madison: The Truth Behind the Legend. 2019. (Real Revolutionaries Ser.). (ENG., Illus.). 64p. (J). (gr. 5-9). lib. bdg. 34.65 (978-0-7565-6252-6(X), 141185, Compass Point Bks.) Capstone.

Snyder, Gail. George Washington. 2004. (Childhoods of the Presidents Ser.). (Illus.). 48p. (J). (gr. 4-18). lib. bdg. 17.95 (978-1-59084-270-6(7)) Mason Crest.

Somervill, Barbara A. The Life & Times of James Madison. 2008. (Profiles in American History Ser.). (Illus.). 48p. (J). (gr. 4-7). lib. bdg. 29.95 (978-1-58415-530-0(2)) Mitchell Lane Pubs.

Sommer, Shelley. John F. Kennedy: His Life & Legacy. 2005. (Illus.). 160p. (J). 16.99 (978-0-06-054135-4(0)) HarperCollins Pubs.

Souza, Pete. Dream Big Dreams: Photographs from Barack Obama's Inspiring & Historic Presidency (Young Readers) 2017. (ENG., Illus.). 96p. (J). (gr. 5-17). 21.99 (978-0-316-51439-2(X)) Little, Brown Bks. for Young Readers.

Spalding, Maddie. How the Executive Branch Works. 2016. (How America Works). (ENG.). 24p. (J). (gr. 3-6). 32.79 (978-1-5038-0903-1(X), 210660) Child's World, Inc, The.

St. George, Judith. So You Want to Be President? Small, David, illus. 2004. (J). (gr. 1-6). 29.95 (978-1-55592-132-3(9)) Weston Woods Studios, Inc.

—So You Want to Be President? The Revised & Updated Edition. Small, David, illus. rev. ed. 2004. 56p. (J). (gr. 2-5). 18.99 (978-0-399-24317-2(8), Philomel Bks.) Penguin Young Readers Group.

Stabler, David. Kid Presidents: True Tales of Childhood from America's Presidents. Horner, Doogie, illus. 2014. (Kid Legends Ser.: 1). 224p. (J). (gr. 3-7). 13.99 (978-1-59474-731-1(8)) Quirk Bks.

Stanley, George E. America in Today's World (1969-2004), 1 vol. 2004. (Primary Source History of the United States Ser.). (ENG., Illus.). 48p. (gr. 5-8). lib. bdg. 33.67 (978-0-8368-5831-0(X), f90bbe7b-9042-429d-92c4-ea9b82b2d8d3, Gareth Stevens Secondary Library) Stevens, Gareth Publishing LLLP.

Steinberg, Don. America Bowl: 44 Presidents vs. 44 Super Bowls in the Ultimate Matchup! 2010. (ENG., Illus.). 96p. (J). (gr. 5-8). 24.94 (978-1-59643-683-1(2), 9781596436831) Roaring Brook Pr.

Stevens, Stewart, Sr. The White House Chandeliers: My Experiences While Working for Seven U. S. Presidents. 2016. (ENG., Illus.). xi, 127p. (gr. 6-17). pap. 25.00 (978-0-9974925-0-7(3)) Lightning Fast Bk. Publishing.

Stier, Catherine. If I Ran for President. Avril, Lynne, illus. 2007. (Albert Whitman Prairie Books Ser.). (ENG.). 32p. (J). (gr. 1-4). 18.80 (978-1-5311-7682-2(8)) Perfection Learning Corp.

—If I Ran for President. Avril, Lynne, illus. 2012. (J). 34.28 (978-1-61913-115-6(3)) Weigl Pubs., Inc.

Stille, Darlene R. The Emergence of Modern America: 1890-1930. 2007. (Presidents of the United States Ser.). (Illus.). 48p. (J). (gr. 4-7). lib. bdg. 29.05 (978-1-59036-747-6(2)); per. 10.95 (978-1-59036-748-3(0)) Weigl Pubs., Inc.

Stine, Megan. Where Is the White House? 2015. (Where Is... ? Ser.). lib. bdg. 16.00 (978-0-606-36591-8(5)) Turtleback.

Stine, Megan & Who HQ. Where Is the White House? Groff, David, illus. 2015. (Where Is? Ser.). 112p. (J). (gr. 3-7). 5.99 (978-0-448-48355-9(6), Penguin Workshop) Penguin Young Readers Group.

—Who Was Richard Nixon? Gutierrez, Manuel, IV & Gutierrez, Manuel, illus. 2020. (Who Was? Ser.). 112p. (J). (gr. 3-7). 5.99 (978-1-5247-8980-0(1), Penguin Workshop) Penguin Young Readers Group.

—Who Was Ulysses S. Grant? Geyer, Mark Edward, illus. 2014. (Who Was? Ser.). 112p. (J). (gr. 3-7). 6.99 (978-0-448-47894-4(3), Penguin Workshop) Penguin Young Readers Group.

Stoltman, Joan. Barack Obama, 1 vol. 2018. (Little Biographies of Big People Ser.). (ENG.). 24p. (gr. 1-2). 24.27 (978-1-5382-1828-0(3), b0e73cd7-4e09-465f-9319-78ac635335da) Stevens, Gareth Publishing LLLP.

Strain Trueit, Trudi. Thomas Jefferson, 1 vol. 2010. (Presidents & Their Times Ser.). (ENG.). 96p. (gr. 6-6). 36.93 (978-0-7614-3622-5(7), 304d3240-2f53-4dd1-b5f5-16559fd45e72) Cavendish Square Publishing LLC.

Strand, Jennifer. Abraham Lincoln. 2016. (Legendary Leaders Ser.). (ENG.). 24p. (J). (gr. -1-2). 49.94 (978-1-68079-402-1(7), 23023, Abdo Zoom-Launch) ABDO Publishing Co.

—Barack Obama. 2016. (Legendary Leaders Ser.). (ENG.). 24p. (J). (gr. -1-2). 49.94 (978-1-68079-403-8(5), 23024, Abdo Zoom-Launch) ABDO Publishing Co.

Sullivan, Anne Marie. Franklin D. Roosevelt. 2004. (Childhood of the Presidents Ser.). (Illus.). 48p. (J). (gr. 4-18). lib. bdg. 17.95 (978-1-59084-279-9(0)) Mason Crest.

Sutcliffe, Jane. Barack Obama. 2010. (History Maker Biographies Ser.). (ENG.). 48p. (gr. 3-6). lib. bdg. 27.93 (978-0-7613-5205-1(8), Lerner Pubns.) Lerner Publishing Group.

—John Adams. 2006. (History Maker Biographies Ser.). (ENG., Illus.). 48p. (gr. 3-6). lib. bdg. 27.93 (978-0-8225-5940-5(4), Lerner Pubns.) Lerner Publishing Group.

—John F. Kennedy. (History Maker Bios Ser.). (J). 2005. (Illus.). 48p. 26.60 (978-0-8225-1546-3(6)) 2004. pap. 8.95 (978-0-8225-2540-0(2)) Lerner Publishing Group. (Lerner Pubns.).

—Ronald Reagan. 2009. pap. 52.95 (978-0-7613-4958-7(8)) 2008. (ENG.). 48p. (gr. 3-6). 27.93 (978-0-8225-8894-8(3), Lerner Pubns.) Lerner Publishing Group.

Swain, Gwenyth. Theodore Roosevelt. 2004. (History Maker Bios Ser.). (J). pap. 8.95 (978-0-8225-2542-4(9)); (ENG., Illus.). 48p. (gr. 3-6). 27.93 (978-0-8225-1548-7(2)) Lerner Publishing Group. (Lerner Pubns.).

Tecco, Betsy Dru. How to Draw the Life & Times of Grover Cleveland. (Kid's Guide to Drawing the Presidents of the United States of America Ser.). 32p. (gr. 4-4). 2009. 50.50 (978-1-61511-142-8(5), PowerKids Pr.) 2005. (ENG.). (YA). 30.27 (978-1-4042-2999-0(X), 20a880ea-d1c0-472f-8f41-a031505053e3) Rosen Publishing Group, Inc., The.

—How to Draw the Life & Times of John Quincy Adams. 2009. (Kid's Guide to Drawing the Presidents of the United States of America Ser.). 32p. (gr. 4-4). 50.50 (978-1-61511-152-7(2), PowerKids Pr.) Rosen Publishing Group, Inc., The.

—How to Draw the Life & Times of Ulysses S. Grant. (Kid's Guide to Drawing the Presidents of the United States of America Ser.). 32p. (gr. 4-4). 2009. 50.50 (978-1-61511-162-6(X), PowerKids Pr.) 2005. (ENG.). (YA). 30.27 (978-1-4042-2995-2(7), 40cb6c01-1985-4211-89fa-35f40be0f4dc) Rosen Publishing Group, Inc., The.

Thomas, Garen. Yes We Can: A Biography of President Barack Obama. 2nd rev. ed. 2008. (ENG., Illus.). 256p. (J). (gr. 3-6). 12.99 (978-0-312-58639-3(6), 900062157) Feiwel & Friends.

Thomas, Peggy. Thomas Jefferson Grows a Nation. Innerst, Stacy, illus. 2015. (ENG.). 48p. (J). (gr. 2-5). 16.95 (978-1-62091-628-5(2), Calkins Creek) Highlights Pr., c/o Highlights for Children, Inc.

Thompson, Ben & Slader, Erik. Not-So-Great Presidents: Commanders in Chief (Epic Fails #3) Foley, Tim, illus. 2019. (Epic Fails Ser.: 3). (ENG.). 160p. (J). pap. 6.99 (978-1-250-15059-2(0), 900182548) Roaring Brook Pr.

Thompson, William & Thompson, Dorcas. George W. Bush. 2004. (Childhoods of the Presidents Ser.). (Illus.). 48p. (J). (gr. 4-18). lib. bdg. 17.95 (978-1-59084-281-2(2)) Mason Crest.

Thomson, Sarah L. What Lincoln Said. Ransome, James E., illus. 2009. 32p. (J). (gr. k-3). lib. bdg. 18.89 (978-0-06-084820-0(0)) HarperCollins Pubs.

Thorburn, Mark. The Executive Branch: Leading the Nation, 1 vol. 2008. (Federal Government Ser.). (ENG., Illus.). 128p. (gr. 6-7). lib. bdg. 37.27 (978-1-59845-060-6(3), f867d6dc-6527-407e-9499-868d6a71f02f, MyReportLinks.com Bks.) Enslow Publishing, LLC.

—The President & the Executive Branch: How Our Nation Is Governed, 1 vol. 2013. (Constitution & the United States Government Ser.). (ENG., Illus.). 104p. (gr. 5-6). 35.93 *(978-0-7660-4063-2(1),* 4fc2a62a-fdbc-4313-babc-764cf15ee975) Enslow Publishing, LLC.

Thornton, Brian. The Everything Kids' Presidents Book: Puzzles, Games & Trivia - for Hours of Presidential Fun. 2007. (Everything(r) Kids Ser.). (ENG., Illus.). 144p. per. 15.99 *(978-1-59869-262-4(3))* Adams Media Corp.

Time for Kids Editors. Presidents of the United States. 2006. (Time for Kids Ser.). (ENG., Illus.). 72p. (J). (gr. 2-6). pap. 7.99 *(978-0-06-081556-1(6),* Collins) HarperCollins Pubs.

—Presidents of the United States. 2017. (America Handbooks, a Time for Kids Ser.). (ENG., Illus.). 80p. (J). (gr. 3-7). pap. 9.95 *(978-1-61893-427-7(9),* Time For Kids) Time Inc. Bks.

—Time for Kids: Ronald Reagan: From Silver Screen to Oval Office. 2005. (Time for Kids Ser.). (ENG., Illus.). 48p. (J). (gr. 2-4). per. 3.99 *(978-0-06-057626-4(X))* HarperCollins Pubs.

Time for Kids Magazine Staff. Franklin D. Roosevelt - A Leader in Troubled Times. 2005. (Time for Kids Ser.). (ENG., Illus.). 48p. (J). (gr. 2-4). per. 3.99 *(978-0-06-057615-8(4))* HarperCollins Pubs.

—Presidents of the United States. 2006. (Time for Kids Ser.). (Illus.). 70p. (J). (gr. 2-6). lib. bdg. 18.89 *(978-0-06-081555-4(8))* HarperCollins Pubs.

—Presidents of the United States. 2017. (America Handbooks, a Time for Kids Ser.). (ENG., Illus.). 80p. (J). (gr. 3-7). 15.95 *(978-1-68330-000-7(9),* Time For Kids) Time Inc. Bks.

Tracosas, L. J. White House Winners: What You Don't Know about the Presidents. Lynch, Josh, illus. 2017. 64p. (J). *(978-1-338-15978-3(X))* Scholastic, Inc.

Troupe, Thomas Kingsley. If I Were the President [Scholastic]. Heyworth, Heather, illus. 2010. (Dream Big! Ser.). 24p. pap. 0.62 *(978-1-4048-6196-1(3),* Picture Window Bks.) Capstone.

Trumbauer, Lisa. Abraham Lincoln & the Civil War. rev. ed. 2016. (Life in the Time Of Ser.). (ENG.). 32p. (J). (gr. 1-3). pap. 8.29 *(978-1-4846-3822-4(0),* 134722, Heinemann) Capstone.

—Set in Stone. 2005. (Yellow Umbrella Fluent Level Ser.). (ENG.). 16p. (gr. k-1). pap. 35.70 *(978-0-7368-5308-8(1),* Capstone Pr.) Capstone.

United States Presidents, 45 vols. 2016. (United States Presidents *2017 Ser.). (ENG.). 40p. (J). (gr. 2-5). lib. bdg. 1603.80 *(978-1-68078-080-2(8),* 21777, Big Buddy Bks.) ABDO Publishing Co.

Upadhyay, Ritu. John F Kennedy the Making of a Leader. 2005. 44p. (J). lib. bdg. 15.00 *(978-1-4242-0851-7(3))* Fitzgerald Bks.

Upadhyay, Ritu & Time for Kids Editors. The Making of a Leader. 2005. (Time for Kids Ser.). (ENG., Illus.). 48p. (J). (gr. 2-4). pap. 3.99 *(978-0-06-057602-8(2))* HarperCollins Pubs.

Vander Hook, Sue. Franklin D. Roosevelt: 32nd U. S. President, 1 vol. 2008. (Essential Lives Set 2 Ser.). (ENG., Illus.). 112p. (YA). (gr. 6-12). lib. bdg. 41.36 *(978-1-60453-041-4(3),* 6663, Essential Library) ABDO Publishing Co.

Venezia, Mike. Andrew Jackson. Venezia, Mike, illus. 2005. (Getting to Know the U. S. Presidents Ser.). (ENG., Illus.). 32p. (J). (gr. 3-4). 28.00 *(978-0-516-22612-5(6),* Children's Pr.) Scholastic Library Publishing.

—Andrew Johnson: Seventeenth President. Venezia, Mike, illus. 2005. (Getting to Know the U. S. Presidents Ser.). (ENG., Illus.). 32p. (J). (gr. 3-7). lib. bdg. 28.00 *(978-0-516-22622-4(3),* Children's Pr.) Scholastic Library Publishing.

—Benjamin Harrison, 23. Venezia, Mike, illus. 2006. (Getting to Know the U. S. Presidents Ser.). (ENG., Illus.). 32p. (J). (gr. 3-6). lib. bdg. 22.44 *(978-0-516-22628-6(2))* Scholastic Library Publishing.

—Calvin Coolidge: Thirtieth President 1923-1929, 30. Venezia, Mike, illus. 2007. (Getting to Know the U. S. Presidents Ser.). (ENG., Illus.). 32p. (J). (gr. 3-6). lib. bdg. 22.44 *(978-0-516-22634-7(7))* Scholastic Library Publishing.

—Chester A. Arthur. Venezia, Mike, illus. 2006. (Getting to Know the U. S. Presidents Ser.). (ENG., Illus.). 32p. (J). (gr. 3-7). lib. bdg. 28.00 *(978-0-516-22626-2(6),* Children's Pr.) Scholastic Library Publishing.

—Chester A. Arthur: Twenty-First President, 1881-1885. Venezia, Mike, illus. 2006. (Getting to Know the U. S. Presidents Ser.). (ENG., Illus.). 32p. (J). (gr. 3-7). pap. 7.95 *(978-0-516-25401-2(4),* Children's Pr.) Scholastic Library Publishing.

—Dwight D. Eisenhower: Thirty-Fourth President 1953-1961. Venezia, Mike, illus. 2007. (Getting to Know the U. S. Presidents Ser.). (Illus.). 32p. (J). (gr. 3-4). 28.00 *(978-0-516-22638-5(X),* Children's Pr.) Scholastic Library Publishing.

—Franklin Pierce: Fourteenth President. Venezia, Mike, illus. 2005. (Getting to Know the U. S. Presidents Ser.). (ENG., Illus.). 32p. (J). (gr. 3-7). lib. bdg. 28.00 *(978-0-516-22619-4(3),* Children's Pr.) Scholastic Library Publishing.

—Gerald R. Ford: Thirty-Eighth President, 1974-1977. Venezia, Mike, illus. 2007. (Getting to Know the U. S. Presidents Ser.). (ENG., Illus.). 32p. (J). (gr. 3-4). 28.00 *(978-0-516-22642-2(8),* Children's Pr.) Scholastic Library Publishing.

—Getting to Know the U. S. Presidents, 6 bks., Set. Venezia, Mike, illus. Incl. Chester A. Arthur. lib. bdg. 28.00 *(978-0-516-22626-2(6),* Children's Pr.); Grover Cleveland: Twenty-Second & Twenty-Fourth President, 1885-1889, 1893-1897. lib. bdg. 28.00 *(978-0-516-22627-9(4),* Children's Pr.); James A. Garfield. lib. bdg. 28.00 *(978-0-516-22625-5(8),* Children's Pr.); Rutherford B. Hayes: Nineteenth President, 1877-1881. lib. bdg. 28.00 *(978-0-516-22624-8(X),* Children's Pr.); William McKinley. lib. bdg. 28.00 *(978-0-516-22629-3(0),* Children's Pr.); 23. Benjamin Harrison. lib. bdg. 22.44 *(978-0-516-22628-6(2));* 32p. (J). (gr. 3-6). (Illus.). 2006. Set lib. bdg. 162.00 o.p. *(978-0-516-25409-8(X),* Children's Pr.) Scholastic Library Publishing.

—Getting to Know the U. S. Presidents, 6 bks., Set. Venezia, Mike, illus. Incl. Dwight D. Eisenhower: Thirty-Fourth President 1953-1961. 28.00 *(978-0-516-22638-5(X),* Children's Pr.); Harry S. Truman: Thirty-Third President. 28.00 *(978-0-516-22637-8(1),* Children's Pr.); Lyndon B. Johnson: Thirty-Sixth President, 1963-1969. 28.00 *(978-0-516-22640-8(1),* Children's Pr.); Richard M. Nixon: Thirty-Seventh President, 1969-1974. 28.00 *(978-0-516-22641-5(X),* Children's Pr.); 32. Franklin D. Roosevelt: Thirty-Second President 1933-1945. 22.44 *(978-0-516-22636-1(3));* 32. John F. Kennedy: Thirty-Fifth President 1961-1963. 22.44 *(978-0-516-22639-2(8));* (Illus.). 32p. (J). (gr. 3-6). 2007. 2007. 162.00 o.p. *(978-0-531-17733-4(5),* Children's Pr.) Scholastic Library Publishing.

—Getting to Know the U. S. Presidents: Bill Clinton. Venezia, Mike, illus. 2007. (Getting to Know the U. S. Presidents Ser.). (ENG., Illus.). 32p. (J). (gr. 3-4). 28.00 *(978-0-516-22646-0(0),* Children's Pr.) Scholastic Library Publishing.

—Getting to Know the U. S. Presidents: George Bush. Venezia, Mike, illus. 2008. (Getting to Know the U. S. Presidents Ser.). (ENG., Illus.). 32p. (J). (gr. 3-4). pap. 7.95 *(978-0-516-25536-1(3),* Children's Pr.) Scholastic Library Publishing.

—Getting to Know the U. S. Presidents: Gerald R. Ford. Venezia, Mike, illus. 2008. (Getting to Know the U. S. Presidents Ser.). (ENG., Illus.). 32p. (J). (gr. 3-4). pap. 7.95 *(978-0-516-25597-2(5),* Children's Pr.) Scholastic Library Publishing.

—Getting to Know the U. S. Presidents: John Tyler. Venezia, Mike, illus. 2005. (Getting to Know the U. S. Presidents Ser.). (ENG., Illus.). 32p. (J). (gr. 3-4). per. 7.95 *(978-0-516-27484-3(8),* Children's Pr.) Scholastic Library Publishing.

—Getting to Know the U. S. Presidents: Richard M. Nixon. Venezia, Mike, illus. 2007. (Getting to Know the U. S. Presidents Ser.). (ENG., Illus.). 32p. (J). (gr. 3-4). pap. 7.95 *(978-0-531-17949-9(4),* Children's Pr.) Scholastic Library Publishing.

—Getting to Know the U. S. Presidents: Thomas Jefferson, 3. Venezia, Mike, illus. 2004. (Getting to Know the U. S. Presidents Ser.). (ENG., Illus.). 32p. (J). (gr. 3-6). 22.44 *(978-0-516-22608-8(8))* Scholastic Library Publishing.

—Getting to Know the U. S. Presidents: William Henry Harrison. Venezia, Mike, illus. 2005. (Getting to Know the U. S. Presidents Ser.). (ENG., Illus.). 32p. (J). (gr. 3-4). per. 7.95 *(978-0-516-27483-6(X),* Children's Pr.) Scholastic Library Publishing.

—Grover Cleveland: Twenty-Second & Twenty-Fourth President, 1885-1889, 1893-1897. Venezia, Mike, illus. 2006. (Getting to Know the U. S. Presidents Ser.). (ENG., Illus.). 32p. (J). (gr. 3-7). pap. 7.95 *(978-0-516-25402-9(2));* lib. bdg. 28.00 *(978-0-516-22627-9(4))* Scholastic Library Publishing. (Children's Pr.).

—Harry S. Truman: Thirty-Third President. Venezia, Mike, illus. 2007. (Getting to Know the U. S. Presidents Ser.). (Illus.). 32p. (J). (gr. 3-4). 28.00 *(978-0-516-22637-8(1),* Children's Pr.) Scholastic Library Publishing.

—James A. Garfield. Venezia, Mike, illus. 2006. (Getting to Know the U. S. Presidents Ser.). (ENG., Illus.). 32p. (J). (gr. 3-7). lib. bdg. 28.00 *(978-0-516-22625-5(8),* Children's Pr.) Scholastic Library Publishing.

—James Buchanan: Fifteenth President. Venezia, Mike, illus. 2005. (Getting to Know the U. S. Presidents Ser.). (ENG., Illus.). 32p. (J). (gr. 3-7). lib. bdg. 28.00 *(978-0-516-22620-0(7),* Children's Pr.) Scholastic Library Publishing.

—James K. Polk: Eleventh President, 1845-1849. Venezia, Mike, illus. 2005. (Getting to Know the U. S. Presidents Ser.). (ENG., Illus.). 32p. (J). (gr. 3-4). 28.00 *(978-0-516-22616-3(9),* Children's Pr.) Scholastic Library Publishing.

—Jimmy Carter: Thirty-Ninth President 1977-1981. Venezia, Mike, illus. 2007. (Getting to Know the U. S. Presidents Ser.). (ENG., Illus.). 32p. (J). (gr. 3-4). 28.00 *(978-0-516-22643-9(6),* Children's Pr.) Scholastic Library Publishing.

—John Tyler: Tenth President, 1841-1845. Venezia, Mike, illus. 2005. (Getting to Know the U. S. Presidents Ser.). (ENG., Illus.). 32p. (J). (gr. 3-4). 28.00 *(978-0-516-22615-6(0),* Children's Pr.) Scholastic Library Publishing.

—Martin Van Buren. Venezia, Mike, illus. 2005. (Getting to Know the U. S. Presidents Ser.). (ENG., Illus.). 32p. (J). (gr. 3-4). 28.00 *(978-0-516-22613-2(4),* Children's Pr.) Scholastic Library Publishing.

—Millard Fillmore: Thirteenth President. Venezia, Mike, illus. 2005. (Getting to Know the U. S. Presidents Ser.). (ENG., Illus.). 32p. (J). (gr. 3-7). lib. bdg. 28.00 *(978-0-516-22618-7(5),* Children's Pr.) Scholastic Library Publishing.

—Millard Fillmore: Thirteenth President, 1850-1853. Venezia, Mike, illus. 2006. (Getting to Know the U. S. Presidents Ser.). (ENG., Illus.). 32p. (J). (gr. 3-7). per. 7.95 *(978-0-516-25487-6(1),* Children's Pr.) Scholastic Library Publishing.

—Ronald Reagan: Fortieth President, 1981-1989. Venezia, Mike, illus. 2007. (Getting to Know the U. S. Presidents Ser.). (ENG., Illus.). 32p. (J). (gr. 3-4). 28.00 *(978-0-516-22644-6(4),* Children's Pr.) Scholastic Library Publishing.

—Rutherford B. Hayes: Nineteenth President, 1877-1881. Venezia, Mike, illus. 2006. (Getting to Know the U. S. Presidents Ser.). (Illus.). 32p. (J). (gr. 3-7). pap. 7.95 *(978-0-516-25404-3(9));* (ENG., lib. bdg. 28.00 *(978-0-516-22624-8(X))* Scholastic Library Publishing. (Children's Pr.).

—Ulysses S. Grant. Venezia, Mike, illus. 2005. (Getting to Know the U. S. Presidents Ser.). (ENG., Illus.). 32p. (J). (gr. 3-7). lib. bdg. 28.00 *(978-0-516-22623-1(1),* Children's Pr.) Scholastic Library Publishing.

—Warren G. Harding: Twenty-Ninth President, 1921-1923. Venezia, Mike, illus. 2006. (Getting to Know the U. S. Presidents Ser.). (ENG., Illus.). 32p. (J). (gr. 3-7). lib. bdg. 28.00 *(978-0-516-22633-0(9))* Scholastic Library Publishing.

—William Henry Harrison. Venezia, Mike, illus. 2005. (Getting to Know the U. S. Presidents Ser.). (ENG., Illus.). 32p. (J). (gr. 3-4). 28.00 *(978-0-516-22614-9(2),* Children's Pr.) Scholastic Library Publishing.

—William Howard Taft: Twenty-Seventh President. Venezia, Mike, illus. 2007. (Getting to Know the U. S. Presidents Ser.). (Illus.). 32p. (J). (gr. 3-7). pap. 7.95 *(978-0-516-25239-1(9),* Children's Pr.) Scholastic Library Publishing.

—William McKinley. Venezia, Mike, illus. 2006. (Getting to Know the U. S. Presidents Ser.). (ENG., Illus.). 32p. (J). (gr. 3-7). lib. bdg. 28.00 *(978-0-516-22629-3(0),* Children's Pr.) Scholastic Library Publishing.

—Woodrow Wilson: Twenty-Eighth President. Venezia, Mike, illus. 2007. (Getting to Know the U. S. Presidents Ser.). (Illus.). 32p. (J). (gr. 3-7). pap. 7.95 *(978-0-516-25462-3(6),* Children's Pr.) Scholastic Library Publishing.

—Zachary Taylor: Twelfth President, 1849-1850. Venezia, Mike, illus. 2005. (Getting to Know the U. S. Presidents Ser.). (ENG., Illus.). 32p. (J). (gr. 3-4). 28.00 *(978-0-516-22617-0(7),* Children's Pr.) Scholastic Library Publishing.

Vescia, Monique. The Emancipation Proclamation, 1 vol. 2016. (Let's Find Out! Primary Sources Ser.). (ENG., Illus.). 32p. (J). (gr. 2-3). lib. bdg. 26.06 *(978-1-5081-0405-6(0),* bf2c8f3c-c00f-498d-9c78-61f20b774f67) Rosen Publishing Group, Inc., The.

Vierow, Wendy. The 1864 Presidential Election: A War-Weary Nation Reelects President Abraham Lincoln, 1 vol. 2004. (Headlines from History Ser.). (ENG., Illus.). 24p. (J). (gr. 3-3). lib. bdg. 26.27 *(978-0-8239-6224-2(5),* 102e5709-9d05-4831-ae6d-ef5ba17c89f) Rosen Publishing Group, Inc., The.

Waxman, Laura Hamilton. Franklin D. Roosevelt. 2004. (History Maker Bios Ser.). (J). pap. 6.95 *(978-0-8225-2539-4(9),* Lerner Pubns.) Lerner Publishing Group.

—Gerald R. Ford. 2009. pap. 52.95 *(978-0-7613-4954-9(5))* 2008. (ENG.). 48p. (gr. 3-6). 27.93 *(978-0-8225-7985-4(5),* Lerner Pubns.) Lerner Publishing Group.

—Jimmy Carter. 2006. (History Maker Biographies Ser.). (ENG., Illus.). 48p. (gr. 3-6). lib. bdg. 27.93 *(978-0-8225-5939-9(0),* Lerner Pubns.) Lerner Publishing Group.

—Woodrow Wilson. 2006. (History Maker Biographies Ser.). (ENG., Illus.). 48p. (gr. 3-6). lib. bdg. 27.93 *(978-0-8225-6053-1(4),* Lerner Pubns.) Lerner Publishing Group.

Wearing, Judy. Abraham Lincoln. 2010. (My Life Ser.). 24p. (J). (gr. 2-4). lib. bdg. 25.70 *(978-1-61690-056-4(3))* Weigl Pubs., Inc.

—Abraham Lincoln: My Life. 2010. pap. 9.95 *(978-1-61690-057-1(1))* Weigl Pubs., Inc.

Welch, Catherine A. George H. W. Bush. 2009. pap. 52.95 *(978-0-7613-4952-5(9))* 2008. (ENG., Illus.). 48p. (J). (gr. 3-6). 27.93 *(978-0-8225-8895-5(1),* Lerner Pubns.) Lerner Publishing Group.

West, David. George Washington: The Life of an American Patriot. 2009. (Graphic Nonfiction Biographies Ser.). (Illus.). 48p. (YA). (gr. 4-5). 58.50 *(978-1-61513-017-7(9),* Rosen Reference) Rosen Publishing Group, Inc., The.

Weston Woods Staff, creator. What to Do about Alice? 2011. 38.75 *(978-0-545-29822-3(9))* Weston Woods Studios, Inc.

Whitelaw, Nancy. Andrew Jackson: Frontier President. 2004. (Notable Americans Ser.). (Illus.). 128p. (J). (gr. 6-12). 23.95 *(978-1-883846-67-1(6),* First Biographies) Reynolds, Morgan Inc.

Wilhelm, Jeffrey. Ulysses S. Grant: From Failure to Hero. 2012. (Social Studies). (ENG.). 32p. (J). pap. 8.00 *(978-1-63437-839-0(3))* American Reading Co.

Wilson, Natashya. How to Draw the Life & Times of Herbert Hoover. (Kid's Guide to Drawing the Presidents of the United States of America Ser.). 32p. (gr. 4-4). 2009. 50.50 *(978-1-61511-144-2(1),* PowerKids Pr.) 2005. (ENG., Illus.). (YA). 30.27 *(978-1-4042-3007-1(6),* 9cbd2f0b-2164-4f30-98fe-11fb269a035d) Rosen Publishing Group, Inc., The.

—How to Draw the Life & Times of William Howard Taft. 2009. (Kid's Guide to Drawing the Presidents of the United States of America Ser.). 32p. (gr. 4-4). 50.50 *(978-1-61511-165-7(4),* PowerKids Pr.) Rosen Publishing Group, Inc., The.

Wilson, Natashya & Natashya, Wilson. How to Draw the Life & Times of James Earl Carter Jr, 1 vol. 2005. (Kid's Guide to Drawing the Presidents of the United States of America Ser.). (ENG., Illus.). 32p. (YA). (gr. 4-4). 30.27 *(978-1-4042-3015-6(7),* 450dbaf6-dfdc-48fe-a6c2-97f364a6ac78) Rosen Publishing Group, Inc., The.

Winget, Mary Mueller. Gerald R. Ford. 2007. (Presidential Leaders Ser.). (Illus.). 112p. (J). (gr. 3-7). lib. bdg. 29.27 *(978-0-8225-1509-8(1),* Twenty-First Century Bks.) Lerner Publishing Group.

Winter, Jonah. JFK. Ford, A. G., illus. 2013. (ENG.). 32p. (J). (gr. -1-3). 17.99 *(978-0-06-176807-1(3),* Tegen, Katherine Bks) HarperCollins Pubs.

Winters, Kay. Abe Lincoln: Abe Lincoln. Carpenter, Nancy, illus. 2003. (ENG.). 40p. (J). (gr. k-3). 19.99 *(978-0-689-82554-5(4),* Simon & Schuster Bks. For Young Readers) Simon & Schuster Bks. For Young Readers.

—Abe Lincoln: The Boy Who Loved Books. Carpenter, Nancy, illus. 2004. 38p. (J). (gr. -1-3). reprint ed. 17.00 *(978-0-7567-7969-6(3))* DIANE Publishing Co.

—Abe Lincoln: The Boy Who Loved Books. Carpenter, Nancy, illus. 2006. (ENG.). 40p. (J). (gr. k-3). reprint ed. 8.99 *(978-1-4169-1268-2(1),* Aladdin) Simon & Schuster Children's Publishing.

Wittekind, Erika. James Madison's Presidency. 2016. (Presidential Powerhouses Ser.). (ENG., Illus.). 104p. (YA). (gr. 6-12). 35.99 *(978-1-4677-7929-6(6),* e13b2ba0-3b43-4bfa-ba26-961be1313ce5); E-Book 54.65 *(978-1-4677-8599-0(7))* Lerner Publishing Group. (Lerner Pubns.).

Wong, Angi Ma. Barack Obama: Historymaker. 2009. (Illus.). 104p. (J). *(978-1-928753-26-1(8))* Pacific Heritage Bks.

Wong, Angi Ma, illus. Meet President Obama: America's 44th President. 2009. 32p. (J). *(978-1-928753-28-5(0))* Pacific Heritage Bks.

Wood, Ethel, compiled by. The Presidency. 2004. (Historical Reader Ser.). (Illus.). 240p. (gr. 6-12). 13.32 *(978-0-618-04821-2(9),* 2-00153) Holt McDougal.

World Book, Inc. Staff, contrib. by. The World Book of America's Presidents, 2 vols. 2005. (Illus.). (gr. 5-12). 99.00 *(978-0-7166-3698-4(0))* World Bk., Inc.

Wukovits, John F. George W Bush: People in the News. 2004. (Illus.). 111p. (J). (gr. 4-8). reprint ed. 22.00 *(978-0-7567-7902-3(2))* DIANE Publishing Co.

Yomtov, Nel. Andrew Jackson: Heroic Leader or Cold-Hearted Ruler?, 1 vol. 2013. (Perspectives on History Ser.). (ENG., Illus.). 32p. (J). (gr. 3-6). 27.99 *(978-1-4765-0245-8(5),* 122299); pap. 7.95 *(978-1-4765-3409-1(8),* 123540) Capstone.

Young, Bev. Presidential Cookies. 2nd ed. 2005. Orig. Title: Presidential Cookies the Lure & the Lore. (ENG., Illus.). 168p. (YA). 23.95 *(978-0-9729095-3-2(2),* SAN 255-1077) Presidential Publishing.

Young, Jeff C. Dwight D. Eisenhower: Soldier & President. 2004. (Notable Americans Ser.). (Illus.). 128p. (YA). (gr. 6-12). 23.95 *(978-1-883846-76-3(5),* First Biographies) Reynolds, Morgan Inc.

Zahensky, Kenneth, ed. George W. Bush, 1 vol. 2017. (Pivotal Presidents: Profiles in Leadership Ser.). (ENG., Illus.). 80p. (J). (gr. 8-8). 36.47 *(978-1-68048-629-2(2),* 313237e8-c2d5-4974-8ba2-eee0eb5e0ae8, Britannica Educational Publishing) Rosen Publishing Group, Inc., The.

Zamora, Dulce. How to Draw the Life & Times of Franklin Pierce. (Kid's Guide to Drawing the Presidents of the United States of America Ser.). 32p. (gr. 4-4). 2009. 50.50 *(978-1-61511-137-4(9),* PowerKids Pr.) 2005. (ENG.). (YA). 30.27 *(978-1-4042-2991-4(4),* 891fb2eb-8678-46c5-89ea-bbe363fddea6) Rosen Publishing Group, Inc., The.

—How to Draw the Life & Times of John Fitzgerald Kennedy. 2009. (Kid's Guide to Drawing the Presidents of the United States of America Ser.). 32p. (gr. 4-4). 50.50 *(978-1-61511-151-0(4),* PowerKids Pr.) Rosen Publishing Group, Inc., The.

—How to Draw the Life & Times of John Tyler. 2009. (Kid's Guide to Drawing the Presidents of the United States of America Ser.). 32p. (gr. 4-4). 50.50 *(978-1-61511-153-4(0),* PowerKids Pr.) Rosen Publishing Group, Inc., The.

Zeiger, Jennifer. Cornerstones of Freedom, Third Series: Barack Obama. 2012. (Cornerstones of Freedom, Third Ser.). (ENG.). 64p. (J). (gr. 4-6). lib. bdg. 30.00 *(978-0-531-23050-3(3),* Children's Pr.) Scholastic Library Publishing.

Zuchora-Walske, Christine. Andrew Jackson's Presidency. 2016. (Presidential Powerhouses Ser.). (ENG., Illus.). 104p. (YA). (gr. 6-12). 35.99 *(978-1-4677-7926-5(1),* 78407cea-eed3-4c5d-9bd1-0b769822ca4e, Lerner Pubns.) Lerner Publishing Group.

Zumbusch, Amelie von. Barack Obama: Man of Destiny, 1 vol. 2010. (Making History: the Obamas Ser.). (ENG., Illus.). 24p. (J). (gr. 2-3). pap. 9.25 *(978-1-4358-9866-0(4),* e200cb41-050a-4dda-87d4-a9846743869d); lib. bdg. 26.27 *(978-1-4358-9387-0(5),* 3e3364d2-8945-4a03-bc46-b5f5f79e1823) Rosen Publishing Group, Inc., The. (PowerKids Pr.).

—Making History: The Obamas, 8 vols. Incl. Barack Obama: Man of Destiny. lib. bdg. 26.27 *(978-1-4358-9387-0(5),* 3e3364d2-8945-4a03-bc46-b5f5f79e1823); Barack Obama's Family Tree: Roots of Achievement. lib. bdg. 26.27 *(978-1-4358-9390-0(5),* c4826398-32e9-4a8a-be59-60f8cdd62981); First Family: The Obamas in the White House. lib. bdg. 26.27 *(978-1-4358-9389-4(1),* 2248e056-c7f7-4e7f-b083-bcbee019cd64); Michelle Obama: Our First Lady. lib. bdg. 26.27 *(978-1-4358-9388-7(3),* 62b0413a-3e96-4376-9e00-b445bdcb7d73); (J). (gr. 2-3). (Making History: the Obamas Ser.). (ENG., Illus.). 24p. 2010. Set lib. bdg. 105.08 *(978-1-4358-9407-5(3),* 36d46a30-a7a4-4bff-beb4-bdb093b45c13, PowerKids Pr.) Rosen Publishing Group, Inc., The.

20 Fun Facts about the White House. 2013. (Fun Fact File: US History! Ser.). 32p. (J). (gr. 3-6). pap. 63.00 *(978-1-4339-9205-6(1))* Stevens, Gareth Publishing LLLP.

PRESIDENTS—UNITED STATES—ASSASSINATION

Gunderson, Jessica. President Mckinley's Killer & the America He Left Behind: The Assassin, the Crime, Teddy Roosevelt's Rise, & the Dawn of the American Century. 2018. (Assassins' America Ser.). (ENG., Illus.). 64p. (J). (gr. 4-9). lib. bdg. 30.65 *(978-0-7565-5714-0(3),* 137213, Compass Point Bks.) Capstone.

Gunderson, Jessica & Tougas, Joseph. Assassins' America: Four Killers, Four Murdered Presidents, & the Country They Left Behind. 2018. (ENG.). 208p. (J). (gr. 4-9). pap., pap., pap. 9.95 *(978-1-62370-981-5(4),* 137226, Capstone Young Readers) Capstone.

Salandria, Vincent J. False Mystery: Essays on the Assassination of JFK. Kelin, John, ed. 2004. 25.00 *(978-0-9754941-0-3(4))* Square Deal Pr.

Smith, Brendan Powell. Assassination! The Brick Chronicle of Attempts on the Lives of Twelve US Presidents. 2013. (ENG., Illus.). 272p. 19.95 *(978-1-62087-998-6(0),* 620998) Skyhorse Publishing Co., Inc.

—Assassination! The Brick Chronicle Presents Attempts on the Lives of Twelve US Presidents. 2016. (ENG., Illus.). 272p. pap. 19.99 *(978-1-5107-0544-9(9))* Skyhorse Publishing Co., Inc.

Spradlin, Michael P. Close Calls: How Eleven US Presidents Escaped from the Brink of Death. 2020. (ENG., Illus.). 128p. (J). 18.99 *(978-1-5476-0023-6(3),* 900195172, Bloomsbury Children's Bks.) Bloomsbury Publishing USA.

Tougas, Joe. President Garfield's Killer & the America He Left Behind: The Assassin, the Crime, the Hapless Doctors, & a President's Slow, Grim Death. 2018. (Assassins' America Ser.). (ENG., Illus.). 64p. (J). (gr. 4-9). lib. bdg. 30.65 *(978-0-7565-5715-7(1),* 137214, Compass Point Bks.) Capstone.

Wilson, Antoine. The Assassination of William McKinley. 2009. (Library of Political Assassinations Ser.). 64p. (gr. 5-5). 58.50 *(978-1-60853-830-0(3))* Rosen Publishing Group, Inc., The.

PRESIDENTS—UNITED STATES—CHILDREN

see Children of Presidents

PRESIDENTS—UNITED STATES—ELECTION

Anderson, Holly Lynn. The Presidential Election Process. 2016. (Illus.). 64p. (J). *(978-1-61900-094-0(6))* Eldorado Ink.

Anderson, Jennifer Joline. Exploring Voting & Elections. 2019. (Searchlight Books (tm) — Getting into Government Ser.). (ENG., Illus.). 32p. (J). (gr. 3-5). 30.65 *(978-1-5415-5584-6(8),* edfc52c7-b514-41c7-ad60-9a07e9eac03c); pap. 9.99 *(978-1-5415-7481-6(8),* a06ae5c0-7f8a-407a-82ca-0142bda7f976) Lerner Publishing Group. (Lerner Pubns.).

Beyer, Mark. The Election of 1800: Congress Helps Settle a Three-Way Vote, 1 vol. 2003. (Primary Sources of Life in the New American Nation Ser.). (ENG., Illus.). 32p. (gr. 4-5). pap. 10.00 *(978-0-8239-4255-8(4),* fe1b84cf-fcb7-471d-8dbe-062a4f707a3d) Rosen Publishing Group, Inc., The.

—The Election Of 1800: Congress Helps Settle a Three-Way Vote. 2009. (Life in the New American Nation Ser.). 32p. (gr. 4-4). 47.90 *(978-1-61514-282-8(7))* Rosen Publishing Group, Inc., The.

Biskup, Agnieszka. Obama: The Historic Election of America's 44th President, 1 vol. Hayden, Seitu, illus. 2011. (American Graphic Ser.). (ENG.). 32p. (J). (gr. 3-9). pap. 8.10 *(978-1-4296-7339-6(7),* 116882) Capstone.

—Obama: The Historic Election of America's 44th President. Hayden, William, illus. 2011. (American Graphic Ser.). (ENG.). 32p. (J). (gr. 3-4). pap. 49.60 *(978-1-4296-7340-2(0),* 16837, Capstone Pr.) Capstone.

Blashfield, Jean F. Hillary Clinton, 1 vol. 2011. (Leading Women Ser.). (ENG.). 96p. (YA). (gr. 7-7). 42.64 *(978-0-7614-4954-6(X),* e653b8cd-2fce-4ce2-be4a-065c33d4a87f) Cavendish Square Publishing LLC.

Bradford Edwards, Sue. The Debate about the Electoral College. 2018. (Pros & Cons Ser.). (ENG., Illus.). 48p. (J). (gr. 5-6). pap. 11.95 *(978-1-63517-598-1(4),* 1635175984); lib. bdg. 34.21 *(978-1-63517-526-4(7),* 1635175267) North Star Editions. (Focus Readers).

Burgan, Michael. TV Shapes Presidential Politics in the Kennedy-Nixon Debates: 4D an Augmented Reading Experience. 2018. (Captured Television History 4D Ser.). (ENG., Illus.). 64p. (J). (gr. 5-9). pap. 8.99 *(978-0-7565-5827-7(1),* 138352, Compass Point Bks.) Capstone.

Buttigieg, Chasten. I Have Something to Tell You — For Young Adults: A Memoir. 2023. (ENG., Illus.). 224p. (YA). (gr. 7). 18.99 *(978-1-6659-0437-7(2),* Atheneum Bks. for Young Readers) Simon & Schuster Children's Publishing.

Carole Marsh. Presidential Elections. 2004. (Presidents on Parade Ser.). lib. bdg. 29.95 *(978-0-635-02221-9(4))*; 48p. (gr. 3-8). pap. 7.95 *(978-0-635-02220-2(6))* Gallopade International.

Connors, Kathleen. What Is the Electoral College?, 1 vol. 2017. (Look at Your Government Ser.). (ENG., Illus.). 32p. (J). (gr. 2-2). pap. 11.50 *(978-1-4824-6063-6(7),* a184aa0b-d3e1-4f17-91fd-2e8b635003f6) Stevens, Gareth Publishing LLLP.

Corso, Phil. The Electoral College, 1 vol. 2019. (U. S. Presidential Elections: How They Work Ser.). (ENG.). 32p. (gr. 4-5). pap. 11.60 *(978-1-7253-1074-2(0),* 312969ff-bb62-4ba6-ae0a-9f625160136f, PowerKids Pr.) Rosen Publishing Group, Inc., The.

Edwards, Sue Bradford. The Debate about the Electoral College. 2018. (Illus.). 48p. (J). *(978-1-63517-742-8(1),* Focus Readers) North Star Editions.

—The Debate about the Electoral College. 2018. 48p. (J). *(978-1-4896-9616-8(4),* AV2 by Weigl) Weigl Pubs., Inc.

Election 2004: Choosing America's President. 2004. (Illus.). 22p. (J). *(978-0-439-68921-2(X))* Scholastic, Inc.

Emmett, Dan & Maynard, Charles. I Am a Secret Service Agent: My Life Spent Protecting the President. 2018. (ENG., Illus.). 224p. (YA). pap. 17.99 *(978-1-250-18180-0(1),* 900190380, St. Martin's Griffin) St. Martin's Pr.

Gibson, Karen Bush. The Historic Fight for the 2008 Democratic Presidential Nomination: The Obama View. 2009. (Monumental Milestones Ser.). (Illus.). 48p. (YA). (gr. 4-7). lib. bdg. 29.95 *(978-1-58415-732-8(1))* Mitchell Lane Pubs.

Goldman, David J. Presidential Losers. 2004. (Middle Grade Nonfiction Ser.). (ENG., Illus.). 72p. (gr. 5-12). 25.26 *(978-0-8225-0100-8(7),* Carolrhoda Bks.) Lerner Publishing Group.

Greenhaven Press Staff, ed. Mitt Romney. 2012. (People in the News Ser.). (ENG., Illus.). 128p. (gr. 7-10). lib. bdg. 33.95 *(978-1-4205-0877-2(6),* Lucent Bks.) Cengage Gale.

Gunderson, Jessica. The Election Of 1860: A Nation Divides on the Eve of War. 2016. (Presidential Politics Ser.). (ENG.). 48p. (J). pap. 54.70 *(978-1-4914-8737-2(2),* 24425) Capstone.

Gutman, Dan. Election! A Kid's Guide to Picking Our President 2012. 2012. (ENG.). 162p. (J). (gr. 2-6). pap. 11.99 *(978-1-4532-7066-0(3),* Open Road Media Young Readers) Open Road Integrated Media, Inc.

Havelin, Kate. Victoria Woodhull: Fearless Feminist. 2006. (Trailblazer Biographies Ser.). (ENG., Illus.). 112p. (gr. 5-9). lib. bdg. 31.93 *(978-0-8225-5986-3(2),* Lerner Pubns.) Lerner Publishing Group.

Heing, Bridey, ed. Critical Perspectives on the Electoral College, 1 vol. 2019. (Analyzing the Issues Ser.). (ENG.). 232p. (gr. 8-8). 50.93 *(978-1-9785-0331-1(8),* f11bfec0-fa08-49a7-bb6f-09cb9d8fb693) Enslow Publishing, LLC.

Idzikowski, Lisa, ed. The Electoral College & the Popular Vote, 1 vol. 2017. (Introducing Issues with Opposing Viewpoints Ser.). (ENG.). 120p. (YA). (gr. 7-10). 43.63 *(978-1-5345-0193-5(2),* 3373069d-372c-4919-b905-1da417d26ce4) Greenhaven Publishing LLC.

King, Margaret. The Electoral College. 2018. (TIME(r): Informational Text Ser.). (ENG., Illus.). 48p. (J). (gr. 7-8). pap. 13.99 *(978-1-4258-5013-5(8))* Teacher Created Materials, Inc.

Klein, Adria F. Barack Obama. 2009. pap. 13.25 *(978-1-60559-055-4(X))* Hameray Publishing Group, Inc.

Klepeis, Alicia Z. Understanding the Electoral College. 2018. (What's up with Your Government? Ser.). (ENG.). 32p. (J). (gr. 4-7). 20.80 *(978-1-5311-8625-8(4))* Perfection Learning Corp.

—Understanding the Electoral College, 1 vol. 2017. (What's up with Your Government? Ser.). (ENG., Illus.). 32p. (J). (gr. 4-5). 27.93 *(978-1-5383-2228-4(5),* f4269108-a6e3-4574-bfbc-4fe2c8e6985a); pap. 11.00 *(978-1-5383-2324-3(9),* ccbe5972-ff8c-41f1-a10b-71458c60d659) Rosen Publishing Group, Inc., The. (PowerKids Pr.).

Krasner, Barbara. A Timeline of Presidential Elections. 2016. (Presidential Politics Ser.). (ENG., Illus.). 48p. (J). (gr. 3-6). lib. bdg. 29.99 *(978-1-4914-8239-1(7),* 130710) Capstone.

Krasner, Barbara, et al. Presidential Politics. 2016. (Presidential Politics Ser.). (ENG., Illus.). 48p. (J). (gr. 3-6). 123.29 *(978-1-4914-8738-9(0),* 24426, Stone Arch Bks.) Capstone.

Krull, Kathleen. A Woman for President: The Story of Victoria Woodhull. Dyer, Jane, illus. 2006. (J). (gr. 2-7). 14.60 *(978-0-7569-8179-2(4))* Perfection Learning Corp.

Mattern, Joanne. President Donald Trump. 2017. (Rookie Biographies(tm) Ser.). (ENG., Illus.). 32p. (J). lib. bdg. 25.00 *(978-0-531-23226-2(3),* Children's Pr.) Scholastic Library Publishing.

Morris-Lipsman, Arlene. Presidential Races: The Battle for Power in the United States. 2007. (People's History Ser.). (ENG., Illus.). 112p. (gr. 5-12). lib. bdg. 33.26 *(978-0-8225-6783-7(0))* Lerner Publishing Group.

National Geographic Learning. Reading Expeditions (Social Studies: Voices from America's Past): the Spirit of a New Nation. 2007. (Avenues Ser.). (ENG., Illus.). 40p. (J). pap. 21.95 *(978-0-7922-8684-4(7))* CENGAGE Learning.

Obama, Barack. & Nelson, Kadir. Change Has Come: An Artist Celebrates Our American Spirit. Nelson, Kadir, illus. 2009. (ENG., Illus.). 64p. (J). (gr. 1). 12.99 *(978-1-4169-8955-4(2),* Simon & Schuster Bks. For Young Readers) Simon & Schuster Bks. For Young Readers.

Orr, Tamra B. Obama vs. Mccain & the Historic Election. 2017. (Perspectives Library: Modern Perspectives Ser.). (ENG., Illus.). 32p. (J). (gr. 4-7). lib. bdg. 32.07 *(978-1-63472-860-7(2),* 209866) Cherry Lake Publishing.

See, Betty. Electing the President: The Electoral Process in Action. 2005. (ENG.). 48p. pap. 14.95 *(978-1-59363-067-6(0))* Prufrock Pr.

St. George, Judith. So You Want to Be President? Small, David, illus. 2004. (J). (gr. 1-6). 29.95 *(978-1-55592-132-3(9))* Weston Woods Studios, Inc.

Stier, Catherine. If I Ran for President. Avril, Lynne, illus. 2007. (Albert Whitman Prairie Books Ser.). (ENG.). 32p. (J). (gr. 1-4). 18.80 *(978-1-5311-7682-2(8))* Perfection Learning Corp.

—If I Ran for President. Avril, Lynne, illus. 2012. (J). 34.28 *(978-1-61913-115-6(3))* Weigl Pubs., Inc.

Streissguth, Tom, contrib. by. The 2016 Presidential Election. 2017. (Special Reports Set 3 Ser.). (ENG., Illus.). 112p. (J). (gr. 6-12). lib. bdg. 41.36 *(978-1-5321-1336-9(6),* 27544, Essential Library) ABDO Publishing Co.

Tracy, Kathleen. The Historic Fight for the 2008 Democratic Presidential Nomination: The Clinton View. 2009. (Monumental Milestones Ser.). (Illus.). 48p. (YA). (gr. 4-7). lib. bdg. 29.95 *(978-1-58415-731-1(3))* Mitchell Lane Pubs.

Vierow, Wendy. The 1864 Presidential Election: A War-Weary Nation Reelects President Abraham Lincoln. 2009. (Headlines from History Ser.). 24p. (gr. 3-3). 42.50 *(978-1-61513-239-3(2),* PowerKids Pr.) Rosen Publishing Group, Inc., The.

Wagner, Heather Lehr. How the President Is Elected. 2007. (U. Government: How It Works). (ENG., Illus.). 95p. (gr. 5-9). lib. bdg. 30.00 *(978-0-7910-9418-1(9),* P127246, Facts On File) Infobase Holdings, Inc.

Yomtov, Nel. Sarah Palin: Political Rebel. D'Ottavi, Francesca, illus. 2011. (American Graphic Ser.). (ENG.). 32p. (J). (gr. 3-4). pap. 48.60 *(978-1-4296-7342-6(7),* 16838, Capstone Pr.) Capstone.

—Sarah Palin: Political Rebel, 1 vol. D'Ottavi, Francesca, illus. 2011. (American Graphic Ser.). (ENG.). 32p. (J). (gr. 3-9). pap. 8.10 *(978-1-4296-7341-9(9),* 116883, Capstone Pr.) Capstone.

Yomtov, Nelson. Sarah Palin: Political Rebel, 1 vol. D'Ottavi, Francesca, illus. 2011. (American Graphic Ser.). (ENG.). 32p. (J). (gr. 3-9). lib. bdg. 31.32 *(978-1-4296-6018-1(X),* 114955, Capstone Pr.) Capstone.

Zacharias, Jared, ed. Amendment XII: the Presidential Election Process, 1 vol. 2008. (Constitutional Amendments: Beyond the Bill of Rights Ser.). (ENG., Illus.). 144p. (gr. 10-12). lib. bdg. 44.83 *(978-0-7377-4123-0(6),* cd1027e1-5dde-4674-b08d-430202fe9555, Greenhaven Publishing) Greenhaven Publishing LLC.

PRESIDENTS—UNITED STATES—FAMILY

Davis, Gibbs. First Kids. Comport, Sally Wern, illus. 2004. (Step into Reading Ser.). (ENG.). 48p. (J). (gr. 2-4). pap. 4.99 *(978-0-375-82218-6(6),* Random Hse. Bks. for Young Readers) Random Hse. Children's Bks.

Katirgis, Jane. Celebrating the Obama Family in Pictures, 1 vol. 2009. (Obama Family Photo Album Ser.). (ENG., Illus.). 32p. (gr. 3-3). lib. bdg. 26.60 *(978-0-7660-3653-6(7),* ba36c440-f581-4b87-aec2-7c703937a9ed) Enslow Publishing, LLC.

Marsh, Carole. Barack Obama - America's 44th President. 2008. (Here & Now Ser.). (Illus.). 40p. (J). (gr. 2-9). pap. 9.99 *(978-0-635-06848-4(6))* Gallopade International.

O'Connor, Jane. If the Walls Could Talk: Family Life at the White House. Hovland, Gary, illus. 2004. (ENG.). 48p. (J). (gr. 1-4). 19.99 *(978-0-689-86863-4(4),* Simon & Schuster/Paula Wiseman Bks.) Simon & Schuster/Paula Wiseman Bks.

Snyder, Gail. Sasha. 2007. (Obamas Ser.). (Illus.). 64p. (YA). (gr. 3-6). pap. 9.95 *(978-1-4222-1487-9(7))*; (gr. 4-7). lib. bdg. 19.95 *(978-1-4222-1480-0(X))* Mason Crest.

Weston Woods Staff, creator. George Washington's Mother. 2011. 38.75 *(978-0-439-72669-6(7))*; 18.95 *(978-0-439-72667-2(0))* Weston Woods Studios, Inc.

White House Insiders. 2014. (White House Insiders Ser.). 24p. (J). (gr. 2-5). pap. 41.70 *(978-1-4824-1595-7(X))* Stevens, Gareth Publishing LLLP.

Zumbusch, Amelie von. Barack Obama's Family Tree: Roots of Achievement, 1 vol. 2010. (Making History: the Obamas Ser.). (ENG., Illus.). 24p. (J). (gr. 2-3). pap. 9.25 *(978-1-4358-9872-1(9),* 699fd69a-374d-485e-9674-bd8fd2dbac80); lib. bdg. 26.27 *(978-1-4358-9390-0(5),* c4826398-32e9-4a8a-be59-60f8cdd62981) Rosen Publishing Group, Inc., The. (PowerKids Pr.).

—First Family: The Obamas in the White House, 1 vol. 2010. (Making History: the Obamas Ser.). (ENG., Illus.). 24p. (J). (gr. 2-3). pap. 9.25 *(978-1-4358-9870-7(2),* 3b0d7460-ff6f-422c-9b8d-54dffd4e98f1); lib. bdg. 26.27 *(978-1-4358-9389-4(1),* 2248e056-c7f7-4e7f-b083-bcbee019cd64) Rosen Publishing Group, Inc., The. (PowerKids Pr.).

PRESIDENTS—UNITED STATES—FICTION

Alger, Horatio. From Canal Boy to President: Or the Boyhood & Manhood of James A. Garfield. 2007. (ENG.). 196p. pap. 19.99 *(978-1-4346-2511-3(7))* Creative Media Partners, LLC.

Angleberger, Tom. Fake Mustache: Or, How Jodie o'Rodeo & Her Wonder Horse (and Some Nerdy Kid) Saved the U. S. Presidential Election from a Mad Genius Criminal Mastermind. 2013. (ENG.). 208p. (J). (gr. 3-7). pap. 7.95 *(978-1-4197-1163-3(6),* 1013303, Amulet Bks.) Abrams, Inc.

Bailey, Michael. Cartoon Nation, 6 bks., Set. Incl. Citizenship. Skog, Jason. Brown, Kelly, illus. 31.32 *(978-1-4296-1331-6(9),* 94598); Political Elections. Miller, Davis Worth & Brevard, Katherine M. Barnett, Charles, III, illus. 31.32 *(978-1-4296-1333-0(5),* 94604); Political Parties. Burgan, Michael & Hoena, Blake A. Barnett, Charles et al, illus. lib. bdg. 31.32 *(978-1-4296-1334-7(3),* 94607); 32p. (J). (gr. 3-9). (Cartoon Nation Ser.). (ENG.). 2008. 93.96 o.p. *(978-1-4296-1675-1(X),* 166725, Capstone Pr.) Capstone.

Barnett, Mac. President Taft Is Stuck in the Bath. Van Dusen, Chris, illus. 2016. (ENG.). 32p. (J). (gr. -1-3). 7.99 *(978-0-7636-6556-2(8))* Candlewick Pr.

Blundell, Gerald Lee. Bunkalunken Goes to Washington & Other Stories, 1 vol. 2010. 138p. pap. 24.95 *(978-1-4489-5234-2(4))* America Star Bks.

Cabot, Meg. All-American Girl. 2008. (All-American Girl Ser.: Vol. 1). 398p. (YA). (gr. 7-12). 19.65 *(978-1-4178-2386-4(0))* Turtleback.

—Ready or Not. (All-American Girl Ser.: 2). (ENG.). 2008. 336p. (YA). (gr. 8). pap. 10.99 *(978-0-06-147996-0(9),* HarperTeen) 2005. 256p. (J). (gr. 7-18). 16.99 *(978-0-06-072450-4(1))* HarperCollins Pubs.

Calabrese, Diane Marie. My Dad's off to War. Swope, Brenda, illus. 2011. 28p. pap. 24.95 *(978-1-4560-0942-7(7))* America Star Bks.

Cavanah, Frances. Abe Lincoln Gets His Chance. 2007. 72p. per. *(978-1-4068-4447-4(0))* Echo Library.

Cobot, Meg. All-American Girl. 2004. 416p. (J). (gr. 7-18). pap. 44.00 incl. audio *(978-0-8072-2281-2(X),* Listening Library) Random Hse. Audio Publishing Group.

DeVillers, Julia. Cleared for Takeoff. Pooler, Paige, illus. 2012. (Liberty Porter, First Daughter Ser.: 3). (ENG.). 224p. (J). (gr. 3-7). pap. 7.99 *(978-1-4169-9131-1(X),* Simon & Schuster/Paula Wiseman Bks.) Simon & Schuster/Paula Wiseman Bks.

—Liberty Porter, First Daughter, 1. Pooler, Paige, illus. 2009. (Liberty Porter, First Daughter Ser.: 1). (ENG.). 176p. (J). (gr. 3-7). 15.99 *(978-1-4169-9126-7(3),* Aladdin) Simon & Schuster Children's Publishing.

—Liberty Porter, First Daughter. Pooler, Paige, illus. 2010. (Liberty Porter, First Daughter Ser.: 1). (ENG.). 192p. (J). (gr. 3-7). pap. 7.99 *(978-1-4169-9127-4(1),* Simon & Schuster/Paula Wiseman Bks.) Simon & Schuster/Paula Wiseman Bks.

—New Girl in Town, 2. Pooler, Paige, illus. 2010. (Liberty Porter, First Daughter Ser.: 2). (ENG.). 208p. (J). (gr. 3-7). 17.99 *(978-1-4169-9128-1(X))* Simon & Schuster, Inc.

Edwards, Myrtice J. Dirty Sally. 2007. 44p. per. 18.95 *(978-1-4327-0774-3(4))* Outskirts Pr., Inc.

Fosberry, Jennifer. Isabella: Girl in Charge. Litwin, Mike, illus. 2016. (ENG.). 32p. (J). (gr. k-4). 16.99 *(978-1-4926-4173-5(1),* 9781492641735, Sourcebooks Jabberwocky) Sourcebooks, Inc.

Freeman, Martha. The Case of the Diamond Dog Collar, 2. 2nd ed. 2012. (First Kids Mysteries Ser.: 2). (ENG.). 144p. (J). (gr. 2-4). 21.19 *(978-0-8234-2337-8(9))* Holiday Hse., Inc.

—The Case of the Rock 'N' Roll Dog, 1. 2012. (First Kids Mysteries Ser.: 1). (ENG., Illus.). 128p. (J). (gr. 2-4). 21.19 *(978-0-8234-2267-8(4))* Holiday Hse., Inc.

Gilchrist, Jan Spivey. Obama: The Day the World Danced. 2009. (Illus.). 32p. (J). (gr. k-3). 18.99 *(978-0-9824095-0-3(8))* Pegasus Bks. for Children.

Gingrich, Callista. Hail to the Chief. Arciero, Susan, illus. 2016. (Ellis the Elephant Ser.: 6). (ENG.). 40p. (J). (gr. -1-4). 16.99 *(978-1-62157-479-8(2),* Regnery Kids) Regnery Publishing.

Gould, Jane H. John Adams, 1 vol. 2012. (Jr. Graphic Founding Fathers Ser.). (ENG., Illus.). 24p. (J). (gr. 2-3). pap. 11.60 *(978-1-4488-7993-9(0),* 430b8510-95b3-4ae5-9485-c78445f12b59); lib. bdg. 28.93 *(978-1-4488-7899-4(3),* cf2b8171-d3ee-44b1-9eb5-299a81407429) Rosen Publishing Group, Inc., The. (PowerKids Pr.).

Hill, Genita S. President Obama's Ghost. 2012. 28p. pap. 24.95 *(978-1-4626-4404-9(X))* America Star Bks.

Hutton, John. Flowers for Mr. President. 2012. (Illus.). (J). *(978-0-9789608-3-4(1))* Salem Academy & College.

James, Tina. Sarabeth Palmer: 1963-1964. 2010. 91p. (J). *(978-0-615-37484-0(0))* Afrolez Productions, LLC.

Kelaita, Lynda. Some Houses Are White. 2009. 32p. pap. 10.95 *(978-1-935125-44-0(3))* Robertson Publishing.

Kennedy Center, The. Chasing George Washington. Hoyt, Ard, illus. 2011. (ENG.). 80p. (J). (gr. 2-5). pap. 5.99 *(978-1-4169-4861-2(9),* Simon & Schuster Bks. For Young Readers) Simon & Schuster Bks. For Young Readers.

—Teddy Roosevelt & the Treasure of Ursa Major. Hoyt, Ard, illus. 2011. (ENG.). 128p. (J). (gr. 2-5). pap. 7.99 *(978-1-4169-4860-5(0),* Simon & Schuster Bks. For Young Readers) Simon & Schuster Bks. For Young Readers.

Kennedy Center, The, et al. Chasing George Washington. Hoyt, Ard, illus. 2009. (ENG.). 80p. (J). (gr. 2-5). 12.99 *(978-1-4169-4858-2(9),* Simon & Schuster Bks. For Young Readers) Simon & Schuster Bks. For Young Readers.

Krause, Robert. The President's Counting Book: The Future Generations of America. 2011. 36p. pap. 18.41 *(978-1-4269-6049-9(2))* Trafford Publishing.

Limbaugh, Rush & Adams Limbaugh, Kathryn. Rush Revere & the Presidency. 2016. (Rush Revere Ser.: 5). (ENG., Illus.). 272p. (gr. 4-7). 21.00 *(978-1-5011-5689-2(6),* Threshold Editions) Threshold Editions.

Marciano, John Bemelmans. Madeline at the White House. (Madeline Ser.). (Illus.). (J). (gr. -1-2). 2020. 34p. bds. 9.99 *(978-0-593-11800-9(6),* Viking Books for Young Readers) 2016. 48p. pap. 9.99 *(978-1-101-99780-2(X),* Puffin Books) 2011. 48p. 19.99 *(978-0-670-01228-2(9),* Viking Books for Young Readers) Penguin Young Readers Group.

—Madeline at the White House. 2016. (Madeline Ser.). lib. bdg. 19.65 *(978-0-606-38845-0(1))* Turtleback.

Marie, Cherry. The President Eats Vegetables & So Do I! 2012. 44p. pap. 12.00 *(978-0-9853259-0-9(9))* Professional Publishing Hse. LLC.

Mcdonald, Megan. Stink: The Incredible Shrinking Kid. Reynolds, Peter H., illus. 2010. (Stink Ser.: No. 1). (ENG.). 112p. (J). (gr. 1-5). 31.36 *(978-1-59961-686-5(6),* 13833, Chapter Bks.) Spotlight.

McNamara, Margaret. Presidents' Day: Ready-To-Read Level 1. Gordon, Mike, illus. 2010. (Robin Hill School Ser.). (ENG.). 32p. (J). (gr. -1-1). pap. 4.99 *(978-1-4169-9170-0(0),* Simon Spotlight) Simon Spotlight.

Meddaugh, Susan. White House Dog. 2011. (Martha Speaks: Chapter Bks.). (ENG., Illus.). 96p. (J). (gr. 1-4). 18.69 *(978-0-547-39359-9(8))*; pap. 5.99 *(978-0-547-21076-6(0))* Houghton Mifflin Harcourt Publishing Co.

Nave, Jeff. Obama's Pajamas. 2008. 44p. pap. 18.99 *(978-1-4389-3150-0(6))* AuthorHouse.

Osborne, Mary Pope. Abe Lincoln at Last! Murdocca, Sal, illus. 2013. (Magic Tree House (R) Merlin Mission Ser.: 19). 144p. (J). (gr. 2-5). 6.99 *(978-0-375-86797-2(X),* Random Hse. Bks. for Young Readers) Random Hse. Children's Bks.

—Abe Lincoln at Last! 2013. (Magic Tree House Merlin Missions Ser.: 19). lib. bdg. 16.00 *(978-0-606-35563-6(4))* Turtleback.

Pollock, Hal. Monster for President. Parisi, Anthony, illus. 2008. 28p. 14.95 *(978-0-9816554-1-3(6))* Esquire Publishing, Inc.

Rolle Williams, Joyce. Chris's Story: A Family Voting Secret Revealed. 2008. 24p. pap. 12.99 *(978-1-4389-4258-2(3))* AuthorHouse.

Roy, Ron. Capital Mysteries #11: the Secret at Jefferson's Mansion. Bush, Timothy, illus. 2009. (Capital Mysteries Ser.: 11). (ENG.). 96p. (J). (gr. 1-4). 6.99 *(978-0-375-84533-8(X),* Random Hse. Bks. for Young Readers) Random Hse. Children's Bks.

—Capital Mysteries #14: Turkey Trouble on the National Mall. Bush, Timothy, illus. 2012. (Capital Mysteries Ser.: 14). 96p. (J). (gr. 1-4). 6.99 *(978-0-307-93220-4(6),* Random Hse. Bks. for Young Readers) Random Hse. Children's Bks.

—The Election-Day Disaster. Bush, Timothy, illus. 2008. (Capital Mysteries Ser.: No. 10). 87p. (gr. 1-4). 15.00 *(978-0-7569-8802-9(0))* Perfection Learning Corp.

Roy, Ronald. Capital Mysteries #14: Turkey Trouble on the National Mall, 14. Bush, Timothy, illus. 2012. (Capital Mysteries Ser.). (ENG.). 96p. (J). (gr. 1-4). lib. bdg. 17.44 *(978-0-375-87004-0(0))* Random House Publishing Group.

Ruiz, Rachel. When Penny Met POTUS. Manwill, Melissa & Manwill, Melissa, illus. 2016. (Fiction Picture Bks.). (ENG.). 32p. (J). (gr. -1-3). lib. bdg. 27.99 *(978-1-5158-0218-1(3),* 132451, Picture Window Bks.) Capstone.

Schmidt, Gary D. First Boy. 2007. (ENG.). 224p. (YA). (gr. 5-9). pap. 14.99 *(978-0-312-37149-4(7),* 900044687) Square Fish.

Smith, Lane. Madam President. Smith, Lane, illus. 2008. (ENG., Illus.). 40p. (J). (gr. -1-3). 16.99 *(978-1-4231-0846-7(9))* Hyperion Pr.

—Madam President. 2011. (J). (gr. 1-4). 29.95 *(978-0-545-10688-7(5))* Weston Woods Studios, Inc.

Stier, Catherine. If I Ran for President. Avril, Lynne, illus. 2007. (ENG.). 32p. (J). (gr. -1-3). pap. 7.99 *(978-0-8075-3544-8(3),* 807535443) Whitman, Albert & Co.

Sun Edit and Book Design, ed. Abraham Lincoln & the Forest of Little Pigeon Creek. 2007. (Illus.). 56p. (J). 19.95 *(978-0-9798739-0-4(8))* AmenTales Entertainment, LLC.

Tubridy, Ryan. Patrick & the President. Lynch, P. J., illus. 2017. (ENG.). 40p. (J). (gr. 1-4). 16.99 *(978-0-7636-8949-0(1))* Candlewick Pr.

Walter, Aaron T. Mr Lincoln's Hat. 2008. 75p. pap. 16.95 *(978-1-60672-852-9(0))* PublishAmerica, Inc.

Wells, Rosemary. Lincoln & His Boys. Lynch, P. J., illus. 2008. (ENG.). 96p. (J). (gr. 3-7). 16.99 *(978-0-7636-3723-1(8))* Candlewick Pr.

Widdemer, Mabel Cleland. James Monroe, Good Neighbor Boy: Childhood of Famous Americans Series. Rawson, Maurice, illus. 2011. 200p. 44.95 *(978-1-258-07964-2(X))* Literary Licensing, LLC.

Worley, Michelle. Buster Goes to the White House, 1 vol. 2009. 48p. pap. 16.95 *(978-1-61546-352-7(6))* PublishAmerica, Inc.

PRESIDENTS—UNITED STATES—POETRY

Katz, Susan. The President's Stuck in the Bathtub: Poems about the Presidents. Neubecker, Robert, illus. 2012. (ENG.). 64p. (J). (gr. 1-4). 18.99 *(978-0-547-18221-6(X),* 1055967, Clarion Bks.) HarperCollins Pubs.

Raczka, Bob. Presidential Misadventures: Poems That Poke Fun at the Man in Charge. Burr, Dan E., illus. 2015. (ENG.). 48p. (J). (gr. 3-7). 25.99 *(978-1-59643-980-1(7),* 900127795) Roaring Brook Pr.

PRESIDENTS—UNITED STATES—POWER

see Executive Power

PRESIDENTS—UNITED STATES—SPOUSES

see Presidents' Spouses

PRESIDENTS' SPOUSES

Anthony, Carl Sferrazza. America's Most Influential First Ladies. 2003. (Illus.). 160p. (gr. 5-18). lib. bdg. 19.95 *(978-1-881508-69-4(2))* Oliver Pr., Inc.

Appelt, Kathi. Miss Lady Bird's Wildflowers: How a First Lady Changed America. Hein, Joy Fisher, illus. 2005. 40p. (J). lib. bdg. 17.89 *(978-0-06-001108-6(4))* HarperCollins Pubs.

Ashby, Ruth. John & Abigail Adams, 1 vol. 2004. (Presidents & First Ladies Ser.). (ENG., Illus.). 48p. (gr. 5-8). lib. bdg. 33.67 *(978-0-8368-5755-9(0),* 21feeb52-5560-4f47-8b3a-496dbf55c165, World Almanac Library) Stevens, Gareth Publishing LLLP.

—Woodrow & Edith Wilson, 1 vol. 2004. (Presidents & First Ladies Ser.). (ENG., Illus.). 48p. (gr. 5-8). lib. bdg. 33.67 *(978-0-8368-5759-7(3),* 08a66539-4499-45c2-9cb6-cafc5a450a33, World Almanac Library) Stevens, Gareth Publishing LLLP.

Bader, Bonnie. Who Was Jacqueline Kennedy? Qiu, Joseph J. M., illus. 2016. (Who Was... ? Ser.). (ENG.). 112p. (J). (gr. 3-7). 16.00 *(978-0-606-39327-0(7))* Turtleback.

Bausum, Ann. Our Country's First Ladies (Direct Mail Edition) 2007. (ENG., Illus.). 128p. (J). (gr. 5-9). 19.95 *(978-1-4263-0006-6(9))* National Geographic Society.

Belton, Blair. Abigail Adams in Her Own Words, 1 vol., Vol. 1. 2014. (Eyewitness to History Ser.). (ENG.). 32p. (J). (gr. 4-5). 29.27 *(978-1-4339-9870-6(X),* 423d331f-8a98-4e8d-be19-7a76ddf90e8d); pap. 11.50 *(978-1-4339-9871-3(8),* 7372aa95-6085-46ff-a3fb-f0f124267522) Stevens, Gareth Publishing LLLP.

Blashfield, Jean F. Hillary Clinton, 1 vol. 2011. (Leading Women Ser.). (ENG.). 96p. (YA). (gr. 7-7). 42.64 *(978-0-7614-4954-6(X),* e653b8cd-2fce-4ce2-be4a-065c33d4a87f) Cavendish Square Publishing LLC.

Blohm, Craig E. Hillary Clinton. 2016. (ENG.). 80p. (J). 38.60 *(978-1-60152-950-3(3))* ReferencePoint Pr., Inc.

Bodden, Valerie. Historic Clinton: Historic Leader. 2009. (Essential Lives Set 4 Ser.). (ENG., Illus.). 112p. (YA). (gr. 6-12). lib. bdg. 41.36 *(978-1-60453-699-7(3),* 6689, Essential Library) ABDO Publishing Co.

—Michelle Obama: First Lady & Role Model. 1 vol. 2009. (Essential Lives Set 4 Ser.). (ENG., Illus.). 112p. (YA). (gr. 6-12). lib. bdg. 41.36 *(978-1-60453-703-1(5),* 6697, Essential Library) ABDO Publishing Co.

Brill, Marlene Targ. Michelle Obama. 2009. (Illus.). 48p. (J). pap. 8.95 *(978-0-7613-5053-8(5))* Lerner Publishing Group.

—Michelle Obama: From Chicago's South Side to the White House. 2009. (Gateway Biographies Ser.). (ENG., Illus.). 48p. (gr. 4-8). 26.60 *(978-0-7613-5033-0(0))* Lerner Publishing Group.

Brophy, David B. Michelle Obama: Meet the First Lady. 2008. 128p. (J). pap. 6.99 *(978-0-06-177990-9(3))* HarperCollins Pubs.

Brown, Jonatha A. Eleanor Roosevelt, 1 vol. 2004. (Gente Que Hay Que Conocer (People We Should Know) Ser.). 24p. (gr. 2-4). (SPA.). pap. 9.15 *(978-0-8368-4591-4(9),* 671df8da-2871-48e5-958d-a951d674cb08); (SPA.). lib. bdg. 24.67 *(978-0-8368-4584-6(6),* 1c0e69f6-59b5-4893-a2b8-cb7079546560); (ENG., Illus.). lib. bdg. 24.67 *(978-0-8368-4468-9(8),* 7d17ffdd-908f-4bd8-81b7-cad97ccbf7c6) Stevens, Gareth Publishing LLLP. (Weekly Reader Leveled Readers).

Bryan, Bethany. Melania Trump: Model & First Lady, 1 vol. 2017. (Leading Women Ser.). (ENG.). 112p. (YA). (gr. 7-7). 41.64 *(978-1-5026-3180-0(6),* ff5e7096-f03c-4465-bb2b-0a6a313da3e8) Cavendish Square Publishing LLC.

Cardillo, Margaret. Just Being Jackie. Denos, Julia, illus. 2018. (ENG.). 32p. (J). (gr. -1-3). 17.99 *(978-0-06-248502-1(4),* Balzer & Bray) HarperCollins Pubs.

Ching, Jacqueline. Abigail Adams: A Revolutionary Woman. 2009. (Library of American Lives & Times Ser.). 112p. (gr. 5-5). 69.20 *(978-1-60853-469-2(3))* Rosen Publishing Group, Inc., The.

Cohen, Della. Eleanor Roosevelt: Proud & Tall. 2005. (Illus.). 16p. (J). pap. *(978-0-7367-2879-9(1))* Zaner-Bloser, Inc.

Colbert, David. Michelle Obama: An American Story. 2008. (ENG., Illus.). 160p. (J). (gr. 3-7). pap. 7.99 *(978-0-547-24770-0(2),* 1100646, Clarion Bks.) HarperCollins Pubs.

Collard, Sneed B., III. Eleanor Roosevelt: Making the World a Better Place, 1 vol. 2009. (American Heroes Ser.). (ENG.). 48p. (gr. 3-3). lib. bdg. 32.64 *(978-0-7614-3069-8(5),* 1b05b04c-6b03-4112-934f-2eeace2a1983) Cavendish Square Publishing LLC.

—Lady Bird Johnson, 1 vol. 2010. (American Heroes Ser.). (ENG.). 48p. (gr. 3-3). 32.64 *(978-0-7614-4056-7(9),* 1b484198-89c3-48ec-b434-f596e2cfb712) Cavendish Square Publishing LLC.

Connors, Kathleen. What's It Like to Be the First Lady?, 1 vol. 2014. (White House Insiders Ser.). (ENG.). 24p. (J). (gr. 2-3). 24.27 *(978-1-4824-1090-7(7),* 2089b38b-8338-4070-bd05-be8998e582be) Stevens, Gareth Publishing LLLP.

Cooper, Ilene. Eleanor Roosevelt, Fighter for Justice: Her Impact on the Civil Rights Movement, the White House, & the World. 2018. (ENG., Illus.). 192p. (J). (gr. 5-9). 17.99 *(978-1-4197-2295-0(6),* 1108501, Abrams Bks. for Young Readers) Abrams, Inc.

Corey, Shana. Michelle Obama: First Lady, Going Higher. Bernardin, James, illus. 2018. (Step into Reading Ser.). 48p. (J). (gr. k-3). pap. 5.99 *(978-1-5247-7229-1(1),* Random Hse. Bks. for Young Readers) Random Hse. Children's Bks.

Doak, Robin S. Hillary Clinton. 2013. (True Book: Biographies Ser.). (ENG., Illus.). 48p. (J). (gr. 3-5). lib. bdg. 21.19 *(978-0-531-21906-5(2),* Children's Pr.); pap. 6.95 *(978-0-531-23877-6(6))* Scholastic Library Publishing.

Donnelly, Shannon. Eleanor Roosevelt. Wolek, Guy, illus. 2005. (Heroes of America Ser.). 236p. (gr. 3-8). lib. bdg. 27.07 *(978-1-59679-260-9(4),* Abdo & Daughters) ABDO Publishing Co.

Dorling Kindersley Publishing Staff. First Ladies. 2017. (Eyewitness Bks.). lib. bdg. 20.85 *(978-0-606-39894-7(5))* Turtleback.

Driscoll, Laura. Hillary Clinton: An American Journey. Wood, Judith V., illus. 2008. (ENG.). 48p. (J). (gr. 3-6). 16.19 *(978-0-448-44787-2(8))* Penguin Young Readers Group.

Edwards, Roberta. Michelle Obama: Primera Dama y Primera Mamá. Call, Ken, illus. 2010. (SPA.). 48p. (gr. 3-5). pap. 9.99 *(978-1-60396-946-8(2))* Santillana USA Publishing Co., Inc.

Egan, Jill. Hillary Rodham Clinton, 1 vol. 2009. (People We Should Know (Second Series) Ser.). (ENG., Illus.). 48p. (J). (gr. 3-5). lib. bdg. 33.67 *(978-1-4339-2188-9(X),* 42b88186-030f-4473-842e-b1101580a9ad, Gareth Stevens Learning Library) Stevens, Gareth Publishing LLLP.

Endsley, Kezia. Michelle Obama: 44th First Lady & Health & Education Advocate, 1 vol. 2014. (Leading Women Ser.). (ENG.). 112p. (YA). (gr. 7-7). lib. bdg. 41.64 *(978-1-62712-975-6(8),* 424f474b-768b-42a2-be45-b14edf9bfe03) Cavendish Square Publishing LLC.

Epstein, Dwayne. Hillary Clinton, 1 vol. 2009. (People in the News Ser.). (ENG., Illus.). 128p. (gr. 7-7). 41.03 *(978-1-4205-0268-8(9),* d39b223e-42d3-45d4-a896-84157b4a51bf, Lucent Pr.) Greenhaven Publishing LLC.

Favor, Lesli J. Eva Perón, 1 vol. 2011. (Leading Women Ser.). (ENG.). 96p. (YA). (gr. 7-7). 42.64 *(978-0-7614-4962-1(0),* 45b3cf21-59b9-44ad-a63a-82c2334b62f3) Cavendish Square Publishing LLC.

Feinberg, Barbara Silberdick. Eleanor Roosevelt: Everything She Could Be. 2003. (Gateway Biography Ser.: 4). (Illus.). 48p. lib. bdg. 23.90 *(978-0-7613-2623-6(5),* Millbrook Pr.) Lerner Publishing Group.

Fleming, Candace. Our Eleanor: A Scrapbook Look at Eleanor Roosevelt's Remarkable Life. 2005. (ENG., Illus.). 192p. (J). (gr. 4-8). 24.99 *(978-0-689-86544-2(9),* Atheneum Bks. for Young Readers) Simon & Schuster Children's Publishing.

Freedman, Jeri. Hillary Rodham Clinton: Profile of a Leading Democrat. 2009. (Career Profiles Ser.). 112p. (gr. 9-10). 63.90 *(978-1-61511-794-9(6))* Rosen Publishing Group, Inc., The.

Glass, Maya. Abigail Adams: Destacada Primera Dama, 1 vol. 2003. (Grandes Personajes en la Historia de Los Estados Unidos (Famous People in American History) Ser.). (SPA.). 32p. (gr. 3-4). pap. 10.00 *(978-0-8239-4218-3(X),* 949fb9de-18b2-4dbb-a839-a4b1bcd6c026, Rosen Classroom); (Illus.). lib. bdg. 29.13 *(978-0-8239-4124-7(8),* 740cfa49-5442-4662-a607-a94262265dbf, Editorial Buenas Letras) Rosen Publishing Group, Inc., The.

—Abigail Adams: Destacada Primera Dama (Abigail Adams: Famous First Lady) 2009. (Grandes personajes en la historia de los Estados Unidos (Famous People in American History) Ser.). (SPA.). 32p. (gr. 2-3). 47.90 *(978-1-61512-787-0(9),* Editorial Buenas Letras) Rosen Publishing Group, Inc., The.

—Abigail Adams: Famous First Lady. (Primary Sources of Famous People in American History Ser.). 32p. 2009. (gr. 2-3). 47.90 *(978-1-60851-643-8(1))* 2003. (ENG., Illus.). (gr. 3-4). pap. 10.00 *(978-0-8239-4172-8(8),* 47a00333-0202-42ce-b8df-2362feca04ab) 2003. (SPA & ENG., Illus.). (J). (gr. 2-3). lib. bdg. 29.13 *(978-0-8239-4148-3(5),* f091600b-d29f-4034-8e84-0a87de754ab5) 2003. (ENG., Illus.). (J). (gr. 3-4). lib. bdg. 29.13 *(978-0-8239-4100-1(0),* c0e820be-d588-41b8-ac14-8ec0d74e31d3) Rosen Publishing Group, Inc., The.

—Abigail Adams: Famous First Lady / Destacada Primera Dama. 2009. (Famous People in American History/Grandes personajes en la historia de los Estados Unidos Ser.). (ENG & SPA.). 32p. (gr. 2-3). 47.90 *(978-1-61512-535-7(3),* Editorial Buenas Letras) Rosen Publishing Group, Inc., The.

Gormley, Beatrice. Laura Bush: America's First Lady. 2005. 122p. (J). lib. bdg. 15.00 *(978-1-59054-921-6(X))* Fitzgerald Bks.

Guernsey, JoAnn B. Hillary Rodham Clinton. 2005. (Biography Ser.). (Illus.). 112p. (J). (gr. 6-18). pap. 7.95 *(978-0-8225-9613-4(X))* Lerner Publishing Group.

Guernsey, Joann Bren. Hillary Rodham Clinton. 2005. (Biography Ser.). (Illus.). 112p. (J). (gr. 3-7). lib. bdg. 29.27 *(978-0-8225-2372-7(8),* Lerner Pubns.) Lerner Publishing Group.

Haldy, Emma E. Eleanor Roosevelt. Bane, Jeff, illus. 2016. (My Early Library: My Itty-Bitty Bio Ser.). (ENG.). 24p. (J). (gr. k-1). 30.64 *(978-1-63470-483-0(5),* 207663) Cherry Lake Publishing.

—Eleanor Roosevelt SP. Bane, Jeff, illus. 2018. (My Early Library: Mi Mini Biografía (My Itty-Bitty Bio) Ser.). (SPA.). 24p. (J). (gr. k-1). lib. bdg. 30.64 *(978-1-5341-3002-9(0),* 212056) Cherry Lake Publishing.

Hally, Ashleigh. Rosalynn Carter. 2012. (Illus.). 24p. (J). *(978-1-935884-74-3(3));* pap. *(978-1-935884-80-4(8))* State Standards Publishing, LLC.

Harness, Cheryl. Hillary Clinton: American Woman of the World. (Real-Life Story Ser.). (ENG., Illus.). (J). (gr. 3-7). 2017. 208p. pap. 7.99 *(978-1-4814-6058-3(7))* 2016. 192p. 17.99 *(978-1-4814-6057-6(9))* Simon & Schuster Children's Publishing. (Aladdin).

Hopkinson, Deborah. Michelle. Ford, A. G., illus. 2009. 32p. (J). (gr. -1-2). 17.99 *(978-0-06-182739-6(8))* HarperCollins Pubs.

Hubbard-Brown, Janet. Eleanor Roosevelt: First Lady. 2009. (Women of Achievement Ser.). (ENG.). 128p. (gr. 6-12). 35.00 *(978-1-60413-076-8(8),* P160529, Facts On File) Infobase Holdings, Inc.

Hudson, Amanda. Michelle Obama, 1 vol. 2009. (People We Should Know (Second Series) Ser.). (ENG.). 48p. (J). (gr. 3-5). pap. 11.50 *(978-1-4339-2192-6(8),* 52e0e14d-5612-4f8c-b7d3-6032009fc9db); lib. bdg. 33.67 *(978-1-4339-2187-2(1),* 39091c59-0022-40d8-9376-30ac82a88229) Stevens, Gareth Publishing LLLP. (Gareth Stevens Learning Library).

Hull, Mary E. Mary Todd Lincoln: Civil War's First Lady, 1 vol. 2014. (Legendary American Biographies Ser.). (ENG.). 96p. (gr. 6-6). 29.60 *(978-0-7660-6480-5(8),* 2334efaa-2847-413e-92a3-b06892d78510); pap. 13.88 *(978-0-7660-6481-2(6),* 77e849a6-625a-4e25-a5bb-d16442ad7740) Enslow Publishing, LLC.

Jones, Lynda. Mrs. Lincoln's Dressmaker: The Unlikely Friendship of Elizabeth Keckley & Mary Todd Lincoln. 2009. (Illus.). 80p. (J). (gr. 5-9). 18.95 *(978-1-4263-0377-7(7),* National Geographic Kids) Disney Publishing Worldwide.

Katirgis, Jane. Celebrating First Lady Michelle Obama in Pictures, 1 vol. 2009. (Obama Family Photo Album Ser.). (ENG., Illus.). 32p. (gr. 3-3). lib. bdg. 26.60 *(978-0-7660-3652-9(9),* d9e0b307-d964-40e1-94b0-d84e91fa5515) Enslow Publishing, LLC.

Kawa, Katie. Hillary Clinton, 1 vol. 2016. (Superwomen Role Models Ser.). (ENG., Illus.). 32p. (J). (gr. 3-4). 27.93 *(978-1-5081-4806-7(6),* 398639c2-17e4-4da6-9549-286742a74876, PowerKids Pr.) Rosen Publishing Group, Inc., The.

Kelley, True. Who Was Abigail Adams? 2014. (Who Was... ? Ser.). lib. bdg. 16.00 *(978-0-606-34166-0(8))* Turtleback.

Kelley, True & Who HQ. Who Was Abigail Adams? O'Brien, John, illus. 2014. (Who Was? Ser.). 112p. (J). (gr. 3-7). 6.99 *(978-0-448-47890-6(0),* Penguin Workshop) Penguin Young Readers Group.

Kent, Zachary A. Dolley Madison: The Enemy Cannot Frighten a Free People, 1 vol. 2008. (Americans: the Spirit of a Nation Ser.). (ENG., Illus.). 128p. (gr. 5-6). lib. bdg. 35.93 *(978-0-7660-3356-6(2),* 578bdc34-0b85-4900-a190-8fc4d183b93a) Enslow Publishing, LLC.

Kerley, Barbara. What to Do about Alice? 2011. (J). (gr. 2-5). 29.95 *(978-0-545-29679-3(X))* Weston Woods Studios, Inc.

Kimmelman, Leslie. Hot Dog! Eleanor Roosevelt Throws a Picnic. Juhasz, Victor, illus. 2014. (ENG.). 40p. (J). (gr. 3-6). 16.99 *(978-1-58536-830-3(X),* 203013) Sleeping Bear Pr.

Klein, Dvora. Eleanor Roosevelt. 2009. pap. 13.25 *(978-1-60559-059-2(2))* Hameray Publishing Group, Inc.

Krull, Kathleen. Hillary Rodham Clinton: Dreams Taking Flight. Bates, Amy June, illus. 2015. (ENG.). 48p. (J). (gr. k-5). 17.99 *(978-1-4814-5113-0(8),* Simon & Schuster Bks. For Young Readers) Simon & Schuster Bks. For Young Readers.

—Mary Todd Lincoln: I'm Usually the Smartest Person in the Room. Baddeley, Elizabeth, illus. 2015. (Women Who Broke the Rules Ser.). (ENG.). 48p. (J). (gr. 1-4). pap. 6.99 *(978-0-8027-3825-7(7),* 9780802738257, Bloomsbury USA Childrens) Bloomsbury Publishing USA.

—Women Who Broke the Rules: Dolley Madison. Johnson, Steve & Fancher, Lou, illus. 2015. (Women Who Broke the Rules Ser.). (ENG.). 48p. (J). (gr. 1-4). 16.99 *(978-0-8027-3793-9(5),* 900139089, Bloomsbury USA Childrens) Bloomsbury Publishing USA.

Lakin, Patricia. Abigail Adams: First Lady of the American Revolution. Bandelin, Debra & Dacey, Bob, illus. 2006. 48p. (J). lib. bdg. 15.00 *(978-1-4242-1560-7(9))* Fitzgerald Bks.

—Abigail Adams: First Lady of the American Revolution (Ready-To-Read Level 3) Dacey, Bob & Bandelin, Debra, illus. 2006. (Ready-To-Read Stories of Famous Americans Ser.). (ENG.). 48p. (J). (gr. 1-3). pap. 4.99 *(978-0-689-87032-3(9),* Simon Spotlight) Simon Spotlight.

Larkin, Tanya. What Was Cooking in Dolley Madison's White House? 2009. (Cooking Throughout American History Ser.). 24p. (gr. 3-3). 42.50 *(978-1-61511-950-9(7),* PowerKids Pr.) Rosen Publishing Group, Inc., The.

—What Was Cooking in Edith Roosevelt's White House? 2009. (Cooking Throughout American History Ser.). 24p. (gr. 3-3). 42.50 *(978-1-61511-951-6(5),* PowerKids Pr.) Rosen Publishing Group, Inc., The.

—What Was Cooking in Julia Grant's White House? 2009. (Cooking Throughout American History Ser.). 24p. (gr. 3-3). 42.50 *(978-1-61511-952-3(3),* PowerKids Pr.) Rosen Publishing Group, Inc., The.

—What Was Cooking in Martha Washington's Presidential Mansion? 2009. (Cooking Throughout American History Ser.). 24p. (gr. 3-3). 42.50 *(978-1-61511-953-0(1),* PowerKids Pr.) Rosen Publishing Group, Inc., The.

Lassieur, Allison. Eleanor Roosevelt: Activist for Social Change. 2006. (Great Life Stories Ser.). (ENG., Illus.). 112p. (J). (gr. 6-8). lib. bdg. 30.50 *(978-0-531-13871-7(2),* Watts, Franklin) Scholastic Library Publishing.

Leaf, Christina. Michelle Obama: Health Advocate. 2019. (Women Leading the Way Ser.). (ENG., Illus.). 24p. (J). (gr. k-3). lib. bdg. 26.95 *(978-1-62617-942-4(5),* Blastoff! Readers) Bellwether Media.

—Michelle Obama: Health Advocate. 2019. (Women Leading the Way Ser.). (ENG., Illus.). 24p. (J). (gr. k-3). pap. 7.99 *(978-1-61891-502-3(9),* 12153, Blastoff! Readers) Bellwether Media.

Lee, Sally. Eleanor Roosevelt, 1 vol. 2010. (First Ladies Ser.). (ENG.). 24p. (J). (gr. -1-2). pap. 7.29 *(978-1-4296-5603-0(4),* 114106); (gr. k-1). pap. 43.74 *(978-1-4296-5604-7(2),* 15474, Capstone Pr.) Capstone.

—Hillary Clinton, 1 vol. 2010. (First Ladies Ser.). (ENG.). 24p. (J). (gr. -1-2). lib. bdg. 27.32 *(978-1-4296-5327-5(2),* 113736, Capstone Pr.) Capstone.

—Martha Washington, 1 vol. 2010. (First Ladies Ser.). (ENG.). 24p. (J). (gr. -1-2). pap. 7.29 *(978-1-4296-5605-4(0),* 114107); (gr. -1-2). lib. bdg. 27.32 *(978-1-4296-5011-3(7),* 112960); (gr. k-1). pap. 43.74 *(978-1-4296-5606-1(9),* 15475) Capstone. (Capstone Pr.).

Loh-Hagan, Virginia. The Real Dolley Madison. 2018. (History Uncut Ser.). (ENG., Illus.). 32p. (J). (gr. 4-8). lib. bdg. 32.07 *(978-1-5341-2952-8(9),* 211852, 45th Parallel Press) Cherry Lake Publishing.

—The Real Edith Wilson. 2019. (History Uncut Ser.). (ENG.). 32p. (J). (gr. 4-8). pap. 14.21 *(978-1-5341-3990-9(7),* 212789); (Illus.). lib. bdg. 32.07 *(978-1-5341-4334-0(3),* 212788) Cherry Lake Publishing. (45th Parallel Press).

Machajewski, Sarah. Michelle Obama, 1 vol. 2016. (Superwomen Role Models Ser.). (ENG., Illus.). 32p. (J). (gr. 3-4). 27.93 *(978-1-5081-4812-8(0),* 8d67cc38-9de9-4c10-90bc-efee1f99a1f6, PowerKids Pr.) Rosen Publishing Group, Inc., The.

Maloof, Torrey. Abigail Adams & the Women Who Shaped America. rev. ed. 2016. (Social Studies: Informational Text Ser.). (ENG., Illus.). 32p. (gr. 4-8). pap. 11.99 *(978-1-4938-3080-0(5))* Teacher Created Materials, Inc.

Mapua, Jeff. Bill & Hillary Clinton, 1 vol. 2014. (Making a Difference: Leaders Who Are Changing the World Ser.). 48p. (YA). (gr. 5-5). (ENG.). 28.41 *(978-1-62275-425-0(5),* e10cbf68-8220-4825-b884-6f256183833c); (ENG.). pap. 15.05 *(978-1-62275-427-4(1),* 09ac0fd0-2ff9-48a5-ad53-c10d0c1c31c3); pap. 84.30 *(978-1-62275-428-1(X))* Rosen Publishing Group, Inc., The.

—Hillary Clinton, 1 vol. 2014. (Britannica Beginner Bios Ser.). (ENG., Illus.). 32p. (J). (gr. 2-3). 26.06 *(978-1-62275-689-6(4),* c6a1ac5c-edfc-4d9f-8b71-fe87854a49f1, Britannica Educational Publishing) Rosen Publishing Group, Inc., The.

Mara, Wil. Laura Bush. 2003. (Rookie Biographies Ser.). (ENG., Illus.). 32p. (J). (gr. 1-2). 20.50 *(978-0-516-22854-9(4),* Children's Pr.) Scholastic Library Publishing.

Marcovitz, Hal. Michelle. 2007. (Obamas Ser.). 64p. (YA). (gr. 3-6). pap. 9.95 *(978-1-4222-1485-5(0));* (gr. 4-7). lib. bdg. 19.95 *(978-1-4222-1478-7(8))* Mason Crest.

Markel, Michelle. Hillary Rodham Clinton: Some Girls Are Born to Lead. Pham, LeUyen, illus. 2016. (ENG.). 40p. (J). (gr. -1-3). 17.99 *(978-0-06-238122-4(9),* Balzer & Bray) HarperCollins Pubs.

Marsh, Carole. Abigail Adams. 2004. 12p. (gr. k-4). 2.95 *(978-0-635-02372-8(5))* Gallopade International.

—Michelle Obama: Biography FunBook. 2009. (J). (gr. 2-9). pap. 3.99 *(978-0-635-07054-8(5))* Gallopade International.

—The Obama Family - Life in the White House: President Barack Obama, First Lady Michelle Obama, First Children Malia & Sasha. 2008. (Here & Now Ser.). 32p. (J). (gr. 2-9). pap. 8.99 *(978-0-635-07051-7(0))* Gallopade International.

Marsico, Katie. Eleanor Roosevelt: First Lady & Human Rights Advocate, 1 vol. 2008. (Essential Lives Set 2 Ser.). (ENG., Illus.). 112p. (YA). (gr. 6-12). lib. bdg. 41.36 *(978-1-60453-040-7(5),* 6661, Essential Library) ABDO Publishing Co.

Mattern, Joanne. Eleanor Roosevelt: More Than a First Lady. 2009. (Women Who Shaped History Ser.). 24p. (gr. 2-3). 42.50 *(978-1-60854-817-0(1),* PowerKids Pr.) Rosen Publishing Group, Inc., The.

—What's So Great about Michelle Obama. 2009. (What's So Great About... ? Ser.). 32p. (J). (gr. 2-4). lib. bdg. 25.70 *(978-1-58415-833-2(6))* Mitchell Lane Pubs.

McPherson, Stephanie. My Dear Husband: Important Letters of Abigail Adams. 2009. (Great Moments in American History Ser.). 32p. (gr. 3-3). 47.90 *(978-1-61513-134-1(5))* Rosen Publishing Group, Inc., The.

Mcpherson, Stephanie Sammartino. Martha Washington: Legendary First Lady of the United States, 1 vol. 2014. (Legendary American Biographies Ser.). (ENG.). 96p. (gr. 6-6). 29.60 *(978-0-7660-6475-1(1),* afd97b4a-9287-4fc5-a030-e63ea9ca3b05) Enslow Publishing, LLC.

Mulhall, Jill K. Abigail Adams, 1 vol. rev. ed. 2004. (Social Studies: Informational Text Ser.). (ENG.). 24p. (gr. 4-8). pap. 10.99 *(978-0-7439-8786-8(1))* Teacher Created Materials, Inc.

Nault, Jennifer. Michelle Obama. 2009. (Remarkable People Ser.). (Illus.). 24p. (J). (gr. 4-6). pap. 8.95 *(978-1-60596-666-3(5));* lib. bdg. 24.45 *(978-1-60596-665-6(7))* Weigl Pubs., Inc.

Nelson, Maria. The Life of Abigail Adams, 1 vol. 2012. (Famous Lives Ser.). (ENG., Illus.). 24p. (J). (gr. 1-2). pap. 9.15 *(978-1-4339-6339-1(6),* 47a08088-2d38-41f7-be23-c2a7404f9a73); lib. bdg. 25.27 *(978-1-4339-6337-7(X),* 9ae33957-f040-42d7-af87-41dd7887e637) Stevens, Gareth Publishing LLLP.

—The Life of Abigail Adams / la Vida de Abigail Adams, 1 vol. 2012. (Famous Lives / Vidas Extraordinarias Ser.). (ENG & SPA., Illus.). 24p. (J). (gr. 1-2). 25.27 *(978-1-4339-6649-1(2),* 1f21cfb0-b1a6-4f79-947f-b12fa4d16635) Stevens, Gareth Publishing LLLP.

Oliver, Alison. Be Bold, Baby: Michelle Obama. Oliver, Alison, illus. 2018. (Be Bold, Baby Ser.). (ENG., Illus.). 20p. (J). (— 1). bds. 9.99 *(978-1-328-51989-4(9),* 1720769, Clarion Bks.) HarperCollins Pubs.

Our Presidents & First Ladies of the White House. 119.40 *(978-0-8249-6046-9(7),* Ideals Pubns.) Worthy Publishing.

Raatma, Lucia. Jacqueline Kennedy, 1 vol. 2010. (First Ladies Ser.). (ENG.). 24p. (J). (gr. -1-2). lib. bdg. 27.32 *(978-1-4296-5009-0(5),* 112958, Capstone Pr.) Capstone.

—Michelle Obama, 1 vol. 2010. (First Ladies Ser.). (ENG.). 24p. (J). (gr. -1-2). pap. 7.29 *(978-1-4296-5599-6(2),* 114104); (gr. k-1). pap. 43.74 *(978-1-4296-5600-9(X),* 15472) Capstone. (Capstone Pr.).

Rajczak Nelson, Kristen. Melania Trump: First Lady of the United States, 1 vol. 2018. (Junior Biographies Ser.). (ENG.). 24p. (gr. 3-4). 24.27 *(978-0-7660-9739-1(0),* bff3ff1b-52c5-4c7a-b8b5-034c18ce9ca5) Enslow Publishing, LLC.

Ransom, Candice. Martha Washington. Ritz, Karen, illus. 2003. (On My Own Biographies Ser.). 48p. (J). 25.26 *(978-0-87614-918-8(2),* Carolrhoda Bks.); (ENG.). (gr. 2-4). per. 8.99 *(978-0-87614-107-6(6),* 4c0f38f4-4630-4dd2-a209-c0d6e8fec56b, First Avenue Editions) Lerner Publishing Group.

Rappaport, Doreen. Eleanor, Quiet No More: The Life of Eleanor Roosevelt. Kelley, Gary, illus. 2009. (Big Words Book Ser.: 4). (ENG.). 48p. (J). (gr. -1-3). 16.99 *(978-0-7868-5141-6(4))* Little, Brown Bks. for Young Readers.

Riddolls, Tom & Wearing, Judy. Hillary Clinton. 2009. (Remarkable People Ser.). (Illus.). 24p. (J). (gr. 4-6). pap. 8.95 *(978-1-60596-621-2(5));* lib. bdg. 24.45 *(978-1-60596-620-5(7))* Weigl Pubs., Inc.

Rinaldo, Denise. Eleanor Roosevelt: With a Discussion of Respect. 2003. (Values in Action Ser.). (J). *(978-1-59203-063-7(7))* Learning Challenge, Inc.

Rosenstock, Barb. Leave It to Abigail! The Revolutionary Life of Abigail Adams. Baddeley, Elizabeth, illus. 2020. (ENG.). 40p. (J). (gr. -1-3). 18.99 *(978-0-316-41571-2(5))* Little, Brown Bks. for Young Readers.

Ruiz, Rachel. When Hillary Rodham Clinton Played Ice Hockey. Doneva, Steliyana, illus. 2017. (Leaders Doing Headstands Ser.). (ENG.). 32p. (J). (gr. 1-4). lib. bdg. 28.65 *(978-1-5158-1573-0(0),* 136243, Picture Window Bks.) Capstone.

Sabin, Francene & Macken, JoAnn Early. Abigail Adams: Young Patriot. Miyake, Yoshi, illus. 2007. 55p. (J). pap. *(978-0-439-88003-9(3))* Scholastic, Inc.

Schwartz, Heather E. Michelle Obama: Political Icon. 2020. (Boss Lady Bios (Alternator Books (r)) Ser.). (ENG., Illus.). 32p. (J). (gr. 3-6). 30.65 *(978-1-5415-9707-5(9),* 4af4e01e-075b-4761-8eac-25b4a12854ed, Lerner Pubns.) Lerner Publishing Group.

Shamir, Ruby. What's the Big Deal about First Ladies. Faulkner, Matt, illus. (What's the Big Deal About Ser.). (J). 2020. 64p. (gr. 1-4). 13.99 *(978-0-593-11486-5(8))* 2017. 32p. (gr. -1-3). 17.99 *(978-0-399-54724-9(X))* Penguin Young Readers Group. (Philomel Bks.).

Shea, John M. Eleanor Roosevelt in Her Own Words, 1 vol. 2015. (Eyewitness to History Ser.). (ENG., Illus.). 32p. (J).

(gr. 4-5). pap. 11.50 *(978-1-4824-4062-1(8)*, 888c0b4d-7e1e-43d7-9749-856bf6736276) Stevens, Gareth Publishing LLLP.

Shepherd, Jodie. Hillary Clinton. 2015. (Rookie Biographies(r) Ser.). (ENG., Illus.). 32p. (J). lib. bdg. 23.00 *(978-0-531-20592-1(4))* Scholastic Library Publishing.

Shulman, Holly. Dolley Madison: Her Life, Letters, & Legacy. 2009. (Library of American Lives & Times Ser.). 112p. (gr. 5-5). 69.20 *(978-1-60853-477-7(4))* Rosen Publishing Group, Inc., The.

Stine, Megan. Who Is Michelle Obama? 2013. (Who Is... ? Ser.). lib. bdg. 14.75 *(978-0-606-32131-0(4))* Turtleback.

Stine, Megan & Who HQ. Who Is Michelle Obama? O'Brien, John, illus. 2013. (Who Was? Ser.). 112p. (J). (gr. 3-7). 5.99 *(978-0-448-47863-0(3)*, Penguin Workshop) Penguin Young Readers Group.

Stoltman, Joan. Eleanor Roosevelt, 1 vol. 2018. (Little Biographies of Big People Ser.). (ENG.). 24p. (gr. 1-2). 24.27 *(978-1-5382-1832-7(1)*, 3e5db8ca-c8eb-442a-baff-08b4749ee825) Stevens, Gareth Publishing LLLP.

—Hillary Clinton, 1 vol. 2017. (Little Biographies of Big People Ser.). (ENG.). 24p. (J). (gr. 1-2). pap. 9.15 *(978-1-5382-0927-1(6)*, 45d15419-e1ba-485e-aecd-492bac53ea80) Stevens, Gareth Publishing LLLP.

—Hillary Clinton, 1 vol. Garcia, Ana Maria, tr. 2017. (Pequeñas Biografías de Grandes Personajes (Little Biographies of Big People) Ser.). (SPA.). 24p. (J). (gr. 1-2). pap. 9.15 *(978-1-5382-1558-6(6)*, 223ef883-505a-47a7-9806-85242aebbfaf); lib. bdg. 24.27 *(978-1-5382-1531-9(4)*, c288e1b0-b83a-4715-865d-2d96d21028a1) Stevens, Gareth Publishing LLLP.

—Melania Trump, 1 vol. 2018. (Little Biographies of Big People Ser.). (ENG.). 24p. (gr. 1-2). 24.27 *(978-1-5382-2896-8(3)*, cf72c0f3-d525-4ee7-b5c3-d4ef7527e10b) Stevens, Gareth Publishing LLLP.

—Michelle Obama, 1 vol. 2017. (Little Biographies of Big People Ser.). (ENG.). 24p. (J). (gr. 1-2). pap. 9.15 *(978-1-5382-0929-5(2)*, fbc15435-d338-4ce0-8dfa-22308002b351) Stevens, Gareth Publishing LLLP.

—Michelle Obama, 1 vol. Garcia, Ana Maria, tr. 2017. (Pequeñas Biografías de Grandes Personajes (Little Biographies of Big People) Ser.). (SPA.). 24p. (J). (gr. 1-2). pap. 9.15 *(978-1-5382-1555-5(1)*, 827c2c46-0ae9-4e2d-82a1-1ea660a36de8); lib. bdg. 24.27 *(978-1-5382-1528-9(4)*, 72bafb7a-6a09-4f74-becc-105367d5c6c9) Stevens, Gareth Publishing LLLP.

Strand, Jennifer. Eleanor Roosevelt. 2017. (First Ladies (Launch!) Ser.). (ENG., Illus.). 24p. (J). (gr. -1-2). lib. bdg. 31.36 *(978-1-5321-2019-0(2)*, 25288, Abdo Zoom-Launch) ABDO Publishing Co.

—Jacqueline Kennedy. 2017. (First Ladies (Launch!) Ser.). (ENG., Illus.). 24p. (J). (gr. -1-2). lib. bdg. 31.36 *(978-1-5321-2016-9(8)*, 25282, Abdo Zoom-Launch) ABDO Publishing Co.

—Lady Bird Johnson. 2018. (First Ladies (Launch!) Ser.). (ENG., Illus.). 24p. (J). (gr. -1-2). lib. bdg. 31.36 *(978-1-5321-2284-2(5)*, 28335, Abdo Zoom-Launch) ABDO Publishing Co.

—Laura Bush. 2017. (First Ladies (Launch!) Ser.). (ENG., Illus.). 24p. (J). (gr. -1-2). lib. bdg. 31.36 *(978-1-5321-2015-2(X)*, 25280, Abdo Zoom-Launch) ABDO Publishing Co.

—Martha Washington. 2017. (First Ladies (Launch!) Ser.). (ENG., Illus.). 24p. (J). (gr. -1-2). lib. bdg. 31.36 *(978-1-5321-2020-6(6)*, 25290, Abdo Zoom-Launch) ABDO Publishing Co.

—Mary Todd Lincoln. 2018. (First Ladies (Launch!) Ser.). (ENG., Illus.). 24p. (J). (gr. -1-2). lib. bdg. 31.36 *(978-1-5321-2285-9(3)*, 28337, Abdo Zoom-Launch) ABDO Publishing Co.

—Melania Trump. 2018. (First Ladies (Launch!) Ser.). (ENG., Illus.). 24p. (J). (gr. -1-2). lib. bdg. 31.36 *(978-1-5321-2286-6(1)*, 28339, Abdo Zoom-Launch) ABDO Publishing Co.

—Michelle Obama. 2017. (First Ladies (Launch!) Ser.). (ENG., Illus.). 24p. (J). (gr. -1-2). lib. bdg. 31.36 *(978-1-5321-2017-6(6)*, 25284, Abdo Zoom-Launch) ABDO Publishing Co.

—Nancy Reagan. 2017. (First Ladies (Launch!) Ser.). (ENG., Illus.). 24p. (J). (gr. -1-2). lib. bdg. 31.36 *(978-1-5321-2018-3(4)*, 25286, Abdo Zoom-Launch) ABDO Publishing Co.

Summers, Portia. Hillary Clinton: Politician & Activist, 1 vol. 2017. (Junior Biographies Ser.). (ENG.). 24p. (gr. 3-4). lib. bdg. 24.27 *(978-0-7660-8670-8(4)*, 59cfec20-341d-41a9-96cc-64292ade5e0c) Enslow Publishing, LLC.

Sutcliffe, Jane. Abigail Adams. 2006. (History Maker Biographies Ser.). (ENG., Illus.). 48p. (gr. 3-6). lib. bdg. 27.93 *(978-0-8225-5942-9(0)*, Lerner Pubns.) Lerner Publishing Group.

Taylor-Butler, Christine. Michelle Obama. 2015. (ENG.). 48p. (J). pap. 6.95 *(978-0-531-21206-6(8)*, Orchard Bks.) Scholastic Library Publishing.

Thompson, Gare. Who Was Eleanor Roosevelt? Wolf, Elizabeth, illus. 2004. (Who Was... ? Ser.). 106p. (gr. 3-7). 15.00 *(978-0-7569-2829-2(X))* Perfection Learning Corp.

—Who Was Eleanor Roosevelt? 2004. (Who Was... ? Ser.). (gr. 3-6). lib. bdg. 16.00 *(978-0-613-72563-7(8))* Turtleback.

Thompson, Gare & Who HQ. Who Was Eleanor Roosevelt? Wolf, Elizabeth, illus. 2004. (Who Was? Ser.). 112p. (J). (gr. 3-7). pap. 5.99 *(978-0-448-43509-1(8)*, Penguin Workshop) Penguin Young Readers Group.

Time for Kids Editors. Abigail Adams: Eyewitness to America's Birth. 2009. (Time for Kids Ser.). (ENG.). 48p. (J). (gr. 2-4). 15.99 *(978-0-06-057629-5(4))*; pap. 3.99 *(978-0-06-057628-8(6)*, Collins) HarperCollins Pubs.

Time for Kids Magazine Staff. Time for Kids: Eleanor Roosevelt: First Lady of the World. 2005. (Time for Kids Ser.). (ENG., Illus.). 48p. (J). (gr. 2-4). per. 3.99 *(978-0-06-057613-4(8))* HarperCollins Pubs.

Tracy, Kathleen. The Historic Fight for the 2008 Democratic Presidential Nomination: The Clinton View. 2009. (Monumental Milestones Ser.). (Illus.). 48p. (YA). (gr. 4-7). lib. bdg. 29.95 *(978-1-58415-731-1(3))* Mitchell Lane Pubs.

Uschan, Michael V. Michelle Obama, 1 vol. 2010. (People in the News Ser.). (ENG., Illus.). 112p. (gr. 7-7). 41.03 *(978-1-4205-0209-1(3)*, a36bfb24-c866-43d1-b0fe-08faaaaf913e, Lucent Pr.) Greenhaven Publishing LLC.

Warner, Sally. Smart about the First Ladies: Smart about History. Buller, Jon et al, illus. 2004. (Smart about History Ser.). 48p. (J). (gr. k-4). mass mkt. 7.99 *(978-0-448-43724-8(4)*, Grosset & Dunlap) Penguin Young Readers Group.

Weakland, Mark. When Eleanor Roosevelt Learned to Jump a Horse. Joseph, John, illus. 2019. (Leaders Doing Headstands Ser.). (ENG.). 32p. (J). (gr. 1-4). pap. 7.95 *(978-1-5158-3050-4(0)*, 138685, Picture Window Bks.) Capstone.

Wells, Catherine. Hillary Clinton. 2007. (Political Profiles Ser.). (Illus.). 112p. (YA). (gr. 5-9). lib. bdg. 27.95 *(978-1-59935-047-9(5))* Reynolds, Morgan Inc.

Weston Woods Staff, creator. What to Do about Alice? 2011. 38.75 *(978-0-545-29822-3(9))* Weston Woods Studios, Inc.

Wheeler, Jill C. Hillary Rodham Clinton. 2003. (Breaking Barriers Ser.). 64p. (gr. 3-8). lib. bdg. 27.07 *(978-1-57765-741-5(1)*, Abdo & Daughters) ABDO Publishing Co.

Whiting, Jim. The Life & Times of Abigail Adams. 2007. (Profiles in American History Ser.). (Illus.). 48p. (J). (gr. 4-7). lib. bdg. 29.95 *(978-1-58415-527-0(2))* Mitchell Lane Pubs.

Winget, Mary. Eleanor Roosevelt. (Biography Ser.). (Illus.). 2005. 112p. (gr. 6-12). lib. bdg. 27.93 *(978-0-8225-4985-7(9))* 2003. 48p. (J). pap. 8.95 *(978-0-8225-4801-0(1)*, Lerner Pubns.) 2003. 48p. (J). (gr. 3-5). lib. bdg. 26.60 *(978-0-8225-4675-7(2))* Lerner Publishing Group.

Winter, Jonah. Hillary. ón, Raul, illus. 2016. 40p. (J). (gr. -1-3). 17.99 *(978-0-553-53388-0(6)*, Schwartz & Wade Bks.) Random Hse. Children's Bks.

Yasuda, Anita. Lady Bird Johnson. 2010. (My Life Ser.). 24p. (J). (gr. 2-4). lib. bdg. 25.70 *(978-1-61690-062-5(8))* Weigl Pubs., Inc.

—Lady Bird Johnson: My Life. 2010. pap. 9.95 *(978-1-61690-063-2(6))* Weigl Pubs., Inc.

Zumbusch, Amelie von. Michelle Obama: Our First Lady, 1 vol. 2010. (Making History: the Obamas Ser.). (ENG., Illus.). 24p. (J). (gr. 2-3). pap. 9.25 *(978-1-4358-9868-4(0)*, 468c9a7f-e11e-4215-9610-71d2c13860bd); lib. bdg. 26.27 *(978-1-4358-9388-7(3)*, 62b0413a-3e96-4376-9e00-b445bdcb7d73) Rosen Publishing Group, Inc., The. (PowerKids Pr.).

PRESLEY, ELVIS, 1935-1977

Alagna, Magdalena. Elvis Presley. 2009. (Rock & Roll Hall of Famers Ser.). 112p. (gr. 5-8). 63.90 *(978-1-60852-474-7(4)*, Rosen Reference) Rosen Publishing Group, Inc., The.

Christensen, Bonnie. Elvis: The Story of the Rock & Roll King. Christensen, Bonnie, illus. 2015. (ENG., Illus.). 32p. (J). (gr. 1-4). 18.99 *(978-0-8050-9447-3(4)*, 900077612, Holt, Henry & Co. Bks. For Young Readers) Holt, Henry & Co.

Clayton, Marie. Elvis Presley: Unseen Archives. (Unseen Archives Ser.). (Illus.). 384p. *(978-0-7525-8335-8(2))* Parragon, Inc.

Doll, Susan. Elvis Presley: With Profiles of Muddy Waters & Mick Jagger. 2006. (Biographical Connections Ser.). (Illus.). 112p. (J). *(978-0-7166-1823-2(0))* World Bk., Inc.

Eanes, Jim. Elvis in Virginia. 2003. (Illus.). 78p. (YA). per. 15.95 *(978-0-9717295-2-0(2))* E & H Publishing Co., Inc.

Edgers, Geoff. Who Was Elvis Presley? O'brien, John, illus. 2007. (Who Was... ? Ser.). 105p. (gr. 2-5). 15.00 *(978-0-7569-8164-8(6))* Perfection Learning Corp.

Edgers, Geoff & Who HQ. Who Was Elvis Presley? O'Brien, John, illus. 2007. (Who Was? Ser.). 112p. (J). (gr. 3-7). pap. 6.99 *(978-0-448-44642-4(1)*, Penguin Workshop) Penguin Young Readers Group.

Hampton, Wilborn. Elvis Presley: A Twentieth Century Life. 2007. (ENG., Illus.). 192p. (YA). (gr. 7). 26.16 *(978-1-4287-4879-8(2))* Follett School Solutions.

Harper, Betty. Color My World Vol. 1: Early Elvis (Coloring Book) Harper, Betty, illus. 2004. (Illus.). 32p. (J). 4.95 *(978-0-932117-42-7(2))* Osborne Enterprises Publishing.

Micklos, John & Micklos, John, Jr. Elvis Presley: Fighting for the Right to Rock, 1 vol. 2017. (Rebels with a Cause Ser.). (ENG.). 128p. (J). (gr. 8-8). 38.93 *(978-0-7660-9258-7(5)*, 5908d67d-754a-4219-b3d7-6ea667662142); pap. 20.95 *(978-0-7660-9549-6(5)*, b5ea81c8-5ee6-4f61-97e4-afe4efbaaad3) Enslow Publishing, LLC.

—Elvis Presley: I Want to Entertain People, 1 vol. 2010. (American Rebels Ser.). (ENG., Illus.). 160p. (YA). (gr. 9-10). 38.60 *(978-0-7660-3382-5(1)*, 9ac42541-9ac9-4a42-be15-4e574dc78d7e) Enslow Publishing, LLC.

Saddleback Educational Publishing Staff, ed. Elvis Presley, 1 vol. unabr. ed. 2007. (Graphic Biographies Ser.). (ENG., Illus.). 25p. (YA). (gr. 4-12). pap. 9.75 *(978-1-59905-221-2(0))* Saddleback Educational Publishing, Inc.

Snyder, R. Bradley, et al. What Every Child Needs to Know about Elvis Presley. 2014. (ENG.). 22p. (J). (-k). bds. 8.95 *(978-1-940705-00-2(2))* Need To Know Publishing.

Watson, Stephanie. Elvis Presley: Rock & Roll's King, 1 vol. 2012. (Lives Cut Short Set 2 Ser.). (ENG.). 112p. (YA). (gr. 6-12). 41.36 *(978-1-61783-482-0(3)*, 11199, Essential Library) ABDO Publishing Co.

Winter, Jonah. Elvis Is King! Red Nose Studio, illus. 2019. 40p. (J). (gr. -1-3). 18.99 *(978-0-399-55470-4(X)*, Schwartz & Wade Bks.) Random Hse. Children's Bks.

PRESS

see Journalism; Newspapers; Periodicals

PRESSURE GROUPS

see Lobbying

PRESSURE SUITS

see Astronauts—Clothing

PREVENTION OF ACCIDENTS

see Accidents—Prevention

PREVENTION OF CRUELTY TO ANIMALS

see Animals—Treatment

PREVENTION OF FIRE

see Fire Prevention

PREVENTIVE MEDICINE

see Bacteriology; Health; Immunity; Public Health

PRICE, HOMER (FICTITIOUS CHARACTER)—FICTION

McCloskey, Robert. Homer Price. l.t. ed. 2004. (Beeler Mystery Ser.). 158p. 29.95 *(978-1-58118-123-4(X))* LRS.

—Homer Price. l.t. ed. (J). (gr. 4-6). reprint ed. 10.00 *(978-0-89064-072-2(6))* National Assn. for Visually Handicapped.

PRIESTLEY, JOSEPH, 1733-1804

Bowden, Mary Ellen & Rosner, Linda. Joseph Priestley, Radical Thinker. 2005. (ENG.). 72p. pap. 19.95 *(978-0-941901-38-3(6))* Chemical Heritage Foundation.

Conley, Kate A. Joseph Priestly & the Discovery of Oxygen. 2005. (Uncharted, Unexplored, & Unexplained Ser.). (Illus.). 48p. (J). (gr. 4-8). lib. bdg. 29.95 *(978-1-58415-367-2(9))* Mitchell Lane Pubs.

PRIMARY EDUCATION

see Education, Elementary

PRIMATES

see also Apes; Human Beings; Lemurs; Monkeys

Aronin, Miriam. Aye-Aye: An Evil Omen. 2008. (Uncommon Animals Ser.). (Illus.). 32p. (YA). (gr. 2-5). lib. bdg. 28.50 *(978-1-59716-731-4(2)*, 1284368) Bearport Publishing Co., Inc.

Bové, Jennifer. I Wish I Was a Gorilla. 2018. (Illus.). 31p. (J). *(978-1-5444-0104-1(3))* Harper & Row Ltd.

Chimps & Monkeys Are Not Pets! 2013. (When Pets Attack! Ser.). 32p. (J). (gr. 3-6). pap. 63.00 *(978-1-4339-9290-2(6))* Stevens, Gareth Publishing LLLP.

Clark, Willow. Bush Babies, 1 vol. 2012. (Up a Tree Ser.). (ENG., Illus.). 24p. (J). (gr. 2-3). pap. 9.25 *(978-1-4488-6335-8(X)*, 33ac2d1b-5177-4595-abb3-d3446f1b6242, PowerKids Pr.); lib. bdg. 26.27 *(978-1-4488-6188-0(8)*, 6d58368b-ff95-4248-9cda-642dcb422a5a) Rosen Publishing Group, Inc., The.

Cooper, Sharon Katz. L Is for Lemur: ABCs of Endangered Primates. 2016. (E for Endangered Ser.). (ENG., Illus.). 32p. (J). (gr. -1-2). lib. bdg. 27.99 *(978-1-4914-8034-2(3)*, 130542, Capstone Pr.) Capstone.

Corwin, Jeff. The World of Primates. 2014. (Wildlife & Nature Identification Ser.). (ENG., Illus.). 2p. (J). (gr. -1-12). 7.95 *(978-1-58355-865-2(9))* Waterford Pr., Inc.

De La Bédoyère, Camilla. Monkeys & Apes, 1 vol. 2014. (Animal Q & A Ser.). (ENG., Illus.). 24p. (J). (gr. 2-2). lib. bdg. 26.27 *(978-1-4777-9190-5(6)*, 40781a2d-f132-48c8-b1cc-6c0b401cabbe, Windmill Bks.) Rosen Publishing Group, Inc., The.

Kalman, Bobbie. Baby Primates. 2013. (ENG., Illus.). 24p. (J). *(978-0-7787-1007-3(6))*; pap. *(978-0-7787-1011-0(4))* Crabtree Publishing Co.

—Les Singes et Autres Primates. Sjonger, Rebecca, illus. 2012. (FRE.). 32p. (J). pap. 9.95 *(978-2-89579-440-0(5))* Bayard Canada CAN. Dist: Crabtree Publishing Co.

Kalman, Bobbie & Levigne, Heather. Les Primates. 2005. (Petit Monde Vivant Ser.). (FRE., Illus.). 32p. (J). pap. 9.95 *(978-2-89579-051-8(5))* Bayard Canada Livres CAN. Dist: Crabtree Publishing Co.

Keats Curtis, Jennifer. Primate School, 1 vol. 2015. (ENG., Illus.). 32p. (J). (gr. 2-5). 17.95 *(978-1-62855-555-4(6))* Arbordale Publishing.

Levy, Janey. The Unsightly Aye-Aye, 1 vol. 2019. (Nature's Freak Show: Ugly Beasts Ser.). (ENG.). 24p. (gr. 2-3). pap. 9.15 *(978-1-5382-4622-1(8)*, 9e6d6426-ccbc-411f-b068-0157c507057e) Stevens, Gareth Publishing LLLP.

Moore Niver, Heather. Chimps & Monkeys Are Not Pets!, 1 vol. 2013. (When Pets Attack! Ser.). (ENG.). 32p. (J). (gr. 3-4). 29.27 *(978-1-4339-9288-9(4)*, 3e94a709-0a01-4309-95a1-811d49709d02); pap. 11.50 *(978-1-4339-9289-6(2)*, 52e3bca3-edb2-42e8-9027-b0f1a764d9e9) Stevens, Gareth Publishing LLLP.

Morgan, Sally. Small Primates. 2004. (J). lib. bdg. *(978-1-59389-178-7(4))* Cherrytree Bks.

Oldfield, Dawn Bluemel. Tarsier. 2016. (Weird but Cute Ser.). (ENG., Illus.). 24p. (J). (gr. -1-3). 26.99 *(978-1-943553-28-0(9))* Bearport Publishing Co., Inc.

Ottaviani, Jim. Primates: The Fearless Science of Jane Goodall, Dian Fossey, & Biruté Galdikas. Wicks, Maris, illus. 2015. (ENG.). 144p. (YA). (gr. 7). pap. 14.99 *(978-1-250-06293-2(4)*, 900142635) Square Fish.

Owings, Lisa & Leaf, Christina. Tarsier. 2014. (Extremely Weird Animals Ser.). (ENG., Illus.). 24p. (J). (gr. 3-8). lib. bdg. 27.95 *(978-1-62617-079-7(7)*, Pilot Bks.) Bellwether Media.

Paterson, Samantha. Primates. 2007. (Life Science (Weigl Hardcover) Ser.). (Illus.). 32p. (J). (gr. 4-7). lib. bdg. 26.00 *(978-1-59036-709-4(X))*; per. 9.95 *(978-1-59036-710-0(3))* Weigl Pubs., Inc.

—The Science of Primates. 2003. (Living Science Ser.). (Illus.). 32p. (J). (gr. 1-3). pap. 9.95 *(978-1-930954-36-6(0))* Weigl Pubs., Inc.

Rafferty, John P. Primates, 1 vol. 2011. (Britannica Guide to Predators & Prey Ser.). (ENG., Illus.). 296p. (YA). (gr. 10-10). lib. bdg. 55.29 *(978-1-61530-339-7(1)*, 4bb449d5-e5cf-41f1-9f9e-698b2dcb525d) Rosen Publishing Group, Inc., The.

Rafferty, John P., ed. Primates, 4 vols. 2011. (Britannica Guide to Predators & Prey Ser.). (ENG., Illus.). 296p. (YA). (gr. 10-10). 110.58 *(978-1-61530-455-4(X)*, 944d9395-dd1b-4432-aacb-896cb6056f9b) Rosen Publishing Group, Inc., The.

Redmond, Ian. Gorilas. Anderson, Peter & Brightling, Geoff, illus. 2003. (SPA.). 64p. 14.95 *(978-84-372-2323-0(7))* Altea, Ediciones, S.A. - Grupo Santillana ESP. Dist: Santillana USA Publishing Co., Inc.

Rich, Mari. Rescuing Primates: Gorillas, Chimps, & Monkeys. 2017. (Illus.). 64p. (J). *(978-1-4222-3877-6(6))* Mason Crest.

Sjonger, Rebecca & Kalman, Bobbie. Monkeys & Other Primates. 2005. (What Kind of Animal Is It? Ser.). (ENG., Illus.). 32p. (J). (gr. 1-2). pap. *(978-0-7787-2223-6(6))*; lib. bdg. *(978-0-7787-2165-9(5))* Crabtree Publishing Co.

Stefoff, Rebecca. The Primate Order, 1 vol. 2007. (Family Trees Ser.). (ENG., Illus.). 96p. (gr. 6-6). lib. bdg. 36.93 *(978-0-7614-1816-0(4)*, e85361ac-2144-41cc-a071-4f18b8414af3) Cavendish Square Publishing LLC.

Van Eck, Thomas. Tarsiers in the Dark, 1 vol. 2012. (Creatures of the Night Ser.). (ENG., Illus.). 24p. (J). (gr. 1-2). pap. 9.15 *(978-1-4339-6382-7(5)*, 58f95b4a-65c9-453a-a379-6fbed62dcff9); lib. bdg. 25.27 *(978-1-4339-6380-3(9)*, fc350b8f-6f9b-4c8d-9cd6-6e9d954043c7) Stevens, Gareth Publishing LLLP.

Webster, Christine. Jane Goodall. 2019. (J). pap. *(978-1-7911-1131-1(9)*, AV2 by Weigl) Weigl Pubs., Inc.

Willis, John. Baboon. 2016. (J). *(978-1-4896-5369-7(4))* Weigl Pubs., Inc.

PRIMATES—FICTION

Browne, Anthony. One Gorilla: a Counting Book. Browne, Anthony, illus. 2015. (ENG., Illus.). 26p. (J). (— 1). bds. 8.99 *(978-0-7636-7915-6(1))* Candlewick Pr.

Cotter, Amelia. Breakfast with Bigfoot. Swinford, Charles, illus. 2013. 30p. pap. 11.95 *(978-1-61876-017-3(3))* Lake Ridge Pr.

Doman, Glenn. Nose Is Not Toes. 2010. (Gentle Revolution Ser.). (ENG., Illus.). 144p. (J). 15.95 *(978-0-7570-0208-3(0))* Square One Pubs.

Fontes, Justine & Fontes, Ron. Casebook: Bigfoot, 1 vol. 2009. (Top Secret Graphica Mysteries Ser.). (ENG., Illus.). 48p. (YA). (gr. 4-4). 33.93 *(978-1-60754-594-1(2)*, bd5f014b-7bcb-49d5-9529-2832f6a60019); pap. 12.75 *(978-1-60754-595-8(0)*, 3a36ccf3-f909-4bfe-aa0c-ea62e096eb46) Rosen Publishing Group, Inc., The. (Windmill Bks.).

MacHale, D. J. The Lost City of Faar. 2003. (Pendragon Ser.: 2). (ENG.). 400p. (J). (gr. 5-9). pap. 10.99 *(978-0-7434-3732-5(2)*, Aladdin) Simon & Schuster Children's Publishing.

Mullarkey, Lisa. Gabriela. Franco, Paula, illus. 2016. (Chicas Poni (Pony Girls) Ser.).Tr. of Gabriela. (SPA.). 112p. (J). (gr. 1-4). lib. bdg. 38.50 *(978-1-61479-623-7(8)*, 25056, Calico Chapter Bks.) ABDO Publishing Co.

Newton-Perry, Linda. The Little Red Car & Bigfoot. 2009. 70p. pap. 15.95 *(978-0-557-08449-4(0))* Lulu Pr., Inc.

Star, Nancy. Mystery of the Snow Day Bigfoot. Bernardin, James, illus. 2005. (Calendar Club Mysteries Ser.: Vol. 3). 77p. (J). pap. 3.95 *(978-0-439-67262-7(7))* Scholastic, Inc.

Sundance/Newbridge LLC Staff. The Abominable Snowman. 2005. (Choose Your Own Adventure Ser.). (gr. 4-8). pap. 5.50 *(978-0-7608-9693-8(3))* Sundance/Newbridge Educational Publishing.

PRIME MINISTERS

Aboff, Marcie. Golda Meir Iron Lady of Israel. 2016. (Spring Forward Ser.). (J). (gr. 2). *(978-1-4900-9454-0(7))* Benchmark Education Co.

Darraj, Susan Muaddi. Silvio Berlusconi: Prime Minister of Italy. 2005. (Major World Leaders Ser.). (ENG., Illus.). 112p. (J). (gr. 6-12). 30.00 *(978-0-7910-8260-7(1)*, P114244, Facts On File) Infobase Holdings, Inc.

Kennedy Henzel, Cynthia. Jacinda Ardern: Prime Minister of New Zealand: Prime Minister of New Zealand. 2019. (World Leaders Set 2 Ser.). (ENG., Illus.). 48p. (J). (gr. 5-6). 34.21 *(978-1-64185-361-3(1)*, 1641853611, Focus Readers) North Star Editions.

Moening, Kate. Angela Merkel: Chancellor of Germany. 2019. (Women Leading the Way Ser.). (ENG., Illus.). 24p. (J). (gr. k-3). pap. 7.99 *(978-1-61891-721-8(8)*, 12302); lib. bdg. 26.95 *(978-1-64487-098-3(3))* Bellwether Media. (Blastoff! Readers).

Naden, Corinne. Benazir Bhutto, 1 vol. 2011. (Leading Women Ser.). (ENG., Illus.). 96p. (J). (gr. 7-7). 42.64 *(978-0-7614-4952-2(3)*, 4cb4dc26-f281-494e-b9ea-ec4657c25e37) Cavendish Square Publishing LLC.

Stewart, J. J. Justin Trudeau: Prime Minister of Canada. 2018. (World Leaders Ser.). (ENG., Illus.). 48p. (J). (gr. 5-6). pap. 11.95 *(978-1-63517-624-7(7)*, 1635176247); lib. bdg. 34.21 *(978-1-63517-552-3(6)*, 1635175526) North Star Editions. (Focus Readers).

Sylvan, Lu. Vladimir Putin. 2015. (Newsmakers Ser.). (ENG., Illus.). 48p. (J). (gr. 4-8). lib. bdg. 35.64 *(978-1-62403-645-3(7)*, 17189) ABDO Publishing Co.

Willett, Edward. Angela Merkel: Chancellor of Germany. 2018. (World Leaders Ser.). (ENG., Illus.). 48p. (J). (gr. 5-6). pap. 11.95 *(978-1-63517-622-3(0)*, 1635176220); lib. bdg. 34.21 *(978-1-63517-550-9(X)*, 163517550X) North Star Editions. (Focus Readers).

PRIME MINISTERS—CANADA

Furgang, Kathy. Justin Trudeau: Prime Minister of Canada, 1 vol. 2018. (Junior Biographies Ser.). (ENG.). 24p. (gr. 3-4). 24.27 *(978-0-7660-9743-8(9)*, 9c07704b-0bda-4f54-908f-50bd70d322b9) Enslow Publishing, LLC.

Hancock, Pat. The Kids Book of Canadian Prime Ministers. Mantha, John, illus. 2005. (Kids Book Of Ser.). 56p. (J). (gr. 3-7). 19.95 *(978-1-55337-740-5(0))* Kids Can Pr., Ltd. CAN. Dist: Hachette Bk. Group.

Hughes, Susan. Lester B. Pearson, 1 vol. 2004. (Canadians Ser.). (ENG., Illus.). 64p. (J). (gr. 5-8). pap. 6.95 *(978-1-55041-504-9(2)*, 1dd61774-e760-4560-8d5d-daa8b23b004c) Trifolium Bks., Inc. CAN. Dist: Firefly Bks., Ltd.

PRIME MINISTERS—GREAT BRITAIN

Collins, Thomas M. Tony Blair. 2005. (Biography Ser.). (Illus.). 112p. (J). (gr. 6-18). pap. 7.95 *(978-0-8225-9622-6(9))*; 29.27 *(978-0-8225-2373-4(6)*, Lerner Pubns.) Lerner Publishing Group.

Daynes, Katie. Winston Churchill. Tomlins, Karen, illus. 2006. (Usborne Famous Lives Gift Bks.). 64p. (J). (gr. 2-5). 8.99 *(978-0-7945-1258-3(5)*, Usborne) EDC Publishing.

Hamilton, Janice. Winston Churchill. 2006. (and E Biography Ser.). (Illus.). 112p. (J). (gr. 3-7). lib. bdg. 27.93 *(978-0-8225-3419-8(3)*, Twenty-First Century Bks.) Lerner Publishing Group.

Labrecque, Ellen & Who HQ. Who Was Winston Churchill? Hoare, Jerry, illus. 2015. (Who Was? Ser.). 112p. (J). (gr.

3-7). 6.99 *(978-0-448-48300-9(9)*, Penguin Workshop) Penguin Young Readers Group.

Lee, Stephen J. Gladstone & Disraeli. 2005. (Questions & Analysis in History Ser.). (ENG., Illus.). 208p. (C). 125.00 *(978-0-415-32356-7(8)*, RU27027); per. 35.95 *(978-0-415-32357-4(6)*, RU27028) Routledge.

Ridley, Sarah. Winston Churchill: ...And World War II. 2013. (History Makers Ser.). (ENG., Illus.). 24p. (J). (gr. 2-4). lib. bdg. 25.65 *(978-1-59771-393-1(7))* Sea-To-Sea Pubns.

Trussell-Cullen, Alan. Winston Churchill. 2009. pap. 13.25 *(978-1-60559-072-1(X))* Hameray Publishing Group, Inc.

Vander Hook, Sue. Winston Churchill: British Prime Minister & Statesman, 1 vol. 2009. (Essential Lives Set 3 Ser.). (ENG., Illus.). 112p. (YA). (gr. 6-12). lib. bdg. 41.36 *(978-1-60453-523-5(7)*, 6675, Essential Library) ABDO Publishing Co.

PRIME MINISTERS—INDIA

Prasad, H.Y. Sharada. Indira Gandhi. 2013. 56p. 10.00 *(978-0-14-333288-6(0))* Penguin Group India IND. Dist: Penguin Publishing Group.

Schupack, Sara. Indira Gandhi, 1 vol. 2013. (Leading Women Ser.). (ENG.). 96p. (YA). (gr. 7-7). pap. 20.99 *(978-1-62712-113-2(7)*, 1ad29198-afee-4a3d-88ce-23789b2bad47); (Illus.). 42.64 *(978-0-7614-4955-3(8)*, f0416d76-ffca-4e20-b244-bec6da55bf97) Cavendish Square Publishing LLC.

PRIME MINISTERS—ISRAEL

Abrams, Dennis. Ehud Olmert. 2008. (Modern World Leaders Ser.). (ENG., Illus.). 136p. (gr. 7-12). 30.00 *(978-0-7910-9761-8(7)*, P159142, Facts On File) Infobase Holdings, Inc.

Blashfield, Jean F. Golda Meir, 1 vol. 2011. (Leading Women Ser.). (ENG.). 96p. (YA). (gr. 7-7). 42.64 *(978-0-7614-4960-7(4)*, c65113b7-d6a4-4fbf-a51d-859173c00522) Cavendish Square Publishing LLC.

Finkelstein, Norman H. Ariel Sharon. 128p. (J). (gr. 6-18). 20.95 *(978-1-58013-205-3(7)*, Kar-Ben Publishing); 2005. (Illus.). 112p. (YA). (gr. 7-12). lib. bdg. 29.27 *(978-0-8225-2370-3(1)*, Lerner Pubns.) Lerner Publishing Group.

Krasner, Barbara. Goldie Takes a Stand! Golda Meir's First Crusade. Garrity-Riley, Kelsey, illus. 2014. (ENG.). 32p. (J). (gr. k-4). 17.95 *(978-1-4677-1200-2(0))* Lerner Publishing Group.

—Goldie Takes a Stand: Golda Meir's First Crusade. Garrity-Riley, Kelsey, illus. 2014. (ENG.). 32p. (J). (gr. k-4). 7.95 *(978-1-4677-1201-9(9)*, c426fcc0-d82b-4759-a9b0-3ae07363554b, Kar-Ben Publishing) Lerner Publishing Group.

Sommers, Michael. Ehud Olmert: Prime Minister of Israel. 2009. (Newsmakers Ser.). 112p. (gr. 9-10). 63.90 *(978-1-60851-131-0(6))* Rosen Publishing Group, Inc., The.

PRIMERS

see also Alphabet Books

Baby's First Words. 2003. (Illus.). (J). bds. 7.98 *(978-0-7525-8651-9(3))* Parragon, Inc.

Beck, Isabel L., et al. Trophies Kindergarten: A Big, Big Van. 2003. (Trophies Ser.). (gr. k-6). 13.80 *(978-0-15-329546-1(5))* Harcourt Schl. Pubs.

—Trophies Kindergarten: A Bug Can Tug. 2003. (Trophies Ser.). (gr. k-6). 13.80 *(978-0-15-329609-3(7))* Harcourt Schl. Pubs.

—Trophies Kindergarten: A Hat I Like. 2003. (Trophies Ser.). (gr. k-6). 13.80 *(978-0-15-329551-5(1))* Harcourt Schl. Pubs.

—Trophies Kindergarten: But I Can. 2003. (Trophies Ser.). (gr. k-6). 13.80 *(978-0-15-329605-5(4))* Harcourt Schl. Pubs.

—Trophies Kindergarten: Come In. 2003. (Trophies Ser.). (gr. k-6). 13.80 *(978-0-15-329547-8(3))* Harcourt Schl. Pubs.

—Trophies Kindergarten: First Day at School. 2003. (Trophies Ser.). (gr. k-6). 13.80 *(978-0-15-329516-4(3))* Harcourt Schl. Pubs.

—Trophies Kindergarten: Hop In! 2003. (Trophies Ser.). (gr. k-6). 13.80 *(978-0-15-329548-5(1))* Harcourt Schl. Pubs.

—Trophies Kindergarten: Hop on Top. 2003. (Trophies Ser.). (gr. k-6). 13.80 *(978-0-15-329545-4(7))* Harcourt Schl. Pubs.

—Trophies Kindergarten: I Am. 2003. (Trophies Ser.). (gr. k-6). 13.80 *(978-0-15-329525-6(2))* Harcourt Schl. Pubs.

—Trophies Kindergarten: I Can See It! 2003. (Trophies Ser.). (gr. k-6). 13.80 *(978-0-15-329543-0(0))* Harcourt Schl. Pubs.

—Trophies Kindergarten: I Have, You Have. 2003. (Trophies Ser.). (gr. k-6). 13.80 *(978-0-15-329536-2(8))* Harcourt Schl. Pubs.

—Trophies Kindergarten: I Nap. 2003. (Trophies Ser.). (gr. k-6). 13.80 *(978-0-15-329528-7(7))* Harcourt Schl. Pubs.

—Trophies Kindergarten: In a Sub. 2003. (Trophies Ser.). (gr. k-6). 13.80 *(978-0-15-329611-6(9))* Harcourt Schl. Pubs.

—Trophies Kindergarten: Is It a Fish? 2003. (Trophies Ser.). (gr. k-6). 13.80 *(978-0-15-329607-9(0))* Harcourt Schl. Pubs.

—Trophies Kindergarten: Is It for Me? 2003. (Trophies Ser.). (gr. k-6). 13.80 *(978-0-15-329549-2(X))* Harcourt Schl. Pubs.

—Trophies Kindergarten: It Is Fun. 2003. (Trophies Ser.). (gr. k-6). 13.80 *(978-0-15-329608-6(9))* Harcourt Schl. Pubs.

—Trophies Kindergarten: Kip the Ant. 2003. (Trophies Ser.). (gr. k-6). 13.80 *(978-0-15-329539-3(2))* Harcourt Schl. Pubs.

—Trophies Kindergarten: Little Cat, Big Cat. 2003. (Trophies Ser.). (gr. k-6). 13.80 *(978-0-15-329552-2(X))* Harcourt Schl. Pubs.

—Trophies Kindergarten: My Bus. 2003. (Trophies Ser.). (gr. k-6). 13.80 *(978-0-15-329522-5(8))* Harcourt Schl. Pubs.

—Trophies Kindergarten: My Pig. 2003. (Trophies Ser.). (gr. k-6). 13.80 *(978-0-15-329535-5(X))* Harcourt Schl. Pubs.

—Trophies Kindergarten: Pet Day. 2003. (Trophies Ser.). (gr. k-6). 13.80 *(978-0-15-329519-5(8))* Harcourt Schl. Pubs.

—Trophies Kindergarten: Sid Hid. 2003. (Trophies Ser.). (gr. k-6). 13.80 *(978-0-15-329610-9(0))* Harcourt Schl. Pubs.

—Trophies Kindergarten: Sit on My Chair. 2003. (Trophies Ser.). (gr. k-6). 13.80 *(978-0-15-329534-8(1))* Harcourt Schl. Pubs.

—Trophies Kindergarten: Soup. 2003. (Trophies Ser.). (gr. k-6). 13.80 *(978-0-15-329537-9(6))* Harcourt Schl. Pubs.

—Trophies Kindergarten: Tap, Tap, Tap. 2003. (Trophies Ser.). (gr. k-6). 13.80 *(978-0-15-329532-4(5))* Harcourt Schl. Pubs.

—Trophies Kindergarten: The Big Ram. 2003. (Trophies Ser.). (gr. k-6). 13.80 *(978-0-15-329540-9(6))* Harcourt Schl. Pubs.

—Trophies Kindergarten: The Dig. 2003. (Trophies Ser.). (gr. k-6). 13.80 *(978-0-15-329538-6(4))* Harcourt Schl. Pubs.

—Trophies Kindergarten: The Mat. 2003. (Trophies Ser.). (gr. k-6). 13.80 *(978-0-15-329526-3(0))* Harcourt Schl. Pubs.

—Trophies Kindergarten: The Park. 2003. (Trophies Ser.). (gr. k-6). 13.80 *(978-0-15-329533-1(3))* Harcourt Schl. Pubs.

—Trophies Kindergarten: The Party. 2003. (Trophies Ser.). (gr. k-6). 13.80 *(978-0-15-329523-2(6))* Harcourt Schl. Pubs.

—Trophies Kindergarten: The Salad. 2003. (Trophies Ser.). (gr. k-6). 13.80 *(978-0-15-329524-9(4))* Harcourt Schl. Pubs.

—Trophies Kindergarten: Up, up, Up. 2003. (Trophies Ser.). (gr. k-6). 13.80 *(978-0-15-329606-2(2))* Harcourt Schl. Pubs.

—Trophies Kindergarten: We Can Fix. 2003. (Trophies Ser.). (gr. k-6). 13.80 *(978-0-15-329550-8(3))* Harcourt Schl. Pubs.

—Trophies Kindergarten: We Go. 2003. (Trophies Ser.). (gr. k-6). 13.80 *(978-0-15-329527-0(9))* Harcourt Schl. Pubs.

—Trophies Kindergarten: What Can Hop? 2003. (Trophies Ser.). (gr. k-6). 13.80 *(978-0-15-329541-6(4))* Harcourt Schl. Pubs.

—Trophies Kindergarten: What Is in the Box? 2003. (Trophies Ser.). (gr. k-6). 13.80 *(978-0-15-329544-7(9))* Harcourt Schl. Pubs.

—Trophies Kindergarten: Where's My Teddy? 2003. (Trophies Ser.). (gr. k-6). 13.80 *(978-0-15-329517-1(1))* Harcourt Schl. Pubs.

Biddle, Steve & Biddle, Megumi. The Crane's Gift. 2003. (ENG.). 32p. pap. 7.33 *(978-0-582-46143-7(X))* Pearson ESL.

Brown, Jane. Who Has Four Feet? l.t. ed. 2005. (Sadlier Phonics Reading Program: Vol. 1). (Illus.). 8p. (gr. -1-1). 23.00 net. *(978-0-8215-7340-2(3))* Sadlier, William H. Inc.

Crawford, Sheryl Ann Saunders & Sanderson, Ian. Easy-to-Read Mini-Book Plays, 15 bks., Set. 2003. (ENG.). 64p. pap. 10.95 *(978-0-439-20155-1(1))* Scholastic, Inc.

Epstein, Brad M. Columbia University 101: My First Text-Board-Book. l.t. ed. 2005. (101 — My First Text-Board Books). (Illus.). 20p. (J). bds. *(978-0-9727702-1-7(6))* Michaelson Entertainment.

Evans, Mary. Cats! Cats! Cats!, 2. Kovalcik, Terry, illus. l.t. ed. 2005. (Sadlier Phonics Reading Program). 8p. (gr. -1-1). 23.00 net. *(978-0-8215-7348-8(9))* Sadlier, William H. Inc.

—Good Pets, Vol. 3. l.t. ed. 2005. (Sadlier Phonics Reading Program). (Illus.). 8p. (gr. -1-1). 23.00 net. *(978-0-8215-7350-1(0))* Sadlier, William H. Inc.

Goldish, Meish. How Many Are Here? Meyerhoff, Jill, illus. l.t. ed. 2005. (Sadlier Phonics Reading Program). 8p. (gr. -1-1). 23.00 net. *(978-0-8215-7344-0(6))* Sadlier, William H. Inc.

—Nice Vine, Quite Fine, Vol. 2. Sargent, Claudia Karabaic, illus. l.t. ed. 2005. (Little Books & Big Bks.: Vol. 7). 8p. (gr. k-2). 23.00 net. *(978-0-8215-7516-1(3))* Sadlier, William H. Inc.

—Zack Can Fix It!, Vol. 4. Scruton, Clive, illus. l.t. ed. 2005. (Sadlier Phonics Reading Program). 8p. (gr. -1-1). 23.00 net. *(978-0-8215-7359-4(4))* Sadlier, William H. Inc.

Grosset & Dunlap. Dick & Jane Fun Wherever We Are. 2004. (Dick & Jane Ser.). (Illus.). 144p. (J). (gr. -1-1). 10.99 *(978-0-448-43614-2(0)*, Grosset & Dunlap) Penguin Young Readers Group.

Harcourt School Publishers Staff. Horizons, Grade 1: Time for Kids Readers. 3rd ed. 2003. (Harcourt Horizons Ser.). pap., tchr. ed. 51.20 *(978-0-15-334646-0(9))* Harcourt Schl. Pubs.

—Horizons, Grade K: Time for Kids Readers. 3rd ed. 2003. (Harcourt Horizons Ser.). pap., tchr. ed. 54.10 *(978-0-15-334645-3(0))* Harcourt Schl. Pubs.

—Trophies Collection. 3rd ed. 2003. (Trophies Ser.). Grade 1. (gr. 1-18). tchr. ed. 596.00 *(978-0-15-327375-9(5))*Grade 2. (gr. 2-18). tchr. ed. 392.80 *(978-0-15-327376-6(3))*Grade 3. (gr. 3-18). tchr. ed. 392.80 *(978-0-15-327377-3(1))*Grade 4. (gr. 4-18). tchr. ed. 419.20 *(978-0-15-327378-0(X))*Grade 5. (gr. 5-18). tchr. ed. 419.20 *(978-0-15-327379-7(8))*Theme 6. (gr. 6-18). tchr. ed. 436.00 *(978-0-15-329239-2(3))* Harcourt Schl. Pubs.

HarperCollins Publishers Ltd. Staff, et al. An I Can Read Halloween Treat, Set. Zimmer, Dirk, illus. 2004. (I Can Read Bks.). (J). (gr. k-3). pap. 11.99 *(978-0-06-054237-5(3)*, Harper Trophy) HarperCollins Pubs.

Herridon, Lynne. Peter & the Wolf. 2003. (ENG.). 32p. pap. 10.00 *(978-0-582-51233-7(6))* Pearson ESL.

Hiebert, Elfrieda H. Ready Read. (J). (gr. -1-3). pap. 179.95 *(978-0-8136-1861-6(4))* Modern Curriculum Pr.

—Ready Read, Stage 1 Take Home Books. (J). (gr. -1-3). pap. 43.50 *(978-0-8136-3277-3(3))* Modern Curriculum Pr.

—Ready Read, Stage 2 Take Home Books, 50 bks. , Set. 2003. (J). (gr. -1-3). pap. 48.50 *(978-0-8136-3278-0(1))* Modern Curriculum Pr.

Hofmeister, Alan, et al. Dash Has Fun. (Reading for All Learners Ser.). (Illus.). (J). pap. *(978-1-56861-145-7(5))* Swift Learning Resources.

Jensen, Patricia. The Mess. Lewis, Anthony, illus. 2003. (My First Reader Ser.). (ENG.). 32p. (J). 18.50 *(978-0-516-22932-4(X)*, Children's Pr.) Scholastic Library Publishing.

Martin, Tyler. I Have a Question, Vol. 4. Williams, Toby, illus. l.t. ed. 2005. (Sadlier Phonics Reading Program). 8p. (gr. -1-1). 23.00 net. *(978-0-8215-7356-3(X))* Sadlier, William H. Inc.

Martinucci, Suzanne. At Space Camp, Vol. 2. l.t. ed. 2005. (Little Books & Big Bks.: Vol. 6). (Illus.). 8p. (gr. k-2). 23.00 net. *(978-0-8215-7515-4(5))* Sadlier, William H. Inc.

Marzollo, Jean. I Spy a Dinosaur's Eye (Scholastic Reader, Level 1) Wick, Walter, photos by. 2003. (Scholastic Reader, Level 1 Ser.). (ENG., Illus.). 32p. (J). (gr. -1-3). pap. 3.99 *(978-0-439-52471-1(7)*, Cartwheel Bks.) Scholastic, Inc.

MCP Staff. Ready Reader S1. 2003. (J). (gr. -1-3). pap. 227.95 *(978-0-8136-1432-8(5))* Modern Curriculum Pr.

—Stage Two - Early. 2003. (J). (gr. -1-3). pap. 227.95 *(978-0-8136-1433-5(3))* Modern Curriculum Pr.

Michaels, David. Bye-Bye, Katy, Vol. 3. Platt, Pierre, illus. l.t. ed. 2005. (Sadlier Phonics Reading Program). 8p. (gr. -1-1). 23.00 net. *(978-0-8215-7354-9(3))* Sadlier, William H. Inc.

Miranda, Anne. The Best Place. l.t. ed. 2005. (Little Books & Big Bks.: Vol. 5). (Illus.). 8p. (gr. k-2). 23.00 net. *(978-0-8215-7514-7(7))* Sadlier, William H. Inc.

—Looking at Lizards, Vol. 2. l.t. ed. 2005. (Sadlier Phonics Reading Program). (Illus.). 8p. (gr. -1-1). 23.00 net. *(978-0-8215-7346-4(2))* Sadlier, William H. Inc.

—Peach Tree Street, Vol. 2. Lodge, Katherine, illus. l.t. ed. 2005. (Little Books & Big Bks.: Vol. 10). 8p. (gr. k-2). 23.00 net. *(978-0-8215-7519-2(8))* Sadlier, William H. Inc.

—Weather Wise, Vol. 3. l.t. ed. 2005. (Sadlier Phonics Reading Program). (Illus.). 8p. (gr. -1-1). 23.00 net. *(978-0-8215-7351-8(9))* Sadlier, William H. Inc.

Montardre, Hélène. The Cat & the Dog. 2003. (Illus.). 8p. (J). bds. 7.95 *(978-1-58728-483-0(9)*, Two-Can Publishing) T&N Children's Publishing.

—Night & Day. 2003. (Illus.). 8p. (J). bds. 7.95 *(978-1-58728-481-6(2)*, Two-Can Publishing) T&N Children's Publishing.

Nicholas, Melissa. Pumpkin Days, Vol. 3. l.t. ed. 2005. (Sadlier Phonics Reading Program). (Illus.). 8p. (gr. -1-1). 23.00 net. *(978-0-8215-7352-5(7))* Sadlier, William H. Inc.

—Stop by a Pond. Gram, Patrick, illus. l.t. ed. 2005. (Little Books & Big Bks.: Vol. 3). 8p. (gr. k-2). 23.00 net. *(978-0-8215-7512-3(0))* Sadlier, William H. Inc.

—Who Is My Mom? Cassels, Jean, illus. l.t. ed. 2005. (Sadlier Phonics Reading Program). 8p. (gr. -1-1). 23.00 net. *(978-0-8215-7341-9(1))* Sadlier, William H. Inc.

O'Keefe, Ruth A. Starter One Hundred One, Bk. 8. AEVAC, Inc. Staff, ed. (Structured Beginning Reading Program Ser.). 96p. (J). stu. ed. 3.50 *(978-0-913356-14-2(X))* AEVAC, Inc.

Olivia, Cynthia. In January & June, Vol. 4. l.t. ed. 2005. (Sadlier Phonics Reading Program: Vol. 16). (Illus.). 8p. (gr. -1-1). 23.00 net. *(978-0-8215-7355-6(1))* Sadlier, William H. Inc.

Packard, Mary. Surprise! Huang, Benrei, illus. 2003. (My First Reader Ser.). (ENG.). 32p. (J). 18.50 *(978-0-516-22937-9(0)*, Children's Pr.) Scholastic Library Publishing.

Paul, Kate. The Best Ride, Vol. 2. l.t. ed. 2005. (Sadlier Phonics Reading Program). (Illus.). 8p. (gr. -1-1). 23.00 net. *(978-0-8215-7345-7(4))* Sadlier, William H. Inc.

Penguin Young Readers. Dick & Jane: Away We Go. 2004. (Dick & Jane Ser.: Vol. 7). (Illus.). 32p. (J). (gr. k-1). mass mkt. 5.99 *(978-0-448-43406-3(7)*, Penguin Young Readers) Penguin Young Readers Group.

—Dick & Jane: Fun with Dick & Jane. 2004. (Dick & Jane Ser.: Vol. 12). (Illus.). 32p. (J). (gr. 1-2). mass mkt. 4.99 *(978-0-448-43411-7(3)*, Penguin Young Readers) Penguin Young Readers Group.

—Dick & Jane: We Play. 2004. (Dick & Jane Ser.: Vol. 11). (Illus.). 32p. (J). (gr. k-1). mass mkt. 4.99 *(978-0-448-43410-0(5)*, Penguin Young Readers) Penguin Young Readers Group.

—Dick & Jane: Who Can Help? 2004. (Dick & Jane Ser.: Vol. 8). (Illus.). 32p. (J). (gr. 1-2). mass mkt. 4.99 *(978-0-448-43407-0(5)*, Penguin Young Readers) Penguin Young Readers Group.

—We See. 2004. (Dick & Jane Ser.: Vol. 9). (Illus.). 32p. (J). (gr. 1-2). mass mkt. 4.99 *(978-0-448-43408-7(3)*, Penguin Young Readers) Penguin Young Readers Group.

—We Work. 2004. (Dick & Jane Ser.: Vol. 10). (Illus.). 32p. (J). (gr. 1-2). mass mkt. 4.99 *(978-0-448-43409-4(1)*, Penguin Young Readers) Penguin Young Readers Group.

Practice Power School Bus Book: Preschool. 2003. 24p. (J). (gr. -1). spiral bd. *(978-1-930355-41-5(6))* Bright of America.

Reading Friends Staff. Peanut Single. (J). *(978-0-8136-3813-3(5))* Modern Curriculum Pr.

—Run Single. (J). *(978-0-8136-3787-7(2))* Modern Curriculum Pr.

Rothman, Cynthia Anne. Funny Bugs. Lester, Mike, illus. l.t. ed. 2005. (Little Books & Big Bks.: Vol. 4). 8p. (gr. k-2). 23.00 net. *(978-0-8215-7513-0(9))* Sadlier, William H. Inc.

—I Love to Read, 3. l.t. ed. 2005. (Sadlier Phonics Reading Program). (Illus.). 8p. (gr. -1-1). 23.00 net. *(978-0-8215-7353-2(5))* Sadlier, William H. Inc.

—Violets & Vegetables, Vol. 4. l.t. ed. 2005. (Sadlier Phonics Reading Program). (Illus.). 8p. (gr. -1-1). 23.00 net. *(978-0-8215-7357-0(8))* Sadlier, William H. Inc.

—What Does Sam Sell? Alley, R. W., illus. l.t. ed. 2005. (Sadlier Phonics Reading Program). 8p. (gr. -1-1). 23.00 net. *(978-0-8215-7342-6(X))* Sadlier, William H. Inc.

—Yes, You Can, Vol. 4. l.t. ed. 2005. (Sadlier Phonics Reading Program). (Illus.). 8p. (gr. -1-1). 23.00 net. *(978-0-8215-7358-7(6))* Sadlier, William H. Inc.

School Zone Publishing. Beginning Reading. 2003. (ENG.). (J). cd-rom 19.99 *(978-1-58947-921-0(1))*; (gr. k-1). cd-rom 19.99 *(978-1-58947-923-4(8))*; (gr. 1-2). cd-rom 19.99 *(978-1-58947-924-1(6))*; (gr. 1-2). cd-rom 19.99 *(978-1-58947-922-7(X))* School Zone Publishing Co.

Schumacher, Stef. Amazing Blue Animals, Vol. 2. l.t. ed. 2005. (Little Books & Big Bks.: Vol. 9). (Illus.). 8p. (gr. k-2). 23.00 net. *(978-0-8215-7518-5(X))* Sadlier, William H. Inc.

Smith, Dodie. 101 Dalmatians. 2003. (ENG., Illus.). 32p. (C). pap. 28.73 *(978-0-582-52979-3(4))* Pearson ESL.

Stanley, Mandy. First Words. 2018. (Kingfisher Board Bks.). (ENG.). 10p. (J). bds. 4.99 *(978-0-7534-7464-8(6)*, 900192051, Kingfisher) Roaring Brook Pr.

—On the Farm. 2018. (Kingfisher Board Bks.). (ENG.). 10p. (J). bds. 4.99 *(978-0-7534-7447-1(6)*, 900192010, Kingfisher) Roaring Brook Pr.

Steck-Vaughn Staff. At-Home Workbooks: Reading. 2004. (Illus.). (gr. 3). pap., wbk. ed. 5.99 *(978-0-7398-8526-0(X))* Steck-Vaughn.

Stuart, Matt. Who Can Run Fast? l.t. ed. 2005. (Little Books & Big Bks.: Vol. 1). (Illus.). 8p. (gr. k-2). 23.00 net. *(978-0-8215-7510-9(4))* Sadlier, William H. Inc.

Taylor, Beth. Tina's Toys. l.t. ed. 2005. (Sadlier Phonics Reading Program). (Illus.). 8p. (gr. -1-1). 23.00 net. *(978-0-8215-7343-3(8))* Sadlier, William H. Inc.

Thryce, Marc & Robinson, Tim. Look at the Pictures. l.t. ed. 2005. (Little Books & Big Bks.: Vol. 2). (Illus.). 8p. (gr. k-2). 23.00 net. *(978-0-8215-7511-6(2))* Sadlier, William H. Inc.

Titzer, Robert C. A Book Your Baby Can Read! Dozier, Brendan et al, photos by. 2003. (Early Language Development Ser.: Vol. 2). (Illus.). 14p. (J). pap. 7.95 *(978-0-9657510-5-6(8)*, 0-9657510-5-8) Infant Learning Co., The.

—A Book Your Baby Can Read! Early Language Development Series. Dozier, Lisa et al, photos by. 2003. (Early Language Development Ser.: Vol. 3). (Illus.). 14p. (J). pap. 7.95 *(978-0-9657510-9-4(0)*, 0-9657510-9-0) Infant Learning Co., The.

—A Book Your Baby Can Read! 5 Book Set: Early Language Development Series, 5 vols., Vol. 1. 2003. (Illus.). 80p. (J). pap. 29.95 *(978-1-931026-05-5(X)*, 1-931026-05-X) Infant Learning Co., The.

—A Book Your Baby Can Read! Review: Early Language Development Series. Dozier, Brendan et al, photos by. 2003. (Early Language Development Ser.). (Illus.). 14p. (J). pap. 7.95 *(978-1-931026-04-8(1)*, 1-931026-04-1) Infant Learning Co., The.

—A Book Your Baby Can Read! Starter: Early Language Development Series, 1, Starter Book. Dozier, Lisa et al, photos by. 2003. (Book Your Baby Can Read!: Starter Book). (Illus.). 14p. (J). pap. 7.95 *(978-1-931026-03-1(3)*, 1-931026-03-3) Infant Learning Co., The.

Williams, Rozanne. Mr. Noisy's Book of Patterns. 2017. (Learn-To-Read Ser.). (ENG., Illus.). (J). pap. 3.49 *(978-1-68310-217-5(7))* Pacific Learning, Inc.

Winter, Max. Did You Know?, Vol. 2. Rechin, Kevin, illus. l.t. ed. 2005. (Little Books & Big Bks.: Vol. 8). 8p. (gr. k-2). 23.00 net. *(978-0-8215-7517-8(1))* Sadlier, William H. Inc.

PRIMITIVE ART

see Art, Primitive

PRINCE EDWARD ISLAND

Dodge, Sandra. Minegoo: The Mi'Kmaq Creation Story of Prince Edward Island, 1 vol. 2017. (ENG., Illus.). 32p. (J). (gr. 1-3). pap. 13.95 *(978-1-927502-85-3(3)*, 00655614-2d5c-4300-9e01-71f2589f9fae) Acorn Pr., The CAN. Dist: Baker & Taylor Publisher Services (BTPS).

MacDonald, Hugh. I is for Island: A Prince Edward Island Alphabet. Jones, Brenda, illus. 2012. (Discover Canada Province by Province Ser.). (ENG.). 40p. (J). (gr. 1-3). 16.95 *(978-1-58536-367-4(7)*, 202347) Sleeping Bear Pr.

PRINCE EDWARD ISLAND—FICTION

Boudreau, Hélène. Keep Out!, 1 vol. Lucas, Diane, illus. 2010. (ENG.). 80p. (J). (gr. 1-3). pap. 8.95 *(978-1-55109-753-4(2))* Nimbus Publishing, Ltd. CAN. Dist: Orca Bk. Pubs. USA.

Chronicles of Avonlea. 2004. 142p. (YA). pap. 7.95 *(978-1-57646-893-7(3))* Quiet Vision Publishing.

Helldorfer, M. C. Anne of Green Gables. Beier, Ellen, illus. 2003. 40p. (J). (gr. -1-2). pap. 7.99 *(978-0-440-41614-2(0)*, Dragonfly Bks.) Random Hse. Children's Bks.

MacDonald, George. Princess & the Goblin. 2006. 128p. per. 10.95 *(978-1-59818-653-6(1))* Aegypan.

—The Princess & the Goblin. 2010. 222p. pap. 13.95 *(978-0-557-47296-3(2))* Lulu Pr., Inc.

Montgomery, L. M. Along the Shore: Tales by the Sea. (YA). 22.95 *(978-0-8488-2655-0(8))* Amereon Ltd.

—Ana la de la Isla. 4th ed. (Ana la de Tejas Verdes Ser.: 3).Tr. of Anne of the Island. (SPA., Illus.). 240p. (YA). (gr. 5-8). *(978-84-7888-635-7(4)*, SAL5036) Emece Editores ESP. Dist: Lectorum Pubns., Inc.

—Anne of Avonlea. 2018. (ENG., Illus.). 250p. (J). (gr. 3-7). pap. *(978-93-5297-101-5(9))* Alpha Editions.

—Anne of Avonlea. (ENG., Illus.). (J). 2018. 400p. pap. 17.95 *(978-1-376-49928-5(2))* 2015. 27.95 *(978-1-297-91573-4(9))* Creative Media Partners, LLC.

—Anne of Avonlea. 2005. pap. *(978-1-905432-15-8(1))* Dodo Pr.

—Anne of Avonlea. 2005. (Aladdin Classics Ser.). (ENG., Illus.). 416p. (J). (gr. 4-7). pap. 5.99 *(978-1-4169-0328-4(3)*, Aladdin) Simon & Schuster Children's Publishing.

—Anne of Avonlea. 2018. (Anne of Green Gables: the Complete Collection: 2). (ENG.). 336p. (J). (gr. 6-12). 8.99 *(978-1-78226-444-6(2)*, 5ab6e735-475a-4e0f-a18b-99628df1f473) Sweet Cherry Publishing GBR. Dist: Baker & Taylor Publisher Services (BTPS).

—Anne of Avonlea. 2018. (ENG., Illus.). 276p. (YA). 24.99 *(978-1-5287-0644-5(7)*, Classic Bks. Library) The Editorium, LLC.

—Anne of Avonlea. 2019. (ENG.). 262p. (J). pap. 11.89 *(978-1-7278-8486-9(8))* CreateSpace Independent Publishing Platform.

—Anne of Avonlea. (ENG.). 2019. 268p. (J). pap. 12.99 *(978-1-7018-6034-6(1))* 2019. 386p. (J). pap. 22.99 *(978-1-0899-1022-0(3))* 2019. 386p. (J). pap. 22.99 *(978-1-0830-1790-1(X))* 2019. 546p. (J). pap. 36.99 *(978-1-0825-6163-4(0))* 2019. 386p. (J). pap. 22.99 *(978-1-0807-5704-6(X))* 2019. 546p. (J). pap. 35.99 *(978-1-0800-7977-3(7))* 2019. 818p. (J). pap. 46.99 *(978-1-0781-0625-2(8))* 2019. 544p. (J). pap. 35.99 *(978-1-0780-6471-2(7))* 2019. 546p. (J). pap. 31.99 *(978-1-0753-6837-0(5))* 2019. 386p. (YA). pap. 22.99 *(978-1-0726-8331-5(8))* 2019. 546p. (YA). pap. 30.99 *(978-1-0707-5140-5(5))* 2019. 268p. (YA). pap. 18.99 *(978-1-0705-9376-0(1))* 2019. 568p. (YA). pap. 33.99 *(978-1-0987-6527-9(3))* 2019. 364p. (YA). pap. 19.99 *(978-1-0968-7536-9(5))* 2019. 268p. (YA). pap. 16.99 *(978-1-0954-6547-9(3))* 2019. 546p. (YA). pap. 34.99 *(978-1-0916-4683-4(X))* 2019. 506p. (YA). pap. 29.99 *(978-1-7965-5870-8(2))* 2019. (Illus.). 546p. (YA). pap. 34.99 *(978-1-7929-7537-0(6))* 2018. (Illus.). 240p. (YA). pap. 15.99 *(978-1-7919-1487-5(X))* Independently Published.

—Anne of Avonlea. 2019. (ENG.). 252p. (J). pap. 27.99 *(978-1-7077-7448-7(X))* Independently Published.

—Anne of Avonlea. 2012. (World Classics Ser.). (ENG.). 228p. pap. 19.99 *(978-1-909438-94-1(4)*, Sovereign) Bollinger, Max GBR. Dist: Gardners Bks. Ltd., Lightning Source UK, Ltd.

—Anne of Avonlea. l.t. ed. 2006. (ENG.). pap. *(978-1-4068-3173-3(5))* Echo Library.

—Anne of Green Gables. 400p. 2005. 33.95 *(978-1-4218-0660-0(6)*, 1st World Library - Literary Society) 2004. per. 16.95 *(978-1-59540-110-6(5))* 1st World Publishing, Inc.

—Anne of Green Gables, 1 vol. Castelao, Patricia, illus. 2011. (Calico Illustrated Classics Ser.: No. 4). (ENG.). 112p. (J). (gr. 2-5). 38.50 *(978-1-61641-612-6(2)*, 4039, Calico Chapter Bks.) ABDO Publishing Co.

—Anne of Green Gables. 2009. 292p. 27.99 *(978-1-60512-375-2(7))*; pap. 14.99 *(978-1-60512-475-9(3))* Akasha Publishing, LLC. (Akasha Classics).

—Anne of Green Gables. 2012. (World Classics Ser.). (ENG.). 260p. pap. 19.99 *(978-1-909438-96-5(0)*, Sovereign) Bollinger, Max GBR. Dist: Lightning Source UK, Ltd.

—Anne of Green Gables. 2008. 316p. 28.99 *(978-0-554-32848-5(8))* 2008. 316p. pap. 29.99

(978-0-554-23545-5(5)) 2007. (ENG.). 312p. pap. 24.99 *(978-1-4264-4662-7(4))* Creative Media Partners, LLC.
—Anne of Green Gables. 2008. (Anne of Green Gables Ser.). (ENG.). 366p. (J). (gr. 4-7). pap. 9.95 *(978-0-9782552-6-8(7))* Davenport Pr. CAN. Dist: Independent Pubs. Group.
—Anne of Green Gables. 2007. per. 6.99 *(978-1-4209-2922-5(4))* Digireads.com Publishing.
—Anne of Green Gables. 2007. 284p. per. *(978-1-4065-6399-3(4))* Dodo Pr.
—Anne of Green Gables. 2007. 572p. *(978-1-84702-773-3(3))* 2006. pap. *(978-1-4068-2170-3(5))* 2006. pap. *(978-1-4068-3174-0(3))* Echo Library.
—Anne of Green Gables. 2009. 242p. pap. 8.58 *(978-0-217-43952-7(7))* General Bks. LLC.
—Anne of Green Gables. 2005. (My First Classics Ser.). 112p. (J). (gr. k-3). pap., pap. 4.99 *(978-0-06-079147-6(0),* HarperFestival) HarperCollins Pubs.
—Anne of Green Gables. 2005. 21.99 *(978-1-4142-5125-7(4))* IndyPublish.com.
—Anne of Green Gables. 2004. reprint ed. pap. 27.95 *(978-1-4191-0717-7(8))*; pap. 1.99 *(978-1-4192-0717-4(2))* Kessinger Publishing, LLC.
—Anne of Green Gables. l.t. ed. 2009. (World Classics Ser.). (ENG.). 384p. pap. 21.95 *(978-1-59688-123-5(2))* Large Print Bk. Co., The.
—Anne of Green Gables. 2003. (ENG.). 320p. (gr. 5-7). 5.95 *(978-0-451-52882-7(4),* Signet) Penguin Publishing Group.
—Anne of Green Gables. 2008. (Puffin Classics Ser.). (Illus.). 464p. (J). (gr. 3-7). 8.99 *(978-0-14-132159-2(8),* Puffin Books) Penguin Young Readers Group.
—Anne of Green Gables. 2003. 320p. (J). (gr. 4-7). 12.60 *(978-0-7569-1848-4(0))* Perfection Learning Corp.
—Anne of Green Gables. 2008. (Modern Library Classics Ser.). (ENG.). 320p. pap. 11.00 *(978-0-8129-7903-9(6),* Modern Library) Random House Publishing Group.
—Anne of Green Gables. 2014. (Official Anne of Green Gables Ser.: 1). 352p. (YA). (gr. 5-12). pap. 13.99 *(978-1-4022-8894-4(8))* Sourcebooks, Inc.
—Anne of Green Gables. 2009. 224p. pap. 15.45 *(978-1-4385-1847-3(1),* Bk. Jungle) Standard Publications, Inc.
—Anne of Green Gables. 2008. 316p. pap. 16.95 *(978-1-60096-101-4(0))*; pap. 16.95 *(978-1-60096-565-4(2))* The Editorium, LLC.
—Anne of Green Gables: Norton Critical Edition. Rubio, Mary Henley & Waterston, Elizabeth, eds. 2007. (Norton Critical Editions Ser.: 0). (ENG., Illus.). 464p. (C). (gr. 9-12). per. 16.00 net. *(978-0-393-92695-8(8),* 92695) Norton, W. W. & Co., Inc.
—The Anne of Green Gables Collection: Six Complete & Unabridged Novels in One Volume. 2013. 1140p. *(978-1-78139-344-4(3))* Benediction Classics.
—Anne of the Island. 2018. (ENG., Illus.). 240p. (J). (gr. 2-5). pap. *(978-93-5297-102-2(7))* Alpha Editions.
—Anne of the Island. 2017. (ENG., Illus.). (J). 28.99 *(978-1-366-55836-7(7))* Blurb, Inc.
—Anne of the Island. 2017. (ENG., Illus.). (J). 25.95 *(978-1-374-89884-4(8))*; pap. 15.95 *(978-1-374-89883-7(X))* Capital Communications, Inc.
—Anne of the Island. (ENG., Illus.). (J). 2017. pap. 15.90 *(978-1-375-53109-2(3))* 2015. 26.95 *(978-1-297-59159-4(3))* Creative Media Partners, LLC.
—Anne of the Island. 2008. (Anne of Green Gables Ser.). (ENG.). 272p. (J). (gr. 4-7). pap. 9.95 *(978-0-9782552-8-2(3))* Davenport Pr. CAN. Dist: Independent Pubs. Group.
—Anne of the Island. 2006. (ENG.). pap. *(978-1-4068-2171-0(3))* Echo Library.
—Anne of the Island. 2010. (Puffin Classics Ser.). (ENG.). 368p. (J). (gr. 5-7). pap. 7.99 *(978-0-14-132736-5(7),* Puffin Books) Penguin Young Readers Group.
—Anne of the Island. 2018. (Anne of Green Gables: the Complete Collection: 3). (ENG.). 312p. (J). (gr. 6-12). 8.99 *(978-1-78226-445-3(0),* 6a902ad3-6883-4c7e-8532-21673815d7a9) Sweet Cherry Publishing GBR. Dist: Baker & Taylor Publisher Services (BTPS).
—Anne of the Island. 2018. (ENG., Illus.). 258p. (YA). 24.99 *(978-1-5287-0650-6(1),* Classic Bks. Library) The Editorium, LLC.
—Anne of the Island. 2019. (ENG.). 250p. (J). pap. 11.89 *(978-1-7278-8584-2(8))* CreateSpace Independent Publishing Platform.
—Anne of the Island. (ENG.). (J). 2019. 252p. pap. 11.99 *(978-1-7018-6205-0(0))* 2019. 352p. pap. 19.99 *(978-1-0899-1090-9(8))* 2019. 788p. pap. 45.99 *(978-1-0828-3158-4(1))* 2019. 498p. pap. 33.99 *(978-1-0825-6062-0(6))* 2019. 788p. pap. 45.99 *(978-1-0804-7520-9(6))* 2019. 466p. pap. 32.99 *(978-1-0799-0876-3(5))* 2019. 740p. pap. 43.99 *(978-1-0776-6557-6(1))* 2019. 498p. pap. 31.99 *(978-1-0753-6839-4(1))* 2019. 352p. pap. 19.99 *(978-1-0726-8332-2(6))* 2019. 526p. pap. 29.99 *(978-1-0985-3618-3(5))* 2019. 342p. pap. 19.99 *(978-1-0968-7543-7(8))* 2019. 252p. pap. 17.99 *(978-1-0705-9734-8(1))* 2019. 500p. pap. 29.99 *(978-1-0707-5185-6(5))* 2019. 498p. pap. 32.99 *(978-1-0916-4685-8(6))* 2019. 462p. pap. 25.99 *(978-1-7965-5869-2(9))* 2019. 136p. pap. 8.60 *(978-1-7953-3769-4(9))* 2018. (Illus.). 224p. pap. 14.99 *(978-1-7919-1456-1(X))* Independently Published.
—Anne of the Island. 2019. (ENG.). 232p. (J). pap. 27.99 *(978-1-7077-7514-9(1))* Independently Published.
—Anne of the Island. 2012. (World Classics Ser.). (ENG.). 212p. pap. 19.99 *(978-1-909438-92-7(8),* Sovereign) Bollinger, Max GBR. Dist: Lightning Source UK, Ltd.
—Anne of the Island. l.t. ed. 2006. (ENG.). pap. *(978-1-4068-3175-7(1))* Echo Library.
—Anne of the Island. 2004. reprint ed. pap. 1.99 *(978-1-4192-0718-1(0))*; pap. 30.95 *(978-1-4179-0885-1(8))* Kessinger Publishing, LLC.
—Anne of the Island. l.t. ed. 2004. 396p. 26.00 *(978-1-58287-640-5(1))* North Bks.
—Emily Climbs: Emily of New Moon Series. 2014. (Emily Ser.: 2). (ENG.). 368p. (YA). (gr. 5-12). pap. 13.99 *(978-1-4022-8915-6(4))* Sourcebooks, Inc.
—Emily's Quest. 2014. (Emily Ser.: 3). (ENG.). 256p. (YA). (gr. 5-12). pap. 12.99 *(978-1-4022-8918-7(9))* Sourcebooks, Inc.
—Jane of Lantern Hill. 2014. (ENG.). 272p. (YA). (gr. 5-12). pap. 11.99 *(978-1-4022-8930-9(8))* Sourcebooks, Inc.
—Kilmeny of the Orchard. 2018. (ENG., Illus.). 118p. (J). (gr. 4-7). pap. *(978-93-5297-106-0(X))* Alpha Editions.
—Kilmeny of the Orchard. 2010. 146p. pap. 16.95 *(978-1-60444-108-6(9))* IndoEuropeanPublishing.com.
—Kilmeny of the Orchard. 2004. 100p. (YA). pap. 7.95 *(978-1-57646-894-4(1))* Quiet Vision Publishing.
—Kilmeny of the Orchard. 2018. (ENG., Illus.). 124p. (J). (gr. 4-7). 14.99 *(978-1-5154-3231-9(9))* Wilder Pubns., Corp.
—Kilmeny of the Orchard. 2019. (ENG.). (J). 248p. pap. 15.99 *(978-1-6967-9912-6(0))*; 248p. pap. 11.99 *(978-1-6999-8624-0(X))*; 122p. pap. 7.99 *(978-1-7018-6677-5(3))*; 248p. pap. 15.99 *(978-1-6910-9073-0(5))*; 248p. pap. 15.99 *(978-1-6949-7534-8(7))*; 332p. pap. 19.99 *(978-1-6862-7332-2(0))*; 376p. pap. 25.00 *(978-1-0895-1503-6(0))*; 332p. pap. 19.99 *(978-1-0859-0762-0(7))*; 252p. pap. 15.99 *(978-1-0803-9449-4(4))*; 252p. pap. 18.99 *(978-1-0830-6207-9(7))*; 122p. pap. 9.99 *(978-1-0805-1773-2(1))*; 252p. pap. 18.99 *(978-1-0784-0836-3(X))*; 332p. pap. 19.99 *(978-1-0776-9765-2(1))*; 252p. pap. 15.99 *(978-1-0761-2348-0(1))*; 334p. pap. 19.99 *(978-1-0727-4932-5(7))*; 166p. pap. 12.99 *(978-1-0705-1744-5(5))*; 376p. pap. 22.99 *(978-1-0997-7222-1(2))*; 230p. pap. 13.99 *(978-1-0989-2774-5(5))*; 252p. pap. 15.99 *(978-1-0974-8816-2(0))*; 252p. pap. 15.99 *(978-1-0934-3789-8(8))*; 252p. pap. 16.99 *(978-1-0917-4648-0(6))*; 252p. pap. 14.99 *(978-1-7969-7320-4(3))* Independently Published.
—Kilmeny of the Orchard. 2019. (ENG.). (J). 112p. pap. 15.99 *(978-1-7077-9097-5(3))*; 84p. pap. 5.99 *(978-1-7036-1459-6(3))* Independently Published.
—Magic for Marigold. 2014. (ENG.). 336p. (YA). (gr. 5-12). pap. 13.99 *(978-1-4022-8921-7(9))* Sourcebooks, Inc.
—Pat of Silver Bush. 2014. (ENG.). 368p. (YA). (gr. 5-12). pap. 13.99 *(978-1-4022-8924-8(3))* Sourcebooks, Inc.
—Rainbow Valley. 2004. reprint ed. pap. 1.99 *(978-1-4192-4385-1(3))*; 210p. pap. 24.95 *(978-1-4191-4385-4(9))* Kessinger Publishing, LLC.
—Rainbow Valley. 2005. (Twelve-Point Ser.). lib. bdg. 25.00 *(978-1-58287-333-6(X))*; lib. bdg. 26.00 *(978-1-58287-825-6(0))* North Bks.
—Rainbow Valley. 2004. 184p. (YA). pap. 8.95 *(978-1-57646-890-6(9))* Quiet Vision Publishing.
—Rilla of Ingleside. l.t. ed. 2007. (ENG.). 314p. pap. 24.99 *(978-1-4346-5286-7(6))* Creative Media Partners, LLC.
—Rilla of Ingleside. 2004. 224p. (YA). pap. 10.95 *(978-1-57646-891-3(7))* Quiet Vision Publishing.
—Rilla of Ingleside. 2006. 384p. pap. 25.45 *(978-1-59462-427-8(5),* Bk. Jungle) Standard Publications, Inc.
—The Story Girl. Date not set. 22.95 *(978-0-8488-2372-6(9))* Amereon Ltd.
—The Story Girl. 2004. reprint ed. pap. 1.99 *(978-1-4192-8361-1(8))* Kessinger Publishing, LLC.
—The Story Girl. 2005. (Twelve-Point Ser.). lib. bdg. 24.00 *(978-1-58287-336-7(4))*; lib. bdg. 25.00 *(978-1-58287-828-7(5))* North Bks.
—A Tangled Web. 2009. (Voyageur Classics Ser.). (ENG.). 296p. pap. 24.99 *(978-1-55488-403-2(9))* Dundurn Pr. CAN. Dist: Ingram Publisher Services.
Montgomery, Lucy Maud. Anne of Avonlea. 2019. (ENG.). (J). (gr. 3-7). 276p. pap. 12.95 *(978-0-368-78940-3(3))*; 96p. pap. 12.71 *(978-0-368-28129-7(9))* Blurb, Inc.
—Anne of Avonlea. (ENG.). (gr. 3-7). 2020. 170p. (YA). pap. 9.99 *(978-1-6594-8477-9(4))* 2018. (Illus.). 594p. (J). pap. 34.99 *(978-1-7916-6454-1(7))* Independently Published.
—Anne of Avonlea. Blake, Sheba, ed. 2020. (ENG.). 254p. (YA). (gr. 3-7). pap. 14.99 *(978-1-222-29341-8(2))* Indy Pub.
—Anne of Avonlea. 2008. (ENG., Illus.). 268p. (J). (gr. 3-7). 18.99 *(978-1-4341-1489-1(9),* Waking Lion Press) The Editorium, LLC.
—Anne of Green Gables. 2013. (Word Cloud Classics Ser.). (ENG.). 264p. (YA). pap. 14.99 *(978-1-60710-728-6(7),* Canterbury Classics) Printers Row Publishing Group.
—Anne of Green Gables: Stories for Young Readers, 1 vol. Smith, David Preston, illus. 2008. (ENG.). 46p. (J). (gr. 1-3). pap. 12.95 *(978-1-55109-662-9(5),* 3b164d3e-d44c-49e5-9188-05373178fc3d) Nimbus Publishing, Ltd. CAN. Dist: Baker & Taylor Publisher Services (BTPS).
—Anne of the Island. 2019. (ENG.). (J). (gr. 2-5). 276p. pap. 12.95 *(978-0-368-79656-2(6))*; 94p. pap. 12.55 *(978-0-368-28130-3(2))* Blurb, Inc.
—Anne of the Island. 2018. (ENG.). 328p. (J). (gr. 2-5). 44.95 *(978-0-343-91137-9(X))*; pap. 27.95 *(978-0-343-91136-2(1))* Creative Media Partners, LLC.
—Anne of the Island. 2019. (ENG.). (J). (gr. 2-5). 734p. pap. 46.99 *(978-1-6881-5126-0(5))*; 736p. pap. 43.99 *(978-1-0968-8163-6(2))*; 448p. pap. 25.99 *(978-1-0932-8992-3(9))* Independently Published.
—Kilmeny of the Orchard. 2019. (ENG.). 264p. (J). (gr. 4-7). 25.95 *(978-0-469-78399-7(0))*; pap. 15.95 *(978-0-469-78398-0(2))* Creative Media Partners, LLC. (Wentworth Pr.).
Montgomery, Lucy Maud & Grandma's Treasures. Anne of Avonlea. 2019. (ENG.). 252p. (YA). (gr. 3-7). *(978-1-7948-2437-9(5))* Lulu Pr., Inc.
Montgomery, Lucy Maud & Treasures, Grandma's. Anne of Avonlea. 2019. (ENG.). 252p. (YA). (gr. 3-7). pap. *(978-1-7948-2462-1(6))* Lulu Pr., Inc.
Rath, Tom H. Donkey Oatie's Impossible Dream. MacAdam, Reegory, illus. 2012. 24p. pap. *(978-0-9866065-5-7(3))* Wood Islands Prints.
Stretch, Ian. Marty the Mailbox. McNevin, Dale, illus. 2009. 24p. pap. 10.95 *(978-1-4251-8435-3(9))* Trafford Publishing.

PRINCES

Ariganello, Lisa. Henry the Navigator: Prince of Portuguese Exploration. 2006. (In the Footsteps of Explorers Ser.). (ENG., Illus.). 32p. (J). (gr. 4-7). pap. *(978-0-7787-2469-8(7))*; lib. bdg. *(978-0-7787-2433-9(6))* Crabtree Publishing Co.
Braun, Eric. Prince: The Man, the Symbol, the Music. 2017. (Gateway Biographies Ser.). (ENG.). 48p. (J). (gr. 4-8). 12.99 *(978-1-5124-3861-1(8))*; 39.99 *(978-1-5124-3860-4(X))*; (Illus.). 31.99 *(978-1-5124-3456-9(6),* 0dbaac1c-fa77-45e4-a8c8-e7eaf94a8897); (Illus.). E-Book 47.99 *(978-1-5124-3457-6(4))* Lerner Publishing Group. (Lerner Pubns.).
Cartlidge, Cherese. Prince Harry, 1 vol. 2012. (People in the News Ser.). (ENG., Illus.). 104p. (gr. 7-7). lib. bdg. 41.03 *(978-1-4205-0760-7(5),* 733bf655-d0c6-4537-920d-d913cdd056a5, Lucent Pr.) Greenhaven Publishing LLC.
Diemer, Lauren & Kissock, Heather. Prince William & Kate Middleton. 2013. (J). *(978-1-62127-392-9(X))* Weigl Pubs., Inc.
Dyan, Penelope. A Royal Residence — A Kid's Guide to Windsor Castle. Weigand, John D., photos by. 2011. (Illus.). 40p. pap. 12.95 *(978-1-935630-65-4(2))* Bellissima Publishing, LLC.
Hurwicz, Claude. Henry the Navigator. 2009. (Primary Source Library of Famous Explorers Ser.). 24p. (gr. 4-4). 42.50 *(978-1-60854-124-9(X),* PowerKids Pr.) Rosen Publishing Group, Inc., The.
Kenney, Karen Latchana. Real-Life Princes. 2019. (Bumba Books (r) — Real-Life Royalty Ser.). (ENG., Illus.). 24p. (J). (gr. -1-1). 26.65 *(978-1-5415-5728-4(X),* d08da931-4e8f-4936-a4a9-6141a43c645a); pap. 8.99 *(978-1-5415-7357-4(9),* f4296d2c-3f1c-491d-afc3-6f43d286f145) Lerner Publishing Group. (Lerner Pubns.).
Lee, Sally. Princes & Princesses, 1 vol. 2013. (Royalty Ser.). (ENG.). 24p. (J). (gr. -1-2). lib. bdg. 27.32 *(978-1-62065-124-7(6),* 120817, Capstone Pr.) Capstone.
McDaniel, Sarita. Princes, 1 vol. 2019. (Meet the Royals Ser.). (ENG.). 24p. (gr. 1-2). pap. 10.35 *(978-1-9785-1185-9(X),* b04bf3ec-79de-4077-82c7-ae5a534aa2d5) Enslow Publishing, LLC.
Sherman, Jill. Prince Harry & Meghan: Royals for a New Era. 2018. (Gateway Biographies Ser.). (ENG., Illus.). 48p. (J). (gr. 4-8). lib. bdg. 31.99 *(978-1-5415-3945-7(1),* 6469d094-5193-422f-bf97-bf204b3eee32, Lerner Pubns.) Lerner Publishing Group.
Timmons, Angie. Kate Middleton & Prince William, 1 vol. 2019. (Power Couples Ser.). (ENG.). 112p. (gr. 7-7). pap. 18.65 *(978-1-5081-8884-1(X),* 8c1b23b5-9e74-412b-9e2a-73d11cf6791f) Rosen Publishing Group, Inc., The.
Tracy, Kathleen. Prince William of Wales. 2011. (Blue Banner Biography Ser.). (YA). (gr. 4-7). 25.70 *(978-1-61228-191-9(5))* Mitchell Lane Pubs.

PRINCES—FICTION

Adventures in Flatfrost. 2014. (Kingdom of Wrenly Ser.: 5). (ENG., Illus.). 128p. (J). (gr. k-4). pap. 6.99 *(978-1-4814-1388-6(0),* Little Simon) Little Simon.
Albright, Emily. The Heir & the Spare. 2016. (ENG.). 287p. (YA). 17.99 *(978-1-4405-9010-8(9),* Simon & Schuster Bks. For Young Readers) Simon & Schuster Bks. For Young Readers.
Amerikaner, Susan, et al. Disney Princess Storybook Collection. 2015. (Illus.). 300p. (J). *(978-1-4847-5331-6(3),* 1394934) Disney Publishing Worldwide.
Anderson, Hans Christian. The Little Mermaid Retold. Charlotte, J. M., illus. 2013. 48p. 18.00 *(978-0-9895422-0-3(3))* MHC Ministries.
Ant, Exupery. Journee avec le Petit Prince. pap. 10.95 *(978-2-07-054268-0(8))* Gallimard, Editions FRA. Dist: Distribooks, Inc.
—L apprends a compter avec Le. pap. 10.95 *(978-2-07-054270-3(X))* Gallimard, Editions FRA. Dist: Distribooks, Inc.
anthony, chance. The Princess of Du'val. 2010. 36p. pap. 7.14 *(978-0-557-03816-9(2))* Lulu Pr., Inc.
Arthur, Felix & Capon, Jenny. Golden Prince. 2012. (IPP Single Titles Ser.). (Illus.). 32p. (J). (gr. -1-1). pap. 7.99 *(978-0-9567122-3-3(1))* Lerner Publishing Group.
At Your Service. 2014. (Mix Ser.). (ENG., Illus.). 272p. (J). (gr. 4-8). pap. 7.99 *(978-1-4814-0283-5(8),* Aladdin) Simon & Schuster Children's Publishing.
Avery, et al. The Tale of Princess Fluffy & Prince Rupert. 2012. (ENG.). 28p. (J). pap. 19.99 *(978-1-4685-3594-5(3))* AuthorHouse.
Baker, E. D. Dragon's Breath: Read-Along/Homework Pack, 6 vols. unabr. ed. 2005. (Frog Princess Ser.: 2). (SPA.). (J). (gr. 5-8). 78.75 *(978-1-4193-3563-1(4),* 42041) Recorded Bks., Inc.
Baker, Sara, illus. Ready to Read Sleeping Beauty. 2007. (Ready to Read Ser.). 31p. (J). (gr. k-2). *(978-1-84610-441-1(6))* Make Believe Ideas.
Banghart, Tracy. Grace & Fury. 2019. (Grace & Fury Ser.: 1). (ENG.). 336p. (YA). (gr. 9-17). pap. 10.99 *(978-0-316-47142-8(9))* Little, Brown Bks. for Young Readers.
Beck, Patricia. Prince Hasmir's High Seas Adventure. 2011. 24p. pap. 15.99 *(978-1-4628-6151-4(2))* Xlibris Corp.
—Princess Feldings & the Academy of Queens. 2010. 28p. 13.99 *(978-1-4490-1376-9(7))* AuthorHouse.
Bell, Hilari. The Prophecy. 2006. (ENG., Illus.). 208p. (J). (gr. 5-9). 15.99 *(978-0-06-059943-0(X))* HarperCollins Pubs.
Beneath the Stone Forest. 2014. (Kingdom of Wrenly Ser.: 6). (ENG., Illus.). 128p. (J). (gr. k-4). pap. 6.99 *(978-1-4814-1391-6(0),* Little Simon) Little Simon.
Bentley, Douglas W. What Will It Take for a Toad to Kiss a Monkey: The Adventures of Princess Gracie & Prince Wallaby. Bentley, Julia Faye, illus. 2008. 52p. per. 24.95 *(978-1-4137-8849-5(1))* America Star Bks.
Bishop, Anne. Anne Bishop's Christmas Dram: The Gift of Three. 2013. 28p. pap. 24.95 *(978-1-4626-8276-8(6))* America Star Bks.
Black, Holly. The Cruel Prince. 2023. (YA). 45.00 *(978-1-955876-16-2(9))* LitJoy Crate.
—The Cruel Prince. 2018. (Folk of the Air Ser.: 1). (ENG.). (YA). (gr. 9-17). 416p. pap. 12.99 *(978-0-316-31031-4(X))*; (Illus.). 384p. 19.99 *(978-0-316-31027-7(1))* Little, Brown Bks. for Young Readers.
Blevins, Wiley. Cinderella & the Vampire Prince. Cox, Steve, illus. 2016. (Scary Tales Retold Ser.). (ENG.). 24p. (J). (gr. k-3). lib. bdg. 27.99 *(978-1-63440-090-9(9),* 36876e97-b32f-433d-82e1-3754e7a21e9e) Red Chair Pr.
—Rapunzel & the Werewolf. Cox, Steve, illus. 2017. (Scary Tales Retold Ser.). (ENG.). 24p. (J). (gr. k-3). lib. bdg. 27.99 *(978-1-63440-167-8(0),* 708c337e-1f1e-459a-a99c-51a30e017a25) Red Chair Pr.
Bolger, Kevin. Sir Fartsalot Hunts the Booger. Gilpin, Stephen, illus. 2009. (ENG.). 224p. (J). (gr. 4-6). 18.69 *(978-1-59514-176-7(6),* Razorbill) Penguin Young Readers Group.
Boulton, M. T. Megan Button & the Brim-Tree. 2012. 106p. pap. *(978-1-909039-06-3(3))* Legend Pr.
Brandon, Wendy. The Frog Prince: Board Book & Puppet Theater. Beckes, Shirley V., illus. 2004. (J). *(978-1-883043-46-9(8))* Straight Edge Pr., The.
Braswell, Liz. Part of Your World (a Twisted Tale) A Twisted Tale. 2018. (Twisted Tale Ser.). (ENG., Illus.). 480p. (YA). (gr. 7-12). 18.99 *(978-1-368-01381-9(3),* Disney-Hyperion) Disney Publishing Worldwide.
Bredin, Henrietta & McEwen, Priscilla. The Prince & the Goosegirl: A Story with Activities Based on the Opera by Humperdinck. 2006. (Illus.). 30p. (J). (gr. k-4). reprint ed. pap. 17.00 *(978-1-4223-5538-1(1))* DIANE Publishing Co.
Brenna, Beverley. Falling for Henry, 1 vol. 2011. (ENG.). 281p. (YA). (gr. 7-12). pap. 12.95 *(978-0-88995-442-7(9),* 1a9698cb-c2aa-4fcf-b2b8-c1e4914d9bbb) Trifolium Bks., Inc. CAN. Dist: Firefly Bks., Ltd.
Brubacher, Melody. The Adventures of Princess Penelope. 2012. 68p. pap. 31.99 *(978-1-4691-9274-1(8))* Xlibris Corp.
Buck, Alicia. Out of the Ashes. 2015. 281p. (YA). pap. 17.99 *(978-1-4621-1727-7(9))* Cedar Fort, Inc./CFI Distribution.
Bunting, Eve. Party at the Pond. Masse, Josée, illus. 2011. (I AM a READER!: Frog & Friends Ser.). (ENG.). 40p. (J). (gr. 1-2). lib. bdg. 9.95 *(978-1-58536-549-4(1),* 202222) Sleeping Bear Pr.
Burden, Meg. The King Commands. 2010. (Tales of the Borderlands Ser.: Bk. 2). 312p. (YA). (gr. 7-18). pap. 8.95 *(978-0-9798824-1-8(9))* Brown Barn Bks.
Burkart, Jeffrey. The Hidden Prince. 2011. (YA). 16.95 *(978-0-9825713-3-0(X))* Clifton Carriage House Pr.
Burkart, Jeffrey E., retold by. The Hidden Prince. 2003. (Illus.). 32p. (J). 9.99 incl. audio compact disk *(978-0-570-07174-7(7))* Concordia Publishing Hse.
Burks, David W. Full Circle: The Story of Outlaw-Prince Edwin, High King of England. 2007. 124p. 20.95 *(978-0-595-70485-9(9))*; per. 10.95 *(978-0-595-46753-2(9))* iUniverse, Inc.
Burnett, Frances. The Lost Prince. 2007. 228p. per. 14.95 *(978-1-60312-338-9(5))*; 26.95 *(978-1-60312-676-2(7))* Aegypan.
—The Lost Prince. (J). 25.95 *(978-0-8488-0691-0(3))* Amereon Ltd.
Burnham, Niki. Royally Crushed; Royally Jacked; Spin Control; Do-Over. 2011. (ENG.). 624p. (YA). (gr. 7). pap. 11.99 *(978-1-4424-0648-3(8),* Simon Pulse) Simon Pulse.
Burns, Jennifer N. Magic in Time: Fairy Tale Stories. 2012. 198p. 24.95 *(978-1-4759-3965-1(5))*; pap. 14.95 *(978-1-4759-3964-4(7))* iUniverse, Inc.
Busch, Jean. Aiden & the Frog Prince, 1 vol. 2009. 48p. pap. 16.95 *(978-1-60836-892-1(0))* America Star Bks.
Carney, Karin. Prince Braden's Animal Kingdom. 2011. 40p. pap. 18.95 *(978-1-4357-9406-1(0))* Lulu Pr., Inc.
Cass, Kiera. The Elite. (Selection Ser.: 2). (ENG.). (YA). (gr. 8). 2014. 352p. pap. 12.99 *(978-0-06-205997-0(1))* 2013. 336p. 19.99 *(978-0-06-205996-3(3))* HarperCollins Pubs. (HarperTeen).
—The Elite. 2014. (Selection Ser.: 2). (YA). lib. bdg. 20.85 *(978-0-606-35489-9(1))* Turtleback.
—La Elite / the Elite, Vol. 1. 2013. (SelecciÓn / the Selection Ser.: 2). (SPA.). 224p. (YA). (gr. 8-12). pap. 20.95 *(978-84-9918-613-9(0))* Penguin Random House Grupo Editorial ESP. Dist: Penguin Random Hse. LLC.
—La Elite/ the Elite, Vol. 2. 2017. (SelecciÓn / the Selection Ser.: 2). (SPA.). 224p. (J). (gr. 8-12). pap. 12.95 *(978-84-16240-61-6(2))* Penguin Random House Grupo Editorial ESP. Dist: Penguin Random Hse. LLC.
—Happily Ever After: Companion to the Selection Series. 2016. (Selection Ser.). (YA). lib. bdg. 20.85 *(978-0-606-38919-8(9))* Turtleback.
—Happily Ever after: Companion to the Selection Series. 2015. (Selection Novella Ser.). (ENG., Illus.). 416p. (YA). (gr. 8). 18.99 *(978-0-06-241408-3(9),* HarperTeen) HarperCollins Pubs.
—The One. 2014. (Selection Ser.: 3). (ENG.). 336p. (YA). (gr. 8). 19.99 *(978-0-06-205999-4(8),* HarperTeen) HarperCollins Pubs.
—The Selection. (Selection Ser.: 1). (ENG.). (YA). (gr. 8). 2013. 352p. pap. 12.99 *(978-0-06-205994-9(7))* 2012. 336p. 19.99 *(978-0-06-205993-2(9))* HarperCollins Pubs. (HarperTeen).
—The Selection, Book 1. (ENG.). 336p. pap. *(978-0-00-746669-6(2),* HarperCollins Children's Bks.) HarperCollins Pubs. Ltd.
—The Selection. 2013. (Selection Ser.: 1). (YA). lib. bdg. 20.85 *(978-0-606-35488-2(3))* Turtleback.
—The Selection. 2013. (Selection Ser.: Vol. 1). (CHI & ENG.). 288p. (YA). (gr. 8). pap. *(978-986-133-471-4(8))* Yuan Shen Pr. Co., Ltd.
—The Selection Stories: the Prince & the Guard. 2014. (Selection Novella Ser.). (ENG.). 240p. (YA). (gr. 8). pap. 15.99 *(978-0-06-231832-9(2),* HarperTeen) HarperCollins Pubs.
Cerami, Matteo, et al. The Planet of the Grand Buffoon: Book 14, No. 14. Elyum Studio, Elyum, illus. 2014. (Little Prince Ser.: 14). (ENG.). 48p. (J). (gr. 4-8). lib. bdg. 26.65 *(978-0-7613-8764-0(1),* 28f17286-fecf-4033-8c5a-e2343978cf59, Graphic Universe™) Lerner Publishing Group.
Christopher, John. Beyond the Burning Lands. 2015. (Sword of the Spirits Ser.: 2). (ENG., Illus.). 272p. (J). (gr. 5-9). pap. 7.99 *(978-1-4814-1994-9(3),* Aladdin) Simon & Schuster Children's Publishing.
Clarke, Jane. Prince Albert's Birthday. Chatterton, Martin, illus. 2005. 24p. (J). lib. bdg. 23.65 *(978-1-59646-748-4(7))* Dingles & Co.

Clausen, Andrew. Prince Caspian. 2003. stu. ed., ring bd. 14.99 *(978-1-58609-195-8(6))* Progeny Pr.

Cochran, Robert. The Sword & the Dagger: A Novel. 2020. (ENG.). 400p. (YA). pap. 19.99 *(978-0-7653-8384-6(5),* 900155635, Tor Teen) Doherty, Tom Assocs., LLC.

Coe, Mary. The Prince of Betherland. 2007. 100p. pap. 9.95 *(978-1-4303-2521-5(6))* Lulu Pr., Inc.

Coe, Mary E. The Prince of Betherland. 2008. 117p. 24.95 *(978-0-557-03112-2(5))* Lulu Pr., Inc.

—The Prince of Betherland A Wonderful World of Fantasy. 2009. 66p. pap. 9.95 *(978-0-557-08499-9(7))* Lulu Pr., Inc.

—The Prince of Betherland a Wonderful World of Fantasy. 2009. 112p. pap. 9.95 *(978-0-557-09297-0(3))* Lulu Pr., Inc.

Coia, Kristina. Lymeria. 2007. 120p. (YA). per. 10.95 *(978-0-595-45268-2(X))* iUniverse, Inc.

Coleman, Alice Scovell. Engraved in Stone. Armand, Anjale Renee, illus. 2003. 152p. (J). 14.95 *(978-0-9729846-0-7(7))* Tiara Bks. LLC.

Corp, Carey & Langdon, Lorie. Doon, 1 vol. 2014. (Doon Novel Ser.: 1). (ENG.). 416p. (YA). pap. 12.99 *(978-0-310-74239-5(0))* Blink.

Cowey, James. William Snottengrout - Gangor's Reign. 2006. 104p. per. *(978-1-84667-006-0(3))* Derwent Pr., The.

Craik, Dinah. The Little Lame Prince & His Traveling Cloak. 2005. reprint ed. pap. 20.95 *(978-1-4179-1940-6(X))* Kessinger Publishing, LLC.

—The Little Lame Prince & the Adventures of a Brownie. Date not set. lib. bdg. 25.95 *(978-0-8488-2095-4(9))* Amereon Ltd.

Craik, Maria Dinah. The Little Lame Prince. 2008. 120p. 21.99 *(978-0-554-31012-1(0))* Creative Media Partners, LLC.

Cummins, Molly. The Jewel of Fez. 2006. 141p. pap. 24.95 *(978-1-4241-1044-5(0))* PublishAmerica, Inc.

Curtis, Jillian M. The Little Prince & His Magic Wand. 2005. (Illus.). 28p. (J). 24.95 *(978-1-59858-015-0(9))*; pap. 16.95 *(978-1-59858-010-5(8))* Dog Ear Publishing, LLC.

Daffern, Brian. Prince Albert Bk. 2: The Beast School. 2005. 160p. (YA). per. 10.95 *(978-0-9709104-6-2(0))* Hickory Tales Publishing.

—Prince Albert Bk. 3: The Realm Pirates. 2004. 192p. (YA). per. 13.95 *(978-0-9709104-7-9(9))* Hickory Tales Publishing.

—Prince Albert in a Can. Bk. 1. 2004. 256p. (YA). per. 13.95 *(978-0-9709104-5-5(2))* Hickory Tales Publishing.

Dahl, Michael. Dungeon of Seven Dooms, 1 vol. 2011. (Good vs Evil Ser.). (ENG.). 48p. (J). (gr. 5-9). lib. bdg. 23.99 *(978-1-4342-2091-2(5),* 102837, Stone Arch Bks.) Capstone.

D'Amico, Carol. Vince, Boy Prince: And the Secrets of How Anyone Can Become a True Prince (or Princess), 1 vol. Cerniga, Kira, illus. 2010. 18p. pap. 24.95 *(978-1-4489-7373-6(2))* PublishAmerica, Inc.

Davison, Gail. Prince Alexander. PellerinUndo, Joel Ray, illus. 2016. (ENG.). 28p. (J). pap. 28.22 *(978-1-5245-1787-8(9))* Xlibris Corp.

Day with the Little Prince. 2015. (Little Prince Ser.). (ENG., Illus.). 10p. (J). (— 1). bds. 7.99 *(978-0-544-69958-8(0),* 1627787, Clarion Bks.) HarperCollins Pubs.

De Haan, Linda & Nijland, Stern. King & King. De Haan, Linda & Nijland, Stern, illus. 2003. (ENG., Illus.). 32p. (J). (gr. k-3). 17.99 *(978-1-58246-061-1(2),* Tricycle Pr.) Random Hse. Children's Bks.

De Los Santos, Elizabeth G. The Secret House. 2011. 18p. pap. 16.95 *(978-1-4626-4409-4(0))* America Star Bks.

de Saint-Exupéry, Antoine. Der Kleine Prinz. 2021.Tr. of Petit Prince. (J). pap. *(978-1-63843-360-6(7))* Carpentino, Michela.

De Saint-Exupéry, Antoine. The Little Prince. 2015.Tr. of Petit Prince. (HEB.). (J). *(978-965-13-1323-3(4))* Am Oved Pubs., Ltd.

—The Little Prince.Tr. of Petit Prince. 17.95 *(978-0-89190-331-4(3))* Amereon Ltd.

—The Little Prince. 2018.Tr. of Petit Prince. (ENG., Illus.). 134p. (J). (gr. 2-4). pap. 5.99 *(978-1-388-18744-6(2))*; pap. 6.95 *(978-0-464-97851-0(3))* Blurb, Inc.

—The Little Prince. 2010.Tr. of Petit Prince. (ENG.). (gr. -1-18). cd-rom 16.95 *(978-2-89517-071-6(1),* 9782895170716) Editions Alexandre Stanke CAN. Dist: Baker & Taylor Publisher Services (BTPS).

—The Little Prince. 2003.Tr. of Petit Prince. (Illus.). (J). *(978-0-15-204730-6(1))* Harcourt Trade Pubs.

—The Little Prince. Kahler, Evan & Woods, Katherine, trs. 2016.Tr. of Petit Prince. (ENG., Illus.). (J). (gr. 3-7). *(978-1-77323-014-6(X))* Rehak, David.

—The Little Prince. Hill, Rowland, tr. Gormand, Caroline, illus. 2016.Tr. of Petit Prince. (ENG.). (J). (gr. 3-6). pap. *(978-2-89687-592-4(1))* chouetteditions.com.

de Saint-Exupéry, Antoine. The Little Prince. 2021.Tr. of Petit Prince. (J). pap. *(978-1-63843-362-0(3))* Carpentino, Michela.

De Saint-Exupéry, Antoine. The Little Prince. lt. ed. 2005.Tr. of Petit Prince. (ENG.). 168p. (J). (gr. 5-8). pap. 15.99 *(978-0-7862-7539-7(1))* Cengage Gale.

de Saint-Exupéry, Antoine. Little Prince 75th Anniversary Edition: Includes the History & Making of the Classic Story. 75th ed. 2018. (ENG., Illus.). 224p. (J). (gr. 5-7). 24.99 *(978-1-328-47975-4(7),* 1715417, Clarion Bks.) HarperCollins Pubs.

—The Little Prince Deluxe Pop-Up Book with Audio. deluxe ed. 2015. (Little Prince Ser.).Tr. of Petit Prince. (ENG., Illus.). 72p. (gr. 5-7). pap. 35.00 *(978-0-544-65649-9(0),* 1622859, Clarion Bks.) HarperCollins Pubs.

De Saint-Exupéry, Antoine. Le Petit Prince. 2016. (FRE., Illus.). (J). pap. *(978-5-521-00151-4(4))* Books on Demand.

—Le Petit Prince. 2021. (J). *(978-1-63843-357-6(7))*; pap. *(978-1-63843-356-9(9))* Carpentino, Michela.

—Le Petit Prince. 2010. (CHI., Illus.). 128p. (J). (gr. 3-7). *(978-986-7897-01-5(3))* Ecus Publishing Hse.

—Le Petit Prince. 2010. (CHI.). 132p. (J). (gr. 5-8). pap. *(978-986-189-225-2(7))* Grimm Cultural Ent., Co., Ltd.

—Le Petit Prince. 2012. (FRE.). 105p. pap. ***(978-1-300-29490-0(6))*** Lulu Pr., Inc.

—Le Petit Prince. 2012. (FRE.). 96p. (J). (gr. 5-8). 19.99 ***(978-1-63823-080-9(3))*** Meirovich, Igal.

—Le Petit Prince. Gormand, Caroline, illus. 2016. (FRE.). (J). (gr. 3-6). pap. *(978-2-89687-593-1(X))* chouetteditions.com.

—El Principito. (SPA., Illus.). 120p. (J). 10.95 *(978-84-206-3628-3(2),* AZ6282) Alianza Editorial, S. A. ESP. Dist: Continental Bk. Co., Inc.

—El Principito. 2018. (Brújula y la Veleta Ser.). (SPA.). 64p. (J). (gr. 4-7). pap. 9.95 *(978-987-718-488-4(5))* Ediciones Lea S.A. ARG. Dist: Independent Pubs. Group.

—El Principito. (Coleccion Centro Literario). (SPA.). (J). pap., stu. ed. 7.95 *(978-958-02-0475-6(6),* CAR005) Editorial Voluntad S.A. COL. Dist: Continental Bk. Co., Inc.

—El Principito. 2003. (SPA., Illus.). 96p. (YA). (gr. 5-8). *(978-84-7888-438-4(6),* SAL7382) Emece Editores ESP. Dist: Lectorum Pubns., Inc.

—El Principito. (SPA.). (J). pap. 10.95 *(978-950-04-0048-0(0))* Emecé Editores S.A. ARG. Dist: Planeta Publishing Corp.

De Saint Exupéry, Antoine, compiled by. The Little Prince: The Coloring Portfolio. 2016.Tr. of Petit Prince. (ENG., Illus.). 128p. 19.95 *(978-2-37495-014-3(X),* 1355701) Cernunnos FRA. Dist: Hachette Bk. Group.

De Saint-Exupéry, Antoine & Hemerman, Ilana. The Little Prince. 2013.Tr. of Petit Prince. (HEB.). (J). *(978-965-13-0883-3(4))*; 90p. *(978-965-13-2376-8(0))* Am Oved Pubs., Ltd.

Despain, Bree. The Eternity Key. 2015. (Into the Dark Ser.). (ENG.). 368p. (YA). (gr. 7-12). 18.99 *(978-1-60684-467-0(9),* f2df1f02-5404-4294-9108-285867af6c12); E-Book 29.32 *(978-1-5124-0179-0(X))* Lerner Publishing Group. (Carolrhoda Lab™).

—The Immortal Throne. 2016. (Into the Dark Ser.: 3). (ENG.). 344p. (YA). (gr. 7-12). 18.99 *(978-1-5124-0583-5(3),* 5f021e9e-aee4-4c3d-8519-1d2047ef1597); E-Book 29.32 *(978-1-5124-0897-3(2))* Lerner Publishing Group. (Carolrhoda Lab™).

—The Shadow Prince. (Into the Dark Ser.: Bk. 1). (ENG.). 496p. (YA). (gr. 7-12). 2015. pap. 9.99 *(978-1-60684-567-7(5),* af40ef41-9789-4250-8f17-2560460d2edc) 2014. 18.99 *(978-1-60684-247-8(1),* 5511e0e1-6e32-400a-aaae-d7ec6209d1a6) Lerner Publishing Group. (Carolrhoda Lab™).

Dharma Publishing Staff. The Power of a Promise: A Story about the Power of Keeping Promises. 2010. 36p. (gr. -1-7). pap. 8.95 *(978-0-89800-603-2(1))* Dharma Publishing.

Disney Books. The Little Mermaid ReadAlong Storybook & CD. 2013. (Read-Along Storybook & CD Ser.). (ENG., Illus.). 32p. (J). (gr. -1-k). pap. 6.99 *(978-1-4231-6889-8(5),* Disney Press Books) Disney Publishing Worldwide.

Disney Press Staff. Valley of Vipers. 2010. 144p. pap. 4.99 *(978-1-4231-1007-1(2))* Disney Pr.

Dixon, Ken. Cobweb Jack & the Sacred Khunjar. 2009. 210p. pap. 28.50 *(978-1-4092-8919-7(2))* Lulu Pr., Inc.

Doeden, Matt. Beauty & the Beast: An Interactive Fairy Tale Adventure. Miramon, Sabrina, illus. 2018. (You Choose: Fractured Fairy Tales Ser.). (ENG.). 112p. (J). (gr. 3-7). lib. bdg. 32.65 *(978-1-5435-3007-0(9),* 138604, Capstone Pr.) Capstone.

Donaldson, Julia. Princess Mirror-Belle & the Flying Horse: Two Books in One, 2 Bks in 1. Monks, Lydia, illus. 2017. (Princess Mirror-Belle Ser.). (ENG.). 192p. (J). (gr. k-2). 8.99 *(978-1-5098-3890-5(2))* Pan Macmillan GBR. Dist: Independent Pubs. Group.

Dower, Laura. Sunny & the Secret Passage. 2013. (Palace Puppies Ser.: 4). (J). lib. bdg. 14.75 *(978-0-606-35108-9(6))* Turtleback.

Downey, Glen. Rebel Prince. Okum, David, illus. 2007. 48p. (J). lib. bdg. 23.08 *(978-1-4242-1642-0(7))* Fitzgerald Bks.

Drischel, Candy L. Restless with the Dark Moon Rising. 2008. 105p. pap. 19.95 *(978-1-60610-421-7(7))* America Star Bks.

Drobeck, Ronald D. My Name Is Prince Albert. 2012. 152p. (gr. 4-6). 30.95 *(978-1-4582-0205-5(4))*; pap. 12.99 *(978-1-4582-0203-1(8))* Author Solutions, LLC. (Abbott Pr.).

Dugan, David J. The Missing Prince of Distria. 2008. 36p. pap. 24.95 *(978-1-60563-587-3(1))* America Star Bks.

Dumas, Alexandre. Barbie & the Three Musketeers: A Junior Novelization. Choi, Allan, illus. 2009. 93p. (J). *(978-0-545-09413-9(5))* Scholastic, Inc.

Duncan, Emily A. Ruthless Gods: A Novel. 2020. (Something Dark & Holy Ser.: 2). (ENG., Illus.). 544p. (YA). 18.99 *(978-1-250-19569-2(1),* 900193806, Wednesday Bks.) St. Martin's Pr.

Eltoukhy, G.N. Sheherazade Chronicles of the Fairy Tales. 2012. 32p. pap. 17.25 *(978-1-4669-3708-6(4))* Trafford Publishing.

Engelbreit, Mary. Mary Engelbreit's Nutcracker. 2014. (ENG., Illus.). 40p. (J). (gr. -1-3). 9.99 *(978-0-06-222417-0(4),* HarperCollins) HarperCollins Pubs.

Essama, Molly Jane. The Prince & the Three Ugly Hags. 2010. 28p. pap. 16.95 *(978-1-4490-5587-5(7))* AuthorHouse.

Everett, Felicity & Rawson, Christopher. Stories of Princes & Princesses. 2004. (Young Reading Ser.). (Illus.). 48p. (J). (gr. 2-18). pap. 5.95 *(978-0-7945-0449-6(3),* Usborne) EDC Publishing.

Faye Morningstar. Little Dream Athe: The Sand Prince. 2012. 20p. pap. 17.99 *(978-1-4772-9540-3(2))* AuthorHouse.

Filak, Stacey. The Queen Underneath. 2018. (ENG.). 288p. (YA). 16.99 *(978-1-62414-560-5(4),* 900191141) Page Street Publishing Co.

Foster, Jackie. Land of Anear, 1 vol. 2010. 27p. pap. 24.95 *(978-1-61546-634-4(7))* America Star Bks.

Gaichies, Sarah. Angela & the Prince. 2011. (FRE & ENG., Illus.). 96p. pap. 32.26 *(978-1-4567-8999-2(6))* AuthorHouse.

Gaydos, Nora. Now I'm Growing! Prince of the Potty - Little Steps for Big Kids! Gutierrez, Akemi, illus. 2011. (ENG.). 30p. (J). (gr. -1-17). 8.99 *(978-1-60169-077-7(0))* Innovative Kids.

George, Jessica Day. Princess of Glass. 2011. (Twelve Dancing Princesses Ser.). (ENG.). 272p. (YA). (gr. 7). pap. 10.99 *(978-1-59990-659-1(7),* 900074740, Bloomsbury USA Childrens) Bloomsbury Publishing USA.

Un Giorno Con Il Piccolo Principe. Ediz. Illustrata. pap. 13.95 *(978-88-451-2269-9(7))* Fabbri Editori - RCS Libri ITA. Dist: Distribooks, Inc.

Gordon, Mike, illus. The Frog Prince. rev. ed. 2007. (Young Reading CD Packs Ser.). 48p. (J). (gr. -1-3). 9.99 incl. audio compact disk *(978-0-7945-1868-4(0),* Usborne) EDC Publishing.

Gormley, Greg. The Prince & the Pee. Mould, Chris, illus. 2018. (ENG.). 32p. (J). (gr. -1-2). 16.99 *(978-0-7636-9916-1(0))* Candlewick Pr.

Gow, Kailin. Diary of a Discount Donna: A Fashion Fables Book: A Novel. 2005. 274p. (YA). per. 10.95 *(978-1-59748-858-7(5))* Sparklesoup LLC.

Gravel, Elise. The Worst Book Ever. 2019. (ENG., Illus.). 48p. 17.95 *(978-1-77046-363-9(1),* 900208055) Drawn & Quarterly Pubns. CAN. Dist: Macmillan.

Gribble, Julie. Bubblegum Princess. Hanson, Lori, illus. 2013. 32p. (J). 16.99 *(978-0-9890914-0-4(6))* NY Media Works, LLC.

Grimm, Brothers. The Frog Prince. Schroeder, Binette, illus. 2013. (ENG.). 32p. (J). (gr. -1-3). 17.95 *(978-0-7358-4140-6(3))* North-South Bks., Inc.

Grimm, Jacob & Grimm, Wilhelm K. The Frog Prince/ El Principe Sapo. 2004. (Illus.). (J). *(978-1-933530-21-5(9))* Bingo Bks., Inc.

Guerrera, Jeannette D. The Pot of Gold. 2012. 20p. pap. 17.99 *(978-1-4685-5883-8(8))* AuthorHouse.

Guillain, Charlotte. Ratpunzel, 1 vol. Beacon, Dawn, illus. 2014. (Animal Fairy Tales Ser.). (ENG.). 24p. (J). (gr. -1-2). lib. bdg. 23.99 *(978-1-4109-6112-9(5),* 124739, Raintree) Capstone.

Haack, Daniel. Prince & Knight. Lewis, Stevie, illus. 2018. (ENG.). 40p. (J). (gr. -1-3). 17.99 *(978-1-4998-0552-9(7))* Little Bee Books Inc.

Haack, Daniel & Galupo, Isabel. Maiden & Princess. Human, Becca, illus. 2019. (ENG.). 40p. (J). (gr. -1-3). 17.99 *(978-1-4998-0776-9(7))* Little Bee Books Inc.

Hale, Shannon. Book of a Thousand Days. 2017. (ENG.). 336p. (YA). pap. 10.99 *(978-1-68119-315-1(9),* 900165753, Bloomsbury USA Childrens) Bloomsbury Publishing USA.

Hall, Frank. The Prince Who Did Not Want to be King. 2011. 132p. 28.95 *(978-1-4497-1440-6(4))*; (J). pap. 11.95 *(978-1-4497-1438-3(2))* Author Solutions, LLC. (WestBow Pr.).

Hardy, S. F. The Empress' New Hair. 2012. 40p. pap. 10.00 *(978-0-9849360-9-0(2))* G Publishing LLC.

Harkrader, Lisa. The Tadpole Prince. 2016. (Spring Forward Ser.). (J). (gr. 2). *(978-1-4900-9473-1(3))* Benchmark Education Co.

Harris, Brenda. Ride Like the Wind. 2011. (Illus.). 40p. (J). pap. 12.95 *(978-1-936076-93-2(4))* Innovo Publishing, LLC.

Harrison, Mette Ivie. The Princess & the Hound. 2007. 410p. (YA). (gr. 7-18). lib. bdg. 18.89 *(978-0-06-113188-2(1),* Eos) HarperCollins Pubs.

Hart, Caryl. The Princess & the Christmas Rescue. Warburton, Sarah, illus. 2017. (ENG.). 32p. (J). (gr. -1-2). 16.99 *(978-0-7636-9632-0(3))* Candlewick Pr.

Hawkins, Loreatha V. The Prince & the Musical Castle. 2009. 32p. pap. 14.49 *(978-1-4389-7678-5(X))* AuthorHouse.

Healy, Christopher. The Hero's Guide to Being an Outlaw. Harris, Todd, illus. 2014. (Hero's Guide Ser.: 3). (ENG.). 528p. (J). (gr. 3-7). 16.99 *(978-0-06-211848-6(X),* Walden Pond Pr.) HarperCollins Pubs.

—The Hero's Guide to Saving Your Kingdom. Harris, Todd, illus. 2013. (Hero's Guide Ser.: 1). (ENG.). 480p. (J). (gr. 3-7). pap. 7.99 *(978-0-06-211745-8(9),* Walden Pond Pr.) HarperCollins Pubs.

Hensley, Judith Victoria. Sir Thomas the Eggslayer. 2008. 156p. pap. 14.95 *(978-0-9795103-8-0(4))* Ascended Ideas.

Herbauts, Anne. Prince Silencio. 2006. (ENG., Illus.). 32p. (J). (gr. -1-3). 14.95 *(978-1-59270-055-4(1))* Enchanted Lion Bks., LLC.

Hewitt, Megan. Eagle Rises. 2013. (ENG.). 118p. (J). pap. 12.99 *(978-1-300-55242-0(5))* Lulu Pr., Inc.

Hill, Leah. The Adventures of Prince Phillip & the Fairytale Creatures: The Giant Problem. 2013. (ENG.). 26p. (J). pap. 10.95 *(978-1-4787-0696-0(1))* Outskirts Pr., Inc.

Hinuss, Roy L. Her Royal Slyness. Hunt, Matt, illus. 2018. 136p. (J). *(978-1-5490-5505-8(4))* ETT Imprint.

—Once upon a Prank. Hunt, Matt, illus. 2018. 120p. (J). *(978-1-5490-5506-5(2))* ETT Imprint.

—Once upon a Prank. 2018. (Prince Not-So Charming Ser.). (Illus.). 120p. (J). lib. bdg. 16.00 *(978-0-606-41110-3(0))* Turtleback.

—Prince Not-So Charming: Her Royal Slyness. Hunt, Matt, illus. 2018. (Prince Not-So Charming Ser.: 2). (ENG.). 144p. (J). pap. 15.99 *(978-1-250-14240-5(7),* 900180219) Imprint IND. Dist: Macmillan.

Hodgson, Mona. The Princess Twins & the Birthday Party, 1 vol. Olson, Julie, illus. 2016. (I Can Read! / Princess Twins Ser.). (ENG.). 32p. (J). pap. 4.99 *(978-0-310-75067-3(9))* Zonderkidz.

Hofmeyr, Dianne. Eye of the Moon. 2011. (ENG.). 336p. (J). (gr. 3-7). pap. 9.99 *(978-1-4424-1188-3(0),* Aladdin) Simon & Schuster Children's Publishing.

Homberg, Ruth. The Little Mermaid. 2013. (Disney Princess Step into Reading Ser.). lib. bdg. 13.55 *(978-0-606-32202-7(7))* Turtleback.

Hong, Chen Jiang. The Tiger Prince. Waters, Alyson, tr. 2018. (ENG., Illus.). 40p. (J). (gr. -1-3). 18.95 *(978-1-68137-294-5(0),* NYR Children's Collection) New York Review of Bks., Inc., The.

Howard, Richard & Mortensen, Viggo. The Little Prince. De Saint-Exupéry, Antoine, illus. 70th ed. 2013.Tr. of Petit Prince. 83p. (J). *(978-0-544-10910-0(4))* Harcourt.

Howell, Laura. Princess & the Pea. 2009. (Young Reading 1 Ser.). 48p. (J). 6.99 *(978-0-7945-2587-3(3),* Usborne) EDC Publishing.

Hoyt, Holly. The Purple Widow. 2009. 314p. 28.25 *(978-1-60860-688-7(0),* Eloquent Bks.) Strategic Book Publishing & Rights Agency (SBPRA).

Hurley, Jeanette Clinger. The Crystal Prince: Love Is the Only Way. 2010. (Illus.). 77p. pap. 32.95 *(978-0-578-03963-3(X))* Outskirts Pr., Inc.

Ibbotson, Eva. The Dragonfly Pool, 9 vols. 2008. (YA). 122.75 *(978-1-4361-5209-9(7))*; 92.75 *(978-1-4361-5205-1(4))*; 90.75 *(978-1-4361-5207-5(0))*; 1.25 *(978-1-4361-5202-0(X))*; 256.75 *(978-1-4361-5206-8(2))*; 120.75 *(978-1-4361-5211-2(9))* Recorded Bks., Inc.

Ifueko, Jordan. Raybearer. (Raybearer Ser.). (ENG., Illus.). (YA). (gr. 7-17). 2021. 400p. pap. 10.99 *(978-1-4197-3983-5(2),* 1297003) 2020. 368p. 18.99 *(978-1-4197-3982-8(4),* 1297001) Abrams, Inc.

Illustrated Stories of Princes & Princesses. 2015. (Illustrated Stories Ser.). (ENG.). (J). 19.99 *(978-0-7945-3416-5(3),* Usborne) EDC Publishing.

Jacques, Brian. The Angel's Command. 2005. (Castaways of the Flying Dutchman Ser.). (ENG., Illus.). 384p. (J). (gr. 3-7). 9.99 *(978-0-14-240285-6(0),* Firebird) Penguin Young Readers Group.

—The Angel's Command. 2003. (Castaways of the Flying Dutchman Ser.: No. 2). 1.00 *(978-1-4175-5393-8(6))* Recorded Bks., Inc.

Jardine, Kathy & Jardine, Ashley. The Durples: Go to School. 2010. 28p. pap. 17.99 *(978-1-4490-3405-4(5))* AuthorHouse.

Jay, Stacey. Princess of Thorns. 2016. (ENG.). 400p. (YA). (gr. 9). pap. 9.99 *(978-0-385-74323-5(8),* Ember) Random Hse. Children's Bks.

Jeffers, Susan. The Nutcracker. Jeffers, Susan, illus. 2007. (Illus.). 40p. (J). (gr. -1-3). 17.89 *(978-0-06-074387-1(5))* HarperCollins Pubs.

—The Nutcracker. 2007. (ENG., Illus.). 40p. (J). (gr. -1-3). 18.99 *(978-0-06-074386-4(7),* HarperCollins) HarperCollins Pubs.

Jesus, Opal De. The Golden Apple Kingdom, 1 vol. 2009. 48p. pap. 16.95 *(978-1-60749-414-0(0))* America Star Bks.

Jones, Christianne C. Beauty & the Beast, 1 vol. Muehlenhardt, Amy, illus. 2013. (My First Classic Story Ser.). (ENG.). 32p. (J). (gr. k-3). pap. 7.10 *(978-1-4795-1851-7(4),* 123440, Picture Window Bks.) Capstone.

Jordan, Annie Laurie. Bogwaddle Pond. La Grange, Myrtle, illus. 2004. 25p. pap. 24.95 *(978-1-4137-2013-6(7))* PublishAmerica, Inc.

Joyce, Sandie May. Little Miss Alice & the Bookworm. 2007. 65p. pap. 24.95 *(978-1-4357-0328-5(6))* Lulu Pr., Inc.

Jungman, Ann. The Footballing Frog: Band 14/Ruby (Collins Big Cat) Burnett, Seb, illus. 2007. (Collins Big Cat Ser.). (ENG.). 80p. (J). (gr. 3-4). pap. 11.99 *(978-0-00-723087-7(7))* HarperCollins Pubs. Ltd. GBR. Dist: Independent Pubs. Group.

Justis, Jon. Pumpkin & the Great Dragon Caper. 2012. 32p. pap. 24.95 *(978-1-4626-9733-5(X))* America Star Bks.

Kagawa, Julie. The Iron King. Chan, Lidia, illus. 2017. (Iron King Ser.). (SPA.). (YA). (gr. 7-12). pap. 19.99 *(978-1-948216-67-8(1))* TidalWave Productions.

—The Iron King. 2010. (Iron Fey Ser.: 1). (J). lib. bdg. 20.85 *(978-0-606-14909-9(0))* Turtleback.

—The Iron Legends. 2012. (Iron Fey Ser.: 5). (J). lib. bdg. 20.85 *(978-0-606-26516-4(3))* Turtleback.

—The Lost Prince. 2012. (Iron Fey Ser.: 5). (J). lib. bdg. 20.85 *(978-0-606-26946-9(0))* Turtleback.

Kale, Ann Stephanian. Marco & Princess Gina. Kale, Ann Stephanian, illus. 2003. (Illus.). 24p. (J). (gr. k-3). pap. 10.00 *(978-0-9704131-5-4(7))* Abril BookStore & Publishing.

Kats, Jewel. Cinderella's Magical Wheelchair: An Empowering Fairy Tale. Kinra, Richa, illus. 2012. (J). 24p. 29.95 *(978-1-61599-113-6(1))*; 20p. pap. 16.95 *(978-1-61599-112-9(3))* Loving Healing Pr., Inc.

—Prince Preemie: A Tale of a Tiny Puppy Who Arrives Early. Lenart, Claudia, illus. 2016. 28p. (J). pap. *(978-1-61599-306-2(1))* Loving Healing Pr., Inc.

Klingele, Lindsey. The Broken World. (ENG.). (YA). (gr. 8). 2018. 448p. pap. 9.99 *(978-0-06-238037-1(0))* 2017. 432p. 17.99 *(978-0-06-238036-4(2))* HarperCollins Pubs. (HarperTeen).

Kneblik, Debi. The Shipwreck of Knottingburg. 2009. (J). pap. 12.00 *(978-1-61623-985-5(9))* Independent Pub.

Koch, Claus. The Three Little Wolves & the Big Bad Boar. 2011. 68p. pap. 9.99 *(978-1-4520-5321-9(9))* AuthorHouse.

Kuhl, Debra. Black Bert the Pirate, 1 vol. 2009. 83p. pap. 19.95 *(978-1-60749-968-8(1))* America Star Bks.

L. Prince Cloud & Princess Evergreen, 1 vol. 2010. 26p. pap. 24.95 *(978-1-4512-9016-5(0))* America Star Bks.

Lagonegro, Melissa. Outside My Window (Disney Tangled) Orpinas, Jean-Paul et al, illus. 2010. (Step into Reading Ser.). (ENG.). 32p. (J). (gr. k-3). pap. 5.99 *(978-0-7364-2688-6(4),* RH/Disney) Random Hse. Children's Bks.

Lance, John & Narvarro. Priscilla Holmes & the Case of the Glass Slipper. 2011. 24p. pap. 14.99 *(978-0-9826594-9-6(0))* 4RV Pub.

Laney, Matt. The Four Guardians. 2019. (Pride Wars Ser.). (ENG., Illus.). 368p. (J). (gr. 5-7). 16.99 *(978-1-328-70738-3(5),* 1673039); pap. 7.99 *(978-0-358-22942-1(1),* 1766222) HarperCollins Pubs. (Clarion Bks.).

—The Spinner Prince. 2019. (Pride Wars Ser.). (ENG.). 352p. (J). (gr. 5-7). pap. 7.99 *(978-1-328-61309-7(7),* 1733493, Clarion Bks.) HarperCollins Pubs.

Laviera, Tato. Mayanito's New Friends / Los Nuevos Amigos de Mayanito. Utomo, Gabhor, illus. 2017. (ENG & SPA.). 32p. (J). (gr. 2-4). 17.95 *(978-1-55885-855-8(5),* Piñata Books) Arte Publico Pr.

Leake, Jessica. Through the White Wood. 2019. (ENG.). 416p. (YA). (gr. 9). 17.99 *(978-0-06-266629-1(0),* HarperTeen) HarperCollins Pubs.

Lehman, Marcus. 5 Novelettes by Marcus Lehman Slipcased: Adopted Princess, Bustenai, Out of the Depths, Rabenu Gershom & Unpaid Ransom. Mindel, Nissan, tr. from GER. Kleiman, Zalman, illus. 2012. (ENG.). (YA). 64.95 *(978-0-8266-0033-2(6))* Kehot Pubn. Society.

Lerangis, Peter. The Promise. 2016. (Seven Wonders Journals: 4). 92p. (J). lib. bdg. 12.35 *(978-0-606-38133-8(3))* Turtleback.

Lewison, Wendy Cheyette. The Prince & the Potty. Motoyama, Keiko, illus. 2006. (ENG.). 40p. (J). (gr. -1-3). 16.99 *(978-0-689-87808-4(7),* Simon & Schuster Bks. For Young Readers) Simon & Schuster Bks. For Young Readers.

Liessner, Richard. The Foot Prince. Liessner, Richard, illus. 2006. (Illus.). 24p. (J). 9.95 *(978-0-9766129-5-7(X))* Raindrop Bks.

Limke, Jeff. Jason: Quest for the Golden Fleece [a Greek Myth]. Seeley, Tim, illus. 2008. (Graphic Myths & Legends Ser.). (ENG.). 48p. (J). (gr. 4-8). per. 9.99 *(978-0-8225-6571-0(4),* d859bf86-0417-49f6-82c3-46591ace4d91, Graphic Universe™) Lerner Publishing Group.

Livan, Paco. WHAT A SNOUT! 2007. (ENG., Illus.). 48p. (J). 18.95 *(978-84-96788-87-9(3))* OQO, Editora ESP. Dist: Baker & Taylor Bks.

Lobel, Arnold. The Arnold Lobel Treasury. 2014. (ENG., Illus.). 160p. (J). (gr. 1-4). pap. 14.99 *(978-0-486-78078-8(3),* 780783) Dover Pubns., Inc.

Louise, Martha. Why Kings & Queens Don't Wear Crowns. Sevig-Fajardo, Mari Elise, tr. from NOR. Nyhus, Svein, illus. 2005. Orig. Title: Hvorfor de kongelige ikke har krone på Hodet. 32p. (J). 17.95 *(978-1-57534-037-1(2),* CSC 100) Skandisk, Inc.

Love, D. Anne. The Secret Prince. 2012. (ENG.). 240p. (J). (gr. 3-7). pap. 11.99 *(978-1-4424-5931-1(X),* McElderry, Margaret K. Bks.) McElderry, Margaret K. Bks.

Low, Vicki. First Emperor. Mayhew, Sara E., illus. 2007. 48p. (J). lib. bdg. 23.08 *(978-1-4242-1626-0(5))* Fitzgerald Bks.

Maas, Sarah J. Throne of Glass. 2013. (Throne of Glass Ser.: 1). (YA). lib. bdg. 22.10 *(978-0-606-31888-4(7))* Turtleback.

—Throne of Glass Collector's Edition. 2018. (Throne of Glass Ser.: 1). (ENG.). 432p. *(978-1-5476-0132-5(9),* 423824) Bloomsbury Publishing Plc.

MacDonald, George. The Light Princess. 2004. reprint ed. pap. 1.99 *(978-1-4192-7001-7(X))* Kessinger Publishing, LLC.

—Light Princess & Other Fairy Stories. 2006. 132p. per. 10.95 *(978-1-59818-618-5(3));* 24.95 *(978-1-59818-236-1(6))* Aegypan.

—The Princess & the Goblin. 2nd ed. 2011. (Puffin Classics Ser.). (ENG., Illus.). 256p. (J). (gr. 5-7). 7.99 *(978-0-14-133248-2(4),* Puffin Books) Penguin Young Readers Group.

Maguire, Gregory. Egg & Spoon. 2014. (ENG., Illus.). 496p. (YA). (gr. 7). 17.99 *(978-0-7636-7220-1(3))* Candlewick Pr.

Manjula Padmanabhan, illus. Unprincess! 2005. 98p. (J). *(978-0-14-333495-8(6),* Puffin) Penguin Publishing Group.

Marinsky, Jane, illus. The Goat-Faced Girl: A Classic Italian Folktale. 2009. (ENG.). 32p. (J). (gr. 1-4). 16.95 *(978-1-56792-393-3(3))* Godine, David R. Pub.

Martin, Rafe. Birdwing. 2007. (ENG.). 384p. (J). (gr. 7-12). pap. 7.99 *(978-0-439-21168-0(9),* Levine, Arthur A. Bks.) Scholastic, Inc.

Mass, Wendy. Rapunzel: The One with All the Hair. 2005. (Illus.). 205p. (J). *(978-0-439-80014-3(5))* Scholastic, Inc.

—Rapunzel, the One with All the Hair: a Wish Novel (Twice upon a Time #1) 2012. (Twice upon a Time Ser.: 1). (ENG.). 208p. (J). (gr. 3-7). pap. 7.99 *(978-0-439-79659-0(8),* Scholastic Pr.) Scholastic, Inc.

—Sleeping Beauty: The One Who Took the Really Long Nap. 2012. (Twice upon a Time Ser.: 2). lib. bdg. 17.20 *(978-0-606-26530-0(9))* Turtleback.

—Sleeping Beauty, the One Who Took the Really Long Nap: a Wish Novel (Twice upon a Time #2) 2018. (Twice upon a Time Ser.: 2). (ENG.). 176p. (J). (gr. 3-7). pap. 7.99 *(978-0-439-79658-3(X),* Scholastic Pr.) Scholastic, Inc.

McGee, Katharine. American Royals. (American Royals Ser.: 1). (ENG.). (YA). (gr. 9). 2020. 464p. pap. 12.99 *(978-1-9848-3020-3(1),* Ember) 2019. 448p. 18.99 *(978-1-9848-3017-3(1),* Random Hse. Bks. for Young Readers) Random Hse. Children's Bks.

—American Royals II: Majesty. (American Royals Ser.: 2). (ENG.). (YA). (gr. 9). 2022. 400p. pap. 12.99 *(978-1-9848-3024-1(4),* Ember) 2020. 384p. 18.99 *(978-1-9848-3021-0(X),* Random Hse. Bks. for Young Readers) Random Hse. Children's Bks.

—American Royals III: Rivals. 2022. (American Royals Ser.: 3). (ENG.). 400p. (YA). (gr. 9). 19.99 *(978-0-593-42970-9(2));* lib. bdg. 22.99 *(978-0-593-42971-6(0))* Random Hse. Children's Bks. (Random Hse. Bks. for Young Readers).

—American Royals (Spanish Edition) 2021. (American Royals Ser.). (SPA.). 282p. (YA). (gr. 8-12). pap. 22.99 *(978-84-272-1650-1(5))* Penguin Random House Grupo Editorial ESP. Dist: Penguin Random Hse. LLC.

McKee, David. El Principe Pedro y el oso de Peluche. (SPA.). (J). 7.95 *(978-958-04-6258-3(5))* Norma S.A. COL. Dist: Distribuidora Norma, Inc.

McKnight, Gillian. To Catch a Prince. 2010. (ENG.). 240p. (YA). (gr. 7). pap. 11.99 *(978-1-4424-2718-1(3),* Simon Pulse) Simon Pulse.

McMakin, Jordan. Prince Ezrick & the Morpheas Curse, 4 vols. 2005. (Illus.). 304p. (J). per. 11.95 *(978-0-9764184-0-5(1))* Canterwine Pr.

McMurtrie, Kevin. The Prince That Always Wore His Top Hat. 2013. 40p. pap. 16.26 *(978-1-4669-9602-1(1))* Trafford Publishing.

McRoberts, Eddison. Sneaking Treats: A Halloween Hunt. Gadra, Jessica, illus. 2012. 48p. 19.95 *(978-1-62137-136-6(0))* Virtualbookworm.com Publishing, Inc.

Meet the Little Prince (Padded Board Book) 2015. (Little Prince Ser.). (ENG., Illus.). 10p. (J). (— 1). bds. 7.99 *(978-0-544-70902-7(0),* 1628913, Clarion Bks.) HarperCollins Pubs.

Meister, Cari. Three Horses, 4 vols. 2018. (Three Horses Ser.). (ENG.). 56p. (J). (gr. k-2). 95.96 *(978-1-5158-2963-8(4),* 28422); pap., pap., pap. 19.80 *(978-1-5158-2964-5(2),* 28423) Capstone. (Picture Window Bks.).

Meyer, Dana. A Gift for Prince Eli. 2012. 24p. pap. 24.95 *(978-1-4626-5575-5(0))* America Star Bks.

Meyer, Julia & Tabler, Marie. One Pea. Tabler, Marie, illus. 2013. (Illus.). 36p. 14.95 *(978-1-62314-139-4(7))* ePub Bud.

Mihai, Adriana. The Inner of the Diamond Shoes. 2011. 28p. pap. 24.95 *(978-1-4560-0979-3(6))* America Star Bks.

Miller, Michael & Strickland, AdriAnne. Shadow Run. 2018. (ENG.). 416p. (YA). (gr. 7). pap. 10.99 *(978-0-399-55256-4(1),* Ember) Random Hse. Children's Bks.

Miller, Penelope. Farbedrook. 2008. 96p. pap. *(978-1-84748-104-7(3))* Athena Pr.

Millman, Selena. More Than a Hero. 2006. 92p. (YA). per. 11.37 *(978-1-4243-2351-7(7))* Independent Publisher Services.

—The Prince & Me. 2006. 146p. (YA). per. 11.20 *(978-1-4243-2353-1(3))* Independent Publisher Services.

Mirabelli, Eugene. The Queen of the Rain Was in Love with the Prince of the Sky. 2008. pap. 5.00 *(978-0-935891-08-9(0))* Spring Harbor Pr.

Moeling, Nell. The Secret Adventures of Prince Justin & the Dragon. 2010. 40p. 17.99 *(978-1-4520-4996-0(3))* AuthorHouse.

Molina, Angeles. El Principe Que No Queria Ser Principe. 2007. (SPA.). 64p. 14.95 *(978-0-8477-0455-2(6))* Univ. of Puerto Rico Pr.

Monnar, Ana. Heart of Stone. Michaud, Nancy, illus. 2007. 24p. (J). per. 11.99 *(978-0-9768035-5-3(0))* Readers Are Leaders U.S.A.

Motayne, Maya. Nocturna. (Nocturna Ser.: 1). (ENG.). (YA). (gr. 8). 2020. 496p. pap. 11.99 *(978-0-06-284274-9(9))* 2019. (Illus.). 480p. 18.99 *(978-0-06-284273-2(0))* HarperCollins Pubs. (Balzer & Bray).

Mulock, Miss. The Little Lame Prince & Other Tales. 2007. 304p. 24.95 *(978-1-4344-9379-8(2))* Wildside Pr., LLC.

Mulrain, Sabrina. A Prince's Happy Ever After. 2011. 40p. pap. 24.95 *(978-1-4560-3251-7(8))* America Star Bks.

Munsch, Robert. The Paper Bag Princess. Martchenko, Michael, illus. (Classic Munsch Ser.). (J). (gr. -1-2). 2018. 32p. 19.95 *(978-1-77321-030-8(0))* 2018. 32p. pap. 6.95 *(978-1-77321-029-2(7))* 10th ed. 2009. (ENG.). 28p. bds. 7.99 *(978-1-55451-211-9(5),* 9781554512119) Annick Pr., Ltd. CAN. Dist: Publishers Group West (PGW).

Nevis, Lance. The Pollywog Prince. Laible MBA, Steve William, ed. Piper, Tom, illus. 2012. 46p. pap. 10.99 *(978-0-9850142-8-5(8))* Kodel Group, LLC, The.

Nguy, Hoa X. The Bamboo Girl. 2007. 84p. (J). pap. 20.00 *(978-0-8059-7562-8(4))* Dorrance Publishing Co., Inc.

Nielsen, Jennifer A. The False Prince. 2012. (Ascendance Trilogy: Bk. 1). (ENG.). (J). (gr. 5-8). 64.99 *(978-1-61707-596-4(5))* Findaway World, LLC.

—The False Prince. 2012. (Ascendance Trilogy: Bk. 1). (Illus.). 342p. (J). pap. *(978-0-545-43347-1(9),* Scholastic Pr.) Scholastic, Inc.

—The False Prince. 2013. (Ascendance Trilogy Ser.: 1). lib. bdg. 18.40 *(978-0-606-31491-6(1))* Turtleback.

—The False Prince (the Ascendance Series, Book 1) (ENG.). 352p. 2013. (Ascendance Ser.: 1). (YA). (gr. 3-7). pap. 8.99 *(978-0-545-28414-1(7),* Scholastic Paperbacks) 2012. (Ascendance Ser.: 1). (Illus.). (YA). (gr. 3-7). 18.99 *(978-0-545-28413-4(9),* Scholastic Pr.) 2012. (Ascendance Trilogy: Bk. 1). E-Book 17.99 *(978-0-545-39249-5(7))* Scholastic, Inc.

Norris, Johanna. The Day Prince Snot Nose Made Friends. 2011. 36p. (gr. -1). pap. 11.32 *(978-1-4567-3283-7(8))* AuthorHouse.

North, Laura. Cinderella's Big Foot. Remphry, Martin, illus. 2014. (Tadpoles: Fairytale Twists Ser.). (ENG.). 32p. (J). (gr. 1-2). *(978-0-7787-0440-9(8));* pap. *(978-0-7787-0448-5(3))* Crabtree Publishing Co.

—Sleeping Beauty — 100 Years Later. Northfield, Gary, illus. 2014. (Tadpoles: Fairytale Twists Ser.). (ENG.). 32p. (J). (gr. 1-2). *(978-0-7787-0444-7(0));* pap. *(978-0-7787-0479-9(3))* Crabtree Publishing Co.

O'Connell, Tyne. A Royal Match. 2011. (Calypso Chronicles Ser.). (ENG.). 512p. (YA). pap. 9.99 *(978-1-59990-751-2(8),* 9781599907512, Bloomsbury USA Childrens) Bloomsbury Publishing USA.

Oppenheim, Joanne. The Prince's Bedtime. Latimer, Miriam, illus. 2019. (ENG.). 32p. (J). (gr. -1-2). pap. 9.99 *(978-1-78285-419-7(3))* Barefoot Bks., Inc.

—The Prince's Breakfast. Latimer, Miriam, illus. 2019. (ENG.). 32p. (J). (gr. -1-2). pap. 9.99 *(978-1-78285-417-3(7))* Barefoot Bks., Inc.

—El Principe No Duerme. Latimer, Miriam, illus. 2014. (SPA.). 32p. (J). (gr. -1-2). pap. 9.99 *(978-1-78285-077-9(5))* Barefoot Bks., Inc.

Oppenheim, Joanne F. The Prince's Bedtime. Latimer, Miriam, illus. 32p. (J). (gr. -1-3). 2007. pap. 7.99 *(978-1-84686-106-2(3))* 2006. (ENG.). 16.99 *(978-1-84148-597-3(7))* Barefoot Bks., Inc.

Oppenheim, Joanne F. & Barefoot Books Staff. The Prince's Breakfast. Latimer, Miriam, illus. 2014. 32p. (J). (gr. -1-2). 16.99 *(978-1-78285-074-8(0));* 9.99 *(978-1-78285-075-5(9))* Barefoot Bks., Inc.

Oppenheim, Joanne F. & Latimer, Muriam. The Prince's Bedtime. Latimer, Muriam, illus. 2007. (Illus.). 32p. (J). (gr. -1-2). 9.99 *(978-1-84686-096-6(2))* Barefoot Bks., Inc.

Pacat, C. S. Kings Rising. 2016. (Captive Prince Trilogy Ser.: 3). (ENG., Illus.). 356p. pap. 17.00 *(978-0-425-27399-9(7),* Berkley) Penguin Publishing Group.

Pace, Terri L. The Christmas Dream, 1 vol. 2009. 116p. pap. 19.95 *(978-1-60813-532-5(2))* America Star Bks.

Parker, Danny & Shield, Guy. Plastic Palace, Volume 4. 2017. (Lola's Toy Box Ser.: 4). (ENG., Illus.). 96p. (J). (gr. k-2). pap. 6.99 *(978-1-76012-439-7(7))* Hardie Grant Children?s Publishing AUS. Dist: Independent Pubs. Group.

Parker, Vic, ed. The Prince & the Dragon & Other Stories, 1 vol. 2015. (Scary Fairy Tales Ser.). (ENG.). 40p. (J). (gr. 3-4). pap. 15.05 *(978-1-4824-3097-4(5),* 6de99058-98b4-4690-a573-0b875e271afe) Stevens, Gareth Publishing LLLP.

Patten, Linda D. Princess Alese & the Kingdom of Serenity. 2013. 20p. pap. 13.77 *(978-1-4669-8724-1(3))* Trafford Publishing.

Pearson, Kimberly Ann. Mystling Glen Book I: The Tale of A Prince. 2009. 207p. pap. 14.95 *(978-1-4327-4169-3(1))* Outskirts Pr., Inc.

Peattie, Cindy. A Cinderella Atlas. Mountford, Karl, illus. 2017. (Text Connections Guided Close Reading Ser.). (J). (gr. 1). *(978-1-4900-1819-5(0))* Benchmark Education Co.

Pef. Belle lisse poire du prince De. pap. 16.95 *(978-2-07-054806-4(6))* Gallimard, Editions FRA. Dist: Distribooks, Inc.

Perrotti, P. J. Jason & the Enchanted Forest. 2004. 48p. pap. 16.95 *(978-1-4137-4593-1(8))* America Star Bks.

Peterson, Alyson. Ian Quicksilver: The Warrior's Return. 2015. vii, 309p. (YA). pap. 17.99 *(978-1-4621-1629-4(9))* Cedar Fort, Inc./CFI Distribution.

Il Piccolo Principe e I Suoi Amici. Ediz. Illustrata. pap. 13.95 *(978-88-451-2266-8(2))* Fabbri Editori - RCS Libri ITA. Dist: Distribooks, Inc.

Picoult, Jodi & van Leer, Samantha. Between the Lines. (ENG., Illus.). 368p. (YA). (gr. 7). 2013. pap. 15.99 *(978-1-4516-3581-2(8))* 2012. 19.99 *(978-1-4516-3575-1(3))* Atria/Emily Bestler Bks. (Atria/Emily Bestler Bks.).

—Off the Page. Gilbert, Yvonne, illus. 2015. (YA). lib. bdg. *(978-0-553-53557-0(9),* Delacorte Pr) Random House Publishing Group.

—Off the Page. Gilbert, Yvonne, illus. 2016. (ENG.). 368p. (YA). (gr. 7). pap. 10.99 *(978-0-553-53559-4(5),* Ember) Random Hse. Children's Bks.

Pierce, Tamora. In the Hand of the Goddess. 2014. (Song of the Lioness Ser.: 2). (ENG., Illus.). 288p. (YA). (gr. 7). 21.99 *(978-1-4814-3960-2(X),* Atheneum Bks. for Young Readers) Simon & Schuster Children's Publishing.

—Tempests & Slaughter (the Numair Chronicles, Book One) (Numair Chronicles Ser.: 1). (ENG.). (YA). (gr. 7). 2019. 496p. pap. 11.99 *(978-0-375-84712-7(X),* Ember) 2018. 480p. 18.99 *(978-0-375-84711-0(1),* Random Hse. Bks. for Young Readers) 2018. 480p. lib. bdg. 21.99 *(978-0-375-94711-7(6),* Random Hse. Bks. for Young Readers) Random Hse. Children's Bks.

Podd, Gloria. A Royal Runt. 2013. 20p. pap. 24.95 *(978-1-63004-012-3(6))* America Star Bks.

Prince Apple Head Humpledink. 2006. 38p. (J). 13.68 *(978-1-4116-7232-1(1))* Lulu Pr., Inc.

Proulx, Roxanna Darling. The Princes of Pleasant Valley: A Day in the Life of Zyler & Xavier, 1 vol. Sandon, Gina, illus. 2010. 46p. 24.95 *(978-1-4489-7641-6(3))* PublishAmerica, Inc.

Prue, Sally. Big Bad Troll. Woodward, Jonathan, illus. 2016. (Reading Ladder Level 2 Ser.). (ENG.). 48p. (gr. k-2). pap. 4.99 *(978-1-4052-7825-6(0),* Reading Ladder) Farshore GBR. Dist: HarperCollins Pubs.

Publications International Ltd. Staff. Disney Adventure Look & Find. 2013. (gr. 1-3). 7.98 *(978-1-4127-7146-7(3),* 1412771463) Phoenix International Publications, Inc.

Publications International Ltd. Staff, creator. Barbie as the Island Princess. 2007. (Play-A-Sound Bks.). (Illus.). 9.98 *(978-1-4127-7413-0(6))* Publications International, Ltd.

Publications International Ltd. Staff, ed. Disney Princess: Cinderella. 2008. (J). 12.98 *(978-1-4127-8475-7(1))* Publications International, Ltd.

Puchner, Willy. ABC of Fantastic Princes. 2015. (ENG., Illus.). 64p. (J). (gr. -1-2). 19.95 *(978-0-7358-4198-7(5))* North-South Bks., Inc.

Quinn, Jordan. The Bard & the Beast. McPhillips, Robert, illus. 2015. (Kingdom of Wrenly Ser.: 9). (ENG.). 128p. (J). (gr. k-4). pap. 6.99 *(978-1-4814-4396-8(8),* Little Simon) Little Simon.

—The False Fairy. McPhillips, Robert, illus. 2016. (Kingdom of Wrenly Ser.: 11). (ENG.). 128p. (J). (gr. k-4). pap. 6.99 *(978-1-4814-8586-9(5),* Little Simon) Little Simon.

—Let the Games Begin! McPhillips, Robert, illus. 2015. (Kingdom of Wrenly Ser.: 7). (ENG.). 128p. (J). (gr. k-4). pap. 6.99 *(978-1-4814-2379-3(7),* Little Simon) Little Simon.

—The Lost Stone. McPhillips, Robert, illus. 2014. (Kingdom of Wrenly Ser.: 1). (ENG.). 128p. (J). (gr. k-4). pap. 6.99 *(978-1-4424-9690-3(8),* Little Simon) Little Simon.

—The Lost Stone. 2014. (Kingdom of Wrenly Ser.: 1). lib. bdg. 16.00 *(978-0-606-35443-1(3))* Turtleback.

—The Pegasus Quest. McPhillips, Robert, illus. 2016. (Kingdom of Wrenly Ser.: 10). (ENG.). 128p. (J). (gr. k-4). pap. 6.99 *(978-1-4814-5870-2(1),* Little Simon) Little Simon.

—The Scarlet Dragon. McPhillips, Robert, illus. 2014. (Kingdom of Wrenly Ser.: 2). (ENG.). 128p. (J). (gr. k-4). pap. 6.99 *(978-1-4424-9693-4(2),* Little Simon) Little Simon.

—The Scarlet Dragon. 2014. (Kingdom of Wrenly Ser.: 2). lib. bdg. 16.00 *(978-0-606-35444-8(1))* Turtleback.

—Sea Monster! McPhillips, Robert, illus. 2014. (Kingdom of Wrenly Ser.: 3). (ENG.). 128p. (J). (gr. k-4). pap. 6.99 *(978-1-4814-0072-5(X),* Little Simon) Little Simon.

—The Secret World of Mermaids. McPhillips, Robert, illus. 2015. (Kingdom of Wrenly Ser.: 8). (ENG.). 128p. (J). (gr. k-4). pap. 6.99 *(978-1-4814-3122-4(6),* Little Simon) Little Simon.

—The Sorcerer's Shadow. McPhillips, Robert, illus. 2017. (Kingdom of Wrenly Ser.: 12). (ENG.). 128p. (J). (gr. k-4). 17.99 *(978-1-5344-0000-9(1));* pap. 6.99 *(978-1-4814-9999-6(8))* Little Simon. (Little Simon).

—The Thirteenth Knight. McPhillips, Robert, illus. 2018. (Kingdom of Wrenly Ser.: 13). (ENG.). 128p. (J). (gr. k-4). 17.99 *(978-1-5344-1275-0(1));* pap. 6.99 *(978-1-5344-1274-3(3))* Little Simon. (Little Simon).

—The Witch's Curse. McPhillips, Robert, illus. 2014. (Kingdom of Wrenly Ser.: 4). (ENG.). 128p. (J). (gr. k-4). pap. 6.99 *(978-1-4814-0075-6(4),* Little Simon) Little Simon.

Rattle, Alison. The Beloved. 2016. (ENG.). 304p. (YA). (gr. 11). pap. 12.99 *(978-1-4714-0379-8(3))* Bonnier Publishing GBR. Dist: Independent Pubs. Group.

Ray, Michelle. Falling for Hamlet. 2012. (ENG.). 368p. (YA). (gr. 10-17). pap. 19.99 *(978-0-316-10161-5(3),* Poppy) Little, Brown Bks. for Young Readers.

Redwine, C. J. The Blood Spell. (Ravenspire Ser.: 4). (ENG.). 448p. (YA). (gr. 8). 2020. pap. 10.99 *(978-0-06-265302-4(4))* 2019. 17.99 *(978-0-06-265301-7(6))* HarperCollins Pubs. (Balzer & Bray).

Reeder, Marilou. The Daring Prince Dashing. West, Karl, illus. 2015. (ENG.). 32p. (J). (gr. -1-k). 16.99 *(978-1-63450-161-3(6),* Sky Pony Pr.) Skyhorse Publishing Co., Inc.

RH Disney. The Princess & the Frog Little Golden Book (Disney Princess & the Frog) RH Disney, illus. 2009. (Little Golden Book Ser.). (ENG., Illus.). 24p. (J). (gr. -1-2). 5.99 *(978-0-7364-2628-2(0),* Golden/Disney) Random Hse. Children's Bks.

Rhodes, Morgan. Crystal Storm: A Falling Kingdoms Novel. (Falling Kingdoms Ser.: 5). (Illus.). (YA). (gr. 7). 2017. 416p. pap. 11.99 *(978-1-59514-823-0(X))* 2016. 368p. 18.99 *(978-1-59514-822-3(1))* Penguin Young Readers Group. (Razorbill).

—Gathering Darkness: A Falling Kingdoms Novel. 2015. (Falling Kingdoms Ser.: 3). 448p. (YA). (gr. 7). 11.99 *(978-1-59514-706-6(3),* Razorbill) Penguin Young Readers Group.

—Immortal Reign: A Falling Kingdoms Novel. 2018. (Falling Kingdoms Ser.: 6). (YA). (gr. 7). 416p. pap. 11.99 *(978-1-59514-825-4(6));* 400p. 18.99 *(978-1-59514-824-7(8))* Penguin Young Readers Group. (Razorbill).

Rigaud, Debbie. Truly Madly Royally. 2019. (ENG.). 304p. (YA). (gr. 7-7). pap. 9.99 *(978-1-338-33272-8(4))* Scholastic, Inc.

Riggs, Kate. Princes & Princesses. 2013. (Illus.). 24p. (J). 25.65 *(978-1-60818-243-5(6),* Creative Education) Creative Co., The.

Riley, Analynn. Legend of the Mountains & the Valleys: The Nine Gifts of Theodosia, the Final Question, Keneim's Quest, Yedda Sings. 2013. 152p. (J). (gr. 4-6). 30.95 *(978-1-4497-8372-3(4));* pap. 13.95 *(978-1-4497-8371-6(6))* Author Solutions, LLC. (WestBow Pr.).

Riley, Kana. The Princess & the Wise Woman. Williams, Jenny, illus. 2012. (ENG.). 24p. (J). (gr. k-2). pap. 6.97 *(978-0-8136-2371-9(5),* Modern Curriculum Pr.) Savvas Learning Co.

Rios, Yuri M. The Kingdom of Ice. Rios, Margarita, tr. 2012. 26p. pap. 9.99 *(978-1-61897-223-1(5),* Strategic Bk. Publishing) Strategic Book Publishing & Rights Agency (SBPRA).

Robin, Ink & Rivard, Joanna. A Real Prince Is Hard to Find: A Modern Fairy Tale. 2013. (ENG., Illus.). 32p. (J). (gr. -1-3). 16.99 *(978-1-61963-215-8(2),* 9781619632158, Bloomsbury USA Childrens) Bloomsbury Publishing USA.

Robinson, Hilary. Beauty & the Pea. Sanfilippo, Simona, illus. 2013. (ENG.). 32p. (J). *(978-0-7787-1155-1(2))* Crabtree Publishing Co.

Rogerson, Margaret. An Enchantment of Ravens. (ENG., Illus.). (YA). (gr. 9). 2018. 320p. pap. 12.99 *(978-1-4814-9759-6(6))* 2017. 304p. 19.99 *(978-1-4814-9758-9(8))* McElderry, Margaret K. Bks. (McElderry, Margaret K. Bks.).

Roscoe, Charlie. The Red Prince. Cole, Tom Clohosy, illus. 2016. (ENG.). 32p. (J). (-k). 16.99 *(978-0-7636-8912-4(2),* Templar) Candlewick Pr.

Rutkoski, Marie. The Cabinet of Wonders: The Kronos Chronicles: Book I. 2013. (Kronos Chronicles Ser.: 1). (ENG.). 288p. (J). (gr. 5-9). pap. 21.99 *(978-1-250-01804-5(8),* 900087537) Square Fish.

—The Celestial Globe: The Kronos Chronicles: Book II. 2013. (Kronos Chronicles Ser.: 2). (ENG.). 320p. (J). (gr. 5-9). pap. 23.99 *(978-1-250-02732-0(2),* 900098304) Square Fish.

Ryan, Rob. The Invisible Kingdom. 2016. (Invisible Kingdom Trilogy Ser.). (ENG., Illus.). 64p. (J). 19.95 *(978-1-56656-077-1(2),* Crocodile Bks.) Interlink Publishing Group, Inc.

Saint-Exupery, Antoine De. The Little Prince. Adreani, Manuela, illus. 2018. (ENG.). 80p. (J). (gr. 3). 16.95 *(978-88-544-1254-5(6))* White Star Publishers ITA. Dist: Sterling Publishing Co., Inc.

Saint-Exupéry, Antoine de. Il Piccolo Principe. Ediz. Illustrata. (ITA.). pap. 17.95 *(978-88-452-4741-5(4))* Fabbri Editori - RCS Libri ITA. Dist: Distribooks, Inc.

Saint-exupery, Antoine De. El Principito / the Little Prince. Carril, Bonifacio Del, tr. 2016. (SPA., 96p. (J). (gr. 5-12). Illus.). 20.95 *(978-84-7888-640-1(0));* pap. 8.95 *(978-84-9838-149-8(5))* Publicaciones y Ediciones Salamandra, S.A. ESP. Dist: Penguin Random Hse. LLC.

Saint-Exupéry, Antoine de. El Principito (edición oficial en tapa blanda con solapas) 2016. (SPA.). 96p. (J). (gr. 5-12). pap. 11.95 *(978-84-7888-719-4(9))* Publicaciones y Ediciones Salamandra, S.A. ESP. Dist: Penguin Random Hse. LLC.

Salisbury, Melinda. The Sin Eater's Daughter (Unabridged Edition), 1 vol. unabr. ed. 2015. (ENG.). 2p. (J). (gr. 9). audio compact disk 39.99 *(978-0-545-83830-6(4))* Scholastic, Inc.

Sanderson, Ruth. The Enchanted Wood. 2016. (Ruth Sanderson Collection). (ENG., Illus.). 32p. (J). (gr. 1-2). 17.95 *(978-1-56656-057-3(8),* Crocodile Bks.) Interlink Publishing Group, Inc.

Schlitt, Jayme & Schlitt, Ron. Rags, Riches & the Robe. 2010. 32p. 17.25 *(978-1-4269-4666-0(X))* Trafford Publishing.

Schnee, Silke. Prince Noah & the School Pirates. Sistig, Heike, illus. 2016. (Prince Noah Book Ser.). (ENG.). 32p. (J). 16.00 *(978-0-87486-765-7(7))* Plough Publishing Hse.

—The Prince Who Was Just Himself. Sistig, Heike, illus. 2015. (Prince Noah Book Ser.). 32p. (J). (gr. -1-4). 16.00 *(978-0-87486-682-7(0))* Plough Publishing Hse.

Scieszka, Jon. The Frog Prince. Johnson, Steve, illus. 2014. 32p. pap. 7.00 *(978-1-61003-314-5(0))* Center for the Collaborative Classroom.

—The Frog Prince, Continued. 2003. (Live Oak Readalong Ser.). (Illus.). (J). 25.95 incl. audio *(978-1-59112-229-6(5));* 28.95 incl. audio compact disk *(978-1-59112-515-0(4))* Live Oak Media.

—The Frog Prince, Continued. Johnson, Steve, illus. 2003. pap. 39.95 incl. audio compact disk *(978-1-59112-522-8(7))* Live Oak Media.

—The Frog Prince, Continued, 4 bks. 2003. (Live Oak Readalong Ser.). (J). pap. 37.95 incl. audio *(978-1-59112-230-2(9))* Live Oak Media.

Scott, Jeff. Becoming the King: Where's my Father? 2006. 222p. (J). per. 17.95 *(978-0-9787624-0-7(1))* TDO Enterprises.

Seredy, Kate. The Chestry Oak. 2015. (Illus.). 253p. (J). pap. 12.95 *(978-1-930900-81-3(3))* Purple Hse. Pr.

Sharp, Laura. The Key Prince. 2012. 24p. pap. 24.95 *(978-1-4626-8959-0(0))* America Star Bks.

Shepherd, Megan. Midnight Beauties. 2019. (Grim Lovelies Ser.). (ENG.). 448p. (YA). (gr. 9). 17.99 *(978-1-328-81190-5(5),* 1688554, Clarion Bks.) HarperCollins Pubs.

Shirer, Priscilla & Detwiler, Gina. The Prince Warriors & the Unseen Invasion. 2016. (Prince Warriors Ser.). (ENG., Illus.). 304p. (J). (gr. 3-7). 12.99 *(978-1-4336-9020-4(9),* 005777486, B&H Kids) B&H Publishing Group.

Sierra, JulieAnn. Legacy & the Dark Prince, 1 vol. 2009. 209p. pap. 24.95 *(978-1-61582-693-3(9))* America Star Bks.

Skye, Evelyn. The Crown's Game. 2017. (Crown's Game Ser.: 1). (ENG.). 432p. (YA). (gr. 8). pap. 9.99 *(978-0-06-242259-0(6),* Balzer & Bray) HarperCollins Pubs.

—The Crown's Game. 2017. (Crown's Game Ser.: bk.1). (ENG.). (YA). lib. bdg. 20.85 *(978-0-606-39645-5(4))* Turtleback.

Smith, Earl. Mainu & the Prince of Bakara: And Other Stories from Africa. 2012. (Illus.). 120p. (YA). (gr. 3-7). pap. 14.95 *(978-1-893731-04-2(9),* Mandolin Hse.) Kush Univ. Pr.

Smith, Nerissia. Prince de'Mario's Adventure, 1 vol. Dartes, Staci, illus. 2009. 29p. pap. 24.95 *(978-1-61582-972-9(5))* America Star Bks.

Smith, Sindy. Indy the Unicorn Prince. Smith, Sindy, illus. 2012. (Illus.). 46p. 29.95 *(978-1-4626-9864-6(6))* America Star Bks.

—Indy the Unicorn Prince. 2012. 48p. pap. 24.95 (978-1-4626-7519-7(0)) America Star Bks.
Sonneveld, Stephen. The Prince of Destiny. 2007. 56p. pap. 30.50 (978-0-615-16784-8(5)) Splendid Torch.
Springer, Nancy. The Oddling Prince. 2018. (ENG.). 288p. pap. 15.95 (978-1-61696-289-0(5), 1f718c3b-b6fe-4af0-bf7d-93daec670fa0) Tachyon Pubns.
Stanley, Diane. Bella at Midnight. Ibatoulline, Bagram, illus. 2007. (ENG.). 304p. (J). (gr. 3-7). pap. 7.99 (978-0-06-077575-9(0), HarperCollins) HarperCollins Pubs.
—The Chosen Prince. 2015. (ENG.). 368p. (J). (gr. 3-7). 16.99 (978-0-06-224897-8(9), HarperCollins) HarperCollins Pubs.
Stockham, Jess, illus. The Princess & the Pea. 2010. (Flip-Up Fairy Tales Ser.). 24p. (J). (gr. -1-2). (978-1-84643-332-0(0)) Child's Play International Ltd.
Styles, Walker. Something Smells Fishy. Whitehouse, Ben, illus. 2016. (Rider Woofson Ser.: 2). (ENG.). 128p. (J). (gr. k-4). 16.99 (978-1-4814-5742-2(X)); pap. 5.99 (978-1-4814-5741-5(1)) Little Simon. (Little Simon).
—Something Smells Fishy. 2016. (Rider Woofson Ser.: 2). lib. bdg. 16.00 (978-0-606-38263-2(1)) Turtleback.
Surette, Janet H. The Prince & the Gift: A Tale of True Beauty. 2010. 44p. pap. 14.95 (978-1-4497-0662-3(2), WestBow Pr.) Author Solutions, LLC.
Teis, Kyra. The Magic Flute, 1 vol. Teis, Kyra, illus. 2008. (ENG., Illus.). 32p. (J). (gr. k-9). 17.95 (978-1-59572-058-0(8)) Star Bright Bks., Inc.
Testa, Maggie. Daniel Plays Ball. 2014. (Daniel Tiger's Neighborhood Ready-To-Read Ser.). lib. bdg. 13.55 (978-0-606-36114-9(6)) Turtleback.
Thomas, Rhiannon. A Wicked Thing. (ENG.). (YA). (gr. 9). 2016. 368p. pap. 9.99 (978-0-06-230354-7(6)) 2015. 352p. 17.99 (978-0-06-230353-0(8)) HarperCollins Pubs. (HarperTeen).
Ting, Renee & Dulemba, Elizabeth O., illus. The Prince's Diary, 1 vol. 2005. (Cinderella Ser.). (ENG.). 32p. (J). (gr. 1-4). 16.95 (978-1-885008-27-5(9), leelowshens, Shen's Bks.) Lee & Low Bks., Inc.
Tish, Aunty. Kiddiwink Kingdom. 2006. (Illus.). 58p. (J). per. 19.95 (978-1-59800-587-5(1)) Outskirts Pr., Inc.
Toybox Innovations, creator. Disney's Enchanted. 2007. (Disney's Read along Collection). (Illus.). 24p. (J). (gr. -1-3). pap. (978-0-7634-2197-7(9)) Walt Disney Records.
Travels with the Little Prince (Tabbed Board Book) 2015. (Little Prince Ser.). (ENG., Illus.). 10p. (J). (— 1). bds. 7.99 (978-0-544-70901-0(2), 1628912, Clarion Bks.) HarperCollins Pubs.
Turner, Megan Whalen. A Conspiracy of Kings. (Queen's Thief Ser.: 4). (ENG.). (YA). (gr. 8). 2017. 368p. pap. 10.99 (978-0-06-264299-8(5)) 2011. 352p. pap. 7.99 (978-0-06-187095-8(1)) 2010. 336p. 17.99 (978-0-06-187093-4(5)) HarperCollins Pubs. (Greenwillow Bks.).
—A Conspiracy of Kings, 6 vols. 2010. (Queen's Thief Ser.: BK.4). (YA). 88.75 (978-1-4498-4573-5(8)); 1.25 (978-1-4498-4574-2(6)); (ENG.). 230.75 (978-1-4498-4569-8(X)); (ENG.). 73.75 (978-1-4498-4570-4(3));No. 4. (ENG.). 90.75 (978-1-4498-4571-1(1)) Recorded Bks., Inc.
Twain, Mark, pseud. The Prince & the Pauper. (J). 19.95 (978-0-8488-0849-5(5)) Amereon Ltd.
—The Prince & the Pauper. (J). 9.95 (978-1-56156-311-1(0)) Kidsbooks, LLC.
—The Prince & the Pauper. 2006. (Aladdin Classics Ser.). (ENG.). 352p. (J). pap. 8.99 (978-1-4169-2805-8(7), Aladdin) Simon & Schuster Children's Publishing.
Twain, Mark, pseud & Clemens, Samuel L. The Prince & the Pauper. 2013. (Works of Mark Twain). 425p. reprint ed. lthr. 79.00 (978-0-7812-1120-8(4)) Reprint Services Corp.
Twain, Mark, pseud & Stead, Philip C. The Purloining of Prince Oleomargarine. Stead, Erin, illus. 160p. (J). (gr. 3-7). 2021. pap. 9.99 (978-0-593-30382-5(2), Yearling) 2017. 24.99 (978-0-553-52322-5(8), Doubleday Bks. for Young Readers) Random Hse. Children's Bks.
Valentino, Serena. Beast Within, the-Villains, Book 2. 2014. (Villains Ser.). (ENG., Illus.). 224p. (YA). (gr. 7-12). 17.99 (978-1-4231-5912-4(8), Disney Press Books) Disney Publishing Worldwide.
Vaugelade, Anais. The War. Rouffiac, Marie-Christine & Streissguth, Thomas, trs. from FRE. Vaugelade, Anais, illus. 2005. (Picture Bks.). (Illus.). 32p. (J). (gr. k-2). 15.25 (978-1-57505-562-6(7)) Lerner Publishing Group.
Viguié, Debbie & Viguié, Debbie. Violet Eyes. 2010. (Once upon a Time Ser.). (ENG.). 224p. (YA). (gr. 7-18). mass mkt. 7.99 (978-1-4169-8676-8(6), Simon Pulse) Simon Pulse.
Wakeman, Lars. Prince Harry the Hairy Prince: A hairy fairy Tale. 2011. 24p. (gr. -1). pap. 12.56 (978-1-4269-6304-9(1)) Trafford Publishing.
Wallace Ii, James C. & Wallace, Amanda D. The Emerald Slippers of Oz. 2013. 156p. pap. 14.99 (978-0-578-12511-4(0)) Scientia Est Vox Pr.
Wang, Jen. The Prince & the Dressmaker. 2018. (ENG., Illus.). 288p. (YA). 25.99 (978-1-250-15985-4(7), 900185795); pap. 17.99 (978-1-62672-363-4(X), 900154833) Roaring Brook Pr. (First Second Bks.).
Ward, Nick. The Tadpole Prince. 2003. (Illus.). 32p. (YA). (978-1-84365-016-4(9), Pavilion Children's Books) Pavilion Bks.
Watt, Fiona. That's Not My Prince. Wells, Rachel, illus. 2013. (Usborne Touchy-Feely Board Bks.). (ENG.). 10p. (J). 9.99 (978-0-7945-2838-6(4), Usborne) EDC Publishing.
Westerfeld, Scott. Behemoth. Thompson, Keith, illus. (Leviathan Trilogy Ser.). (ENG.). (YA). (gr. 7). 2011. 512p. pap. 14.99 (978-1-4169-7176-4(9)) 2010. 496p. 18.99 (978-1-4169-7175-7(0)) Simon Pulse. (Simon Pulse).
—Behemoth. l.t. ed. 2010. (Leviathan Trilogy: Bk. 2). (ENG., Illus.). 540p. 23.99 (978-1-4104-3066-3(9)) Thorndike Pr.
—Behemoth. 2011. (Leviathan Ser.: 2). lib. bdg. 24.50 (978-0-606-22407-9(6)) Turtleback.
—Goliath, 8 vols. 2011. (YA). 124.75 (978-1-4618-0613-4(5)); 305.75 (978-1-4618-0618-9(6)); 122.75 (978-1-4618-0614-1(3)); 1.25 (978-1-4640-3062-8(6)); 122.75 (978-1-4618-0617-2(8)) Recorded Bks., Inc.
—Goliath. Thompson, Keith, illus. (Leviathan Trilogy Ser.). (ENG.). (YA). (gr. 7). 2012. 576p. pap. 14.99 (978-1-4169-7178-8(5)) 2011. 560p. 24.99 (978-1-4169-7177-1(7)) Simon Pulse. (Simon Pulse).
—Goliath. 2012. (Leviathan Ser.: 3). lib. bdg. 24.50 (978-0-606-26355-9(1)) Turtleback.
—Leviathan. Thompson, Keith, illus. (Leviathan Trilogy Ser.). (ENG.). (YA). (gr. 7-18). 2010. 464p. pap. 14.99 (978-1-4169-7174-0(2)) 2009. 448p. 24.99 (978-1-4169-7173-3(4)) Simon Pulse. (Simon Pulse).
—Leviathan. l.t. ed. 2010. (Leviathan Trilogy: Bk. 1). (ENG.). 525p. 23.95 (978-1-4104-2572-0(X)) Thorndike Pr.
—Leviathan (Boxed Set) Leviathan; Behemoth; Goliath. Thompson, Keith, illus. 2012. (Leviathan Trilogy Ser.). (ENG.). 1552p. (YA). (gr. 7). pap. 44.99 (978-1-4424-8377-4(6), Simon Pulse) Simon Pulse.
Weston Woods Staff, creator. Harold's Fairy Tale. 2011. 18.95 (978-0-439-72704-4(9)); 38.75 (978-0-439-72706-8(5)) Weston Woods Studios, Inc.
—James Marshall's Cinderella. 2011. 38.75 (978-0-439-84886-2(5)) Weston Woods Studios, Inc.
White, Lia. Alkis. 2010. (ENG., Illus.). 106p. pap. (978-1-84748-715-5(7)) Athena Pr.
Whitmore, Gary. Prince Luna & the Space Dreamers. 2011. (ENG.). 204p. pap. 8.50 (978-1-4565-8438-2(3)) CreateSpace Independent Publishing Platform.
Wiggins, Bethany. The Dragon's Curse (a Transference Novel) 2018. (Transference Trilogy Ser.: 2). 336p. (YA). (gr. 7). 17.99 (978-0-399-55101-7(8), Crown Books For Young Readers) Random Hse. Children's Bks.
Wilde, Oscar. The Happy Prince & Other Tales. Charles Robinson, illus. 2012. 84p. pap. 3.47 (978-1-60386-460-2(1), Watchmaker Publishing) Wexford College Pr.
—Le Prince Hereux. (FRE.). (J). pap. 15.95 (978-2-07-051629-2(6)) Gallimard, Editions FRA. Dist: Distribooks, Inc.
Williams, Allix Elise. The Adventures of Prince Thaddeus: The Glamorous Guest. 2010. 56p. pap. 11.49 (978-1-4520-5437-7(1)) AuthorHouse.
Willis, Jeanne. Prince Charmless. Ross, Tony, illus. 2014. (ENG.). 32p. (J). (gr. -1-k). pap. 14.99 (978-1-84939-778-0(3)) Andersen Pr. GBR. Dist: Independent Pubs. Group.
Wilson, Diane. To Ride the Gods' Own Stallion. 2010. 256p. (J). (gr. 4-10). pap. 11.99 (978-1-4022-4028-7(7)) Sourcebooks, Inc.
Wilson, Tony. The Princess & the Packet of Frozen Peas, 1 vol. Degennaro, Sue, illus. 2018. (ENG.). 32p. (J). (gr. -1-3). pap. 7.95 (978-1-68263-051-8(X)) Peachtree Publishing Co. Inc.
—The Princess & the Packet of Frozen Peas. 2018. (J). lib. bdg. 18.40 (978-0-606-41012-0(0)) Turtleback.
Wisher, Mark. Don't kiss the Prince. 2010. 33p. pap. 21.50 (978-1-4457-7238-7(8)) Lulu Pr., Inc.
Wonlah, Ivis. King Ola's Pepper Jar. 2012. 28p. pap. 16.09 (978-1-4669-1600-5(1)) Trafford Publishing.
Wu, Nicholas. The Princess & the Pea, 1 vol. rev. ed. 2013. (Literary Text Ser.). (ENG., Illus.). 20p. (gr. 1-2). 7.99 (978-1-4333-5489-2(6)) Teacher Created Materials, Inc.
—The Princess & the Pea: A Retelling of Hans Christian Andersen's Story, 1 vol. rev. ed. 2013. (Literary Text Ser.). (ENG., Illus.). 20p. (J). (gr. 1-2). lib. bdg. 15.96 (978-1-4807-1145-7(4)) Teacher Created Materials, Inc.
Wyss, Tyan. The Solitaire Prince. 2006. 168p. (YA). per. 12.95 (978-1-58939-906-8(4)) Virtualbookworm.com Publishing, Inc.
Yun, Monokuro. The Sign: A Novel. 2019. 188p. (gr. 7-12). pap. 14.95 (978-1-64279-116-7(4)) Morgan James Publishing.

PRINCES AND PRINCESSES

see Princes; Princesses

PRINCESSES

Abdo, Kenny. Meghan Markle. 2018. (Star Biographies Ser.). (ENG., Illus.). 24p. (J). (gr. 2-8). lib. bdg. 31.36 (978-1-5321-2546-1(1), 30101, Abdo Zoom-Fly) ABDO Publishing Co.
Ahrens, Niki. Disney Princess Celebrations: Party Planning the Princess Way. 2020. (J). (978-1-5415-7798-5(1)) Lerner Publishing Group.
Antal, Lara. Princess Diana: Royal Activist & Fashion Icon, 1 vol. 2016. (Leading Women Ser.). (ENG., Illus.). 128p. (YA). (gr. 7-7). 41.64 (978-1-5026-1987-7(3), c1402693-8723-47cb-80ef-2b7d694bca74) Cavendish Square Publishing LLC.
Au, May Parker. Princess Huilua & Kamapuaa. 2007.Tr. of Ke Kamalii Wahine o Huilua a me Kamapuaa. (ENG & HAW.). (J). lib. bdg. (978-0-9773495-4-8(3)) Na Kamalei Koolauloa Early Education Program.
Bingham, Hettie. Real-Life Stories: Kate, Duchess of Cambridge. 2018. (Real-Life Stories Ser.). (ENG.). 32p. (J). (gr. 4-6). pap. 12.99 (978-0-7502-8946-7(5), Wayland) Hachette Children's Group GBR. Dist: Hachette Bk. Group.
Boothroyd, Jennifer. Disney Princess Top 10s: From Ariel to Rapunzel. 2019. (My Top 10 Disney Ser.). (ENG., Illus.). 32p. (J). (gr. 1-4). pap. 8.99 (978-1-5415-4661-5(X), Lerner Pubns.) Lerner Publishing Group.
Cabot, Meg. Princess Lessons. McLaren, Chesley, illus. 2003. (Princess Diaries Guidebook Ser.). (ENG.). 144p. (YA). (gr. 8-18). 15.99 (978-0-06-052677-1(7), HarperTeen) HarperCollins Pubs.
Chapman, Kelly. Princess with a Purpose. Lyon, Tammie, illus. ldr.'s ed. 2009. pap. 12.99 (978-0-7369-2743-7(3)) Harvest Hse. Pubs.
Custance, Petrice. Kate Middleton. 2018. (Superstars! Ser.). (ENG., Illus.). 32p. (J). (gr. 4-4). (978-0-7787-4831-1(6)); pap. (978-0-7787-4846-5(4)) Crabtree Publishing Co.
Davidson, Susanna & Daynes, Katie. Little Princess Treasury. McNicholas, Shelagh & Cascio, Maria Cristina Lo, illus. 2006. (English Heritage Ser.). 96p. (J). 7.99 (978-0-7945-1442-6(1), Usborne) EDC Publishing.
Diemer, Lauren & Kissock, Heather. Prince William & Kate Middleton. 2013. (J). (978-1-62127-392-9(X)) Weigl Pubs., Inc.
Eckel, Jessie, illus. How to Be a Princess in 7 Days or Less. 2005. (How to be A Ser.). 32p. (J). (gr. 3-5). 12.95 (978-0-7534-5921-8(3), Kingfisher) Roaring Brook Pr.
English Heritage Staff. My Life as a Princess. 2005. (Illus.). 32p. pap. 19.95 (978-1-85074-984-4(1)) Historic England Publishing GBR. Dist: Casemate Academic.
Flowerpot Press, creator. Princesses Coloring Book. 2013. (Sockheadz Ser.). (ENG., Illus.). 72p. (J). (gr. -1-3). 4.99 (978-1-77093-543-3(6)) Flowerpot Pr.
Gamble, Adam & Jasper, Mark. Good Night Princesses. Gardner, Louise, illus. 2016. (Good Night Our World Ser.). (ENG.). 20p. (J). (— 1). bds. 9.95 (978-1-60219-225-6(1)) Good Night Bks.
Greenwall, Jessica. First Sticker Book Princesses. Finn, Rebecca, illus. 2013. (First Sticker Bks). 16p. (J). pap. 6.99 (978-0-7945-3357-1(4), Usborne) EDC Publishing.
Grimm, Jacob & Grimm, Wilhelm. The Twelve Dancing Princesses. Mcclintock, Barbara, illus. 2017. (J). (978-0-439-89402-9(6), Scholastic Pr.) Scholastic, Inc.
Jaycox, Jaclyn. A Princess Alphabet: The ABCs of Royalty! Eriza, Gustavo, illus. 2016. (Alphabet Connection Ser.). (ENG.). 32p. (J). (gr. -1-2). lib. bdg. 27.99 (978-1-4795-6885-7(6), 128864, Picture Window Bks.) Capstone.
Kats, Jewel. The Princess & the Ruby: An Autism Fairy Tale. Kinra, Richa, illus. 2013. 42p. 26.95 (978-1-61599-193-8(X)); (J). (gr. 3-7). pap. 16.95 (978-1-61599-175-4(1)) Loving Healing Pr., Inc.
Kenney, Karen Latchana. Real-Life Princesses. 2019. (Bumba Books (r) — Real-Life Royalty Ser.). (ENG., Illus.). 24p. (J). (gr. -1-1). pap. 8.99 (978-1-5415-7358-1(7), c3a25eac-106d-4c34-ad80-0cdf8be8501f); lib. bdg. 26.65 (978-1-5415-5729-1(8), f2e6cd8d-4ee9-4d5e-af0c-6b3d40a5a431) Lerner Publishing Group. (Lerner Pubns.).
Krajnik, Elizabeth. Meghan Markle: American Royal, 1 vol. 2018. (Junior Biographies Ser.). (ENG.). 24p. (J). (gr. 3-4). pap. 10.35 (978-1-9785-0589-6(2), 83d09069-cf23-48a5-b192-17b053d16f01); lib. bdg. 24.27 (978-1-9785-0591-9(4), 5a341e21-227d-4c35-8d92-8b804d37ab4e) Enslow Publishing, LLC.
Labrecque, Ellen & Who HQ. Who Was Princess Diana? Hoare, Jerry, illus. 2017. (Who Was? Ser.). 112p. (J). (gr. 3-7). 5.99 (978-0-448-48855-4(8), Penguin Workshop) Penguin Young Readers Group.
Lajiness, Katie. Kate Middleton, 1 vol. 2015. (Big Buddy Pop Biographies Ser.). (ENG., Illus.). 32p. (J). (gr. 2-5). 34.21 (978-1-68078-055-0(7), 19037, Big Buddy Bks.) ABDO Publishing Co.
Lee, Sally. Princes & Princesses, 1 vol. 2013. (Royalty Ser.). (ENG.). 24p. (J). (gr. -1-2). lib. bdg. 27.32 (978-1-62065-124-7(6), 120817, Capstone Pr.) Capstone.
Maloof, Torrey. Mary Musgrove: Bringing People Together. rev. ed. 2016. (Social Studies: Informational Text Ser.). (ENG., Illus.). 32p. (gr. 2-4). pap. 10.99 (978-1-4938-2557-8(7)) Teacher Created Materials, Inc.
McDaniel, Sarita. Princesses, 1 vol. 2019. (Meet the Royals Ser.). (ENG.). 24p. (gr. 1-2). pap. 10.35 (978-1-9785-1189-7(2), d55f67c3-ee52-45de-9320-62cebbfefa63) Enslow Publishing, LLC.
McDonnell, Peter. The Last Princess. 2005. (Illus.). 16p. (978-0-7367-2910-9(0)) Zaner-Bloser, Inc.
Miller, Eileen Rudisill. Princess Coloring Book. 2012. (Dover Fantasy Coloring Bks.). (ENG.). 32p. (J). (gr. -1-3). pap. 3.99 (978-0-486-49917-8(0), 499170) Dover Pubns., Inc.
Morley, Jacqueline. Do You Want to Be an Ancient Egyptian Princess? 2015. (Do You Want to Be... Ser.). (Illus.). 32p. (gr. 3-6). 28.50 (978-1-909645-33-2(8)) Book Hse. GBR. Dist: Black Rabbit Bks.
Owings, Lisa. Diana: The People's Princess, 1 vol. 2012. (Lives Cut Short Set 2 Ser.). (ENG.). 112p. (YA). (gr. 6-12). lib. bdg. 41.36 (978-1-61783-545-2(5), 11205, Essential Library) ABDO Publishing Co.
Pohl, Amelia E. Mary Musgrove: Georgia, My State Biographies. l.t. ed. 2008. (ENG., Illus.). 24p. (J). (gr. k-2). 22.60 (978-1-935077-02-2(3), Everett Pr.) State Standards Publishing, LLC.
Publications International Ltd. Staff, ed. Disney Princess: My Own Carriage. 2014. 12p. (J). bds. 12.98 (978-1-4508-7381-9(2), 66a3c624-31ec-4290-ae22-6fd5a90376b3) Phoenix International Publications, Inc.
Robinson, Michelle. Happy Birthday to You, Princess. Gausden, Vicki, illus. 2019. (ENG.). 32p. (J). pap. 6.99 (978-0-00-824221-3(6), HarperCollins Children's Bks.) HarperCollins Pubs. Ltd. GBR. Dist: HarperCollins Pubs.
Ryland Peters and Small Staff, creator. Now I Am a Princess. 2008. (ENG., Illus.). 48p. (978-1-84597-741-2(6)) Ryland Peters & Small.
Scholastic Editors. Princess Leia. 2016. (Backstories Ser.: Vol. 7). (ENG., Illus.). 128p. (J). (gr. 3-7). 16.00 (978-0-606-39146-7(0)) Turtleback.
Shirley, Rebekah Joy. I Want to Be a Princess, 1 vol. 2011. (Let's Play Dress Up Ser.). (ENG., Illus.). 24p. (J). (gr. 2-3). pap. 11.60 (978-1-61533-394-3(0), 512673ac-2f55-4932-9de4-071a431f0cfb, Windmill Bks.) Rosen Publishing Group, Inc., The.
Summers, Portia. Kate Middleton: Duchess of Cambridge, 1 vol. 2017. (Junior Biographies Ser.). (ENG., Illus.). 24p. (gr. 3-4). pap. 10.35 (978-0-7660-8781-1(6), d159fb85-35ae-4564-8f37-9c2882ba19cf); lib. bdg. 24.27 (978-0-7660-8672-2(0), f76c4301-d564-474e-ba07-1519728c1a0c) Enslow Publishing, LLC.
Timmons, Angie. Kate Middleton & Prince William, 1 vol. 2019. (Power Couples Ser.). (ENG.). 112p. (gr. 7-7). pap. 18.65 (978-1-5081-8884-1(X), 8c1b23b5-9e74-412b-9e2a-73d11cf6791f) Rosen Publishing Group, Inc., The.
Trussell-Cullen, Alan. Princess Diana. 2009. pap. 13.25 (978-1-60559-068-4(1)) Hameray Publishing Group, Inc.
Waldherr, Kris. Bad Princess: True Tales from Behind the Tiara. Waldherr, Kris, illus. 2018. (ENG., Illus.). 128p. (J). (gr. 4-7). 12.99 (978-1-338-04798-1(1), Scholastic Nonfiction) Scholastic, Inc.
Webster, Angela. In the Presence of a King. Mitchell, Jerica Webster, illus. 2012. (ENG.). 66p. pap. 28.99 (978-1-4685-5442-7(5)) AuthorHouse.
Woodworth, Viki. Princess Mazes. 2012. (Dover Kids Activity Books: Fantasy Ser.). (ENG.). 48p. (J). (gr. 1-4). pap. 4.99 (978-0-486-49058-8(0), 490580) Dover Pubns., Inc.
Yim Bridges, Shirin. Qutlugh Terkan Khatun of Kirman. Nguyen, Albert, illus. 2010. (Thinking Girl's Treasury of Real Princesses Ser.). (ENG.). 24p. (J). (gr. 3-8). 18.95 (978-0-9845098-3-6(6)) Goosebottom Bks. LLC.

PRINCESSES—FICTION

Abbott, Tony. The Hidden Stairs & the Magic Carpet. Jessell, Tim, illus. 2004. (Secrets of Droon Ser.: No. 1). 80p. (gr. 2-5). 15.00 (978-0-7569-3939-7(9)) Perfection Learning Corp.
Acton, Vanessa. Next in Line. 2018. (Suddenly Royal Ser.). (ENG.). 112p. (YA). (gr. 6-12). 26.65 (978-1-5415-2571-9(X), 2d11ff65-650a-44e8-88d7-645ec2e008b7, Darby Creek) Lerner Publishing Group.
Adeniyi, Bab. The Servant, the King, & the Princess. 2012. 28p. pap. 15.99 (978-1-4691-4989-9(3)) Xlibris Corp.
Adkinson, Gma Mary. Growing up with Princess Lizzy: Little Life Lessons. 2012. (ENG.). 50p. pap. 16.95 (978-1-4787-1993-9(1)) Outskirts Pr., Inc.
The Adventures of Marc John Jefferies: The Missing Princess. l.t. ed. 2004. (Illus.). 110p. (YA). per. (978-0-9747218-3-5(2), 100, Young Women Programming) Harper Kids Hse.
Aikins, Dave, illus. Dora Saves the Snow Princess. 2008. (Dora the Explorer Ser.: 27). (ENG.). 24p. (J). (gr. -1-2). pap. 3.99 (978-1-4169-5866-6(5), Simon Spotlight/Nickelodeon) Simon Spotlight/Nickelodeon.
Al-Zeheri, Ali. The Princess & the Gold. 2009. 32p. pap. 12.99 (978-1-4490-2091-0(7)) AuthorHouse.
Alexander. Phonic Comics: Princess School - Level 1. 2011. (ENG., Illus.). 24p. (J). (gr. 1-17). pap. 3.99 (978-1-60169-110-1(6)) Innovative Kids.
Alford, Wade. The Princess & the Golden Ring. 2011. 16p. 8.99 (978-1-4520-9132-7(3)) AuthorHouse.
Allchin, Rosalind. The Frog Princess. 2004. (Illus.). (J). (gr. k-3). spiral bd. (978-0-616-14557-9(8)) Canadian National Institute for the Blind/Institut National Canadien pour les Aveugles.
Allem, Jolyia. The Maiden & the Prince: A Tale of Devotion. 2009. 16p. pap. 8.75 (978-1-4490-2350-8(9)) AuthorHouse.
Alward, Amy. Going Viral. (Potion Diaries). (ENG., Illus.). 352p. (gr. 7). 2018. (J). pap. 11.99 (978-1-4814-4385-2(2)) 2017. (YA). 18.99 (978-1-4814-4384-5(4)) Simon & Schuster Bks. For Young Readers. (Simon & Schuster Bks. For Young Readers).
—Royal Tour. 2017. (Potion Diaries). (ENG., Illus.). 432p. (YA). (gr. 7). pap. 11.99 (978-1-4814-4382-1(8), Simon & Schuster Bks. For Young Readers) Simon & Schuster Bks. For Young Readers.
Amerikaner, Susan, et al. Disney Princess Storybook Collection. 2015. (Illus.). 300p. (J). (978-1-4847-5331-6(3), 1394934) Disney Publishing Worldwide.
Amin, Ahmed. The Mountains of Kohqaf. 2013. 88p. (gr. 4-6). pap. 11.25 (978-1-4907-0959-8(2)) Trafford Publishing.
Amirkhan, Michele. Princess Elian's Quest. 2008. 112p. 20.95 (978-0-595-50870-9(7)); pap. 10.95 (978-0-595-51400-7(6)) iUniverse, Inc.
Amore, Sandra. The Princess Who Lived on the 174th Floor. 2011. 58p. pap. 18.68 (978-1-4653-5854-7(4)) Xlibris Corp.
Anderson, Cassie. Extraordinary: a Story of an Ordinary Princess. 2019. (ENG., Illus.). 200p. (J). (gr. 3-7). pap. 12.99 (978-1-5067-1027-3(1), Dark Horse Books) Dark Horse Comics.
Andrews, Julie & Hamilton, Emma Walton. A Fairy Merry Christmas. 2012. (Passport to Reading Level 1 Ser.). (J). lib. bdg. 14.75 (978-0-606-26692-5(5)) Turtleback.
—A Spooky, Sparkly Halloween. 2016. (Very Fairy Princess Ser.). (J). lib. bdg. 16.00 (978-0-606-38317-2(4)) Turtleback.
—Valentines from the Heart. 2015. (Very Fairy Princess Ser.). (Illus.). (J). lib. bdg. 16.00 (978-0-606-37466-8(3)) Turtleback.
—The Very Fairy Princess: A Winter Wonderland Surprise. 2015. (Very Fairy Princess Ser.). (J). lib. bdg. 16.00 (978-0-606-37465-1(5)) Turtleback.
—The Very Fairy Princess: Teacher's Pet. 2013. (Passport to Reading Level 1 Ser.). (J). lib. bdg. 14.75 (978-0-606-31741-2(4)) Turtleback.
Andrews, Julie & Hamilton, Emma Walton. The Very Fairy Princess. Davenier, Christine, illus. 2010. (Very Fairy Princess Ser.). (ENG.). 32p. (J). (gr. -1-3). 18.99 (978-0-316-04050-1(9)) Little, Brown Bks. for Young Readers.
—The Very Fairy Princess: a Spooky, Sparkly Halloween. Davenier, Christine, illus. 2015. (ENG.). 32p. (J). (gr. -1-3). 18.00 (978-0-316-28304-5(5)) Little, Brown Bks. for Young Readers.
—The Very Fairy Princess Follows Her Heart. Davenier, Christine, illus. 2013. (Very Fairy Princess Ser.). (ENG.). 32p. (J). (gr. -1-3). 16.99 (978-0-316-18559-2(0)) Little, Brown Bks. for Young Readers.
—The Very Fairy Princess Sparkles in the Snow. Davenier, Christine, illus. 2013. (Very Fairy Princess Ser.). (ENG.). 32p. (J). (gr. -1-3). 18.00 (978-0-316-21963-1(0)) Little, Brown Bks. for Young Readers.
—The Very Fairy Princess: Teacher's Pet. Davenier, Christine, illus. 2013. (Passport to Reading Level 1 Ser.). (ENG.). 32p. (J). (gr. -1-3). 4.99 (978-0-316-21959-4(2)) Little, Brown Bks. for Young Readers.
Angelo, Linda. The Three Secrets of Happiness. 2012. (ENG.). 31p. (J). pap. 14.95 (978-1-4327-9349-4(7)) Outskirts Pr., Inc.
Angleberger, Tom. The Princess & the Pit Stop. Santat, Dan, illus. 2018. (ENG.). 48p. (J). (gr. k-2). 16.99 (978-1-4197-2848-8(2), 1123601, Abrams Bks. for Young Readers) Abrams, Inc.
anthony, chance. The Princess of Du'val. 2010. 36p. pap. 7.14 (978-0-557-03816-9(2)) Lulu Pr., Inc.
Argenta, Joan. The Wicked Princess Torment. 2009. (Illus.). 40p. pap. 16.99 (978-1-4389-4345-9(8)) AuthorHouse.
Arias, Carlos Ballesteros. The Magic Forest. 2006. (J). pap. 8.00 (978-0-8059-7022-7(3)) Dorrance Publishing Co., Inc.
Armstrong, Ashley Sage-Taylor. The Adventures of Starlight & Sunny: Book Four in the Adventures of Starlight & Sunny Series, ?Princesses Don't Need a Job !? How to Be an Indepen. 2013. 52p. pap. (978-1-927863-02-2(3)) Armstrong, Ashley.
Armstrong Nhp, Ashley Sage-Taylor. The Adventures of Starlight & Sunny: Book One in, the Adventures of Starlight & Sunny Series, ?the Princess Path?, How to Be True with

Good Deeds. 2013. 46p. pap. *(978-0-9919517-7-2(8))*
Armstrong, Ashley.
Aronson, Sarah. Halfway to Happily Ever after (the Wish List #3) 2018. (Wish List Ser.: 3). (ENG., Illus.). 192p. (J). (gr. 3-7). 14.99 *(978-0-545-94162-4(8),* Scholastic Pr.) Scholastic, Inc.
—Keep Calm & Sparkle on! (the Wish List #2) 2017. (Wish List Ser.: 2). (ENG.). 192p. (J). (gr. 3-7). 14.99 *(978-0-545-94159-4(8),* Scholastic Pr.) Scholastic, Inc.
Aryal, Kusum. The Magic Mermaid Girl. 2011. 36p. pap. *(978-1-4269-8836-3(2))* Trafford Publishing (UK) Ltd.
At Your Service. 2014. (Mix Ser.). (ENG., Illus.). 272p. (J). (gr. 4-8). pap. 7.99 *(978-1-4814-0283-5(8),* Aladdin) Simon & Schuster Children's Publishing.
Attaway-Young, Andrea & Lane Durbin, Deborah. The Secret Treasure - A Fairy Tale. 2010. (ENG.). 40p. 9.95 *(978-1-934363-70-6(7))* Zoe Life Christian Communications.
Auch, Mary Jane. The Princess & the Pizza. Auch, Herm, illus. 2003. (ENG.). 32p. (J). (gr. -1-3). 7.99 *(978-0-8234-1798-8(0))* Holiday Hse., Inc.
Auerbach, Annie. Cindy Big Hair: A Twisted (and Teased & Braided) Cinderella Story. Maxey, David, illus. 2005. 16p. (J). 12.95 *(978-1-58117-387-1(3),* Intervisual/Piggy Toes) Bendon, Inc.
Avery, et al. The Tale of Princess Fluffy & Prince Rupert. 2012. (ENG.). 28p. (J). pap. 19.99 *(978-1-4685-3594-5(3))* AuthorHouse.
Aveyard, Victoria. Cruel Crown. 2016. (Red Queen Novella Ser.). (ENG.). 208p. (YA). (gr. 8-12). pap. 15.99 *(978-0-06-243534-7(5),* HarperTeen) HarperCollins Pubs.
—Glass Sword. l.t. ed. 2016. (Red Queen Ser.: 2). 656p. 24.95 *(978-1-4104-8668-4(0))* Cengage Gale.
—Glass Sword. 2016. (CHI.). 448p. (YA). (gr. 8). pap. *(978-957-33-3248-0(5))* Crown Publishing Co., Ltd.
—Glass Sword. (Red Queen Ser.: 2). (ENG.). 464p. (YA). (gr. 8). 2018. pap. 14.99 *(978-0-06-231067-5(4))* 2016. 19.99 *(978-0-06-231066-8(6))* HarperCollins Pubs. (HarperTeen).
—Glass Sword. 2022. (YA). 40.00 ***(978-1-955876-26-1(6))*** LitJoy Crate.
—Glass Sword. 2018. (Red Queen Ser.: 2). (YA). lib. bdg. 24.50 *(978-0-606-41028-1(7))* Turtleback.
—King's Cage. 2017. (Red Queen Ser.: 3). (ENG., Illus.). 528p. (YA). (gr. 8). 19.99 *(978-0-06-231069-9(0),* HarperTeen) HarperCollins Pubs.
—Red Queen. l.t. ed. 2016. (Red Queen Ser.: 1). 562p. (YA). 24.95 *(978-1-4104-8669-1(9))* Cengage Gale.
—Red Queen. (Red Queen Ser.: 1). (YA). (gr. 8). 2016. (ENG.). 416p. pap. 12.99 *(978-0-06-231064-4(X))* 2015. (ENG.). 400p. 19.99 *(978-0-06-231063-7(1))* 2015. 400p. pap. 12.00 *(978-0-06-236271-1(2))* HarperCollins Pubs. (HarperTeen).
—Red Queen. 2023. (YA). 40.00 ***(978-1-955876-25-4(8))*** LitJoy Crate.
—Red Queen. 2016. (Red Queen Ser.: 1). 416p. lib. bdg. 22.10 *(978-0-606-38918-1(0))* Turtleback.
—Red Queen 2-Book Hardcover Box Set: Red Queen & Glass Sword. 2016. (Red Queen Ser.). (ENG.). 864p. (YA). (gr. 8). 37.98 *(978-0-06-256866-3(3),* HarperTeen) HarperCollins Pubs.
Award, Anna. Princess Tales. Davies, Kate, illus. 2017. (ENG.). 96p. (J). 15.00 *(978-1-84135-523-8(2))* Award Pubns. Ltd. GBR. Dist: Parkwest Pubns., Inc.
Ayaz, Huda. Freeze-Land: A New Beginning. 2013. 110p. pap. 11.99 *(978-1-4808-0267-4(0))* Archway Publishing.
AZ Books Staff. Cinderella. Zyl, Olga, ed. 2012. (Classic Fairy Tales Ser.). (ENG.). 10p. (J). (gr. -1-k). bds. 9.95 *(978-1-61889-007-8(7))* AZ Bks. LLC.
Baer, Jill. Just One of the Princes. 2014. (Sofia the First World of Reading Ser.). (Illus.). 32p. (J). lib. bdg. 13.55 *(978-0-606-35263-5(5))* Turtleback.
Baker, E. D. Dragon's Breath: Read-Along/Homework Pack, 6 vols. unabr. ed. 2005. (Frog Princess Ser.: 2). (SPA.). (J). (gr. 5-8). 78.75 *(978-1-4193-3563-1(4),* 42041) Recorded Bks., Inc.
—More Than a Princess. (More Than a Princess Ser.). (ENG.). (J). 2019. 304p. pap. 8.99 *(978-1-5476-0211-7(2),* 900203281) 2018. 288p. 16.99 *(978-1-68119-768-5(5),* 900185875) Bloomsbury Publishing USA. (Bloomsbury Children's Bks.).
—Power of a Princess. 2019. (More Than a Princess Ser.). (ENG.). 304p. (J). 16.99 *(978-1-68119-769-2(3),* 900185870, Bloomsbury Children's Bks.) Bloomsbury Publishing USA.
—Princess Between Worlds: A Tale of the Wide-Awake Princess. 2017. (Wide-Awake Princess Ser.). (ENG.). 240p. (J). pap. 8.99 *(978-1-68119-279-6(9),* 900165499, Bloomsbury USA Childrens) Bloomsbury Publishing USA.
—Princess in Disguise: A Tale of the Wide-Awake Princess. (Wide-Awake Princess Ser.: 4). (ENG., 2016. Illus.). 240p. (J). pap. 8.99 *(978-1-61963-934-8(3),* 900152548) 2015. 224p. (YA). (gr. 3-6). 16.99 *(978-1-61963-573-9(9),* 900140973) Bloomsbury Publishing USA. (Bloomsbury USA Childrens).
—Unlocking the Spell: A Tale of the Wide-Awake Princess. 2014. (Wide-Awake Princess Ser.: 2). (ENG.). 288p. (YA). (gr. 5-6). pap. 9.99 *(978-1-61963-194-6(6),* 900125844, Bloomsbury USA Childrens) Bloomsbury Publishing USA.
—The Wide-Awake Princess. 2012. (Wide-Awake Princess Ser.: 1). (ENG.). 288p. (J). (gr. 5-14). pap. 8.99 *(978-1-59990-658-4(9),* 900074739, Bloomsbury USA Childrens) Bloomsbury Publishing USA.
Baker, Sara, illus. Ready to Read Sleeping Beauty. 2007. (Ready to Read Ser.). 31p. (J). (gr. k-2). *(978-1-84610-441-1(6))* Make Believe Ideas.
Barbera, Katia. Iron Horse, 1 vol. 2010. 16p. 24.95 *(978-1-4489-4634-1(4))* PublishAmerica, Inc.
Barbieri, Sandra Birriel. Cristal & the Secret of the Enchanted Forest: Cristal y el Secreto Del Bosque Encantado. 2013. 64p. pap. 23.99 *(978-1-4525-6512-5(0))* Balboa Pr.
Bardhan-Quallen, Sudipta. Pirate Princess. McElmurry, Jill, illus. 2012. (ENG.). 40p. (J). (gr. -1-3). 17.99 *(978-0-06-114242-0(5),* HarperCollins) HarperCollins Pubs.
—Snoring Beauty. Manning, Jane, illus. 2014. (J). *(978-0-06-087405-6(8))* Harper & Row Ltd.
—Snoring Beauty. Manning, Jane, illus. 2014. (ENG.). 32p. (J). (gr. -1-3). 17.99 *(978-0-06-087403-2(1),* HarperCollins) HarperCollins Pubs.
Barnes, Susan. Kelly Karate: Discovers the Ice Princess. 2004. 138p. (J). (gr. 4-8). pap. 5.95 *(978-0-9705777-3-3(7))* McBook Pubs., LLC.
Barnhill, Kelly. Iron Hearted Violet. Bruno, Iacopo, illus. 2014. (ENG.). 448p. (J). (gr. 3-7). pap. 8.99 *(978-0-316-05675-5(8))* Little, Brown Bks. for Young Readers.
Barrett, Tracy. Marabel & the Book of Fate. 2018. (Marabel Novel Ser.). (ENG.). 304p. (J). (gr. 3-7). 16.99 *(978-0-316-43399-0(3))* Little, Brown Bks. for Young Readers.
—The Missing Heir. 2012. (Sherlock Files Ser.: 4). (J). lib. bdg. 19.65 *(978-0-606-26131-9(1))* Turtleback.
Barties, Veronica. The Princess & the Frogs. Palacios, Sara, illus. 2016. (ENG.). 40p. (J). (gr. -1-3). 17.99 *(978-0-06-236591-0(6),* Balzer & Bray) HarperCollins Pubs.
Batt, Tanya Robyn. The Princess & White Bear. Ceccoli, Nicoletta, illus. 2008. 40p. (J). (gr. -1-3). 17.99 *(978-1-84686-228-1(0))* Barefoot Bks., Inc.
Baxter, Nicola. My Book of Princess Stories. Lyon, Belinda, illus. 2012. 80p. (J). (gr. k-4). pap. 9.99 *(978-1-84322-801-1(7))* Anness Publishing GBR. Dist: National Bk. Network.
—Princess & the Jewels. Chaffey, Samantha, illus. 2018. 12p. (J). (gr. -1-12). 7.99 *(978-1-84322-626-0(X),* Armadillo) Anness Publishing GBR. Dist: National Bk. Network.
—Princess Stories. Smith, Helen, illus. 2013. (ENG.). 80p. (J). (gr. k-4). pap. 9.99 *(978-1-84322-954-4(4))* Anness Publishing GBR. Dist: National Bk. Network.
Baxter, Nicola & Manson, Beverly. Storybook of Fairy Princesses: Six Tales from an Enchanted Secret World. 2013. (Illus.). 80p. (J). (gr. 2-8). pap. 9.99 *(978-1-84322-898-1(X))* Anness Publishing GBR. Dist: National Bk. Network.
Bealer-Wynton, Cheryl. Blinky's Island. 2008. 60p. pap. 6.50 *(978-1-4303-1146-1(0))* Lulu Pr., Inc.
Beaton, Kate. The Princess & the Pony. Beaton, Kate, illus. 2015. (ENG., Illus.). 40p. (J). (gr. -1-3). 17.99 *(978-0-545-63708-4(2))* Scholastic, Inc.
Beck, Patricia. Princess Feldings & the Academy of Queens. 2010. 28p. 13.99 *(978-1-4490-1376-9(7))* AuthorHouse.
Bell, Juliet Clare & Chapman, Laura Kate. The Kite Princess. 2012. (Illus.). (J). 16.99 *(978-1-84686-803-0(3))* Barefoot Bks., Inc.
Bell, Rebecca. Princess Sara. Bell, Rebecca, illus. 2005. (Illus.). 34p. (J). 9.95 *(978-1-934138-07-6(X))* Bouncing Ball Bks., Inc.
Benjamin, A. H. Wanted: Prince Charming. Florin, Fabiano, illus. 2014. (Race Ahead with Reading Ser.). (ENG.). 32p. (J). (gr. 2-2). *(978-0-7787-1313-5(X))* Crabtree Publishing Co.
Bentley, Douglas W. What Will It Take for a Toad to Kiss a Monkey: The Adventures of Princess Gracie & Prince Wallaby. Bentley, Julia Faye, illus. 2008. 52p. per. 24.95 *(978-1-4137-8849-5(1))* America Star Bks.
Benton, Lynne. The Sad Princess. Catling, Andy, illus. 2009. (Tadpoles Ser.). (ENG.). 24p. (J). (gr. k-2). pap. *(978-0-7787-3903-6(1))* Crabtree Publishing Co.
Berger, Glenn. Princess Chantik & the Outside World. 2012. 92p. pap. 39.99 *(978-0-615-61495-3(7))* Marcabru Publishing.
Bergman, Mara. The Twelve Dancing Princesses: Band 13/Topaz (Collins Big Cat) 2017. (Collins Big Cat Tales Ser.). (ENG., Illus.). 48p. (J). (gr. 2-3). pap. 9.99 *(978-0-00-817938-0(7))* HarperCollins Pubs. Ltd. GBR. Dist: Independent Pubs. Group.
Bernhardt, William. Princess Alice & the Dreadful Dragon. McGhee, Kerry, illus. 2007. 27p. (J). 19.99 *(978-1-930709-65-2(X))* HAWK Publishing Group.
Bernreuter, Bob J. The Gift. 2006. (Illus.). 25p. (J). *(978-1-4120-7546-6(7))* Trafford Publishing.
Berrios, Frank. A Day in the Sun. 2014. lib. bdg. 13.55 *(978-0-606-35546-9(4))* Turtleback.
Berrow, G. M. Twilight Sparkle & the Crystal Heart Spell. 2013. (My Little Pony Chapter Bks.). (J). lib. bdg. 16.00 *(978-0-606-31733-7(3))* Turtleback.
Berry, Erick. The Winged Girl of Knossos. 2017. (ENG., Illus.). 220p. (J). (gr. 3-7). pap. 15.95 *(978-1-58988-120-4(6))* Dry, Paul Bks., Inc.
Bianchi, John & Edwards, Frank B. Princess Frownsalot, 1 vol. rev. ed. 2004. (ENG., Illus.). 127p. (J). pap. 4.95 *(978-1-894323-25-3(4))* Pokeweed Pr. CAN. Dist: Ingram Publisher Services.
Biggs, K. E. The Dawn of Hope. 2010. 112p. pap. 10.99 *(978-1-4490-8931-3(3))* AuthorHouse.
Bilgrey, Marc. And Don't Forget to Rescue the Other Princess. 2009. 252p. 25.95 *(978-1-59414-744-9(2),* Five Star) Cengage Gale.
Binder, Mark. Kings, Wolves, Princesses & Lions: 28 Illustrated Stories for Young Readers. 2012. (ENG., Illus.). 122p. (J). pap. 14.99 *(978-0-9824707-8-7(9))* Light Pubns.
Birney, Betty G. The Princess & the Peabodys. 2007. (ENG.). 256p. (J). (gr. 5-9). 15.99 *(978-0-06-084720-3(4))* HarperCollins Pubs.
Bishop, Jennie. The Three Gifts of Christmas. McDaniels, Preston, illus. 2009. 32p. (J). (gr. 3-18). 15.99 incl. audio compact disk *(978-1-59317-378-4(4))* Warner Pr., Inc.
Blair, Eric. The Frog Prince: A Retelling of the Grimm's Fairy Tale, 1 vol. Ouren, Todd, illus. 2013. (My First Classic Story Ser.). (ENG.). 32p. (J). (gr. k-3). pap. 7.10 *(978-1-4795-1853-1(0),* 123443, Picture Window Bks.) Capstone.
Blevins, Wiley. The Princess & the Poison Pea. Cox, Steve, illus. 2017. (Scary Tales Retold Ser.). (ENG.). 24p. (J). (gr. k-3). pap. 6.99 *(978-1-63440-170-8(0),* 1e625a92-dd6c-461f-855c-8bc07f2d6894); lib. bdg. 27.99 *(978-1-63440-166-1(2),* 986a4545-bd42-4178-9a49-2644d76af4f0) Red Chair Pr.
—Snow White & the Seven Trolls. Cox, Steve, illus. 2016. (Scary Tales Retold Ser.). (ENG.). 24p. (J). (gr. k-3). lib. bdg. 27.99 *(978-1-63440-105-0(0),* 1063d101-1205-4866-b1fc-251762cc5060) Red Chair Pr.
—Ten Missing Princesses. Cox, Steve, illus. 2017. (Scary Tales Retold Ser.). (ENG.). 24p. (J). (gr. k-3). pap. 6.99 *(978-1-63440-172-2(7),* 97967ed0-13a8-4453-839f-022d2bc5b970); lib. bdg. 27.99 *(978-1-63440-168-5(9),* 1aaeb31e-b7b1-4f1d-805e-10da6b4e6aaf) Red Chair Pr.
Bliss, Emily. Unicorn Princesses 2: Flash's Dash. Hanson, Sydney, illus. 2017. (Unicorn Princesses Ser.: 2). (ENG.). 128p. (J). 15.99 *(978-1-68119-329-8(9),* 900170030, Bloomsbury USA Childrens) Bloomsbury Publishing USA.
—Unicorn Princesses 3: Bloom's Ball. Hanson, Sydney, illus. 2017. (Unicorn Princesses Ser.: 3). (ENG.). 128p. (J). pap. 5.99 *(978-1-68119-334-2(5),* 900170042, Bloomsbury USA Childrens) Bloomsbury Publishing USA.
—Unicorn Princesses 4: Prism's Paint. Hanson, Sydney, illus. 2017. (Unicorn Princesses Ser.: 4). (ENG.). 128p. (J). pap. 5.99 *(978-1-68119-338-0(8),* 900170045, Bloomsbury USA Childrens) Bloomsbury Publishing USA.
—Unicorn Princesses 5: Breeze's Blast. Hanson, Sydney, illus. 2018. (Unicorn Princesses Ser.: 5). (ENG.). 128p. (J). 16.99 *(978-1-68119-650-3(6),* 900179833); pap. 5.99 *(978-1-68119-649-7(2),* 900179849) Bloomsbury Publishing USA. (Bloomsbury USA Childrens).
—Unicorn Princesses 6: Moon's Dance. Hanson, Sydney, illus. 2018. (Unicorn Princesses Ser.: 6). (ENG.). 128p. (J). pap. 6.99 *(978-1-68119-652-7(2),* 900179844, Bloomsbury USA Childrens) Bloomsbury Publishing USA.
—Unicorn Princesses 7: Firefly's Glow. Hanson, Sydney, illus. 2018. (Unicorn Princesses Ser.: 7). (ENG.). 128p. (J). 16.99 *(978-1-68119-927-6(0),* 900192376); pap. 5.99 *(978-1-68119-926-9(2),* 900192401) Bloomsbury Publishing USA. (Bloomsbury Children's Bks.).
—Unicorn Princesses 8: Feather's Flight. Hanson, Sydney, illus. 2018. (Unicorn Princesses Ser.: 8). (ENG.). 128p. (J). 16.99 *(978-1-68119-930-6(0),* 900192387); pap. 5.99 *(978-1-68119-929-0(7),* 900192375) Bloomsbury Publishing USA. (Bloomsbury Children's Bks.).
Block, Betty Mitchell. The Magic Pork Chop Bone. 2013. (ENG.). 76p. (YA). pap. 8.95 *(978-1-4787-1482-8(4))* Outskirts Pr., Inc.
Bloomsbury USA. Lift-The-Flap Friends: Princess. 2017. (ENG.). 14p. (J). bds. 9.99 *(978-1-68119-240-6(3),* 900164377, Bloomsbury Activity Bks.) Bloomsbury Publishing USA.
Blythe, Gary, illus. A Treasury of Princess Stories. 2009. (ENG.). 80p. (J). (gr. 2-5). 19.99 *(978-0-7636-4478-9(1))* Candlewick Pr.
Blyton, Enid. Princess & the Pea. 2012. (ENG., Illus.). 24p. (J). pap. 9.95 *(978-1-84135-608-2(5))* Award Pubns. Ltd. GBR. Dist: Parkwest Pubns., Inc.
—Twelve Dancing Princesses. 2012. (ENG., Illus.). 24p. (J). pap. 9.95 *(978-1-84135-610-5(7))* Award Pubns. Ltd. GBR. Dist: Parkwest Pubns., Inc.
Boada, Francesc, adapted by. Cinderella/Cenicienta: Bilingual Edition. 2005. (Bilingual Fairy Tales Ser.: BILI). (ENG., Illus.). 32p. (J). (gr. -1-7). pap. 8.99 *(978-0-8118-3090-4(X))* Chronicle Bks. LLC.
Bohn, Kendall. Fantasy Adventure. 2008. (Kaleidoscopia Coloring Book Ser.). (Illus.). 56p. (J). (gr. -1-7). 8.95 *(978-0-929636-83-2(X))* Syren Bk. Co.
Bondoux, Anne-Laure. The Princetta. 2008. (ENG.). 448p. (YA). (gr. 6-12). pap. 10.99 *(978-1-59990-098-8(X),* 9781599900988, Bloomsbury USA Childrens) Bloomsbury Publishing USA.
Boujie. A Princess from the Heart. 2009. 66p. pap. 15.99 *(978-1-4415-4413-1(5))* Xlibris Corp.
Boulton, M. T. Megan Button & the Brim-Tree. 2012. 106p. pap. *(978-1-909039-06-3(3))* Legend Pr.
Bow, Erin. The Swan Riders. 2017. (Prisoners of Peace Ser.). (ENG.). 384p. (YA). (gr. 9). pap. 11.99 *(978-1-4814-4275-6(9),* McElderry, Margaret K. Bks.) McElderry, Margaret K. Bks.
Bracken, Beth, et al. The Fate of the Willow Queen. Sawyer, Odessa, illus. 2013. (Faerieground Ser.). (ENG.). 96p. (J). (gr. 5-9). 23.99 *(978-1-4342-4492-5(X),* 120491, Stone Arch Bks.) Capstone.
Bradfield, Roger, illus. The Pickle-Chiffon Pie Olympics. 2011. 64p. (J). (gr. -1-3). 18.95 *(978-1-930900-52-3(X))* Purple Hse. Pr.
Bradman, Tony. Snow White & the Magic Mirror (after Happily Ever After) Warburton, Sarah, illus. 2014. (After Happily Ever After Ser.). (ENG.). 56p. (J). (gr. 3-6). lib. bdg. 25.99 *(978-1-4342-7950-7(2),* 124698, Stone Arch Bks.) Capstone.
Brandon, Demi. Princess Shakina's Locks. 2007. 48p. per. 16.95 *(978-1-4241-7195-8(4))* America Star Bks.
Braswell, Liz. Once upon a Dream: A Twisted Tale. 2017. (Twisted Tale Ser.). (YA). lib. bdg. 20.85 *(978-0-606-39935-7(6))* Turtleback.
—Once upon a Dream-A Twisted Tale. 2017. (Twisted Tale Ser.). (ENG.). 464p. (YA). (gr. 7-12). pap. 10.99 *(978-1-4847-0730-2(3),* Disney Press Books) Disney Publishing Worldwide.
—A Whole New World: A Twisted Tale. 2016. (Twisted Tale Ser.). (YA). lib. bdg. 20.85 *(978-0-606-38511-4(8))* Turtleback.
—A Whole New World-A Twisted Tale. 2016. (Twisted Tale Ser.). (ENG.). 400p. (YA). (gr. 7-12). pap. 9.99 *(978-1-4847-0732-6(X),* Disney-Hyperion) Disney Publishing Worldwide.
Brauner, Susan. The Adventures of Sohi: Mystery of Moon Island. 2011. 207p. 28.95 *(978-1-4327-6752-5(6));* pap. 15.95 *(978-1-4327-6536-1(1))* Outskirts Pr., Inc.
Brazier, Yuvonne. Princess Jordan Saves Golden Tree. 2008. 20p. pap. 12.49 *(978-1-4389-3591-1(9))* AuthorHouse.
Breslin, Jayne. The Princess Jelly Tutu Adventures. 2011. (Illus.). 28p. (gr. -1). pap. 14.09 *(978-1-4567-7611-4(8))* AuthorHouse.
Brian, Kate, pseud. The Princess & the Pauper. 2004. 266p. (J). (gr. 5-9). 14.65 *(978-0-7569-3531-3(8))* Perfection Learning Corp.
—The Princess & the Pauper. 2004. (ENG., Illus.). 272p. (YA). reprint ed. mass mkt. 6.99 *(978-0-689-87042-2(6),* Simon Pulse) Simon Pulse.
Brice, Ginny. Princess Maddy & Her Blankie. Gary Ripper, illus. 2011. 20p. pap. 24.95 *(978-1-4560-7745-7(7))* America Star Bks.
Brinson, Julie L. Princess Olivia & the Leap Frog, 1 vol. Brinson, Connor J., illus. 2009. 22p. pap. 24.95 *(978-1-60813-802-9(X))* America Star Bks.
Brocklehurst, Ruth. Princess Things to Make & Do. 2005. (Illus.). 32p. (J). pap. 6.95 *(978-0-7945-0908-8(8),* Usborne) EDC Publishing.
Broderick, Kathy. Disney Princess: Belle (Giant First Play -a-Sound) 2010. 10p. (J). bds. 17.98 *(978-1-60553-543-2(5))* Publications International, Ltd.
Brodsky, Irene. The Adventures of Silly Kitty, Princess Jasmine & First Puppy. 2010. (Illus.). 44p. (J). pap. 23.95 *(978-1-4327-5552-2(8))* Outskirts Pr., Inc.
Brody, Jessica. A Dragon in the Castle? 2018. (Illus.). 94p. (J). *(978-1-5444-2142-1(7))* Disney Publishing Worldwide.
—A Dragon in the Castle?, 2. 2019. (Lego Disney Princess Ch Bks). (ENG., Illus.). 96p. (J). (gr. 2-4). 16.79 *(978-1-64310-791-2(7))* Penworthy Co., LLC, The.
Brooke, Jasmine. The Princess & the Pea: Pass the Pea Pressure Test! 2017. (Fairy Tale Fixers: Fixing Fairy Tale Problems with STEM Ser.). 32p. (gr. 3-4). pap. 63.00 *(978-1-5382-0667-6(6))* Stevens, Gareth Publishing LLLP.
Brooks, Amy. Princess Polly's Gay Winter. 2018. (ENG., Illus.). 106p. (YA). (gr. 7-12). pap. *(978-93-5297-533-4(2))* Alpha Editions.
—Princess Polly's Gay Winter. 2004. reprint ed. pap. 1.99 *(978-1-4192-4299-1(7));* pap. 15.95 *(978-1-4191-4299-4(2))* Kessinger Publishing, LLC.
—Princess Polly's Playmates. 2018. (ENG., Illus.). 108p. (YA). (gr. 7-12). pap. *(978-93-5297-534-1(0))* Alpha Editions.
—Princess Polly's Playmates. 2004. reprint ed. pap. 19.95 *(978-1-4191-4300-7(X));* pap. 1.99 *(978-1-4192-4300-4(4))* Kessinger Publishing, LLC.
Brooks, Donna. The Golden Spindle. 2010. 112p. pap. 30.00 *(978-1-60860-852-2(2),* Eloquent Bks.) Strategic Book Publishing & Rights Agency (SBPRA).
—The Magic Amphor. 2009. 100p. pap. 30.00 *(978-1-60693-027-4(3),* Eloquent Bks.) Strategic Book Publishing & Rights Agency (SBPRA).
Brower, Sandra Shane. Princess Zoe & the Mer-Bird. Steele, Andrea M., illus. 2013. 46p. pap. 10.95 *(978-1-936688-77-7(8),* Compass Flower Pr.) AKA:yoLa.
Brown, Carron, ed. The Little Mermaid & the Princess & the Pea: Two Tales & Their Histories, 1 vol. 2009. (World of Fairy Tales Ser.). (ENG., Illus.). 32p. (J). (gr. 1-2). pap. 11.55 *(978-1-60754-638-2(8),* a3d137ff-acb1-4389-bda1-d37f43fac53f); lib. bdg. 27.27 *(978-1-60754-637-5(X),* dca8f046-f575-474d-a9b9-fdc02afe63f7) Rosen Publishing Group, Inc., The. (Windmill Bks.).
—Sleeping Beauty & Snow White & the Seven Dwarfs: Two Tales & Their Histories, 1 vol. 2009. (World of Fairy Tales Ser.). (ENG., Illus.). 32p. (J). (gr. 1-2). pap. 11.55 *(978-1-60754-635-1(3),* 85434d31-dc86-4f19-899e-add68306efa8); lib. bdg. 27.27 *(978-1-60754-634-4(5),* 210ba78f-6bda-4b3c-8798-3c1d39b6a67c) Rosen Publishing Group, Inc., The. (Windmill Bks.).
Brown, E.A. Gossamer. 2012. 24p. pap. 24.95 *(978-1-4626-5043-9(0))* America Star Bks.
Brubacher, Melody. The Adventures of Princess Penelope. 2012. 68p. pap. 31.99 *(978-1-4691-9274-1(8))* Xlibris Corp.
Brundage, Frances, illus. Cinderella: A Fairy Story. 2004. reprint ed. pap. 15.95 *(978-1-4179-8713-9(8))* Kessinger Publishing, LLC.
Brundage, Jerome. The Princess & the Bear: Book I: the Battle for Aradam. 2007. 148p. per. 24.95 *(978-1-4241-6346-5(3))* America Star Bks.
Bryant, Ann. Dancing Princess. Benton, Tim, illus. 2006. (Ballerina Dreams Ser.). 102p. (J). per. 4.99 *(978-0-7945-1297-2(6),* Usborne) EDC Publishing.
—Princess at Silver Spires. 2014. (School Friends Ser.). (ENG.). 145p. (J). (gr. 4-7). pap. 5.99 *(978-0-7945-3152-2(0),* Usborne) EDC Publishing.
Bryant, Gerry. Metamorphosed: Sun's Gift. 2006. (ENG.). 116p. (YA). 20.95 *(978-0-595-67412-1(7));* pap. 10.95 *(978-0-595-36729-0(1))* iUniverse, Inc.
Buckmaster, Heath L. Box of Hair: A Fairy Tale, 3 bks., Bk. 1. (Illus.). (YA). 2007. 102p. pap. 12.99 *(978-0-9771802-5-7(5))* 2008. 108p. lib. bdg. 25.00 *(978-0-9771802-4-0(7))* Transaltar Publishing.
—Box of Hair: A Fairy Tale. 2008. 104p. pap. 12.50 *(978-1-4357-2690-1(1))* Lulu Pr., Inc.
—The Dragons of Tarnack. 2008. 142p. pap. 13.99 *(978-1-4357-4624-4(4))* Lulu Pr., Inc.
—The Venus Diary. 2008. 136p. pap. 13.50 *(978-0-615-20678-3(6));*Bk. 2. 132p. (YA). lib. bdg. 19.95 *(978-0-9771802-6-4(3))* Transaltar Publishing.
Buller, Laura. The Friendship Bridge. 2018. (Illus.). 27p. (J). *(978-1-5490-5626-0(3))* Disney Publishing Worldwide.
—The Friendship Bridge. 2019. (World of Reading Ser.). (ENG., Illus.). 32p. (J). (gr. k-2). 13.89 *(978-1-64310-799-8(2))* Penworthy Co., LLC, The.
—Lost & Found. 2018. (Illus.). 31p. (J). *(978-1-5490-5625-3(5))* Disney Publishing Worldwide.
—Lost & Found. 2019. (World of Reading Ser.). (ENG., Illus.). 32p. (J). (gr. k-2). 13.89 *(978-1-64310-800-1(X))* Penworthy Co., LLC, The.
Burgis, Stephanie. The Princess Who Flew with Dragons. 2019. (Dragon Heart Ser.: 3). (ENG.). 224p. (J). 16.99 *(978-1-5476-0207-0(4),* 900203278, Bloomsbury Children's Bks.) Bloomsbury Publishing USA.
Burgos-Diaz, Mercedes. Meenah, the Mystical Princess of Zantel. 2011. 56p. pap. 8.95 *(978-1-4620-5928-7(7))* iUniverse, Inc.
Burke, Gloreen & Wijesekera, Kaviella. The Girl Who Dreamt She Was a Princess. 2009. (ENG.). 30p. pap. 21.99 *(978-1-4415-2596-3(3))* Xlibris Corp.
Burkhart, Jessica. Bella's Birthday Unicorn. Ying, Victoria, illus. 2014. (Unicorn Magic Ser.: 1). (ENG.). 144p. (J). (gr. 1-4). pap. 6.99 *(978-1-4424-9822-8(6),* Aladdin) Simon & Schuster Children's Publishing.
—The Hidden Treasure. Ying, Victoria, illus. 2015. (Unicorn Magic Ser.: 4). (ENG.). 112p. (J). (gr. 1-4). pap. 6.99 *(978-1-4424-9829-7(3),* Aladdin) Simon & Schuster Children's Publishing.
—Where's Glimmer? Ying, Victoria, illus. 2014. (Unicorn Magic Ser.: 2). (ENG.). 144p. (J). (gr. 1-4). pap. 6.99 *(978-1-4424-9824-2(2),* Aladdin) Simon & Schuster Children's Publishing.

Burnett, Frances. A Little Princess. 2015. (ENG.). 267p. (J). 15.99 *(978-1-78270-105-7(2))* Award Pubns. Ltd. GBR. Dist: Parkwest Pubns., Inc.

—La Petit Princesse.Tr. of Little Princess. (J). pap. 12.95 *(978-2-07-056710-2(9))* Gallimard, Editions FRA. Dist: Distribooks, Inc.

—Petite Princess. pap. 19.95 *(978-2-07-051994-1(5))* Gallimard, Editions FRA. Dist: Distribooks, Inc.

—Titus kommt nicht alle Tage.Tr. of Little Princess. pap. 21.95 *(978-3-423-70196-9(X))* Deutscher Taschenbuch Verlag GmbH & Co KG DEU. Dist: Distribooks, Inc.

Burnett, Frances Hodgson. A Little Princess. 2017. (First Avenue Classics (tm) Ser.). (ENG.). 222p. (J). (gr. 3-8). E-Book 19.99 *(978-1-5124-2605-2(9)*, First Avenue Editions) Lerner Publishing Group.

Burns, Jennifer N. Magic in Time: Fairy Tale Stories. 2012. 198p. 24.95 *(978-1-4759-3965-1(5))*; pap. 14.95 *(978-1-4759-3964-4(7))* iUniverse, Inc.

Burns, Mary Gore. The Magic Room: Mandy & the Lily Pond. 2011. 48p. pap. 17.30 *(978-1-4634-2642-2(9))* AuthorHouse.

Burt, Bethany. I Am Not a Princess!, 1 vol. McCallum, Brenda, illus. 2016. (ENG.). 40p. (J). 16.99 *(978-0-7643-5212-6(1)*, 7563) Schiffer Publishing, Ltd.

Bush, Vicki-Ann. The Queen of IT. Beachamp, Afiyah, illus. 2011. 60p. (J). pap. 9.98 *(978-0-9816949-7-9(7))* Salt of the Earth Pr.

Cabell, Robert W. The Mermaid Adventures of Princess Miranda: Volume One. Cabell, Robert W., illus. 2013. (Illus.). 128p. pap. 7.95 *(978-0-9890974-3-7(9)*, Oceanus Bks.) Warrington Pubns.

Cabot, Meg. From the Notebooks of a Middle-School Princess. 2016. (From the Notebooks of a Middle School Princess Ser.: 1). (J). lib. bdg. 18.40 *(978-0-606-38554-1(1))* Turtleback.

—From the Notebooks of a Middle School Princess: Meg Cabot; Read by Kathleen Mcinerney. 2015. (From the Notebooks of a Middle School Princess Ser.: 1). (ENG., Illus.). 192p. (J). (gr. 3-7). 16.99 *(978-1-250-06602-2(6)*, 900145229) Feiwel & Friends.

—Journal d'une Princesse.Tr. of Princess Diaries. pap. 13.95 *(978-2-01-321853-5(2))* Hachette Groupe Livre FRA. Dist: Distribooks, Inc.

—Party Princess. 2006. (Princess Diaries: Vol. 7). (ENG., Illus.). 304p. (YA). (gr. 7-12). 16.99 *(978-0-06-072453-5(6))* HarperCollins Pubs.

—The Princess Diaries. 2008. (Princess Diaries: 1). (ENG.). 256p. (YA). (gr. 8). pap. 10.99 *(978-0-06-147993-9(4))*Vols. 1-3, Set. 2006. (Princess Diaries: Vol. I). (J). pap., pap. 19.99 *(978-0-06-115389-1(3))* HarperCollins Pubs. (HarperTeen).

—The Princess Diaries. 2008. 20.00 *(978-0-7569-8793-0(8))* Perfection Learning Corp.

—The Princess Diaries. unabr. ed. 2004. (Princess Diaries: Vol. I). 240p. (J). (gr. 7-18). pap. 38.00 incl. audio *(978-0-8072-0669-0(5)*, Listening Library) Random Hse. Audio Publishing Group.

—The Princess Diaries. 2008. (Princess Diaries: 1). (YA). lib. bdg. 20.85 *(978-1-4178-2328-4(3))* Turtleback.

—The Princess Diaries Box Set: The Princess Diaries; Princess in the Spotlight; Princess in Love. 2003. (Princess Diaries). 304p. (gr. 7-18). pap. 19.99 *(978-0-06-058745-1(8))* HarperCollins Pubs.

—Princess Diaries, Volume 6 & a Half: the Princess Present: A Christmas & Holiday Book. 2004. (Princess Diaries: 6.5). (ENG.). 96p. (YA). (gr. 8-18). 12.99 *(978-0-06-075433-4(8)*, HarperTeen) HarperCollins Pubs.

—The Princess Diaries: Volume 7 & 3/4: Valentine Princess. 2006. (Princess Diaries: 7.75). (ENG.). 96p. (YA). (gr. 8-12). 13.99 *(978-0-06-084718-0(2)*, HarperTeen) HarperCollins Pubs.

—The Princess Diaries, Volume II: Princess in the Spotlight Vol. 2. 2008. (Princess Diaries: 2). (ENG.). 256p. (YA). (gr. 8-12). pap. 11.99 *(978-0-06-147994-6(2)*, HarperTeen) HarperCollins Pubs.

—The Princess Diaries, Volume III: Princess in Love, Vol. 3. 2008. (Princess Diaries: 3). (ENG.). 256p. (YA). (gr. 8-12). pap. 10.99 *(978-0-06-147995-3(0)*, HarperTeen) HarperCollins Pubs.

—The Princess Diaries, Volume IV & a Half: Project Princess. 2003. (Princess Diaries: 4.5). (ENG.). 64p. (YA). (gr. 8-18). pap. 9.99 *(978-0-06-057131-3(4)*, HarperTeen) HarperCollins Pubs.

—The Princess Diaries, Volume IV: Princess in Waiting. 2008. (Princess Diaries: 4). (ENG.). 256p. (YA). (gr. 8). pap. 10.99 *(978-0-06-154364-7(0)*, HarperTeen) HarperCollins Pubs.

—The Princess Diaries, Volume IX: Princess Mia, Vol. 9. 2009. (Princess Diaries: 9). (ENG.). 304p. (YA). (gr. 8). pap. 10.99 *(978-0-06-072463-4(3)*, HarperTeen) HarperCollins Pubs.

—The Princess Diaries, Volume V: Princess in Pink. 2008. (Princess Diaries: 5). (ENG.). 288p. (YA). (gr. 8). pap. 10.99 *(978-0-06-154363-0(2)*, HarperTeen) HarperCollins Pubs.

—The Princess Diaries, Volume VI: Princess in Training, Vol. VI. 2008. (Princess Diaries: 6). (ENG.). 304p. (YA). (gr. 8). pap. 10.99 *(978-0-06-154365-4(9)*, HarperTeen) HarperCollins Pubs.

—The Princess Diaries, Volume VII: Party Princess, Vol. VII. 2008. (Princess Diaries: 7). (ENG.). 320p. (YA). (gr. 8). pap. 9.99 *(978-0-06-154374-6(8)*, HarperTeen) HarperCollins Pubs.

—The Princess Diaries, Volume VIII: Princess on the Brink. 2007. (Princess Diaries: 8). (ENG.) 272p. (YA). (gr. 8). pap. 10.99 *(978-0-06-072460-3(9)*, HarperTeen) HarperCollins Pubs.

—The Princess Diaries, Volume X: Forever Princess, Vol. X. 2009. (Princess Diaries: 10). (ENG.). 416p. (YA). (gr. 8). pap. 10.99 *(978-0-06-123294-7(7)*, HarperTeen) HarperCollins Pubs.

—Princess in Love. 2004. (Princess Diaries: Vol. 3). 288p. (J). (gr. 7-18). pap. 38.00 incl. audio *(978-0-8072-2284-3(4)*, Listening Library) Random Hse. Audio Publishing Group.

—Princess in Pink. 2008. (Princess Diaries: 5). 256p. (YA). (gr. 7-12). 20.85 *(978-1-4178-2563-9(4))* Turtleback.

—Princess in the Spotlight. 2008. (Princess Diaries). 222p. (gr. 7-12). 19.00 *(978-0-7569-8794-7(6))* Perfection Learning Corp.

—Princess in the Spotlight. unabr. ed. 2004. (Princess Diaries: Vol. 2). 272p. (J). (gr. 7-18). pap. 38.00 incl. audio *(978-0-8072-1197-7(4)*, S YA 332 SP, Listening Library) Random Hse. Audio Publishing Group.

—Princess in Training. 2005. (Princess Diaries: Vol. 6). (ENG., Illus.). 288p. (J). (gr. 7-18). 16.99 *(978-0-06-009613-7(6))* HarperCollins Pubs.

—Princess Mia. 2008. (Princess Diaries: Vol. 9). (ENG.). 256p. (J). (gr. 7-18). 16.99 *(978-0-06-072461-0(7))* HarperCollins Pubs.

—Princess Mia. 2009. (Princess Diaries: 9). (YA). lib. bdg. 20.85 *(978-0-606-02178-4(7))* Turtleback.

—Princess on the Brink. 2007. (Princess Diaries: Vol. 8). (ENG.). 256p. (J). 16.99 *(978-0-06-072456-6(0))* HarperCollins Pubs.

—Royal Crown: from the Notebooks of a Middle School Princess. Cabot, Meg, illus. 2019. (From the Notebooks of a Middle School Princess Ser.: 4). (ENG., Illus.). 224p. (J). pap. 10.99 *(978-1-250-30868-9(2)*, 900170016) Square Fish.

—Royal Crush. 2018. (From the Notebooks of a Middle School Princess Ser.: 3). (J). lib. bdg. 18.40 *(978-0-606-41094-6(5))* Turtleback.

—Royal Crush: from the Notebooks of a Middle School Princess. Cabot, Meg, illus. 2018. (From the Notebooks of a Middle School Princess Ser.: 3). (ENG., Illus.). 336p. (J). pap. 13.99 *(978-1-250-15869-7(9)*, 900170013) Square Fish.

Cabrera, Aleix. Princess Criseta's Hamster, 1 vol. Bonilla, Rocio, illus. 2017. (Little Princesses Ser.). (ENG.). 32p. (J). (gr. 1-2). 28.93 *(978-1-5081-9398-2(3)*, 7989a69f-66d1-4572-a06c-8db7516317ae); pap. 11.00 *(978-1-5081-9458-3(0)*, a0e6cc6f-574e-4cb5-b0b0-f514983002ef) Rosen Publishing Group, Inc., The. (Windmill Bks.).

—Princess Nika's Dog, 1 vol. Bonilla, Rocio, illus. 2017. (Little Princesses Ser.). (ENG.). 32p. (J). (gr. 1-2). 28.93 *(978-1-5081-9399-9(1)*, 145837bd-3ee8-4dfc-8de3-b7d70713d3db); pap. 11.00 *(978-1-5081-9459-0(9)*, 35b53c9b-3b51-43ab-8460-bb0063895e0b) Rosen Publishing Group, Inc., The. (Windmill Bks.).

—Princess Sucha's Cat, 1 vol. Bonilla, Rocío, illus. 2017. (Little Princesses Ser.). (ENG.). 32p. (J). (gr. 1-2). 28.93 *(978-1-5081-9400-2(9)*, e5877461-e14c-452b-9f98-10ec2e607865); pap. 11.00 *(978-1-5081-9460-6(2)*, 1a11896b-dd84-47b3-a704-ad0c5cecd8d6) Rosen Publishing Group, Inc., The. (Windmill Bks.).

—Princess Suque's Pony, 1 vol. Bonilla, Rocío, illus. 2017. (Little Princesses Ser.). (ENG.). 32p. (J). (gr. 1-2). 28.93 *(978-1-5081-9401-9(7)*, f44ec0c4-9196-4a07-8a80-067799ab665e); pap. 11.00 *(978-1-5081-9461-3(0)*, 85966d3b-ac9d-43dc-9d87-1eb232aba5d2) Rosen Publishing Group, Inc., The. (Windmill Bks.).

Cafaro, Phyllis. Captain Mcfinn & Friends Meet Coral Rose. 2012. (ENG.). 24p. (J). 19.99 *(978-0-9799283-5-2(4)*, 9780979928352) Captain McFinn and Friends LLC, McFinn Pr.

Calhoun, Dia. Avielle of Rhia, 1 vol. 2006. (ENG.). 400p. (J). (gr. 6). 16.99 *(978-0-7614-5320-8(2))* Marshall Cavendish Corp.

Calonita, Jen. Misfits: Royal Academy Rebels, Book 1. (Royal Academy Rebels Ser.: 1). 288p. (J). (gr. 3-7). 2019. pap. 7.99 *(978-1-4926-9390-1(1))* 2018. 16.99 *(978-1-4926-5128-4(1))* Sourcebooks, Inc.

Candlewick Press. Peppa Pig's Pop-Up Princess Castle. Entertainment One, Entertainment, illus. 2017. (Peppa Pig Ser.). (ENG.). 6p. (J). (gr. -1-2). 24.99 *(978-0-7636-9734-1(6)*, Candlewick Entertainment) Candlewick Pr.

Carbone, Courtney. I Am a Princess. Martinez, Heather, illus. 2016. (J). *(978-1-5182-1626-8(9)*, Golden Bks.) Random Hse. Children's Bks.

—I Am a Princess (Star Wars) Martinez, Heather, illus. 2016. (Little Golden Book Ser.). (ENG.). 24p. (J). (-k). 5.99 *(978-0-7364-3605-2(7)*, Golden Bks.) Random Hse. Children's Bks.

—Palace Pets: Snuggle Buddies. 2014. (Step into Reading Level 2 Ser.). lib. bdg. 13.55 *(978-0-606-35193-5(0))* Turtleback.

—Princess Peppa & the Royal Ball. 2018. (Scholastic Readers Ser.). (ENG.). 32p. (J). (gr. -1-k). 13.89 *(978-1-64310-234-4(6))* Penworthy Co., LLC, The.

—Princess Peppa & the Royal Ball (Peppa Pig: Scholastic Reader, Level 1), 1 vol. (Scholastic Reader, Level 1 Ser.). (ENG., 32p. (J). 2017. Illus.). (gr. -1-k). pap. 4.99 *(978-1-338-18258-3(7))* 2005. (gr. 2-5). E-Book 7.99 *(978-1-338-19011-3(3))* Scholastic, Inc.

—Snuggle Buddies (Disney Princess: Palace Pets) RH Disney, illus. 2014. (Step into Reading Ser.). (ENG.). 32p. (J). (gr. -1-1). 5.99 *(978-0-7364-3155-2(1)*, RH/Disney) Random Hse. Children's Bks.

Cardona, Jose & Williams, Don, illus. Mulan (Disney Princess) 2013. (Little Golden Book Ser.). (ENG.). 24p. (J). (-k). 5.99 *(978-0-7364-3053-1(9)*, Golden/Disney) Random Hse. Children's Bks.

Carey, Anna. Rise. 2013. (Eve Ser.: 3). (ENG.). 336p. (YA). (gr. 8). pap. 10.99 *(978-0-06-204858-5(9)*, HarperCollins) HarperCollins Pubs.

—Rise: An Eve Novel. 2013. (Illus.). 320p. (YA). pap. 9.99 *(978-0-06-226273-8(4))* HarperCollins Pubs.

Carey, Janet Lee. Dragon's Keep. 2007. 302p. (J). *(978-1-4287-3929-1(7))* Harcourt Trade Pubs.

Carney, Karin. Princess Bailey & Her Animal Friends. 2011. (Illus.). 46p. pap. 18.95 *(978-0-557-95745-3(1))* Lulu Pr., Inc.

Carroll, Jacquie Lund. The Queen's Jewels. Gillen, Rosemarie, illus. 2013. 26p. pap. 9.99 *(978-1-61286-147-0(4))* Avid Readers Publishing Group.

Carter, David A. Princess Bugs: A Touch-And-Feel Fairy Tale. Carter, David A., illus. 2013. (David Carter's Bugs Ser.). (ENG., Illus.). 16p. (J). (gr. -1-2). 12.99 *(978-1-4424-5055-4(X)*, Little Simon) Little Simon.

Cartwright, Ran. The Adventures of Billy Space Boy, 1 vol. 2010. 208p. pap. 24.95 *(978-1-4489-3901-5(1))* America Star Bks.

Casaluci, Stacy Manning. Miracles Love a Believer. 2011. 32p. pap. 13.00 *(978-1-61204-094-3(2)*, Eloquent Bks.) Strategic Book Publishing & Rights Agency (SBPRA).

Casey, Mark. An African Princess: Deasha's Wild Adventure. 2010. (Illus.). 54p. pap. 11.95 *(978-1-4327-3864-8(X))* Outskirts Pr., Inc.

Cashman, Mary & Whipple, Cynthia. Merrilee Mannerly & Her Magnificent Manners. Johnson, Meredith, illus. 2010. (J). 16.99 *(978-0-615-36448-3(9))* Pink&Brown Publishing, LLP.

Cass, Kiera. The Crown. 2016. (Selection Ser.: 5). (ENG.). 288p. (YA). (gr. 8). 19.99 *(978-0-06-239217-6(4)*, HarperTeen) HarperCollins Pubs.

—Happily Ever After. 2015. (ENG., Illus.). 416p. (YA). *(978-0-00-814366-4(8))* HarperCollins Pubs.

—Happily Ever After: Companion to the Selection Series. 2016. (Selection Ser.). (YA). lib. bdg. 20.85 *(978-0-606-38919-8(9))* Turtleback.

—Happily Ever after: Companion to the Selection Series. 2015. (Selection Novella Ser.). (ENG., Illus.). 416p. (YA). (gr. 8). 18.99 *(978-0-06-241408-3(9)*, HarperTeen) HarperCollins Pubs.

—The Heir. 2015. (ENG.). 368p. (YA). (Selection Ser.: 4). (gr. 8). 19.99 *(978-0-06-234985-9(6)*, HarperTeen); pap. *(978-0-06-239130-8(5))* HarperCollins Pubs.

—The One. 2015. (Selection Ser.: 3). (ENG.). 368p. (YA). (gr. 8). pap. 12.99 *(978-0-06-206000-6(7)*, HarperTeen) HarperCollins Pubs.

Castner, K. D. Daughters of Ruin. 2017. (ENG.). 320p. (YA). (gr. 9). pap. 11.99 *(978-1-4814-3666-3(X)*, McElderry, Margaret K. Bks.) McElderry, Margaret K. Bks.

Chambers, Dori. Princesses' Pink Pillows. 2009. 20p. pap. 10.50 *(978-1-60693-431-9(7)*, Eloquent Bks.) Strategic Book Publishing & Rights Agency (SBPRA).

Charvet, Lilian. Princess Dilly & the Kingdom of Pily: Book 1. 2010. 40p. pap. 20.99 *(978-1-4490-8330-4(7))* AuthorHouse.

Cheetham, Natasha. The Princess of the Sky. 2011. (Illus.). 24p. pap. 14.09 *(978-1-4567-7482-0(4))* AuthorHouse.

Childs, Tera Lynn. Forgive My Fins. 2011. (Forgive My Fins Ser.: 1). (ENG.). 336p. (YA). (gr. 8). pap. 8.99 *(978-0-06-191467-6(3)*, Tegen, Katherine Bks) HarperCollins Pubs.

—Just for Fins. 2013. (Forgive My Fins Ser.: 3). (ENG.). 256p. (YA). (gr. 8). pap. 9.99 *(978-0-06-219208-0(6)*, Tegen, Katherine Bks) HarperCollins Pubs.

Chima, Cinda Williams. The Demon King. 2010. (Seven Realms Novel Ser.: 1). (ENG.). 528p. (YA). (gr. 7-17). pap. 12.99 *(978-1-4231-2136-7(8))* Little, Brown Bks. for Young Readers.

—The Exiled Queen. 2011. (Seven Realms Novel Ser.: 2). (ENG.). 608p. (YA). (gr. 7-17). pap. 11.99 *(978-1-4231-2137-4(6))* Little, Brown Bks. for Young Readers.

—The Gray Wolf Throne. 2012. (Seven Realms Novel Ser.: 3). (ENG.). 544p. (YA). (gr. 7-17). pap. 11.99 *(978-1-4231-2138-1(4))* Little, Brown Bks. for Young Readers.

—Shadowcaster. (YA). 2018. (Shattered Realms Ser.: 2). (ENG.). 576p. (gr. 8). pap. 10.99 *(978-0-06-238098-2(2)*, HarperTeen) 2017. (Shattered Realms Ser.: 2). (ENG., Illus.). 560p. (gr. 8). 18.99 *(978-0-06-238097-5(4)*, HarperTeen) 2017. (Illus.). 560p. *(978-0-06-266291-0(0))* 2017. (Illus.). 551p. *(978-0-06-269044-9(2))* HarperCollins Pubs.

Chinchinian, Harry. The Princess & the Beggar II: Continuing Adventures. Chinchinian, Harry, illus. 2005. (Illus.). 176p. (J). lib. bdg. 18.95 *(978-1-892476-11-1(8))* Plum Tree Pr.

Chiu, Harry. Enve Lopt Unfolded. 2007. 268p. per. 17.95 *(978-0-595-44707-7(4))* iUniverse, Inc.

Chizuru, Mio. The Pirate & the Princess Volume 1: the Timelight Stone: The Timelight Stone. 2007. 110p. (J). pap. 5.99 *(978-1-933164-43-4(3))* Seven Seas Entertainment, LLC.

—The Pirate & the Princess Volume 2: the Red Crystal: The Red Crystal. 2007. 110p. (J). pap. 5.99 *(978-1-933164-44-1(1))* Seven Seas Entertainment, LLC.

Ciccone, Tizania & Linardi, Franca. The Pancake Princess. Bucci, Gino, illus. 2012. 36p. pap. 13.95 *(978-1-61897-720-5(2)*, Strategic Bk. Publishing) Strategic Book Publishing & Rights Agency (SBPRA).

Cinema, Bobby. Princess School. 2012. 68p. 18.66 *(978-1-4669-3968-4(0))*; 18p. pap. 8.66 *(978-1-4669-3967-7(2))* Trafford Publishing.

Claflin, Willy. Rapunzel & the Seven Dwarfs: A Maynard Moose Tale. Stimson, James, illus. 2011. (ENG.). 33p. (J). (gr. -1-3). 18.95 *(978-0-87483-914-2(9))* August Hse. Pubs., Inc.

Claire Hamelin Bruyere. Princess Bonnie & the Dragon. Mary Connors, illus. 2009. 16p. pap. 8.49 *(978-1-4389-8731-6(5))* AuthorHouse.

Clark, Andy S. Heavenly Magic: The Unforgettable Journey of Cassidy, the Valiant. 2013. 64p. pap. 23.95 *(978-1-4497-9874-1(8)*, WestBow Pr.) Author Solutions, LLC.

Clark, Marc. The Princess Fables. Hosford, Eric, illus. 2013. 114p. pap. 5.99 *(978-0-9910345-0-5(3))* Seven C's Productions, Inc.

Clark, Steven & Clark, Justin. The Golden Knight #1: The Boy Is Summoned. Gibson, Taylor, illus. 2011. (ENG.). 80p. (J). pap. 5.99 *(978-0-9647933-9-2(3))* New Horizons Pr.

Clawson, Kimberly. Fun O' Licious. Bellomy, Gail, illus. 2007. (ENG.). 56p. per. 16.95 *(978-1-4241-5556-9(8))* America Star Bks.

Clibbon, Meg. Sparkly Princesses. Clibbon, Lucy, illus. 2010. (My World Of... Ser.). (ENG.). 32p. (J). (gr. k-2). 21.19 *(978-1-84089-542-1(X))* Evans Brothers, Ltd. GBR. Dist: Children's Plus, Inc.

Cocca-Leffler, Maryann. Princess for a Day. 2012. (Penguin Young Readers, L2 Ser.). (ENG.). 32p. (J). (gr. -1-2). 3.99 *(978-0-448-49485-2(X)*, Grosset & Dunlap) Penguin Publishing Group.

Coe, Mary E. The Prince of Betherland. 2008. 117p. 24.95 *(978-0-557-03112-2(5))* Lulu Pr., Inc.

—The Prince of Betherland A Wonderful World of Fantasy. 2009. 66p. pap. 9.95 *(978-0-557-08499-9(7))* Lulu Pr., Inc.

—The Prince of Betherland a Wonderful World of Fantasy. 2009. 112p. pap. 9.95 *(978-0-557-09297-0(3))* Lulu Pr., Inc.

Coh, Smiljana. Princesses on the Run. 2013. (ENG., Illus.). 40p. (J). (gr. -1-1). 15.95 *(978-0-7624-4612-4(9)*, Running Pr. Kids) Running Pr.

Cohen, Warren Lee. Dragon Baked Bread, 32 vols. Ssebulime, John, illus. 2005. (ENG.). 32p. (J). *(978-1-902636-70-2(8))* Clairview Bks.

Coia, Kristina. Lymeria. 2007. 120p. (YA). per. 10.95 *(978-0-595-45268-2(X))* iUniverse, Inc.

Cokal, Susann. The Kingdom of Little Wounds. 2016. (ENG.). 576p. (YA). (gr. 11). pap. 14.99 *(978-0-7636-8757-1(X))* Candlewick Pr.

Cole, Babette. Princess Smartypants Breaks the Rules! 2010. (KOR., Illus.). 32p. (J). *(978-89-522-1360-0(2))* Salrim Pubn.

Cole, Nikki. Princess Hope. 2012. 40p. pap. 14.95 *(978-1-886528-39-0(X))* ASA Publishing Corp.

Coleman, Alice Scovell. Engraved in Stone. Armand, Anjale Renee, illus. 2003. 152p. (J). 14.95 *(978-0-9729846-0-7(7))* Tiara Bks. LLC.

Collins, A. L. Jack & the Korner Princess: New Jack Tales. 2017. (ENG., Illus.). 160p. (J). pap. 14.99 *(978-1-945330-92-6(9))* Telemachus Pr., LLC.

Connors, Colleen. A Real Princess. 2009. 32p. pap. 12.99 *(978-1-4389-6884-1(1))* AuthorHouse.

Cook, Jacqueline. The Little Bear Who Worried Too Much: Suzie Bear Goes to London. 2011. 34p. (gr. 1-4). pap. 13.50 *(978-1-60976-875-1(2)*, Eloquent Bks.) Strategic Book Publishing & Rights Agency (SBPRA).

Coombs, Kate. The Runaway Princess. l.t. ed. 2007. (Literacy Bridge Middle Reader Ser.). 325p. (J). (gr. 3-7). 22.95 *(978-0-7862-9633-0(X))* Thorndike Pr.

Coonan, Candace N. The Break of Dawn: Tales from Fadreama: Book 3. 2012. 364p. (gr. 4-6). pap. 20.33 *(978-1-4669-3567-9(7))* Trafford Publishing.

Cooper, Michelle. A Brief History of Montmaray. 2011. (Montmaray Journals: 1). (ENG.). 336p. (YA). (gr. 7). pap. 8.99 *(978-0-375-85154-4(2)*, Knopf Bks. for Young Readers) Random Hse. Children's Bks.

Corsetto, Danielle. Adventure Time: Pixel Princesses. 2013. lib. bdg. 23.30 *(978-0-606-35464-6(6))* Turtleback.

Coughlin, Jennie Rose. The Purple Scarf. Howes, Bryan Arthur, illus. 2008. 20p. per. 24.95 *(978-1-60441-733-3(1))* America Star Bks.

Coville, Bruce. The Dragonslayers. unabr. ed. 2004. (Words Take Wingtm Ser.). 119p. (J). (gr. 3-6). pap. 29.00 incl. audio *(978-0-8072-7988-5(9)*, S YA 958 SP, Listening Library) Random Hse. Audio Publishing Group.

Coville, Katherine. Briar & Rose & Jack. 2019. (ENG.). 368p. (J). (gr. 5-7). 16.99 *(978-1-328-95005-5(0)*, 1705914, Clarion Bks.) HarperCollins Pubs.

Cox, Greg. Riese: Kingdom Falling. 2013. (ENG., Illus.). 288p. (YA). (gr. 7). pap. 9.99 *(978-1-4424-2970-3(4)*, Simon & Schuster Bks. For Young Readers) Simon & Schuster Bks. For Young Readers.

Coyle, Carmela Lavigna. Do Princesses & Super Heroes Hit the Trails? A National Park Adventure. 2016. (Do Princesses Ser.). (Illus.). 32p. (J). (gr. -1-12). 15.95 *(978-1-63076-244-5(X))* Muddy Boots Pr.

—Do Princesses Become Astronauts? Gordon, Mike, illus. 2019. (Do Princesses Ser.). 32p. (J). (gr. -1-2). 15.95 *(978-1-63076-347-3(0))* Muddy Boots Pr.

—Do Princesses Boogie? Gordon, Mike, illus. 2016. (Do Princesses Ser.). 26p. (J). (gr. -1-2). bds. 7.95 *(978-1-63076-159-2(1))* Taylor Trade Publishing.

—Do Princesses Have Best Friends Forever? Gordon, Mike & Gordon, Carl, illus. 2010. (ENG.). 32p. (J). E-Book *(978-1-58979-543-3(1))* Taylor Trade Publishing.

—Do Princesses Have Best Friends Forever? Gordon, Carl & Gordon, Mike, illus. 2010. (Do Princesses Ser.). (ENG.). 32p. (J). (gr. -1-3). 15.95 *(978-1-58979-542-6(3))* Taylor Trade Publishing.

—Do Princesses Make Happy Campers? Gordon, Mike, illus. 2015. (Do Princesses Ser.). 32p. (J). (gr. -1-2). 15.95 *(978-1-63076-054-0(4))* Taylor Trade Publishing.

—Do Princesses Scrape Their Knees? 2006. (Do Princesses Ser.). (ENG., Illus.). 32p. (J). (gr. -1-2). 15.95 *(978-0-87358-909-3(2))* Cooper Square Publishing Llc.

—Do Princesses Wear Hiking Boots? Gordon, Mike & Gordon, Carl, illus. 2003. (Do Princesses Ser.). (ENG.). 32p. (J). (gr. -1-2). 15.95 *(978-0-87358-828-7(2))* Cooper Square Publishing Llc.

—Do Princesses Wear Hiking Boots? Gordon, Mike & Gordon, Carl, illus. 2014. (ENG.). 96p. (J). (gr. -1-2). spiral bd. 15.95 *(978-1-58979-945-5(3))* Taylor Trade Publishing.

Cronshaw, Joseph. Podge & Dodge. 2009. 32p. pap. 13.50 *(978-1-60693-868-3(1)*, Strategic Bk. Publishing) Strategic Book Publishing & Rights Agency (SBPRA).

Crossman, David. The Legend of Burial Island: A Bean & Ab Mystery. 2009. (ENG.). 201p. (J). (gr. 3-7). pap. 11.95 *(978-0-89272-797-1(7))* Down East Bks.

Croyle, Paula. Today I'll Be a Princess. Brown, Heather, illus. 2015. (ENG.). 12p. (J). bds. 5.99 *(978-1-4494-6057-0(7))* Andrews McMeel Publishing.

Crum, Shutta. Thomas & the Dragon Queen. Wildish, Lee, illus. 2013. (ENG.). 272p. (J). (gr. 4-6). 21.19 *(978-0-375-85703-4(6))* Random House Publishing Group.

Crump, Fred, Jr. Marigold & the Dragon. 2010. 32p. (J). 12.95 *(978-1-934056-73-8(1))* UMI (Urban Ministries, Inc.).

Cummins, Molly. The Jewel of Fez. 2006. 141p. pap. 24.95 *(978-1-4241-1044-5(0))* PublishAmerica, Inc.

Cuyler, Margery. Princess Bess Gets Dressed. Maione, Heather, illus. 2009. (ENG.). 32p. (J). (gr. -1-3). 18.99 *(978-1-4169-3833-0(8)*, Simon & Schuster Bks. For Young Readers) Simon & Schuster Bks. For Young Readers.

Cynthia, A. Sears. A World Divided: The Fairy Princess Chronicles - Book 1. 2012. 656p. *(978-1-4602-0516-7(2))*; pap. *(978-1-4602-0514-3(6))* FriesenPress.

Cyprus, Naomi. Sisters of Glass. (Sisters of Glass Ser.: 1). (ENG.). (J). (gr. 3-7). 2018. 400p. pap. 9.99 *(978-0-06-245849-0(3))* 2017. 384p. 16.99 *(978-0-06-245847-6(7))* HarperCollins Pubs. (HarperCollins).

Dadey, Debbie. The Lost Princess. Avakyan, Tatevik, illus. 2013. (Mermaid Tales Ser.: 5). (ENG.). 128p. (J). (gr. 1-4). 17.99 *(978-1-4424-8258-6(3))*; pap. 6.99 *(978-1-4424-8257-9(5))* Simon & Schuster Children's Publishing. (Aladdin).

—Lost Princess, Bk. 5. Avakyan, Tatevik, illus. 2015. (Mermaid Tales Ser.). (ENG.). 120p. (J). (gr. 1-4). 31.36 *(978-1-61479-326-7(3)*, 17148, Chapter Bks.) Spotlight.

Dalziel, Edward. Rocket Jumper. 2004. (ENG., Illus.). 16p. (gr. -1-3). 24.95 *(978-1-4290-9002-5(2))* Applewood Bks.

D'Angelo, Elaina R. The Magic Book of E, 1 vol. 2010. 48p. pap. 16.95 *(978-1-4489-3949-7(6))* America Star Bks.

Daniels, Sharon. Fifi the Fabulous. 2011. 24p. pap. 15.99 *(978-1-4628-9262-4(0))* Xlibris Corp.

Danson, Lesley, illus. Snow White. 2006. (Flip-Up Fairy Tales Ser.). 24p. (J). (gr. 1-2). *(978-1-84643-023-7(2))* Child's Play International Ltd.

Dao, Julie C. Kingdom of the Blazing Phoenix. 2019. (Rise of the Empress Ser.: 2). 384p. (YA). (gr. 9). pap. 10.99 *(978-1-5247-3834-1(4)*, Penguin Books) Penguin Young Readers Group.

Darlison, Aleesah. Krystal's Charge. Brailsford, Jill, illus. 2017. (Unicorn Riders Ser.). (ENG.). 112p. (J). (gr. 3-5). pap. 5.95 *(978-1-4795-6558-0(X)*, 128548, Picture Window Bks.) Capstone.

DasGupta, Sayantani. Game of Stars (Kiranmala & the Kingdom Beyond #2) (Kiranmala & the Kingdom Beyond Ser.: 2). (ENG.). 384p. (J). (gr. 3-7). 2020. pap. 8.99 *(978-1-338-18574-4(8))* 2019. (Illus.). 17.99 *(978-1-338-18573-7(X))* Scholastic, Inc. (Scholastic Pr.).

—The Serpent's Secret (Kiranmala & the Kingdom Beyond #1) (Kiranmala & the Kingdom Beyond Ser.: 1). (ENG.). 368p. (J). (gr. 3-7). 2019. pap. 8.99 *(978-1-338-18571-3(3))* 2018. 18.99 *(978-1-338-18570-6(5))* Scholastic, Inc. (Scholastic Pr.).

Davidson, S. & Daynes, K. Princess Jewelry Kid Kit (Bag) 2008. (Kid Kits Ser.). 96p. (J). 15.99 *(978-1-60130-104-8(9)*, Usborne) EDC Publishing.

—Princess Jewelry Kid Kit (Box) 2008. (Kid Kits Ser.). 96p. (J). 15.99 *(978-1-60130-115-4(4)*, Usborne) EDC Publishing.

Davidson, Susanna. The Frog Prince. 2005. 48p. (J). (gr. 2-18). 8.95 *(978-0-7945-0969-9(X)*, Usborne) EDC Publishing.

—Princess Handbook. Gordon, Mike, illus. 2006. 80p. (J). (gr. 3-7). 12.99 *(978-0-7945-1329-0(8)*, Usborne) EDC Publishing.

—Princess Polly & the Pony. Hill, Dave, illus. 2007. (First Reading Level 4 Ser.). 48p. (J). 8.99 *(978-0-7945-1756-4(0)*, Usborne) EDC Publishing.

Davies, Kate & Award, Anna. Beauty & the Beast. 2017. (ENG., Illus.). 24p. (J). pap. 6.00 *(978-1-84135-965-6(3))* Award Pubns. Ltd. GBR. Dist: Parkwest Pubns., Inc.

—The Princess & the Pea. 2017. (ENG., Illus.). 24p. (J). pap. 6.00 *(978-1-84135-966-3(1))* Award Pubns. Ltd. GBR. Dist: Parkwest Pubns., Inc.

—The Sleeping Beauty. 2017. (ENG., Illus.). 24p. (J). pap. 6.00 *(978-1-84135-968-7(8))* Award Pubns. Ltd. GBR. Dist: Parkwest Pubns., Inc.

Davies, Kate, et al. The Twelve Dancing Princesses. 2017. (ENG., Illus.). 24p. (J). pap. 6.00 *(978-1-84135-967-0(X))* Award Pubns. Ltd. GBR. Dist: Parkwest Pubns., Inc.

Davis, Marlo. The Morning Princess. 2013. 26p. pap. 16.95 *(978-1-4497-8792-9(4)*, WestBow Pr.) Author Solutions, LLC.

Day George, Jessica. Wednesdays in the Tower. 2013. (Tuesdays at the Castle Ser.). (ENG.). 240p. (J). (gr. 3-6). E-Book 6.39 *(978-1-61963-051-2(6)*, Bloomsbury USA Childrens) Bloomsbury Publishing USA.

De Audrade, Norma. The Frog, the Princess, the Purpurine, & the Silk Threads. 2005. (J). pap. 8.00 *(978-0-8059-6524-7(6))* Dorrance Publishing Co., Inc.

de la Cruz, Melissa. The Ring & the Crown (Extended Edition): the Ring & the Crown, Book 1. 2017. (ENG.). 480p. (J). (gr. 9-12). pap. 10.99 *(978-1-4847-9925-3(9)*, Disney-Hyperion) Disney Publishing Worldwide.

De Lafayette, Madame. The Princess de Montpensier. 2004. reprint ed. pap. 1.99 *(978-1-4192-7870-9(3))* Kessinger Publishing, LLC.

De Saint-Exupéry, Antoine. Le Petit Prince: Avec les dessins de l'auteur. (FRE., Illus.). 64p. (J). (gr. 1-7). audio, audio compact disk 12.95 *(978-2-921997-41-6(X))* Coffragants CAN. Dist: Penton Overseas, Inc.

—El Principito. (SPA.). 10.98 *(978-968-13-2180-2(4))* Editorial Diana, S.A. MEX. Dist: Continental Bk. Co., Inc.

Dean Wafstet, Cindi. Wings of Light. 2005. 31p. 15.00 *(978-1-4116-5567-6(2))* Lulu Pr., Inc.

Deisher, Kathleen E. Beyond the Gloesmur: Book 1 in the Gloesmur Scrolls. Deisher, Kathleen E., illus. 2003. (Gloesmur Scrolls Ser.). (Illus.). 270p. (J). pap. 13.95 *(978-1-892135-00-1(0))* Lamp Post Publishing, Inc.

Dharma Publishing Staff. The Proud Peacock: A Story about Humility. 3rd ed. 2013. (Jataka Tales Ser.). (Illus.). 36p. (gr. -1-7). pap. 8.95 *(978-0-89800-494-6(2))* Dharma Publishing.

Disney. Big Bear, Little Bear. 2012. (Disney Princess Step into Reading Ser.). lib. bdg. 13.55 *(978-0-606-26391-7(8))* Turtleback.

—Disney Princess: Adventure under the Sea. 2008. (J). 13.99 *(978-1-59319-979-1(1))* LeapFrog Enterprises, Inc.

—Frozen Cinestory, Volume 1. 2014. lib. bdg. 26.95 *(978-0-606-36645-8(8))* Turtleback.

—A Mother's Love. 2012. (Disney Princess Step into Reading Ser.). lib. bdg. 13.55 *(978-0-606-26392-4(6))* Turtleback.

Disney Book Group, et al. Clover Time. 2016. (Sofia the First World of Reading Ser.). (Illus.). 32p. (J). lib. bdg. 13.55 *(978-0-606-37534-4(1))* Turtleback.

Disney Book Group Staff. Disney Princess, Set. 2012. (ENG.). 272p. pap. 12.99 *(978-1-4231-5533-1(5))* Disney Pr.

—Enchanting Tale. 2010. (ENG.). 128p. (J). (gr. -1-2). 14.99 *(978-1-4231-1938-8(X))* Disney Pr.

Disney Books. Frozen ReadAlong Storybook & CD. 2013. (Read-Along Storybook & CD Ser.). (ENG., Illus.). 32p. (J). (gr. -1-k). pap. 6.99 *(978-1-4231-7064-8(4)*, Disney Press Books) Disney Publishing Worldwide.

—Princess Bedtime Stories-2nd Edition. 2017. (Storybook Collection). (ENG., Illus.). 304p. (J). (gr. 1-3). 16.99 *(978-1-4847-4711-7(9)*, Disney Press Books) Disney Publishing Worldwide.

Disney Editors. Frozen. 2013. lib. bdg. 14.75 *(978-0-606-32207-2(8))* Turtleback.

—Frozen - Anna's Icy Adventure. 2013. lib. bdg. 14.75 *(978-0-606-32206-5(X))* Turtleback.

—Mulan Is Loyal / Merida Is Brave. 2017. (Disney Princess Step into Reading Ser.). lib. bdg. 16.00 *(978-0-606-40246-0(2))* Turtleback.

Disney Press Editors. Sofia Takes the Lead. 2014. (Sofia the First World of Reading Ser.). (J). lib. bdg. 13.55 *(978-0-606-34102-8(1))* Turtleback.

Disney Princess Holiday: Cinderella So This Is Christmas/Beauty & the Beast One Magical Christmas/Ariel's Christmas under the Sea. unabr. ed. 2005. (Disney's Read along Collection Ser.). (J). pap. *(978-0-7634-1146-6(9))* Walt Disney Records.

Disney Princess Little Golden Book Library (Disney Princess) Tangled; Brave; the Princess & the Frog; the Little Mermaid; Beauty & the Beast; Cinderella, 6 vols. 2016. (Little Golden Book Ser.). (ENG., Ilius.). 144p. (J). (-k). 35.94 *(978-0-7364-3560-4(3)*, Golden/Disney) Random Hse. Children's Bks.

Disney Princess Staff, adapted by. Princess Enchanted Palace: Storybook & Play Castle. 2010. (Playbox Ser.). (ENG., Illus.). 32p. (J). (gr. -1-2). bds. 19.99 *(978-0-7944-2035-2(4))* Reader's Digest Assn., Inc., The.

Disney Princess Super Activity Fun Storybook Collection. 2005. (J). *(978-1-59487-168-9(X))* Artist Studios, Ltd.

Disney Storybook Artists Staff, contrib. by. Princess Adventure Stories. 2013. (Illus.). 300p. (J). *(978-1-4231-2661-4(0))* Disney Pr.

Disney's Read to Me Treasury - Princess. 2011. 400p. *(978-1-4231-2393-4(X))* Disney Pr.

Dixon, Heather. Entwined. 2012. (ENG.). 480p. (YA). (gr. 8). pap. 10.99 *(978-0-06-200104-7(3)*, Greenwillow Bks.) HarperCollins Pubs.

Donaldson, Julia. A Gold Star for Zog. Scheffler, Axel, illus. 2012. (ENG.). 32p. (J). (gr. -1-3). 18.99 *(978-0-545-41724-2(4)*, Levine, Arthur A. Bks.) Scholastic, Inc.

—Princess Mirror-Belle Bind Up 1. Monks, Lydia, illus. 2017. (Princess Mirror-Belle Ser.). (ENG.). 192p. (J). (gr. k-2). pap. 8.99 *(978-1-5098-3872-1(4))* Pan Macmillan GBR. Dist: Independent Pubs. Group.

—Zog & the Flying Doctors. Scheffler, Axel, illus. 2017. (ENG.). 32p. (J). (gr. -1-3). 17.99 *(978-1-338-13417-9(5)*, Levine, Arthur A. Bks.) Scholastic, Inc.

Donne, Alexa. The Stars We Steal. 2020. (ENG.). 400p. (YA). (gr. 7). 17.99 *(978-1-328-94894-6(3)*, 1705521, HarperTeen) HarperCollins Pubs.

Dorantes, Kathleen. Princess So-Wise. 2005. pap. 11.50 *(978-1-59330-330-3(0))* Aventine Pr.

Doty, Mariel. A Different Kind of Princess: Pictures of You. 2010. 260p. 26.50 *(978-1-60911-318-6(7)*, Eloquent Bks.) Strategic Book Publishing & Rights Agency (SBPRA).

Dower, Laura. Sunny & the Secret Passage. 2013. (Palace Puppies Ser.: 4). (J). lib. bdg. 14.75 *(978-0-606-35108-9(6))* Turtleback.

Doyle, Malachy. Tales from Old Ireland. Sharkey, Niamh, illus. 2008. (ENG.). 96p. (J). 21.99 *(978-1-84686-241-0(8))* Barefoot Bks., Inc.

Dreissigacker Martin, Susan. Princess Stephanie Stories: The Road Trip & the New School. 2009. 32p. pap. 18.79 *(978-1-4389-1836-5(4))* AuthorHouse.

Drobeck, Ronald D. My Name Is Prince Albert. 2012. 152p. (gr. 4-6). 30.95 *(978-1-4582-0205-5(4))*; pap. 12.99 *(978-1-4582-0203-1(8))* Author Solutions, LLC. (Abbott Pr.).

Dube, Pierrette. How to Become a Perfect Princess in Five Days, 1 vol. Melanson, Luc, illus. 2009. (Rainy Day Readers Ser.). (ENG.). 32p. (J). (gr. 1-2). 27.27 *(978-1-60754-376-3(1)*, d475ad4c-eaa9-491c-b8ae-c2c376868dd9, Windmill Bks.) Rosen Publishing Group, Inc., The.

Duffy, Carol Ann. The Princess's Blankets. Hyde, Catherine, illus. 2009. (ENG.). 40p. (J). (gr. k-3). 18.99 *(978-0-7636-4547-2(8)*, Templar) Candlewick Pr.

Durkin, Mary Jane. The Shabby Little Princess. 2009. 24p. pap. 14.99 *(978-1-4389-5115-7(9))* AuthorHouse.

Durst, Sarah Beth. Journey Across the Hidden Islands. 2017. (ENG., Illus.). 352p. (J). (gr. 5-7). 16.99 *(978-0-544-70679-8(X)*, 1628641, Clarion Bks.) HarperCollins Pubs.

Duty, William. Boomtown: Darkpit Mountain & the Princess Three, 1 vol. 2010. 76p. pap. 19.95 *(978-1-4489-5971-6(3))* America Star Bks.

Dyan, Penelope. Introducing Fabulous Marie, a Girl with a Good Head on Her Shoulders. Dyan, Penelope, illus. 2009. (Illus.). 44p. pap. 11.95 *(978-1-935118-55-8(2))* Bellissima Publishing, LLC.

Dyer, Sarah. Princess for a Day: A Clementine & Mungo Story. Dyer, Sarah, illus. (Illus.). 32p. (J). (gr. -1-k). 2009. pap. 12.95 *(978-0-7475-8891-7(0))* 2007. 22.95 *(978-0-7475-8753-8(1))* Bloomsbury Publishing Plc GBR. Dist: Independent Pubs. Group.

Dzidrums, Christine. Princess Dessabelle: Tennis Star. Muths, Tohn Fayette, illus. 2013. 50p. pap. 10.99 *(978-1-938438-34-9(5))* Creative Media Publishing.

—Princess Dessabelle Makes a Friend. Muths, Tohn, illus. 2011. 32p. (J). pap. 9.99 *(978-0-9826435-6-3(X))*; 17.99 *(978-0-9826435-7-0(8))* Creative Media Publishing.

East, Jacqueline, illus. Princess Palace: A Three-Demensional Playset. 2006. 8p. (J). (gr. -1-3). 22.95 *(978-1-58117-492-2(6)*, Intervisual/Piggy Toes) Bendon, Inc.

Eberly, Chelsea. Magic Friends. 2014. (Barbie Step into Reading Level 2 Ser.). lib. bdg. 13.55 *(978-0-606-35991-7(5))* Turtleback.

—Magic Friends (Barbie & the Secret Door) 2014. (Step into Reading Ser.). (ENG., Illus.). 32p. (J). (gr. -1-1). 5.99 *(978-0-385-38296-0(0)*, Random Hse. Bks. for Young Readers) Random Hse. Children's Bks.

Edwards, M. J. Dontayan. 2008. 62p. pap. 19.95 *(978-1-60610-026-4(2))* America Star Bks.

Edwards, Mamie. Magical Mix-Ups: Birthdays & Bridesmaids. Hodgkinson, Leigh, illus. 2012. (Magical Mix-Ups Ser.: 1). (ENG.). 96p. (J). (gr. 2-5). pap. 6.99 *(978-0-7636-6272-1(0))* Candlewick Pr.

—Magical Mix-Ups: Pets & Parties. Hodgkinson, Leigh, illus. 2013. (Magical Mix-Ups Ser.: 3). (ENG.). 96p. (J). (gr. 2-5). pap. 6.99 *(978-0-7636-6371-1(9))* Candlewick Pr.

Egbert, Charles. The Story of Princess Olivia: Wherein an Optimistic Slip of a Girl Brings Sunshine into the Lives of Her Royal Parents, the Whiny King & the ... & His Magical Minion, the Mischi. 2013. (ENG.). 144p. (J). (gr. 4-6). 14.95 *(978-1-59373-147-2(7))* Bunker Hill Publishing, Inc.

Elliott, Ruth. The Night Princess, 1 disc. Elliott, Ruth, illus. 2007. (SPA., Illus.). (J). per. 12.99 incl. DVD *(978-0-9795017-1-5(7))* Edu Designs.

Ellis, Larry & Ellis, Denise Brown. Antigua: The Land of Fairies Wizards & Heroes. 2007. (ENG.). 300p. 28.49 *(978-1-4343-1400-0(6))*; per. 17.99 *(978-1-4259-9782-3(1))* AuthorHouse.

Eltoukhy, G.N. Princess & the Enchanted Pegasus. 2012. 28p. pap. 16.09 *(978-1-4669-1831-3(4))* Trafford Publishing.

Emmett, Jonathan. The Princess & the Pig. Bernatene, Poly, illus. 2011. (ENG.). 32p. (J). (gr. k-8). 17.99 *(978-0-8027-2334-5(9)*, 900076370, Bloomsbury USA Childrens) Bloomsbury Publishing USA.

Espinosa, Rod. The Courageous Princess Pocket Manga. 2012. (Illus.). 232p. pap. 14.99 *(978-0-9841107-9-7(8))* Antarctic Pr., Inc.

EsterSonia. Sissi My Story - My life with my loving Owners. 2010. 78p. pap. 33.50 *(978-1-4452-1215-9(3))* Lulu Pr., Inc.

Eubank, Patricia Reeder. The Princess & the Snarls. Eubank, Patricia Reeder, illus. 2006. (ENG., Illus.). 32p. (J). (gr. k-3). 16.95 *(978-0-8249-5536-6(6)*, Ideals Pubns.) Worthy Publishing.

Evans, Rosemary R. The Little Princesses Magial Party. Taylor, Erin, illus. 2012. 40p. (J). 16.95 *(978-1-60743-759-8(7))* Wink Publishing.

Everett, Felicity & Rawson, Christopher. Stories of Princes & Princesses. 2004. (Young Reading Ser.). (Illus.). 48p. (J). (gr. 2-18). pap. 5.95 *(978-0-7945-0449-6(3)*, Usborne) EDC Publishing.

Fackrell, David. Princess, the Collection, Vol. 1. 2005. 78p. pap. 19.99 *(978-1-4116-5820-2(5))* Lulu Pr., Inc.

Fairbanks, Letitia. Princess April Morning-Glory: What Kind of a World Would You Create, If You Had to Do Three Dood Deeds to Make Ii Home Again? Fairbanks, Letitia, illus. 2013. (ENG., Illus.). 66p. pap. 24.00 *(978-0-9887848-0-2(7))* Sandramantos Publishing.

Fairy Tale- Cinderella. 2005. (J). bds. *(978-1-4194-0039-1(8))* Paradise Pr., Inc.

Fairy tales - Cinderella. 2005. (J). bds. *(978-1-4194-0100-8(9))* Paradise Pr., Inc.

Fairy Tales- Sleeping Beauty. 2005. (J). bds. *(978-1-4194-0042-1(8))* Paradise Pr., Inc.

Falconer, Ian. Olivia & the Fairy Princesses. 2013. (CHI.). 40p. (J). (gr. -1-2). *(978-986-189-389-1(X))* Grimm Cultural Ent., Co., Ltd.

—Olivia & the Fairy Princesses. Falconer, Ian, illus. 2012. (ENG., Illus.). 40p. (J). (gr. -1-3). 19.99 *(978-1-4424-5027-1(4)*, Atheneum Bks. for Young Readers) Simon & Schuster Children's Publishing.

—Olivia y Las Princesas. 2012. (SPA., Illus.). 32p. (J). (gr. -1-1). 17.99 *(978-1-933032-82-5(0))* Lectorum Pubns., Inc.

Farley, Christina. The Princess & the Page. 2017. (ENG.). 240p. (J). (gr. 3-7). 17.99 *(978-0-545-92409-2(X)*, Scholastic Pr.) Scholastic, Inc.

Farrant, Natasha. Eight Princesses & a Magic Mirror. Corry, Lydia, illus. 2020. (ENG.). 224p. (J). (gr. 4-7). 19.95 *(978-1-324-01556-7(X)*, 341556, Norton Young Readers) Norton, W. W. & Co., Inc.

Ferris, Jean. Once upon a Marigold. 2004. 275p. (gr. 5). 17.00 *(978-0-7569-3613-6(6))* Perfection Learning Corp.

—Twice upon a Marigold. 2009. (ENG., Illus.). 304p. (J). (gr. 3-7). pap. 6.99 *(978-0-15-206692-5(6)*, 1099004, Clarion Bks.) HarperCollins Pubs.

Fimbres, Lorraine. The Gingerbread Princess. 2012. 28p. pap. 16.09 *(978-1-4669-1404-9(1))* Trafford Publishing.

Finnegan, Delphine. The Big Birthday Surprise! Hall, Susan, illus. 2017. 24p. (J). *(978-1-5182-5213-6(3))* Random Hse., Inc.

Finney, Shad. Princess Nap. 2008. 28p. pap. 15.99 *(978-1-4363-2119-8(0))* Xlibris Corp.

Finney, Wendy & Ross, Tony. Best Friends! (the Not So Little Princess) 2019. (Not-So-Little Princess Colour Readers Ser.: 2). (ENG., Illus.). 64p. (J). (gr. k-2). 9.99 *(978-1-78344-511-0(4))* Penguin Random Hse. AUS. Dist: Independent Pubs. Group.

Fitzgerald, D. M. The True Story of the Big Red Onion. Cudd, Savannah, illus. 2013. 36p. 18.99 *(978-0-9890288-7-5(9))*; pap. 10.99 *(978-0-9890288-5-1(2))* Mindstir Media.

Flaker, Tracey. Around the Corner: Gwenever's Quest. 2006. 55p. pap. 16.95 *(978-1-4241-1886-1(7))* PublishAmerica, Inc.

Flannigan, Liz. Starlight Grey. Docampo, Valeria, illus. 2013. (Magic Stories Ser.). 48p. (J). (gr. 1-4). pap. 8.99 *(978-1-84686-778-1(9))* Barefoot Bks., Inc.

Fleming, Ligia Morales. The Very Special Princess. 2012. (ENG.). 25p. (J). pap. 14.95 *(978-1-4327-9665-5(8))* Outskirts Pr., Inc.

Fletcher, Susan. Alphabet of Dreams. 2008. (ENG., Illus.). 432p. (YA). (gr. 7-12). mass mkt. 7.99 *(978-0-689-85152-0(9)*, Simon Pulse) Simon Pulse.

Flinn, Alex. Cloaked. 2011. 341p. (YA). lib. bdg. 17.89 *(978-0-06-087423-0(6)*, HarperTeen) HarperCollins Pubs.

—A Kiss in Time. 2010. (ENG.). 400p. (YA). (gr. 8-18). pap. 9.99 *(978-0-06-087421-6(X)*, HarperTeen) HarperCollins Pubs.

Floca, Brian, illus. The Hinky-Pink: An Old Tale. 2008. (ENG.). 48p. (J). (gr. -1-3). 16.99 *(978-0-689-87588-5(6)*, Atheneum/Richard Jackson Bks.) Simon & Schuster Children's Publishing.

Flood, Heather. Snowwhere. 2006. (ENG.). 268p. pap. 19.48 *(978-1-84728-391-7(8))* Lulu Pr., Inc.

Ford, Bernette. Princess Puppy. Williams, Sam, illus. 2013. (J). *(978-0-545-53967-8(6)*, Cartwheel Bks.) Scholastic, Inc.

Foster, Jackie. Land of Anear, 1 vol. 2010. 27p. pap. 24.95 *(978-1-61546-634-4(7))* America Star Bks.

Franklin, Ashley. Not Quite Snow White. Glenn, Ebony, illus. 2019. (ENG.). 32p. (J). (gr. -1-3). 17.99 *(978-0-06-279860-2(X)*, HarperCollins) HarperCollins Pubs.

Franz, Kevin. Into the Hidden Lands: A Castle Rose Adventure. Stigler, Marilyn, illus. 2004. 112p. (J). per. 7.99 *(978-0-9747774-0-5(4))* Starbell Bks.

Freeman, Mylo. Princess Arabella at the Museum. 2021. (Princess Arabella Ser.). (ENG., Illus.). 32p. (J). 16.95 *(978-1-913175-06-1(5))* Cassava Republic Pr. GBR. Dist: Consortium Bk. Sales & Distribution.

—Princess Arabella's Birthday. 2009. (Illus.). 32p. (J). (gr. -1-3). 14.95 *(978-0-9815761-7-6(6))* Mackenzie Smiles, LLC.

French, Vivian. The Cherry Pie Princess. Kissi, Marta, illus. 2018. (ENG.). 176p. (J). pap. 5.99 *(978-1-61067-733-2(1))* Kane Miller.

—Princess Charlotte & the Enchanted Rose. Gibb, Sarah, illus. 2007. (Tiara Club Ser.: No. 7). 80p. (J). (gr. 1-4). pap. 3.99 *(978-0-06-112441-9(9)*, Tegen, Katherine Bks) HarperCollins Pubs.

—Princess Katie & the Silver Pony. Gibb, Sarah, illus. 2007. (Tiara Club Ser.: No.2). 80p. (J). (gr. 1-4). 15.99 *(978-0-06-112432-7(X)*, Tegen, Katherine Bks) HarperCollins Pubs.

—The Tiara Club at Ruby Mansions No. 5: Princess Lauren & the Diamond Necklace. 2008. (Tiara Club Ser.). (ENG., Illus.). 80p. (J). (gr. 1-4). pap. 3.99 *(978-0-06-143488-4(4)*, Tegen, Katherine Bks) HarperCollins Pubs.

Frost, Libby. Princess Snowbelle. 2017. (ENG., Illus.). 32p. (J). 16.99 *(978-1-68119-690-9(5)*, 900182161, Bloomsbury USA Childrens) Bloomsbury Publishing USA.

—Princess Snowbelle & the Snow Games. 2018. (ENG., Illus.). 32p. (J). 16.99 *(978-1-5476-0025-0(X)*, 900195204, Bloomsbury Children's Bks.) Bloomsbury Publishing USA.

Funderburg, April. Soul Snatcher. 2009. 84p. pap. 19.95 *(978-1-60749-765-3(4))* America Star Bks.

Gabriel, Elizabeth P. & Gabriel, Pamela P. Ziccah Blows Her Horn. 2008. 24p. pap. 12.99 *(978-1-4389-2447-2(X))* AuthorHouse.

Gaiman, Neil. Cinnamon. Srinivasan, Divya, illus. 2017. (ENG.). 40p. (J). (gr. -1-3). 19.99 *(978-0-06-239961-8(6)*, HarperCollins) HarperCollins Pubs.

—The Sleeper & the Spindle. Riddell, Chris, illus. (ENG.). (YA). (gr. 8). 2019. 72p. pap. 10.99 *(978-0-06-239825-3(3))* 2015. 64p. 19.99 *(978-0-06-239824-6(5))* HarperCollins Pubs. (HarperCollins).

Gallo, Tina. Cinderella: A Wheel-Y Silly Fairy Tale. Scott, Kimberley, illus. 2011. (Little Simon Sillies Ser.). (ENG.). 14p. (J). (gr. -1-1). lib. bdg. 5.99 *(978-1-4424-2106-6(1)*, Little Simon) Little Simon.

Galvin, Laura Gates. Princess Counting Fun. Parisi, Anthony, ed. 2011. (Learning Library). (ENG., Illus.). 24p. (gr. -1). 8.99 *(978-1-60727-265-6(2))* Studio Mouse LLC.

Galvin, Laura Gates & Studio Mouse Editorial. Cinderella: Dreams Do Come True. 2008. (ENG., Illus.). 36p. (J). (gr. -1). 7.99 *(978-1-59069-436-7(8))* Studio Mouse LLC.

—Cinderella & Belle: Kindness Counts. Williams, Tracee, ed. 2008. (ENG., Illus.). 24p. (J). (gr. -1). 4.99 *(978-1-59069-652-1(2))* Studio Mouse LLC.

Gardener, Amanda & Sealey, Nanlie. Butterfly Pavilion. 2013. 24p. pap. 10.99 *(978-1-60820-898-2(2))* MLR Pr., LLC.

Gardner, Sally. Book of Princesses. (ENG., Illus.). 96p. (J). 19.95 *(978-1-85881-350-9(6)*, Orion) Orion Publishing Group, Ltd. GBR. Dist: Trafalgar Square Publishing.

Garey, Barbara J. The Adventures of Princess Naomia, 1 vol. 2009. 32p. pap. 24.95 *(978-1-61546-090-8(X))* America Star Bks.

Gavin, Jamila. Three Indian Princesses: The Stories of Savitri, Damayanti & Sita. 2004. (ENG., Illus.). 112p. (Orig.). (J). pap. 7.50 *(978-0-7497-4613-1(0))* Farshore GBR. Dist: Trafalgar Square Publishing.

Gaydos, Nora. Princess of the Potty - Little Steps for Big Kids! Gutierrez, Akemi, illus. 2011. (ENG.). 30p. (J). (gr. -1-17). 8.99 *(978-1-60169-076-0(2))* Innovative Kids.

George, Jessica Day. Fridays with the Wizards. (Tuesdays at the Castle Ser.). (ENG.). 2017. 256p. (J). pap. 9.99 *(978-1-68119-204-8(7)*, 900162856) 2016. 240p. (YA). 16.99 *(978-1-61963-429-9(5)*, 900135951) Bloomsbury Publishing USA. (Bloomsbury USA Childrens).

—Princess of Glass. 2011. (Twelve Dancing Princesses Ser.). (ENG.). 272p. (YA). (gr. 7). pap. 10.99 *(978-1-59990-659-1(7)*, 900074740, Bloomsbury USA Childrens) Bloomsbury Publishing USA.

—Princess of the Midnight Ball. 2010. (Twelve Dancing Princesses Ser.). (ENG.). 304p. (YA). (gr. 7-9). pap. 10.99 *(978-1-59990-455-9(1)*, 900064161, Bloomsbury USA Childrens) Bloomsbury Publishing USA.

—Thursdays with the Crown. (Tuesdays at the Castle Ser.). (ENG.). 2017. 240p. (J). pap. 8.99 *(978-1-68119-221-5(7)*, 900164100) 2014. 224p. (YA). (gr. 3-6). 16.99 *(978-1-61963-299-8(3)*, 900132430) Bloomsbury Publishing USA. (Bloomsbury USA Childrens).

—Wednesdays in the Tower. 2017. (Tuesdays at the Castle Ser.). (ENG.). 256p. (J). pap. 8.99 *(978-1-68119-219-2(5)*, 900164104, Bloomsbury USA Childrens) Bloomsbury Publishing USA.

Gil, Carmen. It's a Pain to Be a Princess! Brokenbrow, Jon, tr. Montero Galan, Daniel, illus. 2012. (ENG.). 28p. (J). (gr. k-3). 14.95 *(978-84-15241-78-2(X))* Cuento de Luz SL ESP. Dist: Publishers Group West (PGW).

—Que Fastidio Ser Princesa! (It's a Pain to Be a Princess) (It's a Pain to Be a Princess) Montero Galan, Daniel, illus. 2012. (SPA.). 28p. (J). (gr. k-3). 14.95 *(978-84-15241-14-0(3))* Cuento de Luz SL ESP. Dist: Publishers Group West (PGW).

Giles, Katharine. The Princess of Skye, an Archer Adventure. 2013. (ENG.). 280p. (YA). pap. 12.99 *(978-1-939927-79-8(X))* Telemachus Pr., LLC.

Gili, Phillida. Cinderella: A Pop-up Book. Gili, Phillida, illus. 2007. (Illus.). 12p. (J). 25.00 *(978-1-4223-9031-3(4))* DIANE Publishing Co.

Gillespie, Tonnika. The Queen's 3 Jewels. Anderson, Susan, illus. 2009. 20p. pap. 13.99 *(978-1-4389-3925-4(6))* AuthorHouse.

Gillian, Chelsea, et al. Princess ABCs And 123s. rev. ed. 2007. (ENG., Illus.). 24p. (J). (gr. -1-1). 4.99 *(978-1-59069-560-9(7))* Studio Mouse LLC.

Gilligan, Shannon. Princess Island. Arroyo, Fian, illus. 2015. (ENG.). 96p. (J). (gr. 2-2). pap. 7.99 *(978-1-937133-50-4(8))* Chooseco LLC.

Gilman, Phoebe. The Balloon Tree. 2004. (J). (gr. k-3). spiral bd. *(978-0-616-01650-3(6))* Canadian National Institute for the Blind/Institut National Canadien pour les Aveugles.

—The Balloon Tree. 2011. (ENG., Illus.). 32p. (J). (gr. -1-k). 16.95 *(978-1-61608-454-7(5)*, 608454, Sky Pony Pr.) Skyhorse Publishing Co., Inc.

Glass, Calliope. Tiana: The Stolen Jewel. Disney Storybook Artists, illus. 2017. (Disney Princess Ser.). (ENG.). 96p. (J).

(gr. 2-6). lib. bdg. 31.36 (978-1-5321-4122-5(X), 26995, Chapter Bks.) Spotlight.

Glazov, Sheila N. Princess Shayna's Invisible Visible Gift. 2011. (ENG., Illus.). 136p. pap. 19.95 (978-1-61711-035-1(3), P196501) SLACK, Inc.

Gleason, Colleen. The Chess Queen Enigma: A Stoker & Holmes Novel. (ENG.). 360p. (YA). (gr. 7-12). 2016. pap. 9.99 (978-1-4521-5649-1(2)) 2015. (Stoker & Holmes Ser.: 3). 17.99 (978-1-4521-4317-0(X)) Chronicle Bks. LLC.

—The Spiritglass Charade. 2015. (Stoker & Holmes Ser.: 2). (YA). lib. bdg. 20.85 (978-0-606-37441-5(8)) Turtleback.

Glynn, Connie. The Rosewood Chronicles #1: Undercover Princess. (Rosewood Chronicles Ser.: 1). (ENG.). (J). (gr. 3-7). 2019. 464p. pap. 9.99 (978-0-06-284782-9(1)) 2018. 448p. 16.99 (978-0-06-284780-5(5)) HarperCollins Pubs. (HarperCollins).

Golden Books. Nella's Sticker Adventure! (Nella the Princess Knight) Golden Books, illus. 2018. (ENG., Illus.). 64p. (J). (gr. -1-2). pap. 5.99 (978-1-5247-6886-7(3), Golden Bks.) Random Hse. Children's Bks.

Gologan, Trena. Alexandru's Gift. 2008. 35p. pap. 17.00 (978-1-4357-3486-9(6)) Lulu Pr., Inc.

Gonyea, Maria. Princess Maria. 2013. 28p. pap. 13.95 (978-1-4525-8189-7(4), Balboa Pr.) Author Solutions, LLC.

Goodeaux, Cindi Handley. The Adventures of Princess Jellibean. Dasgupta, Sanghamitra, illus. 2018. (ENG.). 52p. (J). (gr. 1-5). pap. 10.99 (978-1-68160-697-2(6)) Crimson Cloak Publishing.

Gordon, Jennifer. Terrible Tales 2: The Bloodcurdling Truth about the Frog Prince, Jack & the Beanstalk, A Very Fowl Duckling, the Ghoulishly Ghoulish Snow White, A Really Crabby Princess, & A Very Squashed Pea. 2011. 110p. (gr. -1-12). 20.95 (978-1-4620-0941-1(7)); pap. 10.95 (978-1-4620-0940-4(9)) iUniverse, Inc.

Gordon, Mike, illus. The Princess & the Pea. rev. ed. 2007. (Young Reading CD Packs Ser.). 48p. (J). (gr. -1-3). 9.99 incl. audio compact disk (978-0-7945-1875-2(3), Usborne) EDC Publishing.

—Stories of Princesses. 2006. 144p. (J). (gr. 4-7). 14.99 (978-0-7945-1385-6(9), Usborne) EDC Publishing.

Gorman, Zac. Thisby Thestoop & the Black Mountain. Bosma, Sam, illus. (ENG.). 336p. (J). (gr. 3-7). 2019. pap. 6.99 (978-0-06-249568-6(2)) 2018. 16.99 (978-0-06-249567-9(4)) HarperCollins Pubs. (HarperCollins).

Gosling, Cherie & Disney Storybook Artists Staff. Mulan Is Loyal: Merida Is Brave. 2017. (Illus.). 24p. (J). (978-1-5379-5745-6(7)) Random Hse., Inc.

Gouveia, Keith. The Goblin Pricess. 2008. 208p. (978-1-897370-49-0(0)) Lachesis Publishing.

Goyer, Katell. Princesses of World. Misstigri, illus. 2009. 3p. (J). (gr. -1-3). 17.99 (978-0-8437-1445-6(X)) Hammond World Atlas Corp.

Grandoit, Jean. In the Quest for Inshalla: Simbies of the Caribbean at the World Under. 2010. 68p. pap. 25.49 (978-1-4520-3900-8(3)) AuthorHouse.

Grant, Cj. The Princess & the Swan. 2012. 48p. pap. 21.88 (978-1-4669-1594-7(3)) Trafford Publishing.

Gravel, Elise. The Worst Book Ever. 2019. (ENG., Illus.). 48p. 17.95 (978-1-77046-363-9(1), 900208055) Drawn & Quarterly Pubns. CAN. Dist: Macmillan.

Green, Rich. Pearlsus. 2007. 140p. 20.95 (978-0-595-91189-9(7)) iUniverse, Inc.

Green with Envy. 2014. (Unicorn Magic Ser.: 3). (ENG., Illus.). 144p. (J). (gr. 1-4). pap. 6.99 (978-1-4424-9826-6(9), Aladdin) Simon & Schuster Children's Publishing.

Greenawalt, Kelly. Princess Truly in I Am Truly. Rauscher, Amariah, illus. 2017. (Princess Truly Ser.). (ENG.). 40p. (J). (gr. -1-k). 17.99 (978-1-338-16720-7(0), Orchard Bks.) Scholastic, Inc.

—Princess Truly in My Magical, Sparkling Curls. Rauscher, Amariah, illus. 2018. (Princess Truly Ser.). (ENG.). 40p. (J). (gr. -1-k). 18.99 (978-1-338-16719-1(7), Orchard Bks.) Scholastic, Inc.

Greene, Stephanie. A Pocketful of Princess Posey: Princess Posey, First Grader Books 1-3. Roth Sisson, Stephanie, illus. 2014. (Princess Posey, First Grader Ser.). 288p. (J). (gr. k-3). 9.99 (978-0-14-751472-1(X), Puffin Books) Penguin Young Readers Group.

—Princess Posey & the Christmas Magic. 2013. (Princess Posey, First Grader Ser.: 7). 96p. (J). (gr. k-3). pap. 5.99 (978-0-14-242734-7(9), Puffin Books) Penguin Young Readers Group.

—Princess Posey & the First-Grade Boys. Roth Sisson, Stephanie, illus. 2014. (Princess Posey, First Grader Ser.: 8). 96p. (J). (gr. k-3). pap. 5.99 (978-0-14-242735-4(7), Puffin Books) Penguin Young Readers Group.

—Princess Posey & the Flower Girl Fiasco. Roth Sisson, Stephanie, illus. 2018. (Princess Posey, First Grader Ser.: 12). 96p. (J). (gr. k-3). 5.99 (978-0-14-751720-3(6), Puffin Books) Penguin Young Readers Group.

Greenway, Beth. A True Princess of Hawai'i. Yee, Tammy, illus. 2017. (ENG.). 32p. (J). (gr. k-3). 17.95 (978-1-62855-948-4(9)) Arbordale Publishing.

—Una Verdadera Princesa de Hawái. Yee, Tammy, illus. 2017. (SPA.). 32p. (J). (gr. 2-3). pap. 11.95 (978-1-62855-950-7(0), 0e9b39f5-7b57-457e-903b-b4620d5a04b2) Arbordale Publishing.

Gregg, Stacy. The Princess & the Foal. 2015. (ENG.). 272p. (J). (gr. 5). pap. 7.99 (978-0-14-751242-0(5), Puffin Books) Penguin Young Readers Group.

Grey, Chelsea Gillian. Princess Colors. 2004. (Early Learning Ser.). (Illus.). 36p. (J). (gr. -1-3). 12.99 incl. audio compact disk (978-1-59069-370-4(1), 1A102) Studio Mouse LLC.

Grey, Mini. The Very Smart Pea & the Princess-To-be. 2011. (ENG.). 32p. (J). (gr. k-3). pap. 7.99 (978-0-375-87370-6(8), Dragonfly Bks.) Random Hse. Children's Bks.

Gribble, Julie. Bubblegum Princess. Hanson, Lori, illus. 2013. 32p. (J). 16.99 (978-0-9890914-0-4(6)) NY Media Works, LLC.

Griffin, Casey. Secrets of a Reluctant Princess. 2017. (ENG.). 320p. (YA). pap. 9.99 (978-1-63375-593-2(2), 9781633755932) Entangled Publishing, LLC.

Grimm, Brothers. The Frog Prince. Schroeder, Binette, illus. 2013. (ENG.). 32p. (J). (gr. -1-3). 17.95 (978-0-7358-4140-6(3)) North-South Bks., Inc.

—Snow White. Greban, Quentin, illus. 2013. (ENG.). 32p. (J). (gr. -1-3). pap. 7.95 (978-0-7358-4116-1(0)) North-South Bks., Inc.

—The Twelve Dancing Princesses. Duntze, Dorothee, illus. 2013. (ENG.). 32p. (J). (gr. -1-2). 17.95 (978-0-7358-4121-5(7)) North-South Bks., Inc.

Grimm, Jacob & Grimm, Wilhelm K. Sleeping Beauty / La Bella Durmiente. 2004. (Illus.). (J). (978-1-933530-18-5(9)) Bingo Bks., Inc.

Grizzard, Sue H. Princess Caylee: An Incredible Birthday Wish Come True. 2009. 44p. pap. 19.95 (978-1-4490-4001-7(2)) AuthorHouse.

Guerrera, Jeannette D. The Pot of Gold. 2012. 20p. pap. 17.99 (978-1-4685-5883-8(8)) AuthorHouse.

Guillain, Charlotte. The Frog Prince Saves Sleeping Beauty. Widdowson, Dan, illus. 2016. (Fairy Tale Mix-Ups Ser.). (ENG.). 24p. (J). (gr. k-2). lib. bdg. 23.99 (978-1-4109-8302-2(1), 132995, Raintree) Capstone.

Gunderson, Jessica. Sleeping Beauty: An Interactive Fairy Tale Adventure. Epelbaum, Mariano, illus. 2018. (You Choose: Fractured Fairy Tales Ser.). (ENG.). 112p. (J). (gr. 3-7). lib. bdg. 32.65 (978-1-5435-3006-3(0), 138603, Capstone Pr.) Capstone.

Guo, Amy. Vhonk. 2012. 588p. pap. 34.95 (978-1-4626-9981-0(2)) America Star Bks.

Guthrie, Savannah & Oppenheim, Allison. Princesses Save the World. Byrne, Eva, illus. 2018. (ENG.). 32p. (J). (gr. -1-2). 17.99 (978-1-4197-3171-6(8), 1201401, Abrams Bks. for Young Readers) Abrams, Inc.

—Princesses Wear Pants. Byrne, Eva, illus. 2017. (ENG.). 32p. (J). (gr. -1-2). 18.99 (978-1-4197-2603-3(X), 1186101) Abrams, Inc.

Haack, Daniel & Galupo, Isabel. Maiden & Princess. Human, Becca, illus. 2019. (ENG.). 40p. (J). (gr. -1-3). 17.99 (978-1-4998-0776-9(7)) Little Bee Books Inc.

Hack, Brittany. The Glitter Princess. 2012. 24p. 24.95 (978-1-4626-6638-6(8)) America Star Bks.

Haddix, Margaret Peterson. Just Ella. 2015. (Palace Chronicles Ser.: 1). (ENG., Illus.). 208p. (YA). (gr. 7). pap. 10.99 (978-1-4814-2021-1(6), Simon & Schuster Bks. For Young Readers) Simon & Schuster Bks. For Young Readers.

—Palace of Lies. 2015. (Palace Chronicles Ser.: 3). (ENG., Illus.). 368p. (YA). (gr. 7). 19.99 (978-1-4424-4281-8(6)) Simon & Schuster Children's Publishing.

—Palace of Mirrors. 2010. (Palace Chronicles Ser.: 2). (ENG.). 320p. (J). (gr. 5-9). pap. 8.99 (978-1-4424-0667-4(4), Simon & Schuster Bks. For Young Readers) Simon & Schuster Bks. For Young Readers.

Haile, Carol J. The Princess Tree: A Tale of Fairies, Elves & Magic. l.t. ed. 2005. (ESK., Illus.). 32p. (J). 19.95 (978-0-9711236-1-8(6)) Firenze Pr.

Hale, Shannon. Book of a Thousand Days. 2017. (ENG.). 336p. (YA). pap. 10.99 (978-1-68119-315-1(9), 900165753, Bloomsbury USA Childrens) Bloomsbury Publishing USA.

—The Forgotten Sisters. 2016. (Princess Academy Ser.: 3). (J). lib. bdg. 18.40 (978-0-606-38441-4(3)) Turtleback.

—The Goose Girl. 2003. (Books of Bayern Ser.: No. 2). (ENG., Illus.). 400p. (YA). (gr. 5-18). 19.99 (978-1-58234-843-8(X), 900021140, Bloomsbury USA Childrens) Bloomsbury Publishing USA.

—Princess Academy. (Princess Academy Ser.: 1). (ENG.). (gr. 5-8). 2005. 320p. (YA). 17.99 (978-1-58234-993-0(2), 900031142) 2nd ed. 2015. 336p. (J). pap. 9.99 (978-1-61963-613-2(1), 900142415) Bloomsbury Publishing USA. (Bloomsbury USA Childrens).

—Princess Academy. 2009. (Princess Academy Ser.: No. 1). 8.86 (978-0-7848-2867-0(9), Everbind) Marco Bk. Co.

—Princess Academy. 2007. (Princess Academy Ser.: No. 1). 314p. (gr. 5-9). 18.00 (978-0-7569-8180-8(8)) Perfection Learning Corp.

—Princess Academy. (Princess Academy Ser.: No. 1). (978-0-439-88811-0(5), Scholastic) Scholastic, Inc.

—Princess Academy. l.t. ed. 2006. (Princess Academy Ser.: No. 1). 339p. (J). (gr. 5-9). 23.95 (978-0-7862-8733-8(0)) Thorndike Pr.

—Princess Academy. 2015. (Princess Academy Ser.: 1). (YA). lib. bdg. 18.40 (978-0-606-36438-6(2)) Turtleback.

—Princess Academy: the Forgotten Sisters. (Princess Academy Ser.: 3). (ENG.). 2016. 352p. (J). pap. 9.99 (978-1-61963-933-1(5), 900152540) 2015. 336p. (YA). (gr. 5-8). 18.99 (978-1-61963-485-5(6), 900138574) Bloomsbury Publishing USA. (Bloomsbury USA Childrens).

Hale, Shannon & Hale, Dean. The Princess in Black. Pham, LeUyen, illus. (Princess in Black Ser.: 1). (ENG.). 96p. (J). (gr. k-3). 2015. pap. 6.99 (978-0-7636-7888-3(0)) 2014. 15.99 (978-0-7636-6510-4(X)) Candlewick Pr.

—The Princess in Black. 2015. (Princess in Black Ser.: 1). lib. bdg. 17.20 (978-0-606-36863-6(9)) Turtleback.

—The Princess in Black & the Hungry Bunny Horde. Pham, LeUyen, illus. 2016. (Princess in Black Ser.: 3). (ENG.). 96p. (J). (gr. k-3). pap. 6.99 (978-0-7636-9089-2(9)); 15.99 (978-0-7636-6513-5(4)) Candlewick Pr.

—The Princess in Black & the Hungry Bunny Horde. Pham, LeUyen, illus. 2016. (Princess in Black Ser.: 3). (ENG.). 85p. (J). (gr. k-3). 17.20 (978-0-606-39109-2(6)) Turtleback.

—The Princess in Black & the Mysterious Playdate. Pham, LeUyen, illus. (Princess in Black Ser.: 5). (ENG.). 96p. (J). (gr. k-3). 2018. pap. 6.99 (978-1-5362-0051-5(4)) 2017. 15.99 (978-0-7636-8826-4(6)) Candlewick Pr.

—The Princess in Black & the Mysterious Playdate. Pham, LeUyen, illus. 2018. (Princess in Black Ser.). (ENG.). 96p. (J). (gr. k-3). lib. bdg. 31.36 (978-1-5321-4223-9(4), 28560, Chapter Bks.) Spotlight.

—The Princess in Black & the Mysterious Playdate. 2018. (Princess in Black Ser.: 5). (J). lib. bdg. 17.20 (978-0-606-40910-0(6)) Turtleback.

—The Princess in Black & the Perfect Princess Party. Pham, LeUyen, illus. (J). (gr. k-3). 2016. (Princess in Black Ser.: 2). (ENG.). 96p. pap. 6.99 (978-0-7636-8758-8(8)) 2015. (Princess in Black Ser.: 2). (ENG.). 96p. 15.99 (978-0-7636-6511-1(8)) 2015. 87p. (978-1-338-11281-8(3)) Candlewick Pr.

—The Princess in Black & the Perfect Princess Party, 2. 2016. (Princess in Black Ser.). (ENG.). 96p. (gr. k-3). 21.19 (978-1-4844-7927-8(0)) Candlewick Pr.

—The Princess in Black & the Perfect Princess Party. Pham, LeUyen, illus. 2018. (Princess in Black Ser.). (ENG.). 96p. (J). (gr. k-3). lib. bdg. 31.36 (978-1-5321-4220-8(X), 28557, Chapter Bks.) Spotlight.

—The Princess in Black & the Perfect Princess Party. 2016. (Princess in Black Ser.: 2). (Illus.). 87p. (J). lib. bdg. 17.20 (978-0-606-37945-8(2)) Turtleback.

—The Princess in Black & the Science Fair Scare. Pham, LeUyen, illus. (Princess in Black Ser.: 6). (ENG.). 96p. (J). (gr. k-3). 2019. pap. 6.99 (978-1-5362-0686-9(5)) 2018. 15.99 (978-0-7636-8827-1(4)) Candlewick Pr.

—The Princess in Black Takes a Vacation. Pham, LeUyen, illus. 2016. (J). (gr. k-3). (Princess in Black Ser.: 4). (ENG.). 96p. 15.99 (978-0-7636-6512-8(6)); 87p. (978-1-5182-4386-8(X)) Candlewick Pr.

—The Princess in Black Takes a Vacation. 2017. (Princess in Black Ser.: 4). (ENG.). (J). (gr. k-3). lib. bdg. 17.20 (978-0-606-39839-8(2)) Turtleback.

—The Princess in Black: Three Smashing Adventures: Books 1-3, 3 vols. Pham, LeUyen, illus. 2017. (Princess in Black Ser.). (ENG.). 288p. (J). (gr. k-3). pap. 20.97 (978-0-7636-9777-8(X)) Candlewick Pr.

Hall, Kirsten. I'm a Princess. DeRosa, Dee, illus. 2004. (My First Reader Ser.). (ENG.). 32p. (J). (gr. k-1). pap. 3.95 (978-0-516-24630-7(5), Children's Pr.) Scholastic Library Publishing.

Halsted, John D., ed. & compiled by. Peachy Princesses & Impetuous Princes - for Girls Only! Halsted, John D., compiled by. 2013. 386p. pap. (978-1-909302-40-2(6)) Abela Publishing.

Hanak, Elizabeth. The Princess of Cliffwood. 2012. 34p. pap. (978-1-105-30501-6(5)) Lulu.com.

Handa, Nimret. Good Night Stories. 2004. (Illus.). 20p. (J). (978-81-291-0373-4(7)) Rupa & Co.

Hanna, Virginie. The Secret Life of Princesses. Delanssay, Cathy, illus. 2009. 26p. (J). (gr. -1-3). 17.99 (978-0-8437-1476-0(X)) Hammond World Atlas Corp.

Hapka, Catherine, pseud. The Enchanted Science Fair. 2014. (Sofia the First Ser.). (J). lib. bdg. 14.75 (978-0-606-35911-5(7)) Turtleback.

—Holiday in Enchancia. 2013. (Sofia the First Ser.). (J). lib. bdg. 24.50 (978-0-606-32289-8(2)) Turtleback.

Hapka, Cathy, pseud. Pretend & Play Kitty: With Real Crown You Can Wear! Borlasca, Hector, illus. 2004. (Role Play Ser.). 10p. (J). (gr. -1-18). bds. 6.99 (978-1-57151-742-5(1)) Playhouse Publishing.

—The Royal Games. 2014. (Sofia the First Ser.). (J). lib. bdg. 13.55 (978-0-606-34098-4(X)) Turtleback.

Hargreaves, Adam, illus. & creator. Little Miss Princess. Hargreaves, Adam, creator. 2011. (Mr. Men & Little Miss Ser.). (ENG.). 32p. (J). (gr. -1-2). mass mkt. 4.99 (978-0-8431-9834-8(6), Grosset & Dunlap) Penguin Young Readers Group.

Hargreaves, Roger. Little Miss Princess & the Very Special Wedding. 2011. (Mr. Men & Little Miss Ser.). (ENG., Illus.). 24p. (J). (gr. -1-3). (978-1-4052-5996-5(5)) Farshore.

Harris, Kandi. Princess, the Future Queen: A Mother's Guidance. Rippon, Jor-El, illus. l.t. ed. 2006. 32p. (J). bds. 12.99 (978-0-9770331-1-9(2)) Harris, K Publishing, Inc.

Harrison, Christy Gremore. Once upon A Monday. 2010. 40p. pap. 16.99 (978-1-4490-5854-8(X)) AuthorHouse.

Harrison, Mette Ivie. The Princess & the Hound. 2008. (ENG.). 432p. (YA). (gr. 8). pap. 8.99 (978-0-06-113189-9(X), HarperTeen) HarperCollins Pubs.

Harrison, Paula. The Ice Diamond. 2014. (Rescue Princesses Ser.: 10). lib. bdg. 14.75 (978-0-606-35422-6(0)) Turtleback.

—The Lost Gold. 2013. (Rescue Princesses Ser.: 7). lib. bdg. 14.75 (978-0-606-32374-1(0)) Turtleback.

—The Magic Rings. 2013. (Rescue Princesses Ser.: 6). lib. bdg. 14.75 (978-0-606-32373-4(2)) Turtleback.

—The Moonlight Mystery. 2013. (Rescue Princesses Ser.: 3). lib. bdg. 14.75 (978-0-606-31988-1(3)) Turtleback.

—Secret Promise. 2013. (Rescue Princesses Ser.: 1). lib. bdg. 14.75 (978-0-606-31986-7(7)) Turtleback.

—The Snow Jewel. 2013. (Rescue Princesses Ser.: 5). lib. bdg. 14.75 (978-0-606-32372-7(4)) Turtleback.

—The Stolen Crystals. 2013. (Rescue Princesses Ser.: 4). lib. bdg. 14.75 (978-0-606-31989-8(1)) Turtleback.

—Wishing Pearl. 2013. (Rescue Princesses Ser.: 2). (ENG., Illus.). 128p. (J). (gr. 2-5). pap. 4.99 (978-0-545-50914-5(9), Scholastic Paperbacks) Scholastic, Inc.

—Wishing Pearl. 2013. (Rescue Princesses Ser.: 2). lib. bdg. 14.75 (978-0-606-31987-4(5)) Turtleback.

Hart, Caryl. The Princess & the Christmas Rescue. Warburton, Sarah, illus. 2017. (ENG.). 32p. (J). (gr. -1-2). 16.99 (978-0-7636-9632-0(3)) Candlewick Pr.

—The Princess & the Giant. Warburton, Sarah, illus. 2015. (ENG.). 32p. (J). (gr. -1-2). 16.99 (978-0-7636-8007-7(9)) Candlewick Pr.

—The Princess & the Presents. Warburton, Sarah, illus. 2014. (ENG.). 32p. (J). (gr. -1-2). 16.99 (978-0-7636-7398-7(6)) Candlewick Pr.

Haskell, Merrie. Handbook for Dragon Slayers. 2013. (ENG.). 336p. (J). (gr. 3-7). 16.99 (978-0-06-200816-9(1), HarperCollins) HarperCollins Pubs.

—The Princess Curse. 2013. (ENG.). 352p. (J). (gr. 3-7). pap. 7.99 (978-0-06-200815-2(3), HarperCollins) HarperCollins Pubs.

Hatley, Shannon. The Young Princess & the Brave Knight. 2012. 28p. pap. 24.95 (978-1-4626-6779-6(1)) America Star Bks.

Hawkins, A. D. The Time Princess. 2013. 208p. pap. (978-1-78299-661-3(3)) FeedARead.com.

Hawkins, Delta Michelle. Cassandra's Journey. 2012. 28p. pap. 24.95 (978-1-4626-9566-9(3)) America Star Bks.

Hawkins, Mia K. The Broken Guild of Twelve Pirates, 1 vol. 2009. 201p. pap. 24.95 (978-1-61546-333-6(X)) PublishAmerica, Inc.

Hayes, Kimberly Wasserman. Princesses & Dinosaurs. 2011. (Illus.). 28p. pap. 14.09 (978-1-4567-8823-0(X)) AuthorHouse.

Heapy, Teresa. Very Little Sleeping Beauty. Heap, Sue, illus. 2016. (Very Little Ser.). (ENG.). 32p. (J). (gr. -1-3). 16.99 (978-0-544-28279-7(5), 1570975, Clarion Bks.) HarperCollins Pubs.

Hegarty, Pat. If I Were a... Princess. Pope, Liz & Pope, Kate, illus. 2008. 12p. (J). (gr. -1). bds. 6.95 (978-1-58925-838-9(X)) Tiger Tales.

Hegerhorst, Bethany. The Baseball Princess: Samantha's Summer & the Unicorn Flu. Abbott, Kristin, illus. 2012. 32p. (J). (978-0-9871281-5-7(9)) Murray Bks.

Heide, Florence Parry. Princess Hyacinth (the Surprising Tale of a Girl Who Floated) Smith, Lane, illus. 2016. 48p. (J). (gr. -1-3). 8.99 (978-0-553-53804-5(7), Dragonfly Bks.) Random Hse. Children's Bks.

Hendesi, Roya. The Ancient Queendom. 2011. 52p. pap. 29.05 (978-1-4568-2783-0(9)) Xlibris Corp.

Herman, Gail & Studio Iboix Staff. Ariel: The Birthday Surprise. 2011. (Disney Princess Ser.). (ENG., Illus.). 96p. (J). (gr. 2-6). 31.36 (978-1-59961-877-7(X), 5177, Chapter Bks.) Spotlight.

Hewitt, Megan. Eagle Rises. 2013. (ENG.). 118p. (J). pap. 12.99 (978-1-300-55242-0(5)) Lulu Pr., Inc.

Hicks, John. Divided World. 2003. 192p. (YA). per. 6.50 (978-0-9742829-1-6(X)) Quiet Man Publishing.

Hidden. 2014. (ENG., Illus.). 384p. (YA). (gr. 7). 17.99 (978-1-4424-8300-2(8), Simon & Schuster/Paula Wiseman Bks.) Simon & Schuster/Paula Wiseman Bks.

Higgins, M. G. Rodeo Princess. 2015. (Gravel Road Ser.). (YA). lib. bdg. 20.80 (978-0-606-37231-2(8)) Turtleback.

Higgins, Wendy. The Great Hunt. 2017. (Eurona Duology Ser.: 1). (ENG.). 448p. (YA). (gr. 8). pap. 9.99 (978-0-06-238134-7(2), HarperTeen) HarperCollins Pubs.

—The Great Pursuit. (Eurona Duology Ser.: 2). (ENG.). (YA). (gr. 8). 2018. 528p. pap. 9.99 (978-0-06-238137-8(7)) 2017. (Illus.). 512p. 17.99 (978-0-06-238136-1(9)) HarperCollins Pubs. (HarperTeen).

Hilburn, L. M. Little Princesses to the Rescue. 2008. 24p. pap. 24.95 (978-1-60672-783-6(4)) America Star Bks.

Hillyer, Lexa. Winter Glass. 2019. (Spindle Fire Ser.: 2). (ENG.). 352p. (YA). (gr. 9). pap. 9.99 (978-0-06-244091-4(8), HarperTeen) HarperCollins Pubs.

Himekawa, Akira. The Legend of Zelda, Vol. 10: Phantom Hourglass. 2010. (Legend of Zelda Ser.: 10). (ENG., Illus.). 192p. (J). (gr. 2-5). pap. 9.99 (978-1-4215-3724-5(9)) Viz Media.

Hinchliffe, Stuart Jarod. Princess Tiffany Arabella & the Time of Dreams. 2009. 196p. 24.50 (978-1-60860-627-6(9), Strategic Bk. Publishing) Strategic Book Publishing & Rights Agency (SBPRA).

Hinkler Books, ed. The Little Princess Tea Party. 2012. 40p. (J). 19.99 (978-1-74308-402-1(1)) Hinkler Bks. Pty, Ltd. AUS. Dist: Ideals Pubns.

—My Treasury of Princess Tales. 2012. 192p. (J). 12.99 (978-1-74308-000-9(X)) Hinkler Bks. Pty, Ltd. AUS. Dist: Ideals Pubns.

Hinkler Books Staff. CD Storybook: Beauty & the Beast; The Little Mermaid; Cinderella; Snow White. rev. ed. 2004. (Illus.). 128p. (J). (gr. 4-12). 14.95 incl. cd-rom (978-1-86515-754-2(6)) Hinkler Bks. Pty, Ltd. AUS. Dist: Penton Overseas, Inc.

Hinuss, Roy L. Her Royal Slyness. Hunt, Matt, illus. 2018. 136p. (J). (978-1-5490-5505-8(4)) ETT Imprint.

—Her Royal Slyness. 2018. (Prince Not-So Charming Ser.). (J). lib. bdg. 16.00 (978-0-606-41109-7(7)) Turtleback.

—Prince Not-So Charming: Her Royal Slyness. Hunt, Matt, illus. 2018. (Prince Not-So Charming Ser.: 2). (ENG.). 144p. (J). pap. 15.99 (978-1-250-14240-5(7), 900180219) Imprint IND. Dist: Macmillan.

Hocking, Amanda. Ascend. l.t. ed. 2012. (Trylle Trilogy: Bk. 3). (ENG.). 412p. (J). (gr. 8-12). 23.99 (978-1-4104-5014-2(7)) Thorndike Pr.

—Ascend: A Trylle Novel. 2012. (Trylle Novel Ser.: 3). (ENG.). 336p. (YA). (gr. 7). pap. 13.99 (978-1-250-00633-2(3), 900081191, St. Martin's Griffin) St. Martin's Pr.

—Switched, 1. 2012. (Trylle Novel Ser.: 1). (ENG.). 336p. (YA). (gr. 9-12). pap. 13.99 (978-1-250-00631-8(7), 900081189, St. Martin's Griffin) St. Martin's Pr.

—Torn. 2012. (Trylle Novel Ser.: 2). (ENG.). 336p. (YA). (gr. 7-12). pap. 20.00 (978-1-250-00632-5(5), 900081190, St. Martin's Griffin) St. Martin's Pr.

—Torn. l.t. ed. 2012. (Trylle Trilogy: Bk. 2). (ENG.). 450p. (J). (gr. 7-12). 23.99 (978-1-4104-5013-5(9)) Thorndike Pr.

Hodge, A. D. The Saucy Bossy Princess. 2012. 32p. (978-1-4602-1304-9(1)); pap. (978-1-4602-1305-6(X)) FriesenPress.

Hodgson, Mona. The Princess Twins & the Puppy, 1 vol. 2015. (I Can Read! / Princess Twins Ser.). (ENG., Illus.). 32p. (J). pap. 4.99 (978-0-310-75064-2(4)) Zonderkidz.

—The Princess Twins Collection, 1 vol. Olson, Julie, illus. 2017. (I Can Read! / Princess Twins Ser.). (ENG.). 128p. (J). 12.99 (978-0-310-75319-3(8)) Zonderkidz.

—The Princess Twins Play in the Garden, 1 vol. 2015. (I Can Read! / Princess Twins Ser.). (ENG., Illus.). 32p. (J). pap. 4.99 (978-0-310-75050-5(4)) Zonderkidz.

Hoena, Blake. The Not-So-Helpless Princess. Cunyat, Pol, illus. 2016. (Thud & Blunder Ser.). (ENG.). 56p. (J). (gr. 1-3). lib. bdg. 23.99 (978-1-4965-3218-3(X), 132413, Stone Arch Bks.) Capstone.

Hoffman, Mary. The Twelve Dancing Princesses. Clara, Miss, illus. 2013. 40p. (J). (gr. 1-5). 17.99 (978-1-84686-966-2(8)) Barefoot Bks., Inc.

Holland, Dwayne K. Princess Laura & the Magic Waterfall. 2010. 42p. pap. 15.50 (978-1-60860-744-0(5), Strategic Bk. Publishing) Strategic Book Publishing & Rights Agency (SBPRA).

Holub, Joan. Isabel Saves the Prince: Based on a True Story of Isabel I of Spain (Ready-To-Read Level 3) Aleshina, Nonna, illus. 2007. (Young Princesses Around the World Ser.). (ENG.). 48p. (J). (gr. 1-3). pap. 13.99 (978-0-689-87197-9(X), Simon Spotlight) Simon Spotlight.

Holub, Joan & Williams, Suzanne. Aphrodite the Diva. 2011. (Goddess Girls Ser.: 6). (ENG.). 288p. (J). (gr. 3-7). pap. 8.99 (978-1-4424-2100-4(2), Aladdin) Simon & Schuster Children's Publishing.

—Artemis the Loyal. 2011. (Goddess Girls Ser.: 7). (ENG.). 288p. (J). (gr. 3-7). pap. 8.99 (978-1-4424-3377-9(9), Aladdin) Simon & Schuster Children's Publishing.

Homberg, Ruth. Across the Sea (Disney Frozen) RH Disney, illus. 2016. (Step into Reading Ser.). (ENG.). 24p. (J). (gr. -1-1). 5.99 (978-0-7364-3398-3(8), RH/Disney) Random Hse. Children's Bks.

—The Little Mermaid. 2013. (Disney Princess Step into Reading Ser.). lib. bdg. 13.55 *(978-0-606-32202-7(7))* Turtleback.

—The Little Mermaid Step into Reading (Disney Princess) RH Disney, illus. 2013. (Step into Reading Ser.). (ENG.). 32p. (J). (gr. -1-1). 5.99 *(978-0-7364-8128-1(1)*, RH/Disney) Random Hse. Children's Bks.

Hopkins, Douglas. Princess June & the Shadow Pirates, 1 vol. 2007. (ENG., Illus.). 32p. (J). (gr. -1-2). per. *(978-1-894294-88-1(2))* Breakwater Bks., Ltd.

Hopper, Celia Brashear. Blade & the Story of the Pearl Princess. 2004. (J). 15.95 *(978-0-9763093-1-4(9))* Creative Bk. Pubs.

Howard, Cheryl L. Mikhael the Mighty: Be True to Who You Are & You Can Never Go Wrong. 2009. 52p. pap. 18.50 *(978-1-60860-760-0(7)*, Strategic Bk. Publishing) Strategic Book Publishing & Rights Agency (SBPRA).

Howard, Peggy Ann. Zorees: Land of Dreams. 2007. (YA). per. 16.95 *(978-0-9795519-0-1(0))* Dream Scape Publishing, LLC.

Howell, Laura. Princess & the Pea. 2009. (Young Reading 1 Ser.). 48p. (J). 6.99 *(978-0-7945-2587-3(3)*, Usborne) EDC Publishing.

Hughes, Carol. The Princess & the Unicorn. 2009. (ENG.). 288p. (J). (gr. 4-6). lib. bdg. 22.44 *(978-0-375-95562-4(3)*, Yearling) Random Hse. Children's Bks.

Hulst, W. G. van de & Hulst, Willem G. van de, illus. The Search for Christmas. 2014. (J). *(978-1-928136-12-5(5))* Inheritance Pubns.

Humphreys, Audrey. The Dragon Princess. 2012. 24p. pap. 24.99 *(978-1-4691-6554-7(6))* Xlibris Corp.

Humphreys, Neil. A Royal Pain in the Class: Princess Incognito. 2019. (Princess Incognito Ser.). 184p. (J). (gr. 2-4). pap. 16.95 *(978-981-4828-68-0(8))* Marshall Cavendish International (Asia) Private Ltd. SGP. Dist: Independent Pubs. Group.

Humphries, Jennifer & DiCampli, Nicki. Rebekah Grace the Practically Perfect Princess. 2012. (Illus.). 34p. (YA). pap. 9.95 *(978-1-60131-138-2(9)*, Castlebridge Bks.) Big Tent Bks.

Hurt, John Washington, reader. Rabbit Ears World Tales. 2007. (J). 34.99 *(978-0-7393-7549-5(0))* Findaway World, LLC.

Hush: An Irish Princess' Tale. 2014. (ENG., Illus.). 336p. (YA). (gr. 7). pap. 11.99 *(978-1-4424-9496-1(4)*, Simon & Schuster/Paula Wiseman Bks.) Simon & Schuster/Paula Wiseman Bks.

I-Haun. Real - Fake Princess. 2006. (Real/Fake Princess Ser.). (ENG., Illus.). 200p. (YA). pap. 9.95 *(978-1-59796-080-9(2))* DrMaster Pubns. Inc.

—Real/Fake Princess, Vol. 4. Zhao, Yun, tr. 2007. (Real/Fake Princess Ser.). (ENG., Illus.). 200p. pap. 9.95 *(978-1-59796-082-3(9))* DrMaster Pubns. Inc.

I-Huan. Real - Fake Princess, Set, Vols. 1-5. 2007. (ENG., Illus.). 200p. (YA). pap. 34.95 *(978-1-59796-074-8(8))* DrMaster Pubns. Inc.

I-Huan & I-Haun. Real Fake Princess, Vol. 3. 2006. (Real/Fake Princess Ser.). (ENG., Illus.). 200p. (YA). pap. 9.95 *(978-1-59796-081-6(0))* DrMaster Pubns. Inc.

Illustrated Stories of Princes & Princesses. 2015. (Illustrated Stories Ser.). (ENG.). (J). 19.99 *(978-0-7945-3416-5(3)*, Usborne) EDC Publishing.

Imagine That Publishing Ltd. Princess Party a Scratch & Sketch Adventure! 2018. (Dover Kids Activity Books: Fantasy Ser.). (ENG.). 80p. (J). (gr. 1-4). 12.99 *(978-0-486-82904-3(9)*, 829049) Dover Pubns., Inc.

An Inner Child Speaks. 2006. (J). 17.99 *(978-0-9779130-0-8(7))* Zy Iman Pubng.

Innis, Amy. The Adventures of Princess Lilyan: The Shimmering Beauty Ball. 2009. 48p. pap. 16.95 *(978-1-60749-318-1(7))* America Star Bks.

Irvine, Patricia McCune. Beyond the Greenest Hill: A Fairy Tale. 2003. 136p. (YA). pap. 11.95 *(978-0-595-26941-9(9))* iUniverse, Inc.

Isadora, Rachel. The Princess & the Pea. 2009. (Illus.). 32p. (J). (gr. -1-3). pap. 7.99 *(978-0-14-241393-7(3)*, Puffin Books) Penguin Young Readers Group.

—The Twelve Dancing Princesses. Isadora, Rachel, illus. 2009. (Illus.). 32p. (J). (gr. k-3). pap. 8.99 *(978-0-14-241450-7(6)*, Puffin Books) Penguin Young Readers Group.

Jackson, Amy. Cassandra & the Night Sky. 2018. (ENG., Illus.). 32p. (J). pap. 10.95 *(978-1-942945-74-1(4)*, 050c55fd-3ef5-48dd-9731-52687da7d266) Night Heron Media.

—Cassandra & the Night Sky. Paredes, Donna, illus. 2017. (ENG.). 32p. (J). 18.95 *(978-1-942945-40-6(X)*, cfabfbd7-de57-4a43-a5b5-40be4e93f2f3) Night Heron Media.

Jackson, Bridgett. The Princess & the Pink Palace: Book Two of Tales from the Creek. 2008. 36p. pap. 16.99 *(978-1-4389-2038-2(5))* AuthorHouse.

Jacobsen, Annie. The Terrible Troll Cat. Hanson, Susan Jo, illus. 2012. 32p. (J). 9.98 *(978-0-9778276-4-0(X))* Pickled Herring Pr.

Jalonen, Nicole. Magical Animal Army Adventures. 2012. 28p. pap. 15.99 *(978-1-4691-7544-7(4))* Xlibris Corp.

James, Kari, adapted by. Barbie & the Magic of Pegasus: A Junior Novelization. 2005. (Illus.). 72p. pap. *(978-0-439-78542-6(1))* Scholastic, Inc.

Jardine, Kathy & Jardine, Ashley. The Durples: Go to School. 2010. 28p. pap. 17.99 *(978-1-4490-3405-4(5))* AuthorHouse.

Jay, Stacey. Of Beast & Beauty. 2014. (ENG.). 400p. (YA). (gr. 9). pap. 9.99 *(978-0-385-74321-1(1)*, Ember) Random Hse. Children's Bks.

—Princess of Thorns. 2016. (ENG.). 400p. (YA). (gr. 9). pap. 9.99 *(978-0-385-74323-5(8)*, Ember) Random Hse. Children's Bks.

Jensen, Michael & King, David Powers. Woven. 2015. (ENG., Illus.). 352p. (YA). (gr. 7). 18.99 *(978-0-545-68572-6(9)*, Scholastic Pr.) Scholastic, Inc.

Jensen, Michael R. & King, David Powers. Woven. 2015. (Illus.). 344p. (J). *(978-0-545-83117-8(2)*, Scholastic Pr.) Scholastic, Inc.

Johnson, Amy. The Princess & the Frog. 2010. (Illus.). 24p. (J). 14.93 *(978-1-4269-3712-5(1))* Trafford Publishing.

Johnson, Esther A. The Princess & the Garden. Taylor, Carolyn, illus. 2012. 34p. pap. 19.99 *(978-1-62419-614-0(4))* Salem Author Services.

Johnson, Jacqueline & Young, Jeanna Stolle. Princess Charity's Courageous Heart, 1 vol. Aranda, Omar, illus. 2012. (Princess Parables Ser.). (ENG.). 32p. (J). 14.99 *(978-0-310-72701-9(4))* Zonderkidz.

—Princess Faith's Mysterious Garden, 1 vol. Aranda, Omar, illus. 2012. (Princess Parables Ser.). (ENG.). 32p. (J). 14.99 *(978-0-310-72703-3(0))* Zonderkidz.

Johnson, Jacqueline Kinney & Young, Jeanna. Princess Grace & Poppy, 1 vol. 2012. (I Can Read! / Princess Parables Ser.). (ENG.). 32p. (J). pap. 4.99 *(978-0-310-72677-7(8))* Zonderkidz.

Johnson, Rachel N. No Ordinary Princess. Hill, Jessie, illus. 2012. 32p. pap. 16.97 *(978-1-61204-993-9(1)*, Strategic Bk. Publishing) Strategic Book Publishing & Rights Agency (SBPRA).

Johnson, Vargie. Catherine the Great the Victorious: What Made Them Famous? 2006. 156p. (J). per. 15.00 *(978-1-931195-96-6(X))* KiwE Publishing, Ltd.

Johnson, Young, et al. Princess Hope & the Hidden Treasure, 1 vol. Aranda, Omar, illus. 2012. (I Can Read! / Princess Parables Ser.). (ENG.). 32p. (J). pap. 4.99 *(978-0-310-73250-1(6))* Zonderkidz.

Johnston, E. K. Spindle. 2017. (ENG.). 384p. (YA). (gr. 9-17). pap. 9.99 *(978-1-4847-7618-6(6))* Hyperion Bks. for Children.

Jokisch, Kimberly. I Have Two Homes. 2009. 24p. pap. 11.99 *(978-1-4389-2823-4(8))* AuthorHouse.

Jones, Allan. The Six Crowns: Sargasso Skies. Chalk, Gary, illus. 2013. (Six Crowns Ser.: 5). (ENG.). 176p. (J). (gr. 3-7). 16.99 *(978-0-06-200636-3(3)*, Greenwillow Bks.) HarperCollins Pubs.

Jones, Cheri. The Adventures of a Mermaid Princess. 2013. 76p. (gr. -1). pap. 10.84 *(978-1-4907-0598-9(8))* Trafford Publishing.

Jones, Frewin. The Faerie Path #2: the Lost Queen: Book Two of the Faerie Path. 2008. (Faerie Path Ser.: 2). (ENG.). 352p. (YA). (gr. 8). pap. 9.99 *(978-0-06-087107-9(5)*, HarperTeen) HarperCollins Pubs.

—Faerie Path #5: the Enchanted Quest. 2010. (Faerie Path Ser.: 5). (ENG.). 368p. (YA). (gr. 8-18). 16.99 *(978-0-06-087158-1(X)*, HarperTeen) HarperCollins Pubs.

—Faerie Path #6: the Charmed Return. 2011. (Faerie Path Ser.: 6). (ENG.). 368p. (YA). (gr. 8-18). 17.99 *(978-0-06-087161-1(X)*, HarperTeen) HarperCollins Pubs.

—The Lost Queen. 2007. (Faerie Path Ser.: Bk. 2). (YA). (gr. 7). 335p. lib. bdg. 17.89 *(978-0-06-087106-2(7))*; (ENG.). 352p. 16.99 *(978-0-06-087105-5(9))* HarperCollins Pubs. (Eos).

—Warrior Princess. 2009. (YA). 346p. lib. bdg. 17.89 *(978-0-06-087144-4(X))*; (ENG.). 352p. (gr. 7-18). 16.99 *(978-0-06-087143-7(1))* HarperCollins Pubs. (Eos).

—Warrior Princess #2: Destiny's Path. 2010. (Warrior Princess Ser.: 2). (ENG.). 352p. (YA). (gr. 8). pap. 8.99 *(978-0-06-087148-2(2)*, HarperTeen) HarperCollins Pubs.

—Warrior Princess #3: the Emerald Flame. 2010. (Warrior Princess Ser.: 3). (ENG.). 352p. (YA). (gr. 8-18). 16.99 *(978-0-06-087149-9(0)*, HarperTeen) HarperCollins Pubs.

Jones, Janey Louise. Princess Poppy: the Sleepover. 2016. (Princess Poppy Picture Bks.). (ENG., Illus.). 32p. (J). (gr. -1-k). pap. 11.99 *(978-0-552-57069-5(9))* Transworld Publishers Ltd. GBR. Dist: Independent Pubs. Group.

Jones, Ursula. The Princess Who Had No Kingdom. 2015. (Illus.). 32p. (J). *(978-1-4896-3882-3(2))* Weigl Pubs., Inc.

Jordan, Apple. A Fairy-Tale Fall. 2010. (Disney Princess Step into Reading Ser.). lib. bdg. 13.55 *(978-0-606-14879-5(5))* Turtleback.

—A Fairy-Tale Fall (Disney Princess) Legramandi, Francesco, illus. 2010. (Step into Reading Ser.). (ENG.). 32p. (J). (gr. k-3). pap. 5.99 *(978-0-7364-2674-9(4)*, RH/Disney) Random Hse. Children's Bks.

—A Princess Can! 2015. (Disney Princess Step into Reading Ser.). lib. bdg. 14.75 *(978-0-606-36390-7(4))* Turtleback.

—A Princess Can! (Disney Princess) Legramandi, Francesco & Matta, Gabriella, illus. 2015. (Step into Reading Ser.). (ENG.). 24p. (J). (gr. -1-1). 5.99 *(978-0-7364-3341-9(4)*, RH/Disney) Random Hse. Children's Bks.

—Winter Wishes (Disney Princess) Marrucchi, Elisa, illus. 2006. (Step into Reading Ser.). (ENG.). 32p. (J). (gr. k-3). per. 5.99 *(978-0-7364-2409-7(1)*, RH/Disney) Random Hse. Children's Bks.

Jordan, Apple, adapted by. The Right Track. 2017. (Illus.). 24p. (J). *(978-1-5182-3645-7(6))* Random Hse., Inc.

Jordan, Sophie. Reign of Shadows. 2016. (Reign of Shadows Ser.: 1). (ENG.). 304p. (YA). (gr. 8). 17.99 *(978-0-06-237764-7(7)*, HarperTeen) HarperCollins Pubs.

Joy, Christine. The Dream Quest. 2013. 162p. pap. *(978-1-78148-790-7(1))* Grosvenor Hse. Publishing Ltd.

Joyce, Melaine. Cinderella. 2009. (Fairydust Fairytales Ser.). (ENG.). 5p. (J). (gr. -1-k). bds. 6.95 *(978-1-84696-964-5(6)*, TickTock Books) Octopus Publishing Group GBR. Dist: Independent Pubs. Group.

—Snow White. 2009. (Fairydust Fairytales Ser.). (ENG.). 5p. (J). (gr. -1-k). bds. 6.95 *(978-1-84696-965-2(4)*, TickTock Books) Octopus Publishing Group GBR. Dist: Independent Pubs. Group.

Joyce, Rita. Wandawillie. 2005. (J). lib. bdg. 17.95 *(978-1-59094-095-2(4))* Jawbone Publishing Corp.

Joyce, Sandie May. The Crying Princess. 2008. 69p. pap. 25.50 *(978-1-4357-6077-6(8))* Lulu Pr., Inc.

Jules, Jacqueline. The Princess & the Ziz. Kahn, Katherine Janus, illus. 2008. 32p. (J). (gr. -1-3). lib. bdg. 17.95 *(978-0-8225-7377-7(6)*, Kar-Ben Publishing) Lerner Publishing Group.

Julius, Jessica. A New Reindeer Friend (Disney Frozen) RH Disney, illus. 2015. (Little Golden Book Ser.). (ENG.). 24p. (J). (-k). 5.99 *(978-0-7364-3351-8(1)*, Golden/Disney) Random Hse. Children's Bks.

—Olaf's Perfect Day (Disney Frozen) The Disney Storybook Art Team, illus. 2015. (Little Golden Book Ser.). (ENG.). 24p. (J). (-k). 5.99 *(978-0-7364-3356-3(2)*, Golden/Disney) Random Hse. Children's Bks.

K. B. Kendricks. Travis Taylor & the Dragon Quest. 2010. 344p. 29.95 *(978-1-4502-0261-9(6))* iUniverse, Inc.

Kaesshaefer, Charles. The Lost Princess. 2004. (J). mass mkt. 10.00 *(978-0-9744407-0-5(1))* Shelbykay Publishing Co.

Kagawa, Julie. The Iron King. Chan, Lidia, illus. 2017. (Iron King Ser.). (SPA.). (YA). (gr. 7-12). pap. 19.99 *(978-1-948216-67-8(1))* TidalWave Productions.

—The Iron King. 2010. (Iron Fey Ser.: 1). (J). lib. bdg. 20.85 *(978-0-606-14909-9(0))* Turtleback.

—The Iron Knight. 2011. (Iron Fey Ser.: 4). (J). lib. bdg. 20.85 *(978-0-606-23259-3(1))* Turtleback.

Kagna, Barbara. Magic of Masara. Gonzalez, Ashley, illus. 2010. 24p. pap. 12.50 *(978-1-4490-5651-3(2))* AuthorHouse.

Kale, Ann Stephanian. Marco & Princess Gina. Kale, Ann Stephanian, illus. 2003. (Illus.). 24p. (J). (gr. k-3). pap. 10.00 *(978-0-9704131-5-4(7))* Abril BookStore & Publishing.

Kanaki, Shiori, illus. Disney Manga: Tangled. 2017. (Disney Manga: Tangled Ser.). 208p. (J). (gr. 1-1). pap. 10.99 *(978-1-4278-5704-0(0)*, 71500e49-a906-4d70-8994-6550c574c7c3, TOKYOPOP Manga) TOKYOPOP, Inc.

Kang, Hildi. Chengli & the Silk Road Caravan. 2012. (ENG.). 176p. (J). (gr. 2-7). pap. 9.99 *(978-1-933718-78-1(1))* Tanglewood Pr.

Kann, Victoria. Pinkalicious: the Princess of Pink Slumber Party. Kann, Victoria, illus. 2012. (I Can Read Level 1 Ser.). (ENG., Illus.). 32p. (J). (gr. -1-3). 16.99 *(978-0-06-198963-6(0)*, HarperCollins) HarperCollins Pubs.

—Pinkalicious: the Princess of Pink Treasury. Kann, Victoria, illus. 2011. (ENG., Illus.). 208p. (J). (gr. -1-3). 19.99 *(978-0-06-210236-2(2)*, HarperCollins) HarperCollins Pubs.

—The Princess of Pink Slumber Party. 2012. (Pinkalicious I Can Read Ser.). (J). lib. bdg. 13.55 *(978-0-606-23581-5(7))* Turtleback.

—Story Time. 2016. (Pinkalicious I Can Read Ser.). (J). lib. bdg. 13.55 *(978-0-606-38758-3(7))* Turtleback.

Karevold, Alison. KenKarta: Battle of the Onoxmon. Malone, Susan Mary, ed. Polinko, Les, illus. 2011. 300p. (J). 25.98 *(978-0-9843166-3-2(9))* Artists' Orchard, LLC, The.

Kats, Jewel. Teddy Bear Princess: A Story about Sharing & Caring. Arts, Richa Kinra, illus. 2012. 24p. (-18). pap. 13.95 *(978-1-61599-163-1(8)*, Marvelous Spirit Pr.) Loving Healing Pr., Inc.

Katz, Bebe Weinberg. A Best Friend for Claudia. 2008. 77p. pap. 19.95 *(978-1-60563-485-2(9))* America Star Bks.

—Princess Claudia & the Freckles. 2007. 48p. per. 16.95 *(978-1-4241-6446-2(X))* America Star Bks.

Kearney, G. M. The Apple Trees of Tschlin. 2008. (J). 15.99 *(978-1-59955-098-5(9))* Cedar Fort, Inc./CFI Distribution.

Keithly, Bryan. Princess Tarang. 2009. 24p. pap. 11.49 *(978-1-4343-7601-5(X))* AuthorHouse.

Kelly, Miles. Big Book of Princess Stories. 2017. (ENG., Illus.). 96p. (J). 17.95 *(978-1-78617-158-0(9))* Miles Kelly Publishing, Ltd. GBR. Dist: Parkwest Pubns., Inc.

Kelly, Richard, ed. Big Book of Princess Stories. 2017. (ENG.). 96p. (J). 17.95 *(978-1-78209-820-1(8))* Miles Kelly Publishing, Ltd. GBR. Dist: Parkwest Pubns., Inc.

—Read & Play - Princess: Read, Play, Puzzlw & Color for Hours! 2017. (ENG.). 40p. (J). pap. 19.95 *(978-1-78209-980-2(8))* Miles Kelly Publishing, Ltd. GBR. Dist: Parkwest Pubns., Inc.

Khoury, Jessica. The Forbidden Wish. 352p. (YA). (gr. 7). 2017. pap. 10.99 *(978-1-59514-768-4(3))* 2016. 17.99 *(978-1-59514-767-7(5))* Penguin Young Readers Group. (Razorbill).

—The Forbidden Wish. 2017. lib. bdg. 20.85 *(978-0-606-40000-8(1))* Turtleback.

Killion, Bette. Princess Rosie's Rainbows. Jacobs, Kim, illus. 2015. 36p. (J). (gr. k-3). 16.95 *(978-1-937786-44-1(7)*, Wisdom Tales) World Wisdom, Inc.

Kimpton, Diana. Pony-Crazed Princess: Princess Ellie's Mystery. Finlay, Lizzie, illus. 3rd rev. ed. 2006. (ENG.). 96p. (gr. 1-4). pap. 3.99 *(978-0-7868-4872-0(3))* Hyperion Pr.

—Pony-Crazed Princess Super Special: Princess Ellie's Summer Vacation. Finlay, Lizzie, illus. 2007. (ENG.). 144p. (gr. 1-4). pap. 4.99 *(978-1-4231-0616-6(4))* Hyperion Pr.

—Princess Ellie Solves a Mystery. Finlay, Lizzie, illus. 8th rev. ed. 2007. (ENG.). 96p. (gr. 1-4). pap. 3.99 *(978-1-4231-0901-3(5))* Hyperion Pr.

—Princess Ellie to the Rescue. Finlay, Lizzie, illus. 2006. (ENG.). 96p. (gr. 1-4). pap. 3.99 *(978-0-7868-4870-6(7))* Hyperion Pr.

—Princess Ellie's Moonlight Mystery. 2015. (Pony-Crazed Princess Ser.). (ENG.). 96p. (J). (gr. k-5). pap. 4.99 *(978-0-7945-3431-8(7)*, Usborne) EDC Publishing.

—Princess Ellie's Royal Jamboree No. 11. Finlay, Lizzie, illus. 11th ed. 2008. (ENG.). 96p. (gr. 1-4). pap. 3.99 *(978-1-4231-1531-1(7))* Hyperion Pr.

—Princess Ellie's Secret No. 2. Finlay, Lizzie, illus. 2nd rev. ed. 2006. (ENG.). 96p. (gr. 1-4). pap. 3.99 *(978-0-7868-4871-3(5))* Hyperion Pr.

—Princess Ellie's Snowy Ride. Finlay, Lizzie, illus. 2007. (Pony-Crazed Princess Ser.). 90p. (J). 11.65 *(978-0-7569-8352-9(5))* Perfection Learning Corp.

—Princess Ellie's Snowy Ride No. 9. Finlay, Lizzie, illus. 9th rev. ed. 2007. (ENG.). 96p. (gr. 1-4). pap. 3.99 *(978-1-4231-0902-0(3))* Hyperion Pr.

—Princess Ellie's Treasure Hunt No. 10. Finlay, Lizzie, illus. 10th ed. 2008. (ENG.). 96p. (gr. -1-3). pap. 3.99 *(978-1-4231-1414-7(0))* Hyperion Pr.

—A Surprise for Princess Ellie. 2015. (Pony-Crazed Princess Ser.). (ENG.). 96p. (J). (gr. k-5). pap. 4.99 *(978-0-7945-3432-5(5)*, Usborne) EDC Publishing.

—A Surprise for Princess Ellie. Finlay, Lizzie, illus. 6th rev. ed. 2006. (ENG.). 96p. (gr. 1-4). pap. 3.99 *(978-0-7868-4875-1(8))* Hyperion Pr.

Kin, Pamphil. The Gorilla Princess. 2012. (ENG.). pap. *(978-1-4675-2345-5(3))* Independent Pub.

The Kind Princess. 2005. (J). 6.50 *(978-0-9773267-1-6(3))* G Publishing LLC.

Kindler, Jennifer. Rita's Fairytale. 2011. 68p. pap. 10.95 *(978-1-4575-0277-4(1))* Dog Ear Publishing, LLC.

King-Smith, Dick. Lady Lollipop. Barton, Jill, illus. (ENG.). 128p. (J). (gr. 2-4). 2011. 18.69 *(978-0-7636-1269-6(3))* 2003. pap. 8.99 *(978-0-7636-2181-0(1))* Candlewick Pr.

Kingsbury, Karen. The Princess & the Three Knights, 1 vol. Grimard, Gabrielle, illus. 2009. (ENG.). 40p. (J). (gr. -1-2). 15.99 *(978-0-310-71641-9(1))* Zonderkidz.

Kiss a Frog, Princess. (Full House Ser.). 96p. (J). (gr. 4-6). pap. 3.25 *(978-0-938753-63-6(0)*, PP2) Parachute Publishing, LLC.

Kladstrup, Kristin. Garden Princess. (ENG.). 272p. (J). (gr. 5). 2015. pap. 7.99 *(978-0-7636-7668-1(3))* 2013. (Illus.). 15.99 *(978-0-7636-5685-0(2))* Candlewick Pr.

Kliever, S. I. A Slave's Quest. 2011. 284p. pap. *(978-1-77069-178-0(2))* Word Alive Pr.

Kmiec, Irka. Princess Ella Bell. 2012. 26p. pap. 14.99 *(978-1-4772-4554-5(5))* AuthorHouse.

Knudsen, Michelle. The Dragon of Trelian. (Trelian Ser.: 1). (ENG.). 416p. (J). (gr. 5). 2017. pap. 9.99 *(978-0-7636-9454-8(1))* 2009. (Illus.). 16.99 *(978-0-7636-3455-1(7))* Candlewick Pr.

—The Mage of Trelian. 2016. (Trelian Ser.: 3). (ENG.). 432p. (J). (gr. 5). 17.99 *(978-0-7636-7436-6(2))* Candlewick Pr.

—The Princess of Trelian. (Trelian Ser.: 2). (ENG.). 448p. (J). (gr. 5). 2017. pap. 9.99 *(978-0-7636-9455-5(X))* 2012. (Illus.). 16.99 *(978-0-7636-5062-9(5))* Candlewick Pr.

Kodaka, Nao, illus. Disney Manga: the Princess & the Frog. 2018. (Disney Manga: the Princess & the Frog Ser.). 144p. (J). (gr. 1-1). pap. 10.99 *(978-1-4278-5805-4(5)*, d01665f8-0bde-448c-873c-a2c43af43635, TOKYOPOP Manga) TOKYOPOP, Inc.

Kopp, Megan. Scary Folktales, 1 vol. 2010. (Scary Stories Ser.). (ENG.). 32p. (J). (gr. 3-9). lib. bdg. 28.65 *(978-1-4296-4571-3(7)*, 103054, Capstone Pr.) Capstone.

Korba, Joanna. Yeh-shen: A Cinderella Tale from China. 2006. (J). pap. *(978-1-4108-6162-7(7))* Benchmark Education Co.

Kornfield, Katie. One Sweet Princess. Anderson, Howard, illus. 2005. (ENG.). 36p. pap. 15.99 *(978-1-4134-8581-3(2))* Xlibris Corp.

Koster, Amy Sky. Cuddly Princess Pals. 2014. lib. bdg. 13.55 *(978-0-606-35552-0(9))* Turtleback.

Krakower, Harold. Sugarland: Princess Sarafina. 2011. 32p. (gr. 1-2). pap. 12.77 *(978-1-4634-0123-8(X))* AuthorHouse.

Kramer, Alan. The Three Little Pigs Wise up & the Princess Prince & the Vegetables. 2011. (Navigators Ser.). (J). pap. *(978-1-61672-962-2(7))* Benchmark Education Co.

Krise, Gale. It's a Colorful Candy Birthday. 2012. 24p. pap. 24.95 *(978-1-4626-7604-0(9))* America Star Bks.

Kronheimer, Ann, illus. Pretty Princesses: Beautiful Princesses to Color! 2014. (ENG.). 96p. (J). (gr. -1-2). 7.99 *(978-1-4424-8385-9(7)*, Little Simon) Little Simon.

Krulik, Nancy. Quit Buggin' Me! #4. Balistreri, Ben, illus. 2018. (Princess Pulverizer Ser.: 4). 144p. (J). (gr. 1-3). 6.99 *(978-0-515-15840-3(2)*, Penguin Workshop) Penguin Young Readers Group.

—Watch That Witch! #5. Rodrigues, Justin, illus. 2019. (Princess Pulverizer Ser.: 5). 144p. (J). (gr. 1-3). 6.99 *(978-1-5247-9092-9(3))*; 15.99 *(978-1-5247-9093-6(1))* Penguin Young Readers Group. (Penguin Workshop).

Kurtz, John, illus. Disney Princess: Look & Find. 2004. (Disney Princess Ser.). 24p. (J). 7.98 *(978-0-7853-7918-8(5)*, 7179200) Phoenix International Publications, Inc.

L. Prince Cloud & Princess Evergreen, 1 vol. 2010. 26p. pap. 24.95 *(978-1-4512-9016-5(0))* America Star Bks.

Lacek, Carolyn. Destiny Awakened. 2009. 52p. pap. 18.25 *(978-1-60860-736-5(4)*, Eloquent Bks.) Strategic Book Publishing & Rights Agency (SBPRA).

Lagonegro, Melissa. Beautiful Brides (Disney Princess) Marrucchi, Elisa, illus. 2011. (Step into Reading Ser.). (ENG.). 32p. (J). (gr. k-3). pap. 4.99 *(978-0-7364-2685-5(X)*, RH/Disney) Random Hse. Children's Bks.

—Friends for a Princess. 2004. (Disney Princess Step into Reading Ser.). (gr. -1-2). lib. bdg. 13.55 *(978-0-613-73713-5(X))* Turtleback.

—Frozen - A Tale of Two Sisters. 2013. (Disney Princess Step into Reading Ser.). lib. bdg. 13.55 *(978-0-606-32205-8(1))* Turtleback.

—Gwen's Great Gizmos (Disney Junior: Sofia the First) RH Disney, illus. 2016. (Little Golden Book Ser.). (ENG.). 24p. (J). (gr. -1-k). 4.99 *(978-0-7364-3448-5(8)*, Golden/Disney) Random Hse. Children's Bks.

—Kingdom of Color (Disney Tangled) Orpinas, Jean-Paul et al, illus. 2010. (Step into Reading Ser.). (ENG.). 32p. (J). (gr. k-3). pap. 5.99 *(978-0-7364-2687-9(6)*, RH/Disney) Random Hse. Children's Bks.

—Outside My Window (Disney Tangled) Orpinas, Jean-Paul et al, illus. 2010. (Step into Reading Ser.). (ENG.). 32p. (J). (gr. k-3). pap. 5.99 *(978-0-7364-2688-6(4)*, RH/Disney) Random Hse. Children's Bks.

—Polite As a Princess (Disney Princess) Harding, Niall & Harchy, Atelier Philippe, illus. 2006. (Pictureback(R) Ser.). (ENG.). 24p. (J). (gr. -1-2). pap. 3.99 *(978-0-7364-2367-0(2)*, RH/Disney) Random Hse. Children's Bks.

Lagonegro, Melissa, adapted by. Ghost Hunt! 2018. (Illus.). 22p. (J). *(978-1-5490-4049-8(9))* Random Hse., Inc.

Lairamore, Dawn. Ivy's Ever After. 2013. (ENG.). 192p. (J). (gr. 3-7). pap. 7.99 *(978-0-8234-2937-0(7))* Holiday Hse., Inc.

Lake, Susan. Ebony & the Five Dwarfs. 2007. 56p. per. 10.00 *(978-1-4257-7841-5(0))* Xlibris Corp.

Lambert, Nat. Magnetic Dressing up Princesses. 2014. (ENG.). 10p. (J). (gr. -1-k). 9.99 *(978-1-78244-799-3(7))* Top That! Publishing PLC GBR. Dist: Independent Pubs. Group.

Lammle, Leslie. Princess Wannabe. Lammle, Leslie, illus. 2014. (ENG., Illus.). 40p. (J). (gr. -1-3). 17.99 *(978-0-06-125197-9(6)*, HarperCollins) HarperCollins Pubs.

Larousse Mexico Staff, ed. Historias de Princesas y Hadas. 2008.Tr. of Princess & Fairy Stories. (ENG., Illus.). 35p. 9.95 *(978-970-22-1449-6(1))* Larousse, Ediciones, S. A. de C. V. MEX. Dist: Houghton Mifflin Harcourt Publishing Co.

Larsen, Sharon G. The Parable of the Chocolate Chips. 2008. (J). *(978-1-59038-912-6(3))* Deseret Bk. Co.

Larson, M. A. The Shadow Cadets of Pennyroyal Academy. 2017. (Pennyroyal Ser.: 2). lib. bdg. 19.65 *(978-0-606-39792-6(2))* Turtleback.

—The Warrior Princess of Pennyroyal Academy. 2018. (Pennyroyal Ser.: 3). lib. bdg. 19.65 *(978-0-606-41312-1(X))* Turtleback.

Larson, Sara B. Dark Breaks the Dawn. (ENG.). 320p. (YA). (gr. 7-7). 2018. pap. 9.99 *(978-1-338-06870-2(9))* 2017. 17.99 *(978-1-338-06869-6(5)*, Scholastic Pr.) Scholastic, Inc.

L.A.S., Alex. Magnificent Sir Johnny & Santa Claus. 2011. 36p. pap. 24.95 *(978-1-4626-3401-9(X))* America Star Bks.

Lascurain, Anna. Apollo in the Moon House. 2006. Orig. Title: The Moonboy. (J). per. 7.99 (978-0-9769612-3-9(7)) Darker Intentions Pr.

LaShea, Riley. Bleeding Through Kingdoms: Cinderella's Rebellion. 2005. 256p. (YA). per. 14.95 (978-0-9766130-1-5(8)) Tattered Essence Publishing LLC.

LeapFrog Staff. Disney Princess Stories - France. 2003. (Illus.). spiral bd. 14.99 (978-1-59319-005-7(0)) LeapFrog Enterprises, Inc.

—Disney Princess Stories - Latin America. 2003. (Illus.). (J). spiral bd. 14.99 (978-1-59319-001-9(8)) LeapFrog Enterprises, Inc.

Lechermeier, Philippe. Princesas/ Princesses: Mini Album. 2008. (SPA.). 108p. 15.95 (978-84-263-6701-3(1)) Vives, Luis Editorial (Edelvives) ESP. Dist: Lectorum Pubns., Inc.

Ledeaux, Lola. If A Dog Could Blog. 2010. 28p. 12.49 (978-1-4520-7575-4(1)) AuthorHouse.

Lendler, Ian. The Absolutely, Positively No Princesses Book. Zemke, Deborah, illus. 2019. (ENG.). 36p. (J). (gr. 1-5). 16.99 (978-1-939547-51-4(2), 62663356-eefe-4f0a-91f2-485f1af574d6) Creston Bks.

—An Undone Fairy Tale. Martin, Whitney, illus. 2005. (ENG.). 32p. (J). (gr. 1-5). 19.99 (978-0-689-86677-7(1), Simon & Schuster Bks. For Young Readers) Simon & Schuster Bks. For Young Readers.

Lenz, Adrienne. The Glitter Ball: Princess Jewels. 2011. 20p. pap. 24.95 (978-1-4560-4147-2(9)) PublishAmerica, Inc.

Leprechaun, Seamus T. The o'Shea Chronicles. 2013. 312p. pap. (978-1-78407-190-5(0)) FeedARead.com.

Leth, Kate. Adventure Time Vol. 4. 2014. lib. bdg. 24.50 (978-0-606-36119-4(7)) Turtleback.

Levenseller, Tricia. Daughter of the Pirate King. 2018. (Daughter of the Pirate King Ser.: 1). (ENG.). 336p. (YA). pap. 10.99 (978-1-250-14422-5(1), 900160921) Square Fish.

Levine, Gail Carson. The Fairy's Return & Other Princess Tales. 2009. (ENG.). 400p. (J). (gr. 3-7). pap. 7.99 (978-0-06-176898-9(7), HarperCollins) HarperCollins Pubs.

—The Princess Tales, Volume 2, No. 2. Elliott, Mark, illus. 2004. (ENG.). 256p. (J). (gr. 2-7). pap. 9.99 (978-0-06-056043-0(6), HarperCollins) HarperCollins Pubs.

—The Two Princesses of Bamarre. (J). 2012. (ENG.). 272p. (gr. 3-7). pap. 9.99 (978-0-06-440966-7(X), HarperCollins) 2004. (Illus.). 304p. (gr. 7-18). reprint ed. pap. 6.99 (978-0-06-057580-9(8)) HarperCollins Pubs.

Lewis, Ellen Parry. An Unremarkable Girl. 2011. 434p. (YA). pap. 19.99 (978-0-9843437-8-2(4)) Metal Lunchbox Publishing.

Liberts, Jennifer. Happy Birthday, Princess! (Disney Princess) Marrucchi, Elisa, illus. 2016. (Step into Reading Ser.). (ENG.). 24p. (J). (gr. -1-1). pap. 4.99 (978-0-7364-3664-9(2), RH/Disney) Random Hse. Children's Bks.

—I Love My Dad. 2018. (Step into Reading - Level 1 Ser.). lib. bdg. 14.75 (978-0-606-40958-2(0)) Turtleback.

—What Is a Princess? (Disney Princess) Harchy, Atelier Philippe, illus. 2016. (Step into Reading Ser.). (ENG.). 24p. (J). (gr. -1-1). pap. 5.99 (978-0-7364-3666-3(9), RH/Disney) Random Hse. Children's Bks.

Liguori, Tara. Silly Milly Is a Princess. 2008. 28p. pap. 24.95 (978-1-60703-349-3(6)) America Star Bks.

Liles, R. D. The Princess & the Troll. 2012. 44p. pap. 21.99 (978-1-4772-8256-4(4)) AuthorHouse.

Lilibeth, Ethel. Princesses Take Baths Too! 2009. 44p. pap. 18.60 (978-1-4389-6626-7(1)) AuthorHouse.

Limke, Jeff. Tristan & Isolde: The Warrior & the Princess [a British Legend]. Randall, Ron, illus. 2009. (Graphic Myths & Legends Ser.). (ENG.). 48p. (J). (gr. 4-8). pap. 9.99 (978-1-58013-889-5(6), 3b9182fb-99e4-4b65-8c7d-c5eba12bd802, Graphic Universe™) Lerner Publishing Group.

Lincoln, Jerri Kay. Dancing with Unicorns. 2013. 254p. pap. 14.99 (978-1-938322-21-1(5)) Ralston Store Publishing.

Linker, Julie. Disenchanted Princess. 2007. (ENG.). 240p. (YA). (gr. 9-18). pap. 11.99 (978-1-4169-3472-1(3), Simon Pulse) Simon Pulse.

Lisa Maria. Princess of the King. 2012. 28p. pap. 17.99 (978-1-4685-5652-0(5)) AuthorHouse.

Little Princess. 2004. (J). (978-0-9767179-6-6(4)) ABC Development, Inc.

Little Sticker Dolly Dressing Princesses. 2017. (Little Sticker Dolly Dressing Ser.). (ENG.). (J). pap. 8.99 (978-0-7945-3919-1(X), Usborne) EDC Publishing.

Littman, Sarah Darer. Charmed, I'm Sure. 2016. (ENG., Illus.). 208p. (J). (gr. 3-7). 17.99 (978-1-4814-5127-7(8), Aladdin) Simon & Schuster Children's Publishing.

—Charmed, I'm Sure. 2017. (ENG., Illus.). 224p. (J). (gr. 3-7). pap. 8.99 (978-1-4814-5126-0(X), Simon & Schuster/Paula Wiseman Bks.) Simon & Schuster/Paula Wiseman Bks.

Livingston, Lesley. The Valiant. 2018. (Valiant Ser.: 1). (ENG.). 400p. (YA). (gr. 7). pap. 9.99 (978-0-448-49379-4(9), Razorbill) Penguin Young Readers Group.

Lodico, Cheryl Madeleine. The Ice Princess Trilogy. 2007. pap. 20.00 (978-0-8059-8967-0(6)) Dorrance Publishing Co., Inc.

Loewen, Nancy. Believe Me, I Never Felt a Pea! The Story of the Princess & the Pea As Told by the Princess. Bernardini, Cristian, illus. 2016. (Other Side of the Story Ser.). (ENG.). 24p. (J). (gr. -1-3). lib. bdg. 27.99 (978-1-4795-8622-6(6), 130444, Picture Window Bks.) Capstone.

Loggia, Wendy. Aurora: The Perfect Party. Studio IBOIX Staff, illus. 2012. (Disney Princess Ser.). (ENG.). 96p. (J). (gr. 2-6). lib. bdg. 31.36 (978-1-59961-181-5(3), 5182, Chapter Bks.) Spotlight.

Lois, Lowry. The Birthday Ball. Feiffer, Jules, illus. 2011. (ENG.). 192p. (J). (gr. 4-6). 21.19 (978-0-547-23869-2(X)) Houghton Mifflin Harcourt Publishing Co.

Lough, Amber. The Blind Wish. 2015. (Jinni Wars Ser.: 2). (ENG.). 320p. (YA). (gr. 7). 17.99 (978-0-385-36980-0(8), Random Hse. Bks. for Young Readers) Random Hse. Children's Bks.

Louis, Robb. Monster in the Moat. 2011. (Illus.). 44p. (gr. -1). pap. 18.46 (978-1-4567-4053-5(9)) AuthorHouse.

Lowery, Mark. Attack of the Woolly Jumper. 2017. (Roman Garstang Disaster Ser.). (ENG., Illus.). 224p. (J). (gr. 4-7). pap. 8.99 (978-1-84812-582-7(8)) Bonnier Publishing GBR. Dist: Independent Pubs. Group.

Lowes, Sarah. The Snow Queen. Clara, Miss, illus. 2013. 64p. (J). 17.99 (978-1-84686-964-8(1)) Barefoot Bks., Inc.

Lowry, Lois. The Birthday Ball. Feiffer, Jules, illus. 2011. (ENG.). 192p. (J). (gr. 5-7). pap. 8.99 (978-0-547-57710-4(9), 1458458, Clarion Bks.) HarperCollins Pubs.

Luiz, Fernando, illus. How to Be a Princess: A Girly Girl Book. 2009. 12p. (J). bds. 6.95 (978-1-58117-850-0(6), Intervisual/Piggy Toes) Bendon, Inc.

Lundquist, Jenny. The Opal Crown. 2014. (ENG., Illus.). 368p. (J). (gr. 7-17). pap. 9.95 (978-0-7624-5422-8(9), Running Pr. Kids) Running Pr.

—The Princess in the Opal Mask. 2013. (ENG.). 352p. (YA). (gr. 8-17). pap. 18.99 (978-0-7624-5109-8(2), Running Pr. Kids) Running Pr.

Lynn, Kelly. The Princess Transformation, 1 vol. 2010. 132p. pap. 24.95 (978-1-4512-1417-8(0)) America Star Bks.

MacDonald, George. The Light Princess. 2008. 48p. pap. 5.99 (978-1-4209-3096-2(6)) Digireads.com Publishing.

—The Light Princess. 2004. reprint ed. pap. 15.95 (978-1-4191-7001-0(5)) Kessinger Publishing, LLC.

—Light Princess & Other Fairy Stories. 2006. 132p. per. 10.95 (978-1-59818-618-5(3)); 24.95 (978-1-59818-236-1(6)) Aegypan.

—The Light Princess & Other Fairy Stories. 2007. 102p. pap. 18.99 (978-1-4346-1408-7(5)) Creative Media Partners, LLC.

—The Princess & Curdie. 2017. (ENG., Illus.). (J). 23.95 (978-1-374-91384-4(7)); (gr. 3-6). pap. 13.95 (978-1-374-91383-7(9)) Capital Communications, Inc.

—The Princess & Curdie. Stratton, Helen, illus. 2003. 162p. pap. 12.99 (978-1-57646-634-6(5)) Quiet Vision Publishing.

—Princess & Curdie. 2006. 136p. per. 10.95 (978-1-59818-617-8(5)); 24.95 (978-1-59818-235-4(8)) Aegypan.

—Princess & Curdie. 2017. (ENG., Illus.). 224p. (gr. 3-6). pap. 16.99 (978-1-62911-817-8(6), 770892) Whitaker Hse.

—The Princess & Curdie. l.t. ed. 2005. 320p. pap. (978-1-84637-020-5(5)) Echo Library.

—Princess & the Goblin. 2006. 128p. 23.95 (978-1-59818-234-7(X)) Aegypan.

—The Princess & the Goblin. 2003. (Illus.). 160p. (J). 19.95 (978-1-81514-970-2(1)) Antique Collectors' Club.

—The Princess & the Goblin. abr. ed. 2007. 191p. (J). (gr. 4-7). per. 8.99 (978-1-59166-799-5(2)) BJU Pr.

—The Princess & the Goblin. 2017. (ENG., Illus.). (J). (-16). 28.99 (978-1-366-56249-4(6)) Blurb, Inc.

—The Princess & the Goblin. 2005. 108p. per. 5.99 (978-1-4209-2557-9(1)) Digireads.com Publishing.

—The Princess & the Goblin. 2007. 152p. per. (978-1-4065-3015-5(8)) Dodo Pr.

—The Princess & the Goblin. l.t. ed. 2005. 292p. pap. (978-1-84637-021-2(3)) Echo Library.

—The Princess & the Goblin. 2007. pap. 5.99 (978-1-59986-657-4(9), FQ Classics) Filiquarian Publishing, LLC.

—The Princess & the Goblin. 2004. reprint ed. pap. 1.99 (978-1-4192-7868-6(1)) Kessinger Publishing, LLC.

—The Princess & the Goblin. 2011. 174p. pap. 4.95 (978-1-61427-173-4(9)) Martino Fine Bks.

—The Princess & the Goblin. Hughes, Arthur, illus. 2003. 136p. pap. 12.99 (978-1-57646-633-9(7)) Quiet Vision Publishing.

—The Princess & the Goblin. 2008. 188p. pap. 12.95 (978-1-60096-531-9(8)); pap. 12.95 (978-1-60096-825-9(2)) The Editorium, LLC.

—The Princess & the Goblin. 2008. 132p. pap. 4.99 (978-1-60459-454-6(3)) Wilder Pubns., Corp.

—The Princess & the Goblin. Kirk, Maria L. & Hughes, Arthur, illus. 2011. 260p. pap. 10.95 (978-1-59915-250-9(9)) Yesterday's Classics.

—The Princess Treasury. 2008. 372p. pap. 12.99 (978-1-60459-458-4(6)) Wilder Pubns., Corp.

MacDonald, George, ed. The Princess & Curdie. Kirk, Maria L. & Hughes, Arthur, illus. 2011. 260p. pap. 10.95 (978-1-59915-251-6(7)) Yesterday's Classics.

—The Princess & the Goblin. 2004. reprint ed. pap. 20.95 (978-1-4191-7868-9(7)) Kessinger Publishing, LLC.

MacGregor, Rose. Princess Bendy. 2012. (Illus.). 12p. pap. 15.99 (978-1-4678-9038-0(3)) AuthorHouse.

MacHale, D. J. The Monster Princess. Boiger, Alexandra, illus. 2010. (ENG.). 40p. (J). (gr. -1-1). 17.99 (978-1-4169-4809-4(0), Aladdin) Simon & Schuster Children's Publishing.

Macinnis, Katherine. Kelsar. 2006. pap. 12.95 (978-1-58939-876-4(9)) Virtualbookworm.com Publishing, Inc.

Magic Wand Disney Princess. 2005. (Illus.). 10p. (J). bds. 16.98 (978-1-4127-3537-7(8), 7263500) Publications International, Ltd.

Maisner, Heather. Diary of a Princess: A Tale from Marco Polo's Travels. Moxley, Sheila, illus. 2006. 26p. (gr. k-4). reprint ed. pap. 8.00 (978-1-4223-5302-8(8)) DIANE Publishing Co.

Malea. Princess Melia. 2007. 145p. (J). pap. 15.95 (978-1-58909-367-6(4)) Bookstand Publishing.

Malia, Tara Campasano. The Special Princess. 2012. (ENG.). 41p. (J). pap. 15.95 (978-1-4327-3831-0(3)); pap. 24.95 (978-1-4327-7627-5(4)) Outskirts Pr., Inc.

Man-Kong, Mary. Sleeping Beauty. 2014. (Disney Princess Step into Reading Ser.). lib. bdg. 13.55 (978-0-606-36001-2(8)) Turtleback.

—Sleeping Beauty Step into Reading (Disney Princess) RH Disney, illus. 2014. (Step into Reading Ser.). (ENG.). 32p. (J). (gr. -1-1). 5.99 (978-0-7364-3226-9(4), RH/Disney) Random Hse. Children's Bks.

—Star Power. 2012. (Barbie Step into Reading Level 2 Ser.). lib. bdg. 13.55 (978-0-606-26550-8(3)) Turtleback.

Manjula Padmanabhan, illus. Unprincess! 2005. 98p. (J). (978-0-14-333495-8(6), Puffin) Penguin Publishing Group.

Markarian, Margie. The Princess & the Cafe on the Moat. Douglass, Chloe, illus. 2018. (ENG.). 32p. (J). (gr. k-3). 16.99 (978-1-58536-397-1(9), 204402) Sleeping Bear Pr.

Marrs, Christie, creator. The Promise Keeper: I B Hoofinit's Horse Tales. l.t. ed. 2003. (Illus.). 53p. (J). mass mkt. 5.99 (978-1-928890-16-4(4)) I. B. Hoofinit Co.

Marsham, Liz & Francis, Suzanne. Ariel Is Fearless/Jasmine Is Helpful (Disney Princess) The Disney Storybook Art Team & Thomas, Jeffrey, illus. 2017. (Step into Reading Ser.). (ENG.). 48p. (J). (gr. -1-1). pap. 5.99 (978-0-7364-3802-5(5), RH/Disney) Random Hse. Children's Bks.

Marsoli, Lisa Ann. The Missing Necklace. 2014. (Sofia the First World of Reading Ser.). (J). lib. bdg. 13.55 (978-0-606-35912-2(5)) Turtleback.

Martin, Alison. Princess of Tabaria. 2004. (Illus.). 104p. pap. (978-1-84401-151-3(8)) Athena Pr.

Martin, Chandra. Sintacs. 2012. 100p. 19.95 (978-1-4626-7833-4(5)) America Star Bks.

Martin, Molly. Princess Sophia Gets Scared, 1 vol. Florian, Mélanie & Florian, Mélanie, illus. 2013. (Princess Heart Ser.). (ENG.). 24p. (J). (gr. -1-1). 6.95 (978-1-4048-8110-5(7), 121883); lib. bdg. 22.65 (978-1-4048-7854-9(8), 120483) Capstone. (Picture Window Bks.).

Marvin, Susan. Birthday Dreamz. 2011. 36p. (gr. -1). pap. 15.99 (978-1-4567-4173-0(X)) AuthorHouse.

Mass, Wendy. Rapunzel: The One with All the Hair. 2005. (Illus.). 205p. (J). (978-0-439-80014-3(5)) Scholastic, Inc.

—Rapunzel, the One with All the Hair: a Wish Novel (Twice upon a Time #1) 2012. (Twice upon a Time Ser.: 1). (ENG.). 208p. (J). (gr. 3-7). pap. 7.99 (978-0-439-79659-0(6), Scholastic Pr.) Scholastic, Inc.

—Sleeping Beauty, the One Who Took the Really Long Nap: a Wish Novel (Twice upon a Time #2) 2018. (Twice upon a Time Ser.: 2). (ENG.). 176p. (J). (gr. 3-7). pap. 7.99 (978-0-439-79658-3(X), Scholastic Pr.) Scholastic, Inc.

Matsumoto, Reiko Odate. The Princess with the Magic Bowl: As retold from the Japanese folk tale By. 2008. 48p. pap. 22.49 (978-1-4389-1225-7(0)) AuthorHouse.

Matter, Sandy. The Great Sea Chase. 2011. 20p. pap. 24.95 (978-1-4626-2488-1(X)) America Star Bks.

Matthews, Caitlín, et al. The Barefoot Book of Princesses. Whelan, Olwyn, illus. 2008. (Barefoot Bks.). 64p. (J). 19.99 (978-1-84686-239-7(6)) Barefoot Bks., Inc.

Mawhinney, Art, illus. Look & Find Disney Princess Worlds of Wonder. 2006. (Look & Find Books). (J). pap. 24.98 (978-1-4127-6490-2(4)) Publications International, Ltd.

McClintock. Little Princess Picture Book. Date not set. (Illus.). 40p. (J). (gr. -1-3). pap. 4.99 (978-0-06-443539-0(3)) HarperCollins Pubs.

McCusker, Tammy. Move over! Princess Coming Through!, 1 vol. Greve, Hannah K., illus. 2009. 34p. pap. 24.95 (978-1-60749-803-2(0)) America Star Bks.

McGee, Katharine. American Royals. (American Royals Ser.: 1). (ENG.). (YA). (gr. 9). 2020. 464p. pap. 12.99 (978-1-9848-3020-3(1), Ember) 2019. 448p. 18.99 (978-1-9848-3017-3(1), Random Hse. Bks. for Young Readers) Random Hse. Children's Bks.

—American Royals II: Majesty. (American Royals Ser.: 2). (ENG.). (YA). (gr. 9). 2022. 400p. pap. 12.99 (978-1-9848-3024-1(4), Ember) 2020. 384p. 18.99 (978-1-9848-3021-0(X), Random Hse. Bks. for Young Readers) Random Hse. Children's Bks.

—American Royals III: Rivals. 2022. (American Royals Ser.: 3). (ENG.). 400p. (YA). (gr. 9). 19.99 (978-0-593-42970-9(2)); lib. bdg. 22.99 (978-0-593-42971-6(0)) Random Hse. Children's Bks. (Random Hse. Bks. for Young Readers).

—American Royals (Spanish Edition) 2021. (American Royals Ser.). (SPA.). 282p. (YA). (gr. 8-12). pap. 22.99 (978-84-272-1650-1(5)) Penguin Random House Grupo Editorial ESP. Dist: Penguin Random Hse. LLC.

McGhee, Heather. The Wild Adventures of a Curious Princess. Myers, Shari, illus. 2008. (J). per. 9.99 (978-0-9788985-9-5(1)) W & B Pubs.

McGowan, Maureen. Cinderella: Ninja Warrior. 2010. 320p. pap. 8.95 (978-1-60747-778-5(5), Pickwick Pr.) Phoenix Bks., Inc.

—Sleeping Beauty: Vampire Slayer. 2010. 320p. pap. 8.95 (978-1-60747-779-2(3), Pickwick Pr.) Phoenix Bks., Inc.

McGriff, Shawna A. Princess Pink: Princess Pink Helps Zion, Melinda, & Jasmine Learn to Communicate about Their Parents' Divorces. 2010. 56p. pap. 24.00 (978-1-4520-3941-1(0)) AuthorHouse.

—Princess Pink: Princess Pink Saves the Girls of Lahappyville. 2010. 44p. pap. 18.49 (978-1-4520-3936-7(4)) AuthorHouse.

—Princess Pink: Sam Loses Her Mother, but She Gains Her Mother's Heart. 2010. 32p. pap. 15.50 (978-1-4520-3937-4(2)) AuthorHouse.

McGuire, Sarah. The Flight of Swans. 2018. (ENG.). 448p. (J). (gr. 4-8). 18.99 (978-1-5124-4027-0(2), 9fb6e720-cb31-4131-933c-4199722cb62f, Carolrhoda Bks.) Lerner Publishing Group.

McKay, Sindy. The Frog Prince/el Príncipe Rana: Spanish/English (We Both Read - Level 1-2) Ulrich, George, illus. 2016. (We Both Read - Level 1-2 Ser.). (ENG & SPA.). 44p. (J). pap. 5.99 (978-1-60115-076-9(8)) Treasure Bay, Inc.

McRoberts, Eddison. Sneaking Treats: A Halloween Hunt. Gadra, Jessica, illus. 2012. 48p. 19.95 (978-1-62137-136-6(0)) Virtualbookworm.com Publishing, Inc.

Mead, Richelle. Bloodlines. 2012. (Bloodlines Ser.: 1). (ENG.). 448p. (YA). (gr. 7-18). pap. 12.99 (978-1-59514-473-7(0), Razorbill) Penguin Young Readers Group.

Meadows, Daisy. Aisha the Princess & the Pea Fairy. 2016. (Illus.). 62p. (J). (978-0-545-88741-0(0)) Scholastic, Inc.

—Eleanor the Snow White Fairy. 2016. (Illus.). 65p. (J). (978-0-545-88738-0(0)) Scholastic, Inc.

—Faith the Cinderella Fairy. 2016. (Illus.). 65p. (J). (978-0-545-88744-1(5)) Scholastic, Inc.

—Gwen the Beauty & the Beast Fairy. 2016. (Illus.). 67p. (J). (978-1-5182-1018-1(X)) Scholastic, Inc.

—Julia the Sleeping Beauty Fairy. 2016. (Illus.). 65p. (J). (978-0-545-88737-3(2)) Scholastic, Inc.

—Lacey the Little Mermaid Fairy. 2016. (Illus.). 65p. (J). (978-0-545-88742-7(9)) Scholastic, Inc.

—Rita the Frog Princess Fairy. 2016. (Illus.). 58p. (J). (978-0-545-88739-7(9)) Scholastic, Inc.

Mebberson, Amy, et al. Disney Princess Comics Collection. 2016. (ENG.). 96p. (J). (gr. 4-7). 20.85 (978-0-606-39073-6(1)) Turtleback.

Mehta, Lila. Anklet for a Princess: A Cinderella Story from India, 1 vol. Tang, Youshan, illus. 2014. (Cinderella Ser.). (ENG.). 32p. (J). (gr. 1-4). pap. 11.95 (978-1-885008-46-6(5), c37ae78d-8b31-41d0-9619-68e32325cb44, Shen's Bks.) Lee & Low Bks., Inc.

Meskill, Elizia. The Heart Pendant: A Princess' Search for True Love Resplendent. 2012. (ENG.). 22p. (J). 21.95 (978-1-4327-8003-6(4)); pap. 13.95 (978-1-4327-7774-6(2)) Outskirts Pr., Inc.

Metzger, Steve. Princess Kitty. Okstad, Ella, illus. 2017. (ENG.). 32p. (J). (gr. -1-3). 17.99 (978-0-06-230662-3(6), HarperCollins) HarperCollins Pubs.

Meyer, Carolyn. Cleopatra Confesses. (ENG.). 304p. (YA). (gr. 7). 2012. pap. 12.99 (978-1-4169-8728-4(2)) 2011. 16.99 (978-1-4169-8727-7(4)) Simon & Schuster/Paula Wiseman Bks. (Simon & Schuster/Paula Wiseman Bks.).

Meyer, Julia & Tabler, Marie. One Pea. Tabler, Marie, illus. 2013. (Illus.). 36p. 14.95 (978-1-62314-139-4(7)) ePub Bud.

Mi-Leing. Chrystal's Castle. 2007. 40p. 18.50 (978-1-4303-2242-9(X)) Lulu Pr., Inc.

Miller, Eileen Rudisill. Princess Super. 2011. (Dover Sticker Bks.). (ENG., Illus.). 8p. (J). (gr. k-5). 7.99 (978-0-486-48382-5(7)) Dover Pubns., Inc.

Miller, Holly & Schwartzkopf, Jere. A Horse Named Princess: Hola Princess Adios Thistle. 2009. 48p. pap. 17.49 (978-1-4343-6976-5(5)) AuthorHouse.

Miller, Samantha A. The Princess & Her Servant. 2012. (ENG.). 24p. pap. 15.99 (978-1-4691-5580-7(X)) Xlibris Corp.

Miller, Sharee. Princess Hair. (ENG., Illus.). (J). (gr. -1-3). 2019. 20p. bds. 7.99 (978-0-316-44119-3(8)) 2018. 32p. 7.99 (978-0-316-44122-3(8)) 2017. 32p. 17.99 (978-0-316-56261-4(0)) Little, Brown Bks. for Young Readers.

Mlynowski, Sarah. Two Peas in a Pod (Whatever After #11) (Whatever After Ser.: 11). (ENG.). 176p. (J). (gr. 3-7). 2019. pap. 6.99 (978-1-338-16291-2(8)) 2018. 14.99 (978-1-338-16289-9(6), Scholastic Pr.) Scholastic, Inc.

Moerbeek, Kees. Cinderella. 2006. (Roly Poly Box Bks.). (Illus.). 24p. (J). spiral bd. (978-1-84643-019-0(4)) Child's Play International Ltd.

Montanari, Eva. Princess Matilda. 2007. (Illus.). 24p. (J). (gr. -1-1). (978-1-84539-259-8(0)) Meadowside Children's Bks.

Montanari, Eva, illus. Princess Matilda. 2007. 24p. (J). (gr. -1-1). (978-1-84539-276-5(0)) Meadowside Children's Bks.

Montes, Graciela. Había una Vez una Princesa. Torres, Elena, illus. 2006. (Alfaguara Infantil Ser.). 26p. (J). 8.95 (978-1-59820-215-1(4), Alfaguara) Santillana USA Publishing Co., Inc.

Moore, Beth. My Child, My Princess: A Parable about the King. Warren, Beverly, illus. 2014. (ENG.). 32p. (J). (gr. -1-3). 9.99 (978-1-4336-8468-5(3), 005673928, B&H Kids) B&H Publishing Group.

Moore, Nathan. The Little Princess & the Backyard Mystery: A Children's Story. 2008. 27p. pap. 24.95 (978-1-60610-805-5(0)) America Star Bks.

Moriarty, Jaclyn. A Corner of White (the Colors of Madeleine, Book 1) 2013. (Colors of Madeleine Ser.: 1). (ENG.). 384p. (YA). (gr. 7-7). 18.99 (978-0-545-39736-0(7), Levine, Arthur A. Bks.) Scholastic, Inc.

Morley, P. Kevin. The Stinky Pirate & the Princess. 2009. 36p. pap. 17.99 (978-1-4490-4062-8(4)) AuthorHouse.

Morningforest, Chris & Raymond, Rebecca. Princess Underdrawers & the Dragon. 2006. (ENG.). 42p. (J). pap. 15.58 (978-1-4116-8837-7(6)) Lulu Pr., Inc.

Morris, J. & J. Little Black Pearl. 2010. 80p. pap. (978-1-905553-51-8(X)) BookPublishingWorld.

Morrissey, Lynda I. Princesses Don't Hit. Money, Greg, illus. 2012. 24p. pap. (978-1-77097-976-5(X)) FriesenPress.

Moss, Yvonne. The Butterfly Princess. 2011. 16p. (gr. -1). pap. 9.49 (978-1-4567-4044-3(X)) AuthorHouse.

Mowery, Peg K. Once upon A Princess. 2006. 16.50 (978-0-8059-9027-0(5)) Dorrance Publishing Co., Inc.

Moxilada, J. L. Jonty Jones Takes Guard. 2005. 242p. pap. 16.88 (978-1-4116-4126-6(4)) Lulu Pr., Inc.

Mulholland, Jane. Ribeye, the Vegetarian Dragon. 2013. 24p. pap. 24.95 (978-1-4626-9935-3(9)) America Star Bks.

Muloch, Miss. The Little Lame Prince & Other Tales. 2007. 304p. per. 16.95 (978-1-4344-9378-1(4)) Wildside Pr., LLC.

Mulrain, Sabrina. A Prince's Happy Ever After. 2011. 40p. pap. 24.95 (978-1-4560-3251-7(8)) America Star Bks.

Munsch, Robert. The Paper Bag Princess. Martchenko, Michael, illus. (Classic Munsch Ser.). (J). (gr. -1-2). 2018. 32p. 19.95 (978-1-77321-030-8(0)) 2018. 32p. pap. 6.95 (978-1-77321-029-2(7)) 10th ed. 2009. (ENG.). 28p. bds. 7.99 (978-1-55451-211-9(5), 9781554512119) Annick Pr., Ltd. CAN. Dist: Publishers Group West (PGW).

Murdock, Catherine Gilbert. Princess Ben. 2009. (ENG.). 352p. (YA). (gr. 7). pap. 9.99 (978-0-547-22325-4(0), 1061789, Clarion Bks.) HarperCollins Pubs.

—Wisdom's Kiss. 2013. (ENG.). 320p. (YA). (gr. 7). pap. 8.99 (978-0-547-85540-0(0), 1501132, Clarion Bks.) HarperCollins Pubs.

Murphy, Emily P. W. The Princess of Booray. Darmawan, Iwan, illus. 2023. (ENG.). (J). (gr. -1-6). 19.99 (978-0-9742891-2-0(4), Cozy Den Pr.) Marriwell Publishing.

Napoli, Donna Jo. Hush: An Irish Princess' Tale. 2007. (ENG., Illus.). 340p. (YA). (gr. 7-12). 18.69 (978-0-689-86176-5(1)) Simon & Schuster, Inc.

Nasir, Safia. Princess Neelam & Other Stories. 2005. 52p. (978-969-542-109-3(1)); (978-91-21-51821-2(1)) Children Pubns.

Nathan, Sarah. Blue-Ribbon Bunny. 2014. (Sofia the First World of Reading Ser.). (J). lib. bdg. 13.55 (978-0-606-35264-2(3)) Turtleback.

—Jasmine: The Missing Coin. Studio IBOIX Staff, illus. 2012. (Disney Princess Ser.). (ENG.). 96p. (J). (gr. 2-6). lib. bdg. 31.36 (978-1-59961-182-2(1), 5183, Chapter Bks.) Spotlight.

—Sofia's Magic Lesson. 2014. (Sofia the First Ser.). (J). lib. bdg. 13.55 (978-0-606-35258-1(9)) Turtleback.

Negrin, Fabian. The Princess & the Rainbow Coat. Waters, Fiona, illus. 2005. 32p. (J). (978-1-84458-411-6(9), Pavilion Children's Books) Pavilion Bks.

Nelson, D. J. The One-Eyed Spotogon. 2012. (Illus.). 24p. pap. 19.82 (978-1-4772-1965-2(X)) AuthorHouse.

Neubert, Oliver. Chantel's Quest for the Silver Leaf. 2012. (Chantel's Quest Ser.). (ENG., Illus.). 200p. (J). (gr. 4-7). pap. 9.95 (978-1-897476-43-7(4)) Simply Read Bks. CAN. Dist: Ingram Publisher Services.

Newton, Chelle. The Butterfly Princess. Padovano, Chris, illus. 2012. 44p. pap. 11.99 (978-1-61286-129-6(6)) Avid Readers Publishing Group.

Nguy, Hoa X. The Bamboo Girl. 2007. 84p. (J). pap. 20.00 *(978-0-8059-7562-8(4))* Dorrance Publishing Co., Inc.

Nichills, Dee. Visit the Rainforest. 2013. 42p. pap. 9.99 *(978-1-60820-857-9(5))* MLR Pr., LLC.

Nielsen, Jennifer A. The Runaway King. 2014. (Ascendance Trilogy Ser.: 2). lib. bdg. 18.40 *(978-0-606-35663-3(0))* Turtleback.

—The Runaway King (the Ascendance Series, Book 2), 1 vol. 2014. (Ascendance Ser.: 2). (ENG.). 352p. (YA). (gr. 3-7). pap. 8.99 *(978-0-545-28416-5(3)*, Scholastic Paperbacks) Scholastic, Inc.

Nielsen, Susin. Princess Puffybottom ... & Darryl. Mueller, Olivia Chin, illus. 2019. 32p. (J). (gr. -1-2). 17.99 *(978-1-101-91925-5(6)*, Tundra Bks.) Tundra Bks. CAN. Dist: Penguin Random Hse. LLC.

Nielson, Kelli S. Stone Mage Wars, Book 1: Journey to the Fringe. 2011. (YA). 17.99 *(978-1-60908-833-0(6))* Deseret Bk. Co.

Nix, Garth. Frogkisser! 2019. (ENG.). 384p. (YA). (gr. 7-7). pap. 12.99 *(978-1-338-05209-1(8))* Scholastic, Inc.

Norsgaard, E. Jaediker. How Krokken & Poppen Made Peace. 2008. 31p. pap. 24.95 *(978-1-60672-426-2(6))* America Star Bks.

North, Laura. Cinderella: The Terrible Truth. Dreidemy, Joëlle, illus. 2014. (Race Ahead with Reading Ser.). (ENG.). 32p. (J). (gr. 2-2). *(978-0-7787-1326-5(1))* Crabtree Publishing Co.

—The Princess & the Frozen Peas. Dreidemy, Joelle, illus. 2014. (Tadpoles: Fairytale Twists Ser.). (ENG.). 32p. (J). (gr. 1-2). *(978-0-7787-0446-1(7))*; pap. *(978-0-7787-0481-2(5))* Crabtree Publishing Co.

—Sleeping Beauty — 100 Years Later. Northfield, Gary, illus. 2014. (Tadpoles: Fairytale Twists Ser.). (ENG.). 32p. (J). (gr. 1-2). *(978-0-7787-0444-7(0))*; pap. *(978-0-7787-0479-9(3))* Crabtree Publishing Co.

North, Ryan. Adventure Time, Vol. 3. 2013. (Adventure Time Graphic Novels Ser.: 3). lib. bdg. 26.95 *(978-0-606-35462-2(X))* Turtleback.

—Adventure Time Volume 2. 2013. (Adventure Time Graphic Novels Ser.: 2). lib. bdg. 26.95 *(978-0-606-35461-5(1))* Turtleback.

North, Ryan & Paroline, Shelli. Adventure Time Vol.4 - Mathematical Edition. 2014. (Illus.). 144p. *(978-1-78276-171-6(3)*, Titan Bks.) Titan Bks. Ltd.

Novel Units. The Little Prince Novel Units Student Packet. 2019. (ENG.). (YA). pap., stu. ed., wbk. ed. 13.99 *(978-1-58130-719-1(5)*, Novel Units, Inc.) Classroom Library Co.

Noyes, Deborah. Red Butterfly: How a Princess Smuggled the Secret of Silk Out of China. Blackall, Sophie, illus. 2019. (ENG.). 32p. (J). (gr. 1-4). 7.99 *(978-1-5362-0376-9(9))* Candlewick Pr.

Nwokolo, Nwanneka. Zara: The Girl Traveller. 2004. (ENG.). 80p. *(978-1-904744-58-0(3))* Troubador Publishing Ltd.

Oakes, Colleen. Queen of Hearts. 2016. (Queen of Hearts Ser.: 1). (ENG.). 320p. (YA). (gr. 8). 17.99 *(978-0-06-240972-0(7)*, HarperTeen) HarperCollins Pubs.

—War of the Cards. (Queen of Hearts Ser.: 3). (ENG.). (YA). (gr. 8). 2018. 368p. pap. 9.99 *(978-0-06-240980-5(8))* 2017. 352p. 17.99 *(978-0-06-240979-9(4))* HarperCollins Pubs. (HarperTeen).

Ofori-Mankata, Dede Akai. 2012. 48p. pap. 21.88 *(978-1-4669-1569-5(2))* Trafford Publishing.

Ohlin, Nancy. Beauty. 2013. (ENG., Illus.). 208p. (YA). (gr. 7). pap. 9.99 *(978-1-4424-7265-5(0)*, Simon Pulse) Simon Pulse.

O'Malley, Kevin. Once upon a Cool Motorcycle Dude. O'Malley, Kevin & Heyer, Carol, illus. 2005. (ENG.). 32p. (J). (gr. 1-5). 17.99 *(978-0-8027-8947-1(1)*, 900034867, Bloomsbury USA Childrens) Bloomsbury Publishing USA.

O'Neill, K. Princess Princess Ever After. 2016. (ENG., Illus.). 56p. (J). 12.99 *(978-1-62010-340-1(0)*, 9781620103401, Lion Forge) Oni Pr., Inc.

Ordal, Stina Langlo. Princess Aasta Event Kit. (J). *(978-1-58234-806-3(5))* Bloomsbury Publishing USA.

Orr, Wendy. The Princess & Her Panther. Stringer, Lauren, illus. 2010. (ENG.). 40p. (J). (gr. -1-3). 16.99 *(978-1-4169-9780-1(6)*, Beach Lane Bks.) Beach Lane Bks.

O'Ryan, Ellie. Belle: The Charming Gift. Liu, Chun & Melaranci, Elisabetta, illus. 2017. (Disney Princess Ser.). (ENG.). 96p. (J). (gr. 2-6). lib. bdg. 31.36 *(978-1-5321-4120-1(3)*, 26993, Chapter Bks.) Spotlight.

—Cinderella: The Great Mouse Mistake. Studio IBOIX Staff, illus. 2011. (Disney Princess Ser.). (ENG.). 96p. (J). (gr. 2-6). 31.36 *(978-1-59961-879-1(6)*, 5179, Chapter Bks.) Spotlight.

—Jasmine: The Jewel Orchard. 2013. (Disney Princess Early Chapter Bks.). (J). lib. bdg. 14.75 *(978-0-606-27068-7(X))* Turtleback.

Ottolenghi, Carol. The Princess & the Pea. 2009. (Keepsake Stories Ser.: 25). (ENG.). 32p. (gr. -1-3). pap. 3.99 *(978-0-7696-5869-8(5)*, 0769658695, Brighter Child) Carson-Dellosa Publishing, LLC.

Owen, Sarah. Sarah the Fairy Princess's Birthday Party. 2009. 32p. pap. 41.50 *(978-1-4452-5921-5(4))* Lulu Pr., Inc.

P. I. Kids. Palace Pets First Look & Find - O/P. 2015. (ENG.). 16p. (J). *(978-1-4508-8634-5(5)*, 1450886345) Publications International, Ltd.

—Palace Pets Little Pop up Song Book O/P. 2014. (ENG.). 10p. (J). *(978-1-4508-8635-2(3)*, 1450886353) Publications International, Ltd.

Page, Nick & Claire. The Autumn Princess. 2006. (Read with Me (Make Believe Ideas) Ser.). (Illus.). 32p. (J). (gr. k-2). *(978-1-84610-171-7(9))* Make Believe Ideas.

Parker, Lisa L. Gray. Princesses Do Not Wear Tattoos. Logan, Desiree, illus. 2011. 48p. pap. 24.95 *(978-1-4560-3281-4(X))* America Star Bks.

Parnell, Fran & Fatus, Sophie. Grim, Grunt & Grizzle-Tail: A Story from Chile. Fatus, Sophie, illus. 2013. (Monster Stories Ser.: 6). (Illus.). 48p. (J). (gr. 1-4). pap. 8.99 *(978-1-84686-910-5(2))* Barefoot Bks., Inc.

Parragon Staff. Disney Princess Sparkling Dreams. 2010. (Disney Twinkly Lights Board Bks.). 6p. (J). (gr. -1-k). bds. *(978-1-4075-9340-1(4))* Parragon, Inc.

Patten, Linda D. Princess Alese & the Kingdom of Serenity. 2013. 20p. pap. 13.77 *(978-1-4669-8724-1(3))* Trafford Publishing.

Patterson, Shannon. The Princess & the Cheese. 2010. 43p. pap. 19.95 *(978-0-557-51615-5(3))* Lulu Pr., Inc.

Patton, Chris. A Totally True Princess Story. Wellman, Mike, ed. St. Aubin, Claude, illus. 2009. 72p. 12.99 *(978-0-615-27602-1(4))* Atomic Basement.

Pau Pau. The Princess' Adventure. 2007. 52p. pap. 16.95 *(978-1-60441-069-3(8))* America Star Bks.

Pearl, Alexa. Tales of Sasha 4: Princess Lessons. Sordo, Paco, illus. 2017. (Tales of Sasha Ser.: 4). (ENG.). 112p. (J). (gr. k-3). pap. 5.99 *(978-1-4998-0399-0(0))* Little Bee Books Inc.

—Tales of Sasha 5: the Plant Pixies. Sordo, Paco, illus. 2017. (Tales of Sasha Ser.: 5). (ENG.). 112p. (J). (gr. k-3). 16.99 *(978-1-4998-0464-5(4))*; pap. 5.99 *(978-1-4998-0463-8(6))* Little Bee Books Inc.

—Tales of Sasha 6: Wings for Wyatt. Sordo, Paco, illus. 2017. (Tales of Sasha Ser.: 6). (ENG.). 112p. (J). (gr. k-3). 16.99 *(978-1-4998-0466-9(0))*; pap. 5.99 *(978-1-4998-0465-2(2))* Little Bee Books Inc.

—Tales of Sasha 7: the Royal Island. Sordo, Paco, illus. 2018. (Tales of Sasha Ser.: 7). (ENG.). 112p. (J). (gr. k-3). 16.99 *(978-1-4998-0603-8(5))*; pap. 5.99 *(978-1-4998-0602-1(7))* Little Bee Books Inc.

—Tales of Sasha 8: Showtime! Sordo, Paco, illus. 2018. (Tales of Sasha Ser.: 8). (ENG.). 112p. (J). (gr. k-3). 16.99 *(978-1-4998-0605-2(1))*; pap. 5.99 *(978-1-4998-0604-5(3))* Little Bee Books Inc.

—Tales of Sasha 9: the Disappearing History. Sordo, Paco, illus. 2018. (Tales of Sasha Ser.: 9). (ENG.). 112p. (J). (gr. k-3). 16.99 *(978-1-4998-0607-6(8))*; pap. 5.99 *(978-1-4998-0606-9(X))* Little Bee Books Inc.

The Pearl Princess. 2004. (Illus.). 32p. 3.99 *(978-1-894998-00-0(6))* Lake, Jack Productions, Inc. CAN. Dist: Hushion Hse. Publishing, Ltd.

Pearson, Mary E. The Beauty of Darkness: The Remnant Chronicles, Book Three. 2017. (Remnant Chronicles Ser.: 3). (ENG.). 688p. (YA). pap. 14.99 *(978-1-250-11531-7(0)*, 900157585) Square Fish.

—The Heart of Betrayal: The Remnant Chronicles, Book Two. 2015. (Remnant Chronicles Ser.: 2). (ENG.). 480p. (YA). (gr. 9). 21.99 *(978-0-8050-9924-9(7)*, 900126079, Holt, Henry & Co. Bks. For Young Readers) Holt, Henry & Co.

—The Heart of Betrayal: The Remnant Chronicles, Book Two. 2016. (Remnant Chronicles Ser.: 2). (ENG.). 496p. (YA). pap. 12.99 *(978-1-250-08002-8(9)*, 900154651) Square Fish.

—The Kiss of Deception: The Remnant Chronicles, Book One. 2014. (Remnant Chronicles Ser.: 1). (ENG.). 496p. (YA). (gr. 9-12). E-Book *(978-1-62779-218-9(X)*, 900141518, Holt, Henry & Co. Bks. For Young Readers) Holt, Henry & Co.

—The Kiss of Deception: The Remnant Chronicles, Book One. 2015. (Remnant Chronicles Ser.: 1). (ENG.). 512p. (YA). (gr. 9-12). pap. 12.99 *(978-1-250-06315-1(9)*, 900142660) Square Fish.

Pef. Belle lisse poire du prince De. pap. 16.95 *(978-2-07-054806-4(6))* Gallimard, Editions FRA. Dist: Distribooks, Inc.

Perelman, Helen. A Candy Fairies Sweet Collection (Boxed Set) Chocolate Dreams; Rainbow Swirl; Caramel Moon; Cool Mint. Waters, Erica-Jane, illus. 2013. (Candy Fairies Ser.). (ENG.). 512p. (J). (gr. 2-5). pap. 23.99 *(978-1-4424-9390-2(9)*, Aladdin) Simon & Schuster Children's Publishing.

—Mini Sweets. Waters, Erica-Jane, illus. 2017. (Candy Fairies Ser.: 20). (ENG.). 128p. (J). (gr. 2-5). pap. 5.99 *(978-1-4814-4683-9(5)*, Simon & Schuster/Paula Wiseman Bks.) Simon & Schuster/Paula Wiseman Bks.

—Rapunzel: A Day to Remember, 1 vol. Studio IBOIX Staff, illus. 2012. (Disney Princess Ser.). (ENG.). 96p. (J). (gr. 2-6). lib. bdg. 31.36 *(978-1-59961-183-9(X)*, 5184, Chapter Bks.) Spotlight.

—A Royal Rescue: A QUIX Book. Chin Mueller, Olivia, illus. 2018. (Royal Sweets Ser.: 1). (ENG.). 80p. (J). (gr. k-3). 16.99 *(978-1-4814-9478-6(3))*; pap. 5.99 *(978-1-4814-9477-9(5))* Simon & Schuster Children's Publishing. (Aladdin).

—Sugar Secrets: A QUIX Book. Chin Mueller, Olivia, illus. 2018. (Royal Sweets Ser.: 2). (ENG.). 80p. (J). (gr. k-3). 16.99 *(978-1-4814-9481-6(3))*; pap. 5.99 *(978-1-4814-9480-9(5))* Simon & Schuster Children's Publishing. (Aladdin).

—Tiana: The Grand Opening. Studio IBOIX Staff, illus. 2011. (Disney Princess Ser.). (ENG.). 96p. (J). (gr. 2-6). 31.36 *(978-1-59961-880-7(X)*, 5180, Chapter Bks.) Spotlight.

Perez, Marlene. Princess Rock & the Royal Inches. 2004. (Shared Connections Ser.). (J). pap. 27.00 *(978-1-4108-1633-7(8))*; instr.'s gde. ed. 27.00 *(978-1-4108-1609-2(5))* Benchmark Education Co.

Perez, Vivian. Stolen Stories for My Nieces. 2007. (ENG.). 68p. per. 19.95 *(978-1-4241-6679-4(9))* America Star Bks.

Peters, Stephanie True. Sleeping Beauty, Magic Master: A Graphic Novel. López, Álex, illus. 2016. (Far Out Fairy Tales Ser.). (ENG.). 40p. (J). (gr. 3-6). lib. bdg. 26.65 *(978-1-4965-3784-3(X)*, 133107, Stone Arch Bks.) Capstone.

Peterson, Alyson. The Cursed Dagger. 2016. 308p. (YA). pap. *(978-1-4621-1865-6(8))* Cedar Fort, Inc./CFI Distribution.

—The Exiled Prince. 2017. (ENG.). (YA). (gr. 8-12). pap. 17.99 *(978-1-4621-2035-2(0)*, Sweetwater Bks.) Cedar Fort, Inc./CFI Distribution.

—Ian Quicksilver: The Warrior's Return. 2015. vii, 309p. (YA). pap. 17.99 *(978-1-4621-1629-4(9))* Cedar Fort, Inc./CFI Distribution.

Petit, Cheryl. Fairy Princess Melina, 1 vol. 2010. 26p. pap. 24.95 *(978-1-4489-7915-8(3))* PublishAmerica, Inc.

Phillips, Deborah. The Parable of the Princesses. 2008. (Illus.). 48p. (J). 19.99 *(978-1-59038-873-0(9))* Deseret Bk. Co.

Phillips, Elizabeth. The Blueberry Princess. Phillips, Elizabeth & Phillips, Andrea, illus. 2008. 25p. pap. 24.95 *(978-1-60672-097-4(X))* America Star Bks.

Phoenix International Staff, illus. Princess Sofia. 2013. (Play-A-Sound Ser.). (ENG.). 14p. (J). bds., bds. *(978-1-4508-6822-8(3)*, 8877f18f-6f50-4b01-bcb0-36932429420b) Phoenix International Publications, Inc.

PI Kids. Disney: Little First Look & Find: 4 Book Set. 2010. (ENG.). 18p. (J). bds., bds., bds. 21.99 *(978-1-4508-0334-2(2)*, 4181, PI Kids) Phoenix International Publications, Inc.

—Disney Princess: First Look & Find. Mawhinney, Art, illus. 2015. (ENG.). 24p. (J). 2.99 *(978-1-4508-9478-4(X)*, 1732, PI Kids) Phoenix International Publications, Inc.

Piggy Toes Press, creator. Disney Princess Bath Book. 2011. (ENG.). (gr. -1-k). 5.95 *(978-1-61524-416-4(6)*, Intervisual/Piggy Toes) Bendon, Inc.

Pippin-Mathur, Courtney. Dragons Rule, Princesses Drool! Pippin-Mathur, Courtney, illus. 2017. (ENG., Illus.). 40p. (J). (gr. -1-3). 17.99 *(978-1-4814-6138-2(9)*, Little Simon) Little Simon.

Pollett, Allan. For My Little Princess. 2010. 24p. pap. 15.99 *(978-1-4500-7583-1(5))* Xlibris Corp.

Posner-Sanchez, Andrea. Dream Big, Princess! (Disney Princess) RH Disney, illus. 2016. (ENG.). 80p. (J). (gr. -1-2). 9.99 *(978-0-7364-3709-7(6)*, RH/Disney) Random Hse. Children's Bks.

—A Frozen Christmas (Disney Frozen) RH Disney, illus. 2015. (ENG.). 12p. (J). (gr. -1 — 1). bds. 8.99 *(978-0-7364-3479-9(8)*, RH/Disney) Random Hse. Children's Bks.

—Good Night, Princess! (Disney Princess) Legramandi, Francesco & Matta, Gabriella, illus. 2012. (Pictureback(R) Ser.). (ENG.). 16p. (J). (gr. -1-2). pap. 5.99 *(978-0-7364-2851-4(8)*, RH/Disney) Random Hse. Children's Bks.

—I Am a Princess (Disney Princess) Matta, Gabriella & Legramandi, Francesco, illus. 2012. (Little Golden Book Ser.). (ENG.). 24p. (J). (gr. k-k). 5.99 *(978-0-7364-2906-1(9)*, Golden/Disney) Random Hse. Children's Bks.

—I Am Ariel (Disney Princess) Batson, Alan, illus. 2018. (Little Golden Book Ser.). (ENG.). 24p. (J). (-k). 5.99 *(978-0-7364-3852-0(1)*, Golden/Disney) Random Hse. Children's Bks.

—Olaf's Frozen Adventure Little Golden Book (Disney Frozen) Chou, Joey, illus. 2017. (Little Golden Book Ser.). (ENG.). 24p. (J). (-k). 4.99 *(978-0-7364-3835-3(1)*, Golden/Disney) Random Hse. Children's Bks.

—The Perfect Tea Party (Disney Junior: Sofia the First) RH Disney, illus. 2013. (Little Golden Book Ser.). (ENG.). 24p. (J). (-k). 5.99 *(978-0-7364-3109-5(8)*, Golden/Disney) Random Hse. Children's Bks.

—A Royal Easter. 2014. (Disney Princess 8x8 Ser.). lib. bdg. 14.75 *(978-0-606-35553-7(7))* Turtleback.

—Teacup to the Rescue! (Disney Princess: Palace Pets) DiCicco, Sue, illus. 2015. (Little Golden Book Ser.). (ENG.). 24p. (J). (-k). 4.99 *(978-0-7364-3364-8(3)*, Golden/Disney) Random Hse. Children's Bks.

Pretty Princess- Royal Party. 2005. (J). bds. *(978-1-4194-0061-2(4))* Paradise Pr., Inc.

Pretty Princess s/s - Beautiful Princess. 2005. (J). bds. *(978-1-4194-0062-9(2))* Paradise Pr., Inc.

Pretty Princess s/s - Fit for a Princess. 2005. (J). bds. *(978-1-4194-0063-6(0))* Paradise Pr., Inc.

Pretty Princess s/s - Wedding Day. 2005. (J). bds. *(978-1-4194-0064-3(9))* Paradise Pr., Inc.

Princesa Stephanie. 2005. (SPA.). (YA). per. 9.95 *(978-0-9764982-8-5(6))* Legacy Publishing Services, Inc.

Princess & Frog. (Ladybird Bks.). (Illus.). 52p. (J). 12.95 incl. audio *(978-0-86685-634-8(X))* International Bk. Ctr., Inc.

The Princess & the Magic Locket. (My Tooth Is Loose!). (Illus.). 32p. (J). *(978-1-4054-1022-9(1))* Parragon, Inc.

Princess Aurora: A Special Day in Her Life. I.t. ed. 2005. (Illus.). 32p. (J). 5.95 *(978-0-9766640-0-0(3)*, 212-279-3492) Attitudes in Dressing, Inc.

Princess Madeline & the Dragon. 2013. (Illus.). 118p. (YA). pap. 5.99 *(978-1-62375-070-1(9)*, Calibum Bks.) MQuills Publishing.

Princess Protection Program Staff. The Palace of Mystery, No. 4. 2010. (Princess Protection Program Ser.). 144p. pap. 4.99 *(978-1-4231-2727-7(7))* Disney Pr.

Princess Rosa's Winter: Level M, 6 vols. 128p. (gr. 2-3). 49.95 *(978-0-7699-0986-8(8))* Shortland Pubns. (U. S. A.) Inc.

Princesses. 2009. (FACT ATLAS Ser.). 72p. (J). 15.99 *(978-0-8416-1101-6(7))* Hammond World Atlas Corp.

The Priness Who Lost Her Smile. 2006. (J). 19.95 *(978-0-9790682-0-1(7))* Clear Braces L.L.C.

Publications International Ltd. Staff. Disney Adventure Look & Find. 2013. (gr. 1-3). 7.98 *(978-1-4127-7146-7(3)*, 1412771463) Phoenix International Publications, Inc.

—Disney Princess PNO BK. 2010. 10p. (J). 16.98 *(978-1-4127-8997-4(4))* Phoenix International Publications, Inc.

—Disney Princess Songs. 2013. 12p. (J). (gr. k-4). bds. 21.99 *(978-1-4127-8016-2(0)*, fdc578c6-8169-40c1-acde-e3e9449607c7) Phoenix International Publications, Inc.

—Giant Look & Find Disney Princess. 2008. 24p. (J). 15.98 *(978-1-4127-8976-9(1)*, PIL Kids) Publications International, Ltd.

—My 1St Libraries Disney Princess. 2011. 12p. 12.98 *(978-1-4508-1303-7(8))* Publications International, Ltd.

Publications International Ltd. Staff, creator. Barbie as the Island Princess. 2007. (Play-A-Sound Bks.). (Illus.). 9.98 *(978-1-4127-7413-0(6))* Publications International, Ltd.

—Disney Princess Board Books & Bookend Set. 2007. (Illus.). (gr. -1-k). bds. 12.98 *(978-1-4127-8844-1(7))* Publications International, Ltd.

—Disney Princess: Musical Pop-up Treasury. 2007. (Disney Princess Ser.). (Illus.). (J). (gr. -1-3). 15.98 *(978-1-4127-7431-4(4))* Publications International, Ltd.

Publications International Ltd. Staff, ed. Disney Princess. (J). 2011. 64p. 9.98 *(978-1-60553-318-6(1)*, PIL Kids) 2007. (SPA.). 10.98 *(978-1-4127-8026-1(8))* Publications International, Ltd.

—Disney Princess: 26 Stories of Virtue. 2010. 12p. (J). 25.98 *(978-1-60553-692-7(X))* Phoenix International Publications, Inc.

—Disney Princess: Cinderella. 2008. (J). 12.98 *(978-1-4127-8475-7(1))* Publications International, Ltd.

—Disney Princess: Dreams Come True (Talking Look & Find) 2010. 16p. (J). bds. 12.98 *(978-1-60553-538-8(9))* Publications International, Ltd.

—Disney Princess: Enchanted Dreams. 2010. 40p. (J). bds. 14.98 *(978-1-60553-685-9(7))* Publications International, Ltd.

—Disney Princess: Follow Your Dreams. 2010. 24p. (J). 19.98 *(978-1-4127-5357-9(0)*, PIL Kids) Publications International, Ltd.

—Disney Princess: Just Like a Princess. 2010. 48p. (J). 2.98 *(978-1-4508-0731-9(3))* Phoenix International Publications, Inc.

—Disney Princess: Please & Thank You. 2011. 12p. (J). bds. *(978-1-4508-0399-1(7))* Phoenix International Publications, Inc.

—Disney Princess: Stories of Virtue. 2010. 10p. (J). bds. 12.98 *(978-1-4508-0164-5(1))* Phoenix International Publications, Inc.

—Disney Princess Ariel. 2011. 14p. (J). bds. 16.98 *(978-1-4127-9206-6(1))* Publications International, Ltd.

—Disney Princess Aurora. 2011. 14p. (J). bds. 16.98 *(978-1-4127-9205-9(3))* Publications International, Ltd.

—Disney Princess (book Block) 2010. (J). 10.98 *(978-1-4508-0672-5(4))* Phoenix International Publications, Inc.

—Disney Princess (Musical Treasury) 2011. 40p. (J). bds. 15.98 *(978-1-4508-1082-1(9))* Publications International, Ltd.

—Disney Princess Picture Puzzles. 2010. 128p. (J). pap. 13.98 *(978-1-60553-131-1(6))* Phoenix International Publications, Inc.

—Disney Princess under the Starry Sky. 2013. 8p. (J). bds. *(978-1-4508-7130-3(5)*, 1450871305) Phoenix International Publications, Inc.

—Disney Princesses. 2009. 16p. (J). bds. 9.98 *(978-1-4127-7696-7(1)*, PIL Kids) Publications International, Ltd.

—Disney Tales of Virtue 5 Book Set. 2008. (J). pap. 4.98 *(978-1-4127-9392-6(0))* Phoenix International Publications, Inc.

—Little Sound the Princess & the Frog. 2009. 24p. (J). bds. 10.98 *(978-1-4127-6446-9(7))* Publications International, Ltd.

—Look & Find: Disney Princess: Magical Moments. 2010. 24p. (J). 7.98 *(978-1-60553-064-2(6))* Phoenix International Publications, Inc.

—Musical Disney Princesas. 2004. (ESP & SPA., Illus.). 38p. (J). bds. 12.98 *(978-0-7853-8630-8(0)*, 7176101) Publications International, Ltd.

—Musical Pop up Disney Princess. 2008. (SPA.). (J). 15.98 *(978-1-4127-8980-6(X))* Publications International, Ltd.

—My First Book Block Set Disey Princess. 2011. 5p. (J). bds. 14.98 *(978-1-4508-1630-4(4))* Phoenix International Publications, Inc.

—Once upon a Time. 2009. 24p. (J). bds. 17.98 *(978-1-4127-5369-2(4)*, PIL Kids) Publications International, Ltd.

—Please & Thank You. 2010. 20p. (J). bds. 10.98 *(978-1-60553-439-8(0)*, PIL Kids) Publications International, Ltd.

—PNO BK Spa Disney Princess. 2009. 12p. 15.98 *(978-1-4127-9243-1(6))* Phoenix International Publications, Inc.

—The Princess & the Frog. 2009. 24p. (J). 16.98 *(978-1-4127-6421-6(1))* Publications International, Ltd.

—Princess Magic. 2010. (My First Look & Find Ser.). (Illus.). 12p. (gr. -1). bds. 7.98 *(978-1-4127-3074-7(0)*, 7227000) Phoenix International Publications, Inc.

—Sofia the First - Sofia's Royal Day: Includes 6 Punch-Out Play Pieces. Phoenix Books Staff, illus. 2015. 14p. (J). bds. *(978-1-4508-8884-4(4)*, 1450888844) Publications International, Ltd.

—A Surprise for Belle. 2010. 12p. (J). bds. 9.98 *(978-1-4127-4454-6(7))* Phoenix International Publications, Inc.

Rabe, Tish. Frozen. 2013. (Disney Princess Step into Reading Ser.). lib. bdg. 13.55 *(978-0-606-32203-4(5))* Turtleback.

Rai, Lori. Princess Sheron & the Frog. I.t. ed. 2004. (Illus.). 20p. (J). 10.00 *(978-0-9717419-5-9(6))* Rai Consulting & Publishing.

Rakos, Lynnda, et al. Princesses, Mermaids & Fairies Coloring Book. 2012. (Dover Fantasy Coloring Bks.). (ENG.). 32p. (J). (gr. -1-2). pap. 3.99 *(978-0-486-48664-2(8)*, 486648) Dover Pubns., Inc.

Ramius, Edward. Yawnywawnys. 2009. 28p. pap. 14.95 *(978-1-4389-3066-4(6))* AuthorHouse.

Randall, Alice. The Diary of B. B. Bright, Possible Princess. 2012. (J). *(978-1-61858-016-0(7))* Turner Publishing Co.

Randall, Alice & Randall Williams, Caroline. The Diary of B. B. Bright, Possible Princess. Strickland, Shadra, illus. 2012. (ENG.). 192p. (J). (gr. 2-6). 27.99 *(978-1-61858-015-3(9))* Turner Publishing Co.

Random House, illus. Fairytale Collection (Barbie) 2011. (Step into Reading Ser.). (ENG.). 160p. (J). (gr. -1-1). pap. 8.99 *(978-0-375-87255-6(8)*, Random Hse. Bks. for Young Readers) Random Hse. Children's Bks.

Random House Disney. Mulan's Perfect Present / Jasmine's New Friends. 2018. (Disney Princess 8x8 Ser.). lib. bdg. 16.00 *(978-0-606-40950-6(5))* Turtleback.

Ratcliff, Charline. The Princess, the Toad & the Whale. 2012. (ENG.). 36p. (J). (-18). pap. 12.95 *(978-1-4787-1672-3(X))* Outskirts Pr., Inc.

The Real Princess: 6 Small Books. (gr. k-2). 23.00 *(978-0-7635-8505-1(X))* Rigby Education.

Redbank, Tennant. Treasure: Ariel's Curious Kitten. 2015. (Disney Princess Palace Pets Ser.). lib. bdg. 16.00 *(978-0-606-36392-1(0))* Turtleback.

Redwine, C. J. The Shadow Queen. 2016. (Ravenspire Ser.: 1). (ENG.). (YA). (gr. 8). 416p. pap. 10.99 *(978-0-06-236025-0(6))*; (Illus.). 400p. 17.99 *(978-0-06-236024-3(8))* HarperCollins Pubs. (Balzer & Bray).

—The Shadow Queen. 2016. (Ravenspire Ser.: 1). (YA). lib. bdg. 20.85 *(978-0-606-39615-8(2))* Turtleback.

Regan, Dian. Cam's Quest: The Continuing Story of Princess Nevermore & the Wizard's Apprentice. 2007. (Junior Library Guild Selection Ser.). 334p. (J). (gr. 4-8). 17.95 *(978-1-58196-056-3(5)*, Darby Creek) Lerner Publishing Group.

—Princess Nevermore. rev. ed. 2007. (Junior Library Guild Selection Ser.). (ENG.). 256p. (J). (gr. 4-8). 17.95 *(978-1-58196-055-6(7)*, Darby Creek) Lerner Publishing Group.

REID, D. H. Fantasies & Dreams. 2008. 208p. pap. 18.95 *(978-0-557-01592-4(8))* Lulu Pr., Inc.

P Q R

Reid, Danielle. The Princess Puppy: Book 1 Picture Perfect Puppyhood Purpose. 2007. (ENG.). 32p. pap. 14.99 *(978-1-4257-4489-2(3))* Xlibris Corp.

Reisner, Molly. Dora's Princess Party. Aikins, Dave, illus. 2009. (Dora the Explorer Ser.). (ENG.). 12p. (J). (gr. -1-1). 6.99 *(978-1-4169-9045-1(3)*, Simon Spotlight/Nickelodeon) Simon Spotlight/Nickelodeon.

Rene, Rochelle. Bella & the Bad Mood Busters: The Bad Mood Blues. 2012. (ENG.). 22p. (J). 24.95 *(978-1-4327-7279-6(1))* Outskirts Pr., Inc.

Rennert, Laura Joy. Emma, the Extra Ordinary Princess. Florian, Melanie, illus. 2009. (J). *(978-0-525-42152-8(1)*, Dutton Juvenile) Penguin Publishing Group.

—Royal Princess Academy: Dragon Dreams. Florian, Melanie, illus. 2012. (Royal Princess Academy Ser.). (ENG.). 112p. (J). (gr. 1-4). 18.69 *(978-0-8037-3750-1(5))* Penguin Young Readers Group.

RH Disney. Ballerina Princess (Disney Princess) Harding, Niall, illus. 2007. (Step into Reading Ser.). (ENG.). 32p. (J). (gr. k-3). pap. 5.99 *(978-0-7364-2428-8(8)*, RH/Disney) Random Hse. Children's Bks.

—Frozen Story Collection (Disney Frozen) RH Disney, illus. 2015. (Step into Reading Ser.). (ENG., Illus.). 160p. (J). (gr. -1-2). pap. 8.99 *(978-0-7364-3435-5(6)*, RH/Disney) Random Hse. Children's Bks.

—Mulan Is Loyal/Merida Is Brave (Disney Princess) RH Disney, illus. 2017. (Step into Reading Ser.). (ENG., Illus.). 48p. (J). (gr. -1-1). pap. 5.99 *(978-0-7364-3803-2(3)*, RH/Disney) Random Hse. Children's Bks.

—Nine Disney Princess Tales (Disney Princess) RH Disney, illus. 2016. (ENG., Illus.). 224p. (J). (-k). 12.99 *(978-0-7364-3617-5(0)*, Golden/Disney) Random Hse. Children's Bks.

—Princess Story Collection (Disney Princess) 2007. (Step into Reading Ser.). (ENG., Illus.). 160p. (J). (gr. k-3). pap. 7.99 *(978-0-7364-2486-8(5)*, RH/Disney) Random Hse. Children's Bks.

—Sleeping Beauty & the Good Fairies (Disney Classic) RH Disney, illus. 2018. (Little Golden Book Ser.). (ENG., Illus.). 24p. (J). (-k). 4.99 *(978-0-7364-3771-4(1)*, Golden/Disney) Random Hse. Children's Bks.

—Sparkle Magic! (Disney Frozen) RH Disney, illus. 2015. (Pictureback(R) Ser.). (ENG., Illus.). 16p. (J). (gr. -1-2). 5.99 *(978-0-7364-3366-2(X)*, RH/Disney) Random Hse. Children's Bks.

—Springtime Friends (Disney Princess) RH Disney, illus. 2017. (ENG., Illus.). 22p. (J). (-k). bds. 6.99 *(978-0-7364-3736-3(3)*, RH/Disney) Random Hse. Children's Bks.

—Sweet & Spooky Halloween (Disney Princess) Marrucchi, Elisa, illus. 2007. (Pictureback(R) Ser.). (ENG.). 24p. (J). (gr. -1-2). pap. 3.99 *(978-0-7364-2453-0(9)*, RH/Disney) Random Hse. Children's Bks.

RH Disney, illus. Five Enchanting Tales (Disney Princess) 2016. (Step into Reading Ser.). (ENG.). 160p. (J). (gr. -1-2). pap. 7.99 *(978-0-7364-3518-5(2)*, Random Hse. Bks. for Young Readers) Random Hse. Children's Bks.

Rhodes, Morgan. Falling Kingdoms: A Falling Kingdoms Novel. 2014. (Falling Kingdoms Ser.: 1). (ENG., Illus.). 448p. (YA). (gr. 7). pap. 11.99 *(978-1-59514-585-7(0)*, Razorbill) Penguin Young Readers Group.

—Immortal Reign: A Falling Kingdoms Novel. 2018. (Falling Kingdoms Ser.: 6). (YA). (gr. 7). 416p. pap. 11.99 *(978-1-59514-825-4(6))*; 400p. 18.99 *(978-1-59514-824-7(8))* Penguin Young Readers Group. (Razorbill).

—Rebel Spring: A Falling Kingdoms Novel. 2014. (Falling Kingdoms Ser.: 2). (ENG.). 432p. (YA). (gr. 7). pap. 11.99 *(978-1-59514-592-5(3)*, Razorbill) Penguin Young Readers Group.

Richards, Kitty. Cinderella: The Lost Tiara. 2012. (Disney Princess Early Chapter Bks.). (J). lib. bdg. 14.75 *(978-0-606-26572-0(4))* Turtleback.

Richemont, Enid. Princess Frog. Bernstein, Galia, illus. 2014. (Tadpoles: Fairytale Twists Ser.). (ENG.). 32p. (J). (gr. 1-2). *(978-0-7787-0443-0(2))*; pap. *(978-0-7787-0452-2(1))* Crabtree Publishing Co.

Rigby Education Staff. Real Prince: Jumbled Tumble. (gr. k-2). 21.00 *(978-0-7635-2423-4(9))* Rigby Education.

Riggs, Kate. Princes & Princesses. 2013. (Illus.). 24p. (J). 25.65 *(978-1-60818-243-5(6)*, Creative Education) Creative Co., The.

Riggs, Ransom. Tales of the Peculiar. Davidson, Andrew, illus. (ENG.). (YA). (gr. 7). 2017. 208p. pap. 14.99 *(978-0-399-53854-4(2)*, Penguin Books) 2016. 192p. 24.99 *(978-0-399-53853-7(4)*, Dutton Books for Young Readers) Penguin Young Readers Group.

Rizzo, Cynthia Marie. Angela & the Princess. 2006. 89p. pap. 19.95 *(978-1-4241-2599-6(5))* America Star Bks.

Robbins, Trina. The Bark in Space: Book 5, No. 5. Page, Tyler, illus. 2013. (Chicagoland Detective Agency Ser.: 5). (ENG.). 64p. (J). (gr. 4-8). pap. 6.95 *(978-1-4677-0725-1(2)*, 659d0711-80dc-41a4-866d-7c460cfaabf5, Graphic Universe™) Lerner Publishing Group.

Robinson, Diane Mae. Sir Princess Petra: The Pen Pieyu Adventures. 2017. (ENG., Illus.). (J). (gr. 4-7). pap. *(978-1-988714-05-9(2))* Robinson, Diane Mae.

—Sir Princess Petra's Mission: The Pen Pieyu Adventures. 2nd ed. 2017. (Pen Pieyu Adventures Ser.: Vol. 3). (ENG., Illus.). (J). (gr. 2-5). pap. *(978-0-9952482-9-8(X))* Robinson, Diane Mae.

Robinson, Hilary. Beauty & the Pea. Sanfilippo, Simona, illus. 2013. (ENG.). 32p. (J). *(978-0-7787-1155-1(2))* Crabtree Publishing Co.

Robinson, Michelle. Goodnight Princess: The Perfect Bedtime Book! 2015. (Goodnight Ser.). (ENG., Illus.). 32p. (J). (gr. -1 — 1). pap. 7.99 *(978-1-4380-0663-5(2))* Sourcebooks, Inc.

Robinson, Rob. The Princess & the Juggler. 2004. 154p. pap. 12.95 *(978-0-595-30831-6(7))* iUniverse, Inc.

Rodriguez, Lourdes. Mandy, Princess of la la Land: The Green Monster. 2013. 52p. pap. 24.99 *(978-1-4817-0077-1(4))* AuthorHouse.

Rodriguez, Marisol. The Princess & the Chocolate Castle. 2012. 24p. pap. 17.99 *(978-1-4685-4911-9(1))* AuthorHouse.

Roehl, Tessa. Tiana's Best Surprise. 2018. (Disney Princess Beginnings Ser.). lib. bdg. 17.20 *(978-0-606-40954-4(8))* Turtleback.

Rogers, Jewels. The Princess & the Dolphin. 2011. 28p. 12.50 *(978-1-4567-3278-3(1))* AuthorHouse.

—The Princess & the Dolphin. 2010. 26p. pap. 16.99 *(978-1-4269-3966-2(3))* Trafford Publishing.

—The Princess & the Parakeet. 2011. 28p. pap. 12.50 *(978-1-4567-5170-8(0))* AuthorHouse.

—The Princess & the Puppy. 2011. 28p. pap. 12.50 *(978-1-4567-3236-3(6))* AuthorHouse.

—The Princess & the Puppy. 2010. 28p. pap. 16.99 *(978-1-4269-4177-1(3))* Trafford Publishing.

—The Princess & the Rabbit. 2011. 28p. pap. 12.50 *(978-1-4567-5171-5(9))* AuthorHouse.

Rogers, Tom, adapted by. The Secret Spell Book. 2017. (Illus.). 31p. (J). *(978-1-5182-3831-4(9))* Disney Publishing Worldwide.

Romansky, Sally Rosenberg. Invincible. Ott, Margot Janet, illus. 2006. (J). pap. 8.95 *(978-0-9723729-4-7(6))* Imagination Stage, Inc.

Rosado, Jessica E. The Princess. 2012. 26p. 24.95 *(978-1-4512-9466-8(2))* America Star Bks.

Rose, Jasmine. The Last Caterpillar Princess. 2011. 16p. pap. 8.64 *(978-1-4634-1953-0(8))* AuthorHouse.

Rose, Marie. Princess Silver Tears & One Feather. l.t. ed. 2006. (Illus.). 32p. (J). lib. bdg. *(978-1-934190-07-4(1))* Ocean Front Bk. Publishing, Inc.

Rosen, Lucy. My Little Pony: Meet Princess Twilight Sparkle. 2014. (Passport to Reading Level 1 Ser.). (J). lib. bdg. 13.55 *(978-0-606-35939-9(7))* Turtleback.

Ross, Tony. Hora de Dormir. 2006. (Little Princess Ser.).Tr. of Bedtime. (SPA.). (J). (gr. -1-k). bds. 7.95 *(978-968-19-1488-2(0)*, AT33282) Lectorum Pubns., Inc.

—I Don't Want to Go to the Hospital! Ross, Tony, illus. 2013. (ENG., Illus.). 32p. (J). (gr. -1-3). 16.95 *(978-1-4677-1155-5(1))* Lerner Publishing Group.

—I Feel Sick! Ross, Tony, illus. 2015. (ENG., Illus.). 32p. (J). (gr. -1-3). 16.99 *(978-1-4677-5797-3(7))* Andersen Pr. GBR. Dist: Lerner Publishing Group.

—I Feel Sick! Ross, Tony, illus. 2015. (Little Princess Ser.). (ENG., Illus.). 32p. (J). (gr. -1-3). E-Book 27.99 *(978-1-4677-5798-0(5))* Lerner Publishing Group.

—I Want a Bedtime Story! Ross, Tony, illus. 2016. (Little Princess Ser.). (ENG., Illus.). 32p. (J). (gr. -1-3). 17.99 *(978-1-5124-1629-9(0)*, 57eb6720-96d2-4012-9b84-66b336bbb929) Lerner Publishing Group.

—I Want a Sister! Ross, Tony, illus. 2013. (ENG., Illus.). 32p. (J). (gr. -1-3). 16.95 *(978-1-4677-2047-2(X))* Andersen Pr. GBR. Dist: Lerner Publishing Group.

—I Want My Dad! Ross, Tony, illus. 2018. (Little Princess Ser.). (ENG., Illus.). 32p. (J). (gr. -1-3). 17.99 *(978-1-5415-1453-9(X)*, 6c777235-f7e2-4b44-b636-3cfe645539db) Lerner Publishing Group.

—I Want My Dummy! 2018. (Little Princess Ser.: 5). (ENG., Illus.). 32p. (J). (-k). pap. 12.99 *(978-1-78344-633-9(1))* Andersen Pr. GBR. Dist: Independent Pubs. Group.

—I Want My Tooth! 2018. (Little Princess Ser.). (ENG., Illus.). 32p. (J). (gr. k-2). pap. 9.99 *(978-1-78344-601-8(3))* Andersen Pr. GBR. Dist: Independent Pubs. Group.

—I Want Snow! Ross, Tony, illus. 2017. (Little Princess Ser.). (ENG., Illus.). 32p. (J). (gr. -1-3). 17.99 *(978-1-5124-8125-9(4)*, e250c5be-8fca-4986-a652-4f29ea729961) Lerner Publishing Group.

—I Want to Do It Myself! Ross, Tony, illus. 2011. (Andersen Press Picture Bks). (ENG., Illus.). 32p. (J). (gr. -1-3). 16.95 *(978-0-7613-7412-1(4))* Lerner Publishing Group.

—I Want to Go Home! Ross, Tony, illus. 2014. (ENG., Illus.). 32p. (J). (gr. -1-3). 16.95 *(978-1-4677-5095-0(6))* Lerner Publishing Group.

—El Tiempo. 2006. (Little Princess Ser.).Tr. of Weather. (SPA.). (J). (gr. -1-k). bds. 7.95 *(978-968-19-1487-5(2)*, AT33281) Lectorum Pubns., Inc.

Ross, Tony & Finney, Wendy. Where's Gilbert? (the Not So Little Princess) 2020. (Not-So-Little Princess Colour Readers Ser.: 3). (ENG., Illus.). 64p. (J). (gr. k-2). 9.99 *(978-1-78344-523-3(8))* Andersen Pr. GBR. Dist: Independent Pubs. Group.

Rothfuss, Patrick. The Adventures of the Princess & Mr. Whiffle: The Thing Beneath the Bed. Taylor, Nate, illus. 2010. 68p. 25.00 *(978-1-59606-313-6(0))* Subterranean Pr.

Rotman, Risa. Azoi Vi Ess Past Fahr a Princessen (Fit for a Princess) Flohr, Perel, tr. Leff, Tova, illus. 2012.Tr. of Fit for a Princess. (YID.). 32p. (J). 11.99 *(978-1-929628-66-7(8))* Hachai Publishing.

Rousseau, Stephanie. Make It Now!: Princesses: Press Out & Play. 2018. (Make It Now! Ser.). (ENG., Illus.). 12p. (J). (gr. -1-3). pap. 8.99 *(978-1-328-71498-5(5)*, 1674064, Clarion Bks.) HarperCollins Pubs.

A Royal Tea. 2014. (Mermaid Tales Ser.: 9). (ENG., Illus.). 112p. (J). (gr. 1-4). pap. 6.99 *(978-1-4814-0254-5(4)*, Aladdin) Simon & Schuster Children's Publishing.

Ruble, Kam. Princess Annado Tandy's Versery Rhymes. McMullen, T. C., illus. l.t. ed. 2007. 88p. (J). per. *(978-0-9779680-4-6(9))* Global Authors Pubns.

Ryan, Brittney. The Legend of Holly Claus. Long, Laurel, illus. 2004. (Julie Andrews Collection). 544p. (J). (gr. 4-18). 16.99 *(978-0-06-058511-2(0)*, Julie Andrews Collection) HarperCollins Pubs.

Ryan, Pam Muñoz. Solimar: The Sword of the Monarchs. 2022. (Illus.). 40p. (J). (gr. 3-7). 17.99 *(978-1-4847-2835-2(1)*, Disney-Hyperion) Disney Publishing Worldwide.

Ryder, Chloe. Princess Ponies 1: a Magical Friend. 2014. (Princess Ponies Ser.). (ENG., Illus.). 128p. (J). (gr. 1-3). pap. 5.99 *(978-1-61963-165-6(2)*, 900123295, Bloomsbury USA Childrens) Bloomsbury Publishing USA.

—Princess Ponies 2: a Dream Come True. 2014. (Princess Ponies Ser.). (ENG., Illus.). 128p. (J). (gr. 1-3). pap. 6.99 *(978-1-61963-167-0(9)*, 900123305, Bloomsbury USA Childrens) Bloomsbury Publishing USA.

—Princess Ponies 3: the Special Secret. 2014. (Princess Ponies Ser.). (ENG., Illus.). 128p. (J). (gr. 2-4). pap. 6.99 *(978-1-61963-237-0(3)*, 900128207, Bloomsbury USA Childrens) Bloomsbury Publishing USA.

—Princess Ponies 4: a Unicorn Adventure! 2014. (Princess Ponies Ser.). (ENG., Illus.). 128p. (J). (gr. 2-4). pap. 6.99 *(978-1-61963-294-3(2)*, 900132055, Bloomsbury USA Childrens) Bloomsbury Publishing USA.

—Princess Ponies 5: an Amazing Rescue. 2015. (Princess Ponies Ser.). (ENG., Illus.). 128p. (J). (gr. 2-4). pap. 6.99 *(978-1-61963-403-9(1)*, 900135708, Bloomsbury USA Childrens) Bloomsbury Publishing USA.

—Princess Ponies 6: Best Friends Forever! 2015. (Princess Ponies Ser.). (ENG., Illus.). 128p. (J). (gr. 2-4). pap. 5.99 *(978-1-61963-405-3(8)*, 900135710, Bloomsbury USA Childrens) Bloomsbury Publishing USA.

Sage, Angie. Flyte. (Septimus Heap Ser.: 2). (J). 2009. 84.49 *(978-1-4361-5831-2(1))* 2008. 1.25 *(978-1-4193-9383-9(9))* 2006. 114.75 *(978-1-4193-9386-0(3))* 2006. 133.75 *(978-1-4193-9390-7(1))* 2006. 131.75 *(978-1-4193-9392-1(8))* 2006. 111.75 *(978-1-4193-9388-4(X))* 2006. 282.75 *(978-1-4193-9387-7(1))* Recorded Bks., Inc.

—Magyk. Zug, Mark, illus. 2007. (Septimus Heap Ser.: Bk. 1). 564p. (gr. 4-7). 18.00 *(978-0-7569-7760-3(6))* Perfection Learning Corp.

—Magyk. (Septimus Heap Ser.: 1). (J). 2008. 79.75 *(978-1-4361-0584-2(6))* 2007. 1.25 *(978-1-4193-2619-6(8))* 2006. 123.75 *(978-1-4193-3807-6(2))* 2005. 126.75 *(978-1-4193-3805-2(6))* 2005. 106.75 *(978-1-4193-2622-6(8))* 2005. 103.75 *(978-1-4193-2624-0(4))* Recorded Bks., Inc.

—Magyk. 2006. (Septimus Heap Ser.: 1). (J). lib. bdg. 18.40 *(978-1-4177-3321-7(7))* Turtleback.

—Septimus Heap. Set. Zug, Mark, illus. 2007. (Septimus Heap Ser.: Bks. 1-2). (J). (gr. 4). pap. 15.99 *(978-0-06-136195-1(X)*, Tegen, Katherine Bks) HarperCollins Pubs.

—Septimus Heap, Book One: Magyk. Zug, Mark, illus. (Septimus Heap Ser.: 1). (ENG.). (J). (gr. 4-18). 2005. 576p. 18.99 *(978-0-06-057731-5(2))* 2005. 576p. lib. bdg. 18.89 *(978-0-06-057732-2(0))* 2006. 608p. reprint ed. pap. 7.99 *(978-0-06-057733-9(9))* HarperCollins Pubs. (Tegen, Katherine Bks).

—Septimus Heap, Book Two: Flyte. Zug, Mark, illus. (Septimus Heap Ser.: 2). (ENG.). 544p. (J). (gr. 4-7). 2007. pap. 8.99 *(978-0-06-057736-0(3))* 2006. 17.99 *(978-0-06-057734-6(7))* HarperCollins Pubs. (Tegen, Katherine Bks).

Saito, Taeko. Kiss the Frog. 2010. (Princess & the Frog Ser.). (JPN., Illus.). (J). bds. *(978-4-06-262548-7(2))* Kodansha America, Inc.

Sanderson, Ruth. The Snow Princess. 2017. (Ruth Sanderson Collection). (ENG., Illus.). 32p. (J). (gr. -1-3). pap. 8.95 *(978-1-56656-098-6(5)*, Crocodile Bks.) Interlink Publishing Group, Inc.

Sauer, Tammi. Princess in Training. Berger, Joe, illus. 2015. (ENG.). 40p. (J). (gr. -1-3). 7.99 *(978-0-544-45609-9(2)*, 1599394, Clarion Bks.) HarperCollins Pubs.

Saxon, Victoria. Frozen (Disney Frozen) Lee, Grace & Cagol, Andrea, illus. 2015. (Little Golden Book Ser.). (ENG.). 24p. (J). (-k). 5.99 *(978-0-7364-3471-3(2)*, Golden/Disney) Random Hse. Children's Bks.

Schlitz, Laura Amy. Princess Cora & the Crocodile. Floca, Brian, illus. (ENG.). 80p. (J). (gr. -1-3). 2019. pap. 8.99 *(978-1-5362-0878-8(7))* 2017. 17.99 *(978-0-7636-4822-0(1))* Candlewick Pr.

Schow, Betsy. Banished. 2018. (Storymakers Ser.: 3). (ENG.). 336p. (YA). (gr. 6-12). pap. 10.99 *(978-1-4926-3602-1(9))* Sourcebooks, Inc.

—Spelled. 2015. (Storymakers Ser.: 0). (ENG.). 352p. (YA). (gr. 6-12). pap. 10.99 *(978-1-4926-0871-4(8)*, 9781492608714) Sourcebooks, Inc.

Schuette, Eva. The Kingdom of the Wild Gootsies: Meet the Wild Gootsies. 2010. 12p. 8.49 *(978-1-4490-8798-2(1))* AuthorHouse.

Scollon, Bill, et al. Sofia's Princess Adventures. 2015. (Illus.). (J). *(978-1-4847-2563-4(8))* Disney Publishing Worldwide.

Scretching, Dorothy/Janis. Story Time with Princess Dorothy. Walters, Steve, ed. Brunot, Katerina, illus. 2012. 32p. (J). 20.00 *(978-0-9719767-4-0(0)*, Crowned Warrior Publishing) Walters, Steve Ministries.

Scribner, Don. Bennie & Thomas & the Rescue at Razor's Edge: Volume I. Scribner, Peter, illus. 2012. 44p. pap. 24.95 *(978-1-4626-8957-6(4))* America Star Bks.

—Bennie & Thomas & the Rescue at Razor's Edge: Volume II. Scribner, Peter, illus. 2012. 48p. pap. 24.95 *(978-1-4626-9472-3(1))* America Star Bks.

Scribner, Meagen & Jensen, Angelina. Princess & the Peasant. 2013. 40p. pap. *(978-1-4602-3308-5(5))* FriesenPress.

Sears, Cynthia A. The Dragon Lord: The Fairy Princess Chronicles - Book 2. 2013. 376p. *(978-1-4602-3081-7(7))* FriesenPress.

Sebastian, Laura. Ash Princess. 2018. (Illus.). 437p. (YA). *(978-0-525-57826-0(9)*, Delacorte Pr) Random House Publishing Group.

—Ash Princess. (Ash Princess Ser.: 1). (ENG.). (YA). (gr. 7). 2019. 464p. pap. 11.99 *(978-1-5247-6709-9(3)*, Ember) 2018. (Illus.). 448p. 18.99 *(978-1-5247-6706-8(9)*, Delacorte Pr.) 2018. (Illus.). 448p. lib. bdg. 21.99 *(978-1-5247-6707-5(7)*, Delacorte Pr.) Random Hse. Children's Bks.

Secuban, Andy S. The Papagayo: Magical Bird of Paradise. 2008. 24p. pap. 12.99 *(978-1-4389-0660-7(9))* AuthorHouse.

Seever, Berni. A Supernatural Tale. 2007. 62p. pap. 20.00 *(978-1-4196-7788-5(8))* CreateSpace Independent Publishing Platform.

Seiss, Ellie. Dora's Princess Pals. 2011. (Dora the Explorer Ser.). (ENG., Illus.). 12p. (J). (gr. -1-k). 5.99 *(978-1-4424-1203-3(8)*, Simon Spotlight/Nickelodeon) Simon Spotlight/Nickelodeon.

Selfors, Suzanne. A Semi-Charming Kind of Life. 2015. (Ever after High Ser.: Bk. 3). (ENG., Illus.). 224p. (J). E-Book *(978-0-316-40135-7(8))* Little Brown & Co.

Senior, Patricia. Pip & the Magic Flute. 2008. (Illus.). 40p. pap. 18.49 *(978-1-4389-0023-0(6))* AuthorHouse.

Sharma, Radhika. The Princess & the Unicorn Prince. 2007. (ENG.). 48p. pap. 19.96 *(978-1-4357-0072-7(4))* Lulu Pr., Inc.

Sholl, Anna. The Faery Tales of Weir. 2006. 116p. per. 9.95 *(978-1-59818-475-4(X))* Aegypan.

Short, Carol. Robert & the Princess. 2008. 16p. pap. 9.94 *(978-1-4389-2203-4(5))* AuthorHouse.

Shughart-Knecht, Kimberly. Princess Kiali & the Purple Box. 2010. 32p. pap. 12.99 *(978-1-4490-0913-7(1))* AuthorHouse.

Shulda, Daron M. Dragon Boots. 2009. 40p. pap. 18.49 *(978-1-4389-7022-6(6))* AuthorHouse.

Siegel, Terri. Goodnight Princess Scharazad. 2005. (J). lib. bdg. 19.95 *(978-0-9754728-5-9(2))* Big Ransom Studio.

Sierra, JulieAnn. Legacy & the Dark Prince, 1 vol. 2009. 209p. pap. 24.95 *(978-1-61582-693-3(9))* America Star Bks.

Silver Dolphin en Español Editors. Tesoros para llevar Disney: Disney Princess CarryAlong Treasury, Spanish-Language Edition. 2004. (SPA., Illus.). 24p. (J). bds. *(978-970-718-239-4(3)*, Silver Dolphin en Español) Advanced Marketing, S. de R. L. de C. V.

Silver Dolphin en Español Editors, creator. Caritas Felices. 2007. (Disney Princesa (Silver Dolphin) Ser.). (Illus.). 10p. (J). (gr. -1). bds. *(978-970-718-390-2(X)*, Silver Dolphin en Español) Advanced Marketing, S. de R. L. de C. V.

—Felices para Siempre/Happily Ever After. 2007. (Illus.). 5p. (J). (gr. k). *(978-970-718-448-0(5)*, Silver Dolphin en Español) Advanced Marketing, S. de R. L. de C. V.

Simon, Charnan. Tressa the Musical Princess. Allen, Joy, illus. 2005. 25p. (J). *(978-1-58987-112-0(X))* Kindermusik International.

Simone, Ni-Ni & Abrams, Amir. Put Your Diamonds Up! 2014. (Hollywood High Ser.: 3). lib. bdg. 20.80 *(978-0-606-35736-4(X))* Turtleback.

Sims, Anthony. Princess Zoe. 2012. (Illus.). 44p. pap. 24.40 *(978-1-4772-2365-9(7))* AuthorHouse.

Sims, C. Bailey. Candlewax. 2012. (ENG., Illus.). 384p. (YA). 18.99 *(978-0-9839877-1-0(8))*; pap. 13.99 *(978-0-9839877-0-3(X))* Terabyte Pr. LLC.

Simson, Dana. Princess Ruby's Rainbow Day. 2003. (Sparkle Bks.). (J). bds. 10.95 *(978-1-74047-206-7(3))* Book Co. Publishing Pty, Ltd., The AUS. Dist: Penton Overseas, Inc.

Skidmore, Lauren. The Fairest Poison. 2016. 216p. (YA). pap. 16.99 *(978-1-4621-1792-5(9))* Cedar Fort, Inc./CFI Distribution.

Skilbeck, Carol. Adventures of Melonhead. 2011. 56p. 24.99 *(978-1-4568-7464-3(0))*; pap. 15.99 *(978-1-4568-7463-6(2))* Xlibris Corp.

Sklyar, Igor. King & the Star. 2005. (Illus.). 50p. pap. *(978-1-84401-048-6(1))* Athena Pr.

Slater, Dashka. Dangerously Ever After. Docampo, Valeria, illus. 2012. 40p. (J). (gr. k-3). 17.99 *(978-0-8037-3374-9(7)*, Dial Bks) Penguin Young Readers Group.

Smith, Ali. The Story of Antigone. 2019. (Save the Story Ser.: 1). (ENG., Illus.). 100p. (J). (gr. 3-7). pap. 12.95 *(978-1-78269-089-4(1)*, Pushkin Children's Bks.) Steerforth Pr.

Smith, Carrie. Cinderella: Classic Tales Edition. Greenhead, Bill, illus. 2011. (Classic Tales Ser.). (J). *(978-1-936258-77-2(3))* Benchmark Education Co.

—The Princess & the Pea: Classic Tales Edition. Harpster, Steve, illus. 2011. (Classic Tales Ser.). (J). *(978-1-936258-76-5(5))* Benchmark Education Co.

Smith, Nerissia. Prince de'Mario's Adventure, 1 vol. Dartes, Staci, illus. 2009. 29p. pap. 24.95 *(978-1-61582-972-9(5))* America Star Bks.

Smyth, Jimmy. The Fairy Princess. 2013. 34p. pap. *(978-0-9569314-5-0(6))* Smith, Jimmy.

Snodgrass, Lady Cecily. The Really Rotten Princess: Ready-To-Read Level 2. Lester, Mike, illus. 2012. (Really Rotten Princess Ser.). (ENG.). 32p. (J). (gr. k-2). 17.99 *(978-1-4424-3326-7(4)*, Simon Spotlight) Simon & Schuster Children's Publishing.

—The Really Rotten Princess: Ready-To-Read Level 2. Lester, Mike, illus. 2012. (Really Rotten Princess Ser.). (ENG.). 32p. (J). (gr. k-2). pap. 4.99 *(978-1-4424-3325-0(6)*, Simon Spotlight) Simon Spotlight.

—The Really Rotten Princess & the Cupcake Catastrophe: Ready-To-Read Level 2. Lester, Mike, illus. 2013. (Really Rotten Princess Ser.). (ENG.). 32p. (J). (gr. k-2). 17.99 *(978-1-4424-8974-5(X))*; pap. 4.99 *(978-1-4424-8973-8(1))* Simon Spotlight. (Simon Spotlight).

Snyder, Laurel. Up & down the Scratchy Mountains. Call, Greg, illus. 2010. 272p. (J). (gr. 3-7). 7.99 *(978-0-375-84720-2(0)*, Yearling) Random Hse. Children's Bks.

Solange, Helene. Lala the Little Princess. 2009. (Illus.). 32p. pap. 14.49 *(978-1-4490-1005-8(9))* AuthorHouse.

Solomon, Barbara. The Girl Who Wanted to Become a Princess. 2013. 50p. pap. 12.99 *(978-1-62839-354-5(8))* Salem Author Services.

Sommer, Carl. The Great Royal Race. Westbrook, Dick, illus. 2014. (J). pap. *(978-1-57537-952-4(X))* Advance Publishing, Inc.

—The Great Royal Race. 2003. (Another Sommer-Time Story Ser.). (Illus.). 48p. (J). (gr. k-4). lib. bdg. 23.95 incl. audio *(978-1-57537-758-2(6))* Advance Publishing, Inc.

—The Great Royal Race. Westbrook, Dick, illus. 2003. (Another Sommer-Time Story Ser.). 48p. (J). (gr. k-4). lib. bdg. 23.95 incl. audio compact disk *(978-1-57537-708-7(X))* Advance Publishing, Inc.

—The Great Royal Race. 2003. (Another Sommer-Time Story Ser.). (Illus.). 48p. (J). (gr. 1-4). 16.95 incl. audio *(978-1-57537-557-1(5))* Advance Publishing, Inc.

—The Great Royal Race. Westbrook, Dick, illus. 2003. (Another Sommer-Time Story Ser.). 48p. (J). (gr. 1-4). 16.95 incl. audio compact disk *(978-1-57537-508-3(7))* Advance Publishing, Inc.

—The Great Royal Race(La Gran Carrera Real) Westbrook, Dick, illus. 2009. (Another Sommer-Time Story Bilingual Ser.). (SPA & ENG.). 48p. (J). lib. bdg. 16.95 *(978-1-57537-152-8(9))* Advance Publishing, Inc.

—The Race. Budwine, Greg, illus. 2009. (Quest for Success Ser.). (ENG.). 56p. (YA). lib. bdg. 12.95 *(978-1-57537-256-3(8))* Advance Publishing, Inc.

—The Race(La Carrera) Budwine, Greg, illus. 2009. (Quest for Success Bilingual Ser.). (SPA & ENG.). 104p. (YA). lib. bdg. 14.95 *(978-1-57537-230-3(4))* Advance Publishing, Inc.

—The Racing Fools. Budwine, Greg, illus. 2009. (Quest for Success Ser.). (ENG.). 56p. (YA). pap. 4.95 *(978-1-57537-281-5(9))* Advance Publishing, Inc.

—The Ugly Princess. Martinez, Jorge, illus. 2016. 32p. (J). *(978-1-57537-948-7(1))* Advance Publishing, Inc.

Somper, Justin. Allies & Assassins. 2014. (Allies & Assassins Ser.: 1). (ENG.). 496p. (YA). (gr. 7-17). 18.00 *(978-0-316-25393-2(6))* Little, Brown Bks. for Young Readers.

Sorenson, Margo. Ambrose & the Princess. Szegedi, Katalin, illus. 2005. (ENG.). 32p. (J). (gr. -1-3). 16.95 *(978-0-8146-3043-3(X))* Liturgical Pr.

Soundprints Staff. My Princess Treasury. (Kindness Counts Ser.). (ENG., Illus.). 24p. (J). 14.99 *(978-1-59069-373-5(6),* 1A200); 14.99 *(978-1-59069-381-0(7),* 1A201) Studio Mouse LLC.

Sperring, Mark. Princess Scallywag & the Brave, Brave Knight. Powell, Claire, illus. 2019. (ENG.). 32p. (J). pap. 6.99 *(978-0-00-832597-8(9),* HarperCollins Children's Bks.) HarperCollins Pubs. Ltd. GBR. Dist: HarperCollins Pubs.

Spudvilas, Anne. Swan Lake. 2019. (ENG.). 48p. (J). (gr. 5-9). 19.99 *(978-1-74331-845-4(6))* Allen & Unwin AUS. Dist: Independent Pubs. Group.

St. James, Leah. Lights of Imani. Morse, Nessa Neilson, illus. 2013. 28p. pap. 9.99 *(978-0-9853123-6-7(X))* Leah St. James Bks.

Stanek, Robert, pseud. The Kingdoms & the Elves of the Reaches Ii (Reader's Choice Edition, Keeper Martin's Tales Book 2) 2008. (Illus.). 244p. pap. 15.95 *(978-1-57545-197-8(2))* RP Media.

Stanfield, Michael. Bucky & Becky - the Magic of Wigglepoo Mountain. 2009. 144p. pap. 14.96 *(978-0-557-02614-2(8))* Lulu Pr., Inc.

Staniszewski, Anna. The Magic Mirror: a Branches Book (Once upon a Fairy Tale #1) Pamintuan, Macky, illus. 2019. (Once upon a Fairy Tale Ser.: 1). (ENG.). 96p. (J). (gr. 1-3). pap. 4.99 *(978-1-338-34971-9(6))* Scholastic, Inc.

Stanley, Diane. The Princess of Cortova. 2013. 311p. (J). lib. bdg. *(978-0-06-204731-1(0))* HarperCollins Pubs.

Staunton, Ted. Morgan on Ice, 1 vol. Slavin, Bill, illus. 2013. (Formac First Novels Ser.). (ENG.). 56p. (J). (gr. 2-3). 14.95 *(978-1-4595-0289-5(2),* 0289) Formac Publishing Co., Ltd. CAN. Dist: Formac Lorimer Bks. Ltd.

Stockham, Jess, illus. Cinderella. (Flip-Up Fairy Tales Ser.). 24p. (J). 2007. (gr. -1-2). *(978-1-84643-091-6(7))* 2006. (gr. 2-2). *(978-1-904550-74-7(6))* Child's Play International Ltd.

—The Frog Prince. 2007. (Flip-Up Fairy Tales Ser.). 24p. (J). *(978-1-84643-143-2(3))*; (gr. 2-2). pap. *(978-1-84643-077-0(1))* Child's Play International Ltd.

—The Princess & the Pea. 2010. (Flip-Up Fairy Tales Ser.). 24p. (J). (gr. -1-2). *(978-1-84643-332-0(0))* Child's Play International Ltd.

Storm, Falcon. The Persnickety Princess (Tales from upon A. Time - Book 1) l.t. ed. 2013. (ENG.). 94p. pap. 9.95 *(978-1-62253-047-2(0))* Evolved Publishing.

Strelow, Michael. The Alyssa Chronicle: The Princess Gardener, Book II. 2018. (ENG., Illus.). 120p. (J). (gr. -1-12). pap. 11.95 *(978-1-78535-835-7(9),* Our Street Bks.) Hunt, John Publishing Ltd. GBR. Dist: National Bk. Network.

—The Princess Gardener. 2018. (ENG., Illus.). 96p. (J). (gr. -1-12). pap. 10.95 *(978-1-78535-674-2(7),* Our Street Bks.) Hunt, John Publishing Ltd. GBR. Dist: National Bk. Network.

Studio Mouse, creator. Kindness Counts. rev. ed. 2008. (Learn-Aloud Bks.). (ENG., Illus.). (J). 12.99 *(978-1-59069-627-9(1))* Studio Mouse LLC.

Studio Mouse, ed. Disney Preincess Best Friends: Flat Learn & Carry 4 Board Books & CD. rev. ed. 2008. 80p. (J). 12.99 *(978-1-59069-553-1(4))* Studio Mouse LLC.

Studio Mouse Staff. Kindness Counts. rev. ed. 2004. (Kindness Counts Ser.). (ENG., Illus.). 36p. (J). (gr. -1-3). 12.99 *(978-1-59069-364-3(7),* 1A500) Studio Mouse LLC.

—Wedding Countdown. 2008. (ENG.). 36p. (J). (gr. -1). 12.99 *(978-1-59069-740-5(5))* Studio Mouse LLC.

Sullivan, Annie. Tiger Queen, 1 vol. 2019. (ENG.). 336p. (YA). 17.99 *(978-0-310-76877-7(2))* Blink.

Sullivan, Chris Mann. Oh No, Not the Shot! 2011. 24p. pap. 11.98 *(978-1-4490-8392-2(7))* AuthorHouse.

Susaeta, Equipo. La bella durmiente - Sleeping beauty. 2011. (Cuentos Bilingües Ser.). (SPA & ENG.). 34p. (J). (gr. k-2). 8.99 *(978-84-305-2453-2(3))* Susaeta Ediciones, S.A. ESP. Dist: Independent Pubs. Group.

Sussman, Elissa. Stray. 2014. (Stray Ser.: 1). (ENG., Illus.). 384p. (YA). (gr. 8). 17.99 *(978-0-06-227455-7(4),* Greenwillow Bks.) HarperCollins Pubs.

Suttles, Teresa. The Little Gray Box. 2013. 22p. pap. 12.95 *(978-1-62646-450-6(2))* Booklocker.com, Inc.

Sutton, S. A. A Hero for Quale. 2009. 72p. pap. 9.99 *(978-1-60860-189-9(7),* Strategic Bk. Publishing) Strategic Book Publishing & Rights Agency (SBPRA).

Sweet, Susan D. & Miles, Brenda S. Princess Penelopea Hates Peas: A Tale of Picky Eating & Avoiding Catastropeas. Docampo, Valeria, illus. 2016. 32p. (J). *(978-1-4338-2046-5(3),* Magination Pr.) American Psychological Assn.

Sweet, Susan D., et al. Jacqueline & the Beanstalk: A Tale of Facing Giant Fears. 2017. (ENG., Illus.). 32p. (J). 15.95 *(978-1-4338-2682-5(8),* Magination Pr.) American Psychological Assn.

Swiderska, Barbara. The Fisherman's Bride. Swiderska, Barbara, illus. (Illus.). 32p. (J). (gr. -1-3). 12.95 *(978-0-87592-018-4(7))* Scroll Pr., Inc.

Sykes, Julie. Bella at the Ball. Morgan, Richard, illus. 2014. 119p. (J). pap. *(978-0-545-69221-2(0))* Scholastic, Inc.

Tanaka, Rika. Disney Manga: Kilala Princess, Volume 2, Vol. 2. Kodaka, Nao, illus. 2016. (Disney Manga: Kilala Princess Ser.: 2). 176p. (J). (gr. 3-1). pap. 10.99 *(978-1-4278-5663-0(X),* 232f6fef-6b9d-4de3-bfdb-8b714763048c, TOKYOPOP Manga) TOKYOPOP, Inc.

Tarnowska, Wafa'. The Seven Wise Princesses: A Medieval Persian Epic. Nilesh, Misty, illus. 2008. (ENG.). 96p. (J). (gr. 5-9). 19.99 *(978-1-84686-250-2(7))* Barefoot Bks., Inc.

Tarver, Monroe S. Tales from the Mapmaker: Imagia & the Magic Pearls. 2009. (ENG.). 99p. (J). (gr. 2-4). 21.19 *(978-0-9723936-5-2(X))* Wizarding World Pr.

Tavares, Victor, illus. Beauty & the Beast. 2007. (Usborne Young Reading: Series Two Ser.). 63p. (J). 8.99 *(978-0-7945-1456-3(1),* Usborne) EDC Publishing.

Taylor, Kay Lovelace. Princess Aisha & the Cave of Judgment. Rhine, Karen C., illus. 2007. 32p. (J). 19.95 *(978-0-9799119-0-3(7))* KLT & Assocs.

Taylor, Roy. Matilda's Magic Wand: Dreamland Adventure. 2008. 36p. (J). pap. 9.00 *(978-0-8059-7716-5(3))* Dorrance Publishing Co., Inc.

Thanos, Jerald. A Princess Christmas. 2009. (ENG.). 32p. pap. 14.49 *(978-1-4389-6752-3(7))* AuthorHouse.

Thomas, Rhiannon. A Wicked Thing. (ENG.). (YA). (gr. 9). 2016. 368p. pap. 9.99 *(978-0-06-230354-7(6))* 2015. 352p. 17.99 *(978-0-06-230353-0(8))* HarperCollins Pubs. (HarperTeen).

Thompson, Cynthia. Princess Esmeralda of the Land of Ur: The Sharing of Gifts Book Two. 2012. 24p. pap. 12.55 *(978-1-4525-0666-1(3))* Balboa Pr.

TIG, Thomas. Illustrated Treasury of Princess Stories. Kelly, Richard, ed. 2017. 384p. (J). 39.95 *(978-1-78209-986-4(7))* Miles Kelly Publishing, Ltd. GBR. Dist: Parkwest Pubns., Inc.

Tintera, Amy. Avenged. (Ruined Ser.: 2). (ENG.). (YA). (gr. 8). 2018. 432p. pap. 9.99 *(978-0-06-239664-8(1))* 2017. 416p. 17.99 *(978-0-06-239663-1(3))* HarperCollins Pubs. (HarperTeen).

—Ruined. (Ruined Ser.: 1). (ENG.). (YA). (gr. 8). 2017. 384p. pap. 10.99 *(978-0-06-239661-7(7))* 2016. 368p. 17.99 *(978-0-06-239660-0(9))* HarperCollins Pubs. (HarperTeen).

Tomlinson, Heather. Aurelie: A Faerie Tale. 2010. (ENG.). 208p. (YA). (gr. 7-12). pap. 18.99 *(978-0-312-60275-8(8),* 900064245) Square Fish.

Top Secret Tiaras. 2009. (Princess Protection Program Ser.: No. 3). (ENG.). 144p. (J). (gr. 3-7). pap. 4.99 *(978-1-4231-2392-7(1))* Disney Pr.

Top That. Press Out & Play Princess Castle. 2008. *(978-1-84666-611-7(2))* Top That! Publishing PLC.

Torseter, Oyvind. The Heartless Troll. Dickson, Kari, tr. 2016. (ENG., Illus.). 120p. (J). (gr. 1-9). 19.95 *(978-1-59270-193-0(0))* Enchanted Lion Bks., LLC.

Townley, Roderick. The Great Good Thing. 2003. (Richard Jackson Books (Econo-Clad) Ser.). 216p. (gr. 5). 16.00 *(978-0-7569-1435-6(3))* Perfection Learning Corp.

Townsend, S. P. The Star of Persia. 2008. 120p. pap. 12.50 *(978-1-84799-532-2(2))* Lulu Pr., Inc.

ToyBox Innovations, creator. Disney Princess: Cinderella/Snow White/Sleeping Beauty. unabr. abr. ed. 2005. (Disney Princess Ser.). (J). pap. *(978-0-7634-1150-3(7))* Walt Disney Records.

Toybox Innovations, creator. Disney's Enchanted. 2007. (Disney's Read along Collection). (Illus.). 24p. (J). (gr. -1-3). pap. *(978-0-7634-2197-7(9))* Walt Disney Records.

Tran, Hensley. Agatha's Stolen Curve. 2013. 80p. (gr. 4-6). 18.95 *(978-1-4759-7312-9(8))*; pap. 8.95 *(978-1-4759-7310-5(1))* iUniverse, Inc.

Trimble, Irene. Winter Fun for Everyone! (Disney Princess) RH Disney, illus. 2015. (Pictureback(R) Ser.). (ENG.). 16p. (J). (gr. -1-2). 5.99 *(978-0-7364-3416-4(X),* RH/Disney) Random Hse. Children's Bks.

Triplett, Ginger. The Stringed Princess. 2012. 56p. pap. 31.99 *(978-1-4771-2102-3(1))* Xlibris Corp.

Tucker, Patricia Wright. The Princess Who Couldn't Laugh. 2012. 24p. pap. 24.95 *(978-1-4626-8133-4(6))* America Star Bks.

Tyrrell, Kevin. Froggy Kisses. Tyrrell, Kayla, illus. 2008. 22p. pap. 24.95 *(978-1-60672-066-0(X))* America Star Bks.

Valle, Anita. Best Princess Coloring Book. 2012. 50p. pap. 10.50 *(978-1-105-54804-8(X))* Lulu Pr., Inc.

Van Fleet, Mara. Little Color Fairies. Van Fleet, Mara, illus. 2012. (ENG., Illus.). 16p. (J). (gr. -1-1). 15.99 *(978-1-4424-3434-9(1),* Simon & Schuster/Paula Wiseman Bks.) Simon & Schuster/Paula Wiseman Bks.

—Night-Night, Princess. Van Fleet, Mara, illus. 2014. (ENG., Illus.). 16p. (J). (gr. -1-1). 14.99 *(978-1-4424-8646-1(5),* Simon & Schuster/Paula Wiseman Bks.) Simon & Schuster/Paula Wiseman Bks.

Vande Velde, Vivian. The Princess Imposter. 2017. (ENG.). 224p. (J). (gr. 3-7). 16.99 *(978-1-338-12147-6(2),* Scholastic Pr.) Scholastic, Inc.

—Wizard at Work. 2004. (ENG., Illus.). 144p. (J). (gr. 5-7). pap. 10.95 *(978-0-15-205309-3(3),* 1195997, Clarion Bks.) HarperCollins Pubs.

Vaun, Missouri. Birthright. 2017. (ENG., Illus.). 264p. pap. 16.95 *(978-1-62639-485-8(7))* Bold Strokes Bks.

Ventura, Marne. The Worry Warriors, 4 vols. Trinidad, Leo, illus. 2016. (Worry Warriors Ser.). (ENG.). 96p. (J). (gr. 2-4). 106.60 *(978-1-4965-3665-5(7),* 25145, Stone Arch Bks.) Capstone.

Vernon, Ursula. Hamster Princess: Harriet the Invincible. 2015. (Hamster Princess Ser.: 1). (Illus.). 256p. (J). (gr. 3-7). 14.99 *(978-0-8037-3983-3(4),* Dial Bks) Penguin Young Readers Group.

—Hamster Princess: Little Red Rodent Hood. 2018. (Hamster Princess Ser.: 6). (Illus.). 224p. (J). (gr. 3-7). 14.99 *(978-0-399-18658-5(1),* Dial Bks) Penguin Young Readers Group.

—Hamster Princess: of Mice & Magic. 2016. (Hamster Princess Ser.: 2). (Illus.). 240p. (J). (gr. 3-7). 13.99 *(978-0-8037-3984-0(2),* Dial Bks) Penguin Young Readers Group.

—Hamster Princess: Ratpunzel. 2016. (Hamster Princess Ser.: 3). (Illus.). 240p. (J). (gr. 3-7). 14.99 *(978-0-8037-3985-7(0),* Dial Bks) Penguin Young Readers Group.

—Hamster Princess: Whiskerella. 2018. (Hamster Princess Ser.: 5). (Illus.). 256p. (J). (gr. 3-7). 14.99 *(978-0-399-18655-4(7),* Dial Bks) Penguin Young Readers Group.

Viguié, Debbie & Viguié, Debbie. Violet Eyes. 2010. (Once upon a Time Ser.). (ENG.). 224p. (YA). (gr. 7-18). mass mkt. 7.99 *(978-1-4169-8676-8(6),* Simon Pulse) Simon Pulse.

Virtue, Queen Petals De. Princess & the Rain. 2012. 28p. pap. 21.99 *(978-1-4691-2744-6(X))* Xlibris Corp.

Vize, Dania. My Princess Dress up Storybook. 2005. (Illus.). 12p. (J). (gr. -1-3). bds. *(978-1-905051-84-7(0))* Make Believe Ideas.

Voigt, Cynthia. The Tale of Elske. 2015. (Tales of the Kingdom Ser.: 4). (ENG., Illus.). 368p. (YA). (gr. 7). 19.99 *(978-1-4814-2189-8(1),* Atheneum Bks. for Young Readers) Simon & Schuster Children's Publishing.

Wadsworth, Peter. The Wicked Witch of the Woods. 2012. (Illus.). 28p. pap. 8.49 *(978-1-78035-481-1(9),* Fastprint Publishing) Upfront Publishing Ltd. GBR. Dist: Printondemand-worldwide.com.

Wagner, Veronica. Sound Storybook Treasury Disney Princess Bedtime. 2017. (ENG., Illus.). 34p. (J). 29.99 *(978-1-5037-1889-0(1),* 2413, PI Kids) Phoenix International Publications, Inc.

Wallace, Becky. The Storyspinner. 2015. (Keepers' Chronicles Ser.). (ENG., Illus.). 432p. (YA). (gr. 9). 17.99 *(978-1-4814-0565-2(9),* McElderry, Margaret K. Bks.) McElderry, Margaret K. Bks.

Ward, Nick. The Tadpole Prince. 2003. (Illus.). 32p. (YA). *(978-1-84365-016-4(9),* Pavilion Children's Books) Pavilion Bks.

Watson, Andi. Princess Decomposia & Count Spatula. 2015. (ENG., Illus.). 176p. (YA). (gr. 8). 19.99 *(978-1-62672-275-0(7),* 900148323, First Second Bks.) Roaring Brook Pr.

Watt, Fiona. That's Not My Princess. Wells, Rachel, illus. 2006. (Usborne Touchy-Feely Board Bks.). 10p. (J). (gr. -1). bds. 9.99 *(978-0-7945-1325-2(5),* Usborne) EDC Publishing.

Watt, J. S. The Hall of Sorrows. 2006. 67p. pap. 16.95 *(978-1-4241-2984-3(2))* PublishAmerica, Inc.

Wax, Wendy. Phonics Comics: Clara the Klutz - Level 2. Sullivan, Mary, illus. 2007. (ENG.). 24p. (J). (gr. 1-17). per. 3.99 *(978-1-58476-565-3(8))* Innovative Kids.

Wax, Wendy A. Musica en Casa: Libro de Cuentos. de Alba, Arlette, tr. 2005. (Disney Princess Ser.). (SPA., Illus.). 38p. (J). (gr. -1-7). incl. audio compact disk *(978-970-718-289-9(X),* Silver Dolphin en Español) Advanced Marketing, S. de R. L. de C. V.

Webb, Holly. Rose & the Lost Princess. 2014. (Rose Ser.: 2). (ENG.). 256p. (J). (gr. 3-6). pap. 10.99 *(978-1-4022-8584-4(1))* Sourcebooks, Inc.

—Rose & the Magician's Mask. 2014. (Rose Ser.: 3). (ENG.). 224p. (J). (gr. 3-6). pap. 10.99 *(978-1-4926-0430-3(5),* 9781492604303) Sourcebooks, Inc.

Webster, Christy. Anna's Best Friends. 2014. (Disney Princess Step into Reading Ser.). lib. bdg. 13.55 *(978-0-606-35547-6(2))* Turtleback.

Weinberg, Jennifer Liberts. Happy Birthday, Princess! 2012. (Disney Princess Step into Reading Ser.). lib. bdg. 13.55 *(978-0-606-23725-3(9))* Turtleback.

—Princess Hearts. 2012. (Disney Princess Step into Reading Ser.). lib. bdg. 13.55 *(978-0-606-26975-9(4))* Turtleback.

—Princess Hearts (Disney Princess) Legramandi, Francesco, illus. 2012. (Step into Reading Ser.). (ENG.). 32p. (J). (gr. -1-1). pap. 5.99 *(978-0-7364-3013-5(X),* RH/Disney) Random Hse. Children's Bks.

—Princesses & Puppies. 2013. (Disney Princess Step into Reading Ser.). lib. bdg. 13.55 *(978-0-606-32201-0(9))* Turtleback.

West, Madeleine. Lily d V. A. P: Little Princess Snow-Bean, Volume 3. 2020. (Lily d V. A. P Ser.: 3). (ENG.). 112p. (J). (gr. k-2). pap. 9.99 *(978-1-76068-302-3(7))* Little Hare Bks. AUS. Dist: Independent Pubs. Group.

What's the Time Fairy Princess? 2014. (Illus.). (J). *(978-1-4351-5497-1(5))* Barnes & Noble, Inc.

White, J. A. The Thickety #4: The Last Spell. Offermann, Andrea, illus. 2017. (Thickety Ser.: 4). (ENG.). 512p. (J). (gr. 5). 16.99 *(978-0-06-238139-2(3),* Tegen, Katherine Bks) HarperCollins Pubs.

White, Kiersten. And I Darken. 2017. (And I Darken Ser.: 1). (ENG.). 528p. (YA). (gr. 7). pap. 10.99 *(978-0-553-52234-1(5),* Ember) Random Hse. Children's Bks.

—Bright We Burn. 2019. (And I Darken Ser.: 3). (ENG., Illus.). 432p. (YA). (gr. 7). pap. 10.99 *(978-0-553-52242-6(6),* Ember) Random Hse. Children's Bks.

—Now I Rise. 2017. (And I Darken Ser.: 2). (ENG.). 480p. (YA). (gr. 7). 18.99 *(978-0-553-52235-8(3),* Delacorte Pr.) Random Hse. Children's Bks.

White, Vernon. Birdhouse. 2010. (ENG., Illus.). 136p. (YA). pap. 10.95 *(978-1-59362-185-8(X),* d54ab0cc-8ea6-44e3-b7d7-e6caca104d40) Slave Labor Bks.

Whitehouse, Howard. The Faceless Fiend: Being the Tale of a Criminal Mastermind, His Masked Minions & a Princess with a Butter Knife, Involving Explosives & a Certain Amount of Pushing & Shoving. Slavin, Bill, illus. 2007. (Mad Misadventures of Emmaline & Rubberbones Ser.). (ENG.). 272p. (J). (gr. 4-7). 7.95 *(978-1-55453-180-6(2))* Kids Can Pr., Ltd. CAN. Dist: Hachette Bk. Group.

Wiggins, Bethany. The Dragon's Curse (a Transference Novel) 2018. (Transference Trilogy Ser.: 2). 336p. (YA). (gr. 7). 17.99 *(978-0-399-55101-7(8),* Crown Books For Young Readers) Random Hse. Children's Bks.

Wildsmith, Sarah. Princess Charming. 2013. (ENG., Illus.). 32p. (-12). pap. 14.99 *(978-1-62380-970-6(3),* Harmony Ink Pr.) Dreamspinner Pr.

Williams, Allix Elise. The Adventures of Prince Thaddeus: The Glamorous Guest. 2010. 56p. pap. 11.49 *(978-1-4520-5437-7(1))* AuthorHouse.

Williams, Brenda. The Real Princess. Fatus, Sophie, illus. 2008. (ENG.). 40p. (J). (gr. -1-3). 16.99 *(978-1-905236-88-6(3))* Barefoot Bks., Inc.

Williams, Brenda & Barefoot Books Staff. Una Princesa Real: Un Cuento Matemagico. Fatus, Sophie, illus. 2014. 40p. (J). (gr. k-4). pap. 8.99 *(978-1-78285-078-6(3))* Barefoot Bks., Inc.

Williams, Sophy. Princess Stories from Around the World. Tym, Kate, illus. 2004. 64p. (J). *(978-1-84458-142-9(X),* Pavilion Children's Books) Pavilion Bks.

Williamson, Judithe Anne. Princess Kara in Her Village, 1 vol. 2009. 107p. pap. 19.95 *(978-1-60813-817-3(8))* America Star Bks.

Wilson, George H. The Arrival of Grand Princess Leandria. 2010. (Illus.). 50p. (J). 15.00 *(978-0-9778477-5-4(6))* A Story Plus Children Bks.

Wilson, Karma. Princess Me. Unzner, Christa, illus. 2007. (ENG.). 32p. (J). (gr. -1-3). 19.99 *(978-1-4169-4098-2(7),* McElderry, Margaret K. Bks.) McElderry, Margaret K. Bks.

Wilson, Tony. The Princess & the Packet of Frozen Peas, 1 vol. Degennaro, Sue, illus. 2018. (ENG.). 32p. (J). (gr. -1-3). pap. 7.95 *(978-1-68263-051-8(X))* Peachtree Publishing Co. Inc.

—The Princess & the Packet of Frozen Peas. 2018. (J). lib. bdg. 18.40 *(978-0-606-41012-0(0))* Turtleback.

Wind, Chuck T. The Test of Love. 2011. 24p. pap. 24.95 *(978-1-4626-2398-3(0))* America Star Bks.

Winter, Barbara. The Golden Scarab. 2007. (Illus.). 48p. (J). lib. bdg. 15.00 *(978-1-4242-1617-8(6))* Dingles & Co.

Wisher, Mark. Don't kiss the Prince. 2010. 33p. pap. 21.50 *(978-1-4457-7238-7(8))* Lulu Pr., Inc.

Wonlah, Ivis. King Ola's Pepper Jar. 2012. 28p. pap. 16.09 *(978-1-4669-1600-5(1))* Trafford Publishing.

Wood, Audrey. The Princess & the Dragon Mask Book. 2003. (Child's Play Library). (Illus.). 10p. (J). *(978-0-85953-717-9(X))* Child's Play International Ltd.

—Princess, the Dragon & Scaredy Cats. (J). audio *(978-0-85953-375-1(1))* Child's Play International Ltd.

Wood, Jane R. Adventures on Amelia Island: A Pirate, a Princess, & Buried Treasure. Blacker, Elizabeth A., illus. Wood, Jane R., photos by. 2007. (ENG.). 132p. (J). (gr. 3-8). pap. 8.99 *(978-0-9792304-0-0(3))* Florida Kids Pr., Inc.

Woods, Valerie. Princess Portia's Enchanted Journey, 1 vol. 2010. 36p. pap. 24.95 *(978-1-4489-9673-5(2))* America Star Bks.

Wooster, Devin Ann. Sing It Out (Barbie in Rock 'n Royals) 2015. (Step into Reading Ser.). (ENG., Illus.). 24p. (J). (gr. -1-1). 4.99 *(978-0-553-52438-3(0),* Random Hse. Bks. for Young Readers) Random Hse. Children's Bks.

Worrall, Linda, illus. Snow White & the Seven Dwarfs: A Story about Vanity. 2006. (J). 6.99 *(978-1-59939-025-3(6))* Cornerstone Pr.

Wright, Peter M. The Stone Prince, 1 vol. 2009. 48p. pap. 16.95 *(978-1-4489-2591-9(6))* America Star Bks.

Wright, Sabrina L. & Griffin, Dexter. Kalilah: the Whispered Promise. 2005. 159p. (J). (gr. 4-7). per. 12.95 *(978-0-9770363-0-1(8))* First-Sight Publishing.

Written By Tori Velle; Illustrated By Al. Tia Tot Rules! Aguila, Alicia del, illus. 2011. 44p. pap. 24.95 *(978-1-4241-7833-9(9))* America Star Bks.

Wronski, Gareth. Holly Farb & the Princess of the Galaxy. 2017. (ENG., Illus.). 320p. (J). (gr. 3-7). 16.99 *(978-1-4814-7177-0(5),* Aladdin) Simon & Schuster Children's Publishing.

Wu, Nicholas. The Princess & the Pea, 1 vol. rev. ed. 2013. (Literary Text Ser.). (ENG., Illus.). 20p. (J). (gr. 1-2). 7.99 *(978-1-4333-5489-2(6))* Teacher Created Materials, Inc.

—The Princess & the Pea: A Retelling of Hans Christian Andersen's Story, 1 vol. rev. ed. 2013. (Literary Text Ser.). (ENG., Illus.). 20p. (J). (gr. 1-2). lib. bdg. 15.96 *(978-1-4807-1145-7(4))* Teacher Created Materials, Inc.

Wunsch, Emma. Banana Pants! (Miranda & Maude #2) von Innerebner, Jessika, illus. 2019. (ENG.). 144p. (J). (gr. 2-5). 12.99 *(978-1-4197-3180-8(7),* 1247401, Amulet Bks.) Abrams, Inc.

—The Princess & the Absolutely Not a Princess (Miranda & Maude #1) von Innerebner, Jessika, illus. 2018. (ENG.). 144p. (J). (gr. 2-5). 12.99 *(978-1-4197-3179-2(3),* 1247301, Amulet Bks.) Abrams, Inc.

—The Princess & the Absolutely Not a Princess (Miranda & Maude #1), Vol. 1. von Innerebner, Jessika, illus. 2019. (Miranda & Maude Ser.). (ENG.). 160p. (J). (gr. 1-4). pap. 6.99 *(978-1-4197-3374-1(5),* 1247303) Abrams, Inc.

—Recess Rebels (Miranda & Maude #3) von Innerebner, Jessika, illus. 2019. (Miranda & Maude Ser.). (ENG.). 144p. (J). (gr. 2-5). 12.99 *(978-1-4197-3737-4(6),* 1278601, Amulet Bks.) Abrams, Inc.

Wyss, Tyan. The Solitaire Prince. 2006. 168p. (YA). per. 12.95 *(978-1-58939-906-8(4))* Virtualbookworm.com Publishing, Inc.

Yolen, Jane & Harris, Robert J. Girl in a Cage. 2004. 234p. (gr. 5-9). 17.00 *(978-0-7569-2946-6(6))* Perfection Learning Corp.

Yolen, Jane & Stemple, Heidi E. Y. Not All Princesses Dress in Pink. Lanquetin, Anne-Sophie, illus. 2010. (ENG.). 32p. (J). (gr. -1-3). 17.99 *(978-1-4169-8018-6(0),* Simon & Schuster Bks. For Young Readers) Simon & Schuster Bks. For Young Readers.

Young, Jeanna Stolle & Johnson, Jacqueline. Princess Hope & the Hidden Treasure, 1 vol. Aranda, Omar, illus. 2012. (Princess Parables Ser.). (ENG.). 32p. (J). 14.99 *(978-0-310-72699-9(9))* Zonderkidz.

Young, Jeanna Stolle & Johnson, Jacqueline Kinney. Princess Grace & the Little Lost Kitten, 1 vol. Aranda, Omar, illus. 2011. (Princess Parables Ser.). (ENG.). 32p. (J). (gr. -1-2). 14.99 *(978-0-310-71640-2(3))* Zonderkidz.

—Princess Joy's Birthday Blessing, 1 vol. Aranda, Omar, illus. 2011. (Princess Parables Ser.). (ENG.). 32p. (J). (gr. -1-2). 14.99 *(978-0-310-71639-6(X))* Zonderkidz.

Yoyo Books Staff. Princess Charlotte Becomes a Magician. 2005. 32p. *(978-90-5843-459-3(1))* YoYo Bks.

Yu, Mimi. The Girl King. (Girl King Ser.). (ENG.). 496p. (YA). 2020. pap. 10.99 *(978-1-5476-0308-4(9),* 900211273) 2019. 17.99 *(978-1-68119-889-7(4),* 900191621) Bloomsbury Publishing USA. (Bloomsbury Young Adult).

Zahler, Diane. Princess of the Wild Swans. 2013. (ENG., Illus.). 240p. (J). (gr. 3-7). pap. 6.99 *(978-0-06-200495-6(6),* HarperCollins) HarperCollins Pubs.

—Sleeping Beauty's Daughters. 2013. 216p. (J). lib. bdg. *(978-0-06-200497-0(2))* Harper & Row Ltd.

—The Thirteenth Princess. 2011. (ENG.). 272p. (J). (gr. 3-7). pap. 6.99 *(978-0-06-182500-2(X),* HarperCollins) HarperCollins Pubs.

—A True Princess. (ENG.). (J). (gr. 3-7). 2012. 208p. pap. 6.99 *(978-0-06-182503-3(4))* 2011. 192p. 15.99 *(978-0-06-182501-9(8))* HarperCollins Pubs. (HarperCollins).

Zellerhoff, Christi. Princesses Can Be Pirates Too! Davis, Amy, illus. 2012. 38p. 17.99 *(978-1-935961-68-0(3))*; pap. 8.99 *(978-1-935961-95-6(0))* Booktrope. (Booktrope Editions).

Zhao, Yun & I-Haun. Real Fake Princess, Vol. 1. 2006. (Real/Fake Princess Ser.). (ENG., Illus.). 200p. (YA). pap. 9.95 *(978-1-59796-079-3(9))* DrMaster Pubns. Inc.

Ziegler, Argentina Palacios, tr. Dora y la Princesa de la Nieve (Dora Saves the Snow Princess) Aikins, Dave, illus. 2008. (Dora la Exploradora Ser.). (SPA.). 24p. (J). (gr. -1-2). pap. 3.99 *(978-1-4169-5870-3(3),* Libros Para Ninos) Libros Para Ninos.

Zimmerman, Diana S. Kandide & the Secret of the Mists, Bk. 1. Gadd, Maxine, illus. 2008. (Calabiyau Chronicles Ser.). 290p. (J). (gr. 4-7). pap. 9.99 *(978-0-9794328-2-8(0))* Noesis Publishing.

PRINTING

see also Books

Abell, Tracy. All about 3D Printing. 2017. (Cutting-Edge Technology Ser.). (ENG., Illus.). 32p. (J). (gr. 3-5). pap. 9.95 *(978-1-63517-065-8(6))*; lib. bdg. 31.35 *(978-1-63517-009-2(5)*, 1635170095) North Star Editions. (Focus Readers).

Beckham, Robert. Who in the World Was the Secretive Printer Unabridged Compact Dis: The Story of Johannes Gutenberg. unabr. ed. 2008. (Who in the World Ser.: 0). (ENG.). 1p. audio compact disk 12.95 *(978-1-933339-27-6(6)*, 333927) Well-Trained Mind Pr.

Bibbo, Molly Suzanne. Stem: 3-D Printing: Adding & Subtracting Fractions (Grade 4) 2017. (Mathematics in the Real World Ser.). (ENG., Illus.). 32p. (gr. 4-5). pap. 11.99 *(978-1-4258-5554-3(7))* Teacher Created Materials, Inc.

Blohm, Craig E., contrib. by. 3D Printing & Medicine. 2018. (ENG.). 80p. (YA). (gr. 5-12). *(978-1-68282-331-6(8))* ReferencePoint Pr., Inc.

Bodden, Valerie. 3-D Printers. 2017. (Modern Engineering Marvels Ser.). (ENG., Illus.). 32p. (J). (gr. 3-6). lib. bdg. 32.79 *(978-1-5321-1087-0(1)*, 25750, Checkerboard Library) ABDO Publishing Co.

Boozarjomehri, Keon Arasteh. 3D Printing at School & Makerspaces, 1 vol. 2017. (Project Learning with 3D Printing Ser.). (ENG.). 128p. (YA). (gr. 9-9). 47.36 *(978-1-5026-3148-0(2)*, 2cee843c-6b84-445c-8c2a-b63b6f52524b); pap. 22.16 *(978-1-5026-3426-9(0)*, 59513437-7243-40ed-8230-a657c733a167) Cavendish Square Publishing LLC.

Brooks, Susie. Printing & Stamping Art, 1 vol. 2017. (Let's Make Art Ser.). (ENG.). 32p. (J). (gr. 2-3). 29.27 *(978-1-5383-2223-9(4)*, f68cc61d-b3de-4cf5-963d-a3d29f496e28); pap. 12.75 *(978-1-5383-2318-2(4)*, 5e7b7188-f3b0-4655-952c-7d8b0cdd0929) Rosen Publishing Group, Inc., The. (PowerKids Pr.).

Carter, Jason. Gutenberg's Bible, 1 vol. 2016. (Let's Find Out! Primary Sources Ser.). (ENG., Illus.). 32p. (J). (gr. 2-3). lib. bdg. 26.06 *(978-1-5081-0403-2(4)*, de363167-e563-4bc8-be88-fcc6b78a4332) Rosen Publishing Group, Inc., The.

Childress, Diana. Johannes Gutenberg & the Printing Press. 2008. (Pivotal Moments in History Ser.). (ENG., Illus.). 160p. (gr. 9-12). lib. bdg. 38.60 *(978-0-8225-7520-7(5))* Lerner Publishing Group.

Chow-Miller, Ian. How Does 3D Printing Work?, 1 vol. 2017. (Project Learning with 3D Printing Ser.). (ENG.). 128p. (YA). (gr. 9-9). 47.36 *(978-1-5026-3156-5(3)*, 38666daf-a524-4085-b424-cab2913538ba); pap. 22.16 *(978-1-5026-3425-2(2)*, 9312bd51-389d-43f9-8b8f-f862fa7fb166) Cavendish Square Publishing LLC.

Diana, Carla. LEO the Maker Prince: Journeys in 3D Printing. 2013. (ENG., Illus.). 64p. 14.99 *(978-1-4571-8314-0(5)*, 9781457183140) O'Reilly Media, Inc.

DK. 3D Printing Projects. 2017. (ENG., Illus.). 96p. (J). (gr. 4-7). pap. 16.99 *(978-1-4654-6476-7(X)*, DK Children) Dorling Kindersley Publishing, Inc.

Flash Kids Editors, Flash Kids, ed. Print Writing Cards: Learning Cards. 2016. (Write-On Wipe-off Handwriting Cards Ser.). (Illus.). 80p. (J). (gr. -1-1). 10.95 *(978-1-4114-7891-6(6)*, Spark Publishing Group) Sterling Publishing Co., Inc.

Garry-McCord, Kathleen & Sonsky, Kim. Stamp It! Brush-Free Art Prints & Paint Projects. Sonsky, Kim, illus. 2006. (Illus.). 48p. (J). *(978-0-439-81340-2(9))* Scholastic, Inc.

Gitlin, Martin. 3D Printing. 2019. (21st Century Skills Innovation Library: Disruptors in Tech Ser.). (ENG., Illus.). 32p. (J). (gr. 4-8). pap. 14.21 *(978-1-5341-5048-5(X)*, 213499); lib. bdg. 32.07 *(978-1-5341-4762-1(4)*, 213498) Cherry Lake Publishing.

GoBo. Santa Baby: Boxed Set: Boxed Set. 2006. 10p. 9.95 *(978-1-932915-37-2(0))* Sandvik Publishing.

Hamilton, John. Books, 1 vol. 2005. (Straight to the Source Ser.). (ENG.). 32p. (gr. k-6). 27.07 *(978-1-59197-543-4(3)*, Checkerboard Library) ABDO Publishing Co.

Hayward, Linda. I Am a Book. Nicklaus, Carol, illus. (Silly Millies Ser.). 32p. (J). (gr. k-2). 2005. pap. 4.99 *(978-0-7613-1826-2(7)*, First Avenue Editions) 2004. lib. bdg. 17.90 *(978-0-7613-2905-3(6)*, Millbrook Pr.) Lerner Publishing Group.

Hiller, Sandra J. The Life of a Colonial Printer. 2013. (Jr. Graphic Colonial America Ser.). 24p. (J). (gr. 3-6). pap. 63.60 *(978-1-4777-1430-0(8))*; (ENG., Illus.). (gr. 2-3). pap. 11.60 *(978-1-4777-1429-4(4)*, be23caad-71d6-435f-9f23-b07576274835); (ENG., Illus.). (gr. 2-3). lib. bdg. 28.93 *(978-1-4777-1306-8(9)*, 23c9fbb2-8719-4e90-ad43-1edd19736cf7) Rosen Publishing Group, Inc., The. (PowerKids Pr.).

Incentive Publications by World Book (Firm) Staff, contrib. by. 3D Printing & Other Industrial Tech. 2019. (Illus.). 48p. (J). *(978-0-7166-2432-5(X))* World Bk., Inc.

Kenney, Karen Latchana. Cutting-Edge 3D Printing. 2018. (Searchlight Books (tm) — Cutting-Edge STEM Ser.). (ENG., Illus.). 32p. (J). (gr. 3-5). 30.65 *(978-1-5415-2346-3(6)*, 9ef29b8d-cb67-4453-bdc1-bc44acca41db, Lerner Pubns.) Lerner Publishing Group.

LaPierre, Yvette. Inside 3D Printers. 2018. (Inside Technology Ser.). (ENG., Illus.). 48p. (J). (gr. 4-8). lib. bdg. 35.64 *(978-1-5321-1788-6(4)*, 30864) ABDO Publishing Co.

McCarthy, Cecilia Pinto. How 3D Printing Will Impact Society. 2018. (Technology's Impact Ser.). (ENG.). 80p. (YA). (gr. 6-12). 39.93 *(978-1-68282-499-3(3))* ReferencePoint Pr., Inc.

Medina, Sarah. Having Fun with Printing, 1 vol. 2007. (Fun Art Projects Ser.). (ENG., Illus.). 24p. (J). (gr. 2-2). lib. bdg. 28.93 *(978-1-4042-3719-3(4)*, bfcd40f4-cbb2-4232-a9ad-44c71839931b, PowerKids Pr.) Rosen Publishing Group, Inc., The.

Miller, Shannon & Hoena, B. A. A 3-D Printing Mission. 2018. (J). *(978-1-68410-228-0(6))* Cantata Learning.

Mismas, L. J., Jr. Write on! Printing: Tutor Kit (English) 2005. (JPN & ENG., Illus.). 20p. (J). bds. incl. DVD *(978-0-9755836-0-9(3)*, 0101) Incredible Kid, LLC.

Nicholson, Sue. Printing, 6 vols. 2005. (QEB Learn Art Ser.). (Illus.). (J). per. 8.95 *(978-1-59566-123-4(9))* QEB Publishing Inc.

Oachs, Emily Rose. The Printing Press. 2019. (Inventions That Changed the World Ser.). (ENG., Illus.). 32p. (J). (gr. 3-7). pap. 8.99 *(978-1-61891-513-9(4)*, 12163, Blastoff! Discovery) Bellwether Media.

Owens, L. L. Benjamin Franklin, 1 vol. 2007. (Essential Lives Set 1 Ser.). (ENG., Illus.). 112p. (YA). (gr. 6-12). lib. bdg. 41.36 *(978-1-59928-840-6(0)*, 6633, Essential Library) ABDO Publishing Co.

Petersen, Christine. The Printer, 1 vol. 2011. (Colonial People Ser.). (ENG.). 48p. (gr. 4-4). 34.07 *(978-0-7614-4802-0(0)*, d3054ccc-85a8-4324-a018-f21131a51dd9) Cavendish Square Publishing LLC.

Project Learning with 3D Printing, 12 vols. 2017. (Project Learning with 3D Printing Ser.). (ENG.). (J). (gr. 9-9). lib. bdg. 284.16 *(978-1-5026-3229-6(2)*, 11989ae9-a51d-4991-9324-12368b1c91d5) Cavendish Square Publishing LLC.

QEB Let's Start! Art National Book Stores Edition: Printing. 2006. (J). per. *(978-1-59566-299-6(5))* QEB Publishing Inc.

Riley, Gail Blasser. Cornerstones of Freedom: Benjamin Franklin & Electricity. 2004. (Cornerstones of Freedom Ser.). (ENG., Illus.). 48p. (J). (gr. 4-7). 26.00 *(978-0-516-24240-8(7))* Scholastic Library Publishing.

Rossi, Renzo. & Pauli, Erika. The Age of the Book, 1 vol. Baldanzi, Alessandro, illus. 2009. (Reading & Writing Ser.). (ENG.). 32p. (gr. 4-4). 31.21 *(978-0-7614-4321-6(5)*, 0bf4e344-1411-43bb-b7b4-eeda2e17f646) Cavendish Square Publishing LLC.

Sabelko, Rebecca. The Printing Press. 2019. (Inventions That Changed the World Ser.). (ENG., Illus.). 32p. (J). (gr. 3-8). lib. bdg. 27.95 *(978-1-62617-970-7(0)*, Blastoff! Discovery) Bellwether Media.

Thiel, Kristin. Applications for 3D Printing, 1 vol. 2017. (Project Learning with 3D Printing Ser.). (ENG.). 128p. (YA). (gr. 9-9). pap. 22.16 *(978-1-5026-3422-1(8)*, a96e4288-b7a7-4d10-80cf-5a2391aa1b90) Cavendish Square Publishing LLC.

Time for Kids Editors. Benjamin Franklin - A Man of Many Talents. 2005. (Time for Kids Ser.). (ENG., Illus.). 48p. (J). (gr. 2-4). pap. 3.99 *(978-0-06-057609-7(X))* HarperCollins Pubs.

Vilardi, Debbie. 3-D Printers. 2018. (21st Century Inventions Ser.). (ENG., Illus.). 24p. (J). (gr. 1-1). pap. 8.95 *(978-1-63517-789-3(8)*, 1635177898) North Star Editions.

—3-D Printers. 2018. (21st Century Inventions Ser.). (ENG., Illus.). 24p. (J). (gr. k-3). lib. bdg. 31.36 *(978-1-5321-6038-7(0)*, 28708, Pop! Cody Koala) Pop!

Walton, Ruth. Let's Read a Book: Find Out about Books & How They Are Made. 2013. (Let's Find Out Ser.). (ENG., Illus.). 32p. (J). (gr. k-5). 28.50 *(978-1-59771-387-0(2))* Sea-To-Sea Pubns.

PRINTING—HISTORY

Heinrichs, Ann. The Printing Press. 2005. (Inventions That Shaped the World Ser.). (Illus.). 80p. (J). (gr. 4-7). 17.60 *(978-0-7569-6860-1(7))* Perfection Learning Corp.

Hurt, Avery Elizabeth. How the Printing Press Changed the World, 1 vol. 2018. (Inventions That Changed the World Ser.). (ENG.). 64p. (gr. 5-5). pap. 16.28 *(978-1-5026-4113-7(5)*, d38ff5c5-251e-4aee-adad-e73515618ee2) Cavendish Square Publishing LLC.

Krensky, Stephen. Breaking into Print: Before & after the Invention of the Printing Press. Christensen, Bonnie, illus. 2003. 30p. (J). (gr. 3-8). reprint ed. 18.00 *(978-0-7567-6843-0(8))* DIANE Publishing Co.

Mattern, Joanne. The Printing Press: An Information Revolution. 2009. (Technology That Changed the World Ser.). 24p. (gr. 2-3). 42.50 *(978-1-60853-276-6(3)*, PowerKids Pr.) Rosen Publishing Group, Inc., The.

Meltzer, Milton. The Printing Press, 1 vol. 2005. (Great Inventions Ser.). (ENG., Illus.). 144p. (YA). (gr. 8-8). lib. bdg. 45.50 *(978-0-7614-1536-7(X)*, 70532e1e-e9f7-4a04-9311-49e5ae6d6ecf) Cavendish Square Publishing LLC.

Mullins, Lisa. Inventing the Printing Press. 2007. (Breakthrough Inventions Ser.). (ENG., Illus.). 32p. (J). (gr. 3-7). lib. bdg. *(978-0-7787-2819-1(6))*; pap. *(978-0-7787-2841-2(2))* Crabtree Publishing Co.

Olson, Kay Melchisedech. Johann Gutenberg & the Printing Press, 1 vol. Smith, Tod G., illus. 2006. (Inventions & Discovery Ser.). (ENG.). 32p. (J). (gr. 3-9). pap. 8.10 *(978-0-7368-9644-3(9)*, 93403, Capstone Pr.) Capstone.

Silva, Patricia & Pauli, Erika. Modern Times, 1 vol. Baldanzi, Alessandro, illus. 2009. (Reading & Writing Ser.). (ENG.). 32p. (gr. 4-4). 31.21 *(978-0-7614-4322-3(3)*, 7dbe8905-aa51-4531-b174-ecbd61167701) Cavendish Square Publishing LLC.

Spilsbury, Louise. Johannes Gutenberg & the Printing Press, 1 vol., 1. 2015. (Inventions That Changed the World Ser.). (ENG.). 32p. (J). (gr. 4-5). pap. 11.00 *(978-1-5081-4631-5(4)*, 847ecd39-5988-4383-afb9-a1dbe2dca860, PowerKids Pr.) Rosen Publishing Group, Inc., The.

World Book, Inc. Staff, contrib. by. Hieroglyphics to Hypertext: A Timeline of the Written Word. 2016. (Illus.). 40p. (J). *(978-0-7166-3546-8(1))* World Bk.-Childcraft International.

PRINTING INDUSTRY

Otfinoski, Steven. 3D Printing: Science, Technology, & Engineering (Calling All Innovators: a Career for You) 2016. (Calling All Innovators: a Career for You Ser.). (ENG., Illus.). 64p. (J). (gr. 5-8). pap. 8.95 *(978-0-531-21988-1(7)*, Children's Pr.) Scholastic Library Publishing.

PRINTS

see also Engraving

AZ Books. Prints. 2013. (Guess What? Ser.). (ENG.). 10p. (J). (— 1). bds. 5.95 *(978-1-61889-315-4(7))* AZ Bks. LLC.

Galat, Joan Marie. Maker Projects for Kids Who Love Printmaking. 2017. (Be a Maker! Ser.). (ENG., Illus.). 32p. (J). (gr. 5). *(978-0-7787-2889-4(7))* Crabtree Publishing Co.

PRINTS—TECHNIQUE

Hanson, Anders. Cool Printmaking: The Art of Creativity for Kids! 2008. (Cool Art Ser.). (ENG.). 32p. (J). (gr. 3-6). 34.21 *(978-1-60453-147-3(9)*, 4584, Checkerboard Library) ABDO Publishing Co.

Hodgson, Sarah. Printmaking Skills Lab. 2018. (Art Skills Lab Ser.). (Illus.). 32p. (J). (gr. 4-4). *(978-0-7787-5224-0(0))*; pap. *(978-0-7787-5237-0(2))* Crabtree Publishing Co.

Luxbacher, Irene. 123 I Can Make Prints! Luxbacher, Irene, illus. 2008. (Starting Art Ser.). (Illus.). 24p. (J). (gr. -1-2). 14.95 *(978-1-55453-040-3(7))* Kids Can Pr., Ltd. CAN. Dist: Hachette Bk. Group.

Rau, Dana Meachen. Printmaking. Petelinsek, Kathleen, illus. 2015. (How-To Library). (ENG.). 32p. (J). (gr. 3-6). lib. bdg. 32.07 *(978-1-63362-373-6(4)*, 206912) Cherry Lake Publishing.

Scrace, Carolyn. Printing & Other Amazing Techiques. 2015. (How to Art Doodle Ser.). (Illus.). 24p. (gr. 3-6). 28.50 *(978-1-909645-51-6(6))* Book Hse. GBR. Dist: Black Rabbit Bks.

—Printing & Other Amazing Techniques. 2015. (ENG., Illus.). 24p. (J). pap. 8.95 *(978-1-910184-38-7(1))* RiverStream Publishing.

PRISON ESCAPES

see Escapes

PRISONS

see also Criminal Law; Escapes

Aldridge, Rebecca, ed. Mass Incarceration, 1 vol. 2017. (Opposing Viewpoints Ser.). (ENG.). 296p. (gr. 10-12). pap. 34.80 *(978-1-5345-0043-3(X)*, cbdc726e-9eec-4c29-b762-0daeb825fc14); lib. bdg. 50.43 *(978-1-5345-0045-7(6)*, 3f9817a6-6912-49fe-8b33-8c1d0909c1ff) Greenhaven Publishing LLC.

Bakker, T. C. Alcatraz Believe It or Not. House, Charles, illus. 2016. 110p. *(978-1-932519-36-5(X))* Golden Gate National Parks Conservancy.

Berlatsky, Noah, ed. America's Prisons, 1 vol. 2010. (Opposing Viewpoints Ser.). (ENG., Illus.). 224p. (gr. 10-12). 50.43 *(978-0-7377-4956-4(3)*, 41bfd607-82ee-4eb7-a668-92491978e5d3, Greenhaven Publishing) Greenhaven Publishing LLC.

—Imprisonment, 1 vol. 2010. (Global Viewpoints Ser.). (ENG., Illus.). 240p. (gr. 10-12). 47.83 *(978-0-7377-4717-1(X)*, c6fdf7d7-02f7-4fd9-9fcc-fbc50457042c); pap. 32.70 *(978-0-7377-4718-8(8)*, 2931980f-9377-465a-a930-3efb6d3f00d4) Greenhaven Publishing LLC. (Greenhaven Publishing).

Bodden, Valerie. Old Jails. 2017. (Creep Out Ser.). (ENG., Illus.). 24p. (J). (gr. 1-4). *(978-1-60818-809-3(4)*, 20188, Creative Education) Creative Co., The.

Burling, Alexis. Occupying Alcatraz: Native American Activists Demand Change. 2017. (Hidden Heroes Ser.). (ENG., Illus.). 112p. (J). (gr. 6-12). 59.93 *(978-1-68079-742-8(5)*, 23927, Essential Library) ABDO Publishing Co.

Burlingame, Jeff. Prisons, 1 vol. 2012. (Controversy! Ser.). (ENG.). 112p. (YA). (gr. 8-8). 39.79 *(978-1-60870-493-4(9)*, 9edebcfe-c76f-4c93-92d6-a2c09da97557) Cavendish Square Publishing LLC.

Chandler, Matt. Alcatraz: A Chilling Interactive Adventure. 2016. (You Choose: Haunted Places Ser.). (ENG., Illus.). 112p. (J). (gr. 3-7). lib. bdg. 32.65 *(978-1-5157-2580-0(4)*, 132923, Capstone Pr.) Capstone.

Costain, Meredith. You Wouldn't Want to Be an 18th-Century British Convict! A Trip to Australia You'd Rather Not Take. Antram, David, illus. 2006. (You Wouldn't Want to Ser.). (ENG.). 32p. (J). (gr. 2-5). pap. 9.95 *(978-0-531-16998-8(7)*, Watts, Franklin) Scholastic Library Publishing.

Dunn, Dinah. Haunted Prisons. 2014. (Scary Places Ser.). 32p. (J). (gr. 4-8). lib. bdg. 25.27 *(978-1-62724-089-5(6))* Bearport Publishing Co., Inc.

Enz, Tammy. Beyond the Bars: Exploring the Secrets of a Police Station. 2010. (Hidden Worlds Ser.). (ENG.). 32p. (J). (gr. 3-9). lib. bdg. 27.32 *(978-1-4296-3377-2(8)*, 95884, Capstone Pr.) Capstone.

Esherick, Joan. Prisoner Rehabilitation: Success Stories & Failures. 2006. (Incarceration Issues Ser.). (Illus.). 111p. (YA). (gr. 7-18). lib. bdg. 22.95 *(978-1-59084-994-1(9))* Mason Crest.

—Women Incarcerated. 2017. 80p. (J). *(978-1-4222-3790-8(7))* Mason Crest.

Evans, Christine. Escaping Alcatraz. 2018. (Great Escapes in History Ser.). (ENG.). 32p. (J). (gr. 3-6). lib. bdg. 35.64 *(978-1-5038-2525-3(6)*, 212346, MOMENTUM) Child's World, Inc, The.

Faryon, Cynthia J. Real Justice: Guilty of Being Weird: The Story of Guy Paul Morin, 1 vol. 2012. (Lorimer Real Justice Ser.). (ENG., Illus.). 144p. (YA). (gr. 9-12). pap. 12.95 *(978-1-4594-0092-4(5)*, 3b40e44c-6d03-446e-936a-8c36c517fb89) James Lorimer & Co. Ltd., Pubs. CAN. Dist: Lerner Publishing Group.

Friedman, Lauri S., ed. Prisons, 1 vol. 2007. (Introducing Issues with Opposing Viewpoints Ser.). (ENG., Illus.). 144p. (gr. 7-10). lib. bdg. 43.63 *(978-0-7377-3578-9(3)*, 66101a1c-822e-48d7-8681-deadbfc1126a, Greenhaven Publishing) Greenhaven Publishing LLC.

Goozh, Judi & Jeweler, Sue. Tell Me about When Moms & Dads Go to Jail. 2018. (Tell Me about Jail Ser.). (Illus.). 48p. (J). pap. 15.95 *(978-1-78592-807-9(4)*, 696735) Kingsley, Jessica Pubs. GBR. Dist: Hachette UK Distribution.

Gordon, Nick. Alcatraz. 2013. (Scariest Places on Earth Ser.). (ENG., Illus.). 24p. (J). (gr. 3-7). lib. bdg. 26.95 *(978-1-60014-945-0(6)*, Torque Bks.) Bellwether Media.

Hoena, Blake. The Tower of London: A Chilling Interactive Adventure. 2016. (You Choose: Haunted Places Ser.). (ENG., Illus.). 112p. (J). (gr. 3-7). lib. bdg. 32.65 *(978-1-5157-2579-4(0)*, 132922, Capstone Pr.) Capstone.

Hyde, Natalie. Alcatraz. 2013. (ENG., Illus.). 48p. (J). *(978-0-7787-1098-1(X))*; pap. *(978-0-7787-1104-9(8))* Crabtree Publishing Co.

Incarceration Issues: Punishment, Reform, & Rehabilitation, 11 vols., Set. Incl. Alternatives to Prison: Rehabilitation & Other Programs. Russell, Craig. 111p. 2008. lib. bdg. 22.95 *(978-1-59084-991-0(4))*; Incarceration Around the World. Russell, Craig. 112p. 2008. lib. bdg. 22.95 *(978-1-59084-988-0(4))*; Political Prisoners. Smith, Roger. 111p. 2008. lib. bdg. 22.95 *(978-1-59084-987-3(6))*; Prison Conditions: Overcrowding, Disease, Violence, & Abuse. Smith, Roger. 111p. 2008. lib. bdg. 22.95 *(978-1-59084-986-6(8))*; Prisoner Rehabilitation: Success Stories & Failures. Esherick, Joan. 111p. 2006. lib. bdg. 22.95 *(978-1-59084-994-1(9))*; Prisoners on Death Row. Smith, Roger. 111p. 2006. lib. bdg. 22.95 *(978-1-59084-989-7(2))*; Social, Monetary, & Moral Costs of Prisons. Libal, Autumn. 111p. 2008. lib. bdg. 22.95 *(978-1-59084-992-7(2))*; Youth in Prison. Smith, Roger & McIntosh, Marsha & Smith. 111p. 2008. lib. bdg. 22.95 *(978-1-59084-990-3(6))*; (YA). (gr. 7-18). (Incarceration Issues Ser.). (Illus.). 111p. 2007. 252.45 *(978-1-59084-984-2(1))* Mason Crest.

Libal, Autumn. The Social, Monetary, & Moral Costs of Prisons. 2008. (Incarceration Issues Ser.). (Illus.). 111p. (YA). (gr. 7-18). lib. bdg. 22.95 *(978-1-59084-992-7(2))* Mason Crest.

Lock, Joan. Infamous Prisons, Vol. 20. Gomez, Manny, ed. 2016. (Crime & Detection Ser.). (Illus.). 96p. (J). (gr. 7). 24.95 *(978-1-4222-3475-4(4))* Mason Crest.

Macdonald, Fiona. You Wouldn't Want to Be in a Medieval Dungeon! Prisoners You'd Rather Not Meet. Antram, David, illus. rev. ed. 2013. (You Wouldn't Want to... Ser.). (ENG.). 32p. (J). 29.00 *(978-0-531-25948-1(X)*, Watts, Franklin) Scholastic Library Publishing.

—You Wouldn't Want to Be in a Medieval Dungeon! Prisoners You'd Rather Not Meet. 2013. (You Wouldn't Want To Ser.). lib. bdg. 20.80 *(978-0-606-31629-3(9))* Turtleback.

MacDonald, Fiona & Macdonald, Fiona. You Wouldn't Want to Be in a Medieval Dungeon! Prisoners You'd Rather Not Meet. Antram, David, illus. 2003. (You Wouldn't Want to Ser.). (ENG.). 32p. (J). 29.00 *(978-0-531-12312-6(X)*, Watts, Franklin) Scholastic Library Publishing.

Markovics, Joyce L. Deserted Prisons. 2016. (Tiptoe into Scary Places Ser.). (ENG., Illus.). 24p. (J). (gr. k-3). 26.99 *(978-1-68402-052-2(2))* Bearport Publishing Co., Inc.

Merino, Noël, ed. Prison, 1 vol. 2009. (Issues on Trial Ser.). (ENG., Illus.). 216p. (gr. 10-12). 49.93 *(978-0-7377-4344-9(1)*, d68df04b-e44c-4656-ae18-8c15ecd631ad, Greenhaven Publishing) Greenhaven Publishing LLC.

Owings, Lisa. Ghosts in Prisons. 2016. (Ghost Stories Ser.). (ENG., Illus.). 24p. (J). (gr. 3-7). 26.95 *(978-1-62617-431-3(8)*, Epic Bks.) Bellwether Media.

Person, Stephen. Ghostly Alcatraz Island. 2010. (HorrorScapes Ser.). 32p. (YA). (gr. 4-7). lib. bdg. 28.50 *(978-1-936087-97-6(9))* Bearport Publishing Co., Inc.

Poole, H. W. Incarceration & Families, Vol. 12. 2016. (Families Today Ser.). (Illus.). 48p. (J). (gr. 5). 20.95 *(978-1-4222-3618-5(8))* Mason Crest.

Rabiger, Joanna. Daily Prison Life, Vol. 20. 2016. (Crime & Detection Ser.: Vol. 20). (ENG., Illus.). 96p. (J). (gr. 7-12). 24.95 *(978-1-4222-3472-3(X))* Mason Crest.

Ricciuti, Edward R. What's Inside a Police Station, 1 vol. 2008. (What's Inside? Ser.). (ENG., Illus.). 32p. (gr. 1-2). pap. 9.23 *(978-0-7614-3349-1(X)*, acab09c2-4bc4-43c8-83b5-4a964cc25d5e) Cavendish Square Publishing LLC.

Russell, Craig. Incarceration Around the World. 2008. (Incarceration Issues Ser.). (Illus.). 112p. (YA). (gr. 7-18). lib. bdg. 22.95 *(978-1-59084-988-0(4))* Mason Crest.

—Prison Conditions Around the World. 2017. 80p. (J). *(978-1-4222-3786-1(9))* Mason Crest.

Schwartz, Heather E. Locked up for Freedom: Civil Rights Protesters at the Leesburg Stockade. 2017. (ENG., Illus.). 64p. (J). (gr. 5-8). lib. bdg. 34.65 *(978-1-4677-8597-6(0)*, 69ff8b45-33fa-4948-8f64-695e7f11ba03, Millbrook Pr.) Lerner Publishing Group.

Smith, Roger. The History of Punishment & Imprisonment. 2017. 80p. (J). *(978-1-4222-3782-3(6))* Mason Crest.

—Political Prisoners. 2017. (Illus.). 80p. (J). *(978-1-4222-3784-7(2))* Mason Crest.

—Prison Conditions: Overcrowding, Disease, Violence, & Abuse. 2008. (Incarceration Issues Ser.). (Illus.). 111p. (YA). (gr. 7-18). lib. bdg. 22.95 *(978-1-59084-986-6(8))* Mason Crest.

—The Treatment of Prisoners & Prison Conditions. 2017. (Prison System Ser.: Vol. 9). (ENG., Illus.). 80p. (J). (gr. 7-12). 24.95 *(978-1-4222-3787-8(7))* Mason Crest.

Spalding, Maddie. Guarding Supermax Prisons. 2016. (Highly Guarded Places Ser.). (ENG.). 24p. (J). (gr. 2-5). 32.79 *(978-1-5038-0807-2(6)*, 210648) Child's World, Inc, The.

Stewart, David. You Wouldn't Want to Be in a Medieval Dungeon! Antram, David, illus. rev. ed. 2013. (You Wouldn't Want to... Ser.). (ENG.). 32p. (J). 29.00 *(978-0-531-25949-8(8)*, Watts, Franklin) Scholastic Library Publishing.

Summers, Jacque. Escaping a POW Camp. 2018. (Great Escapes in History Ser.). (ENG.). 32p. (J). (gr. 3-6). lib. bdg. 35.64 *(978-1-5038-2528-4(0)*, 212344, MOMENTUM) Child's World, Inc, The.

Tower Oliver, Marilyn. The Infamous Alcatraz Prison in United States History, 1 vol. 2014. (In United States History Ser.). (ENG.). 96p. (gr. 5-5). 31.61 *(978-0-7660-6320-4(8)*, d7d7cd27-906b-45d5-a4e8-767f6f9f3764); pap. 13.88 *(978-0-7660-6321-1(6)*, 25736b57-ea59-4a20-a76f-02f9d87b0765) Enslow Publishing, LLC.

Watson, Stephanie. Incarcerated Youth. 2016. (ENG.). 80p. (J). (gr. 5-12). lib. bdg. *(978-1-60152-982-4(1))* ReferencePoint Pr., Inc.

Williams, Dinah. Haunted Prisons. 2017. (Scary Places Ser.). (ENG.). 32p. (J). (gr. 4-8). 7.99 *(978-1-68402-603-6(2))* Bearport Publishing Co., Inc.

Wood, Alix. Ghostly Prisons, 1 vol. 2016. (World's Scariest Places Ser.). (ENG.). 32p. (J). (gr. 4-5). pap. 11.50 *(978-1-4824-5904-3(3)*, 3beecb88-7c28-4459-acb9-89009569b549) Stevens, Gareth Publishing LLLP.

PRISONS—FICTION

Authords, D. K. Being Alone. 2013. 120p. pap. 19.95 *(978-1-63000-114-8(7))* America Star Bks.

Basye, Dale E. Blimpo Vol. 3: The Third Circle of Heck. Dob, Bob, illus. 2011. (Heck Ser.: 3). 464p. (J). (gr. 3-7). pap. 9.99 *(978-0-375-85677-8(3)*, Yearling) Random Hse. Children's Bks.

—Precocia: the Sixth Circle of Heck. Dob, Bob, illus. 2013. (Heck Ser.: 6). 432p. (J). (gr. 3-7). 7.99 *(978-0-375-86807-8(0)*, Yearling) Random Hse. Children's Bks.

Breslin, Theresa. Prisoner in Alcatraz. 2012. (Stoke Books Titles Ser.). (ENG.). 80p. (YA). (gr. 8-12). pap. 6.95 (978-1-78112-124-5(9)); lib. bdg. 22.60 (978-1-78112-125-2(7)) Lerner Publishing Group.

Burch, Robert. Queenie Peavey. l.t. ed. 2003. (LRS Large Print Cornerstone Ser.). 166p. (J). lib. bdg. 29.95 (978-1-58118-115-9(9)) LRS.

Carr, Kathy. Granny, Where Did My Mommy Go? 2008. 24p. pap. 24.95 (978-1-60610-324-1(5)) America Star Bks.

Choyce, Lesley. Book of Michael, 1 vol. 2008. (ENG.). 224p. (YA). (gr. 9-12). pap. 9.95 (978-0-88995-417-5(8), 46f6c2d9-d965-4aff-bb00-a2db42ea87fb) Trifolium Bks., Inc. CAN. Dist: Firefly Bks., Ltd.

Crowder, Melanie. An Uninterrupted View of the Sky. 304p. (YA). (gr. 7). 2019. pap. 10.99 (978-0-14-751250-5(6), Penguin Books) 2017. 17.99 (978-0-399-16900-7(8), Philomel Bks.) Penguin Young Readers Group.

Darke, J. A. The Grin in the Dark. Evergreen, Nelson, illus. 2015. (Spine Shivers Ser.). (ENG.). 128p. (J). (gr. 4-6). lib. bdg. 27.32 (978-1-4965-0217-9(5), 128031, Stone Arch Bks.) Capstone.

Dean, Myers Walter. Monster. 2014. (ENG.). 304p. (J). (gr. 12-12). 14.24 (978-1-63245-060-9(7)) Lectorum Pubns., Inc.

Delaney, Joseph. Ghost Prison. 2014. (ENG.). 112p. (YA). (gr. 6-12). pap. 8.99 (978-1-4926-0174-6(8)) Sourcebooks, Inc.

D'Souza, Barbara. If We Were Snowflakes. 2018. (YA). pap. (978-1-59719-091-6(8)) Pearlsong Pr.

Ducie, Joe. The Rig. 2017. (ENG.). 320p. (J). (gr. 5-7). pap. 8.99 (978-0-544-93674-4(4), 1658346, Clarion Bks.) HarperCollins Pubs.

Finotti, M. C. Paintbrushes & Arrows. 2016. 113p. (J). (978-1-56164-968-6(6)) Pineapple Pr., Inc.

—Paintbrushes & Arrows: A Story of St. Augustine. 2016. 118p. (J). (gr. -1-12). pap. 14.95 (978-1-56164-963-1(5)) Pineapple Pr., Inc.

Fisher, Catherine. Incarceron. 2010. (Playaway Children Ser.). (J). 64.99 (978-1-61637-331-3(8)) Findaway World, LLC.

—Incarceron. 2010. (Incarceron Ser.). (FRE.). 498p. (YA). (gr. 7-12). pap. (978-2-266-17793-1(1)) Le Robert.

—Incarceron. 2011. (ENG.). 448p. (YA). (gr. 7-12). 26.19 (978-0-8037-3396-1(8), Dial) Penguin Publishing Group.

—Incarceron. 2011. (ENG., Illus.). 464p. (YA). (gr. 7-18). pap. 12.99 (978-0-14-241852-9(8), Firebird) Penguin Young Readers Group.

—Incarceron. 2011. (Incarceron Ser.). (ENG.). 442p. (gr. 7-12). 20.00 (978-1-61383-117-5(X)) Perfection Learning Corp.

—INCARCERON. 2010. (SPA.). 512p. (J). (gr. 8-12). pap. 19.99 (978-84-272-0047-0(1)) RBA Libros, S.A. ESP. Dist: Lectorum Pubns., Inc.

—Incarceron. l.t. ed. 2010. (Incarceron Ser.). (ENG.). 526p. 23.99 (978-1-4104-2991-9(1)) Thorndike Pr.

—Incarceron. 2011. lib. bdg. 22.10 (978-0-606-22590-8(0)) Turtleback.

Forbeck, Matt. Dungeons & Dragons: Big Trouble: An Endless Quest Book. 2018. (Endless Quest Ser.). (ENG., Illus.). 128p. (J). (gr. 3-7). 16.99 (978-1-5362-0245-8(2)); pap. 8.99 (978-1-5362-0244-1(4)) Candlewick Pr. (Candlewick Entertainment).

—Dungeons & Dragons: Escape the Underdark: An Endless Quest Book. 2018. (Endless Quest Ser.). (ENG., Illus.). 128p. (J). (gr. 3-7). 16.99 (978-1-5362-0242-7(8), Candlewick Entertainment) Candlewick Pr.

—Dungeons & Dragons: into the Jungle: An Endless Quest Book. 2018. (Endless Quest Ser.). (ENG., Illus.). 128p. (J). (gr. 3-7). 16.99 (978-1-5362-0246-5(0)); pap. 8.99 (978-1-5362-0241-0(X)) Candlewick Pr. (Candlewick Entertainment).

—Dungeons & Dragons: to Catch a Thief: An Endless Quest Book. 2018. (Endless Quest Ser.). (ENG., Illus.). 128p. (J). (gr. 3-7). 16.99 (978-1-5362-0243-4(6), Candlewick Entertainment) Candlewick Pr.

Gaffney, Linda. My Daddy Does GOOD Things, Too! Dabney, Undra & Goettling, Nickalas, illus. 2006. 55p. per. 10.99 (978-0-9787501-0-7(1)) Gaffney, Linda.

Gorman, Zac. Thisby Thestoop & the Black Mountain. Bosma, Sam, illus. (ENG.). 336p. (J). (gr. 3-7). 2019. pap. 6.99 (978-0-06-249568-6(2)) 2018. 16.99 (978-0-06-249567-9(4)) HarperCollins Pubs. (HarperCollins).

Hueller, Andy. Skipping Stones at the Center of the Earth: A Middle Grade Novel. 2011. 241p. (J). pap. 8.99 (978-1-59955-488-4(7), Bonneville Bks.) Cedar Fort, Inc./CFI Distribution.

Kir-on, Callanitte. The 3-D Files: Prisoner on the Loose. 2003. (Illus.). (J). 10.95 (978-1-931681-47-6(3)) Israel Bookshop Pubns.

Lauren, Ruth. Prisoner of Ice & Snow. 2017. (ENG.). 288p. (J). 16.99 (978-1-68119-131-7(8), 900159799, Bloomsbury USA Childrens) Bloomsbury Publishing USA.

McClintock, Norah. El Regreso, 1 vol. 2011. (Spanish Soundings Ser.).Tr. of Back. (SPA.). 112p. (YA). (gr. 8-12). pap. 9.95 (978-1-55469-973-5(8)) Orca Bk. Pubs. USA.

McVoy, Terra Elan. Criminal. 2013. (ENG.). 288p. (YA). (gr. 9). 16.99 (978-1-4424-2162-2(2), Simon Pulse) Simon Pulse.

Messner, Kate. Breakout. (ENG.). 448p. (J). 2019. pap. 9.99 (978-1-68119-538-4(0), 900176499) 2018. (Illus.). 17.99 (978-1-68119-536-0(4), 900176497) Bloomsbury Publishing USA. (Bloomsbury Children's Bks.).

Morgenroth, Kate. Jude. 2006. (ENG., Illus.). 288p. (YA). (gr. 7-12). reprint ed. mass mkt. 8.99 (978-1-4169-1267-5(3), Simon Pulse) Simon Pulse.

Muchamore, Robert. Maximum Security. 2011. (Cherub Ser.: 3). (ENG.). 320p. (YA). (gr. 7). lib. bdg. 19.99 (978-1-4169-9942-3(6), Simon Pulse) Simon Pulse.

Murphy, Shirley Rousseau. The Cat, the Devil, the Last Escape. 2015. (ENG., Illus.). 320p. 24.99 (978-0-06-226910-2(0), Morrow, William & Co.) HarperCollins Pubs.

Myers, Walter Dean. Monster. 2019. (ENG., Illus.). 336p. (YA). (gr. 8). reprint ed. pap. 12.99 (978-0-06-440731-1(4), Amistad) HarperCollins Pubs.

—Monster. unabr. ed. 2004. 281p. (J). (gr. 7-18). pap. 29.00 incl. audio (978-0-8072-8363-9(0), YA188CX, Listening Library) Random Hse. Audio Publishing Group.

—Monster. Myers, Christopher A., illus. 2004. (National Book Award Finalist Ser.). 281p. (YA). (gr. 7-12). lib. bdg. 20.85 (978-0-613-35985-6(2)) Turtleback.

—Monster: A Graphic Novel. Anyabwile, Dawud, illus. 2015. (Monster Ser.). (ENG.). 160p. (J). (gr. 8). pap. 15.99 (978-0-06-227499-1(6), Quill Tree Bks.) HarperCollins Pubs.

Myers, Walter Dean & Sims, Guy A. Monster. Anyabwile, Dawud, illus. 2015. (J). lib. bdg. 20.85 (978-0-606-37629-7(1)) Turtleback.

Phillips, Dee. Doomed on Death Row. 2016. (Cold Whispers II Ser.). (ENG., Illus.). 32p. (J). (gr. 2-6). 28.50 (978-1-944102-35-7(3)) Bearport Publishing Co., Inc.

Pileggi, Leah. Prisoner 88. (J). 2019. 144p. (gr. 5). pap. 7.99 (978-1-58089-561-3(1)) 2013. 142p. 16.95 (978-1-60734-611-1(7)) 2013. (Illus.). 144p. (gr. 5). 16.95 (978-1-58089-560-6(3)) Charlesbridge Publishing, Inc.

Schraff, Anne E. Unbroken. 2012. (Urban Underground — Cesar Chavez High School Ser.: 28). (YA). lib. bdg. 20.80 (978-0-606-26598-0(8)) Turtleback.

Smith, Alexander Gordon. Death Sentence: Escape from Furnace 3. 2012. (Escape from Furnace Ser.: 3). (ENG.). 288p. (YA). (gr. 7-11). pap. 12.99 (978-0-312-67441-0(4), 900072856) Square Fish.

—Execution: Escape from Furnace 5. 2013. (Escape from Furnace Ser.: 5). (ENG.). 336p. (YA). (gr. 7-11). pap. 13.99 (978-1-250-02942-3(2), 900118576) Square Fish.

—Fugitives: Escape from Furnace 4. 2012. (Escape from Furnace Ser.: 4). (ENG.). 304p. (YA). (gr. 7-11). pap. 15.99 (978-1-250-00339-3(3), 900079878) Square Fish.

—Lockdown: Escape from Furnace 1. 2010. (Escape from Furnace Ser.: 1). (ENG.). 304p. (YA). (gr. 7-11). pap. 10.99 (978-0-312-61193-4(5), 900065537) Square Fish.

—Solitary: Escape from Furnace 2. 2011. (Escape from Furnace Ser.: 2). (ENG.). 256p. (YA). (gr. 7-11). pap. 11.99 (978-0-312-67476-2(7), 900072887) Square Fish.

Spinelli, Jerry. The Warden's Daughter. 2018. 368p. (J). (gr. 4-7). 7.99 (978-0-375-83202-4(5), Yearling) Random Hse. Children's Bks.

Stanglin, Jackie A. Mami, Que Es una Carcel? McGuckie, Cierra Jade, illus. 2007. (J). (gr. -1-3). 36p. 19.99 (978-1-59879-429-8(9)); 40p. 13.99 (978-1-59879-428-1(0)) Lifevest Publishing, Inc.

—What Is Jail, Mommy? McGuckie, Cierra Jade, illus. l.t. ed. 2006. 40p. (J). 21.99 (978-1-59879-252-2(0)); (gr. -1-3). 13.99 (978-1-59879-248-5(2)) Lifevest Publishing, Inc.

Stasse, Lisa M. The Forsaken: The Forsaken Trilogy. (ENG., (YA). (gr. 7). 2013. Illus.). 400p. pap. 11.99 (978-1-4424-3266-6(7)) 2012. 384p. 16.99 (978-1-4424-3265-9(9)) Simon & Schuster Bks. For Young Readers. (Simon & Schuster Bks. For Young Readers).

—The Uprising: The Forsaken Trilogy. (ENG., (YA). (gr. 7). 2014. Illus.). 400p. pap. 9.99 (978-1-4424-3269-7(1)) 2013. 384p. 16.99 (978-1-4424-3268-0(3)) Simon & Schuster Bks. For Young Readers. (Simon & Schuster Bks. For Young Readers).

Venable, Alan. The Man in the Iron Mask. 2007. (Classic Adventures Ser.). pap. 9.95 (978-1-4105-0860-7(9)) Building Wings LLC.

Volponi, Paul. Rikers High. 2011. (ENG.). 272p. (YA). (gr. 7-18). 9.99 (978-0-14-241778-2(5), Speak) Penguin Young Readers Group.

PRISONS—UNITED STATES—FICTION

Braun, Eric Mark. Could You Escape Alcatraz? An Interactive Survival Adventure. 2019. (You Choose: Can You Escape? Ser.). (ENG., Illus.). 112p. (J). (gr. 3-7). lib. bdg. 32.65 (978-1-5435-7392-3(4), 140688) Capstone.

Wilson, John. Battle Scars: The American Civil War, Part Two. 2016. (Fields of Conflict Ser.). (ENG.). 192p. (YA). (gr. 8-12). pap. 12.95 (978-1-77203-093-8(7), Wandering Fox) Heritage Hse. CAN. Dist: Orca Bk. Pubs. USA.

PRIVACY, RIGHT OF

Abramovitz, Melissa. Online Predators. 2016. (ENG.). 80p. (J). (gr. 5-12). lib. bdg. (978-1-68282-092-6(0)) ReferencePoint Pr., Inc.

Anton, Carrie. A Smart Girl's Guide: Digital World: How to Connect, Share, Play, & Keep Yourself Safe. Lewis, Stevie, illus. 2017. (American Girl(r) Wellbeing Ser.). (ENG.). 64p. (J). pap. 12.99 (978-1-68337-043-7(0)) American Girl Publishing, Inc.

Berry, Joy. Help Me Be Good about Snooping. 2009. (Help Me Be Good Ser.). 32p. pap. 7.95 (978-1-60577-122-9(8)) Berry, Joy Enterprises.

Carson, Brian & Ramen, Catherine. Understanding Your Right to Freedom from Searches, 1 vol. 2011. (Personal Freedom & Civic Duty Ser.). (ENG., Illus.). 160p. (YA). (gr. 7-7). lib. bdg. 39.80 (978-1-4488-4670-2(6), 5b7c2e9d-6099-49c5-b920-ff4952c87b82) Rosen Publishing Group, Inc., The.

Coddington, Andrew. Mass Government Surveillance: Spying on Citizens, 1 vol. 2017. (Spying, Surveillance, & Privacy in the 21st Century Ser.). (ENG.). 112p. (YA). (gr. 8-8). 44.50 (978-1-5026-2672-1(1), ffd99925-2eeb-4b09-9dcb-1df4d331b902) Cavendish Square Publishing LLC.

Cunningham, Anne C., ed. Privacy & Security in the Digital Age, 1 vol. 2016. (Current Controversies Ser.). (ENG.). 176p. (J). (gr. 10-12). pap. 33.00 (978-1-5345-0032-7(4), 4817c7de-3793-440d-b111-e829d922b4fb); lib. bdg. 48.03 (978-1-5345-0021-1(9), 34c8845d-3296-42cb-a599-86d1086166e1) Greenhaven Publishing LLC. (Greenhaven Publishing).

Eboch, M. M. Big Data & Privacy Rights, 1 vol. 2016. (Essential Library of the Information Age Ser.). (ENG., Illus.). 112p. (J). (gr. 8-12). lib. bdg. 41.36 (978-1-68078-282-0(7), 21719, Essential Library) ABDO Publishing Co.

Espejo, Roman. Civil Liberties. 2009. (Opposing Viewpoints Ser.). (ENG., Illus.). 240p. (YA). (gr. 10-12). pap. 29.45 (978-0-7377-4355-5(7), LML02109-245310);No. 9. pap. 42.95 (978-0-7377-4356-2(5), LML02109-245369) Cengage Gale. (Greenhaven Pr., Inc.).

Freedman, Jeri. America Debates Privacy Versus Security, 1 vol. 2007. (America Debates Ser.). (ENG., Illus.). 64p. (YA). (gr. 5-6). lib. bdg. 37.13 (978-1-4042-1929-8(3), 2eb69dee-61d6-4b38-aa54-f78f558adcd3) Rosen Publishing Group, Inc., The.

Furgang, Kathy & Gatta, Frank. Understanding Your Right to Privacy, 1 vol. 2011. (Personal Freedom & Civic Duty Ser.). (ENG.). 160p. (YA). (gr. 7-7). lib. bdg. 39.80 (978-1-4488-4669-6(2), 16f1d7d6-5513-41d4-a504-f5248c97118b) Rosen Publishing Group, Inc., The.

Garrett, Brandon. The Right to Privacy. 2009. (Individual Rights & Civic Responsibility Ser.). 128p. (gr. 7-12). 63.90 (978-1-61513-515-8(4)) Rosen Publishing Group, Inc., The.

Glenn, Richard A. The Right to Privacy: Rights & Liberties under the Law, 1 vol. 2003. (America's Freedoms Ser.). (ENG.). 448p. (C). 83.00 (978-1-57607-716-0(0), 900312424) ABC-CLIO, LLC.

Grayson, Robert. Managing Your Digital Footprint, 1 vol. 2011. (Digital & Information Literacy Ser.). (ENG., Illus.). 48p. (YA). (gr. 6-6). pap. 12.75 (978-1-4488-2290-4(4), 92da1fac-6980-42e2-9157-3a0ce49c42a4); lib. bdg. 33.47 (978-1-4488-1319-3(0), 92774e04-b8f9-4fb1-865f-13a57e1d60d7) Rosen Publishing Group, Inc., The. (Rosen Reference).

Henderson, Harry. Online Privacy & Government. 2014. (Privacy in the Online World). (ENG., Illus.). 80p. (J). lib. bdg. (978-1-60152-726-4(8)) ReferencePoint Pr., Inc.

Hubbard, Ben. My Digital Rights & Rules. Vaisberg, Diego, illus. 2019. (Digital Citizens Ser.). (ENG.). 32p. (J). (gr. 2-5). 27.99 (978-1-5415-3881-8(1), d99cfe58-3a93-4e25-82ee-796876e676f9, Lerner Pubns.) Lerner Publishing Group.

—My Digital Safety & Security. Vaisberg, Diego, illus. 2019. (Digital Citizens Ser.). (ENG.). 32p. (J). (gr. 2-5). 27.99 (978-1-5415-3882-5(X), f414e323-5400-419d-ad28-1dee81f78148, Lerner Pubns.) Lerner Publishing Group.

Jakubiak, David J. A Smart Kid's Guide to Internet Privacy, 1 vol. 2009. (Kids Online Ser.). (ENG., Illus.). 24p. (J). (gr. 2-3). pap. 9.25 (978-1-4358-3356-2(2), 1300397); lib. bdg. 26.27 (978-1-4042-8118-9(5), 1300397) Rosen Publishing Group, Inc., The. (PowerKids Pr.).

January, Brendan. Information Insecurity: Privacy under Siege. 2015. (ENG., Illus.). 96p. (YA). (gr. 6-12). lib. bdg. 34.65 (978-1-4677-2517-0(X), bd8a68e6-cc49-473a-8510-e0f202122f9e); E-Book 51.99 (978-1-4677-8803-8(1)) Lerner Publishing Group. (Twenty-First Century Bks.).

Jones, Emma. Who Should See What You're Doing Online?, 1 vol. 2017. (Points of View Ser.). (ENG.). 24p. (J). (gr. 3-3). pap. 9.25 (978-1-5345-2485-9(1), 272fdb62-7b6b-4e55-aa31-55303b23c0c0); lib. bdg. 26.23 (978-1-5345-2423-1(1), 0c58035e-abf6-49bb-a225-0a94c4862a29) Greenhaven Publishing LLC.

Kemper, Bitsy. The Right to Privacy: Interpreting the Constitution, 1 vol. 2014. (Understanding the United States Constitution Ser.). (ENG., Illus.). 112p. (J). (gr. 7-7). 38.80 (978-1-4777-7506-6(4), 704bae28-ef9b-4894-be18-577fe308ab5c) Rosen Publishing Group, Inc., The.

Krasner, Barbara, ed. DNA Testing & Privacy, 1 vol. 2019. (Opposing Viewpoints Ser.). (ENG.). 176p. (gr. 10-12). 50.43 (978-1-5345-0500-1(8), 18cfa324-2ecd-4b2e-8011-66148eeeb266) Greenhaven Publishing LLC.

Kuhn, Betsy. Prying Eyes: Privacy in the Twenty-First Century. 2008. (Exceptional Social Studies Titles for Upper Grades). (ENG., Illus.). 160p. (J). (gr. 7-12). lib. bdg. 38.60 (978-0-8225-7179-7(X)) Lerner Publishing Group.

Lynette, Rachel. How to Deal with Secrets, 1 vol. 2008. (Let's Work It Out Ser.). (ENG., Illus.). 24p. (J). (gr. 2-3). lib. bdg. 26.27 (978-1-4042-4519-8(7), 254ae4fe-27d0-4394-a859-4afdf8222167) Rosen Publishing Group, Inc., The.

McHugh, Jeff. Maintaining a Positive Digital Footprint. 2014. (Explorer Junior Library: Information Explorer Junior Ser.). (ENG.). 24p. (J). (gr. 1-4). pap. 12.79 (978-1-63137-809-6(0), 205400); (Illus.). 32.07 (978-1-63137-789-1(2), 205399) Cherry Lake Publishing.

Merino, Noël, ed. Civil Liberties, 1 vol. 2013. (Opposing Viewpoints Ser.). (ENG., Illus.). 256p. (gr. 10-12). lib. bdg. 50.43 (978-0-7377-6304-1(3), bbf6ae9a-5bd1-46ca-947c-da270ae431a2, Greenhaven Publishing) Greenhaven Publishing LLC.

—Civil Liberties, 1 vol. 2013. (Opposing Viewpoints Ser.). (ENG., Illus.). 256p. (gr. 10-12). pap. 34.80 (978-0-7377-6305-8(1), 4b990e98-ad05-4e4b-9051-0a3359690ba5, Greenhaven Publishing) Greenhaven Publishing LLC.

—Privacy, 1 vol. 2015. (Opposing Viewpoints Ser.). (ENG., Illus.). 184p. (gr. 10-12). pap. 34.80 (978-0-7377-7283-8(2), b18954ac-48ea-411a-b19e-180f6138d960, Greenhaven Publishing) Greenhaven Publishing LLC.

—Teens & Privacy, 1 vol. 2011. (Current Controversies Ser.). (ENG.). 192p. (gr. 10-12). pap. 33.00 (978-0-7377-5134-5(7), 5ebcac1a-011b-4c41-b044-870170f8c0cf, Greenhaven Publishing) Greenhaven Publishing LLC.

—Teens & Privacy, 1 vol. 2011. (Current Controversies Ser.). (ENG.). 192p. (gr. 10-12). lib. bdg. 48.03 (978-0-7377-5133-8(9), f1009fe2-2510-40d6-8cac-6e8d08d98efb, Greenhaven Publishing) Greenhaven Publishing LLC.

Mooney, Carla. Online Privacy & Business. 2014. (Privacy in the Online World). (ENG., Illus.). 80p. (J). lib. bdg. (978-1-60152-724-0(1)) ReferencePoint Pr., Inc.

—Online Privacy & Social Media. 2014. (Privacy in the Online World). (ENG., Illus.). 80p. (J). lib. bdg. (978-1-60152-730-1(6)) ReferencePoint Pr., Inc.

Morlock, Rachael. No Unreasonable Searches & Seizures: A Look at the Third & Fourth Amendments, 1 vol. 2018. (Our Bill of Rights Ser.). (ENG.). 32p. (gr. 5-5). pap. 11.00 (978-1-5383-4296-1(0), 84015ef1-3be9-42cf-9487-da495595301b, PowerKids Pr.) Rosen Publishing Group, Inc., The.

Morretta, Alison. How to Maintain Your Privacy Online. 2015. (J). lib. bdg. (978-1-62713-545-0(6)) 2014. (ENG.). 48p. (gr. 5-5). lib. bdg. 33.07 (978-1-5026-0187-2(7), 2afb3f8d-ca81-4781-aba0-5386162eb656) Cavendish Square Publishing LLC.

Ogden, Charlie. Censorship & Privacy. 2018. (Our Values - Level 3 Ser.). 32p. (J). (gr. 5-6). (978-0-7787-4731-4(X)) Crabtree Publishing Co.

Parks, Peggy J. Online Privacy. 2016. (ENG.). 80p. (J). (gr. 5-12). lib. bdg. (978-1-60152-988-6(0)) ReferencePoint Pr., Inc.

Porterfield, Jason. The Third Amendment: The Right to Privacy in the Home, 1 vol. 2011. (Amendments to the United States Constitution: the Bill of Rights Ser.). (ENG., Illus.). 64p. (YA). (gr. 6-6). lib. bdg. 37.13 (978-1-4488-1256-1(9), c65b7d1b-4a76-4763-a116-93973e0541c2) Rosen Publishing Group, Inc., The.

—Third Amendment: Upholding the Right to Privacy, 1 vol. 2011. (Amendments to the United States Constitution: the Bill of Rights Ser.). (ENG.). 64p. (YA). (gr. 6-6). pap. 13.95 (978-1-4488-2304-8(8), f030c4a2-1fe0-422e-9906-b883ae76e358, Rosen Reference) Rosen Publishing Group, Inc., The.

Rustad, Martha E. H. Learning about Privacy. 2015. (Media Literacy for Kids Ser.). (ENG., Illus.). 24p. (J). (gr. -1-2). lib. bdg. 27.32 (978-1-4914-1832-1(X), 127274, Capstone Pr.) Capstone.

Santos, Rita, ed. Critical Perspectives on Privacy Rights & Protections in the 21st Century, 1 vol. 2018. (Analyzing the Issues Ser.). (ENG.). 224p. (gr. 8-8). 50.93 (978-0-7660-9857-2(5), 7cf4c554-9c72-49be-8018-6fbf49ab0a62) Enslow Publishing, LLC.

Scherer, Lauri S., ed. Privacy, 1 vol. 2014. (Introducing Issues with Opposing Viewpoints Ser.). (ENG., Illus.). 120p. (gr. 7-10). lib. bdg. 43.63 (978-0-7377-6927-2(0), 31e9fa16-25a3-43d2-8d9a-3b9bf33d2967, Greenhaven Publishing) Greenhaven Publishing LLC.

Small, Cathleen. Surveillance & Your Right to Privacy, 1 vol. 2017. (Spying, Surveillance, & Privacy in the 21st Century Ser.). (ENG.). 112p. (YA). (gr. 8-8). lib. bdg. 44.50 (978-1-5026-2676-9(4), 890e0c69-c970-4951-8058-ac448fe68056) Cavendish Square Publishing LLC.

Steffens, Bradley. Threats to Civil Liberties: Privacy. 2018. (Threats to Civil Liberties Ser.). (ENG.). 80p. (YA). (gr. 6-12). 39.93 (978-1-68282-451-1(9)) ReferencePoint Pr., Inc.

Stefoff, Rebecca. Security V. Privacy, 1 vol. 2008. (Open for Debate Ser.). (ENG., Illus.). 144p. (YA). (gr. 8-8). lib. bdg. 45.50 (978-0-7614-2578-6(0), 03769338-a097-45e0-8d15-575f505a8f98) Cavendish Square Publishing LLC.

Wilcox, Christine. Thinking Critically: Online Privacy. 2014. (Thinking Critically). (ENG., Illus.). 80p. (J). lib. bdg. (978-1-60152-734-9(9)) ReferencePoint Pr., Inc.

Wilkinson, Colin. Everything You Need to Know about Digital Privacy, 1 vol. 2017. (Need to Know Library). (ENG., Illus.). 64p. (J). (gr. 5-6). 36.13 (978-1-5081-7400-4(8), 2d3da4db-9223-4025-9e18-47b4ad106b42); pap. 13.95 (978-1-5081-7398-4(2), 6b94b7ec-2b2c-400a-92da-2fe21d8df014) Rosen Publishing Group, Inc., The. (Rosen Young Adult).

21st Century Safety & Privacy. 2013. (21st Century Safety & Privacy Ser.). 64p. (J). (gr. 5-8). pap. 64.75 (978-1-4777-1677-9(7)); (gr. 5-8). pap. 388.50 (978-1-4777-1678-6(5)); (ENG.). (gr. 6-6). 185.60 (978-1-4488-9579-3(0), 2edb6323-522d-467a-8988-0b1d388fe070) Rosen Publishing Group, Inc., The.

PRIVATE SCHOOLS—FICTION

Brian, Kate, pseud. Ambition. 2008. (Private Ser.: No. 7). (ENG.). 288p. (YA). (gr. 9-18). pap. 12.99 (978-1-4169-5882-6(7), Simon & Schuster Bks. For Young Readers) Simon & Schuster Bks. For Young Readers.

—Ominous. 2011. (Private Ser.). (ENG.). 224p. (YA). (gr. 9-18). pap. 9.99 (978-1-4169-8472-6(0), Simon & Schuster Bks. For Young Readers) Simon & Schuster Bks. For Young Readers.

—Suspicion. 2009. (Private Ser.: No. 10). (ENG.). 224p. (YA). (gr. 9-18). pap. 9.99 (978-1-4169-5885-7(1), Simon & Schuster Bks. For Young Readers) Simon & Schuster Bks. For Young Readers.

Burkhart, Jessica. Home Sweet Drama, 8. 2010. (Canterwood Crest Ser.: 8). (ENG.). 240p. (J). (gr. 4-8). pap. 7.99 (978-1-4169-9040-6(2)) Simon & Schuster, Inc.

—Jealousy. 2013. (Canterwood Crest Ser.: 17). lib. bdg. 17.20 (978-0-606-27032-8(9)) Turtleback.

—Popular. 2012. (Canterwood Crest Ser.: 14). (ENG.). 272p. (J). (gr. 4-8). pap. 8.99 (978-1-4424-1950-6(4), Aladdin) Simon & Schuster Children's Publishing.

—Rival Revenge. 2010. (Canterwood Crest Ser.: 7). (ENG.). 240p. (J). (gr. 4-8). pap. 7.99 (978-1-4169-9039-0(9), Aladdin) Simon & Schuster Children's Publishing.

Carter, Ally. Cross My Heart & Hope to Spy. 2016. (Gallagher Girls Ser.: 2). (J). lib. bdg. 20.85 (978-0-606-38296-0(8)) Turtleback.

de Campi, Alex. Kat & Mouse: Tripped, Vol.2. Manfredi, Federica, illus. 2007. (Kat & Mouse Manga Ser.: 2). (ENG.). 96p. (J). (gr. 4-1). pap. 5.99 (978-1-59816-549-4(6), e6390ae8-e307-44cd-8793-cc66156010f7, TOKYOPOP Manga) TOKYOPOP, Inc.

Frost, Mark. The Paladin Prophecy: Book 1, Bk. 1. 2014. (Paladin Prophecy Ser.: 1). (ENG.). 528p. (YA). (gr. 7). pap. 10.99 (978-0-375-87106-1(3), Ember) Random Hse. Children's Bks.

Inches, Alison. School Gyrls POW Scrapbook. 2010. (School Gyrls Ser.). (ENG.). 64p. (J). pap. 7.99 (978-1-4424-0865-4(0), Simon Spotlight) Simon Spotlight.

Kingsley, Kate. Kiss & Break Up. 2011. (Young, Loaded, & Fabulous Ser.: 3). (ENG.). 320p. (YA). (gr. 9-18). pap. 9.99 (978-1-4169-9401-5(7), Simon Pulse) Simon Pulse.

—Pretty on the Outside. 2010. (Young, Loaded, & Fabulous Ser.: 1). (ENG.). 320p. (YA). (gr. 9-18). pap. 9.99 (978-1-4169-9399-5(1), Simon Pulse) Simon Pulse.

Mead, Richelle. Bloodlines. 2012. (Bloodlines Ser.: 1). (ENG.). 448p. (YA). (gr. 7-18). pap. 12.99 (978-1-59514-473-7(0), Razorbill) Penguin Young Readers Group.

Middleton, Casey Olsson. Flying the Imaginarium: Book One, Coconut. 2007. 136p. per. 11.50 (978-1-59330-507-9(9)) Aventine Pr.

Money, Mo. Little Sister. 2011. (School Gyrls Ser.). (ENG.). 112p. (J). pap. 5.99 (978-1-4424-0879-1(0), Simon & Schuster/Paula Wiseman Bks.) Simon & Schuster/Paula Wiseman Bks.

Rain, Mandy. Rock 'n' Roll. 2011. (School Gyrls Ser.). (ENG.). 128p. (J). pap. 5.99 (978-1-4424-0878-4(2), Simon & Schuster/Paula Wiseman Bks.) Simon & Schuster/Paula Wiseman Bks.

Reid, Kimberly. Sweet 16 to Life. 2013. 233p. (J). lib. bdg. 20.80 (978-0-606-27166-0(X)) Turtleback.

Rose, Imogen. Initiation: Japanese Language Edition. Galeano, Tomomi, tr. 2013. 482p. pap. 16.99 (978-1-940015-04-0(9)) Imogen Rose.

Shields, Gillian. Eternal. 2012. (Immortal Ser.: 3). (ENG.). 384p. (YA). (gr. 8). pap. 9.99 (978-0-06-200040-8(3), Tegen, Katherine Bks) HarperCollins Pubs.

Simone, Ni-Ni & Abrams, Amir. Get Ready for War. 2013. (Hollywood High Ser.: 2). 423p. (YA). lib. bdg. 20.80 (978-0-606-27305-3(0)) Turtleback.

Stanwood Pier, Arthu. The Jester of St. Timothy's. 2006. pap. 14.95 (978-1-55742-546-1(9)) Wildside Pr., LLC.

Truett, Trudi. Explorer Academy: the Nebula Secret (Book 1) 2019. (Explorer Academy Ser.: 1). (Illus.). 216p. (J). (gr. 3-7). pap. 9.99 (978-1-4263-3810-6(4), Under the Stars) Disney Publishing Worldwide.

von Ziegesar, Cecily. Gossip Girl: It Had to Be You: The Gossip Girl Prequel. 2009. (Gossip Girl Ser.). (ENG.). 432p. (YA). (gr. 10-17). pap. 10.99 (978-0-316-01769-5(8), Poppy) Little, Brown Bks. for Young Readers.

PRIVATEERING

Nick, Charles. Sir Francis Drake (a Wicked History) 2009. (Wicked History Ser.). (ENG., Illus.). 128p. (J). (gr. 6-12). pap. 5.95 (978-0-531-20740-6(4), Watts, Franklin) Scholastic Library Publishing.

PRIZE FIGHTING

see Boxing

PROBABILITIES

Aboff, Marcie. Pigs, Cows, & Probability. 2011. (Data Mania Ser.). (ENG.). 24p. (gr. 1-2). pap. 41.70 (978-1-4296-6468-4(1), Capstone Pr.) Capstone.

Adamson, Thomas K. and Heather. Give Probability a Chance! 2012. (Fun with Numbers Ser.). (ENG.). 32p. (gr. 1-2). pap. 47.70 (978-1-4296-8305-0(8), Capstone Pr.) Capstone.

Benchmark Education Company, LLC Staff, compiled by. Data Analysis & Probability. 2005. spiral bd. 80.00 (978-1-4108-3915-2(X)); spiral bd. 205.00 (978-1-4108-4512-2(5)); spiral bd. 295.00 (978-1-4108-5452-0(3)); spiral bd. 215.00 (978-1-4108-5453-7(1)); spiral bd. 165.00 (978-1-4108-5863-4(4)); spiral bd. 185.00 (978-1-4108-5864-1(2)); spiral bd. 75.00 (978-1-4108-3908-4(7)); spiral bd. 60.00 (978-1-4108-3898-8(6)); spiral bd. 210.00 (978-1-4108-3897-1(8)) Benchmark Education Co.

—Data & Probability. 2005. spiral bd. 185.00 (978-1-4108-3901-5(X)) Benchmark Education Co.

Burrill, Gail F., et al. Probability Models. (Data-Driven Mathematics Ser.). 96p. (YA). (gr. 7-12). pap., stu. ed. 18.95 (978-1-57232-240-0(3)) Seymour, Dale Pubns.

Burton, Margie, et al. We All Scream for Ice Cream. 2011. (Early Connections Ser.). (J). (978-1-61672-544-0(3)) Benchmark Education Co.

Bussell, Linda. PROBABILIDAD con Juegos y Diversión (PROBABILITY with Fun & Games), 1 vol. 2008. (Las Matemáticas en Nuestro Mundo - Nivel 3 (Math in Our World - Level 3) Ser.). (SPA.). 24p. (gr. 3-3). (J). lib. bdg. 24.67 (978-0-8368-9298-7(4), ae050957-934b-4452-bbe6-53608ca225f8); pap. 9.15 (978-0-8368-9397-7(2), 72871399-ebd9-44ff-aa5c-f92fcdc8b290) Stevens, Gareth Publishing LLLP. (Weekly Reader Leveled Readers).

—PROBABILITY with Fun & Games, 1 vol. 2008. (Math in Our World - Level 3 Ser.). (ENG.). 24p. (gr. 3-3). (J). lib. bdg. 24.67 (978-0-8368-9290-1(9), 53568c5b-9ae3-4143-9389-fc460707475e); pap. 9.15 (978-0-8368-9389-2(1), c9907684-67f3-451e-a1eb-6d695031e035) Stevens, Gareth Publishing LLLP. (Weekly Reader Leveled Readers).

Cohen, Marina. Probability. 2010. (ENG., Illus.). 24p. (J). (978-0-7787-5249-3(6)); pap. (978-0-7787-5296-7(8)) Crabtree Publishing Co.

Cushman, Jean. Do You Wanna Bet? Your Chance to Find Out about Probability. Weston, Martha, illus. 2007. (ENG.). 112p. (J). (gr. 5-7). pap. 7.99 (978-0-618-82999-6(7), 100559, Clarion Bks.) HarperCollins Pubs.

Data Mania. 2011. (Data Mania Ser.). (ENG.). 24p. (gr. 1-2). pap. 166.80 (978-1-4296-6469-1(X), Capstone Pr.) Capstone.

Faulkner, Nicholas & Gregersen, Erik, eds. Statistics & Probability, 1 vol. 2017. (Foundations of Math Ser.). (ENG., Illus.). 400p. (J). (gr. 10-10). lib. bdg. 55.59 (978-1-68048-779-4(5), feec8536-3290-4507-8bf0-476670ee5ae8, Britannica Educational Publishing) Rosen Publishing Group, Inc., The.

Ferrie, Chris. Bayesian Probability for Babies. 2019. (Illus.). 24p. (J). (gr. -1-k). bds. 9.99 (978-1-4926-8079-6(6)) Sourcebooks, Inc.

Fischer, James. Game Math. 2013. (Math 24/7 Ser.: 10). 48p. (J). (gr. 5-18). 19.95 (978-1-4222-2907-1(6)) Mason Crest.

Goldstone, Bruce. That's a Possibility! A Book about What Might Happen. 2013. (ENG., Illus.). 32p. (J). (gr. 2-5). 18.99 (978-0-8050-8998-1(5), 900058873, Holt, Henry & Co. Bks. For Young Readers) Holt, Henry & Co.

Gott, Robert. How to Be in the Wrong Place at the Wrong Time. 2007. 96p. (J). (978-1-4207-0731-1(0)) Sundance/Newbridge Educational Publishing.

Hammelef, Danielle S. This Book Beats the Odds: A Collection of Amazing & Startling Odds, 1 vol. 2012. (Super Trivia Collection). (ENG.). 32p. (J). (gr. 3-9). lib. bdg. 28.65 (978-1-4296-8420-0(8), 118493, Capstone Pr.) Capstone.

Leech, Bonnie. Gregor Mendel's Genetic Theory: Understanding & Applying Concepts of Probability. (PowerMath: Advanced Proficiency Plus Ser.). 32p. (gr. 5-5). 2009. 47.90 (978-1-60851-356-7(4)) 2006. (ENG.). pap. 26.25 (978-1-4358-3820-8(3), 56a53214-f6be-45c7-8207-a98dfff3a1d6) Rosen Publishing Group, Inc., The. (PowerKids Pr.).

Leech, Bonnie Coulter. Gregor Mendel's Genetic Theory: Understanding & Applying Concepts of Probability, 1 vol. (Math for the REAL World Ser.). (ENG., Illus.). 32p. (gr. 5-5). 2009. pap. 10.00 (978-1-4042-6063-4(3), 896c90f3-be13-4df4-a40a-404ebde7ee3f) 2006. (YA). lib. bdg. 28.93 (978-1-4042-3355-3(5), 8204e305-b024-42ed-9c4b-308b9367f93d) Rosen Publishing Group, Inc., The.

MacGillivray, Helen & Petocz, Peter. Statistics & Probability in the Australian Curriculum Years 9 And 10. 2013. (ENG.). pap. (978-1-107-65599-7(4)) Cambridge Univ. Pr.

National Geographic Learning. Reading Expeditions (Science: Math Behind the Science): What's the Chance? 2007. (ENG., Illus.). 24p. (J). pap. 15.95 (978-0-7922-4590-2(3)) CENGAGE Learning.

Peters, Elisa. Statistics & Probability, 1 vol. 2014. (Story of Math Ser.). (ENG.). 64p. (YA). (gr. 8-8). 34.29 (978-1-62275-533-2(2), fd2ed37e-aa69-4c48-87ec-162e0bb68061, Britannica Educational Publishing) Rosen Publishing Group, Inc., The.

Roza, Greg. Heads or Tails: Exploring Probability Through Games. 2004. (Math Big Bookstm Ser.). (ENG.). 24p. (gr. 3-4). 43.95 (978-0-8239-7644-7(0)) Rosen Publishing Group, Inc., The.

Sullivan, Erin. Probability. 2011. (Early Connections Ser.). (J). (978-1-61672-648-5(2)) Benchmark Education Co.

Visto, Joy. What Are the Chances? (Making Math Work Ser.). (ENG.). 48p. (J). (gr. 4-7). 2016. pap. 12.00 (978-1-62832-174-6(1), 20909, Creative Paperbacks) 2015. (Illus.). (978-1-60818-573-3(7), 20908, Creative Education) Creative Co., The.

PROBES, SPACE

see Space Probes

PROBLEM CHILDREN

see also Juvenile Delinquency

Chuta, Edith N. Straight Talk to Troubled Kids: Finding Wisdom Underneath Our Pains. 2007. 76p. per. 10.95 (978-0-595-43778-8(8)) iUniverse, Inc.

Hutchinson, Tim. Battle Scars. 2003. 320p. (J). per. 16.95 (978-1-932133-85-1(2)) Writers' Collective, The.

Lavis, Rose Brenda. Here Comes Trouble & Double Trouble. 2010. 28p. pap. 13.99 (978-1-4490-3607-2(4)) AuthorHouse.

Libal, Autumn. Emotional Disturbance. Albers, Lisa et al, eds. 2014. (Living with a Special Need Ser.: 16). 128p. (J). (gr. 7-18). 25.95 (978-1-4222-3034-3(1)) Mason Crest.

—Runaway Train: Youth with Emotional Disturbance. 2004. (Youth with Special Needs Ser.). (Illus.). 128p. (J). 24.95 (978-1-59084-732-9(6)) Mason Crest.

—Runaway Train: Youth with Emotional Disturbance. 2003. (Youth with Special Needs Ser.). (Illus.). 127p. (YA). (gr. 7). pap. 14.95 (978-1-4222-0429-0(4)) Mason Crest.

McCaffrey, Monica & Hames, Annette, eds. Special Brothers & Sisters: Stories & Tips for Siblings of Children with Special Needs, Disability or Serious Illness. 2005. (Illus.). 96p. (gr. 4-7). per. 19.95 (978-1-84310-383-7(4), 692528) Kingsley, Jessica Pubs. GBR. Dist: Hachette UK Distribution.

McIntosh, Kenneth & Livingston, Phyllis. Youth with Conduct Disorder: In Trouble with the World. 2007. (Helping Youth with Mental, Physical, & Social Disabilities Ser.). (Illus.). 128p. (YA). pap. 14.95 (978-1-4222-0440-5(5)) Mason Crest.

McIntyre, Thomas. The Survival Guide for Kids with Behavior Challenges: How to Make Good Choices & Stay Out of Trouble. rev. ed. 2013. (Survival Guides for Kids Ser.). (ENG., Illus.). 192p. (J). (gr. 4-9). pap. 17.99 (978-1-57542-449-1(5)) Free Spirit Publishing Inc.

Musselman, Barbara. My Mad Book: I Get Mad & Granny Says It's Ok. 2009. 40p. pap. 19.99 (978-1-4389-9438-3(9)) AuthorHouse.

Nelson, Julie. Families Change: A Book for Children Experiencing Termination of Parental Rights. Gallagher, Mary, illus. 2006. (ENG.). 32p. (J). (gr. -1-5). pap. 11.99 (978-1-57542-209-1(3), 1137) Free Spirit Publishing Inc.

PROBLEM CHILDREN—FICTION

Byrne, Mary. Only Children Hear Me: Jake Is a Friend You Can Talk To. 2007. 96p. (J). per. 10.95 (978-0-595-44359-8(1)) iUniverse, Inc.

Cook, Julia. It's Hard to Be a Verb! Hartman, Carrie, illus. 2008. (ENG.). 32p. (J). (gr. k-3). pap. 10.95 (978-1-931636-84-1(2), A444) National Ctr. For Youth Issues.

Diggins, Matthew. Andrew & the Secret Gallery. Diggins, Matthew, illus. 2008. (Illus.). 32p. (J). pap. 6.95 (978-1-60108-026-4(3)) Red Cygnet Pr.

Goerzen, Christy. Explore, 1 vol. 2009. (Orca Currents Ser.). (ENG.). 128p. (J). (gr. 4-7). pap. 9.95 (978-1-55469-119-7(2)) Orca Bk. Pubs. USA.

Jones, Debbie Knatt. Maurice ... As Read to the Students in Room D183 & D184. 2013. 150p. pap. 13.95 (978-1-62516-536-7(6), Strategic Bk. Publishing) Strategic Book Publishing & Rights Agency (SBPRA).

Korobov, Kristine. Allison Marisa Burbank Gets into Trouble. Mahanov, Tanya, ed. Rossi, Andrea., illus. 2008. 172p. 26.90 (978-1-4251-8976-1(8)) Trafford Publishing.

Kropp, Paul & Doherty, Catherine. Juvie. (Illus.). 87p. (978-1-897039-16-8(6)) High Interest Publishing (HIP).

O'Reilly, Jane. The Notations of Cooper Cameron. 2019. (ENG.). 320p. (J). (gr. 3-5). pap. 9.99 (978-1-5415-7759-6(0), e174f65c-5fb0-4ec2-a9cd-9c3eac4a066c, Carolrhoda Bks.) Lerner Publishing Group.

Polak, Monique. 121 Express, 1 vol. 2008. (Orca Currents Ser.). (ENG.). 144p. (J). (gr. 4-7). pap. 9.95 (978-1-55143-976-1(X)) Orca Bk. Pubs. USA.

Taylor, Sean & Quarto Generic Staff. A Waste of Good Paper. 2013. (ENG., Illus.). 290p. (J). (gr. 6-9). pap. 8.99 (978-1-84780-268-2(0), Frances Lincoln Children's Bks.) Quarto Publishing Group UK GBR. Dist: Hachette Bk. Group.

PROBLEM SOLVING

Abramson, Marcie. Painless Math Word Problems. 2nd rev. ed. 2010. (Barron's Painless Ser.). (ENG.). 288p. (YA). (gr. 6-9). pap. 11.99 (978-0-7641-4335-9(2), Barron's Educational Series, Inc.) Kaplan Publishing.

Allanson, Patricia. Paralleila's Problem. Allanson, Patricia, illus. 2007. (Illus.). (J). (gr. -1-3). per. 13.99 (978-1-59879-278-2(4)) Lifevest Publishing, Inc.

Amos, Janine. Don't Do That! How Not to Act, 1 vol. 2009. (Best Behavior Ser.). (ENG., Illus.). 32p. (J). (gr. -1-2). pap. 11.55 (978-1-60754-052-6(5), b763b5fa-043f-4306-a4e8-5d824e2de8c4); lib. bdg. 27.27 (978-1-60754-030-4(4), f7e11b05-af93-465b-8e5e-c89d50442841) Rosen Publishing Group, Inc., The. (Windmill Bks.).

—Go Away! What Not to Say, 1 vol. 2009. (Best Behavior Ser.). (ENG., Illus.). 32p. (J). (gr. -1-2). pap. 11.55 (978-1-60754-044-1(4), ae570d48-9928-4c4a-9ca1-2efb8980b23d); lib. bdg. 27.27 (978-1-60754-026-7(6), fca3810e-8a67-49b9-9b58-ebd00d807ac7) Rosen Publishing Group, Inc., The. (Windmill Bks.).

—It Won't Work! Let's Try Again, 1 vol. 2009. (Best Behavior Ser.). (ENG., Illus.). 32p. (J). (gr. -1-2). lib. bdg. 27.27 (978-1-60754-027-4(4), f67a2177-0c2f-4838-a25f-da7eca8abf83, Windmill Bks.) Rosen Publishing Group, Inc., The.

—It's Mine! Let's Try to Share, 1 vol. 2009. (Best Behavior Ser.). (ENG., Illus.). 32p. (J). (gr. -1-2). pap. 11.55 (978-1-60754-048-9(7), 10ca88d0-2a64-479f-a014-1b6d94260452); lib. bdg. 27.27 (978-1-60754-028-1(2), b971e455-bd06-4b45-a375-6f8bed10d6bc) Rosen Publishing Group, Inc., The. (Windmill Bks.).

—Move over! Learning to Share Our Space, 1 vol. 2009. (Best Behavior Ser.). (ENG., Illus.). 32p. (J). (gr. -1-2). pap. 11.55 (978-1-60754-050-2(9), 5a4ebb76-706d-4cba-9ad2-82c2298611ba); lib. bdg. 27.27 (978-1-60754-029-8(0), 3adf2a89-e2bb-425d-a0d9-6eb2947f9abb) Rosen Publishing Group, Inc., The. (Windmill Bks.).

Arrow, Emily. Taking a Spin. Lenoir, Maarten, illus. 2019. (My Feelings, My Choices Ser.). (ENG.). 24p. (J). (gr. -1-2). 33.99 (978-1-68410-406-2(8), 141216) Cantata Learning.

Berda, Chryste. Fun & Games: Blast off to Camp: Time (Grade 2) rev. ed. 2018. (Mathematics in the Real World Ser.). (ENG., Illus.). 32p. (gr. 2-3). pap. 10.99 (978-1-4258-5754-7(X)) Teacher Created Materials, Inc.

Berda, Chryste L. Despegue Al Campamento: Tiempo. rev. ed. 2018. (Mathematics in the Real World Ser.). (SPA., Illus.). 32p. (J). (gr. 2-3). pap. 10.99 (978-1-4258-2871-4(X)) Teacher Created Materials, Inc.

Beth, Georgia & Marzocchi, Alison. Money Matters: School Fundraisers: Problem Solving with Ratios. 2019. (Mathematics in the Real World Ser.). (ENG., Illus.). 32p. (gr. 5-8). pap. 11.99 (978-1-4258-5880-3(5)) Teacher Created Materials, Inc.

Blaine, Dalton. Where Is My Umbrella? Fixing a Problem, 1 vol. 2017. (Computer Science for the Real World Ser.). (ENG.). 8p. (gr. k-1). pap. (978-1-5383-5052-2(1), 8c0d10ff-3d5d-4c1b-a5ba-5a51b188a34a, Rosen Classroom) Rosen Publishing Group, Inc., The.

Boardworks Learning Centers: Figure It Out. 2006. (J). bds. (978-0-9755252-4-1(7)) Evergreen Pr. of Brainerd, LLC.

Booker, Dwayne. My Science Project: Fixing a Problem, 1 vol. 2017. (Computer Science for the Real World Ser.). (ENG.). 16p. (gr. 2-3). pap. (978-1-5383-5208-3(7), e1b7e75e-9faa-4d7b-b2a4-62ddcc4e972c, Rosen Classroom) Rosen Publishing Group, Inc., The.

—Ty's American Flag: Breaking down the Problem, 1 vol. 2017. (Computer Science for the Real World Ser.). (ENG.). 8p. (gr. k-1). pap. (978-1-5383-5032-4(7), 69f54d7c-b993-4101-954a-630e4f915c51, Rosen Classroom) Rosen Publishing Group, Inc., The.

Burstein, John. What Should I Do? Making Good Decisions. 2009. (Slim Goodbody's Life Skills 101 Ser.). (ENG., Illus.). 32p. (J). (gr. 3-6). pap. (978-0-7787-4807-6(3), 1302929); lib. bdg. (978-0-7787-4791-8(3), 1302929) Crabtree Publishing Co.

Canavan, Thomas. Problem Solving: 50 Math Super Puzzles, 1 vol. 2011. (Math Standards Workout Ser.). (ENG., Illus.). 48p. (YA). (gr. 5-5). pap. 12.75 (978-1-4488-6682-3(0), 10f83779-c434-4db6-9a4c-98eb802ce2fc, Rosen Reference) Rosen Publishing Group, Inc., The.

Charles, R., et al. Problem-Solving Experience in Mathematics. 2003. 30.95 (978-0-201-20689-0(7)) Seymour, Dale Pubns.

Colson, Rob. Super Sums: Addition, Subtraction, Multiplication, & Division (Math Everywhere) (Library Edition) 2017. (Math Everywhere Ser.). (ENG., Illus.). 32p. (J). (gr. 5-8). lib. bdg. 27.00 (978-0-531-22884-5(3), Children's Pr.) Scholastic Library Publishing.

Cook-Cottone, Catherine. The brain owner's manual for Kids: Helping the feeling & thinking parts work Together. 2006. (Illus.). (J). pap. 5.00 (978-0-9795773-0-7(6)) Growing & Learning Pr.

Davies, Monika. Spectacular Sports: Playing Like a Girl: Problem Solving (Grade 4) 2017. (Mathematics in the Real World Ser.). (ENG., Illus.). 32p. (J). (gr. 4-5). pap. 11.99 (978-1-4258-5552-9(0)) Teacher Created Materials, Inc.

Dixon, Dale. Which Materials Float? What's the Problem?, 1 vol. 2017. (Computer Science for the Real World Ser.). (ENG.). 16p. (gr. 2-3). pap. (978-1-5383-5202-1(8), d6fda5bf-8fec-451c-b29f-3ba266d18331, Rosen Classroom) Rosen Publishing Group, Inc., The.

Dunham, Bandhu Scott. We Like to Invent! Stark, Ryan, illus. 2010. (J). pap. (978-1-935387-13-8(8)) Hohm Pr.

Dyer, Janice. Designing Positive School Communities. 2018. (Illus.). 48p. (J). (978-1-4271-2037-3(4)) Crabtree Publishing Co.

Ellis, Roman. We Study Wind: Breaking down the Problem, 1 vol. 2017. (Computer Science for the Real World Ser.). (ENG.). 16p. (gr. 2-3). pap. (978-1-5383-5228-1(1), 5fbea256-5ae0-4933-abee-7290a5f29465, Rosen Classroom) Rosen Publishing Group, Inc., The.

—What's Wrong with the Magnet? Fixing a Problem, 1 vol. 2017. (Computer Science for the Real World Ser.). (ENG.). 12p. (gr. 1-2). pap. (978-1-5383-5148-2(X), 288a37b1-8e4d-480a-94c1-fe989728b940, Rosen Classroom) Rosen Publishing Group, Inc., The.

Flash Kids Editors, Flash Kids, ed. Problem Solving: Grade 2 (Flash Skills) 2010. (Flash Skills Ser.). 64p. (J). pap. 3.95 (978-1-4114-3463-9(3), Spark Publishing Group) Sterling Publishing Co., Inc.

Gallagher, Jim. A Hassled Guy's Guide: How to Deal, 1 vol. 2014. (Guy's Guide Ser.). (ENG.). 64p. (gr. 5-7). 19.61 (978-1-62293-005-0(3), 4fab3ef5-ea79-40f4-9074-b3f9919b5a7f) Enslow Publishing, LLC.

Gerber, Larry. Step-By-Step Guide to Problem Solving at School & Work, 1 vol. 2014. (Winning at Work Readiness Ser.). (ENG.). 64p. (J). (gr. 6-6). 36.13 (978-1-4777-7782-4(2), 389da113-75fa-455e-86fc-c1b05a897960) Rosen Publishing Group, Inc., The.

—Step-By-Step Guide to Problem Solving at School & Work. 2014. (Winning at Work Readiness Ser.). (ENG.). 64p. (YA). (gr. 7-12). 23.75 (978-1-5311-8671-5(8)) Perfection Learning Corp.

Giroux, Lindsay Nina. Goldilocks & the Three Bears: A Problem-Solving Story. Trithart, Emma, illus. 2016. (J). (978-0-87659-707-1(X)) Gryphon Hse., Inc.

—We Are Problem Solvers. Archer, Micha, illus. 2016. (J). (978-0-87659-715-6(0)) Gryphon Hse., Inc.

Golden, Pam. Lulu Learns about Reporting: Ending the Tattle Battle. Outohak, Diana, illus. 2007. 28p. (J). pap. 18.95 (978-0-9659650-8-8(2)) Roedway Pr.

Harasymiw, R. P. Problem Solving with Pigs, 1 vol. 2013. (Animal Math Ser.). (ENG.). 24p. (J). (gr. 1-2). pap. 9.15 (978-1-4339-9324-4(4), 5d0db16d-001a-4fe5-a268-8051cf8d7637); (Illus.). lib. bdg. 25.27 (978-1-4339-9323-7(6), c3c3704c-7c10-4e54-99b1-070f7fc39daf) Stevens, Gareth Publishing LLLP.

Harasymiw, Raymond. Problem Solving with Pigs. 2013. (Animal Math Ser.). 24p. (J). (gr. 1-3). pap. 48.90 (978-1-4339-9325-1(2)) Stevens, Gareth Publishing LLLP.

Hillman, Emilee. Train Your Brain with Activities Using Loops. Regan, Dana, illus. 2019. (Think Like a Programmer Ser.). (ENG.). 32p. (gr. 4-4). 63.48 (978-1-5026-4815-0(6)) Cavendish Square Publishing LLC.

—Train Your Brain with Collaboration Activities, 1 vol. Regan, Dana, illus. 2019. (Think Like a Programmer Ser.). (ENG.). 32p. (gr. 4-4). lib. bdg. 30.21 (978-1-5026-4812-9(1), 004e5ff2-0d47-4f68-8cbb-8ee2703dc761) Cavendish Square Publishing LLC.

—Train Your Brain with Problem-Solving Activities, 1 vol. Regan, Dana, illus. 2019. (Think Like a Programmer Ser.). (ENG.). 32p. (gr. 4-4). pap. 11.58 (978-1-5026-4802-0(4), 3f997a22-ee50-4f3e-ac7f-4dd92811e9b9) Cavendish Square Publishing LLC.

Hoena, Blake. Algorithms: Solve a Problem! Sanchez, Sr., illus. 2018. (Code It! Ser.). (ENG.). 24p. (C). (gr. 1-3). lib. bdg. 33.99 (978-1-68410-383-6(5), 140357) Cantata Learning.

Hoffman, Mary Ann. The History of the Maya: Using Computational Skills in Problem Solving, 1 vol. (Math for the REAL World Ser.). 32p. 2010. (ENG., Illus.). (gr. 5-6). pap. 10.00 (978-1-4042-5148-9(0), 1e7bff57-c49d-4b07-8c00-4641958ee3cf) 2009. (gr. 4-5). 47.90 (978-1-60851-421-2(8)) 2004. (ENG., Illus.). (J). (gr. 5-6). lib. bdg. 28.93 (978-1-4042-2942-6(6), 71c20ad2-2cf7-479d-bfd4-96e680dd4092) Rosen Publishing Group, Inc., The. (PowerKids Pr.).

Huffman, Mindy. What's Wrong with the Experiment? Fixing a Problem, 1 vol. 2017. (Computer Science for the Real World Ser.). (ENG.). 16p. (gr. 2-3). pap. (978-1-5383-5232-8(X), 4f3f61c3-31aa-4a88-9f6a-39e1c5d215a8, Rosen Classroom) Rosen Publishing Group, Inc., The.

Johnson, Robin. How Engineers Solve Problems. 2019. (Full STEAM Ahead! - Engineering Everywhere Ser.). (Illus.). 24p. (J). (gr. 1-1). (978-0-7787-6206-5(8)); (ENG.). pap. (978-0-7787-6251-5(3)) Crabtree Publishing Co.

—Mistakes Help Us Learn. 2019. (Full STEAM Ahead! - Engineering Everywhere Ser.). (Illus.). 24p. (J). (gr. 1-1). (978-0-7787-6207-2(6)); (ENG.). pap. (978-0-7787-6252-2(1)) Crabtree Publishing Co.

Kavanaugh, Dorothy. Hassled Girl? Girls Dealing with Feelings, 1 vol. 2014. (Girls Dealing with Feelings Ser.). (ENG.). 64p. (gr. 5-6). 19.61 (978-1-62293-035-7(5), 249574d8-0ffc-4dd8-9c3c-62942aebe303) Enslow Publishing, LLC.

Kelsey, Elin. Wild Ideas: Let Nature Inspire Your Thinking. Kim, Soyeon, illus. 2015. (ENG.). 32p. (J). (gr. k-5). 18.95 (978-1-77147-062-9(3)) Owlkids Bks. Inc. CAN. Dist: Publishers Group West (PGW).

Kerstein, Lauren H. A Week of Switching, Shifting, & Stretching: How to Make My Thinking More Flexible. 2013. (ENG., Illus.). 57p. (J). (gr. -1-5). pap. 18.00 (978-1-937473-89-1(9)) Autism Asperger Publishing Co.

Klimchuk, David. You Can Fix It: Solving Problems, 1 vol. 2019. (Spotlight on Social & Emotional Learning Ser.). (ENG.). 24p. (gr. 4-6). 27.93 (978-1-7253-0707-0(3), 65ffa94b-cff0-43ba-9f9a-e03cbc082fe2, PowerKids Pr.) Rosen Publishing Group, Inc., The.

Kopp, Megan. Above & Beyond with Critical Thinking & Problem Solving. 2016. (Fueling Your Future! Going above & Beyond in the 21st Century Ser.). (ENG., Illus.). 48p. (J). (gr. 5-9). (978-0-7787-2842-9(0)) Crabtree Publishing Co.

Lawson, Lela. Paco's Winter Plan: What's the Problem?, 1 vol. 2017. (Computer Science for the Real World Ser.). (ENG.). 8p. (gr. k-1). pap. (978-1-5383-5024-9(6), 6592e158-fb20-45af-a785-c89f6d4d15b0, Rosen Classroom) Rosen Publishing Group, Inc., The.

Lechner, Judith. Our New Fish Tank: Learning to Estimate & Round Numbers to the Nearest Ones, Tens, & Hundreds Places. 2004. (Math Big Bookstm Ser.). (ENG.). 16p. (gr. 2-3). 37.95 (978-0-8239-7640-9(8)) Rosen Publishing Group, Inc., The.

Leech, Bonnie. Mesopotamia: Creating & Solving World Problems. 2009. (PowerMath: Advanced Proficiency Plus Ser.). 32p. (gr. 5-5). 47.90 (978-1-60851-362-8(9), PowerKids Pr.) Rosen Publishing Group, Inc., The.

Letts KS2, Letts. Maths - Problem Solving & Reasoning Age 7-9 (Letts Wild About) 2015. (Letts Wild about Learning Ser.). (ENG.). 48p. (J). (gr. 2-4). pap. 8.95 (978-1-84419-788-0(3)) HarperCollins Pubs. Ltd. GBR. Dist: Independent Pubs. Group.

Linde, Barbara. Math in Our Solar System: Applying Problem-Solving Strategies. 2009. (PowerMath: Proficiency Plus Ser.). 32p. (gr. 4-5). 47.90 (978-1-60851-413-7(7), PowerKids Pr.) Rosen Publishing Group, Inc., The.

Linde, Barbara M. Math in Our Solar System: Applying Problem-Solving Strategies, 1 vol. (Math for the REAL World Ser.). (ENG.). 32p. (gr. 5-6). 2009. pap. 10.00

(978-1-4042-5135-9(9), 47c1cfe1-7782-47b5-8a24-378e22c6764a) 2004. (Illus.). (J). lib. bdg. 28.93 (978-1-4042-2936-5(1), 381f9a73-425d-4ac2-aeb8-53eda63581f4, PowerKids Pr.) Rosen Publishing Group, Inc., The.

McDonnell, Rory. Word Problems with Wolves, 1 vol. 2017. (Animal Math Ser.). (ENG.). 24p. (J). (gr. 1-2). pap. 9.15 (978-1-5382-0868-7(7), 528811d4-0b4b-40f3-9742-31d35fc5b8ab) Stevens, Gareth Publishing LLLP.

McKee, Rosie. My Pet Dinosaur: Breaking down the Problem, 1 vol. 2017. (Computer Science for the Real World Ser.). (ENG.). 12p. (gr. 1-2). pap. (978-1-5383-5138-3(2), 1a493f59-2fe3-4618-b0ce-a04298622eb0, Rosen Classroom) Rosen Publishing Group, Inc., The.

Messner, Kate. Solve This! Forensics: Super Science & Curious Capers for the Daring Detective in You. 2020. (Illus.). 160p. (J). (gr. 3-7). (ENG.). 26.90 (978-1-4263-3745-1(0)); pap. 16.99 (978-1-4263-3744-4(2)) Disney Publishing Worldwide. (National Geographic Kids).

Middlewood, G. & Debenham, A. 43 Team-Building Activities. 2007. 64p. per. (978-1-903853-57-3(5)) Brilliant Pubns.

Miller, Reagan. Engineers Solve Problems. 2013. (ENG.). 24p. (J). (978-0-7787-0094-4(1)); (Illus.). pap. (978-0-7787-0101-9(8)) Crabtree Publishing Co.

Morlock, Jeremy. Problem-Solving Methods of the Continental Congress, 1 vol. 2018. (Project Learning Through American History Ser.). (ENG.). 32p. (gr. 4-5). 27.93 (978-1-5383-3071-5(7), d0e28d22-98b0-410a-bee5-d3ef709cfccb, PowerKids Pr.) Rosen Publishing Group, Inc., The.

Pezzimenti, Grace. The Pizza Party: Learning Basic Problem-Solving Skills, 1 vol. (Math for the REAL World Ser.). (ENG.). 12p. (gr. 1-2). 2010. pap. 5.90 (978-0-8239-8914-0(3), 94f09161-d216-4d5b-ad80-5c41299b15a9, Rosen Classroom) 2004. 33.50 (978-0-8239-7636-2(X)) Rosen Publishing Group, Inc., The.

Risby, Bonnie Lou. The Great Honey Robbery: Using Critical Thinking to Solve Problems. 2004. (J). pap. 14.95 (978-1-931334-40-2(4)) Pieces of Learning.

Rogers, Seth. Maestros: Tiempo. rev. ed. 2019. (Mathematics in the Real World Ser.). (SPA., Illus.). 24p. (J). (gr. 1-2). pap. 9.99 (978-1-4258-2853-0(1)) Teacher Created Materials, Inc.

—On the Job: Teachers: Time (Grade 1) rev. ed. 2018. (Mathematics in the Real World Ser.). (ENG., Illus.). 24p. (J). (gr. 1-2). pap. 9.99 (978-1-4258-5691-5(8)) Teacher Created Materials, Inc.

Roza, Greg. The Hoover Dam: Applying Problem-Solving Strategies, 1 vol. (Math for the REAL World Ser.). 32p. (gr. 5-5). 2009. (ENG., Illus.). pap. 10.00 (978-1-4042-6065-8(X), 2d3bd40a-2a1b-423d-93d2-bee8580ad777) 2009. 47.90 (978-1-60851-369-7(6), PowerKids Pr.) 2006. (ENG., Illus.). (YA). lib. bdg. 28.93 (978-1-4042-3356-0(3), 9e940dfb-9f90-48d7-b2ac-8d1623a0fa92) Rosen Publishing Group, Inc., The.

Ruffin, Frances E. Let's Have a Bake Sale: Calculating Profit & Unit Cost, 1 vol. (Math for the REAL World Ser.). 24p. (gr. 3-4). 2010. (ENG., Illus.). pap. 8.25 (978-0-8239-8893-8(7), fa375125-9655-49d9-a189-2e4223c37adb, PowerKids Pr.) 2004. 43.95 (978-0-8239-7645-4(9)) Rosen Publishing Group, Inc., The.

Sargent, Brian. Guess the Order. 2006. (Rookie Read-About Math Ser.). (ENG., Illus.). 32p. (J). (gr. 1-2). lib. bdg. 20.50 (978-0-516-24963-6(0), Children's Pr.) Scholastic Library Publishing.

—Slumber Party Problem Solving. 2006. (Rookie Read-About Math Ser.). (ENG., Illus.). 32p. (J). (gr. 1-2). lib. bdg. 20.50 (978-0-516-24962-9(2), Children's Pr.) Scholastic Library Publishing.

Saviola, Joseph A. The Tour de France: Solving Addition Problems Involving Renaming, 1 vol. 2010. (Math for the REAL World Ser.). (ENG., Illus.). 24p. (gr. 3-4). pap. 8.25 (978-0-8239-8851-8(1), 03a082e6-c98b-4d55-b26f-a0d4236285cf, PowerKids Pr.) Rosen Publishing Group, Inc., The.

—The Tour de France: Solving Addition Problems Using Regrouping. (PowerMath: Intermediate Ser.). 24p. (gr. 3-4). 2009. 45.00 (978-1-60851-386-4(6)) 2003. (ENG., Illus.). (J). lib. bdg. 26.27 (978-0-8239-8963-8(1), 072fe429-6804-4fc3-9184-1d96b21d2d8d) Rosen Publishing Group, Inc., The. (PowerKids Pr.).

Shea, Therese. Biosphere 2: Solving Word Problems, 1 vol. (Math for the REAL World Ser.). 32p. 2010. (ENG., Illus.). (gr. 5-6). pap. 10.00 (978-1-4042-5150-2(2), 76ddb5be-672d-47d8-a171-548c3aa362af, PowerKids Pr.) 2009. (gr. 4-5). 47.90 (978-1-60851-406-9(4), PowerKids Pr.) 2004. (ENG., Illus.). (YA). (gr. 5-6). lib. bdg. 28.93 (978-1-4042-2943-3(4), aca59918-3466-41c4-9073-309dbde80213) Rosen Publishing Group, Inc., The.

—The Great Barrier Reef: Using Graphs & Charts to Solve Word Problems, 1 vol. (Math for the REAL World Ser.). 32p. (gr. 5-5). 2009. (ENG., Illus.). pap. 10.00 (978-1-4042-6071-9(4), ba7c1ab5-c71c-44e6-9a99-fcbe8f211cee) 2009. 47.90 (978-1-60851-367-3(X), PowerKids Pr.) 2006. (ENG., Illus.). (YA). lib. bdg. 28.93 (978-1-4042-3359-1(8), 0aeeb309-4508-4453-9e65-b2deb16f62ce) Rosen Publishing Group, Inc., The.

—The Transcontinental Railroad: Using Proportions to Solve Problems, 1 vol. (Math for the REAL World Ser.). 32p. (gr. 5-5). 2009. (ENG., Illus.). pap. 10.00 (978-1-4042-6075-7(7), 785d186d-7453-4085-8f38-992063e03aac) 2009. 47.90 (978-1-60851-370-3(X), PowerKids Pr.) 2006. (ENG., Illus.). (YA). lib. bdg. 28.93 (978-1-4042-3361-4(X), 7d4994a5-4462-4fc6-b218-453874e356dc) Rosen Publishing Group, Inc., The.

Smith, Sarah. Organization & Problem-Solving, Vol. 7. 2018. (Leadership Skills & Character Building Ser.). 64p. (J). (gr. 7). lib. bdg. 31.93 (978-1-4222-3998-8(5)) Mason Crest.

Sohn, Emily. Variables & Experiments. 2019. (iScience Ser.). (ENG., Illus.). 48p. (J). (gr. 5-6). 23.94 (978-1-68450-944-7(0)); pap. 13.26 (978-1-68404-408-5(1)) Norwood Hse. Pr.

Stockland, Patricia M. Debugging: You Can Fix It! Sanchez, Sr., illus. 2018. (Code It! Ser.). (ENG.). 24p. (C). (gr. 1-3). lib. bdg. 33.99 (978-1-68410-388-1(6), 140361) Cantata Learning.

Taylor-Butler, Christine. Understanding Diagrams. 2012. (True Book Ser.). (ENG.). 48p. (J). pap. 6.95 (978-0-531-26239-9(1)) Scholastic Library Publishing.

Weibourn, Shannon. Step Forward with Problem Solving. 2016. (Step Forward! Ser.). (ENG., Illus.). 24p. (J). (gr. 1-4). (978-0-7787-2768-2(8)) Crabtree Publishing Co.

Williams, Zella & Wingard-Nelson, Rebecca. Word Problems Using Addition & Subtraction, 1 vol. 2016. (Mastering Math Word Problems Ser.). (ENG., Illus.). 48p. (gr. 3-4). pap. 12.70 (978-0-7660-8252-6(0), f9a329e2-a738-49e9-b154-dc6f08f0c12c) Enslow Publishing, LLC.

—Word Problems Using Ratios & Proportions, 1 vol. 2016. (Mastering Math Word Problems Ser.). (ENG.). 48p. (gr. 3-4). pap. 12.70 (978-0-7660-8272-4(5), 976a2bd0-8802-4dd2-a49c-cfa6de8c4a7c) Enslow Publishing, LLC.

Wingard-Nelson, Rebecca. Big Truck & Car Word Problems Starring Multiplication & Division: Math Word Problems Solved, 1 vol. 2009. (Math Word Problems Solved Ser.). (ENG., Illus.). 48p. (gr. 3-3). lib. bdg. 27.93 (978-0-7660-2918-7(2), b09ca9dd-535e-4b8d-b8a4-4e7349cddc94) Enslow Publishing, LLC.

—Fun Food Word Problems Starring Fractions: Math Word Problems Solved, 1 vol. 2009. (Math Word Problems Solved Ser.). (ENG., Illus.). 48p. (gr. 3-3). lib. bdg. 27.93 (978-0-7660-2919-4(0), 87e5b65c-bfa9-4a78-b0a1-0397169003a3) Enslow Publishing, LLC.

—Graphing & Probability Word Problems: No Problem!, 1 vol. 2010. (Math Busters Word Problems Ser.). (ENG., Illus.). 64p. (gr. 5-6). lib. bdg. 31.93 (978-0-7660-3372-6(4), a8d18b1e-ff99-457d-ac8f-40cc07ee2072) Enslow Publishing, LLC.

—I Can Do Money Word Problems, 1 vol. 2010. (I Like Money Math! Ser.). (ENG., Illus.). 24p. (gr. k-2). pap. 10.35 (978-0-7660-3659-8(6), bf4458b3-3d77-4a3d-94e8-119404a45788, Enslow Elementary); lib. bdg. 25.27 (978-0-7660-3145-6(4), 497d6c6b-0eac-4c93-8ecf-9e247c114949) Enslow Publishing, LLC.

—Problem Solving & Word Problem Smarts!, 1 vol. 2011. (Math Smarts! Ser.). (ENG., Illus.). 64p. (gr. 5-6). pap. 11.53 (978-1-59845-325-6(4), 26e73e10-9768-4399-9dbe-54d2b24cb3ba); lib. bdg. 31.93 (978-0-7660-3943-8(9), 746cfda1-b97e-49a7-bea3-10dfe366bfe1) Enslow Publishing, LLC.

—Ready for Word Problems & Problem Solving, 1 vol. 2014. (Ready for Math Ser.). (ENG., Illus.). 48p. (gr. 3-3). pap. 11.53 (978-1-4644-0443-6(7), 20a69110-6490-46b2-be9e-fe6b8234a0c1, Enslow Elementary) Enslow Publishing, LLC.

—Sports Word Problems Starring Decimals & Percents: Math Word Problems Solved, 1 vol. 2009. (Math Word Problems Solved Ser.). (ENG., Illus.). 48p. (gr. 3-3). lib. bdg. 27.93 (978-0-7660-2920-0(4), d845e50b-92c1-481e-bf3a-28192d8e1c13) Enslow Publishing, LLC.

WRITE IT! Problem Solving with Numbers & Words, Grades 5-6. 2004. (J). per. 10.95 (978-1-58123-365-0(5)) Larson Learning, Inc.

WRITE IT! Problem Solving with Numbers & Words, Grades 7-8. 2004. (J). per. 10.95 (978-1-58123-367-4(1)) Larson Learning, Inc.

Zuravicky, Orli. Amazing Animals: Multiplying Multidigit Numbers by a One-Digit Number with Regrouping, 1 vol. 2010. (Math for the REAL World Ser.). (ENG., Illus.). 24p. (gr. 3-4). pap. 8.25 (978-0-8239-8861-7(9), 50dd9d7f-a690-4a82-aefb-5c3b432c07bc, PowerKids Pr.) Rosen Publishing Group, Inc., The.

PROCESSIONS

see Parades

PRODUCTION

see Economics; Industries

PRODUCTS, COMMERCIAL

see Commercial Products

PRODUCTS, DAIRY

see Dairy Products

PRODUCTS, WASTE

see Waste Products

PROFESSION, CHOICE OF

see Vocational Guidance

PROFESSIONS

see also Occupations; Vocational Guidance

also names of professions (e.g. Law; Medicine); also Law—Vocational Guidance; music—Vocational guidance

Antill, Sara. 10 Ways I Can Help My Community, 1 vol. 2012. (I Can Make a Difference Ser.). (ENG., Illus.). 24p. (J). (gr. 2-3). pap. 9.25 (978-1-4488-6363-1(5), a06fb6f8-f55a-474b-b499-fe8ab15e6296); lib. bdg. 26.27 (978-1-4488-6202-3(7), e3028fb1-b729-409f-9274-57aeff84d52f) Rosen Publishing Group, Inc., The. (PowerKids Pr.).

Barberi, Gladys. Pink Fire Trucks. Safar, Lina, illus. 2013.Tr. of Los Camiones de Bomberos de Color Rosado. 30p. (J). 16.95 (978-1-60131-145-0(1)) Big Tent Bks.

Bozzo, Linda. Community Helpers of the Past, Present, & Future, 1 vol. 2010. (Imagining the Future Ser.). (ENG., Illus.). 24p. (gr. k-2). lib. bdg. 25.27 (978-0-7660-3435-8(6), 108b0403-8f84-4ea1-979c-c4cb392f95bd, Enslow Elementary) Enslow Publishing, LLC.

Calling All Innovators: A Career for You? (Set Of 4) 2013. (J). 120.00 (978-0-531-27925-0(1)) Scholastic Library Publishing.

Coan, Sharon. Trabajadores de Mi Ciudad. 2nd rev. ed. 2016. (TIME for KIDS(r): Informational Text Ser.). (SPA.). 12p. (gr. -1-k). 7.99 (978-1-4938-3027-5(9)) Teacher Created Materials, Inc.

Cool Careers: Helping Careers, 10 vols., Set. Incl. Construction Worker. Horn, Geoffrey M. (YA). lib. bdg. 28.67 (978-0-8368-9192-8(9), 8108f670-2997-47d7-baf1-023263089434); FBI Agent. Horn, Geoffrey M. lib. bdg. 28.67 (978-0-8368-9193-5(7), d56e76cd-9208-452f-9922-7c4fd17a6164); Meteorologist. Horn, Geoffrey M. (YA). lib. bdg. 28.67 (978-0-8368-9194-2(5), acabdd96-240b-4229-9936-6ae589f7cf88); Mountain Rescuer. Thomas, William David. lib. bdg. 28.67 (978-0-8368-9195-9(3), bd25c45f-06de-4de4-bd70-2c6a4c8dc77a); Sports Therapist. Horn, Geoffrey M. lib. bdg. 28.67 (978-0-8368-9196-6(1), 6b71aba5-04fc-450e-8801-b68fe7757499); Veterinarian. Thomas, William David. lib. bdg. 28.67 (978-0-8368-9197-3(X), 055ce3f6-ef46-47be-b3b0-7e3389d5a623); (gr. 3-3). (Cool Careers: Helping Careers Ser.). (ENG.). 32p. 2008. Set lib. bdg. 143.35 (978-0-8368-9300-7(X), a63197d7-d5b8-4b23-9387-d5291be29860) Stevens, Gareth Publishing LLLP.

Discovering Careers for Your Future - Group 1, 8 bks., Set. Incl. English. Ferguson. lib. bdg. 21.95 (978-0-89434-321-6(1), P053104); Health. Publishing, Ferguson. lib. bdg. 19.95 (978-0-89434-322-3(X), P053105); 96p. (gr. 4-9). 2000. (Illus.). 700p. Set lib. bdg. 127.60 (978-0-89434-363-6(7), Ferguson Publishing Company) Infobase Holdings, Inc.

Downey, Glen R. The 10 Most Extreme Jobs. 2008. 14.99 (978-1-55448-536-9(3)) Scholastic Library Publishing.

Durrie, Karen. Diversión. 2012. (SPA.). (J). 27.13 (978-1-61913-209-2(5)) Weigl Pubs., Inc.

—Fun: Arabic-English Bilingual Edition. 2016. (Community Helpers Ser.). (ENG.). (J). (gr. 3-7). 29.99 (978-1-61913-902-2(2)) Weigl Pubs., Inc.

—Safety. 2011. (ENG.). (J). lib. bdg. 27.13 (978-1-61690-951-2(X)) Weigl Pubs., Inc.

—Seguridad. 2012. (SPA & ENG.). (J). (978-1-61913-211-5(7)) Weigl Pubs., Inc.

Edwards, Clint. Show Me Community Helpers: My First Picture Encyclopedia, 1 vol. 2013. (My First Picture Encyclopedias Ser.). (ENG.). 32p. (J). (gr. -1-2). pap. 8.10 (978-1-4765-3788-7(7), 123748) Capstone.

Harcourt School Publishers Staff. Jobs People Do, No. 6. 2nd ed. 2003. (Illus.). pap. 139.70 (978-0-15-337561-3(2)) Harcourt Schl. Pubs.

—People & Work Big Book No. 6. 2nd ed. 2003. (Illus.). pap. 139.70 (978-0-15-337571-2(X)) Harcourt Schl. Pubs.

Heling, Kathryn. Clothesline Clues to Jobs People Do. 2014. 17.95 (978-1-63419-654-3(6)) Perfection Learning Corp.

Heling, Kathryn & Hembrook, Deborah. Clothesline Clues to Jobs People Do. Davies, Andy Robert, illus. 2012. (ENG.). 40p. (J). (gr. -1-2). 15.99 (978-1-58089-251-3(5)) Charlesbridge Publishing, Inc.

Honders, Christine. What's It Really Like to Be a Mechanic?, 1 vol. 2019. (Jobs Kids Want Ser.). (ENG.). 24p. (gr. 1-2). pap. 9.25 (978-1-5383-4992-2(2), 3db34da8-01cc-4939-a04e-102e6a83e40b, PowerKids Pr.) Rosen Publishing Group, Inc., The.

In the Dark Interactive Packages: Nighttime Jobs. (Pebble Soup Explorations Ser.). (SPA.). (gr. -1-18). 52.00 (978-0-7578-5250-3(5)) Rigby Education.

Jarrell, Jane & Saathoff, Deborah. Off to Work We Go. 2004. 50p. (gr. -1-18). pap., act. bk. ed. 6.99 (978-0-8054-0823-2(1)) B&H Publishing Group.

Job Connection: Tools to Land the Job. 2nd ed. 2004. (YA). per. 11.95 (978-1-891818-33-2(3), 01-WB03) Linx Educational Publishing, Inc.

Kalman, Bobbie. Helpers in My Community. 2010. (My World Ser.). (ENG., Illus.). 24p. (J). (gr. k-2). (978-0-7787-9444-8(X)); (gr. 1-1). pap. (978-0-7787-9488-2(1)) Crabtree Publishing Co.

Mangrum, Allison. Jobs from A to Z. Capaldi, Gina, illus. 2006. 28p. pap. 9.50 (978-1-55501-675-3(8)) Ballard & Tighe Pubs.

Owen, Ruth. Asteroid Hunters. 2015. (Get to Work with Science & Technology Ser.). (ENG., Illus.). 32p. (J). (gr. 2-7). lib. bdg. 29.32 (978-1-910549-36-0(3), 724871c0-96be-4df7-b419-6f5ff860034c) Ruby Tuesday Books Limited GBR. Dist: Lerner Publishing Group.

Reeves, Diane Lindsey. Glamorous Jobs. 2009. (Way Out Work Ser.). (ENG., Illus.). 48p. (gr. 3-5). 29.95 (978-1-60413-129-1(2), P173467, Ferguson Publishing Company) Infobase Holdings, Inc.

Ryski, Dawid. What Do Grown-Ups Do All Day? 2017. (ENG., Illus.). 32p. (J). (gr. -1-2). 19.95 (978-3-89955-799-2(9)) Die Gestalten Verlag DEU. Dist: Ingram Publisher Services.

Thomas, William David. Mountain Rescuer, 1 vol. 2008. (Cool Careers: Helping Careers Ser.). (ENG.). 32p. (gr. 3-3). pap. 11.50 (978-0-8368-9328-1(X), 0564e2d3-24a3-4549-ab7d-a94967e1b592); lib. bdg. 28.67 (978-0-8368-9195-9(3), bd25c45f-06de-4de4-bd70-2c6a4c8dc77a) Stevens, Gareth Publishing LLLP.

Wolfe, Jane. Pull the Lever: Who Does What? Benham, Tors, illus. 2014. (ENG.). 8p. (J). (gr. -1-2). bds. 6.99 (978-1-86147-392-9(3), Armadillo) Anness Publishing GBR. Dist: National Bk. Network.

PROFESSORS

see Teachers

PROGRAMMING (ELECTRONIC COMPUTERS)

see Computer Programming

PROHIBITION

Beyer, Mark. Temperance & Prohibition: The Movement to Pass Anti-Liquor Laws in America, 1 vol. 2005. (Primary Sources of the Progressive Movement Ser.). (ENG., Illus.). 32p. (gr. 3-4). pap. 10.00 (978-1-4042-0861-2(5), 4aaa1a18-e46a-48ec-95e1-aff662d7c87c) Rosen Publishing Group, Inc., The.

—Temperance & Prohibition: The Movement to Pass Anti-liquor Laws in America. 2009. (Progressive Movement 1900-1920: Efforts to Reform America's New Industrial Society Ser.). 32p. (gr. 3-4). 47.90 (978-1-60854-171-3(1)) Rosen Publishing Group, Inc., The.

Blumenthal, Karen. Bootleg: Murder, Moonshine, & the Lawless Years of Prohibition. 2013. (ENG., Illus.). 176p. (YA). (gr. 7-12). pap. 14.99 (978-1-250-03427-4(2), 900120600) Square Fish.

Dunn, John M. Prohibition, 1 vol. 2010. (American History Ser.). (ENG., Illus.). 112p. (gr. 7-7). 41.03 (978-1-4205-0134-6(8), 0fae9234-0eb9-402e-b015-58ffac3f9dc9, Lucent Pr.) Greenhaven Publishing LLC.

Engdahl, Sylvia, ed. Prohibition, 1 vol. 2012. (Perspectives on Modern World History Ser.). (ENG., Illus.). 216p. (gr. 10-12). lib. bdg. 49.43 (978-0-7377-6370-6(1), e644231c-928f-4bf2-be5d-25f854e5e30d, Greenhaven Publishing) Greenhaven Publishing LLC.

Graham, Amy. A Look at the Eighteenth & Twenty-First Amendments, 1 vol. 2008. (Constitution of the United States Ser.). (ENG., Illus.). 128p. (gr. 6-7). lib. bdg. 37.27 (978-1-59845-063-7(8), 7e12c82c-8173-4def-bda7-129f670df00c, MyReportLinks.com Bks.) Enslow Publishing, LLC.

Stoltman, Joan. Prohibition: Social Movement & Controversial Amendment, 1 vol. 2018. (American History Ser.). (ENG.). 104p. (gr. 7-7). 41.03 (978-1-5345-6412-1(8), 08226442-c5cc-4803-8338-0f5416d388d5, Lucent Pr.) Greenhaven Publishing LLC.

Worth, Richard. Prohibition: The Rise & Fall of the Temperance Movement. 2019. (J). pap. (978-1-9785-1539-0(1)) Enslow Publishing, LLC.

—Teetotalers & Saloon Smashers: The Temperance Movement & Prohibition, 1 vol. 2008. (America's Living History Ser.). (ENG., Illus.). 128p. (gr. 5-6). lib. bdg. 35.93 (978-0-7660-2908-8(5), d0e73a04-bdfd-491e-ac05-4eb1c8ec5e17) Enslow Publishing, LLC.

PROHIBITION—FICTION

George, McKelle. Speak Easy, Speak Love. 2017. (ENG.). 432p. (YA). (gr. 8). 17.99 (978-0-06-256092-6(1), Greenwillow Bks.) HarperCollins Pubs.

Larkin, Jillian. Diva. 2013. (Flappers Ser.: 3). (ENG.). 320p. (YA). (gr. 7). pap. 10.99 (978-0-385-74042-5(5), Ember) Random Hse. Children's Bks.

Lisle, Janet Taylor. Black Duck. 2007. (ENG.). 256p. (J). (gr. 5-18). 8.99 (978-0-14-240902-2(2), Puffin Books) Penguin Young Readers Group.

PROJECT APOLLO (U.S.)

Adamson, Thomas K. Apollo 11 Launches a New Era. 2018. (Events That Changed America Ser.). (ENG.). 32p. (J). (gr. 3-6). lib. bdg. 35.64 (978-1-5038-2517-8(5), 212324, MOMENTUM) Child's World, Inc, The.

—Apollo 11 Moon Landing: An Interactive Space Exploration Adventure. 2016. (You Choose: Space Ser.). (ENG., Illus.). 112p. (J). (gr. 3-7). lib. bdg. 32.65 (978-1-4914-8103-5(X), 130587, Capstone Pr.) Capstone.

—The First Moon Landing, 1 vol. Purcell, Gordon & Beatty, Terry, illus. 2006. (Graphic History Ser.). (ENG.). 32p. (J). (gr. 3-9). per. 8.10 (978-0-7368-9654-2(6), 93409) Capstone.

Aldrin, Buzz. Reaching for the Moon. Minor, Wendell, illus. (ENG.). 40p. (J). (gr. 1-4). 2008. 8.99 (978-0-06-055447-7(9)) 2005. 17.99 (978-0-06-055445-3(2)) HarperCollins Pubs. (HarperCollins).

—Reaching for the Moon. Minor, Wendell, illus. unabr. ed. 2005. (Picture Book Readalong Ser.). (gr. k-4). 28.95 incl. audio compact disk (978-1-59519-582-1(3)) Live Oak Media.

—To the Moon & Back: My Apollo 11 Adventure. 2018. (Illus.). 16p. (J). (gr. 3-7). 32.00 (978-1-4263-3249-4(1), National Geographic Kids) Disney Publishing Worldwide.

Anderson, Dale. The First Moon Landing, 1 vol. 2003. (Landmark Events in American History Ser.). (ENG., Illus.). 48p. (gr. 5-8). pap. 15.05 (978-0-8368-5406-0(3), 8331f41a-909d-4aac-b3ea-e6dc480dd8f7, Gareth Stevens Secondary Library) Stevens, Gareth Publishing LLLP.

Anderson, Dale & Hudson Goff, Elizabeth. The First Moon Landing, 1 vol. 2005. (Graphic Histories Ser.). (ENG., Illus.). 32p. (gr. 3-3). pap. 11.50 (978-0-8368-6255-3(4), 491167e5-ee10-48f6-ace4-7d028e5f1452) Stevens, Gareth Publishing LLLP.

—El Primer Alunizaje (the First Moon Landing), 1 vol. 2007. (Historias Gráficas (Graphic Histories) Ser.). (SPA., Illus.). 32p. (gr. 3-3). pap. 11.50 (978-0-8368-7904-9(X), 302c3f42-3b16-49b2-9303-b4d8f8170ff9); lib. bdg. 29.67 (978-0-8368-7897-4(3), 8703cb2d-af44-4bc5-a497-3658ee3652f6) Stevens, Gareth Publishing LLLP.

Apollo: Stepping Stones to the Moon. (Color & Learn Ser.). 36p. (J). (gr. 1-5). pap. (978-1-882210-14-5(X)) Action Publishing, Inc.

Bailey, Gerry & Foster, Karen. Armstrong's Moon Rock. Radford, Karen & Noyes, Leighton, illus. 2008. (Stories of Great People Ser.). (ENG.). 40p. (J). (gr. 3-8). lib. bdg. (978-0-7787-3684-4(9)); (gr. 5-8). pap. (978-0-7787-3706-3(3)) Crabtree Publishing Co.

Bodden, Valerie. Man Walks on the Moon. 2009. (Days of Change Ser.). 48p. (YA). (gr. 4-7). 22.95 (978-1-58341-735-5(4)) Creative Co., The.

—Man Walks on the Moon: Days of Change. 2015. (Odysseys in History Ser.). (ENG., Illus.). 80p. (J). (gr. 7-10). (978-1-60818-528-3(1), 20956, Creative Education) Creative Co., The.

—Man Walks on the Moon: Odysseys in History. 2016. (Odysseys in History Ser.). (ENG.). 80p. (J). (gr. 7-10). pap. 14.99 (978-1-62832-129-6(6), 20957, Creative Paperbacks) Creative Co., The.

—To the Moon. 2011. (Great Expeditions Ser.). (ENG., Illus.). 48p. (J). (gr. 5-8). 35.65 (978-1-60818-068-4(9), 22153, Creative Education); pap. 12.00 (978-0-89812-666-2(5), 22159, Creative Paperbacks) Creative Co., The.

Brindell Fradin, Dennis. The First Lunar Landing, 1 vol. 2010. (Turning Points in U. S. History Ser.). (ENG.). 48p. (gr. 4-4). 34.07 (978-0-7614-4256-1(1), 2a64a349-32a7-41c4-9b47-d4ecef34bf16) Cavendish Square Publishing LLC.

Brouwer, Sigmund. Moon Mission: The Epic 400-Year Journey to Apollo 11. 2019. (ENG., Illus.). 128p. (J). (gr. 7-11). 17.99 (978-1-5253-0036-3(9)) Kids Can Pr., Ltd. CAN. Dist: Hachette Bk. Group.

Brown, Don. Rocket to the Moon! Big Ideas That Changed the World #1. 2019. (Big Ideas That Changed the World Ser.). (ENG., Illus.). 136p. (J). (gr. 3-7). 14.99 (978-1-4197-3404-5(0), 1254701) Abrams, Inc.

Buckley, James, Jr. Michael Collins: Discovering History's Heroes. 2019. (Jeter Publishing Ser.). (ENG.). 160p. (J). (gr. 2-5). 18.99 *(978-1-5344-2480-7(6))*; (Illus.). pap. 7.99 *(978-1-5344-2479-1(2))* Simon & Schuster Children's Publishing. (Aladdin).

Burleigh, Robert. One Giant Leap. Wimmer, Mike, illus. 2014. 40p. (J). (gr. 1-3). 8.99 *(978-0-14-751165-2(8))*, Puffin Books) Penguin Young Readers Group.

Choi, John & McGowen, Tom. Reaching for the Moon: The Cold War Space Race. 2019. (J). *(978-1-9785-1530-7(8))* Enslow Publishing, LLC.

Close, Edward. Moon Missions, 1 vol., 1. 2014. (Discovery Education: Earth & Space Science Ser.). (ENG.). 32p. (gr. 4-5). 28.93 *(978-1-4777-6178-6(0)*, 3a958377-1ebb-4f7a-814b-0b9ad8ffa8bf, PowerKids Pr.) Rosen Publishing Group, Inc., The.

Dell, Pamela. Man on the Moon: How a Photograph Made Anything Seem Possible, 1 vol. 2010. (Captured History Ser.). (ENG.). 64p. (J). (gr. 5-7). pap. 8.95 *(978-0-7565-4447-8(5)*, 115528, Compass Point Bks.) Capstone.

Di Piazza, Domenica. Space Engineer & Scientist Margaret Hamilton. 2017. (STEM Trailblazer Bios Ser.). (ENG., Illus.). 32p. (J). (gr. 2-5). 26.65 *(978-1-5124-3450-7(7)*, 00361086-11f1-4e7d-80a7-8140621d385a, Lerner Pubns.) Lerner Publishing Group.

Dorling Kindersley Publishing Staff. Moon Landings: Level 3. 2019. (ENG., Illus.). 64p. (J). *(978-0-241-35853-5(1))* Dorling Kindersley Publishing, Inc.

Dunn, Joe. Moon Landing, 1 vol. Espinosa, Rod et al, illus. 2007. (Graphic History Ser.). (ENG.). 32p. (J). (gr. 3-8). 32.79 *(978-1-60270-078-9(8)*, 9042, Graphic Planet - Fiction) Magic Wagon.

Dyer, Alan. Mission to the Moon: (Book & DVD) 2009. (ENG., Illus.). 80p. (J). (gr. 3-7). 19.99 *(978-1-4169-7935-7(2)*, Simon & Schuster Bks. For Young Readers) Simon & Schuster Bks. For Young Readers.

Edge, Laura B. Apollo 13: A Successful Failure. 2020. (ENG., Illus.). 136p. (YA). (gr. 6-12). lib. bdg. 37.32 *(978-1-5415-5900-4(2)*, ac06a4cc-af4f-479a-91d1-7c354675f7e7, Twenty-First Century Bks.) Lerner Publishing Group.

Engdahl, Sylvia, ed. The Apollo 11 Moon Landing, 1 vol. 2011. (Perspectives on Modern World History Ser.). (ENG., Illus.). 224p. (gr. 10-12). 49.43 *(978-0-7377-5735-9(X)*, ddcbb0d3-d8df-4659-bfb5-3001aa465dee, Greenhaven Publishing) Greenhaven Publishing LLC.

Floca, Brian. Moonshot: The Flight of Apollo 11. Floca, Brian, illus. 2019. (ENG., Illus.). 56p. (J). (gr. -1-5). 19.99 *(978-1-5344-4030-2(5)*, Atheneum/Richard Jackson Bks.) Simon & Schuster Children's Publishing.

Friend, Robyn C. The Women of Apollo. Katz, David Arthur, illus. l.t. ed. 2006. 80p. (J). 17.95 *(978-1-880599-80-8(5))*; pap. 12.95 *(978-1-880599-79-2(1))* Cascade Pass, Inc.

Gall, Chris. Go for the Moon: A Rocket, a Boy, & the First Moon Landing. Gall, Chris, illus. 2019. (ENG., Illus.). 48p. (J). 19.99 *(978-1-250-15579-5(7)*, 900184774) Roaring Brook Pr.

Gladstone, James. Earthrise: Apollo 8 & the Photo That Changed the World. Lundy, Christy, illus. 2018. (ENG.). 32p. (J). (gr. 2-5). 16.95 *(978-1-77147-316-3(9))* Owlkids Bks. Inc. CAN. Dist: Publishers Group West (PGW).

Goldberg, Jan. James Lovell: The Rescue of Apollo 13, 1 vol. 2003. (Library of Astronaut Biographies Ser.). (ENG., Illus.). 112p. (gr. 5-8). lib. bdg. 39.80 *(978-0-8239-4459-0(X)*, cf5be92f-7a3b-418d-a041-bfde2da85369, Rosen Reference) Rosen Publishing Group, Inc., The.

Green, Carl R. Walking on the Moon: The Amazing APOLLO 11 Mission, 1 vol. 2012. (American Space Missions: Astronauts, Exploration, & Discovery Ser.). (ENG., Illus.). 48p. (gr. 5-7). 27.93 *(978-0-7660-4076-2(3)*, 74153f82-5742-4637-87b7-a4d7636392e5) Enslow Publishing, LLC.

Green, Jen. The Story of the Race to the Moon. Mark Bergin, illus. 2017. (Explorers Ser.). 32p. (gr. 3-6). 31.35 *(978-1-910706-92-3(2))* Book Hse. GBR. Dist: Black Rabbit Bks.

Hamilton, John. Project Apollo. 2018. (Space Race Ser.). (ENG., Illus.). 48p. (J). (gr. 5-9). lib. bdg. 34.21 *(978-1-5321-1831-9(7)*, 30538, Abdo & Daughters) ABDO Publishing Co.

Hasday, Judy L. The Apollo 13 Mission: Overcoming Adversity. 2006. (Illus.). 120p. (J). (gr. 4-8). reprint ed. 25.00 *(978-1-4223-5546-6(2))* DIANE Publishing Co.

Holden, Henry M. Danger in Space: Surviving the Apollo 13 Disaster, 1 vol. 2012. (American Space Missions: Astronauts, Exploration, & Discovery Ser.). (ENG., Illus.). 48p. (gr. 5-7). 27.93 *(978-0-7660-4072-4(0)*, b1131eae-0299-4004-a3b1-7739ee074086) Enslow Publishing, LLC.

Hubbard, Ben. Neil Armstrong & Traveling to the Moon. 2015. (Adventures in Space Ser.). (ENG., Illus.). 48p. (J). (gr. 4-6). 35.99 *(978-1-4846-2515-6(3)*, 130012, Heinemann) Capstone.

Irwin, James. Destination Moon. 15th anniv. ed. 2004. 52p. 16.00 *(978-1-929241-98-9(4))* Send The Light Distribution LLC.

Jazynka, Kitson. National Geographic Readers: Buzz Aldrin (L3) 2018. (Readers Ser.). (ENG., Illus.). 48p. (J). (gr. 3-7). lib. bdg. 14.90 *(978-1-4263-3207-4(6)*, National Geographic Kids) Disney Publishing Worldwide.

Jd, Duchess Harris & Ringstad, Arnold. The First Moon Landing. 2018. (Perspectives on American Progress Ser.). (ENG., Illus.). 48p. (J). (gr. 4-8). lib. bdg. 35.64 *(978-1-5321-1490-8(7)*, 29112) ABDO Publishing Co.

Jefferis, David. Exploring the Moon: 1969-1972. 2019. (Moon Flight Atlas Ser.). (Illus.). 32p. (J). (gr. 5-5). *(978-0-7787-5409-1(X))*; pap. *(978-0-7787-5418-3(9))* Crabtree Publishing Co.

—Project Apollo: the Race to Land on the Moon. 2019. (Moon Flight Atlas Ser.). (Illus.). 32p. (J). (gr. 5-5). *(978-0-7787-5410-7(3))*; pap. *(978-0-7787-5419-0(7))* Crabtree Publishing Co.

Johnson, Katherine. Reaching for the Moon: The Autobiography of NASA Mathematician Katherine Johnson. (ENG., Illus.). (J). (gr. 5). 2020. 272p. pap. 8.99 *(978-1-5344-4084-5(4))* 2019. 256p. 17.99 *(978-1-5344-4083-8(6))* Simon & Schuster Children's Publishing. (Atheneum Bks. for Young Readers).

Keppeler, Eric. Apollo 11 & the First Men on the Moon, 1 vol. 2018. (Real-Life Scientific Adventures Ser.). (ENG.). 32p. (gr. 4-5). 29.27 *(978-1-5081-6842-3(3)*, 75daa6bc-a2bd-4928-83f4-5a1c877e70f4, PowerKids Pr.) Rosen Publishing Group, Inc., The.

Kluger, Jeffrey & Shamir, Ruby. To the Moon! The True Story of the American Heroes on the Apollo 8 Spaceship. 2019. (Illus.). 304p. (J). (gr. 5). 9.99 *(978-1-5247-4103-7(5)*, Puffin Books) Penguin Young Readers Group.

Koestler-Grack, Rachel. Neil Armstrong, 1 vol. 2009. (People We Should Know (Second Series) Ser.). (ENG.). 48p. (J). (gr. 3-5). pap. 11.50 *(978-1-4339-2147-6(2)*, e4006eee-7361-4818-886b-857c8686683d); lib. bdg. 33.67 *(978-1-4339-1948-0(6)*, c5c0766e-8dda-41a3-b758-f5c155112e75) Stevens, Gareth Publishing LLLP. (Gareth Stevens Learning Library).

Lassieur, Allison. The Race to the Moon: An Interactive History Adventure, 1 vol. 2014. (You Choose: History Ser.). (ENG., Illus.). 112p. (J). (gr. 3-7). 32.65 *(978-1-4765-4185-3(X)*, 124290, Capstone Pr.) Capstone.

Loh-Hagan, Virginia. Apollo 13: Mission to the Moon. 2018. (True Survival Ser.). (ENG.). 32p. (J). (gr. 4-8). pap. 14.21 *(978-1-5341-0871-4(8)*, 210848); (Illus.). lib. bdg. 32.07 *(978-1-5341-0772-4(X)*, 210847) Cherry Lake Publishing. (45th Parallel Press).

Lovitt, Charles. My Little Golden Book about the First Moon Landing. Sims, Bryan, illus. 2019. (Little Golden Book Ser.). (ENG.). 24p. (J). (-k). 5.99 *(978-0-525-58007-2(7)*, Golden Bks.) Random Hse. Children's Bks.

Malam, John. Man Walks on the Moon. 2003. (Dates with History Ser.). 45p. (J). lib. bdg. 28.50 *(978-1-58340-407-2(4))* Black Rabbit Bks.

McPherson, Stephanie Sammartino. The First Men on the Moon. 2009. (History Maker Biographies Ser.). (ENG.). 48p. (gr. 3-6). 27.93 *(978-0-7613-4949-5(9)*, Lerner Pubns.) Lerner Publishing Group.

McReynolds, Linda. Eight Days Gone. O'Rourke, Ryan, illus. 2019. 28p. (J). (— 1). bds. 8.99 *(978-1-57091-024-1(3))* Charlesbridge Publishing, Inc.

Mitchell, Edgar & Mahoney, Ellen. Earthrise: My Adventures As an Apollo 14 Astronaut. 2014. (ENG., Illus.). 192p. (YA). (gr. 7). 19.95 *(978-1-61374-901-2(5))* Chicago Review Pr., Inc.

Nagelhout, Ryan. The First Moon Walk, 1 vol. 2014. (Incredible True Adventures Ser.). (ENG.). 32p. (J). (gr. 3-4). pap. 11.50 *(978-1-4824-2038-8(4)*, 3c771659-10cf-426c-baae-192665f12123) Stevens, Gareth Publishing LLLP.

—Neil Armstrong in His Own Words, 1 vol. 2015. (Eyewitness to History Ser.). (ENG., Illus.). 32p. (J). (gr. 4-5). pap. 11.50 *(978-1-4824-4078-2(4)*, e99a42bf-4083-426c-a3dd-dfa2fc1e89f5) Stevens, Gareth Publishing LLLP.

Olson, Elsie. Breakthroughs in Moon Exploration. 2019. (Cosmos Chronicles (Alternator Books (r)) Ser.). (ENG., Illus.). 32p. (J). (gr. 3-6). pap. 10.99 *(978-1-5415-7369-7(2)*, 5ff50d8f-8878-4f7d-ab5d-e8341f177e7e); lib. bdg. 29.32 *(978-1-5415-5596-9(1)*, 49e56b8f-bdaa-4a09-9ea0-63920cff5d63) Lerner Publishing Group. (Lerner Pubns.).

Ottaviani, Jim. T-Minus: The Race to the Moon. Cannon, Zander & Cannon, Kevin, illus. 2009. (ENG.). 128p. (J). (gr. 3-7). pap. 19.99 *(978-1-4169-4960-2(7)*, Aladdin) Simon & Schuster Children's Publishing.

Oxlade, Chris & West, David. The Apollo Missions & Other Adventures in Space, 1 vol. 2011. (Incredible True Adventures Ser.). (ENG., Illus.). 48p. (YA). (gr. 5-5). pap. 12.75 *(978-1-4488-6664-9(2)*, ae16a48b-3a24-4c61-977a-04d14674e3ce); lib. bdg. 34.47 *(978-1-4488-6660-1(X)*, 607a5fbc-cf3d-4888-9f7a-20ba7795eddf) Rosen Publishing Group, Inc., The. (Rosen Reference).

Petruccio, Steven James. Apollo 11: First Men on the Moon Coloring Book. 2019. (Dover Space Coloring Bks.). (ENG.). 32p. (J). (gr. 3-6). pap. 4.99 *(978-0-486-83494-8(8)*, 834948) Dover Pubns., Inc.

Pohlen, Jerome. The Apollo Missions for Kids: The People & Engineering Behind the Race to the Moon, with 21 Activities. 2019. (For Kids Ser.: 71). (Illus.). 160p. (J). (gr. 4). pap. 18.99 *(978-0-912777-17-7(6))* Chicago Review Pr., Inc.

Radomski, Kassandra. The Apollo 13 Mission: Core Events of a Crisis in Space, 1 vol. 2014. (What Went Wrong? Ser.). (ENG., Illus.). 32p. (J). (gr. 3-6). pap. 7.95 *(978-1-4765-5130-2(8)*, 124448, Capstone Pr.) Capstone.

Richards, Patti. The Apollo Missions. 2018. (Destination Space Ser.). (ENG., Illus.). 48p. (J). (gr. 5-6). pap. 11.95 *(978-1-63517-565-3(8)*, 1635175658); lib. bdg. 34.21 *(978-1-63517-493-9(7)*, 1635174937) North Star Editions. (Focus Readers).

—The Apollo Missions. 2018. (Illus.). 48p. (J). pap. *(978-1-4896-9831-5(0)*, AV2 by Weigl) Weigl Pubs., Inc.

Riley, Christopher & Dolling, Phil. Inside Apollo 11, 1 vol. 2017. (Geek's Guide to Space Ser.). (ENG.). 192p. (J). (gr. 9-9). 46.27 *(978-1-4994-6696-6(X)*, 079cca55-62a2-4f68-89b2-60cd0402a04b, Rosen Young Adult) Rosen Publishing Group, Inc., The.

Riley, Christopher & Woods, David. Inside the Lunar Rover, 1 vol. 2017. (Geek's Guide to Space Ser.). (ENG., Illus.). 192p. (J). (gr. 9-9). 46.27 *(978-1-4994-6699-7(4)*, 8a368130-3c2c-4591-b07c-2d9629856238, Rosen Young Adult) Rosen Publishing Group, Inc., The.

Rissman, Rebecca. Houston, We've Had a Problem: The Story of the Apollo 13 Disaster. 2018. (Tangled History Ser.). (ENG.). 112p. (J). (gr. 3-9). pap. 6.95 *(978-1-5157-7964-3(5)*, 136044); lib. bdg. 32.65 *(978-1-5157-7940-7(8)*, 136036) Capstone. (Capstone Pr.).

Robbins, Dean. The Astronaut Who Painted the Moon: the True Story of Alan Bean. Rubin, Sean, illus. 2019. (ENG.). 40p. (J). (gr. -1-3). 17.99 *(978-1-338-25953-7(9)*, Orchard Bks.) Scholastic, Inc.

—Margaret & the Moon. Knisley, Lucy, illus. 2017. 40p. (J). (gr. -1-3). 18.99 *(978-0-399-55185-7(9)*, Knopf Bks. for Young Readers) Random Hse. Children's Bks.

Rocco, John. How We Got to the Moon: The People, Technology, & Daring Feats of Science Behind Humanity's Greatest Adventure. 2020. (Illus.). 264p. (J). (gr. 5). 29.99 *(978-0-525-64741-6(4)*, Crown Books For Young Readers) Random Hse. Children's Bks.

Sandler, Martin W. Apollo 8: The Mission That Changed Everything. 2018. (ENG., Illus.). 176p. (J). (gr. 5). 24.99 *(978-0-7636-9489-0(4))* Candlewick Pr.

Schyffert, Bea Uusma. The Man Who Went to the Far Side of the Moon: The Story of Apollo 11 Astronaut Michael Collins. 2003. (ENG., Illus.). 80p. (J). (gr. -1-7). 16.99 *(978-0-8118-4007-1(7))* Chronicle Bks. LLC.

—The Man Who Went to the Far Side of the Moon: The Story of Apollo 11 Astronaut Michael Collins (NASA Books, Apollo 11 Book for Kids, Children's Astronaut Books) 2019. (ENG.). 80p. (J). (gr. 3-7). pap. 12.99 *(978-1-4521-8023-6(7))* Chronicle Bks. LLC.

Sipe, Nicole. The History of the First Moon Landing. 2018. (Mathematics in the Real World Ser.). (ENG., Illus.). 32p. (J). (gr. 4-8). pap. 11.99 *(978-1-4258-5822-3(8))* Teacher Created Materials, Inc.

Slade, Suzanne. Countdown: 2979 Days to the Moon. Gonzalez, Thomas, illus. 2018. 144p. (J). (gr. 5-9). 22.95 *(978-1-68263-013-6(7))* Peachtree Publishing Co. Inc.

—Daring Dozen: The Twelve Who Walked on the Moon. Marks, Alan, illus. 2019. 48p. (J). (gr. k-4). lib. bdg. 17.99 *(978-1-58089-773-0(8))* Charlesbridge Publishing, Inc.

Smibert, Angie. 12 Incredible Facts about the First Moon Landing. 2016. (Turning Points in US History Ser.). (ENG., Illus.). 32p. (J). (gr. 3-5). 32.80 *(978-1-63235-130-2(7)*, 12-Story Library) Bookstaves, LLC.

Stone, Adam. The Apollo 13 Mission. 2014. (Disaster Stories Ser.). (ENG., Illus.). 24p. (J). (gr. 3-8). 29.95 *(978-1-62617-149-7(1)*, Black Sheep) Bellwether Media.

Tan, Sheri. Handshake in Space: The Apollo-Soyuz Test Project. Bond, Higgins, illus. 2009. 32p. (J). (gr. 1-5). pap. 9.95 incl. audio *(978-1-60727-104-8(4))*; (ENG.). 9.95 *(978-1-60727-115-4(X))*; (ENG.). 17.95 *(978-1-60727-114-7(1))*; pap. 9.95 incl. reel tape *(978-1-59249-203-9(7))* Soundprints.

Thimmesh, Catherine. Team Moon: How 400,000 People Landed Apollo 11 on the Moon. 2006. (ENG., Illus.). 80p. (J). (gr. 5-7). 19.95 *(978-0-618-50757-3(4)*, 510514, Clarion Bks.) HarperCollins Pubs.

Troupe, Thomas Kingsley. Apollo's First Moon Landing: A Fly on the Wall History. Tejido, Jomike, illus. 2018. (Fly on the Wall History Ser.). (ENG.). 32p. (J). (gr. 1-3). lib. bdg. 27.99 *(978-1-5158-1598-3(6)*, 136251, Picture Window Bks.) Capstone.

Tunby, Benjamin. Surviving a Space Disaster: Apollo 13. 2019. (They Survived (Alternator Books (r)) Ser.). (ENG., Illus.). 32p. (J). (gr. 3-6). 29.32 *(978-1-5415-2350-0(4)*, ab165ec4-a23d-4f4c-889b-fa9cfccea128, Lerner Pubns.) Lerner Publishing Group.

Turner, Myra Faye. Events That Changed the Course of History: The Story of Apollo 11 & the Men on the Moon 50 Years Later. Lieneman, Danielle, ed. 2018. (ENG.). 208p. (YA). pap. 19.95 *(978-1-62023-527-0(7)*, 5be831af-1e65-4060-9f68-0aceed51edae) Atlantic Publishing Group, Inc.

—The Story of Apollo 11 & the Men on the Moon 50 Years Later. 2018. (J). lib. bdg. *(978-1-62023-528-7(5))* Atlantic Publishing Group, Inc.

Weakland, Mark. When Neil Armstrong Built a Wind Tunnel. Lozano, Luciano, illus. 2017. (Leaders Doing Headstands Ser.). (ENG.). 32p. (J). (gr. 1-4). lib. bdg. 28.65 *(978-1-5158-1575-4(7)*, 136245, Picture Window Bks.) Capstone.

Wilkinson, Philip. Spacebusters. 2012. (DK Reader Level 3 Ser.). lib. bdg. 13.55 *(978-0-606-26544-7(9))* Turtleback.

—Spacebusters: The Race to the Moon. 2012. (DK Readers Level 3 Ser.). (ENG.). 48p. (J). (gr. 1-3). 16.19 *(978-0-7566-9085-4(4))* Dorling Kindersley Publishing, Inc.

Woolf, Alex. Trailblazers: Neil Armstrong: First Man on the Moon. 2019. (Trailblazers Ser.). (ENG., Illus.). 192p. (J). (gr. 3-7). 7.99 *(978-0-593-12401-7(4)*, Random Hse. Bks. for Young Readers) Random Hse. Children's Bks.

Yomtov, Nel. The Apollo 11 Moon Landing: July 20 1969, 1 vol. Chiu, Andrew, illus. 2014. (24-Hour History Ser.). (ENG.). 48p. (J). (gr. 3-9). pap. 8.95 *(978-1-4329-9298-9(8)*, 124614); lib. bdg. 33.99 *(978-1-4329-9292-7(9)*, 124609) Capstone. (Heinemann).

Zelon, Helen. The Apollo 13 Mission: Surviving an Explosion in Space. 2009. (Space Missions Ser.). 24p. (gr. 3-4). 42.50 *(978-1-60853-116-5(3)*, PowerKids Pr.) Rosen Publishing Group, Inc., The.

Zemlicka, Shannon. Neil Armstrong. 2003. (History Maker Bios Ser.). (Illus.). 48p. (J). (gr. 2-4). 26.60 *(978-0-8225-0395-8(6)*, Lerner Pubns.) Lerner Publishing Group.

Zoehfeld, Kathleen Weidner. Apollo 13 (Totally True Adventures) How Three Brave Astronauts Survived a Space Disaster. Lowe, Wesley, illus. 2015. (Totally True Adventures Ser.). 112p. (J). (gr. 2-5). pap. 6.99 *(978-0-385-39125-2(0)*, Random Hse. Bks. for Young Readers) Random Hse. Children's Bks.

PROJECT APOLLO (U.S.)—FICTION

Baratz-Logsted, Lauren. I Love You, Michael Collins. 2019. (Penworthy Picks Middle School Ser.). (ENG.). 230p. (J). (gr. 4-5). 19.49 *(978-1-64310-918-3(9))* Penworthy Co., LLC, The.

—I Love You, Michael Collins. 2018. (ENG.). 240p. (J). pap. 8.99 *(978-1-250-15845-1(1)*, 900158161) Square Fish.

—I Love You, Michael Collins. 2018. (J). lib. bdg. 18.40 *(978-0-606-41098-4(8))* Turtleback.

Marazano, Richard. The Sons of Ares, 2 vols. Ponzio, Jean-Michel, illus. 2009. (Chimpanzee Complex Ser.: 1). 56p. pap. 13.95 *(978-1-84918-002-3(4))* CineBook GBR. Dist: National Bk. Network.

PROJECT GEMINI (U.S.)

Green, Carl R. Spacewalk: The Astounding Gemini 4 Mission, 1 vol. 2012. (American Space Missions: Astronauts, Exploration, & Discovery Ser.). (ENG., Illus.). 48p. (gr. 5-7). 27.93 *(978-0-7660-4075-5(5)*, 44a3c810-eb1e-47ba-b4d2-b7bf066c1851) Enslow Publishing, LLC.

Hamilton, John. Project Gemini. 2018. (Space Race Ser.). (ENG., Illus.). 48p. (J). (gr. 5-9). lib. bdg. 34.21 *(978-1-5321-1832-6(5)*, 30540, Abdo & Daughters) ABDO Publishing Co.

Zelon, Helen. The Gemini IV Mission: The First American Space Walk. 2009. (Space Missions Ser.). 24p. (gr. 3-4). 42.50 *(978-1-60853-119-6(8)*, PowerKids Pr.) Rosen Publishing Group, Inc., The.

PROJECT MERCURY (U.S.)

Ashby, Ruth. Rocket Man: The Mercury Adventure of John Glenn, 1 vol. 2019. (Illus.). 124p. (J). (gr. 2-5). pap. 7.95 *(978-1-68263-104-1(4))* Peachtree Publishing Co. Inc.

Hamilton, John. Project Mercury. 2018. (Space Race Ser.). (ENG., Illus.). 48p. (J). (gr. 5-9). lib. bdg. 34.21 *(978-1-5321-1833-3(3)*, 30542, Abdo & Daughters) ABDO Publishing Co.

Myrus, Donald. Keeping up with the Astronauts: The Story of Man's Greatest Adventures in Outer Space Including the John Glenn & Scott Carpenter Flights. 2011. 92p. 38.95 *(978-1-258-10348-4(6))* Literary Licensing, LLC.

Pierce, Philip N. & Schuon, Karl. John H Glenn, Astronaut. 2011. 234p. 46.95 *(978-1-258-00503-0(4))* Literary Licensing, LLC.

Stone, Tanya Lee. Almost Astronauts: 13 Women Who Dared to Dream. 2009. (ENG., Illus.). 144p. (J). (gr. 5). 24.99 *(978-0-7636-3611-1(8))* Candlewick Pr.

Zelon, Helen. The Mercury 6 Mission: The First American Astronaut to Orbit Earth. 2009. (Space Missions Ser.). 24p. (gr. 3-4). 42.50 *(978-1-60853-120-2(1)*, PowerKids Pr.) Rosen Publishing Group, Inc., The.

PROJECT METHOD IN TEACHING

Dykstra, Danell. Exploring Design Investigations Through Science Research Projects, 1 vol. 2018. (Project-Based Learning in Science Ser.). (ENG.). 64p. (gr. 5-5). pap. 14.53 *(978-1-5081-8593-2(X)*, 393e39d6-d3a0-465f-92a2-c437b8e988a6, Rosen Reference) Rosen Publishing Group, Inc., The.

Kahn, William A. The Student's Guide to Successful Project Teams. 2008. (ENG., Illus.). 256p. (C). 72.95 *(978-1-84169-893-9(8)*, RT8938X) Routledge.

Lew, Kristi. Exploring Secondary Research Investigations Through Science Research Projects, 1 vol. 2018. (Project-Based Learning in Science Ser.). (ENG.). 64p. (gr. 5-5). pap. 14.53 *(978-1-5081-8480-5(1)*, b51ce62d-6046-4bcb-9671-b0ab3d9aefae, Rosen Reference) Rosen Publishing Group, Inc., The.

PRONGHORN ANTELOPE

Jackson, Tom. Pronghorns. 2008. (Illus.). 52p. (J). *(978-0-7172-6279-3(0))* Grolier, Ltd.

Lunis, Natalie. Pronghorn: Long-Distance Runner! 2010. (Blink of an Eye: Superfast Animals Ser.). 24p. (J). (gr. k-3). lib. bdg. 26.99 *(978-1-936087-94-5(4))* Bearport Publishing Co., Inc.

PROPAGANDA

see also Advertising

Connolly, Sean. Political Messages & Propaganda. 2010. (J). 34.25 *(978-1-59920-349-2(9))* Black Rabbit Bks.

Doeden, Matt. What Is Propaganda? 2019. (Searchlight Books (tm) — Fake News Ser.). (ENG., Illus.). 32p. (J). (gr. 3-5). lib. bdg. 30.65 *(978-1-5415-5576-1(7)*, 35676cfb-1dee-453e-97c7-98bfe2fe8764, Lerner Pubns.) Lerner Publishing Group.

Micklos, Jr., Jr. Understanding Propaganda. 2018. (Cracking the Media Literacy Code Ser.). (ENG., Illus.). 32p. (J). (gr. 3-6). lib. bdg. 27.99 *(978-1-5435-2705-6(1)*, 138141, Capstone Pr.) Capstone.

Roscoe, Kelly & Roberts, Jeremy. Joseph Goebbels, 1 vol., 1. 2015. (Holocaust Ser.). (ENG., Illus.). 112p. (J). (gr. 7-7). 38.80 *(978-1-5081-7049-5(5)*, 7bbb562f-efcc-4ee2-aabe-bb1578e59cdc, Rosen Young Adult) Rosen Publishing Group, Inc., The.

Shoup, Kate. Nazi Propaganda: Jews in Hitler's Germany, 1 vol. 2016. (Public Persecutions Ser.). (ENG., Illus.). 128p. (J). (gr. 9-9). 47.36 *(978-1-5026-2321-6(8)*, a16e22a3-9ffb-4141-bf8d-6feb6fd658b2) Cavendish Square Publishing LLC.

Young-Brown, Fiona. Fake News & Propaganda, 1 vol. 2019. (Dilemmas in Democracy Ser.). (ENG.). 80p. (gr. 7-7). lib. bdg. 37.36 *(978-1-5026-4496-1(7)*, 503f51af-4eec-46c1-b592-48b06910424f) Cavendish Square Publishing LLC.

PROPAGATION OF PLANTS

see Plant Propagation

PROPHETS

Adil, Hajjah Amina & Sperling, Karima. My Little Lore of Light: A Child's Version of Lore of Light. 2005. (Illus.). x, 193p. (J). 22.00 *(978-1-930409-35-4(4))* Islamic Supreme Council of America.

Bible Visuals International Staff, comment. Prophets to God's People Vol. 24: Old Testament. 2006. (Illus.). (J). pap. *(978-1-932381-84-9(8)*, 2024) Bible Visuals International, Inc.

Bible Visuals International Staff, compiled by. Prophets of the Messiah Vol. 32: Old Testament. 2006. (Illus.). (J). pap. *(978-1-932381-91-7(0)*, 2032) Bible Visuals International, Inc.

Burrill, Richard L. My Sweet Lord: The Life-Stories of Muhammad & the Five God-Men of History. 2005. (YA). (gr. 9-12). pap. 19.95 *(978-1-878464-53-8(1))* Anthro Co., The.

Demi. Muhammad. Demi, illus. 2003. (ENG., Illus.). 48p. (J). (gr. 2-5). 24.99 *(978-0-689-85264-0(9)*, McElderry, Margaret K. Bks.) McElderry, Margaret K. Bks.

Gibby, Shauna. Follow the Prophet: A Flashlight Discovery Book. Beech, Bryan, illus. 2019. (J). 16.99 *(978-1-62972-576-5(5))* Deseret Bk. Co.

Krull, Kathleen. They Saw the Future: Oracles, Psychics, Scientists, Great Thinkers, & Pretty Good Guessers. Brooker, Kyrsten, illus. 2014. (ENG.). 112p. (J). (gr. -1-3). pap. 45.99 *(978-1-4814-3623-6(6)*, Atheneum Bks. for Young Readers) Simon & Schuster Children's Publishing.

Stefoff, Rebecca. Prophets & Prophecy, 1 vol. 2008. (Secrets of the Unexplained Ser.). (ENG., Illus.). 96p. (gr. 6-6). lib. bdg. 36.93 *(978-0-7614-2638-7(8)*, f73a53c0-30df-47ce-82f6-1ec895847c7b) Cavendish Square Publishing LLC.

Taib, Saadah. Prophet Adam & Wicked Iblis Activity Book. Rosli, Shazana, illus. 2019. (Prophets of Islam Activity Bks.). (ENG.). 16p. (J). pap. 3.95 *(978-0-86037-639-2(7))* Kube Publishing Ltd. GBR. Dist: Consortium Bk. Sales & Distribution.

—Prophet Ibrahim & the Little Bird Activity Book. Rosli, Shazana, illus. 2020. (Prophets of Islam Activity Bks.). 16p. (J). pap. 3.95 *(978-0-86037-740-5(7))* Kube Publishing Ltd. GBR. Dist: Consortium Bk. Sales & Distribution.
—Prophet Ismail & the ZamZam Well Activity Book. Rosli, Shazana, illus. 2020. (Prophets of Islam Activity Bks.). 16p. (J). pap. 3.95 *(978-0-86037-745-0(8))* Kube Publishing Ltd. GBR. Dist: Consortium Bk. Sales & Distribution.
Van Der Veer, Andrew. Bible Lessons for Juniors, Book 2: Kings & Prophets. 2007. 88p. (J). 6.00 *(978-1-60178-013-3(3))* Reformation Heritage Bks.
Wallis, Mary Alice & Lindstrom, C. G. Prophets & Apostles. 2008. (LDS Puzzle Pals Ser.). 122p. pap. 14.99 *(978-1-59955-126-5(8)*, Cedar Fort, Inc.) Cedar Fort, Inc./CFI Distribution.

PROSODY
see Versification

PROTECTION OF ANIMALS
see Animals—Treatment

PROTECTION OF BIRDS
see Birds—Protection

PROTECTION OF CHILDREN
see Child Welfare

PROTECTION OF ENVIRONMENT
see Environmental Protection

PROTECTION OF GAME
see Game Protection

PROTECTION OF NATURAL SCENERY
see Natural Monuments

PROTECTION OF WILDLIFE
see Wildlife Conservation

PROTESTANT REFORMATION
see Reformation

PROTOZOA

Graham, Ian. Microscopic Scary Creatures. 2009. (Scary Creatures Ser.). (ENG., Illus.). 32p. (J). (gr. 3-5). 27.00 *(978-0-531-21673-6(X)*, Children's Pr.) Scholastic Library Publishing.
Hollar, Sherman. A Closer Look at Bacteria, Algae, & Protozoa, 1 vol. 2011. (Introduction to Biology Ser.). (ENG., Illus.). 88p. (J). (gr. 8-8). lib. bdg. 35.29 *(978-1-61530-534-6(3)*, 8e218640-6333-429a-b2bc-478f4bae9e41) Rosen Publishing Group, Inc., The.

PROVERBS

Alvarez O'Neill, Juan, illus. Grano a grano... Refranes Populares. 2005. (SPA.). (J). 8.95 *(978-0-8477-1554-1(X))* Univ. of Puerto Rico Pr.
Brennan-Nelson, Denise. My Daddy Likes to Say. Donovan, Jane Monroe, illus. 2009. (Likes to Say Ser.). (ENG.). 32p. (J). (gr. 1-4). 15.95 *(978-1-58536-432-9(0)*, 202162) Sleeping Bear Pr.
—My Grandma Likes to Say. Donovan, Jane Monroe, illus. rev. ed. 2007. (Likes to Say Ser.). (ENG.). 32p. (J). (gr. 1-4). 16.95 *(978-1-58536-284-4(0)*, 202095) Sleeping Bear Pr.
The Christian Student Compass: KJV Monthly Version with Book of Proverbs. 2003. (YA). spiral bd. *(978-0-9725804-2-7(5))* Salt Pubs.
Davis, Mary J. My Wisdom Journal: A Discovering of Proverbs for Kids. 2004. (Journals Just for Kids Ser.). (Illus.). 160p. (J). (gr. 4-7). pap. 9.99 *(978-1-885358-73-8(3)*, Legacy Pr.) Rainbow Pubs. & Legacy Pr.
Dent, Sabrina. Proverbs Kids Fun Activity Book. 2006. (Illus.). 40p. (J). 5.99 *(978-0-9796148-0-4(5))* Joint Heir Multimedia.
Fyne, Olga M. You Can't Teach an Old Dog New Tricks Because. 2010. (Illus.). 26p. pap. 9.99 *(978-1-935105-66-4(3))* Avid Readers Publishing Group.
Gonzalez, Ralfka & Ruiz, Ana, illus. My First Book of Proverbs: Mi Primer Libro de Dichos, 1 vol. 2014. (ENG.). 32p. (J). (gr. k-6). pap. 11.95 *(978-0-89239-200-1(2)*, leelowcbp) Lee & Low Bks., Inc.
Herrera, J. Ignacio. 125 Refranes Infantiles. Torcida, Maria Luisa, illus. (SPA.). (J). (gr. 3-5). 12.76 *(978-84-305-9180-0(X)*, SU6580) Susaeta Ediciones, S.A. ESP. Dist: Lectorum Pubns., Inc.
Johnson, Robin. Understanding Sayings. 2015. (Figuratively Speaking Ser.). (ENG., Illus.). 32p. (J). (gr. 4-4). *(978-0-7787-1778-2(X))* Crabtree Publishing Co.
Levin, Jack E. Proverbs for Young People. Levin, Jack E., illus. 2015. (ENG., Illus.). 72p. (J). (gr. -1-3). 18.99 *(978-1-4814-5945-7(7)*, Aladdin) Simon & Schuster Children's Publishing.
Libal, Autumn. Folk Proverbs & Riddles. 2004. (North American Folklore Ser.). (Illus.). 112p. (YA). (gr. 7-18). lib. bdg. 22.95 *(978-1-59084-343-7(6))* Mason Crest.
MacKenzie, Carine. Wise Words to Follow: Words of Wisdom from the Book of Proverbs. rev. ed. 2009. (ENG., Illus.). 24p. (J). 7.99 *(978-1-84550-430-4(5)*, 5a2b129d-1bbe-49b9-bc44-45cbe88cf90e) Christian Focus Pubns. GBR. Dist: Baker & Taylor Publisher Services (BTPS).
—Wise Words to Obey: Words of Wisdom from the Book of Proverbs. rev. ed. 2009. (ENG., Illus.). 24p. (J). 7.99 *(978-1-84550-431-1(3)*, 645c0f6d-a0d3-4451-aa2c-be06d8228e1a) Christian Focus Pubns. GBR. Dist: Baker & Taylor Publisher Services (BTPS).
—Wise Words to Trust: Words of Wisdom from the Book of Proverbs. rev. ed. 2009. (ENG., Illus.). 24p. (J). 7.99 *(978-1-84550-432-8(1)*, 65d144da-aaf2-4e86-8dbc-9a02d9c85230) Christian Focus Pubns. GBR. Dist: Baker & Taylor Publisher Services (BTPS).
Miller, Ann. Proverbs, Prayers, Poems for Children & Teens. 2005. (J). lib. bdg. 14.95 *(978-0-9748165-1-7(5))* Jayli Publishing Co.
Santana, Sr. Sabina Stella. Happy Ending Children's Stories, & More: Poems, Tongue-Twisters, Proverbs, & Brain-Teasers. 2008. 64p. pap. 13.50 *(978-1-4303-1344-1(7))* Lulu Pr., Inc.
Snedeker, Gus. An Apple a Day: Folk Proverbs & Riddles. 2013. (Illus.). 48p. (J). pap. *(978-1-4222-2504-2(6))* Mason Crest.
—An Apple a Day: Folk Proverbs & Riddles. Jabbour, Alan, ed. 2012. (North American Folklore for Youth Ser.). (Illus.). 48p. (J). (gr. 4). 19.95 *(978-1-4222-2493-9(7))* Mason Crest.
Snook, Randy, photos by. Many Ideas Open the Way: A Collection of Hmong Proverbs. 2003. (Illus.). 32p. (J). 16.95 *(978-1-885008-23-7(6)*, Shen's Bks.) Lee & Low Bks., Inc.
Walters, Eric, compiled by. From the Heart of Africa: A Book of Wisdom. 2018. (Illus.). 40p. (J). (gr. 1-4). 17.99 *(978-1-77049-719-1(6)*, Tundra Bks.) Tundra Bks. CAN. Dist: Penguin Random Hse. LLC.
Yoon, JooHee. Up down Inside Out. 2019. (Illus.). 64p. (J). 18.95 *(978-1-59270-280-0(5))* Enchanted Lion Bks., LLC.
365 Days of Wonder: Mr. Browne's Book of Precepts. 2014. (Wonder Ser.). (ENG.). 432p. (J). (gr. 3-7). 14.99 *(978-0-553-49904-9(1)*, Knopf Bks. for Young Readers) Random Hse. Children's Bks.

PRUSSIA (GERMANY)

Heuston, Kimberley. Otto von Bismarck: Iron Chancellor of Germany. (Wicked History Ser.). (ENG., Illus.). (YA). 2010. 128p. (gr. 6-12). pap. 5.95 *(978-0-531-22824-1(X)*, Watts, Franklin) 2009. 224p. (gr. 5-9). 31.00 *(978-0-531-21278-3(5))* Scholastic Library Publishing.

PRYDAIN (IMAGINARY PLACE)—FICTION

Alexander, Lloyd. The Black Cauldron. 2006. (Chronicles of Prydain: Bk. 2). (Illus.). 182p. (gr. 3-7). 17.00 *(978-0-7569-6813-7(5))* Perfection Learning Corp.
—The Black Cauldron. 2004. (Chronicles of Prydain: Bk. 2). 240p. (J). (gr. 4-7). pap. 38.00 incl. audio *(978-1-4000-8636-8(1)*, Listening Library) Random Hse. Audio Publishing Group.
—The Castle of Llyr. 2004. (Chronicles of Prydain: Bk. 3). 208p. (J). (gr. 4-7). pap. 36.00 incl. audio *(978-1-4000-9019-8(9)*, Listening Library) Random Hse. Audio Publishing Group.
—The High King. 2006. (Chronicles of Prydain: Bk. 5). (Illus.). 253p. (gr. 3-7). 17.00 *(978-0-7569-6816-8(X))* Perfection Learning Corp.

PSALMODY
see Church Music; Hymns

PSYCHIATRISTS—FICTION

Henry, April. Shock Point. 2008. 192p. (YA). (gr. 7-18). 9.99 *(978-0-14-241240-4(6)*, Speak) Penguin Young Readers Group.
London, Jonathan. Here Comes Doctor Hippo: A Little Hippo Story. Eduar, Gilles, illus. 2013. (Little Hippo Story Ser.). (ENG.). 32p. (J). (gr. -1-k). pap. 6.95 *(978-1-62091-595-0(2)*, Astra Young Readers) Astra Publishing Hse.
Miller, Mary Beth. Aimee. 2004. (Illus.). 288p. (YA). (gr. 7-18). 8.99 *(978-0-14-240025-8(4)*, Speak) Penguin Young Readers Group.
Wells, Helen. Cherry Ames at Hilton Hospital: Book 13. 2007. (Cherry Ames Nurse Stories Ser.). 200p. (J). (gr. 3-7). 14.95 *(978-0-8261-0421-2(5))* Springer Publishing Co., Inc.

PSYCHIATRY
see also Psychotherapy

Brinkerhoff, Shirley. Drug Therapy & Obsessive-Compulsive Disorders. 2004. (Encyclopedia of Psychiatric Drugs & Their Disorders Ser.). (Illus.). 128p. (YA). lib. bdg. 24.95 *(978-1-59084-569-1(2))* Mason Crest.
—Drug Therapy & Schizophrenia. 2004. (Encyclopedia of Psychiatric Drugs & Their Disorders Ser.). (Illus.). 128p. (YA). lib. bdg. 24.95 *(978-1-59084-574-5(9))* Mason Crest.
Docalavich, Heather. The Future of Antidepressants: The New Wave of Research. 2008. (Antidepressants Ser.). (Illus.). 104p. (YA). (gr. 7-18). lib. bdg. 24.95 *(978-1-4222-0103-9(1))* Mason Crest.
Esherick, Joan. The FDA & Psychiatric Drugs: How a Drug Is Approved. 2004. (Encyclopedia of Psychiatric Drugs & Their Disorders Ser.). (Illus.). 128p. (YA). lib. bdg. 24.95 *(978-1-59084-578-3(1))* Mason Crest.
Libal, Autumn. Drug Therapy & Dissociative Disorders. 2004. (Encyclopedia of Psychiatric Drugs & Their Disorders Ser.). (Illus.). 128p. (YA). lib. bdg. 24.95 *(978-1-59084-564-6(1))* Mason Crest.
—Drug Therapy & Impulse Control Disorders. 2004. (Encyclopedia of Psychiatric Drugs & Their Disorders Ser.). (Illus.). 128p. (YA). lib. bdg. 24.95 *(978-1-59084-566-0(8))* Mason Crest.
Libal, Joyce. Drug Therapy & Mental Disorders Due to a Medical Condition. 2003. (Psychiatric Disorders: Drugs & Psychology for the Mind & Bod Ser.). (Illus.). 126p. (YA). (gr. 8-12). pap. 14.95 *(978-1-4222-0391-0(3))* Mason Crest.
—Drug Therapy for Mental Disorders Caused by a Medical Condition. 2004. (Encyclopedia of Psychiatric Drugs & Their Disorders Ser.). (Illus.). 128p. (J). lib. bdg. 24.95 *(978-1-59084-567-7(6))* Mason Crest.
Parks, Peggy J. Childhood Trauma. 2019. (Emerging Issues in Public Health Ser.). (ENG.). 80p. (J). (gr. 6-12). 41.27 *(978-1-68282-667-6(8))* ReferencePoint Pr., Inc.

PSYCHICAL RESEARCH
see Parapsychology

PSYCHOANALYSIS
see also Dreams; Hypnotism; Mind and Body; Psychology; Psychology, Pathological

Docalavich, Heather. Antidepressants & Psychology: Talk Therapy vs. Medication. (Antidepressants Ser.). (Illus.). 104p. (YA). (gr. 7-18). 2008. lib. bdg. 24.95 *(978-1-4222-0096-4(5))* 2007. pap. 14.95 *(978-1-4222-0405-4(7))* Mason Crest.
Gillam, Scott. Sigmund Freud: Famous Neurologist, 1 vol. 2011. (Essential Lives Set 7 Ser.). (ENG., Illus.). 112p. (YA). (gr. 6-12). lib. bdg. 41.36 *(978-1-61783-004-4(6)*, 6747, Essential Library) ABDO Publishing Co.

PSYCHOLOGICAL WARFARE

Linebarger, Paul M. A. Psychological Warfare. 2010. (ENG.). 336p. pap. 29.95 *(978-0-89556-120-6(4))* Gateways Bks. & Tapes.

PSYCHOLOGY
see also Animal Psychology; Attitude (Psychology); Child Psychology; Educational Psychology; Emotions; Imagination; Individuality; Intellect; Parapsychology; Perception; Personality; Psychoanalysis; Reasoning; Self-acceptance; Senses and Sensation; Social Psychology; Thought and Thinking

Abblett, Mitch R. From Anger to Action: Powerful Mindfulness Tools to Help Teens Harness Anger for Positive Change. 2019. (Instant Help Solutions Ser.). (ENG.). 168p. (YA). (gr. 6-12). pap. 16.95 *(978-1-68403-229-7(6)*, 42297, Instant Help Books) New Harbinger Pubns.
Adson, Patricia R. A Princess & Her Garden: A Fable of Awakening & Arrival. 2nd ed. 2011. (J). *(978-0-935652-93-2(0))* Myers & Briggs Foundation, Inc.
Ahrens, Niki. Strong Like a Girl: A Disney Guide to Powerful Character. 2020. (J). *(978-1-5415-8993-3(9))* Lerner Publishing Group.
Al-Ghani, Kay. Super Shamlal - Living & Learning with Pathological Demand Avoidance. Al-Ghani, Haitham, illus. 2019. (K. I. Al-Ghani Children's Colour Story Bks.). 72p. 19.95 *(978-1-78775-056-2(6)*, 710028) Kingsley, Jessica Pubs. GBR. Dist: Hachette UK Distribution.
Allen, David, et al. Getting Things Done for Teens: Take Control of Your Life in a Distracting World. 2018. (ENG., Illus.). 160p. pap. 17.00 *(978-0-14-313193-9(1)*, Penguin Bks.) Penguin Publishing Group.
Allyn, Pam. Pam Allyn's Best Books for Boys: How to Engage Boys in Reading in Ways That Will Change Their Lives. 2011. (ENG.). 176p. (gr. 8-8). pap. 21.99 *(978-0-545-20455-2(0)*, Teaching Resources) Scholastic, Inc.
Andrus, Aubre & Bluth, Karen. Happiness Hacks: How to Find Energy & Inspiration. Collignon, Veronica, illus. 2017. (Stress-Busting Survival Guides). (ENG.). 48p. (J). (gr. 4-8). lib. bdg. 31.99 *(978-1-5157-6820-3(1)*, 135349, Capstone Pr.) Capstone.
—Project You: More Than 50 Ways to Calm down, de-Stress, & Feel Great. Collignon, Veronica, illus. 2017. (ENG.). 160p. (YA). (gr. 4-8). pap. 14.95 *(978-1-63079-091-2(5)*, 135352, Switch Pr.) Capstone.
Antill, Sara. Zest, 1 vol. 2013. (Character Strength Ser.). 24p. (J). (ENG.). (gr. 2-3). pap. 9.25 *(978-1-4488-9812-1(9)*, 5b0fa2f8-4d9e-4867-ba81-390cd42525b4); (ENG.). (gr. 2-3). lib. bdg. 26.27 *(978-1-4488-9677-6(0)*, 9c904f5d-c84c-4e83-a409-ba48349687ac); (gr. 3-6). pap. 49.50 *(978-1-4488-9813-8(7))* Rosen Publishing Group, Inc., The. (PowerKids Pr.).
Arrow, Emily. Making It Happen. Landry, Noémie Gionet, illus. 2019. (My Feelings, My Choices Ser.). (ENG.). 24p. (J). (gr. -1-2). pap. 7.95 *(978-1-68410-432-1(7)*, 141227) Cantata Learning.
—Trying Again. Stark, Kayla, illus. 2019. (My Feelings, My Choices Ser.). (ENG.). 24p. (J). (gr. -1-2). 33.99 *(978-1-68410-407-9(6)*, 141217) Cantata Learning.
Aspden, K. L. Help! I've Got an Alarm Bell Going off in My Head! How Panic, Anxiety & Stress Affect Your Body. Ra, Zita, illus. 2015. 48p. pap. 13.95 *(978-1-84905-704-2(4)*, 693933) Kingsley, Jessica Pubs. GBR. Dist: Hachette UK Distribution.
Ayer, Eleanor H. Everything You Need to Know about Stress. 2009. (Need to Know Library). 64p. (gr. 5-5). 58.50 *(978-1-60854-089-1(8))* Rosen Publishing Group, Inc., The.
Becnel, Barbara, ed. Gangs & the Abuse of Power: Stanley Tookie Williams Street Peace Series, 8 bks., Vol. 1, Bk. 7. 2008. 24p. (J). 6.95 *(978-0-9753584-7-4(2))* Damamli Publishing Co.
Belanger, Jeff. Paranormal Encounters: A Look at the Evidence, 1 vol. 2011. (Haunted: Ghosts & the Paranormal Ser.). (ENG., Illus.). 224p. (J). (gr. 8-8). lib. bdg. 42.47 *(978-1-4488-4839-3(3)*, 8e84f59c-b232-4bc4-8a74-b6ff4871e6db) Rosen Publishing Group, Inc., The.
Bellamy, Adam. What's Intuition?, 1 vol. 2017. (All about My Senses Ser.). (ENG.). 24p. (gr. k-1). pap. 10.35 *(978-0-7660-8801-6(4)*, 04f46cee-ab5b-45fe-a762-1ad20af79397) Enslow Publishing, LLC.
Berry, Joy. Help Me Be Good about Fighting. 2009. (ENG.). 40p. (J). (gr. k-2). pap. 7.95 *(978-1-60577-128-1(7))* Berry, Joy Enterprises.
—You Can Go for It! 2009. (ENG.). 304p. (J). (gr. 5-7). pap. 12.95 *(978-1-60577-601-9(7))* Berry, Joy Enterprises.
Berry, Joy Wilt. A Book about Fighting. 2005. (Illus.). (J). *(978-0-7172-8584-6(7))* Scholastic, Inc.
Biegel, Gina. Be Mindful & Stress Less: 50 Ways to Deal with Your (Crazy) Life. 2018. 216p. (YA). (gr. 8-12). pap. 16.95 *(978-1-61180-494-2(9))* Shambhala Pubns., Inc.
—Take in the Good: Skills for Staying Positive & Living Your Best Life. Chambers, Breanna, illus. 2020. 208p. (YA). (gr. 8-12). pap. 17.95 *(978-1-61180-771-4(9))* Shambhala Pubns., Inc.
Boyle, Caitlin. Operation Beautiful: One Note at a Time. 2013. (Operation Beautiful Ser.). (ENG.). 192p. (J). (gr. 4-7). 26.19 *(978-0-448-45756-7(3))* Penguin Young Readers Group.
Bradshaw, Cheryl M. How to Like Yourself: A Teen's Guide to Quieting Your Inner Critic & Building Lasting Self-Esteem. 2016. (Instant Help Solutions Ser.). (ENG.). 216p. (YA). (gr. 6-12). pap. 23.95 *(978-1-62625-348-3(X)*, 33483) New Harbinger Pubns.
Brain, Christine. Psychology. 2009. (ENG., Illus.). 384p. pap. 62.50 *(978-0-340-96684-6(X))* Hodder Education Group GBR. Dist: Trans-Atlantic Pubns., Inc.
Brenner, Rebecca. The Kid's User Guide to a Human Life: Book Two: an Open Heart. Kemmerer, Brooke, illus. 2016. (Kid's User Guide Ser.: 2). (ENG.). 56p. (J). pap. 8.95 *(978-1-63047-866-7(0))* Morgan James Publishing.
Brinkerhoff, Shirley. Psychologist. Riggs, Ernestine G. & Gholar, Cheryl, eds. 2013. (Careers with Character Ser.: 18). 96p. (J). (gr. 7-18). 22.95 *(978-1-4222-2764-0(2))* Mason Crest.
Brown Bear Books. The History of Psychology. 2011. (Psychology Ser.). (ENG., Illus.). 112p. (J). (gr. 9-12). lib. bdg. 42.80 *(978-1-936333-15-8(5)*, 16778) Brown Bear Bks.
Burstein, John. Past Tense: Healthy Ways to Manage Stress. 2010. (ENG., Illus.). 32p. (J). pap. *(978-0-7787-4812-0(X))*; lib. bdg. *(978-0-7787-4796-3(4))* Crabtree Publishing Co.
Canetti, Yanitzia. Almost the Same. 2010. 24p. (J). pap. 5.99 *(978-1-59835-146-0(X)*, BrickHouse Education) Cambridge BrickHouse, Inc.
—Casi Iguales. 2010. (SPA.). 24p. (J). pap. *(978-1-59835-144-6(3)*, BrickHouse Education) Cambridge BrickHouse, Inc.
Carducci, Bernardo J. & Kaiser, Lisa. Shyness: The Ultimate Teen Guide. 2015. (It Happened to Me Ser.: 44). (Illus.). 298p. 59.00 *(978-1-4422-3046-0(0))* Rowman & Littlefield Publishers, Inc.
Cardwell, Mike & Flanagan, Cara. Psychology A2: The Complete Companion. 2003. (ENG., Illus.). 344p. pap. *(978-0-7487-7344-2(4))* Nelson Thornes Ltd.
Carle, Eric. Calm with the Very Hungry Caterpillar. Carle, Eric, illus. 2019. (World of Eric Carle Ser.). (ENG., Illus.). 32p. (J). (-k). 9.99 *(978-1-5247-9218-3(7))* Penguin Young Readers Group.
Carlson, Dale. The Teen Brain Book: Who & What Are You? Teasdale, Nancy, ed. Nicklaus, Carol, illus. 2004. (ENG.). 230p. (gr. 7-12). pap. 14.95 *(978-1-884158-29-2(3))* Bick Publishing Hse.
Carlson, Hannah. Addiction: The Brain Disease. 2010. (ENG., Illus.). 224p. (gr. 7-18). pap. 14.95 *(978-1-884158-35-3(8)*, 03db31a0-ebf1-4ef8-b49f-db048b863aec) Bick Publishing Hse.
Chan, Paul D. Why Is Mommy Sad? A Child's Guide to Parental Depression. Faust, Laurie A., illus. 2006. 12p. (J). pap. 6.99 *(978-1-929622-71-9(6))* Current Clinical Strategies Publishing.
Claybourne, Anna. Healthy for Life: Self-Esteem & Mental Health. 2018. (Healthy for Life Ser.). (ENG., Illus.). 32p. (J). (gr. 4-6). pap. 11.99 *(978-1-4451-4980-6(X)*, Franklin Watts) Hachette Children's Group GBR. Dist: Hachette Bk. Group.
Cleveland, Don. How Do We Know How the Brain Works, 1 vol. 2004. (Great Scientific Questions & the Scientists Who Answered Them Ser.). (ENG., Illus.). 112p. (J). (gr. 7-12). lib. bdg. 39.80 *(978-1-4042-0078-4(9)*, 568b474b-da88-4669-b05f-245bc6e90bdc) Rosen Publishing Group, Inc., The.
Cleveland, Donald. How Do We Know How the Brain Works. 2009. (Great Scientific Questions & the Scientists Who Answered Them Ser.). 112p. (gr. 7-12). 63.90 *(978-1-61513-195-2(7))* Rosen Publishing Group, Inc., The.
Collins-Donnelly, Kate. Starving the Exam Stress Gremlin: A Cognitive Behavioural Therapy Workbook on Managing Exam Stress for Young People. 2017. (Gremlin & Thief CBT Workbooks Ser.). (Illus.). 160p. pap. 21.95 *(978-1-84905-698-4(6)*, 693925) Kingsley, Jessica Pubs. GBR. Dist: Hachette UK Distribution.
Collins GCSE, et al. AQA GCSE 9-1 Psychology All-In-One Complete Revision & Practice: Ideal for the 2024 & 2025 Exams. 2017. (ENG.). 232p. (YA). (gr. 9-11). pap. 16.99 *(978-0-00-822744-9(6))* HarperCollins Pubs. Ltd. GBR. Dist: Independent Pubs. Group.
Cope, Andy. The Teenager's Guide to Life, the Universe & Being Awesome: Super-Charge Your Life. 2019. (ENG.). 224p. 14.99 *(978-1-4736-7942-9(7)*, Teach Yourself) Hodder & Stoughton GBR. Dist: Hachette Bk. Group.
Cope, Andy, et al. The Art of Being a Brilliant Teenager. 2014. (ENG., Illus.). 160p. pap. 18.00 *(978-0-85708-576-8(6)*, Capstone) Wiley, John & Sons, Inc.
Coping: Set 1, 12 vols. 2017. (Coping (2017-2020) Ser.). (ENG.). 112p. (gr. 7-7). 240.78 *(978-1-4994-6631-7(5)*, ec9902b0-3249-404b-84f5-21cfd1f018ab, Rosen Young Adult) Rosen Publishing Group, Inc., The.
Cox, Erika. Psychology. 2010. (ENG.). 204p. pap. 13.95 *(978-1-4441-1541-3(3))* Hodder Education Group GBR. Dist: Trans-Atlantic Pubns., Inc.
Dobosz, Ann Marie. The Perfectionism Workbook for Teens: Activities to Help You Reduce Anxiety & Get Things Done. 2016. (ENG., Illus.). 200p. (YA). (gr. 6-12). pap. 21.95 *(978-1-62625-454-1(0)*, 34541) New Harbinger Pubns.
Doeden, Matt. What Are Hoaxes & Lies? 2019. (Searchlight Books (tm) — Fake News Ser.). (ENG., Illus.). 32p. (J). (gr. 3-5). pap. 9.99 *(978-1-5415-7473-1(7)*, 0be83bc0-f777-40a0-8816-808b6e006a83); lib. bdg. 30.65 *(978-1-5415-5578-5(3)*, 58da6e3d-ab85-4334-9bdc-73bcb89e7048) Lerner Publishing Group. (Lerner Pubns.).
Donovan, Sandy. Keep Your Cool! What You Should Know about Stress. 2009. pap. 52.95 *(978-0-7613-4685-2(6))* Lerner Publishing Group.
Doudna, Kelly. We Have the Nerve, Now Let's Observe!, 1 vol. 2007. (Science Made Simple Ser.). (Illus.). 24p. (J). (gr. k-3). lib. bdg. 24.21 *(978-1-59928-624-2(6)*, SandCastle) ABDO Publishing Co.
Douglas, Malachi. The Question: A Survivor's Guide for Tweens & Teens. Francis, Pamela, ed. 2014. (Illus.). 43p. (J). pap. 12.99 *(978-0-9843369-2-0(3))* Clay Jars Publishing.
Duhig, Holly. Change & Resilience. 2018. (Our Values - Level 3 Ser.). (Illus.). 32p. (J). (gr. 5-6). *(978-0-7787-5433-6(2))* Crabtree Publishing Co.
Eason, Sarah. Don't Play Dirty, Gertie, 1 vol. 2013. (You Choose Ser.). (ENG.). 32p. (gr. 2-2). lib. bdg. 27.93 *(978-0-7660-4307-7(X)*, 15c8daf5-0d60-4025-933d-fdb33d44b757, Enslow Elementary) Enslow Publishing, LLC.
Edwards, Nicola. Happy: A Beginner's Book of Mindfulness. import ed. 2020. (ENG., Illus.). 32p. (J). (gr. -1-2). 17.99 *(978-0-593-12119-1(8)*, Rodale Kids) Random Hse. Children's Bks.
Engdahl, Sylvia, ed. Dissociative Disorders, 1 vol. 2012. (Perspectives on Diseases & Disorders Ser.). (ENG., Illus.). 136p. (gr. 10-12). lib. bdg. 45.93 *(978-0-7377-6353-9(1)*, 9c6e7019-9f1c-4e2e-b6c6-374507bb6e21, Greenhaven Publishing) Greenhaven Publishing LLC.
Engel, Christiane. ABC for Me: ABC Mindful Me, Volume 4. 2018. (ABC for Me Ser.: 4). (ENG., Illus.). 36p. (J). (gr. -1-1). bds. 16.95 *(978-1-63322-510-7(0)*, 301672, Walter Foster Jr) Quarto Publishing Group USA.
Esherick, Joan. Balancing Act: A Teen's Guide to Managing Stress. 2006. (Science of Health Ser.). (Illus.). 128p. (YA). 24.95 *(978-1-59084-853-1(5))* Mason Crest.
—Criminal Psychology & Personality Profiling. Noziglia, Carla Miller & Siegel, Jay A., eds. 2013. (Solving Crimes with Science: Forensics Ser.: 12). (Illus.). 112p. (J). (gr. 7-18). 22.95 *(978-1-4222-2863-0(0))* Mason Crest.
Espeland, Pamela. Knowing Me, Knowing You: The I-Sight Way to Understand Yourself & Others. 2004. (Illus.). 128p. (YA). (gr. 8-12). pap. 13.95 *(978-1-57542-090-5(2))* Free Spirit Publishing Inc.
Feltes Taylor, Kimberly & Braun, Eric. How to Take the ACHE Out of Mistakes. Mark, Steve, illus. 2019. (Laugh & Learn(r) Ser.). (ENG.). 128p. (J). (gr. 2-6). pap. 10.99 *(978-1-63198-308-5(3)*, 83085) Free Spirit Publishing Inc.
Gainer, Cindy. I'm Like You, You're Like Me: A Book about Understanding & Appreciating Each Other. Sakamoto, Miki,

P
Q
R

illus. 2011. (ENG.). 48p. (J). (gr. -1-3). 16.99 *(978-1-57542-383-8(9)*, 23838) Free Spirit Publishing Inc.

Glimm, Adele. Gene Hunter: The Story of Neuropsychologist Nancy Wexler. 2005. (Women's Adventures in Science Ser.). (ENG., Illus.). 128p. (YA). (gr. 5-9). lib. bdg. 31.50 *(978-0-531-16778-6(X))* Scholastic Library Publishing.

Globe-Fearon Staff. Changes. (YA). pap. 12.95 *(978-0-8359-0922-8(0))* Globe Fearon Educational Publishing.

Gordon, Sherri Mabry. Are You at Risk for Public Shaming?, 1 vol. 2015. (Got Issues? Ser.). (ENG., Illus.). 112p. (gr. 7-8). lib. bdg. 38.93 *(978-0-7660-7136-0(7)*, 69eea255-003c-4e23-bc3a-ddb15c43d19f) Enslow Publishing, LLC.

—Surviving a First Breakup, 1 vol. 2017. (Teen Survival Guide Ser.). (ENG.). 48p. (gr. 6-6). 29.60 *(978-0-7660-9192-4(9)*, c8689b95-da66-44c6-a03d-b76adf05becd) Enslow Publishing, LLC.

Grant, Jim & Grant, Caleb. What Gritty Kids Do When No One Is Looking. Regan, Dana, illus. 2016. (ENG.). pap. 10.95 *(978-1-63133-078-0(0))* Staff Development for Educators.

Graves, Sue. But What If? A Book about Feeling Worried. Guicciardini, Desideria, illus. 2013. (Our Emotions & Behavior Ser.). (ENG.). 28p. (J). (gr. -1-3). 15.99 *(978-1-57542-444-6(4))* Free Spirit Publishing Inc.

Gray, T. L. Keezy's 10 Awesome Rules for Teenaged Dating! 2011. (ENG., Illus.). 95p. pap. 12.00 *(978-0-9834332-4-8(0))* Vabella Publishing.

Grossman, Laurie & Musumeci's 5th Grade Class, Musumeci's. Master of Mindfulness: How to Be Your Own Superhero in Times of Stress. 2016. (ENG., Illus.). 72p. (J). (gr. k-5). pap. 14.95 *(978-1-62625-464-0(8)*, 34640) New Harbinger Pubns.

Harbo, Christopher. Batman Is Trustworthy. Frampton, Otis, illus. 2018. (DC Super Heroes Character Education Ser.). (ENG.). 24p. (J). (gr. k-2). pap. 4.95 *(978-1-62370-958-7(X)*, 137176, Stone Arch Bks.) Capstone.

—Supergirl Is Patient. Schigiel, Gregg, illus. 2019. (DC Super Heroes Character Education Ser.). (ENG.). 24p. (J). (gr. k-2). lib. bdg. 27.32 *(978-1-5158-4022-0(0)*, 139810, Stone Arch Bks.) Capstone.

Heinrichs, Ann. Forensic Psychologist. 2009. (21st Century Skills Library: Cool Science Careers Ser.). (ENG., Illus.). 32p. (gr. 4-8). lib. bdg. 32.07 *(978-1-60279-309-5(3)*, 200205) Cherry Lake Publishing.

Higgins, Melissa. Celebrating Differences. 2012. (Celebrating Differences Ser.). (ENG.). 24p. (gr. k-1). pap. 166.80 *(978-1-4296-8325-8(2)*, Capstone Pr.) Capstone.

—We All Look Different. 2012. (Celebrating Differences Ser.). (ENG.). 24p. (gr. k-1). pap. 41.70 *(978-1-4296-8323-4(6)*, Capstone Pr.) Capstone.

Hill, Janet. Miss Mink: Life Lessons for a Cat Countess. 2019. (Illus.). 48p. (J). (gr. -1-3). 17.99 *(978-1-77049-922-5(9)*, Tundra Bks.) Tundra Bks. CAN. Dist: Penguin Random Hse. LLC.

Hirschmann, Kris. Understanding Motivation. 2017. (ENG.). 80p. (YA). (gr. 5-12). *(978-1-68282-275-3(3))* ReferencePoint Pr., Inc.

Hollander, Barbara. What Are Wants & Needs?, 1 vol. 2016. (Let's Find Out! Community Economics Ser.). (ENG.). 32p. (J). (gr. 2-3). lib. bdg. 26.06 *(978-1-68048-407-6(9)*, 41ce350f-7cbb-4fe3-83ed-1f17b65dc156) Rosen Publishing Group, Inc., The.

Hollander, Barbara Gottfried. What Are Wants & Needs? 2016. (Let's Find Out! Ser.). (ENG.). 32p. (J). (gr. 3-7). 23.70 *(978-1-5311-8658-6(0))* Perfection Learning Corp.

Holyoke, Nancy & Woodburn, Judy. A Smart Girl's Guide: Worry: How to Feel Less Stressed & Have More Fun. 2016. (American Girl(r) Wellbeing Ser.). (ENG., Illus.). 96p. (J). pap. 12.99 *(978-1-60958-745-1(6))* American Girl Publishing, Inc.

Hoog, Mark. Leadership Journal. 2011. (ENG.). 62p. (J). pap. 9.99 *(978-0-9770391-5-9(3)*, Growing Field) Growing Field Bks.

Huebner, Dawn. What to Do When You Grumble Too Much: A Kid's Guide to Overcoming Negativity. Matthews, Bonnie, illus. 2006. ("What to Do" Guides for Kids Ser.). 88p. (J). (gr. 4-7). per. 15.95 *(978-1-59147-450-0(7)*, Magination Pr.) American Psychological Assn.

Hugel, Bob. I Did It Without Thinking: True Stories about Impulsive Decisions That Changed Lives. 2008. (Scholastic Choices Ser.). (ENG., Illus.). 112p. (J). (gr. 3-7). 27.00 *(978-0-531-13868-7(2)*, Children's Pr.) Scholastic Library Publishing.

Hyde, Natalie. LGBTQ Rights. 2017. (Uncovering the Past: Analyzing Primary Sources Ser.). (Illus.). 48p. (J). (gr. 5-6). *(978-0-7787-3942-5(2))* Crabtree Publishing Co.

Hyman, Bruce M. & Pedrick, Cherry. Obsessive-Compulsive Disorder. 2003. (Twenty-First Century Medical Library). 96p. (gr. 7-18). lib. bdg. 26.90 *(978-0-7613-2758-5(4)*, Twenty-First Century Bks.) Lerner Publishing Group.

Jarvis, Matt Russell, et al. Angles on Psychology. 2nd rev. ed. 2004. (ENG., Illus.). 300p. (YA). pap. 35.75 *(978-0-7487-8032-7(7))* Nelson Thornes Ltd. GBR. Dist: Oxford Univ. Pr., Inc.

Johnson, Spencer. ¿Quién se ha llevado mi queso? Para niños. 2004. (SPA., Illus.). 62p. (J). 20.95 *(978-84-7953-553-7(9))* Ediciones Urano S. A. ESP. Dist: Spanish Pubs., LLC.

Jones, Grace. My Choices. 2017. (Our Values - Level 1 Ser.). (Illus.). 24p. (J). (gr. 5-8). *(978-0-7787-3701-8(2))* Crabtree Publishing Co.

Jones, Kidada. School of Awake: A Girl's Guide to the Universe. Jones, Koa, illus. 2017. (ENG.). 168p. (YA). (gr. 9-13). pap. 18.95 *(978-1-60868-458-8(X))* New World Library.

Kahn, Ada P. & Doctor, Ronald M. Phobias. 2004. (Life Balance Ser.). (ENG., Illus.). 80p. (YA). (gr. 5-8). pap. 6.95 *(978-0-531-15575-2(7)*, Watts, Franklin) Scholastic Library Publishing.

Kalman, Bobbie. ¿Dónde Está? 2008. (SPA.). 24p. (J). pap. *(978-0-7787-8738-9(9))* Crabtree Publishing Co.

—¿Donde Esta? 2008.Tr. of Where Is It? (SPA.). 24p. (J). lib. bdg. *(978-0-7787-8729-7(X))* Crabtree Publishing Co.

—I Can Do It! 2010. (ENG., Illus.). 16p. (J). (gr. k-2). *(978-0-7787-9423-3(7))*; pap. *(978-0-7787-9467-7(9))* Crabtree Publishing Co.

—Today Is a Great Day! 2010. (My World Ser.). (ENG.). 16p. (J). (gr. k-3). *(978-0-7787-9506-3(3))*; pap. *(978-0-7787-9531-5(4))* Crabtree Publishing Co.

—Where Is It? 2007. (Looking at Nature Ser.). (ENG., Illus.). 24p. (J). (gr. -1-2). pap. *(978-0-7787-3341-6(6))* Crabtree Publishing Co.

Kasschau, Richard A., et al. Understanding Psychology. 2006. (Understanding Psychology Ser.). (ENG., Illus.). 704p. (gr. 9-12). stu. ed. 119.28 *(978-0-07-874517-1(9)*, 0078745179) McGraw-Hill Higher Education.

Kinder, Wynne. Calm: Mindfulness for Kids. 2019. (Illus.). 72p. (J). *(978-1-7254-1976-6(9))* Dorling Kindersley Publishing, Inc.

—Calm: Mindfulness for Kids. 2019. (Mindfulness for Kids Ser.). (ENG., Illus.). 72p. (J). (gr. 1-4). pap. 16.99 *(978-1-4654-7090-4(5)*, DK Children) Dorling Kindersley Publishing, Inc.

Krajna, Cheryl. Blurred Lines: News or Advertisements?, 1 vol. 2018. (Young Citizen's Guide to News Literacy Ser.). (ENG.). 32p. (gr. 4-5). 27.93 *(978-1-5383-4497-2(1)*, 8a994da0-7f70-4eb3-956c-4802d399ab51, PowerKids Pr.) Rosen Publishing Group, Inc., The.

Krasner, Barbara, ed. Returning Soldiers & PTSD, 1 vol. 2017. (Current Controversies Ser.). (ENG.). 296p. (gr. 10-12). pap. 33.00 *(978-1-5345-0087-7(1)*, fda6ba1c-fabb-4687-ad55-1c334b886e98) Greenhaven Publishing LLC.

—Toxic Masculinity, 1 vol. 2019. (Opposing Viewpoints Ser.). (ENG.). 176p. (gr. 10-12). pap. 34.80 *(978-1-5345-0505-6(9)*, c224c417-4d90-4f06-96c7-2136defb983b) Greenhaven Publishing LLC.

Kyi, Tanya Lloyd. Under Pressure: The Science of Stress. Tremblay, Marie-Ève, illus. 2019. (ENG.). 76p. (YA). (gr. 6-9). 16.99 *(978-1-5253-0007-3(5))* Kids Can Pr., Ltd. CAN. Dist: Hachette Bk. Group.

La Bella, Laura. Curiosity. 2013. (7 Character Strengths of Highly Successful Students Ser.). 64p. (J). (gr. 5-8). pap. 77.70 *(978-1-4488-9556-4(1))*; (ENG., Illus.). (gr. 6-6). 37.12 *(978-1-4488-9542-7(1)*, 7db3f7f0-e168-4fff-9797-e9293139427c); (ENG., Illus.). (gr. 6-6). pap. 13.95 *(978-1-4488-9555-7(3)*, 90f74c85-7fce-4138-84a4-1ed6d6772961) Rosen Publishing Group, Inc., The.

Lambillion, Paul. Staying Cool. 2004. (Illus.). 196p. pap. 13.95 *(978-0-7171-3598-1(5))* M.H. Gill & Co. U. C. IRL. Dist: Hushion Hse. Publishing, Ltd.

Langwith, Jacqueline, ed. Mood Disorders, 1 vol. 2009. (Perspectives on Diseases & Disorders Ser.). (ENG., Illus.). 168p. (gr. 10-12). lib. bdg. 45.93 *(978-0-7377-4380-7(8)*, 6da7569c-1b67-4be0-92c9-b04cab536f7d, Greenhaven Publishing) Greenhaven Publishing LLC.

Lewis, Anthony. Teddy or Train? 2008. (Pick & Choose Ser.). (Illus.). 12p. (J). (gr. -1). spiral bd. *(978-1-84643-241-5(3))* Child's Play International Ltd.

Lewis, Anthony, illus. Carrots or Peas? 2008. (Pick & Choose Ser.). 12p. (J). (gr. -1). spiral bd. *(978-1-84643-242-2(1))* Child's Play International Ltd.

—Wind or Rain? 2008. (Pick & Choose Ser.). 12p. (J). (gr. -1). spiral bd. *(978-1-84643-240-8(5))* Child's Play International Ltd.

Lynch, Jason. Everyone Has Hope. Hale, Cole, illus. 2011. (J). *(978-0-938467-09-0(3))* Headline Bks., Inc.

MacAllister, Carol L. The Wisdom Tree & the Red Swing: Thinking Outside the Box for Preteens. 2009. (Wisdom Tree & the Red Swing Ser.). (ENG.). 116p. (J). pap. 3.99 *(978-0-9815818-4-2(6)*, 9780981581842) Take Charge Bks.

Marsico, Katie. Depression & Stress, 1 vol. 2013. (Real Teens... Real Issues Ser.). (ENG.). 80p. (YA). (gr. 7-7). 36.93 *(978-1-60870-851-2(9)*, e08062ac-8a4d-466e-b046-207bdf918849) Cavendish Square Publishing LLC.

—Empathy. Bane, Jeff, illus. 2019. (My Early Library: My Mindful Day Ser.). (ENG.). 24p. (J). (gr. k-1). pap. 12.79 *(978-1-5341-4995-3(3)*, 213287); lib. bdg. 30.64 *(978-1-5341-4709-6(8)*, 213286) Cherry Lake Publishing.

—Openness. Bane, Jeff, illus. 2019. (My Early Library: My Mindful Day Ser.). (ENG.). 24p. (J). (gr. k-1). pap. 12.79 *(978-1-5341-4999-1(6)*, 213303); lib. bdg. 30.64 *(978-1-5341-4713-3(6)*, 213302) Cherry Lake Publishing.

McCraty, Rollin, et al. Transforming Stress for Teens: The HeartMath Solution for Staying Cool under Pressure. 2016. (Instant Help Solutions Ser.). (ENG., Illus.). 216p. (YA). (gr. 6-12). pap. 19.95 *(978-1-62625-194-6(0)*, 31946) New Harbinger Pubns.

McGraw-Hill Education Staff. Understanding Psychology Reading Essentials & Study Guide Student Workbook. 2nd ed. 2003. (Understanding Psychology Ser.). (ENG., Illus.). 240p. (gr. 9-12). stu. ed., per. 9.72 *(978-0-07-860607-6(1)*, 0078606071) McGraw-Hill Higher Education.

Meiners, Cheri J. Be Positive! A Book about Optimism. Allen, Elizabeth, illus. 2013. (Being the Best Me(r) Ser.). (ENG.). 40p. (J). (gr. -1-3). pap. 11.99 *(978-1-57542-441-5(X))* Free Spirit Publishing Inc.

Mental X 2003. (Illus.). 32p. (YA). pap. 5.50 *(978-0-9745066-8-5(0))* Sports In Mind.

Mihaly, Mary E. Getting Your Own Way: A Guide to Growing up Assertively. 2014. (ENG.). 176p. pap. 12.95 *(978-1-59077-306-2(3))* Evans, M. & Co., Inc.

Miles, Lisa & Chown, Xanna Eve. How to Survive Being Dumped, 1 vol. 2013. (Girl Talk Ser.). (Illus.). 48p. (J). (gr. 5-5). (ENG.). pap. 12.75 *(978-1-4777-0716-6(6)*, 2dfa00da-a728-4f0e-ba1f-1566aea435a4, Rosen Classroom); (ENG., lib. bdg. 34.41 *(978-1-4777-0704-3(2)*, 1307468d-3216-4ad4-9cc7-e86faa8debf6, Rosen Reference); pap. 70.50 *(978-1-4777-0717-3(4)*, Rosen Reference) Rosen Publishing Group, Inc., The.

Miller, Connie Colwell. You Can Stay in Control: Wild or Calm? 2018. (Making Good Choices Ser.). (ENG., Illus.). 24p. (J). (gr. k-3). pap. 10.99 *(978-1-68152-234-0(9)*, 14777) Amicus.

Mincher, Kevin. The Ultimate Youth Lifestyle: 7 Steps Any Teenager Can Use to Achieve More Success & Happiness. 2017. 64p. (C). pap. 14.95 *(978-0-9956079-0-3(7))* Unstoppable Teen, Ltd. GBR. Dist: Crown Hse. Publishing LLC.

Moe, Barbara. Coping with Rejection. 2009. (Coping Ser.). 192p. (gr. 7-12). 63.90 *(978-1-61512-010-9(6))* Rosen Publishing Group, Inc., The.

—Understanding Negative Body Image. 2009. (Teen Eating Disorder Prevention Book Ser.). 192p. (gr. 7-12). 63.90 *(978-1-61511-242-5(1))* Rosen Publishing Group, Inc., The.

Morgan, Nicola. Blame My Brain. 2007. (Illus.). 192p. (YA). pap. *(978-1-4063-1116-7(2))* Walker Bks., Ltd.

Moss, Wendy L. & Deluca-Acconi, Robin. School Made Easier: A Kid's Guide to Study Strategies & Anxiety-Busting Tools. (Illus.). 128p. 2014. pap. *(978-1-4338-1336-8(X))* 2013. (ENG., 14.95 *(978-1-4338-1335-1(1))* American Psychological Assn. (Magination Pr.).

Mr. Blue. From Underdog to Wonderdog: Top Ten Tricks to Lead Your Pack. 2012. (ENG., Illus.). 52p. (J). (gr. 1-5). pap. 14.95 *(978-1-936354-26-9(8)*, Tremendous Leadership) Tremendous Life Bks.

Mulhall, Jill. Young Adult Literature: The Worlds Inside Us (Grade 6) 2nd rev. ed. 2016. (TIME(r): Informational Text Ser.). (ENG., Illus.). 48p. (J). (gr. 5-8). pap. 13.99 *(978-1-4938-3598-0(X))* Teacher Created Materials, Inc.

Naik, Anita. Coping with Loss: The Life Changes Handbook. 2009. (Really Useful Handbooks Ser.). (ENG., Illus.). 48p. (J). (gr. 5-11). pap. *(978-0-7787-4404-7(3)*, 1294165) Crabtree Publishing Co.

Naik, Anita & Cronin, Ali. Coping with Loss: The Life Changes Handbook. 2009. (Really Useful Handbooks Ser.). (ENG., Illus.). 48p. (J). (gr. 5-11). lib. bdg. *(978-0-7787-4391-0(8)*, 1294165) Crabtree Publishing Co.

—Read the Signals: The Body Language Handbook. 2009. (Really Useful Handbooks Ser.). (ENG., Illus.). 48p. (J). (gr. 5-11). pap. *(978-0-7787-4401-6(9))* Crabtree Publishing Co.

Nance, Andrew Jordan. Puppy Mind. Durk, Jim, illus. 2016. 32p. (J). (gr. -1-2). 18.95 *(978-1-941529-44-7(5)*, Plum Blossom Bks.) Parallax Pr.

Navarre, Sam. Masculinity, Bullying, & Aggression: A Guy's Guide, 1 vol. 2011. (Young Man's Guide to Contemporary Issues Ser.). (ENG.). 104p. (J). (gr. 8-9). lib. bdg. 39.80 *(978-1-4488-5525-4(X)*, fa266102-feec-48ec-a62d-b7e48e4d834f) Rosen Publishing Group, Inc., The.

Neiman, Barbara. The Adopted Teen Workbook: Develop Confidence, Strength, & Resilience on the Path to Adulthood. 2019. (ENG., Illus.). 184p. (YA). (gr. 6-12). pap. 16.95 *(978-1-68403-141-2(9)*, 41412, Instant Help Books) New Harbinger Pubns.

O'Connor, Frances. Frequently Asked Questions about Academic Anxiety, 1 vol. 2007. (FAQ: Teen Life Ser.). (ENG., Illus.). 64p. (YA). (gr. 5-6). lib. bdg. 37.13 *(978-1-4042-1937-3(4)*, abf2ece1-507d-4e1a-ac7b-3e82024f6d0a) Rosen Publishing Group, Inc., The.

Ogden, Charlie. Identity & Gender. 2017. (Our Values - Level 3 Ser.). (Illus.). 32p. (J). (gr. 5-6). *(978-0-7787-3268-6(1))* Crabtree Publishing Co.

Orr, Tamra B. Surprise. 2016. (21st Century Basic Skills Library: Feelings Ser.). (ENG., Illus.). 24p. (J). (gr. k-3). pap. 12.79 *(978-1-63471-246-0(3)*, 208273, Blackbirch Pr., Inc.) Cherry Lake Publishing.

Ortner, Nick & Taylor, Alison. My Magic Breath: Finding Calm Through Mindful Breathing. Ortner, Nick & Polizzi, Michelle, illus. 2018. (ENG.). 32p. (J). (gr. -1-3). 17.99 *(978-0-06-268776-0(X)*, HarperCollins) HarperCollins Pubs.

Parks, Peggy J. Anxiety Disorders. 2011. 96p. (YA). lib. bdg. 41.27 *(978-1-60152-137-8(5))* ReferencePoint Pr., Inc.

—Teens & PTSD. 2017. (ENG., Illus.). 80p. (J). (gr. 5-12). *(978-1-68282-130-5(7))* ReferencePoint Pr., Inc.

Pessin-Whedbee, Brook. Who Are You? The Kid's Guide to Gender Identity. Bardoff, Naomi, illus. 2016. 40p. (J). 18.95 *(978-1-78592-728-7(0)*, 696300) Kingsley, Jessica Pubs. GBR. Dist: Hachette UK Distribution.

Peters, Elisa & Killcoyne, Hope Lourie, eds. Psychology, 1 vol., 1. 2015. (Britannica Guide to the Social Sciences Ser.). (ENG.). 160p. (J). (gr. 10-10). 37.82 *(978-1-62275-552-3(9)*, d0c45c2c-1cf6-4d49-b23d-9595989abee6, Britannica Educational Publishing) Rosen Publishing Group, Inc., The.

Poole, H. W. Post-Traumatic Stress Disorder, Vol. 13. Walters, Anne S., ed. 2015. (Mental Illnesses & Disorders: Awareness & Understanding Ser.). (Illus.). 48p. (J). (gr. 5). 20.95 *(978-1-4222-3374-0(X))* Mason Crest.

Primrose, Alison. Non-Verbal Reasoning, Age 9-11. 2016. (ENG.). 64p. pap., wbk. ed. 14.95 *(978-1-4718-4935-0(X))* Hodder Education Group GBR. Dist: Trans-Atlantic Pubns., Inc.

Psychologie. (Duden-Schuelerduden Ser.). (GER.). 466p. (YA). *(978-3-411-05252-3(X))* Bibliographisches Institut & F. A. Brockhaus AG DEU. Dist: International Bk. Import Service, Inc.

Quill, Charlie. Anger & Anger Management, 4 vols. 2008. (Teen Mental Health Ser.). (ENG.). 48p. (YA). (gr. 5-6). 68.94 *(978-1-60853-293-3(3)*, c1016796-e764-4dd3-a02b-4d3de3b88553) Rosen Publishing Group, Inc., The.

Raatma, Lucia. Making Smart Choices. 2013. (True Book(tm), a — Guides to Life Ser.). (ENG., Illus.). 48p. (J). lib. bdg. 31.00 *(978-0-531-25524-7(7))* Scholastic Library Publishing.

Reade, Clara. Intuition: The Sixth Sense, 1 vol., 1. 2014. (Your Five Senses & Your Sixth Sense Ser.). (ENG.). 24p. (J). (gr. 1-2). 26.27 *(978-1-4777-2858-1(9)*, f9f91476-d4e9-4003-9b13-c39201ecb9ca, PowerKids Pr.) Rosen Publishing Group, Inc., The.

Reber, Deborah. Doable: The Girls' Guide to Accomplishing Just about Anything. 2015. (ENG., Illus.). 208p. (YA). (gr. 7). pap. 12.99 *(978-1-58270-466-1(X)*, Simon Pulse) Simon Pulse.

Rebman, Renée C. Are You Doing Risky Things? Cutting, Bingeing, Snorting, & Other Dangers, 1 vol. 2014. (Got Issues? Ser.). (ENG., Illus.). 112p. (gr. 6-7). lib. bdg. 38.93 *(978-0-7660-5996-2(0)*, c00544f9-c869-4ae2-9b1f-9a3418fd830e) Enslow Publishing, LLC.

Reeves, Diane Lindsey. Making Choices at Home. 2018. (21st Century Junior Library: Smart Choices Ser.). (ENG., Illus.). 24p. (J). (gr. k-2). pap. 12.79 *(978-1-5341-0885-1(8)*, 210904); lib. bdg. 30.64 *(978-1-5341-0786-1(X)*, 210903) Cherry Lake Publishing.

—Making Choices with Friends. 2018. (21st Century Junior Library: Smart Choices Ser.). (ENG.). 24p. (J). (gr. k-2). pap. 12.79 *(978-1-5341-0886-8(6)*, 210908); (Illus.). lib. bdg. 30.64 *(978-1-5341-0787-8(8)*, 210907) Cherry Lake Publishing.

Rice, Dona Herweck. Like Them (Grade 1) 2018. (See Me Read! Everyday Words Ser.). (ENG., Illus.). 12p. (J). (gr. k-1). 6.99 *(978-1-4938-9859-6(0))* Teacher Created Materials, Inc.

Robinson, Matthew. Making Smart Choices about Relationships. 2009. (Making Smart Choices Ser.). 48p. (gr. 5-5). 53.00 *(978-1-61514-340-5(8)*, Rosen Reference) Rosen Publishing Group, Inc., The.

Rodi, Robert & Ross, Laura. Being Transgender, Vol. 10. Jennings, Kevin, ed. 2016. (Living Proud! Growing up LGBTQ Ser.). (Illus.). 64p. (J). (gr. 7). 23.95 *(978-1-4222-3502-7(5))* Mason Crest.

Roegiers, Maud. Take the Time: Mindfulness for Kids. Roegiers, Maud, illus. 2010. (ENG., Illus.). 32p. (J). (gr. -1-3). 14.95 *(978-1-4338-0794-7(7)*, Magination Pr.) American Psychological Assn.

—Take the Time: Mindfulness for Kids. 2010. (Illus.). 32p. (J). (gr. -1-3). pap. 9.95 *(978-1-4338-0796-1(3)*, Magination Pr.) American Psychological Assn.

Roland, James. Careers in Mental Health. 2017. (ENG., Illus.). 80p. (J). (gr. 5-12). *(978-1-68282-108-4(0))* ReferencePoint Pr., Inc.

Rooney, Anne. The History of Psychology, 1 vol. 2016. (History of the Humanities & Social Sciences Ser.). (ENG., Illus.). 216p. (J). (gr. 8-8). lib. bdg. 47.80 *(978-1-4994-6404-7(5)*, 6c2d5ff5-ff85-441b-88f4-cffc213dfdf8) Rosen Publishing Group, Inc., The.

Rosen, Marvin. Demystifying Dreams. 2004. 64p. (YA). pap. 9.95 *(978-0-595-30290-1(4))* iUniverse, Inc.

Russell, Julia, et al. Cambridge International AS & a Level Psychology Coursebook. 2016. (ENG., Illus.). 368p. pap. 72.60 *(978-1-316-60569-1(8))* Cambridge Univ. Pr.

Safran, Sheri. All Kinds of People. Damon, Emma, illus. 2012. (ENG.). 12p. (J). (gr. -1). 12.99 *(978-1-60887-160-5(6))* Insight Editions.

Saidian, Siyavush. Ways to Make Money Working with Your Hands, 1 vol. 2019. (Cash in on Your Skills Ser.). (ENG.). 80p. (gr. 7-7). pap. 18.60 *(978-1-9785-1557-4(X)*, 7e4e6f9d-fb84-413e-ab13-3dfdc99ed658) Enslow Publishing, LLC.

Saltzman, Amy. A Still Quiet Place for Teens: A Mindfulness Workbook to Ease Stress & Difficult Emotions. 2016. (ENG.). 168p. (YA). (gr. 6-12). pap. 21.95 *(978-1-62625-376-6(5)*, 33766) New Harbinger Pubns.

Sargent, Brian. Losing It: The Meaning of Loss, 1 vol. 2014. (ENG., Illus.). 28p. (J). pap., E-Book 9.50 *(978-1-107-68191-0(X))* Cambridge Univ. Pr.

Saxon, Vickie. Be Mindful, Donald! A Mickey & Friends Story. Disney Storybook Artists, illus. 2018. (Disney Learning Everyday Stories Ser.). (ENG.). 32p. (J). (gr. k-3). pap. 8.99 *(978-1-5415-3284-7(8)*, Lerner Pubns.) Lerner Publishing Group.

—Be Mindful, Donald! A Mickey & Friends Story. Disney Storybook Artists, Disney Storybook, illus. 2018. (Disney Learning Everyday Stories Ser.). (ENG.). 32p. (J). (gr. k-3). lib. bdg. 31.99 *(978-1-5415-3255-7(4)*, Lerner Pubns.) Lerner Publishing Group.

Schab, Lisa M. The Self-Esteem Habit for Teens: 50 Simple Ways to Build Your Confidence Every Day. 2018. (Instant Help Solutions Ser.). (ENG.). 200p. (YA). pap. 19.95 *(978-1-62625-919-5(4)*, 39195) New Harbinger Pubns.

Scholastic. The MindUP Curriculum: Grades 3-5 Grades 3-5. 2011. (MindUP Curriculum Ser.). (ENG., Illus.). 160p. (gr. 3-5). pap. 24.99 *(978-0-545-26713-7(7)*, Teaching Resources) Scholastic, Inc.

—The MindUP Curriculum: Grades 6-8 Grade 6-8. 2011. (MindUP Curriculum Ser.). (ENG., Illus.). 160p. (gr. 6-8). pap. 24.99 *(978-0-545-26714-4(5)*, Teaching Resources) Scholastic, Inc.

—The MindUP Curriculum: Grades PreK - 2. 2011. (MindUP Curriculum Ser.). (ENG., Illus.). 160p. (gr. -1-2). pap. 24.99 *(978-0-545-26712-0(9)*, Teaching Resources) Scholastic, Inc.

Sedley, Ben. Stuff That Sucks: A Teen's Guide to Accepting What You Can't Change & Committing to What You Can. 2017. (Instant Help Solutions Ser.). (ENG., Illus.). 96p. (YA). (gr. 6-12). pap. 19.95 *(978-1-62625-865-5(1)*, 38655) New Harbinger Pubns.

Shoesmith, Geoffrey. Psychology: A Complete GCSE Course. 2003. (ENG., Illus.). 424p. (C). pap. 43.00 *(978-0-7188-3002-1(4))* Lutherworth Pr., The GBR. Dist: ISD.

Shone, Rob & Spender, Nick. Solving Crimes Through Criminal Profiling. 2008. (Graphic Forensic Science Ser.). (ENG., Illus.). 48p. (YA). 58.50 *(978-1-4488-1666-8(1)*, Rosen Reference) Rosen Publishing Group, Inc., The.

Silverman, Robin L. & Silverman, Robin Landew. Reaching Your Goals. 2004. (Life Balance Ser.). (ENG.). 80p. (J). 20.50 *(978-0-531-12342-3(1)*, Watts, Franklin) Scholastic Library Publishing.

Skeen, Michelle & Skeen, Kelly. Just As You Are: A Teen's Guide to Self-Acceptance & Lasting Self-Esteem. 2018. (Instant Help Solutions Ser.). (ENG.). 176p. (YA). pap. 17.95 *(978-1-62625-590-6(3)*, 35906) New Harbinger Pubns.

Slavens, Elaine. Fighting: Deal with It Without Coming to Blows, 1 vol. Murray, Steven, illus. 2nd ed. 2010. (Lorimer Deal with It Ser.). (ENG.). 32p. (J). (gr. 4-9). 24.95 *(978-1-55277-501-1(1)*, 22515bca-f1a4-44a7-a633-0635b9123f86) James Lorimer & Co. Ltd., Pubs. CAN. Dist: Lerner Publishing Group.

Small, Cathleen. The Science of Mind Control & Telepathy, 1 vol. 2018. (Science of Superpowers Ser.). (ENG.). 48p. (J). (gr. 4-4). 33.07 *(978-1-5026-3799-4(5)*, e7039b48-2716-40d5-b3cd-142ea1d27eff) Cavendish Square Publishing LLC.

Sokol, Leslie & Fox, Marci G. The Think Confident, Be Confident Workbook for Teens: Activities to Help You Create Unshakable Self-Confidence & Reach Your Goals. 2016. (ENG.). 224p. (YA). (gr. 6-12). pap. 19.95 *(978-1-62625-483-1(4)*, 34831) New Harbinger Pubns.

Spalding, Maddie. 12 Tips for Managing Stress & Anxiety. 2017. 32p. (J). *(978-1-62143-508-2(3))* Pr. Room Editions LLC.

Spangenburg, Ray, et al. Are You Depressed?, 1 vol. 2015. (Got Issues? Ser.). (ENG., Illus.). 128p. (gr. 7-7). lib. bdg. 38.93 *(978-0-7660-6981-7(8),* 8a1df2d2-bea1-4546-8898-ac15e7bf4616) Enslow Publishing, LLC.

Spilsbury, Louise. Family & Friends, 1 vol. 2011. (Healthy & Happy Ser.). (ENG., Illus.). 32p. (J). (gr. 2-2). lib. bdg. 30.27 *(978-1-4488-5275-8(7),* b71ff534-7d95-49ab-af55-3869bc8ec6de) Rosen Publishing Group, Inc., The.

Staley, Erin. Defeating Stress & Anxiety, 1 vol., 1. 2015. (Effective Survival Strategies Ser.). (ENG., Illus.). 64p. (J). (gr. 6-6). 36.13 *(978-1-4994-6195-4(X),* 4d47e79e-effa-4b51-a889-f3f7aa3c8847, Rosen Young Adult) Rosen Publishing Group, Inc., The.

Statt, David A. A Student's Dictionary of Psychology. 2004. (ENG., Illus.). 176p. (C). per. 26.95 *(978-1-84169-342-2(1),* RU37524, Psychology Press) Taylor & Francis Group GBR. Dist: Taylor & Francis Group.

Stewart, Whitney. Mindful Me Activity Book. Peterson, Stacy, illus. 2018. (ENG.). 96p. (J). (gr. 3-7). pap. 9.99 *(978-0-8075-5146-2(5),* 807551465) Whitman, Albert & Co.

Stoll, Scott & Williams, Sara E. Dream It! A Playbook to Spark Your Awesomeness. 2018. (ENG., Illus.). 80p. (J). pap. *(978-1-4338-2795-2(6),* Magination Pr.) American Psychological Assn.

Stuckey, Rachel. Sexual Orientation & Gender Identity. 2015. (Straight Talk About... Ser.). (ENG., Illus.). 48p. (J). (gr. 5-5). *(978-0-7787-2203-8(1))* Crabtree Publishing Co.

Subbiah, Seetha. Did You Hear That? Help for Children Who Hear Voices. 2016. (ENG., Illus.). 120p. *(978-981-314-414-9(9))* World Scientific Publishing Co. Pte Ltd.

Svoboda, Elizabeth. The Life Heroic: How to Unleash Your Most Amazing Self. Hajny, Chris, illus. 2019. (ENG.). 144p. (J). (gr. 4-8). pap. 16.99 *(978-1-942186-25-0(8),* c6774a94-9c2d-4df5-b7f9-a88df75fdee6, Zest Bks.) Lerner Publishing Group.

Szpirglas, Jeff & Saint-Onge, Danielle. Your Changing Brain: A Guidebook. 2017. (Exploring the Brain Ser.). (Illus.). 48p. (J). (gr. 5-6). pap. *(978-0-7787-3511-3(7))* Crabtree Publishing Co.

Testa, Rylan Jay, et al. The Gender Quest Workbook: A Guide for Teens & Young Adults Exploring Gender Identity. 2015. (ENG.). 168p. (YA). (gr. 5-12). pap. 22.95 *(978-1-62625-297-4(1),* 32974) New Harbinger Pubns.

Treays, Rebecca. Understanding Your Brain - Internet Linked. Fox, Christyan, illus. rev. ed. 2004. (Science for Beginners Ser.). 32p. (J). pap. 7.95 *(978-0-7945-0853-1(7),* Usborne) EDC Publishing.

—Understanding Your Senses - Internet Linked. Fox, Christyan, illus. rev. ed. 2004. (Science for Beginners Ser.). 32p. (J). pap. 7.95 *(978-0-7945-0852-4(9),* Usborne) EDC Publishing.

UFlipp. You & Your Military Hero: Building Positive Thinking Skills During Your Hero's Deployment. 2009. 72p. (J). pap. 19.95 *(978-1-59298-268-4(9))* Beaver's Pond Pr., Inc.

Uhl, Xina M. Strengthening Collaborative Project Skills, 1 vol. 2017. (Skills for Success Ser.). (ENG., Illus.). 64p. (J). (gr. 7-7). 36.13 *(978-1-5081-7566-7(7),* dc652daf-495c-4772-9729-06c8cd05247c, Rosen Young Adult) Rosen Publishing Group, Inc., The.

Verde, Susan. I Am Peace: A Book of Mindfulness. Reynolds, Peter H., illus. 2019. (I Am Bks.). (ENG.). 22p. (J). (gr. -1 — 1). bds. 8.99 *(978-1-4197-3152-5(1),* 1192910, Abrams Appleseed) Abrams, Inc.

—I Am Peace: A Book of Mindfulness. 2017. (I Am Bks.). (ENG., Illus.). 32p. (J). (gr. -1-3). 14.95 *(978-1-4197-2701-6(X),* 1192901, Abrams Bks. for Young Readers) Abrams, Inc.

Verdick, Elizabeth. Bye-Bye Time. Heinlen, Marieka, illus. 2008. (Toddler Tools(r) Ser.). (ENG.). 24p. (J). (gr. k — 1). 9.99 *(978-1-57542-299-2(9),* 22992) Free Spirit Publishing Inc.

—Bye-Bye Time / Momento de la Despedida. Heinlen, Marieka, illus. 2017. (Toddler Tools(r) Ser.). (ENG.). 26p. (J). bds. 9.99 *(978-1-63198-151-7(X),* 81517) Free Spirit Publishing Inc.

Vincent, Denis & Francis, Peter. Non-Verbal Reasoning, Age 8-10. 2016. (ENG.). 56p. pap., wbk. ed. 14.95 *(978-1-4718-4934-3(1))* Hodder Education Group GBR. Dist: Trans-Atlantic Pubns., Inc.

Way, Jennifer & Van Duyne, Sara. What You Can Do about Stress & Anxiety, 1 vol. 2015. (Contemporary Diseases & Disorders Ser.). (ENG., Illus.). 128p. (gr. 7-7). 38.93 *(978-0-7660-7042-4(5),* f229b252-e8d9-4840-a7b0-91bf7830b565) Enslow Publishing, LLC.

Weiss, S. I. Coping with the Beauty Myth: A Guide for Real Girls. 2009. (Coping Ser.). 192p. (gr. 7-12). 63.90 *(978-1-61512-014-7(9))* Rosen Publishing Group, Inc., The.

Welbourn, Shannon. Step Forward with Empathy. 2016. (Step Forward! Ser.). (ENG., Illus.). 24p. (J). (gr. 1-4). *(978-0-7787-2786-6(6))* Crabtree Publishing Co.

—Step Forward with Grit. 2016. (Step Forward! Ser.). (ENG., Illus.). 24p. (J). (gr. 1-4). *(978-0-7787-2767-5(X))* Crabtree Publishing Co.

Welch, Edward. Buster's Ears Trip Him Up: When You Fall. Hox, Joe, illus. 2018. (ENG.). 32p. (J). 16.99 *(978-1-948130-25-7(4))* New Growth Pr.

Wilson, Nolan. The Teen's Guide to Getting Ahead: How to Succeed in High School & Beyond. 2008. 192p. (YA). (gr. 8-11). pap. 15.95 *(978-1-897073-92-6(5))* Lobster Pr. CAN. Dist: Orca Bk. Pubs. USA.

Wooster, Patricia. Ignite Your Spark: Discovering Who You Are from the Inside Out. 2017. (ENG., Illus.). 224p. (YA). (gr. 7). pap. 12.99 *(978-1-58270-564-4(X))* Simon Pulse/Beyond Words.

Wroble, Lisa A. Dealing with Stress: A How-To Guide, 1 vol. 2011. (Life: a How-To Guide Ser.). (ENG., Illus.). 128p. (gr. 6-7). lib. bdg. 35.93 *(978-0-7660-3439-6(9),* 779e80ae-34ad-4589-a25b-e29ebd9273df) Enslow Publishing, LLC.

Wyskowski, Lindsay. Living with PTSD. 2018. (Living with Disorders & Disabilities Ser.). (ENG.). 80p. (YA). (gr. 6-12). 39.93 *(978-1-68282-489-4(6))* ReferencePoint Pr., Inc.

Youssef, Jagger. Which Holds More?, 1 vol. 2020. (Time to Compare! Ser.). (ENG.). 24p. (J). (gr. k-k). pap. 9.15 *(978-1-5382-5518-6(9),* 317364b8-c262-477a-a6ca-71a70ff704a) Stevens, Gareth Publishing LLLP.

Zelinger, Laurie & Zelinger, Jordan. Please Explain Anxiety to Me! Simple Biology & Solutions for Children & Parents. Sabella, Elisa, illus. 2010. 38p. 32.95 *(978-1-61599-051-1(8));* 40p. pap. 21.95 *(978-1-61599-029-0(1))* Loving Healing Pr., Inc.

Zelinger, Laurie E. & Zelinger, Jordan. Please Explain "Anxiety" to Me! Simple Biology & Solutions for Children & Parents. Sabella, Elisa, illus. 2014. (J). pap. 15.95 *(978-1-61599-216-4(2))* Loving Healing Pr., Inc.

PSYCHOLOGY, ABNORMAL

see Psychology, Pathological

PSYCHOLOGY, APPLIED

see also Counseling; Interpersonal Relations; Security (Psychology)

Hanson-Harding, Alexandra. Step-By-Step Guide to Win-Win Negotiating Every Day, 1 vol. 2014. (Winning at Work Readiness Ser.). (ENG.). 64p. (YA). (gr. 6-6). 36.13 *(978-1-4777-7790-9(3),* c05fcff9-234e-4db8-98b6-0f1f91b4371e) Rosen Publishing Group, Inc., The.

McIntyre, Thomas. The Survival Guide for Kids with Behavior Challenges: How to Make Good Choices & Stay Out of Trouble. rev. ed. 2013. (Survival Guides for Kids Ser.). (ENG., Illus.). 192p. (J). (gr. 4-9). pap. 17.99 *(978-1-57542-449-1(5))* Free Spirit Publishing Inc.

PSYCHOLOGY, CHILD

see Child Psychology

PSYCHOLOGY, COMPARATIVE

see also Animal Intelligence; Animal Psychology; Animals—Habits and Behavior

Canetti, Yanitzia. Agarrarse: Ellos lo hacen bien nosotros Tambien. 2010. (SPA.). 24p. (J). 5.99 *(978-1-59835-232-0(6),* BrickHouse Education) Cambridge BrickHouse, Inc.

—What They Can Do, We Can Too! Grab. 2010. pap. 5.99 *(978-1-59835-231-3(8),* BrickHouse Education) Cambridge BrickHouse, Inc.

PSYCHOLOGY—DICTIONARIES

Statt, David A. A Student's Dictionary of Psychology. 2004. (ENG., Illus.). 176p. (C). per. 26.95 *(978-1-84169-342-2(1),* RU37524, Psychology Press) Taylor & Francis Group GBR. Dist: Taylor & Francis Group.

PSYCHOLOGY, EDUCATIONAL

see Educational Psychology

PSYCHOLOGY, INDUSTRIAL

see Psychology, Applied

PSYCHOLOGY, MEDICAL

see Psychology, Pathological

PSYCHOLOGY, PATHOLOGICAL

see also Eating Disorders; Mental Illness; Psychiatry; Psychoanalysis

Bell, Samantha. I Talk in My Sleep. 2014. (Tell Me Why Library). (ENG., Illus.). 24p. (J). (gr. 2-5). 29.21 *(978-1-63188-005-6(5),* 205427) Cherry Lake Publishing.

Berry, Joy. Good Answers to Tough Questions Trauma. Bartholomew, illus. 2010. (Good Answers to Tough Questions Ser.). (ENG.). 48p. (J). (gr. k-7). pap. 7.99 *(978-1-60577-507-4(X))* Berry, Joy Enterprises.

Bjornlund, Lydia. Personality Disorders. 2011. 96p. (YA). (gr. 6-10). lib. bdg. 41.27 *(978-1-60152-139-2(1))* ReferencePoint Pr., Inc.

Bonnice, Sherry. Adjustment Disorders. McDonnell, Mary Ann & Esherick, Donald, eds. 2013. (State of Mental Illness & Its Therapy Ser.: 19). (Illus.). 128p. (J). (gr. 7-18). 24.95 *(978-1-4222-2820-3(7))* Mason Crest.

Bonnice, Sherry & Hoard, Carolyn. Cognitive Disorders. McDonnell, Mary Ann & Esherick, Donald, eds. 2013. (State of Mental Illness & Its Therapy Ser.: 19). (Illus.). 128p. (J). (gr. 7-18). 24.95 *(978-1-4222-2823-4(1))* Mason Crest.

Brinkerhoff, Shirley. Anxiety Disorders. McDonnell, Mary Ann & Esherick, Donald, eds. 2013. (State of Mental Illness & Its Therapy Ser.: 19). (Illus.). 128p. (J). (gr. 7-18). 24.95 *(978-1-4222-2821-0(5))* Mason Crest.

—Drug Therapy & Childhood & Adolescent Disorders. (Encyclopedia of Psychiatric Drugs & Their Disorders Ser.). (Illus.). (YA). 2004. 128p. lib. bdg. 24.95 *(978-1-59084-563-9(3))* 2003. 125p. (gr. 4-7). pap. 14.95 *(978-1-4222-0386-6(7))* Mason Crest.

—Obsessive-Compulsive Disorder. 2014. (Illus.). 128p. (J). *(978-1-4222-2819-7(3))* Mason Crest.

—Obsessive-Compulsive Disorder. McDonnell, Mary Ann & Esherick, Donald, eds. 2013. (State of Mental Illness & Its Therapy Ser.: 19). 128p. (J). (gr. 7-18). 24.95 *(978-1-4222-2830-2(4))* Mason Crest.

—Personality Disorders. McDonnell, Mary Ann & Esherick, Donald, eds. 2013. (State of Mental Illness & Its Therapy Ser.: 19). (Illus.). 128p. (J). (gr. 7-18). 24.95 *(978-1-4222-2831-9(2))* Mason Crest.

Carlson, Dale, et al. Out of Order: Young Adult Manual of Mental Illness & Recovery. 2014. (ENG., Illus.). 256p. (YA). pap. 14.95 *(978-1-884158-37-7(4))* Bick Publishing Hse.

Chou, Joey. Crazy by the Letters. Chou, Joey, illus. 2006. (Illus.). 15.99 *(978-0-9788670-0-3(9))* Choo Choo Clan.

Esherick, Joan. Mood Disorders. McDonnell, Mary Ann & Esherick, Donald, eds. 2013. (State of Mental Illness & Its Therapy Ser.: 19). (Illus.). 128p. (J). (gr. 7-18). 24.95 *(978-1-4222-2829-6(0))* Mason Crest.

—Sleep Deprivation & Its Consequences. Bridgemohan, Carolyn & Forman, Sara, eds. 2013. (Young Adult's Guide to the Science of Health Ser.: 15). 128p. (J). (gr. 7-18). 24.95 *(978-1-4222-2815-9(0))* Mason Crest.

—Sleep Disorders. McDonnell, Mary Ann & Esherick, Donald, eds. 2013. (State of Mental Illness & Its Therapy Ser.: 19). 128p. (J). (gr. 7-18). 24.95 *(978-1-4222-2837-1(1))* Mason Crest.

—Smoking-Related Health Issues. 2014. (Illus.). 128p. (J). *(978-1-4222-2803-6(7))* Mason Crest.

—Suicide & Self-Destructive Behaviors. McDonnell, Mary Ann & Forman, Sara, eds. 2013. (Young Adult's Guide to the Science of Health Ser.: 15). 128p. (J). (gr. 7-18). 24.95 *(978-1-4222-2817-3(7))* Mason Crest.

Giddens, Sandra. Obsessive-Compulsive Disorder. 2009. (Teen Mental Health Ser.). 48p. (gr. 5-6). 53.00 *(978-1-60853-297-1(6))* Rosen Publishing Group, Inc., The.

Iorizzo, Carrie. Anxiety & Phobias. 2013. (ENG., Illus.). 48p. (J). *(978-0-7787-0082-1(8));* pap. *(978-0-7787-0088-3(7))* Crabtree Publishing Co.

Libal, Autumn. Dissociative Disorders. McDonnell, Mary Ann & Esherick, Donald, eds. 2013. (State of Mental Illness & Its Therapy Ser.: 19). 128p. (J). (gr. 7-18). 24.95 *(978-1-4222-2824-1(X))* Mason Crest.

—Impulse-Control Disorders. McDonnell, Mary Ann & Esherick, Donald, eds. 2013. (State of Mental Illness & Its Therapy Ser.: 19). (Illus.). 128p. (J). (gr. 7-18). 24.95 *(978-1-4222-2827-2(4))* Mason Crest.

—Postpartum Disorders. McDonnell, Mary Ann & Esherick, Donald, eds. 2013. (State of Mental Illness & Its Therapy Ser.: 19). (Illus.). 128p. (J). (gr. 7-18). 24.95 *(978-1-4222-2832-6(0))* Mason Crest.

—Psychosomatic Disorders. McDonnell, Mary Ann & Esherick, Donald, eds. 2013. (State of Mental Illness & Its Therapy Ser.: 19). (Illus.). 128p. (J). (gr. 7-18). 24.95 *(978-1-4222-2834-0(7))* Mason Crest.

Marcovitz, Hal. Personality Disorders, 1 vol. 2009. (Diseases & Disorders Ser.). (ENG., Illus.). 112p. (gr. 7-7). lib. bdg. 41.53 *(978-1-4205-0115-5(1),* 74959fc9-7f2f-4321-ac36-7c15241afeb5, Lucent Pr.) Greenhaven Publishing LLC.

McIntosh, Kenneth & Livingston, Phyllis. Youth with Impulse-Control Disorders: On the Spur of the Moment. 2007. (Helping Youth with Mental, Physical, & Social Challenges Ser.). (Illus.). 128p. (YA). pap. 14.95 *(978-1-4222-0447-4(2))* Mason Crest.

—Youth with Juvenile Schizophrenia: the Search for Reality. 2007. (Helping Youth with Mental, Physical, & Social Challenges Ser.). (Illus.). 128p. (YA). (gr. 8-12). pap. 14.95 *(978-1-4222-0448-1(0))* Mason Crest.

Metcalf, Tom & Metcalf, Gena, eds. Phobias, 1 vol. 2008. (Perspectives on Diseases & Disorders Ser.). (ENG., Illus.). 136p. (gr. 10-12). lib. bdg. 45.93 *(978-0-7377-4027-1(2),* 2317a504-eae2-4b7c-b2a3-d189061829d0, Greenhaven Publishing) Greenhaven Publishing LLC.

Mooney, Carla. What Is Anxiety Disorder? 2015. (ENG., Illus.). 80p. (J). lib. bdg. *(978-1-60152-920-6(1))* ReferencePoint Pr., Inc.

—What Is Panic Disorder? 2015. (ENG., Illus.). 80p. (J). lthr. *(978-1-60152-924-4(4))* ReferencePoint Pr., Inc.

Osborne, Jill. Sam Feels Better Now! An Interactive Story for Children. Collier, Kevin Scott, illus. 2008. 44p. (J). pap. 15.95 *(978-1-932690-60-6(3))* Loving Healing Pr., Inc.

Owens, Peter. Teens, Health & Obesity. Developed in Association with the Gallup Organization Staff, ed. 2013. (Gallup Youth Survey: Major Issues & Trends Ser.: 14). (Illus.). 112p. (J). (gr. 7-18). 24.95 *(978-1-4222-2961-3(0))* Mason Crest.

Patterson, James & Friedman, Hal. Med Head: My Knock-Down, Drag-Out, Drugged-Up Battle with My Brain. 2010. (YA). lib. bdg. 23.30 *(978-0-606-14538-1(9))* Turtleback.

Pedrick, Cherry, et al. Obsessive-Compulsive Disorder. 2011. (USA TODAY Health Reports: Diseases & Disorders Ser.). (ENG.). 112p. (gr. 6-12). lib. bdg. 34.60 *(978-0-7613-5884-8(6))* Lerner Publishing Group.

Poole, H. W. Anxiety Disorders, Vol. 13. Walters, Anne S., ed. 2015. (Mental Illnesses & Disorders: Awareness & Understanding Ser.). (Illus.). 48p. (J). (gr. 5). 20.95 *(978-1-4222-3377-1(4))* Mason Crest.

—Obsessive-Compulsive Disorder, Vol. 13. Walters, Anne S., ed. 2015. (Mental Illnesses & Disorders: Awareness & Understanding Ser.). (Illus.). 48p. (J). (gr. 5). 20.95 *(978-1-4222-3373-3(1))* Mason Crest.

—Schizophrenia, Vol. 13. Walters, Anne S., ed. 2015. (Mental Illnesses & Disorders: Awareness & Understanding Ser.). (Illus.). 48p. (J). (gr. 5). 20.95 *(978-1-4222-3375-7(8))* Mason Crest.

—Sleep Disorders, Vol. 13. Walters, Anne S., ed. 2015. (Mental Illnesses & Disorders: Awareness & Understanding Ser.). (Illus.). 48p. (J). (gr. 5). 20.95 *(978-1-4222-3376-4(6))* Mason Crest.

Puliafico, Anthony C. & Robin, Joanna A. The OCD Workbook for Kids: Skills to Help Children Manage Obsessive Thoughts & Compulsive Behaviors. 2017. (ENG., Illus.). 144p. (J). (gr. k-5). pap. 25.95 *(978-1-62625-978-2(X),* 39782) New Harbinger Pubns.

Rauf, Don. Personality. 2017. (Freaky Phenomena Ser.: Vol. 8). (ENG., Illus.). 48p. (J). (gr. 5-8). 20.95 *(978-1-4222-3778-6(8))* Mason Crest.

Shea, John M. Self-Injury & Cutting: Stopping the Pain, 1 vol. 2013. (Helpline: Teen Issues & Answers Ser.). (ENG., Illus.). 80p. (YA). (gr. 5-6). lib. bdg. 38.41 *(978-1-4488-9448-2(4),* 6ad61855-2f3d-4de8-93cc-633919557690, Rosen Classroom) Rosen Publishing Group, Inc., The.

Straus, Susan Farber. Healing Days: A Guide for Kids Who Have Experienced Trauma. Bogade, Maria, illus. 2013. 32p. (J). pap. *(978-1-4338-1293-4(2))* American Psychological Assn.

Straus, Susan Farber & Bogade, Maria. Healing Days: A Guide for Kids Who Have Experienced Trauma. 2013. (ENG., Illus.). 32p. (J). *(978-1-4338-1292-7(4))* American Psychological Assn.

Tourneville, Harry. Attention-Deficit Hyperactivity Disorder, 1 vol. 2013. (ENG., Illus.). 48p. (J). pap. *(978-0-7787-0086-9(0))* Crabtree Publishing Co.

Willett, Edward. Frequently Asked Questions about Exercise Addiction. 2009. (FAQ: Teen Life Ser.). 64p. (gr. 5-6). 58.50 *(978-1-61512-577-7(9))* Rosen Publishing Group, Inc., The.

Williams, Mary E., ed. Self-Injury, 1 vol. 2013. (Introducing Issues with Opposing Viewpoints Ser.). (ENG., Illus.). 128p. (gr. 7-10). lib. bdg. 43.63 *(978-0-7377-6280-8(2),* 2b70df2e-b389-48d8-9c69-105f79c8d56b, Greenhaven Publishing) Greenhaven Publishing LLC.

Wintgens, Alison & Johnson, Maggie. Can I Tell You about Selective Mutism? A Guide for Friends, Family & Professionals. Gallow, Robyn, illus. 2012. (Can I Tell You About...? Ser.). 56p. pap. 15.95 *(978-1-84905-289-4(1),* 694659) Kingsley, Jessica Pubs. GBR. Dist: Hachette UK Distribution.

PSYCHOLOGY, PRACTICAL

see Psychology, Applied

PSYCHOLOGY, RELIGIOUS

Rosenberg, concept. Reach Your Goal. 2011. (YID.). 198p. (YA). 21.00 *(978-0-9832102-1-4(7))* Roth Pubs.

PSYCHOLOGY, SOCIAL

see Social Psychology

PSYCHOLOGY—VOCATIONAL GUIDANCE

Shaw, Jessica. Dream Jobs in Sports Psychology, 1 vol. 2017. (Great Careers in the Sports Industry Ser.). (ENG., Illus.). 128p. (J). (gr. 7-7). 44.13 *(978-1-5383-8144-1(3),* ac94670e-c36e-44e0-afec-60f4c492e1b5) Rosen Publishing Group, Inc., The.

PSYCHOPATHOLOGY

see Psychology, Pathological

PSYCHOPATHY

see Psychology, Pathological

PSYCHOSES

see Mental Illness

PSYCHOTHERAPY

Borenstein, Gerri C. Therapy. 2004. (Life Balance Ser.). (ENG.). 80p. (YA). (gr. 5-8). pap. 6.95 *(978-0-531-15585-1(4),* Watts, Franklin) Scholastic Library Publishing.

Collins-Donnelly, Kate. Starving the Anxiety Gremlin: A Cognitive Behavioural Therapy Workbook on Anxiety Management for Young People. 2013. (Gremlin & Thief CBT Workbooks Ser.). (Illus.). 168p. pap. 21.95 *(978-1-84905-341-9(3),* 694225) Kingsley, Jessica Pubs. GBR. Dist: Hachette UK Distribution.

Conte, Paola, et al. Someone to Talk To: Getting Good at Feeling Better. Keay, Claire, illus. 2017. 64p. (J). pap. *(978-1-4338-2672-6(0),* Magination Pr.) American Psychological Assn.

Esherick, Joan. The Journey Toward Recovery: Youth with Brain Injury. 2004. (Youth with Special Needs Ser.). (Illus.). 128p. (YA). 24.95 *(978-1-59084-734-3(2))* Mason Crest.

Fogerty, Ramona. Prince, Labino, & Chrecas from State Parkway. 2005. (YA). per. 24.95 *(978-0-9759889-5-4(6))* Potenial Psychotherapy Counseling & Remedial Service.

Libal, Autumn. Runaway Train: Youth with Emotional Disturbance. 2003. (Youth with Special Needs Ser.). (Illus.). 127p. (YA). (gr. 7). pap. 14.95 *(978-1-4222-0429-0(4))* Mason Crest.

Rashkin, Rachel. Feeling Better: A Kid's Book about Therapy. Adamson, Bonnie, illus. 2005. 48p. (J). (gr. -1-7). pap. 9.95 *(978-1-59147-238-4(5),* Magination Pr.) American Psychological Assn.

Rashkin-Shoot, Rachel. Feeling Better: A Kid's Book about Therapy. Adamson, Bonnie, illus. 2005. (ENG.). 48p. (J). 14.95 *(978-1-59147-237-7(7),* Magination Pr.) American Psychological Assn.

Scarlet, Janina. Superhero Therapy: Mindfulness Skills to Help Teens & Young Adults Deal with Anxiety, Depression, & Trauma. Alves, Wellinton, illus. 2017. (ENG.). 112p. (YA). (gr. 6-12). pap. 21.95 *(978-1-68403-033-0(1),* 40330) New Harbinger Pubns.

Wheeler, Christine. The Tapping Solution for Teenage Girls: How to Stop Freaking Out & Keep Being Awesome. 2016. 296p. (gr. 5-12). pap. 26.99 *(978-1-4019-4892-4(8))* Hay Hse., Inc.

PTOMAINE POISONING

see Food Poisoning

PUBERTY

see also Adolescence

Attwood, Sarah. Making Sense of Sex: A Forthright Guide to Puberty, Sex & Relationships for People with Asperger's Syndrome. 2008. (Illus.). 320p. (J). (gr. 4-12). pap. 23.95 *(978-1-84310-374-5(5),* 691701) Kingsley, Jessica Pubs. GBR. Dist: Hachette UK Distribution.

Bailey, Jacqui. Sex, Puberty, & All That Stuff: A Guide to Growing Up. 2nd rev. ed. 2016. (ENG., Illus.). 124p. (J). (gr. 5-10). pap. 14.99 *(978-1-4380-0857-8(0))* Sourcebooks, Inc.

Blackstone, Margaret & Guest, Elissa Haden. Girl Stuff: A Survival Guide to Growing Up. Pollak, Barbara, illus. 2006. (ENG.). 176p. (J). (gr. 5-8). 24.94 *(978-0-15-201830-6(1))* Houghton Mifflin Harcourt Publishing Co.

Bloom, Naama. HelloFlo: the Guide, Period: The Everything Puberty Book for the Modern Girl. 2017. (Illus.). 176p. (J). (gr. 5). pap. 12.99 *(978-0-399-18729-2(4),* Dutton Books for Young Readers) Penguin Young Readers Group.

Bourgeois, Paulette & Martyn, Kim. Changes in You & Me: A Book about Puberty Mostly for Girls. Phillips, Louise, illus. rev. ed. 2005. (ENG.). 64p. (J). pap. 16.95 *(978-1-55263-670-1(4))* Kollath-Stensaas Pubs.

Byers, Ann. Frequently Asked Questions about Puberty. (FAQ: Teen Life Ser.). 64p. (gr. 5-6). 2009. 58.50 *(978-1-61512-586-9(8))* 2007. (ENG., Illus.). (YA). 37.13 *(978-1-4042-0966-4(2),* aa0ba62e-3e42-4ab0-b3fb-8d66e7d29848) Rosen Publishing Group, Inc., The.

Daldry, Jeremy. Teenage Guy's Survival Guide. 2011. 11.04 *(978-0-7848-3378-0(8),* Everbind) Marco Bk. Co.

—The Teenage Guy's Survival Guide: The Real Deal on Going Out, Growing up, & Other Guy Stuff. 2nd rev. ed. 2018. (ENG., Illus.). 192p. (J). (gr. 7-17). 17.99 *(978-0-316-56142-6(8))* Little, Brown Bks. for Young Readers.

De la Bédoyère, Camilla. Personal Hygiene & Sexual Health. 2010. (Healthy Lifestyles Ser.). 48p. (J). 35.65 *(978-1-60753-087-9(2))* Amicus Learning.

Deak, JoAnn & Deak, Terrence. The Owner's Manual for Driving Your Adolescent Brain. Harrison, Freya, illus. 2013. (ENG.). 80p. (J). (gr. 4-9). pap. 16.99 *(978-1-939775-02-3(7),* 9781939775023, Little Pickle Pr.) Sourcebooks, Inc.

Favor, Leslie. Everything You Need to Know about Growth Spurts & Delayed Growth. 2009. (Need to Know Library). 64p. (gr. 5-5). 58.50 *(978-1-60854-071-6(5))* Rosen Publishing Group, Inc., The.

Firth, Alex. What's Happening to Me? Meredith, Susan, ed. Larkum, Adam, illus. 2007. 48p. (J). (gr. 4-7). pap. 6.99 *(978-0-7945-1514-0(2),* Usborne) EDC Publishing.

Fiscus, Jim. Coping with Growth Spurts & Delayed Growth. 2009. (Coping Ser.). 192p. (gr. 7-12). 63.90 *(978-1-61512-000-0(9))* Rosen Publishing Group, Inc., The.

Gray, Leon. Puberty, 1 vol. 2010. (Being Healthy, Feeling Great Ser.). (ENG.). 32p. (gr. 3-4). (J). pap. 11.60 *(978-1-61532-378-4(3),* 9e0407d1-f010-400f-b717-8aeebb8f0f43, PowerKids Pr.); (YA). lib. bdg. 30.27 *(978-1-61532-370-8(8),* da2f82e2-1a00-43da-8ed7-819a78789a7b) Rosen Publishing Group, Inc., The.

Gresh, Bob, et al. It's Great to Be a Guy! God Has a Plan for You... & Your Body! 2016. (ENG., Illus.). 128p. (J). (gr. 2-6). pap. 12.99 *(978-0-7369-6278-0(6),* 6962780) Harvest Hse. Pubs.

Hartman, Davida. The Growing up Guide for Girls: What Girls on the Autism Spectrum Need to Know! Suggs, Margaret Anne, illus. 2015. (Growing Up Ser.). 72p. (J). 16.95 *(978-1-84905-574-1(2),* 693027) Kingsley, Jessica Pubs. GBR. Dist: Hachette UK Distribution.

Hickman, Ruth. Going Through Puberty: A Boy's Manual for Body, Mind, & Health. 2013. (What Now? Ser.). (ENG.). 128p. (gr. 2-10). pap. 15.99 *(978-0-9884499-1-6(9))* Lesson Ladder.

—Going Through Puberty: A Girl's Manual for Body, Mind, & Health. 2013. (What Now? Ser.). (ENG.). 128p. (gr. 3-10). pap. 15.99 *(978-0-9884499-0-9(0))* Lesson Ladder.

Holmes, Melisa & Hutchison, Patricia. Girlology's There's Something New about You: A Girl's Guide to Growing Up. 2010. (ENG., Illus.). 128p. (J). (gr. 7-11). pap. 12.95 *(978-0-7573-1526-8(7),* HCI Teens) Health Communications, Inc.

Ibrahim, Marawa. The Girl Guide. Erkas, Sinem, illus. 2018. 214p. (J). *(978-1-5490-6729-7(X))* HarperCollins Pubs.

Kahaner, Ellen. Everything You Need to Know about Growing up Female. 2009. (Need to Know Library). 64p. (gr. 5-5). 58.50 *(978-1-60854-070-9(7))* Rosen Publishing Group, Inc., The.

Lluch, Isabel B. The Ultimate Girls' Guide Journal to Feel Confident, Pretty & Happy. 2009. 100p. (J). (gr. 6-7). spiral bd. 9.95 *(978-1-934386-59-0(6))* WS Publishing.

Loewen, Nancy & Skelley, Paula. Tangles, Growth Spurts, & Being You: Questions & Answers about Growing Up. Mora, Julissa, illus. 2015. (Girl Talk Ser.). (ENG.). 32p. (J). (gr. 3-9). lib. bdg. 28.65 *(978-1-4914-1860-4(5),* 127298, Capstone Pr.) Capstone.

Madaras, Lynda. My Body, My Self for Boys. 2nd rev. ed. 2007. (What's Happening to My Body? Ser.). (ENG., Illus.). 128p. (gr. 4-6). pap. 16.99 *(978-1-55704-767-0(7),* William Morrow Paperbacks) HarperCollins Pubs.

—My Body, My Self for Girls. 3rd rev. ed. 2007. (What's Happening to My Body? Ser.). (ENG., Illus.). 160p. (gr. 4-6). pap. 13.99 *(978-1-55704-766-3(9),* William Morrow Paperbacks) HarperCollins Pubs.

—What's Happening to My Body? Book for Boys. 3rd rev. ed. 2007. (What's Happening to My Body? Ser.). (ENG., Illus.). 256p. (gr. 7-9). 24.99 *(978-1-55704-769-4(3),* Morrow, William & Co.) HarperCollins Pubs.

Madaras, Lynda & Madaras, Area. Que Pasa en Mi Cuerpo? el Libro para Muchachos: La Guía de Mayor Venta Sobre el Desarrollo, Escrita para Adolescentes y Preadolescentes. 2012. (What's Happening to My Body? Ser.). (ENG., Illus.). 256p. (gr. 4-18). pap. 14.99 *(978-1-55704-940-7(8),* William Morrow Paperbacks) HarperCollins Pubs.

—Que Pasa en Mi Cuerpo? Libro para Muchachas: La Guía de Mayor Venta Sobre el Desarrollo Escrita para Adolescentes y Preadolescentes. 2011. (What's Happening to My Body? Ser.). (ENG., Illus.). 288p. (gr. 4-18). pap. 14.99 *(978-1-55704-939-1(4),* William Morrow Paperbacks) HarperCollins Pubs.

Madaras, Lynda, et al. What's Happening to My Body? Book for Boys: Revised Edition. 3rd rev. ed. 2007. (What's Happening to My Body? Ser.). (ENG., Illus.). 256p. (gr. 5-7). pap. 16.99 *(978-1-55704-765-6(0),* William Morrow Paperbacks) HarperCollins Pubs.

—What's Happening to My Body? Book for Girls: Revised Edition. 3rd rev. ed. 2007. (What's Happening to My Body? Ser.). (ENG., Illus.). 288p. (gr. 7-9). pap. 16.99 *(978-1-55704-764-9(2),* William Morrow Paperbacks) HarperCollins Pubs.

Mason, Paul. Your Growing Body & Remarkable Reproductive System. 2015. (Your Brilliant Body! Ser.). (ENG., Illus.). 32p. (J). (gr. 4-5). lib. bdg. *(978-0-7787-2196-3(5))* Crabtree Publishing Co.

Mejia Soto, Guillermina. Higiene de la Pubertad. 2003. (SPA.). 80p. pap. 12.48 *(978-970-661-099-7(5))* Edamex, Editores Asociados Mexicanos, S. A. de C. V. MEX. Dist: Giron Bks.

Meredith, Susan. What's Happening to Me? (Girls Edition) Leschnikoff, Nancy, illus. 2006. 48p. (J). pap. 6.99 *(978-0-7945-1267-5(4),* Usborne) EDC Publishing.

Metzger, Julie & Lehman, Robert. Will Puberty Last My Whole Life? REAL Answers to REAL Questions from Preteens about Body Changes, Sex, & Other Growing-Up Stuff. Cerizo, Lia, illus. 2018. 224p. (J). (gr. 4-7). pap. 18.99 *(978-1-63217-179-5(1),* Little Bigfoot) Sasquatch Bks.

Miles, Lisa & Chown, Xanna Eve. How to Survive Zits & Bad Hair Days. 2013. (Girl Talk Ser.). 48p. (J). (gr. 5-8). pap. 70.50 *(978-1-4777-0725-8(5),* Rosen Reference); (ENG., Illus.). pap. 12.75 *(978-1-4777-0724-1(7),* 410515d3-2c77-4108-9686-6acbe012da9a, Rosen Reference); (ENG., Illus.). lib. bdg. 34.41 *(978-1-4777-0709-8(3),* 0cecfa4b-a962-4237-8542-8833a6161404, Rosen Classroom) Rosen Publishing Group, Inc., The.

Moe, Barbara. Coping with Rejection. 2009. (Coping Ser.). 192p. (gr. 7-12). 63.90 *(978-1-61512-010-9(6))* Rosen Publishing Group, Inc., The.

Natterson, Cara. The Care & Keeping of You 2: The Body Book for Older Girls. Masse, Josee, illus. 2013. (American Girl(r) Wellbeing Ser.). (ENG.). 96p. (J). pap. 12.99 *(978-1-60958-042-1(7))* American Girl Publishing, Inc.

—The Care & Keeping of You 2 Journal. Masse, Josee, illus. 2013. (American Girl(r) Wellbeing Ser.). (ENG.). 96p. (J). spiral bd. 8.99 *(978-1-60958-108-4(3))* American Girl Publishing, Inc.

—Guy Stuff: The Body Book for Boys. Player, Micah, illus. 2017. (American Girl(r) Wellbeing Ser.). (ENG.). 112p. (J). pap. 12.99 *(978-1-68337-026-0(0))* American Girl Publishing, Inc.

Nuchi, Adah. Bunk 9's Guide to Growing Up: Secrets, Tips, & Expert Advice on the Good, the Bad, & the Awkward. Hunt, Meg, illus. 2017. (ENG.). 192p. (J). (gr. 3-7). pap. 12.95 *(978-0-7611-9359-3(6),* 19359) Workman Publishing Co., Inc.

Parker, Victoria. Little Book of Growing Up. 2007. (ENG., Illus.). 128p. (J). (gr. 7-17). pap. 6.99 *(978-0-340-93099-1(3))* Hachette Children's Group GBR. Dist: Hachette Bk. Group.

Picone, Linda. My Changing Body. 2010. 150p. (J). (gr. 4-7). pap. 9.95 *(978-1-57749-181-1(5));* (Illus.). pap. 9.95 *(978-1-57749-187-3(4))* Taylor Trade Publishing.

Plaisted, Caroline. Boy Talk. 2011. (ENG., Illus.). 48p. (J). pap. 11.95 *(978-1-926853-90-1(3))* Saunders Bk. Co. CAN. Dist: RiverStream Publishing.

—Girl Talk: Girl Talk: A Survival Guide to Growing Up. 2011. (ENG., Illus.). 48p. (J). pap. 11.95 *(978-1-926853-91-8(1))* Saunders Bk. Co. CAN. Dist: RiverStream Publishing.

Saltz, Gail. Changing You! A Guide to Body Changes & Sexuality. Cravath, Lynne Avril, illus. 2009. 32p. (J). (gr. 1-3). pap. 7.99 *(978-0-14-241479-8(4),* Puffin Books) Penguin Young Readers Group.

Schaefer, Valorie. The Care & Keeping of You 1: The Body Book for Younger Girls. 2016. (American Girl: the Care & Keeping of You Ser.). (ENG.). 104p. (gr. 4-7). 31.19 *(978-1-4844-9774-6(0))* American Girl Publishing, Inc.

Silverthorne, Sandy. Surviving Zits: How to Cope with Your Changing Self. Silverthorne, Sandy, illus. 2006. (Illus.). 96p. (YA). (gr. 3-6). pap. 5.99 *(978-0-7847-1435-5(5),* 42177) Standard Publishing.

Smith, Liz. A Girl's Guide to Growing up - Booklet, 10 per packet. Perry, Gala, illus. 2005. (J). 63.95 *(978-1-55942-207-9(6))* Witcher Productions.

Spilsbury, Louise. Zits & Hormones? Skills to Handle Puberty, 1 vol. 2018. (Life Skills Ser.). (ENG.). 48p. (gr. 5-5). lib. bdg. 30.93 *(978-0-7660-9977-7(6),* 0dcf3707-d879-4ad5-8cff-90ff60fd43d0) Enslow Publishing, LLC.

Stubbs, Lori. Fearfully & Wonderfully Made: A Christian Health & Puberty Guide for Preteen Boys & Girls. Stubbs, Robert Earl, illus. 2nd ed. 2005. 40p. (J). (gr. -1 — 1). pap. 10.00 *(978-1-58597-174-9(X))* Leathers Publishing.

Vermond, Kira. Growing Up, Inside & Out. 2013. 104p. *(978-1-77147-036-0(4))* Owlkids Bks. Inc.

von Holleben, Jan & Helms, Antje. Does This Happen to Everyone? A Budding Adult's Guide to Puberty. 2014. (ENG.). 160p. (gr. 5-12). 24.95 *(978-3-89955-521-9(X))* Die Gestalten Verlag DEU. Dist: Ingram Publisher Services.

Whittaker, Helen. How Toys Roll. 2012. (Toys & Forces Ser.). 32p. (gr. 1-4). lib. bdg. 27.10 *(978-1-59920-468-0(1))* Black Rabbit Bks.

PUBLIC ADMINISTRATION

Bow, James. What Is the Executive Branch? 2013. (ENG.). 32p. (J). *(978-0-7787-0902-2(7));* pap. *(978-0-7787-0907-7(8))* Crabtree Publishing Co.

—What Is the Executive Branch. 2013. (Your Guide to Government Ser.). (ENG.). 32p. (J). (gr. 3-6). 19.75 *(978-1-68065-726-5(7))* Perfection Learning Corp.

Egan, Tracie. The President & the Executive Branch. 2009. (Primary Source Library of American Citizenship Ser.). 32p. (gr. 5-5). 47.90 *(978-1-61511-229-6(4),* Rosen Reference) Rosen Publishing Group, Inc., The.

Hirsch, Rebecca E. How the Executive Branch Works, 1 vol. 2015. (How the US Government Works). (ENG.). 48p. (J). (gr. 4-8). lib. bdg. 35.64 *(978-1-62403-635-4(X),* 17045) ABDO Publishing Co.

Kishel, Ann-Marie. Government Services. 2007. (First Step Nonfiction - Government Ser.). (ENG., Illus.). 24p. (gr. k-2). lib. bdg. 23.93 *(978-0-8225-6397-6(5),* Lerner Pubns.) Lerner Publishing Group.

Merino, Noël, ed. Government Spending, 1 vol. 2013. (Opposing Viewpoints Ser.). (ENG., Illus.). 240p. (gr. 10-12). pap. 34.80 *(978-0-7377-6323-2(X),* c3f59ddd-5596-4b13-b2f7-360685295e72, Greenhaven Publishing) Greenhaven Publishing LLC.

—Government Spending, 1 vol. 2013. (Opposing Viewpoints Ser.). (ENG., Illus.). 240p. (gr. 10-12). lib. bdg. 50.43 *(978-0-7377-6322-5(1),* a9ace156-5a51-459b-b885-497bba1670bd, Greenhaven Publishing) Greenhaven Publishing LLC.

Townsend, Chris. What Does an Officeholder Do?, 1 vol. 2018. (What Does a Citizen Do? Ser.). (ENG.). 48p. (gr. 5-5). 30.93 *(978-0-7660-9881-7(8),* a410a0f6-47e6-4eac-a1a4-b603bd73cc52) Enslow Publishing, LLC.

PUBLIC FINANCE

see Finance, Public

PUBLIC HEALTH

see also Cemeteries; Communicable Diseases; Hospitals; Noise; Refuse and Refuse Disposal; Sanitation; Sewage Disposal; Vaccination; Water—Pollution; Water-Supply

Amidon Lusted, Marcia, ed. Universal Health Care, 1 vol. 2019. (At Issue Ser.). (ENG.). 128p. (gr. 10-12). pap. 28.80 *(978-1-5345-0625-1(X),* 482f2358-d206-47a7-9908-dfd9d2196a8e) Greenhaven Publishing LLC.

Asher, Dana. Epidemiologists: Life Tracking Deadly Diseases. 2009. (Extreme Careers Ser.). 64p. (gr. 5-5). 58.50 *(978-1-61512-392-6(X),* Rosen Reference) Rosen Publishing Group, Inc., The.

Connolly, Sean. The World Health Organization. 2009. (Global Organizations Ser.). (ENG., Illus.). 48p. (J). (gr. 4-7). pap. *(978-1-897563-39-7(6))* Saunders Bk. Co.

Davis, Catherine G. USA TODAY(r) Lifeline Biographies: Spring 2012 New Releases. 2012. (USA TODAY Health Reports: Diseases & Disorders Ser.). 112p. (gr. 6-12). lib. bdg. 138.40 *(978-0-7613-8911-8(3),* Twenty-First Century Bks.) Lerner Publishing Group.

Dodge Cummings, Judy. Epidemics & Pandemics: Real Tales of Deadly Diseases. 2018. (Mystery & Mayhem Ser.). (ENG., Illus.). 128p. (J). (gr. 5-8). 19.95 *(978-1-61930-623-3(9),* a805827d-f0ef-46fc-83de-bb1801c87df6) Nomad Pr.

—EPIDEMICS AND PANDEMICS: REAL TALES OF DEADLY DISEASES. 2018. (Mystery & Mayhem Ser.). (ENG., Illus.). 128p. (J). (gr. 5-8). pap. 9.95 *(978-1-61930-625-7(5),* 9ad5f007-4082-4dcf-99ee-bb72b26affa8) Nomad Pr.

Doyle, Sheri. Designing Healthy Communities. 2018. (Design Thinking for a Better World Ser.). (ENG., Illus.). 48p. (J). (gr. 6-7). *(978-0-7787-4459-7(0));* pap. *(978-0-7787-4463-4(9))* Crabtree Publishing Co.

Espejo, Roman, ed. Should Vaccinations Be Mandatory?, 1 vol. 2014. (At Issue Ser.). (ENG.). 128p. (gr. 10-12). lib. bdg. 41.03 *(978-0-7377-6862-6(2),* bf6063c9-6103-45e4-878c-e4d34c5cda5c, Greenhaven Publishing) Greenhaven Publishing LLC.

Falligant, Erin. Ambulances / Ambulancias. Sánchez, Sr., illus. 2019. (Machines! / ¡Las Máquinas! Ser.). (MUL.). 24p. (J). (gr. -1-2). lib. bdg. 33.99 *(978-1-68410-336-2(3),* 140256) Cantata Learning.

Ferguson, Olivia, ed. Health Care, 1 vol. 2011. (Issues That Concern You Ser.). (ENG., Illus.). 112p. (gr. 7-10). lib. bdg. 43.63 *(978-0-7377-5207-6(6),* 6f11be8d-1d80-4eff-92bd-7778f9b47b69, Greenhaven Publishing) Greenhaven Publishing LLC.

Gagne, Tammy. Battling Against Drug-Resistant Bacteria. 2017. (Science Frontiers Ser.). (ENG., Illus.). 32p. (J). (gr. 3-6). pap. 9.95 *(978-1-63235-390-0(3),* 11875, 12-Story Library) Bookstaves, LLC.

Hamilton, Robert M. Should the Government Pay for Health Care?, 1 vol. 2019. (Points of View Ser.). (ENG.). 24p. (gr. 3-3). pap. 9.25 *(978-1-5345-2997-7(7),* 7c8a9435-fe7b-40c4-89f2-86fb8a9c50e6, KidHaven Publishing) Greenhaven Publishing LLC.

Health Alert Group 3, 12 vols., Set. Incl. Cerebral Palsy. Bjorklund, Ruth. lib. bdg. 35.50 *(978-0-7614-2209-9(9),* 5366b459-5a49-43f4-9e17-d75a4823c184); Down Syndrome. Targ Brill, Marlene. lib. bdg. 35.50 *(978-0-7614-2207-5(2),* 53609adc-4500-4291-aee5-1769ffd96e1e); Epilepsy. Bjorklund, Ruth. lib. bdg. 35.50 *(978-0-7614-2206-8(4),* afb1a2ec-d10d-4799-987e-3e7b7ef6dcc4); Flu. Hoffmann, Gretchen. lib. bdg. 35.50 *(978-0-7614-2208-2(0),* 3e3dd1b2-f051-42a9-9c07-af947933dcfd); Headaches. Petreycik, Rick. lib. bdg. 35.50 *(978-0-7614-2210-5(2),* a73a9a01-00f0-41e2-bea4-c4667e5dd25d); Meningitis. Klosterman, Lorrie. lib. bdg. 35.50 *(978-0-7614-2211-2(0),* ec8ffe3c-5ee0-491b-aabd-7d243537f3b5); (Illus.). 64p. (gr. 4-4). (Health Alert Ser.). (ENG.). 2007. Set lib. bdg. 213.00 *(978-0-7614-2205-1(6),* 59e5548f-68fc-4e08-a72e-75049a6f4aec, Cavendish Square) Cavendish Square Publishing LLC.

Heitkamp, Kristina Lyn, ed. Universal Health Care, 1 vol. 2018. (Current Controversies Ser.). (ENG.). 176p. (gr. 10-12). 48.03 *(978-1-5345-0316-8(1),* 675cfd95-4786-4989-914c-a21843feafe3) Greenhaven Publishing LLC.

Hepplewhite, Peter. Thomas Crapper, Corsets, & Cruel Britannia: A Grim History of the Vexing Victorians!, 1 vol. 2015. (Awfully Ancient Ser.). (ENG., Illus.). 32p. (J). (gr. 5-5). pap. 11.50 *(978-1-4824-3133-9(5),* 15459855-6dea-443b-a4cd-9d101cd4f42b) Stevens, Gareth Publishing LLLP.

Hundley, Kris & Florida, University Of. The Disease Detectives: Unraveling How Viruses Go Viral. 2015. (ENG.). 20p. pap. 5.95 *(978-1-942852-05-6(3),* Gatorbytes) Univ. Pr. of Florida.

Hunnicutt, Susan C., ed. Universal Health Care, 1 vol. 2010. (Opposing Viewpoints Ser.). (ENG., Illus.). 240p. (gr. 10-12). 50.43 *(978-0-7377-4648-8(3),* 62cc7591-539f-4fa7-8937-338aa1a0cb41); pap. 34.80 *(978-0-7377-4649-5(1),* 7547a291-ff5f-45cb-b687-acb027c9e39d) Greenhaven Publishing LLC. (Greenhaven Publishing).

Kidder, Tracy. Mountains Beyond Mountains (Adapted for Young People) The Quest of Dr. Paul Farmer, a Man Who Would Cure the World. 2014. (ENG.). (YA). (gr. 7). lib. bdg. 19.60 *(978-1-68065-029-7(7))* Perfection Learning Corp.

Kidder, Tracy & French, Michael. Mountains Beyond Mountains (Adapted for Young People) The Quest of Dr. Paul Farmer, a Man Who Would Cure the World. 2014. (ENG.). 288p. (YA). (gr. 7). pap. 9.99 *(978-0-385-74319-8(X),* Ember) Random Hse. Children's Bks.

Krasner, Barbara, ed. Harm Reduction: Public Health Strategies, 1 vol. 2018. (Opposing Viewpoints Ser.). (ENG.). 176p. (gr. 10-12). 50.43 *(978-1-5345-0413-4(3),* db19734f-a4c6-431b-a7e2-626d22d0890a) Greenhaven Publishing LLC.

Lerner Publishing Group Staff. USA Today Health Reports Set: Diseases & Disorders, 5 vols., Set. 2011. (YA). (gr. 6-12). lib. bdg. 173.00 *(978-0-7613-7473-2(6))* Lerner Publishing Group.

Markovics, Joyce L. Blitzed by a Blizzard! 2010. (Disaster Survivors Ser.). (Illus.). 32p. (YA). (gr. 4-7). lib. bdg. 28.50 *(978-1-936087-54-9(5))* Bearport Publishing Co., Inc.

Marsico, Katie. The World Health Organization. 2014. (Community Connections: How Do They Help? Ser.). (ENG., Illus.). 24p. (J). (gr. 2-5). 29.21 *(978-1-63188-030-8(6),* 205527) Cherry Lake Publishing.

Mendenhall, Emily & Koon, Adam, eds. Environmental Health Narratives: A Reader for Youth. Adams Burque, Hannah, illus. 2012. (ENG.). 400p. pap. 34.95 *(978-0-8263-5166-1(2),* P208970) Univ. of New Mexico Pr.

Merino, Noël, ed. Health Care, 1 vol. 2014. (Teen Rights & Freedoms Ser.). (ENG., Illus.). 144p. (gr. 10-12). lib. bdg. 43.63 *(978-0-7377-7000-1(7),* 921bf5c4-5e54-4b3c-a86d-739ce9155541, Greenhaven Publishing) Greenhaven Publishing LLC.

—Medical Testing, 1 vol. 2014. (Opposing Viewpoints Ser.). (ENG., Illus.). 224p. (gr. 10-12). pap. 34.80 *(978-0-7377-6960-9(2),* 9803b97e-50d1-432a-a60d-bbc6011e787c, Greenhaven Publishing) Greenhaven Publishing LLC.

—Medical Testing, 1 vol. 2014. (Opposing Viewpoints Ser.). (ENG.). 224p. (gr. 10-12). lib. bdg. 50.43 *(978-0-7377-6959-3(9),* 7e8c0293-c1d9-4507-9e8f-0084d56ae326, Greenhaven Publishing) Greenhaven Publishing LLC.

Mitchell, Kirstin. Madame Anopheles. 2008.Tr. of Seòora Anopheles. (Illus.). 26p. (J). pap. 20.00 *(978-0-9816301-0-6(3))* Alexander, Raine.

Naden, Corinne. Patients' Rights, 1 vol. 2008. (Open for Debate Ser.). (ENG., Illus.). 144p. (YA). (gr. 8-8). lib. bdg. 45.50 *(978-0-7614-2576-2(4),* 4f39b561-94b9-4c84-aeca-7b4241a84c60) Cavendish Square Publishing LLC.

Perritano, John. Health & Medicine, Vol. 9. van Dijk, Ruud, ed. 2016. (Making of the Modern World: 1945 to the Present Ser.). (Illus.). 64p. (J). (gr. 7). 23.95 *(978-1-4222-3639-0(0))* Mason Crest.

Randolph, Joanne. Snowplows. 2009. (Road Machines Ser.). 24p. (gr. k-1). 37.50 *(978-1-60852-466-2(3),* PowerKids Pr.) Rosen Publishing Group, Inc., The.

Ricciuti, Edward R. Qué Hay Dentro de una Ambulancia? / What's Inside an Ambulance?, 1 vol. 2008. (Qué Hay Dentro? / What's Inside? Ser.). (ENG & SPA., Illus.). 32p. (gr. 1-2). lib. bdg. 25.50 *(978-0-7614-2471-0(7),* 432666dd-94a2-4b8c-987c-4ed2c727aec4) Cavendish Square Publishing LLC.

—Qué Hay Dentro de una Ambulancia? (What's Inside an Ambulance?), 1 vol. 2008. (Qué Hay Dentro? (What's Inside?) Ser.). (SPA., Illus.). 32p. (gr. 1-2). lib. bdg. 25.50 *(978-0-7614-2390-4(7),* 2d7391de-093f-42e8-a53f-83a21ba67a6d) Cavendish Square Publishing LLC.

—What's Inside an Ambulance, 1 vol. 2008. (What's Inside? Ser.). (ENG.). 32p. (gr. 1-2). pap. 9.23 *(978-0-7614-3343-9(0),* 45df7333-572a-4295-88bb-b90f71185e49) Cavendish Square Publishing LLC.

Riggs, Kate. Ambulances. 2016. (Seedlings Ser.). (ENG.). 24p. (J). (gr. k-2). pap. 9.99 *(978-1-62832-183-8(0),* 21011, Creative Paperbacks) Creative Co., The.

Roberts, Kathryn, ed. Global Health, 1 vol. 2019. (Global Viewpoints Ser.). (ENG.). 200p. (gr. 10-12). pap. 32.70 *(978-1-5345-0646-6(2),* 6a8667d3-d8d7-4f22-b78e-b6484fa86f15, Greenhaven Publishing) Greenhaven Publishing LLC.

Roza, Greg. How Do Sewers Work?, 1 vol. 2016. (STEM Waterworks Ser.). (ENG.). 32p. (J). (gr. 5-5). pap. 12.75 *(978-1-4994-2003-6(X),* f2054283-5648-4f69-9e25-8ac5ba720812, PowerKids Pr.) Rosen Publishing Group, Inc., The.

Rudolph, Jessica. Erased by a Tornado! 2010. (Disaster Survivors Ser.). (Illus.). 32p. (YA). (gr. 4-7). lib. bdg. 28.50 *(978-1-936087-52-5(9))* Bearport Publishing Co., Inc.

Steffens, Bradley. Gun Violence. 2019. (Emerging Issues in Public Health Ser.). (ENG.). 80p. (J). (gr. 6-12). 41.27 *(978-1-68282-669-0(4))* ReferencePoint Pr., Inc.

Yomtov, Nel. Epidemiologist. 2013. (21st Century Skills Library: Cool STEM Careers Ser.). (ENG., Illus.). 32p. (gr. 4-8). (J). pap. 14.21 *(978-1-62431-031-7(1),* 202481); 32.07 *(978-1-62431-007-2(9),* 202479) Cherry Lake Publishing.

PUBLIC OPINION

see also Attitude (Psychology); Propaganda

also names of countries with the subdivision Foreign Opinion, e.g., United States—Foreign Opinion

Chant, Christopher. Stalemate: U. S. Public Opinion of the War in Vietnam. 2017. (Vietnam War Ser.: Vol. 5). (ENG., Illus.). 80p. (J). (gr. 7-12). 24.95 *(978-1-4222-3891-2(1))* Mason Crest.

Davies, Monika. Life in Numbers: Polls & Surveys. 2018. (TIME(r): Informational Text Ser.). (ENG., Illus.). 48p. (J). (gr. 6-8). pap. 13.99 *(978-1-4258-5005-0(7))* Teacher Created Materials, Inc.

Eboch, M. M., ed. Witch Hunt or Justice? Accusations Against Public Figures, 1 vol. 2018. (Introducing Issues with Opposing Viewpoints Ser.). (ENG.). 120p. (gr. 7-10). 43.63 *(978-1-5345-0426-4(5),* 263f4dd0-0dfc-4166-bfce-ddf03644beb7) Greenhaven Publishing LLC.

Gallup Youth Survey: Major Issues & Trends, 6 vols., Set. 2004. (YA). 137.70 *(978-1-59084-720-6(2))* Mason Crest.

Gordon, Sherri Mabry. Are You at Risk for Public Shaming?, 1 vol. 2015. (Got Issues? Ser.). (ENG., Illus.). 112p. (gr. 7-8). lib. bdg. 38.93 *(978-0-7660-7136-0(7),* 69eea255-003c-4e23-bc3a-ddb15c43d19f) Enslow Publishing, LLC.

Peaceful Protesters, 12 vols. 2017. (Peaceful Protesters Ser.). (ENG.). (J). (gr. 9-9). lib. bdg. 267.00 *(978-1-5026-3226-5(8),* 0c586a6d-cba6-41f9-b70b-9649d4dc91f8) Cavendish Square Publishing LLC.

Public Persecutions, 12 vols. 2016. (Public Persecutions Ser.). (ENG.). 128p. (YA). (gr. 9-9). lib. bdg. 284.16 *(978-1-5026-2357-7(9),* 362ded1a-f05e-455f-b4f9-bd2e5ebe20eb, Cavendish Square) Cavendish Square Publishing LLC.

PUBLIC PLAYGROUNDS

see Playgrounds

PUBLIC RELATIONS

Harmon, Daniel E. Careers As a Marketing & Public Relations Specialist, 1 vol. 2013. (Essential Careers Ser.). (ENG.). 80p. (YA). (gr. 6-6). 37.47 *(978-1-4777-1793-6(5),* 272a2c97-ae58-47e9-8018-f86ab7fd8afe) Rosen Publishing Group, Inc., The.

Vaughan, Jenny. Causes & Campaigns. 2010. (Media Power Ser.). 48p. (YA). (gr. 5-9). 35.65 *(978-1-60753-111-1(9))* Amicus Learning.

PUBLIC SCHOOLS

Collins, Anna. Student Rights in a New Age of Activism, 1 vol. annot. ed. 2019. (Hot Topics Ser.). (ENG.). 104p. (gr. 7-7). pap. 20.99 *(978-1-5345-6816-7(6),* 1436407c-9732-41af-bc24-a22a844c782f); lib. bdg. 41.03 *(978-1-5345-6817-4(4),* eca42a66-856f-4390-8ad2-5fb09080a7f4) Greenhaven Publishing LLC. (Lucent Pr.).

Lassieur, Allison. School 100 Years Ago. 2011. (Amicus Readers. 100 Years Ago (Level 2) Ser.). (ENG.). 24p. (J). (gr. 1-4). lib. bdg. 25.65 *(978-1-60753-164-7(X),* 17054) Amicus.

PUBLIC SERVICE CORPORATIONS

see Public Utilities

PUBLIC SPEAKING

see also Acting; Debates and Debating

Anderson, Chris & Oberweger, Lorin. Thank You for Coming to My Ted Talk: A Teen Guide to Great Public Speaking. 2020. (ENG.). 160p. (J). (gr. 5-7). 16.99 *(978-1-328-99507-0(0),* 1710660, Clarion Bks.) HarperCollins Pubs.

Athans, Sandra K. & Parente, Robin W. Tips & Tricks for Evaluating an Argument & Its Claims, 1 vol. 2014. (Common Core Readiness Guide to Reading Ser.). (ENG.). 64p. (YA). (gr. 6-6). 36.13 *(978-1-4777-7559-2(5),* 438b0b58-4c39-45ea-9115-7c51509714d1) Rosen Publishing Group, Inc., The.

Benjamin, Susan J. Speak with Success: A Student's Step-by-Step Guide to Fearless Public Speaking. 2nd ed. 2007. (Illus.). 186p. (J). (gr. 6-11). per. 14.95 *(978-1-59647-127-6(1))* Good Year Bks.

Bodden, Valerie. Effective Speeches. 2010. (Nonfiction Ser.). 48p. (YA). (gr. 5-18). 23.95 *(978-1-58341-935-9(7),* Creative Education) Creative Co., The.

—Giving a Presentation. 2014. (Classroom How-To Ser.). (ENG.). 48p. (J). (gr. 5-8). *(978-1-60818-280-0(0),* 21296, Creative Education) Creative Co., The.

—Giving a Presentation. Williams, Nate, illus. 2014. (Classroom How-To Ser.). (ENG.). 48p. (J). (gr. 5-8). pap. 12.00 *(978-0-89812-986-1(9),* 21297, Creative Paperbacks) Creative Co., The.

Bullard, Lisa. Ace Your Oral or Multimedia Presentation, 1 vol. 2009. (Ace It! Information Literacy Ser.). (ENG., Illus.). 48p. (gr. 3-3). lib. bdg. 27.93 *(978-0-7660-3391-7(0),* c07fc8b0-ea93-46a6-8d12-19207511807a) Enslow Publishing, LLC.

Burgett, Cindy. Policy Debate, 1 vol. 2007. (National Forensic League Library of Public Speaking & Debate Ser.). (ENG., Illus.). 48p. (J). (gr. 5-5). lib. bdg. 34.47 *(978-1-4042-1024-0(5),* b5065cf0-fd73-4603-bd5c-a7e82421d9a2) Rosen Publishing Group, Inc., The.

Coleman, Miriam. Present It: Understanding Contexts & Audiences, 1 vol. 2012. (Core Skills Ser.). (ENG., Illus.). 32p. (J). (gr. 4-5). 28.93 *(978-1-4488-7455-2(6),* f28786ef-5709-4f9a-8d1b-45b99ba4a420); pap. 11.00 *(978-1-4488-7527-6(7),* bcaf3c68-303d-4e03-bb9a-ed4250aed08f) Rosen Publishing Group, Inc., The. (PowerKids Pr.).

Duffy, Claire. The Australian Schoolkids' Guide to Debating & Public Speaking. 2015. (Illus.). 192p. pap. 26.99 *(978-1-74223-423-6(2),* UNSW Press) NewSouth Publishing AUS. Dist: Independent Pubs. Group.

—The Teen's Guide to Debating & Public Speaking. 2018. (ENG., Illus.). 280p. (YA). pap. 19.99 *(978-1-4597-4178-2(1))* Dundurn Pr. CAN. Dist: Publishers Group West (PGW).

Engleberg, Isa N. & Daly, John A. Presentations in Everyday Life: Strategies for Effective Speaking. 2nd ed. 2004. 544p. (YA). pap. 74.36 *(978-0-618-26016-4(1),* 313251) CENGAGE Learning.

Farris, Christine King. March On! The Day My Brother Martin Changed the World. Ladd, London, illus. 2011. (J). (gr. 2-7). 29.95 *(978-0-545-10689-4(3))* Weston Woods Studios, Inc.

Green, Lyric & Bullard, Lisa. Future Ready Oral & Multimedia Presentations, 1 vol. 2017. (Future Ready Project Skills Ser.). (ENG.). 48p. (gr. 3-4). pap. 12.70 *(978-0-7660-8771-2(9),* ff6e8704-8eef-4dea-9521-8df8765b69e6); lib. bdg. 29.60 *(978-0-7660-8659-3(3),* dd996b0f-14fc-44f4-b219-974e8bf18376) Enslow Publishing, LLC.

Haney, Johannah. Sharpen Your Debate & Speech Writing Skills, 1 vol. 2012. (Sharpen Your Writing Skills Ser.). (ENG., Illus.). 64p. (gr. 6-7). pap. 11.53 *(978-1-59845-341-6(6),* 5bd28e3e-3e17-4f0d-8eea-37bfce6bbc22); lib. bdg. 31.93 *(978-0-7660-3904-9(8),* 255885a4-6bb4-4e05-b793-34a00f20b033) Enslow Publishing, LLC.

Harper, Leslie. Cómo Dar un Discurso, 1 vol. 2014. (Sé un líder de la Comunidad (Be a Community Leader) Ser.). (SPA.). 32p. (J). (gr. 5-5). lib. bdg. 27.93 *(978-1-4777-6917-1(X),* 661093b5-051f-4602-81a7-8cd6ffb3ad7f, PowerKids Pr.) Rosen Publishing Group, Inc., The.

—How to Give a Speech, 1 vol. 2014. (Be a Community Leader Ser.). (ENG.). 32p. (J). (gr. 5-5). lib. bdg. 27.93 *(978-1-4777-6697-2(9),* 5f47c45c-de93-496f-9aa2-d8cf1b79062c, PowerKids Pr.) Rosen Publishing Group, Inc., The.

Ingalls, Ann. Seth & Savannah Build a Speech. Lee, Karen, illus. 2012. (Writing Builders Ser.). 32p. (J). (gr. 2-4). pap. 11.94 *(978-1-60357-391-7(7))*; lib. bdg. 25.27 *(978-1-59953-511-1(4))* Norwood Hse. Pr.

Marx, Jeff. How to Win a High School Election: Advice & Ideas Collected from over 1,000 High School Seniors. 2003. 180p. (gr. 7-12). pap. 14.95 *(978-0-9667824-0-0(2))* Marx, Jeff.

McHugh, Jeff. Speak up! Giving an Oral Presentation. Petelinsek, Kathleen, illus. 2015. (Explorer Junior Library: Information Explorer Junior Ser.). (ENG.). 24p. (J). (gr. 1-4). 32.07 *(978-1-63188-864-9(1),* 206036) Cherry Lake Publishing.

Meany, John & Shuster, Kate. Speak Out: A Guide to Middle School Debate. 2004. (Illus.). 188p. pap. 24.95 *(978-1-932716-02-3(5))* International Debate Education Assn.

Meyer, Susan. Performing & Creating Speeches, Demonstrations, & Collaborative Learning Experiences with Cool New Digital Tools, 1 vol. 2013. (Way Beyond PowerPoint: Making 21st Century Presentations Ser.). (ENG.). 48p. (J). (gr. 6-6). 34.41 *(978-1-4777-1837-7(0),* 557e924e-9671-41a9-b113-a871abfc9a8a); pap. 12.75 *(978-1-4777-1851-3(6),* 90bf3a32-fd43-4a63-aab7-cac62720f94f) Rosen Publishing Group, Inc., The. (Rosen Reference).

Minden, Cecilia & Roth, Kate. How to Write & Give a Speech. 2011. (Explorer Junior Library: How to Write Ser.). (ENG., Illus.). 24p. (gr. 1-4). lib. bdg. 29.21 *(978-1-61080-108-9(3),* 201118) Cherry Lake Publishing.

—Writing & Giving a Speech. 2019. (Write It Right Ser.). (ENG., Illus.). 24p. (J). (gr. 1-4). pap. 12.79 *(978-1-5341-3943-5(5),* 212601); lib. bdg. 30.64 *(978-1-5341-4287-9(8),* 212600) Cherry Lake Publishing.

The National Forensic League Library of Public Speaking & Debate, 10 vols., Set. Incl. Lincoln-Douglas Debate. Woodhouse, Cynthia. (YA). lib. bdg. 34.47 *(978-1-4042-1025-7(3),* e6056f8f-4a10-49d9-a031-46bb02edd5cd); Parliamentary Debate. West, Keith. (YA). lib. bdg. 34.47 *(978-1-4042-1029-5(6),* 208330e9-cb83-4cf9-93f3-daa88863505d); Policy Debate. Burgett, Cindy. (J). lib. bdg. 34.47 *(978-1-4042-1024-0(5),* b5065cf0-fd73-4603-bd5c-a7e82421d9a2); Public Forum Debate. Kline, Jason. (J). lib. bdg. 34.47 *(978-1-4042-1027-1(X),* ea511997-738c-4da7-9b3b-71cfc8cdeb82); Student Congress Debate. Jacobi, Adam J. (J). lib. bdg. 34.47 *(978-1-4042-1026-4(1),* b6f78ccd-85b4-464f-b17f-55e0eadf2c12); (Illus.). 48p. (gr. 5-5). 2007. (National Forensic League Library of Public Speaking & Debate Ser.). (ENG.). 2006. Set lib. bdg. 172.35 *(978-1-4042-0937-4(9),* 63693eb4-4dae-4985-ad40-8b4e85480305) Rosen Publishing Group, Inc., The.

Performing & Creating Speeches, Demonstrations, & Collaborative Learning Experiences with Cool New Digital Tools. 2013. (Way Beyond PowerPoint: Making 21st Century Presentations Ser.). 48p. (J). (gr. 5-8). pap. 70.50 *(978-1-4777-1852-0(4),* Rosen Reference) Rosen Publishing Group, Inc., The.

Rauf, Don. Strengthening Public Speaking Skills, 1 vol. 2017. (Skills for Success Ser.). (ENG.). 64p. (gr. 7-7). 36.13 *(978-1-5081-7570-4(5),* 8f8c4f60-2649-4c43-ad65-7687cbbef439, Rosen Young Adult) Rosen Publishing Group, Inc., The.

Shipp, Catherine Elisabeth. 12 Great Tips on Writing a Speech. 2017. (Great Tips on Writing Ser.). (ENG., Illus.). 32p. (J). (gr. 3-6). 32.80 *(978-1-63235-277-4(X),* 11731, 12-Story Library) Bookstaves, LLC.

Spilsbury, Louise. The Student's Toolbox: Tips for Better Public Speaking. 2018. (Student's Toolbox Ser.). (ENG.). 32p. (J). (gr. 4-7). pap. 12.99 *(978-0-7502-9108-8(7),* Wayland) Hachette Children's Group GBR. Dist: Hachette Bk. Group.

Taylor, Lacy. Public Speaking Student Activity Book. Matthews, Douglas L., ed. 2003. (Illus.). stu. ed., per., wbk. ed. *(978-1-931680-55-4(8),* Expert Systems for Teachers) Teaching Point, Inc.

Truesdell, Ann. Make Your Point: Creating Powerful Presentations. 2013. (Explorer Library: Information Explorer Ser.). (ENG.). 32p. (gr. 4-8). pap. 14.21 *(978-1-62431-043-0(5),* 202529); (Illus.). 32.07 *(978-1-62431-019-5(2),* 202527) Cherry Lake Publishing.

Ventura, Marne. The 12 Most Influential Speeches of All Time. 2018. (Most Influential Ser.). (ENG., Illus.). 32p. (J). (gr. 3-6). 32.80 *(978-1-63235-414-3(4),* 13751, 12-Story Library) Bookstaves, LLC.

PUBLIC UTILITIES

see also Railroads; Telegraph; Telephone; Water-Supply

Kallan, Stuart A. The Gas Crisis. 2007. (Ripped from the Headlines Ser.). 64p. (YA). (gr. 7-12). 23.95 *(978-1-60217-001-8(0))* Erickson Pr.

Peterson, Megan Cooley. How Electricity Gets from Power Plants to Homes. 2016. (Here to There Ser.). (ENG., Illus.). 24p. (J). (gr. -1-2). lib. bdg. 27.32 *(978-1-4914-8434-0(9),* 130864, Capstone Pr.) Capstone.

PUBLIC WORKS

see also Municipal Engineering

Beyer, Mark. Homeland Security & Weapons of Mass Destruction: How Prepared Are We? 2009. (Library of Weapons of Mass Destruction Ser.). 64p. (gr. 5-5). 58.50 *(978-1-60853-952-9(0))* Rosen Publishing Group, Inc., The.

Reyes, Sonja. Inside Public Works: Understanding Government, 1 vol. 2018. (Civics for the Real World Ser.). (ENG.). 12p. (gr. 1-2). pap. *(978-1-5081-3937-9(7),* e8077e17-f7f2-4ce1-ac65-543f6dd1d02a, Rosen Classroom) Rosen Publishing Group, Inc., The.

Silivanch, Annalise. Rebuilding America's Infrastructure, 1 vol. 2010. (In the News Ser.). (ENG.). 64p. (YA). (gr. 6-6). pap. 13.95 *(978-1-4488-1676-7(9),* 623185cb-3d63-4e16-ae4f-1c6777437731); lib. bdg. 37.13 *(978-1-4358-9444-0(8),* d6c1ea75-a8a7-4e21-9baf-63a0225086af) Rosen Publishing Group, Inc., The.

PUBLISHERS AND PUBLISHING

see also Book Industries and Trade; Books; Printing

Anderson, Kirsten. Who Was Robert Ripley? 2015. (Who Was... ? Ser.). lib. bdg. 16.00 *(978-0-606-36596-3(6))* Turtleback.

Anderson, Kirsten & Who HQ. Who Was Robert Ripley? Foley, Tim, illus. 2015. (Who Was? Ser.). 112p. (J). (gr. 3-7). 5.99 *(978-0-448-48298-9(3),* Penguin Workshop) Penguin Young Readers Group.

Boone, Mary. Johannes Gutenberg: Inventor & Craftsman. 2018. (STEM Scientists & Inventors Ser.). (ENG., Illus.). 24p. (J). (gr. 1-3). lib. bdg. 27.99 *(978-1-5435-0648-8(8),* 137411, Capstone Pr.) Capstone.

Bradshaw, Anne, et al, contrib. by. Publishing Secrets: A Comprehensive Guide to Getting Your Book Published in the LDS Market. 2004. (Illus.). 194p. pap. 14.95 *(978-0-9749241-0-6(5))* Golden Wings Enterprises.

Burden, Peter. News of the World? Fake Sheikhs & Royal Trappings. Dillon, Julia & Hiscocks, Dan, eds. 2009. (ENG., Illus.). 320p. pap. 13.95 *(978-1-903070-72-7(4))* Eye Bks. GBR. Dist: Independent Pubs. Group.

Dodge, Hillary. Careers for Tech Girls in Digital Publishing, 1 vol. 2018. (Tech Girls Ser.). (ENG.). 80p. (J). (gr. 7-7). 37.47 *(978-1-5081-8014-2(8),* 696bb33a-044f-4013-85e3-e211c8c3573a); pap. 16.30 *(978-1-5081-8015-9(6),* 4de7bbdb-bb84-4b1b-b45b-bb3e28e51ef7) Rosen Publishing Group, Inc., The. (Rosen Young Adult).

Fox, Kathleen. A Book Is Just Like You! All about the Parts of a Book. Wallace, John, illus. 2012. 32p. (J). 17.95 *(978-1-60213-060-9(4),* Upstart Bks.) Highsmith Inc.

Harmon, Daniel E. Publishing Your E-Book, 1 vol. 2013. (Digital & Information Literacy Ser.). (ENG., Illus.). 48p. (J). (gr. 5-5). 33.47 *(978-1-4488-9513-7(8),* 0bb4b1f8-84d0-49d8-b1df-f8b8bd4823cb) Rosen Publishing Group, Inc., The.

Haugen, David M. & Musser, Susan, eds. Are Books Becoming Extinct?, 1 vol. 2012. (At Issue Ser.). (ENG.). 128p. (gr. 10-12). pap. 28.80 *(978-0-7377-5547-3(4),* 909441ea-3c93-438f-a49f-4a01ae02d31f); lib. bdg. 41.03 *(978-0-7377-5546-6(6),* eccff1b6-dd10-488a-9b81-bccb2b476ae7) Greenhaven Publishing LLC. (Greenhaven Publishing).

Higgins, Melissa. Julian Assange: WikiLeaks Founder, 1 vol. 2011. (Essential Lives Set 7 Ser.). (ENG., Illus.). 112p. (YA). (gr. 6-12). lib. bdg. 41.36 *(978-1-61783-001-3(1),* 6741, Essential Library) ABDO Publishing Co.

Jeff Bezos & Amazon. 2011. (Graphic Nonfiction Biographies Ser.). (ENG.). 48p. (YA). (gr. 5-8). *(978-1-4488-5549-0(7))*; pap. *(978-1-4488-5648-0(5))* Rosen Publishing Group, Inc., The. (Rosen Reference).

Klein, Rebecca T. Career Building Through Using Digital Publishing Tools, 1 vol. 2013. (Digital Career Building Ser.). (Illus.). 64p. (J). (ENG.). (gr. 6-6). pap. 13.95 *(978-1-4777-1741-7(2),* 516e4a0e-22d8-41f8-85d3-dd2f8921f2fe); (ENG., (gr. 6-6). lib. bdg. 37.13 *(978-1-4777-1724-0(2),* 470a33e5-674f-47ec-914e-d025567d0be8); (gr. 7-12). pap. 77.70 *(978-1-4777-1742-4(0))* Rosen Publishing Group, Inc., The.

Markel, Michelle. Balderdash! John Newbery & the Boisterous Birth of Children's Books (Nonfiction Books for Kids, Early Elementary History Books) Carpenter, Nancy, illus. 2017. (ENG.). 44p. (J). 17.99 *(978-0-8118-7922-4(4))* Chronicle Bks. LLC.

PRESS, Celebration. How a Book Gets Published. 2003. (ENG.). (J). (gr. 2-5). pap., stu. ed. 34.95 *(978-0-673-62836-7(1),* Celebration Pr.) Savvas Learning Co.

Priddy, Roger. Wipe Clean: Early Learning Workbook. 2013. (Wipe Clean Learning Bks.). (ENG.). 56p. (J). spiral bd., wbk. ed. 12.95 *(978-0-312-51341-2(0),* 900081399) St. Martin's Pr.

Read, Write & Publish. (J). (gr. 5). 125.25 *(978-0-669-17767-1(9))* Houghton Mifflin Harcourt School Pubs.

Roberts, Russell. John Newbery & the Story of the Newbery Medal. 2003. (Great Achiever Awards Ser.). (Illus.). 48p. (J). (gr. 4-8). lib. bdg. 29.95 *(978-1-58415-201-9(X))* Mitchell Lane Pubs.

Ryan, Peter K. Careers in Electronic Publishing, 1 vol. 2013. (Careers in Computer Technology Ser.). (ENG.). 80p. (YA). (gr. 8-8). 38.47 *(978-1-4488-9590-8(1),* 0280fe4f-da9b-40af-a713-78488fc81847) Rosen Publishing Group, Inc., The.

Sauerwein, Stan. Ma Murray: The Story of Canada's Crusty Queen of Publishing. 2003. (ENG., Illus.). 144p. per. *(978-1-55153-979-9(9))* Heritage Hse.

Ventura, Marne. You Can Work in Publishing. 2018. (You Can Work in the Arts Ser.). (ENG., Illus.). 32p. (J). (gr. 4-6). lib. bdg. 28.65 *(978-1-5435-4145-8(3),* 139099, Capstone Pr.) Capstone.

Walton, Ruth. Let's Read a Book: Find Out about Books & How They Are Made. 2013. (Let's Find Out Ser.). (ENG., Illus.). 32p. (J). (gr. k-5). 28.50 *(978-1-59771-387-0(2))* Sea-To-Sea Pubns.

Watson, Esther. Whatcha Mean, What's a Zine? Todd, Mark, illus. 2006. (ENG.). 112p. (YA). (gr. 7). pap. 14.99 *(978-0-618-56315-9(6),* 496906, Clarion Bks.) HarperCollins Pubs.

Whitelaw, Nancy. Let's Go! Let's Publish! Katharine Graham & the Washington Post. 2004. (Makers of the Media Ser.). (Illus.). 112p. (YA). (gr. 6-12). 21.95 *(978-1-883846-37-4(4),* First Biographies) Reynolds, Morgan Inc.

—William Randolph Hearst & the American Century. rev. exp. ed. 2004. (Makers of the Media Ser.). (Illus.). 128p. (gr. 6-12). 28.95 *(978-1-931798-35-8(4))* Reynolds, Morgan Inc.

PUBLISHERS AND PUBLISHING—FICTION

Chambliss Bertman, Jennifer. Book Scavenger. 2016. (Book Scavenger Ser.: 1). (ENG.). 368p. (J). pap. 8.99 *(978-1-250-07980-0(2),* 900154628) Square Fish.

Clements, Andrew. The School Story. unabr. ed. 2004. (Middle Grade Cassette Librariestm Ser.). 224p. (J). (gr. 3-7). pap. 29.00 incl. audio *(978-0-8072-1000-0(5),* S YA 352 SP, Listening Library) Random Hse. Audio Publishing Group.

Edge, Christopher. Twelve Minutes to Midnight. 2014. (Penelope Tredwell Mysteries Ser.: 1). (ENG.). 256p. (J). (gr. 3-7). 16.99 *(978-0-8075-8133-9(X),* 080758133X) Whitman, Albert & Co.

McGowan, Patricia. House of Friends. 2012. 242p. 46.95 *(978-1-258-23494-2(7))*; pap. 31.95 *(978-1-258-24543-6(4))* Literary Licensing, LLC.

Patterson, James & Grabenstein, Chris. Laugh Out Loud. Ebbeler, Jeff, illus. 2017. (ENG.). 304p. (J). (gr. 3-7). 13.99 *(978-0-316-43146-0(X),* Jimmy Patterson) Little Brown & Co.

Spizman, Robyn Freedman & Johnston, Mark. Secret Agent. 2006. (ENG.). 240p. (J). (gr. 4-7). pap. 11.99 *(978-1-4169-1862-2(0),* Atheneum Bks. for Young Readers) Simon & Schuster Children's Publishing.

Trooboff, Rhoda. A Book for Elie. Radjou, Anna Nazaretz, illus. 2008. (ENG.). 31p. pap. 15.00 *(978-0-9773536-1-3(3))* Tenley Circle Pr.

Webb Quest, By Sara. Aydil Vice, Author of Kiski the Cat. 2008. 70p. pap. 6.96 *(978-1-4357-5152-1(3))* Lulu Pr., Inc.

PUBLISHING

see Publishers and Publishing

PUERTO RICANS

Conley, Kate A. The Puerto Rican Americans. 2003. (Immigrants in America Ser.). (ENG., Illus.). 112p. (J). (gr. 4-7). lib. bdg. 30.85 *(978-1-59018-432-5(7),* Lucent Bks.) Cengage Gale.

Dávila, Lourdes. How Puerto Ricans Made the US Mainland Home, 1 vol. 2018. (Coming to America: the History of Immigration to the United States Ser.). (ENG.). 80p. (gr. 6-6). pap. 16.88 *(978-1-5081-8136-1(5),* 8686813d-d482-4b3b-b30c-811e601cf537, Rosen Central) Rosen Publishing Group, Inc., The.

Hernández, Roger E. & Hernández, Roger E. 1898 to World War II, 1 vol. 2010. (Hispanic America Ser.). (ENG.). 80p. (gr. 5-5). 36.93 *(978-0-7614-4176-2(X),* cd22c781-913c-43d9-a0ab-9cc0282583ea) Cavendish Square Publishing LLC.

Klein, J. M. Sylvia Mendez: Education Equality Activist, 1 vol. 2019. (Barrier-Breaker Bios Ser.). (ENG.). 32p. (gr. 2-2). pap. 11.58 *(978-1-5026-4972-0(1),* e3b45b76-9434-49ca-90d1-ff0fa4ec73ba) Cavendish Square Publishing LLC.

PUERTO RICANS—BIOGRAPHY

Andersen, Richard. Abraham Rodriguez, 1 vol. 2013. (Today's Writers & Their Works). (ENG.). 144p. (YA). (gr. 7-7). pap. 23.34 *(978-1-62712-147-7(1),* 43597786-d061-4c62-8ce9-3519f36cf1a8) Cavendish Square Publishing LLC.

De Jesús, Ada. El Baile de Octavo y Otros Recuerdos / the Eighth Grade Dance & Other Memories. 2019. (ENG & SPA., Illus.). 64p. (J). (gr. 6-9). pap. 9.95 *(978-1-55885-885-5(7))* Arte Publico Pr.

Fischer, David. Roberto Clemente, 1 vol. 2004. (Trailblazers of the Modern World Ser.). (ENG., Illus.). 48p. (gr. 5-8). pap. 15.05 *(978-0-8368-5264-6(8),* 2a03b158-3cee-44eb-ad90-87581211732e); lib. bdg. 33.67 *(978-0-8368-5495-4(0),* 5d1b37e7-1696-4218-9b0d-e9692164a429) Stevens, Gareth Publishing LLLP. (Gareth Stevens Secondary Library).

Marcovitz, Hal. Puerto Ricans. 2009. (Successful Americans Ser.). 64p. (YA). (gr. 9-12). 22.95 *(978-1-4222-0516-7(9))* Mason Crest.

Marquez, Heron. Roberto Clemente: Baseball's Humanitarian Hero. 2005. (Trailblazer Biography Ser.). (Illus.). 112p. (J). (gr. 3-7). lib. bdg. 30.60 *(978-1-57505-767-5(0))* Lerner Publishing Group.

Winter, Jonah. Roberto Clemente: Pride of the Pittsburgh Pirates. ón, Raúl, illus. 2008. (ENG.). 40p. (J). (gr. -1-3). 8.99 *(978-1-4169-5082-0(6),* Atheneum Bks. for Young Readers) Simon & Schuster Children's Publishing.

—Roberto Clemente: Pride of the Pittsburgh Pirates. ón, Raúl, illus. 2005. (ENG.). 40p. (J). (gr. -1-3). 19.99 *(978-0-689-85643-3(1))* Simon & Schuster, Inc.

PUERTO RICANS—FICTION

Delacre, Lulu. Alicia Afterimage, 1 vol. (ENG.). 144p. (YA). (gr. 7-12). 2017. pap. 18.95 *(978-1-62014-578-4(2),* leelowbooks) 2008. 19.95 *(978-1-60060-242-9(8))* Lee & Low Bks., Inc.

Felicie-Soto, Ada. Arturo & the Hidden Treasure, 1 vol. Ortiz, Abimael, illus. 2015. (Arturo & the Hidden Treasure Ser.). (ENG.). 32p. (J). (gr. 2-4). lib. bdg. 29.27 *(978-1-4994-1863-7(9),* e6aa4ee1-b5ce-4a8f-8672-79d5a33ee4d1, PowerKids Pr.) Rosen Publishing Group, Inc., The.

González, Lucía. The Storyteller's Candle: La Velita de Los Cuentos, 1 vol. Delacre, Lulu, illus. 2013. (ENG.). 32p. (J). (gr. 1-6). pap. 11.95 *(978-0-89239-237-7(1),* leelowcbp, Children's Book Press) Lee & Low Bks., Inc.

Gonzalez, Lucia M. & Delacre, Lulu. The Storyteller's Candle. 2008.Tr. of La Velita de los Cuentos. (SPA & ENG., Illus.). 32p. (J). (gr. k-4). 16.95 *(978-0-89239-222-3(3))* Lee & Low Bks., Inc.

Manzano, Sonia. No Dogs Allowed! Muth, Jon J., illus. 2004. (ENG.). 32p. (J). (gr. -1-2). 19.99 *(978-0-689-83088-4(2),* Atheneum Bks. for Young Readers) Simon & Schuster Children's Publishing.

—The Revolution of Evelyn Serrano. 2014. (ENG.). 224p. (YA). (gr. 9). pap. 10.99 *(978-0-545-32506-6(4))* Scholastic, Inc.

Nicholasa, Mohr. El Bronx Remembered. 2014. (Trophy Keypoint Bks). (ENG.). 272p. (J). (gr. 8-12). 13.24 *(978-1-63245-280-1(4))* Lectorum Pubns., Inc.

Older, Daniel José. Shadowhouse Fall (the Shadowshaper Cypher, Book 2) 2017. (Shadowshaper Cypher Ser.: 2). (ENG., Illus.). 368p. (YA). (gr. 9-9). 18.99 *(978-0-545-95282-8(4),* Levine, Arthur A. Bks.) Scholastic, Inc.

Ortiz Cofer, Judith. An Island Like You: Stories of the Barrio. 2009. (ENG.). 256p. (J). (gr. 7-12). pap. 21.19 *(978-0-545-13133-9(2))* Scholastic, Inc.

Ostow, Micol. Emily Goldberg Learns to Salsa. 2007. 208p. (YA). (gr. 7-18). 8.99 *(978-1-59514-144-6(8),* Razorbill) Penguin Young Readers Group.

Rivera, Rafael, et al. Baseball on Mars/Béisbol en Marte. Rivera, Rafael et al, illus. 2009.Tr. of Béisbol en Marte. (SPA & ENG.). 32p. (J). (gr. -1-3). 16.95 *(978-1-55885-521-2(1))* Arte Publico Pr.

Valentin, Karen. Allie's World: Abuela & Abuelo Move: Abuela & Abuelo Move. 2009. 32p. 6.95 *(978-1-60349-021-4(3),* Marimba Bks.) Just Us Bks., Inc.

Velasquez, Eric. Grandma's Gift. Velasquez, Eric, illus. 2013. (ENG., Illus.). 32p. (J). (gr. k-1). pap. 9.99 *(978-0-8027-3536-2(3),* 900120816, Bloomsbury USA Childrens) Bloomsbury Publishing USA.

Watson, J. A. Hatchling Hero: A Sea Turtle Defender's Journal. Olbey, Arpad, illus. 2018. (Science Squad Ser.). (ENG.). 192p. (J). (gr. 3-4). pap. 9.99 *(978-1-63163-161-0(6),* 1631631616, Jolly Fish Pr.) North Star Editions.

PUERTO RICANS—NEW YORK (STATE)—NEW YORK—FICTION

Caraballo, Samuel & Torrecilla, Pablo. Estrellita in the Big City/Estrellita en la Ciudad Grande. Caraballo, Samuel & Torrecilla, Pablo, illus. 2008. (SPA & ENG., Illus.). 32p. (J). (gr. -1-4). 16.95 *(978-1-55885-498-7(3),* Piñata Books) Arte Publico Pr.

Cofer, Judith Ortiz. Call Me Maria. 2011. 8.44 *(978-0-7848-3341-4(9),* Everbind) Marco Bk. Co.

Pfeffer, Susan Beth. The Dead & the Gone. 2010. (Last Survivors Ser.: 2). 321p. lib. bdg. 19.65 *(978-0-606-14464-3(1))* Turtleback.

Velasquez, Eric. Grandma's Records. Velasquez, Eric, illus. 2004. (ENG., Illus.). 32p. (J). (gr. k-3). pap. 9.99 *(978-0-8027-7660-0(4),* 900032898, Bloomsbury USA Childrens) Bloomsbury Publishing USA.

—Grandma's Records. 2014. 32p. pap. 9.00 *(978-1-61003-346-6(9))* Center for the Collaborative Classroom.

—Grandma's Records. 2004. (Illus.). 32p. (J). (gr. k-3). 16.95 *(978-0-8027-8760-6(6))*; 17.85 *(978-0-8027-8761-3(4))* Walker & Co.

PUERTO RICANS—UNITED STATES

Arkham, Thomas. Both Puerto Rican & American. 2012. (J). pap. *(978-1-4222-2333-8(7))* Mason Crest.

—Both Puerto Rican & American. Limón, José E., ed. 2012. (Hispanic Americans: Major Minority Ser.). 64p. (J). (gr. 4). 22.95 *(978-1-4222-2316-1(7))* Mason Crest.

Bryan, Nichol. Puerto Rican Americans, 1 vol. 2004. (One Nation Set 2 Ser.). (ENG.). 32p. (gr. k-6). 27.07 *(978-1-59197-532-8(8)*, Checkerboard Library) ABDO Publishing Co.

Marcovitz, Hal. Puerto Ricans. 2009. (Successful Americans Ser.). 64p. (YA). (gr. 9-12). 22.95 *(978-1-4222-0516-7(9))* Mason Crest.

Taus-Bolstad, Stacy. Puerto Ricans in America. 2005. (In America Ser.). (Illus.). 80p. (J). (gr. 5-8). lib. bdg. 27.93 *(978-0-8225-3953-7(5))* Lerner Publishing Group.

PUERTO RICANS—UNITED STATES—FICTION

Cartaya, Pablo. Marcus Vega Doesn't Speak Spanish. 2018. (ENG.). 272p. (J). (gr. 5). 17.99 *(978-1-101-99726-0(5)*, Viking Books for Young Readers) Penguin Young Readers Group.

Cofer, Judith Ortiz. An Island Like You: Stories of the Barrio. 2011. 9.15 *(978-0-7848-3583-8(7)*, Everbind) Marco Bk. Co.

Flor, Ada Alma. My Name Is Maria Isabel. 2014. (ENG.). 64p. (J). (gr. 12-12). 9.24 *(978-1-63245-189-7(1))* Lectorum Pubns., Inc.

Garcia, Richard. Los Espiritus de Mi Tia Otilia. 2004. (ENG & SPA., Illus.). (J). (gr. k-3). spiral bd. *(978-0-616-14606-4(X))* Canadian National Institute for the Blind/Institut National Canadien pour les Aveugles.

Manzano, Sonia. Miracle on 133rd Street. Priceman, Marjorie, illus. 2015. (ENG.). 48p. (J). (gr. -1-3). 17.99 *(978-0-689-87887-9(7))* Simon & Schuster Children's Publishing.

PUERTO RICO

Alvarez O'Neill, Juan, illus. ¡Vamos a Jugar! 2005. (SPA.). 28p. (J). 8.95 *(978-0-8477-1553-4(1))* Univ. of Puerto Rico Pr.

Bjorklund, Ruth. Puerto Rico, 1 vol. Santoro, Christopher, illus. 2007. (It's My State! (First Edition)(r) Ser.). (ENG.). 80p. (gr. 4-4). lib. bdg. 34.07 *(978-0-7614-2218-1(8)*, 42f3adac-8216-4ea1-ae6f-b2531103c1d6) Cavendish Square Publishing LLC.

—Puerto Rico, 1 vol. 2nd rev. ed. 2013. (It's My State! (Second Edition)(r) Ser.). (ENG.). 80p. (gr. 4-4). pap. 18.64 *(978-1-62712-096-8(3)*, 10a2789c-aec2-4371-97bb-65501862c96e) Cavendish Square Publishing LLC.

Brown, Jonatha A. Puerto Rico & Other Outlying Areas, 1 vol. 2005. (Portraits of the States Ser.). (ENG., Illus.). 32p. (gr. 3-5). pap. 11.50 *(978-0-8368-4693-5(1)*, aa09b7de-2b3f-4da8-a978-e8d97adbf717); lib. bdg. 28.67 *(978-0-8368-4674-4(5)*, 5b3552ea-07ba-476b-bae7-dbf87cb924cc) Stevens, Gareth Publishing LLLP. (Gareth Stevens Learning Library).

Burgan, Michael. Puerto Rico. 2003. (From Sea to Shining Sea Ser.: 2). (ENG., Illus.). 80p. (J). 30.50 *(978-0-516-22398-8(4)*, Children's Pr.) Scholastic Library Publishing.

—Puerto Rico & Other Outlying Areas, 1 vol. 2003. (World Almanac(r) Library of the States Ser.). (ENG., Illus.). 48p. (gr. 4-6). pap. 15.05 *(978-0-8368-5329-2(6)*, c09f45c4-704b-42cb-9917-7e2850b7b6d2); lib. bdg. 33.67 *(978-0-8368-5158-8(7)*, 9f689cff-edaa-4c54-9757-7e46111c4ba4) Stevens, Gareth Publishing LLLP. (Gareth Stevens Learning Library).

—Puerto Rico y Otras Áreas Periféricas (Puerto Rico & Other Outlying Areas), 1 vol. 2003. (World Almanac(r) Biblioteca de Los Estados (World Almanac(r) Library of the States) Ser.). (SPA.). 48p. (gr. 4-6). lib. bdg. 33.67 *(978-0-8368-5726-9(7)*, 143e99dc-fbff-4a14-8c25-211ce284c1ac, Gareth Stevens Learning Library) Stevens, Gareth Publishing LLLP.

Fein, E. How to Draw Puerto Rico's Sights & Symbols. 2009. (Kid's Guide to Drawing America Ser.). 32p. (gr. k-k). 50.50 *(978-1-61511-092-6(5)*, PowerKids Pr.) Rosen Publishing Group, Inc., The.

George, Marian M. A Little Journey to Puerto Rico. 2004. reprint ed. pap. 1.99 *(978-1-4192-0211-7(1))* Kessinger Publishing, LLC.

Hernandez, Romel. Puerto Rico. 2010. (Caribbean Today Ser.). (Illus.). 64p. (YA). (gr. 9-12). 21.95 *(978-1-4222-0628-7(9))* Mason Crest.

Johnston, Joyce. Puerto Rico. (J). 2012. lib. bdg. 25.26 *(978-0-7613-4554-1(X)*, Lerner Pubns.) 2nd exp. rev. ed. 2003. (Illus.). 84p. (gr. 3-6). pap. 6.95 *(978-0-8225-4150-9(5))* Lerner Publishing Group.

Levy, Patricia & Bahrawi, Nazry. Puerto Rico, 1 vol. 2nd rev. ed. 2007. (Cultures of the World (Second Edition)(r) Ser.). (ENG., Illus.). 144p. (gr. 5-5). lib. bdg. 49.79 *(978-0-7614-1970-9(5)*, 86ac2631-8f67-46f8-ab1a-27bc6fbcb983) Cavendish Square Publishing LLC.

Maine, Tyler & Parker, Bridget. Puerto Rico. 2016. (States Ser.). (ENG., Illus.). 32p. (J). (gr. 3-6). lib. bdg. 27.99 *(978-1-5157-0426-3(2)*, 132037, Capstone Pr.) Capstone.

Marcus, Amy. Exploring Puerto Rico with the Five Themes of Geography. (Library of the Western Hemisphere Ser.). 24p. 2009. (gr. 4-4). 42.50 *(978-1-60853-930-7(X)*, PowerKids Pr.) 2004. (ENG., Illus.). (J). (gr. 3-4). lib. bdg. 26.27 *(978-1-4042-2673-9(7)*, 504b4e5a-643d-4c69-8eea-9816744f7395, PowerKids Pr.) 2004. (ENG., Illus.). (gr. 3-4). pap. 8.25 *(978-0-8239-4633-4(9)*, e3691aad-0dce-4b49-9dbb-b6ea159d430b) Rosen Publishing Group, Inc., The.

Milivojevic, JoAnn. Puerto Rico. 2009. pap. 52.95 *(978-0-7613-4733-0(X))* 2005. (Illus.). 48p. (gr. 2-4). 22.60 *(978-1-57505-144-4(3))* Lerner Publishing Group.

Obregon, Jose Maria. Puerto Rico, 1 vol. Brusca, Maria Cristina, tr. 2005. (Bilingual Library of the United States of America Ser.: Set 2). (ENG & SPA., Illus.). 32p. (J). (gr. 2-2). lib. bdg. 28.93 *(978-1-4042-3104-7(8)*, 96992613-0b0d-446c-9cd8-3a86d5d1d36a) Rosen Publishing Group, Inc., The.

Obregón, José María. Puerto Rico. 2009. (Bilingual Library of the United States of America Ser.). (ENG & SPA.). 32p. (gr. 2-2). 47.90 *(978-1-60853-383-1(2)*, Editorial Buenas Letras) Rosen Publishing Group, Inc., The.

Reynolds, Jeff E. Puerto Rico. 2005. (A to Z Ser.). (ENG., Illus.). 40p. (J). (gr. 2-4). pap. 6.95 *(978-0-516-25073-1(6)*, Children's Pr.) Scholastic Library Publishing.

Rodríguez Gonzalez, Tania. Roberto Clemente. 2012. (Superstars of Baseball ENGLISH Ser.). 32p. (J). (gr. 4). 19.95 *(978-1-4222-2697-1(2))*; (SPA., Illus.). 19.95 *(978-1-4222-2644-5(1))* Mason Crest.

Roth, Susan L. & Trumbore, Cindy. Parrots over Puerto Rico, 1 vol. Roth, Susan L., illus. 2013. (ENG., Illus.). 48p. (J). (gr. 1-6). 20.95 *(978-1-62014-004-8(7)*, leelowbooks) Lee & Low Bks., Inc.

Schwabacher, Martin. Puerto Rico, 1 vol. 2003. (Celebrate the States (First Edition) Ser.). (ENG., Illus.). 144p. (gr. 6-6). lib. bdg. 39.79 *(978-0-7614-1313-4(8)*, b2ebd616-cef4-4fad-a793-cac6d6d70ca5) Cavendish Square Publishing LLC.

Schwabacher, Martin & Otfinoski, Steven. Puerto Rico, 1 vol. 2nd rev. ed. 2010. (Celebrate the States (Second Edition) Ser.). (ENG.). 144p. (gr. 6-6). 39.79 *(978-0-7614-4734-4(2)*, 960b3872-37c1-4325-9f04-b5ba94139a8e) Cavendish Square Publishing LLC.

Silva Lee, Alfonso. Mi Isla y Yo: La Naturaleza de Puerto Rico. Hayskar, Bonnie J., ed. Lago, Alexis, illus. 2007. (SPA.). 32p. (J). pap. 8.95 *(978-1-929165-19-3(6))* PANGAEA.

—Mi isla y yo/My Island & I: La naturaleza de Puerto Rico/The Nature of Puerto Rico. Hayskar, Bonnie J., ed. Lago, Alexis, illus. 2003. (SPA & ENG.). 32p. (J). pap. 9.95 *(978-1-929165-12-4(9))* PANGAEA.

Tagliaferro, Linda. Puerto Rico in Pictures. 2nd ed. 2003. (Visual Geography Series, Second Ser.). (ENG., Illus.). 80p. (gr. 5-12). 31.93 *(978-0-8225-0936-3(9))* Lerner Publishing Group.

Yomtov, Nel. Puerto Rico (a True Book: My United States) (Library Edition) 2018. (True Book (Relaunch) Ser.). (ENG., Illus.). 48p. (J). (gr. 3-5). 31.00 *(978-0-531-23577-5(7)*, Children's Pr.) Scholastic Library Publishing.

Zapata, Elizabeth. Puerto Rico. 2006. (Rookie Read-About Geography Ser.). (ENG., Illus.). 32p. (J). (gr. 1-2). lib. bdg. 20.50 *(978-0-516-25387-9(5))* Scholastic Library Publishing.

PUERTO RICO—BIOGRAPHY

Boehme, Gerry. Roberto Clemente: The Pride of Puerto Rico, 1 vol. 2015. (Game-Changing Athletes Ser.). (ENG., Illus.). 112p. (YA). (gr. 9-9). lib. bdg. 44.50 *(978-1-5026-1058-4(2)*, 3aa9be34-255c-44fd-a92e-560d4df6e9ab) Cavendish Square Publishing LLC.

Cotts, Nat. Daddy Yankee. 2009. (Hip-Hop Ser.). (Illus.). 64p. (YA). (gr. 4-7). pap. 7.95 *(978-1-4222-0342-2(5))* Mason Crest.

—Don Omar. 2009. (Hip Hop (Mason Crest Paperback) Ser.). (Illus.). 64p. (YA). (gr. 4-7). pap. 7.95 *(978-1-4222-0346-0(8))* Mason Crest.

Etingoff, Kim. Ivy Queen. 2009. (Hip-Hop 2 Ser.). (Illus.). 64p. (YA). (gr. 7-12). lib. bdg. 22.95 *(978-1-4222-0295-1(X))* Mason Crest.

PUERTO RICO—FICTION

Acevedo, Ari. Juan Bobo Sends the Pig to Mass. Wrenn, Tom, illus. 2008. (Story Cove Ser.). (SPA & ENG.). 24p. (J). (gr. -1-3). pap. 4.95 *(978-0-87483-883-1(5))* August Hse. Pubs., Inc.

Alvarez, Mrinali & Alvarez, Oneill J. Verde Navidad. 2006. (SPA.). 28p. 8.95 *(978-0-8477-1564-0(7))* Univ. of Puerto Rico Pr.

Azmitia, M. The Same Blood, 1 vol. 2018. (YA Verse Ser.). (ENG.). 200p. (YA). (gr. 3-4). 25.80 *(978-1-5383-8252-3(0)*, 873f0b82-85b1-4d42-8166-a153a96bd440); pap. 16.35 *(978-1-5383-8251-6(2)*, 3f5a2881-e090-4972-b7b7-1e5e74b46e79) Enslow Publishing, LLC.

Cartaya, Pablo. Marcus Vega Doesn't Speak Spanish. 2018. (ENG.). 272p. (J). (gr. 5). 17.99 *(978-1-101-99726-0(5)*, Viking Books for Young Readers) Penguin Young Readers Group.

Cofer, Judith Ortiz. Animal Jamboree / La Fiesta de los Animales: Latino Folktales / Leyendas Latinas. Rosales-Yeomans, Natalia, tr. 2012. (SPA & ENG.). (J). pap. 9.95 *(978-1-55885-743-8(5)*, Piñata Books) Arte Publico Pr.

Courage, Nick. Storm Blown. 2019. (ENG.). 352p. (J). (gr. 4-7). 16.99 *(978-0-525-64596-2(9)*, Delacorte Bks. for Young Readers) Random Hse. Children's Bks.

de Jesus Paolicelli, Marisa. There's a Coqui in My Shoe! 2007. (Illus.). 66p. (J). 21.99 *(978-0-9797641-0-3(6))* Caribbean Experience Con Amor, LLC, A.

Delacre, Lulu. Rafi & Rosi. 2004. (Illus.). 64p. (J). lib. bdg. 13.85 *(978-1-4242-0596-7(4))* Fitzgerald Bks.

—Rafi & Rosi. Delacre, Lulu, illus. 2005. (I Can Read Bks.). (Illus.). 64p. (J). (gr. k-3). pap. 3.99 *(978-0-06-009897-1(X)*, Rayo) HarperCollins Pubs.

—Rafi & Rosi, 1 vol. Delacre, Lulu, illus. 2016. (Rafi & Rosi Ser.). (ENG., Illus.). 64p. (J). (gr. k-3). pap. 11.95 *(978-0-89239-377-0(7)*, leelowcbp) Lee & Low Bks., Inc.

—Rafi & Rosi, 1 vol. 2016. (Rafi & Rosi Ser.). (ENG., Illus.). 64p. (J). (gr. k-3). pap. 11.95 *(978-0-89239-379-4(3)*, leelowcbp) Lee & Low Bks., Inc.

—Rafi & Rosi: Music!, 1 vol. Delacre, Lulu, illus. 2019. (Rafi & Rosi Ser.). (ENG., Illus.). 64p. (J). (gr. 2-2). pap. 11.95 *(978-0-89239-431-9(5)*, leelowcbp, Children's Book Press) Lee & Low Bks., Inc.

—Rafi & Rosi Pirates, 1 vol. 2017. (Rafi & Rosi Ser.). (ENG., Illus.). 64p. (J). (gr. k-3). 16.95 *(978-0-89239-381-7(5)*, leelowcbp, Children's Book Press) Lee & Low Bks., Inc.

—Rafi y Rosi, 1 vol. Delacre, Lulu, illus. 2016. (Rafi & Rosi Ser.).Tr. of Rafi & Rosi. (SPA., Illus.). 64p. (J). (gr. k-3). pap. 10.95 *(978-0-89239-378-7(5)*, leelowcbp) Lee & Low Bks., Inc.

—Rafi y Rosi Carnival, 1 vol. 2016. (Rafi & Rosi Ser.).Tr. of Rafi & Rosi Carnival. (SPA., Illus.). 64p. (J). (gr. k-3). pap. 11.95 *(978-0-89239-380-0(7)*, leelowcbp) Lee & Low Bks., Inc.

—Rafi y Rosi ¡Música!, 1 vol. Delacre, Lulu, illus. 2019. (Rafi & Rosi Ser.). (SPA., Illus.). 64p. (J). (gr. k-3). pap. 10.95 *(978-0-89239-432-6(3)*, leelowcbp, Children's Book Press) Lee & Low Bks., Inc.

—Rafi y Rosi ¡Piratas!, 1 vol. Delacre, Lulu, illus. 2017. (Rafi & Rosi Ser.). (SPA., Illus.). 64p. (J). (gr. k-3). 16.95 *(978-0-89239-428-9(5)*, leelowcbp) Lee & Low Bks., Inc.

—Rafi y Rosi Piratas, 1 vol. 2017. (Rafi & Rosi Ser.). (SPA.). 64p. (J). (gr. k-3). pap. 11.95 *(978-0-89239-382-4(3)*, leelowcbp) Lee & Low Bks., Inc.

Enriquez, Jose. Saving the Mango Farm. 2006. 23p. (J). 10.98 *(978-1-4116-5917-9(1))* Lulu Pr., Inc.

Fontanez, Edwin. En esta hermosa Isla. Fontanez, Edwin, illus. 2nd rev. ed. 2005. (SPA., Illus.). 32p. (J). 16.95 *(978-0-9640868-7-6(5))* Exit Studio.

Garza, Carmen Lomas. Vejigante-Masquerader. (J). (gr. 2-4). *(978-0-590-45777-4(2)*, SO7640) Scholastic, Inc.

Guevara, Melva Vizcarrondo. My Grandma, My Hero. 2007. 58p. pap. 10.00 *(978-0-8059-7296-2(X))* Dorrance Publishing Co., Inc.

Heer, Dusty Rhoades. The Forest That Rains Frogs. 2012. (ENG.). 58p. pap. 19.95 *(978-1-4327-9303-6(9))* Outskirts Pr., Inc.

Hooper, Nancy. Everywhere Coquis. Quinones, Jacqueline, tr. Betancourt, Raymond, illus. 2003.Tr. of En Dondequiera Coquies. (ENG.). 48p. (J). 13.95 *(978-0-942929-14-0(4)*, Omni Arts Publishing) Read Street Publishing, Inc.

Jaffe, Nina. La Flor de Oro: Un Mito Taino de Puerto Rico. Ventura, Gabriela Baeza, tr. from ENG. Sanchez, Enrique O., illus. 2006. (SPA.). 32p. (J). (gr. -1-3). 16.95 *(978-1-55885-463-5(0)*, Piñata Books) Arte Publico Pr.

—Sing, Little Sack! ¡ Canta, Saquito!: a Folktale from Puerto Rico. Cruz, Ray, illus. 2006. 48p. (J). (gr. 2-3). reprint ed. 19.00 *(978-1-4223-5573-2(X))* DIANE Publishing Co.

Landrón, Rafael & Landrón, José Rafael. Beba y la Isla Nena: Beba & the Little Island. Ordóñez, María Antonia, illus. 2010. (SPA & ENG.). 32p. (J). *(978-1-934370-05-6(3)*, Campanita Bks.) Editorial Campana.

Martinez, Lisa Bolivar & Martinez, Matthew. Good Night Puerto Rico. Veno, Joe, illus. 2017. (Good Night Our World Ser.). 20p. (J). (— 1). bds. 9.95 *(978-1-60219-508-0(0))* Good Night Bks.

Montes, Marisa. Get Ready for Gabi No. 5: All in the Familia. Cepeda, Joe, illus. 2004. (ENG.). 112p. (J). (gr. 2-5). pap. *(978-0-439-66156-0(0)*, Scholastic Paperbacks) Scholastic, Inc.

Ortiz, Raquel M. & Ventura, Gabriela Baeza. Sofi & the Magic, Musical Mural. Dominguez, Maria, illus. 2015. (SPA & ENG.). (J). 17.95 *(978-1-55885-803-9(2)*, Piñata Books) Arte Publico Pr.

—When Julia Danced Bomba / Cuando Julia Bailaba Bomba. De Vita, Flor, illus. 2019. (ENG & SPA.). 32p. (J). (gr. 1-3). 17.95 *(978-1-55885-886-2(5))* Arte Publico Pr.

Peakler, Nicole Danette. Tayno Ti & the Legend of the Coqui. 2012. 28p. 24.95 *(978-1-4626-5940-1(3))* America Star Bks.

Posada, Jorge. Sí, Puedes (Play Ball!) ón, Raúl, illus. 2010. (SPA.). 32p. (J). (gr. 1-5). 8.99 *(978-1-4169-9826-6(8)*, Simon & Schuster/Paula Wiseman Bks.) Simon & Schuster/Paula Wiseman Bks.

Reisenauer, Cynthia Mauro. Emerita. Reisenauer, Cynthia Mauro, illus. 2007. (Illus.). 48p. (J). 18.95 *(978-0-9726487-5-2(5))* Puddle Jump Pr., Ltd.

Rodriguez, Ed. Kiki Kokí: La Leyenda Encantada Del Coquí (Kiki Kokí: the Enchanted Legend of the Coquí Frog) 2015. (SPA., Illus.). 40p. (J). (gr. -1-3). 9.99 *(978-1-62672-132-6(7)*, 900139881) Roaring Brook Pr.

Romeu, Emma. Gregorio y el Pirata. 2003.Tr. of Gregorio & the Pirate. (SPA., Illus.). 152p. (J). pap. 9.95 *(978-968-19-0553-8(9))* Santillana USA Publishing Co., Inc.

Vicente, Alidis. The Case of the Three Kings / el Caso de Los Reyes Magos: The Flaca Files / Los Expedientes de Flaca. 2016. (Flaca Files / Los Expedientes de Flaca Ser.). (MUL, ENG & SPA., Illus.). 96p. (J). (gr. 3-6). pap. 9.95 *(978-1-55885-822-0(9)*, Piñata Books) Arte Publico Pr.

Wallner, Alexandra. Sergio & the Hurricane. 2006. (Illus.). (J). (gr. 1-3). 14.60 *(978-0-7569-6800-7(3))* Perfection Learning Corp.

PUERTO RICO—HISTORY

Alvarez O'Neill, Juan, illus. Grano a grano... Refranes Populares. 2005. (SPA.). (J). 8.95 *(978-0-8477-1554-1(X))* Univ. of Puerto Rico Pr.

Bjorklund, Ruth. Puerto Rico, 1 vol. 2nd rev. ed. 2013. (It's My State! (Second Edition)(r) Ser.). (ENG.). 80p. (gr. 4-4). 35.93 *(978-1-60870-883-3(7)*, 32cf35da-aff6-46ba-8279-34cde36564cc) Cavendish Square Publishing LLC.

Clinton, Greg. Puerto Rico & the Spanish-American War, 1 vol. 2015. (Expanding America Ser.). (ENG., Illus.). 96p. (YA). (gr. 8-8). 44.50 *(978-1-5026-0972-4(X)*, a88a02e6-28c6-4cee-955a-e503c5193061) Cavendish Square Publishing LLC.

DaSilva-Gordon, Maria. Puerto Rico: Past & Present, 1 vol. 2010. (United States: Past & Present Ser.). (ENG.). 48p. (YA). (gr. 5-5). pap. 12.75 *(978-1-4358-9529-4(0)*, c44ae568-cfec-4832-94ea-e8fc04bdb019); lib. bdg. 34.47 *(978-1-4358-9502-7(9)*, b519cb4b-3a88-4da6-b1c3-8ea343831ba7) Rosen Publishing Group, Inc., The. (Rosen Reference).

Eagen, Rachel. Ponce de Leon: Exploring Florida & Puerto Rico, 1 vol. 2005. (In the Footsteps of Explorers Ser.). (ENG., Illus.). 32p. (J). (gr. 4-5). pap. *(978-0-7787-2448-3(4))* Crabtree Publishing Co.

Ebon Research Systems Staff. Dare to Be Vol. 4: Luis Munoz Marion. l.t. ed. 2003.Tr. of Atrevete Ser... Un Heroe Luis Munoz Marin. (ENG & SPA., Illus.). 14p. (J). 3.99 *(978-0-9648313-7-7(6))* Ebon Research Systems Publishing, LLC.

Foley, Erin. Festivals of the World: Puerto Rico, 1 vol. 2011. (Festivals of the World Ser.). (ENG.). 32p. (gr. 4-4). 31.21 *(978-1-60870-105-6(0)*, dfdd2d59-7ee7-4b06-934a-b0c27382a999) Cavendish Square Publishing LLC.

Friesen, Helen Lepp. Puerto Rico: Isle of Enchantment. 2012. (J). *(978-1-61913-397-6(0))*; pap. *(978-1-61913-398-3(9))* Weigl Pubs., Inc.

Goldsworthy, Steve. Puerto Rico. 2011. (Guide to American States Ser.). (Illus.). 48p. (YA). (gr. 3-6). 29.99 *(978-1-61690-811-9(4))*; (J). *(978-1-61690-487-6(9))* Weigl Pubs., Inc.

—Puerto Rico: Isle of Enchantment. 2016. (J). *(978-1-4896-4932-4(8))* Weigl Pubs., Inc.

Gutner, Howard. True Books: Puerto Rico. 2009. (True Book Ser.). (ENG., Illus.). 48p. (J). (gr. 3-5). pap. 6.95 *(978-0-531-21360-5(9)*, Children's Pr.) Scholastic Library Publishing.

Hamilton, John. Puerto Rico, 1 vol. 2016. (United States of America Ser.). (ENG., Illus.). 48p. (J). (gr. 5-9). 34.21 *(978-1-68078-341-4(6)*, 21667, Abdo & Daughters) ABDO Publishing Co.

Hantula, Richard & Bjorklund, Ruth. Puerto Rico, 1 vol. 3rd rev. ed. 2015. (It's My State! (Third Edition)(r) Ser.). (ENG., Illus.). 80p. (gr. 4-4). 35.93 *(978-1-62713-216-9(3)*, 87888876-c091-40b9-8b18-428f93e21c5e) Cavendish Square Publishing LLC.

Hernandez, Romel. Puerto Rico, Vol. 11. Henderson, James D., ed. 2015. (Discovering the Caribbean: History, Politics, & Culture Ser.). (Illus.). 64p. (J). (gr. 7). lib. bdg. 22.95 *(978-1-4222-3315-3(4))* Mason Crest.

Krajnik, Elizabeth. The People & Culture of Puerto Rico, 1 vol. 2017. (Celebrating Hispanic Diversity Ser.). (ENG., Illus.). 32p. (J). (gr. 4-5). 27.93 *(978-1-5081-6309-1(X)*, e86bf62e-e14e-4b89-9a93-2d9b2eb1f8c1, PowerKids Pr.) Rosen Publishing Group, Inc., The.

Lusted, Marcia Amidon. Puerto Rico: The Isle of Enchantment, 1 vol. 2010. (Our Amazing States Ser.). (ENG.). 24p. (J). (gr. 3-3). pap. 9.25 *(978-1-4488-0775-8(1)*, 8e19b792-de43-44a2-90f5-f864bd4531ba); lib. bdg. 26.27 *(978-1-4488-0668-3(2)*, f5410b50-9f0d-4142-ac9b-c281d6d7f595) Rosen Publishing Group, Inc., The. (PowerKids Pr.).

Milivojevic, JoAnn. Puerto Rico. 2005. (Ticket to Ser.). (Illus.). 48p. (gr. 2-4). 22.60 *(978-1-57505-144-4(3))* Lerner Publishing Group.

Riddering, Karenlie Anne. Puerto Rico: Encanto Oculto. 2nd ed. 2005. (ENG & SPA.). 60p. (YA). *(978-0-9765977-2-8(1))* Riddering, Maggie.

Stille, Darlene R. America the Beautiful: Puerto Rico (Revised Edition) rev. ed. 2014. (ENG., Illus.). 144p. (J). lib. bdg. 40.00 *(978-0-531-28290-8(2))* Scholastic Library Publishing.

Torres, John. We Visit Puerto Rico. 2010. (Your Land & My Land Ser.). (Illus.). 64p. (J). (gr. 3-6). lib. bdg. 33.95 *(978-1-58415-892-9(1))* Mitchell Lane Pubs.

Worth, Richard. Puerto Rico: From Colony to Commonwealth, 1 vol. 2015. (Our Shared History Ser.). (ENG., Illus.). 128p. (gr. 7-7). lib. bdg. 38.93 *(978-0-7660-7004-2(2)*, 2326958b-146d-4865-9928-cb709b8ddaa0) Enslow Publishing, LLC.

Yasuda, Anita. What's Great about Puerto Rico? 2015. (Our Great States Ser.). (ENG., Illus.). 32p. (J). (gr. 2-5). lib. bdg. 26.65 *(978-1-4677-3872-9(7)*, 0e11715e-3506-4366-a747-d7b6e274a26f, Lerner Pubns.) Lerner Publishing Group.

PUFFINS

Austen, Amy. Puffins, 1 vol., 1. 2015. (Ocean Friends Ser.). (ENG., Illus.). 24p. (J). (gr. 1-1). pap. 9.25 *(978-1-5081-4180-8(0)*, 5c36459d-e0d3-450d-b988-55491194d4d4, PowerKids Pr.) Rosen Publishing Group, Inc., The.

Beer, Amy-Jane. Puffins. 2008. (Nature's Children Ser.). (Illus.). 52p. (J). *(978-0-7172-6260-1(X))* Grolier, Ltd.

Beer, Julie. Penguins vs. Puffins. 2017. (Illus.). 64p. (J). (gr. 1-3). 12.99 *(978-1-4263-2869-5(9)*, National Geographic Kids) Disney Publishing Worldwide.

Markovics, Joyce. MIS Patas Son Palmeadas y Anaranjadas (Puffin) 2016. (Pistas de Animales 2/Zoo Clues 2 Ser.). (SPA.). 24p. (J). (gr. -1-3). 26.99 *(978-1-944102-80-7(9))* Bearport Publishing Co., Inc.

Markovics, Joyce L. My Feet Are Webbed & Orange. 2016. (Zoo Clues 2 Ser.). (ENG., Illus.). 24p. (J). (gr. -1-3). 26.99 *(978-1-944102-62-3(0))* Bearport Publishing Co., Inc.

Myers, Maya. National Geographic Readers: Puffins (PreReader) 2019. (Readers Ser.). (ENG.). 24p. (J). (gr. -1-k). lib. bdg. 14.90 *(978-1-4263-3505-1(9)*, National Geographic Kids) Disney Publishing Worldwide.

Owen, Ruth. Puffins, 1 vol. 2013. (Polar Animals: Life in the Freezer Ser.). (ENG., Illus.). 32p. (gr. 2-3). 29.93 *(978-1-4777-0224-6(5)*, f6d9d4a0-4b00-420e-b347-ce82970ba4b0); pap. 11.00 *(978-1-4777-0235-2(0)*, 5639aa14-9c50-4263-a7dd-fde29a0463a9) Rosen Publishing Group, Inc., The. (Windmill Bks.).

Quinlan, Susan E. Puffins. rev. ed. 2009. (Nature Watch Ser.). (ENG.). 48p. (gr. 4-8). 27.93 *(978-1-58013-944-1(2))* Lerner Publishing Group.

Sexton, Colleen. Puffins. 2009. (Oceans Alive Ser.). (ENG., Illus.). 24p. (J). (gr. k-3). lib. bdg. 26.95 *(978-1-60014-251-2(6))* Bellwether Media.

—Puffins. 2009. (Blastoff! Readers Ser.). (ENG., Illus.). 24p. (J). (gr. k-3). 20.00 *(978-0-531-21714-6(0)*, Children's Pr.) Scholastic Library Publishing.

Statts, Leo. Puffins. 2017. (Awesome Birds Ser.). (ENG., Illus.). 24p. (J). (gr. -1-2). lib. bdg. 31.36 *(978-1-5321-2061-9(3)*, 26744, Abdo Zoom-Launch) ABDO Publishing Co.

PUGET SOUND (WASH.)

Marsico, Katie. Puget Sound. 2013. (Explorer Library: Social Studies Explorer Ser.). (ENG.). 32p. (gr. 4-8). (J). pap. 14.21 *(978-1-62431-039-3(7)*, 202513); (Illus.). lib. bdg. 32.07 *(978-1-62431-015-7(X)*, 202511) Cherry Lake Publishing.

PUGET SOUND (WASH.)—FICTION

Arden, Lynne. Guess What Happened to Me, Auntie Kate! Marino, Natalie, illus. 2008. 52p. pap. 18.95 *(978-1-59858-733-3(1))* Dog Ear Publishing, LLC.

Deuker, Carl. Runner. 2007. (ENG.). 224p. (YA). (gr. 7-12). pap. 15.99 *(978-0-618-73505-1(4)*, 410112, Clarion Bks.) HarperCollins Pubs.

PUGILISM

see Boxing

PULASKI, KAZIMIERZ, 1748-1779

Flavius, Brother. Father of the American Cavalry: A Story of Brigadier General Casimir Pulaski. Jagodits, Carolyn Lee, illus. 2011. 96p. 38.95 *(978-1-258-07161-5(4))* Literary Licensing, LLC.

Kajencki, AnnMarie Francis. Count Casimir Pulaski: From Poland to America, a Hero's Fight for Liberty. (Library of American Lives & Times Ser.). 112p. (gr. 5-5). 2009. 69.20 *(978-1-60853-475-3(8))* 2004. (ENG., Illus.). (YA). lib. bdg. 38.27 *(978-1-4042-2646-3(X)*, de08ddf4-14c2-4d95-97f1-c63934929363) Rosen Publishing Group, Inc., The.

PULITZER, JOSEPH, 1847-1911

Whitelaw, Nancy. Joseph Pulitzer & the New York World. rev. exp. ed. 2004. (Makers of the Media Ser.). (Illus.). 128p. (J). lib. bdg. 21.95 *(978-1-931798-36-5(2))* Reynolds, Morgan Inc.

PUMA

Archer, Claire. Pumas, 1 vol. 2014. (Big Cats Ser.). (ENG.). 24p. (J). (gr. -1-2). lib. bdg. 32.79 *(978-1-62970-005-2(3)*, 1228, Abdo Kids) ABDO Publishing Co.

Carr, Aaron. Cougars. 2014. (Illus.). 24p. (J). *(978-1-62127-210-6(9))* Weigl Pubs., Inc.

Cline, Gina. Cougars. Rupp, Kristina, illus. 2013. (1G Predator Animals Ser.). (ENG.). 24p. (J). pap. 9.60 *(978-1-61406-244-8(7))* American Reading Co.

Early Macken, JoAnn. Cougars, 1 vol. (Animals That Live in the Mountains (First Edition) Ser.). (ENG., 24p. (gr. 1-1). 2005. Illus.). pap. 9.15 *(978-0-8368-6324-6(0)*, dccaad8c-8e34-4b2f-9654-ffa688994467) 2005. (Illus.). lib. bdg. 24.27 *(978-0-8368-6317-8(8)*, 6f2a135c-db91-4db9-8fc0-6759411353a1) 2nd rev. ed. 2009. (J). pap. 9.15 *(978-1-4339-2494-1(3)*, 3b1615a1-a791-461a-b98a-529dd3cdb041) 2nd rev. ed. 2009. (J). lib. bdg. 25.27 *(978-1-4339-2411-8(0)*, 50e31d8c-5836-4bb3-8623-9756b4c82587) Stevens, Gareth Publishing LLLP. (Weekly Reader Leveled Readers).

—Cougars / Puma, 1 vol. 2nd rev. ed. 2009. (Animals That Live in the Mountains / Animales de Las Montañas (Second Edition) Ser.). (ENG & SPA.). 24p. (J). (gr. 1-1). pap. 9.15 *(978-1-4339-2501-6(X)*, eab95431-2c22-42c2-add3-a8004eb8f275, Weekly Reader Leveled Readers); lib. bdg. 25.27 *(978-1-4339-2443-9(9)*, 7e34b99e-73b1-467d-8e7d-a41aadd0a042) Stevens, Gareth Publishing LLLP.

Emminizer, Theresa. What If Mountain Lions Disappeared?, 1 vol. 2019. (Life Without Animals Ser.). (ENG.). 24p. (gr. 1-2). 24.27 *(978-1-5382-3816-5(0)*, 546f18cd-bbca-4dc3-a062-ecc8f4a4e389) Stevens, Gareth Publishing LLLP.

Fox-Parrish, et al. Ghost Cats of the Tetons, Bk. 1. 2010. 40p. pap. 18.99 *(978-1-4490-1939-6(0))* AuthorHouse.

—Ghost Cats of the Tetons: Book 2. 2010. 60p. pap. 23.99 *(978-1-4490-2946-3(9))* AuthorHouse.

—Ghost Cats of the Tetons: Book 3: New Horizons. 2010. 48p. pap. 19.49 *(978-1-4490-2947-0(7))* AuthorHouse.

George, Jean Craighead. Summer Moon. 2003. (J). (gr. 3-7). 20.75 *(978-0-8446-7243-4(2))* Smith, Peter Pub., Inc.

Gish, Melissa. Cougars. 2012. (Living Wild Ser.). (ENG., Illus.). 48p. (J). (gr. 4-7). 23.95 *(978-1-60818-167-4(7)*, 21893, Creative Education) Creative Co., The.

Grack, Rachel. Los Pumas. 2018. (Animales Norteamericanos Ser.). (SPA.). 24p. (J). (gr. 1-4). lib. bdg. *(978-1-68151-623-3(3)*, 15231) Amicus.

—Mountain Lions. 2018. (North American Animals Ser.). (ENG.). 24p. (J). (gr. 1-4). pap. 8.99 *(978-1-68152-337-8(X)*, 15122); lib. bdg. *(978-1-68151-417-8(6)*, 15114) Amicus.

Hogan, Christa C. Mountain Lions. 2017. (Animals of North America Ser.). (ENG., Illus.). 32p. (J). (gr. 2-3). pap. 9.95 *(978-1-63517-092-4(3)*, 1635170923, Focus Readers) North Star Editions.

Jackson, Tom. Cougars. 2008. (Nature's Children Ser.). (Illus.). 52p. (J). *(978-0-7172-6220-5(0))* Grolier, Ltd.

Johnson, Jinny. Mountain Lion. 2014. (North American Mammals Ser.). 24p. (gr. 2-5). 28.50 *(978-1-62588-035-2(9))* Black Rabbit Bks.

—Mountain Lion. 2014. (North American Mammals Ser.). (ENG., Illus.). 24p. (J). (gr. -1-4). pap. 8.95 *(978-1-77092-169-6(9))* Saunders Bk. Co. CAN. Dist: RiverStream Publishing.

Karlin, Wade. Pumas, 1 vol. 2012. (Killer Cats Ser.). (ENG., Illus.). 24p. (J). (gr. 2-3). pap. 9.15 *(978-1-4339-7012-2(0)*, dc836361-2938-471d-a11f-2eee29a3cd43); lib. bdg. 25.27 *(978-1-4339-7011-5(2)*, ce1aa234-cc9c-4477-b0f7-75c1a67b00d7) Stevens, Gareth Publishing LLLP.

Kissock, Heather. Cougars. 2018. (J). *(978-1-4896-7996-3(0)*, AV2 by Weigl) Weigl Pubs., Inc.

Loh-Hagan, Virginia. Mountain Lion. Bane, Jeff, illus. 2017. (My Early Library: My Favorite Animal Ser.). (ENG.). 24p. (J). (gr. k-1). lib. bdg. 30.64 *(978-1-63472-841-6(6)*, 209790) Cherry Lake Publishing.

Magby, Meryl. Mountain Lions. 2013. (American Animals Ser.). 24p. (J). (gr. k-5). pap. 49.50 *(978-1-4777-0949-8(5))*; (ENG.). (gr. 2-3). 26.27 *(978-1-4777-0788-3(3)*, db7cf9c9-dfc1-4710-8ecd-47d45baaa33a); (ENG.). (gr. 2-3). pap. 9.25 *(978-1-4777-0948-1(7)*, d8b45903-2ae3-459d-8b72-f41875eb0298) Rosen Publishing Group, Inc., The. (PowerKids Pr.).

Owen, Ruth. Pumas, 1 vol., 1. 2013. (Dr. Bob's Amazing World of Animals Ser.). (ENG.). 32p. (J). (gr. 2-3). 31.27 *(978-1-4777-9032-8(2)*, 222728e2-77a7-4d34-ba01-369df0a3bc00, Windmill Bks.) Rosen Publishing Group, Inc., The.

Owings, Lisa. Mountain Lion Attack. 2012. (Animal Attacks Ser.). (ENG., Illus.). 24p. (J). (gr. 3-7). lib. bdg. 26.95 *(978-1-60014-789-0(5)*, Torque Bks.) Bellwether Media.

Person, Stephen. Cougar: A Cat with Many Names. 2012. (America's Hidden Animal Treasures Ser.). 32p. (J). (gr. 2-7). lib. bdg. 28.50 *(978-1-61772-569-2(2))* Bearport Publishing Co., Inc.

Raatma, Lucia. How Do We Live Together? Mountain Lions. 2010. (Community Connections: How Do We Live Together? Ser.). (ENG., Illus.). 24p. (gr. 2-5). lib. bdg. 29.21 *(978-1-60279-625-6(4)*, 200328) Cherry Lake Publishing.

Randall, Henry. Cougars, 1 vol. 2011. (Cats of the Wild Ser.). (ENG.). 24p. (J). (gr. 1-2). pap. 9.25 *(978-1-4488-2617-9(9)*, 42084ed9-4c8c-4166-b399-1c2982d320a8); lib. bdg. 26.27 *(978-1-4488-2516-5(4)*, 4147cfb6-a43c-4dcc-909f-5557e61bdb1a) Rosen Publishing Group, Inc., The. (PowerKids Pr.).

—Cougars / Pumas, 1 vol. 2011. (Cats of the Wild / Felinos Salvajes Ser.). (SPA & ENG.). 24p. (gr. 1-2). 26.27 *(978-1-4488-3128-9(8)*, 4ff9972a-6718-481f-89eb-3e3c0b0e16f7) Rosen Publishing Group, Inc., The.

Rathburn, Betsy. Mountain Lions. 2017. (North American Animals Ser.). (ENG., Illus.). 24p. (J). (gr. k-3). lib. bdg. 26.95 *(978-1-62617-639-3(6)*, Blastoff! Readers) Bellwether Media.

Read, Tracy C. Exploring the World of Cougars. 2011. (Exploring the World Of Ser.). (ENG., Illus.). 24p. (J). (gr. 3-7). 16.95 *(978-1-55407-785-4(0)*, 99dd4015-99fc-4ff3-a74b-53a1b034ae2b); pap. 6.95 *(978-1-55407-956-8(X)*, a823f94c-f2a7-4cff-94ec-eff3d131b4b0) Firefly Bks., Ltd.

Riggs, Kate. Cougars. 2014. (J). 25.65 *(978-1-60818-347-0(5)*, Creative Education) Creative Co., The.

Ringstad, Arnold. Cougars. 2015. (Wild Cats Ser.). (Illus.). 24p. (J). 27.10 *(978-1-60753-600-0(5))* Amicus Learning.

Schuetz, Kristin. Mountain Lions. 2014. (Backyard Wildlife Ser.). (ENG.). 24p. (J). (gr. k-3). lib. bdg. 26.95 *(978-1-60014-970-2(7)*, Blastoff! Readers) Bellwether Media.

Shaffer, Lindsay. Mountain Lions. 2019. (Animals of the Mountains Ser.). (ENG., Illus.). 24p. (J). (gr. k-3). lib. bdg. 26.95 *(978-1-64487-015-0(0)*, Blastoff! Readers) Bellwether Media.

Shea, Mary Molly. Perilous Pumas, 1 vol. 2017. (Cutest Animals... That Could Kill You! Ser.). (ENG.). 24p. (J). (gr. 2-3). pap. 9.15 *(978-1-5382-1091-8(6)*, ccd48d1b-4f31-4351-a90d-c7ae77d5da7b) Stevens, Gareth Publishing LLLP.

Shores, Erika L. Mountain Lions, 1 vol. 2010. (Wildcats Ser.). (ENG.). 24p. (J). (gr. -1-2). lib. bdg. 27.32 *(978-1-4296-4485-3(0)*, 102957, Capstone Pr.) Capstone.

Taylor, Trace & Sánchez, Lucía M. Pumas. 2006. (1G Animales Depredadores de Norteamérica Ser.). (SPA., Illus.). 32p. (J). (gr. k-2). pap. 8.00 *(978-1-61541-057-6(0))* American Reading Co.

Tomljanovic, Tatiana. Cougars. (J). 2014. *(978-1-4896-0914-4(8))* 2010. (Illus.). 24p. (gr. 2-4). pap. 11.95 *(978-1-60596-950-3(8))* 2010. (Illus.). 24p. (gr. 2-5). lib. bdg. 25.70 *(978-1-60596-949-7(4))* Weigl Pubs., Inc.

Vogel, Elizabeth. Pumas. 2009. (Big Cats (Powerkids Readers) Ser.). 24p. (gr. 1-1). 37.50 *(978-1-61511-571-6(4)*, PowerKids Pr.) Rosen Publishing Group, Inc., The.

von Zumbusch, Amelie. Pumas: Lone Hunters. 2009. (Dangerous Cats Ser.). 24p. (gr. 2-3). 42.50 *(978-1-61512-130-4(7)*, PowerKids Pr.) Rosen Publishing Group, Inc., The.

Zuchora-Walske, Christine. Mountain Lions, 1 vol. 2012. (Big Cats Ser.). (ENG.). 32p. (J). (gr. 3-9). lib. bdg. 28.65 *(978-1-4296-7644-1(2)*, 117242, Capstone Pr.) Capstone.

PUMA—FICTION

Bond, Katherine Grace. The Summer of No Regrets. 2012. (ENG.). 304p. (YA). (gr. 7-12). pap. 18.99 *(978-1-4022-6504-4(2))* Sourcebooks, Inc.

Carr, Roger Vaughan. The Climb. 2007. 96p. (J). pap. *(978-1-4207-0730-4(2))* Sundance/Newbridge Educational Publishing.

Cox, Renee K. Sammie Jane Saves Charlie: Cougar's Rescue. 2009. (Illus.). 56p. pap. 11.95 *(978-1-4327-3129-8(7))* Outskirts Pr., Inc.

Gibbs, Stuart. Lion Down. 2019. (FunJungle Ser.). (ENG., Illus.). 352p. (J). (gr. 3-7). 18.99 *(978-1-5344-2473-9(3)*, Simon & Schuster Bks. For Young Readers) Simon & Schuster Bks. For Young Readers.

Haig-Brown, Roderick. Panther. 2007. (ENG., Illus.). 256p. (YA). pap. *(978-1-55017-341-3(3)*, 2d08933a-d728-4a16-a878-30b9c7295817) Harbour Publishing Co., Ltd.

Isaac, Michael James. How the Cougar Came to Be Called the Ghost Cat/Ta'n Petalu Telui'tut Skite'kmujewe. Christmas, Dozay (Arlene), illus. 2010. (ENG.). 32p. (J). pap. 12.95 ***(978-1-55266-371-4(X)***, 29869) Community Bks. CAN. Dist: Columbia Univ. Pr.

Johnston, Tony. Puma Dreams. LaMarche, Jim, illus. 2019. (ENG.). 48p. (J). (gr. -1-3). 17.99 *(978-1-5344-2979-6(4)*, Simon & Schuster Bks. For Young Readers) Simon & Schuster Bks. For Young Readers.

Jordan, Rosa. The Last Wild Place, 1 vol. 2008. 256p. (J). (gr. 3-7). 15.95 *(978-1-56145-458-7(3))* Peachtree Publishing Co. Inc.

Love, Nicole M. Cool Cougar! Cool Cougar! Cool Cougar! & the Puma Dance. 2012. 24p. pap. 17.99 *(978-1-4685-7541-5(4))* AuthorHouse.

MacDonald, George. A Rough Shaking. 2017. (ENG., Illus.). (J). pap. 16.95 *(978-1-374-88365-9(4))* Capital Communications, Inc.

Mitchell, Todd. The Last Panther. 2019. (ENG.). 256p. (J). (gr. 3-7). 8.99 *(978-0-399-55561-9(7)*, Yearling) Random Hse. Children's Bks.

Mora, Pat. Dona Flor: A Tall Tale about a Giant Woman with a Great Big Heart. ón, Raul, illus. 2010. (ENG.). 32p. (J). (gr. -1-2). pap. 8.99 *(978-0-375-86144-4(0)*, Dragonfly Bks.) Random Hse. Children's Bks.

Nesbit, Troy. Mystery at Rustlers Fort. 2014. (Wilderness Mystery Ser.). (ENG., Illus.). 282p. (J). (gr. 3-7). pap. 12.95 *(978-1-58979-867-0(8))* Taylor Trade Publishing.

Parrish, Amanda. Greyhound Travels: Puma Travels to Italy. 2010. 28p. pap. 12.49 *(978-1-4490-9453-9(8))* AuthorHouse.

Sauer, Tammi. Wordy Birdy Meets Mr. Cougarpants. Mottram, Dave, illus. 2019. (ENG.). 32p. (J). (gr. -1-2). 19.99 *(978-1-5247-1931-9(5)*, Doubleday Bks. for Young Readers) Random Hse. Children's Bks.

Snyder, Adeline. Hunting with Mountain Lions, 1 vol., Vol. 1. 2013. (Animal Attack! Ser.). (ENG.). 32p. (J). (gr. 2-3). 25.27 *(978-1-4824-0516-3(4)*, b8c64b44-a48b-470e-8f7f-5c95a50c93dc) Stevens, Gareth Publishing LLLP.

PUMPKIN

Colella, Jill. Let's Explore Pumpkins! 2020. (Food Field Trips Ser.). (ENG., Illus.). 24p. (J). (gr. -1-2). 26.65 *(978-1-5415-6304-9(2)*, 01dcb7d0-698e-4da6-a4c3-8c21a43065ab, Lerner Pubns.) Lerner Publishing Group.

Dibble, Traci. Pumpkins Come from Seeds. 2017. (1G Our Natural World Ser.). (ENG., Illus.). 24p. (J). pap. 9.60 *(978-1-64053-194-9(7)*, ARC Pr. Bks.) American Reading Co.

Farmer, Jacqueline. Pumpkins. Tildes, Phyllis Limbacher, illus. 2004. 32p. (J). (gr. k-3). pap. 7.95 *(978-1-57091-558-1(X))* Charlesbridge Publishing, Inc.

Felix, Rebecca. We Harvest Pumpkins in Fall. 2013. (21st Century Basic Skills Library: Let's Look at Fall Ser.). (ENG., Illus.). 24p. (gr. k-3). 26.35 *(978-1-61080-906-1(8)*, 202603); E-Book 43.50 *(978-1-61080-981-8(5)*, 202606) Cherry Lake Publishing.

—We Harvest Pumpkins in the Fall. 2013. (21st Century Basic Skills Library: Let's Look at Fall Ser.). (ENG.). 24p. (J). (gr. k-3). pap. 12.79 *(978-1-61080-931-3(9)*, 202605) Cherry Lake Publishing.

Friesen, Helen Lepp. Growing a Pumpkin. 2008. (Discovering & Exploring Science Ser.). (Illus.). 16p. (J). (gr. -1-3). lib. bdg. 12.95 *(978-0-7569-8426-7(2))* Perfection Learning Corp.

Gates, Margo. Emily's Pumpkin. Darcy, Liam, illus. 2019. (Science All Around Me (Pull Ahead Readers — Fiction) Ser.). (ENG.). 16p. (J). (gr. -1-1). pap. 8.99 *(978-1-5415-7338-3(2)*, 9f42e8de-eb9a-49b2-8cd6-956a7a0fb500, Lerner Pubns.) Lerner Publishing Group.

Grack, Rachel. Pumpkin Seed to Pie. 2020. (Beginning to End Ser.). (ENG., Illus.). 24p. (J). (gr. k-3). lib. bdg. 26.95 *(978-1-64487-141-6(6)*, Blastoff! Readers) Bellwether Media.

Griswold, Cliff. The Pumpkin Patch, 1 vol. 2014. (Fun in Fall Ser.). (ENG.). 24p. (J). (gr. k-k). lib. bdg. 24.27 *(978-1-4824-1788-3(X)*, 29bfee53-5a63-4f9b-81e3-4552c86f5854) Stevens, Gareth Publishing LLLP.

Hayes, Amy. A Seed Becomes a Pumpkin, 1 vol. 2015. (Transformations in Nature Ser.). (ENG., Illus.). 24p. (gr. 1-1). pap. 9.23 *(978-1-5026-0814-7(6)*, c5763084-ce65-4a70-85d7-4de5a5e5302b) Cavendish Square Publishing LLC.

Lee, Jackie. Pumpkin. 2015. (See It Grow Ser.). (ENG.). 24p. (J). (gr. -1-3). lib. bdg. 26.99 *(978-1-62724-840-2(4))* Bearport Publishing Co., Inc.

McNeil, Niki, et al. HOCPP 1110 Five Little Pumpkins. 2006. spiral bd. 14.00 *(978-1-60308-110-8(0))* In the Hands of a Child.

Michele, Tracey. Pumpkin Time. 2011. (Learn-Abouts Ser.). (Illus.). 16p. (J). pap. 7.95 *(978-1-59920-589-2(0))* Black Rabbit Bks.

Nelson, Robin. Pumpkins. 2009. pap. 34.95 *(978-0-7613-4118-5(8))*; (ENG., Illus.). 24p. 23.93 *(978-0-7613-4073-7(4)*, Lerner Pubns.) Lerner Publishing Group.

Peters, Katie. Let's Look at Pumpkins. 2020. (Plant Life Cycles (Pull Ahead Readers — Nonfiction) Ser.). (ENG., Illus.). 16p. (J). (gr. -1-1). 27.99 *(978-1-5415-9021-2(X)*, 406cedb6-01f3-4100-8284-7f057fe31615, Lerner Pubns.) Lerner Publishing Group.

Pfeffer, Wendy. From Seed to Pumpkin. Hale, James Graham, illus. (Let's-Read-And-Find-Out Science 1 Ser.). (ENG.). 40p. (J). (gr. -1-3). 2015. pap. 7.99 *(978-0-06-238185-9(7)*, HarperCollins) 2004. 15.99 *(978-0-06-028038-3(7))* HarperCollins Pubs.

Rustad, Martha E. H. Diversión con Calabazas en Otoño (Fall Pumpkin Fun) Enright, Amanda, illus. 2019. (Diversión en Otoño (Fall Fun) (Early Bird Stories (tm) en Español) Ser.). (SPA.). 24p. (J). (gr. k-2). pap. 8.99 *(978-1-5415-4539-7(7)*, c59b7691-7b94-48bd-829a-46981b248a67); lib. bdg. 29.32 *(978-1-5415-4083-5(2)*, 2673506f-7186-4461-962e-aee818da3026) Lerner Publishing Group. (Ediciones Lerner).

—Fall Pumpkin Fun. Enright, Amanda, illus. 2018. (Fall Fun (Early Bird Stories (tm)) Ser.). (ENG.). 24p. (J). (gr. k-2). lib. bdg. 29.32 *(978-1-5415-2004-2(1)*, 49859806-2f42-467d-978d-61ac70dffbbc, Lerner Pubns.) Lerner Publishing Group.

—Fall Pumpkins: Orange & Plump. Enright, Amanda, illus. 2011. (Fall's Here! Ser.). pap. 39.62 *(978-0-7613-8647-6(5)*, Millbrook Pr.) Lerner Publishing Group.

Schuh, Mari. Pumpkins in Fall. 2013. (ENG., Illus.). 24p. (J). lib. bdg. 25.65 *(978-1-62031-060-1(0))* Jump! Inc.

Shores, Erika L. Pumpkins. 2015. (Celebrate Fall Ser.). (ENG., Illus.). 24p. (J). (gr. -1-2). lib. bdg. 22.65 *(978-1-4914-6004-7(0)*, 128930) Capstone.

Sikkens, Crystal. From Seed to Pumpkin. 2019. (Full STEAM Ahead! - Science Starters Ser.). (Illus.). 24p. (J). (gr. 1-1). pap. *(978-0-7787-6236-2(X))* Crabtree Publishing Co.

Sundance/Newbridge LLC Staff. Growing Pumpkins. 2007. (Early Science Ser.). (gr. k-3). 18.95 *(978-1-4007-6179-1(4))*; pap. 6.10 *(978-1-4007-6175-3(1))* Sundance/Newbridge Educational Publishing.

PUMPKIN—FICTION

The Adventures of the Original Pumpkin Patch Pals. l.t. ed. 2005. (Illus.). 32p. (J). 15.00 *(978-0-9770960-1-5(7))* 3 Pals Media, LLC.

Arthur, Sherry. Magical Hallows Eve. 2009. (ENG.). 44p. pap. 24.00 *(978-0-557-07264-4(6))* Lulu Pr., Inc.

Astley, Neville & Baker, Mark. The Pumpkin Contest. 2018. (Illus.). (J). *(978-1-5444-0652-7(5))* Scholastic, Inc.

Atamer, Billie. The Little Purple Pumpkin. 2013. 28p. (gr. -1-3). pap. 11.95 *(978-1-61244-235-8(8))* Halo Publishing International.

Banach, Jo-Ann. Sam the First Christmas Pumpkin: Sam Meets Santa Claus. 2006. (ENG., Illus.). 28p. per. 19.99 *(978-1-4259-0898-0(5))* AuthorHouse.

Bateman, Teresa. Runaway Pumpkins. Coleman, Stephanie Fizer, illus. 2020. 32p. (J). (gr. -1-2). lib. bdg. 16.99 *(978-1-58089-681-8(2))* Charlesbridge Publishing, Inc.

Bauer, Joan. Squashed. 2005. (ENG.). 208p. (YA). (gr. 7-7). pap. 8.99 *(978-0-14-240426-3(8)*, Speak) Penguin Young Readers Group.

—Squashed. 2005. 194p. (gr. 7-12). 18.00 *(978-0-7569-5781-0(8))* Perfection Learning Corp.

Bennett, Elizabeth. The Biggest Pumpkin Ever! Woodruff, Liza, illus. 2007. (J). pap. *(978-0-545-00232-5(X))* Scholastic, Inc.

Bonnell, Kris. Picking a Pumpkin. 2007. (J). pap. 5.95 *(978-1-933727-51-6(9))* Reading Reading Bks., LLC.

Bowman, Crystal. My Happy Pumpkin: God's Love Shining Through Me, 1 vol. 2014. (ENG.). 14p. (J). bds. 6.99 *(978-0-310-73828-2(8))* Zonderkidz.

Boyd, William T. The Pumpkin Fairy. Roberts, Mary Jo, illus. 2003. 32p. (J). (gr. k-1). 14.95 *(978-0-9718161-0-7(7))* Wyatt Pr.

Brown, Desirae. A Pumpkin's Dream, 1 vol. 2009. 29p. pap. 24.95 *(978-1-60836-364-3(3))* America Star Bks.

Brown, Margaret Wise. The Fierce Yellow Pumpkin. Egielski, Richard, illus. (ENG.). 32p. (J). (gr. -1-1). 2003. 16.99 *(978-0-06-024479-8(8))* 2006. reprint ed. pap. 6.99 *(978-0-06-443534-5(2))* HarperCollins Pubs. (HarperCollins).

Butler, Marybeth, illus. Five Little Pumpkins (Rookie Toddler) 2018. (Rookie Toddler Ser.). (ENG.). 14p. (J). (gr. -1 — 1). bds. 6.95 *(978-0-531-12703-2(6)*, Children's Pr.) Scholastic Library Publishing.

Capucilli, Alyssa Satin. Biscuit Visits the Pumpkin Patch: A Fall & Halloween Book for Kids. Schories, Pat, illus. 2004. (ENG.). 16p. (J). (gr. -1-3). 6.99 *(978-0-06-009466-9(4)*, HarperFestival) HarperCollins Pubs.

Cavanaugh, Wendy. Pumpkin in the Sky: Let's bake a pie together, you & I, with Auntie Wendy. Cavanaugh, Wendy & LeVesque, Sherry, photos by. 2011. (Illus.). 32p. (J). spiral bd. 20.00 *(978-0-9743121-1-8(8))* Eastlight Pr.

Chernesky, Felicia Sanzari. The Boy Who Said Nonsense. Anderson, Nicola, illus. 2016. (ENG.). 32p. (J). (gr. -1-3). 16.99 *(978-0-8075-5742-6(0)*, 807557420) Whitman, Albert & Co.

Chitra Soundar. Pattan's Pumpkin: A Traditional Flood Story from Southern India. Lessac, Frané, illus. 2017. (J). *(978-3-692-74397-4(1))* Candlewick Pr.

Clay Iii, J. Percy. Sampson's Pumpkin Playhouse. 2012. 30p. 24.95 *(978-1-4626-7226-4(4))* America Star Bks.

Cody, Christina. The Perfectly Imperfect Pumpkin. 2010. (ENG.). 24p. pap. 12.99 *(978-1-4490-7537-8(1))* AuthorHouse.

Condenzio, Mary. Oliver. 2013. 20p. pap. 24.95 *(978-1-62709-305-7(2))* America Star Bks.

Cooper, Helen S. Pumpkin Soup, Set. unabr. ed. 2013. (Macmillan Young Listeners Story Time Sets Ser.). (ENG.). (J). 12.99 *(978-1-4272-3920-4(7)*, 9781427239204) Macmillan Audio.

Cordone Warner, Debra. Pumpkee & the Day of Harvest. 2010. 38p. pap. 19.99 *(978-0-557-70397-5(2))* Lulu Pr., Inc.

Crespeno, John. Toby: The Mouse Who Lived in a Pumpkin. 2011. 84p. pap. 28.68 *(978-1-4634-1632-4(6))* AuthorHouse.

Cummins, Lucy Ruth. Stumpkin. Cummins, Lucy Ruth, illus. 2018. (ENG., Illus.). 56p. (J). (gr. -1-3). 18.99 *(978-1-5344-1362-7(6)*, Atheneum Bks. for Young Readers) Simon & Schuster Children's Publishing.

Denega, Danielle & Bridwell, Norman. Pumpkin Patch Puppy. 2006. (Illus.). 26p. (J). pap. *(978-0-439-87764-0(4))* Scholastic, Inc.

Dillon, Jana. Jeb Scarecrow's Pumpkin Patch, 1 vol. 2016. (ENG., Illus.). 34p. (J). (gr. k-3). pap. 9.95 *(978-1-4556-2181-1(1)*, Pelican Publishing) Arcadia Publishing.

Dohr, Robert. The Pumpkin Se. Dewyea, Glenn, illus. 2012. 32p. pap. 13.50 *(978-1-61204-337-1(2)*, Strategic Bk. Publishing) Strategic Book Publishing & Rights Agency (SBPRA).

Donde Esta Belo? (Where's Pipkin?) (Granja Oso de Miel Ser.). (SPA.). (J). bds. 4.99 *(978-0-7899-0611-3(2)*, 495053) Editorial Unilit.

Elliott, Rebecca. Trip to the Pumpkin Farm, 11. 2020. (Branches Early Ch Bks). (ENG.). 72p. (J). (gr. 2-3). 15.36 *(978-1-64697-304-0(6))* Penworthy Co., LLC, The.

—Trip to the Pumpkin Farm: a Branches Book (Owl Diaries #11) Elliott, Rebecca, illus. 2019. (Owl Diaries: 11). (ENG., Illus.). 80p. (J). (gr. k-2). pap. 6.99 *(978-1-338-29864-2(X))* Scholastic, Inc.

—Trip to the Pumpkin Farm: a Branches Book (Owl Diaries #11) (Library Edition) Elliott, Rebecca, illus. 2019. (Owl Diaries: 11). (ENG., Illus.). 80p. (J). (gr. k-2). lib. bdg. 24.99 *(978-1-338-29865-9(8))* Scholastic, Inc.

Evans, Alwyn & Davis, Anne. Pumpkin in Hollow Countdown. Capelle, Joanna, illus. 16p. (J). pap. 7.49 *(978-1-86368-045-5(4))* Fremantle Pr. AUS. Dist: Independent Pubs. Group.

Everett, George W. G. W. Frog & the Pumpkin Patch Bandit. 2010. 40p. 16.95 *(978-1-4497-0759-0(9)*, WestBow Pr.) Author Solutions, LLC.

Fisk, Cindy. Hooga Booga Presents the Little Pumpkin. Fisk, David, illus. 2013. 28p. pap. 11.95 *(978-1-938743-02-3(4))* Reimann Bks.

Fronis, Aly. This Little Pumpkin. Flowers, Luke, illus. 2018. (ENG.). 16p. (J). (gr. -1-k). bds. 5.99 *(978-1-4998-0645-8(0))* Little Bee Books Inc.

Fry, Sonali. The Itsy Bitsy Pumpkin. Rescek, Sanja, illus. 2014. (Itsy Bitsy Ser.). (ENG.). 16p. (J). (gr. -1 — 1). bds. 5.99 *(978-1-4814-0505-8(5)*, Little Simon) Little Simon.

Fuerst, Jeffrey B. Peter Pumpkin Eater. Greenhead, Bill, illus. 2010. (Rising Readers Ser.). (J). 3.49 *(978-1-60719-705-8(7))* Newmark Learning LLC.

Galloway, Fhiona, illus. Where's the Pumpkin? 2015. (ENG.). 16p. (J). (gr. -1 — 1). bds. 5.99 *(978-1-4998-0097-5(5))* Little Bee Books Inc.

Geisert, Arthur. Pumpkin Island. 2018. (Clayton County Trilogy Ser.). (Illus.). 40p. (J). 17.95 *(978-1-59270-265-7(1))* Enchanted Lion Bks., LLC.

Geisler, Ruth. Shine, Smiling Pumpkin. 2004. (J). 0.99 *(978-0-9747923-0-9(6))* C T A, Inc.

George, K. Duck, Duck, Dinosaur: Perfect Pumpkin. Vidal, Oriol, illus. 2017. 32p. (J). *(978-1-5182-4363-9(0))* Harper & Row Ltd.

George, Kallie. Duck, Duck, Dinosaur: Perfect Pumpkin. Vidal, Oriol, illus. 2017. (My First I Can Read Ser.). (ENG.). 32p. (J). (gr. -1-3). 16.99 *(978-0-06-235315-3(2))*; pap. 4.99 *(978-0-06-235314-6(4))* HarperCollins Pubs. (HarperCollins).

Ghigna, Charles. Oh My, Pumpkin Pie! Spengler, Ken, illus. 2005. (Step into Reading Ser.). 32p. (J). (gr. -1-1). pap. 5.99 *(978-0-375-82945-1(8)*, Random Hse. Bks. for Young Readers) Random Hse. Children's Bks.

Gilbert, Jeff. Trick or Shriek. 2006. 72p. pap. 5.97 *(978-0-9646781-1-8(X))* Hairball Pr.

Granata, Nancy. The Perfect Porch for Witch Watching. 2008. 52p. pap. 22.49 *(978-1-4389-0107-7(0))* AuthorHouse.

Greening, Rosie. Five Little Pumpkins. Ede, Lara, illus. 2016. (ENG.). 14p. (J). (gr. -1 — 1). bds. 8.99 *(978-1-78598-400-6(4))* Make Believe Ideas GBR. Dist: Scholastic, Inc.

Gruber, Michael. The Legend of the Brog. Gruber, Michael & Graves, Linda, illus. 2005. (J). per. 9.95 *(978-0-9770413-0-5(1))* Gruber Enterprises.

Guile, Gill, illus. Bear Picks a Pumpkin, 1 vol. 2018. (ENG.). 24p. (J). bds. 8.99 *(978-0-310-76621-6(4))* Zonderkidz.

Harkrader, Lisa. A Pumpkin Tale. 2016. (Spring Forward Ser.). (J). (gr. 2). *(978-1-4900-2247-5(3))* Benchmark Education Co.

Harvey, Sharon M. Legend of the Pumpkin Carver. 2010. 100p. pap. 22.95 *(978-1-4327-1214-3(4))* Outskirts Pr., Inc.

Heuiser Hill, Melanie. Giant Pumpkin Suite. 2017. (ENG.). 448p. (J). (gr. 4-7). 18.99 *(978-0-7636-9155-4(0))* Candlewick Pr.

Hill, Eric. Spot's Thanksgiving. Hill, Eric, illus. 2016. (Spot Ser.). (ENG., Illus.). 10p. (J). (gr. -1-k). bds. 6.99 *(978-0-399-24186-4(8),* Warne) Penguin Young Readers Group.

Hillert, Margaret. Pumpkin, Pumpkin: For the Earliest Reader. Starfall Education, photos by. 2006. (ENG., Illus.). 32p. (J). *(978-1-59577-035-6(6))*; pap. *(978-1-59577-036-3(4))* Starfall Education.

Hills, Tad. Duck & Goose, Find a Pumpkin. Hills, Tad, illus. 2009. (Duck & Goose Ser.). (ENG., Illus.). 22p. (J). (gr. -1 — 1). bds. 7.99 *(978-0-375-85813-0(X),* Schwartz & Wade Bks.) Random Hse. Children's Bks.

—Duck & Goose, Find a Pumpkin (Oversized Board Book) Hills, Tad, illus. 2012. (Duck & Goose Ser.). (ENG., Illus.). 22p. (J). (gr. k-k). bds. 10.99 *(978-0-307-98155-4(X))* Random Hse. Children's Bks.

Holloway, Jamie. Let's Go Pumpkin Picking, 1 vol. 2015. (Rosen REAL Readers: STEM & STEAM Collection). (ENG.). 8p. (gr. k-1). pap. 5.46 *(978-1-4994-9542-3(0),* 2b2bd034-9a89-4107-98ce-4d0b3374dc64, Rosen Classroom) Rosen Publishing Group, Inc., The.

Holub, Joan. Pumpkin Countdown. Smith, Jan, illus. 2014. (AV2 Fiction Readalong Ser.: Vol. 147). (ENG.). (J). (gr. -1-2). lib. bdg. 34.28 *(978-1-4896-2410-9(4),* AV2 by Weigl) Weigl Pubs., Inc.

—Pumpkin Countdown. Smith, Jan, illus. 2018. (ENG.). 32p. (J). (gr. -1-3). pap. 7.99 *(978-0-8075-6662-6(4),* 807566624) Whitman, Albert & Co.

Horning, Sandra. The Biggest Pumpkin, 1 vol. Stone-Barker, Holly, illus. 2014. (ENG.). 32p. 16.99 *(978-1-4556-1925-2(6),* Pelican Publishing) Arcadia Publishing.

Horowitz, Dave. The Ugly Pumpkin. Horowitz, Dave, illus. (ENG., Illus.). (J). 2017. 32p. (— 1). bds. 7.99 *(978-1-5247-4084-9(5),* Nancy Paulsen Books) 2008. 40p. (gr. -1-k). pap. 8.99 *(978-0-14-241145-2(0),* Puffin Books) Penguin Young Readers Group.

Howard, Marie. Punkin & the Peanut. 2012. 30p. 24.95 *(978-1-4626-7332-2(5))* America Star Bks.

Inman, George, Jr., et al. The Bumpy Pumpkin. Lyle, Avis, illus. 2004. (ENG.). 18p. (J). 12.95 *(978-0-9754696-0-6(6))* Bumpy Pumpkin.

Jacobson, Jennifer Richard. Andy Shane & the Pumpkin Trick. Carter, Abby, illus. 2007. (Andy Shane Ser.: 2). (ENG.). 64p. (J). (gr. k-3). per. 5.99 *(978-0-7636-3306-6(2))* Candlewick Pr.

—Andy Shane & the Pumpkin Trick. Carter, Abby, illus. 2008. (Andy Shane Ser.). (J). (gr. -1-3). 25.95 incl. audio *(978-1-4301-0313-4(2))*; pap. 16.95 incl. audio *(978-1-4301-0312-7(4))* Live Oak Media.

Jenkins, Emily. Invisible Inkling: Dangerous Pumpkins. Bliss, Harry, illus. 2012. (Invisible Inkling Ser.: 2). (ENG.). 160p. (J). (gr. 1-5). 14.99 *(978-0-06-180223-2(9),* Balzer & Bray) HarperCollins Pubs.

Jennings, Sharon, et al, adapted by. Franklin's Pumpkin. 2004. (Kids Can Read Ser.). (ENG., Illus.). 32p. (J). (gr. 1-2). 3.95 *(978-1-55337-496-1(7))*; 14.95 *(978-1-55337-495-4(9))* Kids Can Pr., Ltd. CAN. Dist: Hachette Bk. Group.

Johnson, Jay, illus. Ten Little Pumpkins. 2012. (J). *(978-0-545-46862-6(0))* Scholastic, Inc.

Kann, Victoria. Pinkalicious & the Pink Pumpkin. Kann, Victoria, illus. 2011. (Pinkalicious Ser.). (ENG., Illus.). 16p. (J). (gr. -1-2). pap. 6.99 *(978-0-06-198961-2(4),* HarperFestival) HarperCollins Pubs.

Karr, Lily. My Pumpkin. Marts, Doreen Mulryan, illus. 2014. (ENG.). 12p. (J). (gr. -1 — 1). bds. 4.99 *(978-0-545-49332-1(3),* Cartwheel Bks.) Scholastic, Inc.

Katz, Karen. Where Is Baby's Pumpkin? Katz, Karen, illus. 2006. (ENG., Illus.). 14p. (J). (gr. -1 — 1). bds. 7.99 *(978-1-4169-0970-5(2),* Little Simon) Little Simon.

Kirby, Ruth M. Claudius Saves the Pumpkin Patch. Larson, Lisa K., illus. 2008. 20p. pap. 24.95 *(978-1-60703-827-6(7))* America Star Bks.

Klay, Sharon Joy. Denny Grows a Giant Pumpkin. 2010. 28p. pap. 12.99 *(978-1-4520-2871-2(0))* AuthorHouse.

Klein, Abby. The Pumpkin Elf Mystery. McKinley, John, illus. 2007. (Ready, Freddy! Ser.: Bk. 11). 95p. (J). (gr. -1-3). 11.65 *(978-0-7569-8301-7(0))* Perfection Learning Corp.

Kleinberg, Naomi. Thomas & the Runaway Pumpkins (Thomas & Friends) Courtney, Richard, illus. 2018. (Little Golden Book Ser.). (ENG.). 24p. (J). (gr. -1-2). 5.99 *(978-0-385-37391-3(0),* Golden Bks.) Random Hse. Children's Bks.

Kramer, K. Out on the Farm with Farmer Jack. 2012. 24p. pap. 15.99 *(978-1-4797-0823-9(2))* Xlibris Corp.

Kroll, Steven. The Biggest Pumpkin Surprise Ever. Bassett, Jeni, illus. 2012. (ENG.). 10p. (J). (gr. -1-k). bds. 6.99 *(978-0-545-40285-9(9),* Cartwheel Bks.) Scholastic, Inc.

Kroner, David & Du Houx, Ramona. Seasons. Du Houx, E. M. Cornell, illus. 2007. 70p. (J). per. 6.95 *(978-1-882190-54-6(8))* Solon Ctr. for Research & Publishing.

Larsen, Kirsten. Dora's Perfect Pumpkin. Miller, Victoria, illus. 2007. (Dora the Explorer Ser.). (ENG.). 24p. (J). (gr. -1-3). pap. 3.99 *(978-1-4169-3438-7(3),* Simon Spotlight/Nickelodeon) Simon Spotlight/Nickelodeon.

Lay, Kathryn. Josh's Halloween Pumpkin, 1 vol. Bratun, Katy, illus. 2008. (ENG.). 32p. (J). (gr. k-3). 16.99 *(978-1-58980-595-8(X),* Pelican Publishing) Arcadia Publishing.

Lemire, Roger. Pumpkin & Lumpkin. 2005. 17.00 *(978-0-8059-9777-4(6))* Dorrance Publishing Co., Inc.

Lesley, Sharon. The Red Scarf & Other Stories. 2010. 165p. pap. 14.95 *(978-1-4457-6720-8(1))* Lulu Pr., Inc.

Lewis, Anne Margaret. The Runaway Pumpkin. Zenz, Aaron, illus. 2018. (ENG.). 22p. (J). (gr. -1-2). bds. 5.99 *(978-1-5107-2764-9(7),* Sky Pony Pr.) Skyhorse Publishing Co., Inc.

—The Runaway Pumpkin: A Halloween Adventure Story. Zenz, Aaron, illus. 2015. (ENG.). 40p. (J). (gr. -1-k). 15.99 *(978-1-63450-214-6(0),* Sky Pony Pr.) Skyhorse Publishing Co., Inc.

Lightburn, Sandra. Pumpkin People, 1 vol. Lightburn, Ron, illus. 2008. (ENG.). 32p. (J). (gr. -1-k). 17.95 *(978-1-55109-681-0(1),* 13b97ce6-9128-4c3d-bb24-cd1b6efa4608) Nimbus Publishing, Ltd. CAN. Dist: Baker & Taylor Publisher Services (BTPS).

Magsamen, Sandra. I Love You, Little Pumpkin. Magsamen, Sandra, illus. 2017. (ENG.). 10p. (J). (gr. -1 — 1). bds. 8.99 *(978-1-338-11085-2(3),* Cartwheel Bks.) Scholastic, Inc.

Mama Doo. Zachary & the Magic Pumpkin Seeds, 1 vol. 2007. (ENG.). 35p. 24.95 *(978-1-4241-8579-5(3))* America Star Bks.

Marshall, Natalie. Five Little Pumpkins: a Fingers & Toes Nursery Rhyme Book. Marshall, Natalie, illus. 2017. (Fingers & Toes Nursery Rhymes Ser.). (ENG.). 12p. (J). (gr. -1 — 1). bds. 6.99 *(978-1-338-09117-5(4),* Cartwheel Bks.) Scholastic, Inc.

McKy, Katie. Pumpkin Town! or, Nothing Is Better & Worse Than Pumpkins. Bernasconi, Pablo, illus. 2008. (ENG.). 32p. (J). (gr. -1-3). pap. 7.99 *(978-0-547-18193-6(0),* 1055964, Clarion Bks.) HarperCollins Pubs.

McNamara, Margaret. How Many Seeds in a Pumpkin? (Mr. Tiffin's Classroom Series) Karas, G. Brian, illus. 2007. (Mr. Tiffin's Classroom Ser.). (ENG.). 40p. (J). (gr. -1-2). 17.99 *(978-0-375-84014-2(1),* Schwartz & Wade Bks.) Random Hse. Children's Bks.

—The Pumpkin Patch. Gordon, Mike, illus. 2005. (Ready-to-Read Ser.). 32p. (J). lib. bdg. 15.00 *(978-1-59054-932-2(5))* Fitzgerald Bks.

—The Pumpkin Patch. Gordon, Mike, illus. 2008. (Robin Hill School Ser.). (J). (gr. -1-1). pap. 16.95 *(978-1-4301-0622-7(0))* Live Oak Media.

—The Pumpkin Patch. Gordon, Mike, illus. 2003. (Ready-To-Read Level 1 Ser.). (ENG.). 32p. (J). (gr. -1-1). lib. bdg. 17.44 *(978-0-689-85875-8(2))* Simon & Schuster, Inc.

McNamara, Margaret & Gordon, Mike. The Pumpkin Patch: Ready-To-Read Level 1. 2003. (Robin Hill School Ser.). (ENG., Illus.). 32p. (J). (gr. -1-1). pap. 4.99 *(978-0-689-85874-1(4),* Simon Spotlight) Simon Spotlight.

McRoberts, Eddison. Sneaking Treats. Gadra, Jessica, illus. 2013. 48p. pap. 9.95 *(978-1-62137-298-1(7))* Virtualbookworm.com Publishing, Inc.

—Sneaking Treats: A Halloween Hunt. Gadra, Jessica, illus. 2012. 48p. 19.95 *(978-1-62137-136-6(0))* Virtualbookworm.com Publishing, Inc.

Mcwherter, Barbara. Little Pumpkin & Sally: It's O. K. to Be Different. 2008. 26p. pap. 24.95 *(978-1-60563-199-8(X))* America Star Bks.

Meyerhoff, Jenny. Pumpkin Spice. Chatelain, Éva & Chatelain, Éva, illus. 2015. (Friendship Garden Ser.: 2). (ENG.). 144p. (J). (gr. 2-5). pap. 5.99 *(978-1-4814-3909-1(X),* Aladdin) Simon & Schuster Children's Publishing.

—Pumpkin Spice. 2015. (Friendship Garden Ser.: 2). lib. bdg. 16.00 *(978-0-606-37833-8(2))* Turtleback.

Minor, Wendell. How Big Could Your Pumpkin Grow? Minor, Wendell, illus. 2013. (Illus.). 32p. (J). (gr. -1-k). 16.99 *(978-0-399-24684-5(3),* Nancy Paulsen Books) Penguin Young Readers Group.

—Pumpkin Heads. Minor, Wendell, illus. 2021. (Illus.). 32p. (J). (gr. -1-2). lib. bdg. 11.99 *(978-1-58089-935-2(8))* Charlesbridge Publishing, Inc.

Mitchell, Carolyn. The Tale of the Pumpkin Seed Squad. 2006. (ENG.). 40p. per. 16.99 *(978-1-4259-7004-8(4))* AuthorHouse.

Mortimer, Anne. Pumpkin Cat. Mortimer, Anne, illus. 2011. (ENG., Illus.). 24p. (J). (gr. -1-2). 14.99 *(978-0-06-187485-7(X),* Tegen, Katherine Bks) HarperCollins Pubs.

Moulton, Mark Kimball. The Very Best Pumpkin. Good, Karen Hillard, illus. 2010. (ENG.). 32p. (J). (gr. -1-3). 16.99 *(978-1-4169-8288-3(4),* Simon & Schuster/Paula Wiseman Bks.) Simon & Schuster/Paula Wiseman Bks.

Noonan, Julia. My Pumpkin. Lawson, Peter, illus. 2005. (My First Reader Ser.). (ENG.). 32p. (J). (gr. k-1). lib. bdg. 18.50 *(978-0-516-24876-9(6),* Children's Pr.) Scholastic Library Publishing.

Numeroff, Laura. It's Pumpkin Day, Mouse! Bond, Felicia, illus. 2019. (If You Give... Ser.). (ENG.). 24p. (J). (gr. -1 — 1). 9.99 *(978-0-694-01429-3(X),* HarperFestival) HarperCollins Pubs.

Palus, Benji Alexander. The Magic Pumpkin. 2013. 314p. (gr. 10-12). 28.95 *(978-1-4759-7046-3(3))*; pap. 18.95 *(978-1-4759-7048-7(X))* iUniverse, Inc.

Papp, Robert, illus. The Pumpkin Head Mystery. 2010. (Boxcar Children Mysteries Ser.: 124). (ENG.). 128p. (J). (gr. 2-5). 14.99 *(978-0-8075-6668-8(3),* 807566683);No. 124. pap. 5.99 *(978-0-8075-6669-5(1),* 807566691) Random Hse. Children's Bks. (Random Hse. Bks. for Young Readers).

Pasillo, Susan. The Perfect Pumpkin. 2006. (J). lib. bdg. 20.95 *(978-1-933732-14-5(8))* Big Ransom Studio.

Patricelli, Leslie. Boo! / ¡Bu! Patricelli, Leslie, illus. 2017. (Leslie Patricelli Board Bks.). (Illus.). 26p. (J). (— 1). bds. 7.99 *(978-0-7636-9314-5(6))* Candlewick Pr.

Perkins, C. Gale. A Pumpkin for God. 2009. 28p. pap. 14.95 *(978-1-4389-4336-7(9))* AuthorHouse.

Peter the Pumpkin-Eater: Individual Title Six-Packs. (Action Packs Ser.). 104p. (gr. 3-5). 44.00 *(978-0-7635-8401-6(0))* Rigby Education.

Potter, Beatrix. Peter Rabbit & the Pumpkin Patch. Palmer, Ruth, illus. 2013. (Peter Rabbit Ser.). (ENG.). 32p. (J). (gr. -1-2). pap. 4.99 *(978-0-7232-7124-6(0),* Warne) Penguin Young Readers Group.

Public Domain, Public. Five Little Pumpkins: A Fall & Halloween Book for Kids. Yaccarino, Dan, illus. 2003. (ENG.). 16p. (J). (gr. -1-k). bds. 9.99 *(978-0-694-01177-3(0),* HarperFestival) HarperCollins Pubs.

The Pumpkin House, 6 Packs. (Literatura 2000 Ser.). (gr. 2-3). 33.00 *(978-0-7635-0182-2(4))* Rigby Education.

Ray, Christie Jones & Ray, Christie Jones. Pick-A-Pick-a-Pumpkin. 2012. (Illus.). 36p. pap. 12.00 *(978-0-9853223-4-2(9))* Rose Water Cottage Pr.

Richardson, George E. The Mysterious Pumpkin Patch. Lee, Joe, illus. 2008. (ENG.). 30p. pap. 14.95 *(978-1-4343-5379-5(6))* AuthorHouse.

Robinson, Sharon. The Littlest Pumpkin. 2012. 24p. 24.95 *(978-1-4626-5963-0(2))* America Star Bks.

Rockwell, Anne. Apples & Pumpkins. Rockwell, Lizzy, illus. (ENG.). 24p. (J). (gr. -1-3). 2012. 7.99 *(978-1-4424-7656-1(7))* 2011. 16.99 *(978-1-4424-0350-5(0))* Simon & Schuster Children's Publishing. (Aladdin).

Rozelaar, Angie. The Great Pumpkin Contest. Rozelaar, Angie, illus. 2019. (ENG., Illus.). 40p. (J). (gr. -1-3). 17.99 *(978-0-06-274137-0(3),* Tegen, Katherine Bks) HarperCollins Pubs.

Rusu, Meredith. The Pumpkin Contest (Peppa Pig: Level 1 Reader), 1 vol. EOne, illus. 2018. (Scholastic Reader, Level 1 Ser.). (ENG.). 32p. (J). (gr. -1-k). pap. 5.99 *(978-1-338-22881-6(1))* Scholastic, Inc.

Savage, Stephen. Seven Orange Pumpkins Board Book. 2015. (Illus.). 28p. (J). (gr. -1 — 1). bds. 7.99 *(978-0-8037-4138-6(3),* Dial Bks) Penguin Young Readers Group.

—Ten Orange Pumpkins: A Counting Book. 2013. (Illus.). 48p. (J). (gr. -1-k). 17.99 *(978-0-8037-3938-3(9),* Dial Bks) Penguin Young Readers Group.

Schulz, Charles M. Waiting for the Great Pumpkin. 2014. (Peanuts Seasonal Collection: 0). (ENG., Illus.). 64p. (J). (gr. 1-12). 9.99 *(978-1-60699-772-7(6),* 699772) Fantagraphics Bks.

Scotton, Rob. Splat the Cat & the Pumpkin-Picking Plan. 2014. (Splat the Cat Ser.). (ENG., Illus.). 24p. (J). (gr. -1-3). pap. 5.99 *(978-0-06-211586-7(3),* HarperFestival) HarperCollins Pubs.

Seal, Kerry. Five Silly Pumpkins: A Pop-up Halloween Book. Smith, Jane, illus. 2009. 10p. (J). 5.95 *(978-1-58117-908-8(1),* Intervisual/Piggy Toes) Bendon, Inc.

Serfozo, Mary. Plumply, Dumply Pumpkin. Petrone, Valeria, illus. 2006. (Classic Board Bks.). (ENG.). 28p. (J). (gr. -1-1). bds. 7.99 *(978-0-689-86277-9(6),* Little Simon) Little Simon.

Shepherd, Anita. Scareboo's Halloween Trick. 2013. 50p. pap. 7.95 *(978-0-9882368-4-4(2))* New Eden Publishing.

Silva, Amanda. The Day That Jack Became a Jack O'Lantern. 2013. 20p. pap. 24.95 *(978-1-62709-387-3(7))* PublishAmerica, Inc.

Simon, Charnan. Pumpkin Fever. Bryan-Hunt, Jan, illus. 2011. (Rookie Ready to Learn Ser.). 40p. (J). (ENG.). pap. 5.95 *(978-0-531-26803-2(9))*; (gr. -1-k). lib. bdg. 23.00 *(978-0-531-25643-5(X))* Scholastic Library Publishing. (Children's Pr.).

Simon, Mary Manz. The Pumpkin Gospel (die-Cut) A Story of a New Start with God. Scudamore, Angelika, illus. 2016. (ENG.). 14p. (J). (gr. -1 — 1). bds. 12.99 *(978-1-4336-9163-8(9),* 006102446, B&H Kids) B&H Publishing Group.

Sobel, Gerrie. Jacob & His Magical Flying Bears, a Halloween Story. Torres, Dottie, illus. 2009. 32p. pap. 12.95 *(978-1-936051-42-7(7))* Peppertree Pr., The.

Sorenson, Verona. The Pumpkin Patch. 2008. 20p. per. 24.95 *(978-1-60441-565-0(7))* America Star Bks.

Stone, Kate & Accord Publishing, Accord. One Spooky Night: A Halloween Adventure. 2011. (ENG.). 36p. (J). pap. 11.99 *(978-1-4494-0330-0(1))* Andrews McMeel Publishing.

Swindle, Stephanie. Pumpkin Pants. 2009. 32p. pap. 13.95 *(978-1-60860-461-6(6),* Strategic Bk. Publishing) Strategic Book Publishing & Rights Agency (SBPRA).

Tegen, Katherine. The Story of the Jack O'Lantern. Dorman, Brandon, illus. 2010. (ENG.). 32p. (J). (gr. -1-3). 12.99 *(978-0-06-143088-6(9),* HarperCollins) HarperCollins Pubs.

Thomas, Jan. Pumpkin Trouble. Thomas, Jan, illus. 2011. (ENG., Illus.). 40p. (J). (gr. -1-3). 9.99 *(978-0-06-169284-0(0),* HarperCollins) HarperCollins Pubs.

Tiger Tales. Five Little Pumpkins. Mantle, Ben, illus. 2010. (ENG.). 24p. (J). (gr. -1-k). bds. 8.95 *(978-1-58925-856-3(8))* Tiger Tales.

Tim's Pumpkin: Individual Title Six-Packs. (gr. k-1). 23.00 *(978-0-7635-9040-6(1))* Rigby Education.

Titherington, Jeanne. Pumpkin Pumpkin. 2015. 24p. pap. 7.00 *(978-1-61003-615-3(8))* Center for the Collaborative Classroom.

Townsend, Tamela Ann. Finding Pumpkin, 1 vol. 2010. 48p. pap. 16.95 *(978-1-4489-5983-9(7))* America Star Bks.

Tremblay, Patrick. Poor, Poor Jack. 2010. (ENG.). 40p. pap. 26.00 *(978-0-557-25375-3(6))* Lulu Pr., Inc.

Trooboff, Rhoda. Punkinhead's Veggie Adventure: And the Strange Contraption in the Kitchen. Easton, Susan, illus. Rosenbaum, Elizabeth, photos by. 2013. (ENG.). 56p. (J). (gr. -1). pap. 15.00 *(978-0-9773536-7-5(2))* Tenley Circle Pr.

Tucker, Daniel Deon. The Littlest Pumpkin, 1 vol. 2009. 48p. pap. 16.95 *(978-1-61546-872-0(2))* PublishAmerica, Inc.

Tucker, Peter. Pumpkin Bunch. 2009. 32p. 16.30 *(978-0-615-21675-1(7))* PT Publishing.

Tucker, Peter E. Pumpkin Bunch. 2009. 36p. pap. 16.99 *(978-1-4389-7883-3(9))* AuthorHouse.

Wallace, Nancy Elizabeth. Pumpkin Day!, 0 vols. Wallace, Nancy Elizabeth, illus. unabr. ed. 2012. (ENG., Illus.). 32p. (J). (gr. k-3). per. 9.99 *(978-0-7614-5327-7(X),* 9780761453277, Two Lions) Amazon Publishing.

Wan, Joyce. You Are My Pumpkin. Wan, Joyce, illus. 2016. (ENG., Illus.). 14p. (J). (— 1). bds. 6.99 *(978-0-545-88092-3(0),* Cartwheel Bks.) Scholastic, Inc.

Washburn, Kim. Pumpkin Patch Blessings, 1 vol. East, Jacqueline, illus. 2016. (ENG.). 18p. (J). bds. 12.99 *(978-0-310-75819-8(X))* Zonderkidz.

Waters, George T. The Perfect Little Pumpkin. Duquet, Guy J., illus. Lt. ed. 2006. 30p. (J). per. 14.95 *(978-1-59879-286-7(5))* Lifevest Publishing, Inc.

Wayne, Richard, ed. Poppin's Pumpkin Patch Parade. Carlson, Patrick, illus. 2016. (ENG.). 32p. (J). pap. 12.98 *(978-0-9801692-1-8(6))* Gemstone Literary.

Weathers, R. F. Jill's Joyful Surprise. 2005. 32p. pap. 18.00 *(978-1-4208-5263-9(9))* AuthorHouse.

Webb, M. St. John. Knock Three Times! 2003. (Children's Classics). (ENG.). 160p. (J). (gr. 3-6). pap. *(978-1-85326-132-9(7))* Wordsworth Editions, Ltd.

West, Paul & Denslow, W. W. The Pearl & the Pumpkin: A Classic Halloween Tale. Denslow, W. W., illus. 2009. (Dover Children's Classics Ser.). (ENG., Illus.). 264p. (J). (gr. 2-5). pap. 12.99 *(978-0-486-47031-3(8))* Dover Pubns., Inc.

Whitlock, Matt. Punk 'n Patch. Whitlock, Matt, illus. 2005. (Illus.). 32p. (J). (gr. -1-3). 16.95 *(978-0-9769057-0-7(1))* Little Hero.

Wiles, Faith R. The Pumpkin who couldn't say BOO!, 1 vol. 2010. 20p. 24.95 *(978-1-4489-4242-8(X))* PublishAmerica, Inc.

William H. Sadlier Staff. Pumpkin Days, Vol. 3. 2005. (Emergent Library: Vol. 1). (gr. -1-1). 24.00 net. *(978-0-8215-8912-0(1))* Sadlier, William H. Inc.

Williamson, Hilary & Adams, Lynne. The Magic Pumpkin. 2007. (ENG.). 16p. 9.99 *(978-1-4357-0321-6(9))* Lulu Pr., Inc.

Winters, Kay. Whooo's That? A Lift-The-Flap Pumpkin Fun Book. Winston, Jeannie, illus. 2009. (ENG.). 14p. (J). (gr. -1 — 1). 9.99 *(978-0-15-206480-8(X),* 1199346, Clarion Bks.) HarperCollins Pubs.

Wunderli, Stephen. Little Boo. Zeltner, Tim, illus. 2014. (ENG.). 32p. (J). (gr. -1-2). 16.99 *(978-0-8050-9708-5(2),* 900097295, Holt, Henry & Co. Bks. For Young Readers) Holt, Henry & Co.

Yaccarino, Dan. Five Little Pumpkins Came Back Board Book. Yaccarino, Dan, illus. 2018. (ENG., Illus.). 16p. (J). (gr. -1 — 1). bds. 6.99 *(978-0-06-284021-9(5),* HarperFestival) HarperCollins Pubs.

Yolen, Jane. Pumpkin Baby. Mitchell, Susan, illus. 2009. (ENG.). 32p. (J). (gr. -1). *(978-1-55470-141-4(4))* Me to We.

Yoon, Salina. Penguin & Pumpkin. 2014. (Penguin Ser.). (ENG., Illus.). 40p. (J). (gr. -1-1). 15.99 *(978-0-8027-3732-8(3),* 900134209); E-Book 6.39 *(978-0-8027-3770-0(6))* Bloomsbury Publishing USA. (Bloomsbury USA Childrens).

PUNCH AND JUDY

see Puppets

PUNCHED CARD SYSTEMS

see Information Storage and Retrieval Systems

PUNCTUATION

Basher, Simon & Budzik, Mary. Basher Basics: Punctuation: The Write Stuff. Basher, Simon, illus. 2010. (Basher Basics Ser.). (ENG., Illus.). 64p. (J). (gr. 3-7). pap. 8.99 *(978-0-7534-6420-5(9),* 900066949, Kingfisher) Roaring Brook Pr.

Blaisdell, Molly. If You Were a Comma [LTD Commodities]. Gray, Sara, illus. 2010. (Word Fun Ser.). 24p. pap. 3.50 *(978-1-4048-6251-7(X),* Picture Window Bks.) Capstone.

—If You Were Quotation Marks, 1 vol. Gray, Sara, illus. 2009. (Word Fun Ser.). (ENG.). 24p. (J). (gr. 2-4). pap. 7.95 *(978-1-4048-5330-0(8),* 95555, Picture Window Bks.) Capstone.

—If You Were Quotation Marks [LTD Commodities]. Gray, Sara, illus. 2010. (Word Fun Ser.). 24p. pap. 3.50 *(978-1-4048-6255-5(2),* Picture Window Bks.) Capstone.

—If You Were Quotation Marks [Readers World]. Gray, Sara, illus. 2010. (Word Fun Ser.). 24p. pap. 2.72 *(978-1-4048-6706-2(6),* Picture Window Bks.) Capstone.

Brus, Mischa & Schlitz, Matt. Little Full Stop: Chinese/English, bk. 3. Schlitz, Matt, ed. Brus, Mischa, illus. 2012.Tr. of French, Chinese, Japanese. (CHI & ENG., Illus.). 34p. (J). (gr. -1-6). 22.75 *(978-0-9751837-8-6(8))* Mambooks AUS. Dist: Ingram Bk. Co.

—Little Full Stop: English, 8 bks., bk. 2. Schlitz, Matt, ed. Brus, Mischa, illus. 2019.Tr. of French, Chinese, Spanish. (ENG., Illus.). 34p. (J). (gr. k-2). *(978-0-9751837-1-7(0))* Mambooks AUS. Dist: Ingram Content Group.

—Puntito Final - Little Full Stop: Spanish/English, bk. 5. Schlitz, Matt, ed. Brus, Mischa, illus. 2021.Tr. of Spanish/English. (ENG, CHI & SPA., Illus.). 32p. (J). (gr. -1-1). *(978-0-9751837-9-3(6))* Mambooks AUS. Dist: Lightning Source Australia Pty Ltd.

Capitalization & Punctuation. 2013. (Core Language Skills Ser.). 24p. (J). (gr. 2-2). pap. 49.50 *(978-1-4777-0981-8(9),* PowerKids Pr.) Rosen Publishing Group, Inc., The.

Capitalization & Punctuation (Gr. 1-3) 2003. (J). *(978-1-58232-050-2(0))* ECS Learning Systems, Inc.

Carter, Andrew. Punctuation & Sentences, 1 vol. 2009. (Grammar Ray: a Graphic Guide to Grammar Ser.). (ENG.). 24p. (J). (gr. 1-1). pap. 9.15 *(978-1-60754-751-8(1),* d885fd3a-44d4-49f8-ae63-0ca68aa8a17c, Windmill Bks.) Rosen Publishing Group, Inc., The.

Cleary, Brian P. The Punctuation Station. Lew-Vriethoff, Joanne, illus. (ENG.). (J). (gr. k-3). 2018. 40p. pap. 8.99 *(978-1-5415-1492-8(0),* 815a06d5-592c-4416-82ab-d6e29b74bc1a, Millbrook Pr.) 2010. 32p. lib. bdg. 16.95 *(978-0-8225-7852-9(2),* 1306583) Lerner Publishing Group.

Collins, Terry. Whatever Says Mark: Knowing & Using Punctuation, 1 vol. Cox, Thomas, illus. 2013. (Language on the Loose Ser.). (ENG.). 24p. (J). (gr. 2-4). 28.65 *(978-1-4048-8318-5(5),* 122439, Picture Window Bks.) Capstone.

Commas & Colons with Your Class. 2013. (Write Right! Ser.). 24p. (J). (gr. 2-5). pap. 48.90 *(978-1-4339-9067-0(9))* Stevens, Gareth Publishing LLLP.

Connors, Kathleen. Punctuation at the Game, 1 vol. 2012. (Word Play Ser.). (ENG., Illus.). 24p. (J). (gr. 1-2). pap. 9.15 *(978-1-4339-7196-9(8),* e637d222-7ee4-4f91-a368-b7528b599cbb); lib. bdg. 25.27 *(978-1-4339-7195-2(X),* 157db101-b4eb-4b65-b6f7-aa947eb9e2a1) Stevens, Gareth Publishing LLLP.

Dahl, Michael. Commas Say Take a Break. Garbutt, Chris, illus. 2019. (Word Adventures: Punctuation Ser.). (ENG.). 32p. (J). (gr. k-3). lib. bdg. 27.99 *(978-1-5158-3861-6(7),* 139586, Picture Window Bks.) Capstone.

—Exclamation Points Say Wow! Garbutt, Chris, illus. 2019. (Word Adventures: Punctuation Ser.). (ENG.). 32p. (J). (gr. k-3). lib. bdg. 27.99 *(978-1-5158-3863-0(3),* 139587, Picture Window Bks.) Capstone.

—Question Marks Say What? Garbutt, Chris, illus. 2019. (Word Adventures: Punctuation Ser.). (ENG.). 32p. (J). (gr. k-3). pap. 7.95 *(978-1-5158-4056-5(5),* 140050, Picture Window Bks.) Capstone.

Green, Samantha. Punctuation, 1 vol. 2019. (Fun with Grammar Ser.). (ENG.). 24p. (gr. 1-2). pap. 10.35 *(978-1-9785-1265-8(1),* 736b1158-bddd-45c9-86f5-177dca861a03) Enslow Publishing, LLC.

Healy, Nicholas M. If You Were a Period [LTD Commodities]. Gray, Sara, illus. 2010. (Word Fun Ser.). 24p. pap. 3.50 *(978-1-4048-6252-4(8),* Picture Window Bks.) Capstone.

Healy, Nick & Healy, Nicholas M. If You Were a Period, 1 vol. Gray, Sara, illus. 2009. (Word Fun Ser.). (ENG.). 24p. (J). (gr. 2-4). lib. bdg. 28.65 *(978-1-4048-5332-4(4),* 95556, Picture Window Bks.) Capstone.

Heinrichs, Ann. Punctuation. 2019. (English Grammar Ser.). (ENG.). 32p. (J). (gr. 2-5). lib. bdg. 35.64 *(978-1-5038-3247-3(3),* 213005) Child's World, Inc, The.

Herman, Gail. Pedaling to Perfect Punctuation, 1 vol. 2009. (Grammar All-Stars: Writing Tools Ser.). (ENG.). 32p. (J). (gr. 2-4). pap. 11.50 *(978-1-4339-2134-6(0),* 4e10fbc2-dd99-4c01-89ad-c10b64d1ca9a); lib. bdg. 28.67 *(978-1-4339-1941-1(9),* 61478b50-fa9d-453c-b8fb-3f5aa08cfad2) Stevens, Gareth Publishing LLLP. (Gareth Stevens Learning Library).

Irving, Nicole. Improve Your Punctuation. 2004. (Better English Ser.). 32p. (YA). (gr. 5-18). lib. bdg. 14.95 *(978-1-58086-326-1(4))* EDC Publishing.

Kenan, Tessa. What Did He Say? A Book about Quotation Marks. Lewis, Anthony, illus. 2015. (Punctuation Station Ser.). (ENG.). 16p. (J). (gr. k-2). *(978-1-60753-727-4(3),* 15260) Amicus.

LD COACH. TEH Learns to Read: Beginning Words & Written Characters, Volume One. 2004. (Illus.). 40p. (J). 34.95 *(978-0-9745938-1-4(8))* LD Coach, LLC.

Lyons, Shelly. If You Were a Question Mark [LTD Commodities]. Gray, Sara, illus. 2010. (Word Fun Ser.). 24p. pap. 3.50 *(978-1-4048-6253-1(6),* Picture Window Bks.) Capstone.

—If You Were a Question Mark [Readers World]. Gray, Sara, illus. 2010. (Word Fun Ser.). 24p. pap. 2.72 *(978-1-4048-6705-5(8),* Picture Window Bks.) Capstone.

—If You Were an Apostrophe, 1 vol. Gray, Sara, illus. 2009. (Word Fun Ser.). (ENG.). 24p. (J). (gr. 2-4). pap. 7.95 *(978-1-4048-5318-8(9),* 95547, Picture Window Bks.) Capstone.

—If You Were an Apostrophe [Readers World]. Gray, Sara, illus. 2010. (Word Fun Ser.). 24p. pap. 2.72 *(978-1-4048-6708-6(2),* Picture Window Bks.) Capstone.

—If You Were an Exclamation Point, 1 vol. Gray, Sara, illus. 2009. (Word Fun Ser.). (ENG.). 24p. (J). (gr. 2-4). pap. 7.95 *(978-1-4048-5327-0(8),* 95553, Picture Window Bks.) Capstone.

—If You Were an Exclamation Point [LTD Commodities]. Gray, Sara, illus. 2010. (Word Fun Ser.). 24p. pap. 3.50 *(978-1-4048-6254-8(4),* Picture Window Bks.) Capstone.

—If You Were an Exclamation Point [Readers World]. Gray, Sara, illus. 2010. (Word Fun Ser.). 24p. pap. 2.72 *(978-1-4048-6707-9(4),* Picture Window Bks.) Capstone.

Mahoney, Emily. Learn Apostrophes with Fairies, 1 vol. 2020. (Grammar Magic! Ser.). (ENG.). 24p. (gr. 2-3). pap. 9.15 *(978-1-5382-4723-5(2),* 0ad4bdca-8f2b-4769-b623-01759692889a) Stevens, Gareth Publishing LLLP.

Meet the Puncs: A Remarkable Punctuation Family, 8 vols. 2004. (Meet the Puncs: a Remarkable Punctuation Family Ser.). (ENG.). 32p. (gr. 2-4). lib. bdg. 114.68 *(978-0-8368-4222-7(7),* e2967f30-cd14-4133-94a0-caef1433ed67, Gareth Stevens Learning Library) Stevens, Gareth Publishing LLLP.

Murray, Kara. Capitalization & Punctuation, 1 vol. 2013. (Core Language Skills Ser.). (ENG.). 24p. (J). (gr. 2-2). 26.27 *(978-1-4777-0803-3(0),* d28f4ea7-8e91-41e1-a465-e261c45a15f8); (Illus.). pap. 9.25 *(978-1-4777-0980-1(0),* 24465b39-7d25-4203-9cea-09d9bffeba64) Rosen Publishing Group, Inc., The. (PowerKids Pr.).

Powell, Marie. Stop Right There: A Book about Periods. Lewis, Anthony, illus. 2015. (Punctuation Station Ser.). (ENG.). 16p. (J). (gr. k-2). lib. bdg. 17.95 *(978-1-60753-730-4(3),* 15257) Amicus.

—Take a Pause, Paul: A Book about Commas. Lewis, Anthony, illus. 2015. (Punctuation Station Ser.). (ENG.). 16p. (J). (gr. k-2). lib. bdg. 17.95 *(978-1-60753-731-1(1),* 15258) Amicus.

—This Is Exciting! A Book about Exclamation Points. Lewis, Anthony, illus. 2015. (Punctuation Station Ser.). (ENG.). 16p. (J). (gr. k-2). lib. bdg. 17.95 *(978-1-60753-728-1(1),* 15259) Amicus.

—We're Going to the Smiths' House: A Book about Apostrophes. Lewis, Anthony, illus. 2015. (Punctuation Station Ser.). (ENG.). 16p. (J). (gr. k-2). lib. bdg. 17.95 *(978-1-60753-729-8(X),* 15261) Amicus.

—What Is That? A Book about Question Marks. Lewis, Anthony, illus. 2015. (Punctuation Station Ser.). (ENG.). 16p. (J). (gr. k-2). lib. bdg. 17.95 *(978-1-60753-732-8(X),* 15262) Amicus.

Rajczak Nelson, Kristen. Commas & Colons with Your Class, 1 vol. 2013. (Write Right! Ser.). (ENG., Illus.). 24p. (J). (gr. 2-3). pap. 9.15 *(978-1-4339-9066-3(0),* fd097f6e-75bb-4f16-8d11-a0d8e9261081); lib. bdg. 25.27 *(978-1-4339-9065-6(2),* 17f86e1b-964e-4a1d-8b9d-f50e2b0af0ce) Stevens, Gareth Publishing LLLP.

Riggs, Kate. Colons & Semicolons. 2016. (Punctuate It! Ser.). (ENG., Illus.). 32p. (J). (gr. 3-6). pap. 10.99 *(978-1-62832-327-6(2),* 20692, Creative Paperbacks) Creative Co., The.

—Quotation Marks & Apostrophes. 2016. (Punctuate It! Ser.). (ENG.). 32p. (J). (gr. 3-6). pap. 10.99 *(978-1-62832-332-0(9),* 20707, Creative Paperbacks) Creative Co., The.

Rozines Roy, Jennifer. Sharpen Your Good Grammar Skills, 1 vol. 2012. (Sharpen Your Writing Skills Ser.). (ENG., Illus.). 64p. (gr. 6-7). lib. bdg. 31.93 *(978-0-7660-3902-5(1),* f3087814-3cef-448e-8965-98d7d2841bf2) Enslow Publishing, LLC.

Soper, Sandra. Punctuation Practice: Capital. (ENG., Illus.). 32p. (J). pap. 4.95 *(978-0-330-32083-2(1),* Pan) Pan Macmillan GBR. Dist: Trafalgar Square Publishing.

Stanton, Lidia. Tricky Punctuation in Cartoons. 2020. (Illus.). 272p. 18.95 *(978-1-78775-402-7(2),* 743651) Kingsley, Jessica Pubs. GBR. Dist: Hachette UK Distribution.

Stride, Lottie. Write Every Time. 2017. (Buster Reference Ser.). (ENG., Illus.). 128p. (J). (gr. 3-7). pap. 8.99 *(978-1-78055-469-3(9))* O'Mara, Michael Bks., Ltd. GBR. Dist: Independent Pubs. Group.

Studio Mouse, creator. Tracing Punctuation! 2005. (Disney's Chicken Little (Studio Mouse) Ser.). (ENG., Illus.). 28p. (J). (gr. -1-3). 14.99 *(978-1-59069-448-0(1),* 1A603) Studio Mouse LLC.

Taplin, Sam. Grammar & Punctuation IR. 2018. (Activity Puzzle Books - English Activity Books* Ser.). (ENG.). 112p. pap. 4.99 *(978-0-7945-4017-3(1),* Usborne) EDC Publishing.

Truss, Lynne. Eats, Shoots & Leaves: Why, Commas Really Do Make a Difference! Timmons, Bonnie, illus. 2006. (ENG.). 32p. (J). (gr. 1-4). 17.99 *(978-0-399-24491-9(3),* G.P. Putnam's Sons Books for Young Readers) Penguin Young Readers Group.

—The Girl's Like Spaghetti: Why, You Can't Manage Without Apostrophes! Timmons, Bonnie, illus. 2007. (ENG.). 32p. (J). (gr. 1-4). 17.99 *(978-0-399-24706-4(8),* G.P. Putnam's Sons Books for Young Readers) Penguin Young Readers Group.

—Twenty-Odd Ducks: Why, Every Punctuation Mark Counts! Timmons, Bonnie, illus. 2008. (ENG.). 32p. (J). (gr. 1-3). 16.99 *(978-0-399-25058-3(1),* G.P. Putnam's Sons Books for Young Readers) Penguin Young Readers Group.

Using Punctuation (Gr. 3+) 2003. (J). *(978-1-58232-129-5(9))* ECS Learning Systems, Inc.

PUNCTUATION—FICTION

Pulver, Robin. Punctuation Takes a Vacation. Reed, Lynn Rowe, illus. 2004. (ENG.). 32p. (J). (gr. k-3). reprint ed. pap. 7.99 *(978-0-8234-1820-6(0))* Holiday Hse., Inc.

—Punctuation Takes a Vacation. Reed, Lynn Rowe, illus. 2009. (J). (gr. 1-3). 29.95 incl. audio compact disk *(978-1-4301-0708-8(1))* Live Oak Media.

Rosenthal, Amy Krouse. Exclamation Mark. Lichtenheld, Tom, illus. 2013. (ENG.). 56p. (J). (gr. -1-3). 17.99 *(978-0-545-43679-3(6),* Scholastic Pr.) Scholastic, Inc.

—Exclamation Mark. Lichtenheld, Tom, illus. 2022. (ENG.). 56p. (J). (gr. -1-3). pap. 7.99 *(978-1-338-82645-6(X),* Scholastic Pr.) Scholastic, Inc.

Rosenthal, Amy Krouse & Lichtenheld, Tom. Exclamation Mark. 2013. 56p. (J). (gr. k-3). pap. 6.95 *(978-0-545-63130-3(0),* Scholastic) Scholastic, Inc.

PUPPET MAKING

D'Cruz, Anna-Marie. Make Your Own Puppets, 1 vol. 2009. (Do It Yourself Projects! Ser.). (ENG.). 24p. (J). (gr. 4-4). pap. 10.40 *(978-1-4358-2919-0(0),* 27ed0efb-78a2-42bc-8eae-2f558abd25e3, PowerKids Pr.) Rosen Publishing Group, Inc., The.

Doney, Meryl. Puppets, 1 vol. 2004. (Crafts from Many Cultures Ser.). (ENG., Illus.). 32p. (gr. 3-5). lib. bdg. 28.67 *(978-0-8368-4047-6(X),* e359802c-08ae-4ab2-9c5d-3f07dc016aa9, Gareth Stevens Learning Library) Stevens, Gareth Publishing LLLP.

Harbo, Christopher L. Sock Puppet Theater Presents Goldilocks & the Three Bears: A Make & Play Production. 2017. (Sock Puppet Theater Ser.). (ENG., Illus.). 32p. (J). (gr. 1-3). lib. bdg. 27.99 *(978-1-5157-6681-0(0),* 135247, Capstone Classroom) Capstone.

—Sock Puppet Theater Presents the Three Billy Goats Gruff: A Make & Play Production. 2017. (Sock Puppet Theater Ser.). (ENG., Illus.). 32p. (J). (gr. 1-3). lib. bdg. 27.99 *(978-1-5157-6682-7(9),* 135248, Capstone Classroom) Capstone.

—Sock Puppet Theater Presents the Three Little Pigs: A Make & Play Production. 2017. (Sock Puppet Theater Ser.). (ENG., Illus.). 32p. (J). (gr. 1-3). lib. bdg. 27.99 *(978-1-5157-6683-4(7),* 135249, Capstone Classroom) Capstone.

Henry, Sally & Cook, Trevor. Making Puppets, 1 vol. 2010. (Make Your Own Art Ser.). (ENG., Illus.). 32p. (J). (gr. 3-4). 30.27 *(978-1-4488-1584-5(3),* 91ded940-cb87-486c-916d-7905a13bfef3); pap. 12.75 *(978-1-4488-1615-6(7),* 43124d92-baaf-40f8-b338-387d8c5f5657) Rosen Publishing Group, Inc., The. (PowerKids Pr.).

Hodge, Susie. Puppets. 2006. (Design & Make Ser.). (Illus.). 32p. (J). (gr. 4-7). lib. bdg. 28.50 *(978-1-58340-954-1(8))* Black Rabbit Bks.

Leigh, Autumn. Making History: A Horse Sock Puppet, 1 vol. 2005. (Content-Area Literacy Collections). (ENG.). 24p. (gr. 3-4). pap. 8.85 *(978-1-4042-5588-3(5),* bc8e3750-8487-4eb2-8d5d-fd9af12da011) Rosen Publishing Group, Inc., The.

Petelinsek, Kathleen. Making Sock Puppets. Petelinsek, Kathleen, illus. 2014. (How-To Library). (ENG., Illus.). 32p. (J). (gr. 3-6). 32.07 *(978-1-63137-782-2(5),* 205371) Cherry Lake Publishing.

Puppets for a Play: Individual Title Six-Packs. (gr. -1-2). 23.00 *(978-0-7635-9000-0(2))* Rigby Education.

Raffaella, Dowling. Make Your Own Finger Puppets! Tips & Techniques for Fabulous Fun. 2009. (Illus.). (J). *(978-1-60311-206-2(5))* Mud Puddle, Inc.

Regan, Lisa. Fun Kits Make Your Own Finger Puppets. 2005. (Fun Kits Ser.). (Illus.). 48p. (J). (gr. k-2). *(978-1-84510-312-5(2))* Top That! Publishing PLC.

Smith, Thomasina. Fantastic Finger Puppets to Make Yourself: 25 Fun Ideas for Your Fingers, Thumbs & Even Feet! 2014. (Illus.). 64p. (J). (gr. -1-12). pap. 9.99 *(978-1-86147-269-4(2),* Armadillo) Anness Publishing GBR. Dist: National Bk. Network.

Toler, Violet M. Churchmouse Tales: Puppet Book, 10 vols. Koefler, Leatha, illus. rev. ed. 2004. Orig. Title: Charlie Church Mouse. (J). (gr. -1-6). pap. 10.95 *(978-0-9749749-0-3(0))* Wayside Pubns.

—Churchmouse Tales: Puppet Plays, 10 vols., Vol. 2. Koefler, Leatha, illus. 2nd rev. ed. 2004. Orig. Title: "Puppet Plays, Adventures of Charlie & His Friends". (J). (gr. -1-6). pap. 10.95 *(978-0-9749749-1-0(9))* Wayside Pubns.

PUPPET PLAYS

Asphyxia. The Grimstones Collection. Asphyxia, illus. 2015. (Grimstones Ser.). (ENG., Illus.). 488p. (J). (gr. 3-7). pap. 17.99 *(978-1-76011-391-9(3))* Allen & Unwin AUS. Dist: Independent Pubs. Group.

Goldsack, Gaby. Little Lion & Daniel: A Finger Puppet Play & Read Story. 2003. (Snuffleheads Ser.). (Illus.). 14p. (J). 7.99 *(978-0-8254-7268-8(7))* Kregel Pubns.

Harbo, Christopher L. Sock Puppet Theater Presents Goldilocks & the Three Bears: A Make & Play Production. 2017. (Sock Puppet Theater Ser.). (ENG., Illus.). 32p. (J). (gr. 1-3). lib. bdg. 27.99 *(978-1-5157-6681-0(0),* 135247, Capstone Classroom) Capstone.

—Sock Puppet Theater Presents the Three Billy Goats Gruff: A Make & Play Production. 2017. (Sock Puppet Theater Ser.). (ENG.). 32p. (J). (gr. 1-2). E-Book 27.99 *(978-1-5157-6686-5(1),* 73564); (Illus.). lib. bdg. 27.99 *(978-1-5157-6682-7(9),* 135248) Capstone. (Capstone Classroom).

—Sock Puppet Theater Presents the Three Little Pigs: A Make & Play Production. 2017. (Sock Puppet Theater Ser.). (ENG.). 32p. (J). (gr. 1-2). E-Book 27.99 *(978-1-5157-6687-2(X),* 73565); (Illus.). lib. bdg. 27.99 *(978-1-5157-6683-4(7),* 135249) Capstone. (Capstone Classroom).

Katz, Leon. The Greek Myths: Puppet Plays for Children from Ovid's Metamorphoses. 2004. (Applause Bks.). (ENG., Illus.). 160p. pap. 12.95 *(978-1-55783-502-4(0),* 1557835020, Applause Theatre & Cinema) Leonard, Hal Corp.

Landes, William-Alan, ed. Punch & Judy. Cruikshank, George, illus. 2003. (Classic Plays Ser.). 24p. (YA). (gr. 4-12). pap. 7.50 *(978-0-88734-290-5(6))* Players Pr., Inc.

The Laughing Place: Individual Title Six-Packs. (Story Steps Ser.). (gr. k-2). 32.00 *(978-0-7635-9836-5(4))* Rigby Education.

Liebenow, Todd. Sensational Shadows. Washburn, Sue, ed. 2003. 110p. (YA). lib. bdg. 22.00 *(978-1-58302-251-1(1))* Creative Ministry Solutions.

Liebenow, Todd, et al. Plug into the Power. Guibord, Charity, illus. 2003. 28p. (YA). spiral bd. 18.00 *(978-1-58302-231-3(7))* Creative Ministry Solutions.

PUPPET SHOWS

see Puppet Theater

PUPPET THEATER

see also Puppet Plays; Puppets; Shadow Shows

Capaccio, George. Puppetry in Theater, 1 vol. 2017. (Exploring Theater Ser.). (ENG.). 96p. (YA). (gr. 7-7). pap. 20.99 *(978-1-5026-3431-3(7),* 6d6da83c-5334-40a7-86f8-a4473358217b); lib. bdg. 44.50 *(978-1-5026-3005-6(2),* 6215f1f5-abe0-4ec4-bbd2-fa81f5b75139) Cavendish Square Publishing LLC.

Carreiro, Carolyn. Make Your Own Puppets & Puppet Theaters. Jourdenais-Martin, Norma Jean, illus. 2005. (ENG.). 64p. (YA). 10.95 *(978-0-8249-6776-5(3),* 1249275); per. 10.95 *(978-0-8249-6770-3(4),* 1249275) Worthy Publishing. (Ideals Pubns.).

House, Behrman. Creative Puppetry for Jewish Kids. 2005. (ENG., Illus.). 204p. (gr. 4-7). per. 26.95 *(978-0-86705-017-2(9),* 36179796-8542-49db-aadc-958bdbdb4b0f) Behrman Hse., Inc.

Lawson, Jennifer. Our New Solar System: A Puppet Show. 2010. 27p. 19.95 *(978-0-557-21389-4(4))* Lulu Pr., Inc.

Schultz, Terry L. & Sorenson, Linda M. The Organic Puppet Theatre. 6th ed. 2004. (Illus.). 92p. (J). 18.95 *(978-0-9749936-0-7(3))* Homelight Pr.

Smith, Thomasina. Fantastic Finger Puppets to Make Yourself: 25 Fun Ideas for Your Fingers, Thumbs & Even Feet! 2014. (Illus.). 64p. (J). (gr. -1-12). pap. 9.99 *(978-1-86147-269-4(2),* Armadillo) Anness Publishing GBR. Dist: National Bk. Network.

PUPPETRY

see Puppet Making; Puppet Theater

PUPPETS

see also Marionettes

Atkinson, Ruth & Atkinson, Brett. Stick Puppet Templates. Atkinson, Ruth & Atkinson, Brett, illus. (Illus.). (J). (gr. k-2). pap. *(978-1-875739-72-1(6))* Wizard Bks.

Banis, Bud. Me & My Shadows -Shadow Puppet Fun ForKids of All Ages: Enhanced with Practical Paper Pastimes. Banis, Bud, illus. 2012. (Illus.). 122p. (J). pap. 14.95 *(978-1-59630-076-7(0),* BeachHouse Bks.) Science & Humanities Pr.

Capaccio, George. Puppetry in Theater, 1 vol. 2017. (Exploring Theater Ser.). (ENG.). 96p. (YA). (gr. 7-7). pap. 20.99 *(978-1-5026-3431-3(7),* 6d6da83c-5334-40a7-86f8-a4473358217b); lib. bdg. 44.50 *(978-1-5026-3005-6(2),* 6215f1f5-abe0-4ec4-bbd2-fa81f5b75139) Cavendish Square Publishing LLC.

Carreiro, Carolyn. Make Your Own Puppets & Puppet Theaters. Jourdenais-Martin, Norma Jean, illus. 2005. (ENG.). 64p. (YA). per. 10.95 *(978-0-8249-6770-3(4),* 1249275, Ideals Pubns.) Worthy Publishing.

Chronicle Books. Baby Llama: Finger Puppet Book. Huang, Yu-Hsuan, illus. 2019. (Baby Animal Finger Puppets Ser.: 17). (ENG.). 12p. (J). (gr. -1 — 1). bds. 7.99 *(978-1-4521-7081-7(9))* Chronicle Bks. LLC.

—Baby Sloth: Finger Puppet Book: (Finger Puppet Book for Toddlers & Babies, Baby Books for First Year, Animal Finger Puppets) Huang, Yu-Hsuan, illus. 2019. (Baby Animal Finger Puppets Ser.: 18). (ENG.). 12p. (J). (gr. -1 — 1). bds. 7.99 *(978-1-4521-8029-8(6))* Chronicle Bks. LLC.

Cummings, Richard. 101 Hand Puppets: A Guide for Puppeteers of All Ages. 2011. 160p. 41.95 *(978-1-258-06260-6(7))* Literary Licensing, LLC.

Doney, Meryl. Puppets, 1 vol. 2004. (Crafts from Many Cultures Ser.). (ENG., Illus.). 32p. (gr. 3-5). lib. bdg. 28.67 *(978-0-8368-4047-6(X),* e359802c-08ae-4ab2-9c5d-3f07dc016aa9, Gareth Stevens Learning Library) Stevens, Gareth Publishing LLLP.

Fontichiaro, Kristin. Using Light to Make Shadow Puppets. 2018. (21st Century Skills Innovation Library: Makers As Innovators Junior Ser.). (ENG., Illus.). 24p. (J). (gr. 2-5). pap. 12.79 *(978-1-5341-0880-6(7),* 210884); lib. bdg. 30.64 *(978-1-5341-0781-6(9),* 210883) Cherry Lake Publishing.

French, Cathy. Make a Safety Puppet. 2011. (Early Connections Ser.). (J). *(978-1-61672-237-1(1))* Benchmark Education Co.

Group/McGraw-Hill, Wright. Puppets: 6 Each of 1 Anthology. 6 vols. (Wildcats Ser.). 32p. (gr. 2-8). *(978-0-322-05632-9(2))* Wright Group/McGraw-Hill.

Lim, Annalees. Fun with Fabric, 1 vol. 2013. (Clever Crafts Ser.). (ENG., Illus.). 24p. (gr. 2-3). 29.93 *(978-1-4777-0180-5(X),* faf6fbce-9ae8-4493-b9c2-500d1424e00b); pap. 11.60 *(978-1-4777-0188-1(5),* 74ee0afb-2223-4727-8a5b-21115ebae08f) Rosen Publishing Group, Inc., The. (Windmill Bks.).

Meltzer, Brad. I Am Jim Henson. Eliopoulos, Christopher, illus. 2017. (Ordinary People Change the World Ser.). 40p. (J). (gr. k-4). 15.99 *(978-0-525-42850-3(X),* Dial Bks) Penguin Young Readers Group.

Nuttall, Gina. Puppets Around the World. 2004. (QEB Start Writing Ser.). (Illus.). 24p. (J). lib. bdg. 15.95 *(978-1-59566-017-6(8))* QEB Publishing Inc.

Petelinsek, Kathleen. Making Sock Puppets. Petelinsek, Kathleen, illus. 2014. (How-To Library). (ENG., Illus.). 32p. (J). (gr. 3-6). 32.07 *(978-1-63137-782-2(5),* 205371) Cherry Lake Publishing.

Puppets, 6 Packs. (Action Packs Ser.). 104p. (gr. 3-5). 44.00 *(978-0-7635-8410-8(X))* Rigby Education.

Rice, Dona Herweck. The Art of Shadow Puppets. rev. ed. 2019. (Smithsonian: Informational Text Ser.). (ENG., Illus.). 24p. (J). (gr. 1-2). pap. 8.99 *(978-1-4938-6652-6(4))* Teacher Created Materials, Inc.

Smith, Thomasina. Fantastic Finger Puppets to Make Yourself: 25 Fun Ideas for Your Fingers, Thumbs & Even Feet! 2014. (Illus.). 64p. (J). (gr. -1-12). pap. 9.99 *(978-1-86147-269-4(2),* Armadillo) Anness Publishing GBR. Dist: National Bk. Network.

Thompson, Kate. Sneaky Snappy Mr Croc. Green, Barry, illus. 2014. (Hand Puppet Bks.). (ENG.). 10p. (J). (gr. -1). 9.99 *(978-1-78244-618-7(4))* Top That! Publishing PLC GBR. Dist: Independent Pubs. Group.

PUPPETS—FICTION

The Adventures of Pinocchio. 2011. 130p. pap. 9.99 *(978-1-61203-094-4(7))* Bottom of the Hill Publishing.

The Adventures of Pinocchio. (Twelve-Point Ser.). 2003. (J). lib. bdg. 25.00 *(978-1-58287-248-3(1))* 2004. 229p. 25.00 *(978-1-58287-732-7(7))* North Bks.

Ajhar, Brian, illus. Pinocchio. 2005. (Rabbit Ears Ser.). 36p. (J). (gr. k-5). 25.65 *(978-1-59679-228-9(0))* Spotlight.

Albee, Sarah. Elmo Says... (Sesame Street) Leigh, Tom, illus. 2009. (Big Bird's Favorites Board Bks.). (ENG.). 24p. (J). (gr. -1 — 1). bds. 4.99 *(978-0-375-84540-6(2),* Random Hse. Bks. for Young Readers) Random Hse. Children's Bks.

Allen, Constance. My Name Is Elmo (Sesame Street) Swanson, Maggie, illus. 2013. (Little Golden Book Ser.). (ENG.). 24p. (J). (-k). 5.99 *(978-0-449-81066-8(6),* Golden Bks.) Random Hse. Children's Bks.

—Shake a Leg! (Sesame Street) Swanson, Maggie, illus. 2010. (Big Bird's Favorites Board Bks.). (ENG.). 24p. (J). (gr. k — 1). bds. 4.99 *(978-0-375-85424-8(X),* Random Hse. Bks. for Young Readers) Random Hse. Children's Bks.

Angleberger, Tom. Darth Paper Strikes Back. 2011. (Origami Yoda Ser.). (ENG., Illus.). 176p. (J). (gr. 3-7). pap. 7.95 *(978-1-4197-0127-6(4));* pap. *(978-1-4197-0254-9(8))* Abrams, Inc.

—Darth Paper Strikes Back. 2011. (Origami Yoda Ser.: 2). (J). 1.25 *(978-1-4640-2485-6(5));* *(978-1-4618-4266-8(2))* Recorded Bks., Inc.

—Darth Paper Strikes Back. (Origami Yoda Files Ser.: 2). (J). 2015. lib. bdg. 18.40 *(978-0-606-39395-9(1))* 2011. lib. bdg. 25.70 *(978-0-606-33075-6(5))* Turtleback.

—Darth Paper Strikes Back: An Origami Yoda Book. 2011. (Origami Yoda Ser.). (ENG., Illus.). 176p. (J). (gr. 3-7). 13.95 *(978-1-4197-0027-9(8),* 697401, Amulet Bks.) Abrams, Inc.

—Emperor Pickletine Rides the Bus. 2014. (Origami Yoda Files Ser.: 6). (J). lib. bdg. 25.70 *(978-0-606-36168-2(5))* Turtleback.

—Princess Labelmaker to the Rescue! (Origami Yoda #5) 2014. (Origami Yoda Ser.). (ENG., Illus.). 208p. (YA). (gr. 3-7). 13.95 *(978-1-4197-1052-0(4),* 1062801, Amulet Bks.) Abrams, Inc.

—The Secret of the Fortune Wookiee (Origami Yoda #3), Vol. 3. 2012. (Origami Yoda Ser.: No. 3). (ENG., Illus.). 208p. (J). (gr. 3-7). 13.95 *(978-1-4197-0392-8(7),* 1013401, Amulet Bks.) Abrams, Inc.

—The Strange Case of Origami Yoda. 2010. pap. *(978-0-8109-9650-2(2))* Abrams, Inc.

—The Strange Case of Origami Yoda, 2 vols. 2010. (Origami Yoda Ser.: 1). (J). 48.75 *(978-1-4498-4583-4(5))* Recorded Bks., Inc.

—Strange Case of Origami Yoda. 2011. (ENG., Illus.). 160p. pap. *(978-0-8109-9877-3(7),* Amulet Bks.) Abrams, Inc.

—The Strange Case of Origami Yoda (Origami Yoda #1) 2010. (Origami Yoda Ser.). (ENG., Illus.). 160p. (J). (gr. 3-7). 13.95 *(978-0-8109-8425-7(3),* 649801) Abrams, Inc.

—Surprise Attack of Jabba the Puppett. 2013. (Origami Yoda Ser.). (ENG., Illus.). 224p. (YA). (gr. 3-7). pap. 7.95 *(978-1-4197-1045-2(1))* Abrams, Inc.

—The Surprise Attack of Jabba the Puppett: An Origami Yoda Book. 2013. (Origami Yoda Ser.: 4). (J). 48.75 *(978-1-4703-9677-0(7));* 50.75 *(978-1-4703-9686-2(6));* 1.25 *(978-1-4703-9695-4(5));* 48.75 *(978-1-4703-9650-3(5));* 168.75 *(978-1-4703-9641-1(6))* Recorded Bks., Inc.

—Surprise Attack of Jabba the Puppett: An Origami Yoda Book. 2013. (Origami Yoda Ser.). (ENG., Illus.). 224p. (YA). (gr. 3-7). 13.95 *(978-1-4197-0858-9(9),* 1013501, Amulet Bks.) Abrams, Inc.

—The Surprise Attack of Jabba the Puppett: An Origami Yoda Book. 2016. (Origami Yoda Files Ser.: 4). (J). lib. bdg. 18.40 *(978-0-606-38208-3(9))* Turtleback.

—The Surprise Attack of Jabba the Puppett (Origami Yoda #4) 2016. (Origami Yoda Ser.). (ENG.). 240p. (YA). (gr. 3-7). pap. 8.99 *(978-1-4197-2030-7(9),* 1013503) Abrams, Inc.

Las Aventuras de Pinocho. (SPA., Illus.). 160p. (YA). 14.95 *(978-84-7281-190-4(5),* AF1905) Auriga, Ediciones S.A. ESP. Dist: Continental Bk. Co., Inc.

Le Aventure di Pinocchio, Level B. (ITA.). (J). pap. 9.95 *(978-0-88436-050-6(4),* 55254) EMC/Paradigm Publishing.

Baroff, Raina. The Chanukah Puppet Show. 2008. 20p. per. 24.95 *(978-1-4241-8612-9(9))* America Star Bks.

Bedard, Michael. Painted Devil. 2007. (ENG.). 240p. (YA). (gr. 7). pap. 13.95 *(978-1-4169-6139-0(9),* Atheneum Bks. for Young Readers) Simon & Schuster Children's Publishing.

Boyne, John. Noah Barleywater Runs Away. Jeffers, Oliver, illus. 2012. (ENG.). 240p. (J). (gr. 3-7). 7.99 *(978-0-385-75264-0(4),* Yearling) Random Hse. Children's Bks.

Brandon, Wendy. Cinderbear: Board Book & Puppet Theater. Winter, Janet, illus. 2004. (J). *(978-1-883043-47-6(6))* Straight Edge Pr., The.

C. Collodi. The Adventures of Pinocchio. 2007. 104p. per. *(978-1-4068-6037-5(9))* Echo Library.

Campillo, Carlo Collodi. Ilustrado por Susana. Las Aventuras de Pinocho. (Coleccion Cuentos Universales). (SPA.). (YA). (gr. 4-18). *(978-84-261-3145-4(X),* JV30301) Juventud, Editorial ESP. Dist: Lectorum Pubns., Inc.
Carsey, Alice, illus. Pinocchio. 2005.Tr. of Avventure di Pinocchio. (ENG.). 136p. (J). (gr. 2-5). 19.95 *(978-1-933327-00-6(6))* Purple Bear Bks., Inc.
—Pinocchio, the Tale of a Puppet. 2011. 140p. pap. 12.99 *(978-1-61203-095-1(5))* Bottom of the Hill Publishing.
Carter, Brynn. The Puppet Explained. 2012. 140p. (gr. -1). pap. 14.95 *(978-1-4685-5617-9(7))* AuthorHouse.
Carter, Scott William. Wooden Bones. (ENG., illus.). 160p. (J). (gr. 3-7). 2013. pap. 6.99 *(978-1-4424-2752-5(3))* 2012. 15.99 *(978-1-4424-2751-8(5))* Simon & Schuster Bks. For Young Readers. (Simon & Schuster Bks. For Young Readers).
Chronicle Books. Hug Me Little Bunny: Finger Puppet Book: (Finger Puppet Books, Baby Board Books, Sensory Books, Bunny Books for Babies, Touch & Feel Books) 2019. (Hug Me Little Animals Ser.). (ENG., Illus.). 10p. (J). (gr. -1 — 1). bds. 9.99 *(978-1-4521-7522-5(5))* Chronicle Bks. LLC.
Chronicle Books & ImageBooks. Little Bat: Finger Puppet Book: (Finger Puppet Book for Toddlers & Babies, Baby Books for Halloween, Animal Finger Puppets) 2010. (Little Finger Puppet Board Bks.). (ENG., Illus.). 12p. (J). (gr. -1 — 1). 7.99 *(978-0-8118-7514-1(8))* Chronicle Bks. LLC.
—Little Turkey: Finger Puppet Book: (Finger Puppet Book for Toddlers & Babies, Baby Books for First Year, Animal Finger Puppets) 2010. (Little Finger Puppet Board Bks.). (ENG., Illus.). 12p. (J). (gr. -1 — 1). 7.99 *(978-0-8118-7513-4(X))* Chronicle Bks. LLC.
Collodi, C. The Adventures of Pinocchio. 2005. 216p. 27.95 *(978-1-4218-0608-2(8),* 1st World Library - Literary Society) 1st World Publishing, Inc.
—The Adventures of Pinocchio. Della Chiesa, Carol, tr. 2007. (ENG.). 160p. per. *(978-1-4065-1463-6(2))* Dodo Pr.
—The Adventures of Pinocchio. 2007. 108p. (gr. 4-7). per. 7.99 *(978-1-60459-012-8(2))* Wilder Pubns., Corp.
—Pinocchio: the Tale of a Puppet. Carsey, Alice, illus. 2007. (ENG.). 196p. per. *(978-1-4065-1462-9(4))* Dodo Pr.
Collodi, Carlo. The Adventures of Pinocchio. 2019.Tr. of Avventure Di Pinocchio. (ENG.). 220p. (YA). (gr. 7). 24.95 *(978-0-469-59358-9(X));* pap. 14.95 *(978-0-469-59357-2(1))* Creative Media Partners, LLC. (Wentworth Pr.).
—The Adventures of Pinocchio. 2019.Tr. of Avventure Di Pinocchio. (ENG.). 262p. (YA). (gr. 7). pap. 18.99 *(978-1-6933-1615-9(3))* Independently Published.
—The Adventures of Pinocchio. 2014.Tr. of Avventure Di Pinocchio. (ENG.). 170p. (YA). (gr. 7). pap. 11.99 *(978-93-5223-173-7(2))* Maple Pr.
—Adventures of Pinocchio. 2009. (Oxford World's Classics Ser.). (ENG., Illus.). 256p. pap. 10.95 *(978-0-19-955398-3(X))* Oxford Univ. Pr., Inc.
—The Adventures of Pinocchio. Innocenti, Roberto, illus. rev. ed. 2004. 192p. (J). (gr. 2-5). 35.00 *(978-1-56846-190-8(9),* 22063) Creative Co., The.
—The Adventures of Pinocchio. Ediz. Illustrata. 2012. (ENG., Illus.). 312p. *(978-88-492-2206-7(8))* Gangemi.
—Le Avventure Di Pinocchio. 2019. (ITA.). (J). 438p. pap. 28.99 *(978-1-6933-1569-5(6));* 442p. pap. 25.99 *(978-1-0706-3834-8(X))* Independently Published.
—Pinocchio. 2017. (ENG., Illus.). (J). pap. 9.99 *(978-1-366-49758-1(9))* Blurb, Inc.
—Pinocchio. Cowley, Joy, ed. Han, Joon-ho, illus. 2015. (World Classics Ser.). (ENG.). 32p. (gr. k-4). 7.99 *(978-1-925246-69-8(8));* 26.65 *(978-1-925246-43-8(4));* 26.65 *(978-1-925246-17-9(5))* ChoiceMaker Pty. Ltd., The AUS. (Big and SMALL). Dist: Lerner Publishing Group.
—Pinocchio. 2017. (ENG., Illus.). 288p. 12.99 *(978-1-5098-4290-2(X),* 900183864, Collector's Library, The) Pan Macmillan GBR. Dist: Macmillan.
—Pinocchio (Illustrated) Brock, Geoffrey, tr. Testa, Fulvio, illus. 2012.Tr. of Avventure di Pinocchio. (ENG.). 184p. (J). (gr. k-4). 24.95 *(978-1-59017-588-0(3),* NYR Children's Collection) New York Review of Bks., Inc., The.
Cooper, Susan. The Magician's Boy. Riglietti, Serena, illus. 2006. (ENG.). 112p. (J). (gr. 3-7). pap. 9.99 *(978-1-4169-1555-3(9),* McElderry, Margaret K. Bks.) McElderry, Margaret K. Bks.
Las Cosas Del Jardin. (SPA.). 24p. 7.95 *(978-84-488-1109-9(7))* Beascoa, Ediciones S.A. ESP. Dist: Distribooks, Inc.
Las Cosas Del Salon. (SPA.). 24p. 7.95 *(978-84-488-1108-2(9))* Beascoa, Ediciones S.A. ESP. Dist: Distribooks, Inc.
Cowing, Sue. Call Me Drog. 2014. (ENG.). 320p. (J). 13.99 *(978-0-00-757804-7(0))* HarperCollins Pubs. Ltd. GBR. Dist: Independent Pubs. Group.
Cox, Jason. Puppet. 2005. (Illus.). 51p. (YA). per. *(978-1-59971-005-1(6))* Aardvark Global Publishing.
Cuno, Sabine. Abre, Cierra y Aprende! Caballero, D., tr. Senner, Katja, illus. 2007. 14p. (J). (gr. -1). *(978-970-718-489-3(2),* Silver Dolphin en Español) Advanced Marketing, S. de R. L. de C. V.
Descoteaux, Chad. Once upon A Crime Syndicate: A mafia fairy Tale. 2006. 151p. pap. 24.95 *(978-1-4241-0893-0(4))* PublishAmerica, Inc.
Disney Editors. Cinderella Takes the Stage. 2017. (Disney Princess Beginnings Ser.). lib. bdg. 17.20 *(978-0-606-39857-2(0))* Turtleback.
Ernie Gets Lost. (J). 5.58 incl. audio NewSound, LLC.
Friedman, Kinky. Curse of the Missing Puppet Head. 2003. lib. bdg. 29.95 *(978-0-9702383-6-8(3),* CMPH01) Vandam Pr., Inc.
Fuchs, Menucha. Menucha V'Simcha Series #11: All Aboard! Hass, Estie, illus. 2008. (Menucha V'Simcha Ser.). 20p. (J). 8.95 *(978-1-932443-82-0(7),* PSHH) Judaica Pr., Inc., The.
Gerth, Melanie. Five Little Ladybugs with Hand Puppet. Beith, Laura Huliska, illus. 2009. (ENG.). 12p. 12.95 *(978-1-58117-889-0(1),* Intervisual/Piggy Toes) Bendon, Inc.
Hillert, Margaret. Let's Have a Play. Flanigan, Ruth, illus. 2016. (BeginningtoRead Ser.). (ENG.). 32p. (J). (gr. k-2). 22.60 *(978-1-59953-818-1(0))* Norwood Hse. Pr.
—Let's Have a Play. Ruth Flanigan, illus. 2016. (Beginning-To-Read Ser.). (ENG.). 32p. (J). (gr. k-2). pap. 13.26 *(978-1-60357-980-3(X))* Norwood Hse. Pr.
—Pinocchio. Dana Regan, illus. 21st ed. 2016. (Beginning-To-Read Ser.). (ENG.). 32p. (J). (gr. k-2). pap. 13.26 *(978-1-60357-912-4(5))* Norwood Hse. Pr.
—Pinocho. Dana Regan, illus. 2018. (Beginning-To-Read Ser.).Tr. of Pinocchio. (SPA.). 32p. (J). (gr. k-2). pap. 13.26 *(978-1-68404-243-2(7))* Norwood Hse. Pr.
Hillert, Margaret, et al. Pinocho. Regan, Dana, illus. 2018. (BeginningtoRead Ser.).Tr. of Pinocchio. (SPA.). 32p. (J). (gr. -1-2). lib. bdg. 22.60 *(978-1-59953-959-1(4))* Norwood Hse. Pr.
Keats, Ezra Jack. Louie. Keats, Ezra Jack, illus. 2004. (ENG., Illus.). 40p. (J). (gr. -1-2). pap. 7.99 *(978-0-14-240080-7(7),* Puffin Books) Penguin Young Readers Group.
—Louie. 2004. (Illus.). 31p. 17.20 *(978-0-613-97780-7(7))* Turtleback.
Langridge, Roger. The Muppet Show Comic Book: The Treasure of Peg-Leg Wilson. Langridge, Roger, illus. 2010. (Muppet Show Ser.). (ENG., Illus.). 112p. (J). 24.99 *(978-1-60886-530-7(4));* (gr. 4-7). pap. 9.99 *(978-1-60886-504-8(5))* BOOM! Studios.
—The Muppet Show Comic Book - Muppet Mash. Langridge, Roger, illus. 2011. (Muppet Show Ser.). (Illus.). 128p. pap. 9.99 *(978-1-60886-611-3(4))* BOOM! Studios.
—On the Road. Langridge, Roger, illus. 2011. (Kaboom! Graphic Novels Ser.). (ENG., Illus.). 112p. (J). (gr. 4-7). 26.19 *(978-1-60886-516-1(9))* BOOM! Studios.
Lawson, Jennifer. Our New Solar System: A Puppet Show. 2010. 27p. 19.95 *(978-0-557-21389-4(1))* Lulu Pr., Inc.
LeLeu, Lisa. Frenchy the Frog Story Starter: Puppet Show Book Story Starter. 2004. (Puppet Show Bks.). (Illus.). 14p. 1.50 *(978-0-9710537-7-9(4))* LeLeu, Lisa Studios! Inc.
—Miss Moo-Moo the Cow Story Starter: Puppet Book Story Starter. 2004. (Puppet Show Bks.). (Illus.). 14p. 1.50 *(978-0-9710537-1-7(5))* LeLeu, Lisa Studios! Inc.
—Scooter the Cat Gift Set: Puppet Book Gift Set with 2 Books. 2004. (Puppet Show Bks.). (Illus.). 30p. 19.95 *(978-0-9710537-0-0(7))* LeLeu, Lisa Studios! Inc.
—Scooter the Cat Story Teller: Puppet Book Story Starter. 2004. (Puppet Show Bks.). (Illus.). 14p. 1.50 *(978-0-9710537-6-2(6))* LeLeu, Lisa Studios! Inc.
Lilly, Evangeline. The Squickerwonkers. Fraser-Allen, Johnny, illus. 2014. 42p. (gr. k-3). 16.99 *(978-1-78329-545-6(7),* Titan Bks.) Titan Bks. Ltd. GBR. Dist: Penguin Random Hse. LLC.
Love, D. Anne. The Puppeteer's Apprentice. 2004. (ENG., Illus.). 192p. (J). (gr. 3-7). reprint ed. pap. 9.99 *(978-0-689-84425-6(5),* McElderry, Margaret K. Bks.) McElderry, Margaret K. Bks.
—The Puppeteer's Apprentice. 2004. (Aladdin Historical Fiction Ser.). 185p. (gr. 3-7). 17.00 *(978-0-7569-4323-3(X))* Perfection Learning Corp.
Madore, Michele. Rudee Goes Bananas for Manners. Gravitt, Bill, illus. 2006. (ENG.). 38p. (J). pap. 6.95 *(978-0-615-17967-4(3))* Manners Toy Co., LLC.
Magsamen, Sandra. Owl Always Love You! Magsamen, Sandra, illus. 2018. (ENG.). 10p. (J). (gr. -1 — 1). bds. 7.99 *(978-0-545-92800-7(1),* Cartwheel Bks.) Scholastic, Inc.
Make Believe Ideas, creator. BJ's Finger Puppet Book Assortment. 2007. (Illus.). (J). (gr. -1-3). *(978-1-84610-675-0(3))* Make Believe Ideas.
McBratney, Sam. Here I Am!: a Finger Puppet Book: A Guess How Much I Love You Book. Jeram, Anita, illus. 2018. (Guess How Much I Love You Ser.). (ENG.). 16p. (J). (— 1). bds. 13.99 *(978-1-5362-0389-9(0))* Candlewick Pr.
McDonald, Megan. When the Library Lights Go Out. Tillotson, Katherine, illus. 2009. (ENG.). 40p. (J). (gr. -1-1). 9.99 *(978-1-4169-8028-5(8),* Atheneum Bks. for Young Readers) Simon & Schuster Children's Publishing.
Melean, Mary & Lascaris, Alexia. The Adventures of Don Quixote of la Mancha. 2011. 44p. pap. 18.46 *(978-1-4567-6131-8(5))* AuthorHouse.
Michael, Melanie. Nerfnerd. Alderton, John, illus. 2011. (J). *(978-0-938467-07-6(7))* Headline Bks., Inc.
Miller, Toby. The Magic Word. 2011. (Illus.). 24p. pap. 14.09 *(978-1-4567-7793-7(9))* AuthorHouse.
Mitchell, Robin & Steedman, Judith. Snowy & Chinook. 2005. (ENG., Illus.). 22p. (J). (gr. -1-3). 15.95 *(978-0-9688768-9-3(7))* Simply Read Bks. CAN. Dist: Ingram Publisher Services.
Monster at the End of This Book. 2009. (ENG.). 24p. 14.99 *(978-1-74181-222-0(4),* Ideals Pubns.) Worthy Publishing.
Murray, M. A., tr. Pinocchio, As First Translated into English by M a Murray & Illustrated by Charles Folkard. Folkard, Charles, illus. 2009. 280p. pap. 11.95 *(978-1-59915-177-9(4))* Yesterday's Classics.
Nickel. Pinocchio. Date not set. (J). 4.99 *(978-0-7214-5404-7(6))* Nickel Pr.
Page, Nick & Page, Claire. Finger Puppet Books Christmas Story. 2008. (Illus.). 12p. (gr. -1-k). bds. *(978-1-84610-821-1(7))* Make Believe Ideas.
Parragon Staff. Pinocchio: The Magical Story. 2010. (Disney Padded Magical Storybks.). (Illus.). 32p. (J). (gr. -1-1). *(978-1-4075-8451-5(0))* Parragon, Inc.
Paterson, Katherine. El Maestro de las Marionetas.Tr. of Master Puppeteer. (SPA., Illus.). (YA). (gr. 5-8). 9.95 *(978-958-04-4382-7(3),* NR8770) Norma S.A. COL. Dist: Distribuidora Norma, Inc.
—The Master Puppeteer. 3rd ed. (J). pap. 3.95 *(978-0-13-800095-0(6))* Prentice Hall (Schl. Div.).
Pilegard, Virginia Walton. The Warlord's Puppeteers, 1 vol. Debon, Nicolas, illus. 2003. (Warlord's Ser.: 4). (ENG.). 32p. (J). (gr. k-3). 16.99 *(978-1-58980-077-9(X),* Pelican Publishing) Arcadia Publishing.
Pinocchio: The Human Body, Sea Life, The Bedroom. (FRE & ENG., Illus.). 24p. (J). (gr. -1-5). pap., stu. ed. 5.95 *(978-88-8148-243-6(6))* EMC/Paradigm Publishing.
Publications International Ltd. Staff, ed. Elmo Goes to the Doctor. 2010. 14p. (J). bds. 16.98 *(978-1-4127-4609-0(4))* Phoenix International Publications, Inc.
The Puppet Show. (Early Intervention Levels Ser.). 21.30 *(978-0-7362-0362-3(1))* CENGAGE Learning.
Rainey, L. E. Sad Sam, Glad Sam. 2006. (Illus.). 32p. (J). 16.95 *(978-0-9785521-0-7(5))* Shoetree Publishers, Inc.
Ruiz, Margarita, illus. Pinocho. (SPA & ENG.). 24p. (J). (gr. -1-5). pap. 5.95 incl. audio compact disk *(978-88-8148-253-5(3))* EMC/Paradigm Publishing.
Schlitz, Laura Amy. Splendors & Glooms. (ENG.). 400p. (J). 2017. (gr. 5-9). pap. 10.99 *(978-0-7636-9449-4(5))* 2012. (Illus.). (gr. 4-7). 17.99 *(978-0-7636-5380-4(2))* Candlewick Pr.
—Splendors & Glooms. 2014. (ENG.). (J). (gr. 4-7). lib. bdg. 18.60 *(978-1-62765-443-2(7))* Perfection Learning Corp.
—Splendors & Glooms. 2014. lib. bdg. 18.40 *(978-0-606-35170-6(1))* Turtleback.
Schreiber, Elisheva. The Miniature Puppet Theater Book. Pollack, Gadi & Markovitch, Evegeny, illus. (J). 14.95 *(978-1-58330-617-8(X))* Feldheim Pubs.
Schusterman, Michelle. Spell & Spindle. Honesta, Kathrin, illus. 2018. (ENG.). 272p. (J). (gr. 3-7). 16.99 *(978-0-399-55070-6(4),* Random Hse. Bks. for Young Readers) Random Hse. Children's Bks.
Sesame Street 5-Minute Stories (Sesame Street) 2017. (ENG., Illus.). 160p. (J). (gr. -1-2). 14.99 *(978-1-5247-1989-0(7),* Random Hse. Bks. for Young Readers) Random Hse. Children's Bks.
Snider, Jesse Blaze. Muppet Snow White. Paroline, Shelli, illus. 2010. (Muppet Show Ser.). 112p. (J). (gr. 3-6). pap. 9.99 *(978-1-60886-574-1(6))* BOOM! Studios.
Stiberth, Elizabeth. Halloween Mystery. 2008. 32p. pap. 14.49 *(978-1-4389-1112-0(2))* AuthorHouse.
Stine, R. L. Dr. Maniac vs. Robby Schwartz (Goosebumps HorrorLand #5) 2008. (Goosebumps Horrorland Ser.: 5). (ENG., Illus.). 160p. (J). (gr. 3-7). pap. 7.99 *(978-0-439-91873-2(1),* Scholastic Paperbacks) Scholastic, Inc.
—Night of the Puppet People. 2015. (Goosebumps Most Wanted Ser.: 8). lib. bdg. 17.20 *(978-0-606-37792-8(1))* Turtleback.
—Revenge of the Living Dummy. 2008. (Goosebumps HorrorLand Ser.: No. 1). 128p. (J). (gr. 4-7). 13.65 *(978-0-7569-8816-6(0))* Perfection Learning Corp.
—Revenge of the Living Dummy. 2008. (Goosebumps HorrorLand Ser.: 1). 128p. (gr. 4-7). lib. bdg. 17.20 *(978-1-4178-1891-4(3))* Turtleback.
—Son of Slappy. 2013. (Goosebumps Most Wanted Ser.: 2). lib. bdg. 17.20 *(978-0-606-31533-3(0))* Turtleback.
—Son of Slappy (Goosebumps Most Wanted #2) 2013. (Goosebumps Most Wanted Ser.: 2). (ENG.). 160p. (J). (gr. 3-7). pap. 7.99 *(978-0-545-41799-0(6),* Scholastic Paperbacks) Scholastic, Inc.
Stone, Jon. The Monster at the End of This Book. Smollin, Michael, illus. 2015. (ENG.). 26p. (J). (— 1). bds. 7.99 *(978-0-553-50873-4(3),* Golden Bks.) Random Hse. Children's Bks.
Tattum, Stephan. Fun Pup. 2005. (J). 4.95 *(978-1-59792-005-6(3))* F.A.S.T. Learning LLC.
Taylor, Laini. Night of Cake & Puppets. Di Bartolo, Jim, illus. 2017. (Daughter of Smoke & Bone Ser.). (ENG.). 256p. (YA). (gr. 10-17). 16.99 *(978-0-316-43919-0(3))* Little, Brown Bks. for Young Readers.
Teitelbaum, Michael. The Cave of No Return. 2015. (Cold Whispers Ser.). (ENG., Illus.). 32p. (J). (gr. 2-6). lib. bdg. 28.50 *(978-1-62724-812-9(9))* Bearport Publishing Co., Inc.
Trimble, Marcia. Peppy's Shadow. Pellegrini, Will, illus. 2003. 32p. (J). (gr. -1-3). 15.95 *(978-1-891577-70-3(0));* pap. 7.95 *(978-1-891577-71-0(9))* Images Pr.
Tyre, Greg R. Fun with Sockie. 2009. 28p. pap. 14.99 *(978-1-4490-0105-6(X))* AuthorHouse.
Wang, Jack & Wang, Holman. Star Wars Epic Yarns: Return of the Jedi. 2015. (ENG., Illus.). 24p. (J). (gr. -1 — 1). 9.95 *(978-1-4521-3500-7(2))* Chronicle Bks. LLC.

PUPPETS AND PUPPET-PLAYS

see Puppet Plays; Puppet Theater; Puppets

PURCHASING

see Shopping

PURIM

Bredeson, Carmen. Purim. 2003. (Rookie Read-About Holidays Ser.). (ENG., Illus.). 32p. (J). (gr. 1-2). pap. 5.95 *(978-0-516-27928-2(9),* Children's Pr.) Scholastic Library Publishing.
Gottlieb, Wendy Ruth. Purr-Im Cat. 2008. (Illus.). 32p. (J). 16.95 *(978-1-932687-91-0(2),* Devora Publishing) Simcha Media Group.
Kress, Camille. Purim! Kress, Camille, illus. 2004. (Illus.). 10p. (gr. -1-k). bds. 5.95 *(978-0-8074-0654-0(6),* 102555) URJ Pr.
Kropf, Latifa Berry. It's Purim Time! Cohen, Tod, photos by. (ENG., Illus.). 24p. (J). 2012. (gr. -1-1). pap. 8.95 *(978-0-7613-8493-9(6),* bdb5af09-9c05-45d3-98a5-736c08353bd8) 2005. (gr. 2-6). lib. bdg. 12.95 *(978-1-58013-153-7(0))* Lerner Publishing Group. (Kar-Ben Publishing).
Pollack, Gadi, illus. & contrib. by. Purimshpiel. Pollack, Gadi, contrib. by. (ENG & HEB.). *(978-1-58330-611-6(0));* (ENG & FRE.). 21.95 *(978-1-58330-601-7(3));* 19.99 *(978-1-58330-596-6(3))* Feldheim Pubs.
Schram, Peninnah. The Purim Costume. Keiser, Tammy L., illus. 2004. 13.95 *(978-0-8074-0874-2(3),* 101312) URJ Pr.
Simon, Norma. Happy Purim Night. Gordon, Ayala, illus. (Festival Series of Picture Storybooks). (J). (gr. -1). vinyl bd. 4.50 *(978-0-8381-0706-5(0),* 10-706) United Synagogue of America Bk. Service.

PURIM—FICTION

Adelson, Leone. The Mystery Bear: A Purim Story. Howland, Naomi, tr. Howland, Naomi, illus. 2004. 32p. (J). (gr. -1-2). 15.00 *(978-0-618-33727-9(X),* Clarion Bks.) HarperCollins Pubs.
Barash, Chris. Is It Purim Yet? 2018. (2019 Av2 Fiction Ser.). (ENG.). 32p. (J). (gr. -1-1). lib. bdg. 34.28 *(978-1-4896-8267-3(8),* AV2 by Weigl) Weigl Pubs., Inc.
—Is It Purim Yet? Psacharopulo, Alessandra, illus. 2017. (Celebrate Jewish Holidays Ser.). (ENG.). 32p. (J). (gr. -1-3). 16.99 *(978-0-8075-3391-8(2),* 807533912) Whitman, Albert & Co.
Cuyler, Margery. Purim Chicken. 2018. (2019 Av2 Fiction Ser.). (ENG.). 32p. (J). (gr. -1-2). lib. bdg. 34.28 *(978-1-4896-8277-2(5),* AV2 by Weigl) Weigl Pubs., Inc.
—Purim Chicken. Pinillos, Puy, illus. 2017. (ENG.). 32p. (J). (gr. -1-3). 16.99 *(978-0-8075-3381-9(5),* 807533815) Whitman, Albert & Co.
Goldin, Barbara Diamond. A Persian Princess. Doneva, Stellyana, illus. 2019. (ENG.). 32p. (J). 17.95 *(978-1-68115-553-1(2),* 06953505-064b-4bca-a82e-6b2556a1d498, Apples & Honey Pr.) Behrman Hse., Inc.
Howland, Naomi. The Better-Than-Best Purim, 0 vols. 2012. (ENG.). 32p. (J). (gr. -1-2). 16.99 *(978-0-7614-6203-3(1),* 9780761462033, Two Lions) Amazon Publishing.
Kushner, Elisabeth. The Purim Superhero. Byrne, Mike, illus. 2013. (ENG.). 32p. (J). (gr. -1-3). 8.99 *(978-0-7613-9062-6(6),* e21c8b88-429e-4a15-bf99-c61687205a7d, Kar-Ben Publishing) Lerner Publishing Group.
Newman, Tracy. Purim Is Coming! Garofoli, Viviana, illus. 2017. (ENG.). 12p. (J). (gr. -1 — 1). bds. 7.99 *(978-1-5124-0827-0(1),* 8ce8b152-c9bb-4654-b45e-04c5bd767de7, Kar-Ben Publishing) Lerner Publishing Group.
Sandbank, Rachella & Shem-Tov, Tami. A Queen in Jerusalem. Ofer, Avi, illus. 2018. (ENG.). 32p. (J). (gr. -1-2). 12.99 *(978-1-5124-4441-4(3),* 53662b24-b791-48fe-a9c3-28ad79f7107d, Kar-Ben Publishing) Lerner Publishing Group.
Schotter, Roni. Purim Play, 0 vols. Hafner, Marylin, illus. 2012. (ENG.). 34p. (J). (gr. -1-3). pap. 6.99 *(978-0-7614-5800-5(X),* 9780761458005, Two Lions) Amazon Publishing.
Simpson, Lesley. The Purim Surprise. Church, Peter, illus. 2004. (Purim Ser.). (ENG.). 32p. (J). (gr. -1-3). pap. 6.95 *(978-1-58013-090-5(9),* Kar-Ben Publishing) Lerner Publishing Group.
Simpson, Martha Seif. Esther's Gragger: A Toyshop Tale of Purim. 2019. (Illus.). 40p. (J). (gr. k-3). 16.95 *(978-1-937786-75-5(7),* Wisdom Tales) World Wisdom, Inc.
Terwilliger, Kelly. Barnyard Purim. Newman, Barbara Johansen, illus. 2012. (Purim Ser.). (ENG.). 32p. (J). (gr. k-3). pap. 7.95 *(978-0-7613-4514-5(0),* Kar-Ben Publishing) Lerner Publishing Group.
Watts, Irene N. A Telling Time, 1 vol. Shoemaker, Kathryn E., illus. 2004. (ENG.). 32p. (J). (gr. 1-3). 17.95 *(978-1-896580-39-5(4))* Tradewind Bks. CAN. Dist: Orca Bk. Pubs. USA.

PURITANS

Kiely Miller, Barbara. Anne Hutchinson, 1 vol. 2007. (Grandes Personajes (Great Americans) Ser.). 24p. (gr. 2-4). (SPA.). pap. 9.15 *(978-0-8368-8337-4(3),* af384a82-389a-4771-b553-52471853289d); (ENG.). pap. 9.15 *(978-0-8368-8324-4(1),* a8df2685-f3b6-403c-834f-c5e9c37c8aad); (SPA., Illus.). lib. bdg. 24.67 *(978-0-8368-8330-5(6),* 14749122-7836-4305-8205-4305cf766f9f); (ENG., Illus.). lib. bdg. 24.67 *(978-0-8368-8317-6(9),* 349e5929-1415-4b48-9fa4-586b925a16be) Stevens, Gareth Publishing LLLP. (Weekly Reader Leveled Readers).
Marsh, Carole. Anne Hutchinson. 2004. 12p. (gr. k-4). 2.95 *(978-0-635-02370-4(9))* Gallopade International.
Nichols, Joan K. A Matter of Conscience: The Trial of Anne Hutchinson. Krovatin, Dan, illus. 2009. (Steck-Vaughn Stories of America Ser.). (ENG.). 112p. (gr. 3-8). pap. 14.20 *(978-0-8114-8073-4(9))* Houghton Mifflin Harcourt Publishing Co.
Owens, L. L. Pilgrims in America. 2006. (Events in American History Ser.). (Illus.). 48p. (J). (gr. -1-1). lib. bdg. 31.36 *(978-1-60044-122-6(X))* Rourke Educational Media.
The Puritans, Algonkians & Roger Williams (NCHS) (J). (gr. 5-8). spiral bd., tchr.'s planning gde. ed. 13.50 *(978-0-382-44447-0(7))* Cobblestone Publishing Co.
The Puritans, Algonkians & Roger Williams (NCHS) Grades 5-8. (J). tchr. ed. 18.00 *(978-0-382-44537-8(6))* Cobblestone Publishing Co.
Riehecky, Janet & Williams, Gianna. La Colonia de Plymouth (the Settling of Plymouth), 1 vol. 2006. (Hitos de la Historia de Estados Unidos (Landmark Events in American History) Ser.). (SPA.). 48p. (gr. 5-8). pap. 12.70 *(978-0-8368-7471-6(4),* c4b0334d-2730-428d-b1e9-b4c540c786ce, Gareth Stevens Learning Library); (Illus.). lib. bdg. 29.67 *(978-0-8368-7464-8(1),* 08ac8c60-625b-40a5-bde2-463bc20e4058, Gareth Stevens Secondary Library) Stevens, Gareth Publishing LLLP.
Tierney, Tom. Cavalier & Puritan Fashions. 2005. (Dover Fashion Coloring Book Ser.). (ENG., Illus.). 48p. (J). (gr. 6-8). pap. 4.99 *(978-0-486-43655-5(1),* 436551) Dover Pubns., Inc.
Wolfe, James & Moe, Barbara. Understanding the Charter of the Massachusetts Bay Colony, 1 vol. 2015. (Primary Sources of American Political Documents Ser.). (ENG., Illus.). 112p. (gr. 7-7). 38.93 *(978-0-7660-6870-4(6),* cf8f12b6-5051-4cd0-bd46-d235ab795a09) Enslow Publishing, LLC.

PURITANS—FICTION

Literature Connections English: The Witch of Blackbird Pond. 2004. (gr. 6-12). *(978-0-395-78592-8(8),* 2-70293) Holt McDougal.
Noyes, Deborah. Angel & Apostle. 2007. 304p. per. 14.95 *(978-1-932961-29-4(1))* Unbridled Bks.
Rees, Celia. Witch Child. unabr. ed. 2004. (Young Adult Cassette Librariestm Ser.). 304p. (J). (gr. 5-9). pap. 40.00 incl. audio *(978-0-8072-1198-4(2),* S YA 343 SP, Listening Library) Random Hse. Audio Publishing Group.
Smith, Mary P. Wells. The Young Puritans in King Philip's War. Bridgman, L. J., illus. 2011. 396p. 54.95 *(978-1-258-05550-9(3))* Literary Licensing, LLC.
Speare, Elizabeth George. The Witch of Blackbird Pond. 2011. (ENG.). 272p. (J). (gr. 5-7). pap. 8.99 *(978-0-547-55029-9(4),* 1450238, Clarion Bks.) HarperCollins Pubs.
—The Witch of Blackbird Pond. 2004. 223p. (J). (gr. 4-7). pap., tchr.'s planning gde. ed. 38.00 incl. audio *(978-0-8072-0862-5(0),* Listening Library) Random Hse. Audio Publishing Group.
Thompson, Paul B. The Devil's Door: A Salem Witchcraft Story, 1 vol. 2011. (Historical Fiction Adventures Ser.). (ENG., Illus.). 160p. (J). (gr. 3-5). 31.93 *(978-0-7660-3387-0(2),* b032300a-5660-4f10-8e33-a57d5745824e); pap. 13.88 *(978-1-59845-214-3(2),* b6288c2c-d77e-4e8d-8d6c-4dae679dbf24) Enslow Publishing, LLC.

PUZZLES

see also Bible Games and Puzzles; Sudoku

Accord Publishing, Accord. Flip & Click Christmas Hangman. 2011. (ENG.). 72p. (J). pap. 4.99 *(978-1-4494-0836-7(2))* Andrews McMeel Publishing.

—Go Fun! Big Book of Puzzles. 2014. (ENG.). 216p. (J). pap. 12.99 *(978-1-4494-4386-3(9))* Andrews McMeel Publishing.

—Stick to It: Pets: A Magnetic Puzzle Book. 2010. (ENG.). 14p. (J). (gr. -1). bds. 16.99 *(978-0-7407-9726-2(3))* Andrews McMeel Publishing.

Adams, Colleen. Tangram Puzzles: Describing & Comparing Attributes of Plane Geometric Shapes, 1 vol. (Math for the REAL World Ser.). 24p. (gr. 3-4). 2009. (ENG., Illus.). pap. 8.25 *(978-0-8239-8921-8(6),* 2cf667e9-c45a-475e-98f7-d06a308ad7be) 2009. 45.00 *(978-1-60851-383-3(1))* 2003. (ENG., Illus.). (J). lib. bdg. 26.27 *(978-0-8239-8976-8(3),* 4160c094-c5fd-44f5-9bc9-8e29526551a2) Rosen Publishing Group, Inc., The. (PowerKids Pr.).

African American Heritage Pictures, Puzzles, & Word Games. 2004. (YA). per. 16.00 *(978-0-9758586-0-8(2))* Jenkins-Simmons, Glenda.

Agee, Jon. Palindromania! Agee, Jon, illus. 2009. (ENG., Illus.). 112p. (J). (gr. 3-8). pap. 11.11 *(978-0-374-40025-5(3),* 900058755) Square Fish.

Aihara, Kazunori, illus. Let's Find Pokémon! Special Complete Edition (2nd Edition) 2017. (Let's Find Pokémon! Special Complete Edition (2nd Edition) Ser.). (ENG.). 88p. (J). 16.99 *(978-1-4215-9579-5(6))* Viz Media.

All Through the Year (Gr. 1-2) 2003. (J). *(978-1-58232-055-7(1))* ECS Learning Systems, Inc.

All Through the Year (Gr. 1-3) 2003. (J). *(978-1-58232-065-6(9))* ECS Learning Systems, Inc.

All Through the Year (Gr. 2-4) 2003. (J). *(978-1-58232-056-4(X))* ECS Learning Systems, Inc.

Allen, Peter, illus. Ancient Egypt Jigsaw Book. 2006. (Jigsaw Bks.). 14p. (J). (gr. k-3). bds. 14.99 *(978-0-7945-1236-1(4),* Usborne) EDC Publishing.

Allen, Robert. Mensa Mighty Mindbusters for Kids. 2003. 256p. (J). (gr. 4-7). per. *(978-1-84222-897-5(8))* Carlton Bks., Ltd.

—Mensa Presents Secret Codes for Kids. 2003. (Illus.). 128p. (J). pap. *(978-1-84222-767-1(X))* Carlton Bks., Ltd.

Alphabet Puzzle Pairs. 2004. (J). pap. *(978-1-59461-051-6(7))* eeBoo Corp.

Amery, H. Bible Stories Jigsaw Book. 2004. 20p. (J). 14.95 *(978-0-7945-0558-5(9))* EDC Publishing.

—Navidad en la Granja Libro Con Paginas Puzzle. 2004. Orig. Title: Christmas Jigsaw Book. (SPA.). 6p. (J). 8.95 *(978-0-7460-5092-7(5))* EDC Publishing.

—The Steam Train Jigsaw Book. 2004. 14p. (J). 8.95 *(978-0-7945-0296-6(2))* EDC Publishing.

Amery, H. & Cartwright, S. ABC Jigsaw Book. rev. ed. 2004. 18p. (J). 14.95 *(978-0-7945-0619-3(4))* EDC Publishing.

—Christmas Jigsaw Book. 2004. (Farmyard Tales Ser.). (ENG.). 1p. (J). bds. 8.95 *(978-0-7945-0219-5(9),* Usborne) EDC Publishing.

—Farm Animal Jigsaw Book. 2004. (Jigsaw Bks.). (ENG., Illus.). 1p. (J). bds. 8.95 *(978-0-7945-0162-4(1),* Usborne) EDC Publishing.

Amery, Heather. Christmas Story Jigsaw Book. 2004. (Jigsaw Bks.). (Illus.). 14p. (J). 8.95 *(978-0-7945-0223-2(7),* Usborne) EDC Publishing.

—Usborne Greek Myths Jigsaw Book. Edwards, Linda, illus. 2006. (Usborne Jigsaw Bks.). 14p. (J). bds. 14.99 *(978-0-7945-1183-8(X),* Usborne) EDC Publishing.

Analogy Challenges Level A. 2004. (J). pap. 12.95 *(978-1-892069-77-1(6))* MindWare Holdings, Inc.

Analogy Challenges Level B. 2004. (J). pap. 12.95 *(978-1-892069-78-8(4))* MindWare Holdings, Inc.

Andrew, Carol B. Little Farm Puppy. 2006. (Illus.). (J). *(978-1-933577-05-0(3))* Learning Wood, LLC.

Andrews McMeel Publishing, Andrews McMeel. Go Fun! Big Book of Brain Games. 2014. (Go Fun! Ser.: 1). (ENG.). 144p. (J). pap. 8.99 *(978-1-4494-6488-2(2))* Andrews McMeel Publishing.

—Go Fun! Big Book of Brain Games 2. 2016. (Go Fun! Ser.: 12). (ENG.). 128p. (J). pap. 8.99 *(978-1-4494-7883-4(2))* Andrews McMeel Publishing.

—Go Fun! Big Book of Crosswords. 2014. (Go Fun! Ser.: 2). (ENG.). 144p. (J). pap. 8.99 *(978-1-4494-6486-8(6))* Andrews McMeel Publishing.

Anholt, Catherine & Anholt, Laurence. Can You Guess? A Lift-the-Flap Birthday Party Book. 2003. (ENG., Illus.). 16p. pap. 7.95 *(978-0-7112-2214-4(2))* Fleming, Randall.

Aniel, Isabel, illus. My First Mazes: Over 50 Fantastic Puzzles. 2017. (My First Activity Bks.). (ENG.). 64p. (J). (gr. -1-2). pap. 8.99 *(978-1-4380-1003-8(6))* Sourcebooks, Inc.

Animal: Puzzles & Games. 2009. (BOREDOM BUSTERS Ser.). 56p. (J). (gr. 2-7). pap. 4.99 *(978-0-8416-1091-0(6))* American Map Corp.

Animal Clues: 6 Small Books. (gr. k-1). 35.00 *(978-0-7635-6226-7(2))* Rigby Education.

Arensen, Shel. The First Christmas: Nativity Puzzle Book with 6 Play Pieces. 2003. (Illus.). 16p. (J). 10.99 *(978-0-8254-5509-4(X))* Kregel Pubns.

Armadillo Press Staff. My Book of Baby Animals: A Fun-Packed Picture & Puzzle Book for Little Ones. 2016. (Illus.). 48p. (J). (gr. -1-12). bds. 9.99 *(978-1-86147-662-3(0),* Armadillo) Anness Publishing GBR. Dist: National Bk. Network.

Artell, Mike. Backyard Bloodsuckers: Questions, Facts & Tongue Twisters about Creepy Crawlers. 2004. (Illus.). 80p. pap. 14.95 *(978-0-673-59248-4(0))* Good Year Bks.

—Hidden Picture Puzzlers. 2018. (Dover Kids Activity Bks.). (ENG.). 128p. (J). (gr. 2-5). pap. 10.99 *(978-0-486-82505-2(1),* 825051) Dover Pubns., Inc.

—Hidden Pictures. 2012. (Dover Children's Activity Bks.). (ENG., Illus.). 64p. (gr. 5). pap. 2.50 *(978-0-486-28153-7(1))* Dover Pubns., Inc.

Artymoska, Aleksandra. Around the World in 80 Puzzles. Artymoska, Aleksandra, illus. 2018. (ENG., Illus.). 96p. (J). (gr. 2-4). 19.99 *(978-1-5362-0308-0(4),* Big Picture Press) Candlewick Pr.

Artymowska, Aleksandra, illus. Find My Rocket: A Marvelous Maze Adventure. 2018. (ENG.). 32p. 16.99 *(978-1-78627-286-7(5),* King, Laurence Publishing) Orion Publishing Group, Ltd. GBR. Dist: Hachette Bk. Group.

Assorted, illus. Puzzle Quest. 2016. (Brain Candy Ser.). (ENG.). 224p. (J). (gr. 4). pap. 12.99 *(978-1-78445-548-4(2))* Top That! Publishing PLC GBR. Dist: Independent Pubs. Group.

Bagley, Val Chadwick. Seek & Find Noah's Ark. 2017. (Illus.). (J). *(978-1-5244-0292-1(3))* Covenant Communications, Inc.

Bailey, Todd, ed. The Clue Searcher's Discovery Guide To: A Clue Search Puzzles Book: the 50 States, 1. 2004. (Illus.). 60p. spiral bd. 14.99 *(978-0-9753879-0-0(1))* ClueSearchPuzzles.com.

Ball, Liz. Frog Fun Hidden Treasures: Hidden Picture Puzzles, Vol. 8. Ball, Liz, illus. 2008. (Hidden Treasures Ser.: Vol. 8). (Illus.). 56p. (YA). pap. 6.95 *(978-0-9678159-8-5(3))* Hidden Pictures.

Ball, Liz, illus. Bible Stories: Find-the-Picture Puzzles. 2004. (Find-the-Picture Puzzle Ser.: 1). 24p. (J). pap. 2.95 *(978-0-8198-1163-9(7),* 332-026) Pauline Bks. & Media.

—Miracles & Parables of Jesus: Find-the-Picture Puzzles. 2004. (Find-the-Picture Puzzle Ser.: 2). 24p. (J). pap. 2.95 *(978-0-8198-4830-7(1),* 332-221) Pauline Bks. & Media.

Bama. What Am I? 2012. (ENG.). 43p. 14.95 *(978-1-4620-6150-1(8),* b63c1afb-7535-4777-a6d0-5bdfc94c2226) iUniverse, Inc.

Barbaresi, Nina. Animal Search-a-Word Puzzles. 2003. (Dover Little Activity Bks.). (ENG., Illus.). 64p. (J). (gr. k-3). 2.99 *(978-0-486-42767-6(6),* 427676) Dover Pubns., Inc.

—Animal Word Puzzles Coloring Book. 81st ed. 2013. (Dover Kids Activity Books: Animals Ser.). (ENG., Illus.). 48p. (J). (gr. 1-4). pap. 4.99 *(978-0-486-26848-4(9),* 268489) Dover Pubns., Inc.

—Horses. 2005. (Dover Little Activity Bks.). (ENG., Illus.). 64p. (J). (gr. 3-5). pap., act. bk. ed. 2.50 *(978-0-486-44195-5(4),* 441954) Dover Pubns., Inc.

—Little Search-a-Word. 2012. (Dover Little Activity Bks.). (ENG., Illus.). 64p. (J). (gr. k-3). pap. 2.50 *(978-0-486-26455-4(6),* 264556) Dover Pubns., Inc.

Barberi, Marco, et al, trs. Sabelotodo: 1000 Desafios para Tu Inteligencia. Bertran, Nuria, illus. 2003. (SPA.). 384p. 35.00 *(978-84-494-2372-7(4),* GML07104-192209) Oceano Grupo Editoria, S.A. ESP. Dist: Cengage Gale.

Baretti, Sonia & Neradova, Maria, illus. My First Dot-To-Dot: Over 50 Fantastic Puzzles. 2017. (My First Activity Bks.). (ENG.). 64p. (J). (gr. -1-2). pap. 8.99 *(978-1-4380-1002-1(8))* Sourcebooks, Inc.

Baron, Celia. Brain Sizzlers. 2004. (Illus.). 48p. (gr. 4-7). pap. 5.95 *(978-0-673-59962-9(0))* Good Year Bks.

—Brain Sizzlers: Puzzles for Critical Thinkers. 2nd ed. 2007. (Illus.). 88p. (J). pap. 7.95 *(978-1-59647-232-7(4))* Good Year Bks.

Barth, Linda J. Hidden New Jersey. Mitchell, Hazel, illus. 2012. 32p. (J). (gr. 1-4). 17.95 *(978-1-934133-23-1(X),* Mackinac Island Press, Inc.) Charlesbridge Publishing, Inc.

Baruzzi, Agnese. Giant Mazes: Search, Find, & Count! 2018. (ENG., Illus.). 56p. (J). (gr. k). 14.95 *(978-1-4549-2936-9(7))* Sterling Publishing Co., Inc.

Batterson, Jason. Beast Academy Guide 3C. Owen, Erich, illus. 2012. 112p. pap. 15.00 *(978-1-934124-44-4(3))* AoPS Inc.

Batterson, Jason & Rogers, Shannon. Beast Academy Practice 3A. 2012. (Illus.). 128p. pap. 12.00 *(978-1-934124-41-3(9))* AoPS Inc.

Baumann, Leigh. Jekyll Island Fun Book. 2008. 64p. (J). pap. 9.95 *(978-0-9769510-1-8(0))* Seascape Pr.

—St. Simons Island Fun Book. 2008. 64p. (J). pap. 9.95 *(978-0-9769510-2-5(9))* Seascape Pr.

Baxter, Nicola & Birkinshaw, Marie. A Treasury for Little Ones: Hours of Fun for Babies & Toddlers - Stories & Rhymes, Puzzles to Solve, & Things to Make & Do. Endersby, Frank, illus. 2014. 80p. (J). (gr. -1-6). 14.99 *(978-1-86147-368-4(0),* Armadillo) Anness Publishing GBR. Dist: National Bk. Network.

Beecroft, Simon & Harvey, Guy. The Tintin & Snowy Big Activity Book. 2011. (ENG., Illus.). 96p. (J). pap. 19.95 *(978-0-86719-761-7(7))* Last Gasp of San Francisco.

Berghof, Michael. The Story of Christmas: Carry-Me Puzzle Book. 2011. 8p. (J). 12.99 *(978-0-7586-2798-8(X))* Concordia Publishing Hse.

Berthel, Alice H. Power Puzzles: John. 2007. (J). per. 12.95 *(978-1-59352-193-6(6))* Christian Services Publishing.

—Power Puzzles: Luke. 2007. (J). per. 12.95 *(978-1-59352-192-9(8))* Christian Services Publishing.

—Power Puzzles: Matthew. 2006. (J). per. 12.95 *(978-1-59352-174-5(0))* Christian Services Publishing.

Best Travel Activity Book Ever! (Backseat Bks.). (Illus.). 256p. (J). pap. 3.95 *(978-0-528-96542-5(5))* Rand McNally.

Beth, Georgia. Fun & Games: Mazes: Perimeter & Area (Grade 4) 2017. (Mathematics in the Real World Ser.). (ENG., Illus.). 32p. (gr. 4-5). pap. 11.99 *(978-1-4258-5561-1(X))* Teacher Created Materials, Inc.

Beylon, Cathy. Easy Beauty & the Beast Sticker Picture Puzzle. 2006. (Dover Little Activity Bks.). (ENG., Illus.). 4p. (J). (gr. -1-2). 1.50 *(978-0-486-44473-4(2))* Dover Pubns., Inc.

—Easy Firehouse Sticker Picture Puzzle. 2005. (Dover Little Activity Bks.). (ENG., Illus.). 4p. (J). (gr. -1-2). 1.50 *(978-0-486-43850-4(3))* Dover Pubns., Inc.

—Easy Nativity Scene Sticker Picture Puzzle. 2012. (Dover Little Activity Bks.). (ENG., Illus.). 4p. (J). (gr. k-3). 2.50 *(978-0-486-44824-4(X),* 44824X) Dover Pubns., Inc.

—Easy Noah's Ark Sticker Picture Puzzle. 2004. (Dover Little Activity Bks.). (ENG., Illus.). 4p. (J). (gr. k-2). 1.50 *(978-0-486-43864-1(3))* Dover Pubns., Inc.

Bixley, Donovan. The Christmas Looky Book. 2023. (ENG., Illus.). 24p. (J). (gr. k-17). pap. 15.99 *(978-1-86971-345-4(1))* Hachette Australia AUS. Dist: Hachette Bk. Group.

Black, Nessa. Biking. 2020. (Spot Outdoor Fun Ser.). (ENG.). 16p. (J). (gr. -1-2). lib. bdg. *(978-1-68151-807-7(4),* 10681) Amicus.

—Camping. 2020. (Spot Outdoor Fun Ser.). (ENG.). 16p. (J). (gr. -1-2). lib. bdg. *(978-1-68151-808-4(2),* 10682) Amicus.

Blair, Beth L. The Everything Kids' Hidden Pictures Book: Hours of Challenging Fun! 2003. (Everything(r) Kids Ser.). (ENG., Illus.). 144p. pap. 9.99 *(978-1-59337-128-9(4),* Everything) Adams Media Corp.

—The Everything Kids' Pirates Puzzle & Activity Book: Set Sail into a Treasure-Trove of Fun! 3rd ed. 2006. (Everything(r) Kids Ser.). (ENG., Illus.). 144p. per., act. bk. ed. 9.99 *(978-1-59337-607-9(3),* Everything) Adams Media Corp.

Blair, Beth L. & Ericsson, Jennifer A. The Everything Kids' Animal Puzzles & Activity Book: Slither, Soar, & Swing Through a Jungle of Fun! 2005. (Everything(r) Kids Ser.). (ENG., Illus.). 144p. pap., act. bk. ed. 15.99 *(978-1-59337-305-4(8),* Everything) Adams Media Corp.

—The Everything Kids' Games & Puzzles Book: Secret Codes, Twisty Mazes, Hidden Pictures, & Lots More - for Hours of Fun! 2013. (Everything(r) Kids Ser.). (ENG.). 144p. pap. 9.99 *(978-1-4405-6087-3(0))* Adams Media Corp.

—The Everything Kids' Hanukkah Puzzle & Activity Book: Games, Crafts, Trivia, Songs, & Traditions to Celebrate the Festival of Lights! 2008. (Everything(r) Kids Ser.). (ENG., Illus.). 144p. pap., act. bk. ed. 9.99 *(978-1-59869-788-9(9),* Everything) Adams Media Corp.

—The Everything Kids' More Amazing Mazes Book: Wind Your Way Through Hours of Adventurous Fun! 2010. (Everything(r) Kids Ser.). (ENG., Illus.). 144p. pap. 16.99 *(978-1-4405-0150-0(5),* Everything) Adams Media Corp.

—The Everything Kids' Mummies, Pharaohs, & Pyramids Puzzle & Activity Book: Discover the Mysterious Secrets of Ancient Egypt. 2008. (Everything(r) Kids Ser.). (ENG.). 144p. pap., act. bk. ed. 11.50 *(978-1-59869-797-1(8),* Everything) Adams Media Corp.

—The Everything Kids' Picture Puzzles Book: Hidden Pictures, Matching Games, Pattern Puzzles, & More! 2014. (Everything(r) Kids Ser.). (ENG.). 144p. pap. 15.99 *(978-1-4405-7067-4(1),* Everything) Adams Media Corp.

Blank, Left. We're Going on a Bear Hunt: Let's Discover Bugs. 2018. (We're Going on a Bear Hunt Ser.). (ENG., Illus.). 32p. (J). (gr. k-3). pap. 9.99 *(978-1-5362-0070-6(0),* Candlewick Entertainment) Candlewick Pr.

Blincoe, Neale. How to Dazzle at Maths Crosswords. 2004. 48p. (J). pap. 30.00 *(978-1-903853-38-2(9))* Brilliant Pubns. GBR. Dist: Parkwest Pubns., Inc.

Block, Cheryl. Think Analogies B1: Learning to Connect Words & Relationships. 2013. (Think Analogies Books ThinkAnalogy Puzzles Software Ser.). 64p. (gr. 6-12). pap. 11.99 *(978-0-89455-792-7(0))* Critical Thinking Co., The.

Bloom, Jonathan. The Must Have Sudoku Holiday Gift 480 Puzzles. 2012. 278p. pap. *(978-0-9814261-5-0(8))* Sudokids.Com.

Blue Ox Technologies Ltd., Blue Ox & York, Christopher. 7 Little Words for Kids: 100 Puzzles. 2014. (ENG.). 112p. (J). pap. 5.99 *(978-1-4494-4200-2(5))* Andrews McMeel Publishing.

Blundell, Kim & Tyler, Jenny. Big Book of Mazes. rev. ed. 2005. 72p. (J). pap. 10.95 *(978-0-7945-0697-1(6),* Usborne) EDC Publishing.

Blythe, Philip. Nature Hunt! Bewildering Puzzles of the Animal Kingdom. Blythe, Philip, illus. 2005. (ENG., Illus.). 32p. pap., act. bk. ed. *(978-1-877003-82-0(4))* Little Hare Bks. AUS. Dist: HarperCollins Pubs. Australia.

Boardworks Learning Centers: Figure It Out. 2006. (J). bds. *(978-0-9755252-4-1(7))* Evergreen Pr. of Brainerd, LLC.

Bodach, Vijaya Khisty. What Is Missing? 2008. (Discovering & Exploring Science Ser.). (Illus.). 16p. (J). (gr. -1-3). lib. bdg. 12.95 *(978-0-7569-8253-9(7))* Perfection Learning Corp.

Bonogofsky-Gronseth, Jimi. Grumpy Cat's Word Play Book. 2018. (Dover Kids Activity Books: Animals Ser.). (ENG.). 64p. (gr. 2-4). pap. 5.99 *(978-0-486-82469-7(1),* 824691) Dover Pubns., Inc.

Book Company Staff. Busy Bugs. 2003. (Puzzles Ser.). (Illus.). (J). bds. 10.95 *(978-1-74047-335-4(3))* Book Co. Publishing Pty, Ltd., The AUS. Dist: Penton Overseas, Inc.

—Ocean Friends. Lassen, Christian R., illus. 2003. (Puzzles Ser.). (J). bds. 14.95 *(978-1-74047-381-1(7))* Book Co. Publishing Pty, Ltd., The AUS. Dist: Penton Overseas, Inc.

Boos, Andre, illus. Amazing Animal Puzzle Stickers: #1, 1 vol. 2005. (Amazing Animal Puzzle Stickers Ser.). (ENG.). 8p. (J). pap. 5.99 *(978-1-59496-063-5(1))* Teora USA LLC.

—Amazing Animal Puzzle Stickers: #3, 1 vol., Vol. 3. 2005. (Amazing Animal Puzzle Stickers Ser.). (ENG.). 8p. (J). pap. 5.99 *(978-1-59496-065-9(8))* Teora USA LLC.

Booth, Karon. Aslan Is on the Move: Romp in Narnia with Study Helps, Art & Play. 2003. (Illus.). 196p. (J). per. *(978-0-941367-13-4(4))* Peach Blossom Pubns.

Brain Games, 8 vols. 2014. (Brain Games Ser.). (ENG.). 32p. (J). (gr. 4-4). 121.08 *(978-1-4777-5457-3(1),* 9e079a37-f436-411e-8e83-44c41cf9c2f7, Windmill Bks.) Rosen Publishing Group, Inc., The.

Brandreth, Gyles. Madcap Book of Brain Teasers. Axworthy, Anni & Miller, Mike, illus. 288p. (J). pap. 6.95 *(978-0-233-99568-7(4))* Andre Deutsch GBR. Dist: Trafalgar Square Publishing.

Brian, Sarah Jane. Brainiac's Mindbenders: Fun Activities for Geniuses of All Ages. 2005. (Activity Journal Ser.). (Illus.). 128p. (J). act. bk. ed. 12.99 *(978-0-88088-591-1(2))* Peter Pauper Pr. Inc.

—Brainiac's Secret Agent: Fun Activities for Spies of All Ages. 2004. (ENG., Illus.). 128p. (J). spiral bd., act. bk. ed. 12.99 *(978-0-88088-446-4(0),* fcd2348a-df74-4c82-b862-cd446ccbc491) Peter Pauper Pr. Inc.

Bridgewater, Glyn. Dot-To-Dot Ancient World: Join the Dots to Discover the Wonders of Antiquity, with up to 1098 Dots. 2017. (Illus.). 96p. (J). (gr. -1-12). pap. 12.99 *(978-1-78019-511-7(7),* Southwater) Anness Publishing GBR. Dist: National Bk. Network.

—Dot-To-Dot Natural World: Join the Dots to Discover Fascinating Scenes from Nature, with up to 1324 Dots. 2017. (Illus.). 96p. (J). (gr. -1-12). pap. 12.99 *(978-1-78019-512-4(5),* Southwater) Anness Publishing GBR. Dist: National Bk. Network.

British Broadcasting Corporation Staff. When's the Doctor? 2012. (ENG., Illus.). 40p. (YA). 14.99 *(978-1-4059-0849-8(1),* bbfdd1c2-f674-4a70-a218-c1efb8adcc02) Penguin Bks., Ltd. GBR. Dist: Diamond Comic Distributors, Inc.

Brooke, Jasmine. Goldilocks & the Three Bears: Take the Temperature Test & Solve the Porridge Puzzle! 2017. (Fairy Tale Fixers: Fixing Fairy Tale Problems with STEM Ser.). 32p. (gr. 3-4). pap. 63.00 *(978-1-5382-0665-2(X))* Stevens, Gareth Publishing LLLP.

Brooks, Felicity. Big Red Tractor. Cartwright, Stephen, illus. 2006. (Usborne Farmyard Tales Jigsaw Bks.). 10p. (J). (gr. -1-k). bds. 7.99 *(978-0-7945-1130-2(9),* Usborne) EDC Publishing.

—Juega con Gabi. 2006. 10p. (J). bds. 8.99 *(978-0-7460-7387-2(9),* Usborne) EDC Publishing.

—Naughty Woolly. Cartwright, Stephen, illus. 2006. (Usborne Farmyard Tales Jigsaw Bks.). 10p. (J). bds. 7.99 *(978-0-7945-1128-9(7),* Usborne) EDC Publishing.

—Rusty's Friends. Cartwright, Stephen, illus. 2006. (Usborne Farmyard Tales Jigsaw Bks.). 10p. (J). bds. 7.99 *(978-0-7945-1127-2(9),* Usborne) EDC Publishing.

—Tractors Chunky Jigsaw Book. 2005. (Chunky Jigsaw Books Ser.). 14p. (J). 7.95 *(978-0-7945-0861-6(8),* Usborne) EDC Publishing.

—Trains Chunky Jigsaw Book. 2005. (Chunky Jigsaw Books Ser.). 14p. (J). 7.95 *(978-0-7945-0859-3(6),* Usborne) EDC Publishing.

—Usborne Shapes Jigsaw Book. 2008. (Usborne Jigsaw Bks.). (Illus.). 12p. (J). (gr. -1-3). bds. 9.99 *(978-0-7945-2046-5(4),* Usborne) EDC Publishing.

Brooks, Felicity & Tyler, Jenny. The Usborne 1,2,3 Jigsaw Book. Cartwright, Stephen, illus. 2006. (Usborne Jigsaw Bks.). 12p. (J). (gr. -1-k). bds. 15.95 *(978-0-7945-1168-5(6),* Usborne) EDC Publishing.

Brooks, Felicity, et al. The Counting Train. Cartwright, Stephen, illus. 2006. (J). *(978-0-439-89922-2(2))* Scholastic, Inc.

Brown, Jeff. Amazing Washington! A Collection of Puzzlers, Mazes, & Fun! 2005. (Amazing State-by-State Puzzles Ser.). (Illus.). 48p. (J). (gr. 3-7). per. 6.00 *(978-0-87842-508-2(X),* 345) Mountain Pr. Publishing Co., Inc.

Bruning, Matt. Baby Animal Picture Puzzles, 1 vol. 2009. (Look, Look Again Ser.). (ENG.). 32p. (J). (gr. -1-2). lib. bdg. 27.99 *(978-1-4296-3288-1(7),* 95697, Capstone Pr.) Capstone.

—Mighty Machines Picture Puzzles, 1 vol. 2009. (Look, Look Again Ser.). (ENG.). 32p. (J). (gr. -1-2). lib. bdg. 27.99 *(978-1-4296-3289-8(5),* 95698, Capstone Pr.) Capstone.

Bryant-Mole, Karen. Dot-to-Dot Animals. rev. ed. 2004. (Dot to Dot Ser.). (Illus.). 24p. (J). pap. 3.99 *(978-0-7945-0497-7(3))* EDC Publishing.

—Dot-to-Dot in Space. 2004. (Dot to Dot Ser.). (Illus.). 24p. (J). pap. 3.95 *(978-0-7945-0495-3(7))* EDC Publishing.

—Dot-to-Dot Machines. Tyler, Jenny, ed. Round, Graham, illus. rev. ed. 2006. (Dot to Dot Ser.). 22p. (J). (gr. -1-2). pap. 3.99 *(978-0-7945-1495-2(2),* Usborne) EDC Publishing.

—Dot-to-Dot Nature. 2004. (Dot to Dot Ser.). (Illus.). 24p. (J). 3.99 *(978-0-7945-0493-9(0))* EDC Publishing.

Bui, Tak. Spot the Difference. 2012. (Illus.). 48p. (J). (gr. 2-5). pap. 9.95 *(978-1-77049-279-0(8),* Tundra Bks.) Tundra Bks. CAN. Dist: Penguin Random Hse. LLC.

The Bunty Annual 2004. annuals 2004. 128p. (J). 9.95 *(978-0-85116-882-1(5))* Thomson, D.C. & Co., Ltd. GBR. Dist: APG Sales & Distribution Services.

Burchett, Author Walter, BA. Christian children's circle the Word. 2008. (ENG.). 34p. pap. 6.95 *(978-0-557-02505-3(2))* Lulu Pr., Inc.

Burgess, Mark. Mutiny at Crossbones Bay. Cox, Phil Roxbee, ed. Burgess, Mark, illus. 2006. (Usborne Puzzle Adventures Ser.). (Illus.). 48p. (J). (gr. 3-7). pap. 4.99 *(978-0-7945-1407-5(3),* Usborne) EDC Publishing.

Busiere, Agnes. What's Hiding Here? 2016. (ENG., Illus.). 96p. 14.95 *(978-1-77085-823-7(7),* 642e20cb-fdbb-4532-84ad-35192aebd120) Firefly Bks., Ltd.

Buster Books. Odd One Out. 2018. (ENG., Illus.). 96p. (J). (gr. 5). pap. 9.99 *(978-1-5247-9088-2(5),* Penguin Workshop) Penguin Young Readers Group.

Butterfield, Moira. My First Color by Numbers & Shapes: Over 50 Fantastic Puzzles. Muntada, Anna Clariana, illus. 2018. (My First Activity Bks.). (ENG.). 64p. (J). (gr. -1-2). pap. 5.99 *(978-1-4380-1143-1(1))* Sourcebooks, Inc.

—My First Picture Puzzles: Over 50 Fantastic Puzzles. Rimmington, Natasha, illus. 2018. (My First Activity Bks.). (ENG.). 64p. (J). (gr. -1-2). pap. 5.99 *(978-1-4380-1144-8(X))* Sourcebooks, Inc.

Capstone Press. Spot It. 2010. (Spot It Ser.). (ENG.). 32p. lib. bdg. 155.94 *(978-1-4296-5911-6(4),* Capstone Pr.) Capstone.

Carlson, George Leonard & Martin, John. Peter Puzzlemaker: A John Martin Puzzle-Book. 2014. (Dover Kids Activity Bks.). (ENG., Illus.). 112p. (J). (gr. 1-5). pap. 7.99 *(978-0-486-78167-9(4),* 781674) Dover Pubns., Inc.

Carlton Books Staff & Allen, Robert. Mensa Mighty Mystery Puzzles for Kids. 2003. (Illus.). 256p. pap. *(978-1-84222-925-5(7))* Carlton Bks., Ltd.

Carmona, Lisa. Codes & Puzzles. 2018. (ENG., Illus.). 64p. (J). (gr. 1-3). pap., wbk. ed. 4.49 *(978-1-58947-055-2(9),* 31ae6383-ae29-4b85-80cc-bd2c70ced7fe) School Zone Publishing Co.

Carson-Dellosa Publishing Staff. Puzzles & Games for Math, Grade 1. 2010. (Home Workbooks Ser.: 14). (ENG.). 64p. (gr. 1-1). pap. 4.49 *(978-1-60418-791-5(3),* 104360) Carson-Dellosa Publishing, LLC.

Carson-Dellosa Publishing Staff, compiled by. Puzzles & Games for Math, Grade 2. 2010. (Home Workbooks Ser.: 15). (ENG.). 64p. (gr. 2-2). pap. 4.49 *(978-1-60418-798-4(0),* 104367) Carson-Dellosa Publishing, LLC.

Carson, Karen. Horseplay: 50 Puzzles & Games for Horse Lovers. 2004. 68p. (J). pap. 9.95 *(978-1-57779-068-6(5))* Alpine Pubns., Inc.

Cartwright, S. Fairy Jigsaw Puzzle. gif. ed. 2004. (Fairy Jigsaw in A Box Ser.). (Illus.). (J). 11.95 *(978-0-7945-0592-9(9))* EDC Publishing.

Cartwright, Stephen. Abc Floor. Cartwright, Stephen, illus. 2006. (Illus.). 16p. (J). bds. 15.99 *(978-0-7945-1367-2(0),* Usborne) EDC Publishing.

Catlow, Nikalas, illus. Mind Your Own Business! A File of Super Secret Stuff. 2007. (ENG.). 224p. (J). 8.00 *(978-1-84046-763-5(0),* Wizard Books) Icon Bks., Ltd. GBR. Dist: Publishers Group Canada.

Cats & Dogs Picture Puzzle Book. 2017. (Picture Puzzle Bks.). (ENG.). (J). bds. 14.99 *(978-0-7945-3925-2(4),* Usborne) EDC Publishing.

Chamberlain, Kim. The Five-Minute Brain Workout for Kids: 365 Amazing, Fabulous, & Fun Word Puzzles. Chamberlain, Jon, illus. 2015. (ENG.). 416p. (J). (gr. 1-1). pap. 14.99 *(978-1-63450-159-0(4),* Sky Pony Pr.) Skyhorse Publishing Co., Inc.

Chedru, Delphine. Spot It Again! Find More Hidden Creatures. 2011. (ENG., Illus.). 40p. (J). (gr. 1-17). 15.95

(978-0-8109-9736-3(3), 690701, Abrams Bks. for Young Readers) Abrams, Inc.
Child, Jeni. Dot-To-Dot Mystery & Magic: Join the Dots to Discover a World of Enchantment. 2017. (Illus.). 96p. (J). (gr. -1-12). pap. 12.99 *(978-1-78019-513-1(3)*, Southwater) Anness Publishing GBR. Dist: National Bk. Network.
—Dot-To-Dot: under the Sea: Join the Dots to Discover the World below the Waves & on the High Seas. 2017. (Illus.). 96p. (J). (gr. -1-12). pap. 12.99 *(978-1-78019-514-8(1)*, Southwater) Anness Publishing GBR. Dist: National Bk. Network.
Children of the World (Gr. 2-4) 2003. (J). *(978-1-58232-057-1(8))* ECS Learning Systems, Inc.
Children's Puzzle Book. 2003. (J). per. *(978-1-884907-26-5(1))*; per. *(978-1-884907-27-2(X))* Paradise Pr., Inc.
Christmas Dot to Dot: Santa's Big Dot to Dot. 2004. (J). per. 6.95 *(978-1-885920-89-8(X))* Pyramid Publishing, Inc.
The Christmas Puzzle: An Easy-To-sing, Easy-to-stage Kids' Christmas Musical about How We're All Part of God's Picture. 2010. (ENG.). 48p. pap. 5.99 *(978-0-8341-7784-0(6)*, 9780834177840) Lillenas Publishing Co.
Chronicle Books. Space Matching Game: Featuring Photos from the Archives of NASA. 2015. (ENG., Illus.). 56p. (J). (gr. -1-1). 14.99 *(978-1-4521-3390-4(5))* Chronicle Bks. LLC.
Cimmet, Brian. Delicious Word Searches. 2013. (ENG.). 160p. pap. 11.99 *(978-1-4549-0052-8(0)*, Puzzlewright) Sterling Publishing Co., Inc.
Clarke, Catriona. Pirates. McKenna, Terry, illus. 2006. (Beginners Social Studies: Level 2 Ser.). 32p. (J). (gr. 1-3). 4.99 *(978-0-7945-1332-0(8)*, Usborne) EDC Publishing.
Claybourne, Anna. Where's Will? Find Shakespeare Hidden in His Plays. Tilly, illus. 2015. (J). *(978-1-61067-407-2(3))* Kane Miller.
—1001Things to Spot in the Town. 2009. (1001 Things to Spot Ser.). 32p. (J). 9.99 *(978-0-7945-2514-9(8)*, Usborne) EDC Publishing.
Cleary, Brian P. Madam & Nun And 1001: What Is a Palindrome? Gable, Brian, illus. 2012. (Words Are CATegorical (r) Ser.). (ENG.). 32p. (J). (gr. 2-5). lib. bdg. 16.95 *(978-0-7613-4919-8(7)*, 3bd3b287-3ead-4334-b324-5b590fb293ba, Millbrook Pr.) Lerner Publishing Group.
Clifton, Gillian. Puzzle Pieces: Sticking to It. 1 vol. 2017. (Computer Science for the Real World Ser.). (ENG.). 12p. (gr. 1-2). pap. *(978-1-5383-5184-0(6)*, da00823d-a7be-41ff-9d50-ba8d1e3b11eb, Rosen Classroom) Rosen Publishing Group, Inc., The.
Coat, Janik. Who's New at the Zoo. 2017. (ENG., Illus.). 64p. (J). (gr. -1-k). 14.99 *(978-1-78055-455-6(9))* O'Mara, Michael Bks., Ltd. GBR. Dist: Independent Pubs. Group.
Cole, Jeff. Flip & Click Big Book of Games: 100 Games. 2009. (ENG.). 208p. (J). (gr. -1). pap. 11.99 *(978-0-7407-8154-4(5))* Andrews McMeel Publishing.
Cole, Jeff & Stone, Kate. Stick to It - Toys: A Magnetic Puzzle Book. 2011. (ENG., Illus.). 14p. (J). bds. 16.99 *(978-1-4494-0499-4(5))* Andrews McMeel Publishing.
Conceptis, Puzzles. Dot to Dot Puzzles for the Weekend. 2019. (Puzzlewright Junior Dot-To-Dot Ser.: 2). (ENG.). 96p. (J). (gr. 2-6). pap. 6.95 *(978-1-4549-3157-7(4)*, Puzzlewright) Sterling Publishing Co., Inc.
Conceptis Puzzles. Dot-To-Dot Puzzles for Vacation. 2018. (Puzzlewright Junior Dot-To-Dot Ser.: 1). (ENG.). 96p. (J). (gr. 2-6). pap. 6.95 *(978-1-4549-3023-5(3)*, Puzzlewright) Sterling Publishing Co., Inc.
Conley, Erin, ed. Dinomite. 2006. (Spinner Bks.). (ENG., Illus.). 160p. (J). (gr. -1-3). pap. 7.95 *(978-1-57528-948-9(2))* Univ. Games.
—Madcap Mazes. 2005. (Made You Laugh for Kids). (ENG., Illus.). 96p. pap. 5.95 *(978-1-57528-931-1(8))* Univ. Games.
Conrad, Hy. Kids' Whodunits: Catch the Clues!, 1. Blanchard, Sue, illus. 2007. (Jonah Bixby Mystery: Kid Detective! Ser.). (ENG.). 90p. (J). (gr. 2-4). 18.69 *(978-1-4027-3966-8(4))* Sterling Publishing Co., Inc.
Contraire, Bastien. Animals: Hide & Sneak. 2017. (ENG., Illus.). 26p. (gr. -1 — 1). bds. 9.95 *(978-0-7148-7422-7(1))* Phaidon Pr., Inc.
—Food: Hide & Sneak. 2018. (ENG., Illus.). 26p. (gr. -1 — 1). bds. 9.95 *(978-0-7148-7723-5(9))* Phaidon Pr., Inc.
Corr, Christopher. Map of the World Play Scene. 2005. (J). 9.99 *(978-0-7353-0898-5(5))* Galison.
—Whole World: Fun Eco Activities. 2008. (Illus.). 24p. (J). pap. 4.99 *(978-1-84686-220-5(5))* Barefoot Bks., Inc.
Counting Puzzles. Date not set. (Illus.). 96p. (J). 2.98 *(978-0-7525-7519-3(8))* Parragon, Inc.
Creek, Lorie. Who Is This Jesus? A Hidden Picture Book. Creek, Chris, illus. 2012. (J). 18.99 *(978-1-60908-909-2(X))* Deseret Bk. Co.
Critical Thinking-What's Wrong with This Picture? (Gr. 1-3) 2003. (J). *(978-1-58232-066-3(7))* ECS Learning Systems, Inc.
Crompton, Richmal. Just William's Puzzles. 2003. (ENG.). 64p. (J). pap. 3.95 *(978-0-333-62680-1(X))* Macmillan Pubs., Ltd. GBR. Dist: Trafalgar Square Publishing.
Cronin, B. B. The Lost Cousins. 2019. (Illus.). 40p. (J). (gr. -1-2). 19.99 *(978-0-451-47908-2(4)*, Viking Books for Young Readers) Penguin Young Readers Group.
—The Lost House. 2016. (Illus.). 40p. (J). (gr. -1-2). 18.99 *(978-1-101-99921-9(7)*, Viking Books for Young Readers) Penguin Young Readers Group.
Curious Baby Everyday Shapes. 2012. (Curious Baby Curious George Ser.). (ENG., Illus.). 12p. (J). (gr. -1 — 1). bds. 8.99 *(978-0-547-63232-2(0)*, 1467421, Clarion Bks.) HarperCollins Pubs.
Curry, Don, ed. Jungle Fun: Puzzles & Games. 2008. 10p. (J). bds. 9.99 *(978-0-696-23491-0(2))* Meredith Bks.
Curtis, Dolores. Rhyming Pretzels. 2003. pap. 21.00 *(978-0-8059-5907-9(6))* Dorrance Publishing Co., Inc.
D C Thomson Staff, ed. Animals & You Annual 2004. 2003. (Illus.). 128p. (J). 9.95 *(978-0-85116-840-1(X))* Thomson, D.C. & Co., Ltd. GBR. Dist: APG Sales & Distribution Services.
—Bunty Annual for Girls 2004. 2003. (Illus.). 128p. (J). (gr. -1-4). *(978-0-85116-825-8(6))* Thomson, D.C. & Co., Ltd. GBR. Dist: APG Sales & Distribution Services.
Danna, M. Word Search Puzzles for Vacation. 2018. (Puzzlewright Junior Word Search Puzzles Ser.: 4). (ENG.). 96p. (J). (gr. 2-6). pap. 6.95 *(978-1-4549-2960-4(X)*, Puzzlewright) Sterling Publishing Co., Inc.
Danna, Mark. Word Search Puzzles for Clever Kids. 2017. (Puzzlewright Junior Word Search Puzzles Ser.: 1). (ENG.). 96p. (J). (gr. 2-6). pap. 7.95 *(978-1-4549-2280-3(X)*, Puzzlewright) Sterling Publishing Co., Inc.
Daste, Larry. Easy Gingerbread House Sticker Picture Puzzle. 2004. (Dover Little Activity Bks.). (ENG., Illus.). 4p. (J). (gr. k-3). 1.99 *(978-0-486-43895-5(3))* Dover Pubns., Inc.
Daste, Larry, et al. Hidden Picture Mania. Boddy, Joe, illus. 2006. (Dover Kids Activity Bks.). (ENG.). 96p. (J). (gr. 3-6). per. 7.99 *(978-0-486-45911-0(X)*, 45911X) Dover Pubns., Inc.
Davenport, Maxine & Roberts, Cindy, illus. What Can You Spot? 2018. (J). *(978-1-4998-0737-0(6))* Little Bee Books Inc.
David, Juliet. Dot to Dot Coloring & Stickers Bk. 1, 1 vol., 1. Smith, Jan, illus. 2008. (Candle Activity Fun Ser.). 24p. (J). (gr. 4-7). pap. 6.99 *(978-0-8254-7360-9(8)*, Candle Bks.) Lion Hudson PLC GBR. Dist: Kregel Pubns.
David, R. Noahs Ark. 2010. 12p. *(978-965-91286-1-7(4))* Sifrei Bet Shearim Ltd.
David, R., illus. Joseph & His Brothers. 2010. 12p. *(978-965-91286-0-0(6))* Sifrei Bet Shearim Ltd.
Davidson, Susanna & Stowell, Louie. My First Fairyland Book. Raffaella, Ligi, illus. 2012. (My First Book Ser.). 16p. (J). ring bd. 6.99 *(978-0-7945-3227-7(6)*, Usborne) EDC Publishing.
Daynes, Katie. 1001 Things to Spot in the Sea. Gower, Teri, illus. 2009. (1001 Things to Spot Ser.). 32p. (J). (gr. 1). 9.99 *(978-0-7945-2615-3(2)*, Usborne) EDC Publishing.
—1001 Things to Spot in the Sea Sticker Book. 2015. (1001 Things to Spot Sticker Bks.). (ENG.). 32pp + 6p. (J). (gr. k-5). pap. 7.99 *(978-0-7945-3495-0(3)*, Usborne) EDC Publishing.
Del Moral, Susana. El Juego de las Formas. Zaidi, Nadeem, illus. 2005. (Baby Einstein: Libros de Carton Ser.). (SPA.). 6p. (J). (gr. -1). bds. *(978-970-718-303-2(9)*, Silver Dolphin en Español) Advanced Marketing, S. de R. L. de C. V.
Dixon, Andy. Star Quest. Brooks, Felicity, ed. Harris, Nick, illus. rev. ed. 2006. (Usborne Fantasy Puzzle Bks.). 32p. (YA). (gr. 7). pap. 7.99 *(978-0-7945-1099-2(X)*, Usborne) EDC Publishing.
DK. Ultimate Sticker Book: Bulldozer: Over 60 Reusable Full-Color Stickers. 2004. (Ultimate Sticker Book Ser.). (ENG.). 16p. (J). (gr. k-3). pap. 6.99 *(978-0-7566-0563-6(6)*, DK Children) Dorling Kindersley Publishing, Inc.
Doherty, Gillian. Fairyland Jigsaw Bk. Gower, Teri, illus. 2007. 14p. (J). bds. 14.99 *(978-0-7945-1430-3(8)*, Usborne) EDC Publishing.
—1001 Cosas Que Buscar en el Psia de las Hadas. Gower, Teri, illus. 2007. (Titles in Spanish Ser.). 32p. (J). 9.99 *(978-0-7460-8346-8(7)*, Usborne) EDC Publishing.
—1001 Things to Spot in Fairyland. Gower, Teri, illus. 2006. (Usborne 1001 Things to Spot Ser.). 32p. (J). (gr. 1-4). 9.99 *(978-0-7945-1220-0(8)*, Usborne) EDC Publishing.
—1001 Things to Spot Long Ago. 2010. (1001 Things to Spot Ser.). 32p. (J). 9.99 *(978-0-7945-2731-0(0)*, Usborne) EDC Publishing.
—1001 Things to Spot Long Ago. Brooks, Felicity, ed. Gower, Teri, illus. 2006. (Usborne 1001 Things to Spot Ser.). 32p. (J). (gr. 1). lib. bdg. 14.99 *(978-1-58086-963-8(7))* EDC Publishing.
—1001 Things to Spot on the Farm. 2009. (1001 Things to Spot Ser.). 32p. (J). 9.99 *(978-0-7945-2611-5(X)*, Usborne) EDC Publishing.
—1001 Wizard Things to Spot. Gower, Teri, illus. 2008. (Usborne 1001 Things to Spot Ser.). 31p. (J). (gr. 4-7). 9.99 *(978-0-7945-1860-8(5)*, Usborne) EDC Publishing.
Dolby, Karen & Fischel, Emma. Chocolate Island. 2004. (Young Puzzle Adventures Ser.). (Illus.). 32p. (J). (gr. 2-18). pap. 4.95 *(978-0-7945-0231-7(8)*, Usborne); lib. bdg. 12.95 *(978-1-58086-458-9(9))* EDC Publishing.
—Molly's Magic Carpet. 2004. (Young Puzzle Adventures Ser.). (Illus.). 32p. (J). (gr. 2-18). pap. 4.99 *(978-0-7945-0233-1(4)*, Usborne); lib. bdg. 12.99 *(978-1-58086-459-6(7))* EDC Publishing.
—Spooks' Surprise. 2004. (Young Puzzle Adventures Ser.). (Illus.). 32p. (J). (gr. 2-18). pap. 4.95 *(978-0-7945-0234-8(2)*, Usborne) EDC Publishing.
Donahue, Peter. Spot the Differences Picture Puzzles for Kids. 2014. (Dover Kids Activity Bks.). (ENG., Illus.). 64p. (J). (gr. k-5). pap. 9.99 *(978-0-486-78248-5(4)*, 782484) Dover Pubns., Inc.
Donahue, Peter & Whelon, Chuck. Super Fun Mazes. 2018. (Dover Kids Activity Bks.). (ENG.). 96p. (J). (gr. 1-4). pap. 9.99 *(978-0-486-82755-1(0)*, 827550) Dover Pubns., Inc.
Doolittle, John H. Dr. Funster's Creative Thinking Puzzlers A1: Creative Problem-Solving Fun. 2011. (Dr. Funster's Ser.). 45p. (gr. 3-5). pap. 7.99 *(978-0-89455-826-9(9))* Critical Thinking Co., The.
—Dr. Funster's Creative Thinking Puzzlers C1: Creative Problem-Solving Fun. 2003. (Dr. Funster's Ser.). 46p. (gr. 9-12). pap. 7.99 *(978-0-89455-828-3(5))* Critical Thinking Co., The.
Dorling Kindersley Publishing Staff. Leaf It to Cubs. 2008. 16p. (J). (gr. k-5). 2.49 *(978-0-7566-3324-0(9))* Dorling Kindersley Publishing, Inc.
Dover. Game on! Awesome Activities for Clever Kids. 2018. (Dover Kids Activity Bks.). (ENG.). 144p. (J). (gr. 3-6). pap. 12.99 *(978-0-486-82466-6(7)*, 824667) Dover Pubns., Inc.
Dr. Funster's Think-a-Minutes A1: Fast, Fun Brainwork for Higher Grades & Top Test Scores. 2013. (Dr. Funster's Ser.). 48p. (gr. 2-3). pap. 7.99 *(978-0-89455-806-1(4))* Critical Thinking Co., The.
Dr. Funster's Think-a-Minutes B1: Fast, Fun Brainwork for Higher Grades & Top Test Scores. 2008. (Dr. Funster's Ser.). 46p. (gr. 4-5). pap. 7.99 *(978-0-89455-808-5(0))* Critical Thinking Co., The.
Dr. Funster's Think-a-Minutes B2: Fast, Fun Brainwork for Higher Grades & Top Test Scores. 2005. (Dr. Funster's Ser.). 48p. (gr. 4-5). pap. 7.99 *(978-0-89455-809-2(9))* Critical Thinking Co., The.
Dr. Funster's Think-a-Minutes C1: Fast, Fun Brainwork for Higher Grades & Top Test Scores. 2006. (Dr. Funster's Ser.). 45p. (gr. 6-8). pap. 7.99 *(978-0-89455-810-8(2))* Critical Thinking Co., The.
Dr. Funster's Think-a-Minutes C2: Fast, Fun Brainwork for Higher Grades & Top Test Scores. 2005. (Dr. Funster's Ser.). 48p. (gr. 6-8). pap. 7.99 *(978-0-89455-811-5(0))* Critical Thinking Co., The.
Drimmer, Stephanie Warren. Brain Bogglers: Over 100 Games & Puzzles to Reveal the Mysteries of Your Mind. 2017. (Illus.). 176p. (J). (gr. 3-7). pap. 12.99 *(978-1-4263-2423-9(5)*, National Geographic Kids) Disney Publishing Worldwide.
—Brain Games: Big Book of Boredom Busters. 2018. (Illus.). 160p. (J). (gr. 3-7). pap. 12.99 *(978-1-4263-3017-9(0)*, National Geographic Kids) Disney Publishing Worldwide.
—Mastermind: Over 100 Games, Tests, & Puzzles to Unleash Your Inner Genius. 2016. (Illus.). 176p. (J). (gr. 3-7). pap. 12.99 *(978-1-4263-2110-8(4)*, National Geographic Kids) Disney Publishing Worldwide.
Dudziuk, Kasia, et al. My First Activity Book. 2018. (ENG.). 256p. (J). pap. 14.99 *(978-1-78828-303-8(1)*, fc75b1f1-8027-4cf0-95a5-902b2012a5b6) Arcturus Publishing GBR. Dist: Baker & Taylor Publisher Services (BTPS).
Ebert, Andrea & Parchow, Marc, illus. Odd One Out: Over 80 Timed Puzzles to Test Your Skill! 2017. (Challenging... Bks.). (ENG.). 96p. (J). (gr. 3-7). pap. 7.99 *(978-1-4380-1084-7(2))* Sourcebooks, Inc.
Eck, Kristin. Hide-and-Seek Animals. 2004. (Hide-And-Seek Books). (Illus.). (J). lib. bdg. 21.25 *(978-1-4042-2702-6(4)*, PowerKids Pr.) Rosen Publishing Group, Inc., The.
—Hide & Seek Animals. 2009. (Tough Toddler Bks). 16p. (gr. k-k). 42.50 *(978-1-60854-568-1(7)*, PowerKids Pr.) Rosen Publishing Group, Inc., The.
—Hide-and-Seek Clothes. 2004. (Hide-And-Seek Books). (Illus.). (J). lib. bdg. 21.25 *(978-1-4042-2705-7(9)*, PowerKids Pr.) Rosen Publishing Group, Inc., The.
—Hide & Seek Clothes. 2009. (Tough Toddler Bks). 16p. (gr. k-k). 42.50 *(978-1-60854-569-8(5)*, PowerKids Pr.) Rosen Publishing Group, Inc., The.
—Hide-and-Seek Food. 2004. (Hide-And-Seek Books). (Illus.). 16p. (J). lib. bdg. 21.25 *(978-1-4042-2703-3(2)*, PowerKids Pr.) Rosen Publishing Group, Inc., The.
—Hide & Seek Food. 2009. (Tough Toddler Bks). 16p. (gr. k-k). 42.50 *(978-1-60854-570-4(9)*, PowerKids Pr.) Rosen Publishing Group, Inc., The.
—Hide-and-Seek Toys. 2004. (Hide-And-Seek Books). (Illus.). (J). lib. bdg. 21.25 *(978-1-4042-2704-0(0)*, PowerKids Pr.) Rosen Publishing Group, Inc., The.
—Hide & Seek Toys. 2009. (Tough Toddler Bks). 16p. (gr. k-k). 42.50 *(978-1-60854-573-5(3)*, PowerKids Pr.) Rosen Publishing Group, Inc., The.
Editors of Silver Dolphin Books, ed. Highlights: Hidden Pictures: Fun on the Farm. 2017. (Pencil Toppers Ser.). (ENG., Illus.). 64p. (J). (gr. k-k). pap. 9.99 *(978-1-62686-910-3(3)*, Silver Dolphin Bks.) Printers Row Publishing Group.
Editors of Thunder Bay Press, ed. Large Print Dot-To-Dot. 2017. (Large Print Puzzle Bks.). (ENG., Illus.). 256p. pap. 12.99 *(978-1-68412-096-3(9)*, Thunder Bay Pr.) Printers Row Publishing Group.
Elder, Jeremy. Race Against the Clock! Secret Agent. 2011. (Dover Kids Activity Books: Fantasy Ser.). (ENG.). 48p. (gr. -1-8). pap., act. bk. ed. 4.99 *(978-0-486-47992-7(7)*, 479927) Dover Pubns., Inc.
—Space Agent. 2010. (Dover Children's Activity Bks.). (ENG., Illus.). 48p. (J). (gr. 2-5). pap. 4.99 *(978-0-486-47828-9(9))* Dover Pubns., Inc.
Elite Find-a-Word Puzzles. 2003. per. *(978-1-884907-16-6(4))* Paradise Pr., Inc.
Esparza, Thomas, Jr., prod. Esther's Playhouse, Disk D. 2004. (Illus.). (J). cd-rom *(978-1-879817-45-6(4)*, Children) Star Light Pr.
Espinosa, Génie. Spot the Differences: Search & Find Fun. 2019. (Dover Kids Activity Bks.). (ENG.). 96p. (J). (gr. -1-3). pap. 10.99 *(978-0-486-83231-9(7)*, 832317) Dover Pubns., Inc.
Farrell, Alison. Cycle City: (City Books for Kids, Find & Seek Books) 2018. (ENG., Illus.). 40p. (J). (gr. -1-k). 17.99 *(978-1-4521-6334-5(0))* Chronicle Bks. LLC.
Fatus, Sophie. Journey Home from Grandpa's. Fatus, Sophie, illus. 2012. (Illus.). (J). (gr. -1-1). 14.99 *(978-1-84686-745-3(2))* Barefoot Bks., Inc.
Felix the Cat/el Gato Felix: A Fun Surprise. 2005. 32p. (J). pap. *(978-0-9762071-1-5(7))* Big City Publishing.
Fink, Jeri & Paltrowitz, Donna. Gizmo's Tail Twisters. 2004. (Illus.). 36p. (J). per. 8.95 *(978-0-9716567-4-1(6))* Book Web Publishing, Limited.
Fitzpatrick, Joe. The Raggedy Snowman. Flowerpot Press, ed. 2012. (Illus.). 18p. (J). *(978-1-77093-112-1(0))* Flowerpot Children's Pr. Inc.
Flash Kids Editors, ed. Number Puzzles & Games: Grade Pre-K-K (Flash Skills) 2010. (Flash Skills Ser.). (ENG.). 64p. (J). pap. 3.95 *(978-1-4114-3464-6(1)*, Spark Publishing Group) Sterling Publishing Co., Inc.
Ford, Barbara E. Tangrams: The Magnificent Seven Piece Puzzle. 2003. (Illus.). 64p. bds. 19.95 *(978-0-9627337-7-2(6))* Tandora's Box Pr.
Francia, Giada. Alex & Penny's Italy Jigsaw Book. Colombo, Angelo, illus. 2007. (ENG.). 14p. (gr. 1-3). pap. 14.95 *(978-88-544-0242-3(7)*, White Star) Rizzoli International Pubns., Inc.
—Alex & Penny's Wild West Jigsaw Book. Colombo, Angelo, illus. 2007. (ENG.). 14p. (gr. 1-3). pap. 14.95 *(978-88-544-0285-0(0)*, White Star) Rizzoli International Pubns., Inc.
Fremont, Victoria & Flores, Brenda. All Around the World Search-a-Word Puzzles. 2011. (Dover Kids Activity Bks.). (ENG., Illus.). 64p. (gr. 3). 4.00 *(978-0-486-40842-2(6)*, 408426) Dover Pubns., Inc.
Frey, Daniel J., illus. Jacy's Coloring & Activity Book. 2006. 32p. (J). 3.00 *(978-0-9755314-2-6(5))* Majestic Publishing, LLC.
Friel, Helen, des. Midnight Monsters: A Pop-Up Shadow Search. 2018. (ENG., Illus.). 10p. (J). (gr. -1-k). 24.99 *(978-1-78627-320-8(9)*, King, Laurence Publishing) Orion Publishing Group, Ltd. GBR. Dist: Hachette Bk. Group.
Friel, Helen & Friel, Ian, creators. Hoakes Island: A Fiendish Puzzle Adventure. 2018. (ENG.). 64p. (J). (gr. 2-6). 17.99 *(978-1-78627-033-7(1)*, King, Laurence Publishing) Orion Publishing Group, Ltd. GBR. Dist: Hachette Bk. Group.
Frith, Alex. Travel Pocket Puzzle Book. 2015. (Pocket Activity Bks.). (ENG.). 128p. (J). (gr. k-5). pap. 6.99 *(978-0-7945-2743-3(4)*, Usborne) EDC Publishing.
Gallo, Ana. Sleuth & Solve 20+ Mind-Twisting Mysteries: (Mystery Book for Kids & Adults, Puzzle & Brain Teaser Book for All Ages) Escandell, Victor, illus. 2019. (ENG.). 64p. (J). (gr. 3-17). 18.99 *(978-1-4521-7713-7(9))* Chronicle Bks. LLC.
Gardner, Martin. Mind-Boggling Word Puzzles. Myers, V. G., illus. 2010. (Dover Kids Activity Bks.). (ENG.). 96p. (J). (gr. 3-5). pap. 4.99 *(978-0-486-47496-0(8)*, 474968) Dover Pubns., Inc.
George, Joshua. Tiny Town Let's Go Outside. Ribbon, Lemon, illus. 2018. (Tiny Town Build-A-Scene Ser.). (ENG.). 12p. (J). (gr. -1-k). bds. 12.99 *(978-1-78700-381-1(7))* Top That! Publishing PLC GBR. Dist: Independent Pubs. Group.
—Tiny Town Let's Go to the Shops. Ribbon, Lemon, illus. 2018. (Tiny Town Build-A-Scene Ser.). (ENG.). 12p. (J). (gr. -1-k). bds. 12.99 *(978-1-78700-387-3(6))* Top That! Publishing PLC GBR. Dist: Independent Pubs. Group.
Gikow, Louise. What Do You See? Ulrich, George, illus. 2005. (My First Reader Ser.). (ENG.). 32p. (J). (gr. k-1). 18.50 *(978-0-516-25177-6(5)*, Children's Pr.) Scholastic Library Publishing.
Gilpen, Rebecca. Boy's Activity Book. 2013. (Doodle Bks). 96p. (J). pap. 12.99 *(978-0-7945-3171-3(7)*, Usborne) EDC Publishing.
Girel, Stephane, illus. Where Is the Frog? A Children's Book Inspired by Claude Monet. 2013. (Children's Books Inspired by Famous Artworks Ser.). (ENG.). 32p. (J). (gr. -1-3). 14.95 *(978-3-7913-7139-9(8))* Prestel Verlag GmbH & Co KG. DEU. Dist: Penguin Random Hse. LLC.
Godwin, Edward. Logic Puzzles, 1 vol. 2014. (Brain Games Ser.). (ENG., Illus.). 32p. (J). (gr. 4-4). 30.27 *(978-1-4777-5439-9(3)*, 1b089796-65b3-4a91-94e5-75861328ce4d, Windmill Bks.) Rosen Publishing Group, Inc., The.
Greenwald, Todd J., contrib. by. Wizards of Waverly Place Ultimate Puzzle Book. 2009. (Wizards of Waverly Place Ser.). (Illus.). 192p. (J). pap. 4.99 *(978-0-7666-3305-6(5))* Modern Publishing.
Greenwell, Jessica. First Colors Sticker Book. 2015. (Get Ready for School Sticker Bks.). (ENG.). 24+8p. (J). pap. 7.99 *(978-0-7945-3600-8(X)*, Usborne) EDC Publishing.
Group/McGraw-Hill, Wright. And the Winner Is: Level N, 6 vols. 128p. (gr. 3-6). 36.95 *(978-0-322-05885-9(6))* Wright Group/McGraw-Hill.
—Bats about Bats! Level M, 6 vols. (Summer Skies Ser.). 128p. (gr. 3-6). 36.95 *(978-0-322-06724-0(3))* Wright Group/McGraw-Hill.
—Groovy Gran & the Karaoko Kid: Level S, 6 vols. (Whispering Pines Ser.). 128p. (gr. 5-18). 36.95 *(978-0-322-05906-1(2))* Wright Group/McGraw-Hill.
—How not to Catch the Moon: Level L, 6 vols. (Summer Skies Ser.). 128p. (gr. 3-6). 36.95 *(978-0-322-05886-6(4))* Wright Group/McGraw-Hill.
—Samantha's Sea: Level Q, 6 vols. (Whispering Pines Ser.). 128p. (gr. 5-18). 36.95 *(978-0-322-05907-8(0))* Wright Group/McGraw-Hill.
—Survival in Cyberspace: Level T, 6 vols. (Whispering Pines Ser.). 128p. (gr. 5-18). 36.95 *(978-0-322-05904-7(6))* Wright Group/McGraw-Hill.
—Wolf Master: Level R, 6 vols. (Whispering Pines Ser.). 128p. (J). (gr. 5-18). 36.95 *(978-0-322-05900-9(3))* Wright Group/McGraw-Hill.
Guterson, Ben. Winterhouse. Bristol, Chloe, illus. 2018. (Winterhouse Ser.: 1). (ENG.). 400p. (J). pap. 8.99 *(978-1-250-29419-7(3)*, 900174321) Square Fish.
Gutman, Dan. My Weird School: Jokes, Games, & Puzzles. Paillot, Jim, illus. 2018. (My Weird School Ser.). (ENG.). 192p. (J). (gr. 1-5). pap. 5.99 *(978-0-06-279687-5(9)*, HarperCollins) HarperCollins Pubs.
Handford, Martin. Where's Waldo? Destination: Everywhere! 12 Classic Scenes As You've Never Seen Them Before! Handford, Martin, illus. 2017. (Where's Waldo? Ser.). (ENG., Illus.). 32p. (J). (gr. k-4). 19.99 *(978-0-7636-9726-6(5))* Candlewick Pr.
—Where's Waldo? Games on the Go! Puzzles, Activities, & Searches. Handford, Martin, illus. 2018. (Where's Waldo? Ser.). (ENG., Illus.). 64p. (J). (gr. k-4). pap. 14.99 *(978-1-5362-0155-0(3))* Candlewick Pr.
—Where's Waldo? the Incredible Paper Chase. Handford, Martin, illus. 2009. (Where's Waldo? Ser.). (ENG., Illus.). 24p. (J). (gr. k-4). 17.99 *(978-0-7636-4689-9(X))* Candlewick Pr.
—Where's Waldo? the Spectacular Spotlight Search. Handford, Martin, illus. 2018. (Where's Waldo? Ser.). (ENG., Illus.). 16p. (J). (gr. k-4). 18.99 *(978-1-5362-0176-5(6))* Candlewick Pr.
HARCOURT. A Kid's Guide to Washington, D. c: Revised & Updated Edition. Brown, Richard, illus. rev. ed. 2008. (ENG.). 160p. (J). (gr. 1-4). pap. 15.99 *(978-0-15-206125-8(8)*, 1198393, Clarion Bks.) HarperCollins Pubs.
Harper, Charles. Alphabet Children Puzzle Book. 2013. 40p. pap. 19.57 *(978-1-4907-0660-3(7))* Trafford Publishing.
Harrison, Erica, illus. Box of Fairies. 2005. 6p. (J). 11.95 *(978-0-7945-1125-8(2)*, Usborne) EDC Publishing.
Harte, May. Hide-and-Seek Kids. 2004. (Hide-And-Seek Books). (Illus.). (J). lib. bdg. 21.25 *(978-1-4042-2816-0(0)*, PowerKids Pr.) Rosen Publishing Group, Inc., The.
—Hide & Seek Kids. 2009. (Tough Toddler Bks). 16p. (gr. k-k). 42.50 *(978-1-60854-571-1(7)*, PowerKids Pr.) Rosen Publishing Group, Inc., The.
—Hide-and-Seek Pets. 2004. (Hide-And-Seek Books). (J). lib. bdg. 21.25 *(978-1-4042-2815-3(2)*, PowerKids Pr.) Rosen Publishing Group, Inc., The.
—Hide & Seek Pets. 2009. (Tough Toddler Bks). 16p. (gr. k-k). 42.50 *(978-1-60854-572-8(5)*, PowerKids Pr.) Rosen Publishing Group, Inc., The.
Haughom, Lisa, illus. Things That Go! 2010. 16p. (J). *(978-1-58865-542-4(3))* Kidsbooks, LLC.
Helbrough, Emma. Great Planet Earth Search. Milbourne, Anna, ed. Jackson, Ian, illus. 2005. (Great Searches Ser.). 32p. (J). (gr. 3). lib. bdg. 15.95 *(978-1-58086-827-3(4))* EDC Publishing.

Herzog, Brad. I Spy with My Little Eye Baseball: Baseball. Milne, David, illus. 2011. (I Spy with My Little Eye Ser.). (ENG.). 32p. (J). (gr. 1-4). 15.99 *(978-1-58536-496-1(7),* 202195) Sleeping Bear Pr.

Heywood, Rosie. Great Balloon Race. 2004. (Picture Puzzles Ser.). (ENG., Illus.). 1p. (J). (gr. k-3). pap. 6.95 *(978-0-7460-3388-3(5))* EDC Publishing.

—Puzzle Car Race. Haw, Brenda, illus. 2004. (Young Puzzles Ser.). 32p. (J). pap. 6.95 *(978-0-7945-0689-6(5),* Usborne) EDC Publishing.

Heywood, Rosie, ed. Travel Puzzles Sticker Book. Haw, Brenda, illus. rev. ed. 2005. (Travel Puzzles Sticker Book Ser.). 24p. (J). (gr. 1). pap. 6.95 *(978-0-7945-0729-9(8),* Usborne) EDC Publishing.

Hidden Pictures 1-20 (Gr. K-2) 2003. (J). *(978-1-58232-063-2(2))* ECS Learning Systems, Inc.

Highlights. Halloween Hidden Pictures Puzzles to Highlight Clip Strip, 12 vols. 2018. (J). (gr. 1-4). pap. 83.88 *(978-1-68437-348-2(4),* Highlights) Highlights Pr., c/o Highlights for Children, Inc.

Highlights, creator. Barnyard Sticker Puzzles. 2017. (Highlights Sticker Hidden Pictures Ser.). (ENG.). 96p. (J). (gr. -1-k). pap. 9.95 *(978-1-62979-778-6(2),* Highlights) Highlights Pr., c/o Highlights for Children, Inc.

—Dinosaur Puzzles. 2017. (Highlights Hidden Pictures Ser.). (ENG.). 144p. (J). (gr. 1-4). pap. 9.95 *(978-1-62979-780-9(4),* Highlights) Highlights Pr., c/o Highlights for Children, Inc.

—Halloween Hidden Pictures Puzzles to Highlight. 2018. (Highlights Hidden Pictures Puzzles to Highlight Activity Bks.). (Illus.). 32p. (J). (gr. 1-4). pap. 6.99 *(978-1-68437-202-7(X),* Highlights) Highlights Pr., c/o Highlights for Children, Inc.

—Halloween Puzzles. 2014. (Highlights Puzzlemania Activity Bks.). (ENG., Illus.). 144p. (J). (gr. 1-4). pap. 10.99 *(978-1-62979-265-1(9),* Highlights) Highlights Pr., c/o Highlights for Children, Inc.

—Hidden Pictures(r) Two-Player Puzzles. 2018. (Highlights Hidden Pictures Two-Player Puzzles Ser.). 144p. (J). (gr. 1-4). pap. 9.99 *(978-1-62979-943-8(2),* Highlights) Highlights Pr., c/o Highlights for Children, Inc.

—Hide-And-Seek on the Farm: A Hidden Pictures(r) Lift-The-Flap Book. 2018. (Highlights Lift-The-Flap Bks.). (Illus.). 10p. (J). (-k). bds. 12.99 *(978-1-62979-948-3(3),* Highlights) Highlights Pr., c/o Highlights for Children, Inc.

—Horse Puzzles. 2017. (Highlights Hidden Pictures Ser.). (ENG.). 144p. (J). (gr. 1-4). pap. 9.95 *(978-1-62979-841-7(X),* Highlights) Highlights Pr., c/o Highlights for Children, Inc.

—Jumbo Book of Amazing Mazes. 2017. (Highlights Jumbo Books & Pads Ser.). (ENG.). 256p. (J). (gr. 1-4). pap. 12.99 *(978-1-62979-884-4(3),* Highlights) Highlights Pr., c/o Highlights for Children, Inc.

—Jumbo Book of Hidden Pictures. 2017. (Highlights Jumbo Books & Pads Ser.). (ENG.). 256p. (J). (gr. 1-4). pap. 12.99 *(978-1-62979-826-4(6),* Highlights) Highlights Pr., c/o Highlights for Children, Inc.

—Pet Sticker Puzzles. 2017. (Highlights Sticker Hidden Pictures Ser.). (ENG.). 96p. (J). (-k). pap. 9.95 *(978-1-62979-842-4(8),* Highlights) Highlights Pr., c/o Highlights for Children, Inc.

—Things That Go Sticker Puzzles. 2020. (Highlights Sticker Hidden Pictures Ser.). 96p. (J). (-k). pap. 9.95 *(978-1-62979-950-6(5),* Highlights) Highlights Pr., c/o Highlights for Children, Inc.

—Travel Puzzles. 2015. (Highlights Puzzlemania Activity Bks.). (ENG., Illus.). 144p. (J). (gr. 1-4). 9.95 *(978-1-62979-203-3(9),* Highlights) Highlights Pr., c/o Highlights for Children, Inc.

—Winter Puzzles. 2014. (Highlights Puzzlemania Activity Bks.). (ENG., Illus.). 144p. (J). (gr. 1-4). pap. 10.99 *(978-1-62979-266-8(7),* Highlights) Highlights Pr., c/o Highlights for Children, Inc.

—101 Bananas. 2018. (Highlights Hidden Pictures 101 Activity Bks.). 144p. (J). (gr. 1-4). pap. 9.99 *(978-1-62979-942-1(4),* Highlights) Highlights Pr., c/o Highlights for Children, Inc.

—101 Socks. 2018. (Highlights Hidden Pictures 101 Activity Bks.). (Illus.). 144p. (J). (gr. 1-4). pap. 9.99 *(978-1-68437-170-9(8),* Highlights) Highlights Pr., c/o Highlights for Children, Inc.

Highlights Learning, creator. First Grade Big Fun Workbook. 2017. (Highlights Big Fun Activity Workbooks Ser.). (ENG.). 256p. (J). (gr. k-2). pap. 12.99 *(978-1-62979-864-6(9),* Highlights) Highlights Pr., c/o Highlights for Children, Inc.

—Kindergarten Learning Numbers. 2018. (Highlights Learn on the Go Practice Pads Ser.). (Illus.). 64p. (J). (-k). pap. 4.99 *(978-1-68437-163-1(5),* Highlights) Highlights Pr., c/o Highlights for Children, Inc.

—Kindergarten Writing Letters. 2018. (Highlights Learn on the Go Practice Pads Ser.). (Illus.). 64p. (J). (-k). pap. 4.99 *(978-1-68437-162-4(7),* Highlights) Highlights Pr., c/o Highlights for Children, Inc.

—Preschool Colors & Shapes. 2018. (Highlights Learn on the Go Practice Pads Ser.). (Illus.). 64p. (J). (-k). pap. 4.99 *(978-1-68437-161-7(9),* Highlights) Highlights Pr., c/o Highlights for Children, Inc.

—Preschool Tracing. 2018. (Highlights Learn on the Go Practice Pads Ser.). (Illus.). 64p. (J). (-k). pap. 4.99 *(978-1-68437-160-0(0),* Highlights) Highlights Pr., c/o Highlights for Children, Inc.

—Write-On Wipe-off Let's Trace. 2017. (Highlights Write-On Wipe-off Fun to Learn Activity Bks.). (ENG.). 56p. (J). (-k). spiral bd. 12.99 *(978-1-62979-844-8(4),* Highlights) Highlights Pr., c/o Highlights for Children, Inc.

—Write-On Wipe-off Let's Write Letters. 2017. (Highlights Write-On Wipe-off Fun to Learn Activity Bks.). (ENG.). 56p. (J). (-k). spiral bd. 12.99 *(978-1-62979-883-7(5),* Highlights) Highlights Pr., c/o Highlights for Children, Inc.

Highlights USA for Children Staff. Puzzlemania. (Illus.). 48p. (J). pap. 5.95 *(978-0-87534-712-7(6));* pap. 5.95 *(978-0-87534-709-7(6));* pap. 5.95 *(978-0-87534-711-0(8));* pap. 5.95 *(978-0-87534-710-3(X))* Highlights for Children.

Hill, Sandi. Playground Problem Solvers. 2017. (Learn-To-Read Ser.). (ENG., Illus.). (J). (gr. -1-2). pap. 3.49 *(978-1-68310-279-3(7))* Pacific Learning, Inc.

Hills, Laila, illus. Animal Friends. 2017. (J). *(978-1-62885-342-1(5))* Kidsbooks, LLC.

Hinkler Books, ed. Mighty Movers. 2012. (Busy Blocks Ser.). 12p. (J). 5.99 *(978-1-74308-887-6(6))* Hinkler Bks. Pty. Ltd. AUS. Dist: Ideals Pubns.

Hinkler Studios Staff., ed. Sponge Bob Story Vision. 2012. (Story Vision Ser.). 96p. (J). 12.99 *(978-1-74181-226-8(7))* Hinkler Bks. Pty. Ltd. AUS. Dist: Ideals Pubns.

Hinton, Stephanie, illus. Busy Book for Boys: 550 Things to Find. 2014. (J). *(978-1-4351-5358-5(8))* Barnes & Noble, Inc.

—Busy Book for Girls: 550 Things to Find. 2014. (J). *(978-1-4351-5359-2(6))* Barnes & Noble, Inc.

Hockett, Margaret. Punctuation Puzzler - Run-Ons C1. 2005. (Punctuation Puzzler Ser.). 48p. (gr. 7-8). pap. 8.99 *(978-0-89455-819-1(6))* Critical Thinking Co., The.

Hodgson, Rob, text. Monsters! A Scary Top Score Game. 2018. (ENG., Illus.). 111p. (J). (gr. 1-5). 9.99 *(978-1-78627-170-9(2),* King, Laurence Publishing) Orion Publishing Group, Ltd. GBR. Dist: Hachette Bk. Group.

Hogan, Christa C. Wild, Funny Brain Twisters. 2018. (Just for Laughs Ser.). (ENG.). 24p. (J). (gr. 4-6). lib. bdg. *(978-1-68072-332-8(4),* 12107, Hi Jinx) Black Rabbit Bks.

Holm, Sharon Lane. SPARK Game Time! Puzzles & Activities. 2018. (Dover Kids Activity Bks.). (ENG.). 64p. (J). (gr. 1-4). pap. 5.99 *(978-0-486-81910-5(8),* 819108) Dover Pubns., Inc.

Holt, Rinehart and Winston Staff. Science Puzzlers, Twisters & Teasers. 5th ed. 2004. (Illus.). pap. 26.46 *(978-0-03-035192-1(8))* Holt McDougal.

Hood, Karen Jean Matsko. Gaited Horse Activity & Coloring Book. Whispering Pine Press International, ed. Artistic Design Service Staff, illus. 2014. (Hood Activity & Coloring Book Ser.). 160p. (J). bk. 4. spiral bd. 21.95 *(978-1-59649-626-2(2))* Vol. 4. (ENG.). per. 19.95 *(978-1-59210-591-5(2))* Whispering Pine Pr. International, Inc.

—Gaited Horse Activity & Coloring Book-English/German/Spanish Edition. Whispering Pine Press International, Inc. Staff, ed. Artistic Book and Web Design, illus. 2010. (ENG, GER & SPA.). 160p. (J). per. 19.95 *(978-1-59649-522-7(7))* Whispering Pine Pr. International, Inc.

HOP, LLC. Hooked on Learning Puzzles & Mazes. 2006. 64p. 3.79 *(978-1-933863-90-0(0))* HOP, LLC.

Hovanec, Helene & Merrell, Patrick. Chicken Games & Puzzles: 100 Word Games, Picture Puzzles, Fun Mazes, Silly Jokes, Codes, & Activities for Kids. 2012. (Storey's Games & Puzzles Ser.). (ENG.). 144p. (J). (gr. 1-5). pap. 9.95 *(978-1-61212-087-4(3),* 622087) Storey Publishing, LLC.

—The Great Outdoors Games & Puzzles. 2007. (Storey's Games & Puzzles Ser.). (ENG., Illus.). 144p. (J). (gr. 3-7). pap. 9.95 *(978-1-58017-679-8(8),* 67679) Storey Publishing, LLC.

Hovanec, Helene, et al. Pony Play Games & Puzzles. 2008. (Storey's Games & Puzzles Ser.). (ENG., Illus.). 144p. (J). (gr. 1-5). pap. 9.95 *(978-1-60342-063-1(0),* 62063) Storey Publishing, LLC.

I Spy Funhouse. 2003. (J). 129.50 *(978-0-590-66383-0(6))* Scholastic, Inc.

IC4DESIGN & Kamigaki, Hiro. Pierre the Maze Detective: The Search for the Stolen Maze Stone. 2015. (ENG., Illus.). 36p. (J). (gr. 2-6). 19.99 *(978-1-78067-563-3(1),* King, Laurence Publishing) Orion Publishing Group, Ltd. GBR. Dist: Hachette Bk. Group.

IKids, creator. Soft Shapes Chunky Puzzle Playset:outer space (Foam Puzzle & Playset) 2012. (ENG.). 1p. (J). (gr. -1-17). 9.99 *(978-1-60169-271-9(4))* Innovative Kids.

Ikids Staff. Soft Shapes: Dinosaurs (Baby's First Book + Puzzle) Ski, Jenn, illus. 2010. (ENG.). 8p. (J). (gr. -1 — 1). 10.99 *(978-1-60169-043-2(6))* Innovative Kids.

—Soft Shapes: Trucks (Baby's First Book + Puzzle) Ski, Jenn, illus. 2010. (ENG.). 8p. (J). (gr. -1 — 1). 10.99 *(978-1-60169-044-9(4))* Innovative Kids.

—Softs Shapes Ocean. 2011. (ENG., Illus.). 8p. (J). (gr. -1 — 1). 10.99 *(978-1-60169-113-2(0))* Innovative Kids.

Ink, Johnny. Inklings: Kids. 2008. 13p. pap. 12.95 *(978-1-929774-60-9(5))* Greenleaf Book Group.

Jackson, Richard. Snow Scene. Vaccaro Seeger, Laura, illus. 2017. (ENG.). 40p. (J). 17.99 *(978-1-62672-680-2(9),* 900170475) Roaring Brook Pr.

Jackson, Sara. The Saturday Evening Post Spot the Difference Picture Puzzles. 2018. (Dover Kids Activity Bks.). (ENG.). 64p. (gr. 2). pap. 9.99 *(978-0-486-81912-9(4),* 819124) Dover Pubns., Inc.

—Spot the Differences Picture Puzzles for Kids 2. 2017. (Dover Kids Activity Bks.). (ENG., Illus.). 64p. (J). (gr. 1-4). pap. 9.99 *(978-0-486-78249-2(2),* 782492) Dover Pubns., Inc.

James, Danielle & Green, Dan. Where's Rudolf? Find Rudolph & His Festive Helpers in 15 Fun-Filled Puzzles. 2015. (ENG., Illus.). 46p. (J). (gr. 2-5). 14.99 *(978-1-78418-016-4(5))* Blake, John Publishing, Ltd. GBR. Dist: Independent Pubs. Group.

James, Diane. Baa, Baa, Black Sheep. 2004. (Jigsaw Nursery Rhymes Ser.). (ENG., Illus.). 12p. (J). (gr. -1-k). 9.95 *(978-1-58728-625-4(4),* Two-Can Publishing) T&N Children's Publishing.

—Here We Go. 2004. (Jigsaw Rhymes Ser.). (ENG., Illus.). 12p. (J). (gr. -1-k). 9.95 *(978-1-58728-024-5(8),* Two-Can Publishing) T&N Children's Publishing.

—Pat-a-Cake. 2004. (Jigsaw Nursery Rhymes Ser.). (ENG., Illus.). 12p. (J). (gr. -1-k). 9.95 *(978-1-58728-623-0(8),* Two-Can Publishing) T&N Children's Publishing.

—Three Blind Mice. 2004. (Jigsaw Nursery Rhymes Ser.). (ENG., Illus.). 12p. (J). (gr. -1-k). 9.95 *(978-1-58728-626-1(2),* Two-Can Publishing) T&N Children's Publishing.

Janeczko, Paul B., ed. Top Secret: A Handbook of Codes, Ciphers & Secret Writing. LaReau, Jenna, illus. 2006. (ENG.). 144p. (J). (gr. 4-7). per. 11.99 *(978-0-7636-2972-4(3))* Candlewick Pr.

Jay, Aye. The Punk Rock Fun Time Activity Book. 2009. (ENG., Illus.). 48p. pap. 9.95 *(978-1-55022-872-4(2),* 3ab535a3-3663-4173-b1ce-27c6e2be7aee) ECW Pr. CAN. Dist: Baker & Taylor Publisher Services (BTPS).

Jazynka, Kitson. History's Mysteries: Freaky Phenomena: Curious Clues, Cold Cases, & Puzzles from the Past. 2018. (Illus.). 160p. (J). (gr. 3-7). pap. 14.99 *(978-1-4263-3164-0(9));* (ENG., lib. bdg. 24.90 *(978-1-4263-3165-7(7))* Disney Publishing Worldwide. (National Geographic Kids).

Johanson, Sarah Margaret. Caillou: Parade of Colors. Sévigny, Eric, illus. 2012. (Puzzle Bks.). (ENG.). 18p. (J). (gr. -1-1). bds. 12.95 *(978-2-89450-838-1(7))* Caillouet, Gerry.

—Caillou: Parade of Shapes. Sévigny, Eric, illus. 2012. (Puzzle Bks.). (ENG.). 18p. (J). (gr. -1-1). bds. 12.95 *(978-2-89450-839-8(5))* Caillouet, Gerry.

Jones, Bruce Patrick. Celebrity Scenes: Fun & Games with Hollywood Stars. 2015. (Dover Kids Activity Bks.). (ENG.). 48p. (gr. 6). pap. 4.99 *(978-0-486-79349-8(4),* 793494) Dover Pubns., Inc.

Jones, Frankie. Muddle & Match Jobs. Hinton, Stephanie, illus. 2016. 16p. (J). bds. 8.99 *(978-1-61067-491-1(X))* Kane Miller.

Jones, Rob Lloyd. 1001 Pirate Things to Spot. Gower, Teri, illus. 2007. (1001 Things to Spot Ser.). 32p. (J). 9.99 *(978-0-7945-1513-3(4),* Usborne) EDC Publishing.

Jumbo Book of Fun for Kids. 2017. (ENG., Illus.). 320p. (J). (gr. 1-2). pap. 10.99 *(978-1-338-21834-3(4),* 821834) Scholastic, Inc.

Jumbo Book of Kindergarten Fun. 2017. (ENG., Illus.). 320p. (J). (gr. k-k). pap. 10.99 *(978-1-338-16944-7(0))* Scholastic, Inc.

Jumbo Book of Pre-K Fun. 2017. (ENG., Illus.). 320p. (J). (gr. -1 — 1). pap. 10.99 *(978-1-338-16943-0(2),* 816943) Scholastic, Inc.

Jumbo Puzzle Book. 2004. (J). per. *(978-1-57657-006-7(1))* Paradise Pr., Inc.

Junior Puzzles. 2004. 112p. (J). 4.99 *(978-1-85997-389-9(2))* Byeway Bks.

Kalvitis, David. The Greatest Dot-To-Dot Book in the World, Vol. 4. 2003. (ENG.). 48p. (YA). 7.95 *(978-0-9700437-3-3(2))* Monkeying Around.

—The Greatest Dot-To-Dot Super Challenge Book 5, Vol. 5. 2007. (Greatest Dot to Dot! Super Challenge! Ser.). (ENG., Illus.). 48p. (J). (gr. 3-16). 8.95 *(978-0-9700437-4-0(0),* 740) Monkeying Around.

—The Greatest Dot-To-Dot Super Challenge Book 6. 2008. (Greatest Dot to Dot! Super Challenge! Ser.). (ENG.). 48p. (J). (gr. 3-16). 8.95 *(978-0-9700437-5-7(9))* Monkeying Around.

—The Greatest Newspaper Dot-to-Dot! Puzzles, Vol. 7. 2011. (Greatest Newspaper Dot-to-Dot Puzzles Ser.). 40p. (YA). 5.95 *(978-0-9799753-8-7(7))* Monkeying Around.

—The Greatest Newspaper Dot-to-Dot! Puzzles: Volume 5. 2007. (Greatest Newspaper Dot-to-Dot Puzzles Ser.). 40p. (J). (gr. 3-16). pap. 5.95 *(978-0-9799753-6-3(0))* Monkeying Around.

—The Greatest Newspaper Dot-to-Dot! Puzzles: Volume 6. 2007. (Greatest Newspaper Dot-to-Dot Puzzles Ser.). 40p. (J). (gr. 3-16). pap. 5.95 *(978-0-9799753-7-0(9))* Monkeying Around.

Kalz, Jill. Halloween Hide & Seek: Hidden Picture Puzzles, 1 vol. Borlasca, Hector, illus. 2012. (Seek It Out Ser.). (ENG.). 32p. (J). (gr. k-3). 9.95 *(978-1-4048-7728-3(2),* 120452); lib. bdg. 27.32 *(978-1-4048-7495-4(X),* 119533) Capstone. (Picture Window Bks.).

Keating, Nancy & Keating, Laurel. Find Scruncheon & Touton 2: All Around Newfoundland, 1 vol. 2012. (ENG., Illus.). 32p. (J). (gr. k-3). pap. *(978-1-897174-89-0(6))* Breakwater Bks., Ltd.

—Search for Scruncheon & Touton, 1 vol. 2012. (ENG., Illus.). 26p. (J). (gr. -1-3). *(978-1-897174-69-2(1))* Breakwater Bks., Ltd.

Ketch, Jack. Hangman Puzzles for Bright Kids. 2017. (Puzzlewright Junior Hangman Ser.: 4). (ENG.). 96p. (J). (gr. 3-7). pap. 6.95 *(978-1-4549-2713-6(5),* Puzzlewright) Sterling Publishing Co., Inc.

Khan, Sarah. Word Puzzles. 2012. (Wipe-Clean Activity Cards Ser.). 53p. (J). pap. 9.99 *(978-0-7945-3220-8(9),* Usborne) EDC Publishing.

Khanduri, Kamini. The Great World Search. Hancock, David, illus. 2007. (Great Searches (EDC Hardcover) Ser.). 48p. (J). (gr. 3). lib. bdg. 16.99 *(978-1-58086-966-9(1),* Usborne) EDC Publishing.

Khanduri, Kamini, et al. The Usborne Big Book of Picture Puzzles. Groebner, Dominic, illus. 2006. 173p. (J). (gr. 3-7). per. 18.99 *(978-0-7945-1165-4(1),* Usborne) EDC Publishing.

Kids, National Geographic. Weird but True Cool & Crazy Sticker Doodle Book. 2018. (Weird but True Ser.). 160p. (J). pap. 12.99 *(978-1-4263-3023-0(5),* National Geographic Kids) Disney Publishing Worldwide.

Kitch, Anne E. Como Participar en la Liturgia: Un Libro de Actividades para Los Ninos Anglicanos-Episcopales. Martell, Oswald Perez, tr. Perez, Dorothy Thompson, illus. 2008. (SPA.). 48p. (J). pap. 11.95 *(978-0-8192-2331-9(X),* edefa50a-b589-4222-b291-f96aa5d45d3d) Church Publishing, Inc.

Kleven, Dean, illus. Little Einsteins. 2007. (Look & Find Ser.). (J). (gr. -1-3). 7.98 *(978-1-4127-7424-6(1))* Publications International, Ltd.

Kohart, Georgia. A Heritage of the Heart Teaching Companion. 2003. (Illus.). ring bd. 24.95 *(978-0-9706348-1-8(1))* Heritage Heart Farm.

Kraft, Ellen Christiansen. Alphabet Hide & Seek. 2014. (Dover Alphabet Coloring Bks.). (ENG.). 32p. (J). (gr. -1-2). pap. 3.99 *(978-0-486-49471-5(3),* 494713) Dover Pubns., Inc.

Kreloff, Elliot, illus. Matching Puzzle Cards - Numbers. 2012. (ENG.). 36p. (J). (gr. k-12). 9.99 *(978-1-60905-221-8(8))* Blue Apple Bks.

Krings, Antoon. Droles de Petites Betes. (FRE.). pap. 18.95 *(978-2-07-058437-6(2))* Gallimard, Editions FRA. Dist: Distribooks, Inc.

Kumon. My Book of Mazes: Animals. 2006. (Kumon Workbooks Ser.). (ENG., Illus.). 80p. (J). (gr. k-2). per. 7.95 *(978-1-933241-25-8(X))* Kumon Publishing North America, Inc.

Kumon Publishing North America. My Book of Mazes: Around the World. 2007. (ENG., Illus.). 80p. (J). (gr. -1-3). pap. 7.95 *(978-1-933241-40-1(3))* Kumon Publishing North America, Inc.

Kumon Publishing North America, creator. My Book of Pasting: Jigsaw Puzzles. 2006. (Kumon Workbooks Ser.). (Illus.). 80p. (J). (gr. k-2). per. 7.95 *(978-1-933241-29-6(2))* Kumon Publishing North America, Inc.

Kumon Publishing North America, creator. My Book of Easy Mazes. Kumon Publishing North America, . 2006. (Kumon Workbooks Ser.). (ENG., Illus.). 80p. (J). (gr. -1). per. 7.95 *(978-1-933241-24-1(1))* Kumon Publishing North America, Inc.

Kumon Publishing North America, ed. My First Book of Mazes. Kumon Publishing North America, . 2004. (ENG., Illus.). 80p. (J). per. 7.95 *(978-4-7743-0709-1(2))* Kumon Publishing North America, Inc.

Kumon Publshing North America. My Book of Mazes: Things That Go! 2006. (Kumon Workbooks Ser.). (ENG., Illus.). 80p. (J). (gr. -1). per. 7.95 *(978-1-933241-31-9(4))* Kumon Publishing North America, Inc.

Kurtz, John. Grumpy Cat's Road Trip Spot-The-Differences. 2018. (Dover Kids Activity Books: Animals Ser.). (ENG.). 64p. (gr. 2-7). pap. 5.99 *(978-0-486-82470-3(5),* 824705) Dover Pubns., Inc.

—SPARK Amazing America! Word Search. 2017. (Dover Kids Activity Books: U. S. A. Ser.). (ENG.). 64p. (J). (gr. 1-4). pap. 6.99 *(978-0-486-81609-8(5),* 816095) Dover Pubns., Inc.

—SPARK Amazing Animals! Word Search. 2017. (Dover Kids Activity Books: Animals Ser.). (ENG.). 64p. (J). (gr. 1-4). pap. 5.99 *(978-0-486-81770-5(9),* 817709) Dover Pubns., Inc.

—Spot-The-Differences Grumpy Cat Coloring Book. 2017. (Dover Little Activity Bks.). (ENG.). 64p. (J). (gr. k-3). pap. 2.50 *(978-0-486-81959-4(0),* 819590) Dover Pubns., Inc.

Kurtz, John & Activity Books Staff. Claus Kids Activity Book. 2011. (Dover Little Activity Bks.). (ENG.). 64p. (J). (gr. -1-5). 2.00 *(978-0-486-48293-4(6))* Dover Pubns., Inc.

Kutschbach, Doris. Art Detective: Spot the Difference! 2013. (ENG., Illus.). 48p. (J). (gr. 3-7). 14.95 *(978-3-7913-7104-7(5))* Prestel Verlag GmbH & Co KG. DEU. Dist: Penguin Random Hse. LLC.

LaFosse, Michael G. Making Origami Puzzles Step by Step. 2009. (Kid's Guide to Origami Ser.). 24p. (gr. 3-4). 47.90 *(978-1-61511-194-7(8),* PowerKids Pr.) Rosen Publishing Group, Inc., The.

Lamb, Stacy, illus. First Puzzles. 2014. (Usborne Wipe-Clean Ser.). (ENG.). 22p. (J). pap. 7.99 *(978-0-7945-2524-8(5),* Usborne) EDC Publishing.

Lankford, Mary D. Mazes Around the World. Dugan, Karen, illus. 2008. 26p. (J). *(978-0-688-16519-2(2),* Collins) HarperCollins Pubs. Ltd.

Larranaga, Ana, illus. Matching Puzzle Cards - Animals. 2012. (ENG.). 36p. (J). (gr. k-12). 9.99 *(978-1-60905-225-6(0))* Blue Apple Bks.

Laval, Thierry. Mini Look & Find at School (Mini Look & Find) Laval, Thierry, illus. 2017. (Mini Look & Find Ser.). (ENG., Illus.). 14p. (J). (gr. -1-k). 9.95 *(978-0-531-23081-7(3),* Children's Pr.) Scholastic Library Publishing.

Learmonth, Amanda. Color Quest: Color by Numbers: Extreme Puzzle Challenges for Clever Kids. Farnsworth, Lauren, illus. 2018. (Puzzle Masters Ser.). (ENG.). 64p. (J). (gr. 3-6). pap. 9.99 *(978-1-4380-1146-2(6))* Sourcebooks, Inc.

Learn to Juggle. 2004. (How 2 Kits Ser.). (Illus.). 48p. (J). *(978-1-84229-929-6(8))* Top That! Publishing PLC.

LeCompte, David & Padrick, Kendell. Eugene Stillwell Wants to Know!, Pt. 2. 2009. (Eugene Stillwell Wants to Know! Ser.). (ENG.). 96p. (J). (gr. 4-6). pap. 4.95 *(978-1-929945-74-0(4))* Big Guy Bks., Inc.

—Eugene Stillwell Wants to Know! Part III. 2009. (Eugene Stillwell Wants to Know! Ser.). (ENG.). 96p. (J). (gr. 4-6). pap. 4.95 *(978-1-929945-91-7(4))* Big Guy Bks., Inc.

Leichter, Albert. Staunton Treasures Past & Present Connect the Dots. 2005. (J). act. bk. ed. 3.95 *(978-0-9704280-6-6(5))* ClockTower Pubns.

Leigh, S. Puzzle Dungeon. 2004. (Young Puzzles Ser.). (Illus.). 32p. (J). pap. 6.95 *(978-0-7945-0511-0(2),* Usborne) EDC Publishing.

—Puzzle Farm. rev. ed. 2004. (Young Puzzles Ser.). (Illus.). 32p. (J). pap. 6.95 *(978-0-7945-0625-4(9))* EDC Publishing.

—Puzzle Jungle. 2004. (Young Puzzles Ser.). (Illus.). 32p. (J). pap. 6.95 *(978-0-7945-0435-9(3));* lib. bdg. 14.95 *(978-1-58086-534-0(8))* EDC Publishing.

—Puzzle Ocean. 2004. (Young Puzzles Ser.). (Illus.). 32p. (J). pap. 6.95 *(978-0-7945-0436-6(1))* EDC Publishing.

—Puzzle Planet. rev. ed. 2004. (Young Puzzles Ser.). (Illus.). 32p. (J). pap. 6.95 *(978-0-7945-0437-3(X),* Usborne) EDC Publishing.

—Puzzle School. 2004. (Young Puzzles Ser.). (Illus.). 32p. (J). pap. 6.95 *(978-0-7945-0512-7(0))* EDC Publishing.

—Puzzle Town. 2004. (Young Puzzles Ser.). (Illus.). 32p. (J). pap. 6.95 *(978-0-7945-0438-0(8))* EDC Publishing.

Leigh, Susannah. Ciudad Enigma: Lumen Puzzles Infantiles. (SPA., Illus.). (J). pap. *(978-950-724-182-6(5))* Lumen.

—L' Ile Fantastique: Fantastic Island. Gemmell, Kathy & Irving, Nicole, eds. Haw, Brenda, illus. (FRE.). 25p. (J). (gr. 2-3). reprint ed. 17.00 *(978-0-7881-9300-2(7))* DIANE Publishing Co.

—Isla Enigma: Lumen Puzzles Infantiles. (SPA., Illus.). (J). pap. *(978-950-724-183-3(3))* Lumen.

—Puzzle Castle. Waters, Gaby, ed. Haw, Brenda, illus. 2004. (Usborne Young Puzzles Ser.). 32p. (J). (gr. 1). lib. bdg. 14.95 *(978-1-58086-674-3(3));* pap. 6.95 *(978-0-7945-0433-5(7))* EDC Publishing. (Usborne).

—Puzzle Dinosaurs. Tyler, Jenny, ed. Haw, Brenda, illus. 2007. (Young Puzzles Ser.). 32p. (J). pap. 6.99 *(978-0-7945-1778-6(1),* Usborne) EDC Publishing.

—Puzzle Dungeon. Haw, Brenda, illus. 2004. (Young Puzzles Ser.). 32p. (J). (gr. 1). lib. bdg. 14.95 *(978-1-58086-599-9(2))* EDC Publishing.

—Puzzle Farm. Waters, Gaby, ed. Haw, Brenda, illus. 2004. (Young Puzzles Ser.). 32p. (J). (gr. 1). lib. bdg. 14.95 *(978-1-58086-627-9(1),* Usborne) EDC Publishing.

—Puzzle Ocean. Haw, Brenda, illus. 2006. (Young Puzzles Ser.). 32p. (J). (gr. 1). lib. bdg. 14.95 *(978-1-58086-535-7(6))* EDC Publishing.

—Puzzle Palace. Tyler, Jenny, ed. Haw, Brenda, illus. 2005. (Usborne Young Puzzles Ser.). 32p. (J). (gr. -1-3). per. 6.95 *(978-0-7945-1120-3(1),* Usborne) EDC Publishing.

—Puzzle Pirates. Tyler, Jenny, ed. Haw, Brenda, illus. 2006. (Usborne Young Puzzles Ser.). 32p. (J). (gr. 1-4). pap. 6.99 *(978-0-7945-1359-7(X),* Usborne) EDC Publishing.

—Puzzle Pirates. Haw, Brenda, illus. 2006. (Usborne Young Puzzles Ser.). 32p. (J). (gr. 1). lib. bdg. 14.99 *(978-1-58086-973-7(4),* Usborne) EDC Publishing.

—Puzzle Planet. Waters, Gaby, ed. Haw, Brenda, illus. 2006. (Young Puzzles Ser.). 32p. (J). (gr. 1). lib. bdg. 14.95 *(978-1-58086-536-4(4))* EDC Publishing.
—Puzzle Pyramid. Haw, Brenda, illus. 2004. 32p. (J). pap. 6.95 *(978-0-7945-0791-6(3)*, Usborne) EDC Publishing.
—Puzzle School. Haw, Brenda, illus. 2004. (Young Puzzles Ser.). 32p. (Orig.). (J). (gr. 1). lib. bdg. 14.95 *(978-1-58086-600-2(X))* EDC Publishing.
—Puzzle Town. Waters, Gaby, ed. Haw, Brenda, illus. 2006. (Young Puzzles Ser.). 32p. (J). (gr. 1). lib. bdg. 14.95 *(978-1-58086-537-1(2)*, Usborne) EDC Publishing.
—Puzzle Train. Haw, Brenda, illus. 2004. (Young Puzzles Ser.). 32p. (J). (gr. 1). lib. bdg. 14.95 *(978-1-58086-633-0(6)*, Usborne) EDC Publishing.
—Puzzle Train. Waters, Gaby, ed. Haw, Brenda, illus. 2003. (Young Puzzles Ser.). 32p. (J). pap. 6.95 *(978-0-7945-0683-4(6)*, Usborne) EDC Publishing.
—Puzzle World: Combined Volume. Waters, Gaby, ed. Haw, Brenda, illus. 2004. (Young Puzzles Ser.). 96p. (J). pap. 13.95 *(978-0-7945-0688-9(7)*, Usborne) EDC Publishing.
Levin, David H. Bridge Puzzles for Children Vol. 1: Simple Card Play Problems to Introduce Them to This Wonderful Game. 2004. (Illus.). 128p. (J). pap. 14.95 *(978-0-9638001-2-1(4))* Syllogism Pr.
Levin, Freddie. Outer Space Activity Book. 2009. (Dover Little Activity Bks.). (ENG.). 64p. (J). (gr. k-3). pap. 2.99 *(978-0-486-47389-5(9)*, 473899) Dover Pubns., Inc.
Levy, Barbara Soloff. Dot-To-Dot Fun. 2014. (Dover Kids Activity Books: Animals Ser.). (ENG.). 64p. (J). (gr. -1-3). pap. 5.99 *(978-0-486-77962-1(9)*, 779629) Dover Pubns., Inc.
—The Incredible Dot-To-Dot Book. 2014. (Dover Kids Activity Bks.). (ENG.). 48p. (J). (gr. 3-6). pap. 5.99 *(978-0-486-49307-7(5)*, 493075) Dover Pubns., Inc.
—Little Farm Follow-the-Dots. 2005. (Dover Little Activity Bks.). (ENG., Illus.). 64p. (J). (gr. 3-5). pap. 2.50 *(978-0-486-44050-7(8)*, 440508) Dover Pubns., Inc.
—Pets Follow-the-Dots. 2006. (Dover Little Activity Bks.). (ENG., Illus.). 64p. (J). (gr. k-3). per. 2.50 *(978-0-486-44890-9(8)*, 448908) Dover Pubns., Inc.
—Who's Who in the Zoo? Dot-to-Dot Fun. 2007. (Dover Kids Activity Books: Animals Ser.). (ENG., Illus.). 32p. (J). (gr. 1-3). per. 3.99 *(978-0-486-46181-6(5)*, 461815) Dover Pubns., Inc.
Linn, Susie. Princesses. 2016. (My First Sticker Book Ser.). (ENG.). (J). pap. *(978-1-78445-768-6(X))* Top That! Publishing PLC.
Lionni, Leo. What? 2014. (ENG., Illus.). 16p. (J). (— 1). bds. 6.99 *(978-0-385-75406-4(X)*, Knopf Bks. for Young Readers) Random Hse. Children's Bks.
—Where? 2014. (ENG., Illus.). 16p. (J). (— 1). bds. 5.99 *(978-0-385-75407-1(8)*, Knopf Bks. for Young Readers) Random Hse. Children's Bks.
—Who? 2014. (ENG., Illus.). 16p. (J). (— 1). bds. 6.99 *(978-0-385-75405-7(1)*, Knopf Bks. for Young Readers) Random Hse. Children's Bks.
Litchfield, Jo, illus. Box of Trucks. 2004. (Boxed Jigsaws Ser.). 10p. (J). 11.99 *(978-0-7945-0916-3(9)*, Usborne) EDC Publishing.
Little & Large Sticker Activity Bk - Monster Machines. 2008. 24p. pap. *(978-1-84810-059-6(0))* Miles Kelly Publishing, Ltd.
Little & Large Sticker Activity Bugs. 2008. 24p. pap. *(978-1-84810-057-2(4))* Miles Kelly Publishing, Ltd.
Little & Large Sticker Activity Dinosaurs. 2008. 24p. pap. *(978-1-84810-058-9(2))* Miles Kelly Publishing, Ltd.
Little & Large Sticker Activity on the Farm. 2008. 24p. pap. *(978-1-84810-060-2(4))* Miles Kelly Publishing, Ltd.
Little & Large Sticker Activity Pirates. 2008. 24p. pap. *(978-1-84810-061-9(2))* Miles Kelly Publishing, Ltd.
Little & Large Sticker Activity Sharks. 2008. 24p. pap. *(978-1-84810-062-6(0))* Miles Kelly Publishing, Ltd.
Little & Large Sticker Activity Space. 2008. 24p. pap. *(978-1-84810-063-3(9))* Miles Kelly Publishing, Ltd.
Little & Large Sticker Activity Whales & Dolphins. 2008. 24p. pap. *(978-1-84810-064-0(7))* Miles Kelly Publishing, Ltd.
Littlefield, Cindy A. Horse Games & Puzzles: 102 Brainteasers, Word Games, Jokes & Riddles, Picture Puzzlers, Matches & Logic Tests for Horse-Loving Kids. 2004. (Storey's Games & Puzzles Ser.). (ENG., Illus.). 144p. (J). (gr. 3-7). pap. 9.95 *(978-1-58017-538-8(4)*, 67538) Storey Publishing, LLC.
—Sea Life Games & Puzzles. 2006. (Storey's Games & Puzzles Ser.). (ENG., Illus.). 144p. (J). (gr. 3-7). pap. 9.95 *(978-1-58017-624-8(0)*, 67624) Storey Publishing, LLC.
Ljungkvist, Laura. Search & Spot: Animals! 2015. (Search & Spot Book Ser.). (ENG., Illus.). 40p. (J). (gr. -1-3). 16.99 *(978-0-544-54005-7(0)*, 1608732, Clarion Bks.) HarperCollins Pubs.
Lombardo, Giulia & Parchow, Marc, illus. Incredible Puzzles: 150+ Timed Puzzles to Test Your Skill. 2018. (ENG.). 196p. (J). (gr. 3-7). pap. 12.99 *(978-1-4380-1207-0(1))* Sourcebooks, Inc.
Look & Find Ser., 19 bks. (Illus.). (J). lib. bdg. 284.05 *(978-1-56674-907-7(7))* Forest Hse. Publishing Co., Inc.
Lowery, Mike. The Kid's Awesome Activity Book: Games! Puzzles! Mazes! & More! 2018. (ENG., Illus.). 112p. (J). (gr. 1-6). pap. 14.95 *(978-0-7611-8718-9(9)*, 18718) Workman Publishing Co., Inc.
Lucey, Marcia T. Puzzles & Activities for Children Ages 5-7: Year B. 2008. (Catholic Corner Ser.). (Illus.). 67p. (J). (gr. k-2). pap. 14.95 incl. cd-rom *(978-1-58459-373-7(3))* World Library Pubns.
—Puzzles & Activities for Children Ages 7-10: Year B. 2008. (Catholic Corner Ser.). (Illus.). 67p. (J). (gr. 2-5). pap. 14.95 incl. audio compact disk *(978-1-58459-374-4(1))* World Library Pubns.
Lupton, Hugh. Riddle Me This! Riddles & Stories to Challenge Your Mind. Fatus, Sophie, illus. 2003. 64p. (J). 19.99 *(978-1-84148-169-2(6))* Barefoot Bks., Inc.
Machale, Des. Puzzleology: Tough Puzzles for Kids. 2006. (ENG., Illus.). 93p. (J). pap. 16.95 *(978-1-85635-508-7(X))* Mercier Pr., Ltd., The IRL. Dist: Dufour Editions, Inc.
Magma & Laval, Anne. Story Box: Create Your Own Fairy Tales. 2016. (Magma for Laurence King Ser.). (ENG., Illus.). (gr. -1-k). 16.99 *(978-1-85669-980-8(3)*, King, Laurence Publishing) Orion Publishing Group, Ltd. GBR. Dist: Hachette Bk. Group.
Make Believe Ideas. Find-And-Fit: First Words, 1 vol. Lynch, Stuart, illus. 2018. (ENG.). 10p. (J). (gr. -1). 9.99 *(978-1-78692-898-6(1))* Make Believe Ideas GBR. Dist: Scholastic, Inc.
—Instant Einstein: Scratch & Reveal: Epic & Awesome! Make Believe Ideas, illus. 2015. (ENG.). 62p. (J). (gr. 3-7). 7.99 *(978-1-78393-485-0(9))* Make Believe Ideas GBR. Dist: Scholastic, Inc.
Mallet, Lisa & Parchow, Marc, illus. Challenging Mazes: 80 Timed Mazes to Test Your Skill! 2016. (Challenging... Bks.). (ENG.). 96p. (J). (gr. 3-7). pap. 8.99 *(978-1-4380-0788-5(4))* Sourcebooks, Inc.
Manchester, Richard, ed. Colossal Grab a Pencil Pocket Fill-Ins. 2017. (ENG.). 320p. pap. 7.95 *(978-0-88486-644-2(0))* Bristol Park Bks.
Mansfield, Andy. Find the Dots. Mansfield, Andy, illus. 2017. (ENG., Illus.). 14p. (J). (gr. -1-2). 15.00 *(978-0-7636-9558-3(0))* Candlewick Pr.
Maring, Therese, ed. Top-Secret Code Book: Tricky, Fun Codes for You & Your Friends. Lukatz, Casey, illus. 2005. (American Girl Today Ser.). (ENG.). 32p. (J). (gr. 4-7). per. 5.95 *(978-1-59369-018-2(5)*, American Girl) American Girl Publishing, Inc.
Marks, Jennifer L. School Times, 1 vol. 2010. (Spot It Ser.). (ENG.). 32p. lib. bdg. 8.99 *(978-1-4296-5761-7(8)*, Pebble) Capstone.
Martin, Norma. Don Martin Brain Games for Kids. 2007. 68p. pap. 3.95 *(978-1-4343-2848-9(1))* AuthorHouse.
Martin, Peter. Bible People Factfile. Buckingham, Matt, illus. 2014. (ENG.). 48p. (J). (gr. 2-4). 14.99 *(978-0-7459-6388-4(9)*, f4a4ce4c-7eb6-4493-98b8-afa73880217c, Lion Children's) Lion Hudson PLC GBR. Dist: Baker & Taylor Publisher Services (BTPS).
Marzollo, Jean. C'est Moi l'Espion: Défis Suprêmes! Duchesne, Lucie, tr. Wick, Walter, photos by. (I Spy Bks.).Tr. of I Spy Fantasy. (FRE., Illus.). 37p. (J). (gr. -1-3). pap. 16.99 *(978-0-590-24340-7(3))* Scholastic, Inc.
—C'est Moi l'Espion: Du Monde du Mystère. Wick, Walter, photos by. (I Spy Bks.).Tr. of I Spy Mystery: A Book of Picture Riddles. (FRE., Illus.). 37p. (J). (gr. -1-3). pap. 16.99 *(978-0-590-24317-9(9))* Scholastic, Inc.
—I Spy a Butterfly (Scholastic Reader, Level 1) Wick, Walter, photos by. 2007. (Scholastic Reader, Level 1 Ser.). (ENG., Illus.). 32p. (J). (gr. -1-3). pap. 3.99 *(978-0-439-73865-1(2)*, Cartwheel Bks.) Scholastic, Inc.
—I Spy a Christmas Tree. Wick, Walter, photos by. 2010. (I Spy Ser.). (ENG., Illus.). 24p. (J). (gr. -1-3). 9.99 *(978-0-545-22092-7(0)*, Cartwheel Bks.) Scholastic, Inc.
—I Spy a Scary Monster (Scholastic Reader, Level 1) I Spy a Scary Monster. Wick, Walter, photos by. 2005. (Scholastic Reader, Level 1 Ser.). (ENG., Illus.). 32p. (J). (gr. -1-3). pap. 3.99 *(978-0-439-68054-7(9)*, Cartwheel Bks.) Scholastic, Inc.
—I Spy a School Bus (Scholastic Reader, Level 1) Wick, Walter, photos by. 2003. (Scholastic Reader, Level 1 Ser.). (ENG., Illus.). 32p. (J). (gr. -1-3). pap. 3.99 *(978-0-439-52473-5(3)*, Cartwheel Bks.) Scholastic, Inc.
—I Spy a to Z: a Book of Picture Riddles. Wick, Walter, photos by. 2009. (I Spy Ser.). (ENG., Illus.). 56p. (J). (gr. -1-3). 14.99 *(978-0-545-10782-2(2)*, Cartwheel Bks.) Scholastic, Inc.
—I Spy Adventure: 4 Picture Riddle Books. Wick, Walter, illus. Wick, Walter, photos by. 2012. (J). *(978-1-4351-3984-8(4))* Scholastic, Inc.
—I Spy an Egg in a Nest (Scholastic Reader, Level 1) Wick, Walter, photos by. 2011. (Scholastic Reader, Level 1 Ser.). (ENG., Illus.). 32p. (J). (gr. -1-2). pap. 4.95 *(978-0-545-22093-4(9)*, Cartwheel Bks.) Scholastic, Inc.
—I Spy Animals. Wick, Walter, photos by. 2012. (I Spy Ser.). (ENG., Illus.). 14p. (J). (gr. -1-k). pap. 5.99 *(978-0-545-41583-5(7)*, Cartwheel Bks.) Scholastic, Inc.
—I Spy Funny Teeth (Scholastic Reader, Level 1) Wick, Walter, photos by. 2003. (Scholastic Reader, Level 1 Ser.). (ENG., Illus.). 32p. (J). (gr. -1-3). pap. 3.99 *(978-0-439-52472-8(5)*, Cartwheel Bks.) Scholastic, Inc.
—I Spy Little Bunnies (with Foil) Wick, Walter, photos by. 2006. (I Spy Ser.). (ENG., Illus.). 24p. (J). (gr. k — 1). bds. 6.99 *(978-0-439-78535-8(9)*, Cartwheel Bks.) Scholastic, Inc.
—I Spy Merry Christmas (Scholastic Reader, Level 1) Wick, Walter, photos by. 2007. (Scholastic Reader, Level 1 Ser.). (ENG., Illus.). 64p. (J). (gr. -1-3). pap. 5.99 *(978-0-545-03945-1(2)*, Cartwheel Bks.) Scholastic, Inc.
—I Spy Nature. Wick, Walter, photos by. 2006. (Illus.). (J). *(978-0-439-80732-6(8))* Scholastic, Inc.
—I Spy Numbers. Wick, Walter, photos by. 2012. (I Spy Ser.). (ENG., Illus.). 14p. (J). (gr. -1-k). pap. 5.99 *(978-0-545-41585-9(3)*, Cartwheel Bks.) Scholastic, Inc.
—I Spy School. 2012. (I Spy — Scholastic Readers Level 1 Ser.). lib. bdg. 13.55 *(978-0-606-26231-6(8))* Turtleback.
—I Spy Spectacular: a Book of Picture Riddles. Wick, Walter, photos by. 2011. (I Spy Ser.). (ENG., Illus.). 40p. (J). (gr. -1-3). 14.99 *(978-0-545-22278-5(8)*, Cartwheel Bks.) Scholastic, Inc.
—I Spy Ultimate Challenger! A Book of Picture Riddles. Wick, Walter, photos by. 2003. (I Spy Ser.). (ENG., Illus.). 40p. (J). (gr. 2-5). pap. 14.99 *(978-0-439-45401-8(8)*, Cartwheel Bks.) Scholastic, Inc.
Maskel, Hazel. 1001 Things to Spot on Vacation. 2011. (1001 Things to Spot Ser.). 32p. (J). ring bd. 9.99 *(978-0-7945-3087-7(7)*, Usborne) EDC Publishing.
Mawhinney, Art & Disney Storybook Artists Staff, illus. Fairies. 2007. (Look & Find Ser.). 7.98 *(978-1-4127-7423-9(3))* Publications International, Ltd.
Max and Sid, illus. Counting. 2016. (What Can You Spot? Ser.). (ENG.). 18p. (J). (gr. -1 — 1). bds. 7.99 *(978-1-4998-0269-6(2))* Little Bee Books Inc.
—Learning. 2016. (What Can You Spot? Ser.). (ENG.). 18p. (J). (gr. -1 — 1). bds. 7.99 *(978-1-4998-0270-2(6))* Little Bee Books Inc.
Mazurkiewicz, Jessica. Dragons Activity Book. 2011. (Dover Little Activity Bks.). (ENG.). 64p. (J). (gr. k-3). 2.50 *(978-0-486-47521-9(2)*, 475212) Dover Pubns., Inc.
—Winter Fun Activity Book. 2010. (Dover Little Activity Bks.). (ENG., Illus.). 64p. (J). (gr. k-3). pap. 2.50 *(978-0-486-47528-8(X)*, 47528X) Dover Pubns., Inc.
McCurry, Kristen. Alike or Not Alike? A Photo Sorting Game, 1 vol. 2012. (Eye-Look Picture Games Ser.). (ENG.). 32p. (J). (gr. -1-2). lib. bdg. 27.99 *(978-1-4296-7549-9(7)*, 117126, Capstone Pr.) Capstone.
—Up-Close Mysteries: Zoomed-In Photo Puzzles, 1 vol. 2012. (Eye-Look Picture Games Ser.). (ENG.). 32p. (J). (gr. -1-2). lib. bdg. 27.99 *(978-1-4296-7550-5(0)*, 117127, Capstone Pr.) Capstone.
McDonald, Jake, illus. My First Alphabet Dot-To-Dot: Over 50 Fantastic Puzzles. 2019. (My First Activity Bks.). (ENG.). 64p. (J). (gr. -1-2). pap. 8.99 *(978-1-4380-1270-4(5))* Sourcebooks, Inc.
Mcdonald, Jill & Fatus, Sophie. Over in the Meadow Puzzle. Mcdonald, Jill, illus. 2012. (Illus.). (J). (gr. -1-1). 14.99 *(978-1-84686-746-0(0))* Barefoot Bks., Inc.
McEwan-Adkins, Elaine K. The Reading Puzzle: Word Analysis, Grades 4-8. 2008. (ENG., Illus.). 96p. (gr. 4-7). pap. 18.95 *(978-1-4129-5825-7(3)*, B58257P) Corwin Pr.
McKay, Chelsea. A Tangram ABC: Shaping the Alphabet from an Ancient Chinese Puzzle. Firos, Daphne, illus. 2013. 60p. (J). pap. 13.95 *(978-1-939431-04-2(2))* MathWord Pr., LLC.
Mcmahon, Kelly. Mazes, Grade K-1. 2006. (ENG.). 64p. (gr. k-1). pap. 6.99 *(978-1-4206-5990-0(1)*, TCR5990) Teacher Created Resources, Inc.
—More Mazes, Grade K-1. 2006. (ENG.). 64p. (gr. k-1). pap. 6.99 *(978-1-4206-5991-7(X)*, TCR5991) Teacher Created Resources, Inc.
Mega Puzzle Fun. Date not set. 576p. (J). 6.98 *(978-0-7525-9824-6(4))* Parragon, Inc.
Mega Travel Fun. Date not set. 576p. (J). 6.98 *(978-0-7525-9825-3(2))* Parragon, Inc.
Menotti, Andrea. How to Tackle Puzzles, Unravel Riddles, Crack Codes, & Other Ways to Bend Your Brain. 2004. (Illus.). 80p. (J). *(978-0-439-57905-6(8))* Scholastic, Inc.
Milbourne, A. Baby Animals Jigsaw Book. 2004. (SPA.). 14p. (J). 8.95 *(978-0-7945-0448-9(5))* EDC Publishing.
Milbourne, Anna. Familias de Animales Libro Con Paginas Puzzle. Butler, John, illus. 2004. (Titles in Spanish Ser.). (SPA.). 8p. (J). 8.95 *(978-0-7460-6108-4(0)*, Usborne) EDC Publishing.
Miller, D. L. BigFoot Activity Book: Wacky Puzzles, Coloring Pages, Fun Facts & Cool Stickers! 2019. (ENG.). 136p. (J). pap. 9.99 *(978-1-64124-034-5(2)*, 0345B) Fox Chapel Publishing Co., Inc.
—BigFoot Goes on Vacation: A Spectacular Seek & Find Challenge for All Ages! (BigFoot Search & Find Ser.). (ENG., Illus.). 48p. (J). 2019. pap. 9.99 *(978-1-64124-041-3(5)*, 0413) 2018. 14.99 *(978-1-64124-000-0(8)*, 0000B) Fox Chapel Publishing Co., Inc.
—BigFoot Visits the Big Cities of the World: A Spectacular Seek & Find Challenge for All Ages! 2018. (BigFoot Search & Find Ser.). (ENG., Illus.). 48p. (J). (gr. -1-7). 14.99 *(978-1-64124-001-7(6)*, 0017) Fox Chapel Publishing Co., Inc.
Miller, Jonathan, illus. When I Grow Up. 2011. 16p. (J). *(978-1-58865-637-7(3))* Kidsbooks, LLC.
Mitton, Tony & Parker, Ant. Amazing Machines Jigsaw Book. 2018. (Amazing Machines Ser.). (ENG.). 10p. (J). bds. 12.99 *(978-0-7534-7391-7(7)*, 900183782, Kingfisher) Roaring Brook Pr.
Miyamoto, Tetsuya & KenKen Puzzle, LLC. Will Shortz Presents I Can KenKen! Volume 1 Vol. 1: 75 Puzzles for Having Fun with Math. 2008. (ENG.). 112p. (J). pap. 14.99 *(978-0-312-54641-0(6)*, 900055743, St. Martin's Griffin) St. Martin's Pr.
—Will Shortz Presents I Can KenKen! Volume 2 Vol. 2: 75 Puzzles for Having Fun with Math. 2008. (ENG.). 112p. (J). pap. 18.99 *(978-0-312-54642-7(4)*, 900055745, St. Martin's Griffin) St. Martin's Pr.
—Will Shortz Presents I Can KenKen! Volume 3 Vol. 3: 75 Puzzles for Having Fun with Math. 2008. (ENG.). 112p. (J). pap. 18.99 *(978-0-312-54643-4(2)*, 900055747, St. Martin's Griffin) St. Martin's Pr.
Monkey Business: Level K, 6 vols. 128p. (gr. 2-3). 40.50 *(978-0-7699-0994-3(9))* Shortland Pubns. (U. S. A.) Inc.
Moog, Bob. Do I Bug You? A Who Am I? Book. San Francisco School, illus. 2006. (Spinner Books for Kids Ser.). (ENG.). 32p. (J). (gr. -1-12). 9.95 *(978-1-57528-898-7(2))* Univ. Games.
—I-Ballers: Little Books for Big Minds. 2005. (I-Ballers Ser.). (ENG.). pap. 4.95 *(978-1-57528-937-3(7))* Univ. Games.
—Spinner Books: the Grateful Dead. 2006. 240p. pap. *(978-1-57528-897-0(4))* Univ. Games.
Moore, Gareth. The Beautiful Flower Dot-To-Dot Book: 40 Drawings to Complete Yourself. 2018. (ENG.). 96p. pap. 12.99 *(978-1-4721-4047-0(8)*, Robinson) Little, Brown Book Group Ltd. GBR. Dist: Hachette Bk. Group.
—Brain Games: Mighty Book of Mind Benders. 2019. (Illus.). 160p. (J). (gr. 3-7). pap. 12.99 *(978-1-4263-3285-2(8)*, National Geographic Kids) Disney Publishing Worldwide.
—Brain Games for Clever Kids(r). Dickason, Chris, illus. 2014. (Buster Brain Games Ser.). (ENG.). 192p. (J). (gr. 4-6). pap. 7.99 *(978-1-78055-249-1(1))* O'Mara, Michael Bks., Ltd. GBR. Dist: Independent Pubs. Group.
—Brain Gaming for Clever Kids: More Than 100 Puzzles to Exercise Your Mind. Dickason, Chris, illus. 2018. (ENG.). 192p. (J). (gr. 2-6). pap. 6.99 *(978-1-4380-1237-7(3))* Sourcebooks, Inc.
—Explorer Academy Codebreaking Activity Adventure. 2019. (Explorer Academy Ser.). (Illus.). 128p. (J). (gr. 3-7). pap. 12.99 *(978-1-4263-3307-1(2)*, Under the Stars) Disney Publishing Worldwide.
—The Impossible Maze: Find Your Way Out!, 1 vol. 2018. (Puzzle Adventure Stories Ser.). (ENG.). 32p. (J). (gr. 3-3). 30.27 *(978-1-5081-9629-7(X)*, 5d568d65-35ce-4f57-b228-4abb49fde3b6); pap. 12.75 *(978-1-4994-8458-8(5)*, 61257003-b837-4e8a-ad01-f8d9cdb9f4c5) Rosen Publishing Group, Inc., The. (Windmill Bks.).
—The Kids' Book of Mazes 1. 2018. (Buster Puzzle Bks.). (ENG.). 192p. (J). (gr. 1-3). pap. 4.99 *(978-1-78055-500-3(8))* O'Mara, Michael Bks., Ltd. GBR. Dist: Independent Pubs. Group.
—The Kids' Book of Mazes 2. 2018. (Buster Puzzle Bks.). (ENG.). 192p. (J). (gr. 1-3). pap. 4.99 *(978-1-78055-502-7(4))* O'Mara, Michael Bks., Ltd. GBR. Dist: Independent Pubs. Group.
—Math Games for Clever Kids: More Than 100 Puzzles to Exercise Your Mind. Dickason, Chris, illus. 2018. (ENG.). 192p. (J). (gr. 2-6). pap. 7.99 *(978-1-4380-1238-4(1))* Sourcebooks, Inc.
—The Mysterious Woods: Solve Its Secrets!, 1 vol. 2018. (Puzzle Adventure Stories Ser.). (ENG.). 32p. (J). (gr. 3-3). 30.27 *(978-1-5081-9631-0(1)*, 82a958f7-16be-4b5c-9b5c-1aca9a8f0d30); pap. 12.75 *(978-1-5081-9549-8(8)*, 11558349-648c-4313-98fb-f13e6d3244e5) Rosen Publishing Group, Inc., The. (Windmill Bks.).
—Pyramid Puzzles. 2016. (Brain Game Treasure Hunts Ser.). (ENG., Illus.). 32p. (J). (gr. 3-6). 27.99 *(978-1-5124-0622-1(8)*, d414daec-b4e9-492b-bad5-b3474766a87b, Hungry Tomato (r)) Lerner Publishing Group.
—Space Puzzles. 2016. (Brain Game Treasure Hunts Ser.). (ENG., Illus.). 32p. (J). (gr. 3-6). 27.99 *(978-1-5124-0624-5(4)*, d99a5add-e842-4f9c-9052-2fd87c3ac0b1, Hungry Tomato (r)) Lerner Publishing Group.
—Ultimate Dot-To-Dot: Minecraft: 40 Incredible Puzzles with up to 1,000 Dots. 2017. (ENG.). 64p. (J). (gr. 3-7). pap. 9.99 *(978-1-4380-1076-2(1))* Sourcebooks, Inc.
Moran, Paul. Where's the Zombie? A Post-Apocalyptic Zombie Adventure. 2018. (ENG., Illus.). 48p. pap. 10.95 *(978-1-78243-837-3(8))* O'Mara, Michael Bks., Ltd. GBR. Dist: Independent Pubs. Group.
More Time for Bible Puzzles & Games. (Illus.). 32p. (YA). (gr. 5-18). pap. 2.25 *(978-0-87162-664-6(0)*, E9706) Warner Pr., Inc.
More Word Winks: Over 300 Visual Verbal Puzzles. 2004. (J). pap. 12.95 *(978-1-892069-76-4(8))* MindWare Holdings, Inc.
Morgan, Sally. Lonely Planet Kids Brain Teasers 1. Mansfield, Andy, illus. 2018. (Lonely Planet Kids Ser.). (ENG.). 160p. (J). (gr. 1-3). pap. 11.99 *(978-1-78701-315-5(4)*, 5731) Lonely Planet Global Ltd. IRL. Dist: Hachette Bk. Group.
Morris, Michael, illus. Puzzle Cards Letters. gif. ed. 2005. 16p. (J). 9.99 *(978-1-57791-188-3(1))* Brighter Minds Children's Publishing.
—Puzzle Cards Numbers. gif. ed. 2005. 16p. (J). 9.99 *(978-1-57791-187-6(3))* Brighter Minds Children's Publishing.
Mudpuppy Press Staff. Alligator Alphabet Floor Puzzle. 2005. (J). 17.99 *(978-0-7353-1224-1(9))* Galison.
—Dinosaur Block Puzzle. 2005. (J). 12.99 *(978-0-7353-0903-6(5))* Galison.
—Magic Horses 100-piece Puzzle. 2005. (J). 12.99 *(978-0-7353-0512-0(9))* Galison.
My First Hidden Pictures (Gr. K-1) 2003. (J). *(978-1-58232-061-8(6))* ECS Learning Systems, Inc.
My Little Pony Surprize Ink! Clipboard I. 2004. 24p. (J). 9.99 *(978-1-932125-92-4(2))* Giddy Up, LLC.
N. E. Thing Enterprises Staff. Garfield's Magic Eye. (FRE., Illus.). (J). pap. 9.99 *(978-0-590-16004-9(4))* Scholastic, Inc.
—Magic Eye III.Tr. of Oeil Magique III. (FRE., Illus.). (J). pap. 7.99 *(978-0-590-24610-1(0))* Scholastic, Inc.
Napier, Matt. I Spy with My Little Eye Hockey: Hockey. 2008. (I Spy with My Little Eye Ser.). (ENG., Illus.). 32p. (J). (gr. 1-4). 15.99 *(978-1-58536-365-0(0)*, 202150) Sleeping Bear Pr.
National Geographic. The Big Book of Fun! Boredom-Busting Games, Jokes, Puzzles, Mazes, & More Fun Stuff. 2010. (Illus.). 80p. (J). (gr. 1-3). pap. 6.99 *(978-1-4263-0661-7(X)*, National Geographic Kids) Disney Publishing Worldwide.
National Geographic Kids. What in the World? Fun-Tastic Photo Puzzles for Curious Minds. 2014. (Illus.). 48p. (J). (gr. 3-7). 16.99 *(978-1-4263-1517-6(1)*, National Geographic Kids) Disney Publishing Worldwide.
Needham, Kate. Usborne the Great Undersea Search. Brooks, Felicity, ed. Jackson, Ian, illus. rev. ed. 2006. (Great Searches Ser.). 32p. (J). (gr. -1-3). per. 7.99 *(978-0-7945-1228-6(3)*, Usborne) EDC Publishing.
Newman-D'Amico, Fran. Animal Friends Mazes. 2014. (Dover Kids Activity Books: Animals Ser.). (ENG.). 64p. (J). (gr. k-3). pap. 5.99 *(978-0-486-77965-2(3)*, 779653) Dover Pubns., Inc.
—Bugs Activity & Coloring Book. 2007. (Dover Kids Activity Books: Animals Ser.). (ENG., Illus.). 32p. (J). (gr. 1-3). pap. 3.99 *(978-0-486-46199-1(8)*, 461998) Dover Pubns., Inc.
—Busy Backyard Coloring & Activity Book. 2014. (Dover Kids Activity Bks.). (ENG.). 64p. (J). (gr. -1-3). pap. 5.99 *(978-0-486-77957-7(2)*, 779572) Dover Pubns., Inc.
—Fun Farm Animal Mazes. 2006. (Dover Kids Activity Books: Animals Ser.). (ENG., Illus.). 32p. (J). (gr. -1-3). pap. 3.99 *(978-0-486-45184-8(4)*, 451844) Dover Pubns., Inc.
—Girlfriends Activity Book. 2010. (Dover Little Activity Bks.). (ENG., Illus.). 64p. (J). (gr. k-3). pap. 1.50 *(978-0-486-47525-7(5)*, 475255) Dover Pubns., Inc.
—Halloween Fun. 2005. (Dover Halloween Coloring Bks.). (ENG., Illus.). 32p. (J). (gr. k-3). 3.99 *(978-0-486-44699-8(9)*, 446999) Dover Pubns., Inc.
—Little Animal Friends Mazes. 2016. (Dover Little Activity Bks.). (ENG.). 64p. (J). (gr. k-3). pap. 2.50 *(978-0-486-81035-5(6)*, 810356) Dover Pubns., Inc.
—Little Gardener's. 2005. (Dover Kids Activity Bks.). (ENG., Illus.). 32p. (J). (gr. -1-2). pap., act. bk. ed. 3.99 *(978-0-486-43990-7(9)*, 439909) Dover Pubns., Inc.
—My First Book of Puzzle Fun. 2005. (Dover Children's Activity Bks.). (ENG., Illus.). 64p. (J). (gr. -1-2). per. 4.95 *(978-0-486-44075-0(3))* Dover Pubns., Inc.
—SPARK Let's Go! Puzzles & Activities. 2018. (Dover Kids Activity Bks.). (ENG.). 64p. (J). (gr. 1-4). pap. 5.99 *(978-0-486-82026-2(2)*, 820262) Dover Pubns., Inc.
—Spot the Differences Picture Puzzles. 2014. (Dover Little Activity Bks.). (ENG.). 64p. (J). (gr. k-3). pap. 2.50 *(978-0-486-78182-2(8)*, 781828) Dover Pubns., Inc.
—Spot the Differences Puzzle Fun. 2004. (Dover Little Activity Bks.). (ENG., Illus.). 64p. (J). (gr. k-3). pap. 2.99 *(978-0-486-43841-2(4)*, 438414) Dover Pubns., Inc.
Nicholas, Mother Andrea, compiled by. My Little Orthodox Christian Feast Days Activity Book. 2005. (J). spiral bd. 6.95 *(978-0-9773579-0-1(2))* St. Nicholas Monastery.
Nichols, Roy & Corley, Monte. Bible Puzzles: Match-It. 2004. (Illus.). 64p. (J). pap. 9.95 *(978-0-937282-54-0(5)*, RB36154) Rainbow Pubs. & Legacy Pr.
—Bible Puzzles: Pencil Games. 2004. (Illus.). 64p. (J). pap. 9.95 *(978-0-937282-53-3(7)*, B36153) Rainbow Pubs. & Legacy Pr.

Niederman, Derrick. Mind-Stretching Math Puzzles. 2005. (Illus.). 112p. (J). *(978-1-4156-0492-2(4))* Sterling Publishing Co., Inc.

Nilsen, Anna. Pirates: All Aboard for Hours of Puzzling Fun! 2006. (Illus.). 32p. pap. *(978-1-921049-71-2(5))* Little Hare Bks. AUS. Dist: HarperCollins Pubs. Australia.

—Puzzle Heroes: People's Planet. Smith, Dave, illus. 2019. (Puzzle Heroes Ser.). (ENG.). 32p. (J). (gr. 3-7). pap. 11.99 *(978-1-4451-2135-2(2)*, Franklin Watts) Hachette Children's Group GBR. Dist: Hachette Bk. Group.

Noble, Marty. Mandala Mazes. 2010. (Dover Kids Activity Bks.). (ENG.). 48p. (gr. 5). pap. 4.99 *(978-0-486-47653-7(7)*, 476537) Dover Pubns., Inc.

Noodlers: Elusive Illusions. 2004. (J). pap. 12.95 *(978-1-892069-80-1(6))* MindWare Holdings, Inc.

Noodlers: Eye-Bending Icon. 2004. (J). pap. 12.95 *(978-1-892069-79-5(2))* MindWare Holdings, Inc.

Norman, D. Dinosaurs Sticker & Puzzle Kid Kit (Bag) 2007. (Kid Kits Ser.). 24p. (J). pap. 14.99 *(978-1-60130-054-6(9))* EDC Publishing.

Novick, Mary & Hale, Jenny. Farm Animals Jigsaw Book. 2007. (ENG.). bds. *(978-1-921049-99-6(5))* Little Hare Bks. AUS. Dist: HarperCollins Pubs. Australia.

—Zoo Animals Jigsaw Book. 2007. (ENG.). bds. *(978-1-921272-00-4(7))* Little Hare Bks. AUS. Dist: HarperCollins Pubs. Australia.

Oburkova, Eva. Toby's Travels Through Time: Puzzle Adventures in Dinosaur Days, 1 vol. 2007. (Toby's Travels Through Time: Puzzle Adventures in Dinosaur Days Ser.). (ENG., Illus.). 32p. (gr. 1-3). lib. bdg. 30.67 *(978-0-8368-7497-6(8)*, a1709d9a-99ba-47bd-9d58-cae7cfe51748, Gareth Stevens Learning Library) Stevens, Gareth Publishing LLLP.

Okido, Okido. Color Me In! An Activity Book. 2013. (Illus.). 128p. (J). (gr. k-3). pap. 14.95 *(978-0-500-65017-2(9)*, 565017) Thames & Hudson.

Orr, Julie. Hidden Pictures. 2019. (ENG.). 64p. (J). (gr. k-2). pap., wbk. ed. 4.49 *(978-1-58947-054-5(0)*, 32f513be-82f5-4043-b320-56695bcb5352) School Zone Publishing Co.

Osborne, Mary Pope & Boyce, Natalie Pope. Animal Games & Puzzles. Murdocca, Sal, illus. 2015. (Magic Tree House (R) Ser.). 256p. (J). (gr. 2-5). 6.99 *(978-0-553-50840-6(7)*, Random Hse. Bks. for Young Readers) Random Hse. Children's Bks.

—Games & Puzzles from the Tree House: Over 200 Challenges! Murdocca, Sal, illus. 2010. (Magic Tree House (R) Ser.). 256p. (J). (gr. 1-4). act. bk. ed. 6.99 *(978-0-375-86216-8(1)*, Random Hse. Bks. for Young Readers) Random Hse. Children's Bks.

Over 100 Things to Do on a Car Trip. 2017. (Activity Puzzle Bks.). (ENG.). (J). pap. 5.99 *(978-0-7945-3965-8(3)*, Usborne) EDC Publishing.

Overy, Kate. Neat Number Puzzles, 1 vol. Myer, Ed, illus. 2017. (Brain Blasters Ser.). (ENG.). 32p. (J). (gr. 1-2). 30.27 *(978-1-5081-9327-2(4)*, 5d28dfc3-1aab-4382-9588-d7d51409456a); pap. 12.75 *(978-1-5081-9331-9(2)*, 28ea7bba-db3e-4b80-b86f-5c8a75a67f10) Rosen Publishing Group, Inc., The. (Windmill Bks.).

—Perplexing Picture Puzzles, 1 vol. Myer, Ed, illus. 2017. (Brain Blasters Ser.). (ENG.). 32p. (J). (gr. 1-2). 30.27 *(978-1-5081-9328-9(2)*, ec2846bf-719e-4a29-8a72-a6d44677a708); pap. 12.75 *(978-1-5081-9332-6(0)*, 25651af2-6119-492c-a473-74dfadbcf8ff) Rosen Publishing Group, Inc., The. (Windmill Bks.).

—Supersmart Puzzles, 1 vol. Myer, Ed, illus. 2017. (Brain Blasters Ser.). (ENG.). 32p. (J). (gr. 1-2). 30.27 *(978-1-5081-9325-8(8)*, bafcd9f2-fb4a-4bb4-97ca-0f8975558bb5); pap. 12.75 *(978-1-5081-9329-6(0)*, e4fc8968-7ae1-4ef0-9e34-a860e3c54be9) Rosen Publishing Group, Inc., The. (Windmill Bks.).

Pace, Lorenzo. Marching with Martin, 1 vol. 2015. (African American Quartet Ser.). (ENG., Illus.). 48p. (J). (gr. 2-3). 32.93 *(978-1-4777-9285-8(6)*, ed3864cb-7051-4edd-919b-de3609d9330a, Windmill Bks.) Rosen Publishing Group, Inc., The.

Pantone. Pantone: Color Puzzles: 6 Color-Matching Puzzles. Carpenter, Tad, illus. 2013. (Pantone Ser.). (ENG.). 12p. (J). (gr. -1-k). bds. 18.99 *(978-1-4197-0939-5(9)*, 1064410) Abrams, Inc.

Paradis, Anne. Caillou: My Little Bed. Sévigny, Eric, illus. 2012. (ENG.). 10p. (J). (gr. -1-k). 9.99 *(978-2-89450-951-7(0))* Caillouet, Gerry.

Park, Barbara. Junie B. Jones: These Puzzles Hurt My Brain! Book. Brunkus, Denise, illus. 2011. (Junie B. Jones Ser.). (ENG.). 240p. (J). (gr. 1-4). 6.99 *(978-0-375-87123-8(3)*, Random Hse. Bks. for Young Readers) Random Hse. Children's Bks.

Parkes, Lois. Paper Sport: Activities, Games & Puzzles for Sporty Kids. 2012. 44p. pap. 21.99 *(978-1-4771-2582-3(5))* Xlibris Corp.

Parks, Sandra & Black, Howard. Dr. Funster's Visual B1: Creative Problem-Solving Fun. 2003. (Dr. Funster's Ser.). 30p. (gr. 7-9). pap. 4.99 *(978-0-89455-824-5(2))* Critical Thinking Co., The.

—Dr. Funster's Visual C1: Creative Problem-Solving Fun. 2003. (Dr. Funster's Ser.). 30p. (gr. 10-12). pap. 4.99 *(978-0-89455-825-2(0))* Critical Thinking Co., The.

Parri, Celia. Cyfoeth Cudd y Capten: Llyfr Stori a Phosau. 2005. (WEL., Illus.). 28p. pap. *(978-0-86381-397-9(6))* Gwasg Carreg Gwalch.

Pearcey, Alice. The Usborne Castle Jigsaw Book. Milbourne, Anna, ed. Groebner, Dominic, illus. 2006. (Jigsaw Bks.). 14p. (J). (gr. k-3). bds. 14.95 *(978-0-7945-1137-1(6)*, Usborne) EDC Publishing.

Peirce, Lincoln. Big Nate Boredom Buster. Peirce, Lincoln, illus. 2014. (Big Nate Activity Book Ser.: 1). (ENG., Illus.). 224p. (J). (gr. 3-7). pap. 7.99 *(978-0-06-233800-6(5)*, HarperCollins) HarperCollins Pubs.

—Big Nate Boredom Buster: Super Scribbles, Cool Comix, & Lots of Laughs. Peirce, Lincoln, illus. 2011. (Big Nate Activity Book Ser.: 1). (ENG., Illus.). 224p. (J). (gr. 3-7). 10.99 *(978-0-06-206094-5(5)*, HarperCollins) HarperCollins Pubs.

—Big Nate Laugh-O-Rama. Peirce, Lincoln, illus. 2014. (Big Nate Activity Book Ser.: 4). (ENG., Illus.). 224p. (J). (gr. 3-7). pap. 7.99 *(978-0-06-211116-6(7)*, HarperCollins) HarperCollins Pubs.

Penton, ed. A Happy Bugs. 2003. (J). 12.95 *(978-1-74047-216-6(0))* Penton Overseas, Inc.

Penton Overseas, Inc. Staff. U. S. Presidents. 2006. (ENG., Illus.). (J). pap. 7.95 *(978-1-59125-165-1(6))* Penton Overseas, Inc.

Percy, J.P. At Home. 2013. (Can You Guess What I Am? Ser.). (Illus.). 24p. (gr. k-3). lib. bdg. 28.50 *(978-1-59920-893-0(8))* Black Rabbit Bks.

—In the Street. 2013. (Can You Guess What I Am? Ser.). 24p. (gr. k-3). lib. bdg. 28.50 *(978-1-59920-894-7(6))* Black Rabbit Bks.

Perrin, James W., Jr. Back to School Puzzlers: An Awesome Array of Puzzles & Fun! 2004. (Illus.). 58p. (gr. 4-7). pap. 8.95 *(978-0-673-59963-6(9))* Good Year Bks.

—Holiday Puzzlers: An Awesome Array of Puzzles & Fun for November & December. 2005. (Illus.). 58p. (J). (gr. 4-6). per. 8.95 *(978-1-59647-063-7(1))* Good Year Bks.

Perrin, James W. Winter Puzzlers: An Awesome Array of Puzzles & Fun. 2007. pap. 9.95 *(978-1-59647-258-7(8))* Good Year Bks.

Petruccio, Steven James. Construction Site Sticker Picture Puzzle. 2005. (Dover Little Activity Bks.). (ENG., Illus.). 4p. (J). (gr. -1-2). 1.50 *(978-0-486-44156-6(3))* Dover Pubns., Inc.

Phillips, Dave. Americana Mazes. 2011. (Dover Kids Activity Books: U. S. A. Ser.). (ENG.). 48p. (J). (gr. 3-7). pap. 5.99 *(978-0-486-48108-1(5)*, 481085) Dover Pubns., Inc.

—Ancient Treasure Mazes. 2009. (Dover Kids Activity Bks.). (ENG., Illus.). 48p. (J). (gr. 3-7). pap. 4.99 *(978-0-486-46773-3(2)*, 467732) Dover Pubns., Inc.

Phoenix International Staff, illus. Write-and-Erase Look & Find(r) Disney: Packed with 'Find 'Ems & Picture Puzzles! Look, Circle, Wipe Clean, & Play Again! 2014. 20p. (J). bds. *(978-1-4508-8033-6(9)*, 1450880339) Phoenix International Publications, Inc.

PI Kids. Disney Pixar Incredibles 2: Look & Find. 2018. (ENG., Illus.). 24p. (J). 10.99 *(978-1-5037-3044-1(1)*, 2731, PI Kids) Phoenix International Publications, Inc.

—Marvel Avengers: Look & Find. Mawhinney, Art, illus. 2018. (ENG.). 24p. (J). 10.99 *(978-1-5037-3405-0(6)*, 2827, PI Kids) Phoenix International Publications, Inc.

Polinsky, Paige V. Rubik's Cube Creator: Erno Rubik. 2017. (Toy Trailblazers Set 2 Ser.). (ENG., Illus.). 32p. (J). (gr. 3-6). lib. bdg. 32.79 *(978-1-5321-1098-6(7)*, 25772, Checkerboard Library) ABDO Publishing Co.

Poliquin, Rachel. Beastly Puzzles: A Brain-Boggling Animal Guessing Game. Eggenschwiler, Byron, illus. 2019. (ENG.). 32p. (J). (gr. 2-5). 16.99 *(978-1-77138-913-6(3))* Kids Can Pr., Ltd. CAN. Dist: Hachette Bk. Group.

Pomaska, Anna. Dot-to-Dot. 2005. (Dover Kids Activity Bks.). (ENG., Illus.). 32p. (J). (gr. -1-2). pap. 3.99 *(978-0-486-44700-1(6)*, 447006) Dover Pubns., Inc.

Potter, Joe. My First Spot the Difference: Over 50 Fantastic Puzzles. Virgili, Marta Costa, illus. 2018. (My First Activity Bks.). (ENG.). 64p. (J). (gr. -1-2). pap. 6.99 *(978-1-4380-1145-5(8))* Sourcebooks, Inc.

—My First Unicorn Dot-To-Dot: Over 50 Fantastic Puzzles. Buckingham, Faye, illus. 2019. (My First Activity Bks.). (ENG.). 64p. (J). (gr. -1-2). pap. 8.99 *(978-1-4380-1272-8(1))* Sourcebooks, Inc.

Prenting, Ruth & Prenting, Ruth. I Spy ABC: Totally Crazy Letters! Ancutici, Manuela & Ancutici, Manuela, photos by. 2017. (ENG., Illus.). 32p. (J). (gr. -1-2). 14.95 *(978-1-77085-961-6(6)*, 4cfc118d-685a-482b-af46-e0ad2be283fd) Firefly Bks., Ltd.

Priddy, Roger. Dot to Dot for Tiny Tots Wipe Clean Activity Book. 2014. (Dot to Dot Ser.). (ENG.). 56p. (J). (gr. -1 — 1). spiral bd. 12.99 *(978-0-312-51772-4(6)*, 900137837) St. Martin's Pr.

—Maze Book: Follow Me Halloween. 2018. (Finger Mazes Ser.). (ENG., Illus.). 14p. (J). bds. 7.99 *(978-0-312-52723-5(3)*, 900189644) St. Martin's Pr.

—Maze Book: Follow Me Santa. 2018. (Finger Mazes Ser.). (ENG., Illus.). 14p. (J). bds. 8.99 *(978-0-312-52742-6(X)*, 900189899) St. Martin's Pr.

—Puzzle Play Set: MY PLAY FARM: Three Chunky Books & a Giant Jigsaw Puzzle! 2017. (First Learning Play Sets Ser.). (ENG., Illus.). 10p. (J). bds. 18.99 *(978-0-312-52662-7(8)*, 900186526) St. Martin's Pr.

Publications International Ltd. Staff. Brain Games Picture Puzzle 2. 2008. (Brain Games - Picture Puzzles Ser.: 2). (ENG.). 192p. spiral bd. 12.98 *(978-1-4127-1608-6(X)*, 3359800, PIL Kids) Publications International, Ltd.

—Brain Games Picture Puzzle 4. 2008. (Brain Games - Picture Puzzles Ser.: 4). (ENG.). 192p. spiral bd. 12.98 *(978-1-4127-9966-9(X)*, 3360300, PIL Kids) Publications International, Ltd.

—Sound Pooh Clues. 2007. 14p. (J). 16.98 *(978-1-4127-6201-4(4))* Publications International, Ltd.

Publications International Ltd. Staff, creator. Disney Enchanted. 2007. (Interactive Play-A-Sound Ser.). (Illus.). (J). (gr. -1). 15.98 *(978-1-4127-8812-0(9))* Publications International, Ltd.

Publications International Ltd. Staff, ed. Brain Games: Logic Puzzles. 2011. 192p. (J). spiral bd. 8.98 *(978-1-4508-1574-1(X))* Publications International, Ltd.

—Brain Games Kids: Amazing Brain Builder Puzzles. 2010. 192p. (J). 13.98 *(978-1-60553-776-4(4))* Phoenix International Publications, Inc.

—Brain Games Kids: Awesome Brain Builder Puzzles. 2010. 192p. (J). 13.98 *(978-1-60553-777-1(2))* Phoenix International Publications, Inc.

—Brain Games Kids: First Grade. 2010. 192p. (J). spiral bd. 13.98 *(978-1-4508-0054-9(8))* Phoenix International Publications, Inc.

—Brain Games Kids: Kindergarten. 2010. 192p. (J). (gr. k-k). spiral bd. 9.99 *(978-1-4508-0053-2(X)*, 145080053X) Phoenix International Publications, Inc.

—Brain Games Kids: Picture Puzzles. 2011. 192p. (J). spiral bd. 13.98 *(978-1-4508-1711-0(4))* Phoenix International Publications, Inc.

—Brain Games Kids: Preschool. 2010. 192p. (J). spiral bd. 13.98 *(978-1-4508-0052-5(1))* Phoenix International Publications, Inc.

—Brain Games Kids: Super Brain Builder Puzzles. 2010. 192p. (J). 13.98 *(978-1-60553-775-7(6))* Phoenix International Publications, Inc.

—Brain Games Kids: Word Search. 2011. 192p. (J). spiral bd. 13.98 *(978-1-4508-1573-4(1))* Phoenix International Publications, Inc.

—Counting Memory Game Puzzle. 2010. (J). 13.98 *(978-1-60553-350-6(5))* Publications International, Ltd.

—Disney Pixar Cars: First Look & Find & Shaped Puzzle Box Set. 2010. (J). 22.98 *(978-1-4508-0136-2(6))* Publications International, Ltd.

—Disney Pixar Picture Puzzle. 2010. 128p. (J). spiral bd. 12.98 *(978-1-60553-132-8(4))* Phoenix International Publications, Inc.

—Disney Princess First Look & Find & Giant Puzzle. 2010. (J). 22.98 *(978-1-4508-0135-5(8))* Publications International, Ltd.

—Disney Princesses. 2009. 16p. (J). bds. 9.98 *(978-1-4127-7696-7(1)*, PIL Kids) Publications International, Ltd.

—Kindergarten Boot Camp. 2010. (J). 20.98 *(978-1-4508-0069-3(6))* Publications International, Ltd.

—My First U.S. Map Puzzle. 2010. (J). 13.98 *(978-1-60553-306-3(8))* Publications International, Ltd.

—Play-a-Puzzle trade; Book: Alphabet. 2010. 12p. (J). bds. 10.98 *(978-1-60553-799-3(3))* Publications International, Ltd.

—Sesame Street Picture Puzzle. 2010. 128p. (J). spiral bd. 12.98 *(978-1-60553-130-4(8)*, PIL Kids) Publications International, Ltd.

—Solar System Puzzle. 2010. (J). 13.98 *(978-1-60553-351-3(3))* Publications International, Ltd.

Publishing, Standard. Bible Puzzles for Kids (Ages 6-8) 2016. (ENG., Illus.). 144p. (J). (gr. -1-3). per. 16.99 *(978-0-7847-1787-5(7)*, 140193) Standard Publishing.

Puzzability, et al. Bananagrams for Kids. 2010. (ENG., Illus.). 156p. (J). (gr. 2-12). pap. 10.95 *(978-0-7611-5844-8(8)*, 15844) Workman Publishing Co., Inc.

The Puzzle: Individual Title-Six Packs. (Chiquilibros Ser.). (gr. k-1). 23.00 *(978-0-7635-0440-3(8))* Rigby Education.

Puzzles by Joe Edley. Bananagrams! the Official Book: 575 Appealing Word Challenges That Will Drive You Bananas! 2009. (ENG., Illus.). 282p. pap. 10.99 *(978-0-7611-5635-2(6)*, 15635) Workman Publishing Co., Inc.

Radtke, Becky. Little Animals Hidden Pictures. 2006. (Dover Little Activity Bks.). (ENG., Illus.). 64p. (J). (gr. 3-5). per. 2.50 *(978-0-486-44899-2(1)*, 448991) Dover Pubns., Inc.

—Trains Activity Book. 2007. (Dover Little Activity Bks.). (ENG., Illus.). 64p. (J). (gr. k-3). per. 2.50 *(978-0-486-45683-6(8)*, 456838) Dover Pubns., Inc.

Radtke, Becky J. SPARK Theme Park Maze Craze. 2017. (Dover Kids Activity Bks.). (ENG.). 64p. (J). (gr. 1-4). pap. 5.99 *(978-0-486-81587-9(0)*, 815870) Dover Pubns., Inc.

—Unicorns Awesome Activity Book. 2018. (Dover Kids Activity Books: Fantasy Ser.). (ENG.). 48p. (J). (gr. 1-4). pap. 4.99 *(978-0-486-82807-7(7)*, 828077) Dover Pubns., Inc.

Raffin, Deborah. Mitzi's World: Seek & Discover More Than 150 Details in 15 Works of Folk Art. Scott, Jane Wooster, illus. 2009. (ENG.). 32p. (J). (gr. k-2). 18.95 *(978-0-8109-8004-4(5)*, 668801, Abrams Bks. for Young Readers) Abrams, Inc.

Rainbow Publishers Staff. More Bible Puzzles: Life of Jesus. 2004. (Reproducible Activity Books Ser.). (Illus.). 64p. (J). (gr. 4-18). pap. 9.95 *(978-0-937282-57-1(X)*, RB36158) Rainbow Pubs. & Legacy Pr.

—More Bible Puzzles: Memory Verse. 2004. (Reproducible Activity Books Ser.). (Illus.). 64p. (J). (gr. 4-18). pap. 9.95 *(978-0-937282-58-8(8)*, RB36159) Rainbow Pubs. & Legacy Pr.

—More Bible Puzzles: New Testament. 2004. (Reproducible Activity Books Ser.). (Illus.). 64p. (J). (gr. 4-18). pap. 9.95 *(978-0-937282-56-4(1)*, RB36157) Rainbow Pubs. & Legacy Pr.

Rand McNally. Are We There Yet? Awty. 2015. (ENG.). (J). (gr. 4-7). pap. 6.99 *(978-0-528-01340-9(8))* Rand McNally.

Rand McNally, creator. Coast-To-Coast Games. 2015. (ENG.). (J). (gr. 4-7). pap. 6.99 *(978-0-528-01342-3(4))* Rand McNally.

Rao, Lisa. Surf's Up. Merkel, Joe F. & Sazaklis, John, illus. 2007. (Surf's Up Ser.). 32p. (J). (gr. -1-2). 4.99 *(978-0-06-115335-8(4)*, Harper Entertainment) HarperCollins Pubs.

Rath, Robert. Go Wild for Puzzles Glacier National Park. Rath, Robert, illus. 2008. (Illus.). 32p. (J). (gr. k-3). pap. 5.95 *(978-1-56037-428-2(4))* Farcountry Pr.

Read, Howard & Chantler, Chris. Little Howard's Big Book. 2011. (ENG., Illus.). 128p. (J). 15.99 *(978-0-00-739125-7(0))* HarperCollins Pubs. Ltd. GBR. Dist: Independent Pubs. Group.

Really Horrible Facts. 2013. (Really Horrible Facts Ser.). 32p. (J). (gr. k-3). 101.00 *(978-1-61533-868-9(3))*; pap. 40.00 *(978-1-61533-876-4(4))*; pap. 240.00 *(978-1-61533-877-1(2))* Windmill Bks.

Red, White & Blue: The Search for Liberty. 2004. (J). cd-rom 19.95 *(978-1-931203-11-1(3))* Inspired Idea.

Regan, Dana, illus. Hidden Pictures Alphabet. 2004. (ENG.). 32p. (J). pap. 2.99 *(978-1-58947-395-9(7)*, 02197) School Zone Publishing Co.

Regan, Lisa. Brain Boosters: Memory Puzzles. Wood, Steven, illus. 2018. (Brain Boosters Ser.: 5). (ENG.). 96p. (J). pap. 9.99 *(978-1-78888-340-5(3)*, 3372deaa-75b0-400f-a67f-96b7db17f740) Arcturus Publishing GBR. Dist: Baker & Taylor Publisher Services (BTPS).

—Confusing Code Puzzles, 1 vol. Myer, Ed, illus. 2017. (Brain Blasters Ser.). (ENG.). 32p. (J). (gr. 1-2). 30.27 *(978-1-5081-9326-5(6)*, b0f16391-896b-4451-b264-fe14417a8847); pap. 12.75 *(978-1-5081-9330-2(4)*, f6873f0e-4217-400a-935c-ce40042ed59c) Rosen Publishing Group, Inc., The. (Windmill Bks.).

—The Haunted Hotel: Solve Its Mysteries!, 1 vol. 2018. (Puzzle Adventure Stories Ser.). (ENG.). 32p. (J). (gr. 3-3). 30.27 *(978-1-5081-9628-0(1)*, c974c937-722b-4c91-af34-b55f4b8e6451); pap. 12.75 *(978-1-5081-9541-2(2)*, a30721ac-47e1-434b-8ba0-43cc5826bc4d) Rosen Publishing Group, Inc., The. (Windmill Bks.).

—The Inca Adventure: A Quest of Questions!, 1 vol. 2018. (Puzzle Adventure Stories Ser.). (ENG.). 32p. (J). (gr. 3-3). 30.27 *(978-1-5081-9630-3(3)*, 9e817263-aa2e-483f-b2d7-95fd8d03c476); pap. 12.75 *(978-1-5081-9546-7(3)*, f227e931-8920-4929-b995-b7e593093a65) Rosen Publishing Group, Inc., The. (Windmill Bks.).

—The Treasure Hunt: Find the Fortune!, 1 vol. 2018. (Puzzle Adventure Stories Ser.). (ENG.). 32p. (J). (gr. 3-3). 30.27 *(978-1-5081-9632-7(X)*, 623d3386-a3fb-46b3-9e9f-d10a8c17f931); pap. 12.75 *(978-1-5081-9552-8(8)*, 2783bd33-a2c7-4e42-9b58-c6df158edb5b) Rosen Publishing Group, Inc., The. (Windmill Bks.).

Regan, Lisa Regan & Chiacchiera, Moreno. Puzzle Quest. 2016. (ENG., Illus.). 96p. (J). pap. 9.95 *(978-1-78428-206-6(5)*, 3a553753-8226-4b10-9a70-c09255a35ec8) Arcturus Publishing GBR. Dist: Baker & Taylor Publisher Services (BTPS).

Reid, Struan. Pirate Jigsaw Book. Allen, Peter, illus. 2007. (Luxury Jigsaw Bks.). 14p. (J). bds. 14.99 *(978-0-7945-1432-7(4)*, Usborne) EDC Publishing.

Reid, Struan & Stowell, Louie. My First Pirate Book. Allen, Peter, illus. 2012. (My First Book Ser.). 16p. (J). ring bd. 6.99 *(978-0-7945-3228-4(4)*, Usborne) EDC Publishing.

Rhatigan, Joe. The Ultimate Brain Bender Activity Book. Owsley, Anthony, illus. 2017. (Just a Pencil Gets You Many Days of Fun Ser.). (ENG.). 144p. (J). (gr. 2-8). pap., act. bk. ed. 9.99 *(978-1-63322-162-8(8)*, 224366, Moondance) Quarto Publishing Group USA.

Rinaldo, Luana, illus. Matching Puzzle Cards - Colors. 2012. (ENG.). 36p. (J). (gr. k-12). 9.99 *(978-1-60905-220-1(X))* Blue Apple Bks.

Ritchie, Scot. The Everything Kids' Connect the Dots Puzzle & Activity Book: Fun Is As Easy As 1-2-3 with These Cool & Crazy Follow-The-numbers Puzzles. 2008. (Everything(r) Kids Ser.). (ENG., Illus.). 144p. pap., act. bk. ed. 9.99 *(978-1-59869-647-9(5)*, Everything) Adams Media Corp.

—The Everything Kids' More Puzzles Book: From Mazes to Hidden Pictures - & Hours of Fun in Between. 2010. (Everything(r) Kids Ser.). (ENG., Illus.). 144p. pap. 15.99 *(978-1-4405-0647-5(7))* Adams Media Corp.

—Up, up & Away! Ritchie, Scot, illus. 2005. (ENG., Illus.). 32p. pap. *(978-1-921049-01-9(4))* Little Hare Bks. AUS. Dist: HarperCollins Pubs. Australia.

Ritchie, Scott. Ghouliest Ever Puzzle Book: Ghosts & Ghouls. 2008. 32p. (J). pap. *(978-1-921272-62-2(7))* Little Hare Bks. AUS. Dist: HarperCollins Pubs. Australia.

Rivera, Nicole. A Glimpse into Max's World (Max's Mini Puzzle Book) 2011. (ENG.). 40p. pap. 7.99 *(978-1-4610-7663-6(3))* CreateSpace Independent Publishing Platform.

Robson, Kirsteen. Jungle Picture Puzzle Book. 2018. (Picture Puzzle Bks.). (ENG.). 32p. (J). 14.99 *(978-0-7945-4118-7(6)*, Usborne) EDC Publishing.

—My First Maze Book. 2015. (Maze Bks.). (ENG.). 32p. (J). pap. 5.99 *(978-0-7945-3468-4(6)*, Usborne) EDC Publishing.

—Third Big Maze Book. 2015. (Maze Bks.). (ENG.). 64p. (J). (gr. k-5). pap. 9.99 *(978-0-7945-3491-2(0)*, Usborne) EDC Publishing.

Robson, Kirsteen & Smith, Sam. Little Children's Puzzle Pad. 2017. (ENG.). 100p. pap. 9.99 *(978-0-7945-4029-6(5)*, Usborne) EDC Publishing.

Rogers, Kirsteen. Under the Sea Jigsaw Book. Scott, Peter, illus. 2007. (Luxury Jigsaw Bks.). 14p. (J). bds. 14.99 *(978-0-7945-1330-6(1)*, Usborne) EDC Publishing.

Rosart, Sharyn. I Spy the 50 States. 2018. (J). lib. bdg. 29.40 *(978-0-606-41513-2(0))* Turtleback.

Ross, Suzanne. Nature Mazes. 2012. (Dover Little Activity Bks.). (ENG., Illus.). 64p. (J). (gr. k-3). pap. 2.50 *(978-0-486-28221-3(X)*, 28221X) Dover Pubns., Inc.

Roxbee-Cox, Phil. Find the Kitten. Cartwright, Stephen, illus. rev. ed. 2004. (Treasury of Farmyard Tales Ser.). (ENG.). 1p. (J). bds. 3.99 *(978-0-7460-3822-2(4))* EDC Publishing.

Roxbee-Cox, Phil, et al. El Reino de los Juguetes. 2004.Tr. of Magic Toyshop. (SPA., Illus.). 32p. (J). (gr. -1-3). lib. bdg. 14.95 *(978-1-58086-215-8(2)*, EU1202) EDC Publishing.

The Royals: PRINCE WILLIAM & KATE MIDDLETON - Puzzle: PRINCE WILLIAM & KATE MIDDLETON - Puzzle. 2011. 34.95 *(978-1-4507-6248-9(4))* Bluewater Productions, Inc.

Rubik's. How to Solve the Rubik's Cube. 2018. (ENG., Illus.). 64p. (gr. 2). pap. 7.99 *(978-1-4052-9135-4(4))* Farshore GBR. Dist: HarperCollins Pubs.

Russell, Ken & Carter, Philip. Bumper Quiz Book for Kids. (Illus.). 160p. (J). 17.95 *(978-1-85479-300-3(4))* O'Mara, Michael Bks., Ltd. GBR. Dist: Trans-Atlantic Pubns., Inc.

Russo, David Anson. Around the World: The Great Treasure Hunt. Russo, David Anson, illus. 2011. (ENG., Illus.). 28p. (J). (gr. 2-5). pap. 14.99 *(978-1-4424-4343-3(X)*, Simon & Schuster Bks. For Young Readers) Simon & Schuster Bks. For Young Readers.

Russo, M. Great Book of Dot to Dot: Omnibus Edition. Date not set. (J). 19.95 *(978-0-8069-6140-8(6))* Sterling Publishing Co., Inc.

Russo, Monica. Mythical Animals Dot-to-Dot. 2003. (Illus.). 64p. (J). (gr. 5-7). pap. 5.95 *(978-0-8069-9716-2(8))* Sterling Publishing Co., Inc.

Rutherford, Peter, illus. Giant Fun-to-Find Puzzles Busy Animals: Search for Pictures in Eight Exciting Scenes. 2015. 24p. (J). (gr. -1-12). pap. 6.99 *(978-1-86147-460-5(1)*, Armadillo) Anness Publishing GBR. Dist: National Bk. Network.

Sandau, Carol E. 10 Puzzling Pieces. 2010. 80p. pap. 8.95 *(978-1-4502-6244-6(9))* iUniverse, Inc.

Santana, Sr. Sabina Stella. Happy Ending Children's Stories, & More: Poems, Tongue-Twisters, Proverbs, & Brain-Teasers. 2008. 64p. pap. 13.50 *(978-1-4303-1344-1(7))* Lulu Pr., Inc.

Santa's House Activity Fun. Date not set. (Christmas Activity Bks.). (Illus.). 128p. (J). 3.98 *(978-0-7525-6498-2(6))* Parragon, Inc.

Santillan, Jorge & British Broadcasting Company Staff. When's the Doctor? 2nd ed. 2014. (ENG., Illus.). 48p. (YA). pap. 7.99 *(978-1-4059-1720-9(2)*,

42258e50-b7fa-4c38-a789-0e03cc99d024) Penguin Bks., Ltd. GBR. Dist: Diamond Comic Distributors, Inc.

Sauerhofer, Ulrike & Sauerhofer, Ulrike. I Spy 123: Totally Crazy Numbers! Ancutici, Manuela & Ancutici, Manuela, photos by. 2017. (ENG., Illus.). 32p. (J). (gr. -1-2). 14.95 *(978-1-77085-999-9(3),* c45453a1-7b49-4870-9643-7d704bb728e1) Firefly Bks., Ltd.

Saumante, Juliette, illus. Seek & Find - Around the World. 2017. (Seek & Find Ser.). (ENG.). 26p. (J). 12.99 *(978-1-4413-2475-7(5),* b1a05db3-51d7-45a4-9fac-50dde9fd5435) Peter Pauper Pr. Inc.

Schimmell, David. Wizard of Oz. 2011. (Dover Kids Activity Bks.). (ENG., Illus.). 48p. (J). (gr. 2-5). pap., act. bk. ed. 4.99 *(978-0-486-48095-4(X),* 48095X) Dover Pubns., Inc.

Schlegl, William. Parable Puzzlers: Word Puzzles from Jesus' Parables. 2008. 64p. pap. 10.99 *(978-0-7586-1336-3(9))* Concordia Publishing Hse.

Scholastic, Inc. Staff. I Spy Treasure Hunt. 2008. 29.99 *(978-0-439-82069-1(3))* Scholastic, Inc.

School Zone Publishing Company Staff. Numbers, Colors & Shapes, 56 vols. rev. ed. 2018. (ENG.). 52p. (J). (gr. -1-1). 3.49 *(978-0-88743-278-1(6),* 19cfd959-5f2b-4d30-bdb9-aaa0a295495b) School Zone Publishing Co.

—Vocabulary Puzzles 2. (Illus.). (J). 19.99 incl. audio compact disk *(978-0-88743-968-1(3))* School Zone Publishing Co.

School Zone Staff. Big Mazes & More. 2017. (ENG.). 320p. (J). (gr. k-2). pap. 13.99 *(978-1-60159-257-6(4),* f430deb8-3ffa-4a2f-bfed-e0e1fc0ab416) School Zone Publishing Co.

—Dot-To-Dot Numbers. 2004. (ENG.). 32p. (J). pap. 2.99 *(978-1-58947-385-0(X),* 02190) School Zone Publishing Co.

—My First Dot-To-Dots. 2019. (ENG.). 48p. (J). (gr. -1-k). pap. 3.49 *(978-1-60159-246-0(9),* 4c933749-1158-4705-a72c-69190a279aba) School Zone Publishing Co.

—My First Hidden Pictures. 2019. (ENG.). 48p. (J). (gr. -1-k). pap. 3.49 *(978-1-60159-251-4(5),* ec4d1ede-7109-447f-b1f3-b541099c6f62) School Zone Publishing Co.

—My First Mazes. 2019. (ENG.). 48p. (J). (gr. -1-k). pap. 3.49 *(978-1-60159-247-7(7),* ee0cc799-6467-48e8-92ec-fe5918a9b73b) School Zone Publishing Co.

School Zone Staff, ed. Dot-To-Dot Alphabet. 2006. (ENG.). 32p. (J). pap. 2.99 *(978-1-58947-393-5(0),* 02195) School Zone Publishing Co.

—Hidden Pictures Around the World. 2006. (ENG.). 32p. (J). pap. 2.99 *(978-1-58947-387-4(6),* 02192) School Zone Publishing Co.

Schuette, Sarah L. Football Frenzy: A Spot-It Challenge, 1 vol. 2013. (Spot It Ser.). (ENG.). 32p. (J). (gr. -1-2). lib. bdg. 27.99 *(978-1-62065-062-2(2),* 120764, Capstone Pr.) Capstone.

—Hockey Scramble: A Spot-It Challenge, 1 vol. 2013. (Spot It Ser.). (ENG.). 32p. (J). (gr. -1-2). lib. bdg. 27.99 *(978-1-62065-063-9(0),* 120765, Capstone Pr.) Capstone.

—Sports Zone: A Spot-It Challenge, 1 vol. 2012. (Spot It Ser.). (ENG.). 32p. (J). (gr. -1-2). lib. bdg. 27.99 *(978-1-4296-8712-6(6),* 119505, Capstone Pr.) Capstone.

—100th Day: A Spot-It Challenge, 1 vol. 2012. (Spot It Ser.). (ENG., Illus.). 32p. (J). (gr. -1-2). lib. bdg. 27.99 *(978-1-4296-7559-8(4),* 117136, Capstone Pr.) Capstone.

Schuh, Mari. Basketball. 2018. (Spot Ser.). (ENG., Illus.). 16p. (J). (gr. -1-1). pap. 7.99 *(978-1-68152-203-6(9),* 14734) Amicus.

—Football. (Spot Ser.). (ENG., Illus.). 16p. (J). (gr. -1-1). 2018. pap. 9.99 *(978-1-68152-205-0(5),* 14736) 2017. 17.95 *(978-1-68151-086-6(3),* 14617) Amicus.

—Gymnastics. (Spot Ser.). (ENG., Illus.). 16p. (J). (gr. -1-1). 2018. pap. 7.99 *(978-1-68152-206-7(3),* 14737) 2017. 17.95 *(978-1-68151-087-3(1),* 14618) Amicus.

—Hockey. (Spot Ser.). (ENG., Illus.). 16p. (J). (gr. -1-1). 2018. pap. 9.99 *(978-1-68152-207-4(1),* 14738) 2017. 17.95 *(978-1-68151-088-0(X),* 14619) Amicus.

—Soccer. (Spot Ser.). (ENG., Illus.). 16p. (J). (gr. -1-1). 2018. pap. 7.99 *(978-1-68152-208-1(X),* 14739) 2017. 17.95 *(978-1-68151-089-7(8),* 14620) Amicus.

—Swimming. 2019. (Spot Sports Ser.). (ENG.). 16p. (J). (gr. -1-1). pap. 7.99 *(978-1-68152-439-9(2),* 11025) Amicus.

—Tae Kwon Do. 2019. (Spot Sports Ser.). (ENG.). 16p. (J). (gr. -1-1). pap. 7.99 *(978-1-68152-440-5(6),* 11026) Amicus.

—Volleyball. 2019. (Spot Sports Ser.). (ENG.). 16p. (J). (gr. -1-2). lib. bdg. *(978-1-68151-655-4(1),* 10787) Amicus.

Schuh, Mari C. Basketball. 2017. (Spot Sports Ser.). (ENG., Illus.). 16p. (J). (gr. k-3). 17.95 *(978-1-68151-084-2(7))* Amicus Learning.

Schwartz, Linda. Language Critical Thinking, Grades 2-4: Creative Puzzles to Challenge the Brain. Armstrong, Bev & Grayson, Rick, illus. 2005. 64p. (J). pap. 11.99 *(978-0-88160-384-2(8),* LW423, Learning Works, The) Creative Teaching Pr., Inc.

Scott, Peter & Justine, Torode, illus. Box of Bugs. 2005. 6p. (J). 11.95 *(978-0-7945-1023-7(X),* Usborne) EDC Publishing.

Sector, Emma. There Are No Wrong Answers: A Book of Quizzes. Smith, Allie, illus. 2016. (ENG.). 192p. (J). (gr. 3-7). pap. 7.99 *(978-1-4814-5932-7(5),* Aladdin) Simon & Schuster Children's Publishing.

Seuss. Oh, the Places I'll Go! by ME, Myself. 2016. (ENG., Illus.). 64p. (J). (gr. -1-3). 16.99 *(978-0-553-52058-3(X),* Random Hse. Bks. for Young Readers) Random Hse. Children's Bks.

Sewell, Matt. The Big Bird Spot. 2017. (ENG., Illus.). 32p. (J). (gr. 2-4). 15.99 *(978-1-84365-326-4(5),* Pavilion Children's Books) Pavilion Bks. GBR. Dist: HarperCollins Pubs.

Shadow, Jak. The Crime Lord. 2006. (F. E. A. R. Adventures S. Ser.). (ENG., Illus.). 128p. (J). 8.00 *(978-1-84046-693-5(6),* Wizard Books) Icon Bks., Ltd. GBR. Dist: Publishers Group Canada.

Shaw-Russell, Susan. Seek, Sketch & Color — Alphabet. 2013. (Dover Kids Activity Bks.). (ENG.). 64p. (J). (gr. 1-3). pap. 5.99 *(978-0-486-49772-3(0),* 497720) Dover Pubns., Inc.

—Snow White Activity Book. 2012. (Dover Little Activity Bks.). (ENG.). 64p. (J). (gr. k-3). pap. 1.50 *(978-0-486-47226-3(4))* Dover Pubns., Inc.

Shaw-Russell, Susan & Activity Books Staff. Tortoise & the Hare. 2012. (Dover Little Activity Bks.). (ENG., Illus.). 64p. (J). (gr. k-3). pap., act. bk. ed. 1.50 *(978-0-486-47518-9(2))* Dover Pubns., Inc.

Shears, William. My Little Pony. Utopia, illus. 2005. (Look & Find Ser.). 18p. (J). (gr. -1-3). pap. 24.98 *(978-1-4127-3316-8(2),* 7241700) Publications International, Ltd.

Shenk, Mike, et al. The Brainiest Insaniest Ultimate Puzzle Book! 250 Wacky Word Games, Mystifying Mazes, Picture Puzzles, & More to Boggle Your Brain. 2006. (ENG., Illus.). 194p. (J). (gr. 2-7). pap. 14.95 *(978-0-7611-4386-4(6),* 14386) Workman Publishing Co., Inc.

Shulman, Mark. All You Need Is a Pencil: the Wild & Crazy Summer Fun Activity Book. 2018. (All You Need Is a Pencil Ser.: 5). 144p. (J). (gr. 2-5). pap. 7.99 *(978-1-62354-092-0(5))* Charlesbridge Publishing, Inc.

Shurtliff, Norman. Amazing Scriptures: A Book of Mormon Adventure of Comics & Mazes. 2018. (ENG.). pap. 11.99 *(978-1-4621-2213-4(2))* Cedar Fort, Inc./CFI Distribution.

Simon, Francesca. Horrid Henry: Horrid Henry's Gold Medal Games: Colouring, Puzzles & Activities. 2017. (Horrid Henry Ser.). (ENG., Illus.). 24p. (J). (gr. 1-3). pap. 8.99 *(978-1-5101-0127-2(6),* Orion Children's Bks.) Hachette Children's Group GBR. Dist: Hachette Bk. Group.

Simpson, Dana. Rainy Day Unicorn Fun: A Phoebe & Her Unicorn Activity Book. 2017. (ENG.). 144p. (J). pap., act. bk. ed. 11.99 *(978-1-4494-8725-6(4))* Andrews McMeel Publishing.

Sims, L. Puzzle Journey Around the World. 2004. (Puzzle Journey Ser.). 32p. (J). pap. 6.95 *(978-0-7945-0510-3(4))* EDC Publishing.

—Puzzle Journey into Space. 2004. (Puzzle Journey Ser.). 32p. (J). pap. 6.95 *(978-0-7945-0439-7(6))* EDC Publishing.

—Puzzle Journey under the Sea. 2004. (Puzzle Journey Ser.). 32p. (J). pap. 6.95 *(978-0-7945-0481-6(7))* EDC Publishing.

Smart, Jamie. Where's the Doctor? 2017. (Illus.). 40p. (YA). pap. 9.99 *(978-1-4059-0904-4(8),* 14ba51f7-18af-45aa-bc80-7ed27d625b1a) Penguin Bks., Ltd. GBR. Dist: Diamond Comic Distributors, Inc.

SMARTLAB Creative Team. Mega 3D Puzzle Play Dinosaurs. 2010. 3p. mass mkt. 19.99 *(978-1-60380-092-1(1))* becker&mayer! books.

—Mega 3D Puzzle Play Sharks. 2010. 3p. mass mkt. 19.99 *(978-1-60380-094-5(8))* becker&mayer! books.

Smolik, Jane Petrlik. The Great Massachusetts Puzzle Book: Over 75 Puzzles about Life in the Bay State. rev. ed. 2005. (Illus.). 96p. (J). (gr. 2-7). per. 11.95 *(978-0-9664095-5-0(8))* MidRun Pr.

—The Great State of Maine Activity Book: Over 75 Puzzles about Life in Maine. rev. ed. 2006. (Illus.). 96p. (J). (gr. 2-7). per. 11.95 *(978-0-9664095-6-7(6))* MidRun Pr.

Snape, Charles & Snape, Juliet. Brain Busters: Games, Puzzles & More! 2012. (Dover Kids Activity Bks.). (ENG., Illus.). 64p. (J). (gr. 3-5). pap. 9.99 *(978-0-486-48779-3(2),* 487792) Dover Pubns., Inc.

—Mind Twisters: Games, Puzzles & More! 2012. (Dover Kids Activity Bks.). (ENG., Illus.). 64p. (J). (gr. 3-5). pap. 9.99 *(978-0-486-48780-9(6),* 487806) Dover Pubns., Inc.

Somper, Justin. Pyramid Plot. Wingham, Peter, illus. 2004. (Puzzle Adventures Ser.). 48p. (J). pap. 4.95 *(978-0-7945-0139-6(7),* Usborne) EDC Publishing.

Space: Puzzles & Games. 2009. (BOREDOM BUSTERS Ser.). 56p. (J). (gr. 2-7). pap. 4.99 *(978-0-8416-1092-7(4))* American Map Corp.

Spelling Is Fun. 2004. (Play & Learn Pads Ser.). 48p. (J). 3.99 *(978-1-85997-721-7(9))* Byeway Bks.

Sports. 2009. (BOREDOM BUSTERS Ser.). 56p. (J). (gr. 2-7). pap. 4.99 *(978-0-8416-1090-3(8))* American Map Corp.

Stadther, Michael. 101 New Puzzles Clues, Maps, Tantalizing Tales: And Stories of Real Treasure. Stadther, Michael, illus. 2006. (Treasure's Trove Ser.). (ENG., Illus.). 112p. (J). pap. 12.99 *(978-1-4169-2655-9(0))* Treasure Trove, Inc.

Stanley, Stephen. City of Lost Mazes. 2013. (Dover Kids Activity Bks.). (ENG., Illus.). 32p. (J). (gr. 3-8). pap. 5.99 *(978-0-486-49133-2(1),* 491331) Dover Pubns., Inc.

Steinbacher, Philip A. Quotation Quizzlers: Puzzling Your Way Through Famous Quotations. 2003. (J). per. 11.95 *(978-1-883055-60-8(1),* 151) Dandy Lion Pubns.

Stewart, Trenton Lee. The Mysterious Benedict Society: Mr. Benedict's Book of Perplexing Puzzles, Elusive Enigmas, & Curious. Sudyka, Diana, illus. (Mysterious Benedict Society Ser.). (ENG.). 176p. (J). (gr. 3-7). 2016. pap. 9.99 *(978-0-316-39475-8(0))* 2011. 17.99 *(978-0-316-18193-8(5))* Little, Brown Bks. for Young Readers.

Studio Mouse Staff. Spelling Fun. 2011. (Cars Ser.). (ENG., Illus.). 28p. (J). 15.99 *(978-1-59069-938-6(6))* Studio Mouse LLC.

Super Activity Pad. Date not set. 384p. (J). 7.98 *(978-0-7525-9573-3(3))* Parragon, Inc.

Super Puzzle Pad. Date not set. (Illus.). 384p. (J). 7.98 *(978-0-7525-9575-7(X))* Parragon, Inc.

Super Puzzles. 2004. 112p. (J). 4.99 *(978-1-85997-388-2(4))* Byeway Bks.

Super Travel Pad. Date not set. 384p. (J). 7.98 *(978-0-7525-9576-4(8))* Parragon, Inc.

Tallarico, Tony, Sr. Everyday Fun for Kids. 2016. (Dover Little Activity Bks.). (ENG.). 64p. (J). (gr. k-3). pap. 1.99 *(978-0-486-80760-7(6),* 807606) Dover Pubns., Inc.

Tallarico, Tony. Hunt for Hector. 2011. (J). *(978-1-56288-047-7(0))* Checkerboard Pr., Inc.

—Ultimate Sticker Puzzles: License Plates Across the States: Travel Puzzles & Games. Tallarico, Tony, illus. 2005. (Illus.). 24p. (J). (gr. -1-2). mass mkt. 6.99 *(978-0-8431-7737-4(3),* Price Stern Sloan) Penguin Young Readers Group.

Tallarico, Tony J., Jr. English - Spanish Word Search: Sopa de Letras, Vol. 2. 2011. (Dover Bilingual Books for Kids Ser.). (ENG.). 48p. (J). (gr. 2-5). pap. 4.99 *(978-0-486-48098-5(4),* 480984) Dover Pubns., Inc.

—English-Spanish Word Search. 2011. (Dover Bilingual Books for Kids Ser.). (ENG., Illus.). 48p. (J). (gr. 2-5). pap. 4.99 *(978-0-486-48097-8(6),* 480976) Dover Pubns., Inc.

—Presidents Activity Book. 2009. (Dover Little Activity Bks.). (ENG., Illus.). 64p. (J). (gr. k-3). pap. 1.99 *(978-0-486-47388-8(0),* 473880) Dover Pubns., Inc.

—Spot-the-Differences Around the World. 2009. (Dover Kids Activity Bks.). (ENG., Illus.). 48p. (J). (gr. 3-8). pap. 4.99 *(978-0-486-47304-8(X),* 47304X) Dover Pubns., Inc.

—U. S. A. Constitution Activity Book. 2016. (Dover Kids Activity Books: U. S. A. Ser.). (ENG.). 48p. (J). (gr. 3-6). pap. 5.99 *(978-0-486-80934-2(X),* 80934X) Dover Pubns., Inc.

—U. S. A. Secret Code Puzzles for Kids. 2014. (Dover Kids Activity Books: U. S. A. Ser.). (ENG.). 48p. (J). (gr. 3-6). pap. 4.99 *(978-0-486-49459-3(4),* 494594) Dover Pubns., Inc.

—Worldwide Secret Code Puzzles for Kids. 2016. (Dover Kids Activity Bks.). (ENG.). 48p. (J). (gr. 3-5). pap. 5.99 *(978-0-486-79871-4(2),* 798712) Dover Pubns., Inc.

Tallarico, Tony J., Jr. & Tallarico, Tony, Sr. Merry Christmas Activity Book. 2017. (Dover Christmas Activity Books for Kids Ser.). (ENG.). 48p. (J). (gr. 1-4). pap. 4.99 *(978-0-486-81913-6(2),* 819132) Dover Pubns., Inc.

—SPARK Nature Fun Facts Mazes. 2017. (Dover Kids Activity Books: Nature Ser.). (ENG.). 64p. (J). (gr. 1-4). pap. 6.99 *(978-0-486-81582-4(X),* 81582X) Dover Pubns., Inc.

Tatchell, Judy & Rogers, Kirsteen. Dragons Jigsaw Book. Scott, Peter, illus. 2005. (Usborne Jigsaw Bks.). 12p. (J). (gr. -1-3). bds. 14.95 *(978-0-7945-1117-3(1),* Usborne) EDC Publishing.

Tausig, Ben. Mad Tausig vs the Interplanetary Puzzling Peace Patrol. Goopymart, illus. 2007. (ENG.). 94p. (J). (gr. 4-6). per. 7.95 *(978-0-9741319-4-8(6))* 4N Publishing LLC.

Teckentrup, Britta. One Is Not a Pair. Teckentrup, Britta, illus. 2017. (ENG., Illus.). 32p. (J). (-k). 14.99 *(978-0-7636-9319-0(7),* Big Picture Press) Candlewick Pr.

—Where's the Baby? 2018. (ENG., Illus.). 32p. (J). *(978-1-78370-610-5(4))* Candlewick Pr.

Teenage Mutant Ninja Turtles Activity Books. 2004. (J). act. bk. ed. 1.49 *(978-0-7666-1295-2(3),* 99180) Modern Publishing.

Tenah, Ann. Brainiac's Bug Book: Creepy Crawly Activities. McGuinness, Tracy, illus. 2005. (Activity Journals Ser.). 128p. 12.99 *(978-0-88088-362-7(6))* Peter Pauper Pr. Inc.

Teora. Amazing Animal Puzzle Stickers, 1 vol., Vol. 2. Boos, Andre, illus. 2005. (Amazing Animal Puzzle Stickers Ser.). (ENG.). 8p. (J). pap. 5.99 *(978-1-59496-064-2(X))* Teora USA LLC.

The Critical Thinking Co. Dr. Funster's Think-A-Minutes A2: Fast, Fun Brainwork for Higher Grades & Top Test Scores. 2006. (Dr. Funster's Ser.). (ENG.). 48p. (gr. 2-3). pap. 8.99 *(978-0-89455-807-8(2))* Critical Thinking Co., The.

The Puzzle Society, The Puzzle. Pocket Posh Girl Hangman: 100 Puzzles. 2010. (ENG.). 112p. pap. 7.99 *(978-0-7407-9861-0(8))* Andrews McMeel Publishing.

—Pocket Posh Girl Hangman 2: 100 Puzzles. 2011. (ENG.). 112p. pap. 7.99 *(978-1-4494-0733-9(1))* Andrews McMeel Publishing.

—Pocket Posh Girl Sudoku 2 Vol. 2: 100 Puzzles. 2011. (ENG.). 128p. pap. 7.99 *(978-1-4494-0738-4(2))* Andrews McMeel Publishing.

The Puzzling Sports Institute. Slapshot Hockey Quizbook: 50 Fun Games Brought to You by the Puzzling Sports Institute. unabr. ed. 2009. (ENG.). 80p. pap. 8.95 *(978-0-88971-234-8(4),* ea5bfcfc-021b-43f5-90ab-c094d55f05f5) Nightwood Editions CAN. Dist: Harbour Publishing Co., Ltd.

The Times Mind Games. The Times MindGames Number & Logic Puzzles Book 1: 500 Brain-Crunching Puzzles, Featuring 7 Popular Mind Games (the Times Puzzle Books) 2017. (ENG.). 384p. 13.95 *(978-0-00-819030-9(5))* HarperCollins Pubs. Ltd. GBR. Dist: Independent Pubs. Group.

Thomson, Sarah L. The Ring of Honor. 2018. (Secrets of the Seven Ser.). (ENG.). 224p. (J). 17.99 *(978-1-61963-735-1(9),* 900146561, Bloomsbury USA Childrens) Bloomsbury Publishing USA.

Time for Bible Puzzles & Games. (Illus.). 32p. (YA). (gr. 5-18). pap. 2.25 *(978-0-87162-662-2(4),* E9705) Warner Pr., Inc.

Timmerman, Charles. The Everything Large-Print Travel Word Search Book: Find Your Way Through 150 Easy-To-read Puzzles. Lt. ed. 2011. (Everything(r) Ser.). (ENG.). 352p. pap. 15.95 *(978-1-4405-2736-4(9))* Adams Media Corp.

Tonka Sticker Activity Books. 2004. (J). act. bk. ed. 2.99 *(978-0-7666-1142-9(6),* 69685); act. bk. ed. 2.99 *(978-0-7666-1143-6(4),* 69685) Modern Publishing.

Top That Publishing Staff, ed. Brain Workout. 2004. (Illus.). 96p. pap. *(978-1-84510-211-1(8))*; Vol. 2. pap. *(978-1-84510-210-4(X))*; Vol. 3. pap. *(978-1-84510-209-8(6))*; Vol. 4. pap. *(978-1-84510-208-1(8))*; Vol. 5. pap. *(978-1-84510-309-5(2))*; Vol. 6. pap. *(978-1-84510-310-1(6))* Top That! Publishing PLC.

—101 Brainbender Puzzles. 2005. (Illus.). 48p. pap. *(978-1-84510-202-9(9))* Top That! Publishing PLC.

—101 Picture Puzzles. 2005. (Illus.). 48p. pap. *(978-1-84510-201-2(0))* Top That! Publishing PLC.

Toufexis, George. Discovering Washington D. C. Activity Book: Awesome Activities about Our Nation's Capital. 2016. (Dover Kids Activity Books: U. S. A. Ser.). (ENG.). 48p. (J). (gr. 3-6). 5.99 *(978-0-486-80719-5(3),* 807193) Dover Pubns., Inc.

—The Outrageous Human Body Activity Book. 2013. (Dover Children's Science Bks.). (ENG.). 48p. (J). (gr. 3-8). pap. 4.99 *(978-0-486-49116-5(1))* Dover Pubns., Inc.

—World Atlas Activity & Coloring Book. 2014. (Dover Kids Activity Bks.). (ENG.). 64p. (J). (gr. 3-5). 6.99 *(978-0-486-78121-1(6),* 781216) Dover Pubns., Inc.

Trapani, Iza. Rufus & Friends: Rhyme Time. Trapani, Iza, illus. 2008. (Illus.). 40p. (J). (gr. -1-3). pap. 7.95 *(978-1-58089-207-0(8))* Charlesbridge Publishing, Inc.

Tudhope, Simon. Christmas Puzzle Pad. 2017. (Tear-Off Pads Ser.). (ENG.). 204p. pap. 5.99 *(978-0-7945-4140-8(2),* Usborne) EDC Publishing.

Tullet, Hervé & Tullet, Hervé. The Game of Patterns. 2011. (ENG., Illus.). 14p. (gr. -1 — 1). bds. 8.95 *(978-0-7148-6187-6(1))* Phaidon Pr., Inc.

Turnbull, S. Dinosaur Jigsaw Book. 2004. (SPA.). 14p. (J). 8.99 *(978-0-7945-0525-7(2))* EDC Publishing.

Turnbull, Stephanie. Los Dinosaurios Con Cuatro Puzzles Sencillos. Scott, Peter, illus. 2004. (Titles in Spanish Ser.). (SPA.). 6p. (J). 8.95 *(978-0-7460-6109-1(9),* Usborne) EDC Publishing.

Twomey, Emily. Buster's Brilliant Dot to Dot. Twomey, Emily, illus. 2014. (ENG., Illus.). 64p. (J). (gr. k-4). pap. 7.99 *(978-1-78055-201-9(7))* O'Mara, Michael Bks., Ltd. GBR. Dist: Independent Pubs. Group.

—The Kids' Book of Dot to Dot 1. 2018. (Buster Puzzle Bks.). (ENG.). 192p. (J). (gr. 1-5). pap. 4.99 *(978-1-78055-505-8(9))* O'Mara, Michael Bks., Ltd. GBR. Dist: Independent Pubs. Group.

Tyler, Jenny. Dot-to-Dot on the Farm. rev. ed. 2004. (Dot to Dot Ser.). (Illus.). 24p. (J). pap. 3.99 *(978-0-7945-0492-2(2))* EDC Publishing.

Tyler, Jenny & Blundell, Kim. Animal Mazes. rev. ed. 2004. (Maze Fun Ser.). 24p. (J). pap. 5.95 *(978-0-7945-0538-7(4))* EDC Publishing.

—Monster Mazes. rev. ed. 2004. (Maze Fun Ser.). 24p. (J). pap. 5.95 *(978-0-7945-0536-3(8))* EDC Publishing.

Tyo, Courtney. Holiday Puzzles. 2004. 47p. (J). *(978-0-439-68016-5(6))* Scholastic, Inc.

U. S. Kids Editorial Staff. The Best Adventure of the Puzzle Squad. (Illus.). 48p. (J). (gr. k-6). stu. ed. 6.95 *(978-1-885453-75-4(2))* Children's Better Health Institute.

Ungerer, Tomi. One, Two, Where's My Shoe? 2014. (ENG., Illus.). 32p. (gr. -1-k). 14.95 *(978-0-7148-6798-4(5))* Phaidon Pr., Inc.

University Games Staff, compiled by. I-Ballers: Little Books for Big Minds. 2005. (I-Ballers Ser.). (ENG.). pap. 4.95 *(978-1-57528-936-6(9))* Univ. Games.

—Made You Laugh for Kids! Books So Fun You'll Pee Your Pants! 2005. (ENG., Illus.). 224p. (J). (gr. -1-3). pap. 14.95 *(978-1-57528-995-3(4))* Univ. Games.

Vaicikonis, Kris. Puzzle Me-Brain Twisters. 2012. (Illus.). 32p. (J). pap. 4.99 *(978-1-62267-006-2(X))* Bright Connections Media.

Vandenbroucke, Brecht. The Dream of Surrealism 1000 Piece Puzzle: Spot the Artists & Jump down the Rabbit Hole. 2018. (ENG., Illus.). 19.99 *(978-1-78627-313-0(6),* King, Laurence Publishing) Orion Publishing Group, Ltd. GBR. Dist: Hachette Bk. Group.

Vidal, Oriol, illus. Build a Picture Monsters Sticker Book. 2013. (Build a Picture Sticker Bks.). (ENG.). (J). 6.99 *(978-0-7945-2947-5(X),* Usborne) EDC Publishing.

Vidro, Kenn G. Square Pears. 2003. (Illus.). 112p. (J). spiral bd. 7.95 *(978-0-9745308-0-2(8))* Gilbert Square Bks.

Volke, Gordon. Big World Activity Sticker Book, Vol. 2. 2004. (Illus.). 16p. 7.25 *(978-1-84161-130-3(1))* Ravette Publishing, Ltd. GBR. Dist: Parkwest Pubns., Inc.

Volke, Gordon, et al, illus. Panda Patrol Big Activity Book. 2004. 24p. 6.00 *(978-1-84161-111-2(5))* Ravette Publishing, Ltd. GBR. Dist: Parkwest Pubns., Inc.

Wagner, Veronica. Disney Mickey & the Roadster Racers: Go, Go, Go! Look & Find. The Disney Storybook Art Team, illus. 2017. (ENG.). 16p. (J). bds. 12.99 *(978-1-5037-2298-9(8),* 2531, PI Kids) Phoenix International Publications, Inc.

Wallace, MaryAlice & Lindstrom, Charlotte. Scripture Puzzlers: Crosswords, Word Searches, & Other Brain Teasers. 2015. (J). pap. 12.99 *(978-1-4621-1548-8(9),* Horizon Pubs.) Cedar Fort, Inc./CFI Distribution.

Wallis, Mary Alice & Lindstrom, C. G. Prophets & Apostles. 2008. (LDS Puzzle Pals Ser.). 122p. pap. 14.99 *(978-1-59955-126-5(8),* Cedar Fort, Inc.) Cedar Fort, Inc./CFI Distribution.

Ward, Barbara. Connectrix: A Geometric Puzzle Challenge. 2018. (ENG.). 64p. (J). (gr. 3). pap. 14.99 *(978-1-78055-517-1(2))* O'Mara, Michael Bks., Ltd. GBR. Dist: Independent Pubs. Group.

Ward, Simon. Labyrinth: A World of Incredible Mazes! 2018. (ENG., Illus.). 96p. (J). (gr. 1-4). pap. 7.99 *(978-1-4380-1127-1(X))* Sourcebooks, Inc.

Watt, F. & Wells, R. Farm Animals. 2004. 14p. (J). 9.95 *(978-0-7945-0561-5(9))* EDC Publishing.

—Pets. 2004. 14p. (J). 9.95 *(978-0-7945-0621-6(6))* EDC Publishing.

—Things That Go. 2004. 14p. (J). 9.95 *(978-0-7945-0622-3(4))* EDC Publishing.

Watt, Fiona. Animales de la Granja. Wells, Rachel, illus. 2004. (SPA.). 14p. (J). 9.95 *(978-0-7460-6113-8(7),* Usborne) EDC Publishing.

—Animals. Wells, Rachel, illus. 2006. 10p. (J). (gr. -1-k). bds. 9.99 *(978-0-7945-1227-9(5),* Usborne) EDC Publishing.

—Baby's Very First Slide & See Animals. 2015. (Baby's Very First Slide & See Board Bks.). (ENG.). 10p. (J). 14.99 *(978-0-7945-3479-0(1),* Usborne) EDC Publishing.

—Christmas Baby. 2005. 10p. (J). 8.95 *(978-0-7945-1185-2(6),* Usborne) EDC Publishing.

—Fairies Jigsaw Book. Cartwright, Stephen & Bird, Glen, illus. 2005. (Osborne Sparkly Jigsaws Ser.). 10p. (J). bds. 14.99 *(978-0-7945-1131-9(7),* Usborne) EDC Publishing.

—Mascotas. Wells, Rachel, illus. 2004. (Titles in Spanish Ser.). (SPA.). 14p. (J). 9.95 *(978-0-7460-6112-1(9),* Usborne) EDC Publishing.

—Mermaids Jigsaw Book. Cartwright, Stephen & Bird, Glen, illus. 2006. (Osborne Sparkly Jigsaws Ser.). 10p. (J). bds. 14.99 *(978-0-7945-1189-0(9),* Usborne) EDC Publishing.

Watt, Fiona & Wells, Rachel. Anifeiliaid y Fferm. 2005. (WEL., Illus.). 10p. *(978-1-84512-000-9(0))* Cymdeithas Lyfrau Ceredigion.

Wax, Wendy. Easter Bunny on the Loose! 2013. (ENG., Illus.). 32p. (J). (gr. -1-3). 7.99 *(978-0-06-223709-5(8),* HarperCollins) HarperCollins Pubs.

Weber, Bob. Go Fun! Slylock Fox Mystery Puzzles. 2015. (Go Fun! Ser.: 6). (ENG.). 128p. (J). pap. 8.99 *(978-1-4494-6900-9(0))* Andrews McMeel Publishing.

—Go Fun! Spot Six Differences. 2015. (Go Fun! Ser.: 7). (ENG.). 128p. (J). pap. 8.99 *(978-1-4494-6901-6(9))* Andrews McMeel Publishing.

Weber, Ken. Five-Minute Mysteries: (repackage), Pack. 2005. (ENG., Illus.). 200p. (gr. 7-12). per. 10.99 *(978-0-7624-2437-5(0),* Running Pr.) Running Pr.

Weller, Alan & Dover Publications Inc. Staff. Spot the Differences, Bk. 1. 2010. (Dover Kids Activity Bks.: Bk. 1). (ENG., Illus.). 64p. (J). (gr. 3-5). pap. 10.99 *(978-0-486-47299-7(X),* 47299X) Dover Pubns., Inc.

—Spot the Differences: Art Masterpieces, Bk. 2. 2010. (Dover Kids Activity Bks.: Bk. 2). (ENG., Illus.). 64p. (J). (gr. 3-5). 10.99 *(978-0-486-47300-0(7),* 473007) Dover Pubns., Inc.

Whelon, Chuck. Alien Invasion! Mazes. 2010. (Dover Kids Activity Books: Fantasy Ser.). (ENG., Illus.). 48p. (J). (gr. k-3).

pap. 4.99 *(978-0-486-47233-1(7),* 472337) Dover Pubns., Inc.

—Treasure Hunter Activity Book. 2011. (Dover Children's Activity Bks.). (ENG., Illus.). 48p. (J). (gr. 2-5). pap. 4.99 *(978-0-486-47878-4(5))* Dover Pubns., Inc.

—Where's the Princess? And Other Fairy Tale Searches. Whelon, Chuck, illus. 2016. (ENG., Illus.). 32p. (J). (gr. k-3). 16.99 *(978-1-4814-4633-4(9),* Aladdin) Simon & Schuster Children's Publishing.

Where Is Curious George? Around the Town: A Look-And-Find Bo. 2015. (Curious George Ser.). (ENG., Illus.). 32p. (J). (gr. -1-3). 9.99 *(978-0-544-38072-1(X),* 1591847, Clarion Bks.) HarperCollins Pubs.

Wick, Walter. Can You See What I See? 100 Fun Finds Read-And-seek (Scholastic Reader, Level 1) Wick, Walter, photos by. 2009. (Scholastic Reader, Level 1 Ser.). (ENG., Illus.). 32p. (J). (gr. -1-3). pap. 3.99 *(978-0-545-07888-7(1))* Scholastic, Inc.

—Can You See What I See? Animals: Read-And-Seek (Scholastic Reader, Level 1) Wick, Walter, photos by. 2007. (Scholastic Reader, Level 1 Ser.). (ENG., Illus.). 32p. (J). (gr. -1-3). pap. 3.99 *(978-0-439-86227-1(2))* Scholastic, Inc.

—Can You See What I See? Cool Collections: Picture Puzzles to Search & Solve. Wick, Walter, photos by. 2004. (Can You See What I See? Ser.). (ENG., Illus.). 40p. (J). (gr. -1-18). 13.99 *(978-0-439-61772-7(3),* Cartwheel Bks.) Scholastic, Inc.

—Can You See What I See? on a Scary Scary Night: Picture Puzzles to Search & Solve. Wick, Walter, photos by. 2008. (Can You See What I See? Ser.). (ENG., Illus.). 40p. (J). (gr. -1-3). 14.99 *(978-0-439-70870-8(2))* Scholastic, Inc.

—Can You See What I See? Out of This World: Picture Puzzles to Search & Solve. Wick, Walter, photos by. 2013. (Can You See What I See? Ser.). (ENG., Illus.). 40p. (J). (gr. -1-3). 14.99 *(978-0-545-24468-8(4),* Cartwheel Bks.) Scholastic, Inc.

—Can You See What I See? the Night Before Christmas: Picture Puzzles to Search & Solve. Wick, Walter, photos by. 2005. (Can You See What I See? Ser.). (ENG., Illus.). 40p. (J). (gr. k-3). 13.99 *(978-0-439-76927-3(2),* Cartwheel Bks.) Scholastic, Inc.

—Can You See What I See? Toyland Express: Picture Puzzles to Search & Solve. Wick, Walter, photos by. 2011. (Can You See What I See? Ser.). (ENG., Illus.). 40p. (J). (gr. 1-2). 14.99 *(978-0-545-24483-1(8))* Scholastic, Inc.

—Can You See What I See? Treasure Ship: Picture Puzzles to Search & Solve. Wick, Walter, photos by. 2010. (Can You See What I See? Ser.). (ENG., Illus.). 40p. (J). (gr. -1-3). 14.99 *(978-0-439-02643-7(1),* Cartwheel Bks.) Scholastic, Inc.

—Hey, Seymour! Wick, Walter, illus. 2015. (ENG., Illus.). 32p. (J). (gr. -1-k). 18.99 *(978-0-545-50216-0(0),* Scholastic Pr.) Scholastic, Inc.

Wick, Walter, photos by. I Spy: Interactive Sound Book of Picture Riddles. 2003. (Illus.). 30p. (J). 15.98 *(978-0-7853-8424-3(3))* Publications International, Ltd.

The Wiggles Coloring & Activity Books. 2004. (J). act. bk. ed. 0.99 *(978-0-7666-1048-4(9),* 99530); act. bk. ed. 0.99 *(978-0-7666-1049-1(7),* 99530); act. bk. ed. 0.99 *(978-0-7666-1047-7(0),* 99530) Modern Publishing.

The Wiggles Giant Coloring & Activity Books. 2004. (J). act. bk. ed. 1.99 *(978-0-7666-1051-4(9),* 49220); act. bk. ed. 1.99 *(978-0-7666-1050-7(0),* 49220) Modern Publishing.

Williams, Carla. Big Puzzles for Little Hands: Children of the Bible. 2004. (Illus.). 96p. (J). (gr. -1-2). pap. 11.95 *(978-1-885358-49-3(0))* Rainbow Pubs. & Legacy Pr.

—Big Puzzles for Little Hands: Jesus' Life & Lessons. 2004. (Illus.). 96p. (J). (gr. -1-2). pap. 11.95 *(978-1-885358-79-0(2))* Rainbow Pubs. & Legacy Pr.

—Big Puzzles for Little Hands: The Bible Tells Me So. 2004. (Illus.). 96p. (J). (gr. -1-2). pap. 11.95 *(978-1-885358-80-6(6))* Rainbow Pubs. & Legacy Pr.

Woods, Christopher & McClintic, Ben, illus. Where's Hanuman? 2009. (ENG.). 32p. (J). (gr. 3-18). 9.95 *(978-0-9779785-8-8(3),* d6880c06-8af8-4892-9a7d-ab6fb30eb25e) Torchlight Publishing.

Word Winks: Over 300 Visual Verbal Puzzles. 2004. (J). pap. 12.95 *(978-1-892069-75-7(X))* MindWare Holdings, Inc.

World Book-Childcraft International Staff, contrib. by. Brain Games: A Supplement to Childcraft — The How & Why Library. 2010. (J). *(978-0-7166-0624-6(0))* World Bk., Inc.

Wos, Joe. Maze-O-zoic: 50 Dinosaur Mazes. 2018. 64p. (J). (gr. 1-4). pap. 6.99 *(978-1-4380-1227-8(6))* Sourcebooks, Inc.

Wynne, Patricia J. Easy Dinosaur Mazes. 2006. (Dover Kids Activity Books: Dinosaurs Ser.). (ENG., Illus.). 48p. (J). (gr. -1-3). per. 4.99 *(978-0-486-45363-7(4),* 453634) Dover Pubns., Inc.

Xu, Bing. Look! What Do You See? An Art Puzzle Book of American & Chinese Songs. Stadtlander, Becca, illus. 2017. 48p. (J). (gr. 2-5). 18.99 *(978-0-451-47377-6(9),* Viking Books for Young Readers) Penguin Young Readers Group.

Young, Caroline. Big Bug Search. Jackson, Ian, illus. rev. ed. 2005. 32p. (J). pap. 7.99 *(978-0-7945-1045-9(0),* Usborne) EDC Publishing.

Young, Caroline & Needham, Kate. Great Wildlife Search: Big Bug Search, Great Animal Search & Great Undersea Search. Jackson, Ian, illus. 2004. (Great Searches Ser.). 112p. (J). pap. 15.99 *(978-0-7945-0892-0(8),* Usborne) EDC Publishing.

Young, Jay, creator. Secret Ziga Zaga. 2003. (Ziga Zaga Ser.). 192p. (YA). *(978-1-84347-034-2(9),* Pavilion Children's Books) Pavilion Bks.

Yoyo Books Staff. Animals Around Me: Animal Jigsaw Fun. 2004. 12p. bds. *(978-90-5843-550-7(4))* YoYo Bks.

—Baby Animals: Animal Jigsaw Fun. 2004. 12p. bds. *(978-90-5843-551-4(2))* YoYo Bks.

—An Exciting Day Trip: Princess Charlotte's Picture Puzzles. 2005. 32p. *(978-90-5843-456-2(7))* YoYo Bks.

—Farm Animals: Animal Jigsaw Fun. 2004. 12p. bds. *(978-90-5843-549-1(0))* YoYo Bks.

—A Magic Gift: Princess Charlotte's Picture Puzzles. 2005. 32p. *(978-90-5843-457-9(5))* YoYo Bks.

—Wild Animals: Animal Jigsaw Fun. 2004. 12p. bds. *(978-90-5843-552-1(0))* YoYo Bks.

Zourelias, Diana. Fairyland Hidden Pictures. 2006. (Dover Fantasy Coloring Bks.). (ENG., Illus.). 32p. (J). (gr. 3). pap. 3.99 *(978-0-486-45187-9(9),* 451879) Dover Pubns., Inc.

—SPARK Adorable Animals Find It! Color It! 2016. (Dover Kids Activity Books: Animals Ser.). (ENG.). 64p. (J). (gr. 1-4). pap. 5.99 *(978-0-486-81067-6(4),* 810674) Dover Pubns., Inc.

—SPARK Things That Go Find It! Color It! 2017. (Dover Kids Activity Bks.). (ENG.). 64p. (J). (gr. 1-4). pap. 5.99 *(978-0-486-81383-7(5),* 813835) Dover Pubns., Inc.

—SPARK U. S. A. Fun Find it! Color It! 2017. (Dover Kids Activity Books: U. S. A. Ser.). (ENG.). 64p. (J). (gr. 1-4). pap. 5.99 *(978-0-486-81893-1(4),* 818934) Dover Pubns., Inc.

3D Circus Puzzle Book. 12p. (J). *(978-2-89393-867-7(1))* Phidal Publishing, Inc./Editions Phidal, Inc.

PYLE, ERNIE, 1900-1945

Boomhower, Ray E. The Soldier's Friend: A Life of Ernie Pyle. 2006. (Illus.). 134p. 17.95 *(978-0-87195-200-4(9))* Indiana Historical Society.

Shone, Rob. War Correspondents, 1 vol. Forsey, Chris, illus. 2008. (Graphic Careers Ser.). (ENG.). 48p. (J). (gr. 5-5). lib. bdg. 37.13 *(978-1-4042-1449-1(6),* a6d745c4-f2f5-41b5-82e5-d10e71cb82f6); per. 14.05 *(978-1-4042-1450-7(X),* 24c5c00b-755c-4c08-903b-1cd3c3ae1a7c) Rosen Publishing Group, Inc., The.

PYRAMIDS

Biskup, Agnieszka. Egypt's Mysterious Pyramids: An Isabel Soto Archaeology Adventure. Stewart, Roger, illus. 2012. (Graphic Expeditions Ser.). (ENG.). 32p. (gr. 3-4). pap. 47.70 *(978-1-4296-8472-9(0),* Capstone Pr.) Capstone.

Bodden, Valerie. Pyramids. 2008. (Built to Last Ser.). (Illus.). 24p. (J). (gr. 3-7). lib. bdg. 24.25 *(978-1-58341-563-4(7),* Creative Education) Creative Co., The.

Chisholm, Jane & Reid, Straun. Who Built the Pyramids? Stitt, Sue, illus. 2004. (Starting Point History Ser.). 32p. (J). (gr. 1). lib. bdg. 12.95 *(978-1-58086-629-3(8),* Usborne) EDC Publishing.

George, Enzo. The Pyramids of Giza. 2017. (Crypts, Tombs, & Secret Rooms Ser.). 48p. (gr. 4-5). pap. 84.30 *(978-1-5382-0642-3(0))* Stevens, Gareth Publishing LLLP.

Great Pyramids & the Sphinx. (Butterfly Bks.). (ARA., Illus.). 46p. (YA). (gr. 5-8). 9.95 *(978-0-86685-400-9(2))* International Bk. Ctr., Inc.

Hansen, Grace. Great Pyramid of Giza. 2017. (World Wonders Ser.). (ENG., Illus.). 24p. (J). (gr. -1-2). lib. bdg. 32.79 *(978-1-5321-0440-4(5),* 26566, Abdo Kids) ABDO Publishing Co.

Harris, Nicholas. Pyramid. Dennis, Peter, illus. 2006. 31p. (J). *(978-0-7607-7526-4(5))* backpackbook.

Harris, Nicolas. Pyramids Through Time, 1 vol. 2009. (Fast Forward Ser.). (ENG.). 32p. (YA). (gr. 4-4). lib. bdg. 28.93 *(978-1-4358-2801-8(1),* 954c210c-e9f6-406c-97ab-1f5a5c11f3ca) Rosen Publishing Group, Inc., The.

Herbst, Judith. Lands of Mystery. 2004. (Unexplained Ser.). (Illus.). 48p. (J). pap. 7.95 *(978-0-8225-2407-6(4));* (ENG., (gr. 5-12). lib. bdg. 26.60 *(978-0-8225-1630-9(6))* Lerner Publishing Group.

Hoobler, Dorothy & Hoobler, Thomas. Where Are the Great Pyramids? 2015. (Where Is...? Ser.). lib. bdg. 16.00 *(978-0-606-37547-4(3))* Turtleback.

Hoobler, Dorothy, et al. Where Are the Great Pyramids? Hoare, Jerry, illus. 2015. (Where Is? Ser.). 112p. (J). (gr. 3-7). 5.99 *(978-0-448-48409-9(9),* Penguin Workshop) Penguin Young Readers Group.

Hyman, Teresa L. The Pyramids of Giza. 2004. (Great Structures in History Ser.). (ENG., Illus.). 48p. (J). (gr. 3-7). lib. bdg. 27.50 *(978-0-7377-1560-6(X),* Greenhaven Pr., Inc.) Cengage Gale.

Hynson, Colin. The Building of the Great Pyramid. 2006. (Stories from History Ser.). (ENG., Illus.). 48p. (J). (gr. 3-6). 21.19 *(978-0-7696-4708-1(1))* School Specialty, Incorporated.

Kenney, Karen Latchana. Mysteries of the Egyptian Pyramids. 2017. (Ancient Mysteries (Alternator Books (r)) Ser.). (ENG., Illus.). 32p. (J). (gr. 3-6). 29.32 *(978-1-5124-4014-0(0),* 0f69f067-65d0-4bad-b157-0e70704f010e, Lerner Pubns.) Lerner Publishing Group.

Keyes, Anna. Pharaohs, Pyramids Mummies & Faraones, pirámides y Momias: 6 English, 6 Spanish Adaptations. 2011. (ENG & SPA.). (J). 101.00 net. *(978-1-4108-5732-3(8))* Benchmark Education Co.

Kissock, Heather. Pyramids. 2011. (J). *(978-1-61690-435-7(6))* Weigl Pubs., Inc.

Kissock, Heather, ed. Pyramids. 2011. (J). (gr. 4-6). pap. 12.95 *(978-1-61690-771-6(1),* AV2 by Weigl); (Illus.). 24p. (gr. 2-5). 27.13 *(978-1-61690-767-9(3))* Weigl Pubs., Inc.

Leardi, Jeanette. The Great Pyramid: Egypt's Tomb for All Time. 2006. (Castles, Palaces, & Tombs Ser.). (Illus.). 32p. (YA). (gr. 2-5). lib. bdg. 28.50 *(978-1-59716-266-1(3))* Bearport Publishing Co., Inc.

Levy, Janey. The Great Pyramid of Giza: Measuring Length, Area, Volume, & Angles. 2009. (PowerMath: Advanced Proficiency Plus Ser.). 32p. (gr. 5-5). 47.90 *(978-1-60851-368-0(8),* PowerKids Pr.) Rosen Publishing Group, Inc., The.

Macdonald, Fiona. Solving the Mysteries of the Pyramids, 1 vol. 2009. (Digging into History Ser.). (ENG.). 32p. (gr. 3-3). lib. bdg. 32.64 *(978-0-7614-3106-0(3),* cf67327d-b174-4b77-b2b0-2fa3c78f5193) Cavendish Square Publishing LLC.

Malam, John. Pyramids. 2010. (100 Things You Should Know About Ser.). (Illus.). 32p. (YA). (gr. 4-6). lib. bdg. 19.95 *(978-1-4222-1525-8(3))* Mason Crest.

—Pyramids, 1 vol. 2014. (100 Facts You Should Know Ser.). (ENG., Illus.). 48p. (J). (gr. 4-5). lib. bdg. 33.60 *(978-1-4824-2185-9(2),* 0d7bf422-7e5f-4c23-ab6e-191ce7f8b0a5) Stevens, Gareth Publishing LLLP.

Malam, John & Macdonald, Fiona. Pyramids. 2013. (Illus.). 48p. (J). *(978-1-4351-5096-6(1))* Barnes & Noble, Inc.

Mann, Elizabeth. The Great Pyramid: The Story of the Farmers, the God-King & the Most Astonding Structure Ever Built. Turco, Laura Lo, illus. 2006. (Wonders of the World Book Ser.). (ENG.). 48p. (J). (gr. 4-8). pap. 14.95 *(978-1-931414-11-1(4),* c832d9b7-5982-498c-8d04-569a65d0876e) Mikaya Pr.

Marsh, Laura. National Geographic Readers: Pyramids (Level 1) 2017. (Readers Ser.). (Illus.). 32p. (J). (gr. -1-k). pap. 4.99 *(978-1-4263-2690-5(4),* National Geographic Kids) Disney Publishing Worldwide.

Matthews, Sheelagh. Pyramids of Giza. 2007. (Structural Wonders Ser.). (Illus.). 32p. (J). (gr. 4-6). lib. bdg. 26.00 *(978-1-59036-725-4(1));* per. 9.95 *(978-1-59036-726-1(X))* Weigl Pubs., Inc.

McCall, Henrietta. Pyramid. 2015. (Time Shift History Ser.). (Illus.). 32p. (gr. 3-6). 31.35 *(978-1-905638-63-5(9))* Book Hse. GBR. Dist: Black Rabbit Bks.

McNeil, Niki, et al. Pyramids of Egypt. 2007. (In the Hands of a Child: Project Pack Continent Study Ser.). (Illus.). 47p. spiral bd. 12.00 *(978-1-60308-071-2(6))* In the Hands of a Child.

Meachen Rau, Dana. Bookworms: The Inside Story, 12 vols., Set. Incl. Castle. lib. bdg. 25.50 *(978-0-7614-2272-3(2),* adab9f74-2818-438e-ba0f-67058d410319); Igloo. lib. bdg. 25.50 *(978-0-7614-2273-0(0),* b4264f9e-e40b-4791-87cc-23c1251e18a5); Log Cabin. lib. bdg. 25.50 *(978-0-7614-2274-7(9),* 0eb1f358-eb38-4d47-8e2b-9fc2cb65a564); Pyramid. lib. bdg. 25.50 *(978-0-7614-2275-4(7),* 10863ddc-9eee-46aa-abac-fc1eac1dec26); Skyscraper. lib. bdg. 25.50 *(978-0-7614-2276-1(5),* 21c7e684-e08a-4a1d-ba8f-a7294f9995c3); Tepee. lib. bdg. 25.50 *(978-0-7614-2277-8(3),* 36db5006-1580-4f2f-8b71-a10cc6b6c655); (Illus.). 32p. (gr. k-1). (Inside Story Ser.). (ENG.). 2007. Set lib. bdg. 153.00 *(978-0-7614-2271-6(4),* 26d3d7dd-7d58-4920-aa34-ec2e62335409, Cavendish Square) Cavendish Square Publishing LLC.

—Pyramid, 1 vol. (Inside Story Ser.). (ENG.). 32p. (gr. k-1). 2008. pap. 9.23 *(978-0-7614-3302-6(3),* 8551f0d9-3bed-4dc2-b29f-483317cadaf8) 2007. (Illus.). lib. bdg. 25.50 *(978-0-7614-2275-4(7),* 10863ddc-9eee-46aa-abac-fc1eac1dec26) Cavendish Square Publishing LLC.

Mellett, Peter. Find Out about Pyramids. 2013. (Illus.). 64p. (J). (gr. -1-12). pap. 9.99 *(978-1-84322-979-7(X),* Armadillo) Anness Publishing GBR. Dist: National Bk. Network.

Millard, Anne. Misterios de las Piramides. (Coleccion Misterios De). (SPA., Illus.). 48p. (YA). (gr. 5-8). 19.95 *(978-84-348-5690-5(5),* SM6076) SM Ediciones ESP. Dist: AIMS International Bks., Inc., Lectorum Pubns., Inc.

Moore, Gareth. Pyramid Puzzles. 2016. (Brain Game Treasure Hunts Ser.). (ENG., Illus.). 32p. (J). (gr. 3-6). 27.99 *(978-1-5124-0622-1(8),* d414daec-b4e9-492b-bad5-b3474766a87b, Hungry Tomato (r)) Lerner Publishing Group.

Naden, Corinne J. & Blue, Rose. Ancient Egyptians & the Pyramids. 2003. (J). *(978-1-58417-310-6(6));* pap. *(978-1-58417-311-3(4))* Lake Street Pubs.

Neuschwander, Cindy. Mummy Math: an Adventure in Geometry. Langdo, Bryan, illus. 2009. (Matt & Bibi Math Adventures Ser.). (ENG.). 32p. (J). (gr. 2-5). pap. 8.99 *(978-0-312-56117-8(2),* 900058847) Square Fish.

O'Donnell, Kerri. The Pyramids of Egypt. (Reading Room Collection 2 Ser.). 24p. (gr. 3-4). 2009. 42.50 *(978-1-60851-996-5(1),* PowerKids Pr.) 2003. (ENG.). 43.95 *(978-0-8239-8730-6(2))* Rosen Publishing Group, Inc., The.

Orr, Joel N. Structure Is Destiny: The Dandelion Paradox. 2004. (ALB.). (YA). per. 19.95 *(978-0-9634168-9-6(8))* ZEM Pr.

Peterson, Megan Cooley. The Egyptian Pyramids: How Did They Get Built? 2018. (History's Mysteries Ser.). (ENG.). 32p. (J). (gr. 4-6). pap. 9.99 *(978-1-64466-256-4(6),* 12277); (Illus.). lib. bdg. *(978-1-68072-409-7(6),* 12276) Black Rabbit Bks. (Bolt).

Peterson, Sheryl. Egyptian Pyramids. 2005. (Ancient Wonders of the World Ser.). (Illus.). 32p. (J). (gr. 4-7). lib. bdg. 18.95 *(978-1-58341-359-3(6),* Creative Education) Creative Co., The.

The Pyramids of Giza. 2014. (Great Idea Ser.). (ENG.). 48p. (J). (gr. 4-6). lib. bdg. 26.60 *(978-1-59953-593-7(9))* Norwood Hse. Pr.

Raum, Elizabeth. Egyptian Pyramids. 2014. (Ancient Wonders Ser.). (ENG., Illus.). 32p. (J). (gr. 2-5). 28.50 *(978-1-60753-466-2(5),* 15922) Amicus.

Riggs, Kate. Egyptian Pyramids. 2009. (Places of Old Ser.). 24p. (J). (gr. 1-5). lib. bdg. 24.25 *(978-1-58341-707-2(9),* Creative Education) Creative Co., The.

Samuels, Charlie. What Were the Pyramids?, 1 vol. 2017. (Mysteries in History: Solving the Mysteries of the Past Ser.). (ENG.). 48p. (gr. 5-5). lib. bdg. 33.07 *(978-1-5026-2798-8(1),* 042975b5-1409-459a-af85-31d5d8da78ef) Cavendish Square Publishing LLC.

Schimel, Lawrence. If You Were a Kid Building a Pyramid (If You Were a Kid) Ely, Jenn, illus. 2017. (If You Were a Kid Ser.). (ENG.). 32p. (J). (gr. 2-4). pap. 7.95 *(978-0-531-23949-0(7),* Children's Pr.) Scholastic Library Publishing.

Steele, Philip & Philip, Steele. Las Piramides Fueron Construidas. 2006. (Enciclopedia Me Pregunto Por Que). (SPA., Illus.). 32p. (J). (gr. 3-5). 12.99 *(978-84-241-2171-6(6),* EV2033) Everest Editora ESP. Dist: Lectorum Pubns., Inc.

Strom, Laura Layton. The Egyptian Science Gazette. 2008. (Illus.). 36p. (J). pap. *(978-0-531-18813-2(2))* Children's Pr., Ltd.

Sullivan, Erin Ash. Pyramids. 2011. (Early Connections Ser.). (J). *(978-1-61672-594-5(X))* Benchmark Education Co.

—Pyramids: Set Of 6. 2011. (Early Connections Ser.). (J). pap. 37.00 net. *(978-1-4108-1067-0(4))* Benchmark Education Co.

Taplin, Sam. Mummies & Pyramids. 2004. (Discovery Program Ser.). (Illus.). 48p. (J). pap. 8.95 *(978-0-7945-0317-8(9),* Usborne); lib. bdg. 16.95 *(978-1-58086-479-4(1))* EDC Publishing.

Weakland, Mark. Scooby-Doo! & the Pyramids of Giza: The Phantom Pharaohs. Brizuela, Dario, illus. 2018. (Unearthing Ancient Civilizations with Scooby-Doo! Ser.). (ENG.). 32p. (J). (gr. 3-6). lib. bdg. 27.99 *(978-1-5157-7513-3(5),* 135893, Capstone Pr.) Capstone.

World Book, Inc. Staff, contrib. by. The Mysteries of Egypt's Pyramids: The Secrets of the Pharaoh. 2015. (Illus.). 48p. (J). *(978-0-7166-2677-0(2))* World Bk., Inc.

Zuchora-Walske, Christine. Engineering the Pyramids of Giza. 2017. (Building by Design Set 2 Ser.). (ENG., Illus.). 48p. (J). (gr. 4-8). lib. bdg. 35.64 *(978-1-5321-1376-5(5),* 27674) ABDO Publishing Co.

Zuravicky, Orli. Exploring Pyramids Around the World: Making Models of Geometric Solids, 1 vol. 2003. (PowerMath: Proficiency Ser.). (ENG., Illus.). 32p. (J). (gr. 4-5). lib. bdg. 28.93 *(978-0-8239-8992-8(5),* 5b92d1b2-80fa-4330-b2d9-d9049261cd92, PowerKids Pr.) Rosen Publishing Group, Inc., The.

PYTHAGOREAN THEOREM

Ellis, Julie. Pythagoras & the Ratios: A Math Adventure. Peacock, Phyllis Hornung, illus. 2010. (Charlesbridge Math Adventures Ser.). (ENG.). 32p. (J). (gr. 2-5). pap. 7.99 *(978-1-57091-776-9(0));* (gr. k-3). 22.44 *(978-1-57091-775-2(2))* Charlesbridge Publishing, Inc.

—What's Your Angle, Pythagoras? Hornung, Phyllis, illus. 2004. (Charlesbridge Math Adventures Ser.). (ENG.). 32p. (J). (gr. 2-5). pap. 7.99 *(978-1-57091-150-7(9))* Charlesbridge Publishing, Inc.

Q

QUACKS AND QUACKERY

Farndon, John. Quacks & con Artists: The Dubious History of Doctors. Dean, Venitia, illus. 2017. (Sickening History of Medicine Ser.). (ENG.). 32p. (J). (gr. 3-6). E-Book 42.65 *(978-1-5124-2712-7(8));* E-Book 42.65 *(978-1-5124-3635-8(6),* 9781512436358); E-Book 4.99 *(978-1-5124-3636-5(4),* 9781512436365) Lerner Publishing Group. (Hungry Tomato (r)).

Perish, Patrick. Are Aliens Real? 2013. (Unexplained: What's the Evidence? Ser.). (ENG.). 32p. (J). (gr. 2-5). lib. bdg. 28.50 *(978-1-60753-383-2(9),* 16360) Amicus.

QUACKS AND QUACKERY—FICTION

Fagan, Cary. The Boy in the Box: Master Melville's Medicine Show. 2012. (ENG., Illus.). 288p. (J). (gr. 5-7). 16.99 *(978-0-547-75268-6(7),* 1487593, Clarion Bks.) HarperCollins Pubs.

Thompson, Lauren. Little Quack Counts. Anderson, Derek, illus. 2009. (Super Chubbies Ser.). (ENG.). 26p. (J). (gr. -1 — 1). bds. 5.99 *(978-1-4169-6093-5(7),* Little Simon) Little Simon.

—Little Quack Loves Colors. Anderson, Derek, illus. 2009. (Super Chubbies Ser.). (ENG.). 26p. (J). (gr. -1 — 1). bds. 6.99 *(978-1-4169-6094-2(5),* Little Simon) Little Simon.

QUAILS

World Book, Inc. Staff, contrib. by. Quail & Other Galliforms. 2005. (World Book's Animals of the World Ser.). (Illus.). 64p. (J). *(978-0-7166-1266-7(6))* World Bk., Inc.

QUAILS—FICTION

Dharma Publishing. The Hunter & the Quail: The Story about the Power of Cooperation. 2010. 36p. (gr. -1-7). pap. 8.95 *(978-0-89800-602-5(3))* Dharma Publishing.

Oldenburg, Richard. How the Quail Earned His Topknot. 2010. 30p. pap. 12.50 *(978-1-60911-668-2(2),* Eloquent Bks.) Strategic Book Publishing & Rights Agency (SBPRA).

Root, Laura L. Quail in My Garden: Book One of Adventures in My Garden. 2012. 64p. pap. 26.99 *(978-1-4490-6963-6(0))* AuthorHouse.

Sparks, Favre. Agnes, the Eggless Quail. 2009. 28p. pap. 16.50 *(978-1-60693-491-3(0),* Strategic Bk. Publishing) Strategic Book Publishing & Rights Agency (SBPRA).

QUAKERS

see also Society of Friends

Boothroyd, Jennifer. William Penn: A Life of Tolerance. 2006. (Pull Ahead Bks.). (Illus.). 32p. (J). (gr. 3-7). lib. bdg. 22.60 *(978-0-8225-6387-7(8),* Lerner Pubns.) Lerner Publishing Group.

Burton, Margie, et al. Friends. 2011. (Early Connections Ser.). (J). *(978-1-61672-489-4(7))* Benchmark Education Co.

Friends General Conference (U.S.), Religious Education Committee Staff, contrib. by. Lives That Speak: Stories of Twentieth-Century Quakers. 2004. (Illus.). viii, 168p. (J). *(978-1-888305-32-6(0))* QuakerPress.

Levy, Janey. William Penn: Shaping a Nation. (American History Milestones Ser.). 32p. 2009. (gr. 5-5). 47.90 *(978-1-61511-376-7(2))* 2009. (ENG.). (J). (gr. 5-5). lib. bdg. 28.93 *(978-1-4358-3016-5(4),* 24bd2188-de6c-4b3d-aa82-521f8e6f5069) 2009. (Illus.). (J). 60.00 *(978-1-4358-0196-7(2),* 1291824) 2008. (ENG., Illus.). (J). (gr. 5-5). pap. 10.00 *(978-1-4358-0195-0(4),* 513f85ca-cd43-44e9-a265-065502d0d251) Rosen Publishing Group, Inc., The. (PowerKids Pr.).

Marsh, Carole. William Penn. 2003. 12p. (gr. k-4). 2.95 *(978-0-635-02358-2(X))* Gallopade International.

Marsico, Katie. Lucretia Mott: Abolitionist & Women's Rights Leader, 1 vol. 2008. (Essential Lives Set 2 Ser.). (ENG., Illus.). 112p. (YA). (gr. 6-12). lib. bdg. 41.36 *(978-1-60453-039-1(1),* 6659, Essential Library) ABDO Publishing Co.

Mierka, Gregg A. Nathanael Greene: The General Who Saved the Revolution. 2006. (J). pap. *(978-1-59556-017-9(3));* (Illus.). 88p. (gr. 5-11). lib. bdg. 23.95 *(978-1-59556-012-4(2))* OTTN Publishing.

Rand, Carol. Lydia Darragh: Quaker Patriot. Marshall, Dan, illus. (J). 15.95 *(978-0-945912-33-0(1))* Pippin Pr.

Yolen, Jane. Friend: The Story of George Fox & the Quakers. 2nd ed. 2005. (Illus.). xii, 179p. (J). *(978-1-888305-41-8(X))* QuakerPress.

QUANTUM THEORY

see also Chemistry; Force and Energy; Radiation; Relativity (Physics); Thermodynamics

Farber, Ryan Jeffrey. Parallel Universes Explained, 1 vol. 2018. (Mysteries of Space Ser.). (ENG.). 80p. (gr. 7-7). 38.93 *(978-1-9785-0457-8(8),* 043308e0-27d3-44f6-aebc-cd2c3e180d32) Enslow Publishing, LLC.

Ferrie, Chris. The Cat in the Box. 2019. (Illus.). 48p. 17.99 *(978-1-4926-7123-7(1))* Sourcebooks, Inc.

—Quantum Entanglement for Babies. 2017. (Illus.). (J). *(978-1-4926-5608-1(9))*; (Baby University Ser.: 0). 24p. (gr. -1-k). bds. 9.99 *(978-1-4926-5623-4(2))* Sourcebooks, Inc.

—Quantum Information for Babies. 2018. (Baby University Ser.: 0). (Illus.). 24p. (J). (gr. -1-k). bds. 9.99 *(978-1-4926-5630-2(5))* Sourcebooks, Inc.

—Quantum Physics for Babies. 2017. (Baby University Ser.: 0). (Illus.). 24p. (J). (gr. -1-k). bds. 9.99 *(978-1-4926-5622-7(4))* Sourcebooks, Inc.

Hagler, Gina. Discovering Quantum Mechanics, 1 vol. 2014. (Scientist's Guide to Physics Ser.). (ENG.). 112p. (YA). (gr. 7-7). 39.80 *(978-1-4777-8002-2(5),* a4b20576-1797-423f-bbc0-f2442b6af0ee, Rosen Young Adult) Rosen Publishing Group, Inc., The.

McPartland, Randall. Understanding Quantum Physics. 2015. (J). lib. bdg. *(978-1-62713-433-0(6))* 2014. (ENG.). 48p. (YA). (gr. 8-8). 33.07 *(978-1-5026-0145-2(1),* 9ea8c1f2-8625-4b2b-9600-efd3d40a36d2) Cavendish Square Publishing LLC.

Scientific American Staff. Beyond Extreme Physics. 2009. (Scientific American Cutting-Edge Science Ser.). 160p. (gr. 9-9). 63.90 *(978-1-60853-073-1(6))* Rosen Publishing Group, Inc., The.

—Extreme Physics. 2009. (Scientific American Cutting-Edge Science Ser.). 176p. (gr. 9-9). 63.90 *(978-1-60853-076-2(0))* Rosen Publishing Group, Inc., The.

Shoup, Kate. Quantum Mechanics, 1 vol. 2018. (Great Discoveries in Science Ser.). (ENG.). 128p. (gr. 9-9). 47.36 *(978-1-5026-4382-7(0),* dfcdaa75-ba66-4478-ab6b-880a36ca8e5c) Cavendish Square Publishing LLC.

Spiro, Ruth. Baby Loves Quantum Physics! Chan, Irene, illus. 2017. (Baby Loves Science Ser.: 4). 22p. (J). (— 1). bds. 8.99 *(978-1-58089-769-3(X))* Charlesbridge Publishing, Inc.

Topp, Patricia. This Strange Quantum World & You. 2006. (Illus.). 68p. (J). (gr. 4-7). per. 10.95 *(978-1-60002-195-4(6),* 2844) Mountain Valley Publishing, LLC.

Willett, Edward. The Basics of Quantum Physics: Understanding the Photoelectric Effect & Line Spectra, 1 vol. 2004. (Library of Physics Ser.). (ENG., Illus.). 48p. (YA). (gr. 7-7). lib. bdg. 34.47 *(978-1-4042-0334-1(6),* dacdd3a4-a34f-4933-8cc1-fc881d39010c) Rosen Publishing Group, Inc., The.

QUARANTINE

see Communicable Diseases

QUARTER HORSE

Criscione, Rachel Damon. The Quarter Horse. 2009. (Library of Horses Ser.). 24p. (gr. 3-3). 42.50 *(978-1-60853-724-2(2),* PowerKids Pr.) Rosen Publishing Group, Inc., The.

Frazel, Ellen. The American Quarter Horse. 2011. (Horse Breed Roundup Ser.). (ENG., Illus.). 24p. (J). (gr. 3-8). lib. bdg. 27.95 *(978-1-60014-653-4(8),* Pilot Bks.) Bellwether Media.

Linde, Barbara M. Quarter Horses, 1 vol. 2012. (Horsing Around Ser.). (ENG.). 24p. (J). (gr. 2-3). pap. 9.15 *(978-1-4339-6470-1(8),* 7a7c496f-df88-4aa6-b55e-5a4a6a2e1981); lib. bdg. 25.27 *(978-1-4339-6468-8(6),* 2c72cc7a-c4e3-4630-b104-e64cddf7613e) Stevens, Gareth Publishing LLLP. (Gareth Stevens Learning Library).

Meister, Carl. American Quarter Horses. 2018. (Favorite Horse Breeds Ser.). (ENG.). 24p. (J). (gr. 1-4). pap. 8.99 *(978-1-68152-341-5(8),* 15142) Amicus.

Parise-Peterson, Amanda. American Quarter Horses. 2018. (Horse Breeds Ser.). (ENG.). 32p. (J). (gr. 3-9). lib. bdg. 28.65 *(978-1-5435-0032-5(3),* 136984, Capstone Pr.) Capstone.

Scheff, Matt. Andrew Luck, 1 vol. 2015. (Football's Greatest Stars Ser.). (ENG., Illus.). 32p. (J). (gr. 3-9). 32.79 *(978-1-62403-825-9(5),* 18020, SportsZone) ABDO Publishing Co.

Stone, Lynn M. American Quarter Horses. 2007. (Eye to Eye with Horses (High Interest) Ser.). (Illus.). 24p. (J). (gr. 3-6). lib. bdg. 27.07 *(978-1-60044-579-8(9))* Rourke Educational Media.

QUASARS

Owen, Ruth. Quasars, 1 vol. 2012. (Explore Outer Space Ser.). (ENG., Illus.). 32p. (J). (gr. 2-3). 29.93 *(978-1-4488-8076-8(9),* 015a5da8-c1c7-4d2d-9685-cd3a4278350b); pap. 11.00 *(978-1-61533-605-0(2),* 8101875f-e0db-48d0-93f6-074026a117b1) Rosen Publishing Group, Inc., The. (Windmill Bks.).

World Book, Inc. Staff, contrib. by. Quasars & Black Holes. 2010. (Illus.). 64p. (J). *(978-0-7166-9552-3(9))* World Bk., Inc.

QUASI-STELLAR RADIO SOURCES

see Quasars

QUASIMODO (FICTITIOUS CHARACTER)—FICTION

The Hunchback of Notre Dame. (Read-Along Ser.). (J). 7.99 incl. audio *(978-1-55723-992-1(4))* Walt Disney Records.

QUEBEC (PROVINCE)

Arsenault, Elaine. F Is for French: A Quebec Alphabet. Benoit, Renné, illus. 2013. (Discover Canada Province by Province Ser.). (ENG.). 40p. (J). (gr. 1-4). 17.95 *(978-1-58536-435-0(5),* 202351) Sleeping Bear Pr.

Malarek, Victor. Hey Malarek! The True Story of a Street Kid Who Made It. 2nd ed. 2012. (ENG.). 244p. pap. 22.95 *(978-1-4594-0047-4(X),* 0047) James Lorimer & Co. Ltd., Pubs. CAN. Dist: Formac Lorimer Bks. Ltd.

QUEBEC (PROVINCE)—FICTION

Autio, Karen. Second Watch, 1 vol. 2005. (ENG., Illus.). 208p. (J). (gr. 4-7). per. 8.95 *(978-1-55039-151-0(8))* Sono Nis Pr. CAN. Dist: Orca Bk. Pubs. USA.

Brouwer, Sigmund. La Revanche des Loups Gris, 1 vol. Gingras, Gaston, tr. from ENG. Griffiths, Dean, illus. 2011. (Loups Gris Ser.: 2). (FRE.). 72p. (J). (gr. 1-3). pap. 6.95 *(978-1-4598-0011-3(7))* Orca Bk. Pubs. USA.

Bruchac, Joseph. The Winter People. 2004. (Illus.). 176p. (J). (gr. 3-7). 8.99 *(978-0-14-240229-0(X),* Puffin Books) Penguin Young Readers Group.

Burgess, Barbara. The Magic Manuscript: The Nine Companions. 2013. 234p. pap. 12.99 *(978-0-9918574-3-2(7))* Sulby Hall Publishing.

Grant, Robert. Jack in the Bush or A Summer on a Salmon River. 2005. pap. 33.95 *(978-1-4179-5573-2(2))* Kessinger Publishing, LLC.

Gunderson, Jessica. Passage to Fortune: Searching for Saguenay. Kurtz, Rory, illus. 2016. (Discovering the New World Ser.). (ENG.). 96p. (J). (gr. 3-5). lib. bdg. 26.65 *(978-1-4965-3481-1(6),* 132579, Stone Arch Bks.) Capstone.

Henty, George. With Wolfe in Canad: The Winning of a Continent. 2011. 378p. pap. 19.95 *(978-1-61179-149-5(9))* Fireship Pr.

Jardine Stoddart, Heidi. Return to the Sea PB, 1 vol. 2007. (ENG., Illus.). 32p. (J). (gr. 1-3). pap. 11.95 *(978-1-55109-606-3(4),* b6138e5e-db88-4d57-acde-dd66efa3a6d4) Nimbus Publishing, Ltd. CAN. Dist: Baker & Taylor Publisher Services (BTPS).

Littell, William Adams. Guillaume. 2008. 74p. pap. 10.00 *(978-0-8059-7757-8(0))* Dorrance Publishing Co., Inc.

Noel, Michel. Good for Nothing, 1 vol. 2004. (ENG.). 324p. (YA). (gr. 7-10). pap. 14.99 *(978-0-88899-616-9(0),* Libros Tigrillo) Groundwood Bks. CAN. Dist: Publishers Group West (PGW).

Parker, Gilbert. Wild Youth. 2009. 108p. pap. 9.95 *(978-1-60664-359-4(2))* Rodgers, Alan Bks.

Perkyns, Dorothy. Bridget's Black '47. 2009. (ENG.). 160p. (J). (gr. 5-18). pap. 12.99 *(978-1-55488-400-1(4))* Dundurn Pr. CAN. Dist: Publishers Group West (PGW).

Pignat, Caroline. Wild Geese, 1 vol. 2010. (ENG., Illus.). 335p. (J). (gr. 5-9). pap. 12.95 *(978-0-88995-432-8(1),* 5892848d-5e36-48df-8137-257e91a4ebc2) Trifolium Bks., Inc. CAN. Dist: Firefly Bks., Ltd.

Polak, Monique. The Middle of Everywhere, 1 vol. 2009. (ENG., Illus.). 208p. (YA). (gr. 8-12). pap. 14.95 *(978-1-55469-090-9(0))* Orca Bk. Pubs. USA.

Pont, Beattie. Grandma, Tell Me More: Fishing with Grandpa. 2013. 80p. (gr. 2-4). pap. 19.95 *(978-1-4817-2073-1(2))* AuthorHouse.

Roberts, Dw. Pep Squad Mysteries Book: Trouble on Avalanche Mountain. 2008. (ENG., Illus.). 101p. pap. 8.99 *(978-0-557-16575-9(X))* Lulu Pr., Inc.

Wallace, Karen. Raspberries on the Yangtze. 2013. (ENG.). 160p. (J). pap. 8.99 *(978-1-4711-2122-7(4),* Simon & Schuster Children's) Simon & Schuster, Ltd. GBR. Dist: Simon & Schuster, Inc.

White, Tara. Where I Belong, 1 vol. 2015. (ENG., Illus.). 112p. (YA). (gr. 8-12). pap. 12.95 *(978-1-896580-77-7(7))* Tradewind Bks. CAN. Dist: Orca Bk. Pubs. USA.

Yeager, Jackie. Flip the Silver Switch. 2018. (Crimson Five Ser.: 2). (ENG., Illus.). 296p. (J). (gr. 4-7). 15.99 *(978-1-944995-69-0(2))* Amberjack Publishing Co.

QUEBEC (QUEBEC)—FICTION

Gingras, Marie Claude. Let's Spend Summer with Fred. 2012. 198p. 24.95 *(978-1-4626-4413-1(9))* America Star Bks.

Henty, George. With Wolfe in Canada: The Winning of a Continent. 2006. per. 8.95 *(978-1-57646-980-4(8))* Quiet Vision Publishing.

Hotte, Sylvain. Power Forward: A Novel. Roberts, Casey, tr. 2012. (Break Away Ser.). (ENG., Illus.). 180p. (YA). (gr. 8). pap. 16.95 *(978-1-926824-42-0(3),* P209065) Baraka Bks. CAN. Dist: Eurospan Group, The.

Kovacs, Deborah. Catie Copley's Great Escape. Williams, Jared T., illus. 2009. (ENG.). 32p. (J). (gr. -1-3). 17.95 *(978-1-56792-379-7(8))* Godine, David R. Pub.

QUEBEC CAMPAIGN, 1759, 1759—FICTION

Altsheler, Joseph A. The French & Indian War Novels: The Lords of the Wild & The Sun of Quebec, Vol. 3. 2008. (J). reprint ed. 428p. *(978-1-84677-590-1(6))*; 424p. pap. *(978-1-84677-589-5(2))* Leonaur Ltd.

—The Sun of Quebec: A Story of a Great Crisis. 2006. (French & Indian War Ser.: Vol. 6). 324p. (J). reprint ed. 29.95 *(978-1-4218-2337-9(3))*; pap. 14.95 *(978-1-4218-2437-6(X))* 1st World Publishing, Inc. (1st World Library - Literary Society).

—The Sun of Quebec: A Story of a Great Crisis. (French & Indian War Ser.: Vol. 6). (J). reprint ed. 25.95 *(978-0-8488-0907-2(6))* Amereon Ltd.

—The Sun of Quebec: A Story of a Great Crisis. 2007. (French & Indian War Ser.: Vol. 6). 280p. (J). reprint ed. per. *(978-1-4065-6552-2(0))* Dodo Pr.

—The Sun of Quebec: A Story of a Great Crisis. 2007. (French & Indian War Ser.: Vol. 6). 196p. (J). reprint ed. per. *(978-1-4068-1689-1(2))* Echo Library.

—The Sun of Quebec: A Story of a Great Crisis. 2010. (French & Indian War Ser.: Vol. 6). (Illus.). 176p. (J). (gr. 4-7). reprint ed. pap. 19.99 *(978-1-153-72258-2(5))* General Bks. LLC.

—The Sun of Quebec: A Story of a Great Crisis. 2011. (French & Indian War Ser.: Vol. 6). (J). (gr. 4-7). reprint ed. *(978-1-164-50609-6(9))* Kessinger Publishing, LLC.

—The Sun of Quebec: A Story of a Great Crisis. Wrenn, Charles L., illus. (French & Indian War Ser.: Vol. 6). 356p. (J). reprint ed. 2010. (gr. 4-7). pap. 25.56 *(978-1-163-19471-3(9))* 2008. 46.95 *(978-1-4366-7287-0(2))* 2007. per. 31.95 *(978-1-4325-9779-5(5))* Kessinger Publishing, LLC.

—The Sun of Quebec: A Story of a Great Crisis. 2012. (French & Indian War Ser.: Vol. 6). 276p. (J). (gr. 4-7). reprint ed. pap. *(978-3-8472-3211-7(8))* tredition Verlag.

QUEENS

see Kings, Queens, Rulers, etc.

QUERIES

see Questions and Answers

QUESTIONS AND ANSWERS

Abbott, Simon, illus. 100 Questions about Bugs: And All the Answers, Too! 2018. (100 Questions Ser.). (ENG.). 48p. (J). 7.99 *(978-1-4413-2618-8(9),* ff72d12a-2883-49e2-9efd-5a780a2d627c) Peter Pauper Pr. Inc.

—100 Questions about Colonial America: And All the Answers Too! 2018. (100 Questions Ser.). (ENG.). 48p. (J). 7.99 *(978-1-4413-2616-4(2),* bc12b992-f6ed-4bb7-a845-5c51d3fed4e5) Peter Pauper Pr. Inc.

—100 Questions about Outer Space: And All the Answers, Too! 2018. (100 Questions Ser.). (ENG.). 48p. (J). 7.99 *(978-1-4413-2617-1(0),* dacc02d3-1a11-49e1-bbdd-d08555de9f53) Peter Pauper Pr. Inc.

—100 Questions about the Human Body: And All the Answers Too! 2019. (100 Questions Ser.). (ENG.). 48p. (J). 7.99 *(978-1-4413-3101-4(8),* ea01589f-e28b-4ef0-b339-1865856b3f87) Peter Pauper Pr. Inc.

Alcraft, Rob. Collins Big Cat Phonics for Letters & Sounds - Big Questions: Band 07/Turquoise, Bd. 7. 2018. (Collins Big Cat Phonics Ser.). (ENG., Illus.). 24p. (J). pap. 6.99 *(978-0-00-825182-6(7))* HarperCollins Pubs. Ltd. GBR. Dist: Independent Pubs. Group.

Amazing Questions & Answers. 2003. 512p. 9.98 *(978-1-4054-0738-0(7))* Parragon, Inc.

American Girl Editorial Staff. Coconut Quiz Book: Tear & Share Quizzes for You & a Friend. 2004. (ENG., Illus.). 80p. (J). pap. 7.95 *(978-1-58485-912-3(1))* American Girl Publishing, Inc.

Anthony, Erin. I-Ballers: Little Books for Big Minds. 2005. (I-Ballers Ser.). (ENG.). pap. 4.95 *(978-1-57528-938-0(5))* Univ. Games.

Avista Products. Blackbook Directory & Yearbook 2010-11: Black Business Year in Review, vol. 1. annuals aut. collector's ed. 2011. (ENG., Illus.). 160p. 65.00 *(978-0-9798741-0-9(6))* Avista Products.

AZ Books Staff. Countries & People. Borovik, Alija et al, eds. 2013. (Little Genius Ser.). (ENG.). 150p. (J). (gr. 1-3). bds. 19.95 *(978-1-61889-139-6(1))* AZ Bks. LLC.

—History & Discoveries. Shumovich, Nadegda et al, eds. 2013. (Little Genius Ser.). (ENG.). 150p. (J). (gr. 1-3). bds. 19.95 *(978-1-61889-138-9(3))* AZ Bks. LLC.

—Wild Nature. Kokash, Elena et al, eds. 2013. (Little Genius Ser.). (ENG.). 150p. (J). (gr. 1-3). bds. 19.95 *(978-1-61889-140-2(5))* AZ Bks. LLC.

Beaumont, Holly. Why Do Monkeys & Other Mammals Have Fur? 2015. (Animal Body Coverings Ser.). (ENG., Illus.). 24p. (J). (gr. 1-3). pap. 6.99 *(978-1-4846-2539-2(0),* 130024, Heinemann) Capstone.

—Why Do Owls & Other Birds Have Feathers? 2015. (Animal Body Coverings Ser.). (ENG., Illus.). 24p. (J). (gr. 1-3). pap. 6.99 *(978-1-4846-2538-5(2),* 130023, Heinemann) Capstone.

Becker, H. The Personality Quiz Book for You & Your BFFs: Learn All about Your Friends! 2017. (ENG., Illus.). 112p. (J). (gr. 5-8). pap. 7.99 *(978-1-4926-5324-0(1))* Sourcebooks, Inc.

—The Personality Quiz Book Just for You: Learn All about You! 2017. (ENG., Illus.). 112p. (J). (gr. 5-8). pap. 8.99 *(978-1-4926-5321-9(7))* Sourcebooks, Inc.

Beilenson, Suzanne. Quiz Book: Who R U? 2008. (Activity Book Ser.). 160p. (J). (gr. k-5). spiral bd. 12.99 *(978-1-59359-807-5(6))* Peter Pauper Pr. Inc.

Berger, Melvin & Berger, Gilda. Are Mountains Getting Taller? Questions & Answers about the Changing Earth. Carter, Robin, illus. 2003. (Question & Answer Ser.). (ENG.). 48p. (J). pap. 5.95 *(978-0-439-26673-4(4),* Scholastic Reference) Scholastic, Inc.

—The Byte-Sized World of Technology (Fact Attack #2) Rocco, Frank & Watanabe-Rocco, Sarah, illus. 2017. (ENG.). 96p. (J). (gr. 1-3). pap. 7.99 *(978-1-338-04186-6(X))* Scholastic, Inc.

—Dangerous Animals (Scholastic True or False) 2009. (Scholastic True or False Ser.: 5). (ENG.). 48p. (J). (gr. 2-5). pap. 4.99 *(978-0-545-00395-7(4),* Scholastic Reference) Scholastic, Inc.

—Hurricanes Have Eyes but Can't See: And Other Amazing Facts about Wild Weather. 2003. (Illus.). 48p. (J). *(978-0-439-54980-6(9))* Scholastic, Inc.

—Pets. 2009. (Scholastic True or False Ser.: 6). (ENG.). 48p. (J). (gr. k-3). pap. 16.19 *(978-0-545-00396-4(2))* Scholastic, Inc.

—Reptiles (Scholastic True or False) 2008. (Scholastic True or False Ser.: 3). (ENG.). 48p. (J). (gr. 2-5). pap. 4.99 *(978-0-545-00393-3(8),* Scholastic Reference) Scholastic, Inc.

Biggest Ever Book of Questions & Answers. 2003. 256p. (J). 12.98 *(978-1-4054-1710-5(2))* Parragon, Inc.

Bodden, Valerie. Preparing for an Exam. 2014. (Classroom How-To Ser.). (ENG.). 48p. (J). (gr. 5-8). *(978-1-60818-282-4(7),* 21302, Creative Education) Creative Co., The.

Bone, Emily. Lift-The-Flap First Questions & Answers Why Do We Need Bees? 2017. (Lift-The-Flap First Questions & Answers Ser.). (ENG.). 12p. 14.99 *(978-0-7945-4030-2(9),* Usborne) EDC Publishing.

Boyer, Crispin. This or That? The Wacky Book of Choices to Reveal the Hidden You. 2014. (Illus.). 176p. (J). (gr. 3-7). pap. 12.99 *(978-1-4263-1557-2(0),* National Geographic Kids) Disney Publishing Worldwide.

—What Would Happen? Serious Answers to Silly Questions. 2017. (Illus.). 176p. (J). (gr. 3-7). pap. 14.99 *(978-1-4263-2770-4(6),* National Geographic Kids) Disney Publishing Worldwide.

Braun, Eric. Awesome, Disgusting, Unusual Facts about Animals. 2018. (Our Gross, Awesome World Ser.). (ENG.). 24p. (J). (gr. 4-6). pap. 8.99 *(978-1-64466-304-2(X),* 12511); (Illus.). lib. bdg. 28.50 *(978-1-68072-609-1(9),* 12510) Black Rabbit Bks. (Hi Jinx).

—Incredible Animal Trivia: Fun Facts & Quizzes. 2018. (Trivia Time! (Alternator Books (r)) Ser.). (ENG., Illus.). 32p. (J). (gr. 3-6). lib. bdg. 29.32 *(978-1-5124-8330-7(3),* 1412e299-c8ba-4962-9d84-301b6f0045cb, Lerner Pubns.) Lerner Publishing Group.

Brennan, Linda Crotta. We Have Earthquakes. 2014. (Tell Me Why Library). (ENG., Illus.). 24p. (J). (gr. 2-5). 29.21 *(978-1-63188-011-7(X),* 205451) Cherry Lake Publishing.

—We Have Tornadoes. 2014. (Tell Me Why Library). (ENG., Illus.). 24p. (J). (gr. 2-5). 29.21 *(978-1-63188-012-4(8),* 205455) Cherry Lake Publishing.

Brynie, Faith Hickman. 101 Questions..., 6 vols. Holm, Sharon Lane, illus. Incl. 101 Questions about Blood & Circulation with Answers Straight from the Heart. 2001. lib. bdg. 27.90 *(978-0-7613-1455-4(5))*; 101 Questions about Food & Digestion: That Have Been Eating at You until Now. 2002. lib. bdg. 30.60 *(978-0-7613-2309-9(0))*; 101 Questions about Your Immune System You Felt Defenseless to Answer until Now. 2000. lib. bdg. 30.60 *(978-0-7613-1569-8(1))*; 101 Questions about Your Skin That Got under Your Skin... until Now. 2000. lib. bdg. 30.60 *(978-0-7613-1259-8(5))*; 176p. (gr. 7-12). (Illus.). 2004. 139.50 o.p. *(978-0-7613-3139-1(5),* Twenty-First Century Bks.) Lerner Publishing Group.

—101 Questions about Sex & Sexuality: With Answers for the Curious, Cautious, & Confused. Holm, Sharon, illus. 2003. (101 Questions... Ser.). (ENG.). 176p. (gr. 7-12). lib. bdg. 30.60 *(978-0-7613-2310-5(4),* Twenty-First Century Bks.) Lerner Publishing Group.

Burchett, Author Walter, BA. Christian children's questions & answers abraham & keturah to israel & rachel Volume 2. 2009. 32p. pap. 14.28 *(978-0-557-08256-8(0))* Lulu Pr., Inc.

—Christian children's questions & answers adam & eve to abraham & sarah Volume 1. 2009. 36p. pap. 14.44 *(978-0-557-08219-3(6))* Lulu Pr., Inc.

—Christian children's questions & answers birth of christ Volume 5. 2009. 33p. pap. 14.32 *(978-0-557-08275-9(7))* Lulu Pr., Inc.

—Christian children's questions & answers joseph (coat of many colors) Volume 3. 2009. 32p. pap. 14.28 *(978-0-557-08276-6(5))* Lulu Pr., Inc.

—Christian children's questions & answers moses Volume 4. 2009. (ENG.). 32p. pap. 14.28 *(978-0-557-08123-3(8))* Lulu Pr., Inc.

—Christian children's questions & answers resurrection of christ Volume 7. 2009. 32p. pap. 14.28 *(978-0-557-08245-2(5))* Lulu Pr., Inc.

Calhoun, Kelly. Colas Enroscadas (Twisty Tails) Camaleón (Chameleon) 2016. (Adivina (Guess What) Ser.). (SPA., Illus.). 24p. (J). (gr. k-2). 30.64 *(978-1-63471-453-2(9),* 208875) Cherry Lake Publishing.

—Crines Majestuosas (Majestic Manes) Caballo (Horse) 2016. (Adivina (Guess What) Ser.). (SPA., Illus.). 24p. (J). (gr. k-2). 30.64 *(978-1-63471-450-1(4),* 208863) Cherry Lake Publishing.

—Fast & Flightless: Ostrich. 2015. (Guess What Ser.). (ENG., Illus.). 24p. (J). (gr. k-2). 30.64 *(978-1-63362-627-0(X),* 206664) Cherry Lake Publishing.

—Ferocidad Felina (Fiercely Feline) León (Lion) 2016. (Adivina (Guess What) Ser.). (SPA., Illus.). 24p. (J). (gr. k-2). 30.64 *(978-1-63471-448-8(2),* 208855) Cherry Lake Publishing.

—Fiercely Feline: Lion. 2015. (Guess What Ser.). (ENG., Illus.). 24p. (J). (gr. k-2). pap. 12.79 *(978-1-63362-713-0(6),* 206673) Cherry Lake Publishing.

—Majestic Manes: Horse. 2015. (Guess What Ser.). (ENG., Illus.). 24p. (J). (gr. k-2). pap. 12.79 *(978-1-63362-711-6(X),* 206685) Cherry Lake Publishing.

—Nadadores Escamosos (Scaly Swimmers) Cocodrilo (Crocodile) 2016. (Adivina (Guess What) Ser.). (SPA., Illus.). 24p. (J). (gr. k-2). 30.64 *(978-1-63471-451-8(2),* 208867) Cherry Lake Publishing.

—Poised & Pink: Flamingo. 2015. (Guess What Ser.). (ENG., Illus.). 24p. (J). (gr. k-2). pap. 12.79 *(978-1-63362-715-4(2),* 206689) Cherry Lake Publishing.

—Saltarines de Alta Velocidad (High-Speed Hoppers) Canguro (Kangaroo) 2016. (Adivina (Guess What) Ser.). (SPA., Illus.). 24p. (J). (gr. k-2). 30.64 *(978-1-63471-449-5(0),* 208859) Cherry Lake Publishing.

—Scaly Swimmers: Crocodile. 2015. (Guess What Ser.). (ENG., Illus.). 24p. (J). (gr. k-2). 30.64 *(978-1-63362-629-4(6),* 206692) Cherry Lake Publishing.

—Slinky Sliders: Rattlesnake. 2015. (Guess What Ser.). (ENG., Illus.). 24p. (J). (gr. k-2). pap. 12.79 *(978-1-63362-721-5(7),* 206697) Cherry Lake Publishing.

—Twisty Tails: Chameleon. 2015. (Guess What Ser.). (ENG., Illus.). 24p. (J). (gr. k-2). 30.64 *(978-1-63362-628-7(8),* 206708) Cherry Lake Publishing.

—Velocidad Sin Vuelo (Fast & Flightless) Avestruz (Ostrich) 2016. (Adivina (Guess What) Ser.). (SPA., Illus.). 24p. (J). (gr. k-2). 30.64 *(978-1-63471-446-4(6),* 208847) Cherry Lake Publishing.

Callella, Trisha. I Have, Who Has? Language Arts Grades 1-2. Taylor, Jennifer, ed. Peterson, Barbara, illus. 2007. (J). per. 19.99 *(978-1-59198-429-0(7))* Creative Teaching Pr., Inc.

Campbell's Comstant Quiz Companion: The Middle/High School Book of Lists, Terms, & Questions. 2004. (YA). per. 24.95 *(978-0-944322-39-0(5))* Patrick's Pr.

Canavan, Thomas. Do Plants Really Eat Insects? Questions & Answers about the Science of Plants. 2013. (Science F. A. Q. Ser.). (Illus.). 32p. (gr. 3-6). 31.35 *(978-1-78212-392-7(X))* Arcturus Publishing GBR. Dist: Black Rabbit Bks.

—Does It Really Rain Frogs? Questions & Answers about Planet Earth. 2013. (Science F. A. Q. Ser.). (Illus.). 32p. (gr. 3-6). 31.35 *(978-1-78212-393-4(8))* Arcturus Publishing GBR. Dist: Black Rabbit Bks.

—What Makes You Hiccup? Questions & Answers about the Human Body. 2013. (Science F. A. Q. Ser.). (Illus.). 32p. (gr. 3-6). 31.35 *(978-1-78212-394-1(6))* Arcturus Publishing GBR. Dist: Black Rabbit Bks.

—Why Do Ice Cubes Float? Questions & Answers about the Science of Everyday Materials. 2013. (Science F. A. Q. Ser.). (Illus.). 32p. (gr. 3-6). 31.35 *(978-1-78212-396-5(2))* Arcturus Publishing GBR. Dist: Black Rabbit Bks.

—Why Do Zebras Have Stripes? Questions & Answers about Animals. 2013. (Science F. A. Q. Ser.). 32p. (gr. 3-6). 31.35 *(978-1-78212-397-2(0))* Arcturus Publishing GBR. Dist: Black Rabbit Bks.

Card, Michael. Tell Me Why: Eternal Answers to Children's Timeless Questions. 2004. (Tell Me Ser.). (Illus.). 48p. (gr. -1-3). 17.99 *(978-1-58134-031-0(1))* Crossway.

Carle, Eric. De la Cabeza a Los Pies: From Head to Toe (Spanish Edition) Carle, Eric, illus. 2007.Tr. of From Head to Toe. (SPA., Illus.). 32p. (J). (gr. -1-3). pap. 9.99 *(978-0-06-051313-9(6))* HarperCollins Español.

—From Head to Toe Big Book. Carle, Eric, illus. 2007. (ENG., Illus.). 32p. (J). (gr. -1-k). pap. 24.99 *(978-0-06-111972-9(5),* HarperFestival) HarperCollins Pubs.

Carson, Mary Kay. Who Was Susan B. Anthony Vote? And Other Questions about Women's Suffrage. 2015. (Good Question! Ser.). (ENG., Illus.). 32p. (J). (gr. 2). pap. 5.95 *(978-1-4549-1242-2(1))* Sterling Publishing Co., Inc.

Chadow, Alysa. US States. 2003. pap. 14.00 *(978-0-8059-6054-9(6))* Dorrance Publishing Co., Inc.

Charman, Andrew. I Wonder Why Leaves Change Color: And Other Questions about Plants. 2012. (I Wonder Why Ser.). (ENG., Illus.). (J). (gr. k-3). pap. 6.99 *(978-0-7534-6697-1(X),* 900076411, Kingfisher) Roaring Brook Pr.

A Child's First Library of Learning, 30 bks. Incl. Animal Friends. Time-Life Staff. (Illus.). 88p. (gr. -1-4). 1999. 14.95 *(978-0-8094-4849-4(1))*; Animals in Action. (Illus.). 88p. (gr. -1-2). 1999. 14.95 *(978-0-8094-4869-2(6))*; Dangerous Animals. Time-Life Books Editors. Kinney, Karin, ed. (Illus.). 88p. (gr. -1-3). 1996. 16.00 *(978-0-8094-9480-4(9))*; Everyday Life. Ctl. (Illus.). 88p. (gr. -1-4). 1999. 14.95 *(978-0-8094-4865-4(3))*; Explorers & Adventurers. Time-Life Books Editors. Fallow, Allan, ed. (Illus.). 88p. (gr. -1-3). 1996. lib. bdg. *(978-0-8094-9482-8(5))*; Famous Places. Gakken Co. Ltd. Editors. Time-Life Books Editors, tr. (Illus.). 88p. (gr. 1-4). 1999. 14.95 *(978-0-8094-4893-7(9))*; Feelings & Manners. Time-Life Books Editors. Fallow, Allan, ed. (Illus.). 88p. (gr. -1-3). 1997. 14.95 *(978-0-8094-9483-5(3))*; Flowers & Trees. Time-Life Staff. (Illus.). 88p. (gr. 1-4). 1999. 14.95 *(978-0-8094-4857-9(2))*; Health & Safety. Time-Life Books Editors. 1996. *(978-0-8094-9479-8(5))*; How Things Work in Your Home. Time-Life Books Editors. (Illus.). 88p. (gr. 1-4). 1999. 14.95 *(978-0-8094-4873-9(4))*; Insect World. Time-Life Books Editors. (Illus.). 88p. (gr. -1-3). 1999. 14.95 *(978-0-8094-4841-8(6))*; Science Starter. Time-Life Books Editors. (Illus.). 88p. (gr. 1-4). 1999. 14.95 *(978-0-8094-4881-4(5))*; Sky & Earth. Time-Life Books Editors. (Illus.). 88p. (gr. 1-4). 1999. 14.95 *(978-0-8094-4837-1(8))*; Things Around Us. Time-Life Staff. (Illus.). 88p. (gr. -1-2). 1999. 14.95 *(978-0-8094-4845-6(9))*; Things to Do. Gakken Co. Ltd. Editors & Time-Life Books Editors. (Illus.). 88p. (gr. 1-4). 1999. 14.95 *(978-0-8094-4897-5(1))*; Wheels & Wings. Gakken Co. Ltd. Editors. Time-Life Books Editors, tr. (Illus.). 88p. (gr. 1-4). 1999. 14.95 *(978-0-8094-4861-6(0))*; Where Things Come From. Time-Life Books Editors. Fallow, Allan, ed. (Illus.). 88p. (gr. -1-3). 1997. *(978-0-8094-9484-2(1))*; Wind & Weather. Gakken Co. Ltd. Editors. Time-Life Books Editors, tr. (Illus.). 88p. (gr. 1-4). 1999. 14.95 *(978-0-8094-4829-6(7))*; World We Live In. Gakken Co. Ltd. Editors. Time-Life Books Editors, tr. (Illus.). 88p. (gr. 1-4). 1999. 14.95 *(978-0-8094-4885-2(8))*; (J). 403.88 *(978-0-8094-9499-6(X))* Time-Life, Inc.

Ciencias. (Enciclopedias Everest Internacional Ser.). (SPA., Illus.). (YA). (gr. 5-8). 41.95 *(978-84-241-9405-5(5))*, EV7495) Everest Editora ESP. Dist: Lectorum Pubns., Inc.

Cobb, Vicki. What's the BIG Idea? Amazing Science Questions for the Curious Kid. 2013. (ENG., Illus.). 208p. (J). (gr. 2-5). pap. 12.95 *(978-1-62087-685-5(X)*, 620685, Sky Pony Pr.) Skyhorse Publishing Co., Inc.

Craats, Rennay. Construction Q & A. 2013. (J). *(978-1-62127-412-4(8))*; pap. *(978-1-62127-418-6(7))* Weigl Pubs., Inc.

Crompton, Samuel Willard. 100 Relationships That Shaped World History. 2015. (100 Ser.). 100p. (J). (gr. 3-10). pap. 7.95 *(978-0-912517-40-7(9))* Sourcebooks, Inc.

D C Thomson Staff, ed. Bunty Annual for Girls 2004. 2003. (Illus.). 128p. (J). (gr. -1-4). *(978-0-85116-825-8(6))* Thomson, D.C. & Co., Ltd. GBR. Dist: APG Sales & Distribution Services.

Daniels, Kathryn. A Bluestocking Guide - Justice: Companion Workbook to Richard J. Maybury's Book Whatever Happened to Justice? Williams, Jane A., ed. 2004. (Bluestocking Guide Ser.). (ENG.). (YA). pap. 15.95 *(978-0-942617-45-0(2))* Bluestocking Pr.

—A Bluestocking Guide - the Money Mystery: Based on Richard J. Maybury's book the Money Mystery. Williams, Jane A., ed. 2004. (Bluestocking Guide Ser.). (ENG.). 31p. (YA). pap. 8.95 *(978-0-942617-49-8(5))* Bluestocking Pr.

Davis, Graeme. The Unauthorized Harry Potter Quiz Book: 165 Questions Ranging from the Sorcerer's Stone to the Deathly Hallows. 2008. 76p. pap. 15.38 *(978-1-934840-44-3(0))* Nimble Bks. LLC.

Davis, Kenneth C. Don't Know Much about Abraham Lincoln, Vol. 4. Shepperson, Rob, illus. 2003. (Don't Know Much About Ser.). 144p. (J). (gr. 3-7). pap. 4.99 *(978-0-06-442127-0(9))* HarperCollins Pubs.

—Don't Know Much about Abraham Lincoln Abraham Lincoln, Vol. 4. Shepperson, Rob, illus. 2004. (Don't Know Much About Ser.). 144p. (J). (gr. 2-5). 15.89 *(978-0-06-028820-4(5))* HarperCollins Pubs.

—Don't Know Much about American History. Faulkner, Matt, illus. 2003. (ENG.). 224p. (J). (gr. 3-7). pap. 7.99 *(978-0-06-440836-3(1)*, HarperCollins) HarperCollins Pubs.

—Don't Know Much About American History. 2004. (Don't Know Much about Ser.). 224p. (J). (gr. 4-7). pap. 40.00 incl. audio *(978-0-8072-2092-4(2)*, Listening Library) Random Hse. Audio Publishing Group.

—Don't Know Much about Planet Earth. unabr. ed. 2004. (Don't Know Much about Ser.). 144p. (J). (gr. 4-7). pap. 29.00 incl. audio *(978-0-8072-0660-7(1)*, Listening Library) Random Hse. Audio Publishing Group.

—Don't Know Much about Sitting Bull Sitting Bull, Vol. 2. 2003. (Don't Know Much about Ser.). (Illus.). 144p. (J). (gr. 3-7). 16.89 *(978-0-06-028818-1(3))* HarperCollins Pubs.

—Don't Know Much about Space. unabr. ed. 2004. (Don't Know Much about Ser.). 144p. (J). (gr. 4-7). pap. 29.00 incl. audio *(978-0-8072-0661-4(X)*, Listening Library) Random Hse. Audio Publishing Group.

—Don't Know Much about the 50 States. Andriani, Renée, illus. 2004. (ENG.). 64p. (J). (gr. 1-4). pap. 11.99 *(978-0-06-446227-3(7)*, HarperCollins) HarperCollins Pubs.

—Don't Know Much about the Presidents. Martin, Pedro, illus. rev. ed. 2009. (ENG.). 64p. (J). (gr. k-4). pap. 7.99 *(978-0-06-171823-6(8)*, HarperCollins) HarperCollins Pubs.

Daynes, Katie. Lift-The-Flap Questions & Answers about Nature IR. 2018. (Lift-The Flap Questions & Answers Ser.). (ENG.). 14p. (J). 14.99 *(978-0-7945-4121-7(6)*, Usborne) EDC Publishing.

—Lift-The-Flap Very First Questions & Answers What Are Germs? 2017. (Lift-The-Flap Very First Questions & Answers Ser.). (ENG.). 12p. 12.99 *(978-0-7945-4093-7(7)*, Usborne) EDC Publishing.

—Lift-The-Flap Very First Questions & Answers What Are Stars. 2018. (Lift-The-Flap Very First Questions & Answers Ser.). (ENG.). 12p. (J). 12.99 *(978-0-7945-4211-5(5)*, Usborne) EDC Publishing.

—Questions & Answers. 2013. (Usborne Lift the Flap Bks.). (ENG., Illus.). 14p. (J). 14.99 *(978-0-7945-3207-9(1)*, Usborne) EDC Publishing.

De La Bedoyere C. Why Why Why Cant Penguins Fly. 2008. 32p. pap. *(978-1-84810-000-8(0))* Miles Kelly Publishing, Ltd.

De la Bédoyère, Camilla. Why Why Why Are Orang-Utans So Hairy? 2008. (Why Why Why Ser.). (Illus.). 32p. (J). (gr. 4-7). pap. *(978-1-84810-003-9(5))* Miles Kelly Publishing, Ltd.

—Why Why Why Did Dinosaurs Lay Eggs? 2008. (Why Why Why Ser.). (Illus.). 32p. (J). (gr. -1-3). pap. *(978-1-84810-001-5(9))* Miles Kelly Publishing, Ltd.

Dewin, Howard, told to. The Dog: Why Do Dogs Love to Sniff?: The Do's & Don'ts of the Dogs. 2007. (Illus.). 29p. (J). pap. *(978-0-439-02255-2(X))* Scholastic, Inc.

DiSiena, Laura Lyn & Eliot, Hannah. Chickens Don't Fly: And Other Fun Facts. Oswald, Pete, illus. 2014. (Did You Know? Ser.). (ENG.). 32p. (J). (gr. -1-3). pap. 7.99 *(978-1-4424-9326-1(7)*, Little Simon) Little Simon.

Disiena, Laura Lyn & Eliot, Hannah. Hippos Can't Swim. 2014. (Did You Know? Ser.). lib. bdg. 16.00 *(978-0-606-35424-0(7))* Turtleback.

DiSiena, Laura Lyn & Eliot, Hannah. Hippos Can't Swim: And Other Fun Facts. Oswald, Pete, illus. 2014. (Did You Know? Ser.). (ENG.). 32p. (J). (gr. -1-3). pap. 8.99 *(978-1-4424-9324-7(0)*, Little Simon) Little Simon.

—Rainbows Never End: And Other Fun Facts. Oswald, Pete, illus. 2014. (Did You Know? Ser.). (ENG.). 32p. (J). (gr. -1-3). 17.99 *(978-1-4814-0277-4(3))*; pap. 7.99 *(978-1-4814-0275-0(7))* Little Simon. (Little Simon).

—Saturn Could Sail: And Other Fun Facts. Oswald, Pete & Spurgeon, Aaron, illus. 2014. (Did You Know? Ser.). (ENG.). 32p. (J). (gr. -1-3). 17.99 *(978-1-4814-1429-6(1))*; pap. 7.99 *(978-1-4814-1428-9(3))* Little Simon. (Little Simon).

DK. Did You Know? Amazing Answers to the Questions You Ask. 2014. (Why? Ser.). (ENG., Illus.). 160p. (J). (gr. 1-3). 21.99 *(978-1-4654-2045-9(2)*, DK Children) Dorling Kindersley Publishing, Inc.

Dockrey, Donna. Tell Me about A Place Called Heaven. 2009. (ENG.). 32p. pap. 14.50 *(978-0-557-23820-0(X))* Lulu Pr., Inc.

Duden, Jane. Why Do Bears Sleep All Winter? [Chicago]: A Book about Hibernation. 2010. (Why in the World? Ser.). (ENG.). 24p. pap. 6.95 *(978-1-4296-5183-7(0)*, Capstone Pr.) Capstone.

Editors of Brain Quest. Brain Quest America: 850 Questions & Answers to Challenge the Mind. Teacher-Approved! 4th rev. ed. 2013. (Brain Quest Smart Cards Ser.). (ENG.). 152p. (J). (gr. 4-7). 11.95 *(978-0-7611-7239-0(4)*, 17239) Workman Publishing Co., Inc.

—Brain Quest for the Car: 1,100 Questions & Answers All about America. 4th rev. ed. 2013. (Brain Quest Smart Cards Ser.). (ENG.). 152p. (J). (gr. 2-7). 11.95 *(978-0-7611-7401-1(X)*, 17401) Workman Publishing Co., Inc.

Editors of Klutz & Phillips, Karen. It's All about Us (... Especially Me!) 2013. (ENG.). 126p. (J). (gr. 3). 16.99 *(978-0-545-49280-5(7))* Klutz.

Egmont. World's Greatest Who What Where When Quiz Book for Kids. 2003. (ENG., Illus.). 112p. (J). pap. 3.99 *(978-0-603-56100-9(4))* Farshore GBR. Dist: Trafalgar Square Publishing.

Esbaum, Jill. National Geographic Little Kids First Big Book of How. 2016. (National Geographic Little Kids First Big Bks.). (Illus.). 128p. (J). (gr. -1-k). 14.99 *(978-1-4263-2329-4(8)*, National Geographic Kids) Disney Publishing Worldwide.

—National Geographic Little Kids First Big Book of Why 2. 2018. (National Geographic Little Kids First Big Bks.: 2). (Illus.). 128p. (J). (gr. -1-k). 14.99 *(978-1-4263-2999-9(7)*, National Geographic Kids) Disney Publishing Worldwide.

FAQ: Teen Life: Set 6, 12 vols. Incl. Frequently Asked Questions about Drinking & Driving. Cefrey, Holly. lib. bdg. 37.13 *(978-1-4042-1809-3(2)*, 7a13dfc4-c054-4194-814a-690e047319be); Frequently Asked Questions about Exercise Addiction. Willett, Edward. lib. bdg. 37.13 *(978-1-4042-1806-2(8)*, 1d1f5373-784d-4f64-9738-601cef83419d); Frequently Asked Questions about Human Papillomavirus. Gonzalez, Lissette. lib. bdg. 37.13 *(978-1-4042-1813-0(0)*, 22830166-0573-4d37-8c91-b949428581f0); Frequently Asked Questions about Migraines & Headaches. Cobb, Allan B. lib. bdg. 37.13 *(978-1-4042-1814-7(9)*, 4ab4cb94-2051-4431-9b58-af31d4d8ed08); Frequently Asked Questions about Peer Pressure. Juzwiak, Richard. lib. bdg. 37.13 *(978-1-4042-1805-5(X)*, 42016b3a-20e2-4bc5-bd34-abe969908251); Frequently Asked Questions about Suicide. Giddens, Sandra. lib. bdg. 37.13 *(978-1-4042-1811-6(4)*, ce427455-e483-484b-aab1-a66c920d2ce7); (Illus.). 64p. (YA). (gr. 5-6). 2008. (FAQ: Teen Life Ser.). (ENG.). 2008. Set lib. bdg. 222.78 *(978-1-4042-1887-1(4)*, 951b6996-928a-4887-83a0-5a917cefc704) Rosen Publishing Group, Inc., The.

Far from the Madding Crowd: Teaching Unit. 2003. 92p. (YA). ring bd. *(978-1-58049-471-7(4)*, TU4714) Prestwick Hse., Inc.

Farnsworth, Lauren. Quiz Book for Clever Kids(r). Dickason, Chris, illus. 2015. (Buster Brain Games Ser.). (ENG.). 192p. (J). (gr. 4-6). pap. 7.99 *(978-1-78055-314-6(5))* O'Mara, Michael Bks., Ltd. GBR. Dist: Independent Pubs. Group.

Feyh, Janelle. Does God Have a Remote Control? Feyh, Alexa & Deghand, Tim, illus. l.t. ed. 2003. 66p. (J). per. 11.95 *(978-1-932344-26-4(8))* Thornton Publishing, Inc.

Franco, Betsy. Q&a a Day for Me: A 3-Year Journal for Teens. 2014. (Q&a a Day Ser.). (Illus.). 368p. (YA). 16.95 *(978-0-8041-8664-3(2)*, Potter Style) Crown Publishing Group, The.

Freedman, Deborah K. Tacoma's Twenty-One Tales: Every Student Should Be Able to Tell, Teachers, Too! 2010. (Illus.). 48p. (J). *(978-0-09-846234-8(2))* Tacoma Historical Society.

Freedman, E. b., et al. What Does Being Jewish Mean? Read-Aloud Responses to Questions Jewish Children Ask about History, Culture, & Religion. 2003. (ENG.). 160p. pap. 12.95 *(978-0-7432-5413-7(9)*, Touchstone) Touchstone.

Frost, Adam. The Awesome Book of Awesomeness. Bramall, Dan, illus. 2015. (ENG.). 112p. (J). (gr. 2-4). pap. 9.99 *(978-1-61963-793-1(6)*, 900148771, Bloomsbury Activity Bks.) Bloomsbury Publishing USA.

Gaarder, Jostein. Questions Asked. Bartlett, Don, tr. Duezakin, Akin, illus. 2017. 72p. (J). (gr. -1-2). 14.00 *(978-0-914671-66-4(9)*, Elsewhere Editions) Steerforth Pr.

Gaff, Jackie. I Wonder Why the Sahara Is Cold at Night. 2014. 32p. pap. 7.00 *(978-1-61003-351-0(5))* Center for the Collaborative Classroom.

Ganeri, Anita. I Wonder Why the Sea Is Salty. 2014. 32p. pap. 7.00 *(978-1-61003-352-7(3))* Center for the Collaborative Classroom.

—I Wonder Why the Sea Is Salty: And Other Questions about the Oceans. 2011. (I Wonder Why Ser.). (ENG., Illus.). 32p. (J). (gr. k-3). pap. 6.99 *(978-0-7534-6521-9(3)*, 900070301, Kingfisher) Roaring Brook Pr.

—I Wonder Why the Wind Blows. 2011. (I Wonder Why Ser.). (ENG., Illus.). 32p. (J). (gr. k-3). pap. 6.99 *(978-0-7534-6522-6(1)*, 900070349, Kingfisher) Roaring Brook Pr.

Gardeski, Christina Mia. Cats: Questions & Answers. 2016. (Pet Questions & Answers Ser.). (ENG., Illus.). 24p. (J). (gr. -1-2). lib. bdg. 27.32 *(978-1-5157-0356-3(8)*, 131990, Capstone Pr.) Capstone.

—Dogs: Questions & Answers. 2016. (Pet Questions & Answers Ser.). (ENG., Illus.). 24p. (J). (gr. -1-2). lib. bdg. 27.32 *(978-1-5157-0355-6(X)*, 131989, Capstone Pr.) Capstone.

—Hamsters: Questions & Answers. 2016. (Pet Questions & Answers Ser.). (ENG., Illus.). 24p. (J). (gr. -1-2). pap. 6.95 *(978-1-5157-0359-4(2)*, 131992); lib. bdg. 27.32 *(978-1-5157-0352-5(5)*, 131986) Capstone. (Capstone Pr.).

—Pet Birds: Questions & Answers. 2016. (Pet Questions & Answers Ser.). (ENG., Illus.). 24p. (J). (gr. -1-2). lib. bdg. 27.32 *(978-1-5157-0354-9(1)*, 131988, Capstone Pr.) Capstone.

—Pet Fish: Questions & Answers. 2016. (Pet Questions & Answers Ser.). (ENG., Illus.). 24p. (J). (gr. -1-2). lib. bdg. 27.32 *(978-1-5157-0353-2(3)*, 131987, Capstone Pr.) Capstone.

George, Lynn. What Do You Know about Colonial America? 2009. (20 Questions: History Ser.). 24p. (gr. 2-3). 42.50 *(978-1-60854-955-9(0)*, PowerKids Pr.) Rosen Publishing Group, Inc., The.

—What Do You Know about the American Revolution? (20 Questions: History Ser.). 24p. (gr. 2-3). 2009. 42.50 *(978-1-60854-957-3(7)*, PowerKids Pr.) 2007. (ENG., Illus.). (J). lib. bdg. 26.27 *(978-1-4042-4186-2(8)*, ccb2f8ed-9200-4177-8f4d-46934cb5def3) Rosen Publishing Group, Inc., The.

—What Do You Know about the Civil War? 2009. (20 Questions: History Ser.). 24p. (gr. 2-3). 42.50 *(978-1-60854-958-0(5)*, PowerKids Pr.) Rosen Publishing Group, Inc., The.

—What Do You Know about the Gold Rush? (20 Questions: History Ser.). 24p. (gr. 2-3). 2009. 42.50 *(978-1-60854-959-7(3)*, PowerKids Pr.) 2007. (ENG.). (J). lib. bdg. 26.27 *(978-1-4042-4188-6(4)*, ad488f51-2869-4076-a58c-cd1a883b3fe5) Rosen Publishing Group, Inc., The.

Graham, Buck. My First Big Book of Questions & Answers: Things That Go. 2005. (Illus.). 10p. bds. 9.98 *(978-0-7853-7227-1(X)*, 7171500) Publications International, Ltd.

Graham, Monty Dr. My First Big Book of Questions & Answers: Under the Sea. 2005. (Illus.). 10p. bds. 9.98 *(978-0-7853-7228-8(8)*, 7171400) Publications International, Ltd.

Gray, Susan H. Bats Sleep Upside Down. 2015. (Tell Me Why Library). (ENG., Illus.). 24p. (J). (gr. 2-5). 29.21 *(978-1-63362-608-9(3)*, 206616) Cherry Lake Publishing.

—Bears Hibernate. 2015. (Tell Me Why Library). (ENG., Illus.). 24p. (gr. 2-5). pap. 12.79 *(978-1-63362-029-2(8)*, 205873) Cherry Lake Publishing.

—Camels Have Humps. 2014. (Tell Me Why Library). (ENG., Illus.). 24p. (J). (gr. 2-5). 29.21 *(978-1-63188-001-8(2)*, 205411) Cherry Lake Publishing.

—Dolphins Breathe Air. 2015. (Tell Me Why Library). (ENG., Illus.). 24p. (gr. 2-5). pap. 12.79 *(978-1-63362-030-8(1)*, 205877) Cherry Lake Publishing.

—Snakes Shed Their Skin. 2015. (Tell Me Why Library). (ENG., Illus.). 24p. (J). (gr. 2-5). 29.21 *(978-1-63362-616-4(4)*, 206648) Cherry Lake Publishing.

Great Americans. Date not set. (Mini Question & Answers America Ser.). 32p. (J). 3.98 *(978-0-7525-9872-7(4))* Parragon, Inc.

Great Historic Debates & Speeches, 8 vols., Set. 2004. (Great Historic Debates & Speeches Ser.). (ENG.). (J). (gr. 5-8). 148.52 *(978-1-4042-0350-1(8)*, 7feb0985-1b77-4c87-9001-cf23c0358ea7) Rosen Publishing Group, Inc., The.

Great Scientific Questions & the Scientists Who Answered Them: Sets 1 - 2, 18 vols. 2004. (Great Scientific Questions & the Scientists Who Answered Them Ser.). (ENG., Illus.). 112p. (gr. 7-12). lib. bdg. 358.20 *(978-1-4042-0356-3(7)*, 692abd0f-e42c-4b52-9e1c-ac7dbd00e263) Rosen Publishing Group, Inc., The.

Guy, Only A. Hard Questions about Christianity. 2013. 150p. pap. 7.99 *(978-1-939670-03-8(9))* VIP Ink Publishing, L.L.C.

—Hard Questions about the End Times. 2013. 80p. pap. 7.99 *(978-1-939670-00-7(4))* VIP Ink Publishing, L.L.C.

Ham, Ken & Hodge, Bodie. Answers Book for Kids Vol 7: 22 Questions from Kids on Evolution & Millions of Years. 2017. (Answers Book for Kids Ser.: 7). (ENG., Illus.). 48p. (J). (gr. 4-6). 7.99 *(978-1-68344-066-6(8)*, Master Books) New Leaf Publishing Group.

Hamilton, Gina L. Light Q & A. 2013. (J). *(978-1-62127-415-5(2))*; pap. *(978-1-62127-421-6(7))* Weigl Pubs., Inc.

Harness, Cheryl. Ye Olde Weird but True: 300 Outrageous Facts from History. 2013. (Weird but True Ser.). 208p. (J). (gr. 3-7). (ENG.). lib. bdg. 16.90 *(978-1-4263-1383-7(7)*, National Geographic Children's Bks.); (Illus.). pap. 8.99 *(978-1-4263-1382-0(9)*, National Geographic Kids) Disney Publishing Worldwide.

Harte, May. Hide & Seek Kids. 2009. (Tough Toddler Bks). 16p. (gr. k-k). 42.50 *(978-1-60854-571-1(7)*, PowerKids Pr.) Rosen Publishing Group, Inc., The.

Hazan, Maurice, creator. Dime quien Es: Spanish Dialogues Level 1. (SPA.). (J). 134.95 *(978-1-932770-43-8(7)*, SG4) Symtalk, Inc.

—Dime quien Es: Spanish Dialogues Level 2. (SPA.). (J). 134.95 *(978-1-932770-45-2(3)*, SG6) Symtalk, Inc.

—Dime quien Es: Spanish Dialogues Level 3. (SPA.). (YA). 199.95 *(978-1-932770-55-1(0)*, SG16) Symtalk, Inc.

Heimberg, Justin & Gomberg, David. Radically Repulsive: Over 400 Crazy Questions! 2010. (Would You Rather... ? Ser.). (ENG., Illus.). 216p. (J). (gr. 2-18). pap. 9.95 *(978-1-934734-42-1(X))* Seven Footer Pr.

Herrington, Lisa M. Cheetahs & Leopards. 2015. (Rookie Read-About Science: What's the Difference? Ser.). (ENG., Illus.). 32p. (J). lib. bdg. 25.00 *(978-0-531-21481-7(8)*, Children's Pr.) Scholastic Library Publishing.

Higgins, Kitty; Leon. Trivia Pursuit. Leon, Karen, illus. 2004. (Reader's Theater Content-Area Concepts Ser.). (ENG.). (J). (gr. 4). 5.00 net. *(978-1-4108-1140-0(9))* Benchmark Education Co.

Hill, Sandi. Did You Know? 2017. (Learn-To-Read Ser.). (ENG., Illus.). (J). (gr. -1-2). pap. 3.49 *(978-1-68310-317-2(3))* Pacific Learning, Inc.

Hirschmann, Kris & Herndon, Ryan. Test Your Smarts! 2009. (Illus.). 80p. (J). *(978-0-545-12042-5(X))* Scholastic, Inc.

Holub, Joan. Why Do Birds Sing? DiVito, Anna, illus. 2004. (Penguin Young Readers, Level 3 Ser.). 48p. (J). (gr. 1-3). mass mkt. 4.99 *(978-0-14-240106-4(4)*, Penguin Young Readers) Penguin Young Readers Group.

—Why Do Birds Sing? DiVito, Anna, illus. 2004. (Easy-to-Read Ser.). 47p. 14.00 *(978-0-7569-3114-8(2))* Perfection Learning Corp.

—Why Do Snakes Hiss? And Other Questions about Snakes, Lizards, & Turtles. DiVito, Anna, illus. 2004. (Penguin Young Readers, Level 3 Ser.). 48p. (J). (gr. 1-3). mass mkt. 4.99 *(978-0-14-240105-7(6)*, Penguin Young Readers) Penguin Young Readers Group.

Honovich, Nancy. 1,000 Facts about Insects. 2018. (1,000 Facts About Ser.). (ENG., Illus.). 96p. (J). (gr. 3-7). lib. bdg. 24.90 *(978-1-4263-2994-4(6)*, National Geographic Kids) Disney Publishing Worldwide.

Hughes-Odgers, Kyle. Can a Skeleton Have an X-Ray? Hughes-Odgers, Kyle, illus. 2016. (Illus.). 32p. (J). (gr. -1-k). 16.99 *(978-1-925162-69-1(9))* Fremantle Pr. AUS. Dist: Independent Pubs. Group.

Humberstone, E. C. The Usborne First Book of Knowledge. 2004. (Explainers Ser.). (ENG.). 1p. (J). 16.95 *(978-0-7460-1963-4(7)*, Usborne) EDC Publishing.

Hunt, Santana. Name That Mammal!, 1 vol. 2016. (Guess That Animal! Ser.). (ENG.). 24p. (J). (gr. 1-2). lib. bdg. 24.27 *(978-1-4824-4746-0(0)*, 7a75dcb3-a611-44eb-ac91-7f2d4aad4b2b) Stevens, Gareth Publishing LLLP.

Irving, Harry. Picture-Word Quizzes Assessment Sheets & Solution Book: For the Children's Picture-Word & Simple Sentence Book. Graphics Factory, illus. 2009. 196p. pap. 17.14 *(978-1-4269-0667-1(6))* Trafford Publishing.

Jacobs, Marian B. Why Can Airplanes Fly?, 1 vol. 2003. (Library of Why Ser.). (ENG., Illus.). 24p. (J). (gr. 3-4). lib. bdg. 26.27 *(978-0-8239-5274-8(6)*, afce5b9d-a9c6-43a5-8c5a-4b8290ee05c1, PowerKids Pr.) Rosen Publishing Group, Inc., The.

—Why Did the Dinosaurs Become Extinct?, 1 vol. 2003. (Library of Why Ser.). (ENG., Illus.). 24p. (J). (gr. 3-4). lib. bdg. 26.27 *(978-0-8239-5276-2(2)*, 6e20a8ef-5418-416b-84d8-a62340cc2972, PowerKids Pr.) Rosen Publishing Group, Inc., The.

—Why Does It Rain?, 1 vol. 2003. (Library of Why Ser.). (ENG., Illus.). 24p. (J). (gr. 3-4). lib. bdg. 25.27 *(978-0-8239-5273-1(8)*, df8e6c12-ab40-4221-b8b7-bffa4708f492, PowerKids Pr.) Rosen Publishing Group, Inc., The.

Jacobs, Pat. I Wonder Why Penguins Can't Fly: And Other Questions about Polar Lands. 2011. (I Wonder Why Ser.). (ENG., Illus.). 32p. (J). (gr. k-3). pap. 6.99 *(978-0-7534-6530-1(2)*, 900070299, Kingfisher) Roaring Brook Pr.

James, Emily. Do Goldfish Fly? A Question & Answer Book about Animal Movements. 2016. (Animals, Animals! Ser.). (ENG., Illus.). 32p. (J). (gr. -1-2). lib. bdg. 27.99 *(978-1-5157-2666-1(5)*, 133067, Capstone Pr.) Capstone.

—Do Whales Have Whiskers? A Question & Answer Book about Animal Body Parts. 2016. (Animals, Animals! Ser.). (ENG., Illus.). 32p. (J). (gr. -1-2). lib. bdg. 27.99 *(978-1-5157-2664-7(9)*, 133065, Capstone Pr.) Capstone.

Jenkins, Steve & Page, Robin. What Do You Do with a Tail Like This? A Caldecott Honor Award Winner. Calvo, Carlos, tr. Jenkins, Steve, illus. (ENG., Illus.). 32p. (J). (gr. -1-3). 2008. pap. 7.95 *(978-0-618-99713-8(X)*, 1028080) 2003. 17.99 *(978-0-618-25628-0(8)*, 510233) HarperCollins Pubs. (Clarion Bks.).

Jones, Tom. Ask the Astronaut: A Galaxy of Astonishing Answers to Your Questions on Spaceflight. 2016. (Illus.). 224p. (gr. 5-12). pap. 12.95 *(978-1-58834-537-0(6)*, Smithsonian Bks.) Smithsonian Institution Scholarly Pr.

Jordan, Apple. The Cat: Why Do Cats Purr? & Other True Facts. 2007. (Illus.). 30p. (J). pap. *(978-0-545-00088-8(2))* Scholastic, Inc.

Kain, Kathleen. All about Holidays: With Inspector McQ. Mahan, Ben, illus. 2004. (Early Literacy Library). 32p. (J). (gr. 2-5). 219.00 *(978-0-7166-1647-4(5))* World Bk., Inc.

—All about Pets. Miyake, Yoshi, illus. 2004. (Treasure Tree Ser.). 32p. (J). *(978-0-7166-1626-9(2))* World Bk., Inc.

Kaye, Megan. Do You Know Who You Are? Singer, Allison, ed. 2014. (ENG., Illus.). 192p. (YA). (gr. 8-12). pap. 15.99 *(978-1-4654-1649-0(8)*, DK Children) Dorling Kindersley Publishing, Inc.

Keppeler, Jill. 20 Fun Facts about Astronomy, 1 vol. 2017. (Fun Fact File: Earth Science Ser.). (ENG.). 32p. (J). (gr. 2-3). pap. 11.50 *(978-1-5382-1173-1(4)*, 78e1f8bc-ab36-4dea-a9ff-0d82b32c2ff2) Stevens, Gareth Publishing LLLP.

Ketchum, Ron, illus. Rochestrivia: 2,000 Amazing questions & answers all about Rochester NY, it's people & surrounding Towns. l.t. ed. 2005. 250p. per. 19.95 *(978-0-930249-01-4(1))* LL Cameron Group, LLC.

Khan, Sarah. Dinosaur Trivia. 2018. (Activity Puzzle Book - Trivia Bks.). (ENG.). 112p. pap. 4.99 *(978-0-7945-4011-1(2),* Usborne) EDC Publishing.
Kids' Questions Classroom Collection. 2010. (Kids' Questions Ser.). 24p. pap. 125.10 *(978-1-4048-6625-6(6),* Picture Window Bks.) Capstone.
Kiefer, Jeanne. Jobs for Kids: A Smart Kid's Q & A Guide. Green, Anne Canevari, illus. 2003. (Single Titles Ser.). 112p. (gr. 5-8). lib. bdg. 25.90 *(978-0-7613-2611-3(1),* Millbrook Pr.) Lerner Publishing Group.
Lawrence, Paul R. Question Quest HSPA Math Geometry Companion. 2003. (Illus.). (YA). pap. 8.95 *(978-1-931104-16-6(6))* L L Teach.
Le Compte, David & Rolland, Carol. Eugene Stillwell Wants to Know! Padrick, Kendell, ed. 2007. (Eugene Stillwell Wants to Know! Ser.). (ENG., Illus.). 96p. (J). (gr. 4-6). per. 4.95 *(978-1-929945-71-9(X))* Big Guy Bks., Inc.
LeCompte, David & Padrick, Kendell. Eugene Stillwell Wants to Know!, Pt. 2. 2009. (Eugene Stillwell Wants to Know! Ser.). (ENG.). 96p. (J). (gr. 4-6). pap. 4.95 *(978-1-929945-74-0(4))* Big Guy Bks., Inc.
Leipe, Ulla. Lo Que los Ninos Quieren Saber. Limmer, Hannes, illus. (SPA.). 180p. (YA). 11.95 *(978-84-241-5501-8(7),* EV867) Everest Editora ESP. Dist: Continental Bk. Co., Inc.
Levy, Janey. 20 Fun Facts about Fossils, 1 vol. 2017. (Fun Fact File: Earth Science Ser.). (ENG.). 32p. (J). (gr. 2-3). pap. 11.50 *(978-1-5382-1181-6(5),* 53eb242a-8410-4f6c-af83-62b13891412c) Stevens, Gareth Publishing LLLP.
Little Kids Book of Why, 1 vol. 2014. (Little Kids Books of Why Ser.). (ENG.). 48p. (gr. 5-6). pap. 17.90 *(978-1-4914-1935-9(0))* Capstone.
Lluch, Alex A. Let's Leap Ahead 1st Grade Trivia. 2013. 216p. (J). (gr. k). pap. 9.95 *(978-1-61351-045-2(4))* WS Publishing.
—Let's Leap Ahead 2nd Grade Trivia. 2013. 216p. (J). (gr. 1). pap. 9.95 *(978-1-61351-046-9(2))* WS Publishing.
—Let's Leap Ahead 2nd Grade Trivia Notepad: The Game of 300 Questions for You & Your Friends! 2013. 70p. (J). (gr. 1). pap. 3.95 *(978-1-61351-060-5(8))* WS Publishing.
—Let's Leap Ahead 3rd Grade Trivia. 2013. 216p. (J). (gr. 2). pap. 9.95 *(978-1-61351-047-6(0))* WS Publishing.
—Let's Leap Ahead 3rd Grade Trivia Notepad: The Game of 300 Questions for You & Your Friends! 2013. 70p. (J). (gr. 2). pap. 3.95 *(978-1-61351-061-2(6))* WS Publishing.
—Let's Leap Ahead 4th Grade Trivia. 2013. 216p. (J). (gr. 3). pap. 9.95 *(978-1-61351-048-3(9))* WS Publishing.
Lluch, Isabel B. & Lluch, Emily. B. F. F. Best Friends Forever: Quizzes for You & Your Friends. 2012. 80p. (J). (gr. 6). pap. 6.95 *(978-1-936061-55-6(4))* WS Publishing.
—B. F. F. Quizzes. 2013. 128p. (J). (gr. 6). pap. 7.95 *(978-1-61351-030-8(6))* WS Publishing.
—IGirl: B. F. F. Quizzes for You & Your Friends. 2012. 130p. (J). (gr. 6). pap. 4.95 *(978-1-936061-95-2(3))* WS Publishing.
—IGirl: My B. F. F. s: My B. F. F. S. 2013. 80p. (J). (gr. 6). pap. 7.95 *(978-1-61351-016-2(0))* WS Publishing.
—IGirl: My Keepsake: My Keepsake. 2013. 80p. (J). (gr. 6). pap. 7.95 *(978-1-61351-015-5(2))* WS Publishing.
Llull, Maria. I-Ballers: Little Books for Big Minds. 2005. (ENG., Illus.). 60p. (J). (gr. 4-7). pap. 4.95 *(978-1-57528-939-7(3))* Univ. Games.
MacDonald, Margaret. Job Quiz. 2011. (Learn-Abouts: Level 10 Ser.). (Illus.). 16p. (J). pap. 7.95 *(978-1-59920-599-1(8))* Black Rabbit Bks.
Macheske, Felicia. Blue & Bumpy: Blue Crab. 2016. (Guess What Ser.). (ENG., Illus.). 24p. (J). (gr. k-2). 30.64 *(978-1-63470-717-6(6),* 207579) Cherry Lake Publishing.
—Busy Buddies: Dog. 2017. (Guess What Ser.). (ENG., Illus.). 24p. (J). (gr. k-2). lib. bdg. 30.64 *(978-1-63472-851-5(3),* 209830) Cherry Lake Publishing.
—Hefty Hulks: Rhinoceros. 2017. (Guess What Ser.). (ENG., Illus.). 24p. (J). (gr. k-2). lib. bdg. 30.64 *(978-1-63472-169-1(1),* 209248) Cherry Lake Publishing.
—Lanky Legs: Praying Mantis. 2016. (Guess What Ser.). (ENG., Illus.). 24p. (J). (gr. k-2). 30.64 *(978-1-63470-720-6(6),* 207591) Cherry Lake Publishing.
—Wiggling Whiskers: Rabbit. 2017. (Guess What Ser.). (ENG., Illus.). 24p. (J). (gr. k-2). lib. bdg. 30.64 *(978-1-63472-857-7(2),* 209854) Cherry Lake Publishing.
Maclaine, James. Big Picture Book of General Knowledge IR. 2018. (Big Picture Books* Ser.). (ENG.). 32p. 14.99 *(978-0-7945-3960-3(2),* Usborne) EDC Publishing.
—Lift-The-Flap General Knowledge IR. 2015. (Lift-The-Flap Board Bks.). (ENG.). 16p. (J). (gr. k-5). 14.99 *(978-0-7945-3418-9(X),* Usborne) EDC Publishing.
Malloy, Devin. SpookyTalk: Conversation Cards for the Entire Family. 2008. (Tabletalk Conversation Cards Ser.). (Illus.). (J). (gr. 4-7). 6.00 *(978-1-57281-635-0(X))* U.S. Games Systems, Inc.
—WeatherTalk: Conversation Cards for the Entire Family. 2008. (Tabletalk Conversation Cards Ser.). (Illus.). (J). (gr. 4-7). 6.00 *(978-1-57281-632-9(5))* U.S. Games Systems, Inc.
Manning, Mick. Que Hay Debajo de la Cama? Cortes, Eunice, tr. Granström, Brita, illus. 2003. (Descubriendo Mi Mundo Ser.). (SPA.). 32p. (J). *(978-970-690-588-8(X))* Planeta Mexicana Editorial S. A. de C. V.
Marek, Hillary. The smart ass guide to ridiculous Questions. 2010. 139p. pap. 11.06 *(978-0-557-30904-7(2))* Lulu Pr., Inc.
Marsico, Katie. Chameleons Change Color. 2015. (Tell Me Why Library). (ENG., Illus.). 24p. (J). (gr. 2-5). pap. 12.79 *(978-1-63362-699-7(7),* 206621) Cherry Lake Publishing.
—Elephants Have Trunks. 2014. (Tell Me Why Library). (ENG., Illus.). 24p. (J). (gr. 2-5). 29.21 *(978-1-63188-002-5(0),* 205415) Cherry Lake Publishing.
—Giraffes Have Long Necks. 2014. (Tell Me Why Library). (ENG., Illus.). 24p. (J). (gr. 2-5). 29.21 *(978-1-63188-003-2(9),* 205419) Cherry Lake Publishing.
—I Cry. 2014. (Tell Me Why Library). (ENG., Illus.). 24p. (J). (gr. 2-5). 29.21 *(978-1-63188-004-9(7),* 205423) Cherry Lake Publishing.
—I Throw Up. 2014. (Tell Me Why Library). (ENG., Illus.). 24p. (J). (gr. 2-5). 29.21 *(978-1-63188-006-3(3),* 205431) Cherry Lake Publishing.
Martin, Isabel. Birds: A Question & Answer Book, 1 vol. 2014. (Animal Kingdom Questions & Answers Ser.). (ENG.). 24p. (J). (gr. -1-2). 27.32 *(978-1-4914-0561-1(9),* 125899); (Illus.). pap. 6.95 *(978-1-4914-0629-8(1),* 125933) Capstone. (Capstone Pr.).
—Fish: A Question & Answer Book, 1 vol. 2014. (Animal Kingdom Questions & Answers Ser.). (ENG., Illus.). 24p. (J). (gr. -1-2). pap. 6.95 *(978-1-4914-0631-1(3),* 125935, Capstone Pr.) Capstone.
Martin, Mary-Jane. Let Me Put It This Way. 2004. (Illus.). 32p. 11.95 *(978-0-9730583-1-4(5))* Lion & Mouse Tales, Inc. CAN. Dist: Hushion Hse. Publishing, Ltd.
Mason, Paul & Barnham, Kay. Questions You Never Thought You'd Ask. 2013. (Questions You Never Thought You'd Ask Ser.). (ENG.). 32p. (J). (gr. 3-5). pap., pap., pap. 35.80 *(978-1-4109-5208-0(8),* 19619, Raintree) Capstone.
Matheson, Murdoch H. Building Wealth for Teens: Answers to Questions Teens Care About. 2007. 116p. 24.65 *(978-1-4251-2358-1(9))* Trafford Publishing.
Maurice, creator. The Spanish Question Game. (SPA.). (YA). 134.95 *(978-1-932770-48-3(8),* SG9) Symtalk, Inc.
Maynard, Chris. I Wonder Why Planes Have Wings: And Other Questions about Transportation. 2012. (I Wonder Why Ser.). (ENG., Illus.). 32p. (J). (gr. k-3). pap. 6.99 *(978-0-7534-6703-9(8),* 900076420, Kingfisher) Roaring Brook Pr.
Meister, Cari. Totally Wacky Facts about Animals. 2015. (Mind Benders Ser.). (ENG., Illus.). 240p. (J). (gr. 3-6). pap., pap. 7.95 *(978-1-4914-6525-7(5),* 129024, Capstone Pr.) Capstone.
—Totally Wacky Facts about Land Animals. 2015. (Mind Benders Ser.). (ENG., Illus.). 112p. (J). (gr. 3-6). lib. bdg. 23.99 *(978-1-4914-6522-6(0),* 129021, Capstone Pr.) Capstone.
—Totally Wacky Facts about Sea Animals. 2015. (Mind Benders Ser.). (ENG., Illus.). 112p. (J). (gr. 3-6). lib. bdg. 23.99 *(978-1-4914-6521-9(2),* 129020, Capstone Pr.) Capstone.
Miles Kelly Staff. Animals. 2003. (Info Bank Ser.). (Illus.). 96p. (J). 7.95 *(978-1-84236-153-5(8))* Miles Kelly Publishing, Ltd. GBR. Dist: Independent Pubs. Group.
—Geography. 2003. (Info Bank Ser.). (Illus.). 96p. (J). 7.95 *(978-1-84236-055-2(8))* Miles Kelly Publishing, Ltd. GBR. Dist: Independent Pubs. Group.
—History. 2003. (Info Bank Ser.). (Illus.). 96p. (J). 7.95 *(978-1-84236-056-9(6))* Miles Kelly Publishing, Ltd. GBR. Dist: Independent Pubs. Group.
—How Things Work. 2003. (Ask Me a Question Ser.). (Illus.). 20p. spiral bd. 7.95 *(978-1-84236-127-6(9))* Miles Kelly Publishing, Ltd. GBR. Dist: Independent Pubs. Group.
—Nature. 2003. (Ask Me a Question Ser.). (Illus.). 20p. spiral bd. 7.95 *(978-1-84236-125-2(2))* Miles Kelly Publishing, Ltd. GBR. Dist: Independent Pubs. Group.
—Our Planet. 2003. (Ask Me a Question Ser.). (Illus.). 20p. (J). spiral bd. 7.95 *(978-1-84236-128-3(7))* Miles Kelly Publishing, Ltd. GBR. Dist: Independent Pubs. Group.
—People & Places. 2003. (Ask Me a Question Ser.). (Illus.). 20p. spiral bd. 7.95 *(978-1-84236-126-9(0))* Miles Kelly Publishing, Ltd. GBR. Dist: Independent Pubs. Group.
—Science. 2003. (Info Bank Ser.). (Illus.). 96p. (J). 7.95 *(978-1-84236-152-8(X))* Miles Kelly Publishing, Ltd. GBR. Dist: Independent Pubs. Group.
Morlock, Theresa. 20 Fun Facts about Rocks & Gems, 1 vol. 2017. (Fun Fact File: Earth Science Ser.). (ENG.). 32p. (J). (gr. 2-3). pap. 11.50 *(978-1-5382-1189-2(0),* 88cd9cbe-ec6b-49fb-9bb1-04abb719d0ee) Stevens, Gareth Publishing LLLP.
Mortimer, J. R. This or That? 2: More Wacky Choices to Reveal the Hidden You. 2014. (Illus.). 176p. (J). (gr. 3-7). pap. 12.99 *(978-1-4263-1719-4(0),* National Geographic Kids) Disney Publishing Worldwide.
Most, Bernard. Dinosaur Questions. 2008. (Illus.). (J). pap. *(978-0-15-206475-4(3),* Red Wagon Bks.) Harcourt Children's Bks.
—Dinosaur Questions. 2009. (ENG., Illus.). 36p. (J). (gr. -1-3). pap. 6.99 *(978-0-15-206691-8(8),* 1099012, Clarion Bks.) HarperCollins Pubs.
The Moves Make the Man: Teaching Unit. 2003. 73p. (YA). ring bd. *(978-1-58049-433-5(1),* TU4331) Prestwick Hse., Inc.
Munrriz, Mercedes & Munárriz Guezala, Mercedes. Por Qué? Martinez, Rocio, illus. 2003. (SPA.). 16p. (J). *(978-84-667-2627-6(6))* Grupo Anaya, S.A. ESP. Dist: Lectorum Pubns., Inc.
—Qué Es? Martinez, Rocio, illus. 2003. (SPA.). 16p. (J). *(978-84-667-2626-9(8))* Grupo Anaya, S.A. ESP. Dist: Lectorum Pubns., Inc.
Murphy, Glenn. Why Is Snot Green? And Other Extremely Important Questions (and Answers) 2009. (ENG., Illus.). 240p. (J). (gr. 3-6). pap. 13.99 *(978-1-59643-500-1(3),* 900057452) Square Fish.
My Big Book of Questions & Answers. 2003. 512p. (J). 9.98 *(978-1-4054-0758-8(1))* Parragon, Inc.
National Geographic Kids. National Geographic Kids Quiz Whiz: 1,000 Super Fun, Mind-Bending, Totally Awesome Trivia Questions. 2012. (ENG., Illus.). 176p. (J). (gr. 3-7). pap. 9.99 *(978-1-4263-1018-8(8),* National Geographic Kids); lib. bdg. 18.90 *(978-1-4263-1019-5(6),* National Geographic Children's Bks.) Disney Publishing Worldwide.
—National Geographic Kids Quiz Whiz 2: 1,000 Super Fun Mind-Bending Totally Awesome Trivia Questions. 2013. (Quiz Whiz Ser.: 2). (Illus.). 176p. (J). (gr. 3-7). pap. 9.99 *(978-1-4263-1356-1(X),* National Geographic Kids) Disney Publishing Worldwide.
—National Geographic Kids Quiz Whiz 3: 1,000 Super Fun Mind-Bending Totally Awesome Trivia Questions. 2014. (Quiz Whiz Ser.: 3). 176p. (J). (gr. 3-7). pap. 9.99 *(978-1-4263-1484-1(1),* National Geographic Kids) Disney Publishing Worldwide.
—National Geographic Kids Quiz Whiz 4: 1,000 Super Fun Mind-Bending Totally Awesome Trivia Questions. 2014. (Quiz Whiz Ser.: 4). (Illus.). 176p. (J). (gr. 3-7). pap. 9.99 *(978-1-4263-1709-5(3),* National Geographic Kids) Disney Publishing Worldwide.
—Weird but True! Collector's Set, 3 vols., Set. 2012. (Weird but True Ser.). (Illus.). 624p. (J). (gr. 1-3). 24.99 *(978-1-4263-1194-9(X),* National Geographic Kids) Disney Publishing Worldwide.
—Weird but True 1: Expanded Edition, Vol .1. enl. ed. 2018. (Weird but True Ser.: 2). (Illus.). 216p. (J). (gr. 3-7). pap. 8.99 *(978-1-4263-3104-6(5),* National Geographic Kids) Disney Publishing Worldwide.
—Weird but True 2: Expanded Edition, Vol .2. enl. ed. 2018. (Weird but True Ser.: 4). (Illus.). 216p. (J). (gr. 3-7). pap. 8.99 *(978-1-4263-3106-0(1),* National Geographic Kids) Disney Publishing Worldwide.
—Weird but True 3: Expanded Edition. enl. ed. 2018. (Weird but True Ser.: 4). (Illus.). 216p. (J). (gr. 3-7). pap. 8.99 *(978-1-4263-3108-4(8),* National Geographic Kids) Disney Publishing Worldwide.
—Weird but True 4: Expanded Edition. enl. ed. 2018. (Weird but True Ser.: 6). (Illus.). 216p. (J). (gr. 3-7). pap. 8.99 *(978-1-4263-3110-7(X),* National Geographic Kids) Disney Publishing Worldwide.
—Weird but True 5, Vol .5. enl. ed. 2018. (Weird but True Ser.: 6). (Illus.). 216p. (J). (gr. 3-7). pap. 8.99 *(978-1-4263-3112-1(6),* National Geographic Kids) Disney Publishing Worldwide.
—Weird but True 6: Expanded Edition. enl. ed. 2018. (Weird but True Ser.: 7). (Illus.). 216p. (J). (gr. 3-7). pap. 8.99 *(978-1-4263-3114-5(2),* National Geographic Kids) Disney Publishing Worldwide.
—Weird but True 7: Expanded Edition. enl. ed. 2018. (Weird but True Ser.: 8). (Illus.). 216p. (J). (gr. 3-7). pap. 8.99 *(978-1-4263-3116-9(9),* National Geographic Kids) Disney Publishing Worldwide.
—Weird but True 8: Expanded Edition, Vol .8. enl. ed. 2018. (Weird but True Ser.: 9). (Illus.). 216p. (J). (gr. 3-7). pap. 8.99 *(978-1-4263-3118-3(5),* National Geographic Kids) Disney Publishing Worldwide.
—Weird but True 9: Expanded Edition. enl. ed. 2018. (Weird but True Ser.). (Illus.). 216p. (J). (gr. 3-7). pap. 8.99 *(978-1-4263-3120-6(7),* National Geographic Kids) Disney Publishing Worldwide.
National Parents Council. The Whiz Quiz Book - 3rd Edition: For Children & Grown-Up Children. 3rd rev. ed. 2017. (ENG.). 128p. (J). pap. 12.00 *(978-1-84889-297-2(7),* Collins Pr., The) M.H. Gill & Co. U. C. IRL. Dist: Dufour Editions, Inc.
National Parents Council - Primary Staff. The Whiz Quiz Book: For Children & Grown-Up Children. 2006. (ENG.). 117p. (J). per. 10.95 *(978-1-903464-98-4(6),* Collins Pr., The) M.H. Gill & Co. U. C. IRL. Dist: Dufour Editions, Inc.
National Parents Council - Primary Staff, ed. More Whiz Quiz: For Children & Grown-up Children. 2008. (ENG.). 126p. (J). per. 11.95 *(978-1-905172-50-4(8),* Collins Pr., The) M.H. Gill & Co. U. C. IRL. Dist: Dufour Editions, Inc.
Nau, Myrna. Questions & Answers about Ellis Island, 1 vol. 2018. (Eye on Historical Sources Ser.). (ENG.). 32p. (gr. 4-4). 27.93 *(978-1-5383-4111-7(5),* 65f028bf-13d2-49a4-bbe1-c9107d451c8f, PowerKids Pr.) Rosen Publishing Group, Inc., The.
Nicholaus, Bret & Lowrie, Paul. KidChat: 222 Creative Questions to Spark Conversations. 2nd rev. ed. 2004. (Illus.). 128p. (J). pap. 9.95 *(978-0-9755801-0-3(8),* KCR) Questmarc Publishing.
—KidChat Too! All-New Questions to Fuel Young Minds & Mouths. 2004. (Illus.). 128p. (J). pap. 9.95 *(978-0-9755801-1-0(6),* KCT) Questmarc Publishing.
O'Neill, Amanda. I Wonder Why Spiders Spin Webs: And Other Questions about Creepy Crawlies. 2011. (I Wonder Why Ser.). (ENG., Illus.). 32p. (J). (gr. k-3). pap. 6.99 *(978-0-7534-6524-0(8),* 900070351, Kingfisher) Roaring Brook Pr.
Orr, Tamra B. I See Falling Stars. 2015. (Tell Me Why Library). (ENG., Illus.). 24p. (gr. 2-5). pap. 12.79 *(978-1-63362-035-3(2),* 205897) Cherry Lake Publishing.
Overdeck, Laura. Bedtime Math: the Truth Comes Out. Paillot, Jim, illus. 2015. (Bedtime Math Ser.). (ENG.). 96p. (J). (gr. -1-2). 18.99 *(978-1-250-04775-5(7),* 900132482) Feiwel & Friends.
Oxlade, Chris. Why Why Why Do Tornadoes Spin. 2008. 32p. pap. *(978-1-84810-004-6(3))* Miles Kelly Publishing, Ltd.
—Why Why Why Does My Heart Begin to Race? 2008. 32p. pap. *(978-1-84810-002-2(7))* Miles Kelly Publishing, Ltd.
Paquette, Ammi-Joan & Thompson, Laurie Ann. Two Truths & a Lie: It's Alive! Weber, Lisa K., illus. 2018. (ENG.). 176p. (J). (gr. 3-7). pap. 10.99 *(978-0-06-241881-4(5),* Walden Pond Pr.) HarperCollins Pubs.
Parker, Janice. Machines Q & A. 2013. (J). *(978-1-62127-416-2(0));* pap. *(978-1-62127-422-3(5))* Weigl Pubs., Inc.
—Weather Q & A. 2013. (J). *(978-1-62127-417-9(9));* pap. *(978-1-62127-423-0(3))* Weigl Pubs., Inc.
Payne, Jan & Wilder, Steven. It Can Rain Frogs & Fish: And Other Facts about Planet Earth, 1 vol. 2016. (True or False? Ser.). (ENG.). 48p. (gr. 3-3). pap. 12.70 *(978-0-7660-7732-4(2),* 247dbf0b-29ff-4fa8-9009-8b4fac0bf708) Enslow Publishing, LLC.
Peters, Celeste A. Health Q & A. 2013. (J). *(978-1-62127-414-8(4));* pap. *(978-1-62127-420-9(9))* Weigl Pubs., Inc.
Pfister, Marcus. Questions, Questions. 2014. (ENG., Illus.). 32p. (J). (gr. -1 — 1). bds. 8.95 *(978-0-7358-4170-3(5),* 9780735841703) North-South Bks., Inc.
Phillips, Karen, ed. What about You? 2009. (Illus.). 50p. (J). (gr. 3). 16.95 *(978-1-59174-612-6(4))* Klutz.
Pocrass, Kate. Quotes & Questions: A Journal for Your Kid's Quotable Moments. 2019. (ENG., Illus.). 224p. 12.95 *(978-1-4521-7036-7(3))* Chronicle Bks. LLC.
Potts, Kimberly. Boost Your Guy-Q: Quizzes to Test Your Guy Smarts. 2007. (ENG., Illus.). 160p. (gr. 8-12). per. 13.99 *(978-1-59869-230-3(5))* Adams Media Corp.
Powell, Michael. Do My Ears Ever Stop Growing? And 70 Other Questions That Keep You Awake at Night. 2009. (Illus.). 158p. (J). *(978-1-4351-1200-1(8))* Metro Bks.
Q & A: Life's Mysteries Solved!, 12 vols. 2016. (Q & a: Life's Mysteries Solved! Ser.). 32p. (ENG.). (gr. 3-4). lib. bdg. 169.62 *(978-1-4824-4606-7(5),* 45efa3d5-9629-4045-9027-969fee68016d); (gr. 4-3). pap. 63.00 *(978-1-4824-5298-3(7))* Stevens, Gareth Publishing LLLP.
Questions & Answers of the Natural World. 2003. (Illus.). 256p. (J). 12.98 *(978-1-4054-1682-5(3))* Parragon, Inc.
Questmarc Publishing, creator. Chat Pack for Kids: Creative Questions to Ignite the Imagination. 2009. (J). 9.95 *(978-0-9755801-5-8(9))* Questmarc Publishing.
Raum, Elizabeth. Blue-Ringed Octopuses. 2015. (Poisonous Animals Ser.). (ENG., Illus.). 32p. (J). (gr. 2-5). lib. bdg. 19.95 *(978-1-60753-785-4(0),* 15301) Amicus.
—Box Jellyfish. 2015. (Poisonous Animals Ser.). (ENG., Illus.). 32p. (J). (gr. 2-5). lib. bdg. 19.95 *(978-1-60753-786-1(9),* 15302) Amicus.
—Poison Dart Frogs. 2015. (Poisonous Animals Ser.). (ENG., Illus.). 32p. (J). (gr. 2-5). lib. bdg. 19.95 *(978-1-60753-787-8(7),* 15303) Amicus.
Richmond, Ben. Why Is the Sea Salty? And Other Questions about Oceans. Azhderian, Cecelia, illus. 2014. (Good Question! Ser.). 32p. (J). (gr. 1). pap. 5.95 *(978-1-4549-0677-3(4))* Sterling Publishing Co., Inc.
Ripley, Catherine. How? The Most Awesome Question & Answer Book about Nature, Animals, People, Places — And You! Ritchie, Scot, illus. 2019. (ENG.). 192p. (J). (gr. -1-4). pap. 17.95 *(978-1-77147-384-2(3))* Owlkids Bks. Inc. CAN. Dist: Publishers Group West (PGW).
Ristuccia, Christine & Ristuccia, James. The Entire World of WH? Questions. 2004. (J). 39.99 *(978-0-9723457-9-8(5))* Say It Right.
—The Entire World of WH? Questions Flip Book. 2004. (Illus.). 9p. (J). spiral bd. 14.99 *(978-0-9723457-8-1(7))* Say It Right.
Russell, Ken & Carter, Philip. Bumper Quiz Book for Kids. (Illus.). 160p. (J). 17.95 *(978-1-85479-300-3(4))* O'Mara, Michael Bks., Ltd. GBR. Dist: Trans-Atlantic Pubns., Inc.
Russo, Kristin J. Human Body Facts or Fibs. 2018. (Facts or Fibs? Ser.). (ENG., Illus.). 32p. (J). (gr. 3-9). pap. 7.95 *(978-1-5435-0207-7(5),* 137129); lib. bdg. 28.65 *(978-1-5435-0203-9(2),* 137125) Capstone. (Capstone Pr.).
Schwartz, Heather E. Incredible Tech Trivia: Fun Facts & Quizzes. 2018. (Trivia Time! (Alternator Books (r)) Ser.). (ENG., Illus.). 32p. (J). (gr. 3-6). lib. bdg. 29.32 *(978-1-5124-8332-1(X),* b604beb4-0a2a-4a42-82d4-26b3ef2e1d05, Lerner Pubns.) Lerner Publishing Group.
Seip, Shannon Payette. The Pop Quiz Book: Tons of Trivia! Sheuer, Lauren, illus. 2008. (American Girl Library). (ENG.). 80p. (gr. 3-7). spiral bd. 7.95 *(978-1-58485-844-7(3),* American Girl) American Girl Publishing, Inc.
Settel, Joanne. Your Amazing Skin from Outside In. Timmons, Bonnie, illus. 2018. (Your Amazing Body Bks.). (ENG.). 96p. (J). (gr. 3-7). 18.99 *(978-1-4814-2205-5(7))* Simon & Schuster Children's Publishing.
Shand, Jennifer. Why Do Feet Get So Stinky? 2015. (Why Do... ? Ser.). lib. bdg. 19.65 *(978-1-4867-0623-5(1))* Turtleback.
Shea, Therese M. Do Cows Have Two Stomachs? And Other FAQs about Animals, 1 vol. 2016. (Q & a: Life's Mysteries Solved! Ser.). (ENG.). 32p. (J). (gr. 3-4). lib. bdg. 28.27 *(978-1-4824-4778-1(9),* dd185cad-8af6-44f1-84e6-22677b43627d) Stevens, Gareth Publishing LLLP.
Shulman, Mark. Are You "Normal"? More Than 100 Questions That Will Test Your Weirdness. 2011. (Illus.). 176p. (J). (gr. 3-7). pap. 12.95 *(978-1-4263-0837-6(X),* National Geographic Kids) Disney Publishing Worldwide.
Slade, Suzanne. Who Invented Basketball? And Other Questions Kids Have about Sports, 1 vol. Pillo, Cary, illus. 2010. (Kids' Questions Ser.). (ENG.). 24p. (J). (gr. k-2). pap. 7.49 *(978-1-4048-6730-7(9),* 115555, Picture Window Bks.) Capstone.
Smith, Jeremy. Why Why Why... Did Pirates Bury Their Treasure? 2010. (Why Why Why Ser.). (Illus.). 32p. (J). (gr. 1-3). lib. bdg. 18.95 *(978-1-4222-1576-0(8))* Mason Crest.
Smith, Sam & Tudhope, Simon. General Knowledge Trivia Questions. 2018. (Activity Puzzle Book - Trivia Bks.). (ENG.). 112p. (J). pap. 4.99 *(978-0-7945-4012-8(0),* Usborne) EDC Publishing.
Smurd, John & Smidlap, Harley. The 707 Book: (707 Questions-707 Answers) 2008. 140p. pap. 11.95 *(978-0-595-50820-4(0))* iUniverse, Inc.
Solomon, Iris L. & Solomon, Ron. Friendz Pakz: Friends. 2003. (YA). (gr. 3-18). 4.99 *(978-1-930680-04-3(X),* SSP-08FR) Swingset Pr., LLC.
—Friendz Pakz: Future. 2003. (YA). (gr. 3-18). 4.99 *(978-1-930680-05-0(8),* SSP-08FT) Swingset Pr., LLC.
—Friendz Pakz: Love. 2003. (YA). (gr. 3-18). 4.99 *(978-1-930680-07-4(4),* SSP-08LV) Swingset Pr., LLC.
Steele, Philip. I Wonder Why Countries Fly Flags. 2012. (I Wonder Why Ser.). (ENG., Illus.). 32p. (J). (gr. k-3). 6.99 *(978-0-7534-6793-0(3),* 900085101, Kingfisher) Roaring Brook Pr.
Stewart, M. Why Did T Rex Have Short Arms Dinosaurs. 2014. (Good Question! Ser.). (ENG., Illus.). 32p. (J). (gr. 1). pap. 6.95 *(978-1-4549-0679-7(0))* Sterling Publishing Co., Inc.
Stiekel, Bettina, ed. The Nobel Book of Answers: A the Dalai Lama, Mikhail Gorbachev, Shimon Peres. 2010. (ENG.). 272p. (J). (gr. 5-9). pap. 12.99 *(978-1-4424-2193-6(2),* Atheneum Bks. for Young Readers) Simon & Schuster Children's Publishing.
Stock, Gregory. Kids Book of Questions Review. 2nd rev. expurg. ed. (ENG.). (J). pap. 79.50 *(978-0-7611-3625-5(8),* 23625) Workman Publishing Co., Inc.
Stott, Carole. I Wonder Why Stars Twinkle. Tremblay, Marie-Ave, illus. 2011. (I Wonder Why Ser.). (ENG.). 32p. (J). (gr. k-3). pap. 6.99 *(978-0-7534-6520-2(5),* 900070300, Kingfisher) Roaring Brook Pr.
Susaeta, Equipo. 1000 PREGUNTAS Y RESPUESTAS. (SPA., Illus.). 96p. (J). (gr. 3-5). *(978-84-305-8671-4(7),* SU2565) Susaeta Ediciones, S.A. ESP. Dist: Lectorum Pubns., Inc.
Taylor, Barbara. I Wonder Why Zippers Have Teeth. 2012. (I Wonder Why Ser.). (ENG., Illus.). 32p. (J). (gr. k-3). 6.99 *(978-0-7534-6801-2(8),* 900085121, Kingfisher) Roaring Brook Pr.
Tears of a Tiger: Teaching Unit. 2003. 88p. (YA). ring bd. *(978-1-58049-429-8(3),* TU4293) Prestwick Hse., Inc.
Thomas Nelson Publishing Staff. Solomon Says Bible Trivia: Anything Goes: Test Your Bible Knowledge in this Wacky Game Show! 2008. cd-rom 24.95 *(978-0-9754280-9-2(8))* Nelson, Thomas Inc.
—Solomon Says Bible Trivia for Kids: Amazing Animals: Learn about Animals of the Bible. 2008. cd-rom 24.95 *(978-1-4003-1336-5(8))* Nelson, Thomas Inc.
Tiede, Karen. Carve Smart. 2004. 189p. (YA). pap. 19.95 *(978-0-7414-2093-0(7))* Infinity Publishing.

Time for Kids Editors. Big Book of Answers: 1,001 Facts Kids Want to Know. 2015. (Time for Kids Big Bks.). (ENG., Illus.). 192p. (J). (gr. 3-17). 19.95 *(978-1-61893-150-4(4)*, Time For Kids) Time Inc. Bks.
—Big Book of Where. 2013. (Time for Kids Big Bks.). (ENG., Illus.). 192p. (J). (gr. 3-17). 19.95 *(978-1-61893-042-2(7)*, Time For Kids) Time Inc. Bks.
—Kids Ask - We Answer. 2013. (Time for Kids Ser.). (ENG., Illus.). 96p. (J). (gr. -1-1). 14.95 *(978-1-61893-093-4(1)*, Time For Kids) Time Inc. Bks.
—Space. 2014. (Time for Kids X-Why-Z Ser.). (ENG., illus.). 96p. (J). (gr. -1-1). 14.95 *(978-1-61893-126-9(1)*, Time For Kids) Time Inc. Bks.
—Time for Kids Big Book of How. 2011. 192p. (J). pap. 11.99 *(978-1-60320-907-6(7))* Time Inc. Bks.
Time for Kids Magazine Staff. TIME for Kids Big Book of What. 2012. (ENG.). 192p. (J). (gr. 3-17). pap. 11.99 *(978-1-60320-943-4(3))* Time Inc. Bks.
The Time-Life Library of First Questions & Answers, 18 bks. Incl. Are There Diamonds in My Backyard? First Questions & Answers about the Earth. Time-Life for Children Staff. Mark, Sara, ed. 1995. 14.95 *(978-0-7835-0902-0(2))*; Did Triceratops Have Polka Dots? First Questions & Answers about Dinosaurs. Time-Life Books Editors. Fallow, Allan, ed. 1995. 14.95 *(978-0-7835-0903-7(0))*; Do Bears Give Bear Hugs? First Questions & Answers about Animals. Time-Life Books Editors. Fallow, Allan, ed. 1994. 14.95 *(978-0-7835-0870-2(0))*; Do Buildings Have Bones? First Questions & Answers about Buildings. Time-Life Books Editors. Mark, Sara, ed. 1995. 14.95 *(978-0-7835-0900-6(6))*; Do Fish Drink? First Questions & Answers about Water. Time-Life Books Editors. Kagan, Neil, ed. 1993. 14.95 *(978-0-7835-0850-4(6))*; Do Mommies Have Mommies? First Questions & Answers about Families. Time-Life Books Editors. Fallow, Allan, ed. 1994. 14.95 *(978-0-7835-0874-0(3))*; Do Skyscrapers Touch the Sky? First Questions & Answers about Cities. Time-Life Books Editors. Fallow, Allan, ed. 1994. 14.95 *(978-0-7835-0886-3(7))*; How Big Is the Ocean? First Questions & Answers about the Beach. Time-Life Books Editors. Fallow, Allan, ed. 1994. 14.95 *(978-0-7835-0897-9(2))*; How Far Can a Butterfly Fly? First Questions & Answers about Bugs. Time-Life Books Editors. Lesk, Sara M., ed. 1994. 14.95 *(978-0-7835-0882-5(4))*; What Makes Popcorn Pop? First Questions & Answers about Food. Ward, Elizabeth, ed. 1994. 14.95 *(978-0-7835-0862-7(X))*; Where Does the Sun Sleep? First Questions & Answers about Bedtime. Time-Life Books Editors. Kagan, Neil, ed. 1993. 14.95 *(978-0-7835-0866-5(2))*; Who Named My Street Magnolia? First Questions & Answers about Neighborhoods. Time-Life Books Editors. Mark, Sara, ed. 1995. 14.95 *(978-0-7835-0898-6(0))*; Why Are Wagons Red? First Questions & Answers about Transportation. Time-Life Books Editors. Lesk, Sara M., ed. 1994. 14.95 *(978-0-7835-0878-8(6))*; Why Do Balls Bounce? First Questions & Answers about How Things Work. Time-Life Books Editors. Fallow, Allan, ed. 1995. 14.95 *(978-0-7835-0901-3(4))*; Why Do Roosters Crow? First Questions & Answers about Farms. Time-Life Books Editors. Fallow, Allan, ed. & Pedro Paul & Kavanagh, Jim, illus. 1995. 14.95 *(978-0-7835-0899-3(9))*; Why Is the Grass Green? First Questions & Answers about Nature. Time-Life Books Editors. Kagan, Neil, ed. 1993. 14.95 *(978-0-7835-0858-0(1))*; (Illus.). 48p. (J). (gr. k-2). *(978-0-7835-0894-8(8))* Time-Life, Inc.
Todo Sobre Nuestro Mundo. (Coleccion Todo Sobre...). (SPA.). (J). (gr. k-1). *(978-84-243-2966-2(X)*, FH5249) Publicaciones Fher, S.A.
Townsend, John. Gone Missing. 2009. (Amazing Mysteries Ser.). (ENG.). 32p. (J). (gr. 3-6). 28.50 *(978-1-59920-364-5(2)*, 19253, Smart Apple Media) Black Rabbit Bks.
Traynor, Tracy & Pérez, María. Spanish with Abby & Zak, 1 vol. Hambleton, Laura, illus. 2008. (Abby & Zak Ser.). (ENG & SPA.). 48p. (J). (gr. k-2). pap. 16.95 *(978-1-84059-515-4(9))* Milet Publishing.
Trotter, Pamela D., III. Lantern on a Hitching Post: African-American Heritage Quiz Book 2003. 114p. (YA). per. 12.00 *(978-0-9754540-0-8(5))* Arrinton Pubns.
Tudhope, Simon. Animal Trivia. 2018. (Activity Puzzle Books - Trivia Bks.). (ENG.). 112p. (J). pap. 4.99 *(978-0-7945-4010-4(4)*, Usborne) EDC Publishing.
University Games Staff. More 30 Second Mysteries for Kids. 2007. (Spinner Books for Kids Ser.). (ENG.). 160p. (J). (gr. 4-7). pap. 7.95 *(978-1-57528-839-0(7))* Univ. Games.
Very First Questions & Answers: What Is Poop? 2017. (Lift-The-Flap Very First Questions & Answers* Ser.). (ENG.). (J). bds. 12.99 *(978-0-7945-3971-9(8)*, Usborne) EDC Publishing.
Wagner, Kathi & Wagner, Aubrey. The Everything Kids Bible Trivia Book: Stump Your Friends & Family with Your Bible Knowledge. 2004. (Everything(r) Kids Ser.). (ENG., Illus.). 144p. pap. 15.99 *(978-1-59337-031-2(8))* Adams Media Corp.
Walpole, Brenda. I Wonder Why the Sun Rises: And Other Questions about Time & Seasons. Tremblay, Marie-Ave, illus. 2011. (I Wonder Why Ser.). (ENG.). 32p. (J). (gr. k-3). pap. 6.99 *(978-0-7534-6529-5(9)*, 900070356, Kingfisher) Roaring Brook Pr.
—I Wonder Why the Sun Rises & Other Questions about Time & Seasons. 2008. (I Wonder Why Ser.). (Illus.). 32p. (gr. k-3). 17.00 *(978-0-7569-9054-1(8))* Perfection Learning Corp.
Warner, Ask Quinney. Date not set. 160p. (J). (gr. 3-7). pap. 4.99 *(978-0-06-440762-5(4))* HarperCollins Pubs.
Waxman, Laura Hamilton. Why Did the Pilgrims Come to the New World? & Other Questions about the Plymouth Colony. 2010. (Six Questions of American History Ser.). 48p. (J). pap. 9.95 *(978-0-7613-6123-7(5))* Lerner Publishing Group.
Williams, Brian. What about HIST. 2008. 40p. pap. *(978-1-84810-068-8(X))* Miles Kelly Publishing, Ltd.
—What about People & Places. 2008. 40p. pap. *(978-1-84810-072-5(8))* Miles Kelly Publishing, Ltd.
—What about Planet Earth. 2008. 40p. pap. *(978-1-84810-073-2(6))* Miles Kelly Publishing, Ltd.
—What about the Natural World. 2008. 40p. pap. *(978-1-84810-071-8(X))* Miles Kelly Publishing, Ltd.
—What about the Universe. 2008. 40p. pap. *(978-1-84810-075-6(2))* Miles Kelly Publishing, Ltd.
—What about World Wonders. 2008. 40p. pap. *(978-1-84810-076-3(0))* Miles Kelly Publishing, Ltd.
Williams, Jane A. A Bluestocking Guide - Building a Personal Model for Success: Companion Workbook to Richard J. Maybury's Uncle Eric Talks about Personal, Career, & Financial Security. Daniels, Kathryn, ed. 2004. (Bluestocking Guide Ser.). (ENG.). 47p. (YA). pap. 10.95 *(978-0-942617-39-9(8))* Bluestocking Pr.
—A Bluestocking Guide - Political Philosophies: Companion Workbook to Richard J. Maybury's Are You Liberal? Conservative? or Confused? Daniels, Kathryn, ed. 2004. (Bluestocking Guide Ser.). (ENG.). 63p. (YA). pap. 12.95 *(978-0-942617-47-4(9))* Bluestocking Pr.
Williams, Jane A. & Daniels, Kathryn, eds. Economics - A Free Market Reader. 2004. (ENG.). 127p. (J). pap. 12.95 *(978-0-942617-44-3(4))* Bluestocking Pr.
Windeatt, Mary Fabyan & Ignatz, Marie. Vocabulary Quiz Workbook: Based on 6 Great Saints' Lives by Mary Fabyan Windeatt. Lester, Mary Frances, ed. 2004. (ENG.). 200p. (gr. 2-5). pap., wbk. ed. 21.95 *(978-0-89555-743-8(6)*, 1841) TAN Bks.
Witherspoon Press Staff, contrib. by. Belonging to God: A First Catechism. 2003. (J). *(978-1-57153-036-3(3)*, Witherspoon Pr.) Curriculum Publishing, Presbyterian Church (U. S. A.).
Workman Publishing. You Gotta Be Kidding! The Crazy Book of "Would You Rather... ?" Questions. 2006. (ENG., Illus.). 416p. (J). (gr. 4-12). pap. 8.95 *(978-0-7611-4365-9(3)*, 14365) Workman Publishing Co., Inc.
World Book, Inc. Staff, contrib. by. Are There Monsters under My Bed? World Book Answers Your Questions about Random Stuff. 2019. (Illus.). 96p. (J). *(978-0-7166-3831-5(2))* World Bk., Inc.
—If the World Is Round, Then Why Is the Ground Flat? World Book Answers Your Questions about Science. 2019. (Illus.). 96p. (J). *(978-0-7166-3827-8(4))* World Bk., Inc.
—Planet Earth. 2019. (Illus.). 96p. (J). *(978-0-7166-3732-5(4))* World Bk., Inc.
—Weather. 2019. (J). *(978-0-7166-3770-7(7))* World Bk., Inc.
—Where in the World Can I... A Supplement to Childcraft, the How & Why Library. 2019. 160p. (J). *(978-0-7166-0637-6(2))* World Bk., Inc.
Young, Jay. Magic World of Learning. Tucker, Sian, illus. 2003. 32p. *(978-1-903174-42-5(2)*, Pavilion Children's Books) Pavilion Bks.
Young, Jay, creator. Ziga Zaga. 2003. (Illus.). 144p. *(978-1-903174-64-7(3)*, Pavilion Children's Books) Pavilion Bks.
Zakarin, Debra Mostow. Who's Your Superstar BFF? 2010. 112p. pap. 4.95 *(978-1-60747-775-4(0)*, Pickwick Pr.) Phoenix Bks., Inc.
—Who's Your Superstar Soul Mate? 2010. 112p. pap. 4.95 *(978-1-60747-776-1(9)*, Pickwick Pr.) Phoenix Bks., Inc.
Zoehfeld, Kathleen Weidner. How Deep Is the Ocean? Puybaret, Eric, illus. 2016. (Let's-Read-And-Find-Out Science 2 Ser.). (ENG.). 40p. (J). (gr. -1-3). pap. 6.99 *(978-0-06-232819-9(0)*, HarperCollins) HarperCollins Pubs.
The 5 W's (Gr. 1-3) 2003. (J). *(978-1-58232-075-5(6))* ECS Learning Systems, Inc.
20 Questions: History, 4 vols., Set. 2007. (20 Questions: History Ser.). (ENG.). (J). (gr. 2-3). lib. bdg. 52.54 *(978-1-4042-4242-5(2)*, 70a1330d-c12a-4ea7-a907-8f38a7130fd9) Rosen Publishing Group, Inc., The.

QUILTS

Alyce, Kathie. Flip Flop Block Quilts, 1 vol. 2010. (ENG., Illus.). 64p. 22.95 *(978-1-57432-675-8(9)*, 1574326759, American Quilter's Society) Collector Bks.
Avion, Nicole. The Happy Quilt, 1 vol. 2006. (Neighborhood Readers Ser.). (ENG.). 16p. (gr. 1-2). pap. 6.50 *(978-1-4042-7176-0(7)*, ab9bdcef-0527-45f7-8443-359ac65796c2, Rosen Classroom) Rosen Publishing Group, Inc., The.
Cardon, Jenny Wilding. The Little Box of Baby Quilts. 2007. (Little Box Of... Ser.). (ENG.). 20p. 22.95 *(978-1-56477-699-0(9)*, That Patchwork Place) Martingale & Co.
CICO Kidz. My First Quilting Book: 35 Easy & Fun Sewing Projects. 2012. (ENG., Illus.). 128p. (J). (gr. 7-11). pap. 14.95 *(978-1-908170-84-2(0)*, 1908170840, CICO Books) Ryland Peters & Small GBR. Dist: WIPRO.
Herkert, Barbara. Sewing Stories: Harriet Powers' Journey from Slave to Artist. Brantley-Newton, Vanessa, illus. 2015. 40p. (J). (gr. -1-3). 17.99 *(978-0-385-75462-0(0)*, Knopf Bks. for Young Readers) Random Hse. Children's Bks.
Hicks, Kyra E. Martha Ann's Quilt for Queen Victoria. Fődi, Lee Edward, illus. 2012. 32p. (J). pap. 12.95 *(978-0-9824796-8-1(9))* Black Threads Pr.
—Martha Ann's Quilt for Queen Victoria. Fodi, Lee Edward, illus. 2006. 28p. (J). (gr. -1-3). 16.95 *(978-1-933285-59-7(1))* Brown Books Publishing Group.
Hime, Stanley E. Stanley's Quilt Book / Sue Stays Busy. 2011. 60p. pap. 20.00 *(978-1-935271-88-8(1))* Published by Westview, Inc.
Howard, Judy. Heavenly Patchwork: Quilt Stories Stitched with Love. 2006. (Illus.). 150p. 9.95 *(978-0-9762375-0-1(4))* Dorcas Publishing.
Leisure Arts, creator. Cool Stuff Teach Me to Quilt. 2005. (ENG.). 52p. pap. 10.95 *(978-1-57486-635-3(4))* Leisure Arts, Inc.
McKinney, Louise Chessi. The Journey to Freedom on the Underground Railroad. 2006. (ENG.). 32p. pap. 14.99 *(978-1-4257-2304-0(7))* Xlibris Corp.
Pecorella, Jane. How a Quilt Is Built: Learning to Measure an Object Using Inches, 1 vol. 2010. (Math for the REAL World Ser.). (ENG.). 16p. (gr. 2-3). pap. 7.05 *(978-0-8239-8924-9(0)*, 1ec37b8c-74ed-4e06-bbe7-b9b1db5cf079, Rosen Classroom) Rosen Publishing Group, Inc., The.
Plumley, Amie Petronis & Lisle, Andria. Sewing School (r) Quilts: 15 Projects Kids Will Love to Make; Stitch up a Patchwork Pet, Scrappy Journal, T-Shirt Quilt, & More. Burks, Justin Fox, photos by. 2018. (Sewing School Ser.). (ENG., Illus.). 160p. (J). (gr. 3-7). spiral bd. 18.95 *(978-1-61212-859-7(9)*, 622859) Storey Publishing, LLC.
Polydoros, Lori & Benchmark Education Co., LLC. Storytelling on Fabrics: Quilts, Tapestries, Story Cloths, & More. 2014. (Text Connections Ser.). (J). (gr. 3). *(978-1-4509-9646-4(9))* Benchmark Education Co.
Rubin, Susan Goldman. The Quilts of Gee's Bend. 2017. (ENG., Illus.). 56p. (J). (gr. 3-7). 22.99 *(978-1-4197-2131-1(3)*, 1088101, Abrams Bks. for Young Readers) Abrams, Inc.
Sayre, Hilda L. Kids, Quilts & Reading. 2008. 48p. pap. 24.95 *(978-1-4241-9645-6(0))* America Star Bks.
Schmidt, Carol. Creative Haven Patchwork Quilt Designs Coloring Book. 2014. (Adult Coloring Books: Art & Design Ser.). (ENG., Illus.). 64p. (gr. 3). pap. 6.99 *(978-0-486-78031-3(7)*, 780317) Dover Pubns., Inc.
Sturgill, Ruthy. Christmas Tree Advent Calendar: A Country Quilted & Appliquéd Project. 2006. 96p. pap. 24.95 *(978-1-59800-539-4(1))* Outskirts Pr., Inc.
Waldvogel, Merikay. Childhood Treasures: Doll Quilts by & for Children. 2008. (ENG.). 140p. pap. 24.95 *(978-1-56148-599-4(3)*, Good Bks.) Skyhorse Publishing Co., Inc.

QUILTS—FICTION

Avion, Nicole. Un Tapiz de felicidad, 1 vol. 2006. (Lecturas Del Barrio (Neighborhood Readers) Ser.). (SPA.). 16p. (gr. 1-2). pap. 6.50 *(978-1-4042-7178-4(3)*, 7cea9aa7-1fbc-40a1-83fd-a11e25076cd9, Rosen Classroom) Rosen Publishing Group, Inc., The.
Barnett, Mac. The Case of the Case of Mistaken Identity. Rex, Adam, illus. (Brixton Brothers Ser.: 1). (ENG.). (J). (gr. 3-7). 2010. 208p. pap. 7.99 *(978-1-4169-7816-9(X))* 2009. 192p. 15.99 *(978-1-4169-7815-2(1))* Simon & Schuster Bks. For Young Readers. (Simon & Schuster Bks. For Young Readers).
Beckman, David. Mika & the Queen's Quilt. 2012. 62p. pap. 17.95 *(978-1-62709-809-0(7))* America Star Bks.
Blomgren, Jennifer. The Tale of Alice's Quilt. 2008. (That Patchwork Place Ser.). (ENG., Illus.). 95p. (YA). (gr. 8-12). per. 14.95 *(978-1-56477-833-8(9)*, That Patchwork Place) Martingale & Co.
Bourgeois, Paulette. Oma's Quilt. 2004. (Illus.). (J). (gr. k-3). spiral bd. *(978-0-616-11099-7(5))*; spiral bd. *(978-0-616-11100-0(2))* Canadian National Institute for the Blind/Institut National Canadien pour les Aveugles.
Bowman, Andy. The Quilt. Travis, Stephanie, illus. 25p. (J). (gr. 1-6). pap. 6.95 *(978-1-931650-04-5(7))*; lib. bdg. 14.95 *(978-1-931650-05-2(5))* Coastal Publishing Carolina, Inc.
Brodine, Linda. Gramma Please Tell Us a Story. 2012. (ENG.). (J). pap. 12.99 *(978-1-4675-1215-2(X))* Independent Pub.
Burnett, Jenifer. My Jungle Quilt. Burnett, Jenifer, illus. 2006. (Illus.). 32p. (J). 19.99 *(978-0-9777570-0-8(5))* Summerside Lane.
Chema. Patch's Country Quilt. Chema, illus. 2013. (Illus.). 54p. 25.95 *(978-1-60571-188-1(8))*; 50p. pap. 17.95 *(978-1-60571-187-4(X))* Northshire Pr.
Coerr, Eleanor. The Josefina Story Quilt. Degen, Bruce, illus. 2003. (I Can Read! Level 3 Ser.). 64p. (J). (gr. 2-4). lib. bdg. 13.55 *(978-0-8335-2723-3(1))* Turtleback.
Courtney, Kateri. Welby & the Knobby King. 2003. pap. 14.95 *(978-0-9743588-0-2(0))* Castlegate Pr.
Crane, Carol. Handkerchief Quilt. Palmer, Gary, illus. 2010. (ENG.). 32p. (J). (gr. 1-4). 15.95 *(978-1-58536-344-5(8)*, 202134) Sleeping Bear Pr.
Dallas, Sandra. The Quilt Walk. 2012. (ENG., Illus.). 216p. (J). (gr. 4-7). 15.95 *(978-1-58536-800-6(8)*, 202339) Sleeping Bear Pr.
Fitzgerald, Gyleen Xavier. The Dream: A Magical Journey in Colourful Stitches. 2005. (ENG., Illus.). 90p. (J). (gr. 4-7). 29.95 *(978-0-9768215-1-9(6))* FPI Publishing.
Garsee, Linmarie. Annabelle's Vacation with Grandma Hayley: A Mountain Quiltfest Adventure. 2012. 50p. pap. 21.99 *(978-1-4772-7737-9(4))* AuthorHouse.
Geras, Adèle. Apricots at Midnight: And Other Stories from a Patchwork Quilt. 2005. (Illus.). 189p. (J). (gr. -1-17). pap. 5.95 *(978-1-903015-29-2(4))* Barn Owl Bks, London GBR. Dist: Independent Pubs. Group.
Gerdner, Linda & Langford, Sarah. Grandfather's Story Cloth. Loughridge, Stuart, illus. 2008. (Grandfather's Story Cloth Ser.). 32p. (J). (gr. 2-4). 16.95 *(978-1-885008-34-3(1)*, Shen's Bks.) Lee & Low Bks., Inc.
Good, Merle. Reuben & the Quilt. Moss, P. Buckley, illus. rev. ed. 2016. (ENG.). 32p. (J). (gr. -1-3). 16.99 *(978-1-68099-151-2(5)*, Good Bks.) Skyhorse Publishing Co., Inc.
Griffith, Michelle & Conder, Jen. Rosie's Quilt. 2006. (Illus.). (J). 4.99 *(978-0-9789969-4-9(1))* Michelle's Designs.
Hansen, Susan. The Flying Quilt. 2011. pap. 9.95 *(978-0-7414-6469-9(1))* Infinity Publishing.
Hopkinson, Deborah. Sweet Clara & the Freedom Quilt. Ransome, James, illus. 25th ed. 2018. 40p. (J). (gr. -1-2). 16.99 *(978-0-679-82311-7(5)*, Knopf Bks. for Young Readers) Random Hse. Children's Bks.
Johnston, Tony. That Summer. Moser, Barry, illus. 2007. (ENG.). 32p. (J). (gr. 1-4). pap. 6.00 *(978-0-15-205856-2(7)*, 1197587, Clarion Bks.) HarperCollins Pubs.
Keys, Dalen. Just a Quilt? Sponaugle, Kim, illus. 2nd ed. 2012. (ENG.). 32p. (J). 16.00 *(978-1-886068-56-8(9))* Fruitbearer Publishing, LLC.
Kim, Cecil. Friendship Quilt. Jeong, HaJin, illus. rev. ed. 2014. (MySELF Bookshelf Ser.). (ENG.). 32p. (J). (gr. k-2). lib. bdg. 25.27 *(978-1-59953-650-7(1))* Norwood Hse. Pr.
Latham, Irene. Leaving Gee's Bend: A Novel. 2017. (ENG.). 192p. (gr. 5). pap. 11.95 *(978-1-58838-332-7(6)*, 8873, NewSouth Bks.) NewSouth, Inc.
Marsh, Carole. The Mystery on the Underground Railroad. 2009. (Real Kids, Real Places Ser.). (Illus.). 146p. (J). lib. bdg. 18.99 *(978-0-635-06991-7(1)*, Marsh, Carole Mysteries) Gallopade International.
—The Mystery on the Underground Railroad (Hardcover) 2003. 160p. (gr. 2-8). 14.95 *(978-0-635-02110-6(2))* Gallopade International.
McKissack, Patricia C. Stitchin' & Pullin' A Gee's Bend Quilt. Cabrera, Cozbi A., illus. 2016. (ENG.). 48p. (J). (gr. k-4). 19.65 *(978-0-606-39338-6(2))* Turtleback.
O'Connor, Crystal Ball. Katherine's Quilt. 2007. (J). 18.95 *(978-0-9774038-4-4(X))* Monarch Pubs.
Polacco, Patricia. The Keeping Quilt. 2007. 18.00 *(978-0-7569-1720-3(4))* Perfection Learning Corp.
—The Keeping Quilt: 25th Anniversary Edition. Polacco, Patricia, illus. 25th ed. 2013. (ENG., Illus.). 64p. (J). (gr. -1-3). 18.99 *(978-1-4424-8237-1(0)*, Simon & Schuster/Paula Wiseman Bks.) Simon & Schuster/Paula Wiseman Bks.
Stroud, Bettye. The Patchwork Path: A Quilt Map to Freedom. Bennett, Erin Susanne, illus. 2007. (ENG.). 32p. (J). (gr. k-3). pap. 7.99 *(978-0-7636-3519-0(7))* Candlewick Pr.
Wang, Sarah. My Quilt. 2009. (Illus.). 24p. pap. 11.49 *(978-1-4490-3422-1(5))* AuthorHouse.
Werner, Teresa Orem. A Quilt of Wishes. Tremlin, Nathan, illus. l.t. ed. 2005. 26p. (J). 16.95 *(978-1-59879-147-1(8))* Lifevest Publishing, Inc.
Wessel-Estes, Pam. A Quilt & a Home. 2012. 36p. pap. 14.95 *(978-1-4575-1489-0(3))*; 24.95 *(978-1-4575-1490-6(7))* Dog Ear Publishing, LLC.
Woodson, Jacqueline. Show Way. Talbott, Hudson, illus. 2005. (ENG.). 48p. (J). (gr. -1-3). 18.99 *(978-0-399-23749-2(6)*, G.P. Putnam's Sons Books for Young Readers) Penguin Young Readers Group.

QUIMBY, RAMONA (FICTITIOUS CHARACTER)—FICTION

Cleary, Beverly. Beezus & Ramona. Rogers, Jacqueline, illus. 2020. (Ramona Ser.: 1). (ENG.). 208p. (J). (gr. 3-7). 17.99 *(978-0-688-21076-2(7))*; pap. 7.99 *(978-0-380-70918-2(X))* HarperCollins Pubs. (HarperCollins).
—Beezus & Ramona. 2011. 9.01 *(978-0-7848-3570-8(5)*, Everbind) Marco Bk. Co.
—Beezus & Ramona. (Ramona Quimby Ser.). 142p. (J). (gr. 3-5). pap. 4.99 *(978-0-8072-1441-1(8)*, Listening Library) Random Hse. Audio Publishing Group.
—Beezus & Ramona. Darling, Louis, illus. (gr. 3-5). pap. *(978-0-545-24980-5(5))* Scholastic, Inc.
—Beezus & Ramona. (Ramona Quimby Ser.: 1). (J). 2013. lib. bdg. 17.20 *(978-0-88103-289-5(1))* 2010. lib. bdg. 16.00 *(978-0-606-15072-9(2))* Turtleback.
—Beezus & Ramona Movie Tie-In Edition. Rogers, Jacqueline, illus. movie tie-in ed. 2010. (Ramona Ser.: 1). (ENG.). 208p. (J). (gr. 3-7). pap. 5.99 *(978-0-06-191461-4(4)*, HarperFestival) HarperCollins Pubs.
—The Ramona 4-Book Collection, Volume 1 Vol. 1: Beezus & Ramona, Ramona & Her Father, Ramona the Brave, Ramona the Pest, Vol. 1. Rogers, Jacqueline, illus. 2020. (Ramona Ser.). (ENG.). 848p. (J). (gr. 3-7). pap. 31.96 *(978-0-06-124647-0(6)*, HarperCollins) HarperCollins Pubs.
—Ramona & Her Family. (J). Random House Publishing Group.
—Ramona & Her Father. 2009. 8.32 *(978-0-88483-705-3(X)*, Everbind) Marco Bk. Co.
—Ramona & Her Father. (Ramona Quimby Ser.). 186p. (J). (gr. 3-5). pap. 4.99 *(978-0-8072-1439-8(6)*, Listening Library) Random Hse. Audio Publishing Group.
—Ramona & Her Father: A Newbery Honor Award Winner. Rogers, Jacqueline, illus. 2020. (Ramona Ser.: 4). (ENG.). 192p. (J). (gr. 3-7). 16.99 *(978-0-688-22114-0(9))*; pap. 7.99 *(978-0-380-70916-8(3))* HarperCollins Pubs. (HarperCollins).
—Ramona & Her Mother. (Ramona Quimby Ser.). 208p. (J). (gr. 3-5). pap. 4.99 *(978-0-8072-1435-0(3)*, Listening Library) Random Hse. Audio Publishing Group.
—Ramona & Her Mother: A National Book Award Winner. Rogers, Jacqueline, illus. 2020. (Ramona Ser.: 5). (ENG.). 224p. (J). (gr. 3-7). 16.99 *(978-0-688-22195-9(5))*; reprint ed. pap. 7.99 *(978-0-380-70952-6(X))* HarperCollins Pubs. (HarperCollins).
—Ramona Empieza el Curso: A Newbery Honor Award Winner, 1 vol. Rogers, Jacqueline, illus. 2006.Tr. of Ramona Quimby, Age 8. (SPA.). 224p. (J). (gr. 3-7). pap. 7.99 *(978-0-688-15487-5(5)*, MR7554) HarperCollins Español.
—Ramona Forever. Rogers, Jacqueline, illus. 2020. (Ramona Ser.: 7). (ENG.). 208p. (J). (gr. 3-7). 16.99 *(978-0-688-03785-7(2))*; reprint ed. pap. 9.99 *(978-0-380-70960-1(0))* HarperCollins Pubs. (HarperCollins).
—Ramona Forever. (Ramona Quimby Ser.). 182p. (J). (gr. 3-5). pap. 4.99 *(978-0-8072-1437-4(X)*, Listening Library) Random Hse. Audio Publishing Group.
—Ramona Forever. 2013. (Ramona Quimby Ser.: 7). (J). (gr. 3-6). lib. bdg. 17.20 *(978-0-8085-5273-4(2))* Turtleback.
—Ramona la Chinche. Palacios, Argentina, tr. Darling, Louis, illus. 2006. (Ramona Quimby Spanish Ser.: 2).Tr. of Ramona the Pest. (SPA.). 181p. (J). (gr. 4-7). lib. bdg. 16.00 *(978-0-613-00464-0(7))* Turtleback.
—Ramona la Chinche: Ramona the Pest (Spanish Edition), 1 vol. Rogers, Jacqueline, illus. 2006.Tr. of Ramona the Pest. (SPA.). 192p. (J). (gr. 3-7). pap. 7.99 *(978-0-688-14888-1(3)*, MR2295) HarperCollins Español.
—Ramona la Valiente. 2003.Tr. of Ramona the Brave. (SPA., Illus.). 124p. (J). pap. 15.95 *(978-84-239-7099-5(X)*, AV2133) Espasa Calpe, S.A. ESP. Dist: Distribooks, Inc.
—Ramona Quimby, Age 8. (Ramona Quimby Ser.). (J). (gr. 3-5). Random House Publishing Group.
—Ramona Quimby, Age 8. (Ramona Quimby Ser.). 190p. (J). (gr. 3-5). pap. 4.99 *(978-0-8072-1436-7(1)*, Listening Library) Random Hse. Audio Publishing Group.
—Ramona Quimby, Age 8: A Newbery Honor Award Winner. Rogers, Jacqueline, illus. 2020. (Ramona Ser.: 6). (ENG.). 208p. (J). (gr. 3-7). 18.99 *(978-0-688-00477-4(6))*; pap. 7.99 *(978-0-380-70956-4(2))* HarperCollins Pubs. (HarperCollins).
—Ramona the Brave. Rogers, Jacqueline, illus. 2020. (Ramona Ser.: 3). (ENG.). 208p. (J). (gr. 3-7). 16.99 *(978-0-688-22015-0(0))*; pap. 9.99 *(978-0-380-70959-5(7))* HarperCollins Pubs. (HarperCollins).
—Ramona the Brave. (Ramona Quimby Ser.). 190p. (J). (gr. 3-5). pap. 4.99 *(978-0-8072-1440-4(X)*, Listening Library) Random Hse. Audio Publishing Group.
—Ramona the Pest. Rogers, Jacqueline, illus. 2020. (Ramona Ser.: 2). (ENG.). 240p. (J). (gr. 3-7). 16.99 *(978-0-688-21721-1(4))*; pap. 7.99 *(978-0-380-70954-0(6))* HarperCollins Pubs. (HarperCollins).
—Ramona the Pest. (Ramona Quimby Ser.). (J). (gr. 3-5). Random House Publishing Group.
—Ramona the Pest. (Ramona Quimby Ser.). 192p. (J). (gr. 3-5). pap. 4.99 *(978-0-8072-1438-1(8)*, Listening Library) Random Hse. Audio Publishing Group.
—Ramona y Su Padre. 10th ed. 2003.Tr. of Ramona & Her Father. (SPA., Illus.). 136p. (J). (gr. 3-5). 15.95 *(978-84-239-9020-7(6)*, EC1443) Espasa Calpe, S.A. ESP. Dist: Lectorum Pubns., Inc., Distribooks, Inc.

—Ramona's World. Rogers, Jacqueline, illus. 2020. (Ramona Ser.: 8). (ENG.). 240p. (J). (gr. 3-7). 17.99 (978-0-688-16816-2(7)); pap. 7.99 (978-0-380-73272-2(6)) HarperCollins Pubs. (HarperCollins).

—Ramona's World. unabr. ed. 2004. (Ramona Quimby Ser.). 194p. (J). (gr. 3-7). pap. 29.00 incl. audio (978-0-8072-8169-7(7), Listening Library) Random Hse. Audio Publishing Group.

—Ramona's World. 2013. (Ramona Quimby Ser.: 8). (J). (gr. 3-6). lib. bdg. 17.20 (978-0-613-35794-4(9)) Turtleback.

Novel Units. Ramona Forever Novel Units Student Packet. 2019. (ENG.). (J). (gr. 3-5). pap., wbk. ed. 13.99 (978-1-58130-691-0(1), Novel Units, Inc.) Classroom Library Co.

—Ramona Forever Novel Units Teacher Guide. 2019. (ENG.). (J). (gr. 3-5). pap., wbk. ed. 12.99 (978-1-58130-690-3(3), Novel Units, Inc.) Classroom Library Co.

—A Ramona Quimby, Age 8 Novel Units Student Packet. 2019. (Ramona Quimby Ser.). (ENG.). (J). (gr. 3-5). pap. 13.99 (978-1-56137-708-4(2), NU7082SP, Novel Units, Inc.) Classroom Library Co.

—A Ramona Quimby, Age 8 Novel Units Teacher Guide. 2019. (ENG.). (J). (gr. 3-5). pap. 12.99 (978-1-56137-448-9(2), Novel Units, Inc.) Classroom Library Co.

—Ramona the Brave Novel Units Teacher Guide. 2019. (Ramona Quimby Ser.). (ENG.). (J). (gr. 3-5). pap. 12.99 (978-1-56137-444-1(X), Novel Units, Inc.) Classroom Library Co.

QUIZ BOOKS

see Questions and Answers

QUOTATIONS

see also Proverbs

Beilenson, Evelyn. A Warm & Fuzzy Christmas. Giordano, illus. 2013. (ENG.). 80p. 5.95 (978-1-4413-1358-4(3)) Peter Pauper Pr. Inc.

Bodden, Michelle. Well My Teacher Said. Williams, Brittney, illus. 2007. 32p. (J). 14.95 (978-0-9753089-2-9(0)) Water Daughter Publishing.

Brady, Tom, et al. Tom Brady. 2015. (Quotes from the Greatest Athletes Ser.). (ENG., Illus.). 24p. (J). lib. bdg. 12.95 (978-1-4896-3381-1(2), AV2 by Weigl) Weigl Pubs., Inc.

Carlson, Dale. Who Said What? Philosophy Quotes for Teens. Nicklaus, Carol, illus. 2003. (ENG.). 224p. (gr. 7-12). pap. 14.95 (978-1-884158-28-5(5)) Bick Publishing Hse.

Celebrate Freedom: Songs, Symbols, & Sayings of the United States. 2003. (Scott Foresman Social Study Ser.). (Illus.). 32p. (gr. k-2). (978-0-328-03672-1(2)); 48p. (gr. 3-6). (978-0-328-03674-5(9)) Addison-Wesley Educational Pubs., Inc. (Scott Foresman).

Crosby, Sidney, et al. Sidney Crosby. 2015. (Quotes from the Greatest Athletes Ser.). (ENG., Illus.). 24p. (J). lib. bdg. 12.95 (978-1-4896-3377-4(4), AV2 by Weigl) Weigl Pubs., Inc.

Dean, James & Dean, Kimberly. Pete the Cat's Groovy Guide to Life. Dean, James, illus. 2015. (Pete the Cat Ser.). (ENG., Illus.). 48p. (J). (gr. -1-3). 12.99 (978-0-06-235135-7(4), HarperCollins) HarperCollins Pubs.

Engelbreit, Mary. The Blessings of Friendship Treasury, 1 vol. 2014. (ENG., Illus.). 40p. (J). 15.99 (978-0-310-74509-9(8)) Zonderkidz.

Farina von Buchwald, Martin & Prado Farina, Gabriela. The Joy of Giving. Avendano, Dolores, illus. Testino, Mario et al, photos by. 2005. 89p. (J). 18.00 (978-0-9777266-0-8(6)) von Buchwald, Martin Farina.

Foldvary-Anderson, Carol. Words of Love Stained Glass Coloring Book. 2011. (Dover Romance Coloring Bks.). (ENG., Illus.). 32p. (gr. 3-8). pap. 6.99 (978-0-486-47707-7(X), 47707X) Dover Pubns., Inc.

Hamm, Mia, et al. Mia Hamm. 2015. (Quotes from the Greatest Athletes Ser.). (ENG., Illus.). 24p. (J). lib. bdg. 12.95 (978-1-4896-3365-1(0), AV2 by Weigl) Weigl Pubs., Inc.

Hudson, Katura J. Afro-Bets Quotes for Kids: Words for Kids to Live By. Simpson, Howard, illus. 2004. (Afro-Bets Ser.). 64p. (J). (gr. k-4). pap. 5.95 (978-0-940975-89-7(0), Sankofa Bks.) Just Us Bks., Inc.

I Love Babies. 2004. per. 9.95 (978-0-9754779-1-5(9)) Chosen Word Publishing.

Jordan, Michael. Michael Jordan. 2015. (Quotes from the Greatest Athletes Ser.). (ENG., Illus.). 24p. (J). lib. bdg. 12.95 (978-1-4896-3369-9(3), 1393457, AV2 by Weigl) Weigl Pubs., Inc.

Kamerling, Yvonne. TLC for Teenagers & their Parents: Inspirational Quotes, Poetry, Touching Stories. 2004. 122p. (YA). 22.95 (978-0-595-66340-8(0)) iUniverse, Inc.

Kerrigan, Michael. Greeks, 1 vol. 2011. (Ancients in Their Own Words Ser.). (ENG.). 64p. (gr. 6-6). 35.50 (978-1-60870-065-3(8), 26f71200-8804-4204-afbb-05b17e907c5a) Cavendish Square Publishing LLC.

—Mesopotamians, 1 vol. 2011. (Ancients in Their Own Words Ser.). (ENG.). 64p. (gr. 6-6). 35.50 (978-1-60870-066-0(6), 3e38e915-0e5e-474e-94b0-938d6bba3d39) Cavendish Square Publishing LLC.

—Romans, 1 vol. 2011. (Ancients in Their Own Words Ser.). (ENG., Illus.). 64p. (gr. 6-6). 35.50 (978-1-60870-067-7(4), 7b54880f-f286-4ed0-909a-1a46e3c457dd) Cavendish Square Publishing LLC.

Kuchler, Bonnie Louise, compiled by. Just Kids: Pictures, Poems & Other Silly Animal Stuff Just for Kids! 2003. (ENG., Illus.). 32p. tchr. ed. 12.95 (978-1-57223-598-4(5), 5985) Willow Creek Pr., Inc.

Manning, Peyton, et al. Peyton Manning. 2015. (Quotes from the Greatest Athletes Ser.). (ENG., Illus.). 24p. (J). lib. bdg. 12.95 (978-1-4896-3373-6(1), AV2 by Weigl) Weigl Pubs., Inc.

Ogburn, Jacqueline. Little Treasures. Raschka, Chris, illus. 2012. (ENG.). 32p. (J). (gr. -1-3). 16.99 (978-0-547-42862-8(6), 1432026, Clarion Bks.) HarperCollins Pubs.

Peckham, Kim. The Sensational Quotational Devotional: Youthful Devotionals Found in Famous, Funny, & Inspiring Quotes. 2018. 373p. (J). pap. (978-0-8163-6410-7(9)) Pacific Pr. Publishing Assn.

Petrie, H. D., photos by. All God's Creatures; Jesus Loves Me. 2005. (Illus.). 32p. (J). spiral bd. (978-0-9774115-0-4(8)) AGC Outreach Ministry.

Pocrass, Kate. Quotes & Questions: A Journal for Your Kid's Quotable Moments. 2019. (ENG., Illus.). 224p. 12.95 (978-1-4521-7036-7(3)) Chronicle Bks. LLC.

Scholastic. Inspirational African American Quotes Poster Set, Set. 2016. (ENG.). (J). (gr. 3-6). 9.99 (978-1-338-10862-0(X), 810862) Teacher's Friend Pubns., Inc.

—Inspirational Quotes Poster Set. 2016. (ENG.). (J). (gr. 3-6). 9.99 (978-1-338-10510-0(8), 810510) Teacher's Friend Pubns., Inc.

Seabrook, Lochlainn. The Quotable Nathan Bedford Forrest: Selections from the Writings & Speeches of the Confederacy's Most Brilliant Cavalryman. 2012. (Illus.). 130p. pap. 12.95 (978-0-9838185-5-7(X)) Sea Raven Pr.

Seduction by Shakespeare: Advice, Observations & Quotes on Love, Lust, Beauty & Desire. 2004. 128p. (YA). (gr. 11-18). per. 11.95 (978-0-9674898-6-5(5)) TCB-Cafe Publishing.

Venus & Serena Williams. 2015. (Quotes from the Greatest Athletes Ser.). (ENG., Illus.). 24p. (J). lib. bdg. 12.95 (978-1-4896-3385-9(5), AV2 by Weigl) Weigl Pubs., Inc.

Waycott, Flora, illus. She Believed She Could, So She Did: A Journal of Powerful Quotes from Powerful Women. 2018. 208p. (J). (gr. 3-7). pap. 12.95 (978-1-4549-2837-9(9)) Sterling Publishing Co., Inc.

Weiner, Miriam. Shakespeare's Seasons. Whitt, Shannon, illus. 2012. (ENG.). 32p. (J). (gr. -1). 16.99 (978-1-935703-57-0(9)) Downtown Bookworks.

365 Days of Wonder: Mr. Browne's Book of Precepts. 2014. (Wonder Ser.). (ENG.). 432p. (J). (gr. 3-7). 14.99 (978-0-553-49904-9(1), Knopf Bks. for Young Readers) Random Hse. Children's Bks.

R

RABBIS

Finkelman, Shimon. The Story of Reb Moshe: A Biography for Young Readers. 2015. (Illus.). 303p. (J). (978-1-4226-1665-9(7), ArtScroll Series) Mesorah Pubns., Ltd.

Lumer, Marc, illus. When Miracles Happened- Wondrous Stories of Tzaddikim. 2009. 22p. (J). (978-1-56871-484-4(X)) Targum Pr., Inc.

Mindel, Nissan. Maharal to the Rescue. Ayache, Avraham, illus. 2010. 67p. (YA). 10.95 (978-0-8266-0032-5(8)) Kehot Pubn. Society.

Rose, Or N. Abraham Joshua Heschel: Man of Spirit, Man of Action. 2003. (ENG., Illus.). 80p. pap. 9.95 (978-0-8276-0758-3(X)) Jewish Pubn. Society.

Sasso, Sandy Eisenberg. Regina Persisted. Lucas, Margaux, illus. 2018. (ENG.). 32p. (J). 17.95 (978-1-68115-540-1(0), da407696-8acb-4483-8e12-4aed1ba27cfd, Apples & Honey Pr.) Behrman Hse., Inc.

Simon, Solomon & Bial, Morrison D. The Rabbi's Bible Vol. 1: Torah. (J). (gr. 5-6). pap., stu. ed. 3.95 (978-0-87441-319-9(2));Wkbk. 2. pap., stu. ed. 3.95 (978-0-87441-320-5(6)) Behrman Hse., Inc.

RABBITS

Alderton, David. How to Look after Your Pet Rabbit: A Practical Guide to Caring for Your Pet, in Step-By-Step Photographs. 2014. (Illus.). 20p. (J). (gr. -1-3). 8.99 (978-1-84322-834-9(3), Armadillo) Anness Publishing GBR. Dist: National Bk. Network.

Anderson, Jessica Lee. Rabbits / Conejos. Mason, Suzie, illus. 2018. (Pets! / ILas Mascotas! Ser.). (MUL.). 24p. (J). (gr. -1-2). lib. bdg. 33.99 (978-1-68410-253-2(7), 138451) Cantata Learning.

Antol, Jenna. "Do" The Once Forgotten Little Bunny Who Grew to Become a World Record Holder. 2012. (ENG.). 36p. (J). pap. 14.95 (978-1-4787-1593-1(6)) Outskirts Pr., Inc.

Barnes, J. Lou. Pet Rabbits, 1 vol. 2006. (Pet Pals Ser.). (ENG., Illus.). 32p. (gr. 3-5). lib. bdg. 28.67 (978-0-8368-6781-7(5), d7ad00bd-6ec7-4f54-8e74-1fa2f6066ca7, Gareth Stevens Learning Library) Stevens, Gareth Publishing LLLP.

Beck, Angela. Rabbits: Keeping & Caring for Your Pet, 1 vol. 2013. (Keeping & Caring for Your Pet Ser.). (ENG.). 72p. (gr. 6-7). pap. 11.53 (978-1-4644-0297-5(3), 8dd43ac2-a4e7-4994-957b-89e166d06c79); lib. bdg. 31.93 (978-0-7660-4183-7(2), 5e4cd192-523d-472d-9de6-e615bb5b50fb) Enslow Publishing, LLC.

Beer, Amy-Jane. Pet Rabbits. 2009. (Illus.). 52p. (J). (978-0-7172-8050-6(0)) Grolier, Ltd.

Bekkering, Annalise. Rabbits. (J). 2012. 12.95 (978-1-61913-265-8(6)) 2012. 27.13 (978-1-61913-068-5(8)) 2007. (Illus.). 24p. (gr. -1-3). lib. bdg. 24.45 (978-1-59036-679-0(4)) Weigl Pubs., Inc.

—Rabbits. Hudak, Heather C., ed. 2007. (Backyard Animals Ser.). (Illus.). 24p. (J). (gr. -1-3). pap. 8.95 (978-1-59036-680-6(8)) Weigl Pubs., Inc.

Betances, Roberto. Rabbits Eat Poop!, 1 vol. 2017. (Nature's Grossest Ser.). (ENG.). 24p. (J). (gr. 1-2). pap. 9.15 (978-1-5382-0949-3(7), d62632de-c20d-43f1-b63b-7a419bdb651f) Stevens, Gareth Publishing LLLP.

Biniok, Janice. Rabbits. (J). 2009. (Illus.). 112p. 14.95 (978-1-932904-40-6(9)) 2008. (978-1-932904-32-1(8)) Eldorado Ink.

Bissell, Robert, illus. Robert Bissell's Rabbits & Bears. 2013. (ENG.). (J). 7.95 (978-0-7649-6476-3(3)) Pomegranate Communications, Inc.

Bjorklund, Ruth. Rabbits, 1 vol. 2008. (Great Pets Ser.). (ENG., Illus.). 48p. (gr. 3-3). lib. bdg. 32.64 (978-0-7614-2708-7(2), 98bfa265-c5d5-494f-92d3-2b8adc6d15a3) Cavendish Square Publishing LLC.

Bodden, Valerie. Rabbits. 2006. (My First Look at: Pets Ser.). (Illus.). 24p. (J). (gr. -1-3). lib. bdg. 15.95 (978-1-58341-460-6(6), Creative Education) Creative Co., The.

Brooks, Marigold. Angora Rabbits, 1 vol. 2017. (Wild & Woolly Ser.). (ENG.). 24p. (J). (gr. 3-3). 25.27 (978-1-5383-2525-4(X), 404f1627-ceeb-41a7-ade2-ea92fd9ff51c, PowerKids Pr.) Rosen Publishing Group, Inc., The.

Bunnies. 2003. (Three Minute Tales Ser.). 32p. (J). 5.98 (978-0-7525-8914-5(8)); 7.95 (978-0-7525-4758-9(5)) Parragon, Inc.

Burstein, John. Rabbits, 1 vol. 2008. (Slim Goodbody's Inside Guide to Pets Ser.). (ENG., Illus.). 32p. (gr. 3-5). lib. bdg. 28.67 (978-0-8368-8958-1(4), 6a9236b4-f006-4141-90a2-7f87be512c9e, Gareth Stevens Learning Library) Stevens, Gareth Publishing LLLP.

Butterfield, Moira. Rabbit. (Illus.). 32p. lib. bdg. 24.25 (978-1-930643-93-2(4)) Chrysalis Education.

Carr, Aaron. El Conejo. 2012. (SPA.). (J). (978-1-61913-185-9(4)) Weigl Pubs., Inc.

—Rabbit. 2011. (J). (978-1-61690-924-6(2)); (978-1-61690-570-5(0)) Weigl Pubs., Inc.

Chung, Liz. Inside Rabbit Burrows, 1 vol. 2015. (Inside Animal Homes Ser.). (ENG., Illus.). 24p. (J). (gr. 2-3). pap. 9.25 (978-1-4994-0876-8(5), d7fe1a3a-685b-4072-b320-352f231eff15, PowerKids Pr.) Rosen Publishing Group, Inc., The.

—Madrigueras de Conejos (Inside Rabbit Burrows), 1 vol. 2015. (Las Casas de Los Animales (Inside Animal Homes) Ser.). (SPA.). 24p. (J). (gr. 2-3). 25.27 (978-1-4994-0565-1(0), 33bed930-a018-45e2-a2a0-555a443bd2fb, PowerKids Pr.) Rosen Publishing Group, Inc., The.

Colson, Mary. The Truth about Rabbits: What Rabbits Do When You're Not Looking. 2017. (Pets Undercover! Ser.). (ENG., Illus.). 32p. (J). (gr. 2-4). lib. bdg. 32.65 (978-1-4109-8608-5(X), 134510, Raintree) Capstone.

Coppendale, Jean. Rabbit. 2004. (QEB You & Your Pet Ser.). (Illus.). 32p. (J). lib. bdg. 18.95 (978-1-59566-053-4(4)) QEB Publishing Inc.

Dittmer, Lori. Rabbits. 2018. (Seedlings: Backyard Animals Ser.). (ENG.). 24p. (J). (gr. k-2). pap. 8.99 (978-1-62832-601-7(8), 19930, Creative Paperbacks); (gr. -1-k). (978-1-60818-974-8(0), 19921, Creative Education) Creative Co., The.

DK. Baby Touch & Feel: Bunny. 2011. (Baby Touch & Feel Ser.). (ENG.). 14p. (J). (gr. -1 — 1). bds. 7.99 (978-0-7566-8987-2(2), DK Children) Dorling Kindersley Publishing, Inc.

Early Macken, JoAnn. Jackrabbits, 1 vol. (Animals That Live in the Desert (First Edition) Ser.). (ENG., 24p. (gr. 1-1). 2006. Illus.). lib. bdg. 25.27 (978-0-8368-4828-1(4), fcb87a1d-9833-4812-b32a-2c18757267f0) 2nd rev. ed. 2009. (J). pap. 9.15 (978-1-4339-2450-7(1), 97b96490-e70a-41c8-a0c7-8155278d9ad2) 2nd rev. ed. 2009. (J). lib. bdg. 25.27 (978-1-4339-2194-0(4), 15627dfc-9afd-4b32-9b13-3e7c8f8e652c) Stevens, Gareth Publishing LLLP. (Weekly Reader Leveled Readers).

—Jackrabbits / Liebres Americanas, 1 vol. 2nd rev. ed. 2009. (Animals That Live in the Desert / Animales Del Desierto (Second Edition) Ser.). (SPA & ENG.). 24p. (J). (gr. 1-1). pap. 9.15 (978-1-4339-2458-3(7), 518e0de1-68a3-426a-a8ce-572538d65bc4, Weekly Reader Leveled Readers); lib. bdg. 25.27 (978-1-4339-2131-5(6), 329d02f6-87f0-4797-9455-b38a11b9954a) Stevens, Gareth Publishing LLLP.

—Rabbits, 1 vol. 2003. (Let's Read about Pets Ser.). (ENG., Illus.). 24p. (gr. k-2). pap. 9.15 (978-0-8368-3849-7(1), 195f6edf-29d0-48a4-9a2e-6f526a298b27, Weekly Reader Leveled Readers) Stevens, Gareth Publishing LLLP.

Elora, Grace. Bunnies. 2011. (Cute & Cuddly: Baby Animals Ser.). (Illus.). 24p. (gr. k-2). 69.20 (978-1-4339-6149-6(0)); (ENG., pap. 9.15 (978-1-4339-4504-5(5), b8d4903a-cef3-40f9-a98c-009e01b56978); (ENG., (J). 25.27 (978-1-4339-4503-8(7), 8f3a3374-c087-465c-9eee-da1def1fb6be) Stevens, Gareth Publishing LLLP.

Endres, Hollie. Rabbits. 2007. (Farm Animals Ser.). (ENG., Illus.). 24p. (J). (gr. k-3). lib. bdg. 26.95 (978-1-60014-085-3(8)) Bellwether Media.

Fletcher, Ann L. Angora Rabbits, the Complete Owner's Guide, Includes English, French, Giant, Satin & German Breeds. Care, Breeding, Wool, Farming, Lifespan, Colors. 2013. (Illus.). 158p. (J). pap. (978-1-909820-07-4(5)) EKL Publishing.

Foran, Jill. Caring for Your Rabbit. 2005. (Caring for Your Pet Ser.). (Illus.). 32p. (J). (gr. 4-7). lib. bdg. 26.00 (978-1-59036-034-7(6)) Weigl Pubs., Inc.

—Caring for Your Rabbit. Marshall, Diana & Nault, Jennifer, eds. 2003. (Caring for Your Pet Ser.). (Illus.). 32p. (J). pap. 9.95 (978-1-59036-064-4(8)) Weigl Pubs., Inc.

—Rabbit. (Caring for My Pet Ser.). (Illus.). (J). (gr. 3-7). 2014. (ENG.). lib. bdg. 28.55 (978-1-4896-0620-4(3), AV2 by Weigl) 2008. 32p. pap. 9.95 (978-1-59036-909-8(2)) 2008. 32p. lib. bdg. 26.00 (978-1-59036-908-1(4)) Weigl Pubs., Inc.

Foran, Jill & Gillespie, Katie. Rabbit. 2019. (J). (978-1-7911-1924-9(7), AV2 by Weigl) Weigl Pubs., Inc.

Gagne, Tammy. Caring for Rabbits: A 4D Book. 2018. (Expert Pet Care Ser.). (ENG., Illus.). 24p. (J). (gr. 1-3). lib. bdg. 27.99 (978-1-5435-2743-8(4), 138201, Capstone Pr.) Capstone.

Gillespie, Katie. Rabbits. 2017. (Illus.). 24p. (J). (978-1-4896-4503-6(9), AV2 by Weigl) Weigl Pubs., Inc.

Glaser, Rebecca. Bunnies Hop. 2017. (Amicus Ink Board Bks.). (Illus.). 14p. (J). (gr. -1 — 1). bds. 7.99 (978-1-68152-199-2(7), 14730) Amicus.

Glover, David & Glover, Penny. Owning a Pet Rabbit. 2008. (Owning a Pet Ser.). (Illus.). 32p. (J). (gr. 2-5). lib. bdg. 24.25 (978-1-59771-055-8(5)) Sea-To-Sea Pubns.

Graubart, Norman D. How to Track a Rabbit, 1 vol. 2014. (Scatalog: a Kid's Field Guide to Animal Poop Ser.). (ENG., Illus.). 24p. (J). (gr. 2-3). lib. bdg. 27.27 (978-1-4777-5434-4(2), 1882a072-609e-4109-8356-dbbc29411ea0, Windmill Bks.) Rosen Publishing Group, Inc., The.

Gray, Leon. Flemish Giant Rabbit: The World's Biggest Bunny. 2013. (Even More SuperSized! Ser.). (Illus.). 24p. (J). (gr. k-3). lib. bdg. 26.99 (978-1-61772-729-0(6)) Bearport Publishing Co., Inc.

Green, Jen. Rabbits. 2008. (Illus.). 52p. (J). (978-0-7172-6280-9(4)) Grolier, Ltd.

Gregory, Josh. Rabbits. 2016. (Nature's Children Ser.). (ENG., Illus.). 48p. (J). pap. 6.95 (978-0-531-21934-8(8), Children's Pr.) Scholastic Library Publishing.

Guillain, Charlotte. Rabbits: Animal Family Albums. Elsom, Clare, illus. 2013. (Animal Family Albums Ser.). (ENG.). 32p. (J). (gr. 2-4). pap. 8.29 (978-1-4109-4943-1(5), 120933, Raintree) Capstone.

Haakonsen, Jens. Lynx Chase, Hares Dash, 1 vol. 2017. (Hunter & Hunted: Animal Survival Ser.). (ENG.). 24p. (J). (gr. 3-3). 25.27 (978-1-5081-5664-2(6), 17f2f6ae-49fe-4b7b-9cc7-12f4efaf168c, PowerKids Pr.) Rosen Publishing Group, Inc., The.

Hall, Kirsten. My First Reader: Bunny, Bunny. Wilburn, Kathy, illus. 2003. (My First Reader Ser.). (ENG.). 32p. (J). 18.50 (978-0-516-22923-2(0), Children's Pr.) Scholastic Library Publishing.

Harkins, Susan Sales & Harkins, William H. Care for a Pet Bunny. 2008. (How to Convince Your Parents You Can ... Ser.). (Illus.). 32p. (J). (gr. 1-4). lib. bdg. 25.70 (978-1-58415-659-8(7)) Mitchell Lane Pubs.

Heneghan, Judith. Love Your Rabbit, 1 vol. 2013. (Your Perfect Pet Ser.). (ENG., Illus.). 32p. (gr. 3-3). 29.93 (978-1-4777-0187-4(7), 6ad1ede3-64cd-4339-a2a3-7ccf8db62b66); pap. 11.00 (978-1-4777-0202-4(4), 5372c402-bd34-4a2d-9301-5532427bfd39) Rosen Publishing Group, Inc., The. (Windmill Bks.).

Humphrey, Natalie K. Rabbits & Kits, 1 vol. 2020. (Animal Family Ser.). (ENG.). 24p. (gr. k-k). pap. 9.15 (978-1-5382-5582-7(0), b6f4cc44-7635-4555-92dc-b383187ff82e) Stevens, Gareth Publishing LLLP.

Hurley, Jorey. Hop. Hurley, Jorey, illus. 2019. (Classic Board Bks.). (ENG., Illus.). 34p. (J). (gr. -1 — 1). bds. 7.99 (978-1-5344-2988-8(3), Little Simon) Little Simon.

—Hop. Hurley, Jorey, illus. 2016. (ENG., Illus.). 40p. (J). (gr. -1-2). 17.99 (978-1-4814-3272-6(9), Simon & Schuster/Paula Wiseman Bks.) Simon & Schuster/Paula Wiseman Bks.

Jackman, Vernon. Bunnies & Butterflies in the Backyard & the Pirates Who Know Where They Live: Stories That Help Children Learn & Remember Their Address & Telephone Number. Theagene, Jeannisse, illus. l.t. ed. 2010. (ENG.). 32p. (J). pap. 6.99 (978-0-9829371-1-2(3)) New Kid Safety.

Jacobs, Pat. Rabbit Pals. 2017. (Pet Pals Ser.). (Illus.). 32p. (J). (gr. 3-3). (978-0-7787-3561-8(3)) Crabtree Publishing Co.

Johnson, Jinny. Rabbit. 2014. (My New Pet Ser.). (ENG.). 24p. (J). (gr. k-3). lib. bdg. 28.50 (978-1-62588-028-4(6), 17357) Black Rabbit Bks.

—Rabbit. 2014. (My New Pet Ser.). (ENG., Illus.). 24p. (J). (gr. -1-3). pap. 8.95 (978-1-77092-210-5(5)) Saunders Bk. Co. CAN. Dist: RiverStream Publishing.

—Rabbits. 2008. (Get to Know Your Pet Ser.). (ENG.). 32p. (J). (gr. 2-5). 28.50 (978-1-59920-090-3(2), 19271, Smart Apple Media) Black Rabbit Bks.

—Rabbits. 2009. (Get to Know Your Pet Ser.). (ENG., Illus.). 32p. (J). (gr. 4-7). pap. (978-1-897563-32-8(9)) Saunders Bk. Co.

Jopp, Kelsey. Bunnies. 2019. (Animal Babies Ser.). (ENG., Illus.). 16p. (J). (gr. k-1). 25.64 (978-1-64185-743-7(9), 1641857439, Focus Readers) North Star Editions.

Jordan, Apple. Guess Who Hops, 1 vol. 2nd rev. ed. 2012. (Guess Who? Ser.). (ENG., Illus.). 32p. (gr. k-1). 24.07 (978-1-60870-427-9(0), 27d3cebc-34a3-4675-9b13-0d2cedaa9931) Cavendish Square Publishing LLC.

Kalman, Bobbie. Baby Bunnies. 2010. (ENG., Illus.). 24p. (J). (978-0-7787-3958-6(9)); pap. (978-0-7787-3977-7(5)) Crabtree Publishing Co.

Kalman, Bobbie, photos by. Les Bébés Lapins. 2012. (FRE., Illus.). 24p. (J). pap. 9.95 (978-2-89579-441-7(3)) Bayard Canada CAN. Dist: Crabtree Publishing Co.

Kawa, Katie. Cuddly Rabbits, 1 vol. 2011. (Pet Corner Ser.). (Illus.). 24p. (gr. k-k). (ENG.). (J). 25.27 (978-1-4339-5615-7(2), ce43db9f-0249-4019-8b9d-6b2da29ea8cc); (ENG., (J). pap. 9.15 (978-1-4339-5617-1(9), 4822c223-294a-4fd8-8548-755a93288216); 69.20 (978-1-4339-6885-3(1)) Stevens, Gareth Publishing LLLP.

—Cuddly Rabbits / Conejos Encantadores, 1 vol. 2011. (Pet Corner / Rincón de Las Mascotas Ser.). (SPA & ENG., Illus.). 24p. (J). (gr. k-k). lib. bdg. 25.27 (978-1-4339-5619-5(5), 367cc856-7c8e-4765-9a98-69045b32a999) Stevens, Gareth Publishing LLLP.

Kennard, Pippa & Kennard, Pippa. Bunny Island. Fukuda, Yukihiro & Fukuda, Yukihiro, photos by. 2015. (ENG., Illus.). 32p. (J). (gr. -1-1). pap. 4.99 (978-1-77085-657-8(9), 92e37a85-6b03-43b3-ab95-b2db0ea9539c) Firefly Bks., Ltd.

Knott, Marie, ed. Why Waabooz Has Long Ears. 2007. (Illus.). 27p. (J). pap. 8.95 net. (978-0-9779895-2-2(6)) Knott, Joan.

Lambert, Hines. Hunting Rabbits, 1 vol. 2013. (Let's Go Hunting Ser.). (ENG., Illus.). 32p. (J). (gr. 4-5). 28.93 (978-1-4488-9662-2(2), 2cb6cf89-0ba1-4a27-a55a-6701d30cac43); pap. 11.00 (978-1-4488-9782-7(3), 09fc47d0-bc2c-4c0d-acc5-792974269609) Rosen Publishing Group, Inc., The. (PowerKids Pr.).

Leach, Michael. Hare, 1 vol. 2008. (Animal Neighbors Ser.). (ENG.). 32p. (gr. 3-3). pap. 11.60 (978-1-4042-4574-7(X), fe58a56f-3f9b-4d5c-b46a-82f2bf61cc52, Rosen Classroom); (Illus.). (J). lib. bdg. 28.93 (978-1-4358-4997-6(3), eedad408-0498-4ba8-8020-fbe915739542, PowerKids Pr.) Rosen Publishing Group, Inc., The.

Leaf, Christina. Jackrabbits. 2015. (North American Animals Ser.). (ENG., Illus.). 24p. (J). (gr. k-3). lib. bdg. 26.95 (978-1-62617-191-6(2), Blastoff! Readers) Bellwether Media.

—Rabbit or Hare? 2019. (Spotting Differences Ser.). (ENG., Illus.). 24p. (J). (gr. k-3). lib. bdg. 26.95 (978-1-64487-035-8(5), Blastoff! Readers) Bellwether Media.

Leighton, Christina. Cottontail Rabbits. 2017. (North American Animals Ser.). (ENG., Illus.). 24p. (J). (gr. k-3). lib. bdg. 26.95 (978-1-62617-566-2(7), Blastoff! Readers) Bellwether Media.

Lord, Cynthia. Borrowing Bunnies: A Surprising True Tale of Fostering Rabbits. Mitchell, Hazel, illus. Bald, John, photos by. 2019. (ENG.). 40p. (J). 17.99 (978-0-374-30841-4(1),

900186026, Farrar, Straus & Giroux (BYR)) Farrar, Straus & Giroux.
Los Conejos: Individual Title Six-Packs. (Literatura 2000 Ser.). (SPA.). (gr. 2-3). 33.00 *(978-0-7635-1259-0(1))* Rigby Education.
Lowenstein Niven, Felicia. Learning to Care for Small Mammals, 1 vol. 2010. (Beginning Pet Care with American Humane Ser.). (ENG.). 48p. (gr. 3-3). 27.93 *(978-0-7660-3195-1(0),* c4dbf867-2297-430e-9662-e07b36f64229, Enslow Elementary) Enslow Publishing, LLC.
MacAulay, Kelley & Kalman, Bobbie. Rabbits. Crabtree, Marc, illus. Crabtree, Marc, photos by. 2004. (Pet Care Ser.). (ENG.). 32p. (J). pap. *(978-0-7787-1788-1(7))* Crabtree Publishing Co.
MacAulay, Kelley, et al. Les Lapins. 2011. (Petit Monde Vivant (Small Living World) Ser.: No. 78). (FRE., Illus.). 32p. (J). pap. 9.95 *(978-2-89579-372-4(7))* Bayard Canada Livres CAN. Dist: Crabtree Publishing Co.
MacDonald, Margaret. I Want to Buy a Rabbit. 2011. (Learn-Abouts Ser.). (Illus.). 16p. (J). pap. 7.95 *(978-1-59920-631-8(5))* Black Rabbit Bks.
Macheske, Felicia. Wiggling Whiskers: Rabbit. 2017. (Guess What Ser.). (ENG., Illus.). 24p. (J). (gr. k-2). lib. bdg. 30.64 *(978-1-63472-857-7(2),* 209854) Cherry Lake Publishing.
Mara, Wil. Rabbits, 1 vol. 2014. (Backyard Safari Ser.). (ENG.). 32p. (gr. 3-3). 31.21 *(978-1-62712-310-5(5),* a4c14ec7-381e-4707-93e8-fea19ee324eb) Cavendish Square Publishing LLC.
Markovics, Joyce L. Angora Rabbit. 2016. (Weird but Cute Ser.: 8). (ENG., Illus.). 24p. (J). (gr. -1-3). 26.99 *(978-1-62724-847-1(1))* Bearport Publishing Co., Inc.
Marsico, Katie. How Do We Live Together? Rabbits. 2010. (Community Connections: How Do We Live Together? Ser.). (ENG., Illus.). 24p. (gr. 2-5). lib. bdg. 29.21 *(978-1-60279-622-5(X),* 200329) Cherry Lake Publishing.
Martin, Emmett. Bunnies from Head to Tail, 1 vol. 2020. (Animals from Head to Tail Ser.). (ENG.). 24p. (gr. k-2). pap. 9.15 *(978-1-5382-5530-8(8),* a795e100-5aed-4128-9e93-fc73646a811f) Stevens, Gareth Publishing LLLP.
Matthews, Colin. Cat Poop or Rabbit Poop?, 1 vol. 2019. (Scoop on Poop! Ser.). (ENG.). 24p. (gr. 1-2). 24.27 *(978-1-5382-2953-8(6),* 2634076d-3da2-4cdc-84e1-e51126e3d121) Stevens, Gareth Publishing LLLP.
McBride, Anne. Rabbits, Vol. 12. 2016. (Understanding & Caring for Your Pet Ser.: Vol. 12). (ENG., Illus.). 128p. (J). (gr. 5-8). 25.95 *(978-1-4222-3703-8(6))* Mason Crest.
McDowell, Pamela. Liebres. 2013. (Animales en Mi Patio Ser.). (SPA., Illus.). 24p. (J). (gr. -1-3). lib. bdg. 27.13 *(978-1-62127-597-8(3),* AV2 by Weigl) Weigl Pubs., Inc.
—Rabbits. 2012. (J). 27.13 *(978-1-61913-269-6(9));* pap. *(978-1-61913-273-3(7))* Weigl Pubs., Inc.
McGrath, Barbara Barbieri. The Little Gray Bunny. Kim, Violet, illus. 2013. (Holiday Books: Easter Ser.). 32p. (J). (gr. -1-1). 22.44 *(978-1-58089-394-7(5));* pap. 7.95 *(978-1-58089-395-4(3))* Charlesbridge Publishing, Inc.
McLellan, Joe. Nikik & Wapus Save the People, 1 vol. Traverse, Jackie, illus. 2015. (ENG.). 32p. (J). mass mkt. 10.95 *(978-1-894717-70-0(8),* baddc49e-5bc9-4569-a55f-6ed5d2b298d0) Pemmican Pubns., Inc. CAN. Dist: Firefly Bks., Ltd.
Meachen Rau, Dana. El Conejo en el Huerto (the Rabbit in the Garden), 1 vol. 2008. (Naturaleza (Nature) Ser.). (SPA., Illus.). 24p. (gr. k-1). lib. bdg. 25.50 *(978-0-7614-2413-0(X),* fe1580f4-51d1-4d8b-9492-e835a77efe8c) Cavendish Square Publishing LLC.
—The Rabbit in the Garden, 1 vol. 2007. (Nature Ser.). (ENG., Illus.). 24p. (gr. k-1). lib. bdg. 25.50 *(978-0-7614-2308-9(7),* 26ed28e5-fa10-416a-bf00-d0a51ac21099) Cavendish Square Publishing LLC.
Meade, Jean McCurdy. The Tale of Rebekah Rabbit. Clark, Barbara Hoserman, illus. 2009. 28p. pap. 12.95 *(978-1-59858-970-2(9))* Dog Ear Publishing, LLC.
Meister, Cari. Rabbits. 2014. (Illus.). 24p. (J). lib. bdg. 25.65 *(978-1-62031-125-7(9),* Bullfrog Bks.) Jump! Inc.
Minden, Cecilia. Kits Grow up to Be Rabbits. 2010. (21st Century Basic Skills Library: Animals Grow Up Ser.). (ENG., Illus.). 24p. (gr. k-3). lib. bdg. 26.35 *(978-1-60279-854-0(0),* 200574) Cherry Lake Publishing.
Mitchell, Melanie. Rabbits. 2003. (First Step Nonfiction — Animal Life Cycles Ser.). (ENG., Illus.). 24p. (J). (gr. k-2). pap. 6.99 *(978-0-8225-4605-4(1),* 0a650fbe-bccf-4991-975d-828c39b97b3e) Lerner Publishing Group.
Mitchell, Melanie S. Rabbits. 2005. (First Step Nonfiction Ser.). (Illus.). 24p. (gr. k-2). lib. bdg. 17.27 *(978-0-8225-4604-7(3))* Lerner Publishing Group.
Morgan, Sally. Rabbits. 2012. (Pets Plus Ser.). (Illus.). 32p. (gr. 3-6). lib. bdg. 31.35 *(978-1-59920-700-1(1))* Black Rabbit Bks.
Neuman, Susan B. Hop, Bunny! (1 Hardcover/1 CD) 2017. (National Geographic Kids Ser.). (ENG.). (J). 29.95 *(978-1-4301-2645-4(0))* Live Oak Media.
—Hop, Bunny! (1 Paperback/1 CD) 2017. (National Geographic Kids Ser.). (ENG.). (J). pap. 19.95 *(978-1-4301-2644-7(2))* Live Oak Media.
—Hop, Bunny! (4 Paperbacks/1 CD), 4 vols. 2017. (National Geographic Kids Ser.). (J). pap. 31.95 *(978-1-4301-2646-1(9))* Live Oak Media.
Newman, Aline Alexander. National Geographic Kids Chapters: Rascally Rabbits! And More True Stories of Animals Behaving Badly. 2016. (NGK Chapters Ser.). (Illus.). 112p. (J). (gr. 3-7). pap. 5.99 *(978-1-4263-2308-9(5),* National Geographic Kids) Disney Publishing Worldwide.
Olson, Bethany. Baby Rabbits. 2013. (Super Cute! Ser.). (ENG., Illus.). 24p. (J). (gr. k-3). lib. bdg. 26.95 *(978-1-60014-932-0(4),* Blastoff! Readers) Bellwether Media.
Petrie, Kristin. Cottontail Rabbits, 1 vol. 2015. (Backyard Animals Ser.). (ENG.). 32p. (J). (gr. 3-6). 32.79 *(978-1-62403-659-0(7),* 16816, Checkerboard Library) ABDO Publishing Co.
Pettiford, Rebecca. Arctic Hares. 2019. (Animals of the Arctic Ser.). (ENG., Illus.). 24p. (J). (gr. k-3). 26.95 *(978-1-62617-940-0(9),* Blastoff! Readers) Bellwether Media.
Phillips, Clifton C. Rabbits Rule at Night School. 2008. 28p. pap. 8.99 *(978-1-935105-02-2(7))* Avid Readers Publishing Group.
Phillips, Dee. Snowshoe Hare. 2015. (Arctic Animals: Life Outside the Igloo Ser.). (ENG.). 24p. (J). (gr. -1-3). lib. bdg. 26.99 *(978-1-62724-527-2(8))* Bearport Publishing Co., Inc.
Rabbit's Nap. (Acorn Wood Lift-the-Flap Bks.). (YA). bds. 3.50 net. *(978-1-56021-380-2(9))* W.J. Fantasy, Inc.
Randolph, Joanne. Rabbits. (Classroom Pets Ser.). 24p. (gr. 2-3). 2009. 42.50 *(978-1-61511-858-8(6))* 2006. (ENG., Illus.). (J). lib. bdg. 26.27 *(978-1-4042-3680-6(5),* 677ff52e-bb45-46e3-9322-fd2ba4f6e629) Rosen Publishing Group, Inc., The. (PowerKids Pr.).
Raum, Elizabeth. Le Lapin et Son Terrier. Martí, Romina, illus. 2017. (Animaux Architectes Ser.). (FRE.). 24p. (J). (gr. 1-4). *(978-1-77092-384-3(5),* 17615) Amicus.
—Los Orangutanes y Sus Nidos (Orangutans Build Tree Nests) Romina Martí, illus. 2017. (Animal Builders Ser.). (ENG & SPA.). 24p. (J). (gr. 1-4). 20.95 *(978-1-68151-283-9(1),* Amicus Illustrated) Amicus Learning.
—Rabbits Dig Burrows. Martí, Romina, illus. 2017. (Animal Builders Ser.). (ENG.). 24p. (J). (gr. 1-4). lib. bdg. 20.95 *(978-1-68151-173-3(8),* 14666) Amicus.
—Rabbits Dig Burrows: Animal Builders. Martí, Romina, illus. 2018. (Animal Builders Ser.). 24p. (J). (gr. 1-4). pap. 8.99 *(978-1-68152-154-1(7),* 14785) Amicus.
Rayner, Matthew. Rabbit, 1 vol. 2004. (I Am Your Pet Ser.). (ENG., Illus.). 32p. (gr. 2-4). lib. bdg. 28.67 *(978-0-8368-4105-3(0),* cdf60275-a42d-44e6-be6a-275b66efedb4, Gareth Stevens Learning Library) Stevens, Gareth Publishing LLLP.
Robbins, Lynette. Rabbits & Hares. (J). 2012. 49.50 *(978-1-4488-5170-6(X),* PowerKids Pr.) 2011. (ENG.). 24p. (gr. 2-3). pap. 9.25 *(978-1-4488-5169-0(6),* 0acbafea-afd8-46d0-8b53-163d60f33785, PowerKids Pr.) 2011. (ENG.). 24p. (gr. 2-3). lib. bdg. 26.27 *(978-1-4488-5018-1(5),* 95715d46-65af-4f03-b1e2-cdd49b18f4c7) Rosen Publishing Group, Inc., The.
Rockwood, Leigh. Tell Me the Difference Between a Rabbit & a Hare, 1 vol. 2013. (How Are They Different? Ser.). (ENG., Illus.). 24p. (J). (gr. 2-3). pap. 9.25 *(978-1-4488-9734-6(3),* 73dffdc6-d6ea-4657-b568-ed04a05b763e); lib. bdg. 26.27 *(978-1-4488-9638-7(X),* dda72842-93e0-4494-a7ba-3bf4e04c57a7) Rosen Publishing Group, Inc., The. (PowerKids Pr.).
Royston, Angela. Rabbit. 2004. (J). lib. bdg. 27.10 *(978-1-59389-160-2(1))* Chrysalis Education.
Schuh, Mari. Rabbits. 2018. (Spot Pets Ser.). (ENG.). 16p. (J). (gr. -1-2). *(978-1-68151-370-6(6),* 14950); pap. 7.99 *(978-1-68152-290-6(X),* 14958) Amicus.
Schuh, Mari C. Rabbits. 2015. (Backyard Animals Ser.). (ENG., Illus.). 24p. (J). (gr. -1-2). lib. bdg. 27.32 *(978-1-4914-2086-7(3),* 127566, Capstone Pr.) Capstone.
Sexton, Colleen. Bunnies. 2008. (Watch Animals Grow Ser.). (ENG., Illus.). 24p. (J). (gr. k-3). lib. bdg. 26.95 *(978-1-60014-166-9(8))* Bellwether Media.
—Caring for Your Rabbit. 2010. (Pet Care Library). (ENG., Illus.). 24p. (J). (gr. 2-5). lib. bdg. 26.95 *(978-1-60014-471-4(3),* Blastoff! Readers) Bellwether Media.
Shea, Therese M. Arctic Hares, 1 vol. 2010. (Animals That Live in the Tundra Ser.). (ENG., Illus.). 24p. (J). (gr. 1-1). pap. 9.15 *(978-1-4339-3891-7(X),* ba489a8e-2487-4b49-8d9a-6a77cc63b87e); lib. bdg. 25.27 *(978-1-4339-3890-0(1),* 5136bc2b-771b-4e6a-b6c1-e0714b069ee0) Stevens, Gareth Publishing LLLP.
Sikkens, Crystal. The Life Cycle of a Rabbit. 2019. (Full STEAM Ahead! - Science Starters Ser.). (Illus.). 24p. (J). (gr. 1-1). *(978-0-7787-6200-3(9));* pap. *(978-0-7787-6237-9(8))* Crabtree Publishing Co.
Silverman, Buffy. Dwarf Rabbits. 2018. (Lightning Bolt Books (r) — Little Pets Ser.). (ENG., Illus.). 24p. (J). (gr. 1-3). lib. bdg. 29.32 *(978-1-5415-1029-6(1),* 05fc0335-0078-4fdf-a44a-5a177f41f31b, Lerner Pubns.) Lerner Publishing Group.
Steinkraus, Kyla. Rabbits on the Farm. 2010. (Farm Animals Ser.). (Illus.). 24p. (J). (gr. k-3). 22.79 *(978-1-61590-268-2(6))* Rourke Educational Media.
Stewart, Melissa. Rabbits, 1 vol. 2008. (Animals, Animals Ser.). (ENG., Illus.). 48p. (gr. 5-5). lib. bdg. 32.64 *(978-0-7614-2528-1(4),* 7c8ddf4f-4f63-4c80-b225-36c76719bff0) Cavendish Square Publishing LLC.
Stoltman, Joan. My First Bunny, 1 vol. 2017. (Let's Get a Pet! Ser.). (ENG.). 24p. (gr. 1-2). pap. 9.15 *(978-1-4824-6441-2(1),* 24341616-e4bd-400e-a669-825d527f4080) Stevens, Gareth Publishing LLLP.
Tagliaferro, Linda. Rabbits & Their Burrows [Scholastic]. 2010. (Animal Homes Ser.). 24p. pap. 0.49 *(978-1-4296-5796-9(0),* Capstone Pr.) Capstone.
Terp, Gail. Rabbits. 2016. (Wild Animal Kingdom Ser.). (ENG.). 32p. (J). (gr. 4-6). pap. 9.99 *(978-1-64466-174-1(8),* 10413); (Illus.). 31.35 *(978-1-68072-056-3(2),* 10412) Black Rabbit Bks. (Bolt).
Treselt, Alvin & Ewing, Carolyn. The Rabbit Story.Tr. of Histoire de Lapins. (FRE.). (J). pap. 6.99 *(978-0-590-74143-9(8))* Scholastic, Inc.
Walker, Kathryn. See How Rabbits Grow, 1 vol. 2009. (See How They Grow Ser.). (ENG.). 24p. (J). (gr. 2-2). lib. bdg. 26.27 *(978-1-4358-2831-5(3),* 7d063986-1def-4c2b-957d-d1fcbabe9cd3); (Illus.). pap. 9.25 *(978-1-4358-2879-7(8),* b28140b0-ccc4-4eec-89c1-a00207f55911) Rosen Publishing Group, Inc., The. (PowerKids Pr.).
Wendt, Jennifer. Showing Rabbits at the Fair, 1 vol. 2018. (Blue Ribbon Animals Ser.). (ENG.). 24p. (gr. 2-3). lib. bdg. 24.27 *(978-1-5382-2931-6(5),* a4b1e0f1-2067-4756-bb22-2dad9a22421c) Stevens, Gareth Publishing LLLP.
Why Rabbits Have Long Ears: Individual Title Six-Packs. (Literatura 2000 Ser.). (gr. 2-3). 33.00 *(978-0-7635-0270-6(7))* Rigby Education.
Why the Rabbit Has Such Long Ears: Lap Book. (Pebble Soup Explorations Ser.). (SPA.). 16p. (gr. -1-18). 21.00 *(978-0-7578-1667-3(3))* Rigby Education.
Why the Rabbit Has Such Long Ears: Small Book. (Pebble Soup Explorations Ser.). (SPA.). 16p. (gr. -1-18). 5.00 *(978-0-7578-1707-6(6))* Rigby Education.
Wittrock, Jeni. A Baby Rabbit Story. 2011. (Baby Animals Ser.). (ENG.). 24p. (gr. k-1). pap. 41.70 *(978-1-4296-7100-2(9),* Capstone Pr.) Capstone.
—Pet Rabbits up Close. (Pets up Close Ser.). (ENG.). 24p. (J). (gr. -1-2). 2015. Illus.). pap. 6.95 *(978-1-4914-7766-3(0),* 130169) 2014. 27.32 *(978-1-4914-0584-0(8),* 125922) Capstone. (Capstone Pr.).
World Book, Inc. Staff, contrib. by. Holland Lops & Other Rabbits. 2007. (World Book's Animals of the World Ser.). (Illus.). 64p. (J). *(978-0-7166-1330-5(1))* World Bk., Inc.
Worthington, Niles. A Rabbit's Burrow, 1 vol. 2016. (Animal Builders Ser.). (ENG., Illus.). 24p. (gr. 1-1). pap. 9.22 *(978-1-5026-2086-6(3),* ec6d3b3a-c8b7-4e4a-a8f2-a87088c77c5e) Cavendish Square Publishing LLC.
Zobel, Derek. Rabbits. 2010. (Backyard Wildlife Ser.). (ENG., Illus.). 24p. (J). (gr. k-3). lib. bdg. 26.95 *(978-1-60014-443-1(8),* Blastoff! Readers) Bellwether Media.

RABBITS—FICTION

Aamundsen, Martin Berdahl & Tsm, Crew. Nora & the Little Blue Rabbit. 2017. (ENG., Illus.). 40p. (J). (gr. -1-3). 16.95 *(978-1-58423-639-9(6),* f4b06765-45c3-4601-a41a-ef3ee5798114) Gingko Pr., Inc.
Abramson, Laurin. Coco. Abramson, Stephen, photos by. 2010. (Illus.). 28p. pap. 8.75 *(978-1-935125-95-2(8))* Robertson Publishing.
Acreman, Hayley. Found You Rabbit! Acreman, Hayley, illus. 2011. (ENG., Illus.). 34p. (J). (gr. k-2). pap. 9.95 *(978-1-905762-87-3(9))* Parthian Bks. GBR. Dist: Independent Pubs. Group.
Adams, Alison. Brer Rabbit Hears a Noise: Classic Tales Series. Greenhead, Bill, illus. 2011. (Classic Tales Ser.). (J). *(978-1-936258-64-2(1))* Benchmark Education Co.
Adams, Richard. Watership Down: A Novel. 2005. (ENG., Illus.). 496p. pap. 19.99 *(978-0-7432-7770-9(8),* Scribner) Scribner.
Afetian, "Uncle Ted". The Adventures of Midas & the Little Red Airplane. 2005. (Illus.). 32p. (J). 16.95i *(978-0-9752749-0-3(2))* Snyder-Winston Pr.
Ajdari, Fereshteh. The turtle & the Rabbit: A Story for children, parents & grand Parents. 2009. (ENG.). 26p. pap. 15.99 *(978-1-4415-6424-5(1))* Xlibris Corp.
Albee, Sarah. The Bunny Hop (Sesame Street) Swanson, Maggie, illus. 2004. (Big Bird's Favorites Board Bks.). (ENG.). 24p. (J). (gr. k — 1). bds. 4.99 *(978-0-375-82693-1(9),* Random Hse. Bks. for Young Readers) Random Hse. Children's Bks.
Alexander, Brad. Antiniak: A Different Kind of Village. 2011. (ENG.). 74p. pap. 15.50 *(978-1-257-10163-4(3))* Lulu Pr., Inc.
Ana, Reverend & Binkow, Howard. Howard B. Wigglebottom Learns to Listen. Cornelison, Susan F., illus. 2008. (Howard B. Wigglebottom Ser.). (ENG.). 32p. (J). (gr. -1-3). 15.00 *(978-0-9715390-1-3(4),* df6c8ae2-f1da-4aaa-a6cb-27d0ee9d8149, We Do Listen) We Do Listen Foundation.
—Howard B. Wigglebottom Listens to His Heart. Cornelison, Susan F., illus. 2nd ed. 2008. (Howard B. Wigglebottom Ser.). (ENG.). 32p. (J). (gr. -1-3). 15.00 *(978-0-9715390-2-0(2),* ac6db1e7-fc6b-47b5-b36f-019875126f32, We Do Listen) We Do Listen Foundation.
Anderson, Dee, retold by. Otter Gets Tricked! A Cherokee Trickster Story. I.t. ed. 2004. (Illus.). 32p. (J). pap. 6.00 *(978-0-9755934-1-7(2))* Colonel Davenport Historical Foundation.
Anderson, Derek. How the Easter Bunny Saved Christmas. Anderson, Derek, illus. 2006. (ENG., Illus.). 40p. (J). (gr. -1-3). 19.99 *(978-0-689-87634-9(3),* Simon & Schuster Bks. For Young Readers) Simon & Schuster Bks. For Young Readers.
Anderson, Laurie Halse. New Beginnings, 13 vols., 13. 2012. (Vet Volunteers Ser.: 13). (ENG.). 192p. (J). (gr. 3-7). 7.99 *(978-0-14-241675-4(4),* Puffin) Penguin Young Readers Group.
Andros, Camille. Charlotte the Scientist Finds a Cure. Farley, Brianne, illus. 2019. (Charlotte the Scientist Ser.). (ENG.). 40p. (J). (gr. -1-3). 17.99 *(978-0-544-81376-2(6),* 1642033, Clarion Bks.) HarperCollins Pubs.
—Charlotte the Scientist Is Squished. Farley, Brianne, illus. 2017. (Charlotte the Scientist Ser.). (ENG.). 40p. (J). (gr. -1-3). 17.99 *(978-0-544-78583-0(5),* 1638581, Clarion Bks.) HarperCollins Pubs.
Animal Friends Squeaky- Bunny. 2005. (J). bds. *(978-1-4194-0091-9(6))* Paradise Pr., Inc.
Antonia, Miller, illus. Baby's Very First Little Book of Bunnies. 2011. (Baby's Very First Board Bks). 10p. (J). ring bd. 6.99 *(978-0-7945-2955-0(0),* Usborne) EDC Publishing.
Armantrout, Denise. Pink & Green Story Time: Book One. 2013. 32p. pap. 13.99 *(978-1-4525-7581-0(9),* Balboa Pr.) Author Solutions, LLC.
Arnold, Robyn. Branli Says Bye-Bye to Binky. 2007. (ENG.). 32p. 16.50 *(978-0-615-15292-9(9))* Robyn Z Moon Publishing.
Arnosky, Jim. Rabbits & Raindrops. 2014. 16.00 *(978-1-63419-679-6(1))* Perfection Learning Corp.
Arrington, R. Region. Tommy Hop the Bunny, 1 vol. 2009. 16p. pap. 24.95 *(978-1-4489-2134-8(1))* America Star Bks.
Arzave, Jose. Rabbit the Shepherd. 2013. 24p. pap. 10.99 *(978-1-62509-572-5(4))* Salem Author Services.
Ashby, Gaylene. STORY TIME A Collection of Three Children's Stories. 2008. 28p. 14.95 *(978-1-4357-1929-3(8))* Lulu Pr., Inc.
Asher, Sandy. Too Many Frogs. Graves, Keith, illus. 2005. 32p. (J). (gr. -1-k). 16.99 *(978-0-399-23978-6(2),* Philomel Bks.) Penguin Young Readers Group.
—Why Rabbit's Nose Twitches. 2003. (Illus.). 14.95 *(978-1-59319-019-4(0))* LeapFrog Enterprises, Inc.
Auerbach, Annie. Furry Bunny. Rigo, Laura, illus. 2018. (ENG.). 10p. (J). (gr. -1-k). bds. 7.99 *(978-1-4380-5011-9(9))* Sourcebooks, Inc.
Austin, Jeanne J. Unlikely Friends. 2009. 24p. pap. 14.99 *(978-1-4343-2348-4(X))* AuthorHouse.
Auty, Rob. A Hare's Tale 2 - the Golden Hare. Wood, Chaz, illus. 2013. 102p. pap. *(978-1-908098-90-0(2))* 2QT, Ltd. (Publishing).
Auty, Robert C. A Hare's Tale. 2011. (ENG., Illus.). 80p. pap. 9.99 *(978-1-908098-40-5(6))* 2QT, Ltd. (Publishing) GBR. Dist: Printondemand-worldwide.com.
Award, Anna, et al. The Hare & the Tortoise & The Sick Lion. 2014. (ENG.). 24p. (J). pap. 6.95 *(978-1-84135-954-0(8))* Award Pubns. Ltd. GBR. Dist: Parkwest Pubns., Inc.
AZ Books Staff. Who Is the Hare Looking For? Zajceva, Ira, ed. 2012. (Who Is There Ser.). (ENG.). 10p. (J). (-k). bds. 11.95 *(978-1-61889-040-5(9))* AZ Bks. LLC.
Bachelet, Gilles. Mrs. White Rabbit. 2017. (ENG., Illus.). 32p. (J). 17.00 *(978-0-8028-5483-4(4),* Eerdmans Bks For Young Readers) Eerdmans, William B. Publishing Co.
Baglio, Ben M. Bunny in a Basket. Baum, Ann, illus. 2005. 142p. (J). *(978-0-439-68761-4(6))* Scholastic, Inc.
—Runaway Rascal. 2006. (Illus.). 157p. (J). *(978-0-439-79250-9(9))* Scholastic, Inc.
Baguley, Elizabeth. A Long Way from Home. Chapman, Jane, illus. 2008. 32p. (J). (gr. 4-7). 15.95 *(978-1-58925-074-1(5))* Tiger Tales.
Bailey, Arthur Scott. The Tale of Peter Mink. 2005. pap. 20.95 *(978-0-7661-9699-5(2))* Kessinger Publishing, LLC.
Bailey, Rosemary. Benjamin Bunny A Childrens Story. 2004. 12p. (J). pap. 10.33 *(978-1-4116-1043-9(1))* Lulu Pr., Inc.
Baker, Alan. Gray Rabbit's 123. 2017. (Little Rabbit Bks.). (J). lib. bdg. 18.40 *(978-0-606-39601-1(2))* Turtleback.
Balian, Lorna. Humbug Rabbit. 2004. (Illus.). 32p. (J). 15.95 *(978-1-932065-40-4(7))* Star Bright Bks., Inc.
Banks, Steven. Show Me the Bunny! Greenblatt, C. H. & Reiss, William, illus. 2004. (Spongebob Squarepants Ser.). 32p. (J). 11.65 *(978-0-7569-5643-1(9))* Perfection Learning Corp.
Barlone, M. J. A Mouse & Rabbits Tale. 2010. (Illus.). 40p. pap. 16.99 *(978-1-4490-7771-6(4))* AuthorHouse.
Batsel, Hannah. A Is for Another Rabbit. Batsel, Hannah, illus. 2020. (ENG., Illus.). 32p. (J). (gr. -1-2). 17.99 *(978-1-5415-2950-2(2),* 560c7d12-c42e-4a7b-8ba7-b224ff9b6a7f, Carolrhoda Bks.) Lerner Publishing Group.
Bauman Wispe, Lisa. Fritter's Spring: A Pocono Rabbit's Tale. 2010. pap. 11.95 *(978-0-7414-5796-7(2))* Infinity Publishing.
Baumbach, Rudolph. Summer Legends. 2017. (ENG., Illus.). (J). 23.95 *(978-1-374-87060-4(9));* pap. 13.95 *(978-1-374-87059-8(5))* Capital Communications, Inc.
—Summer Legends. 2004. reprint ed. pap. 1.99 *(978-1-4192-4993-8(2));* pap. 21.95 *(978-1-4191-4993-1(8))* Kessinger Publishing, LLC.
Baxter, Nicola. The Bunny Tales Collection: Twelve Lively Stories of Rascally Rabbits. Shuttleworth, Cathie, illus. 2014. 80p. (J). (gr. -1-3). pap. 9.99 *(978-1-84322-934-6(X),* Armadillo) Anness Publishing GBR. Dist: National Bk. Network.
—Stories for Little Ones. Shuttleworth, Cathie, illus. 2018. (ENG.). 256p. (J). (gr. -1-12). 9.99 *(978-0-85723-894-8(9),* Armadillo) Anness Publishing GBR. Dist: National Bk. Network.
Beachy, Elaine. Biff & Becka's Stupendous Vacation. 2013. 156p. (J). 30.95 *(978-1-4497-9069-1(0));* pap. 13.95 *(978-1-4497-9070-7(4))* Author Solutions, LLC. (WestBow Pr.).
Beckstedt, Cynthia. Hopsy. 2008. 24p. pap. 24.95 *(978-1-4241-9122-2(X))* America Star Bks.
Bell, Cece. Rabbit & Robot. 2014. (Candlewick Sparks Ser.). lib. bdg. 13.55 *(978-0-606-35169-0(8))* Turtleback.
—Rabbit & Robot: The Sleepover. Bell, Cece, illus. 2014. (Candlewick Sparks Ser.). (ENG., Illus.). 56p. (J). (gr. k-4). pap. 5.99 *(978-0-7636-6875-4(3))* Candlewick Pr.
—Rabbit & Robot & Ribbit. Bell, Cece, illus. 2017. (Candlewick Sparks Ser.). (ENG., Illus.). 48p. (J). (gr. k-4). pap. 5.99 *(978-0-7636-9782-2(6))* Candlewick Pr.
Benoist, Cathy & Gilmore, Cathy. El Conejito de Pascua: El Cuento de un Día Extraordinario. Sundy, Jonathan, illus. 2014. (SPA.). 40p. (J). (gr. 4-7). 16.99 *(978-0-7648-2456-2(2),* Libros Liguori) Liguori Pubns.
Bentley, Catherine & Bentley, Dawn. Hoppy Goes to School. Huerta, Catherine, illus. 2006. (Pet Tales Ser.). (ENG.). 32p. (J). 2.95 *(978-1-59249-558-0(3))* Soundprints.
Bentley, Dawn. Hoppy Goes to School. Huerta, Catherine, illus. 2006. (ENG.). 32p. (J). pap. 9.95 *(978-1-59249-559-7(1));* (gr. -1-3). 4.95 *(978-1-59249-556-6(7))* Soundprints.
Bentley, Sue. Chocolate Wishes. 2013. (Magic Bunny Ser.: 1). lib. bdg. 14.75 *(978-0-606-31675-0(2))* Turtleback.
—Chocolate Wishes #1. Swan, Angela, illus. 2013. (Magic Bunny Ser.: 1). (ENG.). 128p. (J). (gr. 1-3). pap. 6.99 *(978-0-448-46727-6(5),* Grosset & Dunlap) Penguin Young Readers Group.
—Classroom Capers. 2014. (Magic Bunny Ser.: 4). lib. bdg. 14.75 *(978-0-606-34134-9(X))* Turtleback.
—Classroom Capers #4. Swan, Angela, illus. 2014. (Magic Bunny Ser.: 4). (ENG.). 128p. (J). (gr. 1-3). 6.99 *(978-0-448-46792-4(5),* Grosset & Dunlap) Penguin Young Readers Group.
—Dancing Days. 2014. (Magic Bunny Ser.: 5). lib. bdg. 14.75 *(978-0-606-34135-6(8))* Turtleback.
—Dancing Days #5. Swan, Angela, illus. 2014. (Magic Bunny Ser.: 5). (ENG.). 128p. (J). (gr. 1-3). 5.99 *(978-0-448-46793-1(3),* Grosset & Dunlap) Penguin Young Readers Group.
—A Splash of Magic. 2013. (Magic Bunny Ser.: 3). lib. bdg. 14.75 *(978-0-606-31677-4(9))* Turtleback.
—A Splash of Magic #3. Swan, Angela, illus. 2013. (Magic Bunny Ser.: 3). (ENG.). 128p. (J). (gr. 1-3). pap. 6.99 *(978-0-448-46729-0(1),* Grosset & Dunlap) Penguin Young Readers Group.
—Vacation Dreams. 2013. (Magic Bunny Ser.: 2). lib. bdg. 16.00 *(978-0-606-31676-7(0))* Turtleback.
—Vacation Dreams #2. Swan, Angela, illus. 2013. (Magic Bunny Ser.: 2). (ENG.). 128p. (J). (gr. 1-3). pap. 6.99 *(978-0-448-46728-3(3),* Grosset & Dunlap) Penguin Young Readers Group.
Berenstain, Jan & Berenstain, Mike. Lift & Flap the Berenstain Bears' Baby Easter Bunny. 2008. (Berenstain Bears Ser.). (ENG., Illus.). 16p. (J). (gr. -1-1). pap. 6.99 *(978-0-06-057420-8(8),* HarperFestival) HarperCollins Pubs.

Berger, Carin. Forever Friends. Berger, Carin, illus. 2010. (ENG., Illus.). 40p. (J). (gr. -1-1). 17.99 *(978-0-06-191528-4(9)*, Greenwillow Bks.) HarperCollins Pubs.

Berglund, Andrea Lloyd. A Good Little Horse: Thunder's Morning Stroll. 2009. 36p. (J). pap. 19.95 *(978-1-4327-3822-8(4))* Outskirts Pr., Inc.

Berkes, Marianne. The Tortoise & Hare's Amazing Race, 1 vol. Morrison, Cathy, illus. 2015. (ENG & SPA.). 32p. (J). (gr. k-3). 17.95 *(978-1-62855-635-3(8))* Arbordale Publishing.

Berner, R. Thomas. The Cottontails & the Jackrabbits. Berner, Paulette L., illus. 2008. 22p. (J). per. 19.95 *(978-0-922993-06-2(8))* Marquette Bks.

Berner, Rotraut Susanne, illus. Hound & Hare, 1 vol. 2011. (ENG.). 80p. (J). (gr. k-4). 18.95 *(978-0-88899-987-0(9))* Groundwood Bks. CAN. Dist: Publishers Group West (PGW).

Berry, Eileen M. Buttercup Hill. Harrald-Pilz, Marilee, illus. 2006. 39p. (J). (gr. -1-3). pap. *(978-1-59166-667-7(8))* BJU Pr.

Bianchi, John, illus. Where Is Here? 2016. (1G Bird, Bunny, & Bear Ser.). (ENG.). 12p. (J). pap. 8.00 *(978-1-61406-592-0(6))* American Reading Co.

Bianco, Margery Williams. The Velveteen Rabbit. Felix, Monique, illus. 2013. (ENG.). 40p. (J). (gr. 2-5). pap. 8.99 *(978-0-89812-831-4(5)*, 22070, Creative Paperbacks) Creative Co., The.

—The Velveteen Rabbit, or, How Toys Become Real. Nicholson, William, illus. 2015. iii, 27p. (J). pap. *(978-1-4677-9307-0(8)*, First Avenue Editions) Lerner Publishing Group.

Billings, David Joseph. Road Trip with Rabbit & Squash. Billings, David Joseph, illus. 2006. (Illus.). 48p. (J). per. *(978-0-9789036-0-2(9))* Billings, David J.

Billingsley, Victoria. Happy Hoppy's Orchestra & Other Stories. 2010. 44p. 16.99 *(978-1-4520-6753-7(8))* AuthorHouse.

Birchall, Mark. Rabbit's Birthday Surprise. Birchall, Mark, illus. 2003. (Illus.). 32p. (J). (gr. -1-3). 15.95 *(978-0-87614-910-2(7)*, Carolrhoda Bks.) Lerner Publishing Group.

—Rabbit's Wooly Sweater. Birchall, Mark, illus. 2003. (Picture Bks.). (Illus.). 32p. (J). (gr. -1-3). 15.95 *(978-1-57505-465-0(5)*, Carolrhoda Bks.) Lerner Publishing Group.

Blackwood, Freya. Great Rabbit Chase. 2017. (Illus.). 32p. (J). *(978-1-74381-164-1(0)*, Scholastic Pr.) Scholastic Australia.

Blake, Linda. My Pet Rabbit. 2012. 24p. 24.95 *(978-1-4626-6187-9(4))* America Star Bks.

Blake, Stéphanie. No Quiero Ir a la Escuela. 2007. (SPA., Illus.). 40p. (gr. k-2). 17.99 *(978-84-8470-268-9(5))* Corimbo, Editorial S.L. ESP. Dist: Lectorum Pubns., Inc.

Blaskowsky, Michael, tr. Sato the Rabbit. 2021. (Sato the Rabbit Ser.: 1). (Illus.). 68p. (J). (gr. 1-4). 17.95 *(978-1-59270-318-0(6))* Enchanted Lion Bks., LLC.

—Sato the Rabbit, a Sea of Tea. 2022. (Sato the Rabbit Ser.: 3). (Illus.). 72p. (J). (gr. 1-4). 17.95 *(978-1-59270-355-5(0))* Enchanted Lion Bks., LLC.

Blumberg, Margie. Sunny Bunnies. Goulding, June, illus. 2008. (ENG.). 32p. (gr. -1-k). 15.95 *(978-0-9624166-4-4(9))* MB Publishing, LLC.

Blunt, Fred. Santa Claus vs. the Easter Bunny. 2019. (ENG.). 32p. (J). (gr. -1-3). 12.99 *(978-1-4926-9164-8(X)*, Sourcebooks Jabberwocky) Sourcebooks, Inc.

Blunt, Fred, illus. The Rabbit's Tale. 2013. (Usborne First Reading: Level 1 Ser.). (ENG.). 32p. (J). (gr. -1-3). 6.99 *(978-0-7945-3346-5(9)*, Usborne) EDC Publishing.

Book Buddy: Rabbit with Story Book. Orig. Title: Child's Play. (Illus.). 10p. (J). (gr. -1-3). reprint ed. *(978-1-881469-47-6(6))* Safari, Ltd.

Book Company Staff. Who Am I: Rabbit. 2003. (Board Bks.). (Illus.). (J). bds. 10.95 *(978-1-74047-308-8(6))* Book Co. Publishing Pty, Ltd., The AUS. Dist: Penton Overseas, Inc.

Brackett, Michael. The Adventures of Bunny & Hare. 2010. 138p. pap. 11.00 *(978-1-60911-296-7(2)*, Eloquent Bks.) Strategic Book Publishing & Rights Agency (SBPRA).

Bradford, Danette J. Eric & Wrinkles Meet the Bunnyworms. Bunker, Thomas, illus. 2012. 28p. pap. 24.95 *(978-1-4560-4261-5(0))* America Star Bks.

Brafman, Joshua. Death Bunny! 2008. 248p. 26.95 *(978-0-595-51446-5(4))*; pap. 16.95 *(978-0-595-52098-5(7))* iUniverse, Inc.

Brandt-Taylor, Diane. The Bunny, the Bear, the Bug & the Bee. Brandt, Michael, illus. 2005. (J). cd-rom 9.88 *(978-0-9773236-0-9(9))* TaySysCo Publishing.

Bray, Sorcha. The Adventures of Powerpup & Wonderboy & the Case of the Wicked Chickens. 2010. 48p. pap. 19.75 *(978-1-4490-7133-2(3))* AuthorHouse.

Brennan, Sarah. The Tale of Rhonda Rabbit. Harrison, Harry, illus. 2012. (ENG.). 32p. (J). 24.95 *(978-1-937160-22-7(X))* Eliassen Creative.

Brenner, Barbara, et al. Bunny Tails. Munsinger, Lynn, illus. 2005. 32p. 15.95 *(978-0-689-03925-6(5)*, Milk & Cookies) ibooks, Inc.

Brett, Jan. The Animals' Santa. Brett, Jan, illus. (Illus.). (J). 2021. 34p. (— 1). bds. 9.99 *(978-1-9848-1680-1(2))* 2014. 40p. (gr. -1-k). 18.99 *(978-0-399-25784-1(5))* Penguin Young Readers Group. (G.P. Putnam's Sons Books for Young Readers).

—The Easter Egg. Brett, Jan, illus. (Illus.). 32p. (J). 2017. (— 1). bds. 9.99 *(978-0-399-54733-1(9))* 2010. (gr. -1-k). 19.99 *(978-0-399-25238-9(X))* Penguin Young Readers Group. (G.P. Putnam's Sons Books for Young Readers).

Brewin, Barbara. Sidney Snail's Wonderful World of Adventure. 2009. (Illus.). 32p. pap. 14.49 *(978-1-4389-4100-4(5))* AuthorHouse.

Bright, Rachel. Walter & the No-Need-To-Worry Suit (the Wonderful World of Walter & Winnie) 2015. (Wonderful World of Walter & Winnie Ser.). (ENG.). 32p. (J). 17.99 *(978-0-00-758594-6(2)*, HarperCollins Children's Bks.) HarperCollins Pubs. Ltd. GBR. Dist: HarperCollins Pubs.

Broster, Marie. Binky Bunny's Day Out & Poems for Children. 2006. (Illus.). 60p. pap. *(978-1-84401-793-5(1))* Athena Pr.

Brown, Margaret Wise. A Baby's Gift: Goodnight Moon & the Runaway Bunny, 2 vols. Hurd, Clement, illus. 2022. (ENG.). 70p. (J). (gr. -1 — 1). pap. 15.99 *(978-0-694-01638-9(1)*, HarperFestival) HarperCollins Pubs.

—Boa Noite Lua. pap. 19.95 *(978-85-336-0713-2(X))* Livraria Martins Editora BRA. Dist: Distribooks, Inc.

—Bonsoir Lune.Tr. of Goodnight Moon. (FRE.). (J). pap. 21.95 *(978-2-211-01028-3(8))* Archimede Editions FRA. Dist: Distribooks, Inc.

—Buenas Noches Conejito. 2006. (Illus.). 24p. (J). (gr. -1-k). 12.95 *(978-1-882077-63-2(6))* Sweetwater Pr.

—Buenas Noches, Luna. 2006.Tr. of Goodnight Moon. (SPA.). (J). (gr. -1-2). lib. bdg. 18.40 *(978-0-613-09961-5(3))* Turtleback.

—El Conejito Andarín: The Runaway Bunny (Spanish Edition), 1 vol. Hurd, Clement, illus. 2006. (SPA.). 48p. (J). (gr. -1-3). pap. 8.99 *(978-0-06-077694-7(3))* HarperCollins Español.

—Good Day, Good Night. Long, Loren, illus. 2017. (ENG.). 40p. (J). (gr. -1-3). 18.99 *(978-0-06-238310-5(8)*, HarperCollins) HarperCollins Pubs.

—Goodnight Moon. Hurd, Clement, illus. (ENG.). 32p. (J). (gr. -1-3). 2005. lib. bdg. 18.89 *(978-0-06-077586-5(6))* 60th anniv. ed. 2007. 18.99 *(978-0-06-077585-8(8))* 60th anniv. ed. 2007. pap. 8.99 *(978-0-06-443017-3(0))* HarperCollins Pubs. (HarperCollins).

—Goodnight Moon. 2007. (J). (gr. -1-2). lib. bdg. 18.40 *(978-0-8085-9386-7(2))* Turtleback.

—Goodnight Moon. Hurd, Clement, illus. (J). pap. 32.75 incl. audio. (gr. -1-3). 24.95 incl. audio Weston Woods Studios, Inc.

—Goodnight Moon 123: A Counting Book. Hurd, Clement, illus. 2007. (J). (ENG.). 32p. (gr. -1-k). 16.99 *(978-0-06-112593-5(8))*; 32p. (gr. -1-k). lib. bdg. 17.89 *(978-0-06-112594-2(6))*; *(978-1-4287-4853-8(9))* HarperCollins Pubs.

—Goodnight Moon 123 Padded Board Book: A Counting Book. Hurd, Clement, illus. 2013. (ENG.). 30p. (J). (gr. -1-k). bds. 9.99 *(978-0-06-224405-5(1)*, HarperFestival) HarperCollins Pubs.

—Goodnight Moon 123/Buenas Noches, Luna 123: A Counting Book/un Libro para Contar. Hurd, Clement, illus. 2007. (ENG & SPA.). 32p. (J). (gr. -1-k). 16.99 *(978-0-06-117325-7(8)*, Rayo) HarperCollins Pubs.

—Goodnight Moon Big Book. Hurd, Clement, illus. 2007. (ENG.). 32p. (J). (gr. -1-3). pap. 24.99 *(978-0-06-111977-4(6)*, HarperCollins) HarperCollins Pubs.

—Goodnight Moon Board Book. Hurd, Clement, illus. 60th anniv. ed. 2007. (ENG.). 34p. (J). (gr. -1 — 1). bds. 8.99 *(978-0-694-00361-7(1)*, HarperFestival) HarperCollins Pubs.

—Goodnight Moon Board Book & Bunny: An Easter & Springtime Book for Kids. Hurd, Clement, illus. 2005. (ENG.). 34p. (J). (gr. -1 — 1). bds. 21.99 *(978-0-06-076027-4(3)*, HarperFestival) HarperCollins Pubs.

—Goodnight Moon Classic Library: Contains Goodnight Moon, the Runaway Bunny, & My World. Hurd, Clement, illus. 2011. (ENG.). 32p. (J). (gr. -1-1). 17.99 *(978-0-06-199823-2(0)*, HarperCollins) HarperCollins Pubs.

—Goodnight Moon Cloth Book. Hurd, Clement, illus. 2012. (ENG.). 8p. (J). (gr. -1 — 1). pap. 14.99 *(978-0-06-076224-7(1)*, HarperFestival) HarperCollins Pubs.

—Margaret Wise Brown's the Whispering Rabbit. Won, Annie, illus. 2017. (J). *(978-1-5182-2279-8(1))*; 24p. 4.99 *(978-0-399-55518-3(8))* Random Hse. Children's Bks. (Golden Bks.).

—Mon Petit Monde (French edition of My World) 2004. 40p. 29.95 *(978-0-320-06689-4(4))* French & European Pubns., Inc.

—My World. 2004. (ENG., Illus.). 32p. (J). (gr. -1 — 1). pap. 7.99 *(978-0-694-01660-0(8)*, HarperCollins) HarperCollins Pubs.

—Over the Moon: a Collection of First Books: Goodnight Moon, the Runaway Bunny, & My World. Hurd, Clement, illus. 2006. (ENG.). 108p. (J). (gr. -1-1). 19.99 *(978-0-06-076162-2(8)*, HarperCollins) HarperCollins Pubs.

—The Runaway Bunny. Hurd, Clement, illus. 2005. (ENG.). 48p. (J). (gr. -1 — 1). lib. bdg. 18.89 *(978-0-06-077583-4(1)*, HarperCollins) HarperCollins Pubs.

—The Runaway Bunny: An Easter & Springtime Book for Kids. Hurd, Clement, illus. 2017. (ENG.). 48p. (J). (gr. -1-3). 21.99 *(978-0-06-077582-7(3))*; pap. 9.99 *(978-0-06-443018-0(9))* HarperCollins Pubs. (HarperCollins).

—The Runaway Bunny Board Book: An Easter & Springtime Book for Kids. Hurd, Clement, illus. 2017. (ENG.). 34p. (J). (gr. -1 — 1). bds. 8.99 *(978-0-06-107429-5(2)*, HarperFestival) HarperCollins Pubs.

—The Runaway Bunny Lap Edition: An Easter & Springtime Book for Kids. Hurd, Clement, illus. 2017. (ENG.). 36p. (J). (gr. -1 — 1). bds. 12.99 *(978-0-694-01671-6(3)*, HarperFestival) HarperCollins Pubs.

Brown, Tiffanie & Duncan, Kathryn. Benny Builds a House. 2012. 16p. pap. 12.95 *(978-1-257-93819-3(3))* Lulu Pr., Inc.

Bruna, Dick. Miffy Dances. 2004. (Illus.). 24p. pap. 4.99 *(978-1-59226-010-2(1))* Big Tent Entertainment, Inc.

—Miffy Says, I Love You! 2004. (Illus.). 12p. bds. 5.99 *(978-1-59226-187-1(6))* Big Tent Entertainment, Inc.

—Miffy the Artist Activity Book. 2018. (ENG., Illus.). 28p. (J). (gr. -1-k). pap. 12.95 *(978-1-84976-578-7(2)*, 1315403) Tate Publishing, Ltd. GBR. Dist: Hachette Bk. Group.

—Miffy the Artist Lift-The-Flap Book. 2016. (ENG., Illus.). 12p. (J). (gr. -1-k). bds. 14.50 *(978-1-84976-395-0(X)*, 1647910) Tate Publishing, Ltd. GBR. Dist: Hachette Bk. Group.

Bryan, Sean. A Boy & His Bunny. Murphy, Tom, illus. 2011. (ENG.). 32p. (J). (gr. -1-k). 14.95 *(978-1-61145-023-1(3)*, 611023, Arcade Publishing) Skyhorse Publishing Co., Inc.

Bryson, Brenda. The Adventures of Roo & Winston. 2007. (ENG.). 82p. pap. *(978-1-4357-0145-8(3))* Lulu Pr., Inc.

—The Adventures of Roo & Winston - Crop Circles. 2009. 64p. pap. 12.43 *(978-0-557-17564-2(X))* Lulu Pr., Inc.

Bugbird, Tim. The Love in My Heart. Wickenden, Nadine, illus. 2014. (ENG.). 28p. (J). (— 1). bds. 7.99 *(978-1-78235-966-1(4))* Make Believe Ideas GBR. Dist: Scholastic, Inc.

Buitrago, Jairo. Two White Rabbits, 1 vol. Amado, Elisa, tr. Yockteng, Rafael, illus. 2015. (ENG.). 56p. (J). (gr. k-2). 19.99 *(978-1-55498-741-2(5))* Groundwood Bks. CAN. Dist: Publishers Group West (PGW).

Bunce, Margaret. Adventures with Nature: A Story about Olivia & Her Little Dog, Jake. 2011. 24p. pap. 12.95 *(978-1-4567-2497-9(5))* AuthorHouse.

Bunnicula. 2005. (J). *(978-1-59564-838-9(0))* Steps To Literacy, LLC.

Bunny's House. Date not set. (Illus.). (J). bds. 4.98 *(978-1-4054-0785-4(9))* Parragon, Inc.

Burgess, Thornton. The Adventures of Peter Cottontail. 2018. (Thornton Burgess Library). (ENG., Illus.). 128p. (J). (gr. 2-5). 22.65 *(978-1-942875-61-1(4)*, a31eb61a-89cf-4eed-bb15-cc7c433e62e6, Seagrass) Quarto Publishing Group USA.

Burgess, Thornton W. The Adventures of Jimmy Skunk. 112p. 2008. per. 9.95 *(978-1-60312-416-4(0))* 2007. 22.95 *(978-1-60312-594-9(9))* Aegypan.

—The Adventures of Lightfoot the Deer. 2008. 108p. (gr. -1-3). 22.95 *(978-1-60664-951-0(5))* Aegypan.

—The Adventures of Old Mr Toad. 2007. 140p. (gr. 4-7). 24.95 *(978-1-60312-637-3(6))*; per. 11.95 *(978-1-60312-379-2(2))* Aegypan.

—The Adventures of Old Mr Toad. 2011. 138p. 25.95 *(978-1-4638-9561-7(5))* Rodgers, Alan Bks.

—The Adventures of Paddy the Beaver. 2008. 108p. per. 9.95 *(978-1-60312-502-4(7))* Aegypan.

—The Adventures of Poor Mrs Quack. 2008. 124p. (gr. 4-7). per. 10.95 *(978-1-60312-417-1(9))* Aegypan.

—Big Book of Animal Stories. 2011. (Dover Children's Classics Ser.). (ENG., Illus.). 272p. (J). (gr. 3-8). 9.95 *(978-0-486-41980-0(0)*, 419800) Dover Pubns., Inc.

—Mrs. Peter Rabbit. (J). 18.95 *(978-0-8488-0390-2(6))* Amereon Ltd.

—Mrs Peter Rabbit. 120p. (gr. -1-3). 2007. per. 10.95 *(978-1-60312-005-0(X))* 2006. 22.95 *(978-1-59818-464-8(4))* Aegypan.

—Mrs Peter Rabbit. 2011. 118p. 23.95 *(978-1-4638-9573-0(9))* Rodgers, Alan Bks.

—Mrs. Peter Rabbit. 2004. reprint ed. pap. 15.95 *(978-1-4191-3581-1(3))*; pap. 1.99 *(978-1-4192-3581-8(8))* Kessinger Publishing, LLC.

—Old Mother West Wind. 2008. 112p. per. 9.95 *(978-1-60312-453-9(5))*; 22.95 *(978-1-60312-551-2(5))* Aegypan.

Burks II, Tony Lamair. The Tale of Imani the Bunny. 2013. 24p. pap. 14.95 *(978-1-62646-460-5(X))* Booklocker.com, Inc.

Burton, Jeffrey. The Itsy Bitsy Bunny. Rescek, Sanja, illus. 2016. (Itsy Bitsy Ser.). (ENG.). 16p. (J). (gr. -1 — 1). bds. 5.99 *(978-1-4814-5621-0(0)*, Little Simon) Little Simon.

Bush, Martha Faircloth. Helping Hurting Children: a Journey of Healing: Children's Workbook. 2013. 174p. pap. 19.95 *(978-1-4497-8527-7(1)*, WestBow Pr.) Author Solutions, LLC.

Butler, Dori. The Tortoise & the Hare: An Aesop's Fable. 2006. (J). pap. *(978-1-4108-6167-2(8))* Benchmark Education Co.

Calvani, Mayra. Humberto, the Bookworm Hamster. Grady, Kit, illus. 2009. 20p. pap. 10.95 *(978-1-935137-92-4(1))* Guardian Angel Publishing, Inc.

Cannon, Sherrill S. Peter & the Whimper-Whineys. 2010. 30p. pap. 13.00 *(978-1-60911-517-3(1)*, Strategic Bk. Publishing) Strategic Book Publishing & Rights Agency (SBPRA).

Capobianco, Sue Murphy. Buttons the Bunny of Button Cove Lane. 2013. (ENG., Illus.). (J). 14.95 *(978-1-62086-377-0(4))* Amplify Publishing Group.

Capucilli, Alyssa Satin. Biscuit Meets the Class Pet. Schories, Pat, illus. 2009. (My First I Can Read Ser.). (ENG.). 32p. (J). (gr. -1-3). 16.99 *(978-0-06-117747-7(4))*; pap. 4.99 *(978-0-06-117749-1(0))* HarperCollins Pubs. (HarperCollins).

—Biscuit Meets the Class Pet. 2009. (Biscuit: My First I Can Read! Ser.). (J). lib. bdg. 13.55 *(978-0-606-06960-1(7))* Turtleback.

Cardarelli, Mario. Bunny, an Orphan's Story. 2008. 44p. pap. 18.99 *(978-1-4389-1597-5(7))* AuthorHouse.

Cardoza, Kristina. Pinky Bunny's First Day of Kindergarten. 2011. 16p. pap. 8.75 *(978-1-4634-8753-9(3))* AuthorHouse.

Carlson, Amanda. Sultenfuss Moose's Lost Slipper. 2006. 26p. 18.03 *(978-1-4116-7729-6(3))* Lulu Pr., Inc.

Carlson, Nancy. Get up & Go! 2008. (Illus.). 32p. (J). (gr. -1-k). pap. 8.99 *(978-0-14-241064-6(0)*, Puffin Books) Penguin Young Readers Group.

—Get up & Go! 2008. (Illus.). (gr. -1-3). 16.00 *(978-0-7569-8922-4(1))* Perfection Learning Corp.

—Harriet & George's Christmas Treat. Carlson, Nancy, illus. 2005. (Picture Bks.). (Illus.). 32p. (J). (gr. k-2). 15.95 *(978-1-57505-506-0(6))* Lerner Publishing Group.

—Harriet & George's Christmas Treat. 2003. (Nancy Carlson Picture Bks.). (ENG., Illus.). 32p. (J). (gr. k-2). pap. 9.99 *(978-1-57505-639-5(9)*, 095cb739-adba-4722-8c24-812dfe50efe7, Carolrhoda Bks.) Lerner Publishing Group.

—Harriet & the Roller Coaster. 20th anniv. ed. 2005. (Nancy Carlson's Neighborhood Ser.). (Illus.). 32p. (gr. k-2). 15.95 *(978-1-57505-053-9(6))* Lerner Publishing Group.

—Harriet & the Roller Coaster, 2nd Edition. 20th anniv. rev. ed. 2003. (Nancy Carlson Picture Bks.). (ENG., Illus.). 32p. (J). (gr. k-2). 9.99 *(978-1-57505-202-1(4)*, cf2be221-f1ca-4ad7-ac76-d165cc58536f, Carolrhoda Bks.) Lerner Publishing Group.

—Loudmouth George & the Big Race. rev. ed. 2004. (Carolrhoda Picture Books Ser.). (ENG., Illus.). 32p. (J). (gr. k-2). 15.95 *(978-1-57505-673-9(9))* Lerner Publishing Group.

—Loudmouth George & the Sixth Grade Bully. 20th anniv. ed. 2005. (Nancy Carlson's Neighborhood Ser.). (Illus.). 32p. (J). (gr. k-2). 15.95 *(978-1-57505-218-2(0))* Lerner Publishing Group.

—Loudmouth George & the Sixth-Grade Bully, 2nd Edition. 2nd anniv. rev. ed. 2003. (Nancy Carlson Picture Bks.). (ENG., Illus.). 32p. (J). (gr. k-2). pap. 9.99 *(978-1-57505-549-7(X)*, 7bb72f75-f453-46b0-a06a-3e3291d31014, Carolrhoda Bks.) Lerner Publishing Group.

—Loudmouth George Earns His Allowance. Carlson, Nancy, illus. 2007. (ENG., Illus.). 32p. (J). (gr. k-2). 15.95 *(978-0-8225-6560-4(9)*, Carolrhoda Bks.) Lerner Publishing Group.

Carrer, Chiara. Otto Carrotto. 2011. (ENG., Illus.). 26p. (YA). (gr. -1-3). 16.00 *(978-0-8028-5393-6(5)*, Eerdmans Bks For Young Readers) Eerdmans, William B. Publishing Co.

Carroll, Kathy. Rabbit & the Amazing Hopping Contest. 2007. (Illus.). 16p. (J). 9.99 *(978-0-9791401-6-7(1))* Abecedarian Bks.

Carrotblanca. Date not set. (J). 7.98 incl. audio *(978-1-57042-320-8(2))* Warner Brothers Records.

Casey, Dawn. A Lullaby for Little One. Fuge, Charles, illus. 2015. (ENG.). 32p. (J). (-k). 12.99 *(978-0-7636-7608-7(X))* Candlewick Pr.

Cate, Annette LeBlanc. The Magic Rabbit. Cate, Annette LeBlanc, illus. 2013. (ENG., Illus.). 32p. (J). (gr. -1-1). 21.19 *(978-0-7636-2672-3(4))*; 7.99 *(978-0-7636-6685-9(8))* Candlewick Pr.

—The Magic Rabbit. 2013. lib. bdg. 17.20 *(978-0-606-31601-9(9))* Turtleback.

Caviezel, Giovanni. It's Easter Time. Pagnoni, Roberta, illus. 2010. 10p. (J). (gr. -1-k). bds. 6.99 *(978-0-7641-6334-0(5))* Sourcebooks, Inc.

—Little Bunny. Rigo, Laura, illus. 2012. (Mini Look at Me Bks.). 10p. (J). (gr. -1). bds. 5.99 *(978-0-7641-6509-2(7))* Sourcebooks, Inc.

Chaconas, Dori. Looking for Easter, 1 vol. Moore, Margie, illus. 2011. (Holiday Books: Easter Ser.). (ENG.). 32p. (J). (gr. -1-3). 21.19 *(978-0-8075-4749-6(2))* Whitman, Albert & Co.

—Looking for Easter. Moore, Margie, illus. 2012. 32p. (J). 34.28 *(978-1-61913-120-0(X))* Weigl Pubs., Inc.

Chafe, Justin. Bunny Rabbit on the Moon. 2007. (Illus.). 28p. (J). 14.95 *(978-0-9787660-0-9(8))* Baboosic Enterprises, LLC.

Chambers, Dori. Princesses' Pink Pillows. 2009. 20p. pap. 10.50 *(978-1-60693-431-9(7)*, Eloquent Bks.) Strategic Book Publishing & Rights Agency (SBPRA).

Chance, C. The Trepets Book Three Rabbit Race Day. Champion, Vanessa, illus. 2007. 112p. per. *(978-0-9551289-2-9(7)*, Bumble Bks.) Dragonfly Bks. & Arts.

Chandler, Pauline. Mr. Rabbit the Farmer. Smith, Eric, illus. 2005. (ENG.). 24p. (J). lib. bdg. 23.65 *(978-1-59646-736-1(3))* Dingles & Co.

Charles Santore. The Velveteen Rabbit (Kohl's Edition) Charles Santore, illus. 2012. (ENG., Illus.). 48p. (J). 5.00 *(978-1-60464-032-8(4)*, Applesauce Pr.) Cider Mill Pr. Bk. Pubs., LLC.

Chase, Kit. Oliver's Tree. Chase, Kit, illus. 2014. (ENG., Illus.). 32p. (J). (gr. -1-k). 17.99 *(978-0-399-25700-1(4)*, G.P. Putnam's Sons Books for Young Readers) Penguin Young Readers Group.

Chattin, A. K. Dust Bunnies, 1 vol. 2009. 48p. pap. 16.95 *(978-1-61582-872-2(9))* America Star Bks.

Chaud, Benjamin. Farewell Floppy. 2015. (ENG., Illus.). 40p. (J). (gr. -1-k). 17.99 *(978-1-4521-3734-6(X))* Chronicle Bks. LLC.

Chavez, Joe. Benny the Bunny & Jesus. 2013. 136p. (J). pap. 9.99 *(978-1-62697-463-0(2))* Salem Author Services.

The Christmas Rabbit. 2009. (J). per. 17.95 net. *(978-0-9749915-2-8(X))* Sawmill Publishing.

Chronicle Books. Baby Bunny: Finger Puppet Book. Huang, Yu-Hsuan, illus. 2017. (Baby Animal Finger Puppets Ser.: 5). (ENG.). 12p. (J). 7.99 *(978-1-4521-5609-5(3))* Chronicle Bks. LLC.

—Hug Me Little Bunny: Finger Puppet Book: (Finger Puppet Books, Baby Board Books, Sensory Books, Bunny Books for Babies, Touch & Feel Books) 2019. (Hug Me Little Animals Ser.). (ENG., Illus.). 10p. (J). (gr. -1 — 1). bds. 9.99 *(978-1-4521-7522-5(5))* Chronicle Bks. LLC.

Chronicle Books & Bundo, Marlon. Last Week Tonight with John Oliver Presents: a Day in the Life of Marlon Bundo. Twiss, Jill, illus. 2018. (Hbo Ser.). (ENG.). 40p. (gr. 1-3). 18.99 *(978-1-4521-7380-1(X))* Chronicle Bks. LLC.

Chronicle Books & ImageBooks. Little Bunny: Finger Puppet Book: (Finger Puppet Book for Toddlers & Babies, Baby Books for First Year, Animal Finger Puppets) 2006. (Little Finger Puppet Board Bks.: FING). (ENG., Illus.). 12p. (J). (gr. -1 — 1). bds. 7.99 *(978-0-8118-5644-7(5))* Chronicle Bks. LLC.

Churchman, Jennifer & Churchman, John. The Easter Surprise. (Sweet Pea & Friends Ser.: 5). (ENG., Illus.). (J). (gr. -1 — 1). 2020. 22p. bds. 8.99 *(978-0-316-53822-0(1))* 2019. 40p. 17.99 *(978-0-316-41166-0(3))* Little, Brown Bks. for Young Readers.

Circle of Friends: The Camelot Rabbitry Series - Volume Three. 2006. (Camelot Rabbitry Ser.: 3). (Illus.). 98p. (J). per. 9.95 *(978-0-9672375-3-4(X))* Camelot Tales.

Clare, Caitlen. A Rabbit Hash Christmas. Haltermon, Becky, illus. 2012. 36p. (J). 10.00 *(978-0-9816123-9-3(3))* Merlot Group, LLC, The.

Clarke, Graham. Fluffy Rabbit & Friends. 2016. (ENG.). 117p. (J). (gr. 1-2). 10.95 *(978-1-78554-339-5(3)*, 07de99a4-7d8a-49e2-a67f-bd3e598c96d1) Austin Macauley Pubs. Ltd. GBR. Dist: Baker & Taylor Publisher Services (BTPS).

Climo, Liz. Please Don't Eat Me. 2019. (ENG., Illus.). 40p. (J). (gr. -1-3). 17.99 *(978-0-316-31525-8(7))* Little, Brown Bks. for Young Readers.

Clymer, Susan. There's a Rabbit in My Backpack. 2007. 100p. pap. 8.50 *(978-1-4303-2959-6(9))* Lulu Pr., Inc.

Cocca-Leffler, Maryann. Easter Bunny in Training. Cocca-Leffler, Maryann, illus. 2009. (Sneak a Peek Ser.). (Illus.). 16p. (J). (gr. -1-3). pap. 6.99 *(978-0-06-125673-8(0))* HarperCollins Pubs.

Coe, Jara & Hardy, Donna. Jack Meets the New Baby. 2010. 32p. 12.99 *(978-1-4520-7420-7(8))* AuthorHouse.

Coe, Victoria J. Fenway & Hattie & the Evil Bunny Gang. 2018. (Fenway & Hattie Ser.: 2). (ENG.). 208p. (J). (gr. 3-7). 8.99 *(978-1-101-99634-8(X)*, Puffin Books) Penguin Young Readers Group.

Coffelt, Soraya. It's Not about You, Mr. Easter Bunny: A Love Letter about the True Meaning of Easter. Seroya, Tea, illus. 2017. (Love Letters Book Ser.). (ENG.). 36p. (J). pap. 8.99 *(978-1-68350-063-6(6))* Morgan James Publishing.

Coll-Seck, Jayden. Roddy the Rabbit, 1 vol., 1. 2015. (Rosen REAL Readers: Social Studies Nonfiction / Fiction: Myself, My Community, My World Ser.). (ENG.). 8p. (J). (gr. k-1). pap. 5.46 *(978-1-5081-1833-6(7)*, 94988bd4-bd10-44fd-8ed6-0f47fb4b610d, Rosen Classroom) Rosen Publishing Group, Inc., The.

Conejito Azul: Es un Valiente Socorrista.Tr. of Little Blue Bunny: Fairy Tale Story of Bunny Rabbit to the Rescue. (SPA.). (J). 2.98 *(978-970-22-0018-5(0))* Larousse, Ediciones, S. A. de C. V. MEX. Dist: Continental Bk. Co., Inc.

Conejito Azul: Salva a los Peces.Tr. of Bunny Rabbit Saves the Fish. (SPA.). (J). 2.98 *(978-970-22-0021-5(0))* Larousse, Ediciones, S. A. de C. V. MEX. Dist: Continental Bk. Co., Inc.

Conejito Azul: Y la Aventura de Pap Conejo.Tr. of Bunny Rabbit-Father's Adventure. (SPA.). (J). 2.98 (978-970-22-0019-2(9)) Larousse, Ediciones, S. A. de C. V. MEX. Dist: Continental Bk. Co., Inc.

Connolly, Patrick. The Adventures of Funny, the Amazing Fish-Bunny. 2013. (ENG.). 70p. (YA). pap. 13.95 (978-1-4787-0440-9(3)) Outskirts Pr., Inc.

Conrad, Liz, illus. Little Bunny. 2009. (My Sparkling Springtime Friends Ser.). (ENG.). 10p. (J). bds. 3.95 (978-1-58117-865-4(4), Intervisual/Piggy Toes) Bendon, Inc.

Constantinople, Louise T. The Adventures of Ralph Ribbit. 2012. (ENG.). 103p. pap. 8.95 (978-1-4327-8853-7(1)) Outskirts Pr., Inc.

Conte, Paola, et al. Some Bunny to Talk To: A Story for Children about Going to Therapy. Beeke, Tiphanie, illus. 2014. 32p. (J). pap. (978-1-4338-1650-5(4), Magination Pr.) American Psychological Assn.

Cook, Sherry & Johnson, Terri. Ronnie Rock. 26. Kuhn, Jesse, illus. I.t. ed. 2006. (Quirkles — Exploring Phonics through Science Ser.: 18). 32p. (J). 7.99 (978-1-933815-17-6(5), Quirkles, The) Creative 3, LLC.

—Vinnie Volcano. 26. Kuhn, Jesse, illus. I.t. ed. 2006. (Quirkles — Exploring Phonics through Science Ser.: 22). 32p. (J). 7.99 (978-1-933815-21-3(3), Quirkles, The) Creative 3, LLC.

Cooper, Helen S. Tatty-Ratty. Cooper, Helen S., illus. 2004. (Illus.). 28p. (J). (gr. k-3). reprint ed. 19.00 (978-0-7567-7214-7(1)) DIANE Publishing Co.

Cooper, Robert. The Light Behind Their Eyes: The Story of Jack & Bunny Rabbit. 2005. 92p. pap. 33.75 (978-1-4184-0722-3(4)) AuthorHouse.

Corse, Nicole. Pet Heroes. 2011. (Scholastic Reader, Level 3 Ser.). (ENG.). 32p. (J). (gr. 1-3). pap. 3.99 (978-0-545-25837-1(5)) Scholastic, Inc.

Cory, David. Little Jack Rabbit's Favorite Bunny Tales. Day, Maurice, illus. 2014. (ENG.). 320p. (J). (gr. 1-5). pap. 12.99 (978-0-486-78556-1(4)) Dover Pubns., Inc.

Cosgrove, Stephen. The Grumpling. James, Robin, illus. 2003. (Serendipity Bks.). (Orig.). (J). (gr. k-4). 12.65 (978-0-7569-5259-4(X)) Perfection Learning Corp.

Coven, Wanda. Heidi Heckelbeck & the Tie-Dyed Bunny. 2014. (Heidi Heckelbeck Ser.: 10). lib. bdg. 16.00 (978-0-606-35429-5(8)) Turtleback.

Covey, Sean. A Place for Everything: Habit 3. Curtis, Stacy, illus. (7 Habits of Happy Kids Ser.: 3). (ENG.). 32p. (J). (gr. -1-1). 2018. 6.99 (978-1-5344-1580-5(7)) 2010. 7.99 (978-1-4169-9425-1(4)) Simon & Schuster Bks. For Young Readers. (Simon & Schuster Bks. For Young Readers).

—A Place for Everything: Habit 3 (Ready-To-Read Level 2) Curtis, Stacy, illus. 2019. (7 Habits of Happy Kids Ser.: 3). (ENG.). 32p. (J). (gr. k-2). 17.99 (978-1-5344-4451-5(3)); pap. 4.99 (978-1-5344-4450-8(5)) Simon Spotlight. (Simon Spotlight).

Cowell, Cressida. That Rabbit Belongs to Emily Brown. Layton, Neal, illus. 2007. (ENG.). 40p. (gr. -1-3). 16.99 (978-1-4231-0645-6(8)) Hyperion Pr.

Craddock, Erik. Dragon Boogie. 2012. (Stone Rabbit Ser.: 7). lib. bdg. 17.20 (978-0-606-23868-7(9)) Turtleback.

—Robot Frenzy. 2013. (Stone Rabbit Ser.: 8). lib. bdg. 17.20 (978-0-606-27004-5(3)) Turtleback.

—Stone Rabbit #5: Ninja Slice. Craddock, Erik, illus. 2010. (Stone Rabbit Ser.: 5). (Illus.). 96p. (J). (gr. 3-7). pap. 6.99 (978-0-375-86723-1(6), Random Hse. Bks. for Young Readers) Random Hse. Children's Bks.

Crann, Jacqueline J. Answers for Xavier: How Did I Get Here Mommy? 2010. 28p. pap. 13.99 (978-1-4490-3872-4(7)) AuthorHouse.

Creamer, Joan Klatil. The Magic Sceptre & Reginald the Rabbit. 2007. (Illus.). 32p. (J). 16.95 (978-0-9778476-5-5(9)) Silver Snowflake Publishing.

Crimi, Carolyn. Henry & the Buccaneer Bunnies. Manders, John, illus. 2009. (ENG.). 40p. (J). (gr. -1-3). pap. 8.99 (978-0-7636-4540-3(0)) Candlewick Pr.

Cronin, Doreen. Rescue Bunnies. Menchin, Scott, illus. 2010. (ENG.). 32p. (J). (gr. -1-3). 16.99 (978-0-06-112871-4(6), Balzer & Bray) HarperCollins Pubs.

Crummel, Susan Stevens. Tumbleweed Stew. Stevens, Janet, illus. 2003. (Green Light Readers Ser.). (ENG.). 32p. (J). (gr. -1-3). pap. 4.99 (978-0-15-204830-3(8), 1194585, Clarion Bks.) HarperCollins Pubs.

—Tumbleweed Stew/Sopa de Matojos: Bilingual English & Spanish. Stevens, Janet, illus. 2009. (Green Light Readers Ser.). (ENG.). 36p. (J). (gr. -1-3). pap. 5.99 (978-0-547-25261-2(7), 1271215, Clarion Bks.) HarperCollins Pubs.

Cummins, Chris. Bigsbie - A Bunny's Tale of Surviving Cancer. 2007. 107p. pap. 15.00 (978-1-4116-5785-4(3)) Lulu Pr., Inc.

Dahl, Michael. Bunny Eats Lunch. 1 vol. Vidal, Oriol, illus. 2010. (Hello Genius Ser.). (ENG.). 20p. (J). (gr. -1 — 1). bds. 7.99 (978-1-4048-5728-5(1), 102305, Picture Window Bks.) Capstone.

Davies, Katie. The Great Rabbit Rescue. Shaw, Hannah, illus. 2011. (Great Critter Capers Ser.). (ENG.). 224p. (J). (gr. 3-7). 12.99 (978-1-4424-2064-9(2), Beach Lane Bks.) Beach Lane Bks.

Davis, Chasta. The Easter Bunny & His Famous Painted Eggs. 2011. 28p. pap. 24.95 (978-1-4512-1649-3(1)) America Star Bks.

Davis, Jacky. Black Belt Bunny. Fleck, Jay, illus. 2017. 40p. (J). (-k). 16.99 (978-0-525-42902-9(6), Dial Bks) Penguin Young Readers Group.

Davis, Kathryn Lynn. Wake up! Wake Up! A Springtime Lift-The-Flap Book. Davis, Kathryn Lynn, illus. 2011. (ENG., Illus.). 14p. (J). (gr. -1 — 1). bds. 5.99 (978-1-4424-1217-0(8), Little Simon) Little Simon.

De Sena, Joseph. The Butterfly & the Bunny's Tail. Anfuso, Dennis, illus. 2007. 60p. per. 19.95 (978-1-4327-0404-9(4)) Outskirts Pr., Inc.

Dean, James & Dean, Kimberly. Pete the Cat: Big Easter Adventure: An Easter & Springtime Book for Kids. Dean, James, illus. 2014. (Pete the Cat Ser.). (ENG., Illus.). 24p. (J). (gr. -1-3). 10.99 (978-0-06-219867-9(X), HarperFestival) HarperCollins Pubs.

—Pete the Cat: Five Little Bunnies: An Easter & Springtime Book for Kids. Dean, James, illus. 2020. (Pete the Cat Ser.). (ENG., Illus.). 24p. (J). (gr. -1-3). 9.99 (978-0-06-286829-9(2), HarperCollins) HarperCollins Pubs.

Degen, Bruce. Snow Joke. 2014. 24p. pap. (978-0-8234-3223-3(8)) Holiday Hse., Inc.

DeLuise, Dom & Carter, Derek. Pouch Potato. 2007. 33p. pap. 9.95 (978-0-9717952-0-4(7)) Bacchus Bks.

Denise, Anika A. Bunny in the Middle. Denise, Christopher, illus. 2019. (ENG.). 40p. (J). 17.99 (978-1-250-12036-6(5), 900173006, Holt, Henry & Co. Bks. For Young Readers) Holt, Henry & Co.

Depken, Kristen L. Here Comes Peter Cottontail. 2012. (Step into Reading Level 2 Ser.). lib. bdg. 13.55 (978-0-606-23719-2(4)) Turtleback.

—Tawny Scrawny Lion. DiCicco, Sue, illus. 2016. (Step into Reading Ser.). 32p. (J). (gr. -1-1). pap. 4.99 (978-1-101-93424-1(7), Random Hse. Bks. for Young Readers) Random Hse. Children's Bks.

deRubertis, Barbara. Jeremy Jackrabbit's Jumping Journey. Alley, R. W., illus. 2010. (Animal Antics a to Z Ser.). 32p. (J). (gr. -1-3). pap. 7.95 (978-1-57565-314-3(1), 68d98f86-9489-46bd-b9a9-7247fa0e0d0c, Kane Press) Astra Publishing Hse.

DeVogt, Rindia M. Tommy Hare & the Color Purple. 1 vol. Trogdon, Kathryn, illus. 2009. (ENG.). 22p. pap. 24.95 (978-1-61582-827-2(3)) America Star Bks.

Dew, Rachel. The Big Bunny Bed. 2009. 12p. pap. 11.50 (978-1-60693-316-9(7), Eloquent Bks.) Strategic Book Publishing & Rights Agency (SBPRA).

Dewdney, Anna. Nobunny's Perfect. 2012. (ENG.). 32p. (J). (gr. -1-k). bds. 7.99 (978-0-670-01408-8(7), Viking Books for Young Readers) Penguin Young Readers Group.

Dharma Publishing Staff. The Rabbit Who Overcame Fear: A Story about Wise Action. 2nd ed. 2013. (Jataka Tales Ser.). (Illus.). 36p. (gr. -1-7). pap. 8.95 (978-0-89800-492-2(6)) Dharma Publishing.

Diabate, Keba & Sumnicht, Patricia. The Hyena & the Rabbit. Sullens, Anais, illus. 2015. (J). pap. 10.00 (978-1-59598-370-1(8)) HenschelHAUS Publishing, Inc.

Dicamillo, Kate. The Miraculous Journey of Edward Tulane. 2012. 22.00 (978-1-61383-813-6(1)) Perfection Learning Corp.

—The Miraculous Journey of Edward Tulane. 2015. lib. bdg. 17.20 (978-0-606-37892-5(8)) Turtleback.

DiCamillo, Kate. The Miraculous Journey of Edward Tulane. Ibatoulline, Bagram, illus. (ENG.). (J). 2015. 240p. (gr. 2-5). pap. 8.99 (978-0-7636-8090-9(7)) 2009. 228p. (gr. 2-5). pap. 14.99 (978-0-7636-4783-4(7)) 2006. 228p. (gr. 1-4). 19.99 (978-0-7636-2589-4(2)) Candlewick Pr.

Dicamillo, Kate. The Miraculous Journey of Edward Tulane. Ibatoulline, Bagram, illus. 2009. 198p. (gr. 8-12). 23.30 (978-1-4178-0763-5(6)) Turtleback.

Diehl, Joan. Don't Call Me Bunny! 2018. (ENG., Illus.). 24p. (J). (gr. 1-4). pap. 9.95 (978-1-55571-905-0(8), Grid Pr.) L & R Publishing, LLC.

Disney Books. Disney Bunnies: an Eggcellent Day. 2017. (ENG., Illus.). 12p. (J). (gr. -1-k). bds. 7.99 (978-1-4847-7369-7(1), Disney Press Books) Disney Publishing Worldwide.

—Disney Bunnies: I Love You, My Bunnies Reissue with Stickers. 2017. (ENG., Illus.). 24p. (J). (gr. -1-k). pap. 4.99 (978-1-4847-7370-3(5), Disney Press Books) Disney Publishing Worldwide.

—Disney Bunnies: Thumper's Fluffy Tail. rev. ed. 2008. (Touch-And-feel Book Ser.). (ENG., Illus.). 12p. (J). (gr. -1-k). bds. 6.99 (978-1-4231-0443-8(9), Disney Press Books) Disney Publishing Worldwide.

—Disney Bunnies: Thumper's Furry Friends. 2010. (Touch-And-feel Book Ser.). (ENG.). 12p. (J). (gr. -1-k). bds. 6.99 (978-1-4231-1840-4(5), Disney Press Books) Disney Publishing Worldwide.

—Thumper Finds an Egg. 2009. (ENG., Illus.). 24p. (J). (gr. -1-k). pap. 3.99 (978-1-4231-1717-9(4), Disney Press Books) Disney Publishing Worldwide.

DiTerlizzi, Tony. Kenny & the Book of Beasts. DiTerlizzi, Tony, illus. (Kenny & the Dragon Ser.). (ENG., Illus.). (J). (gr. 3-7). 2021. 240p. pap. 8.99 (978-1-4424-8650-8(3)) 2020. 224p. 17.99 (978-1-4169-8316-3(3)) Simon & Schuster Bks. For Young Readers. (Simon & Schuster Bks. For Young Readers).

—Kenny & the Dragon. 2008. (Playaway Children Ser.). (J). (gr. 3-7). 39.99 (978-1-60640-958-9(1)) Findaway World, LLC.

—Kenny & the Dragon. DiTerlizzi, Tony, illus. 2012. (Kenny & the Dragon Ser.). (ENG., Illus.). 176p. (J). (gr. 3-7). pap. 8.99 (978-1-4424-3651-0(4), Simon & Schuster Bks. For Young Readers) Simon & Schuster Bks. For Young Readers.

—Kenny & the Dragon. DiTerlizzi, Tony, illus. 2008. (Illus.). 160p. (J). (gr. 3-7). 15.99 Simon & Schuster Children's Publishing.

—Kenny & the Dragon. DiTerlizzi, Tony, illus. 2008. (Kenny & the Dragon Ser.). (ENG., Illus.). 160p. (J). (gr. 3-7). 17.99 (978-1-4169-3977-1(6)) Simon & Schuster, Inc.

Divine, Jill. Wicked Rabbit. 2011. (Illus.). 86p. pap. 12.95 (978-1-4457-3797-3(3)) Lulu Pr., Inc.

Dixon, Bob. Holiday Bunny. 2009. 28p. pap. 13.99 (978-1-4490-0436-1(9)) AuthorHouse.

DK. The Adventures of Brer Rabbit & Friends. Copeland, Eric, illus. 2006. (ENG.). 64p. (J). (gr. 5-12). per. 6.99 (978-0-7566-1813-1(4), DK Children) Dorling Kindersley Publishing, Inc.

Doan, Nicholas. Fat Rabbit Farm: Big T's Big Adventure. 2012. (ENG.). pap. 17.95 (978-1-4675-2918-1(4)) Independent Pub.

Dockray, Tracy. My Life Story. Dockray, Tracy, illus. 2003. (Illus.). 40p. (J). lib. bdg. 15.95 (978-1-58717-218-2(6), SeaStar Bks.) Chronicle Bks. LLC.

Dodd, Emma. Love. Dodd, Emma, illus. (Emma Dodd's Love You Bks.). (ENG., Illus.). (J). (— 1). 2018. 22p. bds. 9.99 (978-0-7636-9941-3(1)) 2016. 24p. 14.99 (978-0-7636-8941-4(6)) Candlewick Pr.

Doerrfeld, Cori. Little Bunny Foo Foo: The Real Story. 2016. (Illus.). 32p. (J). (-k). pap. 8.99 (978-1-101-99774-1(5), Puffin Books) Penguin Young Readers Group.

—The Rabbit Listened. Doerrfeld, Cori, illus. 2018. (ENG., Illus.). 40p. (J). (-k). 18.99 (978-0-7352-2935-8(X), Dial Bks) Penguin Young Readers Group.

Dorfman, Ariel. The Rabbits' Rebellion. Riddell, Chris, illus. 2020. (ENG.). 64p. (J). (gr. 2). 13.95 (978-1-60980-937-9(8), Triangle Square) Seven Stories Pr.

Dossantos, Laurie Staples. The Adventures of Stormy. 2009. 34p. pap. 10.50 (978-1-60693-365-7(5), Eloquent Bks.) Strategic Book Publishing & Rights Agency (SBPRA).

Dotlich, Rebecca Kai. The Knowing Book. Cordell, Matthew, illus. 2016. (ENG.). 32p. (J). (gr. 2). 16.99 (978-1-59078-926-1(1), Astra Young Readers) Astra Publishing Hse.

Doudna, Kelly. Rabbit Ears. Nobens, C. A., illus. 2006. (Fact & Fiction Ser.). 24p. (J). pap. 48.42 (978-1-59679-962-2(5)) ABDO Publishing Co.

Dougherty, Mary. Life Adventures with Fossy. 2004. 7p. (J). pap. 10.58 (978-1-4116-1497-0(6)) Lulu Pr., Inc.

Douglas, Babette. Curly Hare Gets It Straight. Williams, Ted, illus. 2006. (Kiss a Me Teacher Creature Stories Ser.). (J). (gr. -1-3). (978-1-890343-35-4(8)) Kiss A Me Productions, Inc.

Dove, Debra. The Fur Flew. 2010. 42p. pap. 19.99 (978-1-60957-425-3(7)) Salem Author Services.

Driscoll, Laura. Disney Bunnies: Thumper & the Noisy Ducky. 2014. (ENG., Illus.). 12p. (J). (gr. -1 — 1). bds. 6.99 (978-1-4231-8487-4(4), Disney Press Books) Disney Publishing Worldwide.

—Disney Bunnies: Thumper Goes AThumpin' 2015. (ENG., Illus.). 12p. (J). (gr. -1 — 1). bds. 6.99 (978-1-4847-0960-3(8), Disney Press Books) Disney Publishing Worldwide.

Drummond, Ree. Charlie's New Friend. 2014. (I Can Read! Level 1 Ser.). (J). lib. bdg. 13.55 (978-0-606-35041-9(1)) Turtleback.

Dub-u-el. Zoom-Zoom & Slo-Poke. 2005. (J). pap. 15.00 (978-0-8059-6808-8(3)) Dorrance Publishing Co., Inc.

Dudar, Judy. I Spy a Bunny. 1 vol. Rudnicki, Richard, illus. 2012. (ENG.). 32p. (J). (gr. -1-k). pap. 12.95 (978-1-55109-942-2(X), 9bef592f-ef5d-4d41-8ba2-e95dc39eb539) Nimbus Publishing, Ltd. CAN. Dist: Baker & Taylor Publisher Services (BTPS).

Dunbar, Joyce. Tell Me Something Happy Before I Go to Sleep Lap Board Book. Gliori, Debi, illus. 2013. (Lullaby Lights Ser.). (ENG.). 24p. (J). (— 1). bds. 11.99 (978-0-547-94059-5(9), 1516931, Clarion Bks.) HarperCollins Pubs.

Dunrea, Olivier. Gideon & Otto Board Book. Dunrea, Olivier, illus. 2013. (Gossie & Friends Ser.). (ENG., Illus.). 32p. (J). (— 1). bds. 7.99 (978-0-547-98398-1(0), 1524122, Clarion Bks.) HarperCollins Pubs.

Duvall, Deborah L. Rabbit & the Fingerbone Necklace. Jacob, Murv, illus. 2009. (ENG.). 32p. (J). (gr. 1). 19.95 (978-0-8263-4723-7(1), P167927) Univ. of New Mexico Pr.

—Rabbit Goes to Kansas. Jacob, Murv, illus. 2007. (ENG.). 32p. (J). (gr. 1-18). 16.95 (978-0-8263-4181-5(0), P128171) Univ. of New Mexico Pr.

Dyan, Penelope. There's No Business Like Bartholomew Bunny's Business. Dyan, Penelope, illus. 2009. (Illus.). 44p. pap. 11.95 (978-1-935118-54-1(4)) Bellissima Publishing, LLC.

Dyckman, Ame. Wolfie the Bunny. OHora, Zachariah, illus. 2015. (ENG.). 40p. (J). (gr. -1-3). 18.99 (978-0-316-22614-1(9)) Little, Brown Bks. for Young Readers.

Dyess, Hal. The Night the Rabbits Dance: An Easter Story. 2011. 20p. pap. 10.00 (978-1-4567-3613-2(2)) AuthorHouse.

Eaddy, Susan. Poppy's Best Babies. Bonnet, Rosalinde, illus. 2018. 40p. (J). (gr. k-3). 15.99 (978-1-58089-770-9(3)) Charlesbridge Publishing, Inc.

—Poppy's Best Paper (1 Hardcover/1 CD) Bonnet, Rosalinde, illus. 2016. (ENG.). (J). (gr. 1-4). audio compact disk 29.95 (978-1-4301-2187-9(4)) Live Oak Media.

East, Jacqueline, illus. Easter Hop. 2008. (ENG.). 16p. (gr. -1-k). bds. 5.95 (978-1-58117-686-5(4), Intervisual/Piggy Toes) Bendon, Inc.

Eaton, Maxwell, III. Birds vs. Bunnies. 2013. (Flying Beaver Brothers Ser.: 4). lib. bdg. 18.40 (978-0-606-32234-8(5)) Turtleback.

Eaton, Maxwell, III & Eaton, Maxwell. The Flying Beaver Brothers: Birds vs. Bunnies: A Graphic Novel. 2013. (Flying Beaver Brothers Ser.: 4). (Illus.). 96p. (J). (gr. 1-4). pap. 7.99 (978-0-449-81022-4(4), Knopf Bks. for Young Readers) Random Hse. Children's Bks.

Edgeworth, Maria. Rosamond: With Other Tales. by Maria Edgeworth. 2006. 388p. per. 26.99 (978-1-4255-4076-0(7)) Michigan Publishing.

Edmonds, Lin. Patric the Pony & the Race for Freedom. 2011. 32p. pap. 15.50 (978-1-4670-3662-7(5)) AuthorHouse.

—Patric the Pony Finds a Friend. Connors, Mary, illus. 2009. 32p. pap. 12.99 (978-1-4389-5167-6(1)) AuthorHouse.

Edvall, Lilian. The Rabbit Who Couldn't Find His Daddy. Gimbergsson, Sara, illus. 2006. 32p. (J). (gr. -1-3). 15.00 (978-91-29-66429-4(2)) R & S Bks. SWE. Dist: Macmillan.

Edwards, Melvin Neal. Goodee the Rabbit. 2012. 76p. (gr. -1). 20.84 (978-1-4669-5072-6(2)); pap. 10.84 (978-1-4669-5070-2(6)) Trafford Publishing.

Eggleton, Jill. Rabbit & Rooster's Ride: 3-in-1 Package. Taylor, Clive, illus. (Sails Literacy Ser.). 24p. (gr. k-18). 57.00 (978-0-7578-8617-1(5)) Rigby Education.

—Rabbit & Rooster's Ride: 6 Small Books. Taylor, Clive, illus. (Sails Literacy Ser.). 24p. (gr. k-18). 25.00 (978-0-7578-7727-8(3)) Rigby Education.

—Rabbit & Rooster's Ride: Big Book Only. Taylor, Clive, illus. (Sails Literacy Ser.). 24p. (gr. k-18). 27.00 (978-0-7578-6200-7(4)) Rigby Education.

Ehrlin, Carl-Johan Forssén. The Rabbit Who Wants to Fall Asleep: A New Way of Getting Children to Sleep. Maununen, Irina, illus. 2015. (ENG.). 32p. (J). (gr. -1-2). 17.99 (978-0-399-55413-1(0), Crown Books For Young Readers) Random Hse. Children's Bks.

Eisele, Barbara. Miss Thistle & Friends. 2009. 48p. pap. 12.99 (978-1-4490-2007-1(0)) AuthorHouse.

Ekholm, Jan. The Little Red Rascal. 2011. 88p. pap. 30.28 (978-1-4567-9501-6(5)) AuthorHouse.

Elrod, Julie. Splitting Hares. 2008. 36p. pap. 16.50 (978-1-60693-484-5(8), Eloquent Bks.) Strategic Book Publishing & Rights Agency (SBPRA).

Equipo Staff. Este No es Mi Conejito. 2004.Tr. of That's Not My Bunny. (SPA., Illus.). 12p. (J). 7.95 (978-0-7460-4512-1(3)) EDC Publishing.

Eriksen, Craig A. Nollie Gnome & Friends: 1. Return from Holiday. 2008. 52p. pap. 10.50 (978-1-4092-0497-8(9)) Lulu Pr., Inc.

Fable, Aesop. The Tortoise & the Hare. 2012. (J). 29.99 (978-1-61913-103-3(X)) Weigl Pubs., Inc.

Falken, L. C. Snuggle Bunnies. McCue, Lisa, illus. 2018. (ENG.). 18p. (J). (gr. -1 — 1). bds. 6.99 (978-0-7944-4069-5(X), Studio Fun International) Printers Row Publishing Group.

Fanger, Rolf. Benjamin Bunny Learns to Fly. 2004. (Just in Time for Easter Fun! Ser.). (Illus.). 32p. (J). 10.99 (978-1-59384-042-6(X)) Parklane Publishing.

Faria, N. K. The Little Smart Rabbit & the Greedy Wolf: Finding Carrots. 2009. (Illus.). 24p. pap. 11.49 (978-1-4490-1004-1(0)) AuthorHouse.

Farnsworth-Simpson, Patricia Ann. Flick the Karate Pig. 2008. 163p. pap. 16.50 (978-1-4357-2843-1(2)) Lulu Pr., Inc.

Felton, Carol & Felton, Amanda. Where's Harley? 2003. (Math Matters Ser.). (ENG., Illus.). 32p. (J). (gr. k-2). pap. 5.99 (978-1-57565-132-3(7), fda47243-feeb-4e35-991a-dd97993ae003, Kane Press) Astra Publishing Hse.

Fiabe Della Buonanotte. pap. 26.95 (978-88-09-02216-4(5)) Giunti Gruppo Editoriale ITA. Dist: Distribooks, Inc.

Filippis, Dina De. Mrs Nguyen's Garden. 2011. 28p. pap. 15.99 (978-1-4568-3337-4(5)) Xlibris Corp.

Finn, Rebecca, illus. Little Bunny. (Cuddly Cuffstm Ser.). 6p. (J). 6.95 (978-1-58925-767-2(7)) Tiger Tales.

First Bunny Stories. Date not set. (Illus.). (J). bds. 9.98 (978-0-7525-9170-4(3)) Parragon, Inc.

First Contact, 1 vol. 2014. (Your Reading Path Ser.). (Illus.). 96p. (J). (gr. 4-4). pap. (978-1-4814-0037-4(1), 3676b92b-2a22-4699-971d-1cc30e706611, Rosen Classroom) Rosen Publishing Group, Inc., The.

Fleming, Candace. Muncha! Muncha! Muncha! Karas, G. Brian, illus. pap. incl. audio (978-1-59112-465-8(4)); pap. 16.95 incl. audio (978-1-59112-463-4(8)); pap. incl. audio compact disk (978-1-59112-925-7(7)); pap. 18.95 incl. audio compact disk (978-1-59112-923-3(0)) Live Oak Media.

—Muncha! Muncha! Muncha! 2004. (Illus.). (J). 28.95 incl. audio compact disk (978-1-59112-924-0(9)) Live Oak Media.

—Ñam! Ñam! Ñam! Schmidt, Alejandra, tr. from ENG. Karas, G. Brian, illus. 2007. (SPA.). 32p. (J). (gr. -1-2). 15.95 (978-1-933032-35-1(9)) Lectorum Pubns., Inc.

—Tippy-Tippy-Tippy, Hide! 2007. (ENG., Illus.). 40p. (J). (gr. -1-3). 19.99 (978-0-689-87479-6(0), Atheneum Bks. for Young Readers) Simon & Schuster Children's Publishing.

—Tippy-Tippy-Tippy, Splash! Karas, G. Brian, illus. 2014. (ENG.). 40p. (J). (gr. -1-3). 16.99 (978-1-4169-5403-3(1), Atheneum Bks. for Young Readers) Simon & Schuster Children's Publishing.

Fleming, Candace, et al. ¡Ñam! ¡Ñam! ¡Ñam! 2018. 32p. (J). pap. 9.99 (978-1-63245-672-4(9)) Lectorum Pubns., Inc.

Floppy's Friends. 2004. (J). (ENG & VIE.). (978-1-84444-666-7(2)); (ENG & TAM.). (978-1-84444-663-6(8)); (ENG & SPA.). (978-1-84444-662-9(X)); (ENG & SOM.). (978-1-84444-661-2(1)); (ENG & POR.). (978-1-84444-660-5(3)); (ENG & PAN.). (978-1-84444-658-2(1)); (ENG & LAO.). (978-1-84444-657-5(3)); (ENG & HIN.). (978-1-84444-656-8(5)); (ENG & GUJ.). (978-1-84444-655-1(7)); (ENG & FRE.). (978-1-84444-654-4(9)); (ENG & PER.). (978-1-84444-653-7(0)); (CRO & ENG.). (978-1-84444-652-0(2)); (CHI & ENG.). (978-1-84444-651-3(4)); (ARA & ENG.). (978-1-84444-648-3(4)); (ALB & ENG.). (978-1-84444-647-6(6)); (ENG & TUR.). (978-1-84444-664-3(6)) Mantra Lingua.

Flor Ada, Alma. A Surprise for Mother Rabbit. (Stories the Year 'Round Ser.). (Illus.). 28p. (J). (gr. k-3). pap. 8.95 (978-1-58105-214-5(6)) Santillana USA Publishing Co., Inc.

The Flower Pot Bunnies Return. 2006. (J). (978-0-9755390-2-6(7)) Fifth Ave Pr.

Floyd, Lucy. Rabbit & Turtle Go to School/Conejo y Tortuga Van a la Escuela: Bilingual English-Spanish. Ada, Alma Flor & Campoy, F. Isabel, trs. Denise, Christopher, illus. 2010. (Green Light Readers Level 1 Ser.).Tr. of Rabbit & Turtle Go to School. (ENG.). 28p. (J). (gr. -1-3). pap. 5.99 (978-0-547-33898-9(8), 1418429, Clarion Bks.) HarperCollins Pubs.

Foley, James M. Baxter Turns down His Buzz: A Story for Little Kids about ADHD. Ng-Benitez, Shirley, illus. 2016. 32p. (J). 15.95 (978-1-4338-2268-1(7), Magination Pr.) American Psychological Assn.

—Danny & the Blue Cloud: Coping with Childhood Depression. Ng-Benitez, Shirley, illus. 2016. (ENG.). 32p. (J). (978-1-4338-2103-5(6), Magination Pr.) American Psychological Assn.

Fontes, Justine. Clean up, Grumpy Bunny. 2006. (Illus.). (978-0-439-68779-9(9)) Scholastic, Inc.

—Please Say Please, Grumpy Bunny! McQueen, Lucinda, illus. 2007. (J). (978-0-439-02012-1(3)) Scholastic, Inc.

Ford, Bernette. First Snow. Braun, Sébastien, illus. 2005. 32p. (J). (978-0-9547373-3-7(4)) Boxer Bks., Ltd.

—First Snow. Braun, Sébastien, illus. 2018. (ENG.). 28p. (J). (gr. -1-1). bds. 7.95 (978-1-910716-63-2(4)) Boxer Bks., Ltd. GBR. Dist: Sterling Publishing Co., Inc.

Ford, Jessie. My Bunny Puzzle Book. 2012. (ENG., Illus.). 8p. (J). (gr. -1 — 1). 6.95 (978-1-4197-0205-1(X), 1015407, Abrams Appleseed) Abrams, Inc.

Forssen Ehrlin, Carl-Johan. El Conejito Que Quiere Dormirse: un Nuevo Método para Ayudar a Los niños a Dormi R / the Rabbit Who Wants to Fall Asleep: a New Way of Getting Children to Sle. 2015. (SPA.). 32p. (J). (gr. -1-k). 9.95 (978-1-941999-59-2(X), Beascoa) Penguin Random House Grupo Editorial ESP. Dist: Penguin Random Hse. LLC.

Foster, Thelma Louise Elisher. A Brand New House. 2011. 24p. pap. 15.99 (978-1-4568-4803-3(8)) Xlibris Corp.

Franciosa, John F. Little Johnny Lion. 2009. 24p. pap. 11.99 (978-1-4389-8810-8(9)) AuthorHouse.

Francis, Suzanne, adapted by. Zootopia: The Junior Novelization. 2016. (Illus.). 121p. (J). (978-1-5182-0840-9(1)) Random Hse., Inc.

P Q R

Freedman, Claire. The Monster of the Woods! Julian, Russell, illus. 2013. (ENG.). 32p. (J). pap. (978-0-545-51571-9(8), Cartwheel Bks.) Scholastic, Inc.

—Oops-a-Daisy! Hansen, Gaby, illus. 32p. (J). 2004. tchr. ed. 15.95 (978-1-58925-037-6(0)) 2006. reprint ed. 6.95 (978-1-58925-398-8(1)) Tiger Tales.

—You're My Little Bunny. Scott, Gavin, illus. 2010. (ENG.). 20p. (J). (gr. k — 1). bds. 8.99 (978-0-545-20721-8(5), Cartwheel Bks.) Scholastic, Inc.

Fronis, Aly. This Little Bunny. Rescek, Sanja, illus. 2016. (ENG.). 16p. (J). (gr. -1-k). bds. 5.99 (978-1-4998-0105-7(X)) Little Bee Books Inc.

Fry, Sonali. Bang! Clang! 2005. (Ready-to-Read Ser.). (J). pap. 3.99 (978-0-689-87419-2(7), Simon Spotlight) Simon Spotlight.

Fuerst, Jeff. The Lion & the Rabbit: A Fable from India. 2006. (J). pap. (978-1-4108-7156-5(8)) Benchmark Education Co.

Fuller, Suzy. Andrew Discovers A Cottontail. 2005. (Illus.). 30p. (J). per. 9.99 (978-1-932338-77-5(2)) Lifevest Publishing, Inc.

Fumari, Eva. Fuzz Mcflops. Entrekin, Alison, tr. 2015. (ENG., Illus.). 56p. (J). (gr. k-3). pap. 12.95 (978-1-78269-075-7(1), Pushkin Press) Steerforth Pr.

Fusek Peters, Andrew. Rabbit Cooks up a Cunning Plan. Robert, Bruno, illus. 2007. (Traditional Tales with a Twist Ser.). 32p. (J). (gr. 2-2). pap. (978-1-84643-097-8(6)) Child's Play International Ltd.

Galbraith, Kathryn O. Boo, Bunny! Board Book. Mack, Jeff, illus. 2012. (ENG.). 32p. (J). (gr. -1 — 1). bds. 5.99 (978-0-547-81850-4(5), 1496581, Clarion Bks.) HarperCollins Pubs.

Gallagher, Kristin Ellerbusch. Cottontail Rabbits. 2005. (Pull Ahead Bks.). (Illus.). 32p. (gr. k-3). lib. bdg. 22.60 (978-0-8225-3617-8(X)) Lerner Publishing Group.

Ganz, Yaffa. Raise a Rabbit, Grow a Goose. Klineman, Harvey, illus. 2008. 30p. 14.99 (978-1-59826-235-3(1)) Feldheim Pubs.

Gardner, Louise, illus. Five Little Easter Eggs. (ENG.). 10p. (J). 2009. (gr. -1). 5.95 (978-1-58117-849-4(2)) 2008. 9.95 (978-1-58117-682-7(1)) Bendon, Inc. (Intervisual/Piggy Toes).

Garis, Howard R. Bed Time Stories: Uncle Wiggily in the Woods. Wisa, Louis, illus. 2007. 160p. per. (978-1-4065-2772-8(6)) Dodo Pr.

—Bed Time Stories: Uncle Wiggily's Adventures. Wisa, Louis, illus. 2007. 140p. per. (978-1-4065-2773-5(4)) Dodo Pr.

—Bed Time Stories: Uncle Wiggily's Travels. Wisa, Louis, illus. 2007. 160p. per. (978-1-4065-2774-2(2)) Dodo Pr.

—Sammie & Susie Littletail. Wisa, Louis, illus. 2007. 120p. per. (978-1-4065-2770-4(X)) Dodo Pr.

—Uncle Wiggily & Old Mother Hubbard. 2008. 116p. 22.95 (978-1-60664-970-1(1)) Aegypan.

—Uncle Wiggily in the Woods. 2008. 132p. 24.95 (978-1-60664-971-8(X)) Aegypan.

—Uncle Wiggily's Adventures. 2008. 132p. 24.95 (978-1-60664-905-3(1)); pap. 10.95 (978-1-60664-024-1(0)) Aegypan.

—Uncle Wiggily's Travels. 2008. 132p. 24.95 (978-1-60664-906-0(X)); pap. 10.95 (978-1-60664-025-8(9)) Aegypan.

Garis, Howard Roger. Daddy Takes Us to the Garden. 2007. (Illus.). 132p. per. (978-1-4065-2766-7(1)) Dodo Pr.

—Favorite Uncle Wiggily Animal Bedtime Stories. Kliros, Thea, illus. unabr. ed. 2011. (Dover Children's Thrift Classics Ser.). (ENG.). 64p. (J). (gr. 3-8). pap. 4.00 (978-0-486-40101-0(4), 401014) Dover Pubns., Inc.

—Uncle Wiggily Bedtime Stories: In Easy-to-Read Type. Kliros, Thea, illus. unabr. ed. 2011. (Dover Children's Thrift Classics Ser.). (ENG.). 80p. (J). (gr. 3-8). pap. 4.00 (978-0-486-29372-1(6), 293726) Dover Pubns., Inc.

—Uncle Wiggily's Travels. 2005. 26.95 (978-1-4218-1469-8(2)); 164p. pap. 11.95 (978-1-4218-1569-5(9)) 1st World Publishing, Inc. (1st World Library - Literary Society).

Garoche, Camille. The Snow Rabbit. 2015. (Illus.). 56p. (J). (gr. -1-3). 16.95 (978-1-59270-181-0(7)) Enchanted Lion Bks., LLC.

Garrett, Christine. Dream Bunny's Tales - Saving the Land of Dreams. 2009. (Illus.). 48p. pap. 13.95 (978-1-60860-451-7(9), Eloquent Bks.) Strategic Book Publishing & Rights Agency (SBPRA).

Garrido, Felipe. El Coyote Tonto. Gonzalez, Francisco, illus. 2003. (Infantil Alfaguara Ser.).Tr. of Dumb Coyote. (SPA.). 60p. (J). (gr. 3-5). pap. 8.95 (978-968-19-0277-3(7)) Santillana USA Publishing Co., Inc.

Gaster, Valerie Land. Jesus Loves the Easter Bunny. 2011. 20p. 14.50 (978-1-4567-4418-2(6)) AuthorHouse.

Gay, Marie-Louise. Rabbit Blue, 1 vol. 2005. (ENG., Illus.). 32p. (J). (gr. -1-1). 9.95 (978-1-55005-083-7(4), 6430ae68-ae92-407a-9086-d0201a7720d0) Fitzhenry & Whiteside, Ltd. CAN. Dist: Firefly Bks., Ltd.

Gay, Romney. Bonny's Wish. 2011. 36p. pap. 35.95 (978-1-258-06495-2(2)) Literary Licensing, LLC.

Gehl, Laura. Hare & Tortoise Race Across Israel. Goodreau, Sarah, illus. 2015. (ENG.). 32p. (J). (gr. -1-1). E-Book 23.99 (978-1-4677-6202-1(4), Kar-Ben Publishing) Lerner Publishing Group.

Gerrity, Arlene. The Tale of Chicken Noodle & Rabbit Stew Number Two. 2010. 24p. 10.99 (978-1-4251-6258-0(4)) Trafford Publishing.

Gershator, Phillis. Time for a Nap. Walker, David, illus. 2018. (Snuggle Time Stories Ser.: 9). 22p. (J). (— 1). bds. 7.95 (978-1-4549-3130-0(2)) Sterling Publishing Co., Inc.

Gershator, Phillis & Green, Mim. Time for a Hug. Walker, David, illus. 2013. (Snuggle Time Stories Ser.: 1). 22p. (J). (gr. -1-k). bds. 7.99 (978-1-4549-0856-2(4)) Sterling Publishing Co., Inc.

Gershator, Phillis & Walker, David. Time for a Bath. 2016. (Snuggle Time Stories Ser.: 3). (ENG., Illus.). 22p. (J). (— 1). bds. 7.99 (978-1-4549-2069-4(6)) Sterling Publishing Co., Inc.

Giachetti, Julia & Benchmark Education Co. Staff. A Tail for a Tail - Cherokee Trickster Tales. 2014. (Text Connections Ser.). (J). (gr. 5). (978-1-4900-1375-6(X)) Benchmark Education Co.

Ginoschio De Osceola, Ibrahim. Enter the Corn Bunny, Vol. 1. 2007. 56p. per. 8.95 (978-0-595-45273-6(6)) iUniverse, Inc.

Giordano, Anne. Spencer, the Magic Rabbit. 2009. 40p. pap. 16.99 (978-1-4490-3296-8(6)) AuthorHouse.

Glass, Calliope. Disney Bunnies: All Ears. 2016. (ENG., Illus.). 12p. (J). (gr. -1 — 1). bds. 7.99 (978-1-4847-2210-7(8), Disney Press Books) Disney Publishing Worldwide.

Gobo, creator. Up! Goes the Bunny! 2005. (Illus.). 10p. (J). (gr. -1-k). bds. 9.95 (978-1-932915-11-2(7)) Sandvik Innovations, LLC.

Goertzen, Angelina. Tinsel the Christmas Tree. 2009. 32p. pap. 12.49 (978-1-4389-8569-5(X)) AuthorHouse.

Golden Books. Sleepy Bunny (Pat the Bunny) Cloth Book. 2003. (Cloth Book Ser.). (ENG., Illus.). 8p. (J). (gr. -1 — 1). 16.99 (978-0-375-82531-6(2), Golden Bks.) Random Hse. Children's Bks.

Gordon, Janice Knuth. The Eager Bunny. 2009. 60p. (J). pap. 27.95 (978-1-4327-3673-6(6)) Outskirts Pr., Inc.

Gore, Leonid. Danny's First Snow. Gore, Leonid, illus. 2007. (ENG., Illus.). 40p. (J). (gr. -1-3). 19.99 (978-1-4169-1330-6(0), Atheneum Bks. for Young Readers) Simon & Schuster Children's Publishing.

Gough, Julian. Rabbit & Bear: Rabbit's Bad Habits. Field, Jim, illus. 2019. (Rabbit & Bear Ser.: 1). (ENG.). 112p. (J). (gr. 1-3). 9.99 (978-1-68412-588-3(X), Silver Dolphin Bks.) Printers Row Publishing Group.

Graham, Oakley. Tiny Town What Did Busy Bunny Hear? Ribbon, Lemon, illus. 2018. (Tiny Town Touch & Trace Ser.). (ENG.). 10p. (J). (— 1). bds. 7.99 (978-1-78700-378-1(7)) Top That! Publishing PLC GBR. Dist: Independent Pubs. Group.

Grandma's Attic. 2008. (Max & Ruby Ser.). 7p. (J). (gr. -1-k). 9.99 (978-0-448-44895-4(5), Grosset & Dunlap) Penguin Publishing Group.

Grant, V. F. Stories from Grimley Forest. 2011. 48p. (gr. 1-2). pap. 19.50 (978-1-4567-4709-1(6)) AuthorHouse.

Gravett, Emily. Bear & Hare — Where's Bear? Gravett, Emily, illus. 2016. (Bear & Hare Ser.). (ENG., Illus.). 32p. (J). (gr. -1-3). 16.99 (978-1-4814-5615-9(6), Simon & Schuster Bks. For Young Readers) Simon & Schuster Bks. For Young Readers.

—Bear & Hare Go Fishing. Gravett, Emily, illus. 2015. (Bear & Hare Ser.). (ENG., Illus.). 32p. (J). (gr. -1-3). 15.99 (978-1-4814-2289-5(8), Simon & Schuster Bks. For Young Readers) Simon & Schuster Bks. For Young Readers.

—Bear & Hare Snow! Gravett, Emily, illus. 2015. (Bear & Hare Ser.). (ENG., Illus.). 32p. (J). (gr. -1-3). 16.99 (978-1-4814-4514-6(6), Simon & Schuster Bks. For Young Readers) Simon & Schuster Bks. For Young Readers.

—The Rabbit Problem. Gravett, Emily, illus. 2010. (ENG., Illus.). 32p. (J). (gr. -1-3). 24.99 (978-1-4424-1255-2(0), Simon & Schuster Bks. For Young Readers) Simon & Schuster Bks. For Young Readers.

—Wolves. Gravett, Emily, illus. 2006. (ENG., Illus.). 40p. (J). (gr. k-3). 19.99 (978-1-4169-1491-4(9), Simon & Schuster Bks. For Young Readers) Simon & Schuster Bks. For Young Readers.

Grindley, Sally, et al. Pam Mae'r Awyr Yn Las? Stori Gan Sally Grindley. 2005. (WEL., Illus.). 25p. (978-1-85596-265-1(9)) Dref Wen.

Grosset & Dunlap. I Would Like to Actually Keep It. 2011. (Charlie & Lola Ser.). (ENG.). 24p. (J). (gr. k-3). pap. 4.99 (978-0-448-45678-2(8), Grosset & Dunlap) Penguin Young Readers Group.

Gulino, ViTina Corso. Peter Rabbit & My Tulips. Murariu, Lorraine, illus. 2012. 26p. (J). pap. 9.95 (978-1-61863-275-3(2)) Bookstand Publishing.

Hagen, Oddmund. Campo Abierto (Open Field) Santos, Nuria G., tr. from NOR. Dezakin, Akin, illus. 2003. (Rosa y Manzana Ser.). (SPA.). 32p. 16.95 (978-84-89804-42-5(7)) Lóguez Ediciones ESP. Dist: Baker & Taylor Bks.

Hailes, Ronald. The Pink Rabbit. 2009. 24p. pap. 10.96 (978-1-4269-1456-0(3)) Trafford Publishing.

Halcomb, Suzanne. The Mcfee Family Harvest. 2012. 40p. pap. 19.75 (978-1-4269-9647-4(0)) Trafford Publishing.

Hale, Shannon & Hale, Dean. The Princess in Black & the Hungry Bunny Horde. Pham, LeUyen, illus. 2016. (Princess in Black Ser.: 3). (ENG.). 96p. (J). (gr. k-3). pap. 6.99 (978-0-7636-9089-2(9)); 15.99 (978-0-7636-6513-5(4)) Candlewick Pr.

—The Princess in Black & the Hungry Bunny Horde. Pham, LeUyen, illus. 2016. (Princess in Black Ser.: 3). (ENG.). 85p. (J). (gr. k-3). 17.20 (978-0-606-39109-2(6)) Turtleback.

Hamilton, Elizabeth L. Jeremy Rabbit's Honesty Pie. 2003. (Character Critters Ser.: No. 2). (Illus.). 32p. (J). (gr. -1-3). per. 5.95 (978-0-9713749-5-9(3), Character-in-Action) Quiet Impact, Inc.

Hammock, Mary B. Msn Cpnp. Princess Reagan & the Paci Fairy. 2012. 24p. pap. 15.99 (978-1-4797-1074-4(1)) Xlibris Corp.

Hands, Nikki. Lilly Bunny Goes to the Doctor. 2011. 28p. pap. 24.95 (978-1-4626-3638-9(1)) America Star Bks.

Haneberg, Janet. Eggie Rabbit. 2006. 37p. (J). pap. 15.23 (978-1-4116-4157-0(4)) Lulu Pr., Inc.

Hannigan, Katherine. Emmaline & the Bunny. Hannigan, Katherine, illus. 2009. (ENG., Illus.). 112p. (J). (gr. 2-7). 16.99 (978-0-06-162654-8(6), Greenwillow Bks.) HarperCollins Pubs.

Happy Easter, Curious George: Gift Book with Egg-Decorating Stickers! 2010. (Curious George Ser.). (ENG., Illus.). 24p. (J). (gr. -1-3). 9.99 (978-0-547-04825-3(4), 1035143, Clarion Bks.) HarperCollins Pubs.

Harris, Dee. The Croaker Sack Bunny. Bohart, Lisa, illus. 2012. 24p. pap. 12.95 (978-1-61493-043-3(0)) Peppertree Pr., The.

Harris, Donna. Dust Bunnies Do Love Donuts. 2009. 40p. pap. 16.99 (978-1-4490-0628-0(0)) AuthorHouse.

Harris, Joel Chandler. Brer Rabbit & Brer Fox. Smith, Lesley, illus. 2014. (ENG.). 24p. (J). pap. 6.95 (978-1-84135-962-5(9)) Award Pubns. Ltd. GBR. Dist: Parkwest Pubns., Inc.

—Brer Rabbit & the Great Race. Smith, Lesley, illus. 2014. (ENG.). 24p. (J). pap. 6.95 (978-1-84135-963-2(7)) Award Pubns. Ltd. GBR. Dist: Parkwest Pubns., Inc.

—Brer Rabbit & the Honey Pot. Smith, Lesley, illus. 2014. (ENG.). 24p. (J). pap. 6.95 (978-1-84135-961-8(0)) Award Pubns. Ltd. GBR. Dist: Parkwest Pubns., Inc.

—Brer Rabbit & the Tar Baby. Smith, Lesley, illus. 2014. (ENG.). 24p. (J). pap. 6.95 (978-1-84135-964-9(5)) Award Pubns. Ltd. GBR. Dist: Parkwest Pubns., Inc.

Hartzell, Andy. Fox Bunny Funny. 2007. (Illus.). 104p. pap. 10.00 (978-1-891830-97-6(X), 9781891830976) Top Shelf Productions.

Hay, Sam. Rise of the Zombie Rabbit. 2015. (Undead Pets Ser.: 5). lib. bdg. 16.00 (978-0-606-36769-1(1)) Turtleback.

—Rise of the Zombie Rabbit #5. Cooper, Simon, illus. 2015. (Undead Pets Ser.: 5). (ENG.). 112p. (J). (gr. 1-3). 5.99 (978-0-448-47799-2(8), Grosset & Dunlap) Penguin Young Readers Group.

Hayes, Geoffrey. A Night-Light for Bunny. Date not set. 32p. (J). (gr. -1-3). pap. 5.99 (978-0-06-443728-8(0)) HarperCollins Pubs.

—A Night-Light for Bunny. Hayes, Geoffrey, illus. 2004. (Illus.). 32p. (J). (gr. -1-3). 14.99 (978-0-06-029163-1(X)) HarperCollins Pubs.

Hayes, J. B. Freddy the Frog's First Christmas. 2012. 44p. pap. 21.99 (978-1-4772-2870-8(5)) AuthorHouse.

Henkel, Pat. Jeffrey's Great Day. Elliott, Luke, illus. 2012. 16p. pap. 24.95 (978-1-4626-7993-5(5)) America Star Bks.

Henkes, Kevin. Little White Rabbit: An Easter & Springtime Book for Kids. Henkes, Kevin, illus. 2011. (ENG., Illus.). 40p. (J). (gr. -1-3). 16.99 (978-0-06-200642-4(8), Greenwillow Bks.) HarperCollins Pubs.

—Little White Rabbit Board Book: An Easter & Springtime Book for Kids. Henkes, Kevin, illus. 2014. (ENG., Illus.). 34p. (J). (gr. -1-3). bds. 8.99 (978-0-06-231409-3(2), Greenwillow Bks.) HarperCollins Pubs.

—So Happy! Lobel, Anita, illus. 2005. (ENG.). 32p. (J). (gr. -1-3). 16.99 (978-0-06-056483-4(0), Greenwillow Bks.) HarperCollins Pubs.

Henne, R. J. The Talking Rabbit & the Farmer. 2011. 124p. pap. 19.95 (978-1-4560-7337-4(0)) America Star Bks.

Henry, Steve. Here Is Big Bunny. 2017. (I Like to Read Ser.). (ENG.). 32p. (J). (gr. -1-3). 4.99 (978-0-8234-3885-3(6)); 7.99 (978-0-8234-3774-0(4)) Holiday Hse., Inc.

Hensley, Tana. Rosa's Rabbit: Step by Step, 1 vol. 2017. (Computer Science for the Real World Ser.). (ENG.). 8p. (gr. k-1). pap. (978-1-5383-5040-9(8), 60076323-8208-4c53-8afc-6de525e3971c, Rosen Classroom) Rosen Publishing Group, Inc., The.

Hersh, Kristin. Toby Snax. 2016. (ENG., Illus.). 40p. (J). (gr. 1-5). 14.95 (978-1-4773-1127-1(0)) Univ. of Texas Pr.

Herz, Henry. Sherlock Chick & Bunny Watson: The Mislaid Egg. Girouard, Patrick, illus. 2019. (ENG.). 32p. (J). (978-1-4556-2433-1(0), Pelican Publishing) Arcadia Publishing.

Heyward, DuBose. The Country Bunny & the Little Gold Shoes 75th Anniversary Edition: An Easter & Springtime Book for Kids. Flack, Marjorie, illus. 2014. (ENG.). 56p. (J). (gr. -1-3). 17.99 (978-0-544-25197-7(0), 1566548, Clarion Bks.) HarperCollins Pubs.

—Happy Easter, Country Bunny Shaped Board Book: An Easter & Springtime Book for Kids. Flack, Marjorie, illus. 2018. (ENG.). 18p. (J). (— 1). bds. 8.99 (978-1-328-68394-6(X), 1670548, Clarion Bks.) HarperCollins Pubs.

Hillenbrand, Will. Snowman's Story, 0 vols. 2014. (ENG., Illus.). 32p. (J). (gr. -1-2). 16.99 (978-1-4778-4787-9(1), 9781477847879, Two Lions) Amazon Publishing.

Hillert, Margaret. The Baby Bunny. Denny Bond, illus. 2016. (Beginning-To-Read Ser.). (ENG.). 32p. (J). (gr. k-2). pap. 13.26 (978-1-60357-934-6(6)) Norwood Hse. Pr.

—Baby Bunny. (Illus.). (J). 4.95 (978-0-87895-653-1(0)) Modern Curriculum Pr.

—Baby Bunny. 2016. (BeginningtoRead Ser.). (ENG., Illus.). 32p. (J). (gr. k-2). 22.60 (978-1-59953-793-1(1)) Norwood Hse. Pr.

Himmelman, John. Bunjitsu Bunny Jumps to the Moon. Himmelman, John, illus. 2017. (Bunjitsu Bunny Ser.: 3). (ENG., Illus.). 144p. (J). pap. 6.99 (978-1-250-12940-6(0), 900158780) Square Fish.

—Bunjitsu Bunny vs. Bunjitsu Bunny. Himmelman, John, illus. 2018. (Bunjitsu Bunny Ser.: 4). (ENG., Illus.). 128p. (J). pap. 8.99 (978-1-250-17720-9(0), 900158783) Square Fish.

Hirschmann, Kris. Hello, Bunny! Hutto, Victoria, illus. 2010. (Paint Me Pals Ser.). (ENG.). 24p. (J). 9.99 (978-1-4169-7903-6(4), Simon Scribbles) Simon Scribbles.

Ho, Jannie, illus. Bunny Boo Has Lost Her Teddy: A Tiny Tab Book. 2014. (Tiny Tab Ser.). (ENG.). 8p. (J). (— 1). bds. 7.99 (978-0-7636-7274-4(2)) Candlewick Pr.

—Cutie Pie Looks for the Easter Bunny: A Tiny Tab Book. 2015. (Tiny Tab Ser.). (ENG.). 8p. (J). (— 1). bds. 7.99 (978-0-7636-7599-8(7)) Candlewick Pr.

Hobbs, Constance. Bugsy's Special Event. 2008. 64p. pap. 10.50 (978-0-9556783-7-0(4)) Hobbs, Constance GBR. Dist: Lulu Pr., Inc.

Hollar, Cheryl Faye. Billy the Bunny Goes to the State Fair. 2005. (J). pap. 7.97 (978-0-9763826-0-7(1)) Hollar, Cheryl Public Relations.

Holloway, Jamie. Hop's Big Race, 1 vol. 2015. (Rosen REAL Readers: STEM & STEAM Collection). (ENG.). 8p. (gr. k-1). pap. 5.46 (978-1-4994-9602-4(8), b5a09fa6-9c3e-433e-af7c-9d895321d32c, Rosen Classroom) Rosen Publishing Group, Inc., The.

Honigsberg, Peter Jan. Pillow of Dreams. Morse, Tony, illus. 2004. 32p. (gr. k-4). 17.95 (978-1-57143-076-2(8)) RDR Bks.

Hop-along Bunny. 2004. (J). per. (978-1-57657-515-4(2)) Paradise Pr., Inc.

Horse, Harry. Little Rabbit Goes to School, 1 vol. 2011. (Little Rabbit Ser.). (ENG., Illus.). 32p. (J). (gr. -1-k). pap. 7.95 (978-1-56145-574-4(1)) Peachtree Publishing Co. Inc.

—Little Rabbit Lost. 2019. (Little Rabbit Ser.). (ENG., Illus.). 32p. (J). (gr. -1-k). pap. 7.99 (978-1-68263-107-2(9)) Peachtree Publishing Co. Inc.

—Little Rabbit's New Baby, 1 vol. 2016. (Little Rabbit Ser.). (ENG., Illus.). 32p. (J). (gr. -1-k). pap. 7.95 (978-1-56145-915-5(1)) Peachtree Publishing Co. Inc.

—Little Rabbit's New Baby / Book & Doll Package. 2008. (Illus.). 32p. (J). (gr. k-1). pap. 22.90 (978-1-56145-453-2(2)) Peachtree Publishing Co. Inc.

How Rabbit Caught the Sun: Individual Title Six-Packs. (Story Steps Ser.). (gr. k-2). 32.00 (978-0-7635-9811-2(9)) Rigby Education.

Howard, Cheryl L. Duster Dustbunny's Seven Days of the Week & Twelve Months in a Year. 2009. (Illus.). 48p. pap. 17.50 (978-1-60860-787-7(9), Eloquent Bks.) Strategic Book Publishing & Rights Agency (SBPRA).

Howe, Deborah & Howe, James. Bunnicula: A Rabbit-Tale of Mystery. Daniel, Alan, illus. 2006. (Bunnicula & Friends Ser.). (ENG.). 128p. (J). (gr. 3-7). pap. 8.99 (978-1-4169-2817-1(0), Atheneum Bks. for Young Readers) Simon & Schuster Children's Publishing.

—A Rabbit-Tale of Mystery. unabr. ed. 2004. (Bunnicula Ser.). 98p. (J). (gr. 3-7). pap. 29.00 incl. audio (978-0-8072-8204-5(9), YYA139SP, Listening Library) Random Hse. Audio Publishing Group.

Howe, James. Bunnicula Strikes Again! 2004. (Bunnicula Ser.). 116p. (J). (gr. 3-7). pap. 29.00 incl. audio (978-0-8072-8213-7(8), Listening Library) Random Hse. Audio Publishing Group.

—Bunnicula Strikes Again! Daniel, Alan, illus. 2007. (Bunnicula & Friends Ser.). (ENG.). 144p. (J). (gr. 3-7). pap. 7.99 (978-1-4169-3968-9(7), Atheneum Bks. for Young Readers) Simon & Schuster Children's Publishing.

—The Celery Stalks at Midnight. unabr. ed. 2004. (Bunnicula Ser.). 111p. (J). (gr. 3-7). pap. 29.00 incl. audio (978-0-8072-8357-8(6), YA173SP, Listening Library) Random Hse. Audio Publishing Group.

—The Celery Stalks at Midnight, 3. Morrill, Leslie, illus. 2006. (Bunnicula & Friends Ser.). (ENG.). 144p. (J). (gr. 3-7). pap. 7.99 (978-1-4169-2814-0(6)) Simon & Schuster, Inc.

—Harold & Chester Stories. Date not set. (Bunnicula & Friends Ser.). (J). (gr. k-3). (978-0-688-10298-2(0)); lib. bdg. (978-0-688-10299-9(9)) HarperCollins Pubs.

—Hot Fudge. Mack, Jeff, illus. 2006. (Bunnicula & Friends Ser.). 42p. (gr. k-4). 14.00 (978-0-7569-7224-0(8)) Perfection Learning Corp.

—Howliday Inn. unabr. ed. 2004. (Bunnicula Ser.). 195p. (J). (gr. 3-7). pap. 29.00 incl. audio (978-0-8072-8382-0(7), YA179SP, Listening Library) Random Hse. Audio Publishing Group.

—Rabbit-Cadabra! Ready-To-Read Level 3. Mack, Jeff, illus. (Bunnicula & Friends Ser.: 4). (ENG.). 48p. (J). (gr. 1-3). 2007. pap. 4.99 (978-0-689-85752-2(7)) 2006. 17.99 (978-0-689-85727-0(6)) Simon Spotlight. (Simon Spotlight).

—Scared Silly. Mack, Jeff, illus. 2006. (Bunnicula & Friends Ser.). 42p. (gr. 1-3). 14.00 (978-0-7569-7225-7(6)) Perfection Learning Corp.

—Scared Silly: Ready-To-Read Level 3, 3. Mack, Jeff, illus. 2005. (Bunnicula & Friends Ser.: 3). (ENG.). 48p. (J). (gr. 1-3). 17.99 (978-0-689-85726-3(8), Simon Spotlight) Simon & Schuster Children's Publishing.

—Scared Silly: Ready-To-Read Level 3. Mack, Jeff, illus. 2006. (Bunnicula & Friends Ser.: 3). (ENG.). 48p. (J). (gr. 1-3). pap. 4.99 (978-0-689-85751-5(9), Simon Spotlight) Simon Spotlight.

—The Vampire Bunny. Mack, Jeff, illus. 2005. (Bunnicula & Friends Ser.). 41p. (J). (gr. 1-3). 11.65 (978-0-7569-6832-8(1)) Perfection Learning Corp.

—The Vampire Bunny: Ready-To-Read Level 3. Mack, Jeff, illus. (Bunnicula & Friends Ser.: 1). (ENG.). 48p. (J). (gr. 1-3). 2005. pap. 4.99 (978-0-689-85749-2(7)) 2004. 17.99 (978-0-689-85724-9(1)) Simon Spotlight. (Simon Spotlight).

Hucks, Doris. Quackie the Bunny. 2012. 42p. pap. 20.99 (978-1-4772-9527-4(5)) AuthorHouse.

Hudson, Katy. Too Many Carrots. Hudson, Katy, illus. 2016. (ENG., Illus.). 32p. (J). (gr. -1-1). 14.95 (978-1-62370-638-8(6), 131389, Capstone Young Readers) Capstone.

Hurrell, Dianne. Tom Burrows & Friends: Short Stories, Rhymes & Poems. 2010. (ENG., Illus.). 50p. pap. (978-1-84748-782-7(3)) Athena Pr.

Hurt, John Washington, reader. Rabbit Ears World Tales. 2007. (J). 34.99 (978-0-7393-7549-5(0)) Findaway World, LLC.

Hutchings, Tony, illus. A Day on the Farm. 2016. (J). (978-1-4351-6337-9(0)) Barnes & Noble, Inc.

—A Week at the Seaside. 2014. (J). (978-1-4351-5464-3(9)) Barnes & Noble, Inc.

Hyde, Willie. Paddles the Amazing Rabbit. 2012. pap. 8.95 (978-0-7414-8130-6(8)) Infinity Publishing.

—Paddles the Amazing Rabbit - Color. 2012. pap. 13.95 (978-0-7414-8131-3(6)) Infinity Publishing.

Ikeda, Daisaku. The Princess & the Moon. McCaughrean, Geraldine, tr. from JPN. Wildsmith, Brian, illus. 2013. 6.95 (978-1-935523-58-1(9)) World Tribune Pr.

Jacobs, Lily. The Littlest Bunny in Arkansas: An Easter Adventure. Dunn, Robert, illus. 2015. (Littlest Bunny Ser.). (ENG.). 32p. (J). (gr. -1-3). 9.99 (978-1-4926-1027-4(5), Hometown World) Sourcebooks, Inc.

—The Littlest Bunny in Austin. Dunn, Robert, illus. 2016. (Littlest Bunny Ser.). (ENG.). 32p. (J). (gr. -1-3). 9.99 (978-1-4926-3347-1(X), 9781492633471, Hometown World) Sourcebooks, Inc.

—The Littlest Bunny in Bentonville: An Easter Adventure. Dunn, Robert, illus. 2015. (Littlest Bunny Ser.). (ENG.). 32p. (J). (gr. -1-3). 9.99 (978-1-4926-1030-4(5), Hometown World) Sourcebooks, Inc.

—The Littlest Bunny in Boise: An Easter Adventure. Dunn, Robert, illus. 2015. (Littlest Bunny Ser.). (ENG.). 32p. (J). (gr. -1-3). 9.99 (978-1-4926-1033-5(X), Hometown World) Sourcebooks, Inc.

—The Littlest Bunny in Buffalo. Dunn, Robert, illus. 2016. (Littlest Bunny Ser.). (ENG.). 32p. (J). (gr. -1-3). 9.99 (978-1-4926-3346-4(1), 9781492633464, Hometown World) Sourcebooks, Inc.

—The Littlest Bunny in Calgary: An Easter Adventure. Dunn, Robert, illus. 2015. (Littlest Bunny Ser.). (ENG.). 32p. (J). (gr. -1-3). 9.99 (978-1-4926-1039-7(9), Hometown World) Sourcebooks, Inc.

—The Littlest Bunny in California: An Easter Adventure. Dunn, Robert, illus. 2015. (Littlest Bunny Ser.). (ENG.). 32p. (J). (gr. -1-3). 9.99 (978-1-4926-1042-7(9), Hometown World) Sourcebooks, Inc.

—The Littlest Bunny in Canada: An Easter Adventure. Dunn, Robert, illus. 2015. (Littlest Bunny Ser.). (ENG.). 32p. (J). (gr. -1-3). 9.99 (978-1-4926-1045-8(3), Hometown World) Sourcebooks, Inc.

—The Littlest Bunny in Chicago: An Easter Adventure. Dunn, Robert, illus. 2015. (Littlest Bunny Ser.). (ENG.). 32p. (J). (gr.

-1-3). 9.99 *(978-1-4926-1051-9(8)*, Hometown World) Sourcebooks, Inc.

—The Littlest Bunny in Cleveland. Dunn, Robert, illus. 2016. (Littlest Bunny Ser.). (ENG.). 32p. (J). (gr. -1-3). 9.99 *(978-1-4926-3353-2(4)*, 9781492633532, Hometown World) Sourcebooks, Inc.

—The Littlest Bunny in Illinois: An Easter Adventure. Dunn, Robert, illus. 2015. (Littlest Bunny Ser.). (ENG.). 32p. (J). (gr. -1-3). 9.99 *(978-1-4926-1081-6(X)*, Hometown World) Sourcebooks, Inc.

—The Littlest Bunny in Indiana: An Easter Adventure. Dunn, Robert, illus. 2015. (Littlest Bunny Ser.). (ENG.). 32p. (J). (gr. -1-3). 9.99 *(978-1-4926-1084-7(4)*, Hometown World) Sourcebooks, Inc.

—The Littlest Bunny in Nashville. Dunn, Robert, illus. 2016. (Littlest Bunny Ser.). (ENG.). 32p. (J). (gr. -1-3). 9.99 *(978-1-4926-3351-8(8)*, 9781492633518, Hometown World) Sourcebooks, Inc.

—The Littlest Bunny in New Orleans. Dunn, Robert, illus. 2016. (Littlest Bunny Ser.). (ENG.). 32p. (J). (gr. -1-3). 9.99 *(978-1-4926-3350-1(X)*, 9781492633501, Hometown World) Sourcebooks, Inc.

—The Littlest Bunny in Newfoundland. Dunn, Robert, illus. 2016. (Littlest Bunny Ser.). (ENG.). 32p. (J). (gr. -1-3). 9.99 *(978-1-4926-3352-5(6)*, 9781492633525, Hometown World) Sourcebooks, Inc.

—The Littlest Bunny in Ottawa: An Easter Adventure. Dunn, Robert, illus. 2015. (Littlest Bunny Ser.). (ENG.). 32p. (J). (gr. -1-3). 9.99 *(978-1-4926-1174-5(3)*, Hometown World) Sourcebooks, Inc.

—The Littlest Bunny in San Diego. Dunn, Robert, illus. 2016. (Littlest Bunny Ser.). (ENG.). 32p. (J). (gr. -1-3). 9.99 *(978-1-4926-3348-8(8)*, 9781492633488, Hometown World) Sourcebooks, Inc.

—The Littlest Bunny in Utah: An Easter Adventure. Dunn, Robert, illus. 2015. (Littlest Bunny Ser.). (ENG.). 32p. (J). (gr. -1-3). 9.99 *(978-1-4926-1219-3(7)*, Hometown World) Sourcebooks, Inc.

Jacques, Brian. The Long Patrol: A Tale from Redwall. Curless, Allan, illus. 2004. (Redwall Ser.: 10). (ENG.). 368p. (J). (gr. 5-5). 9.99 *(978-0-14-240245-0(1)*, Firebird) Penguin Young Readers Group.

James, Brian. Easter Bunny's on His Way! 2005. pap. *(978-0-439-74530-7(6))* Scholastic, Inc.

James, Catherine. Bobby Cottontail's Gift. Collier, Kevin Scott, illus. 2008. 28p. pap. 10.95 *(978-1-935137-07-8(7))* 2006. 32p. (J). E-Book 9.95 incl. cd-rom *(978-1-933090-24-5(3))* Guardian Angel Publishing, Inc.

James, Eric. Tiny the Alabama Easter Bunny. 2018. (Tiny the Easter Bunny Ser.). (ENG.). 40p. (J). (gr. k-3). 9.99 *(978-1-4926-5903-7(7)*, Hometown World) Sourcebooks, Inc.

—Tiny the Alaska Easter Bunny. 2018. (Tiny the Easter Bunny Ser.). (ENG.). 40p. (J). (gr. k-3). 9.99 *(978-1-4926-5904-4(5)*, Hometown World) Sourcebooks, Inc.

—Tiny the Albuquerque Easter Bunny. 2018. (Tiny the Easter Bunny Ser.). (ENG.). 40p. (J). (gr. k-3). 9.99 *(978-1-4926-5905-1(3)*, Hometown World) Sourcebooks, Inc.

—Tiny the Arizona Easter Bunny. 2018. (Tiny the Easter Bunny Ser.). (ENG.). 40p. (J). (gr. k-3). 9.99 *(978-1-4926-5906-8(1)*, Hometown World) Sourcebooks, Inc.

—Tiny the Arkansas Easter Bunny. 2018. (Tiny the Easter Bunny Ser.). (ENG.). 40p. (J). (gr. k-3). 9.99 *(978-1-4926-5907-5(X)*, Hometown World) Sourcebooks, Inc.

—Tiny the Boston Easter Bunny. 2018. (Tiny the Easter Bunny Ser.). (ENG.). 40p. (J). (gr. k-3). 9.99 *(978-1-4926-5910-5(X)*, Hometown World) Sourcebooks, Inc.

—Tiny the Calgary Easter Bunny. 2018. (Tiny the Easter Bunny Ser.). (ENG.). 40p. (J). (gr. k-3). 9.99 *(978-1-4926-5911-2(8)*, Hometown World) Sourcebooks, Inc.

—Tiny the California Easter Bunny. 2018. (Tiny the Easter Bunny Ser.). (ENG.). 40p. (J). (gr. k-3). 9.99 *(978-1-4926-5912-9(6)*, Hometown World) Sourcebooks, Inc.

—Tiny the Canada Easter Bunny. 2018. (Tiny the Easter Bunny Ser.). (ENG.). 40p. (J). (gr. k-3). 9.99 *(978-1-4926-5913-6(4)*, Hometown World) Sourcebooks, Inc.

—Tiny the Chicago Easter Bunny. 2018. (Tiny the Easter Bunny Ser.). (ENG.). 40p. (J). (gr. k-3). 9.99 *(978-1-4926-5915-0(0)*, Hometown World) Sourcebooks, Inc.

—Tiny the Cincinnati Easter Bunny. 2018. (Tiny the Easter Bunny Ser.). (ENG.). 40p. (J). (gr. k-3). 9.99 *(978-1-4926-5916-7(9)*, Hometown World) Sourcebooks, Inc.

—Tiny the Colorado Easter Bunny. 2018. (Tiny the Easter Bunny Ser.). (ENG.). 40p. (J). (gr. k-3). 9.99 *(978-1-4926-5917-4(7)*, Hometown World) Sourcebooks, Inc.

—Tiny the Delaware Easter Bunny. 2018. (Tiny the Easter Bunny Ser.). (ENG.). 40p. (J). (gr. k-3). 9.99 *(978-1-4926-5919-8(3)*, Hometown World) Sourcebooks, Inc.

—Tiny the Easter Bunny. 2018. (Tiny the Easter Bunny Ser.). (ENG.). 40p. (J). (gr. k-3). 9.99 *(978-1-4926-5902-0(9)*, Hometown World) Sourcebooks, Inc.

—Tiny the Edmonton Easter Bunny. 2018. (Tiny the Easter Bunny Ser.). (ENG.). 40p. (J). (gr. k-3). 9.99 *(978-1-4926-5920-4(7)*, Hometown World) Sourcebooks, Inc.

—Tiny the Georgia Easter Bunny. 2018. (Tiny the Easter Bunny Ser.). (ENG.). 40p. (J). (gr. k-3). 9.99 *(978-1-4926-5922-8(3)*, Hometown World) Sourcebooks, Inc.

—Tiny the Hawaii Easter Bunny. 2018. (Tiny the Easter Bunny Ser.). (ENG.). 40p. (J). (gr. k-3). 9.99 *(978-1-4926-5923-5(1)*, Hometown World) Sourcebooks, Inc.

—Tiny the Idaho Easter Bunny. 2018. (Tiny the Easter Bunny Ser.). (ENG.). 40p. (J). (gr. k-3). 9.99 *(978-1-4926-5924-2(X)*, Hometown World) Sourcebooks, Inc.

—Tiny the Illinois Easter Bunny. 2018. (Tiny the Easter Bunny Ser.). (ENG.). 40p. (J). (gr. k-3). 9.99 *(978-1-4926-5925-9(8)*, Hometown World) Sourcebooks, Inc.

—Tiny the Indiana Easter Bunny. 2018. (Tiny the Easter Bunny Ser.). (ENG.). 40p. (J). (gr. k-3). 9.99 *(978-1-4926-5926-6(6)*, Hometown World) Sourcebooks, Inc.

—Tiny the Iowa Easter Bunny. 2018. (Tiny the Easter Bunny Ser.). (ENG.). 40p. (J). (gr. k-3). 9.99 *(978-1-4926-5927-3(4)*, Hometown World) Sourcebooks, Inc.

—Tiny the Kansas City Easter Bunny. 2018. (Tiny the Easter Bunny Ser.). (ENG.). 40p. (J). (gr. k-3). 9.99 *(978-1-4926-5929-7(0)*, Hometown World) Sourcebooks, Inc.

—Tiny the Kansas Easter Bunny. 2018. (Tiny the Easter Bunny Ser.). (ENG.). 40p. (J). (gr. k-3). 9.99 *(978-1-4926-5928-0(2)*, Hometown World) Sourcebooks, Inc.

—Tiny the Kentucky Easter Bunny. 2018. (Tiny the Easter Bunny Ser.). (ENG.). 40p. (J). (gr. k-3). 9.99 *(978-1-4926-5930-3(4)*, Hometown World) Sourcebooks, Inc.

—Tiny the Las Vegas Easter Bunny. 2018. (Tiny the Easter Bunny Ser.). (ENG.). 40p. (J). (gr. k-3). 9.99 *(978-1-4926-5931-0(2)*, Hometown World) Sourcebooks, Inc.

—Tiny the Los Angeles Easter Bunny. 2018. (Tiny the Easter Bunny Ser.). (ENG.). 40p. (J). (gr. k-3). 9.99 *(978-1-4926-5932-7(0)*, Hometown World) Sourcebooks, Inc.

—Tiny the Louisiana Easter Bunny. 2018. (Tiny the Easter Bunny Ser.). (ENG.). 40p. (J). (gr. k-3). 9.99 *(978-1-4926-5933-4(9)*, Hometown World) Sourcebooks, Inc.

—Tiny the Maine Easter Bunny. 2018. (Tiny the Easter Bunny Ser.). (ENG.). 40p. (J). (gr. k-3). 9.99 *(978-1-4926-5934-1(7)*, Hometown World) Sourcebooks, Inc.

—Tiny the Maryland Easter Bunny. 2018. (Tiny the Easter Bunny Ser.). (ENG.). 40p. (J). (gr. k-3). 9.99 *(978-1-4926-5935-8(5)*, Hometown World) Sourcebooks, Inc.

—Tiny the Massachusetts Easter Bunny. 2018. (Tiny the Easter Bunny Ser.). (ENG.). 40p. (J). (gr. k-3). 9.99 *(978-1-4926-5936-5(3)*, Hometown World) Sourcebooks, Inc.

—Tiny the Michigan Easter Bunny. 2018. (Tiny the Easter Bunny Ser.). (ENG.). 40p. (J). (gr. k-3). 9.99 *(978-1-4926-5937-2(1)*, Hometown World) Sourcebooks, Inc.

—Tiny the Minnesota Easter Bunny. 2018. (Tiny the Easter Bunny Ser.). (ENG.). 40p. (J). (gr. k-3). 9.99 *(978-1-4926-5938-9(X)*, Hometown World) Sourcebooks, Inc.

—Tiny the Mississippi Easter Bunny. 2018. (Tiny the Easter Bunny Ser.). (ENG.). 40p. (J). (gr. k-3). 9.99 *(978-1-4926-5939-6(8)*, Hometown World) Sourcebooks, Inc.

—Tiny the Missouri Easter Bunny. 2018. (Tiny the Easter Bunny Ser.). (ENG.). 40p. (J). (gr. k-3). 9.99 *(978-1-4926-5940-2(1)*, Hometown World) Sourcebooks, Inc.

—Tiny the Montana Easter Bunny. 2018. (Tiny the Easter Bunny Ser.). (ENG.). 40p. (J). (gr. k-3). 9.99 *(978-1-4926-5941-9(X)*, Hometown World) Sourcebooks, Inc.

—Tiny the Nebraska Easter Bunny. 2018. (Tiny the Easter Bunny Ser.). (ENG.). 40p. (J). (gr. k-3). 9.99 *(978-1-4926-5942-6(8)*, Hometown World) Sourcebooks, Inc.

—Tiny the Nevada Easter Bunny. 2018. (Tiny the Easter Bunny Ser.). (ENG.). 40p. (J). (gr. k-3). 9.99 *(978-1-4926-5943-3(6)*, Hometown World) Sourcebooks, Inc.

—Tiny the New England Easter Bunny. 2018. (Tiny the Easter Bunny Ser.). (ENG.). 40p. (J). (gr. k-3). 9.99 *(978-1-4926-5944-0(4)*, Hometown World) Sourcebooks, Inc.

—Tiny the New Hampshire Easter Bunny. 2018. (Tiny the Easter Bunny Ser.). (ENG.). 40p. (J). (gr. k-3). 9.99 *(978-1-4926-5945-7(2)*, Hometown World) Sourcebooks, Inc.

—Tiny the New Jersey Easter Bunny. 2018. (Tiny the Easter Bunny Ser.). (ENG.). 40p. (J). (gr. k-3). 9.99 *(978-1-4926-5946-4(0)*, Hometown World) Sourcebooks, Inc.

—Tiny the New Mexico Easter Bunny. 2018. (Tiny the Easter Bunny Ser.). (ENG.). 40p. (J). (gr. k-3). 9.99 *(978-1-4926-5947-1(9)*, Hometown World) Sourcebooks, Inc.

—Tiny the New York City Easter Bunny. 2018. (Tiny the Easter Bunny Ser.). (ENG.). 40p. (J). (gr. k-3). 9.99 *(978-1-4926-5949-5(5)*, Hometown World) Sourcebooks, Inc.

—Tiny the New York Easter Bunny. 2018. (Tiny the Easter Bunny Ser.). (ENG.). 40p. (J). (gr. k-3). 9.99 *(978-1-4926-5948-8(7)*, Hometown World) Sourcebooks, Inc.

—Tiny the North Carolina Easter Bunny. 2018. (Tiny the Easter Bunny Ser.). (ENG.). 40p. (J). (gr. k-3). 9.99 *(978-1-4926-5950-1(9)*, Hometown World) Sourcebooks, Inc.

—Tiny the North Dakota Easter Bunny. 2018. (Tiny the Easter Bunny Ser.). (ENG.). 40p. (J). (gr. k-3). 9.99 *(978-1-4926-5951-8(7)*, Hometown World) Sourcebooks, Inc.

—Tiny the Ohio Easter Bunny. 2018. (Tiny the Easter Bunny Ser.). (ENG.). 40p. (J). (gr. k-3). 9.99 *(978-1-4926-5952-5(5)*, Hometown World) Sourcebooks, Inc.

—Tiny the Oklahoma Easter Bunny. 2018. (Tiny the Easter Bunny Ser.). (ENG.). 40p. (J). (gr. k-3). 9.99 *(978-1-4926-5953-2(3)*, Hometown World) Sourcebooks, Inc.

—Tiny the Oregon Easter Bunny. 2018. (Tiny the Easter Bunny Ser.). (ENG.). 40p. (J). (gr. k-3). 9.99 *(978-1-4926-5955-6(X)*, Hometown World) Sourcebooks, Inc.

—Tiny the Ottawa Easter Bunny. 2018. (Tiny the Easter Bunny Ser.). (ENG.). 40p. (J). (gr. k-3). 9.99 *(978-1-4926-5956-3(8)*, Hometown World) Sourcebooks, Inc.

—Tiny the Pennsylvania Easter Bunny. 2018. (Tiny the Easter Bunny Ser.). (ENG.). 40p. (J). (gr. k-3). 9.99 *(978-1-4926-5957-0(6)*, Hometown World) Sourcebooks, Inc.

—Tiny the Philadelphia Easter Bunny. 2018. (Tiny the Easter Bunny Ser.). (ENG.). 40p. (J). (gr. k-3). 9.99 *(978-1-4926-5958-7(4)*, Hometown World) Sourcebooks, Inc.

—Tiny the Rhode Island Easter Bunny. 2018. (Tiny the Easter Bunny Ser.). (ENG.). 40p. (J). (gr. k-3). 9.99 *(978-1-4926-5961-7(4)*, Hometown World) Sourcebooks, Inc.

—Tiny the San Francisco Easter Bunny. 2018. (Tiny the Easter Bunny Ser.). (ENG.). 40p. (J). (gr. k-3). 9.99 *(978-1-4926-5962-4(2)*, Hometown World) Sourcebooks, Inc.

—Tiny the South Carolina Easter Bunny. 2018. (Tiny the Easter Bunny Ser.). (ENG.). 40p. (J). (gr. k-3). 9.99 *(978-1-4926-5963-1(0)*, Hometown World) Sourcebooks, Inc.

—Tiny the South Dakota Easter Bunny. 2018. (Tiny the Easter Bunny Ser.). (ENG.). 40p. (J). (gr. k-3). 9.99 *(978-1-4926-5964-8(9)*, Hometown World) Sourcebooks, Inc.

—Tiny the St. Louis Easter Bunny. 2018. (Tiny the Easter Bunny Ser.). (ENG.). 40p. (J). (gr. k-3). 9.99 *(978-1-4926-5965-5(7)*, Hometown World) Sourcebooks, Inc.

—Tiny the Texas Easter Bunny. 2018. (Tiny the Easter Bunny Ser.). (ENG.). 40p. (J). (gr. k-3). 9.99 *(978-1-4926-5968-6(1)*, Hometown World) Sourcebooks, Inc.

—Tiny the Vancouver Easter Bunny. 2018. (Tiny the Easter Bunny Ser.). (ENG.). 40p. (J). (gr. k-3). 9.99 *(978-1-4926-5972-3(X)*, Hometown World) Sourcebooks, Inc.

—Tiny the Vermont Easter Bunny. 2018. (Tiny the Easter Bunny Ser.). (ENG.). 40p. (J). (gr. k-3). 9.99 *(978-1-4926-5973-0(8)*, Hometown World) Sourcebooks, Inc.

—Tiny the Virginia Easter Bunny. 2018. (Tiny the Easter Bunny Ser.). (ENG.). 40p. (J). (gr. k-3). 9.99 *(978-1-4926-5974-7(6)*, Hometown World) Sourcebooks, Inc.

—Tiny the West Virginia Easter Bunny. 2018. (Tiny the Easter Bunny Ser.). (ENG.). 40p. (J). (gr. k-3). 9.99 *(978-1-4926-5977-8(0)*, Hometown World) Sourcebooks, Inc.

—Tiny the Wyoming Easter Bunny. 2018. (Tiny the Easter Bunny Ser.). (ENG.). 40p. (J). (gr. k-3). 9.99 *(978-1-4926-5979-2(7)*, Hometown World) Sourcebooks, Inc.

James, Helen Foster. Auntie Loves You! Brown, Petra, illus. 2018. (ENG.). 32p. (J). (gr. -1-1). 15.99 *(978-1-5341-1011-3(9)*, 204589) Sleeping Bear Pr.

—Grandma Loves You! Brown, Petra, illus. 2013. (ENG.). 32p. (J). (gr. -1 — 1). 15.99 *(978-1-58536-836-5(9)*, 202884) Sleeping Bear Pr.

—Grandpa Loves You! Brown, Petra, illus. 2016. (ENG.). 32p. (J). (gr. -1-1). 15.99 *(978-1-58536-940-9(3)*, 204032) Sleeping Bear Pr.

—Mommy Loves You! Brown, Petra, illus. 2017. (ENG.). 32p. (J). (gr. -1-k). 15.99 *(978-1-58536-941-6(1)*, 204232) Sleeping Bear Pr.

James, Jake. Jake s Short Stories. 2010. 64p. pap. 10.99 *(978-1-60957-640-0(3))* Salem Author Services.

James, Rosalind. Bertie Rides Again. 2012. (Illus.). 126p. 29.99 *(978-1-4771-2272-3(9))* Xlibris Corp.

Jasnoch, Dorothy. Frankie the Bunny: Mystery in the Forest. Korzeniowski, Samson O., ed. Jasnoch, Dorothy, illus. 2013. (Illus.). 32p. 17.99 *(978-1-937752-16-3(X))* Owl About Bks. Pubs.

—Frankie the Bunny: The Fall Scramble Begins. Korzeniowski, Samson O., ed. Jasnoch, Dorothy, illus. 2013. (Illus.). 28p. 17.99 *(978-1-937752-19-4(4))* Owl About Bks. Pubs.

—Frankie the Bunny: Wheels of Fortune. Korzeniowski, Samson O., ed. Jasnoch, Dorothy, illus. 2013. (Illus.). 28p. 17.99 *(978-1-937752-17-0(8))* Owl About Bks. Pubs.

—Frankie the Bunny: Woodland Warning. Korzeniowski, Samson O., ed. Jasnoch, Dorothy, illus. 2013. (Illus.). 28p. 17.99 *(978-1-937752-18-7(6))* Owl About Bks. Pubs.

—Frankie the Bunny Helping the Birds. Korzeniowski, Samson, ed. Jasnoch, Dorothy, illus. 2012. (ENG., Illus.). 28p. pap. 12.99 *(978-1-937752-05-7(4))* Owl About Bks. Pubs.

—Frankie the Bunny the Fall Scramble Begins. Korzeniowski, Samson, ed. Jasnoch, Dorothy, illus. 2012. (Illus.). 28p. pap. 12.99 *(978-1-937752-04-0(6))* Owl About Bks. Pubs.

Jenks, Patricia. I'm Only a Little Bunny. Lehto, Christine, illus. 2013. 34p. 15.99 *(978-1-937165-48-2(5))* Orange Hat Publishing.

Jennings, Richard W. Orwell's Luck. 2006. (ENG.). 160p. (J). (gr. 5-7). pap. 11.95 *(978-0-618-69335-1(1)*, 487654, Clarion Bks.) HarperCollins Pubs.

Jeram, Anita. Bunny My Honey. Jeram, Anita, illus. 2009. (ENG., Illus.). 22p. (J). (gr. k-k). bds. 7.99 *(978-0-7636-4645-5(8))* Candlewick Pr.

—Me Gusta Mi Libro de Cuentos. Mlawer, Teresa, tr. (SPA.). (J). (gr. -1-k). 14.95 *(978-1-930332-29-4(7)*, LC5087) Lectorum Pubns., Inc.

Jin, Susie Lee. Mine! Jin, Susie Lee, illus. 2016. (ENG., Illus.). 40p. (J). (gr. -1-3). 16.99 *(978-1-4814-2772-2(5)*, Simon & Schuster Bks. For Young Readers) Simon & Schuster Bks. For Young Readers.

JJ Rabbit & the Monster: Level K, 6 vols. 128p. (gr. 2-3). 49.95 *(978-0-7699-0981-3(7))* Shortland Pubns. (U. S. A.) Inc.

Johannes, Avril & Branham, Jan. Bunny an Alaskan Hare. 2006. 32p. 7.95 *(978-0-9749360-3-1(0))* Icicle Falls Publishing Co.

Johanson, Rhonda. The Great Tempo Race. 2011. 32p. pap. 21.99 *(978-1-4568-5363-1(5))* Xlibris Corp.

Johnson, Gerald J. J. Buffy Bunny. Miltenberger, Jeri & Miltenberger, Dave, illus. 2011. 32p. pap. 24.95 *(978-1-4512-5292-7(7))* America Star Bks.

Johnson, Jane. Are You Ready for Bed? Hansen, Gaby, illus. 2004. 32p. (J). tchr. ed. 14.95 *(978-1-58925-017-8(6))* Tiger Tales.

—Little Bunny's Bathtime! 2004. (Illus.). 32p. (J). tchr. ed. 15.95 *(978-1-58925-043-7(5))* Tiger Tales.

—Little Bunny's Bedtime. Hansen, Gaby, illus. 2006. Orig. Title: Are You Ready for Bed? 16p. (J). bds. 6.95 *(978-1-58925-773-3(1))* Tiger Tales.

Johnson, Kimberly P. The Adventures of the Itty Bitty Bunny. 2004. (Illus.). 24p. (gr. k-2). 14.95 *(978-1-57197-155-5(6)*, Ivy House Publishing Group) Pentland Pr., Inc.

Johnson, Regan. Little Bunny Kung Fu. Johnson, Regan, illus. 2005. (ENG., Illus.). 32p. (J). (gr. -1 — 1). 14.95 *(978-0-9769417-8-1(3))* Blooming Tree Pr.

Jones, Mary Noble. Itsy Rabbit & Friends: Itsy's First Adventure. Jones, Mary Noble, illus. 2007. (Illus.). 28p. (J). per. 15.00 *(978-0-9796209-8-0(8))* Righter Publishing Co., Inc.

Jones, Nancy. The Grandpaws. 2005. 57p. pap. 16.95 *(978-1-4137-4778-2(7))* America Star Bks.

Jordan, Apple. The Bunny Surprise. 2012. (Step into Reading - Level 1 Ser.). lib. bdg. 13.55 *(978-0-606-23723-9(2))* Turtleback.

Josiah, Iris. Tiny Rabbit. 2012. (Illus.). 28p. (J). pap. *(978-0-9572728-0-4(4))* Tiny Island Pr.

Journey of Egg & Rabbit by Lee Grass Whitefeather. 2004. (YA). cd-rom *(978-0-9767413-5-0(0))* Wakinglion Studio.

Joyce, William. E. Aster Bunnymund & the Warrior Eggs at the Earth's Core! Joyce, William, illus. (Guardians Ser.: 2). (ENG., Illus.). (J). (gr. 2-6). 2018. 288p. pap. 8.99 *(978-1-4424-3051-8(6))*Bk. 2. 2012. 272p. 18.99 *(978-1-4424-3050-1(8))* Simon & Schuster Children's Publishing. (Atheneum Bks. for Young Readers).

Just Bunny & Me: Big Book. (Pebble Soup Explorations Ser.). (SPA.). 16p. (gr. -1-18). 31.00 *(978-0-7578-1666-6(5))* Rigby Education.

Just Bunny & Me: Small Book. (Pebble Soup Explorations Ser.). (SPA.). 16p. (gr. -1-18). 5.00 *(978-0-7578-1706-9(8))* Rigby Education.

Kaplan, Michael. Betty Bunny Didn't Do It. Jorisch, Stéphane, illus. 2013. (Betty Bunny Ser.). 32p. (J). (gr. -1-k). 17.99 *(978-0-8037-3858-4(7)*, Dial Bks) Penguin Young Readers Group.

—Betty Bunny Loves Chocolate Cake. Jorisch, Stéphane, illus. 2011. (Betty Bunny Ser.). 32p. (J). (gr. -1-k). 17.99 *(978-0-8037-3407-4(7)*, Dial Bks) Penguin Young Readers Group.

—Betty Bunny Wants a Goal. Jorisch, Stéphane, illus. 2014. (Betty Bunny Ser.). 32p. (J). (gr. -1-k). 17.99 *(978-0-8037-3859-1(5)*, Dial Bks) Penguin Young Readers Group.

—Betty Bunny Wants Everything. Jorisch, Stéphane, illus. 2012. (Betty Bunny Ser.). 32p. (J). (gr. -1-k). 17.99 *(978-0-8037-3408-1(5)*, Dial Bks) Penguin Young Readers Group.

Kapoor, Natalya. My Favorite Time of Day. 2013. 12p. pap. 12.99 *(978-1-4772-8344-8(7))* AuthorHouse.

Karlik, Danielle. The Kaylee Chronicles: First Day Fright. 2007. 20p. per. 24.95 *(978-1-4241-8346-3(4))* America Star Bks.

Karr, Lily. Easter Parade! 2013. lib. bdg. 14.75 *(978-0-606-31494-7(6))* Turtleback.

—My Easter Bunny! Johnson, Jay, illus. 2012. (ENG.). 12p. (J). (gr. -1 — 1). bds. 4.99 *(978-0-545-37117-9(1)*, Cartwheel Bks.) Scholastic, Inc.

Kaye, Christian Thomas. Rachel the Homely Rabbit: A Story about Kindness. Albright, Audrey, illus. 2011. 30p. pap. 9.95 *(978-1-60844-763-3(4))* Dog Ear Publishing, LLC.

Kaye, Shannie. Funny Bunny. 2013. 20p. pap. 24.95 *(978-1-4241-0079-8(8))* America Star Bks.

Keilbart, L. S. One. Benson, Barbara, illus. 2007. (ENG.). 76p. (J). (gr. k-k). per. *(978-1-85756-610-9(6))* Janus Publishing Co.

Keller, Laurie. Do unto Otters: A Book about Manners. Keller, Laurie, illus. 2007. (ENG., Illus.). 40p. (J). (gr. k-3). 21.99 *(978-0-8050-7996-8(3)*, 900034600, Holt, Henry & Co. Bks. For Young Readers) Holt, Henry & Co.

—Do unto Otters: A Book about Manners. Keller, Laurie, illus. 2009. (ENG., Illus.). 40p. (J). (gr. k-3). pap. 9.99 *(978-0-312-58140-4(8)*, 900061994) Square Fish.

Kennedy, Pamela. No, No, Bunny. Keay, Claire, illus. 2017. (ENG.). 16p. (J). (gr. -1-k). bds. 7.99 *(978-0-8249-1651-0(4))* Worthy Publishing.

—Uh-Oh, Bunny. Keay, Claire, illus. 2017. (ENG.). 16p. (J). (gr. -1-k). bds. 7.99 *(978-0-8249-1650-3(6))* Worthy Publishing.

Kerr, Judith. Cuando Hitler Robó el Conejo Rosa.Tr. of When Hitler Stole Pink Rabbit. (SPA.). 272p. (J). 9.95 *(978-84-204-4791-9(9))* Ediciones Alfaguara ESP. Dist: Santillana USA Publishing Co., Inc.

—Cuando Hitler Robó el Conejo Rosa. 2003.Tr. of When Hitler Stole Pink Rabbit. (SPA.). (YA). (gr. 5-8). pap. *(978-84-345-8586-7(3)*, AF0202) Salvat Editores, S.A. ESP. Dist: Lectorum Pubns., Inc.

Kiefer, Janet Kennedy & Barrett, Jill. Can I Play with You? Freckles Book 2. 2013. 42p. pap. *(978-1-4602-0038-4(1))* FriesenPress.

Killen, Nicola. The Little Rabbit. Killen, Nicola, illus. 2019. (My Little Animal Friend Ser.). (ENG., Illus.). 32p. (J). (gr. -1-3). 17.99 *(978-1-5344-3828-6(9)*, Simon & Schuster/Paula Wiseman Bks.) Simon & Schuster/Paula Wiseman Bks.

Kim, Cecil. Nicknames. Han, SooJin, illus. 2014. (MySELF Bookshelf Ser.). (ENG.). 32p. (J). (gr. k-2). pap. 11.94 *(978-1-60357-699-4(1))*; lib. bdg. 25.27 *(978-1-59953-664-4(1))* Norwood Hse. Pr.

Kim, YeShil. Tortoise & Hare. Kheiriyeh, Rashin, illus. 2014. (MySELF Bookshelf Ser.). (ENG.). 32p. (J). (gr. k-2). pap. 11.94 *(978-1-60357-700-7(9))*; lib. bdg. 25.27 *(978-1-59953-665-1(X))* Norwood Hse. Pr.

Kimura, Yuichi. On the Seesaw Bridge. Hata, Kowshiro, illus. 2011. (ENG.). 36p. (J). (gr. -1-3). 14.95 *(978-1-935654-18-6(7)*, Vertical) Kodansha America, Inc.

Kinder, Connie & Virden, Carole. Dash's Pause: An Adventure in Being Found. 2012. (Illus.). 40p. pap. 20.95 *(978-1-4497-6981-9(0)*, WestBow Pr.) Author Solutions, LLC.

Kintz, Elizabeth. The Magic Hose. 2012. 30p. 16.95 *(978-1-4575-1087-8(1))*; pap. 14.00 *(978-1-4575-0948-3(2))* Dog Ear Publishing, LLC.

Kiser, Dolores White. The Marriage of White Rabbit. 2005. (J). 10.00 net. *(978-0-9766648-3-3(6))* White Kiser, Dolores.

Kline, Trish & Donev, Mary. A Scary Day in the Forest: KA Reader 5. 2007. (Illus.). 32p. (J). per. 20.00 *(978-0-9717234-8-1(6))* Ghost Hunter Productions.

Klise, Kate. Imagine Harry. Klise, M. Sarah, illus. 2007. (ENG.). 32p. (J). (gr. -1-3). 16.00 *(978-0-15-205704-6(8))*, 1197146, Clarion Bks.) HarperCollins Pubs.

—Little Rabbit & the Meanest Mother on Earth. Klise, M. Sarah, illus. 2015. (ENG.). 32p. (J). (gr. -1-3). 6.99 *(978-0-544-45611-2(4))*, 1599396, Clarion Bks.) HarperCollins Pubs.

Knudsen, Michelle. Big Mean Mike. Magoon, Scott, illus. 2012. (ENG.). 40p. (J). (gr. -1-3). 15.99 *(978-0-7636-4990-6(2))* Candlewick Pr.

Knutson, Barbara. Sungura & Leopard: A Swahili Trickster Tale. Knutson, Barbara, illus. 2007. (Illus.). 26p. (J). (gr. -1-3). per. 6.95 *(978-0-8225-6801-8(2))*, First Avenue Editions) Lerner Publishing Group.

Kohake, Beverly. The Funny Bunny. 2008. 32p. pap. 16.95 *(978-1-4303-2736-3(7))* Lulu Pr., Inc.

Kramer, Alan & Kramer, Candice. Brer Rabbit Hears a Big Noise in the Woods: An African /American Folktale. 2006. (J). pap. *(978-1-4108-7163-3(0))* Benchmark Education Co.

Kuenzler, Lou. Collins Big Cat Phonics for Letters & Sounds - the Foolish, Timid Rabbit: Band 03/Yellow, Bd. 3. Bencivenni, Beatrice, illus. 2018. (Collins Big Cat Phonics Ser.). (ENG.). 16p. (J). (gr. k-1). pap. 7.99 *(978-0-00-825155-0(X))* HarperCollins Pubs. Ltd. GBR. Dist: Independent Pubs. Group.

Kumiega, Michelle. The Bunnies Who Learn Not to Bully. 2011. 24p. pap. 24.95 *(978-1-4560-6742-7(7))* America Star Bks.

—The Greedy Bunny. 2008. 28p. pap. 24.95 *(978-1-60672-966-3(7))* America Star Bks.

Kunhardt, Dorothy. Pat the Bunny: First Books for Baby (Pat the Bunny) Pat the Bunny; Pat the Puppy; Pat the Cat, 3 vols. 2015. (Touch-And-Feel Ser.). (Illus.). 20p. (J). (— 1). 29.99 *(978-0-553-50838-3(5))*, Golden Bks.) Random Hse. Children's Bks.

Kurkosky, Tina. Bunny Brothers. 2011. 24p. pap. 24.95 *(978-1-4626-3608-2(X))* America Star Bks.

Kyrja. Rupert's Tales: The Nature of Elements, 1 vol. Pringle-Burke, Lesli, illus. 2017. (ENG.). 72p. (J). (gr. -1-3). 16.99 *(978-0-7643-5387-1(X))*, 7672, Red Feather) Schiffer Publishing, Ltd.

—Rupert's Tales: The Wheel of the Year - Samhain, Yule, Imbolc, & Ostara, 1 vol. 2012. (ENG., Illus.). 64p. 19.99 *(978-0-7643-3987-5(7))*, 4366, Red Feather) Schiffer Publishing, Ltd.

—Rupert's Tales: The Wheel of the Year Activity Book, 1 vol. 2012. (ENG., Illus.). 40p. pap. 9.99 *(978-0-7643-4020-8(4))*, 4367, Red Feather) Schiffer Publishing, Ltd.

—Rupert's Tales: Rupert Helps Clean Up: Rupert Helps Clean Up, 1 vol. 2013. (ENG., Illus.). 64p. (J). (gr. -1-3). 19.99 *(978-0-7643-4284-4(3))*, 4882) Schiffer Publishing, Ltd.

—Rupert's Tales: the Wheel of the Year Beltane, Litha, Lammas, & Mabon: The Wheel of the Year Beltane, Litha, Lammas, & Mabon, 1 vol. 2011. (ENG., Illus.). 64p. 19.99 *(978-0-7643-3689-8(4))*, 4054, Red Feather) Schiffer Publishing, Ltd.

Lade, Linda. Peter Bunny: Adventures in the Kudzu Pat. 2006. 82p. pap. 16.95 *(978-1-4241-3818-0(3))* PublishAmerica, Inc.

Ladybird. Peter Rabbit & the Radish Robber - Ladybird Readers Level 1. 2018. (Ladybird Readers Ser.). (Illus.). 48p. (J). (gr. k-2). pap. 8.99 *(978-0-241-29742-1(7))* Penguin Bks., Ltd. GBR. Dist: Independent Pubs. Group.

Ladybird, Ladybird. Peter Rabbit & the Radish Robber, Level 1. 2018. (Ladybird Readers Ser.). (ENG.). 16p. (J). (gr. k-2). pap. 5.99 *(978-0-241-29735-3(4))* Penguin Bks., Ltd. GBR. Dist: Independent Pubs. Group.

Lamm, Drew C. Cottontail at Clover Crescent. 2005. (Smithsonian's Backyard Ser.). (ENG., Illus.). 32p. (J). (gr. -1-2). 8.95 *(978-1-59249-225-1(8))*, SC5005) Soundprints.

—Cottontail at Clover Crescent. Davis, Allen, illus. 2005. (Smithsonian's Backyard Ser.). (ENG.). 32p. (J). (gr. -1-2). pap. 6.95 *(978-1-59249-112-4(X))*, S5005) Soundprints.

Lane, W. Seth. Riley Rabbit's Quest to the Ark. 2011. 32p. (gr. -1 — 1). pap. 17.25 *(978-1-4269-6178-6(2))* Trafford Publishing.

Langen, Annette. Felix & the Flying Suitcase Adventure. Droop, Constanza, illus. 2003. 47p. (J). 14.99 *(978-1-59384-035-8(7))* Parklane Publishing.

—Felix Explores Planet Earth. Droop, Constanza, illus. 2004. (Perfect for Earth Day Promotions! Ser.). 47p. (J). 14.99 *(978-1-59384-030-3(6))* Parklane Publishing.

—Felix's Christmas Around the World. Droop, Constanza, illus. 2003. 40p. (J). 14.99 *(978-1-59384-036-5(5))* Parklane Publishing.

—Letters from Felix: A Little Rabbit on a World Tour. Droop, Constanza, illus. 2003. 47p. (J). 14.99 *(978-1-59384-034-1(9))* Parklane Publishing.

Langley, C. Kevin. Brer Rabbit Comic. 2009. 16p. pap. 9.80 *(978-0-557-11631-7(7))* Lulu Pr., Inc.

Langreuter, Jutta. So Happy Together! Dahle, Stefanie, illus. 2017. (ENG.). 32p. (J). (gr. -1-3). 17.95 *(978-0-7358-4279-3(5))* North-South Bks., Inc.

Lapytski, Serge & Lapytski, Kristina. The Heart of a Lion! E-Hare. 2011. 84p. pap. 12.84 *(978-1-4567-4281-2(7))* AuthorHouse.

Larwood, Kieran. The Beasts of Grimheart. Wyatt, David, illus. 2019. (Longburrow Ser.). (ENG.). 272p. (J). (gr. 5-7). 16.99 *(978-1-328-69602-1(2))*, 1671320, Clarion Bks.) HarperCollins Pubs.

—The Five Realms: the Beasts of Grimheart. Wyatt, David, illus. 2019. (Five Realms Podkin One Ear Ser.). (ENG.). 320p. (J). (gr. 3-5). 15.95 *(978-0-571-32844-4(X))*, Faber & Faber Children's Bks.) Faber & Faber, Inc.

—The Gift of Dark Hollow. Wyatt, David, illus. 2018. (Longburrow Ser.). (ENG.). 272p. (J). (gr. 5-7). 16.99 *(978-1-328-69601-4(4))*, 1671318, Clarion Bks.) HarperCollins Pubs.

Latimer, Alex. Lion vs. Rabbit, 1 vol. 2017. (ENG., Illus.). 32p. (J). (gr. -1-3). pap. 7.95 *(978-1-56145-898-1(8))* Peachtree Publishing Co. Inc.

Lauterbach, B. L. Home-Grown Experiences. 2008. 68p. pap. 7.95 *(978-1-4327-2620-1(X))* Outskirts Pr., Inc.

Lawson, Robert. Rabbit Hill. l.t. ed. (J). (gr. 4-6). reprint ed. 10.00 *(978-0-89064-076-0(9))* National Assn. for Visually Handicapped.

Layne, Steven. Play with Puppy, 1 vol. Hoyt, Ard, illus. 2018. (ENG.). 32p. (J). (gr. -1-3). 16.99 *(978-1-4556-2374-7(1))*, Pelican Publishing) Arcadia Publishing.

Leathers, Philippa. The Black Rabbit. Leathers, Philippa, illus. 2016. (ENG., Illus.). 40p. (J). (gr. -1-2). 7.99 *(978-0-7636-8879-0(7))* Candlewick Pr.

Leathers, Rain. Purple Mountain. 2008. 36p. pap. 20.95 *(978-1-4327-2685-0(4))* Outskirts Pr., Inc.

Lee, Carol & Bell, Donna. Saying Goodbye to Hare: A Story about Death & Dying to Be Used with Children. Ages 5-9. 2013. (ENG., Illus.). 24p. pap. 6.95 *(978-1-85741-138-6(2))* Southgate Pubs. GBR. Dist: Parkwest Pubns., Inc.

Leeuwen, Jean. Five Funny Bunnies: Three Bouncing Tales, 0 vols. Wilsdorf, Anne, illus. 2012. (ENG.). 40p. (J). (gr. -1-3). 17.99 *(978-0-7614-6114-2(0))*, 9780761461142, Two Lions) Amazon Publishing.

Lester, Helen. Listen, Buddy. Munsinger, Lynn, illus. 2013. (Laugh-Along Lessons Ser.). (ENG.). 32p. (J). (gr. -1-3). 8.99 *(978-0-544-00322-4(5))*, 1526364, Clarion Bks.) HarperCollins Pubs.

Levy, Elizabeth. A Hare-Raising Tale. Gerstein, Mordicai, illus. unabr. ed. 2006. (First Chapter Bks.). (J). (gr. 2-4). pap. 17.95 incl. audio *(978-1-59519-704-7(4))*; pap. 20.95 incl. audio compact disk *(978-1-59519-705-4(2))* Live Oak Media.

Levy, Elizabeth & Coville, Bruce. The Dragon of Doom. Gerstein, Mordicai & Coville, Katherine, illus. 2005. 71p. (J). lib. bdg. 15.00 *(978-1-59054-903-2(1))* Fitzgerald Bks.

Light, Steve. The Bunny Burrow Buyer's Book: A Tale of Rabbit Real Estate. 2016. (ENG., Illus.). 16p. (J). (gr. -1-3). 19.95 *(978-1-57687-752-4(3))*, powerHouse Bks.) powerHse. Bks.

The Lion & the Hare: [an East African Folktale]. 2009. (On My Own Folklore Ser.). (gr. 3-5). pap. 6.95 *(978-1-58013-849-9(7))*, First Avenue Editions) Lerner Publishing Group.

Lispector, Clarice. Misterio do Coelho Pensante. pap. 19.95 *(978-85-325-1061-7(2))* Rocco, Editora, Ltda BRA. Dist: Distribooks, Inc.

Little Bunny. 2003. (Goodnight Mr. Moon Ser.). (Illus.). (J). bds. 2.98 *(978-0-7525-4741-1(0))* Parragon, Inc.

Liv‡n, Paco. THE THING THAT HURTS MOST IN THE WORLD. 2007. (ENG., Illus.). 36p. (J). 17.95 *(978-84-96788-89-3(X))* OQO, Editora ESP. Dist: Baker & Taylor Bks.

Llama, Gram. The Bunny Fuzz Mystery. 2007. 32p. per. 24.95 *(978-1-4241-8371-5(5))* America Star Bks.

Lloyd-Jones, Sally. Bunnys First Spring, 1 vol. McPhail, David, illus. 2015. (ENG.). 32p. (J). 16.99 *(978-0-310-73386-7(3))* Zonderkidz.

—Skip to the Loo, My Darling! a Potty Book. Jeram, Anita, illus. 2016. (ENG.). 32p. (J). (-k). 11.99 *(978-0-7636-7234-8(3))* Candlewick Pr.

Lobel, Gill. Little Bear's Special Wish. Hansen, Gaby, illus. 2004. 32p. (J). tchr. ed. 16.95 *(978-1-58925-034-5(6))* Tiger Tales.

Loewen, Nancy. The Tortoise & the Hare, Narrated by the Silly but Truthful Tortoise. Cox, Russ & Cox, Thomas, illus. 2018. (Other Side of the Fable Ser.). (ENG.). 24p. (J). (gr. -1-3). lib. bdg. 27.99 *(978-1-5158-2867-9(0))*, 138405, Picture Window Bks.) Capstone.

Logan, J. Gavin. Plum Bunny. 2008. 52p. pap. 16.95 *(978-1-60563-654-2(1))* America Star Bks.

Loney, Andrea J. Bunnybear. 2018. (2019 Av2 Fiction Ser.). (ENG.). 32p. (J). (gr. -1-3). lib. bdg. 34.28 *(978-1-4896-8251-2(1))*, AV2 by Weigl) Weigl Pubs., Inc.

Lord, Cynthia. Because of the Rabbit (Scholastic Gold) 2019. (ENG.). 192p. (J). (gr. 3-7). 17.99 *(978-0-545-91424-6(8))*, Scholastic Pr.) Scholastic, Inc.

Lorenzo, Amanda. Clovis Escapes! Bks. 3: Runt Farm. Walker, Mark Evan, illus. 2009. 136p. 12.95 *(978-0-9800952-2-7(0))* BooktiMookti Pr.

Lowell, Susan. The Tortoise & the Jackrabbit: La Tortuga y la Liebre. Harris, Jim, illus. 2004. (New Bilingual Picture Book Ser.). (ENG.). 32p. (J). (gr. -1-3). pap. 7.95 *(978-0-87358-869-0(X))* Cooper Square Publishing Llc.

Luchesi, Dennis. Benji Rabbit. 2013. 24p. pap. 24.95 *(978-1-62709-894-6(1))* America Star Bks.

Lundquist, Mary. Cat & Bunny. 2015. (ENG., Illus.). 32p. (J). (gr. -1-3). 17.99 *(978-0-06-228780-9(X))*, Balzer & Bray) HarperCollins Pubs.

Lyons, P. J. Little Bunny's Bible, 1 vol. Mitchell, Melanie, illus. 2015. (ENG.). 16p. (J). bds. 15.99 *(978-0-310-74444-3(X))* Zonderkidz.

Mϋhle, Jörg. Bathtime for Little Rabbit. Mϋhle, Jörg, illus. 2017. (Little Rabbit Ser.). (ENG., Illus.). 20p. (J). (gr. -1 — 1). bds. 9.99 *(978-1-77657-137-6(1))*, 4c219d98-c57b-45f0-87c2-ae7616a732ac) Gecko Pr. NZL. Dist: Lerner Publishing Group.

—Poor Little Rabbit. Mϋhle, Jörg, illus. 2018. (Little Rabbit Ser.). (ENG., Illus.). 20p. (J). (gr. -1 — 1). bds. 9.99 *(978-1-77657-177-2(0))*, 71597102-d7c6-4ee1-bff0-ab4e56f9d2c4) Gecko Pr. NZL. Dist: Lerner Publishing Group.

Maccarone, Grace. Bunny Race! Long, Ethan, illus. 2009. (J). *(978-0-545-11290-1(7))* Scholastic, Inc.

MacDonald, Margaret Read. Pickin' Peas. Cummings, Pat, illus. 2014. (ENG.). 32p. pap. 8.95 *(978-1-939160-83-6(9))* August Hse. Pubs., Inc.

Mack, Jeff. Good News, Bad News. 2012. (ENG., Illus.). 40p. (J). (gr. -1-1). 16.99 *(978-1-4521-0110-1(8))* Chronicle Bks. LLC.

—Hippo & Rabbit in Brave Like Me (3 More Tales) (Scholastic Reader, Level 1) Mack, Jeff, illus. 2011. (Scholastic Reader, Level 1 Ser.). (ENG., Illus.). 32p. (J). (gr. -1-1). pap. 3.99 *(978-0-545-28360-1(4))*, Cartwheel Bks.) Scholastic, Inc.

—Hippo & Rabbit in Three Short Tales (Scholastic Reader, Level 1) Mack, Jeff, illus. 2011. (Scholastic Reader, Level 1 Ser.). (ENG., Illus.). 32p. (J). (gr. -1-1). pap. 3.99 *(978-0-545-27445-6(1))*, Cartwheel Bks.) Scholastic, Inc.

MacKenzie, Emily. Wanted! Ralfy Rabbit, Book Burglar. 2016. (ENG., Illus.). 32p. (J). 17.99 *(978-1-68119-220-8(9))*, 900164103, Bloomsbury USA Childrens) Bloomsbury Publishing USA.

MacKinnon, Mairi, ed. The Hare & the Tortoise. Howarth, Daniel, illus. 2007. (First Reading Level 4 Ser.). 48p. (J). (gr. -1-3). 8.99 *(978-0-7945-1612-3(2))*, Usborne) EDC Publishing.

Magone, Teresa. Little Bunny Has Belly Surgery. 2012. 38p. pap. 9.50 *(978-0-615-58595-6(7))* Little Bunny Bks.

Maillet, Kevin And Haylie. The Scruzzels: Life on the Farm. 2012. 32p. pap. 19.99 *(978-1-4772-2805-0(5))* AuthorHouse.

Malaspina, Ann. Guinea Fowl & Rabbit Get Justice: An African Folktale. Wendland, Paula, illus. 2013. (Folktales from Around the World Ser.). (ENG.). 24p. (J). (gr. k-3). 32.79 *(978-1-62323-614-4(2))*, 206381) Child's World, Inc, The.

Mancini, Kristen Belmont. A Bunny Named Boo. 2011. 24p. pap. *(978-1-4269-7640-7(2))* Trafford Publishing (UK) Ltd.

Mandara, Melissa. Who would you Be? 2010. 32p. pap. 15.95 *(978-1-4520-1605-4(4))* AuthorHouse.

Mandy, Stanley. Bella: The Birthday Party. Mandy, Stanley, illus. 2010. (ENG., Illus.). 32p. (J). (gr. -1-k). 9.95 *(978-1-58925-850-1(9))* Tiger Tales.

—Bella: The Fairy Ball. Mandy, Stanley, illus. 2010. (ENG., Illus.). 32p. (J). (gr. -1-k). 9.95 *(978-1-58925-851-8(7))* Tiger Tales.

Marcero, Deborah. In a Jar. Marcero, Deborah, illus. 2020. (Illus.). 40p. (J). (gr. -1-2). 18.99 *(978-0-525-51459-6(7))*, G.P. Putnam's Sons Books for Young Readers) Penguin Young Readers Group.

Marie, Barbara. Snowy & Felix Find Christmas. 2009. 24p. pap. 11.49 *(978-1-4389-7392-0(6))* AuthorHouse.

Marino, Gianna. Too Tall Houses. 2012. 40p. (J). (gr. -1-k). 18.99 *(978-0-670-01314-2(5))*, Viking Books for Young Readers) Penguin Young Readers Group.

Marion, L. K. Summer Holiday with Funny Bunny. 2012. 32p. pap. 17.25 *(978-1-4669-6475-4(8))* Trafford Publishing.

Marrone, Amanda. The Multiplying Menace. 1. 2010. (Magic Repair Shop Ser.: 1). (ENG.). 288p. (J). (gr. 3-7). pap. 6.99 *(978-1-4169-9033-8(X))*, Aladdin) Simon & Schuster Children's Publishing.

Marshall, Denise. The Adventures of Hip Hop: Hip Hop & the Blueberry Pancakes. Champagne, Heather, illus. 2012. 36p. pap. 14.75 *(978-1-62212-331-5(X))*, Strategic Bk. Publishing) Strategic Book Publishing & Rights Agency (SBPRA).

—The Adventures of Hip Hop: Hip Hop & the Yellow Hat. Schley, Cheri & Champagne, Heather, illus. 2011. 36p. pap. 14.75 *(978-1-60976-342-8(4))*, Eloquent Bks.) Strategic Book Publishing & Rights Agency (SBPRA).

Martin, Bridgitt. Bunny & the Amazing Gift: God Cares for All His Creation. 2013. 28p. pap. 13.99 *(978-1-4908-0952-6(X))*, WestBow Pr.) Author Solutions, LLC.

Marzot, Janet. Las Liebres Blancas. (SPA.). 32p. (J). 13.95 *(978-84-261-1459-4(8))* Juventud, Editorial ESP. Dist: AIMS International Bks., Inc.

Mason, Christopher. Little Bunny Comfy Pants. 2011. 20p. pap. 24.95 *(978-1-4626-0900-0(7))* America Star Bks.

Massie, Rosemary. Rhymen the Rabbit: Meeting the Forest Ranger. 2011. 28p. pap. 13.95 *(978-1-4634-2572-2(4))* AuthorHouse.

—Rhymen the Rabbit: Save the Forest. 2011. 28p. pap. 13.95 *(978-1-4634-1597-6(4))* AuthorHouse.

Mastrangelo, Judy. What Do Bunnies Do All Day? Mastrangelo, Judy, illus. (Illus.). 32p. (J). pap. 4.95 *(978-0-8249-5370-6(3))*, Ideals Pubns.) Worthy Publishing.

May, Bonnie. The Tale of a Rabbit's Tail. 2008. 66p. pap. 34.50 *(978-1-4357-0313-1(8))* Lulu Pr., Inc.

May, R. B. Charlie Finds a Friend. 2010. 32p. pap. 12.99 *(978-1-4490-6913-1(4))* AuthorHouse.

Mayeux, Gertie P. The Hurricane Bunnies. 2007. (ENG.). 40p. pap. 20.99 *(978-1-4343-3754-2(5))* AuthorHouse.

McBratney, Sam. Guess How Much I Love You. Jeram, Anita, illus. 2005. 34p. (J). bds. 19.95 *(978-0-9769313-1-7(1))* Brailleink.

—Guess How Much I Love You. Jeram, Anita, illus. (Guess How Much I Love You Ser.). (J). (gr. -1 — 1). 2014. (ENG.). 40p. 17.99 *(978-0-7636-7448-9(6))* 2006. 32p. 15.99 *(978-0-7636-3503-9(0))* Candlewick Pr.

—Guess How Much I Love You Lap-Size Board Book. Jeram, Anita, illus. 2013. (Guess How Much I Love You Ser.). (ENG.). 24p. (J). (— 1). bds. 14.99 *(978-0-7636-7006-1(5))* Candlewick Pr.

—Guess How Much I Love You: One More Tickle! A Puppet Book. Jeram, Anita, illus. 2016. (Guess How Much I Love You Ser.). (ENG.). 14p. (J). (gr. k-k). bds. 18.99 *(978-0-7636-8819-6(3))* Candlewick Pr.

—Guess How Much I Love You: Pop-Up. Jeram, Anita, illus. 2011. (Guess How Much I Love You Ser.). (ENG.). 16p. (J). (gr. -1-2). 21.99 *(978-0-7636-5378-1(0))* Candlewick Pr.

—A Nutbrown Hare Storybook Pair Boxed Set, 2 vols. Jeram, Anita, illus. 2008. (Guess How Much I Love You Ser.). (ENG.). 48p. (J). (gr. k-k). bds. 14.99 *(978-0-7636-4265-5(7))* Candlewick Pr.

—A Surprise for the Nutbrown Hares. Jeram, Anita, illus. 2009. (J). *(978-0-7636-4903-6(1))* Candlewick Pr.

McCall, Val. Twelve Rabbits & a Turtle: Bilingual English French. 2012. 46p. pap. 9.95 *(978-1-938367-00-7(6))* Destinee Media.

McCallum, Ann. Rabbits Rabbits Everywhere: A Fibonacci Tale. Kendall, Gideon, illus. (ENG.). 32p. (J). (gr. 1-4). 2008. 16.95 *(978-1-57091-895-7(3))* 2007. per. 7.95 *(978-1-57091-896-4(1))* Charlesbridge Publishing, Inc.

McCann, Shawn, illus. Why the Owl Has Big Ears. 2005. 32p. (J). (gr. -1-3). 8.75 *(978-0-9771466-0-4(X))* Goulasche Pr.

McCarty, Peter. Chloe. McCarty, Peter, illus. 2012. (ENG., Illus.). 40p. (J). (gr. -1-1). 16.99 *(978-0-06-114291-8(3))*, Balzer & Bray) HarperCollins Pubs.

McClellan, Cheryl. The Adventures of Bunny Flu Flu. 2008. (ENG.). 88p. per. 51.99 *(978-1-4363-0268-5(4))* Xlibris Corp.

McCully, Emily Arnold. Pete Likes Bunny. 2016. (I Like to Read Ser.). (ENG., Illus.). 24p. (J). (gr. -1-3). 6.99 *(978-0-8234-3687-3(X))* Holiday Hse., Inc.

McCune, Susan. Rabbit & Turtle, 1 vol., 1. 2015. (Rosen REAL Readers: STEM & STEAM Collection). (ENG.). 8p. (J). (gr. k-1). pap. 5.46 *(978-1-5081-1409-3(9))*, aaa38a43-2ffa-49d7-8ad0-a88ba4792a86, Rosen Classroom) Rosen Publishing Group, Inc., The.

McGill, Erin. I Do Not Like Al's Hat. McGill, Erin, illus. 2017. (ENG., Illus.). 32p. (J). (gr. -1-3). 17.99 *(978-0-06-245576-5(1))*, Greenwillow Bks.) HarperCollins Pubs.

McInnes, Lisa. Evelyn's Special Eggs. Duersch, Gretchen, ed. Schlund, Mackenzie, illus. 2011. 32p. pap. *(978-1-77067-394-6(6))* FriesenPress.

McIntyre, Mel. Flutter Bunnies. Grady, Kit, illus. 2008. 24p. pap. 10.95 *(978-1-933090-68-9(5))* Guardian Angel Publishing, Inc.

McKay, Hilary. Lulu & the Rabbit Next Door. 2014. (Lulu Ser.: 4). (J). lib. bdg. 14.75 *(978-0-606-41566-8(1))* Turtleback.

—Lulu & the Rabbit Next Door. Lamont, Priscilla, illus. 2014. (Lulu Ser.: 4). (ENG.). 112p. (J). (gr. 1-5). 13.99 *(978-0-8075-4816-5(2))*, 807548162) Whitman, Albert & Co.

McKenzie, Tiffany M. The Adventures of Alan & the Man-Eating Rabbits. 2013. 24p. pap. 24.95 *(978-1-63000-143-8(0))* America Star Bks.

McLaren, Meg. Rabbit Magic. McLaren, Meg, illus. 2017. (ENG., Illus.). 40p. (J). (gr. -1-3). 16.99 *(978-0-544-78469-7(3))*, 1638303, Clarion Bks.) HarperCollins Pubs.

McLeod, Cinders. Earn It! McLeod, Cinders, illus. 2017. (Moneybunny Book Ser.). (ENG., Illus.). 32p. (J). (-k). 16.99 *(978-0-399-54444-6(5))*, Nancy Paulsen Books) Penguin Young Readers Group.

—Save It! McLeod, Cinders, illus. 2019. (Moneybunny Book Ser.). (ENG., Illus.). 32p. (J). (-k). 16.99 *(978-1-9848-1240-7(8))*, Nancy Paulsen Books) Penguin Young Readers Group.

—Spend It! McLeod, Cinders, illus. 2019. (Moneybunny Book Ser.). (ENG., Illus.). 32p. (J). (-k). 16.99 *(978-0-399-54446-0(1))*, Nancy Paulsen Books) Penguin Young Readers Group.

McMullan, Kate. One Funny Day. Alley, R. W., illus. 2012. (Pearl & Wagner Ser.: 1). 48p. (J). (gr. 1-3). pap. 4.99 *(978-0-448-45866-3(7))*, Penguin Young Readers) Penguin Young Readers Group.

—Pearl & Wagner: Five Days till Summer. 2014. (Penguin Young Readers: Level 3 Ser.). lib. bdg. 13.55 *(978-0-606-35727-2(0))* Turtleback.

—Pearl & Wagner: Three Secrets. 2013. (Penguin Young Readers: Level 3 Ser.). lib. bdg. 13.55 *(978-0-606-31708-5(2))* Turtleback.

—Pearl & Wagner: Three Secrets. Alley, R. W., illus. 2013. (Pearl & Wagner Ser.: 3). 48p. (J). (gr. 1-3). pap. 4.99 *(978-0-448-46472-5(1))*, Penguin Young Readers) Penguin Young Readers Group.

—Pearl & Wagner: Two Good Friends. Alley, R. W., illus. 2011. (Pearl & Wagner Ser.: 2). 48p. (J). (gr. 1-3). pap. 4.99 *(978-0-448-45690-4(7))*, Penguin Young Readers) Penguin Young Readers Group.

MCP Staff. Little Bunny's Lunch: Short u; Consonants b, h; Blends br, cr; Digraphs ch, sh, th. (J). (gr. 1-2). 38.50 *(978-0-8136-1116-7(4))* Modern Curriculum Pr.

McPhail, David. The Blue Door, 1 vol. 2005. (First Flight Level 1 Ser.). (ENG., Illus.). 32p. (J). (gr. -1-1). pap. 4.95 *(978-1-55041-917-7(X))*, cc7e7e2e-374b-4437-a566-2d22dcd0ab75) éditeur, Annika Parance CAN. Dist: Firefly Bks., Ltd.

—Budgie & Boo. 2009. (ENG., Illus.). 32p. (J). (gr. -1-k). 15.95 *(978-0-8109-8324-3(9))*, 646301, Abrams Bks. for Young Readers) Abrams, Inc.

—Rick Is Sick. McPhail, David, illus. 2004. (Green Light Readers Ser.). (ENG., Illus.). 24p. (J). (gr. -1-3). pap. 5.99 *(978-0-15-205092-4(2))*, 1195376, Clarion Bks.) HarperCollins Pubs.

—Rick Is Sick. 2004. (Green Light Readers Level 1 Ser.). 13.50 *(978-0-613-97286-4(4))* Turtleback.

McQueen, Todd, illus. Bob & Rob & Corn on the Cob. 2014. (ENG.). 40p. (J). (gr. -1-k). 16.95 *(978-1-62873-591-8(0))*, Sky Pony Pr.) Skyhorse Publishing Co., Inc.

Meadows, Daisy. Bella the Bunny Fairy. Ripper, Georgie, illus. 2008. (Rainbow Magic — the Pet Fairies Ser.). 65p. (gr. 7). lib. bdg. 14.75 *(978-1-4178-2996-5(6))* Turtleback.

—Magic Animal Friends: Mia Floppyear's Snowy Adventure: Special 3. 2022. (Magic Animal Friends Ser.). (ENG., Illus.). 176p. (J). (gr. k-2). pap. 8.99 *(978-1-4083-3887-2(4))*, Orchard Bks.) Hachette Children's Group GBR. Dist: Hachette Bk. Group.

Melling, David. Hugless Douglas & the Big Sleepover. 2013. (ENG., Illus.). 32p. (J). *(978-1-58925-116-8(4))* Tiger Tales.

Menard, Michele R. Who Do I Think You Are? 2013. 26p. pap. 10.95 *(978-0-9887969-5-9(3))* Four Menards, The.

Metzger, Steve. Five Little Bunnies Hopping on a Hill. 2006. (J). *(978-0-439-80382-3(9))* Scholastic, Inc.

Meyer, Matthew. Raising Hare: Welcome to Sherwood Acores. 2010. 24p. pap. 11.49 *(978-1-4490-8839-2(2))* AuthorHouse.

Meyer, Susan. Matthew & Tall Rabbit Go Camping. Huntington, Amy, illus. 2008. (ENG.). 32p. (J). (gr. -1-3). 15.95 *(978-0-89272-769-8(1))* Down East Bks.

Meyers, Seth. I'm Not Scared, You're Scared. Sayegh, Rob & Sayegh, Rob, Jr., illus. 2022. (ENG.). 40p. (J). (gr. -1-2). 18.99 *(978-0-593-35237-3(8))* Flamingo Bks.

M.H.Pruitt. The Adventures of Rexie the Bear. 2009. 16p. pap. 8.99 *(978-1-4490-4211-0(2))* AuthorHouse.

Midden, Maribeth Grubb. Rosie: The Patchwork Bunny. Techau, Ashlyn, illus. 2011. 24p. (gr. 1-2). pap. 12.99 *(978-1-4269-5671-3(1))* Trafford Publishing.

Middle, Myra. Rabi's Halloween Adventure. 2012. 28p. pap. 21.99 *(978-1-4691-5380-3(7))* Xlibris Corp.

Miles, David W., creator. But First, We Nap: A Little Book about Nap Time. 2018. (ENG., Illus.). 16p. (J). (gr. -1-k). bds. 9.99 *(978-1-64170-017-7(3))*, 550017) Familius LLC.

Miller, Dorothy North. How Mr Foxy Fox Was Outfoxed. 2009. 32p. pap. 14.95 *(978-0-9825086-1-9(1))* Fiction Publishing, Inc.

Miller, Jayna. Too Much Trick or Treat. Thatch, Nancy, ed. Miller, Jayna, illus. 2005. (Illus.). 29p. (J). per. 19.95 *(978-0-933849-83-9(4))* landmark Hse., Ltd.

Miller, Jennifer. Christmas Tails. Knight, Vanessa, illus. 2009. 56p. pap. 17.26 *(978-1-4251-8987-7(3))* Trafford Publishing.

Miller, Pat Zietlow. Wherever You Go. Wheeler, Eliza, illus. 2019. (ENG.). 26p. (J). (gr. -1 — 1). bds. 7.99 *(978-0-316-48794-8(5))* Little, Brown Bks. for Young Readers.

Milne, Brandi. So Good for Little Bunnies. 2nd rev. ed. 2019. (ENG., Illus.). 48p. 20.00 *(978-1-61404-023-1(0))* Baby Tattoo Bks.

Min, Cat. Shy Willow. 2021. (ENG., Illus.). 48p. (J). (gr. -1-2). 17.99 *(978-1-64614-035-0(4))* Levine Querido.

Minear, Jason. Jr & the Carrot Coaster. 2008. 17p. pap. 24.95 *(978-1-60563-469-2(7))* America Star Bks.

Minich, Eric. Digger & the Search for Home. 2006. 48p. pap. 16.95 *(978-1-4241-0321-8(5))* PublishAmerica, Inc.

Minor, Florence. How to Be a Bigger Bunny: An Easter & Springtime Book for Kids. Minor, Wendell, illus. 2017. (ENG.). 32p. (J). (gr. -1-3). 14.99 *(978-0-06-235255-2(5),* Tegen, Katherine Bks) HarperCollins Pubs.

Miot, Ray. Alexis the Wizard Rabbit: Pascale & Alain Adventures. 2009. 36p. pap. 17.99 *(978-1-4389-3440-2(8))* AuthorHouse.

Miskimen, Cora. Mrs. Hunny Bunny's New Spring Hat. 2008. 32p. pap. 24.95 *(978-1-4241-8939-7(X))* America Star Bks.

Mitter, Matt. Sesame Street: Guess Who, Easter Elmo! Mathieu, Joe, illus. 2nd ed. 2018. (Guess Who! Book Ser.). (ENG.). 10p. (J). (gr. -1-k). 10.99 *(978-0-7944-4197-5(1),* Studio Fun International) Printers Row Publishing Group.

Mitton, Tony & Parker, Ant. Super Submarines. 2014. (Amazing Machines Ser.). (ENG., Illus.). 24p. (J). (gr. -1-k). 5.99 *(978-0-7534-7208-8(2),* 900143121, Kingfisher) Roaring Brook Pr.

—Super Submarines. 2014. (Amazing Machines Ser.). (J). lib. bdg. 16.00 *(978-0-606-36133-0(2))* Turtleback.

Miyakoshi, Akiko. The Way Home in the Night. Miyakoshi, Akiko, illus. 2017. (ENG., Illus.). 32p. (J). (gr. -1-2). 16.95 *(978-1-77138-663-0(0))* Kids Can Pr., Ltd. CAN. Dist: Hachette Bk. Group.

Montefiore, Santa & Montefiore, Simon Sebag. The Royal Rabbits of London. Hindley, Kate, illus. 2018. (Royal Rabbits Ser.: 1). (ENG.). 208p. (J). (gr. 3-7). 16.99 *(978-1-4814-9860-9(6),* Aladdin) Simon & Schuster Children's Publishing.

—The Royal Rabbits of London. Hindley, Kate, illus. 2019. (Royal Rabbits Ser.: 1). (ENG.). 224p. (J). (gr. 3-7). pap. 7.99 *(978-1-4814-9861-6(4),* Aladdin) Simon & Schuster Children's Publishing.

Mooney, Ginger. Grandmother Rabbit's Old Red Hat. 2009. 12p. pap. 9.99 *(978-1-4490-0586-3(1))* AuthorHouse.

Morgan, Michaela. Dear Bunny: A Bunny Love Story. Church, Caroline Jayne, illus. 2006. (Scholastic Bookshelf Ser.). (ENG.). 32p. (J). (gr. k-2). 18.69 *(978-0-439-74834-6(8))* Scholastic, Inc.

Morgan, Ruth. The Funny Easter Bunny. 2003. (Illus.). 22p. per. 1.95 *(978-1-932338-10-2(1))* Lifevest Publishing, Inc.

Moroney, Trace. The Things I Love about Me. 2019. (Things I Love about Ser.). (ENG.). 10p. (J). (— 1). bds. 8.99 *(978-1-76040-931-9(6))* Bonnier Publishing GBR. Dist: Independent Pubs. Group.

Morris, Richard T. Fear the Bunny. Burris, Priscilla, illus. 2019. (ENG.). 40p. (J). (gr. -1-3). 17.99 *(978-1-4814-7800-7(1))* Simon & Schuster Children's Publishing.

Morrison, Toni & Morrison, Slade. The Tortoise or the Hare. Cepeda, Joe, illus. (ENG.). 32p. (J). (gr. -1-3). 2014. 8.99 *(978-1-4169-8335-4(X))* 2010. 19.99 *(978-1-4169-8334-7(1))* Simon & Schuster/Paula Wiseman Bks. (Simon & Schuster/Paula Wiseman Bks.).

Mortimer, Anne. Bunny's Easter Egg. 2010. (ENG., Illus.). 32p. (J). (gr. -1-2). 12.99 *(978-0-06-136664-2(1),* Tegen, Katherine Bks) HarperCollins Pubs.

Moseley, Tabitha. Pearl's Tales a Collection of Children's Stories. 2009. 92p. pap. 17.25 *(978-1-60860-670-2(8),* Strategic Bk. Publishing) Strategic Book Publishing & Rights Agency (SBPRA).

Motto, Bernadine. The Adventures of Fluff the Bunny. 2007. 32p. per. 11.95 *(978-1-59800-908-8(7))* Outskirts Pr., Inc.

Mulvey, Ella. The Rabbit-Hole Golf Course. Briggs, Karen, illus. 2017. (ENG.). 32p. (J). (gr. -1-1). 19.99 *(978-1-925266-29-0(X))* Allen & Unwin AUS. Dist: Independent Pubs. Group.

Mumford, Martha. We're Going on an Egg Hunt: A Lift-The-Flap Adventure. Hughes, Laura, illus. (Bunny Adventures Ser.). (ENG.). (J). 2018. 22p. bds. 7.99 *(978-1-68119-838-5(X),* 900188675) 2017. 24p. 17.99 *(978-1-68119-314-4(0),* 900165670) Bloomsbury Publishing USA. (Bloomsbury USA Childrens).

Murray, Alison. Hare & Tortoise. Murray, Alison, illus. 2016. (ENG., Illus.). 32p. (J). (-k). 18.99 *(978-0-7636-8721-2(9))* Candlewick Pr.

Murray, Rosalie. Bobby & Bun Bun's Afternoon Adventure. Swope, Brenda, illus. 2012. 32p. pap. 24.95 *(978-1-4560-5090-0(7))* America Star Bks.

Murrow, Marjorie. The Surprise in Grandma's Eyes. 2009. (Illus.). 16p. pap. 10.98 *(978-1-4389-8104-8(X))* AuthorHouse.

Mussenbrock, Anne. Easter Notes. 2004. 12p. (J). (gr. -1-k). 5.99 *(978-1-59384-037-2(3))* Parklane Publishing.

My Big Book of Beginner Books about Me. 2011. (Beginner Books(R) Ser.). (ENG., Illus.). 208p. (J). (gr. -1-2). 16.99 *(978-0-307-93183-2(8),* Random Hse. Bks. for Young Readers) Random Hse. Children's Bks.

Myers, Robin. Pinky Rabbit Learns to Share. 2008. 20p. pap. 24.95 *(978-1-60703-937-2(0))* America Star Bks.

Nahorniak, Mike. Kalico Jack. 2016. (ENG., Illus.). (J). 16.95 *(978-1-5069-0333-0(9));* pap. 14.95 *(978-1-5069-0290-6(1))* First Edition Design Publishing.

Nass, Marcia Shoshana. The Rabbit Who Lost His Hop: A Story about Self-Control. Gilgannon-Collins, Denise, illus. 2004. (Early Prevention Ser.: 5). (J). per. 19.95 *(978-1-58815-061-5(5),* 66525) Childswork/Childsplay.

Nathan, Sarah. Blue-Ribbon Bunny. 2014. (Sofia the First World of Reading Ser.). (J). lib. bdg. 13.55 *(978-0-606-35264-2(3))* Turtleback.

Nelson, Sean. Bungles Does the Bunny Op. 2012. 36p. pap. 16.95 *(978-1-4575-1106-6(1))* Dog Ear Publishing, LLC.

—Bungles Loses His Marbles. 2008. 36p. pap. 16.95 *(978-1-59858-605-3(X))* Dog Ear Publishing, LLC.

Nelson, Steve & Rollins, Jack. Here Comes Peter Cottontail. Set. Levy, Pamela R., illus. 2007. (ENG.). 26p. 16.99 *(978-0-8249-6689-8(9),* Ideals Pubns.) Worthy Publishing.

Neutzling, Laura. Grandpa Hugs, 1 vol. 2017. (ENG., Illus.). 20p. (J). bds. 9.99 *(978-0-7180-8940-5(5),* Tommy Nelson) Nelson, Thomas Inc.

Newberry, Clare Turlay. Marshmallow: An Easter & Springtime Book for Kids. Newberry, Clare Turlay, illus. 2008. (ENG., Illus.). 32p. (J). (gr. -1-1). 17.99 *(978-0-06-072486-3(2),* HarperCollins) HarperCollins Pubs.

Nicholas, Nicki. Spring Has Sprung for Peter & Lil. 2012. 24p. pap. 15.50 *(978-1-4669-2211-2(7))* Trafford Publishing.

Nicola A Green. Pumpkin: The easter Bunny. 2010. (Illus.). 48p. pap. *(978-1-907011-10-8(2))* Esteemworld Pubns.

Niddrie, June. E. B. & the Bees. 2010. 32p. pap. 16.10 *(978-0-557-31873-5(4))* Lulu Pr., Inc.

Nieting, Sherry. Adventures in Hope Forest: Isabelle's Search for God. 2011. (Illus.). 24p. (J). pap. 10.95 *(978-1-4497-2518-1(X),* WestBow Pr.) Author Solutions, LLC.

Nolan, Allia Zobel. When God Tucks in the Day. Chung, Chi, illus. 2005. 16p. (J). 12.99 *(978-0-8254-5524-7(3))* Kregel Pubns.

Noruziaan, Bahman. The Lonely Snake: Stories of Inspector Rabbit. 2013. 20p. pap. 13.77 *(978-1-4669-8678-7(6))* Trafford Publishing.

O'Connor, Jane. Fancy Nancy & the Missing Easter Bunny. 2017. (Fancy Nancy Picture Bks.). (J). lib. bdg. 14.75 *(978-0-606-39618-9(7))* Turtleback.

Odierno, Lisa. Bunny Hide-and-Seek. 2009. (Smithsonian Baby Animals Ser.). (ENG., Illus.). 16p. (J). (gr. -1-k). 6.95 *(978-1-60727-092-8(7))* Soundprints.

Odierno, Lisa & Soundprints Staff. Bunny Hide-and-Seek. 2009. (Smithsonian Baby Animals Ser.). (ENG., Illus.). 16p. (J). (gr. -1-k). 6.95 *(978-1-60727-105-5(2))* Soundprints.

Ojo, Loyce. Bath Time. 2015. (ENG., Illus.). 35p. (J). mass mkt. 13.95 *(978-1-78554-304-3(0),* fa8994c8-0382-4a91-a9da-c1dd79f592e5) Austin Macauley Pubs. Ltd. GBR. Dist: Baker & Taylor Publisher Services (BTPS).

Oliver, Lynn. The Birthday Present. 2008. (ENG.). 32p. pap. 21.99 *(978-1-4363-2756-5(3))* Xlibris Corp.

O'Neill, Rachael. Do You Want a Hug, Honey Bunny? O'Neill, Rachael, illus. 2008. (Tiger Tales Ser.). (Illus.). 12p. (J). (gr. -1-k). 8.95 *(978-1-58925-829-7(0))* Tiger Tales.

Osborn, Valerie Huffman. A Week of Bunnies. Osborn, Kimberly, ed. 2007. (ENG., Illus.). 32p. (J). 19.95 *(978-1-932278-25-5(7))* Mayhaven Publishing, Inc.

Osborne, Amber & Osborne, Dwight. Puffy Buffy Jones Jones Osborne Dadoot Da Do. Osborne, Amber, illus. 2006. (Illus.). (J). pap. 11.99 *(978-0-9786431-0-2(0))* AAO Publishing.

O'Toole-Freel, Judy. Zigzag the Rocking Roadrunner. Freel, Mirle, illus. 2012. 40p. 24.95 *(978-1-4626-9970-4(7))* America Star Bks.

Ouchley, Amy Griffin. Swamper: Letters from a Louisiana Swamp Rabbit. 2013. (ENG., Illus.). 72p. (gr. 4-7). 22.50 *(978-0-8071-5074-0(6),* 1763) Louisiana State Univ. Pr.

Overington, Marcus. Lost on Bodmin Moor. 2012. (Illus.). 50p. pap. *(978-1-909039-36-0(5))* Legend Pr.

The Package: KinderConcepts Individual Title Six-Packs. (Kinderstarters Ser.). 8p. (gr. -1-1). 21.00 *(978-0-7635-8737-6(0))* Rigby Education.

Palatini, Margie. Goldie & the Three Hares. Davis, Jack E., illus. 2011. (ENG.). 32p. (J). (gr. -1-2). 17.99 *(978-0-06-125314-0(6),* Tegen, Katherine Bks) HarperCollins Pubs.

Pankiw, Mary. Ruffles Rabbit. 2013. 52p. pap. 19.39 *(978-1-4669-7572-9(5))* Trafford Publishing.

Pappas, Peter. Stu the Rabbit. 2007. (J). *(978-0-9801439-3-5(4))* Town & Country Reprographics.

Parasciuc, Natalia. Beaverlini & Rodney Are Having Fun! 2011. (ENG.). 27p. 12.99 *(978-0-557-84882-9(2))* Lulu Pr., Inc.

Park, Linda Sue. What Does Bunny See? A Book of Colors & Flowers. Smith, Maggie, illus. 2018. (ENG.). 32p. (J). (gr. -1-3). pap. 7.99 *(978-1-328-88611-8(5),* 1698480, Clarion Bks.) HarperCollins Pubs.

Parker, Emma. Mr Grumpy Bunny. 2010. (Illus.). pap. *(978-1-877561-22-1(3))* First Edition Ltd.

Parker, Vic, compiled by. The Fish & the Hare & Other Silly Stories, 1 vol. 2015. (Silly Stories Ser.). (ENG.). 40p. (J). (gr. 2-3). pap. 15.05 *(978-1-4824-4199-4(3),* ab1e5772-9b68-4a07-ad79-1433bbf4329e) Stevens, Gareth Publishing LLLP.

—The Hare-Brained Crocodiles & Other Silly Stories, 1 vol. 2015. (Silly Stories Ser.). (ENG.). 40p. (J). (gr. 2-3). pap. 15.05 *(978-1-4824-4202-1(7),* ce434dd8-ca4a-4dc5-80ba-a76c09f9aff8) Stevens, Gareth Publishing LLLP.

Paul, Ann Whitford. Fiesta Fiasco. Long, Ethan, illus. 2012. pap. 18.95 *(978-1-4301-1099-6(6))* Live Oak Media.

Paul, Dwain. The Fox the Hare the Wolf & the Sheep. 2011. 28p. 16.10 *(978-1-4269-5573-0(1))* Trafford Publishing.

Payton-Wright, Kaye. The Secret Wood. 2010. 28p. pap. 21.99 *(978-1-4535-0321-8(8))* Xlibris Corp.

PC Treasures Staff, prod. Peter Rabbit. 2007. (J). *(978-1-60072-021-5(8))* PC Treasures, Inc.

Pence, Charlotte. Marlon Bundo's Day in the Life of the Vice President. Pence, Karen, illus. 2018. (ENG.). 40p. (J). (gr. -1-3). 18.99 *(978-1-62157-776-8(7),* Regnery Kids) Regnery Publishing.

Perkins, Larry B. Jasper Rabbit. 2005. 33p. per. 8.95 *(978-1-4116-1936-4(6))* Lulu Pr., Inc.

Peter Rabbit Books 800845, 3. 2005. (J). *(978-1-59794-046-7(1))* Environments, Inc.

Peters, Stephanie True. The Robo-Battle of Mega Tortoise vs. Hazard Hare: A Graphic Novel. Cano, Fernando, illus. 2017. (Far Out Fables Ser.). (ENG.). 40p. (J). (gr. 3-6). pap. 4.95 *(978-1-4965-5424-6(8),* 136357); lib. bdg. 25.32 *(978-1-4965-5420-8(5),* 136353) Capstone. (Stone Arch Bks.).

Petersen, David. Snowy Valentine. Petersen, David, illus. 2011. (ENG., Illus.). 32p. (J). (gr. -1-3). 14.99 *(978-0-06-146378-5(7),* HarperCollins) HarperCollins Pubs.

Petreman, Gwen. Caught by Rabroar. 2012. 20p. pap. 11.59 *(978-1-4669-5098-6(6))* Trafford Publishing.

Pevear, Ted F. & Pevear, Linda W. Finding Little Feathers a Hub-A-Son. 2012. 24p. 24.95 *(978-1-4626-5874-9(1))* America Star Bks.

Phillips, Dee & Ticktock Media, Ltd. Staff. What Do Rabbits Do? 2009. (What Do Animals Do? Ser.). (ENG.). 5p. (J). (gr. k — 1). bds. 4.95 *(978-1-84696-961-4(1),* TickTock Books) Octopus Publishing Group GBR. Dist: Independent Pubs. Group.

Pilkey, Dav. The Dumb Bunnies. Pilkey, Dav, illus. (ENG., Illus.). 32p. (J). (gr. -1-3). 2007. 12.99 *(978-0-545-03938-3(X),* Blue Sky Pr., The) 2nd ed. 2005. pap. 7.99 *(978-0-439-66944-3(8),* Scholastic Paperbacks) Scholastic, Inc.

—The Dumb Bunnies' Easter. 2009. (ENG., Illus.). 32p. (J). (gr. -1-3). 16.99 *(978-0-545-03946-8(0),* Blue Sky Pr., The) Scholastic, Inc.

—The Dumb Bunnies' Easter. Pilkey, Dav, illus. 2008. (Scholastic Bookshelf Ser.). (ENG., Illus.). 32p. (J). (gr. -1-3). pap. 6.99 *(978-0-545-00880-8(8),* Scholastic Paperbacks) Scholastic, Inc.

—The Dumb Bunnies Go to the Zoo. Pilkey, Dav, illus. 2009. (ENG., Illus.). 32p. (J). (gr. -1-3). 16.99 *(978-0-545-03937-6(1),* Blue Sky Pr., The) Scholastic, Inc.

—The Dumb Bunnies Go to the Zoo. 2007. (ENG.). 32p. pap. 5.99 *(978-0-439-93049-9(9))* Scholastic, Inc.

—Make Way for Dumb Bunnies. Pilkey, Dav, illus. 2007. (ENG., Illus.). 32p. (J). (gr. -1-3). 10.99 *(978-0-545-03939-0(8),* Blue Sky Pr., The) Scholastic, Inc.

Pinkney, Jerry. The Tortoise & the Hare. 2013. (ENG., Illus.). 40p. (J). (gr. -1-3). 18.99 *(978-0-316-18356-7(3))* Little, Brown Bks. for Young Readers.

Poehler, S. Applecheeks & the Pop E. Tree. 2012. 12p. pap. 15.99 *(978-1-4772-8180-2(0))* AuthorHouse.

Ponti, Claude. En El Coche. 2003. (SPA.). 32p. 15.95 *(978-84-95150-08-0(5))* Corimbo, Editorial S.L. ESP. Dist: Distribooks, Inc.

Por que el conejo tiene las orejas tan Largas? Lap Book. (Pebble Soup Exploraciones Ser.). (SPA.). 16p. (gr. -1-18). 21.00 *(978-0-7578-1691-8(6))* Rigby Education.

Por que el conejo tiene las orejas tan Largas? Small Book. (Pebble Soup Exploraciones Ser.). (SPA.). 16p. (gr. -1-18). 5.00 *(978-0-7578-1731-1(9))* Rigby Education.

Por que los conejos tienen las orejas Largas: Individual Title Six-Packs. (Literatura 2000 Ser.). (SPA.). (gr. 2-3). 33.00 *(978-0-7635-1271-2(0))* Rigby Education.

Portis, Antoinette. Not a Box. Portis, Antoinette, illus. 2006. (Not a Box Ser.). (ENG., Illus.). 32p. (J). (gr. -1 — 1). 17.99 *(978-0-06-112322-1(6));* lib. bdg. 16.89 *(978-0-06-112323-8(4))* HarperCollins Pubs. (HarperCollins).

—Not a Box Board Book. 2011. (Not a Box Ser.). (ENG., Illus.). 28p. (J). (gr. -1 — 1). bds. 9.99 *(978-0-06-199442-5(1),* HarperFestival) HarperCollins Pubs.

Posey, Lee. Night Rabbits, 1 vol. Montgomery, Michael G., illus. 2007. 32p. (J). (gr. -1-3). 7.95 *(978-1-56145-397-9(8))* Peachtree Publishing Co. Inc.

Posey, Sandra Mizumoto. Rabbits with Stars in their Eyes. 2010. 32p. pap. 15.00 *(978-0-557-12242-4(2))* Lulu Pr., Inc.

Posner, Tina. Rabbit Tricks. Corbett, Liza, illus. 2006. 8p. (J). pap. *(978-0-439-73513-1(0))* Scholastic, Inc.

Potter, Beatrix. A Beatrix Potter Treasury. 2007. (Peter Rabbit Ser.). (ENG., Illus.). 192p. (J). (gr. -1-2). 24.99 *(978-0-7232-5957-2(7),* Warne) Penguin Young Readers Group.

—Classic Tale of Peter Rabbit Hardcover: The Classic Edition by the New York Times Bestselling Illustrator, Charles Santore. 2013. (Charles Santore Children's Classics Ser.). (ENG., Illus.). 74p. (J). (gr. -1). 19.95 *(978-1-60433-376-3(6),* Applesauce Pr.) Cider Mill Pr. Bk. Pubs., LLC.

—Cuento - Perico el Conejo. Orig. Title: Tale of Peter Rabbit. (SPA.). 60p. (J). 8.95 *(978-84-7444-725-5(9))* Debate, Editorial ESP. Dist: AIMS International Bks., Inc.

—El Gato Tomas. 2003. (Coleccion el Mundo de Peter Rabbit). (SPA., Illus.). (J). (gr. k-2). pap. *(978-950-07-1722-9(0),* SA30685) Editorial Sudamericana S.A. ARG. Dist: Lectorum Pubns., Inc.

—Jeremias el Pescador. 2003. (Coleccion el Mundo de Peter Rabbit). (SPA., Illus.). (J). (gr. k-2). pap. *(978-950-07-1721-2(2),* SA30686) Editorial Sudamericana S.A. ARG. Dist: Lectorum Pubns., Inc.

—La Oca Carlota. 2003. (Coleccion el Mundo de Peter Rabbit). (SPA., Illus.). (J). (gr. k-2). pap. *(978-950-07-1723-6(9),* SA30687) Editorial Sudamericana S.A. ARG. Dist: Lectorum Pubns., Inc.

—The Peter Rabbit & Friends Treasury. Potter, Beatrix, illus. 2006. (Illus.). 240p. (J). (gr. k-4). reprint ed. 20.00 *(978-1-4223-5452-0(0))* DIANE Publishing Co.

—Peter Rabbit Book & Toy. 2006. (Peter Rabbit Ser.). (ENG., Illus.). 70p. (J). (gr. -1 — 1). 17.99 *(978-0-7232-5356-3(0),* Warne) Penguin Young Readers Group.

—Peter Rabbit Lift-the-Flap Words, Colors, & Numbers. 2007. (Potter Ser.). (ENG., Illus.). 12p. (J). (gr. -1-18). 14.99 *(978-0-7232-5828-5(7),* Warne) Penguin Publishing Group.

—Sgeulachd Bheniamin Coineanach. MacDonald, James, 1st, tr. from ENG. Potter, Beatrix, illus. 2008. Tr. of Tale of Benjamin Bunny. (GAE., Illus.). 64p. (J). *(978-0-9552326-4-0(3))* Grace Note Pubns.

—The Tale of Benjamin Bunny. 2007. (Illus.). 60p. per. *(978-1-4065-5873-9(7))* Dodo Pr.

—The Tale of Benjamin Bunny. 2007. 60p. per. 16.95 *(978-0-548-80107-9(X))* Kessinger Publishing, LLC.

—The Tale of Benjamin Bunny. 2012. (World of Beatrix Potter: Peter Rabbit Ser.). (ENG.). 32p. (J). (gr. -1-1). 16.19 *(978-0-7232-6836-9(3));* (gr. 1-2). pap. 4.99 *(978-0-7232-6814-7(2),* Penguin Young Readers) Penguin Young Readers Group.

—The Tale of Benjamin Bunny. (Illus.). 12p. 4.95 *(978-1-58989-272-9(0))* Thurman Hse., LLC.

—The Tale of Peter Rabbit. 2013. 30p. pap. 12.00 *(978-1-927558-35-5(2))* 2012. 26p. pap. 12.00 *(978-0-9880821-2-0(8))* Birch Tree Publishing.

—The Tale of Peter Rabbit. 2010. (ENG.). 30p. pap. 9.49 *(978-1-4538-2670-6(X))* CreateSpace Independent Publishing Platform.

—The Tale of Peter Rabbit. Hague, Michael, illus. 2003. 29p. (J). (gr. 2-5). reprint ed. 16.00 *(978-0-7567-6968-0(X))* DIANE Publishing Co.

—The Tale of Peter Rabbit, 5 vols. 110th ed. 2012. (Peter Rabbit Ser.). (ENG., Illus.). 72p. (J). (gr. -1-2). 8.99 *(978-0-7232-6769-0(3),* Warne) Penguin Young Readers Group.

—The Tale of Peter Rabbit. McPhail, David, illus. 2014. (ENG.). 28p. (J). (gr. -1 — 1). bds. 6.99 *(978-0-545-65096-0(8),* Cartwheel Bks.) Scholastic, Inc.

—The Tale of Peter Rabbit. (Illus.). 12p. 4.95 *(978-1-58989-271-2(2))* Thurman Hse., LLC.

—The Tale of Peter Rabbit. 2012. (Penguin Young Readers Level 2 Ser.). lib. bdg. 13.55 *(978-0-606-23629-4(5))* Turtleback.

—The Tale of the Flopsy Bunnies. 2012. (World of Beatrix Potter: Peter Rabbit Ser.). (ENG.). 32p. (J). (gr. -1-1). 16.19 *(978-0-7232-6837-6(1))* Penguin Young Readers Group.

—Tickle, Tickle, Peter! A First Touch-And-Feel Book. 2012. (Peter Rabbit Ser.). (ENG.). 10p. (J). (gr. -1 — 1). bds. 9.99 *(978-0-7232-6750-8(2),* Warne) Penguin Young Readers Group.

Potter, Beatrix, illus. The Tale of Peter Rabbit. 2014. (J). pap. *(978-1-4677-5772-0(1),* First Avenue Editions) Lerner Publishing Group.

Powell, Christine. Bootsie's Underground Adventure. 2012. 28p. pap. 24.95 *(978-1-4626-7449-7(6))* America Star Bks.

Powell, Richard. Becky Bunny. Rhodes, Katie, illus. 2004. (Fuzzy Friends Ser.). 10p. (J). 7.95 *(978-1-58925-723-8(5))* Tiger Tales.

Powers-Fish, Amy Rose. Ethics 4 Every Bunny. 2012. (ENG.). 77p. pap. 34.77 *(978-1-105-50495-2(6))* Lulu Pr., Inc.

Poydar, Nancy. Bunny Business. 2003. (ENG., Illus.). 32p. (J). (gr. k-3). tchr. ed. 16.95 *(978-0-8234-1771-1(9))* Holiday Hse., Inc.

Prasadam-Halls, Smriti. I Love You Night & Day. Brown, Alison, illus. 2014. (ENG.). 32p. (J). (gr. -1-1). 16.99 *(978-1-61963-222-6(5),* 900127512, Bloomsbury USA Childrens) Bloomsbury Publishing USA.

Price, Mathew. Polo y Los Conejos. (SPA.). pap. 7.95 *(978-950-07-1978-0(9))* Editorial Sudamericana S.A. ARG. Dist: Distribooks, Inc.

Prignano, Barbara. How Bunnies Got Their Cottontails. 2009. (Illus.). 20p. pap. 11.95 *(978-1-60860-675-7(9),* Eloquent Bks.) Strategic Book Publishing & Rights Agency (SBPRA).

Principe, Tami. The Green Rabbit: Rabbits Aren't Supposed to Be Green! 2012. 32p. pap. 10.95 *(978-1-4626-7509-8(3))* America Star Bks.

Publications International Ltd. Staff, ed. Disney Bunnies. 2009. 16p. (J). bds. 9.98 *(978-1-4127-1721-2(3),* PIL Kids) Publications International, Ltd.

—Disney(r) Sofia the FirstShow-And-Tell Surprise. 2015. 8p. (J). bds. *(978-1-4508-7560-8(2),* 1450875602) Publications International, Ltd.

Puglisi, Salvatore. It's best to be Me. 2008. (ENG.). 36p. pap. 14.99 *(978-1-4196-8330-5(6))* CreateSpace Independent Publishing Platform.

Pyne, Jane. Tommy's Secret. 2009. 86p. pap. 10.49 *(978-1-4389-9102-3(9))* AuthorHouse.

Quayle, Ruth. That Bear Can't Babysit. Friend, Alison, illus. 2018. (ENG.). 32p. (J). (gr. -1-2). 16.99 *(978-0-7636-9952-9(7))* Candlewick Pr.

Rabbit's Spring Adventure. 2012. (Illus.). (J). *(978-1-4351-4584-9(4))* Barnes & Noble, Inc.

Rabe, Tish. Five Little Bunnies. Yaccarino, Dan, illus. 2016. (ENG.). 16p. (J). (gr. -1 — 1). bds. 6.99 *(978-0-06-225339-2(5),* HarperFestival) HarperCollins Pubs.

Ralph the Rabbit. 2003. (Chunky Animal Shaped Boards Ser.). (J). 10p. bds. 9.95 *(978-0-7525-7855-2(3));* (Illus.). bds. 1.98 *(978-0-7525-7776-0(X))* Parragon, Inc.

Ramsey, Byra L. Little Stick. 2009. 28p. pap. 13.99 *(978-1-4490-3371-2(7))* AuthorHouse.

Rand, Johnathan. Freddie Fernortner #9: Attack of the Dust Bunnies from Outer Space. 2008. 96p. (J). pap. 4.99 *(978-1-893699-95-3(1))* AudioCraft Publishing, Inc.

Raschka, Chris. Five for a Little One. Raschka, Chris, illus. 2006. (ENG., Illus.). 48p. (J). (gr. -1-2). 19.99 *(978-0-689-84599-4(5),* Atheneum/Richard Jackson Bks.) Simon & Schuster Children's Publishing.

Rath, Tom H. Donkey Oatie's Field Trip. Gaudet, Christine, illus. 2013. 26p. pap. *(978-0-9918033-4-7(5))* Wood Islands Prints.

Rawlinson, Julia & Warnes, Tim. A Surprise for Rosie. 2005. (Illus.). 32p. (J). 15.95 *(978-1-58925-046-8(X))* Tiger Tales.

Rayner, Abigail. The Backup Bunny. Stones, Greg, illus. 2018. (ENG.). 32p. (J). (gr. -1-3). 17.95 *(978-0-7358-4282-3(5))* North-South Bks., Inc.

Reasoner, Charles, illus. Honey Bunny. 2015. (J). *(978-1-4795-5945-9(8),* Picture Window Bks.) Capstone.

Reitze, Glenn Logan. Ernie the Easter Hippopotamus: A Comic Adventure for Anytime. Reitze, Glenn Logan, illus. 2007. (ENG., Illus.). 48p. (J). lib. bdg. 19.95 *(978-0-88265-040-1(8),* Fine Art Editions) North American International.

Reitze, Glenn Logan, illus. & text. Ernie the Easter Hippotamus: A Comic Adventure for Anytime. Reitze, Glenn Logan, text. 2007. 47p. (J). pap. *(978-0-88265-041-8(6))* North American International.

Reynolds, Aaron. Creepy Carrots! Brown, Peter, illus. 2012. (Creepy Tales! Ser.). (ENG.). 40p. (J). (gr. -1-3). 18.99 *(978-1-4424-0297-3(0),* Simon & Schuster Bks. For Young Readers) Simon & Schuster Bks. For Young Readers.

—Creepy Crayon! Brown, Peter, illus. 2022. (Creepy Tales! Ser.). (ENG.). 48p. (J). (gr. -1-3). 18.99 *(978-1-5344-6588-6(X),* Simon & Schuster Bks. For Young Readers) Simon & Schuster Bks. For Young Readers.

—Creepy Pair of Underwear! Brown, Peter, illus. 2017. (Creepy Tales! Ser.). (ENG.). 48p. (J). (gr. -1-3). 18.99 *(978-1-4424-0298-0(9),* Simon & Schuster Bks. For Young Readers) Simon & Schuster Bks. For Young Readers.

—Creepy Pair of Underwear! 2018. (KOR.). (J). (gr. -1-3). *(978-89-6496-367-8(9))* Toto Bk.

—Las Zanahorias Maléficas. 2015.Tr. of Creepy Carrots. (SPA.). 40p. (J). (gr. k-3). 24.95 *(978-84-16117-13-0(6))* Ediciones Obelisco ESP. Dist: Spanish Pubs., LLC.

Rhae, Sympne. My Name is Johnson? l.t. ed. 2006. (Illus.). 53p. (J). per. 13.75 *(978-0-9770043-9-3(2))* New Global Publishing.

Rice, Dona Herwick. The Tortoise & the Hare, 1 vol. rev. ed. 2008. (Reader's Theater Ser.). (ENG.). 24p. (gr. 1-3). pap. 8.99 *(978-1-4333-0290-9(X))* Teacher Created Materials, Inc.

Richard, Ramonda. Robert the Bully. 2012. 28p. pap. 24.95 *(978-1-4626-7170-0(5))* America Star Bks.

Richmond, Lori. Bunny Business (Mama's Day at Work) 2020. (ENG., Illus.). 32p. (J). (gr. -1-k). 18.99 *(978-0-545-92590-7(8),* Scholastic Pr.) Scholastic, Inc.

—Bunny's Staycation (Mama's Business Trip) 2018. (ENG., Illus.). 32p. (J). (gr. -1-k). 17.99 (978-0-545-92589-1(4), Scholastic Pr.) Scholastic, Inc.

Rigby Education Staff. A Class Pet. (Illus.). 8p. (J). bds. 6.95 (978-0-7635-6439-1(7), 764397C99) Rigby Education.

Risom, Ole. I Am a Bunny. Scarry, Richard, illus. 2004. (Golden Sturdy Book Ser.). (ENG.). 26p. (J). (gr. -1 — 1). bds. 7.99 (978-0-375-82778-5(1), Golden Bks.) Random Hse. Children's Bks.

Ritchie, Alison. The Tortoise & the Hare. Noj, Nahta, illus. 2015. (ENG.). 32p. (J). (-k). 15.99 (978-0-7636-7601-8(2), Templar) Candlewick Pr.

Ritchie, Joseph R. Peter Cottontail's Easter Surprise. Halverson, Lydia, illus. 2006. (ENG.). 18p. (J). (gr. -1-k). bds. 9.95 (978-0-8249-6627-0(9), Ideals Pubns.) Worthy Publishing.

Robaard, Jedda. The Little Rabbit Who Lost Her Hop. 2018. (ENG.). 12p. (J). (gr. -1-k). bds. 7.99 (978-1-4998-0683-0(3)) Little Bee Books Inc.

Robe, Adam D. Moving to Another Foster Home. Robe, Kim A., ed. Gavet, Nathalie, illus. 2009. 16p. pap. 11.99 (978-0-9817403-4-8(0)) Robe Communications, Inc.

—Robbie's Trail Through Adoption. Robe, Kim A., ed. Gavet, Nathalie, illus. 2010. 44p. pap. 23.99 (978-1-935831-03-7(8)) Robe Communications, Inc.

—Robbie's Trail Through Adoption — Activity Book. Robe, Kim A., ed. Gavet, Nathalie, illus. 2010. 36p. pap. 16.99 (978-1-935831-04-4(6)) Robe Communications, Inc.

—Robbie's Trail Through Adoption — Adult Guide. Robe, Kim A., ed. Gavet, Nathalie, illus. 2010. 28p. pap. 16.99 (978-1-935831-05-1(4)) Robe Communications, Inc.

—Robbie's Trail Through Foster Care. Robe, Kim A., ed. Gavet, Nathalie, illus. 2010. 40p. pap. 23.99 (978-1-935831-00-6(3)) Robe Communications, Inc.

—Robbie's Trail Through Foster Care — Activity Book. Robe, Kim A., ed. Gavet, Nathalie, illus. 2010. 36p. pap. 16.99 (978-1-935831-01-3(1)) Robe Communications, Inc.

—Robbie's Trail Through Foster Care — Adult Guide. Robe, Kim A., ed. Gavet, Nathalie, illus. 2010. 28p. pap. 16.99 (978-1-935831-02-0(X)) Robe Communications, Inc.

—Robbie's Trail Through Open Adoption. Robe, Kim A., ed. Gavet, Nathalie, illus. 2010. 44p. pap. 23.99 (978-1-935831-06-8(2)) Robe Communications, Inc.

—Wanting to Belong. Robe, Kim A., ed. Gavet, Nathalie, illus. 2009. 16p. pap. 11.99 (978-0-9817403-6-2(7)) Robe Communications, Inc.

Robe, Kim. Robbie's Trail Through Divorce. Gavet, Nathalie, illus. 2012. 40p. (-18). pap. 23.99 (978-1-935831-11-2(9)) Robe Communications, Inc.

—Robbie's Trail Through Divorce - Activity Book. Gavet, Nathalie, illus. 2012. 28p. (-18). pap. 16.99 (978-1-935831-12-9(7)) Robe Communications, Inc.

—Robbie's Trail Through Divorce - Adult Guide. Gavet, Nathalie, illus. 2012. 28p. (-18). pap. 16.99 (978-1-935831-13-6(5)) Robe Communications, Inc.

Robertson, Susan, illus. Little Bunny. 2005. (Bedtime Babies Ser.). 8p. (J). (gr. -1). per., bds. 6.99 (978-1-57755-503-2(1)) Flying Frog Publishing, Inc.

Robey, Katharine Crawford. Hare & the Big Green Lawn. MacDougall, Larry, illus. 2006. (ENG.). 32p. (J). (gr. -1-3). 15.95 (978-0-87358-889-8(4)) Cooper Square Publishing Llc.

Robinson, Jeanette. Blueberry Bunny. 2012. 32p. pap. 19.99 (978-1-4685-6410-5(2)) AuthorHouse.

Rogers, Carol J. The Adventures of Buttonballs' Trails. 2012. 28p. pap. 19.99 (978-1-4772-4481-4(6)) AuthorHouse.

Rogers, Jewels. The Princess & the Rabbit. 2011. 28p. pap. 12.50 (978-1-4567-5171-5(9)) AuthorHouse.

Rogger. The Fifty-Fifth Bear & the Awkward Rabbits: An Amazing Thick Blue Wood Bear Adventure. 2009. (Illus.). 60p. pap. 21.99 (978-1-4389-1672-9(8)) AuthorHouse.

Rohmann, Eric. My Friend Rabbit: A Picture Book. Rohmann, Eric, illus. 2007. (ENG., Illus.). 32p. (J). (gr. -1-1). pap. 8.99 (978-0-312-36752-7(X), 900042356) Square Fish.

Rosen, Jonathan. Night of the Living Cuddle Bunnies: Devin Dexter #1. (Devin & Dexter Ser.: 1). (ENG.). (J). (gr. 2-7). 2018. 304p. pap. 9.99 (978-1-5107-3487-6(2)) 2017. 256p. 15.99 (978-1-5107-1523-3(1)) Skyhorse Publishing Co., Inc. (Sky Pony Pr.).

Rosenthal, Amy Krouse. Duck! Rabbit! Lichtenheld, Tom, illus. aut. ed. 2009. (J). 16.99 (978-0-8118-3332-0(9)) Chronicle Bks. LLC.

Rosie the Counting Rabbit. (J). (gr. k-2). pap. 9.90 (978-0-669-15888-5(7)); pap. 9.90 (978-0-669-15293-7(5)) Houghton Mifflin Harcourt School Pubs.

Ross, Dave "Persue" & Satenstein, Diane. The Origins of Bunny Kitty: A Tale for All Ages. 2016. (ENG., Illus.). 48p. (J). (gr. -1-3). 14.95 (978-1-58423-652-8(3), 6afdf2e5-4141-49d7-9eec-bd7e851ac767) Gingko Pr., Inc.

Roussey, Christine. My Funny Bunny. 2019. (ENG., Illus.). 32p. (J). (gr. -1-1). 16.99 (978-1-4197-3618-6(3), 1271001, Abrams Bks. for Young Readers) Abrams, Inc.

Rowe, Eva McKenzie & Hodge, Darren. Harrison Bean. 2012. 28p. pap. 24.95 (978-1-4626-6503-7(9)) America Star Bks.

Roy, Ron. Calendar Mysteries #2: February Friend. Gurney, John Steven, illus. 2009. (Calendar Mysteries Ser.: 2). 80p. (J). (gr. 1-4). 6.99 (978-0-375-85662-4(5), Random Hse. Bks. for Young Readers) Random Hse. Children's Bks.

Roy Windham, Windham & Windham, Roy. Uncle Fuddy-Duddy & the Big Bad Bear. 2010. 28p. 16.09 (978-1-4269-3065-2(8)) Trafford Publishing.

Rueda, Claudia. Bunny Slopes: (Winter Books for Kids, Snow Children's Books, Skiing Books for Kids) 2016. (Bunny Interactive Picture Bks.). (ENG., Illus.). 60p. (J). (gr. -1-k). 16.99 (978-1-4521-4197-8(5)) Chronicle Bks. LLC.

—Hungry Bunny. 2018. (Bunny Interactive Picture Bks.). (ENG., Illus.). 64p. (J). (gr. -1-k). 15.99 (978-1-4521-6255-3(7)) Chronicle Bks. LLC.

Rumbaugh, Melinda. Somebunny Loves You! 2015. (ENG., Illus.). 16p. (J). bds. 13.99 (978-0-8249-1950-4(5), Worthy Kids/Ideals) Worthy Publishing.

Rumford, James. Beo-Bunny. 2012. 50p. pap. 14.00 (978-1-891839-09-2(8)) Manoa Pr.

Russell, Rachel. How the Hare Saved the Animals of the Savanna from a Drought. 2011. 48p. pap. 21.99 (978-1-4520-7518-1(2)) AuthorHouse.

Russo, Brian. Yoga Bunny: An Easter & Springtime Book for Kids. Russo, Brian, illus. 2016. (ENG., Illus.). 40p. (J). (gr. -1-3). 18.99 (978-0-06-242952-0(3), HarperCollins) HarperCollins Pubs.

Russo, Marisabina. The Bunnies Are Not in Their Beds. Russo, Marisabina, illus. 2019. (Illus.). 36p. (J). (-k). bds. 8.99 (978-0-525-58226-7(6), Schwartz & Wade Bks.) Random Hse. Children's Bks.

—The Bunnies Are Not in Their Beds. 2013. lib. bdg. 18.40 (978-0-606-26964-3(9)) Turtleback.

Rutt, Preston. Tortoise vs. Hare: The Rematch. Redlich, Ben, illus. 2015. (ENG.). 24p. (J). (gr. -1-3). 7.99 (978-1-85733-722-8(0)) Lerner Publishing Group.

Rylant, Cynthia. Annie & Snowball & the Dress-Up Birthday. 2008. (Annie & Snowball Ready-To-Read Ser.). lib. bdg. 13.55 (978-1-4178-1126-7(9)) Turtleback.

—Annie & Snowball & the Dress-Up Birthday: Ready-To-Read Level 2. Stevenson, Suçie & Stevenson, Suçie, illus. (Annie & Snowball Ser.: 1). (ENG.). 40p. (J). (gr. k-2). 2008. pap. 4.99 (978-1-4169-1459-4(5)) 2007. 17.99 (978-1-4169-0938-5(9)) Simon Spotlight. (Simon Spotlight).

—Annie & Snowball & the Grandmother Night. 2013. (Annie & Snowball Ready-To-Read Ser.). lib. bdg. 13.55 (978-0-606-35183-6(3)) Turtleback.

—Annie & Snowball & the Grandmother Night: Ready-To-Read Level 2. Stevenson, Suçie & Stevenson, Suçie, illus. (Annie & Snowball Ser.: 12). (ENG.). 40p. (J). (gr. k-2). 2013. pap. 4.99 (978-1-4169-7204-4(8)) 2012. 17.99 (978-1-4169-7203-7(X)) Simon Spotlight. (Simon Spotlight).

—Annie & Snowball & the Surprise Day: Ready-To-Read Level 2. Stevenson, Suçie & Stevenson, Suçie, illus. (Annie & Snowball Ser.: 11). (ENG.). 40p. (J). (gr. k-2). 2013. pap. 4.99 (978-1-4169-3948-1(2)) 2012. 17.99 (978-1-4169-3944-3(X)) Simon Spotlight. (Simon Spotlight).

—Annie & Snowball & the Teacup Club: Ready-To-Read Level 2. Stevenson, Suçie & Stevenson, Suçie, illus. (Annie & Snowball Ser.: 3). (ENG.). 40p. (J). (gr. k-2). 2009. pap. 4.99 (978-1-4169-1461-7(7)) 2008. 17.99 (978-1-4169-0940-8(0)) Simon Spotlight. (Simon Spotlight).

—Annie & Snowball & the Thankful Friends. 2012. (Annie & Snowball Ready-To-Read Ser.). lib. bdg. 13.55 (978-0-606-26917-9(7)) Turtleback.

—Annie & Snowball & the Wedding Day: Ready-To-Read Level 2. Stevenson, Suçie & Stevenson, Suçie, illus. (Annie & Snowball Ser.: 13). (ENG.). 40p. (J). (gr. k-2). 2015. pap. 4.99 (978-1-4169-7486-4(5)) 2014. 17.99 (978-1-4169-7485-7(7)) Simon Spotlight. (Simon Spotlight).

—The Case of the Climbing Cat. Karas, G. Brian, illus. 2003. (High-Rise Private Eyes Ser.: No. 2). (J). (gr. -1-3). 25.96 incl. audio (978-1-59112-190-9(6)); pap. 29.95 incl. audio (978-1-59112-191-6(4)) Live Oak Media.

—The Case of the Puzzling Possum. Karas, G. Brian, illus. 2003. (High-Rise Private Eyes Ser.: No. 3). (J). (gr. -1-3). 25.95 incl. audio (978-1-59112-198-5(1)); (gr. k-3). pap. 29.95 incl. audio (978-1-59112-199-2(X)) Live Oak Media.

Sadler, Marilyn. Honey Bunny's Honey Bear. Bollen, Roger, illus. 2007. (Step into Reading Ser.). (ENG.). 32p. (J). (gr. -1-1). per. 4.99 (978-0-375-84326-6(4), Random Hse. Bks. for Young Readers) Random Hse. Children's Bks.

—P. J. Funnybunny's Bag of Tricks. Bollen, Roger, illus. 2005. (Step into Reading Ser.). 32p. 14.00 (978-0-7569-5405-5(3)) Perfection Learning Corp.

—P. J. Funnybunny's Bag of Tricks. Bollen, Roger, illus. 2004. (Step into Reading Ser.). 32p. (J). (gr. -1-1). pap. 4.99 (978-0-375-82444-9(8), Random Hse. Bks. for Young Readers) Random Hse. Children's Bks.

—P. J. Funnybunny's Bag of Tricks. 2004. (Step into Reading Level 2 Ser.). (gr. -1-2). lib. bdg. 13.55 (978-0-613-83535-0(2)) Turtleback.

Sadler, Marilyn & Bollen, Roger. Money, Money, Honey Bunny! 2006. (Bright & Early Books(R) Ser.). (ENG., Illus.). 36p. (J). (gr. -1-k). 9.99 (978-0-375-83370-0(6), Random Hse. Bks. for Young Readers) Random Hse. Children's Bks.

Sakai, Komako. The Snow Day. 2009. (J). pap. (978-0-545-01322-2(4), Levine, Arthur A. Bks.) Scholastic, Inc.

Sakai, Komako, creator. The Velveteen Rabbit. 2012. (Illus.). 40p. (J). (gr. -1). 17.95 (978-1-59270-128-5(0)) Enchanted Lion Bks., LLC.

Sakai, Stan. Usagi Yojimbo Vol. 3: Al Filo de la Vida y la Muerte. 2007. (SPA., Illus.). 200p. reprint ed. pap. 15.95 (978-1-59497-319-2(9)) Public Square Bks.

—Usagi Yojimbo Vol. 4: Estaciones. 2007. (SPA., Illus.). 200p. reprint ed. pap. 15.95 (978-1-59497-320-8(2)) Public Square Bks.

—Usagi Yojimbo Vol. 5: Segadora. 2007. (SPA., Illus.). 256p. reprint ed. pap. 17.95 (978-1-59497-321-5(0)) Public Square Bks.

—Usagi Yojimbo Vol. 6: Primeras Andanzas. 2007. (SPA., Illus.). 128p. reprint ed. pap. 12.95 (978-1-59497-322-2(9)) Public Square Bks.

—Usagi Yojimbo Vol. 7: Samurai (en Español) 2007. (SPA., Illus.). 144p. reprint ed. pap. 14.95 (978-1-59497-323-9(7)) Public Square Bks.

Saltzberg, Barney. Dog & Rabbit. Saltzberg, Barney, illus. 2019. (Illus.). 48p. (J). (gr. -1-2). lib. bdg. 14.99 (978-1-62354-107-1(7)) Charlesbridge Publishing, Inc.

Samson, Lucretia. Hungry Tiger & Clever Rabbit: A Tale from Korea, 1 vol. Bijloo, Adrian, illus. 2016. (ENG.). 24p. (J). pap. 9.95 (978-1-927244-58-6(7)) Clean Slate Pr. Ltd. NZL. Dist: Flying Start Bks.

—Hungry Tiger & Clever Rabbit (Big Book Edition) A Tale from Korea. Bijloo, Adrian, illus. 2016. 24p. (J). pap. (978-1-927244-68-5(4)) Flying Start Bks.

Sandall, Ellie. Everybunny Dance! Sandall, Ellie, illus. 2017. (ENG., Illus.). 32p. (J). (gr. -1-3). 17.99 (978-1-4814-9822-7(3), McElderry, Margaret K. Bks.) McElderry, Margaret K. Bks.

—Everybunny Dream! Sandall, Ellie, illus. 2019. (ENG., Illus.). 32p. (J). (gr. -1-3). 17.99 (978-1-5344-4004-3(6), McElderry, Margaret K. Bks.) McElderry, Margaret K. Bks.

Sande, Hans. Snake in the Grass. Vetleseter, Tonje, tr. from NOR. Moursund, Gry, illus. 2008. 40p. (J). (gr. -1-1). 16.95 (978-0-9815761-0-7(9)) Mackenzie Smiles, LLC.

Santore, Charles. Velveteen Rabbit Board Book: The Classic Edition Board Book. 2014. (Classic Edition Ser.). (ENG., Illus.). 24p. (J). (gr. -1). bds. 8.95 (978-1-60433-461-6(4), Applesauce Pr.) Cider Mill Pr. Bk. Pubs., LLC.

—Velveteen Rabbit Hardcover: The Classic Edition. 2013. (Charles Santore Children's Classics Ser.). (ENG., Illus.). 48p. (J). (gr. -1). 19.95 (978-1-60433-277-3(8), Applesauce Pr.) Cider Mill Pr. Bk. Pubs., LLC.

Santos, Penelope. Bird & Rabbit, 1 vol. 2015. (Rosen REAL Readers: STEM & STEAM Collection). (ENG.). 8p. (gr. k-1). pap. 5.46 (978-1-4994-9493-8(9), 47bea000-ff8f-4d88-93ea-24ce223473e6, Rosen Classroom) Rosen Publishing Group, Inc., The.

Sarfatti, Esther, tr. from ENG. Berto Da la Talla. 2006. (Libro de Capitulos de Arturo Ser.). (Illus.). 55p. (J). (gr. 6-8). per. 4.99 (978-1-930332-94-2(7)) Lectorum Pubns., Inc.

Sargent, Dave & Sargent, Pat. Chrissy Cottontail: Mind Your Mama, 15 bks. Huff, Jeane, illus. 2nd rev. ed. 2003. (Animal Pride Ser.: 7). 42p. (J). 7. pap. 6.95 (978-1-56763-772-4(8)) Vol. 7. lib. bdg. 20.95 (978-1-56763-771-7(X)) Ozark Publishing.

—Fuzzy Bunny, 10 vols., Vol. 19. Robinson, Laura, illus. 2004. (Learn to Read Ser.: 10). 18p. (J). lib. bdg. 20.95 (978-1-56763-833-2(3)); lib. bdg. 10.95 (978-1-56763-834-9(1)) Ozark Publishing.

—Fuzzy Bunny/el conejito Velloso, 10 vols., Vol. 19. Robinson, Laura, illus. 2004. (Learn to Read Ser.: 10). (ENG & SPA.). 18p. (J). pap. 10.95 (978-1-56763-998-8(4)); lib. bdg. 20.95 (978-1-56763-997-1(6)) Ozark Publishing.

—Young Dawn: Friends Care! Woodword, Elaine, illus. 2005. (Young Animal Pride Ser.: 8). 24p. (J). 8. pap. 6.95 (978-1-56763-878-3(3)) Vol. 8. lib. bdg. 20.95 (978-1-56763-877-6(5)) Ozark Publishing.

—Young Dike: Teamwork! Woodward, Elaine, illus. 2003. (Young Animal Pride Ser.: 5). 24p. (J). 5. pap. 6.95 (978-1-56763-872-1(4)) Vol. 5. lib. bdg. 20.95 (978-1-56763-871-4(6)) Ozark Publishing.

—Young Sammy: I'm a Little Stinker!, Vol. 9. Woodword, Elaine, illus. 2005. (Young Animal Pride Ser.). 24p. (J). pap. 10.95 (978-1-56763-880-6(5)) Ozark Publishing.

—Young White Thunder: I'm a Leader!, Vol. 6. Woodword, Elaine, illus. 2005. (Young Animal Pride Ser.). 24p. (J). pap. 10.95 (978-1-56763-874-5(0)) Ozark Publishing.

Sargent, Dave, et al. Young Chrissy: Mind Your Mama!, Vol. 7. 2005. (Young Animal Pride Ser.). (Illus.). 24p. (J). lib. bdg. 20.95 (978-1-56763-875-2(9)) Ozark Publishing.

Sasscer, Abby. Sophie's Stuff. Cayless, Sophie, illus. 2012. 36p. pap. 9.95 (978-0-9854729-1-7(X)) Sasscer, Abby.

Sattler, Jennifer. Dollop & Mrs. Fabulous. 2019. (ENG., Illus.). 32p. (J). (gr. -1-2). lib. bdg. 20.99 (978-0-399-55336-3(3), Knopf Bks. for Young Readers) Random Hse. Children's Bks.

Savage, Doug. Disco Fever. 2017. (Illus.). 142p. (J). (978-1-5379-7394-4(0)) Andrews McMeel Publishing.

—Laser Moose & Rabbit Boy. 2016. (Laser Moose & Rabbit Boy Ser.: 1). (ENG., Illus.). 144p. (J). pap. 9.99 (978-1-4494-7094-4(7)) Andrews McMeel Publishing.

—Laser Moose & Rabbit Boy: Disco Fever. 2017. (Laser Moose & Rabbit Boy Ser.: 2). (ENG., Illus.). 144p. (J). pap. 9.99 (978-1-4494-8687-7(8)) Andrews McMeel Publishing.

Saxon, Victoria. Big Trouble in Little Rodentia. 2016. (Illus.). (J). (978-1-5182-0883-6(5)) Random House Children's Books.

Scaglione, Dapos & Maria. A Unique Bunny. 2005. 65p. pap. 19.95 (978-1-4137-9530-1(7)) America Star Bks.

Scarry, Patsy. Richard Scarry's the Bunny Book. Scarry, Richard, illus. (Big Golden Book Ser.). (J). 2015. 32p. (-k). 9.99 (978-0-385-39090-3(4)) 2005. 24p. (gr. -1-2). 5.99 (978-0-375-83224-6(6)) Random Hse. Children's Bks. (Golden Bks.).

Scarry, Richard. Richard Scarry's Best Little Board Book Ever. Random House, illus. 2013. (ENG.). 24p. (J). (— 1). bds. 5.99 (978-0-449-81901-2(9), Golden Bks.) Random Hse. Children's Bks.

—Richard Scarry's Naughty Bunny. 2018. (Little Golden Book Ser.). (Illus.). 24p. (J). (-k). 5.99 (978-1-5247-6727-3(1), Golden Bks.) Random Hse. Children's Bks.

Scheffler, Axel, illus. Pip & Posy: the New Friend. 2017. (Pip & Posy Ser.). (ENG.). 32p. (J). (-k). 12.99 (978-0-7636-9339-8(1)) Candlewick Pr.

Scheuer, Benjamin. Hundred Feet Tall. Williams, Jemima, illus. 2020. (ENG.). 40p. (J). (gr. -1-3). 17.99 (978-1-5344-3219-2(1), Simon & Schuster Bks. For Young Readers) Simon & Schuster Bks. For Young Readers.

Schexnayder, Paul, illus. In the Time of Shimmer & Light. 2018. (J). (978-1-946160-29-4(6)) Univ. of Louisiana at Lafayette Pr.

Schneider, Cheryl & Olson, Carole. Bunnaby Bunny (L) Toddler Reader. Schneider, Cheryl, illus. deluxe ed. 2006. (Illus.). 20p. (J). bds. 10.00 (978-0-9712816-5-3(3)) Third Week Bks.

Schomp, Virginia. Brer Rabbit & the Goober Patch, 1 vol. 2013. (American Legends & Folktales Ser.). (ENG., Illus.). 32p. (gr. 3-3). pap. 11.58 (978-1-62712-014-2(9), 90310587-4577-48bd-b613-45231a0436f3) Cavendish Square Publishing LLC.

Schulman, Janet. 10 Easter Egg Hunters: A Holiday Counting Book. Davick, Linda, illus. 2012. 26p. (J). (gr. -1 — 1). 6.99 (978-0-375-86637-1(X), Knopf Bks. for Young Readers) Random Hse. Children's Bks.

Schwartz, Amy & Marcus, Leonard S. Oscar: The Big Adventure of a Little Sock Monkey. Schwartz, Amy, illus. 2006. (Illus.). 32p. (J). (gr. -1-2). 16.99 (978-0-06-072622-5(9), Tegen, Katherine Bks) HarperCollins Pubs.

Scieszka, Jon & Barnett, Mac. Battle Bunny. Myers, Matt, illus. 2013. (ENG.). 32p. (J). (gr. k-4). 16.99 (978-1-4424-4673-1(0), Simon & Schuster Bks. For Young Readers) Simon & Schuster Bks. For Young Readers.

Seeger, Laura Vaccaro. Why? 2019. (Illus.). 32p. (J). (gr. -1-3). 18.99 (978-0-8234-4173-0(3), Neal Porter Bks) Holiday Hse., Inc.

Segal, John. Carrot Soup. Segal, John, illus. 2006. (ENG., Illus.). 32p. (J). (gr. -1-3). 19.99 (978-0-689-87702-5(1), McElderry, Margaret K. Bks.) McElderry, Margaret K. Bks.

—Sopa de Zanahoria. Mlawer, Teresa, tr. from ENG. 2006. (Illus.). (gr. -1-k). 12.99 (978-1-933032-13-9(8)) Lectorum Pubns., Inc.

Sena, Keiko. Gracie Meets a Ghost. 2016. (Gracie Wears Glasses Book Ser.). (ENG., Illus.). 32p. (J). (gr. -1-k). 16.99 (978-1-940842-13-4(1)) Museyon.

Seuss. The Eye Book. abr. ed. 2016. (Big Bright & Early Board Book Ser.). (ENG., Illus.). 24p. (J). (gr. -1 — 1). bds. 6.99 (978-0-553-53631-7(1), Random Hse. Bks. for Young Readers) Random Hse. Children's Bks.

Shea, Bob. Race You to Bed. Shea, Bob, illus. 2010. (ENG., Illus.). 40p. (J). (gr. -1-2). 16.99 (978-0-06-170417-8(2), Tegen, Katherine Bks) HarperCollins Pubs.

Shepherd, Anita. Easter Rabbit's Magic. 2013. 48p. pap. 7.95 (978-0-9882368-2-0(6)) New Eden Publishing.

Shields, Gillian. The Littlest Bunny. Lovsin, Polona, illus. 2015. 32p. (J). (978-1-4351-5967-9(5)) Barnes & Noble, Inc.

—When the World Is Ready for Bed (padded Board) Currey, Anna, illus. 2010. (ENG.). 26p. (J). (gr. -1 — 1). bds. 7.99 (978-1-59990-533-4(7), 900068691, Bloomsbury USA Childrens) Bloomsbury Publishing USA.

—When the World Was Waiting for You. Currey, Anna, illus. 2012. (ENG.). 26p. (J). (gr. -1 — 1). bds. 8.99 (978-1-59990-849-6(2), 900081566, Bloomsbury USA Childrens) Bloomsbury Publishing USA.

Singleton, Linda Joy. The Trail of the Ghost Bunny. 2018. (Curious Cat Spy Club Ser.: 6). (ENG.). 272p. (J). (gr. 3-7). pap. 9.99 (978-0-8075-1392-7(X), 080751392X) Whitman, Albert & Co.

Skidmore, Marlene. In Trouble Again! 2010. 24p. pap. 9.99 (978-0-9845208-9-3(9)) Faithful Life Pubs.

—Wesley's Swoo-Foo. 2008. 28p. pap. 9.99 (978-0-9821408-5-7(1)) Faithful Life Pubs.

Skye, Obert. Mutant Bunny Island. Vieira, Eduardo, illus. 2017. (ENG.). 224p. (J). (gr. 3-7). 12.99 (978-0-06-239912-0(8), HarperCollins) HarperCollins Pubs.

—Mutant Bunny Island #3: Buns of Steel. Vieira, Eduardo, illus. 2019. (ENG.). 208p. (J). (gr. 3-7). 12.99 (978-0-06-239917-5(9), HarperCollins) HarperCollins Pubs.

Slater, Jean M. The Adventures of Hopper. Slater, Jean M., illus. 2003. (Illus.). 8p. (J). bds. 16.00 (978-0-9743149-3-8(5)) Slater Software, Inc.

Sledge-Yancy, Barbara. The Red Haired Hare. 2011. 40p. pap. 17.49 (978-1-4568-6647-1(8)) Xlibris Corp.

Small, Lily. Bailey the Bunny: Fairy Animals of Misty Wood. 2018. (Fairy Animals of Misty Wood Ser.: 12). (ENG., Illus.). 144p. (J). pap. 6.99 (978-1-250-12704-4(1), 900175310, Holt, Henry & Co. Bks. For Young Readers) Holt, Henry & Co.

—Bella the Bunny: Fairy Animals of Misty Wood. 2015. (Fairy Animals of Misty Wood Ser.: 2). (ENG., Illus.). 144p. (J). (gr. k-3). pap. 6.99 (978-1-62779-142-7(6), 900137175, Holt, Henry & Co. Bks. For Young Readers) Holt, Henry & Co.

Smart, Jamie. Bunny vs. Monkey: a Graphic Novel. Smart, Jamie, illus. 2016. (Bunny vs. Monkey Ser.: 1). (ENG., Illus.). 64p. (J). (gr. 2-5). pap. 7.99 (978-0-545-86184-7(5), Graphix) Scholastic, Inc.

—Bunny vs. Monkey Book 3. 2018. (Bunny vs. Monkey Ser.: 3). lib. bdg. 18.40 (978-0-606-41145-5(3)) Turtleback.

—Bunny vs. Monkey: Book Three. 2018. (Bunny vs. Monkey Ser.: 3). (ENG.). 64p. (J). (gr. 2-5). pap. 7.99 (978-1-338-17686-5(2)) Scholastic, Inc.

Smith, Carrie. The Lion & the Rabbit: Classic Tales Edition. Greenhead, Bill, illus. 2011. (Classic Tales Ser.). (J). (978-1-936258-65-9(X)) Benchmark Education Co.

—Tortoise & Hare Run a Race: Lap Book Edition. Berchtold, Lauren, illus. 2016. (My First Reader's Theater Tales Ser.). (J). (gr. k). (978-1-5021-5509-2(5)) Benchmark Education Co.

—Tortoise & Hare Run a Race: Small Book Edition. Berchtold, Lauren, illus. 2016. (My First Reader's Theater Tales Ser.). (J). (gr. k). (978-1-5021-5514-6(1)) Benchmark Education Co.

Smith, Kathryn & Scott, Karen. King Murray's Royal Tail: The True Story of an Easter Bunny. 2004. 59p. pap. 8.95 (978-0-595-31090-6(7)) iUniverse, Inc.

Smith, Maggie Caldwell. Tommy Wilson, Junior Veterinarian: The Case of the Wounded Jack Rabbit. McHose, Jean, illus. 2005. 104p. (J). (gr. 3-6). pap. 7.95 (978-1-889159-14-0(X)) Magpie Pr., Pine Mountain Club, CA.

Smith, Stephanie. Snowshoe Hare's Family. Hynes, Robert, illus. 2nd ed. 2007. (Soundprints' Read-and-Discover Ser.). (ENG.). (J). (gr. 1-3). 32p. 12.95 (978-1-931465-44-1(4), PS2053); 48p. pap. 3.95 (978-1-931465-15-1(0), S2003) Soundprints.

Smith, Suzanne C. Peter Cottontail & the Easter Bunny Imposter. Brittingham, Geoffrey, illus. 24p. (J). pap. 3.25 (978-0-8249-5372-0(X), Ideals Pubns.) Worthy Publishing.

Smithem, Beth. Dust Bunny's Mission. 2010. 84p. pap. 10.49 (978-1-4520-1934-5(7)) AuthorHouse.

Snow Rabbit, Spring Rabbit: a Book of Changing Seasons. (ENG.). (J). (gr. -1 — 1). 2013. 24p. bds. 7.99 (978-0-307-97790-8(0)) 2011. 32p. 16.99 (978-0-375-86786-6(4)) Random Hse. Children's Bks. (Knopf Bks. for Young Readers).

Solomon, Chad. Adventures of Rabbit & Bear Paws: The Voyageurs. 2008. (ENG.). 32p. pap. (978-0-9739906-2-1(7)) Little Spirit Bear Productions CAN. Dist: Lone Pine Publishing.

Solotareff, Gregoire. Wolfy. Solotareff, Gregoire, illus. 2018. (ENG., Illus.). 36p. (J). (gr. k-3). 16.99 (978-1-77657-156-7(8), ec1c4bfa-8b2a-4390-b247-9888ff858b66) Gecko Pr. NZL. Dist: Lerner Publishing Group.

Sommer, Carl. Miserable Millie. Vignolo, Enrique, illus. 2014. (J). pap. (978-1-57537-960-9(0)) Advance Publishing, Inc.

Soo, Kean. March Grand Prix: the Fast & the Furriest. Soo, Kean, illus. 2015. (March Grand Prix Ser.). (ENG., Illus.). 144p. (J). (gr. 3-6). pap., pap., pap. 14.95 (978-1-62370-171-0(6), 126928, Capstone Young Readers) Capstone.

Soo, Kean, illus. The Great Desert Rally. 2015. (March Grand Prix Ser.). (ENG.). 48p. (J). (gr. 3-6). lib. bdg. 33.32 (978-1-4342-9641-2(5), 126927, Capstone Young Readers) Capstone.

Speed, Evelyn. Digger Rabbit & the First Easter. 2009. (Illus.). 24p. pap. 11.49 (978-1-4389-6105-7(7)) AuthorHouse.

Spelman, Cornelia. When I Feel Angry. Cote, Nancy, illus. 2012. (J). reprint ed. lib. bdg. 32.71 (978-1-61913-139-2(0)) Weigl Pubs., Inc.

The check digit for ISBN-10 appears in parentheses after the full ISBN-13

Spicer, Candace. Hopper & the Happy Houses. 2012. 18.95 (978-0-7414-6863-5(8)); pap. 11.95 (978-0-7414-6862-8(X)) Infinity Publishing.

Spin & Match - Kings, Cookies, & Quakers: The Cookie Man, New Clothes for the King, the Ugly Baby Duck. 2006. (ENG.). 66p. (J). 9.99 (978-1-59204-203-6(1)) Learning Wrap-Ups, Inc.

Sprick, Marilyn & Lemieux, Aurora, adapted by. The Race: Read Well Level K Unit 13 Storybook. 2003. (Read Well Level K Ser.). (Illus.). 20p. (J). (978-1-57035-684-1(X), 55538) Cambium Education, Inc.

Stapylton, K. E. The Terror of Prism Fading. 2008. (ENG.). 258p. pap. (978-1-4357-5457-7(3)) Lulu Pr., Inc.

Stark, Ulf. The Midsummer Tomte & the Little Rabbits: A Day-By-day Summer Story in Twenty-one Short Chapters, 13 vols. Beard, Susan, tr. Eriksson, Eva, illus. 2016. Orig. Title: Sommar I Stora Skogen. 120p. (J). 24.95 (978-1-78250-244-9(0)) Floris Bks. GBR. Dist: Consortium Bk. Sales & Distribution.

Steig, William. Which Would You Rather Be? 2005. (ENG., Illus.). 32p. (J). (gr. -1-3). reprint ed. 9.99 (978-0-06-443792-9(2), HarperCollins) HarperCollins Pubs.

Stein, David Ezra. Hush, Little Bunny. Stein, David Ezra, illus. 2019. (ENG., Illus.). 40p. (J). (gr. -1-3). 17.99 (978-0-06-284522-1(5), Balzer & Bray) HarperCollins Pubs.

Stephenson, Alan. The Adventures of Roy & Rosie Rabbit. 2011. (Illus.). 48p. pap. 19.51 (978-1-4567-9728-7(X)) AuthorHouse.

Sterling, Cheryl, et al. Some Bunny to Talk To: A Story about Going to Therapy. Beeke, Tiphanie, illus. 2014. 32p. (J). (978-1-4338-1649-9(0), Magination Pr.) American Psychological Assn.

Steve Cormey. The Brothers Foot: A Hare Raising Story. Ronda Eden, illus. 2009. 56p. pap. 21.99 (978-1-4389-4269-8(9)) AuthorHouse.

Stevens, Deon. Frankie's Kingdom: Winning in Face of Uncertainty. 2010. 218p. pap. 19.99 (978-1-4535-5409-8(2)) Xlibris Corp.

Stevens, Terry. The Battle at Longshore Causeway. 2006. 64p. pap. (978-1-84401-751-5(6)) Athena Pr.

Stewart, Paul. Rabbit & Hedgehog Treasury. Riddell, Chris, illus. 2018. (ENG.). 112p. (J). (-2). 21.99 (978-1-78344-674-2(9)) Andersen Pr. GBR. Dist: Independent Pubs. Group.

—Un Regalo de Cumpleanos. Riddell, Chris, illus. (SPA.). 30p. (J). (gr. k-2). (978-84-348-6840-3(7), SM30935) SM Ediciones ESP. Dist: Lectorum Pubns., Inc.

Stewart, Paul & Stewart, Paul. Un Poquito de Invierno. Riddell, Chris, illus. 2003. (SPA.). 30p. (J). (gr. k-2). (978-84-348-6839-7(3), SM30933) SM Ediciones ESP. Dist: Lectorum Pubns., Inc.

Stiegemeyer, Julie. Seven Little Bunnies, 0 vols. Bryant, Laura J., illus. 2012. (ENG.). 34p. (J). (gr. -1-1). 15.99 (978-0-7614-5600-1(7), 9780761456001, Two Lions) Amazon Publishing.

Stocks, David. Moon Rabbit. 2008. 276p. pap. (978-1-84747-838-2(7)) Chipmunkapublishing.

Stone, Kate. Bunnies for Tea. 2013. (ENG., Illus.). 10p. (J). bds. 8.99 (978-1-4494-2887-7(8)) Andrews McMeel Publishing.

Stowell, Louie. Brer Rabbit down the Well. Muszynski, Eva, illus. 2010. (First Reading Level 2 Ser.). 32p. (J). 6.99 (978-0-7945-2674-0(8), Usborne) EDC Publishing.

Strohmenger, Marie. The Smart Bunny: A Story about Big & Small, Smart & Stupid, Winning & Losing. 2007. 24p. per. 24.95 (978-1-4241-8249-7(2)) America Star Bks.

Stroschin, Jane H. Atsa & Ga: A Story from the High Desert. Stich, Carolyn R., illus. 2005. 32p. (J). (gr. k-6). (978-1-883960-29-2(0)) Henry Quill Pr.

Summers, Darien. The Mischievous Hare. 2009. (Illus.). 48p. pap. 9.95 (978-1-4327-4602-5(2)) Outskirts Pr., Inc.

Sumaite, Margarita. The Lost Book. 2019. (ENG., Illus.). 32p. (J). (gr. -1-3). 17.99 (978-1-5344-3818-7(1), McElderry, Margaret K. Bks.) McElderry, Margaret K. Bks.

Surplice, Holly. Peek-A-Boo Bunny: An Easter & Springtime Book for Kids. Surplice, Holly, illus. 2014. (ENG., Illus.). 32p. (J). (gr. -1-3). 9.99 (978-0-06-224265-5(2), HarperCollins) HarperCollins Pubs.

Surplice, Holly, illus. Hush-A-Bye Bunny. 2017. (ENG.). 16p. (J). (-k). bds. 8.99 (978-0-7636-9459-3(2)) Candlewick Pr.

Sutherland, David. Samantha Cardigan & the Genie's Revenge. Roberts, David, illus. 2005. (Red Bananas Ser.). (ENG.). 48p. (J). lib. bdg. (978-0-7787-1070-7(X)) Crabtree Publishing Co.

—Samantha Cardigan & the Ghastly Twirling Sickness. Roberts, David, illus. 2005. (Red Bananas Ser.). (ENG.). 48p. (J). lib. bdg. (978-0-7787-1069-1(6)) Crabtree Publishing Co.

Sutherland, David & Roberts, David. Samantha Cardigan & the Genie's Revenge. 2005. (Red Bananas Ser.). (ENG., Illus.). 48p. (J). (gr. 1-3). (978-0-7787-1086-8(6)) Crabtree Publishing Co.

—Samantha Cardigan & the Ghastly Twirling Sickness. 2005. (Red Bananas Ser.). (ENG., Illus.). 48p. (J). (gr. 1-3). (978-0-7787-1085-1(8)) Crabtree Publishing Co.

Sweeney, Kimberly A. Tippy Meets the Easter Bunny! 2012. 24p. pap. 17.99 (978-1-4685-8460-8(X)) AuthorHouse.

Symes, Ruth Louise. Floppy Ears. Kenyon, Tony, illus. 2005. (ENG.). 32p. (J). (978-1-84255-264-3(3), Orion Children's Bks.) Hachette Children's Group.

Tanaka, Usa. Give Me That! Tanaka, Usa, illus. 2007. (ENG., Illus.). 32p. (J). 15.95 (978-0-9741319-0-0(3)) 4N Publishing LLC.

Taplin, Sam. Are You There Little Bunny? 2018. (Little Peek Through Books* Ser.). (ENG.). 12p. (J). 9.99 (978-0-7945-4269-6(7), Usborne) EDC Publishing.

—Easter Bunny Flap Book. 2019. (Flap Bks.). (ENG.). 10ppp. (J). 7.99 (978-0-7945-3256-7(X), Usborne) EDC Publishing.

Tardif, Elizabeth. A Bunny Named Apple. Buehrle, Jacquelyn, illus. 2011. 28p. pap. 24.95 (978-1-4560-0946-5(X)) America Star Bks.

Tatsuyama, Sayuri. Happy Happy Clover, Vol. 2. Tatsuyama, Sayuri, illus. 2009. (Happy Happy Clover Ser.: 2). (ENG., Illus.). 192p. (J). pap. 9.99 (978-1-4215-2657-7(3)) Viz Media.

—Happy Happy Clover, Vol. 4. Tatsuyama, Sayuri, illus. 2010. (Happy Happy Clover Ser.: 4). (ENG., Illus.). 192p. (J). pap. 7.99 (978-1-4215-2735-2(9)) Viz Media.

Taylor, Chet. Last, but Not Least. 2007. (Illus.). 20p. (J). per. 11.99 (978-0-9797574-8-8(7)) Dragonfly Publishing, Inc.

—Last, but Not Least. Taylor, Chet, illus. l.t. ed. 2004. (Illus.). 20p. (J). 17.99 (978-0-9755888-6-4(9)); lib. bdg. 22.99 (978-0-9755888-1-9(8)) Dragonfly Publishing, Inc.

Tegan, Katherine. The Story of the Easter Bunny. 2007. (ENG., Illus.). 40p. (J). (gr. -1-3). pap. 7.99 (978-0-06-058781-9(4), HarperCollins) HarperCollins Pubs.

Tegen, Katherine. The Story of the Easter Bunny: An Easter & Springtime Book for Kids. Lambert, Sally Anne, illus. 2005. (ENG.). 40p. (J). (gr. -1-3). 12.99 (978-0-06-050711-4(X), HarperCollins) HarperCollins Pubs.

Thomas Nelson Community College Staff. God's Love in My Heart, 1 vol. 2014. (ENG.). 24p. bds. 9.99 (978-0-529-11141-8(1), Tommy Nelson) Nelson, Thomas Inc.

Thompson, Emma. The Spectacular Tale of Peter Rabbit. Taylor, Eleanor, illus. 2014. (Peter Rabbit Ser.). (ENG.). 72p. (J). (gr. -1-2). 20.00 (978-0-7232-7116-1(X), Warne) Penguin Young Readers Group.

Thompson, Emma, et al. Sgeulachd Eile Mu Pheader Rabaid. Taylor, Eleonor, illus. 2012.Tr. of Further Tale of Peter Rabbit. (GLA.). 80p. (J). (978-1-907676-12-3(0)) Grace Note Pubns.

Thompson, Lauren. Good Night, Bunny. Yue, Stephanie, illus. 2018. (ENG.). 32p. (J). (gr. -1-k). 16.99 (978-0-545-60335-5(8), Orchard Bks.) Scholastic, Inc.

—Little Bunny. Butler, John, illus. 2013. (ENG.). 30p. (J). (gr. -1-k). bds. 5.99 (978-1-4424-5851-2(8), Little Simon) Little Simon.

—Wee Little Bunny. Butler, John, illus. 2010. (Wee Little Ser.). (ENG.). 32p. (J). (gr. -1-1). 14.99 (978-1-4169-7937-1(9), Simon & Schuster Bks. For Young Readers) Simon & Schuster Bks. For Young Readers.

Thoughts Staff. Bugsy Rabbit: Furry Tales, No. 1. 2005. 13p. 8.99 (978-1-4116-3331-5(8)) Lulu Pr., Inc.

Tidhar, Lavie. Central Station, 1 vol. unabr. ed. 2017. (ENG.). 9.99 (978-1-5436-2453-3(7), 9781543624533, Audible Studios on Brilliance Audio) Brilliance Publishing, Inc.

Tidholm, Anna-Clara. Knock! Knock! Bradley, MaryChris, tr. 2009. (Illus.). 32p. (J). (gr. -1). 9.95 (978-0-9815761-6-9(8)) Mackenzie Smiles, LLC.

Tildes, Phyllis Limbacher. Bunny's Big Surprise. Tildes, Phyllis Limbacher, illus. 2020. (Illus.). 32p. (J). (-k). lib. bdg. 16.99 (978-1-58089-684-9(7)) Charlesbridge Publishing, Inc.

Tillis, Doris. Rudy the Rabbit. Tillis, Carrie, illus. 2005. 32p. per. 17.95 (978-1-58961-410-9(0)) PageFree Publishing, Inc.

Tireman, Loyd. Baby Jack & Jumping Jack Rabbit. Douglass, Ralph, illus. 2015. (Mesaland Ser.). (ENG.). 48p. (J). 12.95 (978-0-8263-5604-8(4), P475908) Univ. of New Mexico Pr.

—Hop-A-long. Douglass, Ralph, illus. 2015. (Mesaland Ser.). (ENG.). 48p. (J). 12.95 (978-0-8263-5608-6(7), P475979) Univ. of New Mexico Pr.

Todd, Burt Kerr. Bun Bun & Other Tales. 2006. pap. 10.00 (978-1-4257-1857-2(4)) Xlibris Corp.

Todd, Diana. Carrotsville. 2004. 42p. per. 12.95 (978-1-932344-61-5(6)) Thornton Publishing, Inc.

Togden, Ra Chel. The Legendary Rabbit of Death - Volume One [Paperback]. 2013. 108p. pap. (978-1-898185-27-7(1)) Aro Bks. worldwide.

Tommy. Bubba & Cecil. 2009. 52p. pap. 16.95 (978-1-60836-860-0(2)) America Star Bks.

Tonatiuh, Duncan. Pancho Rabbit & the Coyote: A Migrant's Tale. 2013. (ENG., Illus.). 32p. (J). (gr. 1-4). 18.99 (978-1-4197-0583-0(0), 692601, Abrams Bks. for Young Readers) Abrams, Inc.

Tonderum, Angela. Kaycee Kangaroo Lost in Alphabet Forest: Adventures of Kaycee Kangaroo. Carlson, Christine, illus. 2008. 41p. pap. 24.95 (978-1-60672-601-3(3)) America Star Bks.

Tone, Satoe. The Very Big Carrot. 2013. (ENG., Illus.). 26p. (J). 12.00 (978-0-8028-5426-1(5), Eerdmans Bks For Young Readers) Eerdmans, William B. Publishing Co.

Torrel, Wendy. GUARDIAN of DREAMS (1st Edition) Klingbeil, Kendall, illus. l.t. ed. 2004. 32p. (J). 14.95 (978-0-9746890-0-5(9)); pap. 10.95 (978-0-9746890-1-2(7)) White Tulip Publishing.

Turner, Jeffrey. Who Am I? Turner, Jeffrey, illus. 2017. (ENG., Illus.). 40p. (J). (gr. -1-3). 15.99 (978-1-4814-5304-2(1), Aladdin) Simon & Schuster Children's Publishing.

Umansky, Kaye. Sophie in Charge. Currey, Anna, illus. 2005. 30p. (J). 9.95 (978-1-56148-478-2(4), Good Bks.) Skyhorse Publishing Co., Inc.

Underwood, Deborah. Ogilvy. McBeth, T. L., illus. 2019. (ENG.). 40p. (J). 18.99 (978-1-250-15176-6(7), 900183400, Holt, Henry & Co. Bks. For Young Readers) Holt, Henry & Co.

van Genechten, Guido. Floppy. 2004. (Illus.). 28p. (J). (978-1-85269-517-0(X)); (ENG & ALB., pap. (978-1-85269-516-3(1)); (ENG & PAN., pap. (978-1-85269-522-4(6)); (ENG & GUJ., pap. (978-1-85269-520-0(X)); (ENG & YOR., pap. (978-1-85269-530-9(7)); (ENG & VIE., pap. (978-1-85269-529-3(3)); (ENG & TUR., pap. (978-1-85269-527-9(7)); (ENG & TAM., pap. (978-1-85269-526-2(9)); (ENG & SOM., pap. (978-1-85269-525-5(0)); (ENG & POR., pap. (978-1-85269-523-1(4)); (ENG., pap. (978-1-85269-524-8(2)) Mantra Lingua.

—Floppy's Friends. van Genechten, Guido, illus. 2004. (ENG & POL., Illus.). 28p. (J). bds. (978-1-84444-659-9(X)) Mantra Lingua.

—Floppy's Friends. 2004. (J). (CHI & ENG.). 16.95 (978-1-84444-650-6(6)); (BEN & ENG.). 16.95 (978-1-84444-649-0(2)); (ENG & URD.). 16.95 (978-1-84444-665-0(4)) Mantra Lingua GBR. Dist: Chinasprout, Inc.

Van Genechten, Guido. Knight Ricky. 2010. (Ricky Ser.). (ENG., Illus.). 30p. (J). (gr. -1-k). 16.95 (978-1-60537-059-0(2)) Clavis Publishing.

—Ricky. 2008. (ENG., Illus.). 32p. (J). (gr. -1-k). 16.95 (978-1-60537-009-5(6)) Clavis ROM. Dist: Publishers Group West (PGW).

—Ricky & Annie. 2010. (Ricky Ser.). (ENG., Illus.). 30p. (J). (gr. -1-k). 16.95 (978-1-60537-062-0(2)) Clavis Publishing.

—Ricky & the Squirrel. 2010. (Ricky Ser.). (ENG., Illus.). 30p. (J). (gr. -1-k). 16.95 (978-1-60537-078-1(9)) Clavis Publishing.

—Ricky Is Brave. 2011. (Ricky Ser.). (ENG., Illus.). 32p. (J). (gr. -1-k). 16.95 (978-1-60537-097-2(5)) Clavis Publishing.

van Genechten, Guido, tr. from DUT. Floppy in the Dark: Floppy Dans le Noir. 2004. (Illus.). 25p. (J). (978-1-85269-242-1(1)) Mantra Lingua.

Van Oss, Laura. Indigo's Gift: Does Indigo Have a Secret Gift? Wolf, Claudia, illus. 2006. 24p. (J). per. 2.99 (978-1-59958-003-6(9)) Journey Stone Creations, LLC.

Velthuijs, Max. Frog & Hare. (ENG., Illus.). 8p. (J). 6.99 (978-0-86264-995-1(1)) Andersen Pr. GBR. Dist: Trafalgar Square Publishing.

Vernon, Ursula. Hamster Princess: Whiskerella. 2018. (Hamster Princess Ser.: 5). (Illus.). 256p. (J). (gr. 3-7). 14.99 (978-0-399-18655-4(7), Dial Bks) Penguin Young Readers Group.

Vetter Squires, Diane. Basil's New Home: The Garden Rabbit Series - Part One. McAteer, Thomas, illus. 2009. 28p. pap. 13.99 (978-1-4490-0675-4(2)) AuthorHouse.

Vezeau, Sheila. Sky, the Blue Bunny. Ostrowski, Justin, illus. 2012. 16p. pap. 24.95 (978-1-4626-7533-3(6)) America Star Bks.

Voorheis, Tracy. Nibbles... a strawberry Tale. Voorheis, Tracy, illus. 2007. (Illus.). 60p. (J). per. 19.00 (978-0-9787113-0-6(0), Ithaca Pr.) Authors & Artists Publishers of New York, Inc.

Waddell, Martin. Class Six & the Very Big Rabbit: Band 10/White (Collins Big Cat) Ross, Tony, illus. 2005. (Collins Big Cat Ser.). (ENG.). 80p. (J). (gr. 1-3). pap. 10.99 (978-0-00-718629-7(0)) HarperCollins Pubs. Ltd. GBR. Dist: Independent Pubs. Group.

Wade, Maryam. Bently & the Crooked Carrot. 2013. 32p. pap. 24.95 (978-1-63000-801-7(X)) America Star Bks.

—Bently & the Silver Wings. 2011. 24p. pap. 24.95 (978-1-4560-7503-3(9)) America Star Bks.

Wahl, Jan. Rabbits on Mars. Schamber, Kimberly, illus. 2005. 32p. (gr. k-2). 15.25 (978-1-57505-511-4(2)) Lerner Publishing Group.

Wahman, Wendy. Rabbit Stew. 2017. (ENG., Illus.). 32p. (J). (gr. -1-2). 16.95 (978-1-62979-583-6(6), Astra Young Readers) Astra Publishing Hse.

Wallace, Adam. How to Catch the Easter Bunny. Elkerton, Andy, illus. 2017. (How to Catch Ser.: 3). (ENG.). 40p. (J). (gr. k-6). 10.99 (978-1-4926-3817-9(X), 9781492638179) Sourcebooks, Inc.

Wallace, G. Ira. Bunny Tales: The Journey Begins. 2009. 24p. pap. 12.00 (978-1-60860-869-0(7), Strategic Bk. Publishing) Strategic Book Publishing & Rights Agency (SBPRA).

Wallace, Nancy Elizabeth. Pumpkin Day!, 0 vols. Wallace, Nancy Elizabeth, illus. unabr. ed. 2012. (ENG., Illus.). 32p. (J). (gr. k-3). per. 9.99 (978-0-7614-5327-7(X), 9780761453277, Two Lions) Amazon Publishing.

—Recycle Every Day!, 0 vols. Wallace, Nancy Elizabeth, illus. 2012. (ENG., Illus.). 41p. (J). (gr. 1-3). pap. 9.99 (978-0-7614-5290-4(7), 9780761452904, Two Lions) Amazon Publishing.

—Tell-A-Bunny, 0 vols. 2013. (ENG., Illus.). 36p. (J). (gr. 1-3). 7.99 (978-0-7614-5369-7(5), 9780761453697, Two Lions) Amazon Publishing.

—The Valentine Express, 0 vols. 2012. (ENG., Illus.). 32p. (J). (gr. -1-2). pap. 9.99 (978-0-7614-5447-2(0), 9780761454472, Two Lions) Amazon Publishing.

Wallis, Quvenzhané. Shai & Emmie Star in to the Rescue! Miller, Sharee, illus. (Shai & Emmie Story Ser.). (ENG.). 128p. (J). (gr. 1-5). 2019. pap. 6.99 (978-1-4814-5889-4(2)) 2018. 15.99 (978-1-4814-5888-7(4)) Simon & Schuster Bks. For Young Readers. (Simon & Schuster Bks. For Young Readers).

Walton, Rick. Bunny Christmas: A Family Celebration. Miglio, Paige, illus. 2004. 32p. (J). (ENG.). 15.99 (978-0-06-008415-8(4)); lib. bdg. 16.89 (978-0-06-008416-5(2)) HarperCollins Pubs.

—So Many Bunnies Board Book: A Bedtime ABC & Counting Book: an Easter & Springtime Book for Kids. Miglio, Paige, illus. 2018. (ENG.). 32p. (J). (gr. -1 — 1). bds. 7.99 (978-0-688-17364-7(0), HarperFestival) HarperCollins Pubs.

Wang, Dorthea Deprisco. Five Minutes until Bed. 2009. (ENG., Illus.). 14p. (J). (gr. 4-7). 14.99 (978-0-7407-8428-6(5)) Andrews McMeel Publishing.

Ward, Helen. Hare & Tortoise. 2005. (ALB & ENG., Illus.). 32p. (J). pap. (978-1-84444-779-4(0)) Mantra Lingua.

Ward, Helen & Aesop, Aesop. Hare & Tortoise. 2005. (CHI, ENG & MUL., Illus.). 32p. (J). pap. (978-1-84444-784-8(7)) Mantra Lingua.

Warner, Liz. El Conejito Grande. 2007. 40p. per. 21.32 (978-1-4257-5616-1(6)) Xlibris Corp.

Washburn, Kim. Bunny Blessings, 1 vol. East, Jacqueline, illus. 2018. (ENG.). 18p. (J). bds. 8.99 (978-0-310-76209-6(X)) Zonderkidz.

Washington, Donna L. Li'l Rabbit's Kwanzaa: A Kwanzaa Holiday Book for Kids. Evans, Shane W., illus. 2010. (ENG.). 32p. (J). (gr. -1-2). 13.99 (978-0-06-072816-8(7), Tegen, Katherine Bks) HarperCollins Pubs.

Washington, Sharalee Marie Shepherd. Little Bear Rabbit Goes to London. 2012. 80p. 24.99 (978-1-4797-2677-6(X)); pap. 15.99 (978-1-4797-2676-9(1)) Xlibris Corp.

Watase, Yuu. Alice 19th, Vol. 1, 7 vols. 2003. (Alice 19th Ser.: 1). (ENG., Illus.). 192p. pap. 9.95 (978-1-59116-215-5(7)) Viz Media.

Watkins, Rowboat. Big Bunny: (Funny Bedtime Read Aloud Book for Kids, Bunny Book) 2018. (ENG., Illus.). 40p. (J). (gr. -1-k). 16.99 (978-1-4521-6390-1(1)) Chronicle Bks. LLC.

Watson, Wendy. Bedtime Bunnies Padded Board Book. 2018. (ENG., Illus.). 26p. (J). (— 1). bds. 8.99 (978-0-544-85958-6(8), 1648585, Clarion Bks.) HarperCollins Pubs.

Watt, Fiona. Hide-and-Seek Bunnies. Danson, Lesley, illus. 2007. (Touchy-Feely Flap Bks). 10p. (J). (gr. -1-k). bds. 16.99 (978-0-7945-1566-9(5), Usborne) EDC Publishing.

—That's Not My Bunny. Wells, Rachel, illus. 2004. (Touchy-Feely Board Bks.). (SPA & ENG.). 1p. (J). (gr. -1-18). bds. 7.99 (978-0-7460-4179-6(9)) EDC Publishing.

Watts, Robin Queen. The Adventures of Beauty & Sam. 2009. 20p. pap. 10.50 (978-1-4269-1286-3(2)) Trafford Publishing.

Weber, Joanne Markey. Flabby Rabbit. 2011. (ENG.). 26p. pap. 15.99 (978-1-4568-9153-4(7)) Xlibris Corp.

Weber, Rebecca. A Party for Rabbit: Set Of 6. 2010. (Early Connections Ser.). (J). 33.00 net. (978-1-59000-713-6(1)) Benchmark Education Co.

Wedge, Chris. Bunny: A Picture Book Adapted from the Animated Film. Wedge, Chris, illus. 2004. (Illus.). 30p. (J). (gr. k-4). reprint ed. 19.00 (978-0-7567-7460-8(8)) DIANE Publishing Co.

Wehr, Paul. The Animated Bunny's Tail. Wehr, Julian, illus. 2005. 20p. (J). 18.95 (978-0-9748093-1-1(4)) Wehr Animations.

Wehrmeijer, Annelien. Emma & Bo Finger Puppet Book: My Best Friend & Me Finger Puppet Books. van de Liejgraaf, Deborah, illus. 2013. (My Best Friend & Me Ser.). (ENG.). 10p. (J). (gr. k-1). bds. 7.99 (978-0-7641-6635-8(2)) Sourcebooks, Inc.

Weiss, Ellen. Winter Spring Summer Fall: A Touch-and-Feel Seasons Book. Bennett, Andy, illus. 2006. (PBS Kids Ser.). 8p. (J). (gr. -1-k). bds. 6.95 (978-1-57791-312-2(4)) Brighter Minds Children's Publishing.

Weiss, Flo. Little Bit Is Big Enough. 2012. 28p. pap. 16.09 (978-1-4669-4074-1(3)) Trafford Publishing.

Welch, Willy. Grumbly Bunnies. Lyon, Tammie Speer, illus. 2004. 32p. (J). 15.95 (978-1-58089-086-1(5)) Charlesbridge Publishing, Inc.

Wellings, Chris R. Sparkles Meets the Easter Bunny: The Adventures of Sparkles. Hammersley, Karen, illus. 2011. 48p. pap. 24.95 (978-1-4560-7063-2(0)) America Star Bks.

Wells, Rosemary. Bunny Cakes (Edición en Español) Wells, Rosemary, illus. 2014. (Max & Ruby Ser.). (SPA., Illus.). 32p. (J). (gr. -1-k). 8.99 (978-0-14-751586-5(6), Puffin Books) Penguin Young Readers Group.

—Bunny Party. 2003. (Max & Ruby Ser.). (Illus.). 32p. (J). (gr. -1-k). pap. 7.99 (978-0-14-250162-7(X), Puffin Books) Penguin Young Readers Group.

—Emily's First 100 Days of School. Wells, Rosemary, illus. 2005. (ENG., Illus.). 64p. (J). (gr. -1-1). pap. 9.99 (978-0-7868-1354-4(7)) Little, Brown Bks. for Young Readers.

—Emily's First 100 Days of School. 2006. (Illus.). (J). (gr. -1-4). 18.95 (978-0-439-84903-6(9), WPCD654) Weston Woods Studios, Inc.

—Hungry Bunny Tales. 2012. (Max & Ruby Ser.). lib. bdg. 14.75 (978-0-606-23658-4(9)) Turtleback.

—Max & Ruby & Twin Trouble. Wells, Rosemary, illus. 2019. (Max & Ruby Adventure Ser.). (ENG., Illus.). 32p. (J). (gr. -1-3). 17.99 (978-1-5344-4365-5(7), Simon & Schuster Bks. For Young Readers) Simon & Schuster Bks. For Young Readers.

—Max & Ruby Play School. 2003. (All Aboard Reading Ser.). (gr. -1-2). lib. bdg. 13.55 (978-0-613-64064-0(0)) Turtleback.

—Max & Ruby's Bedtime Book. 2010. (Max & Ruby Ser.). (Illus.). 48p. (J). (gr. -1-k). 18.99 (978-0-670-01141-4(X), Viking Books for Young Readers) Penguin Young Readers Group.

—Max & Ruby's Preschool Pranks. 2016. (Max & Ruby Ser.). (Illus.). 40p. (J). (-k). 17.99 (978-0-670-78462-2(1), Viking Books for Young Readers) Penguin Young Readers Group.

—Max & the Fall Parade. 2014. (Max Ruby Ser.). lib. bdg. 13.55 (978-0-606-36192-7(8)) Turtleback.

—Max at School. Grey, Andrew, illus. 2017. (Max & Ruby Ser.). 32p. (J). (gr. 1-2). pap. 4.99 (978-0-515-15743-7(0), Penguin Young Readers) Penguin Young Readers Group.

—Max's ABC. 2008. (Max & Ruby Ser.). 32p. (J). (gr. -1-k). pap. 8.99 (978-0-14-241172-8(8), Puffin Books) Penguin Young Readers Group.

—Max's ABC. 2008. (Max & Ruby Ser.). (Illus.). 26p. (gr. -1-k). 17.00 (978-0-7569-8924-8(8)) Perfection Learning Corp.

—Max's Breakfast. 2004. (Max & Ruby Ser.). (ENG.). 12p. (J). (gr. 1 — 1). bds. 7.99 (978-0-670-88712-5(9), Viking Books for Young Readers) Penguin Young Readers Group.

—Max's Bug. Grey, Andrew, illus. 2017. (Max & Ruby Ser.). 32p. (J). (gr. 1-2). pap. 5.99 (978-0-515-15740-6(6), Penguin Young Readers) Penguin Young Readers Group.

—Max's Christmas. 2013. (Max & Ruby Ser.). (ENG.). 32p. (J). (gr. -1-k). 8.99 (978-0-14-750947-5(5), Puffin Books) Penguin Young Readers Group.

—Max's Christmas. 2013. (Max Ruby Ser.). lib. bdg. 18.40 (978-0-606-32139-6(X)) Turtleback.

—Max's Lunch. Grey, Andrew, illus. 2017. (Max & Ruby Ser.). 32p. (J). (gr. 1-2). pap. 4.99 (978-0-515-15737-6(6), Penguin Young Readers) Penguin Young Readers Group.

—Max's Valentine. 2003. (Max & Ruby Ser.). (ENG., Illus.). 16p. (J). (gr. -1 — 1). bds. 5.99 (978-0-670-03668-4(4), Viking Books for Young Readers) Penguin Young Readers Group.

—Read to Your Bunny: with a Note from T. Berry Brazelton, M. D. Wells, Rosemary, illus. 2003. (ENG., Illus.). 14p. (J). (gr. -1). bds. 7.99 (978-0-439-54337-8(1), Cartwheel Bks.) Scholastic, Inc.

—Ruby's Beauty Shop. Wells, Rosemary, illus. 2004. (Max & Ruby Ser.). (ENG., Illus.). 32p. (J). (gr. -1-k). pap. 8.99 (978-0-14-240194-1(3), Puffin Books) Penguin Young Readers Group.

—Ruby's Tea for Two. 2003. (Max & Ruby Ser.). (ENG.). 16p. (J). (gr. -1 — 1). bds. 6.99 (978-0-670-03652-3(8), Viking Books for Young Readers) Penguin Young Readers Group.

—Sleep, My Bunny. Wells, Rosemary, illus. 2018. (ENG., Illus.). 24p. (J). (-k). 14.99 (978-0-7636-9262-9(X)) Candlewick Pr.

—Sporty Bunny Tales. 2014. (Max & Ruby Ser.). lib. bdg. 14.75 (978-0-606-34464-7(0)) Turtleback.

—Voyage to the Bunny Planet. 2008. (ENG., Illus.). 88p. (J). (gr. -1-2). 18.99 (978-0-670-01103-2(7), Viking Books for Young Readers) Penguin Young Readers Group.

—Voyage to the Bunny Planet. 2011. (J). (gr. -1-2). 29.95 (978-0-545-09458-0(5)) Weston Woods Studios, Inc.

Weninger, Brigitte. Davy Loves His Mommy. Tharlet, Eve, illus. 2014. (ENG.). 32p. (J). (gr. k-3). 15.95 (978-0-7358-4164-2(0)) North-South Bks., Inc.

—Davy Loves the Baby. Tharlet, Eve, illus. 2015. (ENG.). 32p. (J). 15.95 (978-0-7358-4210-6(8)) North-South Bks., Inc.

West, Colin. Helicopter Hare. (ENG., Illus.). 61p. (J). pap. 7.95 (978-0-340-66095-9(3)) Hodder & Stoughton GBR. Dist: Trafalgar Square Publishing.

West, Tracey. Rabbit Hood: Stealing Laughs in Sherwood Forest. 2004. (Illus.). 57p. (978-0-439-56600-1(2)) Scholastic, Inc.

Westerlund, Kate. A Whisper in the Snow. Oral, Feridun, illus. 2018. 32p. (J). (gr. k-2). 17.99 (978-988-8341-52-8(9), Minedition) Penguin Young Readers Group.

Weston, Carrie. What Noise Does a Rabbit Make? Byrne, Richard, illus. 2013. (J). (978-1-4351-6493-2(8)) Barnes & Noble, Inc.

Weston Woods Staff, creator. Emily's First 100 Days of School. 2011. 38.75 (978-0-439-84892-3(X)) Weston Woods Studios, Inc.

—Goodnight Moon. 2011. 18.95 (978-0-439-72684-9(0)); 29.95 (978-0-439-73472-1(X)); 38.75 (978-0-439-72686-3(7)) Weston Woods Studios, Inc.

—Morris's Disappearing. 2011. 18.95 (978-0-439-72855-3(X)) Weston Woods Studios, Inc.

—Morris's Disappearing Bag. 2011. 38.75 (978-0-439-72858-4(4)) Weston Woods Studios, Inc.

—Mr. Rabbit & the Lovely Present. 2011. 18.95 (978-0-439-72859-1(2)); 38.75 (978-0-439-72860-7(6)) Weston Woods Studios, Inc.

—Mr Rabbit & the Lovely Present. 2011. 29.95 (978-0-439-73502-5(5)) Weston Woods Studios, Inc.

Wheelie, P. The Fishing Trip: The tales of Tommy the tortoise & Friends. 2009. (Illus.). 32p. pap. 12.99 (978-1-4389-6414-0(5)) AuthorHouse.

White, Jenny. A Surprise for Junior. 2013. 24p. pap. 17.99 (978-1-4817-0602-5(0)) AuthorHouse.

White, Kathryn. Snowshoe the Hare. Rivers, Ruth, illus. 2005. (Red Go Bananas Ser.). (ENG.). 48p. (J). (gr. 2-3). pap. (978-0-7787-2699-9(1), 1253648) Crabtree Publishing Co.

White, Rebecca. Holly's Not So Plain & Ordinary Day. 2011. 38p. pap. 13.97 (978-1-61204-376-0(3), Strategic Bk. Publishing) Strategic Book Publishing & Rights Agency (SBPRA).

Whitford Paul, Ann. Fiesta Fiasco. 2012. 29.95 (978-1-4301-1100-9(3)) Live Oak Media.

Whitmore, Gary. Prince Luna & the Space Dreamers. 2011. (ENG.). 204p. pap. 8.50 (978-1-4565-8438-2(3)) CreateSpace Independent Publishing Platform.

Wilce, Colin. The Rain & Blossom (Rabbit Brook Tales Volume 2) 2006. (ENG.). 88p. pap. 11.66 (978-1-84728-105-0(2)) Lulu Pr., Inc.

—The Youngsters' Adventure & Thanksgiving (Rabbit Brook Tales Volume 4) 2007. (ENG.). 80p. pap. 17.95 (978-1-84753-202-2(0)) Lulu Pr., Inc.

Wilhelm, Hans. Bunny Trouble Treasury. 2014. (ENG., Illus.). 128p. (J). (gr. k-3). pap. 14.99 (978-0-486-49275-9(3), 492753) Dover Pubns., Inc.

Willard, Nancy. A Starlit Snowfall. Pinkney, Jerry, illus. 2011. (ENG.). 32p. (J). (gr. -1-3). 6.99 (978-0-316-18366-6(0)) Little, Brown Bks. for Young Readers.

Willems, Mo. Knuffle Bunny: a Cautionary Tale. 2004. (Knuffle Bunny Ser.). (ENG., Illus.). 40p. (J). (gr. -1-k). 17.99 (978-0-7868-1870-9(0), Hyperion Books for Children) Disney Publishing Worldwide.

Williams, Brenda. Lin Yi's Lantern. Lacombe, Benjamin, illus. 2012. (ENG.). 32p. (J). (gr. k-3). pap. 9.99 (978-1-84686-793-4(2)) Barefoot Bks., Inc.

Williams, Deborah. Little Rabbit Is Sad. Gedeon, Gloria, illus. l.t. ed. 2005. (ENG.). 12p. (Orig.). (gr. k-1). pap. 7.95 (978-1-879835-99-3(1), Kaeden Bks.) Kaeden Corp.

Williams, Donald & Williams, Ronald. The Adventures of Wacko Rabbit. 2012. (Illus.). (J). 14.95 (978-1-62086-058-8(9)) Amplify Publishing Group.

Williams, Jared T. Rabbit Ninja. Williams, Jared T., illus. 2019. (Illus.). 32p. (J). 17.95 (978-1-56792-628-6(2)) Godine, David R. Pub.

Williams, Larry. The League of Clique. Williams, Larry, illus. 2007. (ENG., Illus.). 80p. per. 19.95 (978-1-4241-5976-5(8)) America Star Bks.

Williams, Margery. The Velveteen Rabbit. Felix, Monique, illus. 2005. 40p. pap. 8.95 (978-0-89812-383-8(6)) Creative Co., The.

—The Velveteen Rabbit. Nicholson, William, illus. 2011. (Dover Children's Classics Ser.). (ENG.). 48p. (J). (gr. k-5). pap. 8.99 (978-0-486-48606-2(0), 486060) Dover Pubns., Inc.

—The Velveteen Rabbit. 2003. (J). 9.99 (978-0-9740847-3-2(5)) GiGi Bks.

—The Velveteen Rabbit. 2005. (ENG., Illus.). 96p. (YA). (gr. -1-1). 13.95 (978-0-7573-0333-3(1)) Health Communications, Inc.

—The Velveteen Rabbit. 2010. (CHI., Illus.). (J). (978-957-762-476-5(6)) Hsin Yi Pubns.

—The Velveteen Rabbit. 2003. (ENG.). 16p. (C). pap. 10.00 (978-0-582-77858-0(1)) Pearson Education.

—The Velveteen Rabbit. Nicholson, William S., illus. 2017. (ENG.). 48p. (J). (gr. k-3). 12.99 (978-1-944686-46-8(0), Racehorse Publishing) Skyhorse Publishing Co., Inc.

—The Velveteen Rabbit. Hague, Michael, illus. 2008. (ENG.). 48p. (J). (gr. -1-2). per. 7.99 (978-0-312-37750-2(9), 900049139) Square Fish.

—The Velveteen Rabbit, 0 vols. Spirin, Gennady, illus. 2012. (ENG.). 48p. (J). (gr. 1-3). 17.99 (978-0-7614-5848-7(4), 9780761458487, Two Lions) Amazon Publishing.

—The Velveteen Rabbit: The Classic Children's Book. Nicholson, William, illus. 2014. 48p. (J). (gr. -1-2). 19.99 (978-0-385-37566-5(2), Doubleday Bks. for Young Readers) Random Hse. Children's Bks.

—The Velveteen Rabbit & Other Stories Book & Charm. 2008. 128p. (J). (gr. 2-5). 6.99 (978-0-06-145942-9(9), HarperFestival) HarperCollins Pubs.

—The Velveteen Rabbit Book & Charm. Nicholson, William, illus. 2006. 40p. (J). (gr. -1-3). pap. 4.99 (978-0-06-076067-0(2), HarperFestival) HarperCollins Pubs.

—The Velveteen Rabbit Coloring Book. Kliros, Thea, illus. 2013. (Dover Classic Stories Coloring Book Ser.). (ENG.). 48p. (J). (gr. 2-5). pap. 4.99 (978-0-486-25924-6(2), 259242) Dover Pubns., Inc.

Williams, Sam. School Bus Bunny Bus. Trotter, Stuart, illus. 2006. (ENG.). 10p. (J). (gr. -1-1). 12.95 (978-1-905417-17-9(9)) Boxer Bks., Ltd. GBR. Dist: Sterling Publishing Co., Inc.

Wilmore, Alex, illus. Sleepy Bunny: Board Books with Plush Ears. 2019. (ENG.). 10p. (J). (gr. -1 — 1). bds. 6.99 (978-1-4380-5071-3(2)) Sourcebooks, Inc.

Wilson, Gerrard. Alice on Top of the World. 2009. 159p. pap. 17.50 (978-0-9561553-0-6(8)) Wilson, Gerrard IRL. Dist: Lulu Pr., Inc.

Wilson, Laurie Harman. The Treasures of Destiny. 2012. 72p. pap. 7.95 (978-0-9848050-3-7(6), Little Creek Bks.) Jan-Carol Publishing, INC.

Winch, John. Run, Hare, Run. 2007. (Illus.). 40p. pap. (978-1-921049-55-2(3)) Little Hare Bks. AUS. Dist: HarperCollins Pubs. Australia.

Winget, Susan. Tucker's Apple-Dandy Day. Winget, Susan, illus. 2006. (Illus.). 40p. (J). (gr. -1-k). 13.89 (978-0-06-054647-2(6)) HarperCollins Pubs.

—Tucker's Four-Carrot School Day. Winget, Susan, illus. 2005. (ENG., Illus.). 40p. (J). (gr. -1-k). 12.99 (978-0-06-054642-7(5)) HarperCollins Pubs.

Winship, Daniel, illus. The Tortoise & the Hare: The Tortoise & the Hare. 2012. (SGN, ARA, BOS, CHI & FRE.). 32p. (J). pap. 19.95 incl. DVD (978-0-9818139-2-9(5)) ASL Tales.

Wise Brown, Margaret. The Golden Egg Book. Weisgard, Leonard, illus. 2015. (Little Golden Book Ser.). 24p. (J). (-k). 4.99 (978-0-385-38476-6(9), Golden Bks.) Random Hse. Children's Bks.

—My World Board Book. 2003. (ENG., Illus.). 36p. (J). (gr. -1 — 1). bds. 9.99 (978-0-694-00862-9(1), HarperFestival) HarperCollins Pubs.

Witkowski, Teri. Bitty Bunny's Slipper Search. Ackley, Peggy Jo, illus. 2009. (J). (978-1-59369-586-6(1), American Girl) American Girl Publishing, Inc.

—Bunny & Piggy at the Beach. Ackley, Peggy Jo, illus. 2005. (J). (978-1-58485-961-1(X)) American Girl Publishing, Inc.

Wolif, T. Hal & His Pal Al: The Easter Bunny's Helpers. 2007. (Illus.). 36p. per. 12.97 (978-1-932344-93-6(4)) Thornton Publishing, Inc.

Wood, David. A Year in the Life of the Kingwood Bunnies. Floeter, Nell, illus. 2010. 54p. pap. 15.95 (978-1-936343-07-2(X)) Peppertree Pr., The.

Wood, Maryrose. Alice's Farm: A Rabbit's Tale. 2021. (ENG.). 368p. (J). pap. 8.99 (978-1-250-79175-7(8), 900208345) Square Fish.

Wulfekotte, Dana. Rabbit & Possum. Wulfekotte, Dana, illus. 2018. (ENG., Illus.). 40p. (J). (gr. -1-3). 17.99 (978-0-06-245581-9(8), Greenwillow Bks.) HarperCollins Pubs.

Wynne-Jones, Tim. On Tumbledown Hill, 1 vol. Petricic, Dusan, illus. 2008. (ENG.). 32p. (J). (gr. k-3). pap. 5.95 (978-0-88995-409-0(7), b535b8c2-8843-44c4-a062-fb6fcb6cb8f6) Red Deer Pr. CAN. Dist: Firefly Bks., Ltd.

Yager, Jan. The Reading Rabbit. Lyman, Mitzi, illus. 32p. (J). 2014. (ENG.). 25.95 (978-1-938998-00-3(6)) 2013. pap. 17.95 (978-1-938998-01-0(4)) Hannacroix Creek Bks., Inc.

Yontz, Barbara J. The Adventures of Baby Z & the Rabbit of Oz. 2012. 24p. pap. 15.99 (978-1-4797-3514-3(0)) Xlibris Corp.

Yoon, Salina. Humpty Dumpty. Yoon, Salina, illus. 2012. (ENG., Illus.). 18p. (J). (gr. -1 — 1). bds. 7.99 (978-1-4424-1411-2(1), Little Simon) Little Simon.

Zangrillo, Marguerite Rochelle. The Bunny with the Polka Dot Nose. 2009. 28p. pap. 15.99 (978-1-4363-8966-2(6)) Xlibris Corp.

Ziegler-Sullivan, Ursula. The Pups Save the Bunnies. 2016. (Illus.). (J). (978-1-5182-1575-9(0)) Random Hse., Inc.

Zobel-Nolan, Allia. Bunnies Are for Kissing. East, Jacqueline, illus. 2009. 24p. (J). (gr. -1-k). 7.95 (978-1-58925-842-6(8)) Tiger Tales.

Zolotow, Charlotte. The Bunny Who Found Easter Gift Edition: An Easter & Springtime Book for Kids. Peterson, Betty F. & Craig, Helen, illus. 2018. (ENG.). 40p. (J). (gr. -1-3). 8.99 (978-1-328-69467-6(4), 1671423, Clarion Bks.) HarperCollins Pubs.

Zuckerman, Linda. A Taste for Rabbit. 2007. (J). (978-0-439-86978-2(1), Levine, Arthur A. Bks.) Scholastic, Inc.

RACCOON

Agusta, Autum. Rita & Rascal. 2013. 116p. (gr. 2-4). 22.25 (978-1-4669-6973-5(3)); pap. 12.25 (978-1-4669-6971-1(7)) Trafford Publishing.

Albertson, Al. Raccoons. 2020. (Animals of the Forest Ser.). (ENG.). 24p. (J). (gr. k-3). lib. bdg. 26.95 (978-1-64487-129-4(7), Blastoff! Readers) Bellwether Media.

Baicker, Karen. Raccoons, 1 vol. 2010. (Amazing Animals Ser.). (ENG.). 48p. (J). (gr. 3-5). pap. 11.50 (978-1-4339-4020-0(5), 063653bb-95fb-439e-98c0-b5257f473394); lib. bdg. 30.67 (978-1-4339-4019-4(1), 8e42329e-8b4e-444b-ae49-3572be7990d6) Stevens, Gareth Publishing LLLP. (Gareth Stevens Learning Library).

—Raccoons. 2007. (J). (978-1-59939-125-0(2), Reader's Digest Young Families, Inc.) Studio Fun International.

Berger, Melvin & Berger, Gilda. Raccoons. 2010. (Illus.). 16p. (J). (978-0-545-24434-3(X)) Scholastic, Inc.

Berne, Emma Carlson. Raccoons, 1 vol. 2014. (Scavengers: Eating Nature's Trash Ser.). (ENG., Illus.). 24p. (J). (gr. 2-3). lib. bdg. 25.27 (978-1-4777-6597-5(2), 4c6c8aa5-c871-4973-a4eb-1cea59f57b95, PowerKids Pr.) Rosen Publishing Group, Inc., The.

Borgert-Spaniol, Megan. Baby Raccoons. 2017. (Super Cute! Ser.). (ENG., Illus.). 24p. (J). (gr. k-3). lib. bdg. 26.95 (978-1-62617-545-7(4), Blastoff! Readers) Bellwether Media.

Bowman, Chris. Raccoons. 2015. (North American Animals Ser.). (ENG., Illus.). 24p. (J). (gr. k-3). lib. bdg. 26.95 (978-1-62617-263-0(3), Blastoff! Readers) Bellwether Media.

Crossingham, John, et al. Les Ratons Laveurs. 2005. (Petit Monde Vivant Ser.). (FRE., Illus.). 32p. (J). pap. 9.95 (978-2-89579-048-8(5)) Bayard Canada Livres CAN. Dist: Crabtree Publishing Co.

Dougherty, Rachel. A Raccoon at the White House: Ready-To-Read Level 2. Sanson, Rachel, illus. 2018. (Tails from History Ser.). (ENG.). 32p. (J). (gr. k-2). 17.99 (978-1-5344-0542-4(9)); pap. 4.99 (978-1-5344-0541-7(0)) Simon Spotlight. (Simon Spotlight).

Einhorn, Kama. Raccoon Rescue. 2019. (True Tales of Rescue Ser.). (ENG., Illus.). 160p. (J). (gr. 3-7). 14.99 (978-1-328-76705-9(1), 1680376, Clarion Bks.) HarperCollins Pubs.

Gagne, Tammy. Backyard Jungle Safari Raccoons: Raccoons. 2015. (ENG., Illus.). 32p. (J). 26.50 (978-1-62469-102-7(1)) Purple Toad Publishing, Inc.

Gish, Melissa. Raccoons. (Living Wild Ser.). (ENG.). 48p. (J). 2016. (gr. 5-9). pap. 12.00 (978-1-62832-171-5(7), 20898, Creative Paperbacks) 2015. (Illus.). (gr. 4-7). (978-1-60818-570-2(2), 20897, Creative Education) Creative Co., The.

Gonzales, Doreen. Raccoons in the Dark, 1 vol. 2009. (Creatures of the Night Ser.). (ENG.). 24p. (gr. 2-3). (YA). pap. 9.25 (978-1-4358-3259-6(0), c6a93620-ed7d-4814-86b5-b5aab5874745); (Illus.): (J). 26.27 (978-1-4042-8101-1(0), 6c1de3d2-d0b1-49cd-8e23-165dbfcdaa60) Rosen Publishing Group, Inc., The.

Green, Emily. Raccoons. 2010. (Backyard Wildlife Ser.). (ENG., Illus.). 24p. (J). (gr. k-3). lib. bdg. 26.95 (978-1-60014-444-8(6), Blastoff! Readers) Bellwether Media.

Green, Jen. Raccoons. 2009. (Illus.). 52p. (J). (978-0-7172-6281-6(2)) Grolier, Ltd.

Helbig-Miller, Theresa. Benny the Raccoon, 1 vol. 2008. (ENG.). 27p. per. 24.95 (978-1-60441-214-7(3)) America Star Bks.

Hurtig, Jennifer. Raccoons. (J). 2012. (978-1-61913-069-2(6)) 2012. (978-1-61913-266-5(4)) 2007. (Illus.). 24p. (gr. -1-3). lib. bdg. 24.45 (978-1-59036-669-1(7)) Weigl Pubs., Inc.

—Raccoons. Hudak, Heather C., ed. 2007. (Backyard Animals Ser.). (Illus.). 24p. (J). (gr. -1-3). pap. 8.95 (978-1-59036-670-7(0)) Weigl Pubs., Inc.

Johnson, Jinny. Raccoon. 2014. (North American Mammals Ser.). (ENG., Illus.). 24p. (J). (gr. 1-4). 28.50 (978-1-62588-036-9(7), 17374) Black Rabbit Bks.

—Raccoon. 2014. (North American Mammals Ser.). (ENG., Illus.). 24p. (J). (gr. -1-4). pap. 8.95 (978-1-77092-171-9(0)) Saunders Bk. Co. CAN. Dist: RiverStream Publishing.

Kalman, Bobbie. Baby Raccoons. 2010. (ENG., Illus.). 24p. (J). (978-0-7787-3963-0(5)); pap. (978-0-7787-3982-1(1)) Crabtree Publishing Co.

—Raccoon Family Adventures. 2016. (Animal Family Adventures Ser.). (ENG., Illus.). 32p. (J). (gr. 1-3). (978-0-7787-2230-4(9)) Crabtree Publishing Co.

Kalman, Bobbie & Crossingham, John. The Life Cycle of a Raccoon. Bedell, Barbara, illus. 2003. (Life Cycle Ser.). (ENG.). 32p. (J). (gr. 3-4). pap. (978-0-7787-0691-5(5)); lib. bdg. (978-0-7787-0661-8(3)) Crabtree Publishing Co.

Kissock, Heather. Raccoons. 2016. 24p. (J). (978-1-4896-5399-4(6)) Weigl Pubs., Inc.

Kite, L. Patricia. Raccoons. Boucher, Jerry, illus. Boucher, Jerry, photos by. 2004. (Early Bird Nature Bks.). 47p. (J). 25.26 (978-0-8225-3049-7(X), Lerner Pubns.) Lerner Publishing Group.

Lake, G. G. Raccoons. 2016. (Woodland Wildlife Ser.). (ENG., Illus.). 24p. (J). (gr. -1-2). lib. bdg. 27.32 (978-1-5157-0817-9(9), 132153, Capstone Pr.) Capstone.

Loh-Hagan, Virginia. Raccoon. Bane, Jeff, illus. 2017. (My Early Library: My Favorite Animal Ser.). (ENG.). 24p. (J). (gr. k-1). lib. bdg. 30.64 (978-1-63472-840-9(8), 209786) Cherry Lake Publishing.

Magby, Meryl. Raccoons. 2013. (American Animals Ser.). (Illus.). 24p. (J). (gr. k-5). pap. 49.50 (978-1-4777-0951-1(7)); (ENG., (gr. 2-3). pap. 9.25 (978-1-4777-0950-4(9), a144ac63-6a56-4c31-bdca-221066362c3e); (ENG., (gr. 2-3). lib. bdg. 26.27 (978-1-4777-0789-0(1), 10b4e2a2-23dd-48d0-b11f-1d37f8664e88) Rosen Publishing Group, Inc., The. (PowerKids Pr.).

El Mapache. 2017. (Animales Del Patio Ser.). (Illus.). 16p. (J). (gr. -1-2). lib. bdg. 17.95 (978-1-68151-275-4(0), 14716) Amicus.

Mattern, Joanne. Raccoons Are Night Animals, 1 vol. 2007. (Night Animals Ser.). (ENG., Illus.). 24p. (gr. 1-3). pap. 9.15 (978-0-8368-7856-1(6), e6bdb6d5-5a8c-440d-9427-d19aa94deacd); lib. bdg. 24.67 (978-0-8368-7849-3(3), 0b6cc7f4-eb92-4b8e-8000-f3459d4eecf3) Stevens, Gareth Publishing LLLP. (Weekly Reader Leveled Readers).

—Raccoons Are Night Animals / Los Mapaches Son Animales Nocturnos, 1 vol. 2007. (Night Animals / Animales Nocturnos Ser.). (SPA & ENG., Illus.). 24p. (gr. 1-3). pap. 9.15 (978-0-8368-8053-3(6), d4f74af0-9cc8-459c-bbff-192916dd01d8); lib. bdg. 24.67 (978-0-8368-8046-5(3), 17348a45-7522-4d80-b35d-8ca6a561a6ee) Stevens, Gareth Publishing LLLP. (Weekly Reader Leveled Readers).

McAneney, Caitie. Look Out for the Raccoon!, 1 vol. 2015. (Surprisingly Scary! Ser.). (ENG., Illus.). 24p. (J). (gr. 2-3). pap. 9.25 (978-1-4994-0882-9(X), d2485cc8-67dd-40e1-9798-ddf5f8ccc0a0, PowerKids Pr.) Rosen Publishing Group, Inc., The.

McGill, Jordan. Mapaches. 2012. (SPA.). (J). (978-1-61913-195-8(1)) Weigl Pubs., Inc.

—Raccoons. 2011. (J). 27.13 (978-1-61690-932-1(3)) Weigl Pubs., Inc.

Nelson, Kristin L. Clever Raccoons. 2005. (Pull Ahead Bks.). (Illus.). 32p. (J). (gr. k-3). lib. bdg. 22.60 (978-0-8225-3763-2(X)) Lerner Publishing Group.

North, Sterling. Rascal, Mi Tremendo Mapache. 2003. (Cuatro Vientos Ser.: Vol. 9). (SPA.). 168p. (gr. 5-12). pap. 13.99 (978-84-279-3109-1(3), NG3492) Lectorum Pubns., Inc.

—Rascal (Puffin Modern Classics) 2004. (Puffin Modern Classics Ser.). (Illus.). 192p. (J). (gr. 3-7). 8.99 (978-0-14-240252-8(4), Puffin Books) Penguin Young Readers Group.

O'Mara, Jack. Raccoons in the Dark, 1 vol. 2012. (Creatures of the Night Ser.). (ENG., Illus.). 24p. (J). (gr. 1-2). pap. 9.15 (978-1-4339-6378-0(7), 2112addc-e565-41ac-b97b-d5431a57f3ec); lib. bdg. 25.27 (978-1-4339-6376-6(0), 9162e3c7-bfd1-4428-a910-9748da4e6137) Stevens, Gareth Publishing LLLP.

O'Shaughnessy, Ruth. Raccoons after Dark, 1 vol. 2015. (Animals of the Night Ser.). (ENG.). 32p. (gr. 3-4). pap. 11.52 (978-0-7660-6762-2(9), ce787fe7-43fb-4c4a-b119-e3e9e668d904); (Illus.). 26.93 (978-0-7660-6764-6(5), 680d43ce-0b3d-41cb-a5e0-df1e2f62ebee) Enslow Publishing, LLC.

Otfinoski, Steven. Raccoons, 1 vol. 2011. (Animals, Animals Ser.). (ENG., Illus.). 48p. (J). (gr. 5-5). 32.64 (978-0-7614-4841-9(1), 4300da33-0d60-4ef4-ae4f-757883fa9132) Cavendish Square Publishing LLC.

Owen, Ruth. Raccoon Cubs. 2011. (Wild Baby Animals Ser.). 24p. (J). (gr. k-3). lib. bdg. 25.65 (978-1-61772-154-0(9)); lib. bdg., E-Book 39.93 (978-1-61772-242-4(1)) Bearport Publishing Co., Inc.

Payne, Donald. The Little Lost Raccoons. 2009. 28p. pap. 12.99 (978-1-4389-6159-0(6)) AuthorHouse.

Petrie, Kristin. Raccoons, 1 vol. 2015. (Backyard Animals Ser.). (ENG.). 32p. (J). (gr. 3-6). 32.79 (978-1-62403-662-0(7), 16822, Checkerboard Library) ABDO Publishing Co.

Read, Tracy C. Exploring the World of Raccoons. 2010. (Exploring the World Of Ser.). (ENG., Illus.). 24p. (J). (gr. 2-5). 16.95 (978-1-55407-626-0(9), 7c2ed2bc-6457-4153-94e7-2656e88a3e79); pap. 6.95 (978-1-55407-617-8(X), 3442d78b-9921-4b06-bc10-270e3c307e0f) Firefly Bks., Ltd.

Riggs, Kate. Amazing Animals: Raccoons. 2017. (Amazing Animals Ser.). (ENG., Illus.). 24p. (J). (gr. 1-3). pap. 9.99 (978-1-62832-365-8(5), 20045, Creative Paperbacks) Creative Co., The.

—Raccoons. 2017. (Amazing Animals Ser.). (ENG., Illus.). 24p. (J). (gr. 1-4). (978-1-60818-757-7(8), 20047, Creative Education) Creative Co., The.

Roza, Greg. Your Neighbor the Raccoon, 1 vol. 2011. (City Critters Ser.). (ENG., Illus.). 24p. (J). (gr. 2-3). pap. 9.25 (978-1-4488-5129-4(7), e47fe582-7dce-4d3a-b120-f56f935b20db); lib. bdg. 27.27 (978-1-4488-5000-6(2), 38e21855-1788-4e19-9d79-c80f1269ccf3) Rosen Publishing Group, Inc., The. (Windmill Bks.).

Rustad, Martha E. H. Raccoons. 2013. (ENG., Illus.). 24p. (J). lib. bdg. 25.65 (978-1-62031-072-4(4)) Jump! Inc.

Schuh, Mari C. Raccoons. 2015. (Backyard Animals Ser.). (ENG., Illus.). 24p. (J). (gr. -1-2). lib. bdg. 27.32 (978-1-4914-2087-4(1), 127567, Capstone Pr.) Capstone.

Storm, Marysa. Raccoons. (Spot Backyard Animals Ser.). (ENG., Illus.). 16p. (J). (gr. -1-2). 2018. pap. 7.99 (978-1-68152-220-3(9), 14751) 2017. 17.95 (978-1-68151-095-8(2), 14632) Amicus.

Terp, Gail. Raccoons. 2016. (Wild Animal Kingdom Ser.). (ENG.). 32p. (J). (gr. 4-6). pap. 9.99 (978-1-64466-173-4(X), 10409); (Illus.). 31.35 (978-1-68072-055-6(4), 10408) Black Rabbit Bks. (Bolt).

Wegman, Marcia. Lula Belle. Wegman, Marcia, illus. 2012. (Illus.). 30p. pap. 16.00 (978-1-932043-82-2(9)) Penfield Bks.

RACCOON—FICTION

Appelt, Kathi. The True Blue Scouts of Sugar Man Swamp. (ENG., Illus.). (J). (gr. 3-7). 2014. 352p. pap. 8.99 (978-1-4424-2108-0(8), Atheneum Bks. for Young Readers) 2013. 336p. 19.99 (978-1-4424-2105-9(3)) Simon & Schuster Children's Publishing.

—The True Blue Scouts of Sugar Man Swamp. 2014. lib. bdg. 19.65 (978-0-606-35793-7(9)) Turtleback.

Arnosky, Jim. Raccoon on His Own. Arnosky, Jim, illus. 2003. (ENG., Illus.). 32p. (J). (gr. -1-k). 8.99 (978-0-14-250071-2(2), Puffin Books) Penguin Young Readers Group.

Baggett, Shirley Reed. Adventures of Bandit: A Little Racoon Goes into the Forbidden Forest. 2011. 16p. (gr. 1-2). pap. 9.99 (978-1-4567-6575-0(2)) AuthorHouse.

Ballard, John. The Shining Thing, 1 vol. Hume, Jeff, illus. 2009. 35p. pap. 19.95 (978-1-61546-655-9(X)) PublishAmerica, Inc.

Bloom, Becky. Leo & Lester. Biet, Pascal, illus. 2003. (J). 32p. 15.95 (978-1-59034-582-5(7)); 33p. pap. (978-1-59034-583-2(5)) Mondo Publishing.

Bluedorn, Johannah. The Story of Mr. Pippin. Bluedorn, Johannah, illus. 2004. (Illus.). 32p. (J). 12.00 (978-0-9743616-8-0(2)) Trivium Pursuit.

Bottiglieri, Tim. Robber Raccoon, 1 vol. Bishop, John E., illus. 2009. 16p. pap. 24.95 (978-1-61546-432-6(8)) America Star Bks.

Braymer, Donna. The Adventures of Rowdy Raccoon. 2006. (J). audio compact disk 5.99 (978-0-9766823-8-7(9)) Sable Creek Pr. LLC.

Brightwood, Laura, illus. King Zargon Rules. Brightwood, Laura, . 2006. (J). (978-0-9789871-0-7(1)) 3-C Institute for Social Development.

—Look What You've Done. Brightwood, Laura, . 2007. (J). DVD (978-1-934409-03-9(0)) 3-C Institute for Social Development.

Brown, Ron. Three-Toes the Raccoon Visits the Farm. 2009. 24p. pap. 10.49 (978-1-4389-9035-4(9)) AuthorHouse.

Burgess, Thornton W. The Adventures of Bobby Coon. (J). 18.95 (978-0-8488-0383-4(3)) Amereon Ltd.

—The Adventures of Bobby Coon. 2006. pap. 10.95 (978-1-59605-767-8(X), Cosimo Classics) Cosimo, Inc.

Burkhart, Lorene. Raccoon Tales: Hip, Flip, Skip & Boo & Their Friend Stu. 2007. (Illus.). (J). 8.95 (978-0-9790975-1-5(7)) Burkhart Bks.

—Raccoon Tales: Hip, Flip, Skip & Boo go to the Zoo. 2007. (Illus.). (J). 8.95 (978-0-9790975-2-2(5)) Burkhart Bks.

Cope, Andrew. Raccoon Rampage. 2013. (Awesome Animals Ser.). (ENG.). 192p. (J). (gr. 4-7). 21.19 (978-1-4380-0302-3(1), B.E.S. Publishing) Peterson's.

Councilman, Janet H. Rocky & His Responsible Band of Cowboys, 1 vol. 2009. pap. 24.95 (978-1-60749-384-6(5)) America Star Bks.

—Rocky the Respectful Raccoon & His Red Sunglasses. 2008. 16p. pap. 24.95 (978-1-60813-100-6(9)) America Star Bks.

Crenshaw, Glenda. Friends of the Enchanted Forest: How they Save Christmas. 2011. 28p. pap. 15.47 (978-1-4520-0512-6(5)) AuthorHouse.

deRubertis, Barbara. Rosie Raccoon's Rock & Roll Raft. Alley, R. W., illus. 2011. (Animal Antics A to Z Ser.). 32p. (J). pap. 45.32 (978-0-7613-7664-4(X)) Astra Publishing Hse.

deRubertis, Barbara & DeRubertis, Barbara. Rosie Raccoon's Rock & Roll Raft. Alley, R. W., illus. 2012. (Animal Antics A to Z Ser.). 32p. (J). (gr. 2 — 1). cd-rom 7.95 (978-1-57565-411-9(3)) Astra Publishing Hse.

Dicamillo, Kate. Francine Poulet Meets the Ghost Raccoon. Van Dusen, Chris, illus. 2016. (Tales from Deckawoo Drive

Ser.: 2). (ENG.). 112p. (J). (gr. 1-4). 16.00 *(978-0-606-39088-0(X))* Turtleback.

Dillemuth, Julie. Lucy in the City: A Story about Spatial Thinking. Wood, Laura, illus. 2015. 40p. (J). pap. *(978-1-4338-1928-5(7))*, Magination Pr.) American Psychological Assn.

DiPucchio, Kelly. Super Manny Cleans Up! Graegin, Stephanie, illus. 2018. (Super Manny Ser.). (ENG.). 40p. (J). (gr. -1-3). 17.99 *(978-1-4814-5962-4(7))* Simon & Schuster Children's Publishing.

—Super Manny Stands Up! Graegin, Stephanie, illus. 2017. (Super Manny Ser.). (ENG.). 40p. (J). (gr. -1-3). 17.99 *(978-1-4814-5960-0(0))* Simon & Schuster Children's Publishing.

Eaton, Maxwell, III & Eaton, Maxwell. The Flying Beaver Brothers & the Crazy Critter Race: (a Graphic Novel) 2015. (Flying Beaver Brothers Ser.: 6). (Illus.). 96p. (J). (gr. 1-4). pap. 7.99 *(978-0-385-75469-9(8))*, Knopf Bks. for Young Readers) Random Hse. Children's Bks.

Elliott, Laura Malone. Hunter's Best Friend at School. Munsinger, Lynn, illus. 2005. (gr. -1-2). 17.00 *(978-0-7569-5786-5(9))* Perfection Learning Corp.

Erickson, John. Moonlight Madness. Holmes, Gerald L., illus. 2011. (Hank the Cowdog Ser.: No. 23). (ENG.). 114p. (J). (gr. 3-6). pap. 5.99 *(978-1-59188-123-0(4))* Maverick Bks., Inc.

—The Secret Laundry Monster Files. Holmes, Gerald L., illus. 2011. (Hank the Cowdog Ser.). (ENG.). 128p. (J). (gr. 3-6). pap. 5.99 *(978-1-59188-139-1(0))* Maverick Bks., Inc.

Friend, Catherine. Eddie the Raccoon: Brand New Readers. Yee, Wong Herbert, illus. 2004. (Brand New Readers Ser.). (ENG.). 32p. (J). (gr. -1-3). pap. 6.99 *(978-0-7636-2334-0(2))* Candlewick Pr.

Hallagin, Janet. The Way of Courage. 2006. 30.99 *(978-1-4257-1249-5(5))*; pap. 20.99 *(978-1-4257-1248-8(7))* Xlibris Corp.

Hamilton, Elizabeth L. Ricky Raccoon's Trustworthiness Tree. I.t. ed. 2005. (Character Critters Ser.: No. 11). (Illus.). 32p. (J). per. 5.95 *(978-0-9754629-8-0(9))*, Character-in-Action) Quiet Impact, Inc.

Hanzik, Sharon. Raccoons Don't Use Spoons. 2009. 24p. pap. 17.95 *(978-1-4327-2815-1(6))* Outskirts Pr., Inc.

Henninger, Robert. The Rangers of the Forest. Higgins, Beatrice, illus. 2003. (ENG.). 82p. pap. 12.95 *(978-1-4120-0368-1(7))* Trafford Publishing.

Hesselbein, Deborah A. Tail Talks. Claycomb, Norma L., illus. 2008. 48p. per. 15.95 *(978-1-59858-560-5(6))* Dog Ear Publishing, LLC.

Hill, Susan. Ruby Bakes a Cake. Moore, Margie, illus. 2004. (My First I Can Read Bks.). 32p. (J). (gr. k-3). lib. bdg. 16.89 *(978-0-06-008976-4(8))* HarperCollins Pubs.

—Ruby Bakes a Cake, 1 vol. Moore, Margie, illus. 2010. (I Can Read! / Ruby Raccoon Ser.). (ENG.). 32p. (J). pap. 4.99 *(978-0-310-72022-5(2))* Zonderkidz.

Jackson, Bobby L. Boon the Raccoon & Easel the Weasel. Rodriguez, Christina, illus. 2004. 32p. (J). pap. 11.95 *(978-1-884242-03-8(0))*, BREW2NED); 19.95 *(978-1-884242-02-1(2))*, BREW2NED) Multicultural Pubns.

James, Shilah & James, Michael. Little Land Adventures - Little Raccoon. Castles, Heather, illus. 2010. 24p. pap. *(978-1-926635-36-1(1))* Adlibbed, Ltd.

Johnson, Joshua C. The Raccoon in My Room. 2010. 20p. 10.49 *(978-1-4520-7273-9(6))* AuthorHouse.

Johnson, Virginia. Officer Rick & the Raccoon — a True Story. 2011. 24p. pap. 11.50 *(978-1-60976-114-1(6))*, Eloquent Bks.) Strategic Book Publishing & Rights Agency (SBPRA).

Kimmel, Eric A. I Want a Real Bike in Oregon. Cleland, Josh, illus. 2018. (ENG.). 32p. (J). (gr. 1-3). 17.99 *(978-1-5132-6127-0(4))*, West Winds Pr.) West Margin Pr.

Krulik, Nancy. Camp Rules! Super Special. John and Wendy, illus. 2007. (Katie Kazoo, Switcheroo Ser.: No. 5). 160p. (J). (gr. 2-4). pap. 7.99 *(978-0-448-44542-7(5))*, Grosset & Dunlap) Penguin Young Readers Group.

Luebs, Robin. Please Pick Me up, Mama! Luebs, Robin, illus. 2009. (ENG., Illus.). 40p. (J). (gr. -1-k). 15.99 *(978-1-4169-7977-7(8))*, Beach Lane Bks.) Beach Lane Bks.

Lyle-Soffe, Shari. The Misadventures of Rooter & Snuffle. Collier, Kevin Scott, illus. 2006. 28p. (J). E-Book 5.00 incl. cd-rom *(978-1-933090-43-6(X))* Guardian Angel Publishing, Inc.

—On the Go with Rooter & Snuffle. Collier, Kevin Scott, illus. 2008. 20p. pap. 9.95 *(978-1-933090-96-2(0))* Guardian Angel Publishing, Inc.

—Trouble Finds Rooter & Snuffle. Collier, Kevin Scott, illus. 2008. 20p. pap. 9.95 *(978-1-933090-72-6(3))* Guardian Angel Publishing, Inc.

Macieiski, Ellen. Little Raccoon's Adventures. 2012. 56p. pap. 24.99 *(978-1-4685-3854-0(3))* AuthorHouse.

Marie, Tina. Raccoon Round-Up at the Diamond R Ranch. 2012. 32p. pap. 24.95 *(978-1-4626-7599-9(9))* America Star Bks.

Mattix, Tracy. Begging for Marshmallows. 2013. 44p. pap. 16.95 *(978-1-63000-542-9(8))* America Star Bks.

Maxwell, Andre L. & Maxwell, Amanda L. The Great Chicken Caper. Carter, Jill, illus. 2012. 34p. (-18). 18.00 *(978-0-9881811-1-3(8))* Maxwell, Andre.

McCorkle, Barbara. Bandit Raccoon. Taylor, David A., illus. I.t. ed. 2006. 39p. (J). 19.95 *(978-1-59879-170-9(2))*; per. 13.99 *(978-1-59879-123-5(0))* Lifevest Publishing, Inc.

McPhail, David. The Searcher & Old Tree. McPhail, David, illus. 2011. (ENG., Illus.). 32p. (J). (gr. -1-2). pap. 7.95 *(978-1-58089-224-7(8))* Charlesbridge Publishing, Inc.

—Waddles. 2011. (ENG., Illus.). 32p. (J). (gr. k-2). 16.95 *(978-0-8109-8415-8(6))*, 648701, Abrams Bks. for Young Readers) Abrams, Inc.

Melton, David. The Wonder Years of Oscar the Raccoon. 2013. (ENG.). 32p. (J). 15.95 *(978-1-4327-9964-9(9))* Outskirts Pr., Inc.

Michaud, Sylvie. Book of Dreams - the Ringtail Family. Michaud, Monique, illus. 2012. 24p. pap. *(978-0-9782955-8-5(7))* Crafty Canuck, Inc.

—Book of Love - the Ringtail Family. Michaud, Monique, illus. 2012. 24p. pap. *(978-1-927471-00-5(1))* Crafty Canuck, Inc.

—Book of Wishes - the Ringtail Family. Michaud, Monique, illus. 2012. 24p. pap. *(978-0-9782955-9-2(5))* Crafty Canuck, Inc.

Nieting, Sherry. Adventures in Hope Forest: Isabelle's Search for God. 2011. (Illus.). 24p. (J). pap. 10.95 *(978-1-4497-2518-1(X))*, WestBow Pr.) Author Solutions, LLC.

Odom, Rebecca. Grandpa & the Raccoon. Tebbit, Jake, illus. 2009. 36p. pap. 24.95 *(978-1-60749-912-1(6))* America Star Bks.

Ondaatje, Griffin. Muddy: The Raccoon Who Stole Dishes. Wolfsgruber, Linda, illus. 2019. (ENG.). 32p. (J). (gr. -1-2). 17.95 *(978-0-7358-4337-0(6))* North-South Bks., Inc.

Otto, Carolyn B. Raccoon at Clear Creek Road. Trachok, Cathy, illus. 2005. (Smithsonian's Backyard Ser.). 32p. (J). (gr. -1-3). pap. 8.95 incl. audio *(978-1-59249-490-3(0))*, SC5008); (ENG.). per. 6.95 *(978-1-59249-481-1(1))*, S5008) Soundprints.

Penn, Audrey. Un Beso en Mi Mano (the Kissing Hand) Harper, Ruth, illus. 2006. (ENG.). 32p. (J). (gr. -1-3). 18.99 *(978-1-933718-01-9(3))* Tanglewood Pr.

—Chester Raccoon & the Acorn Full of Memories. Gibson, Barbara, illus. 2009. (Kissing Hand Ser.). (ENG.). 32p. (J). (gr. -1-3). 16.99 *(978-1-933718-29-3(3))* Tanglewood Pr.

—Chester Raccoon & the Big Bad Bully. Gibson, Barbara, illus. 2008. (Kissing Hand Ser.). (ENG.). 32p. (J). (gr. -1-3). 16.99 *(978-1-933718-15-6(3))* Tanglewood Pr.

—Chester Raccoon & the Big Bad Bully [with CD]. Gibson, Barbara, illus. 2008. (Kissing Hand Ser.). (ENG.). 32p. (J). (gr. -1-3). pap. 12.95 incl. audio compact disk *(978-1-933718-30-9(7))* Tanglewood Pr.

—Chester the Brave. Gibson, Barbara, illus. 2012. (Kissing Hand Ser.). (ENG.). 32p. (J). (gr. -1-3). 16.99 *(978-1-933718-79-8(X))* Tanglewood Pr.

—A Color Game for Chester Raccoon. Gibson, Barbara, illus. 2012. (Kissing Hand Ser.). (ENG.). 14p. (J). (gr. -1-2). bds. 7.95 *(978-1-933718-58-3(7))* Tanglewood Pr.

—The Kissing Hand. Harper, Ruth, illus. 2007. (ENG.). 32p. (J). (gr. -1-3). 28.95 *(978-1-933718-07-1(2))* Tanglewood Pr.

—A Kissing Hand for Chester Raccoon. Gibson, Barbara, illus. 2014. (Kissing Hand Ser.). (ENG.). 14p. (J). (gr. -1-2). bds. 8.99 *(978-1-933718-77-4(3))* Tanglewood Pr.

—A Pocket Full of Kisses. Gibson, Barbara Leonard, illus. 2004. (New Child & Family Press Titles Ser.). 32p. (J). (gr. -1-1). 16.95 *(978-0-87868-894-4(3))*, 8943, Child & Family Pr.) Child Welfare League of America, Inc.

—A Pocket Full of Kisses. Gibson, Barbara, illus. 2006. (Kissing Hand Ser.). (ENG.). 32p. (J). (gr. -1-3). 18.99 *(978-1-933718-02-6(1))* Tanglewood Pr.

Penn, Audrey, et al, illus. The Kissing Hand. 2010. 23.05 *(978-0-7569-9299-6(0))* Natl Bk. Network.

Petrella, Angela & Petrella, Michaelanne. Recipe. Bertino, Mike & Althea, Erin, illus. 2013. 48p. (J). (gr. -1-3). 17.95 *(978-1-936365-84-5(7))*, 84b80642-60f2-456f-a348-8d7ac284d4dc) McSweeney's Publishing.

Phillips, Dixie. One Noble Journey. Sponaugle, Kim, illus. 2009. 16p. pap. 9.95 *(978-1-935137-86-3(7))* Guardian Angel Publishing, Inc.

Pick Me up, Mama! 2014. (ENG., Illus.). 34p. (J). (gr. -1-k). bds. 6.99 *(978-1-4814-1633-7(2))*, Little Simon) Little Simon.

Plant, David J. Hungry Roscoe. 2015. (ENG., Illus.). 40p. (J). (gr. -1-2). 17.95 *(978-1-909263-53-6(2))* Flying Eye Bks. GBR. Dist: Penguin Random Hse. LLC.

Qualls, Millie Marie. Miss Cooney & Her New Home. 2012. 24p. pap. 24.95 *(978-1-4626-7426-8(7))* America Star Bks.

Rankine-Van Wassenhoven, Jacqueline. Three Pumpkin Pies for Three Good Neighbors. 2009. 20p. pap. 11.00 *(978-1-4389-3242-2(1))* AuthorHouse.

Robertson-Eletto, Joanne. Rocky: The Okeeheelee Bandit. 2013. 48p. pap. 20.99 *(978-1-4808-0298-8(0))* Archway Publishing.

Roddy, Lee. The Legend of the White Raccoon. 2008. (D. J. Dillon Adventure Ser.: No. 6). (Illus.). 105p. (J). 7.99 *(978-0-88062-270-7(9))* Mott Media.

Rubin, Adam. Fiesta Secreta de Pizza. Salmieri, Daniel, illus. 2015. 40p. (J). (gr. -1-k). 8.99 *(978-0-14-751560-5(2))*, Puffin Books) Penguin Young Readers Group.

—Secret Pizza Party. Salmieri, Daniel, illus. 2013. 40p. (J). (gr. -1-2). 18.99 *(978-0-8037-3947-5(8))*, Dial Bks) Penguin Young Readers Group.

Rylant, Cynthia. The Case of the Climbing Cat. Karas, G. Brian, illus. 2003. (High-Rise Private Eyes Ser.: No. 2). (J). (gr. -1-3). 25.96 incl. audio *(978-1-59112-190-9(6))*; pap. 29.95 incl. audio *(978-1-59112-191-6(4))* Live Oak Media.

—The Case of the Puzzling Possum. Karas, G. Brian, illus. 2003. (High-Rise Private Eyes Ser.: No. 3). (J). (gr. -1-3). 25.95 incl. audio *(978-1-59112-198-5(1))*; (gr. k-3). pap. 29.95 incl. audio *(978-1-59112-199-2(X))* Live Oak Media.

Sargent, Dave & Sargent, David, Jr. Hoot Owl: Mind Your Mamma, 19 vols., Vol. 9. Lenoir, Jane, illus. 2003. (Feather Tales Ser.: 9). 42p. (J). pap. 10.95 *(978-1-56763-736-6(1))* Ozark Publishing.

Sargent, Dave & Sargent, David M., Jr. Hoot Owl: Mind Your Mamma, 20 vols., Vol. 9. Lenoir, Jane, illus. 2nd ed. 2003. (Feather Tales Ser.: 9). 42p. (J). lib. bdg. *(978-1-56763-735-9(3))* Ozark Publishing.

Sargent, Dave & Sargent, Pat. Roy Raccoon: I Love Adventure, 15 vols., Vol. 1. Huff, Jeane, illus. 2nd rev. ed. 2003. (Animal Pride Ser.: 1). 42p. (J). pap. 10.95 *(978-1-56763-760-1(4))*; lib. bdg. 20.95 *(978-1-56763-759-5(0))* Ozark Publishing.

Schachner, Judy. Dewey Bob. Schachner, Judy, illus. 2015. (Illus.). 32p. (J). (gr. k-3). 17.99 *(978-0-8037-4120-1(0))*, Dial Bks) Penguin Young Readers Group.

Scholastic. Animal Antics e-J First Grade Reader Box Set: Scholastic Early Learners (Guided Reader), 1 vol. 2019. (Scholastic Early Learners Ser.).Tr. of Guided Reader. (ENG.). 256p. (J). (gr. -1-1). 16.99 *(978-1-338-36086-8(8))*, Cartwheel Bks.) Scholastic, Inc.

Sheets, Katherine. Captured by Henrey, 1 vol. 2010. 48p. pap. 16.95 *(978-1-4489-4538-2(0))* America Star Bks.

Spurlock, Necole. Rocky & Rudy's Wild Adventure, 1 vol. 2009. 48p. pap. 16.95 *(978-1-61582-600-1(9))* America Star Bks.

Trish Lynch Marquis. Pesty Neighbor. 2009. 28p. pap. 14.99 *(978-1-4389-9011-8(1))* AuthorHouse.

Ulch, Virginia. I Love You Anyway. 2007. 32p. per. 18.95 *(978-1-59858-433-2(2))* Dog Ear Publishing, LLC.

—Love, Bandit - a Tail of Foster Care. 2007. 36p. per. 18.95 *(978-1-59858-353-3(0))* Dog Ear Publishing, LLC.

Verrett, Michael. The White Alligator Crown Quatro. 2010. 147p. pap. 13.95 *(978-0-557-58121-4(4))* Lulu Pr., Inc.

Weck, Peter. Lima Bear's Halloween. DiSalvo, Len, illus. 2012. (Lima Bear Stories Ser.). 40p. (J). 15.95 *(978-1-933872-16-2(0))* Lima Bear Pr LLC, The.

Young, Skottie. Rocket Raccoon & Groot, Volume 1. 2016. (J). lib. bdg. 30.60 *(978-0-606-38357-8(3))* Turtleback.

RACCOONS

see Raccoon

RACE

Alaskan Iditarod Adventure: Represent & Solve Problems Involving Multiplication, 1 vol. 2014. (Rosen Math Readers Ser.). (ENG., Illus.). 24p. (J). (gr. 3-3). pap. 8.25 *(978-1-4777-4962-3(4))*, 85e014a9-4b71-4722-bf08-836d3b1dd039, PowerKids Pr.) Rosen Publishing Group, Inc., The.

All about Us Interactive Packages: Here I Am. (Pebble Soup Explorations Ser.). (gr. -1-18). 52.00 *(978-0-7578-5227-5(0))* Rigby Education.

All about Us Interactive Packages: Making Friends. (Pebble Soup Explorations Ser.). (gr. -1-18). 52.00 *(978-0-7578-5228-2(9))* Rigby Education.

The Amazing Race, 6 vols., Pack. (Chiquilibros Ser.). (gr. k-1). 23.00 *(978-0-7635-0437-3(8))* Rigby Education.

La carrera increíble: Individual Title-Six Packs. (Chiquilibros Ser.). (SPA.). (gr. k-1). 23.00 *(978-0-7635-8603-4(X))* Rigby Education.

Crayton, Lisa A. Everything You Need to Know about Confronting Racist Behavior, 1 vol. 2018. (Need to Know Library). (ENG.). 64p. (gr. 6-6). 36.13 *(978-1-5081-7915-3(8))*, 750eab12-ea28-42ec-a862-39fd4e65f755) Rosen Publishing Group, Inc., The.

Doeden, Matt. More Than a Game: Race, Gender, & Politics in Sports. 2019. (ENG., Illus.). 64p. (J). (gr. 5-12). lib. bdg. 34.65 *(978-1-5415-4094-1(8))*, 82a60aff-b280-455c-94bf-9444fd815bac, Millbrook Pr.) Lerner Publishing Group.

Higgins, Melissa. Celebrating Differences. 2012. (Celebrating Differences Ser.). (ENG.). 24p. (J). (gr. -1-2). pap., pap., pap. 29.16 *(978-1-4296-8324-1(4))*, 17626, Capstone Pr.) Capstone.

Nelson, David Erik, ed. Race in John Howard Griffin's Black Like Me, 1 vol. 2013. (Social Issues in Literature Ser.). (ENG., Illus.). 144p. (gr. 10-12). pap. 33.00 *(978-0-7377-6374-4(4))*, f71de92a-062e-41b7-9e94-7d5eede16f73); lib. bdg. 48.03 *(978-0-7377-6373-7(6))*, ef3b9f1b-d489-4d90-b035-b2bf5a3c2748) Greenhaven Publishing LLC. (Greenhaven Publishing).

Robinson, Chuck. Critical World Issues: Racism, Vol. 16. 2016. (Critical World Issues Ser.: Vol. 16). (ENG., Illus.). 112p. (J). (gr. 7-12). 25.95 *(978-1-4222-3659-8(5))* Mason Crest.

Rotner, Shelley. All Kinds of People. 2018. (Illus.). 24p. (J). (— 1). bds. 7.99 *(978-0-8234-3972-0(0))* Holiday Hse., Inc.

Sax, Anita. One Step at a Time. Jasuna, Aija, illus. 2013. 24p. (J). 17.95 *(978-1-60131-152-8(4))*, Castlebridge Bks.) Big Tent Bks.

Stephens, Aarti D., ed. Is Racism a Serious Problem?, 1 vol. 2009. (At Issue Ser.). (ENG.). 128p. (gr. 10-12). pap. 28.80 *(978-0-7377-4417-0(0))*, 9745e46d-7742-49f2-a183-8d900ed64735);No. 9. 41.03 *(978-0-7377-4416-3(2))*, af1be06b-9313-4e67-b094-db7870e7e34c) Greenhaven Publishing LLC. (Greenhaven Publishing).

RACE DISCRIMINATION

see also Race Relations

Anderson, Wayne. Fighting Racial Discrimination: Treating All Americans Fairly under the Law. 2009. (Progressive Movement 1900-1920: Efforts to Reform America's New Industrial Society Ser.). 32p. (gr. 3-4). 47.90 *(978-1-60854-164-5(9))* Rosen Publishing Group, Inc., The.

Cushman, Clare & Urofsky, Melvin I. (Irving), eds. Black, White, & Brown: The Landmark School Desegregation Case in Retrospect. rev. ed. 2004. (ENG., Illus.). 258p. (gr. 9-18). 70.00 *(978-1-56802-911-5(X))* CQ Pr.

Dudley Gold, Susan. The Civil Rights Act Of 1964, 1 vol. 2011. (Landmark Legislation Ser.). (ENG.). 128p. (YA). (gr. 8-8). 42.64 *(978-1-60870-040-0(2))*, e28f32c0-3ceb-450e-a7b4-d51afcb1631e) Cavendish Square Publishing LLC.

Eboch, M. M. Race & Economics. 2017. (Race in America Ser.). (ENG.). 112p. (J). (gr. 6-12). 59.93 *(978-1-68078-819-8(1))*, 26220, Essential Library) ABDO Publishing Co.

Esty, Amos. Plessy V. Ferguson. 2012. (Civil Rights Movement Ser.). (Illus.). 112p. (YA). (gr. 7-12). 28.95 *(978-1-59935-182-7(X))* Reynolds, Morgan Inc.

Gale Research Inc. Unlocking Current Issues: Race & the Law. 2018. (Unlocking Current Issues Ser.). (ENG., Illus.). 240p. 51.00 *(978-1-4103-8096-8(3))* Cengage Gale.

Glaser, Jason. The End of Apartheid, 1 vol. 2018. (History Just Before You Were Born Ser.). (ENG.). 32p. (J). (gr. 4-5). 28.27 *(978-1-5382-3026-8(7))*, ca0fbf99-9636-4934-8636-5dd3787b25a1) Stevens, Gareth Publishing LLLP.

Green, Meghan. Racism in America: A Long History of Hate, 1 vol. 2017. (Hot Topics Ser.). (ENG.). 112p. (gr. 7-7). 41.03 *(978-1-5345-6143-4(9))*, e08b177d-ff77-4777-b788-7e5899c5cf77, Lucent Pr.) Greenhaven Publishing LLC.

Greenhaven Press Staff, ed. Multiracial America. 2012. (Opposing Viewpoints Ser.). (ENG., Illus.). 240p. (gr. 10-12). pap. 28.90 *(978-0-7377-6331-7(0))*; lib. bdg. 41.70 *(978-0-7377-6330-0(2))* Cengage Gale. (Greenhaven Pr., Inc.).

Grinapol, Corinne. Racial Profiling & Discrimination: Your Legal Rights, 1 vol. 2015. (Know Your Rights Ser.). (ENG., Illus.). 64p. (J). (gr. 7-7). pap. 13.95 *(978-1-4777-8619-2(8))*, 0127463f-6ab4-425f-8f00-e2b733732cd2, Rosen Young Adult) Rosen Publishing Group, Inc., The.

Grinapol, Corinne. Racial Profiling & Discrimination: Your Legal Rights, 1 vol. 2015. (Know Your Rights Ser.). (ENG., Illus.). 64p. (J). (gr. 7-7). 36.47 *(978-1-4777-8020-6(3))*, 5ceacb72-a9ca-4d3b-a623-3cccceb4ac46, Rosen Young Adult) Rosen Publishing Group, Inc., The.

Hanson-Harding, Alexandra. Are You Being Racially Profiled?, 1 vol. 2015. (Got Issues? Ser.). (ENG., Illus.). 112p. (gr. 7-8). lib. bdg. 38.93 *(978-0-7660-7138-4(3))*, fc4b9f96-a08b-45fe-8e3c-75178277470d) Enslow Publishing, LLC.

Harris, Duchess. Black Lives Matter. 2017. (Protest Movements Ser.). (ENG., Illus.). 48p. (J). (gr. 4-8). lib. bdg. 35.64 *(978-1-5321-1394-9(3))*, 27692) ABDO Publishing Co.

Lentin, Alana. Racism & Ethnic Discrimination, 1 vol. 2011. (Contemporary Issues Ser.). (ENG.). 166p. (YA). (gr. 9-9). lib. bdg. 42.47 *(978-1-4488-1861-7(3))*, 0575b085-4066-4f6a-8cae-caa5d8061328) Rosen Publishing Group, Inc., The.

Lishak, Antony. Racism. 2007. (What's That Got to Do with Me?/Watts Ser.). (Illus.). 32p. (YA). (gr. 4-7). lib. bdg. 28.50 *(978-1-59920-038-5(4))* Black Rabbit Bks.

Lo Bosco, Maryellen. Confronting Racism, 1 vol. 2017. (Speak up! Confronting Discrimination in Your Daily Life Ser.). (ENG., Illus.). 64p. (YA). (gr. 7-7). pap. 13.95 *(978-1-5383-8176-2(1))*, 938354d9-232e-4616-a0a8-44bf707a611a) Rosen Publishing Group, Inc., The.

Lüsted, Marcia Amidon. Lyndon B. Johnson & the Civil Rights ACT, 1 vol. 2017. (Spotlight on the Civil Rights Movement Ser.). (ENG., Illus.). 48p. (J). (gr. 6-6). 33.47 *(978-1-5383-8048-2(X))*, 7e6c6e30-9ee8-43e5-9413-0bf6bf097a92); pap. 12.75 *(978-1-5081-7746-3(5))*, cb9830f6-0104-416a-bb10-efb9ad35aa6c) Rosen Publishing Group, Inc., The.

Maraniss, Andrew. Strong Inside (Young Readers Edition) The True Story of How Perry Wallace Broke College Basketball's Color Line. 2017. (Illus.). 272p. (J). (gr. 5). 10.99 *(978-1-5247-3727-6(5))*, Puffin Books) Penguin Young Readers Group.

Open for Debate - Group 5, 8 vols., Set. Incl. National Health Care. Kowalski, Kathiann M. lib. bdg. 45.50 *(978-0-7614-2943-2(3))*, edaa0977-a53f-47fe-aa23-2e0389c5e727); Political Campaigns. Naden, Corinne. lib. bdg. 45.50 *(978-0-7614-2944-9(1))*, 9d2e64a5-2c0c-4a63-9836-204d64ed8840); Religious Fundamentalism. Fridell, Ron. lib. bdg. 45.50 *(978-0-7614-2945-6(X))*, d9d1f5c0-2b35-4938-9b69-3cde347cd370); Right to Die. Stefoff, Rebecca. lib. bdg. 45.50 *(978-0-7614-2948-7(4))*, bcbd0407-c7ba-4a50-9da6-fe926a35d042); 144p. (YA). (gr. 8-8). (Open for Debate Ser.). (ENG.). 2009. Set lib. bdg. 182.00 *(978-0-7614-2940-1(9))*, dee07674-67e9-492f-9ba3-039659ed2638, Cavendish Square) Cavendish Square Publishing LLC.

Orr, Tamra. Coping with Racial Inequality, 1 vol. 2017. (Coping (2017-2020) Ser.). (ENG., Illus.). 112p. (J). (gr. 7-7). 40.13 *(978-1-5081-7396-0(6))*, dd44a0c7-946c-4929-a399-f55a8518494e, Rosen Young Adult) Rosen Publishing Group, Inc., The.

Parks, Peggy. Racial Discrimination. 2018. (Discrimination in Society Ser.). (ENG.). 80p. (YA). (gr. 6-12). 39.93 *(978-1-68282-385-9(7))* ReferencePoint Pr., Inc.

Pinede, Nadine & Harris, Duchess. Sexism & Race. 2017. (Being Female in America Ser.). (ENG.). 112p. (J). (gr. 6-12). lib. bdg. 41.36 *(978-1-5321-1308-6(0))*, 27516, Essential Library) ABDO Publishing Co.

Rogers, Amy B. What's Racism?, 1 vol. 2017. (What's the Issue? Ser.). (ENG.). 24p. (J). (gr. 3-3). pap. 9.25 *(978-1-5345-2505-4(X))*, f6926bbd-8465-405d-84e3-804755b6c128); lib. bdg. 26.23 *(978-1-5345-2437-8(1))*, d95e1bd6-aa53-420a-9ba1-dfe2bb1256a2) Greenhaven Publishing LLC.

Sanna, Ellyn. Native North American Indians. 2012. (Gallup Guides for Youth Facing Persistent Prejudice Ser.). 64p. (J). (gr. 7-8). 22.95 *(978-1-4222-2469-4(4))*; pap. 9.95 *(978-1-4222-2478-6(3))* Mason Crest.

Seba, Jaime. Gallup Guides for Youth Facing Persistent Prejudice. 2012. (Illus.). 64p. (J). *(978-1-4222-2462-5(7))* Mason Crest.

—Gallup Guides for Youth Facing Persistent Prejudice - The LGBT Community. 2012. (Gallup Guides for Youth Facing Persistent Prejudice Ser.). (Illus.). 64p. (J). (gr. 7-8). 22.95 *(978-1-4222-2467-0(8))* Mason Crest.

Seba, Jaime & Sanna, Ellyn. Gallup Guides for Youth Facing Persistent Prejudice. 2012. (Gallup Guides for Youth Facing Persistent Prejudice Ser.). 64p. (J). (gr. 7-8). 22.95 *(978-1-4222-2465-6(1))* Mason Crest.

Stone, Tanya Lee. Courage Has No Color, the True Story of the Triple Nickles: America's First Black Paratroopers. 2013. (ENG., Illus.). 160p. (J). (gr. 5). pap. 17.99 *(978-0-7636-6548-7(7))*; 24.99 *(978-0-7636-5117-6(6))* Candlewick Pr.

Thomas, Pat. The Skin I'm In: A First Look at Racism. Harker, Lesley, illus. 2003. (First Look At... Ser.). (ENG.). 32p. (J). (gr. -1-2). pap. 8.99 *(978-0-7641-2459-4(5))* Sourcebooks, Inc.

Warner, Jody Nyasha. Viola Desmond Won't Be Budged!, 1 vol. Rudnicki, Richard, illus. (ENG.). 32p. (J). (gr. k-4). 2018. pap. 9.95 *(978-1-77306-035-4(X))* 2010. 18.95 *(978-0-88899-779-1(5))* Groundwood Bks. CAN. Dist: Publishers Group West (PGW).

Watson, Marilyn Myrick. Raul Castro: Arizona's First Hispanic Governor. (J). 2011. (Illus.). 28p. *(978-1-935089-40-7(4))* 2007. *(978-0-9790826-6-5(8))* 2007. *(978-0-9790826-5-8(X))* Acacia Publishing, Inc.

RACE PROBLEMS

see Race Relations

RACE RELATIONS

see also Discrimination; Emigration and Immigration; Multicultural Education

also names of countries, cities, etc. with the subdivision Race Relations, e.g. U. S.—Race Relations

Acho, Emmanuel. Uncomfortable Conversations with a Black Boy: Racism, Injustice, & How You Can Be a Changemaker. 2021. (ENG.). 320p. (J). 17.99 *(978-1-250-80106-7(0))*, 900240846) Roaring Brook Pr.

—Uncomfortable Conversations with a Black Boy: Racism, Injustice, & How You Can Be a Changemaker. 2023. (ENG.).

P Q R

336p. (J). pap. 9.99 *(978-1-250-86610-3(3)*, 900240847) Square Fish.

Aikins, Anne Marie. Racism Deal with It: Deal with It Before It Gets under Your Skin, 1 vol. Murray, Steven, illus. 2004. (Lorimer Deal with It Ser.). (ENG.). 32p. (J). (gr. 4-6). 12.95 *(978-1-55028-844-5(X)*, 844) James Lorimer & Co. Ltd., Pubs. CAN. Dist: Lerner Publishing Group.

Aronson, Marc. Race: A History Beyond Black & White. 2007. (ENG., Illus.). 336p. (YA). (gr. 6-12). 21.99 *(978-0-689-86554-1(6)*, Atheneum Bks. for Young Readers) Simon & Schuster Children's Publishing.

Bridges, Ruby. Through My Eyes: Ruby Bridges. Lundell, Margo, ed. Lundell, Margo, illus. 2018. (Follow Me Around... Ser.). (ENG.). 64p. (J). (gr. 3-4). E-Book 27.00 *(978-0-545-70803-6(6))* Scholastic, Inc.

Capek, Michael & Harris, Duchess. The Charlottesville Protests. 2018. (Special Reports). (ENG., Illus.). 112p. (J). (gr. 6-12). lib. bdg. 41.36 *(978-1-5321-1676-6(4)*, 30604, Essential Library) ABDO Publishing Co.

Cline-Ransome, Lesa. Benny Goodman & Teddy Wilson: Taking the Stage As the First Black-And-White Jazz Band in History. Ransome, James E., illus. 2014. (ENG.). 32p. (J). (gr. 3-7). 18.99 *(978-0-8234-2362-0(X))* Holiday Hse., Inc.

Cooper, John, Jr. & Cooper, John. Season of Rage: Hugh Burnett & the Struggle for Civil Rights. 2005. (ENG., Illus.). 80p. (J). (gr. 5-12). pap. 9.95 *(978-0-88776-700-5(1)*, Tundra Bks.) Tundra Bks. CAN. Dist: Penguin Random Hse. LLC.

Deibel, Zac. Racial Segregation: Plessy V. Ferguson, 1 vol. 2018. (Courting History Ser.). (ENG.). 64p. (gr. 6-6). lib. bdg. 37.36 *(978-1-5026-3589-1(5)*, dd1dbc16-d9e0-402c-90d2-04f0625ec7d1) Cavendish Square Publishing LLC.

Durst Johnson, Claudia, ed. Race in the Poetry of Langston Hughes, 1 vol. 2013. (Social Issues in Literature Ser.). (ENG., Illus.). 168p. (gr. 10-12). pap. 33.00 *(978-0-7377-6981-4(5)*, ee302344-01d8-4d82-bcd4-991c66a188a9); lib. bdg. 48.03 *(978-0-7377-6980-7(7)*, 49783385-d54e-4ccd-b284-90b28a312de2) Greenhaven Publishing LLC. (Greenhaven Publishing).

Edwards, Nicola. Racism. (Illus.). 32p. (YA). (gr. 1-18). lib. bdg. 27.10 *(978-1-932333-06-0(1))* Chrysalis Education.

Fiorelli, June Estep. Fannie Lou Hamer: A Voice for Freedom. 2004. (Avisson Young Adult Ser.). (Illus.). 117p. (J). pap. 19.95 *(978-1-888105-62-9(3))* Avisson Pr., Inc.

Ford, Carin T. The Civil War's African-American Soldiers Through Primary Sources, 1 vol. 2013. (Civil War Through Primary Sources Ser.). (ENG.). 48p. (gr. 4-6). 27.93 *(978-0-7660-4125-7(5)*, 915d7238-d55d-464b-8277-85e0d474ba77); pap. 11.53 *(978-1-4644-0183-1(7)*, 0ff0bfa0-13e7-4d9f-9071-ebe5a4ccbad2) Enslow Publishing, LLC.

Gay, Kathlyn. Cultural Diversity: Conflicts & Challenges. 2003. (It Happened to Me Ser.: 6). (ENG., Illus.). 144p. pap. 55.00 *(978-0-8108-4805-4(8))* Scarecrow Pr., Inc.

Gifford, Clive. Racism. (Illus.). 64p. (YA). (gr. 5-18). lib. bdg. 29.95 *(978-1-931983-83-9(6))* Chrysalis Education.

—Racism, 1 vol. 2006. (Global Issues Ser.: 0). (ENG., Illus.). 64p. (YA). (gr. 6-10). pap. 12.95 *(978-1-55285-745-8(X)*, bfa1b67a-af7f-4349-bd5e-4a5302a3ca65) Whitecap Bks., Ltd. CAN. Dist: Firefly Bks., Ltd.

Gosman, Gillian. Rosa Parks, 1 vol. 2011. (Life Stories Ser.). (ENG., Illus.). 24p. (J). (gr. 3-3). pap. 9.25 *(978-1-4488-2757-2(4)*, 3f49635b-67dd-4cd5-9f8d-2b7d9499b2b9, PowerKids Pr.); lib. bdg. 26.27 *(978-1-4488-3218-7(7)*, bea574e5-5551-4a35-a56a-a70912f05db2); lib. bdg. 26.27 *(978-1-4488-2584-4(9)*, 3797e45e-a80c-45ae-b424-7a783c9d915d, PowerKids Pr.) Rosen Publishing Group, Inc., The.

Hanes, Richard Clay, et al. Prejudice in the Modern World. 2007. (J). *(978-1-4144-0206-2(6))*; *(978-1-4144-0205-5(8))* Cengage Gale.

Harris, Duchess & Conley, Kate. Gender & Race in Sports. 2018. (Race & Sports Ser.). (ENG., Illus.). 112p. (J). (gr. 6-12). lib. bdg. 41.36 *(978-1-5321-1670-4(5)*, 30592, Essential Library) ABDO Publishing Co.

Harris, Duchess & Miller, Michael. Race & Sports Management. 2018. (Race & Sports Ser.). (ENG., Illus.). 112p. (J). (gr. 6-12). lib. bdg. 41.36 *(978-1-5321-1673-5(X)*, 30598, Essential Library) ABDO Publishing Co.

Harris, Duchess & Mooney, Carla. Fighting Stereotypes in Sports. 2018. (Race & Sports Ser.). (ENG., Illus.). 112p. (J). (gr. 6-12). lib. bdg. 41.36 *(978-1-5321-1669-8(1)*, 30590, Essential Library) ABDO Publishing Co.

Harris, Duchess & Streissguth, Tom. Race & College Sports. 2018. (Race & Sports Ser.). (ENG., Illus.). 112p. (J). (gr. 6-12). lib. bdg. 41.36 *(978-1-5321-1672-8(1)*, 30596, Essential Library) ABDO Publishing Co.

Hill, Z. B. Gallup Guides for Youth Facing Persistent Prejudice. 2012. (Gallup Guides for Youth Facing Persistent Prejudice Ser.). 64p. (J). (gr. 7-8). 22.95 *(978-1-4222-2463-2(5))* Mason Crest.

Hudson, Wade & Hudson, Cheryl Willis, eds. The Talk: Conversations about Race, Love & Truth. (Illus.). 160p. (J). (gr. 5). 2021. 7.99 *(978-0-593-12164-1(3)*, Yearling) 2020. 16.99 *(978-0-593-12161-0(9)*, Crown Books For Young Readers) 2020. (ENG., lib. bdg. 19.99 *(978-0-593-12162-7(7)*, Crown Books For Young Readers) Random Hse. Children's Bks.

Jelloun, Tahar. Racisme Explique a Ma Fille. pap. 19.95 *(978-88-7754-206-9(3))* Cideb ITA. Dist: Distribooks, Inc.

Joseph, Frederick. The Black Friend: on Being a Better White Person. (ENG.). (YA). (gr. 7). 2023. 288p. pap. 12.00 *(978-1-5362-2304-0(2))* 2020. 272p. 17.99 *(978-1-5362-1701-8(8))* Candlewick Pr.

Lester, Julius. Let's Talk about Race. Barbour, Karen, illus. 2008. (ENG.). 32p. (J). (gr. -1-3). pap. 8.99 *(978-0-06-446226-6(9)*, HarperCollins) HarperCollins Pubs.

Mancini, Candice L., ed. Racism in the Autobiography of Malcolm X, 1 vol. 2008. (Social Issues in Literature Ser.). (ENG., Illus.). 176p. (gr. 10-12). pap. 33.00 *(978-0-7377-4261-9(5)*, c11e206d-a850-44b5-b6cc-7956a1b11178); lib. bdg. 48.03 *(978-0-7377-4260-2(7)*, b9cdb352-b77e-4921-abad-b6f5038b9070) Greenhaven Publishing LLC. (Greenhaven Publishing).

Marcovitz, Hal. Teens & Race. 2008. (Gallup Youth Survey, Major Issues & Trends Ser.). (Illus.). 112,128p. (YA). (gr. 7-9). lib. bdg. 22.95 *(978-1-59084-721-3(0))* Mason Crest.

Marsico, Katie. Racism. 2008. (21st Century Skills Library: Global Perspectives Ser.). (ENG., Illus.). 32p. (gr. 4-8). lib. bdg. 32.07 *(978-1-60279-134-3(1)*, 200107) Cherry Lake Publishing.

Pederson, Charles E. Racism & Intolerance. 2008. (Man's Inhumanities Ser.). (YA). (gr. 7-12). 23.95 *(978-1-60217-976-9(X))* Erickson Pr

Rodger, Marguerite & Rodger, Jessie. Racism & Prejudice, 1 vol. 2010. (Straight Talk about... Ser.). (ENG.). 48p. (J). (gr. 7-10). pap. *(978-0-7787-2136-9(1))* Crabtree Publishing Co.

Rooney, Anne. Race Hate. 2010. (Voices Ser.). (Illus.). 48p. pap. *(978-0-237-54215-3(3))* Evans Brothers, Ltd.

Schramm, Linda Anette. Don't Let the Ziglers into the Zoo! 2004. 31p. pap. 24.95 *(978-1-4137-1541-5(9))* PublishAmerica, Inc.

Seba, Jaime. Gallup Guides for Youth Facing Persistent Prejudice: Blacks. 2012. (Gallup Guides for Youth Facing Persistent Prejudice Ser.). 64p. (J). (gr. 7-8). 22.95 *(978-1-4222-2464-9(3))* Mason Crest.

Spilsbury, Louise. Racism & Intolerance. Kai, Hanane, illus. 2018. (ENG.). 32p. (J). (gr. 1-2). 9.99 *(978-1-4380-5022-5(4))* Sourcebooks, Inc.

Steele, Philip. Race & Crime. 2016. (Behind the News Ser.). (Illus.). 48p. (J). (gr. 6-9). *(978-0-7787-2588-6(X))* Crabtree Publishing Co.

Sutherland, Johnathan & Canwell, Diane. African Americans in the Vietnam War, 1 vol. 2004. (American Experience in Vietnam Ser.). (ENG., Illus.). 48p. (gr. 5-8). lib. bdg. 33.67 *(978-0-8368-5772-6(0)*, 208cb630-74f5-459d-a36c-dc75d64786d4, Gareth Stevens Secondary Library) Stevens, Gareth Publishing LLLP.

Swan, Bill. Real Justice: Jailed for Life for Being Black: The Story of Rubin Hurricane Carter, 1 vol. 2014. (Lorimer Real Justice Ser.). (ENG., Illus.). 144p. (YA). (gr. 9-12). pap. 12.95 *(978-1-4594-0665-0(6)*, 6dccd4e0-c34e-44c2-bf3f-8a418e48241a) James Lorimer & Co. Ltd., Pubs. CAN. Dist: Lerner Publishing Group.

Thomson Gale Staff. Prejudice in the Modern World. Hanes, Sharon M., ed. rev. ed. 2007. (Prejudice in the Modern World Reference Library). (ENG., Illus.). 256p. (J). 129.00 *(978-1-4144-0208-6(2)*, UXL) Cengage Gale.

—Prejudice in the Modern World - Almanac, 2 vols. Hanes, Richard C. et al, eds. rev. ed. 2007. (Prejudice in the Modern World Reference Library). (ENG.). 462p. (YA). 233.00 *(978-1-4144-0204-8(X)*, UXL) Cengage Gale.

Thomson Gale Staff & Hermsen, Sarah. Prejudice in the Modern World: Biographies. Hanes, Richard C. & Rudd, Kelly, eds. rev. ed. 2007. (Prejudice in the Modern World Reference Library). (ENG., Illus.). 288p. (J). 129.00 *(978-1-4144-0207-9(4)*, UXL) Cengage Gale.

—Prejudice in the Modern World: Cumulative Index. rev. ed. 2007. (Prejudice in the Modern World Reference Library). (ENG.). 34p. (YA). 5.00 *(978-1-4144-0209-3(0)*, UXL) Cengage Gale.

Timmons, Angie. Everything You Need to Know about Racism, 1 vol. 2017. (Need to Know Library). (ENG., Illus.). 64p. (J). (gr. 6-6). pap. 13.95 *(978-1-5081-7675-6(2)*, 68e4823c-5d24-44a1-a72f-aee792d06aeb) Rosen Publishing Group, Inc., The.

Vaughn, Wally G. & Davis, Mattie Campbell, eds. The Selma Campaign, 1963-1965: The Decisive Battle of the Civil Rights Movement. 2006. (ENG., Illus.). 244p. pap. 19.95 *(978-0-912469-44-7(7))* Majority Pr., The.

Weatherford, Carole Boston. Unspeakable: The Tulsa Race Massacre. Cooper, Floyd, illus. 2021. (ENG.). 32p. (J). (gr. 3-6). 17.99 *(978-1-5415-8120-3(2)*, 6b87db4d-4f0f-40cd-b33b-220fb2aea4ae, Carolrhoda Bks.) Lerner Publishing Group.

Where Did the Races Come from? 2003. (BUL.). (YA). 0.75 *(978-1-893345-13-3(0))* Answers In Genesis.

RACE RELATIONS—FICTION

Alexie, Sherman. The Absolutely True Diary of a Part-Time Indian. 2011. 10.36 *(978-0-7848-3391-9(5))* 2009. 14.44 *(978-0-7848-3800-6(3))* Marco Bk. Co. (Everbind).

—The Absolutely True Diary of a Part-Time Indian. Forney, Ellen, illus. 2008. 230p. 25.00 *(978-1-60686-072-4(0))* Perfection Learning Corp.

—The Absolutely True Diary of a Part-Time Indian. 2008. (YA). 1.25 *(978-1-4281-8291-2(8))*; 78.49 *(978-1-4361-0259-9(6))*; 68.75 *(978-1-4281-8300-1(0))*; 57.75 *(978-1-4281-8294-3(2))*; 70.75 *(978-1-4281-8298-1(5))*; 212.75 *(978-1-4281-8295-0(0))*; 55.75 *(978-1-4281-8296-7(9))* Recorded Bks., Inc.

—The Absolutely True Diary of a Part-Time Indian. l.t. ed. 2008. (Thorndike Literacy Bridge Ser.). (ENG., Illus.). 301p. (YA). (gr. 7-12). 23.95 *(978-1-4104-0499-2(4))* Thorndike Pr.

—The Absolutely True Diary of a Part-Time Indian. 2009. (YA). lib. bdg. 28.15 *(978-0-606-07296-0(9))* Turtleback.

—The Absolutely True Diary of a Part-Time Indian (National Book Award Winner) (ENG., Illus.). (YA). (gr. 7-17). 2009. 288p. pap. 16.99 *(978-0-316-01369-7(2))* 2007. 320p. 21.99 *(978-0-316-01368-0(4))* Little, Brown Bks. for Young Readers.

Alkaf, Hanna. The Weight of Our Sky. 2019. (ENG., Illus.). 288p. (YA). (gr. 7). 19.99 *(978-1-5344-2608-5(6)*, Salaam Reads) Simon & Schuster Bks. For Young Readers.

Anholt, Laurence. The Hypnotist. 2016. 352p. (YA). (gr. 7). 13.99 *(978-0-552-57345-0(0))* Transworld Publishers Ltd. GBR. Dist: Independent Pubs. Group.

Armistead, John. The Return of Gabriel. Gregory, Fran, illus. 2004. 218p. (gr. 3-8). 17.45 *(978-0-7569-3460-6(5))* Perfection Learning Corp.

—The $66 Summer: A Novel of the Segregated South. 2nd ed. 2006. (Milkweed Prize for Children's Literature Ser.). (ENG., Illus.). 240p. (J). (gr. 3-8). reprint ed. per. 8.00 *(978-1-57131-663-9(9))* Milkweed Editions.

Badger, Ty. Crayons Alive. 2007. pap. 30.00 *(978-0-8059-8636-5(7))* Dorrance Publishing Co., Inc.

Bandy, Michael S. & Stein, Eric. Northbound: a Train Ride Out of Segregation. Ransome, James E., illus. 2020. (ENG.). 40p. (J). (gr. 1-4). 17.99 *(978-0-7636-9650-4(1))* Candlewick Pr.

Bankole, Adekemi. The Rain Beat Dance. 2011. 32p. pap. 21.99 *(978-1-4568-7346-2(6))* Xlibris Corp.

Banks, Sara Harrell. The Everlasting Now, 1 vol. 2010. 168p. (J). (gr. 3-7). 15.95 *(978-1-56145-525-6(3))* Peachtree Publishing Co. Inc.

Belford, Bibi. Crossing the Line. 2017. (ENG.). 304p. (J). (gr. 4-4). 15.99 *(978-1-5107-0800-6(6)*, Sky Pony Pr.) Skyhorse Publishing Co., Inc.

Beus, Bryan. Westly: A Spider's Tale. Beus, Bryan, illus. 2015. (ENG., Illus.). 176p. (J). (gr. 4-6). 15.99 *(978-1-62972-068-5(2)*, 5136479, Shadow Mountain) Shadow Mountain Publishing.

Bildner, Phil. The Soccer Fence: A Story of Friendship, Hope, & Apartheid in South Africa. Watson, Jesse Joshua, illus. 2014. 40p. (J). (gr. 1-3). 18.99 *(978-0-399-24790-3(4)*, G.P. Putnam's Sons Books for Young Readers) Penguin Young Readers Group.

Blackman, Malorie. Black & White. 2007. (ENG.). 512p. (YA). (gr. 9-12). pap. 13.99 *(978-1-4169-0017-7(9)*, Simon & Schuster Bks. For Young Readers) Simon & Schuster Bks. For Young Readers.

—Naughts & Crosses. 2005. (ENG., Illus.). 400p. (YA). (gr. 9-18). 21.99 *(978-1-4169-0016-0(0)*, Simon & Schuster Bks. For Young Readers) Simon & Schuster Bks. For Young Readers.

Blume, Judy. Iggie's House. 2014. (ENG., Illus.). (J). (gr. 3-7). 160p. 18.99 *(978-1-4814-1410-4(0))*; 176p. pap. 7.99 *(978-1-4814-1104-2(7))* Simon & Schuster Children's Publishing. (Atheneum Bks. for Young Readers).

Bolden, Tonya. Saving Savannah. 2020. (ENG., Illus.). 272p. (YA). 17.99 *(978-1-68119-804-0(5)*, 900187335, Bloomsbury Young Adult) Bloomsbury Publishing USA.

Bond, Victoria. Zora & Me: the Summoner. 2020. (Zora & Me Ser.). (ENG., Illus.). 256p. (J). (gr. 5-9). 17.99 *(978-0-7636-4299-0(1))* Candlewick Pr.

Bond, Victoria & Simon, T. R. Zora & Me. 2011. (Zora & Me Ser.). (ENG., Illus.). 192p. (J). (gr. 5). pap. 8.99 *(978-0-7636-5814-4(6))* Candlewick Pr.

Bowlby, Linda S. Future Hope. Helms, Dana, illus. 2008. 298p. (J). (gr. -1-3). pap. 9.95 *(978-0-9779993-6-1(X))* Red Earth Publishing.

Bradley, John Ed. Call Me by My Name. (ENG.). (YA). (gr. 7). 2015. 288p. pap. 12.99 *(978-1-4424-9794-8(7))* 2014. (Illus.). 272p. 17.99 *(978-1-4424-9793-1(9)*, Atheneum Bks. for Young Readers) Simon & Schuster Children's Publishing.

Brooks, Bruce. The Moves Make the Man. (J). pap., stu. ed. *(978-0-13-017518-2(8))*; 3rd ed. pap. 3.95 *(978-0-13-800079-0(4))* Prentice Hall (Schl. Div.).

—The Moves Make the Man: A Newbery Honor Award Winner. 2003. (ENG.). 256p. (YA). (gr. 8-18). pap. 9.99 *(978-0-06-447022-3(9)*, HarperTeen) HarperCollins Pubs.

Budhos, Marina. The Long Ride. 2019. (Illus.). 208p. (J). (gr. 5). 16.99 *(978-0-553-53422-1(X)*, Lamb, Wendy Bks.) Random Hse. Children's Bks.

Bundy, Tamara. Walking with Miss Millie. 2018. 240p. (J). (gr. 5). 8.99 *(978-0-399-54457-6(7)*, Puffin Books) Penguin Young Readers Group.

Burg, Shana. A Thousand Never Evers. 2009. 320p. (J). (gr. 3-7). 8.99 *(978-0-440-42209-9(4)*, Yearling) Random Hse. Children's Bks.

Cho, John. Troublemaker. (ENG.). 224p. (J). (gr. 3-7). 2023. pap. 7.99 *(978-0-7595-5446-7(3))* 2022. 16.99 *(978-0-7595-5447-4(1))* Little, Brown Bks. for Young Readers.

Choldenko, Gennifer. If a Tree Falls at Lunch Period. 2007. (ENG., Illus.). 224p. (YA). (gr. 9-12). 18.69 *(978-0-15-205753-4(6))* Harcourt Children's Bks.

—If a Tree Falls at Lunch Period. 2009. (ENG., Illus.). 224p. (J). (gr. 5-7). pap. 7.99 *(978-0-15-206644-4(6)*, 1099003, Clarion Bks.) HarperCollins Pubs.

Christopher, Matt. The Basket Counts. 2008. (New Matt Christopher Sports Library). 96p. (J). (gr. 4-6). lib. bdg. 26.60 *(978-1-59953-212-7(3))* Norwood Hse. Pr.

Clements, Andrew. The Jacket. 2014. (ENG.). 96p. (J). (gr. 3-7). 10.24 *(978-1-63245-301-3(0))* Lectorum Pubns., Inc.

Coleman, Evelyn. Freedom Train. 2012. (ENG.). 160p. (J). (gr. 3-7). pap. 7.99 *(978-1-4424-3652-7(2)*, McElderry, Margaret K. Bks.) McElderry, Margaret K. Bks.

—Freedom Train. Riley, David, illus. 2008. (ENG.). 160p. (J). (gr. 3-7). 17.99 *(978-0-689-84716-5(5))* Simon & Schuster, Inc.

Collier, Kristi. Jericho Walls. 2007. (ENG.). 224p. (YA). (gr. 4-9). pap. 10.99 *(978-0-8050-8184-8(4)*, 900040613, Holt, Henry & Co. Bks. For Young Readers) Holt, Henry & Co.

Conkling, Winifred. Sylvia & Aki. 2013. 160p. (J). (gr. 4-7). 7.99 *(978-1-58246-345-2(X)*, Yearling) Random Hse. Children's Bks.

Craft, Jerry. New Kid: A Newbery Award Winner. Craft, Jerry, illus. 2019. (ENG., Illus.). 256p. (J). (gr. 3-7). 22.99 *(978-0-06-269120-0(1))*; pap. 12.99 *(978-0-06-269119-4(8))* HarperCollins Pubs. (Quill Tree Bks.).

Crawford, Ann Fears. Keechee: The Witch of the Woods. 2005. (J). *(978-1-931823-21-0(9))* Halcyon Pr.

Crossan, Sarah. The Weight of Water. 2018. (ENG., Illus.). 240p. (J). pap. 10.99 *(978-1-68119-954-2(8)*, 900194338, Bloomsbury Young Adult) Bloomsbury Publishing USA.

—The Weight of Water. 2018. (J). lib. bdg. 22.10 *(978-0-606-41077-9(5))* Turtleback.

Crowe, Chris. Mississippi Trial 1955. 2003. 240p. (YA). (gr. 7-18). 8.99 *(978-0-14-250192-4(1)*, Speak) Penguin Young Readers Group.

—The Mississippi Trial 1955. 2003. (gr. 7-12). lib. bdg. 16.00 *(978-0-613-86522-7(7))* Turtleback.

Curtis, Christopher Paul & Vega, Eida de la. El Viaje de Charlie. 2019. (SPA.). (J). 12.99 *(978-1-63245-697-7(4))* Lectorum Pubns., Inc.

de la Peña, Matt. Ball Don't Lie. 2007. (ENG.). 304p. (YA). (gr. 9-12). pap. 12.99 *(978-0-385-73425-7(5)*, Ember) Random Hse. Children's Bks.

Deborah, Wiles. Freedom Summer. 2014. (ENG.). 32p. (J). (gr. k-3). 12.24 *(978-1-63245-316-7(9))* Lectorum Pubns., Inc.

Dowell, Frances O'Roark. Trouble the Water. (ENG., Illus.). (J). (gr. 4-8). 2017. 304p. pap. 8.99 *(978-1-4814-2464-6(5))* 2016. 288p. 16.99 *(978-1-4814-2463-9(7))* Simon & Schuster Children's Publishing.

—Trouble the Water. 2017. lib. bdg. 18.40 *(978-0-606-40126-5(1))* Turtleback.

Down, Heather. A Deadly Distance. 2005. (Illus.). 128p. (YA). pap. *(978-0-88878-455-1(4)*, Sandcastle Bks.) Dundurn Pr.

Draper, Sharon. Fire from the Rock. 2008. (ENG.). 240p. (YA). (gr. 7-18). 11.99 *(978-0-14-241199-5(X)*, Speak) Penguin Young Readers Group.

Draper, Sharon M. Blended. (ENG.). 320p. (J). (gr. 3-7). 2020. pap. 8.99 *(978-1-4424-9501-2(4)*, Atheneum Bks. for Young Readers) 2018. (Illus.). 17.99 *(978-1-4424-9500-5(6)*, Atheneum/Caitlyn Dlouhy Books) Simon & Schuster Children's Publishing.

—Copper Sun. 2006. (ENG.). 320p. (YA). (gr. 8-18). 19.99 *(978-0-689-82181-3(6)*, Atheneum Bks. for Young Readers) Simon & Schuster Children's Publishing.

Dunagan, Ted M. The Salvation of Miss Lucretia. 2014. (ENG., Illus.). 192p. 21.95 *(978-1-58838-293-1(1)*, 9085, NewSouth Bks.) NewSouth, Inc.

—Secret of the Satilfa. 2010. (ENG.). 208p. (J). (gr. 3-18). 21.95 *(978-1-58838-249-8(4)*, 8987, NewSouth Bks.) NewSouth, Inc.

—Trouble on the Tombigbee. 2011. (ENG., Illus.). 208p. (J). 21.95 *(978-1-58838-270-2(2)*, 9159, NewSouth Bks.) NewSouth, Inc.

—A Yellow Watermelon. 2014. (ENG.). 240p. (J). pap. 17.95 *(978-1-58838-301-3(6)*, 8630, NewSouth Bks.) NewSouth, Inc.

Edwards, Myrtice J. Dirty Sally. 2007. 44p. per. 18.95 *(978-1-4327-0774-3(4))* Outskirts Pr., Inc.

Ehrenberg, Pamela. Ethan, Suspended. 2009. (ENG.). 272p. (J). (gr. 6-9). pap. 8.50 *(978-0-8028-5317-2(X))* 2007. 266p. (YA). (gr. 7-18). 16.00 *(978-0-8028-5324-0(2)*, Eerdmans Bks For Young Readers) Eerdmans, William B. Publishing Co.

Elkins, Stephen. Ebony & Ivory: Discovering 10 Keys to Racial Harmony. Reisch, Jessie, illus. 2003. 32p. (J). (gr. k-18). 14.99 incl. audio compact disk *(978-0-8054-2674-8(4))* B&H Publishing Group.

Ellis, Deborah & Walters, Eric. Bifocal, 1 vol. 2007. (ENG.). 280p. (YA). (gr. 7-12). per. 12.95 *(978-1-55455-062-3(9)*, 40c1a241-5a17-43bc-857e-e8bb6cabba4f) Fitzhenry & Whiteside, Ltd. CAN. Dist: Firefly Bks., Ltd.

—Bifocal, 1 vol. 2007. (ENG.). 240p. (YA). (gr. 7-12). 17.95 *(978-1-55455-036-4(X)*, 81472636-fc44-4218-a9bb-bdaa0b47264c) Trifolium Bks., Inc. CAN. Dist: Firefly Bks., Ltd.

Elster, Jean Alicia. Who's Jim Hines? 2008. (ENG., Illus.). 146p. pap. 12.95 *(978-0-8143-3402-7(4)*, P158269) Wayne State Univ. Pr.

Emory, Kb. Tyler Tales: What Is My Color/ Different Families. 2012. 36p. pap. 21.99 *(978-1-4797-2504-5(8))* Xlibris Corp.

Engle, Margarita. Jazz Owls: A Novel of the Zoot Suit Riots. Gutierrez, Rudy, illus. 2018. (ENG.). 192p. (YA). (gr. 7). 17.99 *(978-1-5344-0943-9(2))* Simon & Schuster Children's Publishing.

English, Karen. Francie. 2007. (ENG.). 208p. (J). (gr. 4-8). per. 14.99 *(978-0-312-37383-2(X)*, 900045529) Square Fish.

—It All Comes down to This. (ENG.). 368p. (J). (gr. 5-7). 2019. pap. 7.99 *(978-0-358-09853-9(X)*, 1748314) 2017. 16.99 *(978-0-544-83957-1(9)*, 1646119) HarperCollins Pubs. (Clarion Bks.).

Erskine, Kathryn. Seeing Red. 2013. (ENG.). 352p. (YA). E-Book *(978-0-545-57645-1(8))*; (J). (gr. 5-9). 16.99 *(978-0-545-46440-6(4))* Scholastic, Inc. (Scholastic Pr.).

Feinstein, John. Backfield Boys: A Football Mystery in Black & White. 2018. (ENG.). 384p. (YA). pap. 12.99 *(978-1-250-18064-3(3)*, 900172809) Square Fish.

Finnegan, Marco. Lizard in a Zoot Suit. Finnegan, Marco, illus. 2020. (ENG., Illus.). 144p. (YA). (gr. 7-12). 31.99 *(978-1-5415-2365-4(2)*, a6f85d3f-7999-47b7-b6d3-96fccb4d533f, Graphic Universe™) Lerner Publishing Group.

Frank, Steven B. Armstrong & Charlie. (ENG.). (J). (gr. 5-7). 2018. 320p. pap. 7.99 *(978-1-328-94166-4(3)*, 1705033) 2017. 304p. 16.99 *(978-0-544-82608-3(6)*, 1644260) HarperCollins Pubs. (Clarion Bks.).

Friedland, Joyce, ed. Lizzie Bright & the Buckminster Boy: Novel-Ties Study Guide. 2007. 36p. pap. 16.95 *(978-0-7675-3558-8(8))* Learning Links Inc.

Gansworth, Eric. If I Ever Get Out of Here. (ENG.). 368p. (YA). 2015. (gr. 6-11). pap. 12.99 *(978-0-545-41731-0(7))* 2013. (gr. 7). 19.99 *(978-0-545-41730-3(9))* Scholastic, Inc. (Levine, Arthur A. Bks.).

Garcia McCall, Guadalupe. All the Stars Denied, 1 vol. 2018. (ENG.). 336p. (YA). (gr. 6-12). 19.95 *(978-1-62014-281-3(3)*, leelowtu, Tu Bks.) Lee & Low Bks., Inc.

Garlington, William R. The Great Divide: Coloring & Activity Book. 2004. (Illus.). (J). 5.95 *(978-0-9708395-4-1(5))* Legacy Publishing Services, Inc.

—The Great Divide: The Adventures of Billy Bean & Bobby Nut. 2004. (Illus.). 127p. (J). pap. 12.95 *(978-0-9708395-2-7(9))* Legacy Publishing Services, Inc.

Gidwitz, Adam & Bowles, David. The Chupacabras of the Río Grande. Aly, Hatem, illus. 2019. (Unicorn Rescue Society Ser.: 4). 192p. (J). (gr. 2-5). 14.99 *(978-0-7352-3179-5(6)*, Dutton Books for Young Readers) Penguin Young Readers Group.

Going, K. L. The Liberation of Gabriel King. 2007. (ENG.). 160p. (J). (gr. 3-7). 7.99 *(978-0-14-240766-0(6)*, Puffin Books) Penguin Young Readers Group.

—The Liberation of Gabriel King. 2007. 151p. (gr. 3-7). 17.00 *(978-0-7569-7762-7(2))* Perfection Learning Corp.

Gutman, Dan. Jackie & Me. 2005. (Baseball Card Adventures Ser.). (Illus.). 145p. (YA). (gr. 4-8). reprint ed. 20.00 *(978-0-7567-9569-6(9))* DIANE Publishing Co.

—Satch & Me. 2009. (Baseball Card Adventures Ser.). (ENG.). 192p. (J). (gr. 5-9). pap. 9.99 *(978-0-06-059493-0(4)*, HarperCollins) HarperCollins Pubs.

Hale, Marian. Dark Water Rising. 2010. (ENG.). 256p. (J). (gr. 6-8). pap. 8.99 *(978-0-312-62908-3(7)*, 900066872) Square Fish.

Hammonds Reed, Christina. The Black Kids. (ENG.). (YA). (gr. 9). 2022. 400p. pap. 12.99 *(978-1-5344-6273-1(2))* 2020. (Illus.). 368p. 19.99 *(978-1-5344-6272-4(4))* Simon & Schuster Bks. For Young Readers. (Simon & Schuster Bks. For Young Readers).

Harris, E. Lynn. Diaries of a Light-Skinned Colored Boy, No. 1. (Illus.). 160p. (J). (gr. 7-17). 15.99 *(978-0-7868-0632-4(X)*, Jump at the Sun) Hyperion Bks. for Children.

Haugaard, Kay. The Day the Dragon Danced, 1 vol. Barritt, Carolyn Reed, illus. 2006. (ENG.). 32p. (J). (gr. 2-4). 17.95 *(978-1-885008-30-5(9)*, leelowshens, Shen's Bks.) Lee & Low Bks., Inc.

Hay, Barbara. Lesson of the White Eagle. Hay, Peter, illus. 2012. (ENG.). 144p. (YA). pap. 11.99 *(978-1-937054-01-4(2))* RoadRunner Pr.

Hegedus, Bethany. Between Us Baxters. 2009. 306p. (YA). (gr. 7-9). 17.95 *(978-1-934813-02-7(8))* 2011. 9.14 *(978-1-934813-18-8(4))* Westside Bks.

Hemphill, Helen. The Adventurous Deeds of Deadwood Jones. 2011. (ENG.). 232p. (J). (gr. 5-9). pap. 7.95 *(978-1-59078-896-7(6)*, Front Street) Astra Publishing Hse.

Higginbotham, Anastasia. Not My Idea: A Book about Whiteness. 2018. (Ordinary Terrible Things Ser.). (Illus.). 64p. (J). (gr. k-7). 18.95 *(978-1-948340-00-7(3))* Dottir Pr.

Jackson, Linda Williams. Midnight Without a Moon. 2017. (ENG.). 320p. (J). (gr. 5-7). pap. 7.99 *(978-1-328-75363-2(8)*, 1678711); 16.99 *(978-0-544-78510-6(X)*, 1638657) HarperCollins Pubs. (Clarion Bks.).

Johnson, Allen, Jr. My Brother's Story. McMorris, Kelley, illus. 2014. (Blackwater Novels Ser.: Vol. 1). (ENG.). 191p. (J). (gr. 4-7). 14.99 *(978-1-933725-37-6(0))* Premium Pr. America.

Johnston, Tony. Bone by Bone by Bone. 2007. (ENG.). 192p. (YA). (gr. 7-12). 30.99 *(978-1-59643-113-3(X)*, 900031670) Roaring Brook Pr.

Jones-Cisneros, Tiffany. Blaxicana It's a ed World. 2012. 12p. pap. 15.99 *(978-1-4685-6192-0(8))* AuthorHouse.

Jordan, Rosa. Lost Goat Lane, 1 vol. 2004. 192p. (J). (gr. 3-7). 14.95 *(978-1-56145-325-2(0))* Peachtree Publishing Co. Inc.

Kendi, Ibram X. Goodnight Racism. Bayoc, Cbabi, illus. 2022. 32p. (J). (gr. -1-2). 18.99 *(978-0-593-11051-5(X)*, Kokila) Penguin Young Readers Group.

Ketchum, Liza. The Life Fantastic: A Novel in Three Acts. 2017. (ENG.). 256p. (YA). 17.99 *(978-1-4405-9876-0(2)*, Simon Pulse) Simon Pulse.

Krech, Bob. Rebound, 0 vols. 2012. (ENG.). 276p. (YA). (gr. 7-12). pap. 9.99 *(978-0-7614-5543-1(4)*, 9780761455431, Skyscape) Amazon Publishing.

Krensky, Stephen. Play Ball, Jackie! Morse, Joe, illus. 2011. (Single Titles Ser.). (ENG.). 32p. (J). (gr. 2-5). lib. bdg. 16.95 *(978-0-8225-9030-9(1)*, Millbrook Pr.) Lerner Publishing Group.

Larson, Kirby. Liberty. 2018. (Dogs of World War II Ser.). lib. bdg. 18.40 *(978-0-606-41133-2(X))* Turtleback.

Latham, Jennifer. Dreamland Burning. 2018. Tr. of s. (ENG.). 400p. (YA). (gr. 9-17). pap. 11.99 *(978-0-316-38490-2(9))* Little, Brown Bks. for Young Readers.

Les Becquets, Diane. The Stones of Mourning Creek, 0 vols. 2012. (ENG.). 320p. (YA). (gr. 7-12). reprint ed. pap. 9.99 *(978-0-7614-5238-6(9)*, 9780761452386, Skyscape) Amazon Publishing.

Levine, Kristin. The Best Bad Luck I Ever Had. 2010. 288p. (J). (gr. 5-18). 8.99 *(978-0-14-241648-8(7)*, Puffin Books) Penguin Young Readers Group.

—The Lions of Little Rock. 2013. 320p. (J). (gr. 5-9). pap. 8.99 *(978-0-14-242435-3(8)*, Puffin Books) Penguin Young Readers Group.

Levy, Marilyn. Checkpoints. 2009. (ENG.). 256p. (gr. 7). pap. 14.95 *(978-0-8276-0870-2(5))* Jewish Pubn. Society.

Long, Loren & Bildner, Phil. Water, Water Everywhere. Long, Loren, illus. (Sluggers Ser.: 4). (ENG., Illus.). (J). (gr. 3-7). 2010. 288p. pap. 9.99 *(978-1-4169-1890-5(6))* 2009. 272p. 14.99 *(978-1-4169-1866-0(3))* Simon & Schuster Bks. For Young Readers. (Simon & Schuster Bks. For Young Readers).

Lorbiecki, Marybeth. Jackie's Bat. Pinkney, Brian, illus. 2006. (ENG.). 40p. (J). (gr. k-3). 19.99 *(978-0-689-84102-6(7)*, Simon & Schuster Bks. For Young Readers) Simon & Schuster Bks. For Young Readers.

Lupica, Mike. Fast Break. 2016. (ENG.). 288p. (J). (gr. 5). pap. 8.99 *(978-1-101-99783-3(4)*, Puffin Books) Penguin Young Readers Group.

—Fast Break. 2016. (ENG.). 288p. (J). (gr. 5). 19.65 *(978-0-606-39313-3(7))* Turtleback.

Lyon, George Ella. Sonny's House of Spies. 2007. (ENG.). 304p. (J). (gr. 6-9). pap. 14.95 *(978-1-4169-6815-3(6)*, Simon & Schuster/Paula Wiseman Bks.) Simon & Schuster/Paula Wiseman Bks.

Magoon, Kekla. How It Went Down. 2014. (ENG.). 336p. (YA). (gr. 9-12). 19.99 *(978-0-8050-9869-3(0)*, 900122903, Holt, Henry & Co. Bks. For Young Readers) Holt, Henry & Co.

—How It Went Down. 2015. (ENG.). 352p. (YA). (gr. 9). pap. 10.99 *(978-1-250-06823-1(1)*, 900147091) Square Fish.

—How It Went Down. 2015. (YA). lib. bdg. 20.85 *(978-0-606-37593-1(7))* Turtleback.

—The Rock & the River. 2010. (ENG.). 304p. (J). (gr. 5-9). pap. 8.99 *(978-1-4169-7803-9(8)*, Aladdin) Simon & Schuster Children's Publishing.

Mazellan, Ron, illus. We Will Walk. 2005. 16p. (J). pap. *(978-0-7367-2919-2(4))* Zaner-Bloser, Inc.

McKissack, Patricia C. A Friendship for Today. 2008. 172p. (J). pap. *(978-0-545-06563-4(1))* Scholastic, Inc.

McMullan, Margaret. When I Crossed No-Bob. 2009. (ENG.). 224p. (J). (gr. 3-7). pap. 7.99 *(978-0-547-23763-3(4)*, 1083873, Clarion Bks.) HarperCollins Pubs.

—When I Crossed No-Bob. 2008. (ENG.). 224p. (J). (gr. 6-8). 22.44 *(978-0-618-71715-6(3))* Houghton Mifflin Harcourt Publishing Co.

Medearis, Angela Shelf. Singing for Dr. King. Hu, Ying-Hwa & Van Wright, Cornelius, illus. 2004. 32p. (J). lib. bdg. 15.00 *(978-1-4242-0237-9(X))* Fitzgerald Bks.

Meyer, Carolyn. White Lilacs. 2007. (ENG., Illus.). 256p. (J). (gr. 3-7). pap. 8.99 *(978-0-15-205851-7(6)*, 1197572, Clarion Bks.) HarperCollins Pubs.

—White Lilacs. 2006. (Illus.). 242p. (gr. 4-7). 16.95 *(978-0-7569-6683-6(3))* Perfection Learning Corp.

Michelson, Richard. Busing Brewster. Roth, R. G., illus. 2018. (ENG.). 32p. (J). pap. 10.95 *(978-1-56792-644-6(4))* Godine, David R. Pub.

Mickles Sr., Robert T. S. Blood Kin, a Savannah Story. 2007. 108p. per. 9.95 *(978-0-595-45129-6(2))* iUniverse, Inc.

Milton, Nina. Tough Luck. 2013. 180p. pap. *(978-1-909734-13-5(6))* ThornBerry Publishing UK.

Mohamoud, Ashlee. Brown Is Beautiful, 1 vol. 2010. 18p. 24.95 *(978-1-4512-0064-5(1))* PublishAmerica, Inc.

Molnar, Gwen. Hate Cell: A Casey Templeton Mystery. 2009. (Casey Templeton Mystery Ser.: 1). (ENG.). 184p. (YA). (gr. 5). pap. 11.99 *(978-1-55002-850-8(2))* Dundurn Pr. CAN. Dist: Publishers Group West (PGW).

Moses, Sheila P. The Legend of Buddy Bush. 2005. (Illus.). 211p. (gr. 7-12). 17.00 *(978-0-7569-5459-8(2))* Perfection Learning Corp.

—The Legend of Buddy Bush, 3 vols. unabr. ed. 2005. (YA). (gr. 3-7). 54.75 *(978-1-4193-3575-4(8)*, 42043) Recorded Bks., Inc.

—The Return of Buddy Bush. 2005. (ENG., Illus.). 160p. (J). (gr. 7-12). 15.95 *(978-0-689-87431-4(6)*, McElderry, Margaret K. Bks.) McElderry, Margaret K. Bks.

Mullinax, Jerry. Enoree. 2009. (YA). pap. *(978-0-88092-646-1(5))* Royal Fireworks Publishing Co.

Myers, Anna. Tulsa Burning. 2004. (Illus.). 184p. (J). (gr. 3-7). 16.95 *(978-0-8027-8829-0(7))* Walker & Co.

Napoli, Donna Jo. Alligator Bayou. 288p. (YA). (gr. 7). 2010. pap. 8.99 *(978-0-553-49417-4(1))* 2009. (ENG.). lib. bdg. 24.94 *(978-0-385-90891-7(1))* Random Hse. Children's Bks. (Lamb, Wendy Bks.).

Noble, Diana J. Evangelina Takes Flight. 2017. (ENG.). 152p. (J). (gr. 5-8). pap. 10.95 *(978-1-55885-848-0(2)*, Piñata Books) Arte Publico Pr.

Nolan, Han. A Summer of Kings. 2006. 334p. (J). *(978-1-4156-7340-9(3))* Harcourt Trade Pubs.

—A Summer of Kings. 2006. (ENG., Illus.). 352p. (YA). (gr. 7-8). 17.00 *(978-0-15-205108-2(2)*, 1195424, Clarion Bks.) HarperCollins Pubs.

Oh, Ellen. Finding Junie Kim. 2021. (ENG.). 368p. (J). (gr. 3-7). 16.99 *(978-0-06-298798-3(4)*, HarperCollins) HarperCollins Pubs.

Older, Daniel José. Dactyl Hill Squad (Dactyl Hill Squad #1) (Dactyl Hill Squad Ser.: 1). (ENG.). (J). (gr. 3-7). 2019. 288p. pap. 6.99 *(978-1-338-26882-9(1))* 2018. (Illus.). 272p. 16.99 *(978-1-338-26881-2(3))* Scholastic, Inc. (Levine, Arthur A. Bks.).

Olsen, Sylvia. Middle Row, 1 vol. 2008. (Orca Soundings Ser.). (ENG.). 136p. (YA). (gr. 8-12). pap. 9.95 *(978-1-55143-899-3(2))* Orca Bk. Pubs. USA.

Pantoja, Stephen. The Amalaganimals: Eracism Sc. 2010. 33p. pap. 23.90 *(978-0-557-31722-6(3))* Lulu Pr., Inc.

Parkhurst, Liz S. Under One Flag: A Year at Rohwer. Clifton, Tom, illus. 2006. (ENG.). 32p. (J). (gr. 3-7). 16.95 *(978-0-87483-759-9(6)*, 1241971) August Hse. Pubs., Inc.

Parsons, Karyn. How High the Moon. 2019. (ENG.). 320p. (J). (gr. 3-7). 16.99 *(978-0-316-48400-8(8))* Little, Brown Bks. for Young Readers.

Patrick, Denise Lewis. A Matter of Souls. 2018. (ENG.). 192p. (YA). (gr. 6-12). pap. 9.99 *(978-1-5415-1482-9(3)*, 4161e4af-dc7d-4119-a82e-dde17ece88ec, Carolrhoda Lab™) Lerner Publishing Group.

Paul, Volponi. Black & White. 2014. (ENG.). 208p. (YA). 11.24 *(978-1-63245-196-5(4))* Lectorum Pubns., Inc.

Pearsall, Shelley. Trouble Don't Last. 2003. (ENG.). 256p. (J). (gr. 3-7). reprint ed. 7.99 *(978-0-440-41811-5(9)*, Yearling) Random Hse. Children's Bks.

Peck, Richard. The River Between Us. 2003. (ENG.). 164p. (J). (gr. 7-7). 21.19 *(978-0-8037-2735-9(6)*, Dial) Penguin Publishing Group.

—The River Between Us. 2005. (ENG.). 176p. (J). (gr. 3-7). reprint ed. pap. 8.99 *(978-0-14-240310-5(5)*, Puffin Books) Penguin Young Readers Group.

Perkins, Mitali, ed. Open Mic: Riffs on Life Between Cultures in Ten Voices. 2016. (ENG.). 144p. (J). (gr. 7). pap. 8.99 *(978-0-7636-9095-3(3))* Candlewick Pr.

Perkyns, Dorothy. Last Days in Africville. 2005. (Illus.). 144p. (YA). pap., tchr. ed. *(978-0-88878-446-9(5)*, Sandcastle Bks.) Dundurn Pr.

—Last Days in Africville. 2006. (ENG.). 120p. (J). (gr. 4-7). pap. 10.99 *(978-1-55002-630-6(5))* Dundurn Pr. CAN. Dist: Publishers Group West (PGW).

Petruck, Rebecca. Boy Bites Bug. 2019. (ENG.). 272p. (J). (gr. 3-17). pap. 9.99 *(978-1-4197-3481-6(4)*, 1136803, Amulet Bks.) Abrams, Inc.

Phillips, Lyda. Mr Touchdown. 2008. 184p. 23.95 *(978-1-4401-0976-8(1))*; pap. 13.95 *(978-1-60528-029-5(1))* iUniverse, Inc. (iUniverse Star).

Pinkney, Andrea Davis. Boycott Blues: How Rosa Parks Inspired a Nation. Pinkney, Brian, illus. 2008. (ENG.). 40p. (J). (gr. k-3). 18.99 *(978-0-06-082118-0(3)*, Greenwillow Bks.) HarperCollins Pubs.

Polacco, Patricia. Chicken Sunday. 2015. 32p. pap. 8.00 *(978-1-61003-527-9(5))* Center for the Collaborative Classroom.

Powell, Patricia Hruby. Loving vs. Virginia: A Documentary Novel of the Landmark Civil Rights Case (Books about Love for Kids, Civil Rights History Book) Strickland, Shadra, illus. 2017. (ENG.). 260p. (YA). (gr. 7-12). 21.99 *(978-1-4521-2590-9(2))* Chronicle Bks. LLC.

Provoost, Anne. Falling 20th Anniversary Edition. Nieuwenhuizen, John, tr. 2nd ed. 2018. (ENG.). 288p. (YA). (gr. 8). pap. 15.99 *(978-1-76029-392-5(X))* Allen & Unwin AUS. Dist: Independent Pubs. Group.

Raschka, Chris. Yo! Yes?, 1 vol. Raschka, Chris, illus. (ENG., Illus.). 32p. (J). (gr. -1-k). 2020. bds. 8.99 *(978-1-338-58385-4(9)*, Cartwheel Bks.) 2007. pap. 7.99 *(978-0-439-92185-5(6))* Scholastic, Inc.

Reynolds, Aaron. Back of the Bus. Cooper, Floyd, illus. 2010. 32p. (J). (gr. 1-3). 16.99 *(978-0-399-25091-0(3)*, Philomel Bks.) Penguin Young Readers Group.

Reynolds, Jason & Brendan Kiely. All American Boys. 2017. (ENG.). (YA). lib. bdg. 20.85 *(978-0-606-39493-2(1))* Turtleback.

Reynolds, Jason & Kiely, Brendan. All American Boys. 2015. (ENG., Illus.). 320p. (YA). (gr. 7). 19.99 *(978-1-4814-6333-1(0)*, Atheneum/Caitlyn Dlouhy Books) Simon & Schuster Children's Publishing.

Reynolds Naylor, Phyllis. Alice in Charge. (Alice Ser.: 22). (ENG., (YA). (gr. 9). 2011. Illus.). 304p. pap. 8.99 *(978-1-4169-7555-7(1))* 2010. 336p. 16.99 *(978-1-4169-7552-6(7))* Simon & Schuster Children's Publishing. (Atheneum Bks. for Young Readers).

Richards, Elizabeth. Phoenix: A Black City Novel. 2nd ed. 2014. (Black City Novel Ser.: 2). 368p. (YA). (gr. 9). pap. 9.99 *(978-0-14-751137-9(2)*, Speak) Penguin Young Readers Group.

Rinaldi, Ann. The Education of Mary: A Little Miss of Color, 1832. 2005. 176p. (J). pap. *(978-0-7868-1377-3(6))* Hyperion Pr.

Robinet, Harriette Gillem. Walking to the Bus-Rider Blues. 2004. (Jean Karl Bks.). 146p. (gr. 3-7). 16.00 *(978-0-7569-4265-6(9))* Perfection Learning Corp.

Robinson, Sharon. The Hero Two Doors down: Based on the True Story of Friendship Between a Boy & a Baseball Legend. 2017. (ENG.). 208p. (J). (gr. 4-7). pap. 7.99 *(978-0-545-80452-3(3)*, Scholastic Paperbacks) Scholastic, Inc.

Rodman, Mary Ann. Yankee Girl. 2008. (ENG.). 240p. (J). (gr. 4-6). pap. 19.99 *(978-0-312-53576-6(7)*, 900054756) Square Fish.

Rosenberg, Aaron. 42 - The Official Movie Novel. 2013. (ENG.). 160p. (J). (gr. 4-6). 18.69 *(978-0-545-53753-7(3))* Scholastic, Inc.

Rucker, Rhonda. Welcome to Bombingham, 1 vol. 2019. (ENG., Illus.). 272p. (J). (gr. 6-12). 14.95 *(978-1-4556-2492-8(6)*, Pelican Publishing) Arcadia Publishing.

Salcedo, Betsy. Together we Can. 2006. 9.00 *(978-0-8059-9155-0(7))* Dorrance Publishing Co., Inc.

Scattergood, Augusta. Glory Be. 2014. (ENG.). 208p. (J). (gr. 4-7). pap. 7.99 *(978-0-545-33181-4(1)*, Scholastic Pr.) Scholastic, Inc.

Schlick Noe, Katherine. Something to Hold. 2011. (ENG., Illus.). 256p. (J). (gr. 5-7). 17.99 *(978-0-547-55813-4(9)*, 1453477, Clarion Bks.) HarperCollins Pubs.

Schmidt, Gary D. Trouble. 2010. (ENG.). 304p. (YA). (gr. 7). pap. 15.99 *(978-0-547-33133-1(9)*, 1417365, Clarion Bks.) HarperCollins Pubs.

Schraff, Anne. Freedom Knows No Color. 2008. (Passages to History Ser.). 118p. (J). lib. bdg. 13.95 *(978-0-7569-8392-5(4))*; (YA). (gr. 7-12). pap. 8.50 *(978-0-7891-7567-0(3))* Perfection Learning Corp.

Schwartz, Ellen. Stealing Home. 2006. 224p. (J). (gr. 4-7). pap. 9.95 *(978-0-88776-765-4(6)*, Tundra Bks.) Tundra Bks. CAN. Dist: Penguin Random Hse. LLC.

Scott, Lisa Ann. School of Charm. 2014. (ENG.). 304p. (J). (gr. 3-7). 16.99 *(978-0-06-220758-6(X)*, Tegen, Katherine Bks) HarperCollins Pubs.

Sharenow, Robert. My Mother the Cheerleader. 2009. (ENG.). 320p. (YA). (gr. 8). pap. 10.99 *(978-0-06-114898-9(9)*, Balzer & Bray) 2007. 304p. (J). (gr. 7-18). 16.99 *(978-0-06-114896-5(2)*, Geringer, Laura Book) 2007. 304p. (J). (gr. 7-18). lib. bdg. 17.89 *(978-0-06-114897-2(0)*, Geringer, Laura Book) HarperCollins Pubs.

Shen, E. L. The Comeback: A Figure Skating Novel. 2021. (ENG., Illus.). 272p. (J). 16.99 *(978-0-374-31379-1(2)*, 900221649, Farrar, Straus & Giroux (BYR)) Farrar, Straus & Giroux.

Simon, T. R. Zora & Me: the Cursed Ground. 2018. (Zora & Me Ser.). (ENG.). 272p. (J). (gr. 5-9). 16.99 *(978-0-7636-4301-0(7))* Candlewick Pr.

Smadja, Brigitte. Tarte aux Escargots. pap. 17.95 *(978-2-211-03633-7(3))* Archimede Editions FRA. Dist: Distribooks, Inc.

Smith, Sarah. The Other Side of Dark. 2010. (ENG.). 320p. (YA). (gr. 7-18). 16.99 *(978-1-4424-0280-5(6)*, Atheneum Bks. for Young Readers) Simon & Schuster Children's Publishing.

Stanley, Brenda. I Am Nuchu. 2010. 334p. (YA). (gr. 9-18). 16.95 *(978-1-934813-47-8(8))* Westside Bks.

Stanley, George E. Night Fires. 2009. (ENG.). 192p. (J). (gr. 3-7). 15.99 *(978-1-4169-7559-5(4)*, Aladdin) Simon & Schuster Children's Publishing.

—Night Fires. 2011. (ENG.). 192p. (J). (gr. 3-7). pap. 6.99 *(978-1-4169-1250-7(9)*, Simon & Schuster/Paula Wiseman Bks.) Simon & Schuster/Paula Wiseman Bks.

Stephenson, Lynda. Dancing with Elvis. 2006. (ENG.). 331p. (YA). (gr. 7). per. 8.00 *(978-0-8028-5300-4(5)*, Eerdmans Bks For Young Readers) Eerdmans, William B. Publishing Co.

Stiver, Joan. The Door in the Floor: An Underground Railroad Adventure. 2008. 48p. pap. 4.99 *(978-1-4343-2953-0(4))* AuthorHouse.

Stone, Nic. Dear Martin. (ENG.). (gr. 9). 2018. 240p. (YA). pap. 10.99 *(978-1-101-93952-9(4)*, Ember) 2017. 224p. (YA). 18.99 *(978-1-101-93949-9(4)*, Crown Books For Young Readers)1. 2018. 240p. 28.69 *(978-1-5364-4655-5(6)*, Ember) Random Hse. Children's Bks.

—Dear Martin. 2018. lib. bdg. 20.85 *(978-0-606-41555-2(6))* Turtleback.

Swinford, Betty. Secrets. 2006. (Freestyle Fiction 12+ Ser.). (ENG.). 176p. (YA). (gr. 4-7). per. 6.99 *(978-1-84550-127-3(6)*, f843eee1-555f-461c-a118-ae9614e11c7f) Christian Focus Pubns. GBR. Dist: Baker & Taylor Publisher Services (BTPS).

Taschek, Karen. The the Risen Horse. 2010. (ENG.). 248p. (YA). (gr. 7-18). pap. 15.95 *(978-0-8263-4837-1(8)*, P198426) Univ. of New Mexico Pr.

Taylor, Mildred D. The Friendship. 2014. (ENG.). 56p. (J). (gr. 3-7). 11.24 *(978-1-63245-342-6(8))* Lectorum Pubns., Inc.

—Roll of Thunder, Hear My Cry: 40th Anniversary Special Edition. 40th anniv. ed. 2016. (ENG., Illus.). 304p. (J). (gr. 3-7). 19.99 *(978-1-101-99388-0(X)*, Dial Bks) Penguin Young Readers Group.

Thomas, Angie. The Hate U Give. 2017. (YA). lib. bdg. 31.80 *(978-0-606-41493-7(2))* Turtleback.

—The Hate U Give: A Printz Honor Winner. (ENG.). (YA). (gr. 9). 2022. 480p. pap. 16.99 *(978-0-06-249854-0(1))* 2017. 464p. 18.99 *(978-0-06-249853-3(3))* HarperCollins Pubs. (Balzer & Bray).

—The Hate U Give Collector's Edition: A Printz Honor Winner. 2018. (ENG.). 512p. (YA). (gr. 9). 20.99 *(978-0-06-287234-0(6)*, Balzer & Bray) HarperCollins Pubs.

—The Hate U Give Movie Tie-In Edition: A Printz Honor Winner. 2018. (ENG.). 480p. (YA). (gr. 9). 19.99 *(978-0-06-287135-0(8)*, Balzer & Bray) HarperCollins Pubs.

Thomas, Rob. Slave Day. 2018. (ENG.). 256p. (YA). (gr. 7). pap. 10.99 *(978-1-5344-2966-6(2)*, Simon & Schuster Bks. For Young Readers) Simon & Schuster Bks. For Young Readers.

Thompson, Tavia. Made by God Wonderfully. 2013. 28p. pap. 24.95 *(978-1-63000-403-3(0))* America Star Bks.

Thrash, Maggie. Strange Lies. (Strange Ser.: 2). (ENG.). 336p. (YA). (gr. 9). 2018. pap. 11.99 *(978-1-4814-6204-4(0))* 2017. (Illus.). 17.99 *(978-1-4814-6203-7(2))* Simon Pulse. (Simon Pulse).

Tocher, Timothy. Chief Sunrise, John McGraw, & Me. 2004. (ENG.). 168p. (J). (gr. 4-8). 16.95 *(978-0-8126-2711-4(3))* Cricket Bks.

The Troubles of Johnny Cannon. 2014. (ENG., Illus.). 304p. (J). (gr. 3-7). 16.99 *(978-1-4814-0003-9(7)*, Simon & Schuster Bks. For Young Readers) Simon & Schuster Bks. For Young Readers.

Tuck, Pamela M. As Fast As Words Could Fly?, 1 vol. Velasquez, Eric, illus. 2013. (ENG.). 40p. (J). 18.95 *(978-1-60060-348-8(3))* Lee & Low Bks., Inc.

Turner, Ann Warren. Sitting Bull Remembers. Minor, Wendell, illus. 2007. (ENG.). 32p. (J). (gr. 1-4). 16.99 *(978-0-06-051399-3(3))* HarperCollins Pubs.

Twain, Mark, pseud. The Adventures of Huckleberry Finn. abr. ed. 2011. (Go Reader Audiobooks Ser.). (ENG.). (YA). (gr. 7-12). 49.93 *(978-1-61641-434-4(0))* Magic Wagon.

—Las Aventuras de Huckleberry Finn. de Atauri, Ines & de Atauri, Juan Diaz, eds. 2006. (Clasicos Juveniles Ser.).Tr. of Adventures of Huckleberry Finn. (SPA., Illus.). 359p. pap. 17.95 *(978-84-263-5252-1(9))* Vives, Luis Editorial (Edelvives) ESP. Dist: Lectorum Pubns., Inc.

Vander Zee, Ruth. Mississippi Morning. Cooper, Floyd, illus. 2004. 32p. (J). 16.00 *(978-0-8028-5211-3(4))* Eerdmans, William B. Publishing Co.

Vaught, Susan. Things Too Huge to Fix by Saying Sorry. 2016. (ENG., Illus.). 352p. (J). (gr. 5-9). 16.99 *(978-1-4814-2279-6(0)*, Simon & Schuster Bks. For Young Readers) Simon & Schuster Bks. For Young Readers.

—Things Too Huge to Fix by Saying Sorry. 2017. (ENG.). 368p. (J). (gr. 5-9). pap. 8.99 *(978-1-4814-2280-2(4)*, Simon & Schuster/Paula Wiseman Bks.) Simon & Schuster/Paula Wiseman Bks.

Volponi, Paul. Response. 2010. 176p. (YA). (gr. 7-18). 6.99 *(978-0-14-241603-7(7)*, Speak) Penguin Young Readers Group.

—Rooftop. 2007. 199p. 17.00 *(978-0-7569-7958-4(7))* Perfection Learning Corp.

Walker, Brian F. Black Boy White School. 2012. (ENG.). 256p. (YA). (gr. 9). 17.99 *(978-0-06-191483-6(5)*, HarperTeen) HarperCollins Pubs.

Walsh, Ann. Shabash! 2nd ed. 2008. (ENG.). 112p. (J). (gr. 4-8). pap. 11.99 *(978-1-55002-829-4(4))* Dundurn Pr. CAN. Dist: Publishers Group West (PGW).

Walvoord, Linda. Rosetta, Rosetta, Sit by Me!, 0 vols. Velasquez, Eric, illus. 2012. (ENG.). 98p. (J). (gr. 1-3). 14.95 *(978-0-7614-5171-6(4)*, 9780761451716, Two Lions) Amazon Publishing.

Watkins, Steve. Down Sand Mountain. (ENG., Illus.). 336p. (YA). (gr. 7). 2011. pap. 7.99 *(978-0-7636-4835-0(3))* 2008. 16.99 *(978-0-7636-3839-9(0))* Candlewick Pr.

Watts, Jeri. Kizzy Ann Stamps. 2013. (ENG., Illus.). 192p. (J). (gr. 4-7). pap. 8.99 *(978-0-7636-6976-8(8))* Candlewick Pr.

Weatherford, Carole Boston. Freedom on the Menu: The Greensboro Sit-Ins. Lagarrigue, Jerome Lagarrigue, illus. 2007. 32p. (J). (gr. -1-3). pap. 8.99 *(978-0-14-240894-0(8)*, Puffin Books) Penguin Young Readers Group.

—Freedom on the Menu: The Greensboro Sit-Ins. Lagarrigue, Jerome, illus. 2004. (ENG.). 32p. (J). (gr. 1-3). 21.19 *(978-0-8037-2860-8(3))* Penguin Young Readers Group.

Weston Woods Staff, creator. Crow Boy. 2011. 38.75 *(978-0-545-23384-2(4))*; 18.95 *(978-0-545-23383-5(6))*; 29.95 *(978-0-545-23382-8(8))* Weston Woods Studios, Inc.

Wilcox, Katherine A. Let Me Be Myself. 2004. 60p. pap. 25.75 *(978-1-4140-3674-8(4))* AuthorHouse.

Wiles, Deborah. The Aurora County All-Stars. 2009. (ENG., Illus.). 256p. (J). (gr. 2-5). pap. 7.99 *(978-0-15-206626-0(8)*, 1063363, Clarion Bks.) HarperCollins Pubs.

—Freedom Summer: Celebrating the 50th Anniversary of the Freedom Summer. Lagarrigue, Jerome, illus. 50th anniv. ed. 2014. (ENG.). 32p. (J). (gr. -1-3). 17.99 *(978-1-4814-2298-7(7)*, Atheneum Bks. for Young Readers) Simon & Schuster Children's Publishing.

Wolf, Joan M. Runs with Courage. 2017. (ENG.). 224p. (J). (gr. 4-7). pap. 9.99 *(978-1-58536-985-0(3)*, 204116) Sleeping Bear Pr.

Woods, Brenda. The Unsung Hero of Birdsong, USA. 2019. 208p. (J). (gr. 5). 16.99 *(978-1-5247-3709-2(7)*, Nancy Paulsen Books) Penguin Young Readers Group.

Woodson, Jacqueline. Feathers. (ENG.). (J). (gr. 5-18). 2010. 160p. 8.99 *(978-0-14-241550-4(2)*, Puffin Books) 2007. 128p. 17.99 *(978-0-399-23989-2(8)*, G.P. Putnam's Sons Books for Young Readers) Penguin Young Readers Group.

—I Hadn't Meant to Tell You This. 2010. (ENG.). 160p. (YA). (gr. 7-18). 8.99 *(978-0-14-241704-1(1)*, Puffin Books) Penguin Young Readers Group.

—I Hadn't Meant to Tell You This. 2006. 114p. (YA). (gr. 7-12). 13.65 *(978-0-7569-6730-7(9))* Perfection Learning Corp.

—If You Come Softly. 2010. (ENG.). 224p. (YA). (gr. 7-18). 9.99 *(978-0-14-241522-1(7)*, Penguin Books) Penguin Young Readers Group.

Wright, Barbara. Crow. 2013. (ENG.). 320p. (J). (gr. 6-8). lib. bdg. 22.44 *(978-0-375-96928-7(4))* Random Hse. Bks. for Young Readers.

—Crow. 2013. (ENG.). 320p. (J). (gr. 5-7). pap. 9.99 *(978-0-375-87367-6(8)*, Yearling) Random Hse. Children's Bks.

Yee, Paul. What Happened This Summer, 1 vol. 2006. (ENG., Illus.). 128p. (YA). (gr. 8-12). per. 10.95 *(978-1-896580-88-3(2))* Tradewind Bks. CAN. Dist: Orca Bk. Pubs. USA.

RACES OF MAN

see Ethnology

RACIAL BALANCE IN SCHOOLS

see Segregation in Education

RACIALLY MIXED PEOPLE

Barack Obama. 2007. (Political Profiles Ser.). (Illus.). 128p. (YA). (gr. 5-9). lib. bdg. 27.95 *(978-1-59935-045-5(9))* Reynolds, Morgan Inc.

Bourcier, Cammy S. Barack Obama. 2009. (Sharing the American Dream Ser.). (Illus.). 64p. (J). (gr. 7-12). 22.95 *(978-1-4222-0574-7(6))* Mason Crest.

Bradley, Michael. Derek Jeter, 1 vol. 2005. (All-Stars Ser.). (ENG., Illus.). 48p. (gr. 4-4). lib. bdg. 34.07 *(978-0-7614-1626-5(9),* 481b5234-65a9-4bc8-8888-ddd61610278c) Cavendish Square Publishing LLC.
—Tiger Woods, 1 vol. 2005. (All-Stars Ser.). (ENG., Illus.). 48p. (gr. 4-4). lib. bdg. 34.07 *(978-0-7614-1631-9(5),* 0b6d6577-aff2-4a6b-9562-e30c1f79270a) Cavendish Square Publishing LLC.
Brill, Marlene Targ. Barack Obama: Working to Make a Difference. 2006. (J). pap. 6.95 *(978-0-8225-6056-2(9),* First Avenue Editions); (Illus.). 48p. 23.93 *(978-0-8225-3417-4(7))* Lerner Publishing Group.
—Barack Obama (Revised Edition) 2009. pap. 52.95 *(978-0-7613-5031-6(4))* Lerner Publishing Group.
Britton, Tamara L. Barack Obama, 1 vol. 2016. (United States Presidents *2017 Ser.). (ENG., Illus.). 40p. (J). (gr. 2-5). lib. bdg. 35.64 *(978-1-68078-111-3(1),* 21839, Big Buddy Bks.) ABDO Publishing Co.
Brown, Jonatha A. Tiger Woods, 1 vol. 2004. (People We Should Know Ser.). (ENG., Illus.). 24p. (gr. 2-4). pap. 9.15 *(978-0-8368-4320-0(7),* 7b2c36d1-ed6b-4d9f-a6b1-5f013e007c67); lib. bdg. 24.67 *(978-0-8368-4313-2(4),* 2668eccd-5bb3-4d38-a77f-1fb75a2db23c) Stevens, Gareth Publishing LLLP. (Weekly Reader Leveled Readers).
Corey, Shana. Barack Obama: Out of Many, One. 2009. (Step into Reading Ser.). (Illus.). 48p. (J). (gr. k-3). pap. 4.99 *(978-0-375-86339-4(7),* Random Hse. Bks. for Young Readers) Random Hse. Children's Bks.
Davis, William Michael. Barack Obama: The Politics of Hope. 2007. (Illus.). 168p. (J). (gr. 10-18). lib. bdg. 25.95 *(978-1-59556-024-7(6),* 1291988); (gr. 8-18). pap. 16.99 *(978-1-59556-032-2(7),* 1291988) OTTN Publishing.
De Medeiros, Michael. Barack Obama. (J). 2013. *(978-1-62127-388-2(1))* 2008. (Illus.). 24p. (gr. 4-6). pap. 8.95 *(978-1-59036-989-0(0))* 2008. (Illus.). 24p. (gr. 4-6). lib. bdg. 24.45 *(978-1-59036-988-3(2))* Weigl Pubs., Inc.
Doeden, Matt. Tiger Woods. 2005. (Sports Heroes & Legends Ser.). (ENG., Illus.). 112p. (gr. 5-12). lib. bdg. 30.60 *(978-0-8225-3082-4(1))* Lerner Publishing Group.
Donovan, Sandy. Derek Jeter. 2008. pap. 40.95 *(978-1-58013-718-8(0))* 2004. 32p. (J). (gr. 2-5). pap. 6.95 *(978-0-8225-2038-2(9))* 2004. (Illus.). 32p. (J). (gr. 3-4). lib. bdg. 23.93 *(978-0-8225-3674-1(9))* Lerner Publishing Group.
Edwards, Roberta & Who HQ. Who Is Barack Obama? O'Brien, John, illus. 2009. (Who Was? Ser.). 112p. (J). (gr. 3-7). pap. 5.99 *(978-0-448-45330-9(4),* Penguin Workshop) Penguin Young Readers Group.
Falk, Laine. Meet President Barack Obama. 2009. (Scholastic News Nonfiction Readers Ser.). (ENG., Illus.). 24p. (J). (gr. k-3). 21.19 *(978-0-531-23403-7(7),* Children's Pr.) Scholastic Library Publishing.
Feinstein, Stephen. Barack Obama, 1 vol. 2008. (African-American Heroes Ser.). (ENG., Illus.). 24p. (gr. k-2). lib. bdg. 25.27 *(978-0-7660-2893-7(3),* 69df780e-533b-4c3f-82e5-c16548d680f1, Enslow Elementary) Enslow Publishing, LLC.
Feinstein, Stephen & Taylor, Charlotte. Barack Obama: First African-American President, 1 vol. 2015. (Exceptional African Americans Ser.). (ENG.). 24p. (gr. 3-4). pap. 10.35 *(978-0-7660-7122-3(7),* 6d9583a1-f228-4f6b-a009-bf3345f11287); (Illus.). 24.27 *(978-0-7660-7124-7(3),* 30bf2328-d3e3-4cc0-a789-bb42085be796) Enslow Publishing, LLC.
Fields, Julianna. Multiracial Families. 2010. (Changing Face of Modern Families Ser.). (Illus.). 64p. (YA). (gr. 5-18). lib. bdg. 22.95 *(978-1-4222-1494-7(X))* Mason Crest.
Goodman, Michael E. Tiger Woods. 2003. (Ovations Ser.). (Illus.). 32p. (J). *(978-1-58341-246-6(8),* Creative Education) Creative Co., The.
Gormley, Beatrice. Barack Obama: Our Forty-Fourth President. 2015. (Real-Life Story Ser.). (ENG., Illus.). 272p. (J). (gr. 3-7). 17.99 *(978-1-4814-4648-8(7),* Aladdin) Simon & Schuster Children's Publishing.
Greenberg, Keith Elliot. Derek Jeter. 2005. (Sports Heroes & Legends Ser.). (Illus.). 106p. (J). (gr. 3-7). lib. bdg. 27.93 *(978-0-8225-3068-8(6),* Lerner Pubns.) Lerner Publishing Group.
Grimes, Nikki. Barack Obama: Son of Promise, Child of Hope. Collier, Bryan, illus. (ENG.). 48p. (J). (gr. k-3). 2012. 9.99 *(978-1-4424-4092-0(9))* 2008. pap. 19.99 *(978-1-4169-7144-3(0))* Simon & Schuster Bks. For Young Readers. (Simon & Schuster Bks. For Young Readers).
Hansen, Grace. Barack Obama. 2015. (Biografías de Los Presidentes de Los Estados Unidos Ser.). (SPA., Illus.). 24p. (J). (gr. -1-2). pap. 7.95 *(978-1-4966-0403-3(2),* 130251, Capstone Classroom) Capstone.
Hoe, Susan. Rosa Parks. 2007. (Sharing the American Dream Ser.). 64p. (YA). (gr. 7-18). pap. 9.95 *(978-1-4222-0760-4(9))* Mason Crest.
Hoppe, Ludwig Augustin. Die Epiklesis Der Griechischen Und Orientalischen Liturgieen Und Der Römische Consekrationskanon (German Edition) 2010. 350p. pap. 32.75 *(978-1-142-96440-5(X))* Creative Media Partners, LLC.
Howard, Tim. The Keeper: the Unguarded Story of Tim Howard Young Readers' Edition. 2015. (ENG.). 288p. (J). (gr. 3-7). pap. 9.99 *(978-0-06-238758-5(8),* HarperCollins) HarperCollins Pubs.
Kawa, Katie. Barack Obama: First African American President, 1 vol. 2012. (Beginning Biographies Ser.). (ENG., Illus.). 24p. (J). (gr. 1-2). 26.27 *(978-1-4488-8595-4(7),* cf17b6d8-b99a-452b-8894-50f2af33c147, PowerKids Pr.) Rosen Publishing Group, Inc., The.
Klein, Adria F. Barack Obama. 2009. pap. 13.25 *(978-1-60559-055-4(X))* Hameray Publishing Group, Inc.
Lara, Carrie & Battuz, Christine. Marvelous Maravilloso: Me & My Beautiful Family. 2018. (ENG., Illus.). 32p. (J). *(978-1-4338-2856-0(1),* Magination Pr.) American Psychological Assn.
Marcovitz, Hal. The Obama Family Tree. 2007. (Obamas Ser.). (Illus.). 64p. (YA). (gr. 3-6). pap. 9.95 *(978-1-4222-1488-6(5))*; (gr. 4-7). lib. bdg. 19.95 *(978-1-4222-1481-7(8))* Mason Crest.
—Obama Mania. 2007. (Obamas Ser.). (Illus.). 64p. (YA). (gr. 3-6). pap. 9.95 *(978-1-4222-1489-3(3))*; (gr. 4-7). lib. bdg. 19.95 *(978-1-4222-1482-4(6))* Mason Crest.
Mendell, David & Thomson, Sarah L. Obama: A Promise of Change. 2008. (ENG., Illus.). 192p. (J). (gr. 3-7). pap. 6.99 *(978-0-06-169700-5(1),* Amistad) HarperCollins Pubs.
Morlock, Rachael. Barack Obama: A Life of Leadership, 1 vol. annot. ed. 2019. (People in the News Ser.). (ENG.). 104p. (gr. 7-7). pap. 20.99 *(978-1-5345-6840-2(9),* 1dbae1b7-6a06-489e-8227-e56a3ac990bb); lib. bdg. 41.03 *(978-1-5345-6841-9(7),* ca00a648-b9d2-4f3f-ae82-795d317aa70f) Greenhaven Publishing LLC. (Lucent Pr.).
O'Connell, Jack. Derek Jeter: The Yankee Kid. Rains, Rob, ed. 2003. (Super Star Ser.). 96p. (J). pap. 4.95 *(978-1-58261-043-6(6))* Sports Publishing, LLC.
O'Neal, Claire. What's So Great about Barack Obama. 2009. (What's So Great About... ? Ser.). 32p. (J). (gr. 2-4). lib. bdg. 25.70 *(978-1-58415-830-1(1))* Mitchell Lane Pubs.
Poole, H. W. Multiracial Families, Vol. 12. 2016. (Families Today Ser.). (Illus.). 48p. (J). (gr. 5). 20.95 *(978-1-4222-3622-2(6))* Mason Crest.
Poole, Hilary W. Military Families. 2017. (Illus.). 48p. (J). *(978-1-4222-3612-3(9))* Mason Crest.
Roberts, Russell. Alicia Keys: Singer-Songwriter, Musician, Actress, & Producer. 2012. (Transcending Race Ser.). 64p. (J). (gr. 5). 22.95 *(978-1-4222-2727-5(8))* Mason Crest.
Robinson, Tom. Barack Obama: 44th U. S. President. 2009. (J). lib. bdg. 32.79 *(978-1-60453-528-0(8),* Essential Library) ABDO Publishing Co.
Sapet, Kerrily. Halle Berry: Academy Award/Winning Actress. 2012. (Transcending Race Ser.). 64p. (J). (gr. 5). 22.95 *(978-1-4222-2729-9(4))* Mason Crest.
Savage, Jeff. Tiger Woods. (Amazing Athletes Ser.). (Illus.). 32p. 2005. (gr. 3-4). lib. bdg. 22.60 *(978-0-8225-1337-7(4))* 2007. (ENG., (gr. 2-5). per. 7.95 *(978-0-8225-6890-2(X),* First Avenue Editions) Lerner Publishing Group.
Schuman, Michael A. Barack Obama: We Are One People, 1 vol. rev. ed. 2008. (African-American Biography Library). (ENG., Illus.). 160p. (gr. 6-7). lib. bdg. 35.93 *(978-0-7660-3649-9(9),* 38ae7d97-e2eb-4050-b3ef-e12048222213) Enslow Publishing, LLC.
Sheen, Barbara. Derek Jeter, 1 vol. 2008. (People in the News Ser.). (ENG., Illus.). 104p. (gr. 7-7). lib. bdg. 41.03 *(978-1-4205-0089-9(9),* be53a154-7d48-4bc8-86bc-af65cd18882f, Lucent Pr.) Greenhaven Publishing LLC.
—Multiracial Families. 2018. (Changing Families Ser.). 64p. (J). (gr. 6-12). 39.93 *(978-1-68282-361-3(X))* ReferencePoint Pr., Inc.
Smith, Crystal. I Am Hapa. Garcia, Michael Satoshi, photos by. 2016. (Illus.). (J). *(978-0-9973947-0-2(6))* East West Discovery Pr.
Smith, Crystal & Garcia, Michael Satoshi. I Am Hapa! 2016. (CHI, SPA & ENG., Illus.). (J). *(978-0-9913454-6-5(0))* East West Discovery Pr.
Sutcliffe, Jane. Barack Obama. 2010. (History Maker Biographies Ser.). (ENG.). 48p. (gr. 3-6). lib. bdg. 27.93 *(978-0-7613-5205-1(8),* Lerner Pubns.) Lerner Publishing Group.
Torres, John Albert. Derek Jeter. 2004. (Blue Banner Biography Ser.). (Illus.). 32p. (J). lib. bdg. 25.70 *(978-1-58415-333-7(4))* Mitchell Lane Pubs.
Winter, Jonah. Barack. Ford, A. G., illus. 32p. (J). (gr. -1-2). 2010. (ENG.). pap. 8.99 *(978-0-06-170396-6(6),* Tegen, Katherine Bks) 2008. lib. bdg. 18.89 *(978-0-06-170393-5(1))* HarperCollins Pubs.
—Barack, 2 vols. 2009. (J). 38.75 *(978-1-4407-3624-7(3))*; 40.75 *(978-1-4407-3618-6(9))*; 38.75 *(978-1-4407-3620-9(0))*; 40.75 *(978-1-4407-3622-3(7))*; 222.75 *(978-1-4407-3619-3(7))*; 1.25 *(978-1-4407-3625-4(1))* Recorded Bks., Inc.
Wong, Angi Ma. Barack Obama: Historymaker. 2009. (Illus.). 104p. (J). *(978-1-928753-86-5(8))* Pacific Heritage Bks.
Wong, Angi Ma, illus. Meet President Obama: America's 44th President. 2009. 32p. (J). *(978-1-928753-28-5(0))* Pacific Heritage Bks.
Zeiger, Jennifer. Cornerstones of Freedom, Third Series: Barack Obama. 2012. (Cornerstones of Freedom, Third Ser.). (ENG.). 64p. (J). (gr. 4-6). lib. bdg. 30.00 *(978-0-531-23050-3(3),* Children's Pr.) Scholastic Library Publishing.
Zumbusch, Amelie von. Barack Obama: Man of Destiny, 1 vol. 2010. (Making History: the Obamas Ser.). (ENG., Illus.). 24p. (J). (gr. 2-3). pap. 9.25 *(978-1-4358-9866-0(4),* e200cb41-050a-4dda-87d4-a9846743869d); lib. bdg. 26.27 *(978-1-4358-9387-0(5),* 3e3364d2-8945-4a03-bc46-b5f5f79e1823) Rosen Publishing Group, Inc., The. (PowerKids Pr.).

RACIALLY MIXED PEOPLE—FICTION

Anderson, Jessica Lee. Border Crossing. 2009. (ENG.). 160p. (J). (gr. 5-10). pap. 8.00 *(978-1-57131-691-2(4))* Milkweed Editions.
Bacigalupi, Paolo. Zombie Baseball Beatdown. 2014. (ENG.). 320p. (J). (gr. 3-7). pap. 8.99 *(978-0-316-22079-8(5))* Little, Brown Bks. for Young Readers.
Balcarcel, Rebecca. The Other Half of Happy: (Middle Grade Novel for Ages 9-12, Bilingual Tween Book) 2019. (ENG., Illus.). 332p. (J). (gr. 5-9). 16.99 *(978-1-4521-6998-9(5))* Chronicle Bks. LLC.
Barkow, Henriette. That's My Mum. Brazell, Derek, illus. 2004. (J). 24p. *(978-1-85269-604-7(4))*; (ENG & CZE.). 28p. pap. *(978-1-85269-628-3(1))*; (ENG & URD.). 28p. pap. *(978-1-85269-609-2(5))*; (ENG & TUR.). 28p. pap. *(978-1-85269-608-5(7))*; (ENG & SPA.). 28p. pap. *(978-1-85269-606-1(0))*; (ENG & SOM.). 28p. pap. *(978-1-85269-605-4(2))*; (ENG & POR.). 28p. pap. *(978-1-85269-603-0(6))*; (ENG & PAN.). 28p. pap. *(978-1-85269-602-3(8))*; (ENG & GUJ.). 28p. pap. *(978-1-85269-601-6(X))*; (ENG & PER.). 28p. pap. *(978-1-85269-599-6(4))*; (ENG & CHI.). 28p. pap. *(978-1-85269-598-9(6))*; (ENG & VIE.). 28p. pap. *(978-1-85269-802-7(0))*; (GER & ENG.). 28p. pap. *(978-1-85269-803-4(9))*; (ENG & ITA.). 28p. pap. *(978-1-85269-804-1(7))*; (ALB & ENG.). 28p. pap. *(978-1-85269-595-8(1))*; (ENG & YOR.). 28p. pap. *(978-1-84444-381-9(7))*; (ENG & BEN.). 28p. pap. *(978-1-85269-597-2(8))* Mantra Lingua.
—That's My Mum: Ajo Eshte Nena Ime. Brazell, Derek, illus. 2004. (ENG & ARA.). 28p. (J). pap. *(978-1-85269-596-5(X))* Mantra Lingua.
Barnettler, Timothy. The Contagious Yawn: A Journey Around the World. Hoover, William, illus. 2017. 41p. (J). pap. *(978-1-63293-189-4(3))* Sunstone Pr.
Benjamin, Floella. My Two Grandads. Chamberlain, Margaret, illus. 2019. (ENG.). 32p. (J). (gr. k-3). pap. 9.99 *(978-0-7112-4091-9(4),* 324891, Frances Lincoln Children's Bks.) Quarto Publishing Group UK GBR. Dist: Hachette UK Distribution.
—My Two Grannies. Chamberlain, Margaret, illus. 2009. (ENG.). 32p. (J). (gr. k-3). pap. 9.99 *(978-1-84780-034-3(3),* Frances Lincoln Children's Bks.) Quarto Publishing Group UK GBR. Dist: Hachette Bk. Group.
Boteju, Tanya. Kings, Queens, & In-Betweens. 2019. (ENG., Illus.). 384p. (YA). (gr. 7). 19.99 *(978-1-5344-3065-5(2),* Simon Pulse) Simon Pulse.
Bowman, Akemi Dawn. Harley in the Sky. 2020. (ENG.). 416p. (YA). (gr. 7). 19.99 *(978-1-5344-3712-8(6),* Simon Pulse) Simon Pulse.
—Starfish. (ENG.). (YA). (gr. 7). 2018. 368p. pap. 12.99 *(978-1-4814-8773-3(6))* 2017. (Illus.). 352p. 19.99 *(978-1-4814-8772-6(8))* Simon Pulse. (Simon Pulse).
Brazell, Derek. That's My Mum: Voici Ma Mere. Barkow, Henriette, illus. 2004. (ENG & FRE.). 28p. (J). pap. *(978-1-85269-600-9(1))* Mantra Lingua.
Brown, Monica. Marisol McDonald & the Clash Bash-Marisol Mcdonald y la Fiesta Sin Igual, 1 vol. Palacios, Sara, illus. 2013. (Marisol Mcdonald Ser.). (ENG.). 40p. (J). (gr. k-3). 19.95 *(978-0-89239-273-5(8),* leelowcbp) Lee & Low Bks., Inc.
—Marisol Mcdonald Doesn't Match: Marisol Mcdonald No Combina, 1 vol. Palacios, Sara, illus. 2013. (Marisol Mcdonald Ser.). (ENG.). 32p. (J). (gr. k-3). 19.95 *(978-0-89239-235-3(5),* leelowcbp) Lee & Low Bks., Inc.
Budhos, Marina. The Long Ride. 2019. (Illus.). 208p. (J). (gr. 5). 16.99 *(978-0-553-53422-1(X),* Lamb, Wendy Bks.) Random Hse. Children's Bks.
Chan, Crystal. All That I Can Fix. (ENG.). 320p. (YA). (gr. 7). 2019. pap. 12.99 *(978-1-5344-0889-0(4))* 2018. (Illus.). 18.99 *(978-1-5344-0888-3(6))* Simon Pulse. (Simon Pulse).
—Bird. (ENG.). (J). (gr. 3-7). 2015. 320p. pap. 8.99 *(978-1-4424-5091-2(6))* 2014. (Illus.). 304p. 16.99 *(978-1-4424-5089-9(4),* Atheneum Bks. for Young Readers) Simon & Schuster Children's Publishing.
Chari, Sheela. Finding Mighty. 2019. (ENG.). 336p. (J). (gr. 5-9). pap. 9.99 *(978-1-4197-3479-3(2),* 1144603, Amulet Bks.) Abrams, Inc.
Chen, Justina. Nothing but the Truth (and a Few White Lies) 2007. (Justina Chen Novel Ser.). (ENG.). 256p. (J). (gr. 7-17). per. 15.99 *(978-0-316-01131-0(2))* Little, Brown Bks. for Young Readers.
Cheng, Andrea. Shanghai Messenger, 1 vol. Young, Ed, illus. 2005. (ENG.). 40p. (J). (gr. 3-7). pap. 10.95 *(978-1-62014-230-1(9),* leelowbooks); 17.95 *(978-1-58430-238-4(0))* Lee & Low Bks., Inc.
Chung, Arree. Mixed: a Colorful Story. Chung, Arree, illus. 2018. (ENG., Illus.). 40p. (J). 18.99 *(978-1-250-14273-3(3),* 900180378, Holt, Henry & Co. Bks. For Young Readers) Holt, Henry & Co.
Compestine, Ying Chang. Crouching Tiger. Nascimbene, Yan, illus. (ENG.). 40p. (J). (gr. 1-4). 2019. 8.99 *(978-1-5362-0560-2(5))* 2011. 16.99 *(978-0-7636-4642-4(3))* Candlewick Pr.
Crawford, Ken. Bing of the Kobuk. 2019. (Illus.). 144p. (J). *(978-0-8163-6583-8(0))* Pacific Pr. Publishing Assn.
Crutcher, Chris. Whale Talk. 2004. 224p. (J). (gr. 7-18). pap. 38.00 incl. audio *(978-0-8072-2289-8(5),* Listening Library) Random Hse. Audio Publishing Group.
Cruz, Maria Colleen. Border Crossing. 2003. 128p. (J). pap. 9.95 *(978-1-55885-405-5(3),* Piñata Books) Arte Publico Pr.
—Border Crossing. 2006. 122p. (gr. 8-12). 19.95 *(978-0-7569-6587-7(X))* Perfection Learning Corp.
Davol, Marguerite W. Black, White, Just Right! Trivas, Irene, illus. 2019. (ENG.). 32p. (J). (gr. -1-3). pap. 7.99 *(978-0-8075-0788-9(1),* 807507881) Whitman, Albert & Co.
de la Peña, Matt. Mexican WhiteBoy. 2010. (ENG.). 272p. (YA). (gr. 9). pap. 12.99 *(978-0-440-23938-3(9),* Ember) Random Hse. Children's Bks.
De La Peña, Matt. Mexican WhiteBoy. 2010. lib. bdg. 20.85 *(978-0-606-12316-7(4))* Turtleback.
Deen, Natasha. Lark Takes a Bow, 1 vol. Cutler, Marcus, illus. 2018. (Orca Echoes Ser.: 3). (ENG.). 96p. (J). (gr. 1-3). pap. 7.95 *(978-1-4598-1715-9(X))* Orca Bk. Pubs. USA.
del Rosario, Juleah. 500 Words or Less. 2018. (ENG., Illus.). 384p. (YA). (gr. 9). 18.99 *(978-1-5344-1044-2(9),* Simon Pulse) Simon Pulse.
Dellaira, Ava. In Search of Us. 2020. (ENG.). 416p. (YA). pap. 10.99 *(978-1-250-29461-6(4),* 900163346) Square Fish.
Diggs, Taye. Mixed Me! Evans, Shane W., illus. 2015. (ENG.). 40p. (J). (gr. -1-3). 17.99 *(978-1-250-04719-9(6),* 900132069) Feiwel & Friends.
Dilloway, Margaret. Xander & the Lost Island of Monsters. 2017. (J). lib. bdg. 17.20 *(978-0-606-39503-8(2))* Turtleback.
Draper, Sharon M. Blended. (ENG.). 320p. (J). (gr. 3-7). 2020. pap. 8.99 *(978-1-4424-9501-2(4),* Atheneum Bks. for Young Readers) 2018. (Illus.). 17.99 *(978-1-4424-9500-5(6),* Atheneum/Caitlyn Dlouhy Books) Simon & Schuster Children's Publishing.
Edwards, Nicholas. Dog Whisperer: the Rescue: The Rescue. 2009. (Dog Whisperer Ser.: 1). (ENG.). 224p. (J). (gr. 3-7). pap. 10.99 *(978-0-312-36768-8(6),* 900042450) Square Fish.
Elliott, Kate, pseud. Court of Fives. 2016. (Court of Fives Ser.: 1). (ENG., Illus.). 464p. (YA). (gr. 7-17). pap. 12.99 *(978-0-316-36430-0(4))* Little, Brown Bks. for Young Readers.
Engle, Margarita. Lion Island: Cuba's Warrior of Words. (ENG.). (J). (gr. 5). 2017. 192p. pap. 7.99 *(978-1-4814-6113-9(3))* 2016. (Illus.). 176p. 16.99 *(978-1-4814-6112-2(5),* Atheneum Bks. for Young Readers) Simon & Schuster Children's Publishing.
Farish, Terry. Either the Beginning or the End of the World. 2015. (ENG.). 200p. (YA). (gr. 8-12). 18.99 *(978-1-4677-7483-3(9),* b2cbce4f-14d6-4326-9b41-74047d9506c0); E-Book 29.32 *(978-1-4677-8813-7(9))* Lerner Publishing Group. (Carolrhoda Lab™).
Faulkner, Matt. Gaijin: American Prisoner of War. 2014. (ENG., Illus.). 144p. (J). (gr. 3-7). 19.99 *(978-1-4231-3735-1(3))* Little, Brown Bks. for Young Readers.
Fields, Monique. Honeysmoke: A Story of Finding Your Color. Moises, Yesenia, illus. 2019. (ENG.). 32p. (J). 18.99 *(978-1-250-11582-9(5),* 900171765) Imprint IND. Dist: Macmillan.
Finotti, M. C. The Treasure of Amelia Island. (Florida Historical Fiction for Youth Ser.). (Illus.). (J). (gr. -1-12). 2012. 104p. pap. 8.95 *(978-1-56164-536-7(2))* 2008. (ENG., 97p. 14.95 *(978-1-56164-416-2(1))* Pineapple Pr., Inc.
Flood, Pansie Hart. It's Test Day, Tiger Turcotte. Wummer, Amy, tr. Wummer, Amy, illus. 2004. (Young Reader Fiction Ser.). 72p. (J). (gr. 1-4). pap. 6.95 *(978-1-57505-670-8(4))*; lib. bdg. 19.93 *(978-1-57505-056-0(0),* Carolrhoda Bks.) Lerner Publishing Group.
—Tiger's Trouble with Donut Head. Wummer, Amy, illus. 2005. 71p. (J). lib. bdg. 19.93 *(978-1-57505-814-6(6),* Carolrhoda Bks.) Lerner Publishing Group.
Frazier, Sundee T. Brendan Buckley's Sixth-Grade Experiment. 2013. (ENG.). 288p. (J). (gr. 4-7). 7.99 *(978-0-385-74051-7(4),* Yearling) Random Hse. Children's Bks.
—Brendan Buckley's Universe & Everything in It. 2008. (ENG.). 208p. (J). (gr. 3-7). 7.99 *(978-0-440-42206-8(X),* Yearling) Random Hse. Children's Bks.
—The Other Half of My Heart. 2011. 304p. (J). (gr. 3-7). 8.99 *(978-0-440-24006-8(9),* Yearling) Random Hse. Children's Bks.
Frazier, Sundee Tucker. Brendan Buckley's Universe & Everything in It, 1. 2008. (Brendan Buckley Ser.). (ENG.). 208p. (J). (gr. 4-6). lib. bdg. 21.19 *(978-0-385-90445-2(2),* Delacorte Pr.) Random Hse. Children's Bks.
—The Other Half of My Heart. 2011. (ENG.). 304p. (J). (gr. 4-6). lib. bdg. 21.19 *(978-0-385-90446-9(0),* Delacorte Pr.) Random Hse. Children's Bks.
Garcia, Cristina. I Wanna Be Your Shoebox. 2009. (ENG.). 208p. (J). (gr. 3-7). pap. 7.99 *(978-1-4169-7904-3(2),* Simon & Schuster Bks. For Young Readers) Simon & Schuster Bks. For Young Readers.
Gibbs, Stuart. Charlie Thorne & the Last Equation. (Charlie Thorne Ser.). (ENG., Illus.). (J). (gr. 5). 2020. 416p. pap. 8.99 *(978-1-5344-2477-7(6))* 2019. 400p. 17.99 *(978-1-5344-2476-0(8))* 2019. 400p. E-Book *(978-1-5344-2478-4(4))* Simon & Schuster Bks. For Young Readers. (Simon & Schuster Bks. For Young Readers).
—Charlie Thorne & the Last Equation, 1. 2020. (Charlie Thorne Ser.). (ENG.). 416p. (gr. 5-8). 24.94 *(978-1-5364-6985-1(8))* Simon & Schuster, Inc.
Gill, David Macinnis. Soul Enchilada. 2010. (ENG.). 384p. (YA). (gr. 9). pap. 9.99 *(978-0-06-167303-0(X),* Greenwillow Bks.) HarperCollins Pubs.
Goo, Maurene. The Way You Make Me Feel. 2018. (ENG.). 336p. (J). pap. *(978-0-374-31195-7(1))* Farrar, Straus & Giroux.
—The Way You Make Me Feel. 2019. (ENG.). 352p. (YA). pap. 9.99 *(978-1-250-30880-1(1),* 900158638) Square Fish.
Green, Tim & Jeter, Derek. Double Play: Baseball Genius 2. 2018. (Jeter Publishing Ser.). (ENG., Illus.). 352p. (J). (gr. 3-7). 17.99 *(978-1-5344-0668-1(9),* Aladdin) Simon & Schuster Children's Publishing.
—Double Play: Baseball Genius 2. 2019. (Jeter Publishing Ser.). (ENG.). 352p. (J). (gr. 3-7). pap. 8.99 *(978-1-5344-0669-8(7),* Simon & Schuster/Paula Wiseman Bks.) Simon & Schuster/Paula Wiseman Bks.
Griffin, Emily Ziff. Light Years. 2017. (ENG., Illus.). 304p. (YA). (gr. 9-12). 18.99 *(978-1-5072-0005-6(6),* Simon Pulse) Simon Pulse.
Gurtler, Janet. If I Tell. 2011. (ENG.). 256p. (YA). (gr. 7-12). pap. 12.99 *(978-1-4022-6103-9(9))* Sourcebooks, Inc.
Haislip, Phyllis Hall. Between the Lines: A Revolutionary War Slave's Journey to Freedom. 2012. (ENG., Illus.). 190p. (J). pap. 8.95 *(978-1-57249-409-1(3),* White Mane Kids) White Mane Publishing Co., Inc.
Hamilton, Virginia, et al. Plain City. (Barco de Vapor). (SPA.). 176p. (YA). (gr. 5-8). 6.95 *(978-84-348-4686-9(1),* LEC6861) SM Ediciones ESP. Dist: Continental Bk. Co., Inc.
Heathfield, Lisa. Paper Butterflies. 2019. (ENG.). 272p. (YA). (gr. 7-12). pap. 9.99 *(978-1-5415-6042-0(6),* 07431f09-5118-4a8c-a304-97ae7ceefdcd, Carolrhoda Lab™) Lerner Publishing Group.
Hesse, Karen. Aleutian Sparrow. Zerbetz, Evon, illus. 2005. (ENG.). 160p. (J). (gr. 4-9). reprint ed. pap. 8.99 *(978-1-4169-0327-7(5),* McElderry, Margaret K. Bks.) McElderry, Margaret K. Bks.
—Aleutian Sparrow. Zerbetz, Evon, illus. 2005. 156p. (J). (gr. 5-9). 13.65 *(978-0-7569-5589-2(0))* Perfection Learning Corp.
Hiranandani, Veera. The Whole Story of Half a Girl. 2013. (ENG.). 224p. (J). (gr. 4-6). lib. bdg. 21.19 *(978-0-375-98995-7(1),* Delacorte Pr.); 8.99 *(978-0-375-87167-2(5),* Yearling) Random Hse. Children's Bks.
Hopkinson, Nalo. The Chaos. (ENG., 256p. (YA). (gr. 9). 2013. Illus.). pap. 11.99 *(978-1-4424-5926-7(3))* 2012. 16.99 *(978-1-4169-5488-0(0))* McElderry, Margaret K. Bks. (McElderry, Margaret K. Bks.).
Jaffe, Michele. Bad Kitty. 2006. (Bad Kitty Ser.: Bk. 1). (ENG., Illus.). 288p. (YA). (gr. 7-12). 16.99 *(978-0-06-078108-8(4))* HarperCollins Pubs.
—Kitty Kitty. 2008. (Bad Kitty Ser.: Bk. 2). 320p. (YA). (gr. 7-18). lib. bdg. 17.89 *(978-0-06-078114-9(9),* HarperTeen) HarperCollins Pubs.
Johnson, Kristin. Wall of Water. 2017. (Day of Disaster Ser.). (ENG.). 112p. (YA). (gr. 6-12). E-Book 39.99 *(978-1-5124-2786-8(1))*; E-Book 39.99 *(978-1-5124-3515-3(5),* 9781512435153) Lerner Publishing Group. (Darby Creek).
Johnson, Kristin F. Wall of Water. 2017. (Day of Disaster Ser.). (ENG.). 112p. (YA). (gr. 6-12). E-Book 6.99 *(978-1-5124-3516-0(3),* 9781512435160, Darby Creek) Lerner Publishing Group.

Jones, Patrick. Barrier. 2014. (Alternative Ser.). (ENG.). 104p. (YA). (gr. 6-12). pap. 7.95 *(978-1-4677-4481-2(6)*, 8735726f-8fde-40f2-b04a-ba121c0d9533, Darby Creek) Lerner Publishing Group.

—Combat Zone. 2015. (Support & Defend Ser.). (ENG.). 96p. (YA). (gr. 6-12). pap. 7.99 *(978-1-4677-8094-0(4)*, 7fcd07df-4780-48e5-8547-63a22f685b50, Darby Creek) Lerner Publishing Group.

Jubilee Jr., Thomas. The Same As James. Baker, David, illus. 2011. 28p. pap. 24.95 *(978-1-4626-0288-9(6))* America Star Bks.

Keller, Tae. The Science of Breakable Things. (J). (gr. 3-7). 2019. (ENG.). 320p. 8.99 *(978-1-5247-1569-4(7)*, Yearling) 2018. 304p. 17.99 *(978-1-5247-1566-3(2)*, Random Hse. Bks. for Young Readers) Random Hse. Children's Bks.

Keyser, Amber J. The Way Back from Broken. (ENG.). 216p. (YA). (gr. 6-12). 2018. pap. 9.99 *(978-1-5415-1488-1(2)*, 053f47d3-53bb-4099-bb59-532f84376fbd) 2015. E-Book 27.99 *(978-1-4677-8817-5(1))* Lerner Publishing Group. (Carolrhoda Lab™).

Kim, Michelle. Running Through Sprinklers. 2018. (ENG., Illus.). 224p. (J). (gr. 5). 16.99 *(978-1-4814-9528-8(3)*, Atheneum Bks. for Young Readers) Simon & Schuster Children's Publishing.

Krishnaswami, Uma. Step up to the Plate, Maria Singh, 1 vol. 2017. (ENG.). 288p. (J). (gr. 3-7). 21.95 *(978-1-60060-261-0(4)*, leelowtu, Tu Bks.) Lee & Low Bks., Inc.

Landman, Tanya. Hell & High Water. 2017. (ENG.). 320p. (J). (gr. 7). 17.99 *(978-0-7636-8875-2(4))* Candlewick Pr.

Lariviere, Sarah. The Bad Kid. 2016. (ENG., Illus.). 304p. (J). (gr. 3-7). 17.99 *(978-1-4814-3581-9(7)*, Simon & Schuster Bks. For Young Readers) Simon & Schuster Bks. For Young Readers.

Larson, Hope. All Together Now. Larson, Hope, illus. 2020. (Eagle Rock Ser.: 2). (ENG., Illus.). 192p. (J). 21.99 *(978-0-374-31162-9(5)*, 900195864); pap. 12.99 *(978-0-374-31365-4(2)*, 900215357) Farrar, Straus & Giroux. (Farrar, Straus & Giroux (BYR)).

Lawrence, Caroline. The Case of the Deadly Desperados, 1. 2013. (P. K. Pinkerton Novels Ser.: 1). (ENG.). 272p. (J). (gr. 4-6). 21.19 *(978-0-399-25633-2(4))* Penguin Young Readers Group.

—P. K. Pinkerton & the Case of the Deadly Desperados. 2013. (P. K. Pinkerton Ser.: 1). (ENG.). 304p. (J). (gr. 3-7). pap. 8.99 *(978-0-14-242381-3(5)*, Puffin Books) Penguin Young Readers Group.

—P. K. Pinkerton & the Pistol-Packing Widows. 2015. (P. K. Pinkerton Ser.: 3). (ENG.). 320p. (J). (gr. 3-7). 7.99 *(978-0-14-751130-0(5)*, Puffin Books) Penguin Young Readers Group.

Lenzi, Christy. Stone Field: A Novel. 2016. (ENG.). 320p. (YA). 29.99 *(978-1-62672-069-5(X)*, 900134314) Roaring Brook Pr.

Leonard, Connie King. Sleeping in My Jeans. 2018. (ENG.). 240p. (YA). pap. 16.00 *(978-1-947845-00-8(4))* Ooligan Pr.

Lewis, Richard. The Demon Queen. 2012. (ENG.). 240p. (YA). (gr. 7). pap. 11.99 *(978-1-4169-3590-2(8)*, Simon & Schuster Bks. For Young Readers) Simon & Schuster Bks. For Young Readers.

Little, Kimberley Griffiths. The Last Snake Runner. 2006. 201p. (YA). (gr. 7-10). reprint ed. 16.00 *(978-1-4223-5838-2(0))* DIANE Publishing Co.

Magoon, Kekla. Camo Girl. 2012. (ENG.). 224p. (J). (gr. 3-9). pap. 8.99 *(978-1-4169-7805-3(4)*, Aladdin) Simon & Schuster Children's Publishing.

—Camo Girl. 2011. (ENG., Illus.). 224p. (J). (gr. 3-9). 19.99 *(978-1-4169-7804-6(6)*, Simon & Schuster/Paula Wiseman Bks.) Simon & Schuster/Paula Wiseman Bks.

Maldonado, Torrey. Secret Saturdays. 2012. (ENG.). 208p. (YA). (gr. 5-18). 7.99 *(978-0-14-241747-8(5)*, Puffin Books) Penguin Young Readers Group.

—Secret Saturdays. 2012. lib. bdg. 18.40 *(978-0-606-23645-4(7))* Turtleback.

Mawhinney, Lynnette. Lulu the One & Only. Poh, Jennie, illus. 2020. 32p. (J). *(978-1-4338-3159-1(7)*, Magination Pr.) American Psychological Assn.

Mayer, Pamela. Chicken Soup, Chicken Soup. Melmon, Deborah, illus. 2016. (ENG.). 32p. (J). (gr. -1-3). 17.99 *(978-1-4677-8934-9(8)*, d1826602-2ac3-41a4-ba03-fbb1f5545a02, Kar-Ben Publishing) Lerner Publishing Group.

Meshon, Aaron. Take Me Out to the Yakyu. Meshon, Aaron, illus. 2013. (ENG., Illus.). 40p. (J). (gr. -1-3). 19.99 *(978-1-4424-4177-4(1)*, Atheneum Bks. for Young Readers) Simon & Schuster Children's Publishing.

Meyer, Carolyn. Jubilee Journey. 2007. (ENG., Illus.). 288p. (J). (gr. 5-7). pap. 17.95 *(978-0-15-205845-6(1)*, 253003, Clarion Bks.) HarperCollins Pubs.

—Jubilee Journey. 2007. 271p. (gr. 5-9). 14.60 *(978-0-7569-6682-9(5))* Perfection Learning Corp.

Monica Brown. Marisol Mcdonald & the Monster: Marisol Mcdonald y el Monstruo (English & Spanish Edition), 1 vol. 2016. (Marisol Mcdonald Ser.). (ENG., Illus.). 32p. (J). (gr. k-3). 19.95 *(978-0-89239-326-8(2)*, leelowcbp) Lee & Low Bks., Inc.

Monk, Isabell. Hope. Porter, Janice Lee, illus. 2004. (Carolrhoda Picture Books Ser.). 32p. (J). (gr. -1-3). 6.95 *(978-1-57505-792-7(1))* Lerner Publishing Group.

Mora, Pat. Gracias Thanks, 1 vol. Parra, John, illus. 2005. (ENG.). 32p. (J). (gr. k-4). 19.95 *(978-1-60060-258-0(4)*, leelowbooks) Lee & Low Bks., Inc.

Namioka, Lensey. Half & Half. 2005. 136p. (gr. 3-7). 16.00 *(978-0-7569-5680-6(3))* Perfection Learning Corp.

—Half & Half. 2004. 144p. (J). (gr. 3-7). 7.99 *(978-0-440-41890-0(9)*, Yearling) Random Hse. Children's Bks.

Nelson, Marilyn. American Ace. 2016. (ENG.). 128p. (YA). (gr. 7). 17.99 *(978-0-8037-3305-3(4)*, Dial Bks) Penguin Young Readers Group.

Nunn, Malla. When the Ground Is Hard. 2019. (ENG.). 272p. (YA). (gr. 7). 17.99 *(978-0-525-51557-9(7)*, G.P. Putnam's Sons Books for Young Readers) Penguin Young Readers Group.

Olivas, Daniel. Benjamin & the Word: Benjamín y la Palabra. Baeza Ventura, Gabriela, tr. Dyen, Don, illus. 2011. 32p. (J). pap. 7.95 *(978-1-55885-687-5(0)*, Piñata Books) Arte Publico Pr.

—Benjamin & Word Benjamin Y la Palabra. (SPA & ENG., Illus.). 32p. 15.95 *(978-1-55885-413-0(4)*, Piñata Books) Arte Publico Pr.

Osborne, Mary Pope. Adaline Falling Star. unabr. ed. 2004. (Middle Grade Cassette Librariestm Ser.). 176p. (J). (gr. 3-7). pap. 29.00 incl. audio *(978-0-8072-1195-3(8)*, S YA 319 SP, Listening Library) Random Hse. Audio Publishing Group.

Ostow, Micol. Emily Goldberg Learns to Salsa. 2007. 208p. (YA). (gr. 7-18). 8.99 *(978-1-59514-144-6(8)*, Razorbill) Penguin Young Readers Group.

Pan, Emily X. R. The Astonishing Color of After. 2019. (ENG.). 480p. (YA). (gr. 7-17). pap. 11.99 *(978-0-316-46401-7(5))* Little, Brown Bks. for Young Readers.

Paolilli, Paul & Brewer, Dan. Nightlights. Brereton, Alice, illus. 2017. (ENG.). 32p. (J). (gr. -1-3). 16.99 *(978-0-8075-5622-1(X)*, 080755622X) Whitman, Albert & Co.

Park, Linda Sue. Prairie Lotus. 2020. (ENG.). 272p. (J). (gr. 5-7). 16.99 *(978-1-328-78150-5(X)*, 1685061, Clarion Bks.) HarperCollins Pubs.

—Prairie Lotus Signed Edition. 2020. (ENG.). 272p. (J). (gr. 5-7). 16.99 *(978-0-358-36014-8(5)*, Clarion Bks.) HarperCollins Pubs.

Parsons, Karyn. How High the Moon. 2019. (ENG.). 320p. (J). (gr. 3-7). 16.99 *(978-0-316-48400-8(8))* Little, Brown Bks. for Young Readers.

Peck, Richard. The River Between Us. 2003. (ENG.). 164p. (J). (gr. 7-7). 21.19 *(978-0-8037-2735-9(6)*, Dial) Penguin Publishing Group.

—The River Between Us. 2005. (ENG.). 176p. (J). (gr. 3-7). reprint ed. pap. 8.99 *(978-0-14-240310-5(5)*, Puffin Books) Penguin Young Readers Group.

Philbrick, Rodman. Zane & the Hurricane: a Story of Katrina. 2015. (ENG.). 192p. (J). (gr. 5-9). pap. 8.99 *(978-0-545-34239-1(2)*, Blue Sky Pr., The) Scholastic, Inc.

Porter, Sarah. Tentacle & Wing. 2017. (ENG.). 272p. (J). (gr. 5-7). 16.99 *(978-1-328-70733-8(4)*, 1672696, Clarion Bks.) HarperCollins Pubs.

Prendergast, G. S. Cold Falling White. (Nahx Invasions Ser.: 2). (ENG.). 576p. (YA). (gr. 9). 2020. pap. 13.99 *(978-1-4814-8188-5(6))* 2019. 19.99 *(978-1-4814-8187-8(8))* Simon & Schuster Bks. For Young Readers. (Simon & Schuster Bks. For Young Readers).

—Cold Falling White. 2019. (ENG.). 368p. (YA). *(978-1-5011-4714-2(5))* Simon & Schuster Children's Publishing.

—Zero Repeat Forever. 2017. (ENG.). (YA). (gr. 9). pap. 12.99 *(978-1-5344-1808-0(3))* Simon & Schuster.

—Zero Repeat Forever. (Nahx Invasions Ser.: 1). (ENG.). (YA). (gr. 9). 2019. 512p. pap. 13.99 *(978-1-4814-8185-4(1))* 2017. (Illus.). 496p. 17.99 *(978-1-4814-8184-7(3))* Simon & Schuster Bks. For Young Readers. (Simon & Schuster Bks. For Young Readers).

Raffa, Edwina & Rigsby, Annelle. Escape to the Everglades. 2013. (Florida Historical Fiction for Youth Ser.). (ENG., Illus.). 110p. (J). (gr. -1-12). pap. 12.95 *(978-1-56164-619-7(9))* Pineapple Pr., Inc.

—Escape to the Everglades Teacher's Activity Guide. 2006. (ENG., Illus.). 34p. pap., tchr. ed., act. bk. ed. 6.00 *(978-1-56164-362-2(9))* Pineapple Pr., Inc.

Redgate, Riley. Final Draft. (ENG.). (gr. 8-17). 2019. 288p. (YA). pap. 9.99 *(978-1-4197-3487-8(3)*, 1164703) 2018. 272p. 17.99 *(978-1-4197-2872-3(5)*, 1164701, Amulet Bks.) Abrams, Inc.

Resau, Laura. What the Moon Saw. 2008. (ENG.). 272p. (J). (gr. 3-7). pap. 8.99 *(978-0-440-23957-4(5)*, Yearling) Random Hse. Children's Bks.

Rinaldi, Ann. The Education of Mary: A Little Miss of Color, 1832. 2005. 176p. (J). pap. *(978-0-7868-1377-3(6))* Hyperion Pr.

—Mutiny's Daughter. 2005. 218p. (J). (gr. 3-7). 13.65 *(978-0-7569-5602-8(1))* Perfection Learning Corp.

Rivers, Karen. The Encyclopedia of Me. 2012. (ENG., Illus.). 256p. (J). (gr. 4-7). 16.99 *(978-0-545-31028-4(8)*, Levine, Arthur A. Bks.) Scholastic, Inc.

Robinson, Gary. Son Who Returns. 2014. (PathFinders Ser.). (ENG.). 120p. (YA). (gr. 8-12). pap. 9.95 *(978-1-939053-04-6(8)*, 7th Generation) BPC.

Salazar, Aida. The Moon Within (Scholastic Gold), 1 vol. 2019. (ENG., Illus.). 240p. (J). (gr. 3-7). 17.99 *(978-1-338-28337-2(5)*, Levine, Arthur A. Bks.) Scholastic, Inc.

Sanders, Scott Loring. Gray Baby. 2009. (ENG.). 336p. (YA). (gr. 7-18). 17.00 *(978-0-547-07661-4(4)*, 1042029, Clarion Bks.) HarperCollins Pubs.

Scott, Kieran. Pretty Fierce. 2017. (ENG.). 304p. (YA). (gr. 6-12). pap. 10.99 *(978-1-4926-3798-1(X)*, 9781492637981) Sourcebooks, Inc.

Sedgwick, Julian. The Black Dragon. Moffett, Patricia, illus. 2016. (Mysterium Ser.: 1). (ENG.). 352p. (J). (gr. 4-8). E-Book 29.32 *(978-1-4677-9555-5(0)*, Carolrhoda Bks.) Lerner Publishing Group.

—The Palace of Memory. No. 2. Moffett, Patricia, illus. 2017. (Mysterium Ser.: 2). (ENG.). 352p. (J). (gr. 4-8). 18.99 *(978-1-4677-7568-7(1)*, a33df367-d91f-4e23-aeec-f2976f2a8368, Carolrhoda Bks.) Lerner Publishing Group.

—The Wheel of Life & Death. No. 3. Moffett, Patricia, illus. 2018. (Mysterium Ser.: 3). (ENG.). 344p. (J). (gr. 4-8). 18.99 *(978-1-4677-7569-4(X)*, e1dc9978-31c7-4613-afa7-14b9bae2030a, Carolrhoda Bks.) Lerner Publishing Group.

Shin, Sun Yung. Cooper's Lesson. Cogan, Kim & Paek, Min, trs. from ENG. Cogan, Kim, illus. 2004. (ENG & KOR.). 32p. (J). 16.95 *(978-0-89239-193-6(6))* Lee & Low Bks., Inc.

—Cooper's Lesson, 1 vol. 2015. (ENG., Illus.). 32p. (J). (gr. 1-5). pap. 11.95 *(978-0-89239-361-9(0)*, leelowcbp, Children's Book Press) Lee & Low Bks., Inc.

Shumaker, Heather. The Griffins of Castle Cary. 2019. (ENG., Illus.). 320p. (J). (gr. 3-7). 17.99 *(978-1-5344-3088-4(1)*, Simon & Schuster Bks. For Young Readers) Simon & Schuster Bks. For Young Readers.

Shusterman, Neal. Red Rider's Hood. 2006. (Dark Fusion Ser.: 3). (ENG.). 192p. (YA). (gr. 7-18). 7.99 *(978-0-14-240678-6(3)*, Speak) Penguin Young Readers Group.

Skurzynski, Gloria. Mysteries in Our National Parks: Escape from Fear: A Mystery in Virgin Islands National Park. 2008. (Mysteries in Our National Park Ser.). (Illus.). 160p. (J). (gr. 3-7). mass mkt. 4.99 *(978-1-4263-0181-0(2)*, National Geographic Kids) Disney Publishing Worldwide.

Stanley, Brenda. I Am Nuchu. 2010. 334p. (YA). (gr. 9-18). 16.95 *(978-1-934813-47-8(8))* Westside Bks.

Stauffacher, Sue. Animal Rescue Team: Hide & Seek. Lamont, Priscilla, illus. 2011. (Animal Rescue Team Ser.: 3). 160p. (J). (gr. 3-7). 6.99 *(978-0-375-85133-9(X)*, Yearling) Random Hse. Children's Bks.

—Animal Rescue Team: Special Delivery! Lamont, Priscilla, illus. 2011. (Animal Rescue Team Ser.: 2). 176p. (J). (gr. 3-7). 6.99 *(978-0-375-85132-2(1)*, Yearling) Random Hse. Children's Bks.

—Gator on the Loose!, 1. Lamont, Priscilla, illus. 2011. (Animal Rescue Team Ser.). (ENG.). 160p. (J). (gr. 2-5). lib. bdg. 18.69 *(978-0-375-95847-2(9)*, Knopf Bks. for Young Readers) Random Hse. Children's Bks.

—Gator on the Loose! Animal Rescue Team. Lamont, Priscilla, illus. 2011. (Animal Rescue Team Ser.: 1). 160p. (J). (gr. 3-7). 6.99 *(978-0-375-85131-5(3)*, Yearling) Random Hse. Children's Bks.

—Hide & Seek, 3. Lamont, Priscilla, illus. 2012. (Animal Rescue Team Ser.). (ENG.). 160p. (J). (gr. 2-5). lib. bdg. 18.69 *(978-0-375-95849-6(5)*, Knopf Bks. for Young Readers) Random Hse. Children's Bks.

Stehlik, Tania Duprey. Violet, 1 vol. Jovanovic, Vanja Vuleta, illus. 2009. (ENG.). 24p. (J). (gr. -1-2). 15.95 *(978-1-897187-60-9(2))* Second Story Pr. CAN. Dist: Orca Bk. Pubs. USA.

Stellings, Caroline. The Contest, 1 vol. 2009. (ENG.). 160p. (J). (gr. 4-7). pap. 9.95 *(978-0-9779183-5-5(1)*, 7th Generation) BPC.

Stevenson, Sarah Jamila. The Latte Rebellion. 2011. (ENG., Illus.). 336p. (YA). (gr. 9-12). pap. 9.95 *(978-0-7387-2278-8(2)*, 0738722782, Flux) North Star Editions.

Sweeney, Joyce. Waiting for June, 0 vols. 2012. (ENG.). 158p. (YA). (gr. 7-12). pap. 7.99 *(978-0-7614-5329-1(6)*, 9780761453291, Skyscape) Amazon Publishing.

Thompson, Holly. Orchards. 2012. (ENG.). 336p. (YA). (gr. 7-12). lib. bdg. 26.19 *(978-0-385-90806-1(7)*, Delacorte Pr.) Random Hse. Children's Bks.

Tolcser, Sarah. Whisper of the Tide. 2018. (ENG., Illus.). 416p. (YA). 17.99 *(978-1-68119-299-4(3)*, 900165542, Bloomsbury Young Adult) Bloomsbury Publishing USA.

Tucker, Zekita. Don't Call Me N!gga. 2007. per. 0.01 net. *(978-1-60402-249-0(3))* Independent Pub.

Turner, Diane D. My Name Is Oney Judge. Massey, Cal, illus. 2010. (J). pap. *(978-0-88378-321-4(5))* Third World Press.

Wallace, Kali. Shallow Graves. 2017. (ENG.). 384p. (YA). (gr. 9). pap. 9.99 *(978-0-06-236621-4(1)*, Tegen, Katherine Bks) HarperCollins Pubs.

Washington, Kathy. Three Colors of Katie. Farina, Kathy, illus. 2010. (J). (gr. k-2). pap. 9.95 *(978-1-932514-18-6(X))* College of DuPage Pr.

Wenberg, Michael. Stringz. 2010. 216p. (YA). (gr. 6-10). 16.95 *(978-1-934813-33-1(8))* Westside Bks.

Wientge, Kristi. Karma Khullar's Mustache. (ENG., Illus.). (J). (gr. 3-7). 2018. 288p. pap. 8.99 *(978-1-4814-7771-0(4))* 2017. 272p. 16.99 *(978-1-4814-7770-3(6))* Simon & Schuster Bks. For Young Readers. (Simon & Schuster Bks. For Young Readers).

—Karma Khullar's Mustache. 2018. lib. bdg. 18.40 *(978-0-606-41410-4(X))* Turtleback.

Williams, Maggy. "I'm Mixed!" Agresta, Elizabeth, illus. 2018. 38p. (J). pap. *(978-1-61599-359-8(2))* Loving Healing Pr., Inc.

Willis, Meredith Sue. Billie of Fish House Lane. 2006. (J). pap. 12.95 *(978-1-932727-02-9(7))* Montemayor Pr.

Wilson, Diane Lee. Black Storm Comin'. 2006. (ENG.). 240p. (J). (gr. 5-9). pap. 8.99 *(978-0-689-87138-2(4)*, McElderry, Margaret K. Bks.) McElderry, Margaret K. Bks.

—Black Storm Comin'. 2006. (Illus.). 291p. (gr. 5-9). 17.00 *(978-0-7569-6908-0(5))* Perfection Learning Corp.

Wong, Janet S. & Cote, Genevieve. Minn & Jake's Almost Terrible Summer. 2008. (ENG., Illus.). 112p. (J). (gr. 2-5). 16.99 *(978-0-374-34977-6(0)*, 900044565, Farrar, Straus & Giroux (BYR)) Farrar, Straus & Giroux.

Woods, Brenda. The Blossoming Universe of Violet Diamond. 2015. 240p. (J). (gr. 3-7). 8.99 *(978-0-14-751430-1(4)*, Puffin Books) Penguin Young Readers Group.

Woodson, Jacqueline. The House You Pass on the Way. 2010. (ENG.). 160p. (J). (gr. 5-8). pap. 8.99 *(978-0-14-241706-5(8)*, Puffin Books) Penguin Young Readers Group.

—Miracle's Boys. 2010. (ENG.). 176p. (J). (gr. 5-18). 8.99 *(978-0-14-241553-5(7)*, Puffin Books) Penguin Young Readers Group.

Yang, Kelly. New from Here. (ENG.). (J). (gr. 3-7). 2023. 384p. pap. 8.99 *(978-1-5344-8831-6(0))* 2022. (Illus.). 368p. 18.99 *(978-1-5344-8830-4(8))* Simon & Schuster Bks. For Young Readers. (Simon & Schuster Bks. For Young Readers).

Yoon, Nicola. Everything, Everything. (ENG.). (YA). (gr. 7). 2017. 352p. pap. 13.99 *(978-0-553-49667-3(0)*, Ember) 2015. (Illus.). 336p. 18.99 *(978-0-553-49664-2(6)*, Delacorte Pr.) Random Hse. Children's Bks.

—Everything, Everything. 2017. lib. bdg. 22.10 *(978-0-606-40341-2(8))* Turtleback.

Young, Karen Romano. Doodlebug: A Novel in Doodles. 2012. (ENG., Illus.). 128p. (J). (gr. 3-7). pap. 15.99 *(978-1-250-01020-9(9)*, 900084757) Square Fish.

—Stuck in the Middle (of Middle School) A Novel in Doodles. 2014. (ENG., Illus.). 128p. (J). (gr. 3-7). pap. 12.99 *(978-1-250-03997-2(5)*, 900123700) Square Fish.

Zhao, Katie. The Dragon Warrior. 2019. (Dragon Warrior Ser.). (ENG., Illus.). 352p. (J). 16.99 *(978-1-5476-0200-1(7)*, 900203292, Bloomsbury Children's Bks.) Bloomsbury Publishing USA.

Zoboi, Ibi. Pride: A Pride & Prejudice Remix. (ENG.). 304p. (YA). (gr. 8). 2019. pap. 11.99 *(978-0-06-256405-4(6))* 2018. 17.99 *(978-0-06-256404-7(8))* 2018. E-Book *(978-0-06-256407-8(2)*, 9780062564078) HarperCollins Pubs. (Balzer & Bray).

RACKETEERING

Black, Andy. Organized Crime, Vol. 20. Gomez, Manny, ed. 2016. (Crime & Detection Ser.). (Illus.). 96p. (J). (gr. 7). 24.95 *(978-1-4222-3483-9(5))* Mason Crest.

Lankford, Ronald D. & Lankford, Ronald D., Jr., eds. Organized Crime, 1 vol. 2009. (Issues on Trial Ser.). (ENG., Illus.). 184p. (gr. 10-12). 43.78 *(978-0-7377-4180-3(5)*, c2a987df-9361-4562-bc50-5d6aecb75b64, Greenhaven Publishing) Greenhaven Publishing LLC.

Loh-Hagan, Virginia. Yakuza vs. Mafia. 2019. (Battle Royale: Lethal Warriors Ser.). (ENG., Illus.). 32p. (J). (gr. 4-8). pap. 14.21 *(978-1-5341-5055-3(2)*, 213527); lib. bdg. 32.07 *(978-1-5341-4769-0(1)*, 213526) Cherry Lake Publishing. (45th Parallel Press).

RACKETEERING—FICTION

Campbell, Isaiah. The Struggles of Johnny Cannon. 2015. 322p. (J). pap. *(978-1-4814-2632-9(X)*, Simon & Schuster Bks. For Young Readers) Simon & Schuster Bks. For Young Readers.

Estep, Jennifer. Bright Blaze of Magic. 2016. (Black Blade Ser.: 3). (ENG.). 320p. (YA). (gr. 9). pap. 18.00 *(978-1-61773-828-9(X))* Kensington Publishing Corp.

Green, Tim. Deep Zone. 2012. (Football Genius Ser.: 5). (J). lib. bdg. 17.20 *(978-0-606-26854-7(5))* Turtleback.

Hale, Bruce. Murder, My Tweet. 2005. (Chet Gecko Mystery Ser.). (Illus.). 117p. (gr. 3-7). 16.00 *(978-0-7569-5248-8(4))* Perfection Learning Corp.

Higgins, Jack & Richards, Justin. Death Run. 2009. (ENG.). 288p. (YA). (gr. 7-18). 8.99 *(978-0-14-241475-0(1)*, Speak) Penguin Young Readers Group.

Korman, Gordon. Son of the Mob. rev. ed. 2017. (ENG.). 240p. (J). (gr. 7-17). pap. 13.99 *(978-1-4847-9845-4(7))* Little, Brown Bks. for Young Readers.

Larbalestier, Justine. Razorhurst. 2016. (ENG.). 336p. (YA). (gr. 9). pap. 10.99 *(978-1-61695-625-7(9)*, Soho Teen) Soho Pr., Inc.

Maetani, Valynne. Ink & Ashes, 1 vol. 2015. (ENG.). 368p. (YA). (gr. 7-12). 19.95 *(978-1-62014-211-0(2)*, leelowtu, Tu Bks.) Lee & Low Bks., Inc.

Maher, Allison. I, the Spy. 2006. (ENG.). 180p. (J). (gr. 4-7). per. 13.95 *(978-1-897235-04-1(6))* Thistledown Pr., Ltd. CAN. Dist: Univ. of Toronto Pr.

Moore, Graeme. Ruin. 2009. (ENG.). 240p. pap. 21.50 *(978-1-4092-8737-7(8))* Lulu Pr., Inc.

Rylander, Chris. The Fourth Stall Part III, Pt. 3. 2014. (Fourth Stall Ser.: 3). (ENG.). 320p. (J). (gr. 3-7). pap. 7.99 *(978-0-06-212006-9(9)*, Walden Pond Pr.) HarperCollins Pubs.

Zevin, Gabrielle. Because It Is My Blood: A Novel. 2013. (Birthright Ser.: 2). (ENG.). 384p. (YA). (gr. 7). pap. 19.99 *(978-1-250-03422-9(1)*, 900120595) Square Fish.

RADAR

Gregory, Josh. From Bats to... Radar. 2012. (21st Century Skills Innovation Library: Innovations from Nature Ser.). (ENG.). 32p. (gr. 4-8). pap. 14.21 *(978-1-61080-670-1(0)*, 202280); (Illus.). 32.07 *(978-1-61080-496-7(1)*, 202106) Cherry Lake Publishing.

On the Radar: Defend & Protect: Spring 2012 New Releases. 2012. (On the Radar: Defend & Protect Ser.). 32p. (gr. 4-8). lib. bdg. 106.40 *(978-0-7613-8898-2(2)*, Lerner Pubns.) Lerner Publishing Group.

On the Radar: Street Style: Spring 2012 New Releases. 2012. (On the Radar: Street Style Ser.). 32p. (gr. 4-8). lib. bdg. 106.40 *(978-0-7613-8899-9(0)*, Lerner Pubns.) Lerner Publishing Group.

Prentzas, G. S. Radar Guns. 2009. (21st Century Skills Library: Global Products Ser.). (ENG., Illus.). 32p. (gr. 4-8). lib. bdg. 32.07 *(978-1-60279-507-5(X)*, 200322) Cherry Lake Publishing.

Zelon, Helen. The Endeavor SRTM: Mapping the Earth. 2009. (Space Missions Ser.). 24p. (gr. 3-4). 42.50 *(978-1-60853-118-9(X)*, PowerKids Pr.) Rosen Publishing Group, Inc., The.

RADIATION

see also Light; Quantum Theory; Radioactivity; Sound; X-Rays

Allman, Toney. Radiation Sickness, 1 vol. 2013. (Diseases & Disorders Ser.). (ENG., Illus.). 104p. (gr. 7-7). lib. bdg. 41.53 *(978-1-4205-0900-7(4)*, 8ce6912d-f961-417b-8e53-a861cb64f5b9, Lucent Pr.) Greenhaven Publishing LLC.

American Cancer Society Staff. Mission: Sunwise (Story Book) Sunwise (Story Book) Environmental Protection Agency (US), ed. 2010. (ENG., Illus.). 13p. (gr. 4). 4.00 *(978-0-16-085823-9(2)*, Environmental Protection Agency) United States Government Printing Office.

Gastineau, John. Nuclear Radiation with Vernier. 2008. (YA). spiral bd. 25.00 *(978-1-929075-54-6(5))* Vernier Software & Technology.

Greeley, August. Fallout: Nuclear Disasters in Our World. 2009. (Man-Made Disasters Ser.). 24p. (gr. 3-3). 42.50 *(978-1-61514-348-1(3)*, PowerKids Pr.) Rosen Publishing Group, Inc., The.

Jankowski, Connie. All about Light & Sound, 1 vol. rev. ed. 2007. (Science: Informational Text Ser.). (ENG.). 32p. (J). (gr. 3-6). pap. 12.99 *(978-0-7439-0579-4(2))* Teacher Created Materials, Inc.

Solway, Andrew. Exploring Sound, Light, & Radiation, 1 vol. 2007. (Exploring Physical Science Ser.). (ENG., Illus.). 48p. (YA). (gr. 6-6). lib. bdg. 34.47 *(978-1-4042-3746-9(1)*, 00bfa945-8d0e-4dbe-832a-882598e802ba) Rosen Publishing Group, Inc., The.

Woodford, Chris. Light & Radiation. 2004. (Routes of Science Ser.). (Illus.). 40p. (J). (gr. 4-7). 24.95 *(978-1-4103-0297-7(0)*, Blackbirch Pr., Inc.) Cengage Gale.

RADIATION CHEMISTRY

see Radiochemistry

RADICALISM

see also Radicals

Doyle, Eamon, ed. Political Extremism in the United States, 1 vol. 2018. (Current Controversies Ser.). (ENG.). 200p. (J). (gr. 10-12). pap. 33.00 *(978-1-5345-0311-3(0)*, 314046f5-72c8-4394-8036-1639b077063c, Greenhaven Publishing) Greenhaven Publishing LLC.

Jones, Grace. Terrorism & Extremism. 2018. (Our Values - Level 3 Ser.). (Illus.). 32p. (J). (gr. 5-6). *(978-0-7787-5199-1(6))* Crabtree Publishing Co.
Merino, Noël, ed. Extremism, 1 vol. 2014. (Global Viewpoints Ser.). (ENG., Illus.). 240p. (gr. 10-12). 47.83 *(978-0-7377-6908-1(4),* d7538682-5809-47ed-b88a-5689e19cbbe5, Greenhaven Publishing) Greenhaven Publishing LLC.
Perritano, John. Radical Republicans: The Struggle for Equality. 2008. (Graphic America Ser.). (ENG., Illus.). 32p. (J). (gr. 3-6). lib. bdg. *(978-0-7787-4187-9(7))* Crabtree Publishing Co.

RADICALS

see also Reformers; Revolutions; Right and Left (Political Science)

Dheirg, Iosold. The Story of Michael Collins for Children. 2017. (ENG.). 140p. (J). pap. 10.99 *(978-1-78117-491-3(1))* Mercier Pr., Ltd., The IRL. Dist: Casemate Pubs. & Bk. Distributors, LLC.
Higgins, Melissa. Julian Assange: WikiLeaks Founder, 1 vol. 2011. (Essential Lives Set 7 Ser.). (ENG., Illus.). 112p. (YA). (gr. 6-12). lib. bdg. 41.36 *(978-1-61783-001-3(1),* 6741, Essential Library) ABDO Publishing Co.
Robinson, C. L. MATH1on1 Radicals Foundation. 2006. (YA). per. 9.99 *(978-0-9786767-8-0(5))* Robinson, Consuelo.

RADIO

Bonner, Richard. The Boy Inventors' Radio Telephone. 2018. (ENG., Illus.). 164p. (YA). (gr. 7-12). pap. *(978-93-5297-257-9(0))* Alpha Editions.
—Boy Inventors Radio Telephone. 2006. 27.95 *(978-1-4218-3004-9(3));* pap. 12.95 *(978-1-4218-3104-6(X))* 1st World Publishing, Inc.
Brooks, Philip. Radio. 2008. (21st Century Skills Innovation Library: Innovation in Entertainment Ser.). (ENG., Illus.). 32p. (gr. 4-8). lib. bdg. 32.07 *(978-1-60279-217-3(8),* 200148) Cherry Lake Publishing.
Fedunkiw, Marianne. Inventing the Radio. 2007. (Breakthrough Inventions Ser.). (ENG., Illus.). 32p. (J). (gr. 3-7). lib. bdg. *(978-0-7787-2817-7(X));* pap. *(978-0-7787-2839-9(0))* Crabtree Publishing Co.
Kulling, Monica. Making Contact! Marconi Goes Wireless. Rudnicki, Richard, illus. (Great Idea Ser.: 5). 32p. (J). (gr. k-3). 2016. pap. 6.99 *(978-1-101-91842-5(X))* 2013. 17.95 *(978-1-77049-378-0(6))* Tundra Bks. CAN. (Tundra Bks.). Dist: Penguin Random Hse. LLC.
Mattern, Joanne. The Radio: The World Tunes In. 2009. (Technology That Changed the World Ser.). 24p. (gr. 2-3). 42.50 *(978-1-60853-277-3(1),* PowerKids Pr.) Rosen Publishing Group, Inc., The.
Radios, Phones & Telecommunications. 2005. (Inventions Ser.). (Illus.). 30p. (J). pap. 15.95 incl. audio *(978-0-9724983-4-0(6))* Jazwares Distribution, Inc.
Smibert, Angie. 12 Great Moments That Changed Radio History. 2015. (Great Moments in Media Ser.). (ENG., Illus.). 32p. (J). (gr. 3-6). 32.80 *(978-1-63235-026-8(2),* 11596, 12-Story Library) Bookstaves, LLC.
Zannos, Susan. Guglielmo Marconi & Radio Waves. 2004. (Uncharted, Unexplored, & Unexplained Ser.). (Illus.). 48p. (J). (gr. 4-8). lib. bdg. 29.95 *(978-1-58415-265-1(6))* Mitchell Lane Pubs.

RADIO—BROADCASTING

see Radio Broadcasting

RADIO—OPERATORS

see Radio Operators

RADIO ASTRONOMY

see also names of celestial radio sources, e.g. Quasars

Firestone, Mary. SETI Scientist. 2005. (Weird Careers in Science Ser.). (ENG., Illus.). 88p. (gr. 5-8). lib. bdg. 25.00 *(978-0-7910-8701-5(8),* P114396, Facts On File) Infobase Holdings, Inc.
Gitlin, Marty. The Fast Telescope. 2018. lib. bdg. 29.95 *(978-1-68020-164-2(6))* Mitchell Lane Pubs.
Jefferis, David. Star Spotters: Telescopes & Observatories. 2008. (Exploring Our Solar System Ser.). (ENG., Illus.). 32p. (J). (gr. 3-8). lib. bdg. *(978-0-7787-3725-4(X))* Crabtree Publishing Co.

RADIO BROADCASTING

see also Television Broadcasting

Anniss, Matt. Dj-Ing, 1 vol. 2010. (Master This! Ser.). (ENG.). 32p. (J). (gr. 4-4). lib. bdg. 28.93 *(978-1-61532-596-2(4),* 349f1c1d-d343-4527-8e6c-9ac27bd8673f, PowerKids Pr.) Rosen Publishing Group, Inc., The.
Connolly, Sean. Television & Radio. 2009. (Getting the Message Ser.). (ENG.). 48p. (J). (gr. 6-10). 34.25 *(978-1-59920-350-8(2),* 19272, Smart Apple Media) Black Rabbit Bks.
McCarthy, Meghan. Aliens Are Coming! The True Account of the 1938 War of the Worlds Radio Broadcast. 2009. 40p. (J). (gr. -1-2). pap. 8.99 *(978-0-385-73678-7(9),* Dragonfly Bks.) Random Hse. Children's Bks.
Publishing, Ferguson, creator. Broadcasting. 2nd rev. ed. 2003. (Ferguson's Careers in Focus Ser.). (ENG.). 192p. (gr. 6-12). 29.95 *(978-0-89434-440-4(4),* P053176, Ferguson Publishing Company) Infobase Holdings, Inc.
Smibert, Angie. 12 Great Moments That Changed Radio History. 2015. (Great Moments in Media Ser.). (ENG., Illus.). 32p. (J). (gr. 3-6). 32.80 *(978-1-63235-026-8(2),* 11596); pap. 9.95 *(978-1-63235-086-2(6),* 11600) Bookstaves, LLC. (12-Story Library).
Teitelbaum, Michael. Sports Broadcasting. 2008. (21st Century Skills Innovation Library: Innovation in Entertainment Ser.). (ENG., Illus.). 32p. (gr. 4-8). lib. bdg. 32.07 *(978-1-60279-216-6(X),* 200147) Cherry Lake Publishing.
Walters, John. Sports Broadcasting, Vol. 10. Ferrer, Al, ed. 2015. (Careers off the Field Ser.). (Illus.). 64p. (J). (gr. 7). 23.95 *(978-1-4222-3271-2(9))* Mason Crest.

RADIO BROADCASTING—BIOGRAPHY

Howell, Dan & Lester, Phil. Dan & Phil Go Outside. 2016. (ENG., Illus.). 224p. (YA). (gr. 7). 19.99 *(978-1-5247-0145-1(9),* Random Hse. Bks. for Young Readers) Random Hse. Children's Bks.
Pezzi, Bryan. David Suzuki: Ma Vie. Karvonen, Tanjah, tr. from ENG. 2011. (FRE., Illus.). 24p. (YA). (gr. 2-4). *(978-1-77071-429-8(4))* Weigl Educational Pubs. Ltd.

RADIO CHEMISTRY

see Radiochemistry

RADIO JOURNALISM

see Journalism; Radio Broadcasting

RADIO OPERATORS

Broderick, Kevin Joyce. The JipiJapa Hat. 2007. 124p. per. 12.95 *(978-0-595-45071-8(7))* iUniverse, Inc.

RADIO OPERATORS—FICTION

Chapman, Allen. The Radio Boys' First Wireless: Or, Winning the Ferberton Prize. 2017. (ENG., Illus.). (J). 22.95 *(978-1-374-82824-7(6))* Capital Communications, Inc.
—The Radio Boys' First Wireless; or, Winning the Ferberton Prize. 2007. 100p. per. *(978-1-4068-4516-7(7))* Echo Library.

RADIO TELESCOPES

Gitlin, Marty. The Fast Telescope. 2018. lib. bdg. 29.95 *(978-1-68020-164-2(6))* Mitchell Lane Pubs.

RADIOACTIVE SUBSTANCES

see Radioactivity

RADIOACTIVE WASTES

Bell, Samantha S. How Can We Reduce Nuclear Pollution? 2016. (Searchlight Books (tm) — What Can We Do about Pollution? Ser.). (ENG., Illus.). 40p. (J). (gr. 3-5). lib. bdg. 30.65 *(978-1-4677-9516-6(X),* 808d71a5-1a98-40ab-85e3-0895d4366c93, Lerner Pubns.) Lerner Publishing Group.
Friedman, Lauri S., ed. Nuclear Power, 1 vol. 2009. (Introducing Issues with Opposing Viewpoints Ser.). (ENG., Illus.). 144p. (gr. 7-10). 43.63 *(978-0-7377-4482-8(0),* 882707e8-089a-4c94-bcb6-df1312a9a5f6, Greenhaven Publishing) Greenhaven Publishing LLC.
Jakubiak, David J. What Can We Do about Nuclear Waste? (Illus.). 24p. 2012. (J). 49.50 *(978-1-4488-5115-7(7),* PowerKids Pr.) 2011. (ENG., (J). (gr. 2-3). pap. 9.25 *(978-1-4488-5114-0(9),* 66ed02f8-fae5-4874-b22b-50a219072878, PowerKids Pr.) 2011. (ENG., (YA). (gr. 2-3). lib. bdg. 26.27 *(978-1-4488-4983-3(7),* 739b604f-73c0-45f5-a6b2-4f54858a6513) Rosen Publishing Group, Inc., The.
Kiesbye, Stefan, ed. Nuclear & Toxic Waste, 1 vol. 2010. (At Issue Ser.). (ENG., Illus.). 120p. (gr. 10-12). 41.03 *(978-0-7377-4681-5(5),* a7c01785-5ebc-4ad6-9f5e-71c7bca62191); pap. 28.80 *(978-0-7377-4682-2(3),* f997f535-a232-42fc-ba15-78306897a53f) Greenhaven Publishing LLC. (Greenhaven Publishing).

RADIOACTIVITY

see also Electrons; Nuclear Physics; Radiochemistry; Uranium; X-Rays

Barton, Chris. The Day-Glo Brothers: The True Story of Bob & Joe Switzer's Bright Ideas & Brand-New Colors. Persiani, Tony, illus. 2009. (ENG.). 44p. (J). (gr. 2-5). 21.99 *(978-1-57091-673-1(X))* Charlesbridge Publishing, Inc.
Dolz, Jordi Bayarri. Marie Curie & Radioactivity. Dolz, Jordi Bayarri, illus. 2020. (Graphic Science Biographies Ser.). (ENG., Illus.). 40p. (J). (gr. 5-8). 30.65 *(978-1-5415-7821-0(X),* 68139cfc-89c0-492f-83f1-2cc1d24524ae, Graphic Universe™) Lerner Publishing Group.
Idzikowski, Lisa. Pierre & Marie Curie: The Couple Who Pioneered Radioactivity Research. 2019. (J). pap. *(978-1-9785-1461-4(1))* Enslow Publishing, LLC.
Jackson, Tom. Radioactive Elements, 1 vol. 2007. (Elements Ser.). (ENG., Illus.). 32p. (gr. 4-4). lib. bdg. 31.21 *(978-0-7614-1923-5(3),* 2d3a69a6-89ac-414a-90ce-eea7b07bdb45) Cavendish Square Publishing LLC.
Lin, Yoming S. The Curies & Radioactivity, 1 vol. 2011. (Eureka! Ser.). (ENG., Illus.). 24p. (YA). (gr. 2-3). lib. bdg. 26.27 *(978-1-4488-5033-4(9),* d43d97f6-388e-4142-b041-debbe22dca81) Rosen Publishing Group, Inc., The.
Meltzer, Brad. I Am Marie Curie. Eliopoulos, Christopher, illus. 2019. (Ordinary People Change the World Ser.). 40p. (J). (gr. k-4). 16.99 *(978-0-525-55585-8(4),* Dial Bks) Penguin Young Readers Group.
O'Quinn, Amy M. Marie Curie for Kids: Her Life & Scientific Discoveries, with 21 Activities & Experiments. 2016. (For Kids Ser.: 65). (ENG., Illus.). 144p. (J). (gr. 4). pap. 18.99 *(978-1-61373-320-2(8))* Chicago Review Pr., Inc.
Tracy, Kathleen. Pierre & Marie Curie & the Discovery of Radium. 2004. (Uncharted, Unexplored, & Unexplained Ser.). (Illus.). 48p. (J). (gr. 4-8). lib. bdg. 29.95 *(978-1-58415-310-8(5))* Mitchell Lane Pubs.

RADIOCARBON DATING

Duling, Kaitlyn. Carbon Dating, 1 vol. 2018. (Great Discoveries in Science Ser.). (ENG.). 128p. (YA). (gr. 9-9). lib. bdg. 47.36 *(978-1-5026-4383-4(9),* da2a2b68-cf3d-4907-b241-d9f25b5edf04) Cavendish Square Publishing LLC.

RADIOCHEMISTRY

Jackson, Tom. Radioactive Elements, 1 vol. 2007. (Elements Ser.). (ENG., Illus.). 32p. (gr. 4-4). lib. bdg. 31.21 *(978-0-7614-1923-5(3),* 2d3a69a6-89ac-414a-90ce-eea7b07bdb45) Cavendish Square Publishing LLC.

RADIOGRAPHY

see X-Rays

RADISSON, PIERRE ESPRIT, APPROXIMATELY 1636-1710

Bailey, Katharine. Radisson & des Groseilliers: Fur Traders of the North. 2006. (In the Footsteps of Explorers Ser.). (ENG., Illus.). 32p. (J). (gr. 3-7). lib. bdg. *(978-0-7787-2422-3(0),* 1253444); (gr. 4-7). pap. *(978-0-7787-2458-2(1),* 1253444) Crabtree Publishing Co.

RAILROAD CONSTRUCTION

see Railroad Engineering

RAILROAD ENGINEERING

Kallen, Stuart. The Chunnel. 2014. (Great Idea Ser.). (ENG., Illus.). 48p. (J). (gr. 4-6). pap. 13.26 *(978-1-60357-576-8(6))* Norwood Hse. Pr.
Kallen, Stuart A. The Chunnel. 2014. (Great Idea Ser.). (ENG., Illus.). 48p. (J). (gr. 4-6). lib. bdg. 26.60 *(978-1-59953-596-8(3))* Norwood Hse. Pr.
Otfinoski, Steven. High-Speed Trains: from Concept to Consumer (Calling All Innovators: a Career for You) (Library Edition) 2015. (Calling All Innovators: a Career for You Ser.). (ENG.). 64p. (J). (gr. 5-8). lib. bdg. 32.00 *(978-0-531-21899-0(6),* Children's Pr.) Scholastic Library Publishing.

RAILROAD STATIONS

Williams, Dinah. Creepy Stations. 2013. (Scary Places Ser.). 32p. (J). (gr. 4-8). lib. bdg. 28.50 *(978-1-61772-749-8(0))* Bearport Publishing Co., Inc.
Wing, Natasha. When Jackie Saved Grand Central: The True Story of Jacqueline Kennedy's Fight for an American Icon. Boiger, Alexandra, illus. 2017. (ENG.). 48p. (J). (gr. 1-4). 17.99 *(978-0-547-44921-0(6),* 1435124, Clarion Bks.) HarperCollins Pubs.

RAILROADS

see also Freight and Freightage; Railroad Engineering; Subways

Amery, Heather & Doherty, Gillian. Wind-up Train Book. 2008. (Wind-up Bks). 14p. (J). bds. 29.99 *(978-0-7945-2192-9(4),* Usborne) EDC Publishing.
Bender, Lionel. Trains & Trams. 2006. (On the Move Ser.). *(978-1-59389-269-2(1))* Chrysalis Education.
Bone, Emily. Trains. 2011. (Beginner's Science Ser.). 32p. (J). ring bd. 4.99 *(978-0-7945-3112-6(1),* Usborne) EDC Publishing.
Brian, marion. Rolling down the Avenue, 1 vol. Lindsley, Jennifer, illus. 2016. (ENG.). 32p. (J). pap. 9.95 *(978-1-4556-2179-8(X),* Pelican Publishing) Arcadia Publishing.
Brooks, Felicity. Trains lift & Look. Litchfield, Jo, illus. 2005. 12p. (J). 9.99 *(978-0-7945-0935-4(5),* Usborne) EDC Publishing.
Burch, Lynda S. Wicky Wacky Things that Go! Trains 1. Burch, Lynda S., photos by. 2004. (Illus.). 16p. (J). E-Book 9.95 incl. cd-rom *(978-1-933090-02-3(2))* Guardian Angel Publishing, Inc.
Carroll, Colleen. How Artists See Jr. - Trains. 2008. (How Artists See Jr Ser.: 2). (ENG., Illus.). 18p. (J). (gr. -1-k). bds. 7.95 *(978-0-7892-0971-9(3),* 790971, Abbeville Kids) Abbeville Pr., Inc.
Chiu, David. Government Regulation of the Railroads: Fighting Unfair Trade Practices in America, 1 vol. (Progressive Movement 1900 - 1920: Efforts to Reform America's New Industrial Society Ser.). (ENG., Illus.). 32p. 2006. (YA). (gr. 3-4). lib. bdg. 30.47 *(978-1-4042-0190-3(4),* 1a29fdb6-5892-431d-ad05-1fcd0a656a64) 2005. (gr. 4-5). pap. 10.00 *(978-1-4042-0849-0(6),* 5c6b79a1-9c0d-4515-b7c1-7feafc08af7d) Rosen Publishing Group, Inc., The.
Clapper, Nikki Bruno. High-Speed Trains. 2015. (All Aboard! Ser.). (ENG., Illus.). 24p. (J). (gr. -1-2). lib. bdg. 27.32 *(978-1-4914-6039-9(3),* 128953, Capstone Pr.) Capstone.
Colby, Jennifer. Kingfishers to Bullet Trains. 2019. (21st Century Junior Library: Tech from Nature Ser.). (ENG.). 24p. (J). (gr. 2-5). pap. 12.79 *(978-1-5341-3949-7(4),* 212625) Cherry Lake Publishing.
Corrigan, Kathleen. Building a Nation. 2016. (Canada Through Time Ser.). (ENG., Illus.). 32p. (J). (gr. 3-5). lib. bdg. 32.65 *(978-1-4109-8120-2(7),* 131009, Raintree) Capstone.
Cullis, Megan. Big Book of Big Trains. 2013. (Big Bks). 16p. (J). ring bd. 14.99 *(978-0-7945-3378-6(7),* Usborne) EDC Publishing.
Dieker, Wendy Strobel. Los Trenes. 2019. (Máquinas Poderosas Ser.). (SPA.). 16p. (J). (gr. -1-2). *(978-1-68151-888-6(0),* 10833) Amicus.
DiSiena, Laura Lyn & Eliot, Hannah. Trains Can Float: And Other Fun Facts. Oswald, Pete & Spurgeon, Aaron, illus. 2014. (Did You Know? Ser.). (ENG.). 32p. (J). (gr. -1-3). 17.99 *(978-1-4814-0281-1(1),* Little Simon) Little Simon.
DK. The Big Book of Trains. 2016. (DK Big Bks.). (ENG., Illus.). 32p. (J). (gr. k-4). 17.99 *(978-1-4654-5361-7(X),* DK Children) Dorling Kindersley Publishing, Inc.
Donahue, Peter. All Aboard! Trains Stained Glass Coloring Book. 2011. (Dover Planes Trains Automobiles Coloring Ser.). (ENG., Illus.). 32p. (J). (gr. -1-2). pap. 6.99 *(978-0-486-47896-8(3),* 478963) Dover Pubns., Inc.
Dubowski, Mark. Superfast Trains. 2005. (Ultimate Speed Ser.). (Illus.). 32p. (J). (gr. 3-6). lib. bdg. 25.27 *(978-1-59716-084-1(9))* Bearport Publishing Co., Inc.
Dyan, Penelope. Steam Train! All the Way to Canterbury, England. Weigand, John D., photos by. 2011. (Illus.). 40p. pap. 11.95 *(978-1-935630-75-3(X))* Bellissima Publishing, LLC.
Emberley, Ed. Ed Emberley's Drawing Book of Trucks & Trains. Emberley, Ed, illus. 2005. (ENG., Illus.). 32p. (J). (gr. 2-17). pap. 8.99 *(978-0-316-78967-7(4))* Little, Brown Bks. for Young Readers.
Gertsberg, Inna. The Way Downtown: Adventures in Public Transit. Lowery, Mike, illus. 2017. (ENG.). 44p. (J). (gr. -1-3). 17.99 *(978-1-77138-552-7(9))* Kids Can Pr., Ltd. CAN. Dist: Hachette Bk. Group.
Gibbons, Gail. Trains. 2019. (Illus.). 24p. (J). (— 1). bds. 7.99 *(978-0-8234-4169-3(5))* Holiday Hse., Inc.
Goodman, Steve. The Train They Call the City of New Orleans. McCurdy, Michael, illus. pap. incl. audio *(978-1-59112-901-1(X));* pap. 18.95 incl. audio compact disk *(978-1-59112-903-5(6));* pap. 16.95 incl. audio *(978-1-59112-899-1(4));* pap. incl. audio compact disk *(978-1-59112-905-9(2))* Live Oak Media.
Goopar, Rocio Arvea. Ro & Otilo: The Magic Train. 2011. 36p. pap. 15.14 *(978-1-4634-1665-2(2))* AuthorHouse.
Graham, Ian. On the Rails. 2008. (QEB Machines at Work Ser.). (Illus.). 36p. (YA). (gr. 4-7). 19.95 *(978-1-59566-316-0(9))* QEB Publishing Inc.
Hammond Editors, ed. Trains. 2009. (Hammond Undercover Ser.). 72p. (J). (gr. 3-7). pap. 13.99 *(978-0-8416-1496-3(2))* Hammond World Atlas Corp.
Harris, Michael & Parker, Steve. Trains - Railways; Tunnels; Signals; Diesel; Steam: With 10 Easy-to-Do Experiments & 230 Exciting Pictures. 2016. (Illus.). 64p. (J). (gr. -1-12). 12.99 *(978-1-86147-489-6(X),* Armadillo) Anness Publishing GBR. Dist: National Bk. Network.
Higgins, Nadia. Trains / Trenes. Sánchez, Sr., illus. 2019. (Machines! / ¡Las Máquinas! Ser.). (MUL.). 24p. (J). (gr. -1-2). lib. bdg. 33.99 *(978-1-68410-341-6(X),* 140261) Cantata Learning.
Hill, Lee Sullivan. Trains on the Move. 2011. (Lightning Bolt Books Vroom-Vroom Ser.). 32p. pap. 45.32 *(978-0-7613-7620-0(8))* Lerner Publishing Group.
Hyde, Natalie. Transcontinental Railroads. 2017. (Uncovering the Past: Analyzing Primary Sources Ser.). 48p. (J). (gr. 5-6). *(978-0-7787-3941-8(4))* Crabtree Publishing Co.
Ikids Staff. Junior Groovies: Trains (Storybook, Fun Facts & Toys) Voltz, Ralph, illus. 2011. (ENG.). 10p. (J). (gr. -1-1). 12.99 *(978-1-60169-149-1(1))* Innovative Kids.
Isaacs, Sally Senzell. Stagecoaches & Railroads. 2012. (All about America Ser.). (ENG., Illus.). 32p. (J). (gr. 4-7). 26.19 *(978-0-7534-6696-4(1),* 9780753466964) Kingfisher Publications, plc GBR. Dist: Children's Plus, Inc.
Johnson, Jordan. How the Steam Engine Changed the World, 1 vol. 2018. (Inventions That Changed the World Ser.). (ENG.). 64p. (gr. 5-5). pap. 16.28 *(978-1-5026-4116-8(X),* 64ac1cb2-1e20-4b61-af4f-8524e51135ed) Cavendish Square Publishing LLC.
Kraft, Eric. The Transcontinental Railroad: Set Of 6. 2011. (Navigators Ser.). (J). pap. 48.00 net. *(978-1-4108-0436-5(4))* Benchmark Education Co.
Landers, Ace. I Am a Train. Migliari, Paola, illus. 2008. (ENG.). 8p. (J). (gr. -1 — 1). bds. 4.99 *(978-0-545-07962-4(4),* Cartwheel Bks.) Scholastic, Inc.
Langston-George, Rebecca. Orphan Trains: Taking the Rails to a New Life. 2016. (Encounter: Narrative Nonfiction Stories Ser.). (ENG., Illus.). 128p. (J). (gr. 3-6). pap. 6.95 *(978-1-62370-630-2(0),* 131148); lib. bdg. 31.32 *(978-1-4914-8551-4(5),* 131147) Capstone. (Capstone Young Readers).
Leighton, Christina. City Trains. 2017. (Amazing Trains Ser.). (ENG., Illus.). 24p. (J). (gr. k-3). lib. bdg. 26.95 *(978-1-62617-669-0(8),* Blastoff! Readers) Bellwether Media.
—Monorails. 2017. (Amazing Trains Ser.). (ENG., Illus.). 24p. (J). (gr. k-3). lib. bdg. 26.95 *(978-1-62617-672-0(8),* Blastoff! Readers) Bellwether Media.
Lindeen, Mary. Trains. 2007. (Mighty Machines Ser.). (ENG., Illus.). 24p. (J). (gr. k-3). lib. bdg. 26.95 *(978-1-60014-062-4(9))* Bellwether Media.
Matthews, John R. The Railroad. 2006. (Inventions That Shaped the World Ser.). (Illus.). 80p. (J). (gr. 5-8). 17.60 *(978-0-7569-6861-8(5))* Perfection Learning Corp.
—The Railroad. 2006. (Inventions That Shaped the World Ser.). (ENG., Illus.). 80p. (J). (gr. 5-8). per. 9.95 *(978-0-531-16745-8(3),* Watts, Franklin) Scholastic Library Publishing.
Mills, Cindy, illus. Cass Railroad Fun Book. 2007. 32p. (J). pap. 2.95 *(978-0-929915-74-6(7))* Headline Bks., Inc.
Murray, Julie. Trains, 1 vol. 2014. (Transportation Ser.). (ENG.). 24p. (J). (gr. -1-2). lib. bdg. 32.79 *(978-1-62970-082-3(7),* 1706, Abdo Kids) ABDO Publishing Co.
Nagelhout, Ryan. The Unofficial Guide to Building Railroads in Minecraft, 1 vol. 2018. (STEM Projects in Minecraft(r) Ser.). (ENG.). 24p. (J). (gr. 3-3). 25.27 *(978-1-5081-6933-8(0),* 4e3c73ac-81a3-4aa9-8ebe-c64d514ff735, PowerKids Pr.) Rosen Publishing Group, Inc., The.
Nelson, Jo. The Railway Revolution: Band 16/Sapphire (Collins Big Cat) 2016. (Collins Big Cat Ser.). (ENG.). 56p. (J). (gr. 4-5). pap. 12.99 *(978-0-00-816395-2(2))* HarperCollins Pubs. Ltd. GBR. Dist: Independent Pubs. Group.
Oczkus, Lori. Close Reading with Paired Texts, 1 vol. rev. ed. 2015. (Close Reading with Paired Texts). (ENG., Illus.). 128p. (gr. k-k). mass mkt. 24.99 *(978-1-4258-1356-7(9))* Shell Educational Publishing.
O'Mara, John. The Transcontinental Railroad, 1 vol. 2019. (Look at U. S. History Ser.). (ENG.). 32p. (gr. 2-2). pap. 11.50 *(978-1-5382-4887-4(5),* 13648f6a-ab29-4900-b9e1-6d709a35c7fe) Stevens, Gareth Publishing LLLP.
Parker, Lewis K. Cornelius Vanderbilt & the Railroad Industry. 2009. (American Tycoons Ser.). 24p. (gr. 3-3). 42.50 *(978-1-61511-389-7(4),* PowerKids Pr.) Rosen Publishing Group, Inc., The.
Peters, Elisa. Let's Ride the Streetcar! 2014. (Public Transportation Ser.). 24p. (J). (gr. k-2). pap. 49.50 *(978-1-4777-6513-5(1),* PowerKids Pr.) Rosen Publishing Group, Inc., The.
—¡Vamos a Tomar el Tranvía! / Let's Ride the Streetcar!, 1 vol. de la Vega, Eida, ed. 2014. (Transporte Público / Public Transportation Ser.). (SPA & ENG.). 24p. (J). (gr. 1-2). 25.27 *(978-1-4777-6779-5(7),* 830ed458-f9ed-413d-9aff-34c977d56703, PowerKids Pr.) Rosen Publishing Group, Inc., The.
Prior, Jennifer. All Aboard! How Trains Work, 1 vol. 2nd rev. ed. 2011. (TIME for KIDS(r): Informational Text Ser.). (ENG.). 28p. (gr. 3-4). pap. 11.99 *(978-1-4333-3656-0(1))* Teacher Created Materials, Inc.
Rajczak, Michael. The Transcontinental Railroad, 1 vol., Vol. 1. 2013. (What You Didn't Know about History Ser.). (ENG., Illus.). 24p. (J). (gr. 2-3). 25.27 *(978-1-4824-0600-9(4),* 7acf73a1-4ad9-461e-a523-2d300a808728) Stevens, Gareth Publishing LLLP.
Rice, Dona. King's Cross: Partición de Figuras. rev. ed. 2019. (Mathematics in the Real World Ser.). (SPA., Illus.). 24p. (J). (gr. 1-2). pap. 9.99 *(978-1-4258-2856-1(6))* Teacher Created Materials, Inc.
Rickards, Lynne. My First Train Trip. Honor Roberts, Ley, illus. 2016. (Cambridge Reading Adventures Ser.). (ENG.). 16p. pap. 7.95 *(978-1-107-57594-3(X))* Cambridge Univ. Pr.
Riggs, Kate. Bullet Trains. 2010. (Now That's Fast! Ser.). 24p. (J). (gr. -1-3). 16.95 *(978-1-58341-911-3(X),* Creative Education) Creative Co., The.
Rottman, Gordon L. The Most Daring Raid of the Civil War: The Great Locomotive Chase, 1 vol. 2011. (Most Daring Raids in History Ser.). (ENG., Illus.). 64p. (YA). (gr. 7-7). 37.13 *(978-1-4488-1870-9(2),* 39516277-a6d8-4cc8-a833-62e9509030a5) Rosen Publishing Group, Inc., The.
Roza, Greg. The Incredible Story of Trains. 2009. (Kid's Guide to Incredible Technology Ser.). 24p. (gr. 3-4). 42.50 *(978-1-61511-175-6(1),* PowerKids Pr.) Rosen Publishing Group, Inc., The.
Ryan, Phillip. Freight Trains, 1 vol. 2010. (All Aboard! Ser.). (ENG.). 24p. (J). (gr. 1-2). pap. 9.25 *(978-1-4488-1211-0(9),* 93aca36b-0779-49b4-85d6-a19e4adec0ab); lib. bdg. 26.27 *(978-1-4488-0635-5(6),*

7b43ea8d-fe91-444c-bfb6-c5599a15af9f) Rosen Publishing Group, Inc., The.
—Monorails, 1 vol. 2010. (All Aboard! Ser.). (ENG.). 24p. (J). (gr. 1-2). pap. 9.25 *(978-1-4488-1217-2(8),* 1ae031f4-4214-4d15-bb71-dc310ac7d242); lib. bdg. 26.27 *(978-1-4488-0638-6(0),* 1f3611fa-d3bb-4420-bf45-a8cdb7e0a373) Rosen Publishing Group, Inc., The.
—Steam-Powered Trains, 1 vol. 2010. (All Aboard! Ser.). (ENG.). 24p. (J). (gr. 1-2). pap. 9.25 *(978-1-4488-1221-9(6),* 2b876c6a-dfb5-4a51-9113-1b4fd29190dc); lib. bdg. 26.27 *(978-1-4488-0640-9(2),* 11b05c4f-7b64-4e3d-8b93-fbc1a15bebc0) Rosen Publishing Group, Inc., The. (PowerKids Pr.).
—Streetcars, 1 vol. 2010. (All Aboard! Ser.). (ENG.). 24p. (J). (gr. 1-2). pap. 9.25 *(978-1-4488-1219-6(4),* 18006418-ef69-4a1d-a6e2-a62b64e05964); lib. bdg. 26.27 *(978-1-4488-0639-3(9),* 7ceb3945-f60e-4300-859f-c7c767011e59) Rosen Publishing Group, Inc., The. (PowerKids Pr.).
Schumacher, Cassandra. Cornelius Vanderbilt: Railroad Tycoon, 1 vol. 2019. (Great American Entrepreneurs Ser.). (ENG.). 128p. (gr. 9-9). lib. bdg. 47.36 *(978-1-5026-4540-1(8),* 1b23f369-9dfd-4836-aa24-44b958aa9c09) Cavendish Square Publishing LLC.
Shea, Therese. Cornelius Vanderbilt & the Railroad Industry, 1 vol. 2016. (Great Entrepreneurs in U. S. History Ser.). (ENG., Illus.). 32p. (J). (gr. 5-5). pap. 12.75 *(978-1-4994-2119-4(2),* ce97aa07-0ca2-47e5-8225-3d205a299793, PowerKids Pr.) Rosen Publishing Group, Inc., The.
Shields, Amy. National Geographic Readers: Trains. 2011. (Readers Ser.). (Illus.). 32p. (J). (gr. -1-k). pap. 4.99 *(978-1-4263-0777-5(2),* National Geographic Kids) Disney Publishing Worldwide.
Simon, Seymour. Seymour Simon's Book of Trains. 2004. (ENG., Illus.). 40p. (J). (gr. -1-3). reprint ed. pap. 7.99 *(978-0-06-446223-5(4),* HarperCollins) HarperCollins Pubs.
Smith, A. G. Cut & Assemble an Old-Fashioned Train. 2010. (Dover Children's Activity Bks.). (ENG.). 40p. (J). (gr. 6-12). 11.95 *(978-0-486-25324-4(4))* Dover Pubns., Inc.
Smithyman, Kathryn & Kalman, Bobbie. Trains on the Tracks. 2007. (Vehicles on the Move Ser.). (ENG., Illus.). 32p. (J). (gr. 3-7). lib. bdg. *(978-0-7787-3045-3(X))* Crabtree Publishing Co.
Snedden, Robert. Railroads, 1 vol. 2016. (Engineering Eurekas Ser.). (ENG.). 32p. (J). (gr. 3-4). pap. 11.00 *(978-1-4994-3097-4(3),* b76c5eb4-bd20-44d2-8410-61d59db2ee1f, PowerKids Pr.) Rosen Publishing Group, Inc., The.
Spray, Sally. Awesome Engineering Trains, Planes, & Ships. 2018. (Awesome Engineering Ser.). (ENG., Illus.). 32p. (J). (gr. 3-6). pap. 8.10 *(978-1-5435-1342-4(5),* 137773); lib. bdg. 27.99 *(978-1-5435-1336-3(0),* 137767) Capstone. (Capstone Pr.).
St. Louis Union Station: A City Within a City. 2003. 19.95 *(978-0-9748109-0-4(8))* Market 1 Group Inc.
Stein, R. Conrad. The Incredible Transcontinental Railroad: Stories in American History, 1 vol. 2012. (Stories in American History Ser.). (ENG., Illus.). 128p. (gr. 5-6). pap. 13.88 *(978-1-4644-0026-1(1),* ae3c854b-3226-4b6e-824a-325e277f1da0) Enslow Publishing, LLC.
Stockland, Patricia M. Debugging: You Can Fix It! Sanchez, Sr., illus. 2018. (Code It! Ser.). (ENG.). 24p. (C). (gr. 1-3). lib. bdg. 33.99 *(978-1-68410-388-1(6),* 140361) Cantata Learning.
Stone, Kate, illus. ABC Train. 2013. (ENG.). 20p. (J). bds. 10.99 *(978-1-4494-3157-0(7))* Andrews McMeel Publishing.
Summers, Alex. Train. 2017. (Transportation & Me! Ser.). (ENG.). 24p. (gr. -1-1). pap. 9.95 *(978-1-68342-205-1(8),* 9781683422051) Rourke Educational Media.
Taplin, Sam. First Sticker Book Trains. 2013. (First Sticker Bks). 24p. (J). pap. 6.99 *(978-0-7945-3351-9(5),* Usborne) EDC Publishing.
Tiner, John Hudson. Trains. (Illus.). 32p. 2004. pap. 8.95 *(978-0-89812-391-3(7),* Creative Paperbacks) 2003. (J). lib. bdg. 18.95 *(978-1-58341-260-2(3),* Creative Education) Creative Co., The.
Trains. (Color & Learn Ser.). 36p. (J). (gr. 1-5). pap. *(978-1-882210-11-4(5))* Action Publishing, Inc.
Turnbull, S. Los Trenes. 2004. Orig. Title: Trains. (SPA.). (J). lib. bdg. 16.95 *(978-1-58086-500-5(3),* Usborne) EDC Publishing.
Wetterer, Margaret K. Kate Shelley y el Tren de Medianoche. Ritz, Karen, illus. 2005. (Yo Solo - Historia (on My Own - History) Ser.). Tr. of Kate Shelley & the Midnight Express. (SPA.). 48p. (J). (gr. 2-5). per. 6.95 *(978-0-8225-3193-7(3))* Lerner Publishing Group.
—Kate Shelley y el Tren de Medianoche (Kate Shelley & the Midnight Express) Ritz, Karen, illus. 2005. (Yo Solo: Historia (on My Own History) Ser.). (SPA.). 48p. (J). (gr. 2-4). lib. bdg. 25.32 *(978-0-8225-3096-1(1),* 8cc58a61-567f-42b1-b889-500883c52b83, Ediciones Lerner) Lerner Publishing Group.
Windmill Books & Windmill Books. Let's Look at Trains. 2009. (Let's Go! Ser.). (Illus.). 18p. (J). (gr. -1-k). bds. 12.75 *(978-1-60754-419-7(9))* Windmill Bks.
Wittmann, Kelly. Building the Transcontinental Railroad: Race of the Railroad Companies. 2017. (Great Race: Fight to the Finish Ser.). 48p. (gr. 4-5). pap. 84.30 *(978-1-5382-0804-5(0))* Stevens, Gareth Publishing LLLP.

RAILROADS—FICTION

Acosta, Daniel. Iron River, 1 vol. 2018. (ENG.). 224p. (YA). (gr. 9-12). 19.95 *(978-1-941026-93-9(1),* 23353382); pap. 13.95 *(978-1-941026-94-6(X),* 23353382) Lee & Low Bks., Inc. (Cinco Puntos Press).
Albout, Corrine & Mabire, Grégoire. All Aboard. 2011. (One by One Ser.). (Illus.). 14p. bds. *(978-1-84089-687-9(6))* Zero to Ten, Ltd.
Alger, Horatio. The Erie Train Boy. reprint ed. pap. 79.00 *(978-1-4047-3565-1(8))* Classic Textbooks.
Allcroft, Britt, et al. Thomas & the Buzzy Bees. 2017. (Illus.). 23p. (J). *(978-1-5182-3651-8(0))* Random Hse., Inc.
Amery, Heather. The Old Steam Train. Cartwright, Stephen, illus. rev. ed. 2007. (Farmyard Tales Readers Ser.). 16p. (J). (gr. -1-3). pap. 5.99 *(978-0-7945-0804-3(9),* Usborne) EDC Publishing.
—Rusty's Train Ride. Cartwright, Stephen, illus. rev. ed. 2007. (Farmyard Tales Readers Ser.). 16p. (J). (gr. -1-3). pap. 5.99 *(978-0-7945-0802-9(2),* Usborne) EDC Publishing.
Anna, Jennifer. Maxwell Dreams of Trains. Blue, Buster, illus. 2009. (ENG.). 88p. (J). 10.99 *(978-1-883573-05-8(X))* Blue Forge Pr.
Appleton, Victor. Tom Swift & His Electric Locomotive. 2005. 27.95 *(978-1-4218-1087-4(5));* 200p. pap. 12.95 *(978-1-4218-1187-1(1))* 1st World Publishing, Inc. (1st World Library - Literary Society).
—Tom Swift & His Electric Locomotive: Or Two Miles a Minute on the Rails. 2007. (ENG.). 136p. pap. 18.99 *(978-1-4346-1490-2(5))* Creative Media Partners, LLC.
—Tom Swift & His Electric Locomotive or. 2006. pap. *(978-1-4065-0899-4(3))* Dodo Pr.
Awdry, W. Busy, Busy Thomas (Thomas & Friends) Stubbs, Tommy, illus. 2013. (ENG.). 12p. (J). (— 1). bds. 5.99 *(978-0-449-81642-4(7),* Random Hse. Bks. for Young Readers) Random Hse. Children's Bks.
—A Crack in the Track (Thomas & Friends) 2004. (Bright & Early Board Books(TM) Ser.). (ENG., Illus.). 24p. (J). (— 1). bds. 4.99 *(978-0-375-82755-6(2),* Random Hse. Bks. for Young Readers) Random Hse. Children's Bks.
—Day of the Diesels (Thomas & Friends) Golden Books, illus. 2012. (Little Golden Book Ser.). (ENG.). 24p. (J). (gr. k-k). 5.99 *(978-0-307-92989-1(2),* Golden Bks.) Random Hse. Children's Bks.
—Fast Train, Slow Train (Thomas & Friends) 2014. (Big Bright & Early Board Book Ser.). (ENG., Illus.). 24p. (J). (— 1). bds. 6.99 *(978-0-385-37408-8(9),* Random Hse. Bks. for Young Readers) Random Hse. Children's Bks.
—Go, Go, Thomas! 2013. (Thomas & Friends 8X8 Ser.). lib. bdg. 14.75 *(978-0-606-26992-6(4))* Turtleback.
—The Good Sport. Courtney, Richard, illus. 2016. 24p. (J). *(978-1-5182-1481-3(9))* Random Hse., Inc.
—Hero of the Rails (Thomas & Friends) 2010. (Little Golden Book Ser.). (ENG., Illus.). 24p. (J). (gr. -1-k). 5.99 *(978-0-375-85950-2(0),* Golden Bks.) Random Hse. Children's Bks.
—The Lost Ship (Thomas & Friends) Courtney, Richard, illus. 2015. (Step into Reading Ser.). (ENG.). 32p. (J). (gr. -1-1). 5.99 *(978-0-553-52171-9(3),* Random Hse. Bks. for Young Readers) Random Hse. Children's Bks.
—Misty Island Rescue (Thomas & Friends) 2011. (Little Golden Book Ser.). (ENG., Illus.). 24p. (J). (gr. -1-k). 5.99 *(978-0-375-87212-9(4),* Golden Bks.) Random Hse. Children's Bks.
—Not So Fast, Bash & Dash! 2013. (Thomas & Friends Step into Reading Ser.). lib. bdg. 13.55 *(978-0-606-32228-7(0))* Turtleback.
—The Rocket Returns. 2014. (Thomas & Friends Step into Reading Ser.). lib. bdg. 13.55 *(978-0-606-35207-9(4))* Turtleback.
—Santa's Little Engine. 2014. (Thomas & Friends Step into Reading Ser.). lib. bdg. 13.55 *(978-0-606-36014-2(X))* Turtleback.
—Search & Rescue! (Thomas & Friends) Random House, illus. 2012. (Pictureback(R) Ser.). (ENG.). 16p. (J). (gr. -1-2). pap. 4.99 *(978-0-307-93029-3(7),* Random Hse. Bks. for Young Readers) Random Hse. Children's Bks.
—Secret of the Green Engine. 2012. (Thomas & Friends Step into Reading Ser.). lib. bdg. 13.55 *(978-0-606-26804-2(9))* Turtleback.
—Thomas' 123 Book. 2013. (Thomas & Friends 8X8 Ser.). lib. bdg. 13.55 *(978-0-606-26991-9(6))* Turtleback.
—Thomas & Friends: Blue Train, Green Train (Thomas & Friends) Stubbs, Tommy, illus. 2006. (Bright & Early Books(R) Ser.). (ENG.). 36p. (J). (gr. k-k). 9.99 *(978-0-375-83463-9(X),* Random Hse. Bks. for Young Readers) Random Hse. Children's Bks.
—Thomas & Friends: Blue Train, Green Train (Thomas & Friends) Stubbs, Tommy, illus. 2007. (Bright & Early Board Books(TM) Ser.). (ENG.). 24p. (J). (— 1). bds. 4.99 *(978-0-375-83984-9(4),* Random Hse. Bks. for Young Readers) Random Hse. Children's Bks.
—Thomas & Friends: My Red Railway Book Box (Thomas & Friends) Go, Train, GO!; Stop, Train, Stop!; a Crack in the Track!; & Blue Train, Green Train, 4 vols. Stubbs, Tommy, illus. 2008. (Bright & Early Board Books(TM) Ser.). (ENG.). 96p. (J). (— 1). bds. 16.99 *(978-0-375-84322-8(1),* Random Hse. Bks. for Young Readers) Random Hse. Children's Bks.
—Thomas & the Shark (Thomas & Friends) Courtney, Richard, illus. 2013. (Step into Reading Ser.). (ENG.). 32p. (J). (gr. -1-1). pap. 5.99 *(978-0-307-98200-1(9),* Random Hse. Bks. for Young Readers) Random Hse. Children's Bks.
—Thomas & the Volcano. 2015. (Thomas & Friends Step into Reading Ser.). lib. bdg. 14.75 *(978-0-606-36404-1(8))* Turtleback.
—Thomas' Big Book of Beginner Books (Thomas & Friends) Random House, illus. 2013. (Beginner Books(R) Ser.). (ENG.). 224p. (J). (gr. -1-2). 16.99 *(978-0-449-81643-1(5),* Random Hse. Bks. for Young Readers) Random Hse. Children's Bks.
—Thomas's Christmas Delivery (Thomas & Friends) Stubbs, Tommy, illus. 2004. (Sparkle Storybook Ser.). (ENG.). 32p. (J). (gr. -1-2). 8.99 *(978-0-375-82877-5(X),* Random Hse. Bks. for Young Readers) Random Hse. Children's Bks.
—Treasure on the Tracks. 2013. (Thomas & Friends Step into Reading Ser.). lib. bdg. 13.55 *(978-0-606-32229-4(9))* Turtleback.
—A Valentine for Percy. 2015. (Thomas & Friends Step into Reading Ser.). (Illus.). 24p. lib. bdg. 14.75 *(978-0-606-38471-1(5))* Turtleback.
—A Valentine for Percy. Courtney, Richard, illus. 2015. 24p. (J). *(978-1-4806-9757-7(5))* Random Hse., Inc.
Awdry, Wilbert V. Easter Engines. 2012. (Thomas & Friends Step into Reading Ser.). lib. bdg. 13.55 *(978-0-606-23717-8(8))* Turtleback.
—Henry & the Elephant. 2007. (Thomas & Friends Step into Reading Ser.). 13.55 *(978-1-4177-7088-5(0))* Turtleback.
—Risky Rails! 2012. (Thomas & Friends 8X8 Ser.). lib. bdg. 13.55 *(978-0-606-26803-5(0))* Turtleback.
—Thomas & the Shark. 2013. (Thomas & Friends Step into Reading Ser.). lib. bdg. 13.55 *(978-0-606-26996-4(7))* Turtleback.
—Thomas in Charge. 2012. (Thomas & Friends 8X8 Ser.). lib. bdg. 14.75 *(978-0-606-26397-9(7))* Turtleback.
Awdry, Wilbert V. & Random House Editors. Thomas & Percy & the Dragon. 2003. (Thomas & Friends Step into Reading Ser.). (gr. -1-2). lib. bdg. 13.55 *(978-0-613-89791-4(9))* Turtleback.
Bailer, Darice. The Last Rail. 2011. (ENG.). 32p. (J). 9.95 *(978-1-60727-173-4(7))* Soundprints.
—Railroad!, Level 3: A Story of the Transcontinental Railroad. Farnsworth, Bill, illus. 3rd ed. 2004. (Soundprints' Read-and-Discover Ser.). (ENG.). 48p. (J). (gr. 1-4). pap. 3.95 *(978-1-59249-017-2(4),* S2007) Soundprints.
Bandy, Michael S. & Stein, Eric. Northbound: a Train Ride Out of Segregation. Ransome, James E., illus. 2020. (ENG.). 40p. (J). (gr. 1-4). 17.99 *(978-0-7636-9650-4(1))* Candlewick Pr.
Barnett, Mac. It Happened on a Train. Rex, Adam, illus. 2012. (Brixton Brothers Ser.: 3). (ENG.). 304p. (J). (gr. 3-7). pap. 8.99 *(978-1-4169-7820-6(8),* Simon & Schuster Bks. For Young Readers) Simon & Schuster Bks. For Young Readers.
Barton, Chris. Shark vs. Train. Lichtenheld, Tom, illus. 2010. (ENG.). 40p. (J). (gr. -1-3). 18.99 *(978-0-316-00762-7(5))* Little, Brown Bks. for Young Readers.
Baxter, Nicola. The Trouble with Trains. Ball, Geoff, illus. 2012. (ENG.). 24p. (J). (gr. -1-k). pap. 6.99 *(978-1-84322-785-4(1),* Armadillo) Anness Publishing GBR. Dist: National Bk. Network.
Bee, William. Stanley's Train, 1 vol. 2019. (Stanley Picture Bks.: 8). (ENG., Illus.). 32p. (J). (gr. -1-2). 14.95 *(978-1-68263-108-9(7))* Peachtree Publishing Co. Inc.
Beil, Michael D. Lantern Sam & the Blue Streak Bandits. 2015. (ENG., Illus.). 288p. (J). (gr. 3-7). pap. 7.99 *(978-0-385-75320-3(9),* Yearling) Random Hse. Children's Bks.
Bell, P. G. The Train to Impossible Places: a Cursed Delivery. 2019. (Train to Impossible Places Ser.: 1). (ENG.). 400p. (J). pap. 7.99 *(978-1-250-21142-2(5),* 900192256) Square Fish.
Bently, Peter. The Cat, the Mouse, & the Runaway Train. Cox, Steve, illus. 2013. (J). *(978-1-4351-4968-7(8))* Barnes & Noble, Inc.
Benton, Ann. Ferdinand: The Engine Who Went off the Rails. 2009. (Colour Bks.). (ENG., Illus.). 40p. (J). 7.99 *(978-1-84550-444-1(5),* 3899eafe-6fe6-4c4f-8a1d-ad4cf7894d45) Christian Focus Pubns. GBR. Dist: Baker & Taylor Publisher Services (BTPS).
Berry, Ron & Mead, David. All Aboard! Charlie the Can-Do Choo Choo. Sharp, Chris, illus. 2009. (ENG.). 8p. 12.99 *(978-0-8249-1420-2(1),* Ideals Pubns.) Worthy Publishing.
Bingham, Jane. The Story of Trains. King, Colin, illus. 2004. (Young Reading Series Two Ser.). 64p. (J). (gr. 2-18). pap. 5.95 *(978-0-7945-0737-4(9),* Usborne) EDC Publishing.
Blathwayt, Benedict, illus. Great Big Train. 2015. (J). *(978-0-553-51289-2(7))* Knopf, Alfred A. Inc.
Boat, Patty. A Disappointing Homecoming: (A Soldier's Story), 1 vol. 2009. 158p. pap. 24.95 *(978-1-61546-997-0(4))* PublishAmerica, Inc.
Boehnert, Ernest. The Magic Christmas Train. 2010. (ENG.). 24p. pap. 14.93 *(978-1-4269-4447-5(0))* Trafford Publishing.
Bradford, Wade. Mr. Complain Takes the Train. Britt, Stephan, illus. 2021. (ENG.). 32p. (J). (gr. -1-3). 17.99 *(978-0-544-82981-7(6),* 1644038, Clarion Bks.) HarperCollins Pubs.
Braun, Sebastien. Whoosh & Chug! Braun, Sebastien, illus. 2014. (ENG., Illus.). 32p. (J). (gr. -1-3). 16.99 *(978-0-06-207754-7(6),* HarperCollins) HarperCollins Pubs.
Brown, Carron. On the Train: Shine-A-Light. 2015. (ENG., Illus.). 36p. (J). 12.99 *(978-1-61067-365-5(4))* Kane Miller.
Brown, Margaret Wise. The Train to Timbuctoo. Seiden, Art, illus. 2018. (Little Golden Book Ser.). 24p. (J). (-k). 4.99 *(978-0-553-53340-8(1),* Golden Bks.) Random Hse. Children's Bks.
—Two Little Trains. 2003. (ENG., Illus.). 32p. (J). (gr. -1-k). pap. 8.99 *(978-0-06-443568-0(7),* HarperCollins) HarperCollins Pubs.
Bryant, Megan E. The Little Engine That Could: Choo Choo Charlie Saves the Carnival. Ong, Cristina, tr. Ong, Cristina, illus. 2004. (Little Engine That Could Ser.). (ENG.). 32p. (J). (gr. -1-1). 16.19 *(978-0-448-43513-8(6))* Penguin Young Readers Group.
Burleigh, Robert. Night Train, Night Train. Minor, Wendell, illus. 2018. 32p. (J). (-k). lib. bdg. 16.99 *(978-1-58089-717-4(7))* Charlesbridge Publishing, Inc.
Burt, Vicky. Eager Beavers. Lindsey, Jessica, illus. 2012. 28p. pap. 13.99 *(978-1-937129-39-2(X))* Faithful Life Pubs.
C. Larene Hall. Martha's Freedom Train. 2009. 100p. pap. 10.49 *(978-1-4389-7977-9(0))* AuthorHouse.
Cartwright, Stephen. Little Book of Train Stories. rev. ed. 2011. (Farmyard Tales Readers Ser.). 64p. (J). ring bd. 8.99 *(978-0-7945-3070-9(2),* Usborne) EDC Publishing.
Chatton, Julie. Trains: Safe & Sound. 2008. 24p. pap. 13.50 *(978-1-60693-307-7(8),* Eloquent Bks.) Strategic Book Publishing & Rights Agency (SBPRA).
Chin, Amanda. Chaff n' Skaffs: Mai & the Lost Moskivvy. Feldman, Luke, illus. 2009. (ENG.). 36p. (J). (gr. -1-3). 15.95 *(978-1-59702-013-8(3))* Immedium.
Chin, Oliver. Timmy & Tammy's Train of Thought. McPherson, Heath, illus. 2007. (ENG.). 36p. (J). (gr. -1-3). 15.95 *(978-1-59702-008-4(7))* Immedium.
Choo Choo. 2011. (Dora the Explorer Ser.). (Illus.). 10p. (J). bds. 10.98 *(978-0-7853-8278-2(X),* 7182700) Publications International, Ltd.
Cline-Ransome, Lesa. Overground Railroad. Ransome, James E., illus. 2020. 48p. (J). (gr. -1-3). 18.99 *(978-0-8234-3873-0(2))* Holiday Hse., Inc.
Cohen, Deborah Bodin. Engineer Ari & the Passover Rush. Kober, Shahar, illus. 2015. (ENG.). 32p. (J). (gr. k-3). lib. bdg. 17.95 *(978-1-4677-3470-7(5));* E-Book 27.99 *(978-1-4677-6201-4(6))* Lerner Publishing Group. (Kar-Ben Publishing).
—Engineer Ari & the Rosh Hashanah Ride. 2008. (High Holidays Ser.). (Illus.). 32p. (J). (gr. -1-3). lib. bdg. 17.95 *(978-0-8225-8648-7(7),* Kar-Ben Publishing) Lerner Publishing Group.
—Engineer Ari & the Sukkah Express. Kober, Shahar, illus. 2010. (Sukkot & Simchat Torah Ser.). (ENG.). 32p. (J). (gr. k-3). lib. bdg. 17.95 *(978-0-7613-5126-9(4),* Kar-Ben Publishing) Lerner Publishing Group.
—Engineer Arielle & the Israel Independence Day Surprise. Orrelle, Yael Kimhi, illus. 2017. (ENG.). 32p. (J). (gr. k-3). pap. 7.99 *(978-1-5124-2095-1(6),* dd3698d6-6646-4d26-b8b8-9f61ee612b7f, Kar-Ben Publishing) Lerner Publishing Group.
Coleman, Evelyn. Freedom Train. 2012. (ENG.). 160p. (J). (gr. 3-7). pap. 7.99 *(978-1-4424-3652-7(2),* McElderry, Margaret K. Bks.) McElderry, Margaret K. Bks.
Coombs, Charles. Railroad Stories: Young Readers. Geer, Charles H., illus. 2011. 194p. 42.95 *(978-1-258-10208-1(0))* Literary Licensing, LLC.
Cooper, Elisha. Train. Cooper, Elisha, illus. 2013. (ENG., Illus.). 40p. (J). (gr. -1-3). 18.99 *(978-0-545-38495-7(8),* Orchard Bks.) Scholastic, Inc.
Courtney, Richard, illus. Reds Against Blues! 2016. 22p. (J). *(978-1-4806-9772-0(9))* Random Hse., Inc.
Cousins, Lucy. Maisy's Train: A Maisy Shaped Board Book. Cousins, Lucy, illus. 2009. (Maisy Ser.). (ENG., Illus.). 16p. (J). (gr. k-k). bds. 7.99 *(978-0-7636-4251-8(7))* Candlewick Pr.
Cowley, Joy. Mrs. WishyWashy & the Big Tub. 2009. pap. 8.25 *(978-1-60559-233-6(1))* Hameray Publishing Group, Inc.
Crabtree, Sally. Magic Train Ride. Esplugas, Sonia & Esplugas, Sonia, illus. 2007. (ENG.). 32p. (J). (gr. -1-k). 6.99 *(978-1-84686-132-1(2))* Barefoot Bks., Inc.
—Magic Train Ride. Esplugas, Sonia, illus. (Barefoot Singalongs Ser.). (J). 2007. (ENG.). 32p. (gr. -1-k). pap. 9.99 *(978-1-905236-91-6(3))* 2006. 0032p. 16.99 *(978-1-905236-52-7(2))* Barefoot Bks., Inc.
Crebbin, June. El Viaje en Tren. Rubio, Esther, tr. Lambert, Stephen, illus. 2004. (SPA.). (J). 7.95 *(978-1-930332-76-8(9))* Lectorum Pubns., Inc.
Crews, Donald. Freight Train. Crews, Donald, illus. 2003. (SPA & ENG., Illus.). 24p. (J). lib. bdg., bds. 16.89 *(978-0-06-056203-8(X))* HarperCollins Pubs.
—Freight Train: A Caldecott Honor Award Winner. Crews, Donald, illus. 2003. (ENG., Illus.). 24p. (J). (gr. -1-3). 16.99 *(978-0-688-80165-6(X));* pap. 9.99 *(978-0-688-11701-6(5))* HarperCollins Pubs. (Greenwillow Bks.).
—Freight Train/Tren de Carga: A Cledecott Honor Award Winner (Bilingual English-Spanish) Crews, Donald, illus. 2003. (ENG., Illus.). 24p. (J). (gr. -1-3). 17.99 *(978-0-06-056202-1(1))* HarperCollins Español.
—Freight Train/Tren de Carga: A Cledecott Honor Award Winner (Bilingual English-Spanish) Crews, Donald, illus. 2008. (ENG., Illus.). 24p. (J). (gr. -1-3). pap. 9.99 *(978-0-06-056204-5(8),* Greenwillow Bks.) HarperCollins Pubs.
—Freight Train/Tren de Carga Bilingual Board Book. 2016. (ENG., Illus.). 32p. (J). (gr. -1 — 1). bds. 8.99 *(978-0-06-245708-0(X),* Greenwillow Bks.) HarperCollins Pubs.
Crews, Donald & Crews, D. Freight Train. 2003. (J). (gr. k-3). 17.20 *(978-0-8085-3581-2(1))* Turtleback.
Crise, Jeff. The Little Train That Had No Bell. 2011. (ENG.). 25p. pap. 9.95 *(978-1-4327-7673-2(8))* Outskirts Pr., Inc.
Crow, Melinda Melton. Brave Fire Truck, 1 vol. Thompson, Chad, illus. 2011. (Wonder Wheels Ser.). (ENG.). 32p. (J). (gr. -1-1). lib. bdg. 22.65 *(978-1-4342-3029-4(5),* 114523, Stone Arch Bks.) Capstone.
—Busy, Busy Train, 1 vol. Thompson, Chad, illus. 2011. (Wonder Wheels Ser.). (ENG.). 32p. (J). (gr. -1-1). pap. 6.25 *(978-1-4342-3383-7(9),* 116390); lib. bdg. 22.65 *(978-1-4342-3028-7(7),* 114522) Capstone. (Stone Arch Bks.).
—The Long Train Ride, 1 vol. Thompson, Chad, illus. 2012. (Wonder Wheels Ser.). (ENG.). 32p. (J). (gr. -1-1). pap. 6.25 *(978-1-4342-4239-6(0),* 120297); lib. bdg. 22.65 *(978-1-4342-4018-7(5),* 118399) Capstone. (Stone Arch Bks.).
Dale, Penny. Dinosaur Rescue! Dale, Penny, illus. 2016. (Dinosaurs on the Go Ser.). (ENG., Illus.). 24p. (J). (-k). bds. 6.99 *(978-0-7636-8000-8(1))* Candlewick Pr.
Dallas, Sandra. The Quilt Walk. (ENG., Illus.). 216p. (J). (gr. 4-7). 2013. pap. 10.99 *(978-1-58536-799-3(0),* 202373) 2012. 15.95 *(978-1-58536-800-6(8),* 202339) Sleeping Bear Pr.
Dare, Will. How to Scare a Stegosaurus. Epelbaum, Mariano, illus. 2018. (Dino Riders Ser.: 6). (ENG.). 128p. (J). (gr. 2-5). pap. 7.99 *(978-1-4926-6812-1(5),* Sourcebooks Jabberwocky) Sourcebooks, Inc.
Dean, James & Dean, Kimberly. Pete the Cat's Train Trip. Dean, James, illus. 2015. (My First I Can Read Ser.). (ENG., Illus.). 32p. (J). (gr. -1-3). pap. 4.99 *(978-0-06-230385-1(6),* HarperCollins) HarperCollins Pubs.
Demarest, Chris. Train. 2017. (ENG., Illus.). 16p. (J). (— 1). bds. 6.99 *(978-0-544-87608-8(3),* 1651101, Clarion Bks.) HarperCollins Pubs.
Demers, David & Demers, Lee Ann. My Grandpa Loves Trains: A Picture Storybook for Preschoolers. Demers, David, photos by. l.t. ed. 2005. (Illus.). 76p. (J). 27.95 *(978-0-922993-36-9(X))* Marquette Bks.
—My Grandpa Loves Trains: A Storybook for Preschoolers. Demers, David, photos by. l.t. ed. 2005. (Illus.). 76p. (J). per. 19.95 *(978-0-922993-23-9(8))* Marquette Bks.
Dorfman, Craig. I Knew You Could! A Book for All the Stops in Your Life. Ong, Cristina, illus. 2003. (Little Engine That Could Ser.). 32p. (J). (gr. -1-2). 12.99 *(978-0-448-43148-2(3),* Grosset & Dunlap) Penguin Young Readers Group.
Douglas, Ryke Leigh. Molly the Trolley & Bud. 2008. 24p. pap. 11.95 *(978-1-4327-2207-4(7))* Outskirts Pr., Inc.
Down the Track, 6 Packs. (Story Steps Ser.). (gr. k-2). 32.00 *(978-0-7635-9804-4(6))* Rigby Education.
Doyle, Bill H. Swindled! The 1906 Journal of Fitz Morgan. 2006. (Crime Through Time Ser.). (ENG., Illus.). 138p. (J). (gr. 3-6). 18.69 *(978-0-316-05736-3(3))* Little Brown & Co.
Duey, Kathleen & Bale, Karen A. Train Wreck: Kansas 1892. 2016. (Survivors Ser.). (ENG., Illus.). 160p. (J). (gr. 3-7). 17.99 *(978-1-4814-6801-5(4),* Simon & Schuster/Paula Wiseman Bks.) Simon & Schuster/Paula Wiseman Bks.
Durbin, William. Until the Last Spike: The Journal of Sean Sullivan, a Transcontinental Railroad Worker, Nebraska & Points West 1867. 2013. (My Name Is America Ser.). lib. bdg. 17.20 *(978-0-606-32342-0(2))* Turtleback.

P
Q
R

Dyer, Mary E. Secret Whispers. 2008. 99p. pap. 19.95 (978-1-60610-261-9(3)) America Star Bks.

Eaton, Jason Carter. How to Train a Train. Rocco, John, illus. (ENG.). (J). 2016. 28p. (-k). bds. 7.99 (978-0-7636-8899-8(1)) 2013. 48p. (gr. -1-3). 18.99 (978-0-7636-6307-0(7)) Candlewick Pr.

Elaine & Shaun Turner. Owen's Train Ride. 2010. 24p. pap. 15.99 (978-1-4535-0420-8(6)) Xlibris Corp.

Evans, Beryl. Charlie the Choo-Choo: From the World of the Dark Tower. Dameron, Ned, illus. 2016. (ENG.). 24p. (J). (gr. -1). 17.99 (978-1-5344-0123-5(7), Simon & Schuster Bks. For Young Readers) Simon & Schuster Bks. For Young Readers.

Falksen, G. D. The Transatlantic Conspiracy. Iwata, Nat, illus. 2017. 240p. (YA). (gr. 9). pap. 10.99 (978-1-61695-814-5(6), Soho Teen) Soho Pr., Inc.

Fath, Teresa. The Train Track Trolley & the Bell Dogs. 2009. 32p. pap. 21.99 (978-1-4415-4350-9(3)) Xlibris Corp.

Figorito, Marcus. Tara Takes the Train, 1 vol. 2006. (Neighborhood Readers Ser.). (ENG.). 16p. (gr. 1-2). pap. 6.50 (978-1-4042-7208-8(9), 6defb4c6-988b-44df-bcfb-a804e6b6e432, Rosen Classroom) Rosen Publishing Group, Inc., The.

Fiona Fox Staff, ed. The Railway Children. 2012. (ENG., Illus.). 64p. (J). 15.00 (978-1-84135-840-6(1)) Award Pubns. Ltd. GBR. Dist: Parkwest Pubns., Inc.

Francis, Mayann. Mayann's Train Ride, 1 vol. Thiébaux-Heikalo, Tamara, illus. 2015. (ENG.). 32p. (J). (gr. 1-3). 22.95 (978-1-77108-348-5(4), a4074706-9a84-4cfd-adc3-24cd71634181) Nimbus Publishing, Ltd. CAN. Dist: Baker & Taylor Publisher Services (BTPS).

Frank, Hannah. The Train to Baker Street. 2008. 44p. pap. 19.49 (978-1-4389-1026-0(6)) AuthorHouse.

Gail, Ginnie. The Great Pigeon Race. Griffin, Don, illus. 2008. 28p. per. 24.95 (978-1-4241-9457-5(1)) America Star Bks.

Gall, Chris. The Littlest Train. (ENG., Illus.). (J). (gr. -1 — 1). 2018. 24p. bds. 8.99 (978-0-316-44890-1(7)) 2017. 40p. 17.99 (978-0-316-39286-0(3)) Little, Brown Bks. for Young Readers.

Galvin, Laura Gates. I've Been Working on the Railroad. Brown, Dan, illus. 2008. (ENG.). 32p. (J). (gr. k-2). 14.95 (978-1-59249-771-3(3)); 8.95 (978-1-59249-772-0(1)) Soundprints.

Gerald, Tom. Traveling by Train: Read Well Level K Unit 19 Storybook. Weber, Philip A., Jr., illus. 2003. (Read Well Level K Ser.). 20p. (J). (978-1-57035-690-2(4), 55597) Cambium Education, Inc.

Golden Books. Thomas & the Dinosaur (Thomas & Friends) Lapadula, Thomas, illus. 2015. (Little Golden Book Ser.). (ENG.). 24p. (J). (-k). 5.99 (978-0-553-49681-9(6), Golden Bks.) Random Hse. Children's Bks.

—Trains, Cranes & Troublesome Trucks (Thomas & Friends) 2015. (Big Bright & Early Board Book Ser.). (ENG., Illus.). 24p. (J). (— 1). bds. 7.99 (978-0-385-37393-7(7), Random Hse. Bks. for Young Readers) Random Hse. Children's Bks.

Greenburg, Dan. Secrets of Dripping Fang, Book Eight: When Bad Snakes Attack Good Children. Fischer, Scott M., illus. 2007. (Secrets of Dripping Fang Ser.: Bk. 8). (ENG.). 144p. (J). (gr. 3-7). 11.99 (978-0-15-206056-5(1), 1198190, Clarion Bks.) HarperCollins Pubs.

Greene, Graham. The Little Train. Ardizzone, Edward, illus. 2018. (Little Train Ser.: 1). 48p. (J). (gr. -1-k). pap. 14.99 (978-1-78295-281-7(0), Red Fox) Random House Children's Books GBR. Dist: Independent Pubs. Group.

Griffiths, Robert. Adventures of Clive. 2005. 45p. (J). pap. 10.01 (978-1-4116-5332-0(7)) Lulu Pr., Inc.

Hancock, H. Irving. The Young Engineers in Colorado: Or, at Railwood Building in Earnest. 2017. (ENG., Illus.). (J). 23.95 (978-1-374-93144-2(6)); pap. 13.95 (978-1-374-93143-5(8)) Capital Communications, Inc.

Harby, Melanie. All Aboard for Dreamland!, 1 vol. Valerios, Geraldo, illus. 2008. (ENG.). 32p. (J). (gr. -1-k). 17.95 (978-1-896580-48-7(3)) Tradewind Bks. CAN. Dist: Orca Bk. Pubs. USA.

Hasany, Syed M. Stop the Train, Monkey! 2013. 28p. pap. 16.09 (978-1-4669-7792-1(2)) Trafford Publishing.

Hautman, Pete. Invisible. Hautman, Pete, illus. 2006. (ENG., Illus.). 160p. (YA). (gr. 7-12). reprint ed. pap. 10.99 (978-0-689-86903-7(7), Simon & Schuster Bks. For Young Readers) Simon & Schuster Bks. For Young Readers.

Heard, Foreman. Tales of Pinkie Posie. 2008. 76p. pap. 15.90 (978-1-4357-3292-6(8)) Lulu Pr., Inc.

High, Linda Oatman. Tenth Avenue Cowboy. Farnsworth, Bill, illus. 2008. 32p. (J). (gr. 4-7). 17.00 (978-0-8028-5330-1(7), Eerdmans Bks For Young Readers) Eerdmans, William B. Publishing Co.

Hillenbrand, Will. Down by the Station. 2011. (ENG., Illus.). 40p. (J). (gr. -1-1). 22.44 (978-0-15-201804-7(2)) Houghton Mifflin Harcourt Publishing Co.

Hillert, Margaret. Little Puff. Dammer, Mike, illus. 2016. (BeginningtoRead Ser.). (ENG.). 32p. (J). (gr. k-2). 22.60 (978-1-59953-800-6(8)) Norwood Hse. Pr.

—Little Puff. Mike Dammer, illus. 2016. (Beginning-To-Read Ser.). (ENG.). 32p. (J). (gr. k-2). pap. 13.26 (978-1-60357-941-4(9)) Norwood Hse. Pr.

Hope, Laura Lee. Freddie & Flossie & the Train Ride: Ready-To-Read Pre-Level 1. Pyle, Chuck, illus. 2005. (Bobbsey Twins Ser.). (ENG.). 32p. (J). (gr. -1-k). pap. 13.99 (978-1-4169-0269-0(4), Simon Spotlight) Simon Spotlight.

Hopeless, Dennis. Disney Kingdoms: Big Thunder Mountain Railroad #1. Walker, Tigh & Beaulieu, Jean-François, illus. 2016. (Disney Kingdoms: Big Thunder Mountain Railroad Ser.). (ENG.). 24p. (J). (gr. k-5). lib. bdg. 31.36 (978-1-61479-575-9(4), 24356, Graphic Novels) Spotlight.

—Disney Kingdoms: Big Thunder Mountain Railroad #2. Walker, Tigh & Beaulieu, Jean-François, illus. 2016. (Disney Kingdoms: Big Thunder Mountain Railroad Ser.). (ENG.). 24p. (J). (gr. k-5). lib. bdg. 31.36 (978-1-61479-576-6(2), 24357, Graphic Novels) Spotlight.

—Disney Kingdoms: Big Thunder Mountain Railroad #3. Ruiz, Felix & Beaulieu, Jean-François, illus. 2016. (Disney Kingdoms: Big Thunder Mountain Railroad Ser.). (ENG.). 24p. (J). (gr. k-5). lib. bdg. 31.36 (978-1-61479-577-3(0), 24358, Graphic Novels) Spotlight.

—Disney Kingdoms: Big Thunder Mountain Railroad #4. Walker, Tigh & Beaulieu, Jean-François, illus. 2016. (Disney Kingdoms: Big Thunder Mountain Railroad Ser.). (ENG.). 24p. (J). (gr. k-5). lib. bdg. 31.36 (978-1-61479-578-0(9), 24359, Graphic Novels) Spotlight.

—Disney Kingdoms: Big Thunder Mountain Railroad #5. Walker, Tigh et al, illus. 2016. (Disney Kingdoms: Big Thunder Mountain Railroad Ser.). (ENG.). 24p. (J). (gr. k-5). lib. bdg. 31.36 (978-1-61479-579-7(7), 24360, Graphic Novels) Spotlight.

Horsbrugh, Wilma. The Train to Glasgow. Cox, Paul, illus. 2004. (ENG.). 32p. (J). (gr. -1-3). 16.00 (978-0-618-38143-2(0), 100335, Clarion Bks.) HarperCollins Pubs.

Hubbell, Patricia. Trains: Steaming! Pulling! Huffing!, 0 vols. Halsey, Megan & Addy, Sean, illus. 2013. (ENG.). 34p. (J). (gr. -1-1). pap. 9.99 (978-0-7614-5593-6(0), 9780761455936, Two Lions) Amazon Publishing.

James, Eric. All Aboard the Spooky Express! Piwowarski, Marcin, illus. 2017. (Spooky Express Ser.). (ENG.). 32p. (J). (gr. k-6). 9.99 (978-1-4926-5375-2(6), Hometown World) Sourcebooks, Inc.

James, Helen Foster. Santa's Christmas Train. Bolton, Bill, illus. 2019. (ENG.). 26p. (J). (gr. -1-1). bds. 7.99 (978-1-5460-1434-8(9), Worthy Kids/Ideals) Worthy Publishing.

Johnson, Angela. I Dream of Trains. Long, Loren, illus. 2003. (ENG.). 32p. (J). (gr. k-2). 19.99 (978-0-689-82609-2(5), Simon & Schuster Bks. For Young Readers) Simon & Schuster Bks. For Young Readers.

Judd, Jennifer Cole. Circus Train, 0 vols. Matthews, Melanie, illus. 2015. (ENG.). 24p. (J). (gr. -1-2). 14.99 (978-1-4778-2634-8(3), 9781477826348, Two Lions) Amazon Publishing.

Kavan, Barbara. Trainman: Gaining Acceptance ... & Friends ... Through Special Interests. 2010. (Illus.). 40p. (J). pap. 17.95 (978-1-934575-70-3(4)) Autism Asperger Publishing Co.

King, Trey. Mystery on the LEGO Express. Wang, Sean, illus. 2014. 24p. (J). (978-1-4242-6168-0(6)) Scholastic, Inc.

—Mystery on the Lego Express. 2014. (LEGO City 8X8 Ser.). (Illus.). 24p. (J). lib. bdg. 13.55 (978-0-606-36068-5(9)) Turtleback.

Kivel, Lee. The Lonely Train. Tucci, Al, illus. 2005. 36p. (J). per. 14.95 (978-0-9774999-0-8(1)) Kivel, Lee.

Klein, Adria F. Big Train. Cameron, Craig, illus. 2013. (Train Time Ser.). (ENG.). 32p. (J). (gr. -1-1). pap. 5.95 (978-1-4342-4886-2(0), 121886, Stone Arch Bks.) Capstone.

—Big Train Takes a Trip. Cameron, Craig, illus. 2013. (Train Time Ser.). (ENG.). 32p. (J). (gr. -1-1). pap. 35.70 (978-1-4342-6300-1(2), 20273, Stone Arch Bks.) Capstone.

—Circus Train & the Clowns. 2013. (Train Time Ser.). (ENG., Illus.). 32p. (J). (gr. -1-1). pap. 35.70 (978-1-4342-6303-2(7), 20277, Stone Arch Bks.) Capstone.

—City Train, 1 vol. Cameron, Craig, illus. 2013. (Train Time Ser.). (ENG.). 32p. (J). (gr. -1-1). lib. bdg. 22.65 (978-1-4342-4189-4(0), 120161, Stone Arch Bks.) Capstone.

—City Train in Trouble. 2013. (Train Time Ser.). (ENG., Illus.). 32p. (J). (gr. -1-1). pap. 35.70 (978-1-4342-6302-5(9), 20276, Stone Arch Bks.) Capstone.

—Freight Train, 1 vol. Cameron, Craig, illus. 2013. (Train Time Ser.). (ENG.). 32p. (J). (gr. -1-1). pap. 5.95 (978-1-4342-4885-5(2), 121887, Stone Arch Bks.) Capstone.

—The Full Freight Train. 2013. (Train Time Ser.). (ENG., Illus.). 32p. (J). (gr. -1-1). pap. 35.70 (978-1-4342-6301-8(0), 20275, Stone Arch Bks.) Capstone.

Kleinberg, Naomi. Thomas & the Runaway Pumpkins (Thomas & Friends) Courtney, Richard, illus. 2018. (Little Golden Book Ser.). (ENG.). 24p. (J). (gr. -1-2). 5.99 (978-0-385-37391-3(0), Golden Bks.) Random Hse. Children's Bks.

Konen, Leah. Love & Other Train Wrecks. 2018. (ENG.). 368p. (YA). (gr. 8). 17.99 (978-0-06-240250-9(1), Tegen, Katherine Bks) HarperCollins Pubs.

Kropik, Linda Kristine. Christopher the Choo Choo Train. Haezer, Jane, illus. 2011. 24p. pap. 11.50 (978-1-60911-522-7(8), Strategic Bk. Publishing) Strategic Book Publishing & Rights Agency (SBPRA).

Lamkin, Robert J. Tommy's Train. 2008. 44p. pap. 24.95 (978-1-60672-147-6(X)) America Star Bks.

LaReau, Kara. The Uncanny Express (the Unintentional Adventures of the Bland Sisters Book 2) Hill, Jen, illus. 2018. (Unintentional Adventures of the Bland Sisters Ser.). (ENG.). (J). (gr. 3-7). 184p. pap. 7.99 (978-1-4197-3204-1(8), 1139403); 176p. 14.99 (978-1-4197-2568-5(8), 1139401) Abrams, Inc. (Amulet Bks.).

Le Guin, Ursula K. Tom Mouse. 2004. (Illus.). (J). (gr. k-3). spiral bd. (978-0-616-14584-5(5)) Canadian National Institute for the Blind/Institut National Canadien pour les Aveugles.

Lehman, Barbara. Trainstop. 2008. (ENG., Illus.). 32p. (J). (gr. -1-3). 17.99 (978-0-618-75640-7(X), 569198, Clarion Bks.) HarperCollins Pubs.

Light, Steve. Trains Go. 2012. (Vehicles Go! Ser.). (ENG., Illus.). 16p. (J). (gr. -1 — 1). bds. 9.99 (978-0-8118-7942-2(9)) Chronicle Bks. LLC.

Lukas, Catherine & Artifact Group. The. Trouble on the Train. 2007. (Backyardigans Ser.: 6). (ENG., Illus.). 24p. (J). (gr. -1-1). pap. 3.99 (978-1-4169-2818-8(9), Simon Spotlight/Nickelodeon) Simon Spotlight/Nickelodeon.

Lund, Deb. All Aboard the Dinotrain. Fine, Howard, illus. 2009. (ENG.). 40p. (J). (gr. -1-3). pap. 9.99 (978-0-547-24825-7(3), 1100733, Clarion Bks.) HarperCollins Pubs.

—All Aboard the Dinotrain Board Book. Fine, Howard, illus. 2011. (ENG.). 30p. (J). (gr. -1 — 1). bds. 7.99 (978-0-547-55415-0(X), 1452006, Clarion Bks.) HarperCollins Pubs.

Lupa, Mary R. Stacy Takes the Train to School. Andriyevskaya, Yevgeniya, illus. 2009. 20p. (J). pap. 10.95 (978-1-4327-1609-7(3)) Outskirts Pr., Inc.

Lyon, George Ella & Lyon, Benn. Trains Run! Wiggins, Mick, illus. 2019. (ENG.). 40p. (J). (gr. -1-3). 17.99 (978-1-4814-8202-8(5)) Simon & Schuster Children's Publishing.

Macaulay, David. Black & White: A Caldecott Award Winner. 2005. (ENG., Illus.). 32p. (J). (gr. -1-3). 8.99 (978-0-618-63687-7(0), 490567, Clarion Bks.) HarperCollins Pubs.

Mack, Karen. Who Makes the Sound? 2008. 11p. pap. 24.95 (978-1-60610-852-9(2)) America Star Bks.

Mackall, Dandi Daley. Rudy Rides the Rails: A Depression Era Story. Ellison, Chris, illus. rev. ed. 2007. (Tales of Young Americans Ser.). (ENG.). 40p. (J). (gr. 1-4). 17.95 (978-1-58536-286-8(7), 202097) Sleeping Bear Pr.

Mara, Nichole. All Aboard! (an Abrams Extend-A-Book) Let's Ride a Train. Kolb, Andrew, illus. 2017. (Abrams Extend-A-Book Ser.). (ENG.). 10p. (J). (gr. -1 — 1). bds. 9.95 (978-1-4197-2567-8(X), 1180210, Abrams Appleseed) Abrams, Inc.

Marsh, Carole. The Mystery on Alaska's Iditarod Trail. 2009. (Real Kids, Real Places Ser.). 145p. (J). 18.99 (978-0-635-06997-9(0), Marsh, Carole Mysteries) Gallopade International.

McCaughrean, Geraldine. Stop the Train! 2003. (ENG.). 304p. (J). (gr. 5-18). 16.99 (978-0-06-050749-7(7)) HarperCollins Pubs.

McKinnon, Bob. Three Little Engines. Fancher, Lou & Johnson, Steve, illus. 2021. (Little Engine That Could Ser.). 48p. (J). (gr. -1-2). 18.99 (978-1-5247-9335-7(3), Grosset & Dunlap) Penguin Young Readers Group.

McLaughlin, B. G. Reuben Rides the Rails. 2010. (Illus.). 32p. pap. 14.49 (978-1-4490-4448-0(4)) AuthorHouse.

McMullan, Kate. I'm Fast! McMullan, Jim, illus. 2012. (ENG.). 40p. (J). (gr. -1-3). 17.99 (978-0-06-192085-1(1)); lib. bdg. 17.89 (978-0-06-192086-8(X)) HarperCollins Pubs. (Balzer & Bray).

McPhail, J. A. Dawn of Day. Battis, Gwen, illus. 2012. 200p. 17.99 (978-0-9851196-2-1(4)) Rowe Publishing.

Meister, Cari & Stone Arch Books Staff. Train Trip, 1 vol. Janovitz, Marilyn, illus. 2010. (My First Graphic Novel Ser.). (ENG.). 32p. (J). (gr. k-2). pap. 6.25 (978-1-4342-2289-3(6), 103158, Stone Arch Bks.) Capstone.

Metzger, Steve. The Turkey Train. Paillot, Jim, illus. 2013. (ENG.). 32p. (J). (gr. -1-k). 6.99 (978-0-545-49229-4(7), Cartwheel Bks.) Scholastic, Inc.

Miéville, China. Railsea: A Novel. 2013. (ENG., Illus.). 448p. pap. 15.99 (978-0-345-52453-9(5), Del Rey) Random Hse. Worlds.

Mitton, Tony. Terrific Trains. 2017. (Amazing Machines Ser.). (ENG.). 20p. (J). bds. 6.99 (978-0-7534-7372-6(0), 900178406, Kingfisher) Roaring Brook Pr.

Mobley, Jeannie. Bobby Lee Claremont & the Criminal Element. 2017. (ENG., Illus.). 246p. (J). (gr. 3-7). 16.95 (978-0-8234-3781-8(7)) Holiday Hse., Inc.

Murray, Regina Waldron. The Very Exciting Train Ride: An Adventure. 2006. (J). per. 15.95 (978-0-9664042-1-0(1)) Murray, Regina Waldron.

Nelson, Dianne Elizabeth. By Here. 2009. 32p. pap. 14.49 (978-1-4490-0366-1(4)) AuthorHouse.

Nesbit, E. Level 2: the Railway Children. 2nd ed. 2008. (Pearson English Graded Readers Ser.). (ENG., Illus.). 48p. pap. 13.32 (978-1-4058-6964-5(X), Pearson ELT) Pearson Education.

—The Railway Children. 2007. 236p. per. 12.95 (978-1-4218-3945-5(8)); (ENG.). (gr. 4-7). 27.95 (978-1-4218-3845-8(1)) 1st World Publishing, Inc. (1st World Library - Literary Society).

—The Railway Children. 2006. (ENG.). 228p. (gr. 4-7). per. 14.95 (978-1-59818-933-9(6)); 26.95 (978-1-59818-179-1(3)) Aegypan.

—The Railway Children. 2013. 140p. pap. (978-1-908388-94-0(3)) Aziloth Bks.

—The Railway Children. 2008. (Illus.). 176p. (J). 8.99 (978-1-59166-924-1(3)) BJU Pr.

—The Railway Children. 2010. 146p. (gr. 4-7). pap. 8.95 (978-1-61104-337-2(9)) Cedar Lake Pubns.

—The Railway Children. Brock, C. E., illus. (YA). 14.95 (978-0-8118-4933-3(3)) Chronicle Bks. LLC.

—The Railway Children. 2012. (ENG.). 234p. pap. 14.99 (978-1-4812-4818-1(9)) CreateSpace Independent Publishing Platform.

—The Railway Children. 2008. 204p. (gr. 4-7). 27.99 (978-0-554-26706-7(3)); 24.99 (978-0-554-36009-6(8)) Creative Media Partners, LLC.

—The Railway Children. 2008. (gr. 4-7). pap. 5.99 (978-1-4209-3105-1(9)) Digireads.com Publishing.

—The Railway Children. Brock, C. E., illus. 2008. (ENG.). 248p. per. (978-1-4065-9815-5(1)) Dodo Pr.

—The Railway Children. 2007. (ENG.). 204p. per. (978-1-4065-3083-4(2)) Dodo Pr.

—The Railway Children. 2006. pap. (978-1-4068-3505-2(6)) 2005. 348p. pap. (978-1-84637-205-6(4)) Echo Library.

—The Railway Children. Brock, Charles Edmund, illus. 2012. 232p. pap. (978-1-78201-004-3(1)) Evertype.

—The Railway Children. 2010. (Illus.). 118p. pap. 19.99 (978-1-153-71841-7(3)) General Bks. LLC.

—The Railway Children. 2010. 184p. pap. (978-1-4076-1891-3(1)) HardPr.

—The Railway Children. (ENG.). (J). pap. (978-0-340-71497-3(2)) Hodder & Stoughton.

—The Railway Children. 2010. 194p. 30.36 (978-1-169-28328-2(4)) 2010. 194p. pap. 18.36 (978-1-162-70632-0(5)) 2010. 194p. 37.95 (978-1-161-47496-1(X)) 2004. reprint ed. pap. 1.99 (978-1-4192-7972-0(6)) 2004. reprint ed. pap. 22.95 (978-1-4191-7972-3(1)) Kessinger Publishing, LLC.

—The Railway Children. 2006. (Twelve-Point Ser.). lib. bdg. 25.00 (978-1-58287-399-2(2)); lib. bdg. 26.00 (978-1-58287-890-4(0)) North Bks.

—The Railway Children. 2017. (ENG., Illus.). 280p. 12.99 (978-1-5098-4316-9(7), 900184057, Collector's Library, The) Pan Macmillan GBR. Dist: Macmillan.

—The Railway Children. unabr. ed. 2004. (Chrysalis Childrens Classics Ser.). (ENG., Illus.). 128p. (YA). pap. (978-1-84365-050-8(9), Pavilion Children's Books) Pavilion Bks.

—The Railway Children. 2nd ed. 2011. (Puffin Classics Ser.). (Illus.). 304p. (J). (gr. 5-7). pap. 8.99 (978-0-14-132160-8(1), Puffin Books) Penguin Young Readers Group.

—The Railway Children. 2004. (ENG.). 580p. (978-0-9548401-2-9(7)) Shoes & Ships & Sealing Wax Ltd.

—The Railway Children. 2009. 156p. (gr. 4-7). pap. 6.99 (978-1-60459-698-4(8)) Wilder Pubns., Corp.

—The Railway Children. 2011. 200p. (gr. 4-7). pap. (978-3-8424-4120-0(7)) tredition Verlag.

Nesbit, Edith. The Railway Children. 2012. (Oxford Children's Classics Ser.). (ENG.). 240p. 9.95 (978-0-19-275819-4(5)) Oxford Univ. Pr., Inc.

—The Railway Children. 2013. (Vintage Children's Classics Ser.). 320p. (J). (gr. 4-7). pap. 10.99 (978-0-09-957299-2(0)) Penguin Random Hse. GBR. Dist: Independent Pubs. Group.

Ng, Yvonne. The Mighty Steam Engine. Smythe, Richard, illus. 2019. 32p. (J). (gr. 1-3). 17.99 (978-1-68152-237-1(3), 10864) Amicus.

Nolen, Jerdine. Eliza's Freedom Road: An Underground Railroad Diary. Strickland, Shadra, illus. 2011. (ENG.). 160p. (J). (gr. 3-7). 19.99 (978-1-4169-5814-7(2), Simon & Schuster/Paula Wiseman Bks.) Simon & Schuster/Paula Wiseman Bks.

O'Dell, Kathryn L. From Wagon to Train. Chalik, Chris, illus. 2017. (Text Connections Guided Close Reading Ser.). (J). (gr. 2). (978-1-4900-1854-6(9)) Benchmark Education Co.

Ogilvy, Ian. Measle & the Wrathmonk. 2004. 224p. (J). (gr. 4-6). 15.99 (978-0-06-058685-0(0)) HarperCollins Pubs.

Opie, David, illus. Monkey & the Engineer. 2007. 24p. (J). 14.95 (978-0-9793972-6-4(X)) JD Publishing.

Oppel, Kenneth. The Boundless. Tierney, Jim, illus. 2014. (ENG.). 336p. (J). (gr. 3-7). 17.99 (978-1-4424-7288-4(X), Simon & Schuster Bks. For Young Readers) Simon & Schuster Bks. For Young Readers.

Parker, Amy. Night Night, Train, 1 vol. Allyn, Virginia, illus. 2017. (Night Night Ser.). (ENG.). 20p. (J). bds. 9.99 (978-0-7180-8932-0(4), Tommy Nelson) Nelson, Thomas Inc.

Parker, Danny. Molly & Mae: A Friendship Journey. Blackwood, Freya, illus. 2017. (ENG.). 32p. (J). (gr. -1-3). 16.99 (978-1-328-71543-2(4), 1674164, Clarion Bks.) HarperCollins Pubs.

Parker, Emma. All Aboard! 2010. (Illus.). 20p. pap. (978-1-877561-74-0(6)) First Edition Ltd.

Peet, Bill. The Caboose Who Got Loose Book & Cd, 1 vol. 2008. (ENG., Illus.). 48p. (J). (gr. -1-3). audio compact disk 10.99 (978-0-618-95979-2(3), 1021923, Clarion Bks.) HarperCollins Pubs.

Piper, Watty & Penguin / LeapFrog. The Little Engine That Could. Long, Loren, illus. 2008. (J). 13.99 (978-1-59319-938-8(4)) LeapFrog Enterprises, Inc.

Pryor, Bonnie. The Iron Dragon: The Courageous Story of Lee Chin, 1 vol. 2011. (Historical Fiction Adventures Ser.). (ENG., Illus.). 160p. (J). (gr. 3-5). 31.93 (978-0-7660-3389-4(9), 519a6a2e-bc8c-434a-847a-07470adaa637); pap. 13.88 (978-1-59845-215-0(0), 3f96b345-e985-4f22-a311-341cf9f481bc) Enslow Publishing, LLC.

Publications International Ltd. Staff. Chuggington Little Lift & Listen. 2011. 12p. (J). bds. 10.98 (978-1-4508-0504-9(3)) Phoenix International Publications, Inc.

Publications International Ltd. Staff, ed. Interactive Play a Sound Thomas the Tank. 2009. 24p. (J). 17.98 (978-0-7853-1360-1(5), PIL Kids) Publications International, Ltd.

—Record a Story with Thomas & Friends: Good Night, Little Engine. 2011. (Illus.). 20p. (J). bds. 25.98 (978-1-4508-1164-4(7)) Phoenix International Publications, Inc.

Pugliano-Martin, Carol. John Henry: An American Tall Tale. 2006. (J). pap. (978-1-4108-6170-2(8)) Benchmark Education Co.

Rabe, Tish. Huff & Puff. Guile, Gill, illus. 2014. (My First I Can Read Ser.). (ENG.). 24p. (J). (gr. -1-3). 16.99 (978-0-06-230502-2(6)); pap. 4.99 (978-0-06-230501-5(8)) HarperCollins Pubs. (HarperCollins).

—Huff & Puff Have Too Much Stuff! Guile, Gill, illus. 2014. (My First I Can Read Ser.). (ENG.). 24p. (J). (gr. -1-3). pap. 4.99 (978-0-06-230505-3(0), HarperCollins) HarperCollins Pubs.

Raffa, Edwina & Rigsby, Annelle. Kidnapped in Key West. (Florida Historical Fiction for Youth Ser.). (ENG.). (J). (gr. -1-12). 2012. 136p. pap. 9.95 (978-1-56164-537-4(0)) 2008. (Illus.). 127p. 14.95 (978-1-56164-413-1(7)) Pineapple Pr., Inc.

Ramoutar, Tagore. Trains, Engines & Locomotives: I Love Trains. 2013. 38p. pap. (978-1-907837-63-0(9)) Longshot Ventures, Ltd.

Random House. Five Tank Engine Tales (Thomas & Friends) Courtney, Richard, illus. 2015. (Step into Reading Ser.). (ENG.). 160p. (J). (gr. -1-1). pap. 8.99 (978-0-385-38496-4(3), Random Hse. Bks. for Young Readers) Random Hse. Children's Bks.

—The Runaway Kite. 2018. (Thomas & Friends Step into Reading Ser.). lib. bdg. 14.75 (978-0-606-40931-5(9)) Turtleback.

—The Runaway Kite (Thomas & Friends) 2018. (Step into Reading Ser.). (ENG., Illus.). 24p. (J). (gr. -1-2). pap. 4.99 (978-0-399-55768-2(7)); lib. bdg. 12.99 (978-1-5247-6903-1(7)) Random Hse. Children's Bks. (Random Hse. Bks. for Young Readers).

—Thomas & Friends 5-Minute Stories: the Sleepytime Collection (Thomas & Friends) 2016. (ENG., Illus.). 160p. (J). (gr. -1-2). 12.99 (978-0-399-55207-6(3), Random Hse. Bks. for Young Readers) Random Hse. Children's Bks.

Random House Editors. Thomas' Tall Friend. 2016. (Step into Reading Level 2 Ser.). lib. bdg. 14.75 (978-0-606-38883-2(4)) Turtleback.

Reeve, Philip. Station Zero. 2019. (Railhead Ser.). (ENG.). 320p. (YA). (gr. 7-12). lib. bdg. 17.95 (978-1-68446-053-3(0), 140333, Capstone Editions) Capstone.

Rev. Awdry, W. Thomas & Friends: Go, Train, Go! (Thomas & Friends) Stubbs, Tommy, illus. 2006. (Bright & Early Board Books(TM) Ser.). (ENG.). 24p. (J). (— 1). bds. 4.99 (978-0-375-83461-5(3), Random Hse. Bks. for Young Readers) Random Hse. Children's Bks.

—Thomas Saves Easter! (Thomas & Friends) Stubbs, Tommy, illus. 2013. (ENG.). 12p. (J). (-k). bds. 6.99 (978-0-307-98158-5(4), Golden Bks.) Random Hse. Children's Bks.

Rey and others, Rey and. Start Your Engines 5-Minute Stories. 2014. (5-Minute Stories Ser.). (ENG., Illus.). 224p. (J). (gr. -1-3). 12.99 (978-0-544-15881-8(4), 1550258, Clarion Bks.) HarperCollins Pubs.

Rey, H. A. & Rey, Margret. Curious George Takes a Train with Stickers. Weston, Martha, illus. 2010. (Curious George Ser.). (ENG.). 24p. (J). (gr. -1-3). pap. 5.99 (978-0-547-50424-7(1), 1442842, Clarion Bks.) HarperCollins Pubs.

Rice, Dona Herwick. John Henry, 1 vol. rev. ed. 2009. (Reader's Theater Ser.). (ENG.). 24p. (gr. 2-4). pap. 8.99 (978-1-4333-0992-2(0)) Teacher Created Materials, Inc.

Richardson, Arleta. Prairie Homestead. 2016. (Beyond the Orphan Train Ser.: 3). (ENG.). 192p. (J). pap. 7.99 (978-0-7814-1357-2(5), 136204) Cook, David C.

—Whistle-Stop West. 2016. (Beyond the Orphan Train Ser.: 2). (ENG.). 192p. (J). pap. 7.99 (978-1-4347-0956-1(6), 136203) Cook, David C.

Richter, Bernd & Richter, Susan. When Grandma & Grandpa Rode the Alaska Train. 2008. (ENG., Illus.). 16p. (J). bds. 8.95 (978-1-931353-40-3(9)) Saddle Pal Creations, Inc.

Rinker, Sherri Duskey. Steam Train, Dream Train (Books for Young Children, Family Read Aloud Books, Children's Train Books, Bedtime Stories) Lichtenheld, Tom, illus. 2018. (Goodnight, Goodnight Construction Site Ser.). (ENG.). 32p. (J). (gr. -1 — 1). bds. 7.99 (978-1-4521-5217-2(9)) Chronicle Bks. LLC.

—Steam Train, Dream Train Colors. Lichtenheld, Tom, illus. 2016. (Goodnight, Goodnight Construction Site Ser.). (ENG.). 20p. (J). (gr. -1 — 1). bds. 7.99 (978-1-4521-4915-8(1)) Chronicle Bks. LLC.

—Steam Train, Dream Train (Easy Reader Books, Reading Books for Children) Lichtenheld, Tom, illus. 2013. (Goodnight, Goodnight Construction Site Ser.). (ENG.). 40p. (J). (gr. -1-1). 16.99 (978-1-4521-0920-6(6)) Chronicle Bks. LLC.

Rosenbaum, Andria Warmflash. Trains Don't Sleep. Gill, Deirdre, illus. 2017. (ENG.). 40p. (J). (gr. -1-3). 16.99 (978-0-544-38074-5(6), 1591860, Clarion Bks.) HarperCollins Pubs.

Roy, Ron. Capital Mysteries #13: Trapped on the D. C. Train! Bush, Timothy, illus. 2011. (Capital Mysteries Ser.: 13). 96p. (J). (gr. 1-4). 5.99 (978-0-375-85926-7(8), Random Hse. Bks. for Young Readers) Random Hse. Children's Bks.

The Runaway Engine & Other Stories: Individual Title Six-Pack. (Story Steps Ser.). (gr. k-2). 48.00 (978-0-7635-9803-7(8)) Rigby Education.

Sander, Sonia. Scooby-Doo & the International Express. 2009. (Illus.). 32p. (J). pap. (978-0-545-16283-8(1)) Scholastic, Inc.

Santillo, LuAnn. The Tracks. Santillo, LuAnn, ed. 2003. (Half-Pint Kids Readers Ser.). (Illus.). 7p. (J). (gr. -1-1). pap. 1.00 (978-1-59256-080-6(6)) Half-Pint Kids, Inc.

Sayres, Brianna Caplan. Where Do Steam Trains Sleep at Night? Slade, Christian, illus. 2017. (Where Do... Ser.). 26p. (J). (gr. -1 — 1). bds. 8.99 (978-0-553-52100-9(4), Random Hse. Bks. for Young Readers) Random Hse. Children's Bks.

Schaefer, Nikki. The Potty Train. Schaefer, Nikki, illus. 2010. (Illus.). 24p. pap. 10.95 (978-1-61633-043-9(0)) Guardian Angel Publishing, Inc.

Selznick, Brian. The Invention of Hugo Cabret. 2007. (CHI., Illus.). 534p. (J). (978-957-570-894-8(6)) Eastern Publishing Co., Ltd., The.

—The Invention of Hugo Cabret. 2008. (CHI., Illus.). 465p. (J). pap. (978-7-5448-0279-6(5)) Jieli Publishing Hse.

—The Invention of Hugo Cabret. Selznick, Brian, illus. 2007. (ENG., Illus.). 544p. (J). (gr. 4-7). 29.99 (978-0-439-81378-5(6), Scholastic Pr.); 534p. (978-1-4071-0348-8(2)) Scholastic, Inc.

Shaskan, Stephen. Big Choo. 2018. (ENG., illus.). 40p. (J). (gr. -1-k). 16.99 (978-0-545-70857-9(5), Scholastic Pr.) Scholastic, Inc.

Shepherd, David & Plummer, William K. We Were There at the Driving of the Golden Spike. 2013. (ENG., Illus.). 192p. (J). (gr. 3-8). pap. 7.99 (978-0-486-49259-9(1), 492591) Dover Pubns., Inc.

Sherri, Sherri Duskey. Steam Train, Dream Train 1-2-3. Lichtenheld, Tom, illus. 2016. (Goodnight, Goodnight Construction Site Ser.). (ENG.). 20p. (J). (gr. -1 — 1). bds. 7.99 (978-1-4521-4914-1(3)) Chronicle Bks. LLC.

Shortle, Stacy & Mooney, Dean J. M. A Train Ride to Grandma's (with NO Chocolate Donut!) Wulfing, Amy J., illus. 2009. 48p. (J). 18.95 (978-0-9759850-5-2(1)) Maple Leaf Ctr.

Skinner, Daphne. All Aboard! Smath, Jerry, illus. 2007. (Math Matters Ser.). 32p. (J). (gr. 1-3). pap. 5.99 (978-1-57565-239-9(0), e3538b34-f443-4ff3-8b7e-a181e945e25c, Kane Press) Astra Publishing Hse.

Smith, B. M. Evan & Cassie Go on a Train Meet, 1 vol. Smith, Mandy M., illus. 2009. 35p. pap. 24.95 (978-1-60836-552-4(2)) America Star Bks.

Sobel, June. The Goodnight Train. Huliska-Beith, Laura, illus. (Goodnight Train Ser.). (ENG.). 32p. (J). (gr. -1-3). 2017. pap. 7.99 (978-1-328-74002-1(1), 1677042) 2006. 17.99 (978-0-15-205436-6(7), 1196359) HarperCollins Pubs. (Clarion Bks.).

Sobel, June & Huliska-Beith, Laura. The Goodnight Train Rolls On! Huliska-Beith, Laura, illus. 2018. (Goodnight Train Ser.). (ENG., Illus.). 32p. (J). (gr. -1-3). 17.99 (978-1-328-50019-9(5), 1717900, Clarion Bks.) HarperCollins Pubs.

Sommer, Carl. The Little Red Train. James, Kennon, illus. 2014. (J). pap. (978-1-57537-958-6(9)) Advance Publishing, Inc.

—The Little Red Train. 2003. (Another Sommer-Time Story Ser.). (Illus.). 48p. (J). (gr. k-4). lib. bdg. 23.95 incl. audio (978-1-57537-764-3(0)) Advance Publishing, Inc.

—The Little Red Train. James, Kennon, illus. 2003. (Another Sommer-Time Story Ser.). (ENG.). 48p. (J). (gr. k-3). 16.95 incl. audio compact disk (978-1-57537-014-9(X)); lib. bdg. 23.95 incl. audio compact disk (978-1-57537-714-8(4)) Advance Publishing, Inc.

—The Little Red Train. 2003. (Another Sommer-Time Story Ser.). (Illus.). 48p. (J). (gr. 1-4). 16.95 incl. audio (978-1-57537-563-2(X)); 16.95 incl. audio compact disk (978-1-57537-514-4(1)) Advance Publishing, Inc.

—The Little Red Train(El Trenecito Rojo) James, Kennon, illus. 2009. (Another Sommer-Time Story Bilingual Ser.). (SPA & ENG.). 48p. (J). lib. bdg. 16.95 (978-1-57537-158-0(8)) Advance Publishing, Inc.

Spencer, Jamie. The Train to Maine. Reed, Rebecca, illus. 2008. (ENG.). 32p. (J). (gr. -1-3). 15.95 (978-0-89272-767-4(5)) Down East Bks.

Stark, Hannah. Trucker & Train. Kolar, Bob, illus. 2019. (ENG.). 40p. (J). (gr. -1-3). 17.99 (978-0-544-80181-3(4), 1640534, Clarion Bks.) HarperCollins Pubs.

Stephenson, Mary. Naven's Dream. 2011. 24p. pap. 24.95 (978-1-4626-0309-1(2)) America Star Bks.

Stevens, Cat. Peace Train. Reynolds, Peter H., illus. 2021. (ENG.). 40p. (J). (gr. -1-3). 18.99 (978-0-06-305399-1(3), HarperCollins) HarperCollins Pubs.

Stilton, Geronimo. Geronimo Stilton Graphic Novels #13: The Fastest Train in the West, Vol. 13. 2013. (Geronimo Stilton Graphic Novels Ser.: 13). (ENG., Illus.). 56p. (J). (gr. 2-6). 9.99 (978-1-59707-448-3(9), 900123335, Papercutz) Mad Cave Studios.

Stilton, Thea. Thea Stilton & the Mystery on the Orient Express. 2012. (Thea Stilton Ser.: 13). lib. bdg. 19.65 (978-0-606-26757-1(3)) Turtleback.

Stockham, Jess, illus. Down by the Station. (Classic Books with Holes 8x8 with CD Ser.). (ENG.). 16p. (J). 2007. (gr. -1-1). (978-1-904550-68-6(1)) 2003. (978-0-85953-132-0(5)) Child's Play International Ltd.

Sturges, Philemon. I Love Trains. Halpern, Shari, illus. 2003. (ENG.). 32p. (J). (gr. -1-1). pap. 7.99 (978-0-06-443667-0(5), HarperCollins) HarperCollins Pubs.

—I Love Trains! Board Book. Halpern, Shari, illus. 2006. (ENG.). 28p. (J). (gr. -1-1). bds. 6.99 (978-0-06-083774-7(8), HarperFestival) HarperCollins Pubs.

Sweet, Melissa. Tupelo Rides the Rails. 2008. (ENG., Illus.). 40p. (J). (gr. 1-4). 17.00 (978-0-618-71714-9(5), 591982, Clarion Bks.) HarperCollins Pubs.

Terhune, Albert Payson. Caleb Conover: Railroader. (J). 13.95 (978-0-8488-1484-7(3)) Amereon Ltd.

—Lad: A Dog. (J). 24.95 (978-0-8488-1485-4(1)) Amereon Ltd.

Testa, Maggie. A Ride Through the Neighborhood. Style Guide, illus. 2014. (Daniel Tiger's Neighborhood Ser.). (ENG.). 12p. (J). (gr. -1-1). bds. 8.99 (978-1-4424-9839-6(0), Simon Spotlight) Simon Spotlight.

Thomas The Tank Engine & Egmont Staff. Thomas & Friends. 2008. (Illus.). 140p. (978-0-603-56338-6(4)) Farshore.

Titcomb, Gordon. The Last Train. Minor, Wendell, illus. 2010. (ENG.). 32p. (J). (gr. -1-3). 19.99 (978-1-59643-164-5(4), 9781596431645) Roaring Brook Pr.

Top That, ed. Let's Play Magnetic Play Scene Trains. 2008. (978-1-84666-557-8(4)) Top That! Publishing PLC.

Top That!, creator. ABC Train. 2007. (Jigsaw Book Ser.). (Illus.). 18p. (J). (gr. -1-3). bds. (978-1-84666-095-5(5)) Top That! Publishing PLC.

—123 Train. 2007. (Jigsaw Book Ser.). (Illus.). 18p. (J). (gr. -1-3). bds. (978-1-84666-097-9(1)) Top That! Publishing PLC.

Townend, Jack. A Railway ABC. 2015. (ENG., Illus.). 58p. (J). (gr. -1-1). 11.95 (978-1-85177-844-7(6)) V&A Publishing GBR. Dist: Hachette Bk. Group.

Tunnell, Michael O. Mailing May. Rand, Ted, illus. 2015. 32p. pap. 7.00 (978-1-61003-610-8(7)) Center for the Collaborative Classroom.

Vaillard, Fabiola. Tongo: The Wish Train. 2012. 32p. pap. 13.95 (978-1-4633-3431-4(1)) Palibrio.

Vamos, Samantha R. Alphabet Trains. O'Rourke, Ryan, illus. 2015. 32p. (J). (gr. -1-2). lib. bdg. 15.99 (978-1-58089-592-7(1)) Charlesbridge Publishing, Inc.

VanArsdale, Anthony, illus. Journey on a Runaway Train. 2017. (Boxcar Children Great Adventure Ser.: 1). (ENG.). 160p. (J). (gr. 2-5). 6.99 (978-0-8075-0696-7(6), 807506966); 12.99 (978-0-8075-0695-0(8), 807506958) Random Hse. Children's Bks. (Random Hse. Bks. for Young Readers).

Vanoosting, James. Walking Mary. 2005. 144p. (J). (gr. 7-18). lib. bdg. 16.89 (978-0-06-028472-5(2)) HarperCollins Pubs.

Vern, Jules. The Adventures of a Special Correspondent. 2009. 180p. 25.95 (978-1-60664-635-9(4)); pap. 13.95 (978-1-60664-377-8(0)) Rodgers, Alan Bks.

Vinesse, Cecilia. The Summer of Us. 2018. (ENG.). 320p. (YA). (gr. 9-17). 17.99 (978-0-316-39113-9(1), Poppy) Little, Brown Bks. for Young Readers.

Waddell, Barbara. If I Could Catch a Train. 2009. 20p. pap. 9.15 (978-1-4251-8667-8(X)) Trafford Publishing.

Walton, Dana E. Bo John's Train. 2012. 28p. pap. 19.99 (978-1-4772-0818-2(6)) AuthorHouse.

Warner, Gertrude Chandler. Journey on a Runaway Train. 2017. (Boxcar Children Great Adventure Ser.: 1). (J). lib. bdg. 17.20 (978-0-606-40315-3(9)) Turtleback.

Warner, Gertrude Chandler, creator. The Mystery of the Orphan Train. 2005. (Boxcar Children Mysteries Ser.: 105). (ENG., Illus.). 128p. (J). (gr. 2-5). lib. bdg. 14.99 (978-0-8075-5558-3(4), 807555584); per. 6.99 (978-0-8075-5559-0(2), 807555592) Random Hse. Children's Bks. (Random Hse. Bks. for Young Readers).

Warren, Bertie. Sammie's Journey to Freedom. 2006. (ENG.). 52p. per. 16.95 (978-1-4241-5142-4(2)) America Star Bks.

Watt, Fiona. Choo Choo. 2009. (Stroller Bks). 8p. (J). 7.99 (978-0-7945-2496-8(6), Usborne) EDC Publishing.

—Pull-Back Busy Train. Field, Jim, illus. 2013. (Pull-Back Bks). 10p. (J). ring bd. 24.99 (978-0-7945-3333-5(7), Usborne) EDC Publishing.

—That's Not My Train. rev. ed. 2008. (Touchy-Feely Board Bks). 10p. (J). bds. 8.99 (978-0-7945-2168-4(1), Usborne) EDC Publishing.

Watt, Fiona & Wells, Rachel. That's Not My Train: Its Wheels Are Too Slippery. 2004. (Touchy-Feely Board Bks.). (SPA & ENG., Illus.). 1p. (J). (gr. -1-18). bds. 7.95 (978-0-7460-3779-9(1)) EDC Publishing.

Weakly, Chris A. Toby the Little Switch Engine. 2012. 24p. 24.95 (978-1-4626-4884-9(3)) America Star Bks.

Webster, Christy. Get Rolling with Phonics (Thomas & Friends) 12 Step into Reading Books, 12 vols. 2016. (Step into Reading Ser.). (ENG., Illus.). 144p. (J). (gr. -1-2). pap. 12.99 (978-1-101-93726-6(2), Random Hse. Bks. for Young Readers) Random Hse. Children's Bks.

Welch, Julie. Happy Hearts, 1 vol. 2009. 52p. pap. 16.95 (978-1-4489-1971-0(1)) America Star Bks.

Wells, Rosemary. On the Blue Comet. Ibatoulline, Bagram, illus. (ENG.). 336p. (J). (gr. 5). 2012. pap. 9.99 (978-0-7636-5815-1(4)) 2010. 16.99 (978-0-7636-3722-4(X)) Candlewick Pr.

Whipple, Wayne. Radio Boys Cronies. 2004. reprint ed. pap. 15.95 (978-1-4191-4378-6(6)) Kessinger Publishing, LLC.

Wilson, Diane Lee. Tracks. (ENG., (J). (gr. 5-9). 2013. Illus.). 304p. pap. 6.99 (978-1-4424-2014-4(6)) 2012. 288p. 16.99 (978-1-4424-2013-7(8)) McElderry, Margaret K. Bks. (McElderry, Margaret K. Bks.).

Wondriska, William. Puff. 2015. (ENG., Illus.). 32p. (J). (gr. k-4). 16.95 (978-0-7893-2911-0(5)) Universe Publishing.

Woodford, Pamela. Sid, Spark & the Signal Man. 2013. (Brighter Little Minds Ser.). (ENG., Illus.). 18p. (J). 10.95 (978-1-871305-82-1(9)) Orpen Pr. IRL. Dist: Dufour Editions, Inc.

Worthington, Heather Hill. Miles of Smiles: The Story of Roxey, the Long Island Rail Road Dog. Farnsworth, Bill, illus. 2010. (J). (978-0-9792918-4-5(4)); pap. (978-0-9792918-8-3(7)) Blue Marlin Pubns.

Yee, Paul. Ghost Train. Chan, Harvey, illus. 2004. 29p. (J). (gr. k-4). reprint ed. 16.00 (978-0-7567-9083-7(2)) DIANE Publishing Co.

—Ghost Train, 1 vol. Chan, Harvey, illus. 2013. (ENG.). 32p. (J). (gr. 1-5). 14.95 (978-1-55498-389-6(4)) Groundwood Bks. CAN. Dist: Publishers Group West (PGW).

Yin. Coolies. Soentpiet, Chris, illus. 2003. 40p. (J). (gr. 2-5). 8.99 (978-0-14-250055-2(0), Puffin Books) Penguin Young Readers Group.

—Coolies. Soentpiet, Chris K., illus. 2003. (gr. k). 18.00 (978-0-7569-1545-2(7)) Perfection Learning Corp.

RAILROADS—FREIGHT

see Freight and Freightage

RAILROADS—HISTORY

Argyle, Ray. The Boy in the Picture: The Craigellachie Kid & the Driving of the Last Spike. 2010. (ENG., Illus.). 152p. (YA). pap. 19.99 (978-1-55488-787-3(9)) Dundurn Pr. CAN. Dist: Publishers Group West (PGW).

Ashley, Susan. Por Tren (Going by Train), 1 vol. 2003. (¡Vámonos! (Going Places) Ser.). (SPA., Illus.). 24p. (gr. 2-4). lib. bdg. 22.67 (978-0-8368-3737-7(1), 40c3f070-f899-4cf6-ad0a-0d1037dd0e2e, Weekly Reader Leveled Readers) Stevens, Gareth Publishing LLLP.

Bankston, John. Electric Trains & Trolleys (1880-1920) 2012. (J). lib. bdg. 29.95 (978-1-61228-291-6(1)) Mitchell Lane Pubs.

Bingham, Jane. The Story of Trains. King, Colin, illus. 2004. (Young Reading Ser.: Vol. 2). 64p. (J). (gr. 2-18). lib. bdg. 13.95 (978-1-58086-702-3(2), Usborne) EDC Publishing.

Cefrey, Holly. The Inventions of Granville Woods: The Railroad Telegraph System & the Third Rail. 2009. (19th Century American Inventors Ser.). 24p. (gr. 2-3). 42.50 (978-1-60854-952-8(6), PowerKids Pr.) Rosen Publishing Group, Inc., The.

Chiu, David. Government Regulation of the Railroads: Fighting Unfair Trade Practicesin America. 2009. (Progressive Movement 1900-1920: Efforts to Reform America's New Industrial Society Ser.). 32p. (gr. 3-4). 47.90 (978-1-60854-165-2(7)) Rosen Publishing Group, Inc., The.

Crewe, Sabrina & Uschan, Michael V. The Transcontinental Railroad, 1 vol. 2004. (Events That Shaped America Ser.). (ENG., Illus.). 32p. (gr. 3-5). lib. bdg. 28.67 (978-0-8368-3401-7(1), 70444a3d-cb94-4de8-bc09-9003d3471b2f, Gareth Stevens Learning Library) Stevens, Gareth Publishing LLLP.

Curlee, Lynn. Trains. Curlee, Lynn, illus. 2009. (ENG., Illus.). 48p. (J). (gr. 4-6). 19.99 (978-1-4169-4848-3(1), Atheneum Bks. for Young Readers) Simon & Schuster Children's Publishing.

Dolan, Edward F., Jr. & Dolan, Edward F. The Transcontinental Railroad, 1 vol. 2003. (Kaleidoscope: American History Ser.). (ENG., Illus.). 48p. (gr. 4-4). 32.64 (978-0-7614-1455-1(X), d8770898-99bc-4987-8e78-a36217f24914) Cavendish Square Publishing LLC.

Dooling, Sandra. Last Spike in CPR: Defining Moments in Canadian History. 2011. (Illus.). 32p. (gr. 5-8). (978-1-77071-689-6(0)) Weigl Educational Pubs. Ltd.

Dunn, Joeming W. Building the Transcontinental Railroad, 1 vol. Espinosa, Rod, illus. 2008. (Graphic History Ser.). (ENG.). 32p. (J). (gr. 3-8). 32.79 (978-1-60270-180-9(6), 9052, Graphic Planet - Fiction) Magic Wagon.

Dyan, Penelope. The Comeback Kids, Book 12, the Redwood Forest. Weigand, John D., photos by. 2013. (Illus.). 34p. pap. 14.95 (978-1-61477-081-7(6)) Bellissima Publishing, LLC.

Floca, Brian. Locomotive. Floca, Brian, illus. 2013. (ENG., Illus.). 64p. (J). (gr. -1-5). 19.99 (978-1-4169-9415-2(7), Atheneum/Richard Jackson Bks.) Simon & Schuster Children's Publishing.

Gibson, Karen. The Railroad Comes to America (1820-1830) 2012. (Illus.). 47p. (J). lib. bdg. 29.95 (978-1-61228-287-9(3)) Mitchell Lane Pubs.

Gove, Bill. Sky Route to the Quarries: History of the Barre Railroad. 2003. 98p. per. 21.95 (978-1-931271-12-7(7)) Bondcliff Bks.

Graham, Ian. You Wouldn't Want to Work on the Railroad! (Revised Edition) 2014. (You Wouldn't Want to... Ser.). (ENG.). 32p. (J). lib. bdg. 29.00 (978-0-531-21178-6(9), Watts, Franklin) Scholastic Library Publishing.

Halpern, Monica. Railroad Fever (Direct Mail Edition) Building the Transcontinental Railroad 1830-1870. 2004. (Crossroads America Ser.). (ENG., Illus.). 40p. (J). (gr. 5-9). 12.95 (978-0-7922-6767-6(2)) National Geographic Society.

Hansen, Holly T. & Johnson, Jennifer Hunt. Memories of the Railroad, 14 vols. 2003. (Illus.). 21p. 9.95 (978-0-9741172-3-2(4), CMB10) Tapis & Assocs., Inc.

Harasymiw, Therese. The Transcontinental Railroad: Connecting the Nation, 1 vol. 2017. (American History Ser.). (ENG.). 104p. (gr. 7-7). lib. bdg. 41.03 (978-1-5345-6137-3(4), 380169be-2be6-4d7d-97fc-8abc1c3e8eab, Lucent Pr.) Greenhaven Publishing LLC.

Hemenway, Scott. Anthracite Collieries & Railroads of the Western Middle Field. 2008. (978-1-931014-08-3(6)) Garrigues Hse. Pubs.

Hodge, Deborah. The Kids Book of Canada's Railway: And How the CPR Was Built. Mantha, John, illus. 2008. (Kids Book Of Ser.). (ENG.). 48p. (J). (gr. 3-7). pap. 15.99 (978-1-55453-256-8(6)) Kids Can Pr., Ltd. CAN. Dist: Hachette Bk. Group.

Hynson, Colin. A History of Railroads, 1 vol. 2005. (From Past to Present Ser.). (ENG., Illus.). 36p. (gr. 4-6). lib. bdg. 28.67 (978-0-8368-6287-4(2), 2eef6bc8-2377-48d4-b351-a50e897cfdbe, Gareth Stevens Learning Library) Stevens, Gareth Publishing LLLP.

Jarrow, Jesse. Oil, Steel, & Railroads: America's Big Businesses in the Late 1800s. (America's Industrial Society in the 19th Century Ser.). 32p. (gr. 4-4). 2009. 47.90 (978-1-61511-337-8(1)) 2003. (ENG., Illus.). pap. 10.00 (978-0-8239-4276-3(7), a40b88e8-1561-410a-b257-646a9dc4260d) Rosen Publishing Group, Inc., The.

Lightfoot, Gordon. Canadian Railroad Trilogy, 1 vol. Wallace, Ian, illus. 2010. (ENG.). 56p. (J). (gr. k). 24.95 (978-0-88899-953-5(4)) Groundwood Bks. CAN. Dist: Publishers Group West (PGW).

Lohse, Joyce B. General William Palmer: Railroad Pioneer. 2009. (Now You Know Bio Ser.: 12). (Illus.). 104p. (J). pap. 8.95 (978-0-86541-092-3(5)) Filter Pr., LLC.

Lynette, Rachel. The Transcontinental Railroad, 1 vol. 2013. (Pioneer Spirit: the Westward Expansion Ser.). (ENG.). 24p. (J). (gr. 2-3). 26.27 (978-1-4777-0785-2(9), 56fc3c90-8a3f-4d6c-8b10-da957491801a); (Illus.). pap. 9.25 (978-1-4777-0903-0(7), 9e793ea2-5a60-4efb-8f00-26c84803618c) Rosen Publishing Group, Inc., The. (PowerKids Pr.).

Magram, Hannah Straus. Railroads of the West. 2004. (History of the Old West Ser.). (Illus.). 64p. (YA). (gr. 5-18). lib. bdg. 19.95 (978-1-59084-073-3(9)) Mason Crest.

Marsh, Carole. The Transcontinental Railroad: The Big Race to the Golden Spike. 2010. (American Milestones Ser.). (Illus.). 28p. (J). pap. 6.99 (978-0-635-07506-2(7)) Gallopade International.

Marsico, Katie. Trains. 2008. (21st Century Skills Innovation Library: Innovation in Transportation Ser.). (ENG., Illus.). 32p. (gr. 4-8). lib. bdg. 32.07 (978-1-60279-234-0(8), 200164) Cherry Lake Publishing.

Mattern, Joanne. The Birth of the Locomotive (1780-1820) 2012. (Illus.). 47p. (J). (gr. 4-8). lib. bdg. 29.95 (978-1-61228-286-2(5)) Mitchell Lane Pubs.

Morris, Neil. Trains. (Past & Present Ser.). (Illus.). 32p. lib. bdg. 24.25 (978-1-931983-37-2(2)) Chrysalis Education.

Murdico, Suzanne J. Railroads & Steamships: Important Developments in American Transportation. (America's Industrial Society in the 19th Century Ser.). 32p. (gr. 4-4). 2009. 47.90 (978-1-61511-340-8(1)) 2003. (ENG., Illus.). (J). pap. 10.00 (978-0-8239-4278-7(3), 44a84b6b-b256-4ad5-a2e0-5367fe9c4a95) 2003. (ENG., Illus.). (J). lib. bdg. 29.13 (978-0-8239-4024-0(1), 9c5f4762-c197-4003-b7e8-465e5458522a, Rosen Reference) Rosen Publishing Group, Inc., The.

Murphy, Jim. Across America on an Emigrant Train. 2003. (ENG., Illus.). 168p. (J). (gr. 5-7). pap. 10.95 (978-0-395-76483-1(1), 111826, Clarion Bks.) HarperCollins Pubs.

Nardo, Don. The Golden Spike: How a Photograph Celebrated the Transcontinental Railroad. 2015. (Captured History Ser.). (ENG., Illus.). 64p. (J). (gr. 5-9). lib. bdg. 35.32 (978-0-7565-4991-6(4), 127634, Compass Point Bks.) Capstone.

O'Mara, Jack. How Railroads Shaped America. (American History Flashpoints! Ser.). 32p. (gr. 4-4). 2009. 47.90 (978-1-61511-368-2(1), PowerKids Pr.) 2009. (ENG.). (J). lib. bdg. 28.93 (978-1-4358-2993-0(X), cba09714-1cf8-4043-be88-fa0e451987f8, PowerKids Pr.) 2008. (ENG.). pap. 10.00 (978-1-4358-0175-2(X), 4659b592-c23e-48c6-9b36-a3f6fd738e5b, Rosen Classroom) Rosen Publishing Group, Inc., The.

Orr, Tamra. The Railroad & the Civil War (1860s) 2012. (J). lib. bdg. 29.95 (978-1-61228-289-3(X)) Mitchell Lane Pubs.

The Pullman Strike Of 1894. 2006. (American Workers Ser.). (Illus.). 144p. (J). (gr. 5-7). lib. bdg. 26.95 (978-1-931798-89-1(3)) Reynolds, Morgan Inc.

Rajczak, Michael. The Transcontinental Railroad, 1 vol., Vol. 1. 2013. (What You Didn't Know about History Ser.). (ENG., Illus.). 24p. (J). (gr. 2-3). pap. 9.15 (978-1-4824-0599-6(7), d7bf741a-57a6-4e5d-bf04-42184db23724) Stevens, Gareth Publishing LLLP.

Raum, Elizabeth. Orphan Trains: An Interactive History Adventure. 2010. (You Choose: History Ser.). (ENG.). 112p. (J). (gr. 3-4). pap. 41.70 (978-1-4296-6441-7(X), 16181); pap. 6.95 (978-1-4296-6273-4(5), 115419); (Illus.). 32.65 (978-1-4296-5479-1(1), 113879) Capstone. (Capstone Pr.).

Richter, Bernd & Richter, Susan. All Aboard the White Pass & Yukon Route Railroad. 2003. 48p. 9.95 (978-1-931353-11-3(5)) Saddle Pal Creations, Inc.

Roberts, Russell. The Railroad Fuels Westward Expansion (1870s) 2012. (Illus.). 47p. (J). lib. bdg. 29.95 (978-1-61228-290-9(3)) Mitchell Lane Pubs.

Shea, Therese. The Transcontinental Railroad: Using Proportions to Solve Problems, 1 vol. (Math for the REAL World Ser.). 32p. (gr. 5-5). 2009. (ENG., Illus.). pap. 10.00 (978-1-4042-6075-7(7), 785d186d-7453-4085-8f38-992063e03aac) 2009. 47.90 (978-1-60851-370-3(X), PowerKids Pr.) 2006. (ENG., Illus.). (YA). lib. bdg. 28.93 (978-1-4042-3361-4(X), 7d4994a5-4462-4fc6-b218-453874e356dc) Rosen Publishing Group, Inc., The.

Shoup, Kate. Life As an Engineer on the First Railroads in America, 1 vol. 2015. (Life As... Ser.). (ENG.). 32p. (gr. 3-3). pap. 11.58 (978-1-5026-1088-1(4), d7101213-a713-4357-92d2-fb1d357b972a) Cavendish Square Publishing LLC.

Sís, Peter. The Train of States. Sís, Peter, illus. 2004. (Illus.). 64p. (J). (gr. 1-18). 17.99 (978-0-06-057838-1(6)) HarperCollins Pubs.

Staunton, Ted. The Dreadful Truth: Building the Railway. Goff, Brian, illus. 2005. (Dreadful Truth Ser.). (ENG.). 80p. (J). (gr. 3-8). (978-0-88780-690-2(2)) Formac Publishing Co., Ltd.

Stunkard, Geoff. Rail Mail: A Century of American Railroading on Picture Postcards. 2004. (Illus.). 128p. pap. 17.95 (978-0-9748216-0-3(8), QMP608) Quarter Milestones Publishing.

Tracy, Kathleen. The Railroad Grows into an Industry (1840-1850) 2012. (Illus.). 47p. (J). lib. bdg. 29.95 (978-1-61228-288-6(1)) Mitchell Lane Pubs.

The Transcontinental Railroad. 2013. (Pioneer Spirit: the Westward Expansion Ser.). 24p. (J). (gr. 3-6). pap. 49.50

P
Q
R

(978-1-4777-0904-7(5), PowerKids Pr.) Rosen Publishing Group, Inc., The.

Uschan, Michael V. The Transcontinental Railroad, 1 vol. 2003. (Landmark Events in American History Ser.). (ENG., Illus.). 48p. (J). (gr. 5-8). pap. 15.05 *(978-0-8368-5410-7(1)*, 1e383fb5-2ffb-4d1c-a683-741a73060a32); lib. bdg. 33.67 *(978-0-8368-5382-7(2)*, d0f576fb-46eb-4602-be10-44e089049cf0) Stevens, Gareth Publishing LLLP. (Gareth Stevens Secondary Library).

Zollitsch, Mike. Buffalo, Rochester, & Pittsburgh Railway: In Color. 2004. (Illus.). 59.95 *(978-1-58248-092-3(3))* Morning Sun Bks., Inc.

Zuchora-Walske, Christine. The Transcontinental Railroad, 1 vol. 2016. (Wild West Ser.). (ENG., Illus.). 48p. (J). (gr. 4-8). lib. bdg. 35.64 *(978-1-68078-261-5(4)*, 22123) ABDO Publishing Co.

RAILROADS—MODELS

Jefferis, David. Model Trains: Creating Tabletop Railroads. 2018. (Model-Making Mindset Ser.). 32p. (J). (gr. 5-5). *(978-0-7787-5017-8(5))* Crabtree Publishing Co.

RAILROADS—STATIONS

see Railroad Stations

RAILROADS—TRAINS

Allard, Mario, illus. Caillou Takes the Train. 2018. (Clubhouse Ser.). (ENG.). 24p. (J). (gr. -1-1). 3.99 *(978-2-89718-463-6(9))* Caillouet, Gerry.

Amato, William. Bullet Trains. 2009. (High-Tech Vehicles Ser.). 24p. (gr. 2-3). 42.50 *(978-1-61513-304-8(6)*, PowerKids Pr.) Rosen Publishing Group, Inc., The.

—Trenes Bala, 1 vol. 2003. (Vehículos de Alta Tecnología (High-Tech Vehicles) Ser.). (SPA., Illus.). 24p. (J). (gr. 2-2). lib. bdg. 26.27 *(978-0-8239-6881-7(2)*, 7993feec-efca-4c1b-a059-b706a3cbbccf) Rosen Publishing Group, Inc., The.

—Trenes bala (Bullet Trains) 2009. (Vehículos de alta tecnología (High-Tech Vehicles) Ser.). (SPA.). 24p. (gr. 2-3). 42.50 *(978-1-60854-722-7(1)*, Editorial Buenas Letras) Rosen Publishing Group, Inc., The.

Ashley, Susan. Going by Train, 1 vol. 2003. (Going Places (First Edition) Ser.). (ENG., Illus.). 24p. (gr. 2-4). pap. 9.15 *(978-0-8368-3837-4(8)*, ad6d7f75-ec11-4c6d-a460-e342e4265b05, Weekly Reader Leveled Readers) Stevens, Gareth Publishing LLLP.

AZ Books, creator. Talking Train. 2012. (Lively Machines Ser.). (ENG., Illus.). 10p. (J). (gr. -1-k). bds. 10.95 *(978-1-61889-325-3(4))* AZ Bks. LLC.

Bergin, Mark. Trains, 1 vol. Bergin, Mark, illus. 2012. (You Can Draw Ser.). (ENG., Illus.). 32p. (J). (gr. 2-2). pap. 11.50 *(978-1-4339-7478-6(9)*, 52c3d223-6ca5-4079-a195-d17b214d63d8); lib. bdg. 29.27 *(978-1-4339-7477-9(0)*, 0eda7c02-95ef-40aa-a783-01927ea6b030) Stevens, Gareth Publishing LLLP.

Beyer, Mark. Trains of the Past. 2009. (Transportation Through the Ages Ser.). 24p. (gr. 1-1). 42.50 *(978-1-60854-591-9(1)*, PowerKids Pr.) Rosen Publishing Group, Inc., The.

—Trenes del Pasado, 1 vol. 2003. (Transporte Ayer y Hoy (Transportation Through the Ages) Ser.). (SPA., Illus.). 24p. (J). (gr. 1-2). lib. bdg. 26.27 *(978-0-8239-6852-7(9)*, 1bfb12bb-a9b2-4c86-9485-be0187111f13) Rosen Publishing Group, Inc., The.

—Trenes del pasado (Trains of the Past) 2009. (transporte ayer y hoy (Transportation Through the Ages) Ser.). (SPA.). 24p. (gr. 1-2). 42.50 *(978-1-61512-256-1(7)*, Editorial Buenas Letras) Rosen Publishing Group, Inc., The.

Biello, David. Bullet Trains: Inside & Out. 2009. (Technology: Blueprints of the Future Ser.). 48p. (gr. 4-4). 53.00 *(978-1-60853-282-7(8))* Rosen Publishing Group, Inc., The.

—Trenes de Alta Velocidad: Por dentro y por fuera (Bullet Trains: Inside & Out) 2009. (Tecnología: Mapas para el Futuro Ser.). (SPA.). 48p. (gr. 4-4). 53.00 *(978-1-60853-291-9(7)*, Editorial Buenas Letras) Rosen Publishing Group, Inc., The.

Bingham, Jane. The Story of Trains. King, Colin, illus. 2004. (Young Reading Ser.: Vol. 2). 64p. (J). (gr. 2-18). lib. bdg. 13.95 *(978-1-58086-702-3(2)*, Usborne) EDC Publishing.

Bowman, Chris. Trains. 2017. (Mighty Machines in Action Ser.). (ENG., Illus.). 24p. (J). (gr. k-3). lib. bdg. 26.95 *(978-1-62617-610-2(8)*, Blastoff! Readers) Bellwether Media.

Brooks, Felicity, des. Build a Picture Trains Sticker Book. 2012. (Build a Picture Sticker Bks). 24p. (J). pap. 6.99 *(978-0-7945-3261-1(6)*, Usborne) EDC Publishing.

Caravantes, Peggy. The Orphan Trains: A History Perspectives Book. 2013. (Perspectives Library). (ENG., Illus.). 32p. (J). (gr. 4-8). 32.07 *(978-1-62431-420-9(1)*, 202800); pap. 14.21 *(978-1-62431-496-4(1)*, 202802) Cherry Lake Publishing.

Carr, Aaron. Trains. 2014. (Illus.). 24p. (J). *(978-1-4896-3236-4(0))* Weigl Pubs., Inc.

Ciovacco, Justine. All about Trains, 1 vol. 2016. (Let's Find Out! Transportation Ser.). (ENG., Illus.). 32p. (J). (gr. 2-3). lib. bdg. 26.06 *(978-1-68048-446-5(X)*, f6691dac-d91c-42d3-a44d-ca5a8b58b093) Rosen Publishing Group, Inc., The.

Clapper, Nikki Bruno. City Trains. 2015. (All Aboard! Ser.). (ENG., Illus.). 24p. (J). (gr. -1-2). lib. bdg. 27.32 *(978-1-4914-6037-5(7)*, 128951, Capstone Pr.) Capstone.

—Passenger Trains. 2015. (All Aboard! Ser.). (ENG., Illus.). 24p. (J). (gr. -1-2). lib. bdg. 27.32 *(978-1-4914-6040-5(7)*, 128954, Capstone Pr.) Capstone.

Clark, Willow. Trains on the Move, 1 vol. 2010. (Transportation Station Ser.). (ENG.). 24p. (J). (gr. 2-3). pap. 9.25 *(978-1-4358-9750-2(1)*, f4f893a4-2e80-44c5-890f-8306849ff142); (Illus.). lib. bdg. 26.27 *(978-1-4358-9331-3(X)*, 4012aa41-bf42-4f2e-9f66-255a4c910713) Rosen Publishing Group, Inc., The. (PowerKids Pr.).

Coming Soon. Trains. 2018. (Eyediscover Ser.). (ENG., Illus.). 24p. (J). 28.55 *(978-1-4896-8335-9(6)*, AV2 by Weigl) Weigl Pubs., Inc.

Crews, Donald. Freight Train. 2010. (Illus.). (J). *(978-1-4351-1213-1(X))* Barnes & Noble, Inc.

David West. Train. 2006. (Illus.). 32p. (J). pap. *(978-1-4109-2564-0(1))* Steck-Vaughn.

Dawson, Emily C. Trains. 2012. (ENG., Illus.). 24p. (J). lib. bdg. 25.65 *(978-1-62031-022-9(8))* Jump! Inc.

Devera, Czeena. Go Train! 2019. (Watch It Go Ser.). (ENG.). 16p. (J). (gr. -1-2). pap. 11.36 *(978-1-5341-3919-0(2)*, 212507, Cherry Blossom Press) Cherry Lake Publishing.

Dieker, Wendy Strobel. Trains. 2019. (Spot Mighty Machines Ser.). (ENG.). 16p. (J). (gr. -1-2). *(978-1-68151-649-3(7)*, 10781) Amicus.

DK. Ultimate Sticker Book: Train: More Than 60 Reusable Full-Color Stickers. 2005. (Ultimate Sticker Book Ser.). (ENG., Illus.). 16p. (J). (gr. k-3). pap. 6.99 *(978-0-7566-1460-7(0)*, DK Children) Dorling Kindersley Publishing, Inc.

Eason, Sarah. How Does a High-Speed Train Work?, 1 vol. 2010. (How Does It Work? Ser.). (ENG.). 32p. (J). (gr. 3-4). lib. bdg. 28.67 *(978-1-4339-3468-1(X)*, 03899577-85ad-407e-a5e8-9193dcb0ab56); (Illus.). pap. 11.50 *(978-1-4339-3469-8(8)*, 0304f33b-ef33-4ea9-ac2d-7ea97eece700) Stevens, Gareth Publishing LLLP. (Gareth Stevens Learning Library).

Editors of Kingfisher. It's All about. . . Speedy Trains. 2016. (It's All About... Ser.). (ENG.). 32p. (J). pap. 5.99 *(978-0-7534-7287-3(2)*, 900160780, Kingfisher) Roaring Brook Pr.

Farndon, John. Stickmen's Guide to Trains & Automobiles. Paul de Quay, John, illus. 2016. (Stickmen's Guides to How Everything Works). (ENG.). 32p. (J). (gr. 3-6). lib. bdg. 27.99 *(978-1-4677-9360-5(4)*, a5a8eae3-07c9-4d43-8792-c0f812348dd1); E-Book 42.65 *(978-1-4677-9590-6(9))* Lerner Publishing Group. (Hungry Tomato (r)).

Frith, Alex. Look Inside Trains. 2015. (Look Inside Board Bks.). (ENG.). 14p. (J). (gr. k-5). 14.99 *(978-0-7945-3448-6(1)*, Usborne) EDC Publishing.

Goodman, Susan E. Trains! Doolittle, Michael J., illus. 2012. (Step into Reading Ser.). 48p. (J). (gr. 1-4). pap. 5.99 *(978-0-375-86941-9(7)*, Random Hse. Bks. for Young Readers) Random Hse. Children's Bks.

—Trains! 2012. (Step into Reading Level 3 Ser.). lib. bdg. 13.55 *(978-0-606-23859-5(X))* Turtleback.

Gordon, Nick. Monster Trains. 2013. (Monster Machines Ser.). (ENG., Illus.). 24p. (J). (gr. k-3). lib. bdg. 26.95 *(978-1-60014-939-9(1)*, Blastoff! Readers) Bellwether Media.

Hamilton, Robert M. On a Train, 1 vol. 2012. (Going Places (New Edition) Ser.). (ENG.). 24p. (J). (gr. k-k). pap. 9.15 *(978-1-4339-6283-7(7)*, 71a425e6-b89b-4369-8a84-d3e96f0049c9); lib. bdg. 25.27 *(978-1-4339-6281-3(0)*, 0e950fe3-4e8e-40e5-9e50-87be54942ce3) Stevens, Gareth Publishing LLLP.

Hofer, Charles. Bullet Trains. (World's Fastest Machines Ser.). 24p. (gr. 2-3). 2009. 42.50 *(978-1-60854-852-1(X))* 2007. (ENG., Illus.). (J). lib. bdg. 26.27 *(978-1-4042-4174-9(4)*, 39e68f05-ae64-4b4f-afb2-b901fdd7764d) Rosen Publishing Group, Inc., The. (PowerKids Pr.).

Hurst, Vera J. 21st-Century Trains, 1 vol. 2018. (Feats of 21st-Century Engineering Ser.). (ENG.). 48p. (gr. 4-4). 29.60 *(978-0-7660-9709-4(9)*, 6a14947c-2d63-441d-986f-eb98b7a0c84f) Enslow Publishing, LLC.

Isbell, Hannah. Zoom in on Rail Networks, 1 vol. 2017. (Zoom in on Engineering Ser.). (ENG.). 24p. (gr. 2-2). lib. bdg. 25.60 *(978-0-7660-8709-5(3)*, 37d55c9e-1dca-4f67-891b-8f063f43b8fa) Enslow Publishing, LLC.

Jacob, Ellen, et al. My Train Book. Vandenberg, Michael, photos by. 2007. (ENG., Illus.). 16p. (J). (gr. -1-k). bds. 6.99 *(978-0-06-089970-7(0)*, Collins) HarperCollins Pubs.

Johnstone, Michael, et al. Trains. (ENG., Illus.). 32p. (J). mass mkt. 8.99 *(978-0-590-24654-5(2))* Scholastic, Inc.

Juettner, Bonnie. Hybrid Cars. 2009. (Great Idea Ser.). (Illus.). 48p. (J). (gr. 4-6). lib. bdg. 26.60 *(978-1-59953-193-9(3))* Norwood Hse. Pr.

Kate Shelley & the Midnight Express. 9.95 *(978-1-59112-169-5(8))* Live Oak Media.

Kemmeter, Jennifer. Build It! Trains: Make Supercool Models with Your Favorite LEGO(r) Parts. 2018. (Brick Bks.: 12). (ENG., Illus.). 102p. (J). (gr. k-3). 32.99 *(978-1-5132-6114-0(2))*; pap. 17.99 *(978-1-5132-6113-3(4))* West Margin Pr. (Graphic Arts Bks.).

Kluth, Paula & Kluth, Victoria. A Is for All Aboard!, 1 vol. Littlejohn, Brad, illus. 2009. 32p. (J). 16.95 *(978-1-59857-071-7(4))* Brookes Publishing.

Leighton, Christina. Freight Trains. 2017. (Amazing Trains Ser.). (ENG., Illus.). 24p. (J). (gr. k-3). lib. bdg. 26.95 *(978-1-62617-670-6(1)*, Blastoff! Readers) Bellwether Media.

—High-Speed Trains. 2017. (Amazing Trains Ser.). (ENG., Illus.). 24p. (J). (gr. k-3). lib. bdg. 26.95 *(978-1-62617-671-3(X)*, Blastoff! Readers) Bellwether Media.

—Passenger Trains. 2017. (Amazing Trains Ser.). (ENG., Illus.). 24p. (J). (gr. k-3). lib. bdg. 26.95 *(978-1-62617-673-7(6)*, Blastoff! Readers) Bellwether Media.

Litchfield, Jo & Brooks, F. Trains. 2004. (Chunky Board Bks.). (ENG., Illus.). 6p. (J). bds. 4.95 *(978-0-7945-0348-2(9)*, Usborne) EDC Publishing.

MacArthur, Collin. Inside a High-Speed Train, 1 vol. 2014. (Life in the Fast Lane Ser.). (ENG., Illus.). 48p. (gr. 4-4). 33.07 *(978-1-62713-043-1(8)*, 24512908-d9a8-4402-bb38-b08d250e7f12) Cavendish Square Publishing LLC.

Mara, Wil. From Kingfishers to... Bullet Trains. 2012. (21st Century Skills Innovation Library: Innovations from Nature Ser.). (ENG.). 32p. (gr. 4-8). pap. 14.21 *(978-1-61080-672-5(7)*, 202282); (Illus.). 32.07 *(978-1-61080-498-1(8)*, 202108) Cherry Lake Publishing.

Mayfield, Marilee Joy. My First Book of Planes, Trains, & Cars. 2016. (Illus.). 51p. (J). *(978-1-4351-6528-1(4))* Barnes & Noble, Inc.

Maynard, Christopher. High-Speed Trains. 2003. (Need for Speed Ser.). (Illus.). 32p. (J). (gr. 3-6). pap. 7.95 *(978-0-8225-0390-3(5))* Lerner Publishing Group.

—Trains. 2005. (Need for Speed Ser.). (Illus.). 32p. (gr. 3-5). lib. bdg. 23.93 *(978-0-8225-0387-3(5))* Lerner Publishing Group.

Meachen Rau, Dana. En Trenes / Trains, 1 vol. 2010. (¡Viajamos! / We Go! Ser.). (ENG & SPA.). 24p. (gr. k-1). lib. bdg. 25.50 *(978-0-7614-4773-3(3)*, a5d5421c-204f-4ac9-9d52-3b0fe1a5292a) Cavendish Square Publishing LLC.

—Trains, 1 vol. 2010. (We Go! Ser.). (ENG.). 24p. (gr. 3-3). 25.50 *(978-0-7614-4081-9(X)*, 78dda8aa-fca5-4aaa-994a-50ffb6c1398f) Cavendish Square Publishing LLC.

Meister, Cari. Trains. 2019. (Transportation in My Community Ser.). (ENG., Illus.). 32p. (J). (gr. -1-2). lib. bdg. 27.99 *(978-1-9771-0685-8(4)*, 140141, Pebble) Capstone.

Miles, David W. Color Train. 2019. (ENG., Illus.). 14p. (J). (gr. -1-k). bds. 12.99 *(978-1-64170-106-8(4)*, 550106) Familius LLC.

Oxlade, Chris. Trains. 2009. (Mighty Machines Ser.). (Illus.). 31p. (J). (gr. 4-7). pap. 7.95 *(978-1-59920-258-7(1))* Black Rabbit Bks.

Peters, Elisa. Let's Take the Train! 2014. (Public Transportation Ser.). (Illus.). 24p. (J). (gr. k-2). pap. 49.50 *(978-1-4777-6514-2(X)*, PowerKids Pr.) Rosen Publishing Group, Inc., The.

—¡Vamos a Tomar el Tren! / Let's Take the Train!, 1 vol. de la Vega, Eida, ed. 2014. (Transporte Público / Public Transportation Ser.). (SPA & ENG.). 24p. (J). (gr. 1-2). 25.27 *(978-1-4777-6781-8(9)*, 3e6a6f3a-d9b9-438b-9687-58e1d9b15ea4, PowerKids Pr.) Rosen Publishing Group, Inc., The.

Priddy, Roger. My Big Train Book. 2015. (My Big Board Bks.). (ENG.). 10p. (J). (gr. -1 — 1). bds. 7.99 *(978-0-312-51943-8(5)*, 900150606) St. Martin's Pr.

Prior, Jennifer. All Aboard! How Trains Work, 1 vol. 2nd rev. ed. 2014. (TIME for KIDS(r): Informational Text Ser.). (ENG., Illus.). 28p. (J). (gr. 3-4). lib. bdg. 25.96 *(978-1-4807-1071-9(7))* Teacher Created Materials, Inc.

Prunier, James. Trains. Prunier, James, illus. 2012. (ENG., Illus.). 32p. (J). (gr. -1-k). spiral bd. 19.99 *(978-1-85103-400-0(5))* Moonlight Publishing, Ltd. GBR. Dist: Independent Pubs. Group.

Radtke, Becky. Trains Activity Book. 2007. (Dover Little Activity Bks.). (ENG., Illus.). 64p. (J). (gr. k-3). per. 2.50 *(978-0-486-45683-6(8)*, 456838) Dover Pubns., Inc.

Riggs, Kate. Bullet Trains. 2015. (Seedlings Ser.). (ENG.). 24p. (J). (gr. -1-k). *(978-1-60818-519-1(2)*, 21221, Creative Education) Creative Co., The.

—Seedlings: Bullet Trains. 2015. (Seedlings Ser.). (ENG.). 24p. (J). (gr. -1-1). pap. 10.99 *(978-1-62832-119-7(9)*, 21222, Creative Paperbacks) Creative Co., The.

—Trains. 2007. (My First Look at: Vehicles Ser.). (Illus.). 24p. (J). (gr. -1-3). lib. bdg. 24.25 *(978-1-58341-529-0(7)*, Creative Education) Creative Co., The.

Ryan, Phillip. Passenger Trains, 1 vol. 2010. (All Aboard! Ser.). (ENG.). 24p. (J). (gr. 1-2). pap. 9.25 *(978-1-4488-1215-8(1)*, 24bc9909-10a5-4e2f-89e7-a032a0971ea2); lib. bdg. 26.27 *(978-1-4488-0637-9(2)*, 83bc4aea-6eb2-4e11-8b90-71083e69c7b7) Rosen Publishing Group, Inc., The. (PowerKids Pr.).

Schuh, Mari. Trains. 2017. (Transportation Ser.). (ENG., Illus.). 24p. (J). (gr. -1-2). pap. 6.95 *(978-1-5157-7308-5(6)*, 135661, Pebble) Capstone.

Sheffield, S. A Train on the Track: Learning the TR Sound. 2009. (PowerPhonics Ser.). 24p. (gr. 1-1). 39.90 *(978-1-60851-430-4(7)*, PowerKids Pr.) Rosen Publishing Group, Inc., The.

Shields, Amy. Trains (1 Hardcover/1 CD) 2016. (National Geographic Readers: Pre-Reader Ser.). (ENG.). (J). *(978-1-4301-2120-6(3))* Live Oak Media.

—Trains (1 Paperback/1 CD) 2016. (National Geographic Readers: Pre-Reader Ser.). (ENG.). (J). pap. *(978-1-4301-2119-0(X))* Live Oak Media.

Silverman, Buffy. How Do Trains Work? 2016. (Lightning Bolt Books (r) — How Vehicles Work Ser.). (ENG., Illus.). 32p. (J). (gr. 1-3). 29.32 *(978-1-4677-9500-5(3)*, b5c1530e-6ca4-4843-ad21-6c5c2f1fbc29, Lerner Pubns.) Lerner Publishing Group.

Smithyman, Kathryn & Kalman, Bobbie. Trains on the Tracks, 1 vol. rev. ed. 2007. (Vehicles on the Move Ser.). (ENG., Illus.). 32p. (J). (gr. 1-5). pap. *(978-0-7787-3059-0(X))* Crabtree Publishing Co.

—Trenes en las Vias. 2007. (Vehículos en Acción Ser.). (SPA & ENG., Illus.). 32p. (J). lib. bdg. *(978-0-7787-8307-7(3))*; (gr. 4-7). pap. *(978-0-7787-8317-6(0))* Crabtree Publishing Co.

Thomas, Mary Ann. Our Train Trip: Learning to Add Times by the Half Hour, 1 vol. 2010. (Math for the REAL World Ser.). (ENG.). 12p. (gr. 1-2). pap. 5.90 *(978-0-8239-8849-5(X)*, f80b45b5-a444-45e0-b417-6675e2a6d2a8, Rosen Classroom) Rosen Publishing Group, Inc., The.

Turnbull, Stephanie. Trains. 2009. (Discovery History Ser.). 48p. (YA). (gr. 3-18). 8.99 *(978-0-7945-2246-9(7)*, Usborne) EDC Publishing.

Veitch, Catherine. Big Machines Ride Rails!, 1 vol. 2014. (Big Machines Ser.). (ENG.). 24p. (J). (gr. -1-1). 25.99 *(978-1-4846-0589-9(6)*, 126691, Heinemann) Capstone.

Von Finn, Denny. Bullet Trains. 2009. (World's Fastest Ser.). (ENG., Illus.). 24p. (J). (gr. 3-7). lib. bdg. 26.95 *(978-1-60014-286-4(9)*, Torque Bks.) Bellwether Media.

West, David. Trains. 2014. (Mechanic Mike's Machines Ser.). 24p. (gr. k-3). 28.50 *(978-1-62588-060-4(X))* Black Rabbit Bks.

Williams, John Matthew. Trains Go!, 1 vol. 2017. (Ways to Go Ser.). (ENG.). 24p. (J). (gr. k-k). pap. 9.15 *(978-1-5382-1025-3(8)*, 836ea712-da86-4ed7-961c-9d770f2d5ca1) Stevens, Gareth Publishing LLLP.

RAILROADS, UNDERGROUND

see Subways

RAILROADS—VOCATIONAL GUIDANCE

Otfinoski, Steven. High-Speed Trains: from Concept to Consumer (Calling All Innovators: a Career for You) (Library Edition) 2015. (Calling All Innovators: a Career for You Ser.). (ENG.). 64p. (J). (gr. 5-8). lib. bdg. 32.00 *(978-0-531-21899-0(6)*, Children's Pr.) Scholastic Library Publishing.

RAILWAYS

see Railroads

RAIN AND RAINFALL

see also Floods; Meteorology; Snow; Storms

Anderson, Judith. Once There Was a Raindrop. Gordon, Mike, illus. 2010. (Nature's Miracles Ser.). (ENG.). 32p. (J). (gr. k-3). 18.69 *(978-0-7641-4495-0(2)*, B.E.S. Publishing) Peterson's.

Appleby, Alex. It's Rainy!, 1 vol. 2013. (What's the Weather? Ser.). (Illus.). 24p. (J). (gr. k-k). (ENG.). pap. 9.15 *(978-1-4339-9397-8(X)*, 426cff56-be4b-4831-92af-abef6d481e97); (ENG., lib. bdg. 25.27 *(978-1-4339-9396-1(1)*, fc75c5bd-7018-48f7-a368-88b8494e8663); pap. 48.90 *(978-1-4339-9398-5(8))* Stevens, Gareth Publishing LLLP.

—It's Rainy! / ¡Está Lloviendo!, 1 vol. 2013. (What's the Weather? / ¿Qué Tiempo Hace? Ser.). (SPA & ENG., Illus.). 24p. (J). (gr. k-k). 25.27 *(978-1-4339-9460-9(7)*, 7dae9155-2b86-45b5-8f7e-08e0a94ec6ff) Stevens, Gareth Publishing LLLP.

Bauer, Marion Dane. Rain: Ready-To-Read Level 1. Wallace, John, illus. 2004. (Weather Ready-To-Reads Ser.). (ENG.). 32p. (J). (gr. -1-1). pap. 4.99 *(978-0-689-85439-2(0)*, Simon Spotlight) Simon Spotlight.

Bauman, Carey. God Controls the Storm. Bauman, Carey, tr. 2007. (Little Jewel Book Ser.). (Illus.). 24p. (J). (gr. 2). pap. 2.70 *(978-0-7399-2396-2(X))* Rod & Staff Pubs., Inc.

Boerger, Kristin & Boyett, Suzi. Let's Read about Rain, 1 vol. 2007. (Let's Read about Weather Ser.). (ENG., Illus.). 12p. (gr. k-1). lib. bdg. 17.67 *(978-0-8368-7805-9(1)*, 9f7e82b3-9971-480c-80b9-eccc43628edf, Weekly Reader Leveled Readers) Stevens, Gareth Publishing LLLP.

—Llueve (Let's Read about Rain), 1 vol. 2007. (¿Qué Tiempo Hace? (Let's Read about Weather) Ser.). (SPA., Illus.). 12p. (J). (gr. k-1). pap. 5.10 *(978-0-8368-8118-9(4)*, 080a1481-b458-45a4-9709-aa38bcfcc80f, Weekly Reader Leveled Readers); lib. bdg. 17.67 *(978-0-8368-8113-4(3)*, 51543699-d46e-4d13-9358-cd5d202f65dc) Stevens, Gareth Publishing LLLP.

Boothroyd, Jennifer. What Is Today's Weather? 2014. (First Step Nonfiction — Let's Watch the Weather Ser.). (ENG., Illus.). 24p. (J). (gr. k-2). pap. 6.99 *(978-1-4677-4500-0(6)*, 1ef483d3-0a2a-4e3b-96e1-f387e3950e74); lib. bdg. 23.99 *(978-1-4677-3916-0(2)*, 61026b9e-bfff-4bfe-8ceb-6f28ef7ac492, Lerner Pubns.) Lerner Publishing Group.

Branley, Franklyn M. Down Comes the Rain. Fraser, Mary Ann, illus. 2017. (Let's-Read-And-Find-Out Science 2 Ser.). (ENG.). 40p. (J). (gr. -1-3). pap. 7.99 *(978-0-06-238663-2(8)*, HarperCollins) HarperCollins Pubs.

Brinker, Spencer. A Rainy Day. 2018. (Weather Watch Ser.). (ENG., Illus.). 16p. (J). (gr. -1-1). 6.99 *(978-1-64280-135-4(6))* Bearport Publishing Co., Inc.

—A Stormy Day. 2018. (Weather Watch Ser.). (ENG., Illus.). 16p. (J). (gr. -1-1). 16.96 *(978-1-64280-000-5(7))*; 6.99 *(978-1-64280-137-8(2))* Bearport Publishing Co., Inc.

Bundey, Nikki. Rain & People. 2005. (Science of Weather Ser.). (Illus.). 32p. (gr. 4-6). lib. bdg. 21.27 *(978-1-57505-494-0(9))* Lerner Publishing Group.

—Rain & the Earth. 2005. (Science of Weather Ser.). (Illus.). 32p. (gr. 4-6). lib. bdg. 21.27 *(978-1-57505-469-8(8))* Lerner Publishing Group.

Carlson-Berne, Emma. From River to Raindrop: The Water Cycle. 2017. (Start to Finish, Second Ser.). (ENG., Illus.). 24p. (J). (gr. k-3). 23.99 *(978-1-5124-3442-2(6)*, 4901946c-a454-473c-b27e-1314009e947f, Lerner Pubns.); pap. 7.99 *(978-1-5124-5623-3(3)*, 8428878e-bfdd-49d3-9017-abee0a4a0a88) Lerner Publishing Group.

Clay, Kathryn. Rain Showers. 2016. (Celebrate Spring Ser.). (ENG., Illus.). 24p. (J). (gr. -1-2). lib. bdg. 22.65 *(978-1-4914-8303-9(2)*, 130779) Capstone.

Coster, Patience. Rain & Floods, 1 vol. 2010. (Weatherwise Ser.). (ENG.). 32p. (gr. 4-4). (J). pap. 11.60 *(978-1-61532-274-9(4)*, 9ceed20b-1c14-4c7a-8f1c-9aa20d16bb3b, PowerKids Pr.); (Illus.). (YA). lib. bdg. 30.27 *(978-1-61532-261-9(2)*, 048b5c0a-454a-45f3-ac18-97d209d7841b) Rosen Publishing Group, Inc., The.

Cox Cannons, Helen. Rain, 1 vol. 2014. (Weather Wise Ser.). (ENG., Illus.). 24p. (J). (gr. -1-1). pap. 5.99 *(978-1-4846-0555-4(1)*, 126646, Heinemann) Capstone.

D'Aubuisson, Elisabeth. Rainy Days, 1 vol. 2006. (What's the Weather? Ser.). (ENG., Illus.). 24p. (J). (gr. 2-3). lib. bdg. 26.27 *(978-1-4042-3682-0(1)*, c8e12711-da4b-4ca1-90d4-9b3bc4ab2dfe, PowerKids Pr.) Rosen Publishing Group, Inc., The.

d'Aubuisson, Elisabeth. Rainy Days. 2009. (What's the Weather? Ser.). 24p. (gr. 2-3). 42.50 *(978-1-60854-775-3(2)*, PowerKids Pr.) Rosen Publishing Group, Inc., The.

Dawson, Emily C. Wet & Dry Places. 2011. (Amicus Readers. Let's Compare (Level A) Ser.). (ENG.). 24p. (J). (gr. -1-2). lib. bdg. 25.65 *(978-1-60753-004-6(X)*, 17025) Amicus.

Doherty, Gillian. Rainy Day. 2005. (First Discovery Ser.). 24p. (J). 9.99 *(978-0-7945-0867-8(7)*, Usborne) EDC Publishing.

Doubleday Entertainment USA - Weather Watch: Rain. 2006. (J). per. 7.95 *(978-1-59566-230-9(8))*; per. 7.95 *(978-1-59566-231-6(6))* QEB Publishing Inc.

Doudna, Kelly. It Is Raining, 1 vol. 2003. (Weather Ser.). (ENG., Illus.). 24p. (J). (gr. k-3). lib. bdg. 24.21 *(978-1-57765-774-3(8)*, SandCastle) ABDO Publishing Co.

Edison, Erin. Rain, 1 vol. 2011. (Weather Basics Ser.). (ENG.). 24p. (J). (gr. -1-2). pap. 7.29 *(978-1-4296-7079-1(7)*, 116755); (gr. k-1). pap. 43.74 *(978-1-4296-7084-5(3)*, 16677) Capstone. (Capstone Pr.).

Firely, G. M. The Raindrop. Holmes, Joshua D., illus. 2004. 21p. pap. 24.95 *(978-1-4137-3388-4(3))* PublishAmerica, Inc.

Ganeri, Anita. Rain, 1 vol. 2004. (Weather Around You Ser.). (ENG., Illus.). 24p. (J). (gr. 2-4). pap. 9.15 *(978-0-8368-4304-0(5)*, afd8a437-7ef3-41d2-be2f-db001ee0d8ce); lib. bdg. 24.67 *(978-0-8368-4299-9(5)*, 814a488a-c094-421b-b118-6f6c6b704253) Stevens, Gareth Publishing LLLP. (Weekly Reader Leveled Readers).

Gates, Margo. Duck Sees the Rain. Herring, Carol, illus. 2019. (Let's Look at Weather (Pull Ahead Readers — Fiction) Ser.). (ENG.). 16p. (J). (gr. -1-1). 27.99 *(978-1-5415-5839-7(1)*, f68036da-4f21-4b91-a168-3e2c414bc554, Lerner Pubns.) Lerner Publishing Group.

Ghigna, Charles. Raindrops Fall All Around. Watson, Laura, illus. 2015. (Springtime Weather Wonders Ser.). (ENG.).

24p. (J). (gr. -1-2). lib. bdg. 22.65 *(978-1-4795-6030-1(8),* 127289, Picture Window Bks.) Capstone.
Gibbons, Gail. It's Raining! (ENG., Illus.). 32p. (J). (gr. -1-3). 2015. 7.99 *(978-0-8234-3303-2(X))* 2014. 17.95 *(978-0-8234-2924-0(5))* Holiday Hse., Inc.
—It's Raining! (1 Hardcover/1 CD) 2016. (ENG.). (J). (gr. k-3). audio compact disk 29.95 *(978-1-4301-2179-4(3))* Live Oak Media.
—It's Raining! (1 Paperback/1 CD) 2016. (ENG.). (J). (gr. k-3). audio compact disk 19.95 *(978-1-4301-2178-7(5))* Live Oak Media.
—It's Raining! (4 Paperbacks/1 CD) 2016. (ENG.). (J). (gr. k-3). audio compact disk 44.95 *(978-1-4301-2180-0(7))* Live Oak Media.
Hansen, Grace. Rain, 1 vol. 2015. (Weather Ser.). (ENG., Illus.). 24p. (J). (gr. -1-2). 32.79 *(978-1-62970-932-1(8),* 18322, Abdo Kids) ABDO Publishing Co.
Herriges, Ann. Rain. 2006. (Weather Ser.). (ENG., Illus.). 24p. (J). (gr. k-3). pap. 6.99 *(978-0-531-17879-9(X),* Blastoff! Readers); lib. bdg. 26.95 *(978-1-60014-027-3(0))* Bellwether Media.
—Rain. 2011. (Blastoff! Readers Ser.). 24p. (J). pap. 5.95 *(978-0-531-27622-8(8),* Children's Pr.) Scholastic Library Publishing.
Holden, Pam. Water from Rain, 1 vol. 2015. (ENG., Illus.). 16p. (-1). pap. *(978-1-77654-084-6(0),* Red Rocket Readers) Flying Start Bks.
I Feel Cold: Individual Title Six-Packs. (gr. -1-2). 23.00 *(978-0-7635-9015-4(0))* Rigby Education.
Ipcizade, Catherine. The Water Cycle: A 4D Book. 2018. (Cycles of Nature Ser.). (ENG., Illus.). 24p. (J). (gr. -1-2). lib. bdg. 29.32 *(978-1-9771-0039-9(2),* 138181, Capstone Pr.) Capstone.
Jacobs, Marian B. Why Does It Rain?, 1 vol. 2003. (Library of Why Ser.). (ENG., Illus.). 24p. (J). (gr. 3-4). lib. bdg. 25.27 *(978-0-8239-5273-1(8),* df8e6c12-ab40-4221-b8b7-bffa4708f492, PowerKids Pr.) Rosen Publishing Group, Inc., The.
Jango-Cohen, Judith. Why Does It Rain? Feltes, Tess, illus. (On My Own Science Ser.). 2006. 47p. (J). (gr. k-3). per. 6.95 *(978-1-57505-854-2(5))* 2005. (ENG.). 48p. (gr. 2-4). lib. bdg. 25.26 *(978-1-57505-762-0(X))* Lerner Publishing Group. (Millbrook Pr.).
Jennings, Terry J. The Weather: Rain. 2004. (J). lib. bdg. 27.10 *(978-1-59389-143-5(1))* Chrysalis Education.
Landman, Tanya. A Drop of Rain Green Band. Tait, Carys, illus. 2016. (Cambridge Reading Adventures Ser.). (ENG.). 16p. pap. 7.95 *(978-1-107-55060-5(2))* Cambridge Univ. Pr.
Lawrence, Ellen. How Are Rain, Snow, & Hail Alike? 2018. (Weather Wise Ser.). (ENG.). 24p. (J). (gr. -1-3). 7.99 *(978-1-64280-089-0(9))* Bearport Publishing Co., Inc.
Lazo, Caroline Evensen. Frank Gehry. 2005. (First Step Nonfiction Ser.). (Illus.). 112p. (J). (gr. 3-7). lib. bdg. 29.27 *(978-0-8225-2649-0(2),* Lerner Pubns.) Lerner Publishing Group.
Lee, Sally. Rainy Weather: A 4D Book. 2018. (All Kinds of Weather Ser.). (ENG., Illus.). 24p. (J). (gr. -1-2). lib. bdg. 24.65 *(978-1-9771-0184-6(4),* 138708, Pebble) Capstone.
MacDonald, Margaret. Rain. 2011. (Learn-Abouts Ser.). (Illus.). 16p. (J). pap. 7.95 *(978-1-59920-649-3(8))* Black Rabbit Bks.
Mara, Wil. Why Does It Rain?, 1 vol. 2010. (Tell Me Why, Tell Me How Ser.). (ENG.). 32p. (gr. 3-3). 32.64 *(978-0-7614-3991-2(9),* c05579b7-5861-4743-92a1-872870ab1603) Cavendish Square Publishing LLC.
Mizrachi, Esther. Rain. 2016. (Illus.). 32p. (J). pap. *(978-0-545-86281-3(7))* Scholastic, Inc.
Nelson, Robin. El Ciclo Del Agua. 2003. (SPA.). 23p. (J). pap. 5.95 *(978-0-8225-4824-9(0),* Lerner Pubns.) Lerner Publishing Group.
—Un Día lluvioso (A Rainy Day) 2006. (Mi Primer Paso al Mundo Real Ser.). (Illus.). 23p. (J). (gr. -1-3). per. 4.25 *(978-0-8225-6550-5(1),* Ediciones Lerner) Lerner Publishing Group.
—Rainy. (First Step Nonfiction — Kinds of Weather Ser.). (ENG., Illus.). 8p. (J). (gr. k-2). 2005. pap. 5.99 *(978-0-8225-5365-6(1),* 2c4912a3-2822-4a86-88af-95669837d5ab) 2015. E-Book 23.99 *(978-1-5124-1037-2(3))* Lerner Publishing Group.
—The Water Cycle. 2003. (First Step Nonfiction Ser.). (Illus.). 24p. (J). (gr. k-2). lib. bdg. 18.60 *(978-0-8225-4596-5(9))* Lerner Publishing Group.
O'Connell, Bailey. Earth's Rainiest Places, 1 vol. 2014. (Earth's Most Extreme Places Ser.). (ENG.). 24p. (J). (gr. 2-3). pap. 9.15 *(978-1-4824-1910-8(6),* a0e69d26-4d50-4203-8f96-e9d015749eec) Stevens, Gareth Publishing LLLP.
Peters, Katie. Look at the Rain. 2019. (Let's Look at Weather (Pull Ahead Readers — Nonfiction) Ser.). (ENG., Illus.). 16p. (J). (gr. -1-1). pap. 8.99 *(978-1-5415-7323-9(4),* 44224a3b-1d8f-4ff9-aca2-b3152aace4fb); lib. bdg. 27.99 *(978-1-5415-5835-9(9),* 4ecdff1b-df8d-4cfd-8ad2-c35aad74414a) Lerner Publishing Group. (Lerner Pubns.).
Plattner, Josh & Craig, Diane. Hail or Freezing Rain?, 1 vol. 2015. (This or That? Weather Ser.). (ENG., Illus.). 24p. (J). (gr. k-4). 32.79 *(978-1-62403-954-6(5),* 19564, Super SandCastle) ABDO Publishing Co.
Posner, Renee & Quinton, Sasha. Suzy Season Loves Fall. D'Argo, Laura, illus. 2003. (Be Mine Bears Ser.). (J). bds. 4.99 *(978-1-58209-352-9(0))* Bks. Are Fun, Ltd.
Purslow, Frances. Precipitation. 2015. (Illus.). 24p. (J). *(978-1-5105-0054-9(5));* pap. *(978-1-5105-0286-4(6))* SmartBook Media, Inc.
—Precipitation. 2016. (Illus.). 24p. (J). *(978-1-4896-5797-8(5))* Weigl Pubs., Inc.
Rain, Snow, & Hail: Individual Title Six-Packs. (Discovery World Ser.). 16p. (gr. 1-2). 28.00 *(978-0-7635-8466-5(5))* Rigby Education.
René, Ellen. Investigating Why It Rains. (Science Detectives Ser.). 24p. (gr. 2-3). 2009. 42.50 *(978-1-60853-016-8(7),* PowerKids Pr.) 2008. (ENG., Illus.). (J). lib. bdg. 26.27 *(978-1-4042-4483-2(2),* 0a9b1aef-d552-431d-afcc-ce00381d844d) Rosen Publishing Group, Inc., The.
Reyes, Sonja. Looks Like Rain! What's the Problem?, 1 vol. 2017. (Computer Science for the Real World Ser.). (ENG.). 8p. (gr. k-1). pap. *(978-1-5383-5028-7(9),* d519ef39-ea75-4354-852e-bd0f3cf41d7c, Rosen Classroom) Rosen Publishing Group, Inc., The.
Rossiter, Brienna. Rain. 2019. (Weather Ser.). (ENG., Illus.). 16p. (J). (gr. k-1). 25.64 *(978-1-64185-790-1(0),* 1641857900, Focus Readers) North Star Editions.
Rustad, Martha E. H. Today Is a Rainy Day. 2017. (What Is the Weather Today? Ser.). (ENG., Illus.). 24p. (J). (gr. -1-2). lib. bdg. 24.65 *(978-1-5157-4921-9(5),* 134537); (gr. k-2). pap. 6.29 *(978-1-4966-0944-1(1),* 134531) Capstone. (Pebble).
Sayre, April Pulley. Raindrops Roll. Sayre, April Pulley, photos by. 2015. (Weather Walks Ser.). (ENG., Illus.). 40p. (J). (gr. -1-3). 18.99 *(978-1-4814-2064-8(X),* Beach Lane Bks.) Beach Lane Bks.
Schwartz, Heather E. Staying Dry. rev. ed. 2019. (Smithsonian: Informational Text Ser.). (ENG., Illus.). 32p. (J). (gr. 2-3). pap. 10.99 *(978-1-4938-6672-4(9))* Teacher Created Materials, Inc.
Selwyn, Josephine. How Do You Measure Rain & Wind? 2012. (Level F Ser.). (ENG., Illus.). 16p. (J). (gr. k-2). pap. 7.95 *(978-1-927136-56-0(3),* 19415) RiverStream Publishing.
Sherman, Josepha. Splish! Splash! A Book about Rain, 1 vol. Yesh, Jeff, illus. 2003. (Amazing Science: Weather Ser.). (ENG.). 24p. (J). (gr. -1-3). per. 8.95 *(978-1-4048-0339-8(4),* 92637, Picture Window Bks.) Capstone.
Solanet & Bergandi. ¿Que Hace Llover? (Coleccion Primeros Pasos en la Ciencia). (SPA., Illus.). 176p. (J). (gr. 1-3). *(978-950-724-017-1(9),* LMA8215) Lumen ARG. Dist: Lectorum Pubns., Inc.
Staunton, Ted & Clark, Brenda. L' Homme De Boue, Mini Bk. (FRE.). (J). pap. 3.99 *(978-0-590-74821-6(1))* Scholastic, Inc.
Stewart, Melissa. Droughts. Ceolin, Andre, illus. 2017. (Let's-Read-And-Find-Out Science 2 Ser.). (ENG.). 40p. (J). (gr. -1-3). 17.99 *(978-0-06-238666-3(2));* pap. 6.99 *(978-0-06-238665-6(4))* HarperCollins Pubs. (HarperCollins).
—When Rain Falls, 1 vol. Bergum, Constance R., illus. 32p. (J). (gr. -1-3). 2019. pap. 7.95 *(978-1-68263-100-3(1))* 2013. 16.95 *(978-1-56145-438-9(9))* Peachtree Publishing Co. Inc.
Strain Trueit, Trudi. Rainy Days, 1 vol. 2010. (Weather Watch Ser.). (ENG.). 24p. (gr. k-1). 25.50 *(978-0-7614-4012-3(7),* 180a0512-42ef-4b08-a60a-31312b10d240) Cavendish Square Publishing LLC.
Vastola, P. Rain: Learning the AI Sound. 2009. (PowerPhonics Ser.). 24p. (gr. 1-1). 39.90 *(978-1-60851-469-4(2),* PowerKids Pr.) Rosen Publishing Group, Inc., The.
Viswanath, Shoba. One Rainy Day: A Counting Book. P.S., Aswathy, illus. 2018. (ENG.). 24p. (J). (gr. -1). bds. 12.99 *(978-1-77321-091-9(2))* Annick Pr., Ltd. CAN. Dist: Publishers Group West (PGW).
Williams, Judith. How Come It's Raining?, 1 vol. 2014. (How Does Weather Happen? Ser.). (ENG.). 24p. (gr. k-1). pap. 10.35 *(978-0-7660-6381-5(X),* 56650ca3-231f-4c43-b269-307b30fa75f0); lib. bdg. 24.27 *(978-0-7660-6380-8(1),* 4e05ad4f-7579-4bab-80cd-126c493da80e) Enslow Publishing, LLC. (Enslow Elementary).
—¿Por Qué Está Lloviendo? / Why Is It Raining?, 1 vol. 2010. (Me Gusta el Clima / I Like Weather! Ser.). (SPA & ENG.). 24p. (gr. k-2). 26.60 *(978-0-7660-3238-5(8),* f10749e9-67f9-44ec-a81f-b348ac3ffcf5, Enslow Elementary) Enslow Publishing, LLC.
Wilson, Annmarie. What Makes Rain?, 1 vol. 2013. (Nature's Super Secrets Ser.). (ENG.). 24p. (gr. 1-2). 25.27 *(978-1-4339-8170-8(X),* 9133524a-cbb2-4bdc-ad3b-1896fdd89102); pap. 9.15 *(978-1-4339-8171-5(8),* 7d0d176c-b556-4834-bbee-9cd37197adb5) Stevens, Gareth Publishing LLLP.

RAIN AND RAINFALL—FICTION

Abuhamda, Nasser. A Flower in the Rain. 2009. 40p. pap. 14.95 *(978-1-59858-879-8(2))* Dog Ear Publishing, LLC.
Adams, Peter. Why Rain & Fire Are Enemies. 2009. 28p. pap. 21.99 *(978-1-4415-4317-2(1))* Xlibris Corp.
Alumenda, Stephen. Toko & the Lost Kittens. 2004. (Illus.). 24p. pap. *(978-9966-25-170-1(7))* Heinemann Kenya, Limited (East African Educational Publishers Ltd E.A.E.P.) KEN. Dist: Michigan State Univ. Pr.
Ashman, Linda. Rain! Calvo, Carlos, tr. Robinson, Christian, illus. 2013. (ENG.). 32p. (J). (gr. -1-3). 18.99 *(978-0-547-73395-1(X),* 1484490, Clarion Bks.) HarperCollins Pubs.
—Rain! Board Book. Calvo, Carlos, tr. Robinson, Christian, illus. 2017. (ENG.). 30p. (J). (— 1). bds. 7.99 *(978-0-544-88037-5(4),* 1651189, Clarion Bks.) HarperCollins Pubs.
Atteberry, Kevan. Puddles!!! Atteberry, Kevan, illus. 2016. (ENG., Illus.). 32p. (J). (gr. -1-3). 14.99 *(978-0-06-230784-2(3),* HarperCollins) HarperCollins Pubs.
Austin-Lockhart, Lora. Raindrop Rewards. 2007. 88p. per. 16.95 *(978-1-4241-7006-7(0))* PublishAmerica, Inc.
Barney, V. J. My Rainy Day. 2012. 32p. pap. 21.99 *(978-1-4691-5162-5(6))* Xlibris Corp.
BeachHouse Publishing. Geckos Make a Rainbow. Murakami, Jon, illus. 2010. (ENG.). 28p. (J). (gr. -1-1). bds. 8.95 *(978-1-933067-38-4(1))* Beachhouse Publishing, LLC.
Becker, Michele Joy. What If Marshmallows Fell from the Sky. Joslin, Irene, illus. 2009. 32p. pap. 12.99 *(978-1-4389-0152-7(6))* AuthorHouse.
Benchmark Education Co., LLC. It's Raining, It's Pouring Big Book. 2014. (Shared Reading Foundations Ser.). (J). (gr. -1). *(978-1-4509-9440-8(7))* Benchmark Education Co.
Bergens, Teri. Mud Trouble. 2010. 34p. pap. 11.99 *(978-1-60844-302-4(7))* Dog Ear Publishing, LLC.
Berlin, Ethan T. The Hugely-Wugely Spider. Edwards, Karl Newsom, illus. 2018. (ENG.). 40p. (J). 18.99 *(978-0-374-30616-8(8),* 900174319, Farrar, Straus & Giroux (BYR)) Farrar, Straus & Giroux.
The Big Rain. 2003. (Illus.). 32p. (J). mass mkt. *(978-0-9740599-2-1(7),* 3) Omnibus Publishing.
Bluemle, Elizabeth. Tap Tap Boom Boom. Karas, G. Brian, illus. 2014. (ENG.). 32p. (J). (gr. -1-2). 17.99 *(978-0-7636-5696-6(8))* Candlewick Pr.
Boswell, Addie. The Rain Stomper, 0 vols. Velasquez, Eric, illus. 2012. (ENG.). 32p. (J). (gr. -1-3). 16.99 *(978-0-7614-5393-2(8),* 9780761453932, Two Lions) Amazon Publishing.
Brafman, Bonnie. Treasure in Marci's House. 2007. (J). pap. 8.00 *(978-0-8059-7418-8(0))* Dorrance Publishing Co., Inc.
Brouillard, Anne. The Bathtub Prima Donna. Brouillard, Anne, illus. 2004. (Illus.). 24p. (J). (gr. k-4). reprint ed. 13.00 *(978-0-7567-7755-5(0))* DIANE Publishing Co.
Carbone, Peter W. Ben the Raindrop: Strength in Perseverance. 2008. (ENG.). 30p. pap. 14.49 *(978-1-4343-4339-0(1))* AuthorHouse.
Carroll, Claudia. Old Dumpling & the Rainy Day. 2008. (ENG.). 55p. pap. 9.95 *(978-0-557-01565-8(0))* Lulu Pr., Inc.
Carson, Penny & Hess, Amy. Simon's Day of Rain. 2008. 17p. 10.94 *(978-1-4357-2168-5(3))* Lulu Pr., Inc.
Cavaliere, Lisa. Lainey Lemonade's Cupcake Parade. 2008. 32p. pap. 24.95 *(978-1-60474-860-4(5))* America Star Bks.
Celee. The Adventures of Remmy Raindrop: Book I. 2009. 16p. pap. 8.49 *(978-1-4389-3623-9(0))* AuthorHouse.
Cerullo, Claudio V. Isabella's Rainy Day with Her Friends. 2011. 16p. pap. 24.95 *(978-1-4626-2463-8(4))* America Star Bks.
Chang, Grace. Jin Jin & Rain Wizard. Chang, Chong, illus. 2009. (ENG.). 48p. (J). (gr. -1-3). 16.95 *(978-1-59270-086-8(1))* Enchanted Lion Bks., LLC.
Chronicle Books & ImageBooks. Little Zebra: Finger Puppet Book: (Finger Puppet Book for Toddlers & Babies, Baby Books for First Year, Animal Finger Puppets) 2013. (Little Finger Puppet Board Bks.). (ENG., Illus.). 12p. (J). (gr. -1 — 1). bds. 6.99 *(978-1-4521-1252-7(5))* Chronicle Bks. LLC.
Church, Caroline Jayne. Rain, Rain, Go Away. Church, Caroline Jayne, illus. 2013. (ENG., Illus.). 14p. (J). (— 1). bds. 6.99 *(978-0-545-48542-5(8),* Cartwheel Bks.) Scholastic, Inc.
Clark, William. Magic Raindrops. 2013. 24p. pap. 14.93 *(978-1-4669-7414-2(1))* Trafford Publishing.
Cocca-Leffler, Maryann. Let It Rain. Cocca-Leffler, Maryann, illus. 2013. (ENG., Illus.). 24p. (J). (gr. k-3). pap. 16.19 *(978-0-545-45343-1(7))* Scholastic, Inc.
Connor, Naomi. Rainy Day Blues. 2012. 26p. pap. 15.99 *(978-1-4685-7388-6(8))* AuthorHouse.
Coxe, Molly. Wet Hen. 2018. (Bright Owl Bks.). (Illus.). 40p. (J). (gr. -1-2). pap. 6.99 *(978-1-57565-976-3(X),* 77d3b305-c032-4cdf-a608-76806a077898); lib. bdg. 17.99 *(978-1-57565-975-6(1),* ec06995e-175f-408c-b3fe-5446476437b8) Astra Publishing Hse. (Kane Press).
Crisp, Dan, illus. The Ants Go Marching. 2009. (Classic Books with Holes Big Book Ser.). 16p. (J). (gr. -1-1). spiral bd. *(978-1-84643-207-1(3));* (ENG.). *(978-1-84643-256-9(1))* Child's Play International Ltd.
Crow, Melinda Melton. Mud Mess, 1 vol. Rooney, Veronica, illus. 2009. (Truck Buddies Ser.). (ENG.). 32p. (J). (gr. -1-1). pap. 6.25 *(978-1-4342-1753-0(1),* 102225, Stone Arch Bks.) Capstone.
Dennis, Elizabeth. Violet Fairy Gets Her Wings. Smillie, Natalie, illus. 2016. (J). *(978-1-5182-4501-5(3))* Simon & Schuster Children's Publishing.
DePalma, Johnny. The Raindrop Keeper. Crabapple, Molly, illus. 2006. (J). per. 8.50 *(978-0-9791127-1-3(0))* Umbrelly Bks.
—The Raindrop Keeper: (Limited Edition Hardcover) Crabapple, Molly, illus. 2006. 50p. (J). 16.50 *(978-0-9791127-8-2(8))* Umbrelly Bks.
DePalma, Johnny & Crabapple, Molly. The Raindrop Keeper. 2007. (ENG.). 50p. (J). pap. 8.50 *(978-0-615-14065-0(3))* Umbrelly Bks.
Dharma Publishing Staff. The Fish King: A Story about the Power of Goodness. 2nd ed. 2013. 36p. (gr. -1-7). pap. 8.95 *(978-0-89800-491-5(8))* Dharma Publishing.
Dixon, Dale. The Rainy Day: Working in a Loop, 1 vol. 2017. (Computer Kids: Powered by Computational Thinking Ser.). (ENG.). 24p. (J). (gr. 3-4). 25.27 *(978-1-5383-2435-6(0),* da13493d-c9bc-4fef-933a-0dbb2818a582, PowerKids Pr.); pap. *(978-1-5081-3792-4(7),* b503d1c5-7e38-4c0c-953c-daafbf7b9767, Rosen Classroom) Rosen Publishing Group, Inc., The.
Du Lac, Leo J. Dogfish on the Moon: Santa Claus & the Flying Carpet 2. Baker, David, illus. 2012. 26p. 24.95 *(978-1-4560-1036-2(0))* America Star Bks.
Dunrea, Olivier. Gossie & Gertie. 2006. (Illus.). 32p. pap. *(978-1-4063-0119-9(1))* Walker Bks., Ltd.
Dyan, Penelope. I Can't Stand the Rain! Dyan, Penelope, illus. 2012. (Illus.). 34p. pap. 11.95 *(978-1-61477-040-4(9))* Bellissima Publishing, LLC.
Echeverria, Jessica. Dora y el Día lluvioso. Savitsky, Steven, illus. 2009. (Dora la Exploradora Ser.). Orig. Title: Dora & the Rainy Day. (SPA.). 26p. (J). (gr. -1). bds. 5.99 *(978-1-4169-7186-3(6),* Libros Para Ninos) Libros Para Ninos.
Ehlert, Lois. Rain Fish. Ehlert, Lois, illus. 2016. (ENG., Illus.). 40p. (J). (gr. -1-3). 19.99 *(978-1-4814-6152-8(4),* Beach Lane Bks.) Beach Lane Bks.
Farrell, Steve. What Do You Do on a Rainy Day? Bendoly, Lynne, illus. 2013. 48p. pap. 24.95 *(978-1-4626-9685-7(6))* America Star Bks.
Faulks, Ben. Watch Out for Muddy Puddles! Cort, Ben, illus. 2018. (ENG.). 32p. (J). 16.99 *(978-1-68119-627-5(1),* 900179490, Bloomsbury USA Childrens) Bloomsbury Publishing USA.
Fernandes, Eugenie. Kitten's Summer. Fernandes, Eugenie, illus. 2013. (ENG., Illus.). 24p. (J). (gr. -1 — 1). bds. 7.95 *(978-1-55453-721-1(5))* Kids Can Pr., Ltd. CAN. Dist: Hachette Bk. Group.
Feurer, Paige. And Then It Rained on Malcolm. Farr, Rich, illus. 2015. (ENG.). 40p. (J). (gr. -1-k). 16.99 *(978-1-63450-150-7(0),* Sky Pony Pr.) Skyhorse Publishing Co., Inc.
Fienberg, Anna, et al. Once Tashi Met a Dragon. 2014. (Tashi Ser.). (ENG., Illus.). 32p. (J). (gr. k-2). 16.99 *(978-1-74175-887-0(4))* Allen & Unwin AUS. Dist: Independent Pubs. Group.
Foster, Ron, illus. I Like Rain. 2007. 28p. (J). (gr. 1-4). *(978-1-929039-39-5(5))* Ambassador Bks., Inc.
Gorbachev, Valeri. Un Dia de lluvia. Gorbachev, Valeri, illus. 2007. (SPA., Illus.). 40p. (J). (gr. -1-3). pap. 8.95 *(978-958-04-7074-8(X))* Norma S.A. COL. Dist: Distribuidora Norma, Inc.
Grant, Callie. Mud Puddle Hunting Day. Magee, Melanie, illus. 2013. (ENG.). 20p. (J). bds. 8.99 *(978-0-9854090-0-5(2))* Blanchard, Graham.
Gray, Joanna. The Little Raindrop. Kolanovic, Dubravka, illus. 2014. (ENG.). 32p. (J). (gr. -1-k). 16.95 *(978-1-62873-821-6(9),* Sky Pony Pr.) Skyhorse Publishing Co., Inc.
Green, Poppy. It's Raining, It's Pouring. Bell, Jennifer A., illus. 2017. (Adventures of Sophie Mouse Ser.: 10). (ENG.). 128p. (J). (gr. k-4). 17.99 *(978-1-4814-8590-6(3),* Little Simon) Little Simon.
Groth-Fleming, Candace. Professor Fergus Fahrenheit & His Wonderful Weather Machine. Weller, Don, illus. 2009. (ENG.). 36p. (J). (gr. -1-3). pap. 10.99 *(978-1-4424-0220-1(2),* Simon & Schuster Bks. For Young Readers) Simon & Schuster Bks. For Young Readers.
Haley, Patty. William's Wet Week. Sayer, Blair, illus. 2010. (ENG.). 16p. (J). (gr. k-2). pap. 7.95 *(978-1-61181-043-1(4),* Kaeden Bks.) Kaeden Corp.
Hall, Susan, illus. Rain, Rain, Go Away. 2010. (Backyardigans Ser.). (ENG.). 24p. (J). (gr. -1-1). 16.19 *(978-1-4169-8509-9(3))* Simon & Schuster, Inc.
Hergenroeder, Ernie, illus. Little Drop of Water. 2007. 24p. (J). 15.00 *(978-0-9724272-4-1(4))* Katydid Publishing LLC.
Hesse, Karen. Come on, Rain! 2004. (J). (gr. k-3). 29.95 *(978-1-55592-500-0(6))* Weston Woods Studios, Inc.
Higginson, Sheila Sweeny. Drip, Drop! the Rain Won't Stop! Your Turn, My Turn Reader. Yee, Josie, illus. 2010. (Playskool Ser.). (ENG.). 24p. (J). (gr. -1-k). pap. 3.99 *(978-1-4169-9046-8(1),* Simon Spotlight) Simon Spotlight.
Hills, Tad & Hills, Tad. Rocket's Very Fine Day. 2019. (Step into Reading Ser.). (Illus.). 32p. (J). (gr. -1-1). pap. 5.99 *(978-0-525-64494-1(6),* Schwartz & Wade Bks.) Random Hse. Children's Bks.
Hinbest, Wendy. Frizzy Tizzy Camps In. 2011. 20p. pap. 11.95 *(978-1-4583-5826-4(7))* Lulu Pr., Inc.
Hodgson, Mona. Thank You God for Rain, 1 vol. Jahier, Milena, illus. 2008. (I Can Read! / Desert Critters Ser.). (ENG.). 32p. (J). (gr. -1-1). pap. 4.99 *(978-0-310-71741-6(8))* Zonderkidz.
Hodson, Debbie. A Mountain Rainbow. 2004. (Illus.). 31p. (J). per. 10.95 *(978-0-9755771-0-3(7))* IvyStone Pr.
Holub, Joan. Itty Bitty Kitty & the Rainy Play Day. Burks, James, illus. 2016. (ENG.). 32p. (J). (gr. -1-3). 17.99 *(978-0-06-232220-3(6),* HarperCollins) HarperCollins Pubs.
Hope, Laura Lee. Bunny Brown & His Sister Sue Keeping S. 2006. 26.95 *(978-1-4218-2975-3(4));* pap. 11.95 *(978-1-4218-3075-9(2))* 1st World Publishing, Inc.
Husted, Ursula. Making Rain. 2004. 56p. (J). per. 9.95 *(978-0-9753225-0-5(8))* Atomic Fruit Pr.
Hyder, M. A. Donia: Stolen Raindrops or Honour among Thieves. 2011. (Illus.). 364p. pap. 20.53 *(978-1-4567-7428-8(X))* AuthorHouse.
Jackson, Bridgett. The Bobos Save the Day: Book One of Tales from the Creek. 2008. 36p. pap. 14.49 *(978-1-4389-2034-4(2))* AuthorHouse.
Jackson, Richard. This Beautiful Day. Lee, Suzy, illus. 2017. (ENG.). 40p. (J). (gr. -1-3). 15.99 *(978-1-4814-4139-1(6),* Atheneum/Caitlyn Dlouhy Books) Simon & Schuster Children's Publishing.
Jasmine, Jean-Pierre. It's Raining Uber. 2013. 166p. (J). pap. 13.99 *(978-1-4808-0122-6(4))* Archway Publishing.
Jennings, Arleen Naish. God Is in the Rain. 2012. 64p. (gr. 1-2). pap. 8.95 *(978-1-4759-3292-8(8))* iUniverse, Inc.
Kerlikowske, Elizabeth. Before the Rain. 2003. 72p. per. 15.00 *(978-1-882983-90-2(4))* March Street Pr.
Khamis, Johnny. Costi & the Raindrop Adventure. Belanger, Damon, illus. 2007. 32p. (J). (gr. -1-3). 6.95 *(978-1-60005-029-9(8))* Happy About.
Klein-Carroll, Theodora. Tippy & the Runaway Cloud. 2013. 28p. pap. 16.95 *(978-1-4525-7390-8(5),* Balboa Pr.) Author Solutions, LLC.
—Tippy the Raindrop. 2012. 30p. pap. 16.99 *(978-1-4525-5725-0(X))* Balboa Pr.
Kolodny, Cynthia. We Like Puddles. Sagasti, Miriam, illus. 2004. (ENG.). 12p. (gr. k-1). pap. 7.95 *(978-1-57874-040-6(1),* Kaeden Bks.) Kaeden Corp.
Koontz, Robin. Lagartija Lisa - ¡El Cielo Se Está Cayendo! 2012. (Little Birdie Readers Ser.).Tr. of Lizzie Little, the Sky Is Falling! (SPA.). 24p. (gr. 2-3). pap. 9.95 *(978-1-61810-541-7(8),* 9781618105417) Rourke Educational Media.
Koontz, Robin Michal. Lizzie Little, the Sky Is Falling! 2011. (ENG., Illus.). (J). (gr. 2-3). pap. 7.95 *(978-1-63430-981-3(2))* Rourke Educational Media.
Krahn, Maria. Charity Prays for Rain. Eshbach, Ariel, illus. 2014. 32p. (J). *(978-0-7399-2475-4(3))* Rod & Staff Pubs., Inc.
Krauss Melmed, Laura. Rainbabies. 2004. (ENG., Illus.). 32p. (J). (gr. -1-3). pap. 9.99 *(978-0-688-15113-3(2),* HarperCollins) HarperCollins Pubs.
Ladd, Debbie. Puddles. Morejon, Tom, illus. 2006. 32p. (J). pap. 8.95 *(978-0-9727615-4-3(3))* Deb on Air Bks.
Lewis, Anne Margaret. Puddle Jumpers. Cote, Nancy, illus. 2016. (ENG.). 32p. (J). (gr. -1-k). 16.99 *(978-1-63450-185-9(3),* Sky Pony Pr.) Skyhorse Publishing Co., Inc.
Lewis, Kim. Seymour & Henry. Lewis, Kim, illus. 2009. (ENG., Illus.). 32p. (J). (gr. k-k). 15.99 *(978-0-7636-4243-3(6))* Candlewick Pr.
Lichtenheld, Tom. Cloudette. Lichtenheld, Tom, illus. 2011. (ENG., Illus.). 40p. (J). (gr. -1-2). 19.99 *(978-0-8050-8776-5(1),* 900050160, Holt, Henry & Co. Bks. For Young Readers) Holt, Henry & Co.
Liniers. The Big Wet Balloon: Toon Books Level 2. Liniers, illus. 2013. (ENG., Illus.). 32p. (J). (gr. -1-3). 12.99 *(978-1-935179-32-0(2),* TOON Books) Astra Publishing Hse.
—The Big Wet Balloon/ el Globo Grande y Mojado: Toon Books Level 2. Liniers, illus. 2013. (ENG., Illus.). 32p. (J). (gr. -1-3). pap. 7.99 *(978-1-935179-39-9(X),* Toon Books) Astra Publishing Hse.
Liniers, illus. The Big Wet Balloon/el Globo Grande y Mojado: Toon Books Level 2. 2013. (SPA.). 32p. (J). (gr. -1-3). 12.95 *(978-1-935179-40-5(3),* Toon Books) Candlewick Pr.
London, Jonathan. Duck & Hippo in the Rainstorm. Joyner, Andrew, illus. 2017. (Duck & Hippo Ser.: 1). (ENG.). 32p. (J).

P Q R

(gr. -1-2). 17.99 *(978-1-5039-3723-9(2)*, 9781503937239, Two Lions) Amazon Publishing.

MacLeod, Jennifer Tzivia. Fast Asleep in a Little Village in Israel. Beeke, Tiphanie, illus. 2018. (ENG.). 32p. (J). 17.95 *(978-1-68115-539-5(7)*, 73160a0c-1e6a-4190-81ea-4157ce5b2e5a, Apples & Honey Pr.) Behrman Hse., Inc.

Magee, Kanika. Rain, Rain, Come Today. Crosson, Cierra, illus. 2004. (J). *(978-0-9748834-2-7(5))* Ebenezer A.M.E. Church.

Markey, Kevin. Rainmaker. 2012. (Illus.). 230p. (J). lib. bdg. 16.89 *(978-0-06-115229-0(3))* HarperCollins Pubs.

Martin, David. Peep & Ducky Rainy Day. Walker, David M., illus. 2018. (Peep & Ducky Ser.). (ENG.). 24p. (J). (— 1). bds. 6.99 *(978-0-7636-9523-1(8))* Candlewick Pr.

Martin, Emily. Downpour. Shaughnessy, Mara, illus. 2013. (ENG.). 32p. (J). (gr. -1-k). 14.95 *(978-1-62087-545-2(4)*, 620545, Sky Pony Pr.) Skyhorse Publishing Co., Inc.

Mase, Naokata. The Rainy Trip Surprise. Perry, Mia Lynn, tr. Mase, Naokata, illus. 2006. (Illus.). 24p. (J). (gr. -1-1). 19.95 incl. audio compact disk *(978-1-74126-436-4(7))* R.I.C. Pubns. AUS. Dist: SCB Distributors.

Masterson, Carla Jo. What's on the Other Side of the Rainbow? The Secret of the Golden Mirror. Fochtman, Omra Jo, illus. 2006. 40p. (J). 24.95 *(978-1-59975-228-0(X))* Father & Son Publishing.

Matranga, Cindy. It Never Rains in Sunny California. 2010. 32p. pap. 12.99 *(978-1-4389-4816-4(6))* AuthorHouse.

McCanna, Tim. Watersong. Smythe, Richard, illus. 2017. (ENG.). 32p. (J). (gr. -1-3). 18.99 *(978-1-4814-6881-7(2)*, Simon & Schuster/Paula Wiseman Bks.) Simon & Schuster/Paula Wiseman Bks.

McDonald, Kirsten. The Big Rain, 1 vol. Meza, Erika, illus. 2015. (Carlos & Carmen Ser.). (ENG.). 32p. (J). (gr. k-3). 32.79 *(978-1-62402-137-4(9)*, 19071, Calico Chapter Bks) Magic Wagon.

McKee, David. Elmer & the Flood. McKee, David, illus. 2015. (Elmer Ser.). (ENG., Illus.). 32p. (J). (gr. -1-3). 17.99 *(978-1-4677-9312-4(4)*, 4f7d7aeb-5cd4-4210-9ee1-31b4e23e2812); E-Book 27.99 *(978-1-4677-9314-8(0))* Lerner Publishing Group.

Miles, Ryan. The Picnic Nightmare. 2012. 24p. pap. 24.95 *(978-1-4512-7153-9(0))* America Star Bks.

Miyares, Daniel. Float. Miyares, Daniel, illus. 2015. (ENG., Illus.). 48p. (J). (gr. -1-3). 18.99 *(978-1-4814-1524-8(7)*, Simon & Schuster Bks. For Young Readers) Simon & Schuster Bks. For Young Readers.

Morgan, Michaela. Dear Bunny: A Bunny Love Story. Church, Caroline Jayne, illus. 2006. (Scholastic Bookshelf Ser.). (ENG.). 32p. (J). (gr. k-2). 18.69 *(978-0-439-74834-6(8))* Scholastic, Inc.

Moss, Lucille. The Gift Within. Uhouse, Debra, illus. l.t. ed. 2005. 19p. (J). 14.95 *(978-1-59879-063-4(3))* Lifevest Publishing, Inc.

Muhammad, Renay. Daddy Why Do We Have Rain. 2004. (Illus.). (J). cd-rom *(978-0-9754024-1-2(2))* Doses of Reality, Inc.

Murray, Kirsty. Puddle Hunters. Blair, Karen, illus. 2019. (ENG.). 32p. (J). (gr. -1-1). 16.99 *(978-1-76029-674-2(0))* Allen & Unwin AUS. Dist: Independent Pubs. Group.

Nash, Damien K. H. & Nash, Kathy. Big Box, Little Box: The Forecast Calls for Potential Rain! Miller, Steve, illus. 2012. 80p. pap. 13.99 *(978-0-9846507-1-2(7))* Faith Bks. & MORE.

Opal, Paola, illus. Saffy Looks for Rain. 2009. (ENG.). 24p. (J). (gr. k — 1). bds. 7.95 *(978-1-897476-03-1(5))* Simply Read Bks. CAN. Dist: Ingram Publisher Services.

Padilla, Felix M. Smiling at the Rain. Padilla, Eren Star, illus. 32p. (J). (gr. 3-18). 16.00 *(978-0-9710860-4-3(4))* Libros, Encouraging Cultural Literacy.

Pelletier, Jennifer. The Wonderful Imagination of Alish. 2011. 32p. pap. 24.95 *(978-1-4626-2613-7(0))* America Star Bks.

Phelan, Matt. Druthers. Phelan, Matt, illus. 2014. (ENG., Illus.). 32p. (J). (-k). 15.99 *(978-0-7636-5955-4(X))* Candlewick Pr.

Quinn, Jordan. The Witch's Curse. McPhillips, Robert, illus. 2014. (Kingdom of Wrenly Ser.: 4). (ENG.). 128p. (J). (gr. k-4). pap. 6.99 *(978-1-4814-0075-6(4)*, Little Simon) Little Simon.

A Rainbow in our Yard. 2005. (J). bds. *(978-0-9761228-1-4(2))* World of Imagination.

The Rainy Day: Individual Title Two-Packs. (Chiquilibros Ser.). (gr. -1-1). 12.00 *(978-0-7635-8532-7(7))* Rigby Education.

Rath, Tom H. Donkey Oatie's Field Trip. Gaudet, Christine, illus. 2013. 26p. pap. *(978-0-9918033-4-7(5))* Wood Islands Prints.

Ray, Mary Lyn. Red Rubber Boot Day. Stringer, Lauren, illus. 2005. (ENG.). 32p. (J). (gr. -1-3). pap. 7.99 *(978-0-15-205398-7(0)*, 1196251, Clarion Bks.) HarperCollins Pubs.

Rooks, Elizabeth. Rayne: Queen Water Supplier of the World. 2012. 32p. pap. 19.99 *(978-1-4772-2375-8(4))* AuthorHouse.

Rosenthal, Amy Krouse. Uni the Unicorn & the Dream Come True. Barrager, Brigette, illus. (Uni the Unicorn Ser.). (J). 2019. 36p. (— 1). bds. 8.99 *(978-1-9848-4821-5(6))* 2017. 40p. (gr. -1-2). 17.99 *(978-1-101-93659-7(2))* Random Hse. Children's Bks. (Random Hse. Bks. for Young Readers).

Rumford, James. Rain School. 2010. (ENG., Illus.). 32p. (J). (gr. -1-3). 17.99 *(978-0-547-24307-8(3)*, 1099430, Clarion Bks.) HarperCollins Pubs.

Sano, Gina. When Is It Going to Rain? 2017. (ENG., Illus.). 24p. pap. 16.99 *(978-1-5245-2195-0(7))* Xlibris Corp.

Sauvageau-Smestad, Sheila. Rain, Rain, What a Pain! 2006. (Illus.). 37p. (J). per. 17.95 *(978-0-9771971-6-3(6))* W & B Pubs.

Scaletta, Kurtis. Mudville. 272p. (J). 2010. (gr. 3-7). 8.99 *(978-0-375-84472-0(4)*, Yearling) 2009. (ENG.). (gr. 4-6). lib. bdg. 22.44 *(978-0-375-95579-2(8)*, Knopf Bks. for Young Readers) Random Hse. Children's Bks.

Schoeningh, Debby. Little Raindrop. Brown, Margaret, illus. 2012. 24p. pap. 9.95 *(978-0-9746360-7-8(X))* Country Side Pr., The.

Scott, Jeanne Ann. Raining Worms. 2005. 160p. (J). pap. 6.99 net. *(978-1-59975-218-1(2))* Independent Pub.

Scotton, Rob. The Rain Is a Pain. 2012. (Splat the Cat: I Can Read Ser.). (J). lib. bdg. 13.55 *(978-0-606-26861-5(8))* Turtleback.

—Splat the Cat: The Rain Is a Pain. 2012. (I Can Read Level 1 Ser.). (ENG., Illus.). 32p. (J). (gr. -1-3). 16.99 *(978-0-06-209018-8(6)*, HarperCollins) HarperCollins Pubs.

—Splat the Cat: the Rain Is a Pain. Scotton, Rob, illus. 2012. (I Can Read Level 1 Ser.). (ENG., Illus.). 32p. (J). (gr. -1-3). pap. 4.99 *(978-0-06-209017-1(8)*, HarperCollins) HarperCollins Pubs.

Sendak, Jack & Sendak, J. The Happy Rain. Sendak, Maurice, illus. 2004. (Sendak Reissues Ser.). (ENG.). 48p. (J). reprint ed. 13.95 *(978-0-06-028785-6(3))* HarperCollins Pubs.

Sesen, Cihan. Stop the Rain, Issue #1. 2010. 45p. pap. 12.99 *(978-0-557-48426-3(X))* Lulu Pr., Inc.

Shannon, David. The Rain Came Down, 1 vol. Shannon, David, illus. 2009. (ENG., Illus.). (J). (gr. -1-3). pap. 10.99 incl. audio compact disk *(978-0-545-13850-5(7))* Scholastic, Inc.

Sheth, Kashmira. Monsoon Afternoon, 1 vol. Jaeggi, Yoshiko, illus. 2018. 32p. (J). (gr. -1-3). pap. 8.99 *(978-1-68263-061-7(7))* Peachtree Publishing Co. Inc.

Shulevitz, Uri. Rain Rain Rivers. Shulevitz, Uri, illus. 2006. (ENG., Illus.). 32p. (J). (gr. -1-3). reprint ed. pap. 9.99 *(978-0-374-46195-9(3)*, 900012475) Square Fish.

Silverman, Erica. Cowgirl Kate & Cocoa: Rain or Shine. Lewin, Betsy, illus. 2009. (Cowgirl Kate & Cocoa Ser.). (ENG.). 44p. (J). (gr. 1-4). pap. 5.99 *(978-0-15-206602-4(0)*, 1099022, Clarion Bks.) HarperCollins Pubs.

Skyberg, Andrea, creator. Snickeyfritz. 2009. (ENG., Illus.). 48p. (J). 17.99 *(978-0-615-25177-6(3))* Wooden Nickel Pr.

Slade Robinson, Nikki. Muddle & Mo's Rainy Day. 2019. (Illus.). 40p. (J). (gr. -1-k). 16.95 *(978-1-76036-058-0(9)*, 30bf3552-1d6d-4096-8469-caef4a884797) Starfish Bay Publishing Pty Ltd. AUS. Dist: Baker & Taylor Publisher Services (BTPS).

Sonriendole a la Lluvia. (SPA.). (J). *(978-0-9710860-5-0(2))* Libros, Encouraging Cultural Literacy.

Spurr, Elizabeth. In the Rain, 1 vol. Oliphant, Manelle, illus. 2018. (In the Weather Ser.). (ENG.). 22p. (J). (gr. -1 — 1). bds. 7.99 *(978-1-56145-853-0(8))* Peachtree Publishing Co. Inc.

Stojic, Manya. Rain. Stojic, Manya, illus. 2009. (ENG., Illus.). 32p. (J). (gr. -1-2). pap. 8.99 *(978-0-385-73729-6(7)*, Dragonfly Bks.) Random Hse. Children's Bks.

Stranaghan, Crystal J. Then It Rained. Espadaler, Rosa, illus. 2007. 24p. (J). *(978-0-9784047-8-9(5))* Pays et Terroirs.

Strathgryffe, Alexander. The Drizzleys. 2009. (Illus.). 48p. pap. *(978-1-84748-543-4(X))* Athena Pr.

Taft, Jean. Worm Weather. Hunt, Matt, illus. 2015. 32p. (J). (-k). bds. 5.99 *(978-0-448-48740-3(3)*, Grosset & Dunlap) Penguin Young Readers Group.

Talbot, Kathy. Camille's Rainy Day Adventure. 2011. 24p. pap. 8.32 *(978-1-4634-5998-7(X))* AuthorHouse.

Testa, Maggie. Olivia & the Rain Dance. 2012. (Olivia Ready-To-Read Level 1 Ser.). lib. bdg. 13.55 *(978-0-606-23688-1(0))* Turtleback.

Thompson, Carol. Rain. Thompson, Carol, illus. 2014. (Whatever the Weather Ser.: 4). (Illus.). 12p. (J). (gr. k-k). spiral bd. *(978-1-84643-683-3(4))* Child's Play International Ltd.

Thompson, Jan & Sharpe, Jaime. Amara's Magical Playhouse: The Adventure Begins. 2010. 108p. pap. 37.99 *(978-1-4520-8284-4(7))* AuthorHouse.

Tremblay, Carole. Floop's New Umbrella, 1 vol. Beshwaty, Steve, illus. 2009. (Floop Ser.). (ENG.). 24p. (J). (gr. -1-k). 27.27 *(978-1-60754-347-3(8)*, 506866a0-14a4-4c13-9e62-69e155ee53fc); pap. 9.15 *(978-1-60754-348-0(6)*, 1851b8a0-f2cc-431b-bb8e-81d6fdf06de1) Rosen Publishing Group, Inc., The. (Windmill Bks.).

Tukel, Onur. Rainstack!, 0 vols. Tukel, Onur, illus. 2013. (ENG.). 64p. (J). (gr. k-3). 17.99 *(978-1-4778-1655-4(0)*, 9781477816554, Two Lions) Amazon Publishing.

Turcotte, Carolyn E. Little Drip Drop's Big Rainy Day. 2011. 40p. (gr. 1-2). pap. 18.46 *(978-1-4567-4873-9(4))* AuthorHouse.

Tuzee, John, text. Puffy: La Nube Que No Podia Llover. 2005. (SPA.). (J). 8.95 *(978-0-9755348-1-6(5))* Kids Life Pr.

Valent, Fred. The Tiniest Raindrop, 1 vol. 2008. (ENG.). 31p. 24.95 *(978-1-60441-393-9(X))* America Star Bks.

Van Cleve, Kathleen. Drizzle. 2011. (ENG.). 368p. (J). (gr. 3-7). 9.99 *(978-0-14-241113-1(2)*, Puffin Books) Penguin Young Readers Group.

Van Straaten, Harmen. TIM & the FLYING MACHINE. 2008. (ENG.). 28p. (J). (gr. 1-7). 12.95 *(978-1-60136-003-8(7))* Audio Holdings, LLC.

Virtue, Queen Petals De. Princess & the Rain. 2012. 28p. pap. 21.99 *(978-1-4691-2744-6(X))* Xlibris Corp.

Wack, Nancy. Puddle Pirate. 2007. 40p. 20.50 *(978-0-615-16634-6(2))* Wack, Nancy.

Walker, Lisa & Coyne, Adrian. The Boy Who Brought Thunder. 2012. (Illus.). 40p. pap. 12.95 *(978-9987-08-222-3(X))* Mkuki na Nyoka Pubs. TZA. Dist: African Bks. Collective, Ltd.

Walker, Tanisha. Rainbow Tots- 10-28. 2011. (ENG.). 35p. pap. 19.99 *(978-0-557-80890-8(1))* Lulu Pr., Inc.

Waters, Graham. The Raindrops & the Wrong Cloud. 2009. (Illus.). 28p. pap. 15.49 *(978-1-4490-0685-3(X))* AuthorHouse.

Weaver, Griz. A Day in the Rain. 2005. 35p. (J). 12.28 *(978-1-4116-0565-7(9))* Lulu Pr., Inc.

Weinberg, Jennifer Liberts. Doc Mcstuffins: Blame It on the Rain. 2014. (World of Reading Ser.). (J). lib. bdg. 13.55 *(978-0-606-35909-2(5))* Turtleback.

Wenger, Brahm & Green, Alan. Dewey Doo-It Builds a House: A Children's Story about Habitat for Humanity. 2006. (ENG., Illus.). 32p. (J). (gr. -1-2). 17.95 incl. lp *(978-0-9745143-2-1(2))* RandallFraser Publishing.

West, Ella. Rain Fall. 2020. (ENG.). 224p. (J). (gr. 6-9). pap. 14.99 *(978-1-76029-683-4(X)*, A&U Children's) Allen & Unwin AUS. Dist: Independent Pubs. Group.

Westover, Gail. Mrs Mouse's Garden Party in Giggleswick Village. Daly, Karen Anne, illus. 2012. 26p. pap. 9.95 *(978-0-9821507-9-5(2))* Thistlewood Publishing.

Whaley, Michelle Marie. Does It Really Rain Cats & Dogs? Ortiz, Ada, illus. 2008. 36p. pap. 24.95 *(978-1-60563-233-9(3))* America Star Bks.

White, Dianne. Blue on Blue. Krommes, Beth, illus. 2014. (ENG.). 48p. (J). (gr. k-3). 19.99 *(978-1-4424-1267-5(4)*, Beach Lane Bks.) Beach Lane Bks.

White, Sandi. Playing with Rain. 2010. (ENG.). 36p. pap. 21.99 *(978-1-4500-1534-9(4))* Xlibris Corp.

Widner, Jan. Then Came the Rains. 2013. 28p. pap. 16.95 *(978-1-4497-9456-9(4)*, WestBow Pr.) Author Solutions, LLC.

Wilce, Colin. The Rain & Blossom (Rabbit Brook Tales Volume 2) 2006. (ENG.). 88p. pap. 11.66 *(978-1-84728-105-0(2))* Lulu Pr., Inc.

Wilhelm, Hans. I Love Rainy Days! (Scholastic Reader, Level 1: Noodles) Wilhelm, Hans, illus. 2011. (Scholastic Reader, Level 1 Ser.). (ENG., Illus.). 32p. (J). (gr. -1-1). pap. 3.99 *(978-0-545-24503-6(6)*, Cartwheel Bks.) Scholastic, Inc.

Williams, Rozanne. Rain. 2017. (Learn-To-Read Ser.). (ENG., Illus.). (J). pap. 3.49 *(978-1-68310-194-9(4))* Pacific Learning, Inc.

Williamson, Linda. Groundhog Breakfast, Soft Petals, & a Roof That Don't Leak Too Much, 1 vol. Mollett, Irene, illus. 2009. 23p. pap. 24.95 *(978-1-60749-618-2(6))* America Star Bks.

Winters, Kari-Lynn. On My Walk, 1 vol. Leist, Christina, illus. 2010. (On My ... Ser.: 1). (ENG.). 32p. (J). (gr. -1-k). 16.95 *(978-1-896580-61-6(0))* Tradewind Bks. CAN. Dist: Orca Bk. Pubs. USA.

Woodford, Pamela. Watching Raindrops. 2013. (Brighter Little Minds Ser.). (ENG., Illus.). 18p. (J). 10.95 *(978-1-871305-84-5(5))* Orpen Pr. IRL. Dist: Dufour Editions, Inc.

Yildirim, Rabia. Wind, Rain & Snow. 2013. (ENG., Illus.). 53p. (J). (gr. k-1). pap. 9.95 *(978-1-59784-284-6(2)*, Tughra Bks.) Blue Dome, Inc.

Yum, Hyewon. Puddle. 2016. (ENG., Illus.). 40p. (J). 18.99 *(978-0-374-31695-2(3)*, 900147132, Farrar, Straus & Giroux (BYR)) Farrar, Straus & Giroux.

Zalme, Ron, illus. Rainy Day Tales. 2009. (J). *(978-1-59078-734-2(X))* Highlights for Children.

RAIN AND RAINFALL—POETRY

Holmer, Anders. Rain. 2018. (ENG., Illus.). 32p. (J). 17.00 *(978-0-8028-5507-7(5)*, Eerdmans Bks For Young Readers) Eerdmans, William B. Publishing Co.

O'Rourke, Ryan, illus. One Big Rain: Poems for Every Season. 2014. (ENG.). 32p. (J). (gr. 2-5). pap. 7.95 *(978-1-57091-717-2(5))* Charlesbridge Publishing, Inc.

RAIN FOREST ECOLOGY

Alaina, Maria. Rainforest. 2011. (Wonder Readers Early Level Ser.). (ENG.). 16p. (gr. -1-1). pap. 35.94 *(978-1-4296-8171-1(3)*, Capstone Pr.) Capstone.

Algor, Marie. Endangered Rain Forest Animals, 1 vol. 2012. (Save Earth's Animals! Ser.). (ENG., Illus.). 24p. (J). (gr. 2-3). pap. 9.25 *(978-1-4488-7495-8(5)*, 7afae836-4dbc-4901-859e-5a085a48a1cb); lib. bdg. 26.27 *(978-1-4488-7422-4(X)*, 8e980b0e-bcd3-41c9-8700-132c89a44f91) Rosen Publishing Group, Inc., The. (PowerKids Pr.).

Aloian, Molly & Kalman, Bobbie. Cadenas Alimentarias del Bosque Tropical. 2007. (Cadenas Alimentarias Ser.). (SPA., Illus.). 32p. (J). (gr. 3-7). pap. *(978-0-7787-8549-1(1))* Crabtree Publishing Co.

—Un Hábitat de Bosque Tropical. 2007. (Introduction a Los Habitats Ser.). (SPA., Illus.). 32p. (J). (gr. 3-7). lib. bdg. *(978-0-7787-8333-6(2))*; (gr. k-3). pap. *(978-0-7787-8357-2(X))* Crabtree Publishing Co.

—Rainforest Food Chains, 1 vol. 2006. (Food Chains Ser.). (ENG., Illus.). 32p. (J). (gr. -1-3). pap. *(978-0-7787-1997-7(9))* Crabtree Publishing Co.

—A Rainforest Habitat, 1 vol. 2006. (Introducing Habitats Ser.). (ENG., Illus.). 32p. (J). (gr. -1-3). pap. *(978-0-7787-2986-0(9))* Crabtree Publishing Co.

Aspen-Baxter, Linda. Rainforests. 2006. (ENG.). (J). pap. 9.95 *(978-1-59036-447-5(3))* Weigl Pubs., Inc.

Ballard, Carol. The Search for Cures from the Rain Forest, 1 vol. 2005. (Science Quest Ser.). (ENG., Illus.). 32p. (J). (gr. 4-6). lib. bdg. 28.67 *(978-0-8368-4554-9(4)*, 9d72a50d-defe-4099-abb6-74e7245766cd, Gareth Stevens Learning Library) Stevens, Gareth Publishing LLLP.

Barnes, J. Lou. 101 Facts about Rain Forests, 1 vol. 2003. (101 Facts about Our World Ser.). (ENG., Illus.). 32p. (gr. 2-4). lib. bdg. 28.67 *(978-0-8368-3710-0(X)*, 70e6af9c-d469-418e-824f-7db347ca3cee, Gareth Stevens Learning Library) Stevens, Gareth Publishing LLLP.

Benchmark Education Co. Who Do You See? a Rain Forest Rap. 2014. (Shared Reading Foundations Ser.). (J). (gr. -1). 39.00 net. *(978-1-4509-9444-6(X))* Benchmark Education Co.

Benoit, Peter. Tropical Rain Forests. 2011. (True Bks.). 48p. (J). (gr. 3-5). 29.00 *(978-0-531-20554-9(1)*, Children's Pr.) Scholastic Library Publishing.

—A True Book: Tropical Rain Forests. 2011. (True Bk Ser.). (ENG.). 48p. (J). (gr. 3-5). pap. 6.95 *(978-0-531-28103-1(5))* Scholastic Library Publishing.

Bodden, Valerie. Rainforests. 2006. (Our World Ser.). (Illus.). 24p. (J). (gr. -1-3). lib. bdg. 16.95 *(978-1-58341-465-1(7)*, Creative Education) Creative Co., The.

Brown, Carron. Secrets of the Rain Forest. 2015. (ENG., Illus.). 36p. (J). 12.99 *(978-1-61067-325-9(5))* Kane Miller.

Castaldo, Nancy F. Rainforests: An Activity Guide for Ages 6-9. 2003. (ENG., Illus.). 144p. (J). (gr. 2-4). pap. 14.95 *(978-1-55652-476-9(5))* Chicago Review Pr., Inc.

Champion, Neil. Tropical Rain Forests. 2006. (Caring for the Planet Ser.). (Illus.). 48p. (YA). (gr. 5-9). lib. bdg. 32.80 *(978-1-58340-508-6(9))* Black Rabbit Bks.

Cole, Melissa S. Rain Forests. 2003. (Wild America Habitats Ser.). (Illus.). 24p. (J). 21.20 *(978-1-56711-808-7(9)*, Blackbirch Pr., Inc.) Cengage Gale.

Collard, Sneed B., III. In the Rain Forest Canopy, 1 vol. 2007. (Science Adventures Ser.). (ENG., Illus.). 48p. (gr. 4-4). lib. bdg. 32.64 *(978-0-7614-1954-9(3)*, bc7e6cf1-bc45-4030-b1ad-9735ea8337cc) Cavendish Square Publishing LLC.

Davies, Monika. How High in the Rainforest? Rainforest Animal Habitats. Marti, Romina, illus. 2018. (Animals Measure Up Ser.). (ENG.). 24p. (J). (gr. 1-4). pap. 9.99 *(978-1-68152-307-1(8)*, 15021) Amicus.

De la Bédoyère, Camilla. Rainforests. 2010. (Unpredictable Nature Ser.). (Illus.). 48p. (J). (gr. 3-18). lib. bdg. 19.95 *(978-1-4222-2004-7(4))* Mason Crest.

Dellaccio, Tanya. Changing Rain Forest Environments. 2019. (Human Impact on Earth: Cause & Effect Ser.). (ENG.). 32p. (gr. 4-5). 60.00 *(978-1-7253-0137-5(7)*, PowerKids Pr.) Rosen Publishing Group, Inc., The.

deMarin, Layne. Amazon Adventure, 1 vol. 2011. (Wonder Readers Fluent Level Ser.). (ENG.). 16p. (gr. -1-2). (J). pap. 6.25 *(978-1-4296-7907-7(7)*, 118239); pap. 35.94 *(978-1-4296-8069-1(5))* Capstone. (Capstone Pr.).

Do You Really Want to Visit a Rainforest? 2014. (Do You Really Want to Visit Earth's Biomes? Ser.). (ENG., Illus.). 24p. (J). (gr. 1-4). lib. bdg. 27.10 *(978-1-60753-453-2(3)*, 15887) Amicus.

Donohue, Moira Rose. National Geographic Little Kids First Big Book of the Rain Forest. 2018. (ENG., Illus.). 128p. (J). (gr. -1-k). lib. bdg. 24.90 *(978-1-4263-3172-5(X)*, National Geographic Kids) Disney Publishing Worldwide.

Duke, Kate. In the Rainforest. Duke, Kate, illus. 2014. (Let's-Read-And-Find-Out Science 2 Ser.). (ENG., Illus.). 40p. (J). (gr. -1-3). pap. 6.99 *(978-0-06-445197-0(6)*, HarperCollins) HarperCollins Pubs.

Dunphy, Madeleine. Here Is the Tropical Rain Forest. Rothman, Michael, illus. 2006. (Web of Life Ser.: 1). (ENG.). 32p. (J). (gr. -1-3). 16.95 *(978-0-9773795-1-4(5))* Web of Life Children's Bks.

Einspruch, Andrew. Rain Forest Habitats. 2013. (Discovery Education: Habitats Ser.). 32p. (J). (gr. 3-6). pap. 60.00 *(978-1-4777-1484-3(7))*; (ENG.). (gr. 4-5). 28.93 *(978-1-4777-1324-2(7)*, 2c909e26-83cb-4d7e-89b1-37ac44e27119); (ENG.). (gr. 4-5). pap. 11.00 *(978-1-4777-1483-6(9)*, a269e9fb-9efb-4ca5-aba2-eed725e97b4b) Rosen Publishing Group, Inc., The. (PowerKids Pr.).

Ganeri, Anita. Exploring Rain Forests: A Benjamin Blog & His Inquisitive Dog Investigation, 1 vol. 2014. (Exploring Habitats with Benjamin Blog & His Inquisitive Dog Ser.). (ENG., Illus.). 32p. (J). (gr. 3-5). pap. 8.95 *(978-1-4329-8786-2(0)*, 124770, Heinemann) Capstone.

Gardeski, Christina Mia. All about Rain Forests. 2017. (Habitats Ser.). (ENG., Illus.). 24p. (J). (gr. -1-2). lib. bdg. 22.65 *(978-1-5157-7643-7(3)*, 135928, Pebble) Capstone.

Gardner, Robert. Rain Forest Experiments: 10 Science Experiments in One Hour or Less, 1 vol. 2014. (Last Minute Science Projects with Biomes Ser.). (ENG., Illus.). 48p. (gr. 5-6). lib. bdg. 26.93 *(978-0-7660-5937-5(5)*, 913a7198-86a3-488a-8eb9-9f47d4513223) Enslow Publishing, LLC.

Gibbs, Maddie. What Are Tropical Rainforests?, 1 vol. 2018. (Let's Find Out! Biomes Ser.). (ENG.). 32p. (gr. 2-3). lib. bdg. 26.06 *(978-1-5081-0697-5(5)*, 25987f8f-0646-4d57-9f3e-517e8f68dd29, Britannica Educational Publishing) Rosen Publishing Group, Inc., The.

Gray, Leon. Tropical Rain Forests. 2015. (Amazing Biomes Ser.). (ENG., Illus.). 32p. (J). (gr. 3-6). 31.35 *(978-1-78121-246-2(5)*, 16393) Brown Bear Bks.

Green, Jen. Find Out about Rainforests: With 20 Projects & More Than 250 Pictures. 2013. (ENG., Illus.). 64p. (J). (gr. k-8). 9.99 *(978-1-84322-746-5(0)*, Armadillo) Anness Publishing GBR. Dist: National Bk. Network.

—Rain Forest Extremes, 1 vol. 2008. (Extreme Nature Ser.). (ENG., Illus.). 32p. (J). (gr. 2-3). pap. *(978-0-7787-4521-1(X))*; lib. bdg. *(978-0-7787-4504-4(X))* Crabtree Publishing Co.

Groves, Julia, illus. Rainforest. 2018. (Child's Play Library). 36p. (J). (ENG.). *(978-1-84643-936-0(1))*; pap. *(978-1-84643-935-3(3))* Child's Play International Ltd.

Hantula, Richard. Rocks & Fossils, 1 vol. 2007. (Gareth Stevens Vital Science Library: Earth Science Ser.). (ENG., Illus.). 48p. (gr. 5-8). lib. bdg. 29.67 *(978-0-8368-7765-6(9)*, be885f08-b5e8-402a-ad24-4581df0534ec, Gareth Stevens Secondary Library) Stevens, Gareth Publishing LLLP.

Head, Honor. Welcome to the Rain Forest. 2017. (Nature's Neighborhoods: All about Ecosystems Ser.). (ENG., Illus.). 32p. (J). (gr. -1-3). lib. bdg. 30.65 *(978-1-911341-95-6(2)*, 0ec74a94-c7ac-495d-9aee-4fdaa77a7b3e) Ruby Tuesday Books Limited GBR. Dist: Lerner Publishing Group.

Hollar, Sherman. Investigating Earth's Desert, Grassland, & Rainforest Biomes, 1 vol. 2011. (Introduction to Earth Science Ser.). (ENG.). 88p. (J). (gr. 8-8). lib. bdg. 35.29 *(978-1-61530-502-5(5)*, c249f23f-b3ef-45c8-8cd0-7675f376e119) Rosen Publishing Group, Inc., The.

Hudak, Heather C. Map & Track Rain Forests. 2019. (Map & Track Biomes & Animals Ser.). (Illus.). 32p. (J). (gr. 4-5). *(978-0-7787-5370-4(0))*; pap. *(978-0-7787-5382-7(4))* Crabtree Publishing Co.

Hunter, Rebecca. Rain Forests. 2012. (Eco Alert! Ser.). (ENG., Illus.). 32p. (gr. 4-6). lib. bdg. 28.50 *(978-1-59771-297-2(3))* Sea-To-Sea Pubns.

Johansson, Philip. The Tropical Rain Forest: Discover This Wet Biome, 1 vol. 2014. (Discover the World's Biomes Ser.). (ENG.). 48p. (gr. 3-4). 26.93 *(978-0-7660-6420-1(4)*, baa29f45-318f-466e-a901-3e63515d4d88); pap. 11.53 *(978-0-7660-6421-8(2)*, e2b37acb-c483-491f-bd55-72665ec4586a) Enslow Publishing, LLC. (Enslow Elementary).

Johnson, Robin. Rain Forests Inside Out. 2014. (Ecosystems Inside Out Ser.). (ENG., Illus.). 32p. (J). (gr. 4-5). *(978-0-7787-0637-3(0))* Crabtree Publishing Co.

Kalman, Bobbie. Les Forêts Humides. 2012. (FRE.). 32p. (J). pap. 9.95 *(978-2-89579-477-6(4))* Bayard Canada CAN. Dist: Crabtree Publishing Co.

Kite, Lorien. Life in a Rain Forest, 1 vol. 2010. (Nature in Focus Ser.). (ENG., Illus.). 32p. (gr. 3-4). (J). pap. 11.50 *(978-1-4339-3408-7(6)*, 42692fcd-a446-407c-81f2-9b12b130b0e7, Gareth Stevens Learning Library); (YA). lib. bdg. 28.67 *(978-1-4339-3410-0(8)*, b2ac692e-f5b0-4eeb-a840-b8d449db10c9) Stevens, Gareth Publishing LLLP.

Kopp, Megan. What Do You Find in a Rainforest Tree? 2016. (ENG., Illus.). 24p. (J). *(978-0-7787-2261-8(9))* Crabtree Publishing Co.

Levy, Janey. Life in a Rain Forest Ecosystem. 2009. (Science Scope Ser.). 32p. (gr. 5-5). 47.90 *(978-1-60853-054-0(X)*, PowerKids Pr.) Rosen Publishing Group, Inc., The.

Lindeen, Mary. Crayola (r) Rain Forest Colors. 2020. (Crayola (r) Colorful Biomes Ser.). (ENG., Illus.). 32p. (J). (gr. k-3).

29.32 *(978-1-5415-7749-7(3)*, 32031a93-fe63-4d56-bbb1-30fc1eb89f25, Lerner Pubns.) Lerner Publishing Group.

Mason, Paul. Rainforest Research Journal. 2010. (ENG.). 32p. (J). *(978-0-7787-9903-0(4))*; pap. *(978-0-7787-9924-5(7))* Crabtree Publishing Co.

McAllister, Ian & Read, Nicholas. A Bear's Life, 1 vol. 2017. (My Great Bear Rainforest Ser.: 2). (ENG., Illus.). 32p. (J). (gr. 1-3). 19.95 *(978-1-4598-1270-3(0))* Orca Bk. Pubs. USA.

McGinlay, Richard. My First Encyclopedia of the Rainforest: A Great Big Book of Amazing Animals & Plants. 2018. (Illus.). 24p. (J). (gr. -1-12). pap. 7.99 *(978-1-86147-848-1(8)*, Armadillo) Anness Publishing GBR. Dist: National Bk. Network.

McLeish, Ewan. Rain Forest Destruction, 1 vol. 2007. (What If We Do Nothing? Ser.). (ENG., Illus.). 48p. (gr. 5-8). pap. 15.05 *(978-0-8368-8158-5(3)*, e10a8bd6-7f03-4ed5-9658-c3d065ec7847); lib. bdg. 33.67 *(978-0-8368-7758-8(6)*, 5f7da118-09cc-479a-8255-0e8f01c3d6fe) Stevens, Gareth Publishing LLLP. (Gareth Stevens Secondary Library).

McNeil, Niki, et al. Rainforest Habitats. 2007. (In the Hands of a Child: Custom Designed Project Pack Ser.). (Illus.). 93p. spiral bd. 22.50 *(978-1-60308-095-8(3))* In the Hands of a Child.

Moore, Heidi. Rain Forest Food Chains, 1 vol. 2010. (Protecting Food Chains Ser.). (ENG., Illus.). 48p. (J). (gr. 3-6). pap. 9.95 *(978-1-4329-3867-3(3)*, 103379, Heinemann) Capstone.

Morey, Allan. Rain Forest Food Chains. 2003. (What Eats What? Ser.). (J). pap. *(978-1-58417-225-3(8))*; lib. bdg. *(978-1-58417-224-6(X))* Lake Street Pubs.

Murray, Aaron R. Counting in the Rain Forest 1-2-3, 1 vol. 2012. (All about Counting in the Biomes Ser.). (ENG., Illus.). 24p. (-1). pap. 10.35 *(978-1-4644-0063-6(6)*, 67bee4a6-02f1-4ebe-9816-7615aaa5588a, Enslow Publishing); (gr. -1-1). 25.27 *(978-0-7660-4055-7(0)*, 44a30e3e-2dec-480f-bf5e-cc4513e6569f, Enslow Publishing); (gr. -1-1). E-Book 25.27 *(978-1-4645-0970-4(0)*, e8808584-6e31-4311-a0f4-5bc0022eec05) Enslow Publishing, LLC.

O'Hare, Ted. Plants of the Rain Forest. 2004. (Rain Forest Today Discovery Library Ser.). (Illus.). 24p. (gr. 1-4). lib. bdg. 22.79 *(978-1-59515-154-4(0))* Rourke Educational Media.

—Vanishing Rain Forests. 2005. (Rain Forest Today Discovery Library Ser.). (Illus.). 24p. (gr. 1-4). 14.95 *(978-1-59515-156-8(7))* Rourke Educational Media.

Oliver, Carmen. A Voice for the Spirit Bears: How One Boy Inspired Millions to Save a Rare Animal. Dockrill, Katy, illus. 2019. (CitizenKid Ser.). (ENG.). 32p. (J). (gr. 1-4). 18.99 *(978-1-77138-979-2(6))* Kids Can Pr., Ltd. CAN. Dist: Hachette Bk. Group.

Pettiford, Rebecca. Rain Forest Food Chains. 2016. (Who Eats What?). (Illus.). 24p. (J). (gr. 2-5). lib. bdg. 25.65 *(978-1-62031-304-6(9)*, Pogo) Jump! Inc.

Pratt-Serafini, Kristin Joy. A Walk in the Rainforest, 1 vol. (Illus.). (J). 2014. 32p. (gr. k-6). 16.99 *(978-1-878265-99-9(7))* 2007. 26p. (gr. -1 — 1). bds. 7.95 *(978-1-58469-088-7(7))* Sourcebooks, Inc. (Dawn Pubns.).

Pratt-Serafini, Kristin Joy & Crandell, Rachel. The Forever Forest: Kids Save a Tropical Treasure. 2008. (Illus.). 32p. (J). (gr. 1-4). pap. 8.99 *(978-1-58469-102-0(6)*, Dawn Pubns.) Sourcebooks, Inc.

Pyers, Greg. Biodiversity of Rain Forests, 1 vol. Morden, Richard, illus. 2011. (Biodiversity Ser.). (ENG.). 32p. (gr. 4-4). 31.21 *(978-1-60870-073-8(9)*, d7729228-5c99-4bc5-baa3-52ae7853bf97) Cavendish Square Publishing LLC.

The Rain Forest, 6 Packs. (Action Packs Ser.). 128p. (gr. 3-5). 44.00 *(978-0-7635-3311-3(4))* Rigby Education.

Ranson, Erin. Rainforest Wonders. Wood, Hannah, illus. 2007. (Sparkling Slide Nature Bks.). (ENG.). 12p. (J). (gr. -1-k). 9.99 *(978-1-84666-356-7(3)*, Tide Mill Pr.) Top That! Publishing PLC GBR. Dist: Independent Pubs. Group.

Read, Nicholas. The Sea Wolves: Living Wild in the Great Bear Rainforest, 1 vol. McAllister, Ian, photos by. 2010. (ENG., Illus.). 128p. (J). (gr. 4-7). pap. 19.95 *(978-1-55469-206-4(7))* Orca Bk. Pubs. USA.

—The Seal Garden. McAllister, Ian, photos by. 2018. (My Great Bear Rainforest Ser.: 3). (ENG., Illus.). 32p. (J). (gr. 1-3). E-Book *(978-1-4598-1269-7(7))* Orca Bk. Pubs.

—Wolf Island, 1 vol. McAllister, Ian, photos by. 2017. (My Great Bear Rainforest Ser.: 1). (ENG., Illus.). 32p. (J). (gr. 1-3). 19.95 *(978-1-4598-1264-2(6))* Orca Bk. Pubs. USA.

Reid, Hunter. In the Rainforest. Chiu, Alex, illus. 2017. (Fluorescent Pop! Ser.). (ENG.). 14p. (J). (gr. -1-k). bds. 5.99 *(978-1-4998-0420-1(2))* Little Bee Books Inc.

Rice, William B. Amazon Rainforest, 1 vol. 2nd rev. ed. 2013. (TIME for KIDS(r): Informational Text Ser.). (ENG., Illus.). 32p. (J). (gr. 3-5). lib. bdg. 25.96 *(978-1-4807-1080-1(6))* Teacher Created Materials, Inc.

Riggs, Kate. Rainforests. (Seedlings Ser.). 24p. (J). 2016. (ENG., Illus.). (gr. -1-k). *(978-1-60818-744-7(6)*, 20743) 2010. (gr. 1-4). 16.95 *(978-1-58341-829-1(6))* Creative Co., The. (Creative Education).

Roumanis, Alexis. Rainforests. 2014. (Illus.). 24p. (J). *(978-1-4896-3018-6(X))* Weigl Pubs., Inc.

Schomp, Virginia. 24 Hours in a Tropical Rain Forest, 1 vol. 2013. (Day in an Ecosystem Ser.). (ENG.). 48p. (gr. 4-4). pap. 13.93 *(978-1-62712-068-5(8)*, fa2872a9-3ac0-471b-aaa4-c17337aba160) Cavendish Square Publishing LLC.

Schuetz, Kari. Life in a Tropical Rain Forest. 2016. (Biomes Alive! Ser.). (ENG., Illus.). 24p. (J). (gr. k-3). lib. bdg. 26.95 *(978-1-62617-320-0(6)*, Blastoff! Readers) Bellwether Media.

Schwartz, Heather E. Crazy Creatures: Amazing Amazon. 2020. (J). pap. *(978-1-64290-724-7(3))* Teacher Created Materials, Inc.

Scott, Janine. Rain Forest Life. 2011. (Habitats Around the World Ser.). (ENG.). 24p. (J). (gr. k-1). pap. 43.74 *(978-1-4296-7156-9(4)*, 16720); (Illus.). (gr. -1-2). pap. 7.29 *(978-1-4296-7152-1(1)*, 116786) Capstone. (Capstone Pr.).

Senior, Kathryn. Life in a Rain Forest. 2005. (What on Earth? Ser.). (ENG., Illus.). 32p. (J). (gr. 2-4). lib. bdg. 25.50 *(978-0-516-25315-2(8)*, Children's Pr.) Scholastic Library Publishing.

Senisi, Ellen B. All in a Rainforest Day. Marent, Thomas, photos by. (Illus.). (J). 2016. (gr. -1-3). 45.99 *(978-0-9912337-2-4(7))* 2016. (ENG., (gr. -1-3). pap. 7.95 *(978-0-9912337-1-7(9))* 2014. (ENG., 32p. 17.95 *(978-0-9912337-0-0(0))* EdTechLens.

Sidabras, Kimberly. Rainforests, Vol. 5. 2018. (World's Biomes Ser.). (Illus.). 80p. (J). (gr. 7). 33.27 *(978-1-4222-4039-7(8))* Mason Crest.

Smith, Kathie Billingslea. Rainforest Animals. Bonforte, Lisa, illus. 2005. 12p. (J). (gr. k-3). 6.99 *(978-1-57755-509-4(0))* Flying Frog Publishing, Inc.

Snedden, Robert. Who Eats Who in the Rainforest? 2006. (Food Chains in Action Ser.). (Illus.). 32p. (YA). (gr. 4-7). 28.50 *(978-1-58340-961-9(0))* Black Rabbit Bks.

Sobol, Richard. Breakfast in the Rainforest: A Visit with Mountain Gorillas. Sobol, Richard, photos by. 2010. (Traveling Photographer Ser.). (ENG., Illus.). 48p. (J). (gr. 1-4). pap. 7.99 *(978-0-7636-5134-3(6))* Candlewick Pr.

Sovak, Jan. Rain Forest Wildlife. 2008. (Dover Animal Coloring Bks.). (ENG., Illus.). 32p. (J). (gr. 3-8). pap. 6.99 *(978-0-486-41554-3(6)*, 415546) Dover Pubns., Inc.

Stradling, Jan. Rain Forest Life: Level I, 6 vols., Vol. 2. (First Explorers Ser.). 24p. (gr. 1-2). 29.95 *(978-0-7699-1463-3(2))* Shortland Pubns. (U. S. A.) Inc.

Tarbox, A. D. A Rain Forest Food Chain. 2008. (Nature's Bounty Ser.). (Illus.). 43p. 22.95 *(978-1-58341-601-3(3)*, Creative Education) Creative Co., The.

—A Rainforest Food Chain. 2009. (Nature's Bounty Ser.). (ENG.). 48p. (J). (gr. 5-8). pap. 12.00 *(978-0-89812-739-3(4)*, 23015, Creative Paperbacks) Creative Co., The.

—A Rainforest Food Chain: Nature's Bounty. 2nd ed. 2015. (Odysseys in Nature Ser.). (ENG., Illus.). 80p. (J). (gr. 7-10). *(978-1-60818-543-6(5)*, 20977, Creative Education) Creative Co., The.

Topacio, Francine. Creatures in a Wet Rain Forest, 1 vol. 2019. (Wild! Exploring Animal Habitats Ser.). (ENG.). 24p. (gr. 3-3). pap. 9.25 *(978-1-7253-0436-9(8)*, ec1abf61-0a75-45bd-b22e-6d96c7b56404, PowerKids Pr.) Rosen Publishing Group, Inc., The.

Vernon, Caitlyn. Nowhere Else on Earth: Standing Tall for the Great Bear Rainforest, 1 vol. 2011. (ENG., Illus.). 136p. (J). (gr. 4-7). pap. 22.95 *(978-1-55469-303-0(9))* Orca Bk. Pubs. USA.

Welsbacher, Anne. Life in a Rain Forest: The Hawaiian Islands. 2003. (Ecosystems in Action Ser.). (ENG., Illus.). 72p. (gr. 5-9). lib. bdg. 26.60 *(978-0-8225-4685-6(X))* Lerner Publishing Group.

—Protecting Earth's Rain Forests. 2009. pap. 58.95 *(978-0-7613-4697-5(X))* 2008. 72p. (YA). (gr. 4-7). lib. bdg. 30.60 *(978-0-8225-7562-7(0))* Lerner Publishing Group.

Wiley, G. D. Tropical Rain Forests. 2003. (Biomes Around the World Ser.). (J). pap. *(978-1-58417-301-4(7))*; lib. bdg. *(978-1-58417-300-7(9))* Lake Street Pubs.

Wilkes, Angela, et al. Rain Forest Animals. Holmes, Steve, illus. rev. ed. 2004. (Ladders Ser.). 32p. (J). (gr. -1-3). 12.95 *(978-1-58728-606-3(8)*, Two-Can Publishing) T&N Children's Publishing.

Wojahn, Rebecca Hogue & Donald. A Rain Forest Food Chain: A Who-Eats-What Adventures in South America. 2009. pap. 58.95 *(978-0-7613-4660-9(0))* Lerner Publishing Group.

Woolf, Alex. Trekking in the Congo Rainforest. 2014. (Traveling Wild Ser.). 32p. (J). (gr. 3-6). pap. 63.00 *(978-1-4824-1253-6(5))* Stevens, Gareth Publishing LLLP.

World Book, Inc. Staff, contrib. by. Tropical Regions & Rain Forests. 2012. (J). *(978-0-7166-0449-5(3))* World Bk., Inc.

Worth, Bonnie. If I Ran the Rain Forest: All about Tropical Rain Forests. Ruiz, Aristides, illus. 2003. (Cat in the Hat's Learning Library). (ENG.). 48p. (J). (gr. -1-3). 9.99 *(978-0-375-81097-8(8)*, Random Hse. Bks. for Young Readers) Random Hse. Children's Bks.

RAIN FORESTS

Alaina, Maria. The Rain Forest. 2011. (Wonder Readers Early Level Ser.). (ENG.). 16p. (J). (gr. -1-1). pap. 6.25 *(978-1-4296-8057-8(1)*, 118375, Capstone Pr.) Capstone.

—Rainforest. 2011. (Wonder Readers Early Level Ser.). (ENG.). 16p. (gr. -1-1). pap. 35.94 *(978-1-4296-8171-1(3)*, Capstone Pr.) Capstone.

Allan, Tony. Rainforests. 2003. (Illus.). lib. bdg. 28.50 *(978-1-59389-124-4(5))* Chrysalis Education.

Amstutz, Lisa J. Rain Forest Animal Adaptations, 1 vol. 2011. (Amazing Animal Adaptations Ser.). (ENG.). 32p. (J). (gr. -1-2). pap. 8.10 *(978-1-4296-7034-0(7)*, 116744); lib. bdg. 27.99 *(978-1-4296-6028-0(7)*, 114971) Capstone.

Aspen-Baxter, Linda. Rainforests. 2011. (J). (gr. 5-8). pap. 13.95 *(978-1-61690-646-7(4)*, AV2 by Weigl); (Illus.). 32p. (gr. 2-5). 28.55 *(978-1-61690-640-5(5))* Weigl Pubs., Inc.

Bailey, Diane. Saving the Rainforests: Inside the World's Most Diverse Habitat. 2017. (Protecting the Earth's Animals Ser.). (ENG., Illus.). 64p. (J). (gr. 5-8). 23.95 *(978-1-4222-3880-6(6))* Mason Crest.

Bailey, Gerry. Tangled in the Rainforest. Noyes, Leighton, illus. 2014. (Science to the Rescue Ser.). (ENG.). 32p. (J). (gr. 4-4). *(978-0-7787-0432-4(7))* Crabtree Publishing Co.

Banner, Horace. Rain Forest Adventures. rev. ed. 2006. (Adventure Ser.). (ENG., Illus.). 96p. (J). pap. 8.99 *(978-1-85792-627-9(7)*, d9ca2b41-adcb-4410-afa6-b8ccc249e425) Christian Focus Pubns. GBR. Dist: Baker & Taylor Publisher Services (BTPS).

Bartholomew, Linda & Bartholomew, Al. Adventures in the Tropics. Bartholomew, Linda & Bartholomew, Al, photos by. 2005. (Illus.). 76p. (J). 15.00 *(978-0-9764802-1-1(2))* Solutions for Human Services, LLC.

—The Rain Forest Book for Kids. Bartholomew, Linda & Bartholomew, Al, photos by. 2005. (Illus.). 32p. (J). 9.00 *(978-0-9764802-0-4(4))* Solutions for Human Services, LLC.

Benchmark Education Company. Tropical Rain Forests (Teacher Guide) 2005. *(978-1-4108-4649-5(0))* Benchmark Education Co.

Benduhn, Tea. Living in Tropical Rain Forests, 1 vol. 2007. (Life on the Edge Ser.). (ENG., Illus.). 24p. (gr. 2-4). pap. 9.15 *(978-0-8368-8349-7(7)*, 255750a9-1115-4bd4-8574-b4a045c6c3ec); lib. bdg. 24.67 *(978-0-8368-8344-2(6)*, 3f407531-1650-49a6-adef-8e3f8c2ce084) Stevens, Gareth Publishing LLLP. (Weekly Reader Leveled Readers).

Benoit, Peter. Tropical Rain Forests. 2011. (True Bks.). 48p. (J). (gr. 3-5). 29.00 *(978-0-531-20554-9(1)*, Children's Pr.) Scholastic Library Publishing.

—A True Book: Tropical Rain Forests. 2011. (True Bk Ser.). (ENG.). 48p. (J). (gr. 3-5). pap. 6.95 *(978-0-531-28103-1(5))* Scholastic Library Publishing.

Berger, Gilda. Rain Forest. Date not set. (Smart Science Ser.). (Illus.). 16p. (J). (gr. 2-5). pap. 5.95 *(978-1-58273-510-8(7))* Sundance/Newbridge Educational Publishing.

Bodden, Valerie. Rainforests. 2006. (Our World Ser.). (Illus.). 24p. (J). (gr. -1-3). lib. bdg. 16.95 *(978-1-58341-465-1(7)*, Creative Education) Creative Co., The.

Bowman, Lucy. Rainforest (Level 2) - Internet Referenced. 2008. (Beginners Nature Ser.). 32p. (J). 4.99 *(978-0-7945-2141-7(X)*, Usborne) EDC Publishing.

Brannon, Barbara. Discover Tropical Rain Forests. 2005. (J). pap. *(978-1-4108-5130-7(3))* Benchmark Education Co.

Brown, Carron. Secrets of the Rain Forest. 2015. (ENG., Illus.). 36p. (J). 12.99 *(978-1-61067-325-9(5))* Kane Miller.

Callery, Sean. Life Cycles: Rainforest. 2018. (Lifecycles Ser.). (ENG.). 32p. (J). pap. 7.99 *(978-0-7534-7382-5(8)*, 9780753473825, Kingfisher) Roaring Brook Pr.

Castaldo, Nancy F. Rainforests: An Activity Guide for Ages 6-9. 2003. (ENG., Illus.). 144p. (J). (gr. 2-4). pap. 14.95 *(978-1-55652-476-9(5))* Chicago Review Pr., Inc.

Chambers, Jo. Tropical Rainforest. 2007. (Trackers-Math Ser.). (gr. 2-5). pap. 5.00 *(978-1-59055-924-6(X))* Pacific Learning, Inc.

Channing, Margot. Rain Forest. 2014. (Closer Look At... Ser.). (Illus.). 32p. (J). (gr. 3-6). 31.35 *(978-1-904642-71-8(3))* Book Hse. GBR. Dist: Black Rabbit Bks.

Chapman, Simon. In the Jungle. Chapman, Simon, illus. 2005. (Illus.). 116p. (J). lib. bdg. 20.00 *(978-1-4242-0630-8(8))* Fitzgerald Bks.

Chinery, Michael & Michael, Chinery. Las Selvas.Tr. of Rain Forests. (SPA.). 40p. (J). (gr. 3-5). 12.76 *(978-84-241-2052-8(3))* Everest Editora ESP. Dist: Lectorum Pubns., Inc.

Clark Sawyer, J. Los Colores de la Selva Tropical: Hermosos y Brillantes. 2014. (Los Colores Cuentan una Historia Ser.). (SPA.). 24p. (J). (gr. -1-3). lib. bdg. 23.93 *(978-1-62724-468-8(9))* Bearport Publishing Co., Inc.

—Rain Forest Colors: Bright & Beautiful. 2014. (Little Bits: Colors Tell a Story Ser.). (ENG.). 24p. (J). (gr. -1-3). lib. bdg. 26.99 *(978-1-62724-326-1(7))* Bearport Publishing Co., Inc.

Clarke, Ginjer L. Life in the Amazon Rainforest. 2018. (Penguin Young Readers, Level 4 Ser.). (Illus.). 48p. (J). (gr. 3-4). pap. 4.99 *(978-1-5247-8487-4(7)*, Penguin Young Readers) Penguin Young Readers Group.

Clarke, Penny. Scary Creatures of the Rain Forest. 2008. (Scary Creatures Ser.). (ENG., Illus.). 32p. (J). (gr. 2-7). 27.00 *(978-0-531-20544-0(4)*, Children's Pr.) Scholastic Library Publishing.

—Scary Creatures: Scary Creatures of the Rain Forest. 2008. (Scary Creatures Ser.). (ENG., Illus.). 32p. (J). (gr. 2-7). pap. 8.95 *(978-0-531-21010-9(3)*, Watts, Franklin) Scholastic Library Publishing.

Cole, Joanna. The Rainforest. 2014. (Magic School Bus Presents Ser.). lib. bdg. 17.20 *(978-0-606-36332-7(7))* Turtleback.

Cole, Melissa S. Rain Forests. 2003. (Wild America Habitats Ser.). (Illus.). 24p. (J). 21.20 *(978-1-56711-808-7(9)*, Blackbirch Pr., Inc.) Cengage Gale.

Collins, Sarah Jean. God Made the Rain Forest. Collins, Sarah Jean, illus. 2020. (God Made Ser.). (ENG., Illus.). 20p. (J). bds. 7.99 *(978-1-4964-3632-0(6)*, 20_32354, Tyndale Kids) Tyndale Hse. Pubs.

Colson, Mary. What Happens If the Rainforests Disappear? 2015. (Unstable Earth Ser.). (ENG.). 32p. (J). 31.35 *(978-1-62588-163-2(0)*, 19380, Smart Apple Media) Black Rabbit Bks.

Cooper, Jenny, illus. Rainforest to Color. 2013. (Nature Coloring Bks). 32p. (J). pap. 5.99 *(978-0-7945-3306-9(X)*, Usborne) EDC Publishing.

Cowcher, Helen. Rainforest. (Illus.). 40p. (CHI, ENG, URD, TUR & VIE.). 16.95 *(978-1-84059-017-3(3))*; (VIE, ENG, URD, TUR & CHI., 16.95 *(978-1-84059-022-7(X))* Milet Publishing.

Datta, Aparajita & Manjrekar, Nima. Walk the Rainforest with Niwupah. Ramaswamy, Maya, illus. 2004. (J). *(978-81-89020-15-6(3))* Katha.

De la Bédoyère, Camilla. Rainforests. 2010. (Unpredictable Nature Ser.). (Illus.). 48p. (J). (gr. 3-18). lib. bdg. 19.95 *(978-1-4222-2004-7(4))* Mason Crest.

Declus, Jennifer. What Might I Find in a Rainforest. Kalasea, illus. 2004. (ENG.). (J). *(978-0-9743690-1-3(2))* Britt Allcroft Productions.

Delano, Marfe Ferguson. Explore My World Rain Forests. 2017. (Explore My World Ser.). (Illus.). 32p. (J). (gr. -1-k). pap. 4.99 *(978-1-4263-2828-2(1))*; (ENG., lib. bdg. 14.90 *(978-1-4263-2829-9(X))* Disney Publishing Worldwide. (National Geographic Kids).

DK. Eyewitness the Amazon: Step into the World's Largest Rainforest. 2015. (DK Eyewitness Ser.). (ENG., Illus.). 72p. (J). (gr. 3-7). pap. 9.99 *(978-1-4654-3566-8(2)*, DK Children) Dorling Kindersley Publishing, Inc.

Do You Really Want to Visit a Rainforest? 2014. (Do You Really Want to Visit Earth's Biomes? Ser.). (ENG., Illus.). 24p. (J). (gr. 1-4). lib. bdg. 27.10 *(978-1-60753-453-2(3)*, 15887) Amicus.

Donohue, Moira Rose. National Geographic Little Kids First Big Book of the Rain Forest. 2018. (Illus.). 128p. (J). (gr. -1-k). 14.99 *(978-1-4263-3171-8(1))*; (ENG., lib. bdg. 24.90 *(978-1-4263-3172-5(X))* Disney Publishing Worldwide. (National Geographic Kids).

Dunphy, Madeleine. Here Is the Tropical Rain Forest. Rothman, Michael, illus. 2006. (Web of Life Ser.: 1). (ENG.). 32p. (J). (gr. -1-3). 16.95 *(978-0-9773795-1-4(5))*; pap. 9.95 *(978-0-9773795-0-7(7))* Web of Life Children's Bks.

Framingham Community Charter School Grade Students. Rainforest Exhibits: How We Learned about Designing & Creating an Authentic Biome. 2003. 73p. pap. 6.25 *(978-1-4116-0071-3(1))* Lulu Pr., Inc.

Franchino, Vicky. Amazon Rain Forest. 2016. (Community Connections: Getting to Know Our Planet Ser.). (ENG., Illus.). 24p. (J). (gr. 2-5). lib. bdg. 29.21 *(978-1-63470-513-4(0)*, 207783) Cherry Lake Publishing.

Franklin, Yvonne. Las Selvas Lluviosas. rev. ed. 2010. (Science: Informational Text Ser.). (SPA., Illus.). 32p. (gr. 2-4). pap. 11.99 *(978-1-4333-2141-2(6))* Teacher Created Materials, Inc.

Frost, Helen. Tigers [Scholastic]. 2011. (Rain Forest Animals Ser.). 24p. pap. 0.50 *(978-1-4296-6311-3(1)*, Pebble) Capstone.

Fuhr, Ute. Let's Look at the Rainforest. Sautai, Raoul, illus. 2012. (ENG.). 38p. (J). (gr. 1-4). spiral bd. 11.99 *(978-1-85103-360-7(2))* Moonlight Publishing, Ltd. GBR. Dist: Independent Pubs. Group.

Gagne, Tammy. Rain Forest Ecosystems, 1 vol. 2015. (Ecosystems of the World Ser.). (ENG., Illus.). 48p. (J). (gr. 4-8). 35.64 *(978-1-62403-856-3(5)*, 18082) ABDO Publishing Co.

Ganeri, Anita. Exploring Rain Forests: A Benjamin Blog & His Inquisitive Dog Investigation, 1 vol. 2014. (Exploring Habitats with Benjamin Blog & His Inquisitive Dog Ser.). (ENG., Illus.). 32p. (J). (gr. 3-5). pap. 8.95 *(978-1-4329-8786-2(0)*, 124770, Heinemann) Capstone.

Gardeski, Christina Mia. All about Rain Forests. 2017. (Habitats Ser.). (ENG., Illus.). 24p. (J). (gr. -1-2). lib. bdg. 22.65 *(978-1-5157-7643-7(3)*, 135928, Pebble) Capstone.

Gardner, Robert. Rain Forest Experiments: 10 Science Experiments in One Hour or Less, 1 vol. 2014. (Last Minute Science Projects with Biomes Ser.). (ENG., Illus.). 48p. (gr. 5-6). lib. bdg. 26.93 *(978-0-7660-5937-5(5)*, 913a7198-86a3-488a-8eb9-9f47d4513223) Enslow Publishing, LLC.

Gibbs, Maddie. What Are Tropical Rainforests?, 1 vol. 2018. (Let's Find Out! Biomes Ser.). (ENG.). 32p. (gr. 2-3). lib. bdg. 26.06 *(978-1-5081-0697-5(5)*, 25987f8f-0646-4d57-9f3e-517e8f68dd29, Britannica Educational Publishing) Rosen Publishing Group, Inc., The.

Gray, Leon. Tropical Rain Forests. 2015. (Amazing Biomes Ser.). (ENG., Illus.). 32p. (J). (gr. 3-6). 31.35 *(978-1-78121-246-2(5)*, 16393) Brown Bear Bks.

Greeley, August. Fading Forests: The Destruction of Our Rainforests. 2009. (Man-Made Disasters Ser.). 24p. (gr. 3-3). 42.50 *(978-1-61514-347-4(5)*, PowerKids Pr.) Rosen Publishing Group, Inc., The.

Green, Jen. Rain Forest Extremes, 1 vol. 2008. (Extreme Nature Ser.). (ENG., Illus.). 32p. (J). (gr. 2-3). pap. *(978-0-7787-4521-1(X))*; lib. bdg. *(978-0-7787-4504-4(X))* Crabtree Publishing Co.

—Rainforests at Risk. 2006. (Illus.). 32p. (YA). (gr. 4-18). lib. bdg. 27.10 *(978-1-59389-116-9(4))* Chrysalis Education.

Group/McGraw-Hill, Wright. In the Rain Forest, 6 vols. (Wildcats Ser.). 32p. (gr. 2-8). *(978-0-322-00599-0(X))* Wright Group/McGraw-Hill.

—Tropical Treasure: The Rain Forest, 6 vols. (Book2WebTM Ser.). (gr. 4-8). 36.50 *(978-0-322-04432-6(4))* Wright Group/McGraw-Hill.

—La Vida en la Selva Tropical, 6 vols., Vol. 2. (First Explorers. Primeros Exploradores Nonfiction Sets Ser.). (SPA.). (gr. 1-2). 29.95 *(978-0-7699-1487-9(X))* Shortland Pubns. (U. S. A.) Inc.

Guiberson, Brenda Z. Rain, Rain, Rain Forest. 2015. (J). lib. bdg. 18.40 *(978-0-606-37341-8(1))* Turtleback.

Hamilton, Jean. The Secrets of Tropical Rainforests: Hot & Humid & Teeming with Life. Leon, Vicki, ed. 2nd ed. 2005. (Jean-Michel Cousteau Presents Ser.). Orig. Title: Tropical Rainforests. (Illus.). 48p. (J). pap. 9.95 *(978-0-9666490-5-5(2))* London Town Pr.

Harris, Nicholas. Rainforest. 2006. (Panoramas Ser.). (Illus.). 23p. (J). *(978-0-7607-8157-9(5))* backpackbook.

Harrison, James. Rainforests. 2014. 48p. pap. 4.00 *(978-1-61003-362-6(0))* Center for the Collaborative Classroom.

Heinrichs, Ann. The Amazon Rain Forest, 1 vol. 2010. (Nature's Wonders Ser.). (ENG.). 96p. (gr. 6-6). 38.36 *(978-0-7614-3932-5(3)*, 59bbb1cc-d727-4783-8734-a55d01ca45d6) Cavendish Square Publishing LLC.

Hendra, Sue. Rookie Preschool: Rookie Learn about Nauture: Busy Day, Busy Night. 2009. (Rookie Preschool Ser.). (ENG., Illus.). 24p. (J). (gr. -1). 23.00 *(978-0-531-24407-4(5))*; pap. 6.95 *(978-0-531-24582-8(9))* Scholastic Library Publishing. (Children's Pr.).

Hunter, Rebecca. Rain Forests. 2012. (Eco Alert! Ser.). (ENG., Illus.). 32p. (gr. 4-6). lib. bdg. 28.50 *(978-1-59771-297-2(3))* Sea-To-Sea Pubns.

Hyde, Natalie. Amazon Rainforest Research Journal. 2017. (Ecosystems Research Journal Ser.). (Illus.). 32p. (J). (gr. 4-5). *(978-0-7787-3467-3(6))*; (ENG., pap. *(978-0-7787-3492-5(7))* Crabtree Publishing Co.

In the Rain Forest: Level F. 16p. 31.50 *(978-0-322-00376-7(8))* Wright Group/McGraw-Hill.

Iyer, Rani. Endangered Rain Forests: Investigating Rain Forests in Crisis. 2015. (Endangered Earth Ser.). (ENG., Illus.). 32p. (J). (gr. 3-6). lib. bdg. 27.99 *(978-1-4914-2039-3(1)*, 127517, Capstone Pr.) Capstone.

Jackson, Tom. The Magic School Bus Presents: the Rainforest: a Nonfiction Companion to the Original Magic School Bus Series. Bracken, Carolyn, illus. 2014. (Magic School Bus Presents Ser.). (ENG.). 32p. (J). (gr. 1-3). pap. 7.99 *(978-0-545-68585-6(0)*, Scholastic Paperbacks) Scholastic, Inc.

Johnson, Rebecca L. A Walk in the Rain Forest. Saroff, Phyllis V., illus. Braasch, Gary, photos by. 2005. (Biomes of North America Ser.). 48p. (gr. 3-6). 23.93 *(978-1-57505-154-3(0))* Lerner Publishing Group.

Kainen, Dan & Wollard, Kathy. Jungle: A Photicular Book. 2016. (Photicular Ser.). (ENG., Illus.). 24p. 26.99 *(978-0-7611-8953-4(X)*, 18953) Workman Publishing Co., Inc.

Kalman, Bobbie. Baby Animals in Rainforest Habitats. 2011. (ENG.). 24p. (J). pap. *(978-0-7787-7745-8(6))* Crabtree Publishing Co.

—Les Forêts Humides. 2012. (FRE.). 32p. (J). pap. 9.95 *(978-2-89579-477-6(4))* Bayard Canada CAN. Dist: Crabtree Publishing Co.

Kelley, K. C. Trek the Rain Forest. 2018. (Amazing Adventures Ser.). (ENG., Illus.). 16p. (J). (gr. k-2). pap. 7.99 *(978-1-68152-268-5(3)*, 14892) Amicus.

Kelly, Miles. 100 Facts Rainforests. Kelly, Richard, ed. 2nd ed. 2017. 48p. (J). pap. 9.95 *(978-1-78617-066-8(3))* Miles Kelly Publishing, Ltd. GBR. Dist: Parkwest Pubns., Inc.

Kenshole, Fiona. Dolphin Readers 3. Let's Go to the Rainforest. International Edition. Wright, Craig, ed. 2010. (ENG., Illus.). 28p. 5.00 *(978-0-19-440106-7(5))* Oxford Univ. Pr., Inc.

Kite, Lorien. Life in a Rain Forest, 1 vol. 2010. (Nature in Focus Ser.). (ENG., Illus.). 32p. (gr. 3-4). (J). pap. 11.50 *(978-1-4339-3408-7(6),* 42692fcd-a446-407c-81f2-9b12b130b0e7, Gareth Stevens Learning Library); (YA). lib. bdg. 28.67 *(978-1-4339-3410-0(8),* b2ac692e-f5b0-4eeb-a840-b8d449db10c9) Stevens, Gareth Publishing LLLP.

Kraft Rector, Rebecca. The Amazon Rainforest. 2018. (Natural Wonders of the World Ser.). (ENG., Illus.). 32p. (J). (gr. 3-5). pap. 9.95 *(978-1-63517-583-7(6))*; lib. bdg. 31.35 *(978-1-63517-511-0(9),* 1635175119) North Star Editions. (Focus Readers).

Kratter, Paul. The Living Rain Forest: An Animal Alphabet. Kratter, Paul, illus. rev. ed. 2010. (Illus.). 32p. (J). (gr. 1-4). pap. 7.95 *(978-1-58089-393-0(7))* Charlesbridge Publishing, Inc.

Levete, Sarah. Life in the Rain Forest. 2011. (Big Picture: Homes Ser.). (ENG.). 24p. (gr. 1-2). pap. 41.70 *(978-1-4296-6732-6(X),* Capstone Pr.) Capstone.

—Rain Forest. 2011. (ENG., Illus.). 24p. (J). pap. *(978-0-7787-7865-3(7),* 1331580); (gr. 3-6). *(978-0-7787-7843-1(6),* 1331580) Crabtree Publishing Co.

Levy, Janey. Discovering Rain Forests. (World Habitats Ser.). 32p. (gr. 4-5). 2009. 47.90 *(978-1-60854-836-1(8),* PowerKids Pr.) 2007. (ENG., Illus.). (YA). lib. bdg. 28.93 *(978-1-4042-3782-7(8),* cb9bf5b3-3fc7-4b57-9769-cea7f417c0b3) Rosen Publishing Group, Inc., The.

Lindeen, Mary & Sexton, Colleen. Rain Forests. 2007. (Learning about the Earth Ser.). (ENG., Illus.). 24p. (J). (gr. k-3). lib. bdg. 26.95 *(978-1-60014-115-7(3))* Bellwether Media.

Lynette, Rachel. Who Lives in a Wet, Wild Rain Forest?, 1 vol. 2010. (Exploring Habitats Ser.). (ENG.). 24p. (J). (gr. 2-3). pap. 9.25 *(978-1-4488-1283-7(6),* 1cbbfa74-37ee-4b5b-a737-4e805e9108e7); lib. bdg. 26.27 *(978-1-4488-0678-2(X),* 3085d531-d279-4016-a814-aae40c90255a) Rosen Publishing Group, Inc., The. (PowerKids Pr.).

Marianne, Berkes. Over in the Jungle: A Rainforest Rhyme. Jeanette, Canyon, illus. 2008. 26p. (J). (gr. -1). bds. 7.95 *(978-1-58469-108-2(5))* Take Heart Pubns.

Mattern, Joanne. Animals of the Tropical Rain Forest. (Reading Room Collection 1 Ser.). 16p. (gr. 2-3). 2009. 37.50 *(978-1-60851-941-5(4),* PowerKids Pr.) 2005. (ENG., Illus.). (J). lib. bdg. 22.27 *(978-1-4042-3341-6(5),* 7c31fbb2-e629-4075-920a-5b1e49c04d05) Rosen Publishing Group, Inc., The.

McAllister, Ian & Van Tol, Alex. Great Bear Rainforest: A Giant-Screen Adventure in the Land of the Spirit Bear, 1 vol. 2019. (ENG., Illus.). 96p. (J). (gr. 4-7). 29.95 *(978-1-4598-2279-5(X))* Orca Bk. Pubs. USA.

McKenzie, Precious. Rainforests. 2010. (Eye to Eye with Endangered Habitats Ser.). (ENG., Illus.). 24p. (gr. 3-6). pap. 8.95 *(978-1-61590-555-3(3),* 9781615905553) Rourke Educational Media.

McLeish, Ewan. Rain Forest Destruction, 1 vol. 2007. (What If We Do Nothing? Ser.). (ENG., Illus.). 48p. (gr. 5-8). pap. 15.05 *(978-0-8368-8158-5(3),* e10a8bd6-7f03-4ed5-9658-c3d065ec7847, Gareth Stevens Secondary Library) Stevens, Gareth Publishing LLLP.

Meister, Cari. Do You Really Want to Meet a Monkey? Fabbri, Daniele, illus. 2014. (Do You Really Want to Meet ... ? Ser.). (ENG.). 24p. (J). (gr. 1-4). 27.10 *(978-1-60753-456-3(8),* 15897) Amicus.

Messner, Kate. Over & under the Rainforest. Neal, Christopher Silas, illus. 2020. (Over & Under Ser.). (ENG.). 48p. (J). (gr. k-3). 18.99 *(978-1-4521-6940-8(3))* Chronicle Bks. LLC.

Mettler, René, illus. The Jungle. 2012. (ENG.). 36p. (J). (gr. -1-k). spiral bd. 19.99 *(978-1-85103-399-7(8))* Moonlight Publishing, Ltd. GBR. Dist: Independent Pubs. Group.

Morey, Allan. Rain Forest Food Chains. 2003. (What Eats What? Ser.). (J). pap. *(978-1-58417-225-3(8))*; lib. bdg. *(978-1-58417-224-6(X))* Lake Street Pubs.

Morris, Ting & Morris, Neil. Rainforest. Hulse, Gillian, illus. 2006. (Sticky Fingers Ser.). 32p. (J). lib. bdg. 28.50 *(978-1-59771-028-2(8))* Sea-To-Sea Pubns.

Murray, Aaron R. Counting in the Rain Forest 1-2-3, 1 vol. 2012. (All about Counting in the Biomes Ser.). (ENG., Illus.). 24p. (-1). pap. 10.35 *(978-1-4644-0063-6(6),* 67bee4a6-02f1-4ebe-9816-7615aaa5588a, Enslow Publishing); (gr. -1-1). 25.27 *(978-0-7660-4055-7(0),* 44a30e3e-2dec-480f-bf5e-cc4513e6569f, Enslow Publishing); (gr. -1-1). E-Book 25.27 *(978-1-4645-0970-4(0),* e8808584-6e31-4311-a0f4-5bc0022eec05) Enslow Publishing, LLC.

Newland, Sonya. Rain Forest Animals. 2011. (Saving Wildlife Ser.). 32p. (gr. 4-7). lib. bdg. 31.35 *(978-1-59920-660-8(9))* Black Rabbit Bks.

Nichols, Catherine. In the Rain Forest, 1 vol. 2003. (We Can Read about Nature! Ser.). (ENG., Illus.). 32p. (gr. 1-2). 25.50 *(978-0-7614-1432-2(0),* c5bca24b-a11d-47b9-87b2-3f6e73fbd4c4) Cavendish Square Publishing LLC.

O'Hare, Ted. Amazing Rain Forest. 2005. (Rain Forest Today Discovery Library Ser.). (Illus.). 24p. (gr. 1-4). 14.95 *(978-1-59515-151-3(6))* Rourke Educational Media.

—Vanishing Rain Forests. 2005. (Rain Forest Today Discovery Library Ser.). (Illus.). 24p. (gr. 1-4). 14.95 *(978-1-59515-156-8(7))* Rourke Educational Media.

Pierce, Nick. Rain Forest. 2013. (Worldwise Nature Ser.). (ENG., Illus.). 23p. (J). *(978-1-911242-82-6(2))* Book Hse.

Powell, Jillian. Projects with Rainforests, 1 vol. 2014. (Make & Learn Ser.). (ENG., Illus.). 32p. (J). (gr. 4-4). 29.27 *(978-1-4777-7165-5(4),* cc564036-60fa-430b-a96f-7e3b21a07877, PowerKids Pr.) Rosen Publishing Group, Inc., The.

Pratt-Serafini, Kristin Joy. A Walk in the Rainforest, 1 vol. 2014. (Illus.). 32p. (J). (gr. k-6). 16.99 *(978-1-878265-99-9(7),* Dawn Pubns.) Sourcebooks, Inc.

Prebeg, Rick. Into the Jungle. Prebeg, Rick, photos by. 2005. (Illus.). (J). *(978-1-933248-05-9(X))* World Quest Learning.

Pyers, Greg. Biodiversity of Rain Forests, 1 vol. Morden, Richard, illus. 2011. (Biodiversity Ser.). (ENG.). 32p. (gr. 4-4). 31.21 *(978-1-60870-073-8(9),* d7729228-5c99-4bc5-baa3-52ae7853bf97) Cavendish Square Publishing LLC.

Rain Forest Animals Pack [Scholastic]. 2011. (Rain Forest Animals Ser.). 24p. pap. 2.50 *(978-1-4296-6316-8(2),* Pebble) Capstone.

Rainforest. 2003. (J). per. *(978-1-57657-884-1(4))* Paradise Pr., Inc.

Read, Nicholas. A Whale's World, 1 vol. McAllister, Ian, photos by. 2018. (My Great Bear Rainforest Ser.: 4). (ENG., Illus.). 32p. (J). (gr. 1-3). 19.95 *(978-1-4598-1273-4(5))* Orca Bk. Pubs. USA.

—Wolf Island, 1 vol. McAllister, Ian, photos by. 2017. (My Great Bear Rainforest Ser.: 1). (ENG., Illus.). 32p. (J). (gr. 1-3). 19.95 *(978-1-4598-1264-2(6))* Orca Bk. Pubs. USA.

Rice, Howard. Step into the Rainforest, 1 vol. 2nd rev. ed. 2011. (TIME for KIDS(r): Informational Text Ser.). (ENG.). 28p. (gr. 2-3). pap. 10.99 *(978-1-4333-3630-0(8))* Teacher Created Materials, Inc.

Rice, William & Franklin, Yvonne. Rainforests, 1 vol. rev. ed. 2009. (Science: Informational Text Ser.). (ENG.). 32p. (J). (gr. 2-4). pap. 11.99 *(978-1-4333-0319-7(1))* Teacher Created Materials, Inc.

Rice, William B. Amazon Rainforest, 1 vol. 2nd rev. ed. 2012. (TIME for KIDS(r): Informational Text Ser.). (ENG.). 32p. (gr. 3-5). pap. 12.99 *(978-1-4333-3671-3(5))* Teacher Created Materials, Inc.

Riggs, Kate. Rainforests. (Seedlings Ser.). (ENG., Illus.). 24p. (J). 2017. (gr. k-2). pap. 7.99 *(978-1-62832-340-5(X),* 20741, Creative Paperbacks) 2016. (gr. -1-k). *(978-1-60818-744-7(6),* 20743, Creative Education) Creative Co., The.

Rissman, Rebecca. Living & Nonliving in the Rain Forest, 1 vol. 2013. (Is It Living or Nonliving? Ser.). (ENG.). 24p. (J). (gr. k-2). 25.99 *(978-1-4109-5382-7(3),* 123311); pap. 6.95 *(978-1-4109-5389-6(0),* 123329) Capstone. (Raintree).

Robinson, Fay. Into the Rain Forest. Lopez, Paul, illus. 2012. 32p. (J). pap. *(978-0-7166-1652-8(1))* World Bk., Inc.

Romero, Libby. Tropical Rain Forests. 2005. (J). pap. *(978-1-4108-4601-3(6))* Benchmark Education Co.

Ross, Suzanne. BOOST Rain Forest Activity Book. 2013. (Dover Kids Activity Books: Nature Ser.). (ENG.). 48p. (J). (gr. 1-2). pap. 5.99 *(978-0-486-49413-5(6),* 494136) Dover Pubns., Inc.

Roumanis, Alexis. Rainforests. 2014. (Illus.). 24p. (J). *(978-1-4896-3018-6(X))* Weigl Pubs., Inc.

Sandler, Michael. Rain Forests: Surviving in the Amazon. 2005. (X-treme Places Ser.). (Illus.). 32p. (YA). (gr. 2-5). lib. bdg. 28.50 *(978-1-59716-089-6(X))* Bearport Publishing Co., Inc.

Schomp, Virginia. 24 Hours in a Tropical Rain Forest, 1 vol. 2013. (Day in an Ecosystem Ser.). (ENG.). 48p. (gr. 4-4). 34.07 *(978-1-60870-895-6(0),* e43fcae5-30af-414b-b5d3-e5b208550774) Cavendish Square Publishing LLC.

Selvas Tropicales. (SPA.). (YA). (gr. 5-8). *(978-84-236-3191-9(5),* ED5686) Edebé ESP. Dist: Lectorum Pubns., Inc.

Senisi, Ellen B. All in a Rainforest Day. Marent, Thomas, photos by. (Illus.). (J). 2016. (gr. -1-3). 45.99 *(978-0-9912337-2-4(7))* 2016. (ENG., (gr. -1-3). pap. 7.95 *(978-0-9912337-1-7(9))* 2014. (ENG., 32p. 17.95 *(978-0-9912337-0-0(0))* EdTechLens.

Shore, Diane Z. & Calvert, Deanna. Riddle Diddle Rainforest. Bauer, Stephanie, illus. 2019. (Riddle Diddle Dumplings Ser.). (ENG.). 10p. (J). (gr. -1-1). bds. 9.99 *(978-1-68152-500-6(3),* 10868) Amicus.

Sidabras, Kimberly. Rainforests, Vol. 5. 2018. (World's Biomes Ser.). (Illus.). 80p. (J). (gr. 7). 33.27 *(978-1-4222-4039-7(8))* Mason Crest.

Silverman, Buffy. Let's Visit the Rain Forest. 2016. (Lightning Bolt Books (r) — Biome Explorers Ser.). (ENG., Illus.). 32p. (J). (gr. 1-3). 29.32 *(978-1-5124-1195-9(7),* 603af08a-15c4-47ac-9f6a-6a48a787add6, Lerner Pubns.) Lerner Publishing Group.

Simon, Seymour. Tropical Rainforests. 2010. (ENG.). 32p. (J). (gr. k-4). 17.99 *(978-0-06-114253-6(0),* HarperCollins) HarperCollins Pubs.

Smith, Kathie Billingslea. Rainforest Animals. Bonforte, Lisa, illus. 2005. 12p. (J). (gr. k-3). 6.99 *(978-1-57755-509-4(0))* Flying Frog Publishing, Inc.

Spilbury, Louise. Rain Forests. 2015. (Research on the Edge Ser.). (ENG., Illus.). 32p. (J). (gr. 3-8). 31.35 *(978-1-62588-156-4(8),* 19355, Smart Apple Media) Black Rabbit Bks.

Spilsbury, Louise. Surviving the Rainforest, 1 vol. 2016. (Sole Survivor Ser.). (ENG.). 48p. (gr. 4-5). pap. 15.05 *(978-1-4824-5079-8(8),* 51fc0870-513a-4554-acf0-c6fa38d83183) Stevens, Gareth Publishing LLLP.

Spilsbury, Louise & Spilsbury, Richard. In the Rainforest, 1 vol. 2016. (Science on Patrol Ser.). (ENG.). 48p. (J). (gr. 4-5). pap. 15.05 *(978-1-4824-5980-7(9),* 73ea7484-248e-4200-b760-78ace22521eb) Stevens, Gareth Publishing LLLP.

Sundance/Newbridge LLC Staff. The Rain Forest. 2007. (Early Science Ser.). (gr. k-3). 18.95 *(978-1-4007-6486-0(6))*; pap. 6.10 *(978-1-4007-6482-2(3))* Sundance/Newbridge Educational Publishing.

Taylor, Trace & Zorzi, Gina. This Is a Rainforest. 2011. (Power 100 - Ecosystems Ser.). 28p. (J). (gr. k-2). pap. 7.95 *(978-1-61541-225-9(5))* American Reading Co.

Thomson, Ruth. Rain Forests. 2012. (Geography Corner Ser.). (ENG., Illus.). 24p. (J). (gr. k-3). 21.25 *(978-1-4488-6618-2(9),* PowerKids Pr.) Rosen Publishing Group, Inc., The.

Trumbauer, Lisa. Discover the Rain Forest. 2005. (Yellow Umbrella Fluent Level Ser.). (ENG., Illus.). 16p. (gr. k-1). pap. 35.70 *(978-0-7368-5294-4(8),* Capstone Pr.) Capstone.

Vogt, Richard C. Rain Forests. 2009. (Insiders Ser.). (ENG.). 64p. (J). (gr. 3-7). 17.99 *(978-1-4169-3866-8(4),* Simon & Schuster Bks. For Young Readers) Simon & Schuster Bks. For Young Readers.

Vonder Brink, Tracy. Protecting the Amazon Rainforest. 2020. (Saving Earth's Biomes Ser.). (ENG., Illus.). 32p. (J). (gr. 3-5). 31.35 *(978-1-64493-068-7(4),* 1644930684, Focus Readers) North Star Editions.

Watson, Galadriel Findlay. The Amazon Rain Forest: The Largest Rain Forest in the World. 2004. (Illus.). 32p. (J). lib. bdg. 26.00 *(978-1-59036-270-9(5))* Weigl Pubs., Inc.

Weisbacher, Anne. Protecting Earth's Rain Forests. 2009. pap. 58.95 *(978-0-7613-4697-5(X))* 2008. 72p. (YA). (gr. 4-7). lib. bdg. 30.60 *(978-0-8225-7562-7(0))* 2015. (ENG., Illus.). 72p. (J). (gr. 4-7). E-Book 46.65 *(978-1-5124-1050-1(0),* Lerner Pubns.) Lerner Publishing Group.

Woolf, Alex. Trekking in the Congo Rainforest. 2014. (Traveling Wild Ser.). 32p. (J). (gr. 3-6). pap. 63.00 *(978-1-4824-1253-6(5))* Stevens, Gareth Publishing LLLP.

World Book, Inc. Staff, contrib. by. Rain Forest Animals. 2007. (J). *(978-0-7166-7729-1(6))* World Bk., Inc.

Wright, Craig, ed. Dolphin Readers: Level 3: 525-Word Vocabulary Let's Go to the Rainforest Activity Book. 2010. (ENG., Illus.). 14p. act. bk. ed. 5.00 *(978-0-19-440167-8(7))* Oxford Univ. Pr., Inc.

Youssef, Jagger. Rainforests, 1 vol. 2017. (Our Exciting Earth! Ser.). (ENG.). 24p. (J). (gr. k-k). pap. 9.15 *(978-1-5382-0977-6(2),* 7603cef2-90b3-4808-8319-a0c225190553) Stevens, Gareth Publishing LLLP.

RAIN FORESTS—FICTION

Albert, Toni Diana. Saving the Rain Forest with Cammie & Cooper. Bowles, Carol, illus. l.t. ed. 2003. 32p. (J). pap. 7.95 *(978-1-929432-02-8(X),* 800-353-2791) Trickle Creek Bks.

Angello, Mary L. The Legend of the Crystal Skull. 2008. 147p. pap. 15.50 *(978-1-4357-3194-3(8))* Lulu Pr., Inc.

Ballantyne, R. M. The Lighthouse. 2006. pap. *(978-1-4065-0531-3(5))* Dodo Pr.

Branch, Keith. Forest Elves: Protectors of the Rainforest. 2013. (ENG.). 42p. (J). pap. 8.95 *(978-1-4787-0650-2(3))* Outskirts Pr., Inc.

Brett, Jan. The Umbrella: Board Book. Brett, Jan, illus. 2011. (Illus.). 36p. (J). (gr. -1 — 1). bds. 8.99 *(978-0-399-25540-3(0),* G.P. Putnam's Sons Books for Young Readers) Penguin Young Readers Group.

Bucher, Charlotte. Cecil Learns to Smile. 2010. 26p. (J). pap. 19.95 *(978-1-4327-4992-7(7))* Outskirts Pr., Inc.

Bunton, M. Catherine. The Fairy Tale Keeper. 2012. 134p. pap. 8.95 *(978-1-60594-783-9(0))* Aeon Publishing Inc.

Burke, Zoe. Charley Harper's What's in the Rain Forest? A Nature Discovery Book. Harper, Charley, illus. 2013. 34p. (J). 14.95 *(978-0-7649-6584-5(0))* Pomegranate Communications, Inc.

Burns, Ian. Possum & Python. 2005. 23p. 8.00 *(978-1-4116-5490-7(0))* Lulu Pr., Inc.

Courtney, Suzanne Gene. Rainfrog. 2011. 34p. pap. 14.50 *(978-1-61204-189-6(2),* Eloquent Bks.) Strategic Book Publishing & Rights Agency (SBPRA).

Covey, Richard D. & Pappas, Diane H. What's Happening to the Rain Forests? 2009. (Planet Earth Patrol Ser.). (Illus.). (J). *(978-0-545-06103-2(2))* Scholastic, Inc.

Crouch, Cheryl. Troo Makes a Big Splash, 1 vol. Zimmer, Kevin, illus. 2011. (I Can Read! / Rainforest Friends Ser.). (ENG.). 32p. (J). (gr. -1-2). pap. 4.99 *(978-0-310-71810-9(4))* Zonderkidz.

—Troo's Big Climb, 1 vol. Zimmer, Kevin, illus. 2011. (I Can Read! / Rainforest Friends Ser.). (ENG.). 32p. (J). (gr. -1-2). pap. 4.99 *(978-0-310-71808-6(2))* Zonderkidz.

—Troo's Secret Clubhouse, 1 vol. Zimmer, Kevin, illus. 2011. (I Can Read! / Rainforest Friends Ser.). (ENG.). 32p. (J). (gr. -1-2). pap. 4.99 *(978-0-310-71809-3(0))* Zonderkidz.

Del Moral, Susana. Un Paseo Por la Selva. Zaidi, Nadeem, illus. 2005. (Baby Einstein: Libros de Carton Ser.). (SPA.). 10p. (J). (gr. -1). bds. *(978-970-718-306-3(3),* Silver Dolphin en Español) Advanced Marketing, S. de R. L. de C. V.

Earhart, Kristin. Rain Forest Relay. 2015. (Race the Wild Ser.: 1). lib. bdg. 14.75 *(978-0-606-37042-4(0))* Turtleback.

Evans, Leah Beth. A Different Kind of Hero. Gedrich, Colleen, illus. 2007. 40p. (J). per. 14.95 *(978-0-9795045-2-5(X))* Tribute Bks.

Fallon, Karla. Rainforest Moon. 2005. 102p. pap. 9.98 *(978-1-4116-3776-4(3))* Lulu Pr., Inc.

Faye, Charlet. The Chilling Adventures of Marshall McCaw. 2004. (Illus.). 60p. (J). 18.95 *(978-0-9655222-1-2(0))* FayeHouse. Pr. International.

Giancamilli, Vanessa. Gecko Gathering. Kest, Kristin, illus. 2005. (Amazing Animal Adventures Ser.). (ENG.). (J). (gr. -1-2). 36p. 2.95 *(978-1-59249-289-3(4),* S7157); 32p. 9.95 *(978-1-59249-323-4(8),* PS7157); 36p. 15.95 *(978-1-59249-288-6(6),* B7107); 36p. pap. 6.95 *(978-1-59249-290-9(8),* S7107) Soundprints.

Gilman, David. Blood Sun. 2012. (Danger Zone Ser.: 3). (ENG.). 432p. (YA). (gr. 7). pap. 10.99 *(978-0-440-42241-9(8),* Ember) Random Hse. Children's Bks.

Glennon, Michelle. My Big Green Teacher: Take a Deep Breath: Saving Our Rainforests. Glennon, Michelle, illus. 2008. (ENG., Illus.). 32p. (J). 19.95 *(978-0-9797952-0-6(6))* GDG Publishing.

Greenburg, J. C. Andrew Lost #15: in the Jungle. Gerardi, Jan, illus. 2007. (Andrew Lost Ser.: 15). (ENG.). 96p. (J). (gr. 1-4). 4.99 *(978-0-375-83564-3(4),* Random Hse. Bks. for Young Readers) Random Hse. Children's Bks.

Grylls, Bear. The Jungle Challenge. McCann, Emma, illus. 2017. 117p. (J). *(978-1-61067-768-4(4))* Kane Miller.

Hall, Michael. Monkey Time. Hall, Michael, illus. 2019. (ENG., Illus.). 48p. (J). (gr. -1-3). 17.99 *(978-0-06-238302-0(7),* Greenwillow Bks.) HarperCollins Pubs.

Harrison, Paula. The Lost Gold. 2013. (Rescue Princesses Ser.: 7). lib. bdg. 14.75 *(978-0-606-32374-1(0))* Turtleback.

Harvey, M. A. Attack of the Jaguar: Dare to Take the Test. 2004. (Illus.). 128p. (J). pap. *(978-1-84458-051-4(2),* Pavilion Children's Books) Pavilion Bks.

Heer, Dusty Rhoades. The Forest That Rains Frogs. 2012. (ENG.). 58p. pap. 19.95 *(978-1-4327-9303-6(9))* Outskirts Pr., Inc.

Hill, Michelle M. Stanley. 2012. 12p. pap. 15.99 *(978-1-4772-2923-1(X))* AuthorHouse.

Hoch, Jeff. Guess Who Saves the Rain Forest? Hoch, Jeff, ed. Kiedrowski, Steve, illus. Date not set. 39p. (J). (gr. k-5). pap. 7.00 *(978-0-9650629-3-0(7))* Coulee Region Pubns., Inc.

Killion, Bette. Little Lek Longtail Learns to Sleep. Vidal, Beatriz, illus. 2016. 28p. (J). (gr. k-3). 17.95 *(978-1-937786-63-2(3),* Wisdom Tales) World Wisdom, Inc.

Knife & Packer, creator. Rain Forest Rumble. 2016. (Illus.). 94p. (J). pap. 6.99 *(978-1-61067-399-0(9))* Kane Miller.

Krebs, Laurie. Un Recorrido Por la Selva. Wilson, Anne, illus. 2011. (SPA.). 40p. (J). (gr. k-5). pap. 9.99 *(978-1-84686-551-0(4))* Barefoot Bks., Inc.

—We're Roaming in the Rainforest. Wilson, Anne, illus. 40p. (J). 2011. (ENG.). (gr. k-5). pap. 9.99 *(978-1-84686-545-9(X))* 2010. (gr. -1-5). 16.99 *(978-1-84686-331-8(7))* Barefoot Bks., Inc.

Krulik, Nancy. Dogs Don't Have Webbed Feet #7. Braun, Sebastien, illus. 2015. (Magic Bone Ser.: 7). 128p. (J). (gr. 1-3). bds. 6.99 *(978-0-448-48096-1(4),* Grosset & Dunlap) Penguin Young Readers Group.

Lamond, Peter. The Rainforest Family & Those Terrible Toads. Purnell, Teresa, illus. 2011. 92p. pap. 27.25 *(978-1-60976-297-1(5),* Eloquent Bks.) Strategic Book Publishing & Rights Agency (SBPRA).

Laviera, Tato. Mayanito's New Friends / Los Nuevos Amigos de Mayanito. Utomo, Gabhor, illus. 2017. (ENG & SPA.). 32p. (J). (gr. 2-4). 17.95 *(978-1-55885-855-8(5),* Piñata Books) Arte Publico Pr.

Lewis, Axel. Rain Forest Rampage, 1 vol. 2014. (Robot Racers Ser.). (ENG.). 160p. (J). (gr. 2-4). 26.65 *(978-1-4342-6571-5(4),* 124406, Stone Arch Bks.) Capstone.

London, C. Alexander. We Dine with Cannibals. 2013. (Accidental Adventure Ser.: 2). 384p. (J). (gr. 3-7). pap. 7.99 *(978-0-14-242474-2(9),* Puffin Books) Penguin Young Readers Group.

Long, Jan. Azule & the White Hummingbird: The Birth of the White Hummingbird. 2014. (Illus.). 84p. (J). pap. 9.95 *(978-1-63047-171-2(2))* Morgan James Publishing.

Lonsdale, Cathy. Bill the Brush Turkey. 2008. (ENG.). 24p. 13.95 *(978-1-4092-0414-5(6))* Lulu Pr., Inc.

Lumry, Amanda & Hurwitz, Laura. Operation Orangutan. 2007. (Adventures of Riley (Unnumberd) Ser.). (Illus.). 36p. (J). (gr. -1-3). 15.95 *(978-0-9748411-4-4(5))* Eaglemont Pr.

Marsh, Carole. The Mystery in the Amazon Rainforest: South America. (Around the World in 80 Mysteries Ser.). (Illus.). 131p. (J). 2009. lib. bdg. 18.99 *(978-0-635-07017-3(0),* Marsh, Carole Mysteries) 2007. (gr. 3-5). 14.95 *(978-0-635-06212-3(7))*8. 2007. (ENG., (gr. 4-6). 22.44 *(978-0-635-06208-6(9))* Gallopade International.

Martinez-Neal, Juana. Zonia's Rain Forest. Martinez-Neal, Juana, illus. 2021. (ENG.). 40p. (J). (gr. -1-3). 17.99 *(978-1-5362-0845-0(0))* Candlewick Pr.

McFarlane, Susannah. Jump Start. 2015. 123p. (J). *(978-1-61067-444-7(8))* Kane Miller.

—Jump Start: EJ12 Girl Hero. 2016. 128p. (J). pap. 5.99 *(978-1-61067-382-2(4))* Kane Miller.

Meadows, Daisy. Lily the Rain Forest Fairy. 2014. (Rainbow Magic — the Earth Fairies Ser.). lib. bdg. 14.75 *(978-0-606-35834-7(X))* Turtleback.

Menard, Michele R. The Canopy House - Vol 2- Gus & Ester Meet the Neighbors. 2013. 34p. pap. 12.50 *(978-0-9891734-1-4(0))* Four Menards, The.

—The Canopy House - Volume 1. 2013. 38p. pap. 13.50 *(978-0-9887969-7-3(X))* Four Menards, The.

Mitchell, Susan K. The Rainforest Grew All Around, 1 vol. McLennan, Connie, illus. 2007. (ENG.). 32p. (J). (gr. -1-2). pap. 10.95 *(978-0-9777423-8-7(5),* 6ddb7762-8a84-4cdc-800d-ae353865c566) Arbordale Publishing.

Mitton, Tony. Rainforest Adventure. 2015. (Amazing Animals Ser.). (ENG., Illus.). 24p. (J). (gr. -1-1). pap. 6.99 *(978-0-7534-7227-9(9),* 900149031, Kingfisher) Roaring Brook Pr.

Nye, Bill & Mone, Gregory. Lost in the Jungle: Jack & the Geniuses Book #3. Iluzada, Nicholas, illus. (Jack & the Geniuses Ser.). (ENG.). 288p. (J). (gr. 3-7). 2019. pap. 7.99 *(978-1-4197-3485-4(7),* 1158103) 2018. 13.99 *(978-1-4197-2867-9(9),* 1158101) Abrams, Inc. (Amulet Bks.).

Osorio, Rick. The Great Adventure of Sally Rock & the Secret of Man, 1 vol. 2009. 164p. pap. 24.95 *(978-1-60813-596-7(9))* America Star Bks.

Packer. Rain Forest Rumble. Knife, illus. 2016. 94p. (J). *(978-1-61067-479-9(0))* Kane Miller.

Page, P. K. Uirapurú: Based on a Brazilian Legend. 2010. (ENG., Illus.). 32p. (J). 19.95 *(978-0-88982-264-1(6))* Oolichan Bks. CAN. Dist: Univ. of Toronto Pr.

Parente, Peter. Peeper the Kinkajou. l.t. ed. 2004. (Peeper & Friends Ser.). (Illus.). 28p. (J). 15.95 *(978-0-9745052-0-6(X),* Peeper & Friends) Tree Of Life Publishing.

Platt, Richard. The Vanishing Rainforest. van Wyk, Rupert, illus. 2007. (ENG.). 32p. (J). pap. 16.95 *(978-0-7112-2170-3(7),* 314574, White Lion Publishing) Quarto Publishing Group UK GBR. Dist: Hachette UK Distribution.

—The Vanishing Rainforest. van Wyk, Rupert, illus. 2003. (ENG.). 32p. (YA). *(978-0-7112-1960-1(5))* ReiseArt Buchhandlung GmbH.

Riggs, Kate. Sounds of the Forest. Dogi, Fiammetta, illus. 2019. (ENG.). 14p. (J). (gr. -1-k). bds. 8.99 *(978-1-56846-318-6(9),* 18680, Creative Editions) Creative Co., The.

Rundell, Katherine. The Explorer. (ENG.). (J). (gr. 3-7). 2018. 352p. pap. 8.99 *(978-1-4814-1946-8(3))* 2017. (Illus.). 336p. 16.99 *(978-1-4814-1945-1(5))* Simon & Schuster Bks. For Young Readers. (Simon & Schuster Bks. For Young Readers).

Sandusky, Thomas & Hill, Kathy. Peter the Poison Dart Frog, Stories of the Rainforest. Johnson, Gretchen, illus. 2011. 24p. pap. 12.95 *(978-1-936343-85-0(1))* Peppertree Pr., The.

Sarago-Kendrick, Delphine. Nana's Land. Sarago-Kendrick, Delphine, illus. 2004. (Illus.). 44p. (J). pap. *(978-1-875641-90-1(4))* Magabala Bks.

Schlegl, Stacey Lynn. Little Frog. 2008. (J). per. 8.95 *(978-0-9801504-0-7(X))* Jan-Carol Publishing, INC.

Schrefer, Eliot. The Lost Rainforest: Mez's Magic. 2018. (Illus.). 368p. (J). *(978-0-06-283959-6(4))*, Tegen, Katherine Bks) HarperCollins Pubs.

—The Lost Rainforest #1: Mez's Magic. Dziubak, Emilia, illus. 2018. (ENG.). (J). (gr. 3-7). 384p. pap. 6.99 *(978-0-06-249113-8(X))*; 368p. 16.99 *(978-0-06-249107-7(5))* HarperCollins Pubs. (Tegen, Katherine Bks).

—The Lost Rainforest #2: Gogi's Gambit. Dziubak, Emilia, illus. 2019. (ENG.). (J). (gr. 3-7). 368p. pap. 6.99 *(978-0-06-249115-2(6))*; 352p. 16.99 *(978-0-06-249111-4(3))* HarperCollins Pubs. (Tegen, Katherine Bks).

Smith, Dale. What the Orangutan Told Alice: A Rain Forest Adventure. Smith, Dale & Russon, Anne E., photos by. 2003. (Illus.). 192p. (gr. 6-12). pap. 15.95 *(978-0-9651452-8-2(X))* Deer Creek Publishing.

Smith, Roland. Ascent. 2018. (Peak Marcello Adventure Ser.: 3). (ENG.). 240p. (YA). (gr. 7). 17.99 *(978-0-544-86759-8(9))*, 1648549, Clarion Bks.) HarperCollins Pubs.

Stilton, Gerónimo. Rumble in the Jungle. 2013. (Geronimo Stilton Ser.: 53). lib. bdg. 18.40 *(978-0-606-31527-2(6))* Turtleback.

Turner, Tracey. Lost in the Jungle of Doom. 2014. (LOST: Can You Survive? Ser.). (ENG., Illus.). 128p. (J). (gr. 6-6). *(978-0-7787-0727-1(X))* Crabtree Publishing Co.

What's in the Rainforest. 2003. (J). per. *(978-1-57657-933-6(6))* Paradise Pr., Inc.

Whitmore, Andrew. Beast of the Jungle. 2007. 96p. (YA). pap. *(978-1-4207-0728-1(0))* Sundance/Newbridge Educational Publishing.

Witte, Anna. The Parrot Tico Tango. 2005. (ENG., Illus.). 24p. (J). (gr. -1-3). pap. 6.99 *(978-1-905236-11-4(5))* Barefoot Bks., Inc.

—The Parrot Tico Tango. Witte, Anna, illus. 2005. (ENG., Illus.). 24p. (J). (gr. k-3). 15.99 *(978-1-84148-243-9(9))* Barefoot Bks., Inc.

Worth, Bonnie. If I Ran the Rain Forest: All about Tropical Rain Forests. Ruiz, Aristides, illus. 2003. (Cat in the Hat's Learning Library). (ENG.). 48p. (J). (gr. -1-3). 9.99 *(978-0-375-81097-8(8))*, Random Hse. Bks. for Young Readers) Random Hse. Children's Bks.

Young, Judy. Tuki & Moka: A Tale of Two Tamarins. Madsen, Jim, illus. 2013. (Tales of the World Ser.). (ENG.). 32p. (J). (gr. 2-4). 16.99 *(978-1-58536-795-5(8))*, 202890) Sleeping Bear Pr.

RAINFALL

see Rain and Rainfall

RAINFORESTS

see Rain Forests

RALEIGH, WALTER, SIR, 1552?-1618

Daly, Ruth. Explore with Sir Walter Raleigh. 2017. (Travel with the Great Explorers Ser.). (Illus.). 32p. (J). (gr. 4-5). *(978-0-7787-3923-4(6))*; pap. *(978-0-7787-3938-8(4))* Crabtree Publishing Co.

McPherson, Stephanie Sammartino. Sir Walter Raleigh. 2005. (History Maker Bios Ser.). (Illus.). 48p. (J). (gr. 3-7). lib. bdg. 26.60 *(978-0-8225-2945-3(9))*, Lerner Pubns.) Lerner Publishing Group.

Olson, Steven P. Sir Walter Raleigh: Explorer for the Court of Queen Elizabeth. 2009. (Library of Explorers & Exploration Ser.). 112p. (gr. 5-8). 66.50 *(978-1-60853-612-2(2))*, Rosen Reference) Rosen Publishing Group, Inc., The.

Rice, Earle, Jr. The Life & Times of Sir Walter Raleigh. 2006. (Profiles in American History Ser.). (Illus.). 48p. (J). (gr. 3-7). lib. bdg. 29.95 *(978-1-58415-452-5(7))* Mitchell Lane Pubs.

Ward, Nancy. Sir Walter Raleigh: Founding the Virginia Colony, 1 vol. 2006. (In the Footsteps of Explorers Ser.). (ENG., Illus.). 32p. (J). (gr. 4-7). pap. *(978-0-7787-2460-5(3))*, 1253445); lib. bdg. *(978-0-7787-2424-7(7))*, 1253445) Crabtree Publishing Co.

RAMS

see Sheep

RANCH LIFE

see also Cowboys

Ancona, George. Mi Casa: My House. 2005. (Somos Latinos (We Are Latinos) Ser.). (SPA & ENG., Illus.). 32p. (J). (gr. 1-3). pap. 8.95 *(978-0-516-25065-6(5))*, Children's Pr.) Scholastic Library Publishing.

Cameron, Charles. Why Lizzie Johnson Matters to Texas, 1 vol. 2013. (Texas Perspectives Ser.). (ENG., Illus.). 32p. (J). (gr. 4-4). lib. bdg. 28.93 *(978-1-4777-0908-5(8))*, 3dbc605b-a618-4499-8ca8-04f4bd9c2864) Rosen Publishing Group, Inc., The.

—Why Richard King Matters to Texas, 1 vol. 2013. (Texas Perspectives Ser.). (ENG., Illus.). 32p. (J). (gr. 4-4). lib. bdg. 28.93 *(978-1-4777-0910-8(X))*, 93194c6d-ef92-4bb2-a6e0-4a3d11620cd5) Rosen Publishing Group, Inc., The.

Catala, Ellen. On the Ranch. 2003. (Shutterbug Bks.). (Illus.). 16p. pap. 4.10 *(978-0-7398-7641-1(4))* Steck-Vaughn.

Craats, Rennay. Ranching. 2003. (Real Life Stories Ser.). (Illus.). 24p. (J). lib. bdg. 24.45 *(978-1-59036-081-1(8))* Weigl Pubs., Inc.

Drinkard, Lawson. Riding on a Range: Western Activities for Kids. Lee, Fran, illus. 2003. (ENG.). 64p. (YA). pap. 9.99 *(978-1-58685-036-4(9))* Gibbs Smith, Publisher.

Freedman, Russell. In the Days of the Vaqueros. 2008. (ENG., Illus.). 80p. (YA). (gr. 7). pap. 9.99 *(978-0-547-13365-2(0))*, 1048765, Clarion Bks.) HarperCollins Pubs.

Get Inside Series. Incl. Baseball. Almonte, Paul. 80p. 14.95 *(978-1-881889-55-7(6))*; Ranch. Morgenroth, Barbara. 64p. 14.95 *(978-1-881889-56-4(4))*; (Illus.). (J). 1994. 29.90 *(978-1-881889-79-3(3))* Silver Moon Pr.

Gilkerson, Patricia. My Adventure on a Ranch. 2006. 44p. (J). 8.99 *(978-1-59092-282-8(4))* Blue Forge Pr.

Gordon, Sharon. At Home on the Ranch, 1 vol. (At Home Ser.). (ENG.). 32p. (gr. k-2). 2008. pap. 9.23 *(978-0-7614-3313-2(9))*, 19aadf80-098a-4382-a57b-e93d23a2384d) 2007. (Illus.). lib. bdg. 25.50 *(978-0-7614-1962-4(4))*, e8ba57a1-7a95-47b0-a4f0-770bd27b9a71) Cavendish Square Publishing LLC.

—Mi Casa en el Rancho / at Home on the Ranch, 1 vol. 2008. (Mi Casa / at Home Ser.). (ENG & SPA., Illus.). 32p. (gr. k-2). lib. bdg. 25.50 *(978-0-7614-2458-1(X))*, bc03ff33-0068-4c53-8116-10df5a511839) Cavendish Square Publishing LLC.

—Mi Casa en el Rancho (at Home on the Ranch), 1 vol. 2008. (Mi Casa (at Home) Ser.). (SPA., Illus.). 32p. (gr. k-2). lib. bdg. 25.50 *(978-0-7614-2378-2(8))*, 458ba04e-75f3-4b2c-92e3-d546cfc84caa) Cavendish Square Publishing LLC.

James, Will. The Will James Cowboy Book, Vol. 1. rev. ed. (Illus.). 128p. (J). (gr. 4). *(978-0-87842-469-6(5))*, 816) Mountain Pr. Publishing Co., Inc.

Kalman, Bobbie. A Visual Dictionary of the Old West. 2007. (Crabtree Visual Dictionaries Ser.). (ENG., Illus.). 32p. (J). (gr. 3-7). lib. bdg. *(978-0-7787-3503-8(6))* Crabtree Publishing Co.

Keaster, Diane W. Darby - the Cow Dog, 9 vols. Page, Debbie et al, illus. l.t. ed. 2005. (ZC Horses: 9). (ENG.). 68p. (J). per. 7.95 *(978-0-9721496-8-6(6))* ZC Horses Series of Children's Bks.

Letters of a Woman Homesteader. 2003. (Our American Heritage Ser.). (J). pap. 62.00 incl. audio compact disk *(978-1-58472-527-5(3))*, In Audio) Sound Room Pubs., Inc.

Mills, Charles. Attack of the Angry Legend; Stranger in the Shadows; Planet of Joy. 2016. (J). *(978-0-8163-6158-8(4))* Pacific Pr. Publishing Assn.

—Treasure of the Merrilee; Whispers in the Wind; Heart of the Warrior. 2016. (J). *(978-0-8163-6154-0(1))* Pacific Pr. Publishing Assn.

Moody, Ralph. Man of the Family. Shenton, Edward, illus. 2019. 274p. (J). *(978-1-948959-07-0(0))* Purple Hse. Pr.

Nathan, Sandy. Tecolote: The Little Horse That Could. 2011. (Illus.). 44p. (J). pap. 14.95 *(978-0-9762809-9-6(X))* Vilasa Pr.

National Geographic Learning. Reading Expeditions (Social Studies: Voices from America's Past): Missions & Ranchos. 2007. (ENG., Illus.). 40p. (J). pap. 21.95 *(978-0-7922-4548-3(2))* CENGAGE Learning.

Peppas, Lynn. Why Charles Goodnight Matters to Texas, 1 vol. 2013. (Texas Perspectives Ser.). (ENG., Illus.). 32p. (J). (gr. 4-4). lib. bdg. 28.93 *(978-1-4777-0907-8(X))*, 275a14bc-e2cc-4ff3-88dc-bff250ac8e56) Rosen Publishing Group, Inc., The.

Peterson, Cris. Amazing Grazing. Upitis, Alvis, photos by. 2011. (ENG., Illus.). 32p. (J). (gr. k-2). pap. 10.95 *(978-1-59078-868-4(0))*, Astra Young Readers) Astra Publishing Hse.

—Amazing Grazing. 2003. (ENG., Illus.). 32p. (gr. 3-6). 26.19 *(978-1-56397-942-2(X))* Highlights Pr., c/o Highlights for Children, Inc.

Sanford, William R. & Green, Carl R. Richard King: Courageous Texas Cattleman, 1 vol. 2013. (Courageous Heroes of the American West Ser.). (ENG., Illus.). 48p. (J). (gr. 5-7). 25.27 *(978-0-7660-4003-8(8))*, 61d735bd-1176-4a8c-85c5-7ad480486444); pap. 11.53 *(978-1-4644-0088-9(1))*, 96233e19-4fed-4d10-bc24-7ca0d56b1d0e) Enslow Publishing, LLC.

Savage, Candace. Born to Be a Cowgirl: A Spirited Ride Through the Old West. 2004. (Illus.). *(978-1-55054-838-9(7))*, Da Capo Pr. Inc.) Hachette Bks.

Schwartz, Heather. Lizzie Johnson: Texan Cowgirl, 1 vol. rev. ed. 2012. (Social Studies: Informational Text Ser.). (ENG.). 32p. (gr. 3-5). pap. 11.99 *(978-1-4333-5051-1(3))* Teacher Created Materials, Inc.

Sipe, Nicole. Art & Culture: Hawaiian Paniolo: Expressions (Grade 5) 2018. (Mathematics in the Real World Ser.). (ENG., Illus.). 32p. (J). (gr. 4-8). pap. 11.99 *(978-1-4258-5808-7(2))* Teacher Created Materials, Inc.

Urbigkit, Cat. Cattle Kids: A Year on the Western Range. 2007. (ENG., Illus.). 32p. (J). (gr. 2-k). 16.95 *(978-1-59078-508-9(8))*, Astra Young Readers) Astra Publishing Hse.

West, David. Lots of Things You Want to Know About Cowboys. 2015. (Lots of Things You Want to Know About Ser.). (ENG., Illus.). 24p. (J). 28.50 *(978-1-62588-089-5(8))*, 19300, Smart Apple Media) Black Rabbit Bks.

Whitney, Louise Doak & Whitney, Gleaves. B Is for Buckaroo: A Cowboy Alphabet. Guy, Susan, illus. rev. ed. 2003. (Sports Ser.). (ENG.). 40p. (J). (gr. 1-4). 17.95 *(978-1-58536-139-7(9))*, 202000) Sleeping Bear Pr.

Williams, Jack S. Townspeople & Ranchers of the California Mission Frontier. 2009. (People of the California Missions Ser.). 64p. (gr. 4-4). 58.50 *(978-1-60851-161-7(8))*, PowerKids Pr.) Rosen Publishing Group, Inc., The.

Wommack, Linda. Ann Bassett: Colorado's Cattle Queen. 2018. (Illus.). 247p. *(978-0-87004-619-3(5))* Caxton Pr.

RANCH LIFE—FICTION

Abrams, Kelsey. Forever Amigo: An Abby Story. Tejido, Jomike, illus. 2019. (Second Chance Ranch Set 2 Ser.). (ENG.). 120p. (J). (gr. 3-4). pap. 7.99 *(978-1-63163-256-3(6))*, 1631632566); lib. bdg. 27.13 *(978-1-63163-255-6(8))*, 1631632558) North Star Editions. (Jolly Fish Pr.).

—Heart Horse: A Natalie Story. Tejido, Jomike, illus. 2019. (Second Chance Ranch Set 2 Ser.). (ENG.). 120p. (J). (gr. 3-4). pap. 7.99 *(978-1-63163-260-0(4))*, 1631632604); lib. bdg. 27.13 *(978-1-63163-259-4(0))*, 1631632590) North Star Editions. (Jolly Fish Pr.).

—It's Not Destiny. Tejido, Jomike, illus. 2018. (Second Chance Ranch Ser.). (ENG.). 120p. (J). (gr. 3-4). pap. 7.99 *(978-1-63163-145-0(4))*, 1631631454, Jolly Fish Pr.) North Star Editions.

—It's Not Destiny: An Abby Story. Tejido, Jomike, illus. 2018. (Second Chance Ranch Ser.). (ENG.). 120p. (J). (gr. 3-4). lib. bdg. 27.13 *(978-1-63163-144-3(6))*, 1631631446, Jolly Fish Pr.) North Star Editions.

—Taking Chances. Tejido, Jomike, illus. 2018. (Second Chance Ranch Ser.). (ENG.). 120p. (J). (gr. 3-4). pap. 7.99 *(978-1-63163-149-8(7))*, 1631631497, Jolly Fish Pr.) North Star Editions.

—Taking Chances: A Grace Story. Tejido, Jomike, illus. 2018. (Second Chance Ranch Ser.). (ENG.). 120p. (J). (gr. 3-4). lib. bdg. 27.13 *(978-1-63163-148-1(9))*, 1631631489, Jolly Fish Pr.) North Star Editions.

—Two to Tango. Tejido, Jomike, illus. 2018. (Second Chance Ranch Ser.). (ENG.). 120p. (J). (gr. 3-4). pap. 7.99 *(978-1-63163-153-5(5))*, 1631631535, Jolly Fish Pr.) North Star Editions.

—Two to Tango: A Natalie Story. Tejido, Jomike, illus. 2018. (Second Chance Ranch Ser.). (ENG.). 120p. (J). (gr. 3-4). lib. bdg. 27.13 *(978-1-63163-152-8(7))*, 1631631527, Jolly Fish Pr.) North Star Editions.

—Wild Midnight. Tejido, Jomike, illus. 2018. (Second Chance Ranch Ser.). (ENG.). 120p. (J). (gr. 3-4). pap. 7.99 *(978-1-63163-157-3(8))*, 1631631578, Jolly Fish Pr.) North Star Editions.

—Wild Midnight: An Emily Story. Tejido, Jomike, illus. 2018. (Second Chance Ranch Ser.). (ENG.). 120p. (J). (gr. 3-4). lib. bdg. 27.13 *(978-1-63163-156-6(X))*, 163163156X, Jolly Fish Pr.) North Star Editions.

Alphin, Elaine Marie. Dinosaur Hunter. Bolognese, Don, illus. 2004. (I Can Read Bks.). 48p. (gr. 2-4). 14.00 *(978-0-7569-3241-1(6))* Perfection Learning Corp.

Babcock, Nona Burroughs. Little Wolf's Adventure: A Medicine Dream & Warrior Ghosts. 2008. 212p. 24.95 *(978-0-595-49087-5(5))*; pap. 14.95 *(978-0-595-46072-4(0))* iUniverse, Inc.

Baker, Willard F. The Boy Ranchers among the Indians: Or, Trailing the Yaquis. 2017. (ENG., Illus.). (J). pap. 12.95 *(978-1-374-84765-1(8))* Capital Communications, Inc.

—The Boy Ranchers among the Indians; or, Trailing the Yaquis. 2016. (ENG., Illus.). (J). pap. *(978-1-4733-3273-7(7))* Read Bks.

Banks, Radine. Nochi Come Back. 2006. 112p. per. 12.20 *(978-1-4120-8803-9(8))* Trafford Publishing.

Beecher, Elizabeth. Roy Rogers on the Double-R Ranch. Nordli, Ernest, illus. 2011. 78p. 37.95 *(978-1-258-03590-7(1))* Literary Licensing, LLC.

Berla, Kathryn. Beau & Bett: A Modern Retelling of Beauty & the Beast. 2019. (ENG.). 256p. (YA). (gr. 9-12). pap. 12.99 *(978-1-948705-44-8(3))* Amberjack Publishing Co.

Blom, Jen K. Possum Summer. Rayyan, Omar, illus. 2011. (ENG.). 256p. (J). (gr. 3-7). 17.95 *(978-0-8234-2331-6(X))* Holiday Hse., Inc.

Brammer, Ethriam Cash. The Rowdy, Rowdy Ranch / Alla en el Rancho Grande. Cruz, D. Nina, illus. 2003. (ENG & SPA.). 32p. (J). 16.95 *(978-1-55885-409-3(6))*, Piñata Books) Arte Publico Pr.

Brinegar, R. L. Ron. Pokey: The Fastest Horse on the Ranch. 2007. 33p. pap. 8.95 *(978-0-7414-4078-5(4))* Infinity Publishing.

Brouwer, Sigmund. Blazer Drive, 1 vol. 2007. (Orca Sports Ser.). (ENG.). 168p. (J). (gr. 4-7). per. 10.95 *(978-1-55143-717-0(1))* Orca Bk. Pubs. USA.

Burkhart, Kiersi & Keyser, Amber J. The Long Trail Home. 2017. (Quartz Creek Ranch Ser.). (ENG.). 240p. (J). (gr. 4-8). E-Book 42.65 *(978-1-5124-2698-4(9))*, Darby Creek) Lerner Publishing Group.

—One Brave Summer. 2017. (Quartz Creek Ranch Ser.). (ENG.). 224p. (J). (gr. 4-8). E-Book 42.65 *(978-1-5124-0892-8(1))*, Darby Creek) Lerner Publishing Group.

Carkhuff Jr., Sam. The Ranch Race. Crow, Katie, illus. 2012. 36p. 16.99 *(978-1-939054-03-6(6))*; pap. 11.99 *(978-1-939054-02-9(8))* Rowe Publishing.

Carr, Annie Roe. Nan Sherwood at Rose Ranch. 2007. 124p. per. *(978-1-4068-4396-5(2))* Echo Library.

—Nan Sherwood at Rose Ranch or the Old Me. 2007. pap. *(978-1-4065-1295-3(8))* Dodo Pr.

Christian, Diana. The Lucky Seven. 2005. 71p. pap. 19.95 *(978-1-4137-5471-1(6))* America Star Bks.

Citra, Becky. Missing, 1 vol. 2011. (ENG.). 184p. (J). (gr. 4-7). pap. 9.95 *(978-1-55469-345-0(4))* Orca Bk. Pubs. USA.

Clark, Brenda. Spiro Goes West: More Adventures of Spiro the Shooting Star. 2008. 57p. pap. 16.95 *(978-1-60474-770-6(6))* America Star Bks.

Compton, Dawn. Leave 'Em Standing. 2005. (Illus.). pap. 12.95 *(978-1-932196-73-3(0))* WordWright.biz, Inc.

Coolidge, Susan. Clover. 2017. (ENG., Illus.). (J). 23.95 *(978-1-374-96593-5(6))* Capital Communications, Inc.

—Clover. 2016. (ENG., Illus.). (J). 26.95 *(978-1-359-71234-9(8))* Creative Media Partners, LLC.

Coombs, Charles. Ranch Mystery: Young Readers. Priscilla, Louis, illus. 2011. 188p. 42.95 *(978-1-258-09854-4(7))* Literary Licensing, LLC.

Cousins Camp. 2010. 32p. pap. 12.99 *(978-1-4490-8387-8(0))* AuthorHouse.

Curtin, Ann. Dreamcatcher. 2015. 201p. (YA). *(978-1-61271-246-8(0))* Zumaya Pubs. LLC.

Dahlstrom, S. J. Texas Grit: the Adventures of Wilder Good #2. 2014. (Adventures of Wilder Good Ser.: 2). (ENG.). 141p. (J). (gr. 3). pap. 9.95 *(978-1-58988-094-8(3))* Dry, Paul Bks., Inc.

Davis, Susan Page. Sarah's Long Ride. 2007. (Piper Ranch Ser.). 173p. (J). (gr. 3-7). per. 8.99 *(978-1-59166-737-7(2))* BJU Pr.

Dembar Greene, Jacqueline. Walk till You Disappear. Sawyer, Odessa, illus. 2019. (ENG.). 208p. (J). (gr. 3-7). 12.99 *(978-1-5415-5722-2(0))*, bff435b6-3586-44fc-908e-e4371282a43d, Kar-Ben Publishing) Lerner Publishing Group.

Dembo, Jaiden. Finding Strider. 2010. 52p. pap. 15.54 *(978-0-557-39981-9(5))* Lulu Pr., Inc.

Draper, Tricia. Bobby Bear Learns to Be a Cowboy. Babinski, Michael, illus. 2004. 36p. (gr. -1-3). per. 14.95 *(978-1-58961-246-4(9))* PageFree Publishing, Inc.

Drummond, Ree. Charlie Plays Ball. deGroat, Diane, illus. 2015. (Charlie the Ranch Dog Ser.). (ENG.). 40p. (J). (gr. -1-3). 18.99 *(978-0-06-229752-5(X))*, HarperCollins) HarperCollins Pubs.

—Charlie the Ranch Dog. deGroat, Diane, illus. 2011. (Charlie the Ranch Dog Ser.). (ENG.). 40p. (J). (gr. -1-3). 17.99 *(978-0-06-199655-9(6))*, HarperCollins) HarperCollins Pubs.

—Charlie the Ranch Dog. 2013. (I Can Read! Level 1 Ser.). (J). lib. bdg. 13.55 *(978-0-606-31822-8(4))* Turtleback.

—Charlie the Ranch Dog: Charlie Goes to the Doctor. deGroat, Diane, illus. 2014. (I Can Read Level 1 Ser.). (ENG.). 32p. (J). (gr. -1-3). pap. 4.99 *(978-0-06-221917-6(0))*, HarperCollins) HarperCollins Pubs.

—Charlie the Ranch Dog: Charlie's New Friend. deGroat, Diane, illus. 2014. (I Can Read Level 1 Ser.). (ENG.). 32p. (J). (gr. -1-3). 16.99 *(978-0-06-221915-2(4))*; pap. 4.99 *(978-0-06-221914-5(6))* HarperCollins Pubs. (HarperCollins).

—Charlie the Ranch Dog: Stuck in the Mud. deGroat, Diane & Whipple, Rick, illus. 2015. (I Can Read Level 1 Ser.). (ENG.). 32p. (J). (gr. -1-3). 16.99 *(978-0-06-234775-6(6))*; pap. 4.99 *(978-0-06-234774-9(8))* HarperCollins Pubs. (HarperCollins).

—Charlie's Snow Day. 2013. (I Can Read! Level 1 Ser.). (J). lib. bdg. 13.55 *(978-0-606-32161-7(6))* Turtleback.

—Little Ree. Rogers, Jacqueline, illus. 2017. (J). *(978-0-06-266351-1(8))* Harper & Row Ltd.

—Little Ree. Rogers, Jacqueline, illus. 2017. (Little Ree Ser.). (ENG.). 40p. (J). (gr. -1-3). 17.99 *(978-0-06-245318-1(1))*, HarperCollins) HarperCollins Pubs.

—Little Ree #2 (signed Edition) Rogers, Jacqueline, illus. 2018. (Little Ree Ser.). 32p. (J). (gr. -1-3). 17.99 *(978-0-06-282077-8(X))* HarperCollins Pubs.

Edge, Laura Bufano. Wild West Dreams. 2006. (J). pap. *(978-0-88092-623-2(6))*; lib. bdg. *(978-0-88092-622-5(8))* Royal Fireworks Publishing Co.

Erickson, John. The Big Question. Holmes, Gerald L., illus. 2012. 128p. (J). pap. *(978-1-59188-160-5(9))* Maverick Bks.

—The Big Question. Holmes, Gerald L., illus. 2012. (Hank the Cowdog Ser.: Vol. 60). (ENG.). 128p. (J). (gr. 3-6). 15.99 *(978-1-59188-260-2(5))* Maverick Bks., Inc.

—The Case of the Black-Hooded Hangmans. Holmes, Gerald L., illus. 2011. (Hank the Cowdog Ser.). (ENG.). 113p. (J). (gr. 3-6). pap. 5.99 *(978-1-59188-124-7(2))* Maverick Bks., Inc.

—The Case of the Blazing Sky. Holmes, Gerald L., illus. 2011. (Hank the Cowdog Ser.). (ENG.). 129p. (J). (gr. 3-6). pap. 5.99 *(978-1-59188-151-3(X))* Maverick Bks., Inc.

—The Case of the Booby-Trapped Pickup. Holmes, Gerald L., illus. 2011. (Hank the Cowdog Ser.). (ENG.). 129p. (J). (gr. 3-6). pap. 5.99 *(978-1-59188-149-0(8))* Maverick Bks., Inc.

—The Case of the Car-Barkaholic Dog. Holmes, Gerald L., illus. 2011. (Hank the Cowdog Ser.). (ENG.). 115p. (J). (gr. 3-6). pap. 5.99 *(978-1-59188-117-9(X))* Maverick Bks., Inc.

—The Case of the Coyote Invasion. Holmes, Gerald L., illus. 2011. (Hank the Cowdog Ser.: No. 56). (ENG.). 132p. (J). (gr. 3-6). pap. 5.99 *(978-1-59188-156-8(0))* Maverick Bks., Inc.

—The Case of the Deadly Ha-Ha Game. Holmes, Gerald L., illus. 2011. (Hank the Cowdog Ser.). (ENG.). 128p. (J). (gr. 3-6). pap. 5.99 *(978-1-59188-137-7(4))* Maverick Bks., Inc.

—The Case of the Dinosaur Birds. Holmes, Gerald L., illus. 2011. (Hank the Cowdog Ser.). (ENG.). 125p. (J). (gr. 3-6). pap. 5.99 *(978-1-59188-154-4(4))* Maverick Bks., Inc.

—The Case of the Double Bumblebee Sting. Holmes, Gerald L., illus. 2011. (Hank the Cowdog Ser.: No. 22). (ENG.). 114p. (J). (gr. 3-6). pap. 5.99 *(978-1-59188-122-3(6))* Maverick Bks., Inc.

—The Case of the Falling Sky. Holmes, Gerald L., illus. 2011. (Hank the Cowdog Ser.: No. 45). (ENG.). 129p. (J). (gr. 3-6). pap. 5.99 *(978-1-59188-145-2(5))* Maverick Bks., Inc.

—The Case of the Fiddle-Playing Fox. Holmes, Gerald L., illus. 2011. (Hank the Cowdog Ser.: No. 12). (ENG.). 118p. (J). (gr. 3-6). pap. 5.99 *(978-1-59188-112-4(9))* Maverick Bks., Inc.

—The Case of the Haystack Kitties. Holmes, Gerald L., illus. 2011. (Hank the Cowdog Ser.). (ENG.). 123p. (J). (gr. 3-6). pap. 5.99 *(978-1-59188-130-8(7))* Maverick Bks., Inc.

—The Case of the Hooking Bull. Holmes, Gerald L., illus. 2011. (Hank the Cowdog Ser.). (ENG.). 119p. (J). (gr. 3-6). pap. 5.99 *(978-1-59188-118-6(8))* Maverick Bks., Inc.

—The Case of the Kidnapped Collie. Holmes, Gerald L., illus. 2011. (Hank the Cowdog Ser.). (ENG.). 113p. (J). (gr. 3-6). pap. 5.99 *(978-1-59188-126-1(9))* Maverick Bks., Inc.

—The Case of the Measled Cowboy. Holmes, Gerald L., illus. 2011. (Hank the Cowdog Ser.: No. 33). (ENG.). 126p. (J). (gr. 3-6). pap. 5.99 *(978-1-59188-133-9(1))* Maverick Bks., Inc.

—The Case of the Midnight Rustler. Holmes, Gerald L., illus. 2011. (Hank the Cowdog Ser.: No. 19). (ENG.). 113p. (J). (gr. 3-6). pap. 5.99 *(978-1-59188-119-3(6))* Maverick Bks., Inc.

—The Case of the Missing Bird Dog. Holmes, Gerald L., illus. 2011. (Hank the Cowdog Ser.: No. 40). (ENG.). 126p. (J). (gr. 3-6). pap. 5.99 *(978-1-59188-140-7(4))* Maverick Bks., Inc.

—The Case of the Missing Cat. Holmes, Gerald L., illus. 2011. (Hank the Cowdog Ser.: No. 15). (ENG.). 114p. (J). (gr. 3-6). pap. 5.99 *(978-1-59188-115-5(3))* Maverick Bks., Inc.

—The Case of the Monkey Burglar. Holmes, Gerald L., illus. 2011. (Hank the Cowdog Ser.: No. 48). (ENG.). 129p. (J). (gr. 3-6). pap. 5.99 *(978-1-59188-148-3(X))* Maverick Bks., Inc.

—The Case of the Mysterious Voice. Holmes, Gerald L., illus. 2012. (Hank the Cowdog (Quality) Ser.: Vol. 58). (ENG.). 123p. (J). (gr. 3-6). pap. 5.99 *(978-1-59188-158-2(7))* Maverick Bks., Inc.

—The Case of the Night-Stalking Bone Monster. Holmes, Gerald L., illus. 2011. (Hank the Cowdog Ser.). (ENG.). 115p. (J). (gr. 3-6). pap. 5.99 *(978-1-59188-127-8(7))* Maverick Bks., Inc.

—The Case of the Perfect Dog. Holmes, Gerald L., illus. 2012. 127p. (J). *(978-1-59188-259-6(1))* Maverick Bks.

—The Case of the Perfect Dog. Holmes, Gerald L., illus. 2012. (Hank the Cowdog (Quality) Ser.). (ENG.). 127p. (J). (gr. 3-6). pap. 5.99 *(978-1-59188-159-9(5))* Maverick Bks., Inc.

—The Case of the Raging Rottweiler. Holmes, Gerald L., illus. 2011. (Hank the Cowdog Ser.). (ENG.). 131p. (J). (gr. 3-6). pap. 5.99 *(978-1-59188-136-0(6))* Maverick Bks., Inc.

—The Case of the Saddle House Robbery. Holmes, Gerald L., illus. 2011. (Hank the Cowdog Ser.: No. 35). (ENG.). 125p. (J). (gr. 3-6). pap. 5.99 *(978-1-59188-135-3(8))* Maverick Bks., Inc.

—The Case of the Secret Weapon. Holmes, Gerald L., illus. 2011. (Hank the Cowdog Ser.). (ENG.). 125p. (J). (gr. 3-6). pap. 5.99 *(978-1-59188-155-1(2))* Maverick Bks., Inc.

—The Case of the Shipwrecked Tree. Holmes, Gerald L., illus. 2011. (Hank the Cowdog Ser.: No. 41). (ENG.). 119p. (J). (gr. 3-6). pap. 5.99 *(978-1-59188-141-4(2))* Maverick Bks., Inc.

—The Case of the Swirling Killer Tornado. Holmes, Gerald L., illus. 2011. (Hank the Cowdog Ser.). (ENG.). 112p. (J). (gr. 3-6). pap. 5.99 *(978-1-59188-125-4(0))* Maverick Bks., Inc.

—The Case of the Tender Cheeping Chickies. Holmes, Gerald L., illus. 2011. (Hank the Cowdog Ser.). (ENG.). 129p. (J).

P Q R

(gr. 3-6). pap. 5.99 *(978-1-59188-147-6(1))* Maverick Bks., Inc.
—The Case of the Three Rings. Holmes, Gerald L., illus. 2014. 124p. (J). pap. *(978-1-59188-164-3(1))* Maverick Bks., Inc.
—The Case of the Tricky Trap. Holmes, Gerald L., illus. 2011. (Hank the Cowdog Ser.). (ENG.). 126p. (J). (gr. 3-6). pap. 5.99 *(978-1-59188-146-9(3))* Maverick Bks., Inc.
—The Case of the Twisted Kitty. Holmes, Gerald L., illus. 2004. (Hank the Cowdog Ser.: No. 43). 131p. (J). lib. bdg. 17.00 *(978-1-4242-1600-0(1))* Fitzgerald Bks.
—The Case of the Twisted Kitty. Holmes, Gerald L., illus. 2011. (Hank the Cowdog Ser.). (ENG.). 131p. (J). (gr. 3-6). pap. 5.99 *(978-1-59188-143-8(9))* Maverick Bks., Inc.
—The Case of the Vampire Cat. Holmes, Gerald L., illus. 2011. (Hank the Cowdog Ser.). (ENG.). 115p. (J). (gr. 3-6). pap. 5.99 *(978-1-59188-121-6(8))* Maverick Bks., Inc.
—The Case of the Vampire Vacuum Sweeper. Holmes, Gerald L., illus. 2011. (Hank the Cowdog Ser.). (ENG.). 119p. (J). (gr. 3-6). pap. 5.99 *(978-1-59188-129-2(3))* Maverick Bks., Inc.
—The Case of the Vanishing Fishhook. Holmes, Gerald L., illus. 2011. (Hank the Cowdog Ser.: No. 31). (ENG.). 124p. (J). (gr. 3-6). pap. 5.99 *(978-1-59188-131-5(5))* Maverick Bks., Inc.
—The Disappearance of Drover. Holmes, Gerald L., illus. 2011. (Hank the Cowdog Ser.). (ENG.). 122p. (J). (gr. 3-6). pap. 5.99 *(978-1-59188-157-5(9))* Maverick Bks., Inc.
—Drover's Secret Life. Holmes, Gerald L., illus. 2011. (Hank the Cowdog Ser.). (ENG.). 118p. (J). (gr. 3-6). pap. 5.99 *(978-1-59188-153-7(6))* Maverick Bks., Inc.
—The Dungeon of Doom. Holmes, Gerald L., illus. 2004. (Hank the Cowdog Ser.: No. 44). 122p. (J). lib. bdg. 17.00 *(978-1-4242-1601-7(X))* Fitzgerald Bks.
—The Dungeon of Doom. Holmes, Gerald L., illus. 2011. (Hank the Cowdog Ser.). (ENG.). 122p. (J). (gr. 3-6). pap. 5.99 *(978-1-59188-144-5(7))* Maverick Bks., Inc.
—The Fling. Holmes, Gerald L., illus. 2011. (Hank the Cowdog Ser.). (ENG.). 126p. (J). (gr. 3-6). pap. 5.99 *(978-1-59188-138-4(2))* Maverick Bks., Inc.
—The Garbage Monster from Outer Space. Holmes, Gerald L., illus. 2011. (Hank the Cowdog Ser.). (ENG.). 126p. (J). (gr. 3-6). pap. 5.99 *(978-1-59188-132-2(3))* Maverick Bks., Inc.
—The Ghost of Rabbits Past. Holmes, Gerald L., illus. 2013. 128p. (J). pap. *(978-1-59188-162-9(5))* Maverick Bks., Inc.
—Hank the Cowdog & Monkey Business. Holmes, Gerald L., illus. 2011. (Hank the Cowdog Ser.). (ENG.). 110p. (J). (gr. 3-6). pap. 5.99 *(978-1-59188-114-8(5))* Maverick Bks., Inc.
—Lost in the Blinded Blizzard. Holmes, Gerald L., illus. 2011. (Hank the Cowdog Ser.). (ENG.). 115p. (J). (gr. 3-6). pap. 5.99 *(978-1-59188-116-2(1))* Maverick Bks., Inc.
—Moonlight Madness. Holmes, Gerald L., illus. 2011. (Hank the Cowdog Ser.: No. 23). (ENG.). 114p. (J). (gr. 3-6). pap. 5.99 *(978-1-59188-123-0(4))* Maverick Bks., Inc.
—The Mopwater Files. Holmes, Gerald L., illus. 2011. (Hank the Cowdog Ser.). (ENG.). 111p. (J). (gr. 3-6). pap. 5.99 *(978-1-59188-128-5(5))* Maverick Bks., Inc.
—The Original Adventures of Hank the Cowdog. Holmes, Gerald L., illus. (ENG.). 127p. (J). (gr. 3-6). 2012. (Hank the Cowdog Ser.: Vol. 1). 15.99 *(978-1-59188-201-5(X))* 2011. (Hank the Cowdog Ser.: No. 1). pap. 5.99 *(978-1-59188-101-8(3))* Maverick Bks., Inc.
—The Phantom in the Mirror. Holmes, Gerald L., illus. 2011. (Hank the Cowdog Ser.: No. 20). (ENG.). 114p. (J). (gr. 3-6). pap. 5.99 *(978-1-59188-120-9(X))* Maverick Bks., Inc.
—The Quest for the Great White Quail. Holmes, Gerald L., illus. 2011. (Hank the Cowdog Ser.). (ENG.). 123p. (J). (gr. 3-6). pap. 5.99 *(978-1-59188-152-0(8))* Maverick Bks., Inc.
—Ranch Life: Cowboys & Horses. 2017. (Hank's Ranch Life Ser.: Vol. 2). (ENG., Illus.). 74p. (J). pap. 6.99 *(978-1-59188-992-2(8))* Maverick Bks., Inc.
—The Return of the Charlie Monsters. Holmes, Gerald L., illus. 2014. 128p. (J). pap. *(978-1-59188-163-6(3))* Maverick Bks., Inc.
—The Secret Laundry Monster Files. Holmes, Gerald L., illus. 2011. (Hank the Cowdog Ser.). (ENG.). 128p. (J). (gr. 3-6). pap. 5.99 *(978-1-59188-139-1(0))* Maverick Bks., Inc.
—The Secret Pledge. Holmes, Gerald L., illus. 2016. 117p. (J). (Hank the Cowdog Ser.: Vol. 68). (ENG.). (gr. 3-6). 15.99 *(978-1-59188-268-8(0))*; (Hank the Cowdog Ser.: Vol. 68). (ENG.). (gr. 3-6). pap. 5.99 *(978-1-59188-168-1(4))*; *(978-1-5182-4067-6(4))* Maverick Bks., Inc.
—Slim's Good-Bye. Holmes, Gerald L., illus. 2011. (Hank the Cowdog Ser.). (ENG.). 132p. (J). (gr. 3-6). pap. 5.99 *(978-1-59188-134-6(X))* Maverick Bks., Inc.
—The Wounded Buzzard on Christmas Eve. Holmes, Gerald L., illus. 2011. (Hank the Cowdog Ser.: No. 13). (ENG.). 112p. (J). (gr. 3-6). pap. 5.99 *(978-1-59188-113-1(7))* Maverick Bks., Inc.
Erickson, John & Holmes, Gerald L., illus. The Case of the Prowling Bear. 2013. 126p. (J). *(978-1-59188-261-9(3))*; pap. *(978-1-59188-161-2(7))* Maverick Bks.
Erickson, John R. Cowboys & Horses. Holmes, Gerald L., illus. 2017. 74p. (J). *(978-1-5444-0370-0(4))* Maverick Bks., Inc.
Erickson, Mary Ellen. Who Jinxed the CG Ranch? 2009. 196p. 24.95 *(978-1-4401-4218-5(1))*; pap. 14.95 *(978-1-4401-4216-1(5))* iUniverse, Inc.
Estergren, Fred B. Tale of a Dog Called Sunshine, 1 vol. 2009. 201p. pap. 24.95 *(978-1-4489-2575-9(4))* America Star Bks.
Estevis, Anne. Chicken Foot Farm. 2008. 154p. (J). (gr. 6-18). pap. 10.95 *(978-1-55885-505-2(X)*, Piñata Books) Arte Publico Pr.
Farley, Terri. Desert Dancer. 2003. (Phantom Stallion Ser.). (Illus.). 234p. (J). (gr. 5-9). 12.65 *(978-0-7569-3561-0(X))* Perfection Learning Corp.
—Phantom Stallion - Wild Horse Island Bk. 2: The Shining Stallion. 2007. (Phantom Stallion: Wild Horse Island Ser.: 2). (ENG., Illus.). 224p. (J). (gr. 5-9). pap. 4.99 *(978-0-06-081543-1(4))* HarperCollins Pubs.
—Rain Forest Rose Bk. 3. 2007. (Phantom Stallion: Wild Horse Island Ser.: 3). (ENG.). 224p. (J). (gr. 5-18). pap. 4.99 *(978-0-06-088616-5(1))* HarperCollins Pubs.
Fleming, Bryn. Cassie & Jasper: Kidnapped Cattle. 2016. (Range Riders Ser.). (ENG.). 147p. (J). 24.99 *(978-1-943328-66-6(8))*; pap. 10.99 *(978-1-941821-95-4(2))* West Margin Pr. (West Winds Pr.).
—Cassie & Jasper to the Rescue. 2014. (Range Riders Ser.). (ENG.). 128p. (YA). (gr. 3-7). 23.99 *(978-1-941821-04-6(9))*; pap. 9.99 *(978-0-88240-992-4(1))* West Margin Pr. (West Winds Pr.).
—Jasper & Willie: Wildfire. 2015. (Range Riders Ser.). (ENG.). 130p. (J). 28.99 *(978-1-941821-92-3(8))*; pap. 9.99 *(978-1-941821-71-8(5))* West Margin Pr. (West Winds Pr.).
Gabel, Stacey. The New Blue Tractor. Neuman, Richard, illus. 2007. 24p. per. 13.95 *(978-1-59858-424-0(3))* Dog Ear Publishing, LLC.
Garis, Howard R. Curlytops at Uncle Frank's Ranch. 2009. 120p. pap. 10.95 *(978-1-60664-408-9(4))* Rodgers, Alan Bks.
—The Curlytops at Uncle Frank's Ranch; or, Little Folks on Ponyback. 2007. 160p. per. *(978-1-4065-2763-6(7))* Dodo Pr.
Garis, Howard Roger. The Curlytops at Uncle Frank's Ranch. 2005. 26.95 *(978-1-4218-1466-7(8)*, 1st World Library - Literary Society) 1st World Publishing, Inc.
—The Curlytops at Uncle Franks Ranch. 2005. 192p. pap. 11.95 *(978-1-4218-1566-4(4)*, 1st World Library - Literary Society) 1st World Publishing, Inc.
—The Curlytops at Uncle Frank's Ranch. 2004. reprint ed. pap. 21.95 *(978-1-4191-5842-1(2))*; pap. 1.99 *(978-1-4192-5842-8(7))* Kessinger Publishing, LLC.
Garst, Shannon. Silver Spurs for Cowboy Boots. Hargens, Charles, illus. 2011. 194p. 42.95 *(978-1-258-08454-7(6))* Literary Licensing, LLC.
Green, D. L. Sparkling Jewel: a Branches Book (Silver Pony Ranch #1) Wallis, Emily, illus. 2015. (Silver Pony Ranch Ser.: 1). (ENG.). 96p. (J). (gr. 1-3). pap. 5.99 *(978-0-545-79765-8(9))* Scholastic, Inc.
Haesche, Richard, Sr. Ghost Wolf. 2007. (ENG.). 207p. (YA). 10.99 *(978-0-9798536-5-4(6))* Kreative X-Pressions Pubns.
Hanes, Rosann. Diamond H Ranch: Told by: Val - Loyal Ranch Dog. 2010. 28p. pap. 13.99 *(978-1-4490-7714-3(5))* AuthorHouse.
HarperCollins Publishers Ltd. Staff, ed. Home on the Range. Date not set. 40p. (J). (gr. -1-3). pap. 5.99 *(978-0-06-443567-3(9))* HarperCollins Pubs.
Heimbuch, Carol Jo. Twilight Tracks. 2007. 112p. per. 10.95 *(978-1-59330-466-9(8))* Aventine Pr.
Helidoniotis, Kathy. Horse Mad Western. 2008. (ENG.). 272p. *(978-0-7322-8424-4(4))* HarperCollins Pubs. Australia.
Horseshoe Canyon. 2005. (J). 30.00 *(978-1-884270-38-3(7))* Hall, Nancy Inc.
Horvath, Polly. Northward to the Moon. 2012. (My One Hundred Adventures Ser.). (ENG.). 256p. (J). (gr. 6-8). lib. bdg. 22.44 *(978-0-375-96110-6(0))* Random House Publishing Group.
—Northward to the Moon. 2012. (My One Hundred Adventures Ser.: 2). 256p. (J). (gr. 5-8). 7.99 *(978-0-307-92980-8(9)*, Yearling) Random Hse. Children's Bks.
James, Will. Look-See with Uncle Bill. rev. ed. (Illus.). 190p. (J). (gr. 4). pap. *(978-0-87842-458-0(X)*, 814) Mountain Pr. Publishing Co., Inc.
—My First Horse, Vol. 1. rev. ed. (Illus.). 48p. (J). (gr. 4). 16.00 *(978-0-87842-488-7(1)*, 819) Mountain Pr. Publishing Co., Inc.
—Uncle Bill: A Tale of Two Kids & a Cowboy. rev. ed. (Tumbleweed Ser.). (Illus.). 185p. (J). (gr. 4-12). pap. 14.00 *(978-0-87842-380-4(X)*, 694) Mountain Pr. Publishing Co., Inc.
—Young Cowboy. rev. ed. 2004. (Illus.). 88p. (J). (gr. 4-7). 15.00 *(978-0-87842-419-1(9)*, 806) Mountain Pr. Publishing Co., Inc.
Johnston, Jeanna. My Busy Day at the Ranch. 2011. 28p. pap. 15.99 *(978-1-4628-9301-0(5))* Xlibris Corp.
Kelso, Mary Jean. Andy & Spirit in Search & Rescue. Snider, Kc, illus. 2013. 28p. pap. 10.95 *(978-1-61633-408-6(8))* Guardian Angel Publishing, Inc.
Kennedy, Marlane. Tornado Alley. 2014. (Disaster Strikes Ser.: 2). lib. bdg. 14.75 *(978-0-606-35828-6(5))* Turtleback.
Kephart, Beth. Small Damages. 2013. (Illus.). 304p. (YA). (gr. 9). pap. 8.99 *(978-0-14-242641-8(5)*, Speak) Penguin Young Readers Group.
Keyser, Amber J. & Burkhart, Kiersi. The Long Trail Home. 2017. (Quartz Creek Ranch Ser.). (ENG.). 240p. (J). (gr. 4-8). 6.99 *(978-1-5124-3090-5(0)*, 237da2bf-d64a-47f5-9377-07661a1f1425, Darby Creek) Lerner Publishing Group.
Law, Ingrid. Scumble. 2011. 432p. (J). (gr. 3-7). 9.99 *(978-0-14-241962-5(1)*, Puffin Books) Penguin Young Readers Group.
—Scumble. l.t. ed. 2011. (Companion to the Newberry Honor Winner Savvy Ser.). (ENG.). 575p. 23.99 *(978-1-4104-3531-6(8))* Thorndike Pr.
Levis, Caron. This Way, Charlie. Santoso, Charles, illus. 2020. (Feeling Friends Ser.). (ENG.). 40p. (J). (gr. -1-3). 17.99 *(978-1-4197-4206-4(X)*, 1679101, Abrams Bks. for Young Readers) Abrams, Inc.
—This Way, Charlie: Inspired by a Real Animal Friendship. Santoso, Charles, illus. 2020. (J). *(978-1-5344-3063-1(6)*, Atheneum Bks. for Young Readers) Simon & Schuster Children's Publishing.
Lewis, Ali. Timber Creek Station. (ENG., Illus.). 240p. (YA). (gr. 6-12). 2018. pap. 9.99 *(978-1-5415-1485-0(8)*, 47e70c69-8468-4ffd-8046-f0b9cfc5bca9) 2016. E-Book 27.99 *(978-1-4677-8816-8(3))* Lerner Publishing Group. (Carolrhoda Lab™).
Mackall, Dandi Daley. Horse Gentler in Training. 2018. (Winnie: the Early Years Ser.: 1). (ENG., Illus.). 112p. (J). pap. 5.99 *(978-1-4964-3280-3(0)*, 20_31611, Tyndale Kids) Tyndale Hse. Pubs.
—A Horse's Best Friend. 2018. (Winnie: the Early Years Ser.: 2). (ENG., Illus.). 112p. (J). pap. 6.99 *(978-1-4964-3284-1(3)*, 20_31613, Tyndale Kids) Tyndale Hse. Pubs.
Maddox, Jake. Cowgirl Grit. Wood, Katie, illus. 2018. (Jake Maddox Girl Sports Stories Ser.). (ENG.). 72p. (J). (gr. 3-6). lib. bdg. 25.32 *(978-1-4965-5847-3(2)*, 136932, Stone Arch Bks.) Capstone.
—Rodeo Challenge. Aburto, Jesus, illus. 2018. (Jake Maddox Sports Stories Ser.). (ENG.). 72p. (J). (gr. 3-6). lib. bdg. 25.99 *(978-1-4965-5865-7(0)*, 136944, Stone Arch Bks.) Capstone.
Marlow, Susan K. Andi Dreams of Gold, 1 vol. 2018. (Circle C Stepping Stones Ser.: 5). (Illus.). 112p. (J). pap. 7.99 *(978-0-8254-4434-0(9))* Kregel Pubns.
—Andi Far from Home, 1 vol. 2018. (Circle C Stepping Stones Ser.: 6). 112p. (J). pap. 7.99 *(978-0-8254-4435-7(7))* Kregel Pubns.
—Andi Lassos Trouble, 1 vol. 2017. (Circle C Stepping Stones Ser.: 3). (Illus.). 112p. (J). pap. 7.99 *(978-0-8254-4432-6(2))* Kregel Pubns.
—Andi to the Rescue, 1 vol. 2017. (Circle C Stepping Stones Ser.: 4). (Illus.). 112p. (J). pap. 7.99 *(978-0-8254-4433-3(0))* Kregel Pubns.
—Andrea Carter & the Dangerous Decision, 1 vol. 2018. (Circle C Adventures Ser.: 6). 144p. (J). pap. 8.99 *(978-0-8254-4501-9(9))* Kregel Pubns.
—Andrea Carter & the Family Secret, 1 vol. (Circle C Adventures Ser.: 3). 144p. (J). 2018. pap. 8.99 *(978-0-8254-4502-6(7))* 2008. pap. 7.99 *(978-0-8254-3365-8(7))* Kregel Pubns.
—Andrea Carter & the Price of Truth, 1 vol. 2017. (Circle C Adventures Ser.: 6). 144p. (J). pap. 8.99 *(978-0-8254-4505-7(1))* Kregel Pubns.
—Andrea Carter & the Trouble with Treasure, 1 vol. 2017. (Circle C Adventures Ser.: 5). 144p. (J). pap. 8.99 *(978-0-8254-4504-0(3))* Kregel Pubns.
—Andrea Carter's Tales from the Circle C Ranch, 1 vol. 2015. (Illus.). 160p. (J). pap. 7.99 *(978-0-8254-4379-4(2))* Kregel Pubns.
—The Last Ride: An Andrea Carter Book, 1 vol. 2016. (Circle C Milestones Ser.: 3). 176p. (YA). pap. 9.99 *(978-0-8254-4369-5(5))* Kregel Pubns.
—Thick As Thieves: An Andrea Carter Book, 1 vol. 2015. (Circle C Milestones Ser.: 1). 176p. (YA). pap. 9.99 *(978-0-8254-4367-1(9))* Kregel Pubns.
Martinello, Marian L. Ready's Gifts. 2003. (Illus.). 158p. (YA). (gr. 8-18). per. 12.95 *(978-0-9724113-0-1(5))* MindCatcher Pr.
Marusak, Elaine Truly. Truly Tales: Aunt Gertie & Uncle George's Haunted House. 2007. (ENG.). 84p. per. 19.95 *(978-1-4241-5959-8(8))* America Star Bks.
Meddaugh, Susan. Martha & Skits Out West. 2011. (Martha Speaks Ser.). (ENG., Illus.). 96p. (J). (gr. 1-4). pap. 5.99 *(978-0-547-21074-2(4))* Houghton Mifflin Harcourt Publishing Co.
Miller, Paula. One-Eyed Jack. Forrest, Chris, illus. (J). 2007. (ENG.). 133p. (gr. 2-7). pap. 8.95 *(978-0-9769417-0-5(8))* 2006. 144p. 13.95 *(978-0-9718348-8-0(1))* Blooming Tree Pr.
Moeri, Louise. The Devil in Ol' Rosie. 2009. (ENG.). 208p. (J). (gr. 3-6). pap. 10.99 *(978-1-4424-0202-7(4)*, Atheneum Bks. for Young Readers) Simon & Schuster Children's Publishing.
Montgomery, Rutherford G. The Golden Stallion's Victory. (J). 20.95 *(978-0-8488-0133-5(4))* Amereon Ltd.
Nolan, Lucy A. Home on the Range, 0 vols. Reed, Mike, illus. 2010. (Down Girl & Sit Ser.: 4). (ENG.). 64p. (J). (gr. 1-4). 14.99 *(978-0-7614-5649-0(X)*, 9780761456490, Two Lions) Amazon Publishing.
Oldfield, Jenny. Crazy Horse. 2009. (Horses of Half Moon Ranch Ser.: 3). (ENG.). 160p. (J). (gr. 4-7). pap. 9.99 *(978-1-4022-1702-9(1))* Sourcebooks, Inc.
Ore, Stephen. Round Trip: A Novel. 2018. (Illus.). 220p. (YA). pap. *(978-1-937849-49-8(X))* Raven Publishing Inc. of Montana.
Out of the Blue. 2014. (J). pap. *(978-0-8163-5016-2(7))* Pacific Pr. Publishing Assn.
Palmer, Catherine. Fatal Harvest. l.t. ed. 2004. (Matthew 25 Ser.). 496p. (YA). 28.95 *(978-0-7862-6259-5(1))* Thorndike Pr.
Parish, Herman. Go West, Amelia Bedelia! Sweat, Lynn, illus. 2012. (I Can Read Level 2 Ser.). (ENG.). 64p. (J). (gr. k-4). pap. 4.99 *(978-0-06-084363-2(2)*, Greenwillow Bks.) HarperCollins Pubs.
Parry, Rosanne. Heart of a Shepherd. 2010. (ENG.). 176p. (J). (gr. 4-6). lib. bdg. 22.44 *(978-0-375-94802-2(3))* Random House Publishing Group.
—Heart of a Shepherd. 2010. 176p. (J). (gr. 3-7). pap. 7.99 *(978-0-375-84803-2(7)*, Yearling) Random Hse. Children's Bks.
Petruck, Rebecca. Steering Toward Normal. 2014. (ENG.). 336p. (J). (gr. 4-8). 16.95 *(978-1-4197-0732-2(9)*, 1057501, Amulet Bks.) Abrams, Inc.
Prentice-Hall Staff. The Red Pony. 2nd ed. (J). stu. ed. *(978-0-13-717133-0(1))* Prentice Hall (Schl. Div.).
Pyke, Helen Godfrey. Julia. 2012. (J). pap. *(978-0-8163-3400-1(5))* Pacific Pr. Publishing Assn.
Ransom, Jeanie Franz. Cowboy Car. Nedelcu, Ovi, illus. 2017. (ENG.). 40p. (J). (gr. -1-2). 17.99 *(978-1-5039-5097-9(2)*, 9781503950979, Two Lions) Amazon Publishing.
Reiss, Kathryn. Message in a Bottle: A Julie Mystery. 2017. 209p. (J). *(978-1-5182-4315-8(0)*, American Girl) American Girl Publishing, Inc.
Roach, Joyce Gibson, tr. Cowgirl of the Rocking R. 2003. (J). *(978-0-9726573-0-3(4))* Crosswinds Bks.
Runels, Margie "B". Talon. 2009. 12p. pap. 8.49 *(978-1-4490-3248-7(6))* AuthorHouse.
Salisbury, Graham. Banjo. 2019. (ENG.). 224p. (J). (gr. 5). 16.99 *(978-0-375-84264-1(0)*, Lamb, Wendy Bks.) Random Hse. Children's Bks.
Sargent, Dave & Sargent, Pat. Chick: (Chocolate Chestnut) Be Loyal. 30 vols., Vol. 16. Lenoir, Jane, illus. 2003. (Saddle up Ser.: Vol. 16). 42p. (J). pap. 10.95 *(978-1-56763-678-9(0))*; lib. bdg. 23.60 *(978-1-56763-677-2(2))* Ozark Publishing.
—Lily: (Lilac Dun) A Second Chance, 30 vols., Vol. 38. Lenoir, Jane, illus. 2003. (Saddle up Ser.: Vol. 38). 42p. (J). pap. 10.95 *(978-1-56763-698-7(5))*; lib. bdg. 23.60 *(978-1-56763-697-0(7))* Ozark Publishing.
Sclafani, Terry. The Thompson Twins Western Adventure. 2009. 114p. pap. 11.95 *(978-1-4327-3783-2(X))* Outskirts Pr., Inc.
Scott, Elizabeth M. It's Rodeo Time! With Mamma Scottie & the Kids. 2009. 52p. pap. 24.99 *(978-1-4490-1750-7(9))* AuthorHouse.
Shafer, Patty. Annie the Texas Ranch Dog - Danger at Lost Maples. Retzlaff, Shay, illus. 2012. (ENG.). 96p. (J). pap. 9.95 *(978-1-61899-009-9(8)*, Tadpole Pr. 4 Kids) Mystic Harbor Pr., LLC.
—Annie the Texas Ranch Dog - Injured Hero. Retzlaff, Shay, illus. 2012. 96p. (J). pap. 9.95 *(978-1-61899-008-2(X)*, Tadpole Pr. 4 Kids) Mystic Harbor Pr., LLC.
Simmons, Andra. What Anna Loves. Capaldi, Gina, illus. 2006. 24p. (J). (gr. -1-3). 15.95 *(978-1-59714-044-7(9))* Heyday.
Smiley, Jane. The Georges & the Jewels: Book One of the Horses of Oak Valley Ranch. 2010. (Horses of Oak Valley Ranch Ser.: 1). (ENG.). 240p. (J). (gr. 5). 7.99 *(978-0-375-86228-1(5)*, Yearling) Random Hse. Children's Bks.
—A Good Horse, 2. 2011. (Horses of Oak Valley Ranch Ser.: Bk. 2). (ENG., Illus.). 256p. (J). (gr. 6-8). lib. bdg. 21.19 *(978-0-375-96228-8(X))* Random House Publishing Group.
—A Good Horse: Book Two of the Horses of Oak Valley Ranch. 2011. (Horses of Oak Valley Ranch Ser.: 2). (ENG.). 256p. (J). (gr. 5). 8.99 *(978-0-375-86230-4(7)*, Yearling) Random Hse. Children's Bks.
—Pie in the Sky: Book Four of the Horses of Oak Valley Ranch. 2013. (Horses of Oak Valley Ranch Ser.: 4). (ENG.). 272p. (J). (gr. 5). 7.99 *(978-0-375-87131-3(4)*, Yearling) Random Hse. Children's Bks.
—True Blue: Book Three of the Horses of Oak Valley Ranch. 2012. (Horses of Oak Valley Ranch Ser.: 3). (ENG.). 304p. (J). (gr. 5). 8.99 *(978-0-375-86232-8(3)*, Yearling) Random Hse. Children's Bks.
Smith, Andrew. Ghost Medicine. 2010. (ENG.). 384p. (YA). (gr. 8-13). pap. 19.99 *(978-0-312-62912-0(5)*, 900066876) Square Fish.
Standish, Burt L. Frank Merriwell's Ranch. Rudman, Jack, ed. 2003. (Frank Merriwell Ser.). pap. 9.95 *(978-0-8373-9168-7(7))* Merriwell, Frank Inc.
Stier, Catherine. I Am Jax, Protector of the Ranch. Rosa, Francesca, illus. 2020. (Dog's Day Ser.: 1). (ENG.). 96p. (J). (gr. 1-5). 12.99 *(978-0-8075-1663-8(5)*, 807516635) Whitman, Albert & Co.
Stilton, Gerónimo & Stilton, Thea. Thea Stilton & the Mountain of Fire. 2009. (Thea Stilton Ser.: 2). lib. bdg. 19.65 *(978-0-606-00232-5(4))* Turtleback.
Stone, Judith. Billie the Buffalo Goes to Town. 2008. 20p. pap. 12.95 *(978-1-4389-2877-7(7))* AuthorHouse.
Stratemeyer, Edward. Dave Porter at Star Ranch. 2007. 260p. 28.95 *(978-1-4218-4144-1(4)*, 1st World Library - Literary Society) 1st World Publishing, Inc.
Sylvester, Kevin. Neil Flambé & the Duel in the Desert. Sylvester, Kevin, illus. (Neil Flambe Capers Ser.: 6). (ENG., Illus.). 304p. (J). (gr. 3-7). 2017. pap. 8.99 *(978-1-4814-1042-7(3))* 2016. 13.99 *(978-1-4814-1041-0(5))* Simon & Schuster Bks. For Young Readers. (Simon & Schuster Bks. For Young Readers).
Tripp, Valerie. Josefina Story Collection. Tibbles, Jean-Paul, illus. 2008. 420p. pap. 29.95 *(978-1-59369-453-1(9))* American Girl Publishing, Inc.
Van Slyke, Rebecca. Lexie the Word Wrangler. Hartland, Jessie, illus. 2017. 40p. (J). (gr. k-3). 18.99 *(978-0-399-16957-1(1)*, Nancy Paulsen Books) Penguin Young Readers Group.
Van Tol, Alex. A Punta de Cuchillo, 1 vol. 2011. (Spanish Soundings Ser.). (SPA.). 136p. (YA). (gr. 8-12). pap. 9.95 *(978-1-55469-863-9(4))* Orca Bk. Pubs. USA.
Walter, Mildred Pitts. Justin & the Best Biscuits in the World. Stock, Catherine, illus. 2010. (ENG.). 144p. (J). (gr. 3-7). pap. 9.99 *(978-0-06-195891-5(3)*, Amistad) HarperCollins Pubs.
—Justin & the Best Biscuits in the World. 2011. 8.32 *(978-0-7848-3586-9(1)*, Everbind) Marco Bk. Co.
Warner, Gertrude Chandler, creator. A Horse Named Dragon. 2008. (Boxcar Children Mysteries Ser.: 114). (ENG., Illus.). 128p. (J). (gr. 2-5). lib. bdg. 14.99 *(978-0-8075-5571-2(1)*, 807555711); per. 7.99 *(978-0-8075-5572-9(X)*, 080755572X) Random Hse. Children's Bks. (Random Hse. Bks. for Young Readers).
Webster, Frank V. Bob Chester's Grit. 2007. (ENG.). 180p. per. 11.95 *(978-1-4218-3327-9(1))* 1st World Publishing, Inc.
—Bob Chester's Grit: From Ranch to Riches. 2018. (ENG., Illus.). 182p. (YA). (gr. 7-12). pap. *(978-93-86874-83-2(0))* Alpha Editions.
—Comrades of the Saddle. 2007. 176p. 26.95 *(978-1-4218-3229-6(1)*, 1st World Library - Literary Society); (ENG.). per. 11.95 *(978-1-4218-3329-3(8))* 1st World Publishing, Inc.
—Comrades of the Saddle or the Young Rough Riders of the Plains. 2004. reprint ed. pap. 1.99 *(978-1-4192-1372-4(5))* Kessinger Publishing, LLC.
Weldon, Stayton. Whitey on the Ranch. Anderson-Shorter, Susan, illus. 2010. 52p. pap. 12.95 *(978-1-4490-5474-8(9))* AuthorHouse.
Yu, Jennifer. Texas Animal Ranch: Ricky's Secret Friends Series, vols. 6, vol. 2. Yu, Jennifer, illus. 2018. (Ricky's Secret Friends Picturebook Ser.: 6). (ENG & CHI., Illus.). (gr. 1-4). 49.95 *(978-0-9787591-2-4(5))* Direct World Publishing.

RANDOLPH, A. PHILIP (ASA PHILIP), 1889-1979

Miller, Calvin Craig. A. Philip Randolph & the African American Labor Movement. 2005. (Civil Rights Leaders Ser.). (Illus.). 160p. (YA). (gr. 6-12). 26.95 *(978-1-931798-50-1(8))* Reynolds, Morgan Inc.

RANK

see Social Classes

RAP (MUSIC)

Anniss, Matt. The Story of Hip-Hop. 2013. (Pop Histories Ser.). 32p. (gr. 4-7). 31.35 *(978-1-59920-965-4(9))* Black Rabbit Bks.
Baker, Soren. The History of Rap & Hip-Hop, 1 vol. (Music Library). (ENG., Illus.). (gr. 7-10). 2012. 136p. lib. bdg. 41.03 *(978-1-4205-0822-2(9)*, 6bdb5833-bfed-4e27-bf00-bfdc0425defc) 2006. 112p. lib. bdg. 35.08 *(978-1-59018-739-5(3)*, 4a33b9b5-7092-4d0d-8e3a-6cbca653c953) Greenhaven Publishing LLC. (Lucent Pr.).
Bankston, John. Eminem. l.t. ed. 2003. (Blue Banner Biography Ser.). (Illus.). 32p. (J). (gr. 3-8). lib. bdg. 25.70 *(978-1-58415-222-4(2))* Mitchell Lane Pubs.
—Jay-Z. l.t. ed. 2004. (Blue Banner Biography Ser.). (Illus.). 32p. (J). (gr. 3-8). lib. bdg. 25.70 *(978-1-58415-223-1(0))* Mitchell Lane Pubs.
Berlatsky, Noah, ed. Rap Music, 1 vol. 2012. (Introducing Issues with Opposing Viewpoints Ser.). (ENG., Illus.). 200p.

(gr. 7-10). lib. bdg. 43.63 *(978-0-7377-6496-3(1),* 544f311d-ded2-4f99-8064-488762a6e250, Greenhaven Publishing) Greenhaven Publishing LLC.

Boston Weatherford, Carole. The Roots of Rap: 16 Bars on the 4 Pillars of Hip-Hop. Morrison, Frank, illus. 2019. (ENG.). 48p. (J). (gr. -1-3). 18.99 *(978-1-4998-0411-9(3))* Little Bee Books Inc.

Burns, Kate, ed. Rap Music & Culture, 1 vol. 2008. (Current Controversies Ser.). (ENG., Illus.). 192p. (gr. 10-12). 48.03 *(978-0-7377-3964-0(9),* e93bdbc8-f446-40cb-a491-6c989fac94d8); pap. 33.00 *(978-0-7377-3965-7(7),* c64ef4e7-e8a7-45e9-aab3-e96bf66f6aef) Greenhaven Publishing LLC. (Greenhaven Publishing).

Carr, Aaron. Rap. 2015. (J). *(978-1-4896-3589-1(0))* Weigl Pubs., Inc.

Cummings, Judy Dodge. Hip-Hop Culture. 2017. (Hip-Hop Insider Ser.). (ENG., Illus.). 112p. (J). (gr. 6-12). lib. bdg. 41.36 *(978-1-5321-1027-6(8),* 25630, Essential Library) ABDO Publishing Co.

—The Men of Hip-Hop. 2017. (Hip-Hop Insider Ser.). (ENG.). 112p. (J). (gr. 6-12). lib. bdg. 41.36 *(978-1-5321-1031-3(6),* 25638, Essential Library) ABDO Publishing Co.

Dagnino, Michelle. Hip Hop from A to Z: A Fresh Look at the Music, the Culture, & the Message. Baldwin, Alisa, illus. 2007. 192p. (J). (gr. 8-12). pap. *(978-1-897073-36-0(4))* Lobster Pr.

Earl, C. F. Hip-Hop: A Short History. 2012. (J). pap. *(978-1-4222-2545-5(3))*; (Illus.). 48p. (gr. 3-4). 19.95 *(978-1-4222-2519-6(4))* Mason Crest.

Ellis, Carol. Landmark Hip-Hop Hits. 2012. (Illus.). 64p. (J). pap. *(978-1-4222-2134-1(2))*; (gr. 4). 22.95 *(978-1-4222-2121-1(0))* Mason Crest.

Garofoli Zamora, Wendy. Hip-Hop History [Scholastic]. 2010. (Hip-Hop World Ser.). 48p. pap. 1.00 *(978-1-4296-5979-6(3))* Capstone.

Gogerly, Liz. Street Dance. 2011. (On the Radar: Dance Ser.). (ENG., Illus.). 32p. (gr. 4-8). lib. bdg. 26.60 *(978-0-7613-7761-0(1))* Lerner Publishing Group.

Graham Gaines, Ann & Majors, Reggie. The Hip-Hop Scene: The Stars, the Fans, the Music, 1 vol. 2009. (Music Scene Ser.). (ENG., Illus.). 48p. (J). (gr. 5-7). lib. bdg. 27.93 *(978-0-7660-3396-2(1),* 15b601b2-8761-4fa3-ab48-dc9d5759b706) Enslow Publishing, LLC.

Hall, Marcella Runell & Cameron, Andrea. The 10 Most Influential Hip Hop Artists. 2008. 14.99 *(978-1-55448-504-8(5))* Scholastic Library Publishing.

Harper, P. Thandi Hicks. Hip-Hop Development. 2005. *(978-1-887191-02-9(X))* Youth Popular Culture Institute, Inc.

Hatch, Thomas. A History of Hip-Hop: The Roots of Rap. 2005. (High Five Reading - Blue Ser.). (ENG., Illus.). 48p. (gr. 3-4). per. 9.00 *(978-0-7368-5750-5(8))* Capstone.

Hip-Hop Headliners, 16 vols., Set. Incl. Alicia Keys. Shea, Mary Molly. 27.93 *(978-1-4339-4784-1(6),* acb83c56-de2d-4634-b62d-0fc3f5992b68); Beyoncé. Kennon, Michou. lib. bdg. 27.93 *(978-1-4339-4788-9(9),* 3f18dd4f-c807-4912-8fd6-6be85d5b19f8); Black Eyed Peas. Shea, Mary Molly. lib. bdg. 27.93 *(978-1-4339-4792-6(7),* 8ebc06b9-d8d8-4896-8f12-84cb83b4f34); Jay-Z. Nacerous, Roman P. lib. bdg. 27.93 *(978-1-4339-4796-4(X),* f9241b4b-b8b9-4502-aa8c-eee30418ad44); Justin Timberlake. Maimone, Max Q. lib. bdg. 27.93 *(978-1-4339-4800-8(1),* 40d6b74b-e6b2-42d1-9734-52b519879c9c); Mary J. Blige. Maimone, Sofia. 27.93 *(978-1-4339-4804-6(4),* 1391fd88-a999-445e-b3da-c7440c12e297); Queen Latifah. Kennon, Michou. lib. bdg. 27.93 *(978-1-4339-4808-4(7),* 4d494ccf-d9fb-49c7-88a9-dc55103f5049); Usher. Shea, Therese M. 27.93 *(978-1-4339-4812-1(5),* 0147663d-f70b-4386-b541-04fd20c28edf); (J). (gr. 1-1). (Hip-Hop Headliners Ser.). (ENG., Illus.). 32p. 2011. Set lib. bdg. 223.44 *(978-1-4339-4948-7(2),* f2631af3-4ad1-403d-a0d3-19f432418d01) Stevens, Gareth Publishing LLLP.

Hip-Hop World [Capstone Sole Source]. 2010. (Hip-Hop World Ser.). 48p. lib. bdg. 122.60 *(978-1-4296-5866-9(5))* Capstone.

Kalman, Bobbie. Reptile Rap. 2010. (My World Ser.). (ENG.). 16p. (J). (gr. k-3). *(978-0-7787-9512-4(8))*; pap. *(978-0-7787-9537-7(3))* Crabtree Publishing Co.

Kenney, Karen Latchana. Cool Hip-Hop Music: Create & Appreciate What Makes Music Great! 2008. (Cool Music Ser.). (ENG., Illus.). 32p. (J). (gr. 3-6). 34.21 *(978-1-59928-971-7(7),* 366, Checkerboard Library) ABDO Publishing Co.

Llanas, Sheila. The Women of Hip-Hop. 2017. (Hip-Hop Insider Ser.). (ENG., Illus.). 112p. (J). (gr. 6-12). lib. bdg. 41.36 *(978-1-5321-1032-0(4),* 25640, Essential Library) ABDO Publishing Co.

Lusted, Marcia Amidon. Hip-Hop Music. 2017. (Hip-Hop Insider Ser.). (ENG., Illus.). 112p. (J). (gr. 6-12). lib. bdg. 41.36 *(978-1-5321-1030-6(8),* 25636, Essential Library) ABDO Publishing Co.

Mattern, Joanne. Nicki Minaj. 2013. (ENG.). 32p. (gr. 4-8). lib. bdg. 25.70 *(978-1-61228-468-2(X))* Mitchell Lane Pubs.

Morris, Rebecca. Hip-Hop Groups. 2017. (Hip-Hop Insider Ser.). (ENG., Illus.). 112p. (J). (gr. 6-12). lib. bdg. 41.36 *(978-1-5321-1029-0(4),* 25634, Essential Library) ABDO Publishing Co.

Morse, Eric. What Is Hip-Hop? Yi, Anny, illus. 2017. (ENG.). 40p. (J). (gr. -1-2). 15.95 *(978-1-61775-584-2(2),* Black Sheep) Akashic Bks.

Norton, James R. Russell Simmons. 2009. (Library of Hip-Hop Biographies Ser.). 48p. (gr. 5-5). 53.00 *(978-1-60853-704-4(8))* Rosen Publishing Group, Inc., The.

Original Raps for the All Occasion Kid, 3 vols. 2003. (J). Vols. IV-VI. pap. *(978-0-9745630-1-5(3))*Vols. I, II, and III. pap. incl. audio compact disk *(978-0-9745630-0-8(5))*Vols. VII, VIII, IX. pap. *(978-0-9745630-2-2(1))* F & S Music KS Publishing Co.

Saddleback Educational Publishing Staff. Jay-Z. 2013. (Hip-Hop Biographies (Saddleback Publishing) Ser.). (YA). lib. bdg. 23.25 *(978-0-606-31484-8(9))* Turtleback.

Thompson, Kim Mitzo & Hilderbrand, Karen Mitzo. Multiplication Rap. 2008. (Playaway Children Ser.). (J). 44.99 *(978-1-59922-324-7(4))* Findaway World, LLC.

Thompson, Tamara, ed. Rap & Hip-Hop, 1 vol. 2013. (Current Controversies Ser.). (ENG.). 168p. (gr. 10-12). pap. 33.00 *(978-0-7377-6244-0(6),* d771a5b8-5d3c-4c02-a67f-8f10ca30bc7c); lib. bdg. 48.03 *(978-0-7377-6243-3(8),* a55b101d-1085-479c-be91-ff8ca471042) Greenhaven Publishing LLC. (Greenhaven Publishing).

Walker, Ida. Around the World. 2009. (Hip-Hop Ser.). (Illus.). 64p. (YA). (gr. 4-7). pap. 7.95 *(978-1-4222-0350-7(6))*; (gr. 7-12). lib. bdg. 22.95 *(978-1-4222-0293-7(3))* Mason Crest.

Waters, Rosa. Yung Joc. 2009. (Hip Hop (Mason Crest Paperback) Ser.). (Illus.). 64p. (YA). pap. 7.95 *(978-1-4222-0339-2(5))* Mason Crest.

RAP (MUSIC)—FICTION

Goode, Laura. Sister Mischief. 2011. (ENG., Illus.). 384p. (YA). (gr. 9-18). 16.99 *(978-0-7636-4640-0(7))* Candlewick Pr.

Gutman, Dan. Rappy Goes to School. Bowers, Tim, illus. 2016. (ENG.). 40p. (J). (gr. -1-3). 17.99 *(978-0-06-229181-3(5),* HarperCollins) HarperCollins Pubs.

—Rappy the Raptor. Bowers, Tim, illus. 2015. (ENG.). 40p. (J). (gr. -1-3). 17.99 *(978-0-06-229180-6(7),* HarperCollins) HarperCollins Pubs.

Jenkins-Greaves, Shenita. Raptown U. S. A. Rappers. 2013. 24p. pap. 14.95 *(978-1-4669-7717-4(5))* Trafford Publishing.

Morningforest, Chris & Raymond, Rebecca. Mooseman Reindeer & Uncle Utley. 2006. 36p. (J). pap. 15.43 *(978-1-4116-8390-7(0))* Lulu Pr., Inc.

Staunton, Ted. Pov, 1 vol. 2017. (Orca Limelights Ser.). (ENG.). 144p. (J). (gr. 4-7). pap. 9.95 *(978-1-4598-1237-6(9))* Orca Bk. Pubs. USA.

Thomas, Angie. On the Come Up. 2019. 447p. (YA). *(978-0-06-284437-8(7))* Addison Wesley.

—On the Come Up. (ENG.). 464p. (YA). (gr. 8). 2020. pap. 15.99 *(978-0-06-249858-8(4))* 2019. 18.99 *(978-0-06-249856-4(8))* HarperCollins Pubs. (Balzer & Bray).

—On the Come Up. 2019. (YA). lib. bdg. 31.80 *(978-0-606-41391-6(X))* Turtleback.

—On the Come Up 9c Mix Flr. 2019. (ENG.). (J). 170.91 *(978-0-06-285708-8(8),* Balzer & Bray) HarperCollins Pubs.

RAP MUSICIANS

Abrams, Dennis. Beastie Boys. 2007. (ENG., Illus.). 104p. (gr. 7-12). lib. bdg. 30.00 *(978-0-7910-9480-8(4),* P126607, Facts On File) Infobase Holdings, Inc.

Anderson, Wayne A. Jay-Z. 2008. (ENG., Illus.). 112p. (gr. 6-12). per. 12.95 *(978-0-7910-9729-8(3),* P142885); (gr. 7-12). lib. bdg. 30.00 *(978-0-7910-9551-5(7),* P126605) Infobase Holdings, Inc. (Facts On File).

Aswell, Sarah, contrib. by. Kendrick Lamar: Rap Titan. 2017. (Hip-Hop Artists Ser.). (ENG., Illus.). 112p. (J). (gr. 6-12). lib. bdg. 41.36 *(978-1-5321-1329-1(3),* 27537, Essential Library) ABDO Publishing Co.

Azzarelli, Ally. Drake! Hip-Hop Celebrity, 1 vol. 2013. (Sizzling Celebrities Ser.). (ENG.). 48p. (gr. 4-6). pap. 11.53 *(978-1-4644-0275-3(2),* 3996c7d4-201b-42d2-9766-92dafb905bfb); (Illus.). 27.93 *(978-0-7660-4168-4(9),* c4d29352-5a93-4074-a1f0-2ac25ec232e8) Enslow Publishing, LLC.

Bailey, Diane. Chance the Rapper: Independent Innovator. 2017. (Hip-Hop Artists Ser.). (ENG., Illus.). 112p. (J). (gr. 6-12). lib. bdg. 41.36 *(978-1-5321-1325-3(0),* 27533, Essential Library) ABDO Publishing Co.

—Mary J. Blige. 2009. (Library of Hip-Hop Biographies Ser.). 48p. (gr. 5-5). 53.00 *(978-1-60853-694-8(7))*; (ENG.). (J). lib. bdg. 34.47 *(978-1-4358-5055-2(6),* 247b702a-a152-4dde-9a68-f217c101b8b5); (ENG., Illus.). (J). pap. 12.75 *(978-1-4358-5441-3(1),* 6c08e5b0-2df2-4f0b-85bc-11ea0ecc9c59) Rosen Publishing Group, Inc., The.

Bankston, John. Bow Wow. l.t. ed. 2004. (Blue Banner Biography Ser.). (Illus.). 32p. (J). (gr. 3-8). lib. bdg. 25.70 *(978-1-58415-220-0(6))* Mitchell Lane Pubs.

—Eminem. l.t. ed. 2003. (Blue Banner Biography Ser.). (Illus.). 32p. (J). (gr. 3-8). lib. bdg. 25.70 *(978-1-58415-222-4(2))* Mitchell Lane Pubs.

—Ja Rule. l.t. ed. 2004. (Blue Banner Biography Ser.). (Illus.). 32p. (J). (gr. 3-8). lib. bdg. 25.70 *(978-1-58415-221-7(4))* Mitchell Lane Pubs.

—Jay-Z. l.t. ed. 2004. (Blue Banner Biography Ser.). (Illus.). 32p. (J). (gr. 3-8). lib. bdg. 25.70 *(978-1-58415-223-1(0))* Mitchell Lane Pubs.

—Nelly. l.t. ed. 2003. (Blue Banner Biography Ser.). (Illus.). 32p. (J). (gr. 3-8). lib. bdg. 25.70 *(978-1-58415-218-7(4))* Mitchell Lane Pubs.

Baughan, Brian. LL Cool J. 2008. (Hip-Hop Ser.). (Illus.). 64p. (YA). (ENG.). (gr. 3-7). per. 7.95 *(978-1-4222-0271-5(2))*; (gr. 7-12). lib. bdg. 22.95 *(978-1-4222-0121-3(X))* Mason Crest.

Bezdecheck, Bethany. Missy Elliott. 2009. (Library of Hip-Hop Biographies Ser.). 48p. (gr. 5-5). 53.00 *(978-1-60853-697-9(1))*; (ENG.). (J). lib. bdg. 34.47 *(978-1-4358-5056-9(4),* caf636e6-df40-42e3-83e2-0f2dc32fdc91); (ENG., Illus.). (J). pap. 12.75 *(978-1-4358-5442-0(X),* e743b4c5-b51e-484d-9878-90f72ae6709f) Rosen Publishing Group, Inc., The.

Bookout, Summer. Jay-Z, Vol. 11. 2018. (Hip-Hop & R & B: Culture, Music & Storytelling Ser.). (Illus.). 80p. (J). (gr. 7). lib. bdg. 33.27 *(978-1-4222-4181-3(5))* Mason Crest.

—Pitbull, Vol. 11. 2018. (Hip-Hop & R & B: Culture, Music & Storytelling Ser.). (Illus.). 80p. (J). (gr. 7). lib. bdg. 33.27 *(978-1-4222-4184-4(X))* Mason Crest.

Boone, Mary. Akon. 2007. (Blue Banner Biography Ser.). (Illus.). 32p. (J). (gr. 4-5). lib. bdg. 25.70 *(978-1-58415-630-7(9))* Mitchell Lane Pubs.

—50 Cent. 2006. (Blue Banner Biography Ser.). (Illus.). 32p. (YA). (gr. 4-7). lib. bdg. 25.70 *(978-1-58415-523-2(X),* 1259604) Mitchell Lane Pubs.

Brewer Boyd, Christie. Eminem, 1 vol. 2012. (People in the News Ser.). (ENG., Illus.). 104p. (gr. 7-7). lib. bdg. 41.03 *(978-1-4205-0753-9(2),* 888946a8-85bb-46e0-a29e-879351e79d30, Lucent Pr.) Greenhaven Publishing LLC.

—Nicki Minaj, 1 vol. 2012. (People in the News Ser.). (ENG., Illus.). 96p. (gr. 7-7). 41.03 *(978-1-4205-0888-8(1),* 9f3bdb00-1dcf-4097-9bb1-9b621bf9bb47, Lucent Pr.) Greenhaven Publishing LLC.

Bridwell, Norman. Clifford's Birthday Party. 50th anniv. ed. 2013. (Clifford 8x8 Ser.). lib. bdg. 14.75 *(978-0-606-31539-5(X))* Turtleback.

Brown, Risa. Pit Bull. 2014. (Illus.). 32p. (J). 25.70 *(978-1-61228-644-0(5))* Mitchell Lane Pubs.

Brown, Terrell. Mary J. Blige. 2008. (Hip-Hop Ser.). (Illus.). 64p. (YA). (gr. 3-7). per. 7.95 *(978-1-4222-0264-7(X))*; (gr. 7-12). lib. bdg. 22.95 *(978-1-4222-0113-8(9))* Mason Crest.

—Pharell Williams. 2008. (Hip-Hop Ser.). (ENG., Illus.). 64p. (YA). (gr. 3-7). per. 7.95 *(978-1-4222-0275-3(5))* Mason Crest.

—Pharrell Williams. 2008. (Hip-Hop Ser.). (Illus.). 64p. (YA). (gr. 3-7). lib. bdg. 22.95 *(978-1-4222-0125-1(2))* Mason Crest.

—Reverend Run (Run-D. M. C.) 2008. (Hip-Hop Ser.). (Illus.). 64p. (YA). (ENG.). (gr. 3-7). per. 7.95 *(978-1-4222-0277-7(1))*; (gr. 7-12). lib. bdg. 22.95 *(978-1-4222-0127-5(9))* Mason Crest.

Burling, Alexis, contrib. by. Drake: Hip-Hop Superstar. 2017. (Hip-Hop Artists Ser.). (ENG., Illus.). 112p. (J). (gr. 6-12). lib. bdg. 41.36 *(978-1-5321-1327-7(7),* 27535, Essential Library) ABDO Publishing Co.

Burlingame, Jeff. Eminem: Hip-Hop Mogul, 1 vol. 2014. (Hip-Hop Moguls Ser.). (ENG., Illus.). 48p. (gr. 4-6). 18.61 *(978-1-62285-206-2(0),* 514cd1a2-1b83-4309-b0f9-66757e7314e1) Enslow Publishing, LLC.

—Jay-Z: A Biography of a Hip-Hop Icon, 1 vol. 2014. (African-American Icons Ser.). (ENG.). 104p. (gr. 6-7). lib. bdg. 30.61 *(978-0-7660-4232-2(4),* 281ff063-45ff-4a31-aac8-46facb3d0208) Enslow Publishing, LLC.

—Kanye West: Hip-Hop Mogul, 1 vol. 2014. (Hip-Hop Moguls Ser.). (ENG., Illus.). 48p. (gr. 4-6). 18.61 *(978-1-62285-211-6(7),* 079e2e02-238e-4613-8b9b-4025f0820233) Enslow Publishing, LLC.

—50 Cent: Hip-Hop Mogul, 1 vol. 2014. (Hip-Hop Moguls Ser.). (ENG., Illus.). 48p. (gr. 4-6). 18.61 *(978-1-62285-201-7(X),* 37d80df9-a04c-4a34-bf4d-a63a989cf373) Enslow Publishing, LLC.

Carlson-Berne, Emma. Snoop Dogg. 2008. (Hip-Hop Ser.). (Illus.). 64p. (J). (ENG.). (gr. 3-7). per. 7.95 *(978-1-4222-0279-1(8))*; (gr. 7-12). lib. bdg. 22.95 *(978-1-4222-0129-9(5))* Mason Crest.

Collier Hillstrom, Laurie. Jay-Z, 1 vol. 2009. (People in the News Ser.). (ENG., Illus.). 96p. (gr. 7-7). 41.03 *(978-1-4205-0158-2(5),* 2e0e1f79-fcbc-4297-ba70-22fd7a7cd7e1, Lucent Pr.) Greenhaven Publishing LLC.

Cotts, Nat. Daddy Yankee. 2009. (Hip-Hop Ser.). (Illus.). 64p. (YA). (gr. 4-7). pap. 7.95 *(978-1-4222-0342-2(5))*; (gr. 7-12). lib. bdg. 22.95 *(978-1-4222-0288-3(7))* Mason Crest.

—Don Omar. 2009. (Hip Hop (Mason Crest Paperback) Ser.). (Illus.). 64p. (YA). (gr. 4-7). pap. 7.95 *(978-1-4222-0346-0(8))*; (gr. 7-12). lib. bdg. 22.95 *(978-1-4222-0290-6(9))* Mason Crest.

—Pitbull. 2009. (Hip Hop (Mason Crest Paperback) Ser.). (Illus.). 64p. (YA). (gr. 4-7). pap. 7.95 *(978-1-4222-0343-9(3))*; (gr. 7-12). lib. bdg. 22.95 *(978-1-4222-0302-6(6))* Mason Crest.

—Young Jeezy. 2009. (Hip-Hop 2 Ser.). (Illus.). 64p. (YA). (gr. 7-12). lib. bdg. 22.95 *(978-1-4222-0306-4(9))* Mason Crest.

Cummings, Judy Dodge. The Men of Hip-Hop. 2017. (Hip-Hop Insider Ser.). (ENG.). 112p. (J). (gr. 6-12). lib. bdg. 41.36 *(978-1-5321-1031-3(6),* 25638, Essential Library) ABDO Publishing Co.

Doeden, Matt. Will Smith. 2007. (Illus.). 112p. (J). pap. 9.95 *(978-0-8225-7064-6(5))*; (ENG., (gr. 5-12). lib. bdg. 27.93 *(978-0-8225-6608-3(7),* Lerner Pubns.) Lerner Publishing Group.

Duncan, Terri Kaye. Cardi B: Breaking Boundaries & Records, 1 vol. 2019. (Hip-Hop Revolution Ser.). (ENG.). 32p. (gr. 5-5). 26.93 *(978-1-9785-0963-4(4),* 3391de38-a74b-43d1-be3a-3ebd15a9a942) Enslow Publishing, LLC.

—Cardi B: Rapper & Online Star, 1 vol. 2019. (Stars of Hip-Hop Ser.). (ENG.). 32p. (gr. 2-2). 26.93 *(978-1-9785-0955-9(3),* 0c746c2f-783b-4862-b736-a7a912aa545d) Enslow Publishing, LLC.

Earl, C. F. Black Eyed Peas. 2012. (Superstars of Hip-Hop Ser.). 48p. (J). (gr. 3-4). pap. 9.95 *(978-1-4222-2537-0(2))*; (Illus.). 19.95 *(978-1-4222-2511-0(9))* Mason Crest.

—Dr. Dre. 2012. (J). pap. *(978-1-4222-2543-1(7))*; (Illus.). 48p. (gr. 3-4). 19.95 *(978-1-4222-2517-2(8))* Mason Crest.

—Drake. 2012. (Superstars of Hip-Hop Ser.). (Illus.). 48p. (J). (gr. 3-4). 19.95 *(978-1-4222-2516-5(X))*; pap. 9.95 *(978-1-4222-2542-4(9))* Mason Crest.

—Flo Rida. 2012. (Superstars of Hip-Hop Ser.). 48p. (J). (gr. 3-4). pap. 9.95 *(978-1-4222-2551-6(8))*; (Illus.). 19.95 *(978-1-4222-2525-7(9))* Mason Crest.

—Jay-Z. 2012. (Superstars of Hip-Hop Ser.). 48p. (J). (gr. 3-4). pap. 9.95 *(978-1-4222-2546-2(1))*; (Illus.). 19.95 *(978-1-4222-2520-2(8))* Mason Crest.

—Kanye West. 2012. (Superstars of Hip-Hop Ser.). 48p. (J). (gr. 3-4). pap. 9.95 *(978-1-4222-2559-2(3))*; (Illus.). 19.95 *(978-1-4222-2533-2(X))* Mason Crest.

—Lil' Wayne. 2012. (Superstars of Hip-Hop Ser.). 48p. (J). (gr. 3-4). pap. 9.95 *(978-1-4222-2558-5(5))*; (Illus.). 19.95 *(978-1-4222-2532-5(1))* Mason Crest.

—Ludacris. 2012. (J). pap. *(978-1-4222-2549-3(6))*; (Illus.). 48p. (gr. 3-4). 19.95 *(978-1-4222-2523-3(2))* Mason Crest.

—Superstars of Hip Hop: T-Pain. 2012. (J). *(978-1-4222-2555-4(0))* Mason Crest.

—T. I. 2012. (J). pap. *(978-1-4222-2553-0(4))* Mason Crest.

—Timbaland. 2012. (J). *(978-1-4222-2554-7(2))*; (Illus.). 48p. (gr. 3-4). 19.95 *(978-1-4222-2528-8(3))* Mason Crest.

Earl, C. F. & Hill, Z. B. Superstars of Hip Hop - T-Pain. 2012. (Superstars of Hip-Hop Ser.). (Illus.). 48p. (J). (gr. 3-4). 19.95 *(978-1-4222-2529-5(1))* Mason Crest.

Embacher, Eric. Will Smith: The Funny, Funky, & Confident Fresh Prince. 2003. (High Five Reading - Red Ser.). (ENG., Illus.). 48p. (gr. 3-4). per. 9.00 *(978-0-7368-2829-1(X))* Capstone.

Etingoff, Kim. Ivy Queen. 2009. (Hip-Hop Ser.). (Illus.). 64p. (YA). (gr. 4-7). pap. 7.95 *(978-1-4222-0349-1(2))*; (gr. 7-12). lib. bdg. 22.95 *(978-1-4222-0295-1(X))* Mason Crest.

—T. I. 2009. (Hip-Hop 2 Ser.). (Illus.). 64p. (YA). (gr. 7-12). lib. bdg. 22.95 *(978-1-4222-0303-3(4))* Mason Crest.

Feinstein, Stephen. Queen Latifah, 1 vol. 2008. (African-American Heroes Ser.). (ENG., Illus.). 24p. (gr. k-2). lib. bdg. 25.27 *(978-0-7660-2896-8(8),* ab6437ed-c77c-45d2-8fc9-01c833d09f0d) Enslow Publishing, LLC.

—Will Smith, 1 vol. 2008. (African-American Heroes Ser.). (ENG., Illus.). 24p. (J). (gr. k-2). lib. bdg. 25.27 *(978-0-7660-2765-7(1),* 220ce28e-91b7-449f-99a3-4d580e94a611, Enslow Elementary) Enslow Publishing, LLC.

Flores, Chris. Pharrell Williams: Singer & Songwriter, 1 vol. 2016. (Junior Biographies Ser.). (ENG.). 24p. (gr. 3-4). pap. 10.35 *(978-0-7660-8192-5(3),* 929a4e41-97a6-4274-9274-8bbcbc77ebf4) Enslow Publishing, LLC.

Forget, Thomas. Beastie Boys. 2009. (Library of Hip-Hop Biographies Ser.). 48p. (gr. 5-5). 53.00 *(978-1-60853-681-8(5))* Rosen Publishing Group, Inc., The.

Gagne, Tammy. LL Cool J. 2013. (ENG.). 32p. (gr. 4-8). lib. bdg. 25.70 *(978-1-61228-464-4(7))* Mitchell Lane Pubs.

—Will. I. am. 2012. (Illus.). 32p. (J). lib. bdg. 25.70 *(978-1-61228-318-0(7))* Mitchell Lane Pubs.

Gelfand, Dale Evva. Sean Combs. 2007. (ENG., Illus.). 104p. (gr. 7-12). lib. bdg. 30.00 *(978-0-7910-9494-5(4),* P126619, Facts On File) Infobase Holdings, Inc.

Gisnash, Sahara. Salt-N-Pepa. 2009. (Library of Hip-Hop Biographies Ser.). 48p. (gr. 5-5). 53.00 *(978-1-60853-705-1(6))* Rosen Publishing Group, Inc., The.

Golus, Carrie. Tupac Shakur. 2007. (Illus.). 112p. (J). pap. 9.95 *(978-0-8225-7063-9(7))*; (ENG., (gr. 5-12). lib. bdg. 27.93 *(978-0-8225-6609-0(5))* Lerner Publishing Group.

Gorman, John. Queen Latifah, 1 vol. 2007. (Today's Superstars Ser.). (ENG., Illus.). 32p. (gr. 3-3). lib. bdg. 34.60 *(978-0-8368-7652-9(0),* 0b57b0a8-d1bf-477e-837e-f919da321c09) Stevens, Gareth Publishing LLLP.

Gottfried, Barbara. Drake: Acting & Rapping to the Top, 1 vol. 2019. (Hip-Hop Revolution Ser.). (ENG.). 32p. (gr. 5-5). pap. 11.53 *(978-1-9785-1010-4(1),* c74c6488-1426-4a06-91a8-d074052f957b) Enslow Publishing, LLC.

—Drake: Rapper & Actor, 1 vol. 2019. (Stars of Hip-Hop Ser.). (ENG.). 32p. (gr. 2-2). 26.93 *(978-1-9785-0957-3(X),* cf188fca-45e8-4d04-8ece-92947152336f) Enslow Publishing, LLC.

Grucella, Ethan. Kanye West, 1 vol. 2012. (Hip-Hop Headliners Ser.). (ENG., Illus.). 32p. (J). (gr. 1-1). pap. 11.50 *(978-1-4339-6614-9(X),* 1b4771eb-df50-4f47-bd0f-94994ed69cfc); lib. bdg. 27.93 *(978-1-4339-6612-5(3),* e8054e96-2da2-43ef-a99f-5f6787138 1da) Stevens, Gareth Publishing LLLP.

Gunderson, Jessica. Jay-Z: Hip-Hop Icon. Kinsella, Pat, illus. 2012. (American Graphic Ser.). (ENG.). 32p. (gr. 3-4). pap. 47.70 *(978-1-4296-8475-0(5))*; (J). pap. 8.10 *(978-1-4296-7993-0(X),* 118325) Capstone. (Capstone Pr.).

Hamilton, Toby G. Busta Rhymes. 2009. (Hip Hop (Mason Crest Paperback) Ser.). (Illus.). 64p. (YA). (gr. 4-7). pap. 7.95 *(978-1-4222-0333-0(6))*; (gr. 7-12). lib. bdg. 22.95 *(978-1-4222-0284-5(4))* Mason Crest.

—Dmx. 2009. (Hip Hop (Mason Crest Paperback) Ser.). (Illus.). 64p. (YA). (gr. 4-7). pap. 7.95 *(978-1-4222-0340-8(9))*; (gr. 7-12). lib. bdg. 22.95 *(978-1-4222-0289-0(5))* Mason Crest.

—Fat Joe. 2009. (Hip Hop (Mason Crest Paperback) Ser.). (Illus.). 64p. (YA). (gr. 4-7). pap. 7.95 *(978-1-4222-0344-6(1))*; (gr. 7-12). lib. bdg. 22.95 *(978-1-4222-0291-3(7))* Mason Crest.

—Ice Cube. 2009. (Hip Hop 2 Ser.). (Illus.). 64p. (YA). (gr. 4-7). pap. 7.95 *(978-1-4222-0327-9(1))*; (gr. 7-12). lib. bdg. 22.95 *(978-1-4222-0294-4(1))* Mason Crest.

Harris, Ashley Rae. Tupac Shakur: Multi-Platinum Rapper, 1 vol. 2010. (Lives Cut Short Set 1 Ser.). (ENG.). 112p. (YA). (gr. 6-12). lib. bdg. 41.36 *(978-1-60453-791-8(4),* 11191, Essential Library) ABDO Publishing Co.

Head, Tom & Head, Deirdre. Chance the Rapper: Musician & Activist, 1 vol. 2019. (Stars of Hip-Hop Ser.). (ENG.). 32p. (gr. 2-2). pap. 11.53 *(978-1-9785-1003-6(9),* 12fdb770-3c6d-4a9c-b35e-f008a9022ee9) Enslow Publishing, LLC.

—Kanye West: Conquering Music & Fashion. 2019. (Hip-Hop Revolution Ser.). (ENG.). 32p. (gr. 5-5). 63.18 *(978-1-9785-1025-8(X))* Enslow Publishing, LLC.

—Kanye West: Rap Superstar & Fashion Designer, 1 vol. 2019. (Stars of Hip-Hop Ser.). (ENG.). 32p. (gr. 2-2). 26.93 *(978-1-9785-0962-7(6),* c4716e87-71ce-4f4e-b8a4-b416b8432820) Enslow Publishing, LLC.

Heos, Bridget. Jay-Z. 2009. (Library of Hip-Hop Biographies Ser.). 48p. (gr. 5-5). 53.00 *(978-1-60853-682-5(3))*; (ENG.). (J). lib. bdg. 34.47 *(978-1-4358-5052-1(1),* 783df990-1e43-4ee3-8cbb-76942ebca636); (ENG., Illus.). (J). pap. 12.75 *(978-1-4358-5438-3(1),* 02aaa371-03cc-4081-baae-00a436d0948f) Rosen Publishing Group, Inc., The.

Higgins, Melissa, contrib. by. Future: Rap Rising Star. 2017. (Hip-Hop Artists Ser.). (ENG., Illus.). 112p. (J). (gr. 6-12). lib. bdg. 41.36 *(978-1-5321-1328-4(5),* 27536, Essential Library) ABDO Publishing Co.

Hill, Laban Carrick. When the Beat Was Born: DJ Kool Herc & the Creation of Hip Hop. Taylor, Theodore, III, illus. 2013. (ENG.). 32p. (J). (gr. 1-5). 18.99 *(978-1-59643-540-7(2),* 900061866) Roaring Brook Pr.

Hill, Z. B. Eminem. 2012. (Superstars of Hip-Hop Ser.). 48p. (J). (gr. 3-4). pap. 9.95 *(978-1-4222-2544-8(5))*; (Illus.). 19.95 *(978-1-4222-2518-9(6))* Mason Crest.

—LL Cool J. 2012. (J). *(978-1-4222-2548-6(8))*; (Illus.). 48p. (gr. 3-4). 19.95 *(978-1-4222-2522-6(4))* Mason Crest.

—Mary J. Blige. 2012. (J). pap. *(978-1-4222-2538-7(0))* Mason Crest.

—Notorious B.I.G. 2012. (J). *(978-1-4222-2550-9(X))*; (Illus.). 48p. (gr. 3-4). 19.95 *(978-1-4222-2524-0(0))* Mason Crest.

P Q R

—Sean "Diddy" Combs. 2012. (J). pap. (978-1-4222-2540-0(2)); (Illus.). 48p. (gr. 3-4). 19.95 (978-1-4222-2514-1(3)) Mason Crest.

—Snoop Dogg. 2012. (Superstars of Hip-Hop Ser.). (Illus.). 48p. (J). (gr. 3-4). 19.95 (978-1-4222-2515-8(1)) Mason Crest.

—Tupac. 2012. (J). pap. (978-1-4222-2556-1(9)); (Illus.). 48p. (gr. 3-4). 19.95 (978-1-4222-2530-1(5)) Mason Crest.

—50 Cent. 2012. (J). pap. (978-1-4222-2535-6(6)); (Illus.). 48p. (gr. 3-4). 19.95 (978-1-4222-2509-7(7)) Mason Crest.

Hill, Z. B. & Earl, C. F. Mary J. Blige. 2012. (Superstars of Hip-Hop Ser.). (Illus.). 48p. (J). (gr. 3-4). 19.95 (978-1-4222-2512-7(7)) Mason Crest.

Hip-Hop: The Complete Series, 25 bks., Set. Incl. Ashanti. Waters, Rosa. (YA). (gr. 3-7). lib. bdg. 22.95 (978-1-4222-0111-4(2)); LL Cool J. Baughan, Brian. (YA). (gr. 7-12). lib. bdg. 22.95 (978-1-4222-0121-3(X)); Ludacris. Scott, Celicia. (YA). (gr. 7-12). lib. bdg. 22.95 (978-1-4222-0122-0(8)); Mariah Carey. Scott, Celicia. (YA). (gr. 7-12). lib. bdg. 22.95 (978-1-4222-0114-5(7)); Mary J. Blige. Brown, Terrell. (YA). (gr. 7-12). lib. bdg. 22.95 (978-1-4222-0113-8(9)); Missy Elliot. Lawlor, Michelle. (YA). (gr. 7-12). lib. bdg. 22.95 (978-1-4222-0117-6(1)); Nelly. Hooper, James. (YA). (gr. 7-12). lib. bdg. 22.95 (978-1-4222-0123-7(6)); Pharrell Williams. Brown, Terrell. (YA). (gr. 3-7). lib. bdg. 22.95 (978-1-4222-0125-1(2)); Queen Latifah. Snyder, Gail. (YA). (gr. 7-12). lib. bdg. 22.95 (978-1-4222-0126-8(0)); Reverend Run (Run-D. M. C.) Brown, Terrell. (YA). (gr. 7-12). lib. bdg. 22.95 (978-1-4222-0127-5(9)); Snoop Dogg. Carlson-Berne, Emma. (J). (gr. 7-12). lib. bdg. 22.95 (978-1-4222-0129-9(5)); Usher. Lord, Raymond. (YA). (gr. 7-12). lib. bdg. 22.95 (978-1-4222-0131-2(7)); (Illus.). 64p. 2008. 2007. 573.75 (978-1-4222-0108-4(2)) Mason Crest.

Hip-Hop 2, 25 vols., Set. Incl. Around the World. Walker, Ida. (Illus.). (YA). lib. bdg. 22.95 (978-1-4222-0293-7(3)); Busta Rhymes. Hamilton, Toby G. (Illus.). (YA). lib. bdg. 22.95 (978-1-4222-0284-5(4)); Christina Aguilera. Lemmens, Mary Jo. (YA). lib. bdg. 22.95 (978-1-4222-0285-2(2)); Ciara. Simone, Jacquelyn. (Illus.). (YA). lib. bdg. 22.95 (978-1-4222-0286-9(0)); Cypress Hill. Lemmens, Maryjo. (Illus.). (YA). lib. bdg. 22.95 (978-1-4222-0287-6(9)); Daddy Yankee. Cotts, Nat. (Illus.). (YA). lib. bdg. 22.95 (978-1-4222-0288-3(7)); Dmx. Hamilton, Toby G. (Illus.). (YA). lib. bdg. 22.95 (978-1-4222-0289-0(5)); Don Omar. Cotts, Nat. (Illus.). (YA). lib. bdg. 22.95 (978-1-4222-0290-6(9)); Fat Joe. Hamilton, Toby G. (Illus.). (YA). lib. bdg. 22.95 (978-1-4222-0291-3(7)); Game. Sanna, Lindsey. (Illus.). (YA). lib. bdg. 22.95 (978-1-4222-0292-0(5)); Ice Cube. Hamilton, Toby G. (Illus.). (YA). lib. bdg. 22.95 (978-1-4222-0294-4(1)); Ivy Queen. Etingoff, Kim. (Illus.). (YA). lib. bdg. 22.95 (978-1-4222-0295-1(X)); Jennifer Lopez. Lemmens, Maryjo & Lemmens, Maryjo. (Illus.). (J). lib. bdg. 22.95 (978-1-4222-0296-8(8)); Juelz Santana. Rockworth, Janice. (Illus.). (YA). lib. bdg. 22.95 (978-1-4222-0297-5(6)); Lloyd Banks. Sanna, E. J. (Illus.). (YA). lib. bdg. 22.95 (978-1-4222-0299-9(2)); Nas. Rockworth, Janice. (Illus.). (YA). lib. bdg. 22.95 (978-1-4222-0300-2(X)); Outkast. Simone, Jacquelyn. (Illus.). (YA). lib. bdg. 22.95 (978-1-4222-0301-9(8)); Pitbull. Cotts, Nat. (Illus.). (YA). lib. bdg. 22.95 (978-1-4222-0302-6(6)); T. I. Etingoff, Kim. (Illus.). (YA). lib. bdg. 22.95 (978-1-4222-0303-3(4)); Wu-Tang Clan. Rockworth, Janice. (Illus.). (YA). lib. bdg. 22.95 (978-1-4222-0304-0(2)); Xzibit. Lemmens, Maryjo. (Illus.). (YA). lib. bdg. 22.95 (978-1-4222-0305-7(0)); Young Jeezy. Cotts, Nat. (Illus.). (YA). lib. bdg. 22.95 (978-1-4222-0306-4(9)); Yung Joc. Waters, Rosa. (Illus.). (YA). lib. bdg. 22.95 (978-1-4222-0307-1(7)); (gr. 7-12). 2009. 64p. 2007. Set lib. bdg. 573.75 (978-1-4222-0077-3(9)) Mason Crest.

Hip-Hop World [Capstone Sole Source]. 2010. (Hip-Hop World Ser.). 48p. lib. bdg. 122.60 (978-1-4296-5866-9(5)) Capstone.

Hooper, James. Nelly. 2008. (Hip-Hop Ser.). (Illus.). 64p. (YA). (ENG.). (gr. 3-7). per. 7.95 (978-1-4222-0273-9(9)); (gr. 7-12). lib. bdg. 22.95 (978-1-4222-0123-7(6)) Mason Crest.

Idzikowski, Lisa. Nicki Minaj: Musician & Fashion Superstar, 1 vol. 2019. (Stars of Hip-Hop Ser.). (ENG.). 32p. (gr. 2-2). pap. 11.53 (978-1-9785-1040-1(3), 1cc2d483-9391-4240-8356-93d070551731) Enslow Publishing, LLC.

—Nicki Minaj: Shaking up Fashion & Music, 1 vol. 2019. (Hip-Hop Revolution Ser.). (ENG.). 32p. (gr. 5-5). pap. 11.53 (978-1-9785-1041-8(1), c7f9a22c-e272-4ef9-9b33-5b2127460818) Enslow Publishing, LLC.

Isbell, Hannah. Drake: Actor & Rapper, 1 vol. 2017. (Junior Biographies Ser.). (ENG.). 24p. (gr. 3-4). pap. 10.35 (978-0-7660-8789-7(1), f6e3ba55-e187-4cb7-8fc0-79efcb3fc914); lib. bdg. 24.27 (978-0-7660-8668-5(2), 06a9fcd1-81c6-4829-afd6-9fdedd640c63) Enslow Publishing, LLC.

Jones Donatelli, Jen. Sean Diddy Combs: A Biography of a Music Mogul, 1 vol. 2014. (African-American Icons Ser.). (ENG.). 104p. (gr. 6-7). 30.61 (978-0-7660-4296-4(0), 226b79f0-e0b7-4d93-a0bf-ede173ebfaf7); pap. 13.88 (978-1-4644-0537-2(9), 2821aa20-c891-41bb-a66d-311ab03503c4) Enslow Publishing, LLC.

Kallen, Stuart A. Kendrick Lamar. 2020. (ENG.). 64p. (YA). (gr. 6-12). 41.27 (978-1-68282-779-6(8)) ReferencePoint Pr., Inc.

—Nicki Minaj. 2020. (ENG.). 64p. (J). (gr. 6-12). 41.27 (978-1-68282-781-9(X)) ReferencePoint Pr., Inc.

Kampff, Joseph. Jay-Z: Rapper & Businessman, 1 vol. 2015. (Exceptional African Americans Ser.). (ENG., Illus.). 24p. (gr. 3-3). 24.27 (978-0-7660-7254-1(1), d978db1b-99b4-4f3e-8ddc-15ac82208eab) Enslow Publishing, LLC.

Kelley, K. C. Pharrell Williams. 2018. (Amazing Americans: Pop Music Stars Ser.). (ENG.). 24p. (J). (gr. -1-3). lib. bdg. 26.99 (978-1-68402-457-5(9)) Bearport Publishing Co., Inc.

Kennedy, Robert. Drake, 1 vol. 2012. (Hip-Hop Headliners Ser.). (ENG., Illus.). 32p. (J). (gr. 1-1). pap. 11.50 (978-1-4339-6606-4(9), b59e275d-3085-47cd-b12b-3b50587ef16f); lib. bdg. 27.93 (978-1-4339-6604-0(2), c0fec627-3564-4cd9-a9b4-32db00c4c967) Stevens, Gareth Publishing LLLP.

Kennon, Michou. Queen Latifah, 1 vol. 2011. (Hip-Hop Headliners Ser.). (ENG., Illus.). 32p. (J). (gr. 1-1). lib. bdg. 27.93 (978-1-4339-4808-4(7), 4d494ccf-d9fb-49c7-88a9-dc55103f5049) Stevens, Gareth Publishing LLLP.

Kitts, W. L. Travis Scott. 2020. (ENG.). 64p. (YA). (gr. 6-12). 41.27 (978-1-68282-773-4(9)) ReferencePoint Pr., Inc.

Klepeis, Alicia Z. J. Cole: Chart-Topping Rapper. 2017. (Hip-Hop Artists Ser.). (ENG., Illus.). 112p. (J). (gr. 6-12). lib. bdg. 41.36 (978-1-5321-1326-0(9), 27534, Essential Library) ABDO Publishing Co.

Klepeis, Alicia Z., contrib. by. Kanye West: Music Industry Influencer. 2017. (Hip-Hop Artists Ser.). (ENG., Illus.). 112p. (J). (gr. 6-12). lib. bdg. 41.36 (978-1-5321-1330-7(7), 27538, Essential Library) ABDO Publishing Co.

K'NAAN & Sol, Sol. When I Get Older: The Story Behind Wavin' Flag. Gutierrez, Rudy, illus. 2012. (ENG.). 1p. (J). (gr. 1-4). 17.99 (978-1-77049-302-5(6), Tundra Bks.) Tundra Bks. CAN. Dist: Penguin Random Hse. LLC.

Koestler-Grack, Rachel A. Queen Latifah. 2008. (ENG., Illus.). 104p. (gr. 6-12). per. 12.95 (978-0-7910-9730-4(7), P142884, Facts On File) Infobase Holdings, Inc.

Kowalski, Emma. The Story of Roc-A-Fella Records. 2012. (J). pap. (978-1-4222-2132-7(6)); 64p. (gr. 4). 22.95 (978-1-4222-2119-8(9)) Mason Crest.

Krumenauer, Heidi. Flo-Rida. 2010. (Blue Banner Biography Ser.). (Illus.). 32p. (YA). (gr. 4-7). lib. bdg. 25.70 (978-1-58415-906-3(5)) Mitchell Lane Pubs.

La Bella, Laura. Kanye West. 2009. (Library of Hip-Hop Biographies Ser.). 48p. (gr. 5-5). 53.00 (978-1-60853-685-6(8)); (ENG.). (J). lib. bdg. 34.47 (978-1-4358-5053-8(X), 8371f781-ad3a-467e-b475-6feca9a45e1c); (ENG., Illus.). (J). pap. 12.75 (978-1-4358-5439-0(X), 71b141b2-8604-4a7e-bf09-5a048556ec82) Rosen Publishing Group, Inc., The.

Lajiness, Katie. Drake. 2017. (Big Buddy Pop Biographies Set 2 Ser.). (ENG., Illus.). 32p. (J). (gr. 2-5). lib. bdg. 34.21 (978-1-5321-1060-3(X), 25696, Big Buddy Bks.) ABDO Publishing Co.

—Pharrell Williams, 1 vol. 2015. (Big Buddy Pop Biographies Ser.). (ENG., Illus.). 32p. (J). (gr. 2-5). 34.21 (978-1-68078-063-5(8), 19053, Big Buddy Bks.) ABDO Publishing Co.

Lawlor, Michelle. Missy Elliot. 2008. (Hip-Hop Ser.). (Illus.). 64p. (YA). (ENG.). (gr. 3-7). per. 7.95 (978-1-4222-0268-5(2)); (gr. 7-12). lib. bdg. 22.95 (978-1-4222-0117-6(1)) Mason Crest.

Lawson, Carlie. Lil Wayne. 2019. (Hip-Hop & R&B: Culture, Music & Storytelling Ser.). (Illus.). 80p. (J). (gr. 12). lib. bdg. 34.60 (978-1-4222-4365-7(6)) Mason Crest.

—Nicki Minaj. 2019. (Hip-Hop & R&B: Culture, Music & Storytelling Ser.). (Illus.). 80p. (J). (gr. 12). lib. bdg. 34.60 (978-1-4222-4366-4(4)) Mason Crest.

—Post Malone. 2019. (Hip-Hop & R&B: Culture, Music & Storytelling Ser.). (Illus.). 80p. (J). (gr. 12). lib. bdg. 34.60 (978-1-4222-4367-1(2)) Mason Crest.

—Travis Scott. 2019. (Hip-Hop & R&B: Culture, Music & Storytelling Ser.). (Illus.). 80p. (J). (gr. 12). lib. bdg. 34.60 (978-1-4222-4368-8(0)) Mason Crest.

Lemmens, Mary Jo. Cypress Hill. 2009. (Hip Hop (Mason Crest Paperback) Ser.). (Illus.). 64p. (YA). (gr. 4-7). pap. 7.95 (978-1-4222-0345-3(X)) Mason Crest.

Lemmens, Maryjo. Cypress Hill. 2009. (Hip-Hop 2 Ser.). (Illus.). 64p. (YA). (gr. 7-12). lib. bdg. 22.95 (978-1-4222-0287-6(9)) Mason Crest.

—Xzibit. 2009. (Hip Hop (Mason Crest Paperback) Ser.). (Illus.). 64p. (YA). (gr. 4-7). pap. 7.95 (978-1-4222-0337-8(9)); (gr. 7-12). lib. bdg. 22.95 (978-1-4222-0305-7(0)) Mason Crest.

London, Martha. Kendrick Lamar. 2019. (Influential People Ser.). (ENG., Illus.). 32p. (J). (gr. 4-6). 30.65 (978-1-5435-7136-3(0), 140415) Capstone.

Lord, Raymond. Usher. 2008. (Hip-Hop Ser.). (Illus.). 64p. (YA). (gr. 3-7). per. 7.95 (978-1-4222-0180-0(5)) Mason Crest.

Lucas, Eileen. Jay-Z: Excelling in Music & Business. 2019. (Hip-Hop Revolution Ser.). (ENG.). 32p. (gr. 5-5). 63.18 (978-1-9785-1019-7(5)) Enslow Publishing, LLC.

—Jay-Z: Hitmaker & Business Leader. 2019. (Stars of Hip-Hop Ser.). (ENG.). 32p. (gr. 2-2). 63.18 (978-1-9785-1018-0(7)) Enslow Publishing, LLC.

Maimone, Sofia. Mary J. Blige, 1 vol. 2011. (Hip-Hop Headliners Ser.). (ENG., Illus.). 32p. (J). (gr. 1-1). 27.93 (978-1-4339-4804-6(4), 1391fd88-a999-445e-b3da-c7440c12e297); pap. 11.50 (978-1-4339-4805-3(2), 627330a9-d75d-4bb0-8f75-bf75fd56143a) Stevens, Gareth Publishing LLLP.

Marcovitz, Hal. Dr. Dre. 2008. (Hip-Hop Ser.). (ENG., Illus.). 64p. (YA). (gr. 3-7). per. 7.95 (978-1-4222-0267-8(4)) Mason Crest.

—Notorious B. I. G. 2008. (Hip-Hop Ser.). (ENG., Illus.). 64p. (YA). (gr. 3-7). per. 7.95 (978-1-4222-0274-6(7)) Mason Crest.

Mattern, Joanne. Eminem. 2008. (Hip-Hop Ser.). (Illus.). 64p. (YA). per. 7.95 (978-1-4222-0179-4(1)) Mason Crest.

—Ludacris. 2011. (Blue Banner Biography Ser.). (Illus.). 32p. (YA). (gr. 4-7). lib. bdg. 25.70 (978-1-61228-055-4(2)) Mitchell Lane Pubs.

—Nicki Minaj. 2013. (ENG.). 32p. (gr. 4-8). lib. bdg. 25.70 (978-1-61228-468-2(X)) Mitchell Lane Pubs.

MattyB & Thrasher, Travis. That's a Rap. 2016. (ENG., Illus.). 272p. (gr. 5-9). 19.99 (978-1-5011-3379-4(9), Gallery Bks.) Gallery Bks.

Mitchell, Susan. Will Smith, 1 vol. 2007. (Today's Superstars Ser.). (ENG., Illus.). 32p. (gr. 3-3). lib. bdg. 34.60 (978-0-8368-7653-6(9), f9976550-7f7f-41e2-8dfa-9db5734ecf1f) Stevens, Gareth Publishing LLLP.

Moore Niver, Heather. Chance the Rapper: Hip-Hop Artist, 1 vol. 2018. (Junior Biographies Ser.). (ENG.). 24p. (gr. 3-4). 24.27 (978-0-7660-9715-5(3), c4910d85-7d77-4e64-9da1-8c77c0e1782b) Enslow Publishing, LLC.

Morgan, Joe L. Cardi B, Vol. 11. 2018. (Hip-Hop & R & B: Culture, Music & Storytelling Ser.). (Illus.). 80p. (J). (gr. 7). lib. bdg. 33.27 (978-1-4222-4186-8(6)) Mason Crest.

—Chance the Rapper, Vol. 11. 2018. (Hip-Hop & R & B: Culture, Music & Storytelling Ser.). (Illus.). 80p. (J). (gr. 7). lib. bdg. 33.27 (978-1-4222-4179-0(3)) Mason Crest.

Morris, Rebecca. Hip-Hop Groups. 2017. (Hip-Hop Insider Ser.). (ENG., Illus.). 112p. (J). (gr. 6-12). lib. bdg. 41.36 (978-1-5321-1029-0(4), 25634, Essential Library) ABDO Publishing Co.

Murray, Laura K. Iggy Azalea. 2016. (Big Time Ser.). (ENG.). 24p. (J). (gr. 1-3). (978-1-60818-671-6(7), 20790, Creative Education) Creative Co., The.

Nacerous, Roman P. Jay-Z, 1 vol. 2011. (Hip-Hop Headliners Ser.). (ENG., Illus.). 32p. (J). (gr. 1-1). pap. 11.50 (978-1-4339-4797-1(8), 7645e123-cfdf-4ae8-abdc-6a30e55d3b16); lib. bdg. 27.93 (978-1-4339-4796-4(X), f9241b4b-b8b9-4502-aa8c-eee30418ad44) Stevens, Gareth Publishing LLLP.

O'Neal, Claire. T. I. 2009. (Blue Banner Biography Ser.). (Illus.). 32p. (YA). (gr. 4-7). lib. bdg. 25.70 (978-1-58415-769-4(0)) Mitchell Lane Pubs.

Orr, Tamra B. Ice Cube. 2006. (Blue Banner Biography Ser.). (Illus.). 32p. (YA). (gr. 4-7). lib. bdg. 25.70 (978-1-58415-517-1(5)) Mitchell Lane Pubs.

O'Sorus, Roman. Eminem, 1 vol. 2012. (Hip-Hop Headliners Ser.). (ENG., Illus.). 32p. (J). (gr. 1-1). pap. 11.50 (978-1-4339-6610-1(7), 839afbf4-66a2-4a5e-a9fd-15c7ecd980d7); lib. bdg. 27.93 (978-1-4339-6608-8(5), f65f6ed6-a53e-4a6e-b006-607e664001ae) Stevens, Gareth Publishing LLLP.

Oswald, Vanessa. Jay-Z: Building a Hip-Hop Empire, 1 vol. 2018. (People in the News Ser.). (ENG.). 104p. (gr. 7-7). 41.03 (978-1-5345-6335-3(0), 106ca4de-a619-4c9d-a69a-f4d6be10a467, Lucent Pr.) Greenhaven Publishing LLC.

Parrish, Jacqueline. Beyoncé & Jay-Z, 1 vol. 2019. (Power Couples Ser.). (ENG.). 112p. (gr. 7-7). 38.80 (978-1-5081-8879-7(3), d7529c14-47a0-4568-822c-4b1ad02e73c5) Rosen Publishing Group, Inc., The.

Payment, Simone. Queen Latifah. (Library of Hip-Hop Biographies Ser.). 48p. (gr. 5-5). 2009. 53.00 (978-1-60853-703-7(X)) 2006. (ENG., Illus.). (YA). lib. bdg. 34.47 (978-1-4042-0518-5(7), 2f3431c1-5972-45e8-ad9b-397aad27801e) Rosen Publishing Group, Inc., The.

Pearce Shea, Kevin. Snoop Dogg, 1 vol. 2012. (Hip-Hop Headliners Ser.). (ENG., Illus.). 32p. (J). (gr. 1-1). pap. 11.50 (978-1-4339-6622-4(0), 23911daf-aee6-4113-abaf-2e8fd461daae); lib. bdg. 27.93 (978-1-4339-6620-0(4), 214787af-ef7c-40d9-9175-091578ca14ba) Stevens, Gareth Publishing LLLP.

Peppas, Lynn. Drake. 2011. (ENG.). 32p. (J). pap. (978-0-7787-7611-6(5)) Crabtree Publishing Co.

Pettinella, Amy. Queen Latifah: Award-Winning Actress & Hip-Hop Activist, 1 vol. 2014. (Leading Women Ser.). (ENG.). 112p. (YA). (gr. 7-7). lib. bdg. 41.64 (978-1-62712-984-8(7), 4969797f-1bd3-429a-8376-67f3f717b954) Cavendish Square Publishing LLC.

Rockworth, Janice. Juelz Santana. 2009. (Hip Hop (Mason Crest Paperback) Ser.). (Illus.). 64p. (YA). (gr. 4-7). pap. 7.95 (978-1-4222-0341-5(7)); (gr. 7-12). lib. bdg. 22.95 (978-1-4222-0297-5(6)) Mason Crest.

—Nas. 2009. (Hip-Hop 2 Ser.). (Illus.). 64p. (YA). (gr. 7-12). lib. bdg. 22.95 (978-1-4222-0300-2(X)) Mason Crest.

—Wu-Tang Clan. 2009. (Hip-Hop Ser.). (Illus.). 64p. (YA). (gr. 4-7). pap. 7.95 (978-1-4222-0335-4(2)); (gr. 7-12). lib. bdg. 22.95 (978-1-4222-0304-0(2)) Mason Crest.

Roza, Greg. OutKast. 2009. (Library of Hip-Hop Biographies Ser.). 48p. (gr. 5-5). 53.00 (978-1-60853-700-6(5)); (ENG.). (J). lib. bdg. 34.47 (978-1-4358-5057-6(2), 3f0dcd44-7c99-412d-9e78-002f382378fb); (ENG., Illus.). (J). pap. 12.75 (978-1-4358-5443-7(8), 33e3098a-7caa-4e01-af54-a4d5e75ff00d) Rosen Publishing Group, Inc., The.

Saddleback Educational Publishing Staff. Chris Brown. 2013. (Hip-Hop Biographies (Saddleback Publishing) Ser.). (YA). lib. bdg. 23.25 (978-0-606-31482-4(2)) Turtleback.

—Drake. 2013. (Hip-Hop Biographies (Saddleback Publishing) Ser.). (YA). lib. bdg. 23.25 (978-0-606-31483-1(0)) Turtleback.

—Kanye West. 2013. (Hip-Hop Biographies (Saddleback Publishing) Ser.). (YA). lib. bdg. 23.25 (978-0-606-31485-5(7)) Turtleback.

—Lil Wayne. 2013. (Hip-Hop Biographies (Saddleback Publishing) Ser.). (YA). lib. bdg. 23.25 (978-0-606-31486-2(5)) Turtleback.

—50 Cent. 2013. (Hip-Hop Biographies (Saddleback Publishing) Ser.). (YA). lib. bdg. 23.25 (978-0-606-31481-7(4)) Turtleback.

Sanna, E. J. Lloyd Banks. 2009. (Hip Hop (Mason Crest Paperback) Ser.). (Illus.). 64p. (YA). (gr. 4-7). pap. 7.95 (978-1-4222-0336-1(0)); (gr. 7-12). lib. bdg. 22.95 (978-1-4222-0299-9(2)) Mason Crest.

Sanna, Lindsey. The Game. 2009. (Hip-Hop Ser.). (Illus.). 64p. (YA). (gr. 3-7). pap. 7.95 (978-1-4222-0329-3(8)); (gr. 7-12). lib. bdg. 22.95 (978-1-4222-0292-0(5)) Mason Crest.

Schuman, Michael A. Will Smith: A Biography of a Rapper Turned Movie Star, 1 vol. 2013. (African-American Icons Ser.). (ENG.). 104p. (gr. 6-7). pap. 13.88 (978-1-59845-397-3(1), 3f6c7595-e4ed-4a4a-a32b-02a2baff1f66) Enslow Publishing, LLC.

—Will Smith a Biography of a Rapper Turned Movie Star, 1 vol. 2013. (African-American Icons Ser.). (ENG.). 104p. (gr. 6-7). E-Book 30.60 (978-1-4646-1148-3(3), 67648730-7c2a-4b02-99d4-2d6553274f9f) Enslow Publishing, LLC.

Schweitzer, Karen. Soulja Boy Tell 'Em. (Role Model Entertainers Ser.). (Illus.). 64p. (YA). 2010. (gr. 7-12). 22.95 (978-1-4222-0509-9(6)) 2007. pap. 9.95 (978-1-4222-0796-3(X)) Mason Crest.

Scott, Celicia. Ludacris. 2008. (Hip-Hop Ser.). (Illus.). 64p. (YA). (ENG.). (gr. 3-7). per. 7.95 (978-1-4222-0272-2(0)); (gr. 7-12). lib. bdg. 22.95 (978-1-4222-0122-0(8)) Mason Crest.

Shea, Mary Molly. The Black Eyed Peas, 1 vol. 2011. (Hip-Hop Headliners Ser.). (ENG., Illus.). 32p. (J). (gr. 1-1). pap. 11.50 (978-1-4339-4793-3(5), cb874c3c-03ff-49b2-86f5-8e5d84f8c28b); lib. bdg. 27.93 (978-1-4339-4792-6(7), 8ebc06b9-d8d8-4896-8c12-f84cb83b4f34) Stevens, Gareth Publishing LLLP.

Shea, Therese M. Kendrick Lamar: Becoming the Voice of Compton, 1 vol. 2019. (Hip-Hop Revolution Ser.). (ENG.). 32p. (gr. 5-5). 26.93 (978-1-9785-0967-2(7), f5671bff-e46e-4664-b947-6640ac43c24f) Enslow Publishing, LLC.

—Kendrick Lamar: Storyteller of Compton, 1 vol. 2019. (Stars of Hip-Hop Ser.). (ENG.). 32p. (gr. 2-2). 26.93 (978-1-9785-0959-7(6), 84ac844e-1a80-4e63-8bff-20e876fdf69e) Enslow Publishing, LLC.

Sheen, Barbara. Kanye West, 1 vol. 2009. (People in the News Ser.). (ENG.). 96p. (gr. 7-7). 41.03 (978-1-4205-0159-9(3), 16d187aa-131d-4a48-85ab-69a51aad1974, Lucent Pr.) Greenhaven Publishing LLC.

Simone, Jacquelyn. Outkast. 2009. (Hip Hop (Mason Crest Paperback) Ser.). (Illus.). 64p. (YA). (gr. 4-7). pap. 7.95 (978-1-4222-0328-6(X)); (gr. 7-12). lib. bdg. 22.95 (978-1-4222-0301-9(8)) Mason Crest.

Simons, Rae. Kanye West. 2008. (Hip-Hop Ser.). (ENG., Illus.). 64p. (YA). (gr. 3-7). per. 7.95 (978-1-4222-0281-4(X)) Mason Crest.

Snellgrove, Chris. Drake, Vol. 11. 2018. (Hip-Hop & R & B: Culture, Music & Storytelling Ser.). (Illus.). 80p. (J). (gr. 7). lib. bdg. 33.27 (978-1-4222-4180-6(7)) Mason Crest.

Snyder, Gail. Queen Latifah. 2008. (Hip-Hop Ser.). (Illus.). 64p. (YA). (ENG.). (gr. 3-7). per. 7.95 (978-1-4222-0276-0(3)); (gr. 7-12). lib. bdg. 22.95 (978-1-4222-0126-8(0)) Mason Crest.

Steffens, Bradley. Drake. 2020. (ENG.). 64p. (YA). (gr. 6-12). 41.27 (978-1-68282-771-0(2)) ReferencePoint Pr., Inc.

—J. Cole. 2020. (ENG.). 64p. (J). (gr. 6-12). 41.27 (978-1-68282-777-2(1)) ReferencePoint Pr., Inc.

Torres, Jennifer. Eve. 2004. (Blue Banner Biography Ser.). (Illus.). 32p. (J). (gr. 3-8). lib. bdg. 25.70 (978-1-58415-317-7(2)) Mitchell Lane Pubs.

—Mary J. Blige. 2007. (Blue Banner Biography Ser.). (Illus.). 32p. (YA). (gr. 4-7). lib. bdg. 25.70 (978-1-58415-612-3(0)) Mitchell Lane Pubs.

Torres, John A. Jay-Z: Hip-Hop Mogul, 1 vol. 2014. (Hip-Hop Moguls Ser.). (ENG., Illus.). 48p. (gr. 4-6). 18.61 (978-1-62285-191-1(9), 89242e04-de5f-4859-b2f5-39cc87920170) Enslow Publishing, LLC.

—Lil Wayne. 2009. (Blue Banner Biography Ser.). (Illus.). 32p. (YA). (gr. 4-7). lib. bdg. 25.70 (978-1-58415-768-7(2)) Mitchell Lane Pubs.

—Ludacris: Hip-Hop Mogul, 1 vol. 2014. (Hip-Hop Moguls Ser.). (ENG., Illus.). 48p. (gr. 4-6). 18.61 (978-1-62285-196-6(X), dd9c13c5-b5ff-464a-9b6f-d9aefdfb8152) Enslow Publishing, LLC.

—Timbaland. 2008. (Blue Banner Biography Ser.). (Illus.). 32p. (YA). (gr. 4-7). lib. bdg. 25.70 (978-1-58415-671-0(6)) Mitchell Lane Pubs.

Torres, John Albert. P. Diddy. 2004. (Blue Banner Biography Ser.). (Illus.). 32p. (J). (gr. 3-8). lib. bdg. 25.70 (978-1-58415-315-3(6)) Mitchell Lane Pubs.

Tracy, Kathleen. Chris Brown. 2007. (Blue Banner Biography Ser.). (Illus.). 32p. (YA). (gr. 4-7). lib. bdg. 25.70 (978-1-58415-617-8(1)) Mitchell Lane Pubs.

—Queen Latifah. 2004. (Blue Banner Biography Ser.). (Illus.). 32p. (J). (gr. 3-8). lib. bdg. 25.70 (978-1-58415-313-9(X)) Mitchell Lane Pubs.

Traugh, Susan M. Sean Combs, 1 vol. 2010. (People in the News Ser.). (ENG., Illus.). 104p. (gr. 7-7). 41.03 (978-1-4205-0237-4(9), 1598dc89-1611-4398-8f6c-d1702cd2b68e, Lucent Pr.) Greenhaven Publishing LLC.

Uhl, Xina M. Pharrell Williams: Music Industry Star. 2017. (Superstar Stories Ser.). (ENG.). 24p. (J). (gr. 3-6). lib. bdg. 32.79 (978-1-5038-1995-5(7), 211871) Child's World, Inc, The.

Uschan, Michael V. Tupac Shakur. 2007. (Illus.). 104p. (J). (978-7-81590-189-0(1), Lucent Bks.) Cengage Gale.

—Tupac Shakur, 1 vol. 2007. (People in the News Ser.). (ENG., Illus.). 104p. (gr. 7-7). lib. bdg. 41.03 (978-1-59018-987-0(6), c28998a7-9438-4411-b444-a9decab0fd94, Lucent Pr.) Greenhaven Publishing LLC.

—Will Smith, 1 vol. 2009. (People in the News Ser.). (ENG., Illus.). 104p. (gr. 7-7). lib. bdg. 41.03 (978-1-4205-0130-8(5), 7ed2c61a-2cbb-4fb8-8fb0-0a5e83432f89, Lucent Pr.) Greenhaven Publishing LLC.

—50 Cent, 1 vol. 2007. (People in the News Ser.). (ENG., Illus.). 104p. (gr. 7-7). lib. bdg. 41.03 (978-1-4205-0011-0(2), 9216b9a9-cdc8-44b9-9151-1579177a9ca5, Lucent Pr.) Greenhaven Publishing LLC.

Vetere, Lori. Pharrell, Vol. 11. 2018. (Hip-Hop & R & B: Culture, Music & Storytelling Ser.). (Illus.). 80p. (J). (gr. 7). lib. bdg. 33.27 (978-1-4222-4183-7(1)) Mason Crest.

Waters, Rosa. Yung Joc. 2009. (Hip-Hop 2 Ser.). (Illus.). 64p. (YA). (gr. 7-12). lib. bdg. 22.95 (978-1-4222-0307-1(7)) Mason Crest.

Weicker, Gretchen. Kanye West: Hip-Hop Star, 1 vol. 2009. (Hot Celebrity Biographies Ser.). (ENG., Illus.). 48p. (gr. 5-7). pap. 11.53 (978-0-7660-3629-1(4), 01c2395e-3553-4634-ae21-4171a6d01be7); lib. bdg. 27.93 (978-0-7660-3214-9(0), 6d315659-3931-4a4f-8ca4-e9aa065bb613) Enslow Publishing, LLC.

Wells, Peggy Sue. Kanye West. 2008. (Blue Banner Biography Ser.). (Illus.). 32p. (YA). (gr. 4-7). lib. bdg. 25.70 (978-1-58415-677-2(5)) Mitchell Lane Pubs.

—Soulja Boy Tell 'Em. 2008. (Blue Banner Biography Ser.). (Illus.). 32p. (YA). (gr. 4-7). lib. bdg. 25.70 (978-1-58415-676-5(7)) Mitchell Lane Pubs.

Will Smith. 2nd rev. ed. 2010. (ENG., illus.). 104p. (gr. 6-12). 35.00 *(978-1-60413-713-2(4)*, P179341, Facts On File) Infobase Holdings, Inc.

Wittmann, Kelly. Sean Diddy Combs. 2008. (Hip-Hop Ser.). (ENG., illus.). 64p. (YA). (gr. 3-7). per. 7.95 *(978-1-4222-0266-1(6))* Mason Crest.

Wolny, Philip. Ludacris. 2009. (Library of Hip-Hop Biographies Ser.). 48p. (gr. 5-5). 53.00 *(978-1-60853-691-7(2))*; (ENG.). (J). lib. bdg. 34.47 *(978-1-4358-5054-5(8)*, e142388d-e45b-40d0-9ab9-6e833312cfd1); (ENG., illus.). (J). pap. 12.75 *(978-1-4358-5440-6(3)*, 4fc0a51f-593b-463e-8d6d-99beb7599b68) Rosen Publishing Group, Inc., The.

—Sean Combs. (Library of Hip-Hop Biographies Ser.). 48p. (gr. 5-5). 2009. 53.00 *(978-1-60853-706-8(4))* 2006. (ENG., illus.). (YA). lib. bdg. 34.47 *(978-1-4042-0516-1(0)*, fa25e8d4-eb10-44a9-aa56-1b483136d942) Rosen Publishing Group, Inc., The.

RAPE

Anderson, Laurie Halse. Shout. 2019. (ENG.). 304p. (YA). (gr. 9). 18.99 *(978-0-670-01210-7(6)*, Viking Books for Young Readers) Penguin Young Readers Group.

Denton, Michelle. Rape Culture: How Can We End It?, 1 vol. 2017. (Hot Topics Ser.). (ENG.). 104p. (YA). (gr. 7-7). pap. 20.99 *(978-1-5345-6292-9(3)*, b808f388-fa77-4bd2-89bb-e17a27d47ca7); lib. bdg. 41.03 *(978-1-5345-6207-3(9)*, 51b2a8d2-3058-4886-9240-3787614e5f98) Greenhaven Publishing LLC. (Lucent Pr.).

Erickson, Marty. The #MeToo Movement. 2019. (In Focus Ser.). (ENG.). 80p. (J). (gr. 6-12). 41.27 *(978-1-68282-717-8(8)*, BrightPoint Pr.) ReferencePoint Pr., Inc.

Gunton, Sharon, ed. Date & Acquaintance Rape, 1 vol. 2008. (Social Issues Firsthand Ser.). (ENG., illus.). 112p. (gr. 10-12). lib. bdg. 35.38 *(978-0-7377-4250-3(X)*, 695942a6-7819-4443-ab6f-ba598981b0de, Greenhaven Publishing) Greenhaven Publishing LLC.

Harris, Duchess & Head, Tom. The Scottsboro Boys. 2018. (Freedom's Promise Ser.). (ENG., illus.). 48p. (J). (gr. 4-8). lib. bdg. 35.64 *(978-1-5321-1775-6(2)*, 30838) ABDO Publishing Co.

Harris, Duchess & Morris, Rebecca. The Silence Breakers & the #MeToo Movement. 2018. (Special Reports). (ENG., illus.). 112p. (J). (gr. 6-12). lib. bdg. 41.36 *(978-1-5321-1683-4(7)*, 30618, Essential Library) ABDO Publishing Co.

Henneberg, Susan. I Have Been Raped, Now What?, 1 vol. 2015. (Teen Life 411 Ser.). (ENG., illus.). 112p. (J). (gr. 7-7). 38.80 *(978-1-4994-6142-8(9)*, 73634e03-a8d9-44c9-badd-08b868f54f48, Rosen Young Adult) Rosen Publishing Group, Inc., The.

Keyser, Amber J. No More Excuses: Dismantling Rape Culture. 2019. (ENG., illus.). 144p. (YA). (gr. 8-12). 37.32 *(978-1-5415-4020-0(4)*, 0f66f534-2e67-4337-b1be-8f33c7f62b6a, Twenty-First Century Bks.) Lerner Publishing Group.

Landau, Elaine. Date Violence. 2005. (Life Balance Ser.). (ENG., illus.). 80p. (J). (gr. 5-8). pap. 6.95 *(978-0-531-16613-0(9)*, Watts, Franklin) Scholastic Library Publishing.

Mooney, Carla. Everything You Need to Know about Sexual Consent, 1 vol. 2017. (Need to Know Library). (ENG., illus.). 64p. (J). (gr. 5-6). 36.13 *(978-1-5081-7412-7(1)*, 5a1239c5-59f4-48d8-bad2-aa25d6b19c20); pap. 13.95 *(978-1-5081-7410-3(5)*, c6007614-5526-4901-8454-9f172a11b561) Rosen Publishing Group, Inc., The. (Rosen Young Adult).

Orr, Tamra. Frequently Asked Questions about Date Rape. (FAQ: Teen Life Ser.). 64p. (gr. 5-6). 2009. 58.50 *(978-1-61512-572-2(8))* 2007. (ENG., illus.). (YA). lib. bdg. 37.13 *(978-1-4042-1972-4(2)*, c0b5d39b-863e-4013-afa1-b3c0a9698cde) Rosen Publishing Group, Inc., The.

Piehl, Norah, ed. Date Rape, 1 vol. 2012. (Issues That Concern You Ser.). (ENG., illus.). 112p. (gr. 7-10). lib. bdg. 43.63 *(978-0-7377-6287-7(X)*, 86d4005b-99af-4f28-bd91-5983f6c8a90c, Greenhaven Publishing) Greenhaven Publishing LLC.

Rissman, Rebecca. Rape Culture & Sexual Violence. 2017. (Special Reports Set 3 Ser.). (ENG., illus.). 112p. (J). (gr. 6-12). lib. bdg. 41.36 *(978-1-5321-1335-2(8)*, 27543, Essential Library) ABDO Publishing Co.

Schmermund, Elizabeth, ed. Campus Sexual Violence, 1 vol. 2016. (At Issue Ser.). (ENG.). 184p. (YA). (gr. 10-12). pap. 28.80 *(978-1-5345-0037-2(5)*, 48560665-0ddd-4234-bbcb-8fe28e6cf3cb); lib. bdg. 41.03 *(978-1-5345-0018-1(9)*, c91fb451-af3c-4f31-a2b1-9dca807c2709) Greenhaven Publishing LLC. (Greenhaven Publishing).

Uschan, Michael V. The Scottsboro Case, 1 vol. 2004. (Landmark Events in American History Ser.). (ENG., illus.). 48p. (gr. 5-8). lib. bdg. 33.67 *(978-0-8368-5388-9(1)*, 3e142ddb-25bb-4aad-a1f6-2ab370d96d45, Gareth Stevens Secondary Library) Stevens, Gareth Publishing LLLP.

Wilkins, Jessica. Date Rape. 2010. (Straight Talk about... Ser.). (ENG.). 48p. (J). (gr. 7-10). pap. *(978-0-7787-2135-2(3))*; lib. bdg. *(978-0-7787-2128-4(0))* Crabtree Publishing Co.

RAPE—FICTION

Almond, David. The Tightrope Walkers. 2016. (ENG.). 336p. (YA). (gr. 9). pap. 9.99 *(978-0-7636-9104-2(6))* Candlewick Pr.

Anderson, Laurie Halse. Speak. 2011. (ENG.). 224p. (YA). (gr. 7-12). pap. 10.99 *(978-0-312-67439-7(2)*, 900072854) Square Fish.

—Speak: the Graphic Novel. Carroll, Emily, illus. 2nd ed. 2018. (ENG.). 384p. (YA). 21.99 *(978-0-374-30028-9(3)*, 900129381, Farrar, Straus & Giroux (BYR)) Farrar, Straus & Giroux.

Benwell, Fox. Kaleidoscope Song. 2018. (ENG.). 416p. (YA). (gr. 9). pap. 12.99 *(978-1-4814-7768-0(4))* Simon & Schuster.

—Kaleidoscope Song. 2017. (ENG.). 416p. (YA). (gr. 9). 17.99 *(978-1-4814-7767-3(6)*, Simon & Schuster Bks. For Young Readers) Simon & Schuster Bks. For Young Readers.

Blake, Ashley Herring. Girl Made of Stars. (ENG.). 304p. (YA). (gr. 9). 2019. pap. 9.99 *(978-0-358-10822-1(5)*, 1748885) 2018. 17.99 *(978-1-328-77823-9(1)*, 1681853) HarperCollins Pubs. (Clarion Bks.).

Blakemore, Megan Frazer. Good & Gone. 2017. (ENG.). 304p. (YA). (gr. 8). 17.99 *(978-0-06-234842-5(6)*, HarperTeen) HarperCollins Pubs.

Blount, Patty. Someone I Used to Know. 2018. (ENG.). 384p. (YA). (gr. 8-12). pap. 10.99 *(978-1-4926-3281-8(3))* Sourcebooks, Inc.

Buckley, Kate. Choices: A Novel. 2009. 208p. (J). pap. 14.95 *(978-1-935359-12-8(6))* Bk. Pubs. Network.

Butcher, Kristin. The Trouble with Liberty, 1 vol. 2003. (Orca Soundings Ser.). (ENG.). 128p. (YA). (gr. 8-12). pap. 9.95 *(978-1-55143-274-8(9))* Orca Bk. Pubs. USA.

Capin, Hannah. Foul Is Fair: A Novel. 2020. (ENG.). 336p. (YA). 18.99 *(978-1-250-23954-9(0)*, 900211181, Wednesday Bks.) St. Martin's Pr.

Carter, T. E. I Stop Somewhere. 2019. (ENG.). 336p. (YA). pap. 17.99 *(978-1-250-29459-3(2)*, 900174482) Square Fish.

Crockett, Mary. How She Died, How I Lived. 2019. (ENG.). 416p. (YA). (gr. 9-17). pap. 10.99 *(978-0-316-52382-0(8))* Little, Brown Bks. for Young Readers.

Desir, C. Fault Line. 2013. (ENG.). 240p. (YA). (gr. 10). 16.99 *(978-1-4424-6072-0(5)*, Simon Pulse) Simon Pulse.

Downham, Jenny. You Against Me. 2012. (ENG.). 416p. (YA). (gr. 9). pap. 9.99 *(978-0-385-75266-4(0)*, Ember) Random Hse. Children's Bks.

Draper, Sharon M. Darkness Before Dawn. 2014. (Hazelwood High Trilogy Ser. 3 Ser.). (ENG.). 288p. (YA). (gr. k-k). 11.24 *(978-1-63245-162-0(X))* Lectorum Pubns., Inc.

—Darkness Before Dawn. 2013. (Hazelwood High Trilogy Ser.: 3). (ENG., illus.). 256p. (YA). (gr. 7). pap. 10.99 *(978-1-4424-8915-8(4)*, Atheneum Bks. for Young Readers) Simon & Schuster Children's Publishing.

—Darkness Before Dawn. 2013. (Hazelwood High Trilogy Ser.: 3). lib. bdg. 20.85 *(978-0-606-32334-5(1))* Turtleback.

Geras, Adèle & Geras, Adèle. Watching the Roses: The Egerton Hall Novels, Volume Two, Vol. 2. 2005. (ENG.). 192p. (YA). (gr. 7-12). pap. 11.95 *(978-0-15-205531-8(2)*, 1196634, Clarion Bks.) HarperCollins Pubs.

Gray, Mila. Run Away with Me. (ENG.). 368p. (YA). (gr. 11). 2018. pap. 12.99 *(978-1-4814-9097-9(4))* 2017. (Illus.). 17.99 *(978-1-4814-9096-2(6))* Simon Pulse. (Simon Pulse).

Halse Anderson, Laurie. Speak. 2010. (CHI.). (YA). (gr. 7-12). pap. *(978-986-6488-66-5(7))* Ecus Publishing Hse.

—Speak. 2006. 24.50 *(978-0-8446-7292-2(0))* Smith, Peter Pub., Inc.

Hamilton, Elizabeth L. Date with Responsibility. 2004. (Character-in-Action Ser.: No. 2). (Illus.). 384p. (YA). per. 19.95 *(978-0-9713749-0-4(2)*, Character-in-Action) Quiet Impact, Inc.

Hartzler, Aaron. What We Saw. 2015. 336p. (YA). (ENG.). (gr. 9). 17.99 *(978-0-06-233874-7(9)*, HarperTeen); *(978-0-06-243062-5(9))* HarperCollins Pubs.

Kiely, Brendan. Tradition. 2018. (ENG., illus.). 352p. (YA). (gr. 9). 18.99 *(978-1-4814-8034-5(0)*, McElderry, Margaret K. Bks.) McElderry, Margaret K. Bks.

Klein, Alina. Rape Girl. 2012. 132p. (YA). 18.95 *(978-1-60898-123-6(1))*; pap. 9.95 *(978-1-60898-124-3(X))* namelos llc.

Konigsberg, Bill. The Music of What Happens, 1 vol. 2019. (ENG.). 352p. (YA). (gr. 9-9). 17.99 *(978-1-338-21550-2(7)*, Levine, Arthur A. Bks.) Scholastic, Inc.

Krossing, Karen. Punch Like a Girl, 1 vol. 2015. (ENG.). 240p. (YA). (gr. 8-12). pap. 12.95 *(978-1-4598-0828-7(2))* Orca Bk. Pubs. USA.

Lipsyte, Robert. Raiders Night. (YA). (gr. 9-12). 2007. (ENG.). 256p. pap. 10.99 *(978-0-06-059948-5(0))* 2006. 232p. 15.99 *(978-0-06-059946-1(4))* 2006. 232p. lib. bdg. 16.89 *(978-0-06-059947-8(2))* HarperCollins Pubs. (HarperTeen).

Lynch, Chris. Inexcusable. 2005. (ENG., illus.). 176p. (YA). (gr. 7-18). 19.99 *(978-0-689-84789-9(0)*, Atheneum Bks. for Young Readers) Simon & Schuster Children's Publishing.

—Inexcusable: 10th Anniversary Edition. 10th ed. 2015. (ENG., illus.). 192p. (YA). (gr. 8). pap. 11.99 *(978-1-4814-3202-3(8)*, Simon & Schuster Bks. For Young Readers) Simon & Schuster Bks. For Young Readers.

—Irreversible. 2016. (ENG., illus.). 352p. (YA). (gr. 7). 17.99 *(978-1-4814-2985-6(X)*, Simon & Schuster Bks. For Young Readers) Simon & Schuster Bks. For Young Readers.

Maggi, Nicole. What They Don't Know. 2018. 368p. (YA). (gr. 8-12). pap. 10.99 *(978-1-4926-7265-4(3))* Sourcebooks, Inc.

Mather, Janice Lynn. Learning to Breathe. 2018. (ENG., illus.). 336p. (YA). (gr. 9). 19.99 *(978-1-5344-0601-8(8)*, Simon & Schuster Bks. For Young Readers) Simon & Schuster Bks. For Young Readers.

McCullough, Joy. Blood Water Paint. 2019. 320p. (YA). (gr. 9). pap. 11.99 *(978-0-7352-3213-6(X)*, Penguin Books) Penguin Young Readers Group.

McGhee, Alison. What I Leave Behind. (ENG.). (YA). (gr. 9). 2019. 224p. pap. 11.99 *(978-1-4814-7657-7(2))* 2018. (Illus.). 208p. 18.99 *(978-1-4814-7656-0(4))* Simon & Schuster Children's Publishing. (Atheneum Bks. for Young Readers).

Myers, Jason. Dead End. 2011. (ENG.). 384p. (YA). (gr. 10-18). pap. 9.99 *(978-1-4424-1430-3(8)*, Simon Pulse) Simon Pulse.

Padian, Maria. Wrecked. 2017. (ENG.). 368p. (YA). (gr. 9-12). pap. 12.99 *(978-1-61620-745-8(0)*, 73745) Algonquin Young Readers.

Reed, Amy. Nowhere Girls. 2017. (ENG.). (YA). (gr. 9). pap. 12.99 *(978-1-5344-1555-3(6))* Simon & Schuster.

—The Nowhere Girls. (ENG., illus.). (YA). (gr. 9). 2019. 432p. pap. 12.99 *(978-1-4814-8174-8(6))* 2017. 416p. 19.99 *(978-1-4814-8173-1(8))* Simon Pulse. (Simon Pulse).

Scoppettone, Sandra. Happy Endings Are All Alike. 2014. (ENG., illus.). 184p. (gr. 6). pap. 12.95 *(978-1-939601-04-9(5))* Ig Publishing, Inc.

Smith, Amber. The Way I Used to Be. (Way I Used to Be Ser.). (ENG.). 384p. (YA). (gr. 9). 2017. pap. 12.99 *(978-1-4814-4936-6(2))* 2016. (Illus.). 19.99 *(978-1-4814-4935-9(4))* McElderry, Margaret K. Bks. (McElderry, Margaret K. Bks.).

Summers, Courtney. All the Rage: A Novel. 2016. (ENG.). 336p. (YA). pap. 12.99 *(978-1-250-06915-3(7)*, 900096244, St. Martin's Griffin) St. Martin's Pr.

Sutton, Michelle. It's Not about Me. 2012. (Second Glances Ser.). (ENG.). 252p. pap. 12.99 *(978-0-9838836-9-2(6))* Sword of the Spirit Publishing.

Thrace, Mischa. My Whole Truth. 2018. (ENG.). 320p. (YA). (gr. 9-12). pap. 11.99 *(978-1-63583-024-8(9)*, 1635830249, Flux) North Star Editions.

Walton, K. M. Empty. 2013. (ENG., illus.). 272p. (YA). (gr. 9). pap. 12.99 *(978-1-4424-5358-6(3)*, Simon Pulse) Simon Pulse.

Yates, Marie. Frankie & Me: The Third Book in the Dani Moore Trilogy. 2018. (ENG., illus.). 192p. (YA). (gr. 8-17). pap. 11.95 *(978-1-78535-772-5(7)*, Lodestone Bks.) Hunt, John Publishing Ltd. GBR. Dist: National Bk. Network.

—Reggie & Me: The First Book in the Dani Moore Trilogy. 2014. (ENG., illus.). 183p. (J). (gr. -1-12). pap. 11.95 *(978-1-78279-723-4(8)*, Lodestone Bks.) Hunt, John Publishing Ltd. GBR. Dist: National Bk. Network.

—Sammy & Me: The Second Book in the Dani Moore Trilogy. 2017. (ENG., illus.). 184p. (YA). (gr. 8-17). pap. 11.95 *(978-1-78535-502-8(3)*, O Bks.) Hunt, John Publishing Ltd. GBR. Dist: National Bk. Network.

York, Kelley. Modern Monsters. 2015. (Entangled Teen Ser.). (ENG.). 352p. (YA). pap. 9.99 *(978-1-63375-002-9(7)*, 9781633750029) Entangled Publishing, LLC.

RAPHAEL, 1483-1520

Mofford, Juliet. Raphael. 2009. (Art Profiles for Kids Ser.). (Illus.). 48p. (YA). (gr. 4-7). lib. bdg. 29.95 *(978-1-58415-745-8(3))* Mitchell Lane Pubs.

RATS

Albright, Rosie. Detection Rats, 1 vol. 2012. (Animal Detectives Ser.). (ENG., illus.). 24p. (J). (gr. 1-1). pap. 9.25 *(978-1-4488-6256-6(6)*, b1be3fad-2883-4d9f-960b-a5ffbd0cebd9); lib. bdg. 26.27 *(978-1-4488-6149-1(7)*, 535d2172-83cc-4c78-86d9-beeaf443c003) Rosen Publishing Group, Inc., The. (PowerKids Pr.).

—Detection Rats: Ratas Detectoras, 1 vol. Alamán, Eduardo, tr. 2012. (Animal Detectives / Detectives Del Reino Animal Ser.). (SPA & ENG.). 24p. (J). (gr. 1-1). lib. bdg. 26.27 *(978-1-4488-6715-8(0)*, c61ffbf9-0646-4efd-94f6-1cf32833eb06) Rosen Publishing Group, Inc., The.

Armentrout, David & Armentrout, Patricia. The Facts on Rats. 2010. (Let's Talk about Pets Ser.). (Illus.). 24p. (J). (gr. k-4). 28.50 *(978-1-61590-247-7(3))* Rourke Educational Media.

Barrett, Tracy. Rats, 1 vol. 2012. (Animals, Animals Ser.). (ENG., illus.). 48p. (gr. 5-5). 32.64 *(978-0-7614-4877-8(2)*, bb37f821-f267-4927-bebc-6729f9f2c816) Cavendish Square Publishing LLC.

Bergeron, Alain M. & Quintin, Michel. Do You Know Rats?, 1 vol. Sampar, illus. 2013. (Do You Know? Ser.). (ENG.). 64p. (J). (gr. 2-4). pap. 9.95 *(978-1-55455-319-8(9)*, 1ade2265-bbce-4f07-9143-eb7cbdfd70d2) Trifolium Bks., Inc. CAN. Dist: Firefly Bks., Ltd.

Berne, Emma Carlson. Rats: Biting Through Concrete! 2013. (Animal Superpowers Ser.). (Illus.). 24p. (J). (gr. k-5). pap. 49.50 *(978-1-4777-0846-0(4))*; (ENG., (gr. 2-3). lib. bdg. 26.27 *(978-1-4777-0752-4(2)*, 5bf281d0-fe11-4f4f-bea8-6fa45ad62e4d) Rosen Publishing Group, Inc., The. (PowerKids Pr.).

Betances, Roberto. Rats Eat Toenails!, 1 vol. 2017. (Nature's Grossest Ser.). (ENG.). 24p. (J). (gr. 1-2). pap. 9.15 *(978-1-5382-0953-0(5)*, 2d8a42ae-f5ff-4eda-967d-99e03baeac1a) Stevens, Gareth Publishing LLLP.

Carr, Aaron. Rat. 2014. (J). *(978-1-4896-3102-2(X))* Weigl Pubs., Inc.

Chancellor, Deborah. Rats. 2009. (Extreme Pets Ser.). (YA). (gr. 4-7). 28.50 *(978-1-59920-236-5(0))* Black Rabbit Bks.

Colson, Rob. The Pet to Get: Rat. 2017. (Pet to Get Ser.). (ENG., illus.). 32p. (J). (gr. 4-6). pap. 12.99 *(978-0-7502-8929-0(5)*, Wayland) Hachette Children's Group GBR. Dist: Hachette Bk. Group.

Coppendale, Jean. Rats. 2004. (QEB You & Your Pet Ser.). (Illus.). 32p. (J). lib. bdg. 18.95 *(978-1-59566-054-1(2))* QEB Publishing Inc.

Eagen, Rachel. Rats Around Us. 2010. (Creepy Crawlies Ser.). (ENG.). 32p. (J). (gr. 3-6). *(978-0-7787-2501-5(4))*; pap. *(978-0-7787-2508-4(1))* Crabtree Publishing Co.

Fee, Deb. The Life & Times of Sir Ear Alot. 2012. 32p. pap. 19.99 *(978-1-4685-7983-3(5))* AuthorHouse.

Gravel, Elise. The Rat: The Disgusting Critters Series. (Disgusting Critters Ser.). (ENG., illus.). 32p. (J). (gr. 1-4). 2016. pap. 5.99 *(978-1-77049-659-0(9))* 2014. 10.99 *(978-1-77049-658-3(0))* Tundra Bks. CAN. (Tundra Bks.). Dist: Penguin Random Hse. LLC.

Hansen, Grace. Rats, 1 vol. 2015. (Animal Friends Ser.). (ENG., illus.). 24p. (J). (gr. -1-2). 32.79 *(978-1-62970-896-6(8)*, 18236, Abdo Kids) ABDO Publishing Co.

Herriott, Charlotte. Rat vs. Cockroach, 1 vol. 2015. (Bizarre Beast Battles Ser.). (ENG.). 24p. (J). (gr. 2-3). pap. 9.15 *(978-1-4824-2788-2(5)*, fe7b1c4d-00d5-4c7b-a806-788f6795ed46) Stevens, Gareth Publishing LLLP.

Hudd, Emily. Naked Mole-Rats. 2019. (Unique Animal Adaptations Ser.). (ENG., illus.). 32p. (J). (gr. 4-6). 28.65 *(978-1-5435-7161-5(1)*, 140428) Capstone.

Johnson, Jinny. Rats & Mice. 2009. (Get to Know Your Pet Ser.). (J). 28.50 *(978-1-59920-091-0(0))* Black Rabbit Bks.

—Rats & Mice. 2009. (Get to Know Your Pet Ser.). (ENG., Illus.). 32p. (J). (gr. 4-7). pap. *(978-1-897563-33-5(7))* Saunders Bk. Co.

Levy, Janey. The Repulsive Naked Mole Rat, 1 vol. 2019. (Nature's Freak Show: Ugly Beasts Ser.). (ENG.). 24p. (gr. 2-3). pap. 9.15 *(978-1-5382-4618-4(X)*, da9e0723-2bac-4d31-accf-dd276d4a142e) Stevens, Gareth Publishing LLLP.

Lunde, Darrin. Dirty Rats? Gustavson, Adam, illus. 2015. (ENG.). 32p. (J). (gr. -1-2). 16.95 *(978-1-58089-566-8(2))* Charlesbridge Publishing, Inc.

Lynette, Rachel. Rats, 1 vol. 2013. (Monsters of the Animal Kingdom Ser.). (ENG., illus.). 24p. (J). (gr. 2-3). pap. 9.25 *(978-1-4488-9717-9(3)*, 54c2b310-a56a-4796-b081-daae0db22449); lib. bdg. 26.27 *(978-1-4488-9630-1(4)*, ef6999b8-aca1-478a-a7a7-b389f53f4006) Rosen Publishing Group, Inc., The. (PowerKids Pr.).

Marrin, Albert. Oh Rats! The Story of Rats & People. Mordan, C. B., illus. 2014. 112p. (J). (gr. 5). pap. 8.99 *(978-0-14-751281-9(6)*, Puffin Books) Penguin Young Readers Group.

Morgan, Sally. Rats & Mice. 2012. (Pets Plus Ser.). (Illus.). 32p. (gr. 3-6). lib. bdg. 31.35 *(978-1-59920-703-2(6))* Black Rabbit Bks.

Owings, Lisa. Rat Attack. 2012. (Animal Attacks Ser.). (ENG., Illus.). 24p. (J). (gr. 3-7). lib. bdg. 26.95 *(978-1-60014-790-6(9)*, Torque Bks.) Bellwether Media.

Quinton, Sasha. Rat-A-Tat: A Phonics Reader. 2009. (Illus.). pap. *(978-1-936199-04-4(1))* Book Shop, Ltd., The.

Rafferty, John P. Rats, Bats, & Xenarthrans, 1 vol. 2011. (Britannica Guide to Predators & Prey Ser.). (ENG., illus.). 256p. (YA). (gr. 10-10). lib. bdg. 55.29 *(978-1-61530-332-8(4)*, 95127fdd-5a3-4d15-8bfb-b01c038e135f) Rosen Publishing Group, Inc., The.

Rafferty, John P., ed. Rats, Bats, & Xenarthrans, 4 vols. 2011. (Britannica Guide to Predators & Prey Ser.). (ENG., illus.). 256p. (YA). (gr. 10-10). 110.58 *(978-1-61530-456-1(8)*, ef0d386b-6fc9-4143-8fda-139d9c03565c) Rosen Publishing Group, Inc., The.

Rayner, Matthew. Rat, 1 vol. 2004. (I Am Your Pet Ser.). (ENG., Illus.). 32p. (gr. 2-4). lib. bdg. 28.67 *(978-0-8368-8386-2(1)*, 2c01301e-5809-4724-adea-ce77e22a73dc, Gareth Stevens Learning Library) Stevens, Gareth Publishing LLLP.

Savage, Stephen. Rat, 1 vol. 2008. (Animal Neighbors Ser.). (ENG.). 32p. (gr. 3-3). pap. 11.60 *(978-1-4042-4568-6(5)*, 60324a52-78bc-43cc-9896-7edf6e9b7c8a, Rosen Classroom); (Illus.). (J). lib. bdg. 28.93 *(978-1-4358-4991-4(4)*, 8dbfd5a2-65cd-4208-975d-65d83cb90449, PowerKids Pr.) Rosen Publishing Group, Inc., The.

Silverstein, Alvin, et al. Rats: Cool Pets!, 1 vol. 2012. (Far-Out & Unusual Pets Ser.). (ENG., illus.). 48p. (gr. 3-3). 27.93 *(978-0-7660-3882-0(3)*, 7ade7ce9-6eec-4422-87e2-38494c00350c); pap. 11.53 *(978-1-4644-0127-5(6)*, 3222b4c8-0319-4c26-9c41-798f3e2f957e) Enslow Publishing, LLC. (Enslow Elementary).

Simon, Elizabeth. Caring for Your Rat. (Caring for Your Pet Ser.). (Illus.). 32p. (J). 2005. (gr. 4-7). per. 9.95 *(978-1-59036-217-4(9))* 2004. lib. bdg. 26.00 *(978-1-59036-197-9(0))* Weigl Pubs., Inc.

—Rat. 2010. pap. 9.95 *(978-1-61690-080-9(6))*; 32p. (J). (gr. 3-5). lib. bdg. 27.13 *(978-1-61690-079-3(2))* Weigl Pubs., Inc.

Thomas, Isabel. Squeak's Guide to Caring for Your Pet Rats or Mice, 1 vol. Peterson, Rick, illus. 2014. (Pets' Guides). (ENG.). 32p. (J). (gr. 1-3). pap. 7.99 *(978-1-4846-0271-3(4)*, 126321, Heinemann) Capstone.

RATS—FICTION

AaronG, Driftin'. Claude Henry, the Iditarod Mouse: The Adventures Begin. 2007. 108p. (J). per. 9.95 *(978-0-595-44990-3(5))* iUniverse, Inc.

Adeola, Ogechi. Jo & Skippa: I want to be You! 2011. (Illus.). 28p. 12.52 *(978-1-4567-7340-3(2))* AuthorHouse.

Angleberger, Tom. Rat with the Human Face: The Qwikpick Papers. 2015. (Qwikpick Papers). (ENG., illus.). 160p. (J). (gr. 3-7). 12.95 *(978-1-4197-1489-4(9)*, 1098201, Amulet Bks.) Abrams, Inc.

Armstrong, Alan W. Whittington. Schindler, S. D., illus. 2007. 191p. (gr. 3-7). 17.00 *(978-0-7569-7768-9(1))* Perfection Learning Corp.

Avi. The Mayor of Central Park. Floca, Brian, illus. 2003. (ENG.). 208p. (J). (gr. 3-6). 15.99 *(978-0-06-000682-2(X))* HarperCollins Pubs.

—The Mayor of Central Park. Floca, Brian, illus. 2005. 193p. (J). (gr. 3-7). 13.65 *(978-0-7569-5125-2(9))* Perfection Learning Corp.

Bailer, Darice & Domínguez, Madelca. La Ratita Presumida. Curto, Rosa Maria, illus. 2007. (SPA & ENG.). 28p. (J). *(978-0-545-03031-1(5))* Scholastic, Inc.

Barkow, Henriette. The Pied Piper. Dry, Roland, illus. 2004. 32p. (J). (ENG.). *(978-1-85269-990-1(6))*; (SOM & ENG.). pap. *(978-1-85269-995-6(7))*; (ENG & TAM.). pap. *(978-1-85269-906-2(X))*; (ENG & SPA.). pap. *(978-1-85269-901-7(9))*; (ENG & POR.). pap. *(978-1-85269-980-2(9))*; (ENG & POL.). pap. *(978-1-85269-975-8(2))*; (PAN & ENG.). pap. *(978-1-85269-970-3(1))*; (ENG & ITA.). pap. *(978-1-85269-965-9(5))*; (ENG & GUJ.). pap. *(978-1-85269-955-0(8))*; (ENG & GER.). pap. *(978-1-85269-950-5(7))*; (FRE & ENG.). pap. *(978-1-85269-945-1(0))*; (ENG & PER.). pap. *(978-1-85269-940-6(X))*; (ENG & CZE.). pap. *(978-1-85269-935-2(3))*; (ENG & ARA.). pap. *(978-1-85269-920-8(5))*; (URD & ENG.). pap. *(978-1-85269-916-1(7))*; (ENG & ALB.). pap. *(978-1-85269-915-4(9))*; (TUR & ENG.). pap. *(978-1-85269-911-6(6))* Mantra Lingua.

Bartell, Maggie. Ratsquirrel. 2009. (ENG.). 41p. pap. 14.64 *(978-0-557-11816-8(6))* Lulu Pr., Inc.

Beck, W. H. Malcolm at Midnight. Lies, Brian, illus. 2015. (ENG.). 272p. (J). (gr. 3-7). pap. 7.99 *(978-0-544-33666-7(6)*, 1584188, Clarion Bks.) HarperCollins Pubs.

Bessesen, Brooke. Zachary Z. Packrat & His Amazing Collections. Campbell, Jenney, illus. 2008. 40p. (J). pap. 19.95 *(978-1-932082-83-8(2))* Arizona Highways.

Bethel, Ellie. Michael Recycle Meets Litterbug Doug. Colombo, Alexandra, illus. 2009. (Michael Recycle Ser.). 24p. (J). (gr. 1-3). 15.99 *(978-1-60010-392-6(8)*, 9781600103926) Idea & Design Works, LLC.

Blackburn, Sheila M. Stewie Scraps & the Space Racer. 2008. 68p. pap. *(978-1-903853-84-9(2))* Brilliant Pubns.

—Stewie Scraps & the Super Sleigh. 2008. 72p. pap. *(978-1-903853-89-4(3))* Brilliant Pubns.

Blacker, Terence. Ms. Wiz Smells a Rat. 2003. (ENG., illus.). 64p. (J). pap. *(978-0-330-37466-8(4)*, Pan) Pan Macmillan.

Bootman, Colin, illus. The Steel Pan Man of Harlem. 2009. (Carolrhoda Picture Bks.). 32p. (J). (gr. 1-3). 16.95 *(978-0-8225-9026-2(3))* Lerner Publishing Group.

P Q R

Brennan, Sarah. The Tale of Run Run Rat. Harrison, Harry, illus. 2012. (ENG.). 32p. (J). 24.95 *(978-1-937160-25-8(4))* Eliassen Creative.

Brown, Alan James. Incredible Journey of Walter Rat. (ENG., Illus.). 63p. (J). pap. *(978-0-340-72750-8(0))* Hodder & Stoughton.

Brown, Rosie L. Zach & Rob's Journey: The Lost Eggs. 2007. 24p. per. 24.95 *(978-1-4241-8401-9(0))* America Star Bks.

Bryant, Phoebe. What Is That in the Air? A play date with Sayde. 2009. (Illus.). 28p. pap. 12.99 *(978-1-4490-2209-9(X))* AuthorHouse.

Butterworth, Nick. The Whisperer. Butterworth, Nick, illus. 2005. (ENG., Illus.). 32p. (gr. k-3). pap. 15.95 *(978-0-00-712018-5(4),* HarperCollins Children's Bks.) HarperCollins Pubs. Ltd. GBR. Dist: HarperCollins Pubs.

Carballeira, Paula. Paco. Barrio, Blanca, illus. 2003. 32p. (J). 14.95 *(978-84-95730-38-1(3))* Kalandraka Catalunya, Edicions, S.L. ESP. Dist: Independent Pubs. Group.

Casey, Dawn. The Great Race. Wilson, Anne, illus. 2008. (ENG.). 32p. (J). (gr. k-5). pap. 9.99 *(978-1-84686-202-1(7))* Barefoot Bks., Inc.

Cerberus Jones, Cerberus. The Warriors of Brin-Hask: The Gateway. 2017. (ENG.). 160p. (J). pap. 5.99 *(978-1-61067-499-7(5))* Kane Miller.

Chichester Clark, Emma. We Are Not Fond of Rat: Band 02B/Red B (Collins Big Cat Phonics) Chichester Clark, Emma, illus. 2006. (Collins Big Cat Phonics Ser.). (ENG., Illus.). 16p. (J). (gr. -1-1). pap. 6.99 *(978-0-00-723590-2(9))* HarperCollins Pubs. Ltd. GBR. Dist: Independent Pubs. Group.

Chin, Oliver Clyde. The Year of the Rat: Tales from the Chinese Zodiac. Alcorn, Jeremiah, illus. 2019. (Tales from the Chinese Zodiac Ser.). (ENG.). 36p. (J). 15.95 *(978-1-59702-147-0(4))* Immedium.

Cody, Matthew. The Secrets of the Pied Piper 3: the Piper's Apprentice. 2017. (Secrets of the Pied Piper Ser.: 3). (ENG., Illus.). 288p. (J). (gr. 3-7). 16.99 *(978-0-385-75530-6(9),* Knopf Bks. for Young Readers) Random Hse. Children's Bks.

Coomber, Suzanne. Salt & Pepper. 2010. 24p. pap. 12.99 *(978-1-4490-6311-5(X))* AuthorHouse.

Cooper, Velyn. Rusty the Rat. 2012. 48p. pap. 9.89 *(978-1-4669-1133-8(6))* Trafford Publishing.

Cope, Clifford D. Caleb: The mouse Engineer. 2009. 24p. pap. 12.99 *(978-1-4389-9877-0(5))* AuthorHouse.

Cousineau, Craig S. Skippy & Oaf: The Battle Against Oxygen Radicals. 2007. (ENG., Illus.). 48p. (J). (gr. 2-4). per. *(978-1-933255-27-9(7))* DNA Pr.

Cousins, Lucy. Pina Piace Giocare. pap. 18.95 *(978-88-04-48797-5(6))* Mondadori ITA. Dist: Distribooks, Inc.

Cox, Judy. The Case of the Purloined Professor, 0 vols. Rayyan, Omar, illus. 2009. (Tails of Frederick & Ishbu Ser.: 0). (ENG.). 256p. (J). (gr. 5-7). 16.99 *(978-0-7614-5544-8(2),* 9780761455448, Two Lions) Amazon Publishing.

—The Mystery of the Burmese Bandicoot, 1 vol. Rayyan, Omar, illus. 2007. (Tails of frederick & Ishbu Ser.). (ENG.). 224p. (J). (gr. 5-9). lib. bdg. 16.99 *(978-0-7614-5376-5(8))* Marshall Cavendish Corp.

—The Mystery of the Burmese Bandicoot. 2012. 254p. (gr. 4-6). pap. 15.95 *(978-1-4759-3838-8(1))* iUniverse, Inc.

Crangle, Claudine. Priscilla Pack Rat: Making Room for Friendship. Crangle, Claudine, illus. 2017. (Illus.). 32p. (J). 15.95 *(978-1-4338-2335-0(7),* Magination Pr.) American Psychological Assn.

Crompton, Paul. Remarkable for Short. 2005. 113p. pap. 19.95 *(978-1-4241-0287-7(1))* PublishAmerica, Inc.

Daley, Michael J. Rat Trap. 2008. (ENG.) 272p. (J). (gr. 3-7). 16.95 *(978-0-8234-2093-3(0))* Holiday Hse., Inc.

Deacon, Alexis. Cheese Belongs to You! Schwarz, Viviane, illus. 2013. (ENG.). 32p. (J). (gr. -1-1). 15.99 *(978-0-7636-6608-8(4))* Candlewick Pr.

Dean, Barbara. Rattalia's Birthday Stories. 2nd ed. 2013. 132p. *(978-0-9572470-4-8(4));* pap. *(978-0-9572470-5-5(2))* Newpole Bks.

DeKeyser, Stacy. The Brixen Witch. Nickle, John, illus. (ENG.). 208p. (J). (gr. 3-7). 2013. pap. 6.99 *(978-1-4424-3329-8(9))* 2012. 15.99 *(978-1-4424-3328-1(0))* McElderry, Margaret K. Bks. (McElderry, Margaret K. Bks.).

DeMaio, Alison. Tyler, the tiniest Tiger. 2010. 21p. 12.21 *(978-0-557-19780-4(5))* Lulu Pr., Inc.

Derrick, Patricia & O'Neil, Shirley. Rathbone the Rat. Martinez, J-P Loppo, illus. 2007. 32p. (J). (gr. -1-3). 18.95 incl. audio compact disk *(978-1-933818-17-7(4))* Animalations.

Donaldson, Julia. The Highway Rat. Scheffler, Axel, illus. 2013. (ENG.). 32p. (J). (gr. -1-3). 17.99 *(978-0-545-47758-1(1),* Levine, Arthur A. Bks.) Scholastic, Inc.

Doudna, Kelly. Pack Rat. Chawla, Neena, illus. 2006. (Fact & Fiction Ser.). 24p. (J). pap. 48.42 *(978-1-59679-956-1(0))* ABDO Publishing Co.

Drachman, Eric. Bad Rats. Muscarello, James, illus. 2008. (ENG.). 32p. (J). (gr. -1-3). 18.95 incl. lp *(978-0-9703809-4-4(1))* Kidwick Bks.

Egielski, Richard. Slim & Jim. Egielski, Richard, illus. 2005. (Illus.). 37p. (J). (gr. k-4). reprint ed. 16.00 *(978-0-7567-8936-7(2))* DIANE Publishing Co.

Eleanor Russell Brown. Mary Warin's Rats: A Time Warp Adventure. 2009. 24p. pap. 12.99 *(978-1-4389-6456-0(0))* AuthorHouse.

Eriksen, Valanee. Christmas Bells & Hero's Tails. 2015. (Illus.). vi, 90p. (J). pap. 7.99 *(978-1-4621-1737-6(6))* Cedar Fort, Inc./CFI Distribution.

Escott, Jamison. The Clockmaker of Mullen. Escott, Esther, illus. 2004. 24p. (J). pap. 8.95 *(978-1-57733-127-8(3),* Papillon Publishing) Blue Dolphin Publishing, Inc.

Ewers, Joe, illus. The Pied Piper: A Tale about Promises. 2006. (J). 6.99 *(978-1-59939-004-8(3))* Cornerstone Pr.

Fairfield, J. S. Cunning Foe: Faulkil. 2009. 88p. pap. 19.95 *(978-1-61546-603-0(7))* America Star Bks.

Fiedler, Lisa. Hopper's Destiny. To, Vivienne, illus. 2016. (Mouseheart Ser.: 2). (ENG.). 368p. (J). (gr. 3-7). pap. 8.99 *(978-1-4814-2090-7(9),* McElderry, Margaret K. Bks.) McElderry, Margaret K. Bks.

—Mouseheart. To, Vivienne, illus. (Mouseheart Ser.: 1). (ENG.). (J). (gr. 3-7). 2015. 336p. pap. 8.99 *(978-1-4424-8783-3(6))* 2014. 320p. 18.99 *(978-1-4424-8781-9(X))* McElderry, Margaret K. Bks. (McElderry, Margaret K. Bks.).

—Return of the Forgotten. To, Vivienne, illus. 2015. (Mouseheart Ser.: 3). (ENG.). 320p. (J). (gr. 3-7). 16.99 *(978-1-4814-2092-1(5),* McElderry, Margaret K. Bks.) McElderry, Margaret K. Bks.

Flor Ada, Alma & Campoy, F. Isabel. Ratoncito Prez, Cartero. Escriva, Sandra Lopez, illus. 2015. (Santillana USA Ser.).Tr. of New Job for Pérez, the Mouse. (SPA.). 32p. (J). (gr. 6-6). pap. 15.95 *(978-1-63113-547-7(3),* Santillana) Santillana USA Publishing Co., Inc.

Fraser, P. J. The Mouse with the Torch, 1 vol. 2009. 48p. pap. 16.95 *(978-1-4489-2080-8(9))* America Star Bks.

Frederick, Heather Vogel. For Your Paws Only. 2013. (Spy Mice Ser.: 2). (ENG., Illus.). 240p. (J). (gr. 3-6). pap. 6.99 *(978-1-4424-6703-3(7),* Simon & Schuster Bks. For Young Readers) Simon & Schuster Bks. For Young Readers.

—For Your Paws Only. Comport, Sally Wern, illus. 2006. (Spy Mice Ser.: 2). (ENG.). 272p. (J). (gr. 3-6). pap. 5.99 *(978-1-4169-4025-8(1),* Simon & Schuster Bks. For Young Readers) Simon & Schuster Bks. For Young Readers.

Furie, Matt. The Night Riders. 2013. (Illus.). 48p. (J). (gr. -1-3). 8.95 *(978-1-938073-72-4(X),* 54da59fb-b496-483f-a5f6-41367ed7cd06) McSweeney's Publishing.

Geshell, Carmen. The Surf Rats of Waikiki Beach. Pagay, Jeff, illus. 2004. 24p. 10.95 *(978-1-57306-226-8(X))* Bess Pr., Inc.

Grahame, Kenneth. Restless Rat, No. 6. Iosa, Ann, illus. 2010. (Easy Reader Classics Ser.). (ENG.). 32p. (J). (gr. k-3). 16.19 *(978-1-4027-6730-2(7))* Sterling Publishing Co., Inc.

—The Wind in the Willows. Ingpen, Robert R., illus. 2012. (Union Square Kids Illustrated Classics Ser.). (ENG.). 224p. (J). (gr. 2-8). 24.99 *(978-1-4027-8283-1(7))* Sterling Publishing Co., Inc.

Gramberg, J. E. Pakrat Bill. 2006. (ENG.). 36p. per. 21.32 *(978-1-4257-3117-5(1))* Xlibris Corp.

Gravett, Emily. Cyril & Pat. Gravett, Emily, illus. 2019. (ENG., Illus.). 32p. (J). (gr. -1-3). 17.99 *(978-1-5344-3950-4(1),* Simon & Schuster Bks. For Young Readers) Simon & Schuster Bks. For Young Readers.

Green, Teri & Taylor, Sue. The Littlest Soldier, 1 vol. 2009. 94p. pap. 19.95 *(978-1-4489-2714-2(5))* America Star Bks.

Griffiths, Andy. The Cat, the Rat, & the Baseball Bat. Denton, Terry, illus. 2013. (My Readers Ser.). (ENG.). 32p. (J). (gr. -1-1). pap. 4.99 *(978-1-250-02774-0(8),* 900104562) Square Fish.

Guillain, Charlotte. Ratpunzel, 1 vol. Beacon, Dawn, illus. 2014. (Animal Fairy Tales Ser.). (ENG.). 24p. (J). (gr. -1-2). lib. bdg. 23.99 *(978-1-4109-6112-9(5),* 124739, Raintree) Capstone.

Haller, Reese. Giving & Receiving. Haller, Reese, illus. 2007. (Fred the Mouse Ser.). (Illus.). 104p. (J). (gr. 4-7). per. 4.97 *(978-0-9772321-5-4(8))* Personal Power Pr.

Hanna, Nicholas. Coven of Rats. 2007. (ENG.). 223p. pap. 15.95 *(978-0-615-14369-9(5))* Hanna, Nicholas.

Hanson, Mary. How to Save Your Tail* *If You Are a Rat Nabbed by Cats Who Really Like Stories about Magic Spoons, Wolves with Snout-Warts, Big, Hairy Chimney Trolls ... & Cookies, Too. 2008. (ENG., Illus.). 112p. (J). (gr. 1-4). 5.99 *(978-0-440-42228-0(0),* Yearling) Random Hse. Children's Bks.

Harries, Tony. Zeegpaw & the Cat Cult. 2008. 304p. pap. 18.95 *(978-1-4357-0754-2(0))* Lulu Pr., Inc.

Heinz, Brian J. The Barnyard Cat. l.t. ed. 2003. (Illus.). 32p. (J). pap. 6.96 *(978-0-936335-07-0(6))* Ballyhoo BookWorks, Inc.

Henry, Kristina. The Rat Tank, 1 vol. 2011. (ENG., Illus.). 40p. (J). (gr. -1-3). 16.99 *(978-0-7643-3842-7(0),* 4271, Schiffer Publishing Ltd) Schiffer Publishing, Ltd.

Herbert, James. The Rats. 2003. (Rats Ser.: Bk. 1). (ENG.). 208p. (J). 32.50 *(978-0-333-76118-2(9))* Macmillan Pubs., Ltd. GBR. Dist: Trafalgar Square Publishing.

Hofmeister, Alan, et al. The Bat Rat. (Reading for All Learners Ser.). (Illus.). (J). pap. *(978-1-56861-119-8(6))* Swift Learning Resources.

—Mat. (Reading for All Learners Ser.). (Illus.). (J). pap. *(978-1-56861-077-1(7))* Swift Learning Resources.

—Mat & the Nut. (Reading for All Learners Ser.). (Illus.). (J). pap. *(978-1-56861-109-9(9))* Swift Learning Resources.

—Mat at Bat. (Reading for All Learners Ser.). (Illus.). (J). pap. *(978-1-56861-118-1(8))* Swift Learning Resources.

—Mat Did It. (Reading for All Learners Ser.). (Illus.). (J). pap. *(978-1-56861-102-0(1))* Swift Learning Resources.

—Mat Is Wet. (Reading for All Learners Ser.). (Illus.). (J). pap. *(978-1-56861-120-4(X))* Swift Learning Resources.

—Mat the Rat. (Reading for All Learners Ser.). (Illus.). (J). pap. *(978-1-56861-111-2(0))* Swift Learning Resources.

—Nat. (Reading for All Learners Ser.). (Illus.). (J). pap. *(978-1-56861-093-1(9))* Swift Learning Resources.

Jackson, Aaron. Milton Da Rat: A Family Barbeque. 2009. 24p. pap. 12.49 *(978-1-4389-4387-9(3))* AuthorHouse.

Jones, Cerberus. The Warriors of Brin-Hask. 2016. 136p. (J). *(978-1-61067-572-7(X))* Kane Miller.

Jones, Rena. A Dinner Date for Dilly. Nielson, Ginger, illus. 2012. 28p. pap. 14.99 *(978-0-9852661-2-7(0))* 4RV Pub.

Jones, Rene'. A New Friend for Dilly. Nielson, Ginger, illus. 2011. 32p. pap. 14.99 *(978-0-9826423-0-6(X))* 4RV Pub.

Jukes, Carlisle E. The Rhino & the Rat: The Delightful Story of Coco & Max. 2009. 28p. pap. 13.25 *(978-1-4389-6751-6(9))* AuthorHouse.

Kasza, Keiko. The Rat & the Tiger. 2007. (Illus.). 32p. (J). (gr. -1-2). pap. 7.99 *(978-0-14-240900-8(6),* Puffin Books) Penguin Young Readers Group.

Kelso, Mary Jean. Rv Mouse. Snider, K. C., illus. 2010. 24p. pap. 10.95 *(978-1-61633-025-5(2))* Guardian Angel Publishing, Inc.

Kondrat, Lauren. Mischievous Mort. 2010. 40p. pap. 17.91 *(978-0-557-43708-5(3))* Lulu Pr., Inc.

Krensky, Stephen. Snack Attack: Ready-To-Read Level 1. Curtis, Stacy, illus. 2008. (Ready-To-Read Ser.). (ENG.). 32p. (J). (gr. -1-1). pap. 4.99 *(978-1-4169-0238-6(4),* Simon Spotlight) Simon Spotlight.

Kroll, Steven. Stuff! Reduce, Reuse, Recycle: Reduce, Reuse, Recycle, 0 vols. Cox, Steve, illus. 2012. (ENG.). 32p. (J). (gr. -1-3). pap. 9.99 *(978-0-7614-6237-8(6),* 9780761462378, Two Lions) Amazon Publishing.

Ladybird. Anansi Helps a Friend Activity Book - Ladybird Readers Level 1. 2016. (Ladybird Readers Ser.). (ENG.). 16p. (J). (gr. 2-4). pap., act. bk. ed. 5.99 *(978-0-241-25420-2(5))* Penguin Bks., Ltd. GBR. Dist: Independent Pubs. Group.

LaReau, Kara. The Infamous Ratsos. Myers, Matt, illus. 2017. (Infamous Ratsos Ser.). (ENG.). 64p. (J). (gr. k-3). pap. 6.99 *(978-0-7636-9875-1(X))* Candlewick Pr.

—The Infamous Ratsos Are Not Afraid. Myers, Matt, illus. 2018. (Infamous Ratsos Ser.). (ENG.). 96p. (J). (gr. k-3). pap. 5.99 *(978-1-5362-0368-4(8))* Candlewick Pr.

—The Infamous Ratsos: Project Fluffy. Myers, Matt, illus. (Infamous Ratsos Ser.). (ENG.). 96p. (J). (gr. k-3). 2020. pap. 5.99 *(978-1-5362-0880-1(9))* 2018. 14.99 *(978-1-5362-0005-8(0))* Candlewick Pr.

Lewis, Jan, illus. The Pied Piper of Hamelin. 2006. (First Fairy Tales Ser.). 30p. (J). (gr. -1-3). lib. bdg. 28.50 *(978-1-59771-072-5(5))* Sea-To-Sea Pubns.

Liberto, Lorenzo. Matt the Rat & His Magic Cloud / Raton Mateo y Su Nube Magica: A Day at School / un Dia de Escuela. Gomez, Rocio, ed. Torres, Irving, illus. 2003. (Matt the Rat Ser. / La Serie de Ratón Mateo). (ENG & SPA.). 32p. (J). lib. bdg. 20.00 *(978-0-9743668-0-7(3))* Harvest Sun Pr., LLC.

—Matt the Rat & His Sister Maggie (Raton Mateo y Su Hermana Maggie) When I Grow Up (Cuando Yo Crezca) Gomez, Rocio, ed. Torres, Irving, illus. 2003. (Matt the Rat Ser. / La Serie de Ratón Mateo). (SPA & ENG.). 40p. (J). lib. bdg. 20.00 *(978-0-9743668-1-4(1))* Harvest Sun Pr., LLC.

—Matt the Rat Fights Back / Ratón Mateo se Defiende. Gomez, Rocio, tr. from ENG. Torres, Irving, illus. 2005. (Matt the Rat Ser. / La Serie de Ratón Mateo). (ENG & SPA.). 32p. (J). lib. bdg. 20.00 *(978-0-9743668-4-5(6))* Harvest Sun Pr., LLC.

—Save the Planet / Salva el Planeta. Gomez, Rocio, tr. Torres, Irving, illus. 2005. (Matt the Rat Ser. / La Serie de Ratón Mateo). (ENG & SPA.). 32p. (J). lib. bdg. 20.00 *(978-0-9743668-5-2(4))* Harvest Sun Pr., LLC.

Liberto, Lorenzo, et al. Matt the Rat's Incredible Creations / Las Creaciones Increibles de Ratón Mateo. Torres, Irving, illus. 2004. (ENG & SPA.). 32p. (J). lib. bdg. 20.00 *(978-0-9743668-3-8(8))* Harvest Sun Pr., LLC.

—Practice Makes Perfect / la Práctica Hace al Maestro. Torres, Irving, illus. 2004. (ENG & SPA.). 32p. (J). lib. bdg. 20.00 *(978-0-9743668-2-1(X))* Harvest Sun Pr., LLC.

Lieb, Josh. Ratscalibur. 2016. lib. bdg. 19.65 *(978-0-606-38850-4(8))* Turtleback.

Lyons, Maggie. Dewi & the Seeds of Doom. 2012. 70p. pap. 9.99 *(978-1-61244-094-1(0))* Halo Publishing International.

Mariconda, Barbara. Sort It Out!, 1 vol. Rogers, Sherry, illus. 2008. (ENG & SPA.). 32p. (J). (gr. k-1). pap. 10.95 *(978-1-934359-32-7(7),* 17c86867-80a5-4681-b3ea-a6a1ca86f26e); 16.95 *(978-1-934359-11-2(4))* Arbordale Publishing.

Marquez, Sofia. Pepe Perez Mexican Mouse: Pepe Perez Comes to the United States: Book 1, 1 vol. 2010. 20p. 24.95 *(978-1-4489-6600-4(0))* PublishAmerica, Inc.

Mathews, Leslie. Edgar Wants to Be Alone. Dumont, Jean-François, illus. 2015. (ENG.). 26p. (J). 16.00 *(978-0-8028-5457-5(5),* Eerdmans Bks For Young Readers) Eerdmans, William B. Publishing Co.

McDonald, Jill, illus. Ghoulish Gang. 2008. (ENG.). 12p. (J). 9.95 *(978-1-58117-782-4(8),* Intervisual/Piggy Toes) Bendon, Inc.

McFarlane, Brian. Coaching the River Rats. 10th ed. 2008. (Mitchell Brothers Ser.). (ENG.). 198p. (J). (gr. 3-7). pap. *(978-1-55168-302-7(4))* Me to We.

McGranaghan, John. Saturn for My Birthday, 1 vol. Edelson, Wendy, illus. 2008. (ENG.). 32p. (J). (gr. -1-4). 16.95 *(978-1-934359-13-6(0));* pap. 8.95 *(978-1-934359-27-3(0))* Arbordale Publishing.

McPhail, David. Big Brown Bear's Birthday Surprise. 2018. (ENG., Illus.). 32p. (J). (gr. -1-3). pap. 3.99 *(978-1-328-89578-3(5),* 1699659, Clarion Bks.) HarperCollins Pubs.

—Big Brown Bear's Birthday Surprise. O'Connor, John, illus. 2007. (Big Brown Bear Ser.). (ENG.). 32p. (J). (gr. -1-3). 16.00 *(978-0-15-206098-5(7),* 1198317, Clarion Bks.) HarperCollins Pubs.

—Big Brown Bear's up & down Day. McPhail, David, illus. 2005. (Illus.). 42p. (J). (gr. -1-3). reprint ed. 16.00 *(978-0-7567-8542-0(1))* DIANE Publishing Co.

Milford, Diana Viola. Fuzzum & Wuzzum, 1 vol. 2010. 34p. pap. 24.95 *(978-1-4489-9168-6(4))* PublishAmerica, Inc.

Mitchell, Stan R. Oskar & Myer at the Lake. 2013. 24p. pap. 24.95 *(978-1-63000-414-9(6))* America Star Bks.

Morgan, Mary Sue. Swifty. 2008. 24p. pap. 24.95 *(978-1-60441-579-7(7))* America Star Bks.

Morris, Ashara. Let's Find Lucy! 2008. (Illus.). 32p. pap. 17.95 *(978-1-4327-3221-9(8))* Outskirts Pr., Inc.

Nees, Susan. Class Pets. 2013. (Missy's Super Duper Royal Deluxe Ser.: 2). (ENG., Illus.). 80p. (J). (gr. k-2). pap. 4.99 *(978-0-545-43852-0(7))* Scholastic, Inc.

—Class Pets. 2013. (Missy's Super Duper Royal Deluxe Ser.: 2). lib. bdg. 14.75 *(978-0-606-31980-5(8))* Turtleback.

Newbigging, Robert Delford. Robert Rat Has A Problem: A Tale of Broccoli. 2010. 44p. pap. 16.99 *(978-1-4520-2134-8(1))* AuthorHouse.

O'Brien, Robert C. Mrs. Frisby & the Rats of NIMH. 2006. (KOR.). 280p. (J). (gr. 4-7). *(978-89-90794-37-6(4))* Green Bks. Co., Ltd.

—Mrs. Frisby & the Rats of NIMH. (J). 2009. 73.75 *(978-1-4618-3748-0(0))* 2003. 81.75 *(978-1-4025-6007-1(9))* Recorded Bks., Inc.

Ottitoloju/Blazing Ideas ltd, Ololade/Adewunmi, retold by. Kunkuru, Jaba Da Kurege: The Tortoise, the Rat & the Squirrel. 2008. (YOR & ENG., Illus.). 36p. 16.00 *(978-0-9801243-7-8(9))* Blazing Ideas Ltd.

—Mbe, Nkapi na Osa. 2008. (YOR & ENG., Illus.). 36p. 16.00 *(978-0-9801243-3-0(6))* Blazing Ideas Ltd.

Parker, Vic, ed. The Rat Catcher & Other Stories, 1 vol. 2015. (Scary Fairy Tales Ser.). (ENG.). 40p. (J). (gr. 3-4). pap. 15.05 *(978-1-4824-3101-8(7),* d0d1dc09-527d-4ff7-a626-bd2d9e19c97e) Stevens, Gareth Publishing LLLP.

Parkins, Rebecca Katherine. Lilly the Little Lava Mouse. 2009. 180p. pap. 43.49 *(978-1-4389-4330-5(X))* AuthorHouse.

Parsons, Tom. Pinky the Rat at the Brussels Sprout Museum. 2007. 194p. 27.76 *(978-1-4303-1538-4(5))* Lulu Pr., Inc.

Pastis, Stephan. Beginning Pearls. 2013. lib. bdg. 20.85 *(978-0-606-31764-1(3))* Turtleback.

A Path of Clouds: The Book off Rhymes. 2013. 50p. pap. *(978-965-550-241-1(4))* Contento De Semrik.

Pauli, Lorenz. The Fox in the Library. Schärer, Kathrin, illus. 2013. (ENG.). 32p. (J). (gr. -1-3). 17.95 *(978-0-7358-4150-5(0))* North-South Bks., Inc.

Pearce, Jacqueline. The Truth about Rats (and Dogs), 1 vol. 2006. (ENG.). 160p. (J). (gr. 4-7). per. 7.95 *(978-1-55143-473-5(3))* Orca Bk. Pubs. USA.

Petit, Karen. The Mystery of the Stolen Stallion. 2007. (Illus.). 246p. (J). per. 14.95 *(978-0-9794420-4-9(4))* Red Letter Pr.

Pratchett, Terry. The Amazing Maurice & His Educated Rodents. 2008. (ENG.). 368p. (YA). (gr. 8-18). pap. 11.99 *(978-0-06-001235-9(8),* Clarion Bks.) HarperCollins Pubs.

—The Amazing Maurice & His Educated Rodents. 2003. (ENG.). 340p. (gr. 7). 19.00 *(978-0-7569-1458-5(2))* Perfection Learning Corp.

—The Amazing Maurice & His Educated Rodents. 2008. (Discworld Ser.: 33). (YA). (gr. 5-8). 19.65 *(978-0-613-65757-0(8))* Turtleback.

Publications International Ltd. Staff. Look & Find Ratatouille. 2007. 24p. (J). 7.10 *(978-1-4127-6837-5(3),* PIL Kids) Publications International, Ltd.

Ratatouille. 2008. (Disney Pixar Character Storybook Ser.). 48p. *(978-1-4075-1739-1(2))* Parragon, Inc.

Reuker, Heidi. Queen of the Rats. 2007. 56p. per. 16.95 *(978-1-4137-9801-2(2))* America Star Bks.

Roudon Jr., James. The Adventures of Ratsy & Kitten: Which Way is Home? 2007. 56p. per. 16.95 *(978-1-4241-8549-8(1))* America Star Bks.

Russell Brown, Eleanor. The Ring of Rats: An Other World Dimension. 2009. 28p. pap. 12.99 *(978-1-4490-0393-7(1))* AuthorHouse.

Samos (Amos Amir). Nemo the Mole Rat: Stories from the Woodland. 2011. (Illus.). 52p. pap. 23.51 *(978-1-4567-8187-3(1))* AuthorHouse.

Schue, Lori Vankirk. Peapod. 2009. (ENG.). 42p. pap. 16.99 *(978-1-4415-2356-3(1))* Xlibris Corp.

Seidler, Tor. Oh, Rats! Evans, Gabriel, illus. 2020. (ENG.). 336p. (J). (gr. 3-7). pap. 8.99 *(978-1-5344-2685-6(X),* Atheneum Bks. for Young Readers) Simon & Schuster Children's Publishing.

—A Rat's Tale. Marcellino, Fred, illus. 2008. (ENG.). 192p. (J). (gr. 3-7). pap. 11.99 *(978-0-374-40031-6(8),* 900058761, Farrar, Straus & Giroux (BYR)) Farrar, Straus & Giroux.

—A Rat's Tale. 186p. (J). (gr. 3-5). pap. 6.95 *(978-0-8072-1514-2(7),* Listening Library) Random Hse. Audio Publishing Group.

Shaskan, Trisha Speed. Foul Play at Elm Tree Park: Case 3. Shaskan, Stephen, illus. 2018. (Q & Ray Ser.). (ENG.). 48p. (J). (gr. 2-5). 26.65 *(978-1-5124-1149-2(3),* 4ca0215d-12ac-4838-90b8-6d7c4d9f7cbc, Graphic Universe™) Lerner Publishing Group.

—Meteorite or Meteor-Wrong? Case 2. Shaskan, Stephen, illus. 2018. (Q & Ray Ser.). (ENG.). 48p. (J). (gr. 2-5). pap. 9.99 *(978-1-5415-1047-0(X),* 447b5341-8871-4bd0-9db7-4c80dbc326c4);Bk. 2. 26.65 *(978-1-5124-1148-5(5),* ac6051f7-42ca-4332-8dd7-363184dbe085) Lerner Publishing Group. (Graphic Universe™).

Shubuck, Sheila. I Love You All Year Round. Padron, Alicia, illus. 2008. (ENG.). 16p. (J). (gr. -1). 10.95 *(978-1-58117-786-2(0),* Intervisual/Piggy Toes) Bendon, Inc.

Smiley, Mark. A Journey Far Away. 2006. 164p. pap. 13.95 *(978-1-59526-494-7(9))* Aeon Publishing Inc.

Smith, Brooke. Mimi & Maty to the Rescue! Book 1: Roger the Rat Is on the Loose! 2014. (ENG., Illus.). 88p. (J). (gr. k-4). pap. 9.95 *(978-1-62914-619-5(6),* Sky Pony Pr.) Skyhorse Publishing Co., Inc.

—Mimi & Maty to the Rescue! Bk. 1: Book 1: Roger the Rat is on the Loose! Arnold, Alli, illus. 2012. (ENG.). 88p. (J). (gr. 1-4). 14.95 *(978-1-62087-252-9(8),* 620252, Sky Pony Pr.) Skyhorse Publishing Co., Inc.

Smith, Holly C. Tyler the Monkey & Andy the Mouse. 2012. 28p. (-18). pap. 24.95 *(978-1-4626-9501-0(9))* America Star Bks.

Staunton, Ted. Morgan's Pet Plot, 1 vol. Slavin, Bill, illus. 2003. (Formac First Novels Ser.: 24). (ENG.). 64p. (J). (gr. 1-5). 4.95 *(978-0-88780-587-5(6),* 587); 14.95 *(978-0-88780-588-2(4),* 588) Formac Publishing Co., Ltd. CAN. Dist: Formac Lorimer Bks. Ltd.

Stilton, Gerónimo. Geronimo Stilton Heromice #10: Sweet Dreams, Sewer Rats! 2017. (Illus.). 128p. (J). *(978-1-338-18272-9(2))* Scholastic, Inc.

Storad, Conrad J. Desert Night Shift: A Pack Rat Story. Jensen, Nathaniel P., illus. 2006. 48p. (J). (gr. -1-3). 15.95 *(978-1-891795-16-9(3))* RGU Group, The.

Strout, Morgan. Petri's Adventures. 2013. 18p. pap. 8.95 *(978-1-4575-2094-5(X))* Dog Ear Publishing, LLC.

Stuart, Lisa Marie. The Little Cat, the Wonderful Witch, & the Clever Mouse. Potter, Lori, illus. 2008. 60p. pap. 21.95 *(978-1-59858-691-6(2))* Dog Ear Publishing, LLC.

Tauiliili, Pemerika L. The Rat & the Bat: And Other Short Stories. 2009. 88p. pap. 16.99 *(978-1-4490-4389-6(5));* pap. 32.49 *(978-1-4389-2700-8(2))* AuthorHouse.

Thompson, Colin. The Short & Incredibly Happy Life of Riley. Lissiat, Amy, illus. 2006. 32p. (J). *(978-0-7344-0806-8(4),* Lothian Children's Bks.) Hachette Australia.

Tremblay, Carole. Romeo, le Rat Romantique. 2004. (FRE., Illus.). (J). (gr. -1-3). spiral bd. *(978-0-616-07266-0(X))* Canadian National Institute for the Blind/Institut National Canadien pour les Aveugles.

Velazquez, Anna. Stewart's Airplane Adventure. 2008. 40p. pap. 24.95 *(978-1-60441-486-8(3))* America Star Bks.

Velthuijs, Max. Frog & the Stranger. 2014. (ENG., Illus.). 32p. (J). (-k). pap. 12.95 *(978-1-78344-143-3(7))* Andersen Pr. GBR. Dist: Independent Pubs. Group.

Ventura, Marne. Nervous Nellie Fights First-Day Frenzy. Trinidad, Leo, illus. 2016. (Worry Warriors Ser.). (ENG.). 96p. (J). (gr. 2-4). lib. bdg. 25.99 *(978-1-4965-3613-6(4),* 132819, Stone Arch Bks.) Capstone.

Vernon, Ursula. Hamster Princess: Ratpunzel. 2016. (Hamster Princess Ser.: 3). (Illus.). 240p. (J). (gr. 3-7). 14.99 *(978-0-8037-3985-7(0),* Dial Bks) Penguin Young Readers Group.

Wall, Layton E. Rat Fishin' with Ralphie Rat: A Bully Learns a Lesson. 2010. 28p. pap. 12.85 *(978-1-4520-4960-1(2))* AuthorHouse.
Watts, Frances. A Rat in a Stripy Sock. Francis, David, illus. 2018. 24p. pap. 6.99 *(978-0-7333-3460-3(1))* ABC Bks. AUS. Dist: HarperCollins Pubs.
Wendling, Nathalie & Glatzmayer, Thomas. Melanie & Tommy Have Two Pet Rats & One Syndrome. 2010. 48p. pap. *(978-1-926582-67-2(5))* Insomniac Pr.
Wersba, Barbara. Walter: The Story of a Rat. Diamond, Donna, illus. 2012. (ENG.). 64p. (J). (gr. 4-7). pap. 8.95 *(978-1-59078-948-3(2),* Astra Young Readers) Astra Publishing Hse.
—Walter: The Story of a Rat. 2012. (ENG., Illus.). 64p. (gr. 4-6). 24.94 *(978-1-932425-41-3(1))* Highlights Pr., c/o Highlights for Children, Inc.
Westen, Leah. Jack the Tooth Rat. 2009. (Illus.). 28p. pap. 12.50 *(978-1-60693-558-3(5),* Eloquent Bks.) Strategic Book Publishing & Rights Agency (SBPRA).
Winthrop, Elizabeth. The Red-Hot Rattoons. Lewin, Betsy, illus. 2006. (ENG.). 224p. (J). (gr. 3-6). pap. 17.99 *(978-0-8050-7986-9(6),* 900034574, Holt, Henry & Co. Bks. For Young Readers) Holt, Henry & Co.

RAVENS

Berne, Emma Carlson. Ravens, 1 vol. 2014. (Scavengers: Eating Nature's Trash Ser.). (ENG., Illus.). 24p. (J). (gr. 2-3). lib. bdg. 25.27 *(978-1-4777-6612-5(X),* df3a0123-aba2-442d-a755-f5ff8e39924e, PowerKids Pr.) Rosen Publishing Group, Inc., The.
Bradley, James. Ravens & Crows. 2006. (Nature Walk Ser.). (ENG., Illus.). 64p. (gr. 4-6). lib. bdg. 28.00 *(978-0-7910-9115-9(5),* P114528, Facts On File) Infobase Holdings, Inc.
Lajiness, Katie. Ravens: Problem Solvers. 2018. (Awesome Animal Powers Ser.). (ENG., Illus.). 32p. (J). (gr. 2-5). lib. bdg. 34.21 *(978-1-5321-1503-5(2),* 28860, Big Buddy Bks.) ABDO Publishing Co.
Webster, Christine. Ravens. 2009. (Backyard Animals Ser.). (Illus.). 24p. (J). (gr. 3-5). pap. 8.95 *(978-1-60596-083-8(7));* lib. bdg. 24.45 *(978-1-60596-082-1(9))* Weigl Pubs., Inc.

RAVENS—FICTION

Adams, Jennifer. Edgar & the Tattle-Tale Heart: a BabyLit(TM) Book: Inspired by Edgar Allan Poe's the Tell-Tale Heart, 1 vol. Stucki, Ron, illus. 2014. (ENG.). 32p. (J). 16.99 *(978-1-4236-3766-0(6))* Gibbs Smith, Publisher.
—Edgar & the Tree House of Usher: Inspired by Edgar Allan Poe's the Fall of the House of Usher, 1 vol. Stucki, Ron, illus. 2015. (Edgar the Raven Ser.). (ENG.). 32p. (J). (gr. -1-k). 16.99 *(978-1-4236-4043-1(8))* Gibbs Smith, Publisher.
Aiken, Joan. Arabel's Raven. Blake, Quentin, illus. 2007. (ENG.). 160p. (J). (gr. 3-7). pap. 11.95 *(978-0-15-206094-7(4),* 1198305, Clarion Bks.) HarperCollins Pubs.
Al-Ghani, K.I. Ronnie Raven Recycles, 1 vol. 2011. (ENG., Illus.). 44p. (J). (gr. -1-3). 16.99 *(978-0-7643-3840-3(4),* 4270, Schiffer Publishing Ltd) Schiffer Publishing, Ltd.
Anastasio, Dina, retold by. How Raven Became Black & Owl Got Its Spots: Set Of 6. 2010. (Early Connections Ser.). (J). pap. 37.00 net. *(978-1-4108-1093-9(3))* Benchmark Education Co.
Avi. Old Wolf. Floca, Brian, illus. 2015. (ENG.). 160p. (J). (gr. 3-7). 17.99 *(978-1-4424-9921-8(4))* Simon & Schuster Children's Publishing.
Bansch, Helga. Odd Bird Out. 2011. (Gecko Press Titles Ser.). (ENG., Illus.). 32p. pap. 17.95 *(978-1-877467-08-0(1))* Gecko Pr. NZL. Dist: Lerner Publishing Group.
Blaikie, Lynn. Beyond the Northern Lights, 1 vol. 2006. (ENG., Illus.). 24p. (J). (gr. k-2). 16.95 *(978-1-55005-123-0(7),* e6790771-e8ff-475d-af8b-b31524ffbb8c) Trifolium Bks., Inc. CAN. Dist: Firefly Bks., Ltd.
Bouchard, David. I am Raven. Everson, Andy, illus. 2nd ed. 2008. 28p. (J). *(978-0-9784327-0-6(3))* More Than Words Bks., Inc.
Brouillet, Chrystine. Le Corbeau. 2003. (Roman Jeunesse Ser.). (FRE.). 96p. (YA). (gr. 4-7). pap. *(978-2-89021-132-2(0))* Diffusion du livre Mirabel (DLM).
Carlstrom, Nancy White. Raven & River. Van Zyle, Jon, illus. 2011. (ENG.). 32p. pap. 13.95 *(978-1-60223-150-4(8))* Univ. of Alaska Pr.
Collins, Christina. After Zero. 2018. (ENG.). 256p. (J). (gr. 3-7). 16.99 *(978-1-4926-5532-9(5))* Sourcebooks, Inc.
Cotes, Gilles. OGM et Chant de Mais. Begin, Jean-Guy, illus. 2004. (FRE.). 112p. (J). *(978-2-89599-002-4(6))* Editions de la Paix CAN. Dist: World of Reading, Ltd.
Dawson, Willow. The Wolf-Birds. 2015. (ENG., Illus.). 40p. (J). (gr. k-4). 17.95 *(978-1-77147-054-4(2),* Owlkids) Owlkids Bks. Inc. CAN. Dist: Publishers Group West (PGW).
Derubertis, Barbara. Victor Vicuna's Volcano Vacation. Alley, R. W., illus. 2011. (Animal Antics A to Z Set III Ser.). pap. 45.32 *(978-0-7613-8431-1(6))* Astra Publishing Hse.
deRubertis, Barbara. Victor Vicuna's Volcano Vacation. Alley, R. W., illus. 2011. (Animal Antics a to Z Ser.). 32p. (J). (gr. -1-3). pap. 7.95 *(978-1-57565-347-1(8),* e2e7f138-2df7-44ad-b7e3-c5fb2ef2c3ed, Kane Press) Astra Publishing Hse.
deRubertis, Barbara & DeRubertis, Barbara. Victor Vicuna's Volcano Vacation. Alley, R. W., illus. 2012. (Animal Antics A to Z Ser.). 32p. (J). (gr. 2 — 1). cd-rom 7.95 *(978-1-57565-415-7(6))* Astra Publishing Hse.
Drummond, Sarah, illus. Raven & the Red Ball. 2013. (ENG.). 28p. (J). 9.95 *(978-0-7649-6609-5(X))* Pomegranate Communications, Inc.
Galera Staff. Cuervo y la Raposa (Raven & the Fox) (SPA.). 24p. (J). 9.95 *(978-84-246-1601-4(4))* La Galera, S.A. Editorial ESP. Dist: AIMS International Bks., Inc.
George, Jean Craighead. Charlie's Raven. 2006. (ENG., Illus.). 208p. (J). (gr. 5-6). reprint ed. 6.99 *(978-0-14-240547-5(7),* Puffin Books) Penguin Young Readers Group.
Hagen, George. Gabriel Finley & the Lord of Air & Darkness. 2017. 288p. (J). (gr. 4-7). 16.99 *(978-0-399-55347-9(9),* Schwartz & Wade Bks.) Random Hse. Children's Bks.
Harris, Patricia. Raven & the Farmer, 1 vol. 2017. (Raven's Orchard Ser.). (ENG.). 24p. (gr. 1-1). pap. 9.25 *(978-1-5081-6143-1(7),* 8a1a2d83-12d4-4469-af6b-b754bc6c2c0a, PowerKids Pr.) Rosen Publishing Group, Inc., The.
—Raven in the City, 1 vol. 2017. (Raven's Orchard Ser.). (ENG.). 24p. (gr. 1-1). pap. 9.25 *(978-1-5081-6147-9(X),* 727b3b77-3bed-4b0a-b325-10163b357228, PowerKids Pr.) Rosen Publishing Group, Inc., The.
—Raven's Garden, 1 vol. 2017. (Raven's Orchard Ser.). (ENG.). 24p. (gr. 1-1). pap. 9.25 *(978-1-5081-6151-6(8),* 9208d9ee-afef-4741-9ea6-5cb7d514d80, PowerKids Pr.) Rosen Publishing Group, Inc., The.
Johannes, Avril & Branham, Jan. Eeny, Meeny, Miney, Moe, Four Alaskan Ravens. Tessama, C., illus. 2003. 32p. (J). 7.95 *(978-0-9749360-0-0(6))* Icicle Falls Publishing Co.
Lassiter, Rhiannon. Void: Hex; Shadows; Ghosts. 2011. (ENG.). 688p. (YA). (gr. 7). pap. 9.99 *(978-1-4424-2929-1(1),* Simon Pulse) Simon Pulse.
Osborne, Mary Pope. Haunted Castle on Hallows Eve. Murdocca, Sal, illus. 2010. (Magic Tree House (R) Merlin Mission Ser.: 2). 144p. (J). (gr. 2-5). pap. 5.99 *(978-0-375-86090-4(8),* Random Hse. Bks. for Young Readers) Random Hse. Children's Bks.
—Haunted Castle on Hallows Eve. 2010. (Magic Tree House Merlin Missions Ser.: 2). lib. bdg. 16.00 *(978-0-606-13992-2(3))* Turtleback.
Raven's Orchard, 6 vols. 2017. (Raven's Orchard Ser.). 24p. (ENG.). (gr. 1-1). 75.81 *(978-1-5081-6188-2(7),* e2553073-220d-4a0a-a8b4-8098c68168fa); (gr. 4-6). pap. 24.75 *(978-1-5081-6190-5(9))* Rosen Publishing Group, Inc., The. (PowerKids Pr.).
Sophia Hansen, Hansen & Hansen, Sophia. The Crow & the Raven. 2010. 20p. 9.50 *(978-1-4269-2752-2(5))* Trafford Publishing.
Stephenson, Midji. The Ravenous Raven. Gray, Steve, illus. 2015. (J). *(978-1-934656-70-9(4))* Grand Canyon Conservancy.
Stewart, Sharon. Raven Quest. 2005. (ENG.). 320p. (J). (gr. 4-6). 15.95 *(978-1-57505-894-8(4),* Carolrhoda Bks.) Lerner Publishing Group.
van Keuren, Luise. Raven, Stay by Me. 2012. (ENG.). 162p. pap. *(978-1-894377-30-0(3))* Breakwater Bks., Ltd.
Woodruff, Elvira. The Ravenmaster's Secret. 2005. (Escape from the Tower of London Ser.). (Illus.). 225p. (gr. 3-7). 16.00 *(978-0-7569-4791-0(X))* Perfection Learning Corp.

RAYS, ROENTGEN

see X-Rays

RCMP

see Royal Canadian Mounted Police

REACTORS (NUCLEAR PHYSICS)

see Nuclear Reactors

READERS

Here are entered school readers in English. For readers in other languages, use the name of the language with the subdivision Readers, e.g. French Language—Readers.

see also Primers

Level I, 6 vols. (Wonder WorldTM Ser.). 16p. 29.95 *(978-0-7802-1035-6(2))* Wright Group/McGraw-Hill.
Abdo Publishing. Adventures in Extreme Reading, 4 vols. 2013. (Adventures in Extreme Reading Ser.: 6). (ENG.). 112p. (J). (gr. 2-5). lib. bdg. 154.00 *(978-1-61641-918-9(0),* 56, Calico Chapter Bks.) ABDO Publishing Co.
Abnett, Dan. The Battle of Gettysburg: Invasion of the North!, 1 vol. 2006. (Graphic Battles of the Civil War Ser.). (ENG., Illus.). 48p. (gr. 4-5). pap. 14.05 *(978-1-4042-6477-9(9),* 36f99f45-4d64-4388-baa4-333123e7efe7, Rosen Classroom) Rosen Publishing Group, Inc., The.
Accelerated Reader. 2005. cd-rom *(978-1-59455-200-7(2))* Renaissance Learning, Inc.
Accelerated Reader RP Student Subscription. 2004. cd-rom *(978-1-59455-164-2(2))* Renaissance Learning, Inc.
Accelerated Reader RP Student Subscription Renewal. 2004. cd-rom *(978-1-59455-166-6(9))* Renaissance Learning, Inc.
Achieve Now Institute Staff. ESR Anthology, Band 3-5. 2004. pap. 24.08 *(978-0-7398-9889-5(2))* Steck-Vaughn.
ACT Reading Victory Student Textbook. 2nd ed. 2005. per. *(978-1-58894-033-9(0))* Cambridge Educational Services, Inc.
Action Packs: Complete Action Packs Add-to Pack. 492.00 *(978-0-7578-8404-7(0))* Rigby Education.
Action Words Board Books 800670, 5. 2005. (J). bds. *(978-1-59794-011-5(9))* Environments, Inc.
Activity Worksheets. 2004. (J). spiral bd. 29.95 *(978-1-886441-64-4(2))* Zoo-phonics, Inc.
Adams, Alison. Changes in the Kitchen. 2017. (Text Connections Guided Close Reading Ser.). (J). (gr. 1). *(978-1-4900-1803-4(4))* Benchmark Education Co.
Adams, Colleen. At the Toy Store, 1 vol. 2006. (Neighborhood Readers Ser.). (ENG.). 8p. (gr. k-1). pap. 5.15 *(978-1-4042-5732-0(2),* c0b916af-358d-49d9-94dd-62f040e7010c, Rosen Classroom) Rosen Publishing Group, Inc., The.
—The Big Day!, 1 vol. 2006. (Neighborhood Readers Ser.). (ENG.). 8p. (gr. k-1). pap. 5.15 *(978-1-4042-5708-5(X),* 62499b9f-40ab-4c55-a0b2-d9cf2dd19ed8, Rosen Classroom) Rosen Publishing Group, Inc., The.
—Jugando en la nieve (Playing in the Snow) 2007. (Lecturas del barrio (Neighborhood Readers) Ser.). (SPA.). 8p. 29.95 *(978-1-4042-7064-0(7),* Rosen Classroom) Rosen Publishing Group, Inc., The.
—Playing in the Snow. (Neighborhood Readers Ser.). (ENG.). 8p. 2007. 29.95 *(978-1-4042-7059-6(0))* 2006. pap. 5.15 *(978-1-4042-5657-6(1),* 4320a7bb-8d68-4736-8d92-88b1d246c4d7) Rosen Publishing Group, Inc., The. (Rosen Classroom).
—School Is Cool!, 1 vol. 2006. (Neighborhood Readers Ser.). (ENG.). 8p. (gr. k-1). pap. 5.15 *(978-1-4042-5676-7(8),* 3fac01d4-45f2-4a26-b767-fd8629cbff64, Rosen Classroom) Rosen Publishing Group, Inc., The.
Add-On Literature Set, 6 vols., Level C. (Into English! Ser.). (gr. 2-18). 47.88 *(978-1-56334-897-6(7),* SC0201) CENGAGE Learning.
Adler, David A. My Dog, & the Key Mystery. Ackerman, Dena, illus. 2018. 30p. (J). *(978-1-61465-601-2(0))* Menucha Pubs. Inc.
Afzal, Uz. Dance to the Beat. 2005. (Big Cat Ser.). (gr. k-2). pap. 6.50 *(978-1-60457-058-8(X))* Pacific Learning, Inc.
—Dance to the Beat: Band 03/Yellow (Collins Big Cat) Lumb, Steve, illus. 2005. (Collins Big Cat Ser.). (ENG.). 16p. (J). (gr. k-1). pap. 7.99 *(978-0-00-718576-4(6))* HarperCollins Pubs. Ltd. GBR. Dist: Independent Pubs. Group.
Agnew, Leonie. The Battle of Kupe & Te Wheke: a Māori Tale: Band 13/Topaz (Collins Big Cat) Bianchi, Fausto, illus. 2016. (Collins Big Cat Ser.). (ENG.). 32p. (J). (gr. 2-3). pap. 10.99 *(978-0-00-814716-7(7))* HarperCollins Pubs. Ltd. GBR. Dist: Independent Pubs. Group.
Ahearn, Dan. Time for Kids Readers. 2003. (Time for Kids Readers Ser.). (ENG.). pap. 84.96 *(978-0-15-340566-2(X))* Harcourt Schl. Pubs.
Ahmad, Kamil. Up, up, up! the Tale of a Magical Basket. 2017. (Text Connections Guided Close Reading Ser.). (J). (gr. 1). *(978-1-4900-1821-8(2))* Benchmark Education Co.
Aiken, David & Aiken, Zora. Chesapeake Play Day, 1 vol. 2015. (ENG., Illus.). 32p. (J). (gr. -1-3). 14.99 *(978-0-7643-4883-9(3),* 6635) Schiffer Publishing, Ltd.
Aikins, David. The Good, the Bad, & the Krabby! 2015. (SpongeBob Squarepants 8X8 Ser.). lib. bdg. 14.75 *(978-0-606-36397-6(1))* Turtleback.
Akers, Martin, et al. Fran Grabs It - Stop! It's a Frog! - the Best Nest: BuildUp Unit 3 Lap Book. Palacios, Sara & Battuz, Christine, illus. 2015. (Build up Core Phonics Ser.). (J). (gr. 1). *(978-1-4900-2602-2(9))* Benchmark Education Co.
Akinyemi, Rowena. Oxford Bookworms Library: under the Moon: Level 1: 400-Word Vocabulary. 3rd ed. 2008. (ENG., Illus.). 64p. 11.00 *(978-0-19-478922-6(5))* Oxford Univ. Pr., Inc.
al-Qadi, Charlotte. Arif Goes Shopping Pink a Band. Van Wyk, Rupert, illus. 2016. (Cambridge Reading Adventures Ser.). (ENG.). 16p. pap. 7.95 *(978-1-316-60810-4(7))* Cambridge Univ. Pr.
Alagna, Magdalena. Wyatt Earp: Lawman of the American West. 2009. (Primary Sources of Famous People in American History Ser.). (gr. 2-3). 47.90 *(978-1-60851-747-3(0))* Rosen Publishing Group, Inc., The.
The Alamo Journals. 2003. (Illus.). pap. 7.60 *(978-0-7398-7523-0(X))* Steck-Vaughn.
Alarcon, Roben. American Indians in the 1800s, 1 vol. rev. ed. 2005. (Social Studies: Informational Text Ser.). (ENG., Illus.). 24p. (J). (gr. 4-8). pap. 10.99 *(978-0-7439-8913-8(9))* Teacher Created Materials, Inc.
—The Constitution & the Bill of Rights, 1 vol. rev. ed. 2004. (Social Studies: Informational Text Ser.). (ENG.). 24p. (J). (gr. 4-8). pap. 10.99 *(978-0-7439-8783-7(7))* Teacher Created Materials, Inc.
—Librarians Then & Now, 1 vol. rev. ed. 2006. (Social Studies: Informational Text Ser.). (ENG.). 32p. (gr. 2-3). pap. 11.99 *(978-0-7439-9376-0(4))* Teacher Created Materials, Inc.
—Sitting Bull, 1 vol. rev. ed. 2005. (Social Studies: Informational Text Ser.). (ENG.). 24p. (J). (gr. 4-8). pap. 10.99 *(978-0-7439-8914-5(7))* Teacher Created Materials, Inc.
—Teachers Then & Now, 1 vol. rev. ed. 2006. (Social Studies: Informational Text Ser.). (ENG.). 32p. (gr. 2-3). pap. 11.99 *(978-0-7439-9375-3(6))* Teacher Created Materials, Inc.
Albee, Jo. American Heroes, 6 vols., Set. 2003. (Phonics Readers 1-36 Ser.). (ENG.). 8p. (gr. k-1). pap. 29.70 *(978-0-7368-3205-2(X))* Capstone.
Albee, Sarah. Julius Caesar, Cleopatra. 2011. (Readers' & Writers' Genre Workshop Ser.). (YA). pap. *(978-1-4509-3023-9(9))* Benchmark Education Co.
Alcraft, Rob. Collins Big Cat Phonics for Letters & Sounds - Big Questions: Band 07/Turquoise, Bd. 7. 2018. (Collins Big Cat Phonics Ser.). (ENG., Illus.). 24p. (J). pap. 6.99 *(978-0-00-825182-6(7))* HarperCollins Pubs. Ltd. GBR. Dist: Independent Pubs. Group.
Alexander, Heather. Junior Groovies - Bugs! 2010. (ENG., Illus.). 10p. (J). (gr. -1-1). 15.99 *(978-1-60169-019-7(3))* Innovative Kids.
—Wallace & Grace & the Cupcake Caper. Zarrin, Laura, illus. 2018. (Wallace & Grace Ser.). (ENG.). 80p. (J). pap. 7.99 *(978-1-68119-011-2(7),* 900154812, Bloomsbury Children's Bks.) Bloomsbury Publishing USA.
Alexander, Linda. As-Easy-As-ABC-123. 50th ed. 2003. (Illus.). (J). cd-rom *(978-0-9714299-2-5(8))* I Save A Tree.
—As-Easy-As-ABC-123 Bilingual. 2003. (SPA., Illus.). (J). cd-rom *(978-0-9714299-3-2(6))* I Save A Tree.
Alexander, Mark. Whose Toes Are Those?, 1 vol. 2006. (Neighborhood Readers Ser.). (ENG.). 12p. (gr. 1-2). pap. 5.90 *(978-1-4042-7042-8(6),* 4b3ed016-ec9d-49a4-bc1b-b25dceb90361, Rosen Classroom) Rosen Publishing Group, Inc., The.
Alexander, richard. The Inuit: People of the North, 1 vol. 2013. (Rosen Readers Ser.). (ENG.). 24p. (J). (gr. 3-3). pap. 8.25 *(978-1-4777-2548-1(2),* 1010cb9a-913a-4572-907d-f43f9b35c096); pap. 49.50 *(978-1-4777-2549-8(0))* Rosen Publishing Group, Inc., The. (Rosen Classroom).
Alexander's Enrichment Activties. 2006. (J). pap. 5.95 *(978-0-9742806-6-0(6))* Heart to Heart Publishing, Inc.
The Alien, 6 vols., Pack. (gr. 1-2). 25.00 *(978-0-7635-9192-2(0))* Rigby Education.
All Across America. (Guided Reading Levels Ser.). 28.56 *(978-0-7362-1060-7(1))* CENGAGE Learning.
All from a Bottle. (Early Intervention Levels Ser.). 31.86 *(978-0-7362-0662-4(0))* CENGAGE Learning.
All In The Family. 2005. (Little Celebrations Thematic Packages Ser.). (J). (gr. k-3). 133.50 *(978-0-673-75386-1(7))* Celebration Pr.
Allen, Kenny. Bird Builds a House, 1 vol. 2006. (Neighborhood Readers Ser.). (ENG.). 8p. (gr. k-1). pap. 5.15 *(978-1-4042-6690-2(9),* ded695e4-d0ae-4a0d-a6e2-1caeeda12ed7, Rosen Classroom) Rosen Publishing Group, Inc., The.
—A Great Day to Skate, 1 vol. 2006. (Neighborhood Readers Ser.). (ENG.). 8p. (gr. 1-2). pap. 5.15 *(978-1-4042-6819-7(7),* 2c234750-98f6-4792-a959-89e7affe33e5, Rosen Classroom) Rosen Publishing Group, Inc., The.
—My School, 1 vol. 2008. (Real Life Readers Ser.). (ENG.). 8p. (gr. k-1). pap. 5.15 *(978-1-4042-7969-8(5),* 74ce0dbd-de90-4437-ad72-4afedf515922, Rosen Classroom) Rosen Publishing Group, Inc., The.
Allen, Margaret. Jingle Jangles Vol. 2256: Fun, Interactive Reading Selections for Fluency Practice. Walter, LaDawn, ed. Rojas, Mary & Vangsgard, Amy, illus. 2004. 128p. (J). (gr. k-2). pap. 14.99 *(978-1-59198-048-3(8),* 2256) Creative Teaching Pr., Inc.
Almy, Judy. My Name Is Ick: A Rhyming Story of an Alaska Caribou. 2003. 9.95 *(978-1-59433-009-4(3))* Publication Consultants.
Alspach, Kate M. Farts Are Fantastic. 2012. 24p. pap. 15.99 *(978-1-4691-5589-0(3))* Xlibris Corp.
Altobello, Albert & Wadhams, Doyle. The 10 Most Important Civil Rights Decisions. 2008. 14.99 *(978-1-55448-528-4(2))* Scholastic Library Publishing.
Alvarez Garcia, Gloria. Los disfraces. 2005. (SPA.). 6p. 5.99 *(978-84-272-6682-7(0))* Molino, Editorial ESP. Dist: Santillana USA Publishing Co., Inc.
Alvarez, Lourdes M. My First Book Things. Brooks, David, illus. 2005. (My First Book Ser.). 9p. (J). (gr. -1-1). bds. 3.95 *(978-1-933050-10-2(1))* Sweetwater Pr.
Amazing Academy Assort. 2009. (J). *(978-1-84879-339-2(1))* Make Believe Ideas.
Amelia Bedilia Book Set 800916, 3 vols. 2005. (J). pap. *(978-1-59794-081-8(X))* Environments, Inc.
American Bible Society. Lee y Aprende: Mi Primera Biblia (My First Read & Learn Bible) American Bible Society, ed. Duendes Del Sur, illus. 2008. (SPA.). 38p. (J). (gr. -1-k). bds. 9.99 *(978-0-545-05656-4(X),* Scholastic en Espanol) Scholastic, Inc.
American Indian Crafts. 2005. (Book Treks Ser.). (J). (gr. 3-18). stu. ed. 34.95 *(978-0-673-62838-1(8))* Celebration Pr.
American Tract Society Staff, compiled by. The Tract Primer: First Lessons in Sound Doctrine for Young Children. 2007. 112p. per. 11.00 *(978-1-59925-130-1(2))* Solid Ground Christian Bks.
The American Tradition: The EMC Write-in Reader. 2nd ed. (Literature & the Language Arts Ser.). (YA). (gr. 11-18). wbk. ed. 19.99 *(978-0-8219-2918-6(6))* EMC/Paradigm Publishing.
Amery, Heather. Grumpy Goat. Cartwright, Stephen, illus. 2004. 16p. (J). pap. 5.95 *(978-0-7945-0788-6(3),* Usborne) EDC Publishing.
—Market Day. Cartwright, Stephen, illus. 2004. 16p. (J). pap. 5.95 *(978-0-7945-0783-1(2),* Usborne) EDC Publishing.
—Runaway Tractor. Cartwright, Stephen, illus. 2004. 16p. (J). pap. 5.95 *(978-0-7945-0748-0(4),* Usborne) EDC Publishing.
Amery, Heather, et al. First Hundred Words in Maori. 2008. (MAO., Illus.). 40p. pap. 14.00 *(978-1-86969-304-6(3))* Huia Pubs. NZL. Dist: Univ. of Hawaii Pr.
Amos, Eduardo. Amazon Rally. 2007. (ENG.). 99999p. pap. 17.32 *(978-1-4058-5199-2(6))* Pearson Education.
Amos, Ruth. Heroes of the Galaxy. 2018. (Star Wars DK Readers Level 2 Ser.). lib. bdg. 14.75 *(978-0-606-41169-1(0))* Turtleback.
Ana, Moh. Kookaburra Tales # 3: Laugh Not at Others. 2013. 16p. pap. 16.81 *(978-1-4669-3477-1(8))* Trafford Publishing.
Analyzing the Issues: Set 5, 12 vols. 2018. (Analyzing the Issues Ser.). (ENG.). 224-232p. (gr. 8-8). lib. bdg. 305.58 *(978-1-9785-0013-6(0),* a7cb53f0-a1db-4ad2-84a4-64c14d0f779b) Enslow Publishing, LLC.
Anastasio, Dina. Mickey & the Beanstalk (Disney Classic) Golden Books, illus. 2018. (Little Golden Book Ser.). (ENG.). 24p. (J). (-k). 5.99 *(978-0-7364-3785-1(1),* Golden/Disney) Random Hse. Children's Bks.
Anastasio, Dina & Jenkins, Amanda. Jake Digs a Hole, Luke & the Bug Man. 2011. (Readers' & Writers' Genre Workshop Ser.). (YA). pap. *(978-1-4509-3022-2(0))* Benchmark Education Co.
Andersen, Jill. All about Ramps, 1 vol. 2016. (Rosen REAL Readers: STEM & STEAM Collection). (ENG.). 8p. (gr. k-1). pap. 5.46 *(978-1-5081-2371-2(3),* aa741f0c-bf56-4845-8574-f7004ac2e3d0, Rosen Classroom) Rosen Publishing Group, Inc., The.
—Carlos Keeps His Cool at School, 1 vol. 2016. (Rosen REAL Readers: Social Studies Nonfiction / Fiction: Myself, My Community, My World Ser.). (ENG.). 12p. (gr. k-1). pap. 6.33 *(978-1-5081-2533-4(3),* 9c4285bc-bfe9-4655-95da-3953500ff03c, Rosen Classroom) Rosen Publishing Group, Inc., The.
—Chanice Visits the Children's Museum, 1 vol. 2016. (Rosen REAL Readers: Social Studies Nonfiction / Fiction: Myself, My Community, My World Ser.). (ENG.). 8p. (gr. k-1). pap. 5.46 *(978-1-5081-2482-5(5),* 0172e499-1457-48bc-a6db-680ffe8d3677, Rosen Classroom) Rosen Publishing Group, Inc., The.
—The Greatest Gift, 1 vol. 2016. (Rosen REAL Readers: Social Studies Nonfiction / Fiction: Myself, My Community, My World Ser.). (ENG.). 12p. (gr. k-1). pap. 6.33 *(978-1-5081-2541-9(4),* 5bf409a3-4095-4c80-a3f4-1ddc0682a5c4, Rosen Classroom) Rosen Publishing Group, Inc., The.
—The Robins in Our Yard, 1 vol. 2016. (Rosen REAL Readers: STEM & STEAM Collection). (ENG.). 8p. (gr. k-1). pap. 5.46 *(978-1-5081-2631-7(3),* c0a01cc6-0d37-46cf-8b81-964d33a48cf6, Rosen Classroom) Rosen Publishing Group, Inc., The.
—A Walk in the Mountains, 1 vol. 2016. (Rosen REAL Readers: STEM & STEAM Collection). (ENG.). 8p. (gr. k-1). pap. 5.46 *(978-1-5081-2610-2(0),* 71a70456-88ef-4c54-bf7e-c2963034ca7f, Rosen Classroom) Rosen Publishing Group, Inc., The.
—We Are Friends of the Earth, 1 vol. 2016. (Rosen REAL Readers: STEM & STEAM Collection). (ENG.). 8p. (gr. k-1). pap. 5.46 *(978-1-5081-2616-4(X),* c119f7a9-502a-4fde-908c-09637762767d, Rosen Classroom) Rosen Publishing Group, Inc., The.
—We Need Air to Breathe, 1 vol. 2016. (Rosen REAL Readers: STEM & STEAM Collection). (ENG.). 8p. (gr. k-1). pap. 5.46 *(978-1-5081-2395-8(0),* 4674bb25-0652-4320-bce0-451cee813e3b, Rosen Classroom) Rosen Publishing Group, Inc., The.
—Why Birds Chirp, 1 vol. 2016. (Rosen REAL Readers: STEM & STEAM Collection). (ENG.). 8p. (gr. k-1). pap. 5.46 *(978-1-5081-2416-0(7),* c04ee208-46e2-45b5-8932-058b45522f0d, Rosen Classroom) Rosen Publishing Group, Inc., The.
Andersen, Neil. WWW: Surfing with Celebrities. 2007. (Steck-Vaughn BOLDPRINT Anthologies Ser.). (ENG., Illus.). 48p. (gr. 7-9). pap. 16.90 *(978-1-4190-4029-0(4))* Houghton Mifflin Harcourt Publishing Co.
Anderson, Al. Adventures with Bingo Borden. Agora Publications Staff, tr. Kurzyca, Krystyna Emilia, illus. 2010.

77p. (J). pap. 9.50 (978-1-887250-46-7(8)) Agora Pubns., Inc.

Anderson, Hans Christian & Stone Arch Books Staff. Caperucita Roja. Rivas, Victor, illus. 2010. (Graphic Spin en Español Ser.). (SPA.). 40p. (J). (gr. 3-6). pap. 5.95 (978-1-4342-2315-9(9), 103184, Stone Arch Bks.) Capstone.

—Rumpelstiltskin: La Novela Grafica, 1 vol. Alanis, Erik Valdez Y., illus. 2010. (Graphic Spin en Español Ser.). (SPA.). 40p. (J). (gr. 3-6). pap. 5.95 (978-1-4342-2273-2(X), 103136, Stone Arch Bks.) Capstone.

Anderson, James. Around Home. rev. ed. 2011. (Mathematics in the Real World Ser.). (ENG.). 32p. (gr. k-1). pap. 9.99 (978-1-4333-3439-9(9)) Teacher Created Materials, Inc.

—Around Town. rev. ed. 2011. (Mathematics in the Real World Ser.). (ENG.). 32p. (gr. k-1). pap. 9.99 (978-1-4333-3438-2(0)) Teacher Created Materials, Inc.

Anderson, Jo Marie. If I Were a Ladybug, 1 vol. 2017. (I'm a Bug! Ser.). (ENG.). 24p. (gr. 1-1). 25.27 (978-1-5081-5723-6(5), a98d8538-607a-41c4-969d-9cdb3b043280, PowerKids Pr.) Rosen Publishing Group, Inc., The.

Anderson, Lynne. Rocket Ship Shapes. 2011. (Early Connections Ser.). (J). (978-1-61672-596-9(6)) Benchmark Education Co.

Anderson, Nancy. All about Mirrors, 1 vol. 2016. (Rosen REAL Readers: STEM & STEAM Collection). (ENG.). 12p. (gr. 1-2). pap. 6.33 (978-1-5081-2437-5(X), 3f66e785-9eb0-46db-85ad-f15f10e84175, Rosen Classroom) Rosen Publishing Group, Inc., The.

—Building Dikes, 1 vol. 2016. (Rosen REAL Readers: STEM & STEAM Collection). (ENG.). 12p. (gr. 1-2). pap. 6.33 (978-1-5081-2464-1(7), a534b356-3fd2-4e87-849a-4c992edbd505, Rosen Classroom) Rosen Publishing Group, Inc., The.

—Election Day with the Robinsons, 1 vol. 2016. (Rosen REAL Readers: Social Studies Nonfiction / Fiction: Myself, My Community, My World Ser.). (ENG.). 12p. (gr. k-1). pap. 6.33 (978-1-5081-2565-5(1), 5f1c06b2-e322-49c0-a75b-a99c4e2a740c, Rosen Classroom) Rosen Publishing Group, Inc., The.

—Homework Help, 1 vol. 2016. (Rosen REAL Readers: Social Studies Nonfiction / Fiction: Myself, My Community, My World Ser.). (ENG.). 8p. (gr. k-1). pap. 5.46 (978-1-5081-2500-6(7), 2b0b9a21-3041-4f63-9353-694d30092918, Rosen Classroom) Rosen Publishing Group, Inc., The.

—The House near the Pond, 1 vol. 2016. (Rosen REAL Readers: STEM & STEAM Collection). (ENG.). 8p. (gr. k-1). pap. 5.46 (978-1-5081-2595-2(3), 42f3becc-64b0-4c9e-b242-2f2c89dfb632, Rosen Classroom) Rosen Publishing Group, Inc., The.

—Isaiah Has a Stomachache, 1 vol. 2016. (Rosen REAL Readers: Social Studies Nonfiction / Fiction: Myself, My Community, My World Ser.). (ENG.). 8p. (gr. k-1). pap. 5.46 (978-1-5081-2479-5(5), 1eb86cb1-3d35-4692-910c-4ef1bcbbd28e, Rosen Classroom) Rosen Publishing Group, Inc., The.

—The Mirror on the Wall, 1 vol. 2016. (Rosen REAL Readers: STEM & STEAM Collection). (ENG.). 12p. (gr. 1-2). pap. 6.33 (978-1-5081-2652-2(6), 91893401-fb6b-4167-91e3-eb3bb6c01bf2, Rosen Classroom) Rosen Publishing Group, Inc., The.

—The Rocket Express, 1 vol. 2016. (Rosen REAL Readers: Social Studies Nonfiction / Fiction: Myself, My Community, My World Ser.). (ENG.). 8p. (gr. k-1). pap. 5.46 (978-1-5081-2494-8(9), b83ec022-ef83-473c-a314-2d425861bc1d, Rosen Classroom) Rosen Publishing Group, Inc., The.

Anderson, Peggy Perry. Time for Bed, the Babysitter Said. 2012. (ENG., Illus.). 32p. (J). (gr. -1-3). pap. 5.99 (978-0-547-85061-0(1), 1501045, Clarion Bks.) HarperCollins Pubs.

—To the Tub. 2012. (Green Light Readers Level 1 Ser.). (ENG., Illus.). 32p. (J). (gr. -1-3). pap. 4.99 (978-0-547-85053-5(0), 1501029, Clarion Bks.) HarperCollins Pubs.

Anderson, Scoular. Connections 1 Pathfinders. 2017. (Cambridge Reading Adventures Ser.). (ENG., Illus.). 32p. pap. 8.60 (978-1-108-43094-4(5)) Cambridge Univ. Pr.

—Fabulous Creatures - Are They Real?: Band 11/Lime (Collins Big Cat) Anderson, Scoular, illus. 2005. (Collins Big Cat Ser.). (ENG., Illus.). 32p. (J). (gr. 1-3). pap. 10.99 (978-0-00-718639-6(8)) HarperCollins Pubs. Ltd. GBR. Dist: Independent Pubs. Group.

—How to Be a Knight: Band 09/Gold (Collins Big Cat) Anderson, Scoular, illus. 2007. (Collins Big Cat Ser.). (ENG., Illus.). 36p. (J). (gr. 1-2). pap. 9.99 (978-0-00-718675-4(4)) HarperCollins Pubs. Ltd. GBR. Dist: Independent Pubs. Group.

—How to Be a Tudor: Band 14/Ruby (Collins Big Cat) Anderson, Scoular, illus. 2007. (Collins Big Cat Ser.). (ENG., Illus.). 48p. (J). (gr. 3-4). pap. 10.99 (978-0-00-723090-7(7)) HarperCollins Pubs. Ltd. GBR. Dist: Independent Pubs. Group.

—How to Be a Viking: Band 12/Copper (Collins Big Cat) Anderson, Scoular, illus. 2007. (Collins Big Cat Ser.). (ENG., Illus.). 32p. (J). (gr. 2-4). pap. 10.99 (978-0-00-723079-2(6)) HarperCollins Pubs. Ltd. GBR. Dist: Independent Pubs. Group.

—Sticks & Bricks & Bits of Stone White Band. 2016. (Cambridge Reading Adventures Ser.). (ENG., Illus.). 32p. pap. 9.50 (978-1-107-56056-7(X)) Cambridge Univ. Pr.

—Where on Earth?: Band 11/Lime (Collins Big Cat) Anderson, Scoular, illus. 2005. (Collins Big Cat Ser.). (ENG., Illus.). 32p. (J). (gr. 1-3). pap. 10.99 (978-0-00-718633-4(9)) HarperCollins Pubs. Ltd. GBR. Dist: Independent Pubs. Group.

Andover, Max. Octopuses & Squid. 2011. (Illus.). 16p. (J). pap. (978-0-545-24792-4(6)) Scholastic, Inc.

Andrews, Catherine, et al. Elson Readers: Book 4, Teacher's Guide, Bk. 4. 2012. (ENG., Illus.). 193p. (gr. -1-12). tchr. ed. 12.95 (978-1-890623-28-9(8)) Applewood Bks.

Andrews, Jane. Young Reader's Series: The seven little sisters who live on the round ball that floats in the Air. 2008. 152p. pap. 14.95 (978-1-60444-020-1(1)) IndoEuropeanPublishing.com.

Animal Parade Books 800790, 4. 2005. (J). bds. (978-1-59794-021-4(6)) Environments, Inc.

Animal Story Board Books 800556, 5. 2005. (J). bds. (978-1-59794-005-4(4)) Environments, Inc.

Ankers, Angela M. Summerbook Readers: Short a & i words, 3. Lt. ed. 2004. (Illus.). 40p. (J). 5.95 (978-1-933055-00-8(6)) Summerbook Co.

Anthony, David H. Freedom: Life after Slavery, 1 vol. rev. ed. 2011. (Social Studies: Informational Text Ser.). (ENG.). 32p. (gr. 4-8). pap. 11.99 (978-1-4333-1521-3(1)) Teacher Created Materials, Inc.

—Langston Hughes: Harlem Renaissance Writer, 1 vol. rev. ed. 2011. (Social Studies: Informational Text Ser.). (ENG., Illus.). 32p. (gr. 4-8). pap. 11.99 (978-1-4333-1520-6(3)) Teacher Created Materials, Inc.

Anthony, Ross. Please Don't Step on the Ants. Anthony, Ross, illus. 2006. (ENG, CHI, SPA & JPN., Illus.). (J). per. (978-0-9727894-4-8(8)) Arizona Blueberry Studios.

Antologia: Para leer en voz Alta: Student & Teacher Support Resources. 2003. (MacMillan/McGraw-Hill. Estudios Sociales Ser.). (ENG & SPA.). (gr. 1-18). (978-0-02-149464-4(9)); (gr. 2-18). (978-0-02-149465-1(7)); (gr. 3-18). (978-0-02-149466-8(5)) Macmillan/McGraw-Hill Schl. Div.

Apodaca, Blanca. All in a Day's Work: Animator, 1 vol. 2nd rev. ed. 2013. (TIME for KIDS(r): Informational Text Ser.). (ENG., Illus.). 64p. (J). (gr. 4-8). pap. 14.99 (978-1-4333-4907-2(8)) Teacher Created Materials, Inc.

—Behind the Canvas: An Artist's Life, 1 vol. 2nd rev. ed. 2012. (TIME for KIDS(r): Informational Text Ser.). (ENG.). 48p. (gr. 4-5). pap. 13.99 (978-1-4333-4826-6(8)) Teacher Created Materials, Inc.

Appel, Marty. Pinstripe Pride: The Inside Story of the New York Yankees. 2016. lib. bdg. 24.50 (978-0-606-38275-5(5)) Turtleback.

Appleby, Alex. ¡Feliz día de Acción de Gracias! / Happy Thanksgiving!, 1 vol., Vol. 1. 2013. (¡Felices Fiestas! / Happy Holidays! Ser.). (SPA & ENG.). 24p. (J). (gr. k-k). 25.27 (978-1-4339-9968-0(4), 31a1bda4-52b2-47fc-8f72-bd2c48a3ad17) Stevens, Gareth Publishing LLLP.

Appleton-Smith, Laura. Dog Agility. White, Keinyo, illus. 2007. (ENG.). 19p. (J). pap. 8.95 (978-1-60541-012-8(8), Books To Remember) Flyleaf Publishing.

Apte, Sunita. The March. 2005. (Illus.). 16p. pap. (978-0-7367-2923-9(2)) Zaner-Bloser, Inc.

Apte, Sunita, text. Moving Home. 2005. (Illus.). 16p. (978-0-7367-2954-3(2)) Zaner-Bloser, Inc.

Archer, Anita L., et al. REWARDS Plus: Reading Excellence: Reading Strategies Applied to Science Passages. 2006. (Illus.). 200p. (gr. 6-8). pap. 11.49 (978-1-59318-286-1(4)) Cambium Education, Inc.

Archer, Dosh. The Case of the Stolen Drumsticks (Detective Paw of the Law: Time to Read, Level 3) Archer, Dosh, illus. 2018. (Time to Read Ser.: 2). (ENG., Illus.). 48p. (J). (gr. k-2). 12.99 (978-0-8075-1556-3(6), 807515566) Whitman, Albert & Co.

Aree, Bill. The Class Vote, 1 vol. 2008. (Real Life Readers Ser.). (ENG.). 12p. (gr. 1-2). pap. 5.90 (978-1-4042-7929-2(6), 5d88b6fc-d62f-4285-97ac-588565c00175, Rosen Classroom) Rosen Publishing Group, Inc., The.

Arengo, Sue. Classic Tales: Thumbelina. Goulding, Celeste, illus. 2006. (ENG.). 24p. 5.50 (978-0-19-422537-3(2)) Oxford Univ. Pr. GBR. Dist: Oxford Univ. Pr., Inc.

—Classic Tales 2e L4 Cinderella. 2nd ed. 2011. (ENG., Illus.). 24p. pap. 8.80 (978-0-19-423942-4(X)) Oxford Univ. Pr., Inc.

—Classic Tales 2e the Princess & the Pea. 2nd ed. 2011. (ENG., Illus.). 24p. pap. 8.80 (978-0-19-423878-6(4)) Oxford Univ. Pr., Inc.

—Jack & the Beanstalk. Ratto, Cinzia, illus. 2006. (ENG.). 24p. 5.50 (978-0-19-422538-0(0)) Oxford Univ. Pr. GBR. Dist: Oxford Univ. Pr., Inc.

Armour, Cy. Earthquakes!, 1 vol. 2nd rev. ed. 2011. (TIME for KIDS(r): Informational Text Ser.). (ENG.). 24p. (gr. 2-3). pap. 9.99 (978-1-4333-3613-3(8)) Teacher Created Materials, Inc.

—Tornadoes & Hurricanes!, 1 vol. 2nd rev. ed. 2011. (TIME for KIDS(r): Informational Text Ser.). (ENG.). 24p. (gr. 2-3). pap. 9.99 (978-1-4333-3614-0(6)) Teacher Created Materials, Inc.

—Volcanoes!, 1 vol. 2nd rev. ed. 2011. (TIME for KIDS(r): Informational Text Ser.). (ENG.). 24p. (gr. 2-3). pap. 9.99 (978-1-4333-3615-7(4)) Teacher Created Materials, Inc.

Arnold Lobel Book Set 800917, 3 vols. 2005. (J). pap. (978-1-59794-082-5(8)) Environments, Inc.

Arnold, Tedd. Fly Guy Presents: Weather. 2016. (Illus.). (J). (978-1-338-04666-3(7)) Scholastic, Inc.

—Fly Guy Presents: Castles (Scholastic Reader, Level 2) Arnold, Tedd, illus. 2017. (Scholastic Reader, Level 2 Ser.). (ENG.). 32p. (J). (gr. k-2). pap. 5.99 (978-0-545-91738-4(7)) Scholastic, Inc.

—Fly Guy Presents: the White House (Scholastic Reader, Level 2) Arnold, Tedd, illus. 2016. (Scholastic Reader, Level 2 Ser.). (ENG., Illus.). 32p. (J). (gr. k-2). pap. 4.99 (978-0-545-91737-7(9)) Scholastic, Inc.

Arnold, Tedd, illus. Police Officers. 2018. (J). (978-1-5444-0550-6(2)) Scholastic, Inc.

Arnone, T. I. The Magic Kazoo. 2009. (ENG., Illus.). 48p. pap. 25.00 (978-0-557-12017-8(9)) Lulu Pr., Inc.

Arrigan, Mary. Pa Jinglebob & the Grabble Gang. 2006. (Red Bananas Ser.). (ENG., Illus.). 48p. (J). (gr. -1-3). lib. bdg. (978-0-7787-1074-5(2)) Crabtree Publishing Co.

Art Pen Pal. 2003. 31.95 (978-0-673-75796-8(X)) Celebration Pr.

Ashe, Susan. Cuda of the Celts. 2005. (Yellow Go Bananas Ser.). (ENG., Illus.). 48p. (J). (gr. 3-4). (978-0-7787-2742-2(4)) Crabtree Publishing Co.

Ashley, Michele. When Do Trees Look Different? 2012. (Level D Ser.). (ENG., Illus.). 16p. (J). (gr. k-2). pap. 7.95 (978-1-927136-38-6(5), 19433) RiverStream Publishing.

—Who Has Ears Like These? 2012. (Level C Ser.). (ENG., Illus.). 16p. (J). (gr. k-2). pap. 7.95 (978-1-927136-27-0(X), 19450) RiverStream Publishing.

—Who Is This? 2012. (Level A Ser.). (ENG., Illus.). 16p. (J). (gr. k-2). pap. 7.95 (978-1-927136-00-3(8), 19451) RiverStream Publishing.

Asnong, Jocey, illus. Nuptse & Lhotse Go to Iceland. 2015. 40p. (J). (gr. k). 18.00 (978-1-77160-124-5(8)) Rocky Mountain Bks.

Asquith, Ros. Hector & the Cello. 2005. (Big Cat Ser.). pap. 6.50 (978-1-60457-077-9(6)) Pacific Learning, Inc.

Asthma in Action. 2005. (Book Treks Ser.). (J). (gr. 3-18). stu. ed. 34.95 (978-0-673-62843-5(4)) Celebration Pr.

Astro, Ian. Moon School, 1 vol. 2006. (Neighborhood Readers Ser.). (ENG.). 16p. (gr. 1-2). pap. 6.50 (978-1-4042-7196-8(1), 5462beef-9025-4a84-b0cd-78c50d2a7eb8, Rosen Classroom) Rosen Publishing Group, Inc., The.

Astronaut Adventure. (Early Intervention Levels Ser.). 21.30 (978-0-7362-0378-4(8)) CENGAGE Learning.

At School. (Early Intervention Levels Ser.). 3.85 (978-1-56334-952-2(3)); 23.10 (978-0-7362-0000-4(2)) CENGAGE Learning.

At the Fair. (Early Intervention Levels Ser.). 23.10 (978-0-7362-0013-4(4)); Vol. 2. 3.85 (978-1-56334-963-8(9)) CENGAGE Learning.

At the Toyshop: Individual Title Six-Packs. (gr. -1-2). 23.00 (978-0-7635-9005-5(3)) Rigby Education.

Athans, Sandra K. & Parente, Robin W. Tips & Tricks for Determining Point of View & Purpose, 1 vol. 2014. (Common Core Readiness Guide to Reading Ser.). (ENG.). 64p. (J). (gr. 6-6). 36.13 (978-1-4777-7555-4(2), d947b5da-ca60-4d30-8084-35038bdf3a8f, Rosen Reference) Rosen Publishing Group, Inc., The.

—Tips & Tricks for Evaluating Multimedia Content, 1 vol. 2014. (Common Core Readiness Guide to Reading Ser.). (ENG.). 64p. (YA). (gr. 6-6). 36.13 (978-1-4777-7563-9(3), 6ee9edec-8903-4dd0-9662-4156b807b3ba, Rosen Reference) Rosen Publishing Group, Inc., The.

Atkins, Jill. Ned in Bed & Fun at the Park. Wray, Jordan, illus. 2019. (Early Bird Readers — Pink (Early Bird Stories (tm)) Ser.). (ENG.). 32p. (J). (gr. -1-2). 30.65 (978-1-5415-4160-3(X), a5dc0e4e-497c-49a5-b9e5-493d626ea377, Lerner Pubns.) Lerner Publishing Group.

—Peck, Hen, Peck! & Ben's Pet. Vagnozzi, Barbara, illus. 2019. (Early Bird Readers — Pink (Early Bird Stories (tm)) Ser.). (ENG.). 32p. (J). (gr. -1-2). pap. 9.99 (978-1-5415-4623-3(7), e1dab588-16c7-448a-84b6-3728125530ba) Lerner Publishing Group.

—Toad Swims for his Life! Mostyn, David, illus. 2004. (ENG.). 24p. (J). lib. bdg. 23.65 (978-1-59646-712-5(6)) Dingles & Co.

—Up in a Rocket: Band 02A/Red A, Bd. 2A. Ortu, Davide, illus. 2018. (Collins Big Cat Phonics Ser.). (ENG.). 16p. (J). (gr. -1-k). pap. 6.99 (978-0-00-825145-1(2)) HarperCollins Pubs. Ltd. GBR. Dist: Independent Pubs. Group.

Auch, Allison. Women Who Dared: Set Of 6. 2011. (Navigators Ser.). (J). 48.00 net. (978-1-4108-0427-3(5)) Benchmark Education Co.

Aucoin, Lee. Weather, 1 vol. rev. ed. 2009. (Early Literacy Ser.). (ENG., Illus.). 16p. (gr. -1-1). 6.99 (978-1-4333-1456-8(8)); 19.99 (978-1-4333-1457-5(6)) Teacher Created Materials, Inc.

Austen, Elizabeth. Living!, 1 vol. rev. ed. 2014. (Science: Informational Text Ser.). (ENG., Illus.). 24p. (gr. -1-1). pap. 9.99 (978-1-4807-4520-9(0)) Teacher Created Materials, Inc.

—Seeds, 1 vol. rev. ed. 2014. (Science: Informational Text Ser.). (ENG., Illus.). 24p. (gr. k-1). pap. 9.99 (978-1-4807-4522-3(7)) Teacher Created Materials, Inc.

—What Do Living Things Need?, 1 vol. rev. ed. 2014. (Science: Informational Text Ser.). (ENG., Illus.). 24p. (gr. -1-1). pap. 9.99 (978-1-4807-4523-0(5)) Teacher Created Materials, Inc.

Austin, Judi. How Many Cookies? Learning to Subtract 1 from One-Digit Numbers, 1 vol. 2010. (Math for the REAL World Ser.). (ENG., Illus.). 8p. (gr. k-1). pap. 5.15 (978-0-8239-8886-0(4), fe89288e-ffa7-44ec-abda-dd6db8685b94) Rosen Publishing Group, Inc., The.

Avenues Language & Literacy Tests: Level D Posttest Booklet (10-Pack) (Avenues Ser.). 30.00 (978-0-7362-2516-8(1)) CENGAGE Learning.

A Avenues Level: Little Language Book Set (11 Titles) (Avenues Ser.). (gr. k-18). 41.53 (978-0-7362-1790-3(8)) CENGAGE Learning.

A Avenues Level: Teacher Support Pack. (Avenues Ser.). (gr. k-18). 716.47 (978-0-7362-2200-6(6)) CENGAGE Learning.

A Avenues Level: Theme Library (10 Titles), 10 vols. (Avenues Ser.). (gr. k-18). 143.98 (978-0-7362-2108-5(5)) CENGAGE Learning.

Avenues Level B: Leveled Books & ETools. (gr. 1-18). 377.86 (978-0-7362-2535-9(8)) CENGAGE Learning.

Avenues Level B: Literature Anthology Set, 2 vols. (Avenues Ser.). (gr. 1-18). 41.20 (978-0-7362-2022-4(4)) CENGAGE Learning.

Avenues Level B: Teacher Support Pack. (Avenues Ser.). (gr. 1-18). 517.25 (978-0-7362-2202-0(2)) CENGAGE Learning.

Avenues Level B: Theme Library, 12 vols. (Avenues Ser.). (gr. 1-18). 109.16 (978-0-7362-1642-9(4)) CENGAGE Learning.

Avenues Level C: Leveled Books & ETools. (gr. 2-18). 447.46 (978-0-7362-2536-6(6)) CENGAGE Learning.

Avenues Level C: Teacher Support Pack. (Avenues Ser.). (gr. 2-18). 405.33 (978-0-7362-2204-4(9)) CENGAGE Learning.

Avenues Level C: Theme Library (12 Titles), 12 vols. (Avenues Ser.). (gr. 2-18). 182.78 (978-0-7362-1891-7(2)) CENGAGE Learning.

Avenues Level D: Leveled Books & ETools. (gr. 3-18). 553.30 (978-0-7362-2537-3(4)) CENGAGE Learning.

Avenues Level D: Theme Library (16 Titles), 16 vols. (Avenues Ser.). (gr. 3-18). 231.85 (978-0-7362-1684-5(7)) CENGAGE Learning.

Avenues Level E: Leveled Books & ETools. (gr. 4-18). 527.49 (978-0-7362-2538-0(2)) CENGAGE Learning.

Avenues Level E: Theme Library (16 Titles), 16 vols. (Avenues Ser.). (gr. 4-18). 186.23 (978-0-7362-1720-0(7)) CENGAGE Learning.

Avenues Level F: Theme Library (16 Titles), 16 vols. (Avenues Ser.). (gr. 5-18). 220.14 (978-0-7362-1756-9(8)) CENGAGE Learning.

Avenues PreK Level. 388.57 (978-0-7362-2469-7(6)) CENGAGE Learning.

Avion, Nicole. Un Tapiz de felicidad, 1 vol. 2006. (Lecturas Del Barrio (Neighborhood Readers) Ser.). (SPA.). 16p. (gr. 1-2). pap. 6.50 (978-1-4042-7178-4(3), 7cea9aa7-1fbc-40a1-83fd-a11e25076cd9, Rosen Classroom) Rosen Publishing Group, Inc., The.

Award, Anna. Hansel & Gretel. 2012. 24p. (J). 9.95 (978-1-84135-514-6(3)) Award Pubns. Ltd. GBR. Dist: Parkwest Pubns., Inc.

Award, Anna & Aesop, Aesop. The Donkey & the Lapdog with the Lion & the Mouse. Biro, Val, illus. 2014. (ENG.). 24p. (J). pap. 6.95 (978-1-84135-953-3(X)) Award Pubns. Ltd. GBR. Dist: Parkwest Pubns., Inc.

Award, Anna & Biro, Val. The Bear & the Travellers & the Ducks & the Tortoise. 2014. (ENG.). 24p. (J). pap. 6.95 (978-1-84135-959-5(9)) Award Pubns. Ltd. GBR. Dist: Parkwest Pubns., Inc.

Award, Anna, et al. The Eagle & the Man with the Town Mouse & the Country Mouse. 2014. (ENG.). 24p. (J). pap. 6.95 (978-1-84135-958-8(0)) Award Pubns. Ltd. GBR. Dist: Parkwest Pubns., Inc.

—The Farmer & His Sons & The Donkey in the Lion's Skin. 2014. (ENG.). 24p. (J). pap. 6.95 (978-1-84135-960-1(2)) Award Pubns. Ltd. GBR. Dist: Parkwest Pubns., Inc.

—The Fox & the Stork & the Man, His Son & the Donkey. 2014. (ENG.). 24p. (J). pap. 6.95 (978-1-84135-955-7(6)) Award Pubns. Ltd. GBR. Dist: Parkwest Pubns., Inc.

—The Hare & the Tortoise & The Sick Lion. 2014. (ENG.). 24p. (J). pap. 6.95 (978-1-84135-954-0(8)) Award Pubns. Ltd. GBR. Dist: Parkwest Pubns., Inc.

—Monkey & the Fishermen & the Donkey in the Pond. 2014. (ENG.). 24p. (J). pap. 6.95 (978-1-84135-956-4(4)) Award Pubns. Ltd. GBR. Dist: Parkwest Pubns., Inc.

Award Publications Staff. Jack & the Beanstalk. 2012. (ENG., Illus.). 24p. pap. 6.50 (978-1-84135-537-5(2)) Award Pubns. Ltd. GBR. Dist: Parkwest Pubns., Inc.

Away from Home: Fourth Grade Guided Comprehension Level M. (On Our Way to English Ser.). (gr. 4-18). 34.50 (978-0-7578-7155-9(0)) Rigby Education.

Ayder, Earl. The Longest Shortcut. McGrellis, Cynthia, illus. 2005. 40p. pap. 8.53 (978-0-7578-9857-0(2)) Rigby Education.

Baby Animals Board Books 800849, 4 vols. 2005. (J). bds. (978-1-59794-050-4(X)) Environments, Inc.

Baby Faces Board Books 800669, 5. 2005. (J). bds. (978-1-59794-010-8(0)) Environments, Inc.

Baby Love Board Book Set 800703, 4. 2005. (J). bds. (978-1-59794-012-2(7)) Environments, Inc.

Baby Play Board Book Set 800807, 2. 2005. (J). bds. (978-1-59794-044-3(5)) Environments, Inc.

Baby's Birthday: Individual Title Six-Packs. (Literatura 2000 Ser.). (gr. k-1). 28.00 (978-0-7635-0021-4(6)) Rigby Education.

Baby's World Board Books 800848, 4. 2005. (J). bds. (978-1-59794-049-8(6)) Environments, Inc.

Baer, Jill. Just One of the Princes. 2014. (Sofia the First World of Reading Ser.). (Illus.). 32p. (J). lib. bdg. 13.55 (978-0-606-35263-5(5)) Turtleback.

Bage, Grant. The Story of Football: Band 17/Diamond (Collins Big Cat) 2016. (Collins Big Cat Ser.). (ENG.). 56p. (J). (gr. 5-6). pap. 11.99 (978-0-00-816398-3(7)) HarperCollins Pubs. Ltd. GBR. Dist: Independent Pubs. Group.

Baghdasaryan, Rouzanna. Moush Wants to Get Lost. Yulia, Lushnikova, illus. 2010. (ARA.). 32p. (J). pap. 16.95 (978-1-60195-091-8(8)) International Step by Step Assn.

Bagnoli, Christine. Miguel's Family Picnic, 1 vol. 2006. (Neighborhood Readers Ser.). (ENG.). 16p. (gr. 1-2). pap. 6.50 (978-1-4042-7006-0(X), 177b5ffe-840f-4d2a-915e-fb5f9fd5ef22, Rosen Classroom) Rosen Publishing Group, Inc., The.

Bains-Fort. It's Keen to Be Green. 2009. 40p. pap. 23.49 (978-1-4389-9145-0(2)) AuthorHouse.

Baker, Catherine. Collins Big Cat Phonics for Letters & Sounds - Disaster Duck: Band 06/Orange, Bd. 6. Alder, Charlie, illus. 2018. (Collins Big Cat Phonics Ser.). (ENG.). 24p. (J). pap. 6.99 (978-0-00-825173-4(8)) HarperCollins Pubs. Ltd. GBR. Dist: Independent Pubs. Group.

—Collins Big Cat Phonics for Letters & Sounds - Pop Pop Pop!: Band 01B/Pink B, Bd. 1B. Castro, Beatriz, illus. 2018. (Collins Big Cat Phonics Ser.). (ENG.). 16p. (J). (gr. -1-k). pap. 6.99 (978-0-00-825137-6(1)) HarperCollins Pubs. Ltd. GBR. Dist: Independent Pubs. Group.

—Collins Big Cat Phonics for Letters & Sounds - up on Deck: Band 01B/Pink B, Bd. 1B. Corke, Estelle, illus. 2018. (Collins Big Cat Phonics Ser.). (ENG.). 16p. (J). (gr. -1-k). pap. 6.99 (978-0-00-825138-3(X)) HarperCollins Pubs. Ltd. GBR. Dist: Independent Pubs. Group.

Baker, Chris. A Year in Barrowswold Forest: Band 15/Emerald. 2017. (Collins Big Cat Ser.). (ENG.). 48p. (J). pap. 10.99 (978-0-00-820886-8(7)) HarperCollins Pubs. Ltd. GBR. Dist: Independent Pubs. Group.

Baker, Clara B. & Baker, Edna D. Reading for Children: First Book. Betts, George Herbert, ed. 2011. 192p. 42.95 (978-1-258-08279-6(9)) Literary Licensing, LLC.

Baker, Keith. At the Park. 2016. (Mr. & Mrs. Green Ser.). (ENG., Illus.). 32p. (J). (gr. 1-4). pap. 4.99 (978-0-544-55556-3(2), 1610462, Clarion Bks.) HarperCollins Pubs.

Baker, Sara, illus. Ready to Read Sleeping Beauty. 2007. (Ready to Read Ser.). 31p. (J). (gr. k-2). (978-1-84610-441-1(6)) Make Believe Ideas.

Baldwin, James. Fifty Famous Stories Retold. 2008. 100p. pap. 9.50 (978-1-60459-518-5(3)) Wilder Pubns., Corp.

—Old Greek Storie. 2006. (Illus.). pap. (978-1-4065-0511-5(0)) Dodo Pr.

—Old Greek Stories. 2005. 192p. pap. 11.95 (978-1-4218-0155-1(8), 1st World Library - Literary Society) 1st World Publishing, Inc.

—Old Greek Stories. 2004. reprint ed. pap. 1.99 (978-1-4192-3803-1(5)); pap. 19.95 (978-1-4191-3803-4(0)) Kessinger Publishing, LLC.

—Old Greek Stories. 2008. (Illus.). 192p. pap. 9.95 (978-1-59915-296-7(7)) Yesterday's Classics.

Ball, Nate. Forces of Nature. 2015. (Alien in My Pocket Ser.: 6). (J). lib. bdg. 14.75 (978-0-606-37611-2(9)) Turtleback.

Bank Street College. Sacajawea: the Jacabee Readers: The Adventures of Dooley, Abby & Baldy. 2012. (ENG.). 84p. (J).

(gr. 1-3). pap. 9.95 *(978-1-59687-879-2(7)*, Milk & Cookies) ibooks, Inc.
Barbour Publishing Staff, compiled by. What's an Alpha-Beta-Soupa? An Indispensable Guide to College. 2005. 192p. pap. 4.97 *(978-1-59310-664-5(5))* Barbour Publishing, Inc.
Barchers, Suzanne I. A Big Job, 1 vol. rev. ed. 2011. (Phonics Ser.). (ENG., Illus.). 16p. (gr. k-1). 6.99 *(978-1-4333-2413-0(X))* Teacher Created Materials, Inc.
—A Box for Ross, 1 vol. rev. ed. 2011. (Phonics Ser.). (ENG., Illus.). 16p. (gr. k-1). 6.99 *(978-1-4333-2415-4(6))* Teacher Created Materials, Inc.
—Dad Wants a Nap, 1 vol. rev. ed. 2011. (Phonics Ser.). (ENG., Illus.). 16p. (gr. k-1). 6.99 *(978-1-4333-2407-9(5))* Teacher Created Materials, Inc.
—Fix It!, 1 vol. rev. ed. 2011. (Phonics Ser.). (ENG., Illus.). 16p. (gr. k-1). 6.99 *(978-1-4333-2423-9(7))* Teacher Created Materials, Inc.
—Get to Bed, Ren!, 1 vol. rev. ed. 2011. (Phonics Ser.). (ENG.). 16p. (gr. k-1). 6.99 *(978-1-4333-2416-1(4))* Teacher Created Materials, Inc.
—Green Peas in Cream, 1 vol. rev. ed. 2011. (Phonics Ser.). (ENG.). 16p. (gr. k-2). 6.99 *(978-1-4333-2916-6(6))* Teacher Created Materials, Inc.
—Gus in the Tub, 1 vol. rev. ed. 2011. (Phonics Ser.). (ENG., Illus.). 16p. (gr. k-1). 6.99 *(978-1-4333-2419-2(9))* Teacher Created Materials, Inc.
—How Big Is Kip?, 1 vol. rev. ed. 2011. (Phonics Ser.). (ENG., Illus.). 16p. (gr. k-1). 6.99 *(978-1-4333-2410-9(5))* Teacher Created Materials, Inc.
—Kate & Gail, 1 vol. rev. ed. 2011. (Phonics Ser.). (ENG., Illus.). 16p. (gr. k-2). 6.99 *(978-1-4333-2907-4(7))* Teacher Created Materials, Inc.
—Kip Gets Fit, 1 vol. rev. ed. 2011. (Phonics Ser.). (ENG.). 16p. (gr. k-1). 6.99 *(978-1-4333-2412-3(1))* Teacher Created Materials, Inc.
—Kip Gets Sick, 1 vol. rev. ed. 2011. (Phonics Ser.). (ENG., Illus.). 16p. (gr. k-1). 6.99 *(978-1-4333-2422-2(9))* Teacher Created Materials, Inc.
—Kip Wins!, 1 vol. rev. ed. 2011. (Phonics Ser.). (ENG., Illus.). 16p. (gr. k-1). 6.99 *(978-1-4333-2411-6(3))* Teacher Created Materials, Inc.
—Late Kate, 1 vol. rev. ed. 2011. (Phonics Ser.). (ENG.). 16p. (gr. k-2). 6.99 *(978-1-4333-2906-7(9))* Teacher Created Materials, Inc.
—Luce & Duke, 1 vol. rev. ed. 2011. (Phonics Ser.). (ENG., Illus.). 16p. (gr. k-2). 6.99 *(978-1-4333-2919-7(0))* Teacher Created Materials, Inc.
—Main Street Block Party, 1 vol. rev. ed. 2011. (Phonics Ser.). (ENG.). 16p. (gr. k-2). 6.99 *(978-1-4333-2923-4(9))* Teacher Created Materials, Inc.
—Main Street Game Day, 1 vol. rev. ed. 2011. (Phonics Ser.). (ENG.). 16p. (gr. k-2). 6.99 *(978-1-4333-2922-7(0))* Teacher Created Materials, Inc.
—Main Street Parade, 1 vol. rev. ed. 2011. (Phonics Ser.). (ENG.). 16p. (gr. k-2). 6.99 *(978-1-4333-2921-0(2))* Teacher Created Materials, Inc.
—Mike Makes up His Mind, 1 vol. rev. ed. 2011. (Phonics Ser.). (ENG.). 16p. (gr. k-2). 6.99 *(978-1-4333-2911-1(5))* Teacher Created Materials, Inc.
—On a Walk with Ren, 1 vol. rev. ed. 2011. (Phonics Ser.). (ENG., Illus.). 16p. (gr. k-1). 6.99 *(978-1-4333-2417-8(2))* Teacher Created Materials, Inc.
—On My Stoop, 1 vol. rev. ed. 2011. (Phonics Ser.). (ENG., Illus.). 16p. (gr. k-2). 6.99 *(978-1-4333-2920-3(4))* Teacher Created Materials, Inc.
—On the Road with Rose & Bose, 1 vol. rev. ed. 2011. (Phonics Ser.). (ENG.). 16p. (gr. k-2). 6.99 *(978-1-4333-2914-2(X))* Teacher Created Materials, Inc.
—Pack a Bag!, 1 vol. rev. ed. 2011. (Phonics Ser.). (ENG.). 16p. (gr. k-1). 6.99 *(978-1-4333-2409-3(1))* Teacher Created Materials, Inc.
—Pete Has Fast Feet, 1 vol. rev. ed. 2011. (Phonics Ser.). (ENG., Illus.). 16p. (gr. k-2). 6.99 *(978-1-4333-2915-9(8))* Teacher Created Materials, Inc.
—Read with Gus, 1 vol. rev. ed. 2011. (Phonics Ser.). (ENG.). 16p. (gr. k-1). 6.99 *(978-1-4333-2420-8(2))* Teacher Created Materials, Inc.
—Ren in a Mess, 1 vol. rev. ed. 2011. (Phonics Ser.). (ENG.). 16p. (gr. k-1). 6.99 *(978-1-4333-2418-5(0))* Teacher Created Materials, Inc.
—Rose & Bose, 1 vol. rev. ed. 2011. (Phonics Ser.). (ENG., Illus.). 16p. (gr. k-2). 6.99 *(978-1-4333-2913-5(1))* Teacher Created Materials, Inc.
—Rose & Dad, 1 vol. rev. ed. 2011. (Phonics Ser.). (ENG.). 16p. (gr. k-2). 6.99 *(978-1-4333-2912-8(3))* Teacher Created Materials, Inc.
—Spy It!, 1 vol. rev. ed. 2011. (Phonics Ser.). (ENG., Illus.). 16p. (gr. k-2). 6.99 *(978-1-4333-2910-4(7))* Teacher Created Materials, Inc.
—To the Dunes with Luce, 1 vol. rev. ed. 2011. (Phonics Ser.). (ENG., Illus.). 16p. (gr. k-2). 6.99 *(978-1-4333-2918-0(2))* Teacher Created Materials, Inc.
—Top That!, 1 vol. rev. ed. 2011. (Phonics Ser.). (ENG., Illus.). 16p. (gr. k-1). 6.99 *(978-1-4333-2414-7(8))* Teacher Created Materials, Inc.
—Twice as Nice: Long Vowel Storybooks, 1 vol. rev. ed. 2011. (Phonics Ser.). (ENG.). 16p. (gr. k-2). 6.99 *(978-1-4333-2909-8(3))* Teacher Created Materials, Inc.
—What Can I Read?, 1 vol. rev. ed. 2011. (Phonics Ser.). (ENG., Illus.). 16p. (gr. k-2). 6.99 *(978-1-4333-2917-3(4))* Teacher Created Materials, Inc.
—What Can San Do?, 1 vol. rev. ed. 2011. (Phonics Ser.). (ENG., Illus.). 16p. (gr. k-1). 6.99 *(978-1-4333-2408-6(3))* Teacher Created Materials, Inc.
—What Luck!, 1 vol. rev. ed. 2011. (Phonics Ser.). (ENG.). 16p. (gr. k-1). 6.99 *(978-1-4333-2421-5(0))* Teacher Created Materials, Inc.
—You Can Do It!, 1 vol. rev. ed. 2011. (Phonics Ser.). (ENG., Illus.). 16p. (gr. k-1). 6.99 *(978-1-4333-2424-6(5))* Teacher Created Materials, Inc.
Barchers, Suzanne I. & Teacher Created Materials Staff. Big Day for Kate, 1 vol. rev. ed. 2011. (Phonics Ser.). (ENG., Illus.). 16p. (gr. k-2). 6.99 *(978-1-4333-2908-1(5))* Teacher Created Materials, Inc.
Bardswich, Elizabeth & Bardswich, Miriam. Out There - Travel. 2007. (Steck-Vaughn BOLDPRINT Anthologies Ser.). (ENG., Illus.). 48p. (gr. 8-10). pap. 16.90 *(978-1-4190-4030-6(8))* Houghton Mifflin Harcourt Publishing Co.
Barefoot Books. My Big Barefoot Book of Spanish & English Words. Fatus, Sophie, illus. 2016. (ENG.). 48p. (J). (gr. -1-1). 19.99 *(978-1-78285-286-5(7))* Barefoot Bks., Inc.
Barella, Laura, illus. Sleeping Beauty. 2009. (Flip-Up Fairy Tales Ser.). 24p. (J). (gr. -1-2). *(978-1-84643-295-8(2))* Child's Play International Ltd.
Barker, Charles Ferguson. Under Ohio: The Story of Ohio's Rocks & Fossils. 2016. (ENG.). 56p. (J). (gr. 3-8). pap. 17.95 *(978-0-8214-2195-6(6))* Ohio Univ. Pr.
Barker, Lori. How Do They Make That? rev. ed. 2012. (Mathematics in the Real World Ser.). (ENG.). 32p. (gr. 5-8). pap. 11.99 *(978-1-4333-3453-5(4))* Teacher Created Materials, Inc.
—Land Animals. rev. ed. 2012. (Mathematics in the Real World Ser.). (ENG.). 32p. (gr. 5-8). pap. 11.99 *(978-1-4333-3456-6(9))* Teacher Created Materials, Inc.
—Sea Creatures. rev. ed. 2012. (Mathematics in the Real World Ser.). (ENG.). 32p. (gr. 5-8). pap. 11.99 *(978-1-4333-3457-3(7))* Teacher Created Materials, Inc.
—Watch It Grow. rev. ed. 2012. (Mathematics in the Real World Ser.). (ENG.). 32p. (gr. 5-8). pap. 11.99 *(978-1-4333-3454-2(2))* Teacher Created Materials, Inc.
—Where Germs Lurk. rev. ed. 2012. (Mathematics in the Real World Ser.). (ENG.). 32p. (gr. 5-8). pap. 11.99 *(978-1-4333-3455-9(0))* Teacher Created Materials, Inc.
Barker, Lori & Nielsen, Aubrie. What Did I Eat? rev. ed. 2012. (Mathematics in the Real World Ser.). (ENG.). 32p. (gr. 5-8). pap. 11.99 *(978-1-4333-3452-8(6))* Teacher Created Materials, Inc.
Barker, Lori & Quinlan, Nola. On the Road: Ratios & Proportions. rev. ed. 2012. (Mathematics in the Real World Ser.). (ENG.). 32p. (gr. 5-8). pap. 11.99 *(978-1-4333-3450-4(X))* Teacher Created Materials, Inc.
—Our New Car. rev. ed. 2012. (Mathematics in the Real World Ser.). (ENG.). 32p. (gr. 5-8). pap. 11.99 *(978-1-4333-3451-1(8))* Teacher Created Materials, Inc.
Barkley, Callie. Amy on Park Patrol. 2017. (Critter Club Ser.: 17). lib. bdg. 16.00 *(978-0-606-40208-8(X))* Turtleback.
Barlow, Helen. Easy read with grandma Read: Book 1, Stage 1. 2008. (ENG., Illus.). 48p. per. *(978-1-84748-262-4(7))* Athena Pr.
Barnes, Derrick D. Low-Down Bad-Day Blues. Boyd, Aaron, illus. 2004. (Just for You Ser.). (ENG.). 32p. (gr. k-1). pap. 3.99 *(978-0-439-56867-8(6)*, Teaching Resources) Scholastic, Inc.
Barnyard Board Book Set 800784, 5. 2005. (J). bds. *(978-1-59794-019-1(4))* Environments, Inc.
Baron, Jessica. What's in the Garden? Learning to Compare Two Sets of Objects, 1 vol. 2010. (Math for the REAL World Ser.). (ENG., Illus.). 8p. (gr. k-1). pap. 5.15 *(978-0-8239-8860-0(0)*, b191e9d6-405e-412d-b552-eee25bfe1bde) Rosen Publishing Group, Inc., The.
Barone, Bill. So Many Scoops!, 1 vol. 2006. (Neighborhood Readers Ser.). (ENG.). 16p. (gr. 1-2). pap. 6.50 *(978-1-4042-7164-7(3)*, 627af503-9475-4d22-beeb-cf08ae83f6ea, Rosen Classroom) Rosen Publishing Group, Inc., The.
Barr, Brady & Keats Curtis, Jennifer. Hasta la Vista, Cocodrilo: el Diario de Alexa. Detwiler, Susan, illus. 2016. (SPA.). 32p. (J). (gr. 2-3). pap. 11.95 *(978-1-62855-836-4(9)*, 3f8213bc-7d57-4d95-ab47-784cd803357f) Arbordale Publishing.
Barr, Linda. Long Road to Freedom: Journey of the Hmong, 6 vols. 2004. (High Five Reading - Purple Ser.). (ENG.). 64p. (gr. 3-4). pap. 54.00 *(978-0-7368-3870-2(8))* Capstone.
Barraclough, Sue. Farm Animals, 1 vol. 2009. (Me & My World Ser.). (ENG., Illus.). 24p. (J). (gr. -1-2). pap. 9.15 *(978-1-60754-060-1(6)*, 79d793df-0fed-4d67-b49f-b3a7349824d8); lib. bdg. 27.27 *(978-1-60754-056-4(8)*, 34de738d-5b06-4425-9a61-f2ba0d815a36) Rosen Publishing Group, Inc., The. (Windmill Bks.).
—On the Move, 1 vol. 2009. (Me & My World Ser.). (ENG., Illus.). 24p. (J). (gr. -1-2). pap. 9.15 *(978-1-60754-064-9(9)*, c576c3f3-4a86-4168-a56e-48aa81135323); lib. bdg. 27.27 *(978-1-60754-058-8(4)*, faff1053-0eaa-401c-a610-e1e7b269ae5b) Rosen Publishing Group, Inc., The. (Windmill Bks.).
Barrett, Jennifer. Lethal Delivery, Postage Prepaid. (Thumbprint Mysteries Ser.). 32.86 *(978-0-8092-0425-0(8))* McGraw-Hill/Contemporary.
Barretta, Gene. Dear Deer: A Book of Homophones. 2007. (J). (gr. k-3). 29.95 incl. audio compact disk *(978-0-8045-4181-7(7))*; 27.95 incl. audio *(978-0-8045-6958-3(4))* Spoken Arts, Inc.
Barrie, James Matthew. Peter Pan: An Illustrated Classic for Kids & Young Readers (Excellent for Bedtime & Young Readers) eMusic, Tom, ed. Friday, Arthur, illus. 2013. 38p. pap. 6.99 *(978-1-62321-067-0(4))* Tommye-music Corp. DBA Tom eMusic.
Barron's Educational Series & Benton, Lynne. Stranger in the Snow/L'etranger dans la Neige: French/English Edition. Cuthbertson, Ollie, illus. 2010. (Let's Read! French-English Ser.). (ENG.). 32p. (J). (gr. k-3). 17.44 *(978-0-7641-4475-2(8)*, B.E.S. Publishing) Peterson's.
Barron's Educational Series & Rabley, Stephen. A New World/Un Nuevo Mundo: Spanish/English Edition. Lopez, David, illus. 2010. (Let's Read! Spanish-English Ser.). (ENG.). 32p. (J). (gr. k-3). 17.44 *(978-0-7641-4471-4(5)*, B.E.S. Publishing) Peterson's.
Bartch, Lea & Mangrum, Kaylea J. Tucker Goes to Kindergarten. Mangrum, Kaylea J., illus. 2013. (Illus.). 54p. pap. 14.99 *(978-0-9883009-5-8(8))* Mangrum, Kaylea J.
Barton, Chris. Mighty Truck on the Farm. Cummings, Troy, illus. 2018. (I Can Read Level 1 Ser.). (ENG.). 32p. (J). (gr. -1-3). 16.99 *(978-0-06-234467-0(6))*; pap. 4.99 *(978-0-06-234466-3(8))* HarperCollins Pubs. (HarperCollins).
—Mighty Truck on the Farm. 2019. (I Can Read 88 Ser.). (ENG.). 32p. (J). (gr. k-1). 14.96 *(978-1-64310-977-0(4))* Penworthy Co., LLC, The.
Barwick. Sail Main5 Weather Alert Nf. 2003. (Rigby Sails Ser.). (ENG.). 32p. (gr. 5-5). pap. 9.50 *(978-0-7578-8020-9(7))* Rigby Education.
Basic Book Set 800082, 20 vols. 2005. (J). bds. *(978-1-59794-000-9(3))* Environments, Inc.
Bassett, Jennifer. Milo, 1. 2014. (Garnet Oracle Readers Ser.). (Illus.). 40p. pap., stu. ed. 4.50 *(978-1-907575-16-7(2))* Garnet Education GBR. Dist: Garnet Publishing, Ltd.
—Oxford Bookworms Library: the Omega Files DS Short Stories: Level 1: 400-Word Vocabulary. 3rd ed. 2008. (ENG., Illus.). 64p. 11.00 *(978-0-19-478913-4(6))* Oxford Univ. Pr., Inc.
—The Watchers, 4. 2014. (Garnet Oracle Readers Ser.). (Illus.). 32p. pap., stu. ed. 4.50 *(978-1-907575-17-4(0))* Garnet Education GBR. Dist: Garnet Publishing, Ltd.
Bates, Matthew. The Ways We Use Water, 1 vol. 2012. (InfoMax Readers Ser.). (ENG., Illus.). 24p. (J). (gr. 1-1). pap. 8.25 *(978-1-4488-9013-2(6)*, 2f32597b-697b-411c-a780-0a840bf8d20c, Rosen Classroom) Rosen Publishing Group, Inc., The.
Batham, Matthew. Lightsleep. 2006. 167p. pap. *(978-1-904623-39-7(5))* WritersPrintShop.
Batkhuu, Kh. The Doll That Flew Away. Myagmardorj, Enkhtungalag, illus. 2007. (ARA & ENG.). 32p. (J). pap. 12.95 *(978-0-60195-092-5(6))* International Step by Step Assn.
Bauer, David. Adding Arctic Animals, 6 vols., Set. 2003. (Yellow Umbrella Early Level Ser.). (ENG.). 16p. (gr. k-1). pap. 35.70 *(978-0-7368-2990-8(3)*, Capstone Pr.) Capstone.
Baugh, Helen. Collins Big Cat Phonics for Letters & Sounds - a Bee on a Lark: Band 02B/Red B, Bd. 2B. Green, Keri, illus. 2018. (Collins Big Cat Phonics Ser.). (ENG.). 16p. (J). pap. 6.99 *(978-0-00-825148-2(7))* HarperCollins Pubs. Ltd. GBR. Dist: Independent Pubs. Group.
Baxter, Nicola. Trouble in Space: A First Reading Adventure Book. Ball, Geoff, illus. 2015. 24p. (J). (gr. -1-12). pap. 6.99 *(978-1-86147-491-9(1)*, Armadillo) Anness Publishing GBR. Dist: National Bk. Network.
—Trouble in the Jungle: A First Reading Adventure Book. Ball, Geoff, illus. 2015. 24p. (J). (gr. -1-12). pap. 6.99 *(978-1-86147-494-0(6)*, Armadillo) Anness Publishing GBR. Dist: National Bk. Network.
—Trouble on the Ice: First Reading Books for 3-5 Year Olds. Ball, Geoff, illus. 2015. 24p. (J). (gr. -1-12). pap. 6.99 *(978-1-86147-492-6(X)*, Armadillo) Anness Publishing GBR. Dist: National Bk. Network.
BBB Bats Song. (Song Box Ser.). (gr. 1-2). 8.50 incl. audio *(978-0-322-00247-0(8))* Wright Group/McGraw-Hill.
BBB Bats Song Big Book. (Song Box Ser.). (gr. 1-2). 31.50 *(978-0-322-00264-7(8))* Wright Group/McGraw-Hill.
BBB Bats Song Small Books Pack of 6, 6 vols. (Song Box Ser.). (gr. 1-2). 29.50 *(978-0-322-00269-2(9))* Wright Group/McGraw-Hill.
BBC. Doctor Who: Doodle Book. 2016. (ENG.). 128p. (J). pap. 10.99 *(978-1-4059-2652-2(X)*, ed05de52-b317-4254-bbfd-d806a274e250) Penguin Bks., Ltd. GBR. Dist: Diamond Comic Distributors, Inc.
Bear Story Board Books 800655, 5. 2005. (J). bds. *(978-1-59794-007-8(0))* Environments, Inc.
Beardsley, Sally. The 10 Bravest Everyday Heroes. 2007. 14.99 *(978-1-55448-488-1(X))* Scholastic Library Publishing.
Beaton, Clare & Blackstone, Stella. Cerdota Grandota. Beaton, Clare, illus. 2006.Tr. of How Big Is a Pig. (Illus.). 24p. (J). (gr. -1-k). bds. 6.99 *(978-1-84686-018-8(0))* Barefoot Bks., Inc.
Beaver, Simon. Dangerous & Dirty Jobs Low Intermediate Book with Online Access, 1 vol. 2014. (ENG., Illus.). 28p. pap., E-Book, E-Book 9.50 *(978-1-107-64567-7(0))* Cambridge Univ. Pr.
—A Light in the Night: the Moon Beginning Book with Online Access, 1 vol. 2014. (ENG., Illus.). 24p. (J). pap., E-Book, E-Book 9.50 *(978-1-107-64756-5(8))* Cambridge Univ. Pr.
—Slice by Slice: The Story of Pizza Low Intermediate Book with Online Access, 1 vol. 2014. (ENG., Illus.). 24p. (J). pap., E-Book, E-Book 9.50 *(978-1-107-65037-4(2))* Cambridge Univ. Pr.
—Traffic Jams: the Road Ahead Beginning Book with Online Access, 1 vol. 2014. (ENG., Illus.). 24p. (J). pap., E-Book 9.50 *(978-1-107-67468-4(9))* Cambridge Univ. Pr.
—Wild Australia! Beginning Book with Online Access, 1 vol. 2014. (ENG., Illus.). 24p. (J). pap., E-Book 9.50 *(978-1-107-62165-7(8))* Cambridge Univ. Pr.
BeaverSimon. Fantastic Creatures: Monsters, Mermaids, & Wild Men Beginning Book with Online Access, 1 vol. 2014. (ENG., Illus.). 24p. (J). pap., E-Book, E-Book 9.50 *(978-1-107-69637-2(2))* Cambridge Univ. Pr.
—PARIS: CITY OF LIGHT BEGINNING BOOK WITH ONLINE ACCESS, 1 vol. 2014. (ENG., Illus.). 24p. (J). pap., E-Book, E-Book 9.50 *(978-1-107-64577-6(8))* Cambridge Univ. Pr.
—SAVED! HEROES IN EVERYDAY LIFE BEGINNING BOOK WITH ONLINE ACCESS, 1 vol. 2014. (ENG., Illus.). 24p. pap., E-Book 7.50 *(978-1-107-64705-3(3))* Cambridge Univ. Pr.
—SPORT, GAME OR HOBBY? LOW INTERMEDIATE BOOK WITH ONLINE ACCESS, 1 vol. 2014. (ENG., Illus.). 48p. (J). pap., E-Book, E-Book 9.50 *(978-1-107-68658-8(X))* Cambridge Univ. Pr.
—YOUNG AND AMAZING: TEENS AT THE TOP HIGH BEGINNING BOOK WITH ONLINE ACCESS, 1 vol. 2014. (ENG., Illus.). 24p. pap., E-Book 9.50 *(978-1-107-62252-4(2))* Cambridge Univ. Pr.
Because I'm Little, 6 Packs. (gr. -1-2). 23.00 *(978-0-7635-8798-7(2))* Rigby Education.
Beck, Isabel L., et al. Decodable Books Collections. 2003. (Trophies Ser.). (gr. 1-18). 15.60 *(978-0-15-326715-4(1))*; (gr. 1-18). 15.60 *(978-0-15-326747-5(X))*; (gr. 1-18). 15.60 *(978-0-15-326746-8(1))*; (gr. 1-18). 15.60 *(978-0-15-326745-1(3))*; (gr. 1-18). 15.60 *(978-0-15-326743-7(7))*; (gr. 1-18). 15.60 *(978-0-15-326742-0(9))*; (gr. 1-18). 15.60 *(978-0-15-326740-6(2))*; (gr. 1-18). 15.60 *(978-0-15-327353-7(4))*; (gr. 1-18). 15.60 *(978-0-15-326737-6(2))*; (gr. 1-18). 15.60 *(978-0-15-326736-9(4))*; (gr. 1-18). 15.60 *(978-0-15-326735-2(6))*; (gr. 1-18). 15.60 *(978-0-15-326734-5(8))*; (gr. 1-18). 15.60 *(978-0-15-326731-4(3))*; (gr. 1-18). 15.60 *(978-0-15-326728-4(3))*; (gr. 1-18). 15.60 *(978-0-15-326726-0(7))*; (gr. 1-18). 15.60 *(978-0-15-326724-6(0))*; (gr. 1-18). 15.60 *(978-0-15-326723-9(2))*; (gr. 1-18). 15.60 *(978-0-15-326722-2(4))*; (gr. 1-18). 15.60 *(978-0-15-326721-5(6))*; (gr. 1-18). 15.60 *(978-0-15-326720-8(8))*; (gr. 1-18). 15.60 *(978-0-15-326719-2(4))*; (gr. 1-18). 15.60 *(978-0-15-326718-5(6))*; (gr. 1-18). 15.60 *(978-0-15-326717-8(8))*; (gr. 1-18). 15.60 *(978-0-15-326716-1(X))*; (gr. 2-18). 18.40 *(978-0-15-326778-9(X))*; (gr. 2-18). 18.40 *(978-0-15-326774-1(7))*; (gr. 2-18). 18.40 *(978-0-15-326773-4(9))* Harcourt Schl. Pubs.
Beckerman, Menucha. Welcome Home. (My Little World Ser.: Vol. 6). (Illus.). 34p. (J). (gr. k-5). 4.95 *(978-1-931681-11-7(2))* Israel Bookshop Pubns.
Beckwith, Carrie, et al. Reading Detective Beginning: Using Higher-Order Thinking to Improve Reading Comprehension. 2013. (Reading Detective Ser.). 192p. (gr. 3-4). pap. 24.99 *(978-0-89455-769-9(6))* Critical Thinking Co., The.
Beebe, Katherine & Kingsley, Nellie F. The First Year Nature Reader. 2004. reprint ed. pap. 21.95 *(978-1-4191-3072-4(2))* Kessinger Publishing, LLC.
Beech, Linda. Inference. 2005. (Reading Passages That Build Comprehension Ser.). (ENG.). 48p. (gr. 2-3). pap. 10.99 *(978-0-439-55424-4(1)*, Teaching Resources) Scholastic, Inc.
—Reading Passages That Build Comprehension: Context Clues Grades 2-3. 2005. (ENG.). 48p. (gr. 2-3). pap. 10.99 *(978-0-439-55426-8(8)*, Teaching Resources) Scholastic, Inc.
—Reading Passages That Build Comprehension: Main Idea & Details Grades 2-3. 2005. (ENG.). 48p. (gr. 2-3). pap. 10.99 *(978-0-439-55425-1(X)*, Teaching Resources) Scholastic, Inc.
Beecroft, Simon. Join the Rebels. 2010. (DK Readers Level 2 Ser.). (ENG.). 32p. (J). (gr. k-2). 16.19 *(978-0-7566-6312-4(1))* Dorling Kindersley Publishing, Inc.
—Pirates ... & Worse! Dorling Kindersley Publishing Staff, ed. 2009. (Star Wars: the Clone Wars DK Readers Ser.). lib. bdg. 13.55 *(978-0-606-07064-5(8))* Turtleback.
—R2-D2 & Friends. 2008. (Star Wars DK Readers Level 2 Ser.). (Illus.). 32p. lib. bdg. 13.55 *(978-1-4364-5044-7(6))* Turtleback.
Being Kind to Naomi: Social/Emotional Lap Book. (Pebble Soup Explorations Ser.). (gr. -1-18). 16.00 *(978-0-7635-7567-0(4))* Rigby Education.
Belcher, Andy. Life on the Reef. Cambridge Reading Adventures. Orange Band. 2016. (Cambridge Reading Adventures Ser.). (ENG., Illus.). 24p. pap. 8.80 *(978-1-107-56022-2(5))* Cambridge Univ. Pr.
—Motorcycles. Cambridge Reading Adventures. Turquoise Band. 2016. (Cambridge Reading Adventures Ser.). (ENG., Illus.). 24p. pap. 8.80 *(978-1-107-57624-7(5))* Cambridge Univ. Pr.
Belcher, Andy & Belcher, Angie. The Baby Turtle: Band 03/Yellow (Collins Big Cat) 2007. (Collins Big Cat Ser.). (ENG.). 16p. (J). (gr. k-1). pap. 7.99 *(978-0-00-718659-4(2))* HarperCollins Pubs. Ltd. GBR. Dist: Independent Pubs. Group.
—Rally Challenge: Band 10/White (Collins Big Cat) Belcher, Andy & Belcher, Angie, photos by. 2005. (Collins Big Cat Ser.). (ENG., Illus.). 32p. (J). (gr. 1-3). pap. 9.99 *(978-0-00-718632-7(0))* HarperCollins Pubs. Ltd. GBR. Dist: Independent Pubs. Group.
Belcher, Angie. Collins Big Cat Phonics for Letters & Sounds - the Equator: Band 06/Orange, Bd. 6. 2018. (Collins Big Cat Phonics Ser.). (ENG., Illus.). 24p. (J). (gr. 1-2). pap. 6.99 *(978-0-00-825176-5(2))* HarperCollins Pubs. Ltd. GBR. Dist: Independent Pubs. Group.
—Storyteller Chapter Books: Fluency - 1 Each of 1 Title: Level T. 6.50 *(978-0-7699-1070-3(X))* Shortland Pubns. (U. S. A.) Inc.
Belcher, Angie & Belcher, Andy. Swimming with Dolphins: Band 09/Gold. Belcher, Angie & Belcher, Andy, illus. 2005. (Collins Big Cat Ser.). (ENG.). 24p. (J). (gr. 1-2). pap. 8.99 *(978-0-00-718623-5(1))* HarperCollins Pubs. Ltd. GBR. Dist: Independent Pubs. Group.
Bell, Jessica. My Wild New Yard. 2017. (Text Connections Guided Close Reading Ser.). (J). (gr. 1). *(978-1-4900-1801-0(8))* Benchmark Education Co.
Bell-Martin, Janelle. Mary Had a Little Lamb. 2011. (Early Literacy Ser.). (ENG.). 16p. (gr. k-1). 19.99 *(978-1-4333-2358-4(3))*; 6.99 *(978-1-4333-2357-7(5))* Teacher Created Materials, Inc.
Belle, Magnolia. Silkie Time. 2017. (Illus.). 31p. (J). *(978-1-5182-3827-7(0))* Little Brown & Co.
—We Are Family. 2017. (Illus.). 32p. (J). *(978-1-5182-4449-0(1))* Little Brown & Co.
Bembibre, Cecilia, et al. La Máscara del Zorro, 1 vol. 2014. (SPA., Illus.). 56p. pap. 15.00 incl. audio compact disk *(978-84-9848-195-2(3))* Edinumen, Editorial ESP. Dist: Cambridge Univ. Pr.
—La Niña de Tus Ojos, 1 vol. 2014. (SPA., Illus.). 56p. pap., stu. ed. 15.00 incl. audio compact disk *(978-84-9848-379-6(4))* Edinumen, Editorial ESP. Dist: Cambridge Univ. Pr.
Ben Nighthorse Campbell, Senador Y Artista. 2003. (Notas Biograficas Ser.). pap. 48.95 *(978-0-8136-5913-8(2))* Modern Curriculum Pr.
Benchmark Education Co., LLC. Sight Walk Big Book. 2014. (Shared Reading Foundations Ser.). (J). (gr. -1). *(978-1-4509-9436-1(9))* Benchmark Education Co.
Benchmark Education Company, LLC Staff. Spanish/English Emergent Supplement. 2005. (BookRoom Collection Ser.). (J). spiral bd. 1685.00 *(978-1-4108-5614-2(3))* Benchmark Education Co.
—SpiralUp Reading Passages. 2009. (SpiralUp Phonics Ser.). (J). cd-rom *(978-1-4108-8534-0(8))* Benchmark Education Co.
Benchmark Education Company, LLC Staff, compiled by. Fluency Kits for Independent Practice. 2005. spiral bd. 4150.00 *(978-1-4108-6219-8(4))*; spiral bd. 3345.00 *(978-1-4108-5380-6(2))* Benchmark Education Co.
—Reading First Bookroom COLL. 2005. spiral bd. 11275.00 *(978-1-4108-4157-5(X))* Benchmark Education Co.
—Spanish/English Early/Fluent Supplement. 2005. (J). 2815.00 net. *(978-1-4108-5662-3(3))* Benchmark Education Co.

—Spanish/English Emergent Single Copy Set. 2005. (J). pap. 283.00 net. *(978-1-4108-5616-6(X))* Benchmark Education Co.

Benita's Plan: Fourth Grade Guided Comprehension Level M. (On Our Way to English Ser.). (gr. 4-18). 34.50 *(978-0-7578-7159-7(3))* Rigby Education.

Benjamin, Joseph & Benchmark Education Co., LLC Staff. Ten Red Hens. 2015. (StartUp Ser.). (J). (gr. k). *(978-1-4900-0698-7(2))* Benchmark Education Co.

Bennett, Leonie. Locket Out. Adams, Arlene, illus. 2004. (ENG.). 24p. (J). lib. bdg. 23.65 *(978-1-59646-688-3(X))* Dingles & Co.

—No Problem! Brown, Judy, illus. 2004. (ENG.). 16p. (J). lib. bdg. 23.65 *(978-1-59646-680-7(4))* Dingles & Co.

Bentley, Marla. Summer Sounds Level 1 Beginner/Elementary. 2010. (Cambridge Experience Readers Ser.). (ENG., Illus.). 46p. pap. 14.75 *(978-0-521-18158-7(5))* Cambridge Univ. Pr.

BentleyMarla. Summer Sounds Level 1 Beginner/Elementary. 2010. (Cambridge Experience Readers Ser.). (ENG., Illus.). 46p. pap. 14.75 *(978-84-8323-995-7(7))* Cambridge Univ. Pr.

Benton, Allie. Inside a Factory, 6 vols., Set. 2004. (Phonics Readers Books 37-72 Ser.). (ENG.). 8p. (gr. k-1). pap. 35.70 *(978-0-7368-4057-6(5))* Capstone.

Benton, Celia. Our Flag, 6 vols., Set. 2003. (Phonics Readers 1-36 Ser.). (ENG.). 8p. (gr. k-1). pap. 29.70 *(978-0-7368-3201-4(7))* Capstone.

Benton, Lynne. Stranger in the Snow. Cuthbertson, Ollie, illus. 2010. (Let's Read! Spanish-English Ser.).Tr. of Extrano en la Nieve. (ENG.). 32p. (J). (gr. k-3). 17.44 *(978-0-7641-4473-8(1)*, B.E.S. Publishing) Peterson's.

Berenstain, Jan & Berenstain, Mike. The Berenstain Bears: Safe & Sound! Berenstain, Jan & Berenstain, Mike, illus. 2009. (Berenstain Bears Ser.). (ENG., Illus.). 32p. (J). (gr. -1-3). pap. 4.99 *(978-0-06-057391-1(0)*, HarperFestival) HarperCollins Pubs.

Berenstain, Jan & Berenstain, Stan. The Berenstain Bears' New Pup. Berenstain, Jan, illus. 2017. (I Can Read Level 1 Ser.). (ENG., Illus.). 40p. (J). (gr. -1-3). 9.99 *(978-0-06-257272-1(5)*, HarperCollins) HarperCollins Pubs.

Berenstain, Jan, et al. My Favorite Dog Stories: Learning to Read Box Set. 2014. (I Can Read Level 1 Ser.). (ENG.). (J). (gr. -1-3). pap. 19.99 *(978-0-06-231331-7(2)*, HarperCollins) HarperCollins Pubs.

Berenstain, Mike, et al. Sister Bear & the Golden Rule. 2017. (Illus.). 32p. (J). *(978-1-5182-4500-8(5))* Zonderkidz.

Berenstain, Stan & Berenstain, Jan. The Berenstain Bears & the Ducklings. Berenstain, Mike, illus. 2018. 30p. (J). *(978-1-5444-0097-6(7)*, BRO-adap20180125-161) Harper & Row Ltd.

Bergman, Mara. The Twelve Dancing Princesses: Band 13/Topaz (Collins Big Cat) 2017. (Collins Big Cat Tales Ser.). (ENG., Illus.). 48p. (J). (gr. 2-3). pap. 9.99 *(978-0-00-817938-0(7))* HarperCollins Pubs. Ltd. GBR. Dist: Independent Pubs. Group.

Berres, et al. Sea Hunt. Date not set. (J). *(978-0-89064-249-8(4))* National Assn. for Visually Handicapped.

Berrios, Frank. To Protect & Serve. 2015. (Cars Step into Reading Ser.). lib. bdg. 14.75 *(978-0-606-36393-8(9))* Turtleback.

Bertrand, Diane Gonzales. Cecilia & Miguel Are Best Friends. Ventura, Gabriela Baeza, tr. Muraida, Thelma, illus. 2014.Tr. of Cecilia y Miguel Son Mejores Amigos. (SPA & ENG.). 32p. (J). 17.95 *(978-1-55885-794-0(X))* Arte Publico Pr.

Betances, Brendan. Granny's Garden, 1 vol. 2006. (Neighborhood Readers Ser.). (ENG., Illus.). 12p. (gr. 1-2). pap. 5.90 *(978-1-4042-7022-0(1)*, 6c987002-aa99-4e3a-b706-882f2d6ef41f, Rosen Classroom) Rosen Publishing Group, Inc., The.

Bethune, Helen. Barnaby Dell, 1 vol. rev. ed. 2013. (Literary Text Ser.). (ENG., Illus.). 24p. (J). (gr. 1-3). pap. 8.99 *(978-1-4333-5523-3(X))* Teacher Created Materials, Inc.

Betsy Ross. (Lexile Levels Ser.). 9.09 *(978-1-56334-735-1(0))* CENGAGE Learning.

Betto. Começo, Meio e Fim. Prezoto, Vanessa, illus. 2014. (POR.). 30p. (J). *(978-85-62500-68-8(2))* Rocco, Editora, Ltda.

Bevan, Clare. The Creature in Wide-Mouth Cave, 8 vols. 2005. (QEB Readers). (Illus.). 24p. (J). (gr. -1-3). lib. bdg. 15.95 *(978-1-59566-065-7(8))* QEB Publishing Inc.

—The Jolly Rascal. 2004. (QEB Start Reading Ser.). (Illus.). 24p. (J). lib. bdg. 15.95 *(978-1-59566-013-8(5))* QEB Publishing Inc.

—Said Mouse to Mole. 2004. (QEB Start Reading Ser.). (Illus.). 24p. (J). lib. bdg. 15.95 *(978-1-59566-014-5(3))* QEB Publishing Inc.

—The Wobbly Wand, 8 vols. 2005. (QEB Readers). (Illus.). 24p. (J). (gr. -1-3). lib. bdg. 15.95 *(978-1-59566-073-2(9))* QEB Publishing Inc.

Bianchi, John. Why is Bird Smart? - BIG BOOK. 2011. (1-3Y Big Bks.). (ENG., Illus.). 16p. (J). pap. 9.60 *(978-1-64053-057-7(6)*, Bird, Bunny & Bear) American Reading Co.

Big Book of R Carry-over Stories. 2004. per. 34.99 *(978-0-9760490-4-3(X))* Say It Right.

Big Book Package, 6 bks., Set. 2004. (gr. 3-18). 218.30 *(978-0-673-61079-9(9))* Addison-Wesley Educational Pubs., Inc.

Big Book Tote Bag. (gr. -1-12). 18.13 *(978-0-7362-1101-7(2))* CENGAGE Learning.

Big Books, 22 bks. 2004. (Scott Foresman Reading Ser.). (gr. k-18). 654.90 *(978-0-328-02950-1(5))* Addison-Wesley Educational Pubs., Inc.

Big Books. (Rosen Real Readers Big Bookstm Ser.). (J). 8p. (gr. k-1). 167.70 *(978-1-4042-6291-1(1))*; 2006. 12p. (gr. 1-2). pap. 160.95 *(978-1-4042-6292-8(X))*; 2006. 16p. (gr. 2-3). pap. 184.00 *(978-1-4042-6293-5(8))* Rosen Publishing Group, Inc., The.

Big City Port. (Lexile Levels Ser.). 7.98 *(978-1-56334-693-4(1))* CENGAGE Learning.

Biographies Classroom Library. (gr. k-2). lib. bdg. 90.95 *(978-0-7368-9457-9(8)*, Red Brick Learning) Capstone.

Biographies Complete Unit. (gr. k-2). 520.95 *(978-0-7368-9458-6(6)*, Red Brick Learning) Capstone.

Birch, Beverley. Two Animal Tales from Africa: Band 15/Emerald (Collins Big Cat) 2017. (Collins Big Cat Tales Ser.). (ENG., Illus.). 48p. (J). (gr. 3-4). pap. 12.99 *(978-0-00-817942-7(5))* HarperCollins Pubs. Ltd. GBR. Dist: Independent Pubs. Group.

Bird Talk. 2005. (Book Treks Ser.). (J). (gr. 3-18). stu. ed. 34.95 *(978-0-673-62846-6(9))* Celebration Pr.

Birkhead, Jennifer. Peeping Through the Low, Green Grass. 2011. 28p. pap. 12.03 *(978-1-4490-5490-8(0))* AuthorHouse.

Biro, Val. The Boy Who Cried Wolf & the Goose That Laid the Golden Eggs. Biro, Val, illus. 2014. (ENG.). 24p. (J). pap. 6.95 *(978-1-84135-957-1(2))* Award Pubns. Ltd. GBR. Dist: Parkwest Pubns., Inc.

The Birthday Party. (Early Intervention Levels Ser.). 3.85 *(978-1-56334-953-9(1))* CENGAGE Learning.

Bishop, Celeste. Hace Sol / It's Sunny, 1 vol. 2016. (¿Qué Tiempo Hace? / What's the Weather Like? Ser.). (ENG & SPA., Illus.). 24p. (J). (gr. 1-1). lib. bdg. 25.27 *(978-1-4994-2330-3(6)*, 5aa8873c-8fa0-4d64-8a76-23d926fa4242, PowerKids Pr.) Rosen Publishing Group, Inc., The.

—Hace Sol (It's Sunny), 1 vol. 2016. (¿Qué Tiempo Hace? (What's the Weather Like?) Ser.). (SPA., Illus.). 24p. (J). (gr. 1-1). lib. bdg. 25.27 *(978-1-4994-2326-6(8)*, 4d67c389-7b95-43fb-af6c-5473cc0e649e, PowerKids Pr.) Rosen Publishing Group, Inc., The.

—Hace Viento / It's Windy, 1 vol. 2016. (¿Qué Tiempo Hace? / What's the Weather Like? Ser.). (ENG & SPA., Illus.). 24p. (J). (gr. 1-1). lib. bdg. 25.27 *(978-1-4994-2337-2(3)*, fdc1cc58-0e3a-4bad-9cc0-3ec3a212c05a, PowerKids Pr.) Rosen Publishing Group, Inc., The.

—Hace Viento (It's Windy), 1 vol. 2016. (¿Qué Tiempo Hace? (What's the Weather Like?) Ser.). (SPA., Illus.). 24p. (J). (gr. 1-1). lib. bdg. 25.27 *(978-1-4994-2333-4(0)*, df02b9cb-ce6f-45a4-8f20-2220830d0ea7, PowerKids Pr.) Rosen Publishing Group, Inc., The.

—¿Por Qué Las Plantas Tienen Hojas? / Why Do Plants Have Leaves?, 1 vol., 1. 2015. (Partes de la Planta / Plant Parts Ser.). (ENG & SPA., Illus.). 24p. (J). (gr. 1-1). 25.27 *(978-1-5081-4741-1(8)*, a12a4e4d-a1d7-483f-a194-c3fb3f6a6eb2, PowerKids Pr.) Rosen Publishing Group, Inc., The.

Bishop, Nic. Is There Anyone Out There?: Band 10/White (Collins Big Cat) Bishop, Nic, photos by. 2005. (Collins Big Cat Ser.). (ENG., Illus.). 352p. (J). (gr. 2-3). pap. 10.99 *(978-0-00-718635-8(5))* HarperCollins Pubs. Ltd. GBR. Dist: Independent Pubs. Group.

—Spiders (Nic Bishop: Scholastic Reader, Level 2) Bishop, Nic, photos by. 2012. (Scholastic Reader, Level 2 Ser.). (ENG., Illus.). 32p. (J). (gr. k-2). pap. 3.99 *(978-0-545-23757-4(2)*, Scholastic Paperbacks) Scholastic, Inc.

BishopRoby, Joshua. The World of Animals, 1 vol. rev. ed. 2007. (Science: Informational Text Ser.). (ENG.). 32p. (J). (gr. 3-6). pap. 12.99 *(978-0-7439-0593-0(8))* Teacher Created Materials, Inc.

Bjerregaard, Malynda. Chatter Batter: Four Stories for Speech. 2005. pap. 34.25 *(978-1-4184-9768-2(1))* AuthorHouse.

BJU Staff. Reading Student Text Grd 2 If. 2004. 21.00 *(978-1-57924-170-4(0))* BJU Pr.

—Reading Student Text Grd 2 Whe. 2004. 21.00 *(978-1-57924-171-1(9))* BJU Pr.

—A Reading Student Text Grd 3. 2004. 21.00 *(978-1-57924-172-8(7))* BJU Pr.

—Reading Student Text Grd 3 B. 2004. 21.00 *(978-1-57924-173-5(5))* BJU Pr.

—Reading Student Text Grd 4. 2004. 32.00 *(978-1-57924-348-7(7))* BJU Pr.

—Reading Student Text Grd 5. 2004. 32.00 *(978-1-57924-371-5(1))* BJU Pr.

—Reading Student Text Grd 6. 2004. 32.00 *(978-1-57924-542-9(0))* BJU Pr.

—Reading Worktext Student Grd 2. 2004. pap. 16.50 *(978-1-57924-174-2(3))* BJU Pr.

—Reading Worktext Student Grd 3. 2004. pap. 16.50 *(978-1-57924-175-9(1))* BJU Pr.

—Reading Worktext Student Grd 4. 2004. pap. 16.50 *(978-1-57924-458-3(0))* BJU Pr.

—Reading Worktext Student Grd 5. 2004. pap. 16.50 *(978-1-57924-443-9(2))* BJU Pr.

—Reading Worktext Student Grd 6. 2004. pap. 16.50 *(978-1-57924-543-6(9))* BJU Pr.

Blachowicz, Camille L. Z. Reading Fluency, Reader Level A. 2004. (JT: READING RATE & FLUENCY Ser.). (ENG.). 48p. (gr. 6-12). spiral bd. 29.20 *(978-0-07-861709-6(X)*, 007861709X) McGraw-Hill Education.

—Reading Fluency, Reader's Record A. 2004. (JT: READING RATE & FLUENCY Ser.). (ENG.). 74p. (gr. 6-12). pap. 20.20 *(978-0-07-861712-6(X)*, 007861712X) McGraw-Hill Education.

Black, Amber. A Day with Miss Sassy. 2008. 16p. pap. 24.95 *(978-1-60610-338-8(5))* PublishAmerica, Inc.

Blackman, Malorie. Sinclair the Wonder Bear. Allwright, Deborah, illus. 2nd ed. 2016. (Reading Ladder Level 2 Ser.). (ENG.). 48p. (gr. k-2). pap. 4.99 *(978-1-4052-8203-1(7))* Farshore GBR. Dist: HarperCollins Pubs.

Blackstone, Stella. Bear about Town / Oso en la Ciudad. Harter, Debbie, illus. 2010. (Bear Ser.). (ENG.). 24p. (J). (gr. -1-1). pap. 8.99 *(978-1-84686-377-6(5))* Barefoot Bks., Inc.

—Bear at Home (Oso en Casa) Harter, Debbie, illus. 2010. 24p. (J). (gr. -1-1). pap. 7.99 *(978-1-84686-422-3(4))* Barefoot Bks., Inc.

—Bear in a Square / Oso en un Cuadrado. Harter, Debbie, illus. 2009. (Bear Ser.). (ENG.). 24p. (J). (gr. -1-1). pap. 8.99 *(978-1-84686-387-5(2))* Barefoot Bks., Inc.

—Bear in a Square / Ours Dans un Carre. Harter, Debbie, illus. rev. ed. 2017. (Bear Ser.). (ENG.). 24p. (J). (gr. -1-1). pap. 8.99 *(978-1-78285-330-5(8))* Barefoot Bks., Inc.

Blaine, Dalton. That's Not Fair! Civic Virtues, 1 vol. 2018. (Civics for the Real World Ser.). (ENG.). 8p. (gr. k-1). pap. *(978-1-5383-6314-0(3)*, 7fa6fd30-15d2-4e41-83fe-a016346dd625, Rosen Classroom) Rosen Publishing Group, Inc., The.

Blanche, David. A Day in My Town, 1 vol. 2012. (InfoMax Readers Ser.). (ENG., Illus.). 16p. (J). (gr. k-k). pap. 7.00 *(978-1-4488-8977-8(4)*, 8250f5a8-5096-4fe4-b405-ea6d2c680044, Rosen Classroom) Rosen Publishing Group, Inc., The.

Blane, Francisco. The Little Girl with Curl. Kelley, Gerald, illus. 2009. (Reader's Theater Nursery Rhymes & Songs Set B Ser.). 48p. (J). pap. *(978-1-60859-157-2(3))* Benchmark Education Co.

—Little Jack Horner Eats Pie. Price, Nick, illus. 2009. (Reader's Theater Nursery Rhymes & Songs Set B Ser.). 48p. (J). pap. *(978-1-60859-158-9(1))* Benchmark Education Co.

—Looking for the Muffin Man. 2008. (Reader's Theater Nursery Rhymes & Songs Ser.). (Illus.). 48p. (J). (gr. k-1). pap. *(978-1-60437-966-2(9))* Benchmark Education Co.

—My New Clothes: Lap Book. 2009. (My First Reader's Theater Set B Ser.). (J). 28.00 *(978-1-935441-01-4(9))* Benchmark Education Co.

—One Raining, Pouring Morning. 2008. (Reader's Theater Nursery Rhymes & Songs Ser.). (Illus.). 48p. (J). (gr. k-1). pap. *(978-1-60437-977-8(4))* Benchmark Education Co.

—People at School: Lap Book. 2009. (My First Reader's Theater Set B Ser.). (J). 28.00 *(978-1-935441-00-7(0))* Benchmark Education Co.

—Stripes at the Beach: Lap Book. 2009. (My First Reader's Theater Set B Ser.). (J). 28.00 *(978-1-60634-988-5(0))* Benchmark Education Co.

—Tim Rows a Boat Gently down the Stream. 2008. (Reader's Theater Nursery Rhymes & Songs Ser.). (Illus.). 48p. (J). (gr. k-1). pap. *(978-1-60437-980-8(4))* Benchmark Education Co.

—Up & Down: Lap Book. 2009. (My First Reader's Theater Set B Ser.). (J). 28.00 *(978-1-60634-989-2(9))* Benchmark Education Co.

—Vegetables Are Good! Lap Book. 2009. (My First Reader's Theater Set B Ser.). (J). 28.00 *(978-1-60634-990-8(2))* Benchmark Education Co.

—What Will You Be? Lap Book. 2009. (My First Reader's Theater Set B Ser.). (J). 28.00 *(978-1-60634-993-9(7))* Benchmark Education Co.

Blank Tabletop Pocket Chart Cards. 2004. (J). 4.95 *(978-1-56911-200-7(2))* Learning Resources, Inc.

Blazeman, Christopher. Eagles up Close, 1 vol. 2nd rev. ed. 2011. (TIME for KIDS(r): Informational Text Ser.). (ENG.). 28p. (gr. 2-3). pap. 9.99 *(978-1-4333-3616-4(2))* Teacher Created Materials, Inc.

—Horses up Close, 1 vol. 2nd rev. ed. 2011. (TIME for KIDS(r): Informational Text Ser.). (ENG.). 28p. (gr. 2-3). pap. 9.99 *(978-1-4333-3617-1(0))* Teacher Created Materials, Inc.

—Snakes up Close, 1 vol. 2nd rev. ed. 2011. (TIME for KIDS(r): Informational Text Ser.). (ENG.). 28p. (gr. 2-3). pap. 8.99 *(978-1-4333-3618-8(9))* Teacher Created Materials, Inc.

Blends & Digraphs Set: Level D. (Sing-along Songs Ser.). (gr. -1-2). 48.46 incl. audio compact disk *(978-0-7362-0422-4(9))* CENGAGE Learning.

Blevins, Wiley. Can You See It?, 6 vols., Set. 2003. (Phonics Readers 1-36 Ser.). (ENG.). 8p. (gr. k-1). pap. 29.70 *(978-0-7368-3191-8(6))* Capstone.

—Germs, 6 vols., Set. 2004. (Phonics Readers Books 37-72 Ser.). (ENG.). 8p. (gr. k-1). pap. 35.70 *(978-0-7368-4055-2(9))* Capstone.

—Now & Long Ago, 6 vols., Set. 2003. (Phonics Readers 1-36 Ser.). (ENG.). 8p. (gr. k-1). pap. 29.70 *(978-0-7368-3218-2(1))* Capstone.

—Push or Pull?, 6 vols., Set. 2003. (Phonics Readers 1-36 Ser.). (ENG.). 8p. (gr. k-1). pap. 29.70 *(978-0-7368-3212-0(2))* Capstone.

—Who Am I?, 6 vols., Set. 2003. (Phonics Readers 1-36 Ser.). (ENG.). 8p. (gr. k-1). pap. 29.70 *(978-0-7368-3185-7(1))* Capstone.

Bloch, Joanne. A Few Little Lies. 2009. (Hodder African Readers Ser.). (ENG., Illus.). 96p. pap. 12.95 *(978-0-340-98415-4(5))* Hodder Education Group GBR. Dist: Trans-Atlantic Pubns., Inc.

Block, Cathy Collins & Mangieri, John N. Scholastic Success with Reading & Math Jumbo Workbook, 1 vol. 2005. (ENG.). 320p. (gr. 3-3). pap., wbk. ed. 14.99 *(978-0-439-78602-7(9)*, Teaching Resources) Scholastic, Inc.

Block, Cheryl, et al. Reading Detective Rx: Using Higher-Order Thinking to Improve Reading Comprehension. 2012. (Reading Detective Ser.). 192p. (gr. 6-12). pap. 24.99 *(978-0-89455-801-6(3))* Critical Thinking Co., The.

Bloor, Thomas. The Legend of Blackbeard: Band 15/Emerald (Collins Big Cat) Kravets, Ivan, illus. 2016. (Collins Big Cat Ser.). (ENG.). 48p. (J). pap. 9.95 *(978-0-00-814725-9(6))* HarperCollins Pubs. Ltd. GBR. Dist: Independent Pubs. Group.

Blue & Green Levels Certificate Only. (gr. k-5). 89.00 *(978-0-7578-6540-4(2))* Rigby Education.

Blue, Green, Orange, Turquoise, Purple & Gold Levels Certificate Only. (gr. k-5). 89.00 *(978-0-7578-6538-1(0))* Rigby Education.

Blumenfeld, Samuel L. Blumenfeld's Alpha-Phonics: A Primer for Beginning Readers. 2006. spiral bd. 29.95 *(978-0-9776024-0-7(0))* Blumont Company, The.

Bluming. Hebrew Reading Homework Book: Lamer Shteigin in Ivri. 2003. (YID.). 48p. (J). (gr. 2-4). pap. 10.55 *(978-0-9729232-0-0(9))* Kreizel Enterprises, Inc.

BMX Billy, 6 pack. (Literatura 2000 Ser.). (gr. 1-2). 28.00 *(978-0-7635-0083-2(6))* Rigby Education.

Board Book Classics Set, 8. 2005. (J). bds. *(978-1-59794-009-2(7))* Environments, Inc.

Board Books & Tapes 800865, 4 vols. 2005. (J). *(978-1-59794-051-1(8))* Environments, Inc.

Bodman, Sue & Franklin, Glen. Where Are My Shoes? Yellow Band. Busby, Ailie, illus. 2017. (Cambridge Reading Adventures Ser.). (ENG.). 16p. (J). pap. 6.15 *(978-1-108-43964-0(0))* Cambridge Univ. Pr.

Bodman, Sue & Franklin, Glen F. Finn Saves the Day Orange Band. Austen, Terry, illus. 2017. (Cambridge Reading Adventures Ser.). (ENG.). 16p. (J). pap. 6.15 *(978-1-108-43977-0(2))* Cambridge Univ. Pr.

Body Numbers, 6 pack. (Discovery World Ser.). 16p. (gr. 1-2). 28.00 *(978-0-7635-8467-2(3))* Rigby Education.

Body, Wendy. Zeebo's Numbers, 4 vols. 2005. (QEB Readers). (Illus.). 24p. (J). (gr. -1-3). lib. bdg. 15.95 *(978-1-59566-103-6(4))* QEB Publishing Inc.

—Zia's Colors, 4 vols. 2005. (QEB Readers). (Illus.). 24p. (J). (gr. -1-3). lib. bdg. 15.95 *(978-1-59566-105-0(0))* QEB Publishing Inc.

Body Works. (Guided Reading Levels Ser.). 32.22 *(978-0-7362-1053-9(9))* CENGAGE Learning.

Bolivar, Simon. Champion of Freedom. 2007. (Read on! Special Edition: Level BA Ser.). (Illus.). 23p. pap. 18.51 *(978-1-4190-3527-2(4))* Steck-Vaughn.

Bond, Janice & Fiebelkorn, Claire. Water on Earth, 1 vol. 2012. (InfoMax Readers Ser.). (ENG., Illus.). 24p. (J). (gr. 1-1). pap. 8.25 *(978-1-4488-9034-7(9)*, 6bd646c2-9498-4977-9389-72d3e5ac4172, Rosen Classroom) Rosen Publishing Group, Inc., The.

Bonnell, Kris. The Big Hungry Cat. 2006. (J). pap. 5.95 *(978-1-933727-33-2(0))* Reading Reading Bks., LLC.

—Down in the Sea. 2006. (J). pap. 5.95 *(978-1-933727-38-7(1))* Reading Reading Bks., LLC.

—Frog Fun. 2006. (J). pap. 5.95 *(978-1-933727-39-4(X))* Reading Reading Bks., LLC.

—The Happy Moon. 2006. (J). pap. 5.95 *(978-1-933727-30-1(6))* Reading Reading Bks., LLC.

—Lemonade. 2006. (J). pap. 5.95 *(978-1-933727-31-8(4))* Reading Reading Bks., LLC.

—The Little Boat. 2006. (J). pap. 5.95 *(978-1-933727-34-9(9))* Reading Reading Bks., LLC.

—The Little Sprout. 2007. (J). pap. 5.95 *(978-1-933727-54-7(3))* Reading Reading Bks., LLC.

—Look Up! 2007. (J). pap. 5.95 *(978-1-933727-48-6(9))* Reading Reading Bks., LLC.

—Mother Animals. 2007. (J). pap. 5.95 *(978-1-933727-49-3(7))* Reading Reading Bks., LLC.

—Mudskipper & the Water. 2006. (J). pap. 3.95 *(978-1-933727-21-9(7))* Reading Reading Bks., LLC.

—Pets for Us. 2007. (J). pap. 5.95 *(978-1-933727-50-9(0))* Reading Reading Bks., LLC.

—Picking a Pumpkin. 2007. (J). pap. 5.95 *(978-1-933727-51-6(9))* Reading Reading Bks., LLC.

—Pizza for Carl. 2006. (J). pap. 3.95 *(978-1-933727-27-1(6))* Reading Reading Bks., LLC.

—Presents for Mom. 2007. (J). pap. 6.95 *(978-1-933727-61-5(6))* Reading Reading Bks., LLC.

—Red Apples for Me. 2007. (J). pap. 5.95 *(978-1-933727-52-3(7))* Reading Reading Bks., LLC.

—Robins in the Spring. 2007. (J). pap. 5.95 *(978-1-933727-53-0(5))* Reading Reading Bks., LLC.

—Spring Is Coming! 2007. (J). pap. 6.95 *(978-1-933727-64-6(0))* Reading Reading Bks., LLC.

—Too Big to Play. 2006. (J). pap. 5.95 *(978-1-933727-35-6(7))* Reading Reading Bks., LLC.

—We Like the Beach. 2007. (J). pap. 5.95 *(978-1-933727-55-4(1))* Reading Reading Bks., LLC.

—We Love Pets. 2007. (J). pap. 5.95 *(978-1-933727-56-1(X))* Reading Reading Bks., LLC.

—What Tigers Do. 2006. (J). pap. 5.95 *(978-1-933727-41-7(1))* Reading Reading Bks., LLC.

—Where Can Louis Sleep? 2007. (J). pap. 5.95 *(978-1-933727-57-8(8))* Reading Reading Bks., LLC.

—Where Is a Bear? 2007. (J). pap. 6.95 *(978-1-933727-63-9(2))* Reading Reading Bks., LLC.

—Where Is the Big Cat? 2007. (J). pap. 6.95 *(978-1-933727-62-2(4))* Reading Reading Bks., LLC.

—The White, White Snow. 2007. (J). pap. 5.95 *(978-1-933727-44-8(6))* Reading Reading Bks., LLC.

—Who Can Wiggle? 2006. (J). pap. 5.95 *(978-1-933727-42-4(X))* Reading Reading Bks., LLC.

—Who Has a Hump? 2007. (J). pap. 5.95 *(978-1-933727-58-5(6))* Reading Reading Bks., LLC.

—Yellow Flowers. 2006. (J). pap. 5.95 *(978-1-933727-36-3(5))* Reading Reading Bks., LLC.

Boocock, Charles & Yu, Jennifer. The 10 Most Memorable Court Cases. 2008. 14.99 *(978-1-55448-548-2(7))* Scholastic Library Publishing.

Book Builder. 2004. (Scott Foresman Reading Ser.). (gr. k-18). cd-rom 29.97 *(978-0-673-64103-8(1))*; (gr. 1-18). cd-rom 29.97 *(978-0-673-64104-5(X))*; (gr. 2-18). cd-rom 29.97 *(978-0-673-64105-2(8))*; (gr. 3-18). cd-rom 29.97 *(978-0-673-64106-9(6))* Addison-Wesley Educational Pubs., Inc.

Booking, Walt. Teddy's Tale, 1 vol. 2006. (Neighborhood Readers Ser.). (ENG.). 12p. (gr. 1-2). pap. 5.90 *(978-1-4042-7054-1(X)*, b9bd6f15-8022-48bd-ae11-5544e85a5587, Rosen Classroom) Rosen Publishing Group, Inc., The.

Books, 6 Pack. (Chiquilibros Ser.). (gr. k-1). 23.00 *(978-0-7635-0423-6(8))* Rigby Education.

BookSource Staff, compiled by. Obi-Wan Kenobi: Jedi Knight. 2012. (Star Wars DK Readers Level 3 Ser.). lib. bdg. 13.55 *(978-0-606-26678-9(X))* Turtleback.

—Who Saved the Galaxy? 2012. (Star Wars DK Readers Level 1 Ser.). lib. bdg. 13.55 *(978-0-606-26677-2(1))* Turtleback.

Bookweb 3 & 4 Certificate Only. (Bookweb Ser.). (gr. 4-18). 89.00 *(978-0-7578-6525-1(9))* Rigby Education.

Bookweb 4 Blackline Masters Book, Vol. 4. (Bookweb Ser.). (gr. 4-18). 52.00 *(978-0-7635-5937-3(7))* Rigby Education.

Bookweb 5 & 6 Certificate Only. (Bookweb Ser.). (gr. 6-18). 89.00 *(978-0-7578-6526-8(7))* Rigby Education.

Bookweb 5 Blackline Masters Book, Vol. 5. (Bookweb Ser.). (gr. 5-18). 52.00 *(978-0-7635-5926-7(1))* Rigby Education.

Bookweb 6 Blackline Masters Book, Vol. 6. (Bookweb Ser.). (gr. 6-18). 52.00 *(978-0-7578-1653-6(3))* Rigby Education.

Boomerangs, 6 Pack. (Story Steps Ser.). (gr. k-2). 32.00 *(978-0-7635-9805-1(4))* Rigby Education.

Booth, Jack. The 10 Greatest Accidental Inventions. 2007. (J). 14.99 *(978-1-55448-510-9(X))* Scholastic Library Publishing.

—The 10 Most Amazing Migrations. 2008. (J). 14.99 *(978-1-55448-522-2(3))* Scholastic Library Publishing.

—The 10 Most Daring Heists. 2007. (J). 14.99 *(978-1-55448-486-7(3))* Scholastic Library Publishing.

—The 10 Most Gripping 20th Century War Stories. 2008. 14.99 *(978-1-55448-497-3(9))* Scholastic Library Publishing.

Bot's Bits: Set A Individual Title Six-Packs. (gr. k-3). 29.00 *(978-0-7635-0534-9(X))* Rigby Education.

Bouchard, Natasha. The Incredible Elastigirl (Disney/Pixar the Incredibles 2) Disney Storybook Art Team, Disney Storybook, illus. 2018. (Step into Reading Ser.). (ENG.). 32p. (J). (gr. -1-1). pap. 5.99 *(978-0-7364-3857-5(2)*, RH/Disney) Random Hse. Children's Bks.

Boundaries Washed Away: Fifth Grade Guided Comprehension Level P. (On Our Way to English Ser.). (gr. 5-18). 34.50 *(978-0-7578-6608-1(5))* Rigby Education.

Bourke, Kenna. Deadly Animals High Beginning Book with Online Access, 1 vol. 2014. (ENG., Illus.). 24p. (J). pap., E-Book, E-Book 9.50 *(978-1-107-69371-5(3))* Cambridge Univ. Pr.
—Slime: the Wonderful World of Mucus Low Intermediate Book with Online Access, 1 vol. 2014. (ENG., Illus.). 24p. (J). pap., E-Book, E-Book 9.50 *(978-1-107-67343-4(7))* Cambridge Univ. Pr.
—So Cute! Beginning Book with Online Access, 1 vol. 2014. (ENG., Illus.). 24p. pap., E-Book, E-Book 9.50 *(978-1-107-64649-0(9))* Cambridge Univ. Pr.
BourkeKenna. Jeff Corwin: Wild Man Beginning Book with Online Access, 1 vol. 2014. (ENG., Illus.). 24p. pap., E-Book, E-Book 9.50 *(978-1-107-68039-5(5))* Cambridge Univ. Pr.
—LOST: THE MYSTERY OF AMELIA EARHART HIGH BEGINNING BOOK WITH ONLINE ACCESS, 1 vol. 2014. (ENG., Illus.). 24p. (J). pap., E-Book, E-Book 9.50 *(978-1-107-69335-7(7))* Cambridge Univ. Pr.
Bove, Candace Scobie. Calypso: A Day in the Life of a Puppy. 2012. 24p. 24.95 *(978-1-4626-4122-2(9))* America Star Bks.
Bowers, Linda. Spotlight on Reading Comprehension Making Inferences & Drawing Conclusions. 2005. (Illus.). (J). per. 11.95 *(978-0-7606-0585-1(8))* LinguiSystems, Inc.
Bowers, Linda, et al. Spotlight on Reading Comprehension Characters & Actions. 2005. (J). per. 11.95 *(978-0-7606-0583-7(1))* LinguiSystems, Inc.
—Spotlight on Reading Comprehension Comparing & Contrasting. 2005. (Illus.). (J). per. 11.95 *(978-0-7606-0581-3(5))* LinguiSystems, Inc.
—Spotlight on Reading Comprehension Figurative Language & Exclusion. 2005. (Illus.). (J). per. 11.95 *(978-0-7606-0582-0(3))* LinguiSystems, Inc.
—Spotlight on Reading Comprehension Paraphrasing & Summarizing. 2005. (J). per. 11.95 *(978-0-7606-0584-4(X))* LinguiSystems, Inc.
—Spotlight on Reading Comprehension Sequencing & Problem Solving. 2005. (Illus.). (J). 11.95 *(978-0-7606-0580-6(7))* LinguiSystems, Inc.
Bowler, Bill. Troy. 2nd ed. 2013. (ENG., Illus.). 40p. pap. 11.00 *(978-0-19-424970-6(0))* Oxford Univ. Pr., Inc.
Bowley, Catherine. Giants of the Ocean Gold Band. 2016. (Cambridge Reading Adventures Ser.). (ENG., Illus.). 24p. pap. 8.80 *(978-1-107-55165-7(X))* Cambridge Univ. Pr.
Boyd, David. Marco Polo & the Roc. Ng, Drew, illus. 2007. 48p. (J). lib. bdg. 23.08 *(978-1-4242-1621-5(4))* Fitzgerald Bks.
Boylan, Susan. When Knife Married Fork. 2017. (ENG., Illus.). (gr. k-5). *(978-1-925590-71-5(2))* Vivid Publishing.
Bradford, Chris. Collins Big Cat Phonics for Letters & Sounds - Jake & Jen in the Tomb of Ice: Band 07/Turquoise, Bd. 7. Paul, Korky, illus. 2018. (Collins Big Cat Phonics Ser.). (ENG.). 24p. (J). (gr. 1-2). pap. 6.99 *(978-0-00-825178-9(9))* HarperCollins Pubs. Ltd. GBR. Dist: Independent Pubs. Group.
Bradley, Kathleen. The Boy Who Cried Wolf, 1 vol. rev. ed. 2008. (Reader's Theater Ser.). (ENG.). 24p. (J). (gr. 1-3). pap. 8.99 *(978-1-4333-0297-8(7))* Teacher Created Materials, Inc.
Bradley, Kathleen E. Making Money Grow, 1 vol. 2nd rev. ed. 2013. (TIME for KIDS(r): Informational Text Ser.). (ENG.). 64p. (gr. 4-8). pap. 14.99 *(978-1-4333-4908-9(6))* Teacher Created Materials, Inc.
Bradley, Timothy J. Animal Architects, 1 vol. 2nd rev. ed. 2012. (TIME for KIDS(r): Informational Text Ser.). (ENG., Illus.). 48p. (gr. 4-5). pap. 13.99 *(978-1-4333-4822-8(5))* Teacher Created Materials, Inc.
—Bug Builders, 1 vol. 2nd rev. ed. 2012. (TIME for KIDS(r): Informational Text Ser.). (ENG., Illus.). 48p. (gr. 4-5). pap. 13.99 *(978-1-4333-4821-1(7))* Teacher Created Materials, Inc.
—Danger in the Desert, 1 vol. 2nd rev. ed. 2013. (TIME for KIDS(r): Informational Text Ser.). (ENG., Illus.). 64p. (J). (gr. 4-8). pap. 14.99 *(978-1-4333-4897-6(7))* Teacher Created Materials, Inc.
—Demons of the Deep, 1 vol. 2nd rev. ed. 2013. (TIME for KIDS(r): Informational Text Ser.). (ENG., Illus.). 64p. (J). (gr. 4-8). pap. 14.99 *(978-1-4333-4896-9(9))* Teacher Created Materials, Inc.
—Strange but True: Bizarre Animals, 1 vol. 2nd rev. ed. 2012. (TIME for KIDS(r): Informational Text Ser.). (ENG.). 48p. (gr. 4-5). pap. 13.99 *(978-1-4333-4861-7(6))* Teacher Created Materials, Inc.
—Strange but True: Gross Anatomy, 1 vol. 2nd rev. ed. 2012. (TIME for KIDS(r): Informational Text Ser.). (ENG.). 48p. (gr. 4-6). pap. 13.99 *(978-1-4333-4860-0(8))* Teacher Created Materials, Inc.
—Strange but True Tiny Creatures, 1 vol. 2nd rev. ed. 2012. (TIME for KIDS(r): Informational Text Ser.). (ENG.). 48p. (gr. 4-5). pap. 13.99 *(978-1-4333-4862-4(4))* Teacher Created Materials, Inc.
—Teddy Bear, Teddy Bear, Say Good Night. Medina, Conni & Stark, Kristy, eds. 2009. (Early Literacy Ser.). (ENG., Illus.). 16p. (gr. -1-1). 19.99 *(978-1-4333-1472-8(X))* Teacher Created Materials, Inc.
—Terror in the Tropics, 1 vol. 2nd rev. ed. 2013. (TIME for KIDS(r): Informational Text Ser.). (ENG., Illus.). 64p. (J). (gr. 4-8). pap. 14.99 *(978-1-4333-4898-3(5))* Teacher Created Materials, Inc.
—Wild Cities, 1 vol. 2nd rev. ed. 2012. (TIME for KIDS(r): Informational Text Ser.). (ENG.). 48p. (gr. 4-5). pap. 13.99 *(978-1-4333-4823-5(3))* Teacher Created Materials, Inc.
Bradman, Tom. Hall of the Bulls: Band 10 White/Band 12 Copper (Collins Big Cat Progress) Jackson, Nicholas, illus. 2014. (Collins Big Cat Progress Ser.). (ENG.). 32p. (J). (gr. 2-3). pap. 10.99 *(978-0-00-751927-9(3))* HarperCollins Pubs. Ltd. GBR. Dist: Independent Pubs. Group.
—King Fox Purple Band. Bernstein, Galia, illus. 2016. (Cambridge Reading Adventures Ser.). (ENG.). 24p. pap. 8.80 *(978-1-107-56215-8(5))* Cambridge Univ. Pr.
Bradman, Tony. Baba Yaga, Level 22. pap. *(978-0-19-030001-2(9))* Oxford Univ. Pr., Inc.
—Dilly & the Goody-Goody. Hellard, Susan, illus. 2nd ed. 2016. (Reading Ladder Level 2 Ser.). (ENG.). 48p. (gr. k-2). pap. 4.99 *(978-1-4052-8222-2(3),* Reading Ladder) Farshore GBR. Dist: HarperCollins Pubs.
—The Frog Prince Hops to It, 1 vol. Warburton, Sarah, illus. 2009. (After Happily Ever After Ser.). (ENG.). 56p. (J). (gr. 3-6). 25.99 *(978-1-4342-1303-7(X),* 95628, Stone Arch Bks.) Capstone.
—Hunters of the Sea 3 Explorers. Bacchin, Giorgio, illus. 2017. (Cambridge Reading Adventures Ser.). (ENG.). 40p. pap. 9.80 *(978-1-108-40099-2(X))* Cambridge Univ. Pr.
—The King Who Thought He Was Clever: a Folk Tale from Russia: Band 14/Ruby (Collins Big Cat) Oliver, Juanbjuan, illus. 2017. (Collins Big Cat Tales Ser.). (ENG.). 48p. (J). (gr. 3-4). pap. 12.99 *(978-0-00-817940-3(9))* HarperCollins Pubs. Ltd. GBR. Dist: Independent Pubs. Group.
—Mei & the Pirate Queen White Band. Anderson, Scoular, illus. 2016. (Cambridge Reading Adventures Ser.). (ENG.). 32p. pap. 9.50 *(978-1-316-50090-3(X))* Cambridge Univ. Pr.
—The Mummy Family Find Fame. 2006. (Red Bananas Ser.). (ENG., Illus.). 48p. (J). (gr. -1-3). lib. bdg. *(978-0-7787-1076-9(9))* Crabtree Publishing Co.
—Polly & the Pirates (Reading Ladder Level 3) Davies, James, illus. 2nd ed. 2016. (Reading Ladder Level 3 Ser.). (ENG.). 48p. (gr. k-2). 4.99 *(978-1-4052-8249-9(5),* Reading Ladder) Farshore GBR. Dist: HarperCollins Pubs.
—The Silk Road White Band. Cerisier, Emmanuel, illus. 2016. (Cambridge Reading Adventures Ser.). (ENG.). 15p. pap. 9.50 *(978-1-107-56232-5(5))* Cambridge Univ. Pr.
—Yu & the Great Flood Gold Band. Hitori De, Nicola, illus. 2016. (Cambridge Reading Adventures Ser.). (ENG.). 24p. pap. 8.80 *(978-1-107-56225-7(2))* Cambridge Univ. Pr.
Bradshaw, Georgine & Wrighton, Charlene. Basic Kit - Kindergarten. Clark, Irene, illus. 2005. Orig. Title: Basic Kit II. (J). 249.95 *(978-1-886441-31-6(6))* Zoo-phonics, Inc.
—Kindergarten Zoo-per Kit. Clark, Irene, illus. 2005. (J). 499.95 *(978-1-886441-34-7(0),* ZOP4219) Zoo-phonics, Inc.
—Preschool Zoo-per Kit. Clark, Irene, illus. 2005. (J). 449.95 *(978-1-886441-32-3(4),* ZOP4218) Zoo-phonics, Inc.
Braidich, Victoria. Monday with Meg, 1 vol. 2006. (Neighborhood Readers Ser.). (ENG.). 12p. (gr. k-1). pap. 5.90 *(978-1-4042-6459-5(0),* e3e562d3-16d5-408a-8351-792ecb72cfe9, Rosen Classroom) Rosen Publishing Group, Inc., The.
Brain, Helen. No More Secrets. 2009. (Hodder African Readers Ser.). (ENG., Illus.). 144p. pap. 12.95 *(978-0-340-98419-2(8))* Hodder Education Group GBR. Dist: Trans-Atlantic Pubns., Inc.
Brand New View. (J). (gr. 2-3). pap. 9.90 *(978-0-669-15889-2(5));* pap. 75.00 *(978-0-669-13446-9(5));* pap. 9.90 *(978-0-669-15290-6(0))* Houghton Mifflin Harcourt School Pubs.
Brandon, Amanda. A Box of Socks. Echeverri, Catalina, illus. 2019. (Early Bird Readers — Orange (Early Bird Stories (tm)) Ser.). (ENG.). 32p. (J). (gr. k-3). 30.65 *(978-1-5415-4220-4(7),* 22dbd3de-9f00-4265-b42f-b4de6ca96902); pap. 9.99 *(978-1-5415-7412-0(5),* 3f31309b-9f99-4661-9720-ace784514b95) Lerner Publishing Group. (Lerner Pubns.).
—A Scarf & a Half. Echeverri, Catalina, illus. 2019. (Early Bird Readers — Orange (Early Bird Stories (tm)) Ser.). (ENG.). 32p. (J). (gr. k-3). 30.65 *(978-1-5415-4222-8(3),* e408a382-acb9-4224-ace7-270d7b2bfce3); pap. 9.99 *(978-1-5415-7415-1(X),* d57fb8a7-fa0d-4ec1-b8f7-f5f0df68ce5c) Lerner Publishing Group. (Lerner Pubns.).
Brasch, Nicolas. A Baseball Giant, 1 vol. rev. ed. 2013. (Literary Text Ser.). (ENG., Illus.). 32p. (gr. 2-4). pap. 11.99 *(978-1-4333-5644-5(9))* Teacher Created Materials, Inc.
Brasch, Nicolas & Dawson, Amanda. The Chalk Circle. 2008. (Rigby Focus Forward: Level G Ser.). (Illus.). 24p. (J). (gr. 4-7). pap. *(978-1-4190-3713-9(7),* Rigby) Pearson Education Australia.
Brasch, Nicolas & Nickel, Adam. Dad & Dan Go Camping. 2008. (Rigby Focus Forward: Level G Ser.). (Illus.). 24p. (J). (gr. 4-7). pap. *(978-1-4190-3705-4(6),* Rigby) Pearson Education Australia.
—Dad & Dan Go Fishing. 2008. (Rigby Focus Forward: Level D Ser.). (Illus.). 16p. (J). (gr. 4-7). pap. *(978-1-4190-3668-2(8),* Rigby) Pearson Education Australia.
Brasch, Nicolas & Parton, Daron. The Riddle of the Camel Race. 2008. (Rigby Focus Forward: Level L Ser.). (Illus.). 24p. (J). (gr. -1-3). pap. *(978-1-4190-3820-4(6),* Rigby) Pearson Education Australia.
Braxton, Simone. Sanjay's Civil War Project: Looking at Data, 1 vol. 2017. (Computer Kids: Powered by Computational Thinking Ser.). (ENG.). 24p. (J). (gr. 3-4). 25.27 *(978-1-5383-2428-8(8),* e9658e17-1969-4480-add3-1af55307323f, PowerKids Pr.); pap. *(978-1-5081-3779-5(X),* 266a8312-3314-410f-b295-08c7cd98fe68, Rosen Classroom) Rosen Publishing Group, Inc., The.
Breakwell, Spike & Millar, Colin. Leila's Game 1 Pathfinders. Perez, Moni, illus. 2017. (Cambridge Reading Adventures Ser.). (ENG.). 32p. pap. 8.60 *(978-1-108-40820-2(6))* Cambridge Univ. Pr.
Brett, Jan. The Wild Christmas Reindeer. Brett, Jan, illus. 2018. (ENG., Illus.). 32p. (J). (-k). bds. 8.99 *(978-0-525-51579-1(8),* G.P. Putnam's Sons Books for Young Readers) Penguin Young Readers Group.
Brezinova, Ivona. Dorothy & the Glasses. Llapashtica, Mentor, illus. 2007. 32p. (J). (ARA & ENG.). pap. 12.95 *(978-1-60195-088-8(8));* (POL & ENG.). pap. 12.95 *(978-1-60195-099-4(3))* International Step by Step Assn.
—To Have a Dog. Deisadze, Zaur, illus. 2007. (POL & ENG.). 32p. (J). pap. 12.95 *(978-1-60195-106-9(X))* International Step by Step Assn.
Brian, Janeen. Maya Monkey, 1 vol. rev. ed. 2013. (Literary Text Ser.). (ENG., Illus.). 20p. (gr. k-2). 7.99 *(978-1-4333-5486-1(1))* Teacher Created Materials, Inc.
Bridge, Chris Helene. Read to Me! Bilingual. 2016. (ENG., Illus.). 32p. (J). pap. 9.95 *(978-1-942945-36-9(1),* 9b5bd1bf-e2c4-4b39-b79b-bddcb22ef19d) Night Heron Media.
Brinker, Spencer. A Goat on a Boat. 2019. (Read & Rhyme Level 3 Ser.). (ENG., Illus.). 16p. (J). (gr. -1-1). 24.21 *(978-1-64280-563-5(7))* Bearport Publishing Co., Inc.
—A Knight in a Fight. 2019. (Read & Rhyme Level 3 Ser.). (ENG., Illus.). 16p. (J). (gr. -1-1). 24.21 *(978-1-64280-558-1(0))* Bearport Publishing Co., Inc.
Brinton, Margaret. 100 Little Reading Comprehension Lessons, Grade 1-4: Fun-To-Read Stories with Skill-Building Exercises. Shalansky, Len, illus. 2004. (ENG.). 112p. pap. 12.95 *(978-1-57310-425-8(6))* Teaching & Learning Co.
The British Tradition: The EMC Write-in Reader. 2nd ed. (Literature & the Language Arts Ser.). (YA). (gr. 12-18). wbk. ed. 19.99 *(978-0-8219-2920-9(8))* EMC/Paradigm Publishing.
Brooke, Jasmine. The Princess & the Pea: Pass the Pea Pressure Test! 2017. (Fairy Tale Fixers: Fixing Fairy Tale Problems with STEM Ser.). 32p. (gr. 3-4). pap. 63.00 *(978-1-5382-0667-6(6))* Stevens, Gareth Publishing LLLP.
Brooke, Samantha. Blowing in the Wind. 2018. (Scholastic Readers Ser.). (ENG.). 32p. (J). (gr. -1-k). 13.89 *(978-1-64310-244-3(3))* Penworthy Co., LLC, The.
—Blowing in the Wind. 2018. (Illus.). 32p. (J). *(978-1-5444-0657-2(6))* Scholastic, Inc.
—Blowing in the Wind (the Magic School Bus Rides Again: Scholastic Reader, Level 2), 1 vol. Artful Doodlers Ltd., illus. 2018. (Scholastic Reader, Level 2 Ser.). (ENG.). 32p. (J). (gr. k-2). pap. 4.99 *(978-1-338-25377-1(8))* Scholastic, Inc.
—Rock Man vs. Weather Man. 2018. (Scholastic Readers Ser.). (ENG.). 31p. (J). (gr. -1-k). 13.89 *(978-1-64310-248-1(6))* Penworthy Co., LLC, The.
—Rock Man vs. Weather Man. 2018. (Illus.). 31p. (J). *(978-1-5444-0658-9(4))* Scholastic, Inc.
—Rock Man vs. Weather Man (the Magic School Bus Rides Again: Scholastic Reader, Level 2) Artful Doodlers Ltd., illus. 2018. (Scholastic Reader, Level 2 Ser.). (ENG.). 32p. (J). (gr. k-2). pap. 5.99 *(978-1-338-25378-8(6))* Scholastic, Inc.
Brooks, Felicity. School Look & Say. Litchfield, Jo, illus. 2005. 10p. (J). 7.95 *(978-0-7945-1015-2(9),* Usborne) EDC Publishing.
Brooks, Susie. A Day in the Life of Triceratops. Woodward, Jonathan, illus. 2016. (Reading Ladder Level 3 Ser.). (ENG.). 32p. (gr. 1-4). pap. 4.99 *(978-1-4052-8042-6(5),* Red Shed) Farshore GBR. Dist: HarperCollins Pubs.
Brown Bear Figures It Out. (Early Intervention Levels Ser.). 31.86 *(978-0-7362-0667-9(1))* CENGAGE Learning.
Brown, Jamal. Bess at the Vet: Practicing the Short e Sound, 1 vol. 2016. (Rosen Phonics Readers Ser.). (ENG.). 8p. (J). (gr. -1-2). pap. *(978-1-5081-3270-7(4),* fbc4d94a-0d5c-4163-bc2c-8d1b96081f37, Rosen Classroom) Rosen Publishing Group, Inc., The.
—Harry Has a Hippo: Practicing the H Sound, 1 vol. 2016. (Rosen Phonics Readers Ser.). (ENG., Illus.). 8p. (J). (gr. -1-2). pap. *(978-1-5081-3095-6(7),* 8b2e4a49-ad2e-4f64-8df2-2166d5771528, Rosen Classroom) Rosen Publishing Group, Inc., The.
—Who Took the Book: Practicing the Short Oo Sound, 1 vol. 2016. (Rosen Phonics Readers Ser.). (ENG.). 12p. (J). (gr. -1-2). pap. *(978-1-5081-3578-4(9),* d490d8f5-b720-4873-a6c4-b813117a6d36, Rosen Classroom) Rosen Publishing Group, Inc., The.
Brown, Janet. The Gingerbread Man (Floor Book) My First Reading Book. Morton, Ken, illus. 2013. (ENG.). 24p. (J). (gr. -1-2). pap. 6.99 *(978-1-84322-900-1(5),* Armadillo) Anness Publishing GBR. Dist: National Bk. Network.
—Hansel & Gretel: My First Reading Book. Morton, Ken, illus. 2013. 24p. (J). (gr. -1-4). 5.99 *(978-1-84322-737-3(1),* Armadillo) Anness Publishing GBR. Dist: National Bk. Network.
—Jack & the Beanstalk: My First Reading Book. Morton, Ken, illus. 2013. 24p. (J). (gr. -1-4). 5.99 *(978-1-84322-738-0(X),* Armadillo) Anness Publishing GBR. Dist: National Bk. Network.
—Puss in Boots. Morton, Ken, illus. 2012. 24p. (J). (gr. -1-12). 5.99 *(978-1-84322-848-6(3))* Anness Publishing GBR. Dist: National Bk. Network.
—Puss in Boots (Floor Book) My First Reading Book. Morton, Ken, illus. 2013. (ENG.). 24p. (J). (gr. -1-2). pap. 6.99 *(978-1-84322-902-5(1),* Armadillo) Anness Publishing GBR. Dist: National Bk. Network.
—Red Riding Hood (Floor Book) My First Reading Book. Morton, Ken, illus. 2015. (ENG.). 24p. (J). (gr. -1-1). pap. 6.99 *(978-1-86147-399-8(0),* Armadillo) Anness Publishing GBR. Dist: National Bk. Network.
—Snow White & the Seven Dwarves. Morton, Ken, illus. 2012. 24p. (J). (gr. -1-12). 5.99 *(978-1-84322-850-9(5))* Anness Publishing GBR. Dist: National Bk. Network.
—Snow White & the Seven Dwarves (Floor Book) My First Reading Book. Morton, Ken, illus. 2013. (ENG.). 30p. (J). (gr. -1-2). pap. 6.99 *(978-1-84322-903-2(X),* Armadillo) Anness Publishing GBR. Dist: National Bk. Network.
—Three Little Pigs (Floor Book) My First Reading Book. Morton, Ken, illus. 2015. (ENG.). 24p. (J). (gr. -1-1). pap. 6.99 *(978-1-86147-396-7(6),* Armadillo) Anness Publishing GBR. Dist: National Bk. Network.
—The Ugly Duckling (Floor Book) My First Reading Book. Morton, Ken, illus. 2015. (ENG.). 24p. (J). (gr. -1-1). pap. 6.99 *(978-1-86147-398-1(2),* Armadillo) Anness Publishing GBR. Dist: National Bk. Network.
Brown, Jeff. Flat Stanley & the Firehouse. Pamintuan, Macky, illus. 2011. (I Can Read Level 2 Ser.). (ENG.). 32p. (J). (gr. -1-3). 16.99 *(978-0-06-143006-0(4));* pap. 4.99 *(978-0-06-143009-1(9))* HarperCollins Pubs. (HarperCollins).
—Flat Stanley & the Haunted House. Pamintuan, Macky, illus. 2010. (I Can Read Level 2 Ser.). (ENG.). 32p. (J). (gr. -1-3). 17.99 *(978-0-06-143004-6(8));* pap. 4.99 *(978-0-06-143005-3(6))* HarperCollins Pubs. (HarperCollins).
Brown, Jeffrey. Lucy & Andy Neanderthal: Bad to the Bones. 2018. (Lucy & Andy Neanderthal Ser.: 3). (Illus.). 208p. (J). (gr. 3-7). 12.99 *(978-0-385-38841-2(1),* Crown Books For Young Readers) Random Hse. Children's Bks.
—Lucy & Andy Neanderthal: Bad to the Bones. 2019. (Lucy & Andy Neanderthal Ser.: 3). (Illus.). 208p. (J). (gr. 3-7). pap. 7.99 *(978-0-525-64399-9(0),* Yearling) Random Hse. Children's Bks.
Brown, Kelli. Yellowstone Park, 1 vol. 2006. (Neighborhood Readers Ser.). (ENG.). 16p. (gr. 1-2). pap. 6.50 *(978-1-4042-7132-6(5),* 5f0028f5-caeb-4585-98eb-3235d2106739, Rosen Classroom) Rosen Publishing Group, Inc., The.
Brown, Marcy & Haley, Dennis. We Both Read Bilingual Edition-The Well-Mannered Monster/el Monstruo Debuenos Modales. Raglin, Tim, illus. 2011. (ENG & SPA.). 44p. (J). pap. 5.99 *(978-1-60115-044-8(X))* Treasure Bay, Inc.
Brown, Vanessa. Kentucky. 2009. (Bilingual Library of the United States of America Ser.). (ENG & SPA.). 32p. (gr. 2-2). 47.90 *(978-1-60853-362-6(X),* Editorial Buenas Letras) Rosen Publishing Group, Inc., The.
Browne, Eileen. Wait for Me!, 8 bks. 2005. (QEB Readers). (Illus.). 24p. (J). (gr. -1-3). lib. bdg. 15.95 *(978-1-59566-075-6(5))* QEB Publishing Inc.
Browne, Hetty S. The Child S World. 2017. (ENG., Illus.). (J). 24.95 *(978-1-374-96171-5(X));* pap. 14.95 *(978-1-374-96170-8(1))* Capital Communications, Inc.
Browne, Hetty S. & Sarah Withers. The Child s World. 2007. (ENG.). 192p. pap. 19.99 *(978-1-4264-8460-5(7))* Creative Media Partners, LLC.
Brunel, Aude. Let's Go to Work. Mancek, Marjan, illus. 2007. 32p. (J). (ARA & ENG.). pap. 16.95 *(978-1-60195-089-5(6));* (POL & ENG.). pap. 16.95 *(978-1-60195-101-4(9))* International Step by Step Assn.
Bryant, Sheree, et al. The Glencoe Reader, Course 1. 2003. (Glencoe Literature Grade 7 Ser.). (ENG., Illus.). 340p. (gr. 6-6). stu. ed., per. 8.92 *(978-0-07-845927-6(3),* 0078459273) McGraw-Hill Higher Education.
—The Glencoe Reader, Course 2. 2003. (Glencoe Literature Grade 7 Ser.). (ENG., Illus.). 353p. (gr. 7-7). stu. ed., per. 8.92 *(978-0-07-845928-3(1),* 0078459281) McGraw-Hill Higher Education.
—The Glencoe Reader Course 4, Course 4. 2003. (ENG., Illus.). 382p. (C). (gr. 6-12). stu. ed., per. 8.28 *(978-0-07-845930-6(3),* 0078459303) McGraw-Hill Higher Education.
Bryson, Theresa. Costume Party. 2011. (Early Connections Ser.). (J). *(978-1-61672-346-0(7))* Benchmark Education Co.
—Farm Alarm. 2011. (Early Connections Ser.). (J). *(978-1-61672-350-7(5))* Benchmark Education Co.
—Farm Work. 2011. (Early Connections Ser.). (J). *(978-1-61672-351-4(3))* Benchmark Education Co.
Buchanan, Fannie R. Magic Music Story Interpretations. 2006. (Illus.). pap. 21.95 *(978-1-4286-5945-2(5))* Kessinger Publishing, LLC.
Buckley, James, Jr. & Dorling Kindersley Publishing Staff. Great Explorers. 2018. (ENG., Illus.). 48p. (J). *(978-0-241-31596-5(4))* Dorling Kindersley Publishing, Inc.
Buckley, Arabella. Plant Life in Field & Garden. 2008. 88p. pap. 11.95 *(978-1-59915-273-8(8))* Yesterday's Classics.
Buckley, Arabella B. Wild Life in Woods & Fields (Yesterday's Classics) 2008. (Illus.). 60p. pap. 9.95 *(978-1-59915-271-4(1))* Yesterday's Classics.
Buckley, James. The Moon. 2016. (Smithsonian Ser.). (ENG., Illus.). 48p. (J). (gr. 3-4). pap. 5.99 *(978-0-448-49020-5(X),* Penguin Young Readers) Penguin Young Readers Group.
Budnick, Madeleine. Outside Todo el Dia: Nature in English y Espanol. 2017. (ArteKids Ser.). (ENG., Illus.). 16p. (J). (gr. -1-k). bds. 7.95 *(978-1-59534-830-2(1))* Trinity Univ. Pr.
—Vamos, Body! Head to Toe in English y Espanol. 2017. (ArteKids Ser.). (Illus.). 16p. (J). (gr. -1-k). bds. 7.95 *(978-1-59534-828-9(X))* Trinity Univ. Pr.
Buesser, Jeanne. He Talks Funny: A Heartwarming Story of Everyday Life. 2010. 28p. 12.49 *(978-1-4520-2595-7(9))* AuthorHouse.
Bugs! (18), Vol. 18. (Early Intervention Levels Ser.). 5.31 *(978-0-7362-0614-3(0))* CENGAGE Learning.
Building a Doghouse: Fourth Grade Guided Comprehension Level M. (On Our Way to English Ser.). (gr. 4-18). 34.50 *(978-0-7578-7157-3(7))* Rigby Education.
Buller, Laura. DK Readers L2: Amazing Dogs: Tales of Daring Dogs! 2016. (DK Readers Level 2 Ser.). (ENG., Illus.). 48p. (J). (gr. k-2). pap. 4.99 *(978-1-4654-4596-4(X),* DK Children) Dorling Kindersley Publishing, Inc.
—DK Readers Level 2: the Lion's Tale. 2019. (DK Readers Level 2 Ser.). (ENG., Illus.). 48p. (J). (gr. k-2). pap. 3.99 *(978-1-4654-7913-6(9),* DK Children) Dorling Kindersley Publishing, Inc.
—Sloths. 2019. (Illus.). 48p. (J). *(978-1-5444-3235-9(6))* Dorling Kindersley Publishing, Inc.
Bunney, Anna. Dolphins in the Wild 3 Explorers. 2017. (Cambridge Reading Adventures Ser.). (ENG., Illus.). 32p. pap. 8.60 *(978-1-108-40583-6(5))* Cambridge Univ. Pr.
Buntrock, Susan. Avenues e (Leveled Books): What's It Worth? 2003. (Rise & Shine Ser.). (ENG.). 16p. (C). pap. 11.95 *(978-0-7362-1739-2(8))* CENGAGE Learning.
—Avenues e (Leveled Books): What's It Worth?, 6-Pack. 2003. (Avenues Ser.). (ENG.). (C). pap. 73.95 *(978-0-7362-2160-3(3))* CENGAGE Learning.
Burach, Ross. Truck Full of Ducks. 2018. (ENG., Illus.). 40p. (J). (gr. -1-3). 18.99 *(978-1-338-12936-6(8),* Scholastic Pr.) Scholastic, Inc.
Burchett, Jan & Vogler, Sara. Collins Big Cat Phonics for Letters & Sounds - Tap Tap: Band 01A/Pink A, Bd. 1A. 2018. (Collins Big Cat Ser.). (ENG., Illus.). 16p. (J). pap. 7.99 *(978-0-00-823017-3(X))* HarperCollins Pubs. Ltd. GBR. Dist: Independent Pubs. Group.
Burg, Ann E. The New York Reader. Darnell, K. L., illus. 2008. (State/Country Readers Ser.). (ENG.). 96p. (J). (gr. 1-4). pap. 5.95 *(978-1-58536-349-0(9),* 202136) Sleeping Bear Pr.
Burgess, Melvin. Level 3: Billy Elliot. 2nd ed. 2008. (Pearson English Graded Readers Ser.). (ENG., Illus.). 64p. pap. 13.32 *(978-1-4058-8176-0(3),* Pearson ELT) Pearson Education.
Burke, Anne. That's Entertainment! 2007. (Steck-Vaughn BOLDPRINT Anthologies Ser.). (ENG., Illus.). 48p. (gr. 9-12). pap., stu. ed. 16.90 *(978-1-4190-4035-1(9))* Houghton Mifflin Harcourt Publishing Co.
Burke, David, adapted by. GOLDILOCKS (English to Chinese - Level 2) Learn MANDARIN CHINESE Through Fairy Tales. 2007. (Learn Chinese Through Fairy Tales Ser.). (ENG & CHI., Illus.). (J). per. 14.95 incl. audio compact disk *(978-1-891888-85-4(4))* Slangman Publishing.
Burke, Juliet. Let's Play!, 1 vol. 2012. (InfoMax Readers Ser.). (ENG., Illus.). 16p. (J). (gr. k-k). pap. 7.00 *(978-1-4488-8899-3(9),* d6f976d3-194d-473a-852a-b43eac237abb, Rosen Classroom) Rosen Publishing Group, Inc., The.
Burke, Sandra & Flebotte, Morrigan. The Crusading Communicator. Flebotte, Morrigan, ed. 2004. (Illus.). 2p. (J). per. *(978-0-9735303-8-4(3))* Black Castle Industries, Inc.
—Hercules Novel Study. Flebotte, Morrigan, ed. 2004. (Illus.). (J). per. *(978-0-9735303-1-5(6))* Black Castle Industries, Inc.
Burnett, Gretel. The A-B-C Smarts: Book 2. 2009. 84p. pap. 28.99 *(978-1-4490-4575-3(8))* AuthorHouse.

P
Q
R

Burr, Avril. Naughty Art. 2012. (Illus.). 66p. pap. *(978-1-78281-017-9(X))* Athena Pr.

Burslem, Diana & Freeman, Diana. Bee Alarm!, 1 vol. Webb, Philip, illus. 2013. (ENG.). 24p. (gr. 3-3). pap. *(978-1-77654-020-4(4),* Red Rocket Readers) Flying Start Bks.

Bursztyn, Dina. The Land of Lost Things: El País de las Cosas Perdidas. Bursztyn, Dina, illus. 2011. (SPA & ENG., Illus.). 32p. (J). (gr. -1-3). 16.95 *(978-1-55885-690-5(0),* Piñata Books) Arte Publico Pr.

Burt, Judith. The 10 Most Valuable Elements. 2008. 14.99 *(978-1-55448-540-6(1))* Scholastic Library Publishing.

Burton, Margie, et al. Peaches all the Time. 2011. (Early Connections Ser.). (J). *(978-1-61672-534-1(6))* Benchmark Education Co.

Buster MCluster: Level G. (Wonder Worldtm Ser.). 16p. 29.95 *(978-0-7802-1033-2(6))* Wright Group/McGraw-Hill.

Buster MCluster has Chicken Pox: Level G, 6 vols. (Wonder Worldtm Ser.). 16p. 29.95 *(978-0-7802-4563-1(6))* Wright Group/McGraw-Hill.

Busy Animals Book Set 800896, 6 vols. 2005. (J). pap. *(978-1-59794-071-9(2))* Environments, Inc.

Busy Bear Book Set 800938, 4 vols. 2005. (J). bds. *(978-1-59794-097-9(6))* Environments, Inc.

Busy Bees: Cassette. (Song Box Ser.). (gr. 1-2). 8.50 incl. audio *(978-0-7802-2269-4(5))* Wright Group/McGraw-Hill.

Busy Children Book Set 800897, 6 vols. 2005. (J). pap. *(978-1-59794-072-6(0))* Environments, Inc.

Butler, Nathalie. I Love My Books!, 1 vol. 2017. (Learning with Stories Ser.). (ENG.). 24p. (gr. 1-1). pap. 9.25 *(978-1-5081-6245-2(X),* 0733ad89-ff7b-4dd8-ac7c-1487beef79c8, PowerKids Pr.) Rosen Publishing Group, Inc., The.

Butterfield, Moira. The Life Cycle of the Orca: Band 16/Sapphire. 2017. (Collins Big Cat Ser.). (ENG., Illus.). 56p. (J). pap. 8.99 *(978-0-00-820890-5(5))* HarperCollins Pubs. Ltd. GBR. Dist: Independent Pubs. Group.

Byerly, Robbie. We Can Fix It. 2009. (1B Potato Chip Bks.). (ENG., Illus.). 16p. (J). pap. 9.60 *(978-1-63437-204-6(2))* American Reading Co.

Byerly, Wendy. I See You, Bird! (Big Book) 2015. (1G Big Bks.). (ENG., Illus.). 16p. (J). pap. 8.00 *(978-1-64053-130-7(0),* ARC Pr. Bks.) American Reading Co.

Byrd, Lee Merrill. Birdie's Beauty Parlor: El Salón de Belleza de Birdy. Delgado, Francisco, illus. 2018. (SPA & ENG.). (J). *(978-1-947627-02-4(3),* Cinco Puntos Press) Lee & Low Bks., Inc.

—Birdie's Beauty Parlor / el Salón de Belleza de Birdie, 1 vol. Delgado, Francisco, illus. 2020. (ENG.). 32p. (J). (gr. -1-2). 18.95 *(978-1-947627-28-4(7),* 23353382, Cinco Puntos Press) Lee & Low Bks., Inc.

Cadenhead, MacKenzie. Buggin' Out! 2018. (Marvel Super Hero Adventures Early Chapter Bks.). (J). lib. bdg. 14.75 *(978-0-606-40978-0(5))* Turtleback.

Cadenhead, MacKenzie & Ryan, Sean. Buggin' Out! Laufman, Derek, illus. 2019. (Marvel Super Hero Adventures Ser.). (ENG.). 80p. (J). (gr. 1-5). lib. bdg. 31.36 *(978-1-5321-4312-0(5),* 31842, Chapter Bks.) Spotlight.

—Sand Trap! Brizuela, Dario, illus. 2019. (Marvel Super Hero Adventures Ser.). (ENG.). 80p. (J). (gr. 1-5). lib. bdg. 31.36 *(978-1-5321-4315-1(X),* 31845, Chapter Bks.) Spotlight.

Cadenhead, MacKenzie & Sean Ryan. Sand Trap! 2018. (Marvel Super Hero Adventures Early Chapter Bks.). (J). lib. bdg. 14.75 *(978-0-606-40979-7(3))* Turtleback.

Cain, Marie Mowery. All Eyes on You. 2013. (Big Books, Blue Ser.). (ENG & SPA., Illus.). 16p. pap. 33.00 *(978-1-59246-017-5(8))* Big Books, by George!

—Cool Places. 2013. (Big Books, Red Ser.). (ENG & SPA., Illus.). 16p. pap. 33.00 *(978-1-59246-215-5(4))* Big Books, by George!

—One by One. 2013. (Big Books, Blue Ser.). (ENG & SPA., Illus.). 16p. pap. 33.00 *(978-1-59246-020-5(8))* Big Books, by George!

The Cake: Individual Title Six-Packs. (Story Steps Ser.). (gr. k-2). 29.00 *(978-0-7635-9601-9(9))* Rigby Education.

Calfee, Pat. Issy Books Set 1, 5 bks. Gee, Isybilla, illus. 2013. 60p. (J). pap. 24.95 *(978-1-938406-13-3(3),* Compass) Raphel Marketing, Inc.

—Issy Books Set 2, 5 bks. Gee, Isybilla, illus. 2013. 60p. (J). pap. 24.95 *(978-1-938406-14-0(1),* Compass) Raphel Marketing, Inc.

—Issy Books Set 3, 10 books. Gee, Isybilla, illus. 2013. 120p. (J). pap. 39.95 *(978-1-938406-15-7(X),* Compass) Raphel Marketing, Inc.

Callan, Mary Ann. Spunky Chunks. 2011. 266p. 31.99 *(978-1-4363-7523-8(1));* pap. 21.99 *(978-1-4363-7522-1(3))* Xlibris Corp.

Called to a Cause. 2003. (Illus.). pap. 5.60 *(978-0-7398-7516-2(7))* Steck-Vaughn.

Callella, Trisha. Developing Reading Fluency, Grade 2: Using Modeled Reading, Phrasing, & Repeated Oral Reading. Fisch, Teri L., ed. Iosa, Ann W., illus. 2003. (Developing Reading Fluency Ser.). 96p. (J). (gr. 2-3). pap. 14.99 *(978-1-57471-995-6(5),* 2248) Creative Teaching Pr., Inc.

—Developing Reading Fluency, Grade 3: Using Modeled Reading, Phrasing, & Repeated Oral Reading. Fisch, Teri L., ed. Yamada, Jane, illus. 2003. (Developing Reading Fluency Ser.). 96p. (J). (gr. 3-4). pap. 14.99 *(978-1-57471-996-3(3),* 2240) Creative Teaching Pr., Inc.

—Developing Reading Fluency, Grade 4: Using Modeled Reading, Phrasing, & Repeated Oral Reading. Fisch, Teri L., ed. Iosa, Ann W., illus. 2003. (Developing Reading Fluency Ser.). 96p. (J). (gr. 4-5). pap. 14.99 *(978-1-57471-997-0(1),* 2250) Creative Teaching Pr., Inc.

Callen, Sharon. Anna Goes to Zambia, 1 vol. rev. ed. 2013. (Literary Text Ser.). (ENG., Illus.). 20p. (gr. 1-2). (J). lib. bdg. 15.96 *(978-1-4807-1151-8(9));* 7.99 *(978-1-4333-5495-3(0))* Teacher Created Materials, Inc.

—Boris & Bea, 1 vol. rev. ed. 2013. (Literary Text Ser.). (ENG., Illus.). 24p. (J). (gr. 1-3). pap. 8.99 *(978-1-4333-5530-1(2))* Teacher Created Materials, Inc.

—Boris Keeps Fit, 1 vol. rev. ed. 2013. (Literary Text Ser.). (ENG., Illus.). 20p. (gr. 1-2). 7.99 *(978-1-4333-5492-2(6))* Teacher Created Materials, Inc.

—Boris the Bassett, 1 vol. rev. ed. 2013. (Literary Text Ser.). (ENG., Illus.). 12p. (gr. 1-2). (J). lib. bdg. 12.96 *(978-1-4807-1133-4(0));* 6.99 *(978-1-4333-5454-0(3))* Teacher Created Materials, Inc.

—Duck Pond Fun, 1 vol. rev. ed. 2013. (Literary Text Ser.). (ENG., Illus.). 12p. (gr. k-2). 6.99 *(978-1-4333-5445-8(4))* Teacher Created Materials, Inc.

—Grandpa & Me, 1 vol. rev. ed. 2013. (Literary Text Ser.). (ENG., Illus.). 12p. (gr. 1-2). (J). lib. bdg. 12.96 *(978-1-4807-1132-7(2));* 6.99 *(978-1-4333-5453-3(5))* Teacher Created Materials, Inc.

—How to Be a Kitten, 1 vol. rev. ed. 2013. (Literary Text Ser.). (ENG., Illus.). 12p. (J). (gr. k-2). 6.99 *(978-1-4333-5457-1(8))* Teacher Created Materials, Inc.

—Life at the Top, 1 vol. rev. ed. 2013. (Literary Text Ser.). (ENG., Illus.). 20p. (gr. 1-2). (J). lib. bdg. 15.96 *(978-1-4807-1143-3(8));* 7.99 *(978-1-4333-5487-8(X))* Teacher Created Materials, Inc.

—Maddy's Mad Hair Day, 1 vol. rev. ed. 2013. (Literary Text Ser.). (ENG., Illus.). 12p. (J). (gr. k-2). 6.99 *(978-1-4333-5450-2(0));* lib. bdg. 12.96 *(978-1-4807-1129-7(2))* Teacher Created Materials, Inc.

—Max, 1 vol. rev. ed. 2013. (Literary Text Ser.). (ENG., Illus.). 12p. (J). (gr. k-2). 6.99 *(978-1-4333-5452-6(7))* Teacher Created Materials, Inc.

—My Life as a Bee, 1 vol. rev. ed. 2013. (Literary Text Ser.). (ENG., Illus.). 20p. (gr. k-2). (J). lib. bdg. 15.96 *(978-1-4807-1139-6(X));* 7.99 *(978-1-4333-5483-0(7))* Teacher Created Materials, Inc.

—Safari Camp, 1 vol. rev. ed. 2013. (Literary Text Ser.). (ENG., Illus.). 20p. (gr. 1-2). (J). lib. bdg. 15.96 *(978-1-4807-1150-1(0));* 7.99 *(978-1-4333-5494-6(2))* Teacher Created Materials, Inc.

—Seb's Train, 1 vol. rev. ed. 2013. (Literary Text Ser.). (ENG., Illus.). 12p. (J). (gr. k-2). 6.99 *(978-1-4333-5446-5(2));* lib. bdg. 12.96 *(978-1-4807-1125-9(X))* Teacher Created Materials, Inc.

—Splash Down!, 1 vol. rev. ed. 2013. (Literary Text Ser.). (ENG., Illus.). 12p. (gr. k-2). (J). lib. bdg. 12.96 *(978-1-4807-1135-8(7));* 6.99 *(978-1-4333-5456-4(X))* Teacher Created Materials, Inc.

—What Can You See?, 1 vol. rev. ed. 2013. (Literary Text Ser.). (ENG., Illus.). 20p. (gr. 1-2). (J). lib. bdg. 15.96 *(978-1-4807-1146-4(2));* 7.99 *(978-1-4333-5490-8(X))* Teacher Created Materials, Inc.

Callery, Sean. The Celts: Band 14/Ruby (Collins Big Cat) 2015. (Collins Big Cat Ser.). (ENG., Illus.). 48p. (J). (gr. 3-4). pap. 10.99 *(978-0-00-812782-4(4))* HarperCollins Pubs. Ltd. GBR. Dist: Independent Pubs. Group.

Cámara, Noemí, et al. Los Fantasmas de Goya, 1 vol. 2014. (SPA., Illus.). 64p. pap. 15.00 incl. audio compact disk *(978-84-9848-200-3(3))* Edinumen, Editorial ESP. Dist: Cambridge Univ. Pr.

Cambridge University Press Staff. Joey's Quiet War & Other Stories. (J). pap. 8.50 *(978-0-13-177460-5(3))* Globe Fearon Educational Publishing.

Cameron, Andrea. The 10 Most Revolutionary Songs. 2008. 14.99 *(978-1-55448-493-5(6))* Scholastic Library Publishing.

Campbell, Dorthina A. Step Forward Strategies for Struggling Readers: Student Resource Guide. 2005. 59p. (J). stu. ed., per. 8.99 *(978-0-9768208-0-2(3))* Edutech Learning Resource Ctr.

Campbell, Kathy. Let's Draw a Bear with Squares. 2009. (Let's Draw with Shapes Ser.). 24p. (gr. k-k). 42.50 *(978-1-61514-202-6(9),* PowerKids Pr.) Rosen Publishing Group, Inc., The.

—Let's Draw a Fish with Triangles. 2009. (Let's Draw with Shapes Ser.). 24p. (gr. k-k). 42.50 *(978-1-61514-207-1(X),* PowerKids Pr.) Rosen Publishing Group, Inc., The.

—Let's Draw a Frog with Ovals. 2009. (Let's Draw with Shapes Ser.). 24p. (gr. k-k). 42.50 *(978-1-61514-208-8(8),* PowerKids Pr.) Rosen Publishing Group, Inc., The.

Camping Out, 6 vols. (Multicultural Programs Ser.). 16p. (gr. 1-3). 24.95 *(978-0-7802-9203-1(0))* Wright Group/McGraw-Hill.

Canetti, Yanitzia. Abecedario de Profesiones y Oficios. 2009. (SPA.). 40p. (J). pap. 8.99 *(978-1-59835-122-4(2),* BrickHouse Education) Cambridge BrickHouse, Inc.

—ABeCedario Salvaje. 2009. (SPA.). 40p. (J). (gr. -1-3). pap. 7.99 *(978-1-59835-117-0(6))* Cambridge BrickHouse, Inc.

Caple, Kathy. Termite Tales: Brand New Readers. Caple, Kathy, illus. 2009. (Brand New Readers Ser.). (ENG., Illus.). 48p. (J). (gr. -1-3). pap. 6.99 *(978-0-7636-3901-3(X))* Candlewick Pr.

Capozzi, Suzy. I Am Brave: A Positive Power Story. Unten, Eren, illus. 2018. (Rodale Kids Curious Readers/Level 2 Ser.: 4). 32p. (J). (gr. -1-1). pap. 4.99 *(978-1-62336-954-5(1),* 9781623369545, Rodale Kids) Random Hse. Children's Bks.

—I Am Helpful. Unten, Eren, illus. 2018. (Rodale Kids Curious Readers/Level 2 Ser.: 6). 32p. (J). (gr. -1-1). pap. 4.99 *(978-1-62336-960-6(6),* 9781623369606, Rodale Kids) Random Hse. Children's Bks.

—I Am Kind: A Positive Power Story. Unten, Eren & Unten, Eren, illus. 2017. (Rodale Kids Curious Readers/Level 2 Ser.: 2). 32p. (J). (gr. -1-1). pap. 4.99 *(978-1-62336-878-4(2),* 9781623368784, Rodale Kids) Random Hse. Children's Bks.

—I Am Smart. Unten, Eren, illus. 2018. (Rodale Kids Curious Readers/Level 2 Ser.: 5). 32p. (J). (gr. -1-1). pap. 4.99 *(978-1-62336-957-6(6),* 9781623369576, Rodale Kids) Random Hse. Children's Bks.

—I Am Strong: A Positive Power Story. Unten, Eren, illus. 2018. (Rodale Kids Curious Readers/Level 2 Ser.: 3). 32p. (J). (gr. -1-1). pap. 4.99 *(978-1-62336-951-4(7),* 9781623369514, Rodale Kids) Random Hse. Children's Bks.

—I Am Thankful: A Positive Power Story. Unten, Eren & Unten, Eren, illus. 2017. (Rodale Kids Curious Readers/Level 2 Ser.: 1). 32p. (J). (gr. -1-1). pap. 4.99 *(978-1-62336-876-0(6),* 9781623368760, Rodale Kids) Random Hse. Children's Bks.

Capucilli, Alyssa Satin. Biscuit & the Baby. Schories, Pat, illus. 2005. (My First I Can Read Ser.). (ENG.). 32p. (J). (gr. -1 — 1). pap. 4.99 *(978-0-06-009461-4(3),* HarperCollins) HarperCollins Pubs.

—Biscuit Flies a Kite. Schories, Pat, illus. 2017. (My First I Can Read Ser.). (ENG.). 32p. (J). (gr. -1-3). pap. 4.99 *(978-0-06-223700-2(4),* HarperCollins) HarperCollins Pubs.

—Biscuit's Day at the Farm. Schories, Pat, illus. 2007. (My First I Can Read Ser.). (ENG.). 32p. (J). (gr. -1 — 1). pap. 4.99 *(978-0-06-074169-3(4),* HarperCollins) HarperCollins Pubs.

—Biscuit's Day at the Farm. 2007. (Biscuit: My First I Can Read! Ser.). (J). lib. bdg. 13.55 *(978-1-4177-9810-0(6))* Turtleback.

Carangelo, Audrey & Hess, Debra. Radiation, Rats, & Mutant Monsters! 2007. (Read on! Special Edition: Level RA Ser.). (Illus.). 23p. (J). (gr. 4-7). pap. 18.51 *(978-1-4190-3506-7(1))* Steck-Vaughn.

—Teenage Plant Food. 2007. (Read on! Special Edition: Level BA Ser.). (Illus.). 23p. (J). (gr. 4-7). pap. 18.51 *(978-1-4190-3524-1(X))* Steck-Vaughn.

Carbone, Courtney. Butterfly Battle! (DC Super Hero Girls) Orum, Pernille, illus. 2018. (Step into Reading Ser.). (ENG.). 32p. (J). (gr. -1-1). pap. 4.99 *(978-1-5247-6917-8(7),* Random Hse. Bks. for Young Readers) Random Hse. Children's Bks.

—Rock Stars! (Sunny Day) Hall, Susan, illus. 2018. (Step into Reading Ser.). (ENG.). 24p. (J). (gr. -1-1). pap. 4.99 *(978-1-5247-6862-1(6),* Random Hse. Bks. for Young Readers) Random Hse. Children's Bks.

—The Safety First! (Peppa Pig: Level 1 Reader) EOne, illus. 2015. (ENG.). 32p. (J). (gr. -1-k). E-Book 8.99 *(978-1-338-29114-8(9))* Scholastic, Inc.

—Stick with Me! (Sunny Day) Random House, illus. 2018. (Step into Reading Ser.). (ENG.). 24p. (J). (gr. -1-1). pap. 4.99 *(978-0-525-57814-7(5),* Random Hse. Bks. for Young Readers) Random Hse. Children's Bks.

—This Makes Me Jealous: Dealing with Feelings. Kushnir, Hilli, illus. 2019. (Rodale Kids Curious Readers/Level 2 Ser.: 6). 32p. (J). (gr. -1-1). pap. 4.99 *(978-1-63565-077-8(1),* 9781635650778, Rodale Kids) Random Hse. Children's Bks.

Cardenas, Ernesto A. Where Does Fruit Come From? 2009. 23.95 *(978-1-60698-056-9(4));* pap. 4.95 *(978-1-60698-054-5(8))* Milo Educational Bks. & Resources.

Carle, Eric. The Eric Carle Ready-To-Read Collection (Boxed Set) Have You Seen My Cat?; the Greedy Python; Pancakes, Pancakes!; Rooster Is off to See the World; a House for Hermit Crab; Walter the Baker. Carle, Eric, illus. 2014. (World of Eric Carle Ser.). (ENG., Illus.). 160p. (J). (gr. -1-2). pap. 15.99 *(978-1-4814-1632-0(4),* Simon Spotlight) Simon Spotlight.

—Rooster Is off to See the World. 2013. (Eric Carle Ready-To-Read Ser.). lib. bdg. 13.55 *(978-0-606-32063-4(6))* Turtleback.

Carlos & Carmen, 4 vols. 2015. (Carlos & Carmen Ser.: 4). (ENG., Illus.). 32p. (J). (gr. k-3). lib. bdg. 131.16 *(978-1-62402-136-7(0),* 19069, Calico Chapter Bks) Magic Wagon.

Carlson-Berne, Emma. My Class Campaign: Working As a Team, 1 vol. 2017. (Computer Kids: Powered by Computational Thinking Ser.). (ENG.). 24p. (J). (gr. 4-5). 25.27 *(978-1-5383-2414-1(8),* ac22d566-682c-4bbc-b191-d22b506b76e1, PowerKids Pr.) Rosen Publishing Group, Inc., The.

Carlson Berne, Emma. My Class Campaign: Working As a Team, 1 vol. 2017. (Computer Science for the Real World Ser.). (ENG.). 24p. (J). (gr. 4-5). pap. *(978-1-5383-5307-3(5),* d0ef7332-99d9-4db9-921e-af3d06588577, Rosen Classroom) Rosen Publishing Group, Inc., The.

Carlson, Lavelle. Can a Toucan Hoot Too? A Phonemic Awareness Tale, 10 vols. Adams, Lucas, illus. 2003. 32p. (J). (gr. -1-1). per. 16.95 *(978-0-9725803-0-4(1))* Children's Publishing.

Carmen's Star Party. (Early Intervention Levels Ser.). 31.86 *(978-0-7362-0622-8(1))* CENGAGE Learning.

Carmen's Star Party (20), Vol. 20. (Early Intervention Levels Ser.). 5.31 *(978-0-7362-0610-5(8))* CENGAGE Learning.

Carnelos, Melissa. The 10 Most Amazing Animal Heroes. 2008. 14.99 *(978-1-55448-516-1(9))* Scholastic Library Publishing.

Carney, Elizabeth. National Geographic Readers: Animals in the City (L2) 2019. (Readers Ser.). (Illus.). 32p. (J). (gr. 1-3). pap. 4.99 *(978-1-4263-3331-6(5),* National Geographic Kids) Disney Publishing Worldwide.

—National Geographic Readers: Mars. 2014. (Readers Ser.). (Illus.). 48p. (J). (gr. 1-3). pap. 4.99 *(978-1-4263-1747-7(6),* National Geographic Kids) Disney Publishing Worldwide.

—National Geographic Readers: Mummies. 2009. (Readers Ser.). (Illus.). 32p. (J). (gr. 1-3). (ENG.). 14.90 *(978-1-4263-0529-0(X));* pap. 4.99 *(978-1-4263-0528-3(1))* Disney Publishing Worldwide. (National Geographic Kids).

Carosella, Melissa. Dolley Madison: First Lady of the United States. rev. ed. 2011. (Social Studies: Informational Text Ser.). (ENG.). 32p. (gr. 4-8). pap. 11.99 *(978-1-4333-1504-6(1))* Teacher Created Materials, Inc.

—The Fight for Freedom: Ending Slavery in America. rev. ed. 2011. (Social Studies: Informational Text Ser.). (ENG., Illus.). 32p. (J). (gr. 4-8). pap. 11.99 *(978-1-4333-1519-0(X))* Teacher Created Materials, Inc.

—Founding Mothers: Women Who Shaped America. rev. ed. 2011. (Social Studies: Informational Text Ser.). (ENG.). 32p. (gr. 4-8). pap. 11.99 *(978-1-4333-1505-3(X))* Teacher Created Materials, Inc.

—Frederick Douglass: Leader of the Abolitionist Movement. rev. ed. 2011. (Social Studies: Informational Text Ser.). (ENG., Illus.). 32p. (J). (gr. 4-8). pap. 11.99 *(978-1-4333-1518-3(1))* Teacher Created Materials, Inc.

—Hillary Rodham Clinton: First Lady, Senator, & Secretary of State. rev. ed. 2011. (Social Studies: Informational Text Ser.). (ENG.). 32p. (gr. 4-8). pap. 11.99 *(978-1-4333-1508-4(4))* Teacher Created Materials, Inc.

—Still Marching Strong: Women in Modern America. rev. ed. 2011. (Social Studies: Informational Text Ser.). (ENG.). 32p. (gr. 4-8). pap. 11.99 *(978-1-4333-1509-1(2))* Teacher Created Materials, Inc.

Carr, Denis. The 10 Most Significant Medical Breakthroughs. 2008. 14.99 *(978-1-55448-491-1(X))* Scholastic Library Publishing.

Carr, Elias. Ava y el Picnic Raquitico. Garton, Michael, illus. 2016. (SPA.). (J). *(978-1-5064-2095-0(8))* 1517 Media.

—Hal y el Nuevo Compañero. Garton, Michael, illus. 2016. (SPA.). (J). *(978-1-5064-2098-1(2))* 1517 Media.

—Rufus y Su Cola Enojada. Garton, Michael, illus. 2016. (SPA.). (J). *(978-1-5064-2096-7(6))* 1517 Media.

Carrington, Jim. Sang Kancil & the Farmer Gold Band. Oliver, Juanbjuan, illus. 2017. (Cambridge Reading Adventures Ser.). (ENG.). 24p. pap. 7.35 *(978-1-108-40574-4(6))* Cambridge Univ. Pr.

—Sang Kancil & the Tiger. Oliver, Juanbjuan, illus. 2016. (Cambridge Reading Adventures Ser.). (ENG.). 16p. pap. 7.95 *(978-1-107-55092-6(0))* Cambridge Univ. Pr.

Carroll. Lbd Gka Nf Fun for All Seasons. 2009. (C). pap. 8.53 *(978-1-4189-3337-1(6))* Rigby Education.

Carroll, Claudia. Missy Mouse & the Rocket Ship. 2008. (ENG.). 39p. pap. 9.95 *(978-0-557-01769-0(6))* Lulu Pr., Inc.

Carson Dellosa Education, compiled by. First Grade Skills. 2010. (Home Workbooks Ser.: 4). (ENG.). 64p. (gr. 1-1). pap. 4.49 *(978-1-60418-784-7(0),* 104353) Carson-Dellosa Publishing, LLC.

—Phonics for Kindergarten, Grade K. 2010. (Home Workbooks Ser.: 12). (ENG.). 64p. (gr. k-k). pap. 4.49 *(978-1-60418-774-8(3),* 104343) Carson-Dellosa Publishing, LLC.

—Scissors Skills, Grades PK - 1. 2010. (Home Workbooks Ser.: 17). (ENG.). 64p. (gr. -1-1). pap. 4.49 *(978-1-60418-766-3(2),* 104335) Carson-Dellosa Publishing, LLC.

Carson-Dellosa Publishing Staff. All about Me, Grades Pk - 1. 2010. (Home Workbooks Ser.: 1). (ENG.). 64p. (gr. -1-1). pap. 4.49 *(978-1-60418-767-0(0),* 104336) Carson-Dellosa Publishing, LLC.

—Beginning Math, Grade 1. 2010. (Home Workbooks Ser.: 2). (ENG.). 64p. (gr. 1-1). pap. 4.49 *(978-1-60418-790-8(5),* 104359) Carson-Dellosa Publishing, LLC.

—Beginning Reading, Grades K. 2010. (Home Workbooks Ser.: 3). (ENG.). 64p. (gr. k-k). pap. 4.49 *(978-1-60418-773-1(5),* 104342) Carson-Dellosa Publishing, LLC.

—Letters & Sounds, Grades K - 1. 2010. (Home Workbooks Ser.: 7). (ENG.). 64p. (gr. k-1). pap. 4.49 *(978-1-60418-779-3(4),* 104348) Carson-Dellosa Publishing, LLC.

—Phonics for First Grade. 2010. (Home Workbooks Ser.: 11). (ENG.). 64p. (gr. 1-1). pap. 4.49 *(978-1-60418-785-4(9),* 104354) Carson-Dellosa Publishing, LLC.

—Printing Practice for Beginners. 2010. (Home Workbooks Ser.: 13). (ENG.). 64p. (gr. k-1). pap. 4.49 *(978-1-60418-780-9(8),* 104349) Carson-Dellosa Publishing, LLC.

—Puzzles & Games for Math, Grade 1. 2010. (Home Workbooks Ser.: 14). (ENG.). 64p. (gr. 1-1). pap. 4.49 *(978-1-60418-791-5(3),* 104360) Carson-Dellosa Publishing, LLC.

—Reading Comprehension, Grade 3. 2010. (Home Workbooks Ser.: 16). (ENG.). 64p. (gr. 3-3). pap. 4.49 *(978-1-60418-800-4(6),* 104369) Carson-Dellosa Publishing, LLC.

—Shapes, Grades PK - K. 2010. (Home Workbooks Ser.: 18). (ENG.). 64p. (gr. -1-k). pap. 4.49 *(978-1-60418-764-9(6),* 104333) Carson-Dellosa Publishing, LLC.

Carson-Dellosa Publishing Staff, compiled by. Puzzles & Games for Math, Grade 2. 2010. (Home Workbooks Ser.: 15). (ENG.). 64p. (gr. 2-2). pap. 4.49 *(978-1-60418-798-4(0),* 104367) Carson-Dellosa Publishing, LLC.

Carson, Janet. Camping with Colleen, 1 vol. 2006. (Neighborhood Readers Ser.). (ENG.). 8p. (gr. 1-2). pap. 5.15 *(978-1-4042-6803-6(0),* adc39570-42c8-4f35-85de-98d263d1f369, Rosen Classroom) Rosen Publishing Group, Inc., The.

Carter, Cathy. You Are My Very Best Friend: The Adventures of Mike & Gabe (in English & Spanish) 2012. 26p. 24.95 *(978-1-4626-7072-7(5))* America Star Bks.

Carus, Andre W. Flint Holds Fire, Level D. Incl. Great Beginnings. 1982. pap., wbk. ed. *(978-0-89688-292-8(6),* 88-292); Headway Level D Real Phonics Workbook A. *(978-0-89688-294-2(2),* 88-294); Level D. tchr.'s training gde. ed. *(978-0-89688-456-4(2),* 88-456); Level D. pap., wbk. ed. *(978-0-89688-462-5(7),* 88-462); Level D. suppl. ed. *(978-0-89688-468-7(6),* 88-468); Level D. suppl. ed. (J). (gr. 2-6). *(978-0-89688-451-9(1),* 88-451) Open Court Publishing Co.

Casey, Dawn. Tales of Two Dragons: Band 15/Emerald. Kawa, Cosei, illus. 2015. (Collins Big Cat Ser.). (ENG.). 48p. (J). (gr. 3-4). pap. 11.99 *(978-0-00-812784-8(0))* HarperCollins Pubs. Ltd. GBR. Dist: Independent Pubs. Group.

—The White Mouse: a Folk Tale from the Panchatantra: Band 13/Topaz (Collins Big Cat) Masukawa, Masako, illus. 2016. (Collins Big Cat Ser.). (ENG.). 32p. (J). pap. 9.99 *(978-0-00-814721-1(3))* HarperCollins Pubs. Ltd. GBR. Dist: Independent Pubs. Group.

Castle, Patricia. In the Garden, 1 vol. 2012. (InfoMax Readers Ser.). (ENG., Illus.). 16p. (J). (gr. k-k). pap. 7.00 *(978-1-4488-8944-0(8),* 56d7730e-32bf-47e8-a065-c19667a233ae, Rosen Classroom) Rosen Publishing Group, Inc., The.

Castor, Harriet. Charlotte Bronte: Band 18/Pearl (Collins Big Cat) Pinteño, Ismael, illus. 2016. (Collins Big Cat Ser.). (ENG.). 80p. (J). (gr. 5-6). pap. 12.99 *(978-0-00-816405-8(3))* HarperCollins Pubs. Ltd. GBR. Dist: Independent Pubs. Group.

—The Incredible Present. Young, Norman, illus. 2004. (Usborne Young Reading: Series Two Ser.). 64p. (J). (gr. k-4). 8.99 *(978-0-7945-1785-4(4),* Usborne) EDC Publishing.

The Cat-Flap Trap: Individual Title Six-Packs. (Story Steps Ser.). (gr. k-2). 32.00 *(978-0-7635-9824-2(0))* Rigby Education.

Catron, John. Stories of Many Cultures. 2008. (ENG.). 136p. (gr. 10-11). pap. 21.50 *(978-0-340-96629-7(7))* Hodder Education Group GBR. Dist: Trans-Atlantic Pubns., Inc.

Caulson, Kathleen. Power Reading: Games. Caulson, Kathleen, illus. 2005. (Illus.). (J). 76p. (gr. 2-4). 29.95 *(978-1-883186-98-2(6),* PPMXG2-3); 88p. (gr. 4-5). 79.95 *(978-1-883186-99-9(4),* PPMXG45) National Reading Styles Institute, Inc.

—Power Reading: Games/Mixed P1. 2005. (Illus.). 76p. (J). (gr. k-2). 29.95 *(978-1-883186-97-5(8),* PPMXGP1) National Reading Styles Institute, Inc.

CD & the Giant Cat: Individual Title Six-Packs. (Action Packs Ser.). 120p. (gr. 3-5). 44.00 *(978-0-7635-8426-9(6))* Rigby Education.
Celebrating Children Set 800827, 7. 2005. (J). *(978-1-59794-024-5(0))* Environments, Inc.
Celebrations Grade Level Libraries: I Like Me! 2005. (Little Celebrations Ser.). (J). (gr. k-3). 74.50 *(978-0-673-77743-0(X))* Celebration Pr.
Celebrations Grade Level Libraries: Jamberry. 2005. (Little Celebrations Ser.). (J). (gr. k-3). 82.95 *(978-0-673-75782-1(X))* Celebration Pr.
Celebrations Grade Level Libraries: The Best Bug Parade. 2005. (Little Celebrations Ser.). (J). (gr. k-3). 82.95 *(978-0-673-77590-0(9))* Celebration Pr.
Cemek, Kim. Preschool Songs & Fingerplays: Building Language Experience Through Rhythm & Movement. 2006. (Early Learning Ser.). (Illus.). 128p. (J). (gr. -1-1). per. 13.99 *(978-1-59198-223-4(5))* Creative Teaching Pr., Inc.
Certificate Only. (gr. k-5). 89.00 *(978-0-7578-6542-8(9))*; (gr. 3-5). 89.00 *(978-0-7578-6524-4(0))*; (gr. 3-5). 89.00 *(978-0-7578-6523-7(2))*; (gr. 4-5). 89.00 *(978-0-7578-6536-7(4))*; (gr. 4-5). 89.00 *(978-0-7578-6535-0(6))* Rigby Education.
Chambers, Catherine. Draw the World Turquoise Band. 2016. (Cambridge Reading Adventures Ser.). (ENG., Illus.). 24p. pap. 8.80 *(978-1-107-57684-1(9))* Cambridge Univ. Pr.
—What's for Lunch? White Band. 2017. (Cambridge Reading Adventures Ser.). (ENG., Illus.). 24p. pap. 8.60 *(978-1-108-41187-5(8))* Cambridge Univ. Pr.
Champman, Joan. Val's Vacation, 1 vol. 2006. (Neighborhood Readers Ser.). (ENG.). 16p. (gr. 1-2). pap. 6.50 *(978-1-4042-6990-3(8),* 811719e2-1d1b-4665-9465-9d71a2df88fe, Rosen Classroom) Rosen Publishing Group, Inc., The.
Chandler, Pauline. Mr. Rabbit the Farmer. Smith, Eric, illus. 2005. (ENG.). 24p. (J). lib. bdg. 23.65 *(978-1-59646-736-1(3))* Dingles & Co.
A Change in Plans: Fourth Grade Guided Comprehension Level M. (On Our Way to English Ser.). (gr. 4-18). 34.50 *(978-0-7578-7156-6(9))* Rigby Education.
Chapman, Cindy. Where Is Your Home?, 6 vols., Set. 2003. (Phonics Readers 1-36 Ser.). (ENG.). 8p. (gr. k-1). pap. 29.70 *(978-0-7368-3208-3(4))* Capstone.
Chapman, Joan. A Cloud Called Cleo, 1 vol. 2006. (Neighborhood Readers Ser.). (ENG.). 12p. (gr. 1-2). pap. 5.90 *(978-1-4042-7050-3(7),* 9681a169-6e6d-4385-acb4-4caf92e594ea, Rosen Classroom) Rosen Publishing Group, Inc., The.
—Heavy & Light: Learning to Compare Weights of Objects, 1 vol. 2010. (Math for the REAL World Ser.). (ENG., Illus.). 8p. (gr. k-1). pap. 5.15 *(978-0-8239-8844-0(9),* d813d4e2-b543-4c4e-97a3-f529b5258d53) Rosen Publishing Group, Inc., The.
—The Lonely Crayon, 1 vol. 2006. (Neighborhood Readers Ser.). (ENG.). 16p. (gr. 1-2). pap. 6.50 *(978-1-4042-7212-5(7),* e24dbcf7-1148-4c8a-a161-214c18d75c98, Rosen Classroom) Rosen Publishing Group, Inc., The.
Chapman, Simon. Himalayas Bottom to Top: Band 18/Pearl. 2017. (Collins Big Cat Ser.). (ENG., Illus.). 80p. (J). pap. 9.99 *(978-0-00-820900-1(6))* HarperCollins Pubs. Ltd. GBR. Dist: Independent Pubs. Group.
Charbonneau, Joelle. The Testing. 2015. (Testing Ser.: 1). lib. bdg. 20.85 *(978-0-606-36831-5(0))* Turtleback.
Charlesworth, Liza. Dog & Frog: An Animal Friends Reader. Smith, Ian, illus. 2015. 16p. (J). *(978-0-545-85962-2(X))* Scholastic, Inc.
—Fish School: An Animal Friends Reader. Smith, Ian, illus. 2015. 16p. (J). pap. *(978-0-545-85963-9(8))* Scholastic, Inc.
—Meet Our Class Pets. Smith, Ian, illus. 2017. 16p. (J). *(978-1-338-18028-2(2))* Scholastic, Inc.
—Night on the Farm: An Animal Friends Reader. Smith, Ian, illus. 2015. 16p. (J). pap. *(978-0-545-85964-6(6))* Scholastic, Inc.
—Please & Thank You. Forshaw, Louise, illus. 2017. 16p. (J). *(978-1-338-18029-9(0))* Scholastic, Inc.
—Science Vocabulary Reader Set: Life Cycles: Exciting Nonfiction Books That Build Kids' Vocabularies. 2007. (Science Vocabulary Readers Ser.). (ENG.). 24p. (gr. 1-3). 84.99 *(978-0-545-01597-4(9))* Scholastic, Inc.
—Science Vocabulary Reader Set: Wild Weather. 2007. (Science Vocabulary Readers Ser.). (ENG., Illus.). (gr. 1-2). 74.99 *(978-0-545-01598-1(7))* Scholastic, Inc.
—Six Silly Chicks: An Animal Friends Reader. Smith, Ian, illus. 2015. 16p. (J). pap. *(978-0-545-85966-0(2))* Scholastic, Inc.
—Wake up, Rooster! An Animal Friends Reader. Smith, Ian, illus. 2015. 16p. (J). pap. *(978-0-545-85971-4(9))* Scholastic, Inc.
Charlie & Champ. 2nd ed. 2004. (J). 4.95 *(978-0-943864-57-0(7))* Davenport, May Pubs.
Charlotte's Web Page: Individual Title Six-Packs. (Action Packs Ser.). 104p. (gr. 3-5). 44.00 *(978-0-7635-2987-1(7))* Rigby Education.
Chatterton, Martin. The Mummy Family Find Fame. Bradman, Tony, illus. 2nd ed. 2016. (Reading Ladder Level 3 Ser.). (ENG.). 48p. (gr. k-2). pap. 4.99 *(978-1-4052-8241-3(X),* Reading Ladder) Farshore GBR. Dist: HarperCollins Pubs.
Cheung, Lisa. The 10 Most Destructive Ecosystem Invaders. 2008. 14.99 *(978-1-55448-489-8(8))* Scholastic Library Publishing.
Chewy Books 800779, 2. 2005. (J). *(978-1-59794-040-5(2))* Environments, Inc.
Chichester Clark, Emma. We Are Not Fond of Rat: Band 02B/Red B (Collins Big Cat Phonics) Chichester Clark, Emma, illus. 2006. (Collins Big Cat Phonics Ser.). (ENG., Illus.). 16p. (J). (gr. -1-1). pap. 6.99 *(978-0-00-723590-2(9))* HarperCollins Pubs. Ltd. GBR. Dist: Independent Pubs. Group.
Chicken Food: 3-in-1 Package. (Sails Literacy Ser.). 24p. (gr. 2-18). 57.00 *(978-0-7578-3213-0(X))* Rigby Education.
Chicken Food: Big Book Only. (Sails Literacy Ser.). 24p. (gr. 2-18). 27.00 *(978-0-7635-6999-0(2))* Rigby Education.
Children & Families Books 800716, 10. 2005. (J). *(978-1-59794-014-6(3))* Environments, Inc.
Children's Feelings Books 800829, 14. 2005. (J). *(978-1-59794-026-9(7))* Environments, Inc.
Children's World Books 800828, 10. 2005. (J). *(978-1-59794-025-2(9))* Environments, Inc.
Child's World Tapes Book Set 800912, 3 vols. 2005. (J). pap. *(978-1-59794-077-1(1))* Environments, Inc.
Chile Fever. (Lexile Levels Ser.). 9.09 *(978-1-56334-733-7(4))* CENGAGE Learning.
Chilek, Laurie. ¡Qué miedo! ¡un tobogán! (the Scary Slide) 2007. (Lecturas del barrio (Neighborhood Readers) Ser.). (SPA.). 8p. 29.95 *(978-1-4042-7291-0(7),* Rosen Classroom) Rosen Publishing Group, Inc., The.
—The Scary Slide. (Neighborhood Readers Ser.). (ENG.). 8p. 2007. 29.95 *(978-1-4042-7290-3(9))* 2006. pap. 5.15 *(978-1-4042-6698-8(4),* e09289fb-1535-4af0-b2de-37eb9a15ee15) Rosen Publishing Group, Inc., The. (Rosen Classroom).
Chinery, Michael. Animales Salvajes. (Enciclopedias Everest Internacional Ser.). (SPA., Illus.). 320p. (J). (gr. 3-5). *(978-84-241-9399-7(7),* EV1502) Everest Editora ESP. Dist: Lectorum Pubns., Inc.
Chinery, Michael & Michael, Chinery. Enciclopedia de los Animales Salvajes, 8 vols. Tr. of Wild World of Animals. (SPA.). 346p. (J). (gr. 3-5). 100.00 *(978-84-241-2059-7(0))* Everest Editora ESP. Dist: Lectorum Pubns., Inc.
Chiquilibros: Add-to Packs. (Smart Start Ser.). (gr. k-1). 37.00 *(978-0-7635-4062-3(5))*; 37.00 *(978-0-7635-4066-1(8))*; 37.00 *(978-0-7635-4064-7(1))*; 76.00 *(978-0-7635-4068-5(4))* Rigby Education.
Chiquilibros: Chiquicuentos Complete Package. (gr. -1-1). 250.00 *(978-0-7635-8570-9(X))* Rigby Education.
Chiquilibros: Chiquicuentos Grupo A Add-to Pack. (gr. -1-1). 125.00 *(978-0-7635-8566-2(1))* Rigby Education.
Chiquilibros: Chiquicuentos Grupo B Add-to Pack. (gr. -1-1). 125.00 *(978-0-7635-8567-9(X))* Rigby Education.
Chiquilibros: Cuentos listos Complete Packages. (gr. k-1). 250.00 *(978-0-7635-4067-8(6))*; 151.00 *(978-0-7635-4065-4(X))*; 151.00 *(978-0-7635-4061-6(7))*; 151.00 *(978-0-7635-4063-0(3))* Rigby Education.
Chronicle Books & ImageBooks. Little Polar Bear: Finger Puppet Book: (Finger Puppet Book for Toddlers & Babies, Baby Books for First Year, Animal Finger Puppets) 2009. (Little Finger Puppet Board Bks.: FING). (ENG., Illus.). 12p. (J). (gr. -1 — 1). bds. 7.99 *(978-0-8118-6974-4(1))* Chronicle Bks. LLC.
Ciencias. (Enciclopedias Everest Internacional Ser.). (SPA., Illus.). (YA). (gr. 5-8). 41.95 *(978-84-241-9405-5(5),* EV7495) Everest Editora ESP. Dist: Lectorum Pubns., Inc.
Citra, Becky. Jeremy & the Golden Fleece, 1 vol. Milne, Jessica, illus. 2007. (Orca Echoes Ser.). (ENG.). 64p. (J). (gr. 1-3). per. 6.95 *(978-1-55143-657-9(4))* Orca Bk. Pubs. USA.
A City Divided. 2003. (Illus.). pap. 7.60 *(978-0-7398-7526-1(4))* Steck-Vaughn.
Civardi, Anne. The Complete Book of First Experiences. Cartwright, Stephen, illus. 2005. (Usborne First Experiences Ser.). 144p. (J). (gr. -1-3). 19.95 *(978-0-7945-1012-1(4),* Usborne) EDC Publishing.
Clark, Julie. The 10 Greatest Breakthroughs in Space Exploration. 2008. (J). 14.99 *(978-1-55448-520-8(7))* Scholastic Library Publishing.
—The 10 Most Essential Chemical Messengers in the Body. 2008. 14.99 *(978-1-55448-541-3(X))* Scholastic Library Publishing.
Clark, Lisa. The 10 Most Revolting Parasites. 2008. (J). 14.99 *(978-1-55448-521-5(5))* Scholastic Library Publishing.
Clark, Sarah Kartchner. Doctors Then & Now, 1 vol. rev. ed. 2006. (Social Studies: Informational Text Ser.). (ENG.). 32p. (gr. 2-3). pap. 11.99 *(978-0-7439-9373-9(X))* Teacher Created Materials, Inc.
—Nurses Then & Now, 1 vol. rev. ed. 2006. (Social Studies: Informational Text Ser.). (ENG.). 32p. (gr. 2-3). pap. 11.99 *(978-0-7439-9374-6(8))* Teacher Created Materials, Inc.
Clarke, Catriona. The Life Cycle of a Polar Bear: Band 14/Ruby. 2017. (Collins Big Cat Ser.). (ENG., Illus.). 48p. (J). pap. 11.99 *(978-0-00-820881-3(6))* HarperCollins Pubs. Ltd. GBR. Dist: Independent Pubs. Group.
—Living in an Earthquake Zone: Band 13/Topaz. 2017. (Collins Big Cat Ser.). (ENG., Illus.). 32p. (J). pap. 9.99 *(978-0-00-820878-3(6))* HarperCollins Pubs. Ltd. GBR. Dist: Independent Pubs. Group.
Clarke, Ella. I Am So Beautiful, 1 vol. rev. ed. 2013. (Literary Text Ser.). (ENG., Illus.). 20p. (gr. k-2). (J). lib. bdg. 15.96 *(978-1-4807-1141-9(1))*; 7.99 *(978-1-4333-5485-4(3))* Teacher Created Materials, Inc.
—When I Grow Up, 1 vol. rev. ed. 2013. (Literary Text Ser.). (ENG., Illus.). 12p. (J). (gr. k-2). 6.99 *(978-1-4333-5448-9(9))*; lib. bdg. 12.96 *(978-1-4807-1127-3(6))* Teacher Created Materials, Inc.
Clarke, Evelyn. Crisis. 2007. (Steck-Vaughn BOLDPRINT Anthologies Ser.). (ENG., Illus.). 48p. (gr. 9-12). pap. 16.90 *(978-1-4190-4034-4(0))* Houghton Mifflin Harcourt Publishing Co.
Clarke, Jane. The Amazing Adventures of Batbird: Band 11/Lime (Collins Big Cat) Schon, Nick, illus. 2005. (Collins Big Cat Ser.). (ENG.). 32p. (J). (gr. 2-3). pap. 10.99 *(978-0-00-718637-2(1))* HarperCollins Pubs. Ltd. GBR. Dist: Independent Pubs. Group.
—Chewy Hughie: Band 07/Turquoise (Collins Big Cat) McConnell, Sarah, illus. 2006. (Collins Big Cat Ser.). (ENG.). 24p. (J). (gr. 2-2). pap. 8.99 *(978-0-00-718692-1(4))* HarperCollins Pubs. Ltd. GBR. Dist: Independent Pubs. Group.
—Collins Big Cat Phonics for Letters & Sounds - Tusks: Band 04/Blue, Bd. 4. Claude, Jean, illus. 2018. (Collins Big Cat Phonics Ser.). (ENG.). 16p. (J). (gr. k-1). pap. 6.99 *(978-0-00-825162-8(2))* HarperCollins Pubs. Ltd. GBR. Dist: Independent Pubs. Group.
—Collins Big Cat Phonics for Letters & Sounds - Where Did My Dingo Go?: Band 05/Green, Bd. 5. Fox, Woody, illus. 2018. (Collins Big Cat Phonics Ser.). (ENG.). 24p. (J). (gr. k-1). pap. 6.99 *(978-0-00-825168-0(1))* HarperCollins Pubs. Ltd. GBR. Dist: Independent Pubs. Group.
—I'm Not Wearing That! Mostyn, David, illus. 2005. (ENG.). 24p. (J). lib. bdg. 23.65 *(978-1-59646-716-3(9))* Dingles & Co.
—Prince Albert's Birthday. Chatterton, Martin, illus. 2005. 24p. (J). lib. bdg. 23.65 *(978-1-59646-748-4(7))* Dingles & Co.
Clarke, M. The Story of Troy. 2007. (Illus.). 184p. per. *(978-1-4065-1381-3(4))* Dodo Pr.
Clarke, Michael. The Story of Troy. 2017. (ENG., Illus.). (J). 23.95 *(978-1-374-81990-0(5))*; pap. 13.95 *(978-1-374-81989-4(1))* Capital Communications, Inc.
Clarke, Zoë. Collins Big Cat Phonics for Letters & Sounds - Big Mud Run: Band 02A/Red A, Bd. 2A. 2018. (Collins Big Cat Phonics Ser.). (ENG., Illus.). 16p. (J). (gr. -1-k). pap. 6.99 *(978-0-00-825144-4(4))* HarperCollins Pubs. Ltd. GBR. Dist: Independent Pubs. Group.
—Collins Big Cat Phonics for Letters & Sounds - Map Man: Band 01A/Pink A, Bd. 1A. Clester, Shane, illus. 2018. (Collins Big Cat Phonics Ser.). (ENG.). 16p. (J). (gr. -1-k). pap. 6.99 *(978-0-00-825131-4(2))* HarperCollins Pubs. Ltd. GBR. Dist: Independent Pubs. Group.
Clarke, Zoe. Collins Big Cat Phonics for Letters & Sounds - Mess on the Rocks: Band 01B/Pink B, Bd. 1B. Ortega, Nathalie, illus. 2018. (Collins Big Cat Ser.). (ENG.). 16p. (J). pap. 6.99 *(978-0-00-823019-7(6))* HarperCollins Pubs. Ltd. GBR. Dist: Independent Pubs. Group.
Clarke, Zoë. Collins Big Cat Phonics for Letters & Sounds - Pip Pip Pip: Band 01A/Pink A, Bd. 1A. Armino, Monica, illus. 2018. (Collins Big Cat Phonics Ser.). (ENG.). 16p. (J). (gr. -1-k). pap. 6.99 *(978-0-00-825133-8(9))* HarperCollins Pubs. Ltd. GBR. Dist: Independent Pubs. Group.
—Collins Big Cat Phonics for Letters & Sounds - Sip It: Band 01A/Pink A, Bd. 1A. 2018. (Collins Big Cat Phonics Ser.). (ENG., Illus.). 16p. (J). (gr. -1-k). pap. 6.99 *(978-0-00-825134-5(7))* HarperCollins Pubs. Ltd. GBR. Dist: Independent Pubs. Group.
—Collins Big Cat Phonics for Letters & Sounds - Tip It: Band 01A/Pink A, Bd. 1A. Roberts, Ley Honor, illus. 2018. (Collins Big Cat Phonics Ser.). (ENG.). 16p. (J). (gr. -1-k). pap. 6.99 *(978-0-00-825132-1(0))* HarperCollins Pubs. Ltd. GBR. Dist: Independent Pubs. Group.
—The Modern Pentathlon: Band 04 Blue/Band 16 Sapphire (Collins Big Cat Progress) 2012. (Collins Big Cat Progress Ser.). (ENG., Illus.). 48p. (J). (gr. 4-5). pap. 6.99 *(978-0-00-742884-7(7))* HarperCollins Pubs. Ltd. GBR. Dist: Independent Pubs. Group.
Class Collection: Fourth Grade. (On Our Way to English Ser.). (gr. 4-18). cd-rom 29.95 *(978-0-7578-4368-6(9))* Rigby Education.
Classic Storytapes Book Set 800911, 3 vols. 2005. (J). pap. *(978-1-59794-076-4(3))* Environments, Inc.
Classification (Gr. 1-2) 2003. (J). *(978-1-58232-040-3(3))* ECS Learning Systems, Inc.
Clausen, Andrew. Prince Caspian. 2003. stu. ed., ring bd. 14.99 *(978-1-58609-195-8(6))* Progeny Pr.
Cleaning up the Park: Individual Title Six-Packs. (gr. -1-2). 23.00 *(978-0-7635-8817-5(2))* Rigby Education.
Cleary, Brian P. Sounds Like Reading, 8 vols., Set. Miskimins, Jason, illus. Incl. Whose Shoes Would You Choose? A Long Vowel Sounds Book with Consonant Digraphs. (Illus.). 32p. (J). (gr. -1-2). 2009. lib. bdg. 23.99 *(978-0-8225-7640-2(6),* a906f38f-c5ca-456c-bae7-1fe65f5a9888, Millbrook Pr.); 2009. lib. bdg. *(978-0-7613-9502-7(4),* Millbrook Pr.) Lerner Publishing Group.
Clemens, Micki. The 10 Most Ingenious Fictional Detectives. 2007. (Illus.). (J). 14.99 *(978-1-55448-514-7(2))* Scholastic Library Publishing.
Clendenin, Arlene M. & Clendenin, Bernard S. The Adventures of the Yellow Beak Bird & the Flying Cats: Yellow Beak Bird & the Flying Cats. 2013. 48p. pap. 11.99 *(978-0-9897662-1-0(7))* Clendenin Fine Art Concepts.
Clifton, Gillian. My Family Goes Green! Defining the Problem, 1 vol. 2017. (Computer Kids: Powered by Computational Thinking Ser.). (ENG.). 24p. (J). (gr. 3-4). 25.27 *(978-1-5383-2417-2(2),* b712597e-e8e2-43da-bb38-b5487ce3a066, PowerKids Pr.); pap. *(978-1-5081-3782-5(X),* 7bbf8402-347e-493c-a292-7c20224984c5, Rosen Classroom) Rosen Publishing Group, Inc., The.
Climbing: Individual Title Six-Packs. (Literatura 2000 Ser.). (gr. k-1). 28.00 *(978-0-7635-0047-4(X))* Rigby Education.
Clinton, Althea L. & Madsen, Eleanor. A Treasury of Bedtime Stories: More Than 40 Classic Tales for Sweet Dreams! Peat, Fern Bisel, illus. 2017. (Children's Classic Collections). (ENG.). 96p. (J). (gr. -1-3). 12.99 *(978-1-944686-07-9(X),* Racehorse Publishing) Skyhorse Publishing Co., Inc.
Clish, Marian L. Fish Don't Swim in a Tree. Clish, Lori, illus. (J). (gr. k-3). pap. 7.95 *(978-1-928632-12-2(2))* Writers Marketplace:Consulting, Critiquing & Publishing.
Cloudcatcher, 6 Packs. (Action Packs Ser.). 104p. (gr. 3-5). 44.00 *(978-0-7635-8412-2(6))* Rigby Education.
CloverLouise. Bullring Kid & Country Cowboy Level 4 Intermediate. 2009. (Cambridge Experience Readers Ser.). (ENG., Illus.). 96p. pap. 14.75 *(978-84-8323-495-2(5))* Cambridge Univ. Pr.
Clyne, Margaret & Griffiths, Rachel. Let's Make Music. 2004. (ENG., Illus.). 16p. (J). (gr. 1-1). pap. 10.92 *(978-0-7652-5155-8(8),* Celebration Pr.) Savvas Learning Co.
Coan, Sharon. Special Me, 1 vol. 2009. (Early Literacy Ser.). (ENG., Illus.). 16p. (gr. k-1). 6.99 *(978-1-4333-1469-8(X))* Teacher Created Materials, Inc.
—Yo Soy Especial. rev. ed. 2010. (Early Literacy Ser.).Tr. of Special Me. (SPA., Illus.). 16p. (gr. k-1). 6.99 *(978-1-4333-1944-0(6))*; 19.99 *(978-1-4333-1945-7(4))* Teacher Created Materials, Inc.
Cochran, Kate & Benchmark Education Co., LLC Staff. Why Mice Hide. 2015. (BuildUp Ser.). (J). (gr. 1). *(978-1-4900-0728-1(8))* Benchmark Education Co.
Coe, Catherine. Collins Big Cat Phonics for Letters & Sounds - Bad Luck, Dad: Band 01B/Pink B, Bd. 1B. Taylor, Erin, illus. 2018. (Collins Big Cat Phonics Ser.). (ENG.). 16p. (J). pap. 6.99 *(978-0-00-825140-6(1))* HarperCollins Pubs. Ltd. GBR. Dist: Independent Pubs. Group.
—Collins Big Cat Phonics for Letters & Sounds - Mog & Mim: Band 01B/Pink B, Bd. 1B. Brown, Judy, illus. 2018. (Collins Big Cat Phonics Ser.). (ENG.). 16p. (J). (gr. -1-k). pap. 6.99 *(978-0-00-825139-0(8))* HarperCollins Pubs. Ltd. GBR. Dist: Independent Pubs. Group.
—Collins Big Cat Phonics for Letters & Sounds - Wow Cow!: Band 02B/Red B, Bd. 2B. Mosedale, Julian, illus. 2018. (Collins Big Cat Phonics Ser.). (ENG.). 16p. (J). (gr. -1-k). pap. 6.99 *(978-0-00-825149-9(5))* HarperCollins Pubs. Ltd. GBR. Dist: Independent Pubs. Group.
—Collins Big Cat Phonics for Letters & Sounds - Zip & Zigzag: Band 02A/Red A, Bd. 2A. Elkerton, Andy, illus. 2018. (Collins Big Cat Phonics Ser.). (ENG.). 16p. (J). (gr. -1-k). pap. 6.99 *(978-0-00-825143-7(6))* HarperCollins Pubs. Ltd. GBR. Dist: Independent Pubs. Group.
Cofreros, Felipe. Sam's Wish. 2007. 28p. per. 21.99 *(978-1-4257-8486-7(0))* Xlibris Corp.
Cohen, Della. Whoppers! 2005. (Illus.). 32p. (J). *(978-0-669-51412-4(8))* Great Source Education Group, Inc.
Cohn, Jessica. Hand to Earth Saving the Environment, 1 vol. 2nd rev. ed. 2012. (TIME for KIDS(r): Informational Text Ser.). (ENG.). 48p. (gr. 4-5). pap. 13.99 *(978-1-4333-4868-6(3))* Teacher Created Materials, Inc.
—Hand to Heart: Improving Communities, 1 vol. 2nd rev. ed. 2012. (TIME for KIDS(r): Informational Text Ser.). (ENG.). 48p. (gr. 4-5). pap. 11.99 *(978-1-4333-4866-2(7))* Teacher Created Materials, Inc.
—Hand to Paw - Protecting Animals, 1 vol. 2nd rev. ed. 2012. (TIME for KIDS(r): Informational Text Ser.). (ENG.). 48p. (gr. 4-5). pap. 13.99 *(978-1-4333-4867-9(5))* Teacher Created Materials, Inc.
—The Medieval Islamic World, 1 vol. rev. ed. 2012. (Social Studies: Informational Text Ser.). (ENG.). 32p. (gr. 4-8). pap. 11.99 *(978-1-4333-5003-0(3))* Teacher Created Materials, Inc.
—Muhammad: Prophet of Islam, 1 vol. rev. ed. 2012. (Social Studies: Informational Text Ser.). (ENG.). 32p. (gr. 4-8). pap. 11.99 *(978-1-4333-5004-7(1))* Teacher Created Materials, Inc.
Cohn, Jessica & Kuligowski, Stephanie. Fearless! Stunt People, 1 vol. 2nd rev. ed. 2013. (TIME for KIDS(r): Informational Text Ser.). (ENG.). 64p. (gr. 4-8). pap. 14.99 *(978-1-4333-4941-6(8))* Teacher Created Materials, Inc.
—Wild Work! Animal Trainers, 1 vol. 2nd rev. ed. 2013. (TIME for KIDS(r): Informational Text Ser.). (ENG.). 64p. (gr. 4-8). pap. 14.99 *(978-1-4333-4942-3(6))* Teacher Created Materials, Inc.
Coirault, Christine. Colors. 2008. (Gymboree Play & Music Ser.). (ENG., Illus.). 24p. (J). (gr. -1). bds. *(978-1-55470-039-4(6))* Me to We.
—Numbers: Learn to Count in Five Languages (English, Spanish, French, German, Italian) 2008. (Gymboree Play & Music Ser.). (ENG., Illus.). 24p. (J). (gr. -1). bds. *(978-1-55470-032-5(9))* Magma.
Coldwell, Lamar. Baron's Book Hunt, 1 vol. 2016. (Rosen REAL Readers: Social Studies Nonfiction / Fiction: Myself, My Community, My World Ser.). (ENG.). 8p. (gr. k-1). pap. 5.46 *(978-1-5081-2476-4(0),* d20cda05-84be-43ad-8be6-33d71f1396c4, Rosen Classroom) Rosen Publishing Group, Inc., The.
—Building with Strong Materials, 1 vol. 2016. (Rosen REAL Readers: STEM & STEAM Collection). (ENG.). 12p. (gr. 1-2). pap. 6.33 *(978-1-5081-2449-8(3),* d690fac5-9fed-4d4a-9128-14260b40f225, Rosen Classroom) Rosen Publishing Group, Inc., The.
—Camillia Captures el Cuco, 1 vol. 2016. (Rosen REAL Readers: Social Studies Nonfiction / Fiction: Myself, My Community, My World Ser.). (ENG.). 12p. (gr. k-1). pap. 6.33 *(978-1-5081-2556-3(2),* 8c929133-0f19-49a6-952a-e62e55039db2, Rosen Classroom) Rosen Publishing Group, Inc., The.
—Constitution Day, 1 vol. 2016. (Rosen REAL Readers: Social Studies Nonfiction / Fiction: Myself, My Community, My World Ser.). (ENG.). 8p. (gr. k-1). pap. 5.46 *(978-1-5081-2287-6(3),* 835495ca-f2fd-4da0-9080-de7504cffc1d, Rosen Classroom) Rosen Publishing Group, Inc., The.
—The Day My Brother Got Lost, 1 vol. 2016. (Rosen REAL Readers: Social Studies Nonfiction / Fiction: Myself, My Community, My World Ser.). (ENG.). 12p. (gr. k-1). pap. 6.33 *(978-1-5081-2530-3(9),* 59d79429-fc55-418c-8e24-30d76a9d7425, Rosen Classroom) Rosen Publishing Group, Inc., The.
—A Law for People, 1 vol. 2016. (Rosen REAL Readers: Social Studies Nonfiction / Fiction: Myself, My Community, My World Ser.). (ENG.). 8p. (gr. k-1). pap. 5.46 *(978-1-5081-2503-7(1),* 44ebd88f-415e-41b2-a623-67e657b4edae, Rosen Classroom) Rosen Publishing Group, Inc., The.
—A River Runs Through This Valley, 1 vol. 2016. (Rosen REAL Readers: Social Studies Nonfiction / Fiction: Myself, My Community, My World Ser.). (ENG.). 8p. (gr. k-1). pap. 5.46 *(978-1-5081-2521-1(X),* 4422013c-824f-4b13-9074-5b0450871615, Rosen Classroom) Rosen Publishing Group, Inc., The.
—The Stone House, 1 vol. 2016. (Rosen REAL Readers: STEM & STEAM Collection). (ENG.). 12p. (gr. 1-2). pap. 6.33 *(978-1-5081-2664-5(X),* e3b6d5ef-ea48-42e6-a403-5b6cbe04d7ee, Rosen Classroom) Rosen Publishing Group, Inc., The.
—The Sun on Our Roof, 1 vol. 2016. (Rosen REAL Readers: Social Studies Nonfiction / Fiction: Myself, My Community, My World Ser.). (ENG.). 12p. (gr. k-1). pap. 6.33 *(978-1-5081-2574-7(0),* 669365f0-f95d-4d99-a318-9d4eec3e578d, Rosen Classroom) Rosen Publishing Group, Inc., The.
—The Tuning Fork, 1 vol. 2016. (Rosen REAL Readers: STEM & STEAM Collection). (ENG.). 12p. (gr. k-1). pap. 6.33 *(978-1-5081-2428-3(0),* 591e7d6c-357c-4c53-add6-7cf05324b2ce, Rosen Classroom) Rosen Publishing Group, Inc., The.
Cole, Bob. Power Reading: Chapter Books/Wizard of OZ. Sirrell, Terri, illus. 2004. 94p. (J). (gr. 3-4). vinyl bd. 39.95 *(978-1-883186-64-7(1),* PPCL1) National Reading Styles Institute, Inc.
—Power Reading: Chapter/Sci-Fi/Dr. Little. Sirrell, Terri, illus. 2004. 25p. (J). (gr. 3-4). vinyl bd. 39.95 *(978-1-883186-63-0(3),* PPSF1) National Reading Styles Institute, Inc.
—Power Reading: Chapter/Sci-Fi/Dr. Little 2. Ford, David, illus. 2005. 25p. (J). (gr. 3-4). vinyl bd. 39.95 *(978-1-883186-76-0(5),* PPSF4) National Reading Styles Institute, Inc.
—Power Reading: Chapter/Sci-Fi/Superhero. Ford, David, illus. 2004. 25p. (J). (gr. 3-4). vinyl bd. 39.95 *(978-1-883186-62-3(5),* PPSF2) National Reading Styles Institute, Inc.

—Power Reading: Chapter/Sci-Fi/Time Warp. Ford, David, illus. 2004. 25p. (J). (gr. 4-18). vinyl bd. 39.95 *(978-1-883186-60-9(9)*, PPSF3) National Reading Styles Institute, Inc.

—Power Reading: Chapter/Sci-Fi/Time Warp 2. Ford, David, illus. 2005. 52p. (J). (gr. 4-18). vinyl bd. 39.95 *(978-1-883186-75-3(7)*, PPSF5) National Reading Styles Institute, Inc.

—Power Reading: Classics/Jungle Book. Connor, Robin, illus. 2004. 94p. (J). (gr. 4-18). vinyl bd. 39.95 *(978-1-883186-61-6(7)*, PPCL2) National Reading Styles Institute, Inc.

—Power Reading: Classics/Treasure Island. Lee, Joe, illus. 2004. 94p. (J). (gr. 5-6). vinyl bd. 39.95 *(978-1-883186-59-3(5)*, PPCL3) National Reading Styles Institute, Inc.

—Power Reading: Comic Book/Dr. Little. Sirrell, Terri, illus. 2005. 36p. (J). (gr. 2-4). vinyl bd. *(978-1-883186-77-7(3)*, PPSFC1) National Reading Styles Institute, Inc.

—Power Reading: Comic Book/Jungle Book. Connor, Robin, illus. 2005. 62p. (J). (gr. 3-18). vinyl bd. 39.95 *(978-1-883186-74-6(9)*, PPCLC2) National Reading Styles Institute, Inc.

—Power Reading: Comic Book/Time Warp. Ford, David, illus. 2005. 36p. (J). (gr. 3-4). vinyl bd. 29.95 *(978-1-883186-69-2(2)*, PPSFC3) National Reading Styles Institute, Inc.

—Power Reading: Comic Book/Time Warp 2. Ford, David, illus. 2005. 36p. (J). (gr. 3-4). vinyl bd. 29.95 *(978-1-933533-01-8(3)*, PPSFC3A) National Reading Styles Institute, Inc.

—Power Reading: Comic Book/Wizard of OZ. Sirrell, Terri, illus. 2005. 60p. (J). (gr. 3-4). vinyl bd. 39.95 *(978-1-883186-80-7(3)*, PPCLC1) National Reading Styles Institute, Inc.

—Power Reading: Nail-Biters! 2. Morton, Vivian, illus. 2005. 94p. (J). (gr. 6-18). vinyl bd. 89.95 *(978-1-883186-25-8(0)*, PPNB2) National Reading Styles Institute, Inc.

Cole, Bob & Sirrell, Terri. Power Reading: Comic Book/Dr. Little 2. 2005. (Illus.). 36p. (J). (gr. 2-4). vinyl bd. 29.95 *(978-1-933533-00-1(5)*, PPSFC1A) National Reading Styles Institute, Inc.

Colfer, Eoin. Iron Man: The Gauntlet. 2016. 288p. (J). pap. *(978-1-74381-176-4(4))* Disney Pr.

—The Legend of Spud Murphy. McCoy, Glenn, illus. 2005. (Eoin Colfer's Legend Of... Ser.). 95p. (gr. 2-6). 16.00 *(978-0-7569-6514-3(4))* Perfection Learning Corp.

Coll-Seck, Jayden. The Class Photo, 1 vol., 1. 2015. (Rosen REAL Readers: Social Studies Nonfiction / Fiction: Myself, My Community, My World Ser.). (ENG.). 8p. (J). (gr. k-1). pap. 5.46 *(978-1-5081-1851-0(5)*, 95491da5-e52e-41ee-a573-e950efcdf20c, Rosen Classroom) Rosen Publishing Group, Inc., The.

—Fairy Tale Food, 1 vol., 1. 2015. (Rosen REAL Readers: Social Studies Nonfiction / Fiction: Myself, My Community, My World Ser.). (ENG.). 12p. (J). (gr. k-1). pap. 6.33 *(978-1-5081-1955-5(4)*, 7928f52d-57cc-4952-b7e1-f6d5d75bb980, Rosen Classroom) Rosen Publishing Group, Inc., The.

—The Finger Paint Party, 1 vol., 1. 2015. (Rosen REAL Readers: STEM & STEAM Collection). (ENG.). 8p. (J). (gr. k-1). pap. 5.46 *(978-1-5081-1461-1(7)*, e3e4dea9-c799-47c0-945d-8010f10a9fda, Rosen Classroom) Rosen Publishing Group, Inc., The.

—In Uncle Bill's Shop, 1 vol., 1. 2015. (Rosen REAL Readers: STEM & STEAM Collection). (ENG.). 12p. (J). (gr. k-1). pap. 6.33 *(978-1-5081-1542-7(7)*, c46b9248-4517-46cc-b454-ac888ee87282, Rosen Classroom) Rosen Publishing Group, Inc., The.

—Our School Motto Matters, 1 vol., 1. 2015. (Rosen REAL Readers: Social Studies Nonfiction / Fiction: Myself, My Community, My World Ser.). (ENG.). 12p. (J). (gr. k-1). pap. 6.33 *(978-1-5081-1928-9(7)*, a452ac11-a533-4c17-9d7f-488fecfc8a69, Rosen Classroom) Rosen Publishing Group, Inc., The.

—Principal for a Day, 1 vol., 1. 2015. (Rosen REAL Readers: Social Studies Nonfiction / Fiction: Myself, My Community, My World Ser.). (ENG.). 12p. (J). (gr. k-1). pap. 6.33 *(978-1-5081-1979-1(1)*, 78af2701-d115-4363-ac11-3bc44a9265bf, Rosen Classroom) Rosen Publishing Group, Inc., The.

—The Quilt, 1 vol., 1. 2015. (Rosen REAL Readers: Social Studies Nonfiction / Fiction: Myself, My Community, My World Ser.). (ENG.). 8p. (J). (gr. k-1). pap. 5.46 *(978-1-5081-1887-9(6)*, b6894b86-4a6c-46d0-93f8-b32ef8ad6eab, Rosen Classroom) Rosen Publishing Group, Inc., The.

—Sara Tries Again, 1 vol., 1. 2015. (Rosen REAL Readers: STEM & STEAM Collection). (ENG.). 12p. (J). (gr. k-1). pap. 6.33 *(978-1-5081-1524-3(9)*, ddafe364-b146-492b-9cef-25addec39e60, Rosen Classroom) Rosen Publishing Group, Inc., The.

—Tanya the Chef, 1 vol., 1. 2015. (Rosen REAL Readers: Social Studies Nonfiction / Fiction: Myself, My Community, My World Ser.). (ENG.). 12p. (J). (gr. k-1). pap. 6.33 *(978-1-5081-1393-5(9)*, 4ce18b1a-cb87-462d-acd2-aa95034c88ce, Rosen Classroom) Rosen Publishing Group, Inc., The.

—A Tree's Tale, 1 vol., 1. 2015. (Rosen REAL Readers: STEM & STEAM Collection). (ENG.). 8p. (J). (gr. k-1). pap. 5.46 *(978-1-5081-1397-3(1)*, df168516-ce9e-4285-9bc1-c690d6136d51, Rosen Classroom) Rosen Publishing Group, Inc., The.

—A Turtle for Malia, 1 vol., 1. 2015. (Rosen REAL Readers: STEM & STEAM Collection). (ENG.). 8p. (J). (gr. k-1). pap. 5.46 *(978-1-5081-1441-3(2)*, 36290bef-ecf4-4436-a43a-5512c10a7319, Rosen Classroom) Rosen Publishing Group, Inc., The.

—Who Are the Millers?, 1 vol., 1. 2015. (Rosen REAL Readers: Social Studies Nonfiction / Fiction: Myself, My Community, My World Ser.). (ENG.). 8p. (J). (gr. k-1). pap. 5.46 *(978-1-5081-1383-6(1)*, 8fe51c5f-9160-40b2-8a79-69661220d5de, Rosen Classroom) Rosen Publishing Group, Inc., The.

—Who Is the Man in the Photo?, 1 vol., 1. 2015. (Rosen REAL Readers: Social Studies Nonfiction / Fiction: Myself, My Community, My World Ser.). (ENG.). 8p. (J). (gr. k-1). pap. 5.46 *(978-1-5081-1869-5(8)*, ba68e203-5d5b-4aa3-9821-3cb23b26e7ff, Rosen Classroom) Rosen Publishing Group, Inc., The.

Collection for Readers Bookshelf Collection, 6 units, Set. 2004. (Scott Foresman Reading Ser.). (gr. 3-18). 180.00 *(978-0-328-03135-1(6))*; (gr. 6-18). 180.00 *(978-0-328-03138-2(0))* Addison-Wesley Educational Pubs., Inc.

Collection for Readers Take-Home. 2004. (Scott Foresman Reading Ser.). (gr. 3-18). 48.00 *(978-0-328-02302-8(7))*; (gr. 4-18). 48.00 *(978-0-328-02684-5(0))*; (gr. 5-18). 48.00 *(978-0-328-02685-2(9))*; (gr. 6-18). 48.00 *(978-0-328-02686-9(7))* Addison-Wesley Educational Pubs., Inc.

Collins Easy Learning. Telling the Time Wipe Clean Activity Book: Ideal for Home Learning (Collins Easy Learning KS1) 2018. (Collins Easy Learning KS1 Ser.). (ENG.). 24p. (J). (gr. -1-k). 7.95 *(978-0-00-827538-9(6))* HarperCollins Pubs. Ltd. GBR. Dist: Independent Pubs. Group.

Collins ELT Readers: Amazing Leaders (Level 4), 1 vol. 2014. (Collins English Readers Ser.). (ENG.). 112p. audio compact disk 13.95 *(978-0-00-754507-0(X))* HarperCollins Pubs. Ltd. GBR. Dist: Independent Pubs. Group.

Collins UK. My Balcony Oasis: (Level 10) 2016. (Collins Big Cat Arabic Ser.). (ENG.). 24p. (J). pap. 5.99 *(978-0-00-818582-4(4))* HarperCollins Pubs. Ltd. GBR. Dist: Independent Pubs. Group.

Color It My Way: Individual Title Six-Packs. (Story Steps Ser.). (gr. k-2). 32.00 *(978-0-7635-9611-8(6))* Rigby Education.

Come & Have Fun: KinderWords Individual Title Six-Packs. (Kinderstarters Ser.). 8p. (gr. -1-1). 21.00 *(978-0-7635-8701-7(X))* Rigby Education.

Come on Up: KinderWords Individual Title Six-Packs. (Kinderstarters Ser.). 8p. (gr. -1-1). 21.00 *(978-0-7635-8698-0(6))* Rigby Education.

Come to My House. (Greetings Ser.: Vol. 3). 24p. (gr. 2-3). 31.00 *(978-0-7635-5702-7(1))* Rigby Education.

Comic Book Facts. 2003. (Illus.). pap. 5.60 *(978-0-7398-7514-8(0))* Steck-Vaughn.

Como buenos Amigos: Social/Emotional Lap Book. (Pebble Soup Exploraciones Ser.). (gr. -1-18). 16.00 *(978-0-7578-1782-3(3))* Rigby Education.

Complete Add-on. 2005. (Book Treks Ser.). (J). (gr. 3-18). 152.95 *(978-0-7652-6134-2(0))*; (gr. 4-18). 157.50 *(978-0-7652-6135-9(9))*; (gr. 5-18). 157.50 *(978-0-7652-6136-6(7))* Celebration Pr.

Complete DRA Pack. (Dra Levels Ser.). 752.54 *(978-0-7362-2576-2(5))* CENGAGE Learning.

Complete Early Intervention Pack. (Early Intervention Levels Ser.). 610.07 *(978-0-7362-2557-1(9))* CENGAGE Learning.

The Complete Graphica Collection (2013) 2013. (Graphica Ser.). (ENG., Illus.). 24–48p. (gr. 3-8). 16041.10 *(978-1-4777-0643-5(7)*, Rosen Classroom) Rosen Publishing Group, Inc., The.

Complete Guided Reading Pack. (Guided Reading Levels Ser.). 752.54 *(978-0-7362-2565-6(X))* CENGAGE Learning.

Complete High Five USA Reading Program I. (gr. 4-18). 667.95 incl. audio *(978-0-7368-9580-4(9)*, Red Brick Learning) Capstone.

Complete High Five USA Reading Program I, Books Only. (gr. 4-18). 599.95 *(978-0-7368-9581-1(7)*, Red Brick Learning) Capstone.

Complete High Five USA Reading Program II. (gr. 4-18). 667.95 incl. audio *(978-0-7368-3859-7(7)*, Red Brick Learning) Capstone.

Complete High Five USA Reading Program II, Books Only. (gr. 4-18). 599.95 *(978-0-7368-3861-0(9)*, Red Brick Learning) Capstone.

Complete Letter Books Program. (gr. k-2). 409.95 *(978-0-7368-4127-6(X)*, Red Brick Learning) Capstone.

Complete Lexile Pack. (Lexile Levels Ser.). 967.73 *(978-0-7362-2577-9(3))* CENGAGE Learning.

Complete Pebble Reading Program. (gr. k-2). 2836.95 *(978-0-7368-1489-8(2)*, Pebble) Capstone.

Comprehension Power Readers: Add-on Pack (Reading Level 1-2) 2005. (Comprehension Power Readers Ser.). (J). (gr. 1-18). 166.95 *(978-0-7652-4339-3(3))*; (gr. 2-18). 166.95 *(978-0-7652-4340-9(7))* Modern Curriculum Pr.

Comprehension Power Readers: Add-on Pack (Reading Level 3-4) 2005. (Comprehension Power Readers Ser.). (J). (gr. 3-18). 194.50 *(978-0-7652-4341-6(5))*; (gr. 4-18). 194.50 *(978-0-7652-4342-3(3))* Modern Curriculum Pr.

Comprehension Power Readers: Add-on Pack (Reading Level 5-6) 2005. (Comprehension Power Readers Ser.). (J). (gr. 5-18). 219.95 *(978-0-7652-4343-0(1))*; (gr. 6-18). 219.95 *(978-0-7652-4344-7(X))* Modern Curriculum Pr.

Comprehension Power Readers: Library (Reading Level 1-2) 2005. (Comprehension Power Readers Ser.). (J). (gr. 1-18). 1026.50 *(978-0-7652-4333-1(4))*; (gr. 2-18). 1026.50 *(978-0-7652-4334-8(2))* Modern Curriculum Pr.

Comprehension Power Readers: Library (Reading Level 3-4) 2005. (Comprehension Power Readers Ser.). (J). (gr. 3-18). 1193.50 *(978-0-7652-4335-5(0))*; (gr. 4-18). 1193.50 *(978-0-7652-4336-2(9))* Modern Curriculum Pr.

Comprehension Power Readers: Library (Reading Level 5-6) 2005. (Comprehension Power Readers Ser.). (J). (gr. 5-18). 1334.95 *(978-0-7652-4337-9(7))*; (gr. 6-18). 1334.95 *(978-0-7652-4338-6(5))* Modern Curriculum Pr.

Conklin, Blane. Barack Obama: President of the United States. rev. ed. 2011. (Social Studies: Informational Text Ser.). (ENG.). 32p. (gr. 4-8). pap. 11.99 *(978-1-4333-1522-0(X))* Teacher Created Materials, Inc.

Conklin, Wendy. Battles of the Civil War, 1 vol. rev. ed. 2005. (Social Studies: Informational Text Ser.). (ENG., Illus.). 24p. (gr. 4-8). pap. 10.99 *(978-0-7439-8919-0(8))* Teacher Created Materials, Inc.

—Benjamin Franklin, 1 vol. rev. ed. 2004. (Social Studies: Informational Text Ser.). (ENG.). 24p. (gr. 4-8). pap. 10.99 *(978-0-7439-8755-4(1))* Teacher Created Materials, Inc.

—Civil Rights Movement, 1 vol. rev. ed. 2007. (Social Studies: Informational Text Ser.). (ENG.). 32p. (J). (gr. 4-8). pap. 11.99 *(978-0-7439-0670-8(5))* Teacher Created Materials, Inc.

—Civil War Leaders, 1 vol. rev. ed. 2005. (Social Studies: Informational Text Ser.). (ENG.). 24p. (gr. 4-8). pap. 10.99 *(978-0-7439-8917-6(1))* Teacher Created Materials, Inc.

—The Cold War, 1 vol. rev. ed. 2007. (Social Studies: Informational Text Ser.). (ENG.). 32p. (gr. 4-8). pap. 11.99 *(978-0-7439-0672-2(1))* Teacher Created Materials, Inc.

—Cold War Leaders, 1 vol. rev. ed. 2007. (Social Studies: Informational Text Ser.). (ENG.). 32p. (gr. 4-8). pap. 11.99 *(978-0-7439-0673-9(X))* Teacher Created Materials, Inc.

—Early Congresses, 1 vol. rev. ed. 2004. (Social Studies: Informational Text Ser.). (ENG.). 24p. (gr. 4-8). pap. 10.99 *(978-0-7439-8750-9(0))* Teacher Created Materials, Inc.

—Exploring the New World, 1 vol. rev. ed. 2004. (Social Studies: Informational Text Ser.). (ENG.). 24p. (J). (gr. 4-8). pap. 10.99 *(978-0-7439-8740-0(3))* Teacher Created Materials, Inc.

—Moctezuma: Aztec Ruler, 1 vol. rev. ed. 2007. (Social Studies: Informational Text Ser.). (ENG.). 32p. (J). (gr. 4-8). pap. 11.99 *(978-0-7439-0457-5(5))* Teacher Created Materials, Inc.

—Robert E. Lee, 1 vol. rev. ed. 2005. (Social Studies: Informational Text Ser.). (ENG.). 24p. (gr. 4-8). pap. 10.99 *(978-0-7439-8918-3(X))* Teacher Created Materials, Inc.

Conley, Jennise M. I Think There's a Monster under My Bed! 2013. 28p. 9.99 *(978-1-61061-972-1(2))* My Three Sisters Publishing.

Conn, Marla. At the Aquarium with Dear Dragon, 10 vols. 2019. (Dear Dragon Developing Readers Ser.). (ENG., Illus.). 24p. (J). (gr. k-k). 23.94 *(978-1-68450-997-3(1))* Norwood Hse. Pr.

—At the Bank with Dear Dragon, 10 vols. David Schimmell, illus. 2019. (Dear Dragon Developing Readers Ser.). (ENG.). 24p. (J). (gr. k-k). pap. 11.94 *(978-1-68404-309-5(3))* Norwood Hse. Pr.

—At the Carnival with Dear Dragon, 10 vols. David Schimmell, illus. 2019. (Dear Dragon Developing Readers Ser.). (ENG.). 24p. (J). (gr. k-k). pap. 11.94 *(978-1-68404-311-8(5))* Norwood Hse. Pr.

—At the Dentist with Dear Dragon, 10 vols. David Schimmell, illus. 2019. (Dear Dragon Developing Readers Ser.). (ENG.). 24p. (J). (gr. k-k). pap. 11.94 *(978-1-68404-312-5(3))* Norwood Hse. Pr.

—At the Firehouse with Dear Dragon, 10 vols. David Schimmell, illus. 2019. (Dear Dragon Developing Readers Ser.). (ENG.). 24p. (J). (gr. k-k). pap. 11.94 *(978-1-68404-313-2(1))* Norwood Hse. Pr.

—At the Hospital with Dear Dragon, 10 vols. 2019. (Dear Dragon Developing Readers Ser.). (ENG., Illus.). 24p. (J). (gr. k-k). 23.94 *(978-1-68450-991-1(2))* Norwood Hse. Pr.

—At the Library with Dear Dragon, 10 vols. David Schimmell, illus. 2019. (Dear Dragon Developing Readers Ser.). (ENG.). 24p. (J). (gr. k-k). pap. 11.94 *(978-1-68404-315-6(8))* Norwood Hse. Pr.

—At the Market with Dear Dragon, 10 vols. David Schimmell, illus. 2019. (Dear Dragon Developing Readers Ser.). (ENG.). 24p. (J). (gr. k-k). pap. 11.94 *(978-1-68404-316-3(6))* Norwood Hse. Pr.

—At the Police Station with Dear Dragon, 10 vols. 2019. (Dear Dragon Developing Readers Ser.). (ENG., Illus.). 24p. (J). (gr. k-k). 23.94 *(978-1-68450-988-1(2))* Norwood Hse. Pr.

—At the Pond with Dear Dragon, 10 vols. 2019. (Dear Dragon Developing Readers Ser.). (ENG., Illus.). 24p. (J). (gr. k-k). 23.94 *(978-1-68450-982-9(3))* Norwood Hse. Pr.

—At the Zoo with Dear Dragon, 10 vols. David Schimmell, illus. 2019. (Dear Dragon Developing Readers Ser.). (ENG.). 24p. (J). (gr. k-k). pap. 11.94 *(978-1-68404-318-7(2))* Norwood Hse. Pr.

—Camping with Dear Dragon, 10 vols. David Schimmell, illus. 2019. (Dear Dragon Developing Readers Ser.). (ENG.). 24p. (J). (gr. k-k). pap. 11.94 *(978-1-68404-306-4(9))* Norwood Hse. Pr.

—I See Colors, Dear Dragon, 10 vols. David Schimmell, illus. 2019. (Dear Dragon Developing Readers Ser.). (ENG.). 24p. (J). (gr. k-k). pap. 11.94 *(978-1-68404-320-0(4))* Norwood Hse. Pr.

—I See Shapes, Dear Dragon, 10 vols. David Schimmell, illus. 2019. (Dear Dragon Developing Readers Ser.). (ENG.). 24p. (J). (gr. k-k). pap. 11.94 *(978-1-68404-321-7(2))* Norwood Hse. Pr.

—In the Woods with Dear Dragon, 10 vols. 2019. (Dear Dragon Developing Readers Ser.). (ENG., Illus.). 24p. (J). (gr. k-k). 23.94 *(978-1-68450-980-5(7))* Norwood Hse. Pr.

—Look at the Sky, Dear Dragon, 10 vols. David Schimmell, illus. 2019. (Dear Dragon Developing Readers Ser.). (ENG.). 24p. (J). (gr. k-k). pap. 11.94 *(978-1-68404-324-8(7))* Norwood Hse. Pr.

—Look in My Pocket, Dear Dragon, 10 vols. David Schimmell, illus. 2019. (Dear Dragon Developing Readers Ser.). (ENG.). 24p. (J). (gr. k-k). pap. 11.94 *(978-1-68404-322-4(0))* Norwood Hse. Pr.

—A to Z with Dear Dragon, 10 vols. 2019. (Dear Dragon Developing Readers Ser.). (ENG., Illus.). 24p. (J). (gr. k-k). 23.94 *(978-1-68450-986-7(6))* Norwood Hse. Pr.

—We Are Happy, Dear Dragon, 10 vols. 2019. (Dear Dragon Developing Readers Ser.). (ENG., Illus.). 24p. (J). (gr. k-k). 23.94 *(978-1-68450-979-9(3))* Norwood Hse. Pr.

—We Are Mad, Dear Dragon, 10 vols. 2019. (Dear Dragon Developing Readers Ser.). (ENG., Illus.). 24p. (J). (gr. k-k). 23.94 *(978-1-68450-978-2(5))* Norwood Hse. Pr.

Connelly, Erin. Watch Out for Wolves! 2017. (Text Connections Guided Close Reading Ser.). (J). (gr. 1). *(978-1-4900-1820-1(4))* Benchmark Education Co.

Connolly, Debbie & Danley, Laurie. Passport to Genre: A Literature Enrichment Guide. Mitchell, Judy, ed. Hillam, Corbin, illus. 2006. 64p. (J). pap. 9.95 *(978-1-57310-488-3(4))* Teaching & Learning Co.

Connolly, Ryan. Tom's Field Trip, 1 vol. 2012. (InfoMax Readers Ser.). (ENG., Illus.). 16p. (J). (gr. k-k). pap. 7.00 *(978-1-4488-8971-6(5)*, cad22244-6c58-4383-a655-f840533b0c36, Rosen Classroom) Rosen Publishing Group, Inc., The.

Contemporary Biography, 7 Bks, Set. (Robbie Reader Ser.). (Illus.). (gr. 1-4). lib. bdg. *(978-1-58415-350-4(4))* Mitchell Lane Pubs.

Content Connect! (gr. 3-5). 1081.53 *(978-0-7362-2579-3(X))* CENGAGE Learning.

Content Connect! Picture It! Big Book with Pen & Teacher's Guide. (gr. 4-8). tchr. ed. 54.98 *(978-0-7362-2436-9(X))* CENGAGE Learning.

Context Clues (Gr. 1-3) 2003. (J). *(978-1-58232-080-9(2))* ECS Learning Systems, Inc.

Contreras, Kathleen. Harvesting Friends: Cosechando Amigos. 2018. (ENG & SPA., Illus.). 32p. (J). (gr. 1-4). 17.95 *(978-1-55885-858-9(X))* Arte Publico Pr.

Cook, Julia. Cheaters Never Prosper, Volume 4. DuFalla, Anita, illus. 2016. (Responsible Me! Ser.). (ENG.). 32p. (J). (gr. k-6). pap. 10.95 *(978-1-944882-08-2(1))* Boys Town Pr.

Cooling, Wendy. The Camel Fair: Band 10/White (Collins Big Cat) 2005. (Collins Big Cat Ser.). (ENG.). 32p. (J). (gr. 2-3). pap. 10.99 *(978-0-00-718634-1(7))* HarperCollins Pubs. Ltd. GBR. Dist: Independent Pubs. Group.

Cope, Clifford D. Caleb: The mouse Engineer. 2009. 24p. pap. 12.99 *(978-1-4389-9877-0(5))* AuthorHouse.

Corchin, D. J. I Feel... Awesome. 2020. (I Feel... Ser.). (Illus.). 56p. (J). (gr. -1-3). 14.99 *(978-1-7282-1973-8(6))* Sourcebooks, Inc.

—I Feel... Different. 2020. (I Feel... Ser.). (Illus.). 56p. (J). (gr. -1-3). 14.99 *(978-1-7282-1970-7(1))* Sourcebooks, Inc.

—I Feel... Sick. 2020. (I Feel... Ser.). (Illus.). 56p. (J). (gr. -1-3). 14.99 *(978-1-7282-1952-3(3))* Sourcebooks, Inc.

Corey, Shana. Stuck in the Mud (Thomas & Friends) Courtney, Richard, illus. 2009. (Step into Reading Ser.). (ENG.). 32p. (J). (gr. -1-1). pap. 5.99 *(978-0-375-86177-2(7)*, Random Hse. Bks. for Young Readers) Random Hse. Children's Bks.

Corner Store. (J). 21.95 *(978-0-8136-4337-3(6))*; pap. 13.15 *(978-0-8136-4336-6(8))* Modern Curriculum Pr.

Cosgrove, Stephen. Storybook Readers, 5 bks. Steelhammer, Ilona, illus. (J). lib. bdg. 73.75 *(978-1-56674-921-3(2))* Forest Hse. Publishing Co., Inc.

Cosgrove, Stephen; Hirschfeld. The Golden Spike. Hirschfeld, Pam, ed. 2004. (Reader's Theater Content-Area Concepts Ser.). (ENG.). (J). (gr. 4-5). 5.00 net. *(978-1-4108-1141-7(7))* Benchmark Education Co.

Cottringer, Anne. Hot Dog. Walker, Katherine, illus. 2005. (ENG.). 24p. (J). lib. bdg. 23.65 *(978-1-59646-738-5(X))* Dingles & Co.

Coughlan, Billy. Not Without My Whale. Karabatzia, Villie, illus. 2019. (Early Bird Readers — Green (Early Bird Stories (tm)) Ser.). (ENG.). 32p. (J). (gr. k-3). 30.65 *(978-1-5415-4204-4(5)*, 8f981220-0b58-4e5f-9c0b-823a7ebf46de); pap. 9.99 *(978-1-5415-7409-0(5)*, 31c2d9b7-aeb3-47e4-8c7a-058f9da6326c) Lerner Publishing Group. (Lerner Pubns.).

Cousineau-Peiffer, Trisha. Have You Ever Heard of a Rainbow Farm. Everett-Hawkes, Bonnie, illus. 2006. 32p. (J). 12.95 *(978-0-9792084-1-6(6))* Dream Ridge Pr.

—Have You Ever Heard of a Rainbow Farm: The Missing Color Kittens. Everett-Hawkes, Bonnie, illus. 2007. 48p. (J). per. 15.95 *(978-0-9792084-2-3(4))* Dream Ridge Pr.

Cousins, Lucy. Maisy's House: Complete with Durable Play Scene: A Fold-Out & Play Book. Cousins, Lucy, illus. 2018. (Maisy Ser.). (ENG., Illus.). 16p. (J). (-k). bds. 9.99 *(978-1-5362-0378-3(5))* Candlewick Pr.

Coven, Wanda. Heidi Heckelbeck & the Never-Ending Day. Burris, Priscilla, illus. 2017. (Heidi Heckelbeck Ser.: 21). (ENG.). 128p. (J). (gr. k-4). 17.99 *(978-1-4814-9525-7(9))*; pap. 6.99 *(978-1-4814-9524-0(0))* Little Simon. (Little Simon).

Cowley, Joy. Big Bear & Little Bear: Buttons. Lam, Amy, illus. 2013. (ENG.). 8p. pap. *(978-1-927186-33-6(1)*, Joy Cowley Club) Flying Start Bks.

—Big Bear & Little Bear: Cold Feet. Lam, Amy, illus. 2013. (ENG.). 8p. pap. *(978-1-927186-27-5(7)*, Joy Cowley Club) Flying Start Bks.

—Big Bear & Little Bear: Cookies. Lam, Amy, illus. 2013. (ENG.). 8p. pap. *(978-1-927186-29-9(3)*, Joy Cowley Club) Flying Start Bks.

—Big Bear & Little Bear: Egg. Lam, Amy, illus. 2013. (ENG.). 8p. pap. *(978-1-927186-32-9(3)*, Joy Cowley Club) Flying Start Bks.

—Big Bear & Little Bear: Ice Cream. Lam, Amy, illus. 2013. (ENG.). 8p. pap. *(978-1-927186-21-3(8)*, Joy Cowley Club) Flying Start Bks.

—Big Bear & Little Bear: Jackets. Lam, Amy, illus. 2013. (ENG.). 8p. pap. *(978-1-927186-26-8(9)*, Joy Cowley Club) Flying Start Bks.

—Big Bear & Little Bear: Lemonade. Lam, Amy, illus. 2013. (ENG.). 8p. pap. *(978-1-927186-28-2(5)*, Joy Cowley Club) Flying Start Bks.

—Big Bear & Little Bear: Lollipop. Lam, Amy, illus. 2013. (ENG.). 8p. pap. *(978-1-927186-30-5(7)*, Joy Cowley Club) Flying Start Bks.

—Big Bear & Little Bear: Puddle. Lam, Amy, illus. 2013. (ENG.). 8p. pap. *(978-1-927186-34-3(X)*, Joy Cowley Club) Flying Start Bks.

—Big Bear & Little Bear: Race. Lam, Amy, illus. 2013. (ENG.). 8p. pap. *(978-1-927186-22-0(6)*, Joy Cowley Club) Flying Start Bks.

—Big Bear & Little Bear: Singing. Lam, Amy, illus. 2013. (ENG.). 8p. pap. *(978-1-927186-25-1(0)*, Joy Cowley Club) Flying Start Bks.

—Big Bear & Little Bear: Story. Lam, Amy, illus. 2013. (ENG.). 8p. pap. *(978-1-927186-23-7(4)*, Joy Cowley Club) Flying Start Bks.

—Big Bear & Little Bear: Wind. Lam, Amy, illus. 2013. (ENG.). 8p. pap. *(978-1-927186-20-6(X)*, Joy Cowley Club) Flying Start Bks.

—The Hungry Giant's Shoe Big Book. 2010. 48.25 *(978-1-60559-250-3(1))* Hameray Publishing Group, Inc.

—Meanies in the House Big Book. 2010. 48.25 *(978-1-60559-251-0(X))* Hameray Publishing Group, Inc.

—Miss Doll & Friends: A Surprise for Miss Doll. Bordicchia, Gaia, illus. 2014. (ENG.). 8p. pap. *(978-0-927244-52-7(7)*, Joy Cowley Club) Flying Start Bks.

—Miss Doll & Friends: Tin Clown. Bordicchia, Gaia, illus. 2014. (ENG.). 8p. pap. *(978-0-927244-55-8(1)*, Joy Cowley Club) Flying Start Bks.

—Miss Doll & Friends: Tin Clown¿s Hat. Bordicchia, Gaia, illus. 2014. (ENG.). 8p. pap. *(978-0-927244-79-4(9)*, Joy Cowley Club) Flying Start Bks.

—Miss Doll & Friends: Where Is Fire Engine? Bordicchia, Gaia, illus. 2014. (ENG.). 8p. pap. *(978-0-927244-57-2(8)*, Joy Cowley Club) Flying Start Bks.

—Mrs. Wishy-Washy's Tub. (Story Box Ser.). 8p. 20.95 *(978-0-7802-9365-6(7))* Wright Group/McGraw-Hill.

—Mrs. WishyWashy & the Big Wash. 2009. pap. 8.25 *(978-1-60559-235-0(8))* Hameray Publishing Group, Inc.
—Mrs. WishyWashy & the Big Wash Big Book. 2010. 48.25 *(978-1-60559-247-3(1))* Hameray Publishing Group, Inc.
—Smarty Pants at the Circus Big Book. 2010. 48.25 *(978-1-60559-249-7(8))* Hameray Publishing Group, Inc.
—Space Aliens in Our School. Ming, Choo Hill, illus. 2004. (ENG.). 8p. (J). (gr. 1-1). pap. 4.67 *(978-1-56270-755-2(8),* Dominie Elementary) Savvas Learning Co.
Cox, Katherine. The Missing Fox. 2015. (Scholastic Reader Level 2 Ser.). lib. bdg. 13.55 *(978-0-606-37748-5(4))* Turtleback.
The Craft Stick Project: Fourth Grade Guided Comprehension Level L. (On Our Way to English Ser.). (gr. 4-18). 34.50 *(978-0-7578-7152-8(6))* Rigby Education.
Crawford, Georgina. Archie-Parchie-Piddley-Poo. 2009. (Illus.). 24p. pap. 12.99 *(978-1-4389-7307-4(1))* AuthorHouse.
Crebbin, June. A Cat for Tom. 2005. (ENG.). 32p. pap. 10.00 *(978-0-521-67471-3(9))* Cambridge Univ. Pr.
—Collins Big Cat Phonics for Letters & Sounds - Jump on, Jump off!: Band 04/Blue, Bd. 4. Peluso, Martina, illus. 2018. (Collins Big Cat Phonics Ser.). (ENG.). 16p. (J). (gr. k-1). pap. 7.99 *(978-0-00-825160-4(6))* HarperCollins Pubs. Ltd. GBR. Dist: Independent Pubs. Group.
Crebbin, June, et al. Spike & the Concert. 2005. (Cambridge Reading Ser.). pap. *(978-5-7107-6036-9(6))* Cambridge Univ. Pr.
Cregan, Elizabeth R. C. All about Mitosis & Meiosis, 1 vol. rev. ed. 2007. (Science: Informational Text Ser.). (ENG.). 32p. (gr. 3-6). pap. 12.99 *(978-0-7439-0585-5(7))* Teacher Created Materials, Inc.
—Investigating Electromagnetism, 1 vol. rev. ed. 2007. (Science: Informational Text Ser.). (ENG.). 32p. (gr. 3-6). pap. 12.99 *(978-0-7439-0575-6(X))* Teacher Created Materials, Inc.
—Investigating the Chemistry of Atoms, 1 vol. rev. ed. 2007. (Science: Informational Text Ser.). (ENG.). 32p. (gr. 3-6). pap. 12.99 *(978-0-7439-0569-5(5))* Teacher Created Materials, Inc.
—Pioneers in Cell Biology, 1 vol. rev. ed. 2007. (Science: Informational Text Ser.). (ENG.). 32p. (gr. 3-6). pap. 12.99 *(978-0-7439-0586-2(5))* Teacher Created Materials, Inc.
Crime Solvers. 2017. (Crime Solvers Ser.). 48p. (gr. 6-6). pap. 84.30 *(978-1-5382-0611-9(0))* Stevens, Gareth Publishing LLLP.
Crocodile Tears. (Sails Literacy Ser.). 24p. (gr. k-18). 8.00 *(978-0-7635-7034-7(6))* Rigby Education.
Crocodile's Bag: Level J, 6 vols. 128p. (gr. 2-3). 41.95 *(978-0-7699-0992-9(2))* Shortland Pubns. (U. S. A.) Inc.
Croft, Andy. David Beckham. 3rd rev. ed. 2005. (ENG., Illus.). 32p. pap. *(978-0-340-90072-7(5))* Cambridge Univ. Pr.
Cronick, Mitch. In the Garden. 2005. (Big Cat Ser.). (gr. k-2). pap. 6.50 *(978-1-60457-007-6(5))* Pacific Learning, Inc.
—In the Garden: Band 01A/Pink a (Collins Big Cat) Sharp, Melanie, illus. 2005. (Collins Big Cat Ser.). (ENG.). 192p. (J). (gr. -1-k). pap. 6.99 *(978-0-00-718538-2(3))* HarperCollins Pubs. Ltd. GBR. Dist: Independent Pubs. Group.
Cronin, Doreen. Click, Clack, Moo. Lewin, Betsy, illus. 2018. 30p. (J). (gr. 1-4). 13.89 *(978-1-64310-126-2(9))* Penworthy Co., LLC, The.
—Click, Clack, Moo: Cows That Type. Lewin, Betsy, illus. 2016. (J). *(978-0-605-96664-2(8),* Simon Spotlight) Simon Spotlight.
—Click, Clack, Moo/Ready-To-Read Level 2: Cows That Type. Lewin, Betsy, illus. 2016. (Click Clack Book Ser.). (ENG.). 32p. (J). (gr. k-2). pap. 4.99 *(978-1-4814-6540-3(6),* Simon Spotlight) Simon Spotlight.
—Giggle, Giggle, Quack. Lewin, Betsy, illus. 2018. 30p. (J). (gr. 1-4). 13.89 *(978-1-64310-125-5(0))* Penworthy Co., LLC, The.
—Giggle, Giggle, Quack. 2016. (Simon & Schuster Ready-To-Read Level 2 Ser.). lib. bdg. 13.55 *(978-0-606-39752-0(3))* Turtleback.
Crops. (Guided Reading Levels Ser.). 28.56 *(978-0-7362-1061-4(X))* CENGAGE Learning.
Cross, Gillian. Brother Aelred's Feet: Band 15/Emerald (Collins Big Cat) Stevens, Tim, illus. 2007. (Collins Big Cat Ser.). (ENG.). 40p. (J). (gr. 3-4). pap. 11.99 *(978-0-00-723093-8(1))* HarperCollins Pubs. Ltd. GBR. Dist: Independent Pubs. Group.
—Sam Sorts It Out. Mier, Colin, illus. 2005. (ENG.). 24p. (J). lib. bdg. 23.65 *(978-1-59646-702-6(9))* Dingles & Co.
Crossley-Holland, Kevin. Storm (Reading Ladder Level 3) Marks, Alan, illus. 2nd ed. 2016. (Reading Ladder Level 3 Ser.). (ENG.). 48p. (gr. k-2). 4.99 *(978-1-4052-8236-9(3),* Reading Ladder) Farshore GBR. Dist: HarperCollins Pubs.
Crowe, Sharon. Daniel & the Big Belly Button. 2009. 23p. (J). pap. 17.95 *(978-1-4327-1549-6(6))* Outskirts Pr., Inc.
Crum, Anna-Maria. Trackers of Dynamic Earth: Set Of 6. 2011. (Navigators Ser.). (J). pap. 48.00 net. *(978-1-4108-0441-9(0))* Benchmark Education Co.
Crummel, Susan Stevens. Tumbleweed Stew/Sopa de Matojos: Bilingual English & Spanish. Stevens, Janet, illus. 2009. (Green Light Readers Ser.). (ENG.). 36p. (J). (gr. -1-3). pap. 5.99 *(978-0-547-25261-2(7),* 1271215, Clarion Bks.) HarperCollins Pubs.
Cullimore, Stan. Alien Swap. Schon, Nick, illus. 2005. (ENG.). 24p. (J). lib. bdg. 23.65 *(978-1-59646-744-6(4))* Dingles & Co.
Cumpiano, Ina. Avenues C (Leveled Books): What a Week! 2003. (Rise & Shine Ser.). (ENG.). (C). pap. 15.95 *(978-0-7362-1906-8(4))* CENGAGE Learning.
Cundy, David. Animals Spell Love. Cundy, David, illus. 2016. (ENG., Illus.). 40p. 15.95 *(978-1-56792-586-9(3))* Godine, David R. Pub.
Curious George Builds a Tree House (Reader Level 2) 2017. (Curious George Ser.). (ENG., Illus.). 24p. (J). (gr. -1-3). pap. 4.99 *(978-0-544-86704-8(1),* 1648560, Clarion Bks.) HarperCollins Pubs.
Curious George Builds an Igloo (Reader Level 2), 1 vol. 2013. (Curious George TV Ser.). (ENG., Illus.). 24p. (J). (gr. -1-3). pap. 4.99 *(978-0-544-09666-0(5),* 0a90920f-82c9-45bd-9f3e-96cc49159a36, Clarion Bks.) HarperCollins Pubs.
Curious George Curious about Phonics 12 Book Set. 2008. (Curious George Ser.). (ENG., Illus.). 192p. (J). (gr. -1-3). pap. 14.99 *(978-0-618-95670-8(0),* 1021380, Clarion Bks.) HarperCollins Pubs.
Curious George Race Day (Reader Level 1) 2010. (Curious George TV Ser.). (ENG., Illus.). 24p. (J). (gr. -1-3). pap. 4.99 *(978-0-547-39361-2(X),* 1426984, Clarion Bks.) HarperCollins Pubs.
Curious George Takes a Trip (Reader Level 1) 2007. (Curious George TV Ser.). (ENG., Illus.). 24p. (J). (gr. -1-3). pap. 4.99 *(978-0-618-88403-2(3),* 491698, Clarion Bks.) HarperCollins Pubs.
Currie, Robin. Tuktuk: un Cuento Sobre la Tundra. Saroff, Phyllis, illus. 2016. (SPA.). 32p. (J). (gr. k-1). pap. 11.95 *(978-1-62855-881-4(4),* 2725d00e-b868-4d78-a464-ad4a5ecafa4c) Arbordale Publishing.
Cushing, Christopher. Let's Celebrate!, 1 vol. 2012. (InfoMax Readers Ser.). (ENG., Illus.). 16p. (J). (gr. k-k). pap. 7.00 *(978-1-4488-8962-4(6),* 3f166bb0-9a73-4b8e-bf9a-d0e13a576f6c, Rosen Classroom) Rosen Publishing Group, Inc., The.
Custureri, Mary. Happy Anderson & Connie Clam. Folmsbee, Patricia, illus. 2006. 36p. (J). spiral bd. 24.95 *(978-1-933190-00-6(0))* HighPoint Publishing, Inc.
Cutteridge, J. O. Nelson's West Indian Readers First Primer, Vol. 1. 2014. (ENG., Illus.). 32p. spiral bd. 6.99 *(978-0-17-566001-8(8))* Oxford Univ. Pr., Inc.
Cutting, Robert. Falling Star. Ng, Drew, illus. 2007. 48p. (J). lib. bdg. 23.08 *(978-1-4242-1625-3(7))* Fitzgerald Bks.
—Mars Colony. Jeevan, Dhamindra, illus. 2007. 48p. (J). lib. bdg. 23.08 *(978-1-4242-1630-7(3))* Fitzgerald Bks.
—The 10 Most Revolutionary Inventions. 2007. (J). 14.99 *(978-1-55448-460-7(X))* Scholastic Library Publishing.
Cuxart, Bernardette, illus. Cuentame un Cuento, No. 4. (SPA.). 96p. (J). (gr. k-3). *(978-84-480-1602-9(5),* TM8095) Timun Mas, Editorial S.A. ESP. Dist: Lectorum Pubns., Inc.
Da Guia, Higina. Pajamas O Pijam. 2008. 32p. pap. 18.95 *(978-1-4327-2055-1(4))* Outskirts Pr., Inc.
Da Silva, Rosa. The 10 Most Uncontrollable Functions of the Body. 2008. (J). 14.99 *(978-1-55448-531-4(2))* Scholastic Library Publishing.
Dad & I, Vol. 3. (Early Intervention Levels Ser.). 3.85 *(978-1-56334-977-5(9))* CENGAGE Learning.
Dal Fuoco, Gina. Spaceship Earth, 1 vol. rev. ed. 2007. (Science: Informational Text Ser.). (ENG., Illus.). 32p. (gr. 4-6). pap. 12.99 *(978-0-7439-0565-7(2))* Teacher Created Materials, Inc.
Dale, Elizabeth. Bad Dog & No, Nell, No! Seal, Julia, illus. 2019. (Early Bird Readers — Pink (Early Bird Stories (tm)) Ser.). (ENG.). 32p. (J). (gr. -1-2). pap. 9.99 *(978-1-5415-4619-6(9),* ebbc5649-3428-4764-8d26-d14ecf3b7e00) Lerner Publishing Group.
—Izzy! Wizzy! Forshaw, Louise, illus. 2019. (Early Bird Readers — Yellow (Early Bird Stories (tm)) Ser.). (ENG.). 32p. (J). (gr. -1-2). 30.65 *(978-1-5415-4168-9(5),* 2354fe56-b64a-4c1d-b804-7c3af26990dc, Lerner Pubns.) Lerner Publishing Group.
—My Secret Alien. 2nd ed. 2016. (Reading Ladder Level 2 Ser.). (ENG., Illus.). 48p. (gr. k-2). pap. 4.99 *(978-1-4052-8231-4(2),* Reading Ladder) Farshore GBR. Dist: HarperCollins Pubs.
—Sam the Star & Clown Fun! Wood, Hannah, illus. 2019. (Early Bird Readers — Red (Early Bird Stories (tm)) Ser.). (ENG.). 32p. (J). (gr. -1-2). pap. 9.99 *(978-1-5415-4627-1(X),* 33a7be46-ce26-4765-9918-0363c46e587d) Lerner Publishing Group.
Dale, Jay. Baby Dinosaur Can Play. East, Jacqueline, illus. 2012. (Engage Literacy Red Ser.). (ENG.). 16p. (J). (gr. k-2). pap. 36.94 *(978-1-4296-8937-3(4),* 18364); pap. 6.99 *(978-1-4296-8936-6(6),* 119973) Capstone. (Capstone Pr.).
—Baby Dinosaur Is Hiding. East, Jacqueline, illus. 2012. (Engage Literacy Yellow Ser.). (ENG.). 16p. (J). (gr. k-2). pap. 36.94 *(978-1-4296-8953-3(6),* 18373); pap. 6.99 *(978-1-4296-8952-6(8),* 119981) Capstone. (Capstone Pr.).
—Baby Dinosaur Is Lost. East, Jacqueline, illus. 2012. (Engage Literacy Blue Ser.). (ENG.). 16p. (J). (gr. k-2). pap. 36.94 *(978-1-4296-8973-1(0),* 18382); pap. 6.99 *(978-1-4296-8972-4(2),* 119991) Capstone. (Capstone Pr.).
—Bananas in My Tummy. Hancock, Anna, illus. 2012. (Engage Literacy Yellow Ser.). (ENG.). 16p. (J). (gr. k-2). pap. 36.94 *(978-1-4296-8843-7(2),* 18315); pap. 6.99 *(978-1-4296-8835-2(1),* 119891) Capstone. (Capstone Pr.).
—Big Balloon. 2012. (Engage Literacy Yellow Ser.). (ENG.). 16p. (J). (gr. k-2). pap. 36.94 *(978-1-4296-8963-2(3),* 18378); (Illus.). pap. 6.99 *(978-1-4296-8962-5(5),* 119986) Capstone. (Capstone Pr.).
—Big Green Crocodile, 1 vol. Hancock, Anna, illus. 2012. (Engage Literacy Blue Ser.). (ENG.). 16p. (J). (gr. k-2). pap. 6.99 *(978-1-4296-8984-7(6),* 119997, Capstone Pr.) Capstone.
—Bob Is in the Garden. Draycott, Michelle, illus. 2012. (Wonder Words Ser.). (ENG.). 16p. (J). (gr. k-2). pap. 36.94 *(978-1-4296-8889-5(0),* 18340, Capstone Pr.) Capstone.
—Can You See It? Ball, Natalie, illus. 2012. (Engage Literacy Yellow Ser.). (ENG.). 16p. (J). (gr. k-2). pap. 36.94 *(978-1-4296-8955-7(2),* 18374); pap. 6.99 *(978-1-4296-8954-0(4),* 119982) Capstone. (Capstone Pr.).
—I Can Help My Grandma. 2015. (Engage Literacy Magenta - Extension A Ser.). (ENG.). 16p. (J). (gr. k-2). pap. 6.99 *(978-1-4914-8639-9(2),* 131246) Capstone.
—In My Car. 2012. (Engage Literacy Magenta Ser.). (ENG.). 16p. (J). (gr. k-2). pap. 36.94 *(978-1-4296-8851-2(3),* 18321); (Illus.). pap. 6.99 *(978-1-4296-8850-5(5),* 119928) Capstone. (Capstone Pr.).
—Lazy Old Pirates. Diggory, Nick, illus. 2012. (Wonder Words Ser.). (ENG.). 16p. (J). (gr. k-2). pap. 36.94 *(978-1-4296-8931-1(5),* 18361, Capstone Pr.) Capstone.
—Lea Is Hungry. Gulliver, Amanda, illus. 2012. (Engage Literacy Red Ser.). (ENG.). 16p. (J). (gr. k-2). pap. 36.94 *(978-1-4296-8841-3(6),* 18309); pap. 6.99 *(978-1-4296-8833-8(5),* 119889) Capstone. (Capstone Pr.).
—Lea's Birthday. Gulliver, Amanda, illus. 2012. (Engage Literacy Yellow Ser.). (ENG.). 16p. (J). (gr. k-2). pap. 36.94 *(978-1-4296-8965-6(X),* 18379); pap. 6.99 *(978-1-4296-8964-9(1),* 119987) Capstone. (Capstone Pr.).
—Little Sam. Jackson, Katy, illus. 2012. (Wonder Words Ser.). (ENG.). 16p. (J). (gr. k-2). pap. 36.94 *(978-1-4296-8901-4(3),* 18346, Capstone Pr.) Capstone.
—Look at the Animals. Fleming, Garry, illus. 2012. (Engage Literacy Magenta Ser.). (ENG.). 16p. (J). (gr. k-2). pap. 36.94 *(978-1-4296-8881-9(5),* 18336); pap. 6.99 *(978-1-4296-8880-2(7),* 119943) Capstone. (Capstone Pr.).
—The Monkey & the Bug. Hancock, Anna, illus. 2015. (Engage Literacy Magenta - Extension A Ser.). (ENG.). 16p. (J). (gr. k-2). pap. 6.99 *(978-1-4914-8634-4(1),* 131240) Capstone.
—My Little Toys. 2012. (Engage Literacy Magenta Ser.). (ENG.). 16p. (J). (gr. k-2). pap. 36.94 *(978-1-4296-8877-2(7),* 18334); pap. 6.99 *(978-1-4296-8876-5(9),* 119941) Capstone. (Capstone Pr.).
—My Pets. Richards, Kirsten, illus. 2012. (Wonder Words Ser.). (ENG.). 16p. (J). (gr. k-2). pap. 36.94 *(978-1-4296-8887-1(4),* 18339, Capstone Pr.) Capstone.
—Wonder Words. Gulliver, Amanda, illus. 2012. (Wonder Words Ser.). (ENG.). 16p. (J). (gr. k-2). pap., pap., pap. 137.77 *(978-1-4296-9575-6(7),* 18803, Capstone Pr.) Capstone.
—Wonder Words Classroom Collection. Gulliver, Amanda, illus. 2012. (Wonder Words Ser.). (ENG.). 16p. (J). (gr. k-2). pap., pap. 785.35 *(978-1-4296-9576-3(5),* 18804, Capstone Pr.) Capstone.
Dale, Jay & Scott, Kay. Lazy Old Pirates, 1 vol. Diggory, Nick, illus. 2012. (Wonder Words Ser.). (ENG.). 16p. (J). (gr. k-2). pap. 6.99 *(978-1-4296-8930-4(7),* 119970, Capstone Pr.) Capstone.
—Little Sam, 1 vol. Jackson, Katy, illus. 2012. (Wonder Words Ser.). (ENG.). 16p. (J). (gr. k-2). pap. 6.99 *(978-1-4296-8900-7(5),* 119953, Capstone Pr.) Capstone.
—My Pets, 1 vol. Richards, Kirsten, illus. 2012. (Wonder Words Ser.). (ENG.). 16p. (J). (gr. k-2). pap. 6.99 *(978-1-4296-8886-4(6),* 119946, Capstone Pr.) Capstone.
Dale, Katie. Collins Big Cat Phonics for Letters & Sounds - Watch Out, Nebit!: Band 06/Orange, Bd. 6. Zolotic, Aleksandar, illus. 2018. (Collins Big Cat Phonics Ser.). (ENG.). 24p. (J). (gr. 1-2). pap. 6.99 *(978-0-00-825172-7(X))* HarperCollins Pubs. Ltd. GBR. Dist: Independent Pubs. Group.
—Little Women: Band 18/Pearl (Collins Big Cat) Selivanova, Elena, illus. 2016. (Collins Big Cat Ser.). (ENG.). 80p. (J). pap. 11.99 *(978-0-00-814737-2(X))* HarperCollins Pubs. Ltd. GBR. Dist: Independent Pubs. Group.
Dalton, Annie. Lilac Peabody & Charlie Chase, No. 3. Griff, illus. 2009. (ENG.). 96p. pap. 5.99 *(978-0-00-713773-2(7),* HarperCollins Children's Bks.) HarperCollins Pubs. Ltd. GBR. Dist: HarperCollins Pubs.
—Lilac Peabody & Honeysuckle Hope, No. 4. Griff, illus. 2009. (ENG.). 96p. (gr. 2-4). pap. 5.99 *(978-0-00-713774-9(5),* HarperCollins Children's Bks.) HarperCollins Pubs. Ltd. GBR. Dist: HarperCollins Pubs.
Daniel, Claire. A Winning Attitude. Winborn, Marsha, illus. 2007. 14p. pap. 4.75 *(978-0-15-377381-5(2))* Harcourt Schl. Pubs.
Daronco, Mickey & Ohanesian, Diane. Am I in It? Set Of 6. 2nd rev. ed. 2011. (BuildUp Ser.). (J). pap. 27.00 net. *(978-1-4108-0736-6(3))* Benchmark Education Co.
—The Big Band: Set Of 6. 2nd rev. ed. 2004. (BuildUp Ser.). (J). 27.00 net. *(978-1-4108-1525-5(0))* Benchmark Education Co.
—Look at Me Now! Set Of 6. 2nd rev. ed. 2004. (BuildUp Ser.). (J). pap. 27.00 net. *(978-1-4108-1528-6(5))* Benchmark Education Co.
—A Lot to Sell: Set Of 6. 2nd rev. ed. 2004. (BuildUp Ser.). (J). pap. 27.00 net. *(978-1-4108-1524-8(2))* Benchmark Education Co.
—My Big Day: Set Of 6. 2nd rev. ed. 2004. (BuildUp Ser.). (J). pap. 27.00 net. *(978-1-4108-1532-3(3))* Benchmark Education Co.
—On a Cold Day: Set Of 6. 2nd rev. ed. 2004. (BuildUp Ser.). (J). pap. 27.00 net. *(978-1-4108-1529-3(3))* Benchmark Education Co.
—Play this Game with Me. 2nd rev. ed. 2003. (BuildUp Ser.). (J). pap. 22.00 *(978-1-4108-0759-5(2))* Benchmark Education Co.
—What Might I Spy? Set Of 6. 2nd rev. ed. 2004. (BuildUp Ser.). (J). pap. 27.00 net. *(978-1-4108-1536-1(6))* Benchmark Education Co.
—Will It Float? Set Of 6. 2nd rev. ed. 2004. (BuildUp Ser.). (J). pap. 27.00 net. *(978-1-4108-1531-6(5))* Benchmark Education Co.
Dase, Pam & Dugan, Christine. Hurricane Hunters. rev. ed. 2012. (Mathematics in the Real World Ser.). (ENG.). 32p. (gr. 5-8). pap. 11.99 *(978-1-4333-3462-7(3))* Teacher Created Materials, Inc.
—Tornado Chasers. rev. ed. 2012. (Mathematics in the Real World Ser.). (ENG.). 32p. (gr. 5-8). pap. 11.99 *(978-1-4333-3463-4(1))* Teacher Created Materials, Inc.
David, Jack. F-14 Tomcats. 2008. (Torque Ser.). (ENG.). 24p. (J). (gr. 3-7). 20.00 *(978-0-531-21643-9(8),* Children's Pr.) Scholastic Library Publishing.
—F-15 Eagles. 2008. (Torque Ser.). (ENG.). 24p. (J). (gr. 3-7). 20.00 *(978-0-531-21644-6(6),* Children's Pr.) Scholastic Library Publishing.
Davidson, Susanna. The Musicians of Bremen. Gordon, Mike & Gordon, Carl, illus. 2007. (Usborne First Reading: Level 3 Ser.). 48p. (J). 8.99 *(978-0-7945-1911-7(3),* Usborne) EDC Publishing.
—The Story of Hanukkah. 2007. (Young Reading Series 1 Gift Bks). 48p. (J). 8.99 *(978-0-7945-1781-6(1),* Usborne) EDC Publishing.
Davies, Beth. Batman's Missions. 2015. (DK Reader Level 3 Ser.). lib. bdg. 13.55 *(978-0-606-36692-2(X))* Turtleback.
Davies, Caroline & Martin, Sharon. Y Frech Goch. 2005. (WEL., Illus.). 12p. pap. *(978-1-86101-079-7(6))* Acen Limited.
Davies, Gill & Freeman, Tina. Friend for Flash. 2004. (Tales from Yellow Barn Farm Ser.). (Illus.). 24p. (J). 3.99 *(978-1-85854-324-6(X))* Brimax Books Ltd. GBR. Dist: Byeway Bks.
Davies, Monika. Surprising Things We Do for Beauty (Grade 8) 2nd rev. ed. 2017. (TIME(r): Informational Text Ser.). (ENG., Illus.). 64p. (J). (gr. 7-8). pap. 13.99 *(978-1-4938-3636-9(6))* Teacher Created Materials, Inc.
Davis, Ashley. The Big Storm, 1 vol. 2006. (Neighborhood Readers Ser.). (ENG.). 16p. (gr. 1-2). pap. 6.50 *(978-1-4042-7192-0(9),* acd57e4e-3518-4d62-8b03-069c49727692, Rosen Classroom) Rosen Publishing Group, Inc., The.
Davis, Cathy Mackey. Lucky el Perro de la Estación de Bomberos. rev. ed. 2007. (Reader's Theater Ser.). (SPA.). 20p. (J). (gr. 1-2). 7.99 *(978-1-4333-0016-5(8))* Teacher Created Materials, Inc.
Davis, Deneena. The 10 Most Essential Natural Resources. 2008. 14.99 *(978-1-55448-549-9(5))* Scholastic Library Publishing.
Davis, Helen J. Good Times with Gregory: Birds: Rescuing a Baby Bird. Davis, Robyn L., illus. 2008. (Good Times with Gregory Ser.). 54p. (J). (gr. -1-4). 12.95 *(978-1-935122-10-4(X))* K&B Products.
Davis, Jim. Garfield y el Deporte. (SPA.). 96p. (J). 9.95 *(978-84-7419-470-8(9),* AU003) Grijalbo Mondadori, S.A.-Junior ESP. Dist: Continental Bk. Co., Inc.
Davis, Mackey Cathy. Postal Workers Then & Now, 1 vol. rev. ed. 2006. (Social Studies: Informational Text Ser.). (ENG.). 32p. (gr. 2-3). pap. 11.99 *(978-0-7439-9381-4(0))* Teacher Created Materials, Inc.
Dawson, Eugene T. Little Valerie Wants to Grow Taller. 2009. 24p. pap. 14.95 *(978-1-4389-7002-8(1))* AuthorHouse.
The Day: Individual Title Six-Packs. (Sails Literacy Ser.). 16p. (gr. k-18). 27.00 *(978-0-7635-4390-7(X))* Rigby Education.
Day & Night. (J). pap. 13.15 *(978-0-8136-4306-9(6))* Modern Curriculum Pr.
The Day of the Dead, 6 packs. (Greetings Ser.: Vol. 1). Tr. of El Dia La Noche. 24p. (gr. 2-3). 31.00 *(978-0-7635-9411-4(3))* Rigby Education.
The Day the Class Chameleon Disappeared: Word Study: Prefixes dis-, un-, ex-, re-, Level B. 2003. ("Plaid" Phonics & Stories Libraries). (gr. 2-3). 38.50 *(978-0-8136-9154-1(0))* Modern Curriculum Pr.
Daynes, Katie. Chocolate. Larkum, Adam, illus. 2004. 48p. (J). (gr. 2-18). pap. 5.95 *(978-0-7945-0759-6(X),* Usborne) EDC Publishing.
De Maupassant, Guy. Mon Oncle Jules et Autres Nouvelles, Level D. (FRE., Illus.). (YA). (gr. 7-12). 9.95 *(978-0-88436-044-5(X),* 40281) EMC/Paradigm Publishing.
Dean, James, illus. Sir Pete the Brave. 2016. 32p. (J). *(978-1-5182-0881-2(9))* Harper & Row Ltd.
Dean, James & Dean, Kimberly. Pete the Cat 12-Book Phonics Fun! Includes 12 Mini-Books Featuring Short & Long Vowel Sounds. Dean, James, illus. 2017. (My First I Can Read Ser.). (ENG., Illus.). 144p. (J). (gr. -1-3). pap. 15.99 *(978-0-06-240452-7(0),* HarperCollins) HarperCollins Pubs.
—Pete the Cat & the Surprise Teacher. Dean, James, illus. 2017. (My First I Can Read Ser.). (ENG., Illus.). 32p. (J). (gr. -1-3). 4.99 *(978-0-06-240428-2(8),* HarperCollins) HarperCollins Pubs.
DeAnda, Diane. The Monster in the Mattress & Other Stories: El Monstruo en el Colchón y Otros Cuentos. 2011. (SPA & ENG., Illus.). 90p. (J). (gr. 3-7). pap. 9.95 *(978-1-55885-693-6(5),* Piñata Books) Arte Publico Pr.
Dear Bess, Vol. 6. (Early Intervention Levels Ser.). 3.55 *(978-0-7362-0172-8(6))* CENGAGE Learning.
Defoe, Daniel. Robinson Crusoe Level 4 Intermediate Book with CD-ROM & Audio CD, 1 vol. 2009. (ENG.). 96p. pap. 13.00 incl. cd-rom, audio compact disk *(978-84-8323-550-8(1))* Cambridge Univ. Pr.
DefoeDaniel. Robinson Crusoe: Paperback Student Book Without Answers. 2009. (Cambridge Experience Readers Ser.). (ENG.). 96p. pap. 14.75 *(978-84-8323-553-9(6))* Cambridge Univ. Pr.
Deighton, Jo, adapted by. Ali Baba & the Forty Thieves: Traditional Stories:Cinderella: The Elves & the Shoemaker. (Scheherezade Presents Ser.: No. 11). (Illus.). 48p. (J). pap. *(978-1-85964-101-9(6),* Ithaca Pr.) Garnet Publishing, Ltd.
—Bacbouc the Lazy Tailor: Traditional Stories:Beauty & the Beast: The Red Shoes. (Scheherezade Presents Ser.: No. 12). (Illus.). 48p. (J). pap. *(978-1-85964-102-6(4),* Ithaca Pr.) Garnet Publishing, Ltd.
—Codadad & His Brothers: Traditional Stories:The Grocer, the Student & the Elf: The Ugly Duckling. (Scheherezade Presents Ser.: No. 13). (Illus.). 48p. (J). pap. *(978-1-85964-103-3(2),* Ithaca Pr.) Garnet Publishing, Ltd.
—The Fisherman & the Wicked Genie: Traditional Stories:The Shepherdess & the Chimney Sweep: Seven with One Blow. (Scheherezade Presents Ser.: No. 14). (Illus.). 48p. (J). pap. *(978-1-85964-104-0(0),* Ithaca Pr.) Garnet Publishing, Ltd.
Dellar, Hugh & Walkley, Andrew. Innovations Elementary-Workbook. 2005. (ENG.). 96p. (C). pap., wbk. ed. 18.95 *(978-1-4130-1271-2(X))* Cengage Heinle.
Delude, Kimberly. Freddie the Fly Motormouth: A Story about Learning to Listen, Vol. 1. Martin, Brian, illus. 2017. (Freddie the Fly Ser.). (ENG.). 31p. (J). (gr. k-5). pap. 10.95 *(978-1-944882-17-4(0))* Boys Town Pr.
The Dentist, 2 Packs. (Chiquilibros Ser.). (gr. -1-1). 12.00 *(978-0-7635-8545-7(9))* Rigby Education.
dePaola, Tomie. The Good Samaritan & Other Parables: Gift Edition. 2017. (ENG.). 32p. (J). (gr. 1-4). 18.99 *(978-0-8234-3888-4(0))* Holiday Hse., Inc.
—Strega Nona & Her Tomatoes. 2017. (Simon & Schuster Ready-To-Read Level 1 Ser.). lib. bdg. 13.55 *(978-0-606-40214-9(4))* Turtleback.
—Strega Nona & the Twins. 2017. (Simon & Schuster Ready-To-Read Level 1 Ser.). lib. bdg. 13.55 *(978-0-606-40215-6(2))* Turtleback.
Depken, Kristen L. Let's Plant a Garden! (Barbie) 2018. (Step into Reading Ser.). (ENG., Illus.). 24p. (J). (gr. -1-1). pap. 5.99 *(978-1-5247-6883-6(9),* Random Hse. Bks. for Young Readers) Random Hse. Children's Bks.
—Rubble's Big Wish. Moore, Harry, illus. 2017. 17p. (J). *(978-1-5182-3644-0(8))* Random Hse., Inc.
—Save the Rainbow! (Shimmer & Shine) Aikins, Dave, illus. 2018. (Step into Reading Ser.). (ENG.). 24p. (J). (gr. -1-1). pap. 5.99 *(978-0-525-57751-5(3));* lib. bdg. 12.99 *(978-0-525-57752-2(1))* Random Hse. Children's Bks. (Random Hse. Bks. for Young Readers).
Depree, Helen. Foundations: Upper Emergent - Upper Emergent - Complete Kit, Vol. 2. 2nd ed. (gr. 1-18). 423.95 *(978-0-322-04291-9(7))* Wright Group/McGraw-Hill.

P
Q
R

Derby, Katy. The 10 Most Daring Escapes. 2008. 14.99 *(978-1-55448-487-4(1))* Scholastic Library Publishing.

DeRidder, Mauritz. Journey to Callisto 3 Explorers. Stuart, Jon, illus. 2017. (Cambridge Reading Adventures Ser.). (ENG.). 40p. pap. 11.00 *(978-1-108-40581-2(9))* Cambridge Univ. Pr.

deRubertis, Barbara. Lana Llama's Little Lamb. Alley, R. W., illus. 2011. (Animal Antics A to Z Ser.). (ENG.). 32p. (J). lib. bdg. 22.60 *(978-1-57565-333-4(8))* Astra Publishing Hse.

—Maxwell Moose's Mountain Monster. Alley, R. W., illus. 2011. (Animal Antics A to Z Ser.). (ENG.). 32p. (J). lib. bdg. 22.60 *(978-1-57565-334-1(6))* Astra Publishing Hse.

—Nina Nandu's Nervous Noggin. Alley, R. W.. illus. 2011. (Animal Antics A to Z Ser.). (ENG.). 32p. (J). lib. bdg. 22.60 *(978-1-57565-335-8(4))* Astra Publishing Hse.

deRubertis, Barbara & Roser, Nancy. Let's Read Together: Resource Guide. 2005. (Let's Read Together Ser.). (Illus.). 56p. pap. 12.95 *(978-1-57565-139-2(4))* Astra Publishing Hse.

Dessen, Maci. Bedtime, 1 vol. 2016. (It's Time Ser.). (ENG.). 24p. (gr. 1-1). pap. 9.25 *(978-1-4994-2277-1(6),* 402fdf6a-17a0-481b-bfa2-af62d9bb44c6, PowerKids Pr.) Rosen Publishing Group, Inc., The.

Devera, Czeena. In My Backyard. 2019. (I Can See Ser.). (ENG.). 16p. (J). (gr. -1-2). pap. 11.36 *(978-1-5341-3917-6(6),* 212501, Cherry Blossom Press) Cherry Lake Publishing.

Dhami, Narinder. Monster under the Stairs. Spoor, Mike, illus. 2005. (ENG.). 24p. (J). lib. bdg. 23.65 *(978-1-59646-718-7(5))* Dingles & Co.

—Samosa Thief. Blundell, Tony, illus. 2005. (ENG.). 24p. (J). lib. bdg. 23.65 *(978-1-59646-708-8(8))* Dingles & Co.

Di-Nsteins, The Albert. No Reading Allowed. 2012. 32p. pap. *(978-1-77093-477-1(4))* Flowerpot Children's Pr. Inc.

Diamond, Claudia. Children of Ancient Greece. 2006. (Rosen Real Readers Big Bookstm Ser.). (ENG.). 16p. (gr. 2-3). 37.95 *(978-1-4042-6223-2(7))* Rosen Publishing Group, Inc., The.

Díaz, Alberto. Mis Primeras Palabras/My First Words. 2018. (ENG & SPA.). 26p. (J). (gr. k-k). bds. 23.99 *(978-84-698-3624-8(2))* Grupo Anaya, S.A. ESP. Dist: Lectorum Pubns., Inc.

Diaz, Alexandra. El único Destino (the Only Road) 2016. (SPA., Illus.). (J). (gr. 3-7). 320p. 18.99 *(978-1-4814-8441-1(9))*; 336p. pap. 8.99 *(978-1-4814-8442-8(7))* Simon & Schuster/Paula Wiseman Bks. (Simon & Schuster/Paula Wiseman Bks.).

Dibble, Traci. Bats. 2010. (1-3Y Wild Animals Ser.). (ENG.). 16p. (J). (gr. k-2). pap. 9.60 *(978-1-61541-299-0(9))* American Reading Co.

—Brown Bears. Dibble, Traci, illus. 2012. (1-3Y Animals Ser.). (ENG., Illus.). 16p. (J). (gr. k-2). pap. 9.60 *(978-1-61541-375-1(8))* American Reading Co.

—Cobras. Dibble, Traci, illus. 2011. (1-3Y Wild Animals Ser.). (ENG., Illus.). 16p. (J). (gr. k-2). pap. 9.60 *(978-1-61541-367-6(7))* American Reading Co.

—How Animals Grow Up. 2014. (1-3Y Science Ser.). (ENG., Illus.). 24p. (J). pap. 9.60 *(978-1-64053-137-6(8),* ARC Pr. Bks.) American Reading Co.

Dibble, Traci & Washington, Joi. Wolves. Washington, Joi, illus. 2010. (1-3Y Animals Ser.). (ENG., Illus.). 16p. (J). (gr. k-2). pap. 9.60 *(978-1-61541-363-8(4))* American Reading Co.

Dibels. 2003. (Scott Foresman Reading Ser.). (gr. k-18). *(978-0-328-07800-4(X))*; (gr. k-18). *(978-0-328-07796-0(8))*; (gr. 1-18). *(978-0-328-07801-1(8))*; (gr. 1-18). *(978-0-328-07797-7(6))*; (gr. 2-18). *(978-0-328-07798-4(4))*; (gr. 3-18). *(978-0-328-07799-1(2))* Addison-Wesley Educational Pubs., Inc. (Scott Foresman).

Dickens, Charles. Oliver Twist. 2019. (ENG.). 386p. (J). 17.95 *(978-1-64594-005-0(5))* Athanatos Publishing Group.

—Oliver Twist. (ENG.). (J). 2019. 300p. pap. 20.08 *(978-0-368-26130-5(1))* 2017. (Illus.). 34.99 *(978-1-366-55962-3(2))* Blurb, Inc.

—Oliver Twist. (ENG.). (J). 2019. 476p. pap. 19.89 *(978-1-7275-1067-6(4))* 2018. 242p. pap. 9.99 *(978-1-9780-6381-5(4))* CreateSpace Independent Publishing Platform.

—Oliver Twist. 2015. (ENG., Illus.). (gr. 4-17). (YA). 32.95 *(978-1-344-93563-0(X))*; 726p. (J). 33.95 *(978-1-340-45596-5(X))* Creative Media Partners, LLC.

—Oliver Twist. 2018. (ENG.). 316p. (J). pap. *(978-1-989201-35-0(0))* East India Publishing Co.

—Oliver Twist. 2015. (MAL., Illus.). (J). pap. 18.00 *(978-81-8423-396-4(5))* Greatest Books Pub.

—Oliver Twist. (ENG.). (J). 2020. 556p. (gr. 3-7). pap. 18.79 *(978-1-6555-2146-1(2))* 2019. 716p. (gr. 3-7). pap. 27.99 *(978-1-7018-9021-3(6))* 2019. 444p. pap. 29.99 *(978-1-0893-4087-4(7))* 2019. 534p. pap. 30.99 *(978-1-0988-6823-9(4))* 2018. (Illus.). 332p. pap. 13.40 *(978-1-7909-6873-2(9))* 2018. (Illus.). 332p. pap. 13.40 *(978-1-7908-8297-7(4))* 2018. (Illus.). 332p. pap. 13.40 *(978-1-7907-2249-5(7))* 2018. (Illus.). 470p. pap. 20.33 *(978-1-7268-6440-4(5))* 2018. (Illus.). 470p. pap. 20.33 *(978-1-7268-6441-1(3))* Independently Published.

—Oliver Twist. 2019. (ENG.). 390p. (J). *(978-3-7340-5875-2(9))*; pap. *(978-3-7340-5874-5(0))* Outlook Verlagsgesellschaft mbH.

—Oliver Twist. 2018. (Illus.). 416p. (J). (gr. 5). 16.99 *(978-0-241-33126-2(9))* Penguin Bks., Ltd. GBR. Dist: Independent Pubs. Group.

—Oliver Twist. 2015. (ENG.). 466p. (J). (gr. 3-7). pap. *(978-81-291-2456-2(4))* Rupa & Co.

—Oliver Twist. (ENG., 2018. Illus.). 556p. (J). 36.34 *(978-1-7317-0542-6(5))* 2018. (Illus.). 556p. (J). pap. 24.26 *(978-1-7317-0543-3(3))* 2018. 556p. (J). 19.19 *(978-1-7317-0130-5(6))* 2018. (Illus.). 556p. (J). pap. 12.40 *(978-1-7317-0131-2(4))* 2011. (Illus.). (YA). (gr. 4-17). 22.99 *(978-1-61382-738-3(5))* Simon & Brown.

Dickens, Charles, creator. Oliver Twist. 2020. (ENG.). (J). (gr. 3-7). 322p. pap. *(978-0-461-22637-9(5))*; 680p. pap. *(978-0-461-66307-5(4))*; 468p. pap. *(978-0-371-67750-6(5))*; 342p. pap. *(978-0-371-66289-2(3))* HardPr.

Dickinson, Tom. Bob's Secret Hideaway: Band 03/Yellow. 2014. (Collins Big Cat Ser.). (ENG., Illus.). 32p. (J). (gr. k-1). pap. 7.99 *(978-0-00-753850-8(2))* HarperCollins Pubs. Ltd. GBR. Dist: Independent Pubs. Group.

Dickmann, Nancy. ¡Mira Cómo Crece!, 11 vols., Set. Incl. Vida de la Manzana. (Illus.). pap. 6.29 *(978-1-4329-5286-0(2),* 116011); Vida Del Girasol. pap. 6.29 *(978-1-4329-5289-1(7),* 116015); (J). (gr. -1-1). (¡Mira Cómo Crece! Ser.). (SPA.). 24p. 2011. pap., pap., pap. 37.74 o.p. *(978-1-4329-5293-8(5),* 16375); 116.60 o.p. *(978-1-4329-5281-5(1),* 16374) Capstone. (Heinemann).

Dickson, Sue. Sing, Spell, Read & Write: All Aboard. rev. ed. 2003. (ENG.). (J). (gr. k-k). pap., stu. ed. 12.95 *(978-0-7652-3211-3(1),* Modern Curriculum Pr.) Savvas Learning Co.

—Sing, Spell, Read & Write: On Track. rev. ed. 2003. (ENG.). (J). (gr. k-k). pap., stu. ed. 8.50 *(978-0-7652-3210-6(3),* Modern Curriculum Pr.) Savvas Learning Co.

Did You Hear? Fourth Grade Guided Comprehension Level N. (On Our Way to English Ser.). (gr. 4-18). 34.50 *(978-0-7578-7160-3(7))* Rigby Education.

Dietrich, Sean, illus. Hansel y Gretel: La Novela Grafica. 2010. (Graphic Spin en Español Ser.). (SPA.). 40p. (J). (gr. 3-6). pap. 5.95 *(978-1-4342-2271-8(3),* 103134); lib. bdg. 25.32 *(978-1-4342-1901-5(1),* 102360) Capstone. (Stone Arch Bks.).

DiGugno, Josh. I Heard That! 2017. (Text Connections Guided Close Reading Ser.). (J). (gr. 1). *(978-1-4900-1829-4(8))* Benchmark Education Co.

Dillon, Diane. I Can Be Anything! Don't Tell Me I Can't. Dillon, Diane, illus. 2018. (ENG., Illus.). 32p. (J). (gr. -1-3). 18.99 *(978-1-338-16690-3(5),* Blue Sky Pr., The) Scholastic, Inc.

Ding-a-lings & Flutterbys. (Sails Literacy Ser.). 24p. (gr. k-18). 8.00 *(978-0-7635-7033-0(8))* Rigby Education.

Dining with Prunella. (J). pap. 13.75 *(978-0-8136-4640-4(5))* Modern Curriculum Pr.

Dinosaur Detective: 6 Each of 1 Anthology, 6 vols. (Wildcats Ser.). 32p. (gr. 2-8). *(978-0-322-00586-0(8))* Wright Group/McGraw-Hill.

The dinosaur Hunt: Individual Title, 6 packs. (gr. 1-2). 22.00 *(978-0-7635-9185-4(8))* Rigby Education.

Discover America State by State (Set), 51 vols., Set. 2005. (Discover America State by State Ser.). (ENG., Illus.). (J). (gr. 1-3). 941.45 *(978-1-58536-294-3(8),* 202286) Sleeping Bear Pr.

Discovering Literature: The EMC Write-in Reader. 2nd ed. (Literature & the Language Arts Ser.). (J). (gr. 6-18). wbk. ed. 17.99 *(978-0-8219-2908-7(9))* EMC/Paradigm Publishing.

Disney. Big Hero 6 Step into Reading. 2014. (Step into Reading Level 3 Ser.). lib. bdg. 13.55 *(978-0-606-35996-2(6))* Turtleback.

Disney Book Group. Trapped in the Death Star! 2016. (Star Wars: World of Reading Ser.). (Illus.). 30p. (J). lib. bdg. 14.75 *(978-0-606-39174-0(6))* Turtleback.

Disney Book Group & Geron, Eric. Beauty & the Beast, Level 2: Something More. Disney Book Group, illus. 2017. (World of Reading Ser.). (ENG., Illus.). 32p. (J). (gr. 1-3). pap. 4.99 *(978-1-4847-8284-2(4))* Disney Pr.

Disney Books. World of Reading: Disney Bunnies: Thumper & the Egg-Level 1 Reader. 2018. (World of Reading Ser.). (ENG., Illus.). 32p. (J). (gr. -1-k). pap. 4.99 *(978-1-4847-9965-9(8),* Disney Press Books) Disney Publishing Worldwide.

—World of Reading: Disney Classic Characters Level 1 Boxed Set: Level 1, Set. 2017. (World of Reading Ser.). (ENG., Illus.). 192p. (J). (gr. 1-3). 12.99 *(978-1-4847-9921-5(6),* Disney Press Books) Disney Publishing Worldwide.

Disney Editors. Big Hero 6 Deluxe Step into Reading. 2014. (Step into Reading Level 3 Ser.). lib. bdg. 14.75 *(978-0-606-35997-9(4))* Turtleback.

—Ocean of Color. 2016. (Step into Reading - Level 1 Ser.). lib. bdg. 14.75 *(978-0-606-38890-0(7))* Turtleback.

—Pua & Heihei. 2017. (Disney Princess Step into Reading Ser.). (Illus.). 21p. (J). lib. bdg. 14.75 *(978-0-606-39854-1(6))* Turtleback.

Disney Press Editors. Callie Asks for Help. 2015. (World of Reading Ser.). (J). lib. bdg. 13.55 *(978-0-606-36897-1(3))* Turtleback.

—Cinderella. 2015. (World of Reading Ser.). (J). lib. bdg. 13.55 *(978-0-606-35918-4(4))* Turtleback.

—Ewoks Join the Fight. 2015. (Star Wars: World of Reading Ser.). (J). lib. bdg. 13.55 *(978-0-606-36912-1(0))* Turtleback.

—Lion Guard: Bunga the Wise. 2016. (World of Reading Ser.). (Illus.). 32p. (J). lib. bdg. 13.55 *(978-0-606-37539-9(2))* Turtleback.

—Sheriff Callie's Wild West: Peck's Trail Mix Mix-Up. 2015. (World of Reading Ser.). (J). lib. bdg. 13.55 *(978-0-606-35915-3(X))* Turtleback.

—Use the Force! 2015. (Star Wars: World of Reading Ser.). (J). lib. bdg. 13.55 *(978-0-606-35923-8(0))* Turtleback.

Disney Publishing Staff. Where Is Your Home?, 15 vols. 2003. (It's Fun to Learn Ser.). (Illus.). 32p. (J). (gr. -1-3). 3.99 *(978-1-57973-133-5(3))* Advance Pubs. LLC.

Disney's World of English. 2005. 899.00 incl. DVD *(978-1-59172-090-4(7))*; 899.00 incl. VHS *(978-1-59172-098-0(2))* Lexicon Marketing, LLC.

Dixon, Dale. Our School Play: Showing Events & Processes, 1 vol. 2017. (Computer Kids: Powered by Computational Thinking Ser.). (ENG.). 24p. (J). (gr. 4-5). 25.27 *(978-1-5383-2425-7(3),* e8c2df47-bc7a-4c7c-801c-ecb3366c20c3, PowerKids Pr.); pap. *(978-1-5383-5308-0(3),* 86a33e43-9e3c-4626-98f4-035199aeaf66, Rosen Classroom) Rosen Publishing Group, Inc., The.

Dixon, Dougal. Dinosaur Explorer, 8 vols. 2005. (QEB Readers). (Illus.). 24p. (J). (gr. -1-3). lib. bdg. 15.95 *(978-1-59566-070-1(4))* QEB Publishing Inc.

DK. DK Readers L0: Star Wars: Blast Off! 2010. (DK Readers Pre-Level 1 Ser.). (ENG., Illus.). 32p. (J). (gr. -1-k). pap. 4.99 *(978-0-7566-6692-7(9),* DK Children) Dorling Kindersley Publishing, Inc.

—DK Readers L1: Star Wars: the Clone Wars: Don't Wake the Zillo Beast! Beware the Galaxy's Baddest Beasts! 2011. (DK Readers Level 1 Ser.). (ENG.). 32p. (J). (gr. -1-1). 4.99 *(978-0-7566-8279-8(7),* DK Children) Dorling Kindersley Publishing, Inc.

—DK Readers L2: Star Wars: Lightsaber Battles. 2018. (DK Readers Level 2 Ser.). (ENG., Illus.). 48p. (J). (gr. k-2). pap. 4.99 *(978-1-4654-6758-4(0),* DK Children) Dorling Kindersley Publishing, Inc.

—DK Readers L3: Real-Life Heroes. 2017. (DK Readers Level 3 Ser.). (ENG., Illus.). 64p. (J). (gr. 2-4). pap. 3.99 *(978-1-4654-6244-2(9),* DK Children) Dorling Kindersley Publishing, Inc.

—FUN FLAPS: All about Me! 2008. (Fun Flaps Ser.). (ENG., Illus.). 14p. (J). (gr. -1-k). bds. 6.99 *(978-0-7566-3438-4(5),* DK Children) Dorling Kindersley Publishing, Inc.

—Sloths. 2019. (ENG., Illus.). 48p. (J). *(978-0-241-37926-4(1))* Dorling Kindersley Publishing, Inc.

Do That, Do This! Set B, 6 Pack. (Supersonic Phonics Ser.). (gr. k-3). 29.00 *(978-0-7635-0540-0(4))* Rigby Education.

Do You Like My Pet? (Early Intervention Levels Ser.). 21.30 *(978-0-7362-0369-2(9))*; Vol. 2. 3.55 *(978-0-7362-0090-5(8))* CENGAGE Learning.

The Doctor, 2 Pack. (Chiquilibros Ser.). (gr. -1-1). 12.00 *(978-0-7635-8544-0(0))* Rigby Education.

Doherty, Ellen. Ellis Island. 2011. (Early Connections Ser.). (J). *(978-1-61672-660-7(1))* Benchmark Education Co.

—William's Journal: Set Of 6. 2011. (Early Connections Ser.). (J). pap. 39.00 net. *(978-1-4108-1558-3(7))* Benchmark Education Co.

Dolan, Penny. The Great Chapatti Chase: Band 10/White. Sua, Laura, illus. 2015. (Collins Big Cat Ser.). (ENG.). 32p. (J). (gr. 2-2). pap. 10.99 *(978-0-00-759121-3(7))* HarperCollins Pubs. Ltd. GBR. Dist: Independent Pubs. Group.

—The Signalman: Two Ghost Stories: Band 14/Ruby (Collins Big Cat) Tambellini, Stefano, illus. 2015. (Collins Big Cat Ser.). (ENG.). 48p. (J). (gr. 3-4). pap. 10.99 *(978-0-00-812780-0(8))* HarperCollins Pubs. Ltd. GBR. Dist: Independent Pubs. Group.

The Dome. 2003. (Illus.). pap. 7.60 *(978-0-7398-7525-4(6))* Steck-Vaughn.

Dominguez, Angela. How Are You? / ¿Cómo Estás? 2018. (ENG., Illus.). 32p. (J). 18.99 *(978-1-250-12686-3(X),* 900175268, Holt, Henry & Co. Bks. For Young Readers) Holt, Henry & Co.

—How Do You Say? / ¿Cómo Se Dice? (Spanish Bilingual) Dominguez, Angela, illus. 2016. (SPA., Illus.). 32p. (J). 19.99 *(978-1-62779-496-1(4),* 900152614, Holt, Henry & Co. Bks. For Young Readers) Holt, Henry & Co.

Dominguez, Elaudy. The Mountain Mystery, 1 vol. 2006. (Neighborhood Readers Ser.). (ENG.). 16p. (gr. 1-2). pap. 6.50 *(978-1-4042-7124-1(4),* 396bbca4-e713-4eb4-a6d0-c0c146995eab, Rosen Classroom) Rosen Publishing Group, Inc., The.

Don, Lari. The House of the Nine Doors: Band 12/Copper (Collins Big Cat) McLellan, Stu, illus. 2015. (Collins Big Cat Ser.). (ENG.). 32p. (J). (gr. 3-3). pap. 9.99 *(978-0-00-812772-5(7))* HarperCollins Pubs. Ltd. GBR. Dist: Independent Pubs. Group.

Donaldson, Julia. Follow the Swallow (Reading Ladder Level 2) Ursell, Martin, illus. 2nd ed. 2016. (Reading Ladder Level 2 Ser.). (ENG.). 48p. (gr. k-2). pap. 4.99 *(978-1-4052-8200-0(2),* Reading Ladder) Farshore GBR. Dist: HarperCollins Pubs.

—The Mermaid & the Octopus: Band 04/Blue (Collins Big Cat) 2006. (Collins Big Cat Ser.). (ENG., Illus.). 16p. (J). (gr. 1-1). pap. 7.99 *(978-0-00-718684-6(3))* HarperCollins Pubs. Ltd. GBR. Dist: Independent Pubs. Group.

—The Pot of Gold: Band 08/Purple (Collins Big Cat) 2006. (Collins Big Cat Ser.). (ENG., Illus.). 24p. (J). (gr. 2-2). pap. 9.99 *(978-0-00-718696-9(7))* HarperCollins Pubs. Ltd. GBR. Dist: Independent Pubs. Group.

—The Quick Brown Fox Cub. 2006. (Red Bananas Ser.). (ENG., Illus.). 48p. (J). (gr. -1-3). lib. bdg. *(978-0-7787-1080-6(7))* Crabtree Publishing Co.

—The Quick Brown Fox Cub (Reading Ladder Level 3) Richards, Lucy, illus. 2nd ed. 2016. (Reading Ladder Level 3 Ser.). (ENG.). 48p. (gr. k-2). pap. 4.99 *(978-1-4052-8240-6(1),* Reading Ladder) Farshore GBR. Dist: HarperCollins Pubs.

—Spinderella (Reading Ladder Level 2) Pichon, Liz, illus. 2nd ed. 2016. (Reading Ladder Level 2 Ser.). (ENG.). 48p. (gr. k-2). pap. 4.99 *(978-1-4052-8202-4(9),* Reading Ladder) Farshore GBR. Dist: HarperCollins Pubs.

Donofrio, Antonio R. & Donofrio, Beatrice Batnag. G-String Cordilleran Revelries: Fairy Tales Retold for Centuries to Teach Life's Family Values & Basic Reading Skills with Simple Magic Tricks & I. 2009. 176p. pap. 17.99 *(978-1-4490-0181-0(5))* AuthorHouse.

Donovan, Barbara A. It's All Matter, 6 vols., Set. 2004. (Phonics Readers Books 37-72 Ser.). (ENG.). 8p. (gr. k-1). pap. 35.70 *(978-0-7368-4060-6(5))* Capstone.

—Move It!, 6 vols., Set. 2004. (Phonics Readers Books 37-72 Ser.). (ENG.). 8p. (gr. k-1). pap. 35.70 *(978-0-7368-4085-9(0))* Capstone.

Don't Interrupt! Individual Title Six-Packs. (gr. 1-2). 25.00 *(978-0-7635-9193-9(9))* Rigby Education.

Don't Splash Me!, 6 Packs. (gr. 1-2). 22.00 *(978-0-7635-9160-1(2))* Rigby Education.

Dooley, Virginia. Reading & Math Jumbo Workbook: Grade PreK, 1 vol. 2005. (ENG.). 320p. (gr. -1 — 1). pap., wbk. ed. 14.99 *(978-0-439-78598-3(7),* Teaching Resources) Scholastic, Inc.

Dorling Kindersley Publishing Staff. Ahsoka in Action! 2012. (Star Wars: the Clone Wars DK Readers Ser.). lib. bdg. 13.55 *(978-0-606-31472-5(5))* Turtleback.

—Can You Spot a Jedi? 2014. (Star Wars DK Readers Pre-Level Ser.). lib. bdg. 13.55 *(978-0-606-35323-6(2))* Turtleback.

—The LEGO Batman Movie. 2016. (LEGO DC Universe DK Readers Ser.). lib. bdg. 13.55 *(978-0-606-39895-4(3))* Turtleback.

—Let's Go Riding! 2013. (DK Reader Level 2 Ser.). lib. bdg. 13.55 *(978-0-606-31477-0(6))* Turtleback.

—Moon Landings: Level 3. 2019. (ENG., Illus.). 64p. (J). *(978-0-241-35853-5(1))* Dorling Kindersley Publishing, Inc.

—My Day. 2011. (DK Readers Pre-Level 1: Learning to Read Ser.). (ENG.). 32p. (J). (gr. -1-1). 16.19 *(978-0-7566-8931-5(7))* Dorling Kindersley Publishing, Inc.

Dotson, Jacob. React & Rise Up, 1 vol. 2010. 58p. pap. 16.95 *(978-1-4489-4168-1(7))* America Star Bks.

Doudna, Kelly. Any Day but Today! 2004. (Sight Words Ser.). (ENG., Illus.). 24p. (J). (gr. k-3). lib. bdg. 24.21 *(978-1-59197-464-2(X))* ABDO Publishing Co.

—Just Make Some Art! 2004. (Sight Words Ser.). (ENG., Illus.). 24p. (J). (gr. k-3). lib. bdg. 24.21 *(978-1-59197-481-9(X),* SandCastle) ABDO Publishing Co.

—There Are Ants down There! 2004. (Sight Words Ser.). (ENG., Illus.). 24p. (J). (gr. k-3). lib. bdg. 24.21 *(978-1-59197-473-4(9),* SandCastle) ABDO Publishing Co.

—Was That Fun? 2004. (Sight Words Ser.). (ENG., Illus.). 24p. (J). (gr. k-3). lib. bdg. 24.21 *(978-1-59197-475-8(5),* SandCastle) ABDO Publishing Co.

—When Can You Play Again? 2004. (Sight Words Ser.). (ENG., Illus.). 24p. (J). (gr. k-3). lib. bdg. 24.21 *(978-1-59197-478-9(X),* SandCastle) ABDO Publishing Co.

Dougherty, John. A Midsummer Night's Dream: Band 18/Pearl (Collins Big Cat) Sumberac, Manuel, illus. 2014. (Collins Big Cat Ser.). (ENG.). 192p. (J). (gr. 5-6). pap. 12.99 *(978-0-00-753012-0(9))* HarperCollins Pubs. Ltd. GBR. Dist: Independent Pubs. Group.

Dovey, Belinda. Alphabet Adventures. 2012. 136p. pap. 71.99 *(978-1-4653-7250-5(4))* Xlibris Corp.

Dow, Suzanne. The Bike Race, 1 vol. 2006. (Neighborhood Readers Ser.). (ENG., Illus.). 12p. (gr. 1-2). pap. 5.90 *(978-1-4042-7018-3(3),* afa14103-d655-4f97-9ff0-1d031269bfd0, Rosen Classroom) Rosen Publishing Group, Inc., The.

Down on the Farm. 2005. (Little Celebrations Thematic Packages Ser.). (J). (gr. k-3). 133.50 *(978-0-673-75377-9(8))* Celebration Pr.

Down the Hill: KinderReaders Individual Title Six-Packs. (Kinderstarters Ser.). 8p. (gr. -1-1). 21.00 *(978-0-7635-8654-6(4))* Rigby Education.

Downey, Glen. Escape from East Berlin. Lingas, Leo, illus. 2007. 48p. (J). lib. bdg. 23.08 *(978-1-4242-1635-2(4))* Fitzgerald Bks.

—Miracle Men. Brennan, Anthony, illus. 2007. (Timeline Ser.). 48p. pap. 8.99 *(978-1-4190-4410-6(9))* Steck-Vaughn.

Downey, Glen R. The 10 Greatest Sports Showdowns. 2008. 14.99 *(978-1-55448-535-2(5))* Scholastic Library Publishing.

—The 10 Most Decisive Battles. 2007. 14.99 *(978-1-55448-507-9(X))* Scholastic Library Publishing.

—The 10 Most Extreme Jobs. 2008. 14.99 *(978-1-55448-536-9(3))* Scholastic Library Publishing.

—The 10 Most Memorable TV Moments. 2008. 14.99 *(978-1-55448-544-4(4))* Scholastic Library Publishing.

—The 10 Most Remarkable Writers. 2008. 14.99 *(978-1-55448-553-6(3))* Scholastic Library Publishing.

—The 10 Most Revolutionary Military Inventions. 2008. 14.99 *(978-1-55448-500-0(2))* Scholastic Library Publishing.

—The 10 Most Shocking Sports Scandals. 2007. 14.99 *(978-1-55448-505-5(3))* Scholastic Library Publishing.

—The 10 Most Significant Documents in History. 2008. 14.99 *(978-1-55448-547-5(9))* Scholastic Library Publishing.

—The 10 Most Unforgettable NASCAR Moments. 2008. 14.99 *(978-1-55448-515-4(0))* Scholastic Library Publishing.

—The 10 Smartest Animals. 2007. 14.99 *(978-1-55448-512-3(6))* Scholastic Library Publishing.

Downey, Glen R. & Cond, Sandie. The 10 Coolest Flying Machines. 2008. 14.99 *(978-1-55448-530-7(4))* Scholastic Library Publishing.

Downey, Glen R. & Malara, Maria. The 10 Hottest Hollywood Cars. 2007. 14.99 *(978-1-55448-526-0(6))* Scholastic Library Publishing.

Downey, Tika. The Biggest Snowball, 1 vol. 2006. (Neighborhood Readers Ser.). (ENG.). 16p. (gr. 1-2). pap. 6.50 *(978-1-4042-7200-2(3),* 1472f103-c896-4209-bcf6-3bdf00fadd22, Rosen Classroom) Rosen Publishing Group, Inc., The.

—Tracks in the Snow, 1 vol. 2006. (Neighborhood Readers Ser.). (ENG.). 16p. (gr. 1-2). pap. 6.50 *(978-1-4042-7180-7(5),* 510446d8-1f90-41d2-ac8b-45d75e748255, Rosen Classroom) Rosen Publishing Group, Inc., The.

Downing, Johnette. Mumbo Jumbo, Stay Out of the Gumbo, 1 vol. Lindsley, Jennifer, illus. 2017. (ENG.). 32p. (J). (gr. -1-3). 19.99 *(978-1-4556-2300-6(8),* Pelican Publishing) Arcadia Publishing.

Doyle, Malachy. Hair Scare. Allen, Jonathan, illus. 2005. (ENG.). 24p. (J). lib. bdg. 23.65 *(978-1-59646-724-8(X))* Dingles & Co.

—King Donal's Secret. Watson, Richard, illus. 2005. (ENG.). 24p. (J). lib. bdg. 23.65 *(978-1-59646-740-8(1))* Dingles & Co.

—Rory's Lost His Voice. Semple, David, illus. 2005. (ENG.). 24p. (J). lib. bdg. 23.65 *(978-1-59646-714-9(2))* Dingles & Co.

Dr. Seuss Book Set 800481, 4. 2005. (J). *(978-1-59794-033-7(X))* Environments, Inc.

Dr. Seuss Book Set 800877, 6 vols. 2005. (J). bds. *(978-1-59794-055-9(0))* Environments, Inc.

Dr. Seuss Books & Tapes Book Set 800910, 3 vols. 2005. (J). pap. *(978-1-59794-075-7(5))* Environments, Inc.

The Dragon Compass: Individual Title Six-Packs. (Bookweb Ser.). 32p. (gr. 6-18). 34.00 *(978-0-7578-0898-2(0))* Rigby Education.

The Dragon Inside. 2003. (Illus.). pap. 5.60 *(978-0-7398-7517-9(5))* Steck-Vaughn.

Drake, Carol. The 10 Best Movies from Books. 2007. (J). 14.99 *(978-1-55448-463-8(4))* Scholastic Library Publishing.

—The 10 Most Incredible Ancient Wonders. 2007. (J). 14.99 *(978-1-55448-467-6(7))* Scholastic Library Publishing.

Drawing Conclusions & Inferences (Gr. 1-3) 2003. (J). *(978-1-58232-079-3(9))* ECS Learning Systems, Inc.

Driesel, Amy. Why Gretchen Can't Spell. 2009. 28p. pap. 13.99 *(978-1-4343-6166-0(7))* AuthorHouse.

Drimmer, Stephanie Warren. National Geographic Readers: Roar! 100 Facts about African Animals (L3) 2018. (Readers Ser.). (Illus.). 48p. (J). (gr. 3-7). pap. 4.99 *(978-1-4263-3241-8(6),* National Geographic Kids) Disney Publishing Worldwide.

Driscoll, Laura. El Chico del Despegue. Ramirez, Alma, tr. from ENG. Thornburgh, Rebecca McKillip, illus. 2009. (Math Matters en Espanol Ser.). (SPA.). 32p. (J). (gr. k-2). pap. 5.95 *(978-1-57565-267-2(6))* Astra Publishing Hse.

—I Want to Be a Police Officer. Echeverri, Catalina, illus. 2018. (I Can Read Level 1 Ser.). (ENG.). 32p. (J). (gr. -1-3). 16.99 *(978-0-06-243245-2(1))*; pap. 5.99 *(978-0-06-243243-8(5))* HarperCollins Pubs. (HarperCollins).

Duckworth, Michael. Oxford Bookworms Library: Voodoo Island: Level 2: 700-Word Vocabulary. 3rd ed. 2008. (ENG., Illus.). 64p. 11.00 *(978-0-19-479075-8(4))* Oxford Univ. Pr., Inc.

Dufresne, Michèle. Animal Tricks: Jasper the Cat Set 1. 2004. (Jasper the Cat Set 1 Ser.). (ENG., Illus.). (J). pap. 7.33 *(978-1-58453-278-1(5))* Pioneer Valley Bks.

—At School Set 1. 2004. (ENG.). (J). pap. 40.00 *(978-1-58453-262-0(9))* Pioneer Valley Bks.

—Bella & Rosie Play Hide & Seek: Bella & Rosie Yellow Set. 2003. (Bella & Rosie Set 1 Ser.). (J). pap. 7.67 *(978-1-932570-11-3(X))* Pioneer Valley Bks.

—Bella & Rosie Yellow Set. 2003. (J). pap. 42.67 *(978-1-932570-08-3(X))* Pioneer Valley Bks.

—Bella Is a Bad Dog: Bella & Rosie Yellow Set. 2003. (Bella & Rosie Set 1 Ser.). (J). pap. 7.67 *(978-1-932570-14-4(4))* Pioneer Valley Bks.

—Bella's Birthday: Bella & Rosie Yellow Set. 2003. (Bella & Rosie Set 1 Ser.). (ENG.). (J). pap. 7.67 *(978-1-932570-09-0(8))* Pioneer Valley Bks.

—A Birthday Present for Spaceboy: Spaceboy Set 1. 2003. (Spaceboy Set 1 Ser.). (ENG.). (J). pap. 7.33 *(978-1-932570-03-8(9)*, Pioneer Valley Bks.) Pioneer Valley Bks.

—Casey & the Nest. 2005. (Georgie Giraffe Chapter Ser.). (ENG.). (J). pap. 7.67 *(978-1-932570-47-2(0))* Pioneer Valley Bks.

—The Deer Report. 2005. (The Fawn Chapter Ser.). (J). pap. 7.67 *(978-1-58453-311-5(0))* Pioneer Valley Bks.

—Dinner Time. 2005. (Gilbert the Pig Chapter Ser.). (J). pap. 7.67 *(978-1-58453-298-9(X))* Pioneer Valley Bks.

—The Fawn. 2005. (The Fawn Chapter Ser.). (J). pap. 7.67 *(978-1-58453-309-2(9))* Pioneer Valley Bks.

—Fawn Chapter Books, Set 2005. (ENG.). (J). pap. 29.33 *(978-1-58453-308-5(0))* Pioneer Valley Bks.

—A Friend for Jasper. 2004. (Jasper the Cat Chapter Ser.). (ENG., Illus.). (J). pap. 7.67 *(978-1-58453-284-2(X))* Pioneer Valley Bks.

—Fun in the Snow: Bella & Rosie Yellow Set. 2003. (Bella & Rosie Set 1 Ser.). (J). pap. 7.67 *(978-1-932570-13-7(6))* Pioneer Valley Bks.

—Gilbert Goes on a Picnic. 2004. (Gilbert the Pig Set 2 Ser.). (J). pap. 7.33 *(978-1-58453-221-7(1))* Pioneer Valley Bks.

—Gilbert the Pig Set 2. 2004. (J). pap. *(978-1-58453-220-0(3))* Pioneer Valley Bks.

—Gilbert the Special Pig. 2004. (Gilbert the Pig Set 2 Ser.). (J). pap. 7.33 *(978-1-58453-223-1(8))* Pioneer Valley Bks.

—Going Fishing. 2007. (Artic Adventures Ser.). (Illus.). 20p. (J). pap. 7.67 *(978-1-58453-314-6(5))* Pioneer Valley Bks.

—Grandma's House: Jasper the Cat Set 1. 2004. (Jasper the Cat Set 1 Ser.). (ENG.). (J). pap. 7.33 *(978-1-58453-277-4(7))* Pioneer Valley Bks.

—Help for Rosie: Bella & Rosie Yellow Set. 2003. (Bella & Rosie Set 1 Ser.). (ENG.). (J). pap. 7.67 *(978-1-932570-10-6(1))* Pioneer Valley Bks.

—Jasper & the Kitten. 2004. (Jasper the Cat Chapter Ser.). (J). pap. 7.67 *(978-1-58453-283-5(1))* Pioneer Valley Bks.

—Jasper the Cat Chapter Books. 2004. (J). pap. 29.33 *(978-1-58453-287-3(4))* Pioneer Valley Bks.

—Jasper the Cat Set 1. 2004. (J). pap. 40.00 *(978-1-58453-282-8(3))* Pioneer Valley Bks.

—Jasper the Fat Cat: Jasper the Cat Set 1. 2004. (Jasper the Cat Set 1 Ser.). (ENG.). (J). pap. 7.33 *(978-1-58453-276-7(9))* Pioneer Valley Bks.

—Lemonade for Gilbert. 2004. (Gilbert the Pig Set 2 Ser.). (J). pap. 7.33 *(978-1-58453-222-4(X))* Pioneer Valley Bks.

—Look Out for Space Monster: Spaceboy Set 1. 2003. (Spaceboy Set 1 Ser.). (J). pap. 7.33 *(978-1-932570-04-5(7))* Pioneer Valley Bks.

—The Loose Tooth. 2005. (J). pap. 7.33 *(978-1-932570-31-1(4))* Pioneer Valley Bks.

—Lost in the Woods: Bella & Rosie Yellow Set. 2003. (Bella & Rosie Set 1 Ser.). (J). pap. 7.67 *(978-1-932570-12-0(8))* Pioneer Valley Bks.

—Mom & Dad Set 1. 2003. (J). pap. 40.00 *(978-1-58453-250-7(5))* Pioneer Valley Bks.

—A Mouse in the House. 2004. (Jasper the Cat Set 1 Ser.). (ENG., Illus.). (J). pap. 7.33 *(978-1-58453-281-1(5))* Pioneer Valley Bks.

—My Classroom. 2004. (At School Ser.). (J). pap. 7.33 *(978-1-58453-266-8(1))* Pioneer Valley Bks.

—My School. 2004. (At School Ser.). (J). pap. 7.33 *(978-1-58453-264-4(5))* Pioneer Valley Bks.

Dufresne, Michele. My Teacher. 2004. (At School Ser.). (J). pap. 7.33 *(978-1-58453-263-7(7))* Pioneer Valley Bks.

Dufresne, Michèle. Nap Time for Gilbert. 2004. (Gilbert the Pig Set 2 Ser.). (J). pap. 7.33 *(978-1-58453-224-8(6))* Pioneer Valley Bks.

—Party Clothes: Jasper the Cat Set 1. 2004. (Jasper the Cat Set 1 Ser.). (ENG.). (J). pap. 7.33 *(978-1-58453-279-8(3))* Pioneer Valley Bks.

—Petting Gilbert. 2004. (Gilbert the Pig Set 2 Ser.). (J). pap. 7.33 *(978-1-58453-225-5(4))* Pioneer Valley Bks.

Dufresne, Michele. Reading Partners. 2004. (At School Ser.). (J). pap. 7.33 *(978-1-58453-267-5(X))* Pioneer Valley Bks.

Dufresne, Michèle. The Sky Is Falling. 2004. (Folk Tales Set 1 Ser.). (J). pap. 7.67 *(978-1-58453-273-6(4))* Pioneer Valley Bks.

—Sleep Tight Spaceboy: Spaceboy Set 1. 2003. (Spaceboy Set 1 Ser.). (J). pap. 7.33 *(978-1-932570-02-1(0))* Pioneer Valley Bks.

—The Space Fort. 2005. (J). pap. 7.33 *(978-1-932570-33-5(0))* Pioneer Valley Bks.

—Spaceboy Finds a Friend: Spaceboy Set 1. 2003. (Spaceboy Set 1 Ser.). (ENG.). (J). pap. 7.33 *(978-1-932570-01-4(2))* Pioneer Valley Bks.

—Spaceboy Plays Hide & Seek: SPaceboy Set 1. 2003. (Spaceboy Set 1 Ser.). (ENG.). (J). pap. 7.33 *(978-1-932570-05-2(5))* Pioneer Valley Bks.

—Spaceboy Set 1. 2003. (J). pap. 40.00 *(978-1-932570-00-7(4))* Pioneer Valley Bks.

—Time for School. 2004. (At School Ser.). (J). pap. 7.33 *(978-1-58453-265-1(3))* Pioneer Valley Bks.

—Trouble for Jasper. 2004. (Jasper the Cat Chapter Ser.). (ACO.). (J). pap. 7.67 *(978-1-58453-286-6(6))* Pioneer Valley Bks.

—A Walk at the Farm. 2005. (Gilbert the Pig Chapter Ser.). (ENG.). (J). pap. 7.67 *(978-1-58453-300-9(5))* Pioneer Valley Bks.

Dufresne, Michele. A Walk for Jasper. 2004. (Jasper the Cat Set 1 Ser.). (ENG.). (J). pap. 7.33 *(978-1-58453-280-4(7))* Pioneer Valley Bks.

Dufresne, Michèle. Where Are the Baby Chicks? 2004. (Gilbert the Pig Set 2 Ser.). (J). pap. 7.33 *(978-1-58453-226-2(2))* Pioneer Valley Bks.

—Who's the Boss? 2004. (Jasper the Cat Chapter Ser.). (J). pap. 7.67 *(978-1-58453-285-9(8))* Pioneer Valley Bks.

Dugan, Christine. Between the Wars, 1 vol. rev. ed. 2007. (Social Studies: Informational Text Ser.). (ENG.). 32p. (gr. 4-8). pap. 11.99 *(978-0-7439-0666-1(7))* Teacher Created Materials, Inc.

—Defying Gravity! Rock Climbing, 1 vol. 2nd rev. ed. 2012. (TIME for KIDS(r): Informational Text Ser.). (ENG.). 48p. (gr. 4-5). pap. 13.99 *(978-1-4333-4830-3(6))* Teacher Created Materials, Inc.

—Final Lap! Go-Kart Racing, 1 vol. 2nd rev. ed. 2012. (TIME for KIDS(r): Informational Text Ser.). (ENG.). 48p. (gr. 4-5). pap. 13.99 *(978-1-4333-4832-7(2))* Teacher Created Materials, Inc.

—From Rags to Riches, 1 vol. 2nd rev. ed. 2013. (TIME for KIDS(r): Informational Text Ser.). (ENG., Illus.). 64p. (J). (gr. 4-8). pap. 14.99 *(978-1-4333-4910-2(8))* Teacher Created Materials, Inc.

—Hang Ten! Surfing, 1 vol. 2nd rev. ed. 2012. (TIME for KIDS(r): Informational Text Ser.). (ENG.). 48p. (gr. 4-5). pap. 13.99 *(978-1-4333-4831-0(4))* Teacher Created Materials, Inc.

—Landscape by Design. rev. ed. 2012. (Mathematics in the Real World Ser.). (ENG.). 32p. (gr. 5-8). pap. 11.99 *(978-1-4333-3459-7(3))* Teacher Created Materials, Inc.

—Living in Space, 1 vol. 2nd rev. ed. 2012. (TIME for KIDS(r): Informational Text Ser.). (ENG.). 32p. (gr. 3-5). pap. 12.99 *(978-1-4333-3675-1(8))* Teacher Created Materials, Inc.

—Rome, 1 vol. rev. ed. 2007. (Social Studies: Informational Text Ser.). (ENG.). 32p. (gr. 4-8). pap. 11.99 *(978-0-7439-0432-2(X))* Teacher Created Materials, Inc.

—A Sense of Art. rev. ed. 2012. (Mathematics in the Real World Ser.). (ENG.). 32p. (gr. 5-8). pap. 11.99 *(978-1-4333-3458-0(5))* Teacher Created Materials, Inc.

—Space Exploration, 1 vol. 2nd rev. ed. 2012. (TIME for KIDS(r): Informational Text Ser.). (ENG.). 32p. (gr. 3-5). pap. 12.99 *(978-1-4333-3674-4(X))* Teacher Created Materials, Inc.

—Tonight's Concert. rev. ed. 2012. (Mathematics in the Real World Ser.). (ENG.). 32p. (gr. 5-8). pap. 11.99 *(978-1-4333-3464-1(X))* Teacher Created Materials, Inc.

Dugan, Christine & Lane, Chloe. Pack It Up: Surface Area & Volume. rev. ed. 2012. (Mathematics in the Real World Ser.). (ENG.). 32p. (gr. 5-8). pap. 11.99 *(978-1-4333-3461-0(5))* Teacher Created Materials, Inc.

Duncan, Cynthia L. Kids Say Such Silly Things. 2012. (Illus.). 20p. pap. 12.99 *(978-1-4567-5095-4(X))* AuthorHouse.

Dunrea, Olivier. Gemma & Gus. Dunrea, Olivier, illus. 2017. (Gossie & Friends Ser.). (ENG., Illus.). 32p. (J). (gr. -1-3). pap. 5.99 *(978-0-544-93722-2(8)*, 1658282, Clarion Bks.) HarperCollins Pubs.

Dupasquier, Philippe. La Obra. (Coleccion Aqui Se Trabaja). (SPA., Illus.). 22p. (J). 10.95 *(978-84-207-3799-7(2)*, ANY762) Grupo Anaya, S.A. ESP. Dist: Continental Bk. Co., Inc.

Durant, Alan. Buzz & Bingo in the Starry Sky: Band 10/White (Collins Big Cat) Walker, Sholto, illus. 2005. (Collins Big Cat Ser.). (ENG.). 16p. (J). (gr. 1-3). pap. 10.99 *(978-0-00-718630-3(4))* HarperCollins Pubs. Ltd. GBR. Dist: Independent Pubs. Group.

—Spider Mcdrew & the Egyptians: Band 12/Copper (Collins Big Cat), Bd. 12. Hopman, Philip, illus. 2007. (Collins Big Cat Ser.). (ENG.). 32p. (J). (gr. 2-3). pap. 10.99 *(978-0-00-723076-1(1))* HarperCollins Pubs. Ltd. GBR. Dist: Independent Pubs. Group.

—The Teeth: Band 11 Lime/Band 14 Ruby (Collins Big Cat Progress) 2014. (Collins Big Cat Progress Ser.). (ENG., Illus.). 32p. (J). (gr. 3-4). pap. 8.85 *(978-0-00-751933-0(8))* HarperCollins Pubs. Ltd. GBR. Dist: Independent Pubs. Group.

Duras, Marguerite. Hiroshima Mon Amour, Level B.Tr. of Hiroshima My Love. (FRE.). (YA). (gr. 7-12). 9.95 *(978-0-88436-998-1(6)*, 40308) EMC/Paradigm Publishing.

Dussling, Jennifer. DK Readers L2: Bugs Bugs Bugs! 2011. (DK Readers Level 2 Ser.). (ENG.). 32p. (J). (gr. 1-3). 4.99 *(978-0-7566-7205-8(8)*, DK Children) Dorling Kindersley Publishing, Inc.

Dyan, Penelope. Ba-Ba-Ba-Bad — -The Story of One Mean Moose. Dyan, Penelope, illus. 2012. (Illus.). 34p. pap. 11.95 *(978-1-61477-053-4(0))* Bellissima Publishing, LLC.

—Bake a Cake, Make Two — -and Let Them Eat Cake. Dyan, Penelope, illus. 2008. (Illus.). 44p. pap. 11.95 *(978-1-935118-18-3(8))* Bellissima Publishing, LLC.

—The Comeback Kids — Book 10 — The American Bison. Weigand, John, photos by. 2012. (Illus.). 34p. pap. 14.95 *(978-1-61477-063-3(8))* Bellissima Publishing, LLC.

—Don't Wake up the Bear! Dyan, Penelope, illus. 2013. (Illus.). 34p. pap. 11.95 *(978-1-61477-094-7(8))* Bellissima Publishing, LLC.

—Fat Rat, Fat Cat — -Because Cats & Rats Are Also People. Dayn, Penelope, illus. 2008. 40p. pap. 11.95 *(978-1-935118-11-4(0))* Bellissima Publishing, LLC.

—Go Far Star Car — Even Though Cars Are Not People. Dyan, Penelope, illus. 2008. (Illus.). 44p. pap. 11.95 *(978-1-935118-12-1(9))* Bellissima Publishing, LLC.

—Go Run, Have Fun — -Because Everyone Likes Fun. Dyan, Penelope, illus. 2008. (Illus.). 44p. pap. 11.95 *(978-1-935118-15-2(3))* Bellissima Publishing, LLC.

—Go to Rat House, Go to Cat House — Even Though Houses Are Not People. Dyan, Penelope, illus. 2008. (Illus.). 44p. pap. 11.95 *(978-1-935118-14-5(5))* Bellissima Publishing, LLC.

—I Love You! Dyan, Penelope, illus. 2012. (Illus.). 34p. pap. 11.95 *(978-1-61477-050-3(6))* Bellissima Publishing, LLC.

—If You Snooze! Dyan, Penelope, illus. 2012. (Illus.). 34p. pap. 11.95 *(978-1-61477-059-6(X))* Bellissima Publishing, LLC.

—In Gracie's Yard! Dyan, Penelope, illus. 2012. (Illus.). 34p. pap. 11.95 *(978-1-61477-067-1(0))* Bellissima Publishing, LLC.

—Jump Frog, Funny Frog — -Because Frogs Are Funny. Dyan, Penelope, illus. 2008. (Illus.). 44p. pap. 11.95 *(978-1-935118-19-0(6))* Bellissima Publishing, LLC.

—Mikey & Me & the Spider — -the Continuing Story of a Girl & Her Dog. Dyan, Penelope, illus. 2010. (Illus.). 50p. pap. 14.95 *(978-1-935118-95-4(1))* Bellissima Publishing, LLC.

—Molly Moose Is on the Loose. Dyan, Penelope, illus. 2012. (Illus.). 34p. pap. 11.95 *(978-1-61477-025-1(5))* Bellissima Publishing, LLC.

—Olympic Gold — Because Everyone Loves a Winner! Dyan, Penelope, illus. 2008. (Illus.). 44p. pap. 11.95 *(978-1-935118-20-6(X))* Bellissima Publishing, LLC.

—Respect! Dyan, Penelope, illus. 2012. (Illus.). 34p. pap. 11.95 *(978-1-61477-058-9(1))* Bellissima Publishing, LLC.

—Sticks — the for Boys Only Version — Because Sticks Are Also People. Dyan, Penelope, illus. 2008. (Illus.). 52p. pap. 11.95 *(978-1-935118-13-8(7))* Bellissima Publishing, LLC.

—The Sunny Side! Dyan, Penelope, illus. 2012. (Illus.). 34p. pap. 11.95 *(978-1-61477-057-2(3))* Bellissima Publishing, LLC.

—Teeth! Dyan, Penelope, illus. 2012. (Illus.). 34p. pap. 11.95 *(978-1-61477-060-2(3))* Bellissima Publishing, LLC.

—That Fat Elephant — -Because Everyone Likes Elephants. Dyan, Penelope, illus. 2008. (Illus.). 44p. pap. 11.95 *(978-1-935118-16-9(1))* Bellissima Publishing, LLC.

—That Fat Rat Family — Because All Families Aren't Rats. Dyan, Penelope, illus. 2008. (Illus.). 44p. pap. 11.95 *(978-1-935118-17-6(X))* Bellissima Publishing, LLC.

—There's a Flea in My Te. Dyan, Penelope, illus. 2012. (Illus.). 34p. pap. 11.95 *(978-1-61477-047-3(6))* Bellissima Publishing, LLC.

—There's a Skunk in My Trunk. Dyan, Penelope, illus. 2012. (Illus.). 34p. pap. 11.95 *(978-1-61477-045-9(X))* Bellissima Publishing, LLC.

—There's a Teddy Bear in My Heart! Dyan, Penelope, illus. 2012. (Illus.). 34p. pap. 11.95 *(978-1-61477-048-0(4))* Bellissima Publishing, LLC.

—What Is a Telephant? Dyan, Penelope, illus. 2013. (Illus.). 34p. pap. 11.95 *(978-1-61477-112-8(X))* Bellissima Publishing, LLC.

—Where Is Lucy? Dyan, Penelope, illus. 2013. (Illus.). 34p. pap. 11.95 *(978-1-61477-120-3(0))* Bellissima Publishing, LLC.

—The White Elephant No One Wants. Dyan, Penelope, illus. 2012. (Illus.). 34p. pap. 11.95 *(978-1-61477-024-4(7))* Bellissima Publishing, LLC.

—Who Cut the Cheese? a for Boys Only Book. Dyan, Penelope, illus. 2008. (Illus.). 44p. pap. 11.95 *(978-1-935118-22-0(6))* Bellissima Publishing, LLC.

—Why Angels Sing! Dyan, Penelope, illus. 2012. (Illus.). 34p. pap. 11.95 *(978-1-61477-065-7(4))* Bellissima Publishing, LLC.

—Work It Out! Dyan, Penelope, illus. 2012. (Illus.). 34p. pap. 11.95 *(978-1-61477-056-5(5))* Bellissima Publishing, LLC.

DynaNotes Grade 9 Reading Review Guide. 2006. (YA). pap. *(978-1-933854-29-8(4))* DynaStudy, Inc.

DynaNotes Grade 9 Reading Review Guide Transparency Set. 2006. (YA). trans. *(978-1-933854-33-5(2))* DynaStudy, Inc.

Early Emergent Guided Reading, Vol. 1. (gr. k-18). 372.95 *(978-0-7802-2770-5(0))* Wright Group/McGraw-Hill.

Early In The Morning. (Early Intervention Levels Ser.). 23.10 *(978-0-7362-0039-4(8))*; Vol. 4. 3.85 *(978-1-56334-986-7(8))* CENGAGE Learning.

Early Reading Comprehension. 2004. (Reading comprehension, ERC MRC Ser.). (gr. 2-4). pap. 8.65 *(978-0-8388-0621-0(X))* Educators Publishing Service, Inc.

Eastman, P. D. Are You My Mother?/¿Eres Tú Mi Mamá? (Bilingual Edition) 2016. (SPA., Illus.). 72p. (J). (gr. 1-4). 17.99 *(978-0-553-53990-5(6)*, Random Hse. Bks. for Young Readers) Random Hse. Children's Bks.

—¿Eres Tú Mi Mamá? (Are You My Mother? Spanish Edition) 2016. (Beginner Books(R) Ser.). (SPA., Illus.). 72p. (J). (gr. -1-2). 9.99 *(978-0-553-53989-9(2)*, Random Hse. Bks. for Young Readers) Random Hse. Children's Bks.

—Go, Dog. Go! Eastman, P. D., illus. 2008. (ENG., Illus.). 64p. pap. *(978-0-00-722546-0(6))* HarperCollins Pubs. Ltd.

Eclipse: Individual Title, 6 pack. (Story Steps Ser.). (gr. k-2). 32.00 *(978-0-7635-9810-5(0))* Rigby Education.

Editors of the American Heritage Di, Editors of. Where Am I Hiding?/¿Donde Me Escondo? Bilingual English-Spanish. Zagarenski, Pamela, illus. 2005. (Good Beginnings Ser.).Tr. of Where Am I Hiding? (ENG.). 8p. (J). (gr. -1 — 1). bds. 4.99 *(978-0-618-51176-1(8)*, J02902, Clarion Bks.) HarperCollins Pubs.

Educational Solutions Staff & Gattegno, Caleb. Primary 3. (J). 84.00 *(978-0-87825-170-4(7))*; tchr. ed. 6.85 *(978-0-87825-205-3(3))* Educational Solutions, Inc.

Education.com. Tell Me a Story: A Workbook of Story Pages & Activities. 2015. (ENG.). 128p. (J). (gr. 1-1). pap. 7.99 *(978-0-486-80258-9(2)*, 802582) Dover Pubns., Inc.

EduTax, Vol. 1. Date not set. *(978-1-888042-02-3(8))*; *(978-1-888042-03-0(6))* Good Reading Bks.

Edwards, Amelia. Carousel Colors, 1 vol. rev. ed. 2013. (Literary Text Ser.). (ENG., Illus.). 12p. (gr. k-2). 6.99 *(978-1-4333-5447-2(0))* Teacher Created Materials, Inc.

—It's Good Enough to Eat!, 1 vol. rev. ed. 2013. (Literary Text Ser.). (ENG., Illus.). 20p. (gr. 1-2). 7.99 *(978-1-4333-5493-9(4))* Teacher Created Materials, Inc.

—Playground Friends, 1 vol. rev. ed. 2013. (Literary Text Ser.). (ENG., Illus.). 12p. (gr. k-2). (J). lib. bdg. 12.96 *(978-1-4807-1128-0(4))*; 6.99 *(978-1-4333-5449-6(7))* Teacher Created Materials, Inc.

Edwards-Hammond, Arlene. Keys, Please? Please Keys? 2012. 50p. pap. 15.99 *(978-1-4771-0376-0(7))* Xlibris Corp.

Edwards, Jean E. Adventure Tales: For Kids Who Want to Become Better Readers. 2012. 102p. 24.99 *(978-1-4771-4118-2(9))*; pap. 15.99 *(978-1-4771-4117-5(0))* Xlibris Corp.

Edwards, Roberta. Best Friends: The True Story of Owen & Mzee. Schwartz, Carol, illus. 2007. (All Aboard Science Reader Ser.). 32p. (gr. -1-3). 14.00 *(978-0-7569-8167-9(0))* Perfection Learning Corp.

Eeles, Alex. Bedtime on the Farm Red Band. Ortu, Davide, illus. 2016. (Cambridge Reading Adventures Ser.). (ENG.). 16p. pap. 7.95 *(978-1-316-50081-1(0))* Cambridge Univ. Pr.

—The Boy Who Said No Yellow Band. Ortu, Davide, illus. 2017. (Cambridge Reading Adventures Ser.). (ENG.). 16p. pap. 6.15 *(978-1-108-40077-0(9))* Cambridge Univ. Pr.

Eggers, Casey. Avenues C (Leveled Books): a Great Day in the City. 2003. (Rise & Shine Ser.). (ENG.). 16p. (C). pap. 11.95 *(978-0-7362-1894-8(7))* CENGAGE Learning.

Eggleton. Sail Blu Nf Chimpanzees. 2004. (Rigby Sails Early Ser.). (ENG.). 16p. (gr. 1-2). pap. 6.95 *(978-0-7578-9960-7(9))* Rigby Education.

—Sail Blu Nf Fantastic Frogs. 2004. (Rigby Sails Early Ser.). (ENG.). 16p. (gr. 1-2). pap. 6.95 *(978-0-7578-9952-2(8))* Rigby Education.

Eggleton, Jill. Bertha & the Beeman. (Sails Literacy Ser.). 24p. (gr. 1-18). 27.00 *(978-0-7578-6201-4(2))* Rigby Education.

—Bertha & the Beeman: 3-in-1 Package. (Sails Literacy Ser.). 24p. (gr. 1-18). 57.00 *(978-0-7578-8618-8(3))* Rigby Education.

—Big Bill's Bed. Matijasevich, Astrid, illus. 2003. (Rigby Sails Early Ser.). (ENG.). 16p. (gr. 1-2). pap. 6.95 *(978-0-7578-8731-4(7))* Houghton Mifflin Harcourt Publishing Co.

—Big Red Comes to Stay. Cammell, Sandra, illus. 2004. (Rigby Sails Early Ser.). (ENG.). 16p. (gr. 1-2). pap. 6.95 *(978-0-7578-9303-2(1))* Houghton Mifflin Harcourt Publishing Co.

—Billy Mcbrown. Pye, Trevor, illus. (Sails Literacy Ser.). 24p. (gr. 1-18). 27.00 *(978-0-7578-6202-1(0))*;Pack. 57.00 *(978-0-7578-8620-1(5))* Rigby Education.

—A Bird Is a Bird. Chambers, Brent, illus. 2003. (Rigby Sails Early Ser.). (ENG.). 16p. (gr. 1-2). pap. 6.95 *(978-0-7578-8662-1(0))* Houghton Mifflin Harcourt Publishing Co.

—Bubble Trouble: 3-in-1 Package. Webb, Philip, illus. (Sails Literacy Ser.). 24p. (gr. k-18). 57.00 *(978-0-7578-8614-0(0))* Rigby Education.

—Bubble Trouble: 6 Small Books. Webb, Philip, illus. (Sails Literacy Ser.). 24p. (gr. k-18). 25.00 *(978-0-7578-7726-1(5))* Rigby Education.

—Bubble Trouble: Big Book Only. Webb, Philip, illus. (Sails Literacy Ser.). 24p. (gr. k-18). 27.00 *(978-0-7578-6197-0(0))* Rigby Education.

—Clown's Pants. Smith, Craig, illus. 2003. (Rigby Sails Early Ser.). (ENG.). 16p. (gr. 1-2). pap. 6.95 *(978-0-7578-8723-9(6))* Houghton Mifflin Harcourt Publishing Co.

—Clown's Party. Smith, Craig, illus. 2003. (Rigby Sails Early Ser.). (ENG.). 16p. (gr. 1-2). pap. 6.95 *(978-0-7578-8669-0(8))* Houghton Mifflin Harcourt Publishing Co.

—Creatures of the Extreme. 2007. (Connectors Ser.). (gr. 2-5). pap. *(978-1-877453-10-6(2))* Global Education Systems Ltd.

—The Deep Ocean. 2007. (Connectors Ser.). (gr. 2-5). pap. *(978-1-877453-02-1(1))* Global Education Systems Ltd.

—The Dream Catcher. (Sails Literacy Ser.). 24p. (gr. 1-18). 8.00 *(978-0-7635-6983-9(6))* Rigby Education.

—The Eye of the Law. 2007. (Connectors Ser.). (gr. 2-5). pap. *(978-1-877453-14-4(5))* Global Education Systems Ltd.

—Fearless Phil: 3-in-1 Package. McGrath, Raymond, illus. (Sails Literacy Ser.). 24p. (gr. 3-18). 57.00 *(978-0-7578-6996-9(3))* Rigby Education.

—Fearless Phil: 6 Small Books. McGrath, Raymond, illus. (Sails Literacy Ser.). 24p. (gr. 3-18). 25.00 *(978-0-7578-6988-4(2))* Rigby Education.

—Fearless Phil: Big Book Only. McGrath, Raymond, illus. (Sails Literacy Ser.). 24p. (gr. 3-18). 27.00 *(978-0-7578-6980-8(7))* Rigby Education.

—The Fire. Pye, Trevor, illus. 2003. (Rigby Sails Early Ser.). (ENG.). 16p. (gr. 1-2). pap. 6.95 *(978-0-7578-8663-8(9))* Houghton Mifflin Harcourt Publishing Co.

—Flea & Big Bill. Matijasevich, Astrid, illus. 2003. (Rigby Sails Early Ser.). (ENG.). 16p. (gr. 1-2). pap. 6.95 *(978-0-7578-8722-2(8))* Houghton Mifflin Harcourt Publishing Co.

—Flea Goes Out! Matijasevich, Astrid, illus. 2003. (Rigby Sails Early Ser.). (ENG.). 16p. (gr. 1-2). pap. 6.95 *(978-0-7578-8737-6(6))* Houghton Mifflin Harcourt Publishing Co.

—Granny Groggin: 3-in-1 Package. (Sails Literacy Ser.). 24p. (gr. 3-18). 57.00 *(978-0-7578-6997-6(1))* Rigby Education.

—The Ice-Cream Machine. Pye, Trevor, illus. 2003. (Rigby Sails Early Ser.). (ENG.). 16p. (gr. 1-2). pap. 6.95 *(978-0-7578-8728-4(7))* Houghton Mifflin Harcourt Publishing Co.

—Invasive Species. 2007. (Connectors Ser.). (gr. 2-5). pap. *(978-1-877453-04-5(8))* Global Education Systems Ltd.

—Mickey Maloney's Missing Bag. Pye, Trevor, illus. 2004. (Rigby Sails Early Ser.). (ENG.). 16p. (gr. 1-2). pap. 6.95 *(978-0-7578-9299-8(X))* Houghton Mifflin Harcourt Publishing Co.

—Mrs. Mcfee. Webb, Philip, illus. 2009. 39.95 *(978-0-7664-3147-8(9))* Abrams & Co. Pubs., Inc.

—The Mystery of Missing Big Wig, 3 vols., Pack. (Sails Literacy Ser.). 24p. (gr. 3-18). 57.00 *(978-0-7578-6998-3(X))* Rigby Education.

—Nomads. 2007. (Connectors Ser.). (gr. 2-5). pap. *(978-1-877453-12-0(9))* Global Education Systems Ltd.

—Sailor Sam in Trouble. Storey, Jim, illus. 2004. (Rigby Sails Early Ser.). (ENG.). 16p. (gr. 1-2). pap. 6.95 *(978-0-7578-9295-0(7))* Houghton Mifflin Harcourt Publishing Co.

—The Sky Bridge. (Sails Literacy Ser.). 24p. (gr. 1-18). 8.00 *(978-0-7635-6982-2(8))* Rigby Education.

—Tony's Dad. Hawley, Kelvin, illus. 2003. (Rigby Sails Sailing Solo Ser.). (ENG.). 24p. (gr. 1-2). pap. 9.05 *(978-0-7578-3975-7(4))* Rigby Education.

—Treasures. 2007. (Connectors Ser.). (gr. 2-5). pap. *(978-1-877453-17-5(X))* Global Education Systems Ltd.

—Turtle's Trouble. Cammell, Sandra, illus. 2003. (Rigby Sails Early Ser.). (ENG.). 16p. (gr. 1-2). pap. 6.95 *(978-0-7578-8672-0(8))* Houghton Mifflin Harcourt Publishing Co.

—Where Are You, Mouse? McGrath, Raymond, illus. 2003. (Rigby Sails Early Ser.). (ENG.). 16p. (gr. 1-2). pap. 6.95 *(978-0-7578-8741-3(4))* Houghton Mifflin Harcourt Publishing Co.

—The Wonder of the Wind. 2007. (Connectors Ser.). (gr. 2-5). pap. *(978-1-877453-19-9(6))* Global Education Systems Ltd.

El Khatiri, Basma. Momma's Song, 1 vol. Kala, Sabah, illus. 2016. (Stories & Fables from Around the World Ser.). (ENG.). 24p. (J). (gr. 1-2). lib. bdg. 26.27 *(978-1-4777-5694-2(9),* 650c7de1-5de2-4328-bf9b-2c864df9ac3e, Windmill Bks.) Rosen Publishing Group, Inc., The.

Eldridge, Jim. The Refugee Camp 4 Voyagers. Sperling, Tom, illus. 2017. (Cambridge Reading Adventures Ser.). (ENG.). 32p. pap. 8.35 *(978-1-108-40108-1(2))* Cambridge Univ. Pr.

Elephant Walk: Level K, 6 vols. 128p. (gr. 2-3). 40.50 *(978-0-7699-0993-6(0))* Shortland Pubns. (U. S. A.) Inc.

Elizabeth, Shelby. Dabby's Pond, 1 vol. 2006. (Neighborhood Readers Ser.). (ENG.). 16p. (gr. 1-2). pap. 6.50 *(978-1-4042-7148-7(1),* 650957f7-a26e-4377-af2f-59e6e5bfbcc0, Rosen Classroom) Rosen Publishing Group, Inc., The.

Ellis, Julie. Shark & Crab Big Book Edition, 1 vol. Hawley, Kelvin, illus. 2014. (ENG.). 16p. (gr. 1-1). pap. *(978-1-77654-094-5(8),* Red Rocket Readers) Flying Start Bks.

Ellis, Julie & Nickel, Adam. The Giant's Causeway. 2008. (Rigby Focus Forward: Level K Ser.). (Illus.). 24p. (J). (gr. -1-3). pap. *(978-1-4190-3796-2(X),* Rigby) Pearson Education Australia.

Ellis, Julie & Stewart, Christen. Lizzie's Hidden Message. 2008. (Rigby Focus Forward: Level N Ser.). (Illus.). 24p. (J). (gr. 4-7). pap. *(978-1-4190-3839-6(7),* Rigby) Pearson Education Australia.

Ellis, Roman. My Class Government: Sharing & Reusing, 1 vol. 2017. (Computer Kids: Powered by Computational Thinking Ser.). (ENG.). 24p. (J). (gr. 3-4). 25.27 *(978-1-5383-2415-8(6),* 2d4160cb-94ea-4b26-9c4b-c0a4afafaae3, PowerKids Pr.); pap. *(978-1-5383-5314-1(8),* 01b39852-a228-4859-80a3-2894f580bb78, Rosen Classroom) Rosen Publishing Group, Inc., The.

Elson, William. Elson Readers: Book Four, Bk. 4. 2017. (ENG., Illus.). 367p. (gr. -1-12). 21.95 *(978-1-890623-18-0(0))* Applewood Bks.

Elson, William, et al. Elson Readers: Book Eight, Vol. 8. 2017. (ENG., Illus.). 575p. (gr. -1-12). 27.95 *(978-1-890623-22-7(9))* Applewood Bks.

—Elson Readers: Book Five, Bk. 5. 2017. (ENG., Illus.). 439p. (gr. -1-12). 23.95 *(978-1-890623-19-7(9))* Applewood Bks.

—Elson Readers: Book Seven, Bk. 7. 2017. (ENG., Illus.). 549p. (gr. -1-12). 25.95 *(978-1-890623-21-0(0))* Applewood Bks.

—Elson Readers: Book Six, Bk. 6. 2017. (ENG., Illus.). 477p. (gr. -1-12). tchr. ed. 24.95 *(978-1-890623-20-3(2))* Applewood Bks.

Elson, William H. The Elson Readers, Vol. 5. 2004. reprint ed. pap. 1.99 *(978-1-4192-6079-7(0))* Kessinger Publishing, LLC.

Elson, William H. & Keck, Christine M. The Elson Readers - Book V. 2007. 420p. per. *(978-1-4065-2501-4(4))* Dodo Pr.

Elson, William H., et al. The Elson Readers, 9 vols. 2005. (Illus.). (J). pap. *(978-1-890623-23-4(7))* Lost Classics Bk. Co.

Ely, Jennifer W. Mommy Teach Me to Read: Pre-Reader Series 1. 2006. (J). 16.99 *(978-0-9777150-0-8(0))* Growing Little Readers.

Embacher, Eric. Will Smith: The Funny, Funky, & Confident Fresh Prince, 6 vols., Set. 2003. (High Five Reading - Red Ser.). (ENG.). 48p. (gr. 3-4). pap. 54.00 *(978-0-7368-2839-0(7))* Capstone.

Emerald, Ruby & Sapphire Levels Certificate Only. (gr. k-5). 89.00 *(978-0-7578-6537-4(2))* Rigby Education.

Emergent: 1 Each of 8 Big Books, Vol. 3. (Sunshinetm Science Ser.). (gr. 1-2). 250.50 *(978-0-7802-0571-0(5))* Wright Group/McGraw-Hill.

Emergent Vol. 3: 1 Each of 8 Student Books. (Sunshinetm Science Ser.). (gr. 1-2). 48.95 *(978-0-7802-0572-7(3))* Wright Group/McGraw-Hill.

Emma. The Adventures of Blue Flamingo. Emma, illus. 2018. (Adventures of Blue Flamingo Ser.). (ENG., Illus.). 26p. (J). (gr. 1-3). pap. 6.99 *(978-1-63529-973-1(X))* Caliber Comics.

Emmett, Jonathan. Danny Dreadnought Saves the World (Reading Ladder Level 2) Chatterton, Martin, illus. 2016. (Reading Ladder Level 2 Ser.). (ENG.). 48p. (gr. k-2). pap. 4.99 *(978-1-4052-8219-2(3),* Reading Ladder) Farshore GBR. Dist: HarperCollins Pubs.

—The Emperor's New Clones (Reading Ladder Level 3) Chatterton, Martin, illus. 2nd ed. 2017. (Reading Ladder Level 3 Ser.). (ENG.). 48p. (gr. k-2). pap. 4.99 *(978-1-4052-8252-9(5),* Reading Ladder) Farshore GBR. Dist: HarperCollins Pubs.

The Enchanted Little Egg. 2017. (ENG., Illus.). 176p. (J). 9.00 *(978-1-78270-142-2(7))* Award Pubns. Ltd. GBR. Dist: Parkwest Pubns., Inc.

Ende, Michael & Michael, Ende. El Largo Camino Hacia Santa Cruz. Kehn, Regina, illus. (SPA.). 64p. (J). (gr. 3-5). 6.95 *(978-84-241-3354-2(4),* EV3073) Everest Editora ESP. Dist: Lectorum Pubns., Inc.

Endres, Hollie J. The Letter Ee Set: Things That Are Alike, 6 vols. 2004. (Letter Bks.). (ENG.). 8p. (gr. k-1). pap. 29.70 *(978-0-7368-4104-7(0))* Capstone.

—The Letter Hh Set: Homes, 6 vols. 2004. (Letter Bks.). (ENG.). 8p. (gr. k-1). pap. 29.70 *(978-0-7368-4107-8(5))* Capstone.

—The Letter Nn Set: At the Grocery Store, 6 vols. 2004. (Letter Bks.). (ENG.). 8p. (gr. k-1). pap. 29.70 *(978-0-7368-4113-9(X))* Capstone.

—The Letter Xx Set: Things I Can See, 6. 2004. (Letter Bks.). (ENG.). 8p. (gr. k-1). pap. 29.70 *(978-0-7368-4123-8(7))* Capstone.

—The Letter Yy Set: All about Me!, 6 vols. 2004. (Letter Bks.). (ENG.). 8p. (gr. k-1). pap. 29.70 *(978-0-7368-4124-5(5))* Capstone.

—Our Red-White-and-Blue Holidays, 6 vols., Set. 2004. (Phonics Readers Books 37-72 Ser.). (ENG.). 8p. (gr. k-1). pap. 35.70 *(978-0-7368-4054-5(0))* Capstone.

—A Trip to the Repair Shop, 6 vols., Set. 2004. (Letter Bks.). (ENG.). 8p. (gr. k-1). pap. 29.70 *(978-0-7368-4111-5(3))* Capstone.

Energy - English Take Home Book. 2007. (Journeys Ser.). (J). pap. 20.00 *(978-1-4042-9535-3(6),* Rosen Classroom) Rosen Publishing Group, Inc., The.

Engage Literacy Leveled Readers Levels A-P: Bookroom Package with Extensions. 2016. (Engage Literacy Ser.). (ENG.). (gr. k-3). pap., pap., pap. 7955.00 *(978-1-5157-4814-4(6),* 175729, Capstone Pr.) Capstone.

Engelmann, Siegfried & Engelmann, Owen. Funnix Beginning Math. 2011. (J). DVD 32.00 *(978-0-9714798-2-1(8))* Royal Limited Partnership.

—Funnix Beginning Math Workbook. 2011. (J). instr.'s gde. ed. 10.00 *(978-0-9714798-4-5(4))* Royal Limited Partnership.

Engle, Margarita. La Selva (Forest World) Romay, Alexis, tr. 2019. (SPA.). (J). (gr. 5). 224p. pap. 7.99 *(978-1-5344-2930-7(1));* (Illus.). 208p. 17.99 *(978-1-5344-5107-0(2))* Simon & Schuster Children's Publishing. (Atheneum Bks. for Young Readers).

English, Alex. Mine, Mine, Mine Said the Porcupine. Levey, Emma, illus. 2019. (Early Bird Readers — Blue (Early Bird Stories (tm)) Ser.). (ENG.). 32p. (J). (gr. -1-2). 30.65 *(978-1-5415-4173-3(1),* b037c99e-c022-438e-9914-09036213cf0c, Lerner Pubns.) Lerner Publishing Group.

—Pirates Don't Drive Diggers. Beedie, Duncan, illus. 2019. (Early Bird Readers — Orange (Early Bird Stories (tm)) Ser.). (ENG.). 32p. (J). (gr. k-3). 30.65 *(978-1-5415-4221-1(5),* 9ac76b41-4605-4891-9cd5-ca610ae092db); pap. 9.99 *(978-1-5415-7414-4(1),* 19707421-c580-497c-b567-bd6ce5f91e10) Lerner Publishing Group. (Lerner Pubns.).

—Yuck! Said the Yak. Levey, Emma, illus. 2019. (Early Bird Readers — Green (Early Bird Stories (tm)) Ser.). (ENG.). 32p. (J). (gr. k-3). pap. 9.99 *(978-1-5415-7410-6(9),* 4d812eaf-c03e-4c79-ba2f-b142a87854fd, Lerner Pubns.) Lerner Publishing Group.

English for a Changing World Listening Comprehension Manual: Level 3, 6 vols. (Fluency Strand Ser.). (YA). 45.00 *(978-1-4045-1217-7(9))* Wright Group/McGraw-Hill.

English in My Pocket: Add-to Pack of Little Books. 34.00 *(978-0-7635-2931-4(1))* Rigby Education.

English in My Pocket: Add-to Pack of Manipulatives. 42.00 *(978-0-7635-2932-1(X))* Rigby Education.

English-Spanish Book Set 800937, 4 vols. 2005. (J). bds. *(978-1-59794-096-2(8))* Environments, Inc.

English to a Beat! (gr. 2-8). 763.19 *(978-0-7362-2508-3(0))* CENGAGE Learning.

English to a Beat! Folk Tales Single-Copy Set. (gr. 2-8). 95.84 *(978-0-7362-2507-6(2))* CENGAGE Learning.

Ennett, Jonathan. Clever Computers Turquoise Band. 2016. (Cambridge Reading Adventures Ser.). (ENG., Illus.). 24p. pap. 8.80 *(978-1-316-50331-7(3))* Cambridge Univ. Pr.

—Town Underground. 2016. (Cambridge Reading Adventures Ser.). (ENG., Illus.). 24p. pap. 8.80 *(978-1-316-50333-1(X))* Cambridge Univ. Pr.

The Entire World of SH & CH Book of Stories. 2004. per. 34.99 *(978-0-9760490-2-9(3))* Say It Right.

Eric Carle Board Book Set 800489, 3. 2005. (J). bds. *(978-1-59794-003-0(8))* Environments, Inc.

Erin, K. c. The Carnival. 2009. 60p. pap. 23.99 *(978-1-4389-7048-6(X))* AuthorHouse.

Escott, John. Level 2: the Ghost of Genny Castle. 2nd ed. 2008. (Pearson English Graded Readers Ser.). (ENG., Illus.). 48p. pap. 13.32 *(978-1-4058-6953-9(4),* Pearson ELT) Pearson Education.

Esquivel, Rosaura. It's Time for School, 1 vol. 2017. (Let's Tell Time Ser.). (ENG.). 24p. (J). (gr. 1-1). 25.27 *(978-1-5081-5725-0(1),* 6176e84c-af4d-4851-8416-254ee45f3d8e, PowerKids Pr.) Rosen Publishing Group, Inc., The.

Essential Words Reading & Language Arts Activity Book (Elementary) Elementary. 2006. (J). 8.95 *(978-1-933655-01-7(1))* New Leaf Educ., Inc.

Eubanks, Holly L. Through the Eye of the Needle. (J). stu. ed. 18.95 *(978-1-56270-047-8(2))* Dominie Pr., Inc.

—Through the Eye of the Needle: Answer Key. (J). 395.00 *(978-1-56270-049-2(9))* Dominie Pr., Inc.

Evan-Moor Educational Publishers. Language Fundamentals, Grade 1. 2016. (Language Fundamentals Ser.). (ENG., Illus.). 272p. (J). (gr. 1-1). pap., tchr. ed. 29.99 *(978-1-62938-217-3(5))* Evan-Moor Educational Pubs.

—Language Fundamentals, Grade 2. 2016. (Language Fundamentals Ser.). (ENG., Illus.). 272p. (J). (gr. 2-2). pap., tchr. ed. 29.99 *(978-1-62938-218-0(3))* Evan-Moor Educational Pubs.

—Language Fundamentals, Grade 3. 2016. (Language Fundamentals Ser.). (ENG., Illus.). 272p. (J). (gr. 3-3). pap., tchr. ed. 29.99 *(978-1-62938-219-7(1))* Evan-Moor Educational Pubs.

—Language Fundamentals, Grade 4. 2016. (Language Fundamentals Ser.). (ENG., Illus.). 272p. (J). (gr. 4-4). pap., tchr. ed. 29.99 *(978-1-62938-220-3(5))* Evan-Moor Educational Pubs.

—Language Fundamentals, Grade 5. 2016. (Language Fundamentals Ser.). (ENG., Illus.). 272p. (J). (gr. 5-5). pap., tchr. ed. 29.99 *(978-1-62938-221-0(3))* Evan-Moor Educational Pubs.

—Language Fundamentals, Grade 6. 2016. (Language Fundamentals Ser.). (ENG., Illus.). 272p. (J). (gr. 6-6). pap., tchr. ed. 29.99 *(978-1-62938-222-7(1))* Evan-Moor Educational Pubs.

—Skill Sharpeners Reading Grade 1. 2005. (Skill Sharpeners: Reading Ser.). (ENG., Illus.). 144p. (J). (gr. 1-1). pap., tchr. ed. 10.99 *(978-1-59673-037-3(4))* Evan-Moor Educational Pubs.

—Skill Sharpeners Reading Grade 2. 2005. (Skill Sharpeners: Reading Ser.). (ENG., Illus.). 144p. (J). (gr. 2-2). pap., tchr. ed. 10.99 *(978-1-59673-038-0(2),* emc 4530) Evan-Moor Educational Pubs.

—Skill Sharpeners Reading Grade 3. 2005. (Skill Sharpeners: Reading Ser.). (ENG., Illus.). 144p. (J). (gr. 3-3). pap., tchr. ed. 10.99 *(978-1-59673-039-7(0),* emc 4531) Evan-Moor Educational Pubs.

—Skill Sharpeners Reading Grade 4. 2005. (Skill Sharpeners: Reading Ser.). (ENG., Illus.). 144p. (J). (gr. 4-4). pap., tchr. ed. 10.99 *(978-1-59673-040-3(4),* emc 4532) Evan-Moor Educational Pubs.

—Skill Sharpeners Reading Grade 5. 2005. (Skill Sharpeners: Reading Ser.). (ENG., Illus.). 144p. (J). (gr. 5-5). pap., tchr. ed. 10.99 *(978-1-59673-041-0(2),* emc 4533) Evan-Moor Educational Pubs.

—Skill Sharpeners Reading Grade 6+ 2005. (Skill Sharpeners: Reading Ser.). (ENG., Illus.). 144p. (J). (gr. 6-6). pap., tchr. ed. 10.99 *(978-1-59673-042-7(0),* emc 4534) Evan-Moor Educational Pubs.

—Skill Sharpeners Reading Grade K. 2005. (Skill Sharpeners: Reading Ser.). (ENG., Illus.). 144p. (J). (gr. k-k). pap., tchr. ed. 10.99 *(978-1-59673-036-6(6),* emc 4528) Evan-Moor Educational Pubs.

—Skill Sharpeners Reading Grade Pre-K. 2005. (Skill Sharpeners: Reading Ser.). (ENG., Illus.). 144p. (J). (gr. -1 — 1). pap., tchr. ed. 10.99 *(978-1-59673-035-9(8),* emc 4527) Evan-Moor Educational Pubs.

Evans, Shira. National Geographic Kids Readers: Animal Homes (Prereader) 2018. (Readers Ser.). (Illus.). 24p. (J). (gr. -1-k). pap. 5.99 *(978-1-4263-3026-1(X),* National Geographic Kids) Disney Publishing Worldwide.

—National Geographic Readers: Tadpole to Frog (L1/Coreader) 2018. (Readers Ser.). (Illus.). 48p. (J). (gr. -1-k). pap. 4.99 *(978-1-4263-3203-6(3),* National Geographic Kids) Disney Publishing Worldwide.

Eva's Lost & Found Report: Fourth Grade Guided Comprehension Level L. (On Our Way to English Ser.). (gr. 4-18). 34.50 *(978-0-7578-7150-4(X))* Rigby Education.

EventoSusan. YOUR DREAM VACATION HIGH BEGINNING BOOK WITH ONLINE ACCESS, 1 vol. 2014. (ENG., Illus.). 24p. (J). pap., E-Book, E-Book 9.50 *(978-1-107-69043-1(9))* Cambridge Univ. Pr.

Everett-CamplinHelen. Grandad's Magic Gadgets Level 2 Elementary/Lower-intermediate. 2009. (Cambridge Experience Readers Ser.). (ENG.). 64p. pap. 14.75 *(978-84-8323-522-5(6))* Cambridge Univ. Pr.

Every Body Tells a Story: Level Q, 6 vols., Vol. 3. (Explorers Ser.). 32p. (gr. 3-6). 44.95 *(978-0-7699-0621-8(4))* Shortland Pubns. (U. S. A.) Inc.

Every Morning: Lap Book. (Pebble Soup Explorations Ser.). 16p. (gr. -1-18). 21.00 *(978-0-7578-1656-7(8))* Rigby Education.

Every Morning: Small Book. (Pebble Soup Explorations Ser.). 16p. (gr. -1-18). 5.00 *(978-0-7578-1696-3(7))* Rigby Education.

Everyday Assessment with Reading Rods. 2004. (J). lib. bdg. 24.95 *(978-1-56911-176-5(6))* Learning Resources, Inc.

Excuse Me, Sir. (J). 26.20 *(978-0-8136-8396-6(3));* (gr. -1-3). 59.50 *(978-0-8136-7912-9(5))* Modern Curriculum Pr.

Excuses, Excuses: 6 Small Books. (gr. k-3). 24.00 *(978-0-7635-6236-6(X))* Rigby Education.

Explore! (Early Intervention Levels Ser.). 21.42 *(978-0-7362-1051-5(2))* CENGAGE Learning.

The Explorer: Individual Title Six-Packs. (gr. -1-2). 27.00 *(978-0-7635-9448-0(2))* Rigby Education.

Explorers: Fluency - Student Book Set - 1 Each of 12 Titles. (Explorers. Exploradores Nonfiction Sets Ser.). (gr. 3-6). 89.95 *(978-0-7699-0815-1(2))* Shortland Pubns. (U. S. A.) Inc.

Exploring Literature: The EMC Write-in Reader. 2nd ed. (Literature & the Language Arts Ser.). (YA). (gr. 7-18). wbk. ed. 17.99 *(978-0-8219-2910-0(0))* EMC/Paradigm Publishing.

Extensions Through the Library TAKS Reading Preparation Grades 3-5: Curriculum Connected Resources. 2004. (Region IV ESC Resources for Librarian Ser.). spiral bd. *(978-1-933049-05-2(7))* Region 4 Education Service Ctr.

Extensions Through the Library TAKS Reading Preparation Grades 6-8. 2005. spiral bd. *(978-1-933049-46-5(4))* Region 4 Education Service Ctr.

Fabregat, Antonio-Manuel. Los Cuentos de Mi Escuela. (SPA.). 64p. (J). (gr. 4). *(978-84-216-1593-5(9),* BU4751) Bruño, Editorial ESP. Dist: Lectorum Pubns., Inc.

La Fabrica. (Coleccion Aqui Se Trabaja). (SPA., Illus.). (J). 10.95 *(978-84-207-3624-2(4),* ANY765) Grupo Anaya, S.A. ESP. Dist: Continental Bk. Co., Inc.

Fabulas Fabulosas. 2006. (SPA.). (J). *(978-1-933485-24-9(8))* Publicaciones Puertorriquenas, Inc.

Fabulous PH Riddles Blends/Dig. (J). pap. 18.16 *(978-0-8136-0864-8(3))* Modern Curriculum Pr.

Fact & Opinion (Gr. 1-3) 2003. (J). *(978-1-58232-078-6(0))* ECS Learning Systems, Inc.

Fakhouri, Shoua. Ibn Sina: Level 13. 2019. (Collins Big Cat Ser.). (ENG.). 32p. (J). (gr. 4-6). pap. 8.99 *(978-0-00-829944-6(7))* HarperCollins Pubs. Ltd. GBR. Dist: Independent Pubs. Group.

—Omar's First Day at School Pink B Band. Pérez, Moni, illus. 2016. (Cambridge Reading Adventures Ser.). (ENG.). 16p. pap. 7.95 *(978-1-316-60811-1(5))* Cambridge Univ. Pr.

Falletta, Bernadette. We Love to Read Stories Coloring Book & Word Search Puzzles. 2005. 23p. (J). 10.95 *(978-1-4116-6291-9(1))* Lulu Pr., Inc.

Falletta, Bernadette & Lewis, Maria. We Love to Read Stories & Songs. 2005. 27p. (J). 14.95 *(978-1-4116-4734-3(3))* Lulu Pr., Inc.

The Family: Individual Title, 6 pack. (Sails Literacy Ser.). 16p. (gr. k-18). 27.00 *(978-0-7635-4409-6(4))* Rigby Education.

Family Counts. (Early Intervention Levels Ser.). 23.10 *(978-0-7362-0001-1(0))* CENGAGE Learning.

Family Living Board Book Set 800646, 4. 2005. (J). bds. *(978-1-59794-038-2(0))* Environments, Inc.

Family Stories: Individual Packs Pack A. (gr. k-2). 15.40 *(978-0-7362-0491-0(1))* CENGAGE Learning.

Family Stories: Individual Packs Pack B. (gr. k-2). 15.40 *(978-0-7362-0493-4(8))* CENGAGE Learning.

Family Stories: Jumbo Packs. (gr. k-2). 157.08 *(978-0-7362-0051-6(7))* CENGAGE Learning.

Famous Tales. 2016. (Famous Tales Ser.). 24p. (gr. 2-2). pap. 49.50 *(978-1-5081-9273-2(1),* Windmill Bks.) Rosen Publishing Group, Inc., The.

Far Away. (Early Intervention Levels Ser.). 3.85 *(978-0-7362-1865-8(3))* CENGAGE Learning.

Farley, Robin. Mia & the Too Big Tutu. Ivanov, Olga & Ivanov, Aleksey, illus. 2010. (My First I Can Read Ser.). (ENG.). 32p. (J). (gr. -1-3). 16.99 *(978-0-06-173302-4(4),* HarperCollins) HarperCollins Pubs.

Farley, Robin & Ivanov, Aleksey. Pink Slippers: Mia & the Too Big Tutu. 2010. (My First I Can Read Ser.). (ENG., Illus.). 32p. (J). (gr. -1-3). pap. 4.99 *(978-0-06-173301-7(6),* HarperCollins) HarperCollins Pubs.

Farmer's Market. (Early Intervention Levels Ser.). 21.30 *(978-0-7362-2126-9(3))* CENGAGE Learning.

Farming. (Early Intervention Levels Ser.). 50.88 *(978-0-7362-2127-6(1));* 8.48 *(978-0-7362-1900-6(5))* CENGAGE Learning.

Fast Forward! 2003. (Fast Forward! Ser.). Level C. (J). (gr. 1-18). stu. ed., per. 67.95 *(978-1-58830-333-2(0))*Level C. (J). (gr. 1-18). stu. ed., per. 7.95 *(978-1-58830-779-8(4))*Level D. (J). (gr. 2-18). stu. ed., per. 7.95 *(978-1-58830-780-4(8))*Level D. (J). (gr. 2-18). stu. ed., per. 67.95 *(978-1-58830-334-9(9))*Level A. tchr. ed., per., tchr.'s training gde. ed. 39.95 *(978-1-58830-783-5(2))*Level A. (J). (gr. 1-18). stu. ed., per. 67.95 *(978-1-58830-331-8(4))*Level A. (J). (gr. 1-18). stu. ed., per. 7.95 *(978-1-58830-777-4(8))*Level B. tchr. ed., per., tchr.'s training gde. ed. 39.95 *(978-1-58830-784-2(0))*Level B. (J). (gr. 1-18). stu. ed., per. 7.95 *(978-1-58830-778-1(6))*Level B. (J). (gr. 1-18). stu. ed., per. 67.95 *(978-1-58830-332-5(2))*Level E. (J). (gr. 1-18). stu. ed., per. 7.95 *(978-1-58830-781-1(6))*Level E. (J). (gr. 2-18). 369.95 *(978-1-58830-799-6(9))*Level E. (J). (gr. 2-18). stu. ed., per. 67.95 *(978-1-58830-335-6(7))*Level F. (J). (gr. 2-18). 369.95 *(978-1-58830-800-9(6))*Level F. (J). (gr. 2-18). stu. ed., per. 7.95 *(978-1-58830-782-8(4))*Level F. (J). (gr. 2-18). stu. ed., per. 67.95 *(978-1-58830-336-3(5))* Metropolitan Teaching & Learning Co.

Faundez, Anne. A Cloak for Swallow, 4 vols. 2005. (QEB Readers). (Illus.). 24p. (J). (gr. 1-4). lib. bdg. 15.95 *(978-1-59566-093-0(3))* QEB Publishing Inc.

—Imaginary Creatures, 4 vols. 2005. (QEB Readers). (Illus.). 24p. (J). (gr. -1-3). lib. bdg. 15.95 *(978-1-59566-102-9(6))* QEB Publishing Inc.

—Sing a Song of Sixpence, 8 vols. 2005. (QEB Readers). (Illus.). 24p. (J). (gr. -1-3). lib. bdg. 15.95 *(978-1-59566-072-5(0))* QEB Publishing Inc.

Faundez, Anne, et al. QEB Start Reading Multipack (6 Titles) Paperback, 6 vols. 2005. (QEB Start Reading Ser.). (Illus.). 144p. (J). lib. bdg. 40.00 *(978-1-59566-063-3(1))* QEB Publishing Inc.

Favorite Animals Book Set 2 800893, 6 vols. 2005. (J). pap. *(978-1-59794-068-9(2))* Environments, Inc.

Favorite Characters 800885, 6 vols. 2005. (J). pap. *(978-1-59794-060-3(7))* Environments, Inc.

Favorite Characters No. 2 800886, 6 vols. 2005. (J). pap. *(978-1-59794-061-0(5))* Environments, Inc.

The Feast: 3-in-1 Package. (Sails Literacy Ser.). 24p. (gr. 2-18). 57.00 *(978-0-7578-3214-7(8))* Rigby Education.

The Feast: Big Book Only. (Sails Literacy Ser.). 24p. (gr. 2-18). 27.00 *(978-0-7635-6994-5(1))* Rigby Education.

Feldman, Luke, illus. La Bella y la Bestia: La Novela Grafica (a Graphic Novel), 1 vol. 2010. (Graphic Spin en Español Ser.). (SPA.). 40p. (J). (gr. 3-6). pap. 5.95 *(978-1-4342-2269-5(1),* 103132, Stone Arch Bks.) Capstone.

Fenske, Jonathan. Please, No More Nuts! Fenske, Jonathan, illus. 2018. (Penguin Young Readers, Level 2 Ser.). (Illus.). 32p. (J). (gr. 1-2). pap. 4.99 *(978-0-515-15965-3(4),* Penguin Young Readers) Penguin Young Readers Group.

Fentiman, David. The Lego Movie. 2013. (DK Reader Level 3 Ser.). lib. bdg. 13.55 *(978-0-606-35322-9(4))* Turtleback.

—New Adventures. 2015. (Illus.). 47p. (J). *(978-1-4806-9626-6(9))* Dorling Kindersley Publishing, Inc.

Fernandez, Joyce & Marsh, Laura. Eins Is One. 2009. 22p. 15.95 *(978-0-578-00209-5(4))* My Second Language Publishing, USA.

—Eins und Zwei are One & Two. 2009. 22p. 15.95 *(978-0-578-00208-8(6))* My Second Language Publishing, USA.

—Um Is One. 2009. 22p. 15.95 *(978-0-557-05629-3(2))* Lulu Pr., Inc.

—Uno y Dos are One & Two. 2008. 22p. pap. 15.95 *(978-0-615-26150-8(7))* My Second Language Publishing, USA.

Fetzer, Erin & Sonday, Arlene. SS1 Readers L6a-10c. l.t. ed. 2004. (ENG., Illus.). 12p. (J). 59.99 *(978-1-891602-14-6(4))* Winsor Learning, Inc.

Fiction & Nonfiction Packs: Jumbo Packs. (gr. k-2). 438.19 *(978-1-56334-397-1(5))* CENGAGE Learning.

Fiction Readers, 30, Set. 2013. (Book Collection). (SPA., Illus.). 20p. (gr. 1-1). 149.70 *(978-1-4938-0207-4(0))* Teacher Created Materials, Inc.

Fielder, Scott. The 10 Greatest 21st Century Innovations. 2008. 14.99 *(978-1-55448-550-5(9))* Scholastic Library Publishing.

Figorito, Marcus. A Dime's Busy Day, 1 vol. 2006. (Neighborhood Readers Ser.). (ENG.). 12p. (gr. k-1). pap. 5.15 *(978-1-4042-6710-7(7),* 3386d309-e9c1-432a-a56f-ab0733b86176, Rosen Classroom) Rosen Publishing Group, Inc., The.

—Tara Takes the Train, 1 vol. 2006. (Neighborhood Readers Ser.). (ENG.). 16p. (gr. 1-2). pap. 6.50 *(978-1-4042-7208-8(9),* 6defb4c6-988b-44df-bcfb-a804e6b6e432, Rosen Classroom) Rosen Publishing Group, Inc., The.

Find the Sock. (Early Intervention Levels Ser.). 21.30 *(978-0-7362-0394-4(X));* Vol. 6. 3.55 *(978-0-7362-0174-2(2))* CENGAGE Learning.

Findley, Violet. Sea Turtles. 2011. (Illus.). 16p. (J). pap. *(978-0-545-24791-7(8))* Scholastic, Inc.

Fine, Ann. Press Play. Dreidemy, Joëlle, illus. 2nd ed. 2017. (Reading Ladder Level 3 Ser.). (ENG.). 48p. (gr. k-2). pap. 4.99 *(978-1-4052-8242-0(8),* Reading Ladder) Farshore GBR. Dist: HarperCollins Pubs.

Fine, Anne. Magic Ball (Reading Ladder Level 3) Robertson, Matt, illus. 2017. (Reading Ladder Level 3 Ser.). (ENG.). 48p. pap. 4.99 *(978-1-4052-8455-4(2),* Reading Ladder) Farshore GBR. Dist: HarperCollins Pubs.

—Under the Bed (Reading Ladder Level 2) Robertson, Matt, illus. 2nd ed. 2016. (Reading Ladder Level 2 Ser.). (ENG.). 48p. (gr. k-2). pap. 4.99 *(978-1-4052-8220-8(7),* Reading Ladder) Farshore GBR. Dist: HarperCollins Pubs.

Fine, Edith Hope & Pinkerton Josephson, Judith. Armando y la Escuela de Lona Azul: Armando & the Blue Tarp School, 1 vol. Sosa, Hernán, illus. 2014.Tr. of Armando & the Blue Tarp School. (SPA.). 32p. (J). (gr. 3-5). pap. 12.95 *(978-1-60060-449-2(8),* leelowbooks) Lee & Low Bks., Inc.

Finnegan, Delphine. The Big Birthday Surprise! Hall, Susan, illus. 2017. 24p. (J). *(978-1-5182-5213-6(3))* Random Hse., Inc.

Fiorella, Christina. My Boy Kyle. 2010. 20p. 13.99 *(978-1-4520-6519-9(5))* AuthorHouse.

First Adventures Book Set 800918, 3 vols. 2005. (J). pap. *(978-1-59794-083-2(6))* Environments, Inc.

First Chapter Book Set 2 800899, 6 vols. 2005. (J). pap. *(978-1-59794-074-0(7))* Environments, Inc.

First Chapter Book Set 800898, 3 vols. 2005. (J). *(978-1-59794-073-3(9))* Environments, Inc.

A First Clay Gathering (Review Multiple Meanings), Level C. 2003. ("Plaid" Phonics & Stories Libraries). 43.50 *(978-0-8136-9234-0(2))* Modern Curriculum Pr.

First Fables Book Set 800915, 6 vols. 2005. (J). pap. *(978-1-59794-080-1(1))* Environments, Inc.

First I can Read Set 800882, 4 vols. 2005. (J). pap. *(978-1-59794-057-3(7))* Environments, Inc.

First Nature Books 800939, 4. 2005. (J). bds. *(978-1-59794-030-6(5))* Environments, Inc.

The First Rainbow: Fourth Grade Guided Comprehension Level O. (On Our Way to English Ser.). (gr. 4-18). 34.50 *(978-0-7578-7165-8(8))* Rigby Education.

First Stories (Gr. K-1) 2003. (J). *(978-1-58232-035-9(7))* ECS Learning Systems, Inc.

First Things: Individual Title Six-Packs. (gr. -1-2). 23.00 *(978-0-7635-8799-4(0))* Rigby Education.

Flaherty, Finn. The Flowerpot, 1 vol. 2006. (Neighborhood Readers Ser.). (ENG.). 16p. (gr. 1-2). pap. 6.50 *(978-1-4042-7224-8(0),* 325243fc-8dab-4b1d-b15e-00e86f2558fd, Rosen Classroom) Rosen Publishing Group, Inc., The.

Flor Ada, Alma. Quiero Ayudar! Dominguez, Angela, illus. 2010.Tr. of Let Me Help! (ENG & SPA.). 32p. (J). (gr. -1-3). 16.95 *(978-0-89239-232-2(0))* Lee & Low Bks., Inc.

Flores, Vanessa. Luna Studies Population: Analyzing Data, 1 vol. 2017. (Computer Kids: Powered by Computational Thinking Ser.). (ENG.). 24p. (J). (gr. 4-5). 25.27 *(978-1-5383-2410-3(5),* e51eecf4-5e0d-4f6c-9532-395159c06fa2, PowerKids Pr.); pap. *(978-1-5383-5315-8(6),* b28fcd35-1d14-4584-a57e-3e641794c607, Rosen Classroom) Rosen Publishing Group, Inc., The.

—My Science Flowchart: Following Instructions, 1 vol. 2017. (Computer Kids: Powered by Computational Thinking Ser.). (ENG.). 24p. (J). (gr. 3-4). 25.27 *(978-1-5383-2418-9(0),* 8b4a8e6c-6bce-4f38-b27b-e1838440d131, PowerKids Pr.); pap. *(978-1-5081-3784-9(6),* ea9a838a-5234-4d89-9271-c481a6a4638c, Rosen Classroom) Rosen Publishing Group, Inc., The.

Florie, Christine. Rookie Ready to Learn en Español: la Mariquita Lara. Dalby, Danny Brooks, illus. 2011. (Rookie Ready to Learn Español Ser.). Orig. Title: Rookie Ready to Learn: Lara Ladybug. (SPA.). 32p. (J). pap. 5.95 *(978-0-531-26783-7(0),* Children's Pr.) Scholastic Library Publishing.

Florie, Christine & Dalby, Danny Brooks. La Mariquita Lara. Dalby, Danny Brooks, illus. 2011. (Rookie Ready to Learn Español Ser.). (SPA., Illus.). 32p. (J). lib. bdg. 23.00 *(978-0-531-26115-6(8),* Children's Pr.) Scholastic Library Publishing.

Flounders, Anne. The Corps of Discovery. Flounders, Anne, ed. 2004. (Reader's Theater Content-Area Concepts Ser.). (ENG., Illus.). (J). (gr. 4-5). 5.00 net. *(978-1-4108-2310-6(5),* A23105) Benchmark Education Co.

Flounders, Anne, ed. Return to Earth. Wolk-Stanley, Jessica; Flounders, illus. 2004. (Reader's Theater Content-Area Concepts Ser.). (ENG.). (J). (gr. 3-5). 5.00 net. *(978-1-4108-2306-9(7),* A23067) Benchmark Education Co.

Flounders, Anne; DuFalla, ed. Sumac & the Magic Lake. DuFalla, Anita, illus. 2004. (Reader's Theater Content-Area Concepts Ser.). (ENG.). (J). (gr. 1-2). 5.00 net. *(978-1-4108-2291-8(5),* A22915) Benchmark Education Co.

Floyd, Cassandra. Ce-Ce: The Life of an American Cocker Spaniel. 2005. (ENG.). 76p. pap. 11.49 *(978-1-4208-8531-6(6))* AuthorHouse.

The Flutey Family Fruitcake: Level L, 6 vols. 128p. (gr. 2-3). 41.95 *(978-0-7699-1019-2(X))* Shortland Pubns. (U. S. A.) Inc.

The Fly: Individual Title Six-Pack. (Story Steps Ser.). (gr. k-2). 20.00 *(978-0-7635-9596-8(9))* Rigby Education.

The Flying Machine: KinderConcepts Individual Title Six-Packs. (Kinderstarters Ser.). 8p. (gr. -1-1). 21.00 *(978-0-7635-8719-2(2))* Rigby Education.

Flynn, Warren. Different Voices. 200p. (YA). pap. 13.95 *(978-1-86368-299-2(6))* Fremantle Pr. AUS. Dist: Independent Pubs. Group.

Fogerty, Ramona. Stories That Increase Reading Fluency: Improving Word Recognition & Comprehension. 2005. (J). per. 19.95 *(978-0-9759889-2-3(1))* Potential Psychotherapy Counseling & Remedial Service.

Folklore. Two Strangers. (J). pap. 2.99 *(978-0-8136-2413-6(4))* Modern Curriculum Pr.

—Two Strangers Director's Guide. (J). pap. 5.99 *(978-0-8136-2438-9(X))* Modern Curriculum Pr.

Follett, Katherine. Energy Sources for the 21st Century. 2011. (Readers' & Writers' Genre Workshop Ser.). (J). pap. *(978-1-4509-3029-1(8))* Benchmark Education Co.

Follow That Spy! Individual Title Six-Packs. (Action Packs Ser.). 120p. (gr. 3-5). 44.00 *(978-0-7635-8419-1(3))* Rigby Education.

Follow the Leader: Individual Title Six-Packs. (gr. 1-2). 22.00 *(978-0-7635-9152-6(1))* Rigby Education.

Following Directions (Gr. K-1) 2003. (J). *(978-1-58232-030-4(6))* ECS Learning Systems, Inc.

Fontana, Lynn & Hoge, Patricia, eds. Education Station Reading Anthology, Volume One: A-B, Band 1-2. 2004. (Illus.). 314p. spiral bd. 48.72 *(978-0-7398-9887-1(6))* Steck-Vaughn.

—Education Station Reading Anthology, Volume Two. 2004. (Illus.). Band 1-2. 274p. spiral bd. 52.36 *(978-0-7398-9888-8(4))*Band 3-5. 132p. spiral bd. 21.84 *(978-0-7398-9890-1(6))* Steck-Vaughn.

—Education Station Reading, Volume One: C-E: Student Resource Book. 2004. (Illus.). 248p. per. 7.84 *(978-0-7398-9883-3(3))* Steck-Vaughn.

—Education Station Reading, Volume One: F-H: Student Resource Book. 2004. (Illus.). 248p. per. 9.24 *(978-0-7398-9885-7(X))* Steck-Vaughn.

Fontes, Justine. Cheerios Action Park Adventure. 2005. (Picture Clue Math Reader Ser.). (Illus.). 28p. (J). pap. *(978-0-439-70343-7(3))* Scholastic, Inc.

For the Love of Turtles: Six-Pack. (Greetings Ser.: Vol. 1). 24p. (gr. 2-3). 31.00 *(978-0-7635-9423-7(7))* Rigby Education.

Ford, Ron. Cindy's Backyard Circus, 1 vol. 2006. (Neighborhood Readers Ser.). (ENG.). 16p. (gr. 1-2). pap. 6.50 *(978-1-4042-7136-4(8),* cb52fbf6-0810-40cd-8096-5c6bc991eb81, Rosen Classroom) Rosen Publishing Group, Inc., The.

—El circo de Cindy (Cindy's Backyard Circus), 1 vol. 2006. (Lecturas Del Barrio (Neighborhood Readers) Ser.). (SPA.). 16p. (gr. 1-2). pap. 6.50 *(978-1-4042-7138-8(4),* 296dece9-ef29-49a8-9c72-0ca20e3f5eaa, Rosen Classroom) Rosen Publishing Group, Inc., The.

—What Do You See?, 1 vol. 2006. (Neighborhood Readers Ser.). (ENG.). 12p. (gr. 1-2). pap. 5.90 *(978-1-4042-6831-9(6),* 0cf59628-d769-4364-bac8-d9b566d16e44, Rosen Classroom) Rosen Publishing Group, Inc., The.

Forde, Patricia. Witches Do Not Like Bicycles (Reading Ladder Level 2) Dreidemy, Joëlle, illus. 2nd ed. 2016. (Reading Ladder Level 2 Ser.). (ENG.). 48p. (gr. k-2). pap. 4.99 *(978-1-4052-8218-5(5),* Reading Ladder) Farshore GBR. Dist: HarperCollins Pubs.

Foresman, Scott. Scott Foresman Reading: Practice. 2003. (ENG.). (gr. 1-1). pap. 20.97 net. *(978-0-328-07537-9(X));* (gr. 2-2). pap. 20.97 net. *(978-0-328-07538-6(8));* (gr. 3-3). pap. 20.97 net. *(978-0-328-07539-3(6));* (gr. 4-4). pap. 20.97 net. *(978-0-328-07540-9(X));* (gr. 5-5). pap. 20.97 net. *(978-0-328-07541-6(8));* (gr. 6-6). pap. 20.97 net. *(978-0-328-07542-3(6))* Savvas Learning Co. (Scott Foresman).

The Forest Walk: Individual Title Two-Packs. (Chiquilibros Ser.). (gr. -1-1). 12.00 *(978-0-7635-8527-3(0))* Rigby Education.

Forrest. Sign of Blood. (Thumbprint Mysteries Ser.). 32.86 *(978-0-8092-0408-3(8))* McGraw-Hill/Contemporary.

Forte, Imogene. Ready to Learn Beginning Reading. 2003. (Illus.). 64p. per. 7.95 *(978-0-86530-595-3(1))* Incentive Pubns., Inc.

Forte, Lauren, adapted by. Car Wash Crunch. 2017. (Illus.). 32p. (J). *(978-1-5182-4445-2(9))* Little Brown & Co.

Foster, John. Marathon: Band 06/Orange. 2006. (Collins Big Cat Ser.). (ENG., Illus.). 24p. (J). (gr. 2-2). pap. 8.99 *(978-0-00-718689-1(4))* HarperCollins Pubs. Ltd. GBR. Dist: Independent Pubs. Group.

Foster, Ruth. Nonfiction Reading Comprehension - Science. 2006. (ENG.). 144p. pap. 16.99 *(978-1-4206-8026-3(9))* Teacher Created Resources, Inc.

—Nonfiction Reading Comprehension - Science, Grade 3. 2006. (ENG.). 144p. pap. 16.99 *(978-1-4206-8021-8(8))* Teacher Created Resources, Inc.

—Nonfiction Reading Comprehension - Social Studies, Grades 1-2. 2006. (ENG.). 144p. pap. 16.99 *(978-1-4206-8027-0(7))* Teacher Created Resources, Inc.

—Nonfiction Reading Comprehension - Social Studies, Grades 2-3. 2006. (ENG.). 144p. pap. 16.99 *(978-1-4206-8023-2(4))* Teacher Created Resources, Inc.

—Social Studies, Grade 3. 2006. (Nonfiction Reading Comprehension Ser.). (ENG., Illus.). 144p. per. 16.99 *(978-1-4206-8024-9(2))* Teacher Created Resources, Inc.

Four Cheerful Chipmunks. (Early Intervention Levels Ser.). 28.38 *(978-0-7362-0415-6(6))* CENGAGE Learning.

Four Cheerful Chipmunks (14), Vol. 14. (Early Intervention Levels Ser.). 4.73 *(978-0-7362-0240-4(4))* CENGAGE Learning.

Fowler, Will. Level 4: Shakespeare-His Life & Plays. 2nd ed. 2008. (Pearson English Graded Readers Ser.). (ENG., Illus.). 72p. pap. 12.71 *(978-1-4058-8231-6(X),* Pearson ELT) Pearson Education.

The Fox in the Moon. (Lexile Levels Ser.). 9.09 *(978-1-56334-705-4(9))* CENGAGE Learning.

Fox, Jennifer. Teen Titans, Go: Pizza Power. 2016. (Passport to Reading Level 2 Ser.). (J). lib. bdg. 14.75 *(978-0-606-38326-4(3))* Turtleback.

Foxe, Steve. Meet Blurr. 2016. (Transformers Passport to Reading Ser.). (J). lib. bdg. 13.55 *(978-0-606-39191-7(6))* Turtleback.

Foxley, Janet. Ruby-Rose: Band 14/Ruby (Collins Big Cat), Bd. 14. Bascon, Pedro, illus. 2015. (Collins Big Cat Ser.). (ENG.). 48p. (J). (gr. 3-4). pap. 11.99 *(978-0-00-812779-4(4))* HarperCollins Pubs. Ltd. GBR. Dist: Independent Pubs. Group.

Francis, JennaKay. Michael's Safari. Howarth, Craig, illus. 2013. 12p. pap. 8.95 *(978-1-61633-411-6(8))* Guardian Angel Publishing, Inc.

Franco, Fabiola. El Novio Robado. (SPA.). (J). pap., wbk. ed. 5.95 *(978-0-8219-0034-5(X),* 70654); (Illus.). stu. ed. 6.95 *(978-0-8219-0033-8(1),* 70278) EMC/Paradigm Publishing.

Frederiksen, Barbara. Rippen Ricky Loves the Game: A Book of Perseverance. 2011. 24p. pap. 15.99 *(978-1-4628-2999-6(6))* Xlibris Corp.

Freed, Kira. Classifying Animals. 2017. (Text Connections Guided Close Reading Ser.). (J). (gr. 1). *(978-1-4900-1799-0(2))* Benchmark Education Co.

—Saving Squirt. Zolotic, Aleksander, illus. 2017. (Text Connections Guided Close Reading Ser.). (J). (gr. 2). *(978-1-4900-1834-8(4))* Benchmark Education Co.

Freeman, Maggie. Building High: Band 11/Lime. 2005. (Collins Big Cat Ser.). (ENG.). 320p. (J). (gr. 2-3). pap. 10.99 *(978-0-00-718642-6(8))* HarperCollins Pubs. Ltd. GBR. Dist: Independent Pubs. Group.

Freeman, Trudy. Shaggy Nick. 2011. 28p. pap. 15.99 *(978-1-4653-4763-3(1))* Xlibris Corp.

French, Jackie. Too Many Pears! Portugese/English, 1 vol. 2009. (ENG., Illus.). 32p. (J). pap. 6.95 *(978-1-59572-197-6(5))* Star Bright Bks., Inc.

French, Kathy. Snap, Crackle, & Flow: Set Of 6. 2011. (Navigators Ser.). (J). 48.00 net. *(978-1-4108-0428-0(3))* Benchmark Education Co.

French, Moira. The Swingewood Stories. 2009. 36p. pap. 16.99 *(978-1-4490-4777-1(7))* AuthorHouse.

French, Vivian. Aladdin & the Genies: Band 14/Ruby (Collins Big Cat) Assanelli, Victoria, illus. 2016. (Collins Big Cat Ser.). (ENG.). 48p. (J). pap. 9.95 *(978-0-00-814720-4(5))* HarperCollins Pubs. Ltd. GBR. Dist: Independent Pubs. Group.

—The Lion & the Mouse Green Band. Rogers, Alan, illus. 2016. (Cambridge Reading Adventures Ser.). (ENG.). 16p. pap. 7.95 *(978-1-107-55038-4(6))* Cambridge Univ. Pr.

—Mountain Mona: Band 09/Gold (Collins Big Cat) Fisher, Chris, illus. 2006. (Collins Big Cat Ser.). (ENG.). 24p. (J). (gr. 2-2). pap. 9.99 *(978-0-00-718700-3(9))* HarperCollins Pubs. Ltd. GBR. Dist: Independent Pubs. Group.

Freund, Lisa. The Seven Natural Wonders: Set Of 6. 2010. (Navigators Ser.). (J). pap. 44.00 net. *(978-1-4108-0403-7(8))* Benchmark Education Co.

Fried, Caren Loebel. Legend of the Gourd. 2010. (HAW & ENG.). 36p. (J). 16.95 *(978-1-58178-103-8(2))* Bishop Museum Pr.

Friedman, Laurie. Happy Birthday, Mallory! Schmitz, Tamara, illus. 2006. (Mallory Ser.: 4). (ENG.). 160p. (J). (gr. 2-5). per. 6.99 *(978-0-8225-6502-4(1),* 3d259894-2ff1-4c6f-99b4-6d417ecc0636, Darby Creek) Lerner Publishing Group.

—Mallory Mcdonald, Super Sitter, Bk. 27. Kalis, Jennifer, illus. 2018. (Mallory Ser.). (ENG.). 160p. (J). (gr. 2-5). pap. 7.99 *(978-1-5415-0110-2(1),* 7db40c11-5879-4407-839c-24bfaffc5352, Darby Creek) Lerner Publishing Group.

Friends of All Colors. (J). 26.20 *(978-0-8136-8405-5(6));* (gr. -1-3). 59.50 *(978-0-8136-7930-3(3))* Modern Curriculum Pr.

Friends of All Colours. (J). 26.20 *(978-0-8136-8404-8(8))* Modern Curriculum Pr.

Friendship in Action: Individual Title Six-Packs. (Action Packs Ser.). 120p. (gr. 3-5). 44.00 *(978-0-7635-8390-3(1))* Rigby Education.

Frino, Michael G. Welcome to Waycool School: Where Learning Is Fun & Lessons are Learned by Everyone! 2010. 32p. pap. 17.25 *(978-1-4269-4048-4(3))* Trafford Publishing.

Frog & Toad Book Set 2 800923, 3 vols. 2005. (J). *(978-1-59794-088-7(7))* Environments, Inc.

Frog & Toad Book Set 3 800924, 6 vols. 2005. (J). pap. *(978-1-59794-089-4(5))* Environments, Inc.

Frog & Toad Book Set 800922, 3 vols. 2005. (J). pap. *(978-1-59794-087-0(9))* Environments, Inc.

From Sea to Sea, Level E. Incl. Headway: Level E from Sea to Sea. *(978-0-89688-457-1(0),* 88-457); Level E. pap., wbk. ed. *(978-0-89688-463-2(5),* 88-463); Level E. suppl. ed. Level E. suppl. ed. Level E. suppl. ed. *(978-0-89688-469-4(4),* 88-469); Level E. suppl. ed. (J). (gr. 2-3). *(978-0-89688-452-6(X),* 88-452) Open Court Publishing Co.

From Seed to Plant. (Lexile Levels Ser.). 9.09 *(978-1-56334-719-1(9))* CENGAGE Learning.

From the Lake to Your Faucet: Fourth Grade Guided Comprehension Level L. (On Our Way to English Ser.). (gr. 4-18). 34.50 *(978-0-7578-7153-5(4))* Rigby Education.

Fruchter, Jason, illus. Friends Help Each Other: Ready-To-Read Pre-Level 1. 2014. (Daniel Tiger's Neighborhood Ser.). (ENG.). 32p. (J). (gr. -1-k). pap. 4.99 *(978-1-4814-0366-5(4),* Simon Spotlight) Simon Spotlight.

—Kai-Lan's Carnival. 2010. (Ni Hao, Kai-Lan Ser.). (ENG.). 24p. (J). (gr. -1-1). 16.19 *(978-1-4424-0177-8(X))* Simon & Schuster, Inc.

Fruits & Vegetables I Like to Eat - English Take Home Book. 2007. (Journeys Ser.). (J). pap. 15.00 *(978-1-4042-5462-6(5),* Rosen Classroom) Rosen Publishing Group, Inc., The.

Fry, Edward B. Reading Drills. 2004. pap., tchr. ed., suppl. ed. *(978-0-8092-0358-1(8))* Jamestown.

—Skimming & Scanning. 2004. pap., tchr. ed., suppl. ed. *(978-0-8092-0362-8(6))* Jamestown.

Fry, Jason. DK Readers L4: Star Wars: Rogue One: Secret Mission: Join the Quest to Destroy the Death Star! 2016. (DK Readers Level 4 Ser.). (ENG.). 96p. (J). (gr. 4-7). pap. 3.99 *(978-1-4654-5264-1(8),* DK Children) Dorling Kindersley Publishing, Inc.

Fuerst, Jeffrey B. Baa Baa Black Sheep Sells Her Wool. 2008. (Reader's Theater Nursery Rhymes & Songs Ser.). (Illus.). 48p. (J). (gr. k-1). pap. *(978-1-60437-965-5(0))* Benchmark Education Co.

—Bear Goes over the Mountain. 2008. (Reader's Theater Nursery Rhymes & Songs Ser.). (Illus.). 48p. (J). (gr. k-1). pap. *(978-1-60437-972-3(3))* Benchmark Education Co.

—Bingo. Greenhead, Bill, illus. 2010. (Rising Readers Ser.). (J). 3.49 *(978-1-60719-687-7(5))* Newmark Learning LLC.

—Bingo, Come Home! Greenhead, Bill, illus. 2009. (Reader's Theater Nursery Rhymes & Songs Set B Ser.). 48p. (J). pap. *(978-1-60859-151-0(4))* Benchmark Education Co.

—Chuck, Woodchuck, Chuck! Greenhead, Bill, illus. 2009. (Reader's Theater Nursery Rhymes & Songs Set B Ser.). 48p. (J). pap. *(978-1-60859-152-7(2))* Benchmark Education Co.

—Going Places: Lap Book. 2009. (My First Reader's Theater Set B Ser.). (J). 28.00 *(978-1-4108-8544-9(5))* Benchmark Education Co.

—Hickory Dickory Dock; or, Go, Mouse, Go! 2008. (Reader's Theater Nursery Rhymes & Songs Ser.). (Illus.). 48p. (J). (gr. k-1). pap. *(978-1-60437-960-0(X))* Benchmark Education Co.

—Hot Cross Buns for Everyone. Abbott, Jason, illus. 2009. (Reader's Theater Nursery Rhymes & Songs Set B Ser.). 48p. (J). pap. *(978-1-60859-153-4(0))* Benchmark Education Co.

—Hunting We Will Go. 2008. (Reader's Theater Nursery Rhymes & Songs Ser.). (Illus.). 48p. (J). (gr. k-1). pap. *(978-1-60437-974-7(X))* Benchmark Education Co.

—Itsy Bitsy Spider Climbs Again. 2008. (Reader's Theater Nursery Rhymes & Songs Ser.). (Illus.). 48p. (J). (gr. k-1). pap. *(978-1-60437-968-6(5))* Benchmark Education Co.

—The Itsy Bitty Spider. Collins, Daryll, illus. 2010. (Rising Readers Ser.). (J). 3.49 *(978-1-60719-689-1(1))* Newmark Learning LLC.

—Jack B. Nimble Jumps. Colby, Garry, illus. 2009. (Reader's Theater Nursery Rhymes & Songs Set B Ser.). 48p. (J). pap. *(978-1-60859-154-1(9))* Benchmark Education Co.

—Lazy Mary Gets Up. Kelley, Gerald, illus. 2009. (Reader's Theater Nursery Rhymes & Songs Set B Ser.). 48p. (J). pap. *(978-1-60859-156-5(5))* Benchmark Education Co.

—Look at It Go! Lap Book. 2009. (My First Reader's Theater Set B Ser.). (J). 28.00 *(978-1-935441-02-1(7))* Benchmark Education Co.

—Lunch with Little Miss Muffet. 2008. (Reader's Theater Nursery Rhymes & Songs Ser.). (Illus.). 48p. (J). (gr. k-1). pap. *(978-1-60437-961-7(8))* Benchmark Education Co.

—Miss Mary Mack & the Jumping Elephants. Workman, Terry, illus. 2009. (Reader's Theater Nursery Rhymes & Songs Set B Ser.). 48p. (J). pap. *(978-1-60859-161-9(1))* Benchmark Education Co.

—The Old Gray Mare IS What She Used to Be. Currant, Gary, illus. 2009. (Reader's Theater Nursery Rhymes & Songs Set B Ser.). 48p. (J). pap. *(978-1-60859-162-6(X))* Benchmark Education Co.

—Old MacDonald's Noisy Farm. 2008. (Reader's Theater Nursery Rhymes & Songs Ser.). (Illus.). (J). (gr. k-1). pap. 35.00 *(978-1-60437-967-9(7))* Benchmark Education Co.

—Party Time with Old King Cole. 2008. (Reader's Theater Nursery Rhymes & Songs Ser.). (Illus.). 48p. (J). (gr. k-1). pap. *(978-1-60437-962-4(6))* Benchmark Education Co.

—Peter Piper Picks & Pickles Peppers. 2008. (Reader's Theater Nursery Rhymes & Songs Ser.). (Illus.). 48p. (J). (gr. k-1). pap. *(978-1-60437-970-9(7))* Benchmark Education Co.

—Peter Pumpkin Eater Loses His Appetite. Greenhead, Bill, illus. 2009. (Reader's Theater Nursery Rhymes & Songs Set B Ser.). 48p. (J). pap. *(978-1-60859-164-0(6))* Benchmark Education Co.

—Pies for Simple Simon. Ledger, Bill, illus. 2009. (Reader's Theater Nursery Rhymes & Songs Set B Ser.). 48p. (J). pap. *(978-1-60859-165-7(4))* Benchmark Education Co.

—Run, Three Blind Mice! Walker, Sholto, illus. 2009. (Reader's Theater Nursery Rhymes & Songs Set B Ser.). 48p. (J). pap. *(978-1-60859-168-8(9))* Benchmark Education Co.

—Sing a Song of Sixpence, the King's Special Pie. 2008. (Reader's Theater Nursery Rhymes & Songs Ser.). (Illus.). 48p. (J). (gr. k-1). pap. *(978-1-60437-979-2(0))* Benchmark Education Co.

—Sorting at My Desk: Lap Book. 2009. (My First Reader's Theater Set B Ser.). (J). 28.00 *(978-1-60634-987-8(2))* Benchmark Education Co.

—Visiting Grandma: Lap Book. 2009. (My First Reader's Theater Set B Ser.). (J). 28.00 *(978-1-60634-991-5(0))* Benchmark Education Co.

—Wishing on a Bright Star. 2008. (Reader's Theater Nursery Rhymes & Songs Ser.). (Illus.). 48p. (J). (gr. k-1). pap. *(978-1-60437-971-6(5))* Benchmark Education Co.

—The Woman Who Lived in a Shoe. Greenhead, Bill, illus. 2009. (Reader's Theater Nursery Rhymes & Songs Set B Ser.). 48p. (J). pap. *(978-1-60859-172-5(7))* Benchmark Education Co.

The Fun Bus: 3-in-1 Package. (Sails Literacy Ser.). 24p. (gr. 1-18). 57.00 *(978-0-7578-3207-9(5))* Rigby Education.

The Fun Bus: 6 Small Books. (Sails Literacy Ser.). 24p. (gr. 1-18). 25.00 *(978-0-7578-3183-6(4))* Rigby Education.

The Fun Bus: Big Book Only. (Sails Literacy Ser.). 24p. (gr. 1-18). 27.00 *(978-0-7635-5931-1(8))* Rigby Education.

Fun With Friends. (Early Intervention Levels Ser.). 23.10 *(978-0-7362-0006-6(1))* CENGAGE Learning.

Furgang, Kathy. A Rainbow Party. 2011. (Early Connections Ser.). (J). *(978-1-61672-569-3(9))* Benchmark Education Co.

—A Seat on the Bus: Set Of 6. 2010. (Early Connections Ser.). (J). 37.00 net. *(978-1-4108-1084-7(4))* Benchmark Education Co.

—Shrimp Joins the Team: Set Of 6. 2010. (Early Connections Ser.). (J). pap. 37.00 net. *(978-1-4108-1368-8(1))* Benchmark Education Co.

—Wendy the Water Drop: Set Of 6. 2010. (Early Connections Ser.). (J). pap. 37.00 net. *(978-1-4108-1095-3(X))* Benchmark Education Co.

Fusek Peters, Andrew. Free Running: Band 11 Lime/Band 14 Ruby (Collins Big Cat Progress) 2014. (Collins Big Cat Progress Ser.). (ENG., Illus.). 32p. (J). (gr. 3-4). pap. 9.99 *(978-0-00-751934-7(6))* HarperCollins Pubs. Ltd. GBR. Dist: Independent Pubs. Group.

Futaba, Aoi. Level C, Vol. 4. 2005. (Illus.). 194p. pap. 9.99 *(978-1-58655-726-3(2),* KGNOV-0539) Media Blasters, Inc.

Fyne, Olga. Jerry & Sherry. 2008. (Illus.). 24p. pap. 12.99 *(978-1-4389-3672-7(9))* AuthorHouse.

Gaafar, Mahmoud. Hisham's Room: Level 8 (Collins Big Cat Arabic Reading Programme) 2019. (Collins Big Cat Ser.). (ENG.). 16p. pap. 5.95 *(978-0-00-827889-2(X))* HarperCollins Pubs. Ltd. GBR. Dist: Independent Pubs. Group.

Gabolinscy, Jack. Do Not Disturb, 1 vol. Cashmore-Hingley, Michael, illus. 2013. (ENG.). 27p. (gr. 3-4). pap. 9.99 *(978-1-77654-019-8(0),* Red Rocket Readers) Flying Start Bks.

Gabolinscy, Jack & Harrison, Brian. Not Again. 2008. (Rigby Focus Forward: Level P Ser.). (Illus.). 24p. (J). (gr. 4-7). pap. *(978-1-4190-3859-4(1),* Rigby) Pearson Education Australia.

Gabolinscy, Jack & Oppatt, Karen. Danny's Dream. 2008. (Rigby Focus Forward: Level O Ser.). (Illus.). 24p. pap. *(978-1-4190-3843-3(5),* Rigby) Pearson Education Australia.

Gaertner, Meg. A Spring Pond. 2020. (Spring Is Here Ser.). (ENG., Illus.). 16p. (J). (gr. k-1). pap. 7.95 *(978-1-64493-103-5(6),* 1644931036); lib. bdg. 25.64 *(978-1-64493-024-3(2),* 1644930242) North Star Editions. (Focus Readers).

Galashan, Kathy. Robots. 2005. (ENG., Illus.). 32p. pap. 8.50 *(978-0-340-87311-3(6))* Cambridge Univ. Pr.

Galat, Joan Marie. National Geographic Readers: Cats (Level 1 Coreader) 2017. (Readers Ser.). (Illus.). 48p. (J). (gr. -1-k). pap. 4.99 *(978-1-4263-2883-1(4),* National Geographic Kids) Disney Publishing Worldwide.

Ganeri, Anita. All Kinds of Plants Blue Band. 2016. (Cambridge Reading Adventures Ser.). (ENG., Illus.). 16p. pap. 7.95 *(978-1-316-60579-0(5))* Cambridge Univ. Pr.

—The Book of World Facts Purple Band. 2016. (Cambridge Reading Adventures Ser.). (ENG., Illus.). 24p. pap. 8.80 *(978-1-316-60080-1(7))* Cambridge Univ. Pr.

—From Rags to Bags Gold Band. 2016. (Cambridge Reading Adventures Ser.). (ENG., Illus.). 16p. pap. 7.95 *(978-1-316-50086-6(1))* Cambridge Univ. Pr.

—Get Active! Orange Band. 2017. (Cambridge Reading Adventures Ser.). (ENG., Illus.). 16p. pap. 7.35 *(978-1-108-43973-2(X))* Cambridge Univ. Pr.

P
Q
R

—Super Malls Orange Band. 2016. (Cambridge Reading Adventures Ser.). (ENG., Illus.). 16p. pap. 7.95 *(978-1-316-50335-5(6))* Cambridge Univ. Pr.
—Who Is the Greatest? 2 Wayfarers. 2017. (Cambridge Reading Adventures Ser.). (ENG., Illus.). 32p. pap. 8.60 *(978-1-108-43617-5(X))* Cambridge Univ. Pr.
A Garden: Individual Title Six-Packs. (Sails Literacy Ser.). 16p. (gr. k-18). 27.00 *(978-0-7635-4384-6(5))* Rigby Education.
Gardner, Lindsey, et al. Pan Fydd Popi a Macs yn Fawr. 2005. (WEL., Illus.). 20p. *(978-1-902416-45-8(7))* Cymdeithas Lyfrau Ceredigion.
Garson, Cindy. Welcome to Kristy's Farm: Book I (Black & White Version) 2007. (ENG.). 56p. per. 21.80 *(978-1-84728-321-4(7))* Lulu Pr., Inc.
Gary, Romain. La Vie Devant Soi, Level C. (FRE.). (YA). (gr. 7-12). 9.99 *(978-0-8219-0869-3(3)*, 40326) EMC/Paradigm Publishing.
Garza, Sarah. Action! Making Movies, 1 vol. 2nd rev. ed. 2013. (TIME for KIDS(r): Informational Text Ser.). (ENG.). 64p. (gr. 4-8). pap. 14.99 *(978-1-4333-4949-2(3))* Teacher Created Materials, Inc.
Garza, Xavier. Just One Itsy Bitsy Little Bite / Sólo un Mordadita Chiquitita. de Vita, Flor, illus. 2018. (ENG & SPA.). 32p. (J). (gr. -1-3). 17.95 *(978-1-55885-872-5(5)*, Piñata Books) Arte Publico Pr.
—Maximilian & the Mystery of the Guardian Angel, 1 vol. Garza, Xavier, illus. 2011. (Max's Lucha Libre Adventures Ser.: 1). (ENG., Illus.). 208p. (J). (gr. 3-7). pap. 18.95 *(978-1-933693-98-9(3)*, 23353382, Cinco Puntos Press) Lee & Low Bks., Inc.
—Rooster Joe & the Bully / el Gallo Joe y el Abusón. 2016. (ENG & SPA., Illus.). 128p. (J). (gr. 5-8). pap. 9.95 *(978-1-55885-835-0(0)*, Piñata Books) Arte Publico Pr.
Garza, Xavier & Villarroel, Carolina. Zulema & the Witch Owl/Zulema y la Bruja Lechuza. Garza, Xavier, illus. 2009. (SPA & ENG., Illus.). 32p. (J). (gr. -1-4). 16.95 *(978-1-55885-515-1(7)*, Piñata Books) Arte Publico Pr.
Gates, Margo. Baking Apples. Crowther, Jeff, illus. 2020. (Plant Life Cycles (Pull Ahead Readers — Fiction) Ser.). (ENG.). 16p. (J). (gr. -1-1). 27.99 *(978-1-5415-9026-7(0)*, c752c82b-6352-4d33-893b-873f19da49eb, Lerner Pubns.) Lerner Publishing Group.
—Cam's Walk. Jennings, Sarah, illus. 2021. (My Community (Pull Ahead Readers — Fiction) Ser.). (ENG.). 16p. (J). (gr. -1-1). 27.99 *(978-1-5415-9018-2(X)*, c5990fd8-fbb4-47bc-8343-e7aed5ffc2b3, Lerner Pubns.) Lerner Publishing Group.
—Duck Sees the Rain. Herring, Carol, illus. 2019. (Let's Look at Weather (Pull Ahead Readers — Fiction) Ser.). (ENG.). 16p. (J). (gr. -1-1). 27.99 *(978-1-5415-5839-7(1)*, f68036da-4f21-4b91-a168-3e2c414bc554, Lerner Pubns.) Lerner Publishing Group.
—The Egg. Hunt, Lisa, illus. 2019. (Seasons All Around Me (Pull Ahead Readers — Fiction) Ser.). (ENG.). 16p. (J). (gr. -1-1). 27.99 *(978-1-5415-5876-2(6)*, f267d425-8413-451b-af3e-52cfe3fe5688, Lerner Pubns.) Lerner Publishing Group.
—Emily's Pumpkin. Darcy, Liam, illus. 2019. (Science All Around Me (Pull Ahead Readers — Fiction) Ser.). (ENG.). 16p. (J). (gr. -1-1). pap. 8.99 *(978-1-5415-7338-3(2)*, 9f42e8de-eb9a-49b2-8cd6-956a7a0fb500, Lerner Pubns.) Lerner Publishing Group.
—The Fish. Darcy, Liam, illus. 2019. (Let's Look at Animal Habitats (Pull Ahead Readers — Fiction) Ser.). (ENG.). 16p. (J). (gr. -1-1). 27.99 *(978-1-5415-5863-2(4)*, 174f6919-9ee7-4f38-8e1b-07ffcc680c0f, Lerner Pubns.) Lerner Publishing Group.
—A Good Nut. Herring, Carol, illus. 2019. (Let's Look at Animal Habitats (Pull Ahead Readers — Fiction) Ser.). (ENG.). 16p. (J). (gr. -1-1). 27.99 *(978-1-5415-5865-6(0)*, dcb05530-a226-4737-855b-0b26b518b851, Lerner Pubns.) Lerner Publishing Group.
—Grandpa's Photos. Crowther, Jeff, illus. 2021. (My Community (Pull Ahead Readers — Fiction) Ser.). (ENG.). 16p. (J). (gr. -1-1). 27.99 *(978-1-5415-9019-9(8)*, a7f520aa-7691-429a-ad8e-54164c3a2d4f, Lerner Pubns.) Lerner Publishing Group.
—Hiding from Lightning. Darcy, Liam, illus. 2019. (Let's Look at Weather (Pull Ahead Readers — Fiction) Ser.). (ENG.). 16p. (J). (gr. -1-1). pap. 8.99 *(978-1-5415-7321-5(8)*, 401fd6a4-497c-4211-b28c-a46ec1a24f4b, Lerner Pubns.) Lerner Publishing Group.
—I Look Up. Hunt, Lisa, illus. 2021. (My Community (Pull Ahead Readers — Fiction) Ser.). (ENG.). 16p. (J). (gr. -1-1). 27.99 *(978-1-5415-9017-5(1)*, aced6078-433d-4f7e-b059-926efa2fff98, Lerner Pubns.) Lerner Publishing Group.
—Into the Clouds. Crowther, Jeff, illus. 2019. (Let's Look at Weather (Pull Ahead Readers — Fiction) Ser.). (ENG.). 16p. (J). (gr. -1-1). 27.99 *(978-1-5415-5840-3(5)*, 502ef064-f1f6-4054-ad17-b5b579637c44, Lerner Pubns.) Lerner Publishing Group.
—The Little Penguin. Noschese, Kip, illus. 2019. (Let's Look at Animal Habitats (Pull Ahead Readers — Fiction) Ser.). (ENG.). 16p. (J). (gr. -1-1). pap. 8.99 *(978-1-5415-7308-6(0)*, b786be41-2e0e-4dfc-948a-bf60dfb28f46, Lerner Pubns.) Lerner Publishing Group.
—Making Tea. Noschese, Kip, illus. 2019. (Science All Around Me (Pull Ahead Readers — Fiction) Ser.). (ENG.). 16p. (J). (gr. -1-1). 27.99 *(978-1-5415-5856-4(1)*, a70d4402-ad6f-439e-ab7d-5b3b3c5f5d04, Lerner Pubns.) Lerner Publishing Group.
—Maya Likes the Beach. Hartley, Brian, illus. 2019. (Seasons All Around Me (Pull Ahead Readers — Fiction) Ser.). (ENG.). 16p. (J). (gr. -1-1). 27.99 *(978-1-5415-5873-1(1)*, 9d43d5af-33bc-4bb7-b018-0443403a2874, Lerner Pubns.) Lerner Publishing Group.
—Mia Can See Patterns. Herring, Carol, illus. 2019. (Science All Around Me (Pull Ahead Readers — Fiction) Ser.). (ENG.). 16p. (J). (gr. -1-1). pap. 8.99 *(978-1-5415-7334-5(X)*, 650ab410-cd4b-4d14-85f3-8f036213e2e0, Lerner Pubns.) Lerner Publishing Group.
—Milo & the Ball. Jennings, Sarah, illus. 2019. (Science All Around Me (Pull Ahead Readers — Fiction) Ser.). (ENG.). 16p. (J). (gr. -1-1). 27.99 *(978-1-5415-5853-3(7)*, 15f6f66d-3ae2-4531-83a7-d98afc3ec69f, Lerner Pubns.) Lerner Publishing Group.
—My Baby Elephant. Jennings, Sarah, illus. 2019. (Let's Look at Animal Habitats (Pull Ahead Readers — Fiction) Ser.). (ENG.). 16p. (J). (gr. -1-1). 27.99 *(978-1-5415-5864-9(2)*, 919a2771-d332-4bf1-a2ff-0e5b7a325b2d, Lerner Pubns.) Lerner Publishing Group.
—No Bugs Here. Crowther, Jeff, illus. 2019. (Let's Look at Animal Habitats (Pull Ahead Readers — Fiction) Ser.). (ENG.). 16p. (J). (gr. -1-1). pap. 8.99 *(978-1-5415-7307-9(2)*, 40e28938-5b6a-4ebe-841c-3bf223c53ba9, Lerner Pubns.) Lerner Publishing Group.
—Turtles in the Sun. Hartley, Brian, illus. 2019. (Let's Look at Weather (Pull Ahead Readers — Fiction) Ser.). (ENG.). 16p. (J). (gr. -1-1). 27.99 *(978-1-5415-5842-7(1)*, 42323cb5-f653-4387-aa19-f6d8c3f03a94, Lerner Pubns.) Lerner Publishing Group.
—Up the Tree. Engell, Mette, illus. 2019. (Let's Look at Animal Habitats (Pull Ahead Readers — Fiction) Ser.). (ENG.). 16p. (J). (gr. -1-1). 27.99 *(978-1-5415-5868-7(5)*, ba1fd997-0137-45a8-becb-2d919231ac89, Lerner Pubns.) Lerner Publishing Group.
—Wait, Ride, Walk. Brown, Stephen, illus. 2021. (My Community (Pull Ahead Readers — Fiction) Ser.). (ENG.). 16p. (J). (gr. -1-1). 27.99 *(978-1-5415-9016-8(3)*, e6411612-9034-4135-9369-9b0c030bc0eb, Lerner Pubns.) Lerner Publishing Group.
—A Windy Day. Jennings, Sarah, illus. 2019. (Let's Look at Weather (Pull Ahead Readers — Fiction) Ser.). (ENG.). 16p. (J). (gr. -1-1). 27.99 *(978-1-5415-5843-4(X)*, dd9f6631-c415-4b45-9893-ce5743d87b45, Lerner Pubns.) Lerner Publishing Group.
Gates, Susan. The Big Pancake Blue Band. Rogers, Alan, illus. 2017. (Cambridge Reading Adventures Ser.). (ENG.). 16p. pap. 7.35 *(978-1-108-43972-5(1))* Cambridge Univ. Pr.
—Mole Who was Scared of the Dark. Breakespeare, Andrew, illus. 2005. (ENG.). 24p. (J). lib. bdg. 23.65 *(978-1-59646-710-1(X))* Dingles & Co.
—Pirate!: Band 15/Emerald (Collins Big Cat), Bd. 15. McClellan, Maddy, illus. 2007. (Collins Big Cat Ser.). (ENG.). 48p. (J). (gr. 3-4). pap. 10.99 *(978-0-00-723095-2(8))* HarperCollins Pubs. Ltd. GBR. Dist: Independent Pubs. Group.
Gaydos, Nora. I'M a New Big Sister. Gutierrez, Akemi, illus. 2010. (ENG.). 30p. (J). (gr. -1-17). 6.99 *(978-1-60169-009-8(6))* Innovative Kids.
—Simply Science Independent Volume 1. 2006. (Now I'm Reading!: Independent Ser.). (ENG., Illus.). 74p. (J). (gr. -1-2). 16.99 *(978-1-58476-247-8(0)*, IKIDS) Innovative Kids.
Geatches, Hazel, ed. At the Beach. 2012. (ENG., Illus.). 32p. 11.00 *(978-0-19-464628-4(9))* Oxford Univ. Pr., Inc.
—Cities. 2012. (ENG., Illus.). 40p. pap. 11.00 *(978-0-19-464682-6(3))* Oxford Univ. Pr., Inc.
—Earth. 2012. (ENG., Illus.). 40p. pap., act. bk. ed. 11.00 *(978-0-19-464679-6(3))* Oxford Univ. Pr., Inc.
—Electricity. 2013. (ENG., Illus.). 40p. pap. 11.00 *(978-0-19-464685-7(8))* Oxford Univ. Pr., Inc.
—Eyes. 2012. (ENG., Illus.). 32p. pap. 11.00 *(978-0-19-464629-1(7))* Oxford Univ. Pr., Inc.
—Schools. 2012. (ENG., Illus.). 32p. pap. 11.00 *(978-0-19-464627-7(0))* Oxford Univ. Pr., Inc.
—Sunny & Rainy. 2012. (ENG., Illus.). 40p. pap. 11.00 *(978-0-19-464680-2(7))* Oxford Univ. Pr., Inc.
—Your Body. 2012. (ENG., Illus.). 40p. pap. 11.00 *(978-0-19-464681-9(5))* Oxford Univ. Pr., Inc.
Geiser, Traci Ferguson & Boylan, Maureen McCourt. Leap into Literacy Fall. Cernek, Kim, ed. Mason, Mark & Willardson, David, illus. 2003. 160p. (J). (gr. k-2). pap. 17.99 *(978-1-57471-960-4(2)*, 3376) Creative Teaching Pr., Inc.
—Leap into Literacy Spring. Cernek, Kim, ed. Rojas, Mary & Willardson, David, illus. 2003. 160p. (J). (gr. k-2). pap. 17.99 *(978-1-57471-959-8(9)*, 3375) Creative Teaching Pr., Inc.
—Leap into Literacy Winter. Cernek, Kim, ed. Vaiko, Diane & Willardson, David, illus. 2003. 160p. (J). (gr. k-2). pap. 17.99 *(978-1-57471-958-1(0)*, 3374) Creative Teaching Pr., Inc.
Geistdoerfer, Patrick. Las Ballenas y Otros Mamiferos Marinos / Whales & Other Sea Mammals. Boucher, Joelle, illus. 2018. (Altea Benjamin Ser.). (SPA.). 32p. (J). (gr. 3-7). pap. 10.99 *(978-1-947783-60-7(2)*, Altea) Penguin Random House Grupo Editorial ESP. Dist: Penguin Random Hse. LLC.
Gemmen, Heather. Learn-to-Read Bible. Wilber, Peggy M., ed. 2003. (Rocket Readers Ser.). (Illus.). 448p. (J). (gr. 1-2). 16.99 *(978-0-7814-3975-6(2)*, 0781439752) Cook, David C.
Gentner, Norma L. & Young, Steve. Save a Tree for Me. (Song Box Ser.). (Illus.). 16p. (gr. 1-2). 31.50 *(978-0-7802-2264-9(4))* Wright Group/McGraw-Hill.
George, Chris. Big & Small, 1 vol. 2017. (Early Concepts Ser.). (ENG.). 24p. (gr. 1-1). pap. 9.25 *(978-1-5081-6217-9(4)*, 844fddff-6edc-4af7-b064-423f998de92c, PowerKids Pr.) Rosen Publishing Group, Inc., The.
George, Jean Craighead. Goose & Duck. Lamont, Priscilla, illus. 2008. (I Can Read Level 2 Ser.). (ENG.). 48p. (J). (gr. k-3). 16.99 *(978-0-06-117076-8(3)*, HarperCollins) HarperCollins Pubs.
George, Kallie. Duck, Duck, Dinosaur: Perfect Pumpkin. Vidal, Oriol, illus. 2017. (My First I Can Read Ser.). (ENG.). 32p. (J). (gr. -1-3). 16.99 *(978-0-06-235315-3(2))*; pap. 4.99 *(978-0-06-235314-6(4))* HarperCollins Pubs. (HarperCollins).
—Splash. Cote, Genevieve, illus. 2016. (Tiny Tails Ser.: 3). 44p. (J). (gr. -1-3). 12.95 *(978-1-927018-77-4(3))* Simply Read Bks. CAN. Dist: Ingram Publisher Services.
George, Lynn. The Leaf Pile, 1 vol. 2006. (Neighborhood Readers Ser.). (ENG.). 16p. (gr. 1-2). pap. 6.50 *(978-1-4042-7120-3(1)*, eb28fcd8-46b5-4310-bbff-9d8e2396137c, Rosen Classroom) Rosen Publishing Group, Inc., The.
—Sammy's Sunglasses, 1 vol. 2006. (Neighborhood Readers Ser.). (ENG.). 8p. (gr. k-1). pap. 5.15 *(978-1-4042-5738-2(1)*, cd62b79f-5fd8-46be-875e-c2ff47e12b39, Rosen Classroom) Rosen Publishing Group, Inc., The.
—The Super Sandwich, 1 vol. 2006. (Neighborhood Readers Ser.). (ENG.). 16p. (gr. 1-2). pap. 6.50 *(978-1-4042-7240-8(2)*, e760106b-4d27-47a9-8eec-3d1e8a182c36, Rosen Classroom) Rosen Publishing Group, Inc., The.
Gerber, Paul. Is It Alive?, 1 vol. 2012. (InfoMax Readers Ser.). (ENG., Illus.). 16p. (J). (gr. k-k). pap. 7.00 *(978-1-4488-8965-5(0)*, 3e520b30-20b8-45fb-9021-5f252d54ec0d, Rosen Classroom) Rosen Publishing Group, Inc., The.
Getting Along: Social/Emotional Lap Book. (Pebble Soup Explorations Ser.). (gr. -1-18). 16.00 *(978-0-7635-7563-2(1))* Rigby Education.
Getting Dressed 800638, 3. 2005. (J). bds. *(978-1-59794-036-8(4))* Environments, Inc.
Getting Ready for Bed: KinderConcepts Individual Title Six-Packs. (Kinderstarters Ser.). 8p. (gr. -1-1). 21.00 *(978-0-7635-8729-1(X))* Rigby Education.
Getting Ready for School: KinderConcepts Individual Title Six-Packs. (Kinderstarters Ser.). 8p. (gr. -1-1). 21.00 *(978-0-7635-8730-7(3))* Rigby Education.
Getting the Sequence (Gr. 1-3) 2003. (J). *(978-1-58232-076-2(4))* ECS Learning Systems, Inc.
Getting to Know Your Neighbors: Fourth Grade Guided Comprehension Level N. (On Our Way to English Ser.). (gr. 4-18). 34.50 *(978-0-7578-7161-0(5))* Rigby Education.
Ghosts! 2003. 31.95 *(978-0-673-75801-9(X))* Celebration Pr.
Giant Games. (Early Intervention Levels Ser.). 31.86 *(978-0-7362-0665-5(5))* CENGAGE Learning.
Giant Games (18), Vol. 18. (Early Intervention Levels Ser.). 5.31 *(978-0-7362-0653-2(1))* CENGAGE Learning.
The Giant of Ginger Hill: 3-in-1 Package. (Sails Literacy Ser.). 24p. (gr. 2-18). 57.00 *(978-0-7578-3216-1(4))* Rigby Education.
The Giant of Ginger Hill: 6 Small Books. (Sails Literacy Ser.). 24p. (gr. 2-18). 25.00 *(978-0-7578-3192-8(3))* Rigby Education.
The Giant of Ginger Hill: Big Book Only. (Sails Literacy Ser.). 24p. (gr. 2-18). 27.00 *(978-0-7635-6992-1(5))* Rigby Education.
Gibbs, Maddie. Las Vacas / Cows, 1 vol. 2014. (Amigos de la Granja / Farmyard Friends Ser.). (ENG & SPA.). 24p. (J). (gr. 1-2). 25.27 *(978-1-4994-0265-0(1)*, 662799de-4e6d-48af-9365-b7efcc0ca86b, PowerKids Pr.) Rosen Publishing Group, Inc., The.
—Los Caballos / Horses, 1 vol. 2014. (Amigos de la Granja / Farmyard Friends Ser.). (ENG & SPA.). 24p. (J). (gr. 1-2). 25.27 *(978-1-4994-0267-4(8)*, eda4741d-8d52-467e-8a72-2b5b92b2ec8b, PowerKids Pr.) Rosen Publishing Group, Inc., The.
—Los Patos / Ducks, 1 vol. 2014. (Amigos de la Granja / Farmyard Friends Ser.). (ENG & SPA., Illus.). 24p. (J). (gr. 1-2). 25.27 *(978-1-4994-0269-8(4)*, d10fcef8-8023-47cf-ba69-cb4b08835b6a, PowerKids Pr.) Rosen Publishing Group, Inc., The.
Gibson. Sail Yel Nf Colorful Animals. 2003. (Rigby Sails Early Ser.). (ENG.). 16p. (gr. 1-2). pap. 6.95 *(978-0-7578-8895-3(X))* Rigby Education.
—Sail Yel Nf Out of the Egg. 2003. (Rigby Sails Early Ser.). (ENG.). 16p. (gr. 1-2). pap. 6.95 *(978-0-7578-8892-2(5))* Rigby Education.
Gibson, Brylee. Dinosaur Discoveries. 2007. (Connectors Ser.). (gr. 2-5). pap. *(978-1-877453-13-7(7))* Global Education Systems Ltd.
—Extreme Scientists. 2007. (Connectors Ser.). (gr. 2-5). pap. *(978-1-877453-08-3(0))* Global Education Systems Ltd.
—Megacities. 2007. (Connectors Ser.). (gr. 2-5). pap. *(978-1-877453-07-6(2))* Global Education Systems Ltd.
—Scams. 2007. (Connectors Ser.). (gr. 2-5). pap. *(978-1-877453-01-4(3))* Global Education Systems Ltd.
—Tails, Tails, Tails. 2003. (Rigby Sails Early Ser.). (ENG., Illus.). 16p. (gr. 1-2). pap. 6.95 *(978-0-7578-8904-2(2))* Houghton Mifflin Harcourt Publishing Co.
—Unseen by the Eye. 2007. (Connectors Ser.). (gr. 2-5). pap. *(978-1-877453-00-7(5))* Global Education Systems Ltd.
—Wildlife Detectives. 2007. (Connectors Ser.). (gr. 2-5). pap. *(978-1-877453-18-2(8))* Global Education Systems Ltd.
—Wonders of the World Megastructures. 2007. (Connectors Ser.). (gr. 2-5). pap. *(978-1-877453-20-5(X))* Global Education Systems Ltd.
—The World Beyond Earth. 2007. (Connectors Ser.). (gr. 2-5). pap. *(978-1-877453-11-3(0))* Global Education Systems Ltd.
Gifford, Clive. The Empire Windrush: Band 10 White/Band 14 Ruby (Collins Big Cat Progress) 2014. (Collins Big Cat Progress Ser.). (ENG., Illus.). 32p. (J). (gr. 3-4). pap. 10.99 *(978-0-00-751926-2(5))* HarperCollins Pubs. Ltd. GBR. Dist: Independent Pubs. Group.
—Reading Ladder Level 3- Animal Survivors. Horne, Sarah, illus. 2017. (Reading Ladder Level 3 Ser.). (ENG.). 32p. (gr. 1-3). pap. 4.99 *(978-1-4052-8492-9(7)*, Red Shed) Farshore GBR. Dist: HarperCollins Pubs.
—Romans. Scrutton, Ben, illus. 2016. (Reading Ladder Level 3 Ser.). (ENG.). 32p. (gr. 1-4). pap. 4.99 *(978-1-4052-8043-3(3)*, Red Shed) Farshore GBR. Dist: HarperCollins Pubs.
Gifford, Myrna Ross. Silent E: A Read-and-Sing Book. Cooper, Frances, illus. 2005. 12p. (J). 9.95 *(978-0-9754618-0-8(X))* Action Factor, Inc.
Giglio, Judy. Dreaming of Great Ideas, 6 vols., Set. 2004. (Phonics Readers Books 37-72 Ser.). (ENG.). 8p. (gr. k-1). pap. 35.70 *(978-0-7368-4064-4(8))* Capstone.
—Sounds & How We Hear Them, 6 vols., Set. 2004. (Phonics Readers Books 37-72 Ser.). (ENG.). 8p. (gr. k-1). pap. 35.70 *(978-0-7368-4069-9(9))* Capstone.
Gilchrist, Cherry. Level 3: Princess Diana. 2nd ed. 2008. (Pearson English Graded Readers Ser.). (ENG., Illus.). 60p. pap. 12.71 *(978-1-4058-8201-9(8)*, Pearson ELT) Pearson Education.
Gillen, Kristin M. Raspberries on Tummies. 2011. 32p. pap. 21.99 *(978-1-4568-9436-8(6))* Xlibris Corp.
Gillen, Lisa P. Spring Time. Gillen, Lisa P., illus. Lt. ed. 2006. (Illus.). 12p. (J). (gr. -1-k). pap. 10.95 *(978-1-57332-351-2(9)*, HighReach Learning, Incorporated) Carson-Dellosa Publishing, LLC.
Gillis, Jennifer Blizin. Two Nice Mice. Krejca, Gary, illus. 2006. (Barron's Reader's Clubhouse Level 2 Ser.). (ENG.). 24p. (J). (gr. k-3). 16.19 *(978-0-7641-3295-7(4)*, B.E.S. Publishing) Peterson's.
Gillot, Laurence & Sebaoun, Elisabeth. Half & Half-Swimming with Dolphins. Rocco & Dorémus, Gaëtan, illus. 2010. 32p. (J). pap. 4.99 *(978-1-60115-216-9(7))*; (ENG.). 17.44 *(978-1-60115-215-2(9))* Treasure Bay, Inc.
The Gingerbread Man: 6 Small Books. (gr. k-1). 30.00 *(978-0-7635-6205-2(X))* Rigby Education.
Gino, Alex. You Don't Know Everything, Jilly P! (Scholastic Gold), 1 vol. 2018. (ENG.). 256p. (J). (gr. 3-7). 18.99 *(978-0-545-95624-5(2)*, Scholastic Pr.) Scholastic, Inc.
Giraffe's Sad Tale. (Lexile Levels Ser.). 47.88 *(978-1-56334-392-6(4))* CENGAGE Learning.
Gittings, Clare. What Are You Looking At? Band 15/Emerald. 2007. (Collins Big Cat Ser.). (ENG., Illus.). 48p. (J). (gr. 3-4). pap. 11.99 *(978-0-00-723091-4(5))* HarperCollins Pubs. Ltd. GBR. Dist: Independent Pubs. Group.
Giudice, Stephanie. Wolves Like to Eat. 2017. (1-3Y Mammals Ser.). (ENG., Illus.). 12p. (J). pap. 9.60 *(978-1-64053-089-8(4)*, ARC Pr. Bks.) American Reading Co.
Giulieri, Anne. In the Playhouse. Aranda, Omar, illus. 2012. (Engage Literacy Magenta Ser.). (ENG.). 16p. (J). (gr. k-2). pap. 36.94 *(978-1-4296-8853-6(X)*, 18322, Capstone Pr.) Capstone.
—In the Sea. Aranda, Omar, illus. 2015. (Engage Literacy Magenta - Extension A Ser.). (ENG.). 16p. (J). (gr. k-2). pap. 6.99 *(978-1-4914-8636-8(8)*, 131243) Capstone.
—In the Water, 1 vol. Hancock, Anna, illus. 2012. (Engage Literacy Magenta Ser.). (ENG.). 16p. (J). (gr. k-2). pap. 6.99 *(978-1-4296-8854-3(8)*, 119930); pap. 36.94 *(978-1-4296-8855-0(6)*, 18323) Capstone. (Capstone Pr.).
—My Food. 2012. (Engage Literacy Magenta Ser.). (ENG.). 16p. (J). (gr. k-2). pap. 36.94 *(978-1-4296-8885-7(8)*, 18338); pap. 6.99 *(978-1-4296-8884-0(X)*, 119945) Capstone. (Capstone Pr.).
—Toys That Float. 2015. (Engage Literacy Magenta - Extension A Ser.). (ENG.). 16p. (J). (gr. k-2). pap. 6.99 *(978-1-4914-8635-1(X)*, 131242) Capstone.
Gleisner, Jenna Lee. Back to School! 2017. (Welcoming the Seasons Ser.). (ENG.). 24p. (J). (gr. -1-2). lib. bdg. 32.79 *(978-1-5038-1666-4(4)*, 211497) Child's World, Inc, The.
—A Trip to the Pumpkin Patch. 2017. (Welcoming the Seasons Ser.). (ENG.). 24p. (J). (gr. -1-2). lib. bdg. 32.79 *(978-1-5038-1664-0(8)*, 211494) Child's World, Inc, The.
Glencoe McGraw-Hill Staff, creator. The American Vision Reading Essentials & Study Guide Student Workbook. 2nd ed. 2004. (United States History (hs) Ser.). (ENG., Illus.). 534p. (gr. 9-12). per. 8.52 *(978-0-07-865439-8(4)*, 0078654394) McGraw-Hill Higher Education.
Glencoe Staff. Catch the Wind '83. (J). (gr. 6). *(978-0-02-131880-3(8))* Macmillan Publishing Co., Inc.
—I Can Too '83: Level 5. (J). *(978-0-02-131670-0(8))* Macmillan Publishing Co., Inc.
A Gnu Named Blue. (Early Intervention Levels Ser.). 31.86 *(978-0-7362-0621-1(3))* CENGAGE Learning.
Go, Red Hens! (Early Intervention Levels Ser.). 21.30 *(978-0-7362-0393-7(1))*; Vol. 6. 3.55 *(978-0-7362-0173-5(4))* CENGAGE Learning.
The Goddess of the Volcano: Six-Pack, 6 packs. (Greetings Ser.: Vol. 1). (gr. 3-5). 31.00 *(978-0-7635-1843-1(3))* Rigby Education.
Godfrey. Murder in the Shadows. (Thumbprint Mysteries Ser.). 32.86 *(978-0-8092-0418-2(5))* McGraw-Hill/Contemporary.
Goh, Michelle. The 10 Best Cinderella Stories in Sports. 2008. 14.99 *(978-1-55448-495-9(2))* Scholastic Library Publishing.
Goin, Miriam Busch. Storms (1 Hardcover/1 CD) 2016. (National Geographic Readers: Pre-Reader Ser.). (ENG.). (J). *(978-1-4301-2125-1(4))* Live Oak Media.
—Storms (1 Paperback/1 CD) 2016. (National Geographic Readers: Pre-Reader Ser.). (ENG.). (J). pap. *(978-1-4301-2124-4(6))* Live Oak Media.
Going Home: KinderConcepts Individual Title Six-Packs. (Kinderstarters Ser.). 8p. (gr. -1-1). 21.00 *(978-0-7635-8724-6(9))* Rigby Education.
Going to the Park with GranDaDy: Big Book: Level F. (Visions Ser.). 8p. 20.95 *(978-0-7802-9745-6(8))* Wright Group/McGraw-Hill.
Going West: Fifth Grade Newcomer Books. (On Our Way to English Ser.). (gr. 5-18). 34.50 *(978-0-7578-7277-8(8))* Rigby Education.
Golden, Brenda. Celebrity. 2007. (Steck-Vaughn BOLDPRINT Anthologies Ser.). (ENG., Illus.). 48p. (gr. 8-10). pap., stu. ed. 16.90 *(978-1-4190-4031-3(6))* Houghton Mifflin Harcourt Publishing Co.
The Golden Dragon: Set D Individual Title Six-Packs. (Supersonic Phonics Ser.). (gr. k-3). 29.00 *(978-0-7635-0552-3(8))* Rigby Education.
Goldie's Shortcut. 12p. (J). bds. *(978-2-7643-0051-0(4))* Phidal Publishing, Inc./Editions Phidal, Inc.
Goldilocks & the Three Bears: Take-Home Book. 2005. (Emergent Library: Vol. 2). (YA). (gr. -1-1). 12.60 *(978-0-8215-7260-3(1))* Sadlier, William H. Inc.
Golding, Julia. Pandora's Box: Band 15/Emerald (Collins Big Cat) 2017. (Collins Big Cat Tales Ser.). (ENG., Illus.). 48p. (J). (gr. 3-4). pap. 12.99 *(978-0-00-817944-1(1))* HarperCollins Pubs. Ltd. GBR. Dist: Independent Pubs. Group.
Goldish, Meish. The Empty Pot: A Chinese Legend. Treatner, Meryle, illus. 2005. 14p. pap. 6.00 *(978-0-15-350582-9(6))* Harcourt Schl. Pubs.
—Lights! Camera! Action! 2012. (Discovery Phonics Ser.). (ENG., Illus.). 14p. (J). (gr. 1-3). pap. 10.47 *(978-0-8136-1154-9(7))* Modern Curriculum Pr.
Goldsmith, Rose. Who Lives near the North Pole? 2012. (Level E Ser.). (ENG., Illus.). 16p. (J). (gr. k-2). pap. 7.95 *(978-1-927136-45-4(8)*, 19454) RiverStream Publishing.
Gomboli, Mario. Comer Bien, Saber Comer. (Coleccion Lobo Rojo).Tr. of Eat Well, Know What to Eat. (SPA.). 32p. (J). (gr. k-3). 6.36 *(978-84-216-3458-5(5))* Bruño, Editorial ESP. Dist: Lectorum Pubns., Inc.
—Lavarse Es Divertido. (SPA.). 32p. (J). (gr. k-3). 6.36 *(978-84-216-3459-2(3))* Bruño, Editorial ESP. Dist: Lectorum Pubns., Inc.
Gonzales, Felipe C. Little Folk Stories & Tales by Don Pablo: Bilingual Stories in Spanish & English = Chistes y Cuentos de Don Pablo: Cuentos Bilingües en Español e Inglés. 2010. (SPA & ENG.). (J). pap. 24.95 *(978-0-86534-772-4(7))* Sunstone Pr.
Gonzalez-Jensen, Margarita. The Bird Who Ate Too Much. Wolff, Jason, illus. 2003. (Rigby on Our Way to English Ser.). (ENG.). 24p. (gr. 3-3). pap. 50.70 *(978-0-7578-4208-5(9))* Rigby Education.
González, Lucía. The Storyteller's Candle: La Velita de Los Cuentos, 1 vol. Delacre, Lulu, illus. 2013. (ENG.). 32p. (J).

(gr. 1-6). pap. 11.95 *(978-0-89239-237-7(1)*, leelowcbp, Children's Book Press) Lee & Low Bks., Inc.
Goodhart, Pippa. Dragon Boy (Reading Ladder Level 3) Ursell, Martin, illus. 2nd ed. 2016. (Reading Ladder Level 3 Ser.). (ENG.). 48p. (gr. k-2). pap. 4.99 *(978-1-4052-8238-3(X)*, Reading Ladder) Farshore GBR. Dist: HarperCollins Pubs.
—House that Jack Built. Parker, Andy, illus. 2004. (ENG.). 24p. (J). lib. bdg. 23.65 *(978-1-59646-700-2(2))* Dingles & Co.
Goodnight Board Books Set 800492, 3. 2005. (J). bds. *(978-1-59794-004-7(6))* Environments, Inc.
Goodrum, L. E. Counting with G & Me. 2009. 20p. pap. 24.95 *(978-1-60749-615-1(1))* America Star Bks.
Goodspeed, Horace. Will's Neighborhood, 1 vol. 2012. (InfoMax Readers Ser.). (ENG., Illus.). 16p. (J). (gr. k-k). pap. 7.00 *(978-1-4488-8881-8(6)*, 51d5d97f-149a-4841-a4fe-4146a299c4cf, Rosen Classroom) Rosen Publishing Group, Inc., The.
The Goose Who Acted Like a Cow (18), Vol. 18. (Early Intervention Levels Ser.). 5.31 *(978-0-7362-0615-0(9))* CENGAGE Learning.
Gordon, Sharon. Bookworms: At Home, 12 vols., Set. Incl. At Home by the Ocean. lib. bdg. 25.50 *(978-0-7614-1959-4(4)*, b15cc6b0-6fd4-44ee-b6db-e091ea9212a1); At Home in the City. lib. bdg. 25.50 *(978-0-7614-1960-0(8)*, 034ecede-017b-4330-aaf8-52d806d0f528); At Home in the Desert. lib. bdg. 25.50 *(978-0-7614-1963-1(2)*, 5407d635-0add-4e67-9345-6f1c6ebe66d1); At Home on the Farm. lib. bdg. 25.50 *(978-0-7614-1958-7(6)*, 59754abf-75aa-4f56-a829-7d18465bed14); At Home on the Mountain. lib. bdg. 25.50 *(978-0-7614-1961-7(6)*, bd851989-7051-4d9b-926e-8e41df196b16); At Home on the Ranch. lib. bdg. 25.50 *(978-0-7614-1962-4(4)*, e8ba57a1-7a95-47b0-a4f0-770bd27b9a71); (Illus.). 32p. (gr. k-2). (At Home Ser.). (ENG.). 2007. 153.00 *(978-0-7614-1957-0(8)*, 47820a1a-3224-4fab-a746-607497e29b86, Cavendish Square) Cavendish Square Publishing LLC.
Gorilla Games. (Early Intervention Levels Ser.). 21.30 *(978-0-7362-0363-0(X))*; Vol. 2. 3.55 *(978-0-7362-0084-4(3))* CENGAGE Learning.
Goring, Ruth. Los ángeles de Adriana. Meza, Erika, illus. 2017. 32p. (J). 16.99 *(978-1-5064-2507-8(0)*, Sparkhouse Family) 1517 Media.
Gottesfeld, Jeff. Fight School, 1 vol. 2014. (Red Rhino Ser.). (ENG.). 68p. (J). (gr. 4-7). pap. 9.95 *(978-1-62250-919-5(6))* Saddleback Educational Publishing, Inc.
Gould, Jane. At the Pond. rev. ed. 2011. (Mathematics in the Real World Ser.). (ENG.). 32p. (gr. k-1). pap. 9.99 *(978-1-4333-3430-6(5))* Teacher Created Materials, Inc.
—In the Garden. rev. ed. 2011. (Mathematics in the Real World Ser.). (ENG.). 32p. (gr. k-1). pap. 9.99 *(978-1-4333-3431-3(3))* Teacher Created Materials, Inc.
Gould, Robert. Dinosaurs. 2005. (Big Stuff Ser.: 7). (ENG., Illus.). 16p. (J). bds. 7.95 *(978-1-929945-58-0(2))* Big Guy Bks., Inc.
—Sea Creatures. 2005. (Big Stuff Ser.: 8). (ENG., Illus.). 16p. (J). bds. 7.95 *(978-1-929945-59-7(0))* Big Guy Bks., Inc.
Gould, Sloane. Following the Law: If... Then, 1 vol. 2017. (Computer Kids: Powered by Computational Thinking Ser.). (ENG.). 24p. (J). (gr. 3-4). 25.27 *(978-1-5383-2397-7(4)*, 09e5db1d-47b3-4ecd-b15f-db3fc2ff96a2, PowerKids Pr.); pap. *(978-1-5081-3773-3(0)*, 92ac4fc8-12c3-4d59-8c26-491d90e48b1a, Rosen Classroom) Rosen Publishing Group, Inc., The.
—Jameer Blasts Off! What Will Happen?, 1 vol. 2017. (Computer Science for the Real World Ser.). (ENG.). 16p. (gr. 2-3). pap. *(978-1-5383-5210-6(9)*, 5d608f5b-7154-4671-a879-56cf36c6e4c9, Rosen Classroom) Rosen Publishing Group, Inc., The.
—Kaydra's Cornrows: Over & over Again, 1 vol. 2017. (Computer Science for the Real World Ser.). (ENG.). 12p. (gr. 1-2). pap. *(978-1-5383-5166-6(8)*, 103c9640-0302-4b91-89b3-435a00eb4643, Rosen Classroom) Rosen Publishing Group, Inc., The.
Grace, Elora. Umbrellas Everywhere!, 1 vol. 2006. (Neighborhood Readers Ser.). (ENG.). 8p. (gr. 1-2). pap. 5.15 *(978-1-4042-6791-6(3)*, 6617174c-4804-4004-934c-cad40c81ac46, Rosen Classroom) Rosen Publishing Group, Inc., The.
Graf, Mike & Follett, Dave. Mudslide. 2008. (Rigby Focus Forward: Level M Ser.). (Illus.). 24p. (J). (gr. 4-7). pap. *(978-1-4190-3828-0(1)*, Rigby) Pearson Education Australia.
Graf, Mike & Kaske, Anne. Dinosaur Canyon. Weston, Steve, illus. 2005. 40p. pap. 8.53 *(978-0-7578-9858-7(0))* Houghton Mifflin Harcourt Supplemental Pubs.
Graf, Mike & Morden, Richard. Dirt on My Shoe. 2008. (Rigby Focus Forward: Level L Ser.). (Illus.). 24p. (J). (gr. 4-7). pap. *(978-1-4190-3805-1(2)*, Rigby) Pearson Education Australia.
Graham, Chris. So Many Snakes, 1 vol. 2005. (Rosen REAL Readers Ser.). (ENG., Illus.). 12p. (gr. 1-2). pap. 5.90 *(978-0-8239-8197-7(5)*, 0de2054f-9df9-4d28-b7da-d7981a08c8a3) Rosen Publishing Group, Inc., The.
Graham, Elspeth. Sandwich that Jack Made. Mould, Chris, illus. 2004. (ENG.). 24p. (J). lib. bdg. 23.65 *(978-1-59646-698-2(7))* Dingles & Co.
Graham, Ian. You Wouldn't Want to Climb Mount Everest! A Deadly Journey to the Top of the World. 2010. (You Wouldn't Want to... Ser.). 32p. (J). 29.00 *(978-0-531-20505-1(3)*, Watts, Franklin) Scholastic Library Publishing.
—You Wouldn't Want to Climb Mount Everest! (You Wouldn't Want to...: History of the World) Antram, David, illus. 2010. (You Wouldn't Want To— Ser.). (ENG.). 32p. (J). (gr. 3-18). pap. 9.95 *(978-0-531-13785-7(6)*, Watts, Franklin) Scholastic Library Publishing.
Graham, S. Jewels for the Journey. 2004. pap. 8.99 *(978-1-58158-043-3(6))* McDougal Publishing Co.
Grahame, Kenneth. Oxford Bookworms Library: the Wind in the Willows: Level 3: 1000-Word Vocabulary. 3rd ed. 2008. (ENG., Illus.). 80p. 11.00 *(978-0-19-479137-3(8))* Oxford Univ. Pr., Inc.
—The Wind in the Willows. 2004. 224p. pap. 12.95 *(978-1-59540-046-8(X)*, 1st World Library - Literary Society) 1st World Publishing, Inc.
Grandfather's Dream. (Lexile Levels Ser.). 9.09 *(978-1-56334-707-8(5))* CENGAGE Learning.
Gray, P. J. The Accident Book 2, 1 vol. 2014. (Trippin' Ser.). (ENG.). 64p. (YA). (gr. 9-12). pap. 10.75 *(978-1-62250-932-4(3))* Saddleback Educational Publishing, Inc.
—The Lab, Bk. 3. 2015. (Trippin' Ser.: 3). (YA). lib. bdg. 19.60 *(978-0-606-36835-3(3))* Turtleback.
—Odds Are Yes [2]. 2016. (Boosters Ser.). (ENG.). 48p. (YA). (gr. 9-12). 9.75 *(978-1-68021-129-0(3))* Saddleback Educational Publishing, Inc.
The Great Invention: Individual Title Six-Packs. (gr. -1-2). 27.00 *(978-0-7635-9452-7(0))* Rigby Education.
Greathouse, Lisa. Backstage Pass: Fashion, 1 vol. 2nd rev. ed. 2011. (TIME for KIDS(r): Informational Text Ser.). (ENG.). 32p. (gr. 3-4). pap. 11.99 *(978-1-4333-3661-4(8))* Teacher Created Materials, Inc.
—The Bakery. rev. ed. 2011. (Mathematics in the Real World Ser.). (ENG.). 32p. (gr. k-1). pap. 9.99 *(978-1-4333-3435-1(6))* Teacher Created Materials, Inc.
—Big Digs - Construction Site, 1 vol. 2nd rev. ed. 2011. (TIME for KIDS(r): Informational Text Ser.). (ENG.). 32p. (gr. 3-4). pap. 11.99 *(978-1-4333-3662-1(6))* Teacher Created Materials, Inc.
—Count Me In! School Carnival, 1 vol. 2nd rev. ed. 2011. (TIME for KIDS(r): Informational Text Ser.). (ENG.). 28p. (gr. 2-3). pap. 10.99 *(978-1-4333-3637-9(5))* Teacher Created Materials, Inc.
—Count Me In! Soccer Tournament, 1 vol. 2nd rev. ed. 2011. (TIME for KIDS(r): Informational Text Ser.). (ENG.). 28p. (gr. 2-3). pap. 10.99 *(978-1-4333-3638-6(3))* Teacher Created Materials, Inc.
—Eat Healthy, 1 vol. 2011. (Science: Informational Text Ser.). (ENG., Illus.). 32p. (gr. 3-4). pap. 11.99 *(978-1-4333-3087-2(3))* Teacher Created Materials, Inc.
—Emergency! Be Prepared, 1 vol. 2011. (Science: Informational Text Ser.). (ENG., Illus.). 32p. (gr. 3-4). pap. 11.99 *(978-1-4333-3092-6(X))* Teacher Created Materials, Inc.
—Farm Animals: Classifying & Sorting. rev. ed. 2011. (Mathematics in the Real World Ser.). (ENG.). 32p. (gr. k-1). pap. 9.99 *(978-1-4333-3442-9(9))* Teacher Created Materials, Inc.
—Find Your Sport, 1 vol. 2011. (Science: Informational Text Ser.). (ENG., Illus.). 32p. (gr. 3-4). pap. 11.99 *(978-1-4333-3090-2(3))* Teacher Created Materials, Inc.
—Fun in the Sun. rev. ed. 2011. (Mathematics in the Real World Ser.). (ENG.). 32p. (gr. k-1). pap. 9.99 *(978-1-4333-3433-7(X))* Teacher Created Materials, Inc.
—Games Are Fun. rev. ed. 2011. (Mathematics in the Real World Ser.). (ENG.). 32p. (gr. k-1). pap. 9.99 *(978-1-4333-3437-5(2))* Teacher Created Materials, Inc.
—Get Moving, 1 vol. 2011. (Science: Informational Text Ser.). (ENG.). 32p. (gr. 3-4). pap. 11.99 *(978-1-4333-3089-6(X))* Teacher Created Materials, Inc.
—Healthy Habits, Healthy You, 1 vol. 2011. (Science: Informational Text Ser.). (ENG., Illus.). 32p. (gr. 3-4). pap. 11.99 *(978-1-4333-3091-9(1))* Teacher Created Materials, Inc.
—Johnny Appleseed, 1 vol. rev. ed. 2009. (Reader's Theater Ser.). (ENG.). 24p. (gr. 2-4). pap. 8.99 *(978-1-4333-0990-8(4))* Teacher Created Materials, Inc.
—Make It Healthy, 1 vol. 2011. (Science: Informational Text Ser.). (ENG.). 32p. (gr. 3-4). pap. 11.99 *(978-1-4333-3088-9(1))* Teacher Created Materials, Inc.
—The Pet Store. rev. ed. 2011. (Mathematics in the Real World Ser.). (ENG.). 32p. (gr. k-1). pap. 9.99 *(978-1-4333-3428-3(3))* Teacher Created Materials, Inc.
—Recess Time: Patterns. rev. ed. 2011. (Mathematics in the Real World Ser.). (ENG.). 32p. (gr. k-1). pap. 9.99 *(978-1-4333-3436-8(4))* Teacher Created Materials, Inc.
—The Snack Shop. rev. ed. 2011. (Mathematics in the Real World Ser.). (ENG.). 32p. (gr. k-1). pap. 9.99 *(978-1-4333-3434-4(8))* Teacher Created Materials, Inc.
—Sweet: Inside a Bakery, 1 vol. 2nd rev. ed. 2011. (TIME for KIDS(r): Informational Text Ser.). (ENG.). 32p. (gr. 3-4). pap. 11.99 *(978-1-4333-3663-8(4))* Teacher Created Materials, Inc.
—The Toy Store. rev. ed. 2011. (Mathematics in the Real World Ser.). (ENG.). 32p. (gr. k-1). pap. 9.99 *(978-1-4333-3429-0(1))* Teacher Created Materials, Inc.
—What's for Lunch?, 1 vol. 2nd rev. ed. 2011. (TIME for KIDS(r): Informational Text Ser.). (ENG., Illus.). 28p. (gr. 2-3). pap. 10.99 *(978-1-4333-3639-3(1))* Teacher Created Materials, Inc.
—Wild Animals, Level K. rev. ed. 2011. (Mathematics in the Real World Ser.). (ENG.). 32p. (gr. k-1). pap. 9.99 *(978-1-4333-3443-6(7))* Teacher Created Materials, Inc.
Greathouse, Lisa & Kuligowski, Stephanie. Unsolved! Mysterious Events, 1 vol. 2nd rev. ed. 2012. (TIME for KIDS(r): Informational Text Ser.). (ENG., Illus.). 48p. (gr. 4-5). pap. 13.99 *(978-1-4333-4827-3(6))* Teacher Created Materials, Inc.
—Unsolved! Mysterious Places, 1 vol. 2nd rev. ed. 2012. (TIME for KIDS(r): Informational Text Ser.). (ENG., Illus.). 48p. (gr. 4-5). pap. 13.99 *(978-1-4333-4828-0(4))* Teacher Created Materials, Inc.
Greathouse, Lisa E. Astronomers Through Time, 1 vol. rev. ed. 2007. (Science: Informational Text Ser.). (ENG.). 32p. (gr. 4-6). pap. 12.99 *(978-0-7439-0562-6(8))* Teacher Created Materials, Inc.
Green Footprints: Individual Title Six-Packs. (Literatura 2000 Ser.). (gr. 1-2). 28.00 *(978-0-7635-0053-5(4))* Rigby Education.
Green, Jen. Snow Leopards: Band 11 Lime/Band 12 Copper (Collins Big Cat Progress) 2014. (Collins Big Cat Progress Ser.). (ENG., Illus.). 32p. (J). (gr. 2-3). pap. 10.99 *(978-0-00-751932-3(X))* HarperCollins Pubs. Ltd. GBR. Dist: Independent Pubs. Group.
Green, Ken. Not a Chance. (Thumbprint Mysteries Ser.). 32.86 *(978-0-8092-0422-9(3))* McGraw-Hill/Contemporary.
Green Light Level 1 Book Set 2 800895, 5 vols. 2005. (J). pap. *(978-1-59794-070-2(4))* Environments, Inc.
Green Light Level 1 Book Set 800894, 5 vols. 2005. (J). *(978-1-59794-069-6(0))* Environments, Inc.
Green Light Level 2 Book Set 800914, 6 vols. 2005. (J). pap. *(978-1-59794-079-5(8))* Environments, Inc.
Green, Rico. Super Animals! 2016. (Step into Reading Level 2 Ser.). lib. bdg. 14.75 *(978-0-606-38487-2(1))* Turtleback.
Greene, Janice. Blood & Basketball, 1 vol. unabr. ed. 2010. (Q Reads Ser.). (ENG.). 32p. (YA). (gr. 9-12). pap. 8.50 *(978-1-61651-213-2(X))* Saddleback Educational Publishing, Inc.
—Breaking Point, 1 vol. unabr. ed. 2010. (Q Reads Ser.). (ENG.). 32p. (YA). (gr. 9-12). pap. 8.50 *(978-1-61651-199-9(0))* Saddleback Educational Publishing, Inc.
—The Eye of the Hurricane, 1 vol. unabr. ed. 2010. (Q Reads Ser.). (ENG.). 32p. (YA). (gr. 9-12). pap. 8.50 *(978-1-61651-191-3(5))* Saddleback Educational Publishing, Inc.
—The House on the Hill, 1 vol. unabr. ed. 2010. (Q Reads Ser.). (ENG.). 32p. (YA). (gr. 9-12). pap. 8.50 *(978-1-61651-192-0(3))* Saddleback Educational Publishing, Inc.
—No Way to Run, 1 vol. unabr. ed. 2010. (Q Reads Ser.). (ENG.). 32p. (YA). (gr. 9-12). pap. 8.50 *(978-1-61651-184-5(2))* Saddleback Educational Publishing, Inc.
—Outcast, 1 vol. unabr. ed. 2010. (Q Reads Ser.). (ENG.). 32p. (YA). (gr. 9-12). pap. 8.50 *(978-1-61651-201-9(6))* Saddleback Educational Publishing, Inc.
—The Plot, 1 vol. unabr. ed. 2010. (Q Reads Ser.). (ENG.). 32p. (YA). (gr. 9-12). pap. 8.50 *(978-1-61651-204-0(0))* Saddleback Educational Publishing, Inc.
—The Ritual, 1 vol. unabr. ed. 2010. (Q Reads Ser.). (ENG.). 32p. (YA). (gr. 9-12). pap. 8.50 *(978-1-61651-185-2(0))* Saddleback Educational Publishing, Inc.
Greene, Janice & Thomas, Terri. Read My Lips, 1 vol. unabr. ed. 2010. (Q Reads Ser.). (ENG.). 32p. (YA). (gr. 9-12). pap. 8.50 *(978-1-61651-216-3(4))* Saddleback Educational Publishing, Inc.
Greenley, Amanda & Evans, Linda. Sledmere Stories - Book 1: The Birthday Party; Ali & Sam Help Out; Well Spotted!, Bk. 1. 2005. (ENG., Illus.). 80p. 8.95 *(978-1-84312-152-7(2)*, RX4678) Fulton, David Pubs. GBR. Dist: Taylor & Francis Group.
—Sledmere Stories - Book 2 Bk. 2: The Gameboy; Sophie Gets It Right; Stop Thief! 2005. (ENG., Illus.). 80p. (C). 26.95 *(978-1-84312-153-4(0)*, RX4679) Fulton, David Pubs. GBR. Dist: Taylor & Francis Group.
—Sledmere Stories - Book 3: The Gang; Learning about the Victorians; Ali & Sam's School Trip. 2005. (ENG., Illus.). 80p. (C). 26.95 *(978-1-84312-154-1(9)*, RX4680) Fulton, David Pubs. GBR. Dist: Taylor & Francis Group.
Greer, Eileen. Fuerte y Suave en la Clase de Música / Loud & Quiet in Music Class, 1 vol. 2017. (Opuestos en la Escuela / Opposites at School Ser.). (ENG & SPA., Illus.). 24p. (J). (gr. 1-1). lib. bdg. 25.27 *(978-1-5081-6349-7(9)*, 0bc15c06-53ce-4a55-ab5e-952ca8d2e015, PowerKids Pr.) Rosen Publishing Group, Inc., The.
—Fuerte y Suave en la Clase de Música (Loud & Quiet in Music Class), 1 vol. 2017. (Opuestos en la Escuela (Opposites at School) Ser.). (SPA.). 24p. (J). (gr. 1-1). pap. 9.25 *(978-1-5383-2716-6(3)*, 1ee40878-121f-4879-aef9-dcc778d0cd8c); (Illus.). lib. bdg. 25.27 *(978-1-5081-6345-9(6)*, fa861929-b7fa-47f0-9b35-29784595fe68) Rosen Publishing Group, Inc., The. (PowerKids Pr.).
Greetings! Add-to Pack. 47.00 *(978-0-7635-9407-7(5))* Rigby Education.
Greetings! Cluster Packages. (Saludos Ser.). (gr. 2-3). 135.00 *(978-0-7635-9408-4(3))*; 135.00 *(978-0-7635-9412-1(1))*; 135.00 *(978-0-7635-9416-9(4))*; 135.00 *(978-0-7635-9422-0(9))* Rigby Education.
Greetings! The Earth Is Our Home Complete Package. 385.00 *(978-0-7635-9420-6(2))* Rigby Education.
Gregoire, Maryellen. Escuelas Viejas y Nuevas. 2012. (Wonder Readers Spanish Emergent Ser.). (SPA.). 16p. (J). (gr. -1-1). pap. 37.50 *(978-1-62065-574-0(8)*, 19239) Capstone.
Gregorich, Barbara. Same or Different. deluxe ed. 2018. (ENG., Illus.). 64p. (J). (gr. -1-k). pap., wbk. ed. 4.49 *(978-1-58947-356-0(6)*, d98b0a06-e08d-4a94-80eb-2907cabc894d) School Zone Publishing Co.
Gregory, Cam. When Do I Go to School? 2012. (Level B Ser.). (ENG., Illus.). 16p. (J). (gr. k-2). pap. 7.95 *(978-1-927136-11-9(3)*, 19432) RiverStream Publishing.
—Where Can I Find a Good Friend? 2012. (Level D Ser.). (ENG., Illus.). 16p. (J). (gr. k-2). pap. 7.95 *(978-1-927136-33-1(4)*, 19439) RiverStream Publishing.
—Where Do Tall Trees Grow? 2012. (Level C Ser.). (ENG., Illus.). 16p. (J). (gr. k-2). pap. 7.95 *(978-1-927136-28-7(8)*, 19445) RiverStream Publishing.
—Who Lives Here? 2012. (Level A Ser.). (ENG., Illus.). 16p. (J). (gr. k-2). pap. 7.95 *(978-1-927136-01-0(6)*, 19453) RiverStream Publishing.
—Who Should Follow Signs? 2012. (Level F Ser.). (ENG., Illus.). 16p. (J). (gr. k-2). pap. 7.95 *(978-1-927136-53-9(9)*, 19455) RiverStream Publishing.
—Why Are Polar Bears in Danger? 2012. (Level E Ser.). (ENG., Illus.). 16p. (J). (gr. k-2). pap. 7.95 *(978-1-927136-44-7(X)*, 19458) RiverStream Publishing.
—Why Does the Moon Look Different? 2012. (Level E Ser.). (ENG., Illus.). 16p. (J). (gr. k-2). pap. 7.95 *(978-1-927136-46-1(6)*, 19464) RiverStream Publishing.
—Why Is It Expensive? 2012. (Level A Ser.). (ENG., Illus.). 16p. (J). (gr. k-2). pap. 7.95 *(978-1-927136-02-7(4)*, 19466) RiverStream Publishing.
Gregory, the Mean Dragon (16), Vol. 16. (Early Intervention Levels Ser.). 4.73 *(978-0-7362-0234-3(X))* CENGAGE Learning.
Greve, Meg. Swim for It! DuFalla, Anita, illus. 2011. (Little Birdie Readers Ser.). (ENG.). 24p. (gr. k-1). 28.50 *(978-1-61741-805-1(6))*, 9781617418051) Rourke Educational Media.
Griffey, Harriet. Earthquakes & Other Natural Disasters. 2010. (DK Readers Level 4 Ser.). (ENG.). 48p. (J). (gr. 2-4). 16.19 *(978-0-7566-5933-2(7))* Dorling Kindersley Publishing, Inc.
Griffin, C. R. Runt & the Two Roses. 2011. 24p. pap. 15.99 *(978-1-4628-4589-7(4))* Xlibris Corp.
Griffin, Mary. Our Needs & Wants, 1 vol. 2008. (Real Life Readers Ser.). (ENG.). 8p. (gr. k-1). pap. 5.15 *(978-1-4042-7965-0(2)*, ef49729f-aa3d-4196-ada0-a7bc411c954c, Rosen Classroom) Rosen Publishing Group, Inc., The.
Griffiths, Rachel. What's the Address? 2004. (ENG., Illus.). 16p. (J). (gr. 1-1). pap. 10.92 *(978-0-7652-5163-3(9)*, Celebration Pr.) Savvas Learning Co.
Grimm, Jacob, et al. Hansel & Gretel. 2005. 48p. (J). (gr. 2-18). 8.95 *(978-0-7945-1053-4(1)*, Usborne) EDC Publishing.
Grimm, Wilhelm K., et al. Elves & Shoemaker. 2004. 48p. (J). (gr. 2-18). pap. 5.95 *(978-0-7945-0758-9(1)*, Usborne) EDC Publishing.
Grindley, Sally. Puff Flies. Fuller, Jeremy, illus. 2011. (My Phonics Readers: Level 3 Ser.). 24p. (J). (gr. -1-1). 24.25 *(978-1-84898-514-8(2))* Sea-To-Sea Pubns.
—Queen Ella's Feet. Aguilar, Sandra, illus. 2011. (My Phonics Readers: Level 3 Ser.). 24p. (J). (gr. -1-1). 24.25 *(978-1-84898-513-1(4))* Sea-To-Sea Pubns.
Gro, Wright. Matchword/Prog Set. (Fast Track Reading Ser.). (gr. k-6). 158.95 incl. cd-rom *(978-0-322-03751-9(4))* Wright Group/McGraw-Hill.
Grogan, John. Marley: Marley's Big Adventure. Cowdrey, Richard, illus. 2009. (I Can Read Level 2 Ser.). (ENG.). 32p. (J). (gr. k-3). pap. 4.99 *(978-0-06-185383-8(6)*, HarperCollins) HarperCollins Pubs.
Grogan, John & Hill, Susan. Marley's Big Adventure. Cowdrey, Richard & Halverson, Lydia, illus. 2009. (I Can Read Book 2 Ser.). 32p. (J). (gr. -1-3). 16.99 *(978-0-06-185384-5(4))* HarperCollins Pubs.
Grosset and Dunlap Staff, et al. Fun with Dick & Jane. 2004. (Penguin Young Readers Level 2 Ser.). (gr. k-3). lib. bdg. 13.55 *(978-0-613-72512-5(3))* Turtleback.
Group/McGraw-Hill, Wright. A Friend in the Wild: Level Q, 6 vols. (Whispering Pines Ser.). 128p. (gr. 5-18). 36.95 *(978-0-322-05905-4(4))* Wright Group/McGraw-Hill.
—Gourmet Delights, 6 vols. (Comprehension Strand Ser.). (YA). (gr. 4-8). pap. 54.00 *(978-0-322-06028-9(1))* Wright Group/McGraw-Hill.
—Legends of the Wild West: Level O, 6 vols. (Autumn Leaves Ser.). 128p. (gr. 3-6). 36.95 *(978-0-322-06732-5(4))* Wright Group/McGraw-Hill.
—Mountain Peaks: Complete Set. (Mountain Peaks Ser.). 327.95 *(978-0-322-07966-3(7))* Wright Group/McGraw-Hill.
—Raging Rivers: Classroom Library Set. (Raging Rivers Ser.). 81.50 *(978-0-322-07970-0(5))* Wright Group/McGraw-Hill.
—Raging Rivers: Complete Set. (Raging Rivers Ser.). 327.95 *(978-0-322-07964-9(0))* Wright Group/McGraw-Hill.
—Riverboat Bill: Level H, 6 vols. (Take Twostm Ser.). 16p. 29.95 *(978-0-322-08958-7(1))* Wright Group/McGraw-Hill.
—Story Box, Leveled Books. 79.95 *(978-0-322-02563-9(X))* Wright Group/McGraw-Hill.
—Storyteller: Upper Emergent - Upper Emergent-Early Fluency - Complete Kit. (Storyteller Ser.). (gr. 1-18). 565.50 *(978-1-4045-1042-5(7))* Wright Group/McGraw-Hill.
—Storyteller Chapter Books: Fluency - 1 Each of 4 Titles: Level S. 24.50 *(978-1-4045-0953-5(4))* Wright Group/McGraw-Hill.
—Sunshine: Early Fluency - Groups 1-2; 1 each of 17 titles: Level M. (Sunshine Ser.). 99.50 *(978-0-322-04312-1(3))* Wright Group/McGraw-Hill.
—Take Twos: Upper Emergent - Level H: 1 Each of 4 Lesson Plans: Level H. (Take Twostm Ser.). 31.50 *(978-1-4045-1729-5(4))* Wright Group/McGraw-Hill.
Grubnedor Press. Tuppy the Turtle Puppy. 2007. (Illus.). 32p. (J). 10.95 *(978-0-9795407-0-7(4))* Grubnedor Pr.
Grudzina, Rebecca. Baby Bumblebee. Boyer, Lyn, illus. 2010. (Rising Readers Ser.). (J). 3.49 *(978-1-60719-688-4(3))* Newmark Learning LLC.
—A Baby Bumblebee for Mommy. Boyer, Lyn, illus. 2009. (Reader's Theater Nursery Rhymes & Songs Set B Ser.). 48p. (J). pap. *(978-1-60859-149-7(2))* Benchmark Education Co.
—Pease Porridge, Please! Harrington, David, illus. 2009. (Reader's Theater Nursery Rhymes & Songs Set B Ser.). 48p. (J). pap. *(978-1-60859-163-3(8))* Benchmark Education Co.
—Red Roses, Blue Violets, And... ? Ledger, Bill, illus. 2009. (Reader's Theater Nursery Rhymes & Songs Set B Ser.). 48p. (J). pap. *(978-1-60859-167-1(0))* Benchmark Education Co.
—Tim's Swim. Piwowarski, Marcin, illus. 2017. (Text Connections Guided Close Reading Ser.). (J). (gr. k). *(978-1-4900-1766-2(6))* Benchmark Education Co.
The Grumpy Millionaire: Individual Title Six-Packs. (Bookweb Ser.). 32p. (gr. 5-18). 34.00 *(978-0-7635-3777-7(2))* Rigby Education.
Guess What! Individual Title Six-Packs. (Literatura 2000 Ser.). (gr. k-1). 28.00 *(978-0-7635-0054-2(2))* Rigby Education.
Guess Who? Individual Title Six-Packs. (gr. k-1). 23.00 *(978-0-7635-8856-4(3))* Rigby Education.
Guest, Elissa Haden. Iris & Walter: the Sleepover. Davenier, Christine, illus. alt. ed. 2012. (Iris & Walter Ser.). (ENG.). 44p. (J). (gr. 1-4). pap. 4.99 *(978-0-547-74556-5(7)*, 1486269, Clarion Bks.) HarperCollins Pubs.
—The School Play. 2015. (Iris & Walter — Green Light Reader Ser.). lib. bdg. 13.55 *(978-0-606-36558-1(3))* Turtleback.
Guided Reading Levels, 25 bks., Set, Level A. (Guided Reading Levels Ser.). 92.05 *(978-0-7362-1186-4(1))* CENGAGE Learning.
Guillain, Charlotte. Extreme Animals: Band 10 White/Band 16 Sapphire (Collins Big Cat Progress) 2014. (Collins Big Cat Progress Ser.). (ENG., Illus.). 32p. (J). (gr. 4-5). pap. 10.99 *(978-0-00-751928-6(1))* HarperCollins Pubs. Ltd. GBR. Dist: Independent Pubs. Group.
Guille-Marrett, Emily & Raby, Charlotte. Collins Big Cat Phonics for Letters & Sounds - I Spy Nursery Rhymes: Band 00/Lilac. Enright, Amanda, illus. 2018. (Collins Big Cat Phonics Ser.). (ENG.). 16p. (J). pap. 6.99 *(978-0-00-825123-9(1))* HarperCollins Pubs. Ltd. GBR. Dist: Independent Pubs. Group.
—Collins Big Cat Phonics for Letters & Sounds - My Day, Our World: Band 00/Lilac. 2018. (Collins Big Cat Phonics Ser.). (ENG., Illus.). 16p. (J). (— 1). pap. 6.99 *(978-0-00-825128-4(2))* HarperCollins Pubs. Ltd. GBR. Dist: Independent Pubs. Group.
—Collins Big Cat Phonics for Letters & Sounds - Sound Walk: Band 00/Lilac. Gurrea, Susana, illus. 2018. (Collins Big Cat Phonics Ser.). (ENG.). 16p. (J). (— 1). pap. 6.99

(978-0-00-825127-7(4)) HarperCollins Pubs. Ltd. GBR. Dist: Independent Pubs. Group.

Gunby, Shirley & Laman, Judi-Lynn. Extinct & Endangered: Big Animals Small World - Painting for Peanuts. 2007. (Steck-Vaughn BOLDPRINT Anthologies Ser.). (ENG., Illus.). 48p. (gr. 4-8). pap. 16.90 *(978-1-4190-4023-8(5))* Houghton Mifflin Harcourt Publishing Co.

Gundersheimer (Mister G), Ben. Señorita Mariposa. Rivero, Marcos Almada, illus. 2019. 32p. (J). (-k). 18.99 *(978-1-5247-4070-2(5)*, Nancy Paulsen Books) Penguin Young Readers Group.

Gunn, Barbara. Old MacDonald's Farm: Read Well Level K Unit 7 Storybook. Marier, Chuck, illus. 2004. (Read Well Level K Ser.). 20p. (J). *(978-1-57035-679-7(3))* Cambium Education, Inc.

Gunn, Barbara, et al. Mark & Dan Go West: Read Well Level K Unit 17 Storybook. Weber, Philip A., Jr., illus. 2003. (Read Well Level K Ser.). 20p. (J). *(978-1-57035-688-9(2)*, 55571) Cambium Education, Inc.

Gurney, Stella. Mr. Bickle & the Ghost, 1 vol. Raga, Silvia, illus. 2009. (Get Ready Readers Ser.). (ENG.). 32p. (J). (gr. k-k). lib. bdg. 27.27 *(978-1-60754-260-5(9)*, 51868dc4-4d92-4f96-a2d9-14a54c25f817, Windmill Bks.) Rosen Publishing Group, Inc., The.

Gutman, Dan. My Weird Reading Tips: Tips, Tricks & Secrets by the Author of My Weird School. 2019. (My Weird School Ser.). (ENG., Illus.). 224p. (J). (gr. 1-5). 16.99 *(978-0-06-288240-0(6)*, HarperCollins) HarperCollins Pubs.

—My Weird Reading Tips: Tips, Tricks & Secrets from the Author of My Weird School. 2019. (My Weird School Ser.). (ENG., Illus.). 224p. (J). (gr. 1-5). pap. 6.99 *(978-0-06-288239-4(2)*, HarperCollins) HarperCollins Pubs.

—My Weird School 4 Books In 1! Books 1-4, 4 bks. in 1. Paillot, Jim, illus. 2016. (My Weird School Ser.). (ENG.). 384p. (J). (gr. 1-5). 16.99 *(978-0-06-249668-3(9)*, HarperCollins) HarperCollins Pubs.

—My Weird School Goes to the Museum. Paillot, Jim, illus. 2016. 30p. (J). *(978-1-5182-2157-6(2))* Harper & Row Ltd.

—Rappy Goes to Mars. Bowers, Tim, illus. 2017. (I Can Read Level 2 Ser.). (ENG.). 32p. (J). (gr. -1-3). 16.99 *(978-0-06-225269-2(0))*; pap. 4.99 *(978-0-06-225268-5(2))* HarperCollins Pubs. (HarperCollins).

—Rappy Goes to the Library. Bowers, Tim, illus. 2017. (I Can Read Level 2 Ser.). (ENG.). 32p. (J). (gr. -1-3). pap. 4.99 *(978-0-06-225265-4(8)*, HarperCollins) HarperCollins Pubs.

—Rappy Goes to the Supermarket. Bowers, Tim, illus. 2017. (I Can Read Level 2 Ser.). (ENG.). 32p. (J). (gr. -1-3). 4.99 *(978-0-06-225262-3(3)*, HarperCollins) HarperCollins Pubs.

Gutner, Howard. True Books: Egypt. 2009. (True Book Ser.). (ENG.). 48p. (J). pap. 6.95 *(978-0-531-21356-8(0)*, Children's Pr.) Scholastic Library Publishing.

Guy, Ginger Foglesong. Siesta Board Book: Bilingual English-Spanish. Moreno, Rene King, illus. 2009. (ENG.). 34p. (J). (gr. -1 — 1). bds. 7.99 *(978-0-06-168884-3(3))* HarperCollins Español.

Gwent (Wales), Staff Development Unit Staff & Acen Staff, contrib. by. Croeso I Gartref Llew. 2005. (WEL., Illus.). 8p. pap. *(978-1-874049-34-0(3))* Acen Limited.

—Nos Da, Arthur. 2005. (WEL., Illus.). 8p. pap. *(978-1-874049-31-9(9))* Acen Limited.

Haas, Jessie. Bramble & Maggie Give & Take. Friend, Alison, illus. 2015. (Candlewick Sparks Ser.). (ENG.). 56p. (J). (gr. k-4). pap. 5.99 *(978-0-7636-7787-9(6))* Candlewick Pr.

Hager, Janet. Truly Julie. 2012. 26p. 14.95 *(978-1-4626-6121-3(1))* America Star Bks.

Haladay, Max. Max Gets Mad, 1 vol. 2006. (Neighborhood Readers Ser.). (ENG.). 8p. (gr. 1-2). pap. 5.15 *(978-1-4042-6811-1(1)*, 937b21d8-5e4c-4b3c-8801-b2ad27c26bb7, Rosen Classroom) Rosen Publishing Group, Inc., The.

Hall, Kirsten. Hide-and-Seek: All about Location. Luedecke, Bev, illus. 2005. (Beastieville Ser.). (ENG.). 32p. (J). (gr. k-1). pap. 3.95 *(978-0-516-25519-4(3)*, Children's Pr.) Scholastic Library Publishing.

Hall, Marcella Runell & Cameron, Andrea. The 10 Most Influential Hip Hop Artists. 2008. 14.99 *(978-1-55448-504-8(5))* Scholastic Library Publishing.

Hall, Ralph. Crabs Blue Band. Belcher, Andy, photos by. 2017. (Cambridge Reading Adventures Ser.). (ENG., Illus.). 16p. pap. 6.15 *(978-1-108-43537-6(8))* Cambridge Univ. Pr.

Hallett, R. B. The 10 Most Decisive Battles on American Soil. 2008. 14.99 *(978-1-55448-538-3(X))* Scholastic Library Publishing.

Halls, Smriti. Norman the Naughty Knight & the Flying Horse (Reading Ladder Level 2) Smith, Ian, illus. 2017. (Reading Ladder Level 2 Ser.). (ENG.). 48p. (gr. k-2). pap. 4.99 *(978-1-4052-8453-0(6)*, Reading Ladder) Farshore GBR. Dist: HarperCollins Pubs.

—Norman the Naughty Knight (Reading Ladder Level 2) Smith, Ian, illus. 2016. (Reading Ladder Level 2 Ser.). (ENG.). 48p. (gr. k-2). pap. 4.99 *(978-1-4052-8214-7(2)*, Reading Ladder) Farshore GBR. Dist: HarperCollins Pubs.

Hama, Larry. The Battle of First Bull Run: The War Begins!, 1 vol. 2006. (Graphic Battles of the Civil War Ser.). (ENG., Illus.). 48p. (gr. 4-5). pap. 14.05 *(978-1-4042-6476-2(0)*, 5a9f1503-6cb6-4333-ba2e-51e98cec6b65, Rosen Classroom) Rosen Publishing Group, Inc., The.

—The Battle of Shiloh: Surprise Attack!, 1 vol. 2006. (Graphic Battles of the Civil War Ser.). (ENG., Illus.). 48p. (gr. 4-5). pap. 14.05 *(978-1-4042-6478-6(7)*, 47c54eba-6131-4a1d-9181-d5c3a3bcc55e, Rosen Classroom) Rosen Publishing Group, Inc., The.

Hambleton, Laura. Collins Big Cat Phonics for Letters & Sounds - Fantastic Yak: Band 02A/Red A, Bd. 2. Hambleton, Laura, illus. 2018. (Collins Big Cat Phonics Ser.). (ENG., Illus.). 16p. (J). (gr. -1-k). pap. 6.99 *(978-0-00-825141-3(X))* HarperCollins Pubs. Ltd. GBR. Dist: Independent Pubs. Group.

—Collins Big Cat Phonics for Letters & Sounds - Pink Boat, Pink Car: Band 02B/Red B, Bd. 2B. Hambleton, Laura, illus. 2018. (Collins Big Cat Phonics Ser.). (ENG., Illus.). 16p. (J). (gr. -1-k). pap. 6.99 *(978-0-00-825147-5(9))* HarperCollins Pubs. Ltd. GBR. Dist: Independent Pubs. Group.

Hamiduddin, Rabab, et al. Arabic Club Readers: Blue Band: Adnan & the Hoopoe. 2014. 16p. spiral bd. 4.99 *(978-1-4085-2489-3(9))* Oxford Univ. Pr., Inc.

—Arabic Club Readers: Blue Band: Majid the Astronaut. 2014. 16p. spiral bd. 4.99 *(978-1-4085-2492-3(9))* Oxford Univ. Pr., Inc.

—Arabic Club Readers: Pink Band: I Have Toys. 2014. (ENG.). 16p. pap. 4.99 *(978-1-4085-2464-0(3))* Oxford Univ. Pr., Inc.

—Arabic Club Readers: Pink Band: in the Jungle. 2014. (ENG.). 16p. pap. 4.99 *(978-1-4085-2465-7(1))* Oxford Univ. Pr., Inc.

—Arabic Club Readers: Red Band: Rain, Rain, Rain, Bk. 11. 2014. (ENG.). 16p. pap. 4.99 *(978-1-4085-2499-2(6))* Oxford Univ. Pr., Inc.

—Arabic Club Readers: Red Band: Time for School. 2014. 16p. spiral bd. 4.99 *(978-1-4085-2454-1(6))* Oxford Univ. Pr., Inc.

—Arabic Readers Club: Blue Band: Nahoula's Story. 2014. 16p. spiral bd. 4.99 *(978-1-4085-2494-7(5))* Oxford Univ. Pr., Inc.

Hammond, Veronica. Wash Those Hands. 2009. (ENG.). 24p. (J). pap. 9.45 *(978-1-4269-1590-1(X))* Trafford Publishing.

Hank's Tank, 6 vols. 8p. (gr. 1). 21.50 *(978-0-322-02061-0(1))* Wright Group/McGraw-Hill.

Hannigan, Paula & Kirkova, Milena. When I'm Big: A Silly Slider Book. 2010. (ENG.). 12p. (J). (gr. -1-1). bds. 14.99 *(978-0-7407-9727-9(1))* Andrews McMeel Publishing.

Hansen, Grace. Ballenas (Whales), 1 vol. 2016. (Vida en el Océano (Ocean Life) Ser.). (SPA., Illus.). 24p. (J). (gr. -1-2). lib. bdg. 32.79 *(978-1-68080-750-9(1)*, 22662, Abdo Kids) ABDO Publishing Co.

—Curiosidades Graciosas de Los Animales! (Animal Facts to Make You Smile!) 2016. (Ver para Creer (Seeing Is Believing) Ser.). (SPA., Illus.). 24p. (J). (gr. -1-2). lib. bdg. 32.79 *(978-1-68080-768-4(4)*, 22698, Abdo Kids) ABDO Publishing Co.

Hanson, Sharon. The 10 Best Love Poems. 2008. 14.99 *(978-1-55448-543-7(6))* Scholastic Library Publishing.

Hapka, Catherine, pseud. Plants vs. Zombies. 2014. (I Can Read! Level 2 Ser.). (J). lib. bdg. 13.55 *(978-0-606-35477-6(8))* Turtleback.

Happy Baby Board Books 800847, 3. 2005. (J). bds. *(978-1-59794-048-1(8))* Environments, Inc.

Happy Tunes Book Set 800944, 5. 2005. (J). bds. *(978-1-59794-031-3(3))* Environments, Inc.

Harcourt Achieve, creator. Avenues. 2005. (Steck-Vaughn Read on! Go Bks.). (Illus.). 108p. (J). per. 8.95 *(978-0-7398-8970-1(2))* Steck-Vaughn.

—Images. 2005. (Steck-Vaughn Read on! Go Bks.). (Illus.). 172p. (J). per. 8.95 *(978-0-7398-8969-5(9))* Steck-Vaughn.

—People. 2005. (Steck-Vaughn Read on! Go Bks.). (Illus.). 88p. (J). per. 8.95 *(978-0-7398-8967-1(2))* Steck-Vaughn.

—Windows. 2005. (Steck-Vaughn Read on! Go Bks.). (Illus.). 152p. (J). per. 8.95 *(978-0-7398-8968-8(0))* Steck-Vaughn.

Harcourt School Publishers, creator. Earth's Changing Crust: Lessons 3-5. 2006. (ENG.). pap. 27.00 *(978-0-15-354803-1(7))* Harcourt Schl. Pubs.

—Ecosystems: Lessons 3-4. 2006. (ENG.). pap. 27.00 *(978-0-15-354818-5(5))* Harcourt Schl. Pubs.

—Energy Transfer & Weather: Lessons 2-3. 2006. (ENG.). pap. 27.00 *(978-0-15-354814-7(2))* Harcourt Schl. Pubs.

—Invisible Pull: Electricity & Magnets. 2009. (ENG., Illus.). 16p. (J). pap. 14.95 *(978-0-15-362219-9(9))* Harcourt Schl. Pubs.

Harcourt School Publishers Staff. Banner Days Level 2-2. 3rd ed. 2003. (Harcourt School Publishers Trophies Ser.). (ENG., Illus.). 448p. (gr. 2-2). pupil's gde. ed. 59.90 *(978-0-15-322475-1(4))* Harcourt Schl. Pubs.

—Horizons Big Book Collection. 2nd ed. 2003. (Illus.). (gr. 1). pap. 840.00 *(978-0-15-337573-6(6))*; (gr. 2). pap. 840.00 *(978-0-15-337581-1(7))* Harcourt Schl. Pubs.

—Horizons Big Book Collection Unit 1. 2nd ed. 2003. (Illus.). pap. 140.00 *(978-0-15-337574-3(4))*; pap. 140.00 *(978-0-15-337812-6(3))* Harcourt Schl. Pubs.

—Horizons Big Book Collection Unit 2. 2nd ed. 2003. (Illus.). pap. 140.00 *(978-0-15-337575-0(2))*; pap. 140.00 *(978-0-15-337813-3(1))* Harcourt Schl. Pubs.

—Horizons Big Book Collection Unit 3. 2nd ed. 2003. (Illus.). pap. 140.00 *(978-0-15-337814-0(X))*; pap. 140.00 *(978-0-15-337577-4(9))* Harcourt Schl. Pubs.

—Horizons Big Book Collection Unit 4. 2nd ed. 2003. (Illus.). pap. 140.00 *(978-0-15-337578-1(7))*; pap. 140.00 *(978-0-15-337815-7(8))* Harcourt Schl. Pubs.

—Horizons Big Book Collection Unit 5. 2nd ed. 2003. (Illus.). pap. 140.00 *(978-0-15-337579-8(5))*; (J). pap. 140.00 *(978-0-15-337816-4(6))* Harcourt Schl. Pubs.

—Horizons Big Book Collection Unit 6. 2nd ed. 2003. (Illus.). pap. 140.00 *(978-0-15-337580-4(9))*; pap. 140.00 *(978-0-15-337817-1(4))* Harcourt Schl. Pubs.

—Horizons ESL Summary. 4th ed. 2004. (gr. 1). pap. 9.30 *(978-0-15-341413-8(8))*; (gr. 2). pap. 9.30 *(978-0-15-341414-5(6))* Harcourt Schl. Pubs.

—Horizons ESL Summary with Ancient Civilizations. 4th ed. 2004. (gr. 3). pap. 12.40 *(978-0-15-341415-2(4))* Harcourt Schl. Pubs.

—Horizons, Grade 2: Time for Kids Readers. 3rd ed. 2003. (Harcourt Horizons Ser.). pap., tchr. ed. 51.20 *(978-0-15-334647-7(7))* Harcourt Schl. Pubs.

—Lets Visit Museum, Above Level Reader Grade K: Harcourt School Publishers Social Studies. 2005. pap. 5.60 *(978-0-15-351872-0(3))* Harcourt Schl. Pubs.

—Little Red Hen Library Book Grade K: Harcourt School Publishers Storytown. 2005. 32p. pap. 8.75 *(978-0-15-352474-5(X))* Harcourt Schl. Pubs.

—Moving into English Big Books: Leveled Library Collection. 2nd ed. 2003. (Illus.). (gr. 2). pap. 508.40 *(978-0-15-337426-5(8))* Harcourt Schl. Pubs.

—Trophies: Lead the Way. 3rd ed. 2003. (Harcourt School Publishers Trophies Ser.). (ENG., Illus.). 784p. (gr. 4-4). 82.50 *(978-0-15-339787-5(X))* Harcourt Schl. Pubs.

—Trophies: Mr. Putter & Tabby, Set 2. 2004. (Illus.). pap. 17.85 *(978-0-15-205375-8(1))* Harcourt Schl. Pubs.

—Trophies: Timeless Treasures. 3rd ed. 2003. (Harcourt School Publishers Trophies Ser.). (ENG., Illus.). 752p. (gr. 6-6). 82.50 *(978-0-15-339789-9(6))* Harcourt Schl. Pubs.

—Trophies Level 1-1: Guess Who. 3rd ed. 2003. (Harcourt School Publishers Trophies Ser.). (ENG., Illus.). 160p. (gr. 1-1). stu. ed. 37.85 *(978-0-15-339776-9(4))* Harcourt Schl. Pubs.

—Trophies Level 1-2: Catch the Dream. 3rd ed. 2003. (Harcourt School Publishers Trophies Ser.). (ENG., Illus.). 176p. (gr. 1-1). stu. ed. 37.85 *(978-0-15-339777-6(2))* Harcourt Schl. Pubs.

—Trophies Level 1-3: Here & There. 3rd ed. 2003. (Harcourt School Publishers Trophies Ser.). (ENG., Illus.). 192p. (gr. 1-1). 40.05 *(978-0-15-339778-3(0))* Harcourt Schl. Pubs.

—Trophies Level 2-2: Banner Days. 3rd ed. 2003. (Harcourt School Publishers Trophies Ser.). (ENG., Illus.). 448p. (gr. 2-2). stu. ed. 58.70 *(978-0-15-339783-7(7))* Harcourt Schl. Pubs.

—Trophies Level 3-1: Changing Patterns. 3rd ed. 2003. (Harcourt School Publishers Trophies Ser.). (ENG., Illus.). 448p. (gr. 3-3). 60.75 *(978-0-15-339784-4(5))* Harcourt Schl. Pubs.

—Trophies Level 3-2: On Your Mark. 3rd ed. 2003. (Harcourt School Publishers Trophies Ser.). (ENG., Illus.). 464p. (gr. 3-3). stu. ed. 60.75 *(978-0-15-339786-8(1))* Harcourt Schl. Pubs.

—Watch This! Level 1-5 Grade 1: Harcourt School Publishers Storytown Florida. 2005. 264p. 23.73 *(978-0-15-352170-6(8))* Harcourt Schl. Pubs.

—Your Health Reader: The Morning. 3rd ed. 2003. (Illus.). pap. 9.40 *(978-0-15-338777-7(7))* Harcourt Schl. Pubs.

Hargis, Alvin. Kingdom of Mystique Series: Book 1. 2007. 25p. pap. 24.95 *(978-1-4241-8635-8(8))* PublishAmerica, Inc.

Hargreaves, Kate. Jammer Star, 1 vol. 2019. (Orca Sports Ser.). (ENG.). 152p. (J). (gr. 4-7). pap. 9.95 *(978-1-4598-1718-0(4))* Orca Bk. Pubs. USA.

Harimann, Sierra. Ice Age: Dawn of the Dinosaurs - Momma Mix-Up. 2009. (I Can Read Level 2 Ser.). (ENG.). 32p. (J). (gr. k-3). pap. 3.99 *(978-0-06-168978-9(5))* HarperCollins Pubs.

Harkness, Karen. Coralee's Best Run Yet. 2007. (Illus.). 40p. (J). per. 7.99 net. *(978-0-9800934-0-7(6))* H&W Publishing Inc.

Harmon, Dan, et al. Monster House - La Casa de los Sustos, 1 vol. 2014. (SPA., Illus.). 40p. pap. 15.00 incl. audio compact disk *(978-84-9848-132-7(5))* Edinumen, Editorial ESP. Dist: Cambridge Univ. Pr.

Harold First Readers 800883, 4 vols. 2005. (J). pap. *(978-1-59794-058-0(5))* Environments, Inc.

Harper, C. J. The Wilderness. 2014. (ENG.). 416p. (YA). pap. 9.99 *(978-0-85707-700-4(7)*, Simon & Schuster Children's) Simon & Schuster, Ltd. GBR. Dist: Simon & Schuster, Inc.

Harper Collins & Auerbach, Annie. Meet Paddington. 2014. (Paddington — I Can Read Ser.). (J). lib. bdg. 13.55 *(978-0-606-35966-5(4))* Turtleback.

Harper, Kathryn. Dressing for the Weather Green Band. Sims, Sean, illus. 2016. (Cambridge Reading Adventures Ser.). (ENG.). 16p. pap. 7.95 *(978-1-316-50324-9(0))* Cambridge Univ. Pr.

—Earthquakes White Band. Dean, Venitia, illus. 2016. (Cambridge Reading Adventures Ser.). (ENG.). 24p. pap. 8.80 *(978-1-316-50342-3(9))* Cambridge Univ. Pr.

—Leopard & His Spots Red Band. Mosedale, Julian, illus. 2016. (Cambridge Reading Adventures Ser.). (ENG.). 16p. pap. 7.95 *(978-1-316-50308-9(9))* Cambridge Univ. Pr.

—Please Stop, Sara! Pink a Band. Nicholls, Paul, illus. 2016. (Cambridge Reading Adventures Ser.). (ENG.). 16p. pap. 7.95 *(978-1-316-50313-3(5))* Cambridge Univ. Pr.

—Seagull Red Band. Villalba, Ana, illus. 2016. (Cambridge Reading Adventures Ser.). (ENG.). 16p. pap. 7.95 *(978-1-316-50310-2(0))* Cambridge Univ. Pr.

—Timbuktu 2 Wayfarers. Peinador, Angeles, illus. 2017. (Cambridge Reading Adventures Ser.). (ENG.). 24p. (J). pap. 7.35 *(978-1-108-41085-4(5))* Cambridge Univ. Pr.

—What Little Kitten Wants Red Band. Bowles, Paula, illus. 2017. (Cambridge Reading Adventures Ser.). (ENG.). 16p. pap. 6.15 *(978-1-108-40569-0(X))* Cambridge Univ. Pr.

—A World of Deserts Gold Band. 2017. (Cambridge Reading Adventures Ser.). (ENG., Illus.). 24p. pap. 7.35 *(978-1-108-40585-0(1))* Cambridge Univ. Pr.

Harper, Reggie. I Study Day & Night: Organizing Data, 1 vol. 2017. (Computer Kids: Powered by Computational Thinking Ser.). (ENG.). 24p. (J). (gr. 4-5). 25.27 *(978-1-5383-2403-5(2)*, 132fdacb-38dc-40f8-9fed-44c199374460, PowerKids Pr.); pap. *(978-1-5081-3765-8(X)*, d248d42b-ebc8-4dee-bbf6-a6b00062a0c9, Rosen Classroom) Rosen Publishing Group, Inc., The.

—Tarik's Telescope: Fixing the Problem, 1 vol. 2017. (Computer Science for the Real World Ser.). (ENG.). 24p. (J). (gr. 3-4). pap. *(978-1-5081-3786-3(2)*, 12d8d64f-8545-47cf-9c5f-b61bcc269d9f, Rosen Classroom); (Illus.). lib. bdg. 25.27 *(978-1-5081-6275-9(1)*, 5863e35d-6b20-4c25-a88f-525e1a2986a6, PowerKids Pr.) Rosen Publishing Group, Inc., The.

Harper, Suzanne. The 10 Most Tragic Romances. 2008. (J). 14.99 *(978-1-55448-546-8(0))* Scholastic Library Publishing.

Harper, Suzanne & Sheppard, Bonnie. The 10 Most Extreme Vacations. 2008. (J). 14.99 *(978-1-55448-534-5(7))* Scholastic Library Publishing.

Harris, Brooke. Baby Gets a Cake. Beckstrand, Jared, illus. 2009. (Reader's Theater Nursery Rhymes & Songs Set B Ser.). 48p. (J). pap. *(978-1-60859-150-3(6))* Benchmark Education Co.

—Brother John, Wake Up! 2008. (Reader's Theater Nursery Rhymes & Songs Ser.). (Illus.). 48p. (J). (gr. k-1). pap. *(978-1-60437-973-0(1))* Benchmark Education Co.

—Fun with Our Friends: Lap Book. 2009. (My First Reader's Theater Set B Ser.). (J). 28.00 *(978-1-4108-8543-2(7))* Benchmark Education Co.

—Healthy Snacks: Lap Book. 2009. (My First Reader's Theater Set B Ser.). (J). 28.00 *(978-1-4108-8545-6(3))* Benchmark Education Co.

—Jack & Jill Play on the Hill. 2008. (Reader's Theater Nursery Rhymes & Songs Ser.). (Illus.). 48p. (J). (gr. k-1). pap. *(978-1-60437-964-8(2))* Benchmark Education Co.

—Little Boy Blue, Where are You? 2008. (Reader's Theater Nursery Rhymes & Songs Ser.). (Illus.). 48p. (J). (gr. k-1). pap. *(978-1-60437-976-1(6))* Benchmark Education Co.

—London Bridge Has Fallen Down. Boyer, Lyn, illus. 2009. (Reader's Theater Nursery Rhymes & Songs Set B Ser.). 48p. (J). pap. *(978-1-60859-159-6(X))* Benchmark Education Co.

—Mary's Garden: How Does it Grow? Xin, Xiao, illus. 2009. (Reader's Theater Nursery Rhymes & Songs Set B Ser.). 48p. (J). pap. *(978-1-60859-160-2(3))* Benchmark Education Co.

—Playing at My House: Lap Book. 2009. (My First Reader's Theater Set B Ser.). (J). 28.00 *(978-1-60634-986-1(4))* Benchmark Education Co.

—The Purple Cow. Hohnstadt, Cedric, illus. 2009. (Reader's Theater Nursery Rhymes & Songs Set B Ser.). 48p. (J). pap. *(978-1-60859-166-4(2))* Benchmark Education Co.

—This Little Pig, That Little Pig. 2008. (Reader's Theater Nursery Rhymes & Songs Ser.). (Illus.). 48p. (J). (gr. k-1). pap. *(978-1-60437-969-3(3))* Benchmark Education Co.

—The Twinkling Stars. Harrington, David, illus. 2009. (Reader's Theater Nursery Rhymes & Songs Set B Ser.). 48p. (J). pap. *(978-1-60859-170-1(0))* Benchmark Education Co.

—Where Has My Little Dog Gone? 2008. (Reader's Theater Nursery Rhymes & Songs Ser.). (Illus.). 48p. (J). (gr. k-1). pap. *(978-1-60437-975-4(8))* Benchmark Education Co.

—Working on the Railroad. 2008. (Reader's Theater Nursery Rhymes & Songs Ser.). (Illus.). 48p. (J). (gr. k-1). pap. *(978-1-60437-981-5(2))* Benchmark Education Co.

Harris, Joel Chandler. Brer Rabbit & Brer Fox. Smith, Lesley, illus. 2014. (ENG.). 24p. (J). pap. 6.95 *(978-1-84135-962-5(9))* Award Pubns. Ltd. GBR. Dist: Parkwest Pubns., Inc.

—Brer Rabbit & the Great Race. Smith, Lesley, illus. 2014. (ENG.). 24p. (J). pap. 6.95 *(978-1-84135-963-2(7))* Award Pubns. Ltd. GBR. Dist: Parkwest Pubns., Inc.

—Brer Rabbit & the Honey Pot. Smith, Lesley, illus. 2014. (ENG.). 24p. (J). pap. 6.95 *(978-1-84135-961-8(0))* Award Pubns. Ltd. GBR. Dist: Parkwest Pubns., Inc.

—Brer Rabbit & the Tar Baby. Smith, Lesley, illus. 2014. (ENG.). 24p. (J). pap. 6.95 *(978-1-84135-964-9(5))* Award Pubns. Ltd. GBR. Dist: Parkwest Pubns., Inc.

Harris, Nic. The Greatest Invention of All Time Low Intermediate Book with Online Access, 1 vol. 2014. (ENG., Illus.). 24p. (J). pap., E-Book 9.50 *(978-1-107-62161-9(5))* Cambridge Univ. Pr.

HarrisNic. EMPIRE: RISE AND FALL LOW INTERMEDIATE BOOK WITH ONLINE ACCESS, 1 vol. 2014. (ENG., Illus.). 24p. (J). pap., E-Book 9.50 *(978-1-107-62844-1(X))* Cambridge Univ. Pr.

—GROWING UP: FROM BABY TO ADULT HIGH BEGINNING BOOK WITH ONLINE ACCESS, 1 vol. 2014. (ENG., Illus.). 24p. (J). pap., E-Book, E-Book 9.50 *(978-1-107-68744-8(6))* Cambridge Univ. Pr.

—HOW COOL IS COLD! LOW INTERMEDIATE BOOK WITH ONLINE ACCESS, 1 vol. 2014. (ENG., Illus.). 24p. (J). pap., E-Book, E-Book 9.50 *(978-1-107-65803-5(9))* Cambridge Univ. Pr.

—MEDICINE: OLD AND NEW LOW INTERMEDIATE BOOK WITH ONLINE ACCESS, 1 vol. 2014. (ENG., Illus.). 24p. (J). pap., E-Book, E-Book 9.50 *(978-1-107-65866-0(7))* Cambridge Univ. Pr.

—THE SCIENCE OF HEAT LOW INTERMEDIATE BOOK WITH ONLINE ACCESS, 1 vol. 2014. (ENG., Illus.). 24p. (J). pap., E-Book 9.50 *(978-1-107-69772-0(7))* Cambridge Univ. Pr.

Harrison, David L. Paul Bunyan: My Story. Kanzler, John, illus. 2008. (Step into Reading Ser.). 48p. (J). (gr. k-3). 4.99 *(978-0-375-84688-5(3)*, Random Hse. Bks. for Young Readers) Random Hse. Children's Bks.

Harrison, Lorraine. My Fourth of July, 1 vol. 2012. (InfoMax Readers Ser.). (ENG., Illus.). 24p. (J). (gr. 1-1). pap. 8.25 *(978-1-4488-9046-0(2)*, 58f9aa3c-4f5d-4661-a81e-57808aac4954, Rosen Classroom) Rosen Publishing Group, Inc., The.

Harrison, Paul. Collins Big Cat Phonics for Letters & Sounds - It Is Hidden: Band 02B/Red B, Bd. 2B. 2018. (Collins Big Cat Phonics Ser.). (ENG., Illus.). 16p. (J). (gr. -1-k). pap. 7.99 *(978-0-00-825151-2(7))* HarperCollins Pubs. Ltd. GBR. Dist: Independent Pubs. Group.

—Collins Big Cat Phonics for Letters & Sounds - This Is My Kit: Band 02A/Red A, Bd. 2A. 2018. (Collins Big Cat Phonics Ser.). (ENG., Illus.). 16p. (J). (gr. -1-k). pap. 6.99 *(978-0-00-825146-8(0))* HarperCollins Pubs. Ltd. GBR. Dist: Independent Pubs. Group.

—Noisy Books, 1 vol. Florin, Fabiano, illus. 2009. (Get Ready Readers Ser.). (ENG.). 32p. (J). (gr. k-k). lib. bdg. 27.27 *(978-1-60754-258-2(7)*, 1735ba23-2ce1-444c-80e1-234ea7574c53, Windmill Bks.) Rosen Publishing Group, Inc., The.

Hart, Melissa. A Guide for Using the Tale of Despereaux in the Classroom. 2005. (ENG.). 48p. pap. 9.99 *(978-1-4206-3164-7(0))* Teacher Created Resources, Inc.

Hartley, Susan. Welcome to Our School. 2004. (Shared Connections Ser.). (J). pap. *(978-1-4108-1626-9(5))*; instr.'s gde. ed. 27.00 *(978-1-4108-1602-3(8))* Benchmark Education Co.

Harvey, Damian. Mr. Fox's Socks. Rescek, Sanja, illus. 2004. (ENG.). 16p. (J). lib. bdg. 23.65 *(978-1-59646-678-4(2))* Dingles & Co.

Harvey, Damien. Dinosaur Rock: Band 01A/Pink a (Collins Big Cat) Ward, Matt, illus. 2005. (Collins Big Cat Ser.). (ENG.). 56p. (J). (gr. -1-k). pap. 7.99 *(978-0-00-718540-5(5))* HarperCollins Pubs. Ltd. GBR. Dist: Independent Pubs. Group.

Harvey, John. My New Skates, 1 vol. 2006. (Neighborhood Readers Ser.). (ENG.). 16p. (gr. 1-2). pap. 6.50 *(978-1-4042-7172-2(4)*, e7690410-2446-4a69-9818-2000b054a2f2, Rosen Classroom) Rosen Publishing Group, Inc., The.

Harvey, Ken. The Leftovers. Hermes, Mary Sue, illus. 2003. (Life in the 'Fridge Ser.). (J). *(978-1-930093-21-8(7))* Brookfield Reader, Inc., The.

Harvey, Paul. Level 1: Surfer! 2nd ed. 2008. (Pearson English Graded Readers Ser.). (ENG.). 32p. pap. 11.99 *(978-1-4058-6969-0(0)*, Pearson ELT) Pearson Education.

Hatched from an Egg. (J). pap. 13.15 *(978-0-8136-4261-1(2))* Modern Curriculum Pr.

Hawes, Alison. At the Market. Cambridge Reading Adventures. Pink B Band. Robert, LeyHonor, illus. 2016. (Cambridge Reading Adventures Ser.). (ENG.). 16p. pap. 7.95 *(978-1-107-54993-7(0))* Cambridge Univ. Pr.

—Collins Big Cat Phonics for Letters & Sounds - in the Fish Tank: Band 02A/Red A, Bd. 2A. John and Gus art, illus. 2018. (Collins Big Cat Phonics Ser.). (ENG.). 16p. (J). (gr. -1-k). pap. 6.99 *(978-0-00-825142-0(8))* HarperCollins Pubs. Ltd. GBR. Dist: Independent Pubs. Group.
—The Enormous Watermelon. Rodriguez, Elba, illus. 2016. (Cambridge Reading Adventures Ser.). (ENG.). 16p. pap. 7.95 *(978-1-107-54924-1(8))* Cambridge Univ. Pr.
—A Hot Day. Lee, Maxine, illus. 2016. (Cambridge Reading Adventures Ser.). (ENG.). 16p. pap. 7.95 *(978-1-316-60069-6(6))* Cambridge Univ. Pr.
—Imani's Library Book Red Band. Busby, Allie, illus. 2017. (Cambridge Reading Adventures Ser.). (ENG.). 16p. pap. 6.15 *(978-1-108-40072-5(8))* Cambridge Univ. Pr.
—Jamila Finds a Friend. Piwowarski, Marcin, illus. 2016. (Cambridge Reading Adventures Ser.). (ENG.). 16p. pap. 7.95 *(978-1-107-54963-0(9))* Cambridge Univ. Pr.
—The Last Lemon Pink B Band. Anegón, Tamara, illus. 2016. (Cambridge Reading Adventures Ser.). (ENG.). 16p. pap. 7.95 *(978-1-107-54909-8(4))* Cambridge Univ. Pr.
—Leela Can Skate Pink B Band. Yoshizumi, Carol, illus. 2016. (Cambridge Reading Adventures Ser.). (ENG.). 16p. pap. 7.95 *(978-1-107-57582-0(6))* Cambridge Univ. Pr.
—My Exercise Diary: Band 02B/Red B (Collins Big Cat) 2006. (Collins Big Cat Ser.). (ENG., Illus.). 16p. (J). (gr. -1-k). pap. 6.99 *(978-0-00-718669-3(X))* HarperCollins Pubs. Ltd. GBR. Dist: Independent Pubs. Group.
—Packing My Bag Pink a Band. Jennings, Sarah, illus. 2016. (Cambridge Reading Adventures Ser.). (ENG.). 16p. pap. 7.95 *(978-1-316-60082-5(3))* Cambridge Univ. Pr.
—Photos Pink a Band. Engel, Christiane, illus. 2017. (Cambridge Reading Adventures Ser.). (ENG.). 16p. pap. 7.95 *(978-1-108-40066-4(3))* Cambridge Univ. Pr.
—School Trip. Mould, Chris, illus. 2004. (ENG.). 24p. (J). lib. bdg. 23.65 *(978-1-59646-694-4(4))* Dingles & Co.
—Weather Report: Band 02A/Red a (Collins Big Cat) Stojic, Manya, illus. 2007. (Collins Big Cat Ser.). (ENG.). 16p. (J). (gr. -1-k). pap. 6.99 *(978-0-00-718655-6(X))* HarperCollins Pubs. Ltd. GBR. Dist: Independent Pubs. Group.
—What Are You Making?: Band 02B/Red B (Collins Big Cat) Elworthy, Antony, illus. 2007. (Collins Big Cat Ser.). (ENG.). 16p. (J). (gr. -1-k). pap. 6.99 *(978-0-00-718657-0(6))* HarperCollins Pubs. Ltd. GBR. Dist: Independent Pubs. Group.
The Hawkers' Amazing Machines. (Early Intervention Levels Ser.). 31.86 *(978-0-7362-0661-7(2))* CENGAGE Learning.
The Hawkers' Amazing Machines (24), Vol. 24. (Early Intervention Levels Ser.). 5.31 *(978-0-7362-0649-5(3))* CENGAGE Learning.
Hawthorne, Philip & Tyler, Jenny. Who's Making That Noise? Cartwright, Stephen, illus. 2005. (Flap Books Ser.). 16p. (J). (gr. 1-18). pap. 7.95 *(978-0-7945-0432-8(9),* Usborne) EDC Publishing.
Haxhia, Miranda. Andy's Cherry Tree. Deisadze, Zaur, illus. 2007. (POL & ENG.). 32p. (J). pap. 12.95 *(978-1-60195-094-9(2))* International Step by Step Assn.
—The Dolls Nose. Kohler, Ursula, illus. 2007. 32p. (J). (ARA & ENG.). pap. 16.95 *(978-1-60195-087-1(X));* (POL & ENG.). pap. 16.95 *(978-1-60195-097-0(7))* International Step by Step Assn.
Hay, Sam. That Dog! Oelofsen, Vian, illus. 2011. (My Phonics Readers: Level 2 Ser.). 24p. (J). (gr. -1-1). 24.25 *(978-1-84898-510-0(X))* Sea-To-Sea Pubns.
—Wish Fish. May, Kate, illus. 2011. (My Phonics Readers: Level 2 Ser.). 24p. (J). (gr. -1-1). 24.25 *(978-1-84898-508-7(8))* Sea-To-Sea Pubns.
Haye, Lucy. ABCD & an Ant's Story. 2005. 23p. pap. 24.95 *(978-1-4137-2537-7(6))* PublishAmerica, Inc.
HB Staff. Alien Vacation. 97th ed. 2003. (Signatures Ser.). (gr. 1-18). pap. 19.20 *(978-0-15-308179-8(1))* Harcourt Schl. Pubs.
—The Baby. 97th ed. 2003. (First-Place Reading Ser.). (gr. 1-18). pap. 16.50 *(978-0-15-308131-6(7))* Harcourt Schl. Pubs.
—Bird's Bad Day. 97th ed. 2003. (First-Place Reading Ser.). (gr. 1-18). pap. 16.50 *(978-0-15-308132-3(5))* Harcourt Schl. Pubs.
—Help! Said Jed. 97th ed. 2003. (First-Place Reading Ser.). (gr. 1-18). pap. 16.50 *(978-0-15-308134-7(1))* Harcourt Schl. Pubs.
—Henry. 97th ed. 2003. (Signatures Ser.). (gr. 1-18). pap. 19.20 *(978-0-15-308184-2(8))* Harcourt Schl. Pubs.
—How the Sky Got It's Stars. 97th ed. 2003. (Signatures Ser.). (gr. 1-18). pap. 19.20 *(978-0-15-308180-4(5))* Harcourt Schl. Pubs.
—I Was Just about to Go to Bed. 97th ed. 2003. (First-Place Reading Ser.). (gr. 1-18). pap. 16.50 *(978-0-15-308145-3(7))* Harcourt Schl. Pubs.
—Just Like You. 97th ed. 2003. (First-Place Reading Ser.). (gr. 1-18). pap. 16.50 *(978-0-15-308127-9(9))* Harcourt Schl. Pubs.
—The King Who Loved to Dance. 97th ed. 2003. (Signatures Ser.). (gr. 1-18). pap. 16.50 *(978-0-15-308161-3(9))* Harcourt Schl. Pubs.
—The Little Chicks Sing. 97th ed. 2003. (Signatures Ser.). (gr. 1-18). pap. 16.50 *(978-0-15-308159-0(7))* Harcourt Schl. Pubs.
—Lunch in Space. 97th ed. 2003. (Signatures Ser.). (gr. 1-18). pap. 19.20 *(978-0-15-308178-1(3))* Harcourt Schl. Pubs.
—My Family Band. 97th ed. 2003. (First-Place Reading Ser.). (gr. 1-18). pap. 16.50 *(978-0-15-308142-2(2))* Harcourt Schl. Pubs.
—My Sister Is My Friend. 97th ed. 2003. (First-Place Reading Ser.). (gr. 1-18). pap., suppl. ed. 16.50 *(978-0-15-308128-6(7))* Harcourt Schl. Pubs.
—My Wild Woolly. 97th ed. 2003. (First-Place Reading Ser.). (gr. 1-18). pap. 16.50 *(978-0-15-308163-7(5))* Harcourt Schl. Pubs.
—One Little Slip. 97th ed. 2003. (First-Place Reading Ser.). (gr. 1-18). pap. 16.50 *(978-0-15-308141-5(4))* Harcourt Schl. Pubs.
—The Perfect Pet. 97th ed. 2003. (First-Place Reading Ser.). (gr. 1-18). pap. 16.50 *(978-0-15-308133-0(3))* Harcourt Schl. Pubs.
—Play Ball! 97th ed. 2003. (Signatures Ser.). (gr. 1-18). pap. 16.50 *(978-0-15-308155-2(4))* Harcourt Schl. Pubs.
—Silly Aunt Tilly. 97th ed. 2003. (Signatures Ser.). (gr. 1-18). pap. 19.20 *(978-0-15-308185-9(6))* Harcourt Schl. Pubs.
—Today Is Monday. 97th ed. 2003. (Signatures Ser.). (gr. 1-18). pap. 16.50 *(978-0-15-308169-9(4))* Harcourt Schl. Pubs.
—What a Shower! 97th ed. 2003. (First-Place Reading Ser.). (gr. 1-18). pap. 16.50 *(978-0-15-308124-8(4))* Harcourt Schl. Pubs.
—Where Babies Play. 97th ed. 2003. (First-Place Reading Ser.). (gr. 1-18). pap. 16.50 *(978-0-15-308136-1(8))* Harcourt Schl. Pubs.
Heads & Tails: Individual Title Six-Packs. (gr. 1-2). 22.00 *(978-0-7635-9154-0(8))* Rigby Education.
Heads or Tails? Fourth Grade Guided Comprehension Level Q. (On Our Way to English Ser.). (gr. 4-18). 34.50 *(978-0-7578-7177-1(1))* Rigby Education.
Heady, Heather. What's at the Beach? Storch, Ellen N., illus. l.t. ed. 2005. 10p. (J). (gr. -1-k). pap. 10.95 *(978-1-57332-355-0(1),* HighReach Learning, Incorporated) Carson-Dellosa Publishing, LLC.
Health & Safety Book Set 800840, 4. 2005. (J). *(978-1-59794-027-6(5))* Environments, Inc.
Health Care Book Set 800842, 6. 2005. (J). *(978-1-59794-028-3(3))* Environments, Inc.
Heaton, Maria. Kangaroos Say Sorry, Too, 1 vol. 2006. (Neighborhood Readers Ser.). (ENG.). 12p. (gr. 1-2). pap. 5.90 *(978-1-4042-7030-5(2),* 9ae5b2ff-1a8c-4467-bfef-5e1a4995d3d1, Rosen Classroom) Rosen Publishing Group, Inc., The.
Heaton, Mark. Ruth Tells the Truth, 1 vol. 2006. (Neighborhood Readers Ser.). (ENG.). 16p. (gr. 1-2). pap. 6.50 *(978-1-4042-7264-4(X),* 1663cb73-ac8b-4eb1-97a8-8085faaae53e, Rosen Classroom) Rosen Publishing Group, Inc., The.
Hecht, Tracey. The Peculiar Possum: The Nocturnals Grow & Read Early Reader, Level 2. Yee, Josie, illus. 2018. (Nocturnals Ser.: 3). (ENG.). 64p. (J). (gr. 1-3). 12.99 *(978-1-944020-19-4(5),* Fabled Films Pr. LLC) Fabled Films LLC.
—The Slithery Shakedown: The Nocturnals Grow & Read Early Reader, Level 2. Yee, Josie, illus. 2018. (Nocturnals Ser.: 2). (ENG.). 64p. (J). (gr. 1-3). pap. 5.99 *(978-1-944020-16-3(0),* Fabled Films Pr. LLC) Fabled Films LLC.
Heckman, Madeline. What Can I Eat? 2017. (1-3Y Science Ser.). (ENG., Illus.). 16p. (J). pap. 8.00 *(978-1-64053-136-9(X),* ARC Pr. Bks.) American Reading Co.
Heddle, Becca. Plants, Pollen & Pollinators: Band 13/Topaz (Collins Big Cat) 2016. (Collins Big Cat Ser.). (ENG., Illus.). 32p. (J). (gr. 2-3). pap. 10.95 *(978-0-00-816385-3(5))* HarperCollins Pubs. Ltd. GBR. Dist: Independent Pubs. Group.
Heddle, Jennifer & Roux, Stéphane. Star Wars Rebels: Sabine's Art Attack, 1 vol. 2015. (World of Reading Level 1 Ser.). (ENG., Illus.). 32p. (J). (gr. -1-3). lib. bdg. 31.36 *(978-1-61479-365-6(4),* 18200) Spotlight.
Hege, Lynnita. The Little Black Hen. Keyes, Tina Misrasi, illus. 2013. 208p. (J). *(978-0-7399-2465-5(6))* Rod & Staff Pubs., Inc.
Heim, Barbara. The Hudson Beavers Build a Lodge. 2013. (ENG.). 44p. (J). 13.95 *(978-1-938586-45-3(X))* Writer's Cramp, Inc.
Helen's Job. (Early Intervention Levels Ser.). 21.30 *(978-0-7362-0360-9(5));* Vol. 2. 3.55 *(978-0-7362-0081-3(9))* CENGAGE Learning.
Help When Needed. 64p. (YA). (gr. 9-12). pap. 9.95 *(978-0-8224-7155-4(8),* 7155) Globe Fearon Educational Publishing.
A Helpful Change. (Early Intervention Levels Ser.). 31.86 *(978-0-7362-0670-9(1))* CENGAGE Learning.
Hemming, Alice. A Gold Star for George. Scott, Kimberley, illus. 2019. (Early Bird Readers — Orange (Early Bird Stories (tm)) Ser.). (ENG.). 32p. (J). (gr. k-3). pap. 9.99 *(978-1-5415-7413-7(3),* f3a42b56-6413-4cc5-a0a4-c95f60c2e3ef, Lerner Pubns.) Lerner Publishing Group.
Hemstock, Whitney M. The ABC's of Traffic Safety. 2010. 34p. pap. 16.95 *(978-0-557-28733-8(2))* Lulu Pr., Inc.
The Hen, the Rooster, & the Bean. (Lexile Levels Ser.). 47.88 *(978-1-56334-393-3(2))* CENGAGE Learning.
Henderson, Judith. Big Words Small Stories: the Missing Donut. McBeth, T. L., illus. 2018. (ENG.). 52p. (J). (gr. k-3). 12.99 *(978-1-77138-788-0(2))* Kids Can Pr., Ltd. CAN. Dist: Hachette Bk. Group.
—Big Words Small Stories: the Traveling Dustball. McBeth, T. L., illus. 2019. (ENG.). 52p. (J). (gr. k-3). 12.99 *(978-1-77138-789-7(0))* Kids Can Pr., Ltd. CAN. Dist: Hachette Bk. Group.
Henkes, Kevin. Crisantemo. 2017.Tr. of Chrysanthemum. (SPA., Illus.). 32p. (J). pap. 9.99 *(978-1-63245-664-9(8))* Lectorum Pubns., Inc.
—Julius, el Rey de la Casa. 2017.Tr. of Julius, the Baby of the World. (SPA., Illus.). 31p. (J). pap. 9.99 *(978-1-63245-668-7(0))* Lectorum Pubns., Inc.
—Lily y Su Bolso de Plastico Morado. 2017.Tr. of Lilly's Purple Plastic Purse. (SPA.). (J). pap. 9.99 *(978-1-63245-667-0(2))* Lectorum Pubns., Inc.
—Owen. 2017. (SPA., Illus.). 24p. (J). pap. 9.99 *(978-1-63245-665-6(6))* Lectorum Pubns., Inc.
—Prudencia Se Preocupa. 2017.Tr. of Wemberly Worried. (SPA.). (J). pap. 9.99 *(978-1-63245-666-3(4))* Lectorum Pubns., Inc.
Henry, Darell W. That Potato Ain't That Big. 2009. (ENG.). 30p. pap. 14.99 *(978-1-4415-8140-2(5))* Xlibris Corp.
Henry, O. Oxford Bookworms Starter. The Ransom of Red Chief. 2nd ed. 2008. (ENG., Illus.). 48p. 11.00 *(978-0-19-423415-3(0))* Oxford Univ. Pr., Inc.
Henry, O. & Escott, John. Oxford Bookworms Playscripts: One Thousand Dollars & Other Plays: Level 2: 700-Word Vocabulary. 2nd ed. 2008. (ENG., Illus.). 64p. 11.00 *(978-0-19-423520-4(3))* Oxford Univ. Pr., Inc.
Henry, Steve. Happy Cat. (I Like to Read Ser.). (ENG.). (J). (gr. -1-3). 2017. 32p. 4.99 *(978-0-8234-3879-2(1))* 2014. (Illus.). 24p. 7.99 *(978-0-8234-3177-9(0))* Holiday Hse., Inc.
Hensley, Sarah M. I Can Be. Teeple, Jackie, illus. l.t. ed. 2006. 12p. (J). (gr. -1-k). pap. 10.95 *(978-1-57332-339-0(X),* HighReach Learning, Incorporated) Carson-Dellosa Publishing, LLC.
Hensley, Sarah M. At the Park. Crowell, Knox, illus. l.t. ed. 2006. 10p. (J). (gr. -1-k). pap. 10.95 *(978-1-57332-354-3(3),* HighReach Learning, Incorporated) Carson-Dellosa Publishing, LLC.
—Water Fun. Crowell, Knox, illus. l.t. ed. 2005. (J). (gr. -1-k). pap. 10.95 *(978-1-57332-342-0(X));* pap. 10.95 *(978-1-57332-343-7(8))* Carson-Dellosa Publishing, LLC. (HighReach Learning, Incorporated).
Hensley, Tana. Keesha Counts Money: Putting Data in Order, 1 vol. 2017. (Computer Science for the Real World Ser.). (ENG.). 12p. (gr. 1-2). pap. *(978-1-5383-5127-7(7),* dca30da9-6761-4316-a829-f2cef0f02df5, Rosen Classroom) Rosen Publishing Group, Inc., The.
Her Story. (J). (gr. 4-6). 84.80 *(978-0-8136-6024-0(6))* Modern Curriculum Pr.
Herbst, Kailee. Lots of Clocks: Learning about Tools That Measure Time, 1 vol. 2010. (Math for the REAL World Ser.). (ENG., Illus.). 8p. (gr. k-1). pap. 5.15 *(978-0-8239-8858-7(9),* b4b1b111-535f-4784-95ea-0d39415d298b) Rosen Publishing Group, Inc., The.
—Who's Short? Who's Tall? Learning to Compare Heights, 1 vol. 2010. (Math for the REAL World Ser.). (ENG., Illus.). 8p. (gr. k-1). pap. 5.15 *(978-0-8239-8856-3(2),* 9f1eaf25-636a-4b38-8a04-42b66ab68df5) Rosen Publishing Group, Inc., The.
Herman, Gail. Scooby-Doo: A Scooby-Rific Reader. 2012. (Illus.). (J). *(978-1-4351-3986-2(0))* Scholastic, Inc.
Hernández, Carlos. It's the Law!, 1 vol. 2012. (InfoMax Readers Ser.). (ENG., Illus.). 24p. (J). (gr. 1-1). pap. 8.25 *(978-1-4488-9073-6(X),* a0ddd50b-65ea-4a28-98bd-69e9693b0c33, Rosen Classroom) Rosen Publishing Group, Inc., The.
Herweck, Diana. All in a Day's Work - Police Officer, 1 vol. 2nd rev. ed. 2013. (TIME for KIDS(r): Informational Text Ser.). (ENG., Illus.). 64p. (J). (gr. 4-8). pap. 14.99 *(978-1-4333-4905-8(1))* Teacher Created Materials, Inc.
—A Day in the Life of a Ballet Dancer, 1 vol. 2nd rev. ed. 2011. (TIME for KIDS(r): Informational Text Ser.). (ENG.). 28p. (gr. 3-4). pap. 11.99 *(978-1-4333-3650-8(2))* Teacher Created Materials, Inc.
—ER Doctor, 1 vol. 2nd rev. ed. 2013. (TIME for KIDS(r): Informational Text Ser.). (ENG., Illus.). 64p. (J). (gr. 4-8). pap. 14.99 *(978-1-4333-4906-5(X))* Teacher Created Materials, Inc.
—In the Game - An Athlete's Life, 1 vol. 2nd rev. ed. 2012. (TIME for KIDS(r): Informational Text Ser.). (ENG.). 48p. (gr. 4-5). pap. 11.99 *(978-1-4333-4824-2(1))* Teacher Created Materials, Inc.
—On the Scene: A CSI's Life, 1 vol. 2nd rev. ed. 2012. (TIME for KIDS(r): Informational Text Ser.). (ENG.). 48p. (gr. 4-5). pap. 13.99 *(978-1-4333-4825-9(X))* Teacher Created Materials, Inc.
Herweck, Don. All about Energy, 1 vol. rev. ed. 2007. (Science: Informational Text Ser.). (ENG.). 32p. (gr. 3-6). pap. 12.99 *(978-0-7439-0571-8(7))* Teacher Created Materials, Inc.
—All about Mechanical Engineering, 1 vol. rev. ed. 2007. (Science: Informational Text Ser.). (ENG.). 32p. (J). (gr. 3-6). pap. 12.99 *(978-0-7439-0577-0(6))* Teacher Created Materials, Inc.
Herweck, Dona. A Day in the Life of a Cowhand, 1 vol. 2nd rev. ed. 2011. (TIME for KIDS(r): Informational Text Ser.). (ENG.). 28p. (gr. 3-4). pap. 11.99 *(978-1-4333-3649-2(9))* Teacher Created Materials, Inc.
—A Day in the Life of a Firefighter, 1 vol. 2nd rev. ed. 2011. (TIME for KIDS(r): Informational Text Ser.). (ENG.). 28p. (gr. 3-4). pap. 11.99 *(978-1-4333-3651-5(0))* Teacher Created Materials, Inc.
—George Washington, 1 vol. 2nd rev. ed. 2011. (TIME for KIDS(r): Informational Text Ser.). (ENG.). 28p. (gr. 2-3). pap. 10.99 *(978-1-4333-3640-9(5))* Teacher Created Materials, Inc.
—Martin Luther King Jr., 1 vol. 2nd rev. ed. 2011. (TIME for KIDS(r): Informational Text Ser.). (ENG.). 28p. (gr. 2-3). pap. 10.99 *(978-1-4333-3641-6(3))* Teacher Created Materials, Inc.
—Susan B. Anthony, 1 vol. 2nd rev. ed. 2011. (TIME for KIDS(r): Informational Text Ser.). (ENG.). 28p. (gr. 2-3). pap. 10.99 *(978-1-4333-3642-3(1))* Teacher Created Materials, Inc.
Herwick Rice, Dona & Bradley, Kathleen. Reconstruction: After the Civil War, 1 vol. rev. ed. 2009. (Reader's Theater Ser.). (ENG.). 32p. (J). (gr. 3-8). pap. 11.99 *(978-1-4333-0547-4(X))* Teacher Created Materials, Inc.
Herwick Rice, Dona & Isecke, Harriet. The Sojourner Truth Story, 1 vol. rev. ed. 2009. (Reader's Theater Ser.). (ENG.). 32p. (gr. 3-8). pap. 11.99 *(978-1-4333-0544-3(5))* Teacher Created Materials, Inc.
Herwick Rice, Dona & Paris, Stephanie. Sal Fink, 1 vol. rev. ed. 2009. (Reader's Theater Ser.). (ENG.). 24p. (gr. 2-4). pap. 8.99 *(978-1-4333-0995-3(5))* Teacher Created Materials, Inc.
Herwick Rice, Dona & Sugarman, Dorothy Alexander. World War I: In Flanders Fields, 1 vol. rev. ed. 2009. (Reader's Theater Ser.). (ENG.). 32p. (gr. 4-8). pap. 11.99 *(978-1-4333-0551-1(8))* Teacher Created Materials, Inc.
Herzog, Joyce. Excursion into Reading Reader: Part of the Little Beginner's Book Series. 2005. (J). spiral bd. 15.00 *(978-1-887225-36-6(6))* Herzog, Joyce.
Hess, Debra. On Trial in Rome: Cicero Versus Caesr. 2007. (Read on! Special Edition: Level AA Ser.). (Illus.). 23p. pap. 18.51 *(978-1-4190-3517-3(7))* Steck-Vaughn.
Hetty Hackett's Farm: 3-in-1 Package. (Sails Literacy Ser.). 24p. (gr. k-18). 57.00 *(978-0-7578-3197-3(4))* Rigby Education.
Hewitt, Sally. Keeping Healthy, 8 vols. 2005. (QEB Readers). (Illus.). 24p. (J). (gr. -1-3). lib. bdg. 15.95 *(978-1-59566-071-8(2))* QEB Publishing Inc.
—The Spick-and-Span Fairy, 8 vols. 2005. (QEB Readers). (Illus.). 24p. (J). (gr. -1-3). lib. bdg. 15.95 *(978-1-59566-066-4(6))* QEB Publishing Inc.
—Where's My Shirt?, 8 vols. 2005. (QEB Readers). (Illus.). 24p. (J). (gr. -1-3). lib. bdg. 15.95 *(978-1-59566-067-1(4))* QEB Publishing Inc.
Hey, Kids! (10-lesson edition All-English version) Book 1 Student's Book (with CD) English Language Teaching. 2003. (Illus.). 112p. spiral bd. incl. audio compact disk *(978-0-7428-1051-8(8))* C C L S Publishing Hse.
Hey, Kids! (10-lesson edition All-English version) Book 2 Student's Book (with CD) English Language Teaching. 2003. (Illus.). 112p. spiral bd. incl. audio compact disk *(978-0-7428-1052-5(6))* C C L S Publishing Hse.
Hiatt, Kay & Stones, Brenda. Collins Primary Literacy - Pupil Book 1B, Bk. 1B. 2008. (Collins Primary Literacy Ser.). (ENG., Illus.). 48p. (J). (gr. 1-1). pap., stu. ed. 9.99 *(978-0-00-722694-8(2))* HarperCollins Pubs. Ltd. GBR. Dist: Independent Pubs. Group.
Hibbert, Clare. DK Readers L1: Star Wars: Tatooine Adventures. 2011. (DK Readers Level 1 Ser.). (ENG.). 48p. (J). (gr. k-4). 4.99 *(978-0-7566-7128-0(0),* DK Children) Dorling Kindersley Publishing, Inc.
Hicks, Diana. American English Primary Colors 2. 2003. (ENG., Illus.). 68p. pap., stu. ed. 17.00 *(978-0-521-53920-3(X))* Cambridge Univ. Pr.
Hide & Seek, 6 Packs. (Chiquilibros Ser.). (gr. k-1). 23.00 *(978-0-7635-0439-7(4))* Rigby Education.
Hiebert. Ready Readers Study Guide to the Big Book Collection. (J). (gr. -1-3). Vol. 1. 314.95 *(978-0-8136-1697-1(2))* Vol. 2. 2003. 422.95 *(978-0-8136-1698-8(0))* Modern Curriculum Pr.
Hiebert, Elfrieda H. Quickreads. 2005. (J). (gr. 2-6). stu. ed. 47.50 *(978-0-7652-4420-8(9));* Vol. 3. stu. ed. 47.50 *(978-0-7652-4424-6(1))* Modern Curriculum Pr.
—Quickreads, Vol. 2. 2003. (ENG.). (J). (gr. 5-8). pap., stu. ed. 47.50 *(978-0-7652-4422-2(5),* Modern Curriculum Pr.) Savvas Learning Co.
—Quickreads: Level B Macintosh Classroom Package. 2005. (J). (gr. 2-18). 1067.50 *(978-0-7652-5115-2(9))* Modern Curriculum Pr.
—Quickreads: Level B Windows Classroom Package. 2005. (J). (gr. 2-18). 1067.50 *(978-0-7652-5112-1(4))* Modern Curriculum Pr.
—Quickreads: Level C Macintosh Classroom Package. 2005. (J). (gr. 3-18). 1067.50 *(978-0-7652-5116-9(7))* Modern Curriculum Pr.
—Quickreads: Level C Windows Classroom Package. 2005. (J). (gr. 3-18). 1067.50 *(978-0-7652-5113-8(2))* Modern Curriculum Pr.
—Quickreads: Level D Macintosh Classroom Package. 2005. (J). (gr. 4-18). 1067.50 *(978-0-7652-5117-6(5))* Modern Curriculum Pr.
—Quickreads: Level D Windows Classroom Package. 2005. (J). (gr. 4-18). 1067.50 *(978-0-7652-5114-5(0))* Modern Curriculum Pr.
—Quickreads: Level E Complete Program. 2005. (J). (gr. 5-18). 351.95 *(978-0-7652-4427-7(6))* Modern Curriculum Pr.
—Quickreads: Macintosh Classroom Program. 2005. (J). (gr. 5-18). 1067.50 *(978-0-7652-6157-1(X))* Modern Curriculum Pr.
—Quickreads: Windows Classroom Program. 2005. (J). (gr. 5-18). 1067.50 *(978-0-7652-6158-8(8))* Modern Curriculum Pr.
Higginson, Sheila Sweeny. Diego rescata al bebé manatí (Diego's Manatee Rescue) McGee, Warner, illus. 2009. (Go, Diego, Go! Ser.). (SPA.). 24p. (J). pap. 3.99 *(978-1-4169-7983-8(2),* Libros Para Ninos) Libros Para Ninos.
High Five Reading - Purple, Set II. 2004. (High Five Reading - Purple Ser.). (ENG.). (gr. 3-4). pap. 45.00 *(978-0-7368-3864-1(3))* Capstone.
High Five USA Reading, Green Level I. (gr. 4-18). 250.95 incl. audio *(978-0-7368-9570-5(1),* Red Brick Learning) Capstone.
High Five USA Reading, Green Level II. (gr. 4-18). 250.95 incl. audio *(978-0-7368-2860-4(5),* Red Brick Learning) Capstone.
High Five USA Reading, Purple Level I. (gr. 4-18). 250.95 incl. audio *(978-0-7368-9516-3(7),* Red Brick Learning) Capstone.
High Five USA Reading, Purple Level II. (gr. 4-18). 250.95 incl. audio *(978-0-7368-3863-4(5),* Red Brick Learning) Capstone.
High Five USA Reading, Red Level I. (gr. 4-18). 250.95 incl. audio *(978-0-7368-9544-6(2),* Red Brick Learning) Capstone.
High Five USA Reading, Red Level II. (gr. 4-18). 250.95 incl. audio *(978-0-7368-2855-0(9),* Red Brick Learning) Capstone.
High Point. (High Point Ser.). (gr. 6-12). 57.61 *(978-0-7362-0969-4(7));* 7.52 *(978-0-7362-0967-0(0));* 7.52 *(978-0-7362-0935-9(2));* tchr. ed. 33.37 *(978-0-7362-0981-6(6));* tchr. ed. 33.37 *(978-0-7362-0949-6(2));* suppl. ed. 57.61 *(978-0-7362-0937-3(9));* tchr.'s assessmt. gde. ed. 27.50 *(978-0-7362-0950-2(6));* instr.'s hndbk. ed. 27.50 *(978-0-7362-0982-3(4));* tchr. ed. 14.19 *(978-0-7362-0936-6(0));* tchr. ed. 14.19 *(978-0-7362-0968-7(9))* CENGAGE Learning.
High Point: Decodable Stories Set, 18 vols. (Reading Basics Ser.). (gr. 3-12). 8.31 *(978-0-7362-1553-4(0))* CENGAGE Learning.
High Point: Reading Basics Package. (gr. 6-12). 160.56 *(978-0-7362-1286-1(8))* CENGAGE Learning.
High Point: The Basics Bookshelf. (gr. 6-12). 487.59 incl. audio compact disk *(978-0-7362-1279-3(5));* 531.44 incl. reel tape *(978-0-7362-1280-9(9));* 443.72 *(978-0-7362-1278-6(7))* CENGAGE Learning.
High Point Diagnosis & Placement Inventory: Test Booklets (10-pack) 19.90 *(978-0-7362-2345-4(2))* CENGAGE Learning.
A High Point Level: The Basics Bookshelf with Teacher's Guide, 6 vols. (High Point Ser.). (gr. 6-12). tchr. ed. 459.28 *(978-0-7362-1281-6(7))* CENGAGE Learning.
Hileman, Jane & Pitt, Marilyn. I Love to Sleep. Bianchi, John, illus. 2013. (1G Potato Chip Bks.). (ENG.). 12p. (J). (gr. k-1). pap. 8.00 *(978-1-59301-797-2(9))* American Reading Co.
—I Want a Dog. Bianchi, John, illus. 2013. (1G Potato Chip Bks.). (ENG.). 12p. (J). (gr. k-1). pap. 8.00 *(978-1-59301-768-2(5))* American Reading Co.
—Time for a Bath. Bianchi, John, illus. 2013. (1G Potato Chip Bks.). (ENG.). 12p. (J). (gr. k-1). pap. 8.00 *(978-1-59301-772-9(3))* American Reading Co.

—You Can't Have It! Bianchi, John, illus. 2012. (1G Potato Chip Bks.). (ENG.). 12p. (J). (gr. k-1). pap. 8.00 *(978-1-59301-767-5(7))* American Reading Co.

Hileman, Jesse & Reher, Matt. Soccer vs Football. 2012. (2R Sports Ser.). (ENG., Illus.). 36p. (J). pap. 8.00 *(978-1-64053-101-7(7),* ARC Pr. Bks.) American Reading Co.

Hill, Oriah. My Day at the Library. 2012. (ENG.). 24p. pap. 15.99 *(978-1-4772-7954-0(7))* AuthorHouse.

Hillert, Margaret. Dear Dragon Learns to Read. Jack Pullan, illus. 2015. (Beginning-To-Read Ser.). (ENG.). 32p. (J). (gr. k-2). pap. 13.26 *(978-1-60357-792-2(0))* Norwood Hse. Pr.

—I Can Do It: For the Earliest Reader. Starfall Education, illus. 2006. (ENG.). 32p. (J). *(978-1-59577-039-4(9));* pap. *(978-1-59577-040-0(2))* Starfall Education.

—Not Too Little to Help, 5 bks. Starfall Education, illus. 2005. (ENG.). 32p. (J). 6.95 *(978-1-59577-026-4(7));* pap. *(978-1-59577-027-1(5))* Starfall Education.

—Penguin, Penguin: For the Earliest Reader, 5 bks. 2005. (ENG., Illus.). 32p. (J). 6.95 *(978-1-59577-020-2(8));* pap. *(978-1-59577-021-9(6))* Starfall Education.

—Pumpkin, Pumpkin: For the Earliest Reader. Starfall Education, photos by. 2006. (ENG., Illus.). 32p. (J). *(978-1-59577-035-6(6));* pap. *(978-1-59577-036-3(4))* Starfall Education.

—Three Little Plays, 5 bks. Starfall Education, illus. 2005. (ENG.). 32p. (J). 6.95 *(978-1-59577-018-9(6));* pap. *(978-1-59577-019-6(4))* Starfall Education.

Hirschfeld, Pam, ed. Under Siege. Leon, Karen; Hirschfeld, illus. 2004. (Reader's Theater Content-Area Concepts Ser.). (ENG.). (J). (gr. 4-5). 5.00 net. *(978-1-4108-1143-1(3))* Benchmark Education Co.

Hirschfeld, Pam; Leon, ed. Across a Stream. Leon, Karen, illus. 2004. (Reader's Theater Content-Area Concepts Ser.). (ENG.). (J). (gr. 4-5). 5.00 net. *(978-1-4108-1142-4(5))* Benchmark Education Co.

—Columbus Meets Isabella & Ferdinand. Leon, Karen, illus. 2004. (Reader's Theater Content-Area Concepts Ser.). (ENG.). (J). (gr. 3-4). 5.00 net. *(978-1-4108-1138-7(7))* Benchmark Education Co.

—Jill Gets Fit. Leon, Karen, illus. 2004. (Reader's Theater Content-Area Concepts Ser.). (ENG.). (J). (gr. 1). 5.00 net. *(978-1-4108-0791-5(6))* Benchmark Education Co.

Hirschfeld, Pam; Urbanovic, ed. Pet Care Kids. Urbanovic, Jackie, illus. 2004. (Reader's Theater Content-Area Concepts Ser.). (ENG.). (J). (gr. 3-5). 5.00 net. *(978-1-4108-1146-2(8))* Benchmark Education Co.

The History Nook. (Early Intervention Levels Ser.). 31.86 *(978-0-7362-0663-1(9))* CENGAGE Learning.

The History Nook (30), Vol. 30. (Early Intervention Levels Ser.). 5.31 *(978-0-7362-0651-8(5))* CENGAGE Learning.

The History of Guitars: Fourth Grade Guided Comprehension Level N. (On Our Way to English Ser.). (gr. 4-18). 34.50 *(978-0-7578-7164-1(X))* Rigby Education.

Hobbs, Ruth & Miller, Lester, contrib. by. A Time to Plant. 2005. (Rod & Staff's Readers Ser.). (Illus.). 256p. (gr. 5-18). 10.85 *(978-0-7399-0405-3(1),* 11501) Rod & Staff Pubs., Inc.

The Hobyahs: 6 Small Books. (gr. k-1). 37.00 *(978-0-7635-6246-5(7))* Rigby Education.

Hoff, Syd. Danny & the Dinosaur: Too Tall. 2015. (I Can Read Level 1 Ser.). (ENG., Illus.). 32p. (J). (gr. -1-3). pap. 4.99 *(978-0-06-228155-5(0),* HarperCollins) HarperCollins Pubs.

Hoffman, Mary. The Sword in the Stone: Band 11 Lime/Band 16 Sapphire (Collins Big Cat Progress) Ginevra, Dante, illus. 2014. (Collins Big Cat Progress Ser.). (ENG.). 32p. (J). (gr. 4-5). pap. 10.99 *(978-0-00-751935-4(4))* HarperCollins Pubs. Ltd. GBR. Dist: Independent Pubs. Group.

Hoffman, Mary Ann. Elbert Takes a Trip, 1 vol. 2006. (Neighborhood Readers Ser.). (ENG., Illus.). 12p. (gr. 1-2). pap. 5.90 *(978-1-4042-6847-0(2),* 63f8bd14-9afd-4550-accd-46efdd3dcaee, Rosen Classroom) Rosen Publishing Group, Inc., The.

—Happy Birthday, Rita Raccoon!, 1 vol. 2006. (Neighborhood Readers Ser.). (ENG.). 16p. (gr. 1-2). pap. 6.50 *(978-1-4042-7140-1(6),* c359758f-dee9-4efc-bd05-5ade7884e97c, Rosen Classroom) Rosen Publishing Group, Inc., The.

—The Maple Tree Mystery. (Neighborhood Readers Ser.). (ENG.). 16p. 2007. 37.95 *(978-1-4042-7342-9(5))* 2006. (gr. 1-2). pap. 6.50 *(978-1-4042-7220-0(8),* d2f72e77-c054-4adc-ba36-4f0206c429a1) Rosen Publishing Group, Inc., The. (Rosen Classroom).

—The Missing Wheel, 1 vol. 2006. (Neighborhood Readers Ser.). (ENG.). 8p. (gr. k-1). pap. 5.15 *(978-1-4042-5668-2(7),* 328db7d9-f44e-4aca-b9a7-c9c58b6f8c15, Rosen Classroom) Rosen Publishing Group, Inc., The.

—El misterio en el árbol (the Maple Tree Mystery) 2007. (Lecturas del barrio (Neighborhood Readers) Ser.). (SPA.). 16p. 37.95 *(978-1-4042-7343-6(3),* Rosen Classroom) Rosen Publishing Group, Inc., The.

—Molly Makes a Milkshake, 1 vol. 2006. (Neighborhood Readers Ser.). (ENG.). 12p. (gr. k-1). pap. 5.90 *(978-1-4042-5768-9(3),* 49278806-c30b-457e-bb7b-8eef7198f326, Rosen Classroom) Rosen Publishing Group, Inc., The.

—A Parrot for Pam, 1 vol. 2006. (Neighborhood Readers Ser.). (ENG.). 8p. (gr. k-1). pap. 5.15 *(978-1-4042-5690-3(3),* 75199843-5e0f-402b-b6b1-1a68bd5ea1bf, Rosen Classroom) Rosen Publishing Group, Inc., The.

—Piñata Party, 1 vol. 2006. (Neighborhood Readers Ser.). (ENG.). 8p. (gr. k-1). pap. 5.15 *(978-1-4042-5720-7(9),* 3cbc62ae-3463-4fde-9ff0-2cb45541f68b, Rosen Classroom) Rosen Publishing Group, Inc., The.

Hoffman, Stephanie. Sharp Teeth, Flat Teeth, 1 vol. 2008. (Real Life Readers Ser.). (ENG.). 12p. (gr. 1-2). pap. 5.90 *(978-1-4042-7917-9(2),* 51ce5e7b-2dca-4d4b-9f63-b2f9c5d24ed5, Rosen Classroom) Rosen Publishing Group, Inc., The.

Hoffmann, Sara E. Ana & the Pet Show. Strange, Katie, illus. 2013. (My Reading Neighborhood: First-Grade Sight Word Stories Ser.). (ENG.). 16p. (J). (gr. -1-1). pap. 6.99 *(978-1-4677-1170-8(5),* 9bddd68a-0c9d-49aa-aa01-5db7327d9e39) Lerner Publishing Group.

—Ben Gives a Gift. Dieterichs, Shelley, illus. 2013. (My Reading Neighborhood: Kindergarten Sight Word Stories Ser.). (ENG.). 16p. (J). (gr. -1-1). pap. 6.99 *(978-1-4677-1164-7(0),* 2f5bdf34-2085-4933-93cb-8aa9fc5ecdab) Lerner Publishing Group.

—Fall Fun for Kit. Roraback, Robin, illus. 2013. (My Reading Neighborhood: Kindergarten Sight Word Stories Ser.). (ENG.). 16p. (J). (gr. -1-1). pap. 6.99 *(978-1-4677-1165-4(9),* 84cfeb8d-f83d-491b-9de8-ac1d9388ce60) Lerner Publishing Group.

—Nan Swims. Roraback, Robin, illus. 2013. (My Reading Neighborhood: Kindergarten Sight Word Stories Ser.). (ENG.). 16p. (J). (gr. -1-1). pap. 6.99 *(978-1-4677-1166-1(7),* d4287f5f-4352-420e-9100-f2ad471fc8d2) Lerner Publishing Group.

—Nia Bakes Cookies. Strange, Katie, illus. 2013. (My Reading Neighborhood: First-Grade Sight Word Stories Ser.). (ENG.). 16p. (J). (gr. -1-1). pap. 6.99 *(978-1-4677-1172-2(1),* 54d04a36-9838-46dc-8ea2-205935d70f37) Lerner Publishing Group.

—A Picnic with Kit. Roraback, Robin, illus. 2013. (My Reading Neighborhood: Kindergarten Sight Word Stories Ser.). (ENG.). 16p. (J). (gr. -1-1). pap. 6.99 *(978-1-4677-1168-5(3),* e92f764a-4122-4d4c-898f-1b08b7dec526) Lerner Publishing Group.

Hofmeister, Alan, et al. Ann & Nan. (Reading for All Learners Ser.). (Illus.). (J). pap. *(978-1-56861-085-6(8))* Swift Learning Resources.

—The Ant & the Bee. (Reading for All Learners Ser.). (Illus.). (J). pap. *(978-1-56861-125-9(0))* Swift Learning Resources.

—The Bad Men. (Reading for All Learners Ser.). (Illus.). (J). pap. *(978-1-56861-117-4(X))* Swift Learning Resources.

—The Bat Rat. (Reading for All Learners Ser.). (Illus.). (J). pap. *(978-1-56861-119-8(6))* Swift Learning Resources.

—The Bee. (Reading for All Learners Ser.). (Illus.). (J). pap. *(978-1-56861-124-2(2))* Swift Learning Resources.

—Ben the Ant. (Reading for All Learners Ser.). (Illus.). (J). pap. *(978-1-56861-123-5(4))* Swift Learning Resources.

—Bud & the Tree. (Reading for All Learners Ser.). (Illus.). (J). pap. *(978-1-56861-135-8(8))* Swift Learning Resources.

—The Bus. (Reading for All Learners Ser.). (Illus.). (J). pap. *(978-1-56861-122-8(6))* Swift Learning Resources.

—Cartons & Clouds. (Reading for All Learners Ser.). (Illus.). (J). pap. *(978-1-56861-195-2(1))* Swift Learning Resources.

—The Creatures of Loon. (Reading for All Learners Ser.). (Illus.). (J). pap. *(978-1-56861-217-1(6))* Swift Learning Resources.

—Freckles & Forests. (Reading for All Learners Ser.). (Illus.). (J). pap. *(978-1-56861-201-0(X))* Swift Learning Resources.

—The Fun Fish. (Reading for All Learners Ser.). (Illus.). (J). pap. *(978-1-56861-121-1(8))* Swift Learning Resources.

—Fun with the Sheet. (Reading for All Learners Ser.). (Illus.). (J). pap. *(978-1-56861-115-0(3))* Swift Learning Resources.

—The Hat. (Reading for All Learners Ser.). (Illus.). (J). pap. *(978-1-56861-105-1(6))* Swift Learning Resources.

—I See Sam. (Reading for All Learners Ser.). (Illus.). (J). pap. *(978-1-56861-073-3(4))* Swift Learning Resources.

—In a Tub. (Reading for All Learners Ser.). (Illus.). (J). pap. *(978-1-56861-128-0(5))* Swift Learning Resources.

—In the Mud. (Reading for All Learners Ser.). (Illus.). (J). pap. *(978-1-56861-127-3(7))* Swift Learning Resources.

—In the Tent. (Reading for All Learners Ser.). (Illus.). (J). pap. *(978-1-56861-132-7(3))* Swift Learning Resources.

—It Is Ann. (Reading for All Learners Ser.). (Illus.). (J). pap. *(978-1-56861-084-9(X))* Swift Learning Resources.

—The Mask. (Reading for All Learners Ser.). (Illus.). (J). pap. *(978-1-56861-139-6(0))* Swift Learning Resources.

—Mat. (Reading for All Learners Ser.). (Illus.). (J). pap. *(978-1-56861-077-1(7))* Swift Learning Resources.

—Mat & the Nut. (Reading for All Learners Ser.). (Illus.). (J). pap. *(978-1-56861-109-9(9))* Swift Learning Resources.

—Mat at Bat. (Reading for All Learners Ser.). (Illus.). (J). pap. *(978-1-56861-118-1(8))* Swift Learning Resources.

—Mat Did It. (Reading for All Learners Ser.). (Illus.). (J). pap. *(978-1-56861-102-0(1))* Swift Learning Resources.

—Mat in the Hat. (Reading for All Learners Ser.). (Illus.). (J). pap. *(978-1-56861-106-8(4))* Swift Learning Resources.

—Mat in the Sun. (Reading for All Learners Ser.). (Illus.). (J). pap. *(978-1-56861-094-8(7))* Swift Learning Resources.

—Mat Is Wet. (Reading for All Learners Ser.). (Illus.). (J). pap. *(978-1-56861-120-4(X))* Swift Learning Resources.

—Mat the Rat. (Reading for All Learners Ser.). (Illus.). (J). pap. *(978-1-56861-111-2(0))* Swift Learning Resources.

—Meet Mit. (Reading for All Learners Ser.). (Illus.). (J). pap. *(978-1-56861-079-5(3))* Swift Learning Resources.

—The Men. (Reading for All Learners Ser.). (Illus.). (J). pap. *(978-1-56861-116-7(1))* Swift Learning Resources.

—Mit & the Weed. (Reading for All Learners Ser.). (Illus.). (J). pap. *(978-1-56861-113-6(7))* Swift Learning Resources.

—Mit Is Wet. (Reading for All Learners Ser.). (Illus.). (J). pap. *(978-1-56861-108-2(0))* Swift Learning Resources.

—Nan & the Man. (Reading for All Learners Ser.). (Illus.). (J). pap. *(978-1-56861-086-3(6))* Swift Learning Resources.

—Nan Sits. (Reading for All Learners Ser.). (Illus.). (J). pap. *(978-1-56861-092-4(0))* Swift Learning Resources.

—Nat. (Reading for All Learners Ser.). (Illus.). (J). pap. *(978-1-56861-093-1(9))* Swift Learning Resources.

—Nell & Ed. (Reading for All Learners Ser.). (Illus.). (J). pap. *(978-1-56861-097-9(1))* Swift Learning Resources.

—The Pond. (Reading for All Learners Ser.). (Illus.). (J). pap. *(978-1-56861-131-0(5))* Swift Learning Resources.

—Ruff. (Reading for All Learners Ser.). (Illus.). (J). pap. *(978-1-56861-137-2(4))* Swift Learning Resources.

—Run, Feet, Run. (Reading for All Learners Ser.). (Illus.). (J). pap. *(978-1-56861-095-5(5))* Swift Learning Resources.

—Sam. (Reading for All Learners Ser.). (Illus.). (J). pap. *(978-1-56861-074-0(2))* Swift Learning Resources.

—Sam Is Mad. (Reading for All Learners Ser.). (Illus.). (J). pap. *(978-1-56861-087-0(4))* Swift Learning Resources.

—Sam Sat. (Reading for All Learners Ser.). (Illus.). (J). pap. *(978-1-56861-083-2(1))* Swift Learning Resources.

—See It. (Reading for All Learners Ser.). (Illus.). (J). pap. *(978-1-56861-080-1(7))* Swift Learning Resources.

—See Mat. (Reading for All Learners Ser.). (Illus.). (J). pap. *(978-1-56861-078-8(5))* Swift Learning Resources.

—See Me. (Reading for All Learners Ser.). (Illus.). (J). pap. *(978-1-56861-076-4(9))* Swift Learning Resources.

—See Sam. (Reading for All Learners Ser.). (Illus.). (J). pap. *(978-1-56861-075-7(0))* Swift Learning Resources.

—See Them. (Reading for All Learners Ser.). (Illus.). (J). pap. *(978-1-56861-107-5(2))* Swift Learning Resources.

—The Seed. (Reading for All Learners Ser.). (Illus.). (J). pap. *(978-1-56861-112-9(9))* Swift Learning Resources.

—Sell the Shell. (Reading for All Learners Ser.). (Illus.). (J). pap. *(978-1-56861-104-4(8))* Swift Learning Resources.

—The Shell. (Reading for All Learners Ser.). (Illus.). (J). pap. *(978-1-56861-103-7(X))* Swift Learning Resources.

—The Ship. (Reading for All Learners Ser.). (Illus.). (J). pap. *(978-1-56861-133-4(1))* Swift Learning Resources.

—Sid. (Reading for All Learners Ser.). (Illus.). (J). pap. *(978-1-56861-088-7(2))* Swift Learning Resources.

—Sid & the Mess. (Reading for All Learners Ser.). (Illus.). (J). pap. *(978-1-56861-090-0(4))* Swift Learning Resources.

—Sis. (Reading for All Learners Ser.). (Illus.). (J). pap. *(978-1-56861-082-5(3))* Swift Learning Resources.

—Sis in a Mess. (Reading for All Learners Ser.). (Illus.). (J). pap. *(978-1-56861-091-7(2))* Swift Learning Resources.

—Sis in the Well. (Reading for All Learners Ser.). (Illus.). (J). pap. *(978-1-56861-098-6(X))* Swift Learning Resources.

—Sit on It. (Reading for All Learners Ser.). (Illus.). (J). pap. *(978-1-56861-081-8(5))* Swift Learning Resources.

—Smash It. (Reading for All Learners Ser.). (Illus.). (J). pap. *(978-1-56861-136-5(6))* Swift Learning Resources.

—Swim with Us. (Reading for All Learners Ser.). (Illus.). (J). pap. *(978-1-56861-140-2(4))* Swift Learning Resources.

—To the Den. (Reading for All Learners Ser.). (Illus.). (J). pap. *(978-1-56861-138-9(2))* Swift Learning Resources.

—A Trip. (Reading for All Learners Ser.). (Illus.). (J). pap. *(978-1-56861-130-3(7))* Swift Learning Resources.

—Up the Path. (Reading for All Learners Ser.). (Illus.). (J). pap. *(978-1-56861-134-1(X))* Swift Learning Resources.

—Up We Go. (Reading for All Learners Ser.). (Illus.). (J). pap. *(978-1-56861-129-7(3))* Swift Learning Resources.

—Was It Wet? (Reading for All Learners Ser.). (Illus.). (J). pap. *(978-1-56861-114-3(5))* Swift Learning Resources.

—We Will Run. (Reading for All Learners Ser.). (Illus.). (J). pap. *(978-1-56861-099-3(8))* Swift Learning Resources.

—We Will See. (Reading for All Learners Ser.). (Illus.). (J). pap. *(978-1-56861-089-4(0))* Swift Learning Resources.

—Who Am I? (Reading for All Learners Ser.). (Illus.). (J). pap. *(978-1-56861-096-2(3))* Swift Learning Resources.

—Will We Win? (Reading for All Learners Ser.). (Illus.). (J). pap. *(978-1-56861-110-5(2))* Swift Learning Resources.

Holden, Barry. The Milky Way BIG BOOK Edition, 1 vol. 2014. (ENG.). 16p. (gr. 2-2). pap. *(978-1-77654-100-3(6),* Red Rocket Readers) Flying Start Bks.

Holden, Pam. About Lighthouses, 1 vol. 2015. (ENG., Illus.). 16p. (-1). pap. *(978-1-77654-077-8(8),* Red Rocket Readers) Flying Start Bks.

—Animal Art, 1 vol. Storey, Jim, illus. 2009. (Red Rocket Readers Ser.). (ENG.). 16p. (gr. 1-1). pap. *(978-1-877419-73-7(7),* Red Rocket Readers) Flying Start Bks.

—Animal Defences, 1 vol. (ENG., Illus.). 16p. pap. *(978-1-77654-135-5(9),* Red Rocket Readers) Flying Start Bks.

—Animal Defenses. 2015. (ENG., Illus.). 16p. (-1). pap. *(978-1-77654-146-1(4),* Red Rocket Readers) Flying Start Bks.

—Are You Hungry?, 1 vol. Hawley, Kelvin, illus. 2009. (Red Rocket Readers Ser.). (ENG.). 16p. (gr. -1-1). pap. *(978-1-877363-23-8(5),* Red Rocket Readers) Flying Start Bks.

—At the Supermarket, 1 vol. 2017. (ENG., Illus.). 17p. (J). pap. *(978-1-77654-216-1(9),* Red Rocket Readers) Flying Start Bks.

—Baby Whale's Mistake, 1 vol. Aziz, Lamia, illus. 2009. (Red Rocket Readers Ser.). (ENG.). 16p. (gr. 2-2). pap. *(978-1-877363-87-0(1))* Flying Start Bks.

—Balloons Fly By, 1 vol. 2015. (ENG., Illus.). 16p. (-1). pap. *(978-1-77654-106-5(5),* Red Rocket Readers) Flying Start Bks.

—Bear Gets Stuck, 1 vol. Whimp, Pauline, illus. 2015. (ENG.). 16p. (-1). pap. *(978-1-77654-127-0(8),* Red Rocket Readers) Flying Start Bks.

—The Big Bad Wolf, 1 vol. Hawley, Kelvin, illus. 2009. (Red Rocket Readers Ser.). (ENG.). 20p. (gr. 2-2). pap. *(978-1-877363-56-6(1),* Red Rocket Readers) Flying Start Bks.

—A Brave Girl, 1 vol. 2015. (ENG., Illus.). 16p. (-1). pap. *(978-1-77654-105-8(7),* Red Rocket Readers) Flying Start Bks.

—Bugs & Beetles, 1 vol. 2015. (ENG., Illus.). 16p. (-2). pap. *(978-1-77654-137-9(5),* Red Rocket Readers) Flying Start Bks.

—Caterpillar to Butterfly, 1 vol. 2015. (ENG., Illus.). 16p. (-1). pap. *(978-1-77654-078-5(6),* Red Rocket Readers) Flying Start Bks.

—Charlie to the Rescue, 1 vol. Hawley, Kelvin, illus. 2015. (ENG.). 16p. (-1). pap. *(978-1-77654-128-7(6),* Red Rocket Readers) Flying Start Bks.

—Close to Home - BIG BOOK, 1 vol. 2016. (ENG.). 16p. (-1). pap. *(978-1-77654-161-4(8),* Red Rocket Readers) Flying Start Bks.

—Come to the Airport, 1 vol. 2017. (ENG., Illus.). 16p. (J). pap. *(978-1-77654-215-4(0),* Red Rocket Readers) Flying Start Bks.

—Come to the City, 1 vol. 2017. (ENG., Illus.). 18p. (J). pap. *(978-1-77654-217-8(7),* Red Rocket Readers) Flying Start Bks.

—Come to the Farm, 1 vol. 2017. (ENG., Illus.). 19p. (J). pap. *(978-1-77654-218-5(5),* Red Rocket Readers) Flying Start Bks.

—Come to the Hospital, 1 vol. 2017. (ENG., Illus.). 20p. (J). pap. *(978-1-77654-219-2(3),* Red Rocket Readers) Flying Start Bks.

—Come to the Zoo, 1 vol. 2017. (ENG., Illus.). 21p. (J). pap. *(978-1-77654-220-8(7),* Red Rocket Readers) Flying Start Bks.

—Cross the River, 1 vol. 2015. (ENG., Illus.). 16p. (-1). pap. *(978-1-77654-107-2(3),* Red Rocket Readers) Flying Start Bks.

—Dance, Dance, Dance!, 1 vol. 2009. (Red Rocket Readers Ser.). (ENG., Illus.). 16p. (gr. 1-1). pap. *(978-1-877490-21-7(0))* Flying Start Bks.

—Dinosaur Hunters, 1 vol. Storey, Jim & Hawley, Kelvin, illus. 2009. (Red Rocket Readers Ser.). (ENG.). 16p. (gr. 2-2). pap. *(978-1-877363-59-7(6),* Red Rocket Readers) Flying Start Bks.

—Dress up Day & Other Stories. 2018. (ENG., Illus.). 136p. (J). lib. bdg. *(978-1-77654-194-2(4),* Red Rocket Readers) Flying Start Bks.

—Everyone Reads - BIG BOOK, 1 vol. Johnson, Deborah, illus. 2016. (ENG.). 16p. (-1). pap. *(978-1-77654-162-1(6),* Red Rocket Readers) Flying Start Bks.

—Farm Friends, 1 vol. Hawley, Kelvin, illus. 2009. (Red Rocket Readers Ser.). (ENG.). 16p. (gr. -1-1). pap. *(978-1-877363-14-6(6),* Red Rocket Readers) Flying Start Bks.

—Fire in the Jungle, 1 vol. Hatam, Samer, illus. 2009. (Red Rocket Readers Ser.). (ENG.). 17p. (gr. 2-2). pap. *(978-1-877363-73-3(1))* Flying Start Bks.

—The Flying Monkey, 1 vol. East, Jacqueline, illus. 2009. (Red Rocket Readers Ser.). (ENG.). 16p. (gr. -1-1). pap. *(978-1-877363-29-0(4),* Red Rocket Readers) Flying Start Bks.

—From Tadpole to Frog, 1 vol. 2015. (ENG., Illus.). 16p. (-1). pap. *(978-1-77654-142-3(1),* Red Rocket Readers) Flying Start Bks.

—From Tadpole to Frog - BIG BOOK, 1 vol. 2016. (ENG.). 16p. (-1). pap. *(978-1-77654-165-2(0),* Red Rocket Readers) Flying Start Bks.

—Fruit for You, 1 vol. Cooper, Jenny, illus. 2009. (Red Rocket Readers Ser.). (ENG.). 16p. (gr. -1-1). pap. *(978-1-877363-01-6(4),* Red Rocket Readers) Flying Start Bks.

—Funny Races, 1 vol. Cashmore-Hingley, Michael, illus. 2015. (ENG.). 16p. (-2). pap. *(978-1-77654-131-7(6),* Red Rocket Readers) Flying Start Bks.

—The Gentle Giant, 1 vol. Hatam, Samer, illus. 2009. (Red Rocket Readers Ser.). (ENG.). 19p. (gr. 2-2). pap. *(978-1-877363-81-8(2))* Flying Start Bks.

—Getting Clean, 1 vol. 2015. (ENG., Illus.). 16p. (-1). pap. *(978-1-77654-108-9(1),* Red Rocket Readers) Flying Start Bks.

—Going Up, 1 vol. Hawley, Kelvin, illus. 2009. (Red Rocket Readers Ser.). (ENG.). 16p. (gr. -1-1). pap. *(978-1-877363-18-4(9),* Red Rocket Readers) Flying Start Bks.

—Good Things from Trees, 1 vol. 2015. (ENG., Illus.). 16p. (-1). pap. *(978-1-77654-079-2(4),* Red Rocket Readers) Flying Start Bks.

—Greedy Gus the Pirate, 1 vol. Whimp, Pauline, illus. 2009. (Red Rocket Readers Ser.). (ENG.). 18p. (gr. 2-2). pap. *(978-1-877363-74-0(X))* Flying Start Bks.

—Happy Birthday, 1 vol. Hawley, Kelvin, illus. 2009. (Red Rocket Readers Ser.). (ENG.). 16p. (gr. -1-1). pap. *(978-1-877363-03-0(0),* Red Rocket Readers) Flying Start Bks.

—Having Fun, 1 vol. 2015. (ENG., Illus.). 16p. (-1). pap. *(978-1-77654-109-6(X),* Red Rocket Readers) Flying Start Bks.

—How Many Legs, 1 vol. 2015. (ENG., Illus.). 16p. (-1). pap. *(978-1-77654-110-2(3),* Red Rocket Readers) Flying Start Bks.

—Huff & Puff!, 1 vol. Storey, Jim, illus. 2009. (Red Rocket Readers Ser.). (ENG.). 16p. (gr. 2-2). pap. *(978-1-877363-58-0(8),* Red Rocket Readers) Flying Start Bks.

—Hunting for Treasure, 1 vol. Whimp, Pauline, illus. 2009. (Red Rocket Readers Ser.). (ENG.). 17p. (gr. 2-2). pap. *(978-1-877363-65-8(0),* Red Rocket Readers) Flying Start Bks.

—I Like to Paint, 1 vol., Set. 2009. (Red Rocket Readers Ser.). (ENG., Illus.). 16p. (gr. -1-1). pap. *(978-1-877435-97-3(X))* Flying Start Bks.

—Jobs People Do Big Book Edition, 1 vol. 2014. (ENG.). 16p. (gr. 1-1). pap. *(978-1-77654-046-4(8),* Red Rocket Readers) Flying Start Bks.

—Keeping Safe, 1 vol. 2015. (ENG., Illus.). 16p. (-2). pap. *(978-1-77654-139-3(1),* Red Rocket Readers) Flying Start Bks.

—King of the Zoo, 1 vol. Cammell, Sandra, illus. 2009. (Red Rocket Readers Ser.). (ENG.). 16p. (gr. -1-1). pap. *(978-1-877363-13-9(8),* Red Rocket Readers) Flying Start Bks.

—Knock, Knock!, 1 vol. Hoit, Richard, illus. 2009. (Red Rocket Readers Ser.). (ENG.). 18p. (gr. 2-2). pap. *(978-1-877363-60-3(X),* Red Rocket Readers) Flying Start Bks.

—Learn about Birds, 1 vol. 2015. (ENG., Illus.). 16p. (-1). pap. *(978-1-77654-080-8(8),* Red Rocket Readers) Flying Start Bks.

—Learning to Swim, 1 vol. 2015. (ENG., Illus.). 16p. (-1). pap. *(978-1-77654-081-5(6),* Red Rocket Readers) Flying Start Bks.

—Let's Play Ball, 1 vol. Webb, Philip, illus. 2009. (Red Rocket Readers Ser.). (ENG.). 16p. (gr. -1-1). pap. *(978-1-877363-17-7(0),* Red Rocket Readers) Flying Start Bks.

—The Long, Long Ride, 1 vol. Storey, Jim, illus. 2009. (Red Rocket Readers Ser.). (ENG.). 22p. (gr. 2-2). pap. *(978-1-877363-76-4(6))* Flying Start Bks.

—Look at My Home, 1 vol. East, Jacqueline, illus. 2009. (Red Rocket Readers Ser.). (ENG.). 16p. (gr. -1-1). pap. *(978-1-877363-04-7(9),* Red Rocket Readers) Flying Start Bks.

—Look in the Mirror, 1 vol. 2015. (ENG., Illus.). 16p. (-1). pap. *(978-1-77654-082-2(4),* Red Rocket Readers) Flying Start Bks.

—Look Outside, 1 vol. 2017. (ENG., Illus.). 23p. (J). pap. *(978-1-77654-222-2(3),* Red Rocket Readers) Flying Start Bks.

—Magic Stone Soup, 1 vol. 2015. (ENG., Illus.). 16p. (-1). pap. *(978-1-77654-075-4(1),* Red Rocket Readers) Flying Start Bks.

—The Mailbox Man, 1 vol. 2015. (ENG., Illus.). 16p. (-1). pap. *(978-1-77654-071-6(9),* Red Rocket Readers) Flying Start Bks.

—Masks, 1 vol. 2009. (Red Rocket Readers Ser.). (ENG., Illus.). 16p. (gr. 1-1). pap. *(978-1-877490-19-4(9))* Flying Start Bks.

—Max Monkey, 1 vol. East, Jacqueline, illus. 2009. (Red Rocket Readers Ser.). (ENG.). 16p. (gr. -1-1). pap. *(978-1-877363-24-5(3)*, Red Rocket Readers) Flying Start Bks.

—Message from Camp, 1 vol. Webb, Philip, illus. 2009. (Red Rocket Readers Ser.). (ENG.). 19p. (gr. 2-2). pap. *(978-1-877363-64-1(2)*, Red Rocket Readers) Flying Start Bks.

—My Hands, 1 vol. Hawley, Kelvin, illus. 2009. (Red Rocket Readers Ser.). (ENG.). 16p. (gr. -1-1). pap. *(978-1-877363-25-2(1)*, Red Rocket Readers) Flying Start Bks.

—Naughty Goldilocks, 1 vol. Holt, Richard, illus. 2009. (Red Rocket Readers Ser.). (ENG.). 16p. (gr. -1-1). pap. *(978-1-877363-08-5(1)*, Red Rocket Readers) Flying Start Bks.

—Noisy Traffic, 1 vol. 2015. (ENG., Illus.). 16p. (-1). pap. *(978-1-77654-111-9(1)*, Red Rocket Readers) Flying Start Bks.

—On the Outside - BIG BOOK, 1 vol. 2016. (ENG.). 16p. (-1). pap. *(978-1-77654-163-8(4)*, Red Rocket Readers) Flying Start Bks.

—Our Puppet Show, 1 vol. 2015. (ENG., Illus.). 16p. (-1). pap. *(978-1-77654-072-3(7)*, Red Rocket Readers) Flying Start Bks.

—Paper Chains, 1 vol. 2009. (Red Rocket Readers Ser.). (ENG., Illus.). 21p. (gr. 2-2). pap. *(978-1-877435-43-0(0))* Flying Start Bks.

—The Paper Trail, 1 vol. Hawley, Kelvin, illus. 2009. (Red Rocket Readers Ser.). (ENG.). 21p. (gr. 2-2). pap. *(978-1-877363-69-6(3))* Flying Start Bks.

—Pass It On, 1 vol. Hawley, Kelvin, illus. 2009. (Red Rocket Readers Ser.). (ENG.). 20p. (gr. 2-2). pap. *(978-1-877363-66-5(9)*, Red Rocket Readers) Flying Start Bks.

—Paulo the Pilot, 1 vol. Whimp, Pauline, illus. 2009. (Red Rocket Readers Ser.). (ENG.). 17p. (gr. 2-2). pap. *(978-1-877363-67-2(7)*, Red Rocket Readers) Flying Start Bks.

—Presents for Grace, 1 vol. Hawley, Kelvin, illus. 2009. (Red Rocket Readers Ser.). (ENG.). 18p. (gr. 2-2). pap. *(978-1-877363-61-0(8)*, Red Rocket Readers) Flying Start Bks.

—A Quick Picnic, 1 vol. Ross, Christine, illus. 2009. (Red Rocket Readers Ser.). (ENG.). 16p. (gr. -1-1). pap. *(978-1-877363-22-1(7)*, Red Rocket Readers) Flying Start Bks.

—The Rainbow Party, 1 vol. Whimp, Pauline, illus. 2009. (Red Rocket Readers Ser.). (ENG.). 20p. pap. *(978-1-877363-82-5(0))* Flying Start Bks.

—Red Riding Hood, 1 vol. Hawley, Kelvin, illus. 2009. (Red Rocket Readers Ser.). (ENG.). 16p. (gr. -1-1). pap. *(978-1-877363-09-2(X)*, Red Rocket Readers) Flying Start Bks.

—Ringing Bells, 1 vol. 2015. (ENG., Illus.). 16p. (-1). pap. *(978-1-77654-083-9(2)*, Red Rocket Readers) Flying Start Bks.

—Sally Snip Snap's Party, 1 vol. Storey, Jim, illus. 2009. (Red Rocket Readers Ser.). (ENG.). 19p. (gr. 2-1). pap. *(978-1-877363-57-3(X)*, Red Rocket Readers) Flying Start Bks.

—See Me Ride, 1 vol. East, Jacqueline, illus. 2009. (Red Rocket Readers Ser.). (ENG.). 16p. (gr. -1-1). pap. *(978-1-877363-30-6(8)*, Red Rocket Readers) Flying Start Bks.

—Show Me a Shape, 1 vol. Cooper, Jenny, illus. 2009. (Red Rocket Readers Ser.). (ENG.). 16p. (gr. -1-1). pap. *(978-1-877363-27-6(8)*, Red Rocket Readers) Flying Start Bks.

—Simple Technology & Other Stories. 2018. (ENG., Illus.). 136p. (J). lib. bdg. *(978-1-77654-204-8(5)*, Red Rocket Readers) Flying Start Bks.

—Sneaky Spider, 1 vol. Storey, Jim, illus. 2009. (Red Rocket Readers Ser.). (ENG.). 17p. (gr. 2-2). pap. *(978-1-877363-83-2(9))* Flying Start Bks.

—So Fast, 1 vol. Webb, Philip, illus. 2009. (Red Rocket Readers Ser.). (ENG.). 16p. (gr. -1-1). pap. *(978-1-877363-20-7(0)*, Red Rocket Readers) Flying Start Bks.

—Stickybeak the Parrot, 1 vol. East, Jacqueline, illus. 2009. (Red Rocket Readers Ser.). (ENG.). 16p. (gr. -1-1). pap. *(978-1-877363-28-3(6)*, Red Rocket Readers) Flying Start Bks.

—Stone Soup, 1 vol. Hawley, Kelvin, illus. 2009. (Red Rocket Readers Ser.). (ENG.). 18p. (gr. 2-2). pap. *(978-1-877363-84-9(7))* Flying Start Bks.

—Surprise from the Sky, 1 vol. Whimp, Pauline, illus. 2009. (Red Rocket Readers Ser.). (ENG.). 21p. (gr. 2-1). pap. *(978-1-877363-68-9(5))* Flying Start Bks.

—The Surprise Visitor, 1 vol. Holt, Richard, illus. 2009. (Red Rocket Readers Ser.). (ENG.). 21p. (gr. 2-2). pap. *(978-1-877363-85-6(5))* Flying Start Bks.

—Thirsty Baby Elephant, 1 vol. 2015. (ENG., Illus.). 16p. (-1). pap. *(978-1-77654-076-1(X)*, Red Rocket Readers) Flying Start Bks.

—Three Billy Goats Gruff, 1 vol. Hawley, Kelvin, illus. 2009. (Red Rocket Readers Ser.). (ENG.). 16p. (gr. -1-1). pap. *(978-1-877363-10-8(3)*, Red Rocket Readers) Flying Start Bks.

—Three Little Pigs, 1 vol. Storey, Jim, illus. 2009. (Red Rocket Readers Ser.). (ENG.). 16p. (gr. -1-1). pap. *(978-1-877363-11-5(1)*, Red Rocket Readers) Flying Start Bks.

—Tin Lizzy, 1 vol. Hawley, Kelvin, illus. 2009. (Red Rocket Readers Ser.). (ENG.). 22p. (gr. 2-2). pap. *(978-1-877363-86-3(3))* Flying Start Bks.

—Too Big & Heavy, 1 vol. Hatam, Samer, illus. 2009. (Red Rocket Readers Ser.). (ENG.). 22p. (gr. 2-2). pap. *(978-1-877363-70-2(7))* Flying Start Bks.

—Toys That Can Go, 1 vol. 2009. (Red Rocket Readers Ser.). (ENG., Illus.). 16p. (gr. -1-1). pap. *(978-1-877435-93-5(7))* Flying Start Bks.

—Trip, Trap!, 1 vol. Hawley, Kelvin, illus. 2009. (Red Rocket Readers Ser.). (ENG.). 22p. (gr. 2-2). pap. *(978-1-877363-62-7(6)*, Red Rocket Readers) Flying Start Bks.

—Trip Trap - BIG BOOK, 1 vol. 2016. (ENG.). 16p. (-2). pap. *(978-1-77654-166-9(9)*, Red Rocket Readers) Flying Start Bks.

—Turtle Is Lost, 1 vol. 2015. (ENG., Illus.). 16p. (-1). pap. *(978-1-77654-074-7(3)*, Red Rocket Readers) Flying Start Bks.

—Two Pirates, 1 vol. Whimp, Pauline, illus. 2009. (Red Rocket Readers Ser.). (ENG.). 23p. (gr. 2-2). pap. *(978-1-877363-71-9(5))* Flying Start Bks.

—The Ugly Troll. Hawley, Kelvin, illus. 2017. 16p. (J). pap. *(978-1-77654-191-1(X)*, Red Rocket Readers) Flying Start Bks.

—Umbrellas Go Up, 1 vol. 2015. (ENG., Illus.). 16p. (-1). pap. *(978-1-77654-073-0(5)*, Red Rocket Readers) Flying Start Bks.

—Watch Me Swim, 1 vol. Hansen, Christine, illus. 2009. (Red Rocket Readers Ser.). (ENG.). 16p. (gr. -1-1). pap. *(978-1-877363-31-3(6)*, Red Rocket Readers) Flying Start Bks.

—Watch Out for Whales, 1 vol. Aziz, Lamia, illus. 2009. (Red Rocket Readers Ser.). (ENG.). 23p. (gr. 2-2). pap. *(978-1-877363-63-4(4)*, Red Rocket Readers) Flying Start Bks.

—Watch the Ball, 1 vol. Whimp, Pauline, illus. 2009. (Red Rocket Readers Ser.). (ENG.). 23p. (gr. 2-2). pap. *(978-1-877363-80-1(4))* Flying Start Bks.

—Water from Rain, 1 vol. 2015. (ENG., Illus.). 16p. (-1). pap. *(978-1-77654-084-6(0)*, Red Rocket Readers) Flying Start Bks.

—Whale Rescue, 1 vol. Aziz, Lamia, illus. 2009. (Red Rocket Readers Ser.). (ENG.). 23p. (gr. 2-2). pap. *(978-1-877363-79-5(0))* Flying Start Bks.

—What Is Black?, 1 vol. 2017. (ENG., Illus.). 16p. (J). pap. *(978-1-77654-223-9(1)*, Red Rocket Readers) Flying Start Bks.

—What Is Blue?, 1 vol. 2017. (ENG., Illus.). 17p. (J). pap. *(978-1-77654-224-6(X)*, Red Rocket Readers) Flying Start Bks.

—What Is Brown?, 1 vol. 2017. (ENG., Illus.). 18p. (J). pap. *(978-1-77654-225-3(8)*, Red Rocket Readers) Flying Start Bks.

—What Is Green?, 1 vol. 2017. (ENG., Illus.). 19p. (J). pap. *(978-1-77654-226-0(6)*, Red Rocket Readers) Flying Start Bks.

—What Is Orange?, 1 vol. 2017. (ENG., Illus.). 20p. (J). pap. *(978-1-77654-227-7(4)*, Red Rocket Readers) Flying Start Bks.

—What Is Red?, 1 vol. 2017. (ENG., Illus.). 21p. (J). pap. *(978-1-77654-228-4(2)*, Red Rocket Readers) Flying Start Bks.

—What Is White?, 1 vol. 2017. (ENG., Illus.). 22p. (J). pap. *(978-1-77654-229-1(0)*, Red Rocket Readers) Flying Start Bks.

—What Is Yellow?, 1 vol. 2017. (ENG., Illus.). 23p. (J). pap. *(978-1-77654-230-7(4)*, Red Rocket Readers) Flying Start Bks.

—When I Grow Up, 1 vol. East, Jacqueline, illus. 2009. (Red Rocket Readers Ser.). (ENG.). 16p. (gr. -1-1). pap. *(978-1-877363-06-1(5)*, Red Rocket Readers) Flying Start Bks.

—Who Swims Here, 1 vol. 2015. (ENG., Illus.). 16p. (-1). pap. *(978-1-77654-112-6(X)*, Red Rocket Readers) Flying Start Bks.

—Who Wins the Race?, 1 vol. 2015. (ENG., Illus.). 16p. (-1). pap. *(978-1-77654-070-9(0)*, Red Rocket Readers) Flying Start Bks.

Holden, Pam & Aesop, Aesop. Clever Crow, 1 vol. Hatam, Samer, illus. (ENG.). 26p. (gr. 3-3). pap. *(978-1-927197-34-9(1)*, Red Rocket Readers) Flying Start Bks.

The Hole in the Hill: Individual Title Six-Packs. (Action Packs Ser.). 104p. (gr. 3-5). 44.00 *(978-0-7635-2993-2(1))* Rigby Education.

Holland, Karen. The Garden Gang. 2010. (Illus.). 32p. pap. 12.99 *(978-1-4490-6532-4(5))* AuthorHouse.

Hollenbeck, Kathleen M. Scholastic Success with Reading & Math Jumbo Workbook, 1 vol. 2005. (ENG.). 320p. (gr. k-k). pap., wbk. ed. 14.99 *(978-0-439-78599-0(5)*, Teaching Resources) Scholastic, Inc.

Holliday, Patricia. I Look in the Mirror. 2005. 17p. (J). 10.52 *(978-1-4116-4656-8(8))* Lulu Pr., Inc.

—You & me makes Two. 2008. 32p. pap. 17.35 *(978-1-4357-5321-1(6))* Lulu Pr., Inc.

Hollingsworth, Tamara. Anne Frank: A Light in the Dark, 1 vol. 2nd rev. ed. 2012. (TIME for KIDS(r): Informational Text Ser.). (ENG.). 48p. (gr. 4-5). pap. 13.99 *(978-1-4333-4865-5(9))* Teacher Created Materials, Inc.

—Helen Keller: A New Vision, 1 vol. 2nd rev. ed. 2012. (TIME for KIDS(r): Informational Text Ser.). (ENG.). 48p. (gr. 4-5). pap. 13.99 *(978-1-4333-4863-1(2))* Teacher Created Materials, Inc.

—Martin Luther: A Reforming Spirit, 1 vol. rev. ed. 2012. (Social Studies: Informational Text Ser.). (ENG.). 32p. (gr. 4-8). pap. 11.99 *(978-1-4333-5010-8(6))* Teacher Created Materials, Inc.

—Nelson Mandela: Leading the Way, 1 vol. 2nd rev. ed. 2012. (TIME for KIDS(r): Informational Text Ser.). (ENG., Illus.). 48p. (gr. 4-5). pap. 11.99 *(978-1-4333-4864-8(0))* Teacher Created Materials, Inc.

—The Reformation: A Religious Revolution, 1 vol. rev. ed. 2012. (Social Studies: Informational Text Ser.). (ENG.). 32p. (gr. 4-8). pap. 11.99 *(978-1-4333-5009-2(2))* Teacher Created Materials, Inc.

—Unforgettable Catastrophes, 1 vol. 2nd rev. ed. 2013. (TIME for KIDS(r): Informational Text Ser.). (ENG., Illus.). 64p. (J). (gr. 4-8). pap. 12.99 *(978-1-4333-4946-1(9))* Teacher Created Materials, Inc.

—Unforgettable Natural Disasters, 1 vol. 2nd rev. ed. 2013. (TIME for KIDS(r): Informational Text Ser.). (ENG.). 64p. (gr. 4-8). pap. 14.99 *(978-1-4333-4944-7(2))* Teacher Created Materials, Inc.

—Unforgettable News Reports, 1 vol. 2nd rev. ed. 2013. (TIME for KIDS(r): Informational Text Ser.). (ENG., Illus.). 64p. (gr. 4-8). pap. 14.99 *(978-1-4333-4945-4(0))* Teacher Created Materials, Inc.

Holmes, Quentin. Real Street Kidz: Art of Authenticity. 2011. 92p. (gr. 3-7). pap. 10.99 *(978-1-4575-0268-2(2))* Dog Ear Publishing, LLC.

HolmesKaren. Slow Motion: Taking Your Time High Beginning Book with Online Access, 1 vol. 2014. (ENG., Illus.). 24p. (J). pap., E-Book, E-Book 7.50 *(978-1-107-69129-2(X))* Cambridge Univ. Pr.

Holt, Rinehart and Winston Staff. Elemental Literature - Elements of Literature. 5th ed. 2003. (Elements of Literature Ser.). (ENG., Illus.). 160p. (gr. 6-6). pap. 17.15 *(978-0-03-035709-1(8))* Houghton Mifflin Harcourt Publishing Co.

—Elements of Literature: Adapted Reader. 5th ed. 2003. (Elements of Literature Ser.). (ENG., Illus.). 168p. (gr. 10-10). pap. 17.15 *(978-0-03-035458-8(7))* Houghton Mifflin Harcourt Publishing Co.

—Elements of Literature: Holt Adapted Reader. 5th ed. 2004. (Elements of Literature Ser.). (ENG.). 184p. (gr. 7-7). pap. 17.15 *(978-0-03-035711-4(X))* Houghton Mifflin Harcourt Publishing Co.

—Elements of Literature: Holt Reader. 5th ed. 2003. (Elements of Literature Ser.). (ENG., Illus.). 424p. (gr. 9-9). pap. 17.15 *(978-0-03-068393-0(9))* Houghton Mifflin Harcourt Publishing Co.

—Elements of Literature - Adapted Reader. 5th ed. 2003. (Elements of Literature Ser.). (ENG., Illus.). 184p. (gr. 12-12). pap. 17.15 *(978-0-03-035461-8(7))* Houghton Mifflin Harcourt Publishing Co.

—Elements of Literature - Holt Adapted Reader. 5th ed. 2003. (Elements of Literature Ser.). (ENG., Illus.). 208p. (gr. 11-11). pap. 17.15 *(978-0-03-035459-5(5))*; (gr. 9-9). pap. 17.15 *(978-0-03-035454-0(4))* Houghton Mifflin Harcourt Publishing Co.

—Elements of Literature 2005 - The Holt Reader. 5th ed. 2003. (Elements of Literature Ser.). (ENG., Illus.). 400p. (gr. 11-11). pap. 17.15 *(978-0-03-068396-1(3))* Houghton Mifflin Harcourt Publishing Co.

—Holt Adapted Reader. 5th ed. 2004. (Elements of Literature Ser.). (ENG., Illus.). 224p. (gr. 8-8). pap. 17.15 *(978-0-03-035712-1(8))* Houghton Mifflin Harcourt Publishing Co.

—Holt Reader. 5th ed. 2003. (Elements of Literature Ser.). (ENG., Illus.). 392p. (gr. 12-12). pap. 17.15 *(978-0-03-068397-8(1))*; 384p. (gr. 7-7). pap. 17.15 *(978-0-03-068391-6(2))* Houghton Mifflin Harcourt Publishing Co.

—The Holt Reader. 5th ed. 2003. (Elements of Literature Ser.). (ENG., Illus.). 368p. (gr. 8-8). pap. 17.15 *(978-0-03-068392-3(0))* Houghton Mifflin Harcourt Publishing Co.

—NY Strategy & Practice for Reading 2004: Science Spectrum. 4th ed. 2004. pap. 12.80 *(978-0-03-074164-7(5))* Holt McDougal.

—OH Strategy & Practice for Reading 2004: Science Spectrum. 2004. pap. 12.80 *(978-0-03-074168-5(8))* Holt McDougal.

—Reader Fourth Course. 4th ed. 2003. (Elements of Literature Ser.). (ENG., Illus.). 408p. (gr. 10-10). pap. 17.15 *(978-0-03-068394-7(7))* Houghton Mifflin Harcourt Publishing Co.

Holt, Sharon & Proudfoot, Dean. Don't Embarrass Me, Dad! 2008. (Rigby Focus Forward: Level H Ser.). (Illus.). 24p. (J). (gr. 4-7). pap. *(978-1-4190-3735-1(8)*, Rigby) Pearson Education Australia.

Holzer, Angela. Fat Freddy. Tucker, Barclay, illus. 2009. 36p. (J). lib. bdg. 8.99 *(978-0-9821563-4-6(0))* Good Sound Publishing.

—My Dog, Eddie. Funk, Debbie, illus. 2009. 36p. (J). lib. bdg. 8.99 *(978-0-9821563-5-3(9))* Good Sound Publishing.

A Home: Individual Title Six-Packs. (Sails Literacy Ser.). 16p. (gr. k-18). 27.00 *(978-0-7635-4387-7(X))* Rigby Education.

A Home for Nellie. 2005. (Book Treks Ser.). (J). (gr. 3-18). stu. ed. 34.95 *(978-0-673-62849-7(3))* Celebration Pr.

Homes & Places. 2005. (Little Celebrations Thematic Packages Ser.). (J). (gr. k-3). 133.50 *(978-0-673-75385-4(9))* Celebration Pr.

Honders, Jamie. Our Community Helpers, 1 vol. 2012. (InfoMax Readers Ser.). (ENG., Illus.). 16p. (J). (gr. k-k). pap. 7.00 *(978-1-4488-8917-4(0)*, e2890ab1-6ecc-4efc-8e10-b7486b015a07, Rosen Classroom) Rosen Publishing Group, Inc., The.

Honest Abe. (Lexile Levels Ser.). 9.09 *(978-1-56334-706-1(7))* CENGAGE Learning.

The Honey Tree, 6 Packs. (Literatura 2000 Ser.). (gr. 2-3). 33.00 *(978-0-7635-0262-1(6))* Rigby Education.

Hook, Francis. Finding the Djinn. 2009. (Hodder African Readers Ser.). (ENG., Illus.). 112p. pap. 12.95 *(978-0-340-99029-2(5))* Hodder Education Group GBR. Dist: Trans-Atlantic Pubns., Inc.

Hoop Dancers. (Early Intervention Levels Ser.). 31.86 *(978-0-7362-0660-0(4))* CENGAGE Learning.

Hopkins, Andy & Potter, Joc. Oxford Bookworms Factfiles: Animals in Danger: Level 1: 400-Word Vocabulary. 3rd ed. 2008. (ENG., Illus.). 64p. pap. 11.00 *(978-0-19-423379-8(0))* Oxford Univ. Pr., Inc.

Horacek, Petr. Who Is the Biggest? Horacek, Petr, illus. 2019. (ENG., Illus.). 16p. (J). (— 1). bds. 8.99 *(978-1-5362-0171-0(5))* Candlewick Pr.

Horsepool, Adam, illus. The Call of the Wild. 2021. (10 Minute Classics Ser.). (ENG.). 32p. (J). (gr. 1-5). 16.99 *(978-1-4867-1825-2(6)*, 0139739a-d69d-4170-8512-32594acbfd9d) Flowerpot Pr.

Hoshino, Felicia. Sora & the Cloud. 2012. (ENG., Illus.). 40p. (J). (gr. -1-3). 15.95 *(978-1-59702-027-5(3))* Immedium.

Hotchkins, Dewayne. Family History, 1 vol. 2016. (Rosen REAL Readers: Social Studies Nonfiction / Fiction: Myself, My Community, My World Ser.). (ENG.). 8p. (gr. k-1). pap. 5.46 *(978-1-5081-2524-2(4)*, cca554f9-e870-4524-8de7-75b1c659f554, Rosen Classroom) Rosen Publishing Group, Inc., The.

—Farmer Jack's Farm Stand, 1 vol. 2016. (Rosen REAL Readers: Social Studies Nonfiction / Fiction: Myself, My Community, My World Ser.). (ENG.). 8p. (gr. k-1). pap. 5.46 *(978-1-5081-2509-9(0)*, a8cdcb25-7411-4f81-b5c0-ba37d27631cb, Rosen Classroom) Rosen Publishing Group, Inc., The.

—Jayla Wins a Flag, 1 vol. 2016. (Rosen REAL Readers: Social Studies Nonfiction / Fiction: Myself, My Community, My World Ser.). (ENG.). 8p. (gr. k-1). pap. 5.46 *(978-1-5081-2473-3(6)*, d2fb2d07-f680-4106-b8ac-08565188974c, Rosen Classroom) Rosen Publishing Group, Inc., The.

—The Polar Bear & the Glacier, 1 vol. 2016. (Rosen REAL Readers: STEM & STEAM Collection). (ENG.). 12p. (gr. 1-2). pap. 6.33 *(978-1-5081-2682-9(8)*, bf7b51ae-0acf-41e0-9fec-ece396974497, Rosen Classroom) Rosen Publishing Group, Inc., The.

—We Buy Vegetables from Mr. Owens, 1 vol. 2016. (Rosen REAL Readers: Social Studies Nonfiction / Fiction: Myself, My Community, My World Ser.). (ENG.). 8p. (gr. k-1). pap. 5.46 *(978-1-5081-2293-7(8)*, b0d0f883-d472-40eb-b938-9efb2d5ac6f0, Rosen Classroom) Rosen Publishing Group, Inc., The.

A House: Individual Title Six-Packs. (Sails Literacy Ser.). 16p. (gr. k-18). 27.00 *(978-0-7635-4425-6(6))* Rigby Education.

House, Catherine. Hanan the Peanut Seller. 2004. (Illus.). 31p. *(978-0-636-06419-5(0))* Maskew Miller Longman.

A House for Sergin: Six-Pack. (Greetings Ser.: Vol. 2). 24p. (gr. 2-3). 31.00 *(978-0-7635-9427-5(X))* Rigby Education.

Housel, Debra J. Immigration, 1 vol. rev. ed. 2007. (Social Studies: Informational Text Ser.). (ENG.). 32p. (gr. 4-8). pap. 11.99 *(978-0-7439-0662-3(4))* Teacher Created Materials, Inc.

—Incredible Invertebrates, 1 vol. 2nd rev. ed. 2011. (TIME for KIDS(r): Informational Text Ser.). (ENG.). 28p. (gr. 3-4). pap. 11.99 *(978-1-4333-3660-7(X))* Teacher Created Materials, Inc.

—Industrial Giants, 1 vol. rev. ed. 2007. (Social Studies: Informational Text Ser.). (ENG.). 32p. (gr. 4-8). pap. 11.99 *(978-0-7439-0661-6(6))* Teacher Created Materials, Inc.

—Industrial Revolution, 1 vol. rev. ed. 2007. (Social Studies: Informational Text Ser.). (ENG.). 32p. (J). (gr. 4-8). pap. 11.99 *(978-0-7439-0660-9(8))* Teacher Created Materials, Inc.

—Inside Ecosystems & Biomes, 1 vol. rev. ed. 2007. (Science: Informational Text Ser.). (ENG., Illus.). 32p. (gr. 3-6). pap. 12.99 *(978-0-7439-0591-6(1))* Teacher Created Materials, Inc.

—Mammal Mania, 1 vol. 2nd rev. ed. 2011. (TIME for KIDS(r): Informational Text Ser.). (ENG.). 28p. (gr. 3-4). pap. 11.99 *(978-1-4333-3658-4(8))* Teacher Created Materials, Inc.

—Pioneering Ecologists, 1 vol. rev. ed. 2007. (Science: Informational Text Ser.). (ENG.). 32p. (J). (gr. 3-6). pap. 12.99 *(978-0-7439-0592-3(X))* Teacher Created Materials, Inc.

—Slithering Reptiles & Amphibians, 1 vol. 2nd rev. ed. 2011. (TIME for KIDS(r): Informational Text Ser.). (ENG.). 28p. (gr. 3-4). pap. 11.99 *(978-1-4333-3659-1(6))* Teacher Created Materials, Inc.

Housel, Debra J. & Rice, Dona Herwick. Buy It! History of Money, 1 vol. 2nd rev. ed. 2012. (TIME for KIDS(r): Informational Text Ser.). (ENG.). 32p. (gr. 3-5). pap. 12.99 *(978-1-4333-3681-2(2))* Teacher Created Materials, Inc.

How Big Is My World? (J). pap. 7.95 *(978-0-8136-0082-6(0))* Modern Curriculum Pr.

How Many Jelly Beans? (Early Intervention Levels Ser.). 21.30 *(978-0-7362-0374-6(5))*; Vol. 2. 3.55 *(978-0-7362-0095-0(9))* CENGAGE Learning.

How the Whale Got His Throat. 2017. (Picture Bks.). (ENG.). (J). 9.99 *(978-0-7945-3869-9(X)*, Usborne) EDC Publishing.

How Things Work Interactive Packages: Looking Closer. (Pebble Soup Explorations Ser.). (gr. -1-18). 52.00 *(978-0-7578-5246-6(7))* Rigby Education.

Howard, Kate. Return of the Djinn. 2016. (LEGO Ninjago Ser.). (ENG.). 32p. (J). (gr. 1-3). pap. 3.99 *(978-0-545-92553-2(3))* Scholastic, Inc.

Howell, Gill. Selkie Child. Keen, Sophie, illus. 2005. (ENG.). 24p. (J). lib. bdg. 23.65 *(978-1-59646-750-7(9))* Dingles & Co.

—Snow King. Cann, Helen, illus. 2005. (ENG.). 24p. (J). lib. bdg. 23.65 *(978-1-59646-742-2(8))* Dingles & Co.

—Tortoise & the Baboon. Woody, illus. 2004. (ENG.). 16p. (J). lib. bdg. 23.65 *(978-1-59646-686-9(3))* Dingles & Co.

Howlett, Bruce & Pitcher, Jeff, creators. Hop, Skip & Jump into Reading Software: For Six Students. 2003. (J). cd-rom *(978-0-9742485-1-6(7))* Sound Reading Solutions.

—Hop, Skip & Jump into Reading Software: For Two Students. 2003. (J). cd-rom *(978-0-9742485-0-9(9))* Sound Reading Solutions.

Howlett, Bruce, et al. Hop, Skip & Jump into Reading. Pitcher, Jeff, illus. 2003. (J). Bk. 1. 9.00 *(978-0-9704183-4-0(5))*Bk. 2. 9.00 *(978-0-9704183-3-3(7)*, Sound Reading)Bk. 3. 9.00 *(978-0-9704183-8-8(8)*, Sound Reading) Sound Reading Solutions.

HSP Staff. Band of Angels Challenge Trade Book Grade 2: Harcourt School Publishers Storytown. 2006. pap. 8.75 *(978-0-15-365114-4(8))* Harcourt Schl. Pubs.

—Eager Challenge Trade Book Grade 6: Harcourt School Publishers Storytown. 2006. pap. 8.75 *(978-0-15-365195-3(4))* Harcourt Schl. Pubs.

—Grandpa Stre Challenge Trade Book Grade 2: Harcourt School Publishers Storytown. 2006. pap. 8.75 *(978-0-15-365112-0(1))* Harcourt Schl. Pubs.

—Loser Challenge Trade Book Grade 6: Harcourt School Publishers Storytown. 2006. pap. 8.75 *(978-0-15-365187-8(3))* Harcourt Schl. Pubs.

—My Rows & Cns Challenge Trade Book Grade 2: Harcourt School Publishers Storytown. 2006. pap. 8.75 *(978-0-15-365118-2(0))* Harcourt Schl. Pubs.

Huang, SuHua. A Faithful Reading Partner: A Story from a Hakka Village. 2012. 28p. pap. 19.99 *(978-1-4685-6267-5(3))* AuthorHouse.

Hudicourt, Caroline. A Mango for Grandpa. Sainsilus, Ismer, illus. 2007. 32p. (J). (ARA & ENG.). pap. 14.95 *(978-1-60195-085-7(3))*; (POL.). pap. 14.95 *(978-1-60195-093-2(4))* International Step by Step Assn.

Hudson, Wade & Hudson, Cheryl Willis, eds. We Rise, We Resist, We Raise Our Voices. 2018. (Illus.). 96p. (J). (gr. 3-7). 18.99 *(978-0-525-58042-3(5)*, Crown Books For Young Readers) Random Hse. Children's Bks.

Huffman, Mindy. Warren Makes a Website: Digital Citizenship, 1 vol. 2017. (Computer Kids: Powered by Computational Thinking Ser.). (ENG.). 24p. (J). (gr. 4-5). 25.27 *(978-1-5383-2438-7(5)*, f9495163-208c-4e57-bceb-2484bccd03c8, PowerKids Pr.); pap. *(978-1-5383-5304-2(0),* 38862442-119c-44fc-af1e-49eef09d4eed, Rosen Classroom) Rosen Publishing Group, Inc., The.

Hughes, A. & Hope, Anthony. Level 5: the Prisoner of Zenda Book & MP3 Pack, Pack. 2nd ed. 2011. (ENG.). x, 86p. (C). pap. 10.99 incl. cd-rom *(978-1-4082-7649-5(6))* Pearson Education.

Hughes, Jon. The Rise of the Sauropods White Band. 2017. (Cambridge Reading Adventures Ser.). (ENG., Illus.). 40p. pap. 8.60 *(978-1-108-40576-8(2))* Cambridge Univ. Pr.

—What Happened to the Dinosaurs?: Band 13/Topaz (Collins Big Cat) Hughes, Jon, illus. 2007. (Collins Big Cat Ser.). (ENG., Illus.). 32p. (J). (gr. 2-4). pap. 10.99 *(978-0-00-723084-6(2))* HarperCollins Pubs. Ltd. GBR. Dist: Independent Pubs. Group.

Hughes, Mónica. The Big Turnip: Band 00/Lilac (Collins Big Cat) Williams, Lisa, illus. 2006. (Collins Big Cat Ser.). (ENG.). 32p. (J). (gr. -1-k). pap. 7.99 *(978-0-00-718644-0(4))* HarperCollins Pubs. Ltd. GBR. Dist: Independent Pubs. Group.

—Cars. 2005. (Big Cat Ser.). (gr. k-2). pap. 6.50 *(978-1-60457-026-7(1))* Pacific Learning, Inc.

—Lights: Band 03/Yellow (Collins Big Cat) 2006. (Collins Big Cat Ser.). (ENG., Illus.). 136p. (J). (gr. 1-1). pap. 7.99 *(978-0-00-718680-8(0))* HarperCollins Pubs. Ltd. GBR. Dist: Independent Pubs. Group.

—Little Mouse Deer & the Crocodile. Moricuchi, Mique, illus. 2004. 24p. (J). lib. bdg. 23.65 *(978-1-59646-684-5(7))* Dingles & Co.

—More Little Mouse Deer Tales. Clemenston, John, illus. 2005. 24p. (J). lib. bdg. 23.65 *(978-1-59646-730-9(4))* Dingles & Co.

—Pushing & Pulling. 2005. (Big Cat Ser.). (gr. k-2). pap. 6.50 *(978-1-60457-025-0(3))* Pacific Learning, Inc.

—Pushing & Pulling: Band 01A/Pink a (Collins Big Cat) Coote, Mark, illus. 2005. (Collins Big Cat Ser.). (ENG.). 16p. (J). (gr. -1-k). pap. 6.99 *(978-0-00-718541-2(3))* HarperCollins Pubs. Ltd. GBR. Dist: Independent Pubs. Group.

—Shapes: Band 01A/Pink a (Collins Big Cat) 2006. (Collins Big Cat Ser.). (ENG., Illus.). 16p. (J). (gr. -1-k). pap. 6.99 *(978-0-00-718649-5(5))* HarperCollins Pubs. Ltd. GBR. Dist: Independent Pubs. Group.

—Stripes. 2005. (Big Cat Ser.). (gr. k-2). pap. 6.50 *(978-1-60457-021-2(0))* Pacific Learning, Inc.

—Stripes: Band 00/Lilac (Collins Big Cat) 2005. (Collins Big Cat Ser.). (ENG.). 16p. (J). (gr. -1-k). pap. 7.99 *(978-0-00-718534-4(0))* HarperCollins Pubs. Ltd. GBR. Dist: Independent Pubs. Group.

Hugo & Splot: Individual Title Six-Packs. (Bookweb Ser.). 32p. (gr. 3-18). 34.00 *(978-0-7635-3936-8(8))* Rigby Education.

The Hummingbirds' Gift. (Lexile Levels Ser.). 9.09 *(978-1-56334-720-7(2))* CENGAGE Learning.

Humphreys, Pauline A. Romance of the Airman. 2005. pap. 43.95 *(978-1-4191-0278-3(8))* Kessinger Publishing, LLC.

The Hungry Chickens: Individual Title Six-Packs. (Literatura 2000 Ser.). (gr. 1-2). 28.00 *(978-0-7635-0136-5(0))* Rigby Education.

Hurley, Trish. The 10 Most Enduring Fashion Trends. 2008. (J). 14.99 *(978-1-55448-524-6(X))* Scholastic Library Publishing.

—The 10 Most Outrageous Outlaws. 2008. 14.99 *(978-1-55448-506-2(1))* Scholastic Library Publishing.

I Am Six. (Early Intervention Levels Ser.). 63.00 *(978-0-7362-2112-2(3))*; 10.50 *(978-0-7362-0513-9(6))* CENGAGE Learning.

I Can Read 50th Anniversary Box Set, Set. 50th anniv. ed. 2007. (I Can Read Level 1 Ser.). (ENG.). (J). (gr. k-3). 14.99 *(978-0-06-123469-9(9),* HarperCollins) HarperCollins Pubs.

I Love My Grandma, Vol. 6. (Early Intervention Levels Ser.). 3.85 *(978-1-56334-970-6(1))* CENGAGE Learning.

I See Tails! (Early Intervention Levels Ser.). 23.10 *(978-0-7362-0009-7(6))*; Vol. 2. 3.85 *(978-1-56334-959-1(0))* CENGAGE Learning.

Iacolina, Mark. Frances Dances. Iacolina, Mark, illus. 2015. (Penguin Young Readers, Level 2 Ser.). (Illus.). 32p. (J). (gr. 1-2). 4.99 *(978-0-448-47929-3(X),* Penguin Young Readers) Penguin Young Readers Group.

Ida B Reading Group Guide. (J). *(978-0-06-074412-0(X))* HarperCollins Pubs.

Ideas of the Modern World, 8 vols., Set. 2003. 205.52 *(978-0-7398-6420-3(3))* Steck-Vaughn.

Idee, Ari. What's Your Snack? 2013. 28p. pap. 9.49 *(978-0-9798991-2-6(5))* Technology & Imagination Pr.

If I Were You. 2003. (Illus.). pap. 5.60 *(978-0-7398-7519-3(1))* Steck-Vaughn.

If You Could Be Anything. 2003. (Illus.). pap. 7.60 *(978-0-7398-7530-8(2))* Steck-Vaughn.

Iggy Iguana's Trip. (Early Intervention Levels Ser.). 21.30 *(978-0-7362-0380-7(X))*; Vol. 3. 3.55 *(978-0-7362-0101-8(7))* CENGAGE Learning.

Ignatow, Amy. The Popularity Papers: Book Seven: the Less-Than-Hidden Secrets & Final Revelations of Lydia Goldblatt & Julie Graham-Chang, Bk. 7. 2015. (Popularity Papers). (ENG., Illus.). 208p. (J). (gr. 3-7). pap. 10.99 *(978-1-4197-1357-6(4),* 1087603, Amulet Bks.) Abrams, Inc.

Ikids Staff. Old MacDonald's Farm. King, Travis, illus. 2010. (ENG.). 20p. (J). (gr. -1-k). 14.99 *(978-1-60169-024-1(X))* Innovative Kids.

I'm Glad I'm Me: Individual Title Six-Packs. (gr. 1-2). 25.00 *(978-0-7635-9194-6(7))* Rigby Education.

I'm not, I'm Not: Individual Title Six-Packs. (gr. 1-2). 22.00 *(978-0-7635-9155-7(6))* Rigby Education.

The Imaginer: Individual Title Six-Packs. (Bookweb Ser.). 32p. (gr. 6-18). 34.00 *(978-0-7578-0900-2(6))* Rigby Education.

In the Bathroom: Individual Title, 6 Packs. (Chiquilibros Ser.). (gr. k-1). 23.00 *(978-0-7635-0452-6(1))* Rigby Education.

In the Box, Vol. 3. (Early Intervention Levels Ser.). 3.55 *(978-0-7362-0098-1(3))* CENGAGE Learning.

In the City Vol. 4: Step K, Level B. (Early Intervention Levels Ser.). 3.85 *(978-1-56334-968-3(X))* CENGAGE Learning.

In the Country: Individual Title Six-Packs. (gr. -1-2). 23.00 *(978-0-7635-8810-6(5))* Rigby Education.

In The Sun. (Early Intervention Levels Ser.). 21.30 *(978-0-7362-0390-6(7))*; Vol. 4. 3.55 *(978-0-7362-0170-4(X))* CENGAGE Learning.

In the Teacup: KinderWords Individual Title, 6 Packs. (Kinderstarters Ser.). 8p. (gr. -1-1). 21.00 *(978-0-7635-8695-9(1))* Rigby Education.

In The Yard. (Early Intervention Levels Ser.). 32.04 *(978-0-7362-2142-9(5))*; 5.34 *(978-0-7362-1694-4(4))* CENGAGE Learning.

Independent Readers Bookshelf Collection, 6 bks., Set. 2004. (gr. 1-18). 99.00 *(978-0-328-00408-9(1))* Addison-Wesley Educational Pubs., Inc.

Inkpen, Mick & Inkpen, Chloe. Hole in the Zoo. 2019. (ENG., Illus.). 32p. (J). (gr. -1 — 1). pap. 9.99 *(978-1-4449-3171-6(7))* Hachette Children's Group GBR. Dist: Hachette Bk. Group.

Instruc, Shurley. Shurley English 1 Kit H/S Ed. 2004. 70.00 *(978-1-58561-048-8(8))* Shurley Instructional Materials, Inc.

—Shurley English 1 Stu Workbook. 2004. pap. 12.00 *(978-1-58561-049-5(6))* Shurley Instructional Materials, Inc.

—Shurley English 2 Kit H/S Ed. 2004. pap. 70.00 *(978-1-58561-044-0(5))* Shurley Instructional Materials, Inc.

—Shurley English 2 Stu Workbook. 2004. pap. 12.00 *(978-1-58561-045-7(3))* Shurley Instructional Materials, Inc.

—Shurley English 3 Kit H/S Ed. 2004. 70.00 *(978-1-58561-040-2(2))* Shurley Instructional Materials, Inc.

—Shurley English 3 Stu Workbook. 2004. pap. 12.00 *(978-1-58561-041-9(0))* Shurley Instructional Materials, Inc.

—Shurley English 4 Kit H/S Ed. 2004. pap. 70.00 *(978-1-58561-036-5(4))* Shurley Instructional Materials, Inc.

—Shurley English 4 Stu Workbook. 2004. pap. 12.00 *(978-1-58561-037-2(2))* Shurley Instructional Materials, Inc.

—Shurley English 5 Kit H/S Ed. 2004. pap. 70.00 *(978-1-58561-032-7(1))* Shurley Instructional Materials, Inc.

—Shurley English 5 Stu Workbook. 2004. pap. 12.00 *(978-1-58561-033-4(X))* Shurley Instructional Materials, Inc.

—Shurley English 6 Stu Workbook. 2004. pap. 12.00 *(978-1-58561-029-7(1))* Shurley Instructional Materials, Inc.

Intervention Handbook. 2004. (Scott Foresman Reading Ser.). (gr. 3-18). 45.68 *(978-0-328-02600-5(X))*; (gr. 4-18). 45.68 *(978-0-328-02601-2(8))*; (gr. 5-18). 45.68 *(978-0-328-02602-9(6))*; (gr. 6-18). tchr. ed. 45.68 *(978-0-328-02603-6(4))* Addison-Wesley Educational Pubs., Inc.

Into English!, 13 vols. (Into English! Ser.). Level C. (gr. k-6). 137.49 *(978-1-56334-803-7(9),* ES0208)Level C. (gr. 2-18). 810.14 *(978-1-56334-825-9(X),* IN0202)Level C. (gr. 2-18). stu. ed., act. bk. ed. 5.84 *(978-1-56334-823-5(3),* LA0201)Level D. (gr. k-6). 110.53 *(978-1-56334-804-4(7),* ES0307)Level D. (gr. 3-18). 648.64 incl. cd-rom *(978-1-56334-843-3(8),* IN0304)Level D. (gr. 3-18). stu. ed., act. bk. ed. 5.84 *(978-1-56334-718-4(0),* LA0301)Level A. (gr. k-6). 116.54 *(978-1-56334-805-1(5),* ES0007)Level B. (gr. k-6). 149.56 *(978-1-56334-802-0(0),* ES0108)Level B. (gr. 1-18). 810.14 *(978-1-56334-807-5(1),* IN0102)Level B. (gr. 1-18). 47.88 *(978-1-56334-896-9(9),* SC0101)Level B. (gr. 1-18). stu. ed., act. bk. ed. 5.84 *(978-1-56334-822-8(5),* LA0101)Level F. (gr. k-6). 112.14 *(978-1-56334-904-1(3),* ES0507)Level F. (gr. 5-18). 648.64 incl. cd-rom *(978-1-56334-875-4(6),* IN0504)Level F. (gr. 5-18). 45.45 *(978-1-56334-900-3(0),* SC0503)Level F. (gr. 5-18). stu. ed., act. bk. ed. 5.84 *(978-1-56334-746-7(6),* LA0501)Level G. (gr. k-6). 99.48 *(978-1-56334-907-2(8),* ES0607)Level G. (gr. 6-18). 626.27 *(978-1-56334-908-9(6),* IN0604)Level G. (gr. 6-18). 44.34 *(978-1-56334-916-4(7),* SC0603)Level G. (gr. 6-18). 648.64 incl. cd-rom *(978-1-56334-901-0(9),* IN0602)Level G. (gr. 6-18). stu. ed., act. bk. ed. 5.84 *(978-1-56334-756-6(3),* LA0601) CENGAGE Learning.

Into English! Portable Packs: Level B. (Into English! Ser.). (gr. 1-5). 286.60 *(978-0-7362-1393-6(7))* CENGAGE Learning.

Into English! Portable Packs: Level C. (Into English! Ser.). (gr. 1-5). 286.60 *(978-0-7362-1394-3(5))* CENGAGE Learning.

Into English! Portable Packs: Level D. (Into English! Ser.). (gr. 1-5). 278.51 *(978-0-7362-1395-0(3))* CENGAGE Learning.

Into English! Portable Packs: Level E. (Into English! Ser.). (gr. 1-5). 278.51 *(978-0-7362-1396-7(1))* CENGAGE Learning.

Into English! Portable Packs: Level F. (Into English! Ser.). (gr. 1-5). 278.51 *(978-0-7362-1397-4(X))* CENGAGE Learning.

Iopeners: Big Book Collection, 20 vols. 2005. (J). (gr. k-18). 525.95 *(978-0-7652-4972-2(3))*; (gr. 1-18). 587.50 *(978-0-7652-4976-0(6))* Modern Curriculum Pr.

Iopeners: Classroom Library. 2005. (J). (gr. k-18). 440.50 *(978-0-7652-4969-2(3))*; (gr. 1-18). 518.50 *(978-0-7652-4973-9(1))*; (gr. 2-18). 518.50 *(978-0-7652-4977-7(4))*; (gr. 3-18). 616.50 *(978-0-7652-4980-7(4))*; (gr. 4-18). 616.50 *(978-0-7652-4983-8(9))*; (gr. 5-18). 694.50 *(978-0-7652-4986-9(3))*; (gr. 6-18). 694.50 *(978-0-7652-4989-0(8))* Modern Curriculum Pr.

Irma Perez, Amada. My Diary from Here/Mi Diario de Aqui Has, 1 vol. 2013.Tr. of My Diary from Here to There. (ENG., Illus.). 32p. (J). (gr. 2-5). pap. 11.95 *(978-0-89239-230-8(4),* leelowcbp) Lee & Low Bks., Inc.

Is Jim In? Set A Individual Title Six-Packs. (Supersonic Phonics Ser.). (gr. k-3). 29.00 *(978-0-7635-0531-8(5))* Rigby Education.

Isabel, Delgado Maria. Chave's Memories / Los Recuerdos de Chave. Yvonne, Symank, illus. 2008. 32p. (J). pap. 7.95 *(978-1-55885-244-0(1),* Piñata Books) Arte Publico Pr.

Isecke, Harriet. Finding Texas: Exploration in New Lands, 1 vol. rev. ed. 2012. (Social Studies: Informational Text Ser.). (ENG.). 32p. (gr. 3-5). pap. 11.99 *(978-1-4333-5042-9(4))* Teacher Created Materials, Inc.

—Lyndon B. Johnson: A Texan in the White House, 1 vol. rev. ed. 2012. (Social Studies: Informational Text Ser.). (ENG.). 32p. (gr. 3-5). pap. 11.99 *(978-1-4333-5052-8(1))* Teacher Created Materials, Inc.

—Stephen F. Austin: The Father of Texas, 1 vol. rev. ed. 2012. (Social Studies: Informational Text Ser.). (ENG.). 32p. (gr. 3-5). pap. 11.99 *(978-1-4333-5045-0(9))* Teacher Created Materials, Inc.

—Susan B. Anthony & Elizabeth Cady Stanton: Early Suffragists. rev. ed. 2011. (Social Studies: Informational Text Ser.). (ENG., Illus.). 32p. (gr. 4-8). pap. 11.99 *(978-1-4333-1506-0(8))* Teacher Created Materials, Inc.

—Texas in the 20th Century: Building Industry & Community, 1 vol. rev. ed. 2012. (Social Studies: Informational Text Ser.). (ENG.). 32p. (gr. 3-5). pap. 11.99 *(978-1-4333-5209-6(5))* Teacher Created Materials, Inc.

—Texas Today: Leading America into the Future, 1 vol. rev. ed. 2012. (Social Studies: Informational Text Ser.). (ENG.). 32p. (gr. 3-5). pap. 11.99 *(978-1-4333-5053-5(X))* Teacher Created Materials, Inc.

—Women's Suffrage: Fighting for Women's Rights. rev. ed. 2011. (Social Studies: Informational Text Ser.). (ENG.). 32p. (gr. 4-8). pap. 11.99 *(978-1-4333-1507-7(6))* Teacher Created Materials, Inc.

¡Ser Amable no Cuesta Nada! Social/Emotional Lap Book. (Pebble Soup Exploraciones Ser.). (SPA.). (gr. -1-18). 16.00 *(978-0-7578-1783-0(1))* Rigby Education.

It's Not Fair: 6 Small Books. (gr. k-3). 24.00 *(978-0-7635-6243-4(2))* Rigby Education.

It's Time: Set 2, 8 vols. 2017. (It's Time Ser.). (ENG.). (J). (gr. 1-1). lib. bdg. 101.08 *(978-1-5081-6319-0(7),* 50bbac0f-311a-40cf-97a2-4a74766cce3b, PowerKids Pr.) Rosen Publishing Group, Inc., The.

Ivanoff, George & Quarmby, Toby. My Best Friend Thinks I'm a Genius. 2008. (Rigby Focus Forward Ser.). (ENG., Illus.). 24p. (gr. 3-8). pap. 11.20 *(978-1-4190-3849-5(4))* Houghton Mifflin Harcourt Publishing Co.

Iversen, Sandra. Alphabet Book Aa. 2009. (Quick60 Alphabet Bks.). (ENG., Illus.). 12p. (J). pap. *(978-1-77540-000-4(X))* Iversen Publishing Ltd.

—Alphabet Book Bb. 2009. (Quick60 Alphabet Bks.). (ENG., Illus.). 12p. (J). pap. *(978-1-77540-001-1(8))* Iversen Publishing Ltd.

—Alphabet Book Cc. 2009. (Quick60 Alphabet Bks.). (ENG., Illus.). 12p. (J). pap. *(978-1-77540-002-8(6))* Iversen Publishing Ltd.

—Alphabet Book Dd. 2009. (Quick60 Alphabet Bks.). (ENG., Illus.). 12p. (J). pap. *(978-1-77540-003-5(4))* Iversen Publishing Ltd.

—Alphabet Book Ee. 2009. (Quick60 Alphabet Bks.). (ENG., Illus.). 12p. (J). pap. *(978-1-77540-004-2(2))* Iversen Publishing Ltd.

—Alphabet Book Ff. 2009. (Quick60 Alphabet Bks.). (ENG., Illus.). 12p. (J). pap. *(978-1-77540-005-9(0))* Iversen Publishing Ltd.

—Alphabet Book Gg. 2009. (Quick60 Alphabet Bks.). (ENG., Illus.). 12p. (J). pap. *(978-1-77540-006-6(9))* Iversen Publishing Ltd.

—Alphabet Book Hh. 2009. (Quick60 Alphabet Bks.). (ENG., Illus.). 12p. (J). pap. *(978-1-77540-007-3(7))* Iversen Publishing Ltd.

—Alphabet Book Ii. 2009. (Quick60 Alphabet Bks.). (ENG., Illus.). 12p. (J). pap. *(978-1-77540-008-0(5))* Iversen Publishing Ltd.

—Alphabet Book Jj. 2009. (Quick60 Alphabet Bks.). (ENG., Illus.). 12p. (J). pap. *(978-1-77540-009-7(3))* Iversen Publishing Ltd.

—Alphabet Book Kk. 2009. (Quick60 Alphabet Bks.). (ENG., Illus.). 12p. (J). pap. *(978-1-77540-010-3(7))* Iversen Publishing Ltd.

—Alphabet Book Ll. 2009. (Quick60 Alphabet Bks.). (ENG., Illus.). 12p. (J). pap. *(978-1-77540-011-0(5))* Iversen Publishing Ltd.

—Alphabet Book Mm. 2009. (ENG., Illus.). 12p. (J). pap. *(978-1-77540-012-7(3))* Iversen Publishing Ltd.

—Alphabet Book Nn. 2009. (Quick60 Alphabet Bks.). (ENG., Illus.). 12p. (J). pap. *(978-1-77540-013-4(1))* Iversen Publishing Ltd.

—Alphabet Book Oo. 2009. (Quick60 Alphabet Bks.). (ENG., Illus.). 12p. (J). pap. *(978-1-77540-014-1(X))* Iversen Publishing Ltd.

—Alphabet Book Pp. 2009. (Quick60 Alphabet Bks.). (ENG., Illus.). 12p. (J). pap. *(978-1-77540-015-8(8))* Iversen Publishing Ltd.

—Alphabet Book Qq. 2009. (Quick60 Alphabet Bks.). (ENG., Illus.). 12p. (J). pap. *(978-1-77540-016-5(6))* Iversen Publishing Ltd.

—Alphabet Book Zz. 2009. (Quick60 Alphabet Bks.). (ENG., Illus.). 12p. (J). pap. *(978-1-77540-025-7(5))* Iversen Publishing Ltd.

—A Day on the Mountain. 2010. (Quick60 Factual Bks.). (ENG., Illus.). 12p. (J). pap. *(978-1-77540-220-6(7))* Iversen Publishing Ltd.

—What Is It? 2009. (ENG., Illus.). 12p. (J). pap. *(978-1-77540-046-2(8))* Iversen Publishing Ltd.

The J-Files: Individual Title, 6 Packs. (Bookweb Ser.). 32p. (gr. 3-18). 34.00 *(978-0-7635-3941-2(4))* Rigby Education.

Jack: 6 Small Books. (gr. k-2). 23.00 *(978-0-7635-8497-9(5))* Rigby Education.

Jackson, Melanie. Tick Tock Terror, 1 vol. 2019. (Orca Currents Ser.). (ENG.). 144p. (J). (gr. 4-7). pap. 9.95 *(978-1-4598-1955-9(1))* Orca Bk. Pubs. USA.

Jackson, Tiffany D. Allegedly. (ENG.). (YA). (gr. 9). 2018. 416p. pap. 15.99 *(978-0-06-242265-1(0))* 2017. 400p. 18.99 *(978-0-06-242264-4(2))* HarperCollins Pubs. (Tegen, Katherine Bks).

Jacobs, Evan. Zombies! 2014. (Red Rhino Ser.). (J). lib. bdg. 18.40 *(978-0-606-36243-6(6))* Turtleback.

Jacobson, Jennifer. Scholastic Success with Reading & Math Jumbo Workbook, 1 vol. 2005. (ENG.). 320p. (gr. 4-4). pap., wbk. ed. 14.99 *(978-0-439-78603-4(7),* Teaching Resources) Scholastic, Inc.

James, Anne. ¡Ataque de las Hormigas! Ramirez, Alma B., tr. from ENG. Lewis, Anthony, illus. 2008. (Science Solves It! en Espanol Ser.). (SPA.). 32p. (J). (gr. -1-3). pap. 5.95 *(978-1-57565-278-8(1))* Astra Publishing Hse.

James Baldwin. Fifty Famous Stories Retold. 2009. (Illus.). 132p. pap. 5.95 *(978-1-60386-206-6(4),* Merchant Bks.) Rough Draft Printing.

James, Eric. Up & Down, 1 vol. 2012. (InfoMax Readers Ser.). (ENG., Illus.). 16p. (J). (gr. k-k). pap. 7.00 *(978-1-4488-8878-8(6),* 76321e24-b733-468c-bd29-cb3c7b9d04b8, Rosen Classroom) Rosen Publishing Group, Inc., The.

James Is Hiding: Individual Title, 6 Packs. (gr. 1-2). 22.00 *(978-0-7635-9162-5(9))* Rigby Education.

James, Karim. The Kids Time to Rhyme: Read & Rhyme at the same Time. 2009. 16p. pap. 14.99 *(978-1-4490-0424-8(5))* AuthorHouse.

James, Lincoln. Sal Sleeps In, 1 vol. 2006. (Neighborhood Readers Ser.). (ENG.). 8p. (gr. k-1). pap. 5.15 *(978-1-4042-5780-1(2),* 3ccfab18-4749-4780-93d3-fc4b7a34c502, Rosen Classroom) Rosen Publishing Group, Inc., The.

—The Street Fair, 1 vol. 2006. (Neighborhood Readers Ser.). (ENG.). 16p. (gr. 1-2). pap. 6.50 *(978-1-4042-7228-6(3),* 72c9d989-d77d-4ed8-987b-1f0ed02c9d13, Rosen Classroom) Rosen Publishing Group, Inc., The.

James, M.r. Oxford Bookworms Library: the Unquiet Grave - Short Stories: Level 4: 1400-Word Vocabulary. 3rd ed. 2008. (ENG., Illus.). 96p. 11.00 *(978-0-19-479191-5(2))* Oxford Univ. Pr., Inc.

James, Wayan. Chalise, Master of Maps, 1 vol. 2016. (Rosen REAL Readers: Social Studies Nonfiction / Fiction: Myself, My Community, My World Ser.). (ENG.). 12p. (gr. k-1). pap. 6.33 *(978-1-5081-2571-6(6),* b31b70ae-c03d-44fb-8ec1-23df2a64c8d4, Rosen Classroom) Rosen Publishing Group, Inc., The.

—Hot Days, Cold Days, 1 vol. 2016. (Rosen REAL Readers: STEM & STEAM Collection). (ENG.). 12p. (gr. k-1). pap. 6.33 *(978-1-5081-2419-1(1),* 777a82b9-4a46-4db2-a293-123a097bd8aa, Rosen Classroom) Rosen Publishing Group, Inc., The.

—The Marble Match, 1 vol. 2016. (Rosen REAL Readers: STEM & STEAM Collection). (ENG.). 8p. (gr. k-1). pap. 5.46 *(978-1-5081-2583-9(X),* f1787a41-08fd-4a40-8c65-c6750401bab4, Rosen Classroom) Rosen Publishing Group, Inc., The.

Jamiol, Paul. Bikers Are Animals: A Children's Book on Motorcycling. Habib, Linda, ed. 2009. 38p. pap. 14.95 *(978-1-60844-232-4(2))* Dog Ear Publishing, LLC.

Jankowski, Connie. All about Light & Sound, 1 vol. rev. ed. 2007. (Science: Informational Text Ser.). (ENG.). 32p. (J). (gr. 3-6). pap. 12.99 *(978-0-7439-0579-4(2))* Teacher Created Materials, Inc.

—Hippocrates: Making the Way for Medicine, 1 vol. rev. ed. 2007. (Science: Informational Text Ser.). (ENG.). 32p. (gr. 3-6). pap. 12.99 *(978-0-7439-0596-1(2))* Teacher Created Materials, Inc.

—Investigating the Human Body, 1 vol. rev. ed. 2007. (Science: Informational Text Ser.). (ENG., Illus.). 32p. (gr. 3-6). pap. 12.99 *(978-0-7439-0595-4(4))* Teacher Created Materials, Inc.

Janovich, Leah. Patty's Pictures. Billin-Frye, Paige, illus. 2010. 16p. (J). *(978-0-545-24820-4(5))* Scholastic, Inc.

Jarman, Julia. Molly & the Giant. Sholto, Walker, illus. 2005. (ENG.). 24p. (J). lib. bdg. 23.65 *(978-1-59646-746-0(0))* Dingles & Co.

—Stowaway!: Band 14/Ruby (Collins Big Cat) Oldroyd, Mark, illus. 2007. (Collins Big Cat Ser.). (ENG.). 48p. (J). (gr. 3-4). pap. 11.99 *(978-0-00-723088-4(5))* HarperCollins Pubs. Ltd. GBR. Dist: Independent Pubs. Group.

Jarrell, Pamela R. A Nice Cool Drink. Teeple, Jackie, illus. l.t. ed. 2005. (J). (gr. -1-k). pap. 10.95 *(978-1-57332-341-3(1))*; pap. 10.95 *(978-1-57332-340-6(3))* Carson-Dellosa Publishing, LLC. (HighReach Learning, Incorporated).

—Planting a Seed. Meier, Kerry L., illus. l.t. ed. 2006. 12p. (J). (gr. -1-k). pap. 10.95 *(978-1-57332-350-5(0),* HighReach Learning, Incorporated) Carson-Dellosa Publishing, LLC.

Jazynka, Kitson. National Geographic Readers: Buzz Aldrin (L3) 2018. (Readers Ser.). (Illus.). 48p. (J). (gr. 3-7). 4.99 *(978-1-4263-3206-7(8),* National Geographic Kids) Disney Publishing Worldwide.

—National Geographic Readers: Gallop! 100 Fun Facts about Horses (L3) 2018. (Readers Ser.). (Illus.). 48p. (J). (gr. 3-7). pap. 4.99 *(978-1-4263-3238-8(6),* National Geographic Kids) Disney Publishing Worldwide.

Jeffries, Katherine. Plants Grow: Lap Book. 2009. (My First Reader's Theater Set B Ser.). (J). 28.00 *(978-1-60634-985-4(6))* Benchmark Education Co.

—Tim's Head, Shoulders, Knees, & Toes. Price, Nick, illus. 2009. (Reader's Theater Nursery Rhymes & Songs Set B Ser.). 48p. (J). pap. *(978-1-60859-169-5(7))* Benchmark Education Co.

Jeffus, Sharon2006, as told by. Artsy Animals: Learn to Read. 2006. (Illus.). 70p. (J). 19.95 *(978-0-9715970-9-9(X))* Visual Manna.

Jenkins, Amanda. Mere Moments A Story of Pearl Harbor, the Day the Towers Fell. 2011. (Readers' & Writers' Genre Workshop Ser.). (J). pap. *(978-1-4509-3019-2(0))* Benchmark Education Co.

—The Strong & the Weak Hammurabi's Code, Tomb Robbers! A Story of Ancient Egypt. 2011. (Readers' & Writers' Genre Workshop Ser.). (YA). pap. *(978-1-4509-3020-8(4))* Benchmark Education Co.

Jenkins, Donna. When I Grow up, I Want to Be a Builder. 2010. 16p. pap. 10.49 *(978-1-4490-6072-5(2))* AuthorHouse.

—When I Grow up, I Want to Be a Football Player. 2010. 16p. pap. 10.49 *(978-1-4490-6496-9(5))* AuthorHouse.

Jenkins, Henry A. The Adventures of Monkey Squirrel & Frogman: Sand Trap. 2009. 16p. pap. 8.49 *(978-1-4343-7827-9(6))* AuthorHouse.

Jenkins, Jennifer Meghan. The 10 Deadliest Predators. 2008. 14.99 *(978-1-55448-502-4(9))* Scholastic Library Publishing.

Jenkins, Meghan. The 10 Most Amazing Birds. 2008. (J). 14.99 *(978-1-55448-532-1(0))* Scholastic Library Publishing.

Jennings, Sharon, et al, adapted by. Franklin's Pond Phantom. 2005. (Kids Can Read Ser.). (ENG., Illus.). 32p. (J). (gr. 1-2). 3.95 *(978-1-55337-719-1(2))*; 14.95 *(978-1-55337-718-4(4))* Kids Can Pr., Ltd. CAN. Dist: Hachette Bk. Group.

Jennings, Terry. Bird Watch, 8 bks. 2005. (QEB Readers). (Illus.). 24p. (J). (gr. -1-3). lib. bdg. 15.95 *(978-1-59566-078-7(X))* QEB Publishing Inc.

—Bugs & Slugs, 8 vols. 2005. (QEB Readers). (Illus.). 24p. (J). (gr. -1-3). lib. bdg. 15.95 *(978-1-59566-069-5(0))* QEB Publishing Inc.

Jessup, Dylan. We're All Americans, 1 vol. 2012. (InfoMax Readers Ser.). (ENG., Illus.). 24p. (J). (gr. 1-1). pap. 8.25 *(978-1-4488-9079-8(9),* 2ca6782d-ecb1-4883-b0b0-e3995b082381, Rosen Classroom) Rosen Publishing Group, Inc., The.

Jinkins, Lisa Heath. PB & J Otter Noodle Stories: Busy Day. 2005. (ENG.). 24p. (J). (gr. -1-1). pap. 3.99 *(978-0-7868-4282-7(2))* Disney Pr.

Jinks, Jenny. The Dog & the Fox. Wood, Hannah, illus. 2019. (Early Bird Readers — Yellow (Early Bird Stories (tm)) Ser.). (ENG.). 32p. (J). (gr. -1-2). 29.32 *(978-1-5415-4171-9(5),*

d70edd4f-ed5f-4894-8f04-16fded5e26ad, Lerner Pubns.) Lerner Publishing Group.
—Nana Ninja. Longcroft, Sean, illus. 2021. (Early Bird Readers — Gold (Early Bird Stories (tm)) Ser.). (ENG.). 32p. (J). (gr. k-3). 30.65 *(978-1-5415-9011-3(2),* 90ce0694-6cba-497e-a8f1-24d7183d35a0, Lerner Pubns.) Lerner Publishing Group.
—Seeds & Stuck in the Tree. Selbert, Kathryn, illus. 2019. (Early Bird Readers — Red (Early Bird Stories (tm)) Ser.). (ENG.). 32p. (J). (gr. -1-2). 30.65 *(978-1-5415-4165-8(0),* f31f1d08-2517-4133-8099-465b2a329ac9, Lerner Pubns.) Lerner Publishing Group.
Johns, Linda & Jones, Melanie Davis. I Can Do It! I Can Bowl!/I Can Ski!/I Can Do It All. Boles, Terry, illus. 2006. (ENG.). 93p. (J). (gr. k-2). pap. 9.95 *(978-0-531-16923-0(5),* Children's Pr.) Scholastic Library Publishing.
Johnson, Bruce. We Both Read-About Dogs. 2009. (ENG., Illus.). 44p. (J). pap. 5.99 *(978-1-60115-238-1(8))* Treasure Bay, Inc.
Johnson, Bruce & McKay, Sindy. Zoo Day/Dia Del Zoologico: Spanish/English Bilingual Edition (We Both Read - Level 1) Johnson, Meredith, illus. 2016. (We Both Read - Level 1 Ser.). (ENG & SPA.). 41p. (J). pap. 5.99 *(978-1-60115-078-3(4))* Treasure Bay, Inc.
Johnson, D. C. & Turner, Sandra. Let's Be Friends. Johnson, D. C. & Johnson, Darnell, illus. 2007. (J). per. 9.95 *(978-1-933556-66-6(8))* Publishers' Graphics, L.L.C.
Johnson, Errol. What's That Sound?, 1 vol. 2006. (Neighborhood Readers Ser.). (ENG., Illus.). 12p. (gr. k-1). pap. 5.90 *(978-1-4042-6738-1(7),* dee34506-d1ee-4047-a2c2-8897615c4ab4, Rosen Classroom) Rosen Publishing Group, Inc., The.
Johnson, Gee. The Octopus. Johnson, Gee, illus. 2010. (2G Marine Life Ser.). (ENG., Illus.). 20p. (J). (gr. k-2). pap. 9.60 *(978-1-61541-221-1(2))* American Reading Co.
Johnson, Gee & Zorzi, Gina. Tiger Sharks. 2015. (2G Marine Life Ser.). (ENG.). 24p. (J). (gr. k-2). pap. 8.00 *(978-1-61541-167-2(4))* American Reading Co.
Johnson, Jennifer. Gettysburg: The Bloodiest Battle of the Civil War. 2009. (24/7 Goes to War Ser.). (ENG.). 64p. (J). (gr. 5-8). lib. bdg. 22.44 *(978-0-531-25528-5(X));* (gr. 6-12). pap. 7.95 *(978-0-531-25453-0(4),* Watts, Franklin) Scholastic Library Publishing.
Johnson, Jo. Grandpa Seashells. 2017. (ENG., Illus.). 32p. (C). pap. 7.95 *(978-0-86388-997-4(2),* Y328929) Routledge.
Johnson, Juliette. Frog & Dog: Practicing the Short O Sound, 1 vol. 2016. (Rosen Phonics Readers Ser.). (ENG., Illus.). 8p. (J). (gr. -1-2). pap. *(978-1-5081-3079-6(5),* d7bb7a2a-fae8-4505-aff7-baa9f6e0e146, Rosen Classroom) Rosen Publishing Group, Inc., The.
Johnson, Margaret. Gone! Level Starter/Beginner American English. 2010. (Cambridge Experience Readers Ser.). (ENG., Illus.). 48p. pap. 14.75 *(978-0-521-14904-4(5))* Cambridge Univ. Pr.
Johnson, Rebecca L. Microquests: Classroom Set. 2008. pap. 43.95 *(978-0-8225-9113-9(8))* Lerner Publishing Group.
—Microquests: Complete Set. 2008. pap. 263.95 *(978-0-8225-9377-5(7))* Lerner Publishing Group.
JohnsonMargaret. Gone! Starter/Beginner. 2009. (Cambridge Experience Readers Ser.). (ENG.). 48p. pap. 14.75 *(978-84-8323-509-6(9))* Cambridge Univ. Pr.
—Parties & Presents: Three Short Stories Level 2 Elementary/Lower-Intermediate. 2010. (Cambridge Experience Readers Ser.). (ENG., Illus.). 62p. pap. 14.75 *(978-84-8323-836-3(5))* Cambridge Univ. Pr.
—Running Wild Level 3 Lower-Intermediate. 2009. (Cambridge Experience Readers Ser.). (ENG.). 80p. pap. 14.75 *(978-84-8323-501-0(3))* Cambridge Univ. Pr.
Jonas, Georgina. Anda (the College Collection Set 1 - for Reluctant Readers), 6, 3. 2016. (College Collection). (ENG., Illus.). 48p. (YA). pap. 4.95 *(978-1-78583-101-0(1))* Crown Hse. Publishing LLC.
—Art Attack (the College Collection Set 1 - for Reluctant Readers), 6, 6. 2016. (College Collection). (ENG., Illus.). 128p. (YA). pap. 6.95 *(978-1-78583-106-5(2))* Crown Hse. Publishing LLC.
—The College Collection Set 1 - for Reluctant Readers, 6. 2016. (College Collection). (ENG., Illus.). 416p. (YA). pap. 24.95 *(978-1-78583-107-2(0))* Crown Hse. Publishing LLC.
—Jim Jam (the College Collection Set 1 - for Reluctant Readers), 6, 1. 2016. (College Collection). (ENG., Illus.). 64p. (YA). pap. 4.95 *(978-1-78583-102-7(X))* Crown Hse. Publishing LLC.
—Luca (the College Collection Set 1 - for Reluctant Readers), 6, 4. 2016. (College Collection). (ENG., Illus.). 64p. (YA). pap. 4.95 *(978-1-78583-103-4(8))* Crown Hse. Publishing LLC.
—Nolan (the College Collection Set 1 - for Reluctant Readers), 6, 5. 2016. (College Collection). (ENG., Illus.). 48p. (YA). pap. 4.95 *(978-1-78583-104-1(6))* Crown Hse. Publishing LLC.
—Woody (the College Collection Set 1 - for Reluctant Readers), 6, 2. 2016. (College Collection). (ENG., Illus.). 64p. (YA). pap. 4.95 *(978-1-78583-105-8(4))* Crown Hse. Publishing LLC.
Jones, Cath. Meg & Rat & Puff! Puff! Puff! Pryce, Adam, illus. 2019. (Early Bird Readers — Pink (Early Bird Stories (tm)) Ser.). (ENG.). 32p. (J). (gr. -1-2). 30.65 *(978-1-5415-4158-0(8),* 38fc0ea5-c23d-470d-b052-032eb0b685e0, Lerner Pubns.) Lerner Publishing Group.
—The Smart Hat. Nicholls, Paul, illus. 2019. (Early Bird Readers — Blue (Early Bird Stories (tm)) Ser.). (ENG.). 32p. (J). (gr. -1-2). pap. 9.99 *(978-1-5415-4614-1(8),* 45322c5b-4f7e-41f8-9904-91f3dc42db3d) Lerner Publishing Group.
Jones, Milo. Snow Friends. Lewis, Stephen, illus. 2010. 16p. (J). pap. *(978-0-545-24823-5(X))* Scholastic, Inc.
Jones, Shelley V. & Gunn, Barbara. Read Well Magazine Unit 20: Slanted Text. 2003. (Read Well Level K Ser.). (Illus.). 8p. (J). *(978-1-59318-104-8(3))* Cambium Education, Inc.
—Shells on the Shore: Read Well Level K Unit 14 Storybook. Jerde, Susan, illus. 2003. (Read Well Level K Ser.). 20p. (J). *(978-1-57035-685-8(8),* 55546) Cambium Education, Inc.
Jones, Stephen Anderton. America Is Good. 2008. 60p. (gr. -1). pap. 22.50 *(978-1-4343-6321-3(X))* AuthorHouse.
Jones, Tammy. At the Shore. 2009. (Sight Word Readers Set A Ser.). (J). 3.49 net. *(978-1-60719-137-7(7))* Newmark Learning LLC.
—Big Pet, Little Pet. 2009. (Sight Word Readers Set A Ser.). (J). 3.49 net. *(978-1-60719-153-7(9))* Newmark Learning LLC.
—Count Around the Room. 2009. (Sight Word Readers Set A Ser.). (J). 3.49 net. *(978-1-60719-157-5(1))* Newmark Learning LLC.
—Count at the Baseball Field. 2009. (Sight Word Readers Set A Ser.). (J). 3.49 net. *(978-1-60719-156-8(3))* Newmark Learning LLC.
—Count on Me. 2009. (Sight Word Readers Set A Ser.). (J). *(978-1-60719-154-4(7))* Newmark Learning LLC.
—I Am Active. 2009. (Sight Word Readers Set A Ser.). (J). *(978-1-60719-139-1(3))* Newmark Learning LLC.
—I Go! 2009. (Sight Word Readers Set A Ser.). (J). 3.49 net. *(978-1-60719-143-8(1))* Newmark Learning LLC.
—I Like the Spring! 2009. (Sight Word Readers Set A Ser.). (J). 3.49 net. *(978-1-60719-138-4(5))* Newmark Learning LLC.
—I Like to Play Sports. 2009. (Sight Word Readers Set A Ser.). (J). 3.49 net. *(978-1-60719-135-3(0))* Newmark Learning LLC.
—In the Water. 2009. (Sight Word Readers Set A Ser.). (J). 3.49 net. *(978-1-60719-142-1(3))* Newmark Learning LLC.
—Jobs Around Town. 2009. (Sight Word Readers Set A Ser.). (J). 3.49 net. *(978-1-60719-158-2(X))* Newmark Learning LLC.
—Look at the Coins. 2009. (Sight Word Readers Set A Ser.). (J). 3.49 net. *(978-1-60719-155-1(5))* Newmark Learning LLC.
—Look at the Shapes. 2009. (Sight Word Readers Set A Ser.). (J). 3.49 net. *(978-1-60719-152-0(0))* Newmark Learning LLC.
—Look at the Sky. 2009. (Sight Word Readers Set A Ser.). (J). 3.49 net. *(978-1-60719-141-4(5))* Newmark Learning LLC.
—Look at the Weather. 2009. (Sight Word Readers Set A Ser.). (J). *(978-1-60719-140-7(7))* Newmark Learning LLC.
—My Family. 2009. (Sight Word Readers Set A Ser.). (J). 3.49 net. *(978-1-60719-148-3(2))* Newmark Learning LLC.
—My Home. 2009. (Sight Word Readers Set A Ser.). (J). 3.49 net. *(978-1-60719-144-5(X))* Newmark Learning LLC.
—My Pet. 2009. (Sight Word Readers Set A Ser.). (J). 3.49 net. *(978-1-60719-145-2(8))* Newmark Learning LLC.
—My Town. 2009. (Sight Word Readers Set A Ser.). (J). *(978-1-60719-147-6(4))* Newmark Learning LLC.
—We Go to School. 2009. (Sight Word Readers Set A Ser.). (J). 3.49 net. *(978-1-60719-146-9(6))* Newmark Learning LLC.
—We Have Fruit. 2009. (Sight Word Readers Set A Ser.). (J). *(978-1-60719-136-0(9))* Newmark Learning LLC.
—We Like Birthdays. 2009. (Sight Word Readers Set A Ser.). (J). 3.49 net. *(978-1-60719-149-0(0))* Newmark Learning LLC.
—What Has Stripes? 2009. (Sight Word Readers Set A Ser.). (J). 3.49 net. *(978-1-60719-151-3(2))* Newmark Learning LLC.
—What Is the Time? 2009. (Sight Word Readers Set A Ser.). (J). 3.49 net. *(978-1-60719-150-6(4))* Newmark Learning LLC.
Jordan, Apple. The Right Track (Disney Frozen: Northern Lights) RH Disney, illus. 2017. (Step into Reading Ser.). (ENG.). 24p. (J). (gr. -1-1). pap. 4.99 *(978-0-7364-3588-8(3),* RH/Disney) Random Hse. Children's Bks.
—Star Song. 2016. (Barbie Step into Reading Level 2 Ser.). lib. bdg. 14.75 *(978-0-606-38885-6(0))* Turtleback.
Jordan, Shirley J. Egypt, 1 vol. rev. ed. 2007. (Social Studies: Informational Text Ser.). (ENG.). 32p. (gr. 4-8). pap. 11.99 *(978-0-7439-0428-5(1))* Teacher Created Materials, Inc.
—Hatshepsut: First Female Pharaoh, 1 vol. rev. ed. 2007. (Social Studies: Informational Text Ser.). (ENG.). 32p. (gr. 4-8). pap. 11.99 *(978-0-7439-0429-2(X))* Teacher Created Materials, Inc.
The Journal: Dear Future II: Individual Title Six-Packs. (Action Packs Ser.). 104p. (gr. 3-5). 44.00 *(978-0-7635-8417-7(7))* Rigby Education.
Joven, C. C. Baseball Buzz. Shems, Ed, illus. 2017. (Sports Illustrated Kids Starting Line Readers Ser.). (ENG.). 32p. (J). (gr. -1-1). lib. bdg. 22.65 *(978-1-4965-4252-6(5),* 133931, Stone Arch Bks.) Capstone.
—Basketball Break. López, Álex, illus. 2017. (Sports Illustrated Kids Starting Line Readers Ser.). (ENG.). 32p. (J). (gr. -1-1). lib. bdg. 22.65 *(978-1-4965-4253-3(3),* 133932, Stone Arch Bks.) Capstone.
Joyce, Jeffrey. A Week with Nate, 1 vol. 2012. (InfoMax Readers Ser.). (ENG., Illus.). 16p. (J). (gr. k-k). pap. 7.00 *(978-1-4488-8908-2(1),* aa9c0e8b-a8c4-41e7-bbf7-8185025e1660, Rosen Classroom) Rosen Publishing Group, Inc., The.
Joyner, Michael. Na Anijoi Sigwa - the Three Pigs. 2015. (ENG & CHR., Illus.). 88p. pap. 11.99 *(978-1-329-31978-3(8))* Lulu Pr., Inc.
—Na Anijoi Wesa Anida Ale Jitaga Usdi - the Three Kittens & Chicken Little. 2016. (ENG & CHR., Illus.). 68p. pap. 10.99 *(978-1-329-93340-8(0))* Lulu Pr., Inc.
—Na Anijoi Wesa Anida Ale Jitaga Usdi / Jalagi-Yonega Didehlogwasdodi - the Three Kittens & Chicken Little / Cherokee-English Dictionary. 2016. (ENG & CHR., Illus.). 42p. pap. 9.99 *(978-1-329-93441-2(5))* Lulu Pr., Inc.
—Na Anijoi Yona - the Three Bears. 2015. (ENG & CHR., Illus.). 60p. pap. 11.99 *(978-1-329-35573-6(3))* Lulu Pr., Inc.
—Na Usdi Agigage Jitaga Agisi - the Little Red Hen. 2015. (ENG & CHR., Illus.). 82p. pap. 11.99 *(978-1-329-22721-7(2))* Lulu Pr., Inc.
Juel, Connie, et al. Ready Readers: Collection. 2005. (J). (gr. 2-18). 698.50 *(978-0-7652-6094-9(8))* Modern Curriculum Pr.
—Ready Readers: Nonfiction Favorites. 2005. (J). (gr. k-18). 699.95 *(978-0-7652-6089-5(1));* (gr. 1-18). 469.95 *(978-0-7652-6093-2(X))* Modern Curriculum Pr.
—Ready Readers: Set 1 Collection. 2005. (J). (gr. k-18). 910.50 *(978-0-7652-6086-4(7));* (gr. 1-18). 793.50 *(978-0-7652-6090-1(5))* Modern Curriculum Pr.
—Ready Readers: Set 2 Collection. 2005. (J). (gr. k-18). 979.95 *(978-0-7652-6087-1(5));* (gr. 1-18). 1325.95 *(978-0-7652-6091-8(3))* Modern Curriculum Pr.
—Ready Readers: Set 3 Collection. 2005. (J). (gr. k-18). 793.50 *(978-0-7652-6088-8(3));* (gr. 1-18). 1138.50 *(978-0-7652-6092-5(1))* Modern Curriculum Pr.
Jules, Jacqueline. Abuela's Special Letters. Smith, Kim, illus. 2018. (Sofia Martinez Ser.). (ENG.). 32p. (J). (gr. k-2). pap. 5.95 *(978-1-5158-0730-8(4),* 133612, Picture Window Bks.) Capstone.
—Shopping Trip Trouble Smith, Kim, illus. 2018. (Sofia Martinez Ser.). (ENG.). 32p. (J). (gr. k-2). pap. 5.95 *(978-1-5158-0731-5(2),* 133613, Picture Window Bks.) Capstone.
Jump & Thump! Individual Title Six-Packs. (gr. -1-2). 23.00 *(978-0-7635-8802-1(4))* Rigby Education.
The Jungle: Individual Title Six-Packs. (Sails Literacy Ser.). 16p. (gr. k-18). 27.00 *(978-0-7635-4388-4(8))* Rigby Education.
Jungle Fun, 6 vols. 2017. (Jungle Fun Ser.). (ENG.). 24p. (gr. 1-1). 75.81 *(978-1-5081-6182-0(8),* 188592bc-f925-4efa-9d08-37e27ce6a746, PowerKids Pr.) Rosen Publishing Group, Inc., The.
Jungman, Ann. The Footballing Frog: Band 14/Ruby (Collins Big Cat) Burnett, Seb, illus. 2007. (Collins Big Cat Ser.). (ENG.). 80p. (J). (gr. 3-4). pap. 11.99 *(978-0-00-723087-7(7))* HarperCollins Pubs. Ltd. GBR. Dist: Independent Pubs. Group.
The junk Box 6 Packs. Individual Title. (gr. 1-2). 22.00 *(978-0-7635-9170-0(X))* Rigby Education.
The Junk-Food Files. 2003. (Illus.). pap. 5.60 *(978-0-7398-7513-1(2))* Steck-Vaughn.
Junyk, Myra. The 10 Greatest Presidents. 2007. (J). 14.99 *(978-1-55448-457-7(X))* Scholastic Library Publishing.
—The 10 Mightiest Rivers. 2008. (J). 14.99 *(978-1-55448-519-2(3))* Scholastic Library Publishing.
—The 10 Most Defining Moments of the Civil War. 2008. (J). 14.99 *(978-1-55448-518-5(5))* Scholastic Library Publishing.
Just Ducky Board Book Set 800794, 3. 2005. (J). bds. *(978-1-59794-023-8(2))* Environments, Inc.
Just My Luck! 6 Packs. Individual Title. (Literatura 2000 Ser.). (gr. 1-2). 28.00 *(978-0-7635-0139-6(5))* Rigby Education.
Just Right: KinderConcepts Individual Title Six-Packs. (Kinderstarters Ser.). 8p. (gr. -1-1). 21.00 *(978-0-7635-8738-3(9))* Rigby Education.
Just the Right Word! (gr. k-3). 106.00 *(978-0-7362-2594-6(3))* CENGAGE Learning.
Justice, Laura M. & Sofka, Amy E. Engaging Children with Print: Building Early Literacy Skills Through Quality Read-Alouds. 2010. (ENG., Illus.). 214p. 79.00 *(978-1-60623-536-2(2));* pap. 32.00 *(978-1-60623-535-5(4))* Guilford Pubns. (Guilford Pr., The).
K Take-Home Readers Blms Set. 2003. (Metro Reading Ser.). (gr. k). *(978-1-58120-608-1(9))* Metropolitan Teaching & Learning Co.
Kachur, Matthew. A Miracle Material: Set Of 6. 2011. (Navigators Ser.). (J). 48.00 net. *(978-1-4108-0430-3(5))* Benchmark Education Co.
Kalar, Bonnie. At Dawn. Spreen, Kathe, illus. Date not set. 8p. (J). (gr. -1-2). pap. *(978-1-891619-24-3(1))* Corona Pr.
—At the Lake. Spreen, Kathe, illus. Date not set. 12p. (J). (gr. -1-2). pap. *(978-1-891619-34-2(9))* Corona Pr.
—At the Pond. Spreen, Kathe, illus. Date not set. 8p. (J). (gr. -1-2). pap. *(978-1-891619-07-6(1))* Corona Pr.
—At the Zoo. Spreen, Kathe, illus. Date not set. 8p. (J). (gr. -1-2). pap. *(978-1-891619-18-2(7))* Corona Pr.
—Beth & Thad. Spreen, Kathe, illus. Date not set. 12p. (J). (gr. -1-2). pap. *(978-1-891619-17-5(9))* Corona Pr.
—The Bird & the Shirt. Spreen, Kathe, illus. Date not set. 12p. (J). (gr. -1-2). pap. *(978-1-891619-30-4(6))* Corona Pr.
—Burt. Spreen, Kathe, illus. Date not set. 8p. (J). (gr. -1-2). pap. *(978-1-891619-31-1(4))* Corona Pr.
—Chuck & the Chick. Spreen, Kathe, illus. Date not set. 8p. (J). (gr. -1-2). pap. *(978-1-891619-16-8(0))* Corona Pr.
—The Clown. Spreen, Kathe, illus. Date not set. 12p. (J). (gr. -1-2). pap. *(978-1-891619-22-9(5))* Corona Pr.
—The Cook & the Crook. Spreen, Kathe, illus. Date not set. 12p. (J). (gr. -1-2). pap. *(978-1-891619-29-8(2))* Corona Pr.
—The Crows. Spreen, Kathe, illus. Date not set. 8p. (J). (gr. -1-2). pap. *(978-1-891619-28-1(4))* Corona Pr.
—A Dream. Spreen, Kathe, illus. Date not set. 12p. (J). (gr. -1-2). pap. *(978-1-891619-23-6(3))* Corona Pr.
—Early Phonetic Readers - Set A, 5 bks., Set. Spreen, Kathe, illus. Incl. Bob. pap. *(978-1-891619-01-4(2));* Cat & the Ant. pap. *(978-1-891619-02-1(0));* Gus on the Bus. pap. *(978-1-891619-03-8(9));* Hen & the Jet. pap. *(978-1-891619-05-2(5));* Tim & Kim. pap. *(978-1-891619-04-5(7));* 8p. (J). (gr. -1-2). 1998. (Illus.). 8.25 *(978-1-891619-00-7(4))* Corona Pr.
—Early Phonetic Readers - Set B, 5 bks., Set. Spreen, Kathe, illus. Incl. At the Pond. pap. *(978-1-891619-07-6(1));* Fran & the Doll. pap. *(978-1-891619-09-0(8));* Fred. pap. *(978-1-891619-10-6(1));* Stan & His Sled. pap. *(978-1-891619-08-3(X));* Trip. pap. *(978-1-891619-11-3(X));* 8p. (J). (gr. -1-2). (Illus.). 8.25 *(978-1-891619-06-9(3))* Corona Pr.
—Early Phonetic Readers - Set C, 20 bks., Set. Spreen, Kathe, illus. Incl. At Dawn. 8p. pap. *(978-1-891619-24-3(1));* At the Zoo. 8p. pap. *(978-1-891619-18-2(7));* Beth & Thad. 12p. pap. *(978-1-891619-17-5(9));* Bird & the Shirt. 12p. pap. *(978-1-891619-30-4(6));* Bright Light. 8p. 5.25 hd *(978-1-891619-32-8(2));* Burt. 8p. pap. *(978-1-891619-31-1(4));* Chuck & the Chick. 8p. pap. *(978-1-891619-16-8(0));* Clown. 12p. pap. *(978-1-891619-22-9(5));* Cook & the Crook. 12p. pap. *(978-1-891619-29-8(2));* Crows. 8p. pap. *(978-1-891619-28-1(4));* Dream. 12p. pap. *(978-1-891619-23-6(3));* Gail Sails. 12p. pap. *(978-1-891619-20-5(9));* Gay & Jay Play. 8p. pap. *(978-1-891619-19-9(5));* Jack. 12p. pap. *(978-1-891619-13-7(6));* Joan's Coat. 12p. pap. *(978-1-891619-21-2(7));* Josh & the Fish. 8p. pap. *(978-1-891619-14-4(4));* Lew & His New Cap. 8p. pap. *(978-1-891619-27-4(6));* Mark at the Farm. 12p. pap. *(978-1-891619-25-0(X));* Scouts. 8p. pap. *(978-1-891619-26-7(8));* Sheep & the Bee. 8p. pap. *(978-1-891619-15-1(2));* (J). (gr. -1-2). (Illus.). 38.50 *(978-1-891619-12-0(8))* Corona Pr.
—Early Phonetic Readers - Set D, 3 bks., Set. Spreen, Kathe, illus. Incl. At the Lake. 12p. pap. *(978-1-891619-34-2(9));* Mike. 8p. pap. *(978-1-891619-35-9(7));* Rose & the Mole. 12p. pap. *(978-1-891619-36-6(5));* (J). (gr. -1-2). (Illus.). 6.25 *(978-1-891619-33-5(0))* Corona Pr.
—Fran & the Doll. Spreen, Kathe, illus. Date not set. 8p. (J). (gr. -1-2). pap. *(978-1-891619-09-0(8))* Corona Pr.
—Fred. Spreen, Kathe, illus. Date not set. 8p. (J). (gr. -1-2). pap. *(978-1-891619-10-6(1))* Corona Pr.
—Gail Sails. Spreen, Kathe, illus. Date not set. 12p. (J). (gr. -1-2). pap. *(978-1-891619-20-5(9))* Corona Pr.
—Gay & Jay Play. Spreen, Kathe, illus. Date not set. 8p. (J). (gr. -1-2). pap. *(978-1-891619-19-9(5))* Corona Pr.
—Joan's Coat. Spreen, Kathe, illus. Date not set. 12p. (J). (gr. -1-2). pap. *(978-1-891619-21-2(7))* Corona Pr.
—Lew & His New Cap. Spreen, Kathe, illus. Date not set. 8p. (J). (gr. -1-2). pap. *(978-1-891619-27-4(6))* Corona Pr.
—Mark at the Farm. Spreen, Kathe, illus. Date not set. 12p. (J). (gr. -1-2). pap. *(978-1-891619-25-0(X))* Corona Pr.
—Mike. Spreen, Kathe, illus. Date not set. 8p. (J). (gr. -1-2). pap. *(978-1-891619-35-9(7))* Corona Pr.
—Rose & the Mole. Spreen, Kathe, illus. Date not set. 12p. (J). (gr. -1-2). pap. *(978-1-891619-36-6(5))* Corona Pr.
—The Sheep & the Bee. Spreen, Kathe, illus. Date not set. 8p. (J). (gr. -1-2). pap. *(978-1-891619-15-1(2))* Corona Pr.
—Stan & His Sled. Spreen, Kathe, illus. Date not set. 8p. (J). (gr. -1-2). pap. *(978-1-891619-08-3(X))* Corona Pr.
—The Trip. Spreen, Kathe, illus. Date not set. 8p. (J). (gr. -1-2). pap. *(978-1-891619-11-3(X))* Corona Pr.
Kalinowski, Delphine. Frog's Fruit Stand, 1 vol. 2006. (Neighborhood Readers Ser.). (ENG.). 8p. (gr. 1-2). pap. 5.15 *(978-1-4042-6807-4(3),* 29147459-03f5-47c5-94ba-59e87f89d790, Rosen Classroom) Rosen Publishing Group, Inc., The.
Kammerer, Heltiare. Pa'a Pono. 2008. (ENG & HAW.). (J). lib. bdg. *(978-0-9773495-7-9(8))* Na Kamalei Koolauloa Early Education Program.
Kann, Victoria. Cherry Blossom. 2015. (Pinkalicious I Can Read Ser.). (J). lib. bdg. 13.55 *(978-0-606-36480-5(3))* Turtleback.
—Pinkalicious & the Babysitter. Kann, Victoria, illus. 2017. (I Can Read Level 1 Ser.). (ENG., Illus.). 32p. (J). (gr. -1-3). 16.99 *(978-0-06-256689-8(X));* pap. 4.99 *(978-0-06-256688-1(1))* HarperCollins Pubs. (HarperCollins).
—Pinkalicious at the Fair. Kann, Victoria, illus. 2018. (I Can Read Level 1 Ser.). (ENG., Illus.). 32p. (J). (gr. -1-3). 16.99 *(978-0-06-256694-2(6));* pap. 5.99 *(978-0-06-256691-1(1))* HarperCollins Pubs. (HarperCollins).
—Story Time. 2016. (Pinkalicious I Can Read Ser.). (J). lib. bdg. 13.55 *(978-0-606-38758-3(7))* Turtleback.
Karsten, Dylan. The Witch & the Wand: Practicing the W Sound, 1 vol. 2016. (Rosen Phonics Readers Ser.). (ENG., Illus.). 12p. (J). (gr. -1-2). pap. *(978-1-5081-3046-8(9),* 7d6a8226-9103-4af2-93ef-bbf8c10a8225, Rosen Classroom) Rosen Publishing Group, Inc., The.
Katschke, Judy. Carlos Gets the Sneezes. 2019. (Branches Early Ch Bks). (ENG.). 96p. (J). (gr. 2-4). 15.96 *(978-1-64310-824-7(7))* Penworthy Co., LLC, The.
—Carlos Gets the Sneezes. 2018. (Magic School Bus Rides Again — Branches Ser.: 2). lib. bdg. 14.75 *(978-0-606-41171-4(2))* Turtleback.
Katz, Ben & Nyman, Debbie. The 10 Greatest Sports Dynasties. 2008. 14.99 *(978-1-55448-525-3(8))* Scholastic Library Publishing.
Kawa, Katie. The Fearless Honey Badger, 1 vol. 2013. (Rosen Readers Ser.). (ENG.). 24p. (J). (gr. 3-3). pap. 8.25 *(978-1-4777-2513-9(X),* 758f81bf-5aca-4183-b577-47f514ecb49b); pap. 49.50 *(978-1-4777-2514-6(8))* Rosen Publishing Group, Inc., The. (Rosen Classroom).
Kelley, K. C. Baby Bears. 2018. (Spot Baby Animals Ser.). (ENG., Illus.). 16p. (J). (gr. -1-2). pap. 7.99 *(978-1-68152-250-0(0),* 14842) Amicus.
—Blast off to Space. 2018. (Amazing Adventures Ser.). (ENG.). 16p. (J). (gr. k-2). lib. bdg. *(978-1-68151-315-7(3),* 14881); (Illus.). pap. 7.99 *(978-1-68152-271-5(3),* 14887) Amicus.
—Flowers. 2018. (Spot Awesome Nature Ser.). (ENG.). 16p. (J). (gr. -1-2). pap. 7.99 *(978-1-68152-247-0(0),* 14822) Amicus.
—Oceans. 2018. (Spot Awesome Nature Ser.). (ENG.). 16p. (J). (gr. -1-2). pap. 7.99 *(978-1-68152-248-7(9),* 14823) Amicus.
—Seasons. 2018. (Spot Awesome Nature Ser.). (ENG.). 16p. (J). (gr. -1-2). pap. 7.99 *(978-1-68152-245-6(4),* 14824) Amicus.
—Space. 2018. (Spot Awesome Nature Ser.). (ENG.). 16p. (J). (gr. -1-2). pap. 7.99 *(978-1-68152-249-4(7),* 14825) Amicus.
—Trees. 2018. (Spot Awesome Nature Ser.). (ENG.). 16p. (J). (gr. -1-2). pap. 7.99 *(978-1-68152-246-3(2),* 14826) Amicus.
—Weather. 2018. (Spot Awesome Nature Ser.). (ENG.). 16p. (J). (gr. -1-2). pap. 7.99 *(978-1-68152-244-9(6),* 14827) Amicus.
Kelly, James Floyd. DK Readers L2: Story of Coding. 2017. (DK Readers Level 2 Ser.). (ENG., Illus.). 48p. (J). (gr. k-2). pap. 3.99 *(978-1-4654-6242-8(2),* DK Children) Dorling Kindersley Publishing, Inc.
Kelly, Maoliosa. My Party. 2005. (Big Cat Ser.). (gr. k-2). pap. 6.50 *(978-1-60457-020-5(2))* Pacific Learning, Inc.
—My Party: Band 00/Lilac (Collins Big Cat) Lumb, Steve, illus. 2005. (Collins Big Cat Ser.). (ENG.). 16p. (J). (gr. -1-k). pap. 7.99 *(978-0-00-718533-7(2))* HarperCollins Pubs. Ltd. GBR. Dist: Independent Pubs. Group.
—What Am I?: Band 00/Lilac (Collins Big Cat) Blake, Beccy, illus. 2007. (Collins Big Cat Ser.). (ENG.). 16p. (J). (gr. -1-k). pap. 7.99 *(978-0-00-718679-2(7))* HarperCollins Pubs. Ltd. GBR. Dist: Independent Pubs. Group.
Kelly, Sharon L. C. M. Coco's Vineyard Vacation: Double Fun on Martha's Vineyard. Galbraith, Alison L., illus. 2005. 40p. (J). 16.95 *(978-0-9766283-0-9(9))* Secret Garden Bookworks.
Kemp, Kristin. Of Mice & Men: An Instructional Guide for Literature. rev. ed. 2015. (Great Works). (ENG., Illus.). 72p. (gr. 9-12). pap. 9.99 *(978-1-4807-8508-3(3))* Shell Educational Publishing.
Kennedy, J. Aday. Stella, the Fire Farting Dragon. Foster, Jack, illus. 2011. 20p. pap. 10.95 *(978-1-61633-149-8(6))* Guardian Angel Publishing, Inc.

PQR

Kennedy, Laura. Pat's Vat Goes Splat: A Lesson in Honesty. 2013. 12p. pap. 10.99 *(978-0-9836230-1-4(5))* Kennedy Enterprises, LLC.

Kennedy, Tim, compiled by. The Road Less Traveled: Seventh Grade Reader. 2004. (Reading to Learn Ser.). (Illus.). v, 265p. (J). *(978-0-87813-852-4(8))* Christian Light Pubns., Inc.

Kenrick, Joanna. Tears of a Friend. 2004. (Shades Ser.). 56p. (J). pap. *(978-0-237-52731-0(6))* Evans Brothers, Ltd.

Kenshole, Fiona. Dolphin Readers 3. Let's Go to the Rainforest. Intenational Edition. Wright, Craig, ed. 2010. (ENG., Illus.). 28p. 5.00 *(978-0-19-440106-7(5))* Oxford Univ. Pr., Inc.

Kernan, Elizabeth. Dolly Takes a Drive, 1 vol. 2006. (Neighborhood Readers Ser.). (ENG., Illus.). 12p. (gr. k-1). pap. 5.90 *(978-1-4042-6754-1(9)*, 97d0c27e-977d-4c3f-9bd7-0535b33db133, Rosen Classroom) Rosen Publishing Group, Inc., The.

—Fred's Bread, 1 vol. 2006. (Neighborhood Readers Ser.). (ENG., Illus.). 16p. (gr. 1-2). pap. 6.50 *(978-1-4042-7010-7(8)*, 089be93a-6d00-4b74-b519-a395f6855a25, Rosen Classroom) Rosen Publishing Group, Inc., The.

—Patty's Pictures, 1 vol. 2006. (Neighborhood Readers Ser.). (ENG.). 12p. (gr. k-1). pap. 5.90 *(978-1-4042-6471-7(X)*, ee545f66-6b81-4a35-8abe-dd574071ee79, Rosen Classroom) Rosen Publishing Group, Inc., The.

Kerrigan, Juliet. Life & Death in an Iron Age Hill Fort: Band 12/Copper (Collins Big Cat) 2015. (Collins Big Cat Ser.). (ENG., Illus.). 32p. (J). (gr. 3-3). pap. 10.99 *(978-0-00-812773-2(5))* HarperCollins Pubs. Ltd. GBR. Dist: Independent Pubs. Group.

—Underwater Treasure: Band 13/Topaz. 2016. (Collins Big Cat Ser.). (ENG.). 32p. (J). (gr. 2-3). pap. 10.99 *(978-0-00-816384-6(7))* HarperCollins Pubs. Ltd. GBR. Dist: Independent Pubs. Group.

Kertell, Lynn Masien. Bob Books - First Stories Box Set | Phonics, Ages 4 & up, Kindergarten (Stage 1: Starting to Read), 1 vol. Sullivan, Dana, illus. 2015. (Bob Bks.). (ENG.). 12p. (J). (gr. -1-1). pap., pap., pap. 17.99 *(978-0-545-73409-7(6))* Scholastic, Inc.

—BOB Books: Beginning Readers Workbook. 2018. (Bob Bks.). (ENG., Illus.). 224p. (J). (gr. -1-k). pap. 12.99 *(978-1-338-22677-5(0))* Scholastic, Inc.

—BOB Books: Developing Readers Workbook. 2018. (Bob Bks.). (ENG.). 224p. (J). (gr. k-2). pap. 12.99 *(978-1-338-22679-9(7))* Scholastic, Inc.

—BOB Books: Emerging Readers Workbook. 2018. (Bob Bks.). (ENG.). 224p. (J). (gr. -1-k). pap. 12.99 *(978-1-338-22678-2(9))* Scholastic, Inc.

—Cupcake Surprise! 2012. (BOB Books: Scholastic Readers Level 1 Ser.). lib. bdg. 13.55 *(978-0-606-23910-3(3))* Turtleback.

Kerven, Rosalind. Sparrow, the Crow & the Pearl. Williamson, Melanie, illus. 2005. (ENG.). 24p. (J). lib. bdg. 23.65 *(978-1-59646-754-5(1))* Dingles & Co.

Kessler, Colleen & Benchmark Education Co. Staff. Rodrigo & the Dogs. 2014. (Text Connections Ser.). (J). (gr. 6). *(978-1-4900-1525-5(6))* Benchmark Education Co.

Khan, Sarah. Birds Lift-the-Flap. Scott, Peter, illus. 2004. (Luxury Lift-the-Flap Ser.). 16p. (J). (gr. 1-18). 11.95 *(978-0-7945-0714-5(X)*, Usborne) EDC Publishing.

Khatreja, Himani. Free the Galaxy. 2015. (LEGO Star Wars DK Reader Ser.). lib. bdg. 13.55 *(978-0-606-37410-1(8))* Turtleback.

The Kids from Quiller's Bend: Individual Title Six-Packs. (Action Packs Ser.). 120p. (gr. 3-5). 44.00 *(978-0-7635-8432-0(0))* Rigby Education.

Kincaid, S. J. Catalyst. 2015. (Insignia Ser.: 3). (ENG.). 432p. (YA). (gr. 8). pap. 10.99 *(978-0-06-209306-6(1)*, Tegen, Katherine Bks) HarperCollins Pubs.

Kindergarten Book Set 800084. 10. 2005. (J). bds. *(978-1-59794-002-3(X))* Environments, Inc.

Kindergarten Ell Picture Book Stories Blms. 2003. (Metro Reading Ser.). (gr. k). 35.99 *(978-1-58120-601-2(1))* Metropolitan Teaching & Learning Co.

Kindergarten Ell Practice Picture Cards Blms. 2003. (Metro Reading Ser.). (gr. k). 41.29 *(978-1-58120-602-9(X))* Metropolitan Teaching & Learning Co.

Kindergarten Ell Program Lap Book. 2003. (Metro Reading Ser.). (J). (gr. k). spiral bd. 116.55 *(978-1-58120-603-6(8))* Metropolitan Teaching & Learning Co.

Kindergarten Ell Program Teacher's Guide. 2003. (Metro Reading Ser.). (gr. k). per. 41.29 *(978-1-58120-607-4(0))* Metropolitan Teaching & Learning Co.

Kindergarten Review 1.1: Take-Home Version. 2004. (Scott Foresman Reading Ser.). (gr. 1-18). stu. ed. 48.00 *(978-0-328-02543-5(7))* Addison-Wesley Educational Pubs., Inc.

Kinderstarters: KinderStarters Complete Package. 1840.00 *(978-0-7635-8909-7(8))* Rigby Education.

King, Emmett. A Kitten Grows. 2007. (Illus.). 8p. pap. 4.75 *(978-0-15-377221-4(2))* Harcourt Schl. Pubs.

King, Kerrigan. At the Aquarium, 1 vol. 2006. (Neighborhood Readers Ser.). (ENG., Illus.). 12p. (gr. k-1). pap. 5.90 *(978-1-4042-6726-8(3)*, d928f38a-259f-4b3e-baa5-57ca4431f765, Rosen Classroom) Rosen Publishing Group, Inc., The.

King, Zelda. The Class Surprise, 1 vol. 2006. (Neighborhood Readers Ser.). (ENG.). 16p. (gr. 1-2). pap. 6.50 *(978-1-4042-6994-1(0)*, ce91d7dc-161e-4b30-94f8-41fcf95a8609, Rosen Classroom) Rosen Publishing Group, Inc., The.

—The Lemonade Stand, 1 vol. 2006. (Neighborhood Readers Ser.). (ENG.). 12p. (gr. k-1). pap. 5.90 *(978-1-4042-6722-0(0)*, 4d6a7b38-4bcc-4173-805d-78800ab03e65, Rosen Classroom) Rosen Publishing Group, Inc., The.

—Let's Bake a Cake, 1 vol. 2006. (Neighborhood Readers Ser.). (ENG.). 16p. (gr. 1-2). pap. 6.50 *(978-1-4042-7260-6(7)*, e35b4f46-e845-4431-b4da-a48e5811135c, Rosen Classroom) Rosen Publishing Group, Inc., The.

—Where's That Cat?, 1 vol. 2006. (Neighborhood Readers Ser.). (ENG.). 12p. (gr. 1-2). pap. 5.90 *(978-1-4042-6851-7(0)*, c9694f86-7ae2-470d-8901-f9810d4ee2f8, Rosen Classroom) Rosen Publishing Group, Inc., The.

Kingdom of the Golden Dragon Bilingual Reading Group Guide. (J). *(978-0-06-072254-8(1))* HarperCollins Pubs.

The King's Cake: 3-in-1 Package. (Sails Literacy Ser.). 24p. (gr. k-18). 57.00 *(978-0-7578-3198-0(2))* Rigby Education.

The King's Cake: Big Book Only. (Sails Literacy Ser.). 24p. (gr. k-18). 27.00 *(978-0-7635-6984-6(4))* Rigby Education.

The King's Ring: KinderReaders Individual Title Six-Packs. (Kinderstarters Ser.). 8p. (gr. -1-1). 21.00 *(978-0-7635-8656-0(0))* Rigby Education.

Kinsner, Kathy. The Amazon: Set Of 6. 2010. (Early Connections Ser.). (J). pap. 39.00 net. *(978-1-4108-1549-1(8))* Benchmark Education Co.

Kipling, Rudyard. Level 2: the Room in the Tower & Other Stories. 2nd ed. 2008. (Pearson English Graded Readers Ser.). (ENG., Illus.). 48p. pap. 13.32 *(978-1-4058-6962-1(3)*, Pearson ELT) Pearson Education.

Kirszner, Laurie G. Casebook: A Good Man Is Hard to Find. pap. 38.95 *(978-0-8384-7942-1(1))*; pap. 28.95 *(978-0-8384-7871-4(9))* Cengage Heinle.

Kita-Bradley, Linda. The Big Snore. 2003. (ENG., Illus.). 22p. pap. *(978-1-894593-25-0(1))* Grass Roots Pr.

—The Big Surprise. 2003. (ENG., Illus.). 28p. pap. *(978-1-894593-24-3(3))* Grass Roots Pr.

Kites, Vol. 3. (Early Intervention Levels Ser.). 3.55 *(978-0-7362-0089-9(4))* CENGAGE Learning.

Kithinji, Gerald, et al. Of Friends, Money & Gossip: 3 Stories & a Play. 2009. (Hodder African Readers Ser.). (ENG., Illus.). 96p. pap. 12.95 *(978-0-340-99027-8(9))* Hodder Education Group GBR. Dist: Trans-Atlantic Pubns., Inc.

Kitzmiller, Brenda. Muddy Mud — an Easy to Read Beginning Reader Book. 2005. 24p. 7.85 *(978-1-4116-2937-0(X))* Lulu Pr., Inc.

Klein, Abby. Stop That Hamster! McKinley, John, illus. 2008. (Ready, Freddy! Ser.: Bk. 12). 95p. (gr. -1-3). 16.00 *(978-0-7569-8300-0(2))* Perfection Learning Corp.

Klein, Judith Anne. Tuxedo Flyer. 2009. 28p. pap. 14.65 *(978-1-4490-0635-8(3))* AuthorHouse.

Klimchuk, Karen. Manuel Makes a Map!, 1 vol. 2013. (Rosen Readers Ser.). (ENG.). 24p. (J). (gr. 2-2). pap. 8.25 *(978-1-4777-2319-7(6)*, b901b21a-deab-4d1a-924b-0e9329470db0); pap. 49.50 *(978-1-4777-2320-3(X))* Rosen Publishing Group, Inc., The. (Rosen Classroom).

Kline, Trish & Donev, Mary. Coming Home: KA Reader 8. 2007. (Illus.). 32p. (J). per. 20.00 *(978-1-934307-01-4(7))* Ghost Hunter Productions.

—Don't Frown, Clown! KA Reader 9. 2007. (Illus.). 32p. (J). per. 20.00 *(978-1-934307-02-1(5))* Ghost Hunter Productions.

—Hoops in the Coop: KA Reader 7. 2007. (Illus.). 32p. (J). per. 20.00 *(978-1-934307-00-7(9))* Ghost Hunter Productions.

Knapman, Timothy. Leisure & Entertainment since 1900: Band 13/Topaz (Collins Big Cat) 2016. (Collins Big Cat Ser.). (ENG.). 32p. (J). (gr. 2-3). pap. 10.99 *(978-0-00-816382-2(0))* HarperCollins Pubs. Ltd. GBR. Dist: Independent Pubs. Group.

Knight, Andrew. Dead Beckoning. (Thumbprint Mysteries Ser.). 32.86 *(978-0-8092-0421-2(5))* McGraw-Hill/Contemporary.

—The Monster in the Loch. (Thumbprint Mysteries Ser.). 32.86 *(978-0-8092-0411-3(8))* McGraw-Hill/Contemporary.

Knighton, Kate, retold by. Phantom of the Opera. 2008. (Young Reading Series 2 Gift Bks). 64p. (J). 8.99 *(978-0-7945-2082-3(0)*, Usborne) EDC Publishing.

Knope, Liz. Carter Visits the U. S. Capitol, 1 vol. 2013. (Rosen Readers Ser.). (ENG.). 24p. (J). (gr. 3-3). pap. 8.25 *(978-1-4777-2531-3(8)*, 5606480f-b5f3-4d92-a0c8-e99d626317a6); pap. 49.50 *(978-1-4777-2532-0(6))* Rosen Publishing Group, Inc., The. (Rosen Classroom).

Know Zone Reading. 2004. (Scott Foresman Reading Ser.). (gr. k-1). cd-rom 29.97 *(978-0-201-68378-3(4))* Addison-Wesley Educational Pubs., Inc.

Knudsen, Michelle. El Caso de Vivian la Vampira. Wummer, Amy, illus. 2008. (Science Solves It! en Espanol Ser.). (SPA.). 32p. (J). (gr. -1-3). pap. 5.95 *(978-1-57565-277-1(3))* Astra Publishing Hse.

—Fish & Frog Big Book: Brand New Readers. Petrone, Valeria, illus. 2010. (Brand New Readers Ser.). (ENG.). 48p. (J). (gr. -1-3). pap. 24.99 *(978-0-7636-4810-7(8))* Candlewick Pr.

Koch, Dorothy Clarke. When the Cows Got Out. 2016. (ENG., Illus.). 32p. (J). (gr. -1). 3.20 *(978-0-7399-2535-5(0))* Rod & Staff Pubs., Inc.

Koch, Dott Clarke. Jacob's House. Koch, William, ed. 2006. (J). incl. audio compact disk *(978-0-9789043-4-0(6))*; pap. *(978-0-9789043-5-7(4))* Wildot Pr.

Kocienda, Genevieve. Aliens: Is Anybody Out There? Low Intermediate Book with Online Access, 1 vol. 2014. (ENG., Illus.). 24p. (J). pap., E-Book, E-Book 9.50 *(978-1-107-66000-7(9))* Cambridge Univ. Pr.

—Do Not Disturb: the Importance of Sleep High Beginning Book with Online Access, 1 vol. 2014. (ENG., Illus.). 24p. pap., E-Book, E-Book 9.50 *(978-1-107-64682-7(0))* Cambridge Univ. Pr.

—Madagascar Low Intermediate Book with Online Access, 1 vol. 2014. (ENG., Illus.). 24p. (J). pap., E-Book, E-Book 9.50 *(978-1-107-62940-0(3))* Cambridge Univ. Pr.

—The Magic of Music Low Intermediate Book with Online Access, 1 vol. 2014. (ENG., Illus.). 24p. (J). pap., E-Book, E-Book 9.50 *(978-1-107-66558-3(2))* Cambridge Univ. Pr.

—On the Move: The Lives of Nomads, 1 vol. 2014. (ENG., Illus.). 28p. pap., E-Book, E-Book 9.50 *(978-1-107-63293-6(5))* Cambridge Univ. Pr.

—Only in America Low Intermediate Book with Online Access, 1 vol. 2014. (ENG., Illus.). 28p. (J). pap., E-Book, E-Book 9.50 *(978-1-107-63700-9(7))* Cambridge Univ. Pr.

—Three in One: the Challenge of the Triathlon Low Intermediate Book with Online Access, 1 vol. 2014. (ENG., Illus.). 24p. (J). pap., E-Book 9.50 *(978-1-107-62255-5(7))* Cambridge Univ. Pr.

KociendaGenevieve. BLIZZARDS: KILLER SNOWSTORM BEGINNING BOOK WITH ONLINE ACCESS, 1 vol. 2014. (ENG., Illus.). 24p. pap., E-Book 9.50 *(978-1-107-62164-0(X))* Cambridge Univ. Pr.

—SUSHI NATION LOW INTERMEDIATE BOOK WITH ONLINE ACCESS, 1 vol. 2014. (ENG., Illus.). 28p. (J). pap., E-Book 9.50 *(978-1-107-63147-2(5))* Cambridge Univ. Pr.

—WATER: VITAL FOR LIFE LOW INTERMEDIATE BOOK WITH ONLINE ACCESS, 1 vol. 2014. (ENG., Illus.). 24p. (J). pap., E-Book, E-Book 9.50 *(978-1-107-62251-7(4))* Cambridge Univ. Pr.

—WEIRD ANIMALS LOW INTERMEDIATE BOOK WITH ONLINE ACCESS, 1 vol. 2014. (ENG., Illus.). 24p. (J). pap., E-Book, E-Book 9.50 *(978-1-107-65664-2(8))* Cambridge Univ. Pr.

—WHAT ARE THE ODDS? FROM SHARK ATTACK TO LIGHTNING STRIKE LOW INTERMEDIATE BOOK WITH ONLINE ACCESS, 1 vol. 2014. (ENG., Illus.). 24p. pap., E-Book, E-Book 9.50 *(978-1-107-66839-3(5))* Cambridge Univ. Pr.

Koh, Frederick. The 10 Mightiest Conquerors. 2008. (J). 14.99 *(978-1-55448-517-8(7))* Scholastic Library Publishing.

—The 10 Most Compelling News Images. 2008. (J). 14.99 *(978-1-55448-533-8(9))* Scholastic Library Publishing.

—The 10 Most Fascinating Cities. 2008. (J). 14.99 *(978-1-55448-499-7(5))* Scholastic Library Publishing.

—The 10 Most Outstanding Entrepreneurs. 2008. (J). 14.99 *(978-1-55448-498-0(7))* Scholastic Library Publishing.

Kondrchek, Jamie & Rasemas, Joe. On My Way to School (De Camino a la Escuela) Vega, Eida de la, tr. Rasemas, Joe, illus. 2009. (Day in the Life Ser.). (SPA & ENG., Illus.). 32p. (J). (gr. -1-1). 25.70 *(978-1-58415-840-0(9))* Mitchell Lane Pubs.

—What Day Is It? (Que Dia Es Hoy?) Vega, Eida de la, tr. Rasemas, Joe, illus. 2009. (Day in the Life Ser.). (SPA & ENG., Illus.). 32p. (J). (gr. -1-1). 25.70 *(978-1-58415-838-7(7))* Mitchell Lane Pubs.

—What Should I Wear Today? (Que Ropa Me Pondre Hoy?) Vega, Eida de la, tr. Rasemas, Joe, illus. 2009. (Day in the Life Ser.). (ENG & SPA., Illus.). 32p. (J). (gr. -1-1). 25.70 *(978-1-58415-839-4(5))* Mitchell Lane Pubs.

Koontz, Robin. Lagartija Lisa - ¡El Cielo Se Está Cayendo! 2012. (Little Birdie Readers Ser.).Tr. of Lizzie Little, the Sky Is Falling! (SPA.). 24p. (gr. 2-3). pap. 9.95 *(978-1-61810-541-7(8)*, 9781618105417) Rourke Educational Media.

Koontz, Robin Michal. Lizzie Little, the Sky Is Falling! 2011. (ENG., Illus.). (J). (gr. 2-3). pap. 7.95 *(978-1-63430-981-3(2))* Rourke Educational Media.

Koponen, Libby. Floods (a True Book: Earth Science) 2009. (True Book (Relaunch) Ser.). (ENG.). 48p. (J). (gr. 3-5). pap. 6.95 *(978-0-531-21351-3(X)*, Children's Pr.) Scholastic Library Publishing.

Korba, Joanna. Yeh-shen: A Cinderella Tale from China. 2006. (J). pap. *(978-1-4108-6162-7(7))* Benchmark Education Co.

Korky Paul: Biography of an Illustrator: Individual Title Six-Packs. (Discovery World Ser.). 24p. (gr. 1-2). 33.00 *(978-0-7635-8471-9(1))* Rigby Education.

Korman, Gordon. Everest: The Climb. 2006. pap. 8.75 *(978-0-15-365176-2(8))* Harcourt Schl. Pubs.

Korringa, Olivia. Miss Olivia Series: Lessons to Start Your Child on the Right Path of Speaking English Correctly. 2009. 28p. pap. 15.99 *(978-1-4415-8751-0(9))* Xlibris Corp.

Kovats, Moira. Tony's Deal. 2003. (ENG., Illus.). 24p. pap. *(978-1-894593-27-4(8))* Grass Roots Pr.

Kramer, Alan. Path from Extinction. Leon, Karen; Kramer, illus. 2004. (Reader's Theater Content-Area Concepts Ser.). (ENG.). (J). (gr. 3-5). 5.00 net. *(978-1-4108-1145-5(X))* Benchmark Education Co.

—The Wizard of Wherever. Leon, Karen; Kramer, illus. 2004. (Reader's Theater Content-Area Concepts Ser.). (ENG.). (J). (gr. 1-2). 5.00 net. *(978-1-4108-0793-9(2))* Benchmark Education Co.

Kramer, Barbara. National Geographic Readers: Nelson Mandela. 2014. (Readers Bios Ser.). (Illus.). 48p. (J). (gr. 1-3). pap. 4.99 *(978-1-4263-1763-7(8)*, National Geographic Kids) Disney Publishing Worldwide.

—National Geographic Readers: Walt Disney (L3) 2017. (Readers Bios Ser.). 48p. (J). (gr. 3-7). pap. 4.99 *(978-1-4263-2673-8(4)*, National Geographic Kids) Disney Publishing Worldwide.

Kramer, Nash. What Goes Fastest? 2012. (Level B Ser.). (ENG., Illus.). 16p. (J). (gr. k-2). pap. 7.95 *(978-1-927136-19-5(9)*, 19421) RiverStream Publishing.

—Why Do You Change in Winter? 2012. (Level F Ser.). (ENG., Illus.). 16p. (J). (gr. k-2). pap. 7.95 *(978-1-927136-57-7(1)*, 19462) RiverStream Publishing.

Kramer, S. A. Baseball's Greatest Hitters: From Ty Cobb to Miguel Cabrera. 2016. (Step into Reading Ser.). (Illus.). 48p. (J). (gr. 2-4). 5.99 *(978-0-553-53910-3(8)*, Random Hse. Bks. for Young Readers) Random Hse. Children's Bks.

Krasinski, Norma. I Am the One That Reads. 2005. (J). per. 16.99 *(978-0-9773962-1-4(5))* Marx Group, The.

—I Am Their Reading Hero. 2005. (J). per. 12.99 *(978-0-9773962-0-7(7))* Marx Group, The.

—Please, Please, Read to Me. 2005. (J). per. 14.99 *(978-0-9773962-2-1(3))* Marx Group, The.

—The Tyler Story. 2005. (J). per. 12.99 *(978-0-9773962-3-8(1))* Marx Group, The.

Krasinski, Norma & Marx, Donald. Kids Reading to Kids: The Phenomenon. 2006. per. 29.95 *(978-0-9773962-4-5(X))* Marx Group, The.

Kratky, Lada. Avenues B (Leveled Books): Hello Duck! 2003. (Rise & Shine Ser.). (ENG.). (C). pap. 9.95 *(978-0-7362-1861-0(0))* CENGAGE Learning.

Kratt, Chris & Kratt, Martin. Wild Animal Babies! (Wild Kratts) 2016. (Step into Reading Ser.). (Illus.). 24p. (J). (gr. -1-1). 5.99 *(978-1-101-93171-4(X)*, Random Hse. Bks. for Young Readers) Random Hse. Children's Bks.

—Wild Insects & Spiders! (Wild Kratts) Random House, illus. 2016. (Step into Reading Ser.). 24p. (J). (gr. -1-1). 5.99 *(978-1-101-93901-7(X)*, Random Hse. Bks. for Young Readers) Random Hse. Children's Bks.

—Wild Predators (Wild Kratts) Random House, illus. 2015. (Step into Reading Ser.). 32p. (J). (gr. -1-1). 4.99 *(978-0-553-52472-7(0)*, Random Hse. Bks. for Young Readers) Random Hse. Children's Bks.

—5 Wild Creature Adventures! (Wild Kratts) Random House, illus. 2017. (Step into Reading Ser.). 160p. (J). (gr. -1-1). 8.99 *(978-1-101-93900-0(1)*, Random Hse. Bks. for Young Readers) Random Hse. Children's Bks.

Krebs, Laurie. Un Recorrido Por la Selva. Wilson, Anne, illus. 2011. (SPA.). 40p. (J). (gr. k-5). pap. 9.99 *(978-1-84686-551-0(4))* Barefoot Bks., Inc.

Kroll, Jennifer. The Cutting Edge: Breakthroughs in Technology, 1 vol. 2nd rev. ed. 2013. (TIME for KIDS(r): Informational Text Ser.). (ENG., Illus.). 64p. (J). (gr. 4-8). pap. 14.99 *(978-1-4333-4947-8(7))* Teacher Created Materials, Inc.

—Mighty Macros: Little Things, Big Results, 1 vol. 2nd rev. ed. 2013. (TIME for KIDS(r): Informational Text Ser.). (ENG.). 64p. (gr. 4-8). pap. 14.99 *(978-1-4333-4948-5(5))* Teacher Created Materials, Inc.

Krpan, Cathy Marks. The 10 Most Phenomenal Modern Buildings. 2008. 14.99 *(978-1-55448-496-6(0))* Scholastic Library Publishing.

Kruk, Halya. The Littlest One. Morchiladze, Manana, illus. 2007. (ARA & ENG.). 32p. (J). pap. 14.95 *(978-1-60195-090-1(X))* International Step by Step Assn.

Krulik, Nancy. Bad Moooove! #3. Balistreri, Ben, illus. 2018. (Princess Pulverizer Ser.: 3). 144p. (J). (gr. 1-3). 6.99 *(978-0-515-15837-3(2)*, Penguin Workshop) Penguin Young Readers Group.

—Crash! 2017. (Kid from Planet Z Ser.: 1). lib. bdg. 16.00 *(978-0-606-40107-4(5))* Turtleback.

Krutop, Lee, creator. Go Out to Play. 2008. (Illus.). 10p. (J). (gr. -1-1). bds. *(978-1-74178-572-2(3))* Brimax Books Ltd.

Kubler, Annie, illus. This Little Piggy / Este Cochinito. 2009. (Baby Board Bks.). (ENG.). 12p. (J). bds. *(978-1-84643-313-9(4))* Child's Play International Ltd.

Kubuitsile, Lauri. Animal Homes Pink a Band. 2016. (Cambridge Reading Adventures Ser.). (ENG., Illus.). 16p. pap. 7.95 *(978-1-316-60071-9(8))* Cambridge Univ. Pr.

—Don't Give up yet! White Band. Perez, Moni, illus. 2017. (Cambridge Reading Adventures Ser.). (ENG.). 24p. pap. 7.35 *(978-1-108-40078-7(7))* Cambridge Univ. Pr.

—For Today, for Tomorrow. Pérez, Moni, illus. 2016. (Cambridge Reading Adventures Ser.). (ENG.). 16p. pap. 7.95 *(978-1-107-55081-0(5))* Cambridge Univ. Pr.

—Oh Bella! Yellow Band. Brown, Steve, illus. 2016. (Cambridge Reading Adventures Ser.). (ENG.). 15p. pap. 7.95 *(978-1-107-55070-4(X))* Cambridge Univ. Pr.

—Sorry Isn't Good Enough Purple Band. Perez, Moni, illus. 2017. (Cambridge Reading Adventures Ser.). (ENG.). 24p. pap. 7.35 *(978-1-108-40081-7(7))* Cambridge Univ. Pr.

—Stars Yellow Band. 2016. (Cambridge Reading Adventures Ser.). (ENG., Illus.). 16p. pap. 7.95 *(978-1-316-50315-7(1))* Cambridge Univ. Pr.

—Tefo & the Lucky Football Boots Gold Band. Pérez, Moni, illus. 2016. (Cambridge Reading Adventures Ser.). (ENG.). 24p. pap. 8.80 *(978-1-107-55141-1(2))* Cambridge Univ. Pr.

Kuenzler, Lou. Collins Big Cat Phonics for Letters & Sounds - the Foolish, Timid Rabbit: Band 03/Yellow, Bd. 3. Bencivenni, Beatrice, illus. 2018. (Collins Big Cat Phonics Ser.). (ENG.). 16p. (J). (gr. k-1). pap. 7.99 *(978-0-00-825155-0(X))* HarperCollins Pubs. Ltd. GBR. Dist: Independent Pubs. Group.

Kuligowski, Stephanie. The Colonization of Texas: Missions & Settlers, 1 vol. rev. ed. 2012. (Social Studies: Informational Text Ser.). (ENG.). 32p. (gr. 3-5). pap. 11.99 *(978-1-4333-5044-3(0))* Teacher Created Materials, Inc.

—Leonardo Da Vinci: Renaissance Artist & Inventor, 1 vol. rev. ed. 2012. (Social Studies: Informational Text Ser.). (ENG.). 32p. (gr. 4-8). pap. 11.99 *(978-1-4333-5008-5(4))* Teacher Created Materials, Inc.

—The Renaissance: A Rebirth of Culture, 1 vol. rev. ed. 2012. (Social Studies: Informational Text Ser.). (ENG.). 32p. (gr. 4-8). pap. 11.99 *(978-1-4333-5007-8(6))* Teacher Created Materials, Inc.

—La Salle: Early Texas Explorer, 1 vol. rev. ed. 2012. (Social Studies: Informational Text Ser.). (ENG.). 32p. (gr. 3-5). pap. 11.99 *(978-1-4333-5043-6(2))* Teacher Created Materials, Inc.

Kumon Publishing North America, creator. Let's Sticker & Paste!, 4 vols. 2005. (Kumon First Steps Workbooks Ser.). (ENG., Illus.). 40p. (J). (gr. -1). pap. 5.95 *(978-1-933241-13-5(6))* Kumon Publishing North America, Inc.

Kumon Staff. Let's Fold!, 4 vols. 2005. (Kumon First Steps Workbooks Ser.). (ENG., Illus.). 40p. (J). (gr. -1). pap., wbk. ed. 5.95 *(978-1-933241-12-8(8))* Kumon Publishing North America, Inc.

Kurtz, John & Kurtz, Sandrina. Storyland: Mr. Rodento Cleans House: A Story Coloring Book. 2015. (ENG., Illus.). 32p. (J). (gr. k-5). pap. 3.99 *(978-0-486-79391-7(5))* Dover Pubns., Inc.

La Rose, Melinda. Surfin' Turf. 2019. (Illus.). 31p. (J). *(978-1-4242-5739-3(5))* Disney Publishing Worldwide.

Labella, Susan. Animal Survivors, 6 bks., Set. Incl. Chameleons & Other Animals with Amazing Skin. (Illus.). 24p. (J). (gr. 1-2). 2005. lib. bdg. 22.00 *(978-0-516-24925-4(8))*; (Scholastic News Nonfiction Readers Ser.). 2005. 108.00 o.p. *(978-0-516-25390-9(5)*, Children's Pr.) Scholastic Library Publishing.

LaBerge, Margaret M. Sara Safety, Personal Safety: Kid's Activity Book. Lucas, Stacey L. & Lopresti, Sarah H., illus. 2004. 21p. (J). pap. *(978-0-9755561-2-2(6))* Reading Resc.

—Sara Safety, School Safety: Kid's Activity Book. Seager, Maryann et al, illus. 2004. (J). pap. *(978-0-9755561-1-5(8))* Reading Resc.

Lacey, Saskia. Surprising Things We Do for Fun (Grade 8) 2nd rev. ed. 2017. (TIME(r): Informational Text Ser.). (ENG., Illus.). 64p. (J). (gr. 6-8). pap. 13.99 *(978-1-4938-3638-3(2))* Teacher Created Materials, Inc.

Ladybird. Aladdin - Ladybird Readers Level 4. 2018. (Ladybird Readers Ser.). (Illus.). 64p. (J). (gr. k-2). pap. 8.99 *(978-0-241-31606-1(5))* Penguin Bks., Ltd. GBR. Dist: Independent Pubs. Group.

—Aladdin Activity Book - Ladybird Readers Level 4. 2019. (Ladybird Readers Ser.). (ENG., Illus.). 16p. (J). (gr. k-2). pap. 5.99 *(978-0-241-31607-8(3))* Penguin Random Hse. GBR. Dist: Independent Pubs. Group.

—Anansi Helps a Friend Activity Book - Ladybird Readers Level 1. 2016. (Ladybird Readers Ser.). (ENG.). 16p. (J). (gr. 2-4). pap., act. bk. ed. 5.99 *(978-0-241-25420-2(5))* Penguin Bks., Ltd. GBR. Dist: Independent Pubs. Group.

—BBC Earth: Deserts - Ladybird Readers Level 1. 2018. (Ladybird Readers Ser.). (Illus.). 48p. (J). (gr. k-2). pap. 8.99

(978-0-241-31608-5(1)) Penguin Bks., Ltd. GBR. Dist: Independent Pubs. Group.

—BBC Earth: Mountains - Ladybird Readers Level 2. 2018. (Ladybird Readers Ser.). (Illus.). 48p. (J). (gr. k-2). pap. 8.99 (978-0-241-31948-2(X)) Penguin Bks., Ltd. GBR. Dist: Independent Pubs. Group.

—Cars - Read It Yourself with Ladybird (non-Fiction) Level 1. 2016. (Read It Yourself with Ladybird Ser.). (ENG.). 32p. (J). 5.99 (978-0-241-24444-9(7)) Penguin Bks., Ltd. GBR. Dist: Independent Pubs. Group.

—Cinderella: Ladybird Readers Level 1, Vol. 1. 2016. (Ladybird Readers Ser.). (Illus.). 48p. (J). (gr. 2-4). pap. 9.99 (978-0-241-25407-3(8)) Penguin Bks., Ltd. GBR. Dist: Independent Pubs. Group.

—Dinosaurs Activity Book - Ladybird Readers Level 2. 2016. (Ladybird Readers Ser.). (ENG.). 16p. (J). (gr. 2-4). pap. 5.99 (978-0-241-25455-4(8)) Penguin Bks., Ltd. GBR. Dist: Independent Pubs. Group.

—Dinosaurs: Ladybird Readers Level 2. 2016. (Ladybird Readers Ser.). (ENG., Illus.). 48p. (J). pap. 9.99 (978-0-241-25447-9(7)) Penguin Bks., Ltd. GBR. Dist: Independent Pubs. Group.

—Emergency Rescue - Read It Yourself with Ladybird (non-Fiction) Level 2. 2016. (Read It Yourself with Ladybird Ser.). (ENG.). 32p. (J). (gr. 2-4). 5.99 (978-0-241-24442-5(0)) Penguin Bks., Ltd. GBR. Dist: Independent Pubs. Group.

—The Enormous Turnip # Ladybird Readers Level 1, Vol. 1. 2016. (Ladybird Readers Ser.). (Illus.). 48p. (J). pap., act. bk. ed. 9.99 (978-0-241-25408-0(6)) Penguin Bks., Ltd. GBR. Dist: Independent Pubs. Group.

—Favourite Pets - Read It Yourself with Ladybird Level 1. 2016. (Read It Yourself with Ladybird Ser.). (ENG.). 32p. (J). 5.99 (978-0-241-23734-2(3)) Penguin Bks., Ltd. GBR. Dist: Independent Pubs. Group.

—How to Use Ladybird Readers. 2016. (Ladybird Readers Ser.). (ENG.). 16p. (J). pap. 5.99 (978-0-241-26230-6(5)) Penguin Bks., Ltd. GBR. Dist: Independent Pubs. Group.

—Jon's Football Team: Ladybird Readers Level 1. 2016. (Ladybird Readers Ser.). (Illus.). 48p. (J). (gr. 2-4). pap. 9.99 (978-0-241-25411-0(6)) Penguin Bks., Ltd. GBR. Dist: Independent Pubs. Group.

—Little Red Riding Hood: Ladybird Readers Level 2, Vol. 2. 2016. (Ladybird Readers Ser.). (Illus.). 48p. (J). (gr. 2-4). pap. 9.99 (978-0-241-25446-2(9)) Penguin Bks., Ltd. GBR. Dist: Independent Pubs. Group.

—Minibeasts - Read It Yourself with Ladybird Level 3. 2016. (Read It Yourself with Ladybird Ser.). (ENG., Illus.). 48p. (J). 5.99 (978-0-241-23737-3(8)) Penguin Bks., Ltd. GBR. Dist: Independent Pubs. Group.

—The Monster Next Door: Ladybird Readers Level 2, Vol. 2. 2016. (Ladybird Readers Ser.). (Illus.). 48p. (J). (gr. 2-4). pap. 9.99 (978-0-241-25444-8(2)) Penguin Bks., Ltd. GBR. Dist: Independent Pubs. Group.

—Our Solar System - Read It Yourself with Ladybird Level 4. 2016. (Read It Yourself with Ladybird Ser.). (ENG.). 48p. (J). (gr. 2-4). 5.99 (978-0-241-23743-4(2)) Penguin Bks., Ltd. GBR. Dist: Independent Pubs. Group.

—Peter Rabbit & the Radish Robber - Ladybird Readers Level 1. 2018. (Ladybird Readers Ser.). (Illus.). 48p. (J). (gr. k-2). pap. 8.99 (978-0-241-29742-1(7)) Penguin Bks., Ltd. GBR. Dist: Independent Pubs. Group.

—The Pied Piper Activity Book - Ladybird Readers Level 4. 2016. (Ladybird Readers Ser.). (ENG.). 16p. (J). pap., act. bk. ed. 5.99 (978-0-241-25373-1(X)) Penguin Bks., Ltd. GBR. Dist: Independent Pubs. Group.

—Planet Earth - Read It Yourself with Ladybird Level 3. 2016. (Read It Yourself with Ladybird Ser.). (ENG., Illus.). 48p. (J). 5.99 (978-0-241-23740-3(8)) Penguin Bks., Ltd. GBR. Dist: Independent Pubs. Group.

—Sam & the Robots Activity Book - Ladybird Readers Level 4. 2016. (Ladybird Readers Ser.). (ENG.). 16p. (J). pap., act. bk. ed. 5.99 (978-0-241-25376-2(4)) Penguin Bks., Ltd. GBR. Dist: Independent Pubs. Group.

—Sharks: Ladybird Readers Level 3, Vol. 3. 2016. (Ladybird Readers Ser.). (Illus.). 64p. (J). (gr. 2-4). pap. 9.99 (978-0-241-25382-3(9)) Penguin Bks., Ltd. GBR. Dist: Independent Pubs. Group.

—Sly Fox & Red Hen. 2016. (Ladybird Readers Ser.). (Illus.). 48p. (J). (gr. 2-4). pap. 9.99 (978-0-241-25443-1(4)) Penguin Bks., Ltd. GBR. Dist: Independent Pubs. Group.

—Snow White - Ladybird Readers Level 3. 2018. (Ladybird Readers Ser.). (Illus.). 64p. (J). (gr. k-2). pap. 8.99 (978-0-241-31955-0(2)) Penguin Bks., Ltd. GBR. Dist: Independent Pubs. Group.

—Space Activity Book - Ladybird Readers Level 4. 2016. (Ladybird Readers Ser.). (ENG.). 16p. (J). (gr. 2-4). pap., act. bk. ed. 5.99 (978-0-241-25377-9(2)) Penguin Bks., Ltd. GBR. Dist: Independent Pubs. Group.

—The Elves & the Shoemaker, Vol. 3. 2016. (Ladybird Readers Ser.). (Illus.). 64p. (J). (gr. 2-4). pap. 9.99 (978-0-241-25385-4(3)) Penguin Bks., Ltd. GBR. Dist: Independent Pubs. Group.

—The Gingerbread Man, Vol. 2. 2016. (Ladybird Readers Ser.). (Illus.). 48p. (J). pap. 9.99 (978-0-241-25442-4(6)) Penguin Bks., Ltd. GBR. Dist: Independent Pubs. Group.

—The Red Knight. 2016. (Ladybird Readers Ser.). (Illus.). 64p. (J). (gr. 2-4). pap. 9.99 (978-0-241-25384-7(5)) Penguin Bks., Ltd. GBR. Dist: Independent Pubs. Group.

—Topsy & Tim: Go to the Zoo Ladybird Readers Level 1. 2016. (Ladybird Readers Ser.). (Illus.). 48p. (J). (gr. 2-4). pap. 9.99 (978-0-241-25414-1(0)) Penguin Bks., Ltd. GBR. Dist: Independent Pubs. Group.

—Topsy & Tim: the Big Race Ladybird Readers Level 2. 2016. (Ladybird Readers Ser.). (Illus.). 48p. (J). (gr. 2-4). pap. 9.99 (978-0-241-25448-6(5)) Penguin Bks., Ltd. GBR. Dist: Independent Pubs. Group.

—Wild Animals - Ladybird Readers Level 2. 2016. (Ladybird Readers Ser.). (Illus.). 48p. (J). (gr. 2-4). pap. 9.99 (978-0-241-25445-5(0)) Penguin Bks., Ltd. GBR. Dist: Independent Pubs. Group.

Ladybird, Ladybird. Ladybird Tales Peter & the Wolf. 2016. (Ladybird Tales Ser.). (Illus.). 48p. (J). (gr. k-2). 9.99 (978-0-7232-9448-1(8)) Penguin Bks., Ltd. GBR. Dist: Independent Pubs. Group.

—Peter Rabbit & the Radish Robber, Level 1. 2018. (Ladybird Readers Ser.). (ENG.). 16p. (J). (gr. k-2). pap. 5.99 (978-0-241-29735-3(4)) Penguin Bks., Ltd. GBR. Dist: Independent Pubs. Group.

Lagonegro, Melissa. Beauty & the Beast. 2017. (Illus.). 24p. (J). (978-1-5182-3646-4(4)) Random Hse., Inc.

—Kingdom of Color (Disney Tangled) Orpinas, Jean-Paul et al, illus. 2010. (Step into Reading Ser.). (ENG.). 32p. (J). (gr. k-3). pap. 5.99 (978-0-7364-2687-9(6), RH/Disney) Random Hse. Children's Bks.

—Outside My Window (Disney Tangled) Orpinas, Jean-Paul et al, illus. 2010. (Step into Reading Ser.). (ENG.). 32p. (J). (gr. k-3). pap. 5.99 (978-0-7364-2688-6(4), RH/Disney) Random Hse. Children's Bks.

Laínez, René Colato. From North to South/Del Norte Al Sur. Cepeda, Joe, illus. 2010.Tr. of Del norte al Sur. (ENG & SPA.). 32p. (J). (gr. k-3). 17.95 (978-0-89239-231-5(2)) Lee & Low Bks., Inc.

Laird, Elizabeth. Where's Toto?/Donde esta Toto? Spanish/English Edition. Martin, Rosa Maria, tr. Ursell, Martin, illus. 2009. (Let's Read! Spanish-English Ser.). (ENG.). 31p. (J). (gr. k-3). 17.44 (978-0-7641-4218-5(6), B.E.S. Publishing) Peterson's.

Laird, Elizabeth & Davison, Roz. Jungle School. Sim, David, illus. 2006. (Green Bananas Ser.). (ENG.). 48p. (J). (gr. -1-3). lib. bdg. (978-0-7787-1026-4(2)) Crabtree Publishing Co.

Lakeshore Learning Materials Staff, contrib. by. Read & Learn Nonfiction: Bold Words & Glossaries, Set of 6 Student Books. 2007. (ELX.). (J). pap. 19.95 (978-1-59746-035-4(4)) Lakeshore Learning Materials.

—Read & Learn Nonfiction: Bold Words & Glossaries Big Book. 2007. (J). pap. 19.95 (978-1-59746-032-3(X)) Lakeshore Learning Materials.

—Read & Learn Nonfiction: Maps, Charts, & Graphs, Set of 6 Student Books. 2007. (J). pap. 19.95 (978-1-59746-034-7(6)) Lakeshore Learning Materials.

—Read & Learn Nonfiction: Maps, Charts, & Graphs Big Book. 2007. (J). pap. 19.95 (978-1-59746-031-6(1)) Lakeshore Learning Materials.

—Read & Learn Nonfiction: Photos, Captions, & Diagrams, Set of 6 Student Books. 2007. (J). pap. 19.95 (978-1-59746-033-0(8)) Lakeshore Learning Materials.

—Read & Learn Nonfiction: Photos, Captions, & Diagrams Big Book. 2007. (J). pap. 19.95 (978-1-59746-030-9(3)) Lakeshore Learning Materials.

—Storyteller Complete Library: CD Version. 2007. (J). 99.50 incl. audio compact disk (978-1-59746-019-4(2)) Lakeshore Learning Materials.

Lakin, Patricia. Max & Mo's Halloween Surprise: Ready-To-Read Level 1. Floca, Brian, illus. 2008. (Max & Mo Ser.). (ENG.). 32p. (J). (gr. -1-1). pap. 4.99 (978-1-4169-2539-2(2), Simon Spotlight) Simon Spotlight.

—Vroom, Zoom, Bud. Atkinson, Cale, illus. 2016. (Penguin Young Readers, Level 1 Ser.). 32p. (J). (gr. k-1). 4.99 (978-0-448-48832-5(9), Penguin Young Readers) Penguin Young Readers Group.

Lalley, Kristine. Show & Tell, 1 vol. 2006. (Neighborhood Readers Ser.). (ENG.). 12p. (gr. k-1). pap. 5.90 (978-1-4042-6465-6(5), e36681c3-624e-4d88-b629-7e0b96cf87b9, Rosen Classroom) Rosen Publishing Group, Inc., The.

Laman, Judi-Lynn. The 10 Most Bizarre Animal Habits. 2008. 14.99 (978-1-55448-542-0(8)) Scholastic Library Publishing.

Lambert, Mark John. The 10 Most Incredible Landforms. 2008. (J). 14.99 (978-1-55448-529-1(0)) Scholastic Library Publishing.

Lambert, Nancy R. Ant-Man Game Over. 2015. (Marvel World of Reading Level 2 Ser.). (J). lib. bdg. 13.55 (978-0-606-37536-8(8)) Turtleback.

Lamplighter Staff. The Boys of Grit Who Changed. 2004. 16.00 (978-1-58474-031-5(0)) Cornerstone Family Ministries/Lamplighter Publishing.

—Clean Your Boots Sir? 2004. 14.00 (978-1-58474-015-5(9)) Cornerstone Family Ministries/Lamplighter Publishing.

—Fireside Readings. 2004. 16.00 (978-1-58474-042-1(6)) Cornerstone Family Ministries/Lamplighter Publishing.

—Hidden Hand. 2004. 22.00 (978-1-58474-107-7(4)) Cornerstone Family Ministries/Lamplighter Publishing.

—Highland Chairman. 2004. 12.00 (978-1-58474-037-7(X)) Cornerstone Family Ministries/Lamplighter Publishing.

—Inheritance. 2004. 15.00 (978-1-58474-009-4(4)) Cornerstone Family Ministries/Lamplighter Publishing.

—Me & Nobbles. 2004. 17.00 (978-1-58474-102-2(3)) Cornerstone Family Ministries/Lamplighter Publishing.

—Melody the Story of a Child. 2004. 16.00 (978-1-58474-016-2(7)) Cornerstone Family Ministries/Lamplighter Publishing.

—Nobody Loves Me. 2004. 15.00 (978-1-58474-035-3(3)) Cornerstone Family Ministries/Lamplighter Publishing.

—Probable Sons. 2004. 15.00 (978-1-58474-033-9(7)) Cornerstone Family Ministries/Lamplighter Publishing.

Lamson, Martha. Oliver. 2008. 28p. pap. 15.99 (978-1-4363-5100-3(6)) Xlibris Corp.

Lancett, Peter. The Past Is Dark. 2008. (Dark Man Ser.). (ENG., Illus.). 48p. pap. (978-1-84167-747-7(7)) Ransom Publishing Ltd.

—The Shadow in the Dark, 1 vol. unabr. ed. 2010. (Dark Man Ser.). (ENG.). 36p. (YA). (gr. 5-12). pap. 8.75 (978-1-61651-021-3(8)) Saddleback Educational Publishing, Inc.

Lanchais, Aurelie, et al. Kto A? 2005. (Who Am I? What Am I? Ser.).Tr. of Who Am I? (RUS, ENG, TUR, VIE & CHI., Illus.). 16p. (J). (gr. -1-1). 9.95 (978-1-84059-232-0(X)) Milet Publishing.

—What Am I? 2005. (Who Am I? What Am I? Ser.). (Illus.). 16p. (J). (gr. -1-1). (URD, ENG, CHI, ARA & BEN.). 9.95 (978-1-84059-248-1(6)); (ARA, ENG, URD, TUR & CHI., 9.95 (978-1-84059-243-6(5)) Milet Publishing.

—Who Am I? 2005. (Who Am I? What Am I? Ser.). (CHI, ENG, VIE, GUJ & RUS., Illus.). 16p. (J). (gr. -1-1). 9.95 (978-1-84059-229-0(X)) Milet Publishing.

Landman, Tanya. A Drop of Rain Green Band. Tait, Carys, illus. 2016. (Cambridge Reading Adventures Ser.). (ENG.). 16p. pap. 7.95 (978-1-107-55060-5(2)) Cambridge Univ. Pr.

—The Fisherman & His Wife: Band 12/Copper (Collins Big Cat) 2017. (Collins Big Cat Tales Ser.). (ENG., Illus.). 32p. (J). (gr. 2-3). pap. 10.99 (978-0-00-817931-1(X)) HarperCollins Pubs. Ltd. GBR. Dist: Independent Pubs. Group.

—The Little Egg: Band 03/Yellow (Collins Big Cat) 2006. (Collins Big Cat Ser.). (ENG., Illus.). 16p. (J). (gr. 1-1). pap. 7.99 (978-0-00-718677-8(0)) HarperCollins Pubs. Ltd. GBR. Dist: Independent Pubs. Group.

Lane, Chloe. Package Design. rev. ed. 2012. (Mathematics in the Real World Ser.). (ENG.). 32p. (gr. 5-8). pap. 11.99 (978-1-4333-3460-3(7)) Teacher Created Materials, Inc.

Lane, Tracy & Benchmark Education Co., LLC Staff. Shade Lake. 2015. (BuildUp Ser.). (J). (gr. 1). (978-1-4900-0725-0(3)) Benchmark Education Co.

Langford, Jane. Hero. Vince, Dawn, illus. 2005. (ENG.). 24p. (J). lib. bdg. 23.65 (978-1-59646-720-0(7)) Dingles & Co.

—An Old Red Hat. Axworthy, Anni, illus. 2004. (ENG.). 24p. (J). lib. bdg. 23.65 (978-1-59646-676-0(6)) Dingles & Co.

Larsen, Becca. Buying & Selling, 1 vol. 2013. (Rosen Readers Ser.). (ENG.). 24p. (J). (gr. 2-2). pap. 8.25 (978-1-4777-2260-2(2), 9cea1a72-defe-4498-a75f-18b20c8ccff3); pap. 49.50 (978-1-4777-2261-9(0)) Rosen Publishing Group, Inc., The. (Rosen Classroom).

LaSala, Paige. Pig Kissing. Gullotti, Pat, illus. 2010. 24p. pap. 12.99 (978-1-4520-2849-1(4)) AuthorHouse.

Last, Shari. Rebel Heroes. 2017. (Star Wars DK Readers Level 3 Ser.). lib. bdg. 13.55 (978-0-606-39898-5(8)) Turtleback.

Latour, Pierre. Where Do Big Machines Work? 2012. (Level B Ser.). (ENG., Illus.). 16p. (J). (gr. k-2). pap. 7.95 (978-1-927136-12-6(1), 19444) RiverStream Publishing.

—Who Eats Who in a Food Chain? 2012. (Level F Ser.). (ENG., Illus.). 16p. (J). (gr. k-2). pap. 7.95 (978-1-927136-58-4(X), 19449) RiverStream Publishing.

—Who Works Here? 2012. (Level C Ser.). (ENG., Illus.). 16p. (J). (gr. k-2). pap. 7.95 (978-1-927136-22-5(9), 19457) RiverStream Publishing.

—Why Can Plants Grow in the Desert? 2012. (Level E Ser.). (ENG., Illus.). 16p. (J). (gr. k-2). pap. 7.95 (978-1-927136-48-5(2), 19460) RiverStream Publishing.

Lavelle, David. Collins Big Cat Phonics for Letters & Sounds - Get Set for Fun: Band 02B/Red B, Bd. 2B. 2018. (Collins Big Cat Phonics Ser.). (ENG.). 16p. (J). (gr. -1-k). pap. 6.99 (978-0-00-825150-5(9)) HarperCollins Pubs. Ltd. GBR. Dist: Independent Pubs. Group.

Lavelle, Sheila. Clever Dog, Webster. 2005. (978-1-901358-00-1(3)) CAMFA.

Lawrence, D. Level 5: British & American Short Stories. 2nd ed. 2008. (ENG.). 88p. pap. 11.99 (978-1-4058-8239-2(5)) Pearson Education.

Leardi, Jeannette. The Brain. 2011. (Readers' & Writers' Genre Workshop Ser.). (J). pap. (978-1-4509-3032-1(8)) Benchmark Education Co.

Learn to Read, Vol. 2. 2006. (J). per. 10.00 (978-0-9774302-1-5(9)) Braun Pubns.

LeBaron, Cecilia. The Cap. 2007. (Illus.). 16p. (J). 5.95 (978-0-9798869-2-8(9)) Crush Publishing.

—The Map. 2007. (Illus.). 16p. (J). 5.95 (978-0-9798869-1-1(0)) Crush Publishing.

—Sam & Val. 2007. (Illus.). 16p. (J). 5.95 (978-0-9798869-3-5(7)) Crush Publishing.

Leblanc, Denise. Mr. Blue, I Have a Question for You. 2013. 36p. pap. 15.95 (978-1-4908-1232-8(6), WestBow Pr.) Author Solutions, LLC.

Lechowick, Silvija D. The Tale of Little Zero & Bully Nine: 1. the Tale of Little Zero & Bully Nine. 2018. (Scientific Fairytales for Children Ser.: 1). (Illus.). 28p. (J). (gr. k-7). 22.97 (978-0-9989929-0-7(9)) BookBaby.

Ledieux, Jack. The Worst Trip EVER! 2017. (Text Connections Guided Close Reading Ser.). (J). (gr. 2). (978-1-4900-1853-9(0)) Benchmark Education Co.

Lee, April. Helping at School, 1 vol. 2012. (InfoMax Readers Ser.). (ENG., Illus.). 16p. (J). (gr. k-k). pap. 7.00 (978-1-4488-8896-2(4), 3ea76b39-1272-4a48-8397-9e0a3deb65a3, Rosen Classroom) Rosen Publishing Group, Inc., The.

—How We Get Around Town, 1 vol. 2012. (InfoMax Readers Ser.). (ENG., Illus.). 16p. (J). (gr. k-k). pap. 7.00 (978-1-4488-8941-9(3), 5e9ca34d-70a0-419f-aa4d-32f009192669, Rosen Classroom) Rosen Publishing Group, Inc., The.

Lee, David. Ellie's Family Album, 1 vol. 2013. (Rosen Readers Ser.). (ENG.). 24p. (J). (gr. 2-2). pap. 8.25 (978-1-4777-2257-2(2), b8f689b9-29d6-4226-8d8f-78efd7fc5b7e); pap. 49.50 (978-1-4777-2258-9(0)) Rosen Publishing Group, Inc., The. (Rosen Classroom).

Lee, Fekany Kimberly. Cell Scientists: Discovering How Cells Work, 1 vol. rev. ed. 2007. (Science: Informational Text Ser.). (ENG.). 32p. (gr. 3-6). pap. 12.99 (978-0-7439-0584-8(9)) Teacher Created Materials, Inc.

Lee, Gisela. China, 1 vol. rev. ed. 2007. (Social Studies: Informational Text Ser.). (ENG.). 32p. (J). (gr. 4-8). pap. 11.99 (978-0-7439-0436-0(2)) Teacher Created Materials, Inc.

Lee, Kimberly Fekany. Looking Inside Cells, 1 vol. rev. ed. 2007. (Science: Informational Text Ser.). (ENG.). 32p. (gr. 3-6). pap. 12.99 (978-0-7439-0583-1(0)) Teacher Created Materials, Inc.

Lee, Quinlan B. Phonics: 12 Book Reading Program, 12 vols. 2006. (Illus.). (978-0-439-78943-1(5)); (978-0-439-78944-8(3)); (978-0-439-78945-5(1)); (978-0-439-78946-2(X)); (978-0-439-78947-9(8)); (978-0-439-78948-6(6)); (978-0-439-78949-3(4)); (978-0-439-78942-4(7)); (978-0-439-78941-7(9)); (978-0-439-78939-4(7)); (978-0-439-78940-0(0)); (978-0-439-78938-7(9)) Scholastic, Inc.

—Phonics Reading Program (Pokémon) 2018. (ENG.). 16p. (J). (gr. -1-3). bds. 12.99 (978-1-338-20744-6(X)) Scholastic, Inc.

Leech, Bonnie. The Names of Numbers: Learning How Numbers Are Represented with Words, 1 vol. 2010. (Math for the REAL World Ser.). (ENG., Illus.). 8p. (gr. k-1). pap. 5.15 (978-0-8239-8884-6(8), 57ba5af2-abc5-4981-b933-7d84014800b7) Rosen Publishing Group, Inc., The.

Lefebvre, Gail. A Week at Snug Bend. 2009. 64p. pap. 19.50 (978-1-60693-627-6(1), Strategic Bk. Publishing) Strategic Book Publishing & Rights Agency (SBPRA).

The Legend of the Bluebonnet: Fourth Grade Guided Comprehension Level L. (On Our Way to English Ser.). (gr. 4-18). 34.50 (978-0-7578-7151-1(8)) Rigby Education.

Lehman, Barbara. Red Again. 2017. (ENG., Illus.). 32p. (J). (gr. -1-3). 16.99 (978-0-544-81859-0(8), 1642244, Clarion Bks.) HarperCollins Pubs.

Lei, Vicki. Mr Grumpy. 2011. 28p. pap. 15.99 (978-1-4568-5587-1(5)) Xlibris Corp.

Leigh, Autumn. The Apple Tree. (Neighborhood Readers Ser.). (ENG.). 16p. 2007. 33.50 (978-1-4042-7328-3(X)) 2006. (gr. 1-2). pap. 6.50 (978-1-4042-7128-9(7), e3b3cedf-a072-4b5b-89a1-89173083a724) Rosen Publishing Group, Inc., The. (Rosen Classroom).

—Door to Door, 1 vol. 2006. (Neighborhood Readers Ser.). (ENG.). 12p. (gr. k-1). pap. 5.90 (978-1-4042-6469-4(8), 7e49d46b-15f2-4557-936d-1c3e673e7a0b, Rosen Classroom) Rosen Publishing Group, Inc., The.

—Far-Out Friends, 1 vol. 2006. (Neighborhood Readers Ser.). (ENG.). 8p. (gr. k-1). pap. 5.15 (978-1-4042-6750-3(6), 239bf85d-6872-464c-8ffc-a93cd277889b, Rosen Classroom) Rosen Publishing Group, Inc., The.

—El manzano (the Apple Tree) 2007. (Lecturas del barrio (Neighborhood Readers) Ser.). (SPA.). 16p. 33.50 (978-1-4042-7329-0(8), Rosen Classroom) Rosen Publishing Group, Inc., The.

—My Teacher, 1 vol. 2008. (Real Life Readers Ser.). (ENG.). 8p. (gr. k-1). pap. 5.15 (978-1-4042-7975-9(X), adc40ba9-50a6-40b5-bdb7-87e31a7d7ce3, Rosen Classroom) Rosen Publishing Group, Inc., The.

—On the Ball: Learning to Identify the Place Values of Ones & Tens, 1 vol. 2010. (Math for the REAL World Ser.). (ENG., Illus.). 8p. (gr. k-1). pap. 5.15 (978-0-8239-8859-4(7), d4c98b27-ecd2-456f-88a7-69c0af5ffbe5) Rosen Publishing Group, Inc., The.

—Signs on the Road: Learning to Identify the Four Basic Geometric Shapes, 1 vol. 2010. (Math for the REAL World Ser.). (ENG., Illus.). 8p. (gr. k-1). pap. 5.15 (978-0-8239-8857-0(0), f5253939-6466-46b7-a4e0-107d37c64b88) Rosen Publishing Group, Inc., The.

Leipe, Ulla. Lo Que los Ninos Quieren Saber. Limmer, Hannes, illus. (SPA.). 180p. (YA). 11.95 (978-84-241-5501-8(7), EV867) Everest Editora ESP. Dist: Continental Bk. Co., Inc.

Lemay, Didi. A Winter Solstice Celebration. Campbell, Jacquie, illus. 2008. 56p. pap. 23.99 (978-1-4389-0998-1(5)) AuthorHouse.

The Lemonade Stand: Individual Title Six-Packs. (gr. -1-2). 27.00 (978-0-7635-9457-2(1)) Rigby Education.

Lems-Tardif, Gina. Pilgrim Children Had Many Chores. 2017. (Learn-To-Read Ser.). (ENG., Illus.). (J). pap. 3.49 (978-1-68310-238-0(X)) Pacific Learning, Inc.

Lend a Hand. (Early Intervention Levels Ser.). 28.38 (978-0-7362-0413-2(X)) CENGAGE Learning.

Lend a Hand (18), Vol. 18. (Early Intervention Levels Ser.). 4.73 (978-0-7362-0238-1(2)) CENGAGE Learning.

Leonard, M. G. Beetle Boy. 2017. lib. bdg. 17.20 (978-0-606-40151-7(2)) Turtleback.

Lerner Publishing Group Staff. History Speaks: Picture Books Plus Reader's Theater, 6 vols., Set. 2011. (J). (gr. 2-4). lib. bdg. 167.58 (978-0-7613-7483-1(3)) Lerner Publishing Group.

LernerClassroom Editors. First Step Nonfiction-Animal Families Teaching Guide. 2009. pap. 7.95 (978-0-8225-5658-9(8)) Lerner Publishing Group.

—First Step Nonfiction-Animal Homes Teaching Guide. 2009. pap. 7.95 (978-0-8225-5672-5(3)) Lerner Publishing Group.

—First Step Nonfiction-Basic Human Needs. 2009. pap., tchr. ed. 7.95 (978-0-8225-1747-4(7)) Lerner Publishing Group.

—On My Own History Teaching Guide. 2009. pap. 7.95 (978-0-8225-5321-2(X)) Lerner Publishing Group.

—Pull Ahead Books-Continents Teaching Guide. 2009. pap. 7.95 (978-0-8225-2349-9(3)) Lerner Publishing Group.

LernerClassroom Editors, ed. Microquests. 2008. pap. 7.95 (978-0-8225-9223-5(1)) Lerner Publishing Group.

Lesespiele. (Duden-Schuelerhilfen Ser.). (GER.). 96p. (J). (gr. 3-4). (978-3-411-02607-4(3)) Bibliographisches Institut & F. A. Brockhaus AG DEU. Dist: International Bk. Import Service, Inc.

Let's Celebrate. (Early Intervention Levels Ser.). 23.10 (978-0-7362-0024-0(X)) CENGAGE Learning.

Let's Eat. 2005. (Little Celebrations Thematic Packages Ser.). (J). (gr. k-3). 133.50 (978-0-673-75379-3(4)) Celebration Pr.

Let's Get Active!, 8 vols. 2017. (Let's Get Active! Ser.). (ENG., Illus.). (J). (gr. 1-1). lib. bdg. 101.08 (978-1-5081-6343-5(X), 0e5cd9bb-989f-4d1f-9461-23d9085f4ca5, PowerKids Pr.) Rosen Publishing Group, Inc., The.

Let's Go Shopping! (Early Intervention Levels Ser.). 23.10 (978-0-7362-0027-1(4)); Vol. 4. 3.85 (978-1-56334-975-1(2)) CENGAGE Learning.

Let's Hear It for Ears! (Early Intervention Levels Ser.). 31.86 (978-0-7362-2134-4(4)); 5.31 (978-0-7362-1915-0(3)) CENGAGE Learning.

Let's Paint!, Vol. 4. (Early Intervention Levels Ser.). 3.85 (978-1-56334-962-1(0)) CENGAGE Learning.

Let's Read Big Book, 3 bks., Set. (Phonics & Friends Ser.). (gr. -1-2). Level C. 14.76 (978-0-7362-1065-2(2))Level D. 14.76 (978-0-7362-1066-9(0))Level B. 14.76 (978-0-7362-1064-5(4)) CENGAGE Learning.

Letter Clusters Big Book, 6 vols. 32p. (gr. k-3). 38.50 (978-0-7802-7194-4(7)) Wright Group/McGraw-Hill.

Level 16 Pack: Set of 17 Titles. (Early Intervention Levels Ser.). 89.99 (978-0-7362-2554-0(4)) CENGAGE Learning.

Level 18 Pack: Set of 13 Titles. (Early Intervention Levels Ser.). 71.47 (978-0-7362-2555-7(2)) CENGAGE Learning.

Level 2 Book Collection 800920, 6 vols. 2005. (J). (978-1-59794-085-6(2)) Environments, Inc.

Level 2 Pack: Set of 16 Titles. (Dra Levels Ser.). 60.09 (978-0-7362-2566-3(8)) CENGAGE Learning.

Level 2 Paperback Book Collection 800921, 6 vols. 2005. (J). pap. (978-1-59794-086-3(0)) Environments, Inc.

Level 3 Books & Tapes Book Set 800927, 6 vols. 2005. (J). pap. (978-1-59794-092-4(5)) Environments, Inc.

Level 3 Pack: Set of 14 Titles. (Dra Levels Ser.). 58.15 (978-0-7362-2567-0(6)) CENGAGE Learning.

Level 3 Pack: Set of 18 Titles. (Early Intervention Levels Ser.). 66.90 (978-0-7362-2548-9(X)) CENGAGE Learning.

Level 3 Paperback Books Set 800928, 6 vols. 2005. (J). pap. *(978-1-59794-093-1(3))* Environments, Inc.

Level 4 Pack: Set of 24 Titles. (Dra Levels Ser.). 89.72 *(978-0-7362-2568-7(4))* CENGAGE Learning.

Level 5 Pack: Set of 19 Titles. (Early Intervention Levels Ser.). 70.45 *(978-0-7362-2549-6(8))* CENGAGE Learning.

Level 6 Pack: Set of 11 Titles. (Early Intervention Levels Ser.). 49.29 *(978-0-7362-2550-2(1))* CENGAGE Learning.

Level 6 Pack: Set of 14 Titles. (Dra Levels Ser.). 51.52 *(978-0-7362-2569-4(2))* CENGAGE Learning.

Level a Big Book Program. (Phonics & Friends Ser.). (gr. -1-2). 651.23 *(978-0-7362-0355-5(9))* CENGAGE Learning.

Level A-C Ell Program Lap Book. 2003. (Metro Reading Ser.). (J). (gr. 12). spiral bd. 116.55 *(978-1-58120-617-3(8))* Metropolitan Teaching & Learning Co.

Level A-C Ell Program Practice Picture Cards Blms. 2003. (Metro Reading Ser.). (gr. 12). 41.29 *(978-1-58120-618-0(6))* Metropolitan Teaching & Learning Co.

Level A Super Classroom Set. (Into English! Ser.). (gr. k-6). 625.88 *(978-1-56334-806-8(3))* CENGAGE Learning.

Level B Pack: Set of 26 Titles. (Guided Reading Levels Ser.). 104.04 *(978-0-7362-2558-8(7))* CENGAGE Learning.

Level D Pack: Set of 21 Titles. (Guided Reading Levels Ser.). 101.29 *(978-0-7362-2560-1(9))* CENGAGE Learning.

Level D Super Classroom Set. (Into English! Ser.). (gr. 3-18). 626.27 *(978-1-56334-849-5(7))* CENGAGE Learning.

Level E Classroom Set. (Phonics & Friends Ser.). (gr. -1-2). 682.59 *(978-0-7362-0601-3(9))* CENGAGE Learning.

Level E Let's Read Little Book Set. (Phonics & Friends Ser.). (gr. -1-2). 14.76 *(978-0-7362-1068-3(7))* CENGAGE Learning.

Level F Classroom Set. (Phonics & Friends Ser.). (gr. -1-2). 682.59 *(978-0-7362-0644-0(2))* CENGAGE Learning.

Level F Let's Read Little Book Set. (Phonics & Friends Ser.). (gr. -1-2). 14.76 *(978-0-7362-1069-0(5))* CENGAGE Learning.

Level F Super Classroom Set. (Into English! Ser.). (gr. 5-18). 626.27 *(978-1-56334-881-5(0))* CENGAGE Learning.

Level L-Set Of 6. 126.23 *(978-0-7565-0862-3(2)*, Compass Point Bks.) Capstone.

Leveled Readers A: Easy, Bookshelf Collection, 30 bks., Set. 2004. (gr. 1-18). 495.00 *(978-0-328-01865-9(1))*; (gr. 2-18). 495.00 *(978-0-328-00411-9(1))*; (gr. 3-18). 495.00 *(978-0-328-00412-6(X))*; (gr. 4-18). 495.00 *(978-0-328-00413-3(8))*; (gr. 5-18). 495.00 *(978-0-328-00414-0(6))*; (gr. 6-18). 495.00 *(978-0-328-00415-7(4))* Addison-Wesley Educational Pubs., Inc.

Leveled Readers B: On-Level, Bookshelf Collection, 30 bks., Set. 2004. (gr. 1-18). 495.00 *(978-0-328-00422-5(7))*; (gr. 2-18). 495.00 *(978-0-328-00423-2(5))*; (gr. 3-18). 495.00 *(978-0-328-00424-9(3))*; (gr. 4-18). 495.00 *(978-0-328-00425-6(1))*; (gr. 5-18). 495.00 *(978-0-328-00426-3(X))*; (gr. 6-18). 495.00 *(978-0-328-00427-0(8))* Addison-Wesley Educational Pubs., Inc.

Leveled Readers C: Challenge, Bookshelf Collection, 6 units, Set. 2004. (Scott Foresman Reading Ser.). (gr. 2-18). 99.00 *(978-0-328-00435-5(9))*; (gr. 6-18). 99.00 *(978-0-328-00439-3(1))* Addison-Wesley Educational Pubs., Inc.

Levels 10-12 Pack: Set of 9 Titles. (Early Intervention Levels Ser.). 46.43 *(978-0-7362-2552-6(8))* CENGAGE Learning.

Levels 12-14 Pack: Set of 10 Titles. (Dra Levels Ser.). 85.63 *(978-0-7362-2571-7(4))* CENGAGE Learning.

Levels 13-15 Pack: Set of 10 Titles. (Early Intervention Levels Ser.). 49.89 *(978-0-7362-2553-3(6))* CENGAGE Learning.

Levels 16-18 Pack: Set of 22 Titles. (Dra Levels Ser.). 115.82 *(978-0-7362-2572-4(2))* CENGAGE Learning.

Levels 20-24 Pack: Set of 12 Titles. (Dra Levels Ser.). 63.31 *(978-0-7362-2573-1(0))* CENGAGE Learning.

Levels 20-24 Pack: Set of 16 Titles. (Early Intervention Levels Ser.). 86.72 *(978-0-7362-2556-4(0))* CENGAGE Learning.

Levels 28-30 Pack: Set of 18 Titles. (Dra Levels Ser.). 114.42 *(978-0-7362-2574-8(9))* CENGAGE Learning.

Levels 38-40 Pack: Set of 14 Titles. (Dra Levels Ser.). 88.02 *(978-0-7362-2575-5(7))* CENGAGE Learning.

Levels 7-8 Pack: Set of 6 Titles. (Early Intervention Levels Ser.). 32.16 *(978-0-7362-2551-9(X))* CENGAGE Learning.

Levels 8-10 Pack: Set of 15 Titles. (Dra Levels Ser.). 85.63 *(978-0-7362-2570-0(6))* CENGAGE Learning.

Levels E-F Pack: Set of 20 Titles. (Guided Reading Levels Ser.). 97.02 *(978-0-7362-2561-8(7))* CENGAGE Learning.

Levels E-F Super Classroom Set. (Phonics & Friends Ser.). (gr. -1-2). 1204.58 *(978-0-7362-0596-2(9))* CENGAGE Learning.

Levels G-J Pack: Set of 24 Titles. (Guided Reading Levels Ser.). 118.32 *(978-0-7362-2562-5(5))* CENGAGE Learning.

Levels K-M Pack: Set of 30 Titles. (Guided Reading Levels Ser.). 172.30 *(978-0-7362-2563-2(3))* CENGAGE Learning.

Levels N-Q Pack: Set of 17 Titles. (Guided Reading Levels Ser.). 106.73 *(978-0-7362-2564-9(1))* CENGAGE Learning.

Levin, Amy. A Bear's Year, 6 vols., Set. 2003. (Phonics Readers 1-36 Ser.). (ENG.). 8p. (gr. k-1). pap. 29.70 *(978-0-7368-3200-7(9))* Capstone.

—Hard Workers, 6 vols., Set. 2003. (Phonics Readers 1-36 Ser.). (ENG.). 8p. (gr. k-1). pap. 29.70 *(978-0-7368-3214-4(9))* Capstone.

—The Vet, 6 vols., Set. 2003. (Phonics Readers 1-36 Ser.). (ENG.). 8p. (gr. k-1). pap. 29.70 *(978-0-7368-3193-2(2))* Capstone.

Levy, Emily, rev. Strategies for Study Success: Highlighting I. 2004. 12.00 *(978-0-9772110-0-5(2))* EBL Coaching.

Levy, Janey. Edwin Visits Earth, 1 vol. 2006. (Neighborhood Readers Ser.). (ENG.). 16p. (gr. 1-2). pap. 6.50 *(978-1-4042-7160-9(0)*, 209947a7-6472-43f9-a407-889f89caad6b, Rosen Classroom) Rosen Publishing Group, Inc., The.

—Jenny in the Jungle, 1 vol. 2006. (Neighborhood Readers Ser.). (ENG.). 8p. (gr. k-1). pap. 5.15 *(978-1-4042-5702-3(0)*, f10f1808-ba27-4c63-8c90-edb3be735942, Rosen Classroom) Rosen Publishing Group, Inc., The.

—The Piggles Picnic, 1 vol. 2006. (Neighborhood Readers Ser.). (ENG.). 12p. (gr. k-1). pap. 5.90 *(978-1-4042-6455-7(8)*, 4dffa697-ee25-4c5a-8f8a-87630102bce9, Rosen Classroom) Rosen Publishing Group, Inc., The.

—Plaga: la Peste Negra (Plague: the Black Death), 1 vol. Sarfatti, Esther, tr. 2015. (Desastres (Doomed) Ser.). (SPA., Illus.). 32p. (J). (gr. 4-5). lib. bdg. 28.27 *(978-1-4824-3248-0(X)*, 69106c09-1ca7-48a8-b418-b03572d64109) Stevens, Gareth Publishing LLLP.

—Play Ball!, 1 vol. 2006. (Neighborhood Readers Ser.). (ENG.). 8p. (gr. k-1). pap. 5.15 *(978-1-4042-5659-0(8)*, 709d2fcb-1a3a-4e01-bf93-a457749fe8c2, Rosen Classroom) Rosen Publishing Group, Inc., The.

—What Would I Wear?, 1 vol. 2006. (Neighborhood Readers Ser.). (ENG.). 8p. (gr. k-1). pap. 5.90 *(978-1-4042-6682-7(8)*, cc799b69-0f30-4426-85b1-3687c9323ff8, Rosen Classroom) Rosen Publishing Group, Inc., The.

Lewis, Rose. The Three Billy Goats Gruff. 2004. (Folk Tales Set 1 Ser.). (ENG.). (J). pap. 7.67 *(978-1-58453-274-3(2))* Pioneer Valley Bks.

Lewman, David. Proud to Be a Ghostbuster. 2016. (Simon & Schuster Ready-To-Read Level 3 Ser.). lib. bdg. 13.55 *(978-0-606-38994-5(6))* Turtleback.

Liberts, Jennifer. Go, Go, Cars! 2019. (Step into Reading Ser.). (ENG.). 32p. (J). (gr. k-1). 14.96 *(978-0-87617-965-9(0))* Penworthy Co., LLC, The.

—Go, Go, Cars! Yamada, Mike, illus. 2018. (Step into Reading Ser.). 32p. (J). (gr. -1-1). 5.99 *(978-0-399-55461-2(0)*, Random Hse. Bks. for Young Readers) Random Hse. Children's Bks.

—Monster Phonics (Blaze & the Monster Machines) 12 Step into Reading Books, 12 vols. Dynamo Limited, illus. 2016. (Step into Reading Ser.). (ENG.). 144p. (J). (gr. -1-1). pap. 12.99 *(978-1-101-94026-6(3)*, Random Hse. Bks. for Young Readers) Random Hse. Children's Bks.

Life Cycles Book Set 800741, 4. 2005. (J). pap. *(978-1-59794-039-9(9))* Environments, Inc.

Light, John. Neighbours Are a Nuisance! 2005. (Illus.). 24p. *(978-1-897968-22-2(1))* Photon Pr.

Light, Kelly. Louise Loves Bake Sales. 2018. (I Can Read Level 1 Ser.). (ENG., Illus.). 32p. (J). (gr. -1-3). 16.99 *(978-0-06-236366-4(2)*, Balzer & Bray) HarperCollins Pubs.

—Louise Loves Bake Sales. Light, Kelly, illus. 2018. (I Can Read Level 1 Ser.). (ENG., Illus.). 32p. (J). (gr. -1-3). pap. 4.99 *(978-0-06-236365-7(4)*, Balzer & Bray) HarperCollins Pubs.

Lin, Joyce, tr. The frog in the Well. Caprio, Pattie, illus. 2008. (ENG & CHI.). 36p. (J). 14.95 *(978-0-9801305-1-5(4))* CE Bilingual Bks. LLC.

Lindeen, Carol K. Farm Tools over Time, 6 vols., Set. 2004. (Phonics Readers Books 37-72 Ser.). (ENG.). 8p. (gr. k-1). pap. 35.70 *(978-0-7368-4084-2(2))* Capstone.

—The Sky at Night, 6 vols., Set. 2004. (Phonics Readers Books 37-72 Ser.). (ENG.). 8p. (gr. k-1). pap. 35.70 *(978-0-7368-4062-0(1))* Capstone.

—What Is a Museum?, 6 vols., Set. 2004. (Phonics Readers Books 37-72 Ser.). (ENG.). 8p. (gr. k-1). pap. 35.70 *(978-0-7368-4076-7(1))* Capstone.

Lindeen, Mary. The Letter Aa Set: Things at School, 6 vols. 2004. (Letter Bks.). (ENG.). 8p. (gr. k-1). pap. 29.70 *(978-0-7368-4100-9(8))* Capstone.

Lindop, Christine. Oxford Bookworms Factfiles: Australia & New Zealand: Level 3: 1000-Word Vocabulary. 3rd ed. 2008. (ENG., Illus.). 80p. 11.00 *(978-0-19-423390-3(1))* Oxford Univ. Pr., Inc.

Lindop, Christine, retold by. Oxford Bookworms Library: the Long White Cloud: Stories from New Zealand: Level 3: 1000-Word Vocabulary. 3rd ed. 2008. (ENG., Illus.). 80p. 11.00 *(978-0-19-479139-7(4))* Oxford Univ. Pr., Inc.

Lindsay, Kenny. A'Choille Fhiadhach (the Wild Wood), 100 vols. 2021. (Lasag Ser.). (ENG.). 74p. (YA). pap. 14.99 *(978-1-910985-75-5(9))* Sandstone Pr. Ltd. GBR. Dist: Casemate Pubs. & Bk. Distributors, LLC.

Lindsay, Kristine. Basic Reading Series - Binder 3. 2004. (J). ring bd. 49.95 *(978-1-58804-371-9(1))* P C I Education.

Lindsey, Cameron. The 10 Best Animal Camouflages. 2008. 14.99 *(978-1-55448-492-8(8))* Scholastic Library Publishing.

—The 10 Most Dangerous Geographic Locations. 2008. 14.99 *(978-1-55448-539-0(8))* Scholastic Library Publishing.

—The 10 Most Terrifying Experiences. 2008. 14.99 *(978-1-55448-551-2(7))* Scholastic Library Publishing.

Lindstrom, Florence M. Meeting New Friends. 2nd ed. 2007. (Illus.). 185p. pap. 8.95 *(978-1-932971-00-2(9))* Christian Liberty Pr.

LinkIt Reading Sudent Resource Book, Level 3. 2006. per. *(978-0-9786500-1-8(8))* Curriculum Concepts International.

Linn, Margot. A Class Play with Ms. Vanilla. Gradisher, Martha, illus. 2005. (I'm Going to Read! Level 3 Ser.: Level 3). (ENG.). 32p. (J). (gr. 1-2). 16.19 *(978-1-4027-2108-3(0))* Sterling Publishing Co., Inc.

Lion King: Simba's Hide & Seek. (My First Read Along Ser.). (J). 7.99 incl. audio *(978-1-55723-747-7(6))* Walt Disney Records.

Lipson, Greta Barclay. Two Sides to Every Story. Hierstein, Judith, illus. 2004. 128p. (J). pap. 14.95 *(978-1-57310-439-5(6))* Teaching & Learning Co.

Litchfield, Jo. First Words Look & Say. Litchfield, Jo, illus. 2005. (Illus.). 18p. (J). 14.99 *(978-0-7945-1024-4(8)*, Usborne) EDC Publishing.

Little Animals Board Books Set 800975, 6. 2005. (J). bds. *(978-1-59794-100-6(X))* Environments, Inc.

Little Bear Book Set 2 800890, 6 vols. 2005. (J). pap. *(978-1-59794-065-8(8))* Environments, Inc.

Little Bear Book Set 800876, 3 vols. 2005. (J). bds. *(978-1-59794-054-2(2))* Environments, Inc.

Little Bear Book Set 800891, 3 vols. 2005. (J). pap. *(978-1-59794-066-5(6))* Environments, Inc.

Little Books Collection: Includes 30 Little Books. 2003. 127.95 *(978-0-7652-0129-4(1))* Modern Curriculum Pr.

Little, Jean. Forward, Shakespeare!, 1 vol. 2005. (Orca Young Readers Ser.). (ENG., Illus.). 112p. (J). (gr. 4-7). per. 5.95 *(978-1-55143-339-4(7))* Orca Bk. Pubs. USA.

Little, Jean & de Vries, Maggie. Once upon a Golden Apple: 25th Anniversary Edition. Gilman, Phoebe, illus. 25th ed. 2016. (ENG.). 26p. (J). (— 1). bds. 7.99 *(978-0-670-07007-7(6)*, Puffin Canada) PRH Canada Young Readers CAN. Dist: Penguin Random Hse. LLC.

A Little Seed: Set A Individual Title Six-Packs. (Smart Start Ser.). (gr. k-1). 23.00 *(978-0-7635-0411-3(4))* Rigby Education.

Littlefield, Angie & Littlefield, Jennifer. The 10 Deadliest Plants. 2007. (J). 14.99 *(978-1-55448-511-6(8))* Scholastic Library Publishing.

Liu, Li. Who Am I? (Big Book) 2010. (1G Big Bks.). (ENG., Illus.). 20p. (J). pap. 8.00 *(978-1-64053-132-1(7)*, ARC Pr. Bks.) American Reading Co.

Live Oak Media PB/CD Readalong Collection. pap. 758.00 incl. audio compact disk *(978-1-59519-235-6(2))*; Vol. 3. pap. 728.00 incl. audio compact disk *(978-1-59519-239-4(5))* Live Oak Media.

Live Oak Media Readalong Collection Set. 2004. cd-rom 84.00 *(978-0-87499-713-2(5))*; cd-rom 84.00 *(978-0-87499-712-5(7))*; Vol. 2. pap. 610.00 incl. audio *(978-1-59519-004-8(X))* Live Oak Media.

Llewellyn, Claire. Asi Nace un Arbol. Mendez, Simon, illus. 2004. (Colección Así Nace... / Starting Life Collection Ser.). (SPA.). 24p. (gr. k-6). pap. 14.95 *(978-1-59437-449-4(X))* Santillana USA Publishing Co., Inc.

—Asi Nace un Pato. Mendez, Simon, illus. 2004. (Colección Así Nace... / Starting Life Collection Ser.). (SPA.). 24p. (gr. k-6). pap. 14.95 *(978-1-59437-448-7(1))* Santillana USA Publishing Co., Inc.

—Asi Nace una Rana. Mendez, Simon, illus. 2003. (Colección Así Nace... / Starting Life Collection Ser.). (SPA.). 24p. (gr. k-6). pap. 14.95 *(978-1-59437-789-1(8))* Santillana USA Publishing Co., Inc.

—Big Bugs Green Band. 2016. (Cambridge Reading Adventures Ser.). (ENG., Illus.). 16p. pap. 7.95 *(978-1-107-55064-3(5))* Cambridge Univ. Pr.

—A Dark Winter Turquoise Band. 2017. (Cambridge Reading Adventures Ser.). (ENG., Illus.). 24p. pap. 7.35 *(978-1-108-43978-7(0))* Cambridge Univ. Pr.

—How Chocolate Is Made Turquoise Band. 2016. (Cambridge Reading Adventures Ser.). (ENG., Illus.). 24p. pap. 8.80 *(978-1-107-57616-2(4))* Cambridge Univ. Pr.

—In the Sea Red Band. Belcher, Andy, photos by. 2016. (Cambridge Reading Adventures Ser.). (ENG., Illus.). 16p. pap. 7.95 *(978-1-107-57578-3(8))* Cambridge Univ. Pr.

—Late for School Yellow Band. Pérez, Moni, illus. 2016. (Cambridge Reading Adventures Ser.). (ENG.). 16p. pap. 7.95 *(978-1-107-57679-7(2))* Cambridge Univ. Pr.

—Looking after Animals. 2016. (Cambridge Reading Adventures Ser.). (ENG., Illus.). 16p. pap. 7.95 *(978-1-316-60582-0(5))* Cambridge Univ. Pr.

—On the Track Blue Band. Ruffle, Mark, illus. 2016. (Cambridge Reading Adventures Ser.). (ENG.). 16p. pap. 7.95 *(978-1-316-50322-5(4))* Cambridge Univ. Pr.

—Our Senses Red Band. 2016. (Cambridge Reading Adventures Ser.). (ENG., Illus.). 16p. pap. 7.95 *(978-1-316-60568-4(X))* Cambridge Univ. Pr.

—The Sun Is up. Cambridge Reading Adventures. Pink a Band. Lopez, Ayesha, illus. 2016. (Cambridge Reading Adventures Ser.). (ENG.). 16p. pap. 7.95 *(978-1-107-54987-6(6))* Cambridge Univ. Pr.

—Water Pink a Band. 2016. (Cambridge Reading Adventures Ser.). (ENG., Illus.). 16p. pap. 7.95 *(978-1-107-57584-4(2))* Cambridge Univ. Pr.

—The Weather Today Red Band. Jonatronix, illus. 2016. (Cambridge Reading Adventures Ser.). (ENG.). 16p. pap. 7.95 *(978-1-107-57676-6(8))* Cambridge Univ. Pr.

Llorente, Pilar Molina. Aura Gris. (SPA.). 80p. (YA). (gr. 5-8). 7.16 *(978-84-216-1636-9(6))* Bruño, Editorial ESP. Dist: Lectorum Pubns., Inc.

Llosa, Mario Vargas. Historia de Mayta. 2005. (SPA., Illus.). 376p. pap. 19.95 *(978-84-204-8415-0(6)*, Alfaguara) Santillana USA Publishing Co., Inc.

Lloyd Jones, Rob. The Story of Spying. 2007. (Young Reading Series 3 Gift Bks). (Illus.). 62p. (J). (gr. 2-5). 8.99 *(978-0-7945-1720-5(X)*, Usborne) EDC Publishing.

Llyfr Lliwio Sali Mali. 2nd ed. 2005. (WEL., Illus.). 24p. pap. *(978-1-902416-88-5(0))* Cymdeithas Lyfrau Ceredigion.

LoaderMandy. Amazing Young Sports People Level 1 Beginner/Elementary. 2010. (Cambridge Experience Readers Ser.). (ENG.). 48p. pap. 14.75 *(978-84-8323-572-0(2))* Cambridge Univ. Pr.

Lobb, Nancy. 16 Extraordinary Native Americans. 2nd ed. 2007. (Illus.). 132p. (YA). (gr. 6-12). tchr. ed., per. 25.00 *(978-0-8251-6282-4(3))* Walch Education.

—16 Extraordinary Young Americans. 2nd ed. 2007. (16 Extraordinary Ser.). (Illus.). 127p. (gr. 6-12). tchr. ed., per. 25.00 *(978-0-8251-6283-1(1))* Walch Education.

Lock, Deborah. Big Trucks. 2013. (DK Reader Pre Level Ser.). lib. bdg. 13.55 *(978-0-606-32459-5(3))* Turtleback.

Lock, Deborah & Dorling Kindersley Publishing Staff. Life in the Stone Age. 2018. (ENG., Illus.). 48p. (J). *(978-0-241-31593-4(X))* Dorling Kindersley Publishing, Inc.

Lockyer, John. How We Communicate, 1 vol. 2018. (ENG., Illus.). 21p. (J). pap. *(978-1-77654-254-3(1)*, Red Rocket Readers) Flying Start Bks.

—The Moon, 1 vol. 2015. (ENG., Illus.). 16p. (-2). pap. *(978-1-77654-140-9(5)*, Red Rocket Readers) Flying Start Bks.

—Paper Making, 1 vol. 2018. (ENG., Illus.). 21p. (J). pap. *(978-1-77654-255-0(X)*, Red Rocket Readers) Flying Start Bks.

—Sound, 1 vol. 2018. (ENG., Illus.). 21p. (J). pap. *(978-1-77654-256-7(8)*, Red Rocket Readers) Flying Start Bks.

—The Sun, 1 vol. 2018. (ENG., Illus.). 21p. (J). pap. *(978-1-77654-257-4(6)*, Red Rocket Readers) Flying Start Bks.

—Vikings, 1 vol. 2018. (ENG., Illus.). 21p. (J). pap. *(978-1-77654-258-1(4)*, Red Rocket Readers) Flying Start Bks.

Lockyer, John & Holden, Pam. Making a Movie, 1 vol. 2009. (Red Rocket Readers Ser.). (ENG., Illus.). 19p. (gr. 2-2). pap. *(978-1-877435-50-8(3)*, Red Rocket Readers) Flying Start Bks.

Lodge, Ali, illus. The Leopard & the Sky God. 2007. (Usborne First Reading: Level 3 Ser.). 48p. (J). (gr. -1-3). 8.99 *(978-0-7945-1838-7(9)*, Usborne) EDC Publishing.

Lofting, Hugh. La Historia del Doctor Dolittle. (SPA.). 136p. 12.95 *(978-84-239-9048-1(6))*; (Illus.). 184p. (YA). (gr. 5-8). 11.95 *(978-84-239-2733-3(4)*, EC2743) Espasa Calpe, S.A. ESP. Dist: Planeta Publishing Corp., Continental Bk. Co., Inc., Lectorum Pubns., Inc.

London, Jack. The Call of the Wild. (ENG.). 112p. (J). 2020. (Arcturus Silhouette Classics Ser.: 5). 12.99 *(978-1-83857-752-0(1)*, 1c3a9d68-a902-4463-b6f9-dae3f0312daf) 2019. (Arcturus Children's Classics Ser.). pap. 6.99 *(978-1-78950-475-0(9)*, d530327a-8b25-4dd8-92ff-46ea2bd0d46d) Arcturus Publishing GBR. Dist: Baker & Taylor Publisher Services (BTPS).

—The Call of the Wild. 2014. (ENG., Illus.). 128p. 17.50 *(978-1-78270-041-8(2))* Award Pubns. Ltd. GBR. Dist: Parkwest Pubns., Inc.

—The Call of the Wild. 2020. (ENG.). (J). (gr. 6). 116p. 16.95 *(978-1-64799-423-5(3))*; 114p. pap. 8.95 *(978-1-64799-422-8(5))* Bibliotech Pr.

—The Call of the Wild. 2019. (ENG.). (J). 84p. (gr. 6). 21.99 *(978-0-368-55922-8(X))*; 84p. (gr. 6). 18.99 *(978-0-368-55923-5(8))*; 76p. (gr. 6). pap. 21.00 *(978-0-368-64463-4(4))*; 84p. (gr. 6). pap. 5.99 *(978-0-368-55921-1(1))*; 76p. (gr. 6). pap. 15.58 *(978-0-368-64461-0(8))*; 76p. (gr. 6). pap. 16.66 *(978-0-368-64462-7(6))*; 112p. (gr. 6). pap. 14.38 *(978-0-368-47555-9(7))*; 112p. (gr. 6). pap. 18.72 *(978-0-368-47547-4(6))*; 100p. (gr. 6). pap. 6.99 *(978-0-368-42660-5(2))*; 108p. (gr. 3-7). pap. 8.52 *(978-0-368-23882-6(2))* Blurb, Inc.

—The Call of the Wild. 2019. (ENG.). 80p. (J). (gr. 6). pap. 7.89 *(978-1-7172-5603-4(1))* CreateSpace Independent Publishing Platform.

—The Call of the Wild. (ENG.). 2018. 236p. (J). (gr. 3-7). 41.95 *(978-0-353-61365-2(7))* 2018. 216p. (J). (gr. 3-7). 41.95 *(978-0-353-60709-5(6))* 2018. 234p. (J). (gr. 3-7). 41.95 *(978-0-353-33661-2(0))* 2018. 236p. (J). (gr. 3-7). pap. 24.95 *(978-0-353-61364-5(9))* 2018. 216p. (J). (gr. 3-7). pap. 24.95 *(978-0-353-60708-8(8))* 2018. 234p. (J). (gr. 3-7). pap. 24.95 *(978-0-353-33660-5(2))* 2018. 286p. (J). (gr. 3-7). 42.95 *(978-0-343-66897-6(1))* 2018. 236p. (J). (gr. 3-7). 41.95 *(978-0-343-67657-5(5))* 2018. 384p. (J). (gr. 3-7). pap. 29.95 *(978-0-344-14100-3(4))* 2018. (Illus.). 236p. (J). 24.95 *(978-0-343-58127-5(2))* 2018. (Illus.). 236p. (J). 24.95 *(978-0-341-71675-4(8))* 2018. (Illus.). 234p. (J). 24.95 *(978-0-343-28907-2(5))* 2018. (Illus.). 216p. (J). 24.95 *(978-0-343-57471-0(3))* 2018. (Illus.). 236p. (J). pap. 14.95 *(978-0-341-71674-7(X))* 2018. (Illus.). 234p. (J). pap. 14.95 *(978-0-343-28906-5(7))* 2018. (Illus.). 216p. (J). pap. 14.95 *(978-0-343-57470-3(5))* 2018. (Illus.). 236p. (J). pap. 14.95 *(978-0-343-58126-8(4))* 2017. (Illus.). (J). pap. 17.95 *(978-1-375-63530-1(1))* 2017. (Illus.). (J). pap. 15.95 *(978-1-375-43328-0(8))* 2017. (Illus.). (YA). (gr. 7). pap. 14.95 *(978-1-376-31581-3(5))* 2017. (Illus.). (YA). (gr. 7). pap. 14.95 *(978-1-376-31907-1(1))* 2017. (Illus.). (YA). (gr. 7). pap. 14.95 *(978-1-375-43706-6(2))* 2015. (Illus.). (YA). (gr. 7). 27.95 *(978-1-297-58719-1(7))* 2015. (Illus.). (YA). (gr. 7). 24.95 *(978-1-297-55263-2(6))* 2015. (Illus.). (YA). (gr. 7). 25.95 *(978-1-297-54339-5(4))* Creative Media Partners, LLC.

—The Call of the Wild. (ENG.). (J). 2020. 102p. pap. *(978-1-77426-017-3(4))* 2019. 86p. (gr. 3-7). pap. *(978-1-989201-53-4(9))* East India Publishing Co.

—The Call of the Wild. (ENG.). (J). 2019. 76p. (gr. 6). pap. 15.99 *(978-1-7072-5297-8(1))* 2019. 288p. (gr. 6). pap. 16.99 *(978-1-6968-4261-7(1))* 2019. 112p. (gr. 6). pap. 12.00 *(978-1-6942-8179-1(5))* 2019. 288p. (gr. 6). pap. 16.99 *(978-1-6947-7921-2(1))* 2019. 104p. (gr. 6). pap. 7.00 *(978-1-6888-2057-9(4))* 2019. 84p. (gr. 6). pap. 8.99 *(978-1-0867-3495-9(5))* 2019. 182p. (gr. 6). pap. 12.99 *(978-1-0869-6900-9(6))* 2019. 100p. (gr. 6). pap. 5.99 *(978-1-0899-7963-0(0))* 2019. 180p. (gr. 6). pap. 12.99 *(978-1-6863-2288-4(7))* 2019. 300p. (gr. 6). pap. 21.99 *(978-1-0898-4708-3(4))* 2019. 136p. (gr. 6). pap. 12.99 *(978-1-0823-4615-6(2))* 2019. 174p. (gr. 6). pap. 13.99 *(978-1-0798-9710-4(0))* 2019. 300p. (gr. 6). pap. 17.99 *(978-1-0778-4330-1(5))* 2019. 174p. (gr. 6). pap. 11.99 *(978-1-0794-1378-6(2))* 2019. 170p. (gr. 6). pap. 14.99 *(978-1-0794-8405-2(1))* 2019. 112p. (gr. 6). pap. 8.99 *(978-1-0710-7867-9(4))* 2019. 170p. (gr. 6). pap. 14.99 *(978-1-0745-6105-5(8))* 2019. 288p. (gr. 6). pap. 16.99 *(978-1-0968-6268-0(9))* 2019. 174p. (gr. 6). pap. 12.99 *(978-1-0988-4290-1(1))* 2019. 170p. (gr. 6). pap. 13.99 *(978-1-0705-2322-4(4))* 2019. 168p. (gr. 6). pap. 12.99 *(978-1-0953-9506-6(8))* 2019. 176p. (gr. 6). pap. 12.99 *(978-1-0921-7111-3(8))* 2019. 182p. (gr. 3-7). pap. 12.99 *(978-1-7962-8296-2(0))* 2019. 108p. (gr. 3-7). pap. 8.95 *(978-1-7966-1461-9(0))* 2019. 170p. (gr. 3-7). pap. 12.99 *(978-1-7950-1776-3(7))* 2019. 170p. (gr. 3-7). pap. 12.99 *(978-1-7944-9508-1(8))* 2018. (Illus.). 176p. (gr. 3-7). pap. 14.99 *(978-1-7920-0645-6(4))* 2018. (Illus.). 204p. (gr. 3-7). pap. 16.99 *(978-1-7915-8480-1(2))* 2018. (Illus.). 68p. (gr. 3-7). pap. 15.00 *(978-1-7294-5390-2(2))* Independently Published.

—The Call of the Wild. 2018. (ENG., Illus.). 214p. (J). (gr. 3-7). pap. *(978-1-387-88088-1(8))* Lulu Pr., Inc.

—The Call of the Wild. 2018. (ENG., 100p. (J). (gr. 3-7). Illus.). *(978-1-77335-121-6(4))*; pap. *(978-1-77335-119-3(2))* Magdalene Pr.

—The Call of the Wild. 2020. (Green Puffin Classics Ser.). (Illus.). 160p. (J). pap. 15.99 *(978-0-241-44076-6(9)*, Puffin) Penguin Bks., Ltd. GBR. Dist: Independent Pubs. Group.

—The Call of the Wild. 2017. (ENG., Illus.). 102p. (YA). (gr. 7). pap. *(978-81-291-2053-3(4))* Rupa & Co.

—The Call of the Wild. (ENG., Illus.). 2018. 82p. (J). (gr. 3-7). 9.95 *(978-1-61382-403-0(3))* 2018. 82p. (J). (gr. 3-7). pap. 4.23 *(978-1-61382-443-6(2))* 2011. (YA). (gr. 7). 12.99 *(978-1-61382-812-0(8))* Simon & Brown.

—The Call of the Wild. Domínguez, Oscar, illus. 2019. 176p. (J). (gr. 6-6). 14.99 *(978-1-63158-393-3(X)*, Racehorse Publishing) Skyhorse Publishing Co., Inc.

—The Call of the Wild. 2018. (ENG., Illus.). 96p. (YA). (gr. 7). pap. 11.99 *(978-1-5287-0566-0(1)*, Classic Bks. Library) The Editorium, LLC.

—The Call of the Wild. 2020. (Mint Editions — Grand Adventures Ser.). (ENG.). 68p. (J). (gr. 3-8). pap. 5.99 *(978-1-5132-6339-7(0)*, West Margin Pr.) West Margin Pr.

—The Call of the Wild. 2018. (ENG., Illus.). 76p. (J). 12.99 *(978-1-5154-2901-2(6))* Wilder Pubns., Corp.

—La Llamada de la Selva. 2019.Tr. of Call of the Wild. (SPA.). 88p. (J). pap. 7.00 *(978-1-0867-9696-4(9))* Independently Published.

London, Jack., creator. Call of the Wild. 2020. (ENG.). 236p. (J). (gr. 6). pap. *(978-0-371-27267-1(X))* HardPr.
London, Jack. & Mitchill, Theodore C. The Call of the Wild. 2019. (ENG.). 164p. (J). (gr. 6). 23.95 *(978-0-530-93716-8(6))*; pap. 13.95 *(978-0-530-93715-1(8))* Creative Media Partners, LLC. (Wentworth Pr.).
London, Jack. & Treasures, Grandma's. The Call of the Wild. 2019. (ENG.). 94p. (J). (gr. 6). pap. *(978-0-359-53583-5(6))* Lulu Pr., Inc.
Long Ago Children. (J). pap. 13.15 *(978-0-8136-4296-3(5))* Modern Curriculum Pr.
Long, David. War School for Dogs: Band 16/Sapphire. 2017. (Collins Big Cat Ser.). (ENG., Illus.). 56p. (J). pap. 12.99 *(978-0-00-820891-2(3))* HarperCollins Pubs. Ltd. GBR. Dist: Independent Pubs. Group.
Longoria, Madelín G. Verdeazul. 2009. (J). *(978-1-59835-132-3(X))* Cambridge BrickHouse, Inc.
Longstaff, Abie. Rumpelstiltskin: Band 09/Gold. Romanet, Caroline, illus. 2015. (Collins Big Cat Ser.). (ENG.). 24p. (J). (gr. 2-2). pap. 9.99 *(978-0-00-759117-6(9))* HarperCollins Pubs. Ltd. GBR. Dist: Independent Pubs. Group.
Look & Learn. (Illus.). (J). (gr. -1-2). lib. bdg. 55.80 *(978-1-56674-928-2(X))* Forest Hse. Publishing Co., Inc.
Looking for Eggs: Individual Title Six-Packs. (gr. 1-2). 22.00 *(978-0-7635-9179-3(3))* Rigby Education.
Looking for Lewis. (J). pap. 13.75 *(978-0-8136-4650-3(2))* Modern Curriculum Pr.
Looking for the Queen. (Early Intervention Levels Ser.). 31.86 *(978-0-7362-0628-0(0))* CENGAGE Learning.
Looking for the Queen (18), Vol. 18. (Early Intervention Levels Ser.). 5.31 *(978-0-7362-0616-7(7))* CENGAGE Learning.
Lopez, Andre. Emily's Electricity Experiments, 1 vol. 2013. (Rosen Readers Ser.). (ENG.). 24p. (J). (gr. 3-3). pap. 8.25 *(978-1-4777-2458-3(3),* 85bff4e2-18b9-4757-815d-09cd725f7f07); pap. 49.50 *(978-1-4777-2459-0(1))* Rosen Publishing Group, Inc., The. (Rosen Classroom).
Lorimer, Janet. The Bad Luck Play, 1 vol. unabr. ed. 2010. (Q Reads Ser.). (ENG.). 32p. (YA). (gr. 9-12). pap. 8.50 *(978-1-61651-198-2(2))* Saddleback Educational Publishing, Inc.
—Beasts, 1 vol. unabr. ed. 2010. (Q Reads Ser.). (ENG.). 32p. (YA). (gr. 9-12). pap. 8.50 *(978-1-61651-212-5(1))* Saddleback Educational Publishing, Inc.
—Ben Cody's Treasure, 1 vol. unabr. ed. 2010. (Q Reads Ser.). (ENG.). 32p. (YA). (gr. 9-12). pap. 8.50 *(978-1-61651-189-0(3))* Saddleback Educational Publishing, Inc.
—Danger on Ice, 1 vol. unabr. ed. 2010. (Q Reads Ser.). (ENG.). 32p. (YA). (gr. 9-12). pap. 8.50 *(978-1-61651-179-1(6))* Saddleback Educational Publishing, Inc.
—Death Grip, 1 vol. unabr. ed. 2010. (Q Reads Ser.). (ENG.). 32p. (YA). (gr. 9-12). pap. 8.50 *(978-1-61651-200-2(8))* Saddleback Educational Publishing, Inc.
—Empty Eyes, 1 vol. unabr. ed. 2010. (Q Reads Ser.). (ENG.). 32p. (YA). (gr. 9-12). pap. 8.50 *(978-1-61651-180-7(X))* Saddleback Educational Publishing, Inc.
—Look to the Light, 1 vol. unabr. ed. 2010. (Q Reads Ser.). (ENG.). 32p. (YA). (gr. 9-12). pap. 8.50 *(978-1-61651-193-7(1))* Saddleback Educational Publishing, Inc.
—The Mystery Quilt, 1 vol. unabr. ed. 2010. (Q Reads Ser.). (ENG.). 32p. (YA). (gr. 9-12). pap. 8.50 *(978-1-61651-183-8(4))* Saddleback Educational Publishing, Inc.
—No Place Like Home, 1 vol. unabr. ed. 2010. (Q Reads Ser.). (ENG.). 32p. (YA). (gr. 9-12). pap. 8.50 *(978-1-61651-203-3(2))* Saddleback Educational Publishing, Inc.
—Ring of Fear, 1 vol. unabr. ed. 2010. (Q Reads Ser.). (ENG.). 32p. (YA). (gr. 9-12). pap. 8.50 *(978-1-61651-194-4(X))* Saddleback Educational Publishing, Inc.
—Ruby's Terrible Secret, 1 vol. unabr. ed. 2010. (Q Reads Ser.). (ENG.). 32p. (YA). (gr. 9-12). pap. 8.50 *(978-1-61651-218-7(0))* Saddleback Educational Publishing, Inc.
—Tug-of-War, 1 vol. unabr. ed. 2010. (Q Reads Ser.). (ENG.). 32p. (YA). (gr. 9-12). pap. 8.50 *(978-1-61651-196-8(6))* Saddleback Educational Publishing, Inc.
Lost: Individual Title, 6 Packs. (Story Steps Ser.). (gr. k-2). 23.00 *(978-0-7635-9817-4(8))* Rigby Education.
Lost! Individual Title, 6 Packs. (gr. k-1). 23.00 *(978-0-7635-9069-7(X))* Rigby Education.
Lost! Set D Individual Title, 6 Packs. (Smart Start Ser.). (gr. k-1). 23.00 *(978-0-7635-0450-2(5))* Rigby Education.
Lovvorn, Ann R. Chocolate Puddles. Reece, James A., illus. 2010. 36p. pap. 15.49 *(978-1-4520-5158-1(5))* AuthorHouse.
Low, Vicki. Cave of Secrets. Roth, Mike, illus. 2007. (Timeline Ser.). 48p. pap. 8.99 *(978-1-4190-4391-8(9))* Steck-Vaughn.
lowe, Jackie & Nash, Marion. Spirals Series: Activities for Home Books, 3 vols. 2005. (Spirals Ser.). (ENG.). (C). 94.95 *(978-1-84312-412-2(2),* RU51880) Fulton, David Pubs. GBR. Dist: Taylor & Francis Group.
Lowry, Lois. Gooney Bird Greene: Three Books in One! Gooney Bird Greene, Gooney Bird & the Room Mother, Gooney the Fabulous. 2016. (Gooney Bird Greene Ser.). (ENG.). 384p. (J). (gr. 1-4). 18.99 *(978-0-544-84824-5(1),* 1647478, Clarion Bks.) HarperCollins Pubs.
Little Bear Book Set 800889, 3 vols. 2005. (J). *(978-1-59794-064-1(X))* Environments, Inc.
Lucy Meets a Dragon, 6 Packs. (Literatura 2000 Ser.). (gr. 2-3). 33.00 *(978-0-7635-0177-8(8))* Rigby Education.
Luen Yang, Gene. Secret Coders: Paths & Portals. 2016. (Secret Coders Ser.: 2). (ENG., Illus.). 96p. (J). pap. 10.99 *(978-1-62672-076-3(2),* 900134877, First Second Bks.) Roaring Brook Pr.
Luke's Adventures: Individual Title Six-Packs. (gr. -1-2). 27.00 *(978-0-7635-9460-2(1))* Rigby Education.
Lumsden, Zoa. The Great Grizzly Race. Suska, Monika, illus. 2019. (Early Bird Readers — Purple (Early Bird Stories (tm)) Ser.). (ENG.). 32p. (J). (gr. k-3). 30.65 *(978-1-5415-4231-0(2),* 3784ef28-44d5-4352-946c-9ca1dca4bcc8); pap. 9.99 *(978-1-5415-7419-9(2),* 6cea8f99-e0a8-4465-915f-f76b6528bb6c) Lerner Publishing Group. (Lerner Pubns.).
Luna, James. Growing up on the Playground / Nuestro Patio de Recreo. Barela-Di Bisceglie, Monica, illus. 2018. (ENG & SPA.). 32p. (J). (gr. -1-3). 17.95 *(978-1-55885-871-8(7),* Piñata Books) Arte Publico Pr.
Luna, James & Villarroel, Carolina. The Runaway Piggy/El Cochinito Fugitivo. Lacámara, Laura, illus. 2010. (SPA.). 32p. (J). (gr. -1-3). 16.95 *(978-1-55885-586-1(6),* Piñata Books) Arte Publico Pr.
Lunch at the Joy House Cafe. (Early Intervention Levels Ser.). 31.86 *(978-0-7362-0666-2(3))* CENGAGE Learning.
Lunch at the Joy House Cafe (24), Vol. 24. (Early Intervention Levels Ser.). 5.31 *(978-0-7362-0654-9(X))* CENGAGE Learning.
Lunch Orders: 6 Small Books. (gr. k-3). 24.00 *(978-0-7635-6238-0(6))* Rigby Education.
The Lunchroom: Individual Title Six-Packs. (gr. -1-2). 27.00 *(978-0-7635-9461-9(X))* Rigby Education.
Lundy, Kathleen Gould. In a Class of Her Own. Alward, Jeff, illus. 2007. 48p. (J). lib. bdg. 23.08 *(978-1-4242-1629-1(X))* Fitzgerald Bks.
Lunis, Natalie. Making a Bug Habitat. 2011. (Early Connections Ser.). (J). *(978-1-61672-561-7(3))* Benchmark Education Co.
Luton, Susan. Bilingual Beginning Skills, Grades PreK-1. 2009. (Bilingual Beginning Skills Ser.). (Illus.). 96p. (J). (gr. -1-3). pap. 14.99 *(978-1-4190-9929-8(9))* Steck-Vaughn.
Lying as Still as I Can: Six-Pack. (Greetings Ser.: Vol. 3). (gr. 2-3). 31.00 *(978-0-7635-9433-6(4))* Rigby Education.
Lyon, Rachel. I Wish I'd Been Born a Unicorn. Ringli, Andrea, illus. 2019. (Early Bird Readers — Green (Early Bird Stories (tm)) Ser.). (ENG.). 32p. (J). (gr. k-3). pap. 9.99 *(978-1-5415-7408-3(7),* 7e4b1cca-74de-4f5f-9695-fbcb104736b5, Lerner Pubns.) Lerner Publishing Group.
—A Royal Mess. Echeverri, Catalina, illus. 2019. (Early Bird Readers — Purple (Early Bird Stories (tm)) Ser.). (ENG.). 32p. (J). (gr. k-3). 30.65 *(978-1-5415-4228-0(2),* 1f61fdbd-9d0d-4876-a230-da8cbc97bb04); pap. 9.99 *(978-1-5415-7420-5(6),* e255fc99-b695-49c6-ac20-b16bec76a867) Lerner Publishing Group. (Lerner Pubns.).
MacAndrewRichard. The Black Pearls Starter/Beginner. 2008. (Cambridge English Readers Ser.). (ENG.). 32p. pap. 14.75 *(978-0-521-73289-5(1))* Cambridge Univ. Pr.
—A Little Trouble in Dublin Level 1 Beginner/Elementary. 2010. (Cambridge Experience Readers Ser.). (ENG., Illus.). 46p. pap. 14.75 *(978-84-8323-695-6(8))* Cambridge Univ. Pr.
—A Little Trouble in the Yorkshire Dales Level 3 Lower Intermediate. 2009. (Cambridge Experience Readers Ser.). (ENG.). 80p. pap. 14.75 *(978-84-8323-584-3(6))* Cambridge Univ. Pr.
—Scotland Level 3 Lower-Intermediate. 2009. (Cambridge Experience Readers Ser.). (ENG., Illus.). 80p. pap. 14.75 *(978-84-8323-579-9(X))* Cambridge Univ. Pr.
Macceca, Michael L. The World of Plants, 1 vol. rev. ed. 2007. (Science: Informational Text Ser.). (ENG.). 32p. (gr. 3-6). pap. 12.99 *(978-0-7439-0589-3(X))* Teacher Created Materials, Inc.
Macceca, Stephanie. George Washington Carver: Agriculture Pioneer, 1 vol. rev. ed. 2007. (Science: Informational Text Ser.). (ENG.). 32p. (gr. 3-6). pap. 12.99 *(978-0-7439-0590-9(3))* Teacher Created Materials, Inc.
Macdonald, Fiona. The Dragon's Bride & Other Dragon Stories: Band 14/Ruby (Collins Big Cat) 2017. (Collins Big Cat Tales Ser.). (ENG., Illus.). 48p. (J). (gr. 3-4). pap. 12.99 *(978-0-00-817939-7(5))* HarperCollins Pubs. Ltd. GBR. Dist: Independent Pubs. Group.
—You Wouldn't Want to Work on a Medieval Cathedral! A Difficult Job That Never Ends. 2010. (You Wouldn't Want to... Ser.). 32p. (J). 29.00 *(978-0-531-20504-4(5),* Watts, Franklin) Scholastic Library Publishing.
MacDonald, Kimber. The Misfits, Level 3. Swain, Wilson, illus. 2006. (ENG.). 24p. (J). (gr. 1-17). per. 3.99 *(978-1-58476-421-2(X),* IKIDS) Innovative Kids.
MacDonald, Margaret. Animal Habitats. 2011. (Learn-Abouts: Level 10 Ser.). (Illus.). 16p. (J). pap. 7.95 *(978-1-59920-598-4(X))* Black Rabbit Bks.
—Boots & Shoes. 2011. (Learn-Abouts: Level 10 Ser.). (Illus.). 16p. (J). pap. 7.95 *(978-1-59920-604-2(8))* Black Rabbit Bks.
—Caves. 2011. (Learn-Abouts Ser.). (Illus.). 16p. (J). pap. 7.95 *(978-1-59920-633-2(1))* Black Rabbit Bks.
—Deciduous & Evergreen Trees. 2011. (Learn-Abouts: Level 10 Ser.). (Illus.). 16p. (J). pap. 7.95 *(978-1-59920-603-5(X))* Black Rabbit Bks.
—Energy from the Sun. 2011. (Learn-Abouts Ser.). (Illus.). 16p. (J). pap. 7.95 *(978-1-59920-634-9(X))* Black Rabbit Bks.
—A Family Tree. 2011. (Learn-Abouts Ser.). (Illus.). 16p. (J). pap. 9.95 *(978-1-59920-613-4(7))* Palgrave Macmillan.
—Fire. 2011. (Learn-Abouts Ser.). (Illus.). 16p. (J). pap. 7.95 *(978-1-59920-618-9(8))* Black Rabbit Bks.
—Glass. 2011. (Learn-Abouts Ser.). (Illus.). 16p. (J). pap. 7.95 *(978-1-59920-636-3(6))* Black Rabbit Bks.
—Homes of the Past. 2011. (Learn-Abouts Ser.). (Illus.). 16p. (J). pap. 7.95 *(978-1-59920-645-5(5))* Black Rabbit Bks.
—How Do Plants Grow? 2011. (Learn-Abouts Ser.). (Illus.). 16p. (J). pap. 9.95 *(978-1-59920-635-6(8))* Palgrave Macmillan.
—I Want to Buy a Rabbit. 2011. (Learn-Abouts Ser.). (Illus.). 16p. (J). pap. 7.95 *(978-1-59920-631-8(5))* Black Rabbit Bks.
—Job Quiz. 2011. (Learn-Abouts: Level 10 Ser.). (Illus.). 16p. (J). pap. 7.95 *(978-1-59920-599-1(8))* Black Rabbit Bks.
—Kitchen Machines. 2011. (Learn-Abouts: Level 10 Ser.). (Illus.). 16p. (J). pap. 7.95 *(978-1-59920-602-8(1))* Black Rabbit Bks.
—Leisure in the Past. 2011. (Learn-Abouts Ser.). (Illus.). 16p. (J). pap. 7.95 *(978-1-59920-629-5(3))* Black Rabbit Bks.
—Meat-Eating Plants. 2011. (Learn-Abouts Ser.). (Illus.). 16p. (J). pap. 7.95 *(978-1-59920-619-6(6))* Black Rabbit Bks.
—Rain. 2011. (Learn-Abouts Ser.). (Illus.). 16p. (J). pap. 7.95 *(978-1-59920-649-3(8))* Black Rabbit Bks.
—Rivers of the World. 2011. (Learn-Abouts Ser.). (Illus.). 16p. (J). pap. 7.95 *(978-1-59920-646-2(3))* Black Rabbit Bks.
—Rules on the Soccer Field. 2011. (Learn-Abouts Ser.). (Illus.). 16p. (J). pap. 7.95 *(978-1-59920-616-5(1))* Black Rabbit Bks.
—Scooters & Skates. 2011. (Learn-Abouts Ser.). (Illus.). 16p. (J). pap. 7.95 *(978-1-59920-650-9(1))* Black Rabbit Bks.
—Toys Long Ago. 2011. (Learn-Abouts: Level 10 Ser.). (Illus.). 16p. (J). pap. 7.95 *(978-1-59920-597-7(1))* Black Rabbit Bks.
—What Are Houses Made Of? 2011. (Learn-Abouts Ser.). (Illus.). 16p. (J). pap. 7.95 *(978-1-59920-620-2(X))* Black Rabbit Bks.
—What Do New Clothes Cost? 2011. (Learn-Abouts Ser.). (Illus.). 16p. (J). pap. 7.95 *(978-1-59920-615-8(3))* Black Rabbit Bks.
—What Do People Do in Winter? 2011. (Learn-Abouts: Level 10 Ser.). (Illus.). 16p. (J). pap. 7.95 *(978-1-59920-601-1(3))* Black Rabbit Bks.
—What Does the Referee Do? 2011. (Learn-Abouts Ser.). (Illus.). 16p. (J). pap. 7.95 *(978-1-59920-632-5(3))* Black Rabbit Bks.
—What Keeps Me Healthy? 2012. (Level B Ser.). (ENG., Illus.). 16p. (J). (gr. k-2). pap. 7.95 *(978-1-927136-13-3(X),* 19425) RiverStream Publishing.
—What Season Is It? 2011. (Learn-Abouts Ser.). (Illus.). 16p. (J). pap. 7.95 *(978-1-59920-617-2(X))* Black Rabbit Bks.
—What Things Did Your Parents Play With? 2012. (Level E Ser.). (ENG., Illus.). 16p. (J). (gr. k-2). pap. 7.95 *(978-1-927136-41-6(5,* 19427) RiverStream Publishing.
—What to Do When You Are Lost. 2011. (Learn-Abouts: Level 10 Ser.). (Illus.). 16p. (J). pap. 7.95 *(978-1-59920-600-4(5))* Black Rabbit Bks.
—When Does This Tree Grow Best? 2012. (Level A Ser.). (ENG., Illus.). 16p. (J). (gr. k-2). pap. 7.95 *(978-1-927136-04-1(0),* 19435) RiverStream Publishing.
—Where Am I? 2012. (Level A Ser.). (ENG., Illus.). 16p. (J). (gr. k-2). pap. 7.95 *(978-1-927136-05-8(9),* 19438) RiverStream Publishing.
—Where Can You Eat This Food? 2012. (Level F Ser.). (ENG., Illus.). 16p. (J). (gr. k-2). pap. 7.95 *(978-1-927136-50-8(4),* 19440) RiverStream Publishing.
—Who Can Save Power? 2012. (Level B Ser.). (ENG., Illus.). 16p. (J). (gr. k-2). pap. 7.95 *(978-1-927136-14-0(8),* 19448) RiverStream Publishing.
—Working as a Team. 2011. (Learn-Abouts Ser.). (Illus.). 16p. (J). pap. 7.95 *(978-1-59920-648-6(X))* Black Rabbit Bks.
Machajewski, Sarah. Our Country's Symbols, 1 vol. 2012. (InfoMax Readers Ser.). (ENG., Illus.). 24p. (J). (gr. 1-1). pap. 8.25 *(978-1-4488-8980-8(4),* 4096fabd-54b7-4f3a-a45b-bf7d62a5cb87, Rosen Classroom) Rosen Publishing Group, Inc., The.
MacKinnon, Mairi. Croc Gets a Shock. Blunt, Fred, illus. 2014. (Usborne Phonics Readers Ser.). (ENG.). (J). (gr. -1-3). pap. 6.99 *(978-0-7945-3395-3(7),* Usborne) EDC Publishing.
Maclaine, James. Elephants IR. 2011. (Beginner's Nature Ser.). 32p. (J). ring bd. 4.99 *(978-0-7945-3122-5(9),* Usborne) EDC Publishing.
MacPhail, Catherine. Jack in Goal: Band 08/Purple (Collins Big Cat) Phillips, Mike, illus. 2019. (Collins Big Cat Ser.). (ENG.). 24p. (J). (gr. k-2). pap. 8.99 *(978-0-00-833896-1(5))* HarperCollins Pubs. Ltd. GBR. Dist: Independent Pubs. Group.
Made in Korea: Six-Pack. (Greetings Ser.: Vol. 3). (gr. 3-5). 31.00 *(978-0-7635-1824-0(7))* Rigby Education.
La Madera. (Coleccion Conceptos de Ciencia en Big Books). (SPA., Illus.). (J). (gr. k-3). 21.95 *(978-0-8136-7426-1(3),* MD7216) Modern Curriculum Pr.
Madson, Trish. C Is for California: A Golden State ABC Primer. 2017. (ENG., Illus.). 20p. (J). (gr. -1 — 1). bds. 12.99 *(978-1-944822-70-5(4),* 552270) Familius LLC.
—T Is for Texas: A Lone Star State ABC Primer. 2017. (ENG., Illus.). 20p. (J). (gr. -1 — 1). bds. 12.99 *(978-1-944822-75-0(5),* 552275) Familius LLC.
—W Is for Washington: An Evergreen State ABC Primer. Miles, David W., illus. 2016. (ENG.). 20p. (J). (gr. -1 — 1). bds. 12.95 *(978-1-944822-02-6(X),* 552202) Familius LLC.
Magazine Level D. 2004. (Reading Central Ser.). (J). (gr. 2-18). 5.95 *(978-1-58830-870-2(7))* Metropolitan Teaching & Learning Co.
Magazine Level E. 2004. (Reading Central Ser.). (J). (gr. 2-18). 5.95 *(978-1-58830-871-9(5))* Metropolitan Teaching & Learning Co.
Magazine Level F. 2004. (Reading Central Ser.). (J). (gr. 2-18). 5.95 *(978-1-58830-872-6(3))* Metropolitan Teaching & Learning Co.
Magee, Wes. Little Dragon. Warburton, Sarah, illus. 2004. (ENG.). 24p. (J). lib. bdg. 23.65 *(978-1-59646-690-6(1))* Dingles & Co.
—Who Likes Pancakes?, 4 vols. 2005. (QEB Readers). (Illus.). 24p. (J). (gr. 1-4). lib. bdg. 15.95 *(978-1-59566-091-6(7))* QEB Publishing Inc.
Maggart, Kaye Wiley & Prentice-Hall Staff. Shining Star, Introductory Level. 2003. (ENG., Illus.). xiv, 289p. (gr. 6-12). 73.20 *(978-0-13-111285-8(6))* Pearson ESL.
Magic Food: Individual Title Six-Packs. (Chiquilibros Ser.). (gr. k-1). 23.00 *(978-0-7635-0441-0(6))* Rigby Education.
Magic Tricks. Date not set. (Illus.). 64p. (J). 5.98 *(978-1-4054-0409-9(4))* Parragon, Inc.
Mahy, Margaret. The Gargling Gorilla: Band 14/Ruby (Collins Big Cat) Phillips, Mike, illus. 2007. (Collins Big Cat Ser.). (ENG.). 112p. (J). (gr. 3-4). pap. 12.99 *(978-0-00-723089-1(3))* HarperCollins Pubs. Ltd. GBR. Dist: Independent Pubs. Group.
The Mail: Individual Title Two-Packs. (Chiquilibros Ser.). (gr. -1-1). 12.00 *(978-0-7635-8541-9(6))* Rigby Education.
Maile, Ruby. When Do You Sleep? 2012. (Level E Ser.). (ENG., Illus.). 16p. (J). (gr. k-2). pap. 7.95 *(978-1-927136-40-9(7),* 19434) RiverStream Publishing.
—Why Are You Having a Party? 2012. (Level B Ser.). (ENG., Illus.). 16p. (J). (gr. k-2). pap. 7.95 *(978-1-927136-10-2(5),* 19459) RiverStream Publishing.
—Why Do You Live Here? 2012. (Level C Ser.). (ENG., Illus.). 16p. (J). (gr. k-2). pap. 7.95 *(978-1-927136-25-6(3),* 19463) RiverStream Publishing.
—Why Should I Eat Fruit? 2012. (Level A Ser.). (ENG., Illus.). 16p. (J). (gr. k-2). pap. 7.95 *(978-1-927136-03-4(2),* 19467) RiverStream Publishing.
Maisy Cloth Books Set 800846, 4. 2005. (J). *(978-1-59794-047-4(X))* Environments, Inc.
Make a Tune. (Early Intervention Levels Ser.). 28.38 *(978-0-7362-0403-3(2))* CENGAGE Learning.
Make a Tune (20), Vol. 20. (Early Intervention Levels Ser.). 4.73 *(978-0-7362-0228-2(5))* CENGAGE Learning.
Make It! (Early Intervention Levels Ser.). 3.55 *(978-0-7362-0078-3(9))*; 21.30 *(978-0-7362-0357-9(5))* CENGAGE Learning.
Malam, John. You Wouldn't Want to Be a Secret Agent During World War II! A Perilous Mission Behind Enemy Lines. 2010. (You Wouldn't Want to... Ser.). 32p. (J). 29.00 *(978-0-531-20474-0(X),* Watts, Franklin) Scholastic Library Publishing.
Malara, Maria. Mysterious Places. 2007. (Steck-Vaughn BOLDPRINT Anthologies Ser.). (ENG., Illus.). 48p. (gr. 4-8). pap. 16.90 *(978-1-4190-4022-1(7))* Houghton Mifflin Harcourt Publishing Co.
Man On The Moon: (Guided Reading Levels Ser.). 8.48 *(978-0-7362-1692-0(8))*; 50.88 *(978-0-7362-2141-2(7))* CENGAGE Learning.
Mangieri, Catherine. A Funny First Day, 1 vol. 2006. (Neighborhood Readers Ser.). (ENG., Illus.). 12p. (gr. 1-2). pap. 5.90 *(978-1-4042-6839-5(1),* 2e68e71c-4053-4ec9-aae2-68c794d91da3, Rosen Classroom) Rosen Publishing Group, Inc., The.
Mann, Rachel. Race to a Fire!, 6 vols., Set. 2003. (Phonics Readers 1-36 Ser.). (ENG.). 8p. (gr. k-1). pap. 29.70 *(978-0-7368-3194-9(0))* Capstone.
—Sun & Rain, 6 vols., Set. 2003. (Phonics Readers 1-36 Ser.). (ENG.). 8p. (gr. k-1). pap. 29.70 *(978-0-7368-3192-5(4))* Capstone.
Manolis, Kay. Blastoff! Readers - Body Systems, 6 vols., Set. Incl. Circulatory System. 20.00 *(978-0-531-21701-6(9))*; Digestive System. 20.00 *(978-0-531-21702-3(7))*; Muscular System. 20.00 *(978-0-531-21703-0(5))*; Nervous System. 20.00 *(978-0-531-21704-7(3))*; Respiratory System. 20.00 *(978-0-531-21705-4(1))*; Skeletal System. 20.00 *(978-0-531-21706-1(X))*; (Illus.). 24p. (J). (gr. k-3). 2009. 2009. Set lib. bdg. 120.00 *(978-0-531-27900-7(6),* Children's Pr.) Scholastic Library Publishing.
Manuel Reeves, Emily. Fiona Flamingo Has Lost Her Pink. 2013. 20p. pap. 10.00 *(978-0-9821506-1-0(X))* Reeves, Emily.
Mara, Wil. National Geographic Readers: Trucks. 2009. (Readers Ser.). (Illus.). 32p. (J). (gr. -1-k). (ENG.). 13.90 *(978-1-4263-0527-6(3))*; pap. 4.99 *(978-1-4263-0526-9(5))* Disney Publishing Worldwide. (National Geographic Kids).
March, Julia. Lego Ninjago - Ninja, Go! 2015. (DK Reader Level 2 Ser.). lib. bdg. 13.55 *(978-0-606-36924-4(4))* Turtleback.
Marchessault, Sara J. Pinky the Dreamer & Her Silver Jet. 2009. 36p. pap. 15.49 *(978-1-4389-9902-9(X))* AuthorHouse.
Markel, Michelle. The Shark That Taught Me English/El Tiburon Que Me Enseno Ingles. Kim, Bo-Young, illus. 2008. (SPA & ENG.). 28p. (J). pap. 8.95 *(978-1-60448-003-0(3))* Lectura Bks.
—The Shark That Taught Me English/El Tiburon Que Me Enseno Ingles. Guerrero, Ernesto, tr. Kim, Bo-Young, illus. 2008. (ENG & SPA.). 28p. (J). (gr. 1-2). 15.95 *(978-1-60448-002-3(5))* Lectura Bks.
Markle, Sandra. Ranger Rick: I Wish I Was an Orca. 2017. (I Can Read Level 1 Ser.). (ENG., Illus.). 32p. (J). (gr. -1-3). 16.99 *(978-0-06-243208-7(7),* HarperCollins) HarperCollins Pubs.
—Ranger Rick: I Wish I Was an Orca. 2017. (I Can Read Level 1 Ser.). (ENG., Illus.). 32p. (J). (gr. -1-3). pap. 4.99 *(978-0-06-243207-0(9),* HarperCollins) HarperCollins Pubs.
Markovics, Joyce. Book Nook. 2019. (Read & Rhyme Level 2 Ser.). (ENG., Illus.). 16p. (J). (gr. -1-1). 24.21 *(978-1-64280-552-9(1))* Bearport Publishing Co., Inc.
—Mice to Slice. 2019. (Read & Rhyme Level 1 Ser.). (ENG., Illus.). 16p. (J). (gr. -1-1). 24.21 *(978-1-64280-542-0(4))* Bearport Publishing Co., Inc.
—Pine to Swine. 2019. (Read & Rhyme Level 1 Ser.). (ENG., Illus.). 16p. (J). (gr. -1-1). 24.21 *(978-1-64280-545-1(9))* Bearport Publishing Co., Inc.
—Ram Jam. 2019. (Read & Rhyme Level 2 Ser.). (ENG., Illus.). 16p. (J). (gr. -1-1). 24.21 *(978-1-64280-551-2(3))* Bearport Publishing Co., Inc.
—Ship Trip. 2019. (Read & Rhyme Level 2 Ser.). (ENG., Illus.). 16p. (J). (gr. -1-1). 24.21 *(978-1-64280-549-9(1))* Bearport Publishing Co., Inc.
Markovics, Pearl & Gambro, Beth. Book Nook. 2020. (Illus.). 16p. (J). pap. 6.99 *(978-1-64280-710-3(9))* Bearport Publishing Co., Inc.
—Mice to Slice: Read & Rhyme Level 1. 2019. (Illus.). 16p. (J). pap. 6.99 *(978-1-64280-706-6(0))* Bearport Publishing Co., Inc.
—Ram Jam. 2020. (Illus.). 16p. (J). pap. 6.99 *(978-1-64280-713-4(3))* Bearport Publishing Co., Inc.
—Ship Trip. 2020. (Illus.). 16p. (J). pap. 6.99 *(978-1-64280-715-8(X))* Bearport Publishing Co., Inc.
Markowitz-Meredith, Susan. Stump Hill: Set Of 6. 2011. (Early Connections Ser.). (J). pap. 39.00 net. *(978-1-4108-1554-5(4))* Benchmark Education Co.
Marks, Melanie. Phonics Comics: Spooky Sara - Level 3, Level 3. Ball, Victoria, illus. 2006. (ENG.). 24p. (J). (gr. 1-17). per. 3.99 *(978-1-58476-473-1(2),* IKIDS) Innovative Kids.
Marsh, Carole. I'm Reading about the Statue of Liberty. 2016. (I'm Reading About Ser.). (ENG., Illus.). (J). lib. bdg. 24.99 *(978-0-635-12207-0(3))*; pap. 7.99 *(978-0-635-12208-7(1))* Gallopade International.
Marsh, Laura. National Geographic Readers: Caterpillar to Butterfly. 2012. (Readers Ser.). (Illus.). 32p. (J). (gr. -1-k). pap. 5.99 *(978-1-4263-0920-5(1),* National Geographic Kids) Disney Publishing Worldwide.
—National Geographic Readers: Deadly Animals Collection. 2019. (Illus.). 144p. (J). (gr. -1-k). pap. 7.99 *(978-1-4263-3515-0(6))*; (ENG., (gr. 1-3). lib. bdg. 17.90 *(978-1-4263-3516-7(4))* Disney Publishing Worldwide. (National Geographic Kids).
—National Geographic Readers: Halloween. 2012. (Readers Ser.). (Illus.). 32p. (J). (gr. -1-k). pap. 4.99 *(978-1-4263-1034-8(X))*; (ENG., lib. bdg. 14.90 *(978-1-4263-1035-5(8))* Disney Publishing Worldwide. (National Geographic Kids).
—National Geographic Readers: Lizards. 2012. (Readers Ser.). (Illus.). 32p. (J). (gr. 1-3). pap. 4.99 *(978-1-4263-0922-9(8),* National Geographic Kids) Disney Publishing Worldwide.

—National Geographic Readers: Owls. 2014. (Readers Ser.). (Illus.). 32p. (J). (gr. -1-k). pap. 5.99 (978-1-4263-1743-9(3), National Geographic Kids) Disney Publishing Worldwide.

—National Geographic Readers: Sea Otters. 2014. (Readers Ser.). (Illus.). 32p. (J). (gr. -1-k). pap. 4.99 (978-1-4263-1751-4(4), National Geographic Kids) Disney Publishing Worldwide.

—National Geographic Readers: Tide Pools (L1) 2019. (Readers Ser.). (Illus.). 32p. (J). (gr. -1-k). pap. 4.99 (978-1-4263-3343-9(9), National Geographic Kids) Disney Publishing Worldwide.

—Ponies (1 Hardcover/1 CD) 2016. (National Geographic Readers: Pre-Reader Ser.). (ENG.). (J). (978-1-4301-2105-3(X)) Live Oak Media.

Marshall, James. George & Martha. 2010. (George & Martha Ser.). (ENG., Illus.). 24p. (J). (gr. -1-3). pap. 4.99 (978-0-547-40624-4(X), 1428502, Clarion Bks.) HarperCollins Pubs.

—George & Martha: Rise & Shine No. 5. 2011. (George & Martha Ser.). (ENG., Illus.). 40p. (J). (gr. -1-3). pap. 4.99 (978-0-547-57687-9(0), 1458448, Clarion Bks.) HarperCollins Pubs.

—George & Martha: the Best of Friends No. 4. 2011. (George & Martha Ser.). (ENG., Illus.). 32p. (J). (gr. -1-3). pap. 4.99 (978-0-547-51988-3(5), 1445281, Clarion Bks.) HarperCollins Pubs.

—George & Martha Two Great Friends. 2010. (George & Martha Ser.). (ENG., Illus.). 32p. (J). (gr. -1-3). pap. 4.99 (978-0-547-40625-1(8), 1428503, Clarion Bks.) HarperCollins Pubs.

Marshall, Natalie. My Turn to Learn Numbers. 2013. (My Turn to Learn Ser.). (ENG., Illus.). 12p. (J). (gr. -1 — 1). bds. 6.99 (978-0-316-25164-8(X)) Little, Brown Bks. for Young Readers.

Marsham, Liz. Batgirl on the Case! 2018. (Justice League Classic: I Can Read! Ser.). (Illus.). 30p. (J). lib. bdg. 13.55 (978-0-606-41049-6(X)) Turtleback.

Marti, Meritxell. Good Night - Buenas Noches, 1 vol. Salomo, Xavier, illus. 2018. 18p. (J). (— 1). bds. 11.99 (978-1-4236-5028-7(X)) Gibbs Smith, Publisher.

Martin, Elena. Look Inside. 2003. (Shutterbug Books: Social Studies). (Illus.). 16p. pap. 4.10 (978-0-7398-7642-8(2)) Steck-Vaughn.

Martin, Elizabeth B. I'm Not a Silly Goose. 2013. (ENG.). (J). pap. 13.00 net. (978-0-578-12913-6(2)) Martin, Elizabeth B.

Martin, Elizabeth B., illus. I'm Not a Silly Goose. Martin, Elizabeth B., . 2014. (ENG.). (J). 9.99 (978-0-9910543-1-2(8)) Martin, Elizabeth B.

Martin, John David. A Time to Plant: Tests. 2005. (Rod & Staff's Readers Ser.). 22p. (gr. 5-18). 1.55 (978-0-7399-0404-6(3), 11511) Rod & Staff Pubs., Inc.

—A Time to Plant: Workbook. 2005. (Rod & Staff's Readers Ser.). 145p. (gr. 5-18). 4.80 (978-0-7399-0402-2(7), 11521) Rod & Staff Pubs., Inc.

Martin, Kevin. Arnold Lobel Wrote Great Stories. 2017. (Text Connections Guided Close Reading Ser.). (J). (gr. 1). (978-1-4900-1800-3(X)) Benchmark Education Co.

Martin, Mary. God Made Nuts. Derstine, Charlene, illus. 2012. 53p. (J). (978-0-7399-2501-0(6)) Rod & Staff Pubs., Inc.

Martin, Mary S. Fishing with Uncle Nathan: Step 4. Petre, Emily, illus. 2016. (Stepping Forward Ser.). (ENG.). 63p. (J). (gr. -1). 3.95 (978-0-7399-2524-9(5)) Rod & Staff Pubs., Inc.

Martinez-Neal, Juana. Alma & How She Got Her Name. Martinez-Neal, Juana, illus. 2018. (ENG., Illus.). 32p. (J). (gr. -1-3). 17.99 (978-0-7636-9355-8(3)) Candlewick Pr.

Martin's mighty Hit: Individual Title Six-Packs. (gr. 1-2). 25.00 (978-0-7635-9144-1(0)) Rigby Education.

Marvel Book Group & Macri, Thomas. This Is Spider-Man. 2012. (Marvel World of Reading Level 1 Ser.). (J). lib. bdg. 13.55 (978-0-606-23787-1(9)) Turtleback.

Marvel Book Group Editors. Thwip! You Are It! 2017. (World of Reading Ser.). (Illus.). (J). lib. bdg. 13.55 (978-0-606-39507-6(5)) Turtleback.

—Tricky Trouble! 2017. (World of Reading Ser.). (Illus.). (J). lib. bdg. 13.55 (978-0-606-39508-3(3)) Turtleback.

Marvel Press Book Group, Marvel Press. World of Reading: Marvel 3-In-1 Listen-along Reader-World of Reading Level 1: 3 Tales of Adventure with CD! 2017. (World of Reading Ser.). (ENG.). 96p. (J). (gr. -1-k). pap. 7.99 (978-1-4847-9948-2(8)) Marvel Worldwide, Inc.

—World of Reading: This Is Miles Morales. 2018. (World of Reading Ser.). (ENG., Illus.). 32p. (J). (gr. 1-3). pap. 4.99 (978-1-368-02863-9(2)) Marvel Worldwide, Inc.

Maryland Reading Success Grade 1. 2003. (Illus.). 32p. (J). 9.95 (978-0-9722452-0-3(0)) New Leaf Educ., Inc.

Maryland Reading Success Grade 2, 3 vols., Vol. 2. 2003. (Illus.). 32p. (J). 9.95 (978-0-9722452-1-0(9)) New Leaf Educ., Inc.

Maryland Reading Success Grade 3, Vol. 3. 2003. (Illus.). 32p. (J). 9.95 (978-0-9722452-5-8(1)) New Leaf Educ., Inc.

Marzollo, Jean. I Spy a Pumpkin (Scholastic Reader, Level 1) Wick, Walter, photos by. 2006. (Scholastic Reader, Level 1 Ser.). (ENG., Illus.). 32p. (J). (gr. -1-3). pap. 3.99 (978-0-439-73863-7(6), Cartwheel Bks.) Scholastic, Inc.

—I Spy Adventure: 4 Picture Riddle Books. Wick, Walter, illus. Wick, Walter, photos by. 2012. (J). (978-1-4351-3984-8(4)) Scholastic, Inc.

—I Spy Lightning in the Sky (Scholastic Reader, Level 1) I Spy Lightning in the Sky. Wick, Walter, illus. 2005. (Scholastic Reader, Level 1 Ser.). (ENG.). 32p. (J). (gr. -1-3). pap. 3.99 (978-0-439-68052-3(2), Cartwheel Bks.) Scholastic, Inc.

Maslen, Bobby Lynn. Bob Books - Advancing Beginners Box Set | Phonics, Ages 4 & up, Kindergarten (Stage 2: Emerging Reader), Set. Maslen, John R., illus. 2006. (Bob Bks.). (ENG.). 16p. (J). (gr. -1-1). 17.99 (978-0-439-84502-1(5), Scholastic Paperbacks) Scholastic, Inc.

—Bob Books - Complex Words Box Set | Phonics, Ages 4 & up, Kindergarten, First Grade (Stage 3: Developing Reader), Set. Maslen, John R., illus. 2006. (Bob Bks.). (ENG.). 24p. (J). (gr. -1-1). 17.99 (978-0-439-84506-9(8), Scholastic Paperbacks) Scholastic, Inc.

—Bob Books - Long Vowels Box Set | Phonics, Ages 4 & up, Kindergarten, First Grade (Stage 3: Developing Reader), 1 vol. Maslen, John R., illus. 2006. (Bob Bks.: No. 5). (ENG.). 16p. (J). (gr. -1-1). pap., pap. 17.99 (978-0-439-86541-8(7), Scholastic Paperbacks) Scholastic, Inc.

Maslen, John R. & Maslen, Bobby Lynn. Bob Books - Set 1: Beginning Readers Box Set | Phonics, Ages 4 & up, Kindergarten (Stage 1: Starting to Read), Set 1. Maslen, John R., illus. 2006. (Bob Bks.). (ENG., Illus.). 12p. (J). (gr. -1-1). 17.99 (978-0-439-84500-7(9)) Scholastic, Inc.

Masoliver, Joaquín. Historias breves para leer elemental, Level 1. 9th ed. (SPA & ENG., Illus.). 150p. (J). 14.95 (978-84-7143-825-6(9), SGS8259) Sociedad General Espanola de Libreria ESP. Dist: Continental Bk. Co., Inc.

Masoliver, Juan Antonio. Historias Breves para Leer, Level 2. (SPA & ENG.). 128p. (J). 14.95 (978-84-7143-732-7(5), SGS4393) Sociedad General Espanola de Libreria ESP. Dist: Continental Bk. Co., Inc.

Mass, Wendy & Brawer, Michael. Space Taxi: Archie's Alien Disguise. 2015. (Space Taxi Ser.: 3). (ENG., Illus.). 128p. (J). (gr. 1-5). pap. 9.99 (978-0-316-24328-5(0)) Little, Brown Bks. for Young Readers.

The Masterpiece: Level M, 6 vols. 128p. (gr. 2-3). 41.95 (978-0-7699-1026-0(2)) Shortland Pubns. (U. S. A.) Inc.

Math in Our World, 14 vols., Set. Incl. ADDING & SUBTRACTING in Math Club. Ayers, Amy. lib. bdg. 24.67 (978-0-8368-8470-8(1), 11260360-a12f-47fb-8913-cd7f1aae9bd2); Counting at the Zoo. Ayers, Amy. lib. bdg. 24.67 (978-0-8368-8469-2(8), 36c9139b-11a9-47fe-9b3a-5067032a5db5); Counting in the City. Sharp, Jean. lib. bdg. 24.67 (978-0-8368-8468-5(X), 04ef9b3b-3822-4f74-928b-07f9f555e442); MEASURING at the Dog Show. Ayers, Amy. lib. bdg. 24.67 (978-0-8368-8474-6(4), f6793012-2417-4a3c-8679-212167eb30c4); PATTERNS on Parade. Freese, Joan. lib. bdg. 24.67 (978-0-8368-8473-9(6), 6f51b3eb-24ff-430e-b55f-43ec61f32411); TABLES & GRAPHS of Healthy Things. Freese, Joan. lib. bdg. 24.67 (978-0-8368-8471-5(X), 66e458b0-93b3-4dc1-bd13-1ade3e9e05f7); USING MATH at the Class Party. Ayers, Amy. lib. bdg. 24.67 (978-0-8368-8475-3(2), f8399466-c15f-4e2c-8bee-0b56ae9caf31); USING MONEY at the Lemonade Stand. Ayers, Amy. lib. bdg. 24.67 (978-0-8368-8472-2(8), 6f742241-06fa-4018-8f8b-da23ce255790); (Illus.). (gr. 1-1). (Math in Our World - Level 1 Ser.). (ENG.). 24p. 2007. Set lib. bdg. 172.02 (978-0-8368-8467-8(1), 60cccaba-9a1b-4a6f-ab78-d1106aca9829, Weekly Reader Leveled Readers) Stevens, Gareth Publishing LLLP.

Matheson, Hughena. The 10 Most Historic Speeches. 2007. 14.99 (978-1-55448-478-2(2)) Scholastic Library Publishing.

Mathis, Pamela. Sound Town the Story of Words. 2010. 32p. pap. 15.99 (978-1-4389-9194-8(0)) AuthorHouse.

Mattern, Joanne. The Annexation of Texas: From Republic to Statehood, 1 vol. rev. ed. 2012. (Social Studies: Informational Text Ser.). (ENG.). 32p. (gr. 3-5). pap. 11.99 (978-1-4333-5048-1(3)) Teacher Created Materials, Inc.

—Geoffrey Chaucer: Medieval Writer, 1 vol. rev. ed. 2012. (Social Studies: Informational Text Ser.). (ENG.). 32p. (gr. 4-8). pap. 11.99 (978-1-4333-5006-1(8)) Teacher Created Materials, Inc.

—Medieval Times: England in the Middle Ages, 1 vol. rev. ed. 2012. (Social Studies: Informational Text Ser.). (ENG.). 32p. (gr. 4-8). pap. 11.99 (978-1-4333-5005-4(X)) Teacher Created Materials, Inc.

—Sam Houston: A Fearless Statesman, 1 vol. rev. ed. 2012. (Social Studies: Informational Text Ser.). (ENG.). 32p. (gr. 3-5). pap. 11.99 (978-1-4333-5049-8(1)) Teacher Created Materials, Inc.

Matthas, Seth. Mateo's Family Traits: Gathering Data, 1 vol. 2017. (Computer Science for the Real World Ser.). (ENG.). 16p. (gr. 2-3). pap. (978-1-5383-5186-4(2), 43b56f38-792c-4883-a722-f6a8a3c5a724, Rosen Classroom) Rosen Publishing Group, Inc., The.

Matthews. Death in the Desert. (Thumbprint Mysteries Ser.). 32.86 (978-0-8092-0416-8(9)) McGraw-Hill/Contemporary.

Matthews, Andrew. Gulliver's Travels: Band 11 Lime/Band 17 Diamond (Collins Big Cat Progress) Horrocks, Steve, illus. 2014. (Collins Big Cat Progress Ser.). (ENG.). 32p. (J). (gr. 5-6). pap. 10.99 (978-0-00-751937-8(0)) HarperCollins Pubs. Ltd. GBR. Dist: Independent Pubs. Group.

Matthews, Layla, et al. Eat at Grandma's? Kids Review a New Restaurant. 2017. (Text Connections Guided Close Reading Ser.). (J). (gr. 2). (978-1-4900-1860-7(3)) Benchmark Education Co.

Matthews, Trisha. I Smell Pancakes!, 1 vol. 2006. (Neighborhood Readers Ser.). (ENG., Illus.). 16p. (gr. 1-2). pap. 6.50 (978-1-4042-7188-3(0), cb94a9ea-f341-4437-9c34-44df44f32d4e, Rosen Classroom) Rosen Publishing Group, Inc., The.

Maule, David. Stealing High Beginning Book with Online Access, 1 vol. 2014. (ENG., Illus.). 24p. (J). pap., E-Book, E-Book 9.50 (978-1-107-67774-6(2)) Cambridge Univ. Pr.

—What Makes a Place Special? Moscow, Egypt, Australia, 1 vol. 2014. (ENG., Illus.). 24p. (J). pap., E-Book 9.50 (978-1-107-63317-9(6)) Cambridge Univ. Pr.

MauleDavid. ARE YOU LISTENING? THE SENSE OF HEARING HIGH BEGINNING BOOK WITH ONLINE ACCESS, 1 vol. 2014. (ENG., Illus.). 24p. (J). pap., E-Book, E-Book 9.50 (978-1-107-63251-6(X)) Cambridge Univ. Pr.

—GENIUS BEGINNING BOOK WITH ONLINE ACCESS, 1 vol. 2014. (ENG., Illus.). 24p. (J). pap., E-Book, E-Book 9.50 (978-1-107-67865-1(X)) Cambridge Univ. Pr.

May I Go Out? (J). 26.20 (978-0-8136-8428-4(5)); 26.20 (978-0-8136-8429-1(3)); (gr. -1-3). 59.50 (978-0-8136-7978-5(8)) Modern Curriculum Pr.

May I Stay Home Today? 6 Small Books. (gr. k-3). 24.00 (978-0-7635-6239-7(4)) Rigby Education.

May, Tallulah. Rainbow Dash: Reading Rainboom! Persico, Zoe, illus. 2018. (J). (978-1-5444-0924-5(9), Golden Bks.) Random Hse. Children's Bks.

Mayer, Mercer. The Fall Festival. 2012. (Illus.). 32p. (J). (978-1-4351-4384-5(1)) HarperCollins Pubs.

—Just a Baby Bird. 2016. (Little Critter: I Can Read! Ser.). (J). lib. bdg. 13.55 (978-0-606-38158-1(9)) Turtleback.

—Little Critter - Snowball Soup: A Winter & Holiday Book for Kids. Mayer, Mercer, illus. 2007. (My First I Can Read Ser.). (ENG., Illus.). 32p. (J). (gr. -1-3). pap. 5.99 (978-0-06-083543-9(5), HarperCollins) HarperCollins Pubs.

—Little Critter Collector's Quintet: Critters Who Care, Going to the Firehouse, This Is My Town, Going to the Sea Park, to the Rescue. Mayer, Mercer, illus. 2017. (My First I Can Read Ser.). (ENG., Illus.). 160p. (J). (gr. -1-3). pap. 19.99 (978-0-06-265349-9(0), HarperCollins) HarperCollins Pubs.

Mayer, Mercer & Mayer, Gina. My Family: A Big Little Critter Book. 2013. (Big Little Critter Ser.: 2). (ENG., Illus.). 98p. (J). 12.95 (978-1-60746-810-3(7), Premiere) FastPrncil, Inc.

—On the Go. 2013. (Big Little Critter Ser.: 4). (ENG., Illus.). 96p. (J). 12.95 (978-1-60746-983-4(9), Premiere) FastPrncil, Inc.

—Staying Well. 2013. (Big Little Critter Ser.: 5). (ENG.). 96p. (J). 12.95 (978-1-60746-732-8(1), Premiere) FastPrncil, Inc.

Mayfield, Christine & Quinn, Kristine M. Hammurabi: Babylonian Ruler, 1 vol. rev. ed. 2007. (Social Studies: Informational Text Ser.). (ENG.). 32p. (gr. 4-8). pap. 11.99 (978-0-7439-0441-4(9)) Teacher Created Materials, Inc.

—Mesopotamia, 1 vol. rev. ed. 2007. (Social Studies: Informational Text Ser.). (ENG.). 32p. (J). (gr. 4-8). pap. 11.99 (978-0-7439-0440-7(0)) Teacher Created Materials, Inc.

Mayfield, Sue. The Four Franks. Parsons, Garry, illus. 2005. (Blue Go Bananas Ser.). (ENG.). 48p. (J). (gr. 1-2). (978-0-7787-2651-7(7)) Crabtree Publishing Co.

Mayhew, Jon. Blood Cave: Band 10 White/Band 16 Sapphire (Collins Big Cat Progress) Bacchin, Giorgio, illus. 2014. (Collins Big Cat Progress Ser.). (ENG.). 32p. (J). (gr. 4-5). pap. 9.99 (978-0-00-751921-7(4)) HarperCollins Pubs. Ltd. GBR. Dist: Independent Pubs. Group.

—Macbeth: Band 18/Pearl (Collins Big Cat) Stone, Adrian, illus. 2014. (Collins Big Cat Ser.). (ENG.). 80p. (J). (gr. 5). pap. 12.99 (978-0-00-753013-7(7)) HarperCollins Pubs. Ltd. GBR. Dist: Independent Pubs. Group.

Mazza, Barbara. How the Short Vowels Got Their Sound. 2007. 28p. per. 17.32 (978-1-4257-2721-5(2)) Xlibris Corp.

McAllister, Margaret. Emily & the Lamb. Vince, Dawn, illus. 2005. (ENG.). 24p. (J). lib. bdg. 23.65 (978-1-59646-756-9(8)) Dingles & Co.

McBratney, Sam. Henry Seamouse. 2005. (978-1-901358-13-1(5)) CAMFA.

McCall, Guadalupe García. El Verano de Las Mariposas, 1 vol. Bowles, David, tr. 2018. Orig. Title: Summer of the Mariposas. (SPA.). 384p. (YA). (gr. 6-12). pap. 16.95 (978-1-62014-786-3(6), leelowtu, Tu Bks.) Lee & Low Bks., Inc.

McCall, Val. Twelve Rabbits & a Turtle: Bilingual English French. 2012. 46p. pap. 9.95 (978-1-938367-00-7(6)) Destinee Media.

McCallum, Rory. The Great Pest Problem: Defining the Problem, 1 vol. 2017. (Computer Kids: Powered by Computational Thinking Ser.). (ENG.). 24p. (J). (gr. 4-5). 25.27 (978-1-5383-2433-2(4), f41bcf02-fff1-48e1-897f-d308da96aae1, PowerKids Pr.); pap. (978-1-5081-3763-4(3), 5f5f5626-90e6-4bbb-95b9-969d2446cd76, Rosen Classroom) Rosen Publishing Group, Inc., The.

—Li Lost His Mitten: Fixing a Problem, 1 vol. 2017. (Computer Science for the Real World Ser.). (ENG.). 8p. (gr. k-1). pap. (978-1-5383-5048-5(3), 3bc98db9-9fd1-45f8-8ea8-03466b808d2f, Rosen Classroom) Rosen Publishing Group, Inc., The.

—Victor's Volcano: Showing Events & Processes, 1 vol. 2017. (Computer Kids: Powered by Computational Thinking Ser.). (ENG.). 24p. (J). (gr. 3-4). 25.27 (978-1-5383-2437-0(7), 284033df-0aed-4a6f-9480-07ef2c4204a4, PowerKids Pr.); pap. (978-1-5081-3787-0(0), 3370bdbd-1a8e-4e9f-8f35-14edcb690166, Rosen Classroom) Rosen Publishing Group, Inc., The.

McCarrier, Andrea, et al. Fact & Fiction 1: Reece to the Rescue; Here Comes a Thunderstorm; Garden Giant; A Sunflower Life Cycle; Mugs Indoors & Outdoors; Cats Are Hunters; Beach Days; Oceans All Around Us, 8 bks., Set. Morley, Amanda et al, illus. 2006. (ENG.). 16p. (J). pap. 120.00 (978-1-893986-25-1(X)) Keep Bks.

McCaughrean, Geraldine & Willey, Bee. Think Again!: Band 11/Lime (Collins Big Cat) 2005. (Collins Big Cat Ser.). (ENG.). 32p. (J). (gr. 1-3). pap. 9.99 (978-0-00-718643-3(6)) HarperCollins Pubs. Ltd. GBR. Dist: Independent Pubs. Group.

McClatchy, Lisa. Eloise & the Big Parade: Ready-To-Read Level 1. Lyon, Tammie, illus. 2007. (Eloise Ser.). (ENG.). 32p. (J). (gr. -1-1). pap. 4.99 (978-1-4169-3523-0(1), Simon Spotlight) Simon Spotlight.

McClenney, Earl H., Jr. Mamma, Is the Maid Goin' Teach? Portriats of Black Women Who Integrated the Public Schools in Richmond, VA. 2005. spiral bd. 10.95 net. (978-0-9618835-5-3(3)) First Associates Publishing.

McClure, Leigh. Molly Makes Electricity: Testing & Checking, 1 vol. 2017. (Computer Kids: Powered by Computational Thinking Ser.). (ENG.). 24p. (J). (gr. 3-4). 25.27 (978-1-5383-2412-7(1), 87370022-74ec-45bc-a1d8-e6a22d29e324, PowerKids Pr.); pap. (978-1-5081-3794-8(3), 7303982e-e2a1-425f-95d8-06352479fd00, Rosen Classroom) Rosen Publishing Group, Inc., The.

McCune, Susan. At the Watering Hole, 1 vol., 1. 2015. (Rosen REAL Readers: STEM & STEAM Collection). (ENG.). 8p. (J). (gr. k-1). pap. 5.46 (978-1-5081-1455-0(2), 3885e076-97ae-4c09-a542-7066ab861505, Rosen Classroom) Rosen Publishing Group, Inc., The.

—Benny & Pops Have a Surprise, 1 vol., 1. 2015. (Rosen REAL Readers: STEM & STEAM Collection). (ENG.). 8p. (J). (gr. k-1). pap. 5.46 (978-1-5081-1475-8(7), c28e498c-e9aa-48d1-bc1c-e8c3f23e2725, Rosen Classroom) Rosen Publishing Group, Inc., The.

—The Choice, 1 vol., 1. 2015. (Rosen REAL Readers: Social Studies Nonfiction / Fiction: Myself, My Community, My World Ser.). (ENG.). 12p. (J). (gr. k-1). pap. 6.33 (978-1-5081-1991-3(0), 4a0073ab-6229-4d47-b85a-512afc176d07, Rosen Classroom) Rosen Publishing Group, Inc., The.

—Every Penny Helps, 1 vol., 1. 2015. (Rosen REAL Readers: Social Studies Nonfiction / Fiction: Myself, My Community, My World Ser.). (ENG.). 12p. (J). (gr. k-1). pap. 6.33 (978-1-5081-1913-5(9), 23ae4f8e-ffb8-48d3-b20b-de820d92d3eb, Rosen Classroom) Rosen Publishing Group, Inc., The.

—A Grandmother's Story, 1 vol., 1. 2015. (Rosen REAL Readers: Social Studies Nonfiction / Fiction: Myself, My Community, My World Ser.). (ENG.). 8p. (J). (gr. k-1). pap. 5.46 (978-1-5081-1522-9(2), adf698e3-8f62-4d3f-919e-659675012233, Rosen Classroom) Rosen Publishing Group, Inc., The.

—Granny's Guacamole, 1 vol., 1. 2015. (Rosen REAL Readers: STEM & STEAM Collection). (ENG.). 12p. (J). (gr. 1-2). pap. 6.33 (978-1-5081-1572-4(9), 61eb7741-115b-43c5-99a7-88399ae14913, Rosen Classroom) Rosen Publishing Group, Inc., The.

—An Inch Taller, 1 vol., 1. 2015. (Rosen REAL Readers: Social Studies Nonfiction / Fiction: Myself, My Community, My World Ser.). (ENG.). 8p. (J). (gr. k-1). pap. 5.46 (978-1-5081-1863-3(9), 2ac8991b-80d0-421c-810c-c3e1bf42ff08, Rosen Classroom) Rosen Publishing Group, Inc., The.

—Our Party at the Park, 1 vol., 1. 2015. (Rosen REAL Readers: Social Studies Nonfiction / Fiction: Myself, My Community, My World Ser.). (ENG.). 8p. (J). (gr. k-1). pap. 5.46 (978-1-5081-1899-2(X), 62951b7b-cff6-46a7-9158-dc2dfeeb10b7, Rosen Classroom) Rosen Publishing Group, Inc., The.

—Paul's Sneakers, 1 vol., 1. 2015. (Rosen REAL Readers: STEM & STEAM Collection). (ENG.). 8p. (J). (gr. k-1). pap. 5.46 (978-1-5081-1514-4(1), cff9d902-e9d8-40fb-9d8b-9d119443e80a, Rosen Classroom) Rosen Publishing Group, Inc., The.

—The Push-Up Test, 1 vol., 1. 2015. (Rosen REAL Readers: STEM & STEAM Collection). (ENG.). 12p. (J). (gr. k-1). pap. 6.33 (978-1-5081-1554-0(0), 539bf55a-1b8a-4ad2-9278-d752a768b4ec, Rosen Classroom) Rosen Publishing Group, Inc., The.

—Space Camp, 1 vol., 1. 2015. (Rosen REAL Readers: STEM & STEAM Collection). (ENG.). 12p. (J). (gr. 1-2). pap. 6.33 (978-1-5081-1626-4(1), 5b077d0d-560a-4dd9-8c39-b194e65f968d, Rosen Classroom) Rosen Publishing Group, Inc., The.

—Taking Turns Talking, 1 vol., 1. 2015. (Rosen REAL Readers: Social Studies Nonfiction / Fiction: Myself, My Community, My World Ser.). (ENG.). 8p. (J). (gr. k-1). pap. 5.46 (978-1-5081-1412-3(9), 8b02a81b-e87e-4028-b2a1-a73a6e901d2d, Rosen Classroom) Rosen Publishing Group, Inc., The.

McDonnell, Ginger. Next Stop: The Caribbean, 1 vol. 2nd rev. ed. 2011. (TIME for KIDS(r): Informational Text Ser.). (ENG.). 24p. (gr. 2-3). pap. 9.99 (978-1-4333-3612-6(X)) Teacher Created Materials, Inc.

—Next Stop - Canada, 1 vol. 2nd rev. ed. 2011. (TIME for KIDS(r): Informational Text Ser.). (ENG.). 24p. (gr. 2-3). pap. 9.99 (978-1-4333-3611-9(1)) Teacher Created Materials, Inc.

—Next Stop - Mexico, 1 vol. 2nd rev. ed. 2011. (TIME for KIDS(r): Informational Text Ser.). (ENG.). 24p. (gr. 2-3). pap. 9.99 (978-1-4333-3610-2(3)) Teacher Created Materials, Inc.

McEwan-Adkins, Elaine K. The Reading Puzzle: Word Analysis, Grades 4-8. 2008. (ENG., Illus.). 96p. (gr. 4-7). pap. 18.95 (978-1-4129-5825-7(3), B58257P) Corwin Pr.

McGraw Hill. The American Vision, StudentWorks Plus CD-ROM. 2nd ed. 2005. (United States History (hs) Ser.). (ENG.). (gr. 9-12). 166.44 (978-0-07-865456-5(4), 0078654564) McGraw-Hill Education.

—In the Spotlight: Vol 1, Levels F-H, Vol. 1. 2006. (Jt Hi-Lo Non-fiction Ser.). (ENG., Illus.). 112p. (gr. 6-12). per. 4.44 (978-0-07-874320-7(6), 0078743206) McGraw-Hill Education.

—Journey Across Time: Early Ages, Student Edition: Student Edition. 2004. (MS World History Ser.). (ENG., Illus.). 794p. (gr. 6-9). stu. ed. 116.60 (978-0-07-824133-8(2), 0078241332) McGraw-Hill Education.

—The Outer Edge Danger Zone. 2005. (Jt: Non-Fiction Reading Ser.). (ENG., Illus.). 120p. (gr. 6-12). per. 30.28 (978-0-07-872905-8(X), 007872905X) McGraw-Hill Education.

McGraw-Hill Staff. Listen!Listen!Letter Sounds in Rhymes Complt Set. (gr. k-1). 210.95 (978-0-322-02636-0(9)) Wright Group/McGraw-Hill.

—Song Box Sets & Resources:Save the Tree for Me Cass. (Song Box Ser.). (gr. 1-2). 8.50 incl. audio (978-0-7802-2265-6(2)) Wright Group/McGraw-Hill.

McGreevy, Joyce. Avenues d (Leveled Books): the Wind Eagle. 2003. (Rise & Shine Ser.). (ENG.). 16p. (Orig.). (C). pap. 17.95 (978-0-7362-1695-1(2)) CENGAGE Learning.

McGuffey, William H. New Mcguffey Fourth Reader. 2006. (ENG.). 204p. pap. 20.99 (978-1-4264-0489-4(1)); pap. 22.99 (978-1-4264-0563-1(4)) Creative Media Partners, LLC.

McGuffey, William Holmes. McGuffey's Third Eclectic Reader. 2017. (ENG., Illus.). (J). 23.95 (978-1-374-99555-0(X)); pap. 13.95 (978-1-374-99554-3(1)) Capital Communications, Inc.

—McGuffey's Third Eclectic Reader. 2017. (ENG., Illus.). (J). pap. 14.95 (978-1-376-29933-5(X)) Creative Media Partners, LLC.

McGuire, Leslie. We Read Phonics-If I Had a Snake. Johnson, Meredith, illus. 2010. (We Read Phonics Ser.). 32p. (J). (gr. 1-5). 9.95 (978-1-60115-333-3(3)); pap. 4.99 (978-1-60115-334-0(1)) Treasure Bay, Inc.

McHale, Scarlett. Brady Makes a Weather Graph, 1 vol. 2013. (InfoMax Readers Ser.). (ENG., Illus.). 24p. (J). (gr. 3-3). pap. 8.25 (978-1-4777-2460-6(5), 26d846c0-5d3a-4250-91d4-658dcbe8357a, Rosen Classroom) Rosen Publishing Group, Inc., The.

McKay, Sindy. The Frog Prince/el Principe Rana: Spanish/English (We Both Read - Level 1-2) Ulrich, George, illus. 2016. (We Both Read - Level 1-2 Ser.). (ENG & SPA.). 44p. (J). pap. 5.99 (978-1-60115-076-9(8)) Treasure Bay, Inc.

—We Both Read Bilingual Edition-About Pets/Acerca de Las Mascotas. 2015.Tr. of Acerca de Las Mascotas. (ENG & SPA., Illus.). 44p. (J). (gr. 1-2). pap. 5.99 (978-1-60115-062-2(8)) Treasure Bay, Inc.

—We Both Read Bilingual Edition-Museum Day/Dia Del Museo. Johnson, Meredith, illus. 2015.Tr. of Dia Del Museo. (ENG & SPA.). 44p. (J). (gr. k-1). pap. 5.99 (978-1-60115-064-6(4)) Treasure Bay, Inc.

—We Both Read Bilingual Edition-Too Many Cats/Demasiados Gatos. Johnson, Meredith, illus. 2011. (ENG & SPA.). 44p. (J). pap. 5.99 (978-1-60115-040-0(7)) Treasure Bay, Inc.

—We Both Read-My Car Trip. Johnson, Meredith, illus. 2005. (We Both Read Ser.). 48p. (J). (gr. -1-2). lib. bdg. 7.99 *(978-1-891327-63-6(1))*; per. 5.99 *(978-1-891327-64-3(X))* Treasure Bay, Inc.
—We Both Read-The Ruby Rose Show. Johnson, Meredith, illus. 2010. (We Both Read Ser.). 44p. (J). (gr. k-3). pap. 5.99 *(978-1-60115-246-6(9))* Treasure Bay, Inc.
—We Read Phonics-Matt & Sid. Reinhart, Larry, illus. 2010. 32p. (J). 9.95 *(978-1-60115-315-9(5))*; pap. 4.99 *(978-1-60115-316-6(3))* Treasure Bay, Inc.
—We Read Phonics-Pat, Cat, & Rat. Johnson, Meredith, illus. 2010. 32p. (J). 9.95 *(978-1-60115-311-1(2))*; pap. 4.99 *(978-1-60115-312-8(0))* Treasure Bay, Inc.
—We Read Phonics-the Garden Crew. Johnson, Meredith, illus. 2011. 32p. (J). 9.95 *(978-1-60115-345-6(7))*; pap. 4.99 *(978-1-60115-346-3(5))* Treasure Bay, Inc.
McManus, Madelyn. Britney Makes a Budget, 1 vol. 2013. (Rosen Readers Ser.). (ENG.). 24p. (J). (gr. 3-3). pap. 8.25 *(978-1-4777-2528-3(8),* 24e4decd-3148-4fd1-a09f-d6aaa1c380c6); pap. 49.50 *(978-1-4777-2529-0(6))* Rosen Publishing Group, Inc., The. (Rosen Classroom).
McMillan, Dawn. Catch of the Day!, 1 vol. Vignolo, Enrique, illus. 2013. (ENG.). 25p. (gr. 3-3). pap. *(978-1-927197-70-7(8),* Red Rocket Readers) Flying Start Bks.
McNee, I. Knights - Internet Referenced. 2005. (Beginners Ser.). 32p. (J). (gr. 1-18). pap. 4.95 *(978-0-7945-0896-8(0),* Usborne) EDC Publishing.
McOmber, Rachel B., ed. McOmber Phonics Storybooks: A Night to Celebrate. rev. ed. (Illus.). (J). *(978-0-944991-71-8(8))* Swift Learning Resources.
—McOmber Phonics Storybooks: Fizz in the Pit. rev. ed. (Illus.). (J). *(978-0-944991-12-1(2))* Swift Learning Resources.
—McOmber Phonics Storybooks: Fizz Mix. rev. ed. (Illus.). (J). *(978-0-944991-11-4(4))* Swift Learning Resources.
—McOmber Phonics Storybooks: Fizz Mud. rev. ed. (Illus.). (J). *(978-0-944991-21-3(1))* Swift Learning Resources.
MCP Staff. The Baby Who Got All the Blame. (J). (gr. 1-2). 38.50 *(978-0-8136-1071-9(0))*; 38.50 *(978-0-8136-9136-7(2))* Modern Curriculum Pr.
—Little Bunny's Lunch: Short u; Consonants b, h; Blends br, cr; Digraphs ch, sh, th. (J). (gr. 1-2). 38.50 *(978-0-8136-1116-7(4))* Modern Curriculum Pr.
—Who Said Boo? Long u; Consonants d, m; Blend dr. (J). 38.50 *(978-0-8136-1091-7(5))* Modern Curriculum Pr.
McRoberts, Richard. The Curious Incident of the Dog in the Night Time. 2005. (Cambridge Wizard English Student Guides). (ENG., Illus.). 64p. pap. 19.95 *(978-0-521-61379-8(5))* Cambridge Univ. Pr.
Meachen Rau, Dana. Guess Who, 6 bks., Set. Incl. Guess Who Grunts. lib. bdg. 25.50 *(978-0-7614-2906-7(9),* 0a8f4823-c6cb-4a5a-ae51-895f67248d94); Guess Who Hunts. lib. bdg. 25.50 *(978-0-7614-2907-4(7),* 19f9df62-bd09-4218-b641-fe6bf1782640); Guess Who Jumps. lib. bdg. 25.50 *(978-0-7614-2908-1(5),* 3f4ab731-404b-4ee6-9a89-580315b53693); Guess Who Purrs. lib. bdg. 25.50 *(978-0-7614-2972-2(7),* e666baf0-caf6-4258-821c-f832f697f141); Guess Who Stings. lib. bdg. 25.50 *(978-0-7614-2973-9(5),* 14a22ff1-f1ef-452b-92f4-38c51e137265); Guess Who Swims. lib. bdg. 25.50 *(978-0-7614-2974-6(3),* 8934e38f-c926-4c45-925a-1edf5fb44664); 32p. (gr. k-1). 2009. (Bookworms: Guess Who 3 Ser.). 24p. 2004. Set lib. bdg. 95.70 net. *(978-0-7614-2905-0(0),* Cavendish Square) Cavendish Square Publishing LLC.
—¿Qué Es un Banco? (What Is a Bank?), 1 vol. 2010. (Dinero y Los Bancos (Money & Banks) Ser.). (SPA., Illus.). 24p. (J). (gr. 2-4). lib. bdg. 24.67 *(978-1-4339-3726-2(3),* 908adb67-827c-4949-aca8-d411140dbed9) Stevens, Gareth Publishing LLLP.
Meadows, Daisy. Alicia the Snow Queen Fairy. 2017. (Illus.). 159p. (J). *(978-1-5182-2779-0(1))* Scholastic, Inc.
Meddaugh, Susan. Haunted House. 2010. (Martha Speaks Ser.). (ENG., Illus.). 24p. (J). (gr. -1-3). pap. 3.99 *(978-0-547-21073-5(6))* Houghton Mifflin Harcourt Publishing Co.
—Martha Speaks: Good Luck, Martha! (Reader) 2012. (Green Light Reader Level 2 Ser.). (ENG., Illus.). 24p. (J). (gr. k-2). 16.19 *(978-0-547-57657-2(9))*; (gr. -1-3). pap. 3.99 *(978-0-547-57658-9(7))* Houghton Mifflin Harcourt Publishing Co.
—Martha Speaks: Haunted House (Reader) 2010. (Green Light Reader Level 2 Ser.). (ENG., Illus.). 24p. (J). (gr. k-2). 16.19 *(978-0-547-39353-7(9))* Houghton Mifflin Harcourt Publishing Co.
—Martha Speaks: Meet Martha (Picture Reader) 2010. (Martha Speaks Ser.). (ENG., Illus.). 24p. (J). (gr. -1-3). 12.99 *(978-0-547-36904-4(2))* Houghton Mifflin Harcourt Publishing Co.
—Meet Martha. 2010. (Martha Speaks Ser.). (ENG., Illus.). 24p. (J). (gr. -1-3). pap. 3.99 *(978-0-547-21079-7(5))* Houghton Mifflin Harcourt Publishing Co.
—Toy Trouble. 2010. (Martha Speaks Ser.). (ENG., Illus.). 24p. (J). (gr. -1-3). pap. 3.99 *(978-0-547-21078-0(7))* Houghton Mifflin Harcourt Publishing Co.
Medina, Conni. Make a Chinese New Year Dragon, 1 vol. 2nd rev. ed. 2011. (TIME for KIDS(r): Informational Text Ser.). (ENG.). 20p. (gr. 1-2). 6.99 *(978-1-4333-3593-8(X))* Teacher Created Materials, Inc.
—Make a Gingerbread Man, 1 vol. 2nd rev. ed. 2011. (TIME for KIDS(r): Informational Text Ser.). (ENG.). 20p. (gr. 1-2). 8.99 *(978-1-4333-3594-5(8))* Teacher Created Materials, Inc.
—Make Papel Picado, 1 vol. 2nd rev. ed. 2011. (TIME for KIDS(r): Informational Text Ser.). (ENG.). 20p. (gr. 1-2). 8.99 *(978-1-4333-3592-1(1))* Teacher Created Materials, Inc.
Medina, Meg. Mango, Abuela y Yo. Dominguez, Angela, illus. 2015. (SPA.). 32p. (J). (gr. k-3). 7.99 *(978-0-7636-8099-2(0))* Candlewick Pr.
Mega Jumbo ABC And 123. 2006. (J). per. 9.95 *(978-1-885920-13-3(X))* Pyramid Publishing, Inc.
Meg's Mad Magnet, 6 vols., Pack,Set C. (Supersonic Phonics Ser.). (gr. k-3). 29.00 *(978-0-7635-0542-4(0))* Rigby Education.
Meissner, David. My Neighborhood: Set Of 6. 2011. (Early Connections Ser.). (J). pap. 39.00 net. *(978-1-4108-1540-8(4))* Benchmark Education Co.
Meister, Cari. Hi-Ho, Tiny. Davis, Rich, illus. 2015. (Tiny Ser.). (ENG.). 32p. (J). (gr. k-1). pap. 4.99 *(978-0-448-48291-0(6),* Penguin Young Readers) Penguin Young Readers Group.
—Rookie Ready to Learn en Español: Me Fascinan Los árboles. Sirrell, Terry, illus. 2011. (Rookie Ready to Learn Español Ser.). Orig. Title: Rookie Ready to Learn: I Love Trees. (SPA.). 40p. (J). pap. 5.95 *(978-0-531-26786-8(5),* Children's Pr.) Scholastic Library Publishing.
—Tiny Goes to the Movies. Davis, Rich, illus. 2016. (Tiny Ser.). 32p. (J). (gr. k-1). pap. 5.99 *(978-0-448-48295-8(9),* Penguin Young Readers) Penguin Young Readers Group.
—Tiny Saves the Day. Davis, Rich, illus. 2016. (Tiny Ser.). 32p. (J). (gr. k-1). 4.99 *(978-0-448-48293-4(2),* Penguin Young Readers) Penguin Young Readers Group.
Mellion, Nicole. Liam's Pets. Filipina, Monika, illus. 2017. (Text Connections Guided Close Reading Ser.). (J). (gr. 1). *(978-1-4900-1802-7(6))* Benchmark Education Co.
Mendoza, Javier, et al. El Mundo. 2008. (Illus.). 32p. (J). pap. 7.99 *(978-1-84686-209-0(4))* Barefoot Bks., Inc.
Meredith, Susan Markowitz. All Work, No Play: Set Of 6. 2010. (Early Connections Ser.). (J). pap. 37.00 net. *(978-1-4108-1072-4(0))* Benchmark Education Co.
Merrell, Billy. Bob's Burgers Mad Libs: World's Greatest Word Game. 2015. (Mad Libs Ser.). (ENG.). 48p. (J). (gr. 3-7). pap. 5.99 *(978-0-8431-8294-1(6),* Mad Libs) Penguin Young Readers Group.
Messner, Kate. Fergus & Zeke. 2018. (Fergus & Zeke Ser.). lib. bdg. 14.75 *(978-0-606-40912-4(2))* Turtleback.
Metal, Liana. Storytime. 2008. 33p. pap. 16.50 *(978-1-4092-2451-8(1))* Lulu Pr., Inc.
Metcalf, Calvin John. The Literary World Seventh Reader. 2007. 308p. 98.99 *(978-1-4280-7591-7(7))*; per. 91.99 *(978-1-4280-7587-0(9))* IndyPublish.com.
Meyers, Terri. Shih Tzu Achoo!! 2009. 24p. pap. 12.99 *(978-1-4389-5696-1(7))* AuthorHouse.
Mi hermanita Annie. (Pebble Soup Exploraciones Ser.). 16p. (gr. -1-18). 31.00 *(978-0-7578-1670-3(3))* Rigby Education.
Mi hermanita Annie: Small Book. (Pebble Soup Exploraciones Ser.). 16p. (gr. -1-18). 5.00 *(978-0-7578-1710-6(6))* Rigby Education.
Michaels, Chris. Finding Stripes. 2010. (Sight Word Readers Ser.). (J). 3.49 *(978-1-60719-626-6(3))* Newmark Learning LLC.
Michaels, Eric. Women of Courage, 6, Set. 2004. (Phonics Readers Books 37-72 Ser.). (ENG.). 16p. (gr. k-1). pap. 35.70 *(978-0-7368-4087-3(7))* Capstone.
Michele, Tracey. African Art. 2011. (Learn-Abouts Ser.). (Illus.). 16p. (J). pap. 7.95 *(978-1-59920-637-0(4))* Black Rabbit Bks.
—Big Cats, Little Cats. 2011. (Learn-Abouts Ser.). (Illus.). 16p. (J). pap. 7.95 *(978-1-59920-595-3(5))* Black Rabbit Bks.
—Bugs & Beetles. 2011. (Learn-Abouts Ser.). (Illus.). 16p. (J). pap. 7.95 *(978-1-59920-611-0(0))* Black Rabbit Bks.
—Clocks. 2011. (Learn-Abouts Ser.). (Illus.). 16p. (J). pap. 7.95 *(978-1-59920-639-4(0))* Black Rabbit Bks.
—Earth's Land & Water. 2011. (Learn-Abouts Ser.). (Illus.). 16p. (J). pap. 7.95 *(978-1-59920-593-9(9))* Black Rabbit Bks.
—Follow the Road Map. 2011. (Learn-Abouts Ser.). (Illus.). 16p. (J). pap. 7.95 *(978-1-59920-638-7(2))* Black Rabbit Bks.
—From Plan to House. 2011. (Illus.). 16p. (J). pap. 7.95 *(978-1-59920-623-3(4))* Black Rabbit Bks.
—Games Around the World. 2011. (Learn-Abouts Ser.). (Illus.). 16p. (J). pap. 7.95 *(978-1-59920-621-9(8))* Black Rabbit Bks.
—Gas & Air. 2011. (Learn-Abouts Ser.). (Illus.). 16p. (J). pap. 7.95 *(978-1-59920-644-8(7))* Black Rabbit Bks.
—Having Fun with Matter. 2011. (Learn-Abouts Ser.). (Illus.). 16p. (J). pap. 7.95 *(978-1-59920-628-8(5))* Black Rabbit Bks.
—The Life Cycle of a Frog. 2011. (Learn-Abouts Ser.). (Illus.). 16p. (J). pap. 7.95 *(978-1-59920-627-1(7))* Black Rabbit Bks.
—The Life of a River. 2011. (Learn-Abouts Ser.). (Illus.). 16p. (J). pap. 9.95 *(978-1-59920-609-7(9))* Palgrave Macmillan.
—Make a Color. 2011. (Learn-Abouts Ser.). (Illus.). 16p. (J). pap. 7.95 *(978-1-59920-596-0(3))* Black Rabbit Bks.
—Make a String Phone. 2011. (Learn-Abouts Ser.). (Illus.). 16p. (J). pap. 7.95 *(978-1-59920-607-3(2))* Black Rabbit Bks.
—Make a Treasure Map. 2011. (Illus.). 16p. (J). pap. 7.95 *(978-1-59920-606-6(4))* Black Rabbit Bks.
—Map the School. 2011. (ENG., Illus.). 16p. (J). pap. 7.95 *(978-1-59920-590-8(4))* Black Rabbit Bks.
—Measure the Weather. 2011. (Learn-Abouts Ser.). (Illus.). 16p. (J). pap. 7.95 *(978-1-59920-641-7(2))* Black Rabbit Bks.
—The Moon. 2011. (Learn-Abouts Ser.). (Illus.). 16p. (J). pap. 7.95 *(978-1-59920-625-7(0))* Black Rabbit Bks.
—Musical Instruments. 2011. (Learn-Abouts Ser.). (Illus.). 16p. (J). pap. 7.95 *(978-1-59920-642-4(0))* Black Rabbit Bks.
—My School, Your School. 2011. (Learn-Abouts Ser.). (ENG., Illus.). 16p. (J). pap. 7.95 *(978-1-59920-605-9(6))* Black Rabbit Bks.
—Old Buildings, New Buildings. 2011. (Learn-Abouts Ser.). (Illus.). 16p. (J). pap. 7.95 *(978-1-59920-591-5(2))* Black Rabbit Bks.
—People Who Help at Car Accidents. 2011. (Learn-Abouts Ser.). (Illus.). 16p. (J). pap. 7.95 *(978-1-59920-608-0(0))* Black Rabbit Bks.
—People Who Work for the City. 2011. (Learn-Abouts Ser.). (Illus.). 16p. (J). pap. 7.95 *(978-1-59920-640-0(4))* Black Rabbit Bks.
—Pumpkin Time. 2011. (Learn-Abouts Ser.). (Illus.). 16p. (J). pap. 7.95 *(978-1-59920-589-2(0))* Black Rabbit Bks.
—Riding a Bike. 2011. (Learn-Abouts Ser.). (Illus.). 16p. (J). pap. 7.95 *(978-1-59920-626-4(9))* Black Rabbit Bks.
—What Do Firefighters Do? 2011. (Learn-Abouts Ser.). (Illus.). 16p. (J). pap. 7.95 *(978-1-59920-592-2(0))* Black Rabbit Bks.
—What Is a Mammal? 2011. (Learn-Abouts Ser.). (Illus.). 16p. (J). pap. 7.95 *(978-1-59920-643-1(9))* Black Rabbit Bks.
—Where Does the Garbage Go? 2011. (Learn-Abouts Ser.). (Illus.). 16p. (J). pap. 7.95 *(978-1-59920-612-7(9))* Black Rabbit Bks.
Midnight Rescue, 6 vols., Pack. (Action Packs Ser.). 120p. (gr. 3-5). 44.00 *(978-0-7635-8391-0(X))* Rigby Education.
Miles, Lisa. Starting to Read. 2004. (Usborne Farmyard Tales Ser.). (ENG., Illus.). 1p. (J). (gr. -1-3). pap. 6.95 *(978-0-7460-3408-8(3))* EDC Publishing.
Milet Publishing Staff. Milet Interactive for Kids - Chinese for English Speakers. 2012. (Milet Interactive for Kids Ser.). (ENG., Illus.). 1p. (J). (gr. k-2). cd-rom 24.95 *(978-1-84059-676-2(7))* Milet Publishing.
Milford, Alison. Collins Big Cat Phonics for Letters & Sounds - the Elf & the Bootmaker: Band 05/Green, Bd. 5. Auriemma, Monica, illus. 2018. (Collins Big Cat Phonics Ser.). (ENG.). 24p. (J). (gr. k-1). pap. 8.99 *(978-0-00-825166-6(5))* HarperCollins Pubs. Ltd. GBR. Dist: Independent Pubs. Group.
—A Finders' Guide to Rocks, Fossils & Soils: Band 13/Topaz. 2017. (Collins Big Cat Ser.). (ENG., Illus.). 32p. (J). pap. 9.99 *(978-0-00-820877-6(8))* HarperCollins Pubs. Ltd. GBR. Dist: Independent Pubs. Group.
The Mill on the Hill, 6 vols., Pack,Set B. (Supersonic Phonics Ser.). (gr. k-3). 29.00 *(978-0-7635-0536-3(6))* Rigby Education.
Millar, Colin & Breakwell, Spike. Movie World 4 Voyagers. 2017. (Cambridge Reading Adventures Ser.). (ENG., Illus.). 48p. pap. 11.00 *(978-1-108-40106-7(6))* Cambridge Univ. Pr.
Miller, Heather. The 10 Most Outstanding American Symbols. 2008. 14.99 *(978-1-55448-508-6(8))* Scholastic Library Publishing.
—The 10 Most Provocative 20th Century Artworks. 2007. (J). 14.99 *(978-1-55448-483-6(9))* Scholastic Library Publishing.
Miller, Kathryn L. Abc's with Sadie: Sadie Goes to the Zoo. 2011. 32p. pap. 17.25 *(978-1-4269-5940-0(0))* Trafford Publishing.
Miller, Marie. Party Time, 1 vol. 2006. (Neighborhood Readers Ser.). (ENG.). 8p. (gr. k-1). pap. 5.15 *(978-1-4042-6706-0(9),* 4015b93f-9d69-4b30-bbc4-3fc5280b507b, Rosen Classroom) Rosen Publishing Group, Inc., The.
Miller, Michael. Hilde und Günter Level Two Reader, 2 books. 2003. (GER., Illus.). 53p. 6.00 *(978-0-9743522-0-6(9),* 0-9743522-0-9) Miller, Michael.
Miller, Mona. Poppy & Branch's Big Adventure. 2017. (Step into Reading Level 3 Ser.). lib. bdg. 14.75 *(978-0-606-39851-0(1))* Turtleback.
Miller, Sara. Vampirina in the Fall. 2018. (Illus.). 32p. (J). *(978-1-5444-0806-4(4))* Disney Publishing Worldwide.
Millett, Peter. The Great Escape White Band. Belli, Alfredo, illus. 2016. (Cambridge Reading Adventures Ser.). (ENG.). 24p. pap. 8.80 *(978-1-107-55158-9(7))* Cambridge Univ. Pr.
—Lost at Sea. Bacchin, Giorgio, illus. 2016. (Cambridge Reading Adventures Ser.). (ENG.). 26p. pap. 8.80 *(978-1-316-50344-7(5))* Cambridge Univ. Pr.
—Meltdown 4 Voyagers. Campos, Leo, illus. 2017. (Cambridge Reading Adventures Ser.). (ENG.). 32p. pap. 8.30 *(978-1-108-43485-0(1))* Cambridge Univ. Pr.
—Power Cut Turquoise Band. Daff, Russ, illus. 2016. (Cambridge Reading Adventures Ser.). (ENG.). 24p. pap. 8.80 *(978-1-316-60586-8(8))* Cambridge Univ. Pr.
—River Rescue 1 Pathfinders. Cerisier, Emmanuel, illus. 2017. (Cambridge Reading Adventures Ser.). (ENG.). 24p. pap. 8.60 *(978-1-108-40071-8(X))* Cambridge Univ. Pr.
—Sandstorm Purple Band. Bacchin, Giorgio, illus. 2016. (Cambridge Reading Adventures Ser.). (ENG.). 24p. pap. 8.80 *(978-1-107-57607-0(5))* Cambridge Univ. Pr.
—Take Zayan with You! Green Band. Daff, Russ, illus. 2016. (Cambridge Reading Adventures Ser.). (ENG.). 16p. pap. 7.95 *(978-1-107-57587-5(7))* Cambridge Univ. Pr.
Millett, Peter & Chambers, Mal. Goal! 2008. (Rigby Focus Forward: Level O Ser.). (Illus.). 24p. (J). (gr. 4-7). pap. *(978-1-4190-3845-7(1),* Rigby) Pearson Education Australia.
Millett, Peter & Scales, Simon. The Game. 2008. (Rigby Focus Forward: Level H Ser.). (Illus.). 24p. (J). (gr. 4-7). pap. *(978-1-4190-3723-8(4),* Rigby) Pearson Education Australia.
Millett, Peter & Texidor, Dee. On the Team. 2008. (Rigby Focus Forward: Level F Ser.). (Illus.). 24p. (J). (gr. 4-7). pap. *(978-1-4190-3698-9(X),* Rigby) Pearson Education Australia.
Millett, Peter & Wallace-Mitchell, Jane. Lions! 2008. (Rigby Focus Forward: Level G Ser.). (Illus.). 24p. (J). (gr. 4-7). pap. *(978-1-4190-3717-7(X),* Rigby) Pearson Education Australia.
Millici, Nate. Star Wars: Finn & Poe Team Up! Parisi, Andrea & Krysinski, Grzegorz, illus. 2017. (World of Reading Level 1 Ser.). (ENG.). 32p. (J). (gr. -1-3). 31.36 *(978-1-5321-4054-9(1),* 25426) Spotlight.
Milligan, Jean F. Inferences for Young Audiences. Kennedy, Allan, illus. 2004. 96p. (J). (gr. 3-7). 14.95 *(978-0-9637825-2-6(5))* Autumn Hse. Publishing.
Mills, Nathan. Living or Nonliving?, 1 vol. 2012. (Rosen Readers Ser.). (ENG., Illus.). 16p. (J). (gr. k-k). pap. 7.00 *(978-1-4488-8746-0(1),* c06efeba-0ac4-4493-9cc0-e906299a6a96, Rosen Classroom) Rosen Publishing Group, Inc., The.
Mills, Nathan & Allyn, Daisy. Around My Neighborhood, 1 vol. 2012. (Rosen Readers Ser.). (ENG., Illus.). 16p. (J). (gr. k-k). pap. 7.00 *(978-1-4488-8646-3(5),* 71ca028e-3189-4367-9dda-cda408983022, Rosen Classroom) Rosen Publishing Group, Inc., The.
Mills, Nathan & Baker, Rick. More or Less?, 1 vol. 2012. (Rosen Readers Ser.). (ENG., Illus.). 16p. (J). (gr. k-k). pap. 7.00 *(978-1-4488-8649-4(X),* cbebaaf9-bd06-4acd-9ace-a5f1d00b2736, Rosen Classroom) Rosen Publishing Group, Inc., The.
Mills, Nathan & Blehn, Mike. Things I Need, Things I Want, 1 vol. 2012. (Rosen Readers Ser.). (ENG., Illus.). 16p. (J). (gr. k-k). pap. 7.00 *(978-1-4488-8728-6(3),* 1f4e8243-f1bf-44d3-9bc7-16739ee96e2f, Rosen Classroom) Rosen Publishing Group, Inc., The.
Mills, Nathan & Christopher, Nick. Time for a Field Trip, 1 vol. 2012. (Rosen Readers Ser.). (ENG., Illus.). 16p. (J). (gr. k-k). pap. 7.00 *(978-1-4488-8752-1(6),* cb2bcd53-1835-4508-a77a-5874a907e1df, Rosen Classroom) Rosen Publishing Group, Inc., The.
Mills, Nathan & Davidson, Amy. My Busy Week, 1 vol. 2012. (Rosen Readers Ser.). (ENG., Illus.). 16p. (J). (gr. k-k). pap. 7.00 *(978-1-4488-8689-0(9),* 0dea7d70-1aa2-4c00-a9e0-15e9fd5b2833, Rosen Classroom) Rosen Publishing Group, Inc., The.
Mills, Nathan & Ericson, Emma. Up or Down?, 1 vol. 2012. (Rosen Readers Ser.). (ENG., Illus.). 16p. (J). (gr. k-k). pap. 7.00 *(978-1-4488-8643-2(0),* 7fb912cd-b423-40ed-8893-b9ce2ee39aa1, Rosen Classroom) Rosen Publishing Group, Inc., The.
Mills, Nathan & Faraday, Daniel. Walk, Run, Skip, & Jump!, 1 vol. 2012. (Rosen Readers Ser.). (ENG., Illus.). 16p. (J). (gr. k-k). pap. 7.00 *(978-1-4488-8680-7(5),* 19d2ecbb-5d2e-4b32-9a9f-d18a62e7eb7d, Rosen Classroom) Rosen Publishing Group, Inc., The.
Mills, Nathan & Frampton, Callie. Tools Tell the Weather, 1 vol. 2012. (Rosen Readers Ser.). (ENG., Illus.). 24p. (J). (gr. 1-1). pap. 8.25 *(978-1-4488-8800-9(X),* 475f84a4-211d-4937-9a2a-cc5f53ea5114, Rosen Classroom) Rosen Publishing Group, Inc., The.
Mills, Nathan & Francis, Bill. Hannah's Four Seasons, 1 vol. 2012. (Rosen Readers Ser.). (ENG., Illus.). 16p. (J). (gr. k-k). pap. 7.00 *(978-1-4488-8740-8(2),* c1b66f27-406d-4deb-8448-5e2f4413896f, Rosen Classroom) Rosen Publishing Group, Inc., The.
Mills, Nathan & Fudoli, Melissa. I Have One More, 1 vol. 2012. (Rosen Readers Ser.). (ENG., Illus.). 16p. (J). (gr. k-k). pap. 7.00 *(978-1-4488-8655-5(4),* 1d7c2e3b-e0f0-4fb6-82fc-e2d298d2e2a2, Rosen Classroom) Rosen Publishing Group, Inc., The.
Mills, Nathan & Goodwin, Josh. How Do I Get There?, 1 vol. 2012. (Rosen Readers Ser.). (ENG., Illus.). 24p. (J). (gr. 1-1). pap. 8.25 *(978-1-4488-8779-8(8),* 018d7396-3ea7-48e5-9aa0-f4dd1aaa00b8, Rosen Classroom) Rosen Publishing Group, Inc., The.
Mills, Nathan & Holtz, Mary Elizabeth. Sabrina's School, 1 vol. 2012. (Rosen Readers Ser.). (ENG., Illus.). 16p. (J). (gr. k-k). pap. 7.00 *(978-1-4488-8719-4(4),* d4d5cd12-8a8c-4e3a-9b68-87c958c15dea, Rosen Classroom) Rosen Publishing Group, Inc., The.
Mills, Nathan & Hume, Desmond. Earth's Water, 1 vol. 2012. (Rosen Readers Ser.). (ENG., Illus.). 24p. (J). (gr. 1-2). pap. 8.25 *(978-1-4488-8818-4(2),* e27b16cf-f8a0-4147-9b24-98e3204f4715, Rosen Classroom) Rosen Publishing Group, Inc., The.
Mills, Nathan & Jamison, Linc. Getting Around Our City, 1 vol. 2012. (Rosen Readers Ser.). (ENG., Illus.). 16p. (J). (gr. k-k). pap. 7.00 *(978-1-4488-8722-4(4),* 6a229458-378f-4f44-9b71-a2c28113cdb2, Rosen Classroom) Rosen Publishing Group, Inc., The.
Mills, Nathan & Kurkowiak, Anne. Tyler's New Friend, 1 vol. 2012. (Rosen Readers Ser.). (ENG., Illus.). 16p. (J). (gr. k-k). pap. 7.00 *(978-1-4488-8731-6(3),* 23a97bb2-0f8a-4ca8-9b75-24d10b240e43, Rosen Classroom) Rosen Publishing Group, Inc., The.
Mills, Nathan & Ludlow, Susan. From Ice to Steam, 1 vol. 2012. (Rosen Readers Ser.). (ENG., Illus.). 24p. (J). (gr. 1-1). pap. 8.25 *(978-1-4488-8812-2(3),* fad63b32-b88e-4731-9e9c-6972bacbb900, Rosen Classroom) Rosen Publishing Group, Inc., The.
Mills, Nathan & Machajewski, Sarah. Symbols of the United States, 1 vol. 2012. (Rosen Readers Ser.). (ENG., Illus.). 24p. (J). (gr. 1-1). pap. 8.25 *(978-1-4488-8761-3(5),* 2abcb7ca-baa6-409b-8a02-9ef028a294de, Rosen Classroom) Rosen Publishing Group, Inc., The.
Mills, Nathan & McCann, Margaret. How We Use Water, 1 vol. 2012. (Rosen Readers Ser.). (ENG., Illus.). 24p. (J). (gr. 1-1). pap. 8.25 *(978-1-4488-8794-1(1),* 3117a6ad-d5ab-43e3-b540-7d9821c92c30, Rosen Classroom) Rosen Publishing Group, Inc., The.
Mills, Nathan & Miller, Andy. Is It Cloth, Clay, or Paper?, 1 vol. 2012. (Rosen Readers Ser.). (ENG., Illus.). 16p. (J). (gr. k-k). pap. 7.00 *(978-1-4488-8707-1(0),* 51e0c7ef-3a4b-4cff-96bb-a2bf17dfabc5, Rosen Classroom) Rosen Publishing Group, Inc., The.
Mills, Nathan & Ridolfi, Isabella. Sue Goes to the Store, 1 vol. 2012. (Rosen Readers Ser.). (ENG., Illus.). 16p. (J). (gr. k-k). pap. 7.00 *(978-1-4488-8737-8(2),* 60c28e5f-c9df-44c0-ba05-d5c1f5370461, Rosen Classroom) Rosen Publishing Group, Inc., The.
Mills, Nathan & Rose, Craig. Carlos Reads a Map, 1 vol. 2012. (Rosen Readers Ser.). (ENG., Illus.). 16p. (J). (gr. k-k). pap. 7.00 *(978-1-4488-8716-3(X),* 013b75bc-0bfc-4704-b126-c00b8a231cf0, Rosen Classroom) Rosen Publishing Group, Inc., The.
—We Help at School, 1 vol. 2012. (Rosen Readers Ser.). (ENG., Illus.). 16p. (J). (gr. k-k). pap. 7.00 *(978-1-4488-8661-6(9),* 35016a5d-44f9-464c-b3fd-ad1aa8e75ccb, Rosen Classroom) Rosen Publishing Group, Inc., The.
Mills, Nathan & Sotherden, Nora. Our Classroom Rules, 1 vol. 2012. (Rosen Readers Ser.). (ENG., Illus.). 16p. (J). (gr. k-k). pap. 7.00 *(978-1-4488-8692-0(9),* 0977b2fa-2b0d-4f23-8448-460740219b75, Rosen Classroom) Rosen Publishing Group, Inc., The.
Mills, Nathan & Stern, Robin. Sara's Seeds, 1 vol. 2012. (Rosen Readers Ser.). (ENG., Illus.). 16p. (J). (gr. k-k). pap. 7.00 *(978-1-4488-8713-2(5),* 24969bea-d328-4f0c-9b99-d49db2428ef3, Rosen Classroom) Rosen Publishing Group, Inc., The.
Mills, Nathan & Swan, Henry. How Animals Live & Grow, 1 vol. 2012. (Rosen Readers Ser.). (ENG., Illus.). 24p. (J). (gr. 1-1). pap. 8.25 *(978-1-4488-8764-4(X),* bcb0ec33-2359-43c7-b3dc-58619b0a18ed, Rosen Classroom) Rosen Publishing Group, Inc., The.
Mills, Nathan & Wesolowski, Harriet. The Songs We Sing: Honoring Our Country, 1 vol. 2012. (Rosen Readers Ser.). (ENG., Illus.). 24p. (J). (gr. 1-2). pap. 8.25 *(978-1-4488-8821-4(2),* 45c822f8-b9c7-4ecb-af47-3e5ded263e4b, Rosen Classroom) Rosen Publishing Group, Inc., The.
Mills, Nathan & White, Ella. Months of the Year, 1 vol. 2012. (Rosen Readers Ser.). (ENG., Illus.). 24p. (J). (gr. 1-1). pap. 8.25 *(978-1-4488-8785-9(2),* a18f0f01-23dc-4ac1-b310-089445da9b55, Rosen Classroom) Rosen Publishing Group, Inc., The.
Mills, Nathan & Wilson, Emily. Good Night, Bears: Learning about Hibernation, 1 vol. 2012. (Rosen Readers Ser.). (ENG., Illus.). 24p. (J). (gr. 1-1). pap. 8.25 *(978-1-4488-8776-7(3),* e4a84e08-48b4-4692-bc3c-ffc9e5754925, Rosen Classroom) Rosen Publishing Group, Inc., The.
Mills, Nathan & Worthy, Shanya. Ana's Community Helpers, 1 vol. 2012. (Rosen Readers Ser.). (ENG., Illus.). 16p. (J). (gr. k-k). pap. 7.00 *(978-1-4488-8698-2(8),* 37289a23-be39-42d9-8ba3-cde0ddec457d, Rosen Classroom) Rosen Publishing Group, Inc., The.
Minden, Cecilia. At the Fish Hut. 2018. (What I Eat Ser.). (ENG.). 16p. (J). (gr. -1-2). pap. 11.36

PQR

(978-1-5341-2867-5(0), 211522, Cherry Blossom Press) Cherry Lake Publishing.

—Beth's Basketball Game. 2018. (Little Blossom Stories Ser.). (ENG.). 16p. (J). (gr. -1-2). pap. 11.36 *(978-1-5341-2862-0(X)*, 211507, Cherry Blossom Press) Cherry Lake Publishing.

—The Bulls Football Team. 2018. (Little Blossom Stories Ser.). (ENG.). 16p. (J). (gr. -1-2). pap. 11.36 *(978-1-5341-2861-3(1)*, 211504, Cherry Blossom Press) Cherry Lake Publishing.

—Buzz Plays Soccer. 2018. (Little Blossom Stories Ser.). (ENG.). 16p. (J). (gr. -1-2). pap. 11.36 *(978-1-5341-2863-7(8)*, 211510, Cherry Blossom Press) Cherry Lake Publishing.

—Cat. 2018. (Learn about Animals Ser.). (ENG., Illus.). 16p. (J). (gr. -1-2). pap. 11.36 *(978-1-5341-2395-3(4)*, 210574) Cherry Lake Publishing.

—Dog. 2018. (Learn about Animals Ser.). (ENG., Illus.). 16p. (J). (gr. -1-2). pap. 11.36 *(978-1-5341-2396-0(2)*, 210577) Cherry Lake Publishing.

—Good Food at the Food Truck. 2018. (What I Eat Ser.). (ENG.). 16p. (J). (gr. -1-2). pap. 11.36 *(978-1-5341-2866-8(2)*, 211519, Cherry Blossom Press) Cherry Lake Publishing.

—Hen. 2018. (Learn about Animals Ser.). (ENG., Illus.). 16p. (J). (gr. -1-2). pap. 11.36 *(978-1-5341-2397-7(0)*, 210580) Cherry Lake Publishing.

—Jump in the Pool. 2018. (Little Blossom Stories Ser.). (ENG.). 16p. (J). (gr. -1-2). pap. 11.36 *(978-1-5341-2864-4(6)*, 211513, Cherry Blossom Press) Cherry Lake Publishing.

—Sam & Jen Get a Pet. 2018. (Little Blossom Stories Ser.). (ENG., Illus.). 16p. (J). (gr. -1-2). pap. 11.36 *(978-1-5341-2398-4(9)*, 210583, Cherry Blossom Press) Cherry Lake Publishing.

—Snacks at the Park. 2018. (What I Eat Ser.). (ENG.). 16p. (J). (gr. -1-2). pap. 11.36 *(978-1-5341-2865-1(4)*, 211516, Cherry Blossom Press) Cherry Lake Publishing.

—Tim & His Bat. 2018. (Little Blossom Stories Ser.). (ENG., Illus.). 16p. (J). (gr. -1-2). pap. 11.36 *(978-1-5341-2401-1(2)*, 210592, Cherry Blossom Press) Cherry Lake Publishing.

—What Can I Get at the Shop? 2018. (What to Put On? Ser.). (ENG.). 16p. (J). (gr. -1-2). pap. 11.36 *(978-1-5341-2870-5(0)*, 211531, Cherry Blossom Press) Cherry Lake Publishing.

—What Can I See in the Fall? 2018. (Seasons Ser.). (ENG.). 16p. (J). (gr. -1-2). pap. 11.36 *(978-1-5341-2873-6(5)*, 211540, Cherry Blossom Press) Cherry Lake Publishing.

—What Can I See in the Spring? 2018. (Seasons Ser.). (ENG.). 16p. (J). (gr. -1-2). pap. 11.36 *(978-1-5341-2874-3(3)*, 211543, Cherry Blossom Press) Cherry Lake Publishing.

—What Can I See in the Summer? 2018. (Seasons Ser.). (ENG.). 16p. (J). (gr. -1-2). pap. 11.36 *(978-1-5341-2875-0(1)*, 211546, Cherry Blossom Press) Cherry Lake Publishing.

—What Can I See in the Winter? 2018. (Seasons Ser.). (ENG.). 16p. (J). (gr. -1-2). pap. 11.36 *(978-1-5341-2876-7(X)*, 211549, Cherry Blossom Press) Cherry Lake Publishing.

—What Is in Your Lunch Box? 2018. (What I Eat Ser.). (ENG.). 16p. (J). (gr. -1-2). pap. 11.36 *(978-1-5341-2868-2(9)*, 211525, Cherry Blossom Press) Cherry Lake Publishing.

—What Shall I Pack for Our Trip? 2018. (What to Put On? Ser.). (ENG.). 16p. (J). (gr. -1-2). pap. 11.36 *(978-1-5341-2872-9(7)*, 211537, Cherry Blossom Press) Cherry Lake Publishing.

—What to Put on for School? 2018. (What to Put On? Ser.). (ENG.). 16p. (J). (gr. -1-2). pap. 11.36 *(978-1-5341-2871-2(9)*, 211534, Cherry Blossom Press) Cherry Lake Publishing.

—What to Put on for the Park? 2018. (What to Put On? Ser.). (ENG.). 16p. (J). (gr. -1-2). pap. 11.36 *(978-1-5341-2869-9(7)*, 211528, Cherry Blossom Press) Cherry Lake Publishing.

Mini Plays & Folktale Plays that Build Reading Skills. 2005. (J). pap. *(978-1-60015-036-4(5))* Steps To Literacy, LLC.

Mis Amigos los Monstruos, 6 vols., Pack. (Literatura 2000 Ser.). (SPA.). (gr. 1-2). 28.00 *(978-0-7635-1047-3(5))* Rigby Education.

The Missing Suit. (Early Intervention Levels Ser.). 28.38 *(978-0-7362-0405-7(9))* CENGAGE Learning.

The Missing Suit (14), Vol. 14. (Early Intervention Levels Ser.). 4.73 *(978-0-7362-0230-5(7))* CENGAGE Learning.

Mitchell, Angela. The Dessert That Wouldn't Wobble. Home, Sarah, illus. 2019. (Early Bird Readers — Purple (Early Bird Stories (tm)) Ser.). (ENG.). 32p. (J). (gr. k-3). 30.65 *(978-1-5415-4232-7(0)*, 94afd683-5639-40f2-9361-16aeaca479e3); pap. 9.99 *(978-1-5415-7417-5(6)*, e293073d-ce2c-4d48-889d-f7d287f32c24) Lerner Publishing Group. (Lerner Pubns.).

Mitchell, David L. A Fun, Cool & Colorful Read: " A Picture Book for Children to Learn Great New Words" 2009. (ENG.). 44p. pap. 21.99 *(978-1-4363-9551-6(8))* Xlibris Corp.

Mitchell-Hughes, Kimberley. The 10 Most Extreme Sports. 2008. 14.99 *(978-1-55448-555-0(X))* Scholastic Library Publishing.

Mitchell, Julie & Chambers, Mal. Bertha. 2008. (Rigby Focus Forward: Level G Ser.). (Illus.). 24p. (J). (gr. 4-7). pap. *(978-1-4190-3703-0(X)*, Rigby) Pearson Education Australia.

—Vega Bay. 2008. (Rigby Focus Forward: Level K Ser.). (Illus.). 24p. pap. *(978-1-4190-3801-3(X)*, Rigby) Pearson Education Australia.

Mitchell, Julie & Konye, Paul. The Bully. 2008. (Rigby Focus Forward: Level K Ser.). (Illus.). 24p. (J). (gr. 4-7). pap. *(978-1-4190-3784-9(6)*, Rigby) Pearson Education Australia.

Mitchell, Julie & McKenzie, Heather. Metal Mouth. 2008. (Rigby Focus Forward: Level H Ser.). (Illus.). 24p. (J). (gr. 4-7). pap. *(978-1-4190-3738-2(2)*, Rigby) Pearson Education Australia.

Mitchell, Lucy Sprague. Here & Now Story Book. Van Loon, Hendrik Willem & Price, Christine, illus. 2015. (ENG.). 256p. (J). (gr. k-3). pap. 7.99 *(978-0-486-79196-8(3))* Dover Pubns., Inc.

Mitchell, Marie & Smith, Mason. Squatch Watch & Other Stories. 2013. 130p. pap. 9.95 *(978-0-692-02010-4(1))* Smith, Mason.

Mitchell, Pratima. Raju's Ride. Waterhouse, Stephen, illus. 2005. (ENG.). 24p. (J). lib. bdg. 23.65 *(978-1-59646-726-2(6))* Dingles & Co.

Modern Staff. Day at Our Dairy Farm. (J). (gr. k-1). 38.95 *(978-0-8136-1358-1(2))* Modern Curriculum Pr.

—Feather for Her Hair Big Book. (J). 22.95 *(978-0-8136-4821-7(1))* Modern Curriculum Pr.

—Positively Me!, 8 bks. (J). (gr. k-2). pap. *(978-0-8136-4801-9(7))* Modern Curriculum Pr.

—Positively Me! Big Book Collection, 3 bks., No. 1. (J). (gr. k-2). *(978-0-8136-4857-6(2))* Modern Curriculum Pr.

Molloy, Bonnie. Ms Flitter-Flutter. 2009. 24p. pap. 9.00 *(978-1-4269-1587-1(X))* Trafford Publishing.

Molly the Perfect Houseguest. Date not set. (Young Global Reader Ser.: Vol. 1). (J). *(978-1-887176-07-1(1))* Global Age Publishing/Global Academy Pr.

Monckeberg, Paulina. Pascualina 2006 Portuguese. 2005. (Pascualina Family of Products Ser.). (ENG.). 272p. (J). spiral bd. 16.99 *(978-956-8222-29-1(4))* Pascualina Producciones S.A.

Montgomery, Anne. Nature Made, 1 vol. rev. ed. 2014. (Science: Informational Text Ser.). (ENG., Illus.). 24p. (J). (gr. k-1). pap. 9.99 *(978-1-4807-4528-5(6))* Teacher Created Materials, Inc.

—Tell Me about It, 1 vol. rev. ed. 2014. (Science: Informational Text Ser.). (ENG., Illus.). 24p. (J). (gr. -1-1). pap. 9.99 *(978-1-4807-4526-1(X))* Teacher Created Materials, Inc.

Montgomery, Mary Sue. A Cloud Is a Cloud Is a What? You've got to be Kidding, 1 vol. 2010. 34p. 24.95 *(978-1-4489-4360-9(4))* PublishAmerica, Inc.

Moon, Nicola. Margarine & Marbles. 2005. (Red Go Bananas Ser.). (ENG., Illus.). 48p. (J). (gr. 2-3). *(978-0-7787-2698-2(3))* Crabtree Publishing Co.

Mooney, Bel. Who Loves Mr. Tubs? Hellard, Susan, illus. 2016. (Reading Ladder Level 2 Ser.). (ENG.). 48p. (gr. k-2). pap. 4.99 *(978-1-4052-8205-5(3)*, Reading Ladder) Farshore GBR. Dist: HarperCollins Pubs.

Moor, Evan. Daily Reading Comprehension, Grade 8. 2013. pap. *(978-1-60823-639-8(0))* Evan-Moor Educational Pubs.

Moore, Elizabeth & Gregory, Helen. Where Do People Work? 2011. (Wonder Readers Emergent Level Ser.). (ENG.). 16p. (gr. -1-1). pap. 35.94 *(978-1-4296-8206-0(X)*, Capstone Pr.) Capstone.

Moore, Inga. Raising Readers House in the Woods. 2014. (ENG.). 56p. (J). 3.40 *(978-0-7636-7913-2(5))* Candlewick Pr.

Moore, Kevin. The Road Maker. 2008. 52p. pap. 31.99 *(978-1-4363-7007-3(8))* Xlibris Corp.

Moore, Monica A. Everyday Heroes. 2006. (ENG.). 52p. per. 12.95 *(978-1-59800-563-9(4))* Outskirts Pr., Inc.

Moore, Phillip. When Did American Astronauts Explore? 2012. (Level C Ser.). (ENG., Illus.). 16p. (J). (gr. k-2). pap. 7.95 *(978-1-927136-26-3(1)*, 19430) RiverStream Publishing.

—When Is This a Home? 2012. (Level A Ser.). (ENG., Illus.). 16p. (J). (gr. k-2). pap. 7.95 *(978-1-927136-07-2(5)*, 19437) RiverStream Publishing.

—Where Does Used Paper Go? 2012. (Level E Ser.). (ENG., Illus.). 16p. (J). (gr. k-2). pap. 7.95 *(978-1-927136-54-6(7)*, 19446) RiverStream Publishing.

—Where Is This Astronaut? 2012. (Level A Ser.). (ENG., Illus.). 16p. (J). (gr. k-2). pap. 7.95 *(978-1-927136-06-5(7)*, 19447) RiverStream Publishing.

Moore, Sharon. The Runaway Kite, 1 vol. 2006. (Neighborhood Readers Ser.). (ENG.). 8p. (gr. k-1). pap. 5.15 *(978-1-4042-6714-5(X)*, 6113cc37-5e03-412c-8ec9-7b9f6bf00abb, Rosen Classroom) Rosen Publishing Group, Inc., The.

—The Starry Sky, 1 vol. 2006. (Neighborhood Readers Ser.). (ENG.). 16p. (gr. 1-2). pap. 6.50 *(978-1-4042-7152-4(X)*, e15cd98a-8be0-4dba-91e4-2e3210928aae, Rosen Classroom) Rosen Publishing Group, Inc., The.

Mora, Pat. Dona Flor: A Tall Tale about a Giant Woman with a Great Big Heart. 6n, Raul, illus. 2010. (ENG.). 32p. (J). (gr. -1-2). pap. 8.99 *(978-0-375-86144-4(0)*, Dragonfly Bks.) Random Hse. Children's Bks.

—Here, Kitty, Kitty! (Ven, Gatita, Ven!) Suarez, Maribel, illus. 2008. (My Family: Mi Familia Ser.). (SPA & ENG.). 24p. (J). (gr. 4-7). lib. bdg. 15.89 *(978-0-06-085045-6(0)*, Rayo) HarperCollins Pubs.

—Here, Kitty, Kitty!/Ven, Gatita, Ven! Bilingual Spanish-English. Suarez, Maribel, illus. 2008. (ENG.). 24p. (J). (gr. -1-3). 16.99 *(978-0-06-085044-9(2))* HarperCollins Español.

More Than a Meal. (Early Intervention Levels Ser.). 28.56 *(978-0-7362-1049-2(0))* CENGAGE Learning.

Morgan, Bernard P. Pszczelarz. Juraszek, Barbara, tr. Parekh, Rikin, illus. 2008. 28p. pap. *(978-1-904312-44-4(6))* MX Publishing, Ltd.

Morgan, Hawys. The Journey of Odysseus: Band 15/Emerald (Collins Big Cat) Bustamante, Martin, illus. 2017. (Collins Big Cat Tales Ser.). (ENG.). 48p. (J). (gr. 3-4). pap. 12.99 *(978-0-00-817941-0(7))* HarperCollins Pubs. Ltd. GBR. Dist: Independent Pubs. Group.

Morgan, Michaela. Band of Friends. Price, Nick, illus. 2005. (ENG.). 24p. (J). lib. bdg. 23.65 *(978-1-59646-734-7(7))* Dingles & Co.

—Mouse with No Name. Mikhail, Jess, illus. 2004. (ENG.). 24p. (J). lib. bdg. 23.65 *(978-1-59646-682-1(0))* Dingles & Co.

—Shy Shark. Gomez, Elena, illus. 2005. (ENG.). 24p. (J). lib. bdg. 23.65 *(978-1-59646-722-4(3))* Dingles & Co.

—Tiger's Tale: Band 10/White (Collins Big Cat) Boon, Debbie, illus. 2005. (Collins Big Cat Ser.). (ENG.). 32p. (J). (gr. 1-3). pap. 9.99 *(978-0-00-718631-0(2))* HarperCollins Pubs. Ltd. GBR. Dist: Independent Pubs. Group.

Morgan, Michaela & Phillips, Mike. Tig in the Dumps: Band 11/Lime (Collins Big Cat) 2005. (Collins Big Cat Ser.). (ENG., Illus.). 32p. (J). (gr. 1-3). pap. 10.99 *(978-0-00-718636-5(3))* HarperCollins Pubs. Ltd. GBR. Dist: Independent Pubs. Group.

Morgan, Ruth. Big Liam, Little Liam. Archbold, Tim, illus. 2005. (ENG.). 24p. (J). lib. bdg. 23.65 *(978-1-59646-728-6(2))* Dingles & Co.

—Jess & the Bean Root. Vagnozzi, Barbara, illus. 2005. (ENG.). 24p. (J). lib. bdg. 23.65 *(978-1-59646-732-3(0))* Dingles & Co.

Morgan, Sally. Collins Big Cat Phonics for Letters & Sounds - Beetles Around the World: Band 06/Orange, Bd. 5. 2018. (Collins Big Cat Phonics Ser.). (ENG., Illus.). 24p. (J). (gr. k-1). pap. 7.99 *(978-0-00-825170-3(3))* HarperCollins Pubs. Ltd. GBR. Dist: Independent Pubs. Group.

—Food Chains: Band 14/Ruby. 2016. (Collins Big Cat Ser.). (ENG.). 48p. (J). pap. 11.99 *(978-0-00-816389-1(8))* HarperCollins Pubs. Ltd. GBR. Dist: Independent Pubs. Group.

—How Do We Move?, 8 bks. 2005. (QEB Readers). (Illus.). 24p. (J). (gr. -1-3). lib. bdg. 15.95 *(978-1-59566-077-0(1))* QEB Publishing Inc.

—The Incredible Life of Sir David Attenborough: Band 16/Sapphire, Bd. 16. 2017. (Collins Big Cat Ser.). (ENG.). 56p. (J). pap. 12.99 *(978-0-00-820889-9(1))* HarperCollins Pubs. Ltd. GBR. Dist: Independent Pubs. Group.

Morlock, Rachael. Malia the Mechanic: Sharing & Reusing, 1 vol. 2017. (Computer Kids: Powered by Computational Thinking Ser.). (ENG.). 24p. (J). (gr. 4-5). 25.27 *(978-1-5383-2411-0(3)*, 94e1dae7-cb4a-48d0-84ea-f163c8a7abe3, PowerKids Pr.); pap. *(978-1-5081-3755-9(2)*, 7a0db659-0ff6-49ca-9e9b-5833b4a861e6, Rosen Classroom) Rosen Publishing Group, Inc., The.

—My Dad Develops Software: Careers in Computers, 1 vol. 2017. (Computer Kids: Powered by Computational Thinking Ser.). (ENG.). 24p. (J). (gr. 4-5). 25.27 *(978-1-5383-2416-5(4)*, 33b6b7ad-5945-45f9-87ec-131a7f7e9e1c, PowerKids Pr.); pap. *(978-1-5383-5301-1(6)*, c6b4321c-4087-43d4-95bd-595d67df50a7, Rosen Classroom) Rosen Publishing Group, Inc., The.

—Rafi's Research Paper: Breaking down the Problem, 1 vol. 2017. (Computer Kids: Powered by Computational Thinking Ser.). (ENG.). 24p. (J). (gr. 4-5). 25.27 *(978-1-5383-2427-1(X)*, c06e76c4-7e90-40ec-b3d3-9dad92c546b1, PowerKids Pr.); pap. *(978-1-5383-5312-7(1)*, ae5a845a-f7cd-4acc-a577-c949fc8a5f6c, Rosen Classroom) Rosen Publishing Group, Inc., The.

—Which Sources Should I Use? Breaking down the Problem, 1 vol. 2017. (Computer Kids: Powered by Computational Thinking Ser.). (ENG.). 24p. (J). (gr. 4-5). 25.27 *(978-1-5383-2449-3(0)*, 1186495a-fea4-452b-a505-3506a7dbfa0f, PowerKids Pr.); pap. *(978-1-5383-5311-0(3)*, 4a740568-4571-4e99-9af0-08a39c178eeb, Rosen Classroom) Rosen Publishing Group, Inc., The.

Morlock, Theresa. Our Assembly Line: Working at the Same Time, 1 vol. 2017. (Computer Kids: Powered by Computational Thinking Ser.). (ENG.). 24p. (J). (gr. 4-5). 25.27 *(978-1-5383-2421-9(0)*, 739ec87d-00f7-49da-a405-ba7a47e2ab64, PowerKids Pr.); pap. *(978-1-5081-3753-5(6)*, 3ac85e73-905e-48aa-89e9-22e55b51427a, Rosen Classroom) Rosen Publishing Group, Inc., The.

The Morning: Individual Title, 2 packs. (Chiquilibros Ser.). (gr. -1-1). 12.00 *(978-0-7635-8531-0(9))* Rigby Education.

Morpurgo, Michael. It's a Dog's Life (Reading Ladder Level 2) George, Hannah, illus. 2016. (Reading Ladder Level 2 Ser.). (ENG.). 48p. (gr. k-2). pap. 4.99 *(978-1-4052-8256-7(8)*, Reading Ladder) Farshore GBR. Dist: HarperCollins Pubs.

Mortensen, Lori. Our Moon. 2018. (Let's Learn Ser.). (ENG., Illus.). 16p. (gr. -1-2). lib. bdg. 28.50 *(978-1-64156-176-1(9)*, 9781641561761) Rourke Educational Media.

Morton, Carlene. Alpha Betti. Lucas, Margeaux, illus. 2007. (ENG.). (J). (gr. -1-3). 17.95 *(978-1-932146-69-1(5)*, Upstart Bks.) Highsmith Inc.

Morton, Ken, illus. The Three Billy Goats Gruff: My First Reading Book. 2013. (ENG.). 24p. (J). (gr. -1-12). 5.99 *(978-1-84322-832-5(7)*, Armadillo) Anness Publishing GBR. Dist: National Bk. Network.

Moses, Antoinette. Vinnie's Vacation Level 1 Beginner/Elementary American English Edition. 2012. (Cambridge Experience Readers Ser.). (ENG., Illus.). 48p. pap. 14.75 *(978-1-107-62130-5(5))* Cambridge Univ. Pr.

Moses, Brian. Cookie Crumbs, 4 vols. 2005. (QEB Readers). (Illus.). 24p. (J). (gr. -1-3). lib. bdg. 15.95 *(978-1-59566-099-2(2))* QEB Publishing Inc.

MosesAntoinette. The Girl at the Window Starter/Beginner. 2007. (Cambridge English Readers Ser.). (ENG., Illus.). 32p. pap. 14.75 *(978-0-521-70585-1(1))* Cambridge Univ. Pr.

Moskal, Greg. Give the Band a Hand, 1 vol. 2006. (Neighborhood Readers Ser.). (ENG.). 12p. (gr. 1-2). pap. 5.90 *(978-1-4042-6859-3(6)*, b1040092-2b86-4c63-ad01-c47bbbeed227, Rosen Classroom) Rosen Publishing Group, Inc., The.

Mother Goose Asks Why? A Family Guide Introducing Science Through Great Children's Literature. 2005. (J). spiral bd. *(978-0-9753985-6-2(3))* Mother Goose Programs.

Mowat, Diane, retold by. Oxford Bookworms Library: a Pair of Ghostly Hands & Other Stories: Level 3: 1000-Word Vocabulary. 3rd ed. 2008. (ENG., Illus.). 80p. 11.00 *(978-0-19-479125-0(4))* Oxford Univ. Pr., Inc.

Mr. Putter Book Set 800926, 6 vols. 2005. (J). pap. *(978-1-59794-091-7(7))* Environments, Inc.

Mr Verdi's New Path: Individual Title Six-Packs. (gr. k-1). 23.00 *(978-0-7635-8859-5(8))* Rigby Education.

Mr. Worm. 2008. (ENG & SPA., Illus.). 64p. (J). 14.95 *(978-0-9787462-6-1(0))* Heritage Publishing Co.

Mrs Sheep's Garden. (Early Intervention Levels Ser.). 31.86 *(978-0-7362-0619-8(1))* CENGAGE Learning.

Mud Pie: Individual Title Six-Packs. (Literatura 2000 Ser.). (gr. -1-1). 28.00 *(978-0-7635-0034-4(8))* Rigby Education.

Muench-Williams, Heather. I Want a Pet. Teeple, Jackie, illus. I.t. ed. 2006. 12p. (J). (gr. -1-k). pap. 10.95 *(978-1-57332-353-6(5)*, HighReach Learning, Incorporated) Carson-Dellosa Publishing, LLC.

Mugford, Simon. Collins Big Cat Phonics for Letters & Sounds - from the Top: Band 03/Yellow, Bd. 3. 2018. (Collins Big Cat Phonics Ser.). (ENG., Illus.). 16p. (J). (gr. k-1). pap. 6.99 *(978-0-00-825157-4(6))* HarperCollins Pubs. Ltd. GBR. Dist: Independent Pubs. Group.

Muhall, Jill K. & Alarcon, Jill. Causes of the Revolution, 1 vol. rev. ed. 2004. (Social Studies: Informational Text Ser.). (ENG., Illus.). 24p. (J). (gr. 4-8). pap. 10.99 *(978-0-7439-8785-1(3))* Teacher Created Materials, Inc.

Muir, Suzanne. Animal Homes. 2007. (Steck-Vaughn BOLDPRINT Anthologies Ser.). (ENG., Illus.). 48p. (gr. 4-6). pap. 16.90 *(978-1-4190-4018-4(9))* Houghton Mifflin Harcourt Publishing Co.

Mulhall, Jill K. Declaration of Independence, 1 vol. rev. ed. 2004. (Social Studies: Informational Text Ser.). (ENG.). 24p. (gr. 4-8). pap. 10.99 *(978-0-7439-8746-2(2))* Teacher Created Materials, Inc.

—Expanding the Nation, 1 vol. rev. ed. 2005. (Social Studies: Informational Text Ser.). (ENG.). 24p. (gr. 4-8). pap. 10.99 *(978-0-7439-8905-3(8))* Teacher Created Materials, Inc.

—James Madison, 1 vol. rev. ed. 2005. (Social Studies: Informational Text Ser.). (ENG.). 24p. (gr. 4-8). pap. 10.99 *(978-0-7439-8908-4(2))* Teacher Created Materials, Inc.

—Thomas Jefferson, 1 vol. rev. ed. 2004. (Social Studies: Informational Text Ser.). (ENG.). 24p. (gr. 4-8). pap. 10.99 *(978-0-7439-8747-9(0))* Teacher Created Materials, Inc.

—The War of 1812, 1 vol. rev. ed. 2005. (Social Studies: Informational Text Ser.). (ENG.). 24p. (J). (gr. 4-8). pap. 10.99 *(978-0-7439-8907-7(4))* Teacher Created Materials, Inc.

Mullarkey, Lisa. Daisy the Cow. Franco, Paula, illus. 2017. (Farmyard Friends Ser.). (ENG.). 32p. (J). (gr. -1-3). 49.94 *(978-1-62402-990-5(6)*, 26386, Calico Chapter Bks) Magic Wagon.

—Patches the Cat. Franco, Paula, illus. 2019. (Farmyard Friends Ser.). (ENG.). 32p. (J). (gr. -1-3). lib. bdg. 32.79 *(978-1-5321-3486-9(X)*, 31891, Calico Chapter Bks) Magic Wagon.

—Sweet Pea the Sheep. Franco, Paula, illus. 2019. (Farmyard Friends Ser.). (ENG.). 32p. (J). (gr. -1-3). lib. bdg. 32.79 *(978-1-5321-3489-0(4)*, 31897, Calico Chapter Bks) Magic Wagon.

Mullican, Jody. What Can It Be? Gray, Stacy A., illus. I.t. ed. 2006. 12p. (J). (gr. -1-k). pap. 10.95 *(978-1-57332-352-9(7)*, HighReach Learning, Incorporated) Carson-Dellosa Publishing, LLC.

Mullican, Judy. Mary & Marsha Make Cookies. Storch, Ellen N., illus. I.t. ed. 2005. 18p. (J). (gr. -1-k). pap. 10.95 *(978-1-57332-346-8(2)*, HighReach Learning, Incorporated) Carson-Dellosa Publishing, LLC.

—Someone New in the Neighborhood. Storch, Ellen N. & Gillen, Lisa P., illus. I.t. ed. 2005. 20p. (J). (gr. -1-k). pap. 10.95 *(978-1-57332-356-7(X)*, HighReach Learning, Incorporated) Carson-Dellosa Publishing, LLC.

Multicultural Book Set 800717, 10. 2005. (J). *(978-1-59794-015-3(1))* Environments, Inc.

Multicultural Celebrations II, 6 bks. (J). (gr. 2-4). pap. 34.95 *(978-0-8136-2353-5(7))* Modern Curriculum Pr.

Multicultural Nonfiction Photo Books, 6 vols. (Content Collections). (gr. k-2). 180.30 *(978-0-7362-2268-6(5))* CENGAGE Learning.

Munson, Victoria. Creepy-Crawlies, 1 vol. 2018. (My First Book of Nature Ser.). (ENG., Illus.). 24p. (J). (gr. 2-2). 26.27 *(978-1-5081-9607-5(9)*, 7bfbdedf-a453-49f7-82aa-bf0200005c27, Windmill Bks.) Rosen Publishing Group, Inc., The.

Munton, Gill. Lost. Set. Archbold, Tim, illus. 2016. (ENG.). 16p. (J). pap. *(978-0-19-837207-3(8))* Oxford Univ. Pr., Inc.

Murdock, Kita Helmetag. Future Flash. 2017. (ENG.). 192p. (J). (gr. 2-7). pap. 9.99 *(978-1-5107-1011-5(6)*, Sky Pony Pr.) Skyhorse Publishing Co., Inc.

Murphy, Eileen. 3 Big Steps. Montgomery, Violet, illus. 2008. 25p. pap. 24.95 *(978-1-60563-310-7(0))* America Star Bks.

Murphy, Frank. Brave Clara Barton. Green, Sarah, illus. 2018. (Step into Reading Ser.). 48p. (J). (gr. k-3). pap. 4.99 *(978-1-5247-1557-1(3)*, Random Hse. Bks. for Young Readers) Random Hse. Children's Bks.

Murray, Helen. The Lego Movie. 2013. (DK Reader Level 2 Ser.). lib. bdg. 13.55 *(978-0-606-35321-2(6))* Turtleback.

Murray, W. We Have Fun. 2nd ed. (Series S705: No. 2). (Illus.). 30p. (J). (gr. -1-5). pap., stu. ed. 1.95 *(978-0-7214-3063-8(5)*, Dutton Juvenile) Penguin Publishing Group.

—Workbook 1: For Use with Books 1a/1b/1c. 2nd ed. (Key Words Readers Ser.: A Series, No. 641-1a). (Illus.). 30p. (J). (gr. -1-5). pap., stu. ed. 1.95 *(978-0-7214-3062-1(7)*, S705, Dutton Juvenile) Penguin Publishing Group.

—Workbook 3: To Be Used with Books 3a, 3b, 3c. 2nd ed. (Key Words Readers Ser.: A Series, No. 641-3a). (Illus.). 30p. (J). (gr. -1-5). pap., stu. ed. 1.95 *(978-0-7214-3064-5(3)*, Dutton Juvenile) Penguin Publishing Group.

—Workbook 4: To Be Used with Books 4a, 4b, 4c. 2nd ed. (Key Words Readers Ser.: A Series, No. 641-4a). (Illus.). 30p. (J). (gr. -1-5). pap., stu. ed. 1.95 *(978-0-7214-3065-2(1)*, Dutton Juvenile) Penguin Publishing Group.

—Workbook 6: To Be Used with Books 6A, 6B, 6C) 2nd ed. (Key Words Readers Ser.: Series S705, No. 6). (Illus.). 30p. (J). (gr. -1-5). pap., stu. ed. 1.95 *(978-0-7214-3067-6(8)*, Dutton Juvenile) Penguin Publishing Group.

Murtagh, Ciaran. Collins Big Cat Phonics for Letters & Sounds - Space Science: Band 07/Turquoise, Bd. 7. 2018. (Collins Big Cat Phonics Ser.). (ENG., Illus.). 24p. (J). (gr. 1-2). pap. 6.99 *(978-0-00-825181-9(9))* HarperCollins Pubs. Ltd. GBR. Dist: Independent Pubs. Group.

—The Making of Mozart: Band 12/Copper. 2017. (Collins Big Cat Ser.). (ENG., Illus.). 32p. (J). pap. 7.99 *(978-0-00-820876-9(X))* HarperCollins Pubs. Ltd. GBR. Dist: Independent Pubs. Group.

My Big Buddy. (J). 26.20 *(978-0-8136-8447-5(1))*; 26.20 *(978-0-8136-8446-8(3))*; 52.45 *(978-0-8136-8014-9(X))* Modern Curriculum Pr.

My Box: Individual Title-Six Packs. (Chiquilibros Ser.). (gr. k-1). 23.00 *(978-0-7635-0435-9(1))* Rigby Education.

My Brother. (Early Intervention Levels Ser.). 23.10 *(978-0-7362-0015-8(0))*; Vol. 4. 3.85 *(978-1-56334-965-2(5))* CENGAGE Learning.

My Child's First Reading Book. 2005. per. *(978-0-9742195-2-3(5))* Den Publishing Co.

My Day. (Early Intervention Levels Ser.).Tr. of Mi dia. 23.10 *(978-0-7362-0014-1(2))*; Vol. 3. 3.85 *(978-1-56334-964-5(7))* CENGAGE Learning.

My Family Board Book Set 800645, 6. 2005. (J). bds. *(978-1-59794-037-5(2))* Environments, Inc.

My Fish. (Early Intervention Levels Ser.). 21.30 (978-0-7362-0359-3(1)) CENGAGE Learning.
My Nest, 6 vols. 8p. (gr. k-1). 21.50 (978-0-322-02063-4(8)) Wright Group/McGraw-Hill.
My Place: Individual Title Six-Pack. (Story Steps Ser.). (gr. k-2). 20.00 (978-0-7635-9572-2(1)) Rigby Education.
My Planet, 6 Packs. (Chiquilibros Ser.). (gr. k-1). 23.00 (978-0-7635-0446-5(7)) Rigby Education.
My Pony. (Early Intervention Levels Ser.). 23.10 (978-0-7362-0018-9(5)); Vol. 2. 3.85 (978-1-56334-967-6(1)) CENGAGE Learning.
My Trip: Individual Title Six-Packs. (Sails Literacy Ser.). 16p. (gr. k-18). 27.00 (978-0-7635-4430-0(2)) Rigby Education.
My Two, Very, Special Friends, 1. 2006. (Illus.). 19p. (J). per. 4.00 (978-0-9788386-1-4(0)) Taylor, Y. H.
Mystery Clues. 2005. (YA). ring bd. 49.95 (978-1-58804-403-7(3)) P C I Education.
Myth or Mystery? Individual Title Six-Packs. (Action Packs Ser.). 104p. (gr. 3-5). 44.00 (978-0-7635-8415-3(0)) Rigby Education.
Nadin, Joanna. Snow White & Rose Red: Band 12/Copper (Collins Big Cat) 2017. (Collins Big Cat Tales Ser.). (ENG., Illus.). 32p. (J). (gr. 2-8). pap. 9.99 (978-0-00-817929-8(8)) HarperCollins Pubs. Ltd. GBR. Dist: Independent Pubs. Group.
—The Stepmonster. 2nd ed. 2016. (Reading Ladder Level 3 Ser.). (ENG., Illus.). 48p. (gr. k-2). pap. 4.99 (978-1-4052-8221-5(5), Reading Ladder) Farshore GBR. Dist: HarperCollins Pubs.
Nap Time, 6 Packs. (Kinderstarters Ser.). 8p. (gr. -1-1). 21.00 (978-0-7635-8647-8(1)) Rigby Education.
Narváez, Concha López & Salmeron, Carmelo. Tomas Es Distinto a los Demas.Tr. of Tomas Is Different from the Others. (SPA.). 64p. (J). (gr. 2-4). (978-84-216-3432-5(1)) Bruño, Editorial ESP. Dist: Lectorum Pubns., Inc.
National Geographic Editors. Creepy Crawly Collection. 2012. lib. bdg. 18.40 (978-0-606-26822-6(7)) Turtleback.
National Geographic Kids. National Geographic Readers: Planet Earth Collection: Readers That Grow with You. 2014. (Illus.). 128p. (J). (gr. 1-3). pap. 7.99 (978-1-4263-1813-9(8), National Geographic Kids) Disney Publishing Worldwide.
National Geographic Learning. Avenues C (Leveled Books): What a Week!, 6-Pack. 2003. (Avenues Ser.). (ENG.). (C). pap. 95.95 (978-0-7362-2129-0(8)) CENGAGE Learning.
—Avenues e (Leveled Books): Your Great State. 2003. (Avenues Ser.). (ENG.). 16p. (C). pap. 12.95 (978-0-7362-1737-8(1)) CENGAGE Learning.
—Avenues e (Leveled Books): Your Great State, 6-Pack. 2003. (Avenues Ser.). (ENG.). (C). pap. 77.95 (978-0-7362-2159-7(X)) CENGAGE Learning.
—English to a Beat! Practice Book. 2004. (ENG.). (C). (gr. 2-8). pap. 12.95 (978-0-7362-2498-7(X)) CENGAGE Learning.
—World Windows 1 (Science): Parts of a Tree: Content Literacy, Nonfiction Reading, Language & Literacy. 2011. (World Windows Ser.). (ENG., Illus.). 16p. (J). pap., stu. ed. 10.95 (978-1-133-31082-2(6)) Cengage Heinle.
Nations, Susan & Alonso, Melissa. Primary Literacy Responses: Core Tasks for Readers & Writers. 2014. (Maupin House Ser.). (ENG.). 224p. pap. 29.95 (978-1-62521-520-8(7)) Capstone.
Naughton, Diane. Bones: And the Stories They Tell, 1 vol. 2014. (ENG., Illus.). 28p. (J). pap., E-Book, E-Book 9.50 (978-1-107-67054-9(3)) Cambridge Univ. Pr.
—Our Green Future, 1 vol. 2014. (ENG., Illus.). 28p. (J). pap., E-Book 9.50 (978-1-107-67286-4(4)) Cambridge Univ. Pr.
—Secrets to a Long Life Intermediate Book with Online Access, 1 vol. 2014. (ENG., Illus.). 28p. (J). pap., E-Book, E-Book 9.50 (978-1-107-68378-5(5)) Cambridge Univ. Pr.
—True Colors Intermediate Book with Online Access, 1 vol. 2014. (ENG., Illus.). 28p. (J). pap., E-Book 9.50 (978-1-107-66068-7(8)) Cambridge Univ. Pr.
—Venice: The Floating City, 1 vol. 2014. (ENG., Illus.). 28p. (J). pap., E-Book 9.50 (978-1-107-62163-3(1)) Cambridge Univ. Pr.
—What Are You Afraid of? Fears & Phobias Intermediate Book with Online Access, 1 vol. 2014. (ENG., Illus.). 28p. (J). pap., E-Book 9.50 (978-1-107-65051-0(8)) Cambridge Univ. Pr.
Nayer, Judy. 25 Easy Bilingual Nonfiction Mini-Books. 2005. (ENG.). 64p. (gr. k-1). pap. 11.99 (978-0-439-70544-8(4), Teaching Resources) Scholastic, Inc.
Neasi, Barbara J. Rookie Ready to Learn en Español: Muchas Veces Yo. Ochoa, Ana, illus. 2011. (Rookie Ready to Learn Español Ser.). Orig. Title: Rookie Ready to Learn: So Many Me's. (SPA.). 40p. (J). pap. 5.95 (978-0-531-26789-9(X), Children's Pr.) Scholastic Library Publishing.
Necklaces. (Early Intervention Levels Ser.). 21.30 (978-0-7362-0371-5(0)); Vol. 3. 3.55 (978-0-7362-0092-9(4)) CENGAGE Learning.
Nees, Susan. School Play. 2013. (Missy's Super Duper Royal Deluxe Ser.: 3). lib. bdg. 14.75 (978-0-606-32366-6(X)) Turtleback.
Neher, Anna-Luise. A Tale from the Trunk No. 2: With Words! Words! Words! 2009. 56p. pap. 10.82 (978-1-4251-8284-7(4)) Trafford Publishing.
The Neighborhood Picnic, 6 vols. (Multicultural Programs Ser.). 16p. (gr. 1-3). 24.95 (978-0-7802-9217-8(0)) Wright Group/McGraw-Hill.
Neighborhood Soup. (J). 21.95 (978-0-8136-4267-3(1)); (gr. 2). 23.50 (978-0-8136-8830-5(2)) Modern Curriculum Pr.
Nelid, Piper. Baking Bread with Grandpa, 1 vol., 1. 2015. (Rosen REAL Readers: STEM & STEAM Collection). (ENG.). 12p. (J). (gr. 1-2). pap. 6.33 (978-1-5081-1569-4(9), 4c2e9d20-e284-48db-afce-d415ad6f0057, Rosen Classroom) Rosen Publishing Group, Inc., The.
—The Coolest Fourth of July of All Time, 1 vol., 1. 2015. (Rosen REAL Readers: Social Studies Nonfiction / Fiction: Myself, My Community, My World Ser.). (ENG.). 12p. (J). (gr. k-1). pap. 6.33 (978-1-5081-1937-1(6), 5c989a22-c81f-4782-b800-2c94fc177a7f, Rosen Classroom) Rosen Publishing Group, Inc., The.
—Emilio & the Baby Pig, 1 vol., 1. 2015. (Rosen REAL Readers: STEM & STEAM Collection). (ENG.). 8p. (J). (gr. k-1). pap. 5.46 (978-1-5081-1404-8(8), 1f0639a1-cde5-492e-a011-33dab066c02c, Rosen Classroom) Rosen Publishing Group, Inc., The.
—Father's Day with My Forever Dad, 1 vol., 1. 2015. (Rosen REAL Readers: Social Studies Nonfiction / Fiction: Myself, My Community, My World Ser.). (ENG.). 8p. (J). (gr. k-1). pap. 5.46 (978-1-5081-1389-8(0), de568b76-790e-4c92-ad90-f2ae33d92039, Rosen Classroom) Rosen Publishing Group, Inc., The.
—First Place, 1 vol., 1. 2015. (Rosen REAL Readers: Social Studies Nonfiction / Fiction: Myself, My Community, My World Ser.). (ENG.). 12p. (J). (gr. k-1). pap. 6.33 (978-1-5081-1988-3(0), 2d73165e-3625-4b20-86fb-de7d9223c3ce, Rosen Classroom) Rosen Publishing Group, Inc., The.
—The Green Building, 1 vol., 1. 2015. (Rosen REAL Readers: Social Studies Nonfiction / Fiction: Myself, My Community, My World Ser.). (ENG.). 8p. (J). (gr. k-1). pap. 5.46 (978-1-5081-1860-2(4), 4ea41f3b-a4c3-49d7-8ac9-dc16fc87874d, Rosen Classroom) Rosen Publishing Group, Inc., The.
—The New Kid, 1 vol., 1. 2015. (Rosen REAL Readers: Social Studies Nonfiction / Fiction: Myself, My Community, My World Ser.). (ENG.). 12p. (J). (gr. k-1). pap. 6.33 (978-1-5081-1919-7(8), 8c46d0b3-fa75-4224-8ce1-d1ef42307bf3, Rosen Classroom) Rosen Publishing Group, Inc., The.
—Racing Day, 1 vol., 1. 2015. (Rosen REAL Readers: STEM & STEAM Collection). (ENG.). 8p. (J). (gr. k-1). pap. 5.46 (978-1-5081-1472-7(2), ceccb516-1ff9-40c4-b04c-d9e3479b60d2, Rosen Classroom) Rosen Publishing Group, Inc., The.
—Rick Gets a Cast, 1 vol., 1. 2015. (Rosen REAL Readers: STEM & STEAM Collection). (ENG.). 12p. (J). (gr. k-1). pap. 6.33 (978-1-5081-1551-9(6), 89fb22ee-a32e-41d9-9d0d-b403af39107d, Rosen Classroom) Rosen Publishing Group, Inc., The.
—Sarah the Great, 1 vol., 1. 2015. (Rosen REAL Readers: Social Studies Nonfiction / Fiction: Myself, My Community, My World Ser.). (ENG.). 8p. (J). (gr. k-1). pap. 5.46 (978-1-5081-1842-8(6), 13df625c-764a-4953-ba79-e1632c9fbafe, Rosen Classroom) Rosen Publishing Group, Inc., The.
—Seesaw Fun, 1 vol., 1. 2015. (Rosen REAL Readers: STEM & STEAM Collection). (ENG.). 12p. (J). (gr. 1-2). pap. 6.33 (978-1-5081-1623-3(7), 13171169-7f53-4a58-bd40-ed420f f1ec35, Rosen Classroom) Rosen Publishing Group, Inc., The.
—A Special Dinner with My Moms, 1 vol., 1. 2015. (Rosen REAL Readers: Social Studies Nonfiction / Fiction: Myself, My Community, My World Ser.). (ENG.). 8p. (J). (gr. k-1). pap. 5.46 (978-1-5081-1510-6(9), 5264e8f6-b286-4f19-8603-bd1a24b8c086, Rosen Classroom) Rosen Publishing Group, Inc., The.
Nelson, Jo. Copernicus, Galileo & Newton: Band 18/Pearl. Bustamante, Martin, illus. 2014. (Collins Big Cat Ser.). (ENG.). 80p. (J). (gr. 5). pap. 12.99 (978-0-00-753017-5(X)) HarperCollins Pubs. Ltd. GBR. Dist: Independent Pubs. Group.
Nelvana Ltd, illus. Read with Ranger Rob: My Pet Ranger. 2019. (Ranger Rob Ser.). (ENG.). 32p. (J). (gr. -1). 3.99 (978-2-89802-007-0(9), CrackBoom! Bks.) Chouette Publishing CAN. Dist: Publishers Group West (PGW).
—Read with Ranger Rob - Scent Trail. 2019. (Ranger Rob Ser.). (ENG.). 32p. (J). (gr. -1). 3.99 (978-2-89802-005-6(2), CrackBoom! Bks.) Chouette Publishing CAN. Dist: Publishers Group West (PGW).
Nesbit, E. The Story of the Treasure Seekers: Being the Adventures of the Bastable Children in Search of A Fortune. 2006. 132p. (gr. 4-7). per. 10.95 (978-1-59818-963-6(8)); 24.95 (978-1-59818-172-2(6)) Aegypan.
Neuman, Susan B. Hop, Bunny! Explore the Forest. 2014. (Readers Ser.). (Illus.). 24p. (J). (gr. -1-k). pap. 5.99 (978-1-4263-1739-2(5), National Geographic Kids) Disney Publishing Worldwide.
—National Geographic Readers: Hang on Monkey! 2014. (Readers Ser.). 24p. (J). (gr. -1-k). pap. 4.99 (978-1-4263-1755-2(7), National Geographic Kids) Disney Publishing Worldwide.
—National Geographic Readers: Jump Pup! 2014. (Readers Ser.). 24p. (J). (gr. -1-k). pap. 4.99 (978-1-4263-1508-4(2), National Geographic Kids) Disney Publishing Worldwide.
—National Geographic Readers: Swim Fish! Explore the Coral Reef. 2014. (Readers Ser.). (Illus.). 24p. (J). (gr. -1-k). pap. 5.99 (978-1-4263-1510-7(4), National Geographic Kids) Disney Publishing Worldwide.
Newcomb, Kristene. Molly Q's Trash Travels Through the Water Cycle. Paschall, Patricia, ed. Newcomb, Kristene, illus. 2007. (Illus.). 32p. (J). per. 8.00 (978-0-9760790-9-5(7)) Folsom Fallies Pr.
Newmark Learning, compiled by. Rising Readers Set A Sets Of 6. 2009. (Rising Readers Ser.). (J). (gr. -1-k). 1005.12 net. (978-1-60719-110-0(5)) Newmark Learning LLC.
—Sight Word Readers 12 copy set with Rack Set A. 2009. (Sight Word Readers Set A Ser.). (J). 1095.12 net. (978-1-60719-159-9(8)) Newmark Learning LLC.
Nicholson, Nancy. Devotional Stories for Little Folks Too. 2007. (J). per. (978-0-9771236-1-2(8)) For Little Folks.
Nielsen, Aubrie. After School. rev. ed. 2011. (Mathematics in the Real World Ser.). (ENG.). 32p. (gr. k-1). pap. 9.99 (978-1-4333-3440-5(2)) Teacher Created Materials, Inc.
—At School. rev. ed. 2011. (Mathematics in the Real World Ser.). (ENG.). 32p. (gr. k-1). pap. 9.99 (978-1-4333-3441-2(0)) Teacher Created Materials, Inc.
Nine Days a Queen Reading Group Guide. (J). (978-0-06-077997-9(7)) HarperCollins Pubs.
Nixon & Brush. Champagne with a Corpse. (Thumbprint Mysteries Ser.). 32.86 (978-0-8092-0420-5(7)) McGraw-Hill/Contemporary.
No Place Like Home. (Lexile Levels Ser.). 47.88 (978-1-56334-094-9(1)) CENGAGE Learning.
No Queen Today! 3-in-1 Package. (Sails Literacy Ser.). 24p. (gr. 2-18). 57.00 (978-0-7578-3217-8(2)) Rigby Education.
No Queen Today! 6 Small Books. (Sails Literacy Ser.). 24p. (gr. 2-18). 25.00 (978-0-7578-3193-5(1)) Rigby Education.
No Queen Today! Big Book Only. (Sails Literacy Ser.). 24p. (gr. 2-18). 27.00 (978-0-7635-6995-2(X)) Rigby Education.
No Secrets. 64p. (YA). (gr. 6-12). pap. (978-0-8224-2381-2(2)) Globe Fearon Educational Publishing.
No Time To Lose. 2003. (Illus.). pap. 7.60 (978-0-7398-7533-9(7)) Steck-Vaughn.
Noble, Trinka Hakes. The New Jersey Reader. Darnell, K. L., illus. 2009. (State/Country Readers Ser.). (ENG.). 96p. (J). (gr. 1-4). 12.95 (978-1-58536-438-1(X), 202166) Sleeping Bear Pr.
—The Pennsylvania Reader. Darnell, K. L., illus. rev. ed. 2007. (State/Country Readers Ser.). (ENG.). 96p. (J). (gr. 1-4). 12.95 (978-1-58536-320-9(0), 202124) Sleeping Bear Pr.
Noonan, Diana. On the Move, 6 vols. (Wonder Worldtm Ser.). 16p. 29.95 (978-0-7802-2014-0(5)) Wright Group/McGraw-Hill.
Northcott, Richard. In the Mountains. 2013. (ENG., Illus.). 40p. pap. 11.00 (978-0-19-464687-1(4)) Oxford Univ. Pr., Inc.
Not Too Messy, Not Too Neat. (J). (gr. 3-5). 75.00 (978-0-669-13694-4(8)) Houghton Mifflin Harcourt School Pubs.
Not When It's Hot. (Early Intervention Levels Ser.). 21.30 (978-0-7362-0387-6(7)) CENGAGE Learning.
Novel Units. Amos Fortune, Free Man Novel Units Student Packet. 2019. (ENG.). (J). pap. 13.99 (978-1-58130-506-7(0), Novel Units, Inc.) Classroom Library Co.
—Black Beauty Novel Units Student Packet. 2019. (ENG.). (J). pap. 13.99 (978-1-58130-852-5(3), Novel Units, Inc.) Classroom Library Co.
—The Color Purple Novel Units Student Packet. 2019. (ENG.). (YA). pap. 13.99 (978-1-58130-508-1(7), Novel Units, Inc.) Classroom Library Co.
—Edgar Allan Poe: A Collection of Stories Novel Units Student Packet. 2019. (ENG.). (YA). pap. 13.99 (978-1-58130-510-4(9), Novel Units, Inc.) Classroom Library Co.
—Ender's Game Novel Units Student Packet. 2019. (ENG.). (YA). (gr. 7-8). pap., stu. ed. 13.99 (978-1-58130-512-8(5), Novel Units, Inc.) Classroom Library Co.
—Fair Weather Novel Units Student Packet. 2019. (ENG.). (J). pap. 13.99 (978-1-58130-514-2(1), Novel Units, Inc.) Classroom Library Co.
—The Five People You Meet in Heaven Novel Units Student Packet. 2019. (ENG.). (YA). (gr. 9-12). pap., stu. ed. 13.99 (978-1-58130-854-9(X), Novel Units, Inc.) Classroom Library Co.
—The Glory Field Novel Units Student Packet. 2019. (ENG.). (YA). pap. 13.99 (978-1-58130-516-6(8), Novel Units, Inc.) Classroom Library Co.
—The Hound of the Baskervilles Novel Units Student Packet. 2019. (ENG.). (YA). pap. 13.99 (978-1-58130-856-3(6), Novel Units, Inc.) Classroom Library Co.
—The Hunchback of Notre Dame Novel Units Student Packet. 2019. (ENG.). (YA). pap. 13.99 (978-1-58130-858-7(2), Novel Units, Inc.) Classroom Library Co.
—Loser Novel Units Student Packet. 2019. (ENG.). (J). pap. 13.99 (978-1-58130-518-0(4), Novel Units, Inc.) Classroom Library Co.
—The Magician's Nephew Novel Units Student Packet. 2019. (ENG.). (J). pap. 13.99 (978-1-58130-860-0(4), Novel Units, Inc.) Classroom Library Co.
—Red Scarf Girl Novel Units Student Packet. 2019. (ENG.). (J). pap. 13.99 (978-1-58130-862-4(0), Novel Units, Inc.) Classroom Library Co.
—Riding Freedom Novel Units Student Packet. 2019. (ENG.). (J). pap. 13.99 (978-1-58130-864-8(7), Novel Units, Inc.) Classroom Library Co.
—The School Story Novel Units Student Packet. 2019. (ENG.). (J). pap. 13.99 (978-1-58130-520-3(6), Novel Units, Inc.) Classroom Library Co.
—Sideways Stories from Wayside School Novel Units Student Packet. 2019. (ENG.). (J). pap. 13.99 (978-1-58130-866-2(3), Novel Units, Inc.) Classroom Library Co.
—Small Steps: The Year I Got Polio Novel Units Student Packet. 2019. (Small Steps Ser.). (ENG.). (J). pap. 13.99 (978-1-58130-522-7(2), Novel Units, Inc.) Classroom Library Co.
—The Time Machine Novel Units Student Packet. 2019. (ENG.). (J). pap. 13.99 (978-1-58130-526-5(5), Novel Units, Inc.) Classroom Library Co.
—Touching Spirit Bear Novel Units Student Packet. 2019. (ENG.). (J). pap. 13.99 (978-1-58130-528-9(1), Novel Units, Inc.) Classroom Library Co.
—Uncle Tom's Cabin Novel Units Student Packet. 2019. (ENG.). (YA). pap. 13.99 (978-1-58130-870-9(1), Novel Units, Inc.) Classroom Library Co.
—When My Name Was Keoko Novel Units Student Packet. 2019. (ENG.). (J). pap. 13.99 (978-1-58130-872-3(8), Novel Units, Inc.) Classroom Library Co.
—Winterdance Novel Units Student Packet. 2019. (ENG.). (J). pap. 13.99 (978-1-58130-874-7(4), Novel Units, Inc.) Classroom Library Co.
—Yolanda 's Genius Novel Units Student Packet. 2019. (ENG.). (J). pap., stu. ed. 13.99 (978-1-58130-530-2(3), Novel Units, Inc.) Classroom Library Co.
Nutrition Adventures with the Nutri Gang, Race Day, Issue #1: The Nutri Gang. 2007. (J). 2.99 (978-0-9792383-0-7(7)) KJ Pubns.
Nuttall, Gina. Is Lion Sick?, 4 vols. 2005. (QEB Readers). (Illus.). 24p. (J). (gr. -1-3). lib. bdg. 15.95 (978-1-59566-100-5(X)) QEB Publishing Inc.
Nye, Kimara. The Four Little Pigs. Bruchnalski, Marcin, illus. 2019. (Early Bird Readers — Purple (Early Bird Stories (tm)) Ser.). (ENG.). 32p. (J). (gr. k-3). 30.65 (978-1-5415-4227-3(4), 60cefd4f-6003-46ef-a1b5-4f0a01fafd6e); pap. 9.99 (978-1-5415-7422-9(2), 22486836-c7a2-484e-b99a-2e87d84aedc9) Lerner Publishing Group. (Lerner Pubns.).
Nyman, Debbie & Wortzman, Ricki. The 10 Best Plays. 2008. 14.99 (978-1-55448-503-1(7)) Scholastic Library Publishing.
—The 10 Most Notable Elected Female Leaders. 2008. 14.99 (978-1-55448-527-7(4)) Scholastic Library Publishing.
—The 10 Most Outstanding Women. 2007. 14.99 (978-1-55448-468-3(5)) Scholastic Library Publishing.
O'Brien, Kathryn. I'd Be Your Princess: A Royal Tale of Godly Character. Garland, Michael, illus. 2007. 28p. (J). (gr. -1-3). 6.99 (978-0-7847-1964-0(0)) Standard Publishing.
O'Brien, Renee McMullen. The Amazing Mocha & His Courageous Journey. O'Brien, Renee McMullen, illus. 2009. (Illus.). 28p. pap. 12.95 (978-1-936051-60-1(5)) Peppertree Pr., The.
Oceanak, Karla. Finicky. Spanjer, Kendra, illus. 2012. (Aldo Zelnick Comic Novel Ser.: 6). (ENG.). 160p. (J). (gr. 3-7). 12.95 (978-1-934649-24-4(4)) Bailiwick Pr.
O'Connell, Mary. Dear Reader: A Novel. 2018. (ENG.). 304p. (YA). pap. 22.99 (978-1-250-07709-7(5), 900152687) Flatiron Bks.
O'Connor, Jane. Fancy Nancy's 12-Book Fantastic Phonics Fun! Includes 12 Mini-Books Featuring Short & Long Vowel Sounds, 12 vols. Glasser, Robin Preiss, illus. 2013. (My First I Can Read Ser.). (ENG.). 120p. (J). (gr. -1-3). 14.99 (978-0-06-208633-4(2), HarperCollins) HarperCollins Pubs.
—It's Backward Day! 2016. (Fancy Nancy - I Can Read! Ser.). (Illus.). 32p. (J). lib. bdg. 13.55 (978-0-606-38175-8(9)) Turtleback.
—Nancy Makes Her Mark. 2018. (Illus.). 32p. (J). (978-1-5444-1102-6(2)) Harper & Row Ltd.
Oczkus, Lori. Close Reading with Paired Texts. rev. ed. 2015. (Close Reading with Paired Texts). (ENG., Illus.). 128p. (gr. 3-3). pap. 24.99 (978-1-4258-1359-8(3)) Shell Educational Publishing.
—Close Reading with Paired Texts, Level 5. rev. ed. 2015. (Close Reading with Paired Texts). (ENG., Illus.). 128p. (gr. 5-5). pap. 19.99 (978-1-4258-1361-1(5)) Shell Educational Publishing.
—Disappearing Rainforests Level 2. rev. ed. 2015. (Close Reading with Paired Texts). (ENG., Illus.). 128p. (gr. 2-2). pap. 19.99 (978-1-4258-1358-1(5)) Shell Educational Publishing.
O'Dea, Lori. Super Dog. Greenhead, Bill, illus. 2017. (Text Connections Guided Close Reading Ser.). (J). (gr. k). (978-1-4900-1770-9(4)) Benchmark Education Co.
O'Dell, Kathryn. Life Online: the Digital Age Low Intermediate Book with Online Access, 1 vol. 2014. (ENG., Illus.). 28p. (J). pap., E-Book, E-Book 9.50 (978-1-107-65069-5(0)) Cambridge Univ. Pr.
—The Science of Light Low Intermediate Book with Online Access, 1 vol. 2014. (ENG., Illus.). 28p. (J). pap., E-Book, E-Book 9.50 (978-1-107-68198-9(7)) Cambridge Univ. Pr.
O'DellKathryn. THE SCIENCE OF DARKNESS LOW INTERMEDIATE BOOK WITH ONLINE ACCESS, 1 vol. 2014. (ENG., Illus.). 28p. (J). pap., E-Book 9.50 (978-1-107-65493-8(9)) Cambridge Univ. Pr.
—SHARK ATTACK LOW INTERMEDIATE BOOK WITH ONLINE ACCESS, 1 vol. 2014. (ENG., Illus.). 28p. (J). pap., E-Book, E-Book 9.50 (978-1-107-66183-7(8)) Cambridge Univ. Pr.
—SHOOT TO KILL: WHY WE HUNT HIGH BEGINNING BOOK WITH ONLINE ACCESS, 1 vol. 2014. (ENG., Illus.). 24p. (J). pap., E-Book 9.50 (978-1-107-62253-1(0)) Cambridge Univ. Pr.
—SURVIVAL GUIDE: LOST IN THE MOUNTAINS LOW INTERMEDIATE BOOK WITH ONLINE ACCESS, 1 vol. 2014. (ENG., Illus.). 28p. (J). pap., E-Book, E-Book 9.50 (978-1-107-64328-4(7)) Cambridge Univ. Pr.
Odenthal, Ingrid. The Warm Heart. 2009. 20p. pap. 12.49 (978-1-4490-5188-4(X)) AuthorHouse.
O'Donnell, Kerri. A Giraffe Can Laugh, 1 vol. 2006. (Neighborhood Readers Ser.). (ENG.). 8p. (gr. k-1). pap. 5.90 (978-1-4042-5762-7(4), b71f483b-6704-48dc-8dfa-7e55531f80e2, Rosen Classroom) Rosen Publishing Group, Inc., The.
—King of the Swamp, 1 vol. 2006. (Neighborhood Readers Ser.). (ENG.). 16p. (gr. 1-2). pap. 6.50 (978-1-4042-7216-3(X), d590fcdc-2d06-4b6b-b5d3-28afe239a0b7, Rosen Classroom) Rosen Publishing Group, Inc., The.
—Sue Helps Out, 1 vol. 2006. (Neighborhood Readers Ser.). (ENG.). 8p. (gr. k-1). pap. 5.15 (978-1-4042-5684-2(9), 2240ecad-c101-4ba9-b621-3e67016ecc34, Rosen Classroom) Rosen Publishing Group, Inc., The.
—When Sue Is Sad, 1 vol. 2006. (Neighborhood Readers Ser.). (ENG.). 8p. (gr. k-1). pap. 5.15 (978-1-4042-5653-8(9), 6f6c3f8c-f7e6-4080-81c8-37fa0b142903, Rosen Classroom) Rosen Publishing Group, Inc., The.
—Whose Hat Is That?, 1 vol. 2006. (Neighborhood Readers Ser.). (ENG.). 8p. (gr. k-1). pap. 5.15 (978-1-4042-5647-7(4), 8e1b8c15-95f3-4558-ae09-f2e9bd841039, Rosen Classroom) Rosen Publishing Group, Inc., The.
O'Donnell, Patrick. Did Dinosaurs Have Dentists?, 1 vol. Mehlen, Erik, illus. 2018. (ENG.). 32p. (J). (gr. -1-3). 14.99 (978-0-7643-5602-5(X), 9906) Schiffer Publishing, Ltd.
O'Donoghue, Chris. Charlie's Reading Rescue: Improve an Older Child's Reading. 2011. (Illus.). 188p. pap. 10.50 (978-1-60976-573-6(7), Eloquent Bks.) Strategic Book Publishing & Rights Agency (SBPRA).
Oe, Patricia Daly. Blue Mouse, Yellow Mouse. Oe, Patricia Daly, illus. 2007. (R. I. C. Story Chest Ser.). (Illus.). 20p. (J). (gr. -1-k). 11.95 incl. audio compact disk (978-1-74126-439-5(1)) R.I.C. Pubns. AUS. Dist: SCB Distributors.
Ofelia, Dumas Lachtman. Big Enough Bastante Grande. Enrique, Sanchez, illus. 2008. 32p. (J). pap. 7.95 (978-1-55885-239-6(5)) Arte Publico Pr.
O'Gorman, Neil. Plants & Their Environments, 1 vol. 2008. (Real Life Readers Ser.). (ENG.). 16p. (gr. 2-3). pap. 7.05 (978-1-4358-0067-0(2), ba207a28-f723-4ea3-8065-e768d2bb41b1, Rosen Classroom) Rosen Publishing Group, Inc., The.
The Old Toad. (Early Intervention Levels Ser.). 28.38 (978-0-7362-0398-2(2)) CENGAGE Learning.
The Old Toad (8), Vol. 8. (Early Intervention Levels Ser.). 4.73 (978-0-7362-0223-7(4)) CENGAGE Learning.
Olien, Jessica. Adrift: An Odd Couple of Polar Bears. Olien, Jessica, illus. 2017. (ENG., Illus.). 40p. (J). (gr. -1-3). 17.99 (978-0-06-245177-4(4), Balzer & Bray) HarperCollins Pubs.
Olivas, John D. Endeavour's Long Journey/la Larga Travesía de Endeavour. Roski, Gayle G., illus. 2016. (SPA.). 40p. (J). 19.95 (978-0-9973947-2-6(2)) East West Discovery Pr.
Olker, Constance. The Punctuation Pals Go to the Baseball Park. Guzman, Minerva, illus. 2005. (Punctuation Pals Ser.). 44p. (J). per. 18.95 (978-1-933449-15-9(2)) Nightengale Pr.

—The Punctuation Pals Go to the Beach. Guzman, Minerva, illus. 2005. (Punctuation Pals Ser.). 36p. (J). per. 18.95 *(978-1-933449-12-8(8))* Nightengale Pr.
—The Punctuation Pals Go to the Moon. 2005. (Illus.). 64p. (J). per. 24.95 *(978-1-933449-13-5(6))* Nightengale Pr.
—The Punctuation Pals Meet at School. 2005. (Illus.). 40p. (J). per. 18.95 *(978-1-933449-07-4(1))* Nightengale Pr.
Olsen, Jan Z. Mat Man Opposites. Delaney, Molly, illus. 2009. (ENG.). stu. ed. 13.75 *(978-1-891627-94-1(5))* Handwriting Without Tears.
O'Mara, Blanche. A Year with Carmen, 1 vol. 2006. (Neighborhood Readers Ser.). (ENG.). 12p. (gr. 1-2). pap. 5.90 *(978-1-4042-6835-7(9),* 11fe4f7a-ad96-4325-a4e8-112ecc614d48, Rosen Classroom) Rosen Publishing Group, Inc., The.
On a Roll: How Communities Build State Parks. 2005. (Book Treks Ser.). (J). 37.95 *(978-0-7652-3254-0(5))* Celebration Pr.
On Our Way to English: Complete Package - Grade 4. (gr. 4-18). 2195.00 *(978-0-7578-6971-6(8))* Rigby Education.
On Our Way to English: Complete Package - Grade 5. (gr. 5-18). 2195.00 *(978-0-7578-6972-3(6))* Rigby Education.
On Our Way to English: Complete Package - Kindergarten. (gr. k-18). 1895.00 *(978-0-7578-6967-9(X))* Rigby Education.
On the Go. 2005. (Little Celebrations Thematic Packages Ser.). (J). (gr. k-3). 133.50 *(978-0-673-75383-0(2))* Celebration Pr.
On This Earth. (Early Intervention Levels Ser.). 23.10 *(978-0-7362-0037-0(1))* CENGAGE Learning.
On Your Mark: Grade 1 Reading Fluency Booklet. (gr. 1-18). 57.19 *(978-0-7362-2474-1(2))* CENGAGE Learning.
On Your Mark: Grade 2 Reading Fluency Booklet. (gr. 2-18). 57.19 *(978-0-7362-2475-8(0))* CENGAGE Learning.
On Your Mark: Grade 3 Reading Fluency Booklet. (gr. 3-18). 57.19 *(978-0-7362-2476-5(9))* CENGAGE Learning.
On Your Mark: Grade 4 Reading Fluency Booklet. (gr. 4-18). 57.19 *(978-0-7362-2477-2(7))* CENGAGE Learning.
On Your Mark: Grade 5 Reading Fluency Booklet. (gr. 5-18). 57.19 *(978-0-7362-2478-9(5))* CENGAGE Learning.
On Your Mark: Grade 6 Reading Fluency Booklet. (gr. 6-18). 57.19 *(978-0-7362-2479-6(3))* CENGAGE Learning.
On Your Mark: Grade 7 Reading Fluency Booklet. (gr. 7-18). 57.19 *(978-0-7362-2480-2(7))* CENGAGE Learning.
On Your Mark: Grade 8 Reading Fluency Booklet. (gr. 8-18). 57.19 *(978-0-7362-2481-9(5))* CENGAGE Learning.
One Afternoon. (Early Intervention Levels Ser.). 47.88 *(978-0-7362-2121-4(2))* CENGAGE Learning.
One Piece At A Time. 2003. (Illus.). pap. 5.60 *(978-0-7398-7511-7(6))* Steck-Vaughn.
One, Two, Three, Four. (Early Intervention Levels Ser.). 23.10 *(978-0-7362-0035-6(5))*; Vol. 6. 3.85 *(978-1-56334-983-6(3))* CENGAGE Learning.
O'Neill, John R. Mahatma Gandhi, Nelson Mandela. 2011. (Readers' & Writers' Genre Workshop Ser.). (YA). pap. *(978-1-4509-3024-6(7))* Benchmark Education Co.
O'Neill, Rachael, illus. My First Library: With Nine Colorful Books. (J). *(978-1-85479-804-6(9))* O'Mara, Michael Bks., Ltd.
Open Court Staff. Intermediate Think Storybook: Level 4. (J). pap. *(978-0-89688-693-3(X),* 88693) Open Court Publishing Co.
Optometrist: Individual Title Six-Packs. (Bookweb Ser.). 32p. (gr. 3-18). 34.00 *(978-0-7635-3946-7(5))* Rigby Education.
Oral Language Flip Chart: Time to Speak & Listen. 2004. (gr. k-18). suppl. ed. 109.15 *(978-0-328-02214-4(4))* Addison-Wesley Educational Pubs., Inc.
Orange & Red Levels Certificate Only. (Discovery World Ser.). (gr. 1-2). 89.00 *(978-0-7578-6527-5(5))* Rigby Education.
Orca Book Publishers, ed. Orca Young Readers Collection, 24 vols. 2011. (Orca Young Readers Ser.). (ENG.). 128p. (J). (gr. 2-6). pap. 190.80 *(978-1-55469-387-0(X))* Orca Bk. Pubs. USA.
Orme, David. Blitz. 2007. (Sharp Shades Ser.). (ENG., Illus.). 64p. (J). (gr. 6-8). pap. 8.99 *(978-0-237-53444-8(4))* Evans Brothers, Ltd. GBR. Dist: Independent Pubs. Group.
—Bugs & Spiders. 2010. (Fact to Fiction Grafx Ser.). (Illus.). 36p. (J). lib. bdg. 16.95 *(978-1-60686-465-4(3))* Perfection Learning Corp.
—Bugs & Spiders. Mongiovi, Jorge, illus. 2010. (Fact to Fiction Ser.). 36p. pap. 7.45 *(978-0-7891-7990-6(3))* Perfection Learning Corp.
—Deadly Virus, Set. 2008. (Starchasers Ser.). (ENG., Illus.). 48p. pap. *(978-1-84167-767-5(1))* Ransom Publishing Ltd.
—Don't Try This at Home. 2008. (Trailblazers Ser.). (ENG., Illus.). 36p. pap. *(978-1-84167-652-4(7))* Ransom Publishing Ltd.
—Extreme Science. 2009. (Fact to Fiction Ser.). (Illus.). 36p. (J). lib. bdg. 16.95 *(978-0-7569-9279-8(6))* Perfection Learning Corp.
—Extreme Sports. 2011. (Fact to Fiction Grafx Ser.). (ENG., Illus.). 36p. (J). (gr. 4-7). lib. bdg. 17.45 *(978-1-61384-019-1(5))* Perfection Learning Corp.
—Fashion. 2008. (Trailblazers Ser.). (ENG., Illus.). 36p. pap. *(978-1-84167-650-0(0))* Ransom Publishing Ltd.
—Fear. 2011. (Fact to Fiction Grafx Ser.). (ENG., Illus.). 36p. (J). (gr. 4-7). lib. bdg. 17.45 *(978-1-61384-018-4(7))* Perfection Learning Corp.
—Great Journeys. 2008. (Trailblazers Ser.). (ENG., Illus.). 36p. pap. *(978-1-84167-653-1(5))* Ransom Publishing Ltd.
—How to Be a Pop Star. 2007. (Trailblazers Ser.). (ENG., Illus.). 36p. pap. *(978-1-84167-594-7(6))* Ransom Publishing Ltd.
—Lost Animals. Mongiovi, Jorge, illus. 2010. (Fact to Fiction Grafx Ser.). 36p. pap. 7.45 *(978-0-7891-7993-7(8))* Perfection Learning Corp.
—Manga. 2007. (Trailblazers Ser.). (ENG., Illus.). 36p. pap. *(978-1-84167-593-0(8))* Ransom Publishing Ltd.
—Plague. 2004. (Shades Ser.). (ENG.). 58p. (J). pap. 7.99 *(978-0-237-52729-7(4))* Evans Brothers, Ltd. GBR. Dist: Independent Pubs. Group.
—Plagues. 2010. (Fact to Fiction Grafx Ser.). (Illus.). 36p. (J). pap. 7.45 *(978-0-7891-7997-5(0))* Perfection Learning Corp.
—Sea Killers. 2007. (Trailblazers Ser.). (ENG., Illus.). 36p. pap. *(978-1-84167-592-3(X))* Ransom Publishing Ltd.
—Speed. 2009. (Fact to Fiction Ser.). (Illus.). 36p. (J). 16.95 *(978-0-7569-9283-5(4))* Perfection Learning Corp.
—Spies. 2010. (Fact to Fiction Grafx Ser.). (Illus.). 36p. (J). lib. bdg. 16.95 *(978-1-60686-473-9(4))* Perfection Learning Corp.
—Spies. Martin, Jan, illus. 2010. (Fact to Fiction Grafx Ser.). 36p. pap. 7.45 *(978-0-7891-7998-2(9))* Perfection Learning Corp.
—Strange Creatures. Lindblad, Stefan, illus. 2010. (Fact to Fiction Grafx Ser.). 36p. pap. 7.45 *(978-0-7891-7994-4(6))* Perfection Learning Corp.
—Weird Places. 2007. (Trailblazers Ser.). (ENG., Illus.). 36p. pap. *(978-1-84167-589-3(X))* Ransom Publishing Ltd.
Orme, David & Orme, David. Science Fiction. 2008. (Trailblazers Ser.). (ENG., Illus.). 36p. pap. *(978-1-84167-693-7(4))* Ransom Publishing Ltd.
Orme David, David. Extreme Sports. 2007. (Trailblazers Ser.). (ENG., Illus.). 36p. pap. *(978-1-84167-590-9(3))* Ransom Publishing Ltd.
Orme, Helen. Death. 2007. (Trailblazers Ser.). (ENG., Illus.). 36p. pap. *(978-1-84167-591-6(1))* Ransom Publishing Ltd.
—Lost! Brett, Cathy, illus. 2007. (Siti's Sisters Ser.). (ENG.). 36p. (J). per. *(978-1-84167-598-5(9))* Ransom Publishing Ltd.
Ormiston, Rickey. My Dog Wiggles. 2010. 20p. 11.49 *(978-1-4490-9824-7(X))* AuthorHouse.
Orozco, José-Luis & Orozco, José-Luis. Rin, Rin, Rin/Do, Re, Mi (Bilingual) (Bilingual Edition) Libro Ilustrado en Español e Inglés / a Picture Book in Spanish & English. Diaz, David, illus. 2005. (SPA.). 32p. (J). (gr. -1-k). 3.99 *(978-0-439-75531-3(X),* Orchard Bks.) Scholastic, Inc.
Orshoski, Paul. We Read Phonics-Bugs on the Bus. Noiset, Michele, illus. 2010. 32p. (J). 9.95 *(978-1-60115-325-8(2))*; pap. 4.99 *(978-1-60115-326-5(0))* Treasure Bay, Inc.
—We Read Phonics-Dad Does It All. Ebbeler, Jeffrey, illus. 2011. 32p. (J). 9.95 *(978-1-60115-341-8(4))*; (YA). pap. 4.99 *(978-1-60115-342-5(2))* Treasure Bay, Inc.
Ortells, Estela. En Africa. (Coleccion Pequeno Simon). (SPA., Illus.). 32p. (J). 7.95 *(978-84-7189-177-8(8),* ORT342) Ortells, Alfredo Editorial S.L. ESP. Dist: Continental Bk. Co., Inc.
—En el Aire. (Coleccion Pequeno Simon). (SPA., Illus.). 32p. (J). 7.95 *(978-84-7189-173-0(5),* ORT328) Ortells, Alfredo Editorial S.L. ESP. Dist: Continental Bk. Co., Inc.
—En el Colegio. (Coleccion Pequeno Simon). (SPA., Illus.). 32p. (J). 7.95 *(978-84-7189-170-9(0),* ORT327) Ortells, Alfredo Editorial S.L. ESP. Dist: Continental Bk. Co., Inc.
—En el Rio. (Coleccion Pequeno Simon). (SPA., Illus.). 32p. (J). 7.95 *(978-84-7189-169-3(7),* ORT346) Ortells, Alfredo Editorial S.L. ESP. Dist: Continental Bk. Co., Inc.
—En Japon. (Coleccion Pequeno Simon). (SPA., Illus.). 32p. (J). 7.95 *(978-84-7189-176-1(X),* ORT331) Ortells, Alfredo Editorial S.L. ESP. Dist: Continental Bk. Co., Inc.
—En la India. (Coleccion Pequeno Simon). (SPA., Illus.). 32p. (J). 7.95 *(978-84-7189-175-4(1),* ORT330) Ortells, Alfredo Editorial S.L. ESP. Dist: Continental Bk. Co., Inc.
—En la Montana. (Coleccion Pequeno Simon). (SPA., Illus.). 32p. (J). 7.95 *(978-84-7189-167-9(0),* ORT343) Ortells, Alfredo Editorial S.L. ESP. Dist: Continental Bk. Co., Inc.
—En la Nieve. (Coleccion Pequeno Simon). (SPA., Illus.). 32p. (J). 7.95 *(978-84-7189-172-3(7),* ORT344) Ortells, Alfredo Editorial S.L. ESP. Dist: Continental Bk. Co., Inc.
—En la Playa. (Coleccion Pequeno Simon). (SPA., Illus.). 32p. (J). 7.95 *(978-84-7189-168-6(9),* ORT347) Ortells, Alfredo Editorial S.L. ESP. Dist: Continental Bk. Co., Inc.
—El Pequeno Castor. (Coleccion Pequeno Simon). (SPA., Illus.). 32p. (J). 7.95 *(978-84-7189-171-6(9),* ORT329) Ortells, Alfredo Editorial S.L. ESP. Dist: Continental Bk. Co., Inc.
—Y los Chihuhuas. (Coleccion Pequeno Simon). (SPA., Illus.). 32p. (J). 7.95 *(978-84-7189-174-7(3),* ORT345) Ortells, Alfredo Editorial S.L. ESP. Dist: Continental Bk. Co., Inc.
O'Ryan, Ray. Cosmic Blackout! Kraft, Jason, illus. 2017. (Galaxy Zack Ser.: 16). (ENG.). 128p. (J). (gr. k-4). 17.99 *(978-1-4814-9990-3(4))*; pap. 5.99 *(978-1-4814-9989-7(0))* Little Simon. (Little Simon).
Oscar & Tatiana: Individual Title Six-Packs. (Literatura 2000 Ser.). (gr. 2-3). 33.00 *(978-0-7635-0267-6(7))* Rigby Education.
Oscar y Tatiana: Individual Title Six-Packs. (Literatura 2000 Ser.). (gr. 2-3). 33.00 *(978-0-7635-1268-2(0))* Rigby Education.
Osteen, Victoria. Unexpected Treasures. Palmisciano, Diane, illus. 2009. (ENG.). 32p. (J). (gr. -1-3). 19.99 *(978-1-4169-5550-4(X),* Little Simon Inspirations) Little Simon Inspirations.
Otfinoski, Steve. Coin Collecting for Kids. Graham, Jack, illus. 2007. (ENG.). 12p. (J). (gr. 2-7). spiral bd. 17.99 *(978-1-58476-624-7(7),* IKIDS) Innovative Kids.
Otter, Otter. (Early Intervention Levels Ser.). 21.30 *(978-0-7362-0381-4(8))*; Vol. 4. 3.55 *(978-0-7362-0102-5(5))* CENGAGE Learning.
Otter, Otter. (J). 26.20 *(978-0-8136-8416-1(1))*; (gr. -1-3). 59.50 *(978-0-8136-7954-9(0))* Modern Curriculum Pr.
Ottolenghi, Carol. The Princess & the Pea. 2009. (Keepsake Stories Ser.: 25). (ENG.). 32p. (gr. -1-3). pap. 3.99 *(978-0-7696-5869-8(5),* 0769658695, Brighter Child) Carson-Dellosa Publishing, LLC.
—Puss in Boots (El Gato Con Botas) 2009. (Keepsake Stories Ser.: 2). (ENG.). 32p. (gr. -1-2). pap. 3.99 *(978-0-7696-5863-6(6),* 0769658636, Brighter Child) Carson-Dellosa Publishing, LLC.
—Sleeping Beauty. 2009. (Brighter Child Keepsake Story Ser.). (ENG.). 32p. (gr. k-2). 16.19 *(978-0-7696-5866-7(0))* School Specialty, Incorporated.
—The Three Billy Goats Gruff. 2009. (Keepsake Stories Ser.: 26). (ENG.). 32p. (gr. -1-3). pap. 3.99 *(978-0-7696-5868-1(7),* 0769658687, Brighter Child) Carson-Dellosa Publishing, LLC.
—The Three Billy Goats Gruff (Los Tres Chivitos) 2009. (Keepsake Stories Ser.: 27). (ENG.). 32p. (gr. -1-2). pap. 3.99 *(978-0-7696-5864-3(4),* 0769658644, Brighter Child) Carson-Dellosa Publishing, LLC.
Our Adobe House: 6 Small Books. (Greetings Ser.: Vol. 2). 24p. (gr. 2-3). 31.00 *(978-0-7635-9428-2(8))* Rigby Education.
Our Adobe House: Big Book. (Greetings Ser.: Vol. 2). 24p. (gr. 2-3). 31.00 *(978-0-7635-5860-4(5))* Rigby Education.
Our New Baby, 6 Packs. (gr. -1-2). 27.00 *(978-0-7635-9469-5(5))* Rigby Education.
Ousley, Pamela. Amy & the Pacifier. 2009. 24p. pap. 15.99 *(978-1-4415-1364-9(7))* Xlibris Corp.
Over the Edge: Magazine Anthology: Level 7, 6 vols. (Comprehension Strand Ser.). (gr. 4-8). 54.00 *(978-0-322-06043-2(5))* Wright Group/McGraw-Hill.
Owen, Anna. A Day Out: Band 02A/Red a (Collins Big Cat) Hammond, Andy, illus. 2005. (Collins Big Cat Ser.). (ENG.). 80p. (J). (gr. -1-k). pap. 6.99 *(978-0-00-718555-9(3))* HarperCollins Pubs. Ltd. GBR. Dist: Independent Pubs. Group.
Owen, Karen. As Quiet As a Mouse. Golubeva, Evgenia, illus. 2019. (Early Bird Readers — Purple (Early Bird Stories (tm)) Ser.). (ENG.). 32p. (J). (gr. k-3). 30.65 *(978-1-5415-4224-2(X),* b86f0cb2-2d79-445c-8403-245c1b6207f6); pap. 9.99 *(978-1-5415-7421-2(4),* 7ab98954-7f51-43e1-8346-0c7f37861472) Lerner Publishing Group. (Lerner Pubns.).
Owen, Ruth. Is It Living or Non-Living? 2017. (Get Started with STEM Ser.). (ENG., Illus.). 32p. (J). (gr. k-3). 9.99 *(978-1-78856-116-7(3),* 89dc4c11-46b9-4d34-b25c-65801a4d0441) Ruby Tuesday Books Limited GBR. Dist: Lerner Publishing Group.
Owings, Jeff. Tiny Todd: Swooped Away. 2009. 20p. pap. 10.49 *(978-1-4490-1214-4(0))* AuthorHouse.
—Tiny Todd: Tiny Todd's First Pet. 2009. 20p. pap. 10.49 *(978-1-4490-1216-8(7))* AuthorHouse.
Oxford, ed. Arabic Club Readers: Pink Band: My House. 2014. (ENG.). 16p. 4.99 *(978-1-4085-2462-6(7))* Oxford Univ. Pr., Inc.
Oxlade, Chris. Mighty Machines, 8bks. 2005. (QEB Readers). (Illus.). 24p. (J). (gr. -1-3). lib. bdg. 15.95 *(978-1-59566-079-4(8))* QEB Publishing Inc.
—The Mobile Continent White Band. 2016. (Cambridge Reading Adventures Ser.). (ENG., Illus.). 32p. pap. 9.50 *(978-1-316-60067-2(X))* Cambridge Univ. Pr.
—Skyscrapers 3 Explorers. 2017. (Cambridge Reading Adventures Ser.). (ENG., Illus.). 32p. pap. 8.60 *(978-1-108-41189-9(4))* Cambridge Univ. Pr.
Pace, Marisa. My Body Systems: Working As a Team, 1 vol. 2017. (Computer Kids: Powered by Computational Thinking Ser.). (ENG.). 24p. (J). (gr. 3-4). 25.27 *(978-1-5383-2413-4(X),* 867575f1-7cd4-4ba0-8ed2-7e78849abf72, PowerKids Pr.); pap. *(978-1-5081-3768-9(4),* df45d385-6e24-425b-a8ff-65adb497bd71, Rosen Classroom) Rosen Publishing Group, Inc., The.
Paderewski, Elliot. A Baby Brother, 1 vol. 2016. (Rosen REAL Readers: STEM & STEAM Collection). (ENG.). 12p. (gr. 1-2). pap. 6.33 *(978-1-5081-2655-3(0),* 73c1a7d6-8fa0-4131-add2-72ade7f46a87, Rosen Classroom) Rosen Publishing Group, Inc., The.
—Born on the Fourth of July, 1 vol. 2016. (Rosen REAL Readers: Social Studies Nonfiction / Fiction: Myself, My Community, My World Ser.). (ENG.). 8p. (gr. k-1). pap. 5.46 *(978-1-5081-2506-8(6),* 1c808ab9-8e0a-44b9-b13f-2b6cc493e069, Rosen Classroom) Rosen Publishing Group, Inc., The.
—Children Have Basic Rights, 1 vol. 2016. (Rosen REAL Readers: Social Studies Nonfiction / Fiction: Myself, My Community, My World Ser.). (ENG.). 12p. (gr. k-1). pap. 6.33 *(978-1-5081-2320-0(9),* baaa2d89-8b23-48fc-a40a-766fbfc95623, Rosen Classroom) Rosen Publishing Group, Inc., The.
—Dwayne's Water Fund, 1 vol. 2016. (Rosen REAL Readers: Social Studies Nonfiction / Fiction: Myself, My Community, My World Ser.). (ENG.). 12p. (gr. k-1). pap. 6.33 *(978-1-5081-2568-6(6),* 3185d983-9697-4deb-8dcc-ea832904638e, Rosen Classroom) Rosen Publishing Group, Inc., The.
—The Mystery Plant, 1 vol. 2016. (Rosen REAL Readers: STEM & STEAM Collection). (ENG.). 12p. (gr. 1-2). pap. 6.33 *(978-1-5081-2670-6(4),* 78c7e722-9e46-4a68-9725-1c75ff57d700, Rosen Classroom) Rosen Publishing Group, Inc., The.
—Waterfall Power, 1 vol. 2016. (Rosen REAL Readers: Social Studies Nonfiction / Fiction: Myself, My Community, My World Ser.). (ENG.). 12p. (gr. k-1). pap. 6.33 *(978-1-5081-2577-8(5),* e537972d-982f-4889-8737-357d0adfe34a, Rosen Classroom) Rosen Publishing Group, Inc., The.
—Why Babies Cry, 1 vol. 2016. (Rosen REAL Readers: STEM & STEAM Collection). (ENG.). 12p. (gr. 1-2). pap. 6.33 *(978-1-5081-2440-5(X),* 4c1106d8-7f91-4e95-9338-7a3bd05c82ad, Rosen Classroom) Rosen Publishing Group, Inc., The.
Paéz, Enrique. Devuelveme el Anillo, Pelo Cepillo. (SPA.). (YA). (gr. 5-8). 112p. *(978-84-216-2561-3(6),* BU7584); 12th ed. (Illus.). 144p. *(978-84-216-1800-4(8),* BU5113) Bruño, Editorial ESP. Dist: Lectorum Pubns., Inc.
Page, Nick & Page, Claire. The Good Samaritan. Loy, Nikki, illus. 2006. (Read with Me (Make Believe Ideas) Ser.). 31p. (J). (gr. k-2). *(978-1-84610-174-8(3))* Make Believe Ideas.
—Read with Me Jack & the Beanstalk: Sticker Activity Book. Goodberry, Jo, illus. 2006. (Read with Me (Make Believe Ideas) Ser.). 12p. (J). (gr. k-2). pap. *(978-1-84610-180-9(8))* Make Believe Ideas.
—Read with Me Jonah the Moaner: Sticker Activity Book. Loy, Nikki, illus. 2006. (Read with Me (Make Believe Ideas) Ser.). 12p. (J). (gr. k-2). pap. *(978-1-84610-183-0(2))* Make Believe Ideas.
—Read with Me Rumpelstiltskin: Sticker Activity Book. Baker, Sara, illus. 2006. (Read with Me (Make Believe Ideas) Ser.). 12p. (J). (gr. k-2). pap. *(978-1-84610-182-3(4))* Make Believe Ideas.
—Read with Me Snow White: Sticker Activity Book. Willey, Bee, illus. 2006. (Read with Me (Make Believe Ideas) Ser.). 12p. (J). (gr. k-2). pap. *(978-1-84610-179-3(4))* Make Believe Ideas.
—Read with Me the Elves & the Shoemaker: Sticker Activity Book. Baker, Sara, illus. 2006. (Read with Me (Make Believe Ideas) Ser.). 12p. (J). (gr. k-2). pap. *(978-1-84610-177-9(8))* Make Believe Ideas.
—Read W/Me 6v. 2006. (Illus.). (J). (gr. -1-3). *(978-5-558-47727-6(X))* Make Believe Ideas.
—The Runaway Son. Baker, Sara, illus. 2006. (Read with Me Ser.). 31p. (J). (gr. k-2). *(978-1-84610-176-2(X))* Make Believe Ideas.
Page, Nick & Claire. Noah & the Ark. 2006. (Read with Me (Make Believe Ideas) Ser.). (Illus.). 32p. (J). (gr. k-2). *(978-1-84610-168-7(9))* Make Believe Ideas.
Page, Philip & Pettit, Marilyn. Much Ado about Nothing. 2005. (ENG., Illus.). 64p. pap. *(978-0-340-88808-7(3))* Cambridge Univ. Pr.
Page, Robin. What Do You Do with a Tail Like This? Jenkins, Steve, illus. 2011. (J). (gr. -1-3). 29.95 *(978-0-545-10698-6(2))* Weston Woods Studios, Inc.
Pahn, Latosha. Come go on a Read along Ride with Me: Read along Ride. 2008. 68p. pap. 9.95 *(978-1-4184-4896-7(6))* AuthorHouse.
Palazzolo, Fran. Wise Owl's First Sounds & Sight Words. 2009. 248p. pap. 88.50 *(978-0-557-08128-8(9))* Lulu Pr., Inc.
—Wise Owl's Vowels. 2009. 290p. pap. 98.95 *(978-0-557-07812-7(1))* Lulu Pr., Inc.
Pan y Canela: Super Classroom Set. (SPA.). (gr. k-2). 1289.61 *(978-0-7362-0445-3(8))* CENGAGE Learning.
Pandora's Box: Level M, 6 vols. 128p. (gr. 2-3). 41.95 *(978-0-7699-1027-7(0))* Shortland Pubns. (U. S. A.) Inc.
Panec, D. J. We Both Read - Changing Places. Elkerton, Andy, illus. 2017. (ENG.). 41p. (J). 9.95 *(978-1-60115-297-8(3))* Treasure Bay, Inc.
Panev, Aleksandar. Queen Nzinga. Steffibauer, Thomas, illus. 2007. 48p. (J). lib. bdg. 23.08 *(978-1-4242-1641-3(9))* Fitzgerald Bks.
Panman, Sandra & Panman, Richard. The Active Reader for Writers. Panman, Sandra, ed. 3rd rev. ed. 2004. 288p. (C). (gr. 9-12). pap. 24.95 *(978-0-912813-30-1(X))* Active Learning Corp.
Pantaleo, Steve. WWE Tag Teams & Team-Ups. 2019. (DK Readers Level 2 Ser.). (Illus.). (J). (gr. k-2). (ENG.). 48p. pap. 4.99 *(978-1-4654-7972-3(4),* DK Children); 46p. *(978-1-5444-3012-6(4))* Dorling Kindersley Publishing, Inc.
Papaloizos, Theodore C. My Greek Reader. Frangouli, Rena, illus. 2004. (GRE & ENG.). 124p. (Orig.). (YA). (gr. 2). pap. *(978-0-932416-46-9(2))* Papaloizos Pubns., Inc.
The Paper Trail: Individual Title Six-Packs. (gr. 1-2). 25.00 *(978-0-7635-9137-3(8))* Rigby Education.
Paprocki, Beth. Storyland: the Marvelous Mccrittersons — Road Trip to Grandma's: A Story Coloring Book. Paprocki, Greg, illus. 2015. (ENG.). 32p. (J). (gr. k-5). pap. 3.99 *(978-0-486-79383-2(4))* Dover Pubns., Inc.
Parent, Nancy. Disney Junior Fancy Nancy: Nancy Makes Her Mark. Disney Storybook Art Team, Disney Storybook, illus. 2018. (I Can Read Level 1 Ser.). (ENG.). 32p. (J). (gr. -1-3). 16.99 *(978-0-06-288865-5(X),* HarperCollins) HarperCollins Pubs.
Parent, Nancy, adapted by. Chez Nancy. 2018. (Illus.). 32p. (J). *(978-1-5444-0825-5(0))* Harper & Row Ltd.
Paris, Stephanie. Drag! Friction & Resistance, 1 vol. 2nd rev. ed. 2013. (TIME for KIDS(r): Informational Text Ser.). (ENG., Illus.). 64p. (J). (gr. 4-8). pap. 14.99 *(978-1-4333-4940-9(X))* Teacher Created Materials, Inc.
—Drugs & Alcohol, 1 vol. 2nd rev. ed. 2012. (TIME for KIDS(r): Informational Text Ser.). (ENG., Illus.). 48p. (gr. 4-6). pap. 13.99 *(978-1-4333-4859-4(4))* Teacher Created Materials, Inc.
—Engineering Feats & Failures. 2nd rev. ed. 2012. (TIME for KIDS(r): Informational Text Ser.). (ENG., Illus.). 48p. (gr. 4-6). pap. 13.99 *(978-1-4333-4871-6(3))* Teacher Created Materials, Inc.
—Pecos Bill & Slue-Foot Sue, 1 vol. rev. ed. 2009. (Reader's Theater Ser.). (ENG.). 24p. (gr. 2-4). pap. 8.99 *(978-1-4333-0991-5(2))* Teacher Created Materials, Inc.
—Pop! Air & Water Pressure, 1 vol. 2nd rev. ed. 2013. (TIME for KIDS(r): Informational Text Ser.). (ENG., Illus.). 64p. (J). (gr. 4-8). pap. 14.99 *(978-1-4333-4939-3(6))* Teacher Created Materials, Inc.
—Straight Talk: Smoking, 1 vol. 2nd rev. ed. 2012. (TIME for KIDS(r): Informational Text Ser.). (ENG., Illus.). 48p. (gr. 4-5). pap. 13.99 *(978-1-4333-4858-7(6))* Teacher Created Materials, Inc.
—Straight Talk - The Truth about Food , 1 vol. 2nd rev. ed. 2012. (TIME for KIDS(r): Informational Text Ser.). (ENG.). 48p. (gr. 4-5). pap. 13.99 *(978-1-4333-4857-0(8))* Teacher Created Materials, Inc.
—Technology Feats & Failures. 2nd rev. ed. 2012. (TIME for KIDS(r): Informational Text Ser.). (ENG.). 48p. (gr. 4-5). pap. 13.99 *(978-1-4333-4869-3(1))* Teacher Created Materials, Inc.
—Vroom! Speed & Acceleration, 1 vol. 2nd rev. ed. 2013. (TIME for KIDS(r): Informational Text Ser.). (ENG.). 64p. (gr. 4-8). pap. 14.99 *(978-1-4333-4938-6(8))* Teacher Created Materials, Inc.
—20th Century: Race to the Moon, 1 vol. 2nd rev. ed. 2013. (TIME for KIDS(r): Informational Text Ser.). (ENG., Illus.). 64p. (J). (gr. 4-8). pap. 14.99 *(978-1-4333-4899-0(3))* Teacher Created Materials, Inc.
Paris, Stephanie & Kuligowski, Stephanie. 22nd Century - Future of Space, 1 vol. 2nd rev. ed. 2013. (TIME for KIDS(r): Informational Text Ser.). (ENG., Illus.). 64p. (J). (gr. 4-8). pap. 14.99 *(978-1-4333-4901-0(9))* Teacher Created Materials, Inc.
Parish, Herman. Amelia Bedelia I Can Read Box Set #2: Books Are a Ball. Avril, Lynne, illus. 2017. (I Can Read Level 1 Ser.). (ENG.). 160p. (J). (gr. -1-3). pap. 29.95 *(978-0-06-244357-1(7),* Greenwillow Bks.) HarperCollins Pubs.
Parish, Peggy. Amelia Bedelia. Siebel, Fritz, illus. 2017. (I Can Read Level 2 Ser.). (ENG.). 72p. (J). (gr. -1-3). 9.99 *(978-0-06-257279-0(2),* Greenwillow Bks.) HarperCollins Pubs.
—Amelia Bedelia 5-Book I Can Read Box Set #1: Amelia Bedelia Hit the Books. Siebel, Fritz et al, illus. 5th ed. 2016. (I Can Read Level 2 Ser.). (ENG.). 320p. (J). (gr. -1-3). pap. 25.95 *(978-0-06-244356-4(9),* Greenwillow Bks.) HarperCollins Pubs.
Parker, Christi E. Abraham Lincoln, 1 vol. rev. ed. 2005. (Social Studies: Informational Text Ser.). (ENG.). 24p. (gr. 4-8). pap. 10.99 *(978-0-7439-8916-9(3))* Teacher Created Materials, Inc.

—American Revolution, 1 vol. rev. ed. 2004. (Social Studies: Informational Text Ser.). (ENG.). 24p. (gr. 4-8). pap. 10.99 (978-0-7439-8748-6(9)) Teacher Created Materials, Inc.

—Civil War Is Coming, 1 vol. rev. ed. 2005. (Social Studies: Informational Text Ser.). (ENG.). 24p. (gr. 4-8). pap. 10.99 (978-0-7439-8915-2(5)) Teacher Created Materials, Inc.

—George Washington, 1 vol. rev. ed. 2004. (Social Studies: Informational Text Ser.). (ENG.). 24p. (gr. 4-8). pap. 10.99 (978-0-7439-8749-3(7)) Teacher Created Materials, Inc.

—Pioneer Trails, 1 vol. rev. ed. 2005. (Social Studies: Informational Text Ser.). (ENG.). 24p. (gr. 4-8). pap. 10.99 (978-0-7439-8909-1(0)) Teacher Created Materials, Inc.

Parker, Helen. Weird Weapons Intermediate Book with Online Access, 1 vol. 2014. (ENG., Illus.). 28p. (J). pap., E-Book, E-Book 9.50 (978-1-107-65200-2(6)) Cambridge Univ. Pr.

Parker, Ian. Ride On: Bikes & Riders Who Rule. 2007. (Steck-Vaughn BOLDPRINT Anthologies Ser.). (ENG., Illus.). 48p. (gr. 6-9). pap. 16.90 (978-1-4190-4026-9(X)) Houghton Mifflin Harcourt Publishing Co.

Parker, John. Sucked In. 2008. (Lightning Strikes Ser.). (ENG.). 96p. (J). pap. (978-1-921150-62-3(9)) Walker Bks. Australia Pty, Ltd.

Parker, Richard Green. Parker's Second Reader: National Series of Selections for Reading Designe. 2007. (ENG.). 166p. pap. 19.99 (978-1-4346-0596-2(5)) Creative Media Partners, LLC.

Parnell, Declan. Blueprint for Pablo, 1 vol., 1. 2015. (Rosen REAL Readers: STEM & STEAM Collection). (ENG.). 12p. (J). (gr. 1-2). pap. 6.33 (978-1-5081-1575-5(3), d6c68144-70de-42ee-8f28-71d64c1183ee, Rosen Classroom) Rosen Publishing Group, Inc., The.

—Dwayne Leads the Song, 1 vol., 1. 2015. (Rosen REAL Readers: Social Studies Nonfiction / Fiction: Myself, My Community, My World Ser.). (ENG.). 12p. (J). (gr. k-1). pap. 6.33 (978-1-5081-1925-8(2), 557d8cbc-d86c-4184-a81f-3594a89a220c, Rosen Classroom) Rosen Publishing Group, Inc., The.

—The Fast Canoe, 1 vol., 1. 2015. (Rosen REAL Readers: Social Studies Nonfiction / Fiction: Myself, My Community, My World Ser.). (ENG.). 8p. (J). (gr. k-1). pap. 5.46 (978-1-5081-1830-5(2), 7a5ad14c-3959-4c59-bd6a-a413a65e4eb1, Rosen Classroom) Rosen Publishing Group, Inc., The.

—Hooray for Bubbles!, 1 vol., 1. 2015. (Rosen REAL Readers: STEM & STEAM Collection). (ENG.). 12p. (J). (gr. 1-2). pap. 6.33 (978-1-5081-1593-9(1), 4ff22afc-1ed7-4665-b2bf-30694a949dc8, Rosen Classroom) Rosen Publishing Group, Inc., The.

—Ping Cleans Her Room, 1 vol., 1. 2015. (Rosen REAL Readers: Social Studies Nonfiction / Fiction: Myself, My Community, My World Ser.). (ENG.). 8p. (J). (gr. k-1). pap. 5.46 (978-1-5081-1382-9(3), 7c9fb9a6-c4b3-4495-bc2c-26fb1a1a756d, Rosen Classroom) Rosen Publishing Group, Inc., The.

—Sammy's Big Trip, 1 vol., 1. 2015. (Rosen REAL Readers: Social Studies Nonfiction / Fiction: Myself, My Community, My World Ser.). (ENG.). 8p. (J). (gr. k-1). pap. 5.46 (978-1-5081-1415-4(3), b6ff9813-94cb-4977-b220-3454bcf952f7, Rosen Classroom) Rosen Publishing Group, Inc., The.

—Speedy & Pete, 1 vol., 1. 2015. (Rosen REAL Readers: STEM & STEAM Collection). (ENG.). 8p. (J). (gr. k-1). pap. 5.46 (978-1-5081-1438-3(2), 0919e4be-bdee-4ff7-9f0f-97c2a81a764f, Rosen Classroom) Rosen Publishing Group, Inc., The.

—Teresa's Construction Challenge, 1 vol., 1. 2015. (Rosen REAL Readers: STEM & STEAM Collection). (ENG.). 12p. (J). (gr. k-1). pap. 6.33 (978-1-5081-1539-7(7), a48b6d04-bca6-4c3d-9f0d-86c9d7901dcb, Rosen Classroom) Rosen Publishing Group, Inc., The.

Parr, todd. Otto Goes to the Beach. 2014. (Passport to Reading Level 1 Ser.). (J). lib. bdg. 14.75 (978-0-606-35303-8(8)) Turtleback.

Parramón, José María. Mi Escuela. Borday, Irene, illus. (Coleccion Estoy En...).Tr. of My School. (SPA.). 32p. (J). (gr. k-3). 6.36 (978-84-342-1004-2(5)) Parramon Ediciones S.A. ESP. Dist: Lectorum Pubns., Inc.

Parramón, José María & Bordoy, Irene. Mi Escuela.Tr. of My School. (SPA., Illus.). (J). (gr. -1-1). 6.95 (978-958-04-1276-2(6)) Norma S.A. COL. Dist: Distribuidora Norma, Inc.

Parsons, Garry. The Football Ghosts. Doyle, Malachy, illus. 2nd ed. 2016. (Reading Ladder Level 3 Ser.). (ENG.). 48p. (gr. k-2). pap. 4.99 (978-1-4052-8243-7(6), Reading Ladder) Farshore GBR. Dist: HarperCollins Pubs.

Parsons, Garry & Donaldson, Julia. The Wrong Kind of Bark (Reading Ladder Level 3) 2nd ed. 2016. (Reading Ladder Level 3 Ser.). (ENG., Illus.). 48p. (gr. k-2). pap. 4.99 (978-1-4052-8237-6(1), Reading Ladder) Farshore GBR. Dist: HarperCollins Pubs.

Partners: Individual Title Six-Packs. (gr. -1-2). 23.00 (978-0-7635-8820-5(2)) Rigby Education.

A Party for the Alley Cats: 3-in-1 Package. (Sails Literacy Ser.). 24p. (gr. 2-18). 57.00 (978-0-7578-6832-0(0)) Rigby Education.

A Party for the Alley Cats: 6 Small Books. (Sails Literacy Ser.). 24p. (gr. 2-18). 25.00 (978-0-7578-6828-3(2)) Rigby Education.

A Party for the Alley Cats: Big Book Only. (Sails Literacy Ser.). 24p. (gr. 2-18). 27.00 (978-0-7578-6820-7(7)) Rigby Education.

Pascal, Francine. Con las Riendas Firmes. Orig. Title: Lucy Takes the Reins. (SPA.). 168p. (J). 6.95 (978-84-272-4645-4(5)) Molino, Editorial ESP. Dist: AIMS International Bks., Inc.

Pasqualin, Marcia A. Good Ozzy, Bad Bella: Sight Words for First Readers. 2010. 24p. 14.93 (978-1-4269-4194-8(3)) Trafford Publishing.

El pastel Perfecto: Individual Title Six-Packs. (Literatura 2000 Ser.). (SPA.). (gr. k-1). 28.00 (978-0-7635-1026-8(2)) Rigby Education.

Patchett, Fiona. Puss in Boots. 2005. 48p. (J). (gr. 2-18). 8.95 (978-0-7945-0970-5(3), Usborne) EDC Publishing.

Patricelli, Leslie. Boo! / ¡Bu! Patricelli, Leslie, illus. 2017. (Leslie Patricelli Board Bks.). (Illus.). 26p. (J). (— 1). bds. 7.99 (978-0-7636-9314-5(6)) Candlewick Pr.

Pat's Train: KinderReaders, 6 Packs. (Kinderstarters Ser.). 8p. (gr. -1-1). 21.00 (978-0-7635-8655-3(2)) Rigby Education.

Patterson, Marie. Early American Indian Tribes, 1 vol. rev. ed. 2004. (Social Studies: Informational Text Ser.). (ENG.). 24p. (J). (gr. 4-8). pap. 10.99 (978-0-7439-8744-8(6)) Teacher Created Materials, Inc.

—Pocahontas, 1 vol. rev. ed. 2004. (Social Studies: Informational Text Ser.). (ENG.). 24p. (J). (gr. 4-8). pap. 10.99 (978-0-7439-8745-5(4)) Teacher Created Materials, Inc.

Paul. Best Friends. 2012. 24p. pap. 17.99 (978-1-4772-0755-0(4)) AuthorHouse.

Paul Ahrens-Gray & Ericka Grogan. Fish. 2005. (Illus.). 60p. (J). pap., act. bk. ed. 4.95 (978-1-59867-001-1(8)) Global Learning, Inc.

Paul, Ann Whitford. Word Builder. Cyrus, Kurt, illus. 2009. (ENG.). 32p. (J). (gr. k-2). 19.99 (978-1-4169-3981-8(4), Simon & Schuster Bks. For Young Readers) Simon & Schuster Bks. For Young Readers.

Paulo the Pilot: Individual Title Six-Packs. (gr. 1-2). 22.00 (978-0-7635-9187-8(4)) Rigby Education.

Pavón Córdoba, María del Mar. ¡Selena, Seleeena! 2005. (Caballo Alado Series-Al Galope Ser.). (SPA., Illus.). 24p. (J). (gr. k-2). pap. 5.95 (978-84-7864-885-6(2)) Combel Editorial, S.A. ESP. Dist: Independent Pubs. Group.

Pearce, Kevin. I'm Special Because..., 1 vol. 2006. (Neighborhood Readers Ser.). (ENG.). 8p. (gr. 1-2). pap. 5.15 (978-1-4042-6815-9(4), 7216dec1-07ff-4238-ab63-114088c74fd2, Rosen Classroom) Rosen Publishing Group, Inc., The.

Pearl, Nancy. Book Crush: For Kids & Teens — Recommended Reading for Every Mood, Moment, & Interest. 2007. (Illus.). 304p. per. 16.95 (978-1-57061-500-9(4)) Sasquatch Bks.

Pearson, Mary E. Rookie Ready to Learn en Español: Puedo Hacer de Todo. Shelly, Jeff, illus. 2011. (Rookie Ready to Learn Español Ser.). Orig. Title: Rookie Ready to Learn: I Can Do It All. (SPA.). 40p. (J). pap. 5.95 (978-0-531-26787-5(3), Children's Pr.) Scholastic Library Publishing.

Pearson, Mary E. & Shelly, Jeff. Puedo Hacer de Todo. Shelly, Jeff, illus. 2011. (Rookie Ready to Learn Español Ser.).Tr. of I Can Do It All. (SPA., Illus.). 40p. (J). lib. bdg. 23.00 (978-0-531-26119-4(0), Children's Pr.) Scholastic Library Publishing.

Peattie, Cindy. A Cinderella Atlas. Mountford, Karl, illus. 2017. (Text Connections Guided Close Reading Ser.). (J). (gr. 1). (978-1-4900-1819-5(0)) Benchmark Education Co.

Peattie, Cindy & Benchmark Education Co. Staff. The Secret Language of Elephants. 2014. (Text Connections Ser.). (J). (gr. 5). (978-1-4900-1367-1(9)) Benchmark Education Co.

Pecci, Mary. Pecci Reading Series: Primer. 2008. (Pecci Reading Ser.). pap. 9.95 (978-0-943220-16-1(5)) Pecci Educational Pubs.

Peirce, Lincoln. Big Nate on a Roll. 2015. (Big Nate Ser.: 3). (J). lib. bdg. 17.20 (978-0-606-36958-9(9)) Turtleback.

Penguin, Izy. Grandma Bendy. Penguin, Izy, illus. 2019. (Early Bird Readers — Green (Early Bird Stories (tm)) Ser.). (ENG., Illus.). 32p. (J). (gr. k-3). 30.65 (978-1-5415-4205-1(3), 9a3e0ab1-eba1-4cc7-abb3-04d91f4bcddb); pap. 9.99 (978-1-5415-7407-6(9), 073e4e65-24df-400b-b706-45022531f0a0) Lerner Publishing Group. (Lerner Pubns.).

Penguin Young Readers. Dick & Jane: Go Away, Spot, 5 vols. 2003. (Dick & Jane Ser.: 5). (Illus.). 32p. (J). (gr. 1-2). mass mkt. 4.99 (978-0-448-43404-9(0), Penguin Young Readers) Penguin Young Readers Group.

—Dick & Jane: Go, Go, Go, 6 vols. 2003. (Dick & Jane Ser.: 6). (Illus.). 32p. (J). (gr. k-1). pap. 4.99 (978-0-448-43405-6(9), Penguin Young Readers) Penguin Young Readers Group.

—Dick & Jane: Guess Who, 4 vols. 2003. (Dick & Jane Ser.: 4). (Illus.). 32p. (J). (gr. 1-2). mass mkt. 4.99 (978-0-448-43403-2(2), Penguin Young Readers) Penguin Young Readers Group.

—Dick & Jane: Jump & Run, 3 vols. 2003. (Dick & Jane Ser.: 3). (Illus.). 32p. (J). (gr. k-1). pap. 5.99 (978-0-448-43402-5(4), Penguin Young Readers) Penguin Young Readers Group.

—Dick & Jane: Something Funny, 2 vols. 2003. (Dick & Jane Ser.: 2). (Illus.). 32p. (J). (gr. k-1). mass mkt. 5.99 (978-0-448-43401-8(6), Penguin Young Readers) Penguin Young Readers Group.

—We Look. 2003. (Dick & Jane Ser.: 1). (Illus.). 32p. (J). (gr. k-1). pap. 5.99 (978-0-448-43400-1(8), Penguin Young Readers) Penguin Young Readers Group.

Penovi, Celina. The Clumsy Stork - la Cigüeña Despistad. 2009. 32p. pap. 17.50 (978-1-4490-2746-9(6)) AuthorHouse.

The People, Places & Principles of English Language Skills, Chapter 1, Activities. 2003. (978-1-928629-79-5(2)) Paradigm Accelerated Curriculum.

The People, Places & Principles of English Language Skills, Chapter 1, Text. 2003. (978-1-928629-69-6(5)) Paradigm Accelerated Curriculum.

The People, Places & Principles of English Language Skills, Chapter 10, Activities. 2003. (978-1-928629-88-7(1)) Paradigm Accelerated Curriculum.

The People, Places & Principles of English Language Skills, Chapter 10, Text. 2003. (978-1-928629-78-8(4)) Paradigm Accelerated Curriculum.

The People, Places & Principles of English Language Skills, Chapter 2, Activities. 2003. (978-1-928629-80-1(6)) Paradigm Accelerated Curriculum.

The People, Places & Principles of English Language Skills, Chapter 2, Text. 2003. (978-1-928629-70-2(9)) Paradigm Accelerated Curriculum.

The People, Places & Principles of English Language Skills, Chapter 3, Activities. 2003. (978-1-928629-81-8(4)) Paradigm Accelerated Curriculum.

The People, Places & Principles of English Language Skills, Chapter 3, Text. 2003. (978-1-928629-71-9(7)) Paradigm Accelerated Curriculum.

The People, Places & Principles of English Language Skills, Chapter 4, Activities. 2003. (978-1-928629-82-5(2)) Paradigm Accelerated Curriculum.

The People, Places & Principles of English Language Skills, Chapter 4, Text. 2003. (978-1-928629-72-6(5)) Paradigm Accelerated Curriculum.

The People, Places & Principles of English Language Skills, Chapter 5, Activities. 2003. (978-1-928629-83-2(0)) Paradigm Accelerated Curriculum.

The People, Places & Principles of English Language Skills, Chapter 5, Text. 2003. (978-1-928629-73-3(3)) Paradigm Accelerated Curriculum.

The People, Places & Principles of English Language Skills, Chapter 6, Activities. 2003. (978-1-928629-84-9(9)) Paradigm Accelerated Curriculum.

The People, Places & Principles of English Language Skills, Chapter 6, Text. 2003. (978-1-928629-74-0(1)) Paradigm Accelerated Curriculum.

The People, Places & Principles of English Language Skills, Chapter 7, Activities. 2003. (978-1-928629-85-6(7)) Paradigm Accelerated Curriculum.

The People, Places & Principles of English Language Skills, Chapter 7, Text. 2003. (978-1-928629-75-7(X)) Paradigm Accelerated Curriculum.

The People, Places & Principles of English Language Skills, Chapter 8, Activities. 2003. (978-1-928629-86-3(5)) Paradigm Accelerated Curriculum.

The People, Places & Principles of English Language Skills, Chapter 8, Text. 2003. (978-1-928629-76-4(8)) Paradigm Accelerated Curriculum.

The People, Places & Principles of English Language Skills, Chapter 9, Activities. 2003. (978-1-928629-87-0(3)) Paradigm Accelerated Curriculum.

Peppas, Lynn. Tractors at Work. 2010. (Vehicles on the Move Ser.). (ENG.). 32p. (J). (gr. k-3). pap. (978-0-7787-3064-4(6)) Crabtree Publishing Co.

Peppers. (Early Intervention Levels Ser.). 23.10 (978-0-7362-0021-9(5)); Vol. 4. 3.85 (978-1-56334-971-3(X)) CENGAGE Learning.

Perritano, John. Fault Lines. 2015. (Red Rhino Nonfiction Ser.). (J). lib. bdg. 20.80 (978-0-606-37201-5(6)) Turtleback.

Perry, Daniel. The Case of the Missing Shoes. 2013. 28p. pap. 9.95 (978-1-4787-2649-4(0)) Outskirts Pr., Inc.

Perry, Kathy J. Feebs to the Rescue. Bruno, Elizabeth, ed. Perry, Kathy J., illus. 2018. (Bandana Acres Ser.: 1). (ENG., Illus.). 50p. (J). (gr. 1-3). pap. 11.00 (978-0-9981291-7-4(8), Chickadee Words) Chickadee Words, LLC.

—Feebs to the Rescue: Night of the Coon. Bruno, Elizabeth, ed. Perry, Kathy J., illus. 2018. (Bandana Acres Ser.: 1). (ENG., Illus.). 50p. (J). (gr. 1-3). 18.00 (978-0-9981291-2-9(7), Chickadee Words) Chickadee Words, LLC.

Peters, Elisa. It's a Bird! 2009. (Everyday Wonders Ser.). 24p. (gr. 1-1). 42.50 (978-1-61512-321-6(0), PowerKids Pr.) Rosen Publishing Group, Inc., The.

—It's a Caterpillar! 2009. (Everyday Wonders Ser.). 24p. (gr. 1-1). 42.50 (978-1-61512-322-3(9), PowerKids Pr.) Rosen Publishing Group, Inc., The.

—It's a Dragonfly! 2009. (Everyday Wonders Ser.). 24p. (gr. 1-1). 42.50 (978-1-61512-323-0(7), PowerKids Pr.) Rosen Publishing Group, Inc., The.

—It's a Sunflower! 2009. (Everyday Wonders Ser.). 24p. (gr. 1-1). 42.50 (978-1-61512-324-7(5), PowerKids Pr.) Rosen Publishing Group, Inc., The.

—It's an Apple Tree! 2009. (Everyday Wonders Ser.). 24p. (gr. 1-1). 42.50 (978-1-61512-325-4(3), PowerKids Pr.) Rosen Publishing Group, Inc., The.

—It's Snow! 2009. (Everyday Wonders Ser.). 24p. (gr. 1-1). 42.50 (978-1-61512-326-1(1), PowerKids Pr.) Rosen Publishing Group, Inc., The.

Peters, Katie. Urban Places. 2021. (My Community (Pull Ahead Readers — Nonfiction) Ser.). (ENG., Illus.). 16p. (J). (gr. -1-1). 27.99 (978-1-5415-9012-0(0), 170fbd88-c342-4cc7-bb82-aeca9815cb41, Lerner Pubns.) Lerner Publishing Group.

Petersen, Null Casey. Games Around the World, 1 vol. 2nd rev. ed. 2011. (TIME for KIDS(r): Informational Text Ser.). (ENG.). 28p. (gr. 3-4). pap. 11.99 (978-1-4333-3653-9(7)) Teacher Created Materials, Inc.

—Markets Around the World, 1 vol. 2nd rev. ed. 2011. (TIME for KIDS(r): Informational Text Ser.). (ENG.). 28p. (gr. 3-4). pap. 11.99 (978-1-4333-3652-2(9)) Teacher Created Materials, Inc.

Petersen, Null Kathleen C. Theater Actors Then & Now, 1 vol. rev. ed. 2006. (Social Studies: Informational Text Ser.). (ENG.). 32p. (gr. 2-3). pap. 11.99 (978-0-7439-9379-1(9)) Teacher Created Materials, Inc.

—Writers Then & Now, 1 vol. rev. ed. 2006. (Social Studies: Informational Text Ser.). (ENG.). 32p. (gr. 2-3). pap. 11.99 (978-0-7439-9380-7(2)) Teacher Created Materials, Inc.

Petty, Kate. Don't Wake Stanley, 8 bks. 2005. (QEB Readers). (Illus.). 24p. (J). (gr. -1-3). lib. bdg. 15.95 (978-1-59566-074-9(7)) QEB Publishing Inc.

Pfeiffer, Judith, illus. We Didn't Know. 2012. 8p. (J). (978-0-7367-2742-6(6)) Zaner-Bloser, Inc.

Phan, Sandy. American Indians in Texas: Conflict & Survival, 1 vol. rev. ed. 2012. (Social Studies: Informational Text Ser.). (ENG., Illus.). 32p. (J). (gr. 3-5). pap. 11.99 (978-1-4333-5040-5(8)) Teacher Created Materials, Inc.

—The Caddo & Comanche: American Indians Tribes in Texas, 1 vol. rev. ed. 2012. (Social Studies: Informational Text Ser.). (ENG.). 32p. (gr. 3-5). pap. 11.99 (978-1-4333-5041-2(6)) Teacher Created Materials, Inc.

—Cecil Rhodes: The Man Who Expanded an Empire, 1 vol. rev. ed. 2012. (Social Studies: Informational Text Ser.). (ENG.). 32p. (gr. 4-8). pap. 11.99 (978-1-4333-5016-0(5)) Teacher Created Materials, Inc.

—Imperialism: Expanding Empires, 1 vol. rev. ed. 2012. (Social Studies: Informational Text Ser.). (ENG.). 32p. (gr. 4-8). pap. 11.99 (978-1-4333-5015-3(7)) Teacher Created Materials, Inc.

Phelps, Bonnie. Story Time with Our Librarian, 1 vol. 2016. (Community Helpers Ser.). (ENG.). 24p. (J). (gr. 1-1). pap. 9.25 (978-1-4994-2708-0(5), f7a9dcf5-85b7-4680-8b09-4f2a02adbdb0, PowerKids Pr.) Rosen Publishing Group, Inc., The.

Phillips, Miriam. Luis Gets Involved: Breaking down the Problem, 1 vol. 2017. (Computer Kids: Powered by Computational Thinking Ser.). (ENG.). 24p. (J). (gr. 3-4). 25.27 (978-1-5383-2409-7(1), 02c66cd3-b396-4d45-a981-a6e8dc01dc34, PowerKids Pr.); pap. (978-1-5081-3783-2(8), 00d3ce44-17fd-458d-aa8a-afebedf1eff2, Rosen Classroom) Rosen Publishing Group, Inc., The.

—Taylor Tracks Animals: Collecting Data, 1 vol. 2017. (Computer Kids: Powered by Computational Thinking Ser.). (ENG.). 24p. (J). (gr. 4-5). 25.27 (978-1-5383-2429-5(6), 7b284379-b71d-4f00-8a00-e5b1d952cffe, PowerKids Pr.); pap. (978-1-5081-3776-4(5), 908640d5-9efa-41b2-9125-fa9462e97771, Rosen Classroom) Rosen Publishing Group, Inc., The.

Phonemic Awareness Pack. (Phonemic Awareness Pack Ser.). (gr. -1-k). 523.57 incl. audio compact disk (978-0-7362-0899-4(2)) CENGAGE Learning.

Phonemic Awareness Pack with Tapes. (Phonemic Awareness Pack Ser.). (gr. -1-k). 538.88 (978-0-7362-0900-7(X)) CENGAGE Learning.

Phonics Decodable Reader 1. 2004. (Scott Foresman Reading Ser.). (gr. 1-18). suppl. ed. 3.35 (978-0-673-65172-3(X)) Addison-Wesley Educational Pubs., Inc.

Phonics Decodable Reader 2. 2004. (Scott Foresman Reading Ser.). (gr. 1-18). suppl. ed. 3.35 (978-0-673-65173-0(8)) Addison-Wesley Educational Pubs., Inc.

Phonics Decodable Reader 3. 2004. (Scott Foresman Reading Ser.). (gr. 1-18). suppl. ed. 3.35 (978-0-673-65174-7(6)) Addison-Wesley Educational Pubs., Inc.

Phonics Decodable Reader 33-41. 2004. (Scott Foresman Reading Ser.). (gr. 1-18). suppl. ed. 7.75 (978-0-673-65180-8(0)) Addison-Wesley Educational Pubs., Inc.

Phonics Decodable Reader 4. 2004. (Scott Foresman Reading Ser.). (gr. 1-18). suppl. ed. 3.35 (978-0-673-65175-4(4)) Addison-Wesley Educational Pubs., Inc.

Phonics Decodable Reader 42-50. 2004. (Scott Foresman Reading Ser.). (gr. 1-18). suppl. ed. 7.75 (978-0-673-65181-5(9)) Addison-Wesley Educational Pubs., Inc.

Phonics Decodable Reader 5. 2004. (Scott Foresman Reading Ser.). (gr. 1-18). suppl. ed. 3.35 (978-0-673-65176-1(2)) Addison-Wesley Educational Pubs., Inc.

Phonics Practice Book. (De Canciones A Cuentos Ser.). (SPA.). (gr. 1-18). 9.13 (978-1-56334-895-2(0)) CENGAGE Learning.

Phonics Readers, Bks. 37-72. (Phonics Readers Ser.). (gr. k-2). 932.95 (978-0-7368-4096-5(6), Red Brick Learning) Capstone.

Phonics Readers Big Books. 2005. (J). pap. 95.00 (978-1-58970-687-3(0)) Lakeshore Learning Materials.

Phonics Readers Bookshelf Collection, 36 bks., Set. 2004. (gr. 1-18). 594.00 (978-0-328-00401-0(4)); (gr. 2-18). 495.00 (978-0-328-00402-7(2)); (gr. 3-18). 495.00 (978-0-328-00403-4(0)) Addison-Wesley Educational Pubs., Inc.

Phonics Readers Student Books. 2005. (J). pap. 29.95 (978-1-58970-685-9(4)) Lakeshore Learning Materials.

Phonics Take-Home Readers. 2004. (Scott Foresman Reading Ser.). (gr. 3-18). 48.00 (978-0-673-61260-1(0)) Addison-Wesley Educational Pubs., Inc.

Pick a Pet. 2005. (Little Celebrations Thematic Packages Ser.). (J). (gr. k-3). 133.50 (978-0-673-75387-8(5)) Celebration Pr.

Picou, Lin. Who's Right. DuFalla, Anita, illus. 2012. (Little Birdie Bks.). (ENG.). 24p. (gr. 2-3). pap. 9.95 (978-1-61810-323-9(7), 9781618103239) Rourke Educational Media.

Picture Perfect Word Book. (gr. -1-2). pap. 206.58 (978-0-7362-2547-2(1)) CENGAGE Learning.

Picture Perfect Word Book. Incl. Picture Perfect Word Book. (J). (gr. -1-1). pap., tchr. ed. 30.00 48.19 (978-0-7362-0176-6(9), P17002) CENGAGE Learning.

Pie Day. (Early Intervention Levels Ser.). 28.38 (978-0-7362-0406-4(7)); Vol. 12. 4.73 (978-0-7362-0231-2(5)) CENGAGE Learning.

Piercy, Jennifer. Ellie's Math Adventure. 2013. 28p. pap. 16.09 (978-1-4669-1909-9(4)) Trafford Publishing.

Pilkey, Dav. Big Dog & Little Dog Making a Mistake/Perrazo y Perrito Se Equivocan: Bilingual English-Spanish. 2017. (Green Light Readers Ser.). (ENG., Illus.). 24p. (J). (gr. -1-3). 12.99 (978-1-328-70262-3(6), 1672397); pap. 5.99 (978-1-328-70263-0(4), 1672398) HarperCollins Pubs. (Clarion Bks.).

Pin It! Fix It! (Early Intervention Levels Ser.). 21.30 (978-0-7362-0389-0(3)); Vol. 6. 3.55 (978-0-7362-0169-8(6)) CENGAGE Learning.

Pindar, Heather. The Great Underwear Robbery. Lombardo, Serena, illus. 2021. (Early Bird Readers — Gold (Early Bird Stories (tm)) Ser.). (ENG.). 32p. (J). (gr. k-3). 30.65 (978-1-5415-9010-6(4), 7079f138-eada-47df-8522-1788b2ee9e10, Lerner Pubns.) Lerner Publishing Group.

—Strictly No Crocs. Batori, Susan, illus. 2019. (Early Bird Readers — Blue (Early Bird Stories (tm)) Ser.). (ENG.). 32p. (J). (gr. -1-2). pap. 9.99 (978-1-5415-4618-9(0), a4d895b3-c5f5-4c10-a6d1-565c7d5f32dd) Lerner Publishing Group.

Pimot, Karen Hutchins. Night Traveler. Pimot, Karen Hutchins, illus. 2007. (Illus.). 24p. per. 12.95 (978-1-934246-97-9(2)) Peppertree Pr., The.

Pirotta, Saviour. George & the Dragon: Band 13/Topaz (Collins Big Cat) Peluso, Martina, illus. 2015. (Collins Big Cat Ser.). (ENG.). 32p. (J). (gr. 2-3). pap. 10.99 (978-0-00-812776-3(X)) HarperCollins Pubs. Ltd. GBR. Dist: Independent Pubs. Group.

Pitt, Marilyn & Hileman, Jane. I Like My Stuff. Bianchi, John, illus. 2013. (1G Potato Chip Bks.). (ENG.). 12p. (J). (gr. k-1). pap. 8.00 (978-1-59301-769-9(3)) American Reading Co.

—Where Is My Boy? Bianchi, John, illus. 2012. (1G Potato Chip Bks.). (ENG.). 12p. (J). (gr. k-1). pap. 8.00 (978-1-59301-766-8(9)) American Reading Co.

—Where Is That Dog? Bianchi, John, illus. 2013. (1G Potato Chip Bks.). (ENG.). 12p. (J). (gr. k-1). pap. 8.00 (978-1-59301-770-5(7)) American Reading Co.

Pitt, Marilyn & Sanchez, Lucia M. La Nevada: Snow Dog. Bianchi, John, illus. 2011. (poder de 50 - Libros papas fritas Ser.). (SPA.). 12p. pap. 33.92 *(978-1-61541-439-0(8))* American Reading Co.

—Perro en Apuros: Let Me In. Bianchi, John, illus. 2011. (poder de 50 - Libros papas fritas Ser.). (SPA.). 12p. pap. 33.92 *(978-1-61541-165-8(8))* American Reading Co.

Pitt, Marilyn & Sánchez, Lucía M. Solos en Casa. Bianchi, John, illus. 2010. (1G Libros Papas Fritas Ser.).Tr. of Home Alone. (SPA.). 12p. (J). (gr. k-1). pap. 9.60 *(978-1-61541-409-3(6))* American Reading Co.

Pitt, Marilyn & Sanchez, Lucia M. La Tormenta: The Storm. Bianchi, John, illus. 2011. (poder de 50 - Libros papas fritas Ser.). (SPA.). 12p. pap. 33.92 *(978-1-61541-441-3(X))* American Reading Co.

Pittis, Arthur M. As My Heart Awakes: A Waldorf Reader for Early Third Grade. Mitchell, David S., ed. Peacock, Ausa M., illus. 2005. (J). bds. 10.00 *(978-1-888365-62-7(5))* Waldorf Publications.

—Fee Fi Fo Fum: A Waldorf Reader for Late Second Grade. Mitchell, David S., ed. Peacock, Ausa M., illus. 2005. (J). bds. 10.00 *(978-1-888365-63-4(3))* Waldorf Publications.

—Sun So Hot I Froze to Death: A Waldorf Reader for Advanced Fourth Grade. Mitchell, David S., ed. Peacock, Ausa M., illus. 2005. (ENG.). (J). bds. 12.00 *(978-1-888365-65-8(X))* Waldorf Publications.

—When I Hear My Heart Wonder: A Waldorf Reader for Late Third Grade. Mitchell, David S., ed. Peacock, Ausa M., illus. 2005. (J). bds. 10.00 *(978-1-888365-66-5(8))* Waldorf Publications.

The Pizza Shop, 2 Packs. (Chiquilibros Ser.). (gr. -1-1). 12.00 *(978-0-7635-8535-8(1))* Rigby Education.

Places: KinderFacts Individual Title Six-Packs. (Kinderstarters Ser.). 8p. (gr. -1-1). 21.00 *(978-0-7635-8746-8(X))* Rigby Education.

Places in My Community, 8 vols. 2016. (Places in My Community Ser.). (ENG.). 00024p. (J). (gr. 1-1). 101.08 *(978-1-4994-2659-5(3),* 289a17a5-33a7-4c14-b7ea-a82ce3eb8bb7, PowerKids Pr.) Rosen Publishing Group, Inc., The.

El Planeta de los Cuentos.Tr. of Planet of Storybook Tales. (SPA.). (J). *(978-84-7773-630-1(8))* Grafalco, S.A.

Platt, Richard. The Golden Age of Baghdad: Band 17/Diamond. 2017. (Collins Big Cat Ser.). (ENG.). 56p. (J). pap. 12.99 *(978-0-00-820895-0(6))* HarperCollins Pubs. Ltd. GBR. Dist: Independent Pubs. Group.

—The Maya: Band 18/Pearl (Collins Big Cat) 2015. (Collins Big Cat Ser.). (ENG., Illus.). 80p. (J). (gr. 5). pap. 11.99 *(978-0-00-812797-8(2))* HarperCollins Pubs. Ltd. GBR. Dist: Independent Pubs. Group.

—Palaces, Peasants & Plagues - England in the 14th Century: Band 18/Pearl (Collins Big Cat) Lawrie, Robin, illus. 2014. (Collins Big Cat Ser.). (ENG.). 80p. (J). (gr. 5). pap. 12.95 *(978-0-00-753016-8(1))* HarperCollins Pubs. Ltd. GBR. Dist: Independent Pubs. Group.

Play the Game You Know. 2005. (Book Treks Ser.). (J). 37.95 *(978-0-7652-3258-8(8))* Celebration Pr.

Pobst, Sandy. Scientific Discovery in the Renaissance: Text Pairs. 2008. (Bridges/Navigators Ser.). (J). (gr. 6). 89.00 *(978-1-4108-8448-0(1))* Benchmark Education Co.

Pocket Chart. (gr. -1-12). 26.27 *(978-0-7362-1100-0(4))* CENGAGE Learning.

Police Work. 2005. (Book Treks Ser.). (J). (gr. 3-18). stu. ed. 34.95 *(978-0-673-62839-8(6))* Celebration Pr.

Pollack, Pam & Belviso, Meg. Gallinas de Aqui para Alla. Adams, Lynn, illus. 2008. (Math Matters en Espanol Ser.). (SPA.). 32p. (J). (gr. -1-3). pap. 5.95 *(978-1-57565-268-9(4))* Astra Publishing Hse.

Popcorn: KinderFacts, 6 Packs. (Kinderstarters Ser.). 8p. (gr. -1-1). 21.00 *(978-0-7635-8747-5(8))* Rigby Education.

Popovic, Novak. Kayla Goes Camping: Practicing the Hard C & K Sound, 1 vol. 2016. (Rosen Phonics Readers Ser.). (ENG., Illus.). 8p. (J). (gr. -1-2). pap. *(978-1-5081-3083-3(3),* 4a8dd317-a6e4-41cf-a4b8-66fb20f3691a, Rosen Classroom) Rosen Publishing Group, Inc., The.

Popper, Lisa. Bunny Bop. 2004. (Illus.). (J). pap. *(978-0-9708947-0-0(8))* Northern Speech Services.

—Danny Dragon. 2004. (Illus.). 16p. (J). pap. *(978-0-9708947-6-2(7))* Northern Speech Services.

—Hanna Hippo. 2004. (Illus.). 16p. (J). pap. *(978-0-9708947-5-5(9))* Northern Speech Services.

—Len & Lil. 2004. (J). pap. *(978-0-9761967-2-3(7))* Northern Speech Services.

—Let' Make Music. 2004. (J). pap. *(978-0-9761967-1-6(9))* Northern Speech Services.

—My Rad Dad. 2005. (ENG.). (J). pap. 69.00 *(978-0-9765497-2-7(7))* Northern Speech Services.

—Nifty Noodle. 2004. (Illus.). 16p. (J). pap. *(978-0-9708947-4-8(0))* Northern Speech Services.

—Patty the Pink Pig. 2004. (J). pap. *(978-0-9761967-0-9(0))* Northern Speech Services.

—Rat Rap. 2004. 16p. (J). pap. *(978-0-9708947-9-3(1))* Northern Speech Services.

—Sammy. 2004. 16p. (J). pap. *(978-0-9708947-8-6(3))* Northern Speech Services.

—Timmy Turtle. 2004. 16p. (J). pap. *(978-0-9708947-7-9(5))* Northern Speech Services.

Posada, Jorge. Sí, Puedes (Play Ball!) ón, Raúl, illus. 2010. (SPA.). 32p. (J). (gr. 1-5). 8.99 *(978-1-4169-9826-6(8),* Simon & Schuster/Paula Wiseman Bks.) Simon & Schuster/Paula Wiseman Bks.

Posner-Sanchez, Andrea. Hello, Olaf! 2015. (Disney Princess Step into Reading Ser.). lib. bdg. 14.75 *(978-0-606-36663-2(6))* Turtleback.

Povey, Jeff. Shift. 2017. (ENG.). 368p. (J). pap. 9.99 *(978-1-4711-1868-5(1),* Simon & Schuster Children's) Simon & Schuster, Ltd. GBR. Dist: Simon & Schuster, Inc.

Powell, Jillian. The First World War: Band 11 Lime/Band 16 Sapphire (Collins Big Cat Progress) 2014. (Collins Big Cat Progress Ser.). (ENG., Illus.). 32p. (J). (gr. 4-5). pap. 11.99 *(978-0-00-751936-1(2))* HarperCollins Pubs. Ltd. GBR. Dist: Independent Pubs. Group.

—Olympic Heroes: Band 05/Green (Collins Big Cat) 2012. (Collins Big Cat Ser.). (ENG., Illus.). 24p. (J). (gr. k-1). pap. 8.99 *(978-0-00-746190-5(9))* HarperCollins Pubs. Ltd. GBR. Dist: Independent Pubs. Group.

—War Art: Band 10 White/Band 17 Diamond (Collins Big Cat Progress) 2014. (Collins Big Cat Progress Ser.). (ENG., Illus.). 32p. (J). (gr. 5-6). pap. 9.99 *(978-0-00-751930-9(3))* HarperCollins Pubs. Ltd. GBR. Dist: Independent Pubs. Group.

Powell, Marie. Sleep, Sheep! 2013. (Word Families Ser.). (ENG.). 16p. (J). (gr. k-2). lib. bdg. 25.65 *(978-1-60753-517-1(3),* 16233) Amicus.

Power Out. (Early Intervention Levels Ser.). 21.42 *(978-0-7362-1056-0(3))* CENGAGE Learning.

Power Reading, 26 vols. 2003. (Illus.). (gr. k-9). vinyl bd. incl. audio *(978-1-883186-37-1(4),* PPS 25); vinyl bd. incl. audio *(978-1-883186-35-7(8),* PPS 25) National Reading Styles Institute, Inc.

Power Reading: Power PAK. 2005. (Illus.). 80p. (J). (gr. 2-4). vinyl bd. 129.95 *(978-1-883186-73-9(0),* PPMX2-3); (gr. 4-5). vinyl bd. 129.95 *(978-1-883186-72-2(2),* PPMX4-5) National Reading Styles Institute, Inc.

Power Reading: Power PAK 4C. 2005. (Illus.). 80p. (J). (gr. 4-5). vinyl bd. 129.95 *(978-1-883186-70-8(6),* PPO4C) National Reading Styles Institute, Inc.

Pre-K Literacy Library. 2003. 430.50 *(978-0-7652-2478-1(X))* Modern Curriculum Pr.

Preece, Phil. Nightmare Park. 2004. (Shades Ser.). 52p. (J). pap. *(978-0-237-52730-3(8))* Evans Brothers, Ltd.

Prentice-Hall Staff. Bridge to Terabithia. 2nd ed. (J). stu. ed. *(978-0-13-717109-5(9))* Prentice Hall (Schl. Div.).

Prereading Activities (K) 2003. (J). *(978-1-58232-045-8(4))* ECS Learning Systems, Inc.

Preschool Books 800083, 10. 2005. (J). bds. *(978-1-59794-001-6(1))* Environments, Inc.

PRESS, Celebration. America's Secret Weapon: The Navajo Code Talkers of World War II. 2003. (ENG.). (J). (gr. 6-8). pap. 37.95 *(978-0-7652-3246-5(4),* Celebration Pr.) Savvas Learning Co.

—Blast Zone: The Eruption & Recovery of Mount St. Helens. 2003. (ENG.). (J). (gr. 6-8). pap. 37.95 *(978-0-7652-3245-8(6),* Celebration Pr.) Savvas Learning Co.

—The Case of the Missing Planet. 2003. (ENG.). (J). (gr. 2-5). pap., stu. ed. 34.95 *(978-0-673-62845-9(0),* Celebration Pr.) Savvas Learning Co.

—Communicating with Animals. 2003. (ENG.). (J). (gr. 6-8). pap. 37.95 *(978-0-7652-3247-2(2),* Celebration Pr.) Savvas Learning Co.

—Hanging Around Bats. 2003. (ENG.). (J). (gr. 2-5). pap., stu. ed. 34.95 *(978-0-673-62834-3(5),* Celebration Pr.) Savvas Learning Co.

—The Hot Shots. 2003. (ENG.). (J). (gr. 6-8). pap. 37.95 *(978-0-7652-3257-1(X),* Celebration Pr.) Savvas Learning Co.

—Hunting Crocodiles with Steve Irwin. 2003. (ENG.). (J). (gr. 2-5). pap., stu. ed. 34.95 *(978-0-673-62080-4(8),* Celebration Pr.) Savvas Learning Co.

—Iopeners: Science Library, 10 vols. 2004. (ENG.). (J). (gr. k-k). 220.95 *(978-0-7652-4970-8(7),* Celebration Pr.) Savvas Learning Co.

—Iopeners: Social Studies Library, 10 vols. 2004. (ENG.). (J). (gr. k-k). 220.95 *(978-0-7652-4971-5(5),* Celebration Pr.) Savvas Learning Co.

—Looking at Lizards. 2003. (ENG.). (J). (gr. 2-5). pap., stu. ed. 34.95 *(978-0-673-62835-0(3),* Celebration Pr.) Savvas Learning Co.

—Remarkable Robots. 2003. (ENG.). (J). (gr. 6-8). pap. 37.95 *(978-0-7652-3243-4(X),* Celebration Pr.) Savvas Learning Co.

—The Renaissance Kids. 2003. (ENG.). (J). (gr. 6-8). pap. 37.95 *(978-0-7652-3255-7(3),* Celebration Pr.) Savvas Learning Co.

—Scream Machines: All about Roller Coasters. 2003. (ENG.). (J). (gr. 6-8). pap. 37.95 *(978-0-7652-3244-1(8),* Celebration Pr.) Savvas Learning Co.

PRESS, Modern Curriculum. Sing, Spell, Read & Write Summer School Intervention Kit: Level 1 Student Pack. 2003. (ENG.). (J). (gr. 1-1). 32.95 *(978-0-7652-3233-5(2),* Modern Curriculum Pr.) Savvas Learning Co.

—Sing, Spell, Read & Write Summer School Intervention Kit: Off We Go. 2003. (ENG.). (J). (gr. 1-1). pap., stu. ed. 12.00 net. *(978-0-7652-3173-4(5),* Modern Curriculum Pr.) Savvas Learning Co.

—Sing, Spell, Read & Write Summer School Intervention Kit: Raceway. 2003. (ENG.). (J). (gr. 1-1). pap., stu. ed. 12.95 *(978-0-7652-3174-1(3),* Modern Curriculum Pr.) Savvas Learning Co.

Price, Sean Stewart & Price, Sean. Attila the Hun: Leader of the Barbarian Hordes. 2009. (Wicked History Ser.). (ENG.). 128p. (J). (gr. 6-12). pap. 5.95 *(978-0-531-20737-6(4),* Watts, Franklin) Scholastic Library Publishing.

Prime Time History, 8 vols., Set. Incl. Crusades: The Two Hundred Years War: The Clash Between the Cross & the Crescent in the Middle East 1096-1291. Harpur, James. lib. bdg. 47.80 *(978-1-4042-1367-8(8),* 9edd92ea-e696-4347-a122-d328e63ac647); Troy: The Myth & Reality Behind the Epic Legend. McCarty, Nick. lib. bdg. 47.80 *(978-1-4042-1365-4(1),* 32d3a0e1-a289-4c81-b3fa-931fedea771a); (Illus.). 128p. (YA). (gr. 10-10). 2008. (Prime Time History Ser.). (ENG.). 2007. Set lib. bdg. 191.20 *(978-1-4042-1487-3(9),* c9596d6a-60e4-4415-aafc-90acf4f3dcb6) Rosen Publishing Group, Inc., The.

Prior, Jennifer. All Aboard! How Trains Work, 1 vol. 2nd rev. ed. 2011. (TIME for KIDS(r): Informational Text Ser.). (ENG.). 28p. (gr. 3-4). pap. 11.99 *(978-1-4333-3656-0(1))* Teacher Created Materials, Inc.

—The Digestive System, 1 vol. 2nd rev. ed. 2012. (TIME for KIDS(r): Informational Text Ser.). (ENG.). 32p. (gr. 3-5). pap. 12.99 *(978-1-4333-3677-5(4))* Teacher Created Materials, Inc.

—The Five Senses, 1 vol. 2nd rev. ed. 2012. (TIME for KIDS(r): Informational Text Ser.). (ENG.). 32p. (gr. 3-5). pap. 12.99 *(978-1-4333-3676-8(6))* Teacher Created Materials, Inc.

—The Human Life Cycle, 1 vol. 2nd rev. ed. 2012. (TIME for KIDS(r): Informational Text Ser.). (ENG.). 32p. (gr. 3-5). pap. 12.99 *(978-1-4333-3678-2(2))* Teacher Created Materials, Inc.

—Take Off! All about Airplanes, 1 vol. 2nd rev. ed. 2011. (TIME for KIDS(r): Informational Text Ser.). (ENG.). 28p. (gr. 3-4). pap. 11.99 *(978-1-4333-3655-3(3))* Teacher Created Materials, Inc.

—Zoom! How Cars Move, 1 vol. 2nd rev. ed. 2011. (TIME for KIDS(r): Informational Text Ser.). (ENG.). 28p. (gr. 3-4). pap. 11.99 *(978-1-4333-3657-7(X))* Teacher Created Materials, Inc.

Pritchard, Gabby. The Great Inventor. Gallego, Pablo, illus. 2016. (Cambridge Reading Adventures Ser.). (ENG.). 16p. pap. 7.95 *(978-1-316-50083-5(7))* Cambridge Univ. Pr.

—The Great Jewelled Egg Mystery Turquoise Band. Franco, Paula, illus. 2016. (Cambridge Reading Adventures Ser.). (ENG.). 16p. pap. 7.95 *(978-1-107-57614-8(8))* Cambridge Univ. Pr.

—Help! Yellow Band. Stuart, Jon, illus. 2017. (Cambridge Reading Adventures Ser.). (ENG.). 16p. pap. 6.15 *(978-1-108-40815-8(X))* Cambridge Univ. Pr.

—Look! It's Baby Duck Red Band. Boden, Lucy, illus. 2016. (Cambridge Reading Adventures Ser.). (ENG.). 16p. pap. 7.95 *(978-1-107-54957-9(4))* Cambridge Univ. Pr.

—Lost! Blue Band. Stuart, Jon, illus. 2016. (Cambridge Reading Adventures Ser.). (ENG.). 16p. pap. 7.95 *(978-1-316-60078-8(5))* Cambridge Univ. Pr.

—Omar in Trouble Orange Band. Pérez, Moni, illus. 2016. (Cambridge Reading Adventures Ser.). (ENG.). 16p. pap. 7.95 *(978-1-316-50329-4(1))* Cambridge Univ. Pr.

—Our Den. Girasole, Alessia, illus. 2016. (Cambridge Reading Adventures Ser.). (ENG.). 16p. pap. 7.95 *(978-1-316-50078-1(0))* Cambridge Univ. Pr.

—Turtle Is a Hero Green Band. Di Baldo, Fabrizio, illus. 2016. (Cambridge Reading Adventures Ser.). (ENG.). 16p. pap. 7.95 *(978-1-107-55046-9(7))* Cambridge Univ. Pr.

Prue, Sally. Big Bad Troll. Woodward, Jonathan, illus. 2016. (Reading Ladder Level 2 Ser.). (ENG.). 48p. (gr. k-2). pap. 4.99 *(978-1-4052-7825-6(0),* Reading Ladder) Farshore GBR. Dist: HarperCollins Pubs.

Publications International Ltd. Staff, ed. Baby Einstein. 2007. (J). 10.98 *(978-1-4127-7467-3(5))* Publications International, Ltd.

—Disney Pixar Cars: Cuentos de Miedo (Little English Spanish Sound Book) 2011. 12p. (J). bds. 10.98 *(978-1-4508-1401-0(8))* Phoenix International Publications, Inc.

—Disney Pixar Cars 2 - World Tour. 2011. 14p. (J). 17.98 *(978-1-4508-1473-7(5))* Phoenix International Publications, Inc.

—Disney Pixar Cars 2 (Look & Find Soft Cover) 2011. 20p. (J). pap. 5.98 *(978-1-4508-1457-7(3))* Publications International, Ltd.

—Disney Pixar Cars 2 Play-a-Sound Book. 2011. 24p. (J). 12.98 *(978-1-4508-0569-8(8))* Phoenix International Publications, Inc.

—Disney Pixar Cars Story Reader 2. 0 Unit. 2011. (J). 30.98 *(978-1-4508-0588-9(4))* Publications International, Ltd.

—Disney Princess Storybook & Magic Bracelet. 2010. 12p. (J). bds. 12.98 *(978-1-4127-9912-6(0))* Phoenix International Publications, Inc.

—Early Learning: My First Library. 2010. 10p. (J). bds. *(978-0-7853-7919-5(3),* 0785379193) Phoenix International Publications, Inc.

—Handy Manny: Fiesta Fun. 2008. (J). bds. 10.98 *(978-1-4127-8867-0(6))* Publications International, Ltd.

—Padded Treasury 160 Spa Sesame Street. 2009. 160p. 12.98 *(978-1-4127-9548-7(6))* Phoenix International Publications, Inc.

—Ring-a-Ling! A Friend Is Here. 2010. 12p. (J). 9.98 *(978-1-4127-7939-5(1))* Phoenix International Publications, Inc.

Publishers, Chelsea House, creator. Scientific American Set. 2007. (Scientific American Ser.). (ENG.). (gr. 5-8). 240.00 *(978-0-7910-9811-0(7),* P179192, Facts On File) Infobase Holdings, Inc.

PuffFlashBang! (Lexile Levels Ser.). 9.09 *(978-1-56334-703-0(2))* CENGAGE Learning.

Pug & Chug: Set C Individual Title Six-Packs. (Supersonic Phonics Ser.). (gr. k-3). 29.00 *(978-0-7635-0544-8(7))* Rigby Education.

Pugliano-Martin, Carol. The Earth on Turtle's Back: Set Of 6. 2011. (Early Connections Ser.). (J). pap. 39.00 net. *(978-1-4108-1555-2(2))* Benchmark Education Co.

—Why Spiders Have Small Waists. 2004. (Shared Connections Ser.). (J). pap. *(978-1-4108-1645-0(1))*; instr.'s gde. ed. 27.00 *(978-1-4108-1621-4(4))* Benchmark Education Co.

Pugliano-Martin, Carol; Flounders. The Day I Followed the Pickle. Flounders, Anne, ed. 2004. (Reader's Theater Content-Area Concepts Ser.). (ENG., Illus.). (J). (gr. 1-2). 5.00 net. *(978-1-4108-2297-0(4),* A22974) Benchmark Education Co.

Pulford, Elizabeth. Billy Brown's Cat. Brown, Daniel, illus. 2012. (Engage Literacy Green Ser.). (ENG.). 16p. (J). (gr. k-2). pap. 36.94 *(978-1-4296-8846-8(7),* 18318, Capstone Pr.) Capstone.

Punter, Russell. Cow Takes a Bow. Blunt, Fred, illus. 2014. (Usborne Phonics Readers Ser.). (ENG.). (J). pap. 6.99 *(978-0-7945-3368-7(X),* Usborne) EDC Publishing.

—Flamingo Plays Bingo. 2019. (Phonics Readers Ser.). (ENG.). 24ppp. (J). pap. 6.99 *(978-0-7945-4396-9(0),* Usborne) EDC Publishing.

—Underpants for Ants. Blunt, Fred, illus. 2014. (Usborne Phonics Readers Ser.). (ENG.). (J). (gr. -1-3). pap. 6.99 *(978-0-7945-3396-0(5),* Usborne) EDC Publishing.

Punter, Russell & MacKinnon, Mairi. Snail Brings the Mail. Blunt, Fred, illus. 2014. (Usborne Phonics Readers Ser.). (ENG.). (J). pap. 6.99 *(978-0-7945-3369-4(8),* Usborne) EDC Publishing.

Purcell, Susan. Goldilocks, 1 vol. 2017. (Fairy-Tale Phonics Ser.). (ENG.). 24p. (J). (gr. 1-1). 26.27 *(978-1-5081-9376-0(2),* c4669a1e-c0e2-49cb-83c1-22b5fdf64649); pap. 9.25 *(978-1-5081-9447-7(5),* a562a763-aaad-476d-a9fd-706d9e57e7fe) Rosen Publishing Group, Inc., The. (Windmill Bks.).

—Little Red Riding Hood, 1 vol. 2017. (Fairy-Tale Phonics Ser.). (ENG.). 24p. (J). (gr. 1-1). 26.27 *(978-1-5081-9375-3(4),* 8ecf9731-429c-434e-9e59-3e09ce9a69ac); pap. 9.25 *(978-1-5081-9448-4(3),* c5bfcf88-df26-49c8-b0bd-84de406096af) Rosen Publishing Group, Inc., The. (Windmill Bks.).

—The Three Little Pigs, 1 vol. 2017. (Fairy-Tale Phonics Ser.). (ENG.). 24p. (J). (gr. 1-1). 26.27 *(978-1-5081-9379-1(7),* 895101ac-e033-4385-82e6-eb9b17ce69c5); pap. 9.25 *(978-1-5081-9451-4(3),* 0ef23af7-2a6b-45a3-85dd-9fda8b9e3233) Rosen Publishing Group, Inc., The. (Windmill Bks.).

Puri, Devi. Sydney Works at the School Store. 2013. (InfoMax Readers Ser.). (ENG.). 24p. (J). (gr. 3-4). pap. 49.50 *(978-1-4777-2589-4(X))*; (Illus.). pap. 8.25 *(978-1-4777-2588-7(1),* 88ee724f-dc1f-4e9b-b26c-fa5f74084891) Rosen Publishing Group, Inc., The. (Rosen Classroom).

Purple & Gold Levels Certificate Only. (gr. k-5). 89.00 *(978-0-7578-6541-1(0))* Rigby Education.

Pyers. Sail Main5 Monkeys, Diverse Animals. 2003. (Rigby Sails Ser.). (ENG.). 32p. (gr. 5-5). pap. 10.20 *(978-0-7578-8019-3(3))* Rigby Education.

Pym, Tasha. Have You Ever?: Band 02A/Red a (Collins Big Cat) Elworthy, Antony, illus. 2007. (Collins Big Cat Ser.). (ENG.). 24p. (J). (gr. -1-k). pap. 7.99 *(978-0-00-718654-9(1))* HarperCollins Pubs. Ltd. GBR. Dist: Independent Pubs. Group.

—Monster Mess: Band 01B/Pink B (Collins Big Cat) Villet, Olivia, illus. 2007. (Collins Big Cat Ser.). (ENG.). 16p. (J). (gr. -1-k). pap. 7.99 *(978-0-00-718650-1(9))* HarperCollins Pubs. Ltd. GBR. Dist: Independent Pubs. Group.

—Super Sculptures: Band 05/Green (Collins Big Cat) 2006. (Collins Big Cat Ser.). (ENG., Illus.). 24p. (J). (gr. 1-1). pap. 8.99 *(978-0-00-718686-0(X))* HarperCollins Pubs. Ltd. GBR. Dist: Independent Pubs. Group.

QEB Start Reading & Writing National Book Stores Edition: Little Red Riding Hood. 2006. (J). per. *(978-1-59566-267-5(7))* QEB Publishing Inc.

QEB Start Reading Set. 2006. (J). per. *(978-1-59566-334-4(7))* QEB Publishing Inc.

Quality Time Easy Readers, 5 bks. (Illus.). (J). lib. bdg. 64.75 *(978-1-56674-925-1(5))* Forest Hse. Publishing Co., Inc.

Quan-D'Eramo, Sandra. The 10 Best TV Game Shows. 2008. 14.99 *(978-1-55448-494-2(4))* Scholastic Library Publishing.

—The 10 Most Amazing Animated Movies. 2007. (J). 14.99 *(978-1-55448-513-0(4))* Scholastic Library Publishing.

Quasar Kids. (J). (gr. 3-5). 75.00 *(978-0-669-13453-7(8))* Houghton Mifflin Harcourt School Pubs.

Queen of the Bean: Individual Title Six-Packs. (Action Packs Ser.). 104p. (gr. 3-5). 44.00 *(978-0-7635-2983-3(4))* Rigby Education.

Quible, Rennie G. Upepo the Rainmaker. 2008. 44p. pap. 17.49 *(978-1-4363-8454-4(0))* Xlibris Corp.

Quick & Quiet. (Early Intervention Levels Ser.). 21.30 *(978-0-7362-0376-0(1))*; Vol. 3. 3.55 *(978-0-7362-0097-4(5))* CENGAGE Learning.

Quintana, Juan. Avenues C (Leveled Books): Farmer's Market. 2003. (Rise & Shine Ser.). (ENG.). 8p. (C). pap. 9.95 *(978-0-7362-1898-6(X))* CENGAGE Learning.

Qusar Kids. (J). (gr. 3-5). pap. 9.90 *(978-0-669-15294-4(3))* Houghton Mifflin Harcourt School Pubs.

Rabe, Tish. Big Snowman, Little Snowman (Disney Frozen) RH Disney, illus. 2013. (Step into Reading Ser.). (ENG.). 32p. (J). (gr. -1-1). 5.99 *(978-0-7364-3119-4(5),* RH/Disney) Random Hse. Children's Bks.

—Have No Fear! Halloween Is Here! (Dr. Seuss/the Cat in the Hat Knows a Lot About. Brannon, Tom, illus. 2016. (Step into Reading Ser.). (ENG.). 24p. (J). (gr. -1-1). 5.99 *(978-1-101-93492-0(1),* Random Hse. Bks. for Young Readers) Random Hse. Children's Bks.

—Innovative Kids Readers: Milly's Silly Suitcase - Level 1. Janovitz, Marilyn, illus. 2006. (J). (gr. -1-1). 6.99 *(978-1-58476-493-9(7))* Innovative Kids.

Rabley, Stephen. Danny's Blog/El Blog de Daniel. Martin, Rosa Maria, tr. Ursell, Martin, illus. 2008. (Let's Read! Spanish-English Ser.).Tr. of El Blog de Daniel. (ENG.). 30p. (J). (gr. k-3). 17.44 *(978-0-7641-4047-1(7),* B.E.S. Publishing) Peterson's.

—Easystart: Maisie & the Dolphin. 2nd ed. 2008. (Pearson English Graded Readers Ser.). (ENG.). 20p. pap. 11.99 *(978-1-4058-6954-6(2),* Pearson ELT) Pearson Education.

—Easystart: Marcel & the Mona Lisa Book & MP3 Pack: Industrial Ecology, Pack. 2nd ed. 2008. (ENG., Illus.). 99999p. pap., pap. 14.65 incl. cd-rom *(978-1-4058-8064-0(3))* Pearson Education.

—The Red Rock/le Rocher Rouge: French/English Edition. Ursell, Martin, illus. 2009. (Let's Read! Bks.). (ENG.). 32p. (gr. 3-7). pap. 4.99 *(978-0-7641-4360-1(3))* Sourcebooks, Inc.

—Red Rock/Roca Roja. Rabley, Stephen & Ursell, Martin, illus. 2009. (Let's Read! Spanish-English Ser.). (ENG.). 32p. (J). (gr. k-3). 17.44 *(978-0-7641-4361-8(1),* B.E.S. Publishing) Peterson's.

Raby, Charlotte. Collins Big Cat Phonics for Letters & Sounds - Pat It: Band 01A/Pink A, Bd. 1A. Blake, Beccy, illus. 2018. (Collins Big Cat Phonics Ser.). (ENG.). 16p. (J). (gr. -1-k). pap. 6.99 *(978-0-00-825129-1(0))* HarperCollins Pubs. Ltd. GBR. Dist: Independent Pubs. Group.

—Collins Big Cat Phonics for Letters & Sounds - Pit Pat: Band 01A/Pink A, Bd. 1A. 2018. (Collins Big Cat Phonics Ser.). (ENG., Illus.). 16p. (J). (gr. -1-k). pap. 6.99 *(978-0-00-825130-7(4))* HarperCollins Pubs. Ltd. GBR. Dist: Independent Pubs. Group.

—Collins Big Cat Phonics for Letters & Sounds - the Dragon King's Daughter: Band 07/Turquoise, Bd. 7. Fusi, Alessandra, illus. 2018. (Collins Big Cat Phonics Ser.). (ENG.). 16p. (J). pap. 6.99 *(978-0-00-825153-6(3))* HarperCollins Pubs. Ltd. GBR. Dist: Independent Pubs. Group.

The Race: Individual Title Six-Packs. (gr. 1-2). 22.00 *(978-0-7635-9165-6(3))* Rigby Education.

Radlauer, Edward. More Readers, 3 bks. (Illus.). (J). (gr. -1-4). lib. bdg. 38.85 *(978-1-56674-922-0(0))* Forest Hse. Publishing Co., Inc.

Ragbag: Set A Individual Title Six-Packs. (Supersonic Phonics Ser.). (gr. k-3). 29.00 *(978-0-7635-0529-5(3))* Rigby Education.

Rainbow Fish Readers 800884, 4 vols. 2005. (J). pap. *(978-1-59794-059-7(3))* Environments, Inc.
Raise a Reader: Language Learning System Level 1. 2006. (SPA.). (J). bds. incl. DVD *(978-0-9785744-0-6(0))* LTL Media LLC.
Rajan, Lisa. Tara Binns: High-Flying Pilot: Band 12/Copper (Collins Big Cat) 2019. (Collins Big Cat Tara Binns Ser.). (ENG., Illus.). 32p. (J). (gr. 2-3). pap. 10.99 *(978-0-00-830656-4(7))* HarperCollins Pubs. Ltd. GBR. Dist: Independent Pubs. Group.
Ralphs, Matt. Space Jump: Band 11 Lime/Band 17 Diamond (Collins Big Cat Progress) 2014. (Collins Big Cat Progress Ser.). (ENG., Illus.). 32p. (J). (gr. 5-6). pap. 10.99 *(978-0-00-751938-5(9))* HarperCollins Pubs. Ltd. GBR. Dist: Independent Pubs. Group.
Ramirez, Iz. Bob the Lizard, 1 vol. Swope, Brenda, illus. 2009. 26p. pap. 24.95 *(978-1-60749-232-0(6))* America Star Bks.
Ramirez, Lasean. Jamal's Wagon, 1 vol. 2016. (Rosen REAL Readers: STEM & STEAM Collection). (ENG.). 8p. (gr. k-1). pap. 5.46 *(978-1-5081-2580-8(5),* c137e669-9919-4c69-8d74-054de5fb11a8, Rosen Classroom) Rosen Publishing Group, Inc., The.
Randolph, Joanne. Electricity in My World, 1 vol. 2006. (Journeys Ser.). (ENG.). 24p. (gr. k-2). pap. 7.05 *(978-1-4042-8418-0(4),* daa15061-dc6f-410e-8b4b-ea2f90ea136e, Rosen Classroom) Rosen Publishing Group, Inc., The.
—Let's Draw a Butterfly with Circles. 2009. (Let's Draw with Shapes Ser.). 24p. (gr. k-k). 42.50 *(978-1-61514-204-0(5),* PowerKids Pr.) Rosen Publishing Group, Inc., The.
—Let's Draw a Horse with Rectangles. 2009. (Let's Draw with Shapes Ser.). 24p. (gr. k-k). 42.50 *(978-1-61514-209-5(6),* PowerKids Pr.) Rosen Publishing Group, Inc., The.
—Let's Draw a Truck with Shapes. 2009. (Let's Draw with Shapes Ser.). 24p. (gr. k-k). 42.50 *(978-1-61514-212-5(6),* PowerKids Pr.) Rosen Publishing Group, Inc., The.
Random House. Mission PAW (PAW Patrol) Lovett, Nate, illus. 2017. (Step into Reading Ser.). (ENG.). 24p. (J). (gr. -1-1). pap. 4.99 *(978-1-5247-6413-5(2),* Random Hse. Bks. for Young Readers) Random Hse. Children's Bks.
—You Can Be a Soccer Player. 2018. (Barbie Step into Reading Level 2 Ser.). lib. bdg. 14.75 *(978-0-606-40927-8(0))* Turtleback.
Random House, illus. Fairytale Collection (Barbie) 2011. (Step into Reading Ser.). (ENG.). 160p. (J). (gr. -1-1). pap. 8.99 *(978-0-375-87255-6(8),* Random Hse. Bks. for Young Readers) Random Hse. Children's Bks.
—Five Puptacular Tales! (PAW Patrol) 2016. (Step into Reading Ser.). (ENG.). 144p. (J). (gr. -1-1). 7.99 *(978-0-399-55300-4(2),* Random Hse. Bks. for Young Readers) Random Hse. Children's Bks.
Rao, Lisa. Iron Man: I Am Iron Man! Guidi, Guido, illus. 2008. (I Can Read Bks.). 32p. (J). (gr. -1-2). pap. 3.99 *(978-0-06-082193-7(0),* Harper Trophy) HarperCollins Pubs.
Rasinski, Timothy V. Daily Word Ladders: Grades 2-3. 2005. (Daily Word Ladders Ser.). (ENG., Illus.). 112p. (gr. 2-3). pap. 15.99 *(978-0-439-51383-8(9),* Teaching Resources) Scholastic, Inc.
Ratcliff, Charline. The Princess, the Toad & the Whale. 2012. (ENG.). 36p. (J). (-18). pap. 12.95 *(978-1-4787-1672-3(X))* Outskirts Pr., Inc.
Rau, Dana Meachen. Neil Armstrong. 2014. (Rookie Biographies(r) Ser.). (ENG.). 32p. (J). lib. bdg. 23.00 *(978-0-531-21063-5(4))* Scholastic Library Publishing.
Raum, Elizabeth & Collins, Terry. You Choose: Historical Eras. 2012. (You Choose: Historical Eras Ser.). (ENG.). 112p. (gr. 3-4). pap. 333.60 *(978-1-4296-9477-3(7),* Capstone Pr.) Capstone.
Ray, Hannah. The Great Big Friend Hunt. 2004. (QEB Start Reading Ser.). (Illus.). 24p. (J). lib. bdg. 15.95 *(978-1-59566-012-1(7))* QEB Publishing Inc.
—Katie's Mom Is a Mermaid, 4 vols. 2005. (QEB Readers). (Illus.). 24p. (J). (gr. -1-3). lib. bdg. 15.95 *(978-1-59566-101-2(8))* QEB Publishing Inc.
Ray, Liz. One Land, Many Cultures, 6 vols., Set. 2004. (Phonics Readers Books 37-72 Ser.). (ENG.). 8p. (gr. k-1). pap. 35.70 *(978-0-7368-4079-8(6))* Capstone.
Ray, Nan. Meet the People. 2004. 66p. (J). per. 8.95 *(978-0-9760280-0-0(X))* You're On!, Inc.
Rayner, Shoo. The Big, Bad City: Band 07/Turquoise. Rayner, Shoo, illus. 2015. (Collins Big Cat Ser.). (ENG., Illus.). 24p. (J). (gr. 2-2). pap. 8.99 *(978-0-00-759109-1(8))* HarperCollins Pubs. Ltd. GBR. Dist: Independent Pubs. Group.
—Cat & Dog Play Hide & Seek. 2005. (Big Cat Ser.). (gr. k-2). pap. 6.50 *(978-1-60457-014-4(8))* Pacific Learning, Inc.
—Cat & Dog Play Hide & Seek Workbook. Moon, Cliff, ed. 2012. (Collins Big Cat Ser.). (ENG.). 24p. (J). (gr. -1-k). pap., wbk. ed. 5.99 *(978-0-00-747432-5(6))* HarperCollins Pubs. Ltd. GBR. Dist: Independent Pubs. Group.
—Collins Big Cat Phonics for Letters & Sounds - Nibble, Nosh & Gnasher: Band 07/Turquoise. Rayner, Shoo, illus. 2018. (Collins Big Cat Phonics Ser.). (ENG., Illus.). 24p. (J). (gr. 1-2). pap. 8.99 *(978-0-00-825179-6(7))* HarperCollins Pubs. Ltd. GBR. Dist: Independent Pubs. Group.
Rayner, Shoo, illus. & concept. Cat & Dog Play Hide & Seek: Band 02A/Red a (Collins Big Cat) Rayner, Shoo, concept. 2006. (Collins Big Cat Ser.). (ENG.). 16p. (J). (gr. -1-k). pap. 7.99 *(978-0-00-718660-0(6))* HarperCollins Pubs. Ltd. GBR. Dist: Independent Pubs. Group.
Rea, Lynn. Tug of War, 1 vol. 2006. (Neighborhood Readers Ser.). (ENG.). 16p. (gr. 1-2). pap. 6.50 *(978-1-4042-7272-9(0),* 8a1bbdc8-e692-4d2a-aa62-174936fd1ca7, Rosen Classroom) Rosen Publishing Group, Inc., The.
Reach a (Read Together Student Books): Community Places. 2010. (Illus.). 8p. (C). pap. 8.95 *(978-0-7362-7993-2(8))* CENGAGE Learning.
Reach a (Read Together Student Books): Family Feelings. 2010. (Illus.). 8p. (C). pap. 8.95 *(978-0-7362-7986-4(5))* CENGAGE Learning.
Reach a (Read Together Student Books): Jobs in Our Community. 2010. (Illus.). 8p. (C). pap. 8.95 *(978-0-7362-7995-6(4))* CENGAGE Learning.
Reach a (Read Together Student Books): Let's Grow! 2010. (Illus.). 8p. (C). pap. 8.95 *(978-0-7362-7990-1(3))* CENGAGE Learning.
Reach a (Read Together Student Books): My Family. 2010. (Illus.). 8p. (C). pap. 8.95 *(978-0-7362-7985-7(7))* CENGAGE Learning.
Reach a (Read Together Student Books): School Places. 2010. (Illus.). 8p. (C). pap. 8.95 *(978-0-7362-7984-0(9))* CENGAGE Learning.
Reach a (Read Together Student Books): School Tools. 2010. (Illus.). 8p. (C). pap. 8.95 *(978-0-7362-7983-3(0))* CENGAGE Learning.
Reach a (Read Together Student Books): up in the Sky. 2010. (Illus.). 8p. (C). pap. 8.95 *(978-0-7362-7998-7(9))* CENGAGE Learning.
Reach a (Read Together Student Books): What Do You See? 2010. (Illus.). 8p. (C). pap. 8.95 *(978-0-7362-7997-0(0))* CENGAGE Learning.
Reach a (Read Together Student Books): What Will He Wear? 2010. (Illus.). 8p. (C). pap. 8.95 *(978-0-7362-7991-8(1))* CENGAGE Learning.
Reach a (Read Together Student Books): What Will I Be? 2010. (Illus.). 8p. (C). pap. 8.95 *(978-0-7362-7996-3(2))* CENGAGE Learning.
Reach a (Read Together Student Books): Where Is He? 2010. (Illus.). 8p. (C). pap. 8.95 *(978-0-7362-7994-9(6))* CENGAGE Learning.
Reaching Higher Additional Resources: English Books (55 Titles) (Reach for Reading Ser.). (gr. 3-5). 260.00 *(978-0-7635-3747-0(0))* Rigby Education.
Reaching Higher Additional Workstations: Without Books. (Reach for Reading Ser.). (gr. 3-5). 285.00 *(978-0-7578-6847-4(9))* Rigby Education.
Reaching up Additional Resources: English Books (75 Titles) (Reach for Reading Ser.). (gr. 1-3). 205.00 *(978-0-7635-3748-7(9))* Rigby Education.
Reaching up Additional Workstations: With Books. (Reach for Reading Ser.). (gr. 1-3). 390.00 *(978-0-7635-3698-5(9))* Rigby Education.
Reaching up Additional Workstations: Without Books. (Reach for Reading Ser.). (gr. 1-3). 285.00 *(978-0-7578-3536-0(8))* Rigby Education.
Read & Spell with Zoo-phonics. 2004. (J). cd-rom 29.95 *(978-1-886441-46-0(4))* Zoo-phonics, Inc.
Read & Spell with Zoo=Phonics Guide for CD-ROM. 2004. (J). 14.95 *(978-1-886441-45-3(6))* Zoo-phonics, Inc.
Read & Write. 2005. (J). pap. 3.99 *(978-1-933200-18-7(9))* Family Bks. at Home.
Read-at-Home Book, Books 1-36. (Phonics Readers Ser.). (gr. k-2). 29.95 *(978-0-7368-3239-7(4),* Red Brick Learning) Capstone.
Read-at-Home Book, Books 37-72. (Phonics Readers Ser.). (gr. k-2). 29.95 *(978-0-7368-4089-7(3),* Red Brick Learning) Capstone.
Read-It! Chapter Books - Swat, 8 bks., Set. 2006. (Read-It! Chapter Books: SWAT Ser.). (ENG.). (gr. 2-4). 149.24 *(978-1-4048-1710-4(7),* Picture Window Bks.) Capstone.
Read-It! Readers. 2005. (Read-It! Readers: Gus the Hedgehog Ser.). (ENG.). 32p. (gr. k-3). 99.95 *(978-1-4048-1526-1(0));* (Illus.). 100.61 *(978-1-4048-0998-7(8))* Capstone. (Picture Window Bks.).
Read-It! Readers - Gus the Hedgehog. 2005. (Read-It! Readers: Gus the Hedgehog Ser.). (ENG., Illus.). 32p. (gr. k-3). 79.96 *(978-1-4048-0995-6(3),* Picture Window Bks.) Capstone.
Read It! Readers: Folk Tales, 6 vols. 2005. (Read-It! Readers: Folk Tales Ser.). (ENG., Illus.). 32p. (gr. k-3). 59.97 *(978-1-4048-0999-4(6),* Picture Window Bks.) Capstone.
Read, Lorna. The Lies They Tell. Date not set. (Sky Bks.). 232p. pap. 54.75 *(978-0-582-08109-3(2))* Addison-Wesley Longman, Ltd. GBR. Dist: Trans-Atlantic Pubns., Inc.
Read on Target Grade 4. 2005. (J). stu. ed., per. 10.95 *(978-1-59230-127-0(4))* Englefield & Assocs., Inc.
Read on Target Grade 5. 2006. (J). pap., stu. ed. 10.95 *(978-1-59230-155-3(X))* Englefield & Assocs., Inc.
Read on Target Grade 6. 2006. (J). stu. ed., per. 10.95 *(978-1-59230-153-9(3))* Englefield & Assocs., Inc.
Reading 2000 Leveled Readers C: Challenge, Bookshelf Collection, 5 units. 2004. (gr. 1-18). 82.50 *(978-0-328-00434-8(0));*Set. (gr. 3-18). 99.00 *(978-0-328-00436-2(7));*Set. (gr. 4-18). 99.00 *(978-0-328-00437-9(5),* Scott Foresman);Set. (gr. 5-18). 99.00 *(978-0-328-00438-6(3))* Addison-Wesley Educational Pubs., Inc.
Reading 2000 Trade Book Library Resource Guide. 2004. (Trade Book Library Resource Guide Ser.). (gr. 6-18). 48.00 *(978-0-673-63003-2(X))* Addison-Wesley Educational Pubs., Inc.
Reading 2002 Big Book Grade Level Package Grade 1.1, 3 bks., Set. 2004. (gr. 1-18). 109.15 *(978-0-328-02951-8(3))* Addison-Wesley Educational Pubs., Inc.
Reading 2002 Collection For Readers Bookshelf Collection. 2004. (gr. 5-18). 180.00 *(978-0-328-03137-5(2));*Units 1-6. (gr. 4-18). 180.00 *(978-0-328-03136-8(4))* Addison-Wesley Educational Pubs., Inc.
Reading 2002 Independent Reader Bookshelf Collection, 36 bks. 2004. (gr. k-18). 594.00 *(978-0-328-02901-3(7))* Addison-Wesley Educational Pubs., Inc.
Reading 2002 Kindergarten Reader Bookshelf Collection, 36 bks. 2004. (gr. k-18). 594.00 *(978-0-328-02903-7(3),* Scott Foresman) Addison-Wesley Educational Pubs., Inc.
Reading 2002 Wordless Story Bookshelf Collection, 36 bks. 2004. (gr. k-18). 594.00 *(978-0-328-02940-2(8))* Addison-Wesley Educational Pubs., Inc.
Reading 2004 Comprehensive Kindergarten Program 2004. 2004. (gr. k-18). *(978-0-328-05065-9(2),* Scott Foresman) Addison-Wesley Educational Pubs., Inc.
Reading 2004 Pupil Edition Grade 1.2. 2004. (gr. 1-18). stu. ed. *(978-0-328-03928-9(4),* Scott Foresman) Addison-Wesley Educational Pubs., Inc.
Reading 2004 Pupil Edition Grade 1.3. 2004. (gr. 1-18). *(978-0-328-03929-6(2),* Scott Foresman) Addison-Wesley Educational Pubs., Inc.
Reading 2004 Pupil Edition Grade 1.4. 2004. (gr. 1-18). *(978-0-328-03930-2(6),* Scott Foresman) Addison-Wesley Educational Pubs., Inc.
Reading 2004 Pupil Edition Grade 2.2. 2nd ed. 2004. (gr. 2-18). stu. ed. *(978-0-328-03934-0(9),* Scott Foresman) Addison-Wesley Educational Pubs., Inc.
Reading at Home: Easy Reading Combo. (gr. k-2). 145.50 *(978-1-56334-413-8(0))* CENGAGE Learning.
Reading at Home: Jumbo Pack. (gr. k-2). 1235.86 *(978-0-7362-1399-8(6))* CENGAGE Learning.
Reading at Home: Phonics Grade 1 Combo. (gr. 1-18). 517.92 *(978-0-7362-1401-8(1))* CENGAGE Learning.
Reading at Home: Sound & Letter Combo. (gr. k-2). 341.12 *(978-0-7362-1400-1(3))* CENGAGE Learning.
Reading Central Level a Kit with 4/C Readers. 2004. (Reading Central Ser.). (J). (gr. 1-18). 299.95 *(978-1-58830-855-9(3))* Metropolitan Teaching & Learning Co.
Reading Central Level a Kit with Paperbks. 2004. (Reading Central Ser.). (J). (gr. 1-18). 364.95 *(978-1-58830-861-0(8))* Metropolitan Teaching & Learning Co.
Reading Central Level a Sh. 2004. (Reading Central Ser.). (J). (gr. 1-18). per. 67.95 *(978-1-58830-168-0(0))* Metropolitan Teaching & Learning Co.
Reading Central Level a Student Handbook. 2004. (Reading Central Ser.). (J). (gr. 1-18). per. 7.95 *(978-1-58830-891-7(X))* Metropolitan Teaching & Learning Co.
Reading Central Level B Kit with 4/C Readers. 2004. (Reading Central Ser.). (J). (gr. 1-18). 299.95 *(978-1-58830-856-6(1))* Metropolitan Teaching & Learning Co.
Reading Central Level B Kit with Paperbks. 2004. (Reading Central Ser.). (J). (gr. 1-18). 364.95 *(978-1-58830-862-7(6))* Metropolitan Teaching & Learning Co.
Reading Central Level B Sh. 2004. (Reading Central Ser.). (J). (gr. 1-18). per. 67.95 *(978-1-58830-169-7(9))* Metropolitan Teaching & Learning Co.
Reading Central Level B Student Handbook. 2004. (Reading Central Ser.). (J). (gr. 1-18). per. 7.95 *(978-1-58830-892-4(8))* Metropolitan Teaching & Learning Co.
Reading Central Level C Kit with 4/C Readers. 2004. (Reading Central Ser.). (J). (gr. 1-18). 299.95 *(978-1-58830-857-3(X))* Metropolitan Teaching & Learning Co.
Reading Central Level C Kit with Paperbks. 2004. (Reading Central Ser.). (J). (gr. 1-18). 364.95 *(978-1-58830-863-4(4))* Metropolitan Teaching & Learning Co.
Reading Central Level C Sh. 2004. (Reading Central Ser.). (J). (gr. 1-18). per. 67.95 *(978-1-58830-192-5(3))* Metropolitan Teaching & Learning Co.
Reading Central Level C Student Handbook. 2004. (Reading Central Ser.). (J). (gr. 1-18). per. 7.95 *(978-1-58830-893-1(6))* Metropolitan Teaching & Learning Co.
Reading Central Level D Kit with 4/C Readers. 2004. (Reading Central Ser.). (J). (gr. 2-18). 299.95 *(978-1-58830-858-0(8))* Metropolitan Teaching & Learning Co.
Reading Central Level D Kit with Paperbks. 2004. (Reading Central Ser.). (J). (gr. 2-18). 369.95 *(978-1-58830-864-1(2))* Metropolitan Teaching & Learning Co.
Reading Central Level D Sh. 2004. (Reading Central Ser.). (J). (gr. 2-18). per. 67.95 *(978-1-58830-193-2(1))* Metropolitan Teaching & Learning Co.
Reading Central Level D Student Handbook. 2004. (Reading Central Ser.). (J). (gr. 2-18). per. 7.95 *(978-1-58830-894-8(4))* Metropolitan Teaching & Learning Co.
Reading Central Level E Kit with 4/C Readers. 2004. (Reading Central Ser.). (J). (gr. 2-18). 299.95 *(978-1-58830-859-7(6))* Metropolitan Teaching & Learning Co.
Reading Central Level E Kit with Paperbks. 2004. (Reading Central Ser.). (J). (gr. 2-18). 369.95 *(978-1-58830-865-8(0))* Metropolitan Teaching & Learning Co.
Reading Central Level E Sh. 2004. (Reading Central Ser.). (J). (gr. 2-18). per. 67.95 *(978-1-58830-194-9(X))* Metropolitan Teaching & Learning Co.
Reading Central Level E Student Handbook. 2004. (Reading Central Ser.). (J). (gr. 2-18). per. 7.95 *(978-1-58830-895-5(2))* Metropolitan Teaching & Learning Co.
Reading Central Level F Kit with 4/C Readers. 2004. (Reading Central Ser.). (J). (gr. 2-18). 299.95 *(978-1-58830-860-3(X))* Metropolitan Teaching & Learning Co.
Reading Central Level F Kit with Paperbks. 2004. (Reading Central Ser.). (J). (gr. 2-18). 369.95 *(978-1-58830-866-5(9))* Metropolitan Teaching & Learning Co.
Reading Central Level F Sh. 2004. (Reading Central Ser.). (J). (gr. 2-18). per. 67.95 *(978-1-58830-196-3(6))* Metropolitan Teaching & Learning Co.
Reading Central Level F Student Handbook. 2004. (Reading Central Ser.). (J). (gr. 2-18). per. 39.95 *(978-1-58830-896-2(0))* Metropolitan Teaching & Learning Co.
Reading First Through Science Grade 4. 2005. (ENG., Illus.). *(978-0-9766802-6-0(2))* Educational Tools, Inc.
Reading Friends Staff. Witches Single. (J). *(978-0-8136-3823-2(2))* Modern Curriculum Pr.
Reading Remedies. 352p. (gr. 1-4). 23.99 *(978-0-513-02100-6(0),* TSD21000) Denison, T. S. & Co., Inc.
Reading Together Intermediate Phase II&III Tutor's Guide Book. 2004. (J). pap. *(978-1-931840-70-5(9))* Learning Together.
Reading Together Tutors Guidebook Phase II&III Grade 3. 2004. (J). pap. *(978-1-931840-66-8(0))* Learning Together.
Reading Worktext Grade 1, Book 2. 2004. 10.50 *(978-0-89084-472-4(0))* BJU Pr.
Ready, Set, Read (Gr. K-1) 2003. (J). *(978-1-58232-033-5(0))* ECS Learning Systems, Inc.
Reaume, Christopher J. The 10 Greatest Threats to Earth. 2008. 14.99 *(978-1-55448-501-7(0))* Scholastic Library Publishing.
Recio, Sili. Si Quisqueya Fuera un Color (If Dominican Were a Color) McCarthy, Brianna, illus. 2020. (SPA.). 32p. (J). (gr. -1-3). 18.99 *(978-1-5344-7709-4(8),* Simon & Schuster Bks. For Young Readers) Simon & Schuster Bks. For Young Readers.
Red Egg & Ginger, 6 Pack. (Greetings Ser.: Vol. 1). 24p. (gr. 2-3). 31.00 *(978-0-7635-9409-1(1))* Rigby Education.
Red, Yellow, Blue & Green Levels Certificate Only. (Sails Literacy Ser.). (gr. 1-6). 89.00 *(978-0-7578-6555-8(0))* Rigby Education.
Redmond, Diane & Mould, Chris. Hercules: Superhero: Band 11/Lime (Collins Big Cat) 2005. (Collins Big Cat Ser.). (ENG.). 288p. (J). (gr. 1-3). pap. 10.99 *(978-0-00-718638-9(X))* HarperCollins Pubs. Ltd. GBR. Dist: Independent Pubs. Group.
Redondo, Kurt. Treasure Map, 1 vol. 2006. (Neighborhood Readers Ser.). (ENG.). 12p. (gr. k-1). pap. 5.90 *(978-1-4042-6463-2(9),* 7eec6135-cdab-44a9-9482-b9a437d5544a, Rosen Classroom) Rosen Publishing Group, Inc., The.
Rees, Celia. The Tear Jar: Band 18/Pearl (Collins Big Cat) 2014. (Collins Big Cat Ser.). (ENG., Illus.). 80p. (J). (gr. 5-6). pap. 10.99 *(978-0-00-753011-3(0))* HarperCollins Pubs. Ltd. GBR. Dist: Independent Pubs. Group.
Reeve, Elizabeth. Sassy: the short stories of being a service Dog. 2010. 35p. pap. 17.00 *(978-0-557-39319-0(1))* Lulu Pr., Inc.
Reher, Matt. Are You in My Family? (Big Book) 2011. (1G Big Bks.). (ENG., Illus.). 28p. (J). pap. 9.60 *(978-1-64053-131-4(9),* ARC Pr. Bks.) American Reading Co.
—Butterflies or Moths. 2013. (2G Bugs Ser.). (ENG., Illus.). 32p. (J). pap. 8.00 *(978-1-63437-975-5(6),* ARC Pr. Bks.) American Reading Co.
—Dan Gets a Call. 2017. (1B Fiction Ser.). (ENG., Illus.). 12p. (J). pap. 9.60 *(978-1-63437-177-3(1))* American Reading Co.
—Frogs & Toads (Big Book) 2011. (1G Big Bks.). (ENG., Illus.). 28p. (J). pap. 9.60 *(978-1-64053-127-7(0),* ARC Pr. Bks.) American Reading Co.
—The Grand Scam. 2015. (1B Fiction Ser.). (ENG., Illus.). 16p. (J). pap. 9.60 *(978-1-63437-190-2(9))* American Reading Co.
—My Pet Snake. 2017. (1G Domestic Animals Ser.). (ENG., Illus.). 24p. (J). pap. 9.60 *(978-1-64053-190-1(4),* ARC Pr. Bks.) American Reading Co.
—That's Fast! 2012. (1-3Y Science Ser.). (ENG., Illus.). 20p. (J). pap. 8.00 *(978-1-64053-189-5(0),* ARC Pr. Bks.) American Reading Co.
—What's So Good about Matt? 2014. (1B Fiction Ser.). (ENG., Illus.). 16p. (J). pap. 9.60 *(978-1-63437-200-8(X))* American Reading Co.
—Who Can I Call? 2016. (1B Fiction Ser.). (ENG., Illus.). 12p. (J). pap. 8.00 *(978-1-63437-048-6(1))* American Reading Co.
Reid, James. Across the Sea, 1 vol. rev. ed. 2013. (Literary Text Ser.). (ENG., Illus.). 12p. (gr. k-2). (J). lib. bdg. 12.96 *(978-1-4807-1130-3(6));* 6.99 *(978-1-4333-5451-9(9))* Teacher Created Materials, Inc.
—Dinosaur House, 1 vol. rev. ed. 2013. (Literary Text Ser.). (ENG., Illus.). 12p. (gr. k-2). 6.99 *(978-1-4333-5459-5(4))* Teacher Created Materials, Inc.
—Edward the Explorer, 1 vol. rev. ed. 2013. (Literary Text Ser.). (ENG., Illus.). 12p. (gr. k-2). 5.99 *(978-1-4333-5455-7(1))* Teacher Created Materials, Inc.
—Ready, Set, Go!, 1 vol. rev. ed. 2013. (Literary Text Ser.). (ENG., Illus.). 20p. (gr. 1-2). (J). lib. bdg. 15.96 *(978-1-4807-1144-0(6));* 7.99 *(978-1-4333-5488-5(8))* Teacher Created Materials, Inc.
—This Is My Story by Frederick G. Frog, 1 vol. rev. ed. 2013. (Literary Text Ser.). (ENG., Illus.). 20p. (gr. k-2). (J). lib. bdg. 15.96 *(978-1-4807-1140-2(3));* 7.99 *(978-1-4333-5484-7(5))* Teacher Created Materials, Inc.
Reid, Rob. Storytime Slam: 15 Lesson Plans for Preschool & Primary Story Programs. 2006. (Illus.). 85p. per. 16.95 *(978-1-932146-52-3(0),* Upstart Bks.) Highsmith Inc.
Reid, Stef. Against the Odds: Band 18/Pearl (Collins Big Cat) Bannister, Philip, illus. 2014. (Collins Big Cat Ser.). (ENG.). 80p. (J). (gr. 5). pap. 11.99 *(978-0-00-753015-1(3))* HarperCollins Pubs. Ltd. GBR. Dist: Independent Pubs. Group.
Reid, Stephanie. My Body. 2011. (Early Literacy Ser.). (ENG.). 16p. (gr. k-1). 19.99 *(978-1-4333-2368-3(0));* 6.99 *(978-1-4333-2367-6(2))* Teacher Created Materials, Inc.
—My Country. rev. ed. 2011. (Early Literacy Ser.). (ENG.). 16p. (gr. -1-1). 19.99 *(978-1-4333-2361-4(3));* 6.99 *(978-1-4333-2360-7(5))* Teacher Created Materials, Inc.
—School. 2011. (Early Literacy Ser.). (ENG.). 16p. (gr. k-1). 19.99 *(978-1-4333-2354-6(0));* 6.99 *(978-1-4333-2353-9(2))* Teacher Created Materials, Inc.
Reilly, Carmel & Ashforth, Kate. A Night Out. 2008. (Rigby Focus Forward: Level E Ser.). (Illus.). 24p. (J). (gr. 4-7). pap. *(978-1-4190-3678-1(5),* Rigby) Pearson Education Australia.
Reilly, Carmel & Culic, Ned. Ben Fox Saves the Day. 2008. (Rigby Focus Forward: Level D Ser.). (Illus.). 24p. (J). (gr. 4-7). pap. *(978-1-4190-3665-1(3),* Rigby) Pearson Education Australia.
Reilly, Carmel & Hopkinson, Courtney. Magic Tricks. 2008. (Rigby Focus Forward: Level F Ser.). (Illus.). 24p. (J). (gr. 4-7). pap. *(978-1-4190-3697-2(1),* Rigby) Pearson Education Australia.
—New Tricks. 2008. (Rigby Focus Forward: Level J Ser.). (Illus.). 24p. (J). (gr. 4-7). pap. *(978-1-4190-3766-5(8),* Rigby) Pearson Education Australia.
Reilly, Carmel & Orsini, Cheryl. Everything Is Changing. 2008. (Rigby Focus Forward: Level I Ser.). (Illus.). 24p. (J). (gr. 4-7). pap. *(978-1-4190-3753-5(6),* Rigby) Pearson Education Australia.
—Saying Goodbye. 2008. (Rigby Focus Forward: Level G Ser.). (Illus.). 24p. (J). (gr. 4-7). pap. *(978-1-4190-3719-1(6),* Rigby) Pearson Education Australia.
Reilly, Carmel & Stewart, Christen. More Like Home. 2008. (Rigby Focus Forward: Level P Ser.). (Illus.). 24p. (J). (gr. 4-7). pap. *(978-1-4190-3854-9(0),* Rigby) Pearson Education Australia.
Reilly, Carmel & Wallace-Mitchell, Jane. Harry Helps Out. 2008. (Rigby Focus Forward: Level E Ser.). (Illus.). 24p. (J). (gr. 4-7). pap. *(978-1-4190-3673-6(4),* Rigby) Pearson Education Australia.
—Mercury & the Woodcutter. 2008. (Rigby Focus Forward: Level J Ser.). (Illus.). 24p. (J). (gr. 4-7). pap. *(978-1-4190-3765-8(X),* Rigby) Pearson Education Australia.
Reilly, Carmel & Young, Karen. Anna Goes to the Zoo. 2008. (Rigby Focus Forward: Level D Ser.). (Illus.). 24p. (J). (gr. 4-7). pap. *(978-1-4190-3663-7(7),* Rigby) Pearson Education Australia.
—Buzz & Zip Get Lost. 2008. (Rigby Focus Forward: Level G Ser.). (Illus.). 24p. (J). (gr. 4-7). pap. *(978-1-4190-3704-7(8),* Rigby) Pearson Education Australia.
—Taking Off. 2008. (Rigby Focus Forward: Level F Ser.). (Illus.). 24p. (J). (gr. 4-7). pap. *(978-1-4190-3690-3(4),* Rigby) Pearson Education Australia.

P
Q
R

Reilly, Carmel, et al. Shipwreck. 2008. (Rigby Focus Forward: Level O Ser.). (Illus.). 24p. (J). (gr. 4-7). pap. *(978-1-4190-3850-1(8)*, Rigby) Pearson Education Australia.

Responding to Literature: The EMC Write-in Reader. 2nd ed. (Literature & the Language Arts Ser.). (YA). (gr. 8-18). wbk. ed. 17.99 *(978-0-8219-2912-4(7))* EMC/Paradigm Publishing.

The Responsible Dr Bones: Social/Emotional Lap Book. (Pebble Soup Explorations Ser.). (gr. -1-18). 16.00 *(978-0-7635-7566-3(6))* Rigby Education.

Rey, H. A. Curious George at the Baseball Game/Jorge el Curioso en el Partido de Béisbol: Bilingual English-Spanish. 2011. (Curious George Ser.). (ENG., Illus.). 24p. (J). (gr. -1-3). pap. 4.99 *(978-0-547-51500-7(6)*, 1444364, Clarion Bks.) HarperCollins Pubs.

—Curious George Makes a Valentine. 2018. (Curious George TV Tie-In Early Reader Ser.). lib. bdg. 14.75 *(978-0-606-40424-2(4))* Turtleback.

—Curious George Shapes (CGTV Pull Tab Board Book) 2008. (Curious George Ser.). (ENG., Illus.). 10p. (J). (gr. -1-k). bds. 6.99 *(978-0-618-89198-6(6)*, 569984, Clarion Bks.) HarperCollins Pubs.

—Curious George Storybook Collection (CGTV) 2010. (Curious George Ser.). (ENG., Illus.). 208p. (J). (gr. -1-3). 13.99 *(978-0-547-39631-6(7)*, 1427356, Clarion Bks.) HarperCollins Pubs.

—A Treasury of Curious GeorgeColeccion de Oro Jorge el Curioso: Bilingual English-Spanish. 2011. (Curious George Ser.). (ENG., Illus.). 208p. (J). (gr. -1-3). 11.99 *(978-0-547-52310-1(6)*, 1446149, Clarion Bks.) HarperCollins Pubs.

Rey, H. A. & Rey, Margret. Home Run. 2012. (Curious George TV Tie-In Early Reader Ser.). lib. bdg. 13.55 *(978-0-606-23985-1(5))* Turtleback.

Reyes, Gabrielle. Winter Friends. 2013. (Illus.). 30p. (J). pap. *(978-0-545-59210-9(0))* Scholastic, Inc.

RH Disney. Belle's Story Collection (Disney Beauty & the Beast) RH Disney, illus. 2017. (Step into Reading Ser.). (ENG., Illus.). 160p. (J). (gr. -1-1). pap. 7.99 *(978-0-7364-3916-9(1)*, RH/Disney) Random Hse. Children's Bks.

—Coco Little Golden Book (Disney/Pixar Coco) The Disney Storybook Art Team, illus. 2017. (Little Golden Book Ser.). (ENG.). 24p. (J). (-k). 5.99 *(978-0-7364-3800-1(9)*, Golden/Disney) Random Hse. Children's Bks.

—Moana Finds the Way (Disney Moana) RH Disney, illus. 2016. (Step into Reading Ser.). (ENG., Illus.). 24p. (J). (gr. -1-1). pap. 5.99 *(978-0-7364-3644-1(8)*, RH/Disney) Random Hse. Children's Bks.

—Pua & Heihei (Disney Moana) RH Disney, illus. 2017. (Step into Reading Ser.). (ENG., Illus.). 24p. (J). (gr. -1-1). pap. 5.99 *(978-0-7364-3684-7(7)*, RH/Disney) Random Hse. Children's Bks.

—Quest for the Heart (Disney Moana) RH Disney, illus. 2016. (Step into Reading Ser.). (ENG., Illus.). 32p. (J). (gr. -1-1). pap. 4.99 *(978-0-7364-3646-5(4)*, RH/Disney) Random Hse. Children's Bks.

—Race Team (Disney/Pixar Cars) RH Disney, illus. 2008. (Step into Reading Ser.). (ENG., Illus.). 32p. (J). (gr. k-3). pap. 5.99 *(978-0-7364-2571-1(3)*, RH/Disney) Random Hse. Children's Bks.

—Toy Story (Disney/Pixar Toy Story) RH Disney, illus. 2009. (Little Golden Book Ser.). (ENG., Illus.). 24p. (J). (gr. -1-2). 5.99 *(978-0-7364-2596-4(9)*, Golden/Disney) Random Hse. Children's Bks.

Rhoades, Jacqueline. Rhoades to Reading Level II. 4th ed. 2004. 102p. (YA). spiral bd., wbk. ed. 19.95 *(978-1-930006-53-9(5))* Rhoades & Assocs.

—Rhoades to Reading Level III. 4th ed. 2004. 286p. (YA). spiral bd., wbk. ed. 29.95 *(978-1-930006-55-3(1))* Rhoades & Assocs.

—Rhoades to Reading Level IV. 4th ed. 2004. 166p. spiral bd., wbk. ed. 19.95 *(978-1-930006-57-7(8)*, 1008) Rhoades & Assocs.

—Rhoades to Reading Level V. 4th ed. 2004. 80p. (YA). spiral bd., wbk. ed. 14.95 *(978-1-930006-59-1(4))* Rhoades & Assocs.

Rhoades, Jacqueline. Rhoades to Reading Level I. 4th ed. 2004. 134p. (YA). spiral bd., wbk. ed. 19.95 *(978-1-930006-51-5(9)*, 1002) Rhoades & Assocs.

Rhodes, Karen. 7 Sensational Stories. 2005. (J). pap. 1.79 *(978-1-59317-084-4(X))* Warner Pr., Inc.

Rhyme Time. 2005. (Little Celebrations Thematic Packages Ser.). (J). (gr. k-3). 133.50 *(978-0-673-75380-9(8))* Celebration Pr.

The Ribbon. (Early Intervention Levels Ser.). 23.10 *(978-0-7362-0016-5(9))*; Vol. 3. 3.85 *(978-1-56334-966-9(3))* CENGAGE Learning.

Ricciuti, Edward R. Bookworms: Ready for School, 12 vols., Set. Incl. We Are a Team. lib. bdg. 25.50 *(978-0-7614-1994-5(2)*, ed3f0415-c9d5-4e5b-a4b0-d3364c724224, Cavendish Square); We Are Kind. lib. bdg. 25.50 *(978-0-7614-1992-1(6)*, 2af08c6d-8c94-46b4-9f91-f2fd93c16f15, Cavendish Square); We Listen. lib. bdg. 25.50 *(978-0-7614-1991-4(8)*, 340b136a-05a4-485f-a0dc-bb04f0184ab3, Cavendish Square); We Share. lib. bdg. 25.50 *(978-0-7614-1993-8(4)*, cf516ef8-930e-4195-be31-78afd19641e2); We Tell the Truth. lib. bdg. 25.50 *(978-0-7614-1996-9(9)*, 3c0d4adf-459b-429d-ab68-1b4edd59e3f8); (Illus.). 24p. (gr. k-1). (Ready for School Ser.). (ENG.). 2007. 153.00 *(978-0-7614-1990-7(X)*, 86c05a7e-1fc7-4bb6-8fc0-d085eeadb040, Cavendish Square) Cavendish Square Publishing LLC.

—Listos para ir a la Escuela, 6 bks., Set. Incl. Compartimos (We Share) lib. bdg. 25.50 *(978-0-7614-2360-7(5)*, 95b3d098-959f-4837-adc1-b57ad7c4c89c); Decimos la Verdad (We Tell the Truth) lib. bdg. 25.50 *(978-0-7614-2362-1(1)*, 5a8a188d-c56f-4227-a124-aa97f30484b7); Escuchamos (We Listen) lib. bdg. 25.50 *(978-0-7614-2359-1(1)*, 7167c3ce-f193-4119-b8d4-bc0322acd3cc); Respetamos Las Reglas (We Follow the Rules) lib. bdg. 25.50 *(978-0-7614-2358-4(3)*, 6b193d7d-bfd1-4c5d-a96e-e53ab0cd5173); Somos Amables (We Are Kind) lib. bdg. 25.50 *(978-0-7614-2356-0(7)*, e418437b-5c6d-47d9-a50a-bdab64062cd0); Somos un Equipo (We Are a Team) lib. bdg. 25.50 *(978-0-7614-2357-7(5)*, 26424f33-a340-4359-91d0-86218711856e); (Illus.). 24p. (gr. k-1). 2008. (Bookworms — Spanish Editions: Listos para Ir a la Escuela Ser.). (SPA.). 2006. lib. bdg. *(978-0-7614-2354-6(0)*, Cavendish Square) Cavendish Square Publishing LLC.

—Ready for School (Listos para Ir a la Escuela), 12 vols. Incl. Compartimos / We Share. lib. bdg. 25.50 *(978-0-7614-2441-3(5)*, 0aed10ef-607e-42e3-87d9-be6bed15e4d0); Decimos la Verdad / We Tell the Truth. lib. bdg. 25.50 *(978-0-7614-2442-0(3)*, a5252380-fd5c-4dcc-a8f1-39511bfe873e); Escuchamos / We Listen. lib. bdg. 25.50 *(978-0-7614-2439-0(3)*, 3349ff25-f0fc-4d63-8fc6-343a928d96ad); Respetamos Las Reglas / We Follow the Rules. lib. bdg. 25.50 *(978-0-7614-2438-3(5)*, 264eb2e7-181b-469e-8f19-280524b8e4bc); Somos Amables / We Are Kind. lib. bdg. 25.50 *(978-0-7614-2435-2(0)*, 031aac6d-734c-4902-9454-43f0da1c4df3); Somos un Equipo / We Are a Team. lib. bdg. 25.50 *(978-0-7614-2436-9(9)*, 3cf0f01b-8774-40f9-8154-3301d5082d2a); (Illus.). 24p. (gr. k-1). (Listos para Ir a la Escuela / Ready for School Ser.). (ENG & SPA.). 2008. Set lib. bdg. 153.00 *(978-0-7614-2434-5(2)*, c369a1cf-c9dc-46c9-9e8b-fe9ce35226bd, Cavendish Square) Cavendish Square Publishing LLC.

—We Tell the Truth, 1 vol. 2008. (Ready for School Ser.). (ENG.). 24p. (gr. k-1). pap. 9.23 *(978-0-7614-3277-7(9)*, f76aef0f-a681-48fe-847e-0d0b9b14e5e9) Cavendish Square Publishing LLC.

Rice, D. M. A Visit to a Car Factory, 1 vol. 2nd rev. ed. 2011. (TIME for KIDS(r): Informational Text Ser.). (ENG.). 24p. (gr. 2-3). pap. 9.99 *(978-1-4333-3607-2(3))* Teacher Created Materials, Inc.

—A Visit to a Farm, 1 vol. 2nd rev. ed. 2011. (TIME for KIDS(r): Informational Text Ser.). (ENG.). 24p. (gr. 2-3). pap. 9.99 *(978-1-4333-3608-9(1))* Teacher Created Materials, Inc.

Rice, Dona. Mohandas Gandhi, 1 vol. 2nd rev. ed. 2012. (TIME for KIDS(r): Informational Text Ser.). (ENG.). 32p. (gr. 3-5). pap. 12.99 *(978-1-4333-3632-9(0))* Teacher Created Materials, Inc.

—Roberto Clemente, 1 vol. 2nd rev. ed. 2012. (TIME for KIDS(r): Informational Text Ser.). (ENG.). 32p. (gr. 3-5). pap. 12.99 *(978-1-4333-3683-6(9))* Teacher Created Materials, Inc.

—What Kind of Weather? 2009. (Early Literacy Ser.). (ENG., Illus.). 16p. (gr. k-1). 19.99 *(978-1-4333-1459-9(2))* Teacher Created Materials, Inc.

Rice, Dona Herweck. American Through & Through, 1 vol. 2011. (Early Literacy Ser.). (ENG.). 16p. (gr. k-1). 6.99 *(978-1-4333-2362-1(1))* Teacher Created Materials, Inc.

—American Through & Through Lap Book, 1 vol. 2011. (Early Literacy Ser.). (ENG.). 16p. (gr. k-1). 19.99 *(978-1-4333-2363-8(X))* Teacher Created Materials, Inc.

—Animal Eyes, 1 vol. 2nd rev. ed. 2011. (TIME for KIDS(r): Informational Text Ser.). (ENG.). 12p. (gr. k-1). 7.99 *(978-1-4333-3578-5(6))* Teacher Created Materials, Inc.

—Animal Mothers & Babies, 1 vol. 2nd rev. ed. 2011. (TIME for KIDS(r): Informational Text Ser.). (ENG.). 12p. (gr. k-1). 7.99 *(978-1-4333-3579-2(4))* Teacher Created Materials, Inc.

—Bad Guys & Gals of the Ancient World, 1 vol. 2nd rev. ed. 2013. (TIME for KIDS(r): Informational Text Ser.). (ENG., Illus.). 64p. (J). (gr. 4-8). pap. 14.99 *(978-1-4333-4904-1(3))* Teacher Created Materials, Inc.

—Bad Guys & Gals of the Wild West, 1 vol. 2nd rev. ed. 2013. (TIME for KIDS(r): Informational Text Ser.). (ENG., Illus.). 64p. (J). (gr. 5-8). pap. 14.99 *(978-1-4333-4903-4(5))* Teacher Created Materials, Inc.

—Bad Guys & Gals on the High Seas, 1 vol. 2nd rev. ed. 2013. (TIME for KIDS(r): Informational Text Ser.). (ENG., Illus.). 64p. (J). (gr. 4-8). pap. 14.99 *(978-1-4333-4902-7(7))* Teacher Created Materials, Inc.

—Batter Up! History of Baseball, 1 vol. 2nd rev. ed. 2012. (TIME for KIDS(r): Informational Text Ser.). (ENG.). 32p. (gr. 3-5). pap. 12.99 *(978-1-4333-3679-9(0))* Teacher Created Materials, Inc.

—A Bee's Life, 1 vol. 2nd rev. ed. 2011. (TIME for KIDS(r): Informational Text Ser.). (ENG.). 20p. (gr. 1-2). 8.99 *(978-1-4333-3588-4(3))* Teacher Created Materials, Inc.

—Big & Little, 1 vol. 2nd rev. ed. 2011. (TIME for KIDS(r): Informational Text Ser.). (ENG.). 12p. (gr. k-1). 7.99 *(978-1-4333-3565-5(4))* Teacher Created Materials, Inc.

—Big Kid School, 1 vol. 2011. (Early Literacy Ser.). (ENG.). 16p. (gr. k-1). 6.99 *(978-1-4333-2355-3(9))*; 19.99 *(978-1-4333-2356-0(7))* Teacher Created Materials, Inc.

—A Butterfly's Life, 1 vol. 2nd rev. ed. 2011. (TIME for KIDS(r): Informational Text Ser.). (ENG.). 20p. (gr. 1-2). 8.99 *(978-1-4333-3587-7(5))* Teacher Created Materials, Inc.

—Colors, 1 vol. 2nd rev. ed. 2011. (TIME for KIDS(r): Informational Text Ser.). (ENG.). 12p. (gr. k-1). 7.99 *(978-1-4333-3566-2(2))* Teacher Created Materials, Inc.

—Delicious & Nutritious. 2011. (Early Literacy Ser.). (ENG.). 16p. (gr. k-1). 19.99 *(978-1-4333-2370-6(2))*; 6.99 *(978-1-4333-2369-0(9))* Teacher Created Materials, Inc.

—A Frog's Life, 1 vol. 2nd rev. ed. 2011. (TIME for KIDS(r): Informational Text Ser.). (ENG.). 20p. (gr. 1-2). 8.99 *(978-1-4333-3586-0(7))* Teacher Created Materials, Inc.

—Going Buggy!, 1 vol. 2nd rev. ed. 2011. (TIME for KIDS(r): Informational Text Ser.). (ENG.). 20p. (gr. 1-2). 8.99 *(978-1-4333-3591-4(3))* Teacher Created Materials, Inc.

—Growing Up, 1 vol. rev. ed. 2014. (Science: Informational Text Ser.). (ENG., Illus.). 24p. (gr. k-1). pap. 9.99 *(978-1-4807-4524-7(3))* Teacher Created Materials, Inc.

—Here Comes the Sun, 1 vol. rev. ed. 2014. (Science: Informational Text Ser.). (ENG., Illus.). 24p. (gr. -1-1). pap. 9.99 *(978-1-4807-4529-2(4))* Teacher Created Materials, Inc.

—Hit It! - History of Tools, 1 vol. 2nd rev. ed. 2012. (TIME for KIDS(r): Informational Text Ser.). (ENG.). 32p. (gr. 3-5). pap. 12.99 *(978-1-4333-3680-5(4))* Teacher Created Materials, Inc.

—Homes Around the World, 1 vol. 2nd rev. ed. 2011. (TIME for KIDS(r): Informational Text Ser.). (ENG.). 20p. (gr. 1-2). 6.99 *(978-1-4333-3598-3(0))* Teacher Created Materials, Inc.

—How Plants Grow, 1 vol. 2nd rev. ed. 2011. (TIME for KIDS(r): Informational Text Ser.). (ENG.). 12p. (gr. k-1). 7.99 *(978-1-4333-3577-8(8))* Teacher Created Materials, Inc.

—I Can, 1 vol. 2nd rev. ed. 2011. (TIME for KIDS(r): Informational Text Ser.). (ENG.). 12p. (gr. k-1). 7.99 *(978-1-4333-3569-3(7))* Teacher Created Materials, Inc.

—I Can Be Anything, 1 vol. rev. ed. 2009. (Early Literacy Ser.). (ENG., Illus.). 16p. (gr. k-1). 6.99 *(978-1-4333-1475-9(4))* Teacher Created Materials, Inc.

—Keeping Fit with Sports, 1 vol. 2nd rev. ed. 2011. (TIME for KIDS(r): Informational Text Ser.). (ENG.). 20p. (gr. 1-2). 6.99 *(978-1-4333-3596-9(4))* Teacher Created Materials, Inc.

—Kids Around the World, 1 vol. 2nd rev. ed. 2011. (TIME for KIDS(r): Informational Text Ser.). (ENG.). 20p. (gr. 1-2). 6.99 *(978-1-4333-3599-0(9))* Teacher Created Materials, Inc.

—Land, 1 vol. 2nd rev. ed. (TIME for KIDS(r): Informational Text Ser.). (ENG., 12p. (gr. k-1). 2013. Illus.). (J). lib. bdg. 15.96 *(978-1-4807-1013-9(X))* 2011. 7.99 *(978-1-4333-3574-7(3))* Teacher Created Materials, Inc.

—My Big Family, 1 vol. 2nd rev. ed. 2011. (TIME for KIDS(r): Informational Text Ser.). (ENG.). 12p. (gr. k-1). 7.99 *(978-1-4333-3570-9(0))* Teacher Created Materials, Inc.

—On the Go, 1 vol. 2nd rev. ed. 2011. (TIME for KIDS(r): Informational Text Ser.). (ENG.). 12p. (gr. k-1). 7.99 *(978-1-4333-3571-6(9))* Teacher Created Materials, Inc.

—Physical Feats & Failures. 2nd rev. ed. 2012. (TIME for KIDS(r): Informational Text Ser.). (ENG.). 48p. (gr. 4-6). pap. 13.99 *(978-1-4333-4870-9(5))* Teacher Created Materials, Inc.

—Places Around the World, 1 vol. 2nd rev. ed. 2011. (TIME for KIDS(r): Informational Text Ser.). (ENG., Illus.). 20p. (gr. 1-2). 8.99 *(978-1-4333-3600-3(6))* Teacher Created Materials, Inc.

—Places to Go, 1 vol. 2nd rev. ed. 2011. (TIME for KIDS(r): Informational Text Ser.). (ENG.). 12p. (gr. k-1). 7.99 *(978-1-4333-3573-0(5))* Teacher Created Materials, Inc.

—Sea Life, 1 vol. 2nd rev. ed. 2011. (TIME for KIDS(r): Informational Text Ser.). (ENG.). 20p. (gr. 1-2). 8.99 *(978-1-4333-3590-7(5))* Teacher Created Materials, Inc.

—Shapes, 1 vol. 2nd rev. ed. 2011. (TIME for KIDS(r): Informational Text Ser.). (ENG.). 12p. (gr. k-1). 7.99 *(978-1-4333-3567-9(0))* Teacher Created Materials, Inc.

—Sort It!, 1 vol. rev. ed. 2014. (Science: Informational Text Ser.). (ENG., Illus.). 24p. (J). (gr. k-1). pap. 9.99 *(978-1-4807-4535-3(9))* Teacher Created Materials, Inc.

—Staying Healthy, 1 vol. 2nd rev. ed. 2011. (TIME for KIDS(r): Informational Text Ser.). (ENG.). 20p. (gr. 1-2). 8.99 *(978-1-4333-3595-2(6))* Teacher Created Materials, Inc.

—Things with Wings, 1 vol. 2nd rev. ed. 2011. (TIME for KIDS(r): Informational Text Ser.). (ENG.). 20p. (gr. 1-2). 6.99 *(978-1-4333-3589-1(1))* Teacher Created Materials, Inc.

—This is Me, 1 vol. 2nd rev. ed. 2011. (TIME for KIDS(r): Informational Text Ser.). (ENG.). 12p. (gr. k-1). 7.99 *(978-1-4333-3568-6(9))* Teacher Created Materials, Inc.

—Too Much Trash!, 1 vol. rev. ed. 2014. (Science: Informational Text Ser.). (ENG., Illus.). 24p. (gr. -1-1). pap. 9.99 *(978-1-4807-4534-6(0))* Teacher Created Materials, Inc.

—Unsolved! History's Mysteries, 1 vol. 2nd rev. ed. 2012. (TIME for KIDS(r): Informational Text Ser.). (ENG.). 48p. (gr. 4-5). pap. 13.99 *(978-1-4333-4829-7(2))* Teacher Created Materials, Inc.

—Water, 1 vol. 2nd rev. ed. 2011. (TIME for KIDS(r): Informational Text Ser.). (ENG.). 12p. (gr. k-1). 7.99 *(978-1-4333-3576-1(X))* Teacher Created Materials, Inc.

—Weather, 1 vol. 2nd rev. ed. 2011. (TIME for KIDS(r): Informational Text Ser.). (ENG.). 12p. (gr. k-1). 7.99 *(978-1-4333-3575-4(1))* Teacher Created Materials, Inc.

—Workers, 1 vol. 2nd rev. ed. 2011. (TIME for KIDS(r): Informational Text Ser.). (ENG.). 12p. (gr. k-1). 7.99 *(978-1-4333-3572-3(7))* Teacher Created Materials, Inc.

Rice, Dona Herweck & Coan, Sharon. Special Me. 2009. (Early Literacy Ser.). (ENG., Illus.). 16p. (gr. k-1). 19.99 *(978-1-4333-1470-4(3))* Teacher Created Materials, Inc.

Rice, Dona Herweck & Petersen, Casey Null. School Around the World, 1 vol. 2nd rev. ed. 2011. (TIME for KIDS(r): Informational Text Ser.). (ENG.). 28p. (gr. 3-4). pap. 11.99 *(978-1-4333-3654-6(5))* Teacher Created Materials, Inc.

Rice, Dona Herweck & Thompson, Chad. Old Mother Hubbard. 2009. (Early Literacy Ser.). (ENG., Illus.). 16p. (gr. k-1). 19.99 *(978-1-4333-1478-0(9))* Teacher Created Materials, Inc.

Rice, Dona Herweck, et al. All about Me. 2009. (Early Literacy Ser.). (ENG., Illus.). 16p. (gr. k-1). 19.99 *(978-1-4333-1468-1(1))* Teacher Created Materials, Inc.

Rice, Dona Herwick. Eating Right, 1 vol. 2nd rev. ed. 2011. (TIME for KIDS(r): Informational Text Ser.). (ENG.). 20p. (gr. 1-2). 8.99 *(978-1-4333-3597-6(2))* Teacher Created Materials, Inc.

—The Fox & the Crow, 1 vol. rev. ed. 2008. (Reader's Theater Ser.). (ENG.). 24p. (gr. 1-3). pap. 8.99 *(978-1-4333-0295-4(0))* Teacher Created Materials, Inc.

—John Henry, 1 vol. rev. ed. 2009. (Reader's Theater Ser.). (ENG.). 24p. (gr. 2-4). pap. 8.99 *(978-1-4333-0992-2(0))* Teacher Created Materials, Inc.

—The Lion & the Mouse, 1 vol. rev. ed. 2008. (Reader's Theater Ser.). (ENG.). 24p. (gr. 1-3). pap. 8.99 *(978-1-4333-0293-0(4))* Teacher Created Materials, Inc.

—The North Wind & the Sun, 1 vol. rev. ed. 2008. (Reader's Theater Ser.). (ENG.). 24p. (gr. 1-3). pap. 8.99 *(978-1-4333-0296-1(9))* Teacher Created Materials, Inc.

—Paul Bunyan, 1 vol. rev. ed. 2009. (Reader's Theater Ser.). (ENG.). 24p. (gr. 2-4). pap. 8.99 *(978-1-4333-0994-6(7))* Teacher Created Materials, Inc.

—The Tortoise & the Hare, 1 vol. rev. ed. 2008. (Reader's Theater Ser.). (ENG.). 24p. (gr. 1-3). pap. 8.99 *(978-1-4333-0290-9(X))* Teacher Created Materials, Inc.

Rice, Dona Herwick & Bradley, Kathleen. Chief Joseph & the Nez Perce, 1 vol. rev. ed. 2009. (Reader's Theater Ser.). (ENG., Illus.). 32p. (gr. 4-8). pap. 11.99 *(978-1-4333-0543-6(7))* Teacher Created Materials, Inc.

—The Goose That Laid the Golden Eggs, 1 vol. rev. ed. 2008. (Reader's Theater Ser.). (ENG., Illus.). 24p. (J). (gr. 1-3). pap. 8.99 *(978-1-4333-0291-6(8))* Teacher Created Materials, Inc.

—Lewis & Clark, 1 vol. rev. ed. 2009. (Reader's Theater Ser.). (ENG., Illus.). 32p. (gr. 4-8). pap. 11.99 *(978-1-4333-0540-5(2))* Teacher Created Materials, Inc.

—Molly Pitcher, 1 vol. rev. ed. 2009. (Reader's Theater Ser.). (ENG., Illus.). 24p. (gr. 2-4). pap. 8.99 *(978-1-4333-0993-9(9))* Teacher Created Materials, Inc.

Rice, Dona Herwick & Housel, Debra. The Grasshopper & the Ants, 1 vol. rev. ed. 2008. (Reader's Theater Ser.). (ENG., Illus.). 24p. (gr. 1-3). pap. 8.99 *(978-1-4333-0292-3(6))* Teacher Created Materials, Inc.

—The Town Mouse & the Country Mouse, 1 vol. rev. ed. 2008. (Reader's Theater Ser.). (ENG., Illus.). 24p. (gr. 1-3). pap. 8.99 *(978-1-4333-0294-7(2))* Teacher Created Materials, Inc.

Rice, Dona Herwick & Isecke, Harriet. Child Labor & the Industrial Revolution, 1 vol. rev. ed. 2009. (Reader's Theater Ser.). (ENG., Illus.). 32p. (gr. 3-8). pap. 11.99 *(978-1-4333-0548-1(8))* Teacher Created Materials, Inc.

—Remember the Alamo, 1 vol. rev. ed. 2009. (Reader's Theater Ser.). (ENG., Illus.). 32p. (gr. 3-8). pap. 11.99 *(978-1-4333-0541-2(0))* Teacher Created Materials, Inc.

Rice, Dona Herwick & Shannon, Catherine. Narcissa Whitman & the Westward Movement, 1 vol. rev. ed. 2009. (Reader's Theater Ser.). (ENG., Illus.). 32p. (J). (gr. 3-8). pap. 11.99 *(978-1-4333-0542-9(9))* Teacher Created Materials, Inc.

Rice, Dona Herwick & Sugarman, Dorothy Alexander. Women's Suffrage, 1 vol. rev. ed. 2009. (Reader's Theater Ser.). (ENG., Illus.). 32p. (J). (gr. 3-8). pap. 11.99 *(978-1-4333-0550-4(X))* Teacher Created Materials, Inc.

—World War II: Battle of Normandy, 1 vol. rev. ed. 2009. (Reader's Theater Ser.). (ENG., Illus.). 32p. (gr. 3-8). pap. 11.99 *(978-1-4333-0553-5(4))* Teacher Created Materials, Inc.

Rice, Donna Herweck. I Can Be Anything. 2009. (Early Literacy Ser.). (ENG., Illus.). 16p. (gr. k-1). 19.99 *(978-1-4333-1476-6(2))* Teacher Created Materials, Inc.

Rice, Howard. Step into the Desert, 1 vol. 2nd rev. ed. 2011. (TIME for KIDS(r): Informational Text Ser.). (ENG.). 28p. (gr. 2-3). pap. 10.99 *(978-1-4333-3629-4(4))* Teacher Created Materials, Inc.

—Step into the Forest, 1 vol. 2nd rev. ed. 2011. (TIME for KIDS(r): Informational Text Ser.). (ENG.). 28p. (gr. 2-3). pap. 10.99 *(978-1-4333-3628-7(6))* Teacher Created Materials, Inc.

—Step into the Rainforest, 1 vol. 2nd rev. ed. 2011. (TIME for KIDS(r): Informational Text Ser.). (ENG.). 28p. (gr. 2-3). pap. 10.99 *(978-1-4333-3630-0(8))* Teacher Created Materials, Inc.

Rice, Katelyn & Kuligowski, Stephanie. Dangerous Catch! Deep Sea Fishers, 1 vol. 2nd rev. ed. 2013. (TIME for KIDS(r): Informational Text Ser.). (ENG.). 64p. (gr. 4-8). pap. 14.99 *(978-1-4333-4943-0(4))* Teacher Created Materials, Inc.

Rice, William B. African Grasslands, 1 vol. 2nd rev. ed. 2012. (TIME for KIDS(r): Informational Text Ser.). (ENG.). 32p. (gr. 3-5). pap. 12.99 *(978-1-4333-3670-6(7))* Teacher Created Materials, Inc.

—Amazon Rainforest, 1 vol. 2nd rev. ed. 2012. (TIME for KIDS(r): Informational Text Ser.). (ENG.). 32p. (gr. 3-5). pap. 12.99 *(978-1-4333-3671-3(5))* Teacher Created Materials, Inc.

—Death Valley Desert, 1 vol. 2nd rev. ed. 2012. (TIME for KIDS(r): Informational Text Ser.). (ENG.). 32p. (gr. 3-5). pap. 12.99 *(978-1-4333-3672-0(3))* Teacher Created Materials, Inc.

—Endangered Animals of the Desert, 1 vol. 2nd rev. ed. 2013. (TIME for KIDS(r): Informational Text Ser.). (ENG., Illus.). 64p. (J). (gr. 4-8). pap. 14.99 *(978-1-4333-4936-2(1))* Teacher Created Materials, Inc.

—Endangered Animals of the Jungle, 1 vol. 2nd rev. ed. 2013. (TIME for KIDS(r): Informational Text Ser.). (ENG.). 64p. (gr. 4-8). pap. 14.99 *(978-1-4333-4937-9(X))* Teacher Created Materials, Inc.

—Endangered Animals of the Sea, 1 vol. 2nd rev. ed. 2013. (TIME for KIDS(r): Informational Text Ser.). (ENG., Illus.). 64p. (J). (gr. 4-8). pap. 14.99 *(978-1-4333-4935-5(3))* Teacher Created Materials, Inc.

—The First Geologists, 1 vol. rev. ed. 2007. (Science: Informational Text Ser.). (ENG.). 32p. (gr. 4-6). pap. 12.99 *(978-0-7439-0554-1(7))* Teacher Created Materials, Inc.

—Jane Goodall, 1 vol. 2nd rev. ed. 2012. (TIME for KIDS(r): Informational Text Ser.). (ENG.). 32p. (gr. 3-5). pap. 12.99 *(978-1-4333-3684-3(7))* Teacher Created Materials, Inc.

—Survival! Desert, 1 vol. 2nd rev. ed. 2012. (TIME for KIDS(r): Informational Text Ser.). (ENG., Illus.). 48p. (gr. 4-5). pap. 13.99 *(978-1-4333-4818-1(7))* Teacher Created Materials, Inc.

—Survival! Jungle, 1 vol. 2nd rev. ed. 2012. (TIME for KIDS(r): Informational Text Ser.). (ENG., Illus.). 48p. (gr. 4-5). pap. 13.99 *(978-1-4333-4820-4(9))* Teacher Created Materials, Inc.

—Survival! Ocean, 1 vol. 2nd rev. ed. 2012. (TIME for KIDS(r): Informational Text Ser.). (ENG., Illus.). 48p. (gr. 4-5). pap. 13.99 *(978-1-4333-4819-8(5))* Teacher Created Materials, Inc.

—The World of Rocks & Minerals, 1 vol. rev. ed. 2007. (Science: Informational Text Ser.). (ENG., Illus.). 32p. (gr. 4-6). pap. 12.99 *(978-0-7439-0553-4(9))* Teacher Created Materials, Inc.

Rice, William B. & Wolfe, Hillary. Blast off to Space Camp, 1 vol. 2nd rev. ed. 2012. (TIME for KIDS(r): Informational Text Ser.). (ENG.). 32p. (gr. 3-5). pap. 12.99 *(978-1-4333-3673-7(1))* Teacher Created Materials, Inc.

Richards, Cassandra. I Help in the Kitchen, 1 vol. Aguilera, Aurora, illus. 2017. (Ways I Help Ser.). (ENG.). 24p. (J). (gr. 1-1). 25.27 *(978-1-5081-5739-7(1)*, be4f55a5-0838-4434-bf14-12d3d5737e26, PowerKids Pr.) Rosen Publishing Group, Inc., The.

Richards, Kitty. Meet the Sparkplugs, Level 3. Simard, Remy, illus. 2006. (ENG.). 24p. (J). (gr. 1-17). per. 3.99 *(978-1-58476-419-9(8)*, IKIDS) Innovative Kids.

—Phonics Comics: Twisted Tales - Level 3, Level 3. Juarez, Fernando, illus. 2006. (ENG.). 24p. (J). (gr. 1-17). per. 3.99 *(978-1-58476-514-1(3)*, IKIDS) Innovative Kids.

Richards, Lucy & Morpurgo, Michael. Mairi's Mermaid (Reading Ladder Level 2) Richards, Lucy, illus. 2nd ed. 2016. (Reading Ladder Level 2 Ser.). (ENG., Illus.). 48p. (gr.

k-2). pap. 4.99 *(978-1-4052-8201-7(0)*, Reading Ladder) Farshore GBR. Dist: HarperCollins Pubs.
Richie's Rocket. (Lexile Levels Ser.). 9.09 *(978-1-56334-736-8(9))* CENGAGE Learning.
Richter, Abigail. I See a Horse!, 1 vol. 2006. (Neighborhood Readers Ser.). (ENG.). 16p. (gr. 1-2). pap. 6.50 *(978-1-4042-7248-4(8)*, 2909f7ab-02d6-4437-81f0-da3b6d82caff, Rosen Classroom) Rosen Publishing Group, Inc., The.
—Mike the Bike, 1 vol. 2006. (Neighborhood Readers Ser.). (ENG.). 16p. (gr. 1-2). pap. 6.50 *(978-1-4042-7168-5(6)*, bc18f98a-65ed-4034-95f0-9fc019eb3a72, Rosen Classroom) Rosen Publishing Group, Inc., The.
Rick & Rosie. (Early Intervention Levels Ser.). 21.30 *(978-0-7362-0365-4(6))*; Vol. 2. 3.55 *(978-0-7362-0086-8(X))* CENGAGE Learning.
Rickards, Lynne. All about Honey Green Band. 2017. (Cambridge Reading Adventures Ser.). (ENG., Illus.). 16p. pap. 6.15 *(978-1-108-40572-0(X))* Cambridge Univ. Pr.
—Baking Bread. Cambridge Reading Adventures. Green Band. 2016. (Cambridge Reading Adventures Ser.). (ENG., Illus.). 17p. pap. 7.95 *(978-1-316-50327-0(5))* Cambridge Univ. Pr.
—The Big City Yellow Band. Roberts, Ley Honor, illus. 2017. (Cambridge Reading Adventures Ser.). (ENG.). 16p. pap. 6.15 *(978-1-108-41079-3(0))* Cambridge Univ. Pr.
—Collins Big Cat Phonics for Letters & Sounds - Noisy Neesha: Band 06/Orange, Bd. 6. Jennings, Sarah, illus. 2018. (Collins Big Cat Phonics Ser.). (ENG.). 24p. (J). (gr. 1-2). pap. 8.99 *(978-0-00-825174-1(6))* HarperCollins Pubs. Ltd. GBR. Dist: Independent Pubs. Group.
—Four Clever Brothers 1 Pathfinders. Bernstein, Galia, illus. 2017. (Cambridge Reading Adventures Ser.). (ENG.). 24p. pap. 7.35 *(978-1-108-41081-6(2))* Cambridge Univ. Pr.
—Games Pink a Band. 2016. (Cambridge Reading Adventures Ser.). (ENG., Illus.). 16p. pap. 7.95 *(978-1-316-60084-9(X))* Cambridge Univ. Pr.
—Hide & Seek Green Band. Pérez, Moni, illus. 2016. (Cambridge Reading Adventures Ser.). (ENG.). 16p. pap. 7.95 *(978-1-107-57599-8(0))* Cambridge Univ. Pr.
—Houses & Homes. Cambridge Reading Adventures. Red Band. 2016. (Cambridge Reading Adventures Ser.). (ENG., Illus.). 16p. pap. 7.95 *(978-1-107-54949-4(3))* Cambridge Univ. Pr.
—I Can Help Pink a Band. 2017. (Cambridge Reading Adventures Ser.). (ENG., Illus.). 16p. pap. 7.95 *(978-1-108-40566-9(5))* Cambridge Univ. Pr.
—My Dad Is a Builder Pink B Band. Hustache, Timothy, illus. 2016. (Cambridge Reading Adventures Ser.). (ENG.). 16p. pap. 7.95 *(978-1-107-54973-9(6))* Cambridge Univ. Pr.
—My First Train Trip. Honor Roberts, Ley, illus. 2016. (Cambridge Reading Adventures Ser.). (ENG.). 16p. pap. 7.95 *(978-1-107-57594-3(X))* Cambridge Univ. Pr.
—Omar Can Help Red Band. Pérez, Moni, illus. 2016. (Cambridge Reading Adventures Ser.). (ENG.). 16p. pap. 7.95 *(978-1-107-57572-1(9))* Cambridge Univ. Pr.
—Playgrounds Yellow Band. 2016. (Cambridge Reading Adventures Ser.). (ENG., Illus.). 16p. pap. 7.95 *(978-1-316-50318-8(6))* Cambridge Univ. Pr.
Rider, Cynthia. Chatterbox Turtle. Petrlik, Andrea, illus. 2004. (ENG.). 24p. (J). lib. bdg. 23.65 *(978-1-59646-696-8(0))* Dingles & Co.
RIGBY. American Journeys: Fourth Grade Class Collection Books. 2003. (Rigby on Our Way to English Ser.). (ENG.). 32p. (gr. 4-4). pap. 50.70 *(978-0-7578-4337-2(9))* Rigby Education.
—Are We There Yet? Second Grade Big Books. 2003. (Rigby on Our Way to English Ser.). (ENG.). 24p. (gr. 2-2). pap. 50.70 *(978-0-7578-1415-0(8))* Rigby Education.
—By the People: Fifth Grade Class Collection Books. 2003. (Rigby on Our Way to English Ser.). (ENG.). 32p. (gr. 5-5). pap. 50.70 *(978-0-7578-4468-3(5))* Rigby Education.
—Can You Help Me Find My Puppy? Kindergarten Big Books. 2003. (Rigby on Our Way to English Ser.). (ENG.). 16p. (gr. k-k). pap. 50.70 *(978-0-7578-1618-5(5))* Rigby Education.
—Diego Saves the Planet! Third Grade Big Books. 2003. (Rigby on Our Way to English Ser.). (ENG.). 24p. (gr. 3-3). pap. 50.70 *(978-0-7578-4212-2(7))* Rigby Education.
—The Early Americas: Fourth Grade Class Collection Books. 2003. (Rigby on Our Way to English Ser.). (ENG.). 32p. (gr. 4-4). pap. 50.70 *(978-0-7578-4341-9(7))* Rigby Education.
—Earth, Moon, & Sun: Fifth Grade Class Collection Books. 2003. (Rigby on Our Way to English Ser.). (ENG.). 32p. (gr. 5-5). pap. 48.75 *(978-0-7578-4473-7(1))* Rigby Education.
—Future Space Explorers: Third Grade Big Books. 2003. (Rigby on Our Way to English Ser.). (ENG.). 24p. (gr. 3-3). pap. 50.70 *(978-0-7578-4211-5(9))* Rigby Education.
—Getting Ready: Kindergarten Big Books. 2003. (Rigby on Our Way to English Ser.). (ENG.). 16p. (gr. k-k). pap. 50.70 *(978-0-7578-1616-1(9))* Rigby Education.
—Golden Opportunities: Fourth Grade Class Collection Books. 2003. (Rigby on Our Way to English Ser.). (ENG.). 32p. (gr. 4-4). pap. 50.70 *(978-0-7578-4343-3(3))* Rigby Education.
—Good News: First Grade Big Books. 2003. (Rigby on Our Way to English Ser.). (ENG.). 16p. (gr. 1-1). pap. 50.70 *(978-0-7578-1505-8(7))* Rigby Education.
—A Growing Nation: Fifth Grade Class Collection Books. 2009. (Rigby on Our Way to English Ser.). (ENG.). 32p. (gr. 5-5). pap. 50.70 *(978-0-7578-4471-3(5))* Rigby Education.
—Ibis & Jaguar's Dinner: Second Grade Big Books. 2003. (Rigby on Our Way to English Ser.). (ENG.). 24p. (gr. 2-2). pap. 50.70 *(978-0-7578-1427-3(1))* Rigby Education.
—In the Deep: Fifth Grade Class Collection Books. 2003. (Rigby on Our Way to English Ser.). (ENG.). 32p. (gr. 5-5). pap. 48.75 *(978-0-7578-4470-6(7))* Rigby Education.
—Just Like Me! First Grade. 2003. (Rigby on Our Way to English Ser.). (ENG.). 24p. (gr. 1-1). pap. 50.70 *(978-0-7578-1513-3(8))* Rigby Education.
—Making a Difference: Third Grade Big Books. 2003. (Rigby on Our Way to English Ser.). (ENG.). 24p. (gr. 3-3). pap. 52.80 *(978-0-7578-4213-9(5))* Rigby Education.
—My Rooster Speaks Korean: Kindergarten Big Books. 2003. (Rigby on Our Way to English Ser.). (ENG.). 16p. (gr. k-k). pap. 50.70 *(978-0-7578-1622-2(3))* Rigby Education.
—Now Hear This! Fifth Grade Class Collection Books. 2003. (Rigby on Our Way to English Ser.). (ENG.). 32p. (gr. 5-5). pap. 50.70 *(978-0-7578-4469-0(3))* Rigby Education.
—Picture Cards: Package of 100 Cards First Grade. 2003. (Rigby on Our Way to English Ser.). (ENG.). 100p. (gr. 1-1). 215.25 *(978-0-7578-1598-0(7))* Rigby Education.
—Picture Cards: Package of 100 Cards Kindergarten. 2003. (Rigby on Our Way to English Ser.). (ENG.). 100p. (gr. k-k). 215.25 *(978-0-7578-1611-6(8))* Rigby Education.
—Picture Cards: Package of 100 Cards Second Grade. 2003. (Rigby on Our Way to English Ser.). (ENG.). 100p. (gr. 2-2). 215.25 *(978-0-7578-1410-5(7))* Rigby Education.
—Picture Cards: Package of 100 Cards Third Grade. 2003. (Rigby on Our Way to English Ser.). (ENG.). 101p. (gr. 3-3). 215.25 *(978-0-7578-4233-7(X))* Rigby Education.
—A Pocketful of Opossums: Second Grade Big Books. 2003. (Rigby on Our Way to English Ser.). (ENG.). 24p. (gr. 2-2). pap. 48.75 *(978-0-7578-1417-4(4))* Rigby Education.
—Pulse of Life: Fifth Grade Class Collection Books. 2003. (Rigby on Our Way to English Ser.). (ENG.). 32p. (gr. 5-5). pap. 48.75 *(978-0-7578-4474-4(X))* Rigby Education.
—Rice All Day: Kindergarten Big Books. 2003. (Rigby on Our Way to English Ser.). (ENG.). 16p. (gr. k-k). pap. 50.70 *(978-0-7578-1620-8(7))* Rigby Education.
—Road to Freedom: Fifth Grade Class Collection Books. 2003. (Rigby on Our Way to English Ser.). (ENG.). 32p. (gr. 5-5). pap. 48.75 *(978-0-7578-4467-6(7))* Rigby Education.
—Rosita's Robot: Third Grade Big Books. 2003. (Rigby on Our Way to English Ser.). (ENG.). 24p. (gr. 3-3). pap. 50.70 *(978-0-7578-4210-8(0))* Rigby Education.
—Tran & the Beautiful Tree: First Grade Big Books. 2003. (Rigby on Our Way to English Ser.). (ENG.). 24p. (gr. 1-1). pap. 50.70 *(978-0-7578-1515-7(4))* Rigby Education.
—Under the Canopy: Fourth Grade Class Collection Books. 2009. (Rigby on Our Way to English Ser.). (ENG.). 32p. (gr. 4-4). pap. 50.70 *(978-0-7578-4342-6(5))* Rigby Education.
—Unearthing the Past: Fourth Grade Class Collection Books. 2003. (Rigby on Our Way to English Ser.). (ENG.). 32p. (gr. 4-4). pap. 48.75 *(978-0-7578-4340-2(9))* Rigby Education.
—Water Detective: Second Grade. 2003. (Rigby on Our Way to English Ser.). (ENG.). 24p. (gr. 2-2). pap. 50.70 *(978-0-7578-1421-1(2))* Rigby Education.
—What Are the Seasons Like? Kindergarten Big Books. 2003. (Rigby on Our Way to English Ser.). (ENG.). 16p. (gr. k-k). pap. 50.70 *(978-0-7578-1624-6(X))* Rigby Education.
—When I Grow Up: Kindergarten Big Books. 2003. (Rigby on Our Way to English Ser.). (ENG.). 16p. (gr. k-k). pap. 50.70 *(978-0-7578-1626-0(6))* Rigby Education.
—Word Wall Starters: Package of 100 Cards Third Grade. 2003. (Rigby on Our Way to English Ser.). (ENG.). 99p. (gr. 3-3). 44.95 *(978-0-7578-4286-3(0))* Rigby Education.
—Word Wall Starters: Package of 115 Cards First Grade. 2003. (Rigby on Our Way to English Ser.). (ENG.). 115p. (gr. 1-1). 51.15 *(978-0-7578-1474-7(3))* Rigby Education.
—Word Wall Starters: Package of 124 Cards Second Grade. 2003. (Rigby on Our Way to English Ser.). (ENG.). 124p. (gr. 2-2). 55.95 *(978-0-7578-1386-3(0))* Rigby Education.
—Word Wall Starters: Package of 65 Cards Kindergarten. 2003. (Rigby on Our Way to English Ser.). (ENG.). 65p. (gr. k-k). 31.00 *(978-0-7578-1562-1(6))* Rigby Education.
Rigby Education Staff. Activity Guide. (Illus.). (gr. k-1). tchr. ed. 18.00 *(978-0-7635-2005-2(5))*; tchr. ed. 18.00 *(978-0-7635-2006-9(3))*; tchr. ed. 18.00 *(978-0-7635-2007-6(1))*; tchr. ed. 18.00 *(978-0-7635-2008-3(X))* Rigby Education.
—A Day on the Farm. (Illus.). 8p. (J). bds. 3.95 *(978-0-7635-6463-6(X)*, 764639C99) Rigby Education.
—Discovery World Org Where Does. (Discovery World Ser.). (Illus.). 12p. (gr. 1-2). 27.00 *(978-0-7635-2698-6(3))* Rigby Education.
—Discovery World Red Biography III. (Discovery World Ser.). 12p. (gr. 1-2). 31.00 *(978-0-7635-2703-7(3))* Rigby Education.
—Everything Changes Big Book: Little Red Riding Hood. (Pebble Soup Explorations Ser.). 16p. (gr. -1-18). 21.00 *(978-0-7635-6482-7(6))* Rigby Education.
—Follow the Paw Prints. (Pebble Soup Explorations Ser.). (Illus.). 16p. (gr. -1-18). 31.00 *(978-0-7635-6446-9(X)*, 764469C99) Rigby Education.
—Jack Big Book. (gr. k-2). 21.00 *(978-0-7635-2409-8(3))* Rigby Education.
—Jumbled Tumble Little Miss. (gr. k-2). 21.00 *(978-0-7635-2415-9(8))* Rigby Education.
—Jumbled Tumble Little Tom. (gr. k-2). 21.00 *(978-0-7635-2414-2(X))* Rigby Education.
—Max. (Sails Literacy Ser.). (Illus.). 16p. (gr. 1-2). 27.00 *(978-0-7635-9906-5(9)*, 699069C99) Rigby Education.
—Roger's Best Friend. (Illus.). 16p. (J). pap. 30.00 *(978-0-7635-6434-6(6)*, 764346C99) Rigby Education.
—Stage 1 Components. (gr. k-3). 57.00 *(978-0-7635-9245-5(5))* Rigby Education.
—Tom Sawyer: Jumbled Tumble. (gr. k-2). 26.00 *(978-0-7635-2424-1(7))* Rigby Education.
—Touching the Moon. (Illus.). 16p. (J). pap. 30.00 *(978-0-7635-6498-8(2)*, 764982C99) Rigby Education.
—Two Eyes That See. (Illus.). 16p. (J). pap. 3.95 *(978-0-7635-7037-8(0)*, 764265C99) Rigby Education.
—Who Works in Your Neighborhood? (Illus.). (J). suppl. ed. 20.00 *(978-0-7635-6453-7(2)*, 764532C99) Rigby Education.
—William Tell. (gr. k-2). 21.00 *(978-0-7635-2426-5(3))* Rigby Education.
Rigby, Robert & Cámara, Noemí. Gol II: Viviendo el Sueño, 1 vol. 2014. (ENG., Illus.). 40p. pap. 15.00 incl. audio compact disk *(978-84-9848-130-3(9))* Edinumen, Editorial ESP. Dist: Cambridge Univ. Pr.
Rigol, Francesc, illus. Dan & Din Learn Numbers. 2009. (Learning with Dan & Din Ser.). 12p. (J). (gr. -1-k). bds. 11.40 *(978-1-60754-402-9(4))* Windmill Bks.
—Dan & Din Learn Shapes. 2009. (Learning with Dan & Din Ser.). 12p. (J). (gr. -1-k). bds. 11.40 *(978-1-60754-400-5(8))* Windmill Bks.
Riley, Cooper. Absolutely Awesome Island Animals. 2009. 24p. pap. 9.95 *(978-0-9740582-4-5(6))* Tiki Tales.
Riley, Kana. The Princess & the Wise Woman. Williams, Jenny, illus. 2012. (ENG.). 24p. (J). (gr. k-2). pap. 6.97 *(978-0-8136-2371-9(5)*, Modern Curriculum Pr.) Savvas Learning Co.
Rimes with Ball 6 Packs. KinderRimes. (Kinderstarters Ser.). (gr. -1-1). 21.00 *(978-0-7635-8667-6(6))* Rigby Education.
Rimes with Cake 6 Packs. KinderRimes. (Kinderstarters Ser.). (gr. -1-1). 21.00 *(978-0-7635-8668-3(4))* Rigby Education.
Rimes with Cap 6 Packs. KinderRimes. (Kinderstarters Ser.). (gr. -1-1). 21.00 *(978-0-7635-8669-0(2))* Rigby Education.
Rimes with Cat 6 Packs. KinderRimes. (Kinderstarters Ser.). (gr. -1-1). 21.00 *(978-0-7635-8670-6(6))* Rigby Education.
Rimes with Clock 6 Packs. KinderRimes. (Kinderstarters Ser.). (gr. -1-1). 21.00 *(978-0-7635-8671-3(4))* Rigby Education.
Rimes with Clown 6 Packs. KinderRimes. (Kinderstarters Ser.). (gr. -1-1). 21.00 *(978-0-7635-8672-0(2))* Rigby Education.
Rimes with Drink 6 Packs. KinderRimes. (Kinderstarters Ser.). (gr. -1-1). 21.00 *(978-0-7635-8673-7(0))* Rigby Education.
Rimes with Goat 6 Packs. KinderRimes. (Kinderstarters Ser.). (gr. -1-1). 21.00 *(978-0-7635-8674-4(9))* Rigby Education.
Rimes with Hay 6 Packs. KinderRimes. (Kinderstarters Ser.). (gr. -1-1). 21.00 *(978-0-7635-8675-1(7))* Rigby Education.
Rimes with Hill 6 Packs. KinderRimes. (Kinderstarters Ser.). (gr. -1-1). 21.00 *(978-0-7635-8676-8(5))* Rigby Education.
Rimes with Jump 6 Packs. KinderRimes. (Kinderstarters Ser.). (gr. -1-1). 21.00 *(978-0-7635-8677-5(3))* Rigby Education.
Rimes with Kick 6 Packs. KinderRimes. (Kinderstarters Ser.). (gr. -1-1). 21.00 *(978-0-7635-8678-2(1))* Rigby Education.
Rimes with King 6 Packs. KinderRimes. (Kinderstarters Ser.). (gr. -1-1). 21.00 *(978-0-7635-8679-9(X))* Rigby Education.
Rimes with Man 6 Packs. KinderRimes. (Kinderstarters Ser.). (gr. -1-1). 21.00 *(978-0-7635-8680-5(3))* Rigby Education.
Rimes with Mice 6 Packs. KinderRimes. (Kinderstarters Ser.). (gr. -1-1). 21.00 *(978-0-7635-8681-2(1))* Rigby Education.
Rimes with Net 6 Packs. KinderRimes. (Kinderstarters Ser.). (gr. -1-1). 21.00 *(978-0-7635-8682-9(X))* Rigby Education.
Rimes with Pig 6 Packs. KinderRimes. (Kinderstarters Ser.). (gr. -1-1). 21.00 *(978-0-7635-8683-6(8))* Rigby Education.
Rimes with Ram 6 Packs. KinderRimes. (Kinderstarters Ser.). (gr. -1-1). 21.00 *(978-0-7635-8684-3(6))* Rigby Education.
Rimes with Ship 6 Packs. KinderRimes. (Kinderstarters Ser.). (gr. -1-1). 21.00 *(978-0-7635-8686-7(2))* Rigby Education.
Rimes with Skate 6 Packs. KinderRimes. (Kinderstarters Ser.). (gr. -1-1). 21.00 *(978-0-7635-8687-4(0))* Rigby Education.
Rimes with Snail 6 Packs. KinderRimes. (Kinderstarters Ser.). (gr. -1-1). 21.00 *(978-0-7635-8688-1(9))* Rigby Education.
Rimes with Track 6 Packs. KinderRimes. (Kinderstarters Ser.). (gr. -1-1). 21.00 *(978-0-7635-8689-8(7))* Rigby Education.
Rimes with Train 6 Packs. KinderRimes. (Kinderstarters Ser.). (gr. -1-1). 21.00 *(978-0-7635-8690-4(0))* Rigby Education.
Rinker, Sherri Duskey. Buenas Noches, ConstruccióN. Buenas Noches, DiversióN. (Goodnight, Goodnight, Construction Site Spanish Language Edition) (Bilingual Children's Book, Spanish Books for Kids) Lazaro, Georgina, tr. Lichtenheld, Tom, illus. 2019. (Goodnight, Goodnight Construction Site Ser.). (SPA.). 32p. (J). (gr. -1 — 1). 16.99 *(978-1-4521-7037-4(1))* Chronicle Bks. LLC.
Ripley, Catherine. Great Math Ideas. 2007. (ENG., Illus.). 16p. (J). (gr. 2-2). pap. 9.47 net. *(978-0-7652-8598-0(3)*, Celebration Pr.) Savvas Learning Co.
The River. (Pebble Soup Explorations Ser.). 16p. (gr. -1-18). 31.00 *(978-0-7578-1660-4(6))* Rigby Education.
The River: Small Book. (Pebble Soup Explorations Ser.). 16p. (gr. -1-18). 5.00 *(978-0-7578-1700-7(9))* Rigby Education.
A River Ran Wild. (Lexile Levels Ser.). 9.09 *(978-1-56334-737-5(7))* CENGAGE Learning.
Rivera, Liz. Miguel's Music (Disney/Pixar Coco) The Disney Storybook Art Team, illus. 2017. (Step into Reading Ser.). (ENG.). 32p. (J). (gr. -1-1). pap. 5.99 *(978-0-7364-3811-7(4)*, RH/Disney) Random Hse. Children's Bks.
RiverStream Readers - Pre-1. 2013. (RiverStream Readers Ser.: PK). 124p. (gr. -1-2). 11.49 *(978-1-62588-900-3(3))* Black Rabbit Bks.
A Robbie Reader Series, 12 Bks, Set. 2004. (Illus.). (gr. 1-4). lib. bdg. 203.40 *(978-1-58415-319-1(9))* Mitchell Lane Pubs.
Robbins, Eliza. The Popcorn Surprise, 1 vol. 2006. (Neighborhood Readers Ser.). (ENG.). 16p. (gr. 1-2). pap. 6.50 *(978-1-4042-7232-3(1)*, d4da17c4-8895-4f94-871d-d6adefbfcb68, Rosen Classroom) Rosen Publishing Group, Inc., The.
—Which Holds More? Learning to Compare Volume, 1 vol. (Math for the REAL World Ser.). (ENG., Illus.). 8p. (gr. k-1). 2010. pap. 5.15 *(978-0-8239-8845-7(7)*, b38b2a62-f5ac-41e5-92b1-de18b12c7112) 2004. 29.95 *(978-0-8239-7631-7(9))* Rosen Publishing Group, Inc., The.
Robbins, Eliza & National Geographic Learning Staff. Nana's New Room, 1 vol. 2006. (Neighborhood Readers Ser.). (ENG.). 12p. (C). (gr. k-1). pap. *(978-1-4042-6734-3(4)*, 5764b975-3cb2-4bde-86ac-dd7bff4ab155, Rosen Classroom) Rosen Publishing Group, Inc., The.
Robbins, Trina & Hess, Debra. Native Princess: Sarah Winnemucca. 2007. (Read on! Special Edition: Level AA Ser.). (Illus.). 23p. pap. 4.84 *(978-1-4190-3515-9(0))* Steck-Vaughn.
Roberto Clemente: Fourth Grade Guided Comprehension Level N. (On Our Way to English Ser.). (gr. 4-18). 34.50 *(978-0-7578-7162-7(3))* Rigby Education.
Robertson, Charmaine. All about Data, 1 vol. 2016. (Rosen REAL Readers: STEM & STEAM Collection). (ENG.). 8p. (gr. k-1). pap. 5.46 *(978-1-5081-2404-7(3)*, 8eaeaddf-7c04-450c-8418-ff50d32aa490, Rosen Classroom) Rosen Publishing Group, Inc., The.
—Bend but Don't Break, 1 vol. 2016. (Rosen REAL Readers: STEM & STEAM Collection). (ENG.). 12p. (gr. 1-2). pap. 6.33 *(978-1-5081-2667-6(4)*, 961e6f27-9479-43f6-96ba-8f00f8badff9, Rosen Classroom) Rosen Publishing Group, Inc., The.
—Building with Flexible Materials, 1 vol. 2016. (Rosen REAL Readers: STEM & STEAM Collection). (ENG.). 12p. (gr. 1-2). pap. 6.33 *(978-1-5081-2452-8(3)*, fcd58708-e439-4974-a7b4-53f794dfb68d, Rosen Classroom) Rosen Publishing Group, Inc., The.
—Hot Rocks, 1 vol. 2016. (Rosen REAL Readers: STEM & STEAM Collection). (ENG.). 8p. (gr. k-1). pap. 5.46 *(978-1-5081-2625-6(9)*, 09959cb3-dd82-4986-a6a0-64fdf2d40d50, Rosen Classroom) Rosen Publishing Group, Inc., The.
—The Landslide, 1 vol. 2016. (Rosen REAL Readers: STEM & STEAM Collection). (ENG.). 12p. (gr. 1-2). pap. 6.33 *(978-1-5081-2676-8(3)*, 879b6e45-90f4-4da8-bd5e-3ca07ce2de9d, Rosen Classroom) Rosen Publishing Group, Inc., The.
Robertson, J. Jean. My Name Is Not... DuFalla, Anita, illus. 2012. (Little Birdie Bks.). (ENG.). 24p. (gr. 1-2). pap. 9.95 *(978-1-61810-320-8(2)*, 9781618103208) Rourke Educational Media.
Robes, Ruth & Almendro, Herminio. Habia una Vez: Libro Segundo de Lectura. (SPA.). (J). pap. 12.95 *(978-84-357-0109-9(3)*, CPR30) Ediciones y Distribuciones Codice, S.A. ESP. Dist: Continental Bk. Co., Inc.
Robins, Maureen Picard. One Land, Many Cultures. 2012. (Little World Social Studies). (ENG.). 24p. (gr. k-2). pap. 9.95 *(978-1-61810-276-8(1)*, 9781618102768) Rourke Educational Media.
Robinson, Hilary. Beauty & the Pea, 1 vol. Sanfilippo, Simona, illus. 2013. (ENG.). 32p. (J). pap. *(978-0-7787-1159-9(5))* Crabtree Publishing Co.
—Cinderella & the Beanstalk, 1 vol. Sanfilippo, Simona, illus. 2013. (ENG.). 32p. (J). pap. *(978-0-7787-1161-2(7))* Crabtree Publishing Co.
—Hansel, Gretel, & the Ugly Duckling. Sanfilippo, Simona, illus. 2013. (ENG.). 32p. (J). pap. *(978-0-7787-1166-7(8))* Crabtree Publishing Co.
—Rapunzel & the Billy Goats, 1 vol. Sanfilippo, Simona, illus. 2013. (ENG.). 32p. (J). pap. *(978-0-7787-1158-2(7))* Crabtree Publishing Co.
Rodgers, Kelly. The Byzantine Empire: A Society That Shaped the World, 1 vol. rev. ed. 2012. (Social Studies: Informational Text Ser.). (ENG.). 32p. (gr. 4-8). pap. 11.99 *(978-1-4333-5001-6(7))* Teacher Created Materials, Inc.
—Justinian I: Byzantine Emperor, 1 vol. rev. ed. 2012. (Social Studies: Informational Text Ser.). (ENG.). 32p. (gr. 4-8). pap. 11.99 *(978-1-4333-5002-3(5))* Teacher Created Materials, Inc.
—Leaders in the Texas Revolution: United for a Cause, 1 vol. rev. ed. 2012. (Social Studies: Informational Text Ser.). (ENG.). 32p. (gr. 3-5). pap. 11.99 *(978-1-4333-5047-4(5))* Teacher Created Materials, Inc.
—The Texas Revolution: Fighting for Independence, 1 vol. rev. ed. 2012. (Social Studies: Informational Text Ser.). (ENG.). 32p. (gr. 3-5). pap. 11.99 *(978-1-4333-5046-7(7))* Teacher Created Materials, Inc.
Roesser, Griffin. Digger Makes a Friend, 1 vol. 2006. (Neighborhood Readers Ser.). (ENG.). 8p. (gr. k-1). pap. 5.15 *(978-1-4042-5774-0(8)*, 15e0d567-6766-4a0a-9e7f-0ed3c808292a, Rosen Classroom) Rosen Publishing Group, Inc., The.
—Who Ate the Turkey?, 1 vol. 2006. (Neighborhood Readers Ser.). (ENG.). 12p. (gr. k-1). pap. 5.90 *(978-1-4042-6457-1(4)*, afed3ba8-a504-4cf7-a0e6-42a7b323526e, Rosen Classroom) Rosen Publishing Group, Inc., The.
Rog, Lori Jamison. Guided Reading Basics: Organizing, Managing, & Implementing a Balanced Literacy Program in K-3. 2003. (ENG., Illus.). 128p. (gr. k-3). pap. 30.67 *(978-1-57110-383-3(X)*, 383) Pembroke Pubs., Ltd. CAN. Dist: Stenhouse Pubs.
Rogers, Jane & Benchmark Education Co., LLC Staff. The Best Nest. 2015. (BuildUp Ser.). (J). (gr. 1). *(978-1-4900-0721-2(0))* Benchmark Education Co.
Roi Visual, illus. Read with Robocar Poli: Hooray for the Heroes! (Level 2: Qualified Reader) Hooray for the Heroes! 2019. (Robocar Poli Ser.). 32p. (J). (gr. -1). 3.99 *(978-2-89802-002-5(8)*, CrackBoom! Bks.) Chouette Publishing CAN. Dist: Publishers Group West (PGW).
Roi Visual, Roi, illus. Read with Robocar Poli: a Visit to the Farm (Level 1: Starting Reader) A Visit to the Farm (Level 1: Starting Reader) 2019. (Robocar Poli Ser.). 32p. (J). (gr. -1). 3.99 *(978-2-924786-99-4(1)*, CrackBoom! Bks.) Chouette Publishing CAN. Dist: Publishers Group West (PGW).
Rollason, Jane. Level 2: Gandhi. 2nd ed. 2008. (Pearson English Graded Readers Ser.). (ENG., Illus.). 32p. pap. 12.71 *(978-1-4058-7693-3(X)*, Pearson ELT) Pearson Education.
Rollason, Jane, adapted by. Amazing Philanthropists: B1 (Collins Amazing People ELT Readers), 1 vol. 2014. (Collins English Readers Ser.). (ENG.). 96p. 13.95 *(978-0-00-754504-9(5))* HarperCollins Pubs. Ltd. GBR. Dist: Independent Pubs. Group.
RollasonJane. Freddie's War Level 6 Advanced. 2010. (Cambridge Experience Readers Ser.). (ENG.). 128p. pap. 14.75 *(978-84-8323-909-4(4))* Cambridge Univ. Pr.
—Killer Bees Level 2 Elementary/Lower-Intermediate. 2009. (Cambridge Experience Readers Ser.). (ENG.). 64p. pap. 14.75 *(978-84-8323-503-4(X))* Cambridge Univ. Pr.
The Roller Coaster: KinderWords Individual Title Six-Packs. (Kinderstarters Ser.). 8p. (gr. -1-1). 21.00 *(978-0-7635-8708-6(7))* Rigby Education.
Roman, Edward. My Busy Year, 1 vol. 2012. (InfoMax Readers Ser.). (ENG., Illus.). 24p. (J). (gr. 1-1). pap. 8.25 *(978-1-4488-9004-0(7)*, a40c6a71-e77d-4fb1-b547-6b8a8cf999ef, Rosen Classroom) Rosen Publishing Group, Inc., The.
Romero, Libby. National Geographic Readers: Animal Architects (L3) 2019. (Readers Ser.). (Illus.). 48p. (J). (gr. 3-7). pap. 4.99 *(978-1-4263-3327-9(7))*; (ENG., lib. bdg. 14.90 *(978-1-4263-3328-6(5))* Disney Publishing Worldwide. (National Geographic Kids).
—National Geographic Readers: Vikings (L2) 2018. (Readers Ser.). (Illus.). 32p. (J). (gr. 1-3). pap. 4.99 *(978-1-4263-3218-0(1)*, National Geographic Kids) Disney Publishing Worldwide.
Rondina, Catherine. The 10 Worst Things about Internet. 2008. 14.99 *(978-1-55448-556-7(8))* Scholastic Library Publishing.
A Rookie Reader(r) — Level C Boxed Set 1 (a Rookie Reader - Boxed Sets), Set. 2005. (Rookie Reader Boxed Sets Ser.). (ENG.). (J). (gr. k-2). 2.99 *(978-0-516-25327-5(1)*, Children's Pr.) Scholastic Library Publishing.
A Rookie Reader: Purple Is Part of a Rainbow, Too Many Balloons, I Love Cats: Level B, Grades K-1. Set 1. 2005. (Rookie Reader Ser.). (ENG.). 96p. (J). (gr. -1-2). 9.95 *(978-0-516-25326-8(3)*, Children's Pr.) Scholastic Library Publishing.
Rookie Reader Boxed Set: All about Me, 1 vol. 2006. (ENG., Illus.). 32p. (J). (gr. k-2). pap., pap. 9.95 *(978-0-531-16924-7(3)*, Children's Pr.) Scholastic Library Publishing.

Rosa-Mendoza, Gladys. My Body/Mi Cuerpo. Butler, Chris, illus. 2007. (English Spanish Foundations Ser.). (ENG & SPA.). 20p. (gr. -1-2). pap. 19.95 (978-1-931398-85-5(2)) Me+Mi Publishing.

Rosado, Maribel. Little Red Hen Is a Good Hen. 2017. (Text Connections Guided Close Reading Ser.). (J). (gr. 1). (978-1-4900-1804-1(2)) Benchmark Education Co.

Rose, Emma. Energy Every Day, 6 vols., Set. 2004. (Phonics Readers Books 37-72 Ser.). (ENG.). 8p. (gr. k-1). pap. 35.70 (978-0-7368-4086-6(9)) Capstone.

—Our Natural Resources, 6 vols., Set. 2004. (Phonics Readers Books 37-72 Ser.). (ENG.). 16p. (gr. k-1). pap. 35.70 (978-0-7368-4070-5(2)) Capstone.

Rose, Mary. Dolphin Readers Starter. My Family. International Edition. 2010. (ENG., Illus.). 20p. 5.00 (978-0-19-440079-4(4)) Oxford Univ. Pr., Inc.

Rosen Common Core Math Readers: Levels a - D. 2013. (Rosen Math Readers Ser.). 16p. (J). (gr. k-1). pap. 1683.00 (978-1-4777-2214-5(9)); pap. 280.50 (978-1-4777-2213-8(0)) Rosen Publishing Group, Inc., The. (Rosen Classroom).

Rosen Common Core Math Readers: Levels d - I. 2013. (Rosen Math Readers Ser.). 24p. (J). (gr. 1-2). pap. 1534.50 (978-1-4777-2219-0(X)); pap. 255.75 (978-1-4777-2220-6(3)) Rosen Publishing Group, Inc., The. (Rosen Classroom).

Rosen, Lucy, et al. The Squeakquel: Meet the 'Munks. 2009. (I Can Read Level 2 Ser.). (ENG., Illus.). 32p. (J). (gr. k-3). pap. 3.99 (978-0-06-184566-6(3)) HarperCollins Pubs.

Rosen, Rachel & Benchmark Education Co., LLC Staff. Rob, Ron, & I. 2015. (StartUp Ser.). (J). (gr. k). (978-1-4900-0697-0(4)) Benchmark Education Co.

—Sit, Sit, Sit. 2015. (StartUp Ser.). (J). (gr. k). (978-1-4900-0689-5(3)) Benchmark Education Co.

Rosen Real Readers Big Books. 855.90 (978-1-4042-6227-0(X)) Rosen Publishing Group, Inc., The.

Rosenthal, Amy Krouse. Cookies Board Book: Bite-Size Life Lessons. Dyer, Jane, illus. 2016. (ENG.). 36p. (J). (gr. -1 — 1). bds. 7.99 (978-0-06-242739-7(3), HarperFestival) HarperCollins Pubs.

Roses Sing on New Snow. (Lexile Levels Ser.). 9.09 (978-1-56334-721-4(0)) CENGAGE Learning.

Ross, Dev. We Both Read Bilingual Edition-Frank & the Giant/Sapi y el Globo. Reinhart, Larry, illus. 2011. (ENG & SPA.). 44p. (J). pap. 5.99 (978-1-60115-042-4(3)) Treasure Bay, Inc.

Ross, Jeff. Shutout, 1 vol. 2019. (Orca Sports Ser.). (ENG.). 160p. (J). (gr. 4-7). pap. 9.95 (978-1-4598-1876-7(8)) Orca Bk. Pubs. USA.

Rosselson, Leon. Tom the Whistling Wonder. Haslam, John, illus. 2005. (ENG.). 24p. (J). lib. bdg. 23.65 (978-1-59646-758-3(4)) Dingles & Co.

Round: Individual Title Six-Packs. (gr. 1-2). 22.00 (978-0-7635-9180-9(7)) Rigby Education.

Roxbee Cox, Phil. Phonics Stories for Young Readers, Vol. 2. 2009. (Phonics Readers Ser.). 96p. (J). 14.99 (978-0-7945-1887-5(7), Usborne) EDC Publishing.

Roy, Alene Adele. The Legend of Dragonfly Pond: Book Three. 2010. (ENG.). 60p. pap. 23.99 (978-1-4490-0834-5(8)) AuthorHouse.

Roy G Biv: Level G. Group 2. (Story Box Ser.). 16p. 31.50 (978-0-322-00333-0(4)) Wright Group/McGraw-Hill.

Roy, James. Queasy Rider. 2008. (Lightning Strikes Ser.). (ENG.). 96p. (J). pap. (978-1-921150-57-9(2)) Walker Bks. Australia Pty. Ltd.

Roza, Greg. A Day for Dad, 1 vol. 2006. (Neighborhood Readers Ser.). (ENG.). 16p. (gr. 1-2). pap. 6.50 (978-1-4042-7268-2(2), e09b164a-f511-409e-8eeb-b617ac4c0562, Rosen Classroom) Rosen Publishing Group, Inc., The.

—El Día de San Valentín (Valentines for Vinnie) 2007. (Lecturas del barrio (Neighborhood Readers) Ser.). (SPA.). 12p. 33.50 (978-1-4042-7301-6(8), Rosen Classroom) Rosen Publishing Group, Inc., The.

—Goal!, 1 vol. 2006. (Neighborhood Readers Ser.). (ENG.). 16p. (gr. 1-2). pap. 6.50 (978-1-4042-7046-6(9), 08747fa9-73fa-4f31-b945-f1530a3ff6fb, Rosen Classroom) Rosen Publishing Group, Inc., The.

—Happy New Year!, 1 vol. 2006. (Neighborhood Readers Ser.). (ENG., Illus.). 16p. (gr. 1-2). pap. 6.50 (978-1-4042-7026-8(4), 8687ac4d-c67d-467d-9fa8-bc57916e13bb, Rosen Classroom) Rosen Publishing Group, Inc., The.

—Lucy's Lunch, 1 vol. 2006. (Neighborhood Readers Ser.). (ENG.). 8p. (gr. k-1). pap. 5.15 (978-1-4042-5649-1(0), 96767313-dc8e-4038-9300-8375d1abaf20, Rosen Classroom) Rosen Publishing Group, Inc., The.

—Out & About, 1 vol. 2006. (Neighborhood Readers Ser.). (ENG.). 8p. (gr. k-1). pap. 5.15 (978-1-4042-5680-4(6), 82a60e4e-85ef-43a0-bb1b-80a4a8974f34, Rosen Classroom) Rosen Publishing Group, Inc., The.

—The Peanut Butter Party, 1 vol. 2006. (Neighborhood Readers Ser.). (ENG., Illus.). 12p. (gr. 1-2). pap. 5.90 (978-1-4042-6827-2(8), c84f875d-6805-4541-95d8-f5f3794dbb5d, Rosen Classroom) Rosen Publishing Group, Inc., The.

—A Piggy Bank for Pedro, 1 vol. 2006. (Neighborhood Readers Ser.). (ENG.). 8p. (gr. k-1). pap. 5.15 (978-1-4042-5714-6(4), a44543a8-a638-4a94-9d39-44dac6499a0e, Rosen Classroom) Rosen Publishing Group, Inc., The.

—Valentines for Vinnie. (Neighborhood Readers Ser.). (ENG.). 12p. 2007. 33.50 (978-1-4042-7300-9(X)) 2006. (gr. 1-2). pap. 5.90 (978-1-4042-6799-2(9), af158d89-bed9-49af-9c39-e9cee6966306) Rosen Publishing Group, Inc., The. (Rosen Classroom).

—Where's the Spaghetti?, 1 vol. 2006. (Neighborhood Readers Ser.). (ENG.). 8p. (gr. k-1). pap. 5.15 (978-1-4042-5655-2(5), 35bc8507-929d-463b-998c-dfe102700fad, Rosen Classroom) Rosen Publishing Group, Inc., The.

Rubin, Elycia. No Biggy! A Story about Overcoming Everyday Obstacles. Talbot, Josh, illus. 2019. (ENG.). 40p. (J). (— 1). pap. 7.99 (978-1-9848-9249-2(5), Dragonfly Bks.) Random Hse. Children's Bks.

Rucker, Jeffrey A. A Trip to the Fire Station, 1 vol. 2005. (Rosen REAL Readers Ser.). (ENG., Illus.). 12p. (gr. 1-2). pap. 5.90 (978-0-8239-8131-1(2), 25667665-b8e0-4cdd-9f09-6fed75f65ee6) Rosen Publishing Group, Inc., The.

Ruffell, Ann & Orme, David. Treachery by Night. 2004. (Shades Ser.). (ENG.). 62p. (J). pap. (978-0-237-52728-0(6)) Evans Brothers, Ltd.

Ruiz-Flores, Lupe. The Battle of the Snow Cones/La Guerra de las Raspas. 2010. (SPA & ENG., Illus.). 32p. (J). (gr. -1-3). 16.95 (978-1-55885-575-5(0), Piñata Books) Arte Publico Pr.

A Rumble & a Grumble: 3-in-1 Package. (Sails Literacy Ser.). 24p. (gr. 1-18). 57.00 (978-0-7578-3210-9(5)) Rigby Education.

Rupp, Kristina. Two Desert Homes. 2016. (1-3Y Ecosystems Ser.). (ENG., Illus.). 20p. (J). pap. 9.60 (978-1-64053-088-1(6), ARC Pr. Bks.) American Reading Co.

Russell, Marcia. A Visit to a Marine Base, 1 vol. 2nd rev. ed. 2011. (TIME for KIDS(r): Informational Text Ser.). (ENG.). 24p. (gr. 2-3). pap. 9.99 (978-1-4333-3609-6(X)) Teacher Created Materials, Inc.

Ruth, Annie. I Can Read. Ruth, Annie, illus. l.t. ed. 2005. (Illus.). 32p. (J). (gr. -1-3). pap. 10.00 (978-0-9656306-7-2(6)) Ruth, A. Creations.

Ruurs, Margriet. Bus to the Badlands, 1 vol. Dávila, Claudia, illus. 2018. (Orca Echoes Ser.). (ENG.). 88p. (J). (gr. 1-3). pap. 6.95 (978-1-4598-1670-1(6)) Orca Bk. Pubs. USA.

Ryan. Lost: Big Book: Level Q. Group 1. (Take-Twostm Ser.). 32p. 38.95 (978-0-322-04485-2(5)) Wright Group/McGraw-Hill.

Ryan, Ann Marie. The Best Gift. Denis, Florencia, illus. 2011. (My Phonics Readers: Level 1 Ser.). 24p. (J). (gr. -1-1). 24.25 (978-1-84898-507-0(X)) Sea-To-Sea Pubns.

Ryan, Margaret. Collins Big Cat Phonics for Letters & Sounds - in the Frog Bog: Band 03/Yellow, Bd. 3. Capriotti, Benedetta, illus. 2018. (Collins Big Cat Phonics Ser.). (ENG.). 16p. (J). (gr. k-1). pap. 6.99 (978-0-00-825154-3(1)) HarperCollins Pubs. Ltd. GBR. Dist: Independent Pubs. Group.

Rylant, Cynthia. The Brownie & Pearl Collection: Brownie & Pearl Step Out; Brownie & Pearl Get Dolled up; Brownie & Pearl Grab a Bite; Brownie & Pearl See the Sights; Brownie & Pearl Go for a Spin; Brownie & Pearl Hit the Hay. Biggs, Brian, illus. 2016. (Brownie & Pearl Ser.). (ENG.). 144p. (J). (gr. -1-k). 12.99 (978-1-4814-8653-8(5), Simon Spotlight) Simon Spotlight.

—Henry & Mudge & a Very Merry Christmas. Stevenson, Suçie, illus. 2005. (Henry & Mudge Ser.). 40p. (gr. -1-3). 14.00 (978-0-7569-5816-9(4)) Perfection Learning Corp.

—Poppleton Se Divierte. Teague, Mark, illus. 2006. (Poppleton Ser.). (SPA.). 48p. pap. 11.73 (978-0-15-356487-1(3)) Harcourt Children's Bks.

Sabo, J. Train Wrecker. 2011. 28p. pap. 24.95 (978-1-4626-4379-0(5)) America Star Bks.

Saffiedine, Amanda. I Don't Understand. 2009. 32p. pap. 12.99 (978-1-4490-1310-3(4)) AuthorHouse.

Sage, Alison. Going on a Plane Purple Band. 2016. (Cambridge Reading Adventures Ser.). (ENG., Illus.). 24p. pap. 8.80 (978-1-316-50088-0(8)) Cambridge Univ. Pr.

Sagner, Sibel. The Show & Tell Day Blue Band. Perez, Moni, illus. 2017. (Cambridge Reading Adventures Ser.). (ENG.). 16p. pap. 6.15 (978-1-108-40191-3(0)) Cambridge Univ. Pr.

Said Mouse to Mole. 2005. (J). per. 8.95 (978-1-59566-139-5(5)) QEB Publishing Inc.

Saltzberg, Barney. I Love Cats. 2006. 20p. pap. 8.99 (978-0-7636-3318-9(6)) Four Blocks.

Salzmann, Mary Elizabeth. Come Home with Me! 2004. (Sight Words Ser.). (ENG., Illus.). 24p. (J). (gr. k-3). lib. bdg. 24.21 (978-1-59197-465-9(8)) ABDO Publishing Co.

—It's Not Good, It's Great! 2003. (Sight Words Ser.). (ENG., Illus.). 24p. (J). (gr. k-3). lib. bdg. 24.21 (978-1-59197-479-6(8), SandCastle) ABDO Publishing Co.

—Out for the Summer! 2004. (Sight Words Ser.). (ENG., Illus.). 24p. (J). (gr. k-3). lib. bdg. 24.21 (978-1-59197-472-7(0), SandCastle) ABDO Publishing Co.

—Snow & More Snow! 2004. (Sight Words Ser.). (ENG., Illus.). 24p. (J). (gr. k-3). lib. bdg. 24.21 (978-1-59197-470-3(4), SandCastle) ABDO Publishing Co.

—They Are the Best! 2004. (Sight Words Ser.). (ENG., Illus.). 24p. (J). (gr. k-3). lib. bdg. 24.21 (978-1-59197-474-1(7), SandCastle) ABDO Publishing Co.

—Who Is This at the Beach? 2004. (Sight Words Ser.). (ENG., Illus.). 24p. (J). (gr. k-3). lib. bdg. 24.21 (978-1-59197-480-2(1), SandCastle) ABDO Publishing Co.

Sam's big Clean-up: Individual Title Six-Packs. (gr. 1-2). 25.00 (978-0-7635-9145-8(9)) Rigby Education.

Sam's Dad: Level M, 6 vols. 128p. (gr. 2-3). 41.95 (978-0-7699-1029-1(7)) Shortland Pubns. (U. S. A.) Inc.

Samson, Tess. Snack Time. 2010. (Sight Word Readers Ser.). (J). 3.49 (978-1-60719-618-1(2)) Newmark Learning LLC.

—What Goes Up? 2010. (Sight Word Readers Ser.). (J). 3.49 (978-1-60719-617-4(4)) Newmark Learning LLC.

Samuel, Adele. Wild World of Sports. 2007. (Steck-Vaughn BOLDPRINT Anthologies Ser.). (ENG., Illus.). 48p. (gr. 4-7). pap. 16.90 (978-1-4190-4020-7(0)) Houghton Mifflin Harcourt Publishing Co.

Samuel, Nigel. Creatures of the Deep. 2007. (Steck-Vaughn BOLDPRINT Anthologies Ser.). (ENG., Illus.). 48p. (gr. 4-7). pap. 16.90 (978-1-4190-4021-4(9)) Houghton Mifflin Harcourt Publishing Co.

—The 10 Coolest Wonders of the Universe. 2008. (Illus.). (J). 14.99 (978-1-55448-490-4(1)) Scholastic Library Publishing.

—The 10 Mightiest Mountains. 2007. (Illus.). (J). 14.99 (978-1-55448-509-3(6)) Scholastic Library Publishing.

Sand Castles: Level I, 6 vols. (Wonder Worldtm Ser.). 16p. 29.95 (978-0-7802-4597-6(0)) Wright Group/McGraw-Hill.

Sandage, Charley. ALL AROUND ARKANSAS Big Book. 2005. (Illus.). (J). pap. (978-0-9794044-2-9(8)) Archeological Assessments, Inc.

Sander, Sonia. Werewolf Watch. 2012. (Scooby Doo Reader Ser.). lib. bdg. 13.55 (978-0-606-23961-5(8)) Turtleback.

Sandler, Michael & Hess, Debra. Checkered Flag! 2007. (Read on! Special Edition: Level AA Ser.). (Illus.). 23p. (J). (gr. 4-7). pap. 4.84 (978-1-4190-3516-6(9)) Steck-Vaughn.

Sandoval, Migs, illus. Beauty & the Beast: Level 3: Learn Chinese Mandarin Through Fairy Tales. 2006. (Learn Chinese Through Fairy Tales Ser.). (ENG & CHI.). 29p. (J). (gr. -1-3). pap. 14.95 incl. audio compact disk (978-1-891888-91-5(9)) Slangman Publishing.

Sands, Nora. Crunch & Munch: Band 05/Green (Collins Big Cat) 2007. (Collins Big Cat Ser.). (ENG., Illus.). 24p. (J). (gr. k-1). pap. 7.99 (978-0-00-718665-5(7)) HarperCollins Pubs. Ltd. GBR. Dist: Independent Pubs. Group.

A Sandwich Person: Level H, 6 vols. (Wonder Worldtm Ser.). 16p. 29.95 (978-0-7802-2028-7(5)) Wright Group/McGraw-Hill.

Sanfilippo, Simona, illus. Rapunzel. 2009. (Flip-Up Fairy Tales Ser.). 24p. (J). (gr. -1-2). (978-1-84643-292-7(8)) Child's Play International Ltd.

Santiago Baca, Jimmy. En Suelo Firme: El Nacimiento de un Poeta. Berástegui, Manu, tr. 2005. (SPA., Illus.). 360p. pap. 25.95 (978-84-204-6424-4(4), Alfaguara) Santillana USA Publishing Co., Inc.

Sargemt, Dave & Sargent, Pat. Batley Needs Glasses, 10 vols., Vol. 12. Robinson, Laura, illus. 2004. (Learn to Read Ser.: 10). 18p. (J). lib. bdg. 20.95 (978-1-56763-819-6(8)) Ozark Publishing.

Sargent, Brian. Altruism: What's in It for Me?, 1 vol. 2014. (ENG., Illus.). 32p. (J). pap., E-Book 9.50 (978-1-107-62262-3(X)) Cambridge Univ. Pr.

—Life on the Edge, 1 vol. 2014. (ENG., Illus.). 28p. (J). pap., E-Book 9.50 (978-1-107-63028-4(2)) Cambridge Univ. Pr.

—Losing It: The Meaning of Loss, 1 vol. 2014. (ENG., Illus.). 28p. (J). pap., E-Book 9.50 (978-1-107-68191-0(X)) Cambridge Univ. Pr.

—Mark Your Territory Intermediate Book with Online Access, 1 vol. 2014. (ENG., Illus.). 28p. pap., E-Book, E-Book 9.50 (978-1-107-65895-0(0)) Cambridge Univ. Pr.

Sargent, Dave & Sargent, Pat. Batley Needs Glasses, 10 vols., Vol. 12. Robinson, Laura, illus. 2004. (Learn to Read Ser.: 10).Tr. of Batley Necesita Anteojos. 18p. (J). pap. 10.95 (978-1-56763-820-2(1)) Ozark Publishing.

SargentBrian. Life in Mumbai High Beginning Book with Online Access, 1 vol. 2014. (ENG., Illus.). 24p. pap., E-Book 9.50 (978-1-107-62167-1(4)) Cambridge Univ. Pr.

—THE TRADITIONS OF DEATH INTERMEDIATE BOOK WITH ONLINE ACCESS, 1 vol. 2014. (ENG., Illus.). 28p. (J). pap., E-Book, E-Book 9.50 (978-1-107-63578-4(0)) Cambridge Univ. Pr.

The Saturday Club. (Early Intervention Levels Ser.). 31.86 (978-0-7362-0623-5(X)) CENGAGE Learning.

The Saturday Club (18), Vol. 18. (Early Intervention Levels Ser.). 5.31 (978-0-7362-0611-2(6)) CENGAGE Learning.

Saviola, Erin. Airplane Jane, 1 vol. 2006. (Neighborhood Readers Ser.). (ENG., Illus.). 16p. (gr. 1-2). pap. 6.50 (978-1-4042-7236-1(4), 44db2dd9-dafd-4b62-96b8-e3b996f08434, Rosen Classroom) Rosen Publishing Group, Inc., The.

—The Biggest Fish, 1 vol. 2006. (Neighborhood Readers Ser.). (ENG.). 8p. (gr. k-1). pap. 5.15 (978-1-4042-6453-3(1), 36bd3c36-253a-465f-bba7-a8430fae70f0, Rosen Classroom) Rosen Publishing Group, Inc., The.

Say Hello! (Early Intervention Levels Ser.). 23.10 (978-0-7362-0004-2(5)); 3.85 (978-1-56334-955-3(8)) CENGAGE Learning.

Sayles, Alayne. Alphie & the Alphabets: A Fun Way to Learn to Read. Platt, Greg, illus. 2005. 44p. (J). spiral bd. 79.95 incl. audio compact disk (978-0-9767506-0-4(0)) Reading Studio Pr.

Saylor-Marchant, Linda. Hip Hop into Reading Series: It's easy to read & rap/read & rap like the President. 2009. (Illus.). (J). pap. 19.95 (978-0-615-24951-3(5)) 44 Enterprises.

Sazaklis, John. Day of Doom. 2013. (Justice League Classic: I Can Read! Ser.). (J). lib. bdg. 13.55 (978-0-606-32162-4(4)) Turtleback.

Scaglione, Joanne & Small, Gail. Life's Little Lessons: An Inch-By-Inch Tale of Success. 2006. (ENG., Illus.). 64p. pap. 29.00 (978-1-57886-336-5(8)) Rowman & Littlefield Education.

Scanlon, Jack. Rainbow Zoo, 1 vol. 2006. (Neighborhood Readers Ser.). (ENG., Illus.). 8p. (gr. k-1). pap. 5.15 (978-1-4042-6686-5(0), 59a8fa80-4f08-4c73-85b0-e625d32b9002, Rosen Classroom) Rosen Publishing Group, Inc., The.

A Scare in the City. (Early Intervention Levels Ser.). 31.86 (978-0-7362-0625-9(6)) CENGAGE Learning.

Schaefer, Elizabeth. Rey Meets BB-8. 2015. (Star Wars: World of Reading Ser.). (J). lib. bdg. 13.55 (978-0-606-38312-7(3)) Turtleback.

Schecter, Deborah. My First Bilingual Little Readers: Level A. 2005. (ENG.). 64p. (gr. k-1). pap. 11.99 (978-0-439-70069-6(8), Teaching Resources) Scholastic, Inc.

Scherm, Deedra. Cinco Panes y un Par de Peces: Una Historia de la Fe y de Dar. Dreyer, Laura, illus. 2008. (SPA.). 20p. (J). (gr. -1-3). bds. 7.99 (978-1-934789-06-3(2)) Lemon Vision Productions.

—Solo uno Como Yo: Una Rima Dulce y Pequenita para Ayudar Hacer Brillar Tu Lucecita. Dreyer, Laura, illus. 2008. (SPA.). 22p. (J). (gr. -1-3). 7.99 (978-1-934789-05-6(4)) Lemon Vision Productions.

Schiavone, Fabio. Ben Makes a Mess: Practicing the Short E Sound, 1 vol. 2016. (Rosen Phonics Readers Ser.). (ENG., Illus.). 8p. (J). (gr. -1-2). pap. (978-1-5081-3089-5(2), 298a60e0-a30c-4e63-be00-ce92e89cabbe, Rosen Classroom) Rosen Publishing Group, Inc., The.

—Vera the Deer: Practicing the EER Sound, 1 vol. 2016. (Rosen Phonics Readers Ser.). (ENG., Illus.). 12p. (J). (gr. -1-2). pap. (978-1-5081-3559-3(2), 6dafa3f1-d4ac-44d9-bcda-8d99ddf207f6, Rosen Classroom) Rosen Publishing Group, Inc., The.

Schifini, Alfredo, et al. Avenues C: Student Anthology. 2003. (Avenues Ser.). (ENG.). (C). (gr. 2-18). 103.95 (978-0-7362-1876-4(9)) CENGAGE Learning.

—Avenues d: Student Anthology. 2003. (Avenues Ser.). (ENG.). 504p. (C). (gr. 3-18). 103.95 (978-0-7362-1673-9(1)) CENGAGE Learning.

—Avenues e: Student Anthology. 2003. (Avenues Ser.). (ENG.). 504p. (C). (gr. 4-18). 103.95 (978-0-7362-1709-5(6)) CENGAGE Learning.

—Avenues F: Student Anthology. 2003. (Avenues Ser.). (ENG.). 512p. (C). (gr. 5-18). 103.95 (978-0-7362-1745-3(2)) CENGAGE Learning.

Scholastic. All about Me/ Todo Sobre Mí (Words Are Fun/Diverpalabras) (Bilingual) (Bilingual Edition) 2017. (Words Are Fun / Diverpalabras Ser.). (SPA.). 12p. (J). (gr. -1 — 1). bds. 8.95 (978-0-531-23071-8(6), Children's Pr.) Scholastic Library Publishing.

—Amazing Animals A-D Kindergarten Box Set - Scholastic Early Learners, 1 vol. 2018. (Scholastic Early Learners Ser.). (ENG.). 256p. (J). (gr. -1-3). 16.99 (978-1-338-29961-8(1)) Scholastic, Inc.

Scholastic Editors. The Rescue Mission. 2015. (Ninjago Readers Ser.: 11). lib. bdg. 13.55 (978-0-606-36373-0(4)) Turtleback.

Scholastic, Inc. Staff. Look at Me! 2017. (Scholastic Early Learners Ser.). (ENG.). 10p. (J). (gr. -1 — 1). bds. 6.99 (978-1-338-16141-0(5), Cartwheel Bks.) Scholastic, Inc.

Scholastic, Inc. Staff & Bermiss, Aamir Lee. I Hate to Be Sick! Wilson-Max, Ken, illus. 2004. (Just for You Ser.). (ENG.). 32p. (gr. k-3). pap. 3.99 (978-0-439-56877-7(3), Teaching Resources) Scholastic, Inc.

Scholastic, Inc. Staff & Chapman, Cindy. Baby Animals, 6 vols., Set. 2003. (Phonics Readers 1-36 Ser.). (ENG.). 8p. (gr. k-1). pap. 29.70 (978-0-7368-3188-8(6)) Capstone.

Scholastic, Inc. Staff & Scholastic, Scholastic Scholastic. Adventures in LEGO City, Set. 2nd ed. 2015. (LEGO City Ser.). (ENG.). (J). (gr. -1-3). 24.99 (978-0-545-80861-3(8)) Scholastic, Inc.

Scholastic, Inc. Staff & Windham, Ryder. Fire Ring Race, 1. 2010. (Star Wars Adventures in Hyperspace Ser.). (ENG.). 96p. (J). (gr. 2-4). 17.44 (978-0-545-21358-5(4)) Scholastic, Inc.

Scholastic News Nonfiction Readers: Kids Like Me (Global Awareness), 5 vols., Set. Incl. This Is the Way We Dress. Behrens, Janice. lib. bdg. 21.19 (978-0-531-21338-4(2)); This Is the Way We Eat Our Food. Falk, Laine. lib. bdg. 21.19 (978-0-531-21339-1(0)); This Is the Way We Go to School. Falk, Laine. lib. bdg. 21.19 (978-0-531-21341-4(2), Children's Pr.); This Is the Way We Help at Home. Miller, Amanda. lib. bdg. 21.19 (978-0-531-21340-7(4)); This Is the Way We Play. Miller, Amanda. lib. bdg. 21.19 (978-0-531-21342-1(0)); 24p. (J). (gr. k-3). 2009. Set lib. bdg. 110.00 (978-0-531-21035-2(9), Children's Pr.) Scholastic Library Publishing.

The School Day, 2, Pack. (Chiquilibros Ser.). (gr. -1-1). 12.00 (978-0-7635-8542-6(4)) Rigby Education.

School Zone. Wonder Words Flash Action Software. 2007. 128p. pap. 15.99 (978-1-58947-112-2(1)) School Zone Publishing Co.

School Zone Publishing Company Staff. Beginning Reading 1-2. deluxe ed. 2019. (ENG.). 64p. (J). (gr. 1-2). pap., wbk. ed. 4.49 (978-1-58947-337-9(X), d680bc01-0363-4089-9210-f6a3413d6c46) School Zone Publishing Co.

School Zone Staff. Readiness. 2005. (ENG.). 56p. (J). 2.79 (978-1-58947-479-6(1)) School Zone Publishing Co.

Schories, Pat, illus. Biscuit & the Big Parade! 2018. 29p. (J). (978-1-5444-0450-9(6)) Harper & Row Ltd.

—Biscuit Flies a Kite. 2017. 29p. (J). (978-0-605-96911-7(6)) Harper & Row Ltd.

Schorr, Titus. Backyard Fun, 1 vol., 1. 2015. (Rosen REAL Readers: STEM & STEAM Collection). (ENG.). 12p. (J). (gr. 1-2). pap. 6.33 (978-1-5081-1566-3(4), 7e8222af-33f2-4d35-998c-3051cd9f10ec, Rosen Classroom) Rosen Publishing Group, Inc., The.

—A Big Change, 1 vol., 1. 2015. (Rosen REAL Readers: STEM & STEAM Collection). (ENG.). 12p. (J). (gr. 1-2). pap. 6.33 (978-1-5081-1584-7(2), 93abc14e-3fda-4762-af0b-7a05fcebb407, Rosen Classroom) Rosen Publishing Group, Inc., The.

—Doing Homework with Dad, 1 vol., 1. 2015. (Rosen REAL Readers: STEM & STEAM Collection). (ENG.). 8p. (J). (gr. k-1). pap. 5.46 (978-1-5081-1507-6(9), c013090e-c8f2-4372-9882-ff80c75b4831, Rosen Classroom) Rosen Publishing Group, Inc., The.

—Field Trip Day, 1 vol., 1. 2015. (Rosen REAL Readers: STEM & STEAM Collection). (ENG.). 8p. (J). (gr. k-1). pap. 5.46 (978-1-5081-1489-5(7), 6bd2ab53-b85d-40c6-8daf-d1fde6b61479, Rosen Classroom) Rosen Publishing Group, Inc., The.

—The Gift, 1 vol., 1. 2015. (Rosen REAL Readers: Social Studies Nonfiction / Fiction: Myself, My Community, My World Ser.). (ENG.). 8p. (J). (gr. k-1). pap. 5.46 (978-1-5081-1875-6(2), 488de9be-6f85-4c77-a96c-e6066336c117, Rosen Classroom) Rosen Publishing Group, Inc., The.

—The Package, 1 vol., 1. 2015. (Rosen REAL Readers: Social Studies Nonfiction / Fiction: Myself, My Community, My World Ser.). (ENG.). 12p. (J). (gr. k-1). pap. 6.33 (978-1-5081-1922-7(8), b7c3fb00-55b2-460f-a4d7-8fbc88e8d483, Rosen Classroom) Rosen Publishing Group, Inc., The.

—The Spelling Bee, 1 vol., 1. 2015. (Rosen REAL Readers: Social Studies Nonfiction / Fiction: Myself, My Community, My World Ser.). (ENG.). 8p. (J). (gr. k-1). pap. 5.46 (978-1-5081-1839-8(6), e3041cf5-2f79-4a8c-80d5-6ad1dc693684, Rosen Classroom) Rosen Publishing Group, Inc., The.

—Star Watch, 1 vol., 1. 2015. (Rosen REAL Readers: STEM & STEAM Collection). (ENG.). 12p. (J). (gr. k-1). pap. 6.33 (978-1-5081-1548-9(6), 6cd50bd0-3f3b-4bc2-bab8-28c5756a652d, Rosen Classroom) Rosen Publishing Group, Inc., The.

—Wings, 1 vol., 1. 2015. (Rosen REAL Readers: Social Studies Nonfiction / Fiction: Myself, My Community, My World Ser.). (ENG.). 12p. (J). (gr. k-1). pap. 6.33 (978-1-5081-1907-4(4), c914baf2-9c83-46c8-99c5-df46b8ffb95f, Rosen Classroom) Rosen Publishing Group, Inc., The.

Schraff, Anne. The Accuser, 1 vol. unabr. ed. 2010. (Q Reads Ser.). (ENG.). 32p. (YA). (gr. 9-12). pap. 8.50 (978-1-61651-188-3(5)) Saddleback Educational Publishing, Inc.

—And We Will Be No More. 2008. (Passages to History Ser.). 127p. (J). (gr. 4-6). lib. bdg. 13.95 (978-0-7569-8395-6(9)) Perfection Learning Corp.

—Black Widow Beauty, 1 vol. unabr. ed. 2010. (Q Reads Ser.). (ENG.). 32p. (YA). (gr. 9-12). pap. 8.50 (978-1-61651-178-4(8)) Saddleback Educational Publishing, Inc.

—Blackout, 1 vol. unabr. ed. 2010. (Q Reads Ser.). (ENG.). 32p. (YA). (gr. 9-12). pap. 8.50 *(978-1-61651-190-6(7))* Saddleback Educational Publishing, Inc.
—The Darkest Secret. 2008. (Passages Ser.). 114p. (YA). (gr. 7-9). lib. bdg. 13.95 *(978-0-7569-8376-5(2))* Perfection Learning Corp.
—The Experiment, 1 vol. unabr. ed. 2010. (Q Reads Ser.). (ENG.). 32p. (YA). (gr. 9-12). pap. 8.50 *(978-1-61651-181-4(8))* Saddleback Educational Publishing, Inc.
—The Haunting of Hawthorne. 2008. (Passages Ser.). 125p. (YA). (gr. 7-9). lib. bdg. 13.95 *(978-0-7569-8379-6(7))* Perfection Learning Corp.
—The Shadow Man. 2008. (Passages Ser.). 134p. (YA). (gr. 7-9). lib. bdg. 13.95 *(978-0-7569-8382-6(7))* Perfection Learning Corp.
—The Shining Mark. 2008. (Passages Ser.). 109p. (J). lib. bdg. 13.95 *(978-0-7569-8383-3(5))* Perfection Learning Corp.
—To Be a Man, 1 vol. unabr. ed. 2010. (Urban Underground Ser.). (ENG.). 181p. (YA). (gr. 9-12). pap. 11.95 *(978-1-61651-008-4(0))* Saddleback Educational Publishing, Inc.
—To Be Somebody. 2008. (Passages Ser.). 120p. (J). (gr. 4-6). lib. bdg. 13.95 *(978-0-7569-8390-1(8))* Perfection Learning Corp.
—Under the Mushroom Cloud. 2008. (Passages to Adventure Ser.). 115p. (J). (gr. 4-6). lib. bdg. 13.95 *(978-0-7569-8399-4(1))* Perfection Learning Corp.
Schreyer, Karmel. Turtles: Ancient Symbol/Modern Survivor Upper Intermediate Book with Online Access, 1 vol. 2014. (ENG., Illus.). 28p. (J). pap., E-Book, E-Book 9.50 *(978-1-107-66057-1(2))* Cambridge Univ. Pr.
SchreyerKarmel. TRAGEDY ON THE SLOPES UPPER INTERMEDIATE BOOK WITH ONLINE ACCESS, 1 vol. 2014. (ENG., Illus.). 28p. pap., E-Book 9.50 *(978-1-107-62159-6(3))* Cambridge Univ. Pr.
—Water Power: The Greatest Force on Earth, 1 vol. 2014. (ENG., Illus.). 28p. (J). pap., E-Book, E-Book 9.50 *(978-1-107-68897-1(3))* Cambridge Univ. Pr.
Schue, Lori Vankirk. Peapod. 2009. (ENG.). 42p. pap. 16.99 *(978-1-4415-2356-3(1))* Xlibris Corp.
Schulz, Charles M. Buon San Valentino, Dolce Babù. pap. 19.95 *(978-88-451-2996-4(9))* Fabbri Editori - RCS Libri ITA. Dist: Distribooks, Inc.
—Tutti Qui, Biscotti! pap. 19.95 *(978-88-451-2810-3(5))* Fabbri Editori - RCS Libri ITA. Dist: Distribooks, Inc.
Schulz, Kathy. Rookie Ready to Learn en Español: Necesito una Ayudita. Iosa, Ann, illus. 2011. (Rookie Ready to Learn Español Ser.). Orig. Title: Rookie Ready to Learn: I Need a Little Help. (SPA.). 32p. (J). pap. 5.95 *(978-0-531-26782-0(2)*, Children's Pr.) Scholastic Library Publishing.
Schwartz, Heather. The French Revolution: Terror & Triumph, 1 vol. rev. ed. 2012. (Social Studies: Informational Text Ser.). (ENG.). 32p. (gr. 4-8). pap. 11.99 *(978-1-4333-5011-5(4))* Teacher Created Materials, Inc.
—Lizzie Johnson: Texan Cowgirl, 1 vol. rev. ed. 2012. (Social Studies: Informational Text Ser.). (ENG.). 32p. (gr. 3-5). pap. 11.99 *(978-1-4333-5051-1(3))* Teacher Created Materials, Inc.
—Marie Antoinette: The Controversial Queen of France, 1 vol. rev. ed. 2012. (Social Studies: Informational Text Ser.). (ENG.). 32p. (gr. 4-8). pap. 11.99 *(978-1-4333-5012-2(2))* Teacher Created Materials, Inc.
Schwarzenegger, Katherine. Maverick & Me. Harris, Phyllis, illus. 2017. (ENG.). 32p. (J). 16.99 *(978-0-8249-5687-5(7))* Worthy Publishing.
Science Fun. 2005. (Little Celebrations Thematic Packages Ser.). (J). (gr. k-3). 133.50 *(978-0-673-75382-3(4))* Celebration Pr.
Science Readers Staff & Van Gorp, Lynn. The World of Genetics, 1 vol. rev. ed. 2007. (Science: Informational Text Ser.). (ENG., Illus.). 32p. (gr. 3-6). pap. 12.99 *(978-0-7439-0597-8(0))* Teacher Created Materials, Inc.
Scooby-Doo Comic Readers: Set, 4 vols. 2015. (Scooby-Doo Comic Readers Ser.: 6). (ENG.). 32p. (J). (gr. -1-3). lib. bdg. 125.44 *(978-1-61479-450-9(2)*, 19429, Graphic Novels) Spotlight.
Scott, Caitlin. Treasure Hunting Set: Looking for Lost Riches, 6 vols. 2003. (High Five Reading - Red Ser.). (ENG.). 48p. (gr. 3-4). pap. 54.00 *(978-0-7368-2835-2(4))* Capstone.
Scott Foresman Early Reading Intervention. 2003. (gr. k-1). *(978-0-328-03826-8(1)*, Scott Foresman) Addison-Wesley Educational Pubs., Inc.
Scott Foresman Family Reading Guide. 2004. (gr. 6-18). 13.50 *(978-0-673-63400-9(0))* Addison-Wesley Educational Pubs., Inc.
Scott Foresman Reading: Additional Resources. 2004. (Scott Foresman Reading Ser.). (gr. 1-18). *(978-0-328-04085-8(1)*, Scott Foresman) Addison-Wesley Educational Pubs., Inc.
Scott Foresman Reading: Links to Reading First. 2004. (Links to Reading Ser.). (gr. k-18). *(978-0-328-05801-3(7))*; (gr. k-18). *(978-0-328-07612-3(0))*; (gr. 1-18). *(978-0-328-05802-0(5))*; (gr. 1-18). *(978-0-328-07613-0(9))*; (gr. 2-18). *(978-0-328-07614-7(7))*; (gr. 2-18). *(978-0-328-05803-7(3))*; (gr. 3-18). *(978-0-328-07615-4(5))*; (gr. 3-18). *(978-0-328-05804-4(1))* Addison-Wesley Educational Pubs., Inc. (Scott Foresman).
Scott Foresman Reading: Technology. 2004. (Fluency Coach Ser.). (gr. 4-18). cd-rom *(978-0-328-09376-2(9)*, Scott Foresman) Addison-Wesley Educational Pubs., Inc.
Scott, Fred & Southworth, Gordon. English for the Thoughtful Child Vol 2, Vol. 2. 2003. (ENG., Illus.). 128p. (J). pap. 18.95 *(978-1-882514-44-1(0))* Greenleaf Pr.
Scott, Jonathan & Scott, Angela. Africa's Big Three: Band 07/Turquoise (Collins Big Cat) Scott, Jonathan & Scott, Angela, illus. 2006. (Collins Big Cat Ser.). (ENG., Illus.). 24p. (J). (gr. 2-2). pap. 8.99 *(978-0-00-718693-8(2))* HarperCollins Pubs. Ltd. GBR. Dist: Independent Pubs. Group.
—Antarctica: Land of the Penguins: Band 10/White (Collins Big Cat) 2005. (Collins Big Cat Ser.). (ENG., Illus.). 32p. (J). (gr. 1-3). pap. 10.99 *(978-0-00-718640-2(1))* HarperCollins Pubs. Ltd. GBR. Dist: Independent Pubs. Group.
—Big Cat Babies: Band 05/Green (Collins Big Cat) Scott, Jonathan & Scott, Angela, illus. 2005. (Collins Big Cat Ser.). (ENG., Illus.). 24p. (J). (gr. k-1). pap. 8.95 *(978-0-00-718594-8(4))* HarperCollins Pubs. Ltd. GBR. Dist: Independent Pubs. Group.
—The Great Migration White Band. 2016. (Cambridge Reading Adventures Ser.). (ENG., Illus.). 32p. pap. 9.50 *(978-1-107-56065-9(9))* Cambridge Univ. Pr.
—Living Dinosaurs: Band 08/Purple (Collins Big Cat) Scott, Jonathan & Scott, Angela, illus. 2007. (Collins Big Cat Ser.). (ENG., Illus.). 24p. (J). (gr. k-1). pap. 9.99 *(978-0-00-718673-0(8))* HarperCollins Pubs. Ltd. GBR. Dist: Independent Pubs. Group.
—The Maasai: Tribe of Warriors: Band 15/Emerald (Collins Big Cat) Scott, Jonathan & Scott, Angela, illus. 2007. (Collins Big Cat Ser.). (ENG., Illus.). 48p. (J). (gr. 3-4). pap. 11.99 *(978-0-00-723097-6(4))* HarperCollins Pubs. Ltd. GBR. Dist: Independent Pubs. Group.
—Scarface: the Real Lion King Gold Band. 2016. (Cambridge Reading Adventures Ser.). (ENG., Illus.). 24p. pap. 8.80 *(978-1-107-56047-5(0))* Cambridge Univ. Pr.
Scott, Jonathan and Angela. Honey & Toto: the Story of a Cheetah Family 1 Pathfinders. 2017. (Cambridge Reading Adventures Ser.). (ENG., Illus.). 24p. pap. 8.60 *(978-1-108-43615-1(3))* Cambridge Univ. Pr.
Scott, Kate. Collins Big Cat Phonics for Letters & Sounds - How the Ear Can Hear: Band 03/Yellow, Bd. 3. 2018. (Collins Big Cat Phonics Ser.). (ENG., Illus.). 16p. (J). (gr. k-1). pap. 6.99 *(978-0-00-825158-1(4))* HarperCollins Pubs. Ltd. GBR. Dist: Independent Pubs. Group.
Scott, Sally. Time for Tea, 1 vol. 2006. (Neighborhood Readers Ser.). (ENG.). 12p. (gr. 1-2). pap. 5.90 *(978-1-4042-6867-8(7)*, aad2967b-bce0-4ed4-987a-2b89a69ee649, Rosen Classroom) Rosen Publishing Group, Inc., The.
Scrapbook of ME: Individual Title Six-Packs. (Story Steps Ser.). (gr. k-2). 32.00 *(978-0-7635-9814-3(3))* Rigby Education.
Scremin, Lauren. The 10 Most Amazing Skyscrapers. 2007. (J). 14.99 *(978-1-55448-480-5(4))* Scholastic Library Publishing.
Sean amables con Naomi: Social/Emotional Lap Book. (Pebble Soup Exploraciones Ser.). (SPA.). (gr. -1-18). 16.00 *(978-0-7578-1787-8(4))* Rigby Education.
A Second Birthday: 6 Small Books. (Greetings Ser.: Vol. 2). 24p. (gr. 2-3). 31.00 *(978-0-7635-9414-5(8))* Rigby Education.
A Second Birthday: Big Book. (Greetings Ser.: Vol. 2). 24p. (gr. 2-3). 31.00 *(978-0-7635-5698-3(X))* Rigby Education.
Second Mrs. Gianconda. (J). pap., stu. ed. *(978-0-13-017583-0(8))* Prentice Hall (Schl. Div.).
See & Say Vinyl Books 800844, 3. 2005. (J). *(978-1-59794-045-0(3))* Environments, Inc.
The Seed: Level A, 6 vols. (Wonder Worldtm Ser.). 16p. 24.95 *(978-0-7802-1048-6(4))* Wright Group/McGraw-Hill.
Seed, Andy. Athletics: Band 04/Blue, Bd. 4. 2018. (Collins Big Cat Phonics Ser.). (ENG., Illus.). 16p. (J). pap. 7.99 *(978-0-00-825163-5(0))* HarperCollins Pubs. Ltd. GBR. Dist: Independent Pubs. Group.
—On the Track: Band 12/Copper. 2017. (Collins Big Cat Ser.). (ENG., Illus.). 32p. (J). pap. 9.99 *(978-0-00-820875-2(1))* HarperCollins Pubs. Ltd. GBR. Dist: Independent Pubs. Group.
—Winter Olympics: Band 10 White/Band 12 Copper (Collins Big Cat Progress) 2014. (Collins Big Cat Progress Ser.). (ENG., Illus.). 32p. (YA). (gr. 7). pap. 9.99 *(978-0-00-751924-8(9))* HarperCollins Pubs. Ltd. GBR. Dist: Independent Pubs. Group.
Sefchovich, Sara. Vivir la Vida. 2005.Tr. of Living Life. (SPA., Illus.). 243p. pap. 14.95 *(978-968-19-0803-4(1))* Aguilar, Altea, Taurus, Alfaguara, S.A. de C.V MEX. Dist: Santillana USA Publishing Co., Inc.
Selleck, Richelle. Little Red Riding Hood. Myer, Ed, illus. 2012. (Little Birdie Bks.). (ENG.). 24p. (gr. 2-3). pap. 9.95 *(978-1-61810-324-6(5)*, 9781618103246) Rourke Educational Media.
Selwyn, Josephine. What Holidays Do You Have? 2012. (Level D Ser.). (ENG., Illus.). 16p. (J). (gr. k-2). pap. 7.95 *(978-1-927136-30-0(X)*, 19422) RiverStream Publishing.
—When Does Water Turn into Ice? 2012. (Level F Ser.). (ENG., Illus.). 16p. (J). (gr. k-2). pap. 7.95 *(978-1-927136-59-1(8)*, 19436) RiverStream Publishing.
—Who Uses This Machine? 2012. (Level C Ser.). (ENG., Illus.). 16p. (J). (gr. k-2). pap. 7.95 *(978-1-927136-29-4(6)*, 19456) RiverStream Publishing.
Sending Messages: Level B, 6 vols. (Wonder Worldtm Ser.). 16p. 24.95 *(978-0-7802-4599-0(7))* Wright Group/McGraw-Hill.
Senior, Kathryn. You Wouldn't Want to Be a Nurse During the American Civil War! A Job That's Not for the Squeamish. 2010. (You Wouldn't Want to... Ser.). 32p. (J). 29.00 *(978-0-531-20506-8(1)*, Watts, Franklin) Scholastic Library Publishing.
Sertori, J. M. Early Kings of England: Band 14/Ruby (Collins Big Cat) 2016. (Collins Big Cat Ser.). (ENG., Illus.). 48p. (J). (gr. 3-4). pap. 12.99 *(978-0-00-816386-0(3))* HarperCollins Pubs. Ltd. GBR. Dist: Independent Pubs. Group.
Set of 10 Big Book Favorites 800714, 10. 2005. (J). bds. *(978-1-59794-013-9(5))* Environments, Inc.
Set of 17 Titles, Vol. 2. (Early Intervention Levels Ser.). 62.45 *(978-0-7362-0998-4(0))* CENGAGE Learning.
Set of 5 Titles. (Early Intervention Levels Ser.). 18.95 *(978-0-7362-0997-7(2))* CENGAGE Learning.
Set of 9 Titles, Vol. 4. (Early Intervention Levels Ser.). 33.15 *(978-0-7362-1000-3(8))* CENGAGE Learning.
Settle, Melissa A. Firefighters Then & Now, 1 vol. rev. ed. 2006. (Social Studies: Informational Text Ser.). (ENG.). 32p. (J). (gr. 2-3). pap. 11.99 *(978-0-7439-9371-5(3))* Teacher Created Materials, Inc.
—Police Then & Now , 1 vol. rev. ed. 2006. (Social Studies: Informational Text Ser.). (ENG., Illus.). 32p. (gr. 2-3). pap. 11.99 *(978-0-7439-9372-2(1))* Teacher Created Materials, Inc.
Seuss. The Big Green Book of Beginner Books. 2009. (Beginner Books(R) Ser.). (ENG., Illus.). 256p. (J). (gr. -1-2). 16.99 *(978-0-375-85807-9(5)*, Random Hse. Bks. for Young Readers) Random Hse. Children's Bks.
—Dr. Seuss's ABC Book & CD, 1 vol. 2005. (ENG., Illus.). 64p. (J). (gr. -1-2). 10.99 *(978-0-375-83496-7(6)*, Random Hse. Bks. for Young Readers) Random Hse. Children's Bks.
Sexton, Colleen. Angelfish. 2009. (Blastoff! Readers Ser.). (ENG., Illus.). 24p. (J). (gr. k-3). 20.00 *(978-0-531-21711-5(6)*, Children's Pr.) Scholastic Library Publishing.
—Frogfish. 2009. (Blastoff! Readers Ser.). (ENG., Illus.). 24p. (J). (gr. k-3). 20.00 *(978-0-531-21712-2(4)*, Children's Pr.) Scholastic Library Publishing.
Shackleton, Caroline. Avalanche! High Intermediate Book with Online Access, 1 vol. 2014. (ENG., Illus.). 28p. pap., E-Book 9.50 *(978-1-107-62157-2(7))* Cambridge Univ. Pr.
—Deep Blue: Discovering the Sea Intermediate Book with Online Access, 1 vol. 2014. (ENG., Illus.). 28p. (J). pap., E-Book, E-Book 9.50 *(978-1-107-69705-8(0))* Cambridge Univ. Pr.
—Down to Earth Intermediate Book with Online Access, 1 vol. 2014. (ENG., Illus.). 28p. pap., E-Book, E-Book 9.50 *(978-1-107-66117-2(X))* Cambridge Univ. Pr.
—Get Smart: Our Amazing Brain Intermediate Book with Online Access, 1 vol. 2014. (ENG., Illus.). 28p. (J). pap., E-Book, E-Book 9.50 *(978-1-107-65063-3(1))* Cambridge Univ. Pr.
—Lift off: Exploring the Universe High Intermediate Book with Online Access, 1 vol. 2014. (ENG., Illus.). 28p. (J). pap., E-Book 9.50 *(978-1-107-69249-7(0))* Cambridge Univ. Pr.
—Money Tree: the Business of Organics High Intermediate Book with Online Access, 1 vol. 2014. (ENG., Illus.). 28p. (J). pap., E-Book 9.50 *(978-1-107-63678-1(7))* Cambridge Univ. Pr.
—Poison: Medicine, Murder, & Mystery High Intermediate Book with Online Access, 1 vol. 2014. (ENG., Illus.). 28p. (J). pap., E-Book 9.50 *(978-1-107-62260-9(3))* Cambridge Univ. Pr.
—Robots: the Next Generation? High Intermediate Book with Online Access, 1 vol. 2014. (ENG., Illus.). 28p. pap., E-Book 9.50 *(978-1-107-67762-3(9))* Cambridge Univ. Pr.
—Trapped! The Aron Ralston Story High Intermediate Book with Online Access, 1 vol. 2014. (ENG., Illus.). 28p. (J). pap., E-Book 9.50 *(978-1-107-66998-7(7))* Cambridge Univ. Pr.
ShackletonCaroline. SKIN UPPER INTERMEDIATE BOOK WITH ONLINE ACCESS, 1 vol. 2014. (ENG., Illus.). 28p. (J). pap., E-Book, E-Book 9.50 *(978-1-107-64189-1(6))* Cambridge Univ. Pr.
—Up in the Air: Our Fight Against Gravity Intermediate Book with Online Access, 1 vol. 2014. (ENG., Illus.). 28p. (J). pap., E-Book, E-Book 9.50 *(978-1-107-63470-1(9))* Cambridge Univ. Pr.
—THE WHEEL LOW INTERMEDIATE BOOK WITH ONLINE ACCESS, 1 vol. 2014. (ENG., Illus.). 28p. (J). pap., E-Book, E-Book 9.50 *(978-1-107-66739-6(9))* Cambridge Univ. Pr.
Shadows: Level H, 6 vols. (Wonder Worldtm Ser.). 16p. 29.95 *(978-0-7802-1049-3(2))* Wright Group/McGraw-Hill.
Shah, Nupur. Let's Go Camping. rev. ed. 2011. (1-3Y in My World Ser.). (ENG., Illus.). 16p. (J). (gr. k-1). pap. 5.99 *(978-1-61541-415-4(0))* American Reading Co.
Shaka: King of the Zulus. (Lexile Levels Ser.). 9.09 *(978-1-56334-749-8(0))* CENGAGE Learning.
Shane & Ned, 6 Packs. (gr. 1-2). 22.00 *(978-0-7635-9171-7(8))* Rigby Education.
Shank, Cathy, et al. Collaborations Literacy. pap., stu. ed. 50.95 *(978-0-8384-9660-2(1))* Cengage Heinle.
Shark Rescue: Level T. Group 2, 6 vols. (Sunshine Ser.). 48p. 44.95 *(978-0-7802-4174-9(6))* Wright Group/McGraw-Hill.
Sharp, Paul. Rookie Ready to Learn en Español: Pablo el Lanzador. Sharp, Paul, illus. 2011. (Rookie Ready to Learn Español Ser.). Orig. Title: Rookie Ready to Learn: Paul the Pitcher. (SPA., Illus.). 40p. (J). pap. 5.95 *(978-0-531-26781-3(4)*, Children's Pr.) Scholastic Library Publishing.
Shava, Ryder. At Work with My Dads, 1 vol., 1. 2015. (Rosen REAL Readers: STEM & STEAM Collection). (ENG.). 12p. (J). (gr. 1-2). pap. 6.33 *(978-1-5081-1581-6(8)*, 9429310f-dc0b-4d83-86de-87124937bc3d, Rosen Classroom) Rosen Publishing Group, Inc., The.
—Bear Wakes Up, 1 vol., 1. 2015. (Rosen REAL Readers: STEM & STEAM Collection). (ENG.). 8p. (J). (gr. k-1). pap. 5.46 *(978-1-5081-1504-5(4)*, fefa993c-7e65-49b4-97af-30d3ef65da82, Rosen Classroom) Rosen Publishing Group, Inc., The.
—The Big Cookout, 1 vol., 1. 2015. (Rosen REAL Readers: Social Studies Nonfiction / Fiction: Myself, My Community, My World Ser.). (ENG.). 8p. (J). (gr. k-1). pap. 5.46 *(978-1-5081-1442-0(0)*, 37844070-f58f-4e42-9889-2afd35d808fd, Rosen Classroom) Rosen Publishing Group, Inc., The.
—Blue Sky Day, 1 vol., 1. 2015. (Rosen REAL Readers: STEM & STEAM Collection). (ENG.). 8p. (J). (gr. k-1). pap. 5.46 *(978-1-5081-1446-8(3)*, 8cffad1a-d0f9-492a-9e19-1694cfaadb59, Rosen Classroom) Rosen Publishing Group, Inc., The.
—Bo's Sand Castle, 1 vol., 1. 2015. (Rosen REAL Readers: STEM & STEAM Collection). (ENG.). 8p. (J). (gr. k-1). pap. 5.46 *(978-1-5081-1465-9(X)*, 12e18a34-5ac9-4fb0-acab-be979f1a2ecd, Rosen Classroom) Rosen Publishing Group, Inc., The.
—Button Eyes, Carrot Nose, 1 vol., 1. 2015. (Rosen REAL Readers: STEM & STEAM Collection). (ENG.). 8p. (J). (gr. k-1). pap. 5.46 *(978-1-5081-1486-4(2)*, 11a28660-2d1e-4f7c-9e5a-975b9d53d157, Rosen Classroom) Rosen Publishing Group, Inc., The.
—The Can Drive, 1 vol., 1. 2015. (Rosen REAL Readers: Social Studies Nonfiction / Fiction: Myself, My Community, My World Ser.). (ENG.). 12p. (J). (gr. k-1). pap. 6.33 *(978-1-5081-1982-1(1)*, e1859b52-6118-48ca-800b-a7a6ed6048ea, Rosen Classroom) Rosen Publishing Group, Inc., The.
—Clara & the Ladybug, 1 vol., 1. 2015. (Rosen REAL Readers: STEM & STEAM Collection). (ENG.). 8p. (J). (gr. k-1). pap. 5.46 *(978-1-5081-1399-7(8)*, 7681a29d-7b54-41c6-856b-0f74cea28f53, Rosen Classroom) Rosen Publishing Group, Inc., The.
—HairCut Day, 1 vol., 1. 2015. (Rosen REAL Readers: Social Studies Nonfiction / Fiction: Myself, My Community, My World Ser.). (ENG.). 8p. (J). (gr. k-1). pap. 5.46 *(978-1-5081-1385-0(8)*, 37f945aa-c901-4fd9-86f9-bb54d4892ccb, Rosen Classroom) Rosen Publishing Group, Inc., The.
—The Lesson, 1 vol., 1. 2015. (Rosen REAL Readers: Social Studies Nonfiction / Fiction: Myself, My Community, My World Ser.). (ENG.). 8p. (J). (gr. k-1). pap. 5.46 *(978-1-5081-1890-9(6)*, 85a8521f-975f-4d2a-8d07-f6d4fcac69b1, Rosen Classroom) Rosen Publishing Group, Inc., The.
—Show & Tell, 1 vol., 1. 2015. (Rosen REAL Readers: Social Studies Nonfiction / Fiction: Myself, My Community, My World Ser.). (ENG.). 12p. (J). (gr. k-1). pap. 6.33 *(978-1-5081-1952-4(X)*, bf91b91c-1ae6-4f81-8f32-b3400557cf3a, Rosen Classroom) Rosen Publishing Group, Inc., The.
—Story Time, 1 vol., 1. 2015. (Rosen REAL Readers: Social Studies Nonfiction / Fiction: Myself, My Community, My World Ser.). (ENG.). 12p. (J). (gr. k-1). pap. 6.33 *(978-1-5081-1949-4(X)*, 30af4389-9d79-4ba2-96b0-c970053f8dcb, Rosen Classroom) Rosen Publishing Group, Inc., The.
—The Talent Show, 1 vol., 1. 2015. (Rosen REAL Readers: Social Studies Nonfiction / Fiction: Myself, My Community, My World Ser.). (ENG.). 8p. (J). (gr. k-1). pap. 5.46 *(978-1-5081-1854-1(X)*, 296630a0-0d84-44cd-a4eb-f45e6af6dcdf, Rosen Classroom) Rosen Publishing Group, Inc., The.
—A Watery World, 1 vol., 1. 2015. (Rosen REAL Readers: STEM & STEAM Collection). (ENG.). 12p. (J). (gr. k-1). pap. 6.33 *(978-1-5081-1527-4(3)*, 79d50cf6-c274-48b2-9427-94df87d5a855, Rosen Classroom) Rosen Publishing Group, Inc., The.
—When I Sat in Lincoln's Lap, 1 vol., 1. 2015. (Rosen REAL Readers: Social Studies Nonfiction / Fiction: Myself, My Community, My World Ser.). (ENG.). 12p. (J). (gr. k-1). pap. 6.33 *(978-1-5081-2003-2(X)*, 5d8db94c-6463-4452-94bf-6322a9f3350a, Rosen Classroom) Rosen Publishing Group, Inc., The.
Shea, Therese. At the Luau, 1 vol. 2006. (Neighborhood Readers Ser.). (ENG.). 16p. (gr. 1-2). pap. 6.50 *(978-1-4042-7002-2(7)*, 0bce0e25-2e2b-46cc-bd07-323051aab55b, Rosen Classroom) Rosen Publishing Group, Inc., The.
—Bear Likes to Share, 1 vol. 2006. (Neighborhood Readers Ser.). (ENG.). 8p. (gr. k-1). pap. 5.15 *(978-1-4042-5696-5(2)*, 3c922660-348b-4775-a9a8-3ca5c1e27aa4, Rosen Classroom) Rosen Publishing Group, Inc., The.
—Carmen's Photo Album, 1 vol. 2006. (Neighborhood Readers Ser.). (ENG.). 12p. (gr. 1-2). pap. 5.90 *(978-1-4042-6795-4(6)*, cd9ce055-4067-420a-a40f-2dab1a5bac4e, Rosen Classroom) Rosen Publishing Group, Inc., The.
—Digger Has a Bath, 1 vol. 2006. (Neighborhood Readers Ser.). (ENG.). 12p. (gr. k-1). pap. 5.90 *(978-1-4042-6467-0(1)*, 7ed76182-de3c-417d-a1b3-edf13b60970a, Rosen Classroom) Rosen Publishing Group, Inc., The.
—Flag Day, 1 vol. 2006. (Neighborhood Readers Ser.). (ENG.). 16p. (gr. 1-2). pap. 6.50 *(978-1-4042-7144-9(9)*, f94e7b63-cca0-4413-b195-edd8742c84a8, Rosen Classroom) Rosen Publishing Group, Inc., The.
—Flags & Fireworks, 1 vol. 2006. (Neighborhood Readers Ser.). (ENG.). 8p. (gr. k-1). pap. 5.15 *(978-1-4042-5726-9(8)*, 5a4d5266-7e2f-453d-9f2b-793b8a527ea6, Rosen Classroom) Rosen Publishing Group, Inc., The.
—A Fuss on the Bus. (Neighborhood Readers Ser.). 2007. (SPA.). 12p. 33.50 *(978-1-4042-7080-0(9))* 2006. (ENG.). 8p. pap. 5.90 *(978-1-4042-5744-3(6)*, a0dba953-3152-48a0-8cb3-39d7d5a6ec0e) Rosen Publishing Group, Inc., The. (Rosen Classroom).
—A House for Mouse, 1 vol. 2006. (Neighborhood Readers Ser.). (ENG.). 8p. (gr. k-1). pap. 5.15 *(978-1-4042-5672-9(5)*, 4a3af609-6796-44e3-b9df-adb3e8d380db, Rosen Classroom) Rosen Publishing Group, Inc., The.
—The Kwanzaa Surprise, 1 vol. 2006. (Neighborhood Readers Ser.). (ENG.). 12p. (gr. k-1). pap. 5.90 *(978-1-4042-6746-6(8)*, 047873d1-d052-4768-9c46-c71bdae65c19, Rosen Classroom) Rosen Publishing Group, Inc., The.
—The Lunch Bunch. (Neighborhood Readers Ser.). (ENG.). 12p. 2007. 33.50 *(978-1-4042-7322-1(0))* 2006. (Illus.). (gr. 1-2). pap. 5.90 *(978-1-4042-7038-1(8)*, bd115bea-fc32-4b0b-89cb-b46e59bd2a0d) Rosen Publishing Group, Inc., The. (Rosen Classroom).
—Un lunch muy especial (the Lunch Bunch) 2007. (Lecturas del barrio (Neighborhood Readers) Ser.). (SPA.). 12p. 33.50 *(978-1-4042-7323-8(9)*, Rosen Classroom) Rosen Publishing Group, Inc., The.
—One More Floor!, 1 vol. 2006. (Neighborhood Readers Ser.). (ENG.). 16p. (gr. 1-2). pap. 6.50 *(978-1-4042-7244-6(5)*, 2dcda1d1-5e34-4ca9-b623-6c75f0c4b4b8, Rosen Classroom) Rosen Publishing Group, Inc., The.
—Sam's New Shoes, 1 vol. 2006. (Neighborhood Readers Ser.). (ENG.). 8p. (gr. k-1). pap. 5.15 *(978-1-4042-5651-4(2)*, c333a900-68f6-4777-9b85-cec010db7840, Rosen Classroom) Rosen Publishing Group, Inc., The.
—The School Bus Mystery, 1 vol. 2006. (Neighborhood Readers Ser.). (ENG.). 16p. (gr. 1-2). pap. 6.50 *(978-1-4042-6982-8(7)*, 3cd2526f-0d62-4b12-bd01-561320c79797, Rosen Classroom) Rosen Publishing Group, Inc., The.
—The Summer Job, 1 vol. 2006. (Neighborhood Readers Ser.). (ENG., Illus.). 12p. (gr. 1-2). pap. 5.90 *(978-1-4042-6855-5(3)*, 33e5bd16-1ab9-472f-953c-3aaccbc60d6d, Rosen Classroom) Rosen Publishing Group, Inc., The.
—A Trip to the White House, 1 vol. 2006. (Neighborhood Readers Ser.). (ENG.). 16p. (gr. 1-2). pap. 6.50 *(978-1-4042-7204-0(6)*, e45cdfbc-8f15-4bce-b753-7d66fa6cae83, Rosen Classroom) Rosen Publishing Group, Inc., The.
Sheehan, P. J. Gabby's Big Game, 1 vol. 2006. (Neighborhood Readers Ser.). (ENG.). 12p. (gr. k-1). pap. 5.90 *(978-1-4042-6758-9(1)*, 96cfb1de-68c6-44b0-9574-73de5d48f6f3, Rosen Classroom) Rosen Publishing Group, Inc., The.
Sheinmel, Courtney. A Case of the Meanies. Bell, Jennifer A., illus. 2012. (Stella Batts Ser.: 4). (ENG.). 160p. (J). (gr. 1-3). pap. 6.99 *(978-1-58536-199-1(2)*, 202257);4. 9.99 *(978-1-58536-198-4(4)*, 202252) Sleeping Bear Pr.

Shepherd Boy & the Giant Color. 2004. pap. 1 50 (978-0-87162-913-5(5)) Warner Pr., Inc.
Sheppard, Bonnie. The 10 Greatest Art Forgers. 2007. (J). 14.99 (978-1-55448-473-7(1)) Scholastic Library Publishing.
Sherman, Patrice. The Enlightenment: A Revolution in Reason, 1 vol. rev. ed. 2012. (Social Studies: Informational Text Ser.). (ENG.). 32p. (gr. 4-8). pap. 11.99 (978-1-4333-5013-9(0)) Teacher Created Materials, Inc.
—George W. Bush: Gobernado de Texas y Presidente de los Estados Unidos / George W. Bush - Texan Governor & U. S. President. 2013. (Primary Source Readers Ser.). (SPA.). lib. bdg. 19.65 (978-0-606-31875-4(5)) Turtleback.
—George W. Bush: Texan Governor & U. S. President, 1 vol. rev. ed. 2012. (Social Studies: Informational Text Ser.). (ENG.). 32p. (gr. 3-5). pap. 11.99 (978-1-4333-5054-2(8)) Teacher Created Materials, Inc.
—John Locke: Philosopher of the Enlightenment, 1 vol. rev. ed. 2012. (Social Studies: Informational Text Ser.). (ENG.). 32p. (gr. 4-8). pap. 11.99 (978-1-4333-5014-6(9)) Teacher Created Materials, Inc.
Shimizu, Michio. Ding Dong. McLaughlin, Sako, tr. Yamamoto, Matsuko, illus. 2009. 32p. 14.95 (978-1-74126-440-1(5)) R.I.C. Pubns. AUS. Dist: SCB Distributors.
Shipton, Paul. Clown School. Blake, Beccy, illus. 2005. (ENG.). 24p. (J). lib. bdg. 23.65 (978-1-59646-752-1(5)) Dingles & Co.
—In the Boat: Band 01A/Pink a (Collins Big Cat) Dunton, Trevor, illus. 2007. (Collins Big Cat Ser.). (ENG.). 24p. (J). (gr. -1-k). pap. 6.99 (978-0-00-718646-4(0)) HarperCollins Pubs. Ltd. GBR. Dist: Independent Pubs. Group.
—What's for Breakfast?: Band 02B/Red B (Collins Big Cat) Stuart, Jon, illus. 2006. (Collins Big Cat Ser.). (ENG.). 16p. (J). (gr. -1-k). pap. 6.99 (978-0-00-718668-6(1)) HarperCollins Pubs. Ltd. GBR. Dist: Independent Pubs. Group.
Shoes, Shoes, Shoes. (Lexile Levels Ser.). 7.98 (978-1-56334-670-5(2)) CENGAGE Learning.
Shore, Diane Z. How to Drive Your Sister Crazy. Rankin, Laura, illus. 2008. (I Can Read Level 2 Ser.). (ENG.). 48p. (J). (gr. k-3). 16.99 (978-0-06-052762-4(5), HarperCollins) HarperCollins Pubs.
Short, Deborah J., et al. Alphachant Phonics: Read-Alone Phonics Stories. 2003. (Summer School Ser.). (ENG.). (C). (gr. -1-k). pap. 21.95 (978-0-7362-2007-1(0)) CENGAGE Learning.
—Avenues a: Practice Book. 2003. (Avenues Ser.). (ENG.). 96p. (C). (gr. k-18). pap. 20.95 (978-0-7362-1786-6(X)) CENGAGE Learning.
—Avenues B: Practice Book. 2003. (Avenues Ser.). (ENG.). 112p. (C). (gr. 1-18). pap. 20.95 (978-0-7362-1835-1(1)) CENGAGE Learning.
—Avenues C: Practice Book. 2003. (Avenues Ser.). (ENG.). 136p. (C). (gr. 2-18). pap. 15.95 (978-0-7362-1884-9(X)) CENGAGE Learning.
—Avenues d: Practice Book. 2003. (Avenues Ser.). (ENG.). 136p. (C). (gr. 3-18). pap. 15.95 (978-0-7362-1678-4(2)) CENGAGE Learning.
—Avenues e: Practice Book. 2003. (Avenues Ser.). (ENG.). 136p. (C). (gr. 4-18). pap. 15.95 (978-0-7362-1714-9(2)) CENGAGE Learning.
—Avenues F: Practice Book. 2003. (Avenues Ser.). (ENG.). 144p. (C). (gr. 5-18). pap. 15.95 (978-0-7362-1750-7(9)) CENGAGE Learning.
—Avenues Level a Unit Progress Test (10-Pack) 2004. (Avenues Ser.). (ENG.). (C). (gr. k-18). pap. 99.95 (978-0-7362-2227-3(8)) CENGAGE Learning.
—Avenues Level C Language & Literacy Post/Test (10-Pack) 2004. (Avenues Ser.). (ENG.). (C). pap. 79.95 (978-0-7362-2514-4(5)) CENGAGE Learning.
—Avenues Level C Unit Progress Test (Intermediate) (10-Pack) 2004. (Avenues Ser.). (ENG.). (C). (gr. 2-18). pap. 185.95 (978-0-7362-2238-9(3)) CENGAGE Learning.
—Avenues Level d Language & Literacy Pre/Test (10-Pack) 2004. (Avenues Ser.). (ENG.). (C). pap. 79.95 (978-0-7362-2515-1(3)) CENGAGE Learning.
—Avenues Level d Unit Progress Test (Advanced) (10-Pack) 2004. (Avenues Ser.). (ENG.). (C). (gr. 3-18). pap. 185.95 (978-0-7362-2252-5(9)) CENGAGE Learning.
—Avenues Level d Unit Progress Test (Beginner) (10-Pack) 2004. (Avenues Ser.). (ENG.). (C). (gr. 3-18). pap. 185.95 (978-0-7362-2246-4(4)) CENGAGE Learning.
—Avenues Level d Unit Progress Test (Intermediate) (10-Pack) 2004. (Avenues Ser.). (ENG.). (C). (gr. 3-18). pap. 185.95 (978-0-7362-2249-5(9)) CENGAGE Learning.
—Avenues Level e Unit Progress Test (Advanced) (10-Pack) 2004. (Avenues Ser.). (ENG.). (C). (gr. 4-18). pap. 185.95 (978-0-7362-2263-1(4)) CENGAGE Learning.
—Avenues Level e Unit Progress Test (Beginner) (10-Pack) 2004. (Avenues Ser.). (ENG.). (C). (gr. 4-18). pap. 185.95 (978-0-7362-2257-0(X)) CENGAGE Learning.
—Avenues Level e Unit Progress Test (Intermediate) (10-Pack) 2004. (Avenues Ser.). (ENG.). (C). (gr. 4-18). pap. 185.95 (978-0-7362-2260-0(X)) CENGAGE Learning.
—Avenues Level F Language & Literacy Post/Test (10-Pack) 2004. (Avenues Ser.). (ENG.). (C). pap. 79.95 (978-0-7362-2520-5(X)) CENGAGE Learning.
—Avenues Level F Unit Progress Test (Advanced) (10-Pack) 2004. (Avenues Ser.). (ENG.). (C). (gr. 5-18). pap. 185.95 (978-0-7362-2284-6(7)) CENGAGE Learning.
—Avenues Level F Unit Progress Test (Beginner) (10-Pack) 2004. (Avenues Ser.). (ENG.). (C). (gr. 5-18). pap. 185.95 (978-0-7362-2278-5(2)) CENGAGE Learning.
—Avenues Level F Unit Progress Test (Intermediate) (10-Pack) 2004. (Avenues Ser.). (ENG.). (C). (gr. 5-18). pap. 185.95 (978-0-7362-2281-5(2)) CENGAGE Learning.
—Lakeside Elementary Student Book. 2003. (Avenues Ser.). (ENG.). (C). (gr. 2-5). pap., stu. ed. 12.95 (978-0-7362-1821-4(1)) CENGAGE Learning.
—My Little Word Books. 2004. (Avenues Ser.). (ENG.). 44p. (C). (gr. -1-2). pap. 12.95 (978-0-7362-2392-8(4)) CENGAGE Learning.
Short Vowels Set: Level B. (Sing-along Songs Ser.). (gr. -1-2). 48.46 incl. audio compact disk (978-0-7362-0420-0(2)) CENGAGE Learning.
Show Me a Snake Hold (16), Vol. 16. (Early Intervention Levels Ser.). 4.73 (978-0-7362-0241-1(2)) CENGAGE Learning.
Show Me a Snake Hole. (Early Intervention Levels Ser.). 28.38 (978-0-7362-0416-3(4)) CENGAGE Learning.
Show What You Know Publishing, ed. Show What You Know on the CSAP 7, Reading/Writing Student Workbook. 2007. (J). per. 13.95 (978-1-59230-246-8(7)) Englefield & Assocs., Inc.
—Show What You Know on the CSAP for Grade 5, Student Workbook. 2007. (J). per. 13.95 (978-1-59230-217-8(3)) Englefield & Assocs., Inc.
—Show What You Know on the CSAP for Grade 9 Reading Student Self-Study Workbook. 2007. (YA). per. 18.95 (978-1-59230-256-7(4)) Englefield & Assocs., Inc.
—Show What You Know on the CSAP Reading & Writing for Grade 6, Student Workbook. 2007. (J). per. 13.95 (978-1-59230-240-6(8)) Englefield & Assocs., Inc.
Shuert, Randy. Randy Ray & Easy Jay: Court Day Adventure. 2011. 28p. pap. 21.99 (978-1-4568-8393-5(3)) Xlibris Corp.
—Randy Ray & Easy Jay: The Wood House Adventure. 2011. 28p. pap. 21.99 (978-1-4568-8395-9(X)) Xlibris Corp.
Shulman, Lisa. The Library, 6 vols., Set. 2004. (Phonics Readers Books 37-72 Ser.). (ENG.). 8p. (gr. k-1). pap. 35.70 (978-0-7368-4056-9(7)) Capstone.
Shurley English 1 H/S/ Ed. 2004. pap. 8.00 (978-1-58561-052-5(6)) Shurley Instructional Materials, Inc.
Shurley English 2 H/S Ed. 2004. pap. 30.00 (978-1-58561-059-4(3)); pap. 8.00 (978-1-58561-053-2(4)) Shurley Instructional Materials, Inc.
Shurley English 3 H/S Ed. 2004. pap. 8.00 (978-1-58561-054-9(2)) Shurley Instructional Materials, Inc.
Si estas Contento, 6 vols., Pack. (Literatura 2000 Ser.). (SPA.). (gr. 1-2). 28.00 (978-0-7635-1078-7(5)) Rigby Education.
Siebert, Anne & Clark, Raymond C. All Around America: The Time Traveler's Talk Show. 2004. (gr. 6-12). pap., wbk. ed. 39.00 incl. cd-rom (978-0-86647-186-2(3)) Pro Lingua Assocs., Inc.
—All Around America Activities: The Time Traveler's Talk Show. 2004. 76p. (gr. 6-12). pap., stu. ed., wbk. ed. 16.50 (978-0-86647-184-8(7)) Pro Lingua Assocs., Inc.
Siegel, Elizabeth. Dinosaurs. 2007. (Steck-Vaughn BOLDPRINT Anthologies Ser.). (ENG., Illus.). 48p. (gr. 4-6). pap. 16.90 (978-1-4190-4019-1(7)) Houghton Mifflin Harcourt Publishing Co.
Sight Word Reproducible Stories. 2005. (J). pap. 9.99 (978-1-58970-702-3(8)) Lakeshore Learning Materials.
Sight Words with Samson. 2006. (J). cd-rom (978-0-9766680-2-2(5)) Knowledge Wand, LLC.
Sigue las Huellas: Big Book. (Pebble Soup Exploraciones Ser.). (SPA.). 16p. (gr. -1-18). 31.00 (978-0-7578-1675-8(4)) Rigby Education.
Sigue las Huellas: Small Book. (Pebble Soup Exploraciones Ser.). (SPA.). 16p. (gr. -1-18). 5.00 (978-0-7578-1715-1(7)) Rigby Education.
Silencio! Individual Title-Six Packs. (Chiquilibros Ser.). (SPA.). (gr. k-1). 23.00 (978-0-7635-8609-6(9)) Rigby Education.
Silva, Sadie. Fen Fixes Her Circuit: Fixing the Problem, 1 vol. 2017. (Computer Kids: Powered by Computational Thinking Ser.). (ENG.). 24p. (J). (gr. 4-5). 25.27 (978-1-5383-2395-3(8), f2c83d4d-a839-43c0-99c8-b8c107bfa666, PowerKids Pr.); pap. (978-1-5383-5309-7(1), fefa31d0-f8e8-4178-9b14-3aeab4a1bc1b, Rosen Classroom) Rosen Publishing Group, Inc., The.
Silver, Connie. A Story Book for Beginning Readers. 2007. 124p. per. 10.95 (978-0-595-46524-8(2)) iUniverse, Inc.
Silverman, Buffy. Lightning Bolt Books: Meet the Animal Groups, 6 vols., Set. Incl. Do You Know about Birds? (Illus.). lib. bdg. 26.60 (978-0-8225-7541-2(8)); Do You Know about Fish? (J). 25.26 (978-0-8225-7540-5(X)); Do You Know about Mammals? (Illus.). 26.60 (978-0-8225-7539-9(6)); 32p. (gr. k-2). 2009. Set lib. bdg. 151.56 (978-0-8225-7538-2(8), Lerner Pubns.) Lerner Publishing Group.
Silverstone, Michael. Paramedics to the Rescue: When Every Second Counts, 6 vols. 2004. (High Five Reading - Purple Ser.). (ENG.). 64p. (gr. 3-4). pap. 54.00 (978-0-7368-3867-2(8)) Capstone.
Simms, Rosie. Read, Think, & Write about It - Binder 1. 2004. (YA). ring bd. 59.95 (978-1-58804-356-6(8)) P C I Education.
—Read, Think, & Write about It - Binder 2. 2004. (YA). ring bd. 59.95 (978-1-58804-357-3(6)) P C I Education.
Simon, Jenne. Lalaloopsy: Chasing Rainbows. 2014. (Scholastic Reader Level 2 Ser.). lib. bdg. 13.55 (978-0-606-35402-8(6)) Turtleback.
Simon, Mary. Oh Oh. 2004. (SPA.). 32p. (J). 2.75 (978-0-570-05186-2(X)) Concordia Publishing Hse.
Simons, Joseph. Under a Living Sky, 1 vol. 2005. (Orca Young Readers Ser.). (ENG., Illus.). 112p. (J). (gr. 4-7). per. 5.95 (978-1-55143-355-4(9)) Orca Bk. Pubs. USA.
Simpson, Louie. My Mom Votes!, 1 vol. 2012. (InfoMax Readers Ser.). (ENG., Illus.). 24p. (J). (gr. 1-1). pap. 8.25 (978-1-4488-9055-2(1), 0eaeb0e1-6144-4aae-9e82-3d16a911dd3e, Rosen Classroom) Rosen Publishing Group, Inc., The.
Sims, Lesley. Midsummer Night's Drem. 2005. (Illus.). 48p. (J). (gr. 2-18). 8.95 (978-0-7945-1077-0(9), Usborne) EDC Publishing.
—Snow white & the seven Dwarfs. 2005. (Illus.). 64p. (J). (gr. 2-18). 8.95 (978-0-7945-1072-5(8), Usborne) EDC Publishing.
—Spider in a Glider. 2019. (Phonics Readers Ser.). (ENG.). 24ppp. (J). pap. 6.99 (978-0-7945-4362-4(6), Usborne) EDC Publishing.
Sing a Song of People. (Early Intervention Levels Ser.). 5.34 (978-0-7362-1895-5(5)); 32.04 (978-0-7362-2125-2(5)) CENGAGE Learning.
Singleton, Sarah. Century. 2008. (ENG.). 224p. (gr. 10-11). pap. 21.50 (978-0-340-96628-0(9)) Hodder Education Group GBR. Dist: Trans-Atlantic Pubns., Inc.
Sink or Float? KinderFacts Individual Title Six-Packs. (Kinderstarters Ser.). 8p. (gr. -1-1). 21.00 (978-0-7635-8749-9(4)) Rigby Education.
SIPPS Beginning Hand-held Sound Cards. 2004. (978-1-57621-455-8(9)) Center for the Collaborative Classroom.
Siwa, JoJo. The Posh Puppy Pageant (JoJo & BowBow #3), Vol. 3. 2019. (JoJo & BowBow Ser.). (ENG., Illus.). 120p. (J). (gr. 1-4). pap. 6.99 (978-1-4197-3602-5(7), 1270103, Amulet Bks.) Abrams, Inc.
—Take the Stage (JoJo & BowBow Book #1) 2018. (JoJo & BowBow Ser.). (ENG., Illus.). 144p. (J). (gr. 1-4). pap. 6.99 (978-1-4197-3601-8(9), 1270003, Amulet Bks.) Abrams, Inc.
Six Fish in a Mix. (Early Intervention Levels Ser.). 21.30 (978-0-7362-0388-3(5)) CENGAGE Learning.
Skittles & Skullbone, 6 Pack, Set D. (gr. k-3). 29.00 (978-0-7635-0547-9(1)) Rigby Education.
Sky Time. (Early Intervention Levels Ser.). 28.38 (978-0-7362-0402-6(4)) CENGAGE Learning.
Sky Time (10), Vol. 10. (Early Intervention Levels Ser.). 4.73 (978-0-7362-0227-5(7)) CENGAGE Learning.
Sky Watch: Level O, 6 vols. (Explorers Ser.). 32p. (gr. 3-6). mac hd 44.95 (978-0-7699-0595-2(1)) Shortland Pubns. (U. S. A.) Inc.
The Sled Ride: Individual Title Two-Packs. (Chiquilibros Ser.). (gr. -1-1). 12.00 (978-0-7635-8526-6(2)) Rigby Education.
Slip & Slide (12), Vol. 12. (Early Intervention Levels Ser.). 4.73 (978-0-7362-0233-6(1)) CENGAGE Learning.
The Smartest One in Class: Individual Title Six-Packs. (gr. -1-2). 27.00 (978-0-7635-9474-9(1)) Rigby Education.
Smith, Aimee & Johnston, Deon. My Hometown Is the Best Place to Visit. 2017. (Text Connections Guided Close Reading Ser.). (J). (gr. 1). (978-1-4900-1824-9(7)) Benchmark Education Co.
Smith, Ben. What Makes the Air Dirty? 2012. (Level C Ser.). (ENG., Illus.). 16p. (J). (gr. k-2). pap. 7.95 (978-1-927136-24-9(5), 19426) RiverStream Publishing.
—Where Can You Find Hard & Soft Things? 2012. (Level E Ser.). (ENG., Illus.). 16p. (J). (gr. k-2). pap. 7.95 (978-1-927136-49-2(0), 19441) RiverStream Publishing.
—Where Did My Grandparents Come From? 2012. (Level C Ser.). (ENG., Illus.). 16p. (J). (gr. k-2). pap. 7.95 (978-1-927136-21-8(0), 19442) RiverStream Publishing.
—Where Do Big Cats Live? 2012. (Level B Ser.). (ENG., Illus.). 16p. (J). (gr. k-2). pap. 7.95 (978-1-927136-17-1(2), 19443) RiverStream Publishing.
—Who Listens to the Weather Forecast? 2012. (Level D Ser.). (ENG., Illus.). 16p. (J). (gr. k-2). pap. 7.95 (978-1-927136-36-2(9), 19452) RiverStream Publishing.
—Why Do We Celebrate? 2012. (Level D Ser.). (ENG., Illus.). 16p. (J). (gr. k-2). pap. 7.95 (978-1-927136-31-7(8), 19461) RiverStream Publishing.
—Why Does This Float? 2012. (Level D Ser.). (ENG., Illus.). 16p. (J). (gr. k-2). pap. 7.95 (978-1-927136-39-3(3), 19465) RiverStream Publishing.
Smith, Carrie. Finding Shapes: Lap Book. 2009. (My First Reader's Theater Set B Ser.). (J). 28.00 (978-1-4108-8542-5(9)) Benchmark Education Co.
—Humpty Dumpty's Fall. 2008. (Reader's Theater Nursery Rhymes & Songs Ser.). (Illus.). 48p. (J). (gr. k-1). pap. (978-1-60437-958-7(8)) Benchmark Education Co.
—The Jumping Monkeys. Harpster, Steve, illus. 2009. (Reader's Theater Nursery Rhymes & Songs Set B Ser.). 48p. (J). pap. (978-1-60859-155-8(7)) Benchmark Education Co.
—Mary Has a Little Lamb. 2008. (Reader's Theater Nursery Rhymes & Songs Ser.). (Illus.). 48p. (J). (gr. k-1). pap. (978-1-60437-978-5(2)) Benchmark Education Co.
—One Silly Hey Diddle Day. 2008. (Reader's Theater Nursery Rhymes & Songs Ser.). (Illus.). 48p. (J). (gr. k-1). pap. (978-1-60437-963-1(4)) Benchmark Education Co.
—We See with Our Eyes: Lap Book. 2009. (My First Reader's Theater Set B Ser.). (J). 28.00 (978-1-60634-992-2(9)) Benchmark Education Co.
—Where Are Bo Peep's Sheep? Abbott, Jason, illus. 2009. (Reader's Theater Nursery Rhymes & Songs Set B Ser.). 48p. (J). pap. (978-1-60859-171-8(9)) Benchmark Education Co.
Smith, David. Nature's Garden. 2009. 132p. 22.50 (978-1-60693-169-1(5), Eloquent Bks.) Strategic Book Publishing & Rights Agency (SBPRA).
Smith, Emily R. Life in the Colonies, 1 vol. rev. ed. 2004. (Social Studies: Informational Text Ser.). (ENG.). 24p. (gr. 4-8). pap. 10.99 (978-0-7439-8742-4(X)) Teacher Created Materials, Inc.
Smith Ford, Deborah. The Little Apple. 2009. 32p. pap. 14.62 (978-1-4251-8806-1(0)) Trafford Publishing.
Smith, Jodene. The Day the Crayons Quit. rev. ed. 2015. (Great Works). (ENG., Illus.). 72p. (gr. k-3). pap. 11.99 (978-1-4807-8506-9(7)) Shell Educational Publishing.
Smith, Kathy. Helping Hannah, 1 vol. 2006. (Neighborhood Readers Ser.). (ENG.). 12p. (C). (gr. k-1). pap. (978-1-4042-6730-5(1), 1f1b260b-ff09-47f5-9183-414c5326aa39, Rosen Classroom) Rosen Publishing Group, Inc., The.
Smith, Michael. My Ducky Buddy. Oliva, Octavio, illus. 2015. (ARA & ENG.). 23p. (J). (978-0-9913454-3-4(6)) East West Discovery Pr.
Smith, Sian. Opposites, 1 vol. 2014. (Opposites Ser.). (ENG.). 24p. (J). (gr. -1-1). pap., pap., pap. 35.94 (978-1-4846-0338-3(9), 21695, Heinemann) Capstone.
—Opposites Big Book, 1 vol. 2014. (Opposites Ser.). (ENG., Illus.). 24p. (J). (gr. -1-1). 26.00 (978-1-4846-0339-0(7), 195266, Heinemann) Capstone.
Smythe, E. Louise. A Primary Reader: Old Time Stories, Fairy Tales & Myths Retold by Children. 2004. reprint ed. pap. 15.95 (978-1-4191-0287-5(7)); pap. 1.99 (978-1-4192-0287-2(1)) Kessinger Publishing, LLC.
Snashall, Sarah. Oxford International English Student Anthology 2. 2014. (ENG., Illus.). 96p. pap. 20.99 (978-0-19-839217-0(6)) Oxford Univ. Pr., Inc.
Snick Snack Sniffle-Nose: Set C Individual Title Six-Packs. (Supersonic Phonics Ser.). (gr. k-3). 29.00 (978-0-7635-0543-1(9)) Rigby Education.
Snider, Brandon T. Meet Quickshadow. 2017. (Transformers Passport to Reading Ser.). (J). lib. bdg. 14.75 (978-0-606-39910-4(0)) Turtleback.
Snowbound! 2003. (Illus.). pap. 7.60 (978-0-7398-7527-8(2)) Steck-Vaughn.
Snyder, Jane. Days of the Week: Learning Ordinal Numbers, 1 vol. 2010. (Math for the REAL World Ser.). (ENG.). 12p. (gr. 1-2). pap. 5.90 (978-0-8239-8913-3(5), 0becf867-7afa-4107-bbc5-f44c333665a4, Rosen Classroom) Rosen Publishing Group, Inc., The.
So Many Things to Do, 6 vols., Pack. (gr. -1-2). 23.00 (978-0-7635-9017-8(7)) Rigby Education.
So, Patty. So Simple Sightwords, 3 vols., 3 discs. 2004. Orig. Title: So Simple Learning: Sightwords. 222p. (J). DVD 189.90 (978-0-9772158-0-5(6)) So Simple Learning.
Socks: Individual Title Six-Packs. (Chiquilibros Ser.). (gr. k-1). 23.00 (978-0-7635-0427-4(0)) Rigby Education.
Soft Cloth Books 800406, 4. 2005. (J). (978-1-59794-032-0(1)) Environments, Inc.
SOft Touch Books 800780, 3. 2005. (J). (978-1-59794-041-2(0)) Environments, Inc.
Solve This! Level J, 6 vols. 128p. (gr. 2-3). 41.95 (978-0-7699-1035-2(1)) Shortland Pubns. (U. S. A.) Inc.
Sometimes: Individual Title Six-Packs. (gr. -1-2). 27.00 (978-0-7635-9476-3(8)); 23.00 (978-0-7635-8803-8(2)) Rigby Education.
Sometimes We're Happy, Sometimes We're Sad: Social/Emotional Lap Book. (Pebble Soup Explorations Ser.). (gr. -1-18). 16.00 (978-0-7635-7574-8(7)) Rigby Education.
Sommer, Cindy. Salvando Las Flores de Camelia, 1 vol. Allen Klein, Laurie, illus. 2016. (SPA.). 32p. (J). (gr. k-1). pap. 11.95 (978-1-62855-872-2(5), 5ad6fc34-bb4d-46a9-94a6-a2ee62c8206b) Arbordale Publishing.
Sows don't Pounce: Decodable Books, 6 vols. (Fast Track Reading Ser.). 24p. (gr. 4-8). 40.95 (978-0-322-05988-7(7)) Wright Group/McGraw-Hill.
Soy Artista: Individual Title Six-Packs. (Literatura 2000 Ser.). (SPA.). (gr. 2-3). 33.00 (978-0-7635-1251-4(6)) Rigby Education.
Soy Chef: Individual Title Six-Packs. (Literatura 2000 Ser.). (SPA.). (gr. 2-3). 33.00 (978-0-7635-1648-2(1)) Rigby Education.
Spanish TAKS MASTER Reading, Gr. 5. 2004. (J). (978-1-57022-472-0(2)) ECS Learning Systems, Inc.
Spanish TAKS MASTER Reading, Gr. 6. 2004. (J). (978-1-57022-500-0(1)) ECS Learning Systems, Inc.
Sparrow, Leilani. Collins Big Cat Phonics for Letters & Sounds - Dig It: Band 01B/Pink B. 2018. (Collins Big Cat Phonics Ser.). (ENG., Illus.). 16p. (J). (gr. -1-k). pap. 6.99 (978-0-00-825136-9(3)) HarperCollins Pubs. Ltd. GBR. Dist: Independent Pubs. Group.
Speaking Out. 2003. (Illus.). pap. 7.60 (978-0-7398-7522-3(1)) Steck-Vaughn.
Speedsters Series. (Illus.). (J). (gr. 2-5). (978-0-525-44950-8(7), Dutton Juvenile) Penguin Publishing Group.
Spider Night! (16), Vol. 16. (Early Intervention Levels Ser.). 4.73 (978-0-7362-0236-7(6)) CENGAGE Learning.
Spielman, Madison. Build It: Skyscrapers, 1 vol. 2nd rev. ed. 2011. (TIME for KIDS(r): Informational Text Ser.). (ENG.). 28p. (gr. 2-3). pap. 9.99 (978-1-4333-3620-1(0)) Teacher Created Materials, Inc.
—Craft It: Hand-Blown Glass, 1 vol. 2nd rev. ed. 2011. (TIME for KIDS(r): Informational Text Ser.). (ENG.). 28p. (gr. 2-3). pap. 9.99 (978-1-4333-3619-5(7)) Teacher Created Materials, Inc.
—Make It - Chocolate, 1 vol. 2nd rev. ed. 2011. (TIME for KIDS(r): Informational Text Ser.). (ENG.). 28p. (gr. 2-3). pap. 9.99 (978-1-4333-3621-8(9)) Teacher Created Materials, Inc.
Spilsbury, Louise. Collins Big Cat Phonics for Letters & Sounds - Blackcurrant Jam: Band 05/Green, Bd. 5. 2018. (Collins Big Cat Ser.). (ENG., Illus.). 24p. (J). pap. 7.99 (978-0-00-823029-6(3)) HarperCollins Pubs. Ltd. GBR. Dist: Independent Pubs. Group.
Spin & Match - Kings, Cookies, & Quakers: The Cookie Man, New Clothes for the King, the Ugly Baby Duck. 2006. (ENG.). 66p. (J). 9.99 (978-1-59204-203-6(1)) Learning Wrap-Ups, Inc.
Spin & Match - Tell Me a Story: The Grasshopper & the Ants, the Fox & the Grapes, the Turtle & the Rabbit. 2006. (ENG.). 66p. (J). 9.99 (978-1-59204-202-9(3)) Learning Wrap-Ups, Inc.
Splawn, "E". Planting Fruitful Seeds. 2011. 32p. pap. 12.77 (978-1-4567-3896-9(8)) AuthorHouse.
Sposito, Pipi, illus. Charles Dickens: Oliver Twist. 2021. (Sweet Cherry Easy Classics Ser.: 2). (ENG.). 96p. (J). 6.95 (978-1-78226-742-3(5), 9e3dd27d-e7ed-41c8-b3cf-7b7f8be87f14) Sweet Cherry Publishing GBR. Dist: Baker & Taylor Publisher Services (BTPS).
Spots, 6 vols., Set C,Pack. (Smart Start Ser.). (gr. k-1). 23.00 (978-0-7635-0436-6(X)) Rigby Education.
Spremulli, Pam. Letter Birds. 2010. (ENG., Illus.). 40p. (J). (gr. k-4). pap. 14.00 (978-1-935557-56-2(4)) PublishingWorks.
Sprick, Jessica. Kangaroos: Read Well Level K Unit 15 Storybook. Crum, Anna-Maria, illus. 2003. (Read Well Level K Ser.). 20p. (J). (978-1-57035-686-5(6), 55554) Cambium Education, Inc.
Sprick, Marilyn. Monkey Business: Read Well Level K Unit 3 Storybook. Nolte, Larry, illus. 2003. (Read Well Level K Ser.). 20p. (J). (978-1-57035-675-9(0)) Cambium Education, Inc.
Sprick, Marilyn, et al. Man's Best Friend: Read Well Level K Unit 5 Storybook. Zilis, Tom, illus. 2003. (Read Well Level K Ser.). 20p. (J). (978-1-57035-677-3(7)) Cambium Education, Inc.
—Read Well K Magazine Prelude F: Plain Text. 2003. (Read Well Level K Ser.). (Illus.). 12p. (J). (978-1-57035-731-2(5)) Cambium Education, Inc.
—Read Well Magazine Prelude A: Plain Text. 2003. (Read Well Level K Ser.). (Illus.). 12p. (J). (978-1-57035-725-1(0)) Cambium Education, Inc.
—Read Well Magazine Prelude A: Slanted Text. 2003. (Read Well Level K Ser.). (Illus.). 12p. (J). (978-1-57035-776-3(5)) Cambium Education, Inc.
—Read Well Magazine Prelude B: Plain Text. 2003. (Read Well Level K Ser.). (Illus.). 12p. (J). (978-1-57035-727-5(7)) Cambium Education, Inc.
—Read Well Magazine Prelude B: Slanted Text. 2003. (Read Well Level K Ser.). (Illus.). 12p. (J). (978-1-57035-777-0(3)) Cambium Education, Inc.
—Read Well Magazine Prelude C: Plain Text. 2004. (Read Well Level K Ser.). (Illus.). 12p. (J). (978-1-57035-728-2(5)) Cambium Education, Inc.

—Read Well Magazine Prelude C: Slanted Text. 2003. (Read Well Level K Ser.). (Illus.). 12p. (J). (978-1-57035-692-6(0)) Cambium Education, Inc.

—Read Well Magazine Prelude D: Plain Text. 2003. (Read Well Level K Ser.). (Illus.). 12p. (J). (978-1-57035-729-9(3)) Cambium Education, Inc.

—Read Well Magazine Prelude D: Slanted Text. 2003. (Read Well Level K Ser.). (Illus.). 12p. (J). (978-1-57035-693-3(9)) Cambium Education, Inc.

—Read Well Magazine Prelude E: Plain Text. 2003. (Read Well Level K Ser.). (Illus.). 12p. (J). (978-1-57035-730-5(7)) Cambium Education, Inc.

—Read Well Magazine Prelude E: Slanted Text. 2003. (Read Well Level K Ser.). (Illus.). 12p. (J). (978-1-57035-694-0(7)) Cambium Education, Inc.

—Read Well Magazine Preude F: Slanted Text. 2003. (Read Well Level K Ser.). (Illus.). 12p. (J). (978-1-57035-695-7(5)) Cambium Education, Inc.

—Read Well Magazine Unit 1: Plain Text. 2003. (Read Well Level K Ser.). (Illus.). 8p. (J). (978-1-57035-735-0(8)) Cambium Education, Inc.

—Read Well Magazine Unit 1: Slanted Text. 2004. (Read Well Level K Ser.). (Illus.). 8p. (J). (978-1-57035-782-4(X)) Cambium Education, Inc.

—Read Well Magazine Unit 10: Plain Text. 2003. (Read Well Level K Ser.). (Illus.). 8p. (J). (978-1-57035-740-4(4)) Cambium Education, Inc.

—Read Well Magazine Unit 10: Slanted Text. 2003. (Read Well Level K Ser.). (Illus.). 8p. (J). (978-1-57035-791-6(9)) Cambium Education, Inc.

—Read Well Magazine Unit 11: Plain Text. 2003. (Read Well Level K Ser.). (Illus.). 8p. (J). (978-1-57035-741-1(2)) Cambium Education, Inc.

—Read Well Magazine Unit 11: Slanted Text. 2003. (Read Well Level K Ser.). (Illus.). 8p. (J). (978-1-57035-792-3(7)) Cambium Education, Inc.

—Read Well Magazine Unit 12: Plain Text. 2004. (Read Well Level K Ser.). (Illus.). 8p. (J). (978-1-57035-742-8(0)) Cambium Education, Inc.

—Read Well Magazine Unit 12: Slanted Text. 2003. (Read Well Level K Ser.). (Illus.). 8p. (J). (978-1-57035-793-0(5)) Cambium Education, Inc.

—Read Well Magazine Unit 14: Plain Text. 2003. (Read Well Level K Ser.). (Illus.). 8p. (J). (978-1-57035-744-2(7)) Cambium Education, Inc.

—Read Well Magazine Unit 15: Plain Text. 2003. (Read Well Level K Ser.). (Illus.). 8p. (J). (978-1-57035-745-9(5)) Cambium Education, Inc.

—Read Well Magazine Unit 15: Slanted Text. 2003. (Read Well Level K Ser.). (Illus.). 8p. (J). (978-1-59318-099-7(3)) Cambium Education, Inc.

—Read Well Magazine Unit 16. 2003. (Read Well Level K Ser.). (Illus.). 8p. (J). (978-1-59318-100-0(0)) Cambium Education, Inc.

—Read Well Magazine Unit 17: Plain Text. 2003. (Read Well Level K Ser.). (Illus.). 8p. (J). (978-1-57035-747-3(1)) Cambium Education, Inc.

—Read Well Magazine Unit 18: Slanted Text. 2003. (Read Well Level K Ser.). (Illus.). 8p. (J). (978-1-59318-102-4(7)) Cambium Education, Inc.

—Read Well Magazine Unit 19: Plain Text. 2003. (Read Well Level K Ser.). (Illus.). 8p. (J). (978-1-57035-749-7(8)) Cambium Education, Inc.

—Read Well Magazine Unit 19: Slanted Text. 2003. (Read Well Level K Ser.). (Illus.). 8p. (J). (978-1-59318-103-1(5)) Cambium Education, Inc.

—Read Well Magazine Unit 2: Plain Text. 2003. (Read Well Level K Ser.). (Illus.). 8p. (J). (978-1-57035-733-6(1)) Cambium Education, Inc.

—Read Well Magazine Unit 2: Slanted Text. 2003. (Read Well Level K Ser.). (Illus.). 8p. (J). (978-1-57035-783-1(8)) Cambium Education, Inc.

—Read Well Magazine Unit 20: Plain Text. 2003. (Read Well Level K Ser.). (Illus.). 8p. (J). (978-1-57035-775-6(7)) Cambium Education, Inc.

—Read Well Magazine Unit 3: Plain Text. 2003. (Read Well Level K Ser.). (Illus.). 8p. (J). (978-1-57035-734-3(X)) Cambium Education, Inc.

—Read Well Magazine Unit 3: Slanted Text. 2003. (Read Well Level K Ser.). (Illus.). 8p. (J). (978-1-57035-784-8(6)) Cambium Education, Inc.

—Read Well Magazine Unit 4: Plain Text. 2003. (Read Well Level K Ser.). (Illus.). 8p. (J). (978-1-57035-732-9(3)) Cambium Education, Inc.

—Read Well Magazine Unit 4: Slanted Text. 2003. (Read Well Level K Ser.). (Illus.). 8p. (J). (978-1-57035-785-5(4)) Cambium Education, Inc.

—Read Well Magazine Unit 5: Plain Text. 2003. (Read Well Level K Ser.). (Illus.). 8p. (J). (978-1-57035-736-7(6)) Cambium Education, Inc.

—Read Well Magazine Unit 6: Plain Text. 2003. (Read Well Level K Ser.). (Illus.). 8p. (J). (978-1-57035-737-4(4)) Cambium Education, Inc.

—Read Well Magazine Unit 6: Slanted Text. 2003. (Read Well Level K Ser.). (Illus.). 8p. (J). (978-1-57035-787-9(0)) Cambium Education, Inc.

—Read Well Magazine Unit 7: Plain Text. 2003. (Read Well Level K Ser.). (Illus.). 8p. (J). (978-1-57035-738-1(2)) Cambium Education, Inc.

—Read Well Magazine Unit 8: Plain Text. 2003. (Read Well Level K Ser.). (Illus.). 8p. (J). (978-1-57035-726-8(9)) Cambium Education, Inc.

—Read Well Magazine Unit 8: Slanted Text. 2003. (Read Well Level K Ser.). (Illus.). 8p. (J). (978-1-57035-789-3(7)) Cambium Education, Inc.

—Read Well Magazine Unit 9: Plain Text. 2003. (Read Well Level K Ser.). (Illus.). 8p. (J). (978-1-57035-739-8(0)) Cambium Education, Inc.

—Read Well Magazine Unit 9: Slanted Text. 2003. (Read Well Level K Ser.). (Illus.). 8p. (J). (978-1-57035-790-9(0)) Cambium Education, Inc.

—Rescue Workers: Read Well Level K Unit 11 Storybook. Zilis, Tom, illus. 2003. (Read Well Level K Ser.). 20p. (J). (978-1-57035-682-7(3), 55511) Cambium Education, Inc.

—Spiders: Read Well Level K Unit 1 Storybook. Shupe, Bobbi & Crum, Anna-Maria, illus. 2003. (Read Well Level K Ser.). 20p. (J). (978-1-57035-673-5(4)) Cambium Education, Inc.

—Spiders: Unit 1 Read Well Level K Teacher's Storybook. Shupe, Bobbi & Crum, Anna-Maria, illus. 2003. (Read Well Level K Ser.). 20p. (J). (978-1-57035-696-4(3)) Cambium Education, Inc.

—Student Workbook 1 (Plain Text) Units 1-9 Plus Review Unit. 2003. (Read Well Level K Ser.). (Illus.). 104p. (J). (978-1-59318-166-6(3)) Cambium Education, Inc.

—Student Workbook 1 (Slant Text) Units 1-9 Plus Review Unit. 2003. (Read Well Level K Ser.). (Illus.). 104p. (J). (978-1-59318-169-7(8)) Cambium Education, Inc.

—Student Workbook 2 (Plain Text) Units 10-18 Plus Review Unit. 2003. (Read Well Level K Ser.). (Illus.). 104p. (J). (978-1-59318-167-3(1)) Cambium Education, Inc.

—Student Workbook 2 (Slant Text) Units 10-18 Plus Review Unit. 2003. (Read Well Level K Ser.). (Illus.). 104p. (J). (978-1-59318-170-3(1)) Cambium Education, Inc.

—Student Workbook 3 (Plain Text) Unit 19 through Vowel Review Unit. 2003. (Read Well Level K Ser.). (J). (978-1-59318-168-0(X)) Cambium Education, Inc.

Spring to Success on the PSSA Grade 5: Test Prep & Skills Practice READING. 2004. 112p. (J). per. 8.00 (978-0-9722452-6-5(X)) New Leaf Educ., Inc.

Spring to Success on the PSSA Grade 8: Test Prep & Skills Practice READING. 2004. 112p. (YA). per. 8.00 (978-0-9722452-2-7(7)) New Leaf Educ., Inc.

The Spy Meeting. (Sails Literacy Ser.). 24p. (gr. 2-18). 27.00 (978-0-7635-6998-3(4));Pack. 57.00 (978-0-7578-3218-5(0)) Rigby Education.

Spyri, Johanna & Ladybird Books Staff. Heidi. Peluso, Martina, illus. 2015. (Ladybird Classics Ser.). 72p. (J). (gr. k-3). 10.99 (978-1-4093-1357-1(3)) Penguin Bks., Ltd. GBR. Dist: Independent Pubs. Group.

Squiggles & Strokes, 6 vols., Pack. (Bookweb Ser.). 32p. (gr. 5-18). 34.00 (978-0-7635-3795-1(0)) Rigby Education.

Stamp, Jeffrey. Red & Slim: One Hot Day. Bohrer, Joe, illus. 2008. 40p. (J). 16.99 (978-0-9794543-0-1(1)) Syllabets, LLC.

Stanek, Robert, pseud. Break Their Bad Habits. deluxe ed. 2009. (Bugville Critters Ser.: No. 9). (Illus.). 24p. 9.99 (978-1-57545-213-5(8), Reagent Pr. Bks. for Young Readers) RP Media.

—Break Their Bad Habits: (the Bugville Critters, Lass's Adventures Series #2) 2009. (Bugville Critters Ser.: No. 9). (Illus.). 52p. (J). pap. 14.95 (978-1-57545-205-0(7), Reagent Pr. Bks. for Young Readers) RP Media.

—Buster Bee's Adventures with Letters & Words. 2008. (ENG., Illus.). 52p. (J). per. 19.95 (978-1-57545-169-5(7)) RP Media.

—Go to Camp. 2010. 34p. pap. 8.99 (978-1-57545-178-7(6), Reagent Pr. Bks. for Young Readers) RP Media.

—Save Their Allowance. 2010. 32p. pap. 8.99 (978-1-57545-175-6(1), Reagent Pr. Bks. for Young Readers) RP Media.

—Stay after School. 2009. (Bugville Critters Ser.: No. 10). (ENG., Illus.). 52p. (J). 14.95 (978-1-57545-206-7(5), Reagent Pr. Bks. for Young Readers) RP Media.

—Visit City Hall. 2009. (Bugville Critters Ser.: No. 12). (ENG., Illus.). 52p. (J). 14.95 (978-1-57545-208-1(1), Reagent Pr. Bks. for Young Readers) RP Media.

Stango, Diane. Too Many Tomatoes, 1 vol. 2006. (Neighborhood Readers Ser.). (ENG.). 12p. (gr. k-1). pap. 5.90 (978-1-4042-6718-3(2), cbbef832-ae95-468b-ac51-12f8d88d36b8, Rosen Classroom) Rosen Publishing Group, Inc., The.

—Vicky's Vegetables, 1 vol. 2006. (Neighborhood Readers Ser.). (ENG.). 16p. (gr. 1-2). pap. 6.50 (978-1-4042-7156-2(2), 357d5fb3-9da0-4339-b007-34702d8176f4, Rosen Classroom) Rosen Publishing Group, Inc., The.

Stango, Diane E. City Life. 2006. (Rosen Real Readers Big Bookstm Ser.). (ENG.). 8p. (gr. k-1). 29.95 (978-1-4042-6210-2(5)) Rosen Publishing Group, Inc., The.

STAR Early Literacy RP Student Subscription. 2004. cd-rom (978-1-59455-175-8(8)) Renaissance Learning, Inc.

STAR Early Literacy RP Student Subscription Renewal. 2004. cd-rom (978-1-59455-176-5(6)) Renaissance Learning, Inc.

STAR Early Literacy RP Subscription Package. 2004. cd-rom (978-1-59455-173-4(1)) Renaissance Learning, Inc.

Star, Ian. Breakfast at the Farm, 1 vol. 2006. (Neighborhood Readers Ser.). (ENG.). 12p. (gr. k-1). pap. 5.90 (978-1-4042-6473-1(6), 4f55841c-54af-4003-bf9b-e3dcb449d863, Rosen Classroom) Rosen Publishing Group, Inc., The.

STAR Reading RP Norms Upgrade. 2004. cd-rom 599.00 (978-1-59455-172-7(3)) Renaissance Learning, Inc.

STAR Reading RP Student Subscription. 2004. cd-rom 0.99 (978-1-59455-169-7(3)) Renaissance Learning, Inc.

STAR Reading RP Student Subscription Renewal. 2004. cd-rom (978-1-59455-170-3(7)) Renaissance Learning, Inc.

STAR Reading RP Subscription Package. 2004. cd-rom (978-1-59455-168-0(5)) Renaissance Learning, Inc.

Starfall Education. Gus the Duck. Starfall Education, ed. 2004. (ENG., Illus.). 8p. (J). pap. (978-1-59577-005-9(4)) Starfall Education.

—Level I Reading & Writing Journal - Block Print: WK201b. Starfall Education, ed. 2011. (ENG., Illus.). 96p. (J). (978-1-59577-045-5(3)) Starfall Education.

—My Horse Glory. Starfall Education, ed. 2004. (ENG., Illus.). 8p. (J). pap. (978-1-59577-013-4(5)) Starfall Education.

—Peg the Hen. Starfall Education, ed. 2004. (ENG., Illus.). 8p. (J). pap. (978-1-59577-002-8(X)) Starfall Education.

—Pete's Sheep. Starfall Education, ed. 2004. (ENG., Illus.). 8p. (J). pap. (978-1-59577-007-3(0)) Starfall Education.

—Robot & Mr. Mole. Starfall Education, ed. 2004. (ENG., Illus.). 8p. (J). pap. (978-1-59577-009-7(7)) Starfall Education.

—Sky Ride. Starfall Education, ed. 2004. (ENG., Illus.). 8p. (J). pap. (978-1-59577-008-0(9)) Starfall Education.

—Soap Boat. Starfall Education, ed. 2004. (ENG., Illus.). 8p. (J). pap. (978-1-59577-011-0(9)) Starfall Education.

Starfall Education, creator. Level II Reading & Writing Journal: Second Edition. 2010. (ENG., Illus.). 96p. (J). 1.95 (978-1-59577-130-8(1)) Starfall Education.

Stark, Barbara. Blue Dinosaur's Friends. l.t. ed. 2006. (Illus.). 24p. (J). E-Book 9.95 incl. cd-rom (978-1-933090-20-7(0)) Guardian Angel Publishing, Inc.

Start It Up! (Early Intervention Levels Ser.). 21.30 (978-0-7362-0391-3(5)); Vol. 6. 3.55 (978-0-7362-0171-1(8)) CENGAGE Learning.

Start Reading. 2013. (Start Reading Ser.). (ENG.). 24p. (gr. k-1). pap. 230.67 (978-1-62065-765-2(1)); pap. 174.75 (978-1-4765-3332-2(6)) Capstone.

Start Reading Classroom Collection. 2013. (Start Reading Ser.). (ENG.). 24p. (gr. k-1). pap. 1048.50 (978-1-4765-3333-9(4)) Capstone.

Starters Two, Red, & Yellow Levels Certificate Only. (gr. k-5). 89.00 (978-0-7578-6539-8(9)) Rigby Education.

Stckvagn. AC Reading for Today. 2004. pap. (978-0-7398-9859-8(0)) Harcourt Schl. Pubs.

Steck-Vaughn, creator. Using Information Resources, Grade 2. 2009. (Using Information Resources Ser.). (Illus.). 64p. pap. 9.99 (978-1-4190-9937-3(X)) Steck-Vaughn.

—Using Information Resources, Grade 3. 2009. (Using Information Resources Ser.). (Illus.). 64p. pap. 9.99 (978-1-4190-9938-0(8)) Steck-Vaughn.

Steck-Vaughn Staff. Cycles Go Bk. FA: Quests. 2004. (Illus.). pap. 8.95 (978-0-7398-8972-5(9)) Steck-Vaughn.

—Cycles Go Bk. GA: Choices. 2004. (Illus.). pap. 8.95 (978-0-7398-8973-2(7)) Steck-Vaughn.

—Cycles Go Bk. HA: Visions. 2004. (Illus.). pap. 8.95 (978-0-7398-8974-9(5)) Steck-Vaughn.

—Cycles Go - Reflections. 2004. (Illus.). pap. 8.95 (978-0-7398-8975-6(3)) Steck-Vaughn.

—Early Reading Program: Professional Development. 2004. pap. 45.00 (978-0-7398-9948-9(1)) Harcourt Schl. Pubs.

—Exactly the Right Egg. 2003. pap. 4.10 (978-0-7398-7631-2(7)) Steck-Vaughn.

—Fact Family Fun. 2003. pap. 4.10 (978-0-7398-7662-6(7)) Steck-Vaughn.

—Language Art & Spelling, 8, Pack. 2004. pap. 68.00 (978-0-7398-9933-5(3)) Harcourt Schl. Pubs.

—Language Arts & Spelling, 8 Packs. 2004. pap. 68.00 (978-0-7398-9929-8(5)); pap. 8.50 (978-0-7398-9848-2(5)); pap., tchr. ed. 10.00 (978-0-7398-9904-5(X)) Harcourt Schl. Pubs.

—Nonfiction Comprehension. 2005. (gr. 3). pap. 12.99 (978-0-7398-8947-3(8)); (gr. 5). pap. 12.99 (978-0-7398-8948-0(6)) Harcourt Schl. Pubs.

—Nonfiction Comprehension, Middle School. 2005. pap. 12.99 (978-0-7398-8949-7(4)) Harcourt Schl. Pubs.

—Primary Grades, Grades 1-3. 2004. (Reader's Theater Ser.). (ENG., Illus.). 160p. (gr. 1-3). pap. 16.99 (978-0-7398-9309-8(2)) Houghton Mifflin Harcourt Publishing Co.

—Reading & Language Arts. 2004. pap. 8.50 (978-0-7398-9845-1(0)) Harcourt Schl. Pubs.

—Reading & Language Arts 8-Pack. 2004. pap. 68.00 (978-0-7398-9926-7(0)) Harcourt Schl. Pubs.

—Reading Comprehension: Building Vocabulary & Measurement. 2003. (Steck-Vaughn Reading Comprehension Ser.). (ENG.). 56p. (gr. k-k). pap., tchr. ed. 33.70 (978-0-7398-8356-3(9)) Houghton Mifflin Harcourt Publishing Co.

—Reading Intermediate, 8, Pack. 2004. pap. 68.00 (978-0-7398-9928-1(7)) Harcourt Schl. Pubs.

—Stuck on You. 2003. pap. 4.10 (978-0-7398-7634-3(1)) Steck-Vaughn.

Steck-Vaughn Staff, creator. Test Fundamentals: Reading: Basic, 8, Pack. 2004. pap. 68.00 (978-0-7398-9932-8(5)) Harcourt Schl. Pubs.

Steel, Abigail. Africa: Band 02A Red a/Band 10 White (Collins Big Cat Phonics Progress) 2013. (Collins Big Cat Phonics Progress Ser.). (ENG., Illus.). 16p. (J). (gr. 1-2). pap. 6.95 (978-0-00-751634-6(7)) HarperCollins Pubs. Ltd. GBR. Dist: Independent Pubs. Group.

Steinberg, Jon L. "Eye" See My Alphabet. 2012. 60p. (-18). pap. 24.99 (978-1-4797-1135-2(7)) Xlibris Corp.

Steiner. Murder Takes a Fast Track. (Thumbprint Mysteries Ser.). 32.86 (978-0-8092-0417-5(7)) McGraw-Hill/Contemporary.

Steiner, Rudolf. Fun Days. (J). pap. 2.75 (978-0-87895-956-3(4)) Modern Curriculum Pr.

Steinkraus, Kyla & Robins, Maureen. Los Problemas Del Intercambio. 2012. (Little Birdie Readers Ser.). (SPA.). 24p. (gr. 2-3). pap. 9.95 (978-1-61810-543-1(4), 9781618105431) Rourke Educational Media.

Stephens, Monique Z. Fantastic Four: The Fantastic Four Versus Doctor Doom. 2005. (Festival Reader Ser.). (Illus.). 32p. (J). (gr. -1-2). 14.99 (978-0-06-082245-3(7), HarperFestival) HarperCollins Pubs.

Stevenson, May. Brilliant Activities for Reading Non-Fiction: Comprehension Activities for 7-11 Year Olds. 2006. (Illus.). 128p. pap. (978-1-903853-46-7(X)) Brilliant Pubns.

Stevenson, Robert Louis. Kidnapped. 2017. (ENG., Illus.). (J). 30.99 (978-1-366-54862-7(0)) Blurb, Inc.

—Kidnapped. 2017. (ENG., Illus.). (J). 24.95 (978-1-374-96355-9(0)); pap. 14.95 (978-1-374-96354-2(2)) Capital Communications, Inc.

—Kidnapped. 2016. (ENG., Illus.). (J). 25.95 (978-1-359-73690-1(5)) Creative Media Partners, LLC.

Stevenson-Spurgon, Barbara J. Have You Ever Made Mud Pies on a Hot Summer Day? This Is a Bitty Book. Ruffin, Aurzella, illus. 2006. 36p. (J). (gr. -1-4). per. 19.95 (978-1-60002-234-0(0), 4073) Mountain Valley Publishing, LLC.

Stewart, Melissa. National Geographic Readers: Water. 2014. (Readers Ser.). (Illus.). 48p. (J). (gr. 1-3). pap. 4.99 (978-1-4263-1474-2(4), National Geographic Kids) Disney Publishing Worldwide.

Stewart, Sue. Oxford Bookworms Factfiles: Recycling: Level 3: 1000-Word Vocabulary. 3rd ed. 2008. (ENG., Illus.). 80p. 11.00 (978-0-19-423389-7(8)) Oxford Univ. Pr., Inc.

Stiles, Amanda. The Runaway Soccer Ball. Torrey, Rich, illus. 2010. 16p. (J). pap. (978-0-545-24819-8(1)) Scholastic, Inc.

Stock, Lisa. DK Readers L2: Star Wars: Rey to the Rescue! Discover Rey's Force Powers! 2017. (DK Readers Level 2 Ser.). (ENG., Illus.). 48p. (J). (gr. k-2). pap. 3.99 (978-1-4654-5580-2(9), DK Children) Dorling Kindersley Publishing, Inc.

—What Is a Droid? 2018. (Star Wars DK Readers Level 1 Ser.). lib. bdg. 14.75 (978-0-606-41168-4(2)) Turtleback.

Stockton, Frank, et al. Level 2: Simply Suspense. 2nd ed. 2008. (Pearson English Graded Readers Ser.). (ENG., Illus.). 56p. pap. 13.32 (978-1-4058-6948-5(8), Pearson ELT) Pearson Education.

Stontz, Karen & Malone, Kelly. Autism & PDD Concepts How Does Becca Bunny Feel? 2004. (J). spiral bd. (978-0-7606-0594-3(7)) LinguiSystems, Inc.

Stop That Noise! KinderWords Individual Title Six-Packs. (Kinderstarters Ser.). 8p. (gr. -1-1). 21.00 (978-0-7635-8694-2(3)) Rigby Education.

Stories & More. 2005. (Little Celebrations Thematic Packages Ser.). (J). (gr. k-3). 133.50 (978-0-673-75376-2(X)) Celebration Pr.

Stories from Many Lands. (J). 3.70 (978-0-8136-2402-0(9)); tchr. ed. 9.30 (978-0-8136-2427-3(4)) Modern Curriculum Pr.

Stories of Ourselves. 2018. (Cambridge International IGCSE Ser.). (ENG., Illus.). 462p. pap. 19.60 (978-1-108-43619-9(6)) Cambridge Univ. Pr.

Storm Warning: KinderConcepts Individual Title Six-Packs. (Kinderstarters Ser.). 8p. (gr. -1-1). 21.00 (978-0-7635-8734-5(6)) Rigby Education.

Stormer, Kate. The Rescue of Little Red. Lowes, Tom, illus. 2005. 91p. (J). (gr. 3-5). per. 5.99 (978-0-9765872-0-0(3)) Caseys World Bks.

Story Box. (gr. 2-18). 8.50 (978-0-7802-3064-4(7)) Wright Group/McGraw-Hill.

Story Center. 2005. (YA). (gr. -1-3). 19.95 (978-0-8215-7557-4(0)) Sadlier, William H. Inc.

Story Center Guide. 2005. (YA). (gr. -1-3). 6.00 (978-0-8215-7558-1(9)) Sadlier, William H. Inc.

The Story of Dona Chila: Six-Pack. (Greetings Ser.: Vol. 3). (gr. 3-5). 31.00 (978-0-7635-1775-5(5)) Rigby Education.

The Story of Jeans, 6 Pack. (Discovery World Ser.). 24p. (gr. 1-2). 33.00 (978-0-7635-8483-2(5)) Rigby Education.

Storytapes Set 800866, 3. 2005. (J). (978-1-59794-029-0(1)) Environments, Inc.

Stowell, Louie. Samurai. Engle, Jason, illus. 2007. (Young Reading Series 3 Gift Bks). 58p. (J). (gr. 2-5). 8.99 (978-0-7945-1719-9(6), Usborne) EDC Publishing.

Streetsweeper, 6 packs. (Bookweb Ser.). 32p. (gr. 3-18). 34.00 (978-0-7635-3943-6(0)) Rigby Education.

String Performers: Individual Title Six-Packs. (gr. k-1). 23.00 (978-0-7635-9029-1(0)) Rigby Education.

Strings, Ropes & Cables, 6 Packs. (gr. k-1). 23.00 (978-0-7635-9024-6(X)) Rigby Education.

Stripland, Rubye Weldon. Lucy Bell, Queen of the Pasture. 2008. 92p. pap. 10.95 (978-1-4357-1472-4(5)) Lulu Pr., Inc.

—Lucy Bell, Queen of the Pasture Book Two. 2008. 100p. pap. 10.95 (978-1-4357-1895-1(X)) Lulu Pr., Inc.

Strong, Jeremy. Bungleman: Band 13/Topaz (Collins Big Cat) Mosedale, Julian, illus. 2007. (Collins Big Cat Ser.). (ENG.). 32p. (J). (gr. 2-3). pap. 10.99 (978-0-00-723083-9(4)) HarperCollins Pubs. Ltd. GBR. Dist: Independent Pubs. Group.

—The Sneezles: Band 10/White (Collins Big Cat) Blundell, Tony, illus. 2005. (Collins Big Cat Ser.). (ENG.). 32p. (J). (gr. 1-3). pap. 10.99 (978-0-00-718628-0(2)) HarperCollins Pubs. Ltd. GBR. Dist: Independent Pubs. Group.

Stuart, Carrie. Chinese New Year, 1 vol. 2006. (Neighborhood Readers Ser.). (ENG.). 12p. (gr. k-1). pap. 5.90 (978-1-4042-6461-8(2), 1c3397a3-2927-432e-96c5-ee9af0868bca, Rosen Classroom) Rosen Publishing Group, Inc., The.

—Lenore's Chores, 1 vol. 2006. (Neighborhood Readers Ser.). (ENG.). 8p. (gr. 1-2). pap. 5.15 (978-1-4042-6823-4(5), eec6a475-0c34-4f4b-9475-9762929c2498, Rosen Classroom) Rosen Publishing Group, Inc., The.

Stuart, Phillip. Stage Fright. 2005. (Young Reading Series 2 Ser.). 64p. (J). (gr. 2-18). pap. 5.95 (978-0-7945-0927-9(4), Usborne) EDC Publishing.

Sturgeon, Kristi. Freckle Juice: An Instructional Guide for Literature. rev. ed. 2015. (Great Works). (ENG., Illus.). 72p. (gr. 3-5). pap. 9.99 (978-1-4807-6993-9(2)) Shell Educational Publishing.

Styles, Walker. The Case of the Missing Tiger's Eye. 2016. (Rider Woofson Ser.: 1). lib. bdg. 16.00 (978-0-606-38262-5(3)) Turtleback.

Suchanek, David. The 10 Most Inspiring Speeches. 2008. 14.99 (978-1-55448-537-6(1)) Scholastic Library Publishing.

Sugar & Spice & All Things Nice: Level M, 6 vols. 128p. (gr. 2-3). 40.50 (978-0-7699-0998-1(1)) Shortland Pubns. (U. S. A.) Inc.

The Sugar Bush: 6 Small Books. (Greetings Ser.: Vol. 1). 24p. (gr. 2-3). 31.00 (978-0-7635-9424-4(5)) Rigby Education.

The Sugar Bush: Big Book. (Greetings Ser.: Vol. 1). 24p. (gr. 2-3). 31.00 (978-0-7635-5706-5(4)) Rigby Education.

Sulky Simon, 6 Packs. (gr. 1-2). 25.00 (978-0-7635-9146-5(7)) Rigby Education.

Sundance/Newbridge LLC Staff. The Abominable Snowman. 2005. (Choose Your Own Adventure Ser.). (gr. 4-8). pap. 5.50 (978-0-7608-9693-8(3)) Sundance/Newbridge Educational Publishing.

—Amazing Water. 2007. (Early Science Ser.). (gr. k-3). 18.95 (978-1-4007-6296-5(0)); pap. 6.10 (978-1-4007-6292-7(8)) Sundance/Newbridge Educational Publishing.

—Animals & Their Babies. 2007. (Early Science Ser.). (gr. k-3). 18.95 (978-1-4007-6215-6(4)); pap. 6.10 (978-1-4007-6211-8(1)) Sundance/Newbridge Educational Publishing.

—Animals in Hiding. 2007. (Early Science Ser.). (gr. k-3). 18.95 (978-1-4007-6350-4(9)) Sundance/Newbridge Educational Publishing.

—An Apple a Day. 2007. (Early Science Ser.). (gr. k-3). 18.95 (978-1-4007-6359-7(2)); pap. 6.10 (978-1-4007-6355-9(X)) Sundance/Newbridge Educational Publishing.

—Being Human. 2007. (Early Science Ser.). (gr. k-3). 18.95 (978-1-4007-6513-3(7)); pap. 6.10 (978-1-4007-6509-6(9)) Sundance/Newbridge Educational Publishing.

—Birds, Birds, Birds. 2004. (Reading PowerWorks Ser.). (gr. 1-3). pap. 6.10 (978-0-7608-9784-3(0)) Sundance/Newbridge Educational Publishing.

—Bubbles, Bubbles Everywhere. 2007. (Early Science Ser.). (gr. k-3). 18.95 (978-1-4007-6206-4(5)); pap. 6.10 (978-1-4007-6202-6(2)) Sundance/Newbridge Educational Publishing.

—Busy As a Bee. 2007. (Early Science Ser.). (gr. k-3). 18.95 (978-1-4007-6594-2(3)); pap. 6.10 (978-1-4007-6590-4(0)) Sundance/Newbridge Educational Publishing.

—A Butterfly Is Born. 2007. (Early Science Ser.). (gr. k-3). 18.95 *(978-1-4007-6224-8(3))*; pap. 6.10 *(978-1-4007-6220-0(0))* Sundance/Newbridge Educational Publishing.
—Design It! Build It! 2007. (Early Science Ser.). (gr. k-3). 18.95 *(978-1-4007-6603-1(6))*; pap. 6.10 *(978-1-4007-6599-7(4))* Sundance/Newbridge Educational Publishing.
—Dollars & Cents. 2004. (Reading PowerWorks Ser.). (gr. 1-3). 37.50 *(978-0-7608-8964-0(3))*; pap. 6.10 *(978-0-7608-8965-7(1))* Sundance/Newbridge Educational Publishing.
—Energy. 2007. (Early Science Ser.). (gr. k-3). 18.95 *(978-1-4007-6549-2(8))*; pap. 6.10 *(978-1-4007-6545-4(5))* Sundance/Newbridge Educational Publishing.
—Exploring Our Oceans. 2004. (Reading PowerWorks Ser.). (gr. 1-3). pap. 6.10 *(978-0-7608-9760-7(3))* Sundance/Newbridge Educational Publishing.
—The Fact Families. 2004. (Reading PowerWorks Ser.). (gr. 1-3). 37.50 *(978-0-7608-9305-0(5))*; pap. 6.10 *(978-0-7608-9306-7(3))* Sundance/Newbridge Educational Publishing.
—Follow the River. 2007. (Early Science Ser.). (gr. k-3). 18.95 *(978-1-4007-6558-4(7))*; pap. 6.10 *(978-1-4007-6554-6(4))* Sundance/Newbridge Educational Publishing.
—For Your Information. 2007. (Early Science Ser.). (gr. k-3). 18.95 *(978-1-4007-6567-6(6))*; pap. 6.10 *(978-1-4007-6563-8(3))* Sundance/Newbridge Educational Publishing.
—From Circles to Cubes. 2004. (Reading PowerWorks Ser.). (gr. 1-3). 37.50 *(978-0-7608-7839-2(0))*; pap. 6.10 *(978-0-7608-7840-8(4))* Sundance/Newbridge Educational Publishing.
—From Peanuts to Peanut Butter. 2007. (Early Science Ser.). (gr. k-3). 18.95 *(978-1-4007-6170-8(0))*; pap. 6.10 *(978-1-4007-6166-1(2))* Sundance/Newbridge Educational Publishing.
—Gravity. 2007. (Early Science Ser.). (gr. k-3). 18.95 *(978-1-4007-6468-6(8))*; pap. 6.10 *(978-1-4007-6464-8(5))* Sundance/Newbridge Educational Publishing.
—Growing Pumpkins. 2007. (Early Science Ser.). (gr. k-3). 18.95 *(978-1-4007-6179-1(4))*; pap. 6.10 *(978-1-4007-6175-3(1))* Sundance/Newbridge Educational Publishing.
—How We Use Electricity. 2007. (Early Science Ser.). (gr. k-3). 18.95 *(978-1-4007-6368-9(1))*; pap. 6.10 *(978-1-4007-6364-1(9))* Sundance/Newbridge Educational Publishing.
—Inventions. 2007. (Early Science Ser.). (gr. k-3). 18.95 *(978-1-4007-6630-7(3))*; pap. 6.10 *(978-1-4007-6626-0(5))* Sundance/Newbridge Educational Publishing.
—Is It Alive? 2007. (Early Science Ser.). (gr. k-3). 18.95 *(978-1-4007-6152-4(2))*; pap. 6.10 *(978-1-4007-6148-7(4))* Sundance/Newbridge Educational Publishing.
—Kids for the Earth. 2007. (Early Science Ser.). (gr. k-3). 18.95 *(978-1-4007-6188-3(3))*; pap. 6.10 *(978-1-4007-6184-5(0))* Sundance/Newbridge Educational Publishing.
—Leaping Frogs. 2007. (Early Science Ser.). (gr. k-3). 18.95 *(978-1-4007-6305-4(3))*; pap. 6.10 *(978-1-4007-6301-6(0))* Sundance/Newbridge Educational Publishing.
—Life in a Pond. 2007. (Early Science Ser.). (gr. k-3). 18.95 *(978-1-4007-6377-1(0))*; pap. 6.10 *(978-1-4007-6373-3(8))* Sundance/Newbridge Educational Publishing.
—Life in a Tree. 2007. (Early Science Ser.). (gr. k-3). 18.95 *(978-1-4007-6459-4(9))*; pap. 6.10 *(978-1-4007-6455-6(6))* Sundance/Newbridge Educational Publishing.
—Light. 2007. (Early Science Ser.). (gr. k-3). 18.95 *(978-1-4007-6314-6(2))*; pap. 6.10 *(978-1-4007-6310-8(X))* Sundance/Newbridge Educational Publishing.
—The Lost Jewels of Nafouti. 2005. (Choose Your Own Adventure Ser.). (gr. 4-8). pap. 5.50 *(978-0-7608-9691-4(7))* Sundance/Newbridge Educational Publishing.
—Make Mine Ice Cream. 2007. (Early Science Ser.). (gr. k-3). 18.95 *(978-1-4007-6522-5(6))*; pap. 6.10 *(978-1-4007-6518-8(8))* Sundance/Newbridge Educational Publishing.
—Matter Is Everything. 2004. (Reading PowerWorks Ser.). (gr. 1-3). 37.50 *(978-0-7608-8900-8(7))*; pap. 6.10 *(978-0-7608-8901-5(5))* Sundance/Newbridge Educational Publishing.
—Mystery of the Maya. 2005. (Choose Your Own Adventure Ser.). (gr. 4-8). pap. 5.50 *(978-0-7608-9692-1(5))* Sundance/Newbridge Educational Publishing.
—One World, Many Cultures. 2004. (Reading PowerWorks Ser.). (gr. 1-3). 37.50 *(978-0-7608-8952-7(X))*; pap. 6.10 *(978-0-7608-8953-4(8))* Sundance/Newbridge Educational Publishing.
—Our American Folklore. 2004. (Reading PowerWorks Ser.). (gr. 1-3). 37.50 *(978-0-7608-9795-9(6))*; pap. 6.10 *(978-0-7608-9796-6(4))* Sundance/Newbridge Educational Publishing.
—Our Natural Resources. 2004. (Reading PowerWorks Ser.). (gr. 1-3). 37.50 *(978-0-7608-9221-3(0))*; pap. 6.10 *(978-0-7608-9222-0(9))* Sundance/Newbridge Educational Publishing.
—Our Sun, Our Weather. 2007. (Early Science Ser.). (gr. k-3). 18.95 *(978-1-4007-6531-7(5))*; pap. 6.10 *(978-1-4007-6527-0(7))* Sundance/Newbridge Educational Publishing.
—Out in Space. 2007. (Early Science Ser.). (gr. k-3). 18.95 *(978-1-4007-6422-8(X))*; pap. 6.10 *(978-1-4007-6418-1(1))* Sundance/Newbridge Educational Publishing.
—Pasta, Please! 2007. (Early Science Ser.). (gr. k-3). 18.95 *(978-1-4007-6332-0(0))*; pap. 6.10 *(978-1-4007-6328-3(2))* Sundance/Newbridge Educational Publishing.
—Predators & Prey. 2007. (Early Science Ser.). (gr. k-3). 18.95 *(978-1-4007-6540-9(4))*; pap. 6.10 *(978-1-4007-6536-2(6))* Sundance/Newbridge Educational Publishing.
—Predicting the Weather. 2004. (Reading PowerWorks Ser.). (gr. 1-3). 37.50 *(978-0-7608-9245-9(8))* Sundance/Newbridge Educational Publishing.
—Properties of Materials. 2007. (Early Science Ser.). (gr. k-3). 18.95 *(978-1-4007-6576-8(5))*; pap. 6.10 *(978-1-4007-6572-0(2))* Sundance/Newbridge Educational Publishing.
—Push & Pull. 2007. (Early Science Ser.). (gr. k-3). 18.95 *(978-1-4007-6134-0(4))*; pap. 6.10 *(978-1-4007-6130-2(1))* Sundance/Newbridge Educational Publishing.
—Rocks & Soil. 2007. (Early Science Ser.). (gr. k-3). 18.95 *(978-1-4007-6441-9(6))*; pap. 6.10 *(978-1-4007-6437-2(8))* Sundance/Newbridge Educational Publishing.
—See, Hear, Touch, Taste, Smell. 2007. (Early Science Ser.). (gr. k-3). 18.95 *(978-1-4007-6197-5(2))*; pap. 6.10 *(978-1-4007-6193-7(X))* Sundance/Newbridge Educational Publishing.
—Seeds Get Around. 2007. (Early Science Ser.). (gr. k-3). 18.95 *(978-1-4007-6341-2(X))*; pap. 6.10 *(978-1-4007-6337-5(1))* Sundance/Newbridge Educational Publishing.
—Simple Machines. 2007. (Early Science Ser.). (gr. k-3). 18.95 *(978-1-4007-6612-3(5))*; pap. 6.10 *(978-1-4007-6608-6(7))* Sundance/Newbridge Educational Publishing.
—Sink or Float? 2007. (Early Science Ser.). (gr. k-3). 18.95 *(978-1-4007-6269-9(3))*; pap. 6.10 *(978-1-4007-6265-1(0))* Sundance/Newbridge Educational Publishing.
—Six Simple Machines. 2004. (Reading PowerWorks Ser.). (gr. 1-3). 37.50 *(978-0-7608-9735-5(2))*; pap. 6.10 *(978-0-7608-9736-2(0))* Sundance/Newbridge Educational Publishing.
—Sound. 2007. (Early Science Ser.). (gr. k-3). 18.95 *(978-1-4007-6395-5(9))*; pap. 6.10 *(978-1-4007-6391-7(6))* Sundance/Newbridge Educational Publishing.
—Spinning a Web. 2007. (Early Science Ser.). (gr. k-3). 18.95 *(978-1-4007-6233-0(2))*; pap. 6.10 *(978-1-4007-6229-3(4))* Sundance/Newbridge Educational Publishing.
—Symbols of America. 2004. (Reading PowerWorks Ser.). (gr. 1-3). 37.50 *(978-0-7608-9257-2(1))* Sundance/Newbridge Educational Publishing.
—Wants & Needs. 2004. (Reading PowerWorks Ser.). (gr. 1-3). 37.50 *(978-0-7608-9819-2(7))*; pap. 6.10 *(978-0-7608-9820-8(0))* Sundance/Newbridge Educational Publishing.
—What's That Sound? 2004. (Reading PowerWorks Ser.). (gr. 1-3). 37.50 *(978-0-7608-9807-9(3))*; pap. 6.10 *(978-0-7608-9808-6(1))* Sundance/Newbridge Educational Publishing.
—A World of Tools. 2007. (Early Science Ser.). (gr. k-3). 18.95 *(978-1-4007-6504-1(8))*; pap. 6.10 *(978-1-4007-6500-3(5))* Sundance/Newbridge Educational Publishing.
Sunflower. (Lexile Levels Ser.). 7.98 *(978-1-56334-672-9(9))* CENGAGE Learning.
Supama. The Science Playground: Fun with Science Concepts & Nature. 2009. (ENG.). 46p. pap. 24.99 *(978-1-4389-3466-2(1))* AuthorHouse.
The Super Supermarket Plan: Individual Title Six-Packs. (gr. k-1). 23.00 *(978-0-7635-8844-1(X))* Rigby Education.
Surfing 6 Packs. KinderConcepts. (Kinderstarters Ser.). 8p. (gr. -1-1). 21.00 *(978-0-7635-8726-0(5))* Rigby Education.
A Surprise for Monica, 6 Packs. (Greetings Ser.: Vol. 2). (gr. 3-5). 31.00 *(978-0-7635-1810-3(7))* Rigby Education.
A Surprise for Mrs O'Malley. (Sails Literacy Ser.). 24p. (gr. 2-18). 27.00 *(978-0-7578-6821-4(5))* Rigby Education.
A Surprise for Mrs O'Malley: 3-in-1 Package. (Sails Literacy Ser.). 24p. (gr. 2-18). 57.00 *(978-0-7578-6833-7(9))* Rigby Education.
Surprise from the Sky, 6 Packs. (gr. 1-2). 25.00 *(978-0-7635-9138-0(6))* Rigby Education.
Sutton, Laurie S. Bug Team Alpha, 6 vols. Clarey, Patricio, illus. 2018. (Bug Team Alpha Ser.). (ENG.). 112p. (J). (gr. 3-6). 159.90 *(978-1-4965-5972-2(X)*, 27621, Stone Arch Bks.) Capstone.
Swann, Tammy & Benchmark Education Co., LLC Staff. Roy Makes a Choice. 2015. (BuildUp Ser.). (J). (gr. 1). *(978-1-4900-0738-0(5))* Benchmark Education Co.
Swartz, Larry & Margolin, Indrani. The 10 Coolest Dance Crazes. 2008. 14.99 *(978-1-55448-523-9(1))* Scholastic Library Publishing.
Swedeen, Staci. The Rumor Report, the Big Jump. 2011. (Readers' & Writers' Genre Workshop Ser.). (YA). pap. *(978-1-4509-3013-0(1))* Benchmark Education Co.
Sweeney, Bernadette. Monster Machines. 2007. (Steck-Vaughn BOLDPRINT Anthologies Ser.). (ENG., Illus.). 48p. (gr. 5-8). pap. 16.90 *(978-1-4190-4024-5(3))* Houghton Mifflin Harcourt Publishing Co.
Sweet, Melissa. Ants (1 Hardcover/1 CD) 2016. (National Geographic Readers: Pre-Reader Ser.). (ENG.). (J). *(978-1-4301-2115-2(7))* Live Oak Media.
—Ants (1 Paperback/1 CD) 2016. (National Geographic Readers: Pre-Reader Ser.). (ENG.). (J). pap. *(978-1-4301-2114-5(9))* Live Oak Media.
Swenlin, Brian & Bardekoff, Jennifer. Magical Mermaids! Aikins, Dave, illus. 2017. 24p. (J). *(978-1-5182-3609-9(X))* Random Hse., Inc.
Swift, Jonathan. Gulliver's Travels. 2019. (ENG.). (J). (gr. 5). 120p. pap. 7.99 *(978-0-368-82650-4(3))*; 218p. pap. 15.31 *(978-0-368-54367-8(6))*; 218p. pap. 17.47 *(978-0-368-54366-1(8))*; 218p. pap. 23.98 *(978-0-368-54365-4(X))*; 140p. pap. 12.68 *(978-0-368-26293-7(6))*; 128p. pap. 12.02 *(978-0-368-26290-6(1))* Blurb, Inc.
—Gulliver's Travels. 2012. (JPN.). (J). *(978-4-16-381340-0(3))* Bungei Shunju.
—Gulliver's Travels. 2019. (ENG.). (J). (gr. 5). 156p. 23.95 *(978-0-469-12861-3(5))*; 118p. 22.95 *(978-0-469-11471-5(1))*; 156p. pap. 13.95 *(978-0-469-12860-6(7))*; 118p. pap. 12.95 *(978-0-469-11470-8(3))* Creative Media Partners, LLC. (Wentworth Pr.).
—Gulliver's Travels. (ENG.). (gr. 5). 2020. 220p. (YA). pap. *(978-1-77426-038-8(7))* 2018. 186p. (J). pap. *(978-1-989201-28-2(8))* East India Publishing Co.
—Gulliver's Travels. (ENG.). (J). 2020. 198p. (gr. 3-7). pap. 9.99 *(978-1-6554-5783-8(7))* 2019. 122p. (gr. 3-7). pap. 15.99 *(978-1-7078-1305-6(1))* 2019. 280p. (gr. 5). pap. 18.99 *(978-1-0891-3846-4(6))* 2019. 338p. (gr. 5). pap. 19.99 *(978-1-6918-0974-5(3))* 2019. 284p. (gr. 5). pap. 15.99 *(978-1-6925-3673-2(7))* 2019. 342p. (gr. 5). pap. 24.99 *(978-1-6940-6926-9(5))* 2019. 558p. (gr. 5). pap. 30.99 *(978-1-6929-2549-9(0))* 2019. 234p. (gr. 5). pap. 15.99 *(978-1-6869-7618-6(6))* 2019. 530p. (gr. 5). pap. 34.99 *(978-1-0774-4237-5(8))* 2019. 340p. (gr. 5). pap. 23.99 *(978-1-0800-7881-3(9))* 2019. 340p. (gr. 5). pap. 23.99 *(978-1-0825-5992-1(X))* 2019. 338p. (gr. 5). pap. 19.99 *(978-1-0859-5899-8(X))* 2019. 562p. (gr. 5). pap. 30.99 *(978-1-0728-1360-6(2))* 2019. 562p. (gr. 5). pap. 30.99 *(978-1-0710-6766-6(4))* 2019. 558p. (gr. 5). pap. 30.99 *(978-1-0707-7411-4(1))* 2019. 668p. (gr. 5). pap. 41.99 *(978-1-7946-4610-0(8))* 2018. 166p. (gr. 5). pap. 8.40 *(978-1-7314-9193-0(X))* 2018. (Illus.). 166p. (gr. 5). pap. 8.40 *(978-1-7902-9600-2(5))* Independently Published.
—Gulliver's Travels. 2020. (ENG.). 220p. (J). (gr. 3-7). pap. *(978-1-716-13563-7(X))* Lulu Pr., Inc.
—Gulliver's Travels. (ENG., Illus.). (J). 2018. 300p. (gr. 5). 28.48 *(978-1-7317-0686-7(3))* 2018. 300p. (gr. 5). pap. 16.42 *(978-1-7317-0687-4(1))* 2011. 15.99 *(978-1-61382-670-6(2))* Simon & Brown.
—Gulliver's Travels. 2012. (ENG., Illus.). 230p. (J). (gr. 5). 17.99 *(978-1-4341-1615-4(8))* The Editorium, LLC.
Swift, Jonathan, creator. Gulliver's Travels. 2020. (ENG.). (J). (gr. 3-7). 392p. pap. *(978-0-461-67010-3(0))*; 230p. pap. *(978-0-371-68273-9(8))* HardPr.
Swift, Jonathan & Priory Books Staff. Gulliver's Travels. *(978-0-7105-0141-7(2))* Haddock, Peter Ltd.
Swigert, Nancy B. Early Intervention Kit Activities Book. 2004. (J). per. *(978-0-7606-0597-4(1))* LinguiSystems, Inc.
Swimming in the Sand. (J). pap. 13.75 *(978-0-8136-3404-3(0))* Modern Curriculum Pr.
Swirnow, Linda. Take on Yellowstone! 2011. 32p. pap. 12.99 *(978-1-4490-2219-8(7))* AuthorHouse.
—What's New at the Zoo? A PhotoPhOnics (c)Reader. 2009. 32p. pap. 12.99 *(978-1-4490-2218-1(9))* AuthorHouse.
Syed, Hafsa N. Piggy Wanted to Learn. 2012. 44p. pap. 11.25 *(978-1-61170-067-1(1))* Robertson Publishing.
Symbols of Our Country, 8 vols. 2016. (Symbols of Our Country Ser.). (ENG.). 00024p. (J). (gr. 1-1). 101.08 *(978-1-4994-2693-9(3)*, a2868806-d20c-44ef-b8e0-0057ea3a7208, PowerKids Pr.) Rosen Publishing Group, Inc., The.
Symington, Martha M. Global Heart Warming: Dream Believe Achieve Series. Sanderson, Jessica B., illus. 2009. 36p. pap. *(978-1-897435-34-2(7))* Agio Publishing Hse.
Szarka, Balazs. European Folk Tales. 2009. 60p. pap. 22.00 *(978-1-60860-432-6(2)*, Eloquent Bks.) Strategic Book Publishing & Rights Agency (SBPRA).
Szymanski, Jennifer. National Geographic Kids Readers: Real Dragons (L1/Coreader) 2018. (Readers Ser.). (Illus.). 48p. (J). (gr. -1-k). pap. 4.99 *(978-1-4263-3046-9(4)*, National Geographic Kids) Disney Publishing Worldwide.
—National Geographic Readers: Here to There (L1/Coreader) 2019. (Readers Ser.). (Illus.). 48p. (J). (gr. -1-k). pap. 4.99 *(978-1-4263-3495-5(8)*, National Geographic Kids) Disney Publishing Worldwide.
—National Geographic Readers: in the Ocean (L1/Coreader) 2018. (Readers Ser.). (Illus.). 48p. (J). (gr. -1-k). pap. 4.99 *(978-1-4263-3235-7(1)*, National Geographic Kids) Disney Publishing Worldwide.
Tabletop Easel. (gr. -1-12). 81.69 *(978-0-7362-0851-2(8))* CENGAGE Learning.
Take a Look at My Family. (Early Intervention Levels Ser.). 28.38 *(978-0-7362-0395-1(8))* CENGAGE Learning.
Take a Look at My Family (8), Vol. 8. (Early Intervention Levels Ser.). 4.73 *(978-0-7362-0220-6(X))* CENGAGE Learning.
Take-Home Books Collection. 2005. (YA). (gr. -1-3). 225.00 *(978-0-8215-7290-0(3))* Sadlier, William H. Inc.
TAKS MASTER Learning with Graphic Organizers, Gr. 3. 2005. (J). *(978-1-57022-550-5(8))* ECS Learning Systems, Inc.
TAKS MASTER Learning with Graphic Organizers, Gr. 4. 2005. (J). *(978-1-57022-551-2(6))* ECS Learning Systems, Inc.
TAKS MASTER Learning with Graphic Organizers, Gr. 5. 2005. (J). *(978-1-57022-552-9(4))* ECS Learning Systems, Inc.
TAKS MASTER Learning with Graphic Organizers, Gr. 6. 2005. (J). *(978-1-57022-553-6(2))* ECS Learning Systems, Inc.
TAKS MASTER Learning with Graphic Organizers, Gr. 7. 2005. (J). *(978-1-57022-554-3(0))* ECS Learning Systems, Inc.
TAKS MASTER Learning with Graphic Organizers, Gr. 8. 2005. (YA). *(978-1-57022-555-0(9))* ECS Learning Systems, Inc.
TAKS MASTER Power Practice, Reading Gr. 3. 2004. (J). *(978-1-57022-541-3(9))* ECS Learning Systems, Inc.
TAKS MASTER Power Practice, Reading Gr. 4. 2004. (J). *(978-1-57022-542-0(7))* ECS Learning Systems, Inc.
TAKS MASTER Power Practice, Reading Gr. 5. 2004. (J). *(978-1-57022-543-7(5))* ECS Learning Systems, Inc.
TAKS MASTER Power Practice, Reading Gr. 6. 2004. (J). *(978-1-57022-544-4(3))* ECS Learning Systems, Inc.
TAKS MASTER Power Practice, Reading Gr. 7. 2004. (J). *(978-1-57022-545-1(1))* ECS Learning Systems, Inc.
TAKS MASTER Power Practice, Reading Gr. 8. 2004. (YA). *(978-1-57022-546-8(X))* ECS Learning Systems, Inc.
TAKS MASTER Practice Test Reading, Gr. 3. 2004. (J). *(978-1-57022-475-1(7))* ECS Learning Systems, Inc.
TAKS MASTER Practice Test Reading, Gr. 4. 2004. (J). *(978-1-57022-528-4(1))* ECS Learning Systems, Inc.
TAKS MASTER Practice Test Reading, Gr. 5. 2004. (J). *(978-1-57022-529-1(X))* ECS Learning Systems, Inc.
TAKS MASTER Practice Test Reading, Gr. 6. 2004. (J). *(978-1-57022-530-7(3))* ECS Learning Systems, Inc.
TAKS MASTER Practice Test Reading, Gr. 7. 2004. (J). *(978-1-57022-531-4(1))* ECS Learning Systems, Inc.
TAKS MASTER Practice Test Reading, Gr. 8. 2004. (YA). *(978-1-57022-532-1(X))* ECS Learning Systems, Inc.
TAKS Open-Ended Reading Response Guide, Grades 9-11 Exit. 2004. (Region IV ESC Resources for Mathematics, Science, Social Studies & Reading Ser.). spiral bd. *(978-1-932797-19-0(X))* Region 4 Education Service Ctr.
TAKS Reading Accelerated Curriculum for Grade 5. 2005. (Region IV ESC Resources for Reading Ser.). spiral bd. *(978-1-933049-06-9(5))* Region 4 Education Service Ctr.
TAKS Reading Accelerated Curriculum Middle School (Volume 1) 2006. spiral bd. *(978-1-933049-18-2(9))* Region 4 Education Service Ctr.
TAKS Reading Preparation Grade 10 - Student Workbook. 2003. (Region IV ESC Resources for Reading Ser.). stu. ed., per. *(978-1-932524-48-2(7))* Region 4 Education Service Ctr.
TAKS Reading Preparation Grade 11 Exit. 2003. (Region IV ESC Resources for Reading Ser.). stu. ed., per., wbk. ed. *(978-1-932524-49-9(5))* Region 4 Education Service Ctr.
TAKS Reading Preparation Grade 4. 2003. (Region IV ESC Resources for Reading Ser.). stu. ed., per., wbk. ed. *(978-1-932524-42-0(8))* Region 4 Education Service Ctr.
TAKS Reading Preparation Grade 5. 2003. (Region IV ESC Resources for Reading Ser.). stu. ed., per., wbk. ed. *(978-1-932524-43-7(6))* Region 4 Education Service Ctr.
TAKS Reading Preparation Grade 6. 2003. (Region IV ESC Resources for Reading Ser.). stu. ed., per., wbk. ed. *(978-1-932524-44-4(4))* Region 4 Education Service Ctr.
TAKS Reading Preparation Grade 8. 2003. (Region IV ESC Resources for Reading Ser.). stu. ed., per., wbk. ed. *(978-1-932524-46-8(0))* Region 4 Education Service Ctr.
TAKS Reading Preparation Grade 9. 2003. (Region IV ESC Resources for Reading Ser.). stu. ed., per., wbk. ed. *(978-1-932524-47-5(9))* Region 4 Education Service Ctr.
TAKS Reading Preparaton Grade 7. 2003. (Region IV ESC Resources for Reading Ser.). stu. ed., per., wbk. ed. *(978-1-932524-45-1(2))* Region 4 Education Service Ctr.
TAKS Readng Preparation Grade 3. 2003. (Region IV ESC Resources for Reading Ser.). stu. ed., per., wbk. ed. *(978-1-932524-41-3(X))* Region 4 Education Service Ctr.
The Tale of the Golden Goose. (Early Intervention Levels Ser.). 31.86 *(978-0-7362-0617-4(5))* CENGAGE Learning.
The Tale of the Golden Goose (18), Vol. 18. (Early Intervention Levels Ser.). 5.31 *(978-0-7362-0605-1(1))* CENGAGE Learning.
Tales of Terror Level 3 Lower-Intermediate. 2009. (Cambridge Experience Readers Ser.). (ENG., Illus.). 80p. pap. 14.75 *(978-84-8323-532-4(3))* Cambridge Univ. Pr.
Tali Drives His Car. (Pebble Soup Explorations Ser.). 16p. (gr. -1-18). 31.00 *(978-0-7578-1663-5(0))* Rigby Education.
Tali Drives His Car: Small Book. (Pebble Soup Explorations Ser.). 16p. (gr. -1-18). 5.00 *(978-0-7578-1703-8(3))* Rigby Education.
Tali Pasea en su Auto. (Pebble Soup Exploraciones Ser.). (SPA.). 16p. (gr. -1-18). 31.00 *(978-0-7578-1687-1(8))* Rigby Education.
Tali pasea en su Auto: Small Book. (Pebble Soup Exploraciones Ser.). (SPA.). 16p. (gr. -1-18). 5.00 *(978-0-7578-1727-4(0))* Rigby Education.
Tall Talk. (Sails Literacy Ser.). 24p. (gr. 2-3). 8.00 *(978-0-7635-7036-1(2))* Rigby Education.
Tatchell, Judy. Bugs & Slugs Lift-the-Flap. 2004. (Luxury Lift-the-Flap Ser.). 16p. (J). (gr. 1-18). 11.95 *(978-0-7945-0762-6(X)*, Usborne) EDC Publishing.
Tavadze, Olesya. Bursunsul & Paskualina. Ivanov, Evgueni, illus. 2007. (POL & ENG.). 32p. (J). pap. 16.95 *(978-1-60195-095-6(0))* International Step by Step Assn.
Taylor, Chad. Drums Save the Day, 1 vol. 2016. (Rosen REAL Readers: STEM & STEAM Collection). (ENG.). 12p. (gr. k-1). pap. 6.33 *(978-1-5081-2649-2(6)*, 20a1a111-4752-425a-87d4-a142d4a88f33, Rosen Classroom) Rosen Publishing Group, Inc., The.
—Drums Send a Signal, 1 vol. 2016. (Rosen REAL Readers: STEM & STEAM Collection). (ENG.). 12p. (gr. k-1). pap. 6.33 *(978-1-5081-2434-4(5)*, 79b6ddc6-bafc-4455-9a6b-e0363b716aac, Rosen Classroom) Rosen Publishing Group, Inc., The.
—Equal under the Law, 1 vol. 2016. (Rosen REAL Readers: Social Studies Nonfiction / Fiction: Myself, My Community, My World Ser.). (ENG.). 12p. (gr. k-1). pap. 6.33 *(978-1-5081-2544-0(9)*, f9497622-af3e-48a2-929d-1f8a7668bb1b, Rosen Classroom) Rosen Publishing Group, Inc., The.
—We Catch Butterflies, 1 vol. 2016. (Rosen REAL Readers: STEM & STEAM Collection). (ENG.). 8p. (gr. k-1). pap. 5.46 *(978-1-5081-2607-2(0)*, 358fdd69-5349-4c6e-b427-b783beb5a483, Rosen Classroom) Rosen Publishing Group, Inc., The.
—When the Ground Shook, 1 vol. 2016. (Rosen REAL Readers: STEM & STEAM Collection). (ENG.). 12p. (gr. 1-2). pap. 6.33 *(978-1-5081-2685-0(2)*, 08d64f13-1a88-45d2-88b7-deba05d54efe, Rosen Classroom) Rosen Publishing Group, Inc., The.
Taylor, Mary Ellen. Maniac Magee. rev. ed. 2015. (Great Works). (ENG., Illus.). 72p. (gr. 4-8). pap. 9.99 *(978-1-4258-8983-8(2))* Shell Educational Publishing.
Taylor, Nicole & Watts, Michael. SpongeBob Squarepants: Wormy. 2014. (ENG.). 32p. (J). pap. incl. audio compact disk *(978-1-909221-71-0(6))* Glasgow, Mary Pubns.
Taylor, Sean. Mojo & Weeza & the New Hat: Band 04/Blue (Collins Big Cat) Mosedale, Julian, illus. 2007. (Collins Big Cat Ser.). (ENG.). 16p. (J). (gr. -1-1). pap. 7.99 *(978-0-00-718662-4(2))* HarperCollins Pubs. Ltd. GBR. Dist: Independent Pubs. Group.
Taylor, Susan. Blast Off!, 1 vol. 2006. (Neighborhood Readers Ser.). (ENG.). 16p. (gr. 1-2). pap. 6.50 *(978-1-4042-6978-1(9)*, 63034de4-c5ad-4989-9e2d-fd6c58498be7, Rosen Classroom) Rosen Publishing Group, Inc., The.
Taylor, Trace. B. 2010. pap. 39.62 *(978-1-61541-090-3(2))* American Reading Co.
—C. 2010. pap. 39.62 *(978-1-61541-102-3(X))* American Reading Co.
—Cats. 2010. pap. 39.62 *(978-1-61541-094-1(5))* American Reading Co.
—China. 2010. pap. 39.62 *(978-1-61541-129-0(1))* American Reading Co.
—D. 2010. pap. 39.62 *(978-1-61541-097-2(X))* American Reading Co.
—Dogs. 2010. pap. 39.62 *(978-1-61541-095-8(3))* American Reading Co.
—F. 2010. pap. 39.62 *(978-1-61541-105-4(4))* American Reading Co.
—G. 2010. pap. 39.62 *(978-1-61541-107-8(0))* American Reading Co.
—H. 2010. pap. 39.62 *(978-1-61541-109-2(7))* American Reading Co.
—In My Garden (Big Book) 2012. (1-3Y Big Bks.). (ENG., Illus.). 20p. (J). pap. 9.60 *(978-1-64053-059-1(2)*, ARC Pr. Bks.) American Reading Co.
—J. 2010. pap. 39.62 *(978-1-61541-111-5(9))* American Reading Co.
—K. 2010. pap. 39.62 *(978-1-61541-113-9(5))* American Reading Co.
—L. 2010. pap. 39.62 *(978-1-61541-096-5(1))* American Reading Co.

—M. 2010. pap. 39.62 *(978-1-61541-091-0(0))* American Reading Co.

—N. 2010. pap. 39.62 *(978-1-61541-115-3(1))* American Reading Co.

—P. 2010. pap. 39.62 *(978-1-61541-117-7(8))* American Reading Co.

—R. 2010. pap. 39.62 *(978-1-61541-119-1(4))* American Reading Co.

—S. 2010. pap. 39.62 *(978-1-61541-099-6(6))* American Reading Co.

—T. 2010. pap. 39.62 *(978-1-61541-103-0(8))* American Reading Co.

Taylor, Trace & SáNchez, LucíA M. BáSquetbol (Basketball) 2011. (ARC Press / el poder de 100 - Deportes (Power 100 - Sports) Ser.). (SPA.). pap. 33.92 *(978-1-61541-468-0(1))* American Reading Co.

—Béisbol (Baseball) 2011. (ARC Press / el poder de 100 - Deportes (Power 100 - Sports) Ser.). (SPA.). pap. 33.92 *(978-1-61541-470-3(3))* American Reading Co.

—China. 2010. pap. 39.62 *(978-1-61541-152-8(6))* American Reading Co.

Taylor, Trace & Sanchez, Lucia M. Delfines (Dolphins) 2011. (poder de 100 - Animales marinos Ser.). (SPA.). 12p. pap. 39.62 *(978-1-61541-283-9(2))* American Reading Co.

—En el bosque (in the Woods) 2011. (Lugares adonde voy Ser.). (SPA.). 16p. pap. 39.62 *(978-1-61541-457-4(6))* American Reading Co.

Taylor, Trace & Sánchez, Lucía M. Escarabajos: Beetles. 2011. (2G - Bichos Ser.). (SPA.). 12p. (J). (gr. k-2). pap. 9.60 *(978-1-61541-422-2(3))* American Reading Co.

Taylor, Trace & Zorzi, Gina. This Is a Desert. 2010. (2G Ecosystems Ser.). (ENG.). 36p. (J). (gr. k-2). pap. 9.60 *(978-1-61541-219-8(0))* American Reading Co.

Taylor, Trace, et al. En el Bosque. 2013. (2Y Lugares Adonde Voy Ser.).Tr. of In the Woods. (SPA.). 12p. (J). (gr. k-2). pap. 9.60 *(978-1-61541-456-7(8))* American Reading Co.

—In the Ocean. Reese, Jonathan, illus. 2012. (1-3Y Ecosystems Ser.). (ENG.). 16p. (J). (gr. k-1). pap. 8.00 *(978-1-59301-438-4(4))* American Reading Co.

—This Is a Forest. 2014. (2G Ecosystems Ser.). (ENG.). 36p. (J). (gr. k-2). pap. 8.00 *(978-1-61541-268-6(9))* American Reading Co.

Te invito a mi Casa: 6 Small Books. (Saludos Ser.: Vol. 3). (SPA.). 24p. (gr. 2-3). 31.00 *(978-0-7635-9529-6(2))* Rigby Education.

Teacher Created Materials. Early America, Set. rev. ed. 2009. (Book Collection). (ENG., Illus.). (J). (gr. 4-6). 55.92 *(978-1-4333-1895-5(4))* Teacher Created Materials, Inc.

—Time for Kids(r) Nonfiction Readers Challenging, 15 bks., Set. rev. ed. 2013. (Book Collection). (ENG., Illus.). (J). (gr. 5-5). 479.40 *(978-1-4333-7498-2(6))* Teacher Created Materials, Inc.

Teacher Created Materials Staff, ed. Kids Learn! Grade PreK-K. 2008. (Kids Learn Ser.). 120p. pap. 9.99 *(978-1-4333-0414-9(7))* Teacher Created Materials, Inc.

—Life Science: Themed Classroom Reader Set. 2007. (Themed Reader Sets Ser.). pap. 909.99 *(978-1-4333-0155-1(5))* Teacher Created Materials, Inc.

—The 20th Century Add-on Pack: Primary Source Readers. 2008. (Primary Source Readers Ser.). 89.99 *(978-1-4333-0049-3(4))* Teacher Created Materials, Inc.

Teagan, Erin. Luciana: Out of This World. 3. 2019. (American Girl Contemporary Ser.). (ENG.). 160p. (J). (gr. 4-6). 17.49 *(978-1-64310-821-6(2))* Penworthy Co., LLC, The.

Teagarden, Janine. A Dog Named Opposite. Kennedy, Kelly, illus. 2010. 16p. (J). *(978-0-545-24821-1(3))* Scholastic, Inc.

Teddy's Colorful World, 6 vols. 2017. (Teddy's Colorful World Ser.). 24p. (ENG.). (gr. 1-1). 75.81 *(978-1-5081-6194-3(1),* 27259d05-a86f-4ae8-b862-419678f1d957); (gr. 4-6). pap. 24.75 *(978-1-5081-6196-7(8))* Rosen Publishing Group, Inc., The. (PowerKids Pr.).

Ted's Red Ball: Set B Individual Title, 6 packs. (Supersonic Phonics Ser.). (gr. k-3). 29.00 *(978-0-7635-0538-7(2))* Rigby Education.

Tell Me How You Feel: Big Book. (Pebble Soup Explorations Ser.). 16p. (gr. -1-18). 31.00 *(978-0-7578-1661-1(4))* Rigby Education.

Tell Me How You Feel: Small Book. (Pebble Soup Explorations Ser.). 16p. (gr. -1-18). 5.00 *(978-0-7578-1701-4(7))* Rigby Education.

Tercio, Ricardo, illus. Jack y Los Frijoles Magicos: La Novela Grafica. 2010. (Graphic Spin en Español Ser.). (SPA.). 40p. (J). (gr. 3-6). pap. 5.95 *(978-1-4342-2272-5(1),* 103135); lib. bdg. 25.99 *(978-1-4342-1902-2(X),* 102361) Capstone. (Stone Arch Bks.).

Terp, Gail. Alex Morgan. 2016. (Women Who Rock Ser.). (ENG., Illus.). 32p. (J). (gr. 4-6). 31.35 *(978-1-68072-067-9(8),* 10426, Bolt) Black Rabbit Bks.

Testa, Maggie. Buddy & Pals. 2018. (Ready-To-Read Ser.). (ENG.). 32p. (J). (gr. -1-1). 13.89 *(978-1-64310-678-6(3))* Penworthy Co., LLC, The.

—Olivia & the Rain Dance. 2012. (Olivia Ready-To-Read Level 1 Ser.). lib. bdg. 13.55 *(978-0-606-23688-1(0))* Turtleback.

Textures: KinderFacts Individual Title Six-Packs. (Kinderstarters Ser.). 8p. (gr. -1-1). 21.00 *(978-0-7635-8750-5(8))* Rigby Education.

Thaler, Mike. The Class Trip from the Black Lagoon (Black Lagoon Adventures #1) Lee, Jared, illus. 2004. (Black Lagoon Adventures Ser.: 1). (ENG.). 64p. (J). (gr. 2-5). pap. 3.99 *(978-0-439-42927-6(7),* Scholastic Paperbacks) Scholastic, Inc.

—The Talent Show from the Black Lagoon (Black Lagoon Adventures #2) Lee, Jared, illus. 2004. (Black Lagoon Adventures Ser.: 2). (ENG.). 64p. (J). (gr. 2-5). 4.99 *(978-0-439-43894-0(2),* Scholastic Paperbacks) Scholastic, Inc.

The Britannica Common Core Library: Set 2, 10 vols. 2014. (Britannica Common Core Library). (ENG.). 32p. (J). (gr. 2-3). lib. bdg. 135.20 *(978-1-62275-676-6(2),* 53028713-6a2d-4655-aa53-1b8cd651836, Britannica Educational Publishing) Rosen Publishing Group, Inc., The.

The Learning Company, The Learning. Learning with Curious George Kindergarten Reading. 2012. (Learning with Curious George Ser.). (ENG., Illus.). 64p. (J). (gr. -1-3). pap. 6.99 *(978-0-547-79096-1(1),* 1492954, Clarion Bks.) HarperCollins Pubs.

The Things I Learn, 12 vols. 2016. (Things I Learn Ser.). (ENG.). 24p. (gr. 1-1). 151.62 *(978-1-4994-2439-3(6),* 4649c9ea-f675-4a6c-a215-a343ce10f2d3, PowerKids Pr.) Rosen Publishing Group, Inc., The.

A Theft in Time: Timedetectors II, 6 Pack. (Action Packs Ser.). 120p. (gr. 3-5). 44.00 *(978-0-7635-8425-2(8))* Rigby Education.

Theme Packs for ELL: Complete Set. (gr. k-6). 203.00 *(978-0-7635-2865-2(X))* Rigby Education.

Theme Packs for ELL: Early Fluent/Fluent Complete Set. (gr. k-6). 184.00 *(978-0-7635-9991-1(3))*; 262.00 *(978-0-7635-9995-9(6))*; 184.00 *(978-0-7635-9999-7(9))*; 218.00 *(978-0-7635-2853-9(6))*; 252.00 *(978-0-7635-2862-1(5))*; 262.00 *(978-0-7635-2857-7(9))* Rigby Education.

Theme Packs for ELL: Early Fluent/Fluent Core Set. (gr. k-6). 175.00 *(978-0-7635-2852-2(8))*; 175.00 *(978-0-7635-9994-2(8))*; 175.00 *(978-0-7635-9987-4(5))*; 175.00 *(978-0-7635-2861-4(7))*; 175.00 *(978-0-7635-2868-3(4))*; 175.00 *(978-0-7635-2856-0(0))* Rigby Education.

Theme Packs for ELL: Early to Fluent Core Set. (gr. k-6). 164.00 *(978-0-7635-2864-5(1))* Rigby Education.

Theme Packs for ELL: Emergent to Early Fluent Core Set. (gr. k-6). 153.00 *(978-0-7635-2866-9(8))* Rigby Education.

Theme Packs for ELL: Emergent/Early Complete Set. (gr. k-6). 148.00 *(978-0-7635-9993-5(X))*; 186.00 *(978-0-7635-9998-0(0))*; 148.00 *(978-0-7635-2851-5(X))*; 218.00 *(978-0-7635-9990-4(5))*; 186.00 *(978-0-7635-9986-7(7))*; 186.00 *(978-0-7635-2860-7(9))* Rigby Education.

Theme Packs for ELL: Emergent/Early Core Set. (gr. k-6). 142.00 *(978-0-7635-9985-0(9))*; 142.00 *(978-0-7635-9989-8(1))*; 142.00 *(978-0-7635-9997-3(2))*; 142.00 *(978-0-7635-2859-1(5))*; 142.00 *(978-0-7635-2855-3(2))* Rigby Education.

Theme Packs for ELL: Theme Pack Complete Set. (gr. k-6). 197.00 *(978-0-7635-2867-6(6))*; 301.00 *(978-0-7635-2869-0(2))* Rigby Education.

Theme Packs for ELL: Theme Pack Super Set. (gr. k-6). 349.00 *(978-0-7635-2850-8(1))*; 349.00 *(978-0-7635-2854-6(4))*; 415.00 *(978-0-7635-2863-8(3))*; 383.00 *(978-0-7635-2858-4(7))*; 344.00 *(978-0-7635-9988-1(3))*; 383.00 *(978-0-7635-9992-8(1))*; 383.00 *(978-0-7635-9996-6(4))* Rigby Education.

Then And Now, 6 Pack. (Discovery World Ser.). 16p. (gr. 1-2). 28.00 *(978-0-7635-8463-4(0))* Rigby Education.

Theobald, Joseph. When Arthur Wouldn't Sleep: Band 06/Orange (Collins Big Cat) Theobald, Joseph, illus. 2006. (Collins Big Cat Ser.). (ENG., Illus.). 24p. (J). (gr. 2-2). pap. 8.99 *(978-0-00-718688-4(6))* HarperCollins Pubs. Ltd. GBR. Dist: Independent Pubs. Group.

There Is No Water! Individual Title Six-Packs. (gr. k-1). 23.00 *(978-0-7635-8849-6(0))* Rigby Education.

There's a Rainbow in the River: Individual Title Six-Packs. (gr. k-1). 23.00 *(978-0-7635-8850-2(4))* Rigby Education.

The Things I Learn. 2016. (Things I Learn Ser.). 24p. (gr. 1-1). pap. 49.50 *(978-1-4994-2492-8(2),* PowerKids Pr.) Rosen Publishing Group, Inc., The.

The Things I Learn: Set 2, 8 vols. 2017. (Things I Learn Ser.). (ENG., Illus.). (J). (gr. 1-1). lib. bdg. 101.08 *(978-1-5081-6325-1(1),* a6526031-fbcd-4049-99f6-4f6c368e5500, PowerKids Pr.) Rosen Publishing Group, Inc., The.

Things to Do. 2005. (Little Celebrations Thematic Packages Ser.). (J). (gr. k-3). 133.50 *(978-0-673-75388-5(3))* Celebration Pr.

Think Twice, Be Nice: Social/Emotional Lap Book. (Pebble Soup Explorations Ser.). (gr. -1-18). 16.00 *(978-0-7635-7570-0(4))* Rigby Education.

This And That, 6 Packs. (gr. -1-2). 23.00 *(978-0-7635-8812-0(1))* Rigby Education.

Thomas, Christine. Language Development Inquiry & Research, 1 vol. 2003. (BrainBuilders Ser.). (ENG.). 48p. (gr. k-4). pap. 5.25 *(978-1-4042-8527-9(X),* fc23a573-875d-41e1-899b-66a8f44b9a97) Rosen Publishing Group, Inc., The.

—Language Development Variety Text, 1 vol. 2003. (BrainBuilders Ser.). (ENG.). 48p. (gr. k-4). pap. 5.25 *(978-1-4042-8525-5(3),* 6ca3adcf-fcab-428b-8908-780c6200c80f) Rosen Publishing Group, Inc., The.

Thomas, Isabel. Collins Big Cat Phonics for Letters & Sounds - Bear Spotting: Band 05/Green, Bd. 5. 2018. (Collins Big Cat Phonics Ser.). (ENG., Illus.). 24p. (J). pap. 8.99 *(978-0-00-825169-7(X))* HarperCollins Pubs. Ltd. GBR. Dist: Independent Pubs. Group.

—Collins Big Cat Phonics for Letters & Sounds - Eggs on Toast: Band 04/Blue, Bd. 4. Byrne, Eva, illus. 2018. (Collins Big Cat Phonics Ser.). (ENG.). 16p. (J). (gr. k-1). pap. 6.99 *(978-0-00-825161-1(4))* HarperCollins Pubs. Ltd. GBR. Dist: Independent Pubs. Group.

—How to Build a House: Band 16/Sapphire (Collins Big Cat) 2016. (Collins Big Cat Ser.). (ENG.). 56p. (J). (gr. 4-5). pap. 12.99 *(978-0-00-816394-5(4))* HarperCollins Pubs. Ltd. GBR. Dist: Independent Pubs. Group.

Thomas, Maribel. Party in the Sky. 2009. 20p. pap. 13.50 *(978-1-60693-364-0(7),* Eloquent Bks.) Strategic Book Publishing & Rights Agency (SBPRA).

Thomas, Mary Ann. The New Neighbors, 1 vol. 2006. (Neighborhood Readers Ser.). (ENG.). 8p. (gr. k-1). pap. 5.15 *(978-1-4042-6694-0(1),* eaf74479-570f-4568-8f7d-95bdf3d1b983, Rosen Classroom) Rosen Publishing Group, Inc., The.

Thomas, Teri. The Barge Ghost, 1 vol. unabr. ed. 2010. (Q Reads Ser.). (ENG.). 32p. (YA). (gr. 9-12). pap. 8.50 *(978-1-61651-211-8(3))* Saddleback Educational Publishing, Inc.

—Bus 99, 1 vol. unabr. ed. 2010. (Q Reads Ser.). (ENG.). 32p. (YA). (gr. 9-12). pap. 8.50 *(978-1-61651-214-9(8))* Saddleback Educational Publishing, Inc.

Thomas, Terri & Greene, Janice. Dimes to Dollars, 1 vol. unabr. ed. 2010. (Q Reads Ser.). (ENG.). 32p. (YA). (gr. 9-12). pap. 8.50 *(978-1-61651-217-0(2))* Saddleback Educational Publishing, Inc.

Thompson, Chad. The Itsy Bitsy Spider. 2009. (Early Literacy Ser.). (ENG., Illus.). 16p. (gr. k-1). 19.99 *(978-1-4333-1455-1(X))*; 6.99 *(978-1-4333-1454-4(1))* Teacher Created Materials, Inc.

—Yankee Doodle. 2011. (Early Literacy Ser.). (ENG.). 16p. (gr. k-1). 19.99 *(978-1-4333-2365-2(6))*; 6.99 *(978-1-4333-2364-5(8))* Teacher Created Materials, Inc.

Thompson, Gare. Shaping the Constitution: Text Pairs. 2008. (Bridges/Navigators Ser.). (J). (gr. 5). 89.00 *(978-1-4108-8422-0(8))* Benchmark Education Co.

Thompson, Lauren. Little Quack's Opposites. Anderson, Derek, illus. 2010. (Super Chubbies Ser.). (ENG.). 26p. (J). (gr. -1 — 1). bds. 5.99 *(978-1-4169-6092-8(9),* Little Simon) Little Simon.

—Mouse Loves Snow. 2018. (Ready-To-Read Ser.). (ENG.). 32p. (J). (gr. -1-1). 13.89 *(978-1-64310-618-2(X))* Penworthy Co., LLC, The.

—Mouse Loves Snow: Ready-To-Read Pre-Level 1. Erdogan, Buket, illus. 2017. (Mouse Ser.). (ENG.). 32p. (J). (gr. -1-k). 17.99 *(978-1-5344-0182-2(2))*; pap. 4.99 *(978-1-5344-0181-5(4))* Simon Spotlight. (Simon Spotlight).

Thompson, Lesley. Zombie Attack. 2nd ed. 2013. (ENG., Illus.). 40p. pap. 11.00 *(978-0-19-424986-7(7))* Oxford Univ. Pr., Inc.

Thompson, Louise. Cold Weather Readers. 2010. 206p. pap. 21.95 *(978-0-557-38162-3(2))* Lulu Pr., Inc.

Thomson, Ruth. Leaves. 2005. (Little Hands (Chrysalis Education) Ser.). (Illus.). 24p. (J). (gr. 1-4). lib. bdg. 22.80 *(978-1-59389-211-1(X))* Chrysalis Education.

—Mountains. 2012. (Geography Corner Ser.). (ENG., Illus.). 24p. (J). (gr. k-3). 21.25 *(978-1-4488-6617-5(0),* PowerKids Pr.) Rosen Publishing Group, Inc., The.

Thomson, Sarah L. Amazing Tigers! 2005. (I Can Read Level 2 Ser.). (ENG., Illus.). 32p. (J). (gr. k-3). pap. 4.99 *(978-0-06-054452-2(X),* HarperCollins) HarperCollins Pubs.

Those Amazingly Useful Ears. (Early Intervention Levels Ser.). 31.86 *(978-0-7362-0669-3(8))* CENGAGE Learning.

Three: KinderFacts Individual Title Six-Packs. (Kinderstarters Ser.). 8p. (gr. -1-1). 21.00 *(978-0-7635-8751-2(6))* Rigby Education.

Ticktock. Snapped by Sam! 2013. (I Love Reading Phonics: Level 5 Ser.). (ENG.). 24p. (J). (gr. k-3). 16.19 *(978-1-84898-775-3(7),* TickTock Books) Octopus Publishing Group GBR. Dist: Children's Plus, Inc.

Tillworth, Mary. Cupcake Challenge! 2015. (Barbie Step into Reading Level 3 Ser.). lib. bdg. 13.55 *(978-0-606-36381-5(5))* Turtleback.

—Old Racers, New Racers. 2017. (Illus.). 24p. (J). *(978-1-5182-5219-8(2))* Random Hse., Inc.

—Zeg & the Egg (Blaze & the Monster Machines) Foley, Niki, illus. 2016. (Step into Reading Ser.). (ENG.). 24p. (J). (gr. -1-1). 4.99 *(978-0-553-53935-6(3),* Random Hse. Bks. for Young Readers) Random Hse. Children's Bks.

Time Capsule, 6 Packs. (Bookweb Ser.). 32p. (gr. 5-18). 34.00 *(978-0-7635-3780-7(2))* Rigby Education.

Time Goes By, 8 vols., Set. Incl. Day at a Zoo. Harrison, Sarah. (J). lib. bdg. 22.60 *(978-1-58013-554-2(4),* 1c1a6444-1558-46fb-a710-1875244d8dbe, Millbrook Pr.); Day in a City. Harris, Nicholas. (J). lib. bdg. 22.60 *(978-1-58013-552-8(8))*; Year at a Construction Site. Harris, Nicholas. (J). lib. bdg. 22.60 *(978-1-58013-549-8(8))*; Year at a Farm. Harris, Nicholas. lib. bdg. 22.60 *(978-1-58013-553-5(6))*; Year in a Castle. Coombs, Rachel. (J). lib. bdg. 22.60 *(978-1-58013-550-4(1))*; Year on a Pirate Ship. Havercroft, Elizabeth. lib. bdg. 22.60 *(978-1-58013-547-4(1))*; (Illus.). 24p. (gr. k-3). 2008. (Time Goes By Ser.). (ENG.). 2008. Set lib. bdg. 113.00 *(978-1-58013-546-7(3))* Lerner Publishing Group.

Timmins, Jeffrey Stewart, illus. Cenicienta: La Novela Grafica. 2010. (Graphic Spin en Español Ser.). (SPA.). 40p. (J). (gr. 3-6). pap. 5.95 *(978-1-4342-2270-1(5),* 103133, Stone Arch Bks.) Capstone.

Timmy: Individual Title Six-Packs. (Literatura 2000 Ser.). (gr. 1-2). 28.00 *(978-0-7635-0067-2(4))* Rigby Education.

Tim's Bedtime: Set D Individual Title Six-Packs. (gr. k-3). 29.00 *(978-0-7635-0548-6(X))* Rigby Education.

Tim's Paintings: Individual Title-Six Packs. (Chiquilibros Ser.). (gr. k-1). 23.00 *(978-0-7635-0430-4(0))* Rigby Education.

Tim's Pumpkin: Individual Title Six-Packs. (gr. k-1). 23.00 *(978-0-7635-9040-6(1))* Rigby Education.

Tin Lizzy: Individual Title Six-Packs. (gr. 1-2). 25.00 *(978-0-7635-9147-2(5))* Rigby Education.

Tina Likes Tools: Lap Book. (Pebble Soup Explorations Ser.). 16p. (gr. -1-18). 21.00 *(978-0-7578-1662-8(2))* Rigby Education.

Tina Likes Tools: Small Book. (Pebble Soup Explorations Ser.). 16p. (gr. -1-18). 5.00 *(978-0-7578-1702-1(5))* Rigby Education.

Tipa, Rob. Treasures of Tāne: Plants of Ngāi Tahu. 2018. (ENG., Illus.). 250p. pap. 40.00 *(978-1-77550-295-1(3),* 12681) Huia Pubs. NZL. Dist: Univ. of Hawaii Pr.

TJ's Tree, 6 Packs. (Literatura 2000 Ser.). (gr. 1-2). 28.00 *(978-0-7635-0116-7(6))* Rigby Education.

To Begin Again: Six-Pack. (Greetings Ser.: Vol. 3). (gr. 3-5). 31.00 *(978-0-7635-2073-1(X))* Rigby Education.

Toliver, K. S. Pam Brown Is Picture Perfect!! 2008. 28p. pap. 12.95 *(978-1-4327-2058-2(9))* Outskirts Pr., Inc.

Tom Sawyer: 6 Small Books. (gr. k-2). 23.00 *(978-0-7635-8507-5(6))* Rigby Education.

Tomblin, Mark. The Itchy-Scratchy Caterpillar. Jones, Doug, illus. 2010. 16p. (J). *(978-0-545-24822-8(1))* Scholastic, Inc.

Tommy's Treasure: Individual Title Six-Packs. (Literatura 2000 Ser.). (gr. 2-3). 33.00 *(978-0-7635-0189-1(1))* Rigby Education.

Tommy's Tummy Ache: Individual Title Six-Packs. (Literatura 2000 Ser.). (gr. -1-1). 28.00 *(978-0-7635-0015-3(1))* Rigby Education.

Tongues: Early Level Satellite Individual Title Six-Packs. (Sails Literacy Ser.). 16p. (gr. 1-2). 27.00 *(978-0-7578-3161-4(3))* Rigby Education.

Top Hat Big Bargains, 21 bks. (J). (gr. 1-6). 275.00 *(978-0-8136-4013-6(X))*; 250.00 *(978-0-8136-4014-3(8))*; 500.00 incl. cd-rom *(978-0-8136-4015-0(6))* Modern Curriculum Pr.

Top That Publishing Staff, ed. What's My Job. 2005. 12p. bds. *(978-1-84510-070-4(0))* Top That! Publishing PLC.

The Tortilla Factory. (Lexile Levels Ser.). 7.98 *(978-1-56334-687-3(7))* CENGAGE Learning.

Toy. 2004. (J). per. *(978-1-57657-474-4(1))* Paradise Pr., Inc.

Tracey, Michele. What Is a Natural Resource? 2012. (Level B Ser.). (ENG., Illus.). 16p. (J). (gr. k-2). pap. 7.95 *(978-1-927136-15-7(6),* 19423) RiverStream Publishing.

—When Can a Flood Happen? 2012. (Level D Ser.). (ENG., Illus.). 16p. (J). (gr. k-2). pap. 7.95 *(978-1-927136-35-5(0),* 19428) RiverStream Publishing.

—When Can I Help in the Classroom? 2012. (Level C Ser.). (ENG., Illus.). 16p. (J). (gr. k-2). pap. 7.95 *(978-1-927136-23-2(7),* 19429) RiverStream Publishing.

Tracking Wildlife with Frank Craighead. 2005. (Book Treks Ser.). (J). 37.95 *(978-0-7652-3252-6(9))* Celebration Pr.

Trade Book Library, 12 bks., Set. 2004. (Trade Book Library). (gr. 6-18). 112.90 *(978-0-673-60781-2(X))* Addison-Wesley Educational Pubs., Inc.

Trade Book Library Grade Level Package, 12 bks., Set. 2004. (Trade Book Library). (gr. 1-18). 112.90 *(978-0-673-60776-8(3))*; (gr. 2-18). 112.90 *(978-0-673-60777-5(1))*; (gr. 3-18). 112.90 *(978-0-673-60778-2(X))*; (gr. 4-18). 112.90 *(978-0-673-60779-9(8))*; (gr. 5-18). 112.90 *(978-0-673-60780-5(1))* Addison-Wesley Educational Pubs., Inc.

Train Time. (Early Intervention Levels Ser.). 31.86 *(978-0-7362-0618-1(3))* CENGAGE Learning.

Travelers & Traders: Level P, 6 vols., Vol. 2. (Explorers Ser.). 32p. (gr. 3-6). 44.95 *(978-0-7699-0611-9(7))* Shortland Pubns. (U. S. A.) Inc.

Traveling in America: Fourth Grade Guided Comprehension Level L. (On Our Way to English Ser.). (gr. 4-18). 34.50 *(978-0-7578-7154-2(2))* Rigby Education.

Treadwell, Harriette Taylor & Free, Margaret. A Furst Readin Book in Ulster Scot. 2011. (Illus.). 124p. pap. *(978-1-904808-68-8(9))* Evertype.

—The Primer. 2009. (Illus.). 118p. pap. *(978-1-904808-26-8(3))* Evertype.

—Reading-Literature: First Reader. Carroll, Sheila, ed. 2012. 150p. pap. 9.95 *(978-0-9818093-9-7(1))* Living Bks. Pr.

—Reading-Literature Second Reader. Richardson, Frederick, illus. 2008. 200p. pap. 9.95 *(978-1-59915-266-0(5))* Yesterday's Classics.

—Reading-Literature Third Reader. Richardson, Frederick, illus. 2008. 264p. pap. 10.95 *(978-1-59915-267-7(3))* Yesterday's Classics.

The Treasure on Fraser Street: Individual Title Six-Packs. (gr. k-1). 23.00 *(978-0-7635-9068-0(1))* Rigby Education.

Treleaven, Lou. Fast Fox & Slow Snail. Creighton-Pester, David, illus. 2019. (Early Bird Readers — Blue (Early Bird Stories (tm)) Ser.). (ENG.). 32p. (J). (gr. -1-2). pap. 9.99 *(978-1-5415-4616-5(4),* 478dbfe9-dd1f-44a2-bd96-fe7ce4a721f0) Lerner Publishing Group.

—Little Fish & Big Fish. Gray, Dean, illus. 2019. (Early Bird Readers — Yellow (Early Bird Stories (tm)) Ser.). (ENG.). 32p. (J). (gr. -1-2). pap. 9.99 *(978-1-5415-4632-5(6),* b908b10e-c898-4f23-9d55-c1ac3bc35e9b) Lerner Publishing Group.

Trewin, Anna, adapted by. Amazing Composers: A2-B1 (Collins Amazing People ELT Readers), 1 vol. 2014. (Collins English Readers Ser.). (ENG.). 80p. pap. 13.95 incl. audio compact disk *(978-0-00-754502-5(9))* HarperCollins Pubs. Ltd. GBR. Dist: Independent Pubs. Group.

Trip to Mini Town. (J). pap. 13.15 *(978-0-8136-4331-1(7))* Modern Curriculum Pr.

Trowell, Michelle. Magnetic My First Words Day's Out. 2008. *(978-1-84666-586-8(8))* Top That! Publishing PLC.

Truman, Dennay H. The Happy Endings. 2007. 65p. per. 8.95 *(978-1-59824-435-9(3))* E-BookTime LLC.

Trumbauer, Lisa. Rookie Ready to Learn en Español: un Diente Está Flojo. Gray, Steve, illus. 2011. (Rookie Ready to Learn Español Ser.). Orig. Title: Rookie Ready to Learn: a Tooth Is Loose. (SPA.). 32p. (J). pap. 5.95 *(978-0-531-26785-1(7),* Children's Pr.) Scholastic Library Publishing.

The Truth about Red Allen. 2003. (Illus.). pap. 7.60 *(978-0-7398-7521-6(3))* Steck-Vaughn.

The Tune of the Hickory Stick. 2004. (YA). per. 10.92 *(978-1-56870-503-3(4))* Hewell Publishing.

Turhan, Sedat. Milet Flashwords English. Hagin, Sally, illus. 2005. (Milet Flashwords Ser.). (ENG.). 60p. (J). (gr. 4-7). 8.95 *(978-1-84059-455-3(1))* Milet Publishing.

Turquoise, Purple & Gold Levels Certificate Only. (Sails Literacy Ser.). (gr. 1-6). 89.00 *(978-0-7578-6556-5(9))* Rigby Education.

Tuxworth, Nicola. Puppies. 2013. (ENG.). 12p. (J). (gr. -1-12). bds. 6.99 *(978-0-7548-2210-3(9))* Anness Publishing GBR. Dist: National Bk. Network.

—Splish Splash. 2013. (ENG.). 12p. (J). (gr. -1 — 1). bds. 6.99 *(978-0-7548-2211-0(7))* Anness Publishing GBR. Dist: National Bk. Network.

Twain, Mark, pseud. A Song for Aunt Polly. Bates, Amy, illus. 2004. (Adventures of Tom Sawyer Ser.: Vol. 1). 32p. (J). *(978-0-7607-3963-1(3))* Barnes & Noble, Inc.

Twin Sisters(r) Staff. Learning with Elmo: Animals. 2010. (J). (gr. k-2). 9.99 *(978-1-59922-402-2(X))* Twin Sisters IP, LLC.

Twine, Alice. Cats of the Wild. 2009. (Baby Animals Ser.). 24p. (gr. 1-1). 42.50 *(978-1-61511-488-7(2),* PowerKids Pr.) Rosen Publishing Group, Inc., The.

Twisters & Drenchers: Magazine Anthology: Level 5, 6 vols. (Comprehension Strand Ser.). (gr. 4-8). 54.00 *(978-0-322-06038-8(9))* Wright Group/McGraw-Hill.

Tyler, Jenny. Baby's Very First Getting Dressed. 2009. (Baby's Very First Board Bks). 10p. (J). (gr. -1). bds. 6.99 *(978-0-7945-2609-2(8),* Usborne) EDC Publishing.

—Baby's Very First Mealtime Book. 2009. (Baby's Very First Board Bks). 10p. (J). (gr. -1). bds. 6.99 *(978-0-7945-2607-8(1),* Usborne) EDC Publishing.

Unbelievable! (Early Intervention Levels Ser.). 31.86 *(978-0-7362-0671-6(X))* CENGAGE Learning.

Uncle Jim: Individual Title Six-Packs. (gr. 1-2). 25.00 *(978-0-7635-9196-0(3))* Rigby Education.

Understanding Literature: The EMC Write-in Reader. 2nd ed. (Literature & the Language Arts Ser.). (YA). (gr. 10-18). wbk. ed. 17.99 *(978-0-8219-2916-2(X))* EMC/Paradigm Publishing.

Unifix Cubes & Flip Books Set 800913, 2 vols. 2005. (J). pap. *(978-1-59794-078-8(X))* Environments, Inc.

Unit Activity Books: 2-Book Set; Consumable Kindergarten. (On Our Way to English Ser.). (gr. k-18). 15.00 (978-0-7578-6766-8(9)) Rigby Education.

Up & Away: Level P, 6 vols., Vol. 2. (Explorers Ser.). 32p. (gr. 3-6). 44.95 (978-0-7699-0607-2(9)) Shortland Pubns. (U. S. A.) Inc.

Upper Emergent Guided Reading, Vol. 3. (gr. 1-18). 435.50 (978-0-7802-9342-7(8)) Wright Group/McGraw-Hill.

Urban, William. Wyatt Earp: The O. K. Corral & the Law of the American West. 2009. (Library of American Lives & Times Ser.). 112p. (gr. 5-5). 69.20 (978-1-60853-512-5(6)) Rosen Publishing Group, Inc., The.

Use Your Head: Social/Emotional Lap Book. (Pebble Soup Explorations Ser.). (gr. -1-18). 16.00 (978-0-7635-7571-7(2)) Rigby Education.

A Vacation Journal: Individual Title Six-Packs. (Discovery World Ser.). 24p. (gr. 1-2). 33.00 (978-0-7635-8469-6(X)) Rigby Education.

Vale, Janice. Going Fast: Band 07/Turquoise. 2007. (Collins Big Cat Ser.). (ENG.). 24p. (J). (gr. 1-2). pap. 8.99 (978-0-00-718671-6(1)) HarperCollins Pubs. Ltd. GBR. Dist: Independent Pubs. Group.

—True Life Survival: Band 12/Copper (Collins Big Cat) Wademan, Spike, illus. 2007. (Collins Big Cat Ser.). (ENG.). 32p. (J). (gr. 2-4). pap. 9.99 (978-0-00-723078-5(8)) HarperCollins Pubs. Ltd. GBR. Dist: Independent Pubs. Group.

—Where Do You Live?: Band 14/Ruby (Collins Big Cat), Bd. 15. 2007. (Collins Big Cat Ser.). (ENG., Illus.). 48p. (J). (gr. 3-4). pap. 10.99 (978-0-00-723098-3(2)) HarperCollins Pubs. Ltd. GBR. Dist: Independent Pubs. Group.

Valentine, Sophie. Zoo Hullabaloo, 1 vol. rev. ed. 2013. (Literary Text Ser.). (ENG., Illus.). 12p. (gr. k-2). (J). lib. bdg. 12.96 (978-1-4807-1137-2(3)); 6.99 (978-1-4333-5458-8(6)) Teacher Created Materials, Inc.

Vallejo, Fernando. El Desbarrancadero. 2005. (SPA.). 197p. pap. 18.95 (978-958-8061-62-7(8), Alfaguara) Santillana USA Publishing Co., Inc.

The Van. (Early Intervention Levels Ser.). 21.30 (978-0-7362-0372-2(9)); Vol. 4. 3.55 (978-0-7362-0093-6(2)) CENGAGE Learning.

Van Dixhorn, Brenda. The Pigeon Books: An Instructional Guide for Literature. rev. ed. 2015. (Great Works). (ENG., Illus.). 72p. (gr. k-3). pap. 9.99 (978-1-4807-6992-2(4)) Shell Educational Publishing.

Van Gorp, Lynn. Gregor Mendel: Genetics Pioneer, 1 vol. rev. ed. 2007. (Science: Informational Text Ser.). (ENG.). 32p. (J). (gr. 3-6). pap. 12.99 (978-0-7439-0598-5(9)) Teacher Created Materials, Inc.

—The World of Elements & Their Properties, 1 vol. rev. ed. 2007. (Science: Informational Text Ser.). (ENG.). 32p. (gr. 3-6). pap. 12.99 (978-0-7439-0581-7(4)) Teacher Created Materials, Inc.

Van Leeuwen, Jean. Amanda Pig, First Grader. Schweninger, Ann, illus. 2009. (Oliver & Amanda Ser.). (ENG.). 48p. (J). (gr. 1-3). mass mkt. 4.99 (978-0-14-241276-3(7), Penguin Young Readers) Penguin Young Readers Group.

Van Lemon, M. Champions of the Garden Games: Winter Fun for Everyone. 2009. 48p. pap. 20.95 (978-1-4490-3580-8(9)) AuthorHouse.

VanLeeuwen. Reading Connection Grade 4. 2003. (Reading Connection Ser.). 96p. (gr. 4-18). 8.95 (978-1-932210-19-4(9)) Rainbow Bridge Publishing.

—Reading Connection Grade 5. 2003. (Reading Connection Ser.). 96p. (gr. 5-18). 8.95 (978-1-932210-20-0(2)) Rainbow Bridge Publishing.

—Reading Connection Grade 6. 2003. (Reading Connection Ser.). 96p. (gr. 6-18). 8.95 (978-1-932210-21-7(0)) Rainbow Bridge Publishing.

Vargo, Sharon, illus. Sugar & Shadow. 2012. 8p. (J). (978-0-7367-2726-6(4)) Zaner-Bloser, Inc.

Vasiliu, Michelle & Orsini, Cheryl. Fire Ready. 2008. (Rigby Focus Forward: Level P Ser.). (Illus.). 24p. (J). (gr. 4-7). pap. (978-1-4190-3855-6(9), Rigby) Pearson Education Australia.

Vaughan, Susan. Let's Eat Lunch: Learning about Picture Graphs, 1 vol. 2010. (Math for the REAL World Ser.). (ENG., Illus.). 8p. (gr. k-1). pap. 5.15 (978-0-8239-8885-3(6), fe902c39-27d2-4222-be19-392f1f264f8a) Rosen Publishing Group, Inc., The.

Veitch, Catherine. Collins Big Cat Phonics for Letters & Sounds - Stunt Jets: Band 03/Yellow, Bd. 3. 2018. (Collins Big Cat Phonics Ser.). (ENG., Illus.). 16p. (J). (gr. k-1). pap. 6.99 (978-0-00-825159-8(2)) HarperCollins Pubs. Ltd. GBR. Dist: Independent Pubs. Group.

Velázquez Press, creator. Velázquez Biliteracy Program PreK Hora de la Comida Set. 2017. (SPA.). (J). (978-1-59495-709-3(6)) Velázquez Pr.

Venezia, Mike. Getting to Know the World's Greatest Inventors & Scientists, 4 vols., Set. Venezia, Mike, illus. Incl. Charles Drew: Doctor Who Got the World Pumped up to Donate Blood. 28.00 (978-0-531-23725-0(7)); Mary Leakey - Archaeologist Who Really Dug Her Work. 28.00 (978-0-531-23727-4(3)); Stephen Hawking: Cosmologist Who Gets a Big Bang Out of the Universe. 28.00 (978-0-531-23728-1(1)); 32p. (J). (gr. 2-5). 2009. (Illus.). 2009. Set lib. bdg. 112.00 (978-0-531-26130-9(1), Watts, Franklin) Scholastic Library Publishing.

Verderosa, Laura. At Grandma's House. 2010. (Sight Word Readers Ser.). (J). 3.49 (978-1-60719-607-5(7)) Newmark Learning LLC.

—At My School. 2010. (Sight Word Readers Ser.). (J). 3.49 (978-1-60719-606-8(9)) Newmark Learning LLC.

—Dad Likes New Clothes. 2010. (Sight Word Readers Ser.). (J). 3.49 (978-1-60719-605-1(0)) Newmark Learning LLC.

—In the Band. 2010. (Sight Word Readers Ser.). (J). 3.49 (978-1-60719-612-9(3)) Newmark Learning LLC.

Verne, Jules. 20,000 Leagues under the Sea. 2018. (ENG., Illus.). 396p. (J). 14.99 (978-1-63158-174-8(0), Racehorse Publishing) Skyhorse Publishing Co., Inc.

Vicary, Tim. Oxford Bookworms Library: Grace Darling: Level 2: 700-Word Vocabulary. 3rd ed. 2008. (ENG., Illus.). 64p. pap. 11.00 (978-0-19-479061-1(4)) Oxford Univ. Pr., Inc.

Vicente, Alidis. The Case of the Three Kings / el Caso de Los Reyes Magos: The Flaca Files / Los Expedientes de Flaca. 2016. (Flaca Files / Los Expedientes de Flaca Ser.). (MUL, ENG & SPA., Illus.). 96p. (J). (gr. 3-6). pap. 9.95 (978-1-55885-822-0(9), Piñata Books) Arte Publico Pr.

—The Shameless Shenanigans of Mister Malo / Las Terribles Travesuras de Mister Malo: The Mister Malo Series / Serie Mister Malo. 2017. (ENG & SPA., Illus.). 115p. (J). (gr. 4-8). pap. 9.95 (978-1-55885-853-4(9), Piñata Books) Arte Publico Pr.

Vicuña, Claudio Orrego. The Surprising Adventures of Balthazar. 2011. (Peace, Justice, Human Rights, & Freedom in Latin America Ser.). (ENG.). 160p. 15.00 (978-1-58966-218-6(0)) Univ. of Scranton Pr.

Villafane-Leon, Ines. A Story for All Seasons: Un Cuento Para Cada Estacion: Immigration of One. 2004. (ENG & SPA.). xiii, 367p. (YA). pap. 22.95 (978-1-882897-78-0(1)) Lost Coast Pr.

Vinci, Victoria. A Party for Piper: Practicing the P Sound, 1 vol. 2016. (Rosen Phonics Readers Ser.). (ENG., Illus.). 8p. (J). (gr. -1-2). pap. (978-1-5081-3071-0(X), 16420d36-b6aa-43dc-b665-5954ea5266bb, Rosen Classroom) Rosen Publishing Group, Inc., The.

—Jake's Jet: Practicing the J Sound, 1 vol. 2016. (Rosen Phonics Readers Ser.). (ENG.). 8p. (J). (gr. -1-2). pap. (978-1-5081-3210-3(0), b2c81d64-c52f-49fb-a3a7-64bc855fe7e4, Rosen Classroom) Rosen Publishing Group, Inc., The.

Viney, Peter. The Case of the Dead Batsman, 7. 2013. (Garnet Oracle Readers Ser.). (Illus.). 40p. pap., stu. ed. 4.50 (978-1-907575-21-1(9)) Garnet Education GBR. Dist: Garnet Publishing, Ltd.

—The Collector, 16. 2014. (Garnet Oracle Readers Ser.). (Illus.). 32p. pap., stu. ed. 4.50 (978-1-907575-31-0(6)) Garnet Education GBR. Dist: Garnet Publishing, Ltd.

—Space Romance, 8. 2014. (Garnet Oracle Readers Ser.). (Illus.). 40p. pap., stu. ed. 4.50 (978-1-907575-22-8(7)) Garnet Education GBR. Dist: Garnet Publishing, Ltd.

—Strawberry & the Sensations, 13. 2014. (Garnet Oracle Readers Ser.). (Illus.). 32p. pap., stu. ed. 4.50 (978-1-907575-28-0(6)) Garnet Education GBR. Dist: Garnet Publishing, Ltd.

—Sunnyvista City, 9. 2014. (Garnet Oracle Readers Ser.). (Illus.). 40p. pap., stu. ed. 4.50 (978-1-907575-24-2(3)) Garnet Education GBR. Dist: Garnet Publishing, Ltd.

—A Tidy Ghost, 17. 2013. (Garnet Oracle Readers Ser.). (Illus.). 40p. pap., stu. ed. 4.50 (978-1-907575-23-5(5)) Garnet Education GBR. Dist: Garnet Publishing, Ltd.

—Underground, 12. 2014. (Garnet Oracle Readers Ser.). (Illus.). 32p. pap., stu. ed. 4.50 (978-1-907575-27-3(8)) Garnet Education GBR. Dist: Garnet Publishing, Ltd.

Vink, Amanda. Kara Is a Chemist: Testing & Checking, 1 vol. 2017. (Computer Kids: Powered by Computational Thinking Ser.). (ENG.). 24p. (J). (gr. 4-5). 25.27 (978-1-5383-2405-9(9), 245d6212-7498-4e53-a451-9dd15d59f058, PowerKids Pr.); pap. (978-1-5081-3758-0(7), 65577954-4ad8-4e79-97a3-5d059494b5db, Rosen Classroom) Rosen Publishing Group, Inc., The.

—Our Rock Hunt: If... Then, 1 vol. 2017. (Computer Kids: Powered by Computational Thinking Ser.). (ENG.). 24p. (J). (gr. 4-5). 25.27 (978-1-5383-2424-0(5), 74fc6aec-2599-45ab-97c9-a7c54cc2bf4e, PowerKids Pr.); pap. (978-1-5081-3751-1(X), 82d42872-ca56-403e-871e-98bae832ad1b, Rosen Classroom) Rosen Publishing Group, Inc., The.

Vizoso Veiga, Xoán Antón. The READING LESSON: Adventures of Huckleberry Finn. 2008. 72p. pap. 13.50 (978-1-4092-0361-2(1)) Lulu Pr., Inc.

von Bissing, Ronimund. La Tierra del Oro Ardiente. (SPA.). (978-84-216-1631-4(5), BU4764) Bruño, Editorial ESP. Dist: Lectorum Pubns., Inc.

Vonthron, Satanta C. Marsy's Perfect Eyesight. Teeple, Jackie, illus. l.t. ed. 2005. (J). (gr. -1-k). pap. 10.95 (978-1-57332-344-4(6)); pap. 10.95 (978-1-57332-345-1(4)) Carson-Dellosa Publishing, LLC. (HighReach Learning, Incorporated).

Voskoboinikov, Valery & Linnamagi, Anne. The Icicle. 2007. (POL & ENG., Illus.). 32p. (J). pap. 16.95 (978-1-60195-100-7(0)) International Step by Step Assn.

Waddell, Martin. Class Six & the Very Big Rabbit: Band 10/White (Collins Big Cat) Ross, Tony, illus. 2005. (Collins Big Cat Ser.). (ENG.). 80p. (J). (gr. 1-3). pap. 10.99 (978-0-00-718629-7(0)) HarperCollins Pubs. Ltd. GBR. Dist: Independent Pubs. Group.

—Something So Big. Canty, Charlotte, illus. 2004. (ENG.). 24p. (J). lib. bdg. 23.65 (978-1-59646-706-4(1)) Dingles & Co.

Wagner, Michael & Vanzet, Gaston. The Mess. 2008. (Rigby Focus Forward: Level E Ser.). (Illus.). 24p. (J). (gr. 4-7). pap. (978-1-4190-3677-4(7), Rigby) Pearson Education Australia.

Wagstaff, Janiel M. Stella Writes an Opinion. 2018. (ENG.). 32p. (gr. k-3). pap. 7.99 (978-1-338-26476-0(1)) Scholastic, Inc.

Waiting in Line: Individual Title Six-Packs. (gr. -1-2). 27.00 (978-0-7635-9480-0(6)) Rigby Education.

Walbruck, Rita M. Auf Heiber Spur, Erlebnisse in Deutschland: Das Ratsel vom Waldsee, Reader 2. (Auf Heisser Spur, Erlebnisse in Deutschland Ser.). (GER., Illus.). 40p. (J). 3.95 (978-0-88436-851-9(3), 45255) EMC/Paradigm Publishing.

Walch Publishing Staff. Assessment Strategies for Reading. 2003. 86p. 24.99 (978-0-8251-4477-6(9)) Walch Education.

Walker, Colin, et al. Explorando el Espacio. (Coleccion Conceptos de Ciencia en Big Books). (SPA., Illus.). (J). (gr. k-3). 12.00 (978-0-8136-6756-0(9), MD7215) Modern Curriculum Pr.

—La Tierra Cambia. (Coleccion Conceptos de Ciencia en Big Books). (SPA., Illus.). (J). (gr. k-3). 12.00 (978-0-8136-6729-4(1), MD7205) Modern Curriculum Pr.

Walker, Nan. Day Camp. 2011. (Early Connections Ser.). (J). (978-1-61672-347-7(5)) Benchmark Education Co.

Walker, Rachel. Be Kind to Bees, 1 vol. 2018. (ENG., Illus.). 21p. (J). pap. (978-1-77654-251-2(7), Red Rocket Readers) Flying Start Bks.

—Book Art, 1 vol. 2015. (ENG., Illus.). 16p. (-2). pap. (978-1-77654-136-2(7), Red Rocket Readers) Flying Start Bks.

—Farming, 1 vol. 2018. (ENG., Illus.). 21p. (J). pap. (978-1-77654-252-9(5), Red Rocket Readers) Flying Start Bks.

—Help Our Oceans, 1 vol. 2015. (ENG., Illus.). 16p. (-2). pap. (978-1-77654-138-6(3), Red Rocket Readers) Flying Start Bks.

—Polar Bear Survival, 1 vol. 2015. (ENG., Illus.). 16p. (-2). pap. (978-1-77654-141-6(3), Red Rocket Readers) Flying Start Bks.

Walker, Theo. Swing, Slither, Swim Low Intermediate Book with Online Access, 1 vol. 2014. (ENG., Illus.). 24p. pap., E-Book 9.50 (978-1-107-69242-8(3)) Cambridge Univ. Pr.

WalkerTheo. THE CITY EXPERIMENT: REBUILDING GREENSBURG, KANSAS LOW INTERMEDIATE BOOK WITH ONLINE ACCESS, 1 vol. 2014. (ENG., Illus.). 24p. (J). pap., E-Book 9.50 (978-1-107-62256-2(5)) Cambridge Univ. Pr.

—EAT UP! BEGINNING BOOK WITH ONLINE ACCESS, 1 vol. 2014. (ENG., Illus.). 24p. (J). pap., E-Book, E-Book 9.50 (978-1-107-68962-6(7)) Cambridge Univ. Pr.

—SUGAR: OUR GUILTY PLEASURE LOW INTERMEDIATE BOOK WITH ONLINE ACCESS, 1 vol. 2014. (ENG., Illus.). 28p. (J). pap., E-Book 9.50 (978-1-107-68146-0(4)) Cambridge Univ. Pr.

Wall, Julia & McKenzie, Heather. Nico's List. 2008. (Rigby Focus Forward: Level M Ser.). (Illus.). 24p. (J). (gr. 4-7). pap. (978-1-4190-3829-7(X), Rigby) Pearson Education Australia.

Wall, Julia & Nickel, Adam. Bruno's Tea. 2008. (Rigby Focus Forward: Level N Ser.). (Illus.). 24p. (J). (gr. 4-7). pap. (978-1-4190-3833-4(8), Rigby) Pearson Education Australia.

Wallace, Clinton. H. The Adventures of Roger Eldemire. 2013. 28p. pap. 9.95 (978-1-4787-2493-3(5)) Outskirts Pr., Inc.

Wallace, Karen. Collins Big Cat Phonics for Letters & Sounds - Maps: Band 04/Blue, Bd. 4. Bacchin, Giorgio, illus. 2018. (Collins Big Cat Phonics Ser.). (ENG.). 16p. (J). (gr. k-1). pap. 6.99 (978-0-00-825165-9(7)) HarperCollins Pubs. Ltd. GBR. Dist: Independent Pubs. Group.

—Flash Harriet & the Loch Ness Monster: Band 13/Topaz (Collins Big Cat) Nayler, Sarah, illus. 2007. (Collins Big Cat Ser.). (ENG.). 32p. (J). (gr. 2-4). pap. 9.99 (978-0-00-723082-2(6)) HarperCollins Pubs. Ltd. GBR. Dist: Independent Pubs. Group.

Waller, Stephen. Level 1: Run for Your Life. 2nd ed. 2008. (Pearson English Graded Readers Ser.). (ENG., Illus.). 32p. pap. 11.99 (978-1-4058-6970-6(4), Pearson ELT) Pearson Education.

Walsh, Kenneth. Our Earth, 1 vol. 2nd rev. ed. 2011. (TIME for KIDS(r): Informational Text Ser.). (ENG.). 28p. (gr. 2-3). pap. 10.99 (978-1-4333-3631-7(6)) Teacher Created Materials, Inc.

—Outer Space, 1 vol. 2nd rev. ed. 2011. (TIME for KIDS(r): Informational Text Ser.). (ENG.). 28p. (gr. 2-3). pap. 10.99 (978-1-4333-3632-4(4)) Teacher Created Materials, Inc.

—The Solar System, 1 vol. 2nd rev. ed. 2011. (TIME for KIDS(r): Informational Text Ser.). (ENG.). 28p. (gr. 2-3). pap. 10.99 (978-1-4333-3633-1(2)) Teacher Created Materials, Inc.

Walter Dragons. (Investigating Ancient Civilizations Ser.). (J). 16.80 (978-0-8136-6342-5(3)) Modern Curriculum Pr.

Wang, Michael. A Stray. 2016. (ENG.). 40p. (J). 14.99 (978-981-4751-30-8(8)) Marshall Cavendish International (Asia) Private Ltd. SGP. Dist: Independent Pubs. Group.

The War Shirt: Six-Pack. (Greetings Ser.: Vol. 2). 24p. (gr. 2-3). 31.00 (978-0-7635-9413-8(X)) Rigby Education.

War Torn. 2003. (Illus.). pap. 5.60 (978-0-7398-7515-5(9)) Steck-Vaughn.

Waring, Rob. Cupid the Dolphin: Footprint Reading Library 4. 2008. (Footprint Reading Library: Level 4 Ser.). (ENG.). 24p. (C). pap. 15.95 (978-1-4240-4463-4(4)) Cengage Heinle.

Warren, Celia. Ready for a Picnic. 2004. (QEB Start Reading Ser.). (Illus.). 24p. (J). lib. bdg. 15.95 (978-1-59566-015-2(1)) QEB Publishing Inc.

Wasson, Dawn K. T. Kuu Tutu. 2008. (ENG & HAW., Illus.). (J). lib. bdg. (978-0-9773495-8-6(6)) Na Kamalei Koolauloa Early Education Program.

Watch me Zoom: Individual Title Six-Packs. (gr. 1-2). 22.00 (978-0-7635-9172-4(6)) Rigby Education.

The Water Caller. 2003. (Illus.). pap. 7.60 (978-0-7398-7529-2(9)) Steck-Vaughn.

Watermelon. (Early Intervention Levels Ser.). 23.10 (978-0-7362-0038-7(X)) CENGAGE Learning.

Waters, Kate. Monarch Butterflies. 2009. (Growing Reader Level 3 Ser.). (Illus.). 32p. (J). pap. (978-0-545-07234-2(4)) Scholastic, Inc.

Watt, Fiona. Fairies. Cartwright, Stephen & Bird, Glen, illus. 2004. 10p. (J). (gr. -1 — 1). per. 15.95 (978-0-7945-0811-1(1), Usborne) EDC Publishing.

—That's Not My Fairy. Wells, Rachel, illus. 2004. 10p. (J). 9.99 (978-0-7945-0793-0(X), Usborne) EDC Publishing.

—Ya Se Hacer Lazos. Cartwright, Stephen, illus. 2005. (SPA.). 10p. (J). 7.95 (978-0-7460-6626-3(0), Usborne) EDC Publishing.

Wax, Wendy. Sugar & Spice. Perrett, Lisa, illus. 2007. (ENG.). 24p. (J). (gr. 1-4). per. 3.99 (978-1-58476-614-8(X), IKIDS) Innovative Kids.

We Both Read-About Bats. 2014. (Illus.). 44p. (J). 9.95 (978-1-60115-267-1(1)) Treasure Bay, Inc.

We Both Read-Museum Day. 2014. (Illus.). 44p. (J). 9.95 (978-1-60115-265-7(5)); pap. 5.99 (978-1-60115-266-4(3)) Treasure Bay, Inc.

We Can: KinderWords Individual Title Six-Packs. (Kinderstarters Ser.). 8p. (gr. -1-1). 21.00 (978-0-7635-8710-9(9)) Rigby Education.

We Clean Up!, 6 Packs. (gr. -1-2). 23.00 (978-0-7635-8813-7(X)) Rigby Education.

Weaver, Jo. Paul Bunyan: A Very Tall Tale, 1 vol. rev. ed. 2013. (Literary Text Ser.). (ENG., Illus.). 20p. (gr. 1-2). (J). lib. bdg. 15.96 (978-1-4807-1153-2(5)); 7.99 (978-1-4333-5497-7(7)) Teacher Created Materials, Inc.

Weaver, Kimberley & Murphy, Allyson. Pack Your Bags... . Go U. S. A. Holdren, Maria K., illus. 2005. (J). 15.99 (978-0-9767351-0-6(5)) Sorella Bks.

Weber, Rebecca. Telling Time Through the Ages: Set Of 6. 2011. (Navigators Ser.). (J). pap. 44.00 net. (978-1-4108-0409-9(7)) Benchmark Education Co.

Webster, Christy. Big Fish, Little Fish (Disney/Pixar Finding Dory) The Disney Storybook Art Team, illus. 2016. (Step into Reading Ser.). (ENG.). 24p. (J). (gr. -1-1). E-Book (978-0-7364-3705-9(3), RH/Disney) Random Hse. Children's Bks.

—Fast As the Flash! 2018. (Step into Reading Level 2 Ser.). lib. bdg. 14.75 (978-0-606-40932-2(7)) Turtleback.

Webster, Grace. Elephant's Ears: Band 03/Yellow. Golden, Emily, illus. 2014. (Collins Big Cat Ser.). (ENG.). 512p. (J). (gr. k-1). pap. 7.99 (978-0-00-753849-2(9)) HarperCollins Pubs. Ltd. GBR. Dist: Independent Pubs. Group.

Wee Whopper: Individual Title Six-Packs. (gr. 1-2). 25.00 (978-0-7635-9139-7(4)) Rigby Education.

Weiland, Peter. So Big yet So Small. Coffey, Kevin, illus. 2012. (J). 14.95 (978-1-937406-16-5(4)) Amplify Publishing Group.

Weir, Jane. Inside the World of Matter, 1 vol. rev. ed. 2007. (Science: Informational Text Ser.). (ENG.). 32p. (gr. 3-6). pap. 12.99 (978-0-7439-0567-1(9)) Teacher Created Materials, Inc.

—Investigating Forces & Motion, 1 vol. rev. ed. 2007. (Science: Informational Text Ser.). (ENG.). 32p. (J). (gr. 3-6). pap. 12.99 (978-0-7439-0573-2(3)) Teacher Created Materials, Inc.

Weiss, Bobbi & Weiss, David. Hiro: Dragon Warrior: Level 2. Short, Robbie, illus. 2007. (ENG.). 24p. (J). (gr. 1-4). per. 3.99 (978-1-58476-616-2(6), IKIDS) Innovative Kids.

Wells, James. Stuffy, the Short-Neck Giraffe Who Liked Peanut Butter. 2006. 9.00 (978-0-8059-9174-1(3)) Dorrance Publishing Co., Inc.

Wells, Rosemary. Max's Half Birthday. Grey, Andrew, illus. 2018. (Max & Ruby Ser.). 32p. (J). (gr. 1-2). pap. 4.99 (978-0-515-15746-8(5), Penguin Young Readers) Penguin Young Readers Group.

Welsh, Clare Helen. Cookie Blast Off! Touliatou, Sophia, illus. 2019. (Early Bird Readers — Purple (Early Bird Stories (tm)) Ser.). (ENG.). 32p. (J). (gr. k-3). 30.65 (978-1-5415-4230-3(4), 9e72767a-c14f-4a97-8281-8df31c261978); pap. 9.99 (978-1-5415-7416-8(8), 141af35e-9336-4262-86c6-06cc791d5ca4) Lerner Publishing Group. (Lerner Pubns.).

Wendorff, Anne. Bear Cubs. 2009. (Blastoff! Readers Ser.). (ENG., Illus.). 24p. (J). (gr. k-3). 20.00 (978-0-531-21626-2(8), Children's Pr.) Scholastic Library Publishing.

—Blastoff! Readers - Watch Animals Grow, 4 vols., Set. Incl. Bear Cubs. 20.00 (978-0-531-21626-2(8)); Eaglets. 20.00 (978-0-531-21627-9(6)); Fawns. 20.00 (978-0-531-21628-6(4)); Lambs. 20.00 (978-0-531-21629-3(2)); (Illus.). 24p. (J). (gr. k-3). 2009. (Blastoff! Readers Ser.). 2009. Set lib. bdg. 80.00 (978-0-531-26129-3(8), Children's Pr.) Scholastic Library Publishing.

—Eaglets. 2009. (Blastoff! Readers Ser.). (ENG., Illus.). 24p. (J). (gr. k-3). 20.00 (978-0-531-21627-9(6), Children's Pr.) Scholastic Library Publishing.

—Fawns. 2009. (Blastoff! Readers Ser.). (ENG., Illus.). 24p. (J). (gr. k-3). 20.00 (978-0-531-21628-6(4), Children's Pr.) Scholastic Library Publishing.

—Lambs. 2009. (Blastoff! Readers Ser.). (ENG., Illus.). 24p. (J). (gr. k-3). 20.00 (978-0-531-21629-3(2), Children's Pr.) Scholastic Library Publishing.

Wendy Lee Jungling; Illustrated By My Fa. Who Do You Want to Be? 2012. 28p. 24.95 (978-1-4626-6873-1(9)) America Star Bks.

Werlin, Nancy. And Then There Were Four. 2018. lib. bdg. 22.10 (978-0-606-41305-3(7)) Turtleback.

Wernham, Sara. The Bird House, 4 Bks., Pack. Stephen, Lib, illus. 2008. (Jolly Phonics Readers, Complete Set Level 4 Ser.). (ENG.). 16p. (J). pap. 14.00 (978-1-84414-054-1(7)) Jolly Learning, Ltd. GBR. Dist: American International Distribution Corp.

—The Enormous Turnip, 6 Bks., Pack. Stephen, Lib & Maddison, Kevin, illus. 2008. (Jolly Phonics Readers, Complete Set Level 4 Ser.). (ENG.). (J). pap. 14.00 (978-1-84414-061-9(X), Jolly Learning) Jolly Learning, Ltd. GBR. Dist: American International Distribution Corp.

—Phonic; Rainforests; Monster Party, 18 vols., Pack, Set. Maddison, Kevin & Wade, Sarah, illus. 2003. (ENG.). (J). pap. 37.50 (978-1-84414-091-6(1), Jolly Learning) Jolly Learning, Ltd. GBR. Dist: American International Distribution Corp.

—Snakes; the Tree That Blinked; the Tree Billy Goats Gruff, 18 Bks., Pack. Maddison, Kevin & Stephen, Lib, illus. 2004. (ENG.). (J). pap. 42.00 (978-1-84414-090-9(3), Jolly Learning) Jolly Learning, Ltd. GBR. Dist: American International Distribution Corp.

—Soccer, 6 Bks., Set. Stephen, Lib & Maddison, Kevin, illus. 2008. (Jolly Phonics Readers, Complete Set Level 4 Ser.). (ENG.). (J). pap. 14.00 (978-1-84414-068-8(7), Jolly Learning) Jolly Learning, Ltd. GBR. Dist: American International Distribution Corp.

—The Tree That Blinked, 6 Bks., Vol. 3. Wade, Sarah, illus. 2004. (Jolly Phonics Readers, Complete Set Level 3 Ser.). (ENG.). (J). pap. 14.00 (978-1-84414-008-4(3), Jolly Learning) Jolly Learning, Ltd. GBR. Dist: American International Distribution Corp.

Wesson, André. Mrs. Applebee & the Sunshine Band, Book 1: Meet the Class! 2007. 48p. pap. 18.50 (978-0-615-14849-6(2)) Se7enth Swan Publishing Group, LLC.

West, Alexandra C. World of Reading: Marvel Super Hero Adventures: These Are the Avengers-Level 1. 2018. (World of Reading Ser.). (ENG., Illus.). 32p. (J). (gr. 1-3). pap. 4.99 (978-1-368-02353-5(3)) Marvel Worldwide, Inc.

West, Colin. Have You Seen the Crocodile? Read & Share. West, Colin, illus. 2003. (Read & Share Ser.). (ENG., Illus.). 32p. (J). (gr. -1-3). pap. 3.99 (978-0-7636-0862-0(9)) Candlewick Pr.

West Indian Reader Bk 2, Bk. 2. 2014. (ENG.). 176p. pap. 7.99 (978-1-4085-2353-7(1)) Oxford Univ. Pr., Inc.

West Indian Reader Bk 3, Bk. 3. 2014. (ENG.). 208p. pap. 8.99 (978-1-4085-2354-4(X)) Oxford Univ. Pr., Inc.

West Indian Reader Introductory. 2014. (ENG.). 96p. pap. 5.99 (978-1-4085-2351-3(5)) Oxford Univ. Pr., Inc.

West, Tracey. Titanium Ninja. 2014. (Ninjago Readers Ser.: 10). lib. bdg. 13.55 (978-0-606-36372-3(6)) Turtleback.

West, William. All about Ants, 1 vol. 2005. (Rosen REAL Readers Ser.). (ENG., Illus.). 12p. (gr. 1-2). pap. 5.90 (978-0-8239-8120-5(7), b8b45e48-22b4-411a-9a49-f5b067494212) Rosen Publishing Group, Inc., The.

Weston Woods Staff, creator. Brave Irene. 2011. 29.95 *(978-0-439-73468-4(1))*; 38.75 *(978-0-439-72666-5(2))*; 18.95 *(978-0-439-72665-8(4))* Weston Woods Studios, Inc.
—Caps for Sale. 2011. 38.75 *(978-0-439-72925-3(4))*; 18.95 *(978-0-439-72924-6(6))* Weston Woods Studios, Inc.
What a Mess!, 6, Pack. (Chiquilibros Ser.). (gr. k-1). 23.00 *(978-0-7635-0410-6(6))* Rigby Education.
What Am I? Individual Title Six-Packs. (Story Steps Ser.). (gr. k-2). 29.00 *(978-0-7635-9593-7(4))* Rigby Education.
What are We Doing? KinderWords Individual Title Six-Packs. (Kinderstarters Ser.). 8p. (gr. -1-1). 21.00 *(978-0-7635-8697-3(8))* Rigby Education.
What can Hurt?, 6 Packs. (gr. 1-2). 22.00 *(978-0-7635-9088-8(6))* Rigby Education.
What Can I Do?, 6 Packs. (Greetings Ser.: Vol. 1). (gr. 2-3). 31.00 *(978-0-7635-9425-1(3))* Rigby Education.
What can Jump?, 6, Pack. (gr. 1-2). 22.00 *(978-0-7635-9114-4(9))* Rigby Education.
What Can Swim?, 6, Pack. (gr. 1-2). 22.00 *(978-0-7635-9089-5(4))* Rigby Education.
What Can We Smell?, 6, Pack. (gr. 1-2). 22.00 *(978-0-7635-9115-1(7))* Rigby Education.
What Can You Do with a Ball of String?, 6, Pack. (gr. k-1). 23.00 *(978-0-7635-9027-7(4))* Rigby Education.
What Can You Taste?, 6, Pack. (gr. 1-2). 22.00 *(978-0-7635-9116-8(5))* Rigby Education.
What Could It Be? Big Book. (Pebble Soup Explorations Ser.). 16p. (gr. -1-18). 31.00 *(978-0-7578-1665-9(7))* Rigby Education.
What Could It Be? Small Book. (Pebble Soup Explorations Ser.). 16p. (gr. -1-18). 5.00 *(978-0-7578-1705-2(X))* Rigby Education.
What Did Ben Want?, 6, Pack. (Chiquilibros Ser.). (gr. k-1). 23.00 *(978-0-7635-0444-1(0))* Rigby Education.
What Did I Use?, 6, Pack. (Discovery World Ser.). 12p. (gr. k-1). 28.00 *(978-0-7635-8448-1(7))* Rigby Education.
What Did They Want?, 6, Pack. (Chiquilibros Ser.). (gr. k-1). 23.00 *(978-0-7635-0445-8(9))* Rigby Education.
What do you Have? Individual Title Six-Packs. (gr. 1-2). 22.00 *(978-0-7635-9173-1(4))* Rigby Education.
What do you Hear? Individual Title Six-Packs. (gr. 1-2). 22.00 *(978-0-7635-9117-5(3))* Rigby Education.
What do you See? Individual Title Six-Packs. (gr. 1-2). 22.00 *(978-0-7635-9100-7(9))* Rigby Education.
What Do You See by the Sea? Take-Home Book. 2005. (Emergent Library: Vol. 2). (YA). (gr. -1-1). 12.60 *(978-0-8215-7252-8(0))* Sadlier, William H. Inc.
What do you Touch? Individual Title Six-Packs. (gr. 1-2). 22.00 *(978-0-7635-9118-2(1))* Rigby Education.
What Does Lucy Like? Take-Home Book. 2005. (Emergent Library: Vol. 2). (YA). (gr. -1-1). 12.60 *(978-0-8215-7256-6(3))* Sadlier, William H. Inc.
What feels Cold?, 6 Packs. (gr. 1-2). 22.00 *(978-0-7635-9101-4(7))* Rigby Education.
What feels Hot?, 6 Packs. (gr. 1-2). 22.00 *(978-0-7635-9102-1(5))* Rigby Education.
What feels Sticky?, 6 Packs. (gr. 1-2). 22.00 *(978-0-7635-9103-8(3))* Rigby Education.
What Gives You Goose Bumps?, 6 Packs. (gr. k-1). 23.00 *(978-0-7635-9044-4(4))* Rigby Education.
What Goes Around & Around?, 6 Packs. (gr. 1-2). 22.00 *(978-0-7635-9119-9(X))* Rigby Education.
What Goes in the Bathtub?, 6 Packs. (Literatura 2000 Ser.). (gr. k-1). 28.00 *(978-0-7635-0017-7(8))* Rigby Education.
What Goes into a Salad? Individual Title Six-Packs. (gr. -1-2). 23.00 *(978-0-7635-8993-6(4))* Rigby Education.
What Goes up & Down?, 6 Packs. (gr. 1-2). 22.00 *(978-0-7635-9120-5(3))* Rigby Education.
What Goes up High?, 6 Packs. (gr. 1-2). 22.00 *(978-0-7635-9090-1(8))* Rigby Education.
What Happens When You Recycle? Individual Title Six-Packs. (Discovery World Ser.). 16p. (gr. 1-2). 28.00 *(978-0-7635-8464-1(9))* Rigby Education.
What I Know: Set 2. 2017. (What I Know Ser.). 24p. (gr. k-k). pap. 48.90 *(978-1-5382-0232-6(8))*; (ENG.). lib. bdg. 145.62 *(978-1-5382-0231-9(X)*, 05f6a441-230f-4fc9-bdec-99495a60e354) Stevens, Gareth Publishing LLLP.
What Is Enormous?, 6 Packs. (gr. 1-2). 22.00 *(978-0-7635-9092-5(4))* Rigby Education.
What Is Fast?, 6 Packs. (gr. 1-2). 22.00 *(978-0-7635-9104-5(1))* Rigby Education.
What Is Fierce?, 6 Packs. (gr. 1-2). 22.00 *(978-0-7635-9093-2(2))* Rigby Education.
What Is He Looking For? KinderWords Individual Title Six-Packs. (Kinderstarters Ser.). 8p. (gr. -1-1). 21.00 *(978-0-7635-8711-6(7))* Rigby Education.
What Is It? (Guided Reading Levels Ser.). 21.42 *(978-0-7362-1047-8(4))* CENGAGE Learning.
What Is Little? (Early Intervention Levels Ser.). 23.10 *(978-0-7362-0003-5(7))* CENGAGE Learning.
What Is Old? Individual Title Six-Packs. (gr. 1-2). 22.00 *(978-0-7635-9096-3(7))* Rigby Education.
What Is Slippery?, 6 Packs. (gr. 1-2). 22.00 *(978-0-7635-9097-0(5))* Rigby Education.
What Is Slow? Individual Title Six-Packs. (gr. 1-2). 22.00 *(978-0-7635-9106-9(8))* Rigby Education.
What Is Soft?, 6 Packs. (gr. 1-2). 22.00 *(978-0-7635-9107-6(6))* Rigby Education.
What Is Tall?, 6 Packs. (gr. 1-2). 22.00 *(978-0-7635-9108-3(4))* Rigby Education.
What Is This? KinderWords, 6 Packs. (Kinderstarters Ser.). 8p. (gr. -1-1). 21.00 *(978-0-7635-8699-7(4))* Rigby Education.
What Is Young?, 6 Packs. (gr. 1-2). 22.00 *(978-0-7635-9109-0(2))* Rigby Education.
What Should You Say? What Should You Do? Social/Emotional Lap Book. (Pebble Soup Explorations Ser.). (gr. -1-18). 16.00 *(978-0-7578-5064-6(0))* Rigby Education.
What Smells Good? Individual Title Six-Packs. (gr. 1-2). 22.00 *(978-0-7635-9121-2(1))* Rigby Education.
What Some People Will Do. 2003. (illus.). pap. 7.60 *(978-0-7398-7535-3(3))* Steck-Vaughn.
What's Around the Corner? Individual Title Six-Packs. (Literatura 2000 Ser.). (gr. 1-2). 28.00 *(978-0-7635-0153-2(0))* Rigby Education.
What's for Lunch? (Peek A Boo Pockets Ser.). 12p. (J). bds. *(978-2-89393-879-0(5))* Phidal Publishing, Inc./Editions Phidal, Inc.
What's in the Castle? (Let's Read about... Ser.). 10p. (J). *(978-2-7643-0073-2(5))* Phidal Publishing, Inc./Editions Phidal, Inc.
What's in the Dollhouse? (Let's Read about... Ser.). 10p. (J). *(978-2-7643-0195-1(2))* Phidal Publishing, Inc./Editions Phidal, Inc.
What's in the Garage? (Let's Read about... Ser.). 10p. (J). *(978-2-7643-0194-4(4))* Phidal Publishing, Inc./Editions Phidal, Inc.
What's on My Farm? (Early Intervention Levels Ser.). 23.10 *(978-0-7362-0007-3(X))* CENGAGE Learning.
What's on the Farm? (Let's Read about... Ser.). 10p. (J). *(978-2-7643-0163-0(4))* Phidal Publishing, Inc./Editions Phidal, Inc.
What's Underneath? Individual Title Six-Packs. (Discovery World Ser.). 16p. (gr. 1-2). 28.00 *(978-0-7635-8465-8(7))* Rigby Education.
Wheels Board Book Set 800789, 3. 2005. (J). bds. *(978-1-59794-042-9(9))* Environments, Inc.
When I Grow Up. (Early Intervention Levels Ser.). 23.10 *(978-0-7362-0025-7(8))* CENGAGE Learning.
When It Snowed: Individual Title, 6 packs. (gr. -1-2). 23.00 *(978-0-7635-9018-5(5))* Rigby Education.
When Lana Was Absent: 6 Small Books. (gr. k-3). 24.00 *(978-0-7635-6240-3(8))* Rigby Education.
When Mr Quinn Snored: Take-Home Book. 2005. (Emergent Library: Vol. 2). (YA). (gr. -1-1). 12.60 *(978-0-8215-7266-5(0))* Sadlier, William H. Inc.
Where are the car Keys? Individual Title Six-Packs. (gr. 1-2). 22.00 *(978-0-7635-9156-4(4))* Rigby Education.
Where Are We Going? (J). 26.20 *(978-0-8136-8392-8(0))*; 26.20 *(978-0-8136-8393-5(9))*; (gr. -1-3). 59.50 *(978-0-8136-7906-8(0))* Modern Curriculum Pr.
Where Are You Going? KinderWords Individual Title Six-Packs. (Kinderstarters Ser.). 8p. (gr. -1-1). 21.00 *(978-0-7635-8712-3(5))* Rigby Education.
Where Does Breakfast Come From?, 6 Packs. (Discovery World Ser.). 16p. (gr. 1-2). 28.00 *(978-0-7635-8454-2(1))* Rigby Education.
Where Is the Treasure? KinderConcepts Individual Title Six-Packs. (Kinderstarters Ser.). 8p. (gr. -1-1). 21.00 *(978-0-7635-8721-5(4))* Rigby Education.
Where We Live Interactive Packages: In My Neighborhood. (Pebble Soup Explorations Ser.). (gr. -1-18). 52.00 *(978-0-7578-5232-9(7))* Rigby Education.
Where We Live Interactive Packages: What People Do. (Pebble Soup Explorations Ser.). (gr. -1-18). 52.00 *(978-0-7578-5234-3(3))* Rigby Education.
Which Egg Is Mine? (Early Intervention Levels Ser.). 23.10 *(978-0-7362-0034-9(7))* CENGAGE Learning.
Which Way, Jack? Individual Title Six-Packs. (Action Packs Ser.). 104p. (gr. 3-5). 44.00 *(978-0-7635-8407-8(X))* Rigby Education.
White, Kiersten. Bright We Burn. 2019. (And I Darken Ser.: 3). (ENG., Illus.). 432p. (YA). (gr. 7). pap. 10.99 *(978-0-553-52242-6(6)*, Ember) Random Hse. Children's Bks.
White, Marco. Freddy's Fishbowl, 1 vol. 2006. (Neighborhood Readers Ser.). (ENG.). 8p. (gr. k-1). pap. 5.15 *(978-1-4042-6702-2(6)*, 2dcef9d1-453d-43b3-9d15-7d948f403479, Rosen Classroom) Rosen Publishing Group, Inc., The.
White, N.m. Unlock Level 1 Listening & Speaking Skills Student's Book & Online Workbook, 1 vol. 2014. (Cambridge Discovery Education Skills Ser.). (ENG., Illus.). 224p. pap., E-Book 50.50 *(978-1-107-67810-1(2))* Cambridge Univ. Pr.
White Paw, Black Paw: KinderReaders Individual Title Six-Packs. (Kinderstarters Ser.). 8p. (gr. -1-1). 21.00 *(978-0-7635-8648-5(X))* Rigby Education.
Whiteford, Rhona & Hachette Children's Group. Complete English, 3 bks. in 1. (ENG., Illus.). 96p. (YA). pap. 15.99 *(978-0-340-71582-6(0))* Hodder & Stoughton GBR. Dist: Trafalgar Square Publishing.
Whiteford, Rhona, et al. Complete English, 4 bks. in 1. (ENG., Illus.). 96p. (YA). pap. 15.99 *(978-0-340-71580-2(4))* Hodder & Stoughton GBR. Dist: Trafalgar Square Publishing.
Who Are We?, 6 Packs. (gr. -1-2). 23.00 *(978-0-7635-8805-2(9))* Rigby Education.
Who Came by Here? (Early Intervention Levels Ser.). 23.10 *(978-0-7362-0031-8(2))* CENGAGE Learning.
Who Lives on a Farm? Individual Title, 6 packs. (Story Steps Ser.). (gr. k-2). 29.00 *(978-0-7635-9570-8(5))* Rigby Education.
Who Looks after Our World? Individual Title Six-Packs. (gr. -1-2). 23.00 *(978-0-7635-8814-4(8))* Rigby Education.
Who Painted the Porcupine. (J). 23.50 *(978-0-8136-3967-3(0))* Modern Curriculum Pr.
Who Will Help Me? Individual Title Six-Packs. (gr. -1-2). 23.00 *(978-0-7635-8795-6(8))* Rigby Education.
Who Will Look Out for Danny? Individual Title Six-Packs. (Action Packs Ser.). 120p. (gr. 3-5). 44.00 *(978-0-7635-8420-7(7))* Rigby Education.
Whoops! Set D Individual Title, 6 packs. (gr. k-3). 29.00 *(978-0-7635-0551-6(X))* Rigby Education.
Who's at the Zoo? (Let's Read about Ser.). 10p. (J). *(978-2-7643-0162-3(6))* Phidal Publishing, Inc./Editions Phidal, Inc.
Who's Coming for a Ride? Individual Title, 6 packs. (Literatura 2000 Ser.). (gr. -1-1). 28.00 *(978-0-7635-0019-1(4))* Rigby Education.
Whose Egg Is This? Individual Title Six-Packs. (Story Steps Ser.). (gr. k-2). 32.00 *(978-0-7635-9607-1(8))* Rigby Education.
Why the Sea Is Salty: Individual Title Six-Packs. (Literatura 2000 Ser.). (gr. 2-3). 33.00 *(978-0-7635-0246-1(4))* Rigby Education.
Whybrow, Ian. The Best Little Bullfrog in the Forest Orange Band. Smillie, Natalie, illus. 2016. (Cambridge Reading Adventures Ser.). (ENG.). 16p. pap. 8.80 *(978-1-107-56018-5(7))* Cambridge Univ. Pr.
—It's Much Too Early! Watson, Laura, illus. 2016. (Cambridge Reading Adventures Ser.). (ENG.). 16p. pap. 7.95 *(978-1-107-56032-1(2))* Cambridge Univ. Pr.
—Little Fennec Fox & Jerboa Turquoise Band. Batori, Susan, illus. 2017. (Cambridge Reading Adventures Ser.). (ENG.). 16p. pap. 6.15 *(978-1-108-43092-0(9))* Cambridge Univ. Pr.
—Sinbad & the Roc Purple Band. Schon, Nick, illus. 2016. (Cambridge Reading Adventures Ser.). (ENG.). 24p. pap. 8.80 *(978-1-316-50340-9(2))* Cambridge Univ. Pr.
—Sinbad Goes to Sea Turquoise Band. Schon, Nick, illus. 2016. (Cambridge Reading Adventures Ser.). (ENG.). 16p. pap. 7.95 *(978-1-316-50338-6(0))* Cambridge Univ. Pr.
—A Tale of Two Sinbads 3 Explorers. Shamshirsaz, Shabab, illus. 2017. (Cambridge Reading Adventures Ser.). (ENG.). 32p. pap. 8.60 *(978-1-108-43097-5(X))* Cambridge Univ. Pr.
Wiggin, Kate Douglas. Rebecca of Sunnybrook Farm. 2008. (Bring the Classics to Life Ser.). (Illus.). 72p. (gr. 1-12). pap., act. bk. ed. 10.95 *(978-1-55576-046-5(5)*, EDCTR-102B) EDCON Publishing Group.
Wilbur's Wild Ride & Other Stories: Individual Title Six-Pack. (Story Steps Ser.). (gr. k-2). 42.00 *(978-0-7635-9598-2(5))* Rigby Education.
Wilcox. The Hidden Men. (Thumbprint Mysteries Ser.). 32.86 *(978-0-8092-0415-1(0))* McGraw-Hill/Contemporary.
Wild Animal Board Book Set 800785, 5. 2005. (J). bds. *(978-1-59794-020-7(8))* Environments, Inc.
Wild Critters. 2005. (Little Celebrations Thematic Packages Ser.). (J). (gr. k-3). 133.50 *(978-0-673-75384-7(0))* Celebration Pr.
Wild Easts Wild West: Level K, 6 vols. 128p. (gr. 2-3). 49.95 *(978-0-7699-0988-2(4))* Shortland Pubns. (U. S. A.) Inc.
Wilde, Kim. Harry's Garden: Band 04/Blue (Collins Big Cat) 2006. (Collins Big Cat Ser.). (ENG., Illus.). 96p. (J). (gr. 1-1). pap. 5.99 *(978-0-00-718676-1(2))* HarperCollins Pubs. Ltd. GBR. Dist: Independent Pubs. Group.
—How to Make a Scarecrow: Band 00/Lilac (Collins Big Cat) 2006. (Collins Big Cat Ser.). (ENG., Illus.). 16p. (J). (gr. -1-k). pap. 6.99 *(978-0-00-718645-7(2))* HarperCollins Pubs. Ltd. GBR. Dist: Independent Pubs. Group.
Wilder, Nellie. Changing Weather, 1 vol. rev. ed. 2014. (Science: Informational Text Ser.). (ENG., Illus.). 24p. (J). (gr. -1-1). pap. 9.99 *(978-1-4807-4531-5(6))* Teacher Created Materials, Inc.
—On Land, 1 vol. rev. ed. 2014. (Science: Informational Text Ser.). (ENG., Illus.). 24p. (gr. k-1). pap. 9.99 *(978-1-4807-4532-2(4))* Teacher Created Materials, Inc.
—What Is the Weather?, 1 vol. rev. ed. 2014. (Science: Informational Text Ser.). (ENG., Illus.). 24p. (J). (gr. k-1). pap. 9.99 *(978-1-4807-4530-8(8))* Teacher Created Materials, Inc.
Wilhelm, Hans. No Kisses, Please! 2004. (Hello Reader! Ser.). (Illus.). (J). pap. *(978-0-439-56420-5(4))* Scholastic, Inc.
Wilhelm, Peggy Jo. The 10 Most Innovative Bands. 2008. 14.99 *(978-1-55448-554-3(1))* Scholastic Library Publishing.
Will, Rebel. Who Lives/Twgn/C. 8p. 20.95 *(978-0-322-00347-7(4))* Wright Group/McGraw-Hill.
Willems, Mo. ¡Hoy Volaré!-An Elephant & Piggie Book, Spanish Edition. 2015. (Elephant & Piggie Book Ser.). (ENG., Illus.). 64p. (J). (gr. 1-k). 9.99 *(978-1-4847-2287-9(6)*, Hyperion Books for Children) Disney Publishing Worldwide.
—¡un Tipo Grande Se Llevó Mi Pelota!-An Elephant & Piggie Book, Spanish Edition. 2015. (Elephant & Piggie Book Ser.). (SPA., Illus.). 64p. (J). (gr. 1-k). 9.99 *(978-1-4847-2285-5(X)*, Hyperion Books for Children) Disney Publishing Worldwide.
William H. Sadlier Staff. Nice Vine, Quite Fine, Vol. 2. 2005. (Early Library). (gr. k-2). 24.00 net. *(978-0-8215-8946-5(6))* Sadlier, William H. Inc.
—Niles Likes to Smile, Vol. 2. 2005. (Early Library). (gr. k-2). 24.00 net. *(978-0-8215-8956-4(3))* Sadlier, William H. Inc.
—What Bear Cubs Like to Do. 2005. (Early Library). (gr. k-2). 24.00 net. *(978-0-8215-8953-3(9))* Sadlier, William H. Inc.
—What Do You See by the Sea? 2005. (Emergent Library: Vol. 2). (gr. -1-1). 24.00 net. *(978-0-8215-8922-9(9))* Sadlier, William H. Inc.
—What Does Lucy Like? 2005. (Emergent Library: Vol. 2). (gr. -1-1). 24.00 net. *(978-0-8215-8926-7(1))* Sadlier, William H. Inc.
—What Does Sam Sell? 2005. (Emergent Library: Vol. 1). (gr. -1-1). 24.00 net. *(978-0-8215-8902-1(4))* Sadlier, William H. Inc.
—When Mr Quinn Snored. 2005. (Emergent Library: Vol. 2). (gr. -1-1). 24.00 net. *(978-0-8215-8936-6(9))* Sadlier, William H. Inc.
—Who Can Run Fast? 2005. (Early Library). (gr. k-2). 24.00 net. *(978-0-8215-8940-3(7))* Sadlier, William H. Inc.
—Who Has Four Feet? Big Book. 2005. (Emergent Library: Vol. 1). (gr. -1-1). 24.00 net. *(978-0-8215-8900-7(8))* Sadlier, William H. Inc.
—Who Is My Mom? 2005. (Emergent Library: Vol. 1). (gr. -1-1). 24.00 net. *(978-0-8215-8901-4(6))* Sadlier, William H. Inc.
—Who Works Here? 2005. (Emergent/Early (Prek-2) Social Studies Package Ser.). 12p. (gr. -1-1). 25.20 *(978-0-8215-7833-9(2))* Sadlier, William H. Inc.
—Why Coyote Howls at Night. 2005. (Fluent Library). (gr. 1-3). 29.34 *(978-0-8215-8960-1(1))* Sadlier, William H. Inc.
—Writing a Research Paper: A Student Guide to Writing a Research Paper. 2005. (Writign a Resarch Paper Ser.). (gr. 7-12). stu. ed. 10.00 net. *(978-0-8215-0761-2(3))* Sadlier, William H. Inc.
William Tell: 6 Small Books. (gr. k-2). 23.00 *(978-0-7635-8506-8(8))* Rigby Education.
Williams, Ben. Look Inside: Your Heart & Lungs, 1 vol. 2nd rev. ed. 2011. (TIME for KIDS(r): Informational Text Ser.). (ENG.). 28p. (gr. 2-3). pap. 10.99 *(978-1-4333-3636-2(7))* Teacher Created Materials, Inc.
—Look Inside - Your Brain, 1 vol. 2nd rev. ed. 2011. (TIME for KIDS(r): Informational Text Ser.). (ENG., Illus.). 28p. (gr. 2-3). pap. 10.99 *(978-1-4333-3634-8(0))* Teacher Created Materials, Inc.
—Your Skeleton & Muscles, 1 vol. 2nd rev. ed. 2011. (TIME for KIDS(r): Informational Text Ser.). (ENG.). 28p. (gr. 2-3). pap. 10.99 *(978-1-4333-3635-5(9))* Teacher Created Materials, Inc.
Williams, Brian. People & Places. 2010. (What About... Ser.). (Illus.). 40p. (J). (gr. 6-8). lib. bdg. 19.95 *(978-1-4222-1563-0(6))* Mason Crest.
Williams, Carolea, ed. Ending Consonants Instant Learning Centers, Vol. 2196. 2004. (Illus.). 32p. (J). (gr. k-2). pap. 9.99 *(978-1-59198-056-8(9)*, CTP 2196) Creative Teaching Pr., Inc.
Williams, Laura E. Father Damien. Kofsky, Kristen, illus. 2009. (ENG.). 60p. (J). (gr. 4). pap. *(978-1-59700-757-3(9))* Island Heritage Publishing.
Williams, Rozanne. Here Is My Cat. 2017. (Learn-To-Read Ser.). (ENG., Illus.). (J). pap. 3.49 *(978-1-68310-328-8(9))* Pacific Learning, Inc.
—I Can Read. 2017. (Learn-To-Read Ser.). (ENG., Illus.). (J). pap. 3.49 *(978-1-68310-196-3(0))* Pacific Learning, Inc.
—I Can Write. 2017. (Learn-To-Read Ser.). (ENG., Illus.). (J). pap. 3.49 *(978-1-68310-197-0(9))* Pacific Learning, Inc.
—I Like Colors. 2017. (Learn-To-Read Ser.). (ENG., Illus.). (J). pap. 3.49 *(978-1-68310-321-9(1))* Pacific Learning, Inc.
—Kids Like. 2017. (Learn-To-Read Ser.). (ENG., Illus.). (J). pap. 3.49 *(978-1-68310-325-7(4))* Pacific Learning, Inc.
—The One & Only Special Me. 2017. (Learn-To-Read Ser.). (ENG., Illus.). (J). pap. 3.49 *(978-1-68310-259-5(2))* Pacific Learning, Inc.
—Oranges for Orange Juice. 2017. (Learn-To-Read Ser.). (ENG., Illus.). (J). pap. 3.49 *(978-1-68310-248-9(7))* Pacific Learning, Inc.
—Under the Sky. 2017. (Learn-To-Read Ser.). (ENG., Illus.). (J). pap. 3.49 *(978-1-68310-199-4(5))* Pacific Learning, Inc.
—What Do You See? 2017. (Learn-To-Read Ser.). (ENG., Illus.). (J). pap. 3.49 *(978-1-68310-200-7(2))* Pacific Learning, Inc.
—Who Will Help? 2017. (Learn-To-Read Ser.). (ENG., Illus.). (J). pap. 3.49 *(978-1-68310-210-6(X))* Pacific Learning, Inc.
Williams, Rozanne Lanczak. The Ants & the Grasshopper, Vol. 4262. Adnet, Bernard, illus. 2005. (Reading for Fluency Ser.). 16p. (J). pap. 3.49 *(978-1-59198-162-6(X))* Creative Teaching Pr., Inc.
—Are We There Yet? Leary, Catherine, illus. 2005. (Science Mini Units Ser.). 8p. (J). pap. 2.49 *(978-1-59198-151-0(4)*, 4251) Creative Teaching Pr., Inc.
—The Big Hungry Bear. Hockerman, Dennis, illus. 2005. (Reading for Fluency Ser.). 8p. (J). pap. 3.49 *(978-1-59198-146-6(8)*, 4246) Creative Teaching Pr., Inc.
—Creepy, Crawly Bugs. Harris, Jennifer Beck, illus. 2005. (Reading for Fluency Ser.). 8p. (J). pap. 3.49 *(978-1-59198-149-7(2)*, 4249) Creative Teaching Pr., Inc.
—Fairy Tale Rock. Christensen, David & Leary, Catherine, illus. 2005. (Reading for Fluency Ser.). 16p. (J). pap. 3.49 *(978-1-59198-153-4(0)*, 4252) Creative Teaching Pr., Inc.
—Here Comes Coco. Banta, Susan, illus. 2005. (Reading for Fluency Ser.). 8p. (J). pap. 3.49 *(978-1-59198-145-9(X)*, 4245) Creative Teaching Pr., Inc.
—Hide & Seek Monsters. Dunne, Kathleen, illus. 2005. (Reading for Fluency Ser.). 16p. (J). pap. 3.49 *(978-1-59198-154-1(9)*, 4254) Creative Teaching Pr., Inc.
—How to Make a Friend. Nobens, Cheryl, illus. 2005. (Reading for Fluency Ser.). 16p. (J). pap. 3.49 *(978-1-59198-155-8(7)*, 4255) Creative Teaching Pr., Inc.
—I Love Mud! Twinem, Neecy, illus. 2005. (Reading for Fluency Ser.). 8p. (J). pap. 3.49 *(978-1-59198-141-1(7)*, 4241) Creative Teaching Pr., Inc.
—Look Closer. Vangsgard, Amy, illus. 2005. (Reading for Fluency Ser.). 8p. (J). pap. 3.49 *(978-1-59198-147-3(6)*, 4247) Creative Teaching Pr., Inc.
—The Mouse Who Cried Cat, Vol. 4263. Mahan, Benton, illus. 2005. (Reading for Fluency Ser.). 16p. (J). pap. 3.49 *(978-1-59198-163-3(8)*, 4263) Creative Teaching Pr., Inc.
—My Pink Piggy Bank. Fletcher, Rusty, illus. 2005. (Reading for Fluency Ser.). 8p. (J). pap. 2.49 *(978-1-59198-144-2(1)*, 4244) Creative Teaching Pr., Inc.
—Pirates Coming Through, 24 vols., Vol. 4257. Pamintuan, Macky, illus. 2005. (Reading for Fluency Ser.). 16p. (J). pap. 3.49 *(978-1-59198-157-2(3)*, 4257) Creative Teaching Pr., Inc.
—Slow & Steady Wins the Race, Vol. 4260. Edwards, Karl, illus. 2005. (Reading for Fluency Ser.). 16p. (J). pap. 3.49 *(978-1-59198-158-9(1)*, 4260) Creative Teaching Pr., Inc.
—Space Trip. Burnett, Lindy, illus. 2005. (Reading for Fluency Ser.). 80p. (J). pap. 32.49 *(978-1-59198-142-8(5)*, 4242) Creative Teaching Pr., Inc.
—The Swim Lesson. Burris, Priscilla, illus. 2005. (Reading for Fluency Ser.). 8p. (J). pap. 3.49 *(978-1-59198-148-0(4)*, 4248) Creative Teaching Pr., Inc.
—The Teacher with the Alligator Purse, Vol. 4259. Richard, Ilene, illus. 2005. (Reading for Fluency Ser.). 16p. (J). pap. 3.49 *(978-1-59198-159-6(X))* Creative Teaching Pr., Inc.
—Today Is Somebody's Birthday. Mahan, Benton, illus. 2005. (Reading for Fluency Ser.). 8p. (J). pap. 2.49 *(978-1-59198-140-4(9)*, 4240) Creative Teaching Pr., Inc.
—What Is the Best Pet?, Vol. 4258. Briles, Patty, illus. 2005. 16p. (J). pap. 3.49 *(978-1-59198-160-2(3)*, 4258) Creative Teaching Pr., Inc.
—What's So Bad about the Big Bad Wolf?, 24 vols. Catalano, Dominic, illus. 2005. (Reading for Fluency Ser.). 8p. (J). pap. 2.49 *(978-1-59198-143-5(3)*, 4243) Creative Teaching Pr., Inc.
—You Can't Catch Me. Edwards, Karl, illus. 2005. (Reading for Fluency Ser.). 8p. (J). pap. 3.49 *(978-1-59198-150-3(6)*, 4250) Creative Teaching Pr., Inc.
Williams, Zachary. Lions at the Library?, 1 vol. 2006. (Neighborhood Readers Ser.). (ENG.). 12p. (gr. 1-2). pap. 5.90 *(978-1-4042-6863-0(4)*, 1a815c85-15cd-4245-b8ba-ba6a36b2df1e, Rosen Classroom) Rosen Publishing Group, Inc., The.
—The Lost Nickel, 1 vol. 2006. (Neighborhood Readers Ser.). (ENG.). 8p. (gr. k-1). pap. 5.15 *(978-1-4042-5786-3(1)*, 8da9b16b-c31f-4375-8494-fba9372d20a9, Rosen Classroom) Rosen Publishing Group, Inc., The.
—What Will It Be?, 1 vol. 2006. (Neighborhood Readers Ser.). (ENG.). 16p. (gr. 1-2). pap. 6.50 *(978-1-4042-7252-1(6)*, 589a3ffa-92ad-4067-9f27-3118f0a5895a, Rosen Classroom) Rosen Publishing Group, Inc., The.
Williamson, Jan. A Special Day in May, 1 vol. 2006. (Neighborhood Readers Ser.). (ENG.). 16p. (gr. 1-2). pap. 6.50 *(978-1-4042-7276-7(3)*, d3870e21-710f-4112-8f2f-b452a6bcbc88, Rosen Classroom) Rosen Publishing Group, Inc., The.
Williams, Rozanne Lanczak. Sing & Read with Greg & Steve All-in-One Pack. 2009. pap. 58.86 *(978-1-60689-164-3(2))* Youngheart Music.
Wilson, Anne, illus. My First Box of Books: 1 2 3 Colours Animals, 3 vols. 2016. 72p. (J). (gr. -1-2). bds. 9.99

(978-1-86147-416-2(4), Armadillo) Anness Publishing GBR. Dist: National Bk. Network.

Wilson, CeCe. Micah Learns to Read, 1 vol. 2015. (Rosen REAL Readers: STEM & STEAM Collection). (ENG.). 8p. (gr. k-1). pap. 5.46 *(978-1-4994-9583-6(8)*, 91ba6eb4-6c58-4733-b816-8b6f78d0205d, Rosen Classroom) Rosen Publishing Group, Inc., The.

Wilson, Jacqueline. Monster Eyeballs. Lewis, Stephen, illus. 2nd ed. 2016. (Reading Ladder Level 2 Ser.). (ENG.). 48p. (gr. k-2). pap. 4.99 *(978-1-4052-8199-7(5))* Farshore GBR. Dist: HarperCollins Pubs.

Wilson, Karma & Chapman, Jane. Bear Snores On. 2009. 34p. pap. 8.50 *(978-0-15-352483-7(9))* Harcourt Schl. Pubs.

Wilson, Mike. The Williams Sisters: Venus & Serena. 2005. (ENG., Illus.). 32p. pap. 8.50 *(978-0-340-84876-0(6))* Cambridge Univ. Pr.

Wilson, Zachary. Rookie Ready to Learn en Español: un Circulo en el Cielo. Adinolfi, JoAnn, illus. 2011. (Rookie Ready to Learn Español Ser.). Orig. Title: Rookie Ready to Learn: a Circle in the Sky. (SPA.). 40p. (J). pap. 5.95 *(978-0-531-26791-2(1)*, Children's Pr.) Scholastic Library Publishing.

Wilson, Zachary & Adinolfi, JoAnn. Un Circulo en el Cielo. Adinolfi, JoAnn, illus. 2011. (Rookie Ready to Learn Español Ser.). (SPA., Illus.). 40p. (J). lib. bdg. 23.00 *(978-0-531-26123-1(9)*, Children's Pr.) Scholastic Library Publishing.

The Wind Eagle. (Guided Reading Levels Ser.). 42.96 *(978-0-7362-2143-6(3))* CENGAGE Learning.

The Wind That Would Not Blow. (Early Intervention Levels Ser.). 31.86 *(978-0-7362-0620-4(5))* CENGAGE Learning.

The Wind That Would Not Blow (28), Vol. 28. (Early Intervention Levels Ser.). 5.31 *(978-0-7362-0608-2(6))* CENGAGE Learning.

Windham Ryder & Dorling Kindersley Publishing Staff. Journey Through Space. 2015. (ENG., Illus.). 48p. (J). *(978-0-241-18633-6(1))* Dorling Kindersley Publishing, Inc.

Windsor. Sail Main4 Comets Nf. 2003. (Rigby Sails Ser.). (ENG.). 32p. (gr. 4-4). pap. 9.50 *(978-0-7578-8507-5(1))* Rigby Education.

Windsor, Herbert C. The Colour Monster. 2009. (Illus.). 32p. pap. 12.99 *(978-1-4490-1056-0(3))* AuthorHouse.

Windsor, Jo. A Long Time Ago: Early Level Satellite Individual Title Six-Packs. (Sails Literacy Ser.). 16p. (gr. 1-2). 27.00 *(978-0-7578-3163-8(X))* Rigby Education.

Wings: KinderWords Individual Title Six-Packs. (Kinderstarters Ser.). 8p. (gr. -1-1). 21.00 *(978-0-7635-8691-1(9))* Rigby Education.

Winter, Barbara. Fight for Rights. Kostic, Dimitri, illus. 2007. 48p. (J). lib. bdg. 23.08 *(978-1-4242-1636-9(2))* Fitzgerald Bks.

—The 10 Most Endangered Animals. 2008. 14.99 *(978-1-55448-552-9(5))* Scholastic Library Publishing.

Wise-Douglas, Terri. The Wonderful World of Cupcakes. Duckworth, Jeffrey, illus. 2011. 28p. pap. 24.95 *(978-1-4626-3570-2(9))* America Star Bks.

The Wise Old Woman. (Lexile Levels Ser.). 9.09 *(978-1-56334-747-4(4))* CENGAGE Learning.

Wood, Alexander. Our Jobs, 1 vol. 2008. (Real Life Readers Ser.). (ENG.). 8p. (gr. k-1). pap. 5.15 *(978-1-4042-8011-3(1)*, d78ff607-a695-4028-82a3-483fd12c5bca, Rosen Classroom) Rosen Publishing Group, Inc., The.

Wood, Cary D. Davis & Pop Go Hiking. Turner, Cecilia, illus. 2014. (ENG.). 30p. (gr. -1-4). 34.95 *(978-1-63047-217-7(4))* Morgan James Publishing.

Wood, D. K. Nightmare at Indian Cave. 2006. pap. 10.00 *(978-1-4257-1640-0(7))* Xlibris Corp.

Wood, Ira. The Fourth of July, 1 vol. 2005. (Rosen REAL Readers Ser.). (ENG., Illus.). 12p. (gr. 1-2). pap. 5.90 *(978-0-8239-8199-1(1)*, 006565c1-8d62-46f5-b63e-087133717240) Rosen Publishing Group, Inc., The.

—The Sandcastle, 1 vol. 2006. (Neighborhood Readers Ser.). (ENG.). 16p. (gr. 1-2). pap. 6.50 *(978-1-4042-6986-6(X)*, 46f49bd2-d0e9-4012-a889-d7165e3f25eb, Rosen Classroom) Rosen Publishing Group, Inc., The.

—Water, Ice, & Steam, 1 vol. 2005. (Rosen REAL Readers Ser.). (ENG., Illus.). 12p. (gr. 1-2). pap. 5.90 *(978-0-8239-6353-9(5)*, 19241861-0961-442d-9575-cb4dddcd1adc) Rosen Publishing Group, Inc., The.

Wood, Lisa. The Human Hotel. 2010. 36p. pap. 15.49 *(978-1-4389-7466-8(3))* AuthorHouse.

Woodcock, Sandra, et al. Being a Model. 2005. (ENG., Illus.). 32p. pap. *(978-0-340-74716-2(1))* Cambridge Univ. Pr.

Woods, Barbara. Avenues F (Leveled Books): the Birth of an Island. 2003. (Rise & Shine Ser.). (ENG.). 16p. (C). pap. 11.95 *(978-0-7362-1760-6(6))* CENGAGE Learning.

—Avenues F (Leveled Books): the Birth of an Island, 6-Pack. 2003. (Avenues Ser.). (ENG.). (C). pap. 73.95 *(978-0-7362-2167-2(0))* CENGAGE Learning.

Woods, Lin. Kenny Can: "Don't Judge Me" 2011. (ENG.). 24p. pap. 15.99 *(978-1-4568-9958-5(9))* Xlibris Corp.

Woods, Sadie. I Help at the Store, 1 vol. Aguilera, Aurora, illus. 2017. (Ways I Help Ser.). (ENG.). 24p. (J). (gr. 1-1). pap. 9.25 *(978-1-5081-5678-9(6)*, 0ebb0784-b51a-45fa-af00-2d9f1a0d16f6, PowerKids Pr.) Rosen Publishing Group, Inc., The.

Woolly, Woolly: Individual Title Six-Packs. (Literatura 2000 Ser.). (gr. 1-2). 28.00 *(978-0-7635-0159-4(X))* Rigby Education.

Wordless Story Book: In My Own Words. 2004. (In My Own Words Reproducible Wordless Story Book Ser.). (gr. -1-k). 29.95 *(978-0-673-65205-8(X))* Addison-Wesley Educational Pubs., Inc.

Wordless Story Books: Take-Home Version. 2004. (gr. k-18). 48.00 *(978-0-328-02301-1(9))* Addison-Wesley Educational Pubs., Inc.

Workers: KinderWords Individual Title Six-Packs. (Kinderstarters Ser.). 8p. (gr. -1-1). 21.00 *(978-0-7635-8714-7(1))* Rigby Education.

World of Language Book Set 800930, 5 vols. 2005. (J). pap. *(978-1-59794-094-8(1))* Environments, Inc.

Wright, Craig. Dolphin Readers: Level 1: 275-Word Vocabulary Meet Molly Activity Book. 2010. (ENG., Illus.). 14p. act. bk. ed. 5.00 *(978-0-19-440144-9(8))* Oxford Univ. Pr., Inc.

—Dolphin Readers: Level 2: 425-Word Vocabulary Double Trouble Activity Book. 2010. (ENG., Illus.). 14p. act. bk. ed. 5.00 *(978-0-19-440152-4(9))* Oxford Univ. Pr., Inc.

—Dolphin Readers: Level 2: 425-Word Vocabulary Matt's Mistake Activity Book. 2010. (ENG., Illus.). 14p. act. bk. ed. 5.00 *(978-0-19-440157-9(X))* Oxford Univ. Pr., Inc.

Wright, Craig, ed. Dolphin Readers: Level 3: 525-Word Vocabulary Just Like Mine Activity Book. 2010. (ENG., Illus.). 14p. act. bk. ed. 5.00 *(978-0-19-440164-7(2))* Oxford Univ. Pr., Inc.

—Dolphin Readers: Level 3: 525-Word Vocabulary Let's Go to the Rainforest Activity Book. 2010. (ENG., Illus.). 14p. act. bk. ed. 5.00 *(978-0-19-440167-8(7))* Oxford Univ. Pr., Inc.

—Dolphin Readers: Level 3: 525-Word Vocabulary New Girl in School Activity Book. 2010. (ENG., Illus.). 14p. act. bk. ed. 5.00 *(978-0-19-440162-3(6))* Oxford Univ. Pr., Inc.

—Dolphin Readers: Level 3: 525-Word Vocabulary Students in Space Activity Book. 2010. (ENG., Illus.). 14p. act. bk. ed. 5.00 *(978-0-19-440160-9(X))* Oxford Univ. Pr., Inc.

—Dolphin Readers: Level 3: 525-Word Vocabulary Things That Fly Activity Book. 2010. (ENG., Illus.). 14p. act. bk. ed. 5.00 *(978-0-19-440166-1(9))* Oxford Univ. Pr., Inc.

—Dolphin Readers: Level 3: 525-Word Vocabulary What Did You Do Yesterday? Activity Book. 2010. (ENG., Illus.). 14p. pap., act. bk. ed. 5.00 *(978-0-19-440161-6(8))* Oxford Univ. Pr., Inc.

—Dolphin Readers: Level 4: 625-Word Vocabulary City Girl, Country Boy Activity Book. 2010. (ENG., Illus.). 16p. act. bk. ed. 5.00 *(978-0-19-440173-9(1))* Oxford Univ. Pr., Inc.

—Dolphin Readers: Level 4: 625-Word Vocabulary in the Ocean Activity Book. 2010. (ENG., Illus.). 16p. act. bk. ed. 5.00 *(978-0-19-440174-6(X))* Oxford Univ. Pr., Inc.

—Dolphin Readers: Level 4: 625-Word Vocabulary Yesterday, Today & Tomorrow Activity Book. 2010. (ENG., Illus.). 16p. act. bk. ed. 5.00 *(978-0-19-440169-2(3))* Oxford Univ. Pr., Inc.

—Dolphin Readers: Starter Level: 175-Word Vocabulary My Family Activity Book. 2010. (ENG.). 16p. act. bk. ed. 5.00 *(978-0-19-440138-8(3))* Oxford Univ. Pr., Inc.

Wright Group. Early Emergent Guided Reading. 2nd ed. 2004. (Wright Group Literacy Ser.). (gr. k-18). 423.95 *(978-0-322-04287-2(9))* Wright Group/McGraw-Hill.

Wright, Holly. Sunflower. 2004. (J). *(978-0-9743690-5-1(5))* Britt Allcroft Productions.

Wrighton, Charlene & Bradshaw, Georgine. Basic Kit - Preschool. Clark, Irene, illus. 2005. Orig. Title: Basis Kit I. (J). 249.95 *(978-1-886441-30-9(8))* Zoo-phonics, Inc.

Wu, Nicholas. The Bears' Story by Baldwin B. Bear, 1 vol. rev. ed. 2013. (Literary Text Ser.). (ENG., Illus.). 20p. (gr. 1-2). (J). lib. bdg. 15.96 *(978-1-4807-1147-1(0))*; 7.99 *(978-1-4333-5491-5(8))* Teacher Created Materials, Inc.

—The Princess & the Pea, 1 vol. rev. ed. 2013. (Literary Text Ser.). (ENG., Illus.). 20p. (gr. 1-2). 7.99 *(978-1-4333-5489-2(6))* Teacher Created Materials, Inc.

—The Princess & the Pea: A Retelling of Hans Christian Andersen's Story, 1 vol. rev. ed. 2013. (Literary Text Ser.). (ENG., Illus.). 20p. (J). (gr. 1-2). lib. bdg. 15.96 *(978-1-4807-1145-7(4))* Teacher Created Materials, Inc.

Wuest, Marcia. Twelve Things to Do at Age 12. 2009. (Readers for Teens Ser.). (ENG.). 26p. pap. 14.75 *(978-0-521-73733-3(8))* Cambridge Univ. Pr.

Yeager, Anne H. American Tall Tales. 2017. (Text Connections Guided Close Reading Ser.). (J). (gr. 2). *(978-1-4900-1839-3(5))* Benchmark Education Co.

A Year Without Rain. (Early Intervention Levels Ser.). 21.42 *(978-0-7362-1048-5(2))* CENGAGE Learning.

Yellow Overalls: Individual Title Six-Packs. (Literatura 2000 Ser.). (gr. 2-3). 33.00 *(978-0-7635-0247-8(2))* Rigby Education.

Yellow Umbrella, Early Level. (gr. k-2). 999.95 *(978-0-7368-3056-0(1)*, Capstone Pr.) Capstone.

Yip & Yap: Consonant y: Level A, 6 vols. (Wright Skills Ser.). 12p. (gr. k-3). 17.95 *(978-0-322-03120-3(6))* Wright Group/McGraw-Hill.

Yolen, Jane. How Do Dinosaurs Laugh Out Loud? Teague, Mark, illus. 2010. (ENG.). 14p. (J). (gr. -1-k). bds. 8.99 *(978-0-545-23652-2(5)*, Cartwheel Bks.) Scholastic, Inc.

Yomtov, Nel. Adventures in Science. O'Neill, Sean et al, illus. 2012. (Adventures in Science Ser.). (ENG.). 32p. (gr. 3-4). pap. 190.80 *(978-1-4296-8470-5(4)*, Capstone Pr.) Capstone.

Yoon, Salina. Penguin Gets Ready for Bed! Yoon, Salina, illus. 2010. (Illus.). 10p. bds. 7.95 *(978-1-60747-751-8(3)*, Pickwick Pr.) Phoenix Bks., Inc.

You do ride Well: Individual Title Six-Packs. (gr. 1-2). 25.00 *(978-0-7635-9197-7(1))* Rigby Education.

Young, Caroline, et al, des. First Picture Word Book. 2004. (First Picture Word Book Ser.). (ENG., Illus.). 16p. (J). bds. 11.95 *(978-0-7945-0645-2(3)*, Usborne) EDC Publishing.

Young Eagles Take to the Sky. 2005. (Book Treks Ser.). (J). (gr. 3-18). stu. ed. 34.95 *(978-0-673-62842-8(6))* Celebration Pr.

Young Explorers in Science. (J). 105.00 *(978-0-8136-4363-2(5))* Modern Curriculum Pr.

Young, Judy. Digger et Daisy Vont Au Docteur (Digger & Daisy Go to the Doctor) Sullivan, Dana, illus. 2016. (Digger & Daisy Ser.). (FRE.). 32p. (J). (gr. k-2). 12.95 *(978-1-62753-949-4(2)*, 204172) Sleeping Bear Pr.

—Digger y Daisy Van a la Ciudad (Digger & Daisy Go to the City) Sullivan, Dana, illus. 2016. (Digger & Daisy Ser.). (SPA.). 32p. (J). (gr. k-2). 9.99 *(978-1-62753-954-8(9)*, 204177) Sleeping Bear Pr.

—Digger y Daisy Van Al Médico (Digger & Daisy Go to the Doctor) Sullivan, Dana, illus. 2016. (Digger & Daisy Ser.). (SPA.). 32p. (J). (gr. k-2). 9.99 *(978-1-62753-953-1(0)*, 204176) Sleeping Bear Pr.

—Digger y Daisy Van Al Zoológico (Digger & Daisy Go to the Zoo) Sullivan, Dana, illus. 2016. (Digger & Daisy Ser.). (SPA.). 32p. (J). (gr. k-2). 9.99 *(978-1-62753-951-7(4)*, 204174) Sleeping Bear Pr.

—Digger y Daisy Van de Picnic (Digger & Daisy Go on a Picnic) Sullivan, Dana, illus. 2016. (Digger & Daisy Ser.). (SPA.). 32p. (J). (gr. k-2). 9.99 *(978-1-62753-952-4(2)*, 204175) Sleeping Bear Pr.

—The Missouri Reader. Darnell, K. L., illus. 2010. (State/Country Readers Ser.). (ENG.). 96p. (J). (gr. 1-4). 12.95 *(978-1-58536-437-4(1)*, 202165) Sleeping Bear Pr.

Young Reader Series, 9 bks., Set. (Illus.). (J). (gr. 3-6). lib. bdg. 121.05 *(978-1-56674-914-5(X))* Forest Hse. Publishing Co., Inc.

Yoyo. Learning Words. 2005. 40p. bds. *(978-90-5843-887-4(2))* YoYo Bks.

Yuen, Kevin. The 10 Most Intense College Football Rivalries. 2008. 14.99 *(978-1-55448-545-1(2))* Scholastic Library Publishing.

Yun's Visit: Fourth Grade Guided Comprehension Level K. (On Our Way to English Ser.). (gr. 4-18). 34.50 *(978-0-7578-7146-7(1))* Rigby Education.

Zamosky, Lisa. Fishers Then & Now, 1 vol. rev. ed. 2006. (Social Studies: Informational Text Ser.). (ENG.). 32p. (gr. 2-3). pap. 11.99 *(978-0-7439-9378-4(0))* Teacher Created Materials, Inc.

—Government Leaders Then & Now, 1 vol. rev. ed. 2006. (Social Studies: Informational Text Ser.). (ENG.). 32p. (J). (gr. 2-3). pap. 11.99 *(978-0-7439-9386-9(1))* Teacher Created Materials, Inc.

—Greece, 1 vol. rev. ed. 2007. (Social Studies: Informational Text Ser.). (ENG.). 32p. (J). (gr. 4-8). pap. 11.99 *(978-0-7439-0434-6(6))* Teacher Created Materials, Inc.

—India, 1 vol. rev. ed. 2007. (Social Studies: Informational Text Ser.). (ENG.). 32p. (J). (gr. 4-8). pap. 11.99 *(978-0-7439-0430-8(3))* Teacher Created Materials, Inc.

—Investigating Simple Organisms, 1 vol. rev. ed. 2007. (Science: Informational Text Ser.). (ENG., Illus.). 32p. (gr. 3-6). pap. 12.99 *(978-0-7439-0587-9(3))* Teacher Created Materials, Inc.

—Mansa Musa: Leader of Mali, 1 vol. rev. ed. 2007. (Social Studies: Informational Text Ser.). (ENG.). 32p. (gr. 4-8). pap. 11.99 *(978-0-7439-0439-1(7))* Teacher Created Materials, Inc.

—Sub-Saharan Africa, 1 vol. rev. ed. 2007. (Social Studies: Informational Text Ser.). (ENG.). 32p. (gr. 4-8). pap. 11.99 *(978-0-7439-0438-4(9))* Teacher Created Materials, Inc.

—World War I, 1 vol. rev. ed. 2007. (Social Studies: Informational Text Ser.). (ENG.). 32p. (gr. 4-8). pap. 11.99 *(978-0-7439-0664-7(0))* Teacher Created Materials, Inc.

Zamosky, Lisa & Conklin, Wendy. World War II, 1 vol. rev. ed. 2007. (Social Studies: Informational Text Ser.). (ENG.). 32p. (gr. 4-8). pap. 11.99 *(978-0-7439-0668-5(3))* Teacher Created Materials, Inc.

Zamosky, Lisa & National Geographic Learning Staff. Farmers Then & Now. rev. ed. 2006. (Social Studies: Informational Text Ser.). (ENG., Illus.). 32p. (gr. 2-3). pap. 11.99 *(978-0-7439-9377-7(2))* Teacher Created Materials, Inc.

Zemke, Deborah. The Curse of Einstein's Pencil. 2017. (Bea Garcia Ser.: 2). lib. bdg. 18.40 *(978-0-606-40084-8(2))* Turtleback.

Zepeda, Gwendolyn. I Kick the Ball: Pateo el Balón. Ventura, Gabriela Baeza, tr. Torrecilla, Pablo, illus. 2011. (SPA & ENG.). 32p. (J). (gr. -1-3). 16.95 *(978-1-55885-688-2(9)*, Piñata Books) Arte Publico Pr.

—Maya & Annie on Saturdays & Sundays: Los Sábados y Domingos de Maya y Annie. 2018. (ENG & SPA., Illus.). 32p. (J). (gr. 1-4). 17.95 *(978-1-55885-859-6(8))* Arte Publico Pr.

Zephaniah, Benjamin. Being Cool: Band 10 White/Band 17 Diamond (Collins Big Cat Progress) Bellemare, Paule Trudel, illus. 2014. (Collins Big Cat Progress Ser.). (ENG.). 32p. (J). (gr. 5-6). pap. 10.99 *(978-0-00-751929-3(X))* HarperCollins Pubs. Ltd. GBR. Dist: Independent Pubs. Group.

Zobel, Derek. Bucket Trucks. 2009. (Blastoff! Readers Ser.). (ENG., Illus.). 24p. (J). (gr. k-3). 20.00 *(978-0-531-21707-8(8)*, Children's Pr.) Scholastic Library Publishing.

—Diggers. 2009. (Blastoff! Readers Ser.). (ENG., Illus.). 24p. (J). (gr. k-3). 20.00 *(978-0-531-21708-5(6)*, Children's Pr.) Scholastic Library Publishing.

—F-22 Raptors. 2008. (Torque Ser.). (ENG.). 24p. (J). (gr. 3-7). 20.00 *(978-0-531-21645-3(4)*, Children's Pr.) Scholastic Library Publishing.

Zoehfeld, Kathleen Weidner. Dinosaurs (1 Hardcover/1 CD) 2016. (National Geographic Readers: Pre-Reader Ser.). (ENG.). (J). *(978-1-4301-2110-7(6))* Live Oak Media.

—Dinosaurs (1 Paperback/1 CD) 2016. (National Geographic Readers: Pre-Reader Ser.). (ENG.). (J). pap. *(978-1-4301-2109-1(2))* Live Oak Media.

Zoo-phonics Quick Tests for the Classroom. 2004. cd-rom *(978-1-886441-41-5(3))* Zoo-phonics, Inc.

Zoom In! Level M, 6 vols. 128p. (gr. 2-3). 40.50 *(978-0-7699-1032-1(7))* Shortland Pubns. (U. S. A.) Inc.

The Zoomer: KinderWords Individual Title Six-Packs. (Kinderstarters Ser.). 8p. (gr. -1-1). 21.00 *(978-0-7635-8709-3(5))* Rigby Education.

Zora, Subhi. The House of Wisdom: Level 11. 2019. (Collins Big Cat Arabic Ser.). (ENG.). 24p. (J). (gr. 3-6). pap. 7.99 *(978-0-00-830499-7(8))* HarperCollins Pubs. Ltd. GBR. Dist: Independent Pubs. Group.

Zorzi, Gina & Sánchez, Lucía M. Desiertos: This Is a Desert. 2012. (2G Ecosistemas Ser.). (SPA.). 36p. (J). (gr. k-2). pap. 9.60 *(978-1-61541-424-6(X))* American Reading Co.

1 Potato, 2 Potato: Individual Title Six-Packs. (Literatura 2000 Ser.). (gr. 2-3). 33.00 *(978-0-7635-0266-9(9))* Rigby Education.

21st Century Debates, 24 bks. 2004. 650.88 *(978-0-7398-6472-2(6))* Harcourt Schl. Pubs.

READING

Here are entered books on methods of teaching reading and general books on the art of reading. Works on teaching retarded readers are entered under Reading—Remedial Teaching. books on the cultural aspects of reading and general discussions of books to read are entered under Books and Reading.

see also Books and Reading

Acid Rain: Level M, 6 vols. (Wonder Worldtm Ser.). 16p. 34.95 *(978-0-7802-2887-0(1))* Wright Group/McGraw-Hill.

Action Sports, 12 vols. 2005. (Action Sports Ser.). (Illus.). 32p. (gr. 4-6). 308.00 *(978-0-7910-7532-6(X)*, Facts On File) Infobase Holdings, Inc.

Adding English/ESL Support. 2004. (Scott Foresman Reading Ser.). (gr. 2-18). 109.15 *(978-0-328-03065-1(1))*; (gr. 3-18). 109.50 *(978-0-328-03066-8(X))*; (gr. 4-18). 109.50 *(978-0-328-03067-5(8))*; (gr. 5-18). 109.50 *(978-0-328-03068-2(6))* Addison-Wesley Educational Pubs., Inc.

The Adventures of Tutankhamen: Level T. Group 2, 6 vols. (Sunshine Ser.). 48p. 44.95 *(978-0-7802-4175-6(4))* Wright Group/McGraw-Hill.

Afflerbach, Peter. Seeing Is Believing. l.t. ed. 2004. (gr. 4-18). 70.40 *(978-0-328-03937-1(3)*, Scott Foresman) Addison-Wesley Educational Pubs., Inc.

After the Dinosaurs: Level P, 6 vols. (Wonder Worldtm Ser.). 48p. 39.95 *(978-0-7802-7084-8(3))* Wright Group/McGraw-Hill.

Against the Odds, 6 vols. (Wildcats Ser.). 32p. (gr. 2-8). *(978-0-322-02443-4(9))* Wright Group/McGraw-Hill.

Alien Monchers: Level 4, 6 vols. (Fluency Strand Ser.). (gr. 4-8). 45.00 *(978-1-4045-1222-1(5))* Wright Group/McGraw-Hill.

All about Ants, 6 vols. (Book2WebTM Ser.). (gr. 4-8). 36.50 *(978-0-322-02977-4(5))* Wright Group/McGraw-Hill.

All about Maps: Level R, 6 vols. (Wonder Worldtm Ser.). 48p. 44.95 *(978-0-7802-7074-9(6))* Wright Group/McGraw-Hill.

All Kinds of Bears, 6 vols. (Book2WebTM Ser.). (gr. 4-8). 36.50 *(978-0-322-02972-9(4))* Wright Group/McGraw-Hill.

All Through the Year, 6 vols. (Multicultural Programs Ser.). 16p. (gr. 1-3). 24.95 *(978-0-7802-9202-4(2))* Wright Group/McGraw-Hill.

Alligator Alley, 6 vols., Vol. 3. (Woodland Mysteriestm Ser.). 133p. (gr. 3-7). 42.50 *(978-0-322-02372-7(6))* Wright Group/McGraw-Hill.

Alliteration Configuration. 2006. (Illus.). 60p. (J). 24.99 *(978-0-9790434-0-6(9))* Jamiram Publishing.

Amaze Us!, 6 vols. (Wildcats Ser.). 32p. (gr. 2-8). *(978-0-322-02442-7(0))* Wright Group/McGraw-Hill.

Amazing Maps: Level Q, 6 vols. (Wonder Worldtm Ser.). 48p. 39.95 *(978-0-7802-2945-7(2))* Wright Group/McGraw-Hill.

American Literature. 2004. (gr. 11-18). cd-rom *(978-0-618-30390-8(1)*, 2-04295) Holt McDougal.

American Literature: EEdition Plus Online (1 Year License) 2004. (gr. 11-18). *(978-0-618-31043-2(6)*, 2-04463) Holt McDougal.

American Literature: EEdition Plus Online (6 Year License) 2004. (gr. 11-18). *(978-0-618-30836-1(9)*, 2-04342) Holt McDougal.

American Literature: The InterActive Reader Plus. 2004. (Language of Literature Ser.). (gr. 11-18). *(978-0-618-30990-0(X)*, 2-04430) Holt McDougal.

American Literature: The InterActive Reader Plus for English Learners. 2004. (gr. 11-18). *(978-0-618-31022-7(3)*, 2-04444) Holt McDougal.

American Literature: The InterActive Reader Plus with Additional Support. 2004. (Language of Literature Ser.). (gr. 11-18). *(978-0-618-31007-4(X)*, 2-04437) Holt McDougal.

And I Mean It, Stanley. 2003. 22.95 *(978-0-673-75905-4(9))* Celebration Pr.

Anderson, Neil J. Active Skills for Reading, Bk. 3. pap. 31.95 *(978-0-8384-7048-0(3))* Cengage Heinle.

Angela's Ashes: Response Journal. 2003. 40p. (YA). *(978-1-58049-991-0(0)*, RJ91) Prestwick Hse., Inc.

Animal Sounds: Big Book: Level C. (Visions Ser.). 8p. 20.95 *(978-0-322-00308-8(3))* Wright Group/McGraw-Hill.

Animal Tracks: Level C, 6 vols. (Wonder Worldtm Ser.). 16p. 24.95 *(978-0-7802-1211-4(8))* Wright Group/McGraw-Hill.

Animals Grow: Level J. (Wonder Worldtm Ser.). 16p. 26.50 *(978-0-7802-3472-7(3))*; 29.95 *(978-0-7802-1191-9(X))* Wright Group/McGraw-Hill.

The Ants & the Grasshopper: R-Controlled Review: Level C, 6 vols. (Wright Skills Ser.). 16p. (gr. k-3). 26.50 *(978-0-322-01501-2(4))* Wright Group/McGraw-Hill.

Appleton-Smith, Laura & Blackaby, Susan. Butterfly Life Cycle. 2014. (Book to Remember Ser.). (ENG., Illus.). 26p. (J). pap. 8.95 *(978-1-60541-153-8(1)*, Books To Remember) Flyleaf Publishing.

Appointment with Action: 6 Each of 1 Anthology, 6 vols. (Wildcats Ser.). 32p. (gr. 2-8). *(978-0-322-00597-6(3))* Wright Group/McGraw-Hill.

Are they here Yet? Short Vowel e: Level A, 6 vols. (Wright Skills Ser.). 12p. (gr. k-3). 17.95 *(978-0-322-03121-0(4))* Wright Group/McGraw-Hill.

Are You a Ladybug?, 6 vols. (Sunshinetm Ser.). 16p. (gr. k-18). 29.50 *(978-0-7802-5430-5(9))* Wright Group/McGraw-Hill.

Around the World in Eighty Days: Response Journal. 2003. 40p. (YA). *(978-1-58049-987-3(2)*, RJ87) Prestwick Hse., Inc.

Ashton, Christine. The Genie of the Bike Lamp: Level P, 6 vols. (Mountain Peaks Ser.). 128p. (gr. 6-18). 36.95 *(978-0-322-05892-7(9))* Wright Group/McGraw-Hill.

At Camp with Gramps: Final Blends -mp, -st: Level B, 6 vols. (Wright Skills Ser.). 16p. (gr. k-3). 17.95 *(978-0-322-01463-3(8))* Wright Group/McGraw-Hill.

Au, Kathryn. Super Qar for Test-Wise Students: Grade 8 5-Pack, 5 vols. (gr. 1-8). 36.95 *(978-0-322-09115-3(2))* Wright Group/McGraw-Hill.

—Super Qar for Test-Wise Students: Grade 8 Kit. (gr. 1-8). 264.95 *(978-0-322-09222-8(1))* Wright Group/McGraw-Hill.

Au, Kathryn & Raphael, Taffy. Super QAR for Test-Wise Students: Grade 6, Student Activity 5-Pack, 5 vols. (ENG.). (gr. 1-8). pap. 36.95 *(978-0-322-09113-9(6))* Wright Group/McGraw-Hill.

—Super QAR for Test-Wise Students: Grade 7, Student Activity 5-Pack, 5 vols. (ENG.). (gr. 1-8). pap. 36.95 *(978-0-322-09114-6(4))* Wright Group/McGraw-Hill.

Auntie Dot's Pot, 6 vols. 8p. (gr. k-1). 21.50 *(978-0-322-02082-5(4))* Wright Group/McGraw-Hill.

Auntie Jan's Plan, 6 vols. 8p. (gr. k-1). 21.50 *(978-0-322-02084-9(0))* Wright Group/McGraw-Hill.

Baby Animals at Home: Level F. 16p. 31.50 *(978-0-322-00372-9(5))* Wright Group/McGraw-Hill.

A Bad Job? Consonant b: Level A, 6 vols. (Wright Skills Ser.). 12p. (gr. k-3). 17.95 *(978-0-322-03113-5(3))* Wright Group/McGraw-Hill.

Barlow, Helen. Easy Read with Grandma Read: Book 1, Stage 3. 2009. (Illus.). 48p. pap. *(978-1-84748-507-6(3))* Athena Pr.

Barney's Horse. 2003. 22.95 *(978-0-673-75907-8(5))* Celebration Pr.

The Baseball Heroes, 6 vols. (Woodland Mysteriestm Ser.). 133p. (gr. 3-7). 42.50 *(978-0-7802-7931-5(X))* Wright Group/McGraw-Hill.

A Basket Full of Surprises: Take-Home Book. 2005. (Emergent Library: Vol. 2). (J). (gr. -1-1). 12.60 *(978-0-8215-7255-9(5))* Sadlier, William H. Inc.

Basketball: Level A, 6 vols. (Wonder Worldtm Ser.). 16p. 24.95 *(978-0-7802-1029-5(8))* Wright Group/McGraw-Hill.

Bath Time: Level A, 6 vols. (Wonder Worldtm Ser.). 16p. 24.95 *(978-0-7802-1195-7(2))* Wright Group/McGraw-Hill.

The Battle of Bowling Street: Level 4, 6 vols. (Fluency Strand Ser.). (gr. 4-8). 45.00 *(978-1-4045-1224-5(1))* Wright Group/McGraw-Hill.

Be a Plant Scientist: Level L, 6 vols. (Take-Twostm Ser.). 16p. 36.95 *(978-0-322-03403-7(5))* Wright Group/McGraw-Hill.

Be Quiet!, 6 Packs. (Chiquilibros Ser.). (gr. k-1). 23.00 *(978-0-7635-0429-8(7))* Rigby Education.

Bearport Publishing. Wildlife Watchers. 2018. (ENG.). 24p. (J). (gr. -1-2). 31.80 *(978-1-78856-077-1(9))* Bearport Publishing Co., Inc.

Beautiful Flowers: Level B, 6 vols. (Wonder Worldtm Ser.). 16p. 24.95 *(978-0-7802-1980-9(5))* Wright Group/McGraw-Hill.

Beck, Isabel L., et al. Julian's Glorious Summer. 2003. (Trophies Ser.). (gr. 3-18). 50.40 *(978-0-15-319277-7(1))* Harcourt Schl. Pubs.

The Bee & the Bug, 6 vols. 8p. (gr. k-1). 21.50 *(978-0-322-02076-4(X))* Wright Group/McGraw-Hill.

The Bee Sting: Digraphs -ck, -ng: Level B, 6 vols. (Wright Skills Ser.). 16p. (gr. k-3). 17.95 *(978-0-322-01476-3(X))* Wright Group/McGraw-Hill.

Behind the Rocks: Level E, 6 vols. (Wonder Worldtm Ser.). 16p. 24.95 *(978-0-7802-1030-1(1))* Wright Group/McGraw-Hill.

Bell, Megan. Brody the Reading Tutor. 2013. 34p. 16.95 *(978-0-9889775-0-1(8))* Bell, Megan.

Benchmark Education Co., LLC. Up in the Sky Big Book. 2014. (Shared Reading Foundations Ser.). (J). (gr. -1). *(978-1-4509-9446-0(6))* Benchmark Education Co.

—We Need a Seed Big Book. 2014. (Shared Reading Foundations Ser.). (J). (gr. -1). *(978-1-4509-9449-1(0))* Benchmark Education Co.

—What Can We Share? Big Book. 2014. (Shared Reading Foundations Ser.). (J). (gr. -1). *(978-1-4509-9424-8(5))* Benchmark Education Co.

—What Do Bears Eat? Big Book. 2014. (Shared Reading Foundations Ser.). (J). (gr. -1). *(978-1-4509-9433-0(4))* Benchmark Education Co.

—What Is That Sound? Big Book. 2014. (Shared Reading Foundations Ser.). (J). (gr. -1). *(978-1-4509-9437-8(7))* Benchmark Education Co.

Benchmark Education Company, LLC Staff. SpiralUp Reading Passages. 2009. (SpiralUp Phonics Ser.). (J). cd-rom *(978-1-4108-8534-0(8))* Benchmark Education Co.

Benchmark Education Company, LLC Staff, compiled by. Comprehension Strategy Posters. 2008. (Comprehension Strategy Posters Ser.). (J). (gr. 3-5). 199.00 *(978-1-4108-8451-0(1))* Benchmark Education Co.

Bennett-Armistead, V. Susan, et al. Beyond Bedtime Stories, 2nd Edition. 2nd ed. 2014. (ENG., Illus.). 224p. pap. 23.99 *(978-0-545-65530-9(7)*, Teaching Resources) Scholastic, Inc.

The Best Children in the World: Big Book: Level H, Group 1. (Story Box Ser.). 16p. 31.50 *(978-0-322-00324-8(5))* Wright Group/McGraw-Hill.

Betty Bline, 6 vols. 8p. (gr. k-1). 21.50 *(978-0-322-02069-6(7))* Wright Group/McGraw-Hill.

Between the Tides: Level F, 6 vols. (Wonder Worldtm Ser.). 16p. 29.95 *(978-0-7802-1982-3(1))* Wright Group/McGraw-Hill.

Bevan, Clare. The Great Big Book of Reading Kindergarten Costco. 2008. (J). pap. *(978-1-59566-622-2(2))* QEB Publishing Inc.

Beyond the Beyond, 6 vols. (Wildcats Ser.). 32p. (gr. 2-8). *(978-0-322-02444-1(7))* Wright Group/McGraw-Hill.

Bickel, Karla. The Reading Machine. Bickel, Karla, illus. I.t. ed. 2004. (Illus.). 16p. (J). (gr. -1-6). pap. 5.00 *(978-1-891452-15-4(0)*, 9) Heart Arbor Bks.

Big & Green: Level A, 6 vols. (Wonder Worldtm Ser.). 16p. 24.95 *(978-0-7802-1031-8(X))* Wright Group/McGraw-Hill.

Big & Little: Level C, Group 1. (Sunshine Ser.). 8p. 20.95 *(978-0-7802-5720-7(0))* Wright Group/McGraw-Hill.

The Big Bigfoot Debate. 2004. (Literacy Think-Togethers Ser.). 16-24p. (gr. 2-3). pap. 39.50 *(978-0-322-06381-5(7))* Wright Group/McGraw-Hill.

Big Blank Piece of Paper. (J). (gr. 2). pap. 12.79 *(978-0-673-80022-0(9)*, Scott Foresman) Addison Wesley Schl.

Big Enough: Level F. (Visions Ser.). 8p. 20.95 *(978-0-322-00312-5(1))* Wright Group/McGraw-Hill.

The Big, Fun Hat: Review of Consonants, Short Vowels, Word Families: Level A, 6 vols. (Wright Skills Ser.). 12p. (gr. k-3). 17.95 *(978-0-322-03125-8(7))* Wright Group/McGraw-Hill.

The Big Round Up: Big Book: Level I. (Wonder Worldtm Ser.). 16p. 26.50 *(978-0-7802-3477-2(4))* Wright Group/McGraw-Hill.

The Big Roundup: Level I, 6 vols. (Wonder Worldtm Ser.). 16p. 29.95 *(978-0-7802-1245-9(2))* Wright Group/McGraw-Hill.

The Big Tan Rat: Short Vowel Word Family Review: Level B, 6 vols. (Wright Skills Ser.). 16p. (gr. k-3). 17.95 *(978-0-322-01458-9(1))* Wright Group/McGraw-Hill.

A Bigger Barger: Level I, Group 1. (Story Box Ser.). 16p. 31.50 *(978-0-322-02464-9(1))* Wright Group/McGraw-Hill.

Bilingual Take-Home Books Collection. 2005. (YA). (gr. -1-1). 113.40 *(978-0-8215-1209-8(9))* Sadlier, William H. Inc.

Billy Drake's Cake, 6 vols. 8p. (gr. k-1). 21.50 *(978-0-322-02085-6(9))* Wright Group/McGraw-Hill.

Bird Beaks: Big Book: Level K. (Wonder Worldtm Ser.). 16p. 26.50 *(978-0-7802-3473-4(1))* Wright Group/McGraw-Hill.

Bird Beaks: Level K, 6 vols. (Wonder Worldtm Ser.). 16p. 34.95 *(978-0-7802-1197-1(9))* Wright Group/McGraw-Hill.

Blachowicz, Camille L. Z. Reading Fluency: Reader, Level C. 2003. (JT: READING RATE & FLUENCY Ser.). (ENG.). 80p. (gr. 6-12). spiral bd. 29.20 *(978-0-07-830908-3(5)*, 0078309085) McGraw-Hill Education.

—Reading Fluency: Reader, Level D. 2003. (JT: READING RATE & FLUENCY Ser.). (ENG.). 74p. (gr. 6-12). pap. 29.20 *(978-0-07-830909-0(3)*, 0078309093) McGraw-Hill Education.

—Reading Fluency: Reader, Level E. 2003. (JT: READING RATE & FLUENCY Ser.). (ENG.). 74p. (gr. 6-12). pap. 29.20 *(978-0-07-830910-6(7)*, 0078309107) McGraw-Hill Education.

—Reading Fluency: Reader, Level F. 2003. (JT: READING RATE & FLUENCY Ser.). (ENG.). 80p. (gr. 6-12). spiral bd. 29.20 *(978-0-07-830911-3(5)*, 0078309115) McGraw-Hill Education.

—Reading Fluency: Reader, Level H. 2003. (JT: READING RATE & FLUENCY Ser.). (ENG.). 80p. (gr. 6-12). spiral bd. 29.20 *(978-0-07-845698-5(3)*, 0078456983) McGraw-Hill Education.

—Reading Fluency: Reader, Level I. 2003. (JT: READING RATE & FLUENCY Ser.). (ENG.). 74p. (gr. 6-12). spiral bd. 29.20 *(978-0-07-845699-2(1)*, 0078456991) McGraw-Hill Education.

—Reading Fluency, Reader's Record, Level C. 2003. (JT: READING RATE & FLUENCY Ser.). (ENG.). 160p. (gr. 6-12). per. 20.20 *(978-0-07-845700-5(9)*, 0078457009) McGraw-Hill Education.

—Reading Fluency, Reader's Record, Level E. 2003. (JT: READING RATE & FLUENCY Ser.). (ENG.). 160p. (gr. 6-12). per. 20.20 *(978-0-07-845702-9(5)*, 0078457025) McGraw-Hill Education.

—Reading Fluency, Reader's Record, Level H' 2003. (JT: READING RATE & FLUENCY Ser.). (ENG.). 160p. (gr. 6-12). per. 20.20 *(978-0-07-845705-0(X)*, 007845705X) McGraw-Hill Education.

—Reading Fluency, Reader's Record, Level I' 2003. (JT: READING RATE & FLUENCY Ser.). (ENG.). 160p. (gr. 6-12). per. 20.20 *(978-0-07-845706-7(8)*, 0078457068) McGraw-Hill Education.

Blanche, Lynn. What Makes It Go? 2004. (ENG., Illus.). 8p. (J). (gr. k-k). pap. 7.56 *(978-0-7652-5138-1(8)*, Celebration Pr.) Savvas Learning Co.

The Blue Fruit Pie: Digraphs ie, ue: Level B, 6 vols. (Wright Skills Ser.). 16p. (gr. k-3). 17.95 *(978-0-322-01481-7(6))* Wright Group/McGraw-Hill.

Bobby Fling, 6 vols. 8p. (gr. k-1). 21.50 *(978-0-322-02068-9(9))* Wright Group/McGraw-Hill.

Boehm, Richard G., et al. Reading Support & Test Preparation: A Child's Place. 2003. (Harcourt Brace Social Studies). (gr. k-7). 27.00 *(978-0-15-312374-0(5))* Harcourt Schl. Pubs.

Boggywooga: Level I, Group 1. (Sunshine Ser.). 16p. 31.50 *(978-0-7802-5754-2(5))* Wright Group/McGraw-Hill.

Bogle's Feet: Level L, Group 1, 6 vols. (Sunshine Ser.). 16p. 36.50 *(978-0-7802-5790-0(1))* Wright Group/McGraw-Hill.

Bonnell, Kris. Clouds Tell the Weather. 2007. (J). pap. 5.95 *(978-1-933727-47-9(0))* Reading Reading Bks., LLC.

—A Friend for Jellyfish. 2006. (J). pap. 3.95 *(978-1-933727-28-8(4))* Reading Reading Bks., LLC.

—A Garden Is Fun. 2006. (J). pap. 5.95 *(978-1-933727-37-0(3))* Reading Reading Bks., LLC.

—A House for Squirrel. 2007. (J). pap. 5.95 *(978-1-933727-46-2(2))* Reading Reading Bks., LLC.

—A Walk with Dad. 2006. (J). pap. 5.95 *(978-1-933727-43-1(8))* Reading Reading Bks., LLC.

Book Treks Add-on Pack, Vol. 4. 2005. (Book Treks Ser.). (J). (gr. 4-8). 100.95 *(978-0-673-61956-3(7))* Modern Curriculum Pr.

Books Only Package. 2005. (Little Celebrations Picture/Text & Literacy Cards Ser.). (J). (gr. k-3). 510.95 *(978-0-673-77194-0(6))*; 633.50 *(978-0-673-77865-9(7))*; 551.95 *(978-0-673-77195-7(4))* Celebration Pr.

A Bottle Garden: Level F, 6 vols. (Wonder Worldtm Ser.). 16p. 29.95 *(978-0-7802-1984-7(8))* Wright Group/McGraw-Hill.

Boyd, Amanda. A Trip Around Town: Learning to Add 3 One-Digit Numbers, 1 vol. 2010. (Math for the REAL World Ser.). (ENG.). 12p. (gr. 1-2). pap. 5.90 *(978-0-8239-8915-7(1)*, 019ed2b9-f7a9-44ab-93d6-9f285dc36ec3, Rosen Classroom) Rosen Publishing Group, Inc., The.

Bozo: Level I, 6 vols. (Wonder Worldtm Ser.). 16p. 29.95 *(978-0-7802-4561-7(X))* Wright Group/McGraw-Hill.

Braun, Cheskel. Learn to Read, Vol. 1. 2006. (YID.). (J). per. 12.00 *(978-0-9774302-0-8(0))* Braun Pubns.

Bread Sets: 1 Each of 3 Big Books. (Sunshinetm Science Ser.). (gr. 1-2). 111.50 *(978-0-7802-2808-5(1))* Wright Group/McGraw-Hill.

Bread Sets: 1 Each of 3 Student Books. (Sunshinetm Science Ser.). (gr. 1-2). 20.95 *(978-0-7802-2809-2(X))* Wright Group/McGraw-Hill.

The Bridge: Level B, Group 2. (Story Box Ser.). 8p. 20.95 *(978-0-7802-9364-9(9))* Wright Group/McGraw-Hill.

Bridge, Chris. Read to Me! 2015. (ENG., Illus.). 32p. (J). 19.95 *(978-1-931721-12-7(2)*, a2ebedd7-39ca-4a7c-8d26-4ff2ace0fea1) Night Heron Media.

Bridges: 6 Each of 1 Anthology, 6 vols. (Wildcats Ser.). 32p. (gr. 2-8). *(978-0-322-02425-0(0))* Wright Group/McGraw-Hill.

Bridges-Across the Gap: Level O, 6 vols. (Wonder Worldtm Ser.). 48p. 39.95 *(978-0-7802-2963-1(0))* Wright Group/McGraw-Hill.

Bright & Beyond - Reading. 2004. (J). *(978-0-9726170-8-6(6))* Pal Toys, LLC.

Brocker, Susan. Across the Oregon Trail: Level R, 6 vols. (Mountain Peaks Ser.). 128p. (gr. 6-18). 36.95 *(978-0-322-05890-3(2))* Wright Group/McGraw-Hill.

Broken Bones, 6 vols. (Sunshinetm Science Ser.). 24p. (gr. 1-2). 31.50 *(978-0-7802-0300-6(3))*; 36.95 *(978-0-7802-0551-2(0))* Wright Group/McGraw-Hill.

Brooks, Bearl. Jumbo Reading Yearbook: Kindergarten. (Jumbo Reading Ser.). 96p. (J). 15.95 *(978-0-8209-0011-7(7)*, B-JECR-R) ESP, Inc.

Brotherly Love Little Book: Early Reading Fluency, Level A. 2004. (ENG.). pap. 6.00 *(978-0-7398-8158-3(2))* Steck-Vaughn.

Bryan, Lynn. Where Do Plants Grow? 2004. (ENG., Illus.). 8p. (J). (gr. k-k). pap. 7.56 *(978-0-7652-5145-9(0)*, Celebration Pr.) Savvas Learning Co.

Bryant, Sheree, et al. The Glencoe Reader World Literature. 2003. (Glencoe Literature Grade 7 Ser.). (ENG., Illus.). 300p. (gr. 10-12). stu. ed., per. 8.92 *(978-0-07-845934-4(6)*, 0078459346) McGraw-Hill Higher Education.

A Bug in a Rug: Consonants c, l, r; Short Vowel u word families: Level A, 6 vols. (Wright Skills Ser.). 12p. (gr. k-3). 17.95 *(978-0-322-01452-7(2))* Wright Group/McGraw-Hill.

Bug-Watching: Big Book: Level B, 6 vols. 8p. 20.95 *(978-0-7802-9744-9(X))* Wright Group/McGraw-Hill.

Building Dreams, Grade 3: American Readers. (J). tchr. ed., wbk. ed. *(978-0-669-05019-6(9))*; wbk. ed. *(978-0-669-05018-9(0))* Houghton Mifflin Harcourt School Pubs.

Building Dreams Reading Kit: American Readers. (J). (gr. 3). *(978-0-669-05026-4(1))* Houghton Mifflin Harcourt School Pubs.

Building Things, 6 vols. (Sunshinetm Ser.). 16p. (gr. k-18). 29.50 *(978-0-7802-5420-6(1))* Wright Group/McGraw-Hill.

Built for Speed Classroom Library. (gr. 4-18). lib. bdg. 24.95 *(978-0-7368-8949-0(3)*, Red Brick Learning) Capstone.

Bump! Bump! Bump!, 6 vols. 8p. (gr. k-1). 21.50 *(978-0-322-02086-3(7))* Wright Group/McGraw-Hill.

The Burglars' Ball: Level Q, 6 vols. (Wonder Worldtm Ser.). 48p. 39.95 *(978-0-7802-2961-7(4))* Wright Group/McGraw-Hill.

The Bush Telegraph: Level T, Group 2, 6 vols. (Sunshine Ser.). 48p. 44.95 *(978-0-7802-4178-7(9))* Wright Group/McGraw-Hill.

Buster: Level E. 8p. 20.95 *(978-0-7802-9742-5(3))* Wright Group/McGraw-Hill.

Buster McCluster: Level G. (Wonder Worldtm Ser.). 16p. 26.50 *(978-0-7802-2828-3(6))* Wright Group/McGraw-Hill.

Busy Bees: 1 Big Book, 6 Each of 1 Student Book, & 1 Cassette. (Song Box Ser.). (gr. 1-2). 68.95 *(978-0-7802-3203-7(8))* Wright Group/McGraw-Hill.

Butler, Heather, ed. Reading for Fluency Resource Guide: Learning to Read Text Accurately & Quickly. 2005. (Reading for Fluency Ser.). (Illus.). 64p. (J). pap. 12.99 *(978-1-59198-166-4(2)*, 4239) Creative Teaching Pr., Inc.

The Buzz in the Box: Consonant z: Level A, 6 vols. (Wright Skills Ser.). 12p. (gr. k-3). 17.95 *(978-0-322-03124-1(9))* Wright Group/McGraw-Hill.

Buzzing Flies: Level C, Group 1. (Sunshine Ser.). 8p. 20.95 *(978-0-7802-5721-4(9))* Wright Group/McGraw-Hill.

By the Pond: Open Vowel Pattern, Words Ending in y with Long i Sound, Ending in o, Ending in e: Level B, 6 vols. (Wright Skills Ser.). 16p. (gr. k-3). 26.50 *(978-0-322-01470-1(0))* Wright Group/McGraw-Hill.

Can I have a Cat? Consonant c: Level A, 6 vols. (Wright Skills Ser.). 12p. (gr. k-3). 17.95 *(978-0-322-03117-3(6))* Wright Group/McGraw-Hill.

Can Kim & Kip Play? Consonant k: Level A, 6 vols. (Wright Skills Ser.). 12p. (gr. k-3). 17.95 *(978-0-322-03132-6(X))* Wright Group/McGraw-Hill.

Carbo Recorded Books: Primary/Intermediate. 2003. (Illus.). (J). (gr. 2-5). pap. 729.00 incl. audio *(978-1-883186-30-2(7)*, NPIS9) National Reading Styles Institute, Inc.

Carson-Dellosa Publishing Staff. Reading Comprehension, Grade 3. 2010. (Home Workbooks Ser.: 16). (ENG.). 64p. (gr. 3-3). pap. 4.49 *(978-1-60418-800-4(6)*, 104369) Carson-Dellosa Publishing, LLC.

Carson, J. You Can Do It! Learning the Y Sound. 2009. (PowerPhonics Ser.). 24p. (gr. 1-1). 39.90 *(978-1-60851-481-6(1)*, PowerKids Pr.) Rosen Publishing Group, Inc., The.

Castellano Boyum, Marie. More Simply Super Storytimes: Programming Ideas for Ages 3-6. 2006. (Illus.). 172p. (J). (gr. -1-1). per. 16.95 *(978-1-932146-29-5(6)*, Upstart Bks.) Highsmith Inc.

Catching Glimpses: American Readers. (J). (gr. 3). *(978-0-669-05027-1(X))*; *(978-0-669-05028-8(8))*; wbk. ed. *(978-0-669-05032-5(6))* Houghton Mifflin Harcourt School Pubs.

Cats: Level F, 6 vols. (Wonder Worldtm Ser.). 16p. 29.95 *(978-0-7802-2889-4(8))* Wright Group/McGraw-Hill.

A Cat's Day: Level A, 6 vols. 8p. 20.95 *(978-0-322-00356-9(3))* Wright Group/McGraw-Hill.

Celebrate Reading! (J). pap., stu. ed. 21.29 *(978-0-673-80011-4(3))*; (J). (gr. 1). pap., stu. ed. 21.29 *(978-0-673-80014-5(8))*; (J). (gr. 1). pap., stu. ed. 21.29 *(978-0-673-80013-8(X))*; (J). (gr. 1). pap., stu. ed. 21.29 *(978-0-673-80012-1(1))*; (J). (gr. 1). pap., stu. ed. 21.29 *(978-0-673-80015-2(6))*; (J). (gr. 1). pap., stu. ed. 21.29 *(978-0-673-80016-9(4))*; (J). (gr. 2). pap., stu. ed. 12.79 *(978-0-673-80021-3(0))*;Bk. C. (J). (gr. 2). pap., stu. ed. 12.79 *(978-0-673-80023-7(7))*;Bk. C. (J). (gr. 3). pap., stu. ed. 13.73 *(978-0-673-80033-6(4))*;Bk. C. (J). (gr. 4). pap., stu. ed. 8.98 *(978-0-673-80043-5(1))*;Bk. C. (J). (gr. 5). pap., stu. ed. 8.98 *(978-0-673-80053-4(9))*;Bk. C. (J). (gr. 5). pap., stu. ed. 8.98 *(978-0-673-80063-3(6))*;Bk. C. (YA). (gr. 7). pap., stu. ed. 14.71 *(978-0-673-80075-6(X))*;Bk. D. (J). (gr. 2). pap., stu. ed. 12.79 *(978-0-673-80024-4(5))*;Bk. D. (J). (gr. 3). pap., stu. ed. 13.73 *(978-0-673-80034-3(2))*;Bk. D. (J). (gr. 4). pap., stu. ed. 8.98 *(978-0-673-80044-2(X))*;Bk. D. (J). (gr. 5). pap., stu. ed. 8.98 *(978-0-673-80054-1(7))*;Bk. D. (J). (gr. 5). pap., stu. ed. 8.98 *(978-0-673-80064-0(4))*;Bk. A. (J). (gr. 3). pap., stu. ed. 13.73 *(978-0-673-80031-2(8))*;Bk. A. (J). (gr. 4). pap., stu. ed. 8.98 *(978-0-673-80051-0(2))*;Bk. A. (J). (gr. 4). pap., stu. ed. 8.98 *(978-0-673-80041-1(5))*;Bk. A. (J). (gr. 5). pap., stu. ed. 8.98 *(978-0-673-80061-9(X))*;Bk. B. (J). (gr. 3). pap., stu. ed. 13.73 *(978-0-673-80032-9(6))*;Bk. B. (J). (gr. 4). pap., stu. ed. 8.98 *(978-0-673-80042-8(3))*;Bk. B. (J). (gr. 5). pap., stu. ed. 8.98 *(978-0-673-80062-6(8))*;Bk. B. (J). (gr. 5). pap., stu. ed. 8.98 *(978-0-673-80052-7(0))*;Bk. E. (J). (gr. 2). pap., stu. ed. 12.79 *(978-0-673-80025-1(3))*;Bk. E. (J). (gr. 3). pap., stu. ed. 13.73 *(978-0-673-80035-0(0))*;Bk. E. (J). (gr. 4). pap., stu. ed. 8.98 *(978-0-673-80045-9(8))*;Bk. E. (J). (gr. 5). pap., stu. ed. 8.98 *(978-0-673-80055-8(5))*;Bk. E. (J). (gr. 5). pap., stu. ed. 8.98 *(978-0-673-80065-7(2))*;Bk. F. (J). (gr. 2). pap., stu. ed. 12.79 *(978-0-673-80026-8(1))*;Bk. F. (J). (gr. 3). pap., stu. ed. 13.73 *(978-0-673-80036-7(9))*;Bk. F. (J). (gr. 4). pap., stu. ed. 8.98 *(978-0-673-80046-6(6))*;Bk. F. (J). (gr. 5). pap., stu. ed. 8.98 *(978-0-673-80066-4(0))*;Bk. F. (J). (gr. 5). pap., stu. ed. 8.98 *(978-0-673-80056-5(3))*;Unit 7A, Bk. A. (YA). (gr. 7). pap., stu. ed. 14.71 *(978-0-673-80071-8(7))*;Unit 7B, Bk. B. (YA). (gr. 7). pap., stu. ed. 14.71 *(978-0-673-80072-5(5))*;Unit 7D, Bk. D. (YA). (gr. 7). pap., stu. ed. 14.71 *(978-0-673-80076-3(8))*;Unit 8A, Bk. A. (YA). (gr. 8). pap., stu. ed. 14.71 *(978-0-673-80081-7(4))*;Unit 8B, Bk. B. (YA). (gr. 8). pap., stu. ed. 14.71 *(978-0-673-80083-1(0))*;Unit 8C, Bk. C. (YA). (gr. 8). pap., stu. ed. 14.71 *(978-0-673-80084-8(9))*;Unit 8D, Bk. D. (YA). (gr. 8). pap., stu. ed. 14.71 *(978-0-673-80085-5(7))* Addison Wesley Schl. (Scott Foresman).

Chad Is the Champ: Digraph ch: Level B, 6 vols. (Wright Skills Ser.). 16p. (gr. k-3). 17.95 *(978-0-322-01472-5(7))* Wright Group/McGraw-Hill.

Challenges Set. 2005. (Challenges Ser.: Vol. 2). (J). (gr. 3-5). tchr. ed. 198.95 *(978-0-7652-2129-2(2))* Modern Curriculum Pr.

Change of Heart: Level 2, 6 vols. (Fluency Strand Ser.). (gr. 4-8). 45.00 *(978-1-4045-1214-6(4))* Wright Group/McGraw-Hill.

Changing Views: American Readers. (J). (gr. 7). *(978-0-669-05084-4(9))*; *(978-0-669-05086-8(5))*; wbk. ed. *(978-0-669-05087-5(3))* Houghton Mifflin Harcourt School Pubs.

Charlesworth, Liza. I Like to Read. Bermejo, Ana, illus. 2017. 16p. (J). *(978-1-338-18030-5(4))* Scholastic, Inc.

Charlie the Pancake Pirate: Level O, 6 vols. (Wonder Worldtm Ser.). 48p. 39.95 *(978-0-7802-2949-5(5))* Wright Group/McGraw-Hill.

Chicchelly, Dana. Preparing for FCAT Reading/ Grade 6. 2007. (J). pap. *(978-1-56765-156-0(9)*, R029W) AMSCO Schl. Pubns., Inc.

Chris's Diary: Level 3, 6 vols. (Fluency Strand Ser.). (gr. 4-8). 45.00 *(978-1-4045-1216-0(0))* Wright Group/McGraw-Hill.

The Circus: Level D, 6 vols. (Wonder Worldtm Ser.). 16p. 24.95 *(978-0-7802-1034-9(4))* Wright Group/McGraw-Hill.

Claire, Elizabeth. Hi! (Illus.). (J). wbk. ed. *(978-0-8056-0122-0(8))* Minerva Bks., Ltd.

Classical Learning Universe. Reading Success: Foundations Student Book: Effective Comprehension Strategies. 2004. *(978-0-9763376-0-7(6))* Classical Learning Universe, LLC.

—Reading Success: Student Book: Effective Comprehension Strategies Level C. 2004. *(978-0-9721733-7-7(4))* Classical Learning Universe, LLC.

Classroom Complete Press, creator. High Frequency Picture Words, Grades PK-2. 2011. (Literacy Skills Ser.). (ENG.). 39.95 *(978-1-55319-514-6(0)*, Classroom Complete Pr.) Rainbow Horizons Publishing, Inc.

—High Frequency Sight Words, Grades PK-2. 2011. (Literacy Skills Ser.). (ENG.). 39.95 *(978-1-55319-513-9(2)*, Classroom Complete Pr.) Rainbow Horizons Publishing, Inc.

—Sight & Picture Words, Grades PK-2. 2011. (Literacy Skills Ser.). (ENG.). 54.95 *(978-1-55319-515-3(9)*, Classroom Complete Pr.) Rainbow Horizons Publishing, Inc.

Clearing Paths: American Readers. (J). (gr. 4). *(978-0-669-05040-0(7))* Houghton Mifflin Harcourt School Pubs.

Clearing Paths Reading Kit: American Readers. (J). (gr. 4). *(978-0-669-05053-0(9))* Houghton Mifflin Harcourt School Pubs.

Clearing Paths Workbook: American Readers. (J). (gr. 4). wbk. ed. *(978-0-669-05048-6(2))* Houghton Mifflin Harcourt School Pubs.

Cleary, Brian P. The Bug in the Jug Wants a Hug. Miskimins, Jason, illus. 2009. (Sounds Like Reading (r) Ser.: 1). (ENG.). (gr. -1-2). pap. 39.62 *(978-0-7613-4700-2(3))* Lerner Publishing Group.

—The Clown in the Gown Drives the Car with the Star. Miskimins, Jason, illus. 2009. (Sounds Like Reading (r) Ser.: 8). (ENG.). (gr. -1-2). pap. 39.62 *(978-0-7613-4707-1(0))* Lerner Publishing Group.

—The Frail Snail on the Trail. Miskimins, Jason, illus. 2009. (Sounds Like Reading (r) Ser.: 4). (ENG.). (gr. -1-2). pap. 39.62 *(978-0-7613-4703-3(8))* Lerner Publishing Group.

—The Nice Mice in the Rice. Miskimins, Jason, illus. 2009. (Sounds Like Reading (r) Ser.: 3). (ENG.). (gr. -1-2). pap. 39.62 *(978-0-7613-4702-6(X))* Lerner Publishing Group.

—The Peaches on the Beaches. Miskimins, Jason, illus. 2009. (Sounds Like Reading (r) Ser.: 7). (ENG.). (gr. -1-2). pap. 39.62 *(978-0-7613-4706-4(2))* Lerner Publishing Group.

—Stop, Drop, & Flop in the Slop. Miskimins, Jason, illus. 2009. (Sounds Like Reading (r) Ser.: 2). (ENG.). (gr. -1-2). pap. 39.62 *(978-0-7613-4701-9(1))* Lerner Publishing Group.

—The Thing on the Wing Can Sing. Miskimins, Jason, illus. 2009. (Sounds Like Reading (r) Ser.: 5). (ENG.). (gr. -1-2). pap. 39.62 *(978-0-7613-4704-0(6))* Lerner Publishing Group.

—Whose Shoes Would You Choose. Miskimins, Jason, illus. 2009. (Sounds Like Reading (r) Ser.: 6). (ENG.). (gr. -1-2). pap. 39.62 *(978-0-7613-4705-7(4))* Lerner Publishing Group.

—Whose Shoes Would You Choose? A Long Vowel Sounds Book with Consonant Digraphs. Miskimins, Jason, illus. 2009. (Sounds Like Reading (r) Ser.: 6). (ENG.). 32p. (J). (gr. -1-2). lib. bdg. 23.99 *(978-0-8225-7640-2(6)*, a906f38f-c5ca-456c-bae7-1fe65f5a9888, Millbrook Pr.) Lerner Publishing Group.

Climbing Up: American Readers. (J). (gr. 1). *(978-0-669-04965-7(4))* Houghton Mifflin Harcourt School Pubs.

The Climbing Wall: Level 7, 6 vols. (Fluency Strand Ser.). (gr. 4-8). 45.00 *(978-1-4045-1244-3(6))* Wright Group/McGraw-Hill.

The Closet in the Hall: Level G, 6 vols. (Wonder Worldtm Ser.). 16p. 29.95 *(978-0-7802-1247-3(9))* Wright Group/McGraw-Hill.

Clothes: Level N, 6 vols. (Wonder Worldtm Ser.). 48p. 34.95 *(978-0-7802-2892-4(8))* Wright Group/McGraw-Hill.

The Coach & the Kid: Level 5, 6 vols. (Fluency Strand Ser.). (gr. 4-8). 45.00 *(978-1-4045-1233-7(0))* Wright Group/McGraw-Hill.

Collecting Cones: Level K, 6 vols. (Wonder Worldtm Ser.). 16p. 34.95 *(978-0-7802-4565-5(2))* Wright Group/McGraw-Hill.

Collins 11+. 11+ Verbal Reasoning Comprehension Practice Workbook: For the 2023 CEM Tests. 2016. (Letts 11+ Success Ser.). (ENG.). 80p. (J). (gr. 5-6). pap. 14.95 *(978-1-84419-901-3(0))* HarperCollins Pubs. Ltd. GBR. Dist: Independent Pubs. Group.

Colors at the Zoo: Take-Home Book. 2005. (Emergent Library: Vol. 2). (YA). (gr. -1-1). 12.60 *(978-0-8215-7269-6(5))* Sadlier, William H. Inc.

Come Back, Amelia Bedelia. 2003. 22.95 *(978-0-673-75911-5(3))* Celebration Pr.

The Common Core Readiness Guide to Reading, 16 vols. 2014. (Common Core Readiness Guide to Reading Ser.). (ENG.). 80p. (YA). (gr. 6-6). 289.04 *(978-1-4777-7599-8(4)*, d514c6ea-d819-4ca9-95a7-d6bcf94f8053, Rosen Reference) Rosen Publishing Group, Inc., The.

Common Core Staff, creator. Higher Scores on Reading & Language Arts Standardized Tests, Grade 4. 2012. (Steck-Vaughn Higher Scores on Reading Standardized Tests Ser.). (ENG., Illus.). 137p. (J). pap. 19.99 *(978-0-547-89849-0(5))* Heinemann-Raintree.

Communities: Level F, 6 vols. (Wonder Worldtm Ser.). 16p. 29.95 *(978-0-7802-1986-1(4))* Wright Group/McGraw-Hill.

Cosmo the ACountant: Level O, 6 vols. (Wonder Worldtm Ser.). 48p. 39.95 *(978-0-7802-2962-4(2))* Wright Group/McGraw-Hill.

Count with Me: Take-Home Book. 2005. (Emergent Library: Vol. 2). (YA). (gr. -1-1). 12.60 *(978-0-8215-7258-0(X))* Sadlier, William H. Inc.

Cousin. My Friend at School: Big Book: Level C. (Visions Ser.). 8p. 20.95 *(978-0-7802-9746-3(6))* Wright Group/McGraw-Hill.

Cox, Phil Roxbee & Cartwright, Stephen. Hen's Pens. 2004. (Phonics Board Bks.). (Illus.). 10p. (J). 4.95 *(978-0-7945-0303-1(9),* Usborne) EDC Publishing.

Crackles: Level P, 6 vols. (Wonder Worldtm Ser.). 48p. 39.95 *(978-0-7802-7072-5(X))* Wright Group/McGraw-Hill.

Cronkite, Walter, frwd. Great American Presidents, 12 vols. 2005. (Great American Presidents Ser.). (Illus.). 112p. (gr. 5-8). 210.00 *(978-0-7910-7595-1(8),* Facts On File) Infobase Holdings, Inc.

The Crook by the Brook: Variant Vowel oo: Level B, 6 vols. (Wright Skills Ser.). 16p. (gr. k-3). 26.50 *(978-0-322-01483-1(2))* Wright Group/McGraw-Hill.

Crossing Boundaries: American Readers. (J). *(978-0-669-05064-6(4));* (gr. 5). *(978-0-669-05054-7(7));* (gr. 5). wbk. ed. *(978-0-669-05060-8(1))* Houghton Mifflin Harcourt School Pubs.

The Crypto Files: Level 6, 6 vols. (Fluency Strand Ser.). (gr. 4-8). 45.00 *(978-1-4045-1236-8(5))* Wright Group/McGraw-Hill.

Cuando el senor Rey ronco: When Mr Quinn Snored. 2005. (Take-Home Bks.). (SPA.). (YA). (gr. -1-3). 15.75 *(978-0-8215-1207-4(2))* Sadlier, William H. Inc.

Cuando el senor Rey ronco/When Mr Quinn Snored. 2005. (Libros en Espanol Para Ninos Ser.). (SPA.). (YA). (gr. -1-1). 11.97 *(978-0-8215-0997-5(7))* Sadlier, William H. Inc.

Cuidando a los animales: Keeping Baby Animals Safe. 2005. (Take-Home Bks.). (SPA.). (YA). (gr. -1-3). 15.75 *(978-0-8215-1206-7(4))* Sadlier, William H. Inc.

Cuidando a los animales/Keeping Baby Animals Safe. 2005. (Libros en Espanol Para Ninos Ser.). (SPA.). (YA). (gr. -1-1). 11.97 *(978-0-8215-0996-8(9))* Sadlier, William H. Inc.

A Cup for a Cub: Consonants c, l, r, Short Vowel u word families: Level A, 6 vols. (Wright Skills Ser.). 12p. (gr. k-3). 17.95 *(978-0-322-01453-4(0))* Wright Group/McGraw-Hill.

Custard: Level F, 6 vols. (Wonder Worldtm Ser.). 16p. 29.95 *(978-0-7802-2894-8(4))* Wright Group/McGraw-Hill.

Cyberspace, 6 vols. (Wildcats Ser.). 32p. (gr. 2-8). *(978-0-322-00600-3(7))* Wright Group/McGraw-Hill.

Czernecki, Stefan. How a Baby Begins. Date not set. 40p. (YA). (gr. 5-9). 15.99 *(978-0-06-025412-4(2))* HarperCollins Pubs.

—Wild Queen. Date not set. 80p. (J). (gr. k-4). 13.99 *(978-0-06-026263-1(X));* lib. bdg. 14.89 *(978-0-06-026264-8(8))* HarperCollins Pubs.

Dance My Dance: Level M, 6 vols. (Take-Twostm Ser.). 32p. 36.95 *(978-0-322-03401-3(9))* Wright Group/McGraw-Hill.

Dangerous Jobs: Level T. Group 1, 6 vols. (Sunshine Ser.). 48p. 44.95 *(978-0-7802-6094-8(5))* Wright Group/McGraw-Hill.

Daniel, Claire. Are You Scared, Jacob? Poole, Helen, illus. 2023. (ENG.). 16p. (J). (gr. -1-1). pap. 33.00 *(978-1-4788-0501-4(3),* a0d520c0-17d2-4d4c-9b6c-9ad2960917b4) Newmark Learning LLC.

—Dylan's Questions. Juan, Juan Bautista, illus. 2023. (ENG.). 16p. (J). (gr. -1-1). pap. 33.00 *(978-1-4788-0519-9(6),* afd848c5-2bcf-4418-9af8-fe300cb9f99a) Newmark Learning LLC.

—I Can Stay Calm. Patton, Julia, illus. 2023. (ENG.). 16p. (J). (gr. -1-1). pap. 5.25 *(978-1-4788-0474-1(2),* 602995e7-8cf9-425b-be40-f7f7ca1f1fd1); pap. 33.00 *(978-1-4788-0511-3(0),* d084f6b9-b2f2-4b7d-a8fd-d1212bd51fe3) Newmark Learning LLC.

Day & Night Little Book: Early Reading Fluency, Level A. 2004. pap. 6.00 *(978-0-7398-8170-5(1))* Steck-Vaughn.

Day & Night Little Book, Grade 1: Early Reading Fluency: Teaching Edition, Level A. 2004. pap. 7.50 *(978-0-7398-8206-1(6))* Steck-Vaughn.

de Lambana, Martha Lucia Martinez. Grafias 1 1: Escritura Asociativa Script: Afianzamiento. (SPA.). (J). (gr. k-6). 12.00 *(978-958-04-5317-8(9))* Norma S.A. COL. Dist: Distribuidora Norma, Inc.

—Grafias 2 2: Escritura Asociativa Script: Transicion. (SPA.). (J). (gr. k-6). 12.00 *(978-958-04-5327-7(6))* Norma S.A. COL. Dist: Distribuidora Norma, Inc.

—Grafias 3 3: Escritura Asociativa Script: Afianzamiento. (SPA.). (J). (gr. k-6). 12.00 *(978-958-04-5328-4(4))* Norma S.A. COL. Dist: Distribuidora Norma, Inc.

Deadbeat: Level O, 6 vols. (Wonder Worldtm Ser.). 48p. 39.95 *(978-0-7802-2947-1(9))* Wright Group/McGraw-Hill.

Dear Pop: Level O, 6 vols. (Wonder Worldtm Ser.). 48p. 39.95 *(978-0-7802-2948-8(7))* Wright Group/McGraw-Hill.

Dear Tom: Level J, 6 vols. (Wonder Worldtm Ser.). 16p. 29.95 *(978-0-7802-4567-9(9))* Wright Group/McGraw-Hill.

Den of Thieves: Level 6, 6 vols. (Fluency Strand Ser.). (gr. 4-8). 45.00 *(978-1-4045-1238-2(1))* Wright Group/McGraw-Hill.

Desert Day: Level B. 8p. 20.95 *(978-0-322-00358-3(X))* Wright Group/McGraw-Hill.

Did You Know? Big Book: Level L. Group 1. (Sunshine Ser.). 24p. 36.50 *(978-0-322-00334-7(2))* Wright Group/McGraw-Hill.

Disney Publishing Staff. I Spy Shapes, 15 vols. 2003. (It's Fun to Learn Ser.). (Illus.). 32p. (J). (gr. -1-3). 3.99 *(978-1-57973-131-1(7))* Advance Pubs. LLC.

The Divers: Level C, 6 vols. (Wonder Worldtm Ser.). 16p. 24.95 *(978-0-7802-1249-7(5))* Wright Group/McGraw-Hill.

Do you Like Rice?, 6 vols. 8p. (gr. k-1). 21.50 *(978-0-322-02058-0(1))* Wright Group/McGraw-Hill.

Do you Remember When?, 6 vols. (Multicultural Programs Ser.). 16p. (gr. 1-3). 24.95 *(978-0-7802-9206-2(5))* Wright Group/McGraw-Hill.

Dolly Fin & Friends: Level 4, 6 vols. (Fluency Strand Ser.). (gr. 4-8). 45.00 *(978-1-4045-1227-6(6))* Wright Group/McGraw-Hill.

Dolphin. 2003. 22.95 *(978-0-673-75914-6(8))* Celebration Pr.

Don't be Late, 6 vols. 8p. (gr. k-1). 21.50 *(978-0-322-02059-7(X))* Wright Group/McGraw-Hill.

Don't Throw it Away: Level G, 6 vols. (Wonder Worldtm Ser.). 16p. 29.95 *(978-0-7802-2896-2(0))* Wright Group/McGraw-Hill.

Dorling Kindersley Publishing Staff. My Day. 2011. (DK Readers Pre-Level 1: Learning to Read Ser.). (ENG.). 32p. (J). (gr. -1-1). 16.19 *(978-0-7566-8931-5(7))* Dorling Kindersley Publishing, Inc.

Doudna, Kelly. Any Day but Today! 2004. (Sight Words Ser.). (ENG., Illus.). 24p. (J). (gr. k-3). lib. bdg. 24.21 *(978-1-59197-464-2(X))* ABDO Publishing Co.

—Just Make Some Art! 2004. (Sight Words Ser.). (ENG., Illus.). 24p. (J). (gr. k-3). lib. bdg. 24.21 *(978-1-59197-481-9(X),* SandCastle) ABDO Publishing Co.

—There Are Ants down There! 2004. (Sight Words Ser.). (ENG., Illus.). 24p. (J). (gr. k-3). lib. bdg. 24.21 *(978-1-59197-473-4(9),* SandCastle) ABDO Publishing Co.

—Was That Fun? 2004. (Sight Words Ser.). (ENG., Illus.). 24p. (J). (gr. k-3). lib. bdg. 24.21 *(978-1-59197-475-8(5),* SandCastle) ABDO Publishing Co.

—When Can You Play Again? 2004. (Sight Words Ser.). (ENG., Illus.). 24p. (J). (gr. k-3). lib. bdg. 24.21 *(978-1-59197-478-9(X),* SandCastle) ABDO Publishing Co.

Douglas. Reading Explorer 4 with Student CD-ROM. 4th ed. 2010. (ENG., Illus.). 224p. (J). pap., stu. ed. incl. cd-rom *(978-1-4240-2939-6(2))* Cengage Heinle.

Down by the Pond: Level H. Group 2. (Story Box Ser.). 16p. 31.50 *(978-0-322-02458-8(7))* Wright Group/McGraw-Hill.

Down to Town: Big Book: Level A. Group 1. (Sunshine Ser.). 8p. 20.95 *(978-0-7802-5705-4(7))* Wright Group/McGraw-Hill.

Dragon! Level F, 6 vols. (Wonder Worldtm Ser.). 16p. 29.95 *(978-0-7802-1199-5(5))* Wright Group/McGraw-Hill.

The Dragon Who Came to Dinner: Schwa Sound: Level C, 6 vols. (Wright Skills Ser.). 16p. (gr. k-3). 26.50 *(978-0-322-01505-0(7))* Wright Group/McGraw-Hill.

Dragon with a Cold: Big Book: Level K. Group 1. (Sunshine Ser.). 16p. 36.50 *(978-0-7802-5792-4(8))* Wright Group/McGraw-Hill.

Dragons Galore: 6 Each of 1 Anthology, 6 vols. (Wildcats Ser.). 32p. (gr. 2-8). *(978-0-322-00582-2(5))* Wright Group/McGraw-Hill.

Ducks: Big Book: Level F. Group 2. (Story Box Ser.). 16p. 20.95 *(978-0-7802-9370-0(3))* Wright Group/McGraw-Hill.

Dupuis, Lynda. Au Pied de la Lettre: Manuel de Lecture, de Vocabulaire, d'expression Orale et Ecrite. rev. ed. 2010. (ENG.). 232p. (C). pap. 77.18 *(978-0-7575-7461-0(0),* P716410) Kendall Hunt Publishing Co.

Dwyer, Judy. Novel Activities. 100p. (J). (gr. 2-6). *(978-1-876367-02-2(4))* Wizard Bks.

Dyan, Penelope. Changes! Dyan, Penelope, illus. 2013. (Illus.). 34p. (J). pap. 11.95 *(978-1-61477-097-8(2))* Bellissima Publishing, LLC.

—Gettin' Dirty! for Boys Only R. Dyan, Penelope, illus. 2013. (Illus.). 34p. pap. 11.95 *(978-1-61477-083-1(2))* Bellissima Publishing, LLC.

—Good Luck Chuck! Dyan, Penelope, illus. 2013. (Illus.). 34p. pap. 11.95 *(978-1-61477-098-5(0))* Bellissima Publishing, LLC.

—Good Night! Dyan, Penelope, illus. 2013. (Illus.). 34p. pap. 11.95 *(978-1-61477-089-3(1))* Bellissima Publishing, LLC.

—Hello Doctor! Dyan, Penelope, illus. 2013. (Illus.). 34p. pap. 11.95 *(978-1-61477-096-1(4))* Bellissima Publishing, LLC.

—Life Is a Dream! Dyan, Penelope, illus. 2013. (Illus.). 34p. pap. 11.95 *(978-1-61477-091-6(3))* Bellissima Publishing, LLC.

Early 1 Package. 2005. (Little Celebrations Emergent & Early Packages Ser.). (J). (gr. k-3). 48.95 *(978-0-673-75373-1(5))* Celebration Pr.

Early 2 Package. 2005. (Little Celebrations Emergent & Early Packages Ser.). (J). (gr. k-3). 50.95 *(978-0-673-75374-8(3))* Celebration Pr.

Early Fluency. (Foundation Ser.). (gr. k-3). 26.50 *(978-0-322-01620-0(7))* Wright Group/McGraw-Hill.

Early Fluency Set 1: 1 Each of 8 Student Books. (Sunshinetm Science Ser.). (gr. 1-2). 55.95 *(978-0-7802-1762-1(4))* Wright Group/McGraw-Hill.

Early Library. 2005. (YA). (gr. -1-3). 239.40 *(978-0-8215-8885-7(0));* Vol. 2. 239.40 *(978-0-8215-8886-4(9))* Sadlier, William H. Inc.

Early Stage 2. 2005. (Little Celebrations Picture/Text & Literacy Cards Ser.). (J). (gr. k-3). 128.50 *(978-0-673-75273-4(9))* Celebration Pr.

Earthquake! Level F, 6 vols. (Wonder Worldtm Ser.). 16p. 29.95 *(978-0-7802-1201-5(0))* Wright Group/McGraw-Hill.

The Earthworm: Level I, 6 vols. (Wonder Worldtm Ser.). 16p. 29.95 *(978-0-7802-1988-5(0))* Wright Group/McGraw-Hill.

Eide, Denise. Knitting Knights: Beyond the Sounds of ABC. Hess, Ingrid, illus. 2017. (J). *(978-1-942154-14-3(3))* Logic of English, Inc.

—Whistling Whales: Beyond the Sounds of ABC. Hess, Ingrid, illus. 2017. (J). *(978-1-942154-13-6(5))* Logic of English, Inc.

Emergent Library, Vol. 2. 2005. (YA). (gr. -1-1). 239.40 *(978-0-8215-8878-9(8));* 239.40 *(978-0-8215-8876-5(1));* 239.40 *(978-0-8215-8877-2(X));* 239.40 *(978-0-8215-8879-6(6))* Sadlier, William H. Inc.

Emergent Package. 2005. (Little Celebrations Emergent & Early Packages Ser.). (J). (gr. k-3). 49.95 *(978-0-673-75372-4(7))* Celebration Pr.

Emergent Stage 1. 2005. (Little Celebrations Picture/Text & Literacy Cards Ser.). (J). (gr. k-3). 128.50 *(978-0-673-75224-6(0))* Celebration Pr.

Emergent Super Big Book Package. 2005. (YA). (gr. -1-3). 900.00 *(978-0-8215-8858-1(3))* Sadlier, William H. Inc.

Emergent Super Little Book. 2005. (YA). (gr. -1-3). 957.60 *(978-0-8215-8857-4(5))* Sadlier, William H. Inc.

Emergent Super Little Book Package. 2005. (YA). (gr. -1-3). 183.00 *(978-0-8215-8856-7(7))* Sadlier, William H. Inc.

Erickson, Karen. MEville to WEville Unit 1: Unit 1 ME, 2 Bks., manual and children's Bk. 2004. 292p. 75.00 *(978-0-9666667-5-5(5))* AbleNet, Inc.

Eruption: 6 Each of 1 Anthology, 6 vols. (Wildcats Ser.). 32p. (gr. 2-8). *(978-0-322-00584-6(1))* Wright Group/McGraw-Hill.

Essential Words Reading & Language Arts Activity Book (Intermediate) Intermediate/Middle School. 2005. (Illus.). 50p. (J). 8.95 *(978-0-9722452-3-4(5))* New Leaf Educ., Inc.

Evaluacion del Desarrollo de la Lectura Leveled Libraries: Extending Stage, Level 40. 2003. (SPA.). tchr. ed. 43.50 *(978-0-7652-2389-0(9))* Modern Curriculum Pr.

Evan-Moor Educational Publishers. Reading Informational Text, Grade 5. 2014. (Reading Informational Text Ser.). (ENG., Illus.). 116p. (J). (gr. 5-5). pap., tchr. ed. 22.99 *(978-1-61368-993-6(4))* Evan-Moor Educational Pubs.

—Reading Paired Text, Grade 4. 2014. (Reading Paired Text Ser.). (ENG., Illus.). 176p. (J). (gr. 4-4). pap., tchr. ed. 23.99 *(978-1-61368-986-8(1))* Evan-Moor Educational Pubs.

Explorers: Fluency - Student Book Set - 1 Each of 12 Titles. (Explorers. Exploradores Nonfiction Sets Ser.). (gr. 3-6). Vol. 2. 89.95 *(978-0-7699-0817-5(9))* Vol. 3. 89.95 *(978-0-7699-0819-9(5))* Shortland Pubns. (U. S. A.) Inc.

Explorers Exploradores Set 1: English - 1 Each of 12 Student Books, 1 Teacher's Resource Book. (Explorers. Exploradores Nonfiction Sets Ser.). (gr. 3-6). 137.95 *(978-0-7699-0576-1(5))* Shortland Pubns. (U. S. A.) Inc.

Explorers Exploradores Set 1: English - 6 Each of 12 Student Books, 1 Teacher's Resource Book. (Explorers. Exploradores Nonfiction Sets Ser.). (gr. 3-6). 558.50 *(978-0-7699-0583-9(8))* Shortland Pubns. (U. S. A.) Inc.

Explorers Exploradores Set 1: Spanish - 1 Each of 12 Student Books. (Explorers. Exploradores Nonfiction Sets Ser.). (gr. 3-6). 89.95 *(978-0-7699-0816-8(0))* Shortland Pubns. (U. S. A.) Inc.

Explorers Exploradores Set 1: Spanish - 6 Each of 12 Student Books, 1 Teacher's Resource Book. (Explorers. Exploradores Nonfiction Sets Ser.). (ENG & SPA.). (gr. 3-6). 558.50 *(978-0-7699-0584-6(6))* Shortland Pubns. (U. S. A.) Inc.

Explorers Exploradores Set 2: English - 1 Each of 12 Student Books, 1 Teacher's Resource Book. (Explorers. Exploradores Nonfiction Sets Ser.). (gr. 3-6). 137.95 *(978-0-7699-0578-5(1))* Shortland Pubns. (U. S. A.) Inc.

Explorers Exploradores Set 2: English - 6 Each of 12 Student Books, 1 Teacher's Resource Book. (Explorers. Exploradores Nonfiction Sets Ser.). (gr. 3-6). 558.50 *(978-0-7699-0585-3(4))* Shortland Pubns. (U. S. A.) Inc.

Explorers Exploradores Set 2: Spanish - 1 Each of 12 Student Books. (Explorers. Exploradores Nonfiction Sets Ser.). (gr. 3-6). 89.95 *(978-0-7699-0818-2(7))* Shortland Pubns. (U. S. A.) Inc.

Explorers Exploradores Set 2: Spanish - 1 Each of 12 Student Books, 1 Teacher's Resource Book. (Explorers. Exploradores Nonfiction Sets Ser.). (gr. 3-6). 137.95 *(978-0-7699-0579-2(X))* Shortland Pubns. (U. S. A.) Inc.

Explorers Exploradores Set 2: Spanish - 6 Each of 12 Student Books, 1 Teacher's Resource Book. (Explorers. Exploradores Nonfiction Sets Ser.). (ENG & SPA.). (gr. 3-6). 558.50 *(978-0-7699-0586-0(2))* Shortland Pubns. (U. S. A.) Inc.

Explorers Exploradores Set 3: English - 1 Each of 12 Student Books, 1 Teacher's Resource Book. (Explorers. Exploradores Nonfiction Sets Ser.). (gr. 3-6). 137.95 *(978-0-7699-0580-8(3))* Shortland Pubns. (U. S. A.) Inc.

Explorers Exploradores Set 3: English - 6 Each of 12 Student Books, 1 Teacher's Resource Book. (Explorers. Exploradores Nonfiction Sets Ser.). (gr. 3-6). 558.50 *(978-0-7699-0587-7(0))* Shortland Pubns. (U. S. A.) Inc.

Explorers Exploradores Set 3: Spanish - 1 Each of 12 Student Books. (Explorers. Exploradores Nonfiction Sets Ser.). (gr. 3-6). 89.95 *(978-0-7699-0820-5(9))* Shortland Pubns. (U. S. A.) Inc.

Explorers Exploradores Set 3: Spanish - 1 Each of 12 Student Books, 1 Teacher's Resource Book. (Explorers. Exploradores Nonfiction Sets Ser.). (gr. 3-6). 137.95 *(978-0-7699-0581-5(1))* Shortland Pubns. (U. S. A.) Inc.

Explorers Exploradores Set 3: Spanish - 6 Each of 12 Student Books, 1 Teacher's Resource Book. (Explorers. Exploradores Nonfiction Sets Ser.). (ENG & SPA.). (gr. 3-6). 558.50 *(978-0-7699-0588-4(9))* Shortland Pubns. (U. S. A.) Inc.

Explorers Exploradores Sets 1,3: English - 1 Each of 36 Student Books, 3 Teacher's Resource Books. (Explorers. Exploradores Nonfiction Sets Ser.). (gr. 3-6). 413.95 *(978-0-7699-0574-7(9))* Shortland Pubns. (U. S. A.) Inc.

Explorers Exploradores Sets 1,3: English - 6 Each of 36 Student Books, 3 Teacher's Resource Books. (Explorers. Exploradores Nonfiction Sets Ser.). (gr. 3-6). 1587.50 *(978-0-7699-0813-7(6))* Shortland Pubns. (U. S. A.) Inc.

Explorers Exploradores Sets 1,3: Spanish - 1 Each of 36 Student Books, 3 Teacher's Resource Books. (Explorers. Exploradores Nonfiction Sets Ser.). (gr. 3-6). 413.95 *(978-0-7699-0575-4(7))* Shortland Pubns. (U. S. A.) Inc.

Explorers Exploradores Sets 1,3: Spanish - 6 Each of 36 Student Books, 3 Teacher's Resource Books. (Explorers. Exploradores Nonfiction Sets Ser.). (SPA.). (gr. 3-6). 1587.50 *(978-0-7699-0814-4(4))* Shortland Pubns. (U. S. A.) Inc.

The Explosive Trek: Level 6, 6 vols. (Fluency Strand Ser.). (gr. 4-8). 45.00 *(978-1-4045-1234-4(9))* Wright Group/McGraw-Hill.

Eyes: Level C, 6 vols. (Wonder Worldtm Ser.). 16p. 24.95 *(978-0-7802-1992-2(9))* Wright Group/McGraw-Hill.

Eyes & Ears Sets: 1 Each of 3 Big Books. (Sunshinetm Science Ser.). (gr. 1-2). 111.50 *(978-0-7802-1445-3(5))* Wright Group/McGraw-Hill.

Eyes & Ears Sets: 1 Each of 3 Student Books. (Sunshinetm Science Ser.). (gr. 1-2). 20.95 *(978-0-7802-1747-8(0))* Wright Group/McGraw-Hill.

Face Painting: Level H, 6 vols. (Wonder Worldtm Ser.). 16p. 29.95 *(978-0-7802-2897-9(9))* Wright Group/McGraw-Hill.

Families, Families: Take-Home Book. 2005. (Lee Bennett Hopkins Worlds of Poetry Classroom Library). (YA). (gr. k-3). 13.50 *(978-0-8215-0566-3(1))* Sadlier, William H. Inc.

Families, Families: Teacher's Theme Resource Folder. 2005. (Lee Bennett Hopkins Worlds of Poetry Classroom Library). (YA). (gr. k-3). 12.00 *(978-0-8215-0515-1(7))* Sadlier, William H. Inc.

Family Reunion, 6 vols. (Multicultural Programs Ser.). 16p. (gr. 1-3). 24.95 *(978-0-7802-9213-0(8))* Wright Group/McGraw-Hill.

Fans: Consonant f: Level A, 6 vols. (Wright Skills Ser.). 12p. (gr. k-3). 17.95 *(978-0-322-03107-4(9))* Wright Group/McGraw-Hill.

The Farm Party: R-Controlled a: Level B, 6 vols. (Wright Skills Ser.). 16p. (gr. k-3). 26.50 *(978-0-322-01486-2(7))* Wright Group/McGraw-Hill.

Faster, Higher, Stronger: The Olympics, 6 vols. (Book2WebTM Ser.). (gr. 4-8). 36.50 *(978-0-322-02984-2(8))* Wright Group/McGraw-Hill.

Fay & Kay by the Bay: Long a Digraphs: Level B, 6 vols. (Wright Skills Ser.). 16p. (gr. k-3). 26.50 *(978-0-322-01478-7(6))* Wright Group/McGraw-Hill.

Feelings Little Book: Early Reading Fluency, Level A. 2004. (gr. 1). pap. 6.00 *(978-0-7398-8159-0(0))* Steck-Vaughn.

Feldman, Jean. Dr Jean Variety Pack. 2007. (J). (gr. -1-3). pap. 56.87 incl. audio compact disk *(978-1-59198-719-2(9))* Creative Teaching Pr., Inc.

Feldman, Reynold & Rumi, M. Jan. WisingUp: A Youth Guide to Good Living. 2004. 192p. (YA). *(978-1-932590-02-9(1))* Wisdom Foundation Publishing.

Felix, the Very Hungry Fish: Take-Home Bk. 2005. (Emergent Library: Vol. 2). (YA). (gr. -1-1). 12.60 *(978-0-8215-7250-4(4))* Sadlier, William H. Inc.

Fences. 2003. 44p. (YA). tchr. ed., ring bd. *(978-1-58049-468-7(4),* TU224) Prestwick Hse., Inc.

Ferguson, Walter F. Speed Learning: The Quest for Excellence. 2004. cd-rom 59.95 *(978-0-9745333-0-8(0))* Mystique International, Ltd.

Fernandez, Cesar. El bibliobus Magico. Torres, Marina, illus. 2004. 88p. pap. 10.00 *(978-84-931888-1-8(6))* Editorial Brief ESP. Dist: Independent Pubs. Group.

Festival Fun: 6 Each of 1 Anthology, 6 vols. (Wildcats Ser.). 32p. (gr. 2-8). *(978-0-322-02424-3(2))* Wright Group/McGraw-Hill.

Fight Deck: Level D, 6 vols. (Wonder Worldtm Ser.). 16p. 24.95 *(978-0-7802-1203-9(7))* Wright Group/McGraw-Hill.

Find Yourself a Friend, 6 vols. (Multicultural Programs Ser.). 16p. (gr. 1-3). 24.95 *(978-0-7802-9210-9(3))* Wright Group/McGraw-Hill.

Finding Places, Grade 1: American Readers. (J). (gr. 1). *(978-0-669-04936-7(0));* wbk. ed. *(978-0-669-04942-8(5))* Houghton Mifflin Harcourt School Pubs.

Fire! Fire! 6 Each of 1 Anthology, 6 vols. (Wildcats Ser.). 32p. (gr. 2-8). *(978-0-322-00581-5(7))* Wright Group/McGraw-Hill.

First Explorers Primeros Exploradores Set. 1: English - 1 Each of 12 Student Books, 1 Each of 12 Lesson Plans. (First Explorers. Primeros Exploradores Nonfiction Sets Ser.). (gr. 1-2). 107.95 *(978-0-7699-1360-5(1))* Shortland Pubns. (U. S. A.) Inc.

First Explorers Primeros Exploradores Set 1: English - 6 Each of 12 Student Books, 1 Each of 12 Lesson Plans: Set 1. (First Explorers. Primeros Exploradores Nonfiction Sets Ser.). (gr. 1-2). 407.50 *(978-0-7699-1364-3(4))* Shortland Pubns. (U. S. A.) Inc.

First Explorers Primeros Exploradores Set 2: English - 6 Each of 12 Student Books, 1 Each of 12 Lesson Plans, (First Explorers. Primeros Exploradores Nonfiction Sets Ser.). (gr. 1-2). 452.50 *(978-0-7699-1365-0(2))* Shortland Pubns. (U. S. A.) Inc.

First Explorers Primeros Exploradores Set. 3: English - 1 Each of 12 Student Books, 1 Each of 12 Lesson Plans. (First Explorers. Primeros Exploradores Nonfiction Sets Ser.). (gr. 1-2). 115.50 *(978-0-7699-1361-2(X))* Shortland Pubns. (U. S. A.) Inc.

First Explorers Primeros Exploradores Sets 1-2: English - 1 Each of 24 Student Books, 1 Each of 24 Lesson Plans. (First Explorers. Primeros Exploradores Nonfiction Sets Ser.). (gr. 1-2). 223.50 *(978-0-7699-1366-7(0))* Shortland Pubns. (U. S. A.) Inc.

First Explorers Primeros Exploradores Sets 1-2: English - 6 Each of 24 Student Books, 1 Each of 24 Lesson Plans. (First Explorers. Primeros Exploradores Nonfiction Sets Ser.). (gr. 1-2). 816.95 *(978-0-7699-1359-9(8))* Shortland Pubns. (U. S. A.) Inc.

Fish: Level E, 6 vols. (Wonder Worldtm Ser.). 16p. 29.95 *(978-0-7802-1994-6(5));* 26.50 *(978-0-7802-7004-6(5))* Wright Group/McGraw-Hill.

Fishing: Level F, 6 vols. (Wonder Worldtm Ser.). 16p. 29.95 *(978-0-7802-1996-0(1))* Wright Group/McGraw-Hill.

The Five Senses: Big Book: Level I. Group 1. (Story Box Ser.). 16p. 31.50 *(978-0-322-02459-5(5))* Wright Group/McGraw-Hill.

Flash Kids Editors, ed. Reading Comprehension: Grade 5 (Flash Skills) 2010. (Flash Skills Ser.). 64p. (J). pap. 3.95 *(978-1-4114-3476-9(5),* Spark Publishing Group) Sterling Publishing Co., Inc.

Flash Kids Editors, Flash Kids, ed. Summer Study, Grade 3. 2016. (Summer Study Ser.). (ENG., Illus.). 160p. (J). (gr. 3-3). pap. 9.95 *(978-1-4114-7859-6(2),* Spark Publishing Group) Sterling Publishing Co., Inc.

—Summer Study, Grade 4. 2016. (Summer Study Ser.). (ENG., Illus.). 160p. (J). (gr. 4-4). pap. 9.95 *(978-1-4114-7860-2(6),* Spark Publishing Group) Sterling Publishing Co., Inc.

—Summer Study, Grade 5. 2016. (Summer Study Ser.). (ENG., Illus.). 160p. (J). (gr. 5-5). pap. 9.95 *(978-1-4114-7861-9(4),* Spark Publishing Group) Sterling Publishing Co., Inc.

Flashkids. Flashkids Reading Fundamentals Grade 4. 2016. (Flash Kids Fundamentals Ser.). (ENG., Illus.). 96p. (J). (gr. 4-4). pap. 7.95 *(978-1-4114-7884-8(3),* Spark Publishing Group) Sterling Publishing Co., Inc.

—Flashkids Reading Fundamentals Grade 5. 2016. (Flash Kids Fundamentals Ser.). (ENG., Illus.). 96p. (J). (gr. 5-5). pap. 7.95 *(978-1-4114-7885-5(1),* Spark Publishing Group) Sterling Publishing Co., Inc.

—Flashkids Reading Fundamentals Grade 6. 2016. (Flash Kids Fundamentals Ser.). (ENG., Illus.). 96p. (J). (gr. 6-6). pap. 7.95 *(978-1-4114-7886-2(X),* Spark Publishing Group) Sterling Publishing Co., Inc.

Flea Treat Little Book: Early Reading Fluency, Level C. 2004. (gr. 3). pap. 6.00 *(978-0-7398-8290-0(2))* Steck-Vaughn.

Fletcher, Barbara. A Rose on the River: Level U, 6 vols. (Mountain Peaks Ser.). 128p. (gr. 6-18). 36.95 *(978-0-322-05888-0(0))* Wright Group/McGraw-Hill.
Flip, Flap, & Fluff: Family Blends: Level B, 6 vols. (Wright Skills Ser.). 16p. (gr. k-3). 17.95 *(978-0-322-01459-6(X))* Wright Group/McGraw-Hill.
The Flood: Level K, 6 vols. (Wonder Worldtm Ser.). 16p. 34.95 *(978-0-7802-4571-6(7))* Wright Group/McGraw-Hill.
Flor Ada, Alma, tr. Take-Home Package: Complete Package. 2003. (Dejame Leer Ser.). (J). 124.95 *(978-0-673-58720-6(7))* Celebration Pr.
Flor Ada, Alma & Campoy, F. Isabel. Colecciones de Libros de la Biblioteca: El Coraje de Sarah Noble. 2003. (Trofeos Ser.). (SPA.). (gr. 6-18). 135.90 *(978-0-15-322124-8(0))* Harcourt Schl. Pubs.
—Colecciones de Libros de la Biblioteca: El Papalote. 2003. (Trofeos Ser.). (SPA.). (gr. 1-18). 81.60 *(978-0-15-319393-4(X))* Harcourt Schl. Pubs.
—Colecciones de Libros de la Biblioteca: Lucita Regresa a Oaxaca. 2003. (Trofeos Ser.). (SPA.). (gr. 3-18). 44.00 *(978-0-15-322094-4(5))* Harcourt Schl. Pubs.
Flores, Debra, et al. Reading Comprehension 1-3: Activities for Understanding. Jennett, Pamela, ed. Grayson, Rick & Iosa, Ann, illus. 2004. 96p. (J). pap. 1.99 *(978-1-59198-045-2(3),* 3384) Creative Teaching Pr., Inc.
—Reading Comprehension 4-6: Activities for Understanding. Jennett, Pamela, ed. Grayson, Rick & Iosa, Ann, illus. 2004. 96p. (J). pap. 12.99 *(978-1-59198-046-9(1),* 3385) Creative Teaching Pr., Inc.
Flour: Level M, 6 vols. (Wonder Worldtm Ser.). 16p. 34.95 *(978-0-7802-1998-4(8))* Wright Group/McGraw-Hill.
Fluency Skills Guide. (Sunshine Skills Guides). 25.95 *(978-0-7802-9858-3(6))* Wright Group/McGraw-Hill.
Fluent Library. 2005. (YA). (gr. -1-3). 119.70 *(978-0-8215-8990-8(3));* Vol. 2. 119.70 *(978-0-8215-8991-5(1))* Sadlier, William H. Inc.
Fluent Stage 3. 2005. (Little Celebrations Picture/Text & Literacy Cards Ser.). (J). (gr. k-3). 128.50 *(978-0-673-77359-3(0))* Celebration Pr.
Fly Away Home: Level K, 6 vols. (Wonder Worldtm Ser.). 16p. 34.95 *(978-0-7802-1205-3(3))* Wright Group/McGraw-Hill.
Follow the Map, 6 vols. 8p. (gr. k-1). 21.50 *(978-0-322-02067-2(0))* Wright Group/McGraw-Hill.
Food Trappers: Level K, 6 vols. (Wonder Worldtm Ser.). 16p. 34.95 *(978-0-7802-1209-1(6))* Wright Group/McGraw-Hill.
Foods of the World, 6 vols. (Book2WebTM Ser.). (gr. 4-8). 36.50 *(978-0-322-02985-9(6))* Wright Group/McGraw-Hill.
Foster, Kelli C. & Erickson, Gina. Get Ready... Get Set... Read!, 5 sets (35 bks.) Russell, Kerri G., illus. (J). lib. bdg. 418.25Set. lib. bdg. 418.25 *(978-1-56674-920-6(4))* Forest Hse. Publishing Co., Inc.
Foundations: Early Emergent-Upper Emergent - 1 Each of 25 Student Books: Level E. 124.95 *(978-0-322-02722-0(5))* Wright Group/McGraw-Hill.
The Four A's: 6 Each of 1 Anthology, 6 vols. (Wildcats Ser.). 32p. (gr. 2-8). *(978-0-322-00595-2(7))* Wright Group/McGraw-Hill.
The Fox: Consonants q, x, z; -ack, -ick, -ill word families: Level A, 6 vols. (Wright Skills Ser.). 12p. (gr. k-3). 17.95 *(978-0-322-01456-5(5))* Wright Group/McGraw-Hill.
Francis, Andre. Cultural Instruments: Big Book: Level R. Group 1. (Take-Twostm Ser.). 32p. 38.95 *(978-0-322-04490-6(1))* Wright Group/McGraw-Hill.
Fredericks, Anthony D. & Lynott, Vicky. Write to Comprehend: Using Writing as a Tool to Build Reading Comprehension. 2007. (Illus.). 138p. per. 19.95 *(978-1-59647-120-7(4))* Good Year Bks.
Frog & Toad All Year. 2003. 31.95 *(978-0-673-75800-2(1))* Celebration Pr.
Frog on a Log: 1 Big Book, 6 Each of 1 Student Book, & 1 Cassette. (Song Box Ser.). (gr. 1-2). 68.95 *(978-0-7802-3204-4(6))* Wright Group/McGraw-Hill.
Frog on a Log: Big Book. (Song Box Ser.). (gr. 1-2). 31.50 *(978-0-7802-2256-4(3))* Wright Group/McGraw-Hill.
From Rocks to Sand: Level L, 6 vols. (Wonder Worldtm Ser.). 16p. 34.95 *(978-0-7802-4575-4(X))* Wright Group/McGraw-Hill.
From the Air: Level F, 6 vols. (Wonder Worldtm Ser.). 16p. 29.95 *(978-0-7802-2000-3(5))* Wright Group/McGraw-Hill.
Fruit Salad: Level D, 6 vols. (Wonder Worldtm Ser.). 16p. 24.95 *(978-0-7802-1241-1(X))* Wright Group/McGraw-Hill.
Fry, Ron. Surefire Tips to Improve Your Reading Skills, 1 vol., 1. 2015. (Surefire Study Success Ser.). (ENG.). 144p. (YA). (gr. 7-8). 38.80 *(978-1-5081-7094-5(0),* f782fa03-8732-441e-86ec-7b6b95573862, Rosen Young Adult) Rosen Publishing Group, Inc., The.
Fuerst, Jeffrey B. A-Hunting We Will Go. Greenhead, Bill, illus. 2010. (Rising Readers Ser.). (J). 3.49 *(978-1-60719-684-6(0))* Newmark Learning LLC.
—Jack Be Nimble. Colby, Garry, illus. 2010. (Rising Readers Ser.). (J). 3.49 *(978-1-60719-698-3(0))* Newmark Learning LLC.
—Lazy Mary. Kelley, Gerald, illus. 2010. (Rising Readers Ser.). (J). 3.49 *(978-1-60719-699-0(9))* Newmark Learning LLC.
Gallinella Rossa. pap. 14.95 *(978-88-04-46594-2(8))* Mondadori ITA. Dist: Distribooks, Inc.
Gant, Linda G. Readers Are Leaders. Gant, Linda G., illus. Date not set. (Illus.). (J). (gr. -1-3). *(978-0-9673625-0-2(4))* Readers Are Leaders.
Gant, Robert, illus. My Big Box of Reading. gif. ed. 2005. 64p. (J). cd-rom 24.95 *(978-1-57791-195-1(4))* Brighter Minds Children's Publishing.
Garbage: Big Book: Level D. (Wonder Worldtm Ser.). 16p. 26.50 *(978-0-7802-7007-7(X))* Wright Group/McGraw-Hill.
Garbage: Level D, 6 vols. (Wonder Worldtm Ser.). 16p. 24.95 *(978-0-7802-2026-3(9))* Wright Group/McGraw-Hill.
Garcia, Ellen. Are You Listening, Jack? Patton, Julia, illus. 2023. (ENG.). 16p. (J). (gr. -1-1). pap. 5.25 *(978-1-4788-0472-7(6),* b73054d2-c606-44d4-a508-01e2c83ea93a); pap. 33.00 *(978-1-4788-0509-0(9),* 887a3926-c0ee-4cb6-a0eb-8d0bba95b07b) Newmark Learning LLC.
—Charlie Is Responsible. Monés, Marc, illus. 2023. (ENG.). 16p. (J). (gr. -1-1). pap. 33.00 *(978-1-4788-0507-6(2),* 9e56f37b-a1ae-4484-8104-85548973df29) Newmark Learning LLC.
—I Can Make a Plan. Juan, Juan Bautista, illus. 2023. (ENG.). 16p. (J). (gr. -1-1). pap. 5.25 *(978-1-4788-0478-9(5),* 378ce7f8-7c9b-4c37-bc30-3f14ad79dd60); pap. 33.00 *(978-1-4788-0515-1(3),* d986474e-f2d7-4ca5-b63d-bec770e5ee61) Newmark Learning LLC.
Gatto con gli Stivali. pap. 14.95 *(978-88-04-44207-3(7))* Mondadori ITA. Dist: Distribooks, Inc.
Geimer, Allan F. I Can Read, You Can Read: Basic Reading Teaching Guide. 140p. (J). pap. 12.95 *(978-1-886358-02-7(8))* Cellular Publishing.
Get Me Out of Here Little Book: Early Reading Fluency, Level C. 2004. pap. 6.00 *(978-0-7398-8296-2(1))* Steck-Vaughn.
Get Smart Skills Staff. HSPT Reading: New Jersey High School Proficiency Test. 2004. 192p. (gr. 11-18). pap. 14.95 *(978-1-932635-31-7(9))* Webster House Publishing LLC.
—PSSA Reading: Pennsylvania System of School Assessment. 2004. 192p. (gr. 11-18). pap. 14.95 *(978-1-932635-28-7(9))* Webster House Publishing LLC.
Getting FIT: Level A, 6 vols. (Wonder Worldtm Ser.). 16p. 24.95 *(978-0-7802-1036-3(0))* Wright Group/McGraw-Hill.
Getting Glasses: Level I, 6 vols. (Wonder Worldtm Ser.). 16p. 29.95 *(978-0-7802-2002-7(1))* Wright Group/McGraw-Hill.
Getting the Sequence (Gr. 4-5) 2004. (J). *(978-1-58232-131-8(0))* ECS Learning Systems, Inc.
Getting There: Level B, 6 vols. (Wonder Worldtm Ser.). 16p. 24.95 *(978-0-7802-1037-0(9))* Wright Group/McGraw-Hill.
Giachetti, Julia. Don't Give Up! Juan, Juan Bautista, illus. 2023. (ENG.). 16p. (J). (gr. -1-1). pap. 33.00 *(978-1-4788-0517-5(X),* 4d4853e6-d717-4892-b36f-466b60f5228e) Newmark Learning LLC.
—My Happy Day. Poole, Helen, illus. 2023. (ENG.). 16p. (J). (gr. -1-1). pap. 33.00 *(978-1-4788-0497-0(1),* f3d32820-a7c0-47ad-b4e8-b11de5b51863); pap. 5.25 *(978-1-4788-0460-4(2),* d464f837-d3b4-467d-a1c3-3d355f18b48f) Newmark Learning LLC.
—Thanks for Sharing, Tommy. Monés, Marc, illus. 2023. (ENG.). 16p. (J). (gr. -1-1). pap. 5.25 *(978-1-4788-0466-6(1),* 7232ac39-7977-4783-ae94-ef7208637623); pap. 33.00 *(978-1-4788-0503-8(X),* 4f9cbb11-272d-4781-943f-377f09b0fc7f) Newmark Learning LLC.
A Giant-Size Hamburger: Level D, 6 vols. (Wonder Worldtm Ser.). 16p. 24.95 *(978-0-7802-1028-8(X))* Wright Group/McGraw-Hill.
Giants in the City: Hard & Soft c & g: Level B, 6 vols. (Wright Skills Ser.). 16p. (gr. k-3). 26.50 *(978-0-322-01489-3(1))* Wright Group/McGraw-Hill.
Giddyoocha! Big Book: Level J. Group 1. (Story Box Ser.). 16p. 31.50 *(978-0-322-02468-7(4))* Wright Group/McGraw-Hill.
The Gig: Level 4, 6 vols. (Fluency Strand Ser.). (gr. 4-8). 45.00 *(978-1-4045-1229-0(2))* Wright Group/McGraw-Hill.
Ginger's War: Level T. Group 3, 6 vols. (Sunshine Ser.). 48p. 44.95 *(978-0-322-01939-3(7))* Wright Group/McGraw-Hill.
Girl Saves Giant: Level P, 6 vols. (Wonder Worldtm Ser.). 48p. 39.95 *(978-0-7802-7070-1(3))* Wright Group/McGraw-Hill.
Glencoe McGraw-Hill Staff, creator. Timed Readings Plus in Social Studies, Vol. 8. 2003. (Jamestown Education Ser.). 118p. (J). per. 17.32 *(978-0-07-845806-4(4),* 9780078458064) Jamestown.
—Timed Readings Plus in Social Studies Book 4, Vol. 4. 2003. (Timed Readings Plus Ser.). 118p. (J). (gr. 4-7). per. 17.32 *(978-0-07-845802-6(1),* 9780078458026) Jamestown.
—Timed Readings Plus in Social Studies Book 5, Vol. 5. 2003. (Timed Readings Plus Ser.). 118p. (J). (gr. 4-7). per. 17.32 *(978-0-07-845803-3(X),* 9780078458033) Jamestown.
—Timed Readings Plus in Social Studies Book 6, Vol. 6. 2003. (Timed Readings Plus Ser.). 118p. (J). (gr. 4-7). per. 17.32 *(978-0-07-845804-0(8),* 9780078458040) Jamestown.
Glencoe Staff. We Can Read. (J). wbk. ed. *(978-0-02-132370-8(4))* Macmillan Publishing Co., Inc.
—We Can Read '83, Level 6. (J). *(978-0-02-131680-9(5))* Macmillan Publishing Co., Inc.
Going Far: American Readers. (J). (gr. 1). *(978-0-669-04964-0(6))* Houghton Mifflin Harcourt School Pubs.
Going on a Field Trip, 6 vols. (Multicultural Programs Ser.). 16p. (gr. 1-3). 24.95 *(978-0-7802-9216-1(2))* Wright Group/McGraw-Hill.
Goober Peas: 1 Big Book, 6 Each of 1 Student Book, & 1 Cassette. (Song Box Ser.). (gr. 1-2). 68.95 *(978-0-7802-0943-5(5))* Wright Group/McGraw-Hill.
Grandma's at the Lake. 2003. 22.95 *(978-0-673-75917-7(2))* Celebration Pr.
Grandma's Heart: Level J, 6 vols. (Wonder Worldtm Ser.). 16p. 29.95 *(978-0-7802-1213-8(4))* Wright Group/McGraw-Hill.
Grandpa Knits Hats: Level E. (Wonder Worldtm Ser.). 16p. 29.95 *(978-0-7802-1038-7(7))* Wright Group/McGraw-Hill.
Great Art & Artists, 6 vols. (Book2WebTM Ser.). (gr. 4-8). 36.50 *(978-0-322-02987-3(2))* Wright Group/McGraw-Hill.
Great Battles Through the Ages, 6 vols. 2005. (Great Battles Through the Ages Ser.). (Illus.). 112p. (gr. 6-12). 180.00 *(978-0-7910-7434-3(X),* Facts On File) Infobase Holdings, Inc.
The Great Big Book of Reading Preschool Costco Edition. 2008. (J). pap. *(978-1-59566-623-9(0))* QEB Publishing Inc.
The Great Monsieur Vertelli: Level R, 6 vols. (Wonder Worldtm Ser.). 48p. 44.95 *(978-0-7802-7083-1(5))* Wright Group/McGraw-Hill.
Grizzly & the Bumble-bee: Big Book: Level K. Group 1. (Sunshine Ser.). 16p. 36.50 *(978-0-7802-5789-4(8))* Wright Group/McGraw-Hill.
Group/McGraw-Hill, Wright. Abraham Lincoln: The Civil War President, 6 vols. (Book2WebTM Ser.). (gr. 4-8). 36.50 *(978-0-322-04462-3(6))* Wright Group/McGraw-Hill.
—Africa: Rich in Land & History, 6 vols. (Book2WebTM Ser.). (gr. 4-8). 36.50 *(978-0-322-04439-5(1))* Wright Group/McGraw-Hill.
—African Art: Level E, 6 vols. (Take Twostm Ser.). 16p. 29.95 *(978-0-322-08988-4(3))* Wright Group/McGraw-Hill.
—Against the Odds: Magazine Anthology - Level 3, 6 vols. (Comprehension Strand Ser.). (gr. 4-8). 54.00 *(978-0-322-06031-9(1))* Wright Group/McGraw-Hill.
—All's Well that End Well: Level N, 6 vols. (Autumn Leaves Ser.). 128p. (gr. 3-6). 36.95 *(978-0-322-06728-8(6))* Wright Group/McGraw-Hill.
—Animal Advocates, 6 vols. (Wildcats Ser.). 32p. (gr. 2-8). *(978-0-322-05861-3(9))* Wright Group/McGraw-Hill.
—Animal Mysteries, 6 vols. (Wildcats Ser.). 32p. (gr. 2-8). *(978-0-322-05859-0(7))* Wright Group/McGraw-Hill.
—Animals Go Mad: Level 2, 6 vols. (Fluency Strand Ser.). (gr. 4-8). 194.95 *(978-1-4045-1292-4(6))* Wright Group/McGraw-Hill.
—Art Show, 6 vols. (D-Man Beans Ser.). 47p. (gr. 4-6). 42.50 *(978-0-322-06262-7(4))* Wright Group/McGraw-Hill.
—Autumn Leaves: Classroom Library Set. (Autumn Leaves Ser.). 81.50 *(978-0-322-07969-4(1))* Wright Group/McGraw-Hill.
—Autumn Leaves: Complete Set. (Autumn Leaves Ser.). 327.95 *(978-0-322-07967-0(5))* Wright Group/McGraw-Hill.
—The Aztec People: Level I, 6 vols. (Take Twostm Ser.). 16p. 29.95 *(978-0-322-08995-2(6))* Wright Group/McGraw-Hill.
—Bad News Good News: Level N, 6 vols. (Autumn Leaves Ser.). 128p. (gr. 3-6). 36.95 *(978-0-322-06733-2(2))* Wright Group/McGraw-Hill.
—Bats about Bats! Level M, 6 vols. (Summer Skies Ser.). 128p. (gr. 3-6). 36.95 *(978-0-322-06724-0(3))* Wright Group/McGraw-Hill.
—Black Tooth the Pirate: Level G, 6 vols. (Take Twostm Ser.). 16p. 29.95 *(978-0-322-08969-3(7))* Wright Group/McGraw-Hill.
—Blow your Top: Magazine Anthology: Level 6, 6 vols. (Comprehension Strand Ser.). (gr. 4-8). 54.00 *(978-0-322-06041-8(9))* Wright Group/McGraw-Hill.
—Bobcat Level: Adventure Journal Set. (Wildcats Ser.). (gr. 2-8). 31.95 *(978-0-322-05791-3(4))* Wright Group/McGraw-Hill.
—Bobcat Level: Lesson Plan Set. (Wildcats Ser.). (gr. 2-8). 96.50 *(978-0-322-06676-2(X))* Wright Group/McGraw-Hill.
—Bobcat Level: Wildcats Bobcat Complete Kit. (Wildcats Ser.). (gr. 2-8). 599.95 *(978-0-322-06484-3(8))* Wright Group/McGraw-Hill.
—Building the Railroads, 6 vols. (Book2WebTM Ser.). (gr. 4-8). 36.50 *(978-0-322-04448-7(0))* Wright Group/McGraw-Hill.
—Burned: Magazine Anthology: Level 7, 6 vols. (Comprehension Strand Ser.). (gr. 4-8). 54.00 *(978-0-322-06044-9(3))* Wright Group/McGraw-Hill.
—Buttons: Collection 1. (Storyteller Interactive Writing Cards Ser.). (gr. k-3). *(978-0-322-09362-1(7))* Wright Group/McGraw-Hill.
—Buzz the Beekeeper: Level 6, 6 vols. (Fluency Strand Ser.). (gr. 4-8). 194.95 *(978-1-4045-1296-2(9))* Wright Group/McGraw-Hill.
—The C & P Pies: Level H, 6 vols. (Take Twostm Ser.). 16p. 29.95 *(978-0-322-08973-0(5))* Wright Group/McGraw-Hill.
—The Calendar: Level G, 6 vols. (Take Twostm Ser.). 16p. 29.95 *(978-0-322-08981-5(6))* Wright Group/McGraw-Hill.
—Celebrating the New Year: Level I, 6 vols. (Take Twostm Ser.). 16p. 29.95 *(978-0-322-08974-7(3))* Wright Group/McGraw-Hill.
—The Chinampa: Level I, 6 vols. (Take Twostm Ser.). 16p. 29.95 *(978-0-322-08996-9(4))* Wright Group/McGraw-Hill.
—Complete Level Sets: Levels 1-2 Complete Set. (Fast Track Reading Ser.). (gr. 4-8). 763.00 *(978-1-4045-0395-3(1))* Wright Group/McGraw-Hill.
—Complete Program Set: Comprehension Strand. (Fast Track Reading Ser.). (gr. 4-8). 2435.00 *(978-1-4045-0406-6(0))* Wright Group/McGraw-Hill.
—Complete Program Set: Fluency Strand. (Fast Track Reading Ser.). (gr. 4-8). 1445.00 *(978-1-4045-0408-0(7))* Wright Group/McGraw-Hill.
—Complete Program Set: Word Work Strand. (Fast Track Reading Ser.). (gr. 4-8). 1299.00 *(978-0-322-07226-8(3))* Wright Group/McGraw-Hill.
—A Day to Remember: Level I, 6 vols. (Take Twostm Ser.). 16p. 29.95 *(978-0-322-08975-4(1))* Wright Group/McGraw-Hill.
—Dog-Sled Racer: Level 5, 6 vols. (Fluency Strand Ser.). (gr. 4-8). 194.95 *(978-1-4045-1295-5(0))* Wright Group/McGraw-Hill.
—Dom's Dragon: Level E, 6 vols. (Take Twostm Ser.). 16p. 29.95 *(978-0-322-08977-8(8))* Wright Group/McGraw-Hill.
—Don't Go Out: Level F, 6 vols. (Take Twostm Ser.). 16p. 29.95 *(978-0-322-08954-9(9))* Wright Group/McGraw-Hill.
—Double Dare., 6 vols. (D-Man Beans Ser.). 47p. (gr. 4-6). 42.50 *(978-0-322-06265-8(9))* Wright Group/McGraw-Hill.
—E-search: Level O, 6 vols. (Autumn Leaves Ser.). 128p. (gr. 3-6). 36.95 *(978-0-322-06730-1(8))* Wright Group/McGraw-Hill.
—Early Emergent Guided Reading Kit 1: Complete Kit. (gr. k-18). 435.96 *(978-1-4045-2057-8(0))* Wright Group/McGraw-Hill.
—Early Emergent Guided Reading Kit 1: Lesson Plans. (gr. k-18). 127.95 *(978-1-4045-2071-4(6))* Wright Group/McGraw-Hill.
—Early Fluency-Fluency Writing Kit. 2004. (Wright Group Literacy Ser.). (gr. k-3). 132.50 *(978-0-322-07021-9(X))* Wright Group/McGraw-Hill.
—Early Fluency Guided Reading Kit 1: Student Books. (Sunshine Ser.). (gr. 2-18). 93.50 *(978-0-322-04217-9(8))* Wright Group/McGraw-Hill.
—Early Fluency Guided Reading Kit 5: Student Books, Vol. 5. (gr. 2-18). 93.50 *(978-0-322-04750-1(1))* Wright Group/McGraw-Hill.
—Early Fluency Kit 1: Complete Kit. (gr. 2-18). 536.95 *(978-1-4045-2062-2(7))* Wright Group/McGraw-Hill.
—Early Fluency Kit 1: Student Books. (gr. 2-18). 94.95 *(978-1-4045-2070-7(8))* Wright Group/McGraw-Hill.
—Explorers: Fluency - Complete Kit. (gr. 3-6). 547.95 *(978-0-322-09171-9(3))* Wright Group/McGraw-Hill.
—Explorers Fluency Complete Kit 2, Vol. 2. (gr. 3-4). 547.95 *(978-0-322-09170-2(5))* Wright Group/McGraw-Hill.
—Explorers Fluency Complete Kit 3, Vol. 3. (gr. 3-4). 547.95 *(978-0-322-09169-6(1))* Wright Group/McGraw-Hill.
—Famous Shipwrecks, 6 vols. (Book2WebTM Ser.). (gr. 4-8). 36.50 *(978-0-322-04458-6(8))* Wright Group/McGraw-Hill.
—FDR & Eleanor: Triumphs & Tragedies, 6 vols. (Book2WebTM Ser.). (gr. 4-8). 36.50 *(978-0-322-04463-0(4))* Wright Group/McGraw-Hill.
—Fibonacci's Cows: Level O, 6 vols. (Mountain Peaks Ser.). 128p. (gr. 6-18). 36.95 *(978-0-322-06737-0(5))* Wright Group/McGraw-Hill.
—Fire at the Museum: Decodable Books, 6 vols. 22nd ed. (Fast Track Reading Ser.). 24p. (gr. 4-8). 40.95 *(978-0-322-05977-1(1))* Wright Group/McGraw-Hill.
—Fire at the Museum Play 11: Decodable Plays, 6 vols. (Fast Track Reading Ser.). 24p. (gr. 4-8). 40.95 *(978-0-322-05991-7(7))* Wright Group/McGraw-Hill.
—First Explorers: Upper Emergent - Complete Kit. (gr. 1-18). 386.50 *(978-0-322-09168-9(3))* Wright Group/McGraw-Hill.
—First Explorers: Upper Emergent - Lesson Plan Set - 1 Each of 12 Lesson Plans. (gr. 1-18). 47.95 *(978-0-322-08418-6(0))* Wright Group/McGraw-Hill.
—First Explorers: Upper Emergent-Early Fluency - Complete Kit. (gr. 1-2). 426.50 *(978-0-322-09167-2(5))* Wright Group/McGraw-Hill.
—First Explorers: Upper Emergent-Early Fluency - Lesson Plan Set - 1 Each of 12 Lesson Plans. (gr. 1-2). 47.95 *(978-0-322-08419-3(9))* Wright Group/McGraw-Hill.
—First Explorers: Upper Emergent-Early Fluency - Student Book Set - 1 Each of 12 Titles. (First Explorers. Primeros Exploradores Nonfiction Sets Ser.). (gr. 1-2). 67.50 *(978-0-7699-1362-9(8))* Shortland Pubns. (U. S. A.) Inc.
—Fluency Guided Reading Kit 3 Vol. 3: Student Books, (gr. 3-6). 112.50 *(978-0-322-04751-8(X))* Wright Group/McGraw-Hill.
—Fossils Reveal Clues about Ancient Life, 6 vols. (Book2WebTM Ser.). (gr. 4-8). 36.50 *(978-0-322-04431-9(6))* Wright Group/McGraw-Hill.
—Found & Lost, 6 vols. (D-Man Beans Ser.). 47p. (gr. 4-6). 42.50 *(978-0-322-06268-9(3))* Wright Group/McGraw-Hill.
—From Plan to House: Level H, 6 vols. (Take Twostm Ser.). 16p. 29.95 *(978-0-322-08999-0(9))* Wright Group/McGraw-Hill.
—Gear Up! Early Emergent - 1 Each of 8 Student Books: Level A. 35.95 *(978-1-4045-2041-7(4))* Wright Group/McGraw-Hill.
—Gear Up! Early Emergent - 1 Each of 8 Student Books: Level B. 35.95 *(978-1-4045-2042-4(2))* Wright Group/McGraw-Hill.
—Gear Up! Early Emergent - 1 Each of 8 Student Books: Level C. 35.95 *(978-1-4045-2043-1(0))* Wright Group/McGraw-Hill.
—Gear Up! Early Emergent - 1 Each of 8 Student Books: Level D. 35.95 *(978-1-4045-2044-8(9))* Wright Group/McGraw-Hill.
—Gear Up! Early Emergent - Complete Kit, Vol. 2. (gr. k-1). 435.95 *(978-1-4045-2058-5(9))* Wright Group/McGraw-Hill.
—Gear Up! Early Fluency - Complete Kit, Vol. 2. (Early Fluency Ser.). (gr. 2-18). 536.95 *(978-1-4045-2064-6(3))* Wright Group/McGraw-Hill.
—Gear Up! Upper Emergent-Early Fluency - 1 Each of 8 Student Books: Level J. 39.50 *(978-1-4045-2051-6(1))* Wright Group/McGraw-Hill.
—Gear Up! Upper Emergent-Early Fluency - 1 Each of 8 Student Books: Level K. (Early Fluency Ser.). 47.50 *(978-1-4045-2052-3(X))* Wright Group/McGraw-Hill.
—Gear Up! Upper Emergent-Early Fluency - 1 Each of 8 Student Books: Level L. (Early Fluency Ser.). 47.50 *(978-1-4045-2053-0(8))* Wright Group/McGraw-Hill.
—Gear Up! Upper Emergent-Early Fluency - 1 Each of 8 Student Books: Level M. (Early Fluency Ser.). 47.50 *(978-1-4045-2054-7(6))* Wright Group/McGraw-Hill.
—Gear Up! Upper Emergent-Early Fluency - 1 Each of 8 Student Books: Level N. (Early Fluency Ser.). 47.50 *(978-1-4045-2056-1(2))* Wright Group/McGraw-Hill.
—Gear Up! Vol. 2: Early Emergent - Gear up! for Guided Reading. (gr. 2-18). 19.50 incl. DVD *(978-1-4045-2079-0(1))* Wright Group/McGraw-Hill.
—Gear Up! Vol. 2: Early Emergent - Gear up! Guided Reading Overview. (gr. 2-18). 19.50 *(978-1-4045-1950-3(5))* Wright Group/McGraw-Hill.
—Gear Up! Vol. 2: Early Fluency - Student Book Set - 1 Each of 16 Titles. (Early Fluency Ser.). (gr. 2-18). 71.95 *(978-1-4045-2072-1(4))* Wright Group/McGraw-Hill.
—Gear Up! Vol. 3: Upper Emergent - Complete Kit. (gr. 1-18). 499.95 *(978-1-4045-2061-5(9))* Wright Group/McGraw-Hill.
—Gear Up! Vol. 3: Upper Emergent - Student Book Set - 1 Each of 16 Titles. (gr. 1-18). 78.95 *(978-1-4045-2069-1(4))* Wright Group/McGraw-Hill.
—Ger Up! Upper Emergent - 1 Each of 8 Student Books: Level E. 39.50 *(978-1-4045-2045-5(7))* Wright Group/McGraw-Hill.
—Ger Up! Upper Emergent - 1 Each of 8 Student Books: Level F. 39.50 *(978-1-4045-2046-2(5))* Wright Group/McGraw-Hill.
—Ger Up! Upper Emergent - 1 Each of 8 Student Books: Level G. 39.50 *(978-1-4045-2048-6(1))* Wright Group/McGraw-Hill.
—Ger Up! Upper Emergent - 1 Each of 8 Student Books: Level H. 39.50 *(978-1-4045-2049-3(X))* Wright Group/McGraw-Hill.
—Ger Up! Upper Emergent - 1 Each of 8 Student Books: Level I. 39.50 *(978-1-4045-2050-9(3))* Wright Group/McGraw-Hill.
—Guided Reading Kits: Upper Emergent Kit 1 (Student Books) (gr. 1-18). 79.95 *(978-0-322-04339-8(5))* Wright Group/McGraw-Hill.
—Guided Reading Kits: Early Emergent Kit 2 Vol. 2: Student Books. (gr. k-18). 66.95 *(978-0-322-04350-3(6))* Wright Group/McGraw-Hill.
—Guided Reading Kits: Early Emergent Kit 4 Vol. 4: Student Books. (gr. k-18). 66.95 *(978-0-322-04348-0(4))* Wright Group/McGraw-Hill.
—Guided Reading Kits: Upper Emergent Kit 1: Student Books. (gr. 1-18). 79.95 *(978-0-322-04347-3(6))* Wright Group/McGraw-Hill.
—Guided Reading Kits: Upper Emergent Kit 2 Vol. 2: Student Books. (gr. 1-18). 79.95 *(978-0-322-04346-6(8))* Wright Group/McGraw-Hill.
—Guided Reading Kits: Upper Emergent Kit 3 Vol. 3: Student Books. (gr. 1-18). 79.95 *(978-0-322-04345-9(X))* Wright Group/McGraw-Hill.
—Helen Keller: Level 3, 6 vols. (Fluency Strand Ser.). (gr. 4-8). 194.95 *(978-1-4045-1293-1(4))* Wright Group/McGraw-Hill.

P
Q
R

—I Want Some Honey: Level E, 6 vols. (Take Twostm Ser.). 16p. 29.95 *(978-0-322-08956-3(5))* Wright Group/McGraw-Hill.

—In the Rain Forest, 6 vols. (Wildcats Ser.). 32p. (gr. 2-8). *(978-0-322-00599-0(X))* Wright Group/McGraw-Hill.

—The Lazy Moon: Level G, 6 vols. (Take Twostm Ser.). 16p. 29.95 *(978-0-322-08982-2(4))* Wright Group/McGraw-Hill.

—Magnificent Masks: 6 Each of 1 Anthology, 6 vols. (Wildcats Ser.). 32p. (gr. 2-8). *(978-0-322-05624-4(1))* Wright Group/McGraw-Hill.

—Make a Raft: Level E, 6 vols. (Take Twostm Ser.). 16p. 29.95 *(978-0-322-08976-1(X))* Wright Group/McGraw-Hill.

—Make me Laugh! 6 Each of 1 Anthology, 6 vols. (Wildcats Ser.). 32p. (gr. 2-8). *(978-0-322-05628-2(4))* Wright Group/McGraw-Hill.

—Maps: Level I, 6 vols. (Take Twostm Ser.). 16p. 29.95 *(978-0-322-08966-2(2))* Wright Group/McGraw-Hill.

—Mira Hacia el Cielo, 6 vols. (First Explorers: Primeros Exploradores Nonfiction Sets Ser.). (SPA.). (gr. 1-2). 29.95 *(978-0-7699-1471-8(3))* Shortland Pubns. (U. S. A.) Inc.

—Mischief & Mayhem: Level O, 6 vols. (Autumn Leaves Ser.). 128p. (gr. 3-6). 36.95 *(978-0-322-06727-1(8))* Wright Group/McGraw-Hill.

—Mosquito Attack: Level 4, 6 vols. (Fluency Strand Ser.). (gr. 4-8). 194.95 *(978-1-4045-1294-8(2))* Wright Group/McGraw-Hill.

—Move it & Shake It! 6 Each of 1 Anthology, 6 vols. (Wildcats Ser.). 32p. (gr. 2-8). *(978-0-322-05621-3(7))* Wright Group/McGraw-Hill.

—Movie Magic, 6 vols. (Wildcats Ser.). 32p. (gr. 2-8). *(978-0-322-05630-5(6))* Wright Group/McGraw-Hill.

—The Music Scene, 6 vols. (Wildcats Ser.). 32p. (gr. 2-8). *(978-0-322-05631-2(4))* Wright Group/McGraw-Hill.

—My Word! what a Bird! Collection 4. (Storyteller Interactive Writing Cards Ser.). (gr. k-3). *(978-0-322-09325-6(2))* Wright Group/McGraw-Hill.

—No Hay Nadie Como Tu, 6 vols. (First Explorers: Primeros Exploradores Nonfiction Sets Ser.). (SPA.). (gr. 1-2). 29.95 *(978-0-7699-1478-7(0))* Shortland Pubns. (U. S. A.) Inc.

—No Room, New Rules, 6 vols. (D-Man Beans Ser.). 47p. (gr. 4-6). 42.50 *(978-0-322-06263-4(2))* Wright Group/McGraw-Hill.

—On the Prowl: 6 Each of 1 Anthology, 6 vols. (Wildcats Ser.). 32p. (gr. 2-8). *(978-0-322-05852-1(X))* Wright Group/McGraw-Hill.

—Outback School: Level E, 6 vols. (Take Twostm Ser.). 16p. 29.95 *(978-0-322-08949-5(2))* Wright Group/McGraw-Hill.

—Panther Level: Wildcats Panther Complete Kit. (Wildcats Ser.). (gr. 2-8). 599.95 *(978-0-322-06490-4(2))* Wright Group/McGraw-Hill.

—Paper Capers: Level N, 6 vols. (Raging Rivers Ser.). 128p. (gr. 3-6). 36.95 *(978-0-322-06726-4(X))* Wright Group/McGraw-Hill.

—Pat's Picture: Level E, 6 vols. (Take Twostm Ser.). 16p. 29.95 *(978-0-322-08989-1(1))* Wright Group/McGraw-Hill.

—Phonics & Word Study Complete Kits: Phonics & Word Study: Level B. (gr. k-3). 429.50 *(978-0-322-03872-1(3))* Wright Group/McGraw-Hill.

—Picture This! 6 Each of 1 Anthology, 6 vols. (Wildcats Ser.). 32p. (gr. 2-8). *(978-0-322-05627-5(6))* Wright Group/McGraw-Hill.

—Pigeon Princess: Level O, 6 vols. (Autumn Leaves Ser.). 128p. (gr. 3-6). 36.95 *(978-0-322-06729-5(4))* Wright Group/McGraw-Hill.

—Pixels & Paint, 6 vols. (Wildcats Ser.). 32p. (gr. 2-8). *(978-0-322-05625-1(X))* Wright Group/McGraw-Hill.

—Plagues: Magazine Anthology: Level 7, 6 vols. (Comprehension Strand Ser.). (gr. 4-8). 54.00 *(978-0-322-09863-3(7))* Wright Group/McGraw-Hill.

—Reading Recovery Kits: Reading Recovery Complete Set. (Reading Recovery Ser.). (J). (gr. k-6). 2754.50 *(978-0-322-04770-9(6))* Wright Group/McGraw-Hill.

—River Wild: 6 Each of 1 Anthology, 6 vols. (Wildcats Ser.). 32p. (gr. 2-8). *(978-0-322-05857-6(0))* Wright Group/McGraw-Hill.

—Rollers & Blades: Level H, 6 vols. (Take Twostm Ser.). 16p. 29.95 *(978-0-322-08964-8(6))* Wright Group/McGraw-Hill.

—The Secret Soccer Ball Maker: Level G, 6 vols. (Take Twostm Ser.). 16p. 29.95 *(978-0-322-08991-4(3))* Wright Group/McGraw-Hill.

—Set 1: Los Alimentos, 6 vols. (First Explorers: Primeros Exploradores Nonfiction Sets Ser.). (SPA.). (gr. 1-2). 29.95 *(978-0-7699-1469-5(1))* Shortland Pubns. (U. S. A.) Inc.

—Set 2: Los Dinosaurios, 6 vols., Vol. 2. (First Explorers: Primeros Exploradores Nonfiction Sets Ser.). (SPA.). (gr. 1-2). 34.95 *(978-0-7699-1484-8(5))* Shortland Pubns. (U. S. A.) Inc.

—Slimed! 6 Each of 1 Anthology, 6 vols. (Wildcats Ser.). 32p. (gr. 2-8). *(978-0-322-05853-8(8))* Wright Group/McGraw-Hill.

—So You Want this Job, do You? Magazine Anthology: Level 6, 6 vols. (Comprehension Strand Ser.). (gr. 4-8). 54.00 *(978-0-322-06042-5(7))* Wright Group/McGraw-Hill.

—Stories on Stage, 6 vols. (Wildcats Ser.). 32p. (gr. 2-8). *(978-0-322-05622-0(5))* Wright Group/McGraw-Hill.

—The Story Box: Early Fluency - Student Book Set - 1 Each of 16 Titles. 2nd ed. (gr. 2-18). 98.50 *(978-0-322-04052-6(3))* Wright Group/McGraw-Hill.

—The Story Box Vol. 3: Early Emergent Kit 3- Lesson Plan Set - 1 Each of 16 Lesson Plans. (gr. k-18). 63.95 *(978-0-322-05929-0(1))* Wright Group/McGraw-Hill.

—Storyteller: Early Emergent - 1 Each of 16 Student Books: Level D. 78.95 *(978-1-4045-1977-0(7))* Wright Group/McGraw-Hill.

—Storyteller: Early Emergent - 1 Each of 3 Student Books: Level A. 14.50 *(978-1-4045-1954-1(8))* Wright Group/McGraw-Hill.

—Storyteller: Early Emergent - 1 Each of 6 Student Books: Level B. 29.50 *(978-1-4045-1962-6(9))* Wright Group/McGraw-Hill.

—Storyteller: Early Emergent - 1 Each of 7 Student Books: Level C. 34.50 *(978-1-4045-1970-1(X))* Wright Group/McGraw-Hill.

—Storyteller: Early Emergent - Student Book Set - 1 Each of 16 Fiction & Nonfiction Titles. (Storyteller Ser.). (gr. k-18). 79.95 *(978-1-4045-1051-7(6))* Wright Group/McGraw-Hill.

—Storyteller: Upper Emergent - 1 Each of 14 Student Books: Level G. 82.95 *(978-1-4045-1983-1(1))* Wright Group/McGraw-Hill.

—Storyteller: Upper Emergent - 1 Each of 15 Student Books: Level E. 88.95 *(978-1-4045-1981-7(5))* Wright Group/McGraw-Hill.

—Storyteller: Upper Emergent - 1 Each of 15 Student Books: Level F. 112.95 *(978-1-4045-1982-4(3))* Wright Group/McGraw-Hill.

—Storyteller: Upper Emergent - 1 Each of 15 Student Books: Level H. 88.95 *(978-1-4045-1984-8(X))* Wright Group/McGraw-Hill.

—Storyteller: Upper Emergent - Complete Kit, Vol. 5. (Storyteller Ser.). (gr. 1-18). 549.50 *(978-1-4045-1041-8(9))* Wright Group/McGraw-Hill.

—Storyteller: Upper Emergent - Lesson Plan Set - 1 Each of 16 Lesson Plans. (Storyteller Ser.). (gr. 1-18). 127.95 *(978-1-4045-1074-6(5))* Wright Group/McGraw-Hill.

—Storyteller: Upper Emergent - Student Book Set - 1 Each of 16 Fiction & Nonfiction Titles. (Storyteller Ser.). (gr. 1-18). 96.50 *(978-1-4045-1058-6(3))* Wright Group/McGraw-Hill.

—Storyteller: Upper Emergent-Early Fluency - 1 Each of 14 Student Books: Level I. 82.95 *(978-1-4045-1985-5(8))* Wright Group/McGraw-Hill.

—Storyteller: Upper Emergent-Early Fluency - 1 Each of 15 Student Books: Level J. 88.95 *(978-1-4045-1986-2(6))* Wright Group/McGraw-Hill.

—Storyteller: Upper Emergent-Early Fluency - 1 Each of 4 Student Books: Level K. 27.50 *(978-1-4045-1987-9(4))* Wright Group/McGraw-Hill.

—Storyteller Vol. 2: Early Emergent - Complete Kit. (Storyteller Ser.). (gr. k-18). 485.50 *(978-1-4045-1036-4(2))* Wright Group/McGraw-Hill.

—Storyteller Chapter Books: Early Fluency-Fluency - 1 Each of 10 Titles: Level O. 61.50 *(978-1-4045-0949-8(6))* Wright Group/McGraw-Hill.

—Storyteller Chapter Books: Early Fluency-Fluency - 1 Each of 11 Titles: Level N. 69.50 *(978-1-4045-0948-1(8))* Wright Group/McGraw-Hill.

—Storyteller Chapter Books: Early Fluency-Fluency - 1 Each of 4 Titles: Level P. 24.50 *(978-1-4045-0950-4(X))* Wright Group/McGraw-Hill.

—Storyteller Chapter Books: Early Fluency-Fluency - 1 Each of 4 Titles: Level Q. 24.50 *(978-1-4045-0951-1(8))* Wright Group/McGraw-Hill.

—Storyteller Chapter Books: Fluency - 1 Each of 2 Title: Level U. 11.95 *(978-1-4045-0955-9(0))* Wright Group/McGraw-Hill.

—Storyteller Chapter Books: Fluency - 1 Each of 2 Titles: Level R. 11.95 *(978-1-4045-0952-8(6))* Wright Group/McGraw-Hill.

—Storyteller Chapter Books: Upper Emergent-Early Fluency - 1 Each of 18 Titles: Level M. 130.95 *(978-1-4045-0947-4(X))* Wright Group/McGraw-Hill.

—Storyteller Chapter Books: Upper Emergent-Early Fluency - 1 Each of 4 Titles: Level J. 27.95 *(978-1-4045-0944-3(5))* Wright Group/McGraw-Hill.

—Storyteller Chapter Books: Upper Emergent-Early Fluency - 1 Each of 8 Titles: Level K. 57.50 *(978-1-4045-0945-0(3))* Wright Group/McGraw-Hill.

—Storyteller Chapter Books: Upper Emergent-Early Fluency - 1 Each of 8 Titles: Level L. 55.50 *(978-1-4045-0946-7(1))* Wright Group/McGraw-Hill.

—Storyteller Upper Emergent Guided Reading Complete Kit 1. (Storyteller Ser.). (gr. 1-18). 549.50 *(978-1-4045-1037-1(0))* Wright Group/McGraw-Hill.

—Storyteller Upper Emergent Guided Reading Complete Kit 2, Vol. 2. (Storyteller Ser.). (gr. 1-18). 549.50 *(978-1-4045-1038-8(9))* Wright Group/McGraw-Hill.

—Storyteller Upper Emergent Guided Reading Complete Kit 3, Vol. 3. (Storyteller Ser.). (gr. 1-18). 549.50 *(978-1-4045-1039-5(7))* Wright Group/McGraw-Hill.

—Storyteller Upper Emergent Guided Reading Kit, Set. (Storyteller Ser.). (gr. 1-18). 93.50 *(978-1-4045-1056-2(7))* Wright Group/McGraw-Hill.

—Storyteller Upper Emergent Guided Reading Kit 3, Set. (Storyteller Ser.). (gr. 1-18). 93.50 *(978-1-4045-1055-5(9))* Wright Group/McGraw-Hill.

—Storyteller Upper Emergent Guided Reading Kit 5, Set. (Storyteller Ser.). (gr. 1-18). 93.50 *(978-1-4045-1057-9(5))* Wright Group/McGraw-Hill.

—Stranger Than Fiction: 6 Each of 1 Anthology, 6 vols. (Wildcats Ser.). 32p. (gr. 2-8). *(978-0-322-05855-2(4))* Wright Group/McGraw-Hill.

—Summer Skies: Classroom Library Set. (Summer Skies Ser.). 81.50 *(978-0-322-07968-7(3))* Wright Group/McGraw-Hill.

—Summer Skies: Complete Set. (Summer Skies Ser.). 327.95 *(978-0-322-07963-2(2))* Wright Group/McGraw-Hill.

—Sunshine: Early Emergent - Group 3: 1 Each of 4 Student Books: Level A. (Sunshine Ser.). 16.95 *(978-0-322-03707-6(7))* Wright Group/McGraw-Hill.

—Sunshine: Early Emergent - Group 3: 1 Each of 4 Student Books: Level C. (Sunshine Ser.). 16.95 *(978-0-322-03709-0(3))* Wright Group/McGraw-Hill.

—Sunshine: Early Emergent - Group 3: 1 Each of 4 Student Books: Level D. (Sunshine Ser.). 16.95 *(978-0-322-03710-6(7))* Wright Group/McGraw-Hill.

—Sunshine: Early Emergent - Group 3:1 Each of 4 Student Books: Level B. (Sunshine Ser.). 16.95 *(978-0-322-03708-3(5))* Wright Group/McGraw-Hill.

—Sunshine: Early Emergent-Upper Emergent - Group 2: 1 Each of 8 Student Books: Level E. (Sunshine Ser.). 39.95 *(978-0-322-04317-6(4))* Wright Group/McGraw-Hill.

—Sunshine: Early Emergent-Upper Emergent - Group 3: 1 Each of 5 Student Books: Level E. (Sunshine Ser.). 24.95 *(978-0-322-03711-3(5))* Wright Group/McGraw-Hill.

—Sunshine: Early Emergent-Upper Emergent - Groups 1-2: 1 Each of 16 Student Books: Level E. (Sunshine Ser.). 79.95 *(978-0-322-04316-9(6))* Wright Group/McGraw-Hill.

—Sunshine: Early Fluency - Enrichment Library: 1 each of 12 titles: Level L. 69.95 *(978-0-322-04025-0(6))* Wright Group/McGraw-Hill.

—Sunshine: Early Fluency - Enrichment Library: 1 each of 5 titles: Level N. (Sunshine Ser.). 29.50 *(978-0-322-04028-1(0))* Wright Group/McGraw-Hill.

—Sunshine: Early Fluency - Enrichment Library, Groups 1-2: 1 each of 11 titles: Level K. (Sunshine Ser.). 69.95 *(978-0-322-04024-3(8))* Wright Group/McGraw-Hill.

—Sunshine: Early Fluency - Group 1: 1 each of 11 titles: Level K. (Sunshine Ser.). 64.50 *(978-0-322-04308-4(5))* Wright Group/McGraw-Hill.

—Sunshine: Early Fluency - Group 1: 1 each of 11 titles: Level L. (Sunshine Ser.). 64.50 *(978-0-322-04311-4(5))* Wright Group/McGraw-Hill.

—Sunshine: Early Fluency - Group 1; 1 each of 11 titles: Level M. (Sunshine Ser.). 64.50 *(978-0-322-04313-8(1))* Wright Group/McGraw-Hill.

—Sunshine: Early Fluency - Group 3: 1 each of 11 Titles: Level N. 64.50 *(978-0-322-05241-3(6))* Wright Group/McGraw-Hill.

—Sunshine: Early Fluency - Group 3: 1 each of 8 Titles: Level K. 46.95 *(978-0-322-05238-3(6))* Wright Group/McGraw-Hill.

—Sunshine: Early Fluency - Groups 1-2: 1 each of 17 titles: Level K. (Sunshine Ser.). 99.50 *(978-0-322-04307-7(7))* Wright Group/McGraw-Hill.

—Sunshine: Early Fluency - Groups 1-2: 1 each of 17 titles: Level L. (Sunshine Ser.). 99.50 *(978-0-322-04309-1(3))* Wright Group/McGraw-Hill.

—Sunshine: Early Fluency-Enrichment Library; 1 each of 7 titles: Level M. (Sunshine Ser.). 40.95 *(978-0-322-04027-4(2))* Wright Group/McGraw-Hill.

—Sunshine: Early Fluency-Group 1; 1 each of 11 titles: Level N. (Sunshine Ser.). 64.50 *(978-0-322-04315-2(8))* Wright Group/McGraw-Hill.

—Sunshine: Early Fluency-Group 3: 1 each of 8 Titles: Level L. 46.95 *(978-0-322-05239-0(4))* Wright Group/McGraw-Hill.

—Sunshine: Early Fluency-Group 3; 1 each of 8 Titles: Level M. 46.95 *(978-0-322-05240-6(8))* Wright Group/McGraw-Hill.

—Sunshine: Early Fluency-Groups 1-2; 1 each of 17 titles: Level N. (Sunshine Ser.). 99.50 *(978-0-322-04314-5(X))* Wright Group/McGraw-Hill.

—Sunshine: Fluency - Group 3: 1 Each of 4 Titles: Level S. (Sunshine Ser.). 29.95 *(978-0-322-05247-5(5))* Wright Group/McGraw-Hill.

—Sunshine: Fluency - Group 3: 1 Each of 4 Titles: Level T. (Sunshine Ser.). 29.95 *(978-0-322-05248-2(3))* Wright Group/McGraw-Hill.

—Sunshine: Fluency - Group 3: 1 each of 6 Titles: Level O. 39.95 *(978-0-322-05242-0(4))* Wright Group/McGraw-Hill.

—Sunshine: Fluency - Group 3: 1 Each of 6 Titles: Level R. (Sunshine Ser.). 44.95 *(978-0-322-05246-8(7))* Wright Group/McGraw-Hill.

—Sunshine: Fluency-Group 3: 1 each of 6 Titles: Level P. 39.95 *(978-0-322-05244-4(0))* Wright Group/McGraw-Hill.

—Sunshine: Fluency-Group 3: 1 each of 6 Titles: Level Q. 39.95 *(978-0-322-05245-1(9))* Wright Group/McGraw-Hill.

—Sunshine: Upper Emergent - Group 1:1 Each of 8 Student Books: Level G. Group 1. (Sunshine Ser.). 39.95 *(978-0-322-04321-3(2))* Wright Group/McGraw-Hill.

—Sunshine: Upper Emergent - Group 1:1 Each of 8 Student Books: Level H. Group 1. (Sunshine Ser.). 39.95 *(978-0-322-04324-4(7))* Wright Group/McGraw-Hill.

—Sunshine: Upper Emergent - Group 2: 1 Each of 8 Student Books: Level G. Group 1. (Sunshine Ser.). 39.95 *(978-0-322-04322-0(0))* Wright Group/McGraw-Hill.

—Sunshine: Upper Emergent - Group 2:1 Each of 7 Student Books: Level F. Group 2. (Sunshine Ser.). 34.95 *(978-0-322-04319-0(0))* Wright Group/McGraw-Hill.

—Sunshine: Upper Emergent - Group 2:1 Each of 9 Student Books: Level H. Group 2. (Sunshine Ser.). 44.95 *(978-0-322-04325-1(5))* Wright Group/McGraw-Hill.

—Sunshine: Upper Emergent - Group 3:1 Each of 12 Student Books: Level H. 59.95 *(978-0-322-03716-8(6))* Wright Group/McGraw-Hill.

—Sunshine: Upper Emergent - Group 3:1 Each of 6 Student Books: Level G. 29.95 *(978-0-322-03714-4(X))* Wright Group/McGraw-Hill.

—Sunshine: Upper Emergent - Group 3:1 Each of 8 Student Books: Level F. Group 3. 24.95 *(978-0-322-03713-7(1))* Wright Group/McGraw-Hill.

—Sunshine: Upper Emergent - Groups 1-2:1 Each of 15 Student Books: Level F. (Sunshine Ser.). 74.95 *(978-0-322-04318-3(2))* Wright Group/McGraw-Hill.

—Sunshine: Upper Emergent - Groups 1-2:1 Each of 16 Student Books: Level G. (Sunshine Ser.). 79.95 *(978-0-322-04320-6(4))* Wright Group/McGraw-Hill.

—Sunshine: Upper Emergent - Nonfiction:1 Each of 3 Student Books: Level G. (Sunshine Ser.). 14.95 *(978-0-322-04304-6(2))* Wright Group/McGraw-Hill.

—Sunshine: Upper Emergent-Enrichment Library: 1 each of 5 student books: Level J. (Sunshine Ser.). 24.95 *(978-0-322-04023-6(X))* Wright Group/McGraw-Hill.

—Sunshine: Upper Emergent-Group 2: 1 each of 5 student books: Level J. 24.95 *(978-0-322-03715-1(8))* Wright Group/McGraw-Hill.

—Sunshine: Upper Emergent-Group 3: 1 each of 10 student books: Level I. 49.95 *(978-0-322-03717-5(4))* Wright Group/McGraw-Hill.

—Sunshine: Upper Emergent-Groups 1-2: 1 each of 16 student books: Level I. (Sunshine Ser.). 79.95 *(978-0-322-04326-8(3))* Wright Group/McGraw-Hill.

—Sunshine: Upper Emergent-Nonfiction: 1 each of 3 student books: Level H. (Sunshine Ser.). 14.95 *(978-0-322-04305-3(0))* Wright Group/McGraw-Hill.

—Sunshine: Upper Emergent-Nonfiction: 1 each of 5 student books: Level I. (Sunshine Ser.). 24.95 *(978-0-322-04306-0(9))* Wright Group/McGraw-Hill.

—Sunshine: Upper Emergent-Nonfiction: 1 each of 5 student books: Level J. (Sunshine Ser.). 24.95 *(978-0-322-04329-9(8))* Wright Group/McGraw-Hill.

—SUNSHINE Early Fluency Guided Reading Kit 5, Vol. 5. 2004. (Wright Group Literacy Ser.). (gr. 2-18). 524.95 *(978-0-322-04746-4(3))* Wright Group/McGraw-Hill.

—Take-Twos: Fluency - 1 each of 12 Titles: Level O. 79.95 *(978-0-322-04576-7(2))* Wright Group/McGraw-Hill.

—Take Twos: Fluency - 1 Each of 4 Titles: Level S. (Take Twostm Ser.). 29.95 *(978-1-4045-0737-1(X))* Wright Group/McGraw-Hill.

—Take Twos: Fluency - 1 Each of 4Ttitles: Level T. (Take Twostm Ser.). 29.95 *(978-1-4045-0738-8(8))* Wright Group/McGraw-Hill.

—Take-Twos: Fluency - Group 1; 1 each of 12 Titles: Level P. 79.95 *(978-0-322-04577-4(0))* Wright Group/McGraw-Hill.

—Take-Twos: Fluency - Group 1; 1 each of 12 Titles: Level Q. 79.95 *(978-0-322-04578-1(9))* Wright Group/McGraw-Hill.

—Take Twos: Fluency - Group 1: 1 each of 12 Titles: Level R. 89.95 *(978-0-322-04579-8(7))* Wright Group/McGraw-Hill.

—Take Twos: Fluency - Group 1: 1 each of 6 Lesson Plans: Level R. 47.95 *(978-0-322-04573-6(8))* Wright Group/McGraw-Hill.

—Take-Twos: Fluency - Group 2; 1 Each of 4 (New) Titles: Level P. (Take Twostm Ser.). 26.95 *(978-1-4045-0731-9(0))* Wright Group/McGraw-Hill.

—Take-Twos: Fluency - Group 2; 1 Each of 4 (New) Titles: Level Q. (Take Twostm Ser.). 26.95 *(978-1-4045-0733-3(7))* Wright Group/McGraw-Hill.

—Take Twos: Fluency - Group 2: 1 Each of 8 (New) Titles: Level R. (Take Twostm Ser.). 59.95 *(978-1-4045-0735-7(3))* Wright Group/McGraw-Hill.

—Take-Twos: Fluency - Groups 1 & 2; 1 Each of 16 Titles: Level P. (Take Twostm Ser.). 106.95 *(978-1-4045-0732-6(9))* Wright Group/McGraw-Hill.

—Take-Twos: Fluency - Groups 1 & 2; 1 Each of 16 Titles: Level Q. (Take Twostm Ser.). 106.95 *(978-1-4045-0734-0(5))* Wright Group/McGraw-Hill.

—Take-Twos: Upper Emergent - 1 Each of 10 Titles: Level J. (Take Twostm Ser.). 49.95 *(978-1-4045-0744-9(2))* Wright Group/McGraw-Hill.

—Take Twos: Upper Emergent - 1 Each of 8 Titles: Level E. (Take Twostm Ser.). 39.95 *(978-1-4045-0739-5(6))* Wright Group/McGraw-Hill.

—Take Twos: Upper Emergent - 1 Each of 8 Titles: Level F. (Take Twostm Ser.). 39.95 *(978-1-4045-0740-1(X))* Wright Group/McGraw-Hill.

—Take Twos: Upper Emergent - 1 Each of 8 Titles: Level H. (Take Twostm Ser.). 39.95 *(978-1-4045-0742-5(6))* Wright Group/McGraw-Hill.

—Take Twos: Upper Emergent - 1 Each of 8 Titles: Level I. (Take Twostm Ser.). 39.95 *(978-1-4045-0743-2(4))* Wright Group/McGraw-Hill.

—Take-Twos Adventure Vol. 3: Fluency - Complete Kit. (gr. 3-4). 492.50 *(978-0-322-09178-8(0))* Wright Group/McGraw-Hill.

—Take-Twos Adventure Vol. 3: Fluency - Student Book Set - 1 Each of 12 Titles. (gr. 3-4). 83.50 *(978-0-322-09306-5(6))* Wright Group/McGraw-Hill.

—Take-Twos Circles & Cycles Vol. 2: Upper Emergent - Student Book Set - 1 Each of 12 Titles. (gr. 1-18). 59.50 *(978-0-322-09314-0(7))* Wright Group/McGraw-Hill.

—Take-Twos Circles & Cycles Vol. 2: Upper Emergent - Upper Emergent - Complete Kit. (gr. 1-18). 366.95 *(978-0-322-09280-8(9))* Wright Group/McGraw-Hill.

—Take-Twos Cultures: Upper Emergent - Complete Kit. (gr. 1-18). 366.95 *(978-0-322-09279-2(5))* Wright Group/McGraw-Hill.

—Take-Twos Cultures: Upper Emergent - Student Book Set - 1 Each of 12 Titles. (Take-Twostm Ser.). (gr. 1-18). 59.50 *(978-0-322-09312-6(0))* Wright Group/McGraw-Hill.

—Take-Twos Earth Links Vol. 3: Upper Emergent - Complete Kit. (gr. 1-18). 366.95 *(978-0-322-09282-2(5))* Wright Group/McGraw-Hill.

—Take-Twos Earth Links Vol. 3: Upper Emergent - Student Book Set - 1 Each of 12 Titles. (Take-Twostm Ser.). (gr. 1-18). 59.50 *(978-0-322-09316-4(3))* Wright Group/McGraw-Hill.

—Take-Twos Finding Out Vol. 6: Fluency - Complete Kit. (gr. 4-6). 501.50 *(978-0-322-09181-8(0))* Wright Group/McGraw-Hill.

—Take-Twos Finding Out Vol. 6: Fluency - Student Book Set - 1 Each of 12 Titles. (Take-Twostm Ser.). (gr. 4-6). 84.95 *(978-0-322-09309-6(0))* Wright Group/McGraw-Hill.

—Take-Twos Land & Air: Early Fluency - Complete Kit. (gr. 2-18). 420.50 *(978-0-322-09172-6(1))* Wright Group/McGraw-Hill.

—Take-Twos Land & Air: Early Fluency - Student Book Set - 1 Each of 12 Titles. (gr. 2-18). 69.95 *(978-0-322-09300-3(7))* Wright Group/McGraw-Hill.

—Take-Twos Making Things Vol. 3: Early Fluency - Complete Kit. (gr. 2-18). 420.50 *(978-0-322-09174-0(8))* Wright Group/McGraw-Hill.

—Take-Twos Making Things Vol. 3: Early Fluency - Student Book Set - 1 Each of 12 Titles. (gr. 2-18). 69.95 *(978-0-322-09302-7(3))* Wright Group/McGraw-Hill.

—Take-Twos Old to New Vol. 4: Fluency - Complete Kit. (gr. 3-4). 492.50 *(978-0-322-09179-5(9))* Wright Group/McGraw-Hill.

—Take-Twos Old to New Vol. 4: Fluency - Student Book Set - 1 Each of 12 Titles. (gr. 3-4). 83.50 *(978-0-322-09307-2(4))* Wright Group/McGraw-Hill.

—Take-Twos Play Time Vol. 4: Upper Emergent - Student Book Set - 1 Each of 12 Titles. (Take-Twostm Ser.). (gr. 1-18). 59.50 *(978-0-322-09318-8(X))* Wright Group/McGraw-Hill.

—Take-Twos Play Time Vol. 4: Upper Emergent - Upper Emergent - Complete Kit. (gr. 1-18). 366.95 *(978-0-322-09283-9(3))* Wright Group/McGraw-Hill.

—Take-Twos Slither, Swim, & Soar: Fluency - Complete Kit. (gr. 3-4). 483.50 *(978-0-322-09176-4(4))* Wright Group/McGraw-Hill.

—Take-Twos Slither, Swim, & Soar: Fluency - Student Book Set - 1 Each of 12 Titles. (gr. 3-4). 81.95 *(978-0-322-09304-1(X))* Wright Group/McGraw-Hill.

—Take-Twos Stories & Legends Vol. 5: Fluency - Complete Kit. (gr. 4-6). 519.50 *(978-0-322-09180-1(2))* Wright Group/McGraw-Hill.

—Take-Twos Stories & Legends Vol. 5: Fluency - Student Book Set - 1 Each of 12 Titles. (Take-Twostm Ser.). (gr. 4-6). 88.50 *(978-0-322-09308-9(2))* Wright Group/McGraw-Hill.

—Teeth: Level G, 6 vols. (Take Twostm Ser.). 16p. 29.95 *(978-0-322-08968-6(9))* Wright Group/McGraw-Hill.

—Tiger Level: Adventure Journal Set. (Wildcats Ser.). (gr. 2-8). 31.95 *(978-0-322-05790-6(6))* Wright Group/McGraw-Hill.

—Tiger Level: Lesson Plan Set. (Wildcats Ser.). (gr. 2-8). 96.50 *(978-0-322-06677-9(8))* Wright Group/McGraw-Hill.

—Tiger Level: Wildcats Tiger Complete Kit. (Wildcats Ser.). (gr. 2-8). 599.95 *(978-0-322-06483-6(X))* Wright Group/McGraw-Hill.

—Tv Times: 6 Each of 1 Anthology, 6 vols. (Wildcats Ser.). 32p. (gr. 2-8). *(978-0-322-05629-9(2))* Wright Group/McGraw-Hill.

—Twig Books: Early Emergent - 1 each of 16 student books: Level A. (Twig Ser.). 66.95 *(978-0-322-04330-5(1))* Wright Group/McGraw-Hill.
—Twig Books: Early Emergent - 1 each of 16 student books: Level B. (Twig Ser.). 66.95 *(978-0-322-04331-2(X))* Wright Group/McGraw-Hill.
—Twig Books: Early Emergent - 1 each of 16 student books: Level C. (Twig Ser.). 66.95 *(978-0-322-04332-9(8))* Wright Group/McGraw-Hill.
—Twig Books: Early Emergent - Upper Emergent - 1 each of 16 student books: Level D. (Twig Ser.). 66.95 *(978-0-322-04333-6(6))* Wright Group/McGraw-Hill.
—Twig Books: Early Emergent - Upper Emergent - 1 each of 16 student books: Level E. (Twig Ser.). 79.95 *(978-0-322-04334-3(4))* Wright Group/McGraw-Hill.
—Twig Books: Student Book Set - 1 Each of 16 Titles. (gr. k-18). 66.95 *(978-0-322-04351-0(4))* Wright Group/McGraw-Hill.
—Twig Books: Upper Emergent - 1 each of 16 student books: Level F. (Twig Ser.). 79.95 *(978-0-322-04335-0(2))* Wright Group/McGraw-Hill.
—Twig Books: Upper Emergent - 1 each of 16 student books: Level G. (Twig Ser.). 79.95 *(978-0-322-04337-4(9))* Wright Group/McGraw-Hill.
—Twig Books: Upper Emergent - 1 each of 16 student books: Level H. (Twig Ser.). 77.95 *(978-0-322-04338-1(7))* Wright Group/McGraw-Hill.
—Twig Books Vol. 3: Early Emergent - Student Book Set - 1 Each of 16 Titles. (gr. k-18). 66.95 *(978-0-322-04349-7(2))* Wright Group/McGraw-Hill.
—Twig Books Vol. 4: Upper Emergent - Student Book Set -1 Each of 16 Titles. (gr. 1-18). 79.95 *(978-0-322-04343-5(3))* Wright Group/McGraw-Hill.
—Upper Emergent Guided Reading Complete Kit 1. (Sunshine Ser.). (gr. 1-18). 486.50 *(978-0-322-04210-0(0))* Wright Group/McGraw-Hill.
—Upper Emergent Guided Reading Kit 5 Vol. 5: Student Books, (gr. 1-18). 79.95 *(978-0-322-03883-7(9))* Wright Group/McGraw-Hill.
—Upper Emergent Guided Reading Kit 6 Vol. 6: Student Books, (gr. 1-18). 79.95 *(978-0-322-03884-4(7))* Wright Group/McGraw-Hill.
—Upper Emergent Kit 1: Complete Kit. (gr. k-1). 499.95 *(978-1-4045-2059-2(7))* Wright Group/McGraw-Hill.
—Upper Emergent Kit 2 Vol. 2: Complete Kit. (gr. 1-18). 499.95 *(978-1-4045-2060-8(0))* Wright Group/McGraw-Hill.
—Vegetarians: Level H, 6 vols. (Take Twostm Ser.). 16p. 29.95 *(978-0-322-08972-3(7))* Wright Group/McGraw-Hill.
—Wear your Art: 6 Each of 1 Anthology, 6 vols. (Wildcats Ser.). 32p. (gr. 2-8). *(978-0-322-05623-7(3))* Wright Group/McGraw-Hill.
—Whispering Pines: Classroom Library Set. (Whispering Pines Ser.). 81.50 *(978-0-322-07971-7(3))* Wright Group/McGraw-Hill.
—Whispering Pines: Complete Set. (Whispering Pines Ser.). 327.95 *(978-0-322-07965-6(9))* Wright Group/McGraw-Hill.
—Wildcats Strand Kits: Animals & Nature Strand. (Wildcats Ser.). (gr. 2-8). 589.95 *(978-0-322-06535-2(6))* Wright Group/McGraw-Hill.
—Wildcats Strand Kits: Arts & Entertainment Strand. (Wildcats Ser.). (gr. 2-8). 589.95 *(978-0-322-06534-5(8))* Wright Group/McGraw-Hill.
—Wildcats Strand Kits: Myths & Misconceptions Strand. (Wildcats Ser.). (gr. 2-8). 589.95 *(978-0-322-06532-1(1))* Wright Group/McGraw-Hill.
—Wildcats Strand Kits: People & Places Strand. (Wildcats Ser.). (gr. 2-8). 589.95 *(978-0-322-06528-4(3))* Wright Group/McGraw-Hill.
—Wildcats Strand Kits: Science & Technology Strand. (Wildcats Ser.). (gr. 2-8). 589.95 *(978-0-322-06529-1(1))* Wright Group/McGraw-Hill.
—Wildcats Strand Kits: Sports & Action Strand. (Wildcats Ser.). (gr. 2-8). 589.95 *(978-0-322-06531-4(3))* Wright Group/McGraw-Hill.
—Wonder World: Early Emergent - Student Book Set - 1 Each of 16 Titles. (gr. k-18). 66.95 *(978-0-322-04341-1(7))* Wright Group/McGraw-Hill.
—Wonder World: Early Fluency - Student Book Set - 1 Each of 16 Titles. (gr. 1-2). 93.50 *(978-0-322-04342-8(5))* Wright Group/McGraw-Hill.
—Wonder World: Upper Emergent - Student Book Set - 1 Each of 16 Titles, Vol. 2. (gr. 1-18). 79.95 *(978-0-322-04340-4(9))* Wright Group/McGraw-Hill.
—Working Like a Dog: 6 Each of 1 Anthology, 6 vols. (Wildcats Ser.). 32p. (gr. 2-8). *(978-0-322-05854-5(6))* Wright Group/McGraw-Hill.
—The Worm Farm: Level E, 6 vols. (Take Twostm Ser.). 16p. 29.95 *(978-0-322-08961-7(1))* Wright Group/McGraw-Hill.
—The Wright Skills: Level A Sets - Short Vowels only: 1 Each of 19 Titles. (Wright Skills Ser.). (gr. k-3). 56.95 *(978-0-322-06473-7(2))* Wright Group/McGraw-Hill.
—The Wright Skills: Level B Sets - 1 Each of 40 Titles (includes long Vowels) (Wright Skills Ser.). (gr. k-3). 143.95 *(978-0-322-03878-3(2))* Wright Group/McGraw-Hill.
—The Wright Skills: Level B Sets - 6 Each of 40 Titles (includes long Vowels) (gr. k-3). 860.50 *(978-0-322-03880-6(4))* Wright Group/McGraw-Hill.
—Young & Wild: 6 Each of 1 Anthology, 6 vols. (Wildcats Ser.). 32p. (gr. 2-8). *(978-0-322-05851-4(1))* Wright Group/McGraw-Hill.
—Zoo Tales: 6 Each of 1 Anthology, 6 vols. (Wildcats Ser.). 32p. (gr. 2-8). *(978-0-322-05856-9(2))* Wright Group/McGraw-Hill.
—The 13th Floor: Level O, 6 vols. (Autumn Leaves Ser.). 128p. (gr. 3-6). 36.95 *(978-0-322-06731-8(6))* Wright Group/McGraw-Hill.
Gruver, Sara. Reading Skills Mini-Lessons. 2003. (ENG.). 96p. pap., tchr. ed. 13.99 *(978-0-7439-3288-2(9))* Teacher Created Resources, Inc.
Guardians of the Garden: Level 3, 6 vols. (Fluency Strand Ser.). (gr. 4-8). 45.00 *(978-1-4045-1218-4(7))* Wright Group/McGraw-Hill.
Guess Who - Group 1, 12 vols. 2005. (Guess Who? Ser.). (ENG., Illus.). 32p. (gr. k-1). lib. bdg. 153.00 *(978-0-7614-1559-6(9),* 8a9e56a4-d56d-4b8d-b8e2-cc70220882c0, Cavendish Square) Cavendish Square Publishing LLC.
Guess Who - Group 2, 12 vols., Set. 2006. (Guess Who? Ser.). (ENG.). (J). (gr. k-1). 153.00 *(978-0-7614-1762-0(1),* 66decf55-4d53-44af-aa07-c7839ff1eac1, Cavendish Square) Cavendish Square Publishing LLC.
Guinea Pig, 6 vols. 8p. (gr. k-1). 21.50 *(978-0-322-02060-3(3))* Wright Group/McGraw-Hill.
Gunn, Barbara. Inuit Tales: Read Well Level K Unit 10 Storybook. Jerde, Susan, illus. 2003. (Read Well Level K Ser.). 20p. (J). *(978-1-57035-681-0(5))* Cambium Education, Inc.
Haddon, Jean. Words: A Computer Lesson. Vargo, Sharon Hawkins, illus. 2003. (Silly Millies Ser.). 32p. (J). (gr. -1-1). pap. 4.99 *(978-0-7613-1797-5(X));* lib. bdg. 17.90 *(978-0-7613-2870-4(X))* Lerner Publishing Group. (Millbrook Pr.).
Hairem Scarem Little Books: Early Reading Fluency, Level C. 2004. pap. 6.00 *(978-0-7398-8293-1(7))* Steck-Vaughn.
Hand Tools: Level N, 6 vols. (Wonder Worldtm Ser.). 48p. 34.95 *(978-0-7802-4577-6(6))* Wright Group/McGraw-Hill.
Haney Perez, Jessica. My First 100 Words Book: A Lift-the-Flap, Pull-Tab Learning Book. March, Chloe, illus. 2005. (Learn to Read Ser.). 10p. (J). 10.95 *(978-1-58117-210-2(9),* Intervisual/Piggy Toes) Bendon, Inc.
Hanrahan, Abigail & McSweeny, Catherine. 50 Quick Play Reading Games. 2004. (J). per. 34.95 *(978-0-7606-0535-6(1))* LinguiSystems, Inc.
Harcourt School Publishers Staff. Assessment & Information Instruction, Grades K-6: Professional Development in Reading - Participant's Guide. 2nd ed. 2003. (Harcourt School Publishers Reading Professional Development Ser.). (ENG.). 40p. (gr. 6-6). pap. 13.90 *(978-0-15-338365-6(8))* Harcourt Schl. Pubs.
—Assessment & Information Instructions, Grades K-6: Professional Development for Reading: Guide to Video. 2nd ed. 2003. pap., tchr. ed. 54.90 *(978-0-15-337406-7(3))* Harcourt Schl. Pubs.
—Be Active!, Grade 3-6: Resource Binder Tabs. 4th ed. 2004. 45.60 *(978-0-15-341284-4(4))* Harcourt Schl. Pubs.
—Be Active!, Grade K-2: Resource Binder Tabs. 4th ed. 2004. 45.60 *(978-0-15-341283-7(6))* Harcourt Schl. Pubs.
—Collections: Phonics Activity Book. 2003. (First-Place Reading Ser.). (Illus.). (gr. k-6). 6.90 *(978-0-15-313423-4(2))* Harcourt Schl. Pubs.
—Flower Garden Lap Book. 3rd ed. 2004. (Trophies Reading Program Ser.). (Illus.). pap. 11.50 *(978-0-15-341029-1(9))* Harcourt Schl. Pubs.
—Herman the Helper Lap Book. 3rd ed. 2003. (Harcourt School Publishers Trophies Ser.). (ENG., Illus.). 32p. (gr. -1 — 1). pap. 14.10 *(978-0-15-340970-7(3))* Harcourt Schl. Pubs.
—Library Package. 2003. (Illus.). (J). (gr. -1). 151.95 *(978-0-15-216666-3(1));* (J). (gr. k-2). 160.95 *(978-0-15-216672-4(6));* (J). (gr. 3-4). 158.00 *(978-0-15-216678-6(5));* (J). (gr. 5-6). 158.00 *(978-0-15-216684-7(X));* (YA). (gr. 7-8). 145.00 *(978-0-15-216690-8(4))* Harcourt Schl. Pubs.
—The Little Quack Lap Book. 3rd ed. 2004. (Trophies Reading Program Ser.). (Illus.). pap. 11.50 *(978-0-15-340969-1(X))* Harcourt Schl. Pubs.
—The Little Red Hen Lap Book. 3rd ed. 2004. (Trophies Reading Program Ser.). (Illus.). pap. 11.50 *(978-0-15-340968-4(1))* Harcourt Schl. Pubs.
—The Months of School. 3rd ed. 2004. (Trophies Reading Program Ser.). (Illus.). (gr. -1). pap. 11.50 *(978-0-15-340896-0(0))* Harcourt Schl. Pubs.
—Trophies. 3rd ed. 2003. (Trophies Ser.). (gr. 1-18). Grade 1-1. tchr. ed. 115.50 *(978-0-15-325022-4(4))*Grade 1-2. tchr. ed. 115.50 *(978-0-15-325023-1(2))*Grade 1-3. tchr. ed. 120.20 *(978-0-15-325024-8(0))*Grade 1-4. tchr. ed. 120.20 *(978-0-15-325025-5(9))*Grade 1-5. tchr. ed. 124.80 *(978-0-15-325026-2(7))* Harcourt Schl. Pubs.
—Trophies Theme 1, Theme 1. 3rd ed. 2003. (Trophies Ser.). (gr. 2-18). tchr. ed. 65.50 *(978-0-15-325030-9(5));* (gr. 2-18). tchr. ed. 65.50 *(978-0-15-325027-9(5));* (gr. 3-18). tchr. ed. 65.50 *(978-0-15-325033-0(X));* (gr. 3-18). tchr. ed. 65.50 *(978-0-15-325036-1(4));* (gr. 4-18). tchr. ed. 69.90 *(978-0-15-325039-2(9));* (gr. 5-18). tchr. ed. 69.90 *(978-0-15-325045-3(3));* (gr. 6-18). tchr. ed. 72.70 *(978-0-15-325051-4(8))* Harcourt Schl. Pubs.
—Trophies Theme 2, Theme 2. 3rd ed. 2003. (Trophies Ser.). (gr. 2-18). tchr. ed. 65.50 *(978-0-15-325028-6(3));* (gr. 2-18). tchr. ed. 65.50 *(978-0-15-325031-6(3));* (gr. 3-18). tchr. ed. 65.50 *(978-0-15-325037-8(2));* (gr. 3-18). tchr. ed. 65.50 *(978-0-15-325034-7(8));* (gr. 4-18). tchr. ed. 69.90 *(978-0-15-325040-8(2));* (gr. 5-18). tchr. ed. 69.90 *(978-0-15-325046-0(1));* (gr. 6-18). tchr. ed. 72.70 *(978-0-15-325052-1(6))* Harcourt Schl. Pubs.
—Trophies Theme 3, Theme 3. 3rd ed. 2003. (Trophies Ser.). (gr. 2-18). tchr. ed. 65.50 *(978-0-15-325032-3(1));* (gr. 2-18). tchr. ed. 65.50 *(978-0-15-325029-3(1));* (gr. 3-18). tchr. ed. 65.50 *(978-0-15-325035-4(6));* (gr. 3-18). tchr. ed. 65.50 *(978-0-15-325038-5(0));* (gr. 4-18). tchr. ed. 69.90 *(978-0-15-325041-5(0));* (gr. 5-18). tchr. ed. 69.90 *(978-0-15-325047-7(X));* (gr. 6-18). tchr. ed. 72.70 *(978-0-15-325053-8(4))* Harcourt Schl. Pubs.
—Trophies Theme 4, Theme 4. 3rd ed. 2003. (Trophies Ser.). (gr. 4-18). tchr. ed. 69.90 *(978-0-15-325042-2(9));* (gr. 5-18). tchr. ed. 69.90 *(978-0-15-325048-4(8));* (gr. 6-18). tchr. ed. 72.70 *(978-0-15-325054-5(2))* Harcourt Schl. Pubs.
—Trophies Theme 5, Theme 5. 3rd ed. 2003. (Trophies Ser.). (gr. 4-18). tchr. ed. 69.90 *(978-0-15-325043-9(7));* (gr. 5-18). tchr. ed. 69.90 *(978-0-15-325049-1(6));* (gr. 6-18). tchr. ed. 72.70 *(978-0-15-325055-2(0))* Harcourt Schl. Pubs.
—Trophies Theme 6, Theme 6. 3rd ed. 2003. (Trophies Ser.). (gr. 4-18). tchr. ed. 69.90 *(978-0-15-325044-6(5));* (gr. 5-18). tchr. ed. 69.90 *(978-0-15-325050-7(X));* (gr. 6-18). tchr. ed. 72.70 *(978-0-15-325056-9(9))* Harcourt Schl. Pubs.
—Trophies Reading Program, Grade K. 3rd ed. 2003. tchr. ed. 135.30 *(978-0-15-339730-1(6))* Harcourt Schl. Pubs.
—Writing Express Espanol, Grade 1. 2nd ed. 2003. (Trofeos Ser.). (SPA.). (gr. 1-18). tchr. ed. 10.10 incl. cd-rom *(978-0-15-324608-1(1))* Harcourt Schl. Pubs.
—1st Place Reading: Title 1 Program Kit. 2nd ed. 2003. (Harcourt Title I Reading Programs Ser.). (gr. 5-18). tchr. ed. 1006.70 *(978-0-15-338009-9(8))* Harcourt Schl. Pubs.
Harner, Jennifer L. Reading & Learning from Informational Text. Petelinsek, Kathleen, illus. 2013. (Explorer Junior Library: Information Explorer Junior Ser.). (ENG.). 24p. (J). (gr. 1-4). 32.07 *(978-1-62431-134-5(2),* 202856); pap. 12.79 *(978-1-62431-266-3(7),* 202858) Cherry Lake Publishing.
Harpster, Steve, illus. First Word Search: Easy First Words. 2011. (First Word Search Ser.). 64p. (J). (gr. -1-1). pap. 4.95 *(978-1-4027-7808-7(2))* Sterling Publishing Co., Inc.
Harry's Hat: Take-Home Book. 2005. (Emergent Library: Vol. 2). (YA). (gr. -1-1). 12.60 *(978-0-8215-7254-2(7))* Sadlier, William H. Inc.
Harvey, Bev. Animal Families, 6 vols. 2005. (Animal Families Ser.). (Illus.). 32p. (gr. 2-4). 138.00 *(978-0-7910-7539-5(7),* Facts On File) Infobase Holdings, Inc.
A Hat for Nan: Consonants b, w; Short Vowel i word families: Level A, 6 vols. (Wright Skills Ser.). 12p. (gr. k-3). 17.95 *(978-0-322-01451-0(4))* Wright Group/McGraw-Hill.
Hats: Big Book: Level B. 8p. 20.95 *(978-0-322-00359-0(8))* Wright Group/McGraw-Hill.
Hats: Level B. 8p. 24.95 *(978-0-7802-8919-2(6))* Wright Group/McGraw-Hill.
Hats: Level G, 6 vols. (Wonder Worldtm Ser.). 16p. 29.95 *(978-0-7802-4579-2(2))* Wright Group/McGraw-Hill.
Hay Making: Level H, 6 vols. (Wonder Worldtm Ser.). 16p. 29.95 *(978-0-7802-1215-2(0))* Wright Group/McGraw-Hill.
HB Staff. All Fall Down. 97th ed. 2003. (First-Place Reading Ser.). (gr. 1-18). pap. 16.50 *(978-0-15-308126-2(0))* Harcourt Schl. Pubs.
Hello: Big Book: Level D. Group 1. (Story Box Ser.). 16p. 20.95 *(978-0-322-00632-4(5))* Wright Group/McGraw-Hill.
Hercules & Other Greek Legends: 6 Each of 1 Anthology, 6 vols. (Wildcats Ser.). 32p. (gr. 2-8). *(978-0-322-00590-7(6))* Wright Group/McGraw-Hill.
Here Comes the Rain! Take-Home Book. 2005. (Emergent Library: Vol. 2). (YA). (gr. -1-1). 12.60 *(978-0-8215-7263-4(6))* Sadlier, William H. Inc.
Heroes: 6 Each of 1 Anthology, 6 vols. (Wildcats Ser.). 32p. (gr. 2-8). *(978-0-322-00579-2(5))* Wright Group/McGraw-Hill.
Hide & Seek: Big Book: Level K. (Wonder Worldtm Ser.). 16p. 26.50 *(978-0-7802-3474-1(X))* Wright Group/McGraw-Hill.
Hide & Seek: Level K, 6 vols. (Wonder Worldtm Ser.). 16p. 34.95 *(978-0-7802-1217-6(7))* Wright Group/McGraw-Hill.
High Tide: Level 7, 6 vols. (Fluency Strand Ser.). (gr. 4-8). 45.00 *(978-1-4045-1242-9(X))* Wright Group/McGraw-Hill.
A Hike in the Trees: Long e Digraphs: Level B, 6 vols. (Wright Skills Ser.). 16p. (gr. k-3). 26.50 *(978-0-322-01479-4(4))* Wright Group/McGraw-Hill.
Hiking with Dad: Level I, 6 vols. (Wonder Worldtm Ser.). 16p. 29.95 *(978-0-7802-2036-2(6))* Wright Group/McGraw-Hill.
Hill, Cheryl E. R is for Reading Books. Pierce, Dave G., illus. 2012. 56p. pap. 17.99 *(978-0-9859770-0-9(0))* N.O.A.H Bks.
Hocus Pocus: 6 Each of 1 Anthology, 6 vols. (Wildcats Ser.). 32p. (gr. 2-8). *(978-0-322-02423-6(4))* Wright Group/McGraw-Hill.
Hohenthal, K. D., creator. The Reading & Writing Connection Journal with Herman the Crab No. 1: What Is the Story About? 2003. 70p. (J). spiral bd. 15.95 *(978-0-9716907-5-2(8),* Ridgewood Publishing) Ridgewood Group, The.
—The Reading & Writing Connection with Herman the Crab No. 2: Story Problem & Solution. 2003. 70p. (J). spiral bd., wbk. ed. 15.95 *(978-0-9716907-6-9(6),* Ridgewood Publishing) Ridgewood Group, The.
—The Reading & Writing Connection with Herman the Crab No. 3: Story Beginning, Middle, End. 2003. 70p. (J). spiral bd., wbk. ed. 15.95 *(978-0-9716907-8-3(2),* Ridgewood Publishing) Ridgewood Group, The.
—The Reading & Writing Connection with Herman the Crab No. 4: Story Problem, Solution, Beginning, Middle, End. 2003. 70p. (J). spiral bd., wbk. ed. 15.95 *(978-0-9716907-9-0(0),* Ridgewood Publishing) Ridgewood Group, The.
Holt, Rinehart and Winston Staff. Elements of Literature: Assessment: Literature, Reading & Vocabulary. 2003. 4th ed. pap. 40.20 *(978-0-03-068518-7(4))* 5th ed. pap. 40.20 *(978-0-03-068519-4(2))* 5th ed. pap. 40.20 *(978-0-03-068517-0(6))* Holt McDougal.
—Holt Reader. 4th ed. 2003. (Elements of Literature Ser.). (ENG., Illus.). 384p. (gr. 6-6). pap. 17.15 *(978-0-03-068389-3(0))* Houghton Mifflin Harcourt Publishing Co.
—Holt Science & Technology: Directed Reading Answer Key. 4th ed. 2004. (Illus.). pap. 11.20 *(978-0-03-037018-2(3))* Holt McDougal.
—Holt Science & Technology: Directed Reading Worksheets. 4th ed. 2004. pap. 15.00 *(978-0-03-036992-6(4));* pap. 15.00 *(978-0-03-036993-3(2));* pap. 15.00 *(978-0-03-036994-0(0))* Holt McDougal.
Holzer, Angela. My Dog, Eddie. Funk, Debbie, illus. 2009. 36p. (J). lib. bdg. 8.99 *(978-0-9821563-5-3(9))* Good Sound Publishing.
Home Pack Collection. 2005. (Nursery Rhymes Build Literacy Ser.). (YA). (gr. -1-3). 48.60 *(978-0-8215-0560-1(2));* (gr. k-3). 48.60 *(978-0-8215-0569-4(6))* Sadlier, William H. Inc.
Hooks, Earnest. Let's go see Mother Wilkerson's Farm. 2011. 72p. pap. 27.08 *(978-1-4389-5072-3(1))* AuthorHouse.
HOP, LLC. Hooked on Phonics Reading Comprehension. 2006. 64p. 3.79 *(978-1-933863-94-8(3))* HOP, LLC.
A House for Me: Big Book: Level F. 16p. 31.50 *(978-0-322-00375-0(X))* Wright Group/McGraw-Hill.
The House on the Hill: Level 5, 6 vols. (Fluency Strand Ser.). (gr. 4-8). 45.00 *(978-1-4045-1228-3(4))* Wright Group/McGraw-Hill.
Houses: Big Book: Level D. Group 1. (Story Box Ser.). 16p. 20.95 *(978-0-7802-7637-6(X))* Wright Group/McGraw-Hill.
Houses: Level M, 6 vols. (Wonder Worldtm Ser.). 16p. 34.95 *(978-0-7802-1219-0(3))* Wright Group/McGraw-Hill.
How a Volcano Is Formed: Level M, 6 vols. (Wonder Worldtm Ser.). 16p. 34.95 *(978-0-7802-2913-6(4))* Wright Group/McGraw-Hill.
How Animals Hide: Level G, 6 vols. (Wonder Worldtm Ser.). 16p. 29.95 *(978-0-7802-4581-5(4))* Wright Group/McGraw-Hill.
How Ants Live, 6 vols. (Sunshinetm Science Ser.). 24p. (gr. 1-2). 36.95 *(978-0-7802-0539-0(1));* 31.50 *(978-0-7802-0288-7(0))* Wright Group/McGraw-Hill.
A Hug Is Warm: Big Book: Level D. Group 1. (Sunshine Ser.). 8p. 20.95 *(978-0-7802-5729-0(4))* Wright Group/McGraw-Hill.
Huggles Can Jungle: Level A. Group 1. (Sunshine Ser.). 8p. 20.95 *(978-0-7802-5707-8(3))* Wright Group/McGraw-Hill.
Huggles Goes Away: Level A. Group 1. (Sunshine Ser.). 8p. 20.95 *(978-0-7802-5708-5(1))* Wright Group/McGraw-Hill.
Hults, Alaska, ed. American History Reader's Theater Vol. 2244: Develop Reading Fluency & Text Comprehension Skills. Hillam, Corbin & Vangsgard, Amy, illus. 2004. 96p. (J). pap. 14.99 *(978-1-59198-039-1(9),* 2244) Creative Teaching Pr., Inc.
—Philosophers to Astronauts Reader's Theater Vol. 2243: Develop Reading Fluency & Text Comprehension Skills. Hillam, Corbin & Vangsgard, Amy, illus. 2004. 96p. (J). pap. 12.99 *(978-1-59198-038-4(0),* 2243) Creative Teaching Pr., Inc.

PQR

I am a Book Worm: Big Book: Level C. Group 1. (Sunshine Ser.). 8p. 20.95 *(978-0-7802-5722-1(7))* Wright Group/McGraw-Hill.
I am a Twin, 6 vols. 8p. (gr. k-1). 21.50 *(978-0-322-02083-2(2))* Wright Group/McGraw-Hill.
I Cannot Fit!, 6 vols. 8p. (gr. k-1). 21.50 *(978-0-322-02071-9(9))* Wright Group/McGraw-Hill.
I Could not Keep Silent: Level T. Group 3, 6 vols. (Sunshine Ser.). 48p. 44.95 *(978-0-322-04601-6(7))* Wright Group/McGraw-Hill.
I Love My Family: Big Book: Level C. Group 1. (Sunshine Ser.). 8p. 20.95 *(978-0-7802-5723-8(5))* Wright Group/McGraw-Hill.
I See You: Level E. 8p. 20.95 *(978-0-322-00342-2(3))* Wright Group/McGraw-Hill.
I Wonder, 6 vols. (Sunshinetm Ser.). 16p. (gr. k-18). 29.50 *(978-0-7802-5423-7(6))* Wright Group/McGraw-Hill.
I Wonder Why? Level G, 6 vols. (Wonder Worldtm Ser.). 16p. 29.95 *(978-0-7802-2016-4(1))* Wright Group/McGraw-Hill.
If I Had a Piece of String. (J). 26.20 *(978-0-8136-8426-0(9));* (gr. -1-3). 59.50 *(978-0-8136-7972-3(9))* Modern Curriculum Pr.
If I Were a Fish. (J). 26.20 *(978-0-8136-8443-7(9));* (gr. -1-3). 59.50 *(978-0-8136-8008-8(5))* Modern Curriculum Pr.
In the Graveyard: Decodable Books, 6 vols. (Fast Track Reading Ser.). 24p. (gr. 4-8). 40.95 *(978-0-322-05986-3(0))* Wright Group/McGraw-Hill.
In the Graveyard Play 12: Decodable Plays, 6 vols. (Fast Track Reading Ser.). 24p. (gr. 4-8). 40.95 *(978-0-322-06000-5(1))* Wright Group/McGraw-Hill.
In the News, 6 vols. (Wildcats Ser.). 32p. (gr. 2-8). *(978-0-322-02437-3(4))* Wright Group/McGraw-Hill.
In the News, 10 vols., Set 2. Incl. Climate Change. Brezina, Corona. lib. bdg. 37.13 *(978-1-4042-1913-7(7),* ce033f3b-9ebc-4b4f-bd33-927192731467); Darfur: African Genocide. Xavier, John. lib. bdg. 37.13 *(978-1-4042-1912-0(9),* c1460c9a-534c-4c82-b437-8f2e8043133d); Green Technology: Earth-Friendly Innovations. Sobha, Geeta. lib. bdg. 37.13 *(978-1-4042-1914-4(5),* cdb65425-01f2-4ef2-8139-bb82aaace90a); Nukes: The Spread of Nuclear Weapons. Minneus, Steve. lib. bdg. 37.13 *(978-1-4042-1916-8(1),* ba946ed1-9ee7-406e-b6ca-7ffd9b6ca863); Oil: The Economics of Fuel. Jovinelly, Joann. lib. bdg. 37.13 *(978-1-4042-1915-1(3),* a88f9a66-8373-458c-9781-2ad0f1d76ce7); (Illus.). 64p. (YA). (gr. 6-6). 2007. (In the News Ser.). (ENG.). 2007. Set lib. bdg. 185.65 *(978-1-4042-1112-4(8),* 14a575df-1acb-45cf-a0fc-1aaf534c7153) Rosen Publishing Group, Inc., The.
In the News: Level O, 6 vols. (Wonder Worldtm Ser.). 48p. 39.95 *(978-0-7802-2959-4(2))* Wright Group/McGraw-Hill.
Incredible Places: 6 Each of 1 Anthology, 6 vols. (Wildcats Ser.). 32p. (gr. 2-8). *(978-0-322-00587-7(6))* Wright Group/McGraw-Hill.
Inventions of Ancient Civilization Collection, 4 pkgs., Set. (J). (gr. 3-6). 327.00 *(978-0-8136-6355-5(5))* Modern Curriculum Pr.
Iris la Bonga & the Helpful Taxi Driver: Level T. Group 1, 6 vols. (Sunshine Ser.). 48p. 44.95 *(978-0-7802-5598-2(4))* Wright Group/McGraw-Hill.
It Takes Time to Grow, 6 vols. (Sunshinetm Ser.). 16p. (gr. k-18). 29.50 *(978-0-7802-5434-3(1))* Wright Group/McGraw-Hill.
It's Noisy at Night: Level F, 6 vols. (Wonder Worldtm Ser.). 16p. 29.95 *(978-0-7802-1039-4(5))* Wright Group/McGraw-Hill.
I've Been Working on the Railroad. (Song Box Ser.). (gr. 1-2). 31.50 *(978-0-7802-0936-7(2));* 8.50 incl. audio *(978-0-7802-0938-1(9))* Wright Group/McGraw-Hill.
I've Been Working on the Railroad: 1 Big Book, 6 Each of 1 Student Book, & 1 Cassette. (Song Box Ser.). (gr. 1-2). 68.95 *(978-0-7802-0939-8(7))* Wright Group/McGraw-Hill.
I've Been Working on the Railroad: 6 Each of 1 Student Book, 6 vols. (Song Box Ser.). (gr. 1-2). 29.50 *(978-0-7802-0937-4(0))* Wright Group/McGraw-Hill.
Jack de Pert at the Supermarket: Level J, 6 vols. (Wonder Worldtm Ser.). 16p. 29.95 *(978-0-7802-1040-0(9))* Wright Group/McGraw-Hill.
Jackman, John. Comprehension: Introductory Pupil Book. 2011. (Collins Primary Focus Ser.). (ENG., Illus.). 128p. (J). (gr. 2-2). pap., stu. ed. 16.99 *(978-0-00-741059-0(X))* HarperCollins Pubs. Ltd. GBR. Dist: Independent Pubs. Group.
—Comprehension: Pupil Book 2, Bk. 2. 2011. (Collins Primary Focus Ser.). (ENG., Illus.). 48p. (J). (gr. 4-4). pap. 16.99 *(978-0-00-741061-3(1))* HarperCollins Pubs. Ltd. GBR. Dist: Independent Pubs. Group.
Jake's Big Day: Long Vowel a, CVCe Pattern: Level B, 6 vols. (Wright Skills Ser.). 16p. (gr. k-3). 17.95 *(978-0-322-01465-7(4))* Wright Group/McGraw-Hill.
Janet & Donald: Decodable Books, 6 vols. (Fast Track Reading Ser.). 24p. (gr. 4-8). 40.95 *(978-0-322-05984-9(4))* Wright Group/McGraw-Hill.
Janet & Donald Play 7: Decodable Plays, 6 vols. (Fast Track Reading Ser.). 24p. (gr. 4-8). 40.95 *(978-0-322-05998-6(4))* Wright Group/McGraw-Hill.
Jean Batter Pioneer of the Sky: Level R, 6 vols. (Wonder Worldtm Ser.). 48p. 44.95 *(978-0-7802-7079-4(7))* Wright Group/McGraw-Hill.
Jen & the Pets: Consonants k, v, y; Short Vowel e Word Families: Level A, 6 vols. (Wright Skills Ser.). 12p. (gr. k-3). 17.95 *(978-0-322-01454-1(9))* Wright Group/McGraw-Hill.

Jennett, Pamela. Discoverers & Inventors Reader's Theater Vol. 2245: Develop Reading Fluency & Test Comprehension Skills. Hults, Alaska, ed. Hilliam, Corbin & Vangsgard, Amy, illus. 2004. 96p. (J). pap. 12.99 *(978-1-59198-040-7(2),* 2245) Creative Teaching Pr., Inc.

Jim Pig is Mad: Short Vowel i: Level A, 6 vols. (Wright Skills Ser.). 12p. (gr. k-3). 17.95 *(978-0-322-03115-9(X))* Wright Group/McGraw-Hill.

Jim's Trumpet: Level K. Group 1. (Sunshine Ser.). 16p. 36.50 *(978-0-7802-5793-1(6))* Wright Group/McGraw-Hill.

Joe's Toe: Long o Digraphs: Level B, 6 vols. (Wright Skills Ser.). 16p. (gr. k-3). 26.50 *(978-0-322-01480-0(8))* Wright Group/McGraw-Hill.

Jog to the Dam: Consonants g, h, j; Short Vowel o word families: Level A, 6 vols. (Wright Skills Ser.). 12p. (gr. k-3). 17.95 *(978-0-322-01448-0(4))* Wright Group/McGraw-Hill.

Joyce, William. Santa Calls Stationery Set. Date not set. (J). 11.95 *(978-0-694-00806-3(0))* HarperCollins Pubs.

Just the Opposite, 12 vols. 2003. (Just the Opposite Ser.). (ENG., Illus.). 24p. (gr. k-1). lib. bdg. 153.00 *(978-0-7614-1567-1(X),* 6f61a562-4469-4a1f-a61c-45be9a55a492, Cavendish Square) Cavendish Square Publishing LLC.

Kalar, Bonnie. Early Phonetic Readers - Set E, 7 bks., set. Spreen, Kathe, illus. Incl. Ann Paints & Plays. pap. *(978-1-891619-40-3(3));* Clair at Home. pap. *(978-1-891619-44-1(6));* Good Day. pap. *(978-1-891619-41-0(1));* Kirk & the Deer. pap. *(978-1-891619-43-4(8));* Miss Lane's Class. pap. *(978-1-891619-38-0(1));* Neal Camps Out. pap. *(978-1-891619-39-7(X));* Trip to the Beach. pap. *(978-1-891619-42-7(X));* 12p. (J). (gr. -1-2). (Illus.). Set pap. 14.50 *(978-1-891619-37-3(3))* Corona Pr.

Kalman, Bobbie. What Is It? 2011. (ENG., Illus.). 16p. (J). pap. *(978-0-7787-9572-8(1));* lib. bdg. *(978-0-7787-9547-6(0))* Crabtree Publishing Co.

Kauzlarich, David. Sociological Classics: A Prentice Hall Pocket Reader. 2004. (ENG.). 144p. (C). pap. 29.00 *(978-0-13-191806-1(0),* Pearson Higher Ed, Prentice Hall) Prentice Hall PTR.

Keen Kite Books, Keen Kite. Year 5 Reading Detectives: Topic Texts with Free Download: Teacher Resources (Reading Detectives) 2018. (ENG.). 88p. pap. 105.00 *(978-0-00-828627-9(2))* HarperCollins Pubs. Ltd. GBR. Dist: Independent Pubs. Group.

Keeping Baby Animals Safe: Take-Home Book. 2005. (Emergent Library: Vol. 2). (YA). (gr. -1-1). 12.60 *(978-0-8215-7264-1(4))* Sadlier, William H. Inc.

Kelly, Sheila M. & Rotner, Shelley. School Days. Rotner, Shelley, photos by. 2020. (ENG., Illus.). 32p. (J). (gr. -1-2). 26.65 *(978-1-5415-5776-5(X),* 02383e8d-5fe8-4935-9616-e5b47e2a2329, Millbrook Pr.) Lerner Publishing Group.

Kertell, Lynn Maslen. My First Bob Books - Pre-Reading Skills Box Set | Phonics, Ages 3 & up, Pre-K (Reading Readiness), 1 vol. Maslen, John R. & Hendra, Sue, illus. 2008. (Bob Bks.). (ENG.). 48p. (J). (gr. -1-k). pap., pap., pap. 17.99 *(978-0-545-01922-4(2),* Cartwheel Bks.) Scholastic, Inc.

Kids Can Learn Franklin Staff, ed. Early Reading. 2004. 32p. pap. *(978-1-55337-604-0(8))* Kids Can Pr., Ltd.

Kimmelman, Leslie. Ben Lost a Tooth. 2004. (ENG., Illus.). 8p. (J). (gr. k-k). pap. 7.56 *(978-0-7652-5132-9(9),* Celebration Pr.) Savvas Learning Co.

—A Dog Named Honey. 2004. (ENG., Illus.). 8p. (J). (gr. k-k). pap. 7.56 *(978-0-7652-5144-2(2),* Celebration Pr.) Savvas Learning Co.

—Star Pictures. 2004. (ENG., Illus.). 8p. (J). (gr. k-k). pap. 7.56 *(978-0-7652-5134-3(5),* Celebration Pr.) Savvas Learning Co.

The King Who Could Knit: Initial Silent Consonants: Level C, 6 vols. (Wright Skills Ser.). 16p. (gr. k-3). 26.50 *(978-0-322-01502-9(2))* Wright Group/McGraw-Hill.

King, Zelda. Try it with Triangles: Learning to Put Triangles Together to Form Other Shapes. 2004. (Math Big Bookstm Ser.). (ENG.). 16p. (gr. 2-3). 37.95 *(978-0-8239-7641-6(6))* Rosen Publishing Group, Inc., The.

The Kitty: Long Vowels e, y, CVCe & Final y Patterns: Level B, 6 vols. (Wright Skills Ser.). 16p. (gr. k-3). 17.95 *(978-0-322-03130-2(3))* Wright Group/McGraw-Hill.

Klees, Amy. 100 Ways I Love to Read. 2008. 24p. pap. 15.99 *(978-1-4363-9383-6(3))* Xlibris Corp.

Koch, Kamla Devi, et al. Teen Stories: Personal Stories for Students Who Are Beginning to Read. (J). tchr. ed. 8.95 *(978-0-916591-20-5(4));* stu. ed. 8.95 *(978-0-916591-19-9(0))* Linmore Publishing, Inc.

L Omino di Panpepato. pap. 14.95 *(978-88-04-44206-6(9))* Mondadori ITA. Dist: Distribooks, Inc.

Lalley, Kristine. How Many Legs? Learning to Multiply Using Repeated Addition. 2009. (PowerMath: Beginning Ser.). 16p. (gr. 2-2). 37.50 *(978-1-60851-373-4(4),* PowerKids Pr.) Rosen Publishing Group, Inc., The.

Language Works Rhyme Time. 8p. (J) *(978-0-8136-3519-4(5))* Modern Curriculum Pr.

Language Works Staff. Message of the Dance. (J). 28.08 *(978-0-8136-3504-0(7))* Modern Curriculum Pr.

Last-Minute Rescue Little Book: Early Reading Fluency, Level C. 2004. pap. 6.00 *(978-0-7398-8300-6(3))* Steck-Vaughn.

Laurence, Jo. How to Be a Wizard at Nursery Rhymes. Ford, Kate, illus. 48p. (J). (gr. 1-3). pap. *(978-1-876367-28-2(8))* Wizard Bks.

Leaf, Munro. How to Be: Six Simple Rules for Being the Best Kid You Can Be. 2015. (Rizzoli Classics Ser.). (ENG., Illus.). 104p. (J). (-k). 19.95 *(978-0-7893-3109-0(8))* Universe Publishing.

LeapFrog Schoolhouse Staff. Read-It-All Books. 2003. (YA). (gr. 3-18). tchr. ed., spiral bd. 19.95 *(978-1-59319-017-0(4),* LeapFrog Schl. Hse.) LeapFrog Enterprises, Inc.

LeapFrog Staff. Sing-along Read-along: Early Reading Set. 2008. (J). pap. 19.99 incl. DVD *(978-1-59319-992-0(9))* LeapFrog Enterprises, Inc.

Learning Co Bks Staff. Best Gift Ever. 2005. (Learn to Read Library). pap. 3.99 *(978-0-7630-8030-3(6))* Houghton Mifflin Harcourt Learning Technology.

—Lucky for Us! 2005. (Learn to Read Library). pap. 3.99 *(978-0-7630-8037-2(3))* Houghton Mifflin Harcourt Learning Technology.

—New Friend. 2005. (Learn to Read Library). pap. 3.99 *(978-0-7630-8032-7(2))* Houghton Mifflin Harcourt Learning Technology.

—Night Noises. 2005. (Learn to Read Library). pap. 3.99 *(978-0-7630-8031-0(4))* Houghton Mifflin Harcourt Learning Technology.

—Starry, Starry Night. 2005. (Learn to Read Library). pap. 3.99 *(978-0-7630-8028-0(4))* Houghton Mifflin Harcourt Learning Technology.

Learning Company Books Staff, ed. Reader Rabbit: Reading Comprehension. 2003. (Illus.). 32p. (J). pap., wbk. ed. *(978-0-7630-7643-6(0))* Magma.

Legler, Caroline. Super Words Early Reading Program, 10 vols. 2005. (Illus.). (J). 16.95 *(978-0-9771233-0-8(8))* Legler, Caroline.

Legs: Big Book: Level C. 8p. 20.95 *(978-0-322-00343-9(1))* Wright Group/McGraw-Hill.

Legs: Level C, 6 vols. 8p. 24.95 *(978-0-7802-9120-1(4))* Wright Group/McGraw-Hill.

Legs, Legs, Legs: Big Book: Level B. (Wonder Worldtm Ser.). 16p. 26.50 *(978-0-7802-2829-0(4))* Wright Group/McGraw-Hill.

Legs, Legs, Legs: Level B, 6 vols. (Wonder Worldtm Ser.). 16p. 24.95 *(978-0-7802-1087-5(5))* Wright Group/McGraw-Hill.

Let's Meet Biographies, 6 vols. 2005. (Let's Meet Biographies Ser.). (Illus.). 32p. (gr. 2-4). 138.00 *(978-0-7910-7317-9(3),* Facts On File) Infobase Holdings, Inc.

Letter Cluster Books Reproducibles. (Foundation Ser.). 64p. (gr. k-3). 26.50 *(978-0-322-01549-4(9))* Wright Group/McGraw-Hill.

Letter Clusters Student Book: 6 Each of 1 Student Book. 32p. (gr. k-3). 31.95 *(978-0-7802-9033-4(X))* Wright Group/McGraw-Hill.

Level C, Vol. 2. (J). 5.99 *(978-0-8136-1703-9(0))* Modern Curriculum Pr.

Levinson, Nancy Smiler. Prairie Friends. Schuett, Stacey, illus. 2003. (I Can Read Bks.). 64p. (J). (gr. k-3). 16.89 *(978-0-06-028002-4(6))* HarperCollins Pubs.

Linde, Barbara M. I Show Respect. Monés, Marc, illus. 2023. (ENG.). 16p. (J). (gr. -1-1). pap. 5.25 *(978-1-4788-0468-0(8),* aaa99dd3-2114-4205-aea6-091a324b1232); pap. 33.00 *(978-1-4788-0505-2(6),* 9e59ebe7-3cde-4c5a-ad46-5f7dac1e4724) Newmark Learning LLC.

—I Take Turns. Patton, Julia, illus. 2023. (ENG.). 16p. (J). (gr. -1-1). pap. 33.00 *(978-1-4788-0513-7(7),* 8d0a1a9f-17ea-4002-80b1-298a1873b591); pap. 5.25 *(978-1-4788-0476-5(9),* eeec199e-1f13-48f8-a899-248979213d38) Newmark Learning LLC.

—I Will Find a Way. Juan, Juan Bautista, illus. 2023. (ENG.). 16p. (J). (gr. -1-1). pap. 33.00 *(978-1-4788-0520-5(X),* 0a992cb7-492c-4022-9f5a-7d48abda18bb); pap. 5.25 *(978-1-4788-0483-3(1),* 8eb123c4-1501-41e8-920e-6e1f3e822218) Newmark Learning LLC.

—Jealous of Josie. Poole, Helen, illus. 2023. (ENG.). 16p. (J). (gr. -1-1). pap. 5.25 *(978-1-4788-0465-9(3),* 02032b3b-6829-4c83-803e-820513c00086); pap. 33.00 *(978-1-4788-0502-1(1),* eed22a30-3194-46b2-9354-e13a8413524c) Newmark Learning LLC.

—A Shopping Trip: Learning to Add Dollars & Cents up to $10.00 Without Regrouping, 1 vol. 2010. (Math for the REAL World Ser.). (ENG.). 16p. (gr. 2-3). pap. 7.05 *(978-0-8239-8900-3(3),* bd150635-7edf-4382-b9b6-c435b7e17e9e, Rosen Classroom) Rosen Publishing Group, Inc., The.

Lindeen, Carol K. From Coast to Coast, 6 vols., Set. 2004. (Phonics Readers Books 37-72 Ser.). (ENG.). 8p. (gr. k-1). pap. 35.70 *(978-0-7368-4061-3(3))* Capstone.

Linder, Don. Where Do Things Go When I Close My Eyes? 2012. (SPA.). (J). pap. 10.00 *(978-1-4675-5390-2(5))* Independent Pub.

Listen: Big Book: Level D. (Visions Ser.). 8p. 20.95 *(978-0-322-00309-5(1))* Wright Group/McGraw-Hill.

Literature Connections English: Fallen Angels. 2004. (gr. 6-12). *(978-0-395-83360-5(4),* 2-70783) Holt McDougal.

Literature Connections English: Jane Eyre. 2004. (gr. 6-12). *(978-0-395-77557-8(4),* 2-80126) Holt McDougal.

Literature Connections English: Julius Caesar. 2004. (gr. 6-12). *(978-0-395-77542-4(6),* 2-80111) Holt McDougal.

Literature Connections English: My Antonia. 2004. (gr. 6-12). *(978-0-395-77539-4(6),* 2-80108) Holt McDougal.

Literature Connections English: Nervous Conditions. 2004. (gr. 6-12). *(978-0-395-77560-8(4),* 2-80129) Holt McDougal.

Little Bear's Friend. 2003. 31.95 *(978-0-673-75802-6(8))* Celebration Pr.

Lizards: Level N, 6 vols. (Wonder Worldtm Ser.). 48p. 34.95 *(978-0-7802-4583-9(0))* Wright Group/McGraw-Hill.

Llueve, Truena y Relampaguea, 6 vols. (Explorers. Exploradores Nonfiction Sets Ser.). (SPA.). 32p. (gr. 3-6). 44.95 *(978-0-7699-0632-4(X))* Shortland Pubns. (U. S. A.) Inc.

Log Man: Level 5, 6 vols. (Fluency Strand Ser.). (gr. 4-8). 45.00 *(978-1-4045-1232-0(2))* Wright Group/McGraw-Hill.

London, S. Keith & Osleeb, Rebecca. Defined Mind. Vocabulary Accelerator: Music-Driven Vocabulary & Comprehension Tools for School / Test / SAT Prep, 1. 2004. 416p. (YA). pap. 25.00 *(978-0-9763767-0-5(9))* Defined Mind, Inc.

Long Ago & Far Away: 6 Each of 1 Anthology, 6 vols. (Wildcats Ser.). 32p. (gr. 2-8). *(978-0-322-00583-9(3))* Wright Group/McGraw-Hill.

Look Here! Level D, 6 vols. (Wonder Worldtm Ser.). 16p. 24.95 *(978-0-7802-1221-3(5))* Wright Group/McGraw-Hill.

Look Out, Dan! Big Book: Level C. Group 2. (Story Box Ser.). 16p. 20.95 *(978-0-7802-9367-0(3))* Wright Group/McGraw-Hill.

Looking for Crabs: Big Books Packages. 2005. (J). (gr. k-3). 75.95 *(978-0-673-77117-9(2))* Celebration Pr.

Looking Out, Climbing up, Going Far Grade 1: American Readers. (J). (gr. 1). wbk. ed. *(978-0-669-04968-8(9))* Houghton Mifflin Harcourt School Pubs.

Loves, June. Pets, 6 vols. 2005. (Pets Ser.). (Illus.). 32p. (gr. 2-4). 138.00 *(978-0-7910-7546-3(X),* Facts On File) Infobase Holdings, Inc.

Madu, Abraham. The Road to take to School Is the Phonics Way: Companion Book for Students. 2003. 98p. pap. 11.95 *(978-0-595-27748-3(9))* iUniverse, Inc.

Magic! Big Book: Level C. 8p. 20.95 *(978-0-322-00623-2(6))* Wright Group/McGraw-Hill.

Magic! Level C, 6 vols. 8p. 24.95 *(978-0-7802-9122-5(0))* Wright Group/McGraw-Hill.

Mai. Many Hands. 2012. 24p. pap. 15.99 *(978-1-4771-4246-2(0))* Xlibris Corp.

Mairi, Mackinnon. Phonics Workbook 1. 2012. (Very First Reading Workbooks Ser.). 36p. (J). pap. 7.99 *(978-0-7945-3115-7(6),* Usborne) EDC Publishing.

—Phonics Workbook 2. 2012. (Very First Reading Workbooks Ser.). 36p. (J). pap. 7.99 *(978-0-7945-3116-4(4),* Usborne) EDC Publishing.

Mai's Big Surprise: Consonant review: Level C, 6 vols. (Wright Skills Ser.). 16p. (gr. k-3). 26.50 *(978-0-322-01490-9(5))* Wright Group/McGraw-Hill.

Major Jump: Big Book: Level B. Group 1. (Sunshine Ser.). 8p. 20.95 *(978-0-7802-5713-9(8))* Wright Group/McGraw-Hill.

Make Believe Ideas. Find It! Make Believe Ideas, illus. 2015. (ENG.). 176p. (J). (gr. -1-3). pap. 8.99 *(978-1-78393-828-5(5))* Make Believe Ideas GBR. Dist: Scholastic, Inc.

Making a TV Documentary: Level R, 6 vols. (Wonder Worldtm Ser.). 48p. 44.95 *(978-0-7802-7082-4(7))* Wright Group/McGraw-Hill.

Making Choices: American Readers. (J). (gr. 6). *(978-0-669-05069-1(5));* wbk. ed. *(978-0-669-05071-4(7))* Houghton Mifflin Harcourt School Pubs.

Making Music: Level B, 6 vols. (Wonder Worldtm Ser.). 16p. 24.95 *(978-0-7802-2008-9(0))* Wright Group/McGraw-Hill.

Mama Goes to School: Big Book: Level D. (Visions Ser.). 8p. 20.95 *(978-0-322-00310-1(5))* Wright Group/McGraw-Hill.

Los Mamíferos Del Mar, 6 vols. (Explorers. Exploradores Nonfiction Sets Ser.). (SPA.). 32p. (gr. 3-6). 44.95 *(978-0-7699-0629-4(X))* Shortland Pubns. (U. S. A.) Inc.

Manners, Jane. Clouds. 2004. (ENG., Illus.). 16p. (J). (gr. 1-1). pap. 10.92 *(978-0-7652-5153-4(1),* Celebration Pr.) Savvas Learning Co.

Los Mapas Del Mundo, 6 vols., Vol. 2. (Explorers. Exploradores Nonfiction Sets Ser.). (SPA.). 32p. (gr. 3-6). 44.95 *(978-0-7699-0646-1(X))* Shortland Pubns. (U. S. A.) Inc.

Marching Along: American Readers. (J). (gr. 2). *(978-0-669-04984-8(0));* wbk. ed. *(978-0-669-04991-6(3))* Houghton Mifflin Harcourt School Pubs.

Maria's Diary: Level R, 6 vols. (Wonder Worldtm Ser.). 48p. 44.95 *(978-0-7802-7067-1(3))* Wright Group/McGraw-Hill.

Mario Mixwell: Level L, 6 vols. (Take-Twostm Ser.). 16p. 36.95 *(978-0-322-03404-4(3))* Wright Group/McGraw-Hill.

The Marketplace: Big Book: Level G. (Visions Ser.). 16p. 20.95 *(978-0-322-00628-7(7))* Wright Group/McGraw-Hill.

Martinez, Jeny. A Walk in the Park. 2011. 32p. pap. 21.99 *(978-1-4568-5229-0(9))* Xlibris Corp.

Marzollo, Jean & Wick, Walter. I Spy a Dinosaur's Eye. 2003. (I Spy — Scholastic Readers Level 1 Ser.). (gr. -1-2). lib. bdg. 13.55 *(978-0-613-72243-8(4))* Turtleback.

Masks: Level E, 6 vols. (Wonder Worldtm Ser.). 16p. 29.95 *(978-0-7802-2010-2(2))* Wright Group/McGraw-Hill.

Mattern, Joanne. At the Football Game: Learning the Symbols , And =, 1 vol. 2010. (Math for the REAL World Ser.). (ENG.). 16p. (gr. 2-3). pap. 7.05 *(978-0-8239-8875-4(9),* 75a3d101-e531-4df0-bad7-8190e0af2c8f, Rosen Classroom) Rosen Publishing Group, Inc., The.

Max Is Sick: Consonants q, x, z; -ack, -ick, -ill word families: Level A, 6 vols. (Wright Skills Ser.). 12p. (gr. k-3). 17.95 *(978-0-322-01457-2(3))* Wright Group/McGraw-Hill.

McDonnell, Flora. Splash. 2004. (CHI & ENG., Illus.). 28p. (J). pap. *(978-1-85269-549-1(8))* Mantra Lingua.

McDougal-Littell Publishing Staff. Literature Connections English: A Place Where the Sea Remembers. 2004. (McDougal Littell Literature Connections Ser.). (ENG.). 208p. (gr. 10-10). 16.25 *(978-0-395-83361-2(2),* 2-70784) Great Source Education Group, Inc.

McDougal-Littell Publishing Staff, creator. Picture Bride & Related Readings. 2006. (Literature Connections Ser.). 314p. (gr. 6-12). *(978-0-395-77540-0(X),* 2-80109) Holt McDougal.

—1984: And Related Readings. 2006. (Literature Connections Ser.). 428p. (YA). (gr. 8-12). *(978-0-395-87471-4(8),* 2-70831) Holt McDougal.

McGraw Hill. Fast Track Reading, Complete Level 3 Set. 2003. (Intervention Ser.). (ENG.). (gr. 3-8). pap. 1951.44 *(978-1-4045-0396-0(X),* 140450396X) McGraw-Hill Education.

—Fast Track Reading, Complete Level 4 Set. 2003. (Intervention Ser.). (ENG.). (gr. 3-8). pap. 1951.44 *(978-1-4045-0397-7(8),* 1404503978) McGraw-Hill Education.

—Fast Track Reading, Complete Level 5 Set. 2003. (Intervention Ser.). (ENG.). (gr. 3-8). pap. 1951.44 *(978-1-4045-0398-4(6),* 1404503986) McGraw-Hill Education.

—Fast Track Reading, Complete Level 6 Set. 2003. (Intervention Ser.). (ENG.). (gr. 3-8). pap. 1951.44 *(978-1-4045-0399-1(4),* 1404503994) McGraw-Hill Education.

—Gear up, Early Emergent Leveled Library 1: Student Books. 2003. (Gear Up Ser.). (ENG.). (gr. k-k). pap. 188.16 *(978-1-4045-2065-3(1),* 1404520651) McGraw-Hill Education.

—Gear up, Early Emergent Leveled Library 2: Student Books, Vol. 2. 2003. (Gear Up Ser.). (ENG.). (gr. k-k). pap. 179.20 *(978-1-4045-2066-0(X),* 140452066X) McGraw-Hill Education.

—Gear up, Upper Emergent Leveled Library 1: Student Books. 2003. (Gear Up Ser.). (ENG.). (gr. 1-1). pap. 207.64 *(978-1-4045-2067-7(8),* 1404520678) McGraw-Hill Education.

—Gear up, Upper Emergent Leveled Library 2: Student Books Vol. 2. 2003. (Gear Up Ser.). (ENG.). (gr. 1-1). pap. 207.64 *(978-1-4045-2068-4(6),* 1404520686) McGraw-Hill Education.

—Timed Readings Plus in Social Studies Book 1: 25 Two-Part Lessons with Questions for Building Reading Speed & Comprehension, Bk. 1. 2003. (JT: READING RATE & FLUENCY Ser.). (ENG.). 120p. (gr. 6-12). per. 30.32 *(978-0-07-845799-9(8),* 0078457998) McGraw-Hill Education.

—Timed Readings Plus Social Studies Book 10: 25 Two-Part Lessons with Questions for Building Reading Speed & Comprehension, Vol. 10. 2003. (JT: READING RATE & FLUENCY Ser.). (ENG.). 120p. (gr. 6-12). per. 30.32 *(978-0-07-845808-8(0),* 0078458080) McGraw-Hill Education.

—Timed Readings Plus Social Studies Book 2 Bk. 3: 25 Two-Part Lessons with Questions for Building Reading Speed & Comprehension, Vol. 2. 2003. (JT: READING RATE & FLUENCY Ser.). (ENG.). 120p. (gr. 6-12). pap. 30.32 *(978-0-07-845800-2(5),* 0078458005) McGraw-Hill Education.

—Timed Readings Plus Social Studies Book 9 Bk. 3: 25 Two-Part Lessons with Questions for Building Reading Speed & Comprehension, Vol. 9. 2003. (JT: READING RATE & FLUENCY Ser.). (ENG.). 120p. (gr. 6-12). pap. 30.32 *(978-0-07-845807-1(2),* 0078458072) McGraw-Hill Education.

McGraw-Hill - Jamestown Education Staff. Timed Readings Plus in Social Studies, Vol. 3. 2003. pap. 17.32 *(978-0-07-845801-9(3),* 9780078458019) Jamestown.

McGraw-Hill Staff. Jo Tries: And Other Selections, 6 vols. (Fast Track Reading Ser.). 24p. (gr. 4-8). 40.95 *(978-0-322-05983-2(6))* Wright Group/McGraw-Hill.

McGraw-Hill, Wright. Treacherous Ice, 6 vols. (Comprehension Strand Ser.). (gr. 4-8). 54.00 *(978-0-322-06032-6(X))* Wright Group/McGraw-Hill.

McKay, Sindy. We Read Phonics-Magic Tricks. Johnson, Meredith, illus. 2011. (We Read Phonics Ser.). 32p. (J). (gr. 1-3). 9.95 *(978-1-60115-337-1(6));* pap. 4.99 *(978-1-60115-338-8(4))* Treasure Bay, Inc.

—We Read Phonics-Matt & Sid. Reinhart, Larry, illus. 2010. 32p. (J). 9.95 *(978-1-60115-315-9(5));* pap. 4.99 *(978-1-60115-316-6(3))* Treasure Bay, Inc.

McNeil, Niki, et al. HOCPP 1118 Beginning Reading. 2006. spiral bd. 30.00 *(978-1-60308-118-4(6))* In the Hands of a Child.

Meeting Challenges: American Readers. (J). (gr. 8). *(978-0-669-05099-8(7)); (978-0-669-05093-6(8))* Houghton Mifflin Harcourt School Pubs.

Meow-Meow Gets Out: Diphthongs ou, ow: Level B, 6 vols. (Wright Skills Ser.). 16p. (gr. k-3). 26.50 *(978-0-322-01484-8(0))* Wright Group/McGraw-Hill.

Mike & His Bride, 6 vols. 8p. (gr. k-1). 21.50 *(978-0-322-02062-7(X))* Wright Group/McGraw-Hill.

Milking: Level H, 6 vols. (Wonder Worldtm Ser.). 16p. 29.95 *(978-0-7802-1207-7(X))* Wright Group/McGraw-Hill.

Minden, Cecilia. Cat. 2018. (Learn about Animals Ser.). (ENG., Illus.). 16p. (J). (gr. -1-2). pap. 11.36 *(978-1-5341-2395-3(4),* 210574) Cherry Lake Publishing.

Mixed-Up Wishing Well Little Book: Early Reading Fluency, Level C. 2004. pap. 6.00 *(978-0-7398-8297-9(X))* Steck-Vaughn.

Modern Staff. Discovery Phonics I: Lively Tales Unlock the Mystery of Long & Short Vowels. 2003. (J). 333.95 *(978-0-8136-1122-8(9))* Modern Curriculum Pr.

Montoya, Martha, creator. Huevos o Pollitos: Take-Home. 2005. (Los Kitos Ser.). (SPA.). (YA). (gr. 1-3). 15.00 *(978-0-8215-8814-7(1))* Sadlier, William H. Inc.

Moon Stars. 2003. 31.95 *(978-0-673-75807-1(9))* Celebration Pr.

Moore, David W. The Good Reader's Kit: the Good Reader's Guide (Hardcover) 2007. (Good Reader's Kit Ser.). (ENG., Illus.). 480p. (C). pap. 67.95 *(978-0-7362-3411-5(X))* CENGAGE Learning.

—The Good Reader's Kit: the Good Reader's Guide (Softcover) 2007. (Good Reader's Kit Ser.). (ENG., Illus.). 480p. (C). pap. 56.95 *(978-0-7362-3410-8(1))* CENGAGE Learning.

Moore, Sheila. Abadaba Alphabet: Learning Letter Sounds. Holsinger, Carol, illus. 2006. 31p. (gr. -1-3). 19.95 *(978-0-9789473-0-9(4))* Abadaba Reading LLC.

Morss, Martha. Advantage Reading Grade 3, Vol. 8114. Hamaguchi, Carla, ed. Tom, Darcy, illus. 2004. (Advantage Workbook Ser.). 112p. 8.99 *(978-1-59198-024-7(0),* CTP 8114) Creative Teaching Pr., Inc.

Moskal, G. I Like Winter: Learning the ER Sound. 2009. (PowerPhonics Ser.). 24p. (gr. 1-1). 39.90 *(978-1-60851-451-9(X),* PowerKids Pr.) Rosen Publishing Group, Inc., The.

Motorbike Racer: Level P, 6 vols. (Wonder Worldtm Ser.). 48p. 39.95 *(978-0-7802-7071-8(1))* Wright Group/McGraw-Hill.

Mountain Gorillas: Level N, 6 vols. (Wonder Worldtm Ser.). 48p. 34.95 *(978-0-7802-2899-3(5))* Wright Group/McGraw-Hill.

Mouse Soup. 2003. 31.95 *(978-0-673-75804-0(4))* Celebration Pr.

Mouse Tales. 2003. 31.95 *(978-0-673-75805-7(2))* Celebration Pr.

Mouse Train: Big Book: Level C. Group 2. (Story Box Ser.). 16p. 20.95 *(978-0-322-00332-3(6))* Wright Group/McGraw-Hill.

Move It: Level E, 6 vols. (Wonder Worldtm Ser.). 16p. 29.95 *(978-0-7802-1223-7(1))* Wright Group/McGraw-Hill.

Moving On: American Readers. (J). (gr. 1). *(978-0-669-04950-3(6));* wbk. ed. *(978-0-669-04956-5(5))* Houghton Mifflin Harcourt School Pubs.

Mrs Grindy's Shoes: Level I. Group 1. (Sunshine Ser.). 16p. 31.50 *(978-0-7802-5756-6(1))* Wright Group/McGraw-Hill.

Murphy, Patricia J. Counting with an Abacus: Learning the Place Values of Ones, Tens, & Hundreds, 1 vol. 2010. (Math for the REAL World Ser.). (ENG.). 16p. (gr. 2-3). pap. 7.05 *(978-0-8239-8880-8(5),* a2b34c3b-5d91-4de8-83e8-908fd59fed5e, Rosen Classroom) Rosen Publishing Group, Inc., The.

My Computer: Level H, 6 vols. (Wonder Worldtm Ser.). 16p. 29.95 *(978-0-7802-1225-1(8))* Wright Group/McGraw-Hill.

My Dad has Asthma: Level L, 6 vols. (Wonder Worldtm Ser.). 16p. 34.95 *(978-0-7802-4587-7(3))* Wright Group/McGraw-Hill.

My Friend Jess: Level H, 6 vols. (Wonder Worldtm Ser.). 16p. 29.95 *(978-0-7802-1227-5(4))* Wright Group/McGraw-Hill.
My Story: Level A, 6 vols. (Wonder Worldtm Ser.). 16p. 24.95 *(978-0-7802-2901-3(0))* Wright Group/McGraw-Hill.
Mythmakers, 6 vols. (Wildcats Ser.). 32p. (gr. 2-8). *(978-0-322-02440-3(4))* Wright Group/McGraw-Hill.
Nana's Sweet Potato Pie, 6 vols. (Multicultural Programs Ser.). 16p. (gr. 1-3). 24.95 *(978-0-7802-9211-6(1))* Wright Group/McGraw-Hill.
A Nap Is not Fun: Short Vowel u: Level A, 6 vols. (Wright Skills Ser.). 12p. (gr. k-3). 17.95 *(978-0-322-03131-9(1))* Wright Group/McGraw-Hill.
National Geographic Learning. Reading Expeditions (Social Studies: Kids Make a Difference): Kids Manage Money. 2007. (Rise & Shine Ser.). (ENG., Illus.). 32p. (J). pap. 18.95 *(978-0-7922-8694-3(4))* CENGAGE Learning.
Native Americans: Level O, 6 vols. (Explorers Ser.). 32p. (gr. 3-6). 44.95 *(978-0-7699-0600-3(1))* Shortland Pubns. (U. S. A.) Inc.
The Neighborhood Clubhouse, 6 vols. (Multicultural Programs Ser.). 16p. (gr. 1-3). 24.95 *(978-0-7802-9212-3(X))* Wright Group/McGraw-Hill.
Nelson. Finding Places: American Readers. (J). *(978-0-669-04947-3(6))* Houghton Mifflin Harcourt School Pubs.
—Looking Out, Climbing Up, Going Far: American Readers. (J). *(978-0-669-04973-2(5))* Houghton Mifflin Harcourt School Pubs.
—Marching Along: American Readers. (J). *(978-0-669-04993-0(X))* Houghton Mifflin Harcourt School Pubs.
—Moving On: American Readers. (J). *(978-0-669-04961-9(1))* Houghton Mifflin Harcourt School Pubs.
—Turning Corners: American Readers. (J). *(978-0-669-05008-0(3))* Houghton Mifflin Harcourt School Pubs.
Nests: Level A, 6 vols. (Wonder Worldtm Ser.). 16p. 24.95 *(978-0-7802-1041-7(7))* Wright Group/McGraw-Hill.
The New Building, 6 vols. (Sunshinetm Ser.). 16p. (gr. k-18). 29.50 *(978-0-7802-5424-4(4))* Wright Group/McGraw-Hill.
New Shoes: Level C, 6 vols. (Wonder Worldtm Ser.). 16p. 24.95 *(978-0-7802-1231-2(2))* Wright Group/McGraw-Hill.
Next Chapters Starter Set. 2005. (J). (gr. 3-5). tchr. ed. 119.95 *(978-0-7652-2126-1(8))* Modern Curriculum Pr.
Nichols, Jennifer. What Should We Wear? 2004. (ENG., Illus.). 8p. (J). (gr. k-k). pap. 6.97 net. *(978-0-7652-5146-6(9),* Celebration Pr.) Savvas Learning Co.
Nighttime: Big Book: Level C. Group 1. (Story Box Ser.). 8p. 20.95 *(978-0-322-00636-2(8))* Wright Group/McGraw-Hill.
No Space to Waste: Level L, 6 vols. 128p. (gr. 2-3). 41.95 *(978-0-7699-1025-3(4))* Shortland Pubns. (U. S. A.) Inc.
No Sweat! Short e Digraph: Level B, 6 vols. (Wright Skills Ser.). 16p. (gr. k-3). 26.50 *(978-0-322-01477-0(8))* Wright Group/McGraw-Hill.
Not what it Seems, 6 vols. (Wildcats Ser.). 32p. (gr. 2-8). *(978-0-322-00602-7(3))* Wright Group/McGraw-Hill.
Notorious Nigel: Level Q, 6 vols. (Wonder Worldtm Ser.). 48p. 39.95 *(978-0-7802-2960-0(6))* Wright Group/McGraw-Hill.
Novel Units. The Wind in the Willows Novel Units Teacher Guide. 2019. (ENG.). (J). pap., tchr. ed., wbk. ed. 12.99 *(978-1-56137-208-9(0),* Novel Units, Inc.) Classroom Library Co.
Nowak, Jennifer. At the Flower Shop: Learning Simple Division by Forming Equal Groups, 1 vol. 2010. (Math for the REAL World Ser.). (ENG.). 16p. (gr. 2-3). pap. 7.05 *(978-0-8239-8930-0(5),* c49a699a-8a7f-4fe8-ae1d-cc850a59e95a, Rosen Classroom) Rosen Publishing Group, Inc., The.
Oatmeal: Level H, 6 vols. (Wonder Worldtm Ser.). 16p. 29.95 *(978-0-7802-1042-4(5))* Wright Group/McGraw-Hill.
Odgers, Sally. Glory Gate: Level Q, 6 vols. (Mountain Peaks Ser.). 128p. (gr. 6-18). 36.95 *(978-0-322-05889-7(9))* Wright Group/McGraw-Hill.
Olivia Agnew's Wild Imagination: Level O, 6 vols. (Wonder Worldtm Ser.). 48p. 39.95 *(978-0-7802-2957-0(6))* Wright Group/McGraw-Hill.
On & off the Road: 6 Each of 1 Anthology, 6 vols. (Wildcats Ser.). 32p. (gr. 2-8). *(978-0-322-02421-2(8))* Wright Group/McGraw-Hill.
On My Street, 6 vols. (Multicultural Programs Ser.). 16p. (gr. 1-3). 24.95 *(978-0-7802-9205-5(7))* Wright Group/McGraw-Hill.
On the Air: Level P, 6 vols. (Wonder Worldtm Ser.). 48p. 39.95 *(978-0-7802-7081-7(9))* Wright Group/McGraw-Hill.
Once I Was a Baby Little Book: Early Reading Fluency, Level A, Bk. 3. 2004. (ENG.). (gr. 1). pap. 6.00 *(978-0-7398-8156-9(6))* Steck-Vaughn.
Oppenheim, Joanne F. & Oppenheim, Stephanie. A Leer y Jugar! con Bebés y Niños Pequeños. Auclair, Joan, illus. 2006.Tr. of Read It! Play It! with Babies & Toddlers. (SPA.). 102p. pap. 10.00 *(978-0-9721050-5-7(0))* Oppenheim Toy Portfolio, Inc.
—Read It! Play It! Auclair, Joan, illus. 2005. 176p. pap. 10.00 *(978-0-9721050-1-9(8))* Oppenheim Toy Portfolio, Inc.
—Read It! Play It! with Babies & Toddlers. 2006. (Illus.). pap. 10.00 *(978-0-9721050-4-0(2))* Oppenheim Toy Portfolio, Inc.
Ornelas, Lourdes. So Can I. 2013. 32p. 25.99 *(978-1-4808-0189-9(5));* pap. 16.99 *(978-1-4808-0187-5(9))* Archway Publishing.
Orphan Train: Medial Digraphs: Level C, 6 vols. (Wright Skills Ser.). 16p. (gr. k-3). 26.50 *(978-0-322-01498-5(0))* Wright Group/McGraw-Hill.
Orshoski, Paul. We Read Phonics-Ant in Her Pants. Ebbeler, Jeffrey, illus. 2010. (ENG.). 32p. (J). pap. 4.99 *(978-1-60115-328-9(7))* Treasure Bay, Inc.
—We Read Phonics-Bugs on the Bus. Noiset, Michele, illus. 2010. 32p. (J). 9.95 *(978-1-60115-325-8(2));* pap. 4.99 *(978-1-60115-326-5(0))* Treasure Bay, Inc.
—We Read Phonics-Sports Dream. Ebbeler, Jeffrey, illus. 2011. (We Read Phonics: Level 5-6 Ser.). 32p. (J). (ENG.). (gr. k-3). 17.44 *(978-1-60115-335-7(X));* (gr. 1-3). pap. 4.99 *(978-1-60115-336-4(8))* Treasure Bay, Inc.
—We Read Phonics-Talent Night. Kulka, Joe, illus. 2011. (We Read Phonics Ser.). 32p. (J). (gr. 1-3). 9.95 *(978-1-60115-339-5(2));* pap. 4.99 *(978-1-60115-340-1(6))* Treasure Bay, Inc.
Osakawa. Hiking in the Wilds: Level Q. Group 1. (Take-Twostm Ser.). 32p. 38.95 *(978-0-322-04488-3(X))* Wright Group/McGraw-Hill.
Ottaway, Jacqueline. Riddle of the Seaplanes (Level S), 6 vols. (Mountain Peaks Ser.). 128p. (gr. 6-18). 36.95 *(978-0-322-05891-0(0))* Wright Group/McGraw-Hill.
Our Granny: Level B. Group 1. (Sunshine Ser.). 8p. 20.95 *(978-0-7802-5715-3(4))* Wright Group/McGraw-Hill.
Out of Luck!, 6 vols. 8p. (gr. k-1). 21.50 *(978-0-322-02081-8(6))* Wright Group/McGraw-Hill.
Out of the Computer: Level 6, 6 vols. (Fluency Strand Ser.). (gr. 4-8). 45.00 *(978-1-4045-1235-1(7))* Wright Group/McGraw-Hill.
Out of the Sunless Land: Level T. Group 2, 6 vols. (Sunshine Ser.). 48p. 44.95 *(978-0-7802-4186-2(X))* Wright Group/McGraw-Hill.
The Ox in the Pit: Consonant x: Level A, 6 vols. (Wright Skills Ser.). 12p. (gr. k-3). 17.95 *(978-0-322-03123-4(0))* Wright Group/McGraw-Hill.
Pacholski, Robert, creator. Aperturas a Lectura. 2003. (SPA., Illus.). (gr. k-3). 78p. stu. ed., wbk. ed. 7.95 *(978-0-9745220-1-2(5));* 9p. tchr. ed. 3.95 *(978-0-9745220-3-6(1))* Aperturas Foundation.
A Pan for Pam: Consonant p: Level A, 6 vols. (Wright Skills Ser.). 12p. (gr. k-3). 17.95 *(978-0-322-03108-1(7))* Wright Group/McGraw-Hill.
A Pan of Jam: Consonant j: Level A, 6 vols. (Wright Skills Ser.). 12p. (gr. k-3). 17.95 *(978-0-322-03109-8(5))* Wright Group/McGraw-Hill.
Papi!: Level T. Group 1, 6 vols. (Sunshine Ser.). 48p. 44.95 *(978-0-7802-5600-2(X))* Wright Group/McGraw-Hill.
Paris, Susan. High Noon: Level P, 6 vols. (Raging Rivers Ser.). 128p. (gr. 3-6). 36.95 *(978-0-322-05894-1(5))* Wright Group/McGraw-Hill.
Parr, Tom. Reading Makes You Feel Good. 2014. 32p. pap. 7.00 *(978-1-61003-382-4(5))* Center for the Collaborative Classroom.
Pearl, Melissa Sherman & Sherman, David A. Sheltering Books: Charities Started by Kids! 2017. (Community Connections: How Do They Help? Ser.). (ENG., Illus.). 24p. (J). (gr. 2-5). lib. bdg. 29.21 *(978-1-63472-846-1(7),* 209810) Cherry Lake Publishing.
Peek, Patsy. Reading Comprehension Practice: Grades 2-8 Practice Worksheets Featuring Story Webs, Newspaper Ads, Fliers. 2012. 64p. (gr. 2-4). pap. 13.95 *(978-1-4772-4933-8(8))* AuthorHouse.
People Dance: Level F, 6 vols. (Wonder Worldtm Ser.). 16p. 29.95 *(978-0-7802-2018-8(8))* Wright Group/McGraw-Hill.
Perritano, John. Mummies in the Library: Divide the Pages. 2013. (iMath Ser.). (ENG., Illus.). 32p. (J). (gr. 3-4). lib. bdg. 22.60 *(978-1-59953-558-6(0))* Norwood Hse. Pr.
Peter Paper Clip, 6 vols. 8p. (gr. k-1). 21.50 *(978-0-322-02065-8(4))* Wright Group/McGraw-Hill.
Phonic Books. Phonic Books Magic Belt: Decodable Books for Older Readers (CVC, Consonant Blends & Consonant Teams) 2014. (Phonic Books Intervention Decodables Ser.). (ENG., Illus.). 192p. (J). (gr. 4-7). 79.00 *(978-1-78369-242-2(1),* Phonic Bks.) DK.
Phonic Books. Phonic Books Talisman 1: Decodable Books for Older Readers (Alternative Vowel Spellings) 2014. (Phonic Books Intervention Decodables Ser.). (ENG., Illus.). 200p. (J). (gr. 4-7). 69.00 ***(978-1-78369-244-6(8),*** Phonic Bks.) DK.
Phonics & Word Study Complete Kits: Phonics & Word Study: Level C. (gr. k-3). 333.95 *(978-0-322-01644-6(4))* Wright Group/McGraw-Hill.
Phonics & Word Study Core Kits: Phonics & Word Study: Level A. (gr. k-3). 153.50 *(978-0-322-01641-5(X))* Wright Group/McGraw-Hill.
Phonics & Word Study Core Kits: Phonics & Word Study: Level B. (gr. k-3). 185.50 *(978-0-322-01643-9(6))* Wright Group/McGraw-Hill.
Phonics & Word Study Core Kits: Phonics & Word Study: Level C. (gr. k-3). 153.50 *(978-0-322-01645-3(2))* Wright Group/McGraw-Hill.
Phonics Plus Staff. Phonics Plus, Bk. F. 2nd ed. (J). 9.55 *(978-0-8136-0396-4(X))* Modern Curriculum Pr.
Photos, Photos: 6 Each of 1 Anthology, 6 vols. (Wildcats Ser.). 32p. (gr. 2-8). *(978-0-322-00580-8(9))* Wright Group/McGraw-Hill.
Picture & Thematic Dictionary Activity Book. (Foundation Ser.). 58p. (gr. k-3). 20.95 *(978-0-322-01561-6(8))* Wright Group/McGraw-Hill.
Pigs & Dogs Play Ball: Consonants b, w; Short Vowel i word families: Level A, 6 vols. (Wright Skills Ser.). 12p. (gr. k-3). 17.95 *(978-0-322-01450-3(6))* Wright Group/McGraw-Hill.
The Pink Tent: Final Blends -nd, -nk, -nt: Level B, 6 vols. (Wright Skills Ser.). 16p. (gr. k-3). 17.95 *(978-0-322-01462-6(X))* Wright Group/McGraw-Hill.
Pippin, Jessica. I Am a Star! Juan, Juan Bautista, illus. 2023. (ENG.). 16p. (J). (gr. -1-1). pap. 33.00 *(978-1-4788-0516-8(1),* b32de0ac-679f-4e9a-bdbf-51c257093f2e) Newmark Learning LLC.
—I Can Be Kind. Monés, Marc, illus. 2023. (ENG.). 16p. (J). (gr. -1-1). pap. 33.00 *(978-1-4788-0504-5(8),* c22c2734-3493-4cf5-ab01-62fff8a3dea3) Newmark Learning LLC.
—I Was So Mad. Poole, Helen, illus. 2023. (ENG.). 16p. (J). (gr. -1-1). pap. 5.25 *(978-1-4788-0462-8(9),* 7d3fc2b0-fe95-40e4-910b-3ffaa98cf047); pap. 33.00 *(978-1-4788-0499-4(8),* c66827fc-7a94-40ab-bbac-e044999542ef) Newmark Learning LLC.
Places to Visit, Places to See: Take-Home Book. 2005. (Lee Bennett Hopkins Worlds of Poetry Classroom Library). (YA). (gr. k-3). 13.50 *(978-0-8215-0568-7(8))* Sadlier, William H. Inc.
Los Planetas, 6 vols., Vol. 2. (Explorers. Exploradores Nonfiction Sets Ser.). (SPA.). 32p. (gr. 3-6). 44.95 *(978-0-7699-0642-3(7))* Shortland Pubns. (U. S. A.) Inc.
Pop, 6 vols. 8p. (gr. k-1). 21.50 *(978-0-322-02073-3(5))* Wright Group/McGraw-Hill.
A Porcupine: Big Book: Level C. (Wonder Worldtm Ser.). 16p. 26.50 *(978-0-7802-3471-0(5))* Wright Group/McGraw-Hill.
A Porcupine: Level C, 6 vols. (Wonder Worldtm Ser.). 16p. 24.95 *(978-0-7802-1189-6(8))* Wright Group/McGraw-Hill.
Potok, Chaim. The Chosen: And Related Readings. 2006. (McDougal Littell Literature Connections Ser.). (ENG.). 416p. (gr. 6-8). 18.50 *(978-0-395-88145-3(5),* 2-70858) Great Source Education Group, Inc.
PowerPhonics Skill Set I: Includes Animals I, Self I & Growing Things, 18 bks. (Illus.). (J). (gr. 1). lib. bdg. 324.00 *(978-0-8239-7204-3(6),* PowerKids Pr.) Rosen Publishing Group, Inc., The.
The Predator. (Song Box Ser.). (gr. 1-2). 8.50 incl. audio *(978-0-7802-2261-8(X))* Wright Group/McGraw-Hill.
The Predator: 1 Big Book, 6 Each of 1 Student Book, & 1 Cassette. (Song Box Ser.). (gr. 1-2). 68.95 *(978-0-7802-3205-1(4))* Wright Group/McGraw-Hill.
The Predator: Big Book. (Song Box Ser.). (gr. 1-2). 31.50 *(978-0-7802-2260-1(1))* Wright Group/McGraw-Hill.
Proof of Magic, 6 vols. (Ragged Island Mysteriestm Ser.). 161p. (gr. 5-7). 42.50 *(978-0-322-01649-1(5))* Wright Group/McGraw-Hill.
Publ, Griffin. Easy Olympic Sports Reader, 6 Bks, Set. 2004. (U. S. Olympic Committee Easy Olympic Sports Readers Ser.). (Illus.). 16p. (J). pap. 17.95 *(978-1-58000-116-8(5))* Griffin Publishing Group.
Publications International Ltd. Staff, ed. Disney Pixar Cars: Story Reader 2. 0 3 Storybook Library. 2011. (J). 19.98 *(978-1-4508-0606-0(6))* Publications International, Ltd.
—Disney Princess: My Own Carriage. 2014. 12p. (J). bds. 12.98 *(978-1-4508-7381-9(2),* 66a3c624-31ec-4290-ae22-6fd5a90376b3) Phoenix International Publications, Inc.
—Let's Learn to Read! 2010. 24p. (J). 16.98 *(978-1-60553-361-2(0))* Publications International, Ltd.
—Preschool Reading & Math Activities. 2010. 128p. 11.98 *(978-1-60553-180-9(4))* Publications International, Ltd.
Pulse- Fun with Reading & Writing. 2006. cd-rom 4.99 *(978-1-60245-040-0(4))* GDL Multimedia, LLC.
Quack! Quack! Quack!, 6 vols. 8p. (gr. k-1). 21.50 *(978-0-322-02074-0(3))* Wright Group/McGraw-Hill.
Que vemos en el mar? What Do You See by the Sea? 2005. (Take-Home Bks.). (SPA.). (YA). (gr. -1-3). 15.75 *(978-0-8215-1202-9(1))* Sadlier, William H. Inc.
Que vemos en el mar?/What Do You See by the Sea? 2005. (Libros en Espanol Para Ninos Ser.). (SPA.). (YA). (gr. -1-1). 11.97 *(978-0-8215-0992-0(6))* Sadlier, William H. Inc.
Queen Jelly Bean: Vowel Digraph Review: Level C, 6 vols. (Wright Skills Ser.). 16p. (gr. k-3). 26.50 *(978-0-322-01499-2(9))* Wright Group/McGraw-Hill.
Queen of the Trail: Decodable Books, 6 vols. (Fast Track Reading Ser.). 24p. (gr. 4-8). 40.95 *(978-0-322-05985-6(2))* Wright Group/McGraw-Hill.
A Quilt for Kristy: Consonant blend review: Level C, 6 vols. (Wright Skills Ser.). 16p. (gr. k-3). 26.50 *(978-0-322-01493-0(X))* Wright Group/McGraw-Hill.
Quinton, Sasha. I-Spy: A Phonics Reader. 2009. (Illus.). *(978-1-936199-06-8(8))* Book Shop, Ltd., The.
—Rat-A-Tat: A Phonics Reader. 2009. (Illus.). pap. *(978-1-936199-04-4(1))* Book Shop, Ltd., The.
—Ring-A-Ding: A Phonics Reader. 2009. (Illus.). pap. *(978-1-936199-00-6(9))* Book Shop, Ltd., The.
—Root-A-Toot: A Phonics Reader. 2009. (Illus.). pap. *(978-1-936199-01-3(7))* Book Shop, Ltd., The.
—Rub-A-Dub: A Phonics Reader. 2009. (Illus.). *(978-1-936199-03-7(3))* Book Shop, Ltd., The.
—Yay-Hooray: A Phonics Reader. 2009. (Illus.). pap. *(978-1-936199-07-5(6))* Book Shop, Ltd., The.
Quit It! Consonant q: Level A, 6 vols. (Wright Skills Ser.). 12p. (gr. k-3). 17.95 *(978-0-322-03122-7(2))* Wright Group/McGraw-Hill.
The Race: Level D. Group 1. (Sunshine Ser.). 8p. 20.95 *(978-0-7802-5733-7(2))* Wright Group/McGraw-Hill.
A Rag for Miss Rat: Consonant r: Level A, 6 vols. (Wright Skills Ser.). 12p. (gr. k-3). 17.95 *(978-0-322-03128-9(1))* Wright Group/McGraw-Hill.
Rasinski, Timothy V. Daily Word Ladders. 2012. (ENG.). 96p. (gr. k-1). pap. 14.99 *(978-0-545-22379-9(2),* Teaching Resources) Scholastic, Inc.
Rat Princess Little Book: Early Reading Fluency, Level C. 2004. pap. 6.00 *(978-0-7398-8299-3(6))* Steck-Vaughn.
Rawson, Christopher. Stories of Giants. Cartwright, Stephen, illus. 2004. (Young Reading Ser.: Vol. 1). 48p. (J). (gr. 2-18). lib. bdg. 13.95 *(978-1-58086-614-9(X),* Usborne) EDC Publishing.
Reach for Reading: Reaching Higher Self-Training Package. (gr. 3-5). 725.00 *(978-0-7578-5931-1(3))* Rigby Education.
Reach for Reading: Reaching up Self-Training Package. (gr. 1-3). 675.00 *(978-0-7578-5932-8(1))* Rigby Education.
Reaching Higher Additional Workstations: With Books. (Reach for Reading Ser.). (gr. 3-5). 425.00 *(978-0-7635-3700-5(4))* Rigby Education.
Read, Write & Publish. (J). (gr. 5). 125.25 *(978-0-669-17767-1(9))* Houghton Mifflin Harcourt School Pubs.
Reader's Theater Program Levels (F-U) Set A, 24 vols - 144 Bks. 2004. (J). pap. 375.00 *(978-1-4108-1512-5(9))* Benchmark Education Co.
Reading & Writing. 2004. (Help with Homework Ser.). 32p. (J). (gr. k-2). wbk. ed. 3.99 *(978-1-904586-24-1(4));* (gr. 1-4). wbk. ed. 3.99 *(978-1-904586-20-3(1))* Byeway Bks.
Reading Fluency Grades K-2. 2005. (J). pap. *(978-1-60015-039-5(X))* Steps To Literacy, LLC.
Reading Is Everywhere, 6 vols. (Sunshinetm Ser.). 16p. (gr. k-18). 29.50 *(978-0-7802-5425-1(2))* Wright Group/McGraw-Hill.
Reading Recovery Kits: Reading Recovery Starter Kit. (Reading Recovery Ser.). (gr. k-6). 367.95 *(978-0-322-00641-6(4))* Wright Group/McGraw-Hill.
Reading Rods Phonemic Awareness Activity Book. 2003. (J). pap. 4.95 *(978-1-56911-117-8(0))* Learning Resources, Inc.
Reading Rods Phonemic Awareness Activity Cards, Set 2. 2003. (J). 19.95 *(978-1-56911-113-0(8))* Learning Resources, Inc.
Reading Rods Prefixes & Suffixes Activity Cards, Set 2. 2003. (J). pap. 19.95 *(978-1-56911-109-3(X))* Learning Resources, Inc.
Reading Rods Readers: Advanced Vowel Mastery Set. 2004. (J). per. 44.95 *(978-1-56911-532-9(X))* Learning Resources, Inc.
Reading Rods Readers: Advanced Vowel Mastery Set Classpack. 2004. (J). per. 249.95 *(978-1-56911-574-9(5))* Learning Resources, Inc.
Reading Rods Readers: Long Vowel Mastery Set Classpack. 2004. (J). per. 184.95 *(978-1-56911-549-7(4))* Learning Resources, Inc.
Reading Rods Readers: Phonics Foundation 1 Classpack. 2003. (J). per. 249.95 *(978-1-56911-575-6(3))* Learning Resources, Inc.
Reading Rods Readers: Phonics Foundation 2 Classpack. 2003. (J). per. 249.95 *(978-1-56911-576-3(1))* Learning Resources, Inc.
Reading Rods Readers: Phonics Foundation Set 1. 2003. (J). pap. 44.95 *(978-1-56911-121-5(9))* Learning Resources, Inc.
Reading Rods Readers: Phonics Foundation Set 2. 2003. (J). pap. 44.95 *(978-1-56911-122-2(7))* Learning Resources, Inc.
Reading Rods Readers: Short Vowel Mastery Set Classpack. 2004. (J). per. 184.95 *(978-1-56911-548-0(6))* Learning Resources, Inc.
Reading Rods Readers: Word Families Foundation Set. 2004. (J). per. 39.95 *(978-1-56911-533-6(8))* Learning Resources, Inc.
Reading Rods Readers: Word Families Foundation Set Classpack. 2004. (J). per. 249.95 *(978-1-56911-573-2(7))* Learning Resources, Inc.
Reading Rods Simple Sentences Activity Cards, Set 2. 2003. (J). pap. 19.95 *(978-1-56911-112-3(X))* Learning Resources, Inc.
Reading Rods Simple Sentences Instruction & Activity Book. 2003. (J). pap. 12.95 *(978-1-56911-110-9(3))* Learning Resources, Inc.
Reading Rods Word Building Activity Book. 2003. (J). pap. 4.95 *(978-1-56911-119-2(7))* Learning Resources, Inc.
Reading Rods Word Building Activity Cards, Set 2. 2003. (J). 19.95 *(978-1-56911-115-4(4))* Learning Resources, Inc.
Reading Rods Word Families Activity Book. 2003. (J). pap. 4.95 *(978-1-56911-118-5(9))* Learning Resources, Inc.
Reading Rods Word Families Activity Cards, Set 2. 2003. (J). 19.95 *(978-1-56911-114-7(6))* Learning Resources, Inc.
Red Fox Cub: Review of Consonants, Short Vowels, Word Families: Level A, 6 vols. (Wright Skills Ser.). 12p. (gr. k-3). 17.95 *(978-0-322-03126-5(5))* Wright Group/McGraw-Hill.
Reeder. Animals of the Arctic & Antarctic: Level O, 6 vols. (Take-Twostm Ser.). 32p. 38.95 *(978-0-322-04489-0(8))* Wright Group/McGraw-Hill.
Rice, Earle, Jr., ed. Great Military Leaders of the 20th Century, 6 vols. 2005. (Great Military Leaders of the 20th Century Ser.). (Illus.). 320p. (gr. 6-12). 120.00 *(978-0-7910-7401-5(3),* Facts On File) Infobase Holdings, Inc.
Rice, Dona Herweck. Like Them (Grade 1) 2018. (See Me Read! Everyday Words Ser.). (ENG., Illus.). 12p. (J). (gr. k-1). 6.99 *(978-1-4938-9859-6(0))* Teacher Created Materials, Inc.
Richardson, Ellis. Common Short Vowel Syllables Level 9: Brown Sequence. rev. ed. Date not set. (Linguistic Pattern Ser.). (Illus.). 64p. (YA). pap. *(978-1-56775-081-2(8))* I S M Teaching Systems, Inc.
—The Sound of Short A Level 4: Green Sequence. rev. ed. Date not set. (Linguistic Pattern Ser.). (Illus.). 64p. (YA). pap. *(978-1-56775-079-9(6))* I S M Teaching Systems, Inc.
—The Sound of Short U Level 8: Brown Sequence. rev. ed. Date not set. (Linguistic Pattern Ser.). (Illus.). 64p. (YA). pap. *(978-1-56775-080-5(X))* I S M Teaching Systems, Inc.
RIGBY. Reading Strategy Cards: Complete Set of 40 Cards (K-5) 2003. (Rigby on Our Way to English Ser.). (ENG.). (gr. 5-5). 83.15 *(978-0-7578-4543-7(6))* Rigby Education.
Rigby Education Staff. Where Do People Live? (Illus.). (J). suppl. ed. 20.00 *(978-0-7635-6445-2(1),* 764451C99) Rigby Education.
Rigg, Diana. Teach a Child to READ in... 3 Simple Steps. Walter, Deborah, illus. 2012. (J). (gr. -1-2). *(978-1-921560-88-0(6))* PLD Organisation Pty. Limited.
Right or Wrong? 6 Each of 1 Anthology, 6 vols. (Wildcats Ser.). 32p. (gr. 2-8). *(978-0-322-00598-3(1))* Wright Group/McGraw-Hill.
Ristuccia, Christine & Ristuccia, James. The Entire World of S & Z Instructional Workbook: A Comprehensive Approach to Remediate Frontal & Lateral Lisps. I.t. ed. 2003. (Illus.). 208p. (J). per. 34.99 *(978-0-9723457-4-3(4))* Say It Right.
Rose, Mary. Week-By-Week Homework for Building Reading Comprehension & Fluency. 2004. (Week-By-Week Homework for Building Reading Comprehension & Fluency Ser.). (ENG.). 96p. (gr. 2-3). pap. 16.99 *(978-0-439-51779-9(6),* Teaching Resources) Scholastic, Inc.
—Week-By-Week Homework for Building Reading Comprehension & Fluency: Grade 1. 2004. (Week-By-Week Homework for Building Reading Comprehension & Fluency Ser.). (ENG.). 96p. (gr. 1-1). pap. 16.99 *(978-0-439-61656-0(5),* Teaching Resources) Scholastic, Inc.
Rosemary, Wells. Listos para leer. 2004. (SPA., Illus.). 32p. (J). (gr. k-1). 14.99 *(978-84-241-8712-5(1))* Everest Editora ESP. Dist: Lectorum Pubns., Inc.
Ross, Val. You Can't Read This: Forbidden Books, Lost Writing, Mistranslations, & Codes. 2006. (Illus.). 152p. (J). (gr. 5-7). 19.95 *(978-0-88776-732-6(X),* Tundra Bks.) Tundra Bks. CAN. Dist: Penguin Random Hse. LLC.
A Royal Deal: Diphthongs oi, oy: Level B, 6 vols. (Wright Skills Ser.). 16p. (gr. k-3). 26.50 *(978-0-322-01485-5(9))* Wright Group/McGraw-Hill.
Rude Luke: Long Vowel u, CVCe Pattern: Level B, 6 vols. (Wright Skills Ser.). 16p. (gr. k-3). 17.95 *(978-0-322-03103-6(6))* Wright Group/McGraw-Hill.
Ruffenach, Jessie E., et al. Learn along with Ashkii: First Grade Level 2. Whitethorne, Bahe, Jr., illus. 2003. (NAV & ENG.). 16p. (J). (gr. -1-3). pap. 7.95 *(978-1-893354-42-5(3))* Salina Bookshelf Inc.
—Learn along with Ashkii: Second Grade Level 1. Whitethorne, Bahe, Jr., illus. 2003. (ENG & NAV.). 16p. (J). (gr. -1-3). pap. 7.95 *(978-1-893354-43-2(1))* Salina Bookshelf Inc.
—Learn along with Ashkii: Second Grade Level 2. Whitethorne, Bahe, Jr., illus. 2003. (NAV & ENG.). 16p. (J). (gr. -1-3). pap. 7.95 *(978-1-893354-44-9(X))* Salina Bookshelf Inc.

—Learn along with Ashkii: Third Grade Level 1. Whitethorne, Bahe, Jr., illus. 2003. (NAV & ENG.). 16p. (J). (gr. 4-7). pap. 7.95 *(978-1-893354-45-6(8))* Salina Bookshelf Inc.
Rumblefish: Response Journal. 2003. 32p. (J). (gr. 7-12). *(978-1-58049-980-4(5)*, RJ80) Prestwick Hse., Inc.
Runaway Hank: Final Blends -ft, -lt: Level C, 6 vols. (Wright Skills Ser.). 16p. (gr. k-3). 26.50 *(978-0-322-01495-4(6))* Wright Group/McGraw-Hill.
Running, 6 vols. (Multicultural Programs Ser.). 16p. (gr. 1-3). 24.95 *(978-0-7802-9215-4(4))* Wright Group/McGraw-Hill.
Sally & the Elephant: Level B, 6 vols. (Wonder Worldtm Ser.). 16p. 24.95 *(978-0-7802-1047-9(6))* Wright Group/McGraw-Hill.
Salzmann, Mary Elizabeth. Come Home with Me! 2004. (Sight Words Ser.). (ENG., Illus.). 24p. (J). (gr. k-3). lib. bdg. 24.21 *(978-1-59197-465-9(8))* ABDO Publishing Co.
—It's Not Good, It's Great! 2003. (Sight Words Ser.). (ENG., Illus.). 24p. (J). (gr. k-3). lib. bdg. 24.21 *(978-1-59197-479-6(8)*, SandCastle) ABDO Publishing Co.
—Out for the Summer! 2004. (Sight Words Ser.). (ENG., Illus.). 24p. (J). (gr. k-3). lib. bdg. 24.21 *(978-1-59197-472-7(0)*, SandCastle) ABDO Publishing Co.
—Snow & More Snow! 2004. (Sight Words Ser.). (ENG., Illus.). 24p. (J). (gr. k-3). lib. bdg. 24.21 *(978-1-59197-470-3(4)*, SandCastle) ABDO Publishing Co.
—They Are the Best! 2004. (Sight Words Ser.). (ENG., Illus.). 24p. (J). (gr. k-3). lib. bdg. 24.21 *(978-1-59197-474-1(7)*, SandCastle) ABDO Publishing Co.
—Who Is This at the Beach? 2004. (Sight Words Ser.). (ENG., Illus.). 24p. (J). (gr. k-3). lib. bdg. 24.21 *(978-1-59197-480-2(1)*, SandCastle) ABDO Publishing Co.
Sam & Nan: Consonants d, f, n, p; Short Vowel a word families: Level A, 6 vols. (Wright Skills Ser.). 12p. (gr. k-3). 17.95 *(978-0-322-01447-3(6))* Wright Group/McGraw-Hill.
Sam & Tat: Consonants m, s, t; Short Vowel a; -am, -at word families: Level A, 6 vols. (Wright Skills Ser.). 12p. (gr. k-3). 17.95 *(978-0-322-01444-2(1))* Wright Group/McGraw-Hill.
Sam Sat: Consonants m, s, t; Short Vowel a: Level A, 6 vols. (Wright Skills Ser.). 12p. (gr. k-3). 17.95 *(978-0-322-03104-3(4))* Wright Group/McGraw-Hill.
Samson, Tess. Going up & Down. 2010. (Sight Word Readers Ser.). (J). 3.49 *(978-1-60719-613-6(1))* Newmark Learning LLC.
Sanseri, Wanda. Play by the Sea. 2003. (J). 5.00 *(978-1-880045-26-8(5))* Back Home Industries.
—SWR Chart Pack. 2003. (J). pap. 9.95 *(978-1-880045-30-5(3))* Back Home Industries.
Sanvageau, Juan. Stories, Fables & Poems for You, Vol. 2.Tr. of Cuentos, Fabulas y Poemas Para Ti. (ENG & SPA., Illus.). 89p. (J). (gr. 3-5). pap. 9.95 *(978-1-893493-01-8(6))* National Educational Systems, Inc.
Saving the Florida Panther, 6 vols., Vol. 4. 2005. (Book Treks Ser.). (Illus.). (J). (gr. 4-8). stu. ed. 35.95 *(978-0-673-61777-4(7))* Celebration Pr.
Scat! Said the Cat: Big Book: Level D. Group 1. (Sunshine Ser.). 8p. 20.95 *(978-0-7802-5734-4(0))* Wright Group/McGraw-Hill.
Scheunemann, Pam. Ape Cape, 1 vol. 2004. (Rhyming Riddles Ser.). (Illus.). 24p. (J). (gr. k-3). lib. bdg. 24.21 *(978-1-59197-457-4(7)*, SandCastle) ABDO Publishing Co.
—Chipper Flipper, 1 vol. 2004. (Rhyming Riddles Ser.). (ENG., Illus.). 24p. (J). (gr. k-3). lib. bdg. 24.21 *(978-1-59197-458-1(5)*, SandCastle) ABDO Publishing Co.
—Cooler Ruler, 1 vol. 2004. (Rhyming Riddles Ser.). (Illus.). 24p. (J). (gr. k-3). lib. bdg. 24.21 *(978-1-59197-459-8(3)*, SandCastle) ABDO Publishing Co.
—Dill Spill, 1 vol. 2004. (Rhyming Riddles Ser.). (Illus.). 24p. (J). (gr. k-3). lib. bdg. 24.21 *(978-1-59197-460-4(7)*, SandCastle) ABDO Publishing Co.
—Loud Crowd, 1 vol. 2004. (Rhyming Riddles Ser.). (Illus.). 24p. (J). (gr. k-3). lib. bdg. 24.21 *(978-1-59197-461-1(5)*, SandCastle) ABDO Publishing Co.
—Overdue Kangaroo, 1 vol. 2004. (Rhyming Riddles Ser.). (ENG., Illus.). 24p. (J). (gr. k-3). lib. bdg. 24.21 *(978-1-59197-462-8(3)*, SandCastle) ABDO Publishing Co.
Scholastic Clubs US Start Readers Non-Fiction (2 Set) Start Reading. 2006. (J). 27.89 *(978-1-59566-326-9(6))* QEB Publishing Inc.
Scholastic, Inc. Staff. Brain Play 1st-3rd. 2008. (J). 29.99 *(978-0-545-05207-8(6))* Scholastic, Inc.
—Brain Play Preschool-1st. 2008. (J). 29.99 *(978-0-439-81350-1(6))* Scholastic, Inc.
Scholastic, Inc. Staff, contrib. by. Entering Pre-K. 2004. (Jumpstart Ser.). (ENG., Illus.). 96p. (J). (gr. -1-k). pap. 6.99 *(978-0-439-38232-8(7))* Scholastic, Inc.
School Zone Publishing. Reading Readiness. 2003. (ENG.). (J). cd-rom 19.99 *(978-1-58947-916-6(5))* School Zone Publishing Co.
School Zone Publishing Company Staff. Reading Comprehension 1. (Illus.). (J). 19.99 incl. audio compact disk *(978-0-88743-942-1(X))* School Zone Publishing Co.
—Reading Skills-1: And Language Activities. (Illus.). (J). 19.99 incl. audio compact disk *(978-0-88743-941-4(1))* School Zone Publishing Co.
Schulz, Charles. Where Did Woodstock Go? Date not set. (ENG.). 100p. (J). 5.95 *(978-0-694-00959-6(8))* HarperCollins Pubs.
Schwartz, Sara Jo & Irvin, Barbara Bando. Second Grade Scholar: Grade 2. Speir, Nancy, illus. rev. ed. 2010. (ENG.). 128p. (J). (gr. k-2). pap. 8.49 *(978-1-58947-012-5(5)*, fe71fca3-49a7-4f76-bc3d-d50da87ea5cc) School Zone Publishing Co.
Scott, Foresman and Company Staff. Fun with Dick & Jane. 2004. (Read with Dick & Jane Ser.). 32p. (J). (gr. -1-2). 21.35 *(978-1-59197-630-1(8))* Spotlight.
Scott, James. The Indian in the Cupboard: Response Journal. 2003. 36p. (YA). *(978-1-58049-976-7(7)*, RJ76) Prestwick Hse., Inc.
—Jane Eyre: A Student Response Journal. 2003. 48p. (YA). *(978-1-58049-984-2(8)*, RJ84) Prestwick Hse., Inc.
Set 3, 4 bks. Incl. Fishing. Yukish, Joseph. Palmer, Kate S., illus. 16p. 2001. pap. 7.95 *(978-1-879835-16-0(9))*; Guess What Kind of Ball. Urmston, Kathleen & Evans, Karen. Kaeden Corp. Staff, ed. Gedeon, Gloria, illus. 16p. 1992. pap. 7.95 *(978-1-879835-15-3(0))*; Lunch. Urmston, Kathleen & Evans, Karen. Kaeden Corp. Staff, ed. Gedeon, Gloria, illus. 12p. 2002. pap. 7.95 *(978-1-879835-14-6(2))*; Our Garage. Urmston, Kathleen. Evans, Karen & Kaeden Corp. Staff, eds. Dragony, Barbara, illus. 12p. 2001. pap. 7.95 *(978-1-879835-17-7(7))*; (gr. k-2)., Kaeden Bks. Set pap. 17.50 o.p. *(978-1-879835-18-4(5))* Kaeden Corp.
Shadows, 6 vols. (Multicultural Programs Ser.). 16p. (gr. 1-3). 24.95 *(978-0-7802-9214-7(6))* Wright Group/McGraw-Hill.
Shake, Rattle, & Roll: Magazine Anthology: Level 4, 6 vols. (Comprehension Strand Ser.). (gr. 4-8). 54.00 *(978-0-322-06034-0(6))* Wright Group/McGraw-Hill.
Shannon, Rosemarie, et al, adapted by. Alphabet Mazes. 2003. (Kids Can Learn with Franklin Ser.). (ENG., Illus.). 32p. (J). (gr. -1-1). pap. 3.95 *(978-1-55337-592-0(0))* Kids Can Pr., Ltd. CAN. Dist: Hachette Bk. Group.
—Measurement. 2003. (Kids Can Learn with Franklin Ser.). (ENG., Illus.). 32p. (J). (gr. k-1). 3.95 *(978-1-55337-595-1(5))* Kids Can Pr., Ltd. CAN. Dist: Hachette Bk. Group.
Shelly's Shell: Digraph sh: Level B, 6 vols. (Wright Skills Ser.). 16p. (gr. k-3). 17.95 *(978-0-322-01471-8(9))* Wright Group/McGraw-Hill.
Shoo! Level C. Group 1. (Sunshine Ser.). 8p. 20.95 *(978-0-7802-5725-2(1))* Wright Group/McGraw-Hill.
Shopping: Big Book: Level A. (Sunshine Ser.). 8p. 20.95 *(978-0-7802-5710-8(3))* Wright Group/McGraw-Hill.
Shortland. Busy Bees. (Song Box Ser.). (gr. 1-2). pap. 31.50 *(978-0-7802-2268-7(7))* Wright Group/McGraw-Hill.
Show And Tell. 2003. (J). per. *(978-1-57657-813-1(5))* Paradise Pr., Inc.
Show And Tell, 6 vols. 8p. (gr. k-1). 21.50 *(978-0-322-02075-7(1))* Wright Group/McGraw-Hill.
Show & Tell: Take-Home Book. 2005. (Emergent Library: Vol. 2). (YA). (gr. -1-1). 12.60 *(978-0-8215-7253-5(9))* Sadlier, William H. Inc.
Sigmond Slitherforth: Level R, 6 vols. (Wonder Worldtm Ser.). 48p. 44.95 *(978-0-7802-7073-2(8))* Wright Group/McGraw-Hill.
The Silly Supper: Medial Consonants: Level C, 6 vols. (Wright Skills Ser.). 16p. (gr. k-3). 26.50 *(978-0-322-01491-6(3))* Wright Group/McGraw-Hill.
Skin, Skin: Level E, 6 vols. (Wonder Worldtm Ser.). 16p. 29.95 *(978-0-7802-1235-0(5))* Wright Group/McGraw-Hill.
Skunk in the Trunk, 6 vols. 8p. (gr. k-1). 21.50 *(978-0-322-02080-1(8))* Wright Group/McGraw-Hill.
The Sky's the Limit, 6 vols. (Wildcats Ser.). 32p. (gr. 2-8). *(978-0-322-00603-4(1))* Wright Group/McGraw-Hill.
Slater, Jean M. Mixed up Morning. Slater, Jean M., illus. 2003. (Illus.). 13p. (J). bds. 16.00 *(978-0-9743149-2-1(7))* Slater Software, Inc.
Sleeping,Dreaming: Level Q, 6 vols. (Wonder Worldtm Ser.). 48p. 39.95 *(978-0-7802-2951-8(7))* Wright Group/McGraw-Hill.
Sloppy Tiger Bedtime: Big Book: Level M. Group 1. (Sunshine Ser.). 24p. 36.50 *(978-0-7802-5791-7(X))* Wright Group/McGraw-Hill.
Slowpoke, 6 vols. 8p. (gr. k-1). 21.50 *(978-0-322-02070-2(0))* Wright Group/McGraw-Hill.
Slug Makes a House Little Book: Early Reading Fluency, Level A. 2004. pap. 6.00 *(978-0-7398-8160-6(4))* Steck-Vaughn.
The Slumber Party Organizer: Level T. Group 1, 6 vols. (Sunshine Ser.). 48p. 44.95 *(978-0-7802-6097-9(X))* Wright Group/McGraw-Hill.
Smelly Armor: Big Book: Level J. Group 2. (Story Box Ser.). 16p. 31.50 *(978-0-322-02470-0(6))* Wright Group/McGraw-Hill.
Smiles, 6 vols. (Multicultural Programs Ser.). 16p. (gr. 1-3). 24.95 *(978-0-7802-9204-8(9))* Wright Group/McGraw-Hill.
Smith, Molly. Be Honest, Jess. Monés, Marc, illus. 2023. (ENG.). 16p. (J). (gr. -1-1). pap. 33.00 *(978-1-4788-0508-3(0)*, 89fff792-b813-49f3-860e-7cd7e2d4f76c) Newmark Learning LLC.
—Be Patient, Maddie. Patton, Julia, illus. 2023. (ENG.). 16p. (J). (gr. -1-1). pap. 33.00 *(978-1-4788-0512-0(9)*, b94fcfea-b53a-4e38-a762-d5938b54893b) Newmark Learning LLC.
—Don't Worry, Mason. Poole, Helen, illus. 2023. (ENG.). 16p. (J). (gr. -1-1). pap. 5.25 *(978-1-4788-0463-5(7)*, a1b758fe-fbb7-4948-a5c7-2424f50879f4); pap. 33.00 *(978-1-4788-0500-7(5)*, 41238337-94ae-4005-961d-bf5c9ec035be) Newmark Learning LLC.
—I Can Follow the Rules. Patton, Julia, illus. 2023. (ENG.). 16p. (J). (gr. -1-1). pap. 5.25 *(978-1-4788-0473-4(4)*, 57267597-e058-4bcb-878c-e9263e0eb302); pap. 33.00 *(978-1-4788-0510-6(2)*, 398378bb-6247-4ac5-a915-1517167e220b) Newmark Learning LLC.
Snake at the Lake: Long Vowel Review: Level C, 6 vols. (Wright Skills Ser.). 16p. (gr. k-3). 26.50 *(978-0-322-01496-1(4))* Wright Group/McGraw-Hill.
Snap Happy Little Book: Early Reading Fluency, Level A, Bk. 1. 2004. pap. 6.00 *(978-0-7398-8157-6(4))* Steck-Vaughn.
Snowball Fight: Level B, 6 vols. (Wonder Worldtm Ser.). 16p. 24.95 *(978-0-7802-1051-6(4))* Wright Group/McGraw-Hill.
Snowman: Level A. Group 2. (Story Box Ser.). 8p. 20.95 *(978-0-322-00320-0(2))* Wright Group/McGraw-Hill.
So, Patty. So Simple at-Home A Month of Ideas: 31 Fun & Simple Activities to Reinforce Your Child's Reading Success! 2007. 36p. (J). spiral bd. *(978-0-9772158-5-0(7))* So Simple Learning.
Sometimes: Level A, 6 vols. (Wonder Worldtm Ser.). 16p. 24.95 *(978-0-7802-2907-5(X))* Wright Group/McGraw-Hill.
Sommer, Carl. Noise! Noise! Noise! Read-along 2003. (Another Sommer-Time Story Ser.). (Illus.). 48p. (J). lib. bdg. 23.95 incl. audio *(978-1-57537-769-8(1))* Advance Publishing, Inc.
Soper, Sandra. Reading & Writing, Bk. 3. rev. ed. (ENG., Illus.). 32p. (J). pap. 5.99 *(978-0-330-32075-7(0)*, Pan) Pan Macmillan GBR. Dist: Trafalgar Square Publishing.
Soup can Telephone: Level K, 6 vols. (Wonder Worldtm Ser.). 16p. 34.95 *(978-0-7802-2912-9(6))* Wright Group/McGraw-Hill.
Spanish Little Book, 6 vols., Pack. 2005. (Libros en Espanol Para Ninos Ser.). (SPA.). (YA). (gr. -1-1). 71.82 *(978-0-8215-0990-6(X))* Sadlier, William H. Inc.
Sparks, Stacey. Clean up, Everybody. Patton, Julia, illus. 2023. (ENG.). 16p. (J). (gr. -1-1). pap. 33.00 *(978-1-4788-0514-4(5)*, fa7e6329-84ab-48b9-994d-11613d7564fb) Newmark Learning LLC.
—Let's Get It Started. Juan, Juan Bautista, illus. 2023. (ENG.). 16p. (J). (gr. -1-1). pap. 33.00 *(978-1-4788-0518-2(8)*, 9c4a1205-983a-45b9-96e0-fa812c0c0f08); pap. 5.25 *(978-1-4788-0481-9(5)*, b728a8bf-acd3-435c-a64e-f3fe0b30f1ed) Newmark Learning LLC.
A Spider Web: Level M, 6 vols. (Wonder Worldtm Ser.). 16p. 34.95 *(978-0-7802-4603-4(9))* Wright Group/McGraw-Hill.
The Sport of Reading: Read Fast, Read Smart, Boost Your Grades. (Illus.). 24p. (J). (gr. 4-18). *(978-0-930251-01-7(6))* BlueChip Pubs.
Spot that Cat! Big Book: Level I. Group 2. (Story Box Ser.). 16p. 31.50 *(978-0-322-02460-1(9))* Wright Group/McGraw-Hill.
Spreading the Word, 6 vols. (Wildcats Ser.). 32p. (gr. 2-8). *(978-0-322-00604-1(X))* Wright Group/McGraw-Hill.
Sprick, Marilyn & Sprick, Jessica. Hey Diddle Diddle: Read Well Level K Unit 16 Storybook. Clark, Steve, illus. 2003. (Read Well Level K Ser.). 20p. (J). *(978-1-57035-687-2(4)*, 55562) Cambium Education, Inc.
Spring to Success on the PSSA Grade 3: Test Prep & Skills Practice READING. 2005. (Illus.). 80p. (J). per. 8.00 *(978-0-9722452-4-1(3))* New Leaf Educ., Inc.
Stamps: Level H, 6 vols. (Wonder Worldtm Ser.). 16p. 29.95 *(978-0-7802-2032-4(3))* Wright Group/McGraw-Hill.
Standish, Russell R. & Standish, Ella. Gwanpa & Nanny's Home. 2003. (Illus.). 128p. (J). pap. 14.95 *(978-0-923309-89-3(6))* Hartland Pubns.
Stanley Stooks: Super Stuntman: Level 7, 6 vols. (Fluency Strand Ser.). (gr. 4-8). 45.00 *(978-1-4045-1245-0(4))* Wright Group/McGraw-Hill.
Starting Off: American Readers. (J). *(978-0-669-04930-5(1))* Houghton Mifflin Harcourt School Pubs.
Steck-Vaughn Staff. Access Reading. 2004. (Steck-Vaughn Access Ser.). (ENG.). 32p. (gr. 9-12). pap., tchr. ed. 8.70 *(978-0-7398-8934-3(6))* Houghton Mifflin Harcourt Publishing Co.
—At-Home Workbooks: Reading. 2004. (Illus.). (gr. 1). pap., wbk. ed. *(978-0-7398-8524-6(3))*; (gr. 2). pap., wbk. ed. *(978-0-7398-8525-3(1))*; (gr. 4). pap., wbk. ed. 5.99 *(978-0-7398-8527-7(8))* Steck-Vaughn.
—Shutterbug: Add to Package. 2004. Level A-I. pap. 141.11 *(978-0-7398-9431-6(5))*Level E-I. pap. 191.90 *(978-0-7398-9432-3(3))*Level H-M. pap. 141.11 *(978-0-7398-9433-0(1))*Level J-M. pap. 191.90 *(978-0-7398-9434-7(X))* Steck-Vaughn.
Steel, Abigail. Comprehension Skills Pupil Book 5. 2017. (ENG.). 64p. (J). pap. 14.99 *(978-0-00-823638-0(0))* HarperCollins Pubs. Ltd. GBR. Dist: Independent Pubs. Group.
Stingrays: Level L, 6 vols. (Wonder Worldtm Ser.). 16p. 34.95 *(978-0-7802-4605-8(5))* Wright Group/McGraw-Hill.
Stone Works: Level M, 6 vols. (Wonder Worldtm Ser.). 16p. 34.95 *(978-0-7802-2909-9(6))* Wright Group/McGraw-Hill.
Stoneman, Sonya. First Aid in Reading. (Illus.). 68p. (J). pap., act. bk. ed. *(978-1-876367-37-4(7))* Wizard Bks.
—First Aid in Reading: Program Book. (Illus.). 180p. (J). pap. *(978-1-876367-24-4(5))* Wizard Bks.
Stop! Big Book: Level E. Group 1. (Story Box Ser.). 16p. 31.50 *(978-0-7802-7638-3(8))* Wright Group/McGraw-Hill.
Stop: Level C. (Wonder Worldtm Ser.). 16p. 24.95 *(978-0-7802-2910-5(X))* Wright Group/McGraw-Hill.
The Story Box: Early Emergent - Group 1:1 Each of 8 Student Books: Level A. 33.50 *(978-1-55911-125-6(9))* Wright Group/McGraw-Hill.
The Story Box: Early Emergent - Group 1:1 Each of 8 Student Books: Level B. 33.50 *(978-1-55911-134-8(8))* Wright Group/McGraw-Hill.
The Story Box: Early Emergent - Group 1:1 Each of 8 Student Books: Level C. 33.50 *(978-1-55911-143-0(7))* Wright Group/McGraw-Hill.
The Story Box: Early Emergent - Group 2:1 Each of 8 Student Books: Level A. 33.50 *(978-0-7802-9927-6(2))* Wright Group/McGraw-Hill.
The Story Box: Early Emergent - Group 2:1 Each of 8 Student Books: Level B. 33.50 *(978-0-7802-9928-3(0))* Wright Group/McGraw-Hill.
The Story Box: Early Emergent - Student Book Set - 1 Each of 16 Titles. (gr. k-18). 66.95 *(978-0-322-03142-5(7))*; Vol. 2. 66.95 *(978-0-7802-9530-8(7))*; Vol. 3. 66.95 *(978-0-7802-9531-5(5))* Wright Group/McGraw-Hill.
The Story Box: Early Emergent-Upper Emergent - Group 1: 1 Each of 8 Student Books: Level D. 33.50 *(978-1-55911-152-2(6))* Wright Group/McGraw-Hill.
The Story Box: Early Emergent-Upper Emergent - Group 1: 1 Each of 8 Student Books: Level E. 39.95 *(978-1-55911-161-4(5))* Wright Group/McGraw-Hill.
The Story Box: Early Emergent-Upper Emergent - Group 2: 1 Each of 8 Student Books: Level C. 33.50 *(978-0-7802-9931-3(0))* Wright Group/McGraw-Hill.
The Story Box: Early Emergent-Upper Emergent - Group 2: 1 Each of 8 Student Books: Level D. 33.50 *(978-0-7802-9932-0(9))* Wright Group/McGraw-Hill.
The Story Box: Early Emergent-Upper Emergent - Group 2: 1 Each of 8 Student Books: Level E. 39.95 *(978-0-7802-9929-0(9))* Wright Group/McGraw-Hill.
The Story Box: Early Fluency - Complete Kit. (gr. 2-18). 537.95 *(978-0-7802-2772-9(7))* Wright Group/McGraw-Hill.
The Story Box: Upper Emergent - Complete Kit. (gr. 1-18). 435.50 *(978-0-7802-2771-2(9))*; Vol. 2. 435.50 *(978-0-7802-9341-0(X))*; Vol. 4. 435.50 *(978-0-322-02574-5(5))*; Vol. 5. 435.50 *(978-0-322-02575-2(3))* Wright Group/McGraw-Hill.
The Story Box: Upper Emergent - Group 1: 1 Each of 8 Student Books: Level I. (Story Box Ser.). 39.95 *(978-0-322-02566-0(4))* Wright Group/McGraw-Hill.
The Story Box: Upper Emergent - Group 1: 1 Each of 8 Student Books: Level J. (Story Box Ser.). 39.95 *(978-0-322-02569-1(9))* Wright Group/McGraw-Hill.
The Story Box: Upper Emergent - Group 1-2: 1 Each of 16 Student Books: Level J. (Story Box Ser.). 79.95 *(978-0-322-02568-4(0))* Wright Group/McGraw-Hill.
The Story Box: Upper Emergent - Group 2: 1 Each of 8 Student Books: Level H. (Story Box Ser.). 39.95 *(978-0-322-02564-6(8))* Wright Group/McGraw-Hill.
The Story Box: Upper Emergent - Group 2: 1 Each of 8 Student Books: Level I. (Story Box Ser.). 39.95 *(978-0-322-02567-7(2))* Wright Group/McGraw-Hill.
The Story Box: Upper Emergent - Group 2: 1 Each of 8 Student Books: Level J. 39.95 *(978-0-322-02571-4(0))* Wright Group/McGraw-Hill.
The Story Box: Upper Emergent - Groups 1: 1 Each of 8 Student Books: Level F. 39.95 *(978-1-55911-170-6(4))* Wright Group/McGraw-Hill.
The Story Box: Upper Emergent - Groups 1: 1 Each of 8 Student Books: Level G. 39.95 *(978-1-55911-179-9(8))* Wright Group/McGraw-Hill.
The Story Box: Upper Emergent - Groups 2: 1 Each of 8 Student Books: Level F. 39.95 *(978-0-7802-9930-6(2))* Wright Group/McGraw-Hill.
The Story Box: Upper Emergent - Groups 2: 1 Each of 8 Student Books: Level G. 39.95 *(978-0-7802-9933-7(7))* Wright Group/McGraw-Hill.
The Story Box: Upper Emergent - Student Book Set - 1 Each of 16 Titles. (gr. 1-18). 79.95 *(978-0-322-03141-8(9))*; Vol. 2. 79.95 *(978-0-7802-9532-2(3))*; Vol. 3. 79.95 *(978-0-7802-9533-9(1))*; Vol. 4. 79.95 *(978-0-322-03139-5(7))*; Vol. 5. 79.95 *(978-0-322-03140-1(0))* Wright Group/McGraw-Hill.
The Story Box Vol. 2: Early Emergent - Early Emergent - Complete Kit. (gr. k-18). 372.95 *(978-0-7802-9339-7(8))* Wright Group/McGraw-Hill.
The Story of My Life: Response Journal. 2003. 40p. (YA). *(978-1-58049-990-3(2)*, RJ90) Prestwick Hse., Inc.
Story Vine: 1 Each of 12 Student Books. (Story Vinestm Ser.). (gr. 3-6). 88.95 *(978-0-7802-9413-4(0))* Wright Group/McGraw-Hill.
Story Vine: 6 Each of 12 Student Books. (Story Vinestm Ser.). (gr. 3-6). 434.50 *(978-0-7802-9414-1(9))* Wright Group/McGraw-Hill.
Stott, Jon C. Gerald Mcdermott & YOU, 1 vol. 2004. (ENG., Illus.). 128p. pap. 40.00 *(978-1-59158-175-8(3)*, 900322223, Libraries Unlimited) ABC-CLIO, LLC.
Stradling, Jan. Lights On: Level K, 6 vols., Vol. 2. (First Explorers Ser.). 24p. (gr. 1-2). 34.95 *(978-0-7699-1461-9(6))* Shortland Pubns. (U. S. A.) Inc.
—Look Up: Level I, 6 vols. (First Explorers Ser.). 24p. (gr. 1-2). 29.95 *(978-0-7699-1447-3(0))* Shortland Pubns. (U. S. A.) Inc.
Strange Days: Level 7, 6 vols. (Fluency Strand Ser.). (gr. 4-8). 45.00 *(978-1-4045-1241-2(1))* Wright Group/McGraw-Hill.
The Stranger from the Sea: Level T. Group 1, 6 vols. (Sunshine Ser.). 48p. 44.95 *(978-0-7802-5601-9(8))* Wright Group/McGraw-Hill.
Strauss, Elizabeth. Beginning Reading 1-2. 2008. (ENG.). 32p. (J). pap. 2.99 *(978-0-88743-756-4(7))* School Zone Publishing Co.
Street Action: 6 Each of 1 Anthology, 6 vols. (Wildcats Ser.). 32p. (gr. 2-8). *(978-0-322-00577-8(9))* Wright Group/McGraw-Hill.
The Strength of Georgia Mills: Level 2, 6 vols. (Fluency Strand Ser.). (gr. 4-8). 45.00 *(978-1-4045-1215-3(2))* Wright Group/McGraw-Hill.
The Summer Mermaid: R-Controlled e, i, u: Level B, 6 vols. (Wright Skills Ser.). 16p. (gr. k-3). 26.50 *(978-0-322-01488-6(3))* Wright Group/McGraw-Hill.
Summer Trips, 6 vols. (Multicultural Programs Ser.). 16p. (gr. 1-3). 24.95 *(978-0-7802-9219-2(7))* Wright Group/McGraw-Hill.
Sunshine: Early Emergent - 1 Each of 32 Big Books: Level A-D. (Sunshine Ser.). 628.50 *(978-0-7802-6775-6(3))* Wright Group/McGraw-Hill.
Sunshine: Early Emergent - 1 Each of 4 Big Books: Level A-D. (Sunshine Ser.). 82.95 *(978-0-7802-6772-5(9))* Wright Group/McGraw-Hill.
Sunshine: Early Emergent - Group 1: 1 Each of 8 Student Books: Level A. (Sunshine Ser.). 33.50 *(978-0-7802-7118-0(1))* Wright Group/McGraw-Hill.
Sunshine: Early Emergent - Group 1: 1 Each of 8 Student Books: Level D. (Sunshine Ser.). 33.50 *(978-0-7802-7124-1(6))* Wright Group/McGraw-Hill.
Sunshine: Early Emergent - Group 1:1 Each of 8 Student Books: Level C. (Sunshine Ser.). 33.50 *(978-0-7802-7122-7(X))* Wright Group/McGraw-Hill.
Sunshine: Early Emergent - Group 2: 1 Each of 8 Student Books: Level A. (Sunshine Ser.). 33.50 *(978-0-7802-7119-7(X))* Wright Group/McGraw-Hill.
Sunshine: Early Emergent - Group 2:1 Each of 8 Student Books: Level B. (Sunshine Ser.). 33.50 *(978-0-7802-7121-0(1))* Wright Group/McGraw-Hill.
Sunshine: Early Emergent - Group 2:1 Each of 8 Student Books: Level C. (Sunshine Ser.). 33.50 *(978-0-7802-7123-4(8))* Wright Group/McGraw-Hill.
Sunshine: Early Emergent - Nonfiction: 1: 1 Each of 4 Student Books: Level A. (Sunshine Ser.). 16.95 *(978-0-7802-3763-6(3))* Wright Group/McGraw-Hill.
Sunshine: Early Emergent - Nonfiction: 1 Each of 4 Student Books: Level C. (Sunshine Ser.). 16.95 *(978-0-7802-3781-0(1))* Wright Group/McGraw-Hill.
Sunshine: Early Emergent - Nonfiction:1 Each of 4 Student Books: Level A. 16.95 *(978-0-7802-3772-8(2))* Wright Group/McGraw-Hill.
Sunshine: Early Emergent - Student Book Set - 1 Each of 16 Titles, Vol. 3. (Wright Group Literacy Ser.). (gr. k-18). 66.95 *(978-0-322-02487-8(0))* Wright Group/McGraw-Hill.
Sunshine: Early Emergent: 1 Each of 8 Student Books: Level B. (Sunshine Ser.). 24.95 *(978-0-7802-7120-3(3))* Wright Group/McGraw-Hill.
Sunshine: Early Emergent-Upper Emergent - 1 Each of 60 Big Books: Level A-J,A-D. (Sunshine Ser.). 1345.50 *(978-0-7802-6779-4(6))* Wright Group/McGraw-Hill.
Sunshine: Early Emergent-Upper Emergent - Group 1: 1 Each of 8 Student Books: Level E. (Sunshine Ser.). 39.95 *(978-0-7802-7126-5(2))* Wright Group/McGraw-Hill.
Sunshine: Early Emergent-Upper Emergent - Nonfiction: 1 Each of 4 Student Books: Level D. (Sunshine Ser.). 16.95 *(978-0-7802-3790-2(0))* Wright Group/McGraw-Hill.
Sunshine: Early Emergent-Upper Emergent - Nonfiction: 1 Each of 4 Student Books: Level E. (Sunshine Ser.). 19.95 *(978-0-7802-6791-6(5))* Wright Group/McGraw-Hill.

Sunshine: Early Fluency - Chapter books, Group 2: 1 each of 2 titles: Level K. 11.95 (978-0-7802-6852-4(0)) Wright Group/McGraw-Hill.
Sunshine: Early Fluency - Chapter books, Group 2: 1 each of 2 titles: Level L. 11.95 (978-0-7802-6853-1(9)) Wright Group/McGraw-Hill.
Sunshine: Early Fluency - Chapter Books, Group 2; 1 each of 2 titles: Level M. 11.95 (978-0-7802-6854-8(7)) Wright Group/McGraw-Hill.
Sunshine: Early Fluency - Fact & Fantasy, Group 1; 1 each of 8 titles: Level L. 46.95 (978-0-7802-8354-1(6)) Wright Group/McGraw-Hill.
Sunshine: Early Fluency - Fact & Fantasy, Group 2; 1 each of 2 titles: Level L. 11.95 (978-0-7802-7876-9(3)) Wright Group/McGraw-Hill.
Sunshine: Early Fluency - Fact & Fantasy, Groups 1-2; 1 each of 10 titles: Level L. 58.50 (978-0-7802-6849-4(0)) Wright Group/McGraw-Hill.
Sunshine: Early Fluency - Group 2: 1 each of 6 titles: Level K. (Sunshine Ser.). 34.95 (978-0-7802-7138-8(6)) Wright Group/McGraw-Hill.
Sunshine: Early Fluency - Group 2; 1 each of 6 titles: Level M. 34.95 (978-0-7802-7140-1(8)) Wright Group/McGraw-Hill.
Sunshine: Early Fluency - Nonfiction, Group 1: 1 each of 8 titles: Level K. 46.95 (978-0-7802-8353-4(8)) Wright Group/McGraw-Hill.
Sunshine: Early Fluency - Nonfiction, Group 2: 1 each of 2 titles: Level K. (Sunshine Ser.). 11.95 (978-0-7802-7875-2(5)) Wright Group/McGraw-Hill.
Sunshine: Early Fluency - Nonfiction, Groups 1-2: 1 each of 10 titles: Level K. 58.50 (978-0-7802-6848-7(2)) Wright Group/McGraw-Hill.
Sunshine: Early Fluency - Student Book Set - 1 Each of 16 Titles. (Wright Group Literacy Ser.). (gr. 2-18). Vol. 2. 93.50 (978-0-322-02491-5(9)) Vol. 3. 93.50 (978-0-322-02492-2(7)) Vol. 4. 93.50 (978-0-322-02493-9(5)) Wright Group/McGraw-Hill.
Sunshine: Early Fluency Fiction. 32p. (gr. 1-5). 46.95 (978-0-7802-6856-2(3)) Wright Group/McGraw-Hill.
Sunshine: Early Fluency-Nonfiction, Group 1; 1 each of 8 titles: Level M. 46.95 (978-0-7802-8355-8(4)) Wright Group/McGraw-Hill.
Sunshine: Early Fluency-Nonfiction, Group 2; 1 each of 2 titles: Level M. 11.95 (978-0-7802-7877-6(1)) Wright Group/McGraw-Hill.
Sunshine: Early Fluency-Nonfiction, Groups 1-2; 1 each of 10 titles: Level M. 58.50 (978-0-7802-6850-0(4)) Wright Group/McGraw-Hill.
Sunshine: Enrichment Library. (Sunshine Ser.). 24p. (gr. 1-5). 91.95 (978-0-7802-9382-3(7)) Wright Group/McGraw-Hill.
Sunshine: Fact & Fantasy, Group 1: 1 each of 8 titles: Level N. 46.95 (978-0-7802-8356-5(2)) Wright Group/McGraw-Hill.
Sunshine: Fact & Fantasy, Group 2: 1 each of 2 titles: Level N. 11.95 (978-0-7802-7878-3(X)) Wright Group/McGraw-Hill.
Sunshine: Fact & Fantasy, Groups 1-2: 1 each of 10 titles: Level N. 58.50 (978-0-7802-6851-7(2)) Wright Group/McGraw-Hill.
Sunshine: Fluency - Chapter books, Group 2: 1 each of 2 titles: Level O. (Sunshine Ser.). 13.50 (978-0-7802-6876-0(8)) Wright Group/McGraw-Hill.
Sunshine: Fluency - Chapter Books, Group 2: 1 Each of 2 Titles: Level R. (Sunshine Ser.). 14.95 (978-0-7802-6879-1(2)) Wright Group/McGraw-Hill.
Sunshine: Fluency - Chapter Books, Group 2: 1 Each of 2 Titles: Level S. (Sunshine Ser.). 14.95 (978-0-7802-6880-7(6)) Wright Group/McGraw-Hill.
Sunshine: Fluency - Chapter Books, Group 2: 1 Each of 2 Titles: Level T. (Sunshine Ser.). 14.95 (978-0-7802-6881-4(4)) Wright Group/McGraw-Hill.
Sunshine: Fluency - Fact & Fantasy, Group 1: 1 each of 8 titles: Level O. 53.50 (978-0-7802-8357-2(0)) Wright Group/McGraw-Hill.
Sunshine: Fluency - Fact & Fantasy, Group 2: 1 each of 2 titles: Level O. 13.50 (978-0-7802-7879-0(8)) Wright Group/McGraw-Hill.
Sunshine: Fluency - Fact & Fantasy, Groups 1-2: 1 each of 10 titles: Level O. (Sunshine Ser.). 66.95 (978-0-7802-6867-8(9)) Wright Group/McGraw-Hill.
Sunshine: Fluency - Group 2: 1 each of 6 titles: Level O. 39.95 (978-0-7802-7143-2(2)) Wright Group/McGraw-Hill.
Sunshine: Fluency - Group 2: 1 Each of 6 Titles: Level R. (Sunshine Ser.). 44.95 (978-0-7802-7220-0(X)) Wright Group/McGraw-Hill.
Sunshine: Fluency - Group 2: 1 Each of 6 Titles: Level S. (Sunshine Ser.). 44.95 (978-0-7802-7222-4(6)) Wright Group/McGraw-Hill.
Sunshine: Fluency - Group 2: 1 Each of 6 Titles: Level T. 44.95 (978-0-7802-7224-8(2)) Wright Group/McGraw-Hill.
Sunshine: Fluency - Nonfiction, Group 1: 1 Each of 8 Titles: Level R. 59.95 (978-0-7802-8360-2(0)) Wright Group/McGraw-Hill.
Sunshine: Fluency - Nonfiction, Group 1: 1 Each of 8 Titles: Level T. (Sunshine Ser.). 59.95 (978-0-7802-8362-6(7)) Wright Group/McGraw-Hill.
Sunshine: Fluency - Nonfiction, Group 2: 1 Each of 2 Titles: Level R. (Sunshine Ser.). 14.95 (978-0-7802-7882-0(8)) Wright Group/McGraw-Hill.
Sunshine: Fluency - Nonfiction, Group 2: 1 Each of 2 Titles: Level T. (Sunshine Ser.). 14.95 (978-0-7802-7884-4(4)) Wright Group/McGraw-Hill.
Sunshine: Fluency - Nonfiction, Groups 1-2: 1 Each of 10 Titles: Level R. (Sunshine Ser.). 74.95 (978-0-7802-6871-5(7)) Wright Group/McGraw-Hill.
Sunshine: Fluency - Nonfiction, Groups 1-2: 1 Each of 10 Titles: Level S. (Sunshine Ser.). 74.95 (978-0-7802-6873-9(3)) Wright Group/McGraw-Hill.
Sunshine: Fluency - Nonfiction, Groups 1-2: 1 Each of 10 Titles: Level T. (Sunshine Ser.). 74.95 (978-0-7802-6874-6(1)) Wright Group/McGraw-Hill.
Sunshine: Fluency - Nonfiction, Groups 2: 1 Each of 2 Titles: Level S. (Sunshine Ser.). 14.95 (978-0-7802-7883-7(6)) Wright Group/McGraw-Hill.
Sunshine: Fluency - Student Book Set - 1 Each of 16 Titles. (Wright Group Literacy Ser.). (gr. 3-6). 112.50 (978-0-322-02494-6(3)); Vol. 2. 112.50 (978-0-322-02495-3(1)) Wright Group/McGraw-Hill.
Sunshine: Fluency-Chapter books, Group 2: 1 each of 2 titles: Level P. (Sunshine Ser.). 13.50 (978-0-7802-6877-7(6)) Wright Group/McGraw-Hill.
Sunshine: Fluency-Chapter books, Groups 2: 1 each of 2 titles: Level Q. (Sunshine Ser.). 13.50 (978-0-7802-6878-4(4)) Wright Group/McGraw-Hill.
Sunshine: Fluency-Fact & Fantasy, Group 1: 1 each of 8 titles: Level P. 53.50 (978-0-7802-8358-9(9)) Wright Group/McGraw-Hill.
Sunshine: Fluency-Fact & Fantasy, Group 2: 1 each of 2 titles: Level P. 13.50 (978-0-7802-7880-6(1)) Wright Group/McGraw-Hill.
Sunshine: Fluency-Fact & Fantasy, Groups 1-2: 1 each of 10 titles: Level P. (Sunshine Ser.). 66.95 (978-0-7802-6868-5(7)) Wright Group/McGraw-Hill.
Sunshine: Fluency Fiction. (Sunshine Ser.). 72p. (gr. 1-5). 84.95 (978-0-7802-6882-1(2)) Wright Group/McGraw-Hill.
Sunshine: Fluency-Group 2: 1 each of 6 titles: Level P. 39.95 (978-0-7802-7145-6(9)) Wright Group/McGraw-Hill.
Sunshine: Fluency-Group 2: 1 each of 6 titles: Level Q. 39.95 (978-0-7802-7218-7(8)) Wright Group/McGraw-Hill.
Sunshine: Fluency-Nonfiction, Group 1: 1 each of 10 titles: Level Q. (Sunshine Ser.). 66.95 (978-0-7802-6870-8(9)) Wright Group/McGraw-Hill.
Sunshine: Fluency-Nonfiction, Group 1: 1 each of 2 titles: Level Q. 13.50 (978-0-7802-7881-3(X)) Wright Group/McGraw-Hill.
Sunshine: Fluency-Nonfiction, Group 1: 1 each of 8 titles: Level Q. 53.50 (978-0-7802-8359-6(7)) Wright Group/McGraw-Hill.
Sunshine: Upper Emergent - Complete Kit, Vol. 3. (Wright Group Literacy Ser.). (gr. 1-18). 486.50 (978-0-322-02479-3(X)) Wright Group/McGraw-Hill.
Sunshine: Upper Emergent - Group 1:1 Each of 8 Student Books: Level F. Group 1. (Sunshine Ser.). 39.95 (978-0-7802-7128-9(9)) Wright Group/McGraw-Hill.
Sunshine: Upper Emergent - Nonfiction:1 Each of 4 Student Books: Level F. Group 1. (Sunshine Ser.). 19.95 (978-0-7802-6792-3(3)) Wright Group/McGraw-Hill.
Sunshine: Upper Emergent - Student Book Set - 1 Each of 16 Titles, Vol. 3. (Wright Group Literacy Ser.). (gr. 1-18). 79.95 (978-0-322-02488-5(9)) Wright Group/McGraw-Hill.
Sunshine: Upper Emergent-Group 1: 1 each of 8 student books: Level I. (Sunshine Ser.). 39.95 (978-0-7802-7134-0(3)) Wright Group/McGraw-Hill.
Sunshine: Upper Emergent-Group 1: 1 each of 8 student books: Level J. (Sunshine Ser.). 39.95 (978-0-7802-7136-4(X)) Wright Group/McGraw-Hill.
Sunshine: Upper Emergent-Group 2: 1 each of 8 student books: Level J. (Sunshine Ser.). 39.95 (978-0-7802-7137-1(8)) Wright Group/McGraw-Hill.
Sunshine Fact & Fantasy Sets: Complete Set - 1 Each of 24 students Books. (Sunshine Ser.). 115.95 (978-0-7802-6785-5(0)) Wright Group/McGraw-Hill.
SUNSHINE Fluency Guided Reading Kit 1. 2004. (Wright Group Literacy Ser.). (gr. 3-6). 604.95 (978-0-322-02624-7(5)) Wright Group/McGraw-Hill.
Sunshine Language Skills Books: 1 Each of 16 Big Books Set 2. (gr. k-1). 474.95 (978-0-7802-8956-7(0)) Wright Group/McGraw-Hill.
Sunshine Language Skills Books: 1 Each of 16 Student Books Set 2. (Sunshine Ser.). (gr. k-1). 91.95 (978-0-7802-8510-1(7)) Wright Group/McGraw-Hill.
Sunshine Language Skills Books: 1 Each of 20 Big Books Sets 1-2. (gr. k-1). 594.50 (978-0-7802-9624-4(9)) Wright Group/McGraw-Hill.
Sunshine Language Skills Books: 1 Each of 20 Student Books Set 1. (gr. k-1). 114.50 (978-0-7802-9623-7(0)) Wright Group/McGraw-Hill.
Sunshine Language Skills Books: 1 Each of 4 Big Books Set 1. (gr. k-1). 125.50 (978-0-7802-8955-0(2)) Wright Group/McGraw-Hill.
Sunshine Language Skills Books: 1 Each of 4 Student Books Set 2. (Sunshine Ser.). (gr. k-1). 22.95 (978-0-7802-6823-4(7)) Wright Group/McGraw-Hill.
Sunshine Language Skills Books: 6 Each of 20 Student Books Sets 1-2. (gr. k-1). 652.50 (978-0-7802-9657-2(5)) Wright Group/McGraw-Hill.
Sunshine Street, 6 vols. (Sunshinetm Ser.). 16p. (gr. k-18). 29.50 (978-0-7802-5443-5(0)) Wright Group/McGraw-Hill.
Surfing: Level J, 6 vols. (Wonder Worldtm Ser.). 16p. 29.95 (978-0-7802-4609-6(8)) Wright Group/McGraw-Hill.
Surfs Up, 6 vols. (Wildcats Ser.). 32p. (gr. 2-8). (978-0-322-00601-0(5)) Wright Group/McGraw-Hill.
Survive!, 6 vols. (Wildcats Ser.). 32p. (gr. 2-8). (978-0-322-02439-7(0)) Wright Group/McGraw-Hill.
The Swimming Pool: Big Book: Level G. (Visions Ser.). 16p. 20.95 (978-0-322-00631-7(7)) Wright Group/McGraw-Hill.
Tails: Level C, 6 vols. (Wonder Worldtm Ser.). 16p. 24.95 (978-0-7802-1052-3(2)) Wright Group/McGraw-Hill.
Tails & Claws: Level E, 6 vols. (Wonder Worldtm Ser.). 16p. 29.95 (978-0-7802-1243-5(6)); 26.50 (978-0-7802-3478-9(2)) Wright Group/McGraw-Hill.
Tails can Tell: Level K, 6 vols. (Wonder Worldtm Ser.). 16p. 34.95 (978-0-7802-2911-2(8)) Wright Group/McGraw-Hill.
Take a Look: 6 Each of 1 Anthology, 6 vols. (Wildcats Ser.). 32p. (gr. 2-8). (978-0-322-02420-5(X)) Wright Group/McGraw-Hill.
Take-Twos: Early Fluency - 1 each of 12 titles: Level K. (Take Twostm Ser.). 69.95 (978-0-322-02642-1(3)) Wright Group/McGraw-Hill.
Take-Twos: Early Fluency - 1 each of 12 titles: Level L. (Take Twostm Ser.). 69.95 (978-0-322-02645-2(8)) Wright Group/McGraw-Hill.
Take-Twos: Early Fluency - 1 each of 12 titles: Level M. (Take Twostm Ser.). 69.95 (978-0-322-02646-9(6)) Wright Group/McGraw-Hill.
Take-Twos: Early Fluency - 1 each of 12 titles: Level N. (Take Twostm Ser.). 69.95 (978-0-322-02644-5(X)) Wright Group/McGraw-Hill.
Taking Care of our World, 6 vols. (Multicultural Programs Ser.). 16p. (gr. 1-3). 24.95 (978-0-7802-9220-8(0)) Wright Group/McGraw-Hill.
TAKS MASTER Student Practice Book, Reading, Grade 2. 2004. (J). (978-1-57022-468-3(4)) ECS Learning Systems, Inc.
Taylor, Trace. N. 2015. (ICP Beginning Letter Bks.). (ENG.). 16p. (J). (gr. k-1). pap. 8.00 (978-1-61541-114-6(3)) American Reading Co.
—P. 2015. (ICP Beginning Letter Bks.). (ENG.). 16p. (J). (gr. k-1). pap. 8.00 (978-1-61541-116-0(X)) American Reading Co.
—S. 2010. (ICP Beginning Letter Bks.). (ENG.). 16p. (J). (gr. k-1). pap. 8.00 (978-1-61541-098-9(8)) American Reading Co.
—T. 2010. (ICP Beginning Letter Bks.). (ENG.). 16p. (J). (gr. k-1). pap. 8.00 (978-1-61541-100-9(3)) American Reading Co.
Tea: Level M, 6 vols. (Wonder Worldtm Ser.). 16p. 34.95 (978-0-7802-4611-9(X)) Wright Group/McGraw-Hill.
Teeth: Big Book: Level G. Group 2. (Story Box Ser.). 16p. 20.95 (978-0-322-00321-7(0)) Wright Group/McGraw-Hill.
Teeth: Level B, 6 vols. (Wonder Worldtm Ser.). 16p. 24.95 (978-0-7802-1053-0(0)) Wright Group/McGraw-Hill.
Teeth: Level R, 6 vols. (Wonder Worldtm Ser.). 48p. 44.95 (978-0-7802-7075-6(4)) Wright Group/McGraw-Hill.
Tell Me No Lies, 6 vols. (Ragged Island Mysteriestm Ser.). 161p. (gr. 5-7). 42.50 (978-0-322-01654-5(1)) Wright Group/McGraw-Hill.
Telling Stories Through Art: Level L, 6 vols. (Take-Twostm Ser.). 16p. 36.95 (978-0-322-03398-6(5)) Wright Group/McGraw-Hill.
Terror Bear Canyon: Level 5, 6 vols. (Fluency Strand Ser.). (gr. 4-8). 45.00 (978-1-4045-1225-2(X)) Wright Group/McGraw-Hill.
Tesoros de Lata: 6 Small Books. (Saludos Ser.: Vol. 3). (SPA.). 24p. (gr. 2-3). 31.00 (978-0-7635-9530-2(6)) Rigby Education.
This Mouth: Level D, 6 vols. (Wonder Worldtm Ser.). 16p. 24.95 (978-0-7802-2034-8(X)) Wright Group/McGraw-Hill.
Thompson, Deanna T. What's So Great about Silent E? The Thoughts of Sunnie Rae. Thompson, Sunnie R., illus. 2010. 28p. pap. 13.99 (978-1-4490-9274-0(8)) AuthorHouse.
Thrills at the Fair: 3-letter blends: Level C, 6 vols. (Wright Skills Ser.). 16p. (gr. k-3). 26.50 (978-0-322-01494-7(8)) Wright Group/McGraw-Hill.
Through the Looking Glass: Response Journal. 2003. 32p. (YA). (978-1-58049-989-7(9), RJ89) Prestwick Hse., Inc.
Thud! Thump! Thud! Digraph th: Level B, 6 vols. (Wright Skills Ser.). 16p. (gr. k-3). 17.95 (978-0-322-01473-2(5)) Wright Group/McGraw-Hill.
Tides: Level L, 6 vols. (Wonder Worldtm Ser.). 16p. 34.95 (978-0-7802-4613-3(6)) Wright Group/McGraw-Hill.
Time Warp: Level T. Group 1, 6 vols. (Sunshine Ser.). 48p. 44.95 (978-0-7802-5602-6(6)) Wright Group/McGraw-Hill.
Tiny Creatures Little Book: Early Reading Fluency, Level C. 2004. pap. 6.00 (978-0-7398-8291-7(0)) Steck-Vaughn.
To Catch a Thief: Level 3, 6 vols. (Fluency Strand Ser.). (gr. 4-8). 45.00 (978-1-4045-1219-1(5)) Wright Group/McGraw-Hill.
To New York: Big Book: Level D. Group 1. (Story Box Ser.). 16p. 20.95 (978-0-322-00637-9(6)) Wright Group/McGraw-Hill.
To the Moon & Beyond: Level T. Group 3, 6 vols. (Sunshine Ser.). 48p. 44.95 (978-0-322-01835-8(8)) Wright Group/McGraw-Hill.
Tofte, Mavis. Doogie Dork's Wish. Tofte, Mavis, illus. 2003. (Illus.). (J). per. 5.75 (978-0-9709906-2-4(6)) Creative Quill Publishing, Inc.
Together, 6 vols. (Sunshinetm Ser.). 16p. (gr. k-18). 29.50 (978-0-7802-5426-8(0)) Wright Group/McGraw-Hill.
Tomato: Level 4, 6 vols. (Fluency Strand Ser.). (gr. 4-8). 45.00 (978-1-4045-1223-8(3)) Wright Group/McGraw-Hill.
Too Many Graphs: Digraph ph: Level B, 6 vols. (Wright Skills Ser.). 16p. (gr. k-3). 17.95 (978-0-322-01475-6(1)) Wright Group/McGraw-Hill.
A Too-Tight Shoes Set, 6 vols. 32p. (gr. 1-3). 26.50 (978-0-7802-8042-7(3)) Wright Group/McGraw-Hill.
Toombs, Robert. Dottie the Bus Driver in Bicycle Safety. Barnett, Linda, illus. 2013. 24p. pap. 9.99 (978-0-9885180-6-3(6)) Mindstir Media.
Touch: Big Book: Level E. 8p. 20.95 (978-0-322-00369-9(5)) Wright Group/McGraw-Hill.
Tracks: Big Book: Level F. 16p. 31.50 (978-0-322-00350-7(4)) Wright Group/McGraw-Hill.
Traffic Light Sandwich: Level J, 6 vols. (Wonder Worldtm Ser.). 16p. 29.95 (978-0-7802-4615-7(2)) Wright Group/McGraw-Hill.
The Tram Ride, 6 vols. 8p. (gr. k-1). 21.50 (978-0-322-02072-6(7)) Wright Group/McGraw-Hill.
The Tree House: Level B. Group 1. (Story Box Ser.). 8p. 20.95 (978-0-7802-7629-1(9)) Wright Group/McGraw-Hill.
Trelease, Jim. Read Aloud Handbook. 5th ed. 2004. 28.25 (978-0-8446-7234-2(3)) Smith, Peter Pub., Inc.
A Truckload of Chocolate: Level 7, 6 vols. (Fluency Strand Ser.). (gr. 4-8). 45.00 (978-1-4045-1243-6(8)) Wright Group/McGraw-Hill.
Tuba Trouble. 2004. (Literacy Think-Togethers Ser.). 16-24p. (gr. 2-3). pap. 39.50 (978-0-322-06368-6(X)) Wright Group/McGraw-Hill.
Tunes for June: Long Vowel u: Level B, 6 vols. (Wright Skills Ser.). 16p. (gr. k-3). 17.95 (978-0-322-01468-8(9)) Wright Group/McGraw-Hill.
Turning Corners: American Readers. (J). (gr. 2). (978-0-669-04999-2(9)) Houghton Mifflin Harcourt School Pubs.
Turning Corners: American Readers 2-2. (J). (gr. 2). wbk. ed. (978-0-669-05004-2(0)) Houghton Mifflin Harcourt School Pubs.
Twain, Mark, pseud. The Prince & the Pauper: Response Journal. 2003. 35p. 19.95 (978-1-58049-986-6(4), RJ86) Prestwick Hse., Inc.
Twig Books: Early Emergent - 1 each of 59 Big Books: Levels A-F Big Books. 1335.95 (978-0-322-00744-4(5)) Wright Group/McGraw-Hill.
Twig Books: Upper Emergent - 1 each of 16 student books: Level I. (gr. 1-2). 79.95 (978-0-322-02653-7(9)) Wright Group/McGraw-Hill.
Twig Books: Upper Emergent - 1 each of 16 student books: Level J. (gr. 1-2). 79.95 (978-0-322-02654-4(7)) Wright Group/McGraw-Hill.
Twig Books: Upper Emergent - Lesson Plan Set - 1 Each of 16 Lesson Plans, Vol. 6. (Twig Ser.). (gr. 1-18). 127.95 (978-0-322-02814-2(0)) Wright Group/McGraw-Hill.
Twig Books: Upper Emergent - Student Book Set - 1 Each of 16 Titles. (Twig Ser.). (gr. 1-18). Vol. 5. 79.95 (978-0-322-02958-3(9)) Vol. 6. 79.95 (978-0-322-02957-6(0)) Wright Group/McGraw-Hill.
Twisters & Other Wind Storms: 6 Each of 1 Anthology, 6 vols. (Wildcats Ser.). 32p. (gr. 2-8). (978-0-322-00591-4(4)) Wright Group/McGraw-Hill.
The Two Runaways, 6 vols., Vol. 2. (Woodland Mysteriestm Ser.). 133p. (gr. 3-7). 42.50 (978-0-7802-7941-4(7)) Wright Group/McGraw-Hill.
Tyler, Jenny & Gee, R. Ready for Reading. 2004. (First Learning Ser.). (ENG., Illus.). 1p. (J). pap., act. bk. ed. 4.99 (978-0-7460-3519-1(5)) EDC Publishing.
Uncle Bill Is Feeling Ill, 6 vols. 8p. (gr. k-1). 21.50 (978-0-322-02078-8(6)) Wright Group/McGraw-Hill.
Uncle Mort's: Level T. Group 3, 6 vols. (Sunshine Ser.). 48p. 44.95 (978-0-322-04600-9(9)) Wright Group/McGraw-Hill.
Under the Clock, 6 vols. 8p. (gr. k-1). 21.50 (978-0-322-02064-1(6)) Wright Group/McGraw-Hill.
Underwater Journey, 6 vols. (Sunshinetm Ser.). 16p. (gr. k-18). 29.50 (978-0-7802-5437-4(6)) Wright Group/McGraw-Hill.
Unidad 1 Superlibro: Comunidades: Vivimos Juntos: Superlibros. 2003. (MacMillan/McGraw-Hill. Estudios Sociales Ser.). (ENG & SPA.). (gr. 2-18). (978-0-02-149441-5(X)) Macmillan/McGraw-Hill Schl. Div.
Up High in the Mountains: 6 Each of 1 Anthology, 6 vols. (Wildcats Ser.). 32p. (gr. 2-8). (978-0-322-02426-7(9)) Wright Group/McGraw-Hill.
Up in a Tree: Level D. Group 1. (Sunshine Ser.). 8p. 20.95 (978-0-7802-5736-8(7)) Wright Group/McGraw-Hill.
Upper Emergent Skills Guide. (Sunshine Skills Guides). 25.95 (978-0-7802-9810-1(1)) Wright Group/McGraw-Hill.
Using the Library: Level N, 6 vols. (Wonder Worldtm Ser.). 48p. 34.95 (978-0-7802-4617-1(9)) Wright Group/McGraw-Hill.
Valentine's Checkup: Take-Home Book. 2005. (Emergent Library: Vol. 2). (YA). (gr. -1-1). 12.60 (978-0-8215-7267-2(9)) Sadlier, William H. Inc.
A Van in the Mud: Consonant v: Level A, 6 vols. (Wright Skills Ser.). 12p. (gr. k-3). 17.95 (978-0-322-03118-0(4)) Wright Group/McGraw-Hill.
Van Ravenswaay, Susan. Reading Is So Easy. 2013. (Illus.). 60p. pap. 19.95 (978-0-9849214-4-7(3)) Mariner Publishing.
Vastola, P. What I Think: Learning the TH Sound. 2009. (PowerPhonics Ser.). 24p. (gr. 1-1). 39.90 (978-1-60851-479-3(X), PowerKids Pr.) Rosen Publishing Group, Inc., The.
Vaughan, Marcia. Story Teller Quilts: Level S, 6 vols. (Raging Rivers Ser.). 128p. (gr. 3-6). 36.95 (978-0-322-05899-6(6)) Wright Group/McGraw-Hill.
A Very Fine Time: Long Vowel i, CVCe Pattern: Level B, 6 vols. (Wright Skills Ser.). 16p. (gr. k-3). 17.95 (978-0-322-01467-1(0)) Wright Group/McGraw-Hill.
Vicary, Tim. Oxford Bookworms Library: the Elephant Man: Level 1: 400-Word Vocabulary. 2006. (ENG., Illus.). 56p. (gr. 4-7). pap. 11.00 (978-0-19-423743-7(5)) Oxford Univ. Pr., Inc.
Visions: Early Emergent - 1 each of 12 Big Books: Levels A-G Big Books. 248.50 (978-0-322-00748-2(8)) Wright Group/McGraw-Hill.
Visions: Early Emergent - 1 Each of 12 Student Books: Level A. (Visions Ser.). 49.95 (978-0-7802-9448-6(3)) Wright Group/McGraw-Hill.
Visions: Early Emergent - 1 Each of 13 Student Books: Level B. (Visions Ser.). 54.50 (978-0-7802-9449-3(1)) Wright Group/McGraw-Hill.
Visions: Early Emergent - 1 Each of 13 Student Books: Level C. 54.50 (978-0-7802-9450-9(5)) Wright Group/McGraw-Hill.
Visions: Early Emergent - Complete Kit. (Visions Ser.). (gr. k-18). 319.50 (978-0-7802-9397-7(5)) Wright Group/McGraw-Hill.
Visions: Early Emergent-Upper Emergent - 1 Each of 12 Student Books: Level D. (Visions Ser.). 49.95 (978-0-7802-9451-6(3)) Wright Group/McGraw-Hill.
Visions: Early Emergent-Upper Emergent - 1 Each of 12 Student Books: Level E. (Visions Ser.). 59.95 (978-0-7802-9452-3(1)) Wright Group/McGraw-Hill.
Visions: Early Emergent-Upper Emergent - 1 Each of 13 Student Books: Level F. (Visions Ser.). 64.95 (978-0-7802-9453-0(X)) Wright Group/McGraw-Hill.
Visions: Upper Emergent - 1 Each of 12 Student Books: Level H. 59.95 (978-0-7802-9454-7(8)) Wright Group/McGraw-Hill.
Visions: Upper Emergent - 1 Each of 13 Student Books: Level G. 64.95 (978-0-7802-9455-4(6)) Wright Group/McGraw-Hill.
Visions: Upper Emergent - Complete Kit. (Visions Ser.). (gr. 1-18). 383.50 (978-0-7802-9398-4(3)) Wright Group/McGraw-Hill.
Visions Enrichment Library: 1 Each of 20 Student Books. (Multicultural Programs Ser.). (gr. 1-3). 83.50 (978-0-7802-9447-9(5)) Wright Group/McGraw-Hill.
The Voyage of the Clowns: Diphthong Review: Level C, 6 vols. (Wright Skills Ser.). 16p. (gr. k-3). 26.50 (978-0-322-01500-5(6)) Wright Group/McGraw-Hill.
Walker, Richard. Your Amazing Body. 2004. (Literacy Think-Togethers Ser.). 16-24p. (gr. 2-3). pap. 39.50 (978-0-322-06376-1(0)) Wright Group/McGraw-Hill.
Warm & Cool Sets: 1 Each of 3 Big Books. (Sunshinetm Science Ser.). (gr. 1-2). 111.50 (978-0-7802-1450-7(1)) Wright Group/McGraw-Hill.
Warming Up: American Readers. (J). (978-0-669-04913-8(1)); (978-0-669-04915-2(8)) Houghton Mifflin Harcourt School Pubs.
Water: Level J, 6 vols. (Wonder Worldtm Ser.). 16p. 29.95 (978-0-7802-2914-3(2)) Wright Group/McGraw-Hill.
Watson, Joy. The Birthday Flood: Level O, 6 vols. (Raging Rivers Ser.). 128p. (gr. 3-6). 36.95 (978-0-322-05896-5(1)) Wright Group/McGraw-Hill.
Waves: Level L, 6 vols. (Wonder Worldtm Ser.). 16p. 34.95 (978-0-7802-4619-5(5)) Wright Group/McGraw-Hill.
We Care for our School: Level K, 6 vols. (Wonder Worldtm Ser.). 16p. 34.95 (978-0-7802-4621-8(7)); 26.50 (978-0-7802-7009-1(6)) Wright Group/McGraw-Hill.
We Look the Same, 6 vols. 8p. (gr. k-1). 21.50 (978-0-322-02079-5(4)) Wright Group/McGraw-Hill.
The Week That Was: Level 3, 6 vols. (Fluency Strand Ser.). (gr. 4-8). 45.00 (978-1-4045-1221-4(7)) Wright Group/McGraw-Hill.
Weeks, Sarah. What Is a Kiss? Date not set. 32p. (J). (gr. -1-2). 15.89 (978-0-06-026256-3(7)) HarperCollins Pubs.

P
Q
R

Wernham, Sara & Lloyd, Sue. Jolly Phonics Activity Book 4: Ai, J, Oa, Ie, Ee, Or, 7 vols. Wade, Sarah, illus. 2010. (Jolly Phonics Activity Books, Set 1-7 Ser.). (ENG.). 7p. (J). pap. *(978-1-84414-156-2(X))* Jolly Learning, Ltd.

What do I See in the Garden: Big Book: Level F. (Wonder Worldtm Ser.). 16p. 29.95 *(978-0-7802-2830-6(8))* Wright Group/McGraw-Hill.

What do I See in the Garden: Level F, 6 vols. (Wonder Worldtm Ser.). 16p. 29.95 *(978-0-7802-1054-7(9))* Wright Group/McGraw-Hill.

What Do You Think? 6 Pack. (Wildcats Ser.). 32p. (gr. 2-8). *(978-0-322-00578-5(7))* Wright Group/McGraw-Hill.

What Else?, 6 vols. (Sunshinetm Ser.). 16p. (gr. k-18). 29.50 *(978-0-7802-5439-8(2))* Wright Group/McGraw-Hill.

What Makes a Dinosaur Sore? (J). (gr. 2-3). 75.00 *(978-0-669-13452-0(X))*; pap. 9.90 *(978-0-669-15894-6(1))*; pap. 9.90 *(978-0-669-15291-3(9))* Houghton Mifflin Harcourt School Pubs.

What Season Is This? Level A, 6 vols. (Wonder Worldtm Ser.). 16p. 24.95 *(978-0-7802-1055-4(7))* Wright Group/McGraw-Hill.

What was This? Level G, 6 vols. (Wonder Worldtm Ser.). 16p. 29.95 *(978-0-7802-2038-6(2))* Wright Group/McGraw-Hill.

What's for Dinner? Level T. Group 1, 6 vols. (Sunshine Ser.). 48p. 44.95 *(978-0-7802-6099-3(6))* Wright Group/McGraw-Hill.

What's in the Bag?, 6 vols. (Multicultural Programs Ser.). 16p. (gr. 1-3). 24.95 *(978-0-7802-9218-5(9))* Wright Group/McGraw-Hill.

What's Inside? Level M, 6 vols. (Wonder Worldtm Ser.). 16p. 34.95 *(978-0-7802-2916-7(9))* Wright Group/McGraw-Hill.

When the Sun Goes Down: Level H, 6 vols. (Wonder Worldtm Ser.). 16p. 29.95 *(978-0-7802-2040-9(4))* Wright Group/McGraw-Hill.

Where Did My Toothbrush Go? (J). (gr. 2-3). 75.00 *(978-0-669-13698-2(0))* Houghton Mifflin Harcourt School Pubs.

Where do all the Birds Go? Level Q, 6 vols. (Wonder Worldtm Ser.). 48p. 39.95 *(978-0-7802-2955-6(X))* Wright Group/McGraw-Hill.

Where do I Sleep? Level Q, 6 vols. (Wonder Worldtm Ser.). 48p. 39.95 *(978-0-7802-2956-3(8))* Wright Group/McGraw-Hill.

Where Is My Caterpillar? Level J, 6 vols. (Wonder Worldtm Ser.). 16p. 29.95 *(978-0-7802-1056-1(5))* Wright Group/McGraw-Hill.

Where's Sylvester's Bed? Level G, 6 vols. (Wonder Worldtm Ser.). 16p. 29.95 *(978-0-7802-1251-0(7))* Wright Group/McGraw-Hill.

Whiskers: Level A, 6 vols. (Wonder Worldtm Ser.). 16p. 24.95 *(978-0-7802-2917-4(7))* Wright Group/McGraw-Hill.

Who Is Quick? Benchmark Assessment for Level A: Level A, 6 vols. (Wright Skills Ser.). 12p. (gr. k-3). 17.95 *(978-0-322-03127-2(3))* Wright Group/McGraw-Hill.

Why do I Need to Know When?, 6 vols. (Multicultural Programs Ser.). 16p. (gr. 1-3). 24.95 *(978-0-7802-9221-5(9))* Wright Group/McGraw-Hill.

The Wigglewaggle-Yipperlick. 2004. (Literacy Think-Togethers Ser.). 16-24p. (gr. 2-3). pap. 31.50 *(978-0-322-06356-3(6))* Wright Group/McGraw-Hill.

Wild Cats: Level P, 6 vols. (Wonder Worldtm Ser.). 48p. 39.95 *(978-0-7802-7069-5(X))* Wright Group/McGraw-Hill.

The Wild Wind: Big Book: Level I. Group 2. (Story Box Ser.). 16p. 31.50 *(978-0-322-02467-0(6))* Wright Group/McGraw-Hill.

Wildlife Watching: Level R, 6 vols. (Wonder Worldtm Ser.). 48p. 44.95 *(978-0-7802-7076-3(2))* Wright Group/McGraw-Hill.

Will Eve Win? Long Vowels e, y, CVCe & Final y Patterns: Level B, 6 vols. (Wright Skills Ser.). 16p. (gr. k-3). 17.95 *(978-0-322-01469-5(7))* Wright Group/McGraw-Hill.

Will it Rain on the Parade? Level J, 6 vols. (Wonder Worldtm Ser.). 16p. 29.95 *(978-0-7802-4623-2(3))* Wright Group/McGraw-Hill.

William H. Sadlier Staff. Ah-choo! 2005. (Fluent Library). (gr. 1-3). 29.34 *(978-0-8215-8962-5(8))* Sadlier, William H. Inc.

—All Mixed Up. 2005. (Early Library). (gr. k-2). 24.00 net. *(978-0-8215-8951-9(2))* Sadlier, William H. Inc.

—A Basket Full of Surprises. 2005. (Emergent Library: Vol. 2). (gr. -1-1). 24.00 net. *(978-0-8215-8925-0(3))* Sadlier, William H. Inc.

—The Best Place. 2005. (Early Library). (gr. k-2). 24.00 net. *(978-0-8215-8944-1(X))* Sadlier, William H. Inc.

—The Best Ride: Big Book, Vol. 2. 2005. (Emergent Library: Vol. 1). (gr. -1-1). 24.00 net. *(978-0-8215-8905-2(9))* Sadlier, William H. Inc.

—Brush, Brush, Brush! 2005. (Emergent (Prek-2) Health Package Ser.). 12p. (gr. -1-1). 25.20 *(978-0-8215-7849-0(9))* Sadlier, William H. Inc.

—The Cheerful King, Vol. 2. 2005. (Fluent Library). (gr. 1-3). 29.34 *(978-0-8215-8967-0(9))* Sadlier, William H. Inc.

—Come Meet Some Seals, Vol. 2. 2005. (Early Library). (gr. k-2). 24.00 net. *(978-0-8215-8959-5(3))* Sadlier, William H. Inc.

—Content Area Readers Library: Early (K-2) 2005. (Content Area Readers Ser.). (gr. -1-2). 465.00 *(978-0-8215-7809-4(X))* Sadlier, William H. Inc.

—Content Area Readers Library: Emergent (PreK-1) 2005. (Content Area Readers Ser.). (gr. -1-2). 498.00 *(978-0-8215-7885-8(5))* Sadlier, William H. Inc.

—Did You Know?, Vol. 2. 2005. (Early Library). (gr. k-2). 24.00 net. *(978-0-8215-8947-2(4))* Sadlier, William H. Inc.

—Discovering Dinosaurs, Vol. 2. 2005. (Fluent Library). (gr. 1-3). 29.34 *(978-0-8215-8966-3(0))* Sadlier, William H. Inc.

—Do You See a Dozen? Big Book, Vol. 2. 2005. (Emergent Library: Vol. 1). (gr. -1-1). 24.00 net. *(978-0-8215-8907-6(5))* Sadlier, William H. Inc.

—Don't Tell! 2005. (Early Library). (gr. k-2). 24.00 net. *(978-0-8215-8954-0(7))* Sadlier, William H. Inc.

—Emergent Library. 2005. (Little Books & Big Books Ser.). (gr. -1-1). 573.00 *(978-0-8215-8861-1(3))*; Vol. 2. 573.00 *(978-0-8215-8871-0(0))* Sadlier, William H. Inc.

—Emergent Library I Big Book Package. 2005. (Little Books & Big Books Ser.). (gr. -1-1). 450.00 *(978-0-8215-8864-2(8))* Sadlier, William H. Inc.

—Emergent Library I Little Book. 2005. (Little Books & Big Books Ser.). (gr. -1-1). 479.00 net. *(978-0-8215-8863-5(X))* Sadlier, William H. Inc.

—Emergent Super Libraries, 2 vols. 2005. (Emergent Libraries Ser.). (gr. -1-1). 1749.00 *(978-0-8215-8855-0(9))* Sadlier, William H. Inc.

—Felix, the Very Hungry Fish. 2005. (Emergent Library: Vol. 2). (gr. -1-1). 24.00 net. *(978-0-8215-8920-5(2))* Sadlier, William H. Inc.

—Good Food. 2005. (Emergent (Prek-2) Health Package Ser.). 12p. (gr. -1-1). 25.20 *(978-0-8215-7847-6(2))* Sadlier, William H. Inc.

—Harry's Hat. 2005. (Emergent Library: Vol. 2). (gr. -1-1). 24.00 net. *(978-0-8215-8924-3(5))* Sadlier, William H. Inc.

—Here Comes the Rain! 2005. (Emergent Library: Vol. 2). (gr. -1-1). 24.00 net. *(978-0-8215-8933-5(4))* Sadlier, William H. Inc.

—How Many Are Here? Big Book. 2005. (Emergent Library: Vol. 1). (gr. -1-1). 24.00 net. *(978-0-8215-8904-5(0))* Sadlier, William H. Inc.

—I Have a Question Vol. 4: Big Book. 2005. (Emergent Library: Vol. 1). (gr. -1-1). 24.00 net. *(978-0-8215-8916-8(4))* Sadlier, William H. Inc.

—I Love to Read, Vol. 3. 2005. (Emergent Library: Vol. 1). (gr. -1-1). 24.00 net. *(978-0-8215-8913-7(X))* Sadlier, William H. Inc.

—In January & June, Vol. 4. 2005. (Emergent Library: Vol. 1). (gr. -1-1). 24.00 net. *(978-0-8215-8915-1(6))* Sadlier, William H. Inc.

—Joey's Rowboat, Vol. 2. 2005. (Early Library). (gr. k-2). 24.00 net. *(978-0-8215-8957-1(1))* Sadlier, William H. Inc.

—Keeping Baby Animals Safe. 2005. (Emergent Library: Vol. 2). (gr. -1-1). 24.00 net. *(978-0-8215-8934-2(2))* Sadlier, William H. Inc.

—Look at the Pictures. 2005. (Early Library). (gr. k-2). 24.00 net. *(978-0-8215-8941-0(5))* Sadlier, William H. Inc.

—A Party for Nine: Big Book, Vol. 2. 2005. (Emergent Library: Vol. 1). (gr. -1-1). 24.00 net. *(978-0-8215-8909-0(1))* Sadlier, William H. Inc.

—Show & Tell. 2005. (Emergent Library: Vol. 2). (gr. -1-1). 24.00 net. *(978-0-8215-8923-6(7))* Sadlier, William H. Inc.

—The Tongue Twister Prize. 2005. (Fluent Library). (gr. 1-3). 29.34 *(978-0-8215-8961-8(X))* Sadlier, William H. Inc.

—Too Small Jill, Vol. 2. 2005. (Fluent Library). (gr. 1-3). 29.34 *(978-0-8215-8965-6(2))* Sadlier, William H. Inc.

—The Trash Can Band. 2005. (Fluent Library). (gr. 1-3). 29.34 *(978-0-8215-8964-9(4))* Sadlier, William H. Inc.

—Ultra-Saver Library Emergent, Early, & Fluent. 2005. (Little Books & Big Books Ser.). (gr. -1-3). 2727.00 *(978-0-8215-8850-5(8))* Sadlier, William H. Inc.

—Valentine's Checkup. 2005. (Emergent Library: Vol. 2). (gr. -1-1). 24.00 net. *(978-0-8215-8937-3(7))* Sadlier, William H. Inc.

—Violets & Vegetables Vol. 4: Big Book. 2005. (Emergent Library: Vol. 1). (gr. -1-1). 24.00 net. *(978-0-8215-8917-5(2))* Sadlier, William H. Inc.

—Weather Wise, Vol. 3. 2005. (Emergent Library: Vol. 1). (gr. -1-1). 24.00 net. *(978-0-8215-8911-3(3))* Sadlier, William H. Inc.

—Zack Can Fix It! Vol. 4: Big Book. 2005. (Emergent Library: Vol. 1). (gr. -1-1). 24.00 net. *(978-0-8215-8919-9(9))* Sadlier, William H. Inc.

Williams, Rozanne. We Can Share at School. 2017. (Learn-To-Read Ser.). (ENG., Illus.). (J). pap. 3.49 *(978-1-68310-242-7(8))* Pacific Learning, Inc.

Williams, Rozanne Lanczak. Mice Are Nice. Moore, Margie, illus. 2005. (Reading for Fluency Ser.). 16p. (J). pap. 3.49 *(978-1-59198-156-5(5)*, 4256) Creative Teaching Pr., Inc.

—Old MacDonald's Funny Farm, Vol. 4261. Starr Taylor, Bridget, illus. 2005. (Reading for Fluency Ser.). 16p. (J). pap. 3.49 *(978-1-59198-161-9(1)*, 4261) Creative Teaching Pr., Inc.

Wilson, Troy. Little Red Reading Hood & the Misread Wolf. Campana, Ilaria, illus. 2019. (ENG.). 32p. (J). (gr. -1-3). 17.99 *(978-0-7624-9266-4(X)*, Running Pr. Kids) Running Pr.

The Witch of Blackbird Pond: Response Journal. 2003. 36p. (YA). *(978-1-58049-993-4(7)*, RJ93) Prestwick Hse., Inc.

Wolf Tracks, 6 vols. (Book2WebTM Ser.). (gr. 4-8). 36.50 *(978-0-322-02971-2(6))* Wright Group/McGraw-Hill.

Wonder World: Early Emergent - 1 Each of 10 Student Books: Level A. 41.95 *(978-0-7802-8265-0(5))* Wright Group/McGraw-Hill.

Wonder World: Early Emergent - 1 Each of 10 Student Books: Level B. 41.95 *(978-0-7802-8266-7(3))* Wright Group/McGraw-Hill.

Wonder World: Early Emergent - 1 Each of 10 Student Books: Level C. 41.95 *(978-0-7802-8267-4(1))* Wright Group/McGraw-Hill.

Wonder World: Early Emergent - 1 Each of 10 Student Books: Level D. 41.95 *(978-0-7802-8268-1(X))* Wright Group/McGraw-Hill.

Wonder World: Early Emergent - 1 Each of 19 Big Books: Levels A-N. 476.95 *(978-0-7802-8530-9(1))* Wright Group/McGraw-Hill.

Wonder World: Early Emergent - Complete Kit. (gr. k-18). 353.50 *(978-0-7802-9042-6(9))* Wright Group/McGraw-Hill.

Wonder World: Early Fluency - 1 Each of 12 Student Books: Level K. 69.95 *(978-0-7802-8275-9(2))* Wright Group/McGraw-Hill.

Wonder World: Early Fluency - 1 Each of 12 Student Books: Level L. 69.95 *(978-0-7802-8276-6(0))* Wright Group/McGraw-Hill.

Wonder World: Early Fluency - 1 Each of 12 Student Books: Level M. 69.95 *(978-0-7802-8277-3(9))* Wright Group/McGraw-Hill.

Wonder World: Early Fluency - Complete Kit. (gr. 1-2). 540.95 *(978-0-7802-9044-0(5))* Wright Group/McGraw-Hill.

Wonder World: Fluency-1 Each of 10 Chapter Books: Level O. (Wonder Worldtm Ser.). (gr. 2-3). 66.95 *(978-0-7802-8279-7(5))* Wright Group/McGraw-Hill.

Wonder World: Fluency-1 Each of 10 Chapter Books: Level P. (Wonder Worldtm Ser.). (gr. 2-3). 66.95 *(978-0-7802-8280-3(9))* Wright Group/McGraw-Hill.

Wonder World: Fluency-1 Each of 10 Chapter Books: Level Q. (Wonder Worldtm Ser.). (gr. 2-3). 66.95 *(978-0-7802-8281-0(7))* Wright Group/McGraw-Hill.

Wonder World: Fluency-1 Each of 10 Chapter Books: Level R. (Wonder Worldtm Ser.). (gr. 2-3). 74.95 *(978-0-7802-8282-7(5))* Wright Group/McGraw-Hill.

Wonder World: Fluency-1 Each of 12 Student Books: Level N. 69.95 *(978-0-7802-8278-0(7))* Wright Group/McGraw-Hill.

Wonder World: Levels O-R. (Wonder Worldtm Ser.). (gr. 2-3). 275.95 *(978-0-7802-8283-4(3))* Wright Group/McGraw-Hill.

Wonder World: Upper Emergent - 1 Each of 12 Student Books: Level E. 59.95 *(978-0-7802-8269-8(8))* Wright Group/McGraw-Hill.

Wonder World: Upper Emergent - 1 Each of 12 Student Books: Level F. 59.95 *(978-0-7802-8270-4(1))* Wright Group/McGraw-Hill.

Wonder World: Upper Emergent - 1 Each of 12 Student Books: Level G. 59.95 *(978-0-7802-8271-1(X))* Wright Group/McGraw-Hill.

Wonder World: Upper Emergent - Complete Kit. (gr. 1-18). 396.95 *(978-0-7802-9043-3(7))* Wright Group/McGraw-Hill.

Wonder World: Upper Emergent - Upper Emergent - Complete Kit, Vol. 2. (gr. 1-18). 396.95 *(978-0-7802-9041-9(0))* Wright Group/McGraw-Hill.

Wonder World: Upper Emergent-1 Each of 12 Student Books: Level H. 59.95 *(978-0-7802-8272-8(8))* Wright Group/McGraw-Hill.

Wonder World: Upper Emergent-1 Each of 12 Student Books: Level I. 59.95 *(978-0-7802-8273-5(6))* Wright Group/McGraw-Hill.

Wonder World: Upper Emergent-1 Each of 12 Student Books: Level J. 59.95 *(978-0-7802-8274-2(4))* Wright Group/McGraw-Hill.

Woodland Mysteries. (gr. 3-7). Set 1. 424.95 *(978-0-7802-7245-3(5))*Set 2. 424.95 *(978-0-7802-8002-1(4))*Set 3. 479.95 *(978-0-322-02629-2(6))* Wright Group/McGraw-Hill.

Woodland Mysteries: Classroom Library Set. (gr. 3-7). 313.95 *(978-0-322-02628-5(8))* Wright Group/McGraw-Hill.

Woodland Mysteries: Complete Boxed Set. (gr. 3-7). 1238.95 *(978-0-322-02625-4(3))* Wright Group/McGraw-Hill.

The Woodlanders Begin, 6 vols., Vol. 3. (Woodland Mysteriestm Ser.). 133p. (gr. 3-7). 42.50 *(978-0-322-02368-0(8))* Wright Group/McGraw-Hill.

Woods, Irons, & Greens: 6 Each of 1 Anthology, 6 vols. (Wildcats Ser.). 32p. (gr. 2-8). *(978-0-322-00589-1(2))* Wright Group/McGraw-Hill.

Word Work Assessment Guide. (Fast Track Reading Ser.). (gr. 4-8). 29.50 *(978-0-322-05948-1(8))* Wright Group/McGraw-Hill.

Workman Publishing & Heos, Bridget. Summer Brain Quest: Between Grades Pre-K & K. Yan, Edison & Wicks, Maris, illus. 2018. (Summer Brain Quest Ser.). (ENG.). 160p. (gr. -1-k). pap. 12.95 *(978-1-5235-0299-8(1)*, 100299) Workman Publishing Co., Inc.

A World Worth Keeping: Level T. Group 1, 6 vols. (Sunshine Ser.). 48p. 44.95 *(978-0-7802-6092-4(9))* Wright Group/McGraw-Hill.

The Wrecks: Level T. Group 2, 6 vols. (Sunshine Ser.). 48p. 44.95 *(978-0-7802-4177-0(0))* Wright Group/McGraw-Hill.

Wrestle Mania: Magazine Anthology: Level 5, 6 vols. (Comprehension Strand Ser.). (gr. 4-8). 54.00 *(978-0-322-06036-4(2))* Wright Group/McGraw-Hill.

Wright Group, Incorporated Staff. Brice & the Whale: Decodable Books, 6 vols. (Fast Track Reading Ser.). 24p. (gr. 4-8). 40.95 *(978-0-322-05981-8(X))* Wright Group/McGraw-Hill.

The Wright Skills: Level B Sets - Long vowels only: 1 Each of 6 Titles. (gr. k-3). 17.95 *(978-0-322-01934-8(6))* Wright Group/McGraw-Hill.

The Wright Skills: Level B Sets - Long vowels only: 6 Each of 6 Titles. (gr. k-3). 109.50 *(978-0-322-01935-5(4))* Wright Group/McGraw-Hill.

The Wright Skills: Level C Sets - 1 Each of 16 Titles. (gr. k-3). 69.95 *(978-0-322-00734-5(8))* Wright Group/McGraw-Hill.

The Wright Skills: Level C Sets - 6 Each of 16 Titles. (gr. k-3). 322.95 *(978-0-322-00813-7(1))* Wright Group/McGraw-Hill.

A Writer's Work: Level N, 6 vols. (Wonder Worldtm Ser.). 48p. 34.95 *(978-0-7802-2918-1(5))* Wright Group/McGraw-Hill.

Yates, Irene. How to Be a Wizard at Reading. 48p. (J). (gr. 2-6). pap. *(978-1-875739-66-0(1))* Wizard Bks.

Zeros And Ones, 6 vols. (Wildcats Ser.). 32p. (gr. 2-8). *(978-0-322-02438-0(2))* Wright Group/McGraw-Hill.

Zone Zoomers: Level 2, 6 vols. (Fluency Strand Ser.). (gr. 4-8). 45.00 *(978-1-4045-1213-9(6))* Wright Group/McGraw-Hill.

The Zoo: Big Book: Level B. (Wonder Worldtm Ser.). 16p. 26.50 *(978-0-7802-2832-0(4))* Wright Group/McGraw-Hill.

The Zoo: Level B, 6 vols. (Wonder Worldtm Ser.). 16p. 24.95 *(978-0-7802-1058-5(1))* Wright Group/McGraw-Hill.

READING—FICTION

Alexander, Kwame. Booked. (Crossover Ser.). (ENG.). (J). (gr. 5-7). 2019. 336p. pap. 9.99 *(978-1-328-59630-7(3)*, 1731272) 2016. 320p. 16.99 *(978-0-544-57098-6(7)*, 1612557) HarperCollins Pubs. (Clarion Bks.).

—Booked. 2016. lib. bdg. 29.40 *(978-0-606-37992-2(4))* Turtleback.

—Surf's Up. Miyares, Daniel, illus. (ENG.). (J). (— 1). 2018. 24p. bds. 7.95 *(978-0-7358-4313-4(9))* 2016. 32p. 18.95 *(978-0-7358-4220-5(5))* North-South Bks., Inc.

Beaty, Andrea. Aaron Slater, Illustrator. Roberts, David, illus. 2021. (Questioneers Ser.). (ENG.). 40p. (J). (gr. k-2). 18.99 *(978-1-4197-5396-1(7)*, 1730501) Abrams, Inc.

Bender, Esther. Elisabeth & the Windmill. 2003. (ENG.). 112p. (J). (gr. 3-7). pap. 6.99 *(978-0-8361-9204-9(4))* Herald Pr.

Bertram, Debbie & Bloom, Susan. The Best Place to Read. Garland, Michael, illus. 2007. 32p. (J). (gr. -1-2). pap. 8.99 *(978-0-375-83757-9(4)*, Dragonfly Bks.) Random Hse. Children's Bks.

—The Best Place to Read. 2007. lib. bdg. 18.40 *(978-1-4177-9097-5(0))* Turtleback.

Biery, Martha. Words Aren't Fair. 2009. 46p. pap. 15.75 *(978-1-60860-793-8(3)*, Eloquent Bks.) Strategic Book Publishing & Rights Agency (SBPRA).

Blum, Denise. Anything Is Possible: The Ben Carson Story. Rea, Nathan, illus. 2015. (ENG.). 28p. (J). pap. 10.00 *(978-0-9899479-1-6(2))* Mainstay Publishing.

Brown, Marc. Arthur's Reading Trick. 2009. (Step into Reading Ser.). (ENG., Illus.). 24p. (J). (gr. k-3). pap. 4.99 *(978-0-375-82977-2(6)*, Random Hse. Bks. for Young Readers) Random Hse. Children's Bks.

Calvani, Mayra. Humberto, the Bookworm Hamster. Grady, Kit, illus. 2009. 20p. pap. 10.95 *(978-1-935137-92-4(1))* Guardian Angel Publishing, Inc.

Capucilli, Alyssa Satin. Biscuit Loves the Library. Schories, Pat, illus. 2014. (My First I Can Read Ser.). (ENG.). 32p. (J). (gr. -1-3). 16.99 *(978-0-06-193507-7(7))*; pap. 4.99 *(978-0-06-193506-0(9))* HarperCollins Pubs. (HarperCollins).

—Biscuit Phonics Fun. 2008. (My First I Can Read Ser.). (ENG., Illus.). 100p. (J). (gr. -1 — 1). 14.99 *(978-0-06-143204-0(0)*, HarperCollins) HarperCollins Pubs.

Carlson, Nancy. I Don't Like to Read! Carlson, Nancy, illus. 2009. (ENG., Illus.). 32p. (J). (gr. k-2). pap. 8.99 *(978-0-14-241451-4(4)*, Puffin Books) Penguin Young Readers Group.

Chichester Clark, Emma. Bears Don't Read! Chichester Clark, Emma, illus. 2016. (Illus.). 32p. (J). 12.99 *(978-1-61067-366-2(2))* Kane Miller.

Cline-Ransome, Lesa. Light in the Darkness: A Story about How Slaves Learned in Secret. Ransome, James E., illus. 2013. (ENG.). 40p. (J). (gr. -1-3). 18.99 *(978-1-4231-3495-4(8))* Little, Brown Bks. for Young Readers.

Cordoza, Sandra Sandlin. Smarticus & the Abc's. 2010. 24p. pap. 11.50 *(978-1-60860-407-4(1)*, Eloquent Bks.) Strategic Book Publishing & Rights Agency (SBPRA).

Coulton, Mia. Danny & Heather Share. Coulton, Mia, photos by. 2003. (ENG., Illus.). 16p. pap. 5.35 *(978-0-9720295-8-2(3))* Maryruth Bks., Inc.

Cuyler, Margery. Hooray for Reading Day! Howard, Arthur, illus. 2008. (Jessica Worries Ser.). (ENG.). 32p. (J). (gr. k-3). 17.99 *(978-0-689-86188-8(5)*, Simon & Schuster Bks. For Young Readers) Simon & Schuster Bks. For Young Readers.

Dail, Maggie. Getting to First Base - Chris Struggles to Read. 2006. 157p. pap. 13.95 *(978-1-4116-8125-5(8))* Lulu Pr., Inc.

Damschroder, Scott. Pinky's Rainy Day: Pinky Padooka takes a trip to Imaginationville. Faust, Laurie, illus. 2004. 36p. (J). lib. bdg. 19.95 *(978-0-9754728-0-4(1))* Big Ransom Studio.

Danziger, Paula. It's a Fair Day, Amber Brown. Ross, Tony, illus. 2003. (Readalongs for Beginning Readers Ser.). (J). 25.95 incl. audio *(978-1-59112-246-3(5))*; pap. 29.95 incl. audio *(978-1-59112-247-0(3))* Live Oak Media.

DeClements, Barthe. Sixth Grade Can Really Kill You. 2008. 160p. (J). (gr. 3-7). 5.99 *(978-0-14-241380-7(1)*, Puffin Books) Penguin Young Readers Group.

Dennis, Kathryn. Too Many Questions. Dennis, Kathryn, illus. 2016. (ENG., Illus.). 32p. (J). 10.99 *(978-1-61067-460-7(X))* Kane Miller.

Dewdney, Anna & Duncan, Reed. Llama Llama Loves to Read. Morrow, J. T., illus. 2018. (Llama Llama Ser.). 40p. (J). (-k). 18.99 *(978-0-670-01397-5(8)*, Viking Books for Young Readers) Penguin Young Readers Group.

Flanagan, Alice K. Blast Off! The Sound of BL. 2017. (Consonant Blends Ser.). (ENG.). 24p. (J). (gr. -1-2). lib. bdg. 32.79 *(978-1-5038-1937-5(X)*, 211533) Child's World, Inc, The.

—I Am Glad: The Sound of GL. 2017. (Consonant Blends Ser.). (ENG.). 24p. (J). (gr. -1-2). lib. bdg. 32.79 *(978-1-5038-1940-5(X)*, 211537) Child's World, Inc, The.

—My Flower Garden: The Sound of FL. 2017. (Consonant Blends Ser.). (ENG.). 24p. (J). (gr. -1-2). lib. bdg. 32.79 *(978-1-5038-1939-9(6)*, 211540) Child's World, Inc, The.

Friden, Chris & Rodriguez Braojos, Alberto. Storytime with Paige. Jaraiz, David, illus. 2008. (J). *(978-0-9758785-8-3(1))*; *(978-0-9801849-4-5(0))* Haydenburn Lane.

Fyne, Olga. My Shadow Is a Copycat. 2009. 56p. pap. 21.99 *(978-1-4389-3671-0(0))* AuthorHouse.

Garson, Cindy. Welcome to Kristy's Farm, Book 2 (Black & White Version) 2007. 104p. pap. 14.00 *(978-1-4303-0366-4(2))* Lulu Pr., Inc.

—Welcome to Kristy's Farm, Book 4. 2007. 104p. pap. 19.50 *(978-1-4303-1000-6(6))* Lulu Pr., Inc.

Gaydos, Nora. Playful Pals, Level 1. Sams, B. B., illus. 2003. (Now I'm Reading!). 128p. (J). (gr. -1-2). 14.99 *(978-1-58476-243-0(8))* Innovative Kids.

Giff, Patricia Reilly. Eleven. (ENG.). (J). 2009. 176p. (gr. 3-7). 7.99 *(978-0-440-23802-7(1)*, Yearling) 2008. 164p. (gr. 4-6). lib. bdg. 21.19 *(978-0-385-90098-0(8)*, Lamb, Wendy Bks.) Random Hse. Children's Bks.

Gikow, Louise. I Can Read. Patience, John, illus. 2004. (My First Reader Ser.). 31p. (J). 18.50 *(978-0-516-24678-9(X)*, Children's Pr.) Scholastic Library Publishing.

Gutman, Dan. Miss Klute Is a Hoot! 2014. (My Weirder School Ser.: 11). (J). lib. bdg. 14.75 *(978-0-606-35503-2(0))* Turtleback.

—My Weirder School #11: Miss Klute Is a Hoot! Paillot, Jim, illus. 2014. (My Weirder School Ser.: 11). (ENG.). 112p. (J). (gr. 1-5). 15.89 *(978-0-06-219845-7(9))*; pap. 6.99 *(978-0-06-219844-0(0))* HarperCollins Pubs. (HarperCollins).

Hardinge, Frances. Fly by Night. 2006. 487p. (J). (gr. 5-9). 16.99 *(978-0-06-087627-2(1))* HarperCollins Pubs.

Hillenbrand, Will. Mighty Reader & the Big Freeze. 2019. (ENG., Illus.). 32p. (J). (gr. -1-3). pap. 7.99 *(978-0-8234-4733-6(2))* Holiday Hse., Inc.

Hillert, Margaret. Dear Dragon Learns to Read. Pullan, Jack, illus. 2015. (BeginningtoRead Ser.). (ENG.). 32p. (J). (gr. k-2). lib. bdg. 22.60 *(978-1-59953-707-8(9))* Norwood Hse. Pr.

Hills, Tad. How Rocket Learned to Read. Hills, Tad, illus. 2010. (Rocket Ser.). (ENG., Illus.). 40p. (J). (gr. -1-2). 17.99 *(978-0-375-85899-4(7))* Random Hse. Children's Bks.

Hirst, Daisy. I Do Not Like Books Anymore! Hirst, Daisy, illus. 2018. (ENG., Illus.). 40p. (J). (gr. -1-2). 17.99 *(978-1-5362-0334-9(3))* Candlewick Pr.

Homberg, Ruth. The Little Mermaid Step into Reading (Disney Princess) RH Disney, illus. 2013. (Step into Reading Ser.). (ENG.). 32p. (J). (gr. -1-1). 5.99 *(978-0-7364-8128-1(1)*, RH/Disney) Random Hse. Children's Bks.

Hunsaker, Debbie. Reading Rug. 2012. 28p. pap. 19.99 *(978-1-4678-7018-4(8))* AuthorHouse.

Hunt, Lynda Mullaly. Fish in a Tree. l.t. ed. 2019. (ENG.). 296p. (J). (gr. 5). pap. 12.99 *(978-1-4328-6397-5(5)*, Large Print Pr.) Thorndike Pr.

—Fish in a Tree. 2017. lib. bdg. 19.65 *(978-0-606-39991-3(7))* Turtleback.

Kamins, Julie Firstenberg. Why Am I at the Red Table? Long, Carlos, illus. 2008. 32p. (J). 13.95 (978-0-9771566-9-6(9)) Librujas.

Kaniecki, Larry. Ho Ho the Elf. 2011. 44p. pap. 21.99 (978-1-4628-6807-0(X)) Xlibris Corp.

Kemnitz, Dianna. Sing with Jack. 2012. 38p. 24.95 (978-1-4626-5656-1(0)) America Star Bks.

Kertell, Lynn Maslen. My First Bob Books - Alphabet Box Set | Phonics, Letter Sounds, Ages 3 & up, Pre-K (Reading Readiness), 1 vol. Maslen, John R. & Hendra, Sue, illus. 2008. (Bob Bks.). (ENG.). 120p. (J). (gr. -1-k). pap., pap., pap. 17.99 (978-0-545-01921-7(4), Cartwheel Bks.) Scholastic, Inc.

Krishnaswami, Uma. Book Uncle & Me, 1 vol. Swaney, Julianna, illus. 2018. (ENG.). 152p. (J). (gr. 2-5). pap. 9.99 (978-1-55498-809-9(8)) Groundwood Bks. CAN. Dist: Publishers Group West (PGW).

Lee, Quinlan B. The Circus Comes to Town. 2005. (Illus.). (J). (978-0-439-77931-9(6)) Scholastic, Inc.

—A Great Day for Soccer. 2005. (Illus.). (J). (978-0-439-77921-0(9)) Scholastic, Inc.

—Sail Away. 2005. (Illus.). (J). (978-0-439-77933-3(2)) Scholastic, Inc.

—Super Spies. 2005. (Illus.). (J). (978-0-439-77923-4(5)) Scholastic, Inc.

Lorton, Sylvia. Johnny's Wish. 2013. 24p. pap. 24.95 (978-1-63004-228-8(5)) America Star Bks.

Maltby, Robert I. Diquan & the Book Monster, 1 vol. 2009. 39p. pap. 24.95 (978-1-61546-964-2(8)) America Star Bks.

Mazurak, Tena. Harley Hits a Homer. 2010. 24p. pap. 12.99 (978-1-4490-9977-0(7)) AuthorHouse.

Mullaly Hunt, Lynda. Fish in a Tree. (J). (gr. 5). 2017. (Illus.). 320p. 8.99 (978-0-14-242642-5(3), Puffin Books) 2015. 288p. 17.99 (978-0-399-16259-6(3), Nancy Paulsen Books) Penguin Young Readers Group.

Papp, Lisa. Madeline Finn & the Library Dog, 1 vol. 2016. (ENG., Illus.). 32p. (J). (gr. -1-3). 17.95 (978-1-56145-910-0(0)) Peachtree Publishing Co. Inc.

Parsons, Corey. I Can Read. 2005. 29p. (J). 9.98 (978-1-4116-6101-1(X)) Lulu Pr., Inc.

Paterson, Katherine. Marvin One Too Many. Clark Brown, Jane, illus. 2003. 28.95 incl. audio compact disk (978-1-59112-635-5(5)); 25.95 incl. audio (978-1-59112-254-8(6)); pap. 31.95 incl. audio compact disk (978-1-59112-636-2(3)); pap. 31.95 incl. audio compact disk (978-1-59112-636-2(3)); (J). pap. 29.95 incl. audio (978-1-59112-255-5(4)) Live Oak Media.

Paul, Sherry. Finn the Foolish Fish: Trouble with Bubbles, Set. Miller, Bob, illus. (See How I Read Ser.). 32p. (Orig.). (J). (gr. -1-2). pap. 14.10 (978-0-675-01084-9(5)) CPI Publishing, Inc.

—Two-B & the Rock 'n' Roll Band, Set. Murphy, Bob, illus. (See How I Read Ser.). 32p. (Orig.). (J). (gr. -1-2). pap. 14.10 (978-0-675-01082-5(9)) CPI Publishing, Inc.

Pearson, Susan. How to Teach a Slug to Read, 0 vols. Slonim, David, illus. 2012. (ENG.). 32p. (J). (gr. k-2). 16.99 (978-0-7614-5805-0(0), 9780761458050, Two Lions) Amazon Publishing.

Play, Laugh, & Learn All Year Long. 2007. (ENG., Illus.). 28p. (J). (gr. -1-1). 16.99 (978-1-59069-503-6(8), 1P1000) Studio Mouse LLC.

Polacco, Patricia. Gracias, Senor Falker. 2006. (SPA., Illus.). 34p. (J). (gr. 2-3). per. 9.99 (978-1-933032-02-3(2), LC34004) Lectorum Pubns., Inc.

—Thank You, Mr. Falker. Polacco, Patricia, illus. 2012. (Illus.). 40p. (J). (gr. k-3). 15.99 (978-0-399-25762-9(4), Philomel Bks.) Penguin Young Readers Group.

Powers, Mark. I Want to Be a Reader! Montag, Maria, illus. 2017. (ENG.). 14p. (J). (— 1). bds. 7.99 (978-1-936669-55-4(2)) Blue Manatee Press.

Shaw, Nancy. Elena's Story. Rodanas, Kristina, illus. 2012. (Tales of the World Ser.). (ENG.). 32p. (J). (gr. 1-4). 16.95 (978-1-58536-528-9(9), 202319) Sleeping Bear Pr.

Spurling, Wesley. Books for Jacob. 2009. 24p. pap. 14.79 (978-1-4389-2231-7(0)) AuthorHouse.

Toles-Stotts, LaShunda. When I Learned to Read. Stotts, Jasmyn & Jayda, illus. l.t. ed. 2005. 36p. (J). per. 11.99 (978-1-59879-071-9(4)) Lifevest Publishing, Inc.

Walker, Kate. I Hate Books! Cox, David, illus. 2007. 88p. (J). (gr. 1-4). 16.95 (978-0-8126-2745-9(8)) Cricket Bks.

Wallace, Suzanne. When I Was a Baby, What Did I Do? What Did I Do? 2012. 28p. pap. 21.99 (978-1-4771-2144-3(7)) Xlibris Corp.

Walter, Mildred Pitts. Alec's Primer. Johnson, Larry, illus. 2005. (ENG.). 32p. (J). (gr. -1-3). 15.95 (978-0-916718-20-6(4)) Vermont Folklife Ctr.

Wang, Adria. My World: My Busy Day. Nicholls, Paul, illus. 2005. 10p. (J). 4.95 (978-1-58117-251-5(6), Intervisual/Piggy Toes) Bendon, Inc.

Williams, Tova. The Boy Who Did Not Want to Read, 1 vol. Suggs, Aisha, illus. 2010. 36p. pap. 24.95 (978-1-4489-5705-7(2)) PublishAmerica, Inc.

Yager, Jan. The Reading Rabbit. Lyman, Mitzi, illus. 32p. (J). 2014. (ENG.). 25.95 (978-1-938998-00-3(6)) 2013. pap. 17.95 (978-1-938998-01-0(4)) Hannacroix Creek Bks., Inc.

READING—REMEDIAL TEACHING

Sandviks HOP, Inc. Staff. Hooked on English. 2007. 199.99 (978-1-60143-752-5(8)) HOP, LLC.

READING—STUDY AND TEACHING

see Reading

READING CLINICS

see Reading—Remedial Teaching

READING INTERESTS

see Books and Reading

READING INTERESTS OF CHILDREN

see Children—Books and Reading

REAGAN, RONALD, 1911-2004

Allen, Susan. The Remarkable Ronald Reagan: Cowboy & Commander in Chief. Harrington, Leslie, illus. 2013. (ENG.). 36p. (J). (gr. 1). 16.99 (978-1-62157-038-7(X)) Regnery Publishing.

Anderson, Michael, contrib. by. Ronald Reagan, 4 vols. 2012. (Pivotal Presidents: Profiles in Leadership Ser.). (ENG., Illus.). 80p. (YA). (gr. 8-8). 72.94 (978-1-61530-958-0(6), dd617cf5-f55d-4034-bafa-3b0e589d19a9); lib. bdg. 36.47 (978-1-61530-944-3(6), 698e3007-eb10-440b-80f9-551da23be232) Rosen Publishing Group, Inc., The.

Baier, Bret & Whitney, Catherine. Three Days in Moscow Young Readers' Edition: Ronald Reagan & the Fall of the Soviet Empire. 2018. (ENG., Illus.). 240p. (J). (gr. 3-7). 17.99 (978-0-06-286445-1(9), HarperCollins) HarperCollins Pubs.

Benge, Janet & Benge, Geoff. Heroes of History - Ronald Reagan: Destiny at His Side. 2010. (ENG.). 224p. (YA). pap. 11.99 (978-1-932096-65-1(5)) Emerald Bks.

Benson, Michael. Ronald Reagan. 2004. (Presidential Leaders Ser.). (Illus.). 112p. (J). 29.27 (978-0-8225-0815-1(X), Lerner Pubns.) Lerner Publishing Group.

Boshier, Rosa. Ronald Reagan: 40th US President, 1 vol. 2013. (Essential Lives Set 8 Ser.). (ENG.). 112p. (YA). (gr. 6-12). lib. bdg. 41.36 (978-1-61783-895-8(0), 6767, Essential Library) ABDO Publishing Co.

Brill, Marlene Targ. America in the 1980s. 2009. (Decades of Twentieth-Century America Ser.). (ENG.). 144p. (gr. 5-12). lib. bdg. 38.60 (978-0-8225-7602-0(3)) Lerner Publishing Group.

Britton, Tamara L. Ronald Reagan, 1 vol. 2016. (United States Presidents *2017 Ser.). (ENG., Illus.). 40p. (J). (gr. 2-5). lib. bdg. 35.64 (978-1-68078-114-4(6), 21845, Big Buddy Bks.) ABDO Publishing Co.

Burgan, Michael. Ronald Reagan. 2011. 128p. pap. 14.99 (978-0-7566-7739-8(4)); (ENG., Illus.). (J). (gr. 5-8). 18.69 (978-0-7566-7075-7(6)) Dorling Kindersley Publishing, Inc.

Gigliotti, Jim. Ronald Reagan, the 40th President. 2016. (First Look at America's Presidents Ser.). (ENG., Illus.). 24p. (J). (gr. -1-3). 26.99 (978-1-944102-69-2(8)) Bearport Publishing Co., Inc.

Margaret, Amy. Ronald Reagan Presidential Library. (Presidential Libraries Ser.). 24p. (gr. 3-3). 2009. 42.50 (978-1-60851-488-5(9)) 2003. (ENG., Illus.). (J). lib. bdg. 26.27 (978-0-8239-6272-3(5), 82b1aa28-ee96-4b10-920c-2b991a063138) Rosen Publishing Group, Inc., The. (PowerKids Pr.).

Marsico, Katie. Ronald Reagan, 1 vol. 2011. (Presidents & Their Times Ser.). (ENG.). 96p. (gr. 6-6). 36.93 (978-0-7614-4814-3(4), a120eb10-6f7c-4e8f-ab7d-8a44a1d07704) Cavendish Square Publishing LLC.

Milton, Joyce & Who HQ. Who Was Ronald Reagan? Wolf, Elizabeth, illus. 2004. (Who Was? Ser.). 112p. (J). (gr. 3-7). pap. 5.99 (978-0-448-43344-8(3), Penguin Workshop) Penguin Young Readers Group.

Mis, M. S. How to Draw the Life & Times of Ronald Reagan. 2009. (Kid's Guide to Drawing the Presidents of the United States of America Ser.). 32p. (gr. 4-4). 50.50 (978-1-61511-158-9(1), PowerKids Pr.) Rosen Publishing Group, Inc., The.

Mis, Melody S. How to Draw the Life & Times of Ronald Reagan, 1 vol. 2005. (Kid's Guide to Drawing the Presidents of the United States of America Ser.). (ENG., Illus.). 32p. (YA). (gr. 4-4). 30.27 (978-1-4042-3016-3(5), 7e454ea0-edb8-4ce5-a3a4-8ec6be2e3e2c) Rosen Publishing Group, Inc., The.

O'Reilly, Bill. The Day the President Was Shot. 2016. (ENG., Illus.). 256p. (J). (gr. 5-9). 19.99 (978-1-62779-699-6(1), 900158363, Holt, Henry & Co. Bks. For Young Readers) Holt, Henry & Co.

Orr, Tamra. Ronald Reagan. 2004. (Childhoods of the Presidents Ser.). (Illus.). 48p. (J). (gr. 4-18). lib. bdg. 17.95 (978-1-59084-280-5(4)) Mason Crest.

Patrick, Denise Lewis. Ronald Reagan: From Silver Screen to Oval Office. 2006. 44p. (J). lib. bdg. 15.00 (978-1-4242-0852-4(1)) Fitzgerald Bks.

Pingry, Patricia A. The Story of Ronald Reagan. Mahan, Ben, illus. 2006. (ENG.). 26p. (J). (gr. -1-k). bds. 7.69 (978-0-8249-6621-8(X), Ideals Pubns.) Worthy Publishing.

Ronald Reagan. annuals Date not set. (Starlog Movie Ser.). (YA). pap. (978-0-934551-04-5(9)) Profile Entertainment, Inc.

Shea, Therese M. Before Ronald Reagan Was President, 1 vol. 2018. (Before They Were President Ser.). (ENG.). 24p. (gr. 2-3). lib. bdg. 24.27 (978-1-5382-2911-8(0), dc9577f9-9282-4610-8848-188518851e6d) Stevens, Gareth Publishing LLLP.

Sutcliffe, Jane. Ronald Reagan. 2009. pap. 52.95 (978-0-7613-4958-7(8)) 2008. (ENG.). 48p. (gr. 3-6). 27.93 (978-0-8225-8894-8(3), Lerner Pubns.) Lerner Publishing Group.

Time for Kids Editors. Time for Kids: Ronald Reagan: From Silver Screen to Oval Office. 2005. (Time for Kids Ser.). (ENG., Illus.). 48p. (J). (gr. 2-4). per. 3.99 (978-0-06-057626-4(X)) HarperCollins Pubs.

Venezia, Mike. Ronald Reagan: Fortieth President, 1981-1989. Venezia, Mike, illus. 2007. (Getting to Know the U. S. Presidents Ser.). (ENG., Illus.). 32p. (J). (gr. 3-4). 28.00 (978-0-516-22644-6(4), Children's Pr.) Scholastic Library Publishing.

Young, Jeff C. Great Communicator: The Story of Ronald Reagan. 2004. (Twentieth Century Leaders Ser.). (Illus.). 128p. (YA). (gr. 6-12). 23.95 (978-1-931798-10-5(9)) Reynolds, Morgan Inc.

REAL ESTATE

see Real Property

REAL ESTATE BUSINESS

Clark, Betty. Choosing a Career in Real Estate. 2009. (World of Work Ser.). 64p. (gr. 5-5). 58.50 (978-1-60854-335-9(8)) Rosen Publishing Group, Inc., The.

REAL PROPERTY

Here are entered general works on real property in the legal sense i.e., ownership of land and buildings (immovable property) as opposed to personal property. Works limited to the buying and selling of real property are entered under Real Estate Business. General works on land without the ownership aspect are entered under Land Ue.

see also Farms; Real Estate Business

Boye, B. D. Our New Home. Boye, B. D., illus. l.t. ed. 2005. (Illus.). 18p. (J). per. 4.99 (978-0-9768078-2-7(3)) Innerchild Publishing, Inc.

Carser, A. R. Donald Trump: 45th US President. 2016. (Essential Lives Set 10 Ser.). (ENG., Illus.). 112p. (J). (gr. 6-12). lib. bdg. 41.36 (978-1-68078-366-7(1), 23222, Essential Library) ABDO Publishing Co.

Mcintosh Wooten, Sara. Donald Trump: From Real Estate to Reality TV, 1 vol. 2009. (People to Know Today Ser.). (ENG., Illus.). 128p. (gr. 6-7). lib. bdg. 35.93 (978-0-7660-2890-6(9), a09fd718-6fc5-411e-b4e3-5311f8d7ffa5) Enslow Publishing, LLC.

Troisi-Paton, Kimberly, ed. Property Rights, 1 vol. 2006. (Bill of Rights Ser.). (ENG., Illus.). 136p. (gr. 10-12). lib. bdg. 44.83 (978-0-7377-3543-7(0), ed017442-299f-4318-947d-cf298c3c634f, Greenhaven Publishing) Greenhaven Publishing LLC.

REALTY

see Real Property

REASONING

see also Intellect; Logic

Beck, Esther & Doudna, Kelly. You'll Cause a Stir When You Infer!, 1 vol. 2007. (Science Made Simple Ser.). (Illus.). 24p. (J). (gr. k-3). lib. bdg. 24.21 (978-1-59928-626-6(2), SandCastle) ABDO Publishing Co.

Berry, Joy. Saying No. 2019. (ENG., Illus.). 34p. (J). (gr. -1-3). pap. 8.99 (978-0-7396-0354-3(X)) Inspired Studios Inc.

Boardworks Learning Centers: Figure It Out. 2006. (J). bds. (978-0-9755252-4-1(7)) Evergreen Pr. of Brainerd, LLC.

Bowers, Linda, et al. No Glamour Language & Reasoning. 2003. (J). per. 41.95 (978-0-7606-0500-4(9)) LinguiSystems, Inc.

Brown, Robin. Practice Papers: Advanced Non-Verbal Reasoning. 2nd ed. (ENG., Illus.). 32p. (YA). pap. 6.99 (978-0-340-72686-0(5)) Hodder & Stoughton GBR. Dist: Trafalgar Square Publishing.

Collins UK. Letts 11+ Success - 11+ Practice Test Papers (Get Ahead) for the CEM Tests Inc. Audio Download. 2017. (Letts 11+ Success Ser.). (ENG.). 104p. (J). (gr. 4-7). pap. 14.99 (978-1-84419-897-9(9)) HarperCollins Pubs. Ltd. GBR. Dist: Independent Pubs. Group.

Collins 11+. Collins 11+ Practice - 11+ Verbal Reasoning Quick Practice Tests Age 9-10 (Year 5): for the 2023 CEM Tests. 2016. (Letts 11+ Success Ser.). (ENG.). 80p. (J). (gr. 4-5). pap. 11.95 (978-1-84419-891-7(X)) HarperCollins Pubs. Ltd. GBR. Dist: Independent Pubs. Group.

Gillham, Bill, et al. Essential Skills, 4 bks. (ENG., Illus.). 128p. (YA). pap. 15.99 (978-0-340-71583-3(9)) Hodder & Stoughton GBR. Dist: Trafalgar Square Publishing.

Head, Alison. Verbal Reasoning, Age 8-10: For 11+, Pre-Test & Independent School Exams Including CEM, GL & ISEB. 2016. (ENG.). 64p. pap., wbk. ed. 34.50 (978-1-4718-4931-2(7)) Hodder Education Group GBR. Dist: Trans-Atlantic Pubns., Inc.

Head, Alison & Pearse, Chris. Verbal Reasoning, Age 9-11. 2016. (ENG.). 64p. pap., wbk. ed. 34.50 (978-1-4718-4932-9(5)) Hodder Education Group GBR. Dist: Trans-Atlantic Pubns., Inc.

Letts KS2, Letts. Maths - Problem Solving & Reasoning Age 7-9 (Letts Wild About) 2015. (Letts Wild about Learning Ser.). (ENG.). 48p. (J). (gr. 2-4). pap. 8.95 (978-1-84419-788-0(3)) HarperCollins Pubs. Ltd. GBR. Dist: Independent Pubs. Group.

Letts 11+, Letts. 11+ Practice Test Papers. 2017. (Letts 11+ Success Ser.). (ENG.). 104p. (J). (gr. 4). pap. 15.99 (978-1-84419-896-2(0)) HarperCollins Pubs. Ltd. GBR. Dist: Independent Pubs. Group.

MacAllister, Carol L. The Wisdom Tree & the Red Swing: Thinking Outside the Box for Preteens. 2009. (Wisdom Tree & the Red Swing Ser.). (ENG.). 116p. (J). pap. 3.99 (978-0-9815818-4-2(6), 9780981581842) Take Charge Bks.

Primrose, Alison. Verbal Reasoning, Age 10-12. 2016. (ENG.). 64p. pap., wbk. ed. 34.50 (978-1-4718-4933-6(3)) Hodder Education Group GBR. Dist: Trans-Atlantic Pubns., Inc.

Rose, Simon. Evaluating Arguments about the Environment. 2018. (State Your Case Ser.). (Illus.). 48p. (J). (gr. 5-6). (978-0-7787-5080-2(9)) Crabtree Publishing Co.

Walch Publishing Staff. Daily Warm-Ups: Analogies. 2007. (gr. 9-12). tchr. ed., spiral bd. 18.99 (978-0-8251-6255-8(6)) Walch Education.

REBUSES

see Riddles

RECLAMATION OF LAND

Here are entered general works on reclamation, including drainage and irrigation.

see also Irrigation; Marshes; Sand

Bjornlund, Lydia D. Deforestation. 2009. (Compact Research Ser.). (YA). (gr. 7-12). 43.93 (978-1-60152-075-3(1)) ReferencePoint Pr., Inc.

Brezina, Corona. Disappearing Forests: Deforestation, Desertification, & Drought, 1 vol. 2009. (Extreme Environmental Threats Ser.). (ENG.). 64p. (gr. 6-6). (YA). lib. bdg. 37.13 (978-1-4358-5018-7(1), ddb2a70f-60bf-4884-9e48-e95e3fe4e952); (Illus.). (J). pap. 13.95 (978-1-4358-5374-4(1), d2bec441-07e6-41ac-a59f-afbc64d1e552) Rosen Publishing Group, Inc., The.

Linde, Barbara M. Deforestation & Desertification: Text Pairs. 2008. (Bridges/Navigators Ser.). (J). (gr. 6). 94.00 (978-1-4108-8432-9(5)) Benchmark Education Co.

RECLAMATION OF LAND—FICTION

Austin, Mike. Junkyard. Austin, Mike, illus. 2014. (ENG., Illus.). 40p. (J). (gr. -1-3). 16.99 (978-1-4424-5961-8(1), Beach Lane Bks.) Beach Lane Bks.

Ward, Helen. The Tin Forest. Anderson, Wayne, illus. 2003. (ENG.). 32p. (J). (gr. -1-2). 8.99 (978-0-14-250156-6(5), Puffin Books) Penguin Young Readers Group.

RECOMMENDED BOOKS

see Best Books

RECONSTRUCTION (U.S. HISTORY, 1865-1877)

Here are entered works dealing with reconstruction in the United States following the Civil War.

Anderson, Dale. The Aftermath of the Civil War, 1 vol. 2004. (World Almanac(r) Library of the Civil War Ser.). (ENG., Illus.). 48p. (gr. 5-8). pap. 15.05 (978-0-8368-5597-5(3), ad27f227-78f5-47db-a4a4-11d6eaec8003); lib. bdg. 33.67 (978-0-8368-5588-3(4), c777ffc3-916f-4e09-bf81-5fbda0f6625d) Stevens, Gareth Publishing LLLP. (Gareth Stevens Secondary Library).

—World Almanac Library of the Civil War, 10 vols. Incl. Aftermath of the Civil War. lib. bdg. 33.67 (978-0-8368-5588-3(4), c777ffc3-916f-4e09-bf81-5fbda0f6625d); Causes of the Civil War. lib. bdg. 33.67 (978-0-8368-5581-4(7), 88052b64-ee89-4168-9b03-c8645b27670f); Civil War at Sea. lib. bdg. 33.67 (978-0-8368-5585-2(X), abaa704c-54ab-437b-a508-a47da1d3dc87); Civil War in the East (1861-July 1863) lib. bdg. 33.67 (978-0-8368-5582-1(5), ea65b134-2894-4b4a-b659-255a776186b0); Civil War in the West (1861-July 1863) lib. bdg. 33.67 (978-0-8368-5583-8(3), a497de3e-669b-4027-92d0-df03b0280971); Home Fronts in the Civil War. lib. bdg. 33.67 (978-0-8368-5587-6(6), f82d4d42-0c19-4e83-844b-321427333a72); Union Victory (July 1863 - 1865) lib. bdg. 33.67 (978-0-8368-5584-5(1), e28734b4-0c65-4c17-9779-244cfe64b88f); (gr. 5-8). (World Almanac(r) Library of the Civil War Ser.). (ENG., Illus.). 48p. 2004. Set lib. bdg. 168.35 (978-0-8368-5580-7(9), 6d23f6f8-b267-4c3a-8417-931f1aeca97a, Gareth Stevens Secondary Library) Stevens, Gareth Publishing LLLP.

Baptiste, Tracey. The Civil War & Reconstruction Eras, 1 vol. 2015. (African American Experience: from Slavery to the Presidency Ser.). (ENG., Illus.). 80p. (J). (gr. 7-8). 35.47 (978-1-68048-039-9(1), e7f0de6d-1523-408b-9831-b566bcc6c36c, Britannica Educational Publishing) Rosen Publishing Group, Inc., The.

Baptiste, Tracey, ed. The Civil War & Reconstruction Eras, 4 vols. 2015. (African American Experience: from Slavery to the Presidency Ser.). (ENG.). 80p. (YA). (gr. 7-8). 70.94 (978-1-68048-040-5(5), 5493c455-171a-4df2-9371-9f612b36021a, Britannica Educational Publishing) Rosen Publishing Group, Inc., The.

Benson, Alana. Great Exit Projects on the Civil War & Reconstruction, 1 vol. 2019. (Great Social Studies Exit Projects Ser.). (ENG.). 64p. (gr. 5-5). 36.13 (978-1-4994-4033-1(2), 217db278-5ca4-4b7a-99f0-9c6d8d765678, Rosen Young Adult) Rosen Publishing Group, Inc., The.

Cooke, Tim. After the War, 1 vol. 2012. (American Civil War: the Right Answer Ser.). (ENG., Illus.). 48p. (J). (gr. 6-8). 34.60 (978-1-4339-7531-8(9), 4f59dc6e-b471-48da-9930-9fb5ab4b06ab); pap. 15.05 (978-1-4339-7532-5(7), f32f003b-b9ac-451e-aa04-226618ca243c) Stevens, Gareth Publishing LLLP. (Gareth Stevens Secondary Library).

Cosson, Jody. Civil War & Reconstruction: 1850-1877. 2007. (Presidents of the United States Ser.). (Illus.). (J). (gr. 4-7). 47p. lib. bdg. 29.05 (978-1-59036-743-8(X)); 48p. per. 10.95 (978-1-59036-744-5(8)) Weigl Pubs., Inc.

Crompton, Sam. Georgia During Reconstruction, 1 vol. 2017. (Spotlight on Georgia Ser.). (ENG.). 32p. (gr. 4-5). pap. 12.75 (978-1-5081-5981-0(5), fbc7b4e9-04bf-4b62-8cee-497d2366da5c, PowerKids Pr.) Rosen Publishing Group, Inc., The.

Dudley, William, ed. Reconstruction, 1 vol. 2003. (At Issue in History Ser.). (ENG., Illus.). 128p. (gr. 10-12). pap. 31.60 (978-0-7377-1357-2(7), b8b08bf2-1fbe-41da-8c2a-269b932e3037, Greenhaven Publishing) Greenhaven Publishing LLC.

Flanagan, Timothy. Reconstruction: A Primary Source History of the Struggle to Unite the North & South after the Civil War, 1 vol. 2004. (Primary Sources in American History Ser.). (ENG., Illus.). 64p. (J). (gr. 5-8). lib. bdg. 37.13 (978-1-4042-0177-4(7), 154ba385-b204-43ac-81c4-6fc934a58a2e) Rosen Publishing Group, Inc., The.

Gates Jr., Henry Louis & Bolden, Tonya. Dark Sky Rising: Reconstruction & the Dawn of Jim Crow (Scholastic Focus) 2019. (ENG., Illus.). 240p. (J). (gr. 4-7). 19.99 (978-1-338-26204-9(1), Scholastic Nonfiction) Scholastic, Inc.

Globe Fearon American History Vol. 1: Prehistory Through Reconstruction. 2003. (American History Ser.). 542p. (YA). (gr. 6-12). 50.95 (978-0-13-024400-0(7)) Globe Fearon Educational Publishing.

Goldstone, Lawrence. Unpunished Murder: Massacre at Colfax & the Quest for Justice (Scholastic Focus) (ENG.). 288p. (gr. 7). 2020. (YA). pap. 9.99 (978-1-338-23946-1(5)) 2018. (Illus.). (J). 17.99 (978-1-338-23945-4(7), Scholastic Nonfiction) Scholastic, Inc.

Greene, Meg & Malvasi, Meg Greene. Into the Land of Freedom: African Americans in Reconstruction. 2004. (People's History Ser.). (ENG., Illus.). 96p. (gr. 5-12). lib. bdg. 33.26 (978-0-8225-4690-0(6)) Lerner Publishing Group.

Grumet, Bridget Hall & Baker, Lawrence W. Primary Sources - Reconstruction Era. 2004. (Reconstruction Era Reference Library). (ENG., Illus.). 256p. (J). lib. bdg. 129.00 (978-0-7876-9219-3(0)) Cengage Gale.

Hakim, Joy. A History of US: Reconstructing America: 1865-1890 a History of US Book Seven. (History of US Ser.: 7). (ENG., Illus.). 208p. (gr. 4-7). 3rd rev. ed. 2006. 24.95 (978-0-19-518900-1(0))Bk. 7. 2nd rev. ed. 2007. per. 15.95 (978-0-19-532721-2(7)) Oxford Univ. Pr., Inc.

Hale, Sarah Elder, ed. Rebuilding a Nation: Picking up the Pieces. 2005. (ENG., Illus.). 48p. (J). (gr. 3-9). 17.95 (978-0-8126-7909-0(1)) Cobblestone Pr.

Howell, Brian. The US Civil War & Reconstruction. 2011. (Explorer Library: Language Arts Explorer Ser.). (ENG., Illus.). 32p. (gr. 4-8). lib. bdg. 32.07 (978-1-61080-201-7(2), 201178) Cherry Lake Publishing.

—The U.S. Civil War & Reconstruction. 2011. (Explorer Library: Language Arts Explorer Ser.). (ENG.). 32p. (gr. 4-8). pap. 14.21 (978-1-61080-289-5(6), 201212) Cherry Lake Publishing.

Howes, Kelly King & Baker, Lawrence W. Almanac, Reconstruction Era. 2004. (Reconstruction Era Reference Library). (ENG., Illus.). 272p. (J). lib. bdg. 129.00 (978-0-7876-9217-9(4), UXL) Cengage Gale.

Howse, Jennifer. Reconstruction. (Illus.). 48p. (J). 2013. (978-1-62127-194-9(3)) 2013. pap. (978-1-62127-200-7(1)) 2008. (gr. 5-8). pap. 10.95 (978-1-59036-879-4(7), 1290894) 2008. (gr. 5-8). lib. bdg. 29.05 (978-1-59036-878-7(9), 1290894) Weigl Pubs., Inc.

Kissock, Heather. Civil War & Reconstruction. 2016. (Illus.). 48p. (J). (978-1-5105-1280-1(2)) SmartBook Media, Inc.

Latta, Susan M. Reconstruction Era, 1 vol. 2014. (African-American History Ser.). (ENG.). 48p. (J). (gr. 4-8).

lib. bdg. 35.64 *(978-1-62403-147-2(1)*, 1175) ABDO Publishing Co.

Maloof, Torrey. Reconstruction: Freedom Delayed. rev. ed. 2017. (Social Studies: Informational Text Ser.). (ENG., Illus.). 32p. (gr. 4-8). pap. 11.99 *(978-1-4938-3806-6(7))* Teacher Created Materials, Inc.

Matuz, Roger & Baker, Lawrence W. Reconstruction Era: Biographies. 2004. (Reconstruction Era Reference Library). (ENG., Illus.). 272p. (J). lib. bdg. 129.00 *(978-0-7876-9218-6(2)*, UXL) Cengage Gale.

Miller, Reagan & Cocca, Lisa Colozza. Reconstruction & the Aftermath of the Civil War. 2011. (ENG.). 48p. (J). pap. *(978-0-7787-5358-2(1))*; lib. bdg. *(978-0-7787-5341-4(7))* Crabtree Publishing Co.

Nelson, Sheila. Americans Divided: The Civil War. 2006. (How America Became America Ser.). (Illus.). 96p. (YA). lib. bdg. 22.95 *(978-1-59084-908-8(6))* Mason Crest.

The New South & the Old West: 1866-1890. 2010. (ENG., Illus.). 136p. (gr. 5-8). 35.00 *(978-1-60413-354-7(6)*, P178885, Facts On File) Infobase Holdings, Inc.

Paris, Stephanie Herweck. Jonathan Clarkson Gibbs: Reconstruction Revolutionary. rev. ed. 2016. (Social Studies: Informational Text Ser.). (ENG.). 32p. (J). (gr. 4-8). pap. 11.99 *(978-1-4938-3540-9(8))* Teacher Created Materials, Inc.

Randolph, Joanne, ed. From Slaves to Soldiers, 1 vol. 2018. (Civil War & Reconstruction: Rebellion & Rebuilding Ser.). (ENG.). 32p. (gr. 4-5). 27.93 *(978-1-5383-4089-9(5)*, 670f1e41-6618-4ada-9e9e-4699604c1f83, PowerKids Pr.) Rosen Publishing Group, Inc., The.

The Reconstruction of the South after the Civil War in United States History, 1 vol. 2014. (In United States History Ser.). (ENG., Illus.). 96p. (gr. 5-6). 31.61 *(978-0-7660-6063-0(2)*, e470890b-4bd1-4e1b-afb4-65be4663df2f) Enslow Publishing, LLC.

Rodgers, Kelly. Civil War & Reconstruction in Florida. rev. ed. 2016. (Social Studies: Informational Text Ser.). (ENG.). 32p. (gr. 3-8). pap. 11.99 *(978-1-4938-3539-3(4))* Teacher Created Materials, Inc.

Ruggiero, Adriane. Reconstruction, 1 vol. 2007. (American Voices From Ser.). (ENG., Illus.). 160p. (gr. 6-6). lib. bdg. 41.21 *(978-0-7614-2168-9(8)*, 6d78edcc-3c8e-45eb-884e-028048c3a98a) Cavendish Square Publishing LLC.

Sebree, Chet'la & Ruggiero, Adriane. Historical Sources on Reconstruction, 1 vol. 2019. (America's Story Ser.). (ENG.). 144p. (gr. 8-8). pap. 22.16 *(978-1-5026-4083-3(X)*, d47c26db-0def-47df-b80b-1bd51d93cb2d) Cavendish Square Publishing LLC.

Stefoff, Rebecca. The Civil War & Reconstruction, 1863-1877, 1 vol. 2003. (North American Historical Atlases Ser.). (ENG., Illus.). 48p. (gr. 5-5). 32.64 *(978-0-7614-1347-9(2)*, 2e3d0af5-5fd6-47eb-aef0-579b0aaea21c) Cavendish Square Publishing LLC.

Streissguth, Tom. Perspectives on Reconstruction. 2018. (Perspectives on US History Ser.). (ENG., Illus.). 32p. (J). (gr. 3-6). 32.80 *(978-1-63235-403-7(9)*, 13725, 12-Story Library) Bookstaves, LLC.

Stroud, Bettye & Schomp, Virginia. The Reconstruction Era, 1 vol. 2007. (Drama of African-American History Ser.). (ENG., Illus.). 80p. (gr. 6-6). lib. bdg. 38.36 *(978-0-7614-2181-8(5)*, 563d4ded-5401-44f3-8d44-514783079efe) Cavendish Square Publishing LLC.

Sutherland, Jonathan. Civil War Victory & the Costly Aftermath. 2017. (Civil War Ser.: Vol. 5). (ENG., Illus.). 79p. (YA). (gr. 7-12). 24.95 *(978-1-4222-3886-8(5))* Mason Crest.

Swartz, Ellen. Reconstruction: Moving Toward Democracy: People of African Descent Define Freedom after the Civil War. 2007. (Illus.). 24p. (J). pap. *(978-1-929768-09-7(5))* R T A Pr.

Uhl, Xina M. & Flanagan, Timothy. A Primary Source Investigation of Reconstruction, 1 vol. 2018. (Uncovering American History Ser.). (ENG.). 64p. (gr. 6-6). pap. 13.95 *(978-1-5081-8405-8(4)*, b6716a0c-44ee-418b-b9fc-be349d9fb5a8, Rosen Reference) Rosen Publishing Group, Inc., The.

Wittman, Susan S. Reconstruction: Outcomes of the Civil War, 1 vol. 2014. (Story of the Civil War Ser.). (ENG., Illus.). 32p. (J). (gr. 3-6). pap. 7.95 *(978-1-4914-0728-8(X)*, 125978, Capstone Pr.) Capstone.

Ziff, Marsha. The Reconstruction of the South after the Civil War in United States History, 1 vol. 2014. (In United States History Ser.). (ENG., Illus.). 96p. (J). (gr. 5-6). pap. 13.88 *(978-0-7660-6064-7(0)*, 7360a8ce-c3af-4e4b-8c55-b90e0a670b72) Enslow Publishing, LLC.

RECONSTRUCTION (U.S. HISTORY, 1865-1877)—FICTION

Asim, Jabari. The Road to Freedom: A Story of the Reconstruction. 2004. 131p. (J). lib. bdg. 16.92 *(978-1-4242-0765-7(7))* Fitzgerald Bks.

Bolden, Tonya. Inventing Victoria. 2019. (ENG., Illus.). 272p. (YA). 17.99 *(978-1-68119-807-1(X)*, 900187338, Bloomsbury Young Adult) Bloomsbury Publishing USA.

LaFaye, A. Stella Stands Alone. 2010. (ENG.). 256p. (YA). (gr. 7). pap. 7.99 *(978-1-4169-8647-8(2)*, Simon & Schuster Bks. For Young Readers) Simon & Schuster Bks. For Young Readers.

Lyons, Kelly Starling. Ellen's Broom. Minter, Daniel, illus. 2012. (ENG.). 32p. (J). (gr. k-3). 17.99 *(978-0-399-25003-3(4)*, G.P. Putnam's Sons Books for Young Readers) Penguin Young Readers Group.

McMullan, Margaret. When I Crossed No-Bob. 2008. (ENG.). 224p. (J). (gr. 6-8). 22.44 *(978-0-618-71715-6(3))* Houghton Mifflin Harcourt Publishing Co.

Osborne, Mary Pope, et al. A Time to Dance: Virginia's Civil War Diary. 2003. (My America Ser.). (ENG.). 112p. (J). 12.95 *(978-0-439-44341-8(5))* Scholastic, Inc.

Westrick, Anne. Brotherhood. 2014. 384p. (J). (gr. 5). pap. 8.99 *(978-0-14-242237-3(1)*, Puffin Books) Penguin Young Readers Group.

RECORD PLAYERS

see Phonograph

RECREATION

Here are entered works on the psychological and social aspects of recreation and works on organized recreational projects.

see also Amusements; Games; Hobbies; Play; Playgrounds; Sports

Amery, Heather. What's Happening at the Seaside? Cartwright, Stephen, illus. rev. ed. 2006. (What's Happening Ser.). 16p. (J). (gr. -1-3). 5.99 *(978-0-7945-1290-3(9)*, Usborne) EDC Publishing.

Beard, Lina & Beard, Adelia B. The American Girl's Handy Book: Making the Most of Outdoor Fun. 2018. (Illus.). 488p. (J). (gr. 4-7). 19.95 *(978-1-4930-3679-0(3)*, Lyons Pr.) Globe Pequot Pr., The.

Benedetti, Debra. Season of Play. Teets, Ashley, illus. 2011. 32p. (J). *(978-0-929915-99-9(2))* Headline Bks., Inc.

Beylon, Cathy. At the Amusement Park. 2004. (Dover Coloring Bks.). (ENG., Illus.). 32p. (J). (gr. -1-2). pap. 2.95 *(978-0-486-43322-6(6))* Dover Pubns., Inc.

Braun, Eric. The Guys' Guide to Making the Outdoors More Awesome, 1 vol. 2014. (Guys' Guides). (ENG., Illus.). 32p. (J). (gr. 3-9). lib. bdg. 28.65 *(978-1-4765-3922-5(7)*, 123921, Capstone Pr.) Capstone.

Brennan, Stephen & Brennan, Lara. The Adventurous Girl's Handbook: For Ages 9 To 99. 2nd ed. 2011. (ENG., Illus.). 208p. (J). (gr. 2-5). pap. 12.95 *(978-1-61608-164-5(3)*, 608164) Skyhorse Publishing Co., Inc.

Butler, Erin K. Extreme Land Sports. 2017. (Sports to the Extreme Ser.). (ENG., Illus.). 32p. (J). (gr. 3-9). lib. bdg. 28.65 *(978-1-5157-7860-8(6)*, 135995, Capstone Pr.) Capstone.

Celebrations, 8 vols. 2016. (Celebrations Ser.). (ENG.). 00024p. (J). (gr. 1-1). 101.08 *(978-1-4994-2627-4(5)*, 9e9b55c1-8ecd-44b0-87d8-43fcb5a41176, PowerKids Pr.) Rosen Publishing Group, Inc., The.

Chissick, Michael. Ladybird's Remarkable Relaxation: How Children (And Frogs, Dogs, Flamingos & Dragons) Can Use Yoga Relaxation to Help Deal with Stress, Grief, Bullying & Lack of Confidence. 2013. (Illus.). 48p. 21.95 *(978-1-84819-146-4(4)*, 694213, Singing Dragon) Kingsley, Jessica Pubs. GBR. Dist: Hachette UK Distribution.

Corwin, Jeff. A Whale of a Time! 2010. (Jeff Corwin Ser.). 112p. (J). (gr. 1-3). 4.99 *(978-0-14-241646-4(0)*, Puffin) Penguin Publishing Group.

Cox, Catherine. Go-Carts, Catapults & Midnight Feasts: 101 Vintage Pastimes for Modern Kids. 2015. (ENG., Illus.). 224p. (J). (gr. k-5). pap. 24.95 *(978-0-7509-6429-6(4))* History Pr. Ltd.,The GBR. Dist: Independent Pubs. Group.

Dezé, Ulrika. Anytime Yoga: Fun & Easy Exercises for Concentration & Calm. Kroug, Simon, illus. 2019. 64p. (J). (gr. -1-2). 16.95 *(978-1-61180-439-3(6)*, Bala Kids) Shambhala Pubns., Inc.

Editors of Klutz. The Encyclopedia of Immaturity Volume 2, Vol. 2. Editors of Klutz, ed. 2009. (ENG., Illus.). 200p. (J). (gr. 3). 19.95 *(978-1-59174-689-8(2))* Klutz.

The Encyclopedia of Immaturity: How to Never Grow Up. 2007. (Illus.). 410p. (J). (gr. 3-7). 19.95 *(978-1-59174-427-6(X))* Klutz.

Fancy Friendship Bracelets. 2009. (Illus.). 60p. (J). (gr. 3). 19.95 *(978-1-59174-692-8(2))* Klutz.

Fuerst, Jeffrey B. Going Places: Lap Book. 2009. (My First Reader's Theater Set B Ser.). (J). 28.00 *(978-1-4108-8544-9(5))* Benchmark Education Co.

Gagliardi, Sue. Get Outside in Spring. 2019. (Get Outside Ser.). (ENG., Illus.). 32p. (J). (gr. 2-3). 31.35 *(978-1-64185-332-3(8)*, 1641853328, Focus Readers) North Star Editions.

Gates, Mariam. Breathe with Me: Using Breath to Feel Strong, Calm, & Happy. 2019. (ENG., Illus.). 32p. (J). 17.95 *(978-1-68364-030-1(6)*, 900220846) Sounds True, Inc.

George, Mike. You Can Relax & Avoid Stress, 1 vol. 2017. (Be Your Best Self Ser.). (ENG., Illus.). 158p. (gr. 9-9). 46.27 *(978-1-4994-6665-2(X)*, 13af2c7b-ba85-4bb0-8abf-616324476f9b, Rosen Young Adult) Rosen Publishing Group, Inc., The.

Glenn, Joshua & Larsen, Elizabeth Foy. Unbored: The Essential Field Guide to Serious Fun. Leone, Tony et al, illus. 2015. (ENG.). 352p. 29.00 *(978-1-60819-641-8(0)*, 325892) Bloomsbury Publishing USA.

—UNBORED Games: Serious Fun for Everyone. Leone, Tony, illus. 2014. (ENG.). 176p. pap. 16.00 *(978-1-62040-706-6(X)*, 260165) Bloomsbury Publishing USA.

Groenendyk, Doretta. Step Outside, 1 vol. 2013. (ENG., Illus.). 32p. (J). (gr. 1-3). pap. 19.95 *(978-1-927502-19-8(5)*, 7ee51e87-4999-4cf7-bdf6-012cd20928d0) Acorn Pr., The CAN. Dist: Baker & Taylor Publisher Services (BTPS).

Hand, Carol. Working in Parks & Recreation in Your Community, 1 vol. 2018. (Careers in Your Community Ser.). (ENG.). 80p. (gr. 7-7). 37.47 *(978-1-4994-6731-4(1)*, e643faf9-dc46-4b41-b931-5f16e657fcca, Rosen Young Adult) Rosen Publishing Group, Inc., The.

Hicks, Kelli. Zip Lines. 2009. (Illus.). 24p. (J). lib. bdg. 27.07 *(978-1-60694-359-5(6))* Rourke Educational Media.

Hip-Hop World [Capstone Sole Source]. 2010. (Hip-Hop World Ser.). 48p. lib. bdg. 122.60 *(978-1-4296-5866-9(5))* Capstone.

Honovich, Nancy. Ultimate Explorer Guide: Explore, Discover, & Create Your Own Adventures with Real National Geographic Explorers As Your Guides! 2017. 160p. (J). (gr. 3-7). pap. 14.99 *(978-1-4263-2709-4(9)*, National Geographic Kids) Disney Publishing Worldwide.

Hughes, Susan. Play Time. 2017. (ENG., Illus.). 14p. (J). (gr. -1). bds. 7.99 *(978-1-55451-951-4(9))* Annick Pr., Ltd. CAN. Dist: Publishers Group West (PGW).

I Like to Visit, 6 vols. 2004. (I Like to Visit Ser.). (ENG.). 24p. (gr. k-2). lib. bdg. 74.01 *(978-0-8368-4450-4(5)*, d7c6d06b-fb18-4d84-814a-1a861a0836d7, Weekly Reader Leveled Readers) Stevens, Gareth Publishing LLLP.

I Like to Visit (Me Gusta Visitar), 10 vols. 2004. (I Like to Visit / Me Gusta Visitar Ser.). (SPA & ENG.). 24p. (gr. k-2). lib. bdg. 123.35 *(978-0-8368-4594-5(3)*, 81f22fe4-948f-4f99-a88c-9622cffc13d7) Stevens, Gareth Publishing LLLP.

Kenney, Karen Latchana. Building a Roller Coaster. 2018. (Sequence Amazing Structures Ser.). (ENG.). 32p. (J). (gr. 2-5). pap. 9.99 *(978-1-68152-350-7(7)*, 15165) Amicus.

Lacey, Saskia. Surprising Things We Do for Fun. 2017. (Time for Kids Nonfiction Readers Ser.). lib. bdg. 22.10 *(978-0-606-40280-4(2))* Turtleback.

Lavelle, David. Collins Big Cat Phonics for Letters & Sounds - Get Set for Fun: Band 02B/Red B, Bd. 2B. 2018. (Collins Big Cat Phonics Ser.). (ENG.). 16p. (J). (gr. -1-k). pap. 6.99 *(978-0-00-825150-5(9))* HarperCollins Pubs. Ltd. GBR. Dist: Independent Pubs. Group.

Mableton, Barry & Ching, Jacqueline. Camping, 1 vol., 1. 2015. (Outdoor Living Ser.). (ENG.). 64p. (J). (gr. 6-6). 36.13 *(978-1-4994-6227-2(1)*, 4c99469d-53b9-443f-80a1-a3c48fdf4a7c, Rosen Young Adult) Rosen Publishing Group, Inc., The.

MacDonald, Margaret. Leisure in the Past. 2011. (Leam-Abouts Ser.). (Illus.). 16p. (J). pap. 7.95 *(978-1-59920-629-5(3))* Black Rabbit Bks.

Martin, Bobi. Theme Parks, 1 vol., 1. 2015. (Role-Playing for Fun & Profit Ser.). (ENG.). 48p. (J). (gr. 5-5). pap. 12.75 *(978-1-4994-3732-4(3)*, 3ac7b5a8-be19-48b0-8f74-0838b8c55451, Rosen Central) Rosen Publishing Group, Inc., The.

Mason, Paul. 25 Fun Things to Do with Your Friends & Family. Sassin, Eva, illus. 2019. (100 Fun Things to Do to Unplug Ser.). (ENG.). 32p. (J). (gr. 3-6). lib. bdg. 27.99 *(978-1-5415-0135-5(7)*, 13fa5f8b-946f-48db-a58f-06805f69a7e0, Hungry Tomato (r)) Lerner Publishing Group.

McConnell, Ruby. A Girl's Guide to the Wild: Be an Adventure-Seeking Outdoor Explorer! Grasseschi, Teresa, illus. 2019. (Her Guide to the Wild Ser.). 272p. (J). (gr. 4-7). pap. 18.99 *(978-1-63217-171-9(6)*, Little Bigfoot) Sasquatch Bks.

Myers, Edward. Let's Build a Playground. 2012. (ENG., Illus.). 48p. (J). (gr. 2-3). pap. 11.00 net. *(978-0-7652-0882-8(2)*, Modern Curriculum Pr.) Savvas Learning Co.

Omoth, Tyler. Busting Boredom in the Great Outdoors. 2017. (Boredom Busters Ser.). (ENG., Illus.). 32p. (J). (gr. 3-9). lib. bdg. 28.65 *(978-1-5157-4703-1(4)*, 134342, Capstone Pr.) Capstone.

Rice, Dona Herweck. Places to Go, 1 vol. 2nd rev. ed. 2013. (TIME for KIDS(r): Informational Text Ser.). (ENG., Illus.). 12p. (J). (gr. k-1). lib. bdg. 15.96 *(978-1-4807-1012-2(1))* Teacher Created Materials, Inc.

Rissman, Rebecca. Counting at the Park, 1 vol. 2012. (I Can Count! Ser.). (ENG.). 24p. (gr. -1-k). pap. 9.95 *(978-1-4329-6700-0(2)*, Heinemann) Capstone.

Rosen, Michael J. Balls! Round 2. Margeson, John, illus. 2008. (Darby Creek Exceptional Titles Ser.). (ENG.). 80p. (J). (gr. 4-8). 18.95 *(978-1-58196-066-2(2)*, Darby Creek) Lerner Publishing Group.

Rustad, Martha Elizabeth Hillman. Family Traditions. 2019. (What Makes a Family Ser.). (ENG., Illus.). 24p. (J). (gr. -1-2). pap. 6.95 *(978-1-9771-1050-3(9)*, 141126); lib. bdg. 27.32 *(978-1-9771-0907-1(1)*, 140509) Capstone. (Pebble).

Salzmann, Mary Elizabeth. Taking Time to Relax. 2004. (Healthy Habits Ser.). (ENG., Illus.). 24p. (J). (gr. k-3). lib. bdg. 24.21 *(978-1-59197-555-7(7)*, SandCastle) ABDO Publishing Co.

Scott, Steph & Akers, Katie. Let's Go Outside: Sticks & Stones - Nature Adventures, Games & Projects for Kids. 2015. (ENG., Illus.). 160p. (gr. -1-2). 12.95 *(978-1-84994-276-8(5)*, Batsford) Pavilion Bks. GBR. Dist: Penguin Random Hse. LLC.

Shava, Ryder. Camping with My Cousins, 1 vol., 1. 2015. (Rosen REAL Readers: Social Studies Nonfiction / Fiction: Myself, My Community, My World Ser.). (ENG.). 8p. (J). (gr. k-1). pap. 5.46 *(978-1-5081-1641-7(5)*, e1250961-920c-44a8-ae4f-d16c1e856ae6, Rosen Classroom) Rosen Publishing Group, Inc., The.

Simon, Mary Manz. My Picnic Basket: And How God Is Always Near. Fenimore, Kristina, illus. 2013. (ENG.). 14p. (J). (gr. -1-k). bds. 9.99 *(978-0-7847-3699-9(5)*, B&H Kids) B&H Publishing Group.

Stratton, Connor. We Play Outside. 2019. (Activities We Do Ser.). (ENG., Illus.). 16p. (J). (gr. k-1). pap. 7.95 *(978-1-64185-871-7(0)*, 1641858710); lib. bdg. 25.64 *(978-1-64185-802-1(8)*, 1641858028) North Star Editions. (Focus Readers).

Thomas, M. Summer at the Beach: Learning the EA Sound. 2009. (PowerPhonics Ser.). 24p. (gr. 1-1). 39.90 *(978-1-60851-472-4(2)*, PowerKids Pr.) Rosen Publishing Group, Inc., The.

Thomsen, Amanda. Backyard Adventure: Get Messy, Get Wet, Build Cool Things, & Have Tons of Wild Fun! 51 Free-Play Activities. 2019. (ENG., Illus.). 160p. (J). (gr. 1-5). pap. 16.95 *(978-1-61212-920-4(X)*, 622920) Storey Publishing, LLC.

Tomio, Jack & Tomio, Stacy. 101 Outdoor Adventures to Have. 2019. (Illus.). 312p. (J). (gr. 3-5). pap. 24.95 *(978-1-4930-4140-4(1)*, Falcon Guides) Globe Pequot Pr., The.

Tomio, Stacy & Keffer, Ken. The Kids' Outdoor Adventure Book: 448 Great Things to Do in Nature Before You Grow Up. 2013. (ENG., Illus.). 224p. (J). (gr. -1-4). pap. 18.95 *(978-0-7627-8352-6(4)*, Falcon Guides) Globe Pequot Pr., The.

Usilton, Theresa A. Let's Go team: Cheer, Dance, & March, 12 vols., Set. 2003. (Let's Go Team Ser.). (Illus.). 64p. (YA). (gr. 5-18). lib. bdg. *(978-1-59084-529-5(3))* Mason Crest.

Verdick, Elizabeth. Calm-Down Time. Heinlen, Marieka, illus. 2010. (Toddler Tools(r) Ser.). (ENG.). 26p. (J). (gr. -1). bds. 9.99 *(978-1-57542-316-6(2)*, 23166) Free Spirit Publishing Inc.

Walsh, Liza Gardner. Muddy Boots: Outdoor Activities for Children. 2015. (Illus.). 136p. (J). (gr. -1-5). 19.95 *(978-1-60893-370-9(9)*, 1388618) Down East Bks.

Webster, Dawn & Yost, Emily. Yellowstone for Kids: A Kid's Guide to Yellowstone National Park. 2016. (Illus.). (J). pap. *(978-0-934948-40-1(2))* Yellowstone Forever.

Winner, Cherie. Ranger Rick Kids' Guide to Camping: All You Need to Know about Having Fun in the Outdoors. 2018. (Ranger Rick Kids' Guides). (ENG., Illus.). 96p. (J). (gr. 3-5). lib. bdg. 34.65 *(978-1-942875-73-4(8)*, 62b2cd83-5ea3-4da3-a780-20b4c42fa428, Walter Foster Jr) Quarto Publishing Group USA.

RECREATIONAL VEHICLES

see Automobiles—Trailers

RECREATIONS, MATHEMATICAL

see Mathematical Recreations

RECREATIONS, SCIENTIFIC

see Scientific Recreations

RECTORS

see Clergy

RECYCLING (WASTE, ETC.)

Here are entered works on the processing of waste paper, cans, bottles, etc.

Allman, Toney. Recycled Tires. 2009. (Great Idea Ser.). (ENG., Illus.). 48p. (J). (gr. 4-6). lib. bdg. 26.60 *(978-1-59953-197-7(6))* Norwood Hse. Pr.

Aloian, Molly. Going Green at School. 2013. (ENG., Illus.). 24p. (J). *(978-0-7787-0264-1(2))*; pap. *(978-0-7787-0283-2(9))* Crabtree Publishing Co.

ALVARADO, Claudia. The plastic Bottle. 2010. 32p. pap. 27.20 *(978-1-4461-2250-1(6))* Lulu Pr., Inc.

Arnold, Tedd. Fly Guy Presents: Garbage & Recycling (Scholastic Reader, Level 2) Arnold, Tedd, illus. 2019. (Scholastic Reader, Level 2 Ser.: 12). (ENG., Illus.). 32p. (J). (gr. k-2). pap. 4.99 *(978-1-338-21719-3(4))* Scholastic, Inc.

Asriningtyas, Visi. What Can We Do with Garbage? Sampah Bisa Diapakan Ya? 2009. (IND & ENG., Illus.). 40p. pap. 16.99 *(978-1-4389-9470-3(2))* AuthorHouse.

Barker, Geoff. How Recycling Works, 1 vol. 2013. (EcoWorks Ser.). 32p. (J). (gr. 3-4). (ENG.). 29.27 *(978-1-4339-9564-4(6)*, 2110b37e-6073-4b9e-8fbd-65319758a7ad); (ENG.). pap. 11.50 *(978-1-4339-9565-1(4)*, 8ae0c5b9-6772-4dc2-abdc-6d85eeadc08a); pap. 63.00 *(978-1-4339-9566-8(2))* Stevens, Gareth Publishing LLLP.

Barnham, Kay. Recycle. 2007. (Environment Action Ser.). (ENG., Illus.). 32p. (J). (gr. 3-7). pap. *(978-0-7787-3669-1(5))* Crabtree Publishing Co.

Barraclough, Sue. Recycling Materials. 2007. (Making a Difference Ser.). (Illus.). 30p. (J). (gr. -1-3). lib. bdg. 27.10 *(978-1-59771-108-1(X))* Sea-To-Sea Pubns.

Berg, Shannon. E-Waste in Guiyu, China. 2019. (21st Century Disasters Ser.). (ENG., Illus.). 32p. (J). (gr. 2-3). pap. 9.95 *(978-1-64185-807-6(9)*, 1641858079); lib. bdg. 31.35 *(978-1-64185-738-3(2)*, 1641857382) North Star Editions. (Focus Readers).

Bethea, Nikole Brooks. Engineering an Awesome Recycling Center with Max Axiom, Super Scientist. Pop Art Studios, illus. 2013. (Graphic Science & Engineering in Action Ser.). (ENG.). 32p. (J). (gr. 3-4). pap. 49.60 *(978-1-62065-700-3(7)*, 19299); pap. 8.10 *(978-1-62065-699-0(X)*, 121697) Capstone. (Capstone Pr.).

Blake, Susannah. Crafts for Accessorizing That Look, 1 vol. 2013. (Eco Chic Ser.). (ENG.). 32p. (gr. 4-6). lib. bdg. 26.61 *(978-0-7660-4313-8(4)*, 73c37536-5e8d-4ccd-a5a8-c3fa9ad56b45) Enslow Publishing, LLC.

Boekhoff, P. M. & Kallen, Stuart A. Recycling. 2004. (Our Environment Ser.). (ENG., Illus.). 48p. (J). (gr. 4-7). 29.15 *(978-0-7377-1517-0(0)*, Kidhaven) Cengage Gale.

Bolte, Mari. Eco Gifts: Upcycled Gifts You Can Make. 2015. (Make It, Gift It Ser.). (ENG., Illus.). 32p. (J). (gr. 3-9). lib. bdg. 28.65 *(978-1-4914-5202-8(1)*, 128784, Capstone Pr.) Capstone.

Bone, Emily & Pratt, Leonie. Recycling Things to Make & Do. 2010. (Activity Book Ser.). 32p. (J). pap. 6.99 *(978-0-7945-2675-7(6)*, Usborne) EDC Publishing.

Brager, Bruce L. How You Can Use Waste Energy to Heat & Light Your Home. 2009. (Tell Your Parents Ser.). (J). (gr. 4-7). 29.95 *(978-1-58415-765-6(8))* Mitchell Lane Pubs.

Bullard, Lisa. Choose to Reuse. Thomas, Wes, illus. 2011. (Planet Protectors Ser.). pap. 39.62 *(978-0-7613-8651-3(3)*, Millbrook Pr.) Lerner Publishing Group.

—Choose to Reuse. Thomas, John Wes, illus. 2011. (Cloverleaf Books (tm) — Planet Protectors Ser.). (ENG.). 24p. (J). (gr. k-2). pap. 8.99 *(978-0-7613-8511-0(8)*, 46b2df66-afc6-4341-b149-19b3ba72bcee); lib. bdg. 25.32 *(978-0-7613-6104-6(9)*, 7460b944-2710-4d73-ba72-50ac36bcb0a4) Lerner Publishing Group. (Millbrook Pr.).

—Go Green by Recycling. Thomas, John Wes, illus. 2018. (Go Green (Early Bird Stories (tm)) Ser.). (ENG.). 24p. (J). (gr. k-2). lib. bdg. 29.32 *(978-1-5415-2013-4(0)*, eb9f9ccd-35ad-47b3-964f-71c8a460fe93, Lerner Pubns.) Lerner Publishing Group.

—Go Green by Reusing. Thomas, John Wes, illus. 2018. (Go Green (Early Bird Stories (tm)) Ser.). (ENG.). 24p. (J). (gr. k-2). pap. 9.99 *(978-1-5415-2715-7(1)*, 73fb9bbb-9577-48b2-98bf-bd1a6a7b1ef1); lib. bdg. 29.32 *(978-1-5415-2012-7(2)*, 4afe41af-bed3-4f77-b0c9-f5058fc8270a, Lerner Pubns.) Lerner Publishing Group.

—Rally for Recycling. Thomas, Wes, illus. 2011. (Planet Protectors Ser.). pap. 39.62 *(978-0-7613-8656-8(4)*, Millbrook Pr.) Lerner Publishing Group.

—Rally for Recycling. Thomas, John Wes, illus. 2011. (Cloverleaf Books (tm) — Planet Protectors Ser.). (ENG.). 24p. (J). (gr. k-2). pap. 8.99 *(978-0-7613-8516-5(9)*, 60001ba1-22ea-4901-b682-7a725ab9d5ee, Millbrook Pr.) Lerner Publishing Group.

Burton, Margie, et al. Reduce, Reuse, & Recycle. 2011. (Early Connections Ser.). (J). *(978-1-61672-503-7(6))* Benchmark Education Co.

Byers, Ann. Reuse It: The History of Modern Recycling, 1 vol. 2017. (History of Conservation: Preserving Our Planet Ser.). (ENG.). 112p. (YA). (gr. 9-9). 44.50 *(978-1-5026-3126-8(1)*, bf3c7cb1-8367-4442-a37f-3b78ac17b691) Cavendish Square Publishing LLC.

Capstone Press. Green Crafts. 2010. (Green Crafts Ser.). (ENG.). 32p. lib. bdg. 159.90 *(978-1-4296-5940-6(8)*, Capstone Pr.) Capstone.

Chapman, Gillian & Robson, Pam. Making Art with Fabric, 1 vol. 2007. (Everyday Art Ser.). (ENG., Illus.). 32p. (YA). (gr. 4-5). lib. bdg. 30.27 *(978-1-4042-3722-3(4)*, ca0213ad-3cc8-4352-8c48-311dc2023a40) Rosen Publishing Group, Inc., The.

—Making Art with Packaging, 1 vol. 2007. (Everyday Art Ser.). (ENG., Illus.). 32p. (YA). (gr. 4-5). lib. bdg. 30.27 *(978-1-4042-3724-7(0)*, c5617d61-ea66-406a-8526-604a929e9e5c) Rosen Publishing Group, Inc., The.

—Making Art with Rocks & Shells, 1 vol. 2007. (Everyday Art Ser.). (ENG., Illus.). 32p. (YA). (gr. 4-5). lib. bdg. 30.27 (978-1-4042-3727-8(5), f6d3d70e-1e6c-496f-8a86-1008851b3321) Rosen Publishing Group, Inc., The.

—Making Art with Sand & Earth, 1 vol. 2007. (Everyday Art Ser.). (ENG., Illus.). 32p. (YA). (gr. 4-5). lib. bdg. 30.27 (978-1-4042-3723-0(2), 9a877ec4-7e47-44cb-83e4-3cf395ff69d4) Rosen Publishing Group, Inc., The.

—Making Art with Wood, 1 vol. 2007. (Everyday Art Ser.). (ENG., Illus.). 32p. (YA). (gr. 4-5). lib. bdg. 30.27 (978-1-4042-3726-1(7), 96ad20ac-e562-40d6-a4e9-0860f5d558e8) Rosen Publishing Group, Inc., The.

Clarke, Zoë. Collins Big Cat Phonics for Letters & Sounds - Tip It: Band 01A/Pink A, Bd. 1A. Roberts, Ley Honor, illus. 2018. (Collins Big Cat Phonics Ser.). (ENG.). 16p. (J). (gr. -1-k). pap. 6.99 (978-0-00-825132-1(0)) HarperCollins Pubs. Ltd. GBR. Dist: Independent Pubs. Group.

Clausen-Grace, Nicki. What Can You Make? 2006. (Science about Me Ser.). (Illus.). 8p. (J). (gr. 3-7). pap. 5.95 (978-1-59515-932-8(0)) Rourke Educational Media.

Close, Edward. What Do We Do with Trash?, 1 vol. 2012. (Discovery Education: the Environment Ser.). (ENG., Illus.). 32p. (J). (gr. 4-5). pap. 11.00 (978-1-4488-7982-3(5), 7f4f345b-ff5d-4cb1-92db-b5b6b6e0fa31); lib. bdg. 28.93 (978-1-4488-7894-9(2), ce3664a3-45d9-4098-ad80-30cac4e3d6e5) Rosen Publishing Group, Inc., The. (PowerKids Pr.).

Constable, Lee. How to Save the Whole Stinkin' Planet: A Garbological Adventure. Hart, James, III, illus. 2019. 256p. (J). (gr. 2-4). 18.99 (978-1-76089-026-1(X), Puffin) Penguin Random Hse. AUS. Dist: Independent Pubs. Group.

David, Sarah B. Reducing Your Carbon Footprint at Home. 2009. (Your Carbon Footprint Ser.). 48p. (gr. 5-5). 53.00 (978-1-60854-910-8(0), Rosen Reference) Rosen Publishing Group, Inc., The.

Davidson, Simon & Gardner, Julia. What Is Waste? Inquiry Box. 2011. (PYP Springboard Ser.). (ENG., Illus.). (gr. -1 — 1). 375.00 (978-1-4441-4733-9(1)) Hodder Education Group GBR. Dist: Trans-Atlantic Pubns., Inc.

D'Cruz, Anna-Marie. Make Your Own Masks, 1 vol. (Do It Yourself Projects! Ser.). (ENG.). 24p. (J). (gr. 4-4). 2009. pap. 10.40 (978-1-4358-2923-7(9), 4cea656d-709e-4634-a2f1-8719a50128e6) 2008. lib. bdg. 28.93 (978-1-4358-2853-7(4), 76b8b4e5-d971-4384-ab94-a474720fca70) Rosen Publishing Group, Inc., The. (PowerKids Pr.).

—Make Your Own Puppets, 1 vol. 2009. (Do It Yourself Projects! Ser.). (ENG.). 24p. (J). (gr. 4-4). pap. 10.40 (978-1-4358-2919-0(0), 27ed0efb-78a2-42bc-8eae-2f558abd25e3, PowerKids Pr.) Rosen Publishing Group, Inc., The.

—Make Your Own Purses & Bags, 1 vol. (Do It Yourself Projects! Ser.). (ENG.). 24p. (J). (gr. 4-4). 2009. pap. 10.40 (978-1-4358-2929-9(8), c52b84c6-270f-46b3-b9fa-eca83e2edc6f) 2008. lib. bdg. 28.93 (978-1-4358-2856-8(9), bd03513d-1a30-4ae1-8e61-0596e809bf59) Rosen Publishing Group, Inc., The. (PowerKids Pr.).

—Make Your Own Shoes & Slippers, 1 vol. (Do It Yourself Projects! Ser.). (ENG.). 24p. (J). (gr. 4-4). 2009. pap. 10.40 (978-1-4358-2921-3(2), 49a5439d-98e2-400c-94d0-9938763f9a8a) 2008. lib. bdg. 28.93 (978-1-4358-2852-0(6), 59480fee-3224-4ddc-8650-f5e37c3c25b2) Rosen Publishing Group, Inc., The. (PowerKids Pr.).

Devera, Czeena. Waste & Recycling Collector. Bane, Jeff, illus. 2018. (Mi Mini Biografía (My Itty-Bitty Bio): My Early Library). (ENG.). 24p. (J). (gr. k-1). pap. 12.79 (978-1-5341-0818-9(1), 210636); lib. bdg. 30.64 (978-1-5341-0719-9(3), 210635) Cherry Lake Publishing.

Dutton, Michael. Amazing Carbon Footprint Facts. 2010. (Dover Nature Coloring Book Ser.). (ENG., Illus.). 32p. (J). (gr. 2-5). pap. 3.99 (978-0-486-47552-3(2)) Dover Pubns., Inc.

Enz, Tammy. Awesome Craft Stick Science. 2016. (Recycled Science Ser.). (ENG., Illus.). 32p. (J). (gr. 3-9). lib. bdg. 28.65 (978-1-5157-0861-2(6), 132164, Capstone Pr.) Capstone.

—Repurpose It: Invent New Uses for Old Stuff. 2012. (Invent It Ser.). (ENG.). 32p. (gr. 3-4). pap. 47.70 (978-1-4296-8457-6(7), Capstone Pr.); (J). pap. 8.10 (978-1-4296-7983-1(2), 118315) Capstone.

Enz, Tammy & Wheeler-Toppen, Jodi. Recycled Science: Bring Out Your Science Genius with Soda Bottles, Potato Chip Bags, & More Unexpected Stuff. 2016. (Recycled Science Ser.). (ENG., Illus.). 112p. (J). (gr. 3-9). pap., pap., pap. 9.95 (978-1-62370-697-5(1), 132172, Capstone Young Readers) Capstone.

Faulkner, Nicholas & Peterson, Judy Monroe. Biodegradability & You, 1 vol. 2018. (How Our Choices Impact Earth Ser.). (ENG.). 64p. (gr. 6-6). 36.13 (978-1-5081-8141-5(1), 55b75ed8-96c7-4747-84b3-be6a054e0e12, Rosen Reference) Rosen Publishing Group, Inc., The.

Faulkner, Nicholas & Watson, Stephanie. Recycling & You, 1 vol. 2018. (How Our Choices Impact Earth Ser.). (ENG.). 64p. (gr. 6-6). 36.13 (978-1-5081-8153-8(5), b0fbd43e-f3f6-4988-b552-31ff6bdaedb1, Rosen Reference) Rosen Publishing Group, Inc., The.

Friday, Megan. Green Crafts: Become an Earth-Friendly Craft Star, Step by Easy Step! 2012. (Craft Star Ser.). (Illus.). 64p. (gr. 2-4). 32.80 (978-1-936309-38-2(6)) Quarto Publishing Group USA.

Friedman, Lauri S. Garbage & Recycling. 2009. (Introducing Issues with Opposing Viewpoints Ser.). (ENG., Illus.). 144p. (J). (gr. 7-10). 36.95 (978-0-7377-4337-1(9), Greenhaven Pr., Inc.) Cengage Gale.

Friedman, Lauri S., ed. Recycling, 1 vol. 2010. (Writing the Critical Essay: an Opposing Viewpoints Guide Ser.). (ENG., Illus.). 112p. (gr. 7-12). 39.93 (978-0-7377-4803-1(6), 49554b2a-98e6-4f09-bb5e-5ddf7fc263c6, Greenhaven Publishing) Greenhaven Publishing LLC.

Fulcher, Roz. Science Around the House: Simple Projects Using Household Recyclables. 2010. (Dover Science for Kids Ser.). (ENG., Illus.). 80p. (J). (gr. 3-5). pap. 6.99 (978-0-486-47645-2(6), 476456) Dover Pubns., Inc.

Fun Fabrics. 2013. (From Trash to Treasure Ser.). 32p. (J). (gr. 3-6). pap. 70.50 (978-1-4777-1363-1(8), PowerKids Pr.) Rosen Publishing Group, Inc., The.

Fyvie, Erica. Trash Revolution: Breaking the Waste Cycle. Slavin, Bill, illus. 2018. (ENG.). 64p. (J). (gr. 3-7). 18.99 (978-1-77138-078-2(0)) Kids Can Pr., Ltd. CAN. Dist: Hachette Bk. Group.

Gagne, Tammy. Recycle Every Day. 2013. (Kids Save the Earth Ser.). (ENG.). 24p. (J). (gr. 1-4). lib. bdg. 27.10 (978-1-60753-520-1(3), 16323) Amicus.

Ganeri, Anita. From Rags to Bags Gold Band. 2016. (Cambridge Reading Adventures Ser.). (ENG., Illus.). 16p. pap. 7.95 (978-1-316-50086-6(1)) Cambridge Univ. Pr.

Gardner, Robert. Recycle: Green Science Projects for a Sustainable Planet, 1 vol. 2011. (Team Green Science Projects Ser.). (ENG., Illus.). 128p. (gr. 5-6). lib. bdg. 35.93 (978-0-7660-3648-2(0), 2564c932-c6ef-4ff1-b24c-493dc36685df) Enslow Publishing, LLC.

Gay, Kathlyn. Buried: Too Much Garbage, 1 vol. 2015. (End of Life As We Know It Ser.). (ENG., Illus.). 144p. (gr. 7-8). lib. bdg. 38.93 (978-0-7660-7276-3(2), f2daf463-6264-42e7-acd7-51b5f9d913e5) Enslow Publishing, LLC.

Goldsmith, Mike. Recycling. 2009. (Now We Know About... Ser.). (ENG., Illus.). 24p. (J). (gr. k-3). pap. (978-0-7787-4739-0(5)); lib. bdg. (978-0-7787-4722-2(0)) Crabtree Publishing Co.

Goldstein, Monica. Children Go Green: Bus trip to Little Stars Elementary. 2010. 23p. (J). pap. 14.95 (978-1-4327-2528-0(9)) Outskirts Pr., Inc.

Gordon, Jo. Reciclar (Recycling) (SPA., Illus.). 32p. (J). 10.95 (978-84-348-3988-5(1)) SM Ediciones ESP. Dist: AIMS International Bks., Inc.

Green Crafts. 2010. (Green Crafts Ser.). (ENG.). 32p. (J). (gr. 3-4). 171.90 (978-1-4296-5460-9(0), 170574) Capstone.

Green, Jen. Garbage & Litter. 2010. (Reduce, Reuse, Recycle! Ser.). 32p. (J). (gr. 1-5). E-Book 50.50 (978-1-4488-0365-1(9)); (ENG.). (J). (gr. 2-3). pap. 11.60 (978-1-61532-243-5(4), bffe139e-d0ac-43cb-b5f9-af9c8174121e, PowerKids Pr.); (ENG., Illus.). (YA). (gr. 2-3). lib. bdg. 30.27 (978-1-61532-234-3(5), 27747281-54b2-485e-8854-383075690a30) Rosen Publishing Group, Inc., The.

—Reducing & Recycling Waste, 1 vol. 2011. (Sherlock Bones Looks at the Environment Ser.). (ENG., Illus.). 32p. (YA). (gr. 5-5). lib. bdg. 29.93 (978-1-61533-382-0(7), 4e69f55f-db19-4080-8921-b19887b80dc6, Windmill Bks.) Rosen Publishing Group, Inc., The.

—Why Should I Recycle? Gordon, Mike, illus. 2005. (Why Should I? Bks.). (ENG.). 32p. (J). (gr. -1-2). pap. 8.99 (978-0-7641-3155-4(9)) Sourcebooks, Inc.

Green, Robert. From Waste to Energy. 2009. (21st Century Skills Library: Power Up! Ser.). (ENG., Illus.). 32p. (gr. 4-8). lib. bdg. 32.07 (978-1-60279-509-9(6), 200324) Cherry Lake Publishing.

Grier, Paul. Recycling Paper. 2013. (InfoMax Readers Ser.). (ENG.). 24p. (J). (gr. 2-3). pap. 49.50 (978-1-4777-2275-6(0)); (Illus.). pap. 8.25 (978-1-4777-2274-9(2), c838cc42-3f62-4c33-8921-91f4bd7a7471) Rosen Publishing Group, Inc., The. (Rosen Classroom).

Haerens, Margaret, ed. Garbage & Recycling, 1 vol. 2011. (Opposing Viewpoints Ser.). (ENG., Illus.). 248p. (gr. 10-12). 50.43 (978-0-7377-5428-5(1), ad45d16e-ac7d-44e9-be00-670d6df9d722, Greenhaven Publishing) Greenhaven Publishing LLC.

Heos, Bridget. Follow That Bottle! A Plastic Recycling Journey. Westgate, Alex, illus. 2016. (Keeping Cities Clean Ser.). (ENG.). 24p. (J). (gr. 1-4). lib. bdg. 20.95 (978-1-60753-964-3(0), 15652) Amicus.

—Follow That Garbage! A Journey to the Landfill. Westgate, Alex, illus. 2016. (Keeping Cities Clean Ser.). (ENG.). 24p. (J). (gr. 1-4). lib. bdg. 20.95 (978-1-60753-963-6(2), 15653) Amicus.

—Follow That Tap Water! A Journey down the Drain. Westgate, Alex, illus. 2016. (Keeping Cities Clean Ser.). (ENG.). 24p. (J). (gr. 1-4). lib. bdg. 20.95 (978-1-60753-965-0(9), 15655) Amicus.

Hewitt, Sally. Reduce & Reuse. 2008. (Rise & Shine Ser.). (ENG., Illus.). 32p. (J). (gr. 3-7). pap. (978-0-7787-4102-2(8)) Crabtree Publishing Co.

—Waste & Recycling. 2008. (Rise & Shine Ser.). (ENG., Illus.). 32p. (J). (gr. 3-7). pap. (978-0-7787-4105-3(2)); lib. bdg. (978-0-7787-4098-8(6)) Crabtree Publishing Co.

Hock, Peggy. Our Earth: Making Less Trash (Scholastic News Nonfiction Readers: Conservation) 2008. (Scholastic News Nonfiction Readers Ser.). (ENG.). 24p. (J). (gr. 1-2). pap. 6.95 (978-0-531-20434-4(0), Children's Pr.) Scholastic Library Publishing.

Holland, Gini. Paper Crafts, 1 vol. 2013. (From Trash to Treasure Ser.). (ENG.). 32p. (J). (gr. 4-5). 30.17 (978-1-4777-1282-5(8), 29b9f470-98b5-4a2c-bc86-95a3ac3fdd24); pap. 12.75 (978-1-4777-1358-7(1), a17f7cd2-6e67-4c37-a154-0ec8171f7bea) Rosen Publishing Group, Inc., The. (PowerKids Pr.).

Hunter, Rebecca. Waste & Recycling. 2012. (Eco Alert! Ser.). (ENG., Illus.). 32p. (J). (gr. 4-6). lib. bdg. 28.50 (978-1-59771-299-6(X)) Sea-To-Sea Pubns.

Icanberry, Mark. LooLeDo. 96p. Bk. 1. 2010. (Illus.). 12.95 (978-1-893327-12-2(4))Bk. 2. 2011. 14.95 (978-1-893327-11-5(6))Bk. 3. 2011. 14.95 (978-1-893327-10-8(8)) Look, Learn & Do Pubns.

Ikids Staff. Why Do We Recycle? Science Made Simple! Pérez, Sara Rojo, illus. 2009. (ENG.). 22p. (J). (gr. -1-1). 9.99 (978-1-58476-935-4(1)) Innovative Kids.

Inskipp, Carol. Reducing & Recycling Waste, 1 vol. 2004. (Improving Our Environment Ser.). (ENG., Illus.). 32p. (gr. 3-5). lib. bdg. 28.67 (978-0-8368-4429-0(7), cac96568-0bcc-4c19-805a-c628b53b5a9f, Gareth Stevens Learning Library) Stevens, Gareth Publishing LLLP.

Jackson, Steve. How Is Paper Recycled?, 1 vol. 2013. (Rosen Readers Ser.). (ENG.). 24p. (J). (gr. 2-2). pap. 8.25 (978-1-4777-2254-1(8), 13cb4f51-30c1-4b62-8946-c40ac39ad017); pap. 49.50 (978-1-4777-2255-8(6)) Rosen Publishing Group, Inc., The. (Rosen Classroom).

James, Lincoln. Where Does the Garbage Go?, 1 vol. 2012. (Everyday Mysteries Ser.). (ENG., Illus.). 24p. (J). (gr. 2-2). pap. 9.15 (978-1-4339-6327-8(2), 4d4c12d6-f6bc-43f4-a0bb-a821e55e0e15); lib. bdg. 25.27 (978-1-4339-6325-4(6), d46122a9-067d-4e1a-a83f-914427034513) Stevens, Gareth Publishing LLLP.

Jewelry. 2013. (From Trash to Treasure Ser.). 32p. (J). (gr. 3-6). pap. 70.50 (978-1-4777-1361-7(1), PowerKids Pr.) Rosen Publishing Group, Inc., The.

Jones, Jen. Cool Crafts with Flowers, Leaves, & Twigs: Green Projects for Resourceful Kids, 1 vol. 2010. (Green Crafts Ser.). (ENG.). 32p. (J). (gr. 3-9). lib. bdg. 28.65 (978-1-4296-4766-3(3), 103297) Capstone.

Kemarskaya, Oksana. Planet Earth Projects. 2011. (Dover Science for Kids Ser.). (ENG., Illus.). 64p. (J). (gr. 3-5). pap. 6.99 (978-0-486-47923-1(4), 479234) Dover Pubns., Inc.

Kings, Gary & Ginger, Richard. Funky Junk: Recycle Rubbish into Art! Green, Barry, illus. 2012. (Dover Children's Activity Bks.). (ENG.). 64p. (J). (gr. 3-5). pap. 9.99 (978-0-486-49022-9(X), 49022X) Dover Pubns., Inc.

Kington, Emily. Rad Recycled Art. 2019. (Wild Art Projects Ser.). (ENG., Illus.). 32p. (J). (gr. 3-6). lib. bdg. 27.99 (978-1-5415-0129-4(2), 9f22b12e-e1ac-4bea-a898-772041e481bd, Hungry Tomato (r)) Lerner Publishing Group.

Kishel, Ann-Marie. Recycle. 2006. (First Step Nonfiction — Conservation Ser.). (ENG., Illus.). 8p. (J). (gr. k-2). pap. 5.99 (978-0-8225-5676-3(6), 793f98bd-41f0-45b7-8576-df74cab7207b) Lerner Publishing Group.

—Reduce. 2006. (First Step Nonfiction — Conservation Ser.). (ENG., Illus.). 8p. (J). (gr. k-2). pap. 5.99 (978-0-8225-5677-0(4), c5620798-90b6-4bdc-aca4-5694856834b9) Lerner Publishing Group.

Kondonassis, Yolanda. Our House Is Round: A Kid's Book about Why Protecting Our Earth Matters. Brush, Joan, illus. 2012. (ENG.). 48p. (J). (gr. -1-k). 16.95 (978-1-61608-588-9(6), 608588, Sky Pony Pr.) Skyhorse Publishing Co., Inc.

Kutner, Laura, et al. The Soda Bottle School: A True Story of Recycling, Teamwork, & One Crazy Idea, 1 vol. 2016. (ENG., Illus.). 32p. (J). (gr. 1-7). pap. 9.95 (978-0-88448-372-4(X), 884372) Tilbury Hse. Pubs.

Labrecque, Ellen. Recycling & Waste. 2017. (21st Century Skills Library: Global Citizens: Environmentalism Ser.). (ENG., Illus.). 32p. (J). (gr. 4-7). lib. bdg. 32.07 (978-1-63472-871-3(8), 209910) Cherry Lake Publishing.

Lanz, Helen. Reduce, Reuse, Recycle. 2012. (Go Green Ser.). (ENG., Illus.). (gr. 3-6). lib. bdg. 28.50 (978-1-59771-303-0(1)) Sea-To-Sea Pubns.

Lawrence, Ellen. Garbage Galore. 2014. (Science Slam: Green World, Clean World Ser.). 24p. (J). (gr. -1-3). lib. bdg. 26.99 (978-1-62724-102-1(7)) Bearport Publishing Co., Inc.

Lepetit, Angie. Trash Magic: A Book about Recycling a Plastic Bottle, 1 vol. 2013. (Earth Matters Ser.). (ENG.). 32p. (J). (gr. -1-2). pap. 8.10 (978-1-62065-743-0(0), 121727); (gr. -1-2). lib. bdg. 27.99 (978-1-62065-049-3(5), 120744); (gr. 1-2). pap. 48.60 (978-1-62065-744-7(9), 19325, Capstone Pr.) Capstone.

Lindeen, Mary. Reduce, Reuse, Recycle. 2017. (Beginning-To-Read Ser.). (ENG.). 32p. (J). (gr. k-2). pap. 13.26 (978-1-68404-095-7(7)); (Illus.). 22.60 (978-1-59953-876-1(8)) Norwood Hse. Pr.

Llewellyn, Claire. Let's Recycle. 2005. (Illus.). 32p. (YA). (gr. 1-18). lib. bdg. 27.10 (978-1-932333-22-0(3)) Chrysalis Education.

Llimós, Anna & Llimós, Anna. Easy Earth-Friendly Crafts in 5 Steps, 1 vol. 2008. (Easy Crafts in 5 Steps Ser.). (ENG., Illus.). 32p. (gr. 3-3). pap. 10.35 (978-0-7660-3761-8(4), 1b90d364-028d-4157-9ff1-bf3468bb8552, Enslow Elementary) Enslow Publishing, LLC.

Lombardo, Jennifer. Should Plastic Bags Be Banned?, 1 vol. 2019. (Points of View Ser.). (ENG.). 24p. (gr. 3-3). lib. bdg. 26.23 (978-1-5345-3194-9(7), 81c015e3-499e-42eb-873a-acb5ed6fd790, KidHaven Publishing) Greenhaven Publishing LLC.

Lord, Michelle. Nature Recycles - How about You?, 1 vol. Morrison, Cathy, illus. 2013. (ENG.). 32p. (J). (gr. -1-4). 17.95 (978-1-60718-615-1(2)); pap. 9.95 (978-1-60718-627-4(6)) Arbordale Publishing.

—Nature Recycles - How about You? (Spanish), 1 vol. Morrison, Cathy, illus. 2013. (SPA & ENG.). 32p. (J). (gr. -1-4). 17.95 (978-1-60718-711-0(6)) Arbordale Publishing.

MacDonald, Margaret. How Can You Re-Use an Egg Carton? 2012. (Level D Ser.). (ENG., Illus.). 16p. (J). (gr. k-2). pap. 7.95 (978-1-927136-34-8(2), 19411) RiverStream Publishing.

MacGregor, Cynthia. Recycling a Can. 2009. (Reading Room Collection 2 Ser.). 24p. (gr. 3-4). 42.50 (978-1-60851-984-2(8), PowerKids Pr.) Rosen Publishing Group, Inc., The.

Maloof, Torrey. We Recycle, 1 vol. rev. ed. 2014. (Science: Informational Text Ser.). (ENG., Illus.). 24p. (gr. 1-2). pap. 9.99 (978-1-4807-4573-5(1)) Teacher Created Materials, Inc.

Malue, Jenna. Recycling Plastic: Understand Place Value, 1 vol. 2014. (Math Masters: Number & Operations in Base Ten Ser.). (ENG., Illus.). 24p. (J). (gr. 2-2). 25.27 (978-1-4777-6427-5(5), 6cacfd0c-4026-462f-acd8-f3d5ad0a19dc); pap. 8.25 (978-1-4777-4651-6(X), c66434b2-cbd6-4407-aef6-31e2ef3b6079) Rosen Publishing Group, Inc., The. (Rosen Classroom).

Mancini, Candice L., ed. Garbage & Recycling, 1 vol. 2010. (Global Viewpoints Ser.). (ENG.). 232p. (gr. 10-12). 47.83 (978-0-7377-5081-2(2), 4c03ee71-c4aa-4dd5-a178-7478dd372abf); (Illus.). pap. 32.70 (978-0-7377-5082-9(0), 74b4e7ef-c6eb-4025-a5d1-badbc71917d7) Greenhaven Publishing LLC. (Greenhaven Publishing).

Martin, Laura C. Recycled Crafts Box: Sock Puppets, Cardboard Castles, Bottle Bugs & 37 More Earth-Friendly Projects & Activities You Can Create. 2004. (ENG., Illus.). 96p. (J). (gr. 3-7). pap. 10.95 (978-1-58017-522-7(8), 67522) Storey Publishing, LLC.

McClintock Miller, Shannon & Hoena, Blake. A Recycled-Art Mission. Brown, Alan, illus. 2019. (Adventures in Makerspace Ser.). (ENG.). 32p. (J). (gr. 3-5). lib. bdg. 30.65 (978-1-4965-7949-2(6), 139758, Stone Arch Bks.) Capstone.

McMullen, Gemma. Recycling Materials, 1 vol. 2016. (Environmental Issues Ser.). (ENG.). 24p. (J). (gr. 2-3). pap. 9.25 (978-1-5345-2049-3(X), 560dcab6-79a1-4707-b1cd-2824cf828bb8); lib. bdg. 26.23 (978-1-5345-2051-6(1), a357ba9a-77df-4862-b6f3-5be2f2931855) Greenhaven Publishing LLC. (KidHaven Publishing).

Meissner, David. Where Does Your Garbage Go? 2011. (Early Connections Ser.). (J). (978-1-61672-608-9(3)) Benchmark Education Co.

Meredith, Susan. Why Should I Recycle? 2010. (What's Happening Ser.). 48p. (J). pap. 6.99 (978-0-7945-2785-3(X), Usborne) EDC Publishing.

Metz, Lorijo. What Can We Do about Trash & Recycling?, 1 vol. 2009. (Protecting Our Planet Ser.). (ENG., Illus.). 24p. (gr. 2-3). (J). pap. 9.25 (978-1-4358-2483-6(0), f5cab69c-03c3-4f44-9173-ef5128423d15, PowerKids Pr.); (YA). lib. bdg. 26.27 (978-1-4042-8082-3(0), 90ca251e-699c-4cc9-809d-b21c8e4d01e3) Rosen Publishing Group, Inc., The.

Miller, Heather. Nifty Thrifty Art Crafts, 1 vol. 2007. (Nifty Thrifty Crafts for Kids Ser.). (ENG., Illus.). 32p. (gr. 3-3). lib. bdg. 26.60 (978-0-7660-2780-0(5), 50f16a6f-3063-4c40-8704-ee3283935999, Enslow Elementary) Enslow Publishing, LLC.

Milner, Sara. A Trip to the Recycling Center, 1 vol. 2016. (PowerKids Readers: My Community Ser.). (ENG.). 24p. (J). (gr. k-k). pap. 9.25 (978-1-4994-2778-3(6), 5497a3d4-36ab-4b58-ad45-09cdd8754906, PowerKids Pr.) Rosen Publishing Group, Inc., The.

Minden, Cecilia. Kids Can Clean up Trash. 2010. (21st Century Basic Skills Library: Kids Can Ser.). (ENG., Illus.). 24p. (gr. k-3). lib. bdg. 26.35 (978-1-60279-870-0(2), 200606) Cherry Lake Publishing.

—Kids Can Recycle. 2010. (21st Century Basic Skills Library: Kids Can Ser.). (ENG., Illus.). 24p. (gr. k-3). lib. bdg. 26.35 (978-1-60279-867-0(2), 200600) Cherry Lake Publishing.

—Kids Can Reuse. 2010. (21st Century Basic Skills Library: Kids Can Ser.). (ENG., Illus.). 24p. (gr. k-3). lib. bdg. 26.35 (978-1-60279-868-7(0), 200602) Cherry Lake Publishing.

—Save the Planet: Reduce, Reuse, & Recycle. 2010. (Explorer Library: Language Arts Explorer Ser.). (ENG.). 32p. (gr. 4-8). pap. 14.21 (978-1-60279-671-3(8), 200918) Cherry Lake Publishing.

—Save the Planet: Reduce, Reuse, & Recycle. 2010. (Explorer Library: Language Arts Explorer Ser.). (ENG., Illus.). 32p. (gr. 4-8). lib. bdg. 32.07 (978-1-60279-662-1(9), 200355) Cherry Lake Publishing.

Mooney, Carla. Recycling. rev. ed. 2014. (Matters of Opinion Ser.). (ENG.). 64p. (J). (gr. 4-6). pap. 14.60 (978-1-60357-583-6(9)); (Illus.). lib. bdg. 27.93 (978-1-59953-603-3(X)) Norwood Hse. Pr.

Moore, Phillip. Where Does Used Paper Go? 2012. (Level E Ser.). (ENG., Illus.). 16p. (J). (gr. k-2). pap. 7.95 (978-1-927136-54-6(7), 19446) RiverStream Publishing.

Morgan, Sally. Old Clothes. 2007. (Dealing with Waste/Watts Ser.). (Illus.). 30p. (J). (gr. 4-7). lib. bdg. 28.50 (978-1-59920-011-8(2)) Black Rabbit Bks.

Morlock, Rachael. Where Does Scrap Metal Go? Sharing & Reusing, 1 vol. 2017. (Computer Science for the Real World Ser.). (ENG.). 24p. (J). (gr. 4-5). pap. (978-1-5081-3754-2(4), 51e68569-9307-4350-a6e0-16a7d600501d, Rosen Classroom) Rosen Publishing Group, Inc., The.

Morlock, Rachael, contrib. by. Where Does Scrap Metal Go? Sharing & Reusing, 1 vol. 2017. (Computer Kids: Powered by Computational Thinking Ser.). (ENG.). 24p. (J). (gr. 4-5). 25.27 (978-1-5383-2448-6(2), b542dc1f-1a42-41c5-b5fa-0d0a45ac3475, PowerKids Pr.) Rosen Publishing Group, Inc., The.

Moser, Elise. What Milly Did: The Remarkable Pioneer of Plastics Recycling, 1 vol. Ritchie, Scot, illus. 2016. (ENG.). 48p. (J). (gr. 3-6). pap. 9.95 (978-1-55498-893-8(4)) Groundwood Bks. CAN. Dist: Publishers Group West (PGW).

National Geographic Learning. World Windows 3 (Science): Taking Care of Earth: Content Literacy, Nonfiction Reading, Language & Literacy. 2011. (World Windows Ser.). (ENG., Illus.). 16p. (J). stu. ed. 10.95 (978-1-133-56615-1(4)) Cengage Heinle.

Orme, Helen. Garbage & Recycling. 2008. (Earth in Danger Ser.). (Illus.). 32p. (YA). (gr. 3-6). lib. bdg. 25.27 (978-1-59716-726-0(6), 1284325) Bearport Publishing Co., Inc.

Owen, Ruth. Fun Fabrics, 1 vol. 2013. (From Trash to Treasure Ser.). (ENG.). 32p. (J). (gr. 4-5). 30.17 (978-1-4777-1284-9(4), c05bc913-03ac-41ae-887f-66fa3d3d9a9c); pap. 12.75 (978-1-4777-1362-4(X), 43755e96-9de7-45b4-af19-c0676ccd38f6) Rosen Publishing Group, Inc., The. (PowerKids Pr.).

—Gifts. 2013. (From Trash to Treasure Ser.). (Illus.). 32p. (J). (gr. 3-6). pap. 70.50 (978-1-4777-1369-3(7)); (ENG., (gr. 4-5). 30.17 (978-1-4777-1287-0(9), 3abbcf31-a3b4-4ef5-a8c4-45235151a013); (ENG., (gr. 4-5). pap. 12.75 (978-1-4777-1368-6(9), d232b95b-e015-424a-b489-cbe3ec7a6130) Rosen Publishing Group, Inc., The. (PowerKids Pr.).

—Jewelry, 1 vol. 2013. (From Trash to Treasure Ser.). (ENG.). 32p. (J). (gr. 4-5). 30.17 (978-1-4777-1283-2(6), aecbd09a-ed4b-4dca-bca3-d1ed27433eff); pap. 12.75 (978-1-4777-1360-0(3), 7c2a7eb6-5339-462e-ac51-539cb811f27a) Rosen Publishing Group, Inc., The. (PowerKids Pr.).

—Nature Crafts. 2013. (From Trash to Treasure Ser.). 32p. (J). (gr. 3-6). pap. 70.50 (978-1-4777-1365-5(4)); (ENG.). (gr. 4-5). 30.17 (978-1-4777-1285-6(2), 94f62422-cd01-46b5-a483-ca39230ac2fe); (ENG.). (gr. 4-5). pap. 12.75 (978-1-4777-1364-8(6), a055ab57-6fb5-4be3-b8ca-8606387b3fc4) Rosen Publishing Group, Inc., The. (PowerKids Pr.).

—Paper Crafts. 2013. (From Trash to Treasure Ser.). 32p. (J). (gr. 3-6). pap. 70.50 *(978-1-4777-1359-4(X)*, PowerKids Pr.) Rosen Publishing Group, Inc., The.

Parks, Peggy J. Garbage & Recycling. 2008. (Ripped from the Headlines Ser.). (YA). (gr. 7-12). 23.95 *(978-1-60217-023-0(1))* Erickson Pr.

—Garbage & Recycling. 2010. (Compact Research Ser.). (YA). (gr. 7-12). 41.27 *(978-1-60152-121-7(9))* ReferencePoint Pr., Inc.

Paul, Miranda. One Plastic Bag: Isatou Ceesay & the Recycling Women of the Gambia. Zunon, Elizabeth, illus. 2015. (ENG.). 32p. (J). (gr. k-3). lib. bdg. 19.99 *(978-1-4677-1608-6(1)*, 3ec140d3-02bb-43c0-9289-c7820c301191, Millbrook Pr.) Lerner Publishing Group.

Persad, Sabbithry. Operation: Reuse It! Reduce, Reuse, Recycle. Campbell, Jenny, illus. 2011. (Garbology Kids Ser.: 2). (ENG.). 40p. (J). (gr. k-2). pap. 8.95 *(978-0-9812439-1-7(6))* Firewater Media Group.

Pohl, Kathleen. What Happens at a Recycling Center?, 1 vol. 2006. (Where People Work Ser.). (ENG., Illus.). 24p. (gr. k-2). pap. 9.15 *(978-0-8368-6895-1(1)*, 896dff2a-40fb-4155-aa15-30a42a9bf7f5); lib. bdg. 24.67 *(978-0-8368-6888-3(9)*, 6151e4e0-3791-4d52-a2e0-7ab5310b07b0) Stevens, Gareth Publishing LLLP. (Weekly Reader Leveled Readers).

—What Happens at a Recycling Center? / ¿Qué Pasa en un Centro de Reciclaje?, 1 vol. 2006. (Where People Work / ¿dónde Trabaja la Gente? Ser.). (Illus.). 24p. (gr. k-2). (ENG & SPA.). (J). lib. bdg. 24.67 *(978-0-8368-7389-4(0)*, 5847d46b-7bb1-4569-b21f-0d6ff7315193); (SPA & ENG., pap. 9.15 *(978-0-8368-7396-2(3)*, 4a25acbb-fe55-4121-87c5-90159d513326) Stevens, Gareth Publishing LLLP. (Weekly Reader Leveled Readers).

Puri, Devi. Recycling, Reusing, & Conserving, 1 vol. 2016. (Global Guardians Ser.). (ENG.). 24p. (J). (gr. 3-3). pap. 9.25 *(978-1-4994-2755-4(7)*, 5ca271c9-cbc3-4e75-85dd-70bae0f4cd5b, PowerKids Pr.) Rosen Publishing Group, Inc., The.

Rabe, Tish. How to Help the Earth-By the Lorax. Ruiz, Aristides et al, illus. 2012. (Step into Reading: Step 3 Ser.). (ENG.). 48p. (J). (gr. k-2). lib. bdg. 16.19 *(978-0-375-96977-5(2))* Random Hse. Bks. for Young Readers.

—How to Help the Earth-By the Lorax. 2012. (Step into Reading Level 3 Ser.). lib. bdg. 13.55 *(978-0-606-23848-9(4))* Turtleback.

—How to Help the Earth-By the Lorax (Dr. Seuss) 2012. (Step into Reading Ser.). (ENG., Illus.). 48p. (J). (gr. k-3). pap. 5.99 *(978-0-375-86977-8(8)*, Random Hse. Bks. for Young Readers) Random Hse. Children's Bks.

Rau, Dana Meachen. Crafting with Recyclables. Petelinsek, Kathleen, illus. 2013. (How-To Library). (ENG.). 32p. (J). (gr. 3-6). 32.07 *(978-1-62431-146-8(6)*, 202904); pap. 14.21 *(978-1-62431-278-6(0)*, 202906) Cherry Lake Publishing.

—Crafting with Recyclables: Even More Projects. Petelinsek, Kathleen, illus. 2016. (How-To Library). (ENG.). 32p. (J). (gr. 3-6). lib. bdg. 32.07 *(978-1-63471-419-8(9)*, 208455) Cherry Lake Publishing.

Reilly, Kathleen M. Planet Earth: Finding Balance on the Blue Marble with Environmental Science Activities for Kids. Casteel, Tom, illus. 2019. (Build It Yourself Ser.). (ENG.). 128p. (J). (gr. 4-6). 22.95 *(978-1-61930-740-7(5)*, 33ec5fae-afee-4647-816d-addb4ac676f1); pap. 17.95 *(978-1-61930-743-8(X)*, 45ddd69d-b67c-4b41-90ff-5575fd96d227) Nomad Pr.

Reynolds, Alison. Let's Use It Again. Hopgood, Andrew, illus. 2009. (Save Our Planet! Ser.). 12p. (J). (gr. -1-3). bds. 11.40 *(978-1-60754-415-9(6))* Windmill Bks.

Rhatigan, Joe. Get a Job at the Landfill. 2016. (Bright Futures Press: Get a Job Ser.). (ENG., Illus.). 32p. (J). (gr. 4-6). 32.07 *(978-1-63471-905-6(0)*, 208941) Cherry Lake Publishing.

Riachi, Ghassan Diab & Mitchell, Anna B. L. I. B. B. Y. The Green Dog. RJI Publishing, ed. Ritzmann, Mary B., illus. 2011.Tr. of L. I. B. B. Y. , el Perro Verde. 32p. (J). mass mkt. 9.95 *(978-1-885184-11-5(5))* RJI Publishing.

Rice, Dona Herweck. Too Much Trash!, 1 vol. rev. ed. 2014. (Science: Informational Text Ser.). (ENG., Illus.). 24p. (gr. -1-1). pap. 9.99 *(978-1-4807-4534-6(0))* Teacher Created Materials, Inc.

Riley, Karen. Agarranderas Plasticas y Otras Cosas: Plastic Rings & Other Things. 2003. (ENG & SPA., Illus.). 16p. (J). (gr. 2-5). pap. 4.50 *(978-0-9708135-2-7(X))* S.C.R.A.P. Gallery.

Rissman, Rebecca. Reducing, Reusing, & Recycling Waste. 2018. (Putting the Planet First Ser.). (Illus.). 32p. (J). (gr. 4-4). *(978-0-7787-5031-4(0))* Crabtree Publishing Co.

Rivera, Andrea. Recycling. 2016. (Our Renewable Earth Ser.). (ENG., Illus.). 24p. (J). (gr. -1-2). lib. bdg. 31.36 *(978-1-68079-940-8(1)*, 24184, Abdo Zoom-Launch) ABDO Publishing Co.

Roca, Nuria. The Three R's: Reuse, Reduce, Recycle. Curto, Rosa M., illus. 2007. (What Do You Know about? Bks.). 36p. (J). (gr. -1-1). pap. 7.99 *(978-0-7641-3581-1(3))* Sourcebooks, Inc.

Rodger, Ellen. Recycling Waste, 1 vol. 2009. (Saving Our World Ser.). (ENG.). 32p. (gr. 4-4). lib. bdg. 31.21 *(978-0-7614-3222-7(1)*, 2ce76b38-1c57-469b-a542-1f5754d7322a) Cavendish Square Publishing LLC.

Ross, Kathy. Earth-Friendly Crafts: Clever Ways to Reuse Everyday Items. Malépart, Céline, illus. 2011. (ENG.). 48p. (gr. 2-5). pap. 7.95 *(978-0-7613-7409-1(4)*, Millbrook Pr.) Lerner Publishing Group.

Ross, Michael Elsohn. Re-Cycles. Moore, Gustav, illus. 2003. (Cycles Ser.). (ENG.). 32p. (J). (gr. 2-4). pap. 7.99 *(978-0-7613-1949-8(2)*, 560a2c58-773d-454d-a23b-ba871ef9e1d2, First Avenue Editions) Lerner Publishing Group.

Rustad, Martha E. H. I Can Reduce Waste. 2019. (Helping the Environment Ser.). (ENG., Illus.). 24p. (J). (gr. -1-2). lib. bdg. 27.32 *(978-1-9771-0312-3(X)*, 139313, Capstone Pr.) Capstone.

Sévigny, Eric, illus. Caillou: As Good As New. 2012. (Ecology Club Ser.). (ENG.). 24p. (J). (gr. -1-1). pap. 5.99 *(978-2-89450-832-9(8))* Caillouet, Gerry.

Shea, John M. Where Does the Recycling Go?, 1 vol. 2012. (Everyday Mysteries Ser.). (ENG., Illus.). 24p. (J). (gr. 2-2). 25.27 *(978-1-4339-6333-9(7)*, e300e315-c160-46d4-9967-9fbdeb65869f); pap. 9.15 *(978-1-4339-6335-3(3)*, 75b80f61-341c-46cb-b78b-3556f4fcef4e) Stevens, Gareth Publishing LLLP.

Shores, Erika L. How Garbage Gets from Trash Cans to Landfills. 2016. (Here to There Ser.). (ENG., Illus.). 24p. (J). (gr. -1-2). lib. bdg. 27.32 *(978-1-4914-8433-3(0)*, 130862, Capstone Pr.) Capstone.

Sirrine, Carol & Jones, Jennifer. Re-Craft: Unique Projects That Look Great (and Save the Planet) 2011. (Craft It Yourself Ser.). (ENG.). 112p. (J). (gr. 3-9). 12.95 *(978-1-4296-6637-4(4)*, 115769, Capstone Young Readers) Capstone.

Solway, Andrew. Waste Disposal. 2009. (World at Risk Ser.). (ENG.). 48p. (J). (gr. 5-9). 34.25 *(978-1-59920-380-5(4)*, 19399, Smart Apple Media) Black Rabbit Bks.

Spilsbury, Louise. Projects with Recycling & Reusing, 1 vol. 2014. (Make & Learn Ser.). (ENG.). 32p. (J). (gr. 4-4). lib. bdg. 29.27 *(978-1-4777-7169-3(7)*, f71a0a4a-5c66-49d3-8f89-e31533249cd0, PowerKids Pr.) Rosen Publishing Group, Inc., The.

—Waste & Recycling Challenges. 2009. (Illus.). 48p. (J). 70.50 *(978-1-4358-5487-1(X)*, Rosen Reference); (ENG., (gr. 5-5). pap. 12.75 *(978-1-4358-5486-4(1)*, 25f3ffa9-c7f9-4330-bcde-21e0c9967f81, Rosen Reference); (ENG., (gr. 5-5). lib. bdg. 34.47 *(978-1-4358-5355-3(5)*, 7e370fac-d619-48e6-8ec4-957f881bfe7b) Rosen Publishing Group, Inc., The.

Staff, Gareth Editorial Staff. Recyclables, 1 vol. 2004. (Let's Create! Ser.). (ENG., Illus.). 32p. (gr. 2-4). lib. bdg. 28.67 *(978-0-8368-4018-6(6)*, ce2d891e-a539-466e-acaa-32f0f4856108, Gareth Stevens Learning Library) Stevens, Gareth Publishing LLLP.

Stamper, Judith Bauer. Sam Helps Recycle. 2010. (J). *(978-1-60617-138-7(0))* Teaching Strategies, LLC.

Stewart, Sue. Oxford Bookworms Factfiles: Recycling: Level 3: 1000-Word Vocabulary. 3rd ed. 2008. (ENG., Illus.). 80p. 11.00 *(978-0-19-423389-7(8))* Oxford Univ. Pr., Inc.

Sundance/Newbridge LLC Staff. Where Does All the Garbage Go? 2007. (Early Science Ser.). (gr. k-3). 18.95 *(978-1-4007-6260-6(X))*; pap. 6.10 *(978-1-4007-6256-9(1))* Sundance/Newbridge Educational Publishing.

Turnbull, Stephanie. Trash & Recycling. 2006. (Beginners Science Ser.). (Illus.). 32p. (J). (gr. 4-7). lib. bdg. 12.99 *(978-1-58086-948-5(3)*, Usborne) EDC Publishing.

—Trash & Recycling. Fox, Christyan, illus. 2006. (Beginners Science: Level 2 Ser.). 32p. (J). (gr. 1-3). 4.99 *(978-0-7945-1400-6(6)*, Usborne) EDC Publishing.

Ventura, Marne. Amazing Recycled Projects You Can Create. 2015. (Imagine It, Build It Ser.). (ENG., Illus.). 32p. (J). (gr. 3-9). lib. bdg. 28.65 *(978-1-4914-4292-0(1)*, 128685, Capstone Pr.) Capstone.

Walker, Kate. Food & Garden Waste, 1 vol. Vanzet, Gaston, illus. 2011. (Recycling Ser.). (ENG.). 32p. (J). (gr. 1-1). 31.21 *(978-1-60870-129-2(8)*, b1ade1b9-57dc-4221-a899-164e143400f2) Cavendish Square Publishing LLC.

Watson, Stephanie. Making Good Choices about Recycling & Reuse. 2009. (J). 77.70 *(978-1-4358-5607-3(4)*, Rosen Reference); (ENG.). 64p. (YA). (gr. 6-6). pap. 13.95 *(978-1-4358-5606-6(6)*, b7aebf9a-55e7-45e5-81db-cb9ec8392e72, Rosen Reference); (ENG., Illus.). 64p. (YA). (gr. 6-6). lib. bdg. 37.13 *(978-1-4358-5312-6(1)*, daa45e5f-85c2-4435-854b-f137897b0622) Rosen Publishing Group, Inc., The.

Weber, Rebecca. Time to Recycle. 2011. (Earth & Space Science Ser.). (ENG.). 24p. (J). (gr. k-1). pap. 43.74 *(978-1-4296-7145-3(9)*, 16714, Capstone Pr.) Capstone.

Weitzman, Elizabeth. 10 Cosas Que Puedes Hacer para Reducir, Reciclar y Reutilizar (Rookie Star: Make a Difference) 2017. (Rookie Star Ser.). (SPA., Illus.). 32p. (J). (gr. 2-3). pap. 5.95 *(978-1-338-18781-6(3)*, Children's Pr.) Scholastic Library Publishing.

—10 Cosas Que Puedes Hacer para Reducir, Reciclar y Reutilizar (Rookie Star: Make a Difference) (Library Edition) 2017. (Rookie Star Ser.). (SPA., Illus.). 32p. (J). (gr. 2-3). lib. bdg. 25.00 *(978-0-531-22860-9(6)*, Children's Pr.) Scholastic Library Publishing.

—10 Things You Can Do to Reduce, Reuse, Recycle. 2016. (Rookie Star — Make a Difference Ser.). (ENG., Illus.). 32p. (J). lib. bdg. 25.00 *(978-0-531-22654-4(9)*, Children's Pr.) Scholastic Library Publishing.

Wheeler-Toppen, Jodi. Amazing Cardboard Tube Science. 2016. (Recycled Science Ser.). (ENG., Illus.). 32p. (J). (gr. 3-9). lib. bdg. 28.65 *(978-1-5157-0860-5(8)*, 132162, Capstone Pr.) Capstone.

Whittaker, Helen. Waste: Information & Projects to Reduce Your Environmental Footprint, 1 vol. Porcellato, Nives & Craig, Andrew, illus. 2012. (Living Green Ser.). (ENG.). 32p. (gr. 4-4). 31.21 *(978-1-60870-577-1(3)*, 86ddb392-c97a-407f-b301-050e6bd51f84) Cavendish Square Publishing LLC.

Wilcox, Charlotte. Earth-Friendly Waste Management. 2009. pap. 58.95 *(978-0-7613-4691-3(0))* 2008. (Illus.). 72p. (YA). (gr. 4-7). lib. bdg. 30.60 *(978-0-8225-7560-3(4))* Lerner Publishing Group.

—Recycling. 2008. pap. 52.95 *(978-0-8225-9329-4(7))* 2007. (ENG., Illus.). 48p. (gr. 4-8). lib. bdg. 27.93 *(978-0-8225-6768-4(7))* Lerner Publishing Group.

Wilder, Nellie. Taking Food to Go. rev. ed. 2019. (Smithsonian: Informational Text Ser.). (ENG., Illus.). 20p. (J). (gr. k-1). 7.99 *(978-1-4938-6634-2(6))* Teacher Created Materials, Inc.

Williams, Nancy Noel. Don't Lose It, Reuse It. 2010. *(978-1-60617-134-9(8))* Teaching Strategies, LLC.

Williams, Zachary & Snyder, Jane. Cleaning up the Park: Learning to Count by Fives, 1 vol. 2010. (Math for the REAL World Ser.). (ENG.). 12p. (gr. 1-2). pap. 5.90 *(978-0-8239-8892-1(9)*, 96df70c3-fcda-4835-ad6a-1ec8dc30fa74, Rosen Classroom) Rosen Publishing Group, Inc., The.

Winnick, Nick. Reduce Waste. 2010. (Being Green Ser.). (Illus.). 32p. (YA). (gr. 3-6). lib. bdg. 27.13 *(978-1-61690-100-4(4))*; (J). (gr. 4-6). pap. 12.95 *(978-1-61690-101-1(2))* Weigl Pubs., Inc.

Young, Clare. Explorar y crear. 2012. (SPA.). 128p. (gr. 13-13). pap. 20.99 *(978-84-261-3887-3(X))* Juventud, Editorial ESP. Dist: Lectorum Pubns., Inc.

Your Carbon Footprint, 12 vols., Set. Incl. On the Move: Green Transportation. Furgang, Kathy & Furgang, Adam. lib. bdg. 34.47 *(978-1-4042-1773-7(8)*, 4350af81-a9f6-4345-845b-09e5923144c1); Reducing Your Carbon Footprint at Home. Ganchy, Sally. lib. bdg. 34.47 *(978-1-4042-1772-0(X)*, c1b55bf1-02c4-4bbb-9886-2f441ed88906); Reducing Your Carbon Footprint at School. Nagle, Jeanne. lib. bdg. 34.47 *(978-1-4042-1774-4(6)*, 65472741-3c09-4ade-b61d-f957ab7e97b8); Reducing Your Carbon Footprint in the Kitchen. Hall, Linley Erin. lib. bdg. 34.47 *(978-1-4042-1776-8(2)*, 72d24f36-8fb5-4098-8c0b-4b96b4418379); Reducing Your Carbon Footprint on Vacation. Roza, Greg. lib. bdg. 34.47 *(978-1-4042-1777-5(0)*, 0fcc1d0b-b782-478d-b5fb-792b5c4b6600); Smart Shopping: Shopping Green. Nagle, Jeanne. lib. bdg. 34.47 *(978-1-4042-1775-1(4)*, c91fdd48-1034-40bb-a5a8-cff6b9d007a2); (Illus.). 48p. (YA). (gr. 5-5). 2008. (Your Carbon Footprint Ser.). (ENG.). 2008. Set lib. bdg. 206.82 *(978-1-4042-1880-2(7)*, 82d1547c-d4b7-4afc-b404-e6497dd88511) Rosen Publishing Group, Inc., The.

Zahn, Peter. Let's Recycle, 1 vol. 2013. (Rosen Math Readers Ser.). (ENG.). 24p. (J). (gr. 1-1). pap. 8.25 *(978-1-4777-2109-4(6)*, a8582d39-3f9e-4fd8-90e8-35cb30ade5ce, Rosen Classroom) Rosen Publishing Group, Inc., The.

—Let's Recycle: Represent & Solve Addition Problems, 1 vol. 2013. (Core Math Skills: Operations & Algebraic Thinking Ser.). (ENG.). 24p. (J). (gr. 1-1). lib. bdg. 26.27 *(978-1-4777-2207-7(6)*, 04483b69-e492-4310-bf73-6354d7202868, PowerKids Pr.) Rosen Publishing Group, Inc., The.

RECYCLING (WASTE, ETC.)—FICTION

A Boy And His Dog & Bozak, Jon. Demo: The Story of the Junkyard Dog. 2007. 56p. (J). 19.99 *(978-0-9794769-1-4(7))* Adibooks.com.

Bacigalupi, Paolo. Ship Breaker (National Book Award Finalist) 2011. (ENG.). 352p. (YA). (gr. 10-17). pap. 12.99 *(978-0-316-05619-9(7))* Little, Brown Bks. for Young Readers.

Belford, Bibi. Canned & Crushed. 2015. (ENG.). 192p. (J). (gr. 2-7). 14.99 *(978-1-63220-435-6(5)*, Sky Pony Pr.) Skyhorse Publishing Co., Inc.

Berenstain, Jan & Berenstain, Mike. The Berenstain Bears Go Green. 2013. (Berenstain Bears Ser.). (Illus.). (J). lib. bdg. 13.55 *(978-0-606-27142-4(2))* Turtleback.

Berenstain, Jan & Mike. The Berenstain Bears Spring Storybook Favorites: Includes 7 Stories Plus Stickers!: a Springtime Book for Kids. Berenstain, Mike, illus. 2019. (Berenstain Bears Ser.). (ENG.). 192p. (J). (gr. -1-3). 13.99 *(978-0-06-288310-0(0)*, HarperCollins) HarperCollins Pubs.

Bergen, Lara. Don't Throw That Away! A Lift-The-Flap Book about Recycling & Reusing. Snyder, Betsy, illus. 2009. (Little Green Bks.). (ENG.). 14p. (J). (gr. -1-1). bds. 8.99 *(978-1-4169-7517-5(9)*, Little Simon) Little Simon.

Berthold, Joy. Peter on Patrol. 2011. 16p. 8.49 *(978-1-4567-1247-1(0))* AuthorHouse.

Bethel, Ellie. Michael Recycle. Colombo, Alexandra, illus. 2008. (Michael Recycle Ser.). 28p. (J). (gr. 1-3). 15.99 *(978-1-60010-224-0(7)*, 9781600102240) Idea & Design Works, LLC.

—Michael Recycle. 2008. (Illus.). (J). *(978-1-84539-281-9(7))*; 23p. *(978-1-84539-282-6(5))* Idea & Design Works, LLC.

—Michael Recycle Meets Litterbug Doug. Colombo, Alexandra, illus. 2009. (Michael Recycle Ser.). 24p. (J). (gr. 1-3). 15.99 *(978-1-60010-392-6(8)*, 9781600103926) Idea & Design Works, LLC.

—Michael Recycle Saves Christmas. Colombo, Alexandra, illus. 2010. (Michael Recycle Ser.). 32p. (J). (gr. 1-3). 15.99 *(978-1-60010-843-3(1)*, 9781600108433) Idea & Design Works, LLC.

Bewley, Elizabeth. Choose to Recycle. Latimer, Miriam, illus. 2009. 10p. 7.95 *(978-1-58117-904-0(9)*, Intervisual/Piggy Toes) Bendon, Inc.

Bookless, Evelyn. Captain Green & the Plastic Scene. Deeptown, Danny, illus. 2019. 32p. (J). (gr. -1-1). 14.99 *(978-981-4794-77-0(5))* Marshall Cavendish International (Asia) Private Ltd. SGP. Dist: Independent Pubs. Group.

Brown, Monica. Maya's Blanket / la Manta de Maya, 1 vol. Diaz, David, illus. 2015. (ENG.). 32p. (J). (gr. k-4). 19.95 *(978-0-89239-292-6(4)*, leelowcbp) Lee & Low Bks., Inc.

Cook, Sherry & Johnson, Terri. X. E. Ecology. 26. Kuhn, Jesse, illus. I.t. ed. 2006. (Quirkles — Exploring Phonics through Science Ser.: 24). 32p. (J). 7.99 *(978-1-933815-23-7(X)*, Quirkles, The) Creative 3, LLC.

Criswell, Ginger. Recycle Michael. 2012. (Illus.). 24p. 12.99 *(978-1-60010-906-5(3))* Idea & Design Works, LLC.

Curious George Plants a Tree. 2010. (Curious George Ser.). (ENG., Illus.). 24p. (J). (gr. -1-3). pap. 5.99 *(978-0-547-29776-7(9)*, 1413169, Clarion Bks.) HarperCollins Pubs.

Day, Nicholas. Junk: a Spectacular Tale of Trash: A Spectacular Tale of Trash. Disbury, Tom, illus. 2018. (ENG.). 32p. (J). (gr. k-3). 16.99 *(978-1-58536-400-8(2)*, 204586) Sleeping Bear Pr.

Donnelly, Rebecca. The Friendship Lie. 2019. (ENG., Illus.). 272p. (J). (gr. 4-7). 15.95 *(978-1-68446-061-8(1)*, 140521, Capstone Editions) Capstone.

Dyan, Penelope. Eileen Green the Recycling Queen. Dyan, Penwlope, illus. 2009. 44p. pap. 11.95 *(978-1-935118-51-0(X))* Bellissima Publishing, LLC.

Elovitz Marshall, Linda. Rainbow Weavery, 1 vol. Chavarri, Elisa, illus. 2016. (ENG.). 40p. (J). (gr. k-4). 20.95 *(978-0-89239-374-9(2)*, leelowcbp) Lee & Low Bks., Inc.

Ghigna, Charles. Recycling Is Fun, 1 vol. Jatkowska, Agnieszka, illus. 2012. (My Little Planet Ser.). (ENG.). 24p. (J). (gr. -1 — 1). 6.95 *(978-1-4048-7229-5(9)*, 118111, Picture Window Bks.) Capstone.

Gilbert, Nikki Murphy. Gilbert Green. 2009. 32p. pap. 14.99 *(978-1-4490-4377-3(1))* AuthorHouse.

Glennon, Michelle. My Big Green Teacher: Please Turn off the Lights. Glennon, Michelle, illus. 2008. (ENG., Illus.). 32p. (J). 19.95 *(978-0-9796625-3-9(2))* GDG Publishing.

—My Big Green Teacher: Seven Generations from Now. Glennon, Michelle, illus. 2008. (Illus.). (J). 19.95 *(978-0-9797952-1-3(4))* GDG Publishing.

—My Big Green Teacher: Taking the Green Road. Glennon, Michelle, illus. 2008. (Illus.). 32p. (J). 19.95 *(978-0-9796625-7-7(5))* GDG Publishing.

—My Big Green Teacher: Recycling: It's Easy Being Green. Glennon, Michelle, illus. 2007. (Illus.). 32p. (J). 19.95 *(978-0-9796625-6-0(7))* GDG Publishing.

Harp, Susan. Evie Goes Clean & Green. Siau, Jon, illus. 2013. 24p. (J). lib. bdg. 14.95 *(978-1-938730-09-2(7))* M.T. Publishing Co., Inc.

Harper, Charise Mericle. Just Grace Goes Green. 2009. (Just Grace Ser.: 4). (ENG., Illus.). 192p. (J). (gr. 1-4). pap. 7.99 *(978-0-547-24821-9(0)*, 1100711, Clarion Bks.) HarperCollins Pubs.

Hasting, Lori A. Green with N. V. 2012. (ENG.). pap. 14.95 *(978-1-4675-4195-4(8))* Independent Pub.

Inches, Alison. The Adventures of a Plastic Bottle: A Story about Recycling. Whitehead, Pete, illus. 2009. (Little Green Bks.). (ENG.). 24p. (J). (gr. -1-1). pap. 4.99 *(978-1-4169-6788-0(5)*, Little Simon) Little Simon.

—The Adventures of an Aluminum Can: A Story about Recycling. Chambers, Mark, illus. 2009. (Little Green Bks.). (ENG.). 24p. (J). (gr. -1-1). pap. 4.99 *(978-1-4169-7221-1(8)*, Little Simon) Little Simon.

Janelle, Nicole & Cholette, Daniel. Naby Recycles. 2012. 32p. pap. 14.60 *(978-1-105-53454-6(5))* Lulu Pr., Inc.

Kann, Victoria. Emeraldalicious: A Springtime Book for Kids. Kann, Victoria, illus. 2013. (Pinkalicious Ser.). (ENG., Illus.). 40p. (J). (gr. -1-3). 19.99 *(978-0-06-178126-1(6))*; lib. bdg. 18.89 *(978-0-06-178127-8(4))* HarperCollins Pubs. (HarperCollins).

Klepeis, Alicia & Ventura, Gabriela Baeza. Francisco's Kites. Undercuffler, Gary, illus. 2015. (SPA & ENG.). (J). 17.95 *(978-1-55885-804-6(0)*, Piñata Books) Arte Publico Pr.

Kroll, Steven. Stuff! Reduce, Reuse, Recycle: Reduce, Reuse, Recycle, 0 vols. Cox, Steve, illus. 2012. (ENG.). 32p. (J). (gr. -1-3). pap. 9.99 *(978-0-7614-6237-8(6)*, 9780761462378, Two Lions) Amazon Publishing.

Kyrja. Rupert's Tales: Rupert Helps Clean Up: Rupert Helps Clean Up, 1 vol. 2013. (ENG., Illus.). 64p. (J). (gr. -1-3). 19.99 *(978-0-7643-4284-4(3)*, 4882) Schiffer Publishing, Ltd.

Lawson, Lela. Robin Recycles: Sharing & Reusing, 1 vol. 2017. (Computer Science for the Real World Ser.). (ENG.). 16p. (gr. 2-3). pap. *(978-1-5383-5220-5(6)*, c3729b65-7161-4572-97ee-041c4b528c2b, Rosen Classroom) Rosen Publishing Group, Inc., The.

Louise, Kate. Pierre the French Bulldog Recycles. Straker, Bethany, illus. 2015. (ENG.). 32p. (J). (gr. -1-k). 14.99 *(978-1-63220-411-0(8)*, Sky Pony Pr.) Skyhorse Publishing Co., Inc.

Meissner, David. The Race to Recycle: Set Of 6. 2010. (Early Connections Ser.). (J). pap. 37.00 net. *(978-1-4108-1361-9(4))* Benchmark Education Co.

Messner, Kate. Marty McGuire Digs Worms! Floca, Brian, illus. 2012. (ENG.). 176p. (J). (gr. -1-3). pap. 5.99 *(978-0-545-14247-2(4)*, Scholastic Pr.) Scholastic, Inc.

Mommy, Tell Me a Story about What Daddy Does. 2nd ed. 2013. 32p. pap. 13.99 *(978-0-9855699-6-9(4))* Richer Life, LLC.

Montgomery, R. A. Your Very Own Robot Goes Cuckoo-Bananas! Newton, Keith, illus. 2010. (ENG.). 80p. (J). (gr. 2-2). pap. 7.99 *(978-1-933390-39-0(5))* Chooseco LLC.

O'Leary, Sara. This Is Sadie. Morstad, Julie, illus. 2015. 32p. (J). (gr. -1-2). 17.99 *(978-1-77049-532-6(0)*, Tundra Bks.) Tundra Bks. CAN. Dist: Penguin Random Hse. LLC.

Pace, Marisa. My Community Project: Sharing & Reusing, 1 vol. 2017. (Computer Science for the Real World Ser.). (ENG.). 12p. (gr. 1-2). pap. *(978-1-5383-5170-3(6)*, 77e52888-97b1-4e60-a02a-175655a8b90c, Rosen Classroom) Rosen Publishing Group, Inc., The.

Papp, Robert, illus. The Clue in the Recycling Bin. 2011. (Boxcar Children Mysteries Ser.: 126). (ENG.). 128p. (J). (gr. 2-5). pap. 6.99 *(978-0-8075-1209-8(5)*, 807512095, Random Hse. Bks. for Young Readers) Random Hse. Children's Bks.

Patterson, Ellie. Michael Recycle & the Tree Top Cops. Colombo, Alexandra, illus. 2012. (Michael Recycle Ser.). (ENG.). 24p. (J). (gr. 1-3). 15.99 *(978-1-61377-161-7(4)*, 9781613771617) Idea & Design Works, LLC.

Perera, Oleene. Timmy Tangelo Goes Green. 2010. 20p. 12.50 *(978-0-557-41286-0(2))* Lulu Pr., Inc.

Readman, Jo. George Saves the World by Lunchtime. Roberts, Ley Honor, illus. 2006. 32p. (J). (gr. k-2). pap. 15.99 *(978-1-903919-50-7(9))* Transworld Publishers Ltd. GBR. Dist: Independent Pubs. Group.

Rey, H. A. Curious George Discovers Recycling. 2017. (Curious George Discovers Ser.). (ENG.). (J). (gr. -1-3). lib. bdg. 17.20 *(978-0-606-39822-0(8))* Turtleback.

—Curious George Plants a Tree. 2009. (Curious George Ser.). (ENG., Illus.). 32p. (J). (gr. -1-3). 14.99 *(978-0-547-15087-1(3)*, 1051758, Clarion Bks.) HarperCollins Pubs.

Reynolds, Paul A. Sydney & Simon: Go Green! Reynolds, Peter H., illus. 2015. (Sydney & Simon Ser.: 2). 48p. (J). (gr. 1-4). lib. bdg. 12.95 *(978-1-58089-677-1(4))* Charlesbridge Publishing, Inc.

Ross, Joel. The Fog Diver. 2015. (Fog Diver Ser.: 1). (ENG.). 336p. (J). (gr. 3-7). 16.99 *(978-0-06-235293-4(8)*, HarperCollins) HarperCollins Pubs.

—The Lost Compass. (Fog Diver Ser.: 2). (ENG.). (J). (gr. 3-7). 2017. 368p. pap. 9.99 *(978-0-06-235309-2(8))* 2016. 352p. 16.99 *(978-0-06-235297-2(0))* HarperCollins Pubs. (HarperCollins).

—The Lost Compass. 2017. (Fog Diver Ser.: Vol. 2). (ENG.). (J). (gr. 3-7). lib. bdg. 17.20 *(978-0-606-40052-7(4))* Turtleback.

Scotto, Michael. Builda the Re-Bicycler. Gabriel, Evette, illus. 2009. (J). *(978-1-935193-22-7(8))* Lincoln Learning Solutions.

Sensel, Joni. The Garbage Monster. Bivins, Christopher, illus. 2003. 24p. (J). (gr. -1-18). 14.95 *(978-0-9701195-2-0(6))* Dream Factory Bks.

Silverman, Toby. The Garbage Grandma. Strapec, Amy, illus. 2005. 23p. (J). 9.50 *(978-0-9793475-0-4(5))* Silverman, Toby.

Sterrett, Nicole. 1-2 Recycling's for You! 2008. 12p. pap. 24.95 *(978-1-60610-223-7(0))* America Star Bks.

Stockham, Jess, illus. Recycling! 2011. (Helping Hands Ser.). 24p. (J). *(978-1-84643-415-0(7))* Child's Play International Ltd.

Trantham, Cary Gordon. The Saving of Sophi: El Rescate de Sofia. 2012. (ENG.). 30p. pap. 19.99 *(978-1-4772-0799-4(6))* AuthorHouse.

Trice, Linda. Kenya's Art. Mitchell, Hazel, illus. 2016. (ENG.). 32p. (J). (gr. -1-3). 16.95 *(978-1-57091-848-3(1))* Charlesbridge Publishing, Inc.

Wallace, Nancy Elizabeth. Recycle Every Day!, 0 vols. Wallace, Nancy Elizabeth, illus. 2012. (ENG., Illus.). 41p. (J). (gr. 1-3). pap. 9.99 *(978-0-7614-5290-4(7))*, 9780761452904, Two Lions) Amazon Publishing.

Warmus, Paul J. Sue's Zoo & the Magic Garden. 2012. pap. 11.95 *(978-0-7414-7200-7(7))* Infinity Publishing.

Weihs, Sally. Big Blue Goes Green. 2012. 24p. pap. 17.99 *(978-1-4685-5587-5(1))* AuthorHouse.

Yee, Wong Herbert. A Brand-New Day with Mouse & Mole. 2012. (Green Light Readers Level 3 Ser.). lib. bdg. 13.55 *(978-0-606-24437-4(9))* Turtleback.

—A Brand-New Day with Mouse & Mole (Reader) 2012. (Mouse & Mole Story Ser.). (ENG., Illus.). 48p. (J). (gr. 1-4). pap. 4.99 *(978-0-547-72209-2(5))*, 1482465, Clarion Bks.) HarperCollins Pubs.

RED CHINA

see China

RED CLOUD, 1822-1909

Drury, Bob & Clavin, Tom. The Heart of Everything That Is: Young Readers Edition. (ENG.). (J). (gr. 5). 2018. 336p. pap. 8.99 *(978-1-4814-6461-1(2))* 2017. (Illus.). 320p. 16.99 *(978-1-4814-6460-4(4))* McElderry, Margaret K. Bks. (McElderry, Margaret K. Bks.).

Goble, Paul. Red Cloud's War: Brave Eagle's Account of the Fetterman Fight. 2015. (Illus.). 48p. (J). (gr. 3-7). 16.95 *(978-1-937786-38-0(2))*, Wisdom Tales) World Wisdom, Inc.

Higgins, Nadia. Defending the Land: Causes & Effects of Red Cloud's War. 2015. (Cause & Effect: American Indian History Ser.). (ENG., Illus.). 32p. (J). (gr. 3-6). pap. 7.95 *(978-1-4914-2210-6(6))*, 127721, Capstone Pr.) Capstone.

Nelson, S. D. Red Cloud: A Lakota Story of War & Surrender. 2017. (ENG., Illus.). 64p. (J). (gr. 3-7). 19.95 *(978-1-4197-2313-1(8))*, 1145401, Abrams Bks. for Young Readers) Abrams, Inc.

Sanford, William R. Oglala Lakota Chief Red Cloud, 1 vol. 2013. (Native American Chiefs & Warriors Ser.). (ENG.). 48p. (gr. 5-7). pap. 11.53 *(978-1-4644-0259-3(0))*, 02d4d6bb-16b0-491c-ab93-c29644f75dfc); (Illus.). (J). 25.27 *(978-0-7660-4096-0(8))*, 6ccbb27b-959e-4d68-ae26-2a990c4a16d8) Enslow Publishing, LLC.

RED CROSS AND RED CRESCENT

see also American Red Cross

Connolly, Sean. The International Red Cross. 2009. (Global Organizations Ser.). (ENG., Illus.). 48p. (J). (gr. 4-7). pap. *(978-1-897563-35-9(3))* Saunders Bk. Co.

Faulkner, Georgene. Red Cross Stories for Children. 2004. reprint ed. pap. 15.95 *(978-1-4179-9875-3(X))* Kessinger Publishing, LLC.

Marsico, Katie. The Red Cross. 2014. (Community Connections: How Do They Help? Ser.). (ENG., Illus.). 24p. (J). (gr. 2-5). 29.21 *(978-1-63188-028-5(4))*, 205519) Cherry Lake Publishing.

McLuskey, Krista. The Red Cross. 2003. (International Organizations Ser.). (Illus.). 32p. (J). (gr. 4-7). lib. bdg. 26.00 *(978-1-59036-019-4(2))* Weigl Pubs., Inc.

Suen, Anastasia. La Cruz Roja, 1 vol. 2003. (Organizaciones de Ayuda (Helping Organizations) Ser.). (SPA., Illus.). 24p. (J). (gr. 2-2). lib. bdg. 26.27 *(978-0-8239-6856-5(1))*, 031274fe-36d8-435d-bbff-38432cae8d8c) Rosen Publishing Group, Inc., The.

—La Cruz Roja (the Red Cross) 2009. (Organizaciones de ayuda (Helping Organizations) Ser.). (SPA.). 24p. (gr. 2-2). 42.50 *(978-1-60851-146-4(4))*, Editorial Buenas Letras) Rosen Publishing Group, Inc., The.

—The Red Cross. 2009. (Helping Organizations Ser.). 24p. (gr. 2-2). 42.50 *(978-1-61513-262-1(7))*, PowerKids Pr.) Rosen Publishing Group, Inc., The.

REDUCING

see Weight Control

REDWALL ABBEY (IMAGINARY PLACE)—FICTION

Jacques, Brian. Mariel of Redwall: A Tale from Redwall. Chalk, Gary, illus. 2003. (Redwall Ser.: 4). (ENG.). 400p. (J). (gr. 5-5). pap. 10.99 *(978-0-14-230239-2(2))*, Firebird) Penguin Young Readers Group.

—Martfox: A Tale from Redwall. 2005. (Redwall Ser.: 11). (ENG.). 400p. (J). (gr. 5-5). reprint ed. 9.99 *(978-0-14-250108-5(5))*, Firebird) Penguin Young Readers Group.

—Martin the Warrior: A Tale from Redwall. 2004. (Redwall Ser.: 6). (ENG., Illus.). 384p. (J). (gr. 5-18). pap. 9.99 *(978-0-14-240055-5(6))*, Firebird) Penguin Young Readers Group.

—Martin the Warrior: The Prisoner & the Tyrant; Actors & Searchers; The Battle of Marshank. unabr. ed. 2004. (Redwall Radio Play Ser.: Bks. 1-3). (J). (gr. 4-7). 10p. pap. 50.00 incl. audio *(978-0-8072-8177-2(8))*, YA124CX); 376p. pap. 58.00 incl. audio *(978-0-8072-8178-9(6))*, YA124SP) Random Hse. Audio Publishing Group. (Listening Library).

—Mattimeo: A Tale from Redwall. Chalk, Gary, illus. 2003. (Redwall Ser.: 3). (ENG.). 448p. (J). (gr. 5-7). pap. 9.99 *(978-0-14-230240-8(6))*, Firebird) Penguin Young Readers Group.

—Salamandastron: A Tale from Redwall. Chalk, Gary, illus. 2003. (Redwall Ser.: 5). (ENG.). 400p. (J). (gr. 5-5). pap. 9.99 *(978-0-14-250152-8(2))*, Firebird) Penguin Young Readers Group.

—Seven Strange & Ghostly Tales. 144p. (J). (gr. 3-5). pap. 5.99 *(978-0-8072-1486-2(8))*, Listening Library) Random Hse. Audio Publishing Group.

—Taggerung: A Tale from Redwall. Chalk, Gary, illus. 2003. (Redwall Ser.: 14). (ENG.). 448p. (J). (gr. 5-18). pap. 9.99 *(978-0-14-250154-2(9))*, Firebird) Penguin Young Readers Group.

REDWOOD

Halter, Loretta. A Voice for the Redwoods. Bartczak, Peter, illus. 2010. (ENG.). 64p. (J). 18.95 *(978-0-9822942-0-8(4))* Nature's Hopes & Heroes.

Mihaly, Christy. California's Redwood Forest. 2018. (Natural Wonders of the World Ser.). (ENG., Illus.). 32p. (J). (gr. 3-5). lib. bdg. 31.35 *(978-1-63517-512-7(7))*, 1635175127, Focus Readers) North Star Editions.

Weaver, Harriett E. There Stand the Giants: The Story of the Redwood Trees. 2011. 70p. 36.95 *(978-1-258-01221-2(9))* Literary Licensing, LLC.

REED, HENRY (FICTITIOUS CHARACTER)—FICTION

Robertson, Keith. Henry Reed, Inc. abr. ed. (J). (gr. 4-7). pap. 15.95 incl. audio *(978-0-670-36801-3(6))* Live Oak Media.

—Henry Reed, Inc., Set. McCloskey, Robert, illus. abr. ed. (J). (gr. 4-7). 24.95 incl. audio *(978-0-670-36800-6(8))* Live Oak Media.

REFERENCE BOOKS

see also Encyclopedias and Dictionaries

Bodden, Valerie. Print & Subscription Sources. 2012. (Research for Writing Ser.). (ENG.). 48p. (J). (gr. 4-7). 23.95 *(978-1-60818-205-3(3))*, 21953, Creative Education) Creative Co., The.

Brown, Liz. Reference Materials. 2007. (Social Studies Essential Skills Ser.). (Illus.). 24p. (J). (gr. 4-7). lib. bdg. 24.45 *(978-1-59036-757-5(X))*; per. 8.95 *(978-1-59036-758-2(8))* Weigl Pubs., Inc.

Child Horizons, 10 vols, Set. Incl. Bible Story Hour. Johnson, Louisa M. (gr. k-4). 1996. 22.95 *(978-0-87392-002-5(3))*; Parade of Stories. Neigoff, Anna, ed. (gr. k-4). 1996. 22.95 *(978-0-87392-005-6(8))*; Plant & Animal Ways. Murphy, Margaret. (gr. 4-6). 1996. 22.95 *(978-0-87392-114-5(3))*; Questions Children Ask. Bonhivert, Edith & Bonhivert, Ernest. (gr. 2-4). 1997. 22.95 *(978-0-87392-010-0(4))*; Story Hour. Bjoland, Ester M. (gr. k-4). 1996. 22.95 *(978-0-87392-003-2(1))*; Words to Know. Bricker, Harry & Beckwith, Yvonne. (gr. k-3). 1997. 22.95 *(978-0-87392-011-7(2))*; (J). 200.00 *(978-0-87392-500-6(9))*, Ferguson Publishing Company) Infobase Holdings, Inc.

Dumont, Thora & Malone, Janet. Nemeth Reference Sheets. 2003. spiral bd. 14.95 *(978-0-939173-56-3(5))* National Braille Pr.

Hamilton, John. Libraries & Reference Materials, 1 vol. 2005. (Straight to the Source Ser.). (ENG.). 32p. (gr. k-6). 27.07 *(978-1-59197-545-8(X))*, Checkerboard Library) ABDO Publishing Co.

Helbrough, Emma. Book of Knowledge. 2004. 208p. (J). lib. bdg. 27.95 *(978-1-58086-612-5(3))*, Usborne) EDC Publishing.

—The Usborne Internet-Linked Book of Knowledge. 2004. (ENG., Illus.). 208p. (J). 19.99 *(978-0-7945-0594-3(5))* EDC Publishing.

Howell, Sara. How to Gather Information, Take Notes, & Sort Evidence, 1 vol., 1. 2013. (Core Writing Skills Ser.). (ENG.). 24p. (J). (gr. 3-3). 26.27 *(978-1-4777-2909-0(7))*, 2fbd70a6-9530-46ce-975c-07e275203741, PowerKids Pr.) Rosen Publishing Group, Inc., The.

Longman Children¿S Picture Dictionary with Audio CD. 2004. (ENG., Illus.). (C). (gr. k-5). pap. 22.40 *(978-962-00-5233-0(1))*, Prentice Hall) Savvas Learning Co.

O'Laughlin, Michael C. By Mac & 'O' You'll Always Know, Mac, Mc, & 'O' Names in Ireland, Scotland & America: With Census Records from the 17th to 20th Century. 2003. (Illus.). 60p. spiral bd. 25.00 net. *(978-0-940134-60-7(8))* Irish Genealogical Foundation.

Rabbat, Suzy. Hit the Books. 2010. (Explorer Library: Information Explorer Ser.). (ENG., Illus.). 32p. (gr. 4-8). lib. bdg. 32.07 *(978-1-60279-641-6(6))*, 200344) Cherry Lake Publishing.

—Super Smart Information Strategies: Hit the Books. 2010. (Explorer Library: Information Explorer Ser.). (ENG.). 32p. (gr. 4-8). pap. 14.21 *(978-1-61080-258-1(6))*, 200906) Cherry Lake Publishing.

Top That Publishing Staff, ed. Survival. 2004. (I-Quest Ser.). (Illus.). 48p. (J). per. *(978-1-84510-176-3(6))* Top That! Publishing PLC.

Watson, Carol. My First Book of Facts. (Illus.). (J). pap. 18.95 *(978-0-590-74341-9(4))* Scholastic, Inc.

REFORM, SOCIAL

see Social Problems

REFORM OF CRIMINALS

see Crime

REFORMATION

see also Europe—History—1492-1789

Carr, Simonetta. John Calvin. Taglietti, Emanuele, illus. 2008. (ENG.). 63p. (J). 18.00 *(978-1-60178-055-3(9))* Reformation Heritage Bks.

—John Knox. Abraxas, Matt, illus. 2014. (ENG.). 64p. (J). 18.00 *(978-1-60178-289-2(6))* Reformation Heritage Bks.

—Julia Gonzaga. 2018. (Christian Biographies for Young Readers Ser.). (ENG., Illus.). 63p. (J). (gr. 3-7). 18.00 *(978-1-60178-678-4(6))* Reformation Heritage Bks.

Chibi, Andrew A. The English Reformation: The Effect on a Nation. 2003. (Studymates Ser.). (ENG., Illus.). 98p. *(978-1-84285-024-4(5))* GLMP Ltd.

Davis, Thomas. John Calvin. 2004. (Spiritual Leaders & Thinkers Ser.). (ENG., Illus.). 120p. (gr. 9-13). 30.00 *(978-0-7910-8100-6(1))*, P114119, Facts On File) Infobase Holdings, Inc.

Flatt, Lizann. Religion in the Renaissance. 2009. (ENG., Illus.). 32p. (J). (gr. 5-7). *(978-0-7787-4597-6(X))*; (gr. 6-9). pap. *(978-0-7787-4617-1(8))* Crabtree Publishing Co.

George, Enzo. The Reformation, 1 vol. 2016. (Primary Sources in World History Ser.). (ENG.). 48p. (gr. 6-6). 33.07 *(978-1-5026-2016-3(2))*, 17e79efd-cd51-471d-a707-5c21078e2a74) Cavendish Square Publishing LLC.

Havemeyer, Janie. Catherine de' Medici: "The Black Queen" Malone, Peter, illus. 2011. (Thinking Girl's Treasury of Dastardly Dames Ser.). (ENG.). 32p. (J). (gr. 3-8). 18.95 *(978-0-9834256-3-2(9))* Goosebottom Bks. LLC.

Hinds, Kathryn. The Church, 1 vol. 2005. (Life in the Renaissance Ser.). (ENG., Illus.). 80p. (gr. 6-6). lib. bdg. 36.93 *(978-0-7614-1679-1(X))*, 0fb0dd84-62dd-45e0-9b39-ff108ea5672d) Cavendish Square Publishing LLC.

Hollingsworth, Tamara. The Reformation: A Religious Revolution, 1 vol. rev. ed. 2012. (Social Studies: Informational Text Ser.). (ENG.). 32p. (gr. 4-8). pap. 11.99 *(978-1-4333-5009-2(2))* Teacher Created Materials, Inc.

Luther, Martin. A Mighty Fortress Is Our God. Jaspersen, Jason, illus. 2017. (ENG.). 32p. (J). 14.99 *(978-1-933737-02-7(6))* Kloria Publishing LLC.

MacKenzie, Catherine. John Calvin: What Is the Truth? rev. ed. 2013. (Little Lights Ser.). (ENG., Illus.). 24p. (J). 7.99 *(978-1-84550-560-8(3))*, 893a01da-0af7-45de-bf5f-42a078868520) Christian Focus Pubns. GBR. Dist: Baker & Taylor Publisher Services (BTPS).

—Martin Luther: What Should I Do? rev. ed. 2013. (Little Lights Ser.). (ENG., Illus.). 24p. (J). 7.99 *(978-1-84550-561-5(1))*, 73c43d0a-3047-4c73-ae23-2834dd3639b9) Christian Focus Pubns. GBR. Dist: Baker & Taylor Publisher Services (BTPS).

Nichols, Stephen J. Reformation ABCs: The People, Places, & Things of the Reformation — From a to Z. Bustard, Ned, illus. 2017. (ENG.). 56p. 16.99 *(978-1-4335-5282-3(5))* Crossway.

Reformation: PowerPoint Presentation in World History. 2005. cd-rom 49.95 net. *(978-1-56004-216-7(8))* Social Studies Schl. Service.

Reformation DBA. 2003. spiral bd. 16.95 *(978-1-56004-167-2(6))* Social Studies Schl. Service.

Rijswijk, Cor van. John Is Not Afraid. 2004. (Illus.). 43p. (J). *(978-1-894666-81-7(X))* Inheritance Pubns.

—Martin Shows the Way. 2004. (Illus.). 43p. (J). *(978-1-894666-80-0(1))* Inheritance Pubns.

Roth-Beck, Meike. The Life & Times of Martin Luther. Ensikat, Klaus, illus. 2017. (ENG.). 44p. (J). *(978-0-8028-5495-7(8))*, Eerdmans Bks For Young Readers) Eerdmans, William B. Publishing Co.

Sengele, Mark. Inside the Reformation. 2012. (Illus.). 72p. (J). 16.99 *(978-0-7586-3120-6(0))* Concordia Publishing Hse.

REFORMATION—FICTION

Alcock, Deborah. The King's Service: A Story of the Thirty Years' War. 2008. (Illus.). 183p. (YA). *(978-1-894666-06-0(2))* Inheritance Pubns.

Basye, Dale E. Rapacia: the Second Circle of Heck. Dob, Bob, illus. 2010. (Heck Ser.: 2). 384p. (J). (gr. 3-7). pap. 7.99 *(978-0-375-84078-4(8))*, Yearling) Random Hse. Children's Bks.

Coats, J. Anderson. R Is for Rebel. 2018. (ENG., Illus.). 256p. (J). (gr. 5). 16.99 *(978-1-4814-9667-4(0))*, Atheneum Bks. for Young Readers) Simon & Schuster Children's Publishing.

Farenhorst, Christine. Wings Like a Dove: The Courage of Queen Jeanne D'Albret. 2006. (Chosen Daughters Ser.). 207p. (YA). (gr. 7). per. 11.99 *(978-0-87552-642-3(X))* P & R Publishing.

Marston, Hope Irvin. Against the Tide: The Valor of Margaret Wilson. 2007. (Chosen Daughters Ser.). 219p. (J). (gr. 3-7). per. 11.99 *(978-1-59638-061-5(6))* P & R Publishing.

Van Halsema, Thea B. This Was John Calvin. 2011. 184p. (gr. 3-7). 42.95 *(978-1-258-05962-0(2))* Literary Licensing, LLC.

Walshe, Elizabeth Hely. Under the Inquisition: A Story of the Reformation in Italy. 2009. (Illus.). 315p. *(978-1-894666-30-5(5))* Inheritance Pubns.

Weinberger, Justin. Reformed. 2017. (ENG.). 208p. (J). (gr. 3-7). 16.99 *(978-0-545-90252-6(5))*, Scholastic Pr.) Scholastic, Inc.

REFORMERS

Archer, Jules. The Unpopular Ones: Fifteen American Men & Women Who Stood up for What They Believed In. 2016. (Jules Archer History for Young Readers Ser.). (ENG., Illus.). 208p. (J). (gr. 6-6). 16.99 *(978-1-63450-200-9(0))*, Sky Pony Pr.) Skyhorse Publishing Co., Inc.

Butler, Mary. Sojourner Truth: From Slave to Activist for Freedom. 2009. (Library of American Lives & Times Ser.). 112p. (gr. 5-5). 69.20 *(978-1-60853-505-7(3))* Rosen Publishing Group, Inc., The.

Chambers, Veronica. Resist: 35 Profiles of Ordinary People Who Rose up Against Tyranny & Injustice. Turnbull, Tracy, illus. 2018. (ENG.). 224p. (J). (gr. 3-7). 16.99 *(978-0-06-279625-7(9))*, HarperCollins) HarperCollins Pubs.

Collins, Kathleen. Sojourner Truth: Defensora de los derechos civiles (Sojourner Truth: Equal Rights Advocate) 2009. (Grandes personajes en la historia de los Estados Unidos (Famous People in American History) Ser.). (SPA.). 32p. (gr. 2-3). 47.90 *(978-1-61512-808-2(5))*, Editorial Buenas Letras) Rosen Publishing Group, Inc., The.

—Sojourner Truth: Equal Rights Advocate. (Primary Sources of Famous People in American History Ser.). 32p. 2009. (gr. 2-3). 47.90 *(978-1-60851-727-5(6))* 2003. (ENG., Illus.). (gr. 3-4). pap. 10.00 *(978-0-8239-4193-3(0))*, a3e0d003-2b16-455d-a83a-e5c1a3908d7c) Rosen Publishing Group, Inc., The.

—Sojourner Truth: Equal Rights Advocate / Defensora de los derechos Civiles. 2009. (Famous People in American History/Grandes personajes en la historia de los Estados Unidos Ser.). (ENG & SPA.). 32p. (gr. 2-3). 47.90 *(978-1-61512-556-2(6))*, Editorial Buenas Letras) Rosen Publishing Group, Inc., The.

Hally, Ashleigh. Lugenia Burns Hope. 2012. (Illus.). 24p. (J). lib. bdg. *(978-1-935884-76-7(X))* State Standards Publishing, LLC.

Hirsch, E. D., Jr., ed. Civil Rights Leaders. 2003. tchr. ed. 9.95 *(978-0-7690-5053-9(0))*; stu. ed. 49.95 *(978-0-7690-2958-0(2))* Pearson Learning.

Kann, Bob. Belle & Bob la Follette: Partners in Politics. 2008. (Badger Biographies Ser.). (ENG., Illus.). 144p. (J). (gr. 3-7). pap. 12.95 *(978-0-87020-407-6(4))* Wisconsin Historical Society.

Kent, Deborah. Elizabeth Cady Stanton: Woman Knows the Cost of Life, 1 vol. 2008. (Americans: the Spirit of a Nation Ser.). (ENG., Illus.). 128p. (gr. 5-6). lib. bdg. 35.93 *(978-0-7660-3357-3(0))*, a08165a5-32e5-45ad-8cb3-d3e3ffca7805) Enslow Publishing, LLC.

Krass, Peter. Sojourner Truth: Antislavery Activist. 2004. (Black Americans of Achievement Legacy Edition Ser.). (ENG., Illus.). 112p. (gr. 6-12). 35.00 *(978-0-7910-8165-5(6))*, P114169, Facts On File) Infobase Holdings, Inc.

Kudlinski, Kathleen. Sojourner Truth. Wooden, Lenny, illus. 2003. (Childhood of Famous Americans Ser.). (ENG.). 160p. (J). (gr. 3-7). mass mkt. 7.99 *(978-0-689-85274-9(6))*, Simon & Schuster/Paula Wiseman Bks.) Simon & Schuster/Paula Wiseman Bks.

Loh-Hagan, Virginia. Girl Activists. 2019. (History's Yearbook Ser.). (ENG., Illus.). 32p. (J). (gr. 4-8). pap. 14.21 *(978-1-5341-5077-5(3))*, 213615); lib. bdg. 32.07 *(978-1-5341-4791-1(8))*, 213614) Cherry Lake Publishing. (45th Parallel Press).

Mattern, Joanne. Sojourner Truth: Early Abolitionist. 2009. (Women Who Shaped History Ser.). 24p. (gr. 2-3). 42.50 *(978-1-60854-821-7(X))*, PowerKids Pr.) Rosen Publishing Group, Inc., The.

McKissack, Patricia C. & McKissack, Fredrick, Jr. Sojourner Truth: Ain't I a Woman? 2003. (Illus.). 186p. (gr. 4-7). 17.20 *(978-0-7857-2515-2(6))* Turtleback.

Osial, Heather L. Californians Who Made a Difference. rev. ed. 2017. (Social Studies: Informational Text Ser.). (ENG., Illus.). 32p. (J). (gr. 3-5). pap. 9.99 *(978-1-4258-3247-6(4))* Teacher Created Materials, Inc.

Pinkney, Andrea Davis. Peace Warriors (Profiles #6) 2013. (Profiles Ser.: 6). (ENG.). 144p. (J). (gr. 4-7). pap. 6.99 *(978-0-545-51857-4(1))*, Scholastic Paperbacks) Scholastic, Inc.

Rappaport, Doreen. Eleanor, Quiet No More: The Life of Eleanor Roosevelt. Kelley, Gary, illus. 2009. (Big Words Book Ser.: 4). (ENG.). 48p. (J). (gr. -1-3). 16.99 *(978-0-7868-5141-6(4))* Little, Brown Bks. for Young Readers.

Ruffin, Frances E. Sojourner Truth: Early Abolitionist. 2009. (American Legends Ser.). 24p. (gr. 3-3). 42.50 *(978-1-61511-387-3(8))*, PowerKids Pr.) Rosen Publishing Group, Inc., The.

—Unsinkable Molly Brown. 2009. (American Legends Ser.). 24p. (gr. 3-3). 42.50 *(978-1-61511-377-4(0))*, PowerKids Pr.) Rosen Publishing Group, Inc., The.

Runstedler, Nancy. Pay It Forward Kids: Small Acts, Big Change, 1 vol. 2013. (Ripple Effects Ser.). (ENG., Illus.). 64p. (YA). (gr. 6-10). 19.95 *(978-1-55455-301-3(6))*, 5c6c46af-048a-40df-8bac-ae0eaef09ed4) Fitzhenry & Whiteside, Ltd. CAN. Dist: Firefly Bks., Ltd.

Shaw, Maura D. Dorothy Day: A Catholic Life of Action. Marchesi, Stephen, illus. 2004. (Spiritual Biographies for Young Readers Ser.). (ENG.). 32p. (J). 12.99 *(978-1-59473-011-5(3))*, 9135644c-888c-415d-a4b2-abbdcd24b83e, Skylight Paths Publishing) LongHill Partners, Inc.

Shetterly, Robert. Americans Who Tell the Truth. 2008. (Illus.). 46p. (gr. 4-6). 18.00 *(978-0-7569-8912-5(4))* Perfection Learning Corp.

Steele, Philip. Activists, 1 vol. 2011. (20th Century Lives Ser.). (ENG., Illus.). 32p. (YA). (gr. 5-5). 30.27 *(978-1-4488-3292-7(6))*, dd57bb80-0f38-4720-92a2-71a168739e3c) Rosen Publishing Group, Inc., The.

Stevenson, Bryan. Just Mercy (Adapted for Young Adults) A True Story of the Fight for Justice. 2018. 288p. (YA). (gr. 7). 18.99 *(978-0-525-58003-4(4))*; (ENG.). lib. bdg. 21.99 *(978-0-525-58004-1(2))* Random Hse. Children's Bks. (Delacorte Pr.).

Stone, Tanya Lee. Elizabeth Leads the Way: Elizabeth Cady Stanton & the Right to Vote. Gibbon, Rebecca, illus. 2010. (ENG.). 32p. (J). (gr. 1-5). pap. 8.99 *(978-0-312-60236-9(7))*, 900064232) Square Fish.

Swain, Gwenyth. Sojourner Truth. Archambault, Matthew, illus. 2005. (On My Own Biography Ser.). 48p. (J). (gr. 1-3). pap. 6.95 *(978-1-57505-827-6(8))* Lerner Publishing Group.

—Sojourner Truth. 2005. (On My Own Biography Ser.). (Illus.). 48p. (J). 25.26 *(978-1-57505-651-7(8))*, Carolrhoda Bks.) Lerner Publishing Group.

Weldon, Christine. Everyone Can Be a Changemaker: The Ashoka Effect, 1 vol. 2018. (Ripple Effects Ser.). (ENG.). 72p. (J). (gr. 5-12). 17.95 *(978-1-55455-357-0(1))*, 7ac6274f-643c-426c-93ff-b6e801c34b9c) Fitzhenry & Whiteside, Ltd. CAN. Dist: Firefly Bks., Ltd.

Wilson, Janet. Our Heroes: How Kids Are Making a Difference, 1 vol. 2014. (Kids Making a Difference Ser.: 3). (ENG., Illus.). 32p. (J). (gr. 2-6). 18.95 *(978-1-927583-41-8(1))* Second Story Pr. CAN. Dist: Orca Bk. Pubs. USA.

—Our Rights: How Kids Are Changing the World, 1 vol. 2013. (Kids Making a Difference Ser.: 2). (ENG., Illus.). 32p. (J). (gr. 4-6). lib. bdg. 18.95 *(978-1-926920-95-5(3))* Second Story Pr. CAN. Dist: Orca Bk. Pubs. USA.

Yousafzai, Malala. Malala's Magic Pencil. Kerascoët, illus. 2017. (ENG.). 48p. (J). (gr. -1-3). 17.99 *(978-0-316-31957-7(0))* Little, Brown Bks. for Young Readers.

REFRIGERATION AND REFRIGERATING MACHINERY

Plumbing, Heating, Air Conditioning & Refrigeration Student Activity. 2004. (YA). cd-rom *(978-1-57078-954-0(1))*, CEV60033) C E V Multimedia, Ltd.

REFUGEES

Abery, Julie. Yusra Swims. Deng, Sally, illus. 2020. 32p. (J). (gr. 1-3). 19.99 *(978-1-56846-329-2(4))*, 18373, Creative Editions) Creative Co., The.

Aykroyd, Clarissa. Refugees. 2005. (Changing Face of North America Ser.). (Illus.). 112p. (YA). lib. bdg. 24.95 *(978-1-59084-692-6(3))* Mason Crest.

Barghoorn, Linda. Hoping for a Home after el Salvador, 1 vol. 2019. (Leaving My Homeland: after the Journey Ser.). (ENG., Illus.). 32p. (J). (gr. 4-4). pap. *(978-0-7787-6500-4(8))*, f4ef5ce5-8ce9-401b-ba1d-444328dc4a7); lib. bdg. *(978-0-7787-6494-6(X))*, b5f2cc13-5c31-4395-8305-396c5ce0459d) Crabtree Publishing Co.

—My New Home after Syria. 2018. (Leaving My Homeland: after the Journey Ser.). (Illus.). 32p. (J). (gr. 4-4). *(978-0-7787-4983-7(5))* Crabtree Publishing Co.

PQR

—A Refugee's Journey from Bhutan. 2018. (Leaving My Homeland Ser.). (Illus.). 32p. (J). (gr. 4-4). (978-0-7787-4684-3(4)) Crabtree Publishing Co.

—A Refugee's Journey from Colombia. 2017. (Leaving My Homeland Ser.). (Illus.). 32p. (J). (gr. 4-4). (978-0-7787-3672-1(5)) Crabtree Publishing Co.

—A Refugee's Journey from el Salvador. 2018. (Leaving My Homeland Ser.). (Illus.). 32p. (J). (gr. 4-4). (978-0-7787-4685-0(2)) Crabtree Publishing Co.

—A Refugee's Journey from Eritrea. 2018. (Leaving My Homeland Ser.). (Illus.). 32p. (J). (gr. 4-4). (978-0-7787-4686-7(0)) Crabtree Publishing Co.

—A Refugee's Journey from Somalia. 2017. (Leaving My Homeland Ser.). (Illus.). 32p. (J). (gr. 4-4). (978-0-7787-3675-2(X)) Crabtree Publishing Co.

—Returning to Afghanistan. 2018. (Leaving My Homeland: after the Journey Ser.). (Illus.). 32p. (J). (gr. 4-4). (978-0-7787-4985-1(1)) Crabtree Publishing Co.

—Returning to Colombia, 1 vol. 2019. (Leaving My Homeland: after the Journey Ser.). (ENG., Illus.). 32p. (J). (gr. 4-4). pap. (978-0-7787-6498-4(2), e2a28c6d-2cb6-4f9d-945b-5c5992097ac3); lib. bdg. (978-0-7787-6486-1(9), ac1ef328-37fc-430d-875b-e027df7515ef) Crabtree Publishing Co.

Barr, Linda. Long Road to Freedom: Journey of the Hmong. 2004. (High Five Reading - Purple Ser.). (ENG., Illus.). 64p. (gr. 3-4). per. 9.00 (978-0-7368-3852-8(X)) Capstone.

Borden, Louise. The Journey That Saved Curious George: The True Wartime Escape of Margret & H. A. Rey. Drummond, Allan, illus. (Curious George Ser.). (ENG.). 80p. (J). (gr. 3-7). 2010. pap. 8.99 (978-0-547-41746-2(2), 1430026) 2005. 17.99 (978-0-618-33924-2(8), 581802) HarperCollins Pubs. (Clarion Bks.).

Bryan, Nichol. Jewish Americans, 1 vol. 2004. (One Nation Set 1 Ser.). (ENG.). 32p. (gr. k-6). 27.07 (978-1-57765-986-0(4), Checkerboard Library) ABDO Publishing Co.

—Somali Americans, 1 vol. 2004. (One Nation Set 1 Ser.). (ENG.). 32p. (gr. k-6). 27.07 (978-1-57765-989-1(9), Checkerboard Library) ABDO Publishing Co.

Bui, Nam. Fish over Diamond. 2012. 138p. 30.99 (978-1-4691-9624-4(7)) Xlibris Corp.

Burlingame, Jeff. The Lost Boys of Sudan, 1 vol. 2012. (Great Escapes Ser.). (ENG.). 80p. (gr. 6-6). 36.93 (978-1-60870-475-0(0), d33ca83f-55e2-4d39-80a5-bc24de6ff0d4) Cavendish Square Publishing LLC.

Cherenfant, Sabine. How Vietnamese Immigrants Made America Home, 1 vol. 2018. (Coming to America: the History of Immigration to the United States Ser.). (ENG.). 80p. (gr. 6-6). 38.80 (978-1-5081-8138-5(1), 4adae765-75b5-4f62-9976-3fb3d914a9e7) Rosen Publishing Group, Inc., The.

Cohen, Sheila & Terman Cohen, Sheila. Mai Ya's Long Journey. 2005. (Badger Biographies Ser.). (ENG., Illus.). 96p. (J). (gr. 3-7). per. 12.95 (978-0-87020-365-7(7)) Wisconsin Historical Society.

Coleman, Lori. Vietnamese in America. 2005. (In America Ser.). (Illus.). 80p. (J). (gr. 5-8). lib. bdg. 27.93 (978-0-8225-3951-3(9)) Lerner Publishing Group.

Creager, Ellen. Life As an Iraqi American. 1 vol. 2017. (One Nation for All: Immigrants in the United States Ser.). (ENG.). 32p. (J). (gr. 4-5). 27.93 (978-1-5383-2244-4(7), 2f97c90c-efb5-4d87-9111-15386318ee50); pap. 11.00 (978-1-5383-2340-3(0), 285ed640-cc5a-44ce-aea6-1afecb54a7a3) Rosen Publishing Group, Inc., The. (PowerKids Pr.).

Dau, John Bul. Lost Boy, Lost Girl: Escaping Civil War in Sudan. 2010. (Illus.). 160p. (YA). (gr. 7-12). (ENG.). 23.90 (978-1-4263-0709-6(8)); 15.95 (978-1-4263-0708-9(X)) Disney Publishing Worldwide. (National Geographic Kids).

DePietro, Frank. Central American Immigrants. 2012. (J). pap. (978-1-4222-2334-5(5)) Mason Crest.

—Central American Immigrants. Limón, José E., ed. 2012. (Hispanic Americans: Major Minority Ser.). 64p. (J). (gr. 4). 22.95 (978-1-4222-2317-8(5)) Mason Crest.

Dolphin, Laurie. Our Journey from Tibet. Johnson, Nancy Jo, photos by. 2006. (Illus.). 40p. (J). (gr. k-4). 16.00 (978-0-7567-9812-3(4)) DIANE Publishing Co.

Eboch, M. M., ed. Migrants & Refugees, 1 vol. 2017. (Global Viewpoints Ser.). (ENG.). 272p. (gr. 10-12). pap. 32.70 (978-1-5345-0116-4(9), 5b5c6283-86c4-4911-9bb1-b434e11281be); lib. bdg. 47.83 (978-1-5345-0118-8(5), 46abc2cc-3dc6-43aa-931e-5bb9fe5e0b33) Greenhaven Publishing LLC.

Ellis, Deborah. Children of War, 1 vol. 2009. (ENG., Illus.). 128p. (J). (gr. 6-7). pap. 12.99 (978-0-88899-908-5(9)) Groundwood Bks. CAN. Dist: Publishers Group West (PGW).

Erickson, Marty. Refugees. 2019. (In Focus Ser.). (ENG.). 80p. (J). (gr. 6-12). 41.27 (978-1-68282-719-2(4), BrightPoint Pr.) ReferencePoint Pr., Inc.

Fulton, Kristen. Flight for Freedom: The Wetzel Family's Daring Escape from East Germany (Berlin Wall History for Kids Book; Nonfiction Picture Books) Kuhlmann, Torben, illus. 2020. (ENG.). 56p. (J). (gr. k-3). 17.99 (978-1-4521-4960-8(7)) Chronicle Bks. LLC.

Gallagher, Jim. Refugees & Asylum. 2020. (ENG.). 80p. (YA). (gr. 6-12). 41.27 (978-1-68282-767-3(4)) ReferencePoint Pr., Inc.

Glynne, Andy. Hamid's Story: A Real-Life Account of His Journey from Eritrea. 2017. (Seeking Refuge Ser.). (ENG., Illus.). 32p. (J). (gr. k-5). 27.99 (978-1-5158-1413-9(0), 135355, Picture Window Bks.) Capstone.

—Juliane's Story: A Real-Life Account of Her Journey from Zimbabwe. 2017. (Seeking Refuge Ser.). (ENG., Illus.). 32p. (J). (gr. k-5). 27.99 (978-1-5158-1414-6(9), 135356, Picture Window Bks.) Capstone.

—Navid's Story: A Real-Life Account of His Journey from Iran. 2017. (Seeking Refuge Ser.). (ENG., Illus.). 32p. (J). (gr. k-5). 27.99 (978-1-5158-1415-3(7), 135357, Picture Window Bks.) Capstone.

Golabek, Mona & Cohen, Lee. The Children of Willesden Lane: A True Story of Hope & Survival During World War II (Young Readers Edition) 2017. (ENG., Illus.). 224p. (J). E-Book (978-0-316-55489-3(8)) Little Brown & Co.

Gravel, Elise. What Is a Refugee? 2019. (ENG., Illus.). 32p. (J). (gr. -1-2). 18.99 (978-0-593-12005-7(1), Schwartz & Wade Bks.) Random Hse. Children's Bks.

Harris, Duchess & Herschbach, Elisabeth. The Refugee Crisis. 2018. (Special Reports). (ENG., Illus.). 112p. (J). (gr. 6-12). lib. bdg. 41.36 (978-1-5321-1681-0(0), 30614, Essential Library) ABDO Publishing Co.

Heing, Bridey. True Stories of Teen Refugees, 1 vol. 2017. (True Teen Stories Ser.). (ENG.). 112p. (YA). (gr. 9-9). pap. 20.99 (978-1-5026-3400-9(7), 2fea3e82-86eb-406e-be52-2971e4384d6d) Cavendish Square Publishing LLC.

Hodge, Deborah. Rescuing the Children: The Story of the Kindertransport. 2012. (Illus.). 64p. (J). (gr. 5). 17.95 (978-1-77049-256-1(9), Tundra Bks.) Tundra Bks. CAN. Dist: Penguin Random Hse. LLC.

Hudak, Heather C. Hoping for a Home after Nigeria, 1 vol. 2019. (Leaving My Homeland: after the Journey Ser.). (ENG., Illus.). 32p. (J). (gr. 4-4). pap. (978-0-7787-6502-8(4), 289deecd-ae47-424d-961e-d0d40467ced1); lib. bdg. (978-0-7787-6496-0(6), 2e7d411b-dda2-4747-b81d-b0dc7b0b6833) Crabtree Publishing Co.

—Immigration & Refugees. 2019. (Get Informed — Stay Informed Ser.). (Illus.). 48p. (J). (gr. 5-6). (978-0-7787-5333-9(6)); pap. (978-0-7787-5347-6(6)) Crabtree Publishing Co.

—My New Home after Iran, 1 vol. 2019. (Leaving My Homeland: after the Journey Ser.). (ENG., Illus.). 32p. (J). (gr. 4-4). pap. (978-0-7787-6501-1(6), 1dd8d112-e994-4d26-a0a6-3f4feac08879); lib. bdg. (978-0-7787-6495-3(8), acc8321d-e3e3-422e-b13d-450154e248bf) Crabtree Publishing Co.

—My New Home after Somalia, 1 vol. 2019. (Leaving My Homeland: after the Journey Ser.). (ENG., Illus.). 32p. (J). (gr. 4-4). pap. (978-0-7787-6503-5(2), 19798fbf-7cf8-4517-93a9-25d28569ba0d); lib. bdg. (978-0-7787-6497-7(4), 321cad7a-4ad5-4e72-8467-ae0ee0889628) Crabtree Publishing Co.

—My New Home after Yemen. 2018. (Leaving My Homeland: after the Journey Ser.). (Illus.). 32p. (J). (gr. 4-4). (978-0-7787-4984-4(3)) Crabtree Publishing Co.

—A Refugee's Journey from Guatemala. 2017. (Leaving My Homeland Ser.). (Illus.). 32p. (J). (gr. 4-4). (978-0-7787-3673-8(3)) Crabtree Publishing Co.

—A Refugee's Journey from Iran. 2018. (Leaving My Homeland Ser.). (Illus.). 32p. (J). (gr. 4-4). (978-0-7787-4687-4(9)) Crabtree Publishing Co.

—A Refugee's Journey from Yemen. 2017. (Leaving My Homeland Ser.). (Illus.). 32p. (J). (gr. 4-4). (978-0-7787-3677-6(6)) Crabtree Publishing Co.

—Returning to Guatemala. 2018. (Leaving My Homeland: after the Journey Ser.). (Illus.). 32p. (J). (gr. 4-4). (978-0-7787-4986-8(X)) Crabtree Publishing Co.

Jacobs Altman, Linda. Escape: Teens on the Run: Primary Sources from the Holocaust, 1 vol. 2010. (True Stories of Teens in the Holocaust Ser.). (ENG., Illus.). 128p. (gr. 9-10). 35.93 (978-0-7660-3270-5(1), 16a24f0b-cc62-468e-842c-5aa7c9118ea4) Enslow Publishing, LLC.

Jal, David & Jacobs, Laura K. David's Journey: The Story of David Jal, One of the Lost Boys of Sudan. Bezesky, Tracy, illus. 2012. (ENG.). 32p. 20.00 (978-1-934478-30-1(X)) Sunray Publishing.

Jamieson, Victoria & Mohamed, Omar. When Stars Are Scattered. Jamieson, Victoria & Geddy, Iman, illus. 2020. (ENG.). 264p. (J). (gr. 4-7). 22.99 (978-0-525-55391-5(6)); pap. 13.99 (978-0-525-55390-8(8)) Penguin Young Readers Group. (Dial Bks).

Kacer, Kathy. To Hope & Back: The Journey of the St. Louis, 1 vol. 2011. (Holocaust Remembrance Series for Young Readers Ser.: 11). (ENG., Illus.). 204p. (J). (gr. 6-8). pap. 14.95 (978-1-897187-96-8(3)) Second Story Pr. CAN. Dist: Orca Bk. Pubs. USA.

Kalman, Bobbie. Refugee Child: My Memories of the 1956 Hungarian Revolution. Bedell, Barbara, illus. 2006. (ENG.). 224p. (J). (gr. 3-7). lib. bdg. (978-0-7787-2760-6(2)) Crabtree Publishing Co.

—Refugee Child Activity Guide. 2006. (ENG., Illus.). 32p. (J). (gr. 3-7). bds. (978-0-7787-2759-0(9)) Crabtree Publishing Co.

Kazerooni, Abbas. On Two Feet & Wings, 0 vols. 2014. (ENG.). 256p. (YA). (gr. 7-12). pap. 9.99 (978-1-4778-2037-7(X), 9781477820377, Skyscape) Amazon Publishing.

Kendall, Martha E. & Keat, Nawuth. Alive in the Killing Fields: Surviving the Khmer Rouge Genocide. 2009. (Illus.). 128p. (J). (gr. 7-12). 15.95 (978-1-4263-0515-3(X), National Geographic Kids) Disney Publishing Worldwide.

King, Norma. Everything You Need to Know about Immigrants & Refugees, 1 vol. 2017. (Need to Know Library). (ENG.). 64p. (J). (gr. 6-6). pap. 13.95 (978-1-5081-7671-8(X), e1df8aaf-669b-4880-b334-ca1c641031d8) Rosen Publishing Group, Inc., The.

Knight, Margy Burns. Who Belongs Here? An American Story. O'Brien, Anne Sibley, illus. 2004. 32p. 19.45 (978-0-7569-2426-3(X)) Perfection Learning Corp.

Knight, Margy Burns, et al. Who Belongs Here? An American Story. 2nd ed. 2004. (Illus.). 40p. (gr. 3-8). 16.95 (978-0-88448-110-2(7)) Tilbury Hse. Pubs.

Krasner, Barbara, ed. Human Migration, 1 vol. 2019. (Opposing Viewpoints Ser.). (ENG.). 200p. (gr. 10-12). pap. 34.80 (978-1-5345-0598-8(9), 8e749bf2-f41f-48f5-aa28-2df975360f13) Greenhaven Publishing LLC.

Kuntz, Doug & Shrodes, Amy. Lost & Found Cat: The True Story of Kunkush's Incredible Journey. Cornelison, Sue, illus. 2019. 48p. (J). (gr. -1-3). pap. 8.99 (978-1-5247-1550-2(6), Dragonfly Bks.) Random Hse. Children's Bks.

Leatherdale, Mary Beth. Stormy Seas: Stories of Young Boat Refugees. Shakespeare, Eleanor, illus. 2017. 64p. (J). (gr. 4). pap. 12.95 (978-1-55451-895-1(4)) Annick Pr., Ltd. CAN. Dist: Publishers Group West (PGW).

Levy, Janey. Refugee Workers. (Extreme Careers Ser.). 64p. (gr. 5-5). 2009. 58.50 (978-1-61512-403-9(9), Rosen Reference) 2007. (ENG., Illus.). (J). lib. bdg. 37.13 (978-1-4042-0960-2(3), c9b984c3-3155-45c9-8a2a-4ac15e17c4a0) Rosen Publishing Group, Inc., The.

Lucas, Lisa. Spectacularly Beautiful: A Refugee's Story. Stein, Laurie, illus. 2018. (ENG.). 32p. (J). (gr. -1-2). 16.99 (978-1-57687-891-0(0), powerHouse Bks.) powerHse. Bks.

Markham, Lauren. The Far Away Brothers (Adapted for Young Adults) Two Teenage Immigrants Making a Life in America. 2019. (ENG.). 288p. (YA). (gr. 7). 17.99 (978-1-9848-2977-1(7), Delacorte Pr.) Random Hse. Children's Bks.

Mason, Helen. A Refugee's Journey from Afghanistan. 2017. (Leaving My Homeland Ser.). (ENG., Illus.). 32p. (J). (gr. 4-4). (978-0-7787-3125-2(1)); pap. (978-0-7787-3129-0(4)) Crabtree Publishing Co.

—A Refugee's Journey from Syria. 2017. (Leaving My Homeland Ser.). (ENG., Illus.). 32p. (J). (gr. 4-4). (978-0-7787-3128-3(6)); pap. (978-0-7787-3184-9(7)) Crabtree Publishing Co.

Matthews, Jenny. Children Growing up with War. Matthews, Jenny, photos by. 2014. (ENG., Illus.). 48p. (J). (gr. 5). 17.99 (978-0-7636-6942-3(3)) Candlewick Pr.

McCarney, Rosemary. Where Will I Live?, 1 vol. 2017. (ENG., Illus.). 24p. (J). (gr. 1-3). 19.95 (978-1-77260-028-5(8)) Second Story Pr. CAN. Dist: Orca Bk. Pubs. USA.

McPherson, Stephanie Sammartino. The Global Refugee Crisis: Fleeing Conflict & Violence. 2019. (ENG., Illus.). 128p. (YA). (gr. 6-12). 37.32 (978-1-5415-2811-6(5), 780aeafb-8b0b-4fd2-ab65-3fb9813b3bcc, Twenty-First Century Bks.) Lerner Publishing Group.

Naidoo, Beverley. Making It Home: Real-Life Stories from Children Forced to Flee. 2005. (Illus.). 117p. (gr. 3-7). 17.00 (978-0-7569-5823-7(7)) Perfection Learning Corp.

Neil Wallace, Sandra & Wallace, Rich. First Generation: 36 Trailblazing Immigrants & Refugees Who Make America Great. Nowicka, Agata, illus. 2018. (ENG.). 96p. (J). (gr. 3-7). 18.99 (978-0-316-51524-5(8)) Little, Brown Bks. for Young Readers.

Parker, Lewis K. Why Vietnamese Immigrants Came to America. 2009. (Coming to America Ser.). 24p. (gr. 2-3). 42.50 (978-1-61511-888-5(8), PowerKids Pr.) Rosen Publishing Group, Inc., The.

Pearl, Melissa Sherman. Paper Beads from Africa: Charities Started by Kids! 2018. (Community Connections: How Do They Help? Ser.). (ENG., Illus.). 24p. (J). (gr. 2-5). pap. 12.79 (978-1-5341-0830-1(0), 210684); lib. bdg. 29.21 (978-1-5341-0731-1(2), 210683) Cherry Lake Publishing.

Perritano, John. The Making of the Modern World: 1945 to the Present: Migration & Refugees, Vol. 9. van Dijk, Ruud, ed. 2016. (Making of the Modern World: 1945 to the Present Ser.: Vol. 9). (ENG.). 64p. (J). (gr. 7-12). 23.95 (978-1-4222-3640-6(4)) Mason Crest.

Rodger, Ellen. Hoping for a Home after Myanmar. 2018. (Leaving My Homeland: after the Journey Ser.). (Illus.). 32p. (J). (gr. 4-4). (978-0-7787-4974-5(6)) Crabtree Publishing Co.

—My New Home after Iraq. 2018. (Leaving My Homeland: after the Journey Ser.). (Illus.). 32p. (J). (gr. 4-4). (978-0-7787-4975-2(4)) Crabtree Publishing Co.

—A Refugee's Journey from Iraq. 2017. (Leaving My Homeland Ser.). (ENG., Illus.). 32p. (J). (gr. 4-4). (978-0-7787-3127-6(8)); pap. (978-0-7787-3157-3(X)) Crabtree Publishing Co.

—A Refugee's Journey from Myanmar. 2017. (Leaving My Homeland Ser.). (Illus.). 32p. (J). (gr. 4-4). (978-0-7787-3674-5(1)) Crabtree Publishing Co.

—A Refugee's Journey from Nigeria. 2018. (Leaving My Homeland Ser.). (Illus.). 32p. (J). (gr. 4-4). (978-0-7787-4688-1(7)) Crabtree Publishing Co.

—A Refugee's Journey from South Sudan. 2017. (Leaving My Homeland Ser.). (Illus.). 32p. (J). (gr. 4-4). (978-0-7787-3676-9(8)) Crabtree Publishing Co.

—A Refugee's Journey from the Democratic Republic of the Congo. 2017. (Leaving My Homeland Ser.). (ENG., Illus.). 32p. (J). (gr. 4-4). (978-0-7787-3126-9(X)); pap. (978-0-7787-3156-6(1)) Crabtree Publishing Co.

—A Refugee's Journey from Ukraine. 2018. (Leaving My Homeland Ser.). (Illus.). 32p. (J). (gr. 4-4). (978-0-7787-4689-8(5)) Crabtree Publishing Co.

Schwartz, Eric. Central American Immigrants to the United States: Refugees from Unrest. 2007. (Hispanic Heritage Ser.). (Illus.). 112p. (YA). (gr. 4-7). lib. bdg. 22.95 (978-1-59084-929-3(9)) Mason Crest.

Senker, Cath & Hachette Children's Group. Refugees, 1 vol. 2011. (Global Issues Ser.). (ENG., Illus.). 48p. (YA). (gr. 6-6). lib. bdg. 34.47 (978-1-4488-1880-8(X), d2567166-c82a-42fb-98d5-1563e52de0b1, Rosen Reference) Rosen Publishing Group, Inc., The.

Skrypuch, Marsha Forchuk. Adrift at Sea: A Vietnamese Boy's Story of Survival. Deines, Brian, illus. 2016. (ENG.). 40p. (J). (gr. 1-4). 19.95 (978-1-77278-005-5(7)) Pajama Pr. CAN. Dist: Publishers Group West (PGW).

Sonneborn, Liz. The Khmer Rouge, 1 vol. 2012. (Great Escapes Ser.). (ENG., Illus.). 80p. (gr. 6-6). 36.93 (978-1-60870-474-3(2), 149e435b-e136-4ed9-b4b5-7f18a6663000) Cavendish Square Publishing LLC.

Spence, Kelly. Yusra Mardini: Refugee Hero & Olympic Swimmer. 2018. (Remarkable Lives Revealed Ser.). (ENG., Illus.). 32p. (J). (gr. 3-3). (978-0-7787-4711-6(5)); pap. (978-0-7787-4726-0(3)) Crabtree Publishing Co.

St. John, Warren. Outcasts United: The Story of a Refugee Soccer Team That Changed a Town. 2013. 240p. (YA). (gr. 7). pap. 10.99 (978-0-385-74195-8(2), Ember) Random Hse. Children's Bks.

Staeger, Rob. Asylees. 2005. (Changing Face of North America Ser.). (Illus.). 112p. (YA). lib. bdg. 24.95 (978-1-59084-685-8(0)) Mason Crest.

Teenage Refugees Speak Out. 2005. (Illus.). (gr. 7-12). lib. bdg. 106.35 (978-0-8239-9331-4(0)) Rosen Publishing Group, Inc., The.

Troupe, Thomas Kingsley. Extreme Stories about Disappearances. 24p. (J). 2019. (Illus.). pap. (978-1-68072-767-8(2)) 2018. (ENG.). (gr. 4-6). pap. 8.99 (978-1-64466-320-2(1), 12575, Hi Jinx) Black Rabbit Bks.

Uschan, Michael V. Human Rights in Focus: Refugees. 2017. (ENG., Illus.). 80p. (J). (gr. 5-12). (978-1-68282-233-3(8)) ReferencePoint Pr., Inc.

Uwiringiyimana, Sandra & Pesta, Abigail. How Dare the Sun Rise: Memoirs of a War Child. (ENG., Illus.). 304p. (YA). (gr. 8). 2018. pap. 11.99 (978-0-06-247015-7(9)) 2017. 19.99 (978-0-06-247014-0(0)) HarperCollins Pubs. (Tegen, Katherine Bks).

Velasquez, Liliana. Dreams & Nightmares: I Fled Alone to the United States When I Was Fourteen. 2017. (Working & Writing for Change Ser.). (ENG., Illus.). 211p. (YA). (gr. 9-12). pap. 22.95 (978-1-60235-939-0(3)) Parlor Pr.

Yousafzai, Malala. We Are Displaced: My Journey & Stories from Refugee Girls Around the World. (ENG., Illus.). (YA). (gr. 9-17). 2021. 224p. pap. 11.99 (978-0-316-52365-3(8)) 2019. 224p. 18.99 (978-0-316-52364-6(X)) 2019. 256p. 20.99 (978-0-316-52948-8(6)) Little, Brown Bks. for Young Readers.

REFUGEES—FICTION

Abdel-Fattah, Randa. The Lines We Cross. (ENG.). 400p. (YA). (gr. 7-7). 2018. pap. 10.99 (978-1-338-28205-4(0)) 2017. 18.99 (978-1-338-11866-7(8), Scholastic Pr.) Scholastic, Inc.

Agosin, Marjorie. I Lived on Butterfly Hill. White, Lee, illus. 2014. (Butterfly Hill Ser.). (ENG.). 464p. (J). (gr. 5-9). 21.99 (978-1-4169-5344-9(2), Atheneum Bks. for Young Readers) Simon & Schuster Children's Publishing.

Anderson, Natalie C. City of Saints & Thieves. 2018. (ENG.). 432p. (YA). (gr. 7). pap. 11.99 (978-0-399-54759-1(2), Speak) Penguin Young Readers Group.

Appelfeld, Aharon. Adam & Thomas. Green, Jeffrey M., tr. Dumas, Philippe, illus. 2017. 160p. (J). (gr. 3-7). pap. 14.95 (978-1-60980-744-3(8), Triangle Square) Seven Stories Pr.

Aslan, Austin. The Islands at the End of the World. 2015. (Islands at the End of the World Ser.). (ENG., Illus.). 384p. (YA). (gr. 7). pap. 10.99 (978-0-385-74403-4(X), Ember) Random Hse. Children's Bks.

Behar, Ruth. Letters from Cuba. 2020. (ENG., Illus.). 272p. (J). (gr. 5). 17.99 (978-0-525-51647-7(6), Nancy Paulsen Books) Penguin Young Readers Group.

Booth, Anne. Refuge. Usher, Sam, illus. 2016. (ENG.). 32p. (J). (gr. -1-3). 15.99 (978-0-316-36172-9(0)) Little, Brown Bks. for Young Readers.

Boyce, Frank Cottrell. The Unforgotten Coat. 2011. (ENG., Illus.). 112p. (J). (gr. 3-7). 16.99 (978-0-7636-5729-1(8)) Candlewick Pr.

—The Unforgotten Coat. 2011. (Playaway Children Ser.). (ENG.). (J). (gr. 4-7). 39.99 (978-1-4558-4539-2(6)) Findaway World, LLC.

Brashares, Ann. The Here & Now. 2014. 242p. (YA). (978-0-385-39008-8(4), Delacorte Pr) Random House Publishing Group.

—The Here & Now. 2015. (ENG.). 256p. (YA). (gr. 7). pap. 10.99 (978-0-385-73683-1(5), Ember) Random Hse. Children's Bks.

Burg, Ann E. Rebekkah's Journey: A World War II Refugee Story. Iskowitz, Joel, illus. 2006. (Tales of Young Americans Ser.). (ENG.). 48p. (J). (gr. 1-4). 17.95 (978-1-58536-275-2(1), 202086) Sleeping Bear Pr.

Casanova, Mary. The Klipfish Code. 2012. (ENG.). 240p. (J). (gr. 5-7). pap. 7.99 (978-0-547-74447-6(1), 1485490, Clarion Bks.) HarperCollins Pubs.

Choyce, Lesley. Refuge Cove. 2004. (Orca Soundings Ser.). 89p. 19.95 (978-0-7569-4325-7(6)) Perfection Learning Corp.

Collins, A. L. Asylum: Refugees of Mars. Tikulin, Tomislav, illus. 2018. (Redworld Ser.). (ENG.). 128p. (J). (gr. 3-8). lib. bdg. 25.99 (978-1-4965-5886-2(3), 137024, Stone Arch Bks.) Capstone.

Conolan, Emily. Touch the Sun: the Freedom Finders. 2019. (Freedom Finders Ser.). (ENG., Illus.). 336p. (J). (gr. 4-8). pap. 10.99 (978-1-76029-492-2(6)) Allen & Unwin AUS. Dist: Independent Pubs. Group.

Cooney, Caroline B. Diamonds in the Shadow. 2009. 240p. (YA). 9.99 (978-1-4000-7424-2(X), WaterBrook Pr.) Crown Publishing Group, The.

—Diamonds in the Shadow. 2007. (ENG.). 228p. (YA). (gr. 7-12). lib. bdg. 26.19 (978-0-385-90278-6(6)) Random House Publishing Group.

—Diamonds in the Shadow. 2009. (ENG.). 240p. (YA). (gr. 7). pap. 9.99 (978-0-385-73262-8(7), Delacorte Bks. for Young Readers) Random Hse. Children's Bks.

Cooper, Michelle. The FitzOsbornes at War. 2013. (Montmaray Journals: 3). (ENG.). 560p. (YA). (gr. 7). pap. 12.99 (978-0-307-93058-3(0), Ember) Random Hse. Children's Bks.

Copp, Mary Wagley. Wherever I Go. Mohammed, Munir D., illus. 2020. (ENG.). 32p. (J). (gr. 1-4). 19.99 (978-1-5344-1919-3(5)) Simon & Schuster Children's Publishing.

Cremer, Andrea. The Inventor's Secret. 2015. (Inventor's Secret Ser.: 1). (ENG.). 416p. (YA). (gr. 7). pap. 10.99 (978-0-14-751438-7(X), Speak) Penguin Young Readers Group.

De Arias, Patricia. Marwan's Journey. Borràs, Laura, illus. 2018. 36p. (J). (gr. k-2). 17.99 (978-988-8341-55-9(3), Minedition) Penguin Young Readers Group.

Del Rizzo, Suzanne. My Beautiful Birds. Del Rizzo, Suzane, illus. 2017. (ENG.). 32p. (J). (gr. 1-3). 18.95 (978-1-77278-010-9(3)) Pajama Pr. CAN. Dist: Publishers Group West (PGW).

Diaz, Alexandra. The Crossroads. (ENG.). (J). (gr. 3-7). 2019. 352p. pap. 8.99 (978-1-5344-1456-3(8)) 2018. (Illus.). 336p. 18.99 (978-1-5344-1455-6(X)) Simon & Schuster/Paula Wiseman Bks. (Simon & Schuster/Paula Wiseman Bks.).

—The Only Road. (ENG.). (J). (gr. 3-7). 2017. 336p. pap. 8.99 (978-1-4814-5751-4(9)) 2016. (Illus.). 320p. 18.99 (978-1-4814-5750-7(0)) Simon & Schuster/Paula Wiseman Bks. (Simon & Schuster/Paula Wiseman Bks.).

—El único Destino (the Only Road) 2016. (SPA., Illus.). (J). (gr. 3-7). 320p. 18.99 (978-1-4814-8441-1(9)); 336p. pap. 8.99 (978-1-4814-8442-8(7)) Simon & Schuster/Paula Wiseman Bks. (Simon & Schuster/Paula Wiseman Bks.).

Ehrmantraut, Brenda. Hope Weavers. Magnuson, Diana, illus. 2009. (J). (978-0-9729833-8-9(4)) Bubble Gum Pr.

PQR

Eldridge, Jim. The Refugee Camp 4 Voyagers. Sperling, Tom, illus. 2017. (Cambridge Reading Adventures Ser.). (ENG.). 32p. pap. 8.35 *(978-1-108-40108-1(2))* Cambridge Univ. Pr.
Elizabeth's Story 1848. 2014. (Secrets of the Manor Ser.: 3). (ENG., Illus.). 160p. (J). (gr. 3-7). pap. 7.99 *(978-1-4814-1840-9(8)*, Simon Spotlight) Simon Spotlight.
Ellis, Deborah. Mud City. 1 vol. 2015. (Breadwinner Ser.: 3). (ENG., Illus.). 168p. (J). (gr. 5-9). pap. 10.99 *(978-1-55498-773-3(3))* Groundwood Bks. CAN. Dist: Publishers Group West (PGW).
—Mud City. 2013. 156p. pap. *(978-1-4596-6445-6(0))* ReadHowYouWant.com, Ltd.
—Parvana's Journey. 2013. 184p. pap. *(978-1-4596-6476-0(0))* ReadHowYouWant.com, Ltd.
Engle, Margarita. Tropical Secrets: Holocaust Refugees in Cuba. 2009. (ENG.). 208p. (YA). (gr. 7-12). 24.99 *(978-0-8050-8936-3(5)*, 900055289, Holt, Henry & Co. Bks. For Young Readers) Holt, Henry & Co.
Farish, Terry. The Good Braider. 0 vols. 2013. (ENG.). 224p. (YA). (gr. 7-12). pap. 9.99 *(978-1-4778-1628-8(3)*, 9781477816288, Skyscape) Amazon Publishing.
—The Good Braider. 2014. (ENG.). 221p. (YA). (gr. 9-12). lib. bdg. 21.80 *(978-1-5311-8306-6(9))* Perfection Learning Corp.
Flores-Galbis, Enrique. 90 Miles to Havana. 2012. (ENG.). 304p. (J). (gr. 4-7). pap. 8.99 *(978-1-250-00559-5(0)*, 900081145) Square Fish.
Fountain, Ele. Refugee 87. 2020. (ENG.). 256p. (J). (gr. 3-7). pap. 8.99 *(978-0-316-42301-4(7))* Little, Brown Bks. for Young Readers.
Fraillon, Zana. The Bone Sparrow. 2016. (ENG.). 240p. (J). (gr. 4-7). 16.99 *(978-1-4847-8151-7(1))* Little, Brown Bks. for Young Readers.
Gibney, Shannon. Dream Country. 2019. (ENG., Illus.). 368p. (YA). (gr. 9). pap. 10.99 *(978-0-7352-3168-9(0)*, Penguin Books) Penguin Young Readers Group.
Goring, Ruth. Adriana's Angels. Meza, Erika, illus. 2017. (J). 16.99 *(978-1-5064-1832-2(5)*, Sparkhouse Family) 1517 Media.
—Los ángeles de Adriana. Meza, Erika, illus. 2017. 32p. (J). 16.99 *(978-1-5064-2507-8(0)*, Sparkhouse Family) 1517 Media.
Gratz, Alan. Refugee. 1 vol. 2017. (ENG.). 352p. (J). (gr. 4-7). 17.99 *(978-0-545-88083-1(1)*, Scholastic Pr.) Scholastic, Inc.
Greder, Armin. The Mediterranean. 2018. (ENG., Illus.). 40p. (J). (gr. 3). 25.99 *(978-1-76063-095-9(0))* Allen & Unwin AUS. Dist: Independent Pubs. Group.
Greene, Janice. No Exit. 1 vol. unabr. ed. 2010. (Q Reads Ser.). (ENG.). 32p. (YA). (gr. 9-12). pap. 8.50 *(978-1-61651-202-6(4))* Saddleback Educational Publishing, Inc.
Hager, Mandy. Into the Wilderness. 2014. (Blood of the Lamb Ser.: 2). (ENG.). 335p. (YA). (gr. 9). 17.99 *(978-1-61614-863-8(2)*, Pyr) Start Publishing LLC.
Halahmy, Miriam. Hidden. 2018. (ENG.). 224p. (YA). (gr. 7). pap. 9.99 *(978-0-8234-4026-9(5))* Holiday Hse., Inc.
—Saving Hanno: The Story of a Refugee Dog. 2019. (ENG.). 112p. (J). (gr. 3-7). 17.99 *(978-0-8234-4165-5(2))* Holiday Hse., Inc.
Harris, Christine. The Silver Path. (Illus.). (J). (ENG & VIE.). 26p. *(978-1-85430-327-1(9)*, 93381); (CHI & ENG.). 32p. *(978-1-85430-323-3(6)*, 93425) Little Tiger Pr. Group.
Hartnett, Sonya. The Midnight Zoo. Offermann, Andrea, illus. 2018. (ENG.). 224p. (J). (gr. 5-9). pap. 8.99 *(978-0-7636-6462-6(6))* Candlewick Pr.
Hiranandani, Veera. The Night Diary. (J). (gr. 3-7). 2019. (Illus.). 288p. 8.99 *(978-0-7352-2852-8(3)*, Puffin Books) 2018. 272p. 17.99 *(978-0-7352-2851-1(5)*, Kokila) Penguin Young Readers Group.
Holm, Anne. I Am David. 2004. (ENG.). 256p. (J). (gr. 3-7). pap. 9.99 *(978-0-15-205160-0(0)*, 1195564, Clarion Bks.) HarperCollins Pubs.
Howard, Ellen. Different Kind of Courage. 2007. (ENG.). 184p. (J). (gr. 3-7). pap. 10.95 *(978-1-4169-6730-9(3)*, Simon & Schuster/Paula Wiseman Bks.) Simon & Schuster/Paula Wiseman Bks.
Kazerooni, Abbas. The Boy with Two Lives. 2016. (ENG.). 256p. (YA). (gr. 7). 12.99 *(978-1-74331-483-8(3))* Allen & Unwin AUS. Dist: Independent Pubs. Group.
Kelly, Kevin. A Horse Called el Dorado. 2005. (ENG.). 144p. (J). pap. 10.95 *(978-0-86278-907-7(9))* O'Brien Pr., Ltd., The IRL. Dist: Dufour Editions, Inc.
Khan, Rukhsana. The Roses in My Carpets. 1 vol. Himler, Ronald, illus. 2004. (ENG.). 32p. (J). (gr. 1-3). pap. 14.95 *(978-1-55005-069-1(9)*, 401ba9c0-37da-4895-8825-a9e2846f9cc6) Fitzhenry & Whiteside, Ltd. CAN. Dist: Firefly Bks., Ltd.
Kullab, Samya. Escape from Syria. Roche, Jackie, illus. 2017. (ENG.). 96p. (gr. 7-12). 19.95 *(978-1-77085-982-1(9)*, d1b74160-dd04-46de-bb91-929f73e88949) Firefly Bks., Ltd.
Lai, Thanhhà. Butterfly Yellow. 2019. (ENG.). 304p. (YA). (gr. 8). 17.99 *(978-0-06-222921-2(4)*, HarperCollins) HarperCollins Pubs.
Langridge, R. Criminy. 2018. (Illus.). 112p. (J). (gr. 5-9). pap. 12.99 *(978-1-5067-0744-0(0)*, Dark Horse Books) Dark Horse Comics.
Lantigua, Lizette M. Mission Libertad. 2012. (ENG.). 192p. (YA). pap. 9.95 *(978-0-8198-4900-7(6))* Pauline Bks. & Media.
Lasenby, Jack. Taur. (Travellers Ser.: No. 2). (Illus.). 160p. (YA). (gr. 8-18). pap. *(978-1-877135-18-7(6)*, Longacre Pr.) Random Hse. New Zealand.
Lewis, Gill. A Story Like the Wind. Weaver, Jo, illus. 2018. (ENG.). 80p. (J). 16.00 *(978-0-8028-5514-5(8)*, Eerdmans Bks For Young Readers) Eerdmans, William B. Publishing Co.
Lombard, Jenny. Drita, My Homegirl. 2008. 144p. (J). (gr. 3-7). 6.99 *(978-0-14-240905-3(7)*, Puffin Books) Penguin Young Readers Group.
—Drita, My Homegirl. 2008. 135p. (J). (gr. 4-6). 13.65 *(978-0-7569-8919-4(1))* Perfection Learning Corp.
Maclear, Kyo. Story Boat. Kheiriyeh, Rashin, illus. 2020. (ENG.). 40p. (J). (gr. -1-2). 17.99 *(978-0-7352-6359-8(0)*, Tundra Bks.) Tundra Bks. CAN. Dist: Penguin Random Hse. LLC.
Maddox, Jake. Skaters Feroces. Aparicio Publishing LLC, Aparicio Publishing, tr. Muñiz, Berenice, illus. 2020. (Jake Maddox Novelas Gráficas Ser.). (SPA.). 72p. (J). (gr. 3-8). pap. 6.95 *(978-1-4965-9314-6(6)*, 142344); lib. bdg. 27.99 *(978-1-4965-9179-1(8)*, 142088) Capstone. (Stone Arch Bks.).
—Strange Boarders. Muñiz, Berenice, illus. 2018. (Jake Maddox Graphic Novels Ser.). (ENG.). 72p. (J). (gr. 3-8). pap. 6.95 *(978-1-4965-6050-6(7)*, 137431); lib. bdg. 27.99 *(978-1-4965-6046-9(9)*, 137427) Capstone. (Stone Arch Bks.).
Manivong, Laura. Escaping the Tiger. 2010. (ENG.). 224p. (J). (gr. 5-18). 15.99 *(978-0-06-166177-8(5))* HarperCollins Pubs.
Marsh, Katherine. Nowhere Boy. 2020. (ENG.). 384p. (J). pap. 8.99 *(978-1-250-21145-3(X)*, 900198061) Square Fish.
Matthews, L. S. Fish. 2006. 183p. (gr. 5-9). 16.50 *(978-0-7569-6626-3(4))* Perfection Learning Corp.
Mazer, Norma Fox. Good Night, Maman. 2010. (ENG., Illus.). 192p. (J). (gr. 5-7). pap. 12.95 *(978-0-15-206173-9(8)*, 1198532, Clarion Bks.) HarperCollins Pubs.
McDougall, Sophia. Mars Evacuees. (ENG.). (J). (gr. 3-7). 2016. 432p. pap. 7.99 *(978-0-06-229400-5(8))* 2015. 416p. 16.99 *(978-0-06-229399-2(0))* HarperCollins Pubs. (HarperCollins).
Mead, Alice. Year of No Rain. 2005. (Illus.). 129p. (gr. 4-7). 15.50 *(978-0-7569-5158-0(5))* Perfection Learning Corp.
Mikaelsen, Ben. Tree Girl. 2005. (ENG.). 240p. (YA). (gr. 8). pap. 11.99 *(978-0-06-009006-7(5)*, HarperTeen) HarperCollins Pubs.
Mitchell, Jane. Without Refuge. 2018. (ENG.). 288p. (J). (gr. 4-7). 16.99 *(978-1-5415-0050-1(4)*, bbf255d3-caab-431e-aef2-238a34400f75, Carolrhoda Bks.) Lerner Publishing Group.
Moon, Young-Sook. Across the Tumen: A North Korean Kkotjebi Boy's Quest. 2014.Tr. of 꽃제비 영대;: 죽음을 넘어 희망을 찾아간 소년;. (ENG.). 128p. pap. 16.99 *(978-1-62412-009-1(1)*, 2715) Seoul Selection KOR. Dist: Univ. of Hawaii Pr.
Morano, John. Makoona. 2nd rev. ed. 2005. (Morano Eco-Adventure Ser.: 2). 236p. (YA). (gr. 8-12). per. 14.99 *(978-1-59092-111-1(9))* Blue Forge Pr.
—Makoona. Anderson, Sarah, illus. 2017. (John Morano Eco-Adventure Ser.: Vol. 2). (ENG.). (YA). (gr. 8-12). pap. 9.99 *(978-1-945760-04-4(4))* Grey Gecko Pr.
Morley, Ben. The Silence Seeker. Pearce, Carl, illus. 2009. (ENG.). 32p. (J). (gr. k-2). pap. 14.99 *(978-1-84853-003-4(X))* Transworld Publishers Ltd. GBR. Dist: Independent Pubs. Group.
Morpurgo, Michael. Shadow. 2014. (ENG.). 208p. (J). (gr. 5-9). pap. 10.99 *(978-1-250-03996-5(7)*, 900123699) Square Fish.
Nagai, Mariko. Under the Broken Sky. 2019. (ENG., Illus.). 304p. (J). 17.99 *(978-1-250-15921-2(0)*, 900185614, Holt, Henry & Co. Bks. For Young Readers) Holt, Henry & Co.
Naidoo, Beverley. The Other Side of Truth. 2008. 252p. (gr. 5-9). 17.00 *(978-0-7569-8941-5(8))* Perfection Learning Corp.
Nanji, Shenaaz. Child of Dandelions. 1 vol. 2008. (ENG., Illus.). 216p. (YA). (gr. 8-12). pap. 9.95 *(978-1-897187-50-0(5)*, 1897187505) Second Story Pr. CAN. Dist: Orca Bk. Pubs. USA.
Novel Units. Lily's Crossing Novel Units Student Packet. 2019. (ENG.). (J). pap. 13.99 *(978-1-58130-645-3(8)*, Novel Units, Inc.) Classroom Library Co.
—Lily's Crossing Novel Units Teacher Guide. 2019. (ENG.). (J). pap. 12.99 *(978-1-58130-644-6(X)*, Novel Units, Inc.) Classroom Library Co.
O'Brien, Anne Sibley. A Path of Stars. O'Brien, Anne Sibley, illus. 2012. (Illus.). 40p. (J). (gr. k-3). 17.99 *(978-1-57091-735-6(3))* Charlesbridge Publishing, Inc.
Ørbeck-Nilssen, Constance. Vanishing Colors. Düzakin, Akin, illus. 2019. (ENG.). 40p. (J). *(978-0-8028-5518-3(0)*, Eerdmans Bks For Young Readers) Eerdmans, William B. Publishing Co.
Osborne, William. Hitler's Secret. 2013. (Illus.). 333p. (YA). *(978-0-545-51533-7(5)*, Chicken Hse., The) Scholastic, Inc.
Padian, Maria. Out of Nowhere. 2015. (ENG.). 352p. (YA). (gr. 7). pap. 10.99 *(978-0-375-86562-6(4)*, Ember) Random Hse. Children's Bks.
Park, Linda Sue. A Long Walk to Water: Based on a True Story. (ENG., Illus.). 128p. (J). (gr. 5-7). 2011. pap. 9.99 *(978-0-547-57731-9(1)*, 1458533) 2010. 18.99 *(978-0-547-25127-1(0)*, 1101512) HarperCollins Pubs. (Clarion Bks.).
—A Long Walk to Water: Based on a True Story. 2009. 8.32 *(978-0-7848-3885-3(2)*, Everbind) Marco Bk. Co.
—A Long Walk to Water: Based on a True Story. 2011. 18.00 *(978-1-61383-124-3(2))* Perfection Learning Corp.
—A Long Walk to Water: Based on a True Story. 2011. lib. bdg. 18.40 *(978-0-606-23406-1(3))* Turtleback.
Paterson, Katherine. The Day of the Pelican. 2010. (ENG.). 160p. (J). (gr. 5-7). pap. 7.99 *(978-0-547-40627-5(4)*, 1428505, Clarion Bks.) HarperCollins Pubs.
Perl, Lila. Isabel's War. 2014. (ENG.). 224p. (J). (gr. 2-7). pap. 12.95 *(978-1-939601-27-8(4))* Ig Publishing, Inc.
Pinkney, Andrea Davis. The Red Pencil. Evans, Shane W., illus. 2014. (ENG.). 336p. (J). (gr. 4-17). 34.99 *(978-0-316-24780-1(4))* Little, Brown Bks. for Young Readers.
Prins, Piet. The Grim Reaper. 2006. (Illus.). 130p. (J). pap. *(978-1-894666-74-9(7))* Inheritance Pubns.
—Hideout in the Swamp. 2006. (Illus.). 136p. (J). pap. *(978-1-894666-73-2(9))* Inheritance Pubns.
Pung, Alice. Marly & the Goat: Marly: Book 3, Bk. 3. 3rd ed. 2016. (Our Australian Girl Ser.: 3). (Illus.). 144p. (J). (gr. 3-7). 14.99 *(978-0-14-330851-5(3))* Penguin Random Hse. AUS. Dist: Independent Pubs. Group.
Ross, Susan. Kiki & Jacques: A Refugee Story. 2019. (ENG.). 144p. (J). (gr. 3-7). pap. 7.99 *(978-0-8234-4180-8(6))* Holiday Hse., Inc.
Sanna, Francesca. The Journey. 2016. (ENG., Illus.). 48p. (J). (gr. k-2). 17.99 *(978-1-909263-99-4(0))* Flying Eye Bks. GBR. Dist: Penguin Random Hse. LLC.
—Me & My Fear. 2018. (ENG., Illus.). 40p. (J). (gr. -1-2). 17.99 *(978-1-911171-53-9(4))* Flying Eye Bks. GBR. Dist: Penguin Random Hse. LLC.
Senzai, N. H. Escape from Aleppo. 2018. (ENG., Illus.). 336p. (J). (gr. 3-7). 17.99 *(978-1-4814-7217-3(8)*, Simon & Schuster/Paula Wiseman Bks.) Simon & Schuster/Paula Wiseman Bks.
—Shooting Kabul. 1. 2010. (Kabul Chronicles Ser.). (ENG., Illus.). 272p. (J). (gr. 3-7). 19.99 *(978-1-4424-0194-5(X))* Simon & Schuster, Inc.
—Shooting Kabul. 2011. (Kabul Chronicles Ser.). (ENG., Illus.). 288p. (J). (gr. 3-7). pap. 8.99 *(978-1-4424-0195-2(8)*, Simon & Schuster/Paula Wiseman Bks.) Simon & Schuster/Paula Wiseman Bks.
Sepetys, Ruta. Salt to the Sea. l.t. ed. 2016. 500p. 24.95 *(978-1-4104-9287-6(7))* Cengage Gale.
—Salt to the Sea. (ENG.). (YA). (gr. 7). 2017. 448p. pap. 12.99 *(978-0-14-242362-2(9)*, Penguin Books) 2016. (Illus.). 400p. 19.99 *(978-0-399-16030-1(2)*, Philomel Bks.) Penguin Young Readers Group.
—Salt to the Sea. 2017. lib. bdg. 22.10 *(978-0-606-40492-1(9))* Turtleback.
Shulevitz, Uri. How I Learned Geography. Shulevitz, Uri, illus. 2008. (ENG., Illus.). 32p. (J). (gr. -1-3). 21.99 *(978-0-374-33499-4(4)*, 900030472, Farrar, Straus & Giroux (BYR)) Farrar, Straus & Giroux.
Simon, Tanya & Simon, Richard. Oskar & the Eight Blessings. Siegel, Mark, illus. 2015. (ENG.). 40p. (J). (gr. -1-3). 19.99 *(978-1-59643-949-8(1)*, 900123918) Roaring Brook Pr.
Skrypuch, Marsha Forchuk. The War Below. 2018. (ENG.). 256p. (J). (gr. 3-7). 17.99 *(978-1-338-23302-5(5)*, Scholastic Pr.) Scholastic, Inc.
Stamper, Vesper. What the Night Sings. 2018. (Illus.). 272p. (YA). (gr. 7). 21.99 *(978-1-5247-0038-6(X)*, Knopf Bks. for Young Readers) Random Hse. Children's Bks.
Staples, Suzanne Fisher. Under the Persimmon Tree. 2008. (Illus.). 281p. (gr. 7-12). 20.00 *(978-0-7569-9004-6(1))* Perfection Learning Corp.
—Under the Persimmon Tree. 2008. (ENG., Illus.). 304p. (YA). (gr. 7-12). pap. 13.99 *(978-0-312-37776-2(2)*, 900049283) Square Fish.
Stein, R. Conrad. Someone Talked! 2011. (ENG.). 146p. (J). pap. 8.95 *(978-1-935178-17-0(2)*, ChironBooks) Coleman/Perrin.
Swindells, Robert. Ruby Tanya. 2005. 256p. (J). (gr. 7). per. 15.99 *(978-0-440-86398-4(8))* Transworld Publishers Ltd. GBR. Dist: Independent Pubs. Group.
TenNapel, Doug. Escape from the Lizzarks: A Graphic Novel, Bk. 1. TenNapel, Doug, illus. 2015. (Nnewts Ser.: 1). (ENG., Illus.). 192p. (J). (gr. 3-7). pap. 12.99 *(978-0-545-67646-5(0)*, Graphix) Scholastic, Inc.
Thor, Annika. A Faraway Island. Schenck, Linda, tr. 2011. (Faraway Island Ser.: 1). 256p. (J). (gr. 3-7). 7.99 *(978-0-375-84495-9(3)*, Yearling) Random Hse. Children's Bks.
—The Lily Pond. Schenck, Linda, tr. (Faraway Island Ser.). 224p. (J). (gr. 4-7). 2012. 7.99 *(978-0-385-74040-1(9)*, Yearling)2. 2013. (ENG.). lib. bdg. 21.19 *(978-0-385-90838-2(5)*, Delacorte Pr.) Random Hse. Children's Bks.
Walter, Jon. Close to the Wind. 2017. (ENG.). 320p. (J). (gr. 5-7). pap. 8.99 *(978-0-545-82275-6(0))* Scholastic, Inc.
Walters, Eric. Walking Home. 2014. (ENG.). 304p. (J). (gr. 5). pap. 10.99 *(978-0-385-68157-5(7))* Doubleday Canada, Ltd. CAN. Dist: Penguin Random Hse. LLC.
Weber, Judith Eichler. Seeking Safety. Martin, John F., illus. 2006. (Adventures in America Ser.). (J). *(978-1-893110-46-5(X))* Silver Moon Pr.
Whitebeach, Terry & Enadio, Sarafino Wani. Trouble Tomorrow. 2017. (ENG.). 224p. (YA). (gr. 8-12). pap. 12.99 *(978-1-76029-146-4(3))* Allen & Unwin AUS. Dist: Independent Pubs. Group.
Whitman, Sylvia. The Milk of Birds. (ENG., Illus.). 384p. (YA). (gr. 9). 2014. pap. 12.99 *(978-1-4424-4683-0(8))* 2013. 16.99 *(978-1-4424-4682-3(X)*, Atheneum Bks. for Young Readers) Simon & Schuster Children's Publishing.
Whitney, Kim Ablon. The Other Half of Life. 2010. 256p. (YA). (gr. 7). mass mkt. 7.99 *(978-0-375-84422-5(8)*, Laurel Leaf) Random Hse. Children's Bks.
Williams, Karen & Mohammed, Khadra. My Name Is Sangoel. Stock, Catherine, illus. 2009. (ENG.). 36p. (J). (gr. 1-5). 17.00 *(978-0-8028-5307-3(2)*, Eerdmans Bks For Young Readers) Eerdmans, William B. Publishing Co.
Williams, Karen Lynn & Mohammed, Khadra. Four Feet, Two Sandals. Chayka, Doug, illus. rev. ed. 2016. 32p. (gr. 2-5). 18.70 *(978-0-8028-5296-0(3))* Kendall Hunt Publishing Co.
Williams, Mary. Brothers in Hope: The Story of the Lost Boys of Sudan. 1 vol. Christie, R. Gregory, illus. 2013. (ENG.). 40p. (J). (gr. 2-5). 20.95 *(978-1-58430-232-2(1)*, leelowbooks) Lee & Low Bks., Inc.
Williams, Michael. Now Is the Time for Running. 2013. (ENG.). 240p. (YA). (gr. 7-17). pap. 10.99 *(978-0-316-07788-0(7))* Little, Brown Bks. for Young Readers.
Williamson, Victoria. The Fox Girl & the White Gazelle. 26 vols. 2018. 272p. (J). 9.95 *(978-1-78250-490-0(7)*, Kelpies) Floris Bks. GBR. Dist: Consortium Bk. Sales & Distribution.
Zeiss, Joyce Burns. Out of the Dragon's Mouth. 2015. (ENG., Illus.). 240p. (YA). (gr. 9-12). pap. 11.99 *(978-0-7387-4196-3(5)*, 0738741965, Flux) North Star Editions.

REFUSE AND REFUSE DISPOSAL

see also Hazardous Wastes; Pollution; Sewage Disposal; Waste Products; Water—Pollution

Addison, D. R. Garbage Trucks at Work. 2009. (Big Trucks Ser.). 24p. (J). (gr. 1-1). 42.50 *(978-1-61511-585-3(4)*, PowerKids Pr.) Rosen Publishing Group, Inc., The.
Alexander, richard. Que Hacen Los Recolectores de Basura? / What Do Garbage Collectors Do?. 1 vol. 2015. (Ayudantes de la Comunidad / Helping the Community Ser.). (ENG & SPA.). 24p. (J). (gr. 1-1). 25.27 *(978-1-4994-0611-5(8)*, be8aac68-8e15-4a0b-a895-f5e0d221c8f0, PowerKids Pr.) Rosen Publishing Group, Inc., The.
—What Do Garbage Collectors Do?. 1 vol. 2015. (Helping the Community Ser.). (ENG., Illus.). 24p. (J). (gr. 1-1). pap. 9.25 *(978-1-4994-0631-3(2)*, b65809ec-5a4c-4cd5-a58b-03a0b95cd8ad, PowerKids Pr.) Rosen Publishing Group, Inc., The.
Arnold, Tedd. Fly Guy Presents: Garbage & Recycling (Scholastic Reader, Level 2) Arnold, Tedd, illus. 2019. (Scholastic Reader, Level 2 Ser.: 12). (ENG., Illus.). 32p. (J). (gr. k-2). pap. 4.99 *(978-1-338-21719-3(4))* Scholastic, Inc.
Barnham, Kay. Recycle. 2007. (Environment Action Ser.). (ENG., Illus.). 32p. (J). (gr. 3-7). pap. *(978-0-7787-3669-1(5))* Crabtree Publishing Co.
Barraclough, Sue. Recycling Materials. 2007. (Making a Difference Ser.). (Illus.). 30p. (J). (gr. -1-3). lib. bdg. 27.10 *(978-1-59771-108-1(X))* Sea-To-Sea Pubns.
Bellamy, Rufus. Waste & Pollution. 2010. (Sustaining Our Environment Ser.). 48p. (J). 35.65 *(978-1-60753-139-5(9))* Amicus Learning.
Bodden, Valerie. The War on Waste. 2010. (Earth Issues Ser.). 48p. (YA). (gr. 5-18). 23.95 *(978-1-58341-985-4(3)*, Creative Education) Creative Co., The.
Bourgeois, Paulette. Garbage Collectors. LaFave, Kim, illus. 2004. 32p. (J). lib. bdg. 15.38 *(978-1-4242-1190-6(5))* Fitzgerald Bks.
—Garbage Collectors. LaFave, Kim, illus. 2003. (Kids Can Read Level 3 Ser.). (ENG.). 32p. (J). (gr. k-3). 16.19 *(978-1-55337-573-9(4))* Kids Can Pr., Ltd. CAN. Dist: Children's Plus, Inc.
Bruno, Nikki. Gross Jobs Working with Garbage: 4D an Augmented Reading Experience. 2019. (Gross Jobs 4D Ser.). (ENG., Illus.). 32p. (J). (gr. 3-9). lib. bdg. 31.99 *(978-1-5435-5487-8(3)*, 139358, Capstone Pr.) Capstone.
—Gross Jobs Working with Water & Sewers: 4D an Augmented Reading Experience. 2019. (Gross Jobs 4D Ser.). (ENG., Illus.). 32p. (J). (gr. 3-9). lib. bdg. 31.99 *(978-1-5435-5488-5(1)*, 139359, Capstone Pr.) Capstone.
Bullard, Lisa. Look Out for Litter. Xin, Xiao, illus. 2011. (Planet Protectors Ser.). pap. 39.62 *(978-0-7613-8654-4(8)*, Millbrook Pr.) Lerner Publishing Group.
—Look Out for Litter. Zheng, Xin, illus. 2011. (Cloverleaf Books (tm) — Planet Protectors Ser.). (ENG.). 24p. (J). (gr. k-2). pap. 8.99 *(978-0-7613-8514-1(2)*, 5a4b4f8b-38ab-4ad0-91f9-1f30b3a7f7a5, Millbrook Pr.) Lerner Publishing Group.
—Rally for Recycling. Thomas, Wes, illus. 2011. (Planet Protectors Ser.). pap. 39.62 *(978-0-7613-8656-8(4)*, Millbrook Pr.) Lerner Publishing Group.
—Rally for Recycling. Thomas, John Wes, illus. 2011. (Cloverleaf Books (tm) — Planet Protectors Ser.). (ENG.). 24p. (J). (gr. k-2). pap. 8.99 *(978-0-7613-8516-5(9)*, 60001ba1-22ea-4901-b682-7a725ab9d5ee, Millbrook Pr.) Lerner Publishing Group.
Burton, Margie, et al. Clean Beaches & Playas Limpias: 6 English, 6 Spanish Adaptations. 2011. (J). spiral bd. 75.00 net. *(978-1-4108-5625-8(9))* Benchmark Education Co.
Carr, Aaron. Garbage Trucks. 2014. (Illus.). 24p. (J). *(978-1-4896-3224-1(7))* Weigl Pubs., Inc.
Close, Edward. What Do We Do with Trash?. 1 vol. 2012. (Discovery Education: the Environment Ser.). (ENG., Illus.). 32p. (J). (gr. 4-5). pap. 11.00 *(978-1-4488-7982-3(5)*, 7f4f345b-ff5d-4cb1-92db-b5b6b6e0fa31); lib. bdg. 28.93 *(978-1-4488-7894-9(2)*, ce3664a3-45d9-4098-ad80-30cac4e3d6e5) Rosen Publishing Group, Inc., The. (PowerKids Pr.).
Constable, Lee. How to Save the Whole Stinkin' Planet: A Garbological Adventure. Hart, James, III, illus. 2019. 256p. (J). (gr. 2-4). 18.99 *(978-1-76089-026-1(X)*, Puffin) Penguin Random Hse. AUS. Dist: Independent Pubs. Group.
Daynes, Katie. The Stinking Story of Garbage. Mayer, Uwe, illus. (Usborne Young Reading: Series Two Ser.). (J). 2006. 64p. (gr. 4-7). per. 5.99 *(978-0-7945-1247-7(X))* 2007. 62p. (gr. -1-3). 8.99 *(978-0-7945-1750-2(1))* EDC Publishing. (Usborne).
Dayton, Connor. Garbage Trucks. (Illus.). 24p. (J). 2012. 49.50 *(978-1-4488-5067-9(3))* 2011. (ENG., (gr. 1-1). pap. 9.25 *(978-1-4488-5066-2(5)*, 35ea8f5b-50d4-481a-864b-ad916e3b1d6e) 2011. (ENG., (gr. 1-1). lib. bdg. 26.27 *(978-1-4488-4958-1(6)*, d9002ded-1fbc-476e-865c-b9ec92a00538) Rosen Publishing Group, Inc., The. (PowerKids Pr.).
Devera, Czeena. Waste & Recycling Collector. Bane, Jeff, illus. 2018. (Mi Mini Biografía (My Itty-Bitty Bio): My Early Library). (ENG.). 24p. (J). (gr. k-1). pap. 12.79 *(978-1-5341-0818-9(1)*, 210636); lib. bdg. 30.64 *(978-1-5341-0719-9(3)*, 210635) Cherry Lake Publishing.
Dieker, Wendy Strobel. Garbage Trucks. 2018. (Spot Mighty Machines Ser.). (ENG.). 16p. (J). (gr. -1-2). pap. 9.99 *(978-1-68152-294-4(2)*, 14984); lib. bdg. *(978-1-68151-374-4(9)*, 14978) Amicus.
Dorion, Christiane. Earth's Garbage Crisis. 1 vol. 2007. (What If We Do Nothing? Ser.). (ENG., Illus.). 48p. (J). (gr. 5-8). pap. 15.05 *(978-0-8368-8153-0(2)*, d45608f7-1f16-4d4f-ac3f-e9beea4635e9); lib. bdg. 33.67 *(978-0-8368-7753-3(5)*, 5f0a2111-63ef-4c86-b249-7f8445a04dce, Gareth Stevens Secondary Library) Stevens, Gareth Publishing LLLP.
Eamer, Claire. What a Waste: Where Does Our Garbage Go? Edlund, Bambi, illus. 2017. (ENG.). 96p. (J). (gr. 3-7). 22.95 *(978-1-55451-919-4(5))* Annick Pr., Ltd. CAN. Dist: Publishers Group West (PGW).
Early Macken, JoAnn. Sanitation Workers. 1 vol. 2010. (People in My Community (Second Edition) Ser.). (ENG.). 24p. (J). (gr. k-2). pap. 9.15 *(978-1-4339-3810-8(3)*, 3900cc00-7f18-4d20-9731-a2fcd3d69a89); lib. bdg. 25.27 *(978-1-4339-3809-2(X)*, 5ee91a61-212b-4918-81a2-ebea9dee3c73) Stevens, Gareth Publishing LLLP.
Elliot, Marion. Recycled Craft Projects for Kids: 50 Fantastic Things to Make from Junk. Shown. 2014. (Illus.). 96p. (J). (gr. 2-7). 13.99 *(978-1-84322-891-2(2)*, Armadillo) Anness Publishing GBR. Dist: National Bk. Network.
Enz, Tammy. Repurpose It: Invent New Uses for Old Stuff. 2012. (Invent It Ser.). (ENG.). 32p. (gr. 3-4). pap. 47.70 *(978-1-4296-8457-6(7)*, Capstone Pr.); (J). pap. 8.10 *(978-1-4296-7983-1(2)*, 118315) Capstone.
Flynn, Riley. Garbage Goes Out! What Happens after That? 2018. (Story of Sanitation Ser.). (ENG., Illus.). 32p. (J). (gr. 3-6). lib. bdg. 27.99 *(978-1-5435-3111-4(3)*, 138707, Capstone Pr.) Capstone.
Flynn, Sarah Wassner. This Book Stinks! Gross Garbage, Rotten Rubbish, & the Science of Trash. 2017. 128p. (J). (gr.

3-7). pap. 14.99 (978-1-4263-2730-8(7), National Geographic Kids) Disney Publishing Worldwide.

Forest, Anne. Sanitation Workers, 1 vol., 1. 2015. (Hands-On Jobs Ser.). (ENG., Illus.). 24p. (J). (gr. 3-4). pap. 9.25 (978-1-5081-4371-0(4), 62e0da69-1c9f-440d-a266-f2dbd705f58c, PowerKids Pr.) Rosen Publishing Group, Inc., The.

Friedman, Lauri S. Garbage & Recycling. 2009. (Introducing Issues with Opposing Viewpoints Ser.). (ENG., Illus.). 144p. (J). (gr. 7-10). 36.95 (978-0-7377-4337-1(9), Greenhaven Pr., Inc.) Cengage Gale.

Furgang, Kathy. Where Does Your Garbage Go? & ¿Adónde va la Basura? 6 English, 6 Spanish Adaptations. 2011. (ENG & SPA.). (J). 75.00 net. (978-1-4108-5635-7(6)) Benchmark Education Co.

Fyvie, Erica. Trash Revolution: Breaking the Waste Cycle. Slavin, Bill, illus. 2018. (ENG.). 64p. (J). (gr. 3-7). 18.99 (978-1-77138-078-2(0)) Kids Can Pr., Ltd. CAN. Dist: Hachette Bk. Group.

Green, Jen. Garbage & Litter. 2010. (Reduce, Reuse, Recycle! Ser.). 32p. (J). (gr. 1-5). E-Book 50.50 (978-1-4488-0365-1(9)); (ENG.). (J). (gr. 2-3). pap. 11.60 (978-1-61532-243-5(4), bffe139e-d0ac-43cb-b5f9-af9c8174121e, PowerKids Pr.); (ENG., Illus.). (YA). (gr. 2-3). lib. bdg. 30.27 (978-1-61532-234-3(5), 27747281-54b2-485e-8854-383075690a30) Rosen Publishing Group, Inc., The.

—Water. 2010. (Reduce, Reuse, Recycle! Ser.). 32p. (J). (gr. 1-5). E-Book 50.50 (978-1-4488-0368-2(3)); (ENG.). (gr. 2-3). pap. 11.60 (978-1-61532-246-6(9), 67428810-de31-4197-b81c-07c13b65647d, PowerKids Pr.); (ENG., Illus.). (gr. 2-3). lib. bdg. 30.27 (978-1-61532-235-0(3), f717bea8-0cff-4bd0-877e-a264202146c6) Rosen Publishing Group, Inc., The.

Haerens, Margaret, ed. Garbage & Recycling, 1 vol. 2011. (Opposing Viewpoints Ser.). (ENG., Illus.). 248p. (gr. 10-12). 50.43 (978-0-7377-5428-5(1), ad45d16e-ac7d-44e9-be00-670d6df9d722, Greenhaven Publishing) Greenhaven Publishing LLC.

Hand, Carol. Working in Trash & Recycling Collection in Your Community, 1 vol. 2018. (Careers in Your Community Ser.). (ENG.). 80p. (gr. 7-7). 37.47 (978-1-4994-6734-5(6), c59a7435-200e-48ba-8f79-bae42c091ece) Rosen Publishing Group, Inc., The.

Harmon, Daniel E. Jobs in Environmental Cleanup & Emergency Hazmat Response, 1 vol. 2010. (Green Careers Ser.). (ENG., Illus.). 80p. (YA). (gr. 6-6). lib. bdg. 38.47 (978-1-4358-3570-2(0), 4e9364fd-9fe0-47fe-8634-46249a9de995) Rosen Publishing Group, Inc., The.

Heos, Bridget. Follow That Bottle! A Plastic Recycling Journey. Westgate, Alex, illus. 2016. (Keeping Cities Clean Ser.). (ENG.). 24p. (J). (gr. 1-4). lib. bdg. 20.95 (978-1-60753-964-3(0), 15652) Amicus.

—Follow That Garbage! A Journey to the Landfill. Westgate, Alex, illus. 2016. (Keeping Cities Clean Ser.). (ENG.). 24p. (J). (gr. 1-4). lib. bdg. 20.95 (978-1-60753-963-6(2), 15653) Amicus.

—Follow That Tap Water! A Journey down the Drain. Westgate, Alex, illus. 2016. (Keeping Cities Clean Ser.). (ENG.). 24p. (J). (gr. 1-4). lib. bdg. 20.95 (978-1-60753-965-0(9), 15655) Amicus.

Hepplewhite, Peter. Loos, Poos, & Number Twos: A Disgusting Journey Through the Bowels of History!, 1 vol. 2015. (Awfully Ancient Ser.). (ENG., Illus.). 32p. (J). (gr. 5-5). pap. 11.50 (978-1-4824-3117-9(3), a62f2339-83b1-433d-ba16-27f5601745c6) Stevens, Gareth Publishing LLLP.

Hewitt, Sally. Waste & Recycling. 2008. (Rise & Shine Ser.). (ENG., Illus.). 32p. (J). (gr. 3-7). pap. (978-0-7787-4105-3(2)); lib. bdg. (978-0-7787-4098-8(6)) Crabtree Publishing Co.

Higgins, Nadia. Garbage Trucks / Camiones de Basura. Sánchez, Sr., illus. 2019. (Machines! / ¡Las Máquinas! Ser.). (MUL.). 24p. (J). (gr. -1-2). lib. bdg. 33.99 (978-1-68410-340-9(1), 140260) Cantata Learning.

Horn, Geoffrey M. Sewer Inspector, 1 vol. 2011. (Dirty & Dangerous Jobs Ser.). (ENG.). 32p. (gr. 3-3). 31.21 (978-1-60870-178-0(6), cb693de3-d23b-49ca-b194-3cf32090da86) Cavendish Square Publishing LLC.

Hudd, Emily. How Long Does It Take for Trash to Decompose? 2019. (How Long Does It Take? Ser.). (ENG., Illus.). 32p. (J). (gr. 3-6). pap. 7.95 (978-1-5435-7542-2(0), 141074); lib. bdg. 29.99 (978-1-5435-7291-9(X), 140608) Capstone.

Inskipp, Carol. Reducing & Recycling Waste, 1 vol. 2004. (Improving Our Environment Ser.). (ENG., Illus.). 32p. (gr. 3-5). lib. bdg. 28.67 (978-0-8368-4429-0(7), cac96568-0bcc-4c19-805a-c628b53b5a9f, Gareth Stevens Learning Library) Stevens, Gareth Publishing LLLP.

Jakab, Cheryl. Waste Management, 1 vol. 2011. (Environment in Focus Ser.). (ENG.). 32p. (gr. 4-4). 31.21 (978-1-60870-093-6(3), 5610ac42-657e-4c9f-a62f-9c2ad15909ca) Cavendish Square Publishing LLC.

James, Lincoln. Where Does the Garbage Go?, 1 vol. 2012. (Everyday Mysteries Ser.). (ENG., Illus.). 24p. (J). (gr. 2-2). pap. 9.15 (978-1-4339-6327-8(2), 4d4c12d6-f6bc-43f4-a0bb-a821e55e0e15); lib. bdg. 25.27 (978-1-4339-6325-4(6), d46122a9-067d-4e1a-a83f-914427034513) Stevens, Gareth Publishing LLLP.

Kallen, Stuart A. Trashing the Planet: Examining Our Global Garbage Glut. 2017. (ENG., Illus.). 104p. (YA). (gr. 6-12). 37.32 (978-1-5124-1314-4(3), cdb91cf4-e5ad-46ec-97fa-442aa2435c76, Twenty-First Century Bks.) Lerner Publishing Group.

Kenan, Tessa. Hooray for Garbage Collectors! 2017. (Bumba Books (r) — Hooray for Community Helpers! Ser.). (ENG., Illus.). 24p. (J). (gr. -1-1). 26.65 (978-1-5124-3352-4(7), 8b4c1b06-6f3d-4f3f-a440-8e4e49b1bf83, Lerner Pubns.); pap. 8.99 (978-1-5124-5552-6(0), c48648f1-0864-4d6d-93e7-650da47aa682) Lerner Publishing Group.

—¡Que Vivan Los Recolectores de Basura! (Hooray for Garbage Collectors!) 2018. (Bumba Books (r) en Español — ¡Que Vivan Los Ayudantes Comunitarios! (Hooray for Community Helpers!) Ser.). (SPA., Illus.). 24p. (J). (gr. -1-1). 26.65 (978-1-5124-9752-6(5), 2c7076a0-f2b5-4635-9fb5-a866f0d590fa, Ediciones Lerner) Lerner Publishing Group.

Knight, M. J. Why Shouldn't I Drop Litter? 2009. (One Small Step Ser.). (YA). (gr. 2-5). 28.50 (978-1-59920-265-5(4)) Black Rabbit Bks.

Knight M J. Why Shouldn't I Drop Litter? 2009. (One Small Step Ser.). (ENG., Illus.). 32p. (J). (gr. -1-3). pap. (978-1-897563-51-9(5)) Saunders Bk. Co.

Landers, Ace. I Am a Garbage Truck. Migliari, Paola, illus. 2008. (ENG.). 8p. (J). (gr. -1 — 1). bds. 4.99 (978-0-545-07963-1(2), Cartwheel Bks.) Scholastic, Inc.

Latham, Donna. Garbage: Follow the Path of Your Trash with Environmental Science Activities for Kids. Casteel, Tom, illus. 2019. (Build It Yourself Ser.). (ENG.). 128p. (J). (gr. 4-6). 22.95 (978-1-61930-744-5(8), 568bd6cc-1b8c-4739-9a54-a54711d56cac); pap. 17.95 (978-1-61930-747-6(2), f4e812b2-c8a8-4871-9a6e-19a0dd649ddc) Nomad Pr.

Lawrence, Ellen. Garbage Galore. 2014. (Science Slam: Green World, Clean World Ser.). 24p. (J). (gr. -1-3). lib. bdg. 26.99 (978-1-62724-102-1(7)) Bearport Publishing Co., Inc.

Leaf, Christina. Garbage Collectors. 2018. (Community Helpers Ser.). (ENG., Illus.). 24p. (J). (gr. k-3). lib. bdg. 26.95 (978-1-62617-898-4(4), Blastoff! Readers) Bellwether Media.

Linde, Barbara M. Pollution, 1 vol. 2013. (Habitat Havoc Ser.). (ENG., Illus.). 32p. (J). (gr. 3-4). lib. bdg. 29.27 (978-1-4339-9926-0(9), dff8dedc-c8ee-4740-93c0-a6e20833174d) Stevens, Gareth Publishing LLLP.

Lindeen, Mary. Garbage Trucks. 2007. (Mighty Machines Ser.). (ENG., Illus.). 24p. (J). (gr. k-3). lib. bdg. 26.95 (978-1-60014-117-1(X)) Bellwether Media.

—Trash That Trash, Elmo & Abby! 2020. (Go Green with Sesame Street (r) Ser.). (ENG., Illus.). 32p. (J). (gr. -1-2). lib. bdg. 27.99 (978-1-5415-7258-4(0), c6ffef89-480d-4da4-89db-9356691679f9, Lerner Pubns.) Lerner Publishing Group.

Loh-Hagan, Virginia. Neighborhood Cleanup. 2017. (D. I. Y. Make It Happen Ser.). (ENG., Illus.). 32p. (J). (gr. 4-8). lib. bdg. 32.07 (978-1-63472-880-5(7), 209946, 45th Parallel Press) Cherry Lake Publishing.

MacCarald, Clara. Turning Poop into Power Fuel, 1 vol. 2017. (Power of Poop Ser.). (ENG.). 32p. (gr. 3-4). pap. 11.52 (978-0-7660-9100-9(7), 58e24ebe-5200-404a-b50e-a4e779275eff) Enslow Publishing, LLC.

Mancini, Candice L., ed. Garbage & Recycling, 1 vol. 2010. (Global Viewpoints Ser.). (ENG.). 232p. (gr. 10-12). 47.83 (978-0-7377-5081-2(2), 4c03ee71-c4aa-4dd5-a178-7478dd372abf); (Illus.). pap. 32.70 (978-0-7377-5082-9(0), 74b4e7ef-c6eb-4025-a5d1-badbc71917d7) Greenhaven Publishing LLC. (Greenhaven Publishing).

McCarthy, Meghan. All That Trash: The Story of the 1987 Garbage Barge & Our Problem with Stuff. McCarthy, Meghan, illus. 2018. (ENG., Illus.). 48p. (J). (gr. -1-3). 19.99 (978-1-4814-7752-9(8), Simon & Schuster/Paula Wiseman Bks.) Simon & Schuster/Paula Wiseman Bks.

McKissick, Katie. The Hidden World of Garbage: Multi-Digit Numbers (Grade 4) 2017. (Mathematics in the Real World Ser.). (ENG., Illus.). 32p. (J). (gr. 4-5). pap. 11.99 (978-1-4258-5546-8(6)) Teacher Created Materials, Inc.

Meissner, David. Where Does Your Garbage Go? 2011. (Early Connections Ser.). (J). (978-1-61672-608-9(3)) Benchmark Education Co.

—Where Does Your Garbage Go? Set Of 6. 2011. (Early Connections Ser.). (J). pap. 37.00 net. (978-1-4108-1077-9(1)) Benchmark Education Co.

Meister, Cari. Garbage Trucks. 2013. (ENG., Illus.). 24p. (J). lib. bdg. 25.65 (978-1-62031-045-8(7)) Jump! Inc.

Meyer, Susan. Getting a Job in Sanitation, 1 vol. 2013. (Job Basics: Getting the Job You Need Ser.). (ENG.). 80p. (YA). (gr. 8-8). 38.41 (978-1-4488-9607-3(X), 87cd22c7-97c7-4370-ac86-06b9c117dfb6) Rosen Publishing Group, Inc., The.

Michele, Tracey. Where Does the Garbage Go? 2011. (Learn-Abouts Ser.). (Illus.). 16p. (J). pap. 7.95 (978-1-59920-612-7(9)) Black Rabbit Bks.

Minden, Cecilia. Kids Can Clean up Trash. 2010. (21st Century Basic Skills Library: Kids Can Ser.). (ENG., Illus.). 24p. (gr. k-3). lib. bdg. 26.35 (978-1-60279-870-0(2), 200606) Cherry Lake Publishing.

Morrison, Marie. Garbage Trucks, 1 vol. 2019. (XL Machines! Ser.). (ENG.). 24p. (gr. 1-2). pap. 9.25 (978-1-7253-1154-1(2), 042e1794-2cdc-4565-bb2b-e7c60b771148, PowerKids Pr.) Rosen Publishing Group, Inc., The.

Murray, Aaron R. Sanitation Workers Help Us, 1 vol. 2012. (All about Community Helpers Ser.). (ENG., Illus.). 24p. (-1). pap. 10.35 (978-1-4644-0058-2(X), 21ffa4f5-f404-41a5-a746-0009729c430a, Enslow Publishing); (gr. -1-1). 25.27 (978-0-7660-4049-6(6), 1f4f847b-c5c6-466a-a16c-f6e2fbae447c, Enslow Publishing); (gr. -1-1). E-Book 25.27 (978-1-4645-0965-0(4), 844ab032-86a6-4a5b-b920-19c9af3d09ac) Enslow Publishing, LLC.

Murray, Julie. Garbage Collectors. 2018. (My Community: Jobs Ser.). (ENG.). 24p. (J). (gr. -1-2). lib. bdg. 31.36 (978-1-5321-0788-7(9), 28137, Abdo Kids) ABDO Publishing Co.

Nevins, Debbie & Foran, Jill. Waste Management. 2017. (J). (978-1-5105-2231-2(X)) SmartBook Media, Inc.

Newman, Barbara Johansen. Glamorous Garbage. 2015. (ENG., Illus.). 40p. (J). (gr. -1-3). 16.95 (978-1-62091-626-1(6), Astra Young Readers) Astra Publishing Hse.

Orme, Helen. Garbage & Recycling. 2008. (Earth in Danger Ser.). (Illus.). 32p. (YA). (gr. 3-6). lib. bdg. 25.27 (978-1-59716-726-0(6), 1284325) Bearport Publishing Co., Inc.

Ostopowich, Melanie. Waste. 2009. (Science Q & A Ser.). (Illus.). 48p. (YA). (gr. 5-8). pap. 10.95 (978-1-60596-065-4(9)); lib. bdg. 29.05 (978-1-60596-064-7(0)) Weigl Pubs., Inc.

Parker, Russ. Waste Management Crisis, 1 vol. 2009. (Planet in Crisis Ser.). (ENG.). 32p. (gr. 5-5). (YA). lib. bdg. 30.47 (978-1-4358-5253-2(2), 46d0b83b-97aa-40e9-bff2-9607e3781be9); (Illus.). (J). pap. 11.00 (978-1-4358-0683-2(2), 970f8463-ec99-4118-a29b-f562488adaa7) Rosen Publishing Group, Inc., The. (Rosen Reference).

Parks, Peggy J. Garbage. 2011. (J). (978-1-60217-031-5(2)) Erickson Pr.

—Garbage & Recycling. 2008. (Ripped from the Headlines Ser.). (YA). (gr. 7-12). 23.95 (978-1-60217-023-0(1)) Erickson Pr.

—Garbage & Recycling. 2010. (Compact Research Ser.). (YA). (gr. 7-12). 41.27 (978-1-60152-121-7(9)) ReferencePoint Pr., Inc.

Pettiford, Rebecca. Garbage Collectors. 2015. (J). lib. bdg. 25.65 (978-1-62031-157-8(7), Bullfrog Bks.) Jump! Inc.

Rabe, Tish. How to Help the Earth-By the Lorax. Ruiz, Aristides et al, illus. 2012. (Step into Reading: Step 3 Ser.). (ENG.). 48p. (J). (gr. k-2). lib. bdg. 16.19 (978-0-375-96977-5(2)) Random Hse. Bks. for Young Readers.

—How to Help the Earth-By the Lorax. 2012. (Step into Reading Level 3 Ser.). lib. bdg. 13.55 (978-0-606-23848-9(4)) Turtleback.

—How to Help the Earth-By the Lorax (Dr. Seuss) 2012. (Step into Reading Ser.). (ENG., Illus.). 48p. (J). (gr. k-3). pap. 5.99 (978-0-375-86977-8(8), Random Hse. Bks. for Young Readers) Random Hse. Children's Bks.

Reilly, Kevin. Waste Management, 1 vol. 2019. (Exploring Infrastructure Ser.). (ENG.). 48p. (gr. 3-4). 29.60 (978-1-9785-0339-7(3), 5a793140-56fe-4cae-a907-41934eb9413c) Enslow Publishing, LLC.

Reynolds, Alison. Let's Use It Again. Hopgood, Andrew, illus. 2009. (Save Our Planet! Ser.). 12p. (J). (gr. -1-3). bds. 11.40 (978-1-60754-415-9(6)) Windmill Bks.

Rhatigan, Joe. Get a Job at the Landfill. 2016. (Bright Futures Press: Get a Job Ser.). (ENG., Illus.). 32p. (J). (gr. 4-6). 32.07 (978-1-63471-905-6(0), 208941) Cherry Lake Publishing.

Riley, Karen. Don't Trash My Planet. 2004. (Illus.). 20p. (J). (gr. k-5). pap. 10.00 (978-0-9708135-4-1(6), "5,000") S.C.R.A.P. Gallery.

Rissman, Rebecca. Reducing, Reusing, & Recycling Waste. 2018. (Putting the Planet First Ser.). (Illus.). 32p. (J). (gr. 4-4). (978-0-7787-5031-4(0)) Crabtree Publishing Co.

Ritchie, Scot. Join the No-Plastic Challenge! A First Book of Reducing Waste. Ritchie, Scot, illus. 2019. (Exploring Our Community Ser.). (ENG., Illus.). 32p. (J). (gr. -1-2). 16.99 (978-1-5253-0240-4(X)) Kids Can Pr., Ltd. CAN. Dist: Hachette Bk. Group.

Rodger, Ellen. Recycling Waste, 1 vol. 2009. (Saving Our World Ser.). (ENG.). 32p. (gr. 4-4). lib. bdg. 31.21 (978-0-7614-3222-7(1), 2ce76b38-1c57-469b-a542-1f5754d7322a) Cavendish Square Publishing LLC.

Roza, Greg. Landfills, 1 vol. 2013. (Habitat Havoc Ser.). (ENG., Illus.). 32p. (J). (gr. 3-4). 29.27 (978-1-4339-9921-5(8), f4d523d8-9551-4ba8-9fb3-ba903a865a72) Stevens, Gareth Publishing LLLP.

Scavengers: Eating Nature's Trash, 12 vols. 2014. (Scavengers: Eating Nature's Trash Ser.). (ENG.). 24p. (J). (gr. 2-3). 151.62 (978-1-4777-6617-0(0), e9074c1d-fdcb-4128-99bf-cf9e5c58a89f, PowerKids Pr.) Rosen Publishing Group, Inc., The.

Schuh, Mari. I Can Pick up Litter. 2019. (Helping the Environment Ser.). (ENG., Illus.). 24p. (J). (gr. -1-2). lib. bdg. 27.32 (978-1-9771-0309-3(X), 139305, Capstone Pr.) Capstone.

Sévigny, Eric, illus. Caillou: As Good As New. 2012. (Ecology Club Ser.). (ENG.). 24p. (J). (gr. -1-1). pap. 5.99 (978-2-89450-832-9(8)) Caillouet, Gerry.

Shores, Erika L. How Garbage Gets from Trash Cans to Landfills. 2016. (Here to There Ser.). (ENG., Illus.). 24p. (J). (gr. -1-2). lib. bdg. 27.32 (978-1-4914-8433-3(0), 130862, Capstone Pr.) Capstone.

Showers, Paul. Where Does the Garbage Go? Chewning, Randy, illus. 2015. (Let's-Read-And-Find-Out Science 2 Ser.). (ENG.). 32p. (J). (gr. -1-3). pap. 6.99 (978-0-06-238200-9(4), HarperCollins) HarperCollins Pubs.

Smith-Llera, Danielle. Trash Vortex: How Plastic Pollution Is Choking the World's Oceans. 2018. (Captured Science History Ser.). (ENG., Illus.). 64p. (J). (gr. 5-9). lib. bdg. 35.32 (978-0-7565-5745-4(3), 137541, Compass Point Bks.) Capstone.

—You Are Eating Plastic Every Day: What's in Our Food? 2019. (Informed! Ser.). (ENG., Illus.). 64p. (J). (gr. 5-9). 37.32 (978-0-7565-6174-1(4), 140657); pap. 8.95 (978-0-7565-6229-8(5), 140930) Capstone. (Compass Point Bks.).

Solway, Andrew. Waste Disposal. 2009. (World at Risk Ser.). (ENG.). 48p. (J). (gr. 5-9). 34.25 (978-1-59920-380-5(4), 19399, Smart Apple Media) Black Rabbit Bks.

Sundance/Newbridge LLC Staff. Where Does All the Garbage Go? 2007. (Early Science Ser.). (gr. k-3). 18.95 (978-1-4007-6260-6(X)); pap. 6.10 (978-1-4007-6256-9(1)) Sundance/Newbridge Educational Publishing.

Tilmont, Amy. Trash Talk: What You Throw Away. 2011. (Second Nature Ser.). (Illus.). 48p. (J). (gr. 5-8). lib. bdg. 26.60 (978-1-59953-459-6(2)) Norwood Hse. Pr.

Turnbull, Stephanie. Collecting. 2015. (Try This! Ser.). (ENG., Illus.). 24p. (J). (gr. 3-6). 27.10 (978-1-62588-371-1(4), 17445) Black Rabbit Bks.

—Trash & Recycling. 2006. (Beginners Science Ser.). (Illus.). 32p. (J). (gr. 4-7). lib. bdg. 12.99 (978-1-58086-948-5(3), Usborne) EDC Publishing.

—Trash & Recycling. Fox, Christyan, illus. 2006. (Beginners Science: Level 2 Ser.). 32p. (J). (gr. 1-3). 4.99 (978-0-7945-1400-6(6), Usborne) EDC Publishing.

Walker, Kate. Clothing, 1 vol. Vanzet, Gaston, illus. 2011. (Recycling Ser.). (ENG.). 32p. (J). (gr. 1-1). 31.21 (978-1-60870-128-5(X), 9f8731f9-aa6c-44f5-b15d-80b847e48693) Cavendish Square Publishing LLC.

—Food & Garden Waste, 1 vol. Vanzet, Gaston, illus. 2011. (Recycling Ser.). (ENG.). 32p. (J). (gr. 1-1). 31.21 (978-1-60870-129-2(8), b1ade1b9-57dc-4221-a899-164e143400f2) Cavendish Square Publishing LLC.

Walsh, Melanie. 10 Things I Can Do to Help My World. Walsh, Melanie, illus. 2012. (ENG., Illus.). 40p. (J). (gr. -1-2). pap. 8.99 (978-0-7636-5919-6(3)) Candlewick Pr.

Ward, Dj & Meisel, Paul. What Happens to Our Trash? 2012. (Let's-Read-And-Find-Out Science 2 Ser.). (ENG., Illus.). 40p. (J). (gr. -1-3). pap. 5.99 (978-0-06-168755-6(3), HarperCollins) HarperCollins Pubs.

Weitzman, Elizabeth. 10 Cosas Que Puedes Hacer para Reducir, Reciclar y Reutilizar (Rookie Star: Make a Difference) 2017. (Rookie Star Ser.). (SPA., Illus.). 32p. (J). (gr. 2-3). pap. 5.95 (978-1-338-18781-6(3), Children's Pr.) Scholastic Library Publishing.

—10 Cosas Que Puedes Hacer para Reducir, Reciclar y Reutilizar (Rookie Star: Make a Difference) (Library Edition) 2017. (Rookie Star Ser.). (SPA., Illus.). 32p. (J). (gr. 2-3). lib. bdg. 25.00 (978-0-531-22860-9(6), Children's Pr.) Scholastic Library Publishing.

—10 Things You Can Do to Reduce, Reuse, Recycle. 2016. (Rookie Star — Make a Difference Ser.). (ENG., Illus.). 32p. (J). lib. bdg. 25.00 (978-0-531-22654-4(9), Children's Pr.) Scholastic Library Publishing.

Wheeler, Adrienne. Waste Disposal, 1 vol. 2017. (Earth's Environment in Danger Ser.). (ENG.). 24p. (J). (gr. 3-3). 25.27 (978-1-5383-2545-2(4), d49fde94-088a-44c8-9dba-80798f1b2b38); pap. 9.25 (978-1-5383-2615-2(9), b1726416-a5d2-4387-ae48-baf73a0909e5) Rosen Publishing Group, Inc., The. (PowerKids Pr.).

Wilcox, Charlotte. Earth-Friendly Waste Management. 2009. pap. 58.95 (978-0-7613-4691-3(0)) 2008. (Illus.). 72p. (YA). (gr. 4-7). lib. bdg. 30.60 (978-0-8225-7560-3(4)) Lerner Publishing Group.

Winnick, Nick. Reducing Waste. 2016. (J). (978-1-5105-2221-3(2)) SmartBook Media, Inc.

REFUSE AND REFUSE DISPOSAL—FICTION

Angleberger, Tom. Poop Fountain! The Qwikpick Papers. 2014. (Qwikpick Papers). (ENG., Illus.). 144p. (J). (gr. 3-7). 12.95 (978-1-4197-0425-3(7), 1013201, Amulet Bks.) Abrams, Inc.

Artifact Group, The. The Trash Planet. 2009. (Backyardigans Ser.: 12). (ENG.). 24p. (J). pap. 3.99 (978-1-4169-6868-9(7), Simon Spotlight/Nickelodeon) Simon Spotlight/Nickelodeon.

Auerbach, Annie. Junkyard Dig! Building from a to Z. Shannon, David et al, illus. 2010. (Jon Scieszka's Trucktown Ser.). (ENG.). 26p. (J). (gr. -1-k). bds. 5.99 (978-1-4169-4187-3(8), Little Simon) Little Simon.

Bildner, Phil. Marvelous Cornelius: Hurricane Katrina & the Spirit of New Orleans. Parra, John, illus. 2015. (ENG.). 44p. (J). (gr. k-3). 16.99 (978-1-4521-2578-7(3)) Chronicle Bks. LLC.

Brimner, Larry Dane. Trash Trouble. Tripp, Christine, illus. 2003. (Rookie Choices Ser.). (ENG.). 32p. (gr. 1-2). pap. 5.95 (978-0-516-27837-7(1), Children's Pr.) Scholastic Library Publishing.

Brooklyn. The Adventures of the Earth Saver Girl: Don't be a Litterbug. 2010. (Illus.). 24p. pap. 8.49 (978-0-9822822-4-3(9)) Wright Bk. Publishing.

Corderoy, Tracey. It's Only One! Neal, Tony, illus. 2020. (ENG.). 32p. (J). (gr. -1-2). 17.99 (978-1-68010-227-7(3)) Tiger Tales.

Covey, Richard D. & Pappas, Diane H. Ugh! Don't Be a Litterbug! 2009. (Illus.). (J). pap. (978-0-545-06102-5(4)) Scholastic, Inc.

Day, Nicholas. Junk: a Spectacular Tale of Trash: A Spectacular Tale of Trash. Disbury, Tom, illus. 2018. (ENG.). 32p. (J). (gr. k-3). 16.99 (978-1-58536-400-8(2), 204586) Sleeping Bear Pr.

DiPucchio, Kelly. Super Manny Cleans Up! Graegin, Stephanie, illus. 2018. (Super Manny Ser.). (ENG.). 40p. (J). (gr. -1-3). 17.99 (978-1-4814-5962-4(7)) Simon & Schuster Children's Publishing.

Donnelly, Rebecca. The Friendship Lie. 2019. (ENG., Illus.). 272p. (J). (gr. 4-7). 15.95 (978-1-68446-061-8(1), 140521, Capstone Editions) Capstone.

Gnoske, Alexandra. Loui Saves the Earth. 2010. 16p. 9.49 (978-1-4520-0034-3(4)) AuthorHouse.

Harp, Susan. Retrieving with Evie. Siau, John, illus. 2007. (ENG.). 24p. (J). lib. bdg. 12.95 (978-1-932439-67-0(6)) M.T. Publishing Co., Inc.

Keene, Carolyn. California Schemin' Book One in the Malibu Mayhem Trilogy. 2011. (Nancy Drew (All New) Girl Detective Ser.: 45). (ENG.). 160p. (J). (gr. 3-7). pap. 7.99 (978-1-4424-2295-7(5), Aladdin) Simon & Schuster Children's Publishing.

Lee, Newman. Creepy Kitchen. Elizabeth, Neering, ed. Dan, Houser, illus. 2012. 40p. (J). pap. 10.00 (978-1-62314-873-7(1)) Fisticuff Publishing.

McMillan, Dawn. Seagull Sid: And the Naughty Things His Seagulls Did! Kinnaird, Ross, illus. 2019. (ENG.). 32p. (gr. 1-5). pap. 8.99 (978-0-486-83247-0(3), 832473) Dover Pubns., Inc.

McMullan, Kate. I Stink! McMullan, Jim, illus. 2006. (ENG.). 40p. (J). (gr. -1-3). reprint ed. pap. 8.99 (978-0-06-443836-0(8), HarperCollins) HarperCollins Pubs.

—I Stink! Board Book. McMullan, Jim, illus. 2005. (ENG.). 34p. (J). (gr. -1-k). bds. 10.99 (978-0-06-074592-9(4), HarperFestival) HarperCollins Pubs.

Morris, Garvin. Dump Dog. Morris, Garvin, illus. (Illus.). (J). 2008. 32p. pap. 6.95 (978-1-60108-022-6(0)) 2007. 40p. (gr. -1-2). 15.95 (978-1-60108-012-7(3)) Red Cygnet Pr.

Mulligan, Andy. Trash. 2011. (ENG., Illus.). 240p. (YA). (gr. 7-12). pap. 11.99 (978-0-385-75216-9(4), Ember) Random Hse. Children's Bks.

Odanaka, Barbara. Smash! Mash! Crash! There Goes the Trash! Hillenbrand, Will, illus. 2006. (ENG.). 32p. (J). (gr. -1-3). 19.99 (978-0-689-85160-5(X), McElderry, Margaret K. Bks.) McElderry, Margaret K. Bks.

Reynolds, Paul A. Sydney & Simon: Go Green! Reynolds, Peter H., illus. 2015. (Sydney & Simon Ser.: 2). 48p. (J). (gr. 1-4). lib. bdg. 12.95 (978-1-58089-677-1(4)) Charlesbridge Publishing, Inc.

The check digit for ISBN-10 appears in parentheses after the full ISBN-13

Sander, Sonia. Smash That Trash! Shannon, David et al, illus. 2009. (Jon Scieszka's Trucktown Ser.). (ENG.). 14p. (J). (gr. -1-k). 7.99 *(978-1-4169-4180-4(0),* Little Simon) Little Simon.
Sensel, Joni. The Garbage Monster. Bivins, Christopher, illus. 2003. 24p. (J). (gr. -1-18). 14.95 *(978-0-9701195-2-0(6))* Dream Factory Bks.
Stewart, Nancy. Bella Saves the Beach. Bell, Samantha, illus. 2013. 24p. 19.95 *(978-1-61633-370-6(7));* pap. 11.95 *(978-1-61633-371-3(5))* Guardian Angel Publishing, Inc.
Wallace, Nancy Elizabeth. Recycle Every Day!, 0 vols. Wallace, Nancy Elizabeth, illus. 2012. (ENG., Illus.). 41p. (J). (gr. 1-3). pap. 9.99 *(978-0-7614-5290-4(7),* 9780761452904, Two Lions) Amazon Publishing.
Ward, Helen. The Tin Forest. Anderson, Wayne, illus. 2003. (ENG.). 32p. (J). (gr. -1-2). 8.99 *(978-0-14-250156-6(5),* Puffin Books) Penguin Young Readers Group.
Weston Woods Staff, creator. I Stink! 2011. 38.75 *(978-0-439-02724-3(1));* 18.95 *(978-0-439-02722-9(5))* Weston Woods Studios, Inc.

REGATTAS

see Rowing; Yachts and Yachting

REIGN OF TERROR

see France—History—Revolution, 1789-1799

REINDEER

Ariel, A. D. Land of Reindeer. 2016. (Spring Forward Ser.). (J). (gr. 2). *(978-1-4900-9462-5(8))* Benchmark Education Co.
Bauer, Jeff. Renos Asombrosos. 2007. (SPA., Illus.). 24p. (J). pap. *(978-0-545-02281-1(9))* Scholastic, Inc.
Best, Arthur. Reindeer, 1 vol. 2018. (Migrating Animals Ser.). (ENG.). 24p. (J). (gr. 1-1). 27.36 *(978-1-5026-3713-0(8),* 5aa37042-5507-48fd-9753-62d0ce9bcd71) Cavendish Square Publishing LLC.
Lynch, Seth. Reindeer at the Zoo, 1 vol. 2019. (Zoo Animals Ser.). (ENG.). 24p. (gr. k-k). pap. 9.15 *(978-1-5382-3942-1(6),* 2b4a0934-6d3a-429b-a4f8-48c6f9fa9f68) Stevens, Gareth Publishing LLLP.
Machajewski, Sarah. Raising Reindeer, 1 vol. 2019. (Unusual Farm Animals Ser.). (ENG.). 24p. (gr. 2-3). pap. 9.25 *(978-1-7253-0910-4(6),* c6c30786-a296-432d-9d92-f3917a49ae44, PowerKids Pr.) Rosen Publishing Group, Inc., The.
Markovics, Joyce L. Caribou: And Reindeer, Too. 2011. (Built for Cold Ser.). 32p. (YA). (gr. 1-4). lib. bdg. 28.50 *(978-1-61772-130-4(1));* (J). (gr. 4-5). lib. bdg., E-Book 49.22 *(978-1-61772-220-2(0))* Bearport Publishing Co., Inc.
Marsico, Katie. Reindeer, 1 vol. 2011. (Day in the Life: Polar Animals Ser.). (ENG.). 24p. (J). (gr. k-2). pap. 6.79 *(978-1-4329-5337-9(0),* 116047, Heinemann) Capstone.
Pettiford, Rebecca. Reindeer. 2019. (Animals of the Arctic Ser.). (ENG., Illus.). 24p. (J). (gr. k-3). lib. bdg. 26.95 *(978-1-62617-939-4(5),* Blastoff! Readers) Bellwether Media.
Phillips, Dee. Reindeer. 2015. (Arctic Animals: Life Outside the Igloo Ser.). (ENG.). 24p. (J). (gr. -1-3). lib. bdg. 26.99 *(978-1-62724-529-6(4))* Bearport Publishing Co., Inc.
Publications International Ltd. Staff, ed. Rudolph the Red-Nosed Reindeer (Look & Find) 2010. 24p. (J). 7.98 *(978-1-60553-958-4(9))* Phoenix International Publications, Inc.
Sandler, Martin W. The Impossible Rescue: The True Story of an Amazing Arctic Adventure. 2014. (ENG.). 176p. (J). (gr. 5). pap. 16.99 *(978-0-7636-7093-1(6))* Candlewick Pr.
Suen, Anastasia. Reindeer. 2020. (Spot Arctic Animals Ser.). (ENG.). 16p. (J). (gr. -1-1). pap. 7.99 *(978-1-68152-526-6(7),* 10725) Amicus.
Watt, Fiona. That's Not My Reindeer... Wells, Rachel, illus. 2014. (Usborne Touchy-Feely Bks.). (ENG.). 10p. (gr. -1). bds. 9.99 *(978-0-7945-3390-8(6),* Usborne) EDC Publishing.

REINDEER—FICTION

Anderson, Derek. How the Easter Bunny Saved Christmas. Anderson, Derek, illus. 2006. (ENG., Illus.). 40p. (J). (gr. -1-3). 19.99 *(978-0-689-87634-9(3),* Simon & Schuster Bks. For Young Readers) Simon & Schuster Bks. For Young Readers.
Anonymous. Rudolph Saves the Day. 2014. (J). lib. bdg. 14.75 *(978-0-606-36126-2(X))* Turtleback.
Bass, William E. Santa Revisits His Secret Little Helper. Salazar, Vivian, illus. 2012. 26p. 24.95 *(978-1-4626-5396-6(0))* America Star Bks.
Baugh, Helen. Rudy's Windy Christmas. Mantle, Ben, illus. 2015. (ENG.). 32p. (J). (gr. -1-3). 16.99 *(978-0-8075-7173-6(3),* 807571733) Whitman, Albert & Co.
Baum, L. Frank. A Kidnapped Santa Claus. 2011. 24p. 12.95 *(978-1-4638-9603-4(4));* pap. 6.95 *(978-1-4638-0070-3(3))* Rodgers, Alan Bks.
Berger, Samantha. Santa's Reindeer Games. Manders, John, illus. 2011. (J). *(978-0-545-36866-7(9))* Scholastic, Inc.
Berry Byrd, Holly. Jingle Bells. Cottage Door Press, ed. Bos, Miriam, illus. 2017. (ENG.). 12p. (J). (gr. -1-k). bds. 10.99 *(978-1-68052-230-3(2),* 1002160) Cottage Door Pr.
Blondin, George. The Legend of the Caribou Boy / Ekwò dǫzhìa Wegondì, 1 vol. Sundberg, Mary Rose, tr. McSwain, Ray, illus. 2009. (ENG & DGR.). 40p. (J). (gr. 1-3). cd-rom 19.95 *(978-1-894778-71-8(5))* Theytus Bks., Ltd. CAN. Dist: Orca Bk. Pubs. USA.
Burgess, Thornton W. The Christmas Reindeer. Chase, Rhoda, illus. 2013. (Dover Children's Classics Ser.). (ENG.). 152p. (J). (gr. k-3). pap. 5.99 *(978-0-486-49153-0(6),* 491536) Dover Pubns., Inc.
Burton, Jeffrey. The Itsy Bitsy Reindeer. Rescek, Sanja, illus. 2016. (Itsy Bitsy Ser.). (ENG.). 16p. (J). (gr. -1 — 1). bds. 5.99 *(978-1-4814-6855-8(3),* Little Simon) Little Simon.
Chandler, Bill & Chandler, Marie. The Reindeer That Couldn't Fly. Kling, Leslie, illus. 2009. 48p. pap. 19.99 *(978-1-933817-40-8(2))* Profits Publishing.
Chronicle Books. Baby Reindeer: Finger Puppet Book: (Finger Puppet Book for Toddlers & Babies, Baby Books for First Year, Animal Finger Puppets) Huang, Yu-Hsuan, illus. 2016. (Baby Animal Finger Puppets Ser.: 4). (ENG.). 12p. (J). (gr. -1 — 1). 7.99 *(978-1-4521-4661-4(6))* Chronicle Bks. LLC.
Curry, Kenneth. Priscilla & the Reindeer. 2007. (Illus.). 22p. (J). 10.95 *(978-0-9798364-5-9(X))* Curry Brothers Publishing Group.
Cuthbert, R M. Reindeer. Cuthbert, R M & Vincent, Allison, illus. 2006. 30p. (J). 12.95 *(978-1-56167-908-9(9))* American Literary Pr.
Daley-Prado, M. The Super Heroes Save Christmas! 2007. 24p. per. 24.95 *(978-1-4241-9123-9(8))* America Star Bks.
Disney Books. Frozen: Reindeers Are Better Than People. 2015. (ENG., Illus.). 12p. (J). (gr. -1-k). bds. 6.99 *(978-1-4847-2469-9(0),* Disney Press Books) Disney Publishing Worldwide.
DiTerlizzi, Angela. Seeking a Santa. Smith, Allie, illus. 2016. (ENG.). 30p. (J). (gr. -1 — 1). bds. 7.99 *(978-1-4814-7674-4(2),* Little Simon) Little Simon.
Dougherty, Brandi. The Littlest Reindeer. Todd, Michelle, illus. 2017. (Littlest Ser.). (ENG.). 24p. (J). (gr. -1-k). pap. 5.99 *(978-1-338-15738-3(8),* Cartwheel Bks.) Scholastic, Inc.
Down, Hayley. Reindeer's Snowy Adventure. Machell, Dawn, illus. 2016. (ENG.). 12p. (J). (gr. -1 — 1). bds. 6.99 *(978-1-78598-437-2(3))* Make Believe Ideas GBR. Dist: Scholastic, Inc.
Eight Jolly Reindeer. 2014. (ENG., Illus.). 16p. (J). (gr. -1 — 1). bds. 6.99 *(978-0-545-65145-5(X),* Cartwheel Bks.) Scholastic, Inc.
Eubank, Patricia Reeder. Countdown to Christmas. 2003. (ENG., Illus.). 14p. (J). (gr. -1-k). bds. 9.95 *(978-0-8249-6505-1(1),* Ideals Pubns.) Worthy Publishing.
Falk, Barbara Bustetter & Hyman, Helen Kandel. Don't Park on the Roof. 2007. 36p. per. 21.32 *(978-1-4257-7096-9(7))* Xlibris Corp.
Foreman, Michael. The Little Reindeer. Foreman, Michael, illus. 2007. (ENG., Illus.). 32p. (J). (gr. -1-2). per. 10.99 *(978-1-84270-582-7(2))* Andersen Pr. GBR. Dist: Independent Pubs. Group.
Fronis, Aly. This Little Reindeer. Flowers, Luke, illus. 2017. (ENG.). 16p. (J). (gr. -1-k). bds. 5.99 *(978-1-4998-0525-3(X))* Little Bee Books Inc.
Greenberg, Nicki. The Naughtiest Reindeer. 2014. (Naughtiest Reindeer Ser.). (ENG., Illus.). 32p. (J). (gr. -1-k). 15.99 *(978-1-74331-304-6(7))* Allen & Unwin AUS. Dist: Independent Pubs. Group.
—Naughtiest Reindeer Takes a Bow. 2018. (Naughtiest Reindeer Ser.: 4). (ENG., Illus.). 32p. (J). (gr. -1-1). 15.99 *(978-1-76029-565-3(5))* Allen & Unwin AUS. Dist: Independent Pubs. Group.
Hansen, Eric. Ian, Ceo, North Pole. 2008. 108p. pap. 9.95 *(978-1-60693-554-5(2),* Eloquent Bks.) Strategic Book Publishing & Rights Agency (SBPRA).
Holt, Gretta Scott. The Reindeer Who Was Afraid to Fly. Jones, Amber & Sullivan, Allen, illus. 2008. (ENG.). 24p. pap. 11.49 *(978-1-4389-1709-2(0))* AuthorHouse.
Inger's Promise: Evaluation Guide. 2006. (J). *(978-1-55942-409-7(5))* Witcher Productions.
Julius, Jessica. A New Reindeer Friend. 2015. lib. bdg. 13.55 *(978-0-606-36680-9(6))* Turtleback.
—A New Reindeer Friend (Disney Frozen) RH Disney, illus. 2015. (Little Golden Book Ser.). (ENG.). 24p. (J). (-k). 5.99 *(978-0-7364-3351-8(1),* Golden/Disney) Random Hse. Children's Bks.
Killen, Nicola. The Little Reindeer. Killen, Nicola, illus. 2017. (My Little Animal Friend Ser.). (ENG., Illus.). 32p. (J). (gr. -1-3). 17.99 *(978-1-4814-8686-6(1),* Simon & Schuster/Paula Wiseman Bks.) Simon & Schuster/Paula Wiseman Bks.
Lester, Vivian. Wee-Dolph, the Tiniest Reindeer. Wiggs, Sue, illus. 22p. (J). (gr. -1-3). pap. 4.00 *(978-1-929785-01-8(1))* Connexions Unlimited.
Levine, Whitney Joy. The Tiniest Reindeer. 2008. 24p. pap. 12.99 *(978-1-4389-3102-9(6))* AuthorHouse.
Madaras, Diana. Kitty Humbug's Christmas Tail. Madaras, Diana & Nielsen, Ric, illus. 2009. 24p. 17.99 *(978-1-892344-56-4(4))* Palomino Publishing.
Magsamen, Sandra. Our Little Deer (Made with Love) Magsamen, Sandra, illus. 2016. (Made with Love Ser.). (ENG., Illus.). 14p. (J). bds. 7.99 *(978-1-338-11081-4(0),* Cartwheel Bks.) Scholastic, Inc.
May, Robert L. Rudolph Shines Again. Caparo, Antonio Javier, illus. (Classic Board Bks.). (ENG.). (J). (gr. -1 — 1). 2018. 42p. bds. 7.99 *(978-1-5344-1839-4(3))* 2015. 40p. 17.99 *(978-1-4424-7498-7(X))* Little Simon. (Little Simon).
Miceli, Robert L. The Adventures of Twilight. 2008. 80p. pap. 22.50 *(978-1-60693-241-4(1),* Strategic Bk. Publishing) Strategic Book Publishing & Rights Agency (SBPRA).
Mlynowski, Sarah. Cold As Ice (Whatever After #6) 2015. (Whatever After Ser.: 6). (ENG.). 176p. (J). (gr. 3-7). pap. 5.99 *(978-0-545-62736-8(2),* Scholastic Pr.) Scholastic, Inc.
Morningforest, Chris & Raymond, Rebecca. Mooseman Reindeer & Uncle Utley. 2006. 36p. (J). pap. 15.43 *(978-1-4116-8390-7(0))* Lulu Pr., Inc.
Moulton, Mark Kimball. Reindeer Christmas. Good, Karen Hillard, illus. 2008. (ENG.). 40p. (J). (gr. -1-3). 15.99 *(978-1-4169-6108-6(9),* Simon & Schuster/Paula Wiseman Bks.) Simon & Schuster/Paula Wiseman Bks.
O., Lila. Lulabelle's Jewels: The Christmas Wish of Mrs. Claus. 2008. 20p. pap. 12.49 *(978-1-4389-3189-0(1))* AuthorHouse.
Penny, Anne. Scraper. 2006. (Illus.). 56p. pap. *(978-1-84401-921-2(7))* Athena Pr.
Posner-Sanchez, Andrea. Olaf's Frozen Adventure Little Golden Book (Disney Frozen) Chou, Joey, illus. 2017. (Little Golden Book Ser.). (ENG.). 24p. (J). (-k). 4.99 *(978-0-7364-3835-3(1),* Golden/Disney) Random Hse. Children's Bks.
Powell-Tuck, Maudie. Last Stop on the Reindeer Express. Mountford, Karl James, illus. 2018. (ENG.). 32p. (J). (gr. -1-2). 18.99 *(978-1-5247-7166-9(X),* Doubleday Bks. for Young Readers) Random Hse. Children's Bks.
Publications International Ltd. Staff, ed. Rudolph the Red-Nosed Reindeer(r): A Flashlight Adventure Sound Book. 2014. 14p. (J). *(978-1-4508-9047-2(4),* 1450890474) Publications International, Ltd.
—Rudolph the Red-Nosed Reindeer (Book & Plush) 2011. 8p. (J). bds. 11.98 *(978-1-4508-2170-4(7))* Publications International, Ltd.
Rasmussen, Liz, illus. Too Fat to Fly. 2007. 32p. (J). 16.95 *(978-0-9793517-0-9(7))* Silver Bells Publishing Hse.
Rees, Douglas. Jeannette Claus Saves Christmas. Latyk, Olivier, illus. 2010. (ENG.). 40p. (J). (gr. k-3). 16.99 *(978-1-4169-2686-3(0),* McElderry, Margaret K. Bks.) McElderry, Margaret K. Bks.
Reindeer. 2003. (Shaped Board Books Ser.). 14p. (J). (gr. -1-k). bds. 9.95 *(978-0-7525-8850-6(8))* Parragon, Inc.
The Reindeer's Big Night. 2003. (J). per. *(978-1-57657-926-8(3))* Paradise Pr., Inc.
Repchuck, Caroline. The Little Reindeer. 2005. (ENG., Illus.). 20p. (J). *(978-1-55168-294-5(X))* Fenn, H. B. & Co., Ltd.
Rigo, Laura. Little Reindeer. 2011. (Mini Look at Me Bks.). (Illus.). 10p. (J). (gr. -1). bds. 7.99 *(978-0-7641-6450-7(3))* Sourcebooks, Inc.
Rivers-Moore, Debbie. Five Christmas Reindeer: A Slide & Count Book. Everitt-Stewart, Andy, illus. 2015. (ENG.). 10p. (J). (gr. -1 — 1). bds. 8.99 *(978-1-4998-0169-9(6))* Little Bee Books Inc.
Rowland, Teresa. Blusher's First Christmas. 2012. 64p. (-18). pap. 20.95 *(978-1-4525-0718-7(X))* Balboa Pr.
Rudolph the Red-Nosed Reindeer. 2004. 4p. (J). 3.95 *(978-0-634-09040-0(2))* Leonard, Hal Corp.
Rudolph the Red-Nosed Reindeer. 2014. (ENG., Illus.). 40p. (J). (gr. -1-1). 18.99 *(978-1-4424-7495-6(5),* Little Simon) Little Simon.
Saunders, Katie, illus. Little Reindeer. 2012. 10p. (J). *(978-1-4351-4314-2(0))* Barnes & Noble, Inc.
Sharp, Rhonda Winchell. The Nine Most Famous Reindeer of All. Vandewater, Rena, illus. 2004. 40p. (J). pap. 15.99 *(978-0-9748047-8-1(9))* Hickory Bark Productions.
Sonnebom, Scott. The Reindeer Games. Lozano, Omar, illus. 2015. (North Police Ser.). (ENG.). 32p. (J). (gr. k-2). lib. bdg. 21.32 *(978-1-4795-6487-3(7),* 128340, Picture Window Bks.) Capstone.
Sorenson, E. Randy. The First Reindeer Couldn't Fly. 2007. (Illus.). 32p. (J). 17.99 *(978-0-615-16939-2(2))* Sorenson, E. Randy.
Stainton, Sue. Christmas Magic. Melhuish, Eva, illus. 2007. 32p. (J). (gr. -1-1). lib. bdg. 16.89 *(978-0-06-078572-7(1),* Tegen, Katherine Bks) HarperCollins Pubs.
Stepp, Shirley. Santa Lost His Cell Phone. 2012. 24p. 24.95 *(978-1-4626-5479-6(7))* America Star Bks.
Sullivan, E. J. Bubba the Redneck Reindeer. Eldredge, Ernie, illus. 2007. 32p. (J). (gr. 4-7). 12.95 *(978-1-60261-008-8(8))* Cliff Road Bks.
Tavares, Matt. Dasher: How a Brave Little Doe Changed Christmas Forever. Tavares, Matt, illus. 2019. (Dasher Ser.). (ENG., Illus.). (J). E-Book 17.99 *(978-1-5362-1490-1(6),* 85751); 40p. (gr. -1-3). 17.99 *(978-1-5362-0137-6(5))* Candlewick Pr.
Tyrell, Melissa. The Little Reindeer. Brooks, Nan, illus. enl. ed. 2005. (ENG.). 10p. (J). (gr. -1-3). 4.95 *(978-1-58117-119-8(6),* Intervisual/Piggy Toes) Bendon, Inc.
Wallace, R. Mike. Saunter. 2009. 36p. pap. 10.75 *(978-1-60693-994-9(7),* Strategic Bk. Publishing) Strategic Book Publishing & Rights Agency (SBPRA).
Walstead, Alice. How to Catch a Reindeer. Elkerton, Andy, illus. 2022. (How to Catch Ser.). 40p. (J). (gr. k-3). 10.99 *(978-1-7282-7613-7(6))* Sourcebooks, Inc.
Watt, Fiona. That's Not My Reindeer: Its Body Is Too Furry. Wells, Rachel, illus. 2008. (Usborne Touchy-Feely Board Bks.). 10p. (J). (gr. -1-k). bds. 9.99 *(978-0-7945-1890-5(7),* Usborne) EDC Publishing.
Wheeler, Lisa. Uncles & Antlers. Floca, Brian, illus. 2014. (ENG.). 40p. (J). (gr. -1-3). 17.99 *(978-1-4814-3018-0(1),* Atheneum Bks. for Young Readers) Simon & Schuster Children's Publishing.
Woolf, Julia, illus. Reindeer Run. 2008. (ENG.). 10p. (J). bds. 4.95 *(978-1-58117-813-5(1),* Intervisual/Piggy Toes) Bendon, Inc.

RELATIVITY (PHYSICS)

see also Quantum Theory

Doeden, Matt. Albert Einstein: Relativity Rock Star. 2020. (Gateway Biographies Ser.). (ENG., Illus.). 48p. (J). (gr. 4-8). pap. 11.99 *(978-1-5415-8885-1(1),* 59af402d-2595-43ea-a3ed-b530aef54dcc); lib. bdg. 31.99 *(978-1-5415-7743-5(4),* 0301db16-7b69-45be-b0d2-41de3eb21e49) Lerner Publishing Group. (Lerner Pubns.).
Kook, Ima. Einstein's Theory of Relativity: Go Too Fast & Strange Things Happen. 2008. (As Dreamed by Itsy Ser.). (Illus.). 24p. (J). pap. 12.00 *(978-1-892298-23-2(6))* Abique Pub.
Manning, Phillip. Theory of Relativity. 2012. (ENG., Illus.). 128p. (gr. 6-12). lib. bdg. 35.00 *(978-1-60413-294-6(9),* P189835, Facts On File) Infobase Holdings, Inc.
Morton, Alan. Einstein's Theories of Relativity, 1 vol. 2005. (Milestones in Modern Science Ser.). (ENG.). 48p. (gr. 6-8). pap. 15.05 *(978-0-8368-5860-0(3),* 8fba2e5f-93b3-4e2d-849e-1a57036498c8); (Illus.). lib. bdg. 33.67 *(978-0-8368-5853-2(0),* 3044b77b-add3-4377-8068-a4d77ab7ff31) Stevens, Gareth Publishing LLLP. (Gareth Stevens Secondary Library).
Parker, Katie. The Theory of Relativity, 1 vol. 2010. (Big Ideas in Science Ser.). (ENG., Illus.). 48p. (gr. 5-5). 34.07 *(978-0-7614-4398-8(3),* c2451e46-6078-4d33-ae72-2adc49bc6091) Cavendish Square Publishing LLC.
Pohlen, Jerome. Albert Einstein & Relativity for Kids: His Life & Ideas with 21 Activities & Thought Experiments. 2012. (For Kids Ser.: 45). (Illus.). 144p. (J). (gr. 4). pap. 18.99 *(978-1-61374-028-6(X))* Chicago Review Pr., Inc.
Rooney, Anne. Albert Einstein & His Theory of Relativity. 2012. (Miracle Makers Ser.). (ENG.). 48p. (YA). (gr. 5-8). 27.95 *(978-1-4488-6038-8(5),* Rosen Reference) Rosen Publishing Group, Inc., The.
Scientific American Staff. Beyond Extreme Physics. 2009. (Scientific American Cutting-Edge Science Ser.). 160p. (gr. 9-9). 63.90 *(978-1-60853-073-1(6))* Rosen Publishing Group, Inc., The.
Tolish, Alexander. Gravity Explained, 1 vol. 2018. (Mysteries of Space Ser.). (ENG.). 80p. (gr. 7-7). 38.93 *(978-0-7660-9950-0(4),* 6f687c8e-4426-49a7-88d1-24013624ca22) Enslow Publishing, LLC.
Whiting, Jim. Space & Time. (Mysteries of the Universe Ser.). (ENG., Illus.). 48p. (J). (gr. 5-9). 2013. pap. 12.00 *(978-0-89812-917-5(6),* 21931, Creative Paperbacks) 2012. 23.95 *(978-1-60818-192-6(8),* 21924, Creative Education) Creative Co., The.
Winterberg, Jenna. Conservation of Mass. 2015. (Science: Informational Text Ser.). (ENG.). 32p. (gr. 4-8). pap. 11.99 *(978-1-4807-4722-7(X))* Teacher Created Materials, Inc.

RELAXATION

see Recreation

RELIGION

see also Belief and Doubt; Faith; God; Indians of North America—Religion; Mythology; Religions; Spiritual Life; Superstition; Theology; Worship

Ajmera, Maya, et al. Faith. 2009. (Global Fund for Children Bks.). (Illus.). 48p. (J). (gr. -1-3). 16.95 *(978-1-58089-177-6(2));* pap. 8.95 *(978-1-58089-178-3(0))* Charlesbridge Publishing, Inc.
Alexander, Audrey. Angels, Demons, & Religious Rituals. 2015. (J). *(978-1-61900-065-0(2))* Eldorado Ink.
Atique, Quazi M. Zahid. The Path of Peace: The Complete Code of Life. 2004. 497p. (YA). pap. 30.00 *(978-0-9766702-0-9(8))* Path of Peace Inc., The.
Attinger, Billy, illus. Baby's First Little Book of Prayers. gif. ed. 2003. (Wee Witness Ser.). 32p. (J). 7.99 *(978-0-7369-1185-6(5))* Harvest Hse. Pubs.
Center for Learning Network Staff. Sexuality: Connecting Mind, Body, & Spirit — Minicourse. 2003. (Religion Ser.). 119p. (YA). tchr. ed., spiral bd. 12.95 *(978-1-56077-745-8(1))* Center for Learning, The.
The Challenge of Choices. 2003. (YA). tchr. ed. *(978-0-9706117-3-4(0));* stu. ed. *(978-0-9706117-2-7(2))* Riverstone Group Publishing.
The Challenge of Choices Strategic Planner. 2003. *(978-0-9706117-4-1(9))* Riverstone Group Publishing.
Clarke, Steve. Themes to InspiRE for KS3, Bk. 1. 2011. (Dynamic Learning Ser.). (ENG., Illus.). 96p. pap. 39.50 *(978-1-4441-2205-3(3))* Hodder Education Group GBR. Dist: Trans-Atlantic Pubns., Inc.
Cowell, Lynn. Brave Beauty: Finding the Fearless You, 1 vol. 2017. (Faithgirlz Ser.). (ENG., Illus.). 320p. (J). 16.99 *(978-0-310-76314-7(2))* Zonderkidz.
Crosby, Jim. Devotions for the Armchair Quarterback. 2004. 109p. per. 12.95 *(978-1-932338-33-1(0))* Lifevest Publishing, Inc.
Damon, Emma. All Kinds of Beliefs. 2004. (J). *(978-1-84444-163-1(6));* (ARA & ENG.). *(978-1-84444-160-0(1))* Mantra Lingua.
—All Kinds of Beliefs. 2003. (J). (ENG & URD.). 17.95 *(978-1-84444-164-8(4));* (CHI & ENG.). 17.95 *(978-1-84444-162-4(8));* (BEN & ENG., Illus.). 17.95 *(978-1-84444-161-7(X))* Mantra Lingua GBR. Dist: Chinasprout, Inc.
Dobson, Shirley. God's Ten Best Coloring Book 50-Unit Merch. 2004. 16p. 64.50 *(978-0-8307-3117-6(2),* Gospel Light) Gospel Light Pubns.
Downey, Michael. Digging Deep: Fostering the Spirituality of Young Men. 2003. (ENG.). 96p. (YA). per. 28.25 *(978-0-88489-803-0(2))* Saint Mary's Press of Minnesota.
Dunning, Lisa. Restless Spirits-Utah's Small Town Ghosts. 2010. 256p. (J). pap. 16.99 *(978-1-59955-371-9(6),* Cedar Fort, Inc.) Cedar Fort, Inc./CFI Distribution.
Encyclopaedia Britannica Publishers, Inc. Staff, contrib. by. Religions Around the World. 2003. (Britannica Learning Library). (Illus.). 64p. (J). (gr. 2-5). 14.95 *(978-1-59339-007-5(6),* 049908-EN-REF) Encyclopaedia Britannica, Inc.
Eugster, Rachel & Whiting, Jim. The Role of Religion in the Early Islamic World, 1 vol. 2012. (Life in the Early Islamic World Ser.). (ENG., Illus.). 48p. (J). pap. *(978-0-7787-2176-5(0));* lib. bdg. *(978-0-7787-2169-7(8))* Crabtree Publishing Co.
Freeman, Lisa Show. The Colors of God. 2010. 28p. 16.95 *(978-1-4269-3063-8(1))* Trafford Publishing.
Fridell, Ron. Religious Fundamentalism, 1 vol. 2009. (Open for Debate Ser.). (ENG.). 144p. (YA). (gr. 8-8). lib. bdg. 45.50 *(978-0-7614-2945-6(X),* d9d1f5c0-2b35-4938-9b69-3cde347cd370) Cavendish Square Publishing LLC.
Friedenthal, Lora & Kavanaugh, Dorothy. Religions of Africa. Ojakorotu, Victor & Rotberg, Robert I., eds. 2013. (Africa: Progress & Problems Ser.: 13). (Illus.). 112p. (J). (gr. 7-18). 24.95 *(978-1-4222-2947-7(5))* Mason Crest.
Fruit of the Spirit Poster Pack. 2004. (gr. 1-6). 19.99 *(978-0-8307-2581-6(4),* Gospel Light) Gospel Light Pubns.
Gallery, Philip D. & Harlow, Janet L. Can You Find Followers of Jesus? Introducing Your Child to the Disciples. 2003. (Illus.). 40p. *(978-2-89507-120-4(9))* Novalis Publishing.
Gerner, Katy. Religions Around the World, 12 vols., Set. Incl. Buddhism. lib. bdg. 21.27 *(978-0-7614-3164-0(0),* ab5846ea-3873-4580-b44f-762b30d18bad); Catholicism. lib. bdg. 21.27 *(978-0-7614-3165-7(9),* f51ee5d8-f71e-489e-b16c-2106cdb4b218); Hinduism. lib. bdg. 21.27 *(978-0-7614-3166-4(7),* b6b7da83-87a8-4e4d-bbd5-31c5d3769e17); Islam. lib. bdg. 21.27 *(978-0-7614-3167-1(5),* a305dd13-5a4d-4ad7-a8f7-08dc14ab69ba); Judaism. 21.27 *(978-0-7614-3170-1(5),* a0bdbba9-a99a-4e69-b79e-842c9143ccb7); Protestantism. lib. bdg. 21.27 *(978-0-7614-3173-2(X),* 984af45c-da6f-4c46-a0da-3f5a8f59f42d); 32p. (gr. 3-3). (Religions Around the World Ser.). (ENG.). 2009. Set lib. bdg. 127.62 *(978-0-7614-3162-6(4),* afe0fca5-62f9-4949-993e-707310e3aae8, Cavendish Square) Cavendish Square Publishing LLC.
Gervais, Josephine. Mommies Are Protecting Their Children. 2013. 20p. pap. 24.95 *(978-1-62709-538-9(1))* America Star Bks.
—Mommies Are Special People. 2013. 24p. pap. 24.95 *(978-1-62709-537-2(3))* America Star Bks.
Green, Edna. My Special Thoughts: Designed for African-American Children. 2004. (J). (gr. -1-5). 10.00 *(978-0-9743019-1-4(4))* My Special Thoughts.
Habitat For Humanity Of The Chesapeake, ed. Peace by Piece: Illustrations by Christian, Jewish & Muslim Children Ages 5-17. 2012. 100p. (J). pap. 24.95 *(978-1-934074-74-9(8))* Apprentice Hse.
Hartz, Paula R. Shinto. 3rd rev. ed. 2009. (World Religions Ser.). Orig. Title: Shinto. (ENG., Illus.). 144p. (gr. 6-12). 40.00 *(978-1-60413-113-0(6),* P163094, Facts On File) Infobase Holdings, Inc.
Hodges, Ted. Religion & World Conflict, 1 vol. 2006. (World History Ser.). (ENG., Illus.). 104p. (J). (gr. 7-7). lib. bdg. 41.53 *(978-1-59018-642-8(7),*

b4593aab-5a2a-4b9c-8eeb-ecd85781925a, Lucent Pr.) Greenhaven Publishing LLC.

Hossler, Margaret. Spenser Rose Is Born. 2003. 32p. 12.99 (978-0-9650491-4-6(0)) Send The Light Distribution LLC.

Kallen, Stuart A. Voodoo. 2005. (Mystery Library). (Illus.). 112p. (YA). (gr. 7-10). lib. bdg. 29.95 (978-1-59018-630-5(3), Lucent Bks.) Cengage Gale.

Kalman, Bobbie. What Is Religion?, 1 vol. 2009. (Our Multicultural World Ser.). (ENG., Illus.). 32p. (J). (gr. 1-4). pap. (978-0-7787-4651-5(8)); lib. bdg. (978-0-7787-4636-2(4)) Crabtree Publishing Co.

Kaplan, Leslie C. Art & Religion in Ancient Egypt, 1 vol. 2003. (Primary Sources of Ancient Civilizations: Egypt, Greece, & Rome Ser.). (ENG.). 24p. (gr. 3-4). pap. 8.25 (978-0-8239-8932-4(1), e60ba784-59da-4704-a55a-4a1db96ee615, PowerKids Pr.) Rosen Publishing Group, Inc., The.

Killcoyne, Hope Lourie & Wolny, Philip, eds. The 100 Most Influential Religious Leaders of All Time, 1 vol., 1. 2016. (Britannica Guide to the World's Most Influential People Ser.). (ENG., Illus.). 376p. (J). (gr. 10-10). 56.59 (978-1-68048-277-5(7), ffaeb020-ef9f-478e-b780-c1095058d60a, Britannica Educational Publishing) Rosen Publishing Group, Inc., The.

Klemp, Joan & Moore, Anthony N. Sounds of HU. Brouhard, Crary & Carrol, Patrick, illus. 2013. (J). pap. (978-1-57043-363-4(1)) Eckankar.

Labosh, Kathy. The Child with Autism Learns the Faith: The Sunday School Guide. 2007. per. 14.00 (978-0-9744341-4-8(0)) Labosh Publishing.

Liardon, Roberts & Goldenberg, Olly. God's Generals for Kids Volume 2: Smith Wigglesworth, vols. 10, vol. 2. 2018. (ENG., Illus.). 168p. pap. 10.99 (978-1-61036-474-4(0), 141574) Bridge-Logos, Inc.

Mackenzie, Carine. Jose el Sonador de Dios Foce, Natalia, tr. Apps, Fred, illus. l.t. ed. 2004. (Biblewise Ser.). (SPA.). 32p. (J). pap. 4.50 (978-1-932789-16-4(2), 45545360-0975-4e2b-93f4-605e93caf8c0, CF4Kids) Christian Focus Pubns. GBR. Dist: Baker & Taylor Publisher Services (BTPS).

Martin, Oscar, Jr., creator. The Creation Story l.t. ed. 2003. (Illus.). 25p. (J). E-Book 19.95 incl. cd-rom (978-0-9748416-0-1(9)) Build Your Story.

McNeil, Niki, et al. HOCPP 1126 the Pilgrims. 2006. spiral bd. 16.00 (978-1-60308-126-9(7)) In the Hands of a Child.

Meisels, Dovid. Shabbos Secrets: The Mysteries Revealed. 2003. (Illus.). 365p. 25.95 (978-1-931681-43-8(0)) Israel Bookshop Pubns.

Miller, Debra A., ed. Politics & Religion, 1 vol. 2013. (Current Controversies Ser.). (ENG., Illus.). 176p. (gr. 10-12). pap. 33.00 (978-0-7377-6885-5(1), 5671de04-0cf1-4249-ae64-b066e9737323); lib. bdg. 48.03 (978-0-7377-6884-8(3), e709936c-99a7-4e35-8b25-c0217e0e4be3) Greenhaven Publishing LLC. (Greenhaven Publishing).

Moehlenpah, Arlo. Creation Versus Evolution: Scientific & Religious Considerations. 2003. 36p. (YA). (978-0-9667054-6-1(7)) Doing Good Ministries.

Nguyen, Hy Thi. Challenges. 2013. 260p. (gr. 10-12). pap. 16.55 (978-1-4817-2404-3(5)) AuthorHouse.

Olsen, Debi W. My Very Own Book about Religious Science. 2004. 32p. (J). 10.95 (978-1-931947-11-4(2)) Ink & Scribe.

Place, Robert Michael. Shamanism. 2008. (Mysteries, Legends, & Unexplained Phenomena Ser.). (ENG., Illus.). 120p. (gr. 7-12). lib. bdg. 29.95 (978-0-7910-9396-2(4), P159099, Facts On File) Infobase Holdings, Inc.

Pochocki, Ethel. Around the Year Once upon a Time Saints. Hatke, Ben, illus. 2009. (ENG.). 211p. (J). (gr. 4-6). pap. 14.95 (978-1-932350-26-5(8)) Ignatius Pr.

Prindle, Twyla D. Can I Have Some Money Please? Hansen, Lorie, illus. 2004. (ENG & SPA.). 20p. (J). (gr. k-4). 7.95 (978-0-9759527-2-6(2)) Prindle Hse. Publishing Co.

—Deception: The Devil Hears Your Prayers Too. 2004. (ENG.). 184p. (YA). pap. 14.95 (978-0-9759527-1-9(4)) Prindle Hse. Publishing Co.

—Teacher's Lounge. 2004. 184p. (YA). 19.95 (978-0-9759527-0-2(6)) Prindle Hse. Publishing Co.

Pundit Baraiya, Gopaldasji. Primer of Jain Principles. Gosalia, Kirit, tr. 2004. 210p. pap. 10.00 (978-0-9748681-0-3(8)) Songadh, Jain Swadhyay Mandir.

Rabbi Schneur Zalman of Liadi. Shulchan Aruch: Hilchot Rosh Hashana thru Lulav -New Edition. 2003. (HEB.). 192p. per. 4.95 (978-0-8266-5189-1(5)) Kehot Pubn. Society.

Religion & Modern Culture: Spiritual Beliefs That Influence North America Today, 13 vols., Set. Incl. Controversial World of Biblical Archaeology: Tomb Raiders, Fakes, & Scholars. McIntosh, Kenneth. (gr. 7-18). lib. bdg. 22.95 (978-1-59084-983-5(3)); Grail, the Shroud, & Other Religious Relics: Secrets & Ancient Mysteries. McIntosh, Kenneth. (gr. 3-7). lib. bdg. 22.95 (978-1-59084-978-1(7), 1248067); Growth of North American Religious Beliefs: Spiritual Diversity. McIntosh, Jonathan S. & McIntosh, Kenneth R. (gr. 7-18). lib. bdg. 22.95 (978-1-59084-975-0(2)); Issues of Church, State, & Religious Liberties: Whose Freedom, Whose Faith? McIntosh, Kenneth & McIntosh, Marsha. (gr. 8-12). lib. bdg. 22.95 (978-1-59084-973-6(6)); Prophecies & End-Time Speculations: The Shape of Things to Come. McIntosh, Kenneth. (gr. 3-7). lib. bdg. 22.95 (978-1-59084-979-8(5), 1248068); Women & Religion: Reinterpreting Scriptures to Find the Sacred Feminine. McIntosh, Kenneth R. (gr. 3-7). lib. bdg. 22.95 (978-1-59084-977-4(9)); (YA). 2007. (Illus.). 112p. 2006. Set lib. bdg. 298.35 (978-1-59084-970-5(1), 1248067) Mason Crest.

Religions of Humanity, Set. 2005. (Religions of Humanity Ser.). 32p. (gr. 6-12). 219.50 (978-0-7910-6621-8(5), Facts On File) Infobase Holdings, Inc.

SL Resources Staff, prod. Inhabit Student Book. 2010. 47p. (YA). 3.99 (978-1-935040-77-4(4)) SL Resources.

—SEQUENCE Student Work Book. 2009. 47p. (YA). 3.99 (978-1-935040-74-3(X)) SL Resources.

Sonnier, Suzanne. Shinto, Spirits, & Shrines: Religion in Japan, 1 vol. 2007. (Lucent Library of Historical Eras Ser.). (ENG., Illus.). 96p. (gr. 7-10). lib. bdg. 41.03 (978-1-4205-0029-5(5), 2ab6c961-ed73-4308-b303-170e93f8da89, Lucent Pr.) Greenhaven Publishing LLC.

Staeger, Rob. Native American Religions. Johnson, Troy, ed. 2013. (Native American Life Ser.: 15). 64p. (J). (gr. 5-18). 19.95 (978-1-4222-2974-3(2)) Mason Crest.

Stanley, Caleb & Dennis, Austin. The Alternative: Awaken Your Dream, Unite Your Community, & Live in Hope, 1 vol. 2019. (ENG., Illus.). 192p. (YA). pap. 16.99 (978-0-310-76588-2(9)) Zondervan.

Whitbread, Henry. Lives of the Great Spiritual Leaders. 2011. (Illus.). 96p. (J). (gr. 4-7). 19.95 (978-0-500-51578-5(6), 551578) Thames & Hudson.

RELIGION—PHILOSOPHY

see also Philosophy and Religion

Crispin, Gerald W. God Speaks Through Dreams: But Who's Listening?, No. 1. Crispin, Gerald W. & Crispin, Vera G., eds. unabr. ed. 2003. (Illus.). 160p. (gr. 10-18). reprint ed. pap. 19.95 (978-0-9744015-1-5(X)) Benchmark Book Craft.

RELIGION—STUDY AND TEACHING

see Religious Education

RELIGION AND PHILOSOPHY

see Philosophy and Religion

RELIGION AND SCIENCE

see also Creation; Evolution; Human Beings—Origin

Answers to Evolution Wall Chart. 2004. (978-1-890947-87-3(3)) Rose Publishing.

Brand, Leonard. God, Science, Friends: Do You Know Jesus? 2019. (Illus.). 185p. (J). pap. (978-0-8163-6518-0(0)) Pacific Pr. Publishing Assn.

Derr, Louise Barrett. Experiencing Bible Science. 2007. 128p. per. 16.95 (978-1-59919-025-9(7)) Elim Publishing.

Engdahl, Sharon & Engdahl, Terry. The Evolution of Creation: A Children's Primer on the Evolution of God's Creation, 1 vol. 2010. 30p. 24.95 (978-1-4489-4228-2(4)) PublishAmerica, Inc.

Giglio, Louie. How Great Is Our God: 100 Indescribable Devotions about God & Science, 1 vol. Anderson, Nicola, illus. 2019. (Indescribable Kids Ser.). (ENG.). 208p. (J). 17.99 (978-1-4002-1552-2(8), Tommy Nelson) Nelson, Thomas Inc.

—Indescribable: 100 Devotions for Kids about God & Science, 1 vol. 2017. (Indescribable Kids Ser.). (ENG., Illus.). 208p. (J). 17.99 (978-0-7180-8610-7(4), Tommy Nelson) Nelson, Thomas Inc.

Gonzalez, David J. There Are No Space Aliens! 12 Biblical Points Disproving Space Aliens. l.t. ed. 2003. 48p. 9.95 (978-0-9741561-0-1(8)) Gonzalez, David J. Ministries.

Hodge, Bodie & Welch, Laura, eds. Dragons: Legends & Lore of Dinosaurs. Looney, Bill, illus. 2009. 24p. (J). 19.99 (978-0-89051-558-7(1), Master Books) New Leaf Publishing Group.

Science & Living in God's World. (J). 10.00 (978-1-931555-49-4(4));Bk. 1. (J). 10.00 (978-1-931555-50-0(8));Bk. 2. (J). 20.00 (978-1-931555-51-7(6));Bk. 3. (J). 22.00 (978-1-931555-52-4(4));Bk. 4. (J). 16.00 (978-1-931555-53-1(2));Bk. 5. (YA). 12.00 (978-1-931555-54-8(0));Bk. 6. (YA). 20.00 (978-1-931555-55-5(9));Bk. 7. (YA). 20.00 (978-1-931555-56-2(7));Bk. 8. (YA). 20.00 (978-1-931555-57-9(5)) Our Lady of Victory Schl.

Syed, Ibrahim. Quranic Inspirations. 2007. 688p. (YA). per. 37.95 (978-0-595-45003-9(2)) iUniverse, Inc.

Walker, Joe. Belief & Science. 2009. (ENG., Illus.). 208p. pap., tchr. ed. 43.50 (978-0-340-97302-8(1)) Hodder Education Group GBR. Dist: Trans-Atlantic Pubns., Inc.

Waunsch, John. My Very, Very First Weather Book. 2013. 56p. 23.99 (978-1-62697-903-1(0)); pap. 12.99 (978-1-62697-764-8(X)) Salem Author Services.

RELIGION AND STATE

see Church and State

RELIGIONS

see also Bahai Faith; Buddhism; Christianity; Confucianism; Hinduism; Judaism; Mythology; Religion; Sects

Adams, Simon. The History of World Religions: Explore the Great Faiths That Shaped Our Civilization. 2016. (Illus.). 64p. (J). (gr. -1-11). 12.99 (978-1-86147-752-1(X), Armadillo) Anness Publishing GBR. Dist: National Bk. Network.

Ajmera, Maya, et al. Faith. 2009. (Global Fund for Children Bks.). (Illus.). 48p. (J). (gr. -1-3). 16.95 (978-1-58089-177-6(2)); pap. 8.95 (978-1-58089-178-3(0)) Charlesbridge Publishing, Inc.

Altson, John & Miliotis, Patti Rae. What Happened to Grandpa? A Child Views the Hereafter Through the World's Major Religions. 2009. 36p. pap. 16.99 (978-1-4343-6743-3(6)) AuthorHouse.

Anderson, Dale. Churches & Religion in the Middle Ages, 1 vol. 2005. (World Almanac(r) Library of the Middle Ages Ser.). (ENG., Illus.). 48p. (gr. 5-8). lib. bdg. 33.67 (978-0-8368-5892-1(1), e2c2661a-e114-4308-9f97-c809f6e1611d, Gareth Stevens Secondary Library) Stevens, Gareth Publishing LLLP.

Atkin, Pippa. Flexi-RE Evaluation, Bk. 3. 2003. (ENG., Illus.). 128p. pap., stu. ed. 15.95 (978-0-7487-6354-2(6)) Nelson Thornes Ltd. GBR. Dist: Trans-Atlantic Pubns., Inc.

Boersma, Heather. Dream Big: 30 Days to Life Beyond All You Could Ask or Imagine. 2012. ix, 119p. (978-1-77069-453-8(6)) Word Alive Pr.

Britannica, Learning Library. Religions Around the World. 2003. (Illus.). 64p. 14.95 (978-1-59339-038-9(6)) Encyclopaedia Britannica, Inc.

Bullard, Lisa. My Religion, Your Religion. Conger, Holli, illus. 2015. (Cloverleaf Books (tm) — Alike & Different Ser.). (ENG.). 24p. (J). (gr. k-2). pap. 8.99 (978-1-4677-6033-1(1), a79f7a2e-5f6a-4c77-9c34-9087b9586544, Millbrook Pr.) Lerner Publishing Group.

Cavell-Clarke, Steffi. Celebrating Different Beliefs. 2017. (Our Values - Level 2 Ser.). (Illus.). 24p. (J). (gr. 2-3). (978-0-7787-3261-7(4)) Crabtree Publishing Co.

Ceanadach, Siusaidh. Let's Talk about Elements & the Pagan Wheel. 2013. (ENG., Illus.). 73p. (J). (gr. -1-12). pap. 9.95 (978-1-78099-561-8(X), Moon Bks.) Hunt, John Publishing Ltd. GBR. Dist: National Bk. Network.

Clarke, Steve. Themes to InspiRE for KS3, Bk. 1. 2011. (Dynamic Learning Ser.). (ENG., Illus.). 96p. pap. 39.50 (978-1-4441-2205-3(3)) Hodder Education Group GBR. Dist: Trans-Atlantic Pubns., Inc.

DK. What Do You Believe? Big Questions about Religion. 2016. (Big Questions Ser.). (ENG., Illus.). 96p. (J). (gr. 2-5). pap. 10.99 (978-1-4654-4386-1(X), DK Children) Dorling Kindersley Publishing, Inc.

Eastwood, Kay. Places of Worship in the Middle Ages. 2003. (Medieval World Ser.). (ENG., Illus.). 32p. (J). (gr. 5). lib. bdg. (978-0-7787-1347-0(4)) Crabtree Publishing Co.

Glossop, Jennifer. The Kids Book of World Religions. Mantha, John, illus. 2013. (Kids Book Of Ser.). (ENG.). 64p. (J). (gr. 3-7). pap. 14.99 (978-1-55453-981-9(1)) Kids Can Pr., Ltd. CAN. Dist: Hachette Bk. Group.

Green, Connie R. & Oldendorf, Sandra Brenneman. Religious Diversity & Children's Literature. 2011. (ENG.). E-Book (978-1-61735-398-7(1)) Information Age Publishing, Inc.

Gunderson, Cory Gideon. Religions of the Middle East. 2003. (World in Conflict-the Middle East Ser.). 32p. (gr. 4-8). 27.07 (978-1-59197-412-3(7), Abdo & Daughters) ABDO Publishing Co.

Hakowski, Maryann. Vine & Branches, ol. 3. Price, Carolyn, illus. 2003. (Resources for Youth Retreats Ser.: Vol. 3). 176p. (J). (gr. 6-7). pap. 24.95 (978-0-88489-323-3(5)) Saint Mary's Press of Minnesota.

Haywood, John. Through the Ages: Gods, Beliefs & Ceremonies. 2008. (Illus.). 64p. (J). (gr. 4-7). pap. 12.99 (978-1-84476-601-7(2)) Anness Publishing GBR. Dist: National Bk. Network.

Henzel, Cynthia Kennedy. Understanding Scientology. 2018. (Understanding World Religions & Beliefs Ser.). (ENG., Illus.). 112p. (J). (gr. 6-12). lib. bdg. 41.36 (978-1-5321-1428-1(1), 28838, Essential Library) ABDO Publishing Co.

Hibbert, Clare. Beliefs & Ideas That Changed the World. 2017. (Revolutions Ser.). (ENG., Illus.). 64p. (J). (gr. 3-6). 19.99 (978-0-7123-5680-0(0)) British Library, The GBR. Dist: Independent Pubs. Group.

Hickman, Clare & Meredith, Sue. The Usborne Encyclopedia of World Religions: Internet-Linked. Rogers, Kirsteen, ed. Rolland, Leonard Le, illus. rev. ed. 2006. (Usborne Encyclopedia of World Religions Ser.). 128p. (J). (gr. 5-9). per. 14.95 (978-0-7945-1059-6(0), Usborne) EDC Publishing.

Kallen, Stuart A. Communication with the Dead. 2009. (Library of Ghosts & Hauntings Ser.). (Illus.). 80p. (J). (gr. 7-12). 43.93 (978-1-60152-089-0(1), 1305811) ReferencePoint Pr., Inc.

Kalman, Bobbie. What Is Religion? 2009. (Our Multicultural World Ser.). (ENG., Illus.). 32p. (J). (gr. 1-4). lib. bdg. (978-0-7787-4636-2(4)) Crabtree Publishing Co.

Kelly, Sheila M. & Rotner, Shelley. Many Ways: How Families Practice Their Beliefs & Religions. Rotner, Shelley, photos by. 2010. (Shelley Rotner's Early Childhood Library). (ENG., Illus.). 32p. (J). (gr. k-3). pap. 11.99 (978-0-7613-6531-0(1), 26e505e7-a336-4b65-80c1-1d44c98609b9, Millbrook Pr.) Lerner Publishing Group.

Lewis, Andy & Orme, Robert. World Religions: Judaism, Christianity & Islam. 2017. (ENG.). 120p. (J). (gr. 6-9). pap. 29.99 (978-0-00-822768-5(3)) HarperCollins Pubs. Ltd. GBR. Dist: Independent Pubs. Group.

Major, Gail Baccelli. What Do You See in Me I am Who I am. Major, Rebekah, illus. 2013. (ENG.). 32p. (J). pap. 9.95 (978-1-939289-22-3(X), Little Creek Bks.) Jan-Carol Publishing, INC.

Mayled, Jon & Ahluwalia, Libby. Philosophy & Ethics. 2003. (ENG., Illus.). 208p. pap. (978-0-7487-7157-8(3)) Nelson Thornes Ltd.

Mead, Jean. What religions are in our Neighbourhood? 2013. (Step up Religion Ser.). (Illus.). 32p. (J). pap. 12.99 (978-0-237-54379-2(6)) Evans Brothers, Ltd. GBR. Dist: Independent Pubs. Group.

Meredith, Susan. The Usborne Book of World Religions. Evans, Cheryl, ed. Hewetson, Nicholas J., illus. 2006. (World Religions (Usborne) Ser.). 64p. (J). (gr. 5). lib. bdg. 17.99 (978-1-58086-908-9(4), Usborne) EDC Publishing.

—The Usborne Book of World Religions. Evans, Cheryl, ed. Hewetson, Nicholas J. & Gower, Jeremy, illus. rev. ed. 2006. (World Cultures Ser.). 64p. (J). (gr. 5). pap. 9.99 (978-0-7945-1027-5(2)) EDC Publishing.

Meredith, Susan & Hickman, Claire. Encyclopedia of World Religions. rev. ed. 2012. (World Cultures Ser.). 128p. (J). pap. 14.99 (978-0-7945-2753-2(1), Usborne) EDC Publishing.

O'Brien, Joanne & Palmer, Martin, eds. World Religions Set, 14 vols., Set. 2009. (ENG.). (gr. 6-12). 560.00 (978-1-60413-649-4(9), P166844, Facts On File) Infobase Holdings, Inc.

Palmer, Martin, et al. Religions of the World: The Illustrated Guide to Origins, Beliefs, Traditions & Festivals. 2nd rev. ed. 2005. (Illustrated Guide to Customs & Beliefs Ser.). (Illus.). 160p. (gr. 6-12). 29.95 (978-0-8160-6258-4(7), Checkmark Bks.) Infobase Holdings, Inc.

Raushenbush, Paul. Teen Spirit: One World, Many Paths. 2004. (ENG., Illus.). 252p. (YA). pap. 11.95 (978-0-7573-0119-3(3), HCI Teens) Health Communications, Inc.

Rogers, Kirsteen & Hickman, Clare. Religiones Del Mundo - Internet Linked. 2005. (Titles in Spanish Ser.). (SPA.). 128p. (J). 19.95 (978-0-7460-5093-4(3), Usborne) EDC Publishing.

Rotner, Shelley & Kelly, Sheila M. Many Ways: How Families Practice Their Beliefs & Religions. Rotner, Shelley, photos by. 2005. (Shelley Rotner's Early Childhood Library). (ENG., Illus.). 32p. (gr. k-3). lib. bdg. 22.60 (978-0-7613-2873-5(4), Millbrook Pr.) Lerner Publishing Group.

Schomp, Virginia. The Ancient Persians, 1 vol. 2010. (Myths of the World Ser.). (ENG.). 96p. (gr. 6-6). 36.93 (978-0-7614-4218-9(9), efe94990-0819-4124-a613-bb0ae45a4c24) Cavendish Square Publishing LLC.

Shanddaramon. Pagan Sabbats of the Northern Hemisphere. 2008. 39p. 18.95 (978-0-615-18601-6(7)) Astor Pr.

Stockstill, Gloria McQueen. To the Town of Bethlehem. Durrell, Julie, illus. 2004. 20p. (J). bds. 5.49 (978-0-7586-0051-6(8)) Concordia Publishing Hse.

Teen Spirit Guide to Modern Shamanism: A Beginner's Map Charting an Ancient Path. 2014. (ENG., Illus.). 147p. (J). (gr. -1-12). pap. 16.95 (978-1-78279-433-2(6), Soul Rocks Bks.) Hunt, John Publishing Ltd. GBR. Dist: National Bk. Network.

Wall, Molly & Mandryk, Jason. Window on the World: An Operation World Prayer Resource. rev. ed. 2018. (Operation World Resources Ser.). (ENG.). 224p. pap. 30.00 (978-0-8308-5783-8(4), IVP Bks.) InterVarsity Pr.

Wallace, Ann Hamilton. The Messenger: Revelations from an Unlikely Prophet. 2003. (ENG., Illus.). 150p. (gr. 9-12). 22.95 (978-0-9724458-0-1(3)) Sonrise Publishing.

What Is Faith? 2006. (Faith Discovery Ser.). (Illus.). 24p. (J). bds. 6.99 (978-0-7847-1396-9(0), 04056) Standard Publishing.

Wills, Anna. Who Believes What? Exploring the World's Major Religions. Tomm, Nora, illus. 2018. (ENG.). 40p. (J). (gr. 4-8). 18.95 (978-1-77147-333-0(9)) Owlkids Bks. Inc. CAN. Dist: Publishers Group West (PGW).

World Religions, 12 vols., Set. Incl. Buddhism. Young, Serinity. lib. bdg. 42.64 (978-0-7614-2114-6(9), 95d0c8b7-316d-41e8-8372-a5babe06774b); Hinduism. Young, Serinity. lib. bdg. 42.64 (978-0-7614-2116-0(5), c5573a4d-37d6-4f4c-81b8-ea04be6f79bc); Islam. Alkouatli, Claire. lib. bdg. 42.64 (978-0-7614-2120-7(3), 00d50c46-932d-4627-8bc3-51008042d4eb); Judaism. Wool, Danny. lib. bdg. 42.64 (978-0-7614-2118-4(1), e3264b64-71b0-42e2-a487-9ad77e1062dc); Protestantism. Eppehimer, Trevor. lib. bdg. 42.64 (978-0-7614-2117-7(3), 75d5e7d4-3aa3-4263-8588-e3440ec8f268); Roman Catholicism. Otfinoski, Steven. lib. bdg. 42.64 (978-0-7614-2119-1(X), 5305c52a-9831-494d-9a04-b32e6a5055b2); (Illus.). 144p. (YA). (gr. 7-7). (World Religions Ser.). (ENG.). 2007. Set lib. bdg. 255.84 (978-0-7614-2113-9(0), e306605f-06fd-4bf7-8f82-4df42fa08252, Cavendish Square) Cavendish Square Publishing LLC.

York Lumbard, Alexis. Everyone Prays: Celebrating Faith Around the World. Sadeghian, Alireza, illus. 2014. 28p. (J). (gr. -1-3). 17.95 (978-1-937786-19-9(6), Wisdom Tales) World Wisdom, Inc.

RELIGIONS—BIOGRAPHY

Here are entered collections of biographies of religious leaders not limited to the Christian religion.

see also Christian Biography

Carr, Simonetta. Marie Durand: Christian Biographies for Young Readers. Abraxas, Matt, illus. 2015. (ENG.). 60p. (J). 18.00 (978-1-60178-390-5(6)) Reformation Heritage Bks.

Grant, Myrna. Gladys Aylward: No Mountain Too High. rev. ed. 2013. (Trail Blazers Ser.). (ENG.). 176p. (J). mass mkt. 8.99 (978-1-85792-594-4(7), e4d61dc8-55a3-4b82-8ba8-ac98ac191d28, CF4Kids) Christian Focus Pubns. GBR. Dist: Baker & Taylor Publisher Services (BTPS).

Kwiatkowski, Gerhard & Lanczkowski, Günter. Religionen: Von Alten Naturreligionen bis zu Modernen Sekten, Ursprung und Geschichte aller Religionen, 1 vol. (Duden-Schuelerduden Ser.). (GER & ENG., Illus.). 467p. (YA). 27.95 (978-3-411-01369-2(9)) Bibliographisches Institut & F. A. Brockhaus AG DEU. Dist: Continental Bk. Co., Inc.

Marty, Martin E., intro. Spiritual Leaders & Thinkers. (Illus.). (gr. 9-13). lib. bdg. 252.45 (978-0-7910-8413-7(2), Facts On File) Infobase Holdings, Inc.

Moore, Kieron. Buddha: an Enlightened Life. Nagulakonda, Rajesh, illus. 2017. (Campfire Graphic Novels Ser.). (ENG.). 160p. (YA). (gr. 7). pap. 16.99 (978-93-81182-29-1(9), Campfire) Steerforth Pr.

Nardo, Don. Founders of Faiths. 2011. (World Religions & Beliefs Ser.). (Illus.). 159p. (J). (gr. 7-12). 28.95 (978-1-59935-147-6(1)) Reynolds, Morgan Inc.

Touger, Malka. A Door That's Never Locked. 2011. (ENG.). 64p. (J). 14.95 (978-0-8266-0131-5(6)) Kehot Pubn. Society.

RELIGIONS—FICTION

Abraham, Michelle Shapiro. Where Is Grandpa Dennis? Fried, Janice, illus. 2009. (J). (978-0-8074-1083-7(7)) URJ Pr.

Adahan, Miriam. Torah Tigers. 2009. 48p. 17.99 (978-1-59826-308-4(0)) Feldheim Pubs.

Alberti, Robert. Mitlanyal: The Gods of Change, Vol. 2. 10th ed. 2004. (Illus.). 184p. (YA). pap. 19.95 (978-0-9725880-3-4(5), mit2) Zottola Publishing, Inc.

Arnold, Edward Ronny. Rashida. 2003. 110p. (YA). pap. 7.99 (978-0-9721216-6-8(8), 0972121668) Computer Classics (R).

Barash, Chris. Is It Sukkot Yet? Psacharopulo, Alessandra, illus. 2016. (Celebrate Jewish Holidays Ser.). (ENG.). 32p. (J). (gr. -1-3). 16.99 (978-0-8075-3388-8(2), 807533882) Whitman, Albert & Co.

Barricks, Jerim. I Want to Know??? 2003. (Illus.). 26p. (J). 10.00 (978-0-9743512-0-9(2)) Barricks, Jeri Ministry.

Bell, Shirley. Boys on the Make. 2007. 54p. 16.95 (978-1-4241-6575-9(X)) America Star Bks.

Benenfeld, Rikki. I Go Visiting. 2007. (Toddler Experience Ser.). (ENG., Illus.). 32p. (J). (gr. -1-k). 11.99 (978-1-929628-33-9(1)) Hachai Publishing.

Blume, Judy. Are You There God? It's Me, Margaret. 149p. (J). (gr. 4-6). pap. 3.50 (978-0-8072-1421-3(3)); (YA). (gr. 5-18). pap. 4.99 (978-0-8072-1508-1(2)) Random Hse. Audio Publishing Group. (Listening Library).

Brooks, Grace. The Asquinn Twins & Grant. 2010. 111p. pap. 9.94 (978-0-557-26972-3(5)) Lulu Pr., Inc.

Bunce, Elizabeth C. StarCrossed. 2011. (ENG.). 368p. (YA). pap. 9.99 (978-0-545-13606-8(7), Levine, Arthur A. Bks.) Scholastic, Inc.

Chancellor, Deborah. The Christmas Story. Downing, Julie, illus. 12p. (J). (gr. -1-18). bds. 6.95 (978-0-8294-1480-6(0)) Loyola Pr.

Chrisagis, Brian. Who & What Am I? Good News Gang. Chrisagis, Shawn, illus. 2006. 24p. (J). 9.99 (978-1-59958-014-2(4)) Journey Stone Creations, LLC.

Chrisagis, Shawn & Chrisagis, Brian. Prejudice in Mandi's Garden: Seeds of Kindness. 2006. 24p. (J). pap. 2.99 (978-1-59958-009-8(8)) Journey Stone Creations, LLC.

Cobb, Judith A. The First Gift. Cowper-Thomas, Wendy, illus. 2008. (J). pap. (978-0-87743-708-6(4)) Baha'i Publishing Trust, U.S.

Cohen, Deborah Bodin. Papa Jethro. Dippold, Jane, illus. 2007. (Jewish Identity Ser.). (ENG.). 32p. (J). (gr. -1-1). per. 7.95 (978-1-58013-252-7(9), Kar-Ben Publishing) Lerner Publishing Group.

Connolly, Ed. Summer Dance of the Fireflies. Flynn, Noel, illus. 2003. (ENG.). 44p. per. 18.95 (978-1-888996-64-7(1)) Red Hen Pr.

Cowper-Thomas, Wendy, illus. Something Important. 2010. (J). (978-0-87743-711-6(4)) Baha'i Publishing Trust, U.S.
Coy, John. Box Out. 2010. (ENG.). 304p. (J). (gr. 7-12). 24.94 (978-0-545-17416-9(3)) Scholastic, Inc.
Coyle, Katie. Vivian Apple at the End of the World. 2016. (ENG.). 288p. (YA). (gr. 7). pap. 8.99 (978-0-544-66867-6(7), 1625492, Clarion Bks.) HarperCollins Pubs.
Dillon, Sally Pierson. Exile of the Chosen: God's Heroes from Solomon to Malachi. 2003. (Pathfinder Junior Book Club Ser.). 223p. (J). pap. 10.99 (978-0-8280-1703-9(4), 58-710) Review & Herald Publishing Assn.
Douglas, Babette. Rosebud. 2004. (J). 9.99 (978-1-890343-12-5(9)) Kiss A Me Productions, Inc.
Finley, Martha. Christmas with Grandma Elsie, Vol. 14. 320p. (gr. 4-7). pap. 5.95 (978-1-58182-108-6(5), Cumberland Hse.) Sourcebooks, Inc.
—Elsie & the Raymonds, Vol. 15. 320p. (gr. 4-7). pap. 5.95 (978-1-58182-110-9(7), Cumberland Hse.) Sourcebooks, Inc.
—Elsie Yachting with the Raymonds, Vol. 16. 320p. (gr. 4-7). pap. 5.95 (978-1-58182-111-6(5), Cumberland Hse.) Sourcebooks, Inc.
—Elsie's Friends at Woodburn, Vol. 13. 320p. (gr. 4-7). pap. 5.95 (978-1-58182-107-9(7), Cumberland Hse.) Sourcebooks, Inc.
Finney, Ruth. A Prayer for Momma. 2007. 38p. pap. 8.00 (978-0-8059-7483-6(0)) Dorrance Publishing Co., Inc.
Fleischman, Sid. The Entertainer & the Dybbuk. 2009. (ENG.). 192p. (J). (gr. 4-9). pap. 6.99 (978-0-06-177140-8(6), Greenwillow Bks.) HarperCollins Pubs.
Gould, M&R. What Would Jesus Do? Purity of Intention. 2008. 35p. pap. 24.95 (978-1-60672-675-4(7)) America Star Bks.
Gregory, Philippa. Stormbringers. van Deelen, Fred, illus. 2013. (Order of Darkness Ser.: 2). (ENG.). 336p. (YA). (gr. 9). pap. 9.99 (978-1-4424-7688-2(5)); 17.99 (978-1-4424-7687-5(7)) Simon Pulse. (Simon Pulse).
Hatcher, John S. Ali's Dream. 2014. (ENG.). 310p. (J). (gr. 6-11). pap. 15.00 (978-1-61851-068-6(1)) Baha'i Publishing.
Hauser, Lisa Kay. 1-2-3, & God Made Me! 2004. (Illus.). 32p. 15.95 (978-1-886864-03-0(9)) Golden Anchor Pr.
—1-2-3, Special Like Me! 2004. (Illus.). 32p. (J). 15.95 (978-1-886864-17-7(9), 1231325) Golden Anchor Pr.
Hautman, Pete. The Cydonian Pyramid. (Klaatu Diskos Ser.: 2). (ENG.). 368p. (YA). (gr. 7). 2014. pap. 8.99 (978-0-7636-6933-1(4)) 2013. 16.99 (978-0-7636-5404-7(3)) Candlewick Pr.
—Godless. (ENG.). 208p. (YA). (gr. 7-12). 2005. pap. 12.99 (978-1-4169-0816-6(1)) 2004. (Illus.). 18.99 (978-0-689-86278-6(4)) Simon & Schuster Bks. For Young Readers. (Simon & Schuster Bks. For Young Readers).
Hawkins, Wanda. Geronimo Discovers Faith. 2007. (Illus.). 24p. (J). per. 12.99 (978-1-59879-336-9(5)) Lifevest Publishing, Inc.
Hawxhurst, Joan C. Bubbe & Gram: My Two Grandmothers. Bynum-Nwulu, Jane, illus. 2003. 32p. (J). (gr. -1-2). 12.95 (978-0-9651284-2-1(3)) Dovetail Publishing.
Hocknell, Barbara. The Mouse Who Attended the Last Supper: And Other Stories. 2007. (Illus.). 48p. per. (978-1-84748-200-6(7)) Athena Pr.
Hodakov, Levi. I Go to the Ohel. Rosenfeld, D. L. & Leverton, Yossi, eds. Benenfeld, Rikki, illus. 2011. (Toddler Experience Ser.). 32p. (J). 11.99 (978-1-929628-61-2(7)) Hachai Publishing.
Holmes, Andy. If You Give a Boy a Bible. 2004. (Illus.). 32p. (J). 10.99 (978-0-8254-5513-1(8)) Kregel Pubns.
Hünermann, Wilhelm. A Crucified Heart: A Novel of St. Herman Joseph. Szanto, Hubert, tr. from GER. 2004. Orig. Title: Der Moench Vom Steinfeld. (Illus.). 176p. (YA). (978-0-9742298-1-2(4)) St. Michael's Abbey.
Jaskwhich, Cynthia Sheperd. Mema Says Good-Bye. Mazibuko, Luthando, illus. 2010. (J). (978-0-87743-710-9(6)) Baha'i Publishing Trust, U.S.
Jenkins, Jerry B. & Lahaye, Tim. The Mark of the Beast: Witness Behind Bars. 2003. (Left Behind Ser.). 146p. (J). 13.65 (978-0-7569-3532-0(6)) Perfection Learning Corp.
Koffsky, Ann. Shabbat Shalom, Hey! Koffsky, Ann, illus. 2015. (ENG., Illus.). 24p. (J). (gr. -1-k). lib. bdg. 9.99 (978-1-4677-4917-6(6), d719be77-c753-4940-809e-dd42198c6358, Kar-Ben Publishing) Lerner Publishing Group.
Koster, Gloria. Little Red Ruthie: A Hanukkah Tale. Eastland, Sue, illus. 2017. (ENG.). 32p. (J). (gr. -1-3). 17.99 (978-0-8075-4646-8(1), 807546461) Whitman, Albert & Co.
Lepard, Jenina. Diamonds in the Rough. 2009. (J). pap. (978-0-87743-713-0(0)) Baha'i Publishing Trust, U.S.
Lieberman, Leanne. Gravity, 1 vol. 2008. (ENG.). 280p. (YA). (gr. 8-12). pap. 12.95 (978-1-55469-049-7(8)) Orca Bk. Pubs. USA.
Littman, Sarah Darer. Confessions of a Closet Catholic. 2006. 208p. (J). (gr. 5-18). reprint ed. 7.99 (978-0-14-240597-0(3), Puffin Books) Penguin Young Readers Group.
Luedke, Robert James. Eye Witness: A Fictional Tale of Absolute Truth. 2005. (Eye Witness Ser.). (ENG., Illus.). 96p. pap. 13.99 (978-0-9758924-0-4(1)); lib. bdg. 24.99 (978-0-9758924-1-1(X)) Head Pr. Publishing.
Madison, Ron. Ned & the World's Religions: As Seen Through the Eyes of Children. Covolo, David, illus. 2008. 36p. (J). 14.95 (978-1-887206-26-6(4)) Ned's Head Productions.
Mahr, Aryeh. Mysteries of the Aleph Beis. 2008. 54p. 17.99 (978-1-59826-211-7(4)) Feldheim Pubs.
Martin, W. Lyon. An Ordinary Girl, A Magical Child. Martin, W. Lyon, illus. 2008. (ENG., Illus.). 48p. (J). lib. bdg. 16.95 (978-0-9796834-3-5(2), Magical Child Bks.) Shades of White.
McO-Campbell, Adrian. The Wildness Within & the Tree of Eyes. 2010. 80p. pap. 38.95 (978-1-4457-1664-0(X)) Lulu Pr., Inc.
Mills, Samuel. The Demon Slayer, 1 vol. 2009. 192p. (YA). pap. 15.00 (978-0-88010-701-3(4)) SteinerBooks, Inc.
—The Fire Bringer, 1 vol. 2009. 128p. (J). pap. 15.00 (978-0-88010-700-6(6)) SteinerBooks, Inc.
Morley, Farah, illus. The Spider & the Doves: The Story of the Hijra. 2012. (ENG.). 30p. (J). (gr. -1-2). 8.95 (978-0-86037-449-7(1)) Kube Publishing Ltd. GBR. Dist: Consortium Bk. Sales & Distribution.
Naibantsky, Danail. Bludnia Sin (the Prodigal Son) Guetov, Dimitar, ed. 2nd unabr. ed. 2004. (BUL.). 228p. per. 9.99 (978-0-9753970-3-9(6)) Capricorn Publishing.
Naughty Krishna. 2003. (J). 2.99 (978-0-9748285-1-0(3)) Anar Bks. LLC.
Newman, Tracy. Simchat Torah Is Coming! Garofoli, Viviana, illus. 2018. (ENG.). 12p. (J). (gr. -1 — 1). bds. 5.99 (978-1-5124-2100-2(6), 388c65f8-ce27-4342-bcf0-20442cb0c9cf, Kar-Ben Publishing) Lerner Publishing Group.
Oppenheim, Shulamith. I Blis: An Islamic Tale. Young, Ed, illus. 2004. 29p. (J). (gr. k-4). reprint ed. 16.00 (978-0-7567-7575-9(2)) DIANE Publishing Co.
Padgett, Anthony. Divinityland. 2010. (Illus.). 20p. 21.50 (978-0-9561587-1-0(4)) Auditors of God, The GBR. Dist: Lulu Pr., Inc.
Pelletier, Cynthia L. & Rabin, Shri. She Who Walks with Tigers, 1 vol. 2010. 80p. pap. 19.95 (978-1-4512-8767-7(4)) America Star Bks.
Peretti, Frank E. The Tombs of Anak, Vol. 3. 2004. (Cooper Kids Adventure Ser.: 3). (ENG.). 144p. (J). (gr. 3-6). pap. 6.99 (978-1-58134-620-6(4)) Crossway.
Powers, Emily. Wendell Has a Cracked Shell. Moody, Jason, illus. 2008. 32p. (gr. -1-18). pap. 14.95 (978-0-9801357-6-3(1)) Tree of Life Publishing Hse.
Rapp, Pat. Noisy Nativity. 2008. 24p. per. 24.95 (978-1-4241-9866-5(6)) America Star Bks.
Rennie-Pattison, Caroline. The Law of Three: A Sarah Martin Mystery. 2007. (Sarah Martin Mystery Ser.: 2). (ENG.). 232p. (YA). (gr. 6). pap. 10.99 (978-1-55002-733-4(6)) Dundurn Pr. CAN. Dist: Publishers Group West (PGW).
Rose, Robert. Godintoxicated Becoming Paranoid. 2007. 260p. pap. 29.95 (978-1-4327-0041-6(3)) Outskirts Pr., Inc.
Sawyers, Carol. Trapped At 13. 2005. 220p. (YA). pap. 14.00 (978-0-9767778-4-7(3), 704-724-1683) Alpha & Omega Publishing.
Sharma, Nick. Shalu, Diwali: The Festival of Lights. 2015. (ENG., Illus.). 38p. (J). (gr. -1-3). 9.95 (978-0-9914804-4-9(9), Shalu Children's Series, The) Penman Productions.
Singer, Marilyn. Brushes with Religion. Date not set. 192p. (YA). (gr. 7-18). mass mkt. 5.99 (978-0-06-440789-2(6)) HarperCollins Pubs.
St. John, Patricia. The Victor. 2003. 176p. 6.49 (978-0-86201-139-0(6)) Scripture Union GBR. Dist: Gabriel Resources.
Steedman, Amy. In God's Garden (Yesterday's Classics) 2006. (J). per. 9.95 (978-1-59915-032-1(8)) Yesterday's Classics.
Stephens, Dawn. The Little Pot. 2009. (Illus.). (J). (gr. -1-3). 17.95 (978-1-933982-11-3(X), bPlus Bks.) Bumble Bee Publishing.
Stevens, Noel. Tin Gods. 2008. 116p. pap. 10.95 (978-0-595-53046-5(X)) iUniverse, Inc.
Taylor, Yvonne. Hartlie: The Streak. Taylor, Yvonne, ed. (Hartlie: Vol. 1). (Illus.). 32p. (J). 10.99 (978-0-9709187-0-3(4)) Peaceable Productions.
Thompson, James A., Jr. The Amarna Experiment. 2003. 128p. (YA). 21.95 (978-0-595-65753-7(2)); pap. 11.95 (978-0-595-28296-8(2)) iUniverse, Inc.
Tika. Baby Love. Standish, Joyce, ed. Burroughs, Derrie, illus. l.t. ed. 2006. 18p. (J). (gr. 1-5). pap. 15.00 (978-0-9716244-1-2(0)) TLS Publishing.
Townsend, Diana. He Saw Their Faith. 2007. 25p. 21.50 (978-0-615-16214-0(2)) Townsend, Diana.
Van Ryk, Laverne. A Garland of Emeralds. 2006. (Illus.). 305p. 31.50 (978-1-4122-0156-8(X)) Trafford Publishing.
Von Schmid. Stolen Child. 2004. 13.00 (978-1-58474-022-3(1)) Cornerstone Family Ministries/Lamplighter Publishing.
Warner, Susan. Daisy. 2007. 316p. pap. 14.99 (978-1-4264-9407-9(6)); 356p. pap. 20.99 (978-1-4264-9788-9(1)) Creative Media Partners, LLC.
Wasserman, Sand. The Sun's Special Blessing: Happens Only Once in 28 Years - French Flap. Koffsky, Ann, illus. 2009. 36p. 12.95 (978-1-934440-76-6(0), Pitspopany Pr.) Simcha Media Group.
—The Sun's Special Blessing: Happens Only Once in 28 Years - HC. Koffsky, Ann, illus. 2009. 36p. 17.95 (978-1-934440-92-6(2), Pitspopany Pr.) Simcha Media Group.
Wiles, Patricia. My Mom's a Mortician: A Novel. 2004. 249p. (J). (978-1-59156-433-1(6)) Covenant Communications.
Williston, Teresa Peirce. Hindu Tales. Squire, Maud Hunt, illus. 2011. 86p. 37.95 (978-1-258-02582-3(5)) Literary Licensing, LLC.
Wittinger, Ellen. Blind Faith. 2007. (ENG.). 304p. (YA). (gr. 7-12). pap. 9.99 (978-1-4169-4906-0(2), Simon & Schuster Bks. For Young Readers) Simon & Schuster Bks. For Young Readers.
Woodson, Jacqueline. Feathers. (ENG.). (J). (gr. 5-18). 2010. 160p. 8.99 (978-0-14-241550-4(2), Puffin Books) 2007. 128p. 17.99 (978-0-399-23989-2(8), G.P. Putnam's Sons Books for Young Readers) Penguin Young Readers Group.
Zeldin, Danny. The Choient Man. 2011. 32p. pap. 14.95 (978-1-4567-5137-1(9)) AuthorHouse.

RELIGIOUS ART
see Art, Medieval; Christian Art and Symbolism; Church Architecture

RELIGIOUS BELIEF
see Belief and Doubt; Faith

RELIGIOUS BIOGRAPHY
see Christian Biography; Religions—Biography

RELIGIOUS CEREMONIES
see Rites and Ceremonies

RELIGIOUS DENOMINATIONS
see Sects

RELIGIOUS EDUCATION
see also Bible—Study; Moral Education

Arthur, Kay & Arndt, Janna. Fast-Forward to the Future: Daniel 7-12. 2008. (Discover 4 Yourself Inductive Bible Studies for Kids Ser.). (ENG., Illus.). 144p. (J). (gr. 2-6). per. 12.99 (978-0-7369-2285-2(7), 6922852) Harvest Hse. Pubs.
Arthur, Kay & Domeij, Scoti. Wrong Way, Jonah! Leite, Eleni, tr. 2003. (Discover-4-Yourself for Kids Ser.). (POR., Illus.). 93p. (J). pap. 8.99 (978-1-888655-71-1(2)) Precept.
The Ascension. (Illus.). (gr. 1-4). 3.00 (978-0-570-05525-9(3), 54-1035) Concordia Publishing Hse.
Barfield, Maggie. The Big Bible Activity Book: 188 Bible Stories to Enjoy Together. Carpenter, Mark, illus. 2017. (ENG.). 96p. (J). 20.99 (978-1-78506-557-6(2), f7404c6e-1e85-40d5-a14f-a77a355c13f9) SPCK Publishing GBR. Dist: Baker & Taylor Publisher Services (BTPS).
Barnabas Fund, Trustees Staff. Brothers & Sisters: Loving Our Persecuted Family. 2012. (ENG., Illus.). 38p. (gr. 1-7). pap. 10.00 (978-0-9853109-7-4(9)) Isaac Publishing.
Beller, Dyan. Creative Bible Crafts: Reproducible Activities. 2004. (Illus.). 64p. (J). (gr. 5-6). pap. 9.95 (978-1-885358-15-8(6), B36240) Rainbow Pubs. & Legacy Pr.
Bishop, Jennie. Jesus Must Be Really Special. Wummer, Amy, illus. 2006. (Heritage Builders Ser.). 32p. (J). 14.99 (978-0-7847-1379-2(6), 04029) Standard Publishing.
Bortins, Robert. My CC ABCs, Cycle 3. Neverov, Leah, illus. 2017. 26p. (J). bds. 10.99 (978-0-9972442-5-0(9)) Classical Conversations, Inc.
Boston, Vicki & Stroh, Debbie. Christ's Kids Create: Volume 2; Favorite Seasonal Craft Ideas, Vol. 2. 2nd ed. 2006. (CPH Teaching Resource Ser.). (Illus.). 64p. pap. 10.99 (978-0-7586-1109-3(9)) Concordia Publishing Hse.
Broslavick, Chris & Pichler, Tony. Totally Lent: A Teen's Journey to Easter 2006. Cannizzo, Karen A., ed. 2005. (Illus.). 64p. (J). 5.95 (978-1-933178-24-0(8), 3566) Pflaum Publishing Group.
Burchett, Author Walter, BA. Christian children's fill in the blank Revised. 2009. 37p. pap. 14.48 (978-0-557-08184-4(X)) Lulu Pr., Inc.
—Christian children's questions & answers abraham & keturah to israel & rachel Volume 2. 2009. 32p. pap. 14.28 (978-0-557-08256-8(0)) Lulu Pr., Inc.
—Christian children's questions & answers adam & eve to abraham & sarah Volume 1. 2009. 36p. pap. 14.44 (978-0-557-08219-3(6)) Lulu Pr., Inc.
—Christian children's questions & answers joseph (coat of many colors) Volume 3. 2009. 32p. pap. 14.28 (978-0-557-08276-6(5)) Lulu Pr., Inc.
—Christian children's questions & answers resurrection of christ Volume 7. 2009. 32p. pap. 14.28 (978-0-557-08245-2(5)) Lulu Pr., Inc.
Cannizzo, Karen & Schippe, Cullen, eds. The Church Welcomes Me: Grade 2, 6 books. 2005. (Faith Activities for Catholic Kids Ser.). (Illus.). 32p. (J). (gr. -1-3). pap. 6.95 (978-1-933178-16-5(7), 2802) Pflaum Publishing Group.
—Jesus Loves Me: Grade 1, 6 books. 2005. (Faith Activities for Catholic Kids Ser.). (Illus.). 32p. (J). (gr. k-2). pap. 6.95 (978-1-933178-15-8(9), 2801) Pflaum Publishing Group.
—Learning the Way: Grade 3, 6 books. 2005. (Faith Activities for Catholic Kids Ser.). (Illus.). 32p. (J). (gr. 2-4). pap. 6.95 (978-1-933178-17-2(5), 2803) Pflaum Publishing Group.
Cannizzo, Karen & Schippe, Cullen W., eds. Discovering the Story of God's People: Grade 6, 6 bks. 2005. (Faith Activities for Catholic Kids Ser.). (Illus.). 32p. pap. 6.95 (978-1-933178-20-2(5), 2806) Pflaum Publishing Group.
—Learning to Celebrate: Grade 5, 6 bks. 2005. (Faith Activities for Catholic Kids Ser.). (Illus.). 32p. pap. 6.95 (978-1-933178-19-6(1), 2805) Pflaum Publishing Group.
Christian, Judy, et al. Scribble, Dribble, & Glue: Bible Art Projects for Kids. 2007. (Illus.). 64p. pap. 10.99 (978-0-7586-1308-0(3)) Concordia Publishing Hse.
Complete 5 Subject Set. 2004. (Switched on Schoolhouse Ser.). (YA). (gr. 8). cd-rom 299.95 (978-0-7403-0591-7(3)) Alpha Omega Pubns., Inc.
CrossTown. (gr. 1-18). stu. ed. 11.25 (978-0-570-00766-1(6), 22-2880); (gr. 3-18). stu. ed. 11.25 (978-0-570-00770-8(4), 22-2884) Concordia Publishing Hse.
David C. Cook Publishing Company Staff, creator. Full Tilt Wacky Games. 2008. (Bible Fun Stuff for Middle School Ser.). (Illus.). 112p. (J). (gr. 6-8). pap. 19.99 (978-1-4347-6855-1(4)) Cook, David C.
—Fun Science That Teaches God's Word for Tweeners. 2008. (BFS Ser.). (Illus.). 120p. (gr. 4-6). per. 19.99 (978-0-7814-4558-0(2)) Cook, David C.
—Stick'em up Bible Crafts. 2008. (Bible Fun Stuff for Preschool Ser.). (Illus.). 112p. (J). (gr. -1-k). pap. 19.99 (978-1-4347-6864-3(3)) Cook, David C.
—Through-the-Bible Crafts. 2008. (Bible Fun Stuff for K-1 Ser.). (Illus.). 112p. (J). (gr. k-1). pap. 19.99 (978-1-4347-6862-9(7)) Cook, David C.
Day by Day. 2004. (gr. k-12). Vol. 1. 50.00 (978-1-58095-847-9(8), WB001) Vol. 2. 50.00 (978-1-58095-848-6(6), WB002) Vol. 3. 50.00 (978-1-58095-849-3(4), WB003) Vol. 4. 50.00 (978-1-58095-850-9(8), WB004) Vol. 5. 50.00 (978-1-58095-851-6(6), WB005) Alpha Omega Pubns., Inc. (Weaver).
Dennis, Rainey. Passport 2 Purity. 2004. 29.99 (978-1-57229-656-5(9)) FamilyLife.
Diagnostic Tests: Student Testing Kit, 5 bks., Set. 2004. (J). (gr. 1-8). suppl. ed. 19.95 (978-0-7403-0096-7(2), AS9922) Alpha Omega Pubns., Inc.
Dios Elige a Su Pueblo: Quarter 1, Level 3. (Caminando con Jesus (Walking with Jesus) Series B).Tr. of God Chooses His People. (SPA.). (J). (gr. 3-4). stu. ed. 3.50 (978-0-570-05152-7(5), 16-3911) Concordia Publishing Hse.
Dios Me Da Su Palabra: Quarter 1, Level 2. (Caminando con Jesus (Walking with Jesus) Series A).Tr. of God Gives Me His Word. (SPA.). (J). (gr. 1-2). stu. ed. 3.50 (978-0-570-05132-9(0), 16-2811) Concordia Publishing Hse.
Dios Me Dio Relaciones: Quarter 3, Level 1. (Caminando con Jesus (Walking with Jesus) Series B).Tr. of God Gave Me Relationships. (SPA.). (J). (gr. -1-k). stu. ed. 3.50 (978-0-570-05112-1(6), 16-1913) Concordia Publishing Hse.
Dios Me Dio un Cuerpo: Quarter 2, Level 1. (Caminando con Jesus (Walking with Jesus) Series B).Tr. of God Gave Me a Body. (SPA.). (J). (gr. -1-k). stu. ed. 3.50 (978-0-570-05111-4(8), 16-1912) Concordia Publishing Hse.
Dios Me Dio un Mundo: Quarter 1, Level 1. (Caminando con Jesus (Walking with Jesus) Series B).Tr. of God Gave Me a World. (SPA.). (J). (gr. -1-k). stu. ed. 3.50 (978-0-570-05110-7(X), 16-1911) Concordia Publishing Hse.
Dios Prepara a Su Pueblo: Quarter 2, Level 3. (Caminando con Jesus (Walking with Jesus) Series B).Tr. of God Prepares His People. (SPA.). (J). (gr. 3-4). stu. ed. 3.50 (978-0-570-05153-4(3), 16-3912) Concordia Publishing Hse.
Ellis, Colette. Credo: I Believe. Avakoff, Caroline, ed. Pelicano, Christopher J., illus. 2009. (Faith & Life Ser.). 121p. (J). pap. 7.95 (978-0-89870-898-1(2)) Ignatius Pr.
El Espiritu Santo (The Holy Spirit) Quarter 1, Level 3. (Caminando con Jesus (Walking with Jesus) Series A). (SPA.). (J). (gr. 3-4). stu. ed. 3.50 (978-0-570-05149-7(5), 16-3811) Concordia Publishing Hse.
Evans, Gwydion, et al. Ar Dîm Duw: Cyfres o Sesiynau Sydd Yn Defnyddio Byd Chwaraeon I Son Am y Ffydd Gristnogol. 2005. (WEL., Illus.). 24p. pap. (978-1-85994-036-5(6)) Cyhoeddiadau'r Gair.
Faith First Development Team, creator. Faith First Grade 6. 2006. (Illus.). 336p. per. 12.50 (978-0-7829-0928-9(0)) RCL Benziger Publishing.
Fears, Melissa. Thank God It's Sunday. 2004. (J). per. 6.95 (978-0-89315-413-4(X)) Lambert Bk. Hse., Inc.
Fischer, Carl. Days of Faith: Student Planner & Assignment Book 2004-2005. Connelly, Gwen & Holmberg, Ansgar, illus. 2004. 108p. (J). spiral bd. 3.25 (978-0-89837-199-4(6), 9805) Pflaum Publishing Group.
Fogg, Paul. I Know That God Loves Me. 2008. (Illus.). 32p. pap. 9.95 (978-0-9814878-3-0(1)) Little Hands Bk. Co., LLC.
Forsyth-Vail, Gail. Love & Help. 2016. (J). pap. (978-1-55896-788-5(5)) Unitarian Universalist Assn.
Gallery, Philip D. Can You Find Saints? Introducing Your Child to Holy Men & Women. Harlow, Janet L., tr. Harlow, Janet L., illus. 2003. 40p. (J). (978-2-89507-437-3(2)) Franciscan Media.
God Is Creator. 2.99 (978-0-7847-0851-4(7)) Standard Publishing.
God Is Eternal. 2.99 (978-0-7847-0854-5(1)) Standard Publishing.
God Is Ever-Present. 2.99 (978-0-7847-0855-2(X)) Standard Publishing.
Gold Mine of Crafts for Kids C. 2004. pap. 16.99 (978-0-8307-2626-4(8)) Gospel Light Pubns.
Grebing, Diane J. & Haas, Jane Elling. Bible Craft Potpourri: 50 Clever Bible Craft Projects. 2007. (Illus.). 62p. pap. 10.99 (978-0-7586-1309-7(1)) Concordia Publishing Hse.
Hakowski, Maryann. Vine & Branches. St. George, Carolyn, illus. 2003. (Resources for Youth Retreats Ser.: Vol. 1). 160p. (YA). (gr. 7-12). spiral bd. 24.95 (978-0-88489-255-7(7)) Saint Mary's Press of Minnesota.
—Vine & Branches, Vol. 2. Stamschror, Robert P., ed. St. George, Carolyn, illus. 2003. (Resources for Youth Retreats Ser.: Vol. 2). 168p. (YA). (gr. 7-12). spiral bd. 24.95 (978-0-88489-278-6(6)) Saint Mary's Press of Minnesota.
Hatfield, Tyrel & Hatfield, Justin. Righteous Roundup: Wanted: Righteous children of God. Hatfield, Tyrel, illus. 2008. (Illus.). (J). cd-rom 99.00 (978-0-9766703-6-0(4)) Little Acorn LLC.
Holford, Karen. I Miss Grandpa: A Story to Help Your Child Understand Death — & Eternal Life. 2004. (Illus.). 32p. (J). 4.97 (978-0-8163-2030-1(6)) Pacific Pr. Publishing Assn.
Hosch, Jenifer. 50 Bible Activities for Creative Minds. 2004. 64p. (gr. 3-6). 10.99 (978-0-7586-0129-2(8)) Concordia Publishing Hse.
Hunt, Jeanne. Celebrating Saints & Seasons: Hundreds of Activities for Catholic Children. 2010. (ENG.). 192p. pap. 15.99 (978-0-86716-959-1(1)) Franciscan Media.
James, Steven. 24 Tandem Bible Hero Story Scripts for Children's Ministry. 2006. (Illus.). 96p. (YA). pap. 10.99 (978-0-7847-1321-1(9), 04312) Standard Publishing.
—24 Tandem Bible Story Scripts for Children's Ministry. 2006. 96p. (YA). pap. 15.99 (978-0-7847-1320-4(0), 42038) Standard Publishing.
Jarrell, Jane & Saathoff, Deborah. Off to Work We Go. 2004. 50p. (gr. -1-18). pap., act. bk. ed. 6.99 (978-0-8054-0823-2(1)) B&H Publishing Group.
Julio, Susan & Schooler, Cindy. Interactive Bible Bulletin Boards: Winter. 2004. 128p. (J). pap. 13.95 (978-1-885358-33-2(4), RB36712) Rainbow Pubs. & Legacy Pr.
Karyn, Henley. I Learn about God. 2004. pap. 2.99 (978-0-7847-0651-0(4)) Standard Publishing.
Kawasaki, Shauna Mooney, illus. My Family Can Be Forever: Sharing Time Activities. 2003. 62p. (J). pap. (978-1-59038-232-5(3)) Deseret Bk. Co.
Kennedy, Nancy B. Make It, Shake It, Mix It Up: 44 Bible Stories Brought to Life with Science. Cannell, Jon, illus. 2008. 61p. pap. 10.99 (978-0-7586-1334-9(2)) Concordia Publishing Hse.
Kitch, Anne E. What We Do in Advent: An Anglican Kids' Activity Book. Perez, Dorothy Thompson, illus. 2006. (ENG.). 48p. (J). (gr. -1-2). pap. 11.95 (978-0-8192-2195-7(3), 171cd8f5-565a-45e1-a5d8-87f153067df1) Church Publishing, Inc.
Larkin, Jean, ed. Celebrate with Jesus: A Child's Book of the Sacraments. Swisher, Elizabeth et al, illus. 2007. 32p. pap. 3.95 (978-1-933178-67-7(1)) Pflaum Publishing Group.
Lewis, Carole. First Place Group Starter Kit. 2004. 179.99 (978-0-8307-3369-9(8), Gospel Light) Gospel Light Pubns.
Little KidsTime 1: Bible Story Pictures. 2004. 104p. 19.99 (978-0-8307-2773-5(6), Gospel Light) Gospel Light Pubns.
Machowski, Marty. Don't Blame the Mud. 2019. (ENG., Illus.). 32p. (J). 16.99 (978-1-948130-96-7(3)) New Growth Pr.
McMickle, Marvin Andrew. Profiles in Black: Phat Facts for Teens. Elster, Jean Alicia, ed. 2008. (Illus.). 176p. (J). pap. 22.00 (978-0-8170-1508-4(6)) Judson Pr.
Meloche, Renee Taft. Heroes for Young Readers Activity Guide for Books 1-4: Educational & Character-Building Lessons for Children. 2006. (Heroes for Young Readers Ser.). (Illus.). 90p. per. 12.99 (978-1-57658-367-8(8)) YWAM Publishing.
Millett, Melanie. Teeny Tiny Talks: Junior Primary: I Will Follow God's Plan for Me, Vol. 1. Millett, Melanie, illus. 2004. (Illus.). (J). per. 12.95 (978-1-55517-778-2(6), Cedar Fort, Inc.) Cedar Fort, Inc./CFI Distribution.
National Consultants for Education, creator. The Treasure of My Catholic Faith: 2nd Grade. 2004. (Treasure of My Catholic Faith Ser.: No. 2). (Illus.). 240p. pap. 14.95 (978-0-9743661-4-2(5)) Circle Pr.
—The Treasure of My Catholic Faith: 4th Grade. 2004. (Treasure of My Catholic Faith Ser.: No. 4). (Illus.). 272p. pap. 14.95 (978-0-9743661-6-6(1)) Circle Pr.

P Q R

—The Treasure of My Catholic Faith: 5th Grade. 2004. (Treasure of My Catholic Faith Ser.: No. 5). (Illus.). 295p. pap. 14.95 (978-0-9743661-7-3(X)) Circle Pr.

—The Treasure of My Catholic Faith: 6th Grade. 2004. (Treasure of My Catholic Faith Ser.: No. 6). (Illus.). 295p. pap. 14.95 (978-0-9743661-8-0(8)) Circle Pr.

Noonan, Joseph. What Is My Vocation? Student Edition. 2005. 7.00 net. (978-0-9774733-0-4(9)) Univ. St. Mary of the Lake, Mundelein Seminary.

Nystrom, Jennifer. Favorite Bible Children: Grades 1 & 2. 2004. (Illus.). 96p. (J). (gr. 1-2). pap. 11.95 (978-1-885358-77-6(6)) Rainbow Pubs. & Legacy Pr.

—Favorite Bible Children: Grades 3 & 4. 2004. (Illus.). 96p. (J). (gr. 3-4). pap. 11.95 (978-1-885358-78-3(4)) Rainbow Pubs. & Legacy Pr.

Olla, Debbie. Confirmation Certificate. 2004. (Illus.). (J). pap. 9.95 (978-0-937997-76-5(5), 504510) Pflaum Publishing Group.

Pearson, Mary R. Bible Learning Games: Reproducible Activities. 2004. (Illus.). 64p. (J). pap. 9.95 (978-0-937282-72-4(3), RB36251); (gr. -1-k). pap. 9.95 (978-0-937282-73-1(1), RB36252); (gr. 1-2). pap. 9.95 (978-0-937282-74-8(X), RB36253); (gr. 3-4). pap. 9.95 (978-0-937282-75-5(8), RB36254) Rainbow Pubs. & Legacy Pr.

El Pecado (Sin) Quarter 1, Level 2. (Caminando con Jesus (Walking with Jesus) Series B). (SPA.). (J). (gr. 1-2). stu. ed. 3.50 (978-0-570-05135-0(5), 16-2911) Concordia Publishing Hse.

Plum, Joan Ensor & Plum, Paul S. I Am Special: Jesus Is Our Friend. Most, Andee, illus. 5th ed. 2007. 112p. (J). (gr. k-1). per. 11.95 (978-1-59276-296-5(4)) Our Sunday Visitor, Publishing Div.

Plum, Paul & Plum, Joanensor. las 3 Year Old Religious Education Program. 2005. (J). bds. 13.95 (978-1-59276-087-9(2)) Our Sunday Visitor, Publishing Div.

Power Twins Handbook Volume One. 2006. (J). spiral bd. (978-0-9742355-1-6(2)) Brda, Tracy.

Rainbow Publishers Staff. Bible Explorer: 52 Week Bible Study. 2004. (Illus.). 64p. (J). (gr. 1-3). pap. 9.95 (978-0-937282-76-2(6), RB36181) Rainbow Pubs. & Legacy Pr.

—Coloring Plus Activities: God's Promises. 2004. (Illus.). 64p. (J). (gr. -1-3). pap. 9.95 (978-0-937282-49-6(9), RB37165) Rainbow Pubs. & Legacy Pr.

—Coloring Plus Activities: Heroes of the Bible. 2004. (Illus.). 64p. (J). (gr. -1-3). pap. 9.95 (978-0-937282-47-2(2), RB37163) Rainbow Pubs. & Legacy Pr.

—Learning Adventures! Summer. 2004. (Learning Adventures! Ser.). (Illus.). 64p. (J). pap. 9.95 (978-1-885358-14-1(8), RB36314) Rainbow Pubs. & Legacy Pr.

—Learning Adventures! Winter. 2004. (Learning Adventures! Ser.). (Illus.). 64p. (J). pap. 9.95 (978-1-885358-12-7(1), RB36312) Rainbow Pubs. & Legacy Pr.

Rashad, Girmen. How Does God See Me? David, Amor, illus. 2008. (Little Christian Ser.). 24p. 9.99 (978-0-9819100-0-0(9)) Elkarez Publishing Co.

Rhydderch, Gwyn, et al. Iesu'r Ffrind: 16 Sesiwn Yn Cyflwyno Bywyd Iesu Ar Gyfer Plant Cynradd Yn Seiliedig Ar Efengyl Luc. 2005. (WEL., Illus.). 120p. pap. (978-1-85994-007-5(2)) Cyhoeddiadau'r Gair.

Roberts, Catrin, et al. Mawredd Mawr Moses! 16 Sesiwn Beiblaidd Ar Gyfer Clwb Plant Neu'r Ysgol Sul. 2005. (WEL., Illus.). 76p. pap. (978-1-85994-034-1(X)) Cyhoeddiadau'r Gair.

Rock, Lois, et al. Beibl y Plant Lleiaf. 2005. (WEL., Illus.). 230p. (978-1-85994-514-8(7)) Cyhoeddiadau'r Gair.

Rossel, Seymour. Torah Portion-by-Portion. 2007. (Illus.). 368p. (J). pap. 15.95 (978-1-891662-94-2(5)) Torah Aura Productions.

Rostrom, Laura Lee. My First Book of Mormon Activity Book. 2012. pap. 3.99 (978-1-59955-958-2(7)) Cedar Fort, Inc./CFI Distribution.

Savitskas, Margaret. Totally Lent! A Kid's Journey to Easter 2006. Larkin, Jean K., ed. 2005. (Illus.). 64p. (J). 5.95 (978-1-933178-25-7(6), 3576) Pflaum Publishing Group.

Savitskas, Margaret & Behe, Mary. Totally Lent! A Child's Journey to Easter 2006. Larkin, Jean K., ed. 2005. (Illus.). 64p. (J). 5.95 (978-1-933178-26-4(4), 3586) Pflaum Publishing Group.

Schippe, Cullen & Cannizzo, Karen, eds. Learning How to Live: Grade 4, 6 bks. 2005. (Faith Activities for Catholic Kids Ser.). (Illus.). 32p. (J). (gr. 3-5). pap. 6.95 (978-1-933178-18-9(3), 2804) Pflaum Publishing Group.

Schlegl, William. Bible Alphabet Puzzles. 2006. (Illus.). 64p. pap. 10.99 (978-0-7586-1300-4(8)) Concordia Publishing Hse.

School of the Bible for Kids: The Most High God. 2003. (ENG & GER.). 238p. ring bd. 79.95 (978-0-9767647-3-1(3)) Kids in Ministry International.

Sewell, Elisabeth. Bible Activity Book. 2010. (ENG., Illus.). 38p. (J). pap. 8.00 (978-0-7152-0907-3(8)) Saint Andrew Pr., Ltd. GBR. Dist: Westminster John Knox Pr., Norwich Bks. & Music.

Shanddaramon. A Pagan Book of ABCs. 2009. (ENG.). 60p. pap. (978-0-557-09532-2(8)) Lulu Pr., Inc.

Sharer, Avigail. Here, There, Everywhere / Kids' True Stories of Finding Hashem in Their Lives. 2012. (ENG.). 159p. (J). pap. (978-1-4226-1179-1(5)) Mesorah Pubns., Ltd.

Silverstru, Emil. The Cave Book. 2008. (Illus.). 84p. (J). (gr. 7-12). 18.99 (978-0-89051-496-2(8), Master Books) New Leaf Publishing Group.

Sonharvest County Fair Starter. 2004. pap. 49.99 (978-0-8307-3008-7(7)) Gospel Light Pubns.

Soul Survivor Guide to Service Projects. 2004. 96p. 19.99 (978-0-8307-3529-7(1), Gospel Light) Gospel Light Pubns.

Soul Survivor Guide to Youth Ministry. 2004. 96p. 19.99 (978-0-8307-3530-3(5), Gospel Light) Gospel Light Pubns.

Soul Survivor Prayer Ministry How to Pray for Others. 2004. 72p. 5.99 (978-0-8307-3527-3(5), Gospel Light) Gospel Light Pubns.

Stobaugh, James. Skills for Literary Analysis Student: Encouraging Thoughtful Christians to be World Changers. 2005. (Broadman & Holman Literature Ser.). 272p. stu. ed. 24.99 (978-0-8054-5897-8(2)) B&H Publishing Group.

Stohs, Anita Reith. Praise God with Paper Cups: 45 Easy Bible Crafts; Grades 1-5. Koehler, Ed, illus. 2005. (CPH Teaching Resource Ser.). 64p. pap. 10.99 (978-0-7586-0842-0(X)) Concordia Publishing Hse.

Story Cards - Year 1. 2003. (Story Hour Ser.). (Illus.). 5.95 (978-1-56212-346-8(7), 001655) Faith Alive Christian Resources.

Story Cards - Year 2. 2003. (Story Hour Ser.). (Illus.). 5.95 (978-1-56212-409-0(9), 001665) Faith Alive Christian Resources.

Stroh, Debbie & Boston, Vicki. Christ's Kids Create: Volume 1. 2006. (CPH Teaching Resource Ser.). (Illus.). 64p. pap. 10.99 (978-0-7586-1106-2(4)) Concordia Publishing Hse.

Sunflower Education Staff. A Golden Thread. 2012. 54p. pap. 11.95 (978-1-937166-13-7(9)) Sunflower Education.

Thurman, Debbie. Sheer Faith: A Teen's Journey to Godly Growth. 2004. 112p. pap. 10.95 (978-0-9676289-3-6(8)) Cedar Hse. Pubs.

Trammell, Fredi. Journey Through the Bible for Kids. 2009. (J). pap. (978-1-61623-151-4(3)) Independent Pub.

Tyrtania, Joachim & Hemrich-Skomer, Denise. Together Time: Cycle A. 2007. (Illus.). 80p. per. 10.95 (978-0-9787087-2-6(5)) Bound by Grace Pr., LLC.

Vacation Bible School - Look & Do Stories. 2004. (Vacation Bible School Ser.). (Illus.). 64p. (J). 9.95 (978-1-885358-02-8(4)) Rainbow Pubs. & Legacy Pr.

Vaisey, Gill & Lewis, Sian. William Booth: Cristion Arbennig Iawn. 2005. (WEL., Illus.). 28p. pap. (978-1-85644-620-4(4)) CAA.

Washington, Linda & Dall, Jeanette. Favorite Bible Children: Ages 2 & 3. 2004. (Illus.). 96p. (J). pap. 11.95 (978-1-885358-75-2(X)) Rainbow Pubs. & Legacy Pr.

—Favorite Bible Children: Ages 4 & 5. 2004. (Illus.). 96p. (J). pap. 11.95 (978-1-885358-76-9(8)) Rainbow Pubs. & Legacy Pr.

Wean, Sarah. Teach Them to Your Children: An Alphabet of Biblical Poems, Verses, & Stories. Sanford, Lori Hood, illus. 2006. 56p. (J). 17.00 (978-0-9787559-5-9(2)) Vision Forum, Inc., The.

Wiliamson, Nancy. 52 Ideas for Special Days. 2004. (Fifty-Two Ways Ser.). (Illus.). 64p. (J). (gr. -1-7). pap. 9.95 (978-0-937282-01-4(4), RB36108) Rainbow Pubs. & Legacy Pr.

Williamson, Nancy. 52 Bible Drills & Quizzes. 2004. (Fifty-Two Ways Ser.). (Illus.). 64p. (J). (gr. -1-7). pap. 9.95 (978-0-937282-66-3(9), RB36168) Rainbow Pubs. & Legacy Pr.

—52 Ways to Teach Bible Reading. 2004. (Fifty-Two Ways Ser.). (Illus.). 64p. (J). (gr. -1-7). pap. 9.95 (978-0-937282-63-2(4), RB36106) Rainbow Pubs. & Legacy Pr.

—52 Ways to Teach Missions. 2004. (Fifty-Two Ways Ser.). (Illus.). 64p. (J). (gr. -1-7). pap. 9.95 (978-0-937282-67-0(7), RB36169) Rainbow Pubs. & Legacy Pr.

—52 Ways to Teach Stewardship. 2004. (Fifty-Two Ways Ser.). (Illus.). 64p. (J). (gr. -1-7). pap. 9.95 (978-1-885358-16-5(4), RB36170) Rainbow Pubs. & Legacy Pr.

Wonderfully Made: God's Plan for Growing Up. (J). (gr. 2-3). 6.99 (978-1-57153-301-2(X)) Curriculum Publishing, Presbyterian Church (U. S. A.).

Woodfield, Elaine. Stories of the Saints V1, 4 vols. Staggenborg, Kim, illus. 2009. (J). pap. 13.95 (978-0-9788376-8-6(1)) Catholic Heritage Curricula.

—Stories of the Saints V2, 4 vols. Staggenborg, Kim, illus. 2009. (J). pap. 0.00 (978-0-9788376-9-3(X)) Catholic Heritage Curricula.

Woodman, Ros. The Proud Prayer. 2018. (Board Books Stories Jesus Told Ser.). (ENG., Illus.). 16p. (J). (gr. -1-3). pap. 0.99 (978-1-85792-173-1(9), 07feba1e-0a85-4496-8967-7cd2fa780db0) Christian Focus Pubns. GBR. Dist: Baker & Taylor Publisher Services (BTPS).

RELIGIOUS FESTIVALS

see Fasts and Feasts

RELIGIOUS FREEDOM

see Freedom of Religion

RELIGIOUS HISTORY

see Church History

RELIGIOUS LIBERTY

see Freedom of Religion

RELIGIOUS LITERATURE

see also Bible As Literature; Catholic Literature

Attinger, Billy, illus. Baby's First Little Book of Prayers. gif. ed. 2003. (Wee Witness Ser.). 32p. (J). 7.99 (978-0-7369-1185-6(5)) Harvest Hse. Pubs.

McLaughlin, Edith M. & Curtis, T. Adrian, eds. American Cardinal Readers Book One, bk. 1. 2014. (American Cardinal Reader Ser.: 1). (ENG., Illus.). 184p. (J). (gr. k-2). reprint ed. 16.95 (978-0-911845-36-5(4), NP9027, Neumann Pr.) TAN Bks.

—American Cardinal Readers Book Three, Bk. 3. 2014. (American Cardinal Reader Ser.: 3). (ENG., Illus.). 256p. (J). (gr. 1-3). reprint ed. 19.95 (978-0-911845-38-9(0), NP9029, Neumann Pr.) TAN Bks.

—American Cardinal Readers Book Two, Bk. 2. 2014. (American Cardinal Reader Ser.: 2). (ENG., Illus.). 224p. (J). (gr. k-2). reprint ed. 18.95 (978-0-911845-37-2(2), NP9028, Neumann Pr.) TAN Bks.

—American Cardinal Readers Primer: Primer. 2014. (ENG., Illus.). 104p. (J). (gr. k-1). reprint ed. 16.95 (978-0-911845-52-5(6), NP9026, Neumann Pr.) TAN Bks.

RELIGIOUS MUSIC

see Church Music

RELIGIOUS ORDERS

see Monasticism and Religious Orders

RELIGIOUS PAINTING

see Christian Art and Symbolism

RELIGIOUS POETRY

see also Carols; Hymns

Appelt, Kathi. I See Moon. Jenkins, Reid Debra & Jenkins, Debra Reid, illus. 2009. (ENG.). 12p. (J). (gr. -1). bds. 8.00 (978-0-8028-5358-5(7), Eerdmans Bks For Young Readers) Eerdmans, William B. Publishing Co.

—I See the Moon. Jenkins, Debra Reid, illus. 2004. 24p. (J). (gr. -1-2). 15.00 (978-0-8028-5118-5(5)) Eerdmans, William B. Publishing Co.

Bartlett, Irene. The Old Testament: Bible Poems for Children. 2007. (Illus.). 92p. per. (978-1-84748-204-4(X)) Athena Pr.

Busch, Melinda Kay. The Fiery Furnace. Koehler, Ed, illus. 2004. (Arch Bks.). 16p. (J). (gr. k-4). 1.99 (978-0-7586-0479-8(3)) Concordia Publishing Hse.

Cotner, June. House Blessings: Prayers, Poems, & Toasts Celebrating Home & Family. 2005. (ENG., Illus.). 164p. (gr. 8-17). 16.95 (978-0-9748486-0-0(3)) Chronicle Bks. LLC.

Draper, Diane E. Expressions from the Experience: Christian Poetry & Short Inspirations. 2003. 87p. (YA). pap. 9.95 (978-0-7414-1482-3(1)) Infinity Publishing.

Fbs: 1ST & 2ND GRADERS' MEMORY VERSES. (J). (gr. 1-2). (978-0-633-00372-2(7)) Lifeway Christian Resources.

Fulton, Stephen (Abdul-Hakeem). 110 Islamic Poems for Children. 2007. 41p. pap. 8.95 (978-0-7414-3963-5(8)) Infinity Publishing.

Krug, Christine Suguitan. Favorite Action Bible Verses. 2003. (Illus.). 48p. (gr. -1-k). 10.99 (978-0-7586-0228-2(6)) Concordia Publishing Hse.

McCauley, Marlene. Song of Kateri: Princess of the Eucharist. McCauley, R. Allan, ed. McCauley, Marlene & Children's Art-Friends of Kateri, illus. unabr. ed. 2005. 300p. (YA). (gr. 4-7). per. 14.95 (978-0-9633633-2-9(8)) Grace Hse. Publishing.

Reese, Amy, illus. Illustrated Psalms of Praise: Psalmos de Albanza Ilustrados. 2005. (SPA & ENG.). 64p. (J). 16.95 (978-1-56854-561-5(4)) Liturgy Training Pubns.

Weisheit, Eldon. 150 Psalms for Teens. 2003. 160p. (YA). 9.49 (978-0-7586-0120-9(4)) Concordia Publishing Hse.

REMBRANDT HARMENSZOON VAN RIJN, 1606-1669

Dunn, Mary. My Adventure with Rembrandt. 2006. 44p. (J). 8.99 (978-1-59092-463-1(0)) Blue Forge Pr.

Mason, Anthony. Rembrandt, 1 vol. 2004. (Lives of the Artists Ser.). (ENG., Illus.). 48p. (gr. 5-8). pap. 15.05 (978-0-8368-5656-9(2), 572fccb5-3188-4518-8d1e-824702e3fcfb); lib. bdg. 33.67 (978-0-8368-5651-4(1), 86a72854-e833-46cb-9ac7-006ad20a662c) Stevens, Gareth Publishing LLLP. (Gareth Stevens Secondary Library).

Mis, Melody S. Rembrandt. 2009. (Meet the Artist Ser.). 24p. (gr. 2-3). 42.50 (978-1-61514-632-1(6), PowerKids Pr.) Rosen Publishing Group, Inc., The.

Pescio, Claudio. Rembrandt. 2008. (Art Masters Ser.). 64p. (YA). (gr. 6-18). lib. bdg. 24.95 net. (978-1-934545-02-7(3)) Oliver Pr., Inc.

Roberts, Russell. Rembrandt. 2008. (Art Profiles for Kids Ser.). (Illus.). 48p. (YA). (gr. 4-7). lib. bdg. 29.95 (978-1-58415-710-6(0)) Mitchell Lane Pubs.

REMEDIAL READING

see Reading—Remedial Teaching

REMINGTON, FREDERIC, 1861-1909

Venezia, Mike. Frederic Remington. Venezia, Mike, illus. 2003. (Getting to Know the World's Greatest Artists Ser.). (ENG., Illus.). 32p. (J). (gr. 3-4). pap. 6.95 (978-0-516-27812-4(6), Children's Pr.) Scholastic Library Publishing.

REMUS, UNCLE (FICTITIOUS CHARACTER)—FICTION

Cloke, Rene. My Best Brer Rabbit Stories. 2012. (Illus.). 80p. 15.00 (978-1-84135-806-2(1)) Award Pubns. Ltd. GBR. Dist: Parkwest Pubns., Inc.

Harris, Joel Chandler. Nights with Uncle Remus. 2008. 288p. 29.95 (978-1-60664-915-2(9)); pap. 15.95 (978-1-60664-035-7(6)) Aegypan.

—Uncle Remus: His Songs & His Sayings. 265p. (J). 18.00 (978-0-9645990-0-0(7)) Historic Pr.-South.

RENAISSANCE

see also Art, Renaissance; Civilization, Medieval; Humanism; Middle Ages

Benchmark Education Company, LLC Staff, compiled by. The Renaissance: Theme Set. 2006. (J). 135.00 (978-1-4108-7142-8(8)) Benchmark Education Co.

Boekhoff, P. M. & Kallen, Stuart A. The Italian Renaissance. 2003. (History of the World Ser.). (Illus.). 48p. (J). (gr. 3-5). 23.70 (978-0-7377-1036-6(5), Kidhaven) Cengage Gale.

Carr, Simonetta. Michelangelo for Kids: His Life & Ideas, with 21 Activities. 2016. (For Kids Ser.: 63). (ENG., Illus.). 144p. (J). (gr. 4). pap. 18.99 (978-1-61373-193-2(0)) Chicago Review Pr., Inc.

Corrick, James A. The Renaissance, 1 vol. 2006. (World History Ser.). (ENG., Illus.). 104p. (gr. 7-7). lib. bdg. 41.53 (978-1-59018-836-1(5), c8f0bfec-29b3-4d2e-b81b-57e78fdcf2f7, Lucent Pr.) Greenhaven Publishing LLC.

Currie, Stephen. The Renaissance. 2012. (Illus.). 96p. (YA). lib. bdg. 43.93 (978-1-60152-189-7(8)) ReferencePoint Pr., Inc.

Day, Nancy. Your Travel Guide to Renaissance Europe. 2005. (Passport to History Ser.). (Illus.). 96p. (gr. 5-8). lib. bdg. 26.50 (978-0-8225-3080-0(5)) Lerner Publishing Group.

Elliott, Lynne. Exploration in the Renaissance, 1 vol. 2009. (Renaissance World Ser.). (ENG., Illus.). 32p. (J). (gr. 5-8). pap. (978-0-7787-4613-3(5)); lib. bdg. (978-0-7787-4593-8(7)) Crabtree Publishing Co.

—The Renaissance in Europe, 1 vol. 2009. (Renaissance World Ser.). (ENG., Illus.). 32p. (J). (gr. 5-8). pap. (978-0-7787-4611-9(9)); lib. bdg. (978-0-7787-4591-4(0)) Crabtree Publishing Co.

Flatt, Lizann. Cities & Statecraft in the Renaissance. 2009. (ENG., Illus.). 32p. (J). (gr. 5-7). (978-0-7787-4595-2(3)); (gr. 6-9). pap. (978-0-7787-4615-7(1)) Crabtree Publishing Co.

—Religion in the Renaissance. 2009. (ENG., Illus.). 32p. (J). (gr. 5-7). (978-0-7787-4597-6(X)); (gr. 6-9). pap. (978-0-7787-4617-1(8)) Crabtree Publishing Co.

George, Enzo. The Renaissance, 1 vol. 2016. (Primary Sources in World History Ser.). (ENG.). 48p. (gr. 6-6). 33.07 (978-1-5026-1809-2(5), 21f3de4b-d7cc-4d24-93ad-3a019e6082ad) Cavendish Square Publishing LLC.

Greenblatt, Miriam. Lorenzo de' Medici & Renaissance Italy, 1 vol. 2003. (Rulers & Their Times Ser.). (ENG., Illus.). 80p. (gr. 6-6). lib. bdg. 36.93 (978-0-7614-1490-2(8), 7c9c2d4e-da0f-463d-b40a-a44f752d3214) Cavendish Square Publishing LLC.

Hancock, Lee. Lorenzo de' Medici: Florence's Great Leader & Patron of the Arts. (Rulers, Scholars, & Artists of the Renaissance Ser.). 112p. (gr. 5-8). 2009. 66.50 (978-1-60852-942-1(8), Rosen Reference) 2004. (ENG., Illus.). (J). lib. bdg. 39.80 (978-1-4042-0315-0(X), ca8076a6-2614-4397-8ac0-414e3eda79d9) Rosen Publishing Group, Inc., The.

Herold, Vickey. Science During the Renaissance. 2006. (J). pap. (978-1-4108-6464-2(2)) Benchmark Education Co.

Hinds, Kathryn. The Church, 1 vol. 2005. (Life in the Renaissance Ser.). (ENG., Illus.). 80p. (gr. 6-6). lib. bdg. 36.93 (978-0-7614-1679-1(X), 0fb0dd84-62dd-45e0-9b39-ff108ea5672d) Cavendish Square Publishing LLC.

—The City, 1 vol. 2005. (Life in the Renaissance Ser.). (ENG., Illus.). 80p. (gr. 6-6). lib. bdg. 36.93 (978-0-7614-1678-4(1), b68cbffc-2e00-48d1-ad8c-b5770275a011) Cavendish Square Publishing LLC.

—The Countryside, 1 vol. (Life in the Roman Empire (2006) Ser.). (ENG., Illus.). 80p. (gr. 6-6). 2006. 36.93 (978-0-7614-1656-2(0), 63ad3ab6-70f1-4ccd-ac4e-4af15599345b) 2005. lib. bdg. 36.93 (978-0-7614-1677-7(3), 634e70fd-a60e-4cb7-ab00-dd70ce87329b) Cavendish Square Publishing LLC.

—The Court, 1 vol. 2005. (Life in the Renaissance Ser.). (ENG., Illus.). 80p. (gr. 6-6). lib. bdg. 36.93 (978-0-7614-1676-0(5), 1232a1ca-e953-4253-8ad1-6f6dfd2df73c) Cavendish Square Publishing LLC.

—Everyday Life in the Renaissance, 1 vol. 2010. (Everyday Life Ser.). (ENG.). 336p. (gr. 6-7). 45.50 (978-0-7614-4483-1(1), 79ab850c-e0ff-4e76-b786-f19f9e83d46a) Cavendish Square Publishing LLC.

Hirsch, E. D., Jr., ed. The Renaissance, Level 5. 2003. tchr. ed. 9.95 (978-0-7690-5074-4(3)); stu. ed. 49.95 (978-0-7690-2853-8(5)) Pearson Learning.

Huntley, Theresa. Women in the Renaissance. 2009. (ENG., Illus.). 32p. (J). (gr. 5-7). (978-0-7787-4598-3(8)); (gr. 6-9). pap. (978-0-7787-4618-8(6)) Crabtree Publishing Co.

Klepeis, Alicia Z. The Renaissance Inventors: With History Projects for Kids. 2018. (the Renaissance for Kids Ser.). (ENG., Illus.). 112p. (J). (gr. 5-10). 22.95 (978-1-61930-683-7(2), 2d7185c5-9482-4b24-963b-79cfb8fe3a3b) Nomad Pr.

Kubesh, Katie & Belletto, Kimm. HOCPP 1056 Renaissance. 2006. spiral bd. 18.50 (978-1-60308-056-9(2)) In the Hands of a Child.

Kuligowski, Stephanie. The Renaissance: A Rebirth of Culture, 1 vol. rev. ed. 2012. (Social Studies: Informational Text Ser.). (ENG.). 32p. (gr. 4-8). pap. 11.99 (978-1-4333-5007-8(6)) Teacher Created Materials, Inc.

MacDonald, Fiona. You Wouldn't Want to Be a Crusader! A War You'd Rather Not Fight. Bergin, Mark, illus. 2005. (You Wouldn't Want to... Ser.). (ENG.). 32p. (J). (gr. 2-5). 29.00 (978-0-531-12412-3(6)); pap. 9.95 (978-0-531-12392-8(8)) Scholastic Library Publishing. (Watts, Franklin).

Morris, Neil. Everyday Life in the Renaissance. 2008. (Uncovering History Ser.). (ENG., Illus.). 48p. (J). (gr. 2-7). 19.95 (978-88-89272-58-9(9)) McRae Bks. Srl ITA. Dist: Independent Pubs. Group.

Murphy, Lauren. Art & Culture of the Renaissance World. 2010. (Ancient Art & Cultures Ser.). 40p. (YA). (gr. 5-8). lib. bdg., E-Book 53.00 (978-1-61532-967-0(6)) Rosen Publishing Group, Inc., The.

Murphy, Lauren & Matthews, Rupert. Art & Culture of the Renaissance World, 1 vol. 2010. (Ancient Art & Cultures Ser.). (ENG., Illus.). 40p. (gr. 6-6). (J). pap. 12.75 (978-1-61532-889-5(0), a2f2c76e-31bf-4f5e-a009-ae0630e78bfa); (YA). lib. bdg. 31.80 (978-1-4358-3593-1(X), cf427b1e-f143-42c4-84f6-5e06fafa1d35) Rosen Publishing Group, Inc., The. (Rosen Reference).

Phillips, John. World History Biographies: Leonardo Da Vinci: The Genius Who Defined the Renaissance. 2008. (National Geographic World History Biographies Ser.). (Illus.). 64p. (J). (gr. 3-7). pap. 7.99 (978-1-4263-0248-0(7), National Geographic Kids) Disney Publishing Worldwide.

Platt, Richard. In the Renaissance. Lawrence, David, illus. 2011. (How They Made Things Work! Ser.). 32p. (YA). (gr. 2-5). lib. bdg. 28.50 (978-1-59771-289-7(2)) Sea-To-Sea Pubns.

Rajczak, Kristen. Renaissance Fairs, 1 vol., 1. 2015. (Role-Playing for Fun & Profit Ser.). (ENG.). 48p. (J). (gr. 5-5). pap. 12.75 (978-1-4994-3720-1(X), 293d8027-d15b-4714-87db-aff624376f29, Rosen Reference) Rosen Publishing Group, Inc., The.

The Renaissance, 1300-1600. 2004. (Stories in History Ser.). (Illus.). 190p. (gr. 6-12). 13.32 (978-0-618-14224-8(X), 2-00244) Holt McDougal.

Romanek, Trudee. Great Ideas of the Renaissance. 2009. (Renaissance World Ser.). (ENG., Illus.). 32p. (J). (gr. 5-7). (978-0-7787-4596-9(1)); (gr. 6-9). pap. (978-0-7787-4616-4(X)) Crabtree Publishing Co.

Roscoe, Kelly. The Italian & Northern Renaissance, 1 vol. 2017. (Power & Religion in Medieval & Renaissance Times Ser.). (ENG., Illus.). 112p. (J). (gr. 10-10). 37.82 (978-1-68048-627-8(6), 7d2c7363-c50b-44da-928d-ab5554f63d01, Britannica Educational Publishing) Rosen Publishing Group, Inc., The.

Rossi, Renzo. In Renaissance Florence with Leonardo, 1 vol. 2009. (Come See My City Ser.). (ENG., Illus.). 48p. (gr. 4-4). lib. bdg. 31.21 (978-0-7614-4329-2(0), cc58e45d-3aa0-44a8-8fb1-fe5c4d3ee51c) Cavendish Square Publishing LLC.

Samuels, Charlie. Timeline of the Renaissance, 1 vol. 2010. (History Highlights: a Gareth Stevens Timeline Ser.). (ENG., Illus.). 48p. (gr. 6-8). (J). pap. 15.05 (978-1-4339-3487-2(6), 6e19a080-a2be-4a0a-9f30-4f1d0d640b85); (YA). lib. bdg. 34.60 (978-1-4339-3486-5(8), c861f173-0cab-4be2-93b4-a3eca2273a5a) Stevens, Gareth Publishing LLLP. (Gareth Stevens Secondary Library).

Simpson, Kathleen. Women in the Renaissance: Text Pairs. 2008. (Bridges/Navigators Ser.). (J). (gr. 6). 89.00 (978-1-4108-8449-7(X)) Benchmark Education Co.

Taylor, Diane C. The Renaissance Thinkers: With History Projects for Kids. 2018. (the Renaissance for Kids Ser.). (ENG., Illus.). 112p. (J). (gr. 5-10). 22.95 (978-1-61930-692-9(1), 3c9390fe-bce0-49a7-bc51-b4d53654767b) Nomad Pr.

Thomson, Melissa & Dean, Ruth. Women of the Renaissance. 2004. (Women in History Ser.). (ENG., Illus.). 128p. (YA). (gr. 7-10). lib. bdg. 33.45 *(978-1-59018-473-8(4)*, Lucent Bks.) Cengage Gale.

Wagner, Heather Lehr. Machiavelli: Renaissance Political Analyst & Author. 2005. (Makers of the Middle Ages & Renaissance Ser.). (ENG., Illus.). 136p. (gr. 5-8). lib. bdg. 32.95 *(978-0-7910-8629-2(1)*, P114345, Facts On File) Infobase Holdings, Inc.

RENAISSANCE—FICTION

Avi. Murder at Midnight. 2011. (ENG.). 256p. (J). (gr. 3-7). pap. 7.99 *(978-0-545-08091-0(6)*, Scholastic Paperbacks) Scholastic, Inc.

Grey, Christopher. Leonardo's Shadow: Or, My Astonishing Life As Leonardo Da Vinci's Servant. 2008. (ENG.). 400p. (YA). (gr. 7). pap. 13.99 *(978-1-4169-0544-8(8)*, Atheneum Bks. for Young Readers) Simon & Schuster Children's Publishing.

Napoli, Donna Jo. The Smile. 2009. 272p. (YA). (gr. 7-18). 7.99 *(978-0-14-241492-7(1)*, Speak) Penguin Young Readers Group.

Osborne, Mary A. Nonna's Book of Mysteries. 2010. (ENG., Illus.). 352p. (gr. 8-17). pap. 16.95 *(978-1-936181-16-2(9))* Lake Street Pr.

Wettersten, Laura. My Faire Lady. 2014. (ENG., Illus.). 352p. (YA). (gr. 7). 17.99 *(978-1-4424-8933-2(2)*, Simon & Schuster Bks. For Young Readers) Simon & Schuster Bks. For Young Readers.

RENOIR, AUGUSTE, 1841-1919

Boutan, Mila. Renoir & Me. 2010. (ENG., Illus.). 48p. (J). (gr. 3-7). pap. 18.95 *(978-1-4081-2384-3(3)*, 900069878, A&C Black Visual Arts) Bloomsbury Publishing Plc GBR. Dist: Macmillan.

Kelley, True. Smart about Art: Pierre-Auguste Renoir: Paintings That Smile. 2005. (Smart about Art Ser.). (Illus.). 32p. (J). (gr. k-4). mass mkt. 7.99 *(978-0-448-43371-4(0)*, Grosset & Dunlap) Penguin Young Readers Group.

Miller, Sabine. Renoir, Vol. 7. 2015. (Great Artists Collection). (Illus.). 64p. (J). (gr. 7). lib. bdg. 23.95 *(978-1-4222-3262-0(X))* Mason Crest.

Nichols, Catherine. Pierre-Auguste Renoir. (Primary Source Library of Famous Artists Ser.). 32p. (gr. 3-4). 2009. 42.50 *(978-1-60854-104-1(5))* 2005. (ENG., Illus.). (J). lib. bdg. 27.60 *(978-1-4042-2765-1(2)*, cc309da8-8b19-4fb3-b670-da92beba1bb0) Rosen Publishing Group, Inc., The. (PowerKids Pr.).

Sellier, Marie. Renoir's Colors. 2010. (ENG., Illus.). 40p. (gr. -1-k). 16.95 *(978-1-60606-003-2(1))* Getty Pubns.

Somervill, Barbara A. Pierre-Auguste Renoir. 2007. (Art Profiles for Kids Ser.). (Illus.). 48p. (YA). (gr. 4-7). lib. bdg. 29.95 *(978-1-58415-566-9(3))* Mitchell Lane Pubs.

Spence, David. The Impressionists: Monet, Cezanne, Renoir, Degas. 2010. (ENG.). 128p. (J). (gr. 4-7). pap. 12.95 *(978-1-84696-217-2(X)*, TickTock Books) Octopus Publishing Group GBR. Dist: Independent Pubs. Group.

—Renoir. 2010. (Great Artists & Their World Ser.). 48p. 32.80 *(978-1-84898-317-5(4))* Black Rabbit Bks.

—Renoir: Color y Naturaleza. (Coleccion Grandes Artistas).Tr. of Renoir: Colot & Nature. (SPA.). (YA). (gr. 5-8). 12.76 *(978-84-8211-137-7(X))* Celeste Ediciones, S.A. ESP. Dist: Lectorum Pubns., Inc.

REPAIRING

see also Building—Repair and Reconstruction

Lüsted, Marcia Amidon. For People Who Love to Fix Things, 1 vol. 2016. (Cool Careers Without College Ser.). (ENG., Illus.). 104p. (J). (gr. 7-7). 41.12 *(978-1-5081-7284-0(6)*, ef7888b6-0a87-4ea0-b05d-8edfca7e5460) Rosen Publishing Group, Inc., The.

Stockland, Patricia M. Debugging: You Can Fix It! Sanchez, Sr., illus. 2018. (Code It! Ser.). (ENG.). 24p. (C). (gr. 1-3). lib. bdg. 33.99 *(978-1-68410-388-1(6)*, 140361) Cantata Learning.

Van Slyke, Marge. Furniture Refinishing in A Class by Yourself. Lambert, Barbara, ed. van der Sterre, Johanna, illus. 2004. 91p. per. 9.95 *(978-0-9755548-0-7(8))* Log Cabin Bks.

REPORT WRITING

Abraham, Philip. Language Development Writing Process, 1 vol. 2003. (BrainBuilders Ser.). (ENG.). 48p. (gr. k-4). pap. 5.25 *(978-1-4042-8520-0(2)*, 9cb1f0dc-d38c-4b5b-8051-002ba8312dce) Rosen Publishing Group, Inc., The.

Asselin, Kristine Carlson. Smart Research Strategies: Finding the Right Sources, 1 vol. 2013. (Research Tool Kit Ser.). (ENG.). 32p. (J). (gr. 3-6). pap. 8.10 *(978-1-62065-790-4(2)*, 121756, Capstone Pr.) Capstone.

—Smart Research Strategies: Finding the Right Sources. 2013. (Research Tool Kit Ser.). (ENG.). 32p. (J). (gr. 3-4). pap. 48.60 *(978-1-62065-791-1(0)*, 19370, Capstone Pr.) Capstone.

—Think for Yourself: Avoiding Plagiarism. 2013. (Research Tool Kit Ser.). (ENG.). 32p. (J). (gr. 3-4). pap. 48.60 *(978-1-62065-793-5(7)*, 19372); pap. 8.10 *(978-1-62065-792-8(9)*, 121757) Capstone. (Capstone Pr.).

Bentley, Nancy. Don't Be a Copycat! Write a Great Report Without Plagiarizing, 1 vol. 2008. (Prime (Elementary) Ser.). (ENG., Illus.). 64p. (gr. 3-3). lib. bdg. 31.93 *(978-0-7660-2860-9(7)*, da7ae078-3bc4-4dcf-8855-dec5c93fe9a1) Enslow Publishing, LLC.

Bodden, Valerie. Giving a Presentation. 2014. (Classroom How-To Ser.). (ENG.). 48p. (J). (gr. 5-8). *(978-1-60818-280-0(0)*, 21296, Creative Education) Creative Co., The.

—Giving a Presentation. Williams, Nate, illus. 2014. (Classroom How-To Ser.). (ENG.). 48p. (J). (gr. 5-8). pap. 12.00 *(978-0-89812-986-1(9)*, 21297, Creative Paperbacks) Creative Co., The.

—Writing a Research Paper. 2014. (Classroom How-To Ser.). (ENG.). 48p. (J). (gr. 5-8). *(978-1-60818-283-1(5)*, 21305, Creative Education) Creative Co., The.

—Writing a Research Paper. Williams, Nate, illus. 2014. (Classroom How-To Ser.). (ENG.). 48p. (J). (gr. 5-8). pap. 12.00 *(978-0-89812-989-2(3)*, 21306, Creative Paperbacks) Creative Co., The.

Books, Checkmark, creator. Research & Information Management: Follow the Fast Track to Career Success. 2nd rev. ed. 2007. (Mastering Career Skills Ser.). (ENG., Illus.). 128p. per. 12.95 *(978-0-8160-7118-0(7)*, P165515, Checkmark Bks.) Infobase Holdings, Inc.

Buzzeo, Toni. R is for Research. Wong, Nicole, illus. 2008. 17.95 *(978-1-60213-032-6(9))*; (J). (gr. 2-4). 17.95 *(978-1-60213-030-2(2))* Highsmith Inc. (Upstart Bks.).

Cefrey, Holly. Researching People, Places, & Events, 1 vol. 2009. (Digital & Information Literacy Ser.). (ENG., Illus.). 48p. (YA). (gr. 6-6). lib. bdg. 33.47 *(978-1-4358-5317-1(2)*, 819a951a-a334-4cce-b644-7f619a15851c, Rosen Reference) Rosen Publishing Group, Inc., The.

Colby, Jennifer. Data in Arguments. 2017. (21st Century Skills Library: Data Geek Ser.). (ENG., Illus.). 32p. (J). (gr. 4-7). lib. bdg. 32.07 *(978-1-63472-707-5(X)*, 210086) Cherry Lake Publishing.

Coleman, Kelly. Choose It! Finding the Right Research Topic. Petelinsek, Kathleen, illus. 2015. (Explorer Junior Library: Information Explorer Junior Ser.). (ENG.). 24p. (J). (gr. 1-4). 32.07 *(978-1-63188-862-5(5)*, 206028) Cherry Lake Publishing.

Coleman, Miriam. Present It: Understanding Contexts & Audiences, 1 vol. 2012. (Core Skills Ser.). (ENG., Illus.). 32p. (J). (gr. 4-5). 28.93 *(978-1-4488-7455-2(6)*, f28786ef-5709-4f9a-8d1b-45b99ba4a420); pap. 11.00 *(978-1-4488-7527-6(7)*, bcaf3c68-303d-4e03-bb9a-ed4250aed08f) Rosen Publishing Group, Inc., The. (PowerKids Pr.).

—Prove It: Gathering Evidence & Integrating Information, 1 vol. 2012. (Core Skills Ser.). (ENG., Illus.). 32p. (J). (gr. 4-5). 28.93 *(978-1-4488-7453-8(X)*, 996e5ed6-112d-474a-a793-22ef52c7e7d3); pap. 11.00 *(978-1-4488-7525-2(0)*, 5a7eef9e-f3d1-48a6-a4f4-c7c49a1fcc02) Rosen Publishing Group, Inc., The. (PowerKids Pr.).

Cornwall, Phyllis. Put It All Together. 2010. (Explorer Library: Information Explorer Ser.). (ENG., Illus.). 32p. (gr. 4-8). lib. bdg. 32.07 *(978-1-60279-643-0(2)*, 200346) Cherry Lake Publishing.

—Super Smart Information Strategies: Put It All Together. 2010. (Explorer Library: Information Explorer Ser.). (ENG.). 32p. (gr. 4-8). pap. 14.21 *(978-1-61080-262-8(4)*, 200908) Cherry Lake Publishing.

Creating Book Reports with Cool New Digital Tools. 2013. (Way Beyond PowerPoint: Making 21st Century Presentations Ser.). 48p. (J). (gr. 5-8). pap. 70.50 *(978-1-4777-1846-9(X)*, Rosen Reference) Rosen Publishing Group, Inc., The.

Digital Photo Activity Kit Deluxe Vivitar 3700 series Lab-10. 2005. (J). cd-rom 1790.00 *(978-1-933229-02-7(0))* APTE, Inc.

Digital Photo Activity Kit Deluxe Vivitar 3700 series Lab-15. 2005. (J). cd-rom 2610.00 *(978-1-933229-03-4(9))* APTE, Inc.

Digital Photo Activity Kit Deluxe Vivitar 3700 series Lab-20. 2005. (J). 3260.00 *(978-1-933229-04-1(7))* APTE, Inc.

Digital Photo Activity Kit Deluxe Vivitar 3700 series Lab-25. 2005. (J). 3924.00 *(978-1-933229-05-8(5))* APTE, Inc.

Digital Photo Activity Kit Deluxe Vivitar 3700 series Lab-30. 2005. (J). 4585.00 *(978-1-933229-06-5(3))* APTE, Inc.

Digital Photo Activity Kit Deluxe Vivitar 3700 series Lab-35. 2005. (J). 5239.00 *(978-1-933229-07-2(1))* APTE, Inc.

Digital Photo Activity Kit Deluxe Vivitar 3700 series Lab-5. 2005. (J). cd-rom 648.95 *(978-1-933229-01-0(2))* APTE, Inc.

Digital Photo Activity Kit Deluxe Vivitar 3700 Series school Version. 2005. (J). cd-rom 133.95 *(978-1-933229-00-3(4))* APTE, Inc.

Digital Photo Activity Kit Deluxe Vivitar 5300 series Lab- 2005. (J). 1759.95 *(978-1-933229-09-6(8))* APTE, Inc.

Digital Photo Activity Kit Deluxe Vivitar 5300 series Lab-10. 2005. (J). 3469.99 *(978-1-933229-10-2(1))* APTE, Inc.

Digital Photo Activity Kit Deluxe Vivitar 5300 series Lab-15. 2005. (J). 5129.95 *(978-1-933229-11-9(X))* APTE, Inc.

Digital Photo Activity Kit Deluxe Vivitar 5300 series Lab-25. 2005. (J). 8123.90 *(978-1-933229-12-6(8))* APTE, Inc.

Digital Photo Activity Kit Deluxe Vivitar 5300 series Lab-30. 2005. (J). 9624.95 *(978-1-933229-14-0(4))* APTE, Inc.

Digital Photo Activity Kit Deluxe Vivitar 5300 series Lab-35. 2005. (J). 11119.95 *(978-1-933229-15-7(2))* APTE, Inc.

Digital Photo Activity Kit Deluxe Vivitar 5300 series Single. 2005. (J). 359.99 *(978-1-933229-08-9(X))* APTE, Inc.

Don't Panic: The Procrastinator's Guide to Writing an Effective Term Paper. 2004. 64p. (YA). per. 9.95 *(978-0-9632123-5-1(4))* Crystal Pr.

DynaNotes Grade 4 Writing TAKS Review Guide Transparency Set. 2006. (J). trans. *(978-1-933854-42-7(1))* DynaStudy, Inc.

DynaNotes Grade 7 Writing TAKS Review Guide. 2006. (J). pap. *(978-1-933854-39-7(1))* DynaStudy, Inc.

DynaNotes Grade 7 Writing TAKS Review Guide Transparency Set. 2006. (J). trans. *(978-1-933854-40-3(5))* DynaStudy, Inc.

Evan-Moor. Easy File Folder Reports Grades 3-6. 2004. (ENG.). 240p. (J). pap. 21.99 *(978-1-55799-963-4(5)*, EMC 6001) Evan-Moor Educational Pubs.

Evergreen: a Guide to Writing with Readings. 7th ed. 2003. (YA). (gr. 6-12). stu. ed. 3.96 incl. cd-rom *(978-0-618-27389-8(1)*, 315696) CENGAGE Learning.

Fandel, Jennifer. Picture Yourself Writing Nonfiction: Using Photos to Inspire Writing. 2011. (See It, Write It Ser.). (ENG.). 32p. (gr. 3-4). pap. 47.70 *(978-1-4296-7208-5(0)*, Capstone Pr.) Capstone.

Fields, Jan. You Can Write Excellent Reports. 2012. (You Can Write Ser.). (ENG.). 24p. (gr. 1-2). pap. 41.70 *(978-1-4296-8384-5(8))*; (Illus.). (J). pap. 7.29 *(978-1-4296-7962-6(X)*, 118294) Capstone. (Capstone Pr.).

Fontichiaro, Kristin. Review It! Helping Peers Create Their Best Work. Petelinsek, Kathleen, illus. 2015. (Explorer Junior Library: Information Explorer Junior Ser.). (ENG.). 24p. (J). (gr. 1-4). 32.07 *(978-1-63188-865-6(X)*, 206040) Cherry Lake Publishing.

Gallion, Sue Lowell. Rick & Rachel Build a Research Report. Chung, Chi, illus. 2014. (Writing Builders Ser.). (ENG.). 32p. (J). (gr. 2-4). pap. 11.94 *(978-1-60357-557-7(X))*; lib. bdg. 25.27 *(978-1-59953-583-8(1))* Norwood Hse. Pr.

Ganeri, Anita. I Can Write Reports. 2013. (I Can Write Ser.). (ENG.). 32p. (gr. 1-3). pap. 8.29 *(978-1-4329-6944-8(7)*, 119870, Heinemann) Capstone.

Gleed, Paul. Bloom's How to Write about William Shakespeare. 2008. (Bloom's How to Write About Ser.). (ENG.). 244p. (gr. 9-18). 45.00 *(978-0-7910-9484-6(7)*, P129244, Facts On File) Infobase Holdings, Inc.

Greek, Joseph. Writing Term Papers with Cool New Digital Tools, 1 vol. 2013. (Way Beyond PowerPoint: Making 21st Century Presentations Ser.). (ENG., Illus.). 48p. (J). (gr. 6-6). 34.41 *(978-1-4777-1835-3(4)*, 11e05faf-7156-4e40-9a7d-36b819904331); pap. 12.75 *(978-1-4777-1853-7(2)*, d34f8a1c-6ef5-49e7-b6b2-3c53ea31a554) Rosen Publishing Group, Inc., The. (Rosen Reference).

Green, Julie. Write It Down. 2010. (Explorer Library: Information Explorer Ser.). (ENG., Illus.). 32p. (gr. 4-8). lib. bdg. 32.07 *(978-1-60279-645-4(9)*, 200348) Cherry Lake Publishing.

Green, Lyric & Bullard, Lisa. Future Ready Oral & Multimedia Presentations, 1 vol. 2017. (Future Ready Project Skills Ser.). (ENG.). 48p. (gr. 3-4). pap. 12.70 *(978-0-7660-8771-2(9)*, ff6e8704-8eef-4dea-9521-8df8765b69e6); lib. bdg. 29.60 *(978-0-7660-8659-3(3)*, dd996b0f-14fc-44f4-b219-974e8bf18376) Enslow Publishing, LLC.

Green, Lyric & Graham Gaines, Ann. Future Ready Research Papers, 1 vol. 2017. (Future Ready Project Skills Ser.). (ENG.). 48p. (gr. 3-4). pap. 12.70 *(978-0-7660-8773-6(5)*, 336adb6c-ce9d-4139-8752-e12631911a58); lib. bdg. 29.60 *(978-0-7660-8661-6(5)*, c176dc63-9873-4626-acdb-0e71b593bfbc) Enslow Publishing, LLC.

Hagler, Gina. Creating Book Reports with Cool New Digital Tools, 1 vol. 2013. (Way Beyond PowerPoint: Making 21st Century Presentations Ser.). (ENG.). 48p. (J). (gr. 6-6). 34.41 *(978-1-4777-1834-6(6)*, c3402fa3-e8d4-46b0-93fb-cda346427193); pap. 12.75 *(978-1-4777-1845-2(1)*, cba9dcbc-1de0-44d3-b14b-d9cf29580476) Rosen Publishing Group, Inc., The. (Rosen Reference).

Hamilton, John. Primary & Secondary Sources, 1 vol. 2005. (Straight to the Source Ser.). (ENG.). 32p. (gr. k-6). 27.07 *(978-1-59197-548-9(4)*, Checkerboard Library) ABDO Publishing Co.

Herman, Gail. Make-A-Splash Writing Rules, 1 vol. 2009. (Grammar All-Stars: Writing Tools Ser.). (ENG.). 32p. (J). (gr. 2-4). pap. 11.50 *(978-1-4339-2136-0(7)*, c15ed5fd-914d-4224-8a50-acb23bb541c7); lib. bdg. 28.67 *(978-1-4339-1943-5(5)*, ab7445df-a43b-49bd-91ae-08f75610f86a) Stevens, Gareth Publishing LLLP. (Gareth Stevens Learning Library).

Hook, Sue Vander. Writing Intriguing Informational Pieces. 2015. (Write This Way Ser.). (ENG., Illus.). 56p. (J). (gr. 6-8). 33.32 *(978-1-4677-7907-4(5)*, e5330acf-7a94-4cf0-9ce7-0ead11e28774, Lerner Pubns.) Lerner Publishing Group.

Houghton, Peggy M., et al. Houghton & Houghton Manual of Style: A Guide to Writing Research Papers. 2009. (J). *(978-0-923568-97-9(2))* Baker College Publishing Co.

Howell, Sara. How to Plan, Revise, & Edit Your Text, 1 vol., 1. 2013. (Core Writing Skills Ser.). (ENG.). 24p. (J). (gr. 3-3). 26.27 *(978-1-4777-2910-6(0)*, 402ce120-0894-4ef9-8108-b7945a10007a, PowerKids Pr.) Rosen Publishing Group, Inc., The.

—How to Write an Explanatory Text, 1 vol., 1. 2013. (Core Writing Skills Ser.). (ENG.). 24p. (J). (gr. 3-3). 26.27 *(978-1-4777-2907-6(0)*, ddf5854b-6e96-4aa2-a885-c7eaa621fff8, PowerKids Pr.) Rosen Publishing Group, Inc., The.

Jarnow, Jill. Writing to Describe, 1 vol. 2005. (Write Now: a Kid's Guide to Nonfiction Writing Ser.). (ENG., Illus.). 24p. (J). (gr. 3-4). lib. bdg. 26.27 *(978-1-4042-2832-0(2)*, 96a32864-c583-4200-aac0-9448c7026ab1, PowerKids Pr.) Rosen Publishing Group, Inc., The.

Jennings, Brien J. What's Your Source? Using Sources in Your Writing. 2018. (All about Media Ser.). (ENG., Illus.). 24p. (J). (gr. 1-3). lib. bdg. 27.99 *(978-1-5435-0220-6(2)*, 137138, Capstone Pr.) Capstone.

Kemmerer, Susan. Research in Increments. 2nd ed. 2004. 75p. pap. 12.95 *(978-0-9758543-1-0(3))* Schoolhouse Publishing.

Levy, Janey. Language Development: Writing Process, 1 vol. 2003. (BrainBuilders Ser.). (ENG.). 48p. (gr. k-4). pap. 5.25 *(978-1-4042-8569-9(5)*, faf1663b-1c3d-42dc-b6d2-c253481d5052) Rosen Publishing Group, Inc., The.

Loewen, Nancy. Just the Facts: Writing Your Own Research Report, 1 vol. Beacon, Dawn, illus. 2009. (Writer's Toolbox Ser.). (ENG.). 32p. (J). (gr. 2-4). pap. 8.95 *(978-1-4048-5702-5(8)*, 102277, Picture Window Bks.) Capstone.

—Just the Facts [Scholastic]: Writing Your Own Research Report. Beacon, Dawn, illus. 2010. (Writer's Toolbox Ser.). 32p. pap. 0.50 *(978-1-4048-6171-8(8)*, Picture Window Bks.) Capstone.

Marlow, Herb. A Student's Guide to Successful Writing. 2005. (J). 24.95 *(978-1-893595-53-8(6))* Four Seasons Bks., Inc.

McDougal-Littell Publishing Staff, creator. Writing Research Reports. 2006. (Illus.). 103p. (gr. 6-12). per. *(978-0-618-05272-1(0)*, 2-22379) Holt McDougal.

McGuinness, Denis E. & Spencer, Lauren. Writing to Describe. 2011. (Illus.). 64p. (J). 77.70 *(978-1-4488-4744-0(3)*, Rosen Reference); (ENG., (J). (gr. 5-5). pap. 13.95 *(978-1-4488-4686-3(2)*, 566273fe-8f3d-406d-8a88-72f2dd643339, Rosen Reference); (ENG., (YA). (gr. 5-5). lib. bdg. 37.13 *(978-1-4488-4680-1(3)*, e27d770d-252f-4b54-8d99-92e12cb33d90) Rosen Publishing Group, Inc., The.

Milton, Bess. Language Development Writing Process, 1 vol. 2003. (BrainBuilders Ser.). (ENG.). 48p. (gr. k-4). pap. 5.25 *(978-1-4042-8559-0(8)*, 71a01898-425f-4e43-8186-53ef04556e5f) Rosen Publishing Group, Inc., The.

Minden, Cecilia. Writing a News Article. Herring, Carol, illus. 2019. (Write It Right Ser.). (ENG.). 24p. (J). (gr. 1-4). pap. 12.79 *(978-1-5341-5008-9(0)*, 213339); lib. bdg. 30.64 *(978-1-5341-4722-5(5)*, 213338) Cherry Lake Publishing.

Minden, Cecilia & Roth, Kate. How to Write a Report. 2011. (Explorer Junior Library: How to Write Ser.). (ENG., Illus.). 24p. (gr. 1-4). lib. bdg. 29.21 *(978-1-61080-105-8(9)*, 201112) Cherry Lake Publishing.

—Writing a Book Report. 2019. (Write It Right Ser.). (ENG., Illus.). 24p. (J). (gr. 1-4). pap. 12.79 *(978-1-5341-3939-8(7)*, 212585); lib. bdg. 30.64 *(978-1-5341-4283-1(5)*, 212584) Cherry Lake Publishing.

—Writing a Report. 2019. (Write It Right Ser.). (ENG., Illus.). 24p. (J). (gr. 1-4). pap. 12.79 *(978-1-5341-3938-1(9)*, 212581); lib. bdg. 30.64 *(978-1-5341-4282-4(7)*, 212580) Cherry Lake Publishing.

Morkane, Sue. Original Writing. 2004. (Routledge a Level English Guides). (ENG., Illus.). 112p. (C). 105.00 *(978-0-415-31911-9(0)*, RU26771); per. 33.95 *(978-0-415-31912-6(9)*, RU26772) Routledge.

Nash, Kimberley. Book Reports: A one-year writing Course. 2006. (ENG., Illus.). 192p. spiral bd., wbk. ed. 33.00 *(978-0-9710950-6-9(X)*, 13030) Resurrection Resources LLC.

—Essays & Research Reports - Level A Level A: A one year writing Course. 2007. (ENG., Illus.). 181p. (gr. 5-7). spiral bd., wbk. ed. 33.00 *(978-0-9653723-6-7(7)*, #12010) Resurrection Resources LLC.

—Essays & Research Reports - Level B: A one year writing Course. 2007. (ENG., Illus.). 247p. spiral bd., wbk. ed. 35.00 *(978-0-9710950-2-1(7)*, 12020) Resurrection Resources LLC.

—Lab Reports: 10 Experiments. 2007. (ENG., Illus.). 140p. spiral bd., wbk. ed. 20.00 *(978-0-9710950-8-3(6))* Resurrection Resources LLC.

Nelson, G. Lynn. Writing & Being: Embracing Your Life Through Creative Journaling. 2nd rev. ed. 2004. (ENG., Illus.). 176p. pap. 16.95 *(978-1-880913-61-1(5))* New World Library.

Owings, Lisa. Share Your Book Report. 2013. (Library Smarts Ser.). (ENG., Illus.). 24p. (J). (gr. -1-2). lib. bdg. 23.99 *(978-1-4677-1504-1(2)*, 4fec3776-a085-4b81-ac0b-47b07ecacd80, Lerner Pubns.) Lerner Publishing Group.

Patrick, Olive. How to Write A+ Reports. 2019. (J). pap. *(978-1-9785-1401-0(8))* Enslow Publishing, LLC.

Priddy, Anna. Bloom's How to Write about Emily Dickinson. 2007. (Bloom's How to Write About Ser.). (ENG.). 262p. (gr. 9-18). 45.00 *(978-0-7910-9492-1(8)*, P129239, Facts On File) Infobase Holdings, Inc.

Proudfit, Benjamin. Writing Book Reports, 1 vol. 2014. (Write Right! Ser.). (ENG.). 24p. (J). (gr. 2-3). 25.27 *(978-1-4824-0804-1(X)*, e660f690-031e-4c4d-b641-ebbe4f46fb49) Stevens, Gareth Publishing LLLP.

—Writing Research Papers, 1 vol. 2014. (Write Right! Ser.). (ENG.). 24p. (J). (gr. 2-3). 25.27 *(978-1-4824-1120-1(2)*, 144fb042-7295-41b2-98d7-686a44d77a0e) Stevens, Gareth Publishing LLLP.

Range, Ellen. Take Note! Taking & Organizing Notes. 2014. (Explorer Junior Library: Information Explorer Junior Ser.). (ENG., Illus.). 24p. (J). (gr. 1-4). 32.07 *(978-1-63137-788-4(4)*, 205395) Cherry Lake Publishing.

Rasinski, Timothy V. Daily Word Ladders: Grades 2-3. 2005. (Daily Word Ladders Ser.). (ENG., Illus.). 112p. (gr. 2-3). pap. 15.99 *(978-0-439-51383-8(9)*, Teaching Resources) Scholastic, Inc.

Rollins, Brenda. How to Write a Book Report: 80 Interactive Screen Pages. 2011. (Writing Skills Ser.). (J). (gr. 3-8). pap. 39.95 *(978-1-55319-506-1(X)*, Classroom Complete Pr.) Rainbow Horizons Publishing, Inc.

—How to Write an Essay: 80 Interactive Screen Pages. 2011. (Writing Skills Ser.). (J). (gr. 3-8). pap. 39.95 *(978-1-55319-507-8(8)*, Classroom Complete Pr.) Rainbow Horizons Publishing, Inc.

Rozines Roy, Jennifer. Sharpen Your Report Writing Skills, 1 vol. 2012. (Sharpen Your Writing Skills Ser.). (ENG., Illus.). 64p. (gr. 6-7). pap. 11.53 *(978-1-59845-338-6(6)*, c1b883b7-24ef-4b54-88c4-dcc8acb33e98); lib. bdg. 31.93 *(978-0-7660-3905-6(6)*, 45746f34-03a8-4b50-8b12-87380f077e0b) Enslow Publishing, LLC.

—Sharpen Your Story or Narrative Writing Skills, 1 vol. 2012. (Sharpen Your Writing Skills Ser.). (ENG., Illus.). 64p. (gr. 6-7). pap. 11.53 *(978-1-59845-340-9(8)*, 0d73a7e3-104d-4a10-a067-b2fa48e94e80); lib. bdg. 31.93 *(978-0-7660-3901-8(3)*, 8d12bb10-274b-49f0-af01-0eac24697272) Enslow Publishing, LLC.

Rustad, Martha E. H. Learning about Nonfiction, 1 vol. 2014. (Language Arts Ser.). (ENG.). 24p. (J). (gr. -1-2). 27.32 *(978-1-4914-0579-6(1)*, 125916, Capstone Pr.) Capstone.

Sharkawy, Azza. Share It! 2014. (Science Sleuths Ser.). (ENG., Illus.). 24p. (J). (gr. 2-2). *(978-0-7787-0781-3(4))* Crabtree Publishing Co.

Shearer, Cynthia & Washington, George. Handwriting by George 28-55: Rules of Civility & Decent Behaviour in Company & Conversation: Rules 28-53 to Draw & Write, 4 vols., Vol. 2. 2009. (ENG.). 62p. (J). pap. 9.95 *(978-1-882514-37-3(8))* Greenleaf Pr.

Silate, Jennifer. Language Development Writing Process, 1 vol. 2003. (BrainBuilders Ser.). (ENG.). 48p. (gr. k-4). pap. 5.25 *(978-1-4042-8564-4(4)*, 074d4a41-e1d8-4995-9ff1-286f966dd8ff) Rosen Publishing Group, Inc., The.

SIRS Discoverer. 2005. (J). mass mkt. *(978-0-89777-566-3(X))* SIRS Publishing, Inc.

SIRS Discoverer: Getting Started Manual Spring 2004. 2003. (YA). cd-rom 1425.00 *(978-0-89777-542-7(2))* SIRS Publishing, Inc.

Spencer, Lauren. A Step-by-Step Guide to Informative Writing. 2009. (Library of Writing Skills Ser.). 48p. (gr. 5-8). 53.00 *(978-1-60853-978-9(4)*, Rosen Reference) Rosen Publishing Group, Inc., The.

Stiles, Mary & Mills, Barbara. A Rookie's Guide to Research. 3rd ed. 2003. 92p. (YA). spiral bd. 10.95 *(978-0-9721404-1-6(7))* Union Creek Communications, Inc.

Tribble. Word for Word. Date not set. (Illus.). 80p. pap. 28.75 *(978-0-582-01663-7(0))* Addison-Wesley Longman, Ltd. GBR. Dist: Trans-Atlantic Pubns., Inc.

Write on Target for Grade 5. 2006. (J). stu. ed., per., wbk. ed. 16.95 *(978-1-59230-159-1(2))* Englefield & Assocs., Inc.
Write on Target Grade 3: Student Workbook. 2005. (J). stu. ed., per. 10.95 *(978-1-59230-151-5(7))* Englefield & Assocs., Inc.
Write on Target Grade 4: Student Workbook. 2005. (J). stu. ed., per. 10.95 *(978-1-59230-149-2(5))* Englefield & Assocs., Inc.
Write on Target Grade 6: Student Workbook. 2005. (J). pap., stu. ed. 10.95 *(978-1-59230-157-7(6))* Englefield & Assocs., Inc.
Writing Term Papers with Cool New Digital Tools. 2013. (Way Beyond PowerPoint: Making 21st Century Presentations Ser.). (Illus.). 48p. (J). (gr. 5-8). pap. 70.50 *(978-1-4777-1854-4(0),* Rosen Reference) Rosen Publishing Group, Inc., The.
Yomtov, Nel. How to Write a Lab Report. Petelinsek, Kathleen, illus. 2013. (Explorer Junior Library: How to Write Ser.). (ENG.). 24p. (J). (gr. 1-4). 29.21 *(978-1-62431-185-7(7),* 203064); pap. 12.79 *(978-1-62431-317-2(5),* 203066) Cherry Lake Publishing.
Zaroulis, Christina. Tackling Your High School Term Paper. 2003. (Students Helping Students Ser.). 80p. (gr. 9-12). pap. 8.95 *(978-0-9719392-1-9(7))* Natavi Guides.

REPORTERS AND REPORTING

see also Journalism

Boomhower, Ray E. The Soldier's Friend: A Life of Ernie Pyle. 2006. (Illus.). 134p. 17.95 *(978-0-87195-200-4(9))* Indiana Historical Society.
Cooper, Candy J. Reporting from Iraq: On the Ground in Fallujah. 2012. pap. *(978-0-545-32799-2(7))* Scholastic, Inc.
Copeland, Cynthia L. Cub. 2020. (ENG., Illus.). 240p. (gr. 3-7). (J). pap. 12.95 *(978-1-61620-848-6(1),* 73848); 24.95 *(978-1-61620-993-3(3),* 73993) Algonquin Young Readers.
Hamilton, John. Real-Time Reporting. 2004. (War in Iraq Ser.). (Illus.). 48p. (gr. 4-8). lib. bdg. 27.07 *(978-1-59197-497-0(6),* Abdo & Daughters) ABDO Publishing Co.
Johnson, Jennifer Hunt & Hansen, Holly T. Father Remembers, 615 vols., Vol. 6. 2003. (Illus.). 30p. 9.95 *(978-0-9729610-5-9(4),* CMB06) Tapis & Assocs., Inc.
—Grandma Remembers, 315 vols., Vol. 3. 2003. (Illus.). 30p. 9.95 *(978-0-9729610-2-8(X),* CMB03) Tapis & Assocs., Inc.
—Grandpa Remembers, 415 vols., Vol. 4. 2003. (Illus.). 30p. 9.95 *(978-0-9729610-3-5(8),* CMB04) Tapis & Assocs., Inc.
—Mother Remembers, 515 vols., Vol. 5. 2003. (Illus.). 30p. 9.95 *(978-0-9729610-4-2(6),* CMB05) Tapis & Assocs., Inc.
—My Memories, 115 vols., Vol. 1. 2003. (Illus.). 29p. 9.95 *(978-0-9729610-0-4(3),* CMB01) Tapis & Assocs., Inc.
—Remembering Grandma, 1115 vols., Vol. 11. 2003. (Illus.). 28p. 9.95 *(978-0-9729610-6-6(2),* CMB12) Tapis & Assocs., Inc.
—Remembering Grandpa, 1215 vols., Vol. 12. 2003. (Illus.). 28p. 9.95 *(978-0-9729610-7-3(0),* CMB12) Tapis & Assocs., Inc.
—Your Memories, 215 vols., Vol. 2. 2003. (Illus.). 29p. 9.95 *(978-0-9729610-1-1(1),* CMB02) Tapis & Assocs., Inc.
Loveless, Antony & Crewe, Sabrina. War Correspondents. 2012. (ENG., Illus.). 32p. (J). lib. bdg. *(978-0-7787-5103-8(1));* (The World's Most Dangerous Jobs Ser.: No. 10). pap. *(978-0-7787-5117-5(1))* Crabtree Publishing Co.
Macfarlane, Colin. Hit the Headlines: Exciting Journalism Activities for Improving Writing & Thinking Skills. 2012. (ENG., Illus.). 192p. (C). pap. 57.95 *(978-0-415-69511-4(2),* Y126804) Routledge.
Mahoney, Ellen. Nellie Bly & Investigative Journalism for Kids: Mighty Muckrakers from the Golden Age to Today, with 21 Activities. 2015. (For Kids Ser.: 56). (ENG., Illus.). 144p. (J). (gr. 4). pap. 16.95 *(978-1-61374-997-5(X))* Chicago Review Pr., Inc.
Minden, Cecilia & Roth, Kate. How to Write an Interview. 2011. (Explorer Junior Library: How to Write Ser.). (ENG., Illus.). 24p. (gr. 1-4). lib. bdg. 29.21 *(978-1-60279-996-7(2),* 200992) Cherry Lake Publishing.
Mooney, Carla. Asking Questions about How the News Is Created. 2015. (21st Century Skills Library: Asking Questions about Media Ser.). (ENG., Illus.). 32p. (J). (gr. 4-8). 32.07 *(978-1-63362-489-4(7),* 206864) Cherry Lake Publishing.
Pettiford, Rebecca. Reporters. 2015. (Illus.). 24p. (J). lib. bdg. 25.65 *(978-1-62031-159-2(3),* Bullfrog Bks.) Jump! Inc.
Rhatigan, Joe. People You Gotta Meet Before You Grow Up: Get to Know the Movers & Shakers, Heroes & Hotshots in Your Hometown. 2014. (ENG., Illus.). 128p. (J). (gr. 2-5). 14.95 *(978-1-62354-004-3(6))* Charlesbridge Publishing, Inc.
Saenger, Diana. Everyone Wants My Job! The ABCs of Entertainment Writing. Fife, Bruce, ed. unabr. ed. 2003. (Writing & Publishing Ser.). (Illus.). 159p. (YA). (gr. 8-12). pap. 15.00 *(978-0-941599-53-5(1))* Piccadilly Bks., Ltd.
Shone, Rob. War Correspondents. 2009. (Graphic Careers Ser.). (ENG.). 48p. (YA). (gr. 5-5). 58.50 *(978-1-61512-894-5(8),* Rosen Reference) Rosen Publishing Group, Inc., The.
—War Correspondents, 1 vol. Forsey, Chris, illus. 2008. (Graphic Careers Ser.). (ENG.). 48p. (J). (gr. 5-5). lib. bdg. 37.13 *(978-1-4042-1449-1(6),* a6d745c4-f2f5-41b5-82e5-d10e71cb82f6); per. 14.05 *(978-1-4042-1450-7(X),* 24c5c00b-755c-4c08-903b-1cd3c3ae1a7c) Rosen Publishing Group, Inc., The.
Wilson, Julius & Benchmark Education Co. Staff. I Was a 21st Century Civil War Reporter. 2014. (Text Connections Ser.). (J). (gr. 5). *(978-1-4900-1378-7(4))* Benchmark Education Co.

REPORTERS AND REPORTING—FICTION

Ace Reporter, 6, Pack. (Bookweb Ser.). 32p. (gr. 3-18). 34.00 *(978-0-7635-3940-5(6))* Rigby Education.
Appleton, Victor. Restricted Access. 2019. (Tom Swift Inventors' Academy Ser.: 3). (ENG., Illus.). 160p. (J). (gr. 3-7). 17.99 *(978-1-5344-3637-4(5),* Simon & Schuster/Paula Wiseman Bks.) Simon & Schuster/Paula Wiseman Bks.
Bauer, Joan. Peeled. 2009. (ENG.). 256p. (YA). (gr. 7-18). 10.99 *(978-0-14-241430-9(1),* Speak) Penguin Young Readers Group.
Bond, Gwenda. Fallout. 2015. (Lois Lane Ser.). (ENG.). 304p. (YA). (gr. 9-12). 16.95 *(978-1-63079-005-9(2),* 127326, Switch Pr.) Capstone.
Cirrone, Dorian. The Big Scoop, 1 vol. Woodruff, Liza, illus. 2006. (Marshall Cavendish Chapter Book Ser.). (ENG.). 74p. (J). (gr. 2-5). 14.99 *(978-0-7614-5323-9(7))* Marshall Cavendish Corp.
—The Missing Silver Dollar, 1 vol. Woodruff, Liza, illus. 2006. (Lindy Blues Ser.). (ENG.). 32p. (J). (gr. -1-3). 14.95 *(978-0-7614-5284-3(2))* Marshall Cavendish Corp.
Daneshvari, Gitty. The School of Fear: the Final Exam. (School of Fear Ser.: 3). (ENG.). (J). (gr. 3-7). 2012. 352p. pap. 18.99 *(978-0-316-18285-0(0))* 2011. (Illus.). 336p. 16.99 *(978-0-316-18287-4(7))* Little, Brown Bks. for Young Readers.
Davis, Christy. Newshounds. 2010. 156p. pap. 12.50 *(978-1-4389-7869-7(3))* AuthorHouse.
Dirkes, Craig. Sucktown, Alaska. 2017. (ENG.). 352p. (YA). (gr. 9-12). 17.95 *(978-1-63079-055-4(9),* 132182, Switch Pr.) Capstone.
Eaton, Walter Pricha. Peanut Cub Reporter: A Boy Scout's Life. 2005. pap. 28.95 *(978-1-885529-74-9(0))* Stevens Publishing.
Ellison, Joy D. Carol & Connie. 2008. 28p. per. 24.95 *(978-1-4241-9276-2(5))* America Star Bks.
Fantaskey, Beth. Isabel Feeney, Star Reporter. 2017. (ENG.). (J). (gr. 5-7). lib. bdg. 18.40 *(978-0-606-39809-1(0))* Turtleback.
Fontes, Justine & Fontes, Ron. Casebook: Bigfoot, 1 vol. 2009. (Top Secret Graphica Mysteries Ser.). (ENG., Illus.). 48p. (YA). (gr. 4-4). 33.93 *(978-1-60754-594-1(2),* bd5f014b-7bcb-49d5-9529-2832f6a60019); pap. 12.75 *(978-1-60754-595-8(0),* 3a36ccf3-f909-4bfe-aa0c-ea62e096eb46) Rosen Publishing Group, Inc., The. (Windmill Bks.).
Garis, Howard Roger. Larry Dexter's Great Search or, the Hunt for the Missing Millionaire. 2007. 196p. per. *(978-1-4065-2768-1(8))* Dodo Pr.
Green, Tim. Football Champ. 2010. (Football Genius Ser.: 3). (ENG.). 304p. (J). (gr. 3-7). pap. 9.99 *(978-0-06-162691-3(0),* HarperCollins) HarperCollins Pubs.
Greene, Janice. The Ritual, 1 vol. unabr. ed. 2010. (Q Reads Ser.). (ENG.). 32p. (YA). (gr. 9-12). pap. 8.50 *(978-1-61651-185-2(0))* Saddleback Educational Publishing, Inc.
Harrington, Kim. Revenge of the Red Club. 2020. (ENG., Illus.). 256p. (J). (gr. 4-8). pap. 8.99 *(978-1-5344-3573-5(5),* Simon & Schuster/Paula Wiseman Bks.) Simon & Schuster/Paula Wiseman Bks.
Ireland, Justina. Scream Site. 2018. (ENG.). 264p. (YA). (gr. 7-12). 15.95 *(978-1-63079-102-5(4),* 138468, Capstone Editions) Capstone.
Jackson, Kyle. Back on Track. Rumble, Simon, illus. 2018. (Mac's Sports Report). (ENG.). 128p. (J). (gr. 3-4). pap. 7.99 *(978-1-63163-224-2(8),* 1631632248); lib. bdg. 27.13 *(978-1-63163-223-5(X),* 163163223X) North Star Editions. (Jolly Fish Pr.).
—Concussion Comeback. Rumble, Simon, illus. 2018. (Mac's Sports Report). (ENG.). 128p. (J). (gr. 3-4). pap. 7.99 *(978-1-63163-228-0(0),* 1631632280); lib. bdg. 27.13 *(978-1-63163-227-3(2),* 1631632272) North Star Editions. (Jolly Fish Pr.).
—Racket Rumors. Rumble, Simon, illus. 2018. (Mac's Sports Report). (ENG.). 128p. (J). (gr. 3-4). pap. 7.99 *(978-1-63163-232-7(9),* 1631632329); lib. bdg. 27.13 *(978-1-63163-231-0(0),* 1631632310) North Star Editions. (Jolly Fish Pr.).
—Sideline Pressure. 2018. (Mac's Sports Report). (ENG., Illus.). 128p. (J). (gr. 3-4). lib. bdg. 27.13 *(978-1-63163-235-8(3),* 1631632353, Jolly Fish Pr.) North Star Editions.
—Sideline Pressure. Rumble, Simon, illus. 2018. (Mac's Sports Report). (ENG.). 128p. (J). (gr. 3-4). pap. 7.99 *(978-1-63163-236-5(1),* 1631632361, Jolly Fish Pr.) North Star Editions.
Judge, Malcolm. Jonny Jakes Investigates the Old School Ghoul. Brown, Alan, illus. 2016. (Middle-Grade Novels Ser.). (ENG.). 240p. (J). (gr. 4-7). lib. bdg. 25.99 *(978-1-4965-2829-2(8),* 131698, Stone Arch Bks.) Capstone.
Karre, Elizabeth. The Campaign. (Opportunity Ser.). (ENG.). 104p. (YA). (gr. 6-12). 2013. pap. 7.95 *(978-1-4677-1498-3(4),* 9166f313-88f6-4b14-b5fe-ebced6f83870, Darby Creek) 2015. E-Book 53.32 *(978-1-4677-6013-3(7),* 9781467760133, Lerner Digital) Lerner Publishing Group.
Krulik, Nancy. What's Black & White & Stinks All Over? #4. Blecha, Aaron, illus. 2011. (George Brown, Class Clown Ser.: 4). (ENG.). 128p. (J). (gr. 2-4). pap. 6.99 *(978-0-448-45370-5(3),* Grosset & Dunlap) Penguin Young Readers Group.
Larson, Kirby. Hattie Ever After. 2014. (Hattie Ser.: 2). (ENG.). 256p. (YA). (gr. 7). pap. 8.99 *(978-0-375-85090-5(2),* Ember) Random Hse. Children's Bks.
Law, Ingrid. Scumble. 2011. 432p. (J). (gr. 3-7). 9.99 *(978-0-14-241962-5(1),* Puffin Books) Penguin Young Readers Group.
—Scumble. l.t. ed. 2011. (Companion to the Newberry Honor Winner Savvy Ser.). (ENG.). 575p. 23.99 *(978-1-4104-3531-6(8))* Thorndike Pr.
LeSourd, Nancy. Attack at Pearl Harbor, 1 vol. 2008. (Liberty Letters Ser.). (ENG.). 224p. (J). pap. 7.99 *(978-0-310-71389-0(7))* Zonderkidz.
Lysiak, Hilde & Lysiak, Matthew. Fire! Fire!: a Branches Book (Hilde Cracks the Case #3) Lew-Vriethoff, Joanne, illus. 2017. (Hilde Cracks the Case Ser.: 3). (ENG.). 96p. (J). (gr. 1-3). pap. 6.99 *(978-1-338-14161-0(9))* Scholastic, Inc.
—Hero Dog!: a Branches Book (Hilde Cracks the Case #1) Lew-Vriethoff, Joanne, illus. 2017. (Hilde Cracks the Case Ser.: 1). (ENG.). 112p. (J). (gr. 1-3). pap. 5.99 *(978-1-338-14155-9(4))* Scholastic, Inc.
—Thief Strikes!: a Branches Book (Hilde Cracks the Case #6) Lew-Vriethoff, Joanne, illus. 2019. (Hilde Cracks the Case Ser.: 6). (ENG.). 96p. (J). (gr. 1-3). pap. 5.99 *(978-1-338-28391-4(X))* Scholastic, Inc.
—Tornado Hits!: a Branches Book (Hilde Cracks the Case #5) Lew-Vriethoff, Joanne, illus. 2018. (Hilde Cracks the Case Ser.: 5). (ENG.). 96p. (J). (gr. 1-3). pap. 5.99 *(978-1-338-26677-1(2))* Scholastic, Inc.
—UFO Spotted!: a Branches Book (Hilde Cracks the Case #4) Lew-Vriethoff, Joanne, illus. 2018. (Hilde Cracks the Case Ser.: 4). (ENG.). 96p. (J). (gr. 1-3). pap. 5.99 *(978-1-338-14164-1(3))* Scholastic, Inc.
—UFO Spotted!: a Branches Book (Hilde Cracks the Case #4) (Library Edition) Lew-Vriethoff, Joanne, illus. 2018. (Hilde Cracks the Case Ser.: 4). (ENG.). 96p. (J). (gr. 1-3). lib. bdg. 24.99 *(978-1-338-14165-8(1))* Scholastic, Inc.
MacLachlan, Patricia. Just Dance. (ENG.). 128p. (J). (gr. 2). 2018. pap. 7.99 *(978-1-4814-7253-1(4))* 2017. (Illus.). 15.99 *(978-1-4814-7252-4(6))* McElderry, Margaret K. Bks. (McElderry, Margaret K. Bks.).
McDonald, Megan. Judy Moody & Friends: Amy Namey in Ace Reporter. Madrid, Erwin, illus. 2014. (Judy Moody & Friends Ser.: 3). (ENG.). 64p. (J). (gr. -1-1). 12.99 *(978-0-7636-5715-4(8))* Candlewick Pr.
Mercer, Sienna. My Sister the Vampire #2: Fangtastic! 2007. (My Sister the Vampire Ser.: 2). (ENG.). 208p. (J). (gr. 3-7). per. 6.99 *(978-0-06-087115-4(6),* HarperCollins) HarperCollins Pubs.
Morrison, Harry Steele. The Adventures of A Boy Reporter. 2004. reprint ed. pap. 1.99 *(978-1-4192-5137-5(6));* pap. 20.95 *(978-1-4191-5137-8(1))* Kessinger Publishing, LLC.
O'Connor, Jane. Fancy Nancy: Nancy Clancy, Late-Breaking News! Glasser, Robin Preiss, illus. 2018. (Nancy Clancy Ser.: 8). (ENG.). 144p. (J). (gr. 1-5). pap. 5.99 *(978-0-06-226972-0(0),* HarperCollins) HarperCollins Pubs.
Parish, Herman. Amelia Bedelia, Cub Reporter. 2012. (I Can Read Level 2 Ser.). (ENG., Illus.). 64p. (J). (gr. -1-3). pap. 4.99 *(978-0-06-209509-1(9),* Greenwillow Bks.) HarperCollins Pubs.
Schindler, Holly. Feral. 2014. (ENG.). 432p. (YA). (gr. 8). 17.99 *(978-0-06-222020-2(9),* HarperTeen) HarperCollins Pubs.
Siegal, Ida. Big News! (Emma Is on the Air #1) Peña, Karla, illus. 2015. (Emma Is on the Air Ser.: 1). (ENG.). 128p. (J). (gr. 2-5). pap. 5.99 *(978-0-545-68692-1(X),* Scholastic Paperbacks) Scholastic, Inc.
Stilton, Thea. A Fashionable Mystery (Thea Stilton Mouseford Academy #8) Stilton, Thea, illus. 2019. (Thea Stilton Mouseford Academy Ser.: 8). (ENG., Illus.). 128p. (J). (gr. 2-5). pap. 7.99 *(978-0-545-87096-2(8),* Scholastic Paperbacks) Scholastic, Inc.
Stork, Francisco X. Disappeared. 2017. (ENG.). 336p. (YA). (gr. 7-7). 17.99 *(978-0-545-94447-2(3),* Scholastic Pr.) Scholastic, Inc.
Strohm, Stephanie Kate. The Date to Save. 2017. (ENG.). 288p. (YA). (gr. 7-7). 17.99 *(978-1-338-14906-7(7))* Scholastic, Inc.
Swallow, Pamela C. Groundhog Gets a Say. Bunkus, Denise, illus. 2007. (ENG.). 40p. (J). (gr. k-3). pap. 8.99 *(978-0-14-240896-4(4),* Puffin Books) Penguin Young Readers Group.
Villanueva, Gail D. My Fate According to the Butterfly. 2019. (ENG.). 240p. (J). (gr. 3-7). 17.99 *(978-1-338-31050-4(X),* Scholastic Pr.) Scholastic, Inc.
Wallace, Rich. Curveball #9, No. 9. 2008. (Winning Season Ser.: 9). 128p. (J). (gr. 3-7). 5.99 *(978-0-14-241092-9(6),* Puffin Books) Penguin Young Readers Group.
Wise, Rachel. Breaking News. 2013. (Dear Know-It-All Ser.: 10). (ENG., Illus.). 160p. (J). (gr. 3-7). 15.99 *(978-1-4424-8965-3(0));* pap. 7.99 *(978-1-4424-8964-6(2))* Simon Spotlight. (Simon Spotlight).
—Cast Your Ballot! 2013. (Dear Know-It-All Ser.: 9). (ENG., Illus.). 160p. (J). (gr. 3-7). 15.99 *(978-1-4424-8793-2(3));* pap. 5.99 *(978-1-4424-8792-5(5))* Simon Spotlight. (Simon Spotlight).

REPRODUCTION

see also Cells; Embryology; Pregnancy; Sex

Ballard, Carol. Understanding Reproduction. (Understanding the Human Body Ser.). (Illus.). 2010. 46p. (J). 70.50 *(978-1-4358-9699-4(8))* 2010. (ENG., 48p. (YA). (gr. 7-7). lib. bdg. 34.47 *(978-1-4358-9682-6(3),* b3d55e8f-a622-4719-9c00-d74becd8d25c) 2009. (ENG., 48p. (YA). (gr. 7-7). pap. 12.75 *(978-1-4358-9688-8(2),* 434f9eb2-e558-4604-80ff-eca602b5af58) Rosen Publishing Group, Inc., The. (Rosen Reference).
Brynie, Faith Hickman. 101 Questions about Reproduction: Or How 1 + 1 = 3 or 4 or More. Holm, Sharon, illus. 2005. (101 Questions... Ser.). (ENG.). 176p. (gr. 7-12). 30.60 *(978-0-7613-2311-2(2))* Lerner Publishing Group.
Doney, Malcolm & Doney, Meryl. Who Made Me? Butterworth, Nick & Inkpen, Mick, illus. 3rd ed. 2014. (ENG.). 32p. (J). (gr. -1). 7.99 *(978-1-78128-138-3(6),* 3082ea49-a87f-4387-992f-0f1cec66de4c, Candle Bks.) Lion Hudson PLC GBR. Dist: Baker & Taylor Publisher Services (BTPS).
The Endocrine System, the Reproductive System, Human Development. 2006. (World Book's Human Body Works). (Illus.). 48p. (J). *(978-0-7166-4431-6(2))* World Bk., Inc.
Harris, Robie H. It's So Amazing! A Book about Eggs, Sperm, Birth, Babies, & Families. Emberley, Michael, illus. 2014. (Family Library). (ENG.). 88p. (J). (gr. 2-5). 22.99 *(978-0-7636-6873-0(7))* Candlewick Pr.
—What's in There? All about Before You Were Born. Bernard Westcott, Nadine, illus. 2013. (Let's Talk about You & Me Ser.). (ENG.). 40p. (J). (-k). 17.99 *(978-0-7636-3630-2(4))* Candlewick Pr.
Heller, Ruth. Chickens Aren't the Only Ones. l.t. ed. (FRE., Illus.). (J). ring bd. 29.95 *(978-0-590-73732-6(5))* Scholastic, Inc.
Holt, Rinehart and Winston Staff. Holt Science & Technology Chapter 26: Life Science: Reproduction & Development. 5th ed. 2004. (Illus.). pap. 12.86 *(978-0-03-030251-0(X))* Holt McDougal.
Jones, Phill. Reproduction & Cloning. 2nd rev. ed. 2012. (ENG.). 136p. (gr. 6-12). 35.00 *(978-1-61753-025-8(5),* P207534, Facts On File) Infobase Holdings, Inc.
Kim, Melissa L. Learning about the Endocrine & Reproductive Systems, 1 vol. 2013. (Learning about the Human Body Systems Ser.). (ENG.). 48p. (gr. 5-6). pap. 11.53 *(978-1-4644-0237-1(X),* ed35bb86-3ab1-474e-b88a-9bdfdd4472fa) Enslow Publishing, LLC.
Klosterman, Lorrie. Reproductive System, 1 vol. 2010. (Amazing Human Body Ser.). (ENG.). 80p. (gr. 6-6). 36.93 *(978-0-7614-4041-3(0),* a4bc4e81-c950-4d9a-afe5-8b063bdb06a4) Cavendish Square Publishing LLC.
Loper, Ami M. The Miracle of Life. Loper, Carol J., illus. 2007. (J). *(978-0-9678798-1-9(7))* Biblical Standards Pubns.
Lowery, Zoe & Bringle, Jennifer. Reproductive Health & Women's Rights, 1 vol. 2017. (Women in the World Ser.). (ENG., Illus.). 112p. (J). (gr. 6-6). 38.80 *(978-1-5081-7445-5(8),* 425946ed-f968-456b-877f-12a7c92c8e53, Rosen Young Adult) Rosen Publishing Group, Inc., The.
Milbourne, Anna. Where Do Baby Animals Come From? 2012. (Picture Bks). 24p. (J). bds. 10.99 *(978-0-7945-3284-0(5),* Usborne) EDC Publishing.
Morley, Margaret Warner. A Song of Life 1922. Forsyth, Robert, illus. 2004. reprint ed. pap. 21.95 *(978-1-4179-7842-7(2))* Kessinger Publishing, LLC.
Saltz, Gail. Amazing You! Getting Smart about Your Private Parts. Cravath, Lynne Avril, illus. 2008. 32p. (J). (gr. -1-2). pap. 8.99 *(978-0-14-241058-5(6),* Puffin Books) Penguin Young Readers Group.
Wanjie, Anne, ed. The Basics of Reproduction, 1 vol. 2013. (Core Concepts Ser.). (ENG., Illus.). 96p. (YA). (gr. 7-7). lib. bdg. 39.77 *(978-1-4777-0549-0(X),* 76329eb5-0758-48f8-850c-c40817ed31f9, Rosen Classroom) Rosen Publishing Group, Inc., The.
Williams, Kara. Fertility Technology: The Baby Debate. 2009. (Focus on Science & Society Ser.). 64p. (gr. 5-6). 58.50 *(978-1-61512-622-4(8))* Rosen Publishing Group, Inc., The.

REPTILES

see also Crocodiles; Lizards; Snakes; Turtles

ABDO Publishing Company Staff & Hansen, Grace. Reptiles, 6 vols. 2014. (Reptiles (Abdo Kids) Ser.: 6). (ENG.). 24p. (J). (gr. -1-2). lib. bdg. 196.74 *(978-1-62970-056-4(8),* 1609, Abdo Kids) ABDO Publishing Co.
Alderton, David. Snakes & Reptiles Around the World. 2014. (Animals Around the World Ser.). (ENG., Illus.). 32p. (J). (gr. 2-5). 31.35 *(978-1-62588-197-7(5),* 19263, Smart Apple Media) Black Rabbit Bks.
Allan, John. Reptiles & Amphibians. 2019. (Amazing Life Cycles Ser.). (ENG., Illus.). 32p. (J). (gr. 1-3). lib. bdg. 29.32 *(978-1-912108-03-9(8),* 973caa4b-71e4-4756-964e-1178c0747870, Hungry Tomato (r)) Lerner Publishing Group.
Allen, Sarah & Sossella, David. 100 Pterosaurs to Fold & Fly. 2018. (Tear-Off Papercraft Pads Ser.). (ENG.). 100p. 7.99 *(978-0-7945-4232-0(8),* Usborne) EDC Publishing.
Allison, Pamela S. Emerald's Journal: A summer with Hatchlings. Cepeda, Joseph C., photos by. 2007. (Illus.). 24p. (J). lib. bdg. 16.95 *(978-0-9793474-1-2(6))* Sand Sage Pr.
Amazing Reptiles, 4 vols. 2014. (Amazing Reptiles Ser.: 8). (ENG.). 48p. (J). (gr. 4-8). lib. bdg. 142.56 *(978-1-62403-367-4(9),* 1179) ABDO Publishing Co.
Amphibians & Reptiles. 2005. (World of Animals Ser.: Vols. 41-50). (J). 499.00 *(978-0-7172-5916-8(1))* Scholastic Library Publishing.
Arnold, Tedd, illus. Fly Guy Presents: Snakes. 2016. (J). *(978-1-5182-0352-7(3))* Scholastic, Inc.
Barraclough, Susan. Snakes & Reptiles: The Scariest Cold-Blooded Creatures on Earth. 2008. (Illus.). 192p. (J). *(978-1-4351-0774-8(8))* Barnes & Noble, Inc.
Baxter, Bethany. Caimans, Gharials, Alligators, & Crocodiles, 1 vol. 2013. (Awesome Armored Animals Ser.). (ENG.). 24p. (J). (gr. 2-3). 26.27 *(978-1-4777-0798-2(0),* 98f12649-55c2-425a-bf59-cf2508b74316); pap. 9.25 *(978-1-4777-0968-9(1),* db41c8e9-a7f1-475f-810d-317f8d8d5792) Rosen Publishing Group, Inc., The. (PowerKids Pr.).
Believe It Or Not, Ripley's, compiled by. Ripley Twists: Snakes & Reptiles. 2015. (Twist Ser.: 14). (ENG., Illus.). 48p. (J). 12.95 *(978-1-60991-141-6(5))* Ripley Entertainment, Inc.
Believe It Or Not!, Ripleys, compiled by. Ripley Twists PB: Snakes & Reptiles. 2018. (Twist Ser.: 14). (ENG.). 48p. (J). pap. 7.99 *(978-1-60991-233-8(0))* Ripley Entertainment, Inc.
Bell, Samantha S. 12 Reptiles Back from the Brink. 2015. (Back from the Brink Ser.). (ENG., Illus.). 32p. (J). (gr. 3-6). 32.80 *(978-1-63235-005-3(X),* 11532, 12-Story Library) Bookstaves, LLC.
Berger, Melvin & Berger, Gilda. Reptiles (Scholastic True or False) 2008. (Scholastic True or False Ser.: 3). (ENG.). 48p. (J). (gr. 2-5). pap. 4.99 *(978-0-545-00393-3(8),* Scholastic Reference) Scholastic, Inc.
Betances, Roberto. Lizard Blood, 1 vol. 2014. (Nature's Grossest Ser.). (ENG., Illus.). 24p. (J). (gr. 1-2). 24.27 *(978-1-4824-1843-9(6),* 9d029716-a939-4c45-aea8-c1e743484d54) Stevens, Gareth Publishing LLLP.
Boothroyd, Jennifer. Scales. 2011. (First Step Nonfiction — Body Coverings Ser.). (gr. k-2). (ENG., Illus.). 24p. (J). pap. 6.99 *(978-0-7613-7829-7(4),* be2e6528-847d-40c2-ba80-aea4778b4c7a); pap. 33.92 *(978-0-7613-8609-4(2))* Lerner Publishing Group.
Bredeson, Carmen. Flying Geckos & Other Weird Reptiles, 1 vol. 2009. (I Like Weird Animals! Ser.). (ENG., Illus.). 24p. (gr. k-2). lib. bdg. 25.27 *(978-0-7660-3126-5(8),* 751d6852-ae8f-4001-a55f-536d36cf6ad7, Enslow Elementary) Enslow Publishing, LLC.
Brett, Flora. A Reptile's View of the World. 2015. (Pet Perspectives Ser.). (ENG., Illus.). 24p. (J). (gr. 1-3). lib. bdg. 27.99 *(978-1-4914-5051-2(7),* 128769, Capstone Pr.) Capstone.
Brookes, Olivia. The Rise of the Reptiles, 1 vol. 2012. (Dinosaur Files Ser.). (ENG.). 32p. (J). (gr. 3-4). pap. 11.00 *(978-1-61533-526-8(9),* 22d9e276-a08f-405c-90ff-1dc877376881); lib. bdg. 29.93 *(978-1-61533-519-0(6),* 6bb7a1b1-9d5d-44aa-a23d-98881c69fb12) Rosen Publishing Group, Inc., The. (Windmill Bks.).
Brown Bear Books. Reptiles & Amphibians. 2011. (Endangered Animals Ser.). (ENG.). 64p. (J). (gr. 8-11). lib. bdg. 39.95 *(978-1-936333-36-3(8),* 16486) Brown Bear Bks.
Buckingham, Suzanne. Meet the Bearded Dragon. (Scales & Tails Ser.). 24p. (gr. 2-3). 2009. 42.50 *(978-1-60852-980-3(0))* 2008. (ENG., Illus.). (J). lib. bdg. 26.27 *(978-1-4042-4500-6(6),* e6245595-d837-46d2-aafc-85ca1a6f1d30) Rosen Publishing Group, Inc., The. (PowerKids Pr.).

—Meet the Iguana. 2009. (Scales & Tails Ser.). 24p. (gr. 2-3). 42.50 *(978-1-60852-983-4(5)*, PowerKids Pr.) Rosen Publishing Group, Inc., The.

Bulletpoints Reptiles & Amphibians. 2005. (Illus.). (J). per. 4.99 *(978-1-933581-05-7(0))* Byeway Bks.

Burnstead, Pat & Worsley, Norman H. Canadian Skin & Scales. 2003. (Illus.). 168p. (YA). (gr. 5-6). pap. *(978-0-9689278-1-6(5))* Simply Wild Pubns., Inc.

Caimans, Gharials, Alligators, & Crocodiles. 2013. (Awesome Armored Animals Ser.). 24p. (J). (gr. k-5). pap. 49.50 *(978-1-4777-0969-6(X)*, PowerKids Pr.) Rosen Publishing Group, Inc., The.

Campbell, Jonathan A. & Lamar, William W. The Venomous Reptiles of the Western Hemisphere, 2 vols. 2004. (ENG., Illus.). 528p. (gr. 17). 184.95 *(978-0-8014-4141-7(2)*, 978-0-8014-4141-7, Comstock Publishing Assocs.) Cornell Univ. Pr.

Caputo, Christine A. Reptiles & Amphibians. 2012. (Illus.). 32p. (J). *(978-0-545-46701-8(2))* Scholastic, Inc.

Cavell-Clarke, Steffi. Reptiles, 1 vol. 2016. (Animal Classification Ser.). (ENG.). 32p. (J). (gr. 3-4). pap. 11.50 *(978-1-5345-2021-9(X)*, 5bb59b18-d365-408d-90ee-b7d98b69b32c); lib. bdg. 28.88 *(978-1-5345-2023-3(6)*, 8a2f0210-1c3c-4fed-8ac0-28bbec2db3cd) Greenhaven Publishing LLC. (KidHaven Publishing).

Clarke, Catriona. Reptiles: Internet-Referenced. 2009. (Beginner's Nature Ser.). 32p. (J). 4.99 *(978-0-7945-2490-6(7)*, Usborne) EDC Publishing.

Cleary, Brian P. Tortoise, Tree Snake, Gator, & Sea Snake: What Is a Reptile? Goneau, Martin, illus. 2012. (Animal Groups Are CATegorical (tm) Ser.). (ENG.). 32p. (J). (gr. k-3). lib. bdg. 26.65 *(978-0-7613-6210-4(X)*, 1ffff0ee-da5d-4b1b-a8fe-78c34f6e59c7, Millbrook Pr.) Lerner Publishing Group.

Cleave, Andrew. Snakes & Reptiles - Pb: A Portrait of the Animal World. 2013. (Portrait of the Animal World Ser.). (Illus.). 80p. pap. 9.95 *(978-1-59764-318-4(1))* New Line Bks.

Costain, Meredith. Reptiles: Cold-Blooded Creatures, 1 vol. 2014. (Discovery Education: Animals Ser.). (ENG.). 32p. (J). (gr. 4-5). 27.93 *(978-1-4777-6936-2(6)*, 8fa8e201-df24-4486-a3d0-5b9f3deacab9); pap. 11.00 *(978-1-4777-6937-9(4)*, bbe70963-1313-4990-acf0-3d5fe169cf1b) Rosen Publishing Group, Inc., The. (PowerKids Pr.).

Crump, Marty. Amphibians & Reptiles: An Introduction to Their Natural History & Conservation, 1 vol. 2011. (ENG., Illus.). 272p. (J). 29.95 *(978-1-935778-20-2(X))* McDonald & Woodward Publishing Co., The.

Dennard, Deborah. Reptiles: Explore the Fascinating Worlds of Alligators & Crocodiles, Lizards, Snakes, Turtles. Dewey, Jennifer Owings, tr. Dewey, Jennifer Owings, illus. 2004. (Our Wild World Ser.). (ENG.). 192p. (J). (gr. 3-6). 16.95 *(978-1-55971-880-6(3))* Cooper Square Publishing Llc.

DK. DKfindout! Reptiles & Amphibians. 2017. (DK Findout! Ser.). (ENG., Illus.). 64p. (J). (gr. 1-4). pap. 10.99 *(978-1-4654-6310-4(0)*, DK Children) Dorling Kindersley Publishing, Inc.

—Ultimate Sticker Book: Reptile: More Than 60 Reusable Full-Color Stickers. 2005. (Ultimate Sticker Book Ser.). (ENG., Illus.). 16p. (J). (gr. k-3). pap. 6.99 *(978-0-7566-0977-1(1)*, DK Children) Dorling Kindersley Publishing, Inc.

DK & Woodward, John. Everything You Need to Know about Snakes. 2013. (Everything You Need to Know Ser.). (ENG.). 80p. (J). (gr. 2-5). 15.99 *(978-1-4654-0246-2(2)*, DK Children) Dorling Kindersley Publishing, Inc.

Dowling, Lucy. Why Why Why... Do Lizards Stick to Walls? 2010. (Why Why Why Ser.). 32p. (J). (gr. 1-3). lib. bdg. 18.95 *(978-1-4222-1582-1(2))* Mason Crest.

Duke, Shirley. Reptiles & Amphibians Explained, 1 vol. 2016. (Distinctions in Nature Ser.). (ENG.). 32p. (gr. 3-3). 30.21 *(978-1-5026-1746-0(3)*, 5b955962-bd65-4a7c-827d-85571e3578c0) Cavendish Square Publishing LLC.

Edwards, Sue Bradford. The Evolution of Reptiles. 2018. (Animal Evolution Ser.). (ENG., Illus.). 112p. (J). (gr. 6-12). lib. bdg. 41.36 *(978-1-5321-1667-4(5)*, 30586, Essential Library) ABDO Publishing Co.

Encyclopaedia Britannica, Inc. Staff, compiled by. Britannica Illustrated Science Library: Reptiles & Dinosaurs, 16 vols. 2008. (Illus.). (J). 29.95 *(978-1-59339-395-3(4))* Encyclopaedia Britannica, Inc.

—My First Britannica: Birds, Insects, Reptiles, & Aquatic Life. 2008. (gr. 7-12). *(978-1-59339-411-0(X))* Encyclopaedia Britannica, Inc.

Encyclopedia Britannica Staff, creator. Reptiles & Dinosaurs. 2011. (Britannica Illustrated Science Library Ser.). (J). 37.44 *(978-1-61535-464-1(6))* Encyclopaedia Britannica, Inc.

Fact Atlas: Reptiles. 2009. (FACT ATLAS Ser.). 72p. (J). 14.95 *(978-0-8416-1096-5(7))* Hammond World Atlas Corp.

Fisher, Diana & Shelly, Jeff, illus. All about Dinosaurs & Reptiles. 2010. (All about Drawing Ser.). 80p. (J). 34.25 *(978-1-936309-07-8(6))* Quarto Publishing Group USA.

Fletcher, Patricia. Why Do Thorny Devils Have Two Heads? And Other Curious Reptile Adaptations, 1 vol. 2017. (Odd Adaptations Ser.). (ENG.). 32p. (J). (gr. 3-4). pap. 11.50 *(978-1-5382-0405-4(3)*, f821a47e-73d9-4591-88dc-44f2d41b787c) Stevens, Gareth Publishing LLLP.

Florence, Debbi Michiko. Betty the Bearded Dragon. Demmer, Melanie, illus. 2019. (My Furry Foster Family Ser.). (ENG.). 72p. (J). (gr. k-2). pap. 7.95 *(978-1-5158-4559-1(1)*, 141147); lib. bdg. 23.99 *(978-1-5158-4476-1(5)*, 140576) Capstone. (Picture Window Bks.).

Gingold, Janet. My Adventure with Reptiles: Advanced My Adventure. 2009. (ENG.). 72p. (J). pap. 9.99 *(978-1-59092-464-8(9))* Blue Forge Pr.

Gish, Melissa. Alligators. 2017. (X-Books: Predators Ser.). (ENG., Illus.). 32p. (J). (gr. 3-6). *(978-1-60818-817-8(5)*, 20384, Creative Education) Creative Co., The.

Graham Gaines, Ann. Kids Top 10 Pet Reptiles & Amphibians, 1 vol. 2014. (American Humane Association Top 10 Pets for Kids Ser.). (ENG.). 48p. (gr. 3-4). 26.93 *(978-0-7660-6645-8(2)*, 1652e1e3-e698-4316-9202-08f032713417); pap. 11.53 *(978-0-7660-6646-5(0)*, c3e68103-d434-40c6-bfbd-f6d39f1b52d4, Enslow Elementary) Enslow Publishing, LLC.

—Top 10 Reptiles & Amphibians for Kids, 1 vol. 2008. (Top Pets for Kids with American Humane Ser.). (ENG., Illus.). 48p. (gr. 3-3). lib. bdg. 27.93 *(978-0-7660-3074-9(1)*, ea5ca672-f92a-4d14-8b13-a1314a8ffd45) Enslow Publishing, LLC.

Green, Jen, et al. Exploring the World of Reptiles & Amphibians, 6 vols. Friel, John P., ed. 2009. (ENG., Illus.). 480p. (gr. 5-8). 210.00 *(978-1-60413-256-4(6)*, P160532, Facts On File) Infobase Holdings, Inc.

Green, Ken. Reptiles - Weird Wildlife, 6 bks., Set. 2003. (Illus.). pap. 48.30 *(978-1-4109-0299-3(4))* Harcourt Schl. Pubs.

Greve, Tom. Reptiles. 2014. 24p. pap. 8.00 *(978-1-61003-376-3(0))* Center for the Collaborative Classroom.

Hall, Julie. Reptiles & Amphibians: Grades 2 & 3. (Illus.). (J). pap., wbk. ed. 4.99 *(978-0-88743-964-3(0))* School Zone Publishing Co.

Hall, Katharine. Amphibians & Reptiles: A Compare & Contrast Book, 1 vol. 2015. (ENG., Illus.). 32p. (J). (gr. 2-3). pap. 11.95 *(978-1-62855-560-8(2)*, cf3200b5-2826-4ba7-a332-5beee66edc6b) Arbordale Publishing.

—Amphibians & Reptiles (Spanish) A Compare & Contrast Book, 1 vol. 2015. Tr. of Amphibians & Reptiles: a Compare & Contrast Book. (SPA., Illus.). 32p. (J). (gr. 2-3). pap. 11.95 *(978-1-62855-569-1(6)*, 134090aa-a19b-4821-acea-fb8d10754bab) Arbordale Publishing.

Hansen, Grace. Komodo Dragons, 1 vol. 2014. (Reptiles (Abdo Kids) Ser.). (ENG., Illus.). 24p. (J). (gr. -1-2). lib. bdg. 32.79 *(978-1-62970-060-1(6)*, 1613, Abdo Kids) ABDO Publishing Co.

Harrington, Jane. Extreme Pets. 2007. (ENG., Illus.). 164p. (J). (gr. 2-5). pap., instr.'s hndbk. ed. 12.99 *(978-0-439-82948-9(8))* Scholastic, Inc.

Harris, Terrell. Slimy, Scaly, Deadly Reptiles & Amphibians, 12 vols., Set. Incl. Amphibians. lib. bdg. 28.67 *(978-1-4339-3441-4(8)*, 81cdd512-15b8-4cbe-8244-3e4558e64533); Crocodiles & Alligators. lib. bdg. 28.67 *(978-1-4339-3435-3(3)*, 9409b779-072e-4923-9f87-2a3c7a15fd8e); Lizards. lib. bdg. 28.67 *(978-1-4339-3426-1(4)*, 58428da1-1f67-4761-9ea9-3544e596a54b); Nonvenomous Snakes. lib. bdg. 28.67 *(978-1-4339-3432-2(9)*, a288c10b-fe8a-4bb5-b663-5fcdaa5d54bc); Turtles. lib. bdg. 28.67 *(978-1-4339-3438-4(8)*, 86b29150-444c-41c0-a127-30bd61400abb); Venomous Snakes. lib. bdg. 28.67 *(978-1-4339-3429-2(9)*, c6407d40-cd4e-46d5-bb30-31bd0cfdd8a3); (Illus.). (J). (gr. 3-4). (Slimy, Scaly, Deadly Reptiles & Amphibians Ser.). (ENG.). 32p. 2010. Set lib. bdg. 172.02 *(978-1-4339-3584-8(8)*, fe57e7c6-2da6-45cd-94ae-f279cf35b82f, Gareth Stevens Learning Library) Stevens, Gareth Publishing LLLP.

Harrison, Paul. Reptiles. (Up Close Ser.). 24p. (gr. 3-3). 2009. 47.90 *(978-1-60854-700-5(0))* 2006. (ENG., Illus.). (J). lib. bdg. 28.93 *(978-1-4042-3763-6(1)*, f5920a4a-6813-4c56-bfeb-8dfa669b9190) Rosen Publishing Group, Inc., The. (PowerKids Pr.).

Harvey, Bev. Reptiles. (Eyes on Nature Ser.). 32p. (J). (gr. 1). pap. *(978-1-882210-54-1(9))* Action Publishing, Inc.

Hibbert, Clare. Sea Creatures & Flying Reptiles, 1 vol. 2018. (Dino Explorers Ser.). (ENG.). 32p. (gr. 3-3). lib. bdg. 26.93 *(978-0-7660-9992-0(X)*, dd80b841-9000-4fc7-8455-7e9c3244d766) Enslow Publishing, LLC.

Himmelman, John. Basic Illustrated Guide to Frogs, Snakes, Bugs, & Slugs. 2013. (Basic Illustrated Ser.). (ENG., Illus.). 104p. (J). (gr. k-5). pap. 12.95 *(978-0-7627-8259-8(5)*, Falcon Guides) Globe Pequot Pr., The.

Hirsch, Rebecca E. Boa Constrictors: Prey-Crushing Reptiles. 2015. (Comparing Animal Traits Ser.). (ENG., Illus.). 32p. (J). (gr. 2-4). 26.65 *(978-1-4677-7981-4(4)*, 2c058dff-2004-4487-a9ff-e0c104ae7781, Lerner Pubns.) Lerner Publishing Group.

—Tuataras: Dinosaur-Era Reptiles. 2015. (Comparing Animal Traits Ser.). (ENG., Illus.). 32p. (J). (gr. 2-4). 26.65 *(978-1-4677-7979-1(2)*, 5e05fb50-da28-4bd7-ab5a-cef3d1a2ca25, Lerner Pubns.) Lerner Publishing Group.

Hirschmann, Kris. Deadliest Reptiles. 2016. (ENG.). 80p. (J). (gr. 5-12). lib. bdg. *(978-1-68282-052-0(1))* ReferencePoint Pr., Inc.

Hoena, Blake. National Geographic Kids Everything Reptiles: Snap up All the Photos, Facts, & Fun. 2016. (National Geographic Kids Everything Ser.). (Illus.). 64p. (J). (gr. 3-7). pap. 12.99 *(978-1-4263-2526-7(6)*, National Geographic Kids) Disney Publishing Worldwide.

Hofmann, Kate. Ranger Rick's Amazing Animals: Reptiles. 2016. (Ranger Rick: Amazing Animals Ser.). (Illus.). 40p. (J). (gr. 2-7). pap. 7.95 *(978-1-63076-202-5(4))* Muddy Boots Pr.

Holt, Rinehart and Winston Staff. Holt Science & Technology Chapter 16: Life Science: Fishes, Amphibians, & Reptiles. 5th ed. 2004. (Illus.). pap. 12.86 *(978-0-03-030221-3(8))* Holt McDougal.

Holub, Joan. Why Do Snakes Hiss? And Other Questions about Snakes, Lizards, & Turtles. DiVito, Anna, illus. 2004. (Penguin Young Readers, Level 3 Ser.). 48p. (J). (gr. 1-3). mass mkt. 4.99 *(978-0-14-240105-7(6)*, Penguin Young Readers) Penguin Young Readers Group.

Housel, Debra J. Slithering Reptiles & Amphibians, 1 vol. 2nd rev. ed. 2011. (TIME for KIDS(r): Informational Text Ser.). (ENG.). 28p. (gr. 3-4). pap. 11.99 *(978-1-4333-3659-1(6))* Teacher Created Materials, Inc.

Howell, Catherine H. National Geographic Kids: Reptiles & Amphibians: Find Adventure! Go Outside! Have Fun! Be a Backyard Ranger & Amphibian Adventurer! 2016. (Illus.). 160p. (J). (gr. 3-7). pap. 12.99 *(978-1-4263-2544-1(4)*, National Geographic Kids) Disney Publishing Worldwide.

—Ultimate Explorer Field Guide: Reptiles & Amphibians: Find Adventure! Go Outside! Have Fun! Be a Backyard Ranger & Amphibian Adventurer! 2016. (ENG., Illus.). 160p. (J). (gr. 3-7). lib. bdg. 22.90 *(978-1-4263-2545-8(2)*, National Geographic Kids) Disney Publishing Worldwide.

Hudak, Heather C. Reptiles & Amphibians. (Animal Facts Ser.). (Illus.). 24p. (J). 2005. (gr. 2-3). per. 8.95 *(978-1-59036-246-4(2))* 2004. lib. bdg. 24.45 *(978-1-59036-204-4(7))* Weigl Pubs., Inc.

Hughes, Jon. Pterosaur! Purple Band. 2016. (Cambridge Reading Adventures Ser.). (ENG., Illus.). 24p. pap. 8.80 *(978-1-107-55108-4(0))* Cambridge Univ. Pr.

Hughes, Sarah Anne. Peterson Field Guide Coloring Books: Reptiles & Amphibians. 2nd ed. 2013. (Peterson Field Guide Color-In Bks.). (ENG., Illus.). 64p. 10.99 *(978-0-544-02695-7(0)*, 1529290, Mariner Bks.) HarperCollins Pubs.

Hunt, Santana. Name That Reptile!, 1 vol. 2016. (Guess That Animal! Ser.). (ENG., Illus.). 24p. (J). (gr. 1-2). lib. bdg. 24.27 *(978-1-4824-4747-7(9)*, 6f0d83c2-d42b-4102-bccb-4b70c2bd43fc) Stevens, Gareth Publishing LLLP.

Hutchinson, Mark. Reptiles. 2011. (Insiders Ser.). (ENG.). 64p. (J). (gr. 3-7). 17.99 *(978-1-4424-3276-5(4)*, Simon & Schuster Bks. For Young Readers) Simon & Schuster Bks. For Young Readers.

Iguanas & Reptiles. 2007. (Illus.). (J). cd-rom 9.99 *(978-0-9795190-5-5(5))* Color & Learn.

Jackson, Tom. Reptiles, 1 vol. 2016. (Animal Mechanicals Ser.). (ENG.). 32p. (gr. 3-3). pap. 11.00 *(978-1-4994-2250-4(4)*, 270ba755-3c6b-40eb-bf71-c9c660f54354, PowerKids Pr.) Rosen Publishing Group, Inc., The.

—World's Biggest Reptiles. Jevtic, Vladimir, illus. 2018. (Extreme Reptiles Ser.). (ENG.). 32p. (J). (gr. 3-6). lib. bdg. 27.99 *(978-1-5415-0091-4(1)*, dd7499dd-e05c-4ecd-bc30-c2185a29e210, Hungry Tomato (r)) Lerner Publishing Group.

—World's Deadliest Reptiles. Jevtic, Vladimir, illus. 2018. (Extreme Reptiles Ser.). (ENG.). 32p. (J). (gr. 3-6). lib. bdg. 27.99 *(978-1-5415-0090-7(3)*, 48c55d9a-dd79-48d7-821e-59b76685d300, Hungry Tomato (r)) Lerner Publishing Group.

—World's Sneakiest Reptiles. Jevtic, Vladimir, illus. 2018. (Extreme Reptiles Ser.). (ENG.). 32p. (J). (gr. 3-6). lib. bdg. 27.99 *(978-1-5415-0092-1(X)*, 3b57661c-4255-4085-b9f6-55443bd77ef0, Hungry Tomato (r)) Lerner Publishing Group.

Jacobs, Pat. Why Do Reptiles Have Scales? And Other Questions about Evolution & Classification, 1 vol. 2016. (Wildlife Wonders Ser.). (ENG.). 32p. (J). (gr. 3-3). pap. 11.00 *(978-1-4994-3209-1(7)*, 301d5009-7869-4ecb-893e-07f1c1f6f2db, PowerKids Pr.) Rosen Publishing Group, Inc., The.

Jacobson, Bray. Reptile Life Cycles. 2017. (Look at Life Cycles Ser.). 32p. (J). (gr. 2-2). 63.00 *(978-1-5382-1052-9(5))* Stevens, Gareth Publishing LLLP.

Jango-Cohen, Judith. Desert Iguanas. (Pull Ahead Bks.). (Illus.). 32p. (J). (gr. k-3). 2005. lib. bdg. 22.60 *(978-0-8225-3635-2(8))* 2003. pap. 5.95 *(978-0-8225-3642-0(0))* Lerner Publishing Group.

Jankowski, Matt. Attack of the Burmese Pythons, 1 vol. 2016. (Animal Invaders: Destroying Native Habitats Ser.). (ENG., Illus.). 24p. (J). (gr. 2-3). pap. 9.15 *(978-1-4824-5659-2(1)*, 1cc01fa5-3575-469f-96e8-7c2ff64a4d1b) Stevens, Gareth Publishing LLLP.

Jaycox, Jaclyn. Reptiles: A 4D Book. 2018. (Little Zoologist Ser.). (ENG., Illus.). 32p. (J). (gr. -1-2). lib. bdg. 30.65 *(978-1-5435-2647-9(0)*, 138107, Pebble) Capstone.

Johnson, Jinny. Pteranodon & Other Flying Reptiles. Rosewarne, Graham, illus. 2007. (Dinosaurs Alive! Ser.). 32p. (J). (gr. 4-7). lib. bdg. 28.50 *(978-1-59920-068-2(6))* Black Rabbit Bks.

Kalman, Bobbie. Baby Reptiles, 1 vol. 2008. (It's Fun to Learn about Baby Animals Ser.). (ENG., Illus.). 24p. (J). (gr. k-3). pap. *(978-0-7787-3973-9(2))* Crabtree Publishing Co.

—¿Qué Son los Reptiles? 2005. (Serie la Ciencia de los Seres Vivos Ser.). (SPA., Illus.). 32p. (J). (gr. 3-4). lib. bdg. *(978-0-7787-8762-4(1))* Crabtree Publishing Co.

—?Qué Son los Reptiles? 2005. (Ciencia de los Seres Vivos Ser.). (SPA., Illus.). 32p. (J). (gr. 3-4). pap. *(978-0-7787-8808-9(3))* Crabtree Publishing Co.

—Reptile Rap. 2010. (My World Ser.). (ENG.). 16p. (J). (gr. k-3). *(978-0-7787-9512-4(8))*; pap. *(978-0-7787-9537-7(3))* Crabtree Publishing Co.

—Les Reptiles. 2011. (FRE., Illus.). 32p. (J). pap. 9.95 *(978-2-89579-394-6(8))* Bayard Canada CAN. Dist: Crabtree Publishing Co.

Kaminski, Mary. Raising Reptiles: Divide Within 100, 1 vol. 2014. (Rosen Math Readers Ser.). (ENG., Illus.). 24p. (J). (gr. 3-3). pap. 8.25 *(978-1-4777-4949-4(7)*, 76bc4dc4-d52c-42a9-8d05-0add4610d3da, PowerKids Pr.) Rosen Publishing Group, Inc., The.

Kaspar, Anna. What's a Reptile?, 1 vol. 2012. (All about Animals Ser.). (ENG.). 24p. (J). (gr. 1-1). pap. 9.25 *(978-1-4488-6226-9(4)*, 673fc136-3078-49fa-9663-98836f423465); lib. bdg. 26.27 *(978-1-4488-6134-7(9)*, e19dad52-b302-4b7d-a450-ccc6f9bfeeb0) Rosen Publishing Group, Inc., The. (PowerKids Pr.).

—What's a Reptile? Qué Es un Reptil?, 1 vol. 2012. (All about Animals / Todo Sobre Los Animales Ser.). (SPA & ENG., Illus.). 24p. (J). (gr. 1-1). lib. bdg. 26.27 *(978-1-4488-6700-4(2)*, eae46282-fa55-45b1-867f-654cc9e20fed, PowerKids Pr.) Rosen Publishing Group, Inc., The.

Keats Curtis, Jennifer & F. Angeli, Nicole. La Dama de Las Siguanas, 1 vol. Jones, Veronica, illus. 2018. (SPA.). 32p. (J). (gr. 2-3). pap. 11.95 *(978-1-60718-311-2(0)*, 04869b23-1f5d-45bd-8f9c-3c4143d9220a) Arbordale Publishing.

—The Lizard Lady, 1 vol. Jones, Veronica, illus. 2018. (ENG.). 32p. (J). (gr. k-3). 17.95 *(978-1-60718-066-1(9)*, 9781607180661); pap. 9.95 *(978-1-60718-091-3(X)*, 9781607180913) Arbordale Publishing.

Kenney, Karen Latchana. Flying Dragons. (Weird & Unusual Animals Ser.). (ENG., Illus.). 24p. (J). (gr. 1-4). 2018. pap. 8.99 *(978-1-68152-187-9(3)*, 16099) 2017. 20.95 *(978-1-68151-156-6(8)*, 14699) Amicus.

Kessler, Colleen. A Project Guide to Reptiles & Birds. 2010. (Life Science Projects for Kids Ser.). (Illus.). 48p. (J). (gr. 4-8). lib. bdg. 29.95 *(978-1-58415-874-5(3))* Mitchell Lane Pubs.

Kingsley, Imogen. Bearded Dragons. 2019. (Lizards in the Wild Ser.). (ENG.). 24p. (J). (gr. 1-4). lib. bdg. *(978-1-68151-554-0(7)*, 14515) Amicus.

Kratt, Chris & Kratt, Martin. Wild Reptiles: Snakes, Crocodiles, Lizards, & Turtles (Wild Kratts) Random House, illus. 2015. (Step into Reading Ser.). 32p. (J). (gr. k-4). 5.99 *(978-0-553-50775-1(3)*, Random Hse. Bks. for Young Readers) Random Hse. Children's Bks.

Lee, Celeste & Herndon, Ryan, compiled by. Guinness World Records, Top 10. 2007. (Illus.). 29p. (J). pap. *(978-0-439-87417-5(3))* Scholastic, Inc.

Levine, Michelle. Reptiles. 2014. (Animal Kingdom Ser.). (ENG., Illus.). 32p. (J). (gr. 2-5). lib. bdg. 28.50 *(978-1-60753-476-1(2)*, 15945) Amicus.

Lewis, Clare. Why Do Snakes & Other Animals Have Scales? 2015. (Animal Body Coverings Ser.). (ENG., Illus.). 24p. (J). (gr. 1-3). pap. 6.99 *(978-1-4846-2540-8(4)*, 130025, Heinemann) Capstone.

Little & Large Sticker Activity - Reptiles & Amphibians. 2006. (J). 3.99 *(978-1-933581-35-4(2))* Byeway Bks.

Lowenstein Niven, Felicia. Learning to Care for Reptiles & Amphibians, 1 vol. 2010. (Beginning Pet Care with American Humane Ser.). (ENG.). 48p. (gr. 3-3). 27.93 *(978-0-7660-3194-4(2)*, 35b8272f-1772-4790-8fa3-b5d12cf8ecc0, Enslow Elementary) Enslow Publishing, LLC.

Loxton, Daniel. Plesiosaur Peril, 0 vols. Loxton, Daniel & Smith, Jim W. W., illus. 2014. (Tales of Prehistoric Life Ser.). (ENG.). 32p. (J). (gr. -1-2). 16.95 *(978-1-55453-633-7(2))* Kids Can Pr., Ltd. CAN. Dist: Hachette Bk. Group.

MacAulay, Kelley & Kalman, Bobbie. Reptiles de Todo Tipo. 2005. (Que Tipo de Animal Es? Ser.). (SPA., Illus.). 32p. (J). (gr. 3-7). pap. *(978-0-7787-8871-3(7))*; lib. bdg. *(978-0-7787-8835-5(0))* Crabtree Publishing Co.

—Reptiles of All Kinds. 2005. (What Kind of Animal Is It? Ser.). (ENG., Illus.). 32p. (J). lib. bdg. *(978-0-7787-2158-1(2))*; pap. *(978-0-7787-2216-8(3))* Crabtree Publishing Co.

Macgregor, Eloise. Sidewinder. 2015. (Desert Animals Searchin' for Shade Ser.). (ENG.). 24p. (J). (gr. -1-3). lib. bdg. 26.99 *(978-1-62724-534-0(0))* Bearport Publishing Co., Inc.

Martin, Isabel. Reptiles: A Question & Answer Book, 1 vol. 2014. (Animal Kingdom Questions & Answers Ser.). (ENG., Illus.). 24p. (J). (gr. -1-2). pap. 6.95 *(978-1-4914-0633-5(X)*, 125937, Capstone Pr.) Capstone.

Mathewson, Robert F. The How & Why Wonder Book of Reptiles & Amphibians. Sweet, Darrell & Allen, Douglas, illus. 2011. 48p. pap. 35.95 *(978-1-258-09940-4(3))* Literary Licensing, LLC.

Mattern, Joanne. Reptiles & Amphibians. 2009. (Reading Room Collection 2 Ser.). 24p. (gr. 3-4). 42.50 *(978-1-60851-986-6(4)*, PowerKids Pr.) Rosen Publishing Group, Inc., The.

—Reptiles y anfibios (Reptiles & Amphibians) 2009. (Reading Room Collection: Spanish Ser.). (SPA.). 24p. (gr. 3-4). 42.50 *(978-1-60854-179-9(7)*, Editorial Buenas Letras) Rosen Publishing Group, Inc., The.

Mattison, Christopher. Reptiles & Amphibians. 2007. (Facts at Your Fingertips Ser.). (Illus.). 64p. (YA). (gr. 7-12). lib. bdg. 35.65 *(978-1-933834-04-7(8))* Brown Bear Books.

McNab, Chris. Endangered Reptiles, 1 vol. 2005. (Nature's Monsters: Reptiles & Amphibians Ser.). (ENG., Illus.). 32p. (gr. 3-5). lib. bdg. 28.67 *(978-0-8368-6171-6(X)*, 460eba2f-7722-4a87-93e6-599ea64261bc, Gareth Stevens Learning Library) Stevens, Gareth Publishing LLLP.

Mertz, Leslie A., et al. Grzimek's Student Animal Life Resource, 2 vols. 2005. (Illus.). xxxix, 427p. (J). *(978-0-7876-9406-7(1))*; *(978-0-7876-9405-0(3))* Cengage Gale. (UXL).

Miller, Derek. Shells, Scales, & Skin, 1 vol. 2018. (Animal Structures Ser.). (ENG.). 24p. (gr. 1-1). 25.93 *(978-1-5026-4251-6(4)*, fe62fd7d-93f9-4029-bd0e-aa8b56ea43b0) Cavendish Square Publishing LLC.

Miller, Jake. The Bearded Dragon. 2009. (Lizard Library). 24p. (gr. 3-3). 42.50 *(978-1-60854-009-9(X)*, PowerKids Pr.) Rosen Publishing Group, Inc., The.

Miller, Mirella S. Sea Turtles Are Awesome. 2018. (Animals Are Awesome Ser.). (ENG., Illus.). 32p. (J). (gr. 3-6). 32.80 *(978-1-63235-437-2(3)*, 13815, 12-Story Library) Bookstaves, LLC.

Mitchell, Susan K. Biggest vs. Smallest Slimy, Scaly Creatures, 1 vol. 2010. (Biggest vs. Smallest Animals Ser.). (ENG., Illus.). 24p. (J). (gr. k-2). 25.27 *(978-0-7660-3579-9(4)*, 590d0b31-fc15-43e8-9759-5783ae81f371, Enslow Elementary) Enslow Publishing, LLC.

Murray, Julie. Reptiles. 2018. (Animal Classes Ser.). (ENG., Illus.). 24p. (J). (gr. k-4). lib. bdg. 31.36 *(978-1-5321-2300-9(0)*, 28367, Abdo Zoom-Dash) ABDO Publishing Co.

National Geographic. National Geographic Readers: Creepy Crawly Collection. 2012. (Readers Ser.). (Illus.). 128p. (J). (gr. -1-k). pap. 7.99 *(978-1-4263-1197-0(4)*, National Geographic Kids) Disney Publishing Worldwide.

National Geographic Kids. National Geographic Kids Reptiles & Amphibians: Sticker Activity Book. 2017. (NG Sticker Activity Bks.). 56p. (J). (gr. -1-k). pap. 6.99 *(978-1-4263-2777-3(3)*, National Geographic Kids) Disney Publishing Worldwide.

O'Donnell, Kerri. Komodo Dragons. 2009. (Ugly Animals Ser.). 24p. (gr. 2-3). 42.50 *(978-1-60854-600-8(4)*, PowerKids Pr.) Rosen Publishing Group, Inc., The.

O'Reilly, Wenda. GO FISH WILDLIFE REPTILES & AMPHIBIANS. 2007. n/ap. pap. 119.40 *(978-1-59960-018-5(8))* Birdcage Pr.

Osborne, Mary Pope & Boyce, Natalie Pope. Snakes & Other Reptiles: A Nonfiction Companion to Magic Tree House Merlin Mission #17: a Crazy Day with Cobras. Murdocca, Sal, illus. 2011. (Magic Tree House (R) Fact Tracker Ser.: 23). 128p. (J). (gr. 2-5). 6.99 *(978-0-375-86011-9(8)*, Random Hse. Bks. for Young Readers) Random Hse. Children's Bks.

Parker, Janice. Reptiles. 2007. (Life Science (Weigl Hardcover) Ser.). (Illus.). 32p. (J). (gr. 4-7). lib. bdg. 26.00 *(978-1-59036-711-7(1))*; per. 8.95 *(978-1-59036-712-4(X))* Weigl Pubs., Inc.

Parker, Steve. 50 Things You Should Know about Fierce Creatures. Marshall, Anne, ed. 2004. (50 Things You Should

Know Ser.). (Illus.). 112p. (J). 14.99 (978-1-84236-301-0(8)) Miles Kelly Publishing, Ltd. GBR. Dist: Independent Pubs. Group.

Parker, Steven. See-Through Reptiles. 2004. 32p. 15.95 (978-0-7624-2290-6(4)) Running Pr.

Phillips, Dee. Reptiles & Amphibians. 2006. (Blue Zoo Guides). (ENG., Illus.). 96p. (J). (gr. -1-2). 18.95 (978-1-58728-561-5(4)) Cooper Square Publishing Llc.

Priddy, Roger. Smart Kids: Reptiles & Amphibians. 2007. (Smart Kids Ser.). (ENG., Illus.). 32p. (J). (gr. -1-2). 10.99 (978-0-312-49921-1(3), 900044124) St. Martin's Pr.

—Smart Kids Reptiles & Amphibians: With More Than 30 Stickers. 2018. (Smart Kids Ser.). (ENG., Illus.). 24p. (J). pap. 5.99 (978-0-312-50603-2(1), 900178652) St. Martin's Pr.

Pterodactylse. 2011. (ENG., Illus.). 24p. (J). pap. 8.95 (978-1-77092-104-7(4)) Saunders Bk. Co. CAN. Dist: Creative Co., The.

Rabe, Tish. Miles & Miles of Reptiles: All about Reptiles. Ruiz, Aristides, illus. 2009. (Cat in the Hat's Learning Library). (ENG.). 48p. (J). (gr. -1-3). 9.99 (978-0-375-82884-3(2), Random Hse. Bks. for Young Readers) Random Hse. Children's Bks.

Rake, Matthew. Prehistoric Sea Beasts. Mendez, Simon, illus. 2017. (If Extinct Beasts Came to Life Ser.). (ENG.). 32p. (J). (gr. 3-6). 7.99 (978-1-5124-1158-4(2), cc477503-e896-49c1-a50c-de9b770a000b); E-Book 42.65 (978-1-5124-3617-4(8), 9781512436174); E-Book 42.65 (978-1-5124-0909-3(X)); E-Book 4.99 (978-1-5124-3618-1(6), 9781512436181) Lerner Publishing Group. (Hungry Tomato (r)).

Rector, Rebecca Kraft. Reptiles, 1 vol. 2018. (Investigate Biodiversity Ser.). (ENG.). 24p. (gr. 2-2). 25.60 (978-1-9785-0188-1(9), 5f5375b4-83b7-4bc9-a3e9-ddee6fbb93ce) Enslow Publishing, LLC.

Reptiles. Date not set. (Question & Answers of the Natural World Ser.). 32p. 4.98 (978-0-7525-4321-5(0)) Parragon, Inc.

Reptiles & Amphibians, 1 vol. 2014. (Animal Q & A Ser.). (ENG., Illus.). 24p. (J). (gr. 2-2). lib. bdg. 26.27 (978-1-4777-9194-3(9), a855a78e-bb6e-4dcc-81cf-1c6765e362e0, Windmill Bks.) Rosen Publishing Group, Inc., The.

Reptiles & Amphibians: Level P, 6 vols., Vol. 3. (Explorers Ser.). 32p. (gr. 3-6). 44.95 (978-0-7699-0614-0(1)) Shortland Pubns. (U. S. A.) Inc.

Los Reptiles Y Los Anfibios, 6 vols., Vol. 3. (Explorers. Exploradores Nonfiction Sets Ser.). (SPA.). (gr. 3-6). (978-0-7699-0650-8(8)) Shortland Pubns. (U. S. A.) Inc.

Richardson, Joy. Reptiles, 1 vol. 2004. (Variety of Life Ser.). (ENG., Illus.). 32p. (gr. 2-4). lib. bdg. 28.67 (978-0-8368-4508-2(0), e69e5cb9-eacd-4e44-8ddc-79f78c421827, Gareth Stevens Learning Library) Stevens, Gareth Publishing LLLP.

Riehecky, Janet. Reptiles. 2017. (My First Animal Kingdom Encyclopedias Ser.). (ENG., Illus.). 32p. (J). (gr. -1-2). lib. bdg. 27.99 (978-1-5157-3928-9(7), 133354, Capstone Pr.) Capstone.

Ringstad, Arnold. Totally Amazing Facts about Reptiles. 2017. (Mind Benders Ser.). (ENG., Illus.). 112p. (J). (gr. 3-6). lib. bdg. 23.99 (978-1-5157-6974-3(7), 135432, Capstone Pr.) Capstone.

Ritchey, Richard I. True Adventures of the Reptileman. 2007. 60p. per. 10.95 (978-0-595-45020-6(2)) iUniverse, Inc.

Rodríguez, Ana María. The Secret of the Squiggly Green Bombers... & More!, 1 vol. 2017. (Animal Secrets Revealed! Ser.). (ENG.). 48p. (gr. 4-4). lib. bdg. 29.60 (978-0-7660-8631-9(3), 4585a1ef-1be2-4811-bfe7-1a0a22ae7be4) Enslow Publishing, LLC.

Rodríguez, Ana María & Rodríguez, Ana María. Secret of the Puking Penguins... & More!, 1 vol. 2008. (Animal Secrets Revealed! Ser.). (ENG., Illus.). 48p. (gr. 5-7). lib. bdg. 27.93 (978-0-7660-2955-2(7), 3ea06338-16db-4c3e-adfe-0005e650f8e5) Enslow Publishing, LLC.

Royston, Angela. Reptiles. (Illus.). 32p. (YA). (gr. 2-18). lib. bdg. 27.10 (978-1-932333-38-1(X)) Chrysalis Education.

Saidian, Siyavush. Staying Safe with Scales & Scutes, 1 vol. 2017. (How Animals Adapt to Survive Ser.). (ENG.). 24p. (J). (gr. 3-3). 25.27 (978-1-5081-6431-9(2), 38de294f-fe56-4e01-bc9f-8c2534fa0598, PowerKids Pr.) Rosen Publishing Group, Inc., The.

Savage, Stephen. Focus on Reptiles, 1 vol. 2011. (Animal Watch Ser.). (ENG.). 32p. (YA). (gr. 3-4). lib. bdg. 29.27 (978-1-4339-5993-6(3), 72a741ae-23a7-4160-a04e-83a70bcc83a3) Stevens, Gareth Publishing LLLP.

Scaly Things: Level N, 6 vols. (Explorers Ser.). 32p. (gr. 3-6). 44.95 (978-0-7699-0594-5(3)) Shortland Pubns. (U. S. A.) Inc.

Schafer, Susan. Invasive Reptiles & Amphibians, 1 vol. 2016. (Invasive Species Ser.). (ENG.). 48p. (gr. 4-4). 33.07 (978-1-5026-1830-6(3), a5a22c0e-46c6-48fa-9125-d71c4d4ce3a1) Cavendish Square Publishing LLC.

School Zone Publishing Company Staff. Reptiles & Amphibians. (Illus.). (J). 19.99 incl. audio compact disk (978-0-88743-978-0(0)) School Zone Publishing Co.

Schuetz, Kari. Reptiles. 2012. (Animal Classes Ser.). (ENG., Illus.). 24p. (J). (gr. k-3). lib. bdg. 26.95 (978-1-60014-776-0(3), Blastoff! Readers) Bellwether Media.

Schuh, Mari. The World's Biggest Reptiles. 2015. (Illus.). 24p. (J). lib. bdg. (978-1-62031-205-6(0)) Jump! Inc.

Shaffer, Jody Jensen. Bearded Dragons, 1 vol. 2014. (Amazing Reptiles Ser.). (ENG.). 48p. (J). (gr. 4-8). lib. bdg. 35.64 (978-1-62403-369-8(5), 1183) ABDO Publishing Co.

Shea, Therese. Really Strange Reptiles, 1 vol. 2016. (Really Strange Adaptations Ser.). (ENG.). 32p. (J). (gr. 5-5). pap. 11.00 (978-1-4994-2792-9(1), 802d9b01-945a-4cdc-b677-c5ab18a3cc01, PowerKids Pr.) Rosen Publishing Group, Inc., The.

Shea, Therese M. Creepy Reptiles, 1 vol. 2012. (Nature's Creepiest Creatures Ser.). (ENG., Illus.). 24p. (J). (gr. 2-3). pap. 9.15 (978-1-4339-6499-2(6), 18e8a30a-208a-4e62-b291-7e5857efa030); lib. bdg. 25.27 (978-1-4339-6497-8(X), eae6bd9a-b1c7-4c73-a52a-e589563ebb07) Stevens, Gareth Publishing LLLP. (Gareth Stevens Learning Library).

Sill, Cathryn. About Reptiles: A Guide for Children, 1 vol. Sill, John, illus. 2003. (About...Ser.). (ENG.). 40p. (J). (gr. k-3). pap. 7.95 (978-1-56145-233-0(5)) Peachtree Publishing Co. Inc.

—About Reptiles / Sobre Los Reptiles: A Guide for Children / una Guía para Niños, 1 vol. Sill, John, illus. 2016. (About... Ser.: 20). 40p. (J). (gr. -1-2). pap. 8.99 (978-1-56145-909-4(7)) Peachtree Publishing Co. Inc.

Silverman, Buffy. ¿Sabes Algo Sobre Reptiles? (Do You Know about Reptiles?) 2012. (Libros Rayo — Conoce Los Grupos de Animales (Lightning Bolt Books (r) — Meet the Animal Groups) Ser.). (SPA., Illus.). 32p. (J). (gr. 1-3). pap. 9.99 (978-0-7613-9378-8(1), f27765fb-e73d-419e-a25f-aee484ad67cb, Ediciones Lerner) Lerner Publishing Group.

Simon, Elizabeth. Caring for Your Iguana. 2005. (Caring for Your Pet Ser.). (Illus.). 32p. (J). per. 9.95 (978-1-59036-215-0(2)); (gr. 4-7). lib. bdg. 26.00 (978-1-59036-195-5(4)) Weigl Pubs., Inc.

Smith, Michael A. The Wild Lives of Reptiles & Amphibians: A Young Herpetologist's Guide. 2020. (Kathie & Ed Cox Jr. Books on Conservation Leadership, Sponsored by the Meadows Center for Water & the Environment, Texas State University Ser.). (ENG., Illus.). 172p. pap. 18.95 (978-1-62349-873-3(2), P632591) Texas A&M Univ. Pr.

Snedden, Robert. Reptiles. (Living Things Ser.). (Illus.). 32p. 2009. (J). (gr. 4-7). pap. 7.95 (978-1-59920-199-3(2)) 2007. (YA). (gr. 3-6). lib. bdg. 28.50 (978-1-59920-082-8(1)) Black Rabbit Bks.

Sol90 Editorial Staff. A Visual Guide to Reptiles & Dinosaurs, 1 vol. 2018. (Visual Exploration of Science Ser.). (ENG.). 104p. (gr. 8-8). 38.80 (978-1-5081-8242-9(6), 51ec6d30-c5c4-4d50-99c3-d8512e7589ca, Rosen Young Adult) Rosen Publishing Group, Inc., The.

Somervill, Barbara A. Monitor Lizard. 2010. (21st Century Skills Library: Animal Invaders Ser.). (ENG., Illus.). 32p. (gr. 4-8). lib. bdg. 32.07 (978-1-60279-627-0(0), 200334) Cherry Lake Publishing.

Spilsbury, Louise. Superstar Reptiles, 1 vol. 2014. (Nature's Got Talent Ser.). (ENG., Illus.). 32p. (J). (gr. 3-3). lib. bdg. 27.93 (978-1-4777-7056-6(9), 7fe658b7-b24e-42ed-902d-adbd52e30c10, PowerKids Pr.) Rosen Publishing Group, Inc., The.

Spirn, Michele. Ripley's Cold-Blooded Creatures. 2004. (Illus.). 60p. (J). (978-0-439-63362-8(1)) Scholastic, Inc.

Squire, Ann O. Reptiles. 2013. (True Book(tm), a — Animal Kingdom Ser.). (ENG.). 48p. (J). 31.00 (978-0-531-21755-9(8)) Scholastic Library Publishing.

Stark, Kristy. Terrarium Pets: Volume (Grade 6) 2019. (Mathematics in the Real World Ser.). (ENG., Illus.). 32p. (gr. 5-8). pap. 11.99 (978-1-4258-5891-9(0)) Teacher Created Materials, Inc.

Stille, Darlene R. The Life Cycle of Reptiles, 1 vol. 2011. (Life Cycles Ser.). (ENG.). 48p. (J). (gr. 3-6). pap. 9.95 (978-1-4329-4989-1(6), 114902, Heinemann) Capstone.

Sullivan, Courtney. Reptiles at the Zoo: Divide Within 100, 1 vol. 2014. (InfoMax Math Readers Ser.). (ENG.). 24p. (J). (gr. 3-3). pap. 8.25 (978-1-4777-4690-5(0), 4703182e-28dc-41fe-b1dc-16890a26315e, Rosen Classroom) Rosen Publishing Group, Inc., The.

Taylor, Barbara. In Focus: Reptiles. 2017. (In Focus Ser.). (ENG.). 64p. (J). 17.99 (978-0-7534-7367-2(4), 9780753473672, Kingfisher) Roaring Brook Pr.

Taylor, Barbara & Green, Jen. Explore the Deadly World of Bugs, Snakes, Spiders, Crocodiles: The Dramatic Lives & Conflicts of the World's Strangest Creatures Shown in 1500 Amazing Close-Up Photographs. 2013. (ENG., Illus.). 512p. (J). (gr. -1-12). pap. 17.99 (978-1-84322-840-0(8), Armadillo) Anness Publishing GBR. Dist: National Bk. Network.

Taylor, Barbara & O'Shea, Mark. The Ultimate Book of Snakes & Reptiles: Discover the Amazing World of Snakes, Crocodiles, Lizards & Turtles. 2015. (Illus.). 256p. (J). (gr. -1-12). pap. 13.99 (978-1-86147-459-9(8), Armadillo) Anness Publishing GBR. Dist: National Bk. Network.

Taylor, Barbara, et al. The Deadly World of Bugs, Snakes, Spiders, Crocodiles: And Hundreds of Other Amazing Reptiles & Insects. 2008. (ENG., Illus.). 512p. (J). (gr. 4-7). 29.99 (978-0-7548-1781-9(4)) Anness Publishing GBR. Dist: National Bk. Network.

Taylor, Trace. Komodo Dragons. 2011. (1-3Y Animals Ser.). (ENG.). 24p. (J). (gr. k-2). pap. 8.00 (978-1-59301-431-5(7)) American Reading Co.

Titmus, Dawn. Reptiles & Amphibians, 1 vol. 2018. (Cool Pets for Kids Ser.). (ENG.). 32p. (J). (gr. 3-3). 27.93 (978-1-5383-3809-4(2), 070dee32-5069-4118-97ec-5c5236ea2d72, PowerKids Pr.) Rosen Publishing Group, Inc., The.

Top That Publishing Staff, ed. How to Draw Monster Reptiles. 2005. (Illus.). 48p. pap. (978-1-84510-745-1(4)) Top That! Publishing PLC.

Twist, Clint. Reptiles & Amphibians Dictionary. 2005. (Illus.). 64p. (J). pap. (978-0-439-66828-6(X)) Scholastic, Inc.

Underwood, Gary. Reptiles, 1 vol. 2010. (Weird, Wild, & Wonderful Ser.). (ENG., Illus.). 24p. (J). (gr. 2-3). lib. bdg. 24.67 (978-1-4339-3572-5(4), 5d0480dd-3165-468c-9313-a0ae83480cb6, Gareth Stevens Learning Library) Stevens, Gareth Publishing LLLP.

Valdez, Patricia. Joan Procter, Dragon Doctor: The Woman Who Loved Reptiles. Sala, Felicita, illus. 2018. 40p. (J). (gr. -1-3). 18.99 (978-0-399-55725-5(3), Knopf Bks. for Young Readers) Random Hse. Children's Bks.

Veitch, Catherine. Reptile Babies. 2013. (Animal Babies Ser.). (ENG.). 24p. (J). (gr. -1-1). pap. 42.70 (978-1-4329-8428-1(4), 20520); (Illus.). pap. 6.95 (978-1-4329-8421-2(7), 124404) Capstone. (Heinemann).

Weakland, Mark. Flying Reptiles: Ranking Their Speed, Strength, & Smarts. 2019. (Dinosaurs by Design Ser.). (ENG.). 32p. (J). (gr. 4-6). pap. 9.99 (978-1-64466-028-7(8), 12701); (Illus.). lib. bdg. (978-1-68072-823-1(7), 12700) Black Rabbit Bks. (Bolt).

Weber, Belinda. Discover Science: Reptiles. 2019. (Discover Science Ser.). (ENG.). 56p. (J). pap. 7.99 (978-0-7534-7534-8(0), 900210383, Kingfisher) Roaring Brook Pr.

—Kingfisher Young Knowledge - Reptiles. 2011. 48p. 11.99 (978-84-96609-99-0(5)) Edilupa Ediciones, S.L. ESP. Dist: Lectorum Pubns., Inc.

West, David. Crocodiles & Other Reptiles, 1 vol. 2017. (Inside Animals Ser.). (ENG.). 24p. (J). (gr. 3-3). 26.27 (978-1-5081-9390-6(8), 369efc62-662e-4650-93bc-c72127931edf); pap. 9.25 (978-1-5081-9426-2(2), 8b401ea4-f224-47bc-a167-94515affcce6) Rosen Publishing Group, Inc., The. (Windmill Bks.).

—Pteranodon: Giant of the Sky, 1 vol. Riley, Terry & Ball, Geoff, illus. 2007. (Graphic Dinosaurs Ser.). (ENG.). 32p. (J). (gr. 4-4). lib. bdg. 30.27 (978-1-4042-3895-4(6), 4675c14b-8a45-47c5-8a28-7fb6365bc24c) Rosen Publishing Group, Inc., The.

Who's Hiding Inside? Reptiles. 2005. (Who's Hiding Inside Ser.). 12p. (J). bds. 7.95 (978-1-58117-307-9(5), Intervisual/Piggy Toes) Bendon, Inc.

Wild about Snakes. 2011. (Wild about Snakes Ser.). (ENG.). 32p. (gr. 3-4). pap. 190.80 (978-1-4296-6427-1(4), Capstone Pr.) Capstone.

Williams, Brian. Amazing Reptiles & Amphibians, 1 vol. 2008. (Amazing Life Cycles Ser.). (ENG., Illus.). 32p. (gr. 3-5). lib. bdg. 28.67 (978-0-8368-8898-0(7), 6714477f-cf2f-49bd-9918-1b18318798f4, Gareth Stevens Learning Library) Stevens, Gareth Publishing LLLP.

Wilsdon, Christina. Ultimate Reptileopedia: The Most Complete Reptile Reference Ever. 2015. (Illus.). 272p. (J). (gr. 3-7). 24.99 (978-1-4263-2102-3(3), National Geographic Kids) Disney Publishing Worldwide.

Winner, Cherie. Everything Reptile. 2014. 64p. pap. 8.00 (978-1-61003-326-8(4)) Center for the Collaborative Classroom.

—Everything Reptile: What Kids Really Want to Know about Reptiles. 2004. (Kids Faqs Ser.). (ENG., Illus.). 64p. (J). (gr. 3-6). pap. 7.95 (978-1-55971-164-7(7)) Cooper Square Publishing Llc.

Woolf, Alex. The Science of Sea Monsters: Prehistoric Reptiles of the Sea (the Science of Dinosaurs) (Library Edition) Rowland, Andy, illus. 2017. (Science Of... Ser.). (ENG.). 32p. (J). (gr. 3). lib. bdg. 29.00 (978-0-531-25832-3(7), Watts, Franklin) Scholastic Library Publishing.

World Book, Inc. Staff, contrib. by. Amphibians & Reptiles of the United States & Canada. 2004. (World Book's Science & Nature Guides Ser.). (Illus.). 80p. (J). (978-0-7166-4209-1(3)) World Bk., Inc.

—Reptiles. 2009. (J). (978-0-7166-0408-2(6)) World Bk., Inc.

Zabludoff, Marc. The Reptile Class, 1 vol. 2007. (Family Trees Ser.). (ENG., Illus.). 96p. (gr. 6-6). lib. bdg. 36.93 (978-0-7614-1820-7(2), 49e657ed-40c6-4e97-9810-bcd7bf62b558) Cavendish Square Publishing LLC.

Zayarny, Jack. Reptiles. 2016. (J). (978-1-5105-1118-7(0)) SmartBook Media, Inc.

REPTILES—FICTION

Busby, Deehna R. Father's Precious Creations Series: Things That Crawl. 2012. 64p. pap. 24.99 (978-1-4685-5030-6(6)) AuthorHouse.

Down, Dale. The Adventures of Dennis the Dimetrodon. 2009. (Illus.). 48p. pap. (978-1-84748-463-5(8)) Athena Pr.

Gibbs, Stuart. Tyrannosaurus Wrecks. (FunJungle Ser.). (ENG., Illus.). (J). (gr. 3-7). 2021. 368p. pap. 8.99 (978-1-5344-4376-1(2)) 2020. 336p. 17.99 (978-1-5344-4375-4(4)) Simon & Schuster Bks. For Young Readers. (Simon & Schuster Bks. For Young Readers).

Hale, Bruce. Farewell, My Lunchbag: A Chet Gecko Mystery. Hale, Bruce, illus. 2009. (Chet Gecko Ser.: 3). (ENG., Illus.). 128p. (J). (gr. 3-7). pap. 6.99 (978-0-15-202629-5(0), 1193357, Clarion Bks.) HarperCollins Pubs.

Hambleton, Laura. Chameleon Races, 1 vol. 2005. (Chameleon Ser.). (ENG., Illus.). 16p. (J). (gr. 5). bds. 7.95 (978-1-84059-422-5(5)); (gr. -1). bds. 8.95 (978-1-84059-433-1(0)) Milet Publishing.

—Chameleon Races, 1 vol. Dai, Hongchao, tr. 2005. (Chameleon Ser.). (ENG., Illus.). 16p. (J). 8.95 (978-1-84059-429-4(2)) Milet Publishing.

—Chameleon Races, 1 vol. Umicini, Roberta, tr. 2005. (Chameleon Ser.). (ENG., Illus.). 16p. (J). bds. 8.95 (978-1-84059-427-0(6)) Milet Publishing.

—Chameleon Races, 1 vol. Erdogan, Faith, tr. 2005. (Chameleon Ser.). (ENG., Illus.). 16p. (J). (gr. -1). bds. 8.95 (978-1-84059-432-4(2)) Milet Publishing.

—Chameleon Swims, 1 vol. Choudhury, Dorbesh, tr. 2005. (Chameleon Ser.). (ENG., Illus.). 16p. (J). (gr. -1). bds. 8.95 (978-1-84059-437-9(3)) Milet Publishing.

Irwin, Bindi & Kunz, Chris. Trouble at the Zoo. 2011. (Bindi's Wildlife Adventures Ser.: 1). (ENG.). 112p. (J). (gr. 3-6). pap. 5.99 (978-1-4022-5514-4(4), Sourcebooks Jabberwocky) Sourcebooks, Inc.

Julie, Aunt. State Symbols of Texas - Paddleduck #8. 2012. (ENG.). 50p. pap. 5.95 (978-1-105-91163-7(2)) Lulu Pr., Inc.

Krulik, Nancy. Free the Worms! John & Wendy, illus. 2008. (Katie Kazoo, Switcheroo Ser.). 78p. (J). 11.65 (978-0-7569-8807-4(1)) Perfection Learning Corp.

Lionni, Leo. Su Propio Color. Mlawer, Teresa, tr. from ENG. 2007. (SPA., Illus.). 32p. (J). (gr. k-2). 12.99 (978-1-933032-14-6(6)) Lectorum Pubns., Inc.

MacHado, Ana Maria. Tiririca, Jararaca y Perereca. Faria, Rosana, illus. 2003. 28p. pap. (978-980-257-283-0(7)) Ekare, Ediciones.

Mohler, Marie. Leonard's Song. 2008. 32p. 18.95 (978-1-4357-1372-7(9)) Lulu Pr., Inc.

O'Ryan, Ray. The Prehistoric Planet. Jack, Colin, illus. 2013. (Galaxy Zack Ser.: 3). (ENG.). 128p. (J). (gr. k-4). 17.99 (978-1-4424-6716-3(9)); pap. 6.99 (978-1-4424-6715-6(0)) Little Simon. (Little Simon).

Rand, Johnathan. American Chillers #27 Kentucky Komodo Dragons. 2009. 208p. (J). pap. 5.99 (978-1-893699-90-8(0)) AudioCraft Publishing, Inc.

Reasoner, Charles. Reptiles. 2009. (Learning Tab Board Bks.). (Illus.). 10p. (J). (gr. -1-k). bds. 9.99 (978-1-934650-80-6(3)) Just For Kids Pr., LLC.

TenNapel, Doug. The Battle for Amphibopolis: a Graphic Novel (Nnewts #3), Vol. 3. 2017. (Nnewts Ser.: 3). (ENG., Illus.). 224p. (J). (gr. 3-7). pap. 12.99 (978-0-545-67670-0(3), Graphix) Scholastic, Inc.

Townsend, Wendy. Lizard Love. 2013. 198p. 18.95 (978-1-60898-151-9(7)) namelos llc.

Vernon, Ursula. Attack of the Ninja Frogs. 2012. (Dragonbreath Ser.: 2). lib. bdg. 17.20 (978-0-606-26666-6(6)) Turtleback.

—Dragonbreath #2: Attack of the Ninja Frogs. 2nd ed. (Dragonbreath Ser.: 2). 208p. (J). (gr. 3-7). 2012. pap. 8.99 (978-0-14-242066-9(2), Puffin Books) 2010. 14.99 (978-0-8037-3365-7(8), Dial Bks) Penguin Young Readers Group.

Wrecks, Billy. Reptile Rumble! 2014. (Step into Reading Level 2 Ser.). lib. bdg. 13.55 (978-0-606-35541-4(3)) Turtleback.

REPTILES, FOSSIL

see also Dinosaurs

Beaumont, Steve. Drawing Pteranodon & Other Flying Reptiles, 1 vol. 2010. (Drawing Dinosaurs Ser.). (ENG., Illus.). 32p. (J). (gr. 3-3). pap. 12.75 (978-1-4488-0428-3(0), b6bc9530-02ab-4ec6-ab35-0ba2485af283); lib. bdg. 30.27 (978-1-61531-904-6(2), 0580b349-d51f-49da-bea3-deaf2cb01812) Rosen Publishing Group, Inc., The.

Brown, Charlotte Lewis. Beyond the Dinosaurs: Monsters of the Air & Sea. Wilson, Phil, illus. 2008. (I Can Read Level 2 Ser.). (ENG.). 32p. (J). (gr. -1-3). pap. 5.99 (978-0-06-053058-7(8), HarperCollins) HarperCollins Pubs.

Brown, Charlotte Lewis & Brown, Charlotte L. Beyond the Dinosaurs: Monsters of the Air & Sea. Wilson, Phil, illus. 2007. (I Can Read Bks.). (ENG.). 32p. (J). (gr. -1-3). 15.99 (978-0-06-053056-3(1)) HarperCollins Pubs.

Connors, Kathleen. Dinosaur Fossils, 1 vol. 2012. (Fossilized! Ser.). (ENG., Illus.). 24p. (J). (gr. 2-3). pap. 9.15 (978-1-4339-6410-7(4), 70d645d6-8337-44bf-9e61-87a7a43da4e3); lib. bdg. 25.27 (978-1-4339-6408-4(2), cb43bcec-0f2a-4f0e-8f03-b404ecc1cacd) Stevens, Gareth Publishing LLLP.

Dodson, Peter. Pterosaurs up Close: Flying Reptiles, 1 vol. Bindon, John, illus. 2011. (Zoom in on Dinosaurs! Ser.). (ENG.). 24p. (gr. k-2). 25.60 (978-0-7660-3332-0(5), 41696d0b-2e5d-4af7-8325-9a807d3dc187) Enslow Publishing, LLC.

Frost, Kathy. Discovering Pterosaurs. 2018. (Sequence Discovering Dinosaurs Ser.). (ENG.). 32p. (J). (gr. 2-5). pap. 9.99 (978-1-68152-355-2(8), 15183); lib. bdg. (978-1-68151-435-2(4), 15177) Amicus.

Gregory, Josh. Ichthyosaur. 2013. (21st Century Junior Library: Dinosaurs Ser.). (ENG., Illus.). 24p. (J). (gr. 2-5). pap. 12.79 (978-1-62431-298-4(5), 202986); lib. bdg. 29.21 (978-1-62431-166-6(0), 202984) Cherry Lake Publishing.

Hamilton, S. L. Sea Reptiles. 2017. (Xtreme Dinosaurs Ser.). (ENG., Illus.). 32p. (J). (gr. 3-9). lib. bdg. 32.79 (978-1-5321-1297-3(1), 27505, Abdo & Daughters) ABDO Publishing Co.

Hughes, Mónica. Swimming Giants. 2007. (I Love Reading Ser.). (Illus.). 24p. (J). (gr. -1-2). lib. bdg. 25.65 (978-1-59716-542-6(5)) Bearport Publishing Co., Inc.

Jeffrey, Gary. Elasmosaurus: The Long-Necked Swimmer, 1 vol. Riley, Terry, illus. 2008. (Graphic Dinosaurs Ser.). (ENG.). 32p. (gr. 4-4). pap. 12.30 (978-1-4042-7715-1(3), 7f38de89-f3b1-4f5c-98d7-e4ee7b8d4baa, PowerKids Pr.) Rosen Publishing Group, Inc., The.

Johnson, Jinny. Flying Reptiles. 2014. (Discovering Dinosaurs Ser.). (ENG., Illus.). 24p. (J). (gr. 2-5). 28.50 (978-1-62588-014-7(6), 17293) Black Rabbit Bks.

—Pteranodon & Other Flying Reptiles. Rosewarne, Graham, illus. 2009. (Dinosaurs Alive! Ser.). 32p. (J). (gr. 4-7). pap. 7.95 (978-1-59920-185-6(2)) Black Rabbit Bks.

Kelly, Harold G. How the Dinosaurs Disappeared. (Reading Room Collection 1 Ser.). 16p. (gr. 2-3). 2009. 37.50 (978-1-60851-945-3(7)) 2005. (ENG., Illus.). (J). lib. bdg. 22.27 (978-1-4042-3340-9(7), 35134a52-a91f-44af-a69a-6fc08183f47e) Rosen Publishing Group, Inc., The. (PowerKids Pr.).

Lunis, Natalie. Ocean Monsters. 2008. (Dino Times Trivia Ser.). (Illus.). 24p. (J). (gr. k-3). lib. bdg. 26.99 (978-1-59716-713-0(4), 1284318) Bearport Publishing Co., Inc.

—Sky Terrors. 2008. (Dino Times Trivia Ser.). (Illus.). 24p. (J). (gr. k-3). lib. bdg. 26.99 (978-1-59716-714-7(2), 1284317) Bearport Publishing Co., Inc.

Miles, Liz. Flying Monsters. 2012. (Illus.). 32p. (J). (978-1-84858-567-6(5)) Arcturus Pubs., Inc.

Myers, Tim. If You Give a T-Rex a Bone. Hovemann, Anisa Claire, illus. 2007. (Sharing Nature with Children Book Ser.). 32p. (J). (gr. -1-5). 16.95 (978-1-58469-097-9(6)) Take Heart Pubns.

Parker, Steve. Did Dinosaurs Lay Eggs? And Other Questions & Answers about Prehistoric Reptiles. Rosewarne, Graham, illus. 2016. 32p. (J). (gr. -1-12). 7.99 (978-1-86147-481-0(4), Armadillo) Anness Publishing GBR. Dist: National Bk. Network.

Riggs, Kate. Pterodactyls. 2012. (J). 25.65 (978-1-60818-117-9(0), Creative Education) Creative Co., The.

Roberts, Russell. Where Did All the Dinosaurs Go? 2005. (Natural Disasters Ser.). (Illus.). 32p. (J). (gr. 1-4). lib. bdg. 25.70 (978-1-58415-420-4(9)) Mitchell Lane Pubs.

Rockwood, Leigh. Plesiosaurus. (J). 2012. 49.50 (978-1-4488-5091-4(6)) 2011. (ENG.). 24p. (gr. 2-3). pap. 9.25 (978-1-4488-5090-7(8), d32b36b5-bcde-4a37-88fc-34a567af9578) 2011. (ENG., Illus.). 24p. (gr. 2-3). lib. bdg. 26.27 (978-1-4488-4970-3(5), db82f174-4178-4c0a-9ce7-4a2d79fb6657) Rosen Publishing Group, Inc., The. (PowerKids Pr.).

—Pteranodon. (Illus.). 24p. (J). 2012. 49.50 (978-1-4488-5081-5(9), 1329103) 2011. (ENG., (gr. 2-3). pap. 9.25 (978-1-4488-5080-8(0), 2343bfa8-e978-4e9b-bb8a-e41b78811409) 2011. (ENG., (gr. 2-3). lib. bdg. 26.27 (978-1-4488-4965-9(9), ce2dd4ee-9854-4c9d-994f-908e14510e0d) Rosen Publishing Group, Inc., The. (PowerKids Pr.).

Slepian, Curtis. Digging up Dinosaurs. rev. ed. 2018. (Smithsonian: Informational Text Ser.). (ENG., Illus.). 32p. (J). (gr. 4-8). pap. 12.99 (978-1-4938-6709-7(1)) Teacher Created Materials, Inc.

Staunton, Joseph. Dinosaurs in the Sky. 2010. (Discover the Dinosaurs Ser.). 32p. (J). (gr. 2-5). 28.50 (978-1-60753-108-1(9)) Amicus Learning.

Staunton, Joseph & Hynson, Colin. Dinosaurs in the Sky. 2011. (Inside Crime Ser.). 48p. (YA). (gr. 5-9). lib. bdg. 34.25 *(978-1-59920-394-2(4))* Black Rabbit Bks.

Thomson, Sarah L. Ancient Animals: Plesiosaur. Plant, Andrew, illus. 2017. (Ancient Animals Ser.). 32p. (J). (gr. 1-4). lib. bdg. 12.99 *(978-1-58089-542-2(5))* Charlesbridge Publishing, Inc.

Wagner, Karen. Mosasaurus: Mighty Ruler of the Sea. 2008. (ENG., Illus.). 36p. (J). (gr. k-2). pap. 6.95 *(978-1-59249-781-2(0))* Soundprints.

—Mosasaurus: Mighty Ruler of the Sea. Carr, Karen, illus. 2008. (ENG.). 36p. (J). (gr. k-2). 8.95 *(978-1-59249-782-9(9))*; 2.95 *(978-1-59249-783-6(7))*; 9.95 *(978-1-59249-784-3(5))*; 14.95 *(978-1-59249-780-5(2))* Soundprints.

West, David. Allosaurus & Other Dinosaurs & Reptiles from the Upper Jurassic, 1 vol. West, David, illus. 2012. (Dinosaurs! Ser.). (ENG., Illus.). 32p. (J). (gr. 3-5). 29.27 *(978-1-4339-6704-7(9),* 640536e3-97c5-4530-8eef-329c4423ab39); pap. 11.50 *(978-1-4339-6705-4(7),* 9b69e3d1-cc57-4654-aa5b-778869995cfd, Gareth Stevens Learning Library) Stevens, Gareth Publishing LLLP.

—Lesothosaurus & Other Dinosaurs & Reptiles from the Lower Jurassic, 1 vol. West, David, illus. 2012. (Dinosaurs! Ser.). (ENG., Illus.). 32p. (J). (gr. 3-5). pap. 11.50 *(978-1-4339-6717-7(0),* f237a850-6583-4747-ba3b-4d4eb337f268, Gareth Stevens Learning Library); lib. bdg. 29.27 *(978-1-4339-6715-3(4),* 858c8796-bc9c-40fe-89cc-0f788f663bd3) Stevens, Gareth Publishing LLLP.

—Prehistoric Sea Reptiles, 1 vol., 1. 2015. (Prehistoric Animals Ser.). (ENG., Illus.). 24p. (J). (gr. 2-3). pap. 9.25 *(978-1-5081-9045-5(3),* bc3649cf-5127-4b53-80d9-f939c29f04b6, Windmill Bks.) Rosen Publishing Group, Inc., The.

—Spinosaurus & Other Dinosaurs & Reptiles from the Upper Cretaceous, 1 vol. West, David, illus. 2012. (Dinosaurs! Ser.). (ENG., Illus.). 32p. (J). (gr. 3-5). 29.27 *(978-1-4339-6719-1(7),* 0b82f069-87c8-4593-8fc7-dcd4aead1a5e); pap. 11.50 *(978-1-4339-6721-4(9),* 0ff005fb-12f6-439f-94b2-1e3b4673c0fa, Gareth Stevens Learning Library) Stevens, Gareth Publishing LLLP.

—Utahraptor & Other Dinosaurs & Reptiles from the Lower Cretaceous, 1 vol. West, David, illus. 2012. (Dinosaurs! Ser.). (ENG., Illus.). 32p. (J). (gr. 3-5). 29.27 *(978-1-4339-6723-8(5),* 5036667d-8ae2-4299-aa55-805a505d3f8a); pap. 11.50 *(978-1-4339-6725-2(1),* a8027fe5-ff21-4f34-8e15-36c9f4f838c0, Gareth Stevens Learning Library) Stevens, Gareth Publishing LLLP.

Woolf, Alex. The Science of Flying Reptiles: the Terrifying Truth about the Pterosaurs (the Science of Dinosaurs) (Library Edition) Beach, Bryan, illus. 2017. (Science Of... Ser.). (ENG.). 32p. (J). (gr. 3). lib. bdg. 29.00 *(978-0-531-25830-9(0),* Watts, Franklin) Scholastic Library Publishing.

Zabludoff, Marc. Kronosaurus, 1 vol. Bollinger, Peter, illus. 2011. (Prehistoric Beasts Ser.). (ENG.). 32p. (gr. 2-2). 32.64 *(978-1-60870-035-6(6),* 6014be4b-28c3-4f01-9f8d-9405a9f223a0) Cavendish Square Publishing LLC.

RESCUE WORK

see also First Aid

Allan, John. Firefighters to the Rescue. 2019. (Math Adventures (Step 1) Ser.). (ENG., Illus.). 32p. (J). (gr. 1-3). lib. bdg. 29.32 *(978-1-912108-46-6(1),* 92569254-2716-4494-8d53-99078cfb9116, Hungry Tomato (r)) Lerner Publishing Group.

—Let's Look at Emergency Vehicles. 2019. (Mini Mechanics Ser.). (ENG., Illus.). 24p. (J). (gr. 1-3). 26.65 *(978-1-5415-5535-8(X),* c7e7a410-d5d4-4472-b7a6-ec1d18917840, Hungry Tomato (r)) Lerner Publishing Group.

Allberti, Frances C. Finding Rover. Gremillion, Barry, illus. 2006. (J). per. *(978-0-9785937-1-1(5))* Open Pages Publishing.

Allman, Toney. Jaws of Life. 2008. (Great Idea Ser.). (Illus.). 48p. (J). (gr. 4-6). lib. bdg. 26.60 *(978-1-59953-191-5(7))* Norwood Hse. Pr.

Andrews Henningfeld, Diane & Haugen, David M., eds. Hurricane Katrina, 1 vol. 2010. (At Issue Ser.). (ENG.). 152p. (gr. 10-12). 41.03 *(978-0-7377-4882-6(6),* d10d4d4a-0c6a-4824-83f3-951fc357b796); pap. 28.80 *(978-0-7377-4883-3(4),* 6c811ff7-5104-4f18-b9ad-ec0a927d8a1a) Greenhaven Publishing LLC. (Greenhaven Publishing).

Animal Rescue. 2014. (Animal Rescue Ser.). 32p. (J). (gr. 3-6). pap. 40.00 *(978-1-4777-7213-3(8),* PowerKids Pr.) Rosen Publishing Group, Inc., The.

Aronson, Marc. Rising Water: The Story of the Thai Cave Rescue. (ENG., Illus.). (J). (gr. 5-9). 2020. 176p. pap. 7.99 *(978-1-5344-4414-0(9))* 2019. 160p. 17.99 *(978-1-5344-4413-3(0))* Simon & Schuster Children's Publishing. (Atheneum Bks. for Young Readers).

Auerbach, Annie. Meet Boulder the Construction-Bot. 2013. (Transformers Passport to Reading Ser.). (J). lib. bdg. 13.55 *(978-0-606-32274-4(4))* Turtleback.

Basner, Shannon. Mojo's Magical Ride: True Story of Courage, Transformation & Love; an Alaskan Dog Rescue Story. 2013. 40p. pap. 24.95 *(978-1-4626-6154-1(8))* America Star Bks.

Best, B. J. Rescue Helicopters. 2017. (Riding to the Rescue! Ser.). (Illus.). 24p. (J). (gr. 1-1). pap. 49.32 *(978-1-5026-2558-8(X))* Cavendish Square Publishing LLC.

Blake, Kevin. Air-Sea Rescue Officers. 2016. (Police: Search & Rescue! Ser.: 6). (ENG., Illus.). 32p. (J). (gr. 2-7). 28.50 *(978-1-943553-12-9(2))* Bearport Publishing Co., Inc.

—City Cops. 2016. (Police: Search & Rescue! Ser.). (ENG., Illus.). 32p. (J). (gr. 2-7). 28.50 *(978-1-943553-11-2(4))* Bearport Publishing Co., Inc.

Bow, James. Rescue Missions. 2008. (Science Solves It Ser.). (ENG., Illus.). 32p. (J). (gr. 3-7). pap. *(978-0-7787-4176-3(1),* 1286290); lib. bdg. *(978-0-7787-4169-5(9),* 1286290) Crabtree Publishing Co.

Bozzo, Linda. Search & Rescue Dog Heroes, 1 vol. 2010. (Amazing Working Dogs with American Humane Ser.). (ENG., Illus.). 48p. (gr. 3-3). 27.93 *(978-0-7660-3201-9(9),* c462f398-b201-4ed3-8da6-1545ca15f3e3) Enslow Publishing, LLC.

Braun, Eric. Trapped Behind Enemy Lines: The Story of the U. S. Army Air Force 807th Medical Evacuation Squadron. 2016. (Encounter: Narrative Nonfiction Stories Ser.). (ENG., Illus.). 224p. (J). (gr. 4-5). lib. bdg. 33.32 *(978-1-4914-8042-7(4),* 130545, Capstone Young Readers) Capstone.

Brown Bear Books. Rescue Squad: Saving Lives. 2012. (Mission Impossible Ser.). (ENG.). 32p. (J). (gr. 4-6). lib. bdg. 31.35 *(978-1-936333-28-8(7),* 16752) Brown Bear Bks.

Brown, Mike. Rescue Services. 2004. (Twentieth-Century Developments in Fashion & Costume Ser.). (Illus.). 64p. (YA). (gr. 7-18). lib. bdg. 19.95 *(978-1-59084-428-1(9))* Mason Crest.

Burgan, Michael. Total Devastation: The Story of Hurricane Katrina. 2016. (Tangled History Ser.). (ENG., Illus.). 112p. (J). (gr. 3-9). lib. bdg. 32.65 *(978-1-4914-8452-4(7),* 130899, Capstone Pr.) Capstone.

Chancellor, Deborah. Sea Rescue. 2013. (Emergency Vehicles Ser.). (Illus.). 24p. (gr. k-3). lib. bdg. 28.50 *(978-1-59920-891-6(1))* Black Rabbit Bks.

Demarest, Chris L. Mayday! Mayday! A Coast Guard Rescue. Demarest, Chris L., illus. 2004. (ENG., Illus.). 40p. (J). (gr. -1-5). 19.99 *(978-0-689-85161-2(8),* McElderry, Margaret K. Bks.) McElderry, Margaret K. Bks.

Doeden, Matt. World War II Escapes & Rescues. 2018. (Heroes of World War II (Alternator Books (r)) Ser.). (ENG., Illus.). 32p. (J). (gr. 3-6). lib. bdg. 30.65 *(978-1-5415-2152-0(8),* 05db5389-d4bd-4cf8-b332-576519f5e983, Lerner Pubns.) Lerner Publishing Group.

Doman, Mary Kate. Rescue Vehicles, 1 vol. 2011. (All about Big Machines Ser.). (ENG., Illus.). 24p. (gr. -1-1). pap. 10.35 *(978-1-59845-244-0(4),* d8efe931-e2d7-4553-90a1-a565d3bb8419); lib. bdg. 25.27 *(978-0-7660-3934-6(X),* 7f3e809f-b811-4dcd-91d3-41452b961477) Enslow Publishing, LLC. (Enslow Publishing).

Emergency! A Lego Adventure in the Real World. 2017. (Illus.). 31p. *(978-1-338-20717-0(2))* Scholastic, Inc.

Fortuna, Lois. Rescue Boats, 1 vol. 2016. (To the Rescue! Ser.). (ENG., Illus.). 24p. (J). (gr. k-k). 24.27 *(978-1-4824-4662-3(6),* 4addb579-f9c4-4888-afa8-25007eea8c44) Stevens, Gareth Publishing LLLP.

Freedman, Jeri. Careers in Emergency Medical Response Teams' Search & Rescue Units. 2009. (Careers in Search & Rescue Operations Ser.). 64p. (gr. 5-8). 58.50 *(978-1-61511-805-2(5),* Rosen Reference) Rosen Publishing Group, Inc., The.

Ganeri, Anita. Survival in the Jungle. 2011. (ENG.). 24p. (J). pap. *(978-0-7787-7880-6(0))*; (gr. 3-6). *(978-0-7787-7858-5(4))* Crabtree Publishing Co.

Gersh, Camilla. Emergency Rescue. 2016. (Illus.). 64p. (J). *(978-1-4806-9867-3(9))* Dorling Kindersley Publishing, Inc.

Gilpin, Daniel. Rescue Vehicles, 1 vol. Pang, Alex, illus. 2011. (Machines Close-Up Ser.). (ENG.). 32p. (gr. 4-4). 31.21 *(978-1-60870-111-7(5),* 2b5c3164-2cb9-466b-80f6-484ba3f35644) Cavendish Square Publishing LLC.

Goldish, Meish. Firefighters to the Rescue. 2011. (Work of Heroes: First Responders in Action Ser.). 32p. (YA). (gr. 1-4). lib. bdg. 28.50 *(978-1-61772-284-4(7))* Bearport Publishing Co., Inc.

—State Troopers. 2016. (Police: Search & Rescue! Ser.). (ENG., Illus.). 32p. (J). (gr. 2-7). 28.50 *(978-1-943553-15-0(7))* Bearport Publishing Co., Inc.

Gonzalez, Lissette. Search & Rescue Specialists. (Dangerous Jobs Ser.). 24p. (gr. 2-3). 2009. 42.50 *(978-1-61512-135-9(8))* 2007. (ENG., Illus.). (J). lib. bdg. 26.27 *(978-1-4042-3779-7(8),* 3270be90-510d-4efb-95d7-2876bdcef9ba) Rosen Publishing Group, Inc., The. (PowerKids Pr.).

Gray, Susan H. Emergency Care. 2008. (21st Century Skills Innovation Library: Innovation in Medicine Ser.). (ENG., Illus.). 32p. (gr. 4-8). lib. bdg. 32.07 *(978-1-60279-230-2(5),* 200161) Cherry Lake Publishing.

Green, Sara. Snow Search Dogs. 2013. (Dogs to the Rescue! Ser.). (ENG., Illus.). 24p. (J). (gr. 3-8). lib. bdg. 27.95 *(978-1-60014-959-7(6),* Pilot Bks.) Bellwether Media.

Gregory, Josh. What Does It Do? Ambulance. 2011. (Community Connections: What Does It Do? Ser.). (ENG., Illus.). 24p. (gr. 2-5). lib. bdg. 29.21 *(978-1-60279-969-1(5),* 200970) Cherry Lake Publishing.

Hamilton, S. L. Search & Rescue Bk. 2. 2015. (Xtreme Jobs Ser.). (ENG., Illus.). 32p. (J). (gr. 3-9). 32.79 *(978-1-62403-759-7(3),* 17752, Abdo & Daughters) ABDO Publishing Co.

Harasymiw, Mark J. Pararescuemen, 1 vol. 2012. (U. S. Special Forces Ser.). (ENG., Illus.). 32p. (J). (gr. 3-4). pap. 11.50 *(978-1-4339-6571-5(2),* e1caeac4-d4b7-4ac0-b69e-ac86616c0ec9); lib. bdg. 29.27 *(978-1-4339-6569-2(0),* 09b57886-b9e9-4d81-b6b8-a87747d34428) Stevens, Gareth Publishing LLLP. (Gareth Stevens Learning Library).

Hoffman, Mary Ann. Hurricane Katrina. 2009. (Nature in the News Ser.). 32p. (gr. 3-4). 42.50 *(978-1-61514-821-9(3),* PowerKids Pr.) Rosen Publishing Group, Inc., The.

Hood, Susan & Sornhiran, Pathana. Titan & the Wild Boars: The True Cave Rescue of the Thai Soccer Team. Phumiruk, Dow, illus. 2019. (ENG.). 48p. (J). (gr. -1-3). 19.99 *(978-0-06-290772-1(7),* HarperCollins) HarperCollins Pubs.

Idzikowski, Lisa. Search-And-Rescue Animals, 1 vol. 2018. (Animals at Work Ser.). (ENG.). 32p. (gr. 3-3). 26.93 *(978-0-7660-9623-3(8),* 92defe24-a7be-43af-b4d1-5aabfe7ec109) Enslow Publishing, LLC.

Jankowski, Susan. True Ocean Rescue Stories, 1 vol. 2011. (True Rescue Stories Ser.). (ENG.). 48p. (gr. 5-7). lib. bdg. 25.27 *(978-0-7660-3665-9(0),* 0d13b1d8-1968-4595-8f21-5e0acb1bb4bd) Enslow Publishing, LLC.

—True Wilderness Rescue Stories, 1 vol. 2011. (True Rescue Stories Ser.). (ENG.). 48p. (gr. 5-7). lib. bdg. 25.27 *(978-0-7660-3666-6(9),* 7e9d8a43-e1d4-4d66-9292-252a9206954b) Enslow Publishing, LLC.

Johnson, Linda Carlson & Johnson, Keri. 9.11 Helping the Heroes: A Salvation Army Story. 2011. (Illus.). (J). *(978-0-89216-130-0(2))* Salvation Army.

Kalman, Bobbie. Bomberos Al Rescate. 2006. (Mi Communidad y Quienes Contribuyen a Ella Ser.). (ENG & SPA., Illus.). 32p. (J). (gr. 3-7). pap. *(978-0-7787-8442-5(8))*; lib. bdg. *(978-0-7787-8428-9(2))* Crabtree Publishing Co.

—Emergency Workers Are on Their Way! 2004. (My Community & Its Helpers Ser.). (ENG., Illus.). 32p. (J). pap. *(978-0-7787-2122-2(1))*; lib. bdg. *(978-0-7787-2094-2(2))* Crabtree Publishing Co.

—Firefighters to the Rescue!, 1 vol. 2004. (My Community & Its Helpers Ser.). (ENG., Illus.). 32p. (J). pap. *(978-0-7787-2124-6(8))* Crabtree Publishing Co.

Kast, Edie. Heroic Animals. 2005. (Illus.). 24p. (J). *(978-0-328-13606-3(9),* Scott Foresman) Addison-Wesley Educational Pubs., Inc.

Katz, Samuel M. Against All Odds: Counterterrorist Hostage Rescues. 2004. (Terrorist Dossiers Ser.). (Illus.). 72p. (J). (gr. 4-7). lib. bdg. 26.60 *(978-0-8225-1567-8(9))* Lerner Publishing Group.

Kids, National Geographic. Doggy Defenders: Stella the Search Dog. 2019. (Doggy Defenders Ser.). (Illus.). 48p. (J). (gr. -1-k). 9.99 *(978-1-4263-3449-8(4),* National Geographic Kids) Disney Publishing Worldwide.

La Bella, Laura. Search & Rescue Swimmers, 1 vol. 2008. (Extreme Careers Ser.). (ENG., Illus.). 64p. (YA). (gr. 5-5). lib. bdg. 37.13 *(978-1-4042-1786-7(X),* a630f377-e969-4dc6-9f5e-797f8f893314) Rosen Publishing Group, Inc., The.

—Search-and-rescue Swimmers. 2009. (Extreme Careers Ser.). 64p. (gr. 5-5). 58.50 *(978-1-61512-405-3(5),* Rosen Reference) Rosen Publishing Group, Inc., The.

Ladybird. Emergency Rescue - Read It Yourself with Ladybird (non-Fiction) Level 2. 2016. (Read It Yourself with Ladybird Ser.). (ENG.). 32p. (J). (gr. 2-4). 5.99 *(978-0-241-24442-5(0))* Penguin Bks., Ltd. GBR. Dist: Independent Pubs. Group.

Lewis, Brenda Ralph. Hostage Rescue with the FBI. 2004. (Rescue & Prevention Ser.). (Illus.). 96p. (YA). (gr. 7-18). lib. bdg. 22.95 *(978-1-59084-403-8(3))* Mason Crest.

—Rescuing Hostages: The FBI. 2017. (Illus.). 80p. (J). *(978-1-4222-3770-0(2))* Mason Crest.

—Wilderness Rescue with the U. S. Search & Rescue Task Force. 2004. (Rescue & Prevention Ser.). (Illus.). 96p. (YA). (gr. 7-18). lib. bdg. 22.95 *(978-1-59084-404-5(1))* Mason Crest.

Lewis, Mark L. Combat Rescues. 2019. (Rescues in Focus Ser.). (ENG., Illus.). 32p. (J). (gr. 2-3). pap. 9.95 *(978-1-64185-840-3(0),* 1641858400, Focus Readers) North Star Editions.

—Mountain Rescues. 2019. (Rescues in Focus Ser.). (ENG., Illus.). 32p. (J). (gr. 2-3). pap. 9.95 *(978-1-64185-842-7(7),* 1641858427); lib. bdg. 31.35 *(978-1-64185-773-4(0),* 1641857730) North Star Editions. (Focus Readers).

—Storm Rescues. 2019. (Rescues in Focus Ser.). (ENG., Illus.). 32p. (J). (gr. 2-3). pap. 9.95 *(978-1-64185-843-4(5),* 1641858435); lib. bdg. 31.35 *(978-1-64185-774-1(9),* 1641857749) North Star Editions. (Focus Readers).

—Underground Rescues. 2019. (Rescues in Focus Ser.). (ENG., Illus.). 32p. (J). (gr. 2-3). pap. 9.95 *(978-1-64185-844-1(3),* 1641858443); lib. bdg. 31.35 *(978-1-64185-775-8(7),* 1641857757) North Star Editions. (Focus Readers).

Litchfield, J. & Brooks, F. Rescue Vehicles. 2004. (ENG., Illus.). 10p. (J). bds. 4.99 *(978-0-7945-0589-9(9))* EDC Publishing.

Martin, Brett S. Search-And-Rescue Robots. 2018. (Robot Innovations Ser.). (ENG., Illus.). 48p. (J). (gr. 4-4). pap. 11.95 *(978-1-64185-278-4(X),* 164185278X, Core Library); lib. bdg. 35.64 *(978-1-5321-1470-0(2),* 29132) ABDO Publishing Co.

Martin, Claudia. My Little Book of Rescue Vehicles. 2016. (Illus.). 64p. (J). *(978-1-4351-6335-5(4))* Barnes & Noble, Inc.

Mattern, Joanne. Emt. 2009. (Working Together Ser.). 24p. (gr. 1-2). 42.50 *(978-1-60854-830-9(9),* PowerKids Pr.) Rosen Publishing Group, Inc., The.

Matthews, Carolyn. True Stories of Rescue & Survival: Canada's Unknown Heroes. 2008. (ENG., Illus.). 176p. (YA). (gr. 6-18). pap. 19.99 *(978-1-55002-851-5(0))* Dundurn Pr. CAN. Dist: Publishers Group West (PGW).

McNab, Chris. Surviving Hostage Rescue Missions. Carney, John, ed. 2014. (Extreme Survival in the Military Ser.: 12). (Illus.). 64p. (J). (gr. 7-18). lib. bdg. 23.95 *(978-1-4222-3090-9(2))* Mason Crest.

Moran, Lisa & Hawley, Mary. Making a Difference SB2 to the Rescue. 2010. (Connect to Literacy Ser.). 8p. pap. *(978-1-4334-0504-4(0))* Millmark Education.

Murray, Aaron R. Firefighters Help Us, 1 vol. 2012. (All about Community Helpers Ser.). (ENG., Illus.). 24p. (-1). pap. 10.35 *(978-1-4644-0053-7(9),* 61b59918-2c0f-49ae-8b6c-a2da0fcc5154); (gr. -1-1). 25.27 *(978-0-7660-4047-2(X),* ff3fcf27-f183-42f9-95f1-0f1fab821bbb) Enslow Publishing, LLC. (Enslow Publishing).

Murray, Julie. Search-And-Rescue Animals. 2019. (Working Animals Ser.). (ENG., Illus.). 24p. (J). (gr. k-4). lib. bdg. 31.36 *(978-1-5321-2733-5(2),* 31673, Abdo Zoom-Dash) ABDO Publishing Co.

National Geographic Kids. 125 Pet Rescues: From Pound to Palace: Homeless Pets Made Happy. 2017. (Illus.). 112p. (J). (gr. 3-7). pap. 12.99 *(978-1-4263-2736-0(6),* National Geographic Kids) Disney Publishing Worldwide.

Newcomb, Tim. Search & Rescue Team, Vol. 12. 2015. (On a Mission Ser.). (Illus.). 48p. (J). (gr. 5). 20.95 *(978-1-4222-3399-3(5))* Mason Crest.

Peppas, Lynn. Superstorm Sandy. 2013. (ENG., Illus.). 48p. (J). *(978-0-7787-1193-3(5))*; pap. *(978-0-7787-1195-7(1))* Crabtree Publishing Co.

Perish, Patrick. Wilderness Rescue Pilot. 2015. (Dangerous Jobs Ser.). (ENG., Illus.). 24p. (J). (gr. 3-7). lib. bdg. 26.95 *(978-1-62617-199-2(8),* Torque Bks.) Bellwether Media.

Perry, Phyllis Jean. Sherlock Hounds: Our Heroic Search & Rescue Dogs. 2006. (Illus.). 32p. (J). pap. *(978-1-59336-728-2(7))* Mondo Publishing.

Petersen, Justin. Search & Rescue Teams: Saving People in Danger. 2016. (Emergency! Ser.). (ENG., Illus.). 32p. (J). (gr. 3-9). lib. bdg. 28.65 *(978-1-4914-8031-1(9),* 130533, Capstone Pr.) Capstone.

Phidal Publishing Staff, ed. Rescue Squad. (Cool Cars Ser.). (J). 16p. *(978-2-7643-0132-6(4))*; 2004. (Illus.). 10p. *(978-2-7643-0209-5(6))* Phidal Publishing, Inc./Editions Phidal, Inc.

Poolos, Jamie. Hostage Rescuers. (Extreme Careers Ser.). 64p. (gr. 5-5). 2009. 58.50 *(978-1-61512-399-5(7),* Rosen Reference) 2007. (ENG., Illus.). lib. bdg. 37.13 *(978-1-4042-0941-1(7),* 8fdbb894-9a6f-4d83-8a1f-c316f0c58f69) Rosen Publishing Group, Inc., The.

Priddy, Roger. My Big Rescue Book. 2004. (Illus.). 10p. (J). *(978-1-84332-215-3(3))* St. Martin's Pr.

Randolph, Joanne. Emergency Helicopters. (To the Rescue! Ser.). 24p. (gr. 1-1). 2009. 42.50 *(978-1-60854-396-0(X))* 2008. (ENG., Illus.). (J). lib. bdg. 26.27 *(978-1-4042-4151-0(5),* aba5c715-76dc-442f-871d-616488408333) Rosen Publishing Group, Inc., The. (PowerKids Pr.).

—Emergency Helicopters/Helicopteros de Emergencia. 2009. (To the Rescue! / ¡Al rescate! Ser.). (ENG & SPA.). 24p. (gr. 1-1). 42.50 *(978-1-60854-402-8(8),* Editorial Buenas Letras) Rosen Publishing Group, Inc., The.

—Emergency Helicopters/Helicopteros de Emergencia, 1 vol. Alaman, Eduardo, tr. 2007. (To the Rescue! / ¡Al Rescate! Ser.). (ENG & SPA., Illus.). 24p. (J). (gr. 1-1). lib. bdg. 26.27 *(978-1-4042-7672-7(6),* 01fabb15-ffae-49fc-9e95-8616b8d83048) Rosen Publishing Group, Inc., The.

Ready, Dee. Firefighters Help. 2013. (Our Community Helpers Ser.). (ENG.). 24p. (J). (gr. k-1). pap. 38.74 *(978-1-62065-846-8(1),* 19419, Pebble) Capstone.

Ready, Dee & Ready, Dee. Firefighters Help, 1 vol. 2013. (Our Community Helpers Ser.). (ENG.). 24p. (J). (gr. -1-2). pap. 6.29 *(978-1-62065-845-1(3),* 121787); lib. bdg. 24.65 *(978-1-62065-082-0(7),* 120782) Capstone. (Capstone Pr.).

Rescue! 6 Each of 1 Anthology, 6 vols. (Wildcats Ser.). 32p. (gr. 2-8). *(978-0-322-00585-3(X))* Wright Group/McGraw-Hill.

Rettung in Not. (Illus.). 40p. (J). *(978-3-411-08181-3(3))* Bibliographisches Institut & F. A. Brockhaus AG DEU. Dist: i. b. d., Ltd.

Riggs, Kate. Rescue Boats. 2016. (Seedlings Ser.). (ENG.). 24p. (J). (gr. k-2). pap. 7.99 *(978-1-62832-188-3(1),* 21031, Creative Paperbacks) Creative Co., The.

—To the Rescue! Williams, Nate, illus. 2016. (ENG.). 14p. (J). (gr. -1 — 1). bds. 7.99 *(978-1-56846-288-2(3),* 20560, Creative Editions) Creative Co., The.

Roleff, Tamara L., ed. The World Trade Center Attack. 2003. (History Firsthand Ser.). (Illus.). 202p. (YA). (gr. 7-10). pap. 21.20 *(978-0-7377-1469-2(7),* Greenhaven Pr., Inc.) Cengage Gale.

Roza, Greg. Careers in the Coast Guard's Search & Rescue Units. 2009. (Careers in Search & Rescue Operations Ser.). 64p. (gr. 5-8). 58.50 *(978-1-61511-808-3(X),* Rosen Reference) Rosen Publishing Group, Inc., The.

Sandler, Martin W. The Impossible Rescue: The True Story of an Amazing Arctic Adventure. 2014. (ENG.). 176p. (J). (gr. 5). pap. 16.99 *(978-0-7636-7093-1(6))* Candlewick Pr.

Sandler, Michael. Pararescuemen in Action. 2008. (Special Ops Ser.). (Illus.). 32p. (J). (gr. 3-6). lib. bdg. 28.50 *(978-1-59716-633-1(2))* Bearport Publishing Co., Inc.

Settle, Jimmy & Rearden, Don. Never Quit: How I Became a Special Ops Pararescue Jumper. 2018. (ENG., Illus.). 304p. (YA). 18.99 *(978-1-250-13961-0(9),* 900179410, St. Martin's Griffin) St. Martin's Pr.

Slingerland, Janet. Rescue Vehicles. 2018. (Vehicles on the Job Ser.). (ENG., Illus.). 24p. (J). (gr. 1-3). 25.27 *(978-1-59953-944-7(6))* Norwood Hse. Pr.

Somervill, Barbara A. First Response - By Air. 2007. (High Interest Bks.). (ENG., Illus.). 48p. (J). (gr. 4-7). pap. 6.95 *(978-0-531-18718-0(7))* Scholastic Library Publishing.

—First Response by Air. 2007. (High Interest Books: Natural Disasters Ser.). (ENG., Illus.). 48p. (J). (gr. 7-9). lib. bdg. 21.19 *(978-0-531-12432-1(0))* Scholastic Library Publishing.

Somerville, Louisa. Rescue Vehicles. Jensen, Hans, illus. (J). mass mkt. 8.99 *(978-0-590-24557-9(0))* Scholastic, Inc.

Staniford, Linda. Rescue at Sea Around the World. 2016. (To the Rescue! Ser.). (ENG., Illus.). 24p. (J). (gr. k-2). lib. bdg. 25.99 *(978-1-4846-2753-2(9),* 131310, Heinemann) Capstone.

Thomas, William David. Wilderness Rescue Pilot, 1 vol. 2011. (Dirty & Dangerous Jobs Ser.). (ENG.). 32p. (gr. 3-3). 31.21 *(978-1-60870-180-3(8),* 798fd31a-fb05-485d-9918-60c40c951448) Cavendish Square Publishing LLC.

Torres, John Albert. Disaster in the Indian Ocean, Tsunami 2004. 2005. (Monumental Milestones Ser.). (Illus.). 48p. (YA). (gr. 4-7). lib. bdg. 29.95 *(978-1-58415-344-3(X))* Mitchell Lane Pubs.

Waeschle, Amy. Daring Avalanche Rescues. 2018. (Rescued! Ser.). (ENG., Illus.). 32p. (J). (gr. 3-9). lib. bdg. 28.65 *(978-1-5435-0115-5(X),* 137068, Capstone Pr.) Capstone.

—Daring Earthquake Rescues. 2018. (Rescued! Ser.). (ENG., Illus.). 32p. (J). (gr. 3-9). lib. bdg. 28.65 *(978-1-5435-0114-8(1),* 137067, Capstone Pr.) Capstone.

—Daring Flood Rescues. 2018. (Rescued! Ser.). (ENG., Illus.). 32p. (J). (gr. 3-9). lib. bdg. 28.65 *(978-1-5435-0113-1(3),* 137066, Capstone Pr.) Capstone.

—Daring Wildfire Rescues. 2018. (Rescued! Ser.). (ENG., Illus.). 32p. (J). (gr. 3-9). lib. bdg. 28.65 *(978-1-5435-0112-4(5),* 137065, Capstone Pr.) Capstone.

Weintraub, Aileen. First Response by Sea. 2007. (High Interest Books: Natural Disasters Ser.). (ENG., Illus.). 48p. (J). (gr. 7-9). lib. bdg. 18.69 *(978-0-531-12434-5(7))* Scholastic Library Publishing.

West, David. Rescue Vehicles. 2015. (Mechanic Mike's Machines Ser.). (ENG.). 24p. (J). (gr. k-3). 28.50 *(978-1-62588-058-1(8),* 19316, Smart Apple Media) Black Rabbit Bks.

Whiting, Jim. FBI Hostage Rescue & Swat Teams. 2014. (U. S. Special Forces Ser.). (ENG., Illus.). 48p. (J). (gr. 5-8). lib.

bdg. 35.65 *(978-1-60818-462-0(5)*, 21430, Creative Education) Creative Co., The.
Wilcox, Christine. Careers in Emergency Response. 2017. (ENG., Illus.). 80p. (J). (gr. 5-12). lib. bdg. *(978-1-68282-104-6(8))* ReferencePoint Pr., Inc.
Williams, Christopher. One Incredible Dog! Kizzy. Friedman, Judith, illus. 2006. (One Incredible Dog! Ser.). (ENG.). 32p. (J). (gr. -1-3). lib. bdg. 15.95 *(978-0-9766805-5-0(6))* Keene Publishing.
World Book, Inc. Staff, contrib. by. Robots in Action. 2019. (Illus.). 48p. (J). *(978-0-7166-4135-3(6))* World Bk., Inc.
Yomtov, Nel. Rescue. 2016. (Military Missions Ser.). (ENG., Illus.). 24p. (J). (gr. 3-7). 26.95 *(978-1-62617-438-2(5)*, Epic Bks.) Bellwether Media.
Young, Jeff C. True Underground Rescue Stories, 1 vol. 2011. (True Rescue Stories Ser.). (ENG.). 48p. (gr. 5-7). 25.27 *(978-0-7660-3676-5(6)*, d9b21d0d-82cd-4664-a112-9922b49ec273) Enslow Publishing, LLC.
Zullo, Allan. Heroes of 9/11. 2011. (Illus.). 181p. (J). pap. *(978-0-545-25506-6(6))* Scholastic, Inc.

RESCUE WORK—FICTION

Adamson, Ged. Shark Dog & the School Trip Rescue! 2018. (ENG., Illus.). 40p. (J). (gr. -1-3). 17.99 *(978-0-06-245718-9(7)*, HarperCollins) HarperCollins Pubs.
AMEET Studio. R2-D2 to the Rescue! 2016. (LEGO Star Wars Chapter Bks.: 4). (ENG.). 64p. (J). (gr. 2-5). lib. bdg. 14.75 *(978-0-606-39152-8(5))* Turtleback.
Anderson, Laurie Halse. Storm Rescue. 2008. (Vet Volunteers Ser.: 6). (ENG.). 144p. (J). (gr. 3-7). 7.99 *(978-0-14-241101-8(9)*, Puffin Books) Penguin Young Readers Group.
Appleton, Victor. Into the Abyss. 2007. (Tom Swift, Young Inventor Ser.). (ENG.). 160p. (gr. 3-7). 27.07 *(978-1-59961-350-5(6))* Spotlight.
Archer, Colleen Rutherford. Collie Rescue. Umana, Maria Gomez, illus. 2004. 112p. (J). pap. *(978-1-894131-67-4(3)*, Virago Press) Penumbra Pr.
Arnett, Dee. Gifted. 2008. 240p. pap. 18.95 *(978-1-4092-0442-8(1))* Lulu Pr., Inc.
Atchison, David C. The Adventures of Black Bart: an Encounter with Regret. 2008. 84p. pap. 7.94 *(978-0-615-23723-7(1))* Black Bart Bks.
Auerbach, Annie. Meet Boulder the Construction-Bot. 2013. (Transformers Passport to Reading Ser.). (J). lib. bdg. 13.55 *(978-0-606-32274-4(4))* Turtleback.
Bailey, Kevin. Anthony Meets the Playground Bully. 2009. 20p. pap. 13.50 *(978-1-60860-072-4(6)*, Eloquent Bks.) Strategic Book Publishing & Rights Agency (SBPRA).
Bailey, Mary R. Vhan Zeely & the Time Prevaricators. 2009. 188p. pap. 12.95 *(978-1-60911-003-1(X)*, Eloquent Bks.) Strategic Book Publishing & Rights Agency (SBPRA).
Ballantyne, R. M. The Lighthouse. 2006. pap. *(978-1-4065-0531-3(5))* Dodo Pr.
—Saved by the Lifeboat. 2004. reprint ed. pap. 1.99 *(978-1-4192-4624-1(0))* Kessinger Publishing, LLC.
Ballock-Dixon, Saige J. & Medina, Sylvia M. Chilean Mines. Eagle, Joy, illus. 2013. 35p. pap. 11.49 *(978-1-939871-00-8(X))* Green Kids Club, Inc.
Baltazar, Armand. Timeless: Diego & the Rangers of the Vastlantic. Baltazar, Armand, illus. 2017. (Timeless Ser.: 1). (ENG., Illus.). 624p. (J). (gr. 3-7). 19.99 *(978-0-06-240236-3(6)*, Tegen, Katherine Bks) HarperCollins Pubs.
Barkley, Callie. Liz & the Nosy Neighbor. Bishop, Tracy, illus. 2018. (Critter Club Ser.: 19). (ENG.). 128p. (J). (gr. k-4). 17.99 *(978-1-5344-2969-7(7))*; pap. 6.99 *(978-1-5344-2968-0(9))* Little Simon. (Little Simon).
Barnes, Jennifer Lynn. The Lovely & the Lost. 2019. (ENG.). 336p. (YA). (gr. 7-17). 17.99 *(978-1-4847-7620-9(8))* Hyperion Pr.
Barnum, P. T. Dick Broadhead: A Story of Perilous Adve. 2006. pap. 30.95 *(978-1-4286-1959-3(3))* Kessinger Publishing, LLC.
Behling, Steve. Nickelodeon PAW Patrol: School Time Adventure. Petrossi, Fabrizio, illus. 2018. (ENG.). 10p. (J). (gr. -1-k). bds. 9.99 *(978-0-7944-4020-6(7)*, Studio Fun International) Printers Row Publishing Group.
Bell, Michele Ashman. Rescue: A Jungle Adventure. 2006. 246p. (J). pap. *(978-1-59811-093-7(4))* Covenant Communications.
Bellis, Jill. The Return of the Magnificent Six: A Christmas Adventure. Farmer, Zoe, illus. 2008. (The Magnificent Six: Vol. 2). 62p. pap. 14.00 *(978-1-58690-073-1(0))* Players Pr., Inc.
Beresford, Elisabeth. Tomsk to the Rescue. 2016. (ENG., Illus.). 15p. (J). (gr. k-6). pap. *(978-0-340-73581-7(3))* Hodder & Stoughton.
Bishop, Debbie. Black Tide: Enter the Game. 2003. (Black Tide Rising Ser.: Vol. 1). (ENG., Illus.). 157p. (J). (gr. -1-12). pap. 7.95 *(978-0-9664737-3-5(6))* Left Field Angel Gate.
Blabey, Aaron. The Bad Guys. (Bad Guys Ser.: 4). 2017. (Illus.). 139p. (J). lib. bdg. 16.00 *(978-0-606-40550-8(X))* 2016. lib. bdg. 16.00 *(978-0-606-40039-8(7))* Turtleback.
—The Bad Guys in Attack of the Zittens (the Bad Guys #4), 1 vol. Blabey, Aaron, illus. 2017. (Bad Guys Ser.: 4). (ENG., Illus.). 144p. (J). (gr. 2-5). pap. 5.99 *(978-1-338-08753-6(3)*, Scholastic Paperbacks) Scholastic, Inc.
—The Bad Guys in Intergalactic Gas (the Bad Guys #5), 1 vol. 2017. (Bad Guys Ser.: 5). (ENG., Illus.). 144p. (J). (gr. 2-5). pap. 5.99 *(978-1-338-18957-5(3)*, Scholastic Paperbacks) Scholastic, Inc.
—The Bad Guys in Mission Unpluckable (the Bad Guys #2), 1 vol. Blabey, Aaron, illus. 2017. (Bad Guys Ser.: 2). (ENG., Illus.). 144p. (J). (gr. 2-5). pap. 5.99 *(978-0-545-91241-9(5)*, Scholastic Pr.) Scholastic, Inc.
—The Bad Guys in the Furball Strikes Back (the Bad Guys #3), 1 vol. Blabey, Aaron, illus. 2017. (Bad Guys Ser.: 3). (ENG., Illus.). 144p. (J). (gr. 2-5). pap. 5.99 *(978-1-338-08749-9(5)*, Scholastic Paperbacks) Scholastic, Inc.
—The Bad Guys (the Bad Guys #1), 1 vol. Blabey, Aaron, illus. 2016. (Bad Guys Ser.: 1). (ENG., Illus.). 144p. (J). (gr. 2-5). pap. 5.99 *(978-0-545-91240-2(7)*, Scholastic Pr.) Scholastic, Inc.
—Mission Unpluckable. 2017. (Bad Guys Ser.: 2). lib. bdg. 16.00 *(978-0-606-40154-8(7))* Turtleback.
Blackburn, Sheila M. Stewie Scraps & the Trolley Cart. 2008. 72p. pap. *(978-1-903853-88-7(5))* Brilliant Pubns.
Blazin' Hot: Picture Book (English) 8x8. 2006. (J). 5.99 *(978-1-933934-29-7(8))* Mighty Kids Media.
Blazin' Hot Picture Book (English) 2005. (Illus.). (J). 5.99 *(978-0-9765953-9-7(7))* Mighty Kids Media.
Botha, Si. Goosala Goop. 2009. 48p. pap. 16.50 *(978-1-60860-124-0(2)*, Strategic Bk. Publishing) Strategic Book Publishing & Rights Agency (SBPRA).
Bracken, Beth & Fraser, Kay. Believe, 1 vol. Sawyer, Odessa, illus. 2014. (Faeriegound Ser.). (ENG.). 288p. (J). (gr. 4-8). 12.95 *(978-1-62370-113-0(9)*, 125670, Capstone Young Readers) Capstone.
Bracken, Beth, et al. The Willow Queen's Gate, 1 vol. Sawyer, Odessa, illus. 2012. (Faeriegound Ser.). (ENG.). 96p. (J). (gr. 5-9). lib. bdg. 23.99 *(978-1-4342-3304-2(9)*, 116268, Stone Arch Bks.) Capstone.
Brightwood, Laura, illus. Ka-ulu the Strong. Brightwood, Laura. 2006. (J). *(978-0-9789871-3-8(6))* 3-C Institute for Social Development.
Brown, Elizabeth Rhea. Sweet Maneuvers. 2013. 36p. pap. 24.95 *(978-1-4626-8977-4(9))* America Star Bks.
Cafaro, Phyllis C. Captain Mcfinn & Friends Encounter the Bully Bunker. 2012. (ENG., Illus.). 24p. (J). 17.99 *(978-0-9859482-2-1(1)*, 9780985948221); pap. 9.99 *(978-0-9859482-3-8(X)*, 9780985948238) Captain McFinn and Friends LLC, McFinn Pr.
Carbone, Courtney. Break the Ice!/Everest Saves the Day! (PAW Patrol) MJ Illustrations, illus. 2017. (Step into Reading Ser.). (ENG.). 48p. (J). (gr. -1-1). pap. 5.99 *(978-1-5247-6400-5(0)*, Random Hse. Bks. for Young Readers) Random Hse. Children's Bks.
Carlson, Claudia. Avi & the Snowy Day. Decker, C. B., illus. 2017. (ENG.). 32p. (J). 9.95 *(978-1-68115-528-9(1)*, 6363aae9-476f-492a-a905-b7d889214a40) Behrman Hse., Inc.
—Avi the Ambulance Goes to School. Carlson, Claudia, illus. 2015. (ENG., Illus.). 32p. (J). pap. 9.95 *(978-1-68115-503-6(6)*, 193dd950-0960-428f-9e07-e9f10212d629) Behrman Hse., Inc.
Caron, Eleonore. Gizmo & Ellen Mysteries: The Case of the Missing Boy. 2012. 24p. pap. 24.95 *(978-1-4626-6747-5(3))* America Star Bks.
Carter, Ally. Not If I Save You First. (ENG.). 304p. (gr. 7). 2019. (J). pap. 10.99 *(978-1-338-13415-5(9))* 2018. (YA). 18.99 *(978-1-338-13414-8(0))* Scholastic, Inc. (Scholastic Pr.).
Cartwheel: A Sequel to Double Eagle. 2013. (ENG.). 252p. (YA). 17.00 *(978-0-9844460-3-2(6))* Bucking Horse Bks.
Castillo, Ina. Red the Super Wiener. 2008. 24p. pap. 24.95 *(978-1-60474-897-0(4))* America Star Bks.
Chandler, Jeff. The New Kitten: A Story about a Foster Puppy, 1 vol. 2009. 48p. pap. 24.95 *(978-1-61546-176-9(0))* America Star Bks.
Charles L. Wilson. The Search Is On: The Wild Adventures of Lester & Dora. 2009. 200p. 24.99 *(978-1-4269-1813-1(5))*; pap. 14.99 *(978-1-4269-1812-4(7))* Trafford Publishing.
Chick, Bryan. The Secret Zoo: Raids & Rescues. 2013. (Secret Zoo Ser.: 5). (ENG.). 272p. (J). (gr. 3-7). 16.99 *(978-0-06-219228-8(0)*, Greenwillow Bks.) HarperCollins Pubs.
Citro, Asia. Unicorn & Germs: Zoey & Sassafras #6. Lindsay, Marion, illus. 2018. (Zoey & Sassafras Ser.: 6). 96p. (J). (gr. 1-5). pap. 5.99 *(978-1-943147-47-2(7)*, 28266b15-d47f-4eb9-a5f7-47058f41d3fc) Innovation Pr., The.
Clover, Peter. Rescue Riders: Fire Alert. l.t. ed. 2007. 108p. per. *(978-1-905665-30-3(X))* Pollinger In Print.
Cohen, Alana. Heroes! (LEGO City: Lift-The-Flap Board Book) White, David & White, Dave, illus. 2011. (LEGO City Ser.). (ENG.). 16p. (J). (gr. -1-k). bds. 9.99 *(978-0-545-27439-5(7))* Scholastic, Inc.
Coleman, Claudia. Yo Yo & the Great Flood. 2008. 100p. pap. 22.95 *(978-1-60145-606-9(9))* Booklocker.com, Inc.
Collier, Kevin Scott. Journeys of Hope, Pearl of Wisdom. Collier, Kevin Scott, illus. 2006. (Illus.). 28p. (J). E-Book 9.95 incl. cd-rom *(978-1-933090-31-3(6))* Guardian Angel Publishing, Inc.
Copeland, Cynthia L. Elin's Island. 2003. (Single Titles Ser.: up). (ENG.). 144p. (YA). (gr. 6-12). lib. bdg. 22.60 *(978-0-7613-2522-2(0)*, Millbrook Pr.) Lerner Publishing Group.
Cox, Renee K. Sammie Jane Saves Charlie: Cougar's Rescue. 2009. (Illus.). 56p. pap. 11.95 *(978-1-4327-3129-8(7))* Outskirts Pr., Inc.
Cronin, Doreen. The Legend of Diamond Lil: A J. J. Tully Mystery. Cornell, Kevin, illus. 2012. (ENG.). 144p. (J). (gr. 1-5). lib. bdg. 15.89 *(978-0-06-198578-2(3)*, Balzer & Bray) HarperCollins Pubs.
—Rescue Bunnies. Menchin, Scott, illus. 2010. (ENG.). 32p. (J). (gr. -1-3). 16.99 *(978-0-06-112871-4(6)*, Balzer & Bray) HarperCollins Pubs.
Cronshaw, Joseph. Podge & Dodge. 2009. 32p. pap. 13.50 *(978-1-60693-868-3(1)*, Strategic Bk. Publishing) Strategic Book Publishing & Rights Agency (SBPRA).
Curious George Snowy Day. 2007. (Curious George Ser.). (ENG., Illus.). 24p. (J). (gr. -1-3). 4.99 *(978-0-618-80043-8(3)*, 489784, Clarion Bks.) HarperCollins Pubs.
Dahlstrom, Kathryn. Peppy's Rescue. Date not set. (Good News Club Ser.). (J). (gr. 4-11). pap. 4.99 *(978-1-55976-826-9(6))* CEF Pr.
Dale, Penny. Dinosaur Rescue! Dale, Penny, illus. 2016. (Dinosaurs on the Go Ser.). (ENG., Illus.). 24p. (J). (-k). bds. 6.99 *(978-0-7636-8000-8(1))* Candlewick Pr.
Dalmatian Press Staff. To the Rescue! 2008. (ENG.). 6p. bds. 4.95 *(978-1-58117-724-4(0)*, Intervisual/Piggy Toes) Bendon, Inc.
Darke, J. A. Attack of the Mud Creatures. Evergreen, Nelson, illus. 2015. (Spine Shivers Ser.). (ENG.). 128p. (J). (gr. 4-6). lib. bdg. 27.32 *(978-1-4965-0220-9(5)*, 128034, Stone Arch Bks.) Capstone.
David, Erica. Extreme Rescue: Crocodile Mission. McGee, Warner, illus. 2009. (Go, Diego, Go! Ser.). (ENG.). 24p. (J). pap. 3.99 *(978-1-4169-8515-0(8)*, Simon Spotlight/Nickelodeon) Simon Spotlight/Nickelodeon.
Davis, Helen J. Good Times with Gregory: Birds: Rescuing a Baby Bird. Davis, Robyn L., illus. 2008. (Good Times with Gregory Ser.). 54p. (J). (gr. -1-4). 12.95 *(978-1-935122-10-4(X))* K&B Products.
Depken, Kristen L. Chase's Space Case (Paw Patrol) Jackson, Mike, illus. 2016. (Step into Reading Ser.). (ENG.). 24p. (J). (gr. -1-1). 4.99 *(978-0-553-53886-1(1)*, Random Hse. Bks. for Young Readers) Random Hse. Children's Bks.
—Dinosaur Rescue! (Jurassic World: Fallen Kingdom) Random House, illus. 2018. (Step into Reading Ser.). (ENG.). 32p. (J). (gr. k-3). pap. 4.99 *(978-0-525-58078-2(6)*, Random Hse. Bks. for Young Readers) Random Hse. Children's Bks.
—Rubble to the Rescue! (Paw Patrol) Jackson, Mike, illus. 2015. (Step into Reading Ser.). (ENG.). 24p. (J). (gr. -1-1). 5.99 *(978-0-553-52290-7(6)*, Random Hse. Bks. for Young Readers) Random Hse. Children's Bks.
Devine, Ginger. The Missing Goose Egg: A Sam the Lamb Mystery. 2009. 32p. pap. 14.95 *(978-1-4389-8839-9(7))* AuthorHouse.
DiCicco, Sue & Mawhinney, Art, illus. Diego y los Dinosaurios. 2008. (Go, Diego, Go! Ser.). Orig. Title: Diego's Great Dinosaur Rescue. (SPA & ENG.). 24p. (J). (gr. -1-2). pap. 3.99 *(978-1-4169-5871-0(1)*, Libros Para Ninos) Libros Para Ninos.
—Diego's Great Dinosaur Rescue. 2008. (Go, Diego, Go! Ser.). (ENG.). 24p. (J). (gr. -1-2). pap. 3.99 *(978-1-4169-5867-3(3)*, Simon Spotlight/Nickelodeon) Simon Spotlight/Nickelodeon.
Disney Press Editors. Awesome Guy to the Rescue! / Bella's Big Break. 2015. (Doc Mcstuffins 8X8 Ser.). (J). lib. bdg. 16.00 *(978-0-606-36899-5(X))* Turtleback.
—Rescue from Jabba's Palace. 2015. (Star Wars: World of Reading Ser.). (J). lib. bdg. 13.55 *(978-0-606-35930-6(3))* Turtleback.
Dixon, Virginia. What Happened to Willie? Thomas, Tim, illus. 2007. 32p. (J). 16.00 *(978-0-9795386-0-5(2))* Grand Productions.
Dormer, Frank W. Firefighter Duckies! Dormer, Frank W., illus. 2017. (ENG., Illus.). 40p. (J). (gr. -1-3). 17.99 *(978-1-4814-6090-3(0)*, Atheneum Bks. for Young Readers) Simon & Schuster Children's Publishing.
Dreyer, Ellen. Starfishers to the Rescue. 2012. (First Chapters: Set 2 Ser.: Vol. 10). (ENG., Illus.). 64p. (J). (gr. 2-3). pap. 9.50 *(978-0-7652-0886-6(5))* Modern Curriculum Pr.
Dyan, Penelope. Vita Mccafee Mckay, Cat Rescuer. Dyan, Penelope, illus. 2009. (Illus.). 44p. pap. 11.95 *(978-1-935118-53-4(6))* Bellissima Publishing, LLC.
Ehlin, Gina. Emma & Friends; Emma Rescues Cali. Ayzenberg, Nina, illus. l.t. ed. 2006. 24p. (J). 17.99 *(978-1-59879-113-6(3))*; per. 10.99 *(978-1-59879-112-9(5))* Lifevest Publishing, Inc.
Eichler, Ken. Swift Eagle's Odyssey with the Buffalo. 2007. 59p. pap. 16.95 *(978-1-60474-199-5(6))* America Star Bks.
Filbin, Sandra A. The Enchanted World: A Tooth Fairy's Tale. 2010. 158p. pap. 14.50 *(978-1-60860-379-4(2)*, Strategic Bk. Publishing) Strategic Book Publishing & Rights Agency (SBPRA).
Flores, Catty, illus. Les Misérables. adapted ed. 2014. (ENG.). 64p. pap. 7.95 *(978-1-906230-79-1(X))* Real Reads Ltd. GBR. Dist: Casemate Pubs. & Bk. Distributors, LLC.
Free Wheelin' Coloring/Activity Book (English) 2005. (Illus.). (J). 2.99 *(978-0-9770455-7-0(9))* Mighty Kids Media.
Gallagher, Diana G. The Great Kitten Challenge, 1 vol. Puglisi, Adriana & Puglisi, Adriana, illus. 2013. (Pet Friends Forever Ser.). (ENG.). 88p. (J). (gr. 1-3). pap. 5.95 *(978-1-4795-1864-7(6)*, 123502, Picture Window Bks.) Capstone.
Gannett, Ruth Stiles & Gannett, Ruth Chrisman. My Father's Dragon. 2019. (ENG., Illus.). 96p. (gr. 1-4). 15.95 *(978-0-486-83749-9(1)*, 837491) Dover Pubns., Inc.
Garis, Howard R. The Curlytops & Their Pets. 2009. 120p. pap. 10.95 *(978-1-60664-341-9(X))* Rodgers, Alan Bks.
Gayton, Sam. Lilliput, 1 vol. Ratterree, Alice, illus. (ENG.). 256p. (J). (gr. 3-7). 2017. pap. 8.95 *(978-1-68263-006-8(4))* 2015. 16.95 *(978-1-56145-806-6(5))* Peachtree Publishing Co. Inc.
Getsinger, Mary. A Dream Come True. 2009. 20p. pap. 9.50 *(978-1-4251-8885-6(0))* Trafford Publishing.
Gianferrari, Maria. Operation Rescue Dog. Uribe, Luisa, illus. 2018. (ENG.). 40p. (J). 17.99 *(978-1-4998-0667-0(1))* Little Bee Books Inc.
Golden Books. PAW Patrol Little Golden Book Favorites, Volume 2 (PAW Patrol) Golden Books, illus. 2018. (Little Golden Book Ser.). (ENG., Illus.). 80p. (J). (-k). 7.99 *(978-1-5247-7272-7(0)*, Golden Bks.) Random Hse. Children's Bks.
—Pirate Pups! (Paw Patrol) Petrossi, Fabrizio, illus. 2016. (Little Golden Book Ser.). (ENG.). 24p. (J). (gr. -1-k). 5.99 *(978-0-553-53888-5(8)*, Golden Bks.) Random Hse. Children's Bks.
—The Pups Save Christmas! (Paw Patrol) Moore, Harry, illus. 2015. (Big Golden Book Ser.). (ENG.). 48p. (J). (gr. -1-2). 10.99 *(978-0-553-52391-1(0)*, Golden Bks.) Random Hse. Children's Bks.
Graham, Bob. How to Heal a Broken Wing. Graham, Bob, illus. 2017. (ENG., Illus.). 40p. (J). (gr. -1-2). 8.99 *(978-0-7636-9841-6(5))* Candlewick Pr.
Gurtler, Janet. Shyanna's Wish. Wood, Katie, illus. 2015. (Mermaid Kingdom Ser.). (ENG.). 96p. (J). (gr. 3-5). 23.99 *(978-1-4342-9696-2(2)*, 127009, Stone Arch Bks.) Capstone.
Haddix, Margaret Peterson. Among the Brave. 2004. (Shadow Children Ser.: Bk. 5). 132p. (J). lib. bdg. 20.00 *(978-1-4242-0392-5(9))* Fitzgerald Bks.
Halahmy, Miriam. Rip to the Rescue. 2020. (ENG.). 208p. (J). (gr. 3-7). 16.99 *(978-0-8234-4441-0(4))* Holiday Hse., Inc.
Hall, Marjory. The Gold-Lined Box. 2003. 224p. 11.95 *(978-0-9714612-6-0(0))* Green Mansion Pr. LLC.
Hamilton, Kersten. Yellow Copter. Petrone, Valeria, illus. 2016. (Red Truck & Friends Ser.). 26p. (J). (— 1). bds. 8.99 *(978-1-101-99796-3(6)*, Viking Books for Young Readers) Penguin Young Readers Group.
Hansen, Amelia, illus. It's Raining Pups & Dogs! 2013. (Sit! Stay! Read! Ser.). (ENG.). 24p. (J). (gr. k). 16.95 *(978-0-940719-16-3(9))* Gryphon Pr., The.
Harley, Stephen. The Christmastime Dog Rescue. 2013. (ENG.). 24p. pap. 19.99 *(978-1-4624-0774-3(9)*, Inspiring Voices) Author Solutions, LLC.
Harpan, Gaile. The Ballad of Omar the Cat. Reddy, Sneha, illus. 2008. 28p. pap. 12.95 *(978-0-9820479-1-0(6))* Peppertree Pr., The.
Hart, Alison. Whirlwind. 2010. (Shadow Horse Ser.). 272p. (YA). (gr. 7-8). pap. 8.99 *(978-0-375-86005-8(3)*, Laurel Leaf) Random Hse. Children's Bks.
Haslett, Katherine A. The Day Amy Met the Prime Minister & Mrs. Blair. 2007. (Illus.). 32p. (J). pap. 8.00 *(978-0-8059-7353-2(2))* Dorrance Publishing Co., Inc.
Henninger, Robert. The Rangers of the Forest. Higgins, Beatrice, illus. 2003. (ENG.). 82p. pap. 12.95 *(978-1-4120-0368-1(7))* Trafford Publishing.
Henry, Steve. Hide! 2018. (I Like to Read Ser.). (Illus.). 32p. (J). (gr. -1-3). 14.99 *(978-0-8234-3773-3(6))* Holiday Hse., Inc.
—Hide! 2019. (I Like to Read Ser.). (ENG.). 30p. (J). (gr. k-1). 17.96 *(978-0-87617-954-3(5))* Penworthy Co., LLC, The.
Henson, Jim & Martin, Craig. Doozers. 2015. (Illus.). (J). *(978-1-4806-9271-8(9)*, Simon Spotlight) Simon Spotlight.
Higginson, Sheila Sweeny. Diego rescata al bebé manatí (Diego's Manatee Rescue) McGee, Warner, illus. 2009. (Go, Diego, Go! Ser.). (SPA.). 24p. (J). pap. 3.99 *(978-1-4169-7983-8(2)*, Libros Para Ninos) Libros Para Ninos.
Hilburn, L. M. Little Princesses to the Rescue. 2008. 24p. pap. 24.95 *(978-1-60672-783-6(4))* America Star Bks.
Holden, Pam. Baby Whale's Mistake, 1 vol. Aziz, Lamia, illus. 2009. (Red Rocket Readers Ser.). (ENG.). 16p. (gr. 2-2). pap. *(978-1-877363-87-0(1))* Flying Start Bks.
Holsather, Kent /Wilson. Sara's Moon. 2007. (Illus.). 176p. (YA). per. 12.95 *(978-0-9729101-3-2(1))* Lonejack Mountain Pr.
Howard, A. G. Ensnared. 2015. (Splintered Ser.: 3). (J). lib. bdg. 19.60 *(978-0-606-37434-7(5))* Turtleback.
Howard, Cheryl L. Mikhael the Mighty: Be True to Who You Are & You Can Never Go Wrong. 2009. 52p. pap. 18.50 *(978-1-60860-760-0(7)*, Strategic Bk. Publishing) Strategic Book Publishing & Rights Agency (SBPRA).
Hughes, Shirley. Alfie Gets in First. 2009. (Alfie Ser.). (Illus.). 32p. (J). (gr. -1-k). pap. 14.99 *(978-1-86230-783-4(0)*, Red Fox) Random House Children's Books GBR. Dist: Independent Pubs. Group.
Hulk to the Rescue. 2003. (J). per. *(978-1-57657-811-7(9))* Paradise Pr., Inc.
Hunt, Bonnie. The Missing Chimp: A Grayson Twins Adventures, 1 vol. 2009. 100p. pap. 19.95 *(978-1-60813-481-6(4))* America Star Bks.
Hurtado, Patricia. The Magical Feline & the White Haven. 2009. 142p. pap. 10.95 *(978-1-60594-325-1(8)*, Llumina Pr.) Aeon Publishing Inc.
Inches, Alison. I Can Save the Earth! One Little Monster Learns to Reduce, Reuse, & Recycle. Garofoli, Viviana, illus. 2008. (Little Green Bks.). (ENG.). 24p. (J). (gr. -1-1). pap. 5.99 *(978-1-4169-6789-7(3)*, Little Simon) Little Simon.
Jackson, Maureen. You Count Too. 2012. 20p. pap. 17.99 *(978-1-4772-1241-7(8))* AuthorHouse.
Jennings, Sharon. Batnapped. *(978-1-897039-30-4(1))* High Interest Publishing (HIP).
Johnson, Gerald J. J. Ellie Saves the Day, 1 vol. Funke, Peggy, illus. 2009. 12p. pap. 24.95 *(978-1-60836-709-2(6))* America Star Bks.
Johnson, Sandi & Fefie, Flora. Zemo to the Rescue: Dorp 7 Rock Band. l.t. ed. 2003. (Illus.). 15p. (J). (gr. k-5). spiral bd. 4.99 *(978-1-929063-25-3(3)*, 327) Moons & Stars Publishing For Children.
Jones, Janey Louise. Superfairies to the Rescue. Poh, Jennie, illus. 2018. (ENG.). 192p. (J). (gr. k-3). pap., pap., pap. 6.95 *(978-1-62370-990-7(3)*, 137403, Capstone Young Readers) Capstone.
Keene, Carolyn. The Bungalow Mystery #3, No. 3. 2014. (Nancy Drew Ser.: 3). 192p. (J). (gr. 3-7). 7.99 *(978-0-448-47971-2(0)*, Grosset & Dunlap) Penguin Young Readers Group.
—The Hidden Staircase #2, No. 2. 2014. (Nancy Drew Ser.: 2). 192p. (J). (gr. 3-7). 9.99 *(978-0-448-47970-5(2)*, Grosset & Dunlap) Penguin Young Readers Group.
—The Mystery at Lilac Inn #4. 2014. (Nancy Drew Ser.: 4). 192p. (J). (gr. 3-7). 10.99 *(978-0-448-47972-9(9)*, Grosset & Dunlap) Penguin Young Readers Group.
—The Secret of the Old Clock #1, Bk. 1. 2014. (Nancy Drew Ser.: 1). 192p. (J). (gr. 3-7). 9.99 *(978-0-448-47969-9(9)*, Grosset & Dunlap) Penguin Young Readers Group.
Kennedy, Marlane. Earthquake Shock. 2014. (Disaster Strikes Ser.: 1). lib. bdg. 14.75 *(978-0-606-35827-9(7))* Turtleback.
Kipling, Rudyard. Captains Courageous. 2008. (Bring the Classics to Life Ser.). (ENG., Illus.). 72p. (gr. 4-12). pap., act. bk. ed. 10.95 *(978-0-931334-66-5(7)*, EDCTR-401B) EDCON Publishing Group.
Korman, Gordon. Escape. 2008. (Island (Playaway Audio) Ser.). (J). 34.99 *(978-1-60514-854-0(7))* Findaway World, LLC.
—Zoobreak. 2009. 230p. (J). *(978-0-545-20027-1(X)*, Scholastic Pr.) Scholastic, Inc.
Krueger, Jim. Secret Alliance, 1 vol., 5. Padilla, Ariel, illus. 2008. (Z Graphic Novels / Tomo Ser.). (ENG.). 160p. (J). pap. 6.99 *(978-0-310-71304-3(8))* Zondervan.
Landers, Ace. Coast Guard to the Rescue. 2018. (Lego 8x8 Ser.). (ENG.). 24p. (J). (gr. -1-k). 13.89 *(978-1-64310-228-3(1))* Penworthy Co., LLC, The.
—Coast Guard to the Rescue. 2018. (LEGO City 8X8 Ser.). (Illus.). 24p. (J). lib. bdg. 14.75 *(978-0-606-41181-3(X))* Turtleback.
Lawson, Tanya. Pawpaw Harry & the Baby Squirrel. 2011. 24p. pap. 12.00 *(978-1-4567-4616-2(2))* AuthorHouse.
Lester, Alison. The Snow Pony. 2006. (ENG., Illus.). 208p. (J). (gr. 5-7). pap. 12.95 *(978-0-618-77125-7(5)*, 489867, Clarion Bks.) HarperCollins Pubs.
Little Airplane Productions & Fogarty, Alexandria, illus. Baby Beaver Rescue. 2009. (Wonder Pets! Ser.). (ENG.). 24p. (J). (gr. -1-2). pap. 3.99 *(978-1-4169-8499-3(2)*, Simon Spotlight/Nickelodeon) Simon Spotlight/Nickelodeon.
Lively, Deborah Dreher. Hateya Sam. 2009. 32p. pap. 13.75 *(978-1-60860-029-8(7)*, Eloquent Bks.) Strategic Book Publishing & Rights Agency (SBPRA).

Lush, Nella. Gracie & Belle Never Again! 2007. 20p. per. 24.95 *(978-1-4241-8373-9(1))* America Star Bks.
Lyle-Soffe, Shari. On the Go with Rooter & Snuffle. Collier, Kevin Scott, illus. 2008. 20p. pap. 9.95 *(978-1-933090-96-2(0))* Guardian Angel Publishing, Inc.
M F Feierabend, J. Olivia Ponty & Friends to the Rescue. 2012. 32p. pap. 32.70 *(978-1-4771-1081-2(X))* Xlibris Corp.
Macdangereuse, T. T. The Untamed Scoundrel. 2014. (Epic Tales from Adventure Time Ser.). lib. bdg. 17.20 *(978-0-606-35718-0(1))* Turtleback.
Mackall, Dandi Daley. Dark Horse. 2009. (Starlight Animal Rescue Ser.: 4). (ENG.). 224p. (J). (gr. 3-7). mass mkt. 6.99 *(978-1-4143-1271-2(7)*, 4600265, Tyndale Kids) Tyndale Hse. Pubs.
Maher, Alex, illus. El Safari de Diego. 2007. (Go, Diego, Go! Ser.).Tr. of Diego's Safari Rescue. (SPA.). 24p. (J). (gr. -1-2). pap. 3.99 *(978-1-4169-5998-4(X)*, Libros Para Ninos) Libros Para Ninos.
Maher, Allison. I, the Spy. 2006. (ENG.). 180p. (J). (gr. 4-7). per. 13.95 *(978-1-897235-04-1(6))* Thistledown Pr., Ltd. CAN. Dist: Univ. of Toronto Pr.
Manning, Matthew K. The League of Laughs. Doescher, Erik, illus. 2018. (You Choose Stories: Justice League Ser.). (ENG.). 112p. (J). (gr. 2-6). pap. 6.95 *(978-1-4965-6556-3(8)*, 138569, Stone Arch Bks.) Capstone.
—U. S. Special Forces: Ghosts of the Night. Enecio, Jeremy, illus. 2016. (U. S. Special Ops Ser.). (ENG.). 96p. (J). (gr. 3-4). E-Book 31.99 *(978-1-4965-3477-4(8)*, 69904, Stone Arch Bks.) Capstone.
—The Ultimate Weapon. Doescher, Erik, illus. 2018. (You Choose Stories: Justice League Ser.). (ENG.). 112p. (J). (gr. 2-6). pap. 6.95 *(978-1-4965-6557-0(6)*, 138570, Stone Arch Bks.) Capstone.
Martinez, Heather, illus. Ready, Set, Tow! 2018. (J). *(978-1-5444-0206-2(6)*, Golden Bks.) Random Hse. Children's Bks.
Mawhinney, Art, illus. Diego's Arctic Rescue. 2009. (Go, Diego, Go! Ser.). (ENG.). 24p. (J). (gr. -1-2). pap. 3.99 *(978-1-4169-8504-4(2)*, Simon Spotlight/Nickelodeon) Simon Spotlight/Nickelodeon.
—Dora & Diego to the Rescue! 2010. (Go, Diego, Go! Ser.). (ENG.). 48p. (J). pap. 5.99 *(978-1-4424-0660-5(7)*, Simon Spotlight/Nickelodeon) Simon Spotlight/Nickelodeon.
Mayer, Mercer. Little Critter: to the Rescue! Mayer, Mercer, illus. 2008. (My First I Can Read Ser.). (ENG., Illus.). 32p. (J). (gr. -1-3). pap. 4.99 *(978-0-06-083547-7(8)*, HarperCollins) HarperCollins Pubs.
—To the Rescue! Mayer, Mercer, illus. 2008. (My First I Can Read Bks.). (ENG., Illus.). 32p. (J). (gr. -1-3). 16.99 *(978-0-06-083548-4(6))* HarperCollins Pubs.
McCully, Emily Arnold. Los Patitos Pasean. 2020. (¡Me Gusta Leer! Ser.). (Illus.). 24p. (J). (gr. -1-3). pap. 8.99 *(978-0-8234-4687-2(5))* Holiday Hse., Inc.
McGrath, Jennifer. Chocolate River Rescue, 1 vol. 2007. (ENG.). 112p. (J). (gr. 4-7). pap. 12.95 *(978-1-55109-600-1(5)*, fb45b529-c96f-4a22-933d-3f4b5ca71b5f) Nimbus Publishing, Ltd. CAN. Dist: Baker & Taylor Publisher Services (BTPS).
McKay, Hilary. Lulu & the Hedgehog in the Rain. 2015. (Lulu Ser.: 5). (J). lib. bdg. 14.75 *(978-0-606-41565-1(3))* Turtleback.
McKee, David. Elmer & Butterfly. McKee, David, illus. 2015. (Elmer Ser.). (ENG., Illus.). 32p. (J). (gr. -1-3). 18.99 *(978-1-4677-6326-4(8)*, 088407ce-7cbf-4fd4-84e9-c3f6660da644) Lerner Publishing Group.
McKendry, Sam. To the Rescue! 2007. 6p. 9.95 *(978-1-58117-562-2(0)*, Intervisual/Piggy Toes) Bendon, Inc.
McKimmie, Chris. Lara of Newtown. 2016. (ENG., Illus.). 32p. (J). (gr. -1-3). 19.99 *(978-1-76011-232-5(1))* Allen & Unwin AUS. Dist: Independent Pubs. Group.
Meintjes, Chris. Angel's Flight. 2009. 156p. 25.99 *(978-1-4269-0843-9(1))*; pap. 15.99 *(978-1-4269-0842-2(3))* Trafford Publishing.
Meister, Cari. The Stranded Orca, 1 vol. Harpster, Steve, illus. 2012. (Ocean Tales Ser.). (ENG.). 32p. (J). (gr. 2-3). lib. bdg. 22.65 *(978-1-4342-4026-2(6)*, 118411, Stone Arch Bks.) Capstone.
Miles, Ellen. Bear. 2009. (Puppy Place Ser.: 14). lib. bdg. 14.75 *(978-0-606-04427-1(2))* Turtleback.
—Champ. 2016. 84p. (J). *(978-1-5182-2778-3(3))* Scholastic, Inc.
—Mocha. 2013. (Puppy Place Ser.: 29). lib. bdg. 14.75 *(978-0-606-32384-0(8))* Turtleback.
Miller, Jeff. The Nerdy Dozen. 2015. (Nerdy Dozen Ser.: 1). (ENG.). 320p. (J). (gr. 3-7). pap. 6.99 *(978-0-06-227263-8(2)*, HarperCollins) HarperCollins Pubs.
Miyazaki, Hayao. Ponyo Film Comic, Vol. 1. movie tie-in ed. 2009. (Ponyo Film Comics Ser.: 1). (ENG., Illus.). 172p. (J). pap. 9.99 *(978-1-4215-3077-2(5))* Viz Media.
—Ponyo Film Comic, Vol. 2. movie tie-in ed. 2009. (Ponyo Film Comics Ser.: 2). (ENG., Illus.). 152p. (J). pap. 9.99 *(978-1-4215-3078-9(3))* Viz Media.
—Ponyo Film Comic, Vol. 3. movie tie-in ed. 2009. (Ponyo Film Comics Ser.: 3). (ENG., Illus.). 152p. (J). pap. 9.99 *(978-1-4215-3079-6(1))* Viz Media.
Moore, Eva. Lucky Ducklings. Carpenter, Nancy, illus. 2013. (ENG.). 32p. (J). (gr. k-2). 16.99 *(978-0-439-44861-1(1)*, Orchard Bks.) Scholastic, Inc.
Morgan, Michaela. Shy Shark. Gomez, Elena, illus. 2005. (ENG.). 24p. (J). lib. bdg. 23.65 *(978-1-59646-722-4(3))* Dingles & Co.
Morris, J. & J. Little Black Pearl. 2010. 80p. pap. *(978-1-905553-51-8(X))* BookPublishingWorld.
Morris, Kim. Tinker Bell & the Great Fairy Rescue. 2010. (ENG.). 32p. 12.99 *(978-1-4231-2925-7(3))* Disney Pr.
Mors, Peter D. & Mors, Terry M. L D the Littlest Dragster. Weiss, Tracy, illus. 2009. 36p. pap. 16.99 *(978-1-4389-7445-3(0))* AuthorHouse.
Myhre, J. A. A Bird, a Girl, & a Rescue: Book Two of the Rwendigo Tales. Masso, Acacia, illus. 2016. (ENG.). 144p. (J). pap. 16.99 *(978-1-942572-69-5(7))* New Growth Pr.
Nelson, James Gary. Smileytooth & Bushwack Plaque. Bumstead, Debbie, illus. 2009. 16p. pap. 9.95 *(978-1-61633-009-5(0))* Guardian Angel Publishing, Inc.
Noland, Charles. The Adventures of Drew & Ellie: The Daring Rescue. Moyer, Tom, illus. 2nd ed. 2006. 92p. (J). per. 7.95 *(978-0-9789297-2-5(1))* TMD Enterprises.
Northrop, Michael. Surrounded by Sharks. 2014. (ENG.). 224p. (YA). (gr. 4-7). 18.99 *(978-0-545-61545-7(3)*, Scholastic Pr.) Scholastic, Inc.
Odgers, Darrel & Odgers, Sally. Bush Rescue. Dawson, Janine, illus. 2016. 89p. (J). *(978-1-61067-563-5(0))* Kane Miller.
Odgers, Sally & Darrel. Bush Rescue: Pup Patrol. Dawson, Janine, illus. 2017. 96p. (J). pap. 4.99 *(978-1-61067-519-2(3))* Kane Miller.
—Storm Rescue: Pup Patrol. Dawson, Janine, illus. 2018. 89p. (J). pap. 4.99 *(978-1-61067-657-1(2))* Kane Miller.
O'Donnell, Liam & O'Donnell, Laura. Duncan: A Brave Rescue. Hynes, Robert, illus. 2004. (Pet Tales Ser.). (ENG.). 32p. (J). (gr. -1-3). 4.95 *(978-1-59249-291-6(6)*, 1B001) Soundprints.
—Duncan: A Brave Rescue. Hynes, Robert, illus. 2005. (Pet Tales Ser.). (ENG.). 32p. (J). (gr. -1-2). 2.95 *(978-1-59249-292-3(4)*, 1B003) Soundprints.
Parker, John. Chaos Mountain. 2007. 96p. (YA). pap. *(978-1-4207-0734-2(5))* Sundance/Newbridge Educational Publishing.
Patron, Susan. Lucky Breaks. Phelan, Matt, illus. 2009. (ENG.). 192p. (J). (gr. 3-7). 16.99 *(978-1-4169-3998-6(9)*, Atheneum Bks. for Young Readers) Simon & Schuster Children's Publishing.
Patterson, James. Maximum Ride Boxed Set #1. 2010. (ENG.). 1392p. (YA). (gr. 5-17). pap. 32.99 *(978-0-316-12825-4(2)*, Jimmy Patterson) Little Brown & Co.
Peters, Tony. Kids on a Case: The Case of the Ten Grand Kidnapping. 2008. 84p. pap. 9.95 *(978-1-60693-173-8(3)*, Eloquent Bks.) Strategic Book Publishing & Rights Agency (SBPRA).
Pickett, Anola. Whisper Island. 2013. (ENG.). 235p. (J). (gr. 3-7). pap. 14.99 *(978-1-4621-1167-1(X)*, Sweetwater Bks.) Cedar Fort, Inc./CFI Distribution.
Pippin, Sheila C. Katrina: Through Mango's Eyes. Pippin, Kristin A. & Pippin, Sheila C., illus. 2007. (J). (gr. -1-5). pap. 12.95 *(978-1-56167-956-0(9))* American Literary Pr.
Publications International Ltd. Staff, ed. Look & Find Wolverine & X Men. 2009. 24p. (J). 7.98 *(978-1-4127-3592-6(0)*, PIL Kids) Publications International, Ltd.
Random House. Sea Patrol to the Rescue! (PAW Patrol) Lovett, Nate, illus. 2018. (Pictureback(R) Ser.). (ENG.). 24p. (J). (gr. -1-2). pap. 5.99 *(978-1-5247-6875-1(8)*, Random Hse. Bks. for Young Readers) Random Hse. Children's Bks.
Ransom, Candice. The Underground Adventure of Arly Dunbar, Cave Explorer. Hammond, Ted & Carbajal, Richard Pimentel, illus. 2011. (History's Kid Heroes Set III Ser.). pap. 51.02 *(978-0-7613-7640-8(2)*, Graphic Universe™) Lerner Publishing Group.
Rees, Douglas. Uncle Pirate to the Rescue. Auth, Tony, illus. 2010. (ENG.). 112p. (J). (gr. 2-5). pap. 6.99 *(978-1-4169-7505-2(5)*, McElderry, Margaret K. Bks.) McElderry, Margaret K. Bks.
Richards, Pat. Bardolph Bedivere Wolf Returns. Richards, Charles, illus. 2007. 42p. (J). *(978-0-9790796-4-1(0))* PJR Assocs., Ltd.
Rigby. Golden Lasso. (gr. k-1). 23.00 *(978-0-7635-9021-5(5))* Rigby Education.
Riner, Kendall F. The Rescue Adventures of Fireman Frank. 2006. (Illus.). 52p. (J). pap. 12.00 *(978-0-9786369-1-3(0))* Warwick Hse. Publishing.
Ripley, Esther. Heroes to the Rescue. 2016. (DK Reader Level 2 Ser.). lib. bdg. 13.55 *(978-0-606-38711-8(0))* Turtleback.
Rocha, K. E. Hidden Rock Rescue (Secrets of Bearhaven #3) 2016. (Secrets of Bearhaven Ser.: 3). (ENG.). 224p. (J). (gr. 3-7). 14.99 *(978-0-545-81305-1(0)*, Scholastic Pr.) Scholastic, Inc.
Roddy, Lee. The Legend of Fire. 2006. (Ladd Family Adventure Ser.: Vol. 2). (Illus.). 133p. (J). (gr. 3-7). per. 7.99 *(978-0-88062-251-6(2))* Mott Media.
Rogers, Wanda Gayle. Miss Bean & the Great Tricycle Rescue: The Great Tricycle Rescue. 2007. (J). 7.95 *(978-1-59872-735-7(4))* Instant Pub.
Rooney, Anne. Muffin, 1 vol. Julian, Sean, illus. 2009. (Go! Readers Ser.). (ENG.). 48p. (J). (gr. 1-2). pap. 13.85 *(978-1-60754-270-4(6)*, cb02cbe0-5b4c-41ea-ab76-789ffa9149f5); lib. bdg. 33.93 *(978-1-60754-269-8(2)*, fec7c290-698f-4b0b-a8d7-8b55c579b74a) Rosen Publishing Group, Inc., The. (Windmill Bks.).
Rosen, Lucy. Blast Off! 2015. (Transformers 8x8 Ser.). (J). lib. bdg. 13.55 *(978-0-606-37228-2(8))* Turtleback.
Ross, Richard. Arctic Airlift. 2005. (Illus.). 36p. (J). 17.00 *(978-0-9763119-0-4(9))* Blue Fox Pr.
Sagerman, Evan. Giraffe Rescue Company. Chou, Joey, illus. 2016. (J). *(978-1-4424-1366-5(2))* Simon & Schuster Children's Publishing.
Salvatierra, Dante. The Latchkey Kids & the Trip Through T. 2005. (ENG.). 234p. pap. 12.99 *(978-1-4116-3814-3(X))* Lulu Pr., Inc.
Sanders, Gaye Lynn. Chameleon Girl. 2008. 60p. pap. 16.95 *(978-1-60703-643-2(6))* America Star Bks.
Sanders, Stephanie & Pauling, Galen T. Q. T. Pie's Rescue Adventure. l.t. ed. 2003. (ENG., Illus.). 36p. (J). (gr. -1-6). mass mkt. 4.99 *(978-0-9670875-3-5(8)*, 313-533-7383) SanPaul Group, LLC, The.
Scholastic. Let's Go, Rescue Trucks! 2018. (Spin Me! Ser.). (ENG.). 12p. (J). (gr. -1 — 1). bds. 7.99 *(978-1-338-25680-2(7)*, Cartwheel Bks.) Scholastic, Inc.
Scribner, Don. Bennie & Thomas & the Rescue at Razor's Edge: Volume I. Scribner, Peter, illus. 2012. 44p. pap. 24.95 *(978-1-4626-8957-6(4))* America Star Bks.
—Bennie & Thomas & the Rescue at Razor's Edge: Volume II. Scribner, Peter, illus. 2012. 48p. pap. 24.95 *(978-1-4626-9472-3(1))* America Star Bks.
Shotz, Jennifer Li. Hurricane Rescue. 2017. (Hero Ser.: 2). (J). lib. bdg. 18.40 *(978-0-606-40134-0(2))* Turtleback.
Simon Spotlight, creator. Dora & Diego's Adventures! 2007. (Dora the Explorer Ser.). (ENG., Illus.). 80p. (J). (gr. -1-2). 7.99 *(978-1-4169-3532-2(0)*, Simon Spotlight/Nickelodeon) Simon Spotlight/Nickelodeon.
Simonson, Louise. The Joker & Harley Quinn's Justice League Jailhouse. Levins, Tim, illus. 2018. (Justice League Ser.). (ENG.). 88p. (J). (gr. 2-6). lib. bdg. 27.32 *(978-1-4965-5980-7(0)*, 137329, Stone Arch Bks.) Capstone.
Sina-Atanda, Moyin. The Phenomenal Four: Four on a Mission to Save the Animals. 2013. 52p. (gr. 4-6). pap. 10.03 *(978-1-4669-7291-9(2))* Trafford Publishing.
Smith, Claude Clayton. The Gull That Lost the Sea. Cathcart, Sharyn, illus. 2008. (ENG.). 34p. pap. 5.95 *(978-0-9667359-7-0(8)*, BeanPole Bks.) OH Industries.
Smith, Geof. Meet Tracker! (PAW Patrol) Fruchter, Jason, illus. 2016. (Step into Reading Ser.). (ENG.). 24p. (J). (gr. -1-1). pap. 4.99 *(978-0-553-52288-4(4)*, Random Hse. Bks. for Young Readers) Random Hse. Children's Bks.
Smith, L. J. Passion. 2008. (Dark Visions Ser.: Bk. 3). (ENG.). 224p. (YA). (gr. 7). pap. 10.99 *(978-1-4169-8483-2(6)*, Simon Pulse) Simon Pulse.
Smith, Lee A. Dobee the Littlest Dragon. 2008. 24p. per. 24.95 *(978-1-60441-165-2(1))* America Star Bks.
Smith, Roland. Jack's Run. 2007. (ENG.). 256p. (J). (gr. 5-9). pap. 6.99 *(978-1-4231-0407-0(2))* Hyperion Pr.
Snider, Brandon T. Dangerous Rescue. 2016. (Transformers 8x8 Ser.). (J). lib. bdg. 13.55 *(978-0-606-37515-3(5))* Turtleback.
Snyder, Maria V. Storm Watcher. 2013. 228p. (gr. 4-8). pap. 9.99 *(978-1-61603-033-9(X))* Leap Bks.
Spradlin, Michael P. Pararescue Corps. Karkavelas, Spiros, illus. 2019. (Pararescue Corps Ser.). (ENG.). 240p. (J). (gr. 4-8). pap., pap., pap. 9.95 *(978-1-4965-8105-1(9)*, 140248, Stone Arch Bks.) Capstone.
—Viper Strike: A 4D Book. Karkavelas, Spiros, illus. 2018. (Pararescue Corps Ser.). (ENG.). 128p. (J). (gr. 4-8). lib. bdg. 27.32 *(978-1-4965-5202-0(4)*, 136214, Stone Arch Bks.) Capstone.
Stainton, Sue. The Lighthouse Cat. Mortimer, Anne, illus. 2004. (ENG.). 32p. (J). (gr. -1-2). 17.99 *(978-0-06-009604-5(7)*, Tegen, Katherine Bks) HarperCollins Pubs.
Stewart, E. J. The Wayfaring Dolphin. 2010. 298p. pap. 16.95 *(978-0-557-33701-9(1))* Lulu Pr., Inc.
Stewart, Whitney. Marshall: A Nantucket Sea Rescue. Lyall, Dennis, illus. 2008. (ENG.). 32p. (J). (gr. -1-2). 2.95 *(978-1-59249-856-7(6))*; 6.95 *(978-1-59249-855-0(8))*; 10.95 *(978-1-59249-857-4(4))* Soundprints.
Sullivan, Steve & Guerdat, Andy. Mission Paw. Lovett, Nate, illus. 2017. 24p. (J). *(978-1-5182-4195-6(6))* Random Hse., Inc.
Sutton, Laurie S. Cosmic Conquest. Doescher, Erik, illus. 2018. (You Choose Stories: Justice League Ser.). (ENG.). 112p. (J). (gr. 2-6). lib. bdg. 32.65 *(978-1-4965-6555-6(X)*, 138568, Stone Arch Bks.) Capstone.
—The Draco. Nathan, James, illus. 2017. (Bug Team Alpha Ser.). (ENG.). 112p. (J). (gr. 3-6). lib. bdg. 26.65 *(978-1-4965-5186-3(9)*, 136189, Stone Arch Bks.) Capstone.
Szymanski, Lois K. A Pony to the Rescue. 2007. (Charming Ponies Ser.). 96p. (J). (gr. 2-5). pap. 4.99 *(978-0-06-128869-2(1)*, HarperFestival) HarperCollins Pubs.
Tabares, Veronica. Monkeys on an Island. Tabares, Bridgitt, illus. 2012. 32p. (J). pap. 14.50 *(978-1-60916-005-0(3))* Sun Break Publishing.
Thomas, Blair L. The Sabatini Prophecy. 2008. (ENG.). 496p. (YA). 8.99 *(978-0-9760237-4-6(1))* Axiom Hse.
Tilert, Heather R. Ming-Ming Saves the Day: Follow the Reader Level 1. 2008. (Wonder Pets! Ser.). (ENG.). 24p. (J). 24.99 *(978-1-4169-6459-9(2)*, Simon Scribbles) Simon Scribbles.
Tillworth, Mary. Up in the Air!/under the Waves! (PAW Patrol) Random House, illus. 2018. (Step into Reading Ser.). (ENG.). 48p. (J). (gr. -1-2). pap. 5.99 *(978-1-5247-7279-6(8)*, Random Hse. Bks. for Young Readers) Random Hse. Children's Bks.
Top That Publishing Staff, ed. Rescue Helicopter. Dronsfield, Paul, illus. 2007. (Story Book Ser.). (ENG.). 33p. (J). (gr. -1). bds. *(978-1-84666-179-2(X)*, Tide Mill Pr.) Top That! Publishing PLC.
Troupe, Thomas Kingsley. A Spaceship Named Judy. Tayal, Amit, illus. 2017. (Star Belchers Ser.). (ENG.). 128p. (J). (gr. 3-6). lib. bdg. 25.99 *(978-1-4965-4871-9(X)*, 135636, Stone Arch Bks.) Capstone.
Truax, Lois. Grandmothers Are Magic. 2010. 28p. pap. 5.95 *(978-1-935355-01-4(5))* New Shelves Bks.
Ursu, Anne. Breadcrumbs. McGuire, Erin, illus. 2013. (ENG.). 336p. (J). (gr. 3-7). pap. 7.99 *(978-0-06-201506-8(0)*, Walden Pond Pr.) HarperCollins Pubs.
Velle, Tori. Jake the Snake. 2009. 40p. pap. 16.99 *(978-1-4490-4431-2(X))* AuthorHouse.
Verba, Joan Marie. Action Alert. 2008. 176p. (YA). pap. 15.95 *(978-0-9653575-8-6(9))* FTL Pubns.
Verne, Jules. The English at the North Pole. 2009. 160p. 24.95 *(978-1-60664-684-7(2))*; pap. 13.95 *(978-1-60664-313-6(4))* Rodgers, Alan Bks.
Vrabel, Beth. Bringing Me Back. 2018. (ENG.). 256p. (J). (gr. 3-7). 16.99 *(978-1-5107-2527-0(X)*, Sky Pony Pr.) Skyhorse Publishing Co., Inc.
Waldron, Douglas E. Cody Sackett of Montana: Tales of Adventure. 2008. 188p. per. 24.95 *(978-1-4241-9781-1(3))* America Star Bks.
Wallace, Bill. Skinny-Dipping at Monster Lake. 2004. 212p. (gr. 3-7). 16.00 *(978-0-7569-3486-6(9))* Perfection Learning Corp.
—Skinny-Dipping at Monster Lake. 2004. (ENG., Illus.). 224p. (J). (gr. 3-7). pap. 6.99 *(978-0-689-85151-3(0)*, Simon & Schuster/Paula Wiseman Bks.) Simon & Schuster/Paula Wiseman Bks.
Waters, Michael. Tommy & his Flying Saucer of Milk. 2009. 32p. pap. 16.95 *(978-1-4357-4802-6(6))* Lulu Pr., Inc.
Watson, Jude. Underworld. 2005. (Star Wars Ser.: No. 3). 137p. (J). lib. bdg. 20.00 *(978-1-4242-0776-3(2))* Fitzgerald Bks.
Watt, Fiona. Busy Helicopter Book. 2012. (Pull-Back Bks). 10p. (J). ring bd. 24.99 *(978-0-7945-3203-1(9)*, Usborne) EDC Publishing.
Wax, Wendy. Diego & Papi to the Rescue. Hom, John, illus. 2007. (Go, Diego, Go! Ser.: 3). (ENG.). 24p. (J). pap. 3.99 *(978-1-4169-2781-5(6)*, Simon Spotlight/Nickelodeon) Simon Spotlight/Nickelodeon.
—Diego y Papi al Rescate. Ziegler, Argentina Palacios, tr. Hom, John, illus. 2008. (Go, Diego, Go! Ser.).Tr. of Diego & Papi to the Rescue. (SPA.). 24p. (J). (gr. -1-2). pap. 3.99 *(978-1-4169-5044-8(3)*, Libros Para Ninos) Libros Para Ninos.
Whitmore, Andrew. Beast of the Jungle. 2007. 96p. (YA). pap. *(978-1-4207-0728-1(0))* Sundance/Newbridge Educational Publishing.
Williams, Geoffrey T. Manatees & Mermaids. 2010. (ENG., Illus.). 64p. (J). (gr. 3-7). 8.95 *(978-0-9800444-3-0(X))* Save Our Seas, Ltd.
Williams, Kelly Ann. Pye. 2010. 36p. pap. 11.50 *(978-1-4452-8438-5(3))* Lulu Pr., Inc.
Wilson, Mark A. The Amazing Gift from the Woods. 2008. 48p. pap. 16.95 *(978-1-60563-056-4(X))* America Star Bks.
Wood, Audrey & Wood, Bruce Robert, illus. Alphabet Rescue. 2006. (J). *(978-0-439-88927-8(8))* Scholastic, Inc.
Wooten, Arthur. Wise Bear William: A New Beginning. Santora, Bud, illus. 2012. 44p. pap. 12.99 *(978-0-9850529-1-1(0))* Galaxias Productions.
Young, Judy. Minnow & Rose: An Oregon Trail Story. Farnsworth, Bill, illus. 2009. (Tales of Young Americans Ser.). (ENG.). 32p. (J). (gr. 1-4). 17.95 *(978-1-58536-421-3(5)*, 202156) Sleeping Bear Pr.
YoYo. Vermonia 4: the Rukan Prophecy, 1 vol. 2011. (Vermonia Ser.: No. 4). (ENG., Illus.). 208p. (J). (gr. 4-6). pap. 12.75 *(978-0-7636-4950-0(3)*, 03e4d4da-9c43-4de6-9266-b739570de8c0, Windmill Bks.) Rosen Publishing Group, Inc., The.
Zajonc, Taylor. The Iron Island. Rodriguez, Geraldine, illus. 2018. (Adventures of Samuel Oliver Ser.). (ENG.). 48p. (J). (gr. 3-7). lib. bdg. 34.21 *(978-1-5321-3373-2(1)*, 31169, Spellbound) Magic Wagon.
Zappa, Shana Muldoon, et al. Scarlet Discovers True Strength, 5. 2016. (Star Darlings Ser.). (ENG., Illus.). 176p. (J). (gr. 3-6). 21.19 *(978-1-4844-7390-0(6))* Disney Pr.
Ziegler-Sullivan, Ursula. Pirate Pups! Petrossi, Fabrizio, illus. 2016. (J). *(978-1-4806-9717-1(6)*, Golden Bks.) Random Hse. Children's Bks.

RESEARCH

see also Discoveries in Science; Learning and Scholarship

also subjects with the subdivision Research, e.g. Agriculture—Research; Medicine—Research

Albee, Michael J. Elements of Research: The Student's Guide to Avoiding Plagiarism in the Information Age. 2003. (Illus.). 140p. per. *(978-0-9745405-0-4(1))* Albee, Michael.
Asselin, Kristine Carlson. Smart Research Strategies: Finding the Right Sources, 1 vol. 2013. (Research Tool Kit Ser.). (ENG.). 32p. (J). (gr. 3-6). pap. 8.10 *(978-1-62065-790-4(2)*, 121756, Capstone Pr.) Capstone.
—Smart Research Strategies: Finding the Right Sources. 2013. (Research Tool Kit Ser.). (ENG.). 32p. (J). (gr. 3-4). pap. 48.60 *(978-1-62065-791-1(0)*, 19370, Capstone Pr.) Capstone.
—Think for Yourself: Avoiding Plagiarism. 2013. (Research Tool Kit Ser.). (ENG.). 32p. (J). (gr. 3-4). pap. 48.60 *(978-1-62065-793-5(7)*, 19372); pap. 8.10 *(978-1-62065-792-8(9)*, 121757) Capstone. (Capstone Pr.).
Bell, Samantha S. Before the Internet. 2020. (What Did We Do? Ser.). (ENG., Illus.). 32p. (J). (gr. 2-3). pap. 9.95 *(978-1-64493-126-4(5)*, 1644931265); lib. bdg. 31.35 *(978-1-64493-047-2(1)*, 1644930471) North Star Editions. (Focus Readers).
Berg, Shannon. Before Computers. 2020. (What Did We Do? Ser.). (ENG., Illus.). 32p. (J). (gr. 2-3). pap. 9.95 *(978-1-64493-121-9(4)*, 1644931214); lib. bdg. 31.35 *(978-1-64493-042-7(0)*, 1644930420) North Star Editions. (Focus Readers).
Bodden, Valerie. Doing Primary Research. 2012. (Research for Writing Ser.). (ENG.). 48p. (J). (gr. 4-7). 23.95 *(978-1-60818-204-6(5)*, 21952, Creative Education) Creative Co., The.
—Writing a Research Paper. 2014. (Classroom How-To Ser.). (ENG.). 48p. (J). (gr. 5-8). *(978-1-60818-283-1(5)*, 21305, Creative Education) Creative Co., The.
—Writing a Research Paper. Williams, Nate, illus. 2014. (Classroom How-To Ser.). (ENG.). 48p. (J). (gr. 5-8). pap. 12.00 *(978-0-89812-989-2(3)*, 21306, Creative Paperbacks) Creative Co., The.
Brinkerhoff, Shirley. Research Scientist. Riggs, Ernestine G. & Gholar, Cheryl, eds. 2013. (Careers with Character Ser.: 18). 96p. (J). (gr. 7-18). 22.95 *(978-1-4222-2765-7(0))* Mason Crest.
Britton, Arthur K. Life at a Polar Research Station, 1 vol. 2013. (Extreme Jobs in Extreme Places Ser.). (ENG., Illus.). 32p. (J). (gr. 3-4). pap. 11.50 *(978-1-4339-8483-9(0)*, 064a0bd4-e9e5-44ff-8bcc-dc0c35ec13ec); lib. bdg. 29.27 *(978-1-4339-8482-2(2)*, fc7c6c94-19c6-45a1-be98-c589bb32321b) Stevens, Gareth Publishing LLLP.
Carlson Berne, Emma. Answer! Analyze Your Data, 1 vol. 2014. (Scientific Method in Action Ser.). (Illus.). 24p. (J). (gr. 3-3). (ENG.). 25.27 *(978-1-4777-2930-4(5)*, 65980130-6256-493a-9f85-c51e66a8c715); (ENG., pap. 9.25 *(978-1-4777-3017-1(6)*, 8875c218-bafb-4b73-b1e0-ac0d026636fb); pap. 49.50 *(978-1-4777-3088-1(5))* Rosen Publishing Group, Inc., The. (PowerKids Pr.).
—Share! Present Your Findings. 2014. (Scientific Method in Action Ser.). (Illus.). 24p. (J). (gr. 3-6). pap. 49.50 *(978-1-4777-3089-8(3)*, PowerKids Pr.) Rosen Publishing Group, Inc., The.
Cefrey, Holly. Researching People, Places, & Events, 1 vol. 2009. (Digital & Information Literacy Ser.). (ENG., Illus.). 48p. (YA). (gr. 6-6). lib. bdg. 33.47 *(978-1-4358-5317-1(2)*, 819a951a-a334-4cce-b644-7f619a15851c, Rosen Reference) Rosen Publishing Group, Inc., The.
Chappell, Rachel. Solving Science Questions: A Book about the Scientific Process. 2007. (Big Ideas for Young Scientists Ser.). (Illus.). 24p. (J). (gr. 2-5). lib. bdg. *(978-1-60044-542-2(X))* Rourke Educational Media.
Colby, Jennifer. Data in Arguments. 2017. (21st Century Skills Library: Data Geek Ser.). (ENG., Illus.). 32p. (J). (gr. 4-7). lib. bdg. 32.07 *(978-1-63472-707-5(X)*, 210086) Cherry Lake Publishing.

Coleman, Kelly. Choose It! Finding the Right Research Topic. Petelinsek, Kathleen, illus. 2015. (Explorer Junior Library: Information Explorer Junior Ser.). (ENG.). 24p. (J). (gr. 1-4). 32.07 (978-1-63188-862-5(5), 206028) Cherry Lake Publishing.

Coleman, Miriam. Find It: Searching for Information, 1 vol. 2012. (Core Skills Ser.). (ENG., Illus.). 32p. (J). (gr. 4-5). 28.93 (978-1-4488-7451-4(3), e959e652-6943-4981-88fb-d380ba799abc); pap. 11.00 (978-1-4488-7536-8(6), 0d42d9aa-ac99-4bbe-8596-8ce4c2f42914) Rosen Publishing Group, Inc., The. (PowerKids Pr.).

—Prove It: Gathering Evidence & Integrating Information, 1 vol. 2012. (Core Skills Ser.). (ENG., Illus.). 32p. (J). (gr. 4-5). 28.93 (978-1-4488-7453-8(X), 996e5ed6-112d-474a-a793-22ef52c7e7d3); pap. 11.00 (978-1-4488-7525-2(0), 5a7eef9e-f3d1-48a6-a4f4-c7c49a1fcc02) Rosen Publishing Group, Inc., The. (PowerKids Pr.).

Doudna, Kelly. Ill Use Information for My Explanation!, 1 vol. 2007. (Science Made Simple Ser.). (Illus.). 24p. (J). (gr. k-3). lib. bdg. 24.21 (978-1-59928-588-7(6), SandCastle) ABDO Publishing Co.

Flatt, Lizann. Collecting Data. 2016. (Get Graphing! Building Data Literacy Skills Ser.). (ENG., Illus.). 24p. (J). (gr. 1-3). (978-0-7787-2633-3(9)) Crabtree Publishing Co.

Fontichiaro, Kristin. Find Out Firsthand: Using Primary Sources. 2012. (Explorer Junior Library: Information Explorer Junior Ser.). (ENG.). 24p. (gr. 1-4). pap. 12.79 (978-1-61080-661-9(1), 202271); (Illus.). 32.07 (978-1-61080-487-5(2), 202097) Cherry Lake Publishing.

—Go Straight to the Source. 2010. (Explorer Library: Information Explorer Ser.). (ENG., Illus.). 32p. (gr. 4-8). lib. bdg. 32.07 (978-1-60279-640-9(8), 200343) Cherry Lake Publishing.

—Super Smart Information Strategies: Go Straight to the Source. 2010. (Explorer Library: Information Explorer Ser.). (ENG.). 32p. (gr. 4-8). pap. 14.21 (978-1-61080-257-4(8), 200905) Cherry Lake Publishing.

—Watch It! Researching with Videos. Petelinsek, Kathleen, illus. 2015. (Explorer Junior Library: Information Explorer Junior Ser.). (ENG.). 24p. (J). (gr. 1-4). 32.07 (978-1-63188-863-2(3), 206032) Cherry Lake Publishing.

Fontichiaro, Kristin & Johnson, Emily. Know What to Ask: Forming Great Research Questions. 2012. (Explorer Library: Information Explorer Ser.). (ENG., Illus.). 32p. (gr. 4-8). 32.07 (978-1-61080-483-7(X), 202093) Cherry Lake Publishing.

Furgang, Adam. Searching Online for Image, Audio, & Video Files, 1 vol. 2009. (Digital & Information Literacy Ser.). (ENG., Illus.). 48p. (YA). (gr. 6-6). lib. bdg. 33.47 (978-1-4358-5318-8(0), b4f69062-0f30-48d6-8f79-c901d282a33b) Rosen Publishing Group, Inc., The.

Graham Gaines, Ann. Master the Library & Media Center, 1 vol. 2009. (Ace It! Information Literacy Ser.). (ENG., Illus.). 48p. (gr. 3-3). lib. bdg. 27.93 (978-0-7660-3393-1(7), 37a32d0f-af8e-4981-abbc-47f5b448a02a) Enslow Publishing, LLC.

Green, Lyric & Graham Gaines, Ann. Future Ready Research Papers, 1 vol. 2017. (Future Ready Project Skills Ser.). (ENG.). 48p. (gr. 3-4). pap. 12.70 (978-0-7660-8773-6(5), 336adb6c-ce9d-4139-8752-e12631911a58); lib. bdg. 29.60 (978-0-7660-8661-6(5), c176dc63-9873-4626-acdb-0e71b593bfbc) Enslow Publishing, LLC.

Hamilton, John. Newspapers, 1 vol. 2005. (Straight to the Source Ser.). (ENG., Illus.). 32p. (gr. k-6). 27.07 (978-1-59197-547-2(6), Checkerboard Library) ABDO Publishing Co.

—Primary & Secondary Sources, 1 vol. 2005. (Straight to the Source Ser.). (ENG.). 32p. (gr. k-6). 27.07 (978-1-59197-548-9(4), Checkerboard Library) ABDO Publishing Co.

Harbo, Christopher L. Frankenstein's Monster & Scientific Methods. Aón, Carlos, illus. 2013. (Monster Science Ser.). (ENG.). 32p. (J). (gr. 3-4). pap. 48.60 (978-1-62065-817-8(8), 19400, Capstone Pr.); pap. 8.10 (978-1-62065-816-1(X), 121774) Capstone.

Harper, Leslie. Cómo Mantenerse Informado. 2014. (Sé un líder de la Comunidad (Be a Community Leader) Ser.). (SPA.). 32p. (J). (gr. 4-6). pap. 60.00 (978-1-4777-6923-2(4), PowerKids Pr.) Rosen Publishing Group, Inc., The.

—Cómo Mantenerse Informados, 1 vol. 2014. (Sé un líder de la Comunidad (Be a Community Leader) Ser.). (SPA.). 32p. (J). (gr. 5-5). lib. bdg. 27.93 (978-1-4777-6921-8(8), 829dbc4b-55b0-4ea3-a1f3-e1095203f601, PowerKids Pr.) Rosen Publishing Group, Inc., The.

Heitkamp, Kristina Lyn. Exploring Field Investigations Through Science Research Projects, 1 vol. 2018. (Project-Based Learning in Science Ser.). (ENG.). 64p. (gr. 5-5). pap. 14.53 (978-1-5081-8474-4(7), 472ea2ee-ca41-4b3b-9a82-59d43e824d5a, Rosen Reference) Rosen Publishing Group, Inc., The.

Howell, Sara. How to Gather Information, Take Notes, & Sort Evidence, 1 vol., 1. 2013. (Core Writing Skills Ser.). (ENG.). 24p. (J). (gr. 3-3). 26.27 (978-1-4777-2909-0(7), 2fbd70a6-9530-46ce-975c-07e275203741, PowerKids Pr.) Rosen Publishing Group, Inc., The.

Hulick, Kathryn. Citizen Science: How Anyone Can Contribute to Scientific Discovery. 2019. (YA). (978-1-68282-736-9(4)) ReferencePoint Pr., Inc.

Jakubiak, David J. A Smart Kid's Guide to Doing Internet Research, 1 vol. 2009. (Kids Online Ser.). (ENG., Illus.). 24p. (J). (gr. 2-3). pap. 9.25 (978-1-4358-3352-4(X), 0d58b0e9-2bf8-4d9e-b25f-682036962e43); lib. bdg. 26.27 (978-1-4042-8116-5(9), b630e9b2-c7ba-41d5-942e-f158f49589e2) Rosen Publishing Group, Inc., The. (PowerKids Pr.).

Jennings, Brien J. What's Your Source? Using Sources in Your Writing. 2018. (All about Media Ser.). (ENG., Illus.). 24p. (J). (gr. 1-3). lib. bdg. 27.99 (978-1-5435-0220-6(2), 137138, Capstone Pr.) Capstone.

Johnson, Emily & Fontichiaro, Kristin. Know What to Ask: Forming Great Research Questions. 2012. (Explorer Library: Information Explorer Ser.). (ENG.). 32p. (gr. 4-8). pap. 14.21 (978-1-61080-657-2(3), 202267) Cherry Lake Publishing.

Keller, Susanna. What Are Primary Sources?, 1 vol. 2018. (Let's Find Out! Social Studies Skills Ser.). (ENG.). 32p. (gr. 2-3). 26.06 (978-1-5081-0703-3(3), a465e8b5-2c06-44b8-9c00-ec3933d0db74, Britannica Educational Publishing) Rosen Publishing Group, Inc., The.

Klein, Rebecca T. & Asselin, Janelle. Cool Careers Without College for People Who Love Reading & Research, 1 vol. 2017. (Cool Careers Without College Ser.). (ENG.). 112p. (gr. 7-7). 41.12 (978-1-5081-7542-1(X), acdb05fa-e512-4010-9699-2bca67475949, Rosen Young Adult) Rosen Publishing Group, Inc., The.

Kopp, Megan. Building Your Knowledge in the Digital World. 2018. (ENG.). (J). (gr. 3-7). (978-1-4271-2042-7(0)); (Illus.). 32p. (gr. 5-5). (978-0-7787-4588-4(0)); (Illus.). 32p. (gr. 5-5). pap. (978-0-7787-4602-7(X)) Crabtree Publishing Co.

Kovacs, Vic. Get into Citizen Science. 2017. (Get-Into-It Guides). (Illus.). 32p. (J). (gr. 4-5). (978-0-7787-3636-3(9)) Crabtree Publishing Co.

Larson, Kirsten. Tools of the Trade: Using Scientific Equipment. 2016. (Let's Explore Science Ser.). (ENG.). 48p. (gr. 5-8). 35.64 (978-1-68191-400-8(X), 9781681914008) Rourke Educational Media.

Linde, Barbara M. Cyberspace Research, 1 vol. 2012. (Cyberspace Survival Guide Ser.). (ENG., Illus.). 32p. (J). (gr. 3-4). 29.27 (978-1-4339-7216-4(6), d9a33596-76a1-4c9c-b08c-ed019cd2fb4c); pap. 11.50 (978-1-4339-7217-1(4), c8c9ba97-16cf-496c-9c2a-7b6ab71f1ebd) Stevens, Gareth Publishing LLLP. (Gareth Stevens Learning Library).

McAneney, Caitie. Make a Research Plan, 1 vol. 2018. (Think Like a Scientist Ser.). (ENG.). 32p. (gr. 3-4). lib. bdg. 26.06 (978-1-5383-0226-2(8), 180b42ef-aaa5-439b-9688-40e32a7f3a41, Britannica Educational Publishing) Rosen Publishing Group, Inc., The.

McIlroy, Michelle. What Are Secondary Sources?, 1 vol. 2018. (Let's Find Out! Social Studies Skills Ser.). (ENG.). 32p. (gr. 2-3). lib. bdg. 26.06 (978-1-5081-0704-0(1), a92751b2-0003-4965-8eb9-6b577dc6c4de, Britannica Educational Publishing) Rosen Publishing Group, Inc., The.

Michalski, Pete & Lily, Henrietta M. Research Project Success Using Digital Tools, 1 vol., 1. 2015. (Digital & Information Literacy Ser.). (ENG.). 48p. (J). (gr. 6-6). 33.47 (978-1-4994-3787-4(0), e4d1e4ee-09bc-4820-b3e6-d177956ff89e); pap. 12.75 (978-1-4994-3785-0(4), b44b1b39-a449-4fcf-8169-263a9d569c7f) Rosen Publishing Group, Inc., The. (Rosen Central).

Morse, Virginia & Nottage, Cindy. Iim: Independent Investigation Method Teacher Manual with Companion CD. 2005. spiral bd. 59.95 incl. cd-rom (978-1-57652-024-6(2)) Active Learning Systems, LLC.

Oehrli, Jo Angela. Ethical Data Use. 2017. (21st Century Skills Library: Data Geek Ser.). (ENG., Illus.). 32p. (J). (gr. 4-7). lib. bdg. 32.07 (978-1-63472-713-6(4), 210110) Cherry Lake Publishing.

Pascaretti, Vicki & Wilkie, Sara. Super Smart Information Strategies: Team Up Online. 2010. (Explorer Library: Information Explorer Ser.). (ENG.). 32p. (gr. 4-8). pap. 14.21 (978-1-61080-264-2(0), 200909) Cherry Lake Publishing.

—Team up Online. 2010. (Explorer Library: Information Explorer Ser.). (ENG., Illus.). 32p. (gr. 4-8). lib. bdg. 32.07 (978-1-60279-644-7(0), 200347) Cherry Lake Publishing.

Rabbat, Suzy. Hit the Books. 2010. (Explorer Library: Information Explorer Ser.). (ENG., Illus.). 32p. (gr. 4-8). lib. bdg. 32.07 (978-1-60279-641-6(6), 200344) Cherry Lake Publishing.

—Super Smart Information Strategies: Hit the Books. 2010. (Explorer Library: Information Explorer Ser.). (ENG.). 32p. (gr. 4-8). pap. 14.21 (978-1-61080-258-1(6), 200906) Cherry Lake Publishing.

Research Tools You Can Use, 22 vols. 2014. (Research Tools You Can Use Ser.). (ENG.). 32p. (J). (gr. 2-3). 312.72 (978-1-62275-759-6(9), 4c4ed158-9f7a-4c38-a84a-27c6b952329a) Rosen Publishing Group, Inc., The.

Rosenzweig, Charlotte, et al. The Path to Research. 2005. (Illus.). 95p. (YA). (gr. 8-18). pap. 8.95 (978-0-9677925-2-1(5)) Long Beach City Schl. District.

Roslund, Samantha. Join Forces: Teaming up Online. 2012. (Explorer Junior Library: Information Explorer Junior Ser.). (ENG., Illus.). 24p. (gr. 1-4). 32.07 (978-1-61080-486-8(4), 202096) Cherry Lake Publishing.

Smith, Paula. Plan & Investigate It!, 1 vol. 2015. (Science Sleuths Ser.). (ENG., Illus.). 24p. (J). (gr. 2-2). pap. (978-0-7787-1546-7(9)) Crabtree Publishing Co.

Somervill, Barbara A. Sorting It Out: Evaluating Data. (Think Like a Scientist Ser.). 24p. (gr. 2-3). 2009. 42.50 (978-1-60854-357-1(9), PowerKids Pr.) 2006. (ENG.). pap. 8.25 (978-1-4358-2682-3(5), fc058202-23bd-47a2-a37a-6be32a7f8bbc, Rosen Classroom) Rosen Publishing Group, Inc., The.

—What Are the Facts? Collecting Information, 1 vol. 2006. (Think Like a Scientist Ser.). (ENG., Illus.). 24p. (YA). (gr. 2-3). lib. bdg. 26.27 (978-1-4042-3484-0(5), 7763489f-16fc-4783-825e-52a18dbb17e0) Rosen Publishing Group, Inc., The.

—What Are the Facts? Collecting Information. (Think Like a Scientist Ser.). 24p. (gr. 2-3). 2009. 42.50 (978-1-60854-358-8(7), PowerKids Pr.) 2006. (ENG.). pap. 8.25 (978-1-4358-2683-0(3), a7eb66ea-5749-41fb-b243-ee0739354128, Rosen Classroom) Rosen Publishing Group, Inc., The.

Truesdell, Ann. Fire Away: Asking Great Interview Questions. 2012. (Explorer Library: Information Explorer Ser.). (ENG.). 32p. (gr. 4-8). pap. 14.21 (978-1-61080-655-8(7), 202265); (Illus.). 32.07 (978-1-61080-481-3(3), 202091) Cherry Lake Publishing.

Vittachi, Nury & Cheung, Step. The First of Everything. 2019. (ENG., Illus.). 240p. (J). pap. (978-981-327-477-8(8)) Write Editions.

Whitley, Peggy & Goodwin, Susan Williams. 99 Jumpstarts for Kids' Science Research, 1 vol. 2005. (ENG., Illus.). 264p. per. 42.00 (978-1-59158-261-8(X), 900308586, Libraries Unlimited) ABC-CLIO, LLC.

Wolny, Philip. Strengthening Research Paper Skills, 1 vol. 2017. (Skills for Success Ser.). (ENG.). 64p. (J). (gr. 7-7). 36.13 (978-1-5081-7572-8(1), 797106d1-fab2-4362-8c32-8a2576f3e856, Rosen Young Adult) Rosen Publishing Group, Inc., The.

RESEARCH—VOCATIONAL GUIDANCE

Books, Checkmark, creator. Research & Information Management: Follow the Fast Track to Career Success. 2nd rev. ed. 2007. (Mastering Career Skills Ser.). (ENG., Illus.). 128p. per. 12.95 (978-0-8160-7118-0(7), P165515, Checkmark Bks.) Infobase Holdings, Inc.

Latta, Sara L. Ice Scientist: Careers in the Frozen Antarctic, 1 vol. 2009. (Wild Science Careers Ser.). (ENG., Illus.). 128p. (gr. 5-6). lib. bdg. 35.93 (978-0-7660-3048-0(2), bfc92540-f7a2-456a-9694-7c881999ee5b) Enslow Publishing, LLC.

Sheen, Barbara. Careers If You Like Research & Analysis. 2019. (Career Exploration Ser.). (ENG.). 80p. (J). (gr. 6-12). 41.27 (978-1-68282-591-4(4)) ReferencePoint Pr., Inc.

RESIDENCES

see Architecture, Domestic; Houses

RESOURCES

see Marine Resources

RESPIRATION

Aleo, Karen. Living Things Need Air. 2019. (What Living Things Need Ser.). (ENG., Illus.). 24p. (J). (gr. -1-2). pap. 6.95 (978-1-9771-1034-3(7), 141110); lib. bdg. 24.65 (978-1-9771-0884-5(9), 140492) Capstone. (Pebble).

Andrews, Barbara. Discover the Respiratory System. 2006. (J). pap. (978-1-4108-6514-4(2)) Benchmark Education Co.

Aparato Respiratorio Soplo de Vida. (Coleccion Mundo Invisible).Tr. of Respiratory System. (SPA.). (YA). (gr. 5-8). pap. 8.00 (978-958-04-3224-1(4)) Norma S.A. COL. Dist: Distribuidora Norma, Inc.

Aparato respiratorio soplo de Vida. (SPA.). (J). 10.00 (978-84-342-1909-0(3)) Parramon Ediciones S.A. ESP. Dist: Distribuidora Norma, Inc.

Bailey, Jacqui. What Happens When You Breathe?, 1 vol. 2008. (How Your Body Works (2008) Ser.). (ENG., Illus.). 32p. (J). (gr. 3-3). lib. bdg. 30.27 (978-1-4042-4428-3(X), a4cc9f2e-0a45-48cb-b557-ae9f446cd109, PowerKids Pr.) Rosen Publishing Group, Inc., The.

Burstein, John. The Remarkable Respiratory System: How Do My Lungs Work? 2009. (Slim Goodbody's Body Buddies Ser.). (ENG., Illus.). 32p. (J). (gr. 3-5). pap. (978-0-7787-4430-6(2)); lib. bdg. (978-0-7787-4416-0(7)) Crabtree Publishing Co.

Castel-Branco, Inês. Breathe. 2018. (Illus.). 40p. (J). (978-1-4338-2872-0(3)) American Psychological Assn.

Caster, Shannon. Lungs, 1 vol. 2010. (Human Body: a Closer Look Ser.). (ENG., Illus.). 24p. (gr. 2-3). (J). pap. 9.25 (978-1-4358-9830-1(3), db460230-a64e-46cb-859a-8804cabada21, PowerKids Pr.); (YA). lib. bdg. 26.27 (978-1-4358-9371-9(9), 9a5893ad-1afc-4710-91e7-d4ba4b8a3bf1) Rosen Publishing Group, Inc., The.

Concord, Parker & Hayhurst, Chris. The Lungs in 3D, 1 vol. 2015. (Human Body In 3D Ser.). (ENG., Illus.). 64p. (J). (gr. 5-6). 36.13 (978-1-4994-3605-1(X), e3375b70-eac8-4f7c-9c3b-9123c7df5d23, Rosen Central) Rosen Publishing Group, Inc., The.

Donavan, Barbara A. Body Systems: Set of 6: Respiratory & Circulatory. 2011. (Navigators Ser.). (J). 48.00 net. (978-1-4108-5084-3(6)) Benchmark Education Co.

Donovan, Barbara A. Body Systems: Respiratory & Circulatory: Text Pairs. 2008. (Bridges/Navigators Ser.). (J). (gr. 5). 89.00 (978-1-4108-8407-7(4)) Benchmark Education Co.

Figorito, Christine. The Lungs in Your Body, 1 vol. 2014. (Let's Find Out! the Human Body Ser.). (ENG.). 32p. (J). (gr. 2-3). 26.06 (978-1-62275-628-5(2), 10715f7a-a146-41d7-9ea3-72e2b890b859, Britannica Educational Publishing) Rosen Publishing Group, Inc., The.

Ford, Jeanne Marie. Life with Cystic Fibrosis. 2018. (Everyday Heroes Ser.). (ENG.). 24p. (J). (gr. 3-6). lib. bdg. 32.79 (978-1-5038-2509-3(4), 212337, MOMENTUM) Child's World, Inc, The.

Furgang, Kathy. My Lungs. 2009. (My Body Ser.). 24p. (gr. 3-3). 42.50 (978-1-61514-690-1(3), PowerKids Pr.) Rosen Publishing Group, Inc., The.

Gates, Mariam. Breathe with Me: Using Breath to Feel Strong, Calm, & Happy. 2019. (ENG., Illus.). 32p. (J). 17.95 (978-1-68364-030-1(6), 900220846) Sounds True, Inc.

Goddu, Krystyna Poray. The Respiratory System. 2018. (Amazing Human Body Ser.). (ENG.). 32p. (gr. 2-7). 9.95 (978-1-68072-685-5(4)); (Illus.). (J). (gr. 4-6). lib. bdg. (978-1-68072-391-5(X), 23161); (J). (gr. 4-6). pap. 9.99 (978-1-64466-238-0(8), 12208) Black Rabbit Bks. (Bolt).

—El Sistema Respiratorio. 2018. (Asombroso Cuerpo Humano Ser.). (SPA.). 32p. (J). (gr. 4-6). lib. bdg. (978-1-68072-961-0(6), 12432, Bolt) Black Rabbit Bks.

—Le Système Respiratoire. 2018. (incroyable Corps Humain Ser.). (FRE.). 32p. (J). (gr. 4-6). (978-1-77092-445-1(0), 12442, Bolt) Black Rabbit Bks.

Green, Emily & Manolis, Kay. The Respiratory System. 2009. (Body Systems Ser.). (ENG., Illus.). 24p. (J). (gr. 2-5). lib. bdg. 26.95 (978-1-60014-246-8(X)) Bellwether Media.

Hansen, Grace. Respiratory System. 2018. (Beginning Science: Body Systems Ser.). (ENG., Illus.). 24p. (J). (gr. -1-2). lib. bdg. 32.79 (978-1-5321-8188-7(4), 29849, Abdo Kids) ABDO Publishing Co.

Hayhurst, Chris. The Lungs: Learning How We Breathe. 2009. (3-D Library of the Human Body Ser.). 48p. (gr. 5-8). 55.90 (978-1-60853-325-1(5), Rosen Reference) Rosen Publishing Group, Inc., The.

Holt, Rinehart and Winston Staff. Holt Science & Technology Chapter 23: Life Science: Circulation & Respiration. 5th ed. 2004. (Illus.). pap. 12.86 (978-0-03-030239-8(0)) Holt McDougal.

Houghton, Gillian. Breath: The Respiratory System. 2009. (Body Works Ser.). 24p. (gr. 2-3). 42.50 (978-1-61511-643-0(5), PowerKids Pr.) Rosen Publishing Group, Inc., The.

—Breath: the Respiratory System, 1 vol. 2006. (Body Works). (ENG., Illus.). 24p. (J). (gr. 2-3). lib. bdg. 26.27 (978-1-4042-3471-0(3), 06097422-7b2e-46e4-9d0e-15460bab8f43) Rosen Publishing Group, Inc., The.

—The Respiratory System, 1 vol. 2006. (Human Body: a Closer Look Ser.). (ENG., Illus.). 24p. (gr. 2-3). pap. 9.25 (978-1-4042-2180-2(8), 233a0fd9-1465-421f-8199-2e06a427ef30, PowerKids Pr.) Rosen Publishing Group, Inc., The.

How Does It Breathe?, 6 Packs. (gr. k-1). 23.00 (978-0-7635-9036-9(3)) Rigby Education.

Jango-Cohen, Judith. El Aparato Respiratorio. Translations.com Staff, tr. 2006. (Libros Sobre el Cuerpo Humano para Madrugadores Ser.). (ENG & SPA., Illus.). 48p. (gr. 2-4). lib. bdg. 26.60 (978-0-8225-6256-6(1)) Lerner Publishing Group.

—The Respiratory System. 2004. (Early Bird Body Systems Ser.). (ENG., Illus.). 48p. (gr. 2-5). lib. bdg. 26.60 (978-0-8225-1250-9(5)) Lerner Publishing Group.

Katschke, Judy. Carlos Gets the Sneezes. Artful Doodlers Ltd. Staff, illus. 2018. (Magic School Bus Rides Again Ser.: 3). (ENG.). 96p. (J). (gr. 2-5). lib. bdg. 15.99 (978-1-338-23212-7(6)) Scholastic, Inc.

Kolpin, Molly. Why Do I Yawn? 2015. (My Silly Body Ser.). (ENG., Illus.). 24p. (J). (gr. -1-2). lib. bdg. 27.32 (978-1-4914-2107-9(X), 127590, Capstone Pr.) Capstone.

Latham, Donna. Respiration & Photosynthesis. rev. ed. 2016. (Sci-Hi: Life Science Ser.). (ENG.). 48p. (J). (gr. 6-10). pap. 8.99 (978-1-4109-8632-0(2), 134718, Raintree) Capstone.

Lee, Justin. The Respiratory System. 2009. (Insider's Guide to the Body Ser.). 48p. (gr. 5-8). 53.00 (978-1-61513-585-1(5), Rosen Reference) Rosen Publishing Group, Inc., The.

Macdonald, Fiona. The Science of Snot & Phlegm: the Slimy Truth about Breathing (the Science of the Body) (Library Edition) 2017. (Science Of... Ser.). (ENG., Illus.). 32p. (J). (gr. 3). lib. bdg. 29.00 (978-0-531-23144-9(5), Watts, Franklin) Scholastic Library Publishing.

Meachen Rau, Dana. My Lungs, 1 vol. 2013. (Bookworms: My Body Ser.). (ENG.). 24p. (gr. 2-2). pap. 9.23 (978-1-62712-035-7(1), 37fdf618-69f6-4781-88cf-f9a33ea0a820); 2nd ed. 24.07 (978-1-60870-435-4(1), 52ac7aa7-ab0f-49ac-be34-7b571d481f64) Cavendish Square Publishing LLC.

Meyer, William. Big Breath: A Guided Meditation for Kids. Jacobs, Brittany, illus. 2019. (ENG.). 32p. (J). (gr. -1-5). 16.95 (978-1-60868-633-9(7)) New World Library.

Nunn, Daniel. Air, 1 vol. 2012. (Why Living Things Need Ser.). (ENG.). 24p. (gr. -1-1). pap. 6.29 (978-1-4329-5919-7(0), 117621, Heinemann) Capstone.

Orr, Tamra B. Respiration. 2009. (Explorer Library: Science Explorer Ser.). (ENG., Illus.). 32p. (gr. 4-8). lib. bdg. 32.07 (978-1-60279-519-8(3), 200292) Cherry Lake Publishing.

Peterson, Judy Monroe. Breathe: Keeping Your Lungs Healthy, 1 vol. 2012. (Healthy Habits Ser.). (ENG., Illus.). 64p. (J). (gr. 5-5). lib. bdg. 37.13 (978-1-4488-6951-0(X), 3234cf0f-6c15-4ada-bb8a-4c75ea9f13c1, Rosen Reference) Rosen Publishing Group, Inc., The.

Pettiford, Rebecca. The Respiratory System. 2019. (Your Body Systems Ser.). (ENG., Illus.). 24p. (J). (gr. k-3). pap. 7.99 (978-1-61891-755-3(2), 12312, Blastoff! Readers) Bellwether Media.

Reina, Mary. A Tour of Your Respiratory System. Jones, Chris, illus. 2012. (First Graphics: Body Systems Ser.). (ENG.). 24p. (J). (gr. 1-2). pap. 37.74 (978-1-4296-9331-8(2), 18556) Capstone.

Rose, Simon. Lungs: All about the Respiratory System. 2017. (Illus.). 32p. (J). (978-1-5105-0896-5(1)) SmartBook Media, Inc.

—Respiratory System. (J). 2018. (Illus.). 32p. pap. (978-1-4896-9923-7(6), AV2 by Weigl) 2014. (978-1-4896-1178-9(9)) Weigl Pubs., Inc.

Rustad, Martha E. H. My Respiratory System: A 4D Book. 2018. (My Body Systems Ser.). (ENG., Illus.). 24p. (J). (gr. -1-2). lib. bdg. 29.32 (978-1-9771-0021-4(X), 138174, Capstone Pr.) Capstone.

Salt, Zelda. 20 Fun Facts about the Respiratory System, 1 vol. 2018. (Fun Fact File: Body Systems Ser.). (ENG.). 32p. (gr. 2-3). lib. bdg. 27.93 (978-1-5382-2925-5(0), 7558f8b8-bbfb-4a94-8a1c-98ac0722c6a3) Stevens, Gareth Publishing LLLP.

Schwinn, Aleaha. What Happens When I Yawn?, 1 vol. 2013. (My Body Does Strange Stuff! Ser.). (ENG., Illus.). 24p. (J). (gr. 1-2). pap. 9.15 (978-1-4339-9358-9(9), 874ec7f7-19a8-40be-aa2c-bece90281da8); lib. bdg. 25.27 (978-1-4339-9357-2(0), e7eaa981-d6a8-4a2a-baee-cf76de0d9f94) Stevens, Gareth Publishing LLLP.

Shea, John M. The Respiratory System, 1 vol. 2012. (Human Body Ser.). (ENG., Illus.). 32p. (J). (gr. 4-5). 29.27 (978-1-4339-6592-0(5), 8ca88b43-33ed-4a15-b3b5-15dcd4935515); pap. 11.50 (978-1-4339-6594-4(1), 011d34a6-2364-4c4d-bfb2-b1f71cf8c310, Gareth Stevens Learning Library) Stevens, Gareth Publishing LLLP.

Simon, Seymour. Lungs: All about Our Respiratory System & More! 2007. (ENG., Illus.). 32p. (J). (gr. k-4). 17.99 (978-0-06-054654-0(9), HarperCollins) HarperCollins Pubs.

Stewart, Melissa. Blasts of Gas: The Secrets of Breathing, Burping, & Passing Gas, 1 vol. Hamlin, Janet, illus. 2010. (Gross & Goofy Body Ser.). (ENG.). 48p. (gr. 3-3). 32.64 (978-0-7614-4155-7(7), 3b95f34b-42d2-4a41-9f61-11c47e7a680e) Cavendish Square Publishing LLC.

—How Do Fish Breathe Underwater?, 1 vol. 2008. (Tell Me Why, Tell Me How Ser.). (ENG., Illus.). 32p. (gr. 3-3). pap. 9.23 (978-0-7614-3365-1(1), 9a9d3308-e568-409c-9ed5-f7aa169883d2) Cavendish Square Publishing LLC.

Stewart, Whitney. Mindful Tots: Tummy Ride. Alejandro, Rocío, illus. 2019. (Mindful Tots Ser.). (ENG.). 14p. (J). (gr. -1-k). bds. 7.99 (978-1-78285-748-8(6)) Barefoot Bks., Inc.

What Happens When I Yawn? 2013. (My Body Does Strange Stuff! Ser.). 24p. (J). (gr. 1-3). pap. 48.90 (978-1-4339-9359-6(7)) Stevens, Gareth Publishing LLLP.

Whittemore, Susan. The Respiratory System. 2009. (Human Body: How It Works). (ENG., Illus.). 112p. (gr. 9-18). 35.00 (978-1-60413-375-2(9), P165428, Facts On File) Infobase Holdings, Inc.

Willard, Christopher & O'Leary, Wendy. Breathing Makes It Better: A Book for Sad Days, Mad Days, Glad Days, & All the Feelings In-Between. 2019. (Illus.). 36p. (J). (gr. -1-2). 16.95 *(978-1-61180-469-0(8)*, Bala Kids) Shambhala Pubns., Inc.

Willard, Christopher & Rechtschaffen, Daniel. Alphabreaths: The ABCs of Mindful Breathing. 2019. (ENG., Illus.). 32p. (J). 18.99 *(978-1-68364-197-1(3)*, 900220906) Sounds True, Inc.

Willard, Christopher & Weisser, Olivia. The Breathing Book. 2020. (ENG., Illus.). 32p. (J). 15.99 *(978-1-68364-306-7(2)*, 900220948) Sounds True, Inc.

World Book, Inc. Staff, contrib. by. The Respiratory System. 2013. (Illus.). 32p. (J). *(978-0-7166-1847-8(8))* World Bk., Inc.

RESTAURANTS

Ancona, George. Let's Eat. 2003. (J). *(978-0-7636-1805-6(5))* Candlewick Pr.

Cohn, Jessica. On the Job in a Restaurant. Scheuer, Lauren, illus. 2016. (Core Content Social Studies — on the Job Ser.). (ENG.). 32p. (J). (gr. 2-5). lib. bdg. 26.65 *(978-1-63440-110-4(7)*, 72869dd4-337d-403f-a47c-aacc4e474aa5) Red Chair Pr.

Colby, Jennifer. Restaurant. 2016. (21st Century Junior Library: Explore a Workplace Ser.). (ENG., Illus.). 24p. (J). (gr. 2-5). 29.21 *(978-1-63471-077-0(0)*, 208387) Cherry Lake Publishing.

Doering Tourville, Amanda. Manners in the Lunchroom. Lensch, Chris, illus. 2009. (Way to Be!: Manners Ser.). 24p. (gr. -1-2). pap. 2.76 *(978-1-4048-6051-3(7)*, Picture Window Bks.) Capstone.

Etingoff, Kim. Eating Out: How to Order in Restaurants. Borus, Joshua, ed. 2013. (Understanding Nutrition: a Gateway to Physical & Mental Health Ser.: 11). (Illus.). 48p. (J). (gr. 5-18). 19.95 *(978-1-4222-2877-7(0))* Mason Crest.

Felix, Rebecca. Ruth Fertel: Ruth's Chris Steak House Creator. 2017. (Female Foodies Ser.). (ENG.). 32p. (J). (gr. 3-6). lib. bdg. 32.79 *(978-1-5321-1267-6(X)*, 27591, Checkerboard Library) ABDO Publishing Co.

Frisch, Aaron & Gilbert, Sara. The Story of McDonald's. 2008. (Built for Success Ser.). (ENG., Illus.). 48p. (J). (gr. 5-8). 22.95 *(978-1-58341-606-8(4)*, 23857) Creative Co., The.

Gilbert, Sara. The Story of Mcdonald's. 2009. (Built for Success Ser.). (ENG., Illus.). 48p. (J). (gr. 5-8). pap. 12.00 *(978-0-89812-756-0(4)*, 23862, Creative Paperbacks) Creative Co., The.

—The Story of McDonald's. 2011. (ENG., Illus.). 48p. (J). (gr. 5-17). pap. *(978-1-897563-04-5(3))* Saunders Bk. Co.

Green, Sara. Dairy Queen. 2016. (Brands We Know Ser.). (ENG., Illus.). 24p. (J). (gr. 3-8). 27.95 *(978-1-62617-407-8(5)*, Pilot Bks.) Bellwether Media.

—McDonald's. 2015. (Brands We Know Ser.). (ENG., Illus.). 24p. (J). (gr. 3-8). lib. bdg. 27.95 *(978-1-62617-209-8(9)*, Pilot Bks.) Bellwether Media.

Harvey, Joanna & Crabtree, Marc. Meet My Neighbor, the Restaurant Owner. 2010. (ENG., Illus.). 24p. (J). pap. *(978-0-7787-4586-0(4))*; lib. bdg. *(978-0-7787-4576-1(7))* Crabtree Publishing Co.

Llanas, Sheila Griffin. Colonel Harland Sanders: KFC Creator. 2014. (Food Dudes Ser.). (ENG.). 32p. (J). (gr. 3-6). 32.79 *(978-1-62403-318-6(0)*, 1398, Checkerboard Library) ABDO Publishing Co.

—Dave Thomas: Wendy's Founder. 2014. (Food Dudes Ser.). (ENG.). 32p. (J). (gr. 3-6). 32.79 *(978-1-62403-319-3(9)*, 1400, Checkerboard Library) ABDO Publishing Co.

—Tom Monaghan: Domino's Pizza Innovator. 2014. (Food Dudes Ser.). (ENG.). 32p. (J). (gr. 3-6). 32.79 *(978-1-62403-316-2(4)*, 1394, Checkerboard Library) ABDO Publishing Co.

Machajewski, Sarah. Cool Careers Without College for People Who Love to Cook & Eat, 1 vol. 2nd ed. 2013. (Cool Careers Without College Ser.). (ENG., Illus.). 144p. (J). (gr. 7-7). 41.12 *(978-1-4777-1820-9(6)*, dd40ac43-d714-46d0-8d0a-37df46cdf4b3) Rosen Publishing Group, Inc., The.

—Discovering STEM at the Restaurant, 1 vol. 2015. (STEM in the Real World Ser.). (ENG., Illus.). 24p. (J). (gr. 2-3). pap. 9.25 *(978-1-4994-0924-6(9)*, a8b2e9a5-a409-4ed5-967c-3ee158a0054e, PowerKids Pr.) Rosen Publishing Group, Inc., The.

Marsico, Katie. Working at a Restaurant. 2008. (21st Century Junior Library: Careers Ser.). (ENG., Illus.). 24p. (gr. 2-5). lib. bdg. 29.21 *(978-1-60279-269-2(0)*, 200174) Cherry Lake Publishing.

Matthews, Layla, et al. Eat at Grandma's? Kids Review a New Restaurant. 2017. (Text Connections Guided Close Reading Ser.). (J). (gr. 2). *(978-1-4900-1860-7(3))* Benchmark Education Co.

Minden, Cecilia. Restaurants by the Numbers. 2007. (21st Century Skills Library: Real World Math Ser.). (ENG.). 32p. (gr. 4-8). lib. bdg. 32.07 *(978-1-60279-009-4(4)*, 200067) Cherry Lake Publishing.

Payment, Simone. Careers in Restaurants, 1 vol. 2013. (Essential Careers Ser.). (ENG., Illus.). 80p. (YA). (gr. 6-6). lib. bdg. 37.47 *(978-1-4488-9475-8(1)*, 27c616a0-4014-474f-9b27-dd939a29516e, Rosen Classroom) Rosen Publishing Group, Inc., The.

Rathlé, Simone & Lee, Tania. Topsy Turvy History of New Orleans & Ten Tiny Turtles: 300 Years & Slowly Counting... Lee, Tania, illus. 2018. (ENG., Illus.). 35p. (J). 16.95 *(978-0-692-98877-0(7))* simoneink, llc.

Rivera, Sheila. Server. 2007. (First Step Nonfiction — Work People Do Ser.). (ENG., Illus.). 8p. (J). (gr. k-2). pap. 5.99 *(978-0-8225-6847-6(0)*, 3f38b14c-c878-4a18-81e0-bf7dea69ac5a) Lerner Publishing Group.

Scherer, Lauri S., ed. Fast Food, 1 vol. 2013. (Introducing Issues with Opposing Viewpoints Ser.). (ENG.). 144p. (gr. 7-10). lib. bdg. 43.63 *(978-0-7377-6922-7(X)*, cea548df-8708-41f2-98fa-51f895450938, Greenhaven Publishing) Greenhaven Publishing LLC.

Schlosser, Eric. Chew on This: Everything You Don't Want to Know about Fast Food. 2007. lib. bdg. 20.85 *(978-1-4177-7657-3(9))* Turtleback.

Senker, Cath. McDonald's: The Business Behind the Golden Arches. 2016. (Big Brands Ser.). (ENG., Illus.). 32p. (J). (gr. 4-6). E-Book 39.99 *(978-1-5124-0593-4(0)*, Lerner Pubns.) Lerner Publishing Group.

Watt, F. Vamos a Comer! 2004.Tr. of Baby's Mealtime. (SPA., Illus.). 16p. (J). (gr. -1). pap. 4.95 *(978-0-7460-4540-4(9))* EDC Publishing.

RESTAURANTS—FICTION

Ackerman, Peter. The Screaming Chef. Dalton, Max, illus. 2017. (ENG.). 32p. (J). 17.95 *(978-1-56792-598-2(7))* Godine, David R. Pub.

Alger, Horatio. Joe's Luck. 2005. 28.95 *(978-1-4218-1455-1(2))*; 264p. pap. 13.95 *(978-1-4218-1555-8(9))* 1st World Publishing, Inc. (1st World Library - Literary Society).

—Joe's Luck: Or, Always Wide Awake. 2006. (ENG.). 176p. pap. 19.99 *(978-1-4264-0883-0(8))*; 170p. pap. 21.99 *(978-1-4264-0864-9(1))* Creative Media Partners, LLC.

—Joe's Luck: Or, Always Wide Awake. 2006. pap. *(978-1-4065-0713-3(X))* Dodo Pr.

Anderson, Peggy Perry. Out to Lunch. 2015. (Green Light Readers Ser.). (ENG., Illus.). 32p. (J). (gr. 1-4). pap. 4.99 *(978-0-544-52858-1(1)*, 1607369, Clarion Bks.) HarperCollins Pubs.

Argueta, Jorge. La Fiesta de Las Tortillas: The Fiesta of the Tortillas. Hayes, Joe & Franco, Sharon, trs. from SPA. Alvarez, Maria Jesus, illus. 2006. (Bilingual Bks). (ENG & SPA.). 32p. (gr. 3-5). 15.95 *(978-1-59820-094-2(1)*, Alfaguara) Santillana USA Publishing Co., Inc.

Arnold, Tedd. There's a Fly Guy in My Soup. 2012. (Fly Guy Ser.: 12). lib. bdg. 17.20 *(978-0-606-26533-1(3))* Turtleback.

—There's a Fly Guy in My Soup (Fly Guy #12) Arnold, Tedd, illus. 2012. (Fly Guy Ser.: 12). (ENG., Illus.). 32p. (J). (gr. -1-3). 6.99 *(978-0-545-31284-4(1)*, Cartwheel Bks.) Scholastic, Inc.

Balaban, Mariah. Scooby-Doo! & the Haunted Diner. 2010. (Illus.). 31p. (J). *(978-0-545-20882-6(3))* Scholastic, Inc.

Barbour, Karen. Little Nino's Pizzeria Big Book. 2015. (ENG., Illus.). 32p. (J). (gr. -1-3). pap. 26.99 *(978-0-544-45608-2(4)*, 1599393, Clarion Bks.) HarperCollins Pubs.

Bayliss, Jessica. Ten after Closing. 2018. (ENG.). 328p. (YA). (gr. 8-12). 16.99 *(978-1-5107-3207-0(1)*, Sky Pony Pr.) Skyhorse Publishing Co., Inc.

Bee, William. Stanley's Diner, 1 vol. 2015. (Stanley Picture Bks.: 4). (ENG., Illus.). 32p. (J). (gr. -1-2). 14.99 *(978-1-56145-802-8(3))* Peachtree Publishing Co. Inc.

Berenstain, Jan & Berenstain, Mike. The Berenstain Bears Go Out to Eat. 2009. (Berenstain Bears Ser.). (J). lib. bdg. 13.55 *(978-0-606-09291-3(9))* Turtleback.

Burach, Ross. There's a Giraffe in My Soup. Burach, Ross, illus. 2016. (ENG., Illus.). 32p. (J). (gr. -1-3). 17.99 *(978-0-06-236014-4(0)*, HarperCollins) HarperCollins Pubs.

Caletti, Deb. The Fortunes of Indigo Skye. (ENG.). (YA). (gr. 7). 2009. 320p. pap. 9.99 *(978-1-4169-1008-4(5))* 2008. 304p. 15.99 *(978-1-4169-1007-7(7))* Simon Pulse. (Simon Pulse).

Callaghan, Cindy. Lost in Rome. 2015. (Mix Ser.). (ENG., Illus.). 208p. (J). (gr. 4-8). 17.99 *(978-1-4814-4282-4(1)*, Aladdin) Simon & Schuster Children's Publishing.

Callen, Sharon. The Curious Café, 1 vol. rev. ed. 2013. (Literary Text Ser.). (ENG., Illus.). 32p. (J). (gr. 2-3). pap. 10.99 *(978-1-4333-5609-4(0))*; lib. bdg. 19.96 *(978-1-4807-1731-2(2))* Teacher Created Materials, Inc.

Cartaya, Pablo. The Epic Fail of Arturo Zamora. 2018. lib. bdg. 19.65 *(978-0-606-40872-1(X))* Turtleback.

Colbert, Brandy. Finding Yvonne. 2018. (ENG.). 288p. (YA). (gr. 9-17). 17.99 *(978-0-316-34905-5(4))* Little, Brown Bks. for Young Readers.

Dairman, Tara. Stars So Sweet: An All Four Stars Book. 2016. (All Four Stars Ser.: 3). 288p. (J). (gr. 3-7). 17.99 *(978-1-101-99648-5(X)*, G.P. Putnam's Sons Books for Young Readers) Penguin Young Readers Group.

Destiny, A. & Helms, Rhonda. Never Too Late. 2015. (Flirt Ser.). (ENG., Illus.). 224p. (YA). (gr. 7). pap. 9.99 *(978-1-4814-5188-8(X)*, Simon Pulse) Simon Pulse.

Devlin, Wende. Old Black Witch! Devlin, Harry, illus. 2012. (ENG.). 32p. (J). (gr. -1-3). 18.95 *(978-1-930900-62-2(7))* Purple Hse. Pr.

Dobkin, Bonnie. Crazy Pizza Day. Dey, Romi, illus. 2010. (J). *(978-1-60617-150-9(X))* Teaching Strategies, LLC.

Dodds, Dayle Ann. Minnie's Diner: A Multiplying Menu. Manders, John, illus. 2007. (ENG.). 40p. (J). (gr. k-3). pap. 8.99 *(978-0-7636-3313-4(5))* Candlewick Pr.

Doudna, Kelly. Penguin Suit. Chawla, Neena, illus. 2006. (Fact & Fiction Ser.). 24p. (J). pap. 48.42 *(978-1-59679-958-5(7))* ABDO Publishing Co.

Durand, Hallie. Dessert First. Davenier, Christine, illus. 2010. (ENG.). 176p. (J). (gr. 2-5). pap. 5.99 *(978-1-4169-6386-8(3)*, Atheneum Bks. for Young Readers) Simon & Schuster Children's Publishing.

—Dessert First, 1. Davenier, Christine, illus. 2009. (ENG.). 160p. (J). (gr. 2-5). 14.99 *(978-1-4169-6385-1(5))* Simon & Schuster, Inc.

—Just Desserts. Davenier, Christine, illus. 2011. (ENG.). 224p. (J). (gr. 2-5). pap. 5.99 *(978-1-4169-6388-2(X)*, Atheneum Bks. for Young Readers) Simon & Schuster Children's Publishing.

—No Room for Dessert. Davenier, Christine, illus. 2012. (ENG.). 192p. (J). (gr. 2-5). pap. 6.99 *(978-1-4424-0361-1(6)*, Atheneum Bks. for Young Readers) Simon & Schuster Children's Publishing.

Fischer, Ellen. If an Armadillo Went to a Restaurant. Wood, Laura, illus. 2014. (ENG.). 32p. (J). (-2). 14.95 *(978-1-938063-39-8(2)*, Mighty Media Kids) Mighty Media Pr.

Ganeshram, Ramin. Stir It Up! 2011. (J). *(978-0-545-16583-9(0))* Scholastic, Inc.

Glass, Calliope. Tiana: The Stolen Jewel. Disney Storybook Artists, illus. 2017. (Disney Princess Ser.). (ENG.). 96p. (J). (gr. 2-6). lib. bdg. 31.36 *(978-1-5321-4122-5(X)*, 26995, Chapter Bks.) Spotlight.

Goldsmann, Henri. Secret Agent Spanky Sheep in the mystery of: the Pooperous Pizza Plunderer. 2006. 140p. pap. 11.99 *(978-1-4116-8094-4(4))* Lulu Pr., Inc.

Grogan, John. Marley: Thanks, Mom & Dad! Cowdrey, Richard, illus. 2011. (Marley Ser.). (ENG.). 24p. (J). (gr. -1-2). 3.99 *(978-0-06-185381-4(X)*, HarperFestival) HarperCollins Pubs.

Guess, Catherine Ritch. Rudy el Puerco Rojo. 2006. (SPA & ENG., Illus.). 32p. 14.95 *(978-1-933341-21-7(1))* CRM.

—Rudy the Red Pig. Haynes, Jason & Oke, Rachel, illus. 2006. (ENG.). 32p. (J). 13.95 *(978-1-933341-13-2(0))* CRM.

Inspector Grub & the Gourmet Mystery: Individual Title Six-Packs. (Bookweb Ser.). 32p. (gr. 4-18). 34.00 *(978-0-7635-3726-5(8))* Rigby Education.

Jakubowski, Michele. Tour of Trouble. Pinelli, Amerigo, illus. 2016. (Sleuths of Somerville Ser.). (ENG.). 144p. (J). (gr. 4-6). lib. bdg. 25.99 *(978-1-4965-3176-6(0)*, 132215, Stone Arch Bks.) Capstone.

Kennedy, Claire. After Hours. 2015. (ENG., Illus.). 256p. (YA). (gr. 9). 17.99 *(978-1-4814-3016-6(5)*, Simon Pulse) Simon Pulse.

Lee, Day's. The Fragrant Garden. Bellemare, Josee, illus. 2005. (ENG.). 32p. (J). (gr. -1-7). per. 11.95 *(978-1-894917-26-1(X)*, Napoleon & Co.) Dundurn Pr. CAN. Dist: Publishers Group West (PGW).

Leonard, Julia Platt. Cold Case. (ENG.). 288p. (J). (gr. 3-7). 2012. pap. 5.99 *(978-1-4424-2010-6(3))* 2011. (Illus.). 15.99 *(978-1-4424-2009-0(X))* Simon & Schuster/Paula Wiseman Bks. (Simon & Schuster/Paula Wiseman Bks.).

Lin, Grace. Dim Sum for Everyone! Lin, Grace, illus. 2014. (Illus.). 24p. (J). (gr. -1-2). bds. 6.99 *(978-0-385-75488-0(4)*, Knopf Bks. for Young Readers) Random Hse. Children's Bks.

London, Jonathan. Froggy Eats Out. 2004. (Illus.). (J). (gr. -1-18). spiral bd. *(978-0-616-11117-8(7))*; spiral bd. *(978-0-616-11118-5(5))* Canadian National Institute for the Blind/Institut National Canadien pour les Aveugles.

—Froggy Eats Out. Remkiewicz, Frank, illus. 2003. (Froggy Ser.). 32p. (J). (gr. -1-k). pap. 7.99 *(978-0-14-250061-3(5)*, Puffin Books) Penguin Young Readers Group.

—Froggy Eats Out. Remkiewicz, Frank, illus. 2003. (Froggy Ser.). 13.65 *(978-0-7569-1464-6(7))* Perfection Learning Corp.

—Froggy Eats Out. 2003. (Froggy Ser.). (gr. k-3). lib. bdg. 17.20 *(978-0-613-67453-9(7))* Turtleback.

Marks, Janae. On Air with Zoe Washington. 2023. (Zoe Washington Ser.). (ENG.). 304p. (J). (gr. 3-7). 19.99 *(978-0-06-321231-2(5)*, Tegen, Katherine Bks) HarperCollins Pubs.

McGuirk, Leslie & Von Bidder, Alex. Wiggens Learns His Manners at the Four Seasons Restaurant. McGuirk, Leslie, illus. 2009. (ENG., Illus.). 32p. (J). (gr. -1-2). 16.99 *(978-0-7636-4014-9(X))* Candlewick Pr.

McMann, Lisa. Crash. 2013. (Visions Ser.: 1). (ENG.). 256p. (YA). (gr. 9). 19.99 *(978-1-4424-0391-8(8)*, Simon Pulse) Simon Pulse.

Menotti, Andrea. Operation Fowl Play. Kennedy, Kelly, illus. 2004. (Spy Five Ser.). 92p. (J). *(978-0-439-70349-9(2))* Scholastic, Inc.

—Operation Master Mole. Kennedy, Kelly, illus. 2004. (Spy Five Ser.). 93p. (J). *(978-0-439-70351-2(4))* Scholastic, Inc.

Miyazawa, Kenji. The Restaurant of Many Colors. Sato, Kunio, illus. 2005. 31p. (J). 17.95 *(978-4-902216-24-0(8))* R.I.C. Publications Asia Co, Inc. JPN. Dist: Continental Enterprises Group, Inc. (CEG).

Murray, Diana. Pizza Pig. 2019. (Step into Reading Ser.). (ENG.). 31p. (J). (gr. k-1). 14.96 *(978-0-87617-968-0(5))* Penworthy Co., LLC, The.

—Pizza Pig. 2018. (Step into Reading Ser.). (Illus.). 32p. (J). (gr. -1-1). pap. 5.99 *(978-1-5247-1334-8(1)*, Random Hse. Bks. for Young Readers) Random Hse. Children's Bks.

Newman, Samantha. Sammy Skizzors & the Rainbow Knight. 2010. 32p. 14.99 *(978-1-4520-9976-7(6))* AuthorHouse.

Newton, Robert. The Punjabi Pappadum. 2003. 160p. (J). pap. *(978-0-7022-3363-0(3))* Univ. of Queensland Pr.

Ockler, Sarah. Bittersweet. 2012. (ENG.). (YA). (gr. 9). 400p. pap. 9.99 *(978-1-4424-3036-5(2))*; 384p. 16.99 *(978-1-4424-3035-8(4))* Simon Pulse. (Simon Pulse).

Oxenbury, Helen. En El Restaurante de Mis Tios. (SPA.). 16p. (J). 7.50 *(978-84-261-1944-5(1))* Juventud, Editorial ESP. Dist: AIMS International Bks., Inc.

Patron, Susan. Lucky for Good. McGuire, Erin, illus. 2012. (ENG.). 224p. (J). (gr. 3-7). pap. 8.99 *(978-1-4169-9059-8(3)*, Atheneum Bks. for Young Readers) Simon & Schuster Children's Publishing.

—Lucky for Good, 3. McGuire, Erin, illus. 2011. (ENG.). 224p. (J). (gr. 3-7). 16.99 *(978-1-4169-9058-1(5))* Simon & Schuster, Inc.

Perelman, Helen. Tiana: The Grand Opening. Studio IBOIX Staff, illus. 2011. (Disney Princess Ser.). (ENG.). 96p. (J). (gr. 2-6). 31.36 *(978-1-59961-880-7(X)*, 5180, Chapter Bks.) Spotlight.

Potter, Ellen. Pish Posh. 2011. (ENG.). 176p. (J). (gr. 3-7). 7.99 *(978-0-14-241906-9(0)*, Puffin Books) Penguin Young Readers Group.

Press, Judy. The Case of the Missing Kiddush Cup. 2018. (J). *(978-1-5415-0015-0(6)*, Kar-Ben Publishing) Lerner Publishing Group.

Random House Staff. You're Fired! 2014. (SpongeBob Squarepants 8X8 Ser.). lib. bdg. 13.55 *(978-0-606-35204-8(X))* Turtleback.

Rosen, Michael. Happy Harry's Cafe. Holland, Richard, illus. 2012. (ENG.). 32p. (J). (gr. -1-2). 16.99 *(978-0-7636-6239-4(9))* Candlewick Pr.

Rubinstein, Elana. Once upon an Apple Cake: a Rosh Hashanah Story. Naalchigar, Jennifer, illus. 2019. (Saralee Siegel Ser.: 1). (ENG.). 112p. (J). 16.95 *(978-1-68115-549-4(4)*, 2d23f6b0-2647-46dc-b5fa-b78fbf8c47a8, Apples & Honey Pr.) Behrman Hse., Inc.

Rylant, Cynthia. The Case of the Missing Monkey. Karas, G. Brian, illus. 2003. (High-Rise Private Eyes Ser.: No. 1). (J). 25.95 incl. audio *(978-1-59112-194-7(9))*; pap. 29.95 incl. audio *(978-1-59112-195-4(7))* Live Oak Media.

—The Case of the Missing Monkey. Karas, G. Brian, illus. 2003. (High-Rise Private Eyes Ser.: 1). 46p. (J). (gr. 1-17). 14.75 *(978-0-613-44194-0(X))* Turtleback.

—The Van Gogh Cafe. 2006. (ENG., Illus.). 64p. (J). (gr. 3-7). pap. 8.99 *(978-0-15-205750-3(1)*, 1197281, Clarion Bks.) HarperCollins Pubs.

—The Van Gogh Café. 2015. 64p. pap. 7.00 *(978-1-61003-500-2(3))* Center for the Collaborative Classroom.

Saunders, Zina, illus. Trouble at the Krusty Krab! 2004. (SpongeBob SquarePants Ser.). (ENG.). 32p. (J). pap. 3.99 *(978-0-689-86838-2(3)*, Simon Spotlight/Nickelodeon) Simon Spotlight/Nickelodeon.

Scott, Elaine. Secrets of the Cirque Medrano. 2008. (Illus.). 216p. (J). (gr. 5-9). 15.95 *(978-1-57091-712-7(4))* Charlesbridge Publishing, Inc.

—The Spanish Web: An Encounter with Picasso. 2004. (Art Encounters Ser.). (J). 15.95 *(978-0-8230-0410-2(4))*; pap. 6.99 *(978-0-8230-0413-3(9))* Watson-Guptill Pubns., Inc.

Scott, Janine. Café Cosmos, 1 vol. Wood, Hannah, illus. 2009. (Treasure Chest Readers Ser.). (ENG.). 24p. (J). (gr. 1-1). pap. 9.15 *(978-1-60754-674-0(4)*, 1dece89f-fea7-4a4b-b784-8d6413382311); lib. bdg. 27.27 *(978-1-60754-673-3(6)*, 16ffcaf2-b162-4e05-83e0-eb19ec85efb5) Rosen Publishing Group, Inc., The. (Windmill Bks.).

Sherrard, Valerie. Chasing Shadows: A Shelby Belgarden Mystery. 2004. (ENG.). 216p. (YA). pap. 9.99 *(978-1-55002-502-6(3))* Dundurn Pr. CAN. Dist: Publishers Group West (PGW).

Slippery, Sloppery Spaghetti: Individual Title Six-Packs. (gr. k-1). 23.00 *(978-0-7635-9025-3(8))* Rigby Education.

Smith, Cynthia Leitich. Blessed. 2011. (Tantalize Ser.: 3). (ENG., Illus.). 480p. (YA). (gr. 9-18). 17.99 *(978-0-7636-4326-3(2))* Candlewick Pr.

—Tantalize. 2008. (Tantalize Ser.: 1). (ENG., Illus.). 336p. (YA). (gr. 9). pap. 9.99 *(978-0-7636-4059-0(X))* Candlewick Pr.

Sorenson, Margo. Spaghetti Smiles, 1 vol. Harrington, David, illus. 2014. (ENG.). 32p. (J). (gr. k-3). 16.99 *(978-1-4556-1922-1(1)*, Pelican Publishing) Arcadia Publishing.

Spinelli, Eileen. The Dancing Pancake. Lew-Vriethoff, Joanne, illus. 2011. 256p. (J). (gr. 3-7). 8.99 *(978-0-375-85348-7(0)*, Yearling) Random Hse. Children's Bks.

Springstubb, Tricia. Mo Wren, Lost & Found. Ross, Heather, illus. 2011. (Fox Street Ser.: 2). (ENG.). 256p. (J). (gr. 3-7). 15.99 *(978-0-06-199039-7(6)*, Balzer & Bray) HarperCollins Pubs.

Stalcup. La Loncheria. Arroyo, illus. 2008. (SPA & ENG.). 28p. (J). pap. 8.95 *(978-1-60448-006-1(8))* Lectura Bks.

Stamper, Judith Bauer. Breakfast at Danny's Diner: A Book about Multiplication. Demarest, Chris, illus. 2003. (All Aboard Math Reader Ser.). 48p. (J). (gr. 2-4). 11.65 *(978-0-7569-1695-4(X))* Perfection Learning Corp.

Stilton, Thea. Thea Stilton: Big Trouble in the Big Apple (Thea Stilton #8) A Geronimo Stilton Adventure, Volume 8. 2011. (Thea Stilton Ser.: 8). (ENG., Illus.). 176p. (J). (gr. 2-5). pap. 8.99 *(978-0-545-22775-9(5)*, Scholastic Paperbacks) Scholastic, Inc.

Surrisi, C. M. A Side of Sabotage: A Quinnie Boyd Mystery. (Quinnie Boyd Mysteries Ser.). (ENG.). 280p. (J). (gr. 4-8). 2019. pap. 9.99 *(978-1-5415-7758-9(2)*, df48a301-f493-4867-acd0-7099f5d7865c) 2018. 16.99 *(978-1-5124-4836-8(2)*, 2f2233a9-53da-4efc-ba4d-e5c7d38d2937) Lerner Publishing Group. (Carolrhoda Bks.).

Sylvester, Kevin. Neil Flambé & the Crusader's Curse. Sylvester, Kevin, illus. 2014. (Neil Flambe Capers Ser.: 3). (ENG., Illus.). 320p. (J). (gr. 3-7). pap. 7.99 *(978-1-4424-4287-0(5)*, Simon & Schuster Bks. For Young Readers) Simon & Schuster Bks. For Young Readers.

—Neil Flambé & the Marco Polo Murders. 2010. (Neil Flambé Capers Ser.: No. 1). (Illus.). 304p. (YA). (gr. 5-9). *(978-1-55470-266-4(6))* Me to We.

—Neil Flambé & the Marco Polo Murders. Sylvester, Kevin, illus. 2012. (Neil Flambe Capers Ser.: 1). (ENG., Illus.). 304p. (J). (gr. 3-7). 14.99 *(978-1-4424-4604-5(8)*, Simon & Schuster Bks. For Young Readers) Simon & Schuster Bks. For Young Readers.

—Neil Flambé & the Tokyo Treasure. Sylvester, Kevin, illus. (Neil Flambe Capers Ser.: 4). (ENG., Illus.). (J). (gr. 3-7). 2014. 368p. pap. 8.99 *(978-1-4424-4289-4(1))* 2012. 352p. 13.99 *(978-1-4424-4288-7(3))* Simon & Schuster Bks. For Young Readers. (Simon & Schuster Bks. For Young Readers).

Tate, Cynthia Wagoner. Gordy's Grimy but Groovy Adventure. 2005. (ENG.). 24p. 12.98 *(978-1-4116-6297-1(0))* Lulu Pr., Inc.

Taylor, Trace. Dogtown Diner. 2010. pap. 39.62 *(978-1-61541-088-0(0))* American Reading Co.

—Dogtown's Got Talent. 2010. pap. 39.62 *(978-1-61541-137-5(2))* American Reading Co.

—Flying over Dogtown. 2010. pap. 39.62 *(978-1-61541-141-2(0))* American Reading Co.

—Hair Day in Dogtown. 2010. pap. 39.62 *(978-1-61541-143-6(7))* American Reading Co.

—Wedding Day in Dogtown. 2010. pap. 39.62 *(978-1-61541-145-0(3))* American Reading Co.

Terrell, Brandon. Limbo's Diner. 2016. (Tartan House Ser.). (ENG., Illus.). 96p. (J). (gr. 3-6). *(978-1-63235-164-7(1)*, 11895, 12-Story Library) Bookstaves, LLC.

Turnage, Sheila. Three Times Lucky. 2013. (Mo & Dale Mysteries Ser.). (Illus.). 336p. (J). (gr. 5). pap. 9.99 *(978-0-14-242605-0(9)*, Puffin Books) Penguin Young Readers Group.

—Three Times Lucky. 2013. (Mo & Dale Mystery Ser.: 1). lib. bdg. 18.40 *(978-0-606-34168-4(4))* Turtleback.

Vinopol, Corinne & Bednarczyk, Angela. ASL Tales & Games for Kids - Biscuit Blvd: Computer Software in American Sign Language. 2004. (J). cd-rom 34.95 *(978-0-9667589-9-3(4))* Institute for Disabilities Research & Training, Inc.

Watts, Julia. Free Spirits. 2009. (ENG.). 176p. (J). (gr. 1). pap. 8.95 *(978-0-9667359-2-5(7)*, BeanPole Bks.) OH Industries.

Weeks, Sarah. Two Eggs, Please. Lewin, Betsy, illus. 2007. (ENG.). 32p. (J). (gr. -1-1). reprint ed. 7.99 *(978-1-4169-2714-3(X)*, Atheneum Bks. for Young Readers) Simon & Schuster Children's Publishing.

Wellington, Monica. Pizza at Sally's. Wellington, Monica, illus. 2006. (Illus.). 32p. (J). (gr. -1-2). 17.99 *(978-0-525-47715-0(2)*, Dutton Books for Young Readers) Penguin Young Readers Group.

Whelan, Gloria. The Boy Who Wanted to Cook. Adams, Steve, illus. 2011. (Tales of the World Ser.). (ENG.). 32p. (J). (gr. 1-4). lib. bdg. 16.95 *(978-1-58536-534-0(3)*, 202216) Sleeping Bear Pr.

Williams, Kathryn. Pizza, Love, & Other Stuff That Made Me Famous: A Novel. 2013. (ENG.). 256p. (YA). (gr. 7-12). pap. 14.99 *(978-1-250-02745-0(4)*, 900098318) Square Fish.

Wynne-Jones, Tim. Lord of the Fries. (Illus.). pap. 6.95 *(978-0-88899-384-7(6))* Groundwood Bks. CAN. Dist: Publishers Group West (PGW).

RETAIL TRADE

see also Advertising; Department Stores; Sales Personnel; Supermarkets

Caraccilo, Dominic. E-Tailing: Careers Selling over the Web. 2009. (Library of E-Commerce & Internet Careers Ser.). 64p. (gr. 5-5). 58.50 *(978-1-60853-587-3(8))* Rosen Publishing Group, Inc., The.

Enz, Tammy. Hidden Worlds, 4 vols., Set. Incl. Behind the Racks: Exploring the Secrets of a Shopping Mall. lib. bdg. 27.32 *(978-1-4296-3386-4(7)*, 95892); Beyond the Bars: Exploring the Secrets of a Police Station. lib. bdg. 27.32 *(978-1-4296-3377-2(8)*, 95884); (J). (gr. 3-9). (Hidden Worlds Ser.). (ENG.). 32p. 2010. 81.96 o.p. *(978-1-4296-3777-0(3)*, 168679, Capstone Pr.) Capstone.

Gilbert, Sara. The Story of Target. 2014. (Built for Success Ser.). (ENG., Illus.). 48p. (J). (gr. 5-8). *(978-1-60818-397-5(1)*, 21290, Creative Education) Creative Co., The.

—The Story of Wal-Mart. 2011. (Built for Success Ser.). (ENG., Illus.). 48p. (J). (gr. 5-8). 34.25 *(978-1-60818-064-6(6)*, 23855) Creative Co., The.

—The Stoy of Wal-Mart. 2012. (Built for Success Ser.). (ENG., Illus.). 48p. (J). (gr. 5-8). pap. 12.00 *(978-0-89812-662-4(2)*, 23860, Creative Paperbacks) Creative Co., The.

Glaser, Jason. Careers in Online Retailing, 1 vol. 2013. (Careers in Computer Technology Ser.). (ENG.). 80p. (YA). (gr. 8-8). 38.47 *(978-1-4488-9595-3(2)*, c6768a9d-825e-42ad-a382-2029eeee7e54) Rosen Publishing Group, Inc., The.

Hidden Worlds [Capstone Sole Source]. 2010. (Hidden Worlds Ser.). 32p. lib. bdg. 101.28 *(978-1-4296-5865-2(7)*, Capstone Pr.) Capstone.

Krieg, Katherine. Sam Walton: Founder of the Walmart Empire, 1 vol. 2013. (Essential Lives Set 8 Ser.). (ENG., Illus.). 112p. (YA). (gr. 6-12). lib. bdg. 41.36 *(978-1-61783-898-9(5)*, 6773, Essential Library) ABDO Publishing Co.

La Bella, Laura. Getting a Job in the Retail Industry, 1 vol. 2016. (Job Basics: Getting the Job You Need Ser.). (ENG., Illus.). 80p. (J). (gr. 8-8). 38.41 *(978-1-4777-8558-4(2)*, 7dd203d2-9273-4f52-bc3c-6e39220b707e) Rosen Publishing Group, Inc., The.

LaCamera, Breanne. E-Commerce. 2019. (21st Century Skills Innovation Library: Disruptors in Tech Ser.). (ENG., Illus.). 32p. (J). (gr. 4-8). pap. 14.21 *(978-1-5341-5041-6(2)*, 213471); lib. bdg. 32.07 *(978-1-5341-4755-3(1)*, 213470) Cherry Lake Publishing.

Meachen Rau, Dana. Grocer, 1 vol. 2008. (Jobs in Town Ser.). (ENG., Illus.). 24p. (gr. k-1). lib. bdg. 25.50 *(978-0-7614-2720-9(1)*, ea0a4810-343f-4d4b-b6a4-51904b124ae0) Cavendish Square Publishing LLC.

Reeves, Diane Lindsey. Get a Job at the Shopping Mall. 2016. (Bright Futures Press: Get a Job Ser.). (ENG., Illus.). 32p. (J). (gr. 4-6). 32.07 *(978-1-63471-908-7(5)*, 208953) Cherry Lake Publishing.

Rissman, Rebecca. ABCs at the Store, 1 vol. 2012. (Everyday Alphabet Ser.). (ENG., Illus.). 32p. (gr. -1-k). pap. 9.95 *(978-1-4109-4734-5(3)*, 119322, Raintree) Capstone.

Shores, Erika L. Sam Walton, 1 vol. 2014. (Business Leaders Ser.). (ENG.). 24p. (J). (gr. -1-2). lib. bdg. 24.65 *(978-1-4765-9642-6(5)*, 125433, Pebble) Capstone.

RETAIL TRADE—VOCATIONAL GUIDANCE

Avitan, Amos. Your Life in Trade: A Contractor's Guide to Success. 2003. (Illus.). 300p. (YA). per. *(978-0-9689715-2-9(0))* Amos Avitan. Inc.

Endsaff, Najoud & Rooney, Anne. Retail Careers. 2010. (In the Workplace Ser.). 48p. (J). 35.65 *(978-1-60753-093-0(7))* Amicus Learning.

Ensaff, Najoud, et al. Retail Careers. 2011. (Been There! Ser.). 32p. (gr. 3-6). lib. bdg. 31.35 *(978-1-59920-473-4(8))* Black Rabbit Bks.

Mooney, Carla. Using Computer Science in Online Retail Careers, 1 vol. 2017. (Coding Your Passion Ser.). (ENG., Illus.). 80p. (J). (gr. 7-7). 37.47 *(978-1-5081-7519-3(5)*, d894d260-c21f-440c-b347-3e125c111d9e, Rosen Young Adult) Rosen Publishing Group, Inc., The.

Santos, Edson. People Who Love to Buy Things, 1 vol. 2006. (Cool Careers Without College (2002-2006) Ser.). (ENG., Illus.). 144p. (YA). (gr. 7-7). lib. bdg. 41.13 *(978-1-4042-0751-6(1)*, a6c84d0e-a368-479c-8c59-bc9bc5b54bcc) Rosen Publishing Group, Inc., The.

RETARDED PERSONS

see People with Mental Disabilities

REVERE, PAUL, 1735-1818

Brandt, Keith & Macken, JoAnn Early. Paul Revere, Son of Liberty. Livingston, Francis, illus. 2007. 50p. (J). *(978-0-439-02017-6(4))* Scholastic, Inc.

Draper, Allison Stark. The Start of the American Revolutionary War: Paul Revere Rides at Midnight. 2009. (Headlines from History Ser.). 24p. (gr. 3-3). 42.50 *(978-1-61513-247-8(3)*, PowerKids Pr.) Rosen Publishing Group, Inc., The.

Edwards, Roberta & Who HQ. Who Was Paul Revere? O'Brien, John, illus. 2011. (Who Was? Ser.). 112p. (J). (gr. 3-7). pap. 6.99 *(978-0-448-45715-4(6)*, Penguin Workshop) Penguin Young Readers Group.

Erlic, Lily. Paul Revere. 2019. (Illus.). 24p. (J). *(978-1-4896-9550-5(8)*, AV2 by Weigl) Weigl Pubs., Inc.

Ford, Barbara. Paul Revere: American Patriot, 1 vol. 2014. (Legendary American Biographies Ser.). (ENG.). 96p. (gr. 6-6). 29.60 *(978-0-7660-6485-0(9)*, 71b83a69-4129-48f5-bc63-b49d99ff4350); pap. 13.88 *(978-0-7660-6486-7(7)*, 16fec7fd-cdf8-4057-83a8-a000c6afe506) Enslow Publishing, LLC.

Golden, Nancy. The British Are Coming! The Midnight Ride of Paul Revere. (Great Moments in American History Ser.). 32p. (gr. 3-3). 2009. 47.90 *(978-1-61513-136-5(1))* 2003. (ENG., Illus.). (J). lib. bdg. 29.13 *(978-0-8239-4378-4(X)*, cf658248-0d7f-4ee9-a293-f9f8a3e053da) Rosen Publishing Group, Inc., The.

Hicks, Dwayne. Paul Revere: American Patriot, 1 vol. 2012. (Beginning Biographies Ser.). (ENG., Illus.). 24p. (J). (gr. 1-2). 26.27 *(978-1-4488-8599-2(X)*, 2aa1337b-5524-4b90-af85-b8dbee02d41d, PowerKids Pr.) Rosen Publishing Group, Inc., The.

Ingram, Scott. Paul Revere. 2003. (Triangle History of the American Revolution Ser.). (Illus.). 104p. (J). 28.70 *(978-1-56711-780-6(5)*, Blackbirch Pr., Inc.) Cengage Gale.

Jeffrey, Gary. Paul Revere & His Midnight Ride, 1 vol. 2011. (Graphic Heroes of the American Revolution Ser.). (ENG.). 24p. (J). (gr. 3-3). pap. 9.15 *(978-1-4339-6020-8(6)*, 0981fe11-ad56-49bb-ba3e-6601372ad8b3, Gareth Stevens Learning Library); lib. bdg. 26.60 *(978-1-4339-6019-2(2)*, c3cd73f3-b213-499a-b80e-d68ebc2109bb) Stevens, Gareth Publishing LLLP.

Kallio, Jamie. 12 Questions about Paul Revere's Ride. 2017. (Examining Primary Sources Ser.). (ENG., Illus.). 32p. (J). (gr. 3-6). 32.80 *(978-1-63235-286-6(9)*, 11755); pap. 9.95 *(978-1-63235-336-8(9)*, 11763) Bookstaves, LLC. (12-Story Library).

Katirgis, Jane & McCarthy, Rose. Meet Paul Revere: Revolutionary Hero, 1 vol. 2019. (Introducing Famous Americans Ser.). (ENG.). 32p. (gr. 3-4). pap. 11.53 *(978-1-9785-1130-9(2)*, aabbf4d0-c3b3-4ca2-86a7-db6ef8ac5f6d) Enslow Publishing, LLC.

Keller, Susanna. The True Story of Paul Revere's Ride, 1 vol. 2013. (What Really Happened? Ser.). (ENG., Illus.). 24p. (J). (gr. 2-3). pap. 9.25 *(978-1-4488-9838-1(2)*, efd634f7-c46f-44be-a810-8952a3a1d7af); lib. bdg. 26.27 *(978-1-4488-9690-5(8)*, b9df1cc6-fbb3-44a4-8594-63505b0e3628) Rosen Publishing Group, Inc., The. (PowerKids Pr.).

Lantos, Jeff. Why Longfellow Lied: The Truth about Paul Revere's Midnight Ride. 2021. (Illus.). 160p. (J). (gr. 3-7). lib. bdg. 18.99 *(978-1-58089-933-8(1))* Charlesbridge Publishing, Inc.

Mack, Molly. The Life of Paul Revere, 1 vol. 2012. (InfoMax Readers Ser.). (ENG., Illus.). 24p. (J). (gr. 1-1). pap. 8.25 *(978-1-4488-9049-1(7)*, ed30d88c-450a-4152-abba-81a56a50f15f, Rosen Classroom) Rosen Publishing Group, Inc., The.

Mara, Wil. Rookie Biographies: Paul Revere. 2005. (Rookie Biographies Ser.). (ENG., Illus.). 32p. (J). (gr. 1-2). pap. 4.95 *(978-0-516-25820-1(6)*, Children's Pr.) Scholastic Library Publishing.

McCarthy, Rose. Paul Revere: Freedom Rider. (Primary Sources of Famous People in American History Ser.). 32p. 2009. (gr. 2-3). 47.90 *(978-1-60851-714-5(4))* 2003. (ENG., Illus.). (gr. 3-4). pap. 10.00 *(978-0-8239-4190-2(6)*, 745cf6da-8ac8-464c-bd8c-b253a4e4e52a) 2003. (ENG., Illus.). (gr. 3-4). lib. bdg. 29.13 *(978-0-8239-4118-6(3)*, 944430a4-16ea-43f1-aea5-c6d0a91b92f5, Rosen Reference) Rosen Publishing Group, Inc., The.

—Paul Revere: Freedom Rider / Jinete de la causa Revolucionaria. 2009. (Famous People in American History/Grandes personajes en la historia de los Estados Unidos Ser.). (ENG & SPA.). 32p. (gr. 2-3). 47.90 *(978-1-61512-553-1(1)*, Editorial Buenas Letras) Rosen Publishing Group, Inc., The.

—Paul Revere: Jinete de la Causa Revolucionaria, 1 vol. 2003. (Grandes Personajes en la Historia de Los Estados Unidos (Famous People in American History) Ser.). (SPA., Illus.). 32p. (gr. 3-4). lib. bdg. 29.13 *(978-0-8239-4142-1(6)*, 0f9c7bc7-d836-46e1-b5f3-3aa567e9dc5a, Editorial Buenas Letras) Rosen Publishing Group, Inc., The.

—Paul Revere: Jinete de la causa revolucionaria (Paul Revere: Freedom Rider) 2009. (Grandes personajes en la historia de los Estados Unidos (Famous People in American History) Ser.). (SPA.). 32p. (gr. 2-3). 47.90 *(978-1-61512-806-8(9)*, Editorial Buenas Letras) Rosen Publishing Group, Inc., The.

—Paul Revere: Jinete de la guerra de Independencia, 1 vol. 2003. (Grandes Personajes en la Historia de Los Estados Unidos (Famous People in American History) Ser.). (SPA.). 32p. (gr. 3-4). pap. 10.00 *(978-0-8239-4236-7(8)*, 7a9dae9c-1087-4ed3-af54-9ea70e742eec, Rosen Classroom) Rosen Publishing Group, Inc., The.

Mills, Nathan & Hicks, Dwayne. Paul Revere: American Patriot, 1 vol. 2012. (Rosen Readers Ser.). (ENG., Illus.). 24p. (J). (gr. 1-2). pap. 8.25 *(978-1-4488-8836-8(0)*, 134af41f-53e0-4456-a0f8-6e74a2a5ae8e, Rosen Classroom) Rosen Publishing Group, Inc., The.

Min, Ellen. The Midnight Ride of Paul Revere: One If by Land, Two If by Sea, 1 vol. 2015. (Spotlight on American History Ser.). (ENG., Illus.). 24p. (J). (gr. 4-6). pap. 11.00 *(978-1-4994-1734-0(9)*, 6ebe0528-c359-4a33-b22f-cde39d20f9ee, PowerKids Pr.) Rosen Publishing Group, Inc., The.

Nelson, Maria. The Life of Paul Revere, 1 vol. 2012. (Famous Lives Ser.). (ENG.). 24p. (J). (gr. 1-2). pap. 9.15 *(978-1-4339-6355-1(8)*, 28f1d255-6234-4269-a325-eee483bc787f); lib. bdg. 25.27 *(978-1-4339-6353-7(1)*, 94adfa60-b92a-4642-bf87-ccb0fbd3bbd7) Stevens, Gareth Publishing LLLP.

—The Life of Paul Revere / la Vida de Paul Revere, 1 vol. 2012. (Famous Lives / Vidas Extraordinarias Ser.). (ENG & SPA., Illus.). 24p. (J). (gr. 1-2). 25.27 *(978-1-4339-6657-6(3)*, aa338b1b-e2d8-4616-9737-e97b8dd61403) Stevens, Gareth Publishing LLLP.

Roop, Peter & Roop, Connie. Let's Ride, Paul Revere! 2004. (Before I Made History Ser.). (Illus.). 60p. (J). pap. *(978-0-439-67623-6(1))* Scholastic, Inc.

Smith, Andrea P. A Day in the Life of Colonial Silversmith Paul Revere. (Illus.). 24p. (J). 2012. 63.60 *(978-1-4488-5217-8(X))* 2011. (ENG., (gr. 2-3). pap. 11.60 *(978-1-4488-5216-1(1)*, 222487a5-1e5c-4e48-abee-09b3e5f95238) 2011. (ENG., (gr. 2-3). lib. bdg. 28.93 *(978-1-4488-5189-8(0)*, 2bb3a4f9-0113-4e50-be2f-9f17eb9f5dd4) Rosen Publishing Group, Inc., The. (PowerKids Pr.).

Weston Woods Staff, creator. And Then What Happened, Paul Revere? 2011. 29.95 *(978-0-439-73467-7(3))*; 38.75 *(978-0-439-72663-4(8))*; 18.95 *(978-0-439-72661-0(1))* Weston Woods Studios, Inc.

Whiting, Jim. The Life & Times of Paul Revere. 2006. (Profiles in American History Ser.). (Illus.). 48p. (J). (gr. 3-7). lib. bdg. 29.95 *(978-1-58415-441-9(1))* Mitchell Lane Pubs.

Winter, Jonah. Paul Revere & the Bell Ringers. Dodson, Bert, illus. 2005. 32p. (J). lib. bdg. 15.00 *(978-1-59054-952-0(X))* Fitzgerald Bks.

—Paul Revere & the Bell Ringers: Ready-To-Read Level 2. Dodson, Bert, illus. 2003. (Ready-To-Read Childhood of Famous Americans Ser.). (ENG.). 32p. (J). (gr. k-2). pap. 4.99 *(978-0-689-85635-8(0)*, Simon Spotlight) Simon Spotlight.

REVERE, PAUL, 1735-1818—FICTION

Egan, Kate. The Midnight Ride of Flat Revere. Pamintuan, Macky, illus. 2016. 134p. (J). *(978-1-5182-2203-0(X))* Harper & Row Ltd.

Hardman, Ron & Hardman, Jessica. Shadow Fox: Sons of Liberty. Barnecut, Suzanne, ed. Harrigan, Mike, illus. 2010. (Shadow Fox Ser.). 186p. (J). (gr. 4-8). 22.99 *(978-0-9819607-1-5(5))* Fox Run Pr., LLC.

—Shadow Fox: Sons of Liberty. Barnecut, Suzanne, ed. Harrigan, Mike, illus. 2010. (Shadow Fox Ser.). 186p. (J). (gr. 4-8). pap. 11.99 *(978-0-9819607-0-8(7))* Fox Run Pr., LLC.

—Shadow Fox: Sons of Liberty Teacher's Edition. Barnecutt, Suzanne, ed. Harrigan, Mike, illus. 2010. (Shadow Fox Ser.: 1). 186p. (J). 34.99 *(978-0-9819607-2-2(3))* Fox Run Pr., LLC.

Lawson, Robert. Mr. Revere & I. 2003. (J). (gr. 4-8). 22.75 *(978-0-8446-7258-8(0))* Smith, Peter Pub., Inc.

Rinaldi, Ann. The Secret of Sarah Revere. 2003. (Great Episodes Ser.). (ENG.). 336p. (J). (gr. 5-7). pap. 9.99 *(978-0-15-204684-2(4)*, 1194115, Clarion Bks.) HarperCollins Pubs.

REVERE, PAUL, 1735-1818—POETRY

Longfellow, Henry. Paul Revere's Ride: The Landlord's Tale. Santore, Charles, illus. 2003. 40p. (J). lib. bdg. 17.89 *(978-0-06-623747-3(5))* HarperCollins Pubs.

Longfellow, Henry Wadsworth. Paul Revere's Ride. 2011. (ENG., Illus.). 32p. (gr. 3-6). 26.19 *(978-1-56397-799-2(0))* Highlights Pr., c/o Highlights for Children, Inc.

Revere, Paul. Paul Revere's Ride. 2010. (Books of American Wisdom Ser.). (ENG.). 32p. 12.95 *(978-1-55709-072-0(6))* Applewood Bks.

REVIEWS

see Book Reviews

REVIVAL OF LETTERS

see Renaissance

REVOLUTION, AMERICAN

see United States—History—Revolution, 1775-1783

REVOLUTION, FRENCH

see France—History—Revolution, 1789-1799

REVOLUTIONS

see also France—History—Revolution, 1789-1799; Hungary—History—Revolution, 1956; Social Conflict; United States—History—Revolution, 1775-1783

The Age of Revolution, 20 vols. 2015. (Age of Revolution Ser.). (ENG.). 168-184p. (YA). (gr. 9-10). 378.20 *(978-1-68048-201-0(7)*, db3841a7-dee6-43ee-be83-6ca391ba6bdf, Britannica Educational Publishing) Rosen Publishing Group, Inc., The.

Arruda, Suzanne Middendorf. Freedom's Martyr: The Story of Jose Rizal, National Hero of the Philippines. 2003. (Avisson Young Adult Ser.). (Illus.). 106p. (J). pap. 19.95 *(978-1-888105-55-1(0))* Avisson Pr., Inc.

Croce, Nicholas, ed. Anarchism, Revolution, & Terrorism, 1 vol. 2014. (Political & Economic Systems Ser.). (ENG.). 232p. (J). (gr. 10-10). 47.59 *(978-1-62275-353-6(4)*, 6e5e3737-bb64-4dc9-aa7a-16283c62c67f) Rosen Publishing Group, Inc., The.

Dodge Cummings, Judy. Rebels & Revolutions: Real Tales of Radical Change in America. 2017. (Mystery & Mayhem Ser.). (ENG., Illus.). 128p. (J). (gr. 4-6). 19.95 *(978-1-61930-547-2(X)*, 0a649428-fd58-42af-8dba-5550571227e2); pap. 9.95 *(978-1-61930-551-9(8)*, 7ed208fc-70b4-4e66-ad8d-04e7a7442e25) Nomad Pr.

Fabiny, Sarah & Who HQ. Who Was Fidel Castro? Hammond, Ted, illus. 2017. (Who Was? Ser.). 112p. (J). (gr. 3-7). 6.99 *(978-0-451-53333-3(X)*, Penguin Workshop) Penguin Young Readers Group.

Gay, Kathlyn. The Aftermath of the Chinese Nationalist Revolution. 2008. (Aftermath of History Ser.). (ENG., Illus.). 160p. (J). (gr. 9-12). lib. bdg. 38.60 *(978-0-8225-7601-3(5))* Lerner Publishing Group.

Hughes, Christopher. Cuba. 2003. (Nations in Conflict Ser.). 48p. (J). 26.19 *(978-1-56711-511-6(X)*, Blackbirch Pr., Inc.) Cengage Gale.

MacCurtain, Fionnuala. The Story of Tomás Mac Curtáin. 2011. (Irish Heros for Children Ser.). (ENG.). 128p. (J). 16.95 *(978-1-85635-716-6(3))* Mercier Pr., Ltd., The IRL. Dist: Dufour Editions, Inc.

Malaspina, Ann. Mao Zedong & the Chinese Revolution, 1 vol. 2015. (People & Events That Changed the World Ser.). (ENG., Illus.). 128p. (gr. 7-8). lib. bdg. 38.93 *(978-0-7660-7292-3(4)*, a6376b76-b4a7-4ec2-b29b-6db67609e41e) Enslow Publishing, LLC.

McNab, Chris. Famous Battles of the Age of Revolution, 1 vol. 2017. (Classic Warfare Ser.). (ENG.). 72p. (YA). (gr. 8-8). lib. bdg. 37.36 *(978-1-5026-3252-4(7)*, cda2c722-c80a-466a-ae3b-757873daefea) Cavendish Square Publishing LLC.

Schmermund, Elizabeth & McGowen, Tom. Maximilien Robespierre & the French Revolution, 1 vol. 2015. (People & Events That Changed the World Ser.). (ENG., Illus.). 128p. (gr. 7-8). lib. bdg. 38.93 *(978-0-7660-7294-7(0)*, 3fd33d38-9369-4036-921d-fb75cf48f097) Enslow Publishing, LLC.

Steele, Philip. Uprisings in the Middle East & North Africa. 2016. (Behind the News Ser.). (Illus.). 48p. (J). (gr. 6-9). *(978-0-7787-2589-3(8))* Crabtree Publishing Co.

World Book, Inc. Staff, contrib. by. The Chinese Revolution. 2010. (Illus.). 64p. (J). *(978-0-7166-1503-3(7))* World Bk., Inc.

REVOLUTIONS—FICTION

Alvarez, Julia. Antes de Ser Libres. Valenzuela, Liliana, tr. from ENG. 2018. Tr. of Before We Were Free. (SPA.). 192p. (YA). (gr. 7). pap. 10.99 *(978-0-525-57977-9(X)*, Ember) Random Hse. Children's Bks.

—Antes de Ser Libres. 2004. Tr. of Before We Were Free. (SPA.). (gr. 7-12). lib. bdg. 17.20 *(978-0-613-71931-5(X))* Turtleback.

—Before We Were Free. 2004. 192p. (J). (gr. 7-18). pap. 38.00 incl. audio *(978-1-4000-9017-4(2)*, Listening Library) Random Hse. Audio Publishing Group.

—Before We Were Free. 2004. (gr. 7-12). lib. bdg. 17.20 *(978-0-613-72269-8(8))* Turtleback.

Braswell, Liz. A Whole New World: A Twisted Tale. 2016. (Twisted Tale Ser.). (YA). lib. bdg. 20.85 *(978-0-606-38511-4(8))* Turtleback.

—A Whole New World-A Twisted Tale. 2016. (Twisted Tale Ser.). (ENG.). 400p. (YA). (gr. 7-12). pap. 9.99 *(978-1-4847-0732-6(X)*, Disney-Hyperion) Disney Publishing Worldwide.

Brennan, Sarah Rees. Tell the Wind & Fire. 2017. (ENG.). 368p. (YA). (gr. 7). pap. 9.99 *(978-0-544-93887-8(9)*, 1658467, Clarion Bks.) HarperCollins Pubs.

Brody, Jessica & Rendell, Joanne. Sky Without Stars. 2019. (System Divine Ser.: 1). (ENG., Illus.). 592p. (YA). (gr. 7). 19.99 *(978-1-5344-1063-3(5)*, Simon Pulse) Simon Pulse.

Clark, Marian. Benji's Sicarii Sword. 2007. 156p. per. 13.99 *(978-1-60266-022-9(0))* Salem Author Services.

De Pauw, Linda Grant. In Search of Molly Pitcher. 2008. 164p. pap. 12.00 *(978-1-4357-0607-1(2))* Lulu Pr., Inc.

Diver, Lucienne. Vamped. 2017. (ENG., Illus.). (YA). pap. 14.95 *(978-1-62268-115-0(0))* Bella Rosa Bks.

Fine, Sarah. Of Dreams & Rust. 2016. (ENG.). 304p. (YA). (gr. 9). pap. 11.99 *(978-1-4424-8362-0(8)*, McElderry, Margaret K. Bks.) McElderry, Margaret K. Bks.

Júlia, Álvarez. Before We Were Free. 2014. (ENG.). 192p. (YA). 11.24 *(978-1-63245-139-2(5))* Lectorum Pubns., Inc.

Kramer, J. Kasper. The Story That Cannot Be Told. 2020. (ENG., Illus.). 400p. (J). (gr. 3-7). pap. 8.99 *(978-1-5344-3069-3(5)*, Atheneum Bks. for Young Readers) Simon & Schuster Children's Publishing.

Marsden, Carolyn. My Own Revolution. 2012. (ENG., Illus.). 192p. (YA). (gr. 7-9). 16.99 *(978-0-7636-5395-8(0))* Candlewick Pr.

Miller, Sarah. The Lost Crown. (ENG., Illus.). 448p. (YA). (gr. 7). 2012. pap. 12.99 *(978-1-4169-8341-5(4))* 2011. 17.99 *(978-1-4169-8340-8(6))* Simon & Schuster Children's Publishing. (Atheneum Bks. for Young Readers).

Mull, Brandon. Beyonders the Complete Set (Boxed Set) A World Without Heroes; Seeds of Rebellion; Chasing the Prophecy. Set. 2013. (Beyonders Ser.). (ENG., Illus.). 1456p. (J). (gr. 3-7). 59.99 *(978-1-4424-8593-8(0)*, Aladdin) Simon & Schuster Children's Publishing.

—Chasing the Prophecy. (Beyonders Ser.: 3). (ENG.). (J). (gr. 3-7). 2014. 528p. pap. 9.99 *(978-1-4169-9797-9(0))* 2013. 512p. 21.99 *(978-1-4169-9796-2(2))* Simon & Schuster Children's Publishing. (Aladdin).

—Seeds of Rebellion. (Beyonders Ser.: 2). (ENG., Illus.). 512p. (J). (gr. 3-7). 2013. pap. 9.99 *(978-1-4169-9795-5(4))* 2012. 21.99 *(978-1-4169-9794-8(6))* Simon & Schuster Children's Publishing. (Aladdin).

—Seeds of Rebellion. 2012. (Beyonders Ser.: Bk. 2). (ENG., Illus.). 512p. (J). pap. 10.99 *(978-1-4424-4965-7(9)*, Simon & Schuster/Paula Wiseman Bks.) Simon & Schuster/Paula Wiseman Bks.

—Seeds of Rebellion. 2013. (Beyonders Ser.: 2). lib. bdg. 19.65 *(978-0-606-27030-4(2))* Turtleback.

—A World Without Heroes. (J). 2011. (Beyonders Ser.: 1). 1.25 *(978-1-4640-0920-4(1))* (Beyonders Ser.: 1). 92.75 *(978-1-4618-0338-6(1))* 2011. (Beyonders Ser.: 1). 124.75 *(978-1-4618-0353-9(5))* 2011. 122.75 *(978-1-4618-0363-8(2))* Recorded Bks., Inc.

—A World Without Heroes. (Beyonders Ser.: 1). (ENG.). (J). (gr. 3-7). 2012. 512p. pap. 9.99 *(978-1-4169-9793-1(8))* 2011. 464p. 21.99 *(978-1-4169-9792-4(X))* Simon & Schuster Children's Publishing. (Aladdin).

—A World Without Heroes. 2011. (Beyonders Ser.: Bk. 1). (ENG.). 464p. (J). pap. 10.99 *(978-1-4424-3530-8(5)*, Simon & Schuster/Paula Wiseman Bks.) Simon & Schuster/Paula Wiseman Bks.

—A World Without Heroes. 2012. (Beyonders Ser.: 1). lib. bdg. 19.65 *(978-0-606-23675-1(9))* Turtleback.

Nagara, Innosanto. M Is for Movement. Nagara, Innosanto, illus. 2019. (ENG., Illus.). 96p. (J). (gr. 3-7). 19.95 *(978-1-60980-935-5(1)*, Triangle Square) Seven Stories Pr.

Ngan, Natasha. Girls of Paper & Fire. (YA). 2019. (ENG.). 416p. (gr. 10-17). pap. 12.99 *(978-0-316-56135-8(5))* 2018. 385p. *(978-0-316-45220-5(3))* 2018. (ENG.). 400p. (gr. 10-17). 19.99 *(978-0-316-56136-5(3))* 2018. 385p. *(978-0-316-53040-8(9))* 2018. 385p. *(978-0-316-45352-3(8))* Little Brown & Co. (Jimmy Patterson).

—Girls of Paper & Fire. 2019. (ENG.). 416p. lib. bdg. 21.80 *(978-1-6636-2724-7(X))* Perfection Learning Corp.

North, Phoebe. Starglass. 2013. (Starglass Sequence Ser.). (ENG., Illus.). 448p. (YA). (gr. 7). 17.99 *(978-1-4424-5953-3(0)*, Simon & Schuster Bks. For Young Readers) Simon & Schuster Bks. For Young Readers.

Purdie, Kathryn. Crystal Blade. (Burning Glass Ser.: 2). (ENG.). (YA). (gr. 9). 2018. 384p. pap. 9.99 *(978-0-06-241240-9(X))* 2017. (Illus.). 368p. 17.99 *(978-0-06-241239-3(6))* HarperCollins Pubs. (Tegen, Katherine Bks).

Richmond, Caroline Tung. Live in Infamy (a Companion to the Only Thing to Fear) 2018. (ENG.). 304p. (YA). (gr. 7). 18.99 *(978-1-338-11109-5(4)*, Scholastic Pr.) Scholastic, Inc.

Rinaldi, Ann. Cast Two Shadows: The American Revolution in the South. 2004. (Great Episodes Ser.). (ENG., Illus.). 304p. (YA). (gr. 7-8). pap. 7.99 *(978-0-15-205077-1(9)*, 1195334, Clarion Bks.) HarperCollins Pubs.

Stasse, Lisa M. The Defiant: The Forsaken Trilogy. 2014. (ENG., Illus.). 352p. (YA). (gr. 7). 17.99 *(978-1-4424-3271-0(3)*, Simon & Schuster Bks. For Young Readers) Simon & Schuster Bks. For Young Readers.

—The Defiant: The Forsaken Trilogy. 2015. (ENG., Illus.). 352p. (YA). (gr. 7). pap. 10.99 *(978-1-4424-3272-7(1))* Simon & Schuster Children's Publishing.

—The Uprising: The Forsaken Trilogy. 2013. (ENG.). 384p. (YA). (gr. 7). 16.99 *(978-1-4424-3268-0(3)*, Simon &

Schuster Bks. For Young Readers) Simon & Schuster Bks. For Young Readers.
Thomas, Rhiannon. A Wicked Thing. 2015. (ENG.). 352p. (YA). (gr. 9). 17.99 *(978-0-06-230353-0(8)*, HarperTeen) HarperCollins Pubs.
Whelan, Gloria. Angel on the Square. 2003. (Russian Saga Ser.: 1). (ENG.). 304p. (J). (gr. 5-9). pap. 9.99 *(978-0-06-440879-0(5)*, HarperCollins) HarperCollins Pubs.
—Angel on the Square. 2004. 288p. (gr. 5-9). 20.00 *(978-0-7569-4062-1(1))* Perfection Learning Corp.

RHETORIC

see also Criticism; Debates and Debating; Letter Writing; Punctuation; Satire; Style, Literary

Abraham, Philip. Language Development Writing Process, 1 vol. 2003. (BrainBuilders Ser.). (ENG.). 48p. (gr. k-4). pap. 5.25 *(978-1-4042-8520-0(2)*, 9cb1f0dc-d38c-4b5b-8051-002ba8312dce) Rosen Publishing Group, Inc., The.
Allen, Susan & Lindaman, Jane. Written Anything Good Lately? Enright, Vicky, illus. (J). 2010. (ENG.). 32p. (gr. k-3). pap. 7.99 *(978-0-7613-5477-2(8)*, 1a59dccf-356f-4a58-aad6-bf08b3dde2ef, First Avenue Editions) 2006. 31p. (gr. 3-7). lib. bdg. 15.95 *(978-0-7613-2426-3(7)*, Millbrook Pr.) Lerner Publishing Group.
Atlee, Nancy. The Absolutely Essential Writing Guide. 2004. (J). per. 13.95 *(978-1-883055-68-4(7))* Dandy Lion Pubns.
Beers. Elements of Literature: Enhanced Online Edition. 5th ed. 2004. (J). (gr. k). 19.93 *(978-0-03-037277-3(1))*; (J). (gr. 2). 19.93 *(978-0-03-037279-7(8))*; (J). (gr. 3). 19.93 *(978-0-03-037281-0(X))*; (J). (gr. 4). 19.93 *(978-0-03-037282-7(8))*; (gr. 5). 19.93 *(978-0-03-037283-4(6))*; (gr. 6). 19.93 *(978-0-03-037284-1(4))* Holt McDougal.
Benke, Karen. Rip the Page! Adventures in Creative Writing. 2010. (Illus.). 256p. (J). (gr. 4-7). pap. 16.95 *(978-1-59030-812-7(3)*, Roost Books) Shambhala Pubns., Inc.
Beutel, Roger & Spencer, Lauren. Writing a Narrative. 2011. 77.70 *(978-1-4488-4747-1(8)*, Rosen Reference); (ENG.). 64p. (gr. 5-5). pap. 13.95 *(978-1-4488-4689-4(7)*, f72188ef-afdc-4f8d-9d20-e2de97140aa9, Rosen Reference); (ENG.). 64p. (YA). (gr. 5-5). lib. bdg. 37.13 *(978-1-4488-4683-2(8)*, 919e3b71-db15-40c6-bf36-5509817d3af6) Rosen Publishing Group, Inc., The.
Bevan, Clare. The Wonderful Gift. 2004. (QEB Start Writing Ser.). (Illus.). 24p. (J). lib. bdg. 15.95 *(978-1-59566-022-0(4))* QEB Publishing Inc.
BJU Press, creator. Worktext for K5: For Christian Schools. 2004. (Illus.). 392p. per. 30.00 *(978-1-57924-845-1(4))* BJU Pr.
BJU Staff. American Republic Activity S 8. 2004. pap. 14.50 *(978-1-57924-333-3(9))* BJU Pr.
—American Republic Student Grd8. 2004. 32.00 *(978-1-57924-312-8(6))* BJU Pr.
—Beginnings Write Now Grd K5. 2004. pap. 5.00 *(978-1-57924-846-8(2))* BJU Pr.
Bodden, Valerie. Dialogue & Characterization. 2017. (Odysseys in Prose Ser.). (ENG., Illus.). 80p. (J). (gr. 7-11). pap. 14.99 *(978-1-62832-323-8(X)*, 20680, Creative Paperbacks) Creative Co., The.
—Imagery & Description. 2017. (Odysseys in Prose Ser.). (ENG., Illus.). 80p. (J). (gr. 7-11). pap. 14.99 *(978-1-62832-324-5(8)*, 20683, Creative Paperbacks) Creative Co., The.
—Narration & Point of View. 2017. (Odysseys in Prose Ser.). (ENG., Illus.). 80p. (J). (gr. 7-11). pap. 14.99 *(978-1-62832-325-2(6)*, 20686, Creative Paperbacks) Creative Co., The.
Bow, James. Evaluating Arguments about Sports & Entertainment. 2018. (State Your Case Ser.). (Illus.). 48p. (J). (gr. 5-6). *(978-0-7787-5078-9(7))* Crabtree Publishing Co.
Bracey, Ronay. Writing ... Take Small Steps: Improve Students' Writing Skills. 2003. spiral bd. *(978-1-933570-84-6(9))* Aardvark Global Publishing.
Brown Conroy, Erin. Writing Skillbuilders Bk. 2: A Fun-Filled Activity Book to Build Strong Handwriting Skills. 2004. (J). spiral bd. 14.95 *(978-0-9740981-7-3(5))* Celtic Cross Communications.
—Writing Skillbuilders Bk. 3: A Fun-Filled Activity Book for Beautiful Cursive Handwriting. 2004. (J). spiral bd. 14.95 *(978-0-9740981-8-0(3))* Celtic Cross Communications.
Cannon Hackett, Teresa. Creative Writing: Using Fairy Tales to Enrich Writing Skills. 2005. (ENG.). 42p. pap. 14.95 *(978-1-59363-025-6(5))* Prufrock Pr.
Capstone Classroom & Stead, Tony. Are You a Cliff Dweller? 2017. (What's the Point? Reading & Writing Expository Text Ser.). (ENG., Illus.). 16p. (J). (gr. 1-1). pap. 6.95 *(978-1-4966-0756-0(2)*, 132391, Capstone Classroom) Capstone.
—Are Your Mother & Father Related? 2017. (What's the Point? Reading & Writing Expository Text Ser.). (ENG., Illus.). 16p. (J). (gr. k-k). pap. 6.95 *(978-1-4966-0760-7(0)*, 132395, Capstone Classroom) Capstone.
—Can a Wolf Raise a Cat? 2017. (What's the Point? Reading & Writing Expository Text Ser.). (ENG., Illus.). 16p. (J). (gr. k-k). pap. 6.95 *(978-1-4966-0759-1(7)*, 132394, Capstone Classroom) Capstone.
—Can Your Dog Do Your Homework? And Other Questions about Animals. 2017. (What's the Point? Reading & Writing Expository Text Ser.). (ENG., Illus.). 16p. (J). (gr. 1-1). pap. 6.95 *(978-1-4966-0753-9(8)*, 132388, Capstone Classroom) Capstone.
—Could a Mouse Push a Car? 2017. (What's the Point? Reading & Writing Expository Text Ser.). (ENG., Illus.). 16p. (J). (gr. 2-2). pap. 6.95 *(978-1-4966-0747-8(3)*, 132382, Capstone Classroom) Capstone.
—Does a Cat Really Have Nine Lives? And Other Interesting Animal Facts. 2017. (What's the Point? Reading & Writing Expository Text Ser.). (ENG., Illus.). 24p. (J). (gr. 4-4). pap. 6.95 *(978-1-4966-0738-6(4)*, 132373, Capstone Classroom) Capstone.
—Does a Rabbit Lay Eggs? 2017. (What's the Point? Reading & Writing Expository Text Ser.). (ENG., Illus.). 16p. (J). (gr. 1-1). pap. 6.95 *(978-1-4966-0755-3(4)*, 132390, Capstone Classroom) Capstone.
—Does an Elephant Float? 2017. (What's the Point? Reading & Writing Expository Text Ser.). (ENG., Illus.). 16p. (J). (gr. 2-2). pap. 6.95 *(978-1-4966-0751-5(1)*, 132386, Capstone Classroom) Capstone.
—How Many Stomachs Do I Have? 2017. (What's the Point? Reading & Writing Expository Text Ser.). (ENG., Illus.). 24p. (J). (gr. 3-3). pap. 6.95 *(978-1-4966-0744-7(9)*, 132379, Capstone Classroom) Capstone.
Carroll, Joyce Armstrong, et al. Writing & Grammar: Communication in Action, 3 vols. 2003. (ENG.). 988p. (YA). (gr. 9-9). 494.00 *(978-0-13-037494-3(6)*, Prentice Hall) Savvas Learning Co.
—Writing & Grammar: Communication in Action, Bronze Level, 3 vols. 2003. (ENG.). 812p. (YA). (gr. 7-7). 406.00 *(978-0-13-037492-9(X))* Prentice Hall Pr.
—Writing & Grammar: Communication in Action, Platinum Level, 3 vols. 2004. 992p. (YA). (gr. 10-18). 496.00 *(978-0-13-116634-9(4))* Prentice Hall Pr.
Chin, Beverly. Grammar for Writing 2007: Level Orange, Consumable. 2007. (Grammar for Writing Ser.). (gr. 10). pap. 17.00 net. *(978-0-8215-0220-4(4))* Sadlier, William H. Inc.
Cleary, Brian P. Skin Like Milk, Hair of Silk: What Are Similes & Metaphors? Gable, Brian, illus. (Words Are CATegorical (r) Ser.). (ENG.). (gr. 2-5). 2011. 32p. (J). pap. 7.99 *(978-0-7613-3945-8(0)*, 808d8ab0-6331-4c22-826d-961a6d6516d8) 2007. pap. 39.62 *(978-0-7613-8361-1(1))* Lerner Publishing Group. (Millbrook Pr.).
Colby, Jennifer. Data in Arguments. 2017. (21st Century Skills Library: Data Geek Ser.). (ENG., Illus.). 32p. (J). (gr. 4-7). lib. bdg. 32.07 *(978-1-63472-707-5(X)*, 210086) Cherry Lake Publishing.
Collins Easy Learning. First Words Age 3-5 Wipe Clean Activity Book: Ideal for Home Learning. 2017. (Collins Easy Learning Preschool Ser.). (ENG.). 24p. (J). (gr. -1-k). 7.95 *(978-0-00-821293-3(7))* HarperCollins Pubs. Ltd. GBR. Dist: Independent Pubs. Group.
Culham, Ruth. 6 + 1 Traits of Writing: The Complete Guide for the Primary Grades. 2005. (6+1 Traits of Writing Ser.). (ENG., Illus.). 304p. (gr. k-2). pap. 29.99 *(978-0-439-57412-9(9))* Scholastic, Inc.
Davidson, Kay. Becoming a Better Writer Using the Simple 6: Grades 3rd - 6th. 2007. pap. 28.95 *(978-1-931334-98-3(6))* Pieces of Learning.
—The Simple 6 for K-2 Writers. 2007. pap. 28.95 *(978-1-931334-97-6(8))* Pieces of Learning.
Diamond, Mark. 6 Tricks to Student Narrative Writing Success: An Easy Guide for Students, Teachers & Parents. l.t. ed. 2005. (ENG., Illus.). 96p. per. 14.95 *(978-0-9771470-0-7(2))* Anyone Can Write bks.
Digital Photo Activity Kit Deluxe Vivitar 3700 series Lab-10. 2005. (J). cd-rom 1790.00 *(978-1-933229-02-7(0))* APTE, Inc.
Digital Photo Activity Kit Deluxe Vivitar 3700 series Lab-15. 2005. (J). cd-rom 2610.00 *(978-1-933229-03-4(9))* APTE, Inc.
Digital Photo Activity Kit Deluxe Vivitar 3700 series Lab-20. 2005. (J). 3260.00 *(978-1-933229-04-1(7))* APTE, Inc.
Digital Photo Activity Kit Deluxe Vivitar 3700 series Lab-25. 2005. (J). 3924.00 *(978-1-933229-05-8(5))* APTE, Inc.
Digital Photo Activity Kit Deluxe Vivitar 3700 series Lab-30. 2005. (J). 4585.00 *(978-1-933229-06-5(3))* APTE, Inc.
Digital Photo Activity Kit Deluxe Vivitar 3700 series Lab-35. 2005. (J). 5239.00 *(978-1-933229-07-2(1))* APTE, Inc.
Digital Photo Activity Kit Deluxe Vivitar 3700 series Lab-5. 2005. (J). cd-rom 648.95 *(978-1-933229-01-0(2))* APTE, Inc.
Digital Photo Activity Kit Deluxe Vivitar 3700 Series school Version. 2005. (J). cd-rom 133.95 *(978-1-933229-00-3(4))* APTE, Inc.
Digital Photo Activity Kit Deluxe Vivitar 5300 series Lab- 2005. (J). 1759.95 *(978-1-933229-09-6(8))* APTE, Inc.
Digital Photo Activity Kit Deluxe Vivitar 5300 series Lab-10. 2005. (J). 3469.99 *(978-1-933229-10-2(1))* APTE, Inc.
Digital Photo Activity Kit Deluxe Vivitar 5300 series Lab-15. 2005. (J). 5129.95 *(978-1-933229-11-9(X))* APTE, Inc.
Digital Photo Activity Kit Deluxe Vivitar 5300 series Lab-25. 2005. (J). 8123.90 *(978-1-933229-12-6(8))* APTE, Inc.
Digital Photo Activity Kit Deluxe Vivitar 5300 series Lab-30. 2005. (J). 9624.95 *(978-1-933229-14-0(4))* APTE, Inc.
Digital Photo Activity Kit Deluxe Vivitar 5300 series Lab-35. 2005. (J). 11119.95 *(978-1-933229-15-7(2))* APTE, Inc.
Digital Photo Activity Kit Deluxe Vivitar 5300 series Single. 2005. (J). 359.99 *(978-1-933229-08-9(X))* APTE, Inc.
DynaNotes Grade 4 Writing TAKS Review Guide. 2006. (J). pap. *(978-1-933854-41-0(3))* DynaStudy, Inc.
DynaNotes Grade 4 Writing TAKS Review Guide Transparency Set. 2006. (J). trans. *(978-1-933854-42-7(1))* DynaStudy, Inc.
DynaNotes Grade 7 Writing TAKS Review Guide. 2006. (J). pap. *(978-1-933854-39-7(1))* DynaStudy, Inc.
DynaNotes Grade 7 Writing TAKS Review Guide Transparency Set. 2006. (J). trans. *(978-1-933854-40-3(5))* DynaStudy, Inc.
Education.com. Write Away: A Workbook of Creative & Narrative Writing Prompts. 2015. (ENG.). 112p. (J). (gr. 3-3). pap. 7.99 *(978-0-486-80267-1(1))* Dover Pubns., Inc.
EMC-Paradigm Publishing Staff. Discovering Literature: Resource. (J). (gr. 6). Unit 8. pap., tchr. ed. *(978-0-8219-2039-8(1))*Unit 9. pap. *(978-0-8219-2040-4(5))*Unit 10. pap., tchr. ed. *(978-0-8219-2041-1(3))*Unit 11. pap., tchr. ed. *(978-0-8219-2042-8(1))*Unit 12. pap. *(978-0-8219-2043-5(0))* EMC/Paradigm Publishing.
Evan-Moor. Writing Centers, Grades 1-2. 2007. (Take It to Your Seat Ser.). (ENG., Illus.). 192p. (J). pap. 24.99 *(978-1-59673-078-6(1)*, EMC 6002) Evan-Moor Educational Pubs.
—Writing Centers Grades 2-3. 2005. (Take It to Your Seat: Writing Centers Ser.). (ENG., Illus.). 192p. (J). (gr. 2-3). pap., tchr. ed. 26.99 *(978-1-59673-079-3(X)*, EMC 6003) Evan-Moor Educational Pubs.
—Writing Centers, Grades 4-5. 2005. (Take It to Your Seat: Writing Centers Ser.). (ENG., Illus.). 192p. (J). (gr. 4-5). pap., tchr. ed. 26.99 *(978-1-59673-081-6(1)*, EMC 6005) Evan-Moor Educational Pubs.
—Writing Centers, Grades 5-6. 2005. (Take It to Your Seat: Writing Centers Ser.). (ENG., Illus.). 192p. (gr. 5-6). pap., tchr. ed. 26.99 *(978-1-59673-082-3(X)*, EMC 6006) Evan-Moor Educational Pubs.
Evan-Moor Educational Publishers. Skill Sharpeners Spell & Write Grade 1. 2005. (Skill Sharpeners: Spell & Write Ser.). (ENG., Illus.). 144p. (J). (gr. 1-1). pap., tchr. ed. 10.99 *(978-1-59673-045-8(5)*, emc 4537) Evan-Moor Educational Pubs.
—Skill Sharpeners Spell & Write Grade 2. 2005. (Skill Sharpeners: Spell & Write Ser.). (ENG., Illus.). 144p. (J). (gr. 2-2). pap., tchr. ed. 10.99 *(978-1-59673-046-5(3)*, emc 4538) Evan-Moor Educational Pubs.
—Skill Sharpeners Spell & Write Grade 3. 2005. (Skill Sharpeners: Spell & Write Ser.). (ENG., Illus.). 144p. (J). (gr. 3-3). pap., tchr. ed. 10.99 *(978-1-59673-047-2(1)*, emc 4539) Evan-Moor Educational Pubs.
—Skill Sharpeners Spell & Write Grade 4. 2005. (Skill Sharpeners: Spell & Write Ser.). (ENG., Illus.). 144p. (J). (gr. 4-4). pap., tchr. ed. 10.99 *(978-1-59673-048-9(X)*, emc 4540) Evan-Moor Educational Pubs.
—Skill Sharpeners Spell & Write Grade 5. 2005. (Skill Sharpeners: Spell & Write Ser.). (ENG., Illus.). 144p. (J). (gr. 5-5). pap., tchr. ed. 10.99 *(978-1-59673-049-6(8)*, emc 4542) Evan-Moor Educational Pubs.
—Skill Sharpeners Spell & Write Grade 6+ 2005. (Skill Sharpeners: Spell & Write Ser.). (ENG., Illus.). 144p. (J). (gr. 6-6). pap., tchr. ed. 10.99 *(978-1-59673-050-2(1)*, emc 4542) Evan-Moor Educational Pubs.
—Skill Sharpeners Spell & Write Grade Pre-K. 2005. (Skill Sharpeners: Spell & Write Ser.). (ENG., Illus.). 144p. (J). (gr. -1 — 1). pap., tchr. ed. 10.99 *(978-1-59673-043-4(9)*, emc 4535) Evan-Moor Educational Pubs.
Evergreen: a Guide to Writing with Readings. 7th ed. 2003. (YA). (gr. 6-12). stu. ed. 36.96 incl. cd-rom *(978-0-618-27389-8(1)*, 315696) CENGAGE Learning.
Festival Fun: 6 Each of 1 Anthology, 6 vols. (Wildcats Ser.). 32p. (gr. 2-8). *(978-0-322-02424-3(2))* Wright Group/McGraw-Hill.
Fire! Fire! 6 Each of 1 Anthology, 6 vols. (Wildcats Ser.). 32p. (gr. 2-8). *(978-0-322-00581-5(7))* Wright Group/McGraw-Hill.
Ford, Jeanne Marie. 12 Great Tips on Writing to Inform. 2017. (Great Tips on Writing Ser.). (ENG., Illus.). 32p. (J). (gr. 3-6). 32.80 *(978-1-63235-278-1(8)*, 11732, 12-Story Library) Bookstaves, LLC.
Giants in the City: Hard & Soft c & g: Level B, 6 vols. (Wright Skills Ser.). 16p. (gr. k-3). 26.50 *(978-0-322-01489-3(1))* Wright Group/McGraw-Hill.
Giff, Patricia Reilly. Writing with Rosie: You Can Write a Story Too. 2018. lib. bdg. 17.20 *(978-0-606-41341-1(3))* Turtleback.
Gould, Judith S. & Gould, Evan Jay. Four Square: A Companion to the Four Square Writing Method: Writing in the Content Areas for Grades 1-4. Mitchell, Judy, ed. Radtke, Becky J., illus. 2004. 112p. (J). pap. 11.95 *(978-1-57310-421-0(3))* Teaching & Learning Co.
—Four Square: A Companion to the Four Square Writing Method: Writing in the Content Areas for Grades 5-9. Mitchell, Judy, ed. Wheeler, Ron, illus. 2004. 112p. (J). pap. 11.95 *(978-1-57310-422-7(1))* Teaching & Learning Co.
Group/McGraw-Hill, Wright. Early Fluency-Fluency Writing Kit. 2004. (Wright Group Literacy Ser.). (gr. k-3). 132.50 *(978-0-322-07021-9(X))* Wright Group/McGraw-Hill.
—Emergent Writing Kit. 2004. (Wright Group Literacy Ser.). (gr. k-3). 79.50 *(978-0-322-06615-1(8))* Wright Group/McGraw-Hill.
—Five Little Frogs: Collection 1. (Storyteller Interactive Writing Cards Ser.). (gr. k-3). *(978-0-322-09363-8(5))* Wright Group/McGraw-Hill.
—Holly's Birthday Cake: Collection 2. (Storyteller Interactive Writing Cards Ser.). (gr. k-3). *(978-0-322-09336-2(8))* Wright Group/McGraw-Hill.
—In the Rain Forest, 6 vols. (Wildcats Ser.). 32p. (gr. 2-8). *(978-0-322-00599-0(X))* Wright Group/McGraw-Hill.
—My Word! what a Bird! Collection 4. (Storyteller Interactive Writing Cards Ser.). (gr. k-3). *(978-0-322-09325-6(2))* Wright Group/McGraw-Hill.
—Ready, Set, Pop! Collection 3. (Storyteller Interactive Writing Cards Ser.). (gr. k-3). *(978-0-322-09348-5(1))* Wright Group/McGraw-Hill.
—River Wild: 6 Each of 1 Anthology, 6 vols. (Wildcats Ser.). 32p. (gr. 2-8). *(978-0-322-05857-6(0))* Wright Group/McGraw-Hill.
—Sand: Collection 3. (Storyteller Interactive Writing Cards Ser.). (gr. k-3). *(978-0-322-09349-2(X))* Wright Group/McGraw-Hill.
Hennessy, Brendan. Essay to Write? 2nd ed. 2004. 93p. pap. *(978-1-85703-835-4(5)*, How To Books) Little, Brown Book Group Ltd.
Hercules & Other Greek Legends: 6 Each of 1 Anthology, 6 vols. (Wildcats Ser.). 32p. (gr. 2-8). *(978-0-322-00590-7(6))* Wright Group/McGraw-Hill.
Heroes: 6 Each of 1 Anthology, 6 vols. (Wildcats Ser.). 32p. (gr. 2-8). *(978-0-322-00579-2(5))* Wright Group/McGraw-Hill.
Herzog, Joyce. Budding Authors: Adventures in Writing. 2005. (J). spiral bd. 10.00 *(978-1-887225-52-6(8))* Herzog, Joyce.
—Budding Authors: Step into Writing. 2005. (J). spiral bd. 10.00 *(978-1-887225-51-9(X))* Herzog, Joyce.
—Budding Authors: Then & Now. 2005. (J). spiral bd. 10.00 *(978-1-887225-53-3(6))* Herzog, Joyce.
—Budding Authors: Twirling Around. Sinclair, Angie et al, eds. 2005. (J). spiral bd. 10.00 *(978-1-887225-56-4(0))* Herzog, Joyce.
—Budding Authors: Writing U. S. History. 2005. (J). spiral bd. 12.00 *(978-1-887225-55-7(2))* Herzog, Joyce.
—Budding Authors: Zooming Ahead. 2005. (J). spiral bd. 10.00 *(978-1-887225-54-0(4))* Herzog, Joyce.
—Draw & Write 2. 2004. (J). spiral bd. 12.00 *(978-1-887225-32-8(3))* Herzog, Joyce.
—Draw & Write I. 2004. (J). spiral bd. 12.00 *(978-1-887225-31-1(5))* Herzog, Joyce.
Hohlt, Janie. Basic Writing 2. 2005. (J). ring bd. 49.95 *(978-1-58804-398-7(6))* P C I Education.
—Basic Writing Binder 2. 2005. (J). ring bd. 49.95 *(978-1-58804-400-6(9))* P C I Education.
Hook, Sue Vander. Writing Intriguing Informational Pieces. 2015. (Write This Way Ser.). (ENG., Illus.). 56p. (J). (gr. 6-8). 33.32 *(978-1-4677-7907-4(5)*, e5330acf-7a94-4cf0-9ce7-0ead11e28774, Lerner Pubns.) Lerner Publishing Group.
Hop, Jog, & Tap: Consonants g, h, j; Short Vowel o word families: Level A, 6 vols. (Wright Skills Ser.). 12p. (gr. k-3). 17.95 *(978-0-322-01449-7(2))* Wright Group/McGraw-Hill.
Howell, Sara. How to Write an Opinion Piece, 1 vol., 1. 2013. (Core Writing Skills Ser.). (ENG.). 24p. (J). (gr. 3-3). 26.27 *(978-1-4777-2906-9(2)*, 97909a41-20c2-40d0-9c5e-8394985e35d5); pap. 9.25 *(978-1-4777-2995-3(X)*, 84698199-ef92-4e21-9647-da824a68ae01) Rosen Publishing Group, Inc., The. (PowerKids Pr.).
Hutson-Nechkash, Peg. Help Me Write: Frames & Rubrics for Classroom Writing Success. 2003. (Illus.). (J). 34.95 *(978-1-932054-12-5(X))* Super Duper Pubns.
In the News, 6 vols. (Wildcats Ser.). 32p. (gr. 2-8). *(978-0-322-02437-3(4))* Wright Group/McGraw-Hill.
In the News, 10 vols., Set 2. Incl. Climate Change. Brezina, Corona. lib. bdg. 37.13 *(978-1-4042-1913-7(7)*, ce033f3b-9ebc-4b4f-bd33-927192731467); Darfur: African Genocide. Xavier, John. lib. bdg. 37.13 *(978-1-4042-1912-0(9)*, c1460c9a-534c-4c82-b437-8f2e8043133d); Green Technology: Earth-Friendly Innovations. Sobha, Geeta. lib. bdg. 37.13 *(978-1-4042-1914-4(5)*, cdb65425-01f2-4ef2-8139-bb82aaace90a); Nukes: The Spread of Nuclear Weapons. Minneus, Steve. lib. bdg. 37.13 *(978-1-4042-1916-8(1)*, ba946ed1-9ee7-406e-b6ca-7ffd9b6ca863); Oil: The Economics of Fuel. Jovinelly, Joann. lib. bdg. 37.13 *(978-1-4042-1915-1(3)*, a88f9a66-8373-458c-9781-2ad0f1d76ce7); (Illus.). 64p. (YA). (gr. 6-6). 2007. (In the News Ser.). (ENG.). 2007. Set lib. bdg. 185.65 *(978-1-4042-1112-4(8)*, 14a575df-1acb-45cf-a0fc-1aaf534c7153) Rosen Publishing Group, Inc., The.
Incredible Places: 6 Each of 1 Anthology, 6 vols. (Wildcats Ser.). 32p. (gr. 2-8). *(978-0-322-00587-7(6))* Wright Group/McGraw-Hill.
Jarnow, Jill. Writing to Instruct. 2009. (Write Now: A Kid's Guide to Nonfiction Writing Ser.). 24p. (gr. 3-4). 42.50 *(978-1-60854-896-5(1)*, PowerKids Pr.) Rosen Publishing Group, Inc., The.
Jones, Molly. 12 Great Tips on Writing to Persuade. 2017. (Great Tips on Writing Ser.). (ENG., Illus.). 32p. (J). (gr. 3-6). 32.80 *(978-1-63235-279-8(6)*, 11733, 12-Story Library) Bookstaves, LLC.
Keppeler, Jill. Speaking with Purpose: Communication. 2019. (Spotlight on Social & Emotional Learning Ser.). (ENG.). 24p. (gr. 4-6). 60.00 *(978-1-7253-0690-5(5)*, PowerKids Pr.) Rosen Publishing Group, Inc., The.
Khan, Hena. How to Say What You Mean, Mean What You Say, & Get What You Want. 2004. (Illus.). 80p. (J). *(978-0-439-57904-9(X))* Scholastic, Inc.
Levy, Janey. Language Development: Writing Process, 1 vol. 2003. (BrainBuilders Ser.). (ENG.). 48p. (gr. k-4). pap. 5.25 *(978-1-4042-8569-9(5)*, faf1663b-1c3d-42dc-b6d2-c253481d5052) Rosen Publishing Group, Inc., The.
Liverman, Debra, ed. Daily Journal Prompts. 2005. 112p. (gr. 1-3). 14.95 *(978-1-56234-625-6(3))*; (gr. 4-6). 14.95 *(978-1-56234-626-3(1))* Education Ctr., Inc. (Mailbox Bks., The).
Loewen, Nancy. Stubborn As a Mule & Other Silly Similes. Watkins, Adam, illus. 2010. (Ways to Say It Ser.). (ENG.). 24p. (J). (gr. 3-5). pap. 7.49 *(978-1-4048-6715-4(5)*, 115515, Picture Window Bks.) Capstone.
—You're Toast & Other Metaphors We Adore, 1 vol. Wu, Donald, illus. 2010. (Ways to Say It Ser.). (ENG.). 24p. (J). (gr. 3-5). pap. 7.49 *(978-1-4048-6717-8(1)*, 115517, Picture Window Bks.) Capstone.
Magee, Wes. Pet the Cat. 2004. (QEB Start Writing Ser.). (Illus.). 24p. (J). lib. bdg. 15.95 *(978-1-59566-023-7(2))* QEB Publishing Inc.
Marlow, Herb. A Student's Guide to Successful Writing. 2005. (J). 24.95 *(978-1-893595-53-8(6))* Four Seasons Bks., Inc.
McCarty, Diane Bischoff. Copywork for Children: For Grades 1-3. 2004. (Illus.). 63p. (J). *(978-0-9712124-1-1(4))* Angel Heart Children's Pr.
McCurry, Kristen. Pick a Picture, Write an Opinion!, 1 vol. 2014. (Little Scribe Ser.). (ENG., Illus.). 32p. (J). (gr. -1-2). lib. bdg. 27.99 *(978-1-4765-4240-9(6)*, 124347, Capstone Pr.) Capstone.
Mechanech Publications Staff. Writing Better with Every Letter: My Handwriting Practice Book. 2004. (Illus.). (J). 112p. (gr. 1-18). pap. *(978-0-9702861-2-3(0))*; Vol. 2. 95p. (gr. 2-18). pap. 10.00 *(978-0-9702861-4-7(7))* Mechanech Pubns.
Milton, Bess. Language Development Writing Process, 1 vol. 2003. (BrainBuilders Ser.). (ENG.). 48p. (gr. k-4). pap. 5.25 *(978-1-4042-8559-0(8)*, 71a01898-425f-4e43-8186-53ef04556e5f) Rosen Publishing Group, Inc., The.
Minden, Cecilia & Roth, Kate. How to Write a News Article. 2012. (Explorer Junior Library: How to Write Ser.). (ENG., Illus.). 24p. (gr. 1-4). lib. bdg. 29.21 *(978-1-61080-308-3(6)*, 201276) Cherry Lake Publishing.
Minden, Cecilia, et al. How to Write a News Article. 2012. (Explorer Junior Library: Language Arts Explorer Junior Ser.). (ENG., Illus.). 24p. (gr. 1-4). pap. 12.79 *(978-1-61080-318-2(3)*, 201278) Cherry Lake Publishing.
Morkane, Sue. Original Writing. 2004. (Routledge a Level English Guides). (ENG., Illus.). 112p. (C). 105.00 *(978-0-415-31911-9(0)*, RU26771); per. 33.95 *(978-0-415-31912-6(9)*, RU26772) Routledge.
Mythmakers, 6 vols. (Wildcats Ser.). 32p. (gr. 2-8). *(978-0-322-02440-3(4))* Wright Group/McGraw-Hill.
Nelson, Linda & Logie, Daniel. Writing Sourcebook: Foundations for Writing. 2004. 80p. 6.95 *(978-1-931181-38-9(1))* Universal Publishing.
Nolan, Chris & Spencer, Lauren. Writing to Persuade. 2011. (Illus.). 63p. (J). 77.70 *(978-1-4488-4749-5(4)*, Rosen Reference); (ENG., 64p. (J). (gr. 5-5). pap. 13.95 *(978-1-4488-4691-7(9)*, 0dfc838b-f962-4e0f-9626-b83d03d9ca25, Rosen Reference); (ENG., 64p. (YA). (gr. 5-5). lib. bdg. 37.13 *(978-1-4488-4685-6(4)*,

P Q R

0e8d6dc2-1c56-4bfd-b3c6-d63b80734456) Rosen Publishing Group, Inc., The.

Olsen, Jan Z. Mat Man Shapes. Delaney, Molly, illus. 2007. (ENG.). 32p. stu. ed. 13.75 (978-1-891627-92-7(9)) Handwriting Without Tears.

Parker, Helen. Wipe Clean Phonics. 2007. (Wipe Clean Ser.). (Illus.). 12p. (J). bds. (978-1-84610-583-8(8)) Make Believe Ideas.

Peha, Steve & Lester, Margot. Be a Better Writer: For School, for Fun, for Anyone Ages 10-15. 2nd ed. 2016. (ENG., Illus.). 351p. (YA). pap. 19.95 (978-0-9972831-0-5(6)) Teaching That Makes Sense.

Perkins, Sally J. & Stoner, Mark R. Making Sense of Messages: A Critical Apprenticeship in Rhetorical Criticism. 2006. (Illus.). 320p. (YA). pap. 67.56 (978-0-618-14488-4(9), 351240) CENGAGE Learning.

Peter Pauper Press, Inc., creator. Handwriting: Learn Cursive! 2015. (Handwriting Ser.). (ENG., Illus.). 96p. (J). pap. 5.99 (978-1-4413-1815-2(1), 9fda01c8-a27d-41d3-ae89-4fc11106f9f8) Peter Pauper Pr. Inc.

Proudfit, Benjamin. Writing Opinion Papers, 1 vol. 2014. (Write Right! Ser.). (ENG.). 24p. (J). (gr. 2-3). 25.27 (978-1-4824-1128-7(8), d99c43de-233a-4d33-85d5-b5476bba787d) Stevens, Gareth Publishing LLLP.

Purslow, Frances. Expository Paragraphs. 2007. (Learning to Write Ser.). (Illus.). 24p. (J). (gr. 4-7). lib. bdg. 24.45 (978-1-59036-735-3(9)); per. 8.95 (978-1-59036-736-0(7)) Weigl Pubs., Inc.

—Narrative Paragraphs. 2007. (Learning to Write Ser.). (Illus.). 24p. (J). (gr. 4-7). lib. bdg. 24.45 (978-1-59036-733-9(2)); per. 8.95 (978-1-59036-734-6(0)) Weigl Pubs., Inc.

—Persuasive Paragraphs. 2007. (Learning to Write Ser.). (Illus.). 24p. (J). (gr. 4-6). lib. bdg. 24.45 (978-1-59036-731-5(6)); per. 8.95 (978-1-59036-732-2(4)) Weigl Pubs., Inc.

Read & Write. 2005. (J). pap. 3.99 (978-1-933200-18-7(9)) Family Bks. at Home.

Real-World Writing. 2005. (YA). ring bd. 69.95 (978-1-58804-389-4(4)) P C I Education.

Right or Wrong? 6 Each of 1 Anthology, 6 vols. (Wildcats Ser.). 32p. (gr. 2-8). (978-0-322-00598-3(1)) Wright Group/McGraw-Hill.

Rollins, Brenda. Master Writing: 240 Interactive Screen Pages Big Box. 2011. (Writing Skills Ser.). (J). (gr. 3-8). pap. 79.95 incl. cd-rom (978-1-55319-508-5(6), Classroom Complete Pr.) Rainbow Horizons Publishing, Inc.

Rondina, Catherine. Don't Touch That Toad & Other Strange Things Adults Tell You. Sylvester, Kevin, illus. 96p. (J). (gr. 2-5). 2014. (ENG.). pap. 8.95 (978-1-55453-455-5(0)) 2010. 14.95 (978-1-55453-454-8(2)) Kids Can Pr., Ltd. CAN. Dist: Hachette Bk. Group.

Rose, Simon. Evaluating Arguments about Food. 2018. (State Your Case Ser.). (Illus.). 48p. (J). (gr. 5-6). (978-0-7787-5077-2(9)) Crabtree Publishing Co.

—Evaluating Arguments about Technology. 2018. (State Your Case Ser.). (Illus.). 48p. (J). (gr. 5-6). (978-0-7787-5079-6(5)) Crabtree Publishing Co.

—Evaluating Arguments about the Environment. 2018. (State Your Case Ser.). (Illus.). 48p. (J). (gr. 5-6). (978-0-7787-5080-2(9)) Crabtree Publishing Co.

Rozines Roy, Jennifer. Sharpen Your Story or Narrative Writing Skills, 1 vol. 2012. (Sharpen Your Writing Skills Ser.). (ENG., Illus.). 64p. (gr. 6-7). pap. 11.53 (978-1-59845-340-9(8), 0d73a7e3-104d-4a10-a067-b2fa48e94e80); lib. bdg. 31.93 (978-0-7660-3901-8(3), 8d12bb10-274b-49f0-af01-0eac24697272) Enslow Publishing, LLC.

Scardamalia, Marlene, et al. Writing for Results. xiii, 167p. (J). (gr. 4-12). (978-0-89688-184-6(9), 88-184) Open Court Publishing Co.

Scholastic. First 100 Words: Scholastic Early Learners (Touch & Lift) 2016. (Scholastic Early Learners Ser.). (ENG.). 12p. (J). (gr. -1 — 1). 6.99 (978-0-545-90330-1(0), Cartwheel Bks.) Scholastic, Inc.

Scholastic, Inc. Staff. Contemporary Cursive Grades 2-4. CHANG, Maria, ed. 2010. (ENG.). 48p. (gr. 2-4). pap. 5.99 (978-0-545-20091-2(1), Teaching Resources) Scholastic, Inc.

Shearer, Cynthia & Washington, George. Handwriting by George 28-55: Rules of Civility & Decent Behaviour in Company & Conversation: Rules 28-53 to Draw & Write, 4 vols., Vol. 2. 2009. (ENG.). 62p. (J). pap. 9.95 (978-1-882514-37-3(8)) Greenleaf Pr.

Show What You Know Publishing, ed. Show What You Know on the CSAP 7, Reading/Writing Student Workbook. 2007. (J). per. 13.95 (978-1-59230-246-8(7)) Englefield & Assocs., Inc.

—Show What You Know on the CSAP for Grade 5, Student Workbook. 2007. (J). per. 13.95 (978-1-59230-217-8(3)) Englefield & Assocs., Inc.

—Show What You Know on the CSAP for Grade 9 Writing Student Self-Study Workbook. 2007. (YA). per. 18.95 (978-1-59230-293-2(9)) Englefield & Assocs., Inc.

—Show What You Know on the CSAP Reading & Writing for Grade 6, Student Workbook. 2007. (J). per. 13.95 (978-1-59230-240-6(8)) Englefield & Assocs., Inc.

Silate, Jennifer. Language Development Writing Process, 1 vol. 2003. (BrainBuilders Ser.). (ENG.). 48p. (gr. k-4). pap. 5.25 (978-1-4042-8564-4(4), 074d4a41-e1d8-4995-9ff1-286f966cd8ff) Rosen Publishing Group, Inc., The.

Spencer, Lauren. A Step-by-Step Guide to Informative Writing. 2009. (Library of Writing Skills Ser.). 48p. (gr. 5-8). 53.00 (978-1-60853-978-9(4), Rosen Reference) Rosen Publishing Group, Inc., The.

Starfall Education. Level I Reading & Writing Journal - Block Print: WK201b. Starfall Education, ed. 2011. (ENG., Illus.). 96p. (J). (978-1-59577-045-5(3)) Starfall Education.

Starfall Education, creator. Level II Reading & Writing Journal: Second Edition. 2010. (ENG., Illus.). 96p. (J). 1.95 (978-1-59577-130-8(1)) Starfall Education.

Stella, Heather. Get Ready for School: Writing Skills. 2017. (Get Ready for School Ser.). (ENG., Illus.). 128p. (J). (gr. 1-4). spiral bd. 12.99 (978-0-316-50255-9(3), Black Dog & Leventhal Pubs. Inc.) Running Pr.

Stobaugh, James. Skills for Rhetoric: Encouraging Thoughtful Christians to Be World Changers. 2003. (YA). 30.50 (978-0-9725890-4-8(X)) For Such A Time As This Ministries.

—Skills for Rhetoric Student. 2005. (Broadman & Holman Literature Ser.). 272p. stu. ed. 24.99 (978-0-8054-5898-5(0)) B&H Publishing Group.

TAKS MASTER Power Practice, Writing Gr. 4. 2005. (J). per. (978-1-57022-547-5(8)) ECS Learning Systems, Inc.

TAKS MASTER Power Practice, Writing, Gr. 7. 2005. (J). per. (978-1-57022-548-2(6)) ECS Learning Systems, Inc.

TAKS MASTER Practice Test, Writing Gr. 4. 2004. (J). (978-1-57022-533-8(8)) ECS Learning Systems, Inc.

TAKS MASTER Practice Test, Writing Gr. 7. 2004. (J). (978-1-57022-534-5(6)) ECS Learning Systems, Inc.

Top That Publishing, creator. Writing My First Words: Early Days Magic Writing Book. 2007. (Illus.). 8p. (gr. -1-k). bds. (978-1-84666-340-6(7)) Top That! Publishing PLC.

Voyages in English: Writing & Grammar. 2004. (gr. 1-18). tchr. ed. (978-0-8294-0980-2(7)); (gr. 1-18). tchr. ed., wbk. ed. (978-0-8294-1383-0(9)); (gr. 1-18). stu. ed. (978-0-8294-0981-9(5)); (gr. 1-18). stu. ed., wbk. ed. (978-0-8294-1382-3(0)); (gr. 2-18). tchr. ed. (978-0-8294-0982-6(3)); (gr. 2-18). tchr. ed., wbk. ed. (978-0-8294-1385-4(5)); (gr. 2-18). stu. ed. (978-0-8294-0983-3(1)); (gr. 2-18). stu. ed., wbk. ed. (978-0-8294-1384-7(7)); (gr. 3-18). (978-0-8294-1303-8(0)); (gr. 3-18). tchr. ed. (978-0-8294-0985-7(8)); (gr. 3-18). tchr. ed., wbk. ed. (978-0-8294-1319-9(7)); (gr. 3-18). stu. ed. (978-0-8294-0986-4(6)); (gr. 3-18). stu. ed., wbk. ed. (978-0-8294-1318-2(9)); (gr. 4-18). tchr. ed., wbk. ed. (978-0-8294-1321-2(9)); (gr. 4-18). stu. ed. (978-0-8294-0988-8(2)) Loyola Pr.

Wach, Martin. An Adventure in Writing. 2007. (Illus.). 32p. (J). (gr. -1-3). per. 14.95 (978-0-929915-54-8(2)) Headline Bks., Inc.

Wasylyk, Thomas M. Second Edition Handwriting: A Self-Improvement Workbook. 2006. (ENG.). 80p. 7.95 (978-1-931181-66-2(7), Item #139) Universal Publishing.

—Second Edition Handwriting: Beginning Cursive Writing. 2006. (ENG.). 80p. 7.95 (978-1-931181-62-4(4), Item # 135) Universal Publishing.

—Second Edition Handwriting: Improving Cursive Writing. 2006. (ENG.). 80p. 7.95 (978-1-931181-63-1(2), Item # 136) Universal Publishing.

—Second Edition Handwriting: Introduction to Cursive. 2006. 80p. 7.95 (978-1-931181-61-7(6), Item # 134) Universal Publishing.

—Second Edition Handwriting: Manuscript Review & Enrichment. 2006. 7.95 (978-1-931181-60-0(8), Item # 133) Universal Publishing.

—Second Edition Handwriting: Manuscript Writing. 2006. 80p. 7.95 (978-1-931181-59-4(4), Item # 132) Universal Publishing.

—Second Edition Handwriting: Reading & Writing Readiness Skills. 2006. 80p. 7.95 (978-1-931181-57-0(8), Item #130) Universal Publishing.

—Second Edition Handwriting: Writing for Learning. 2006. (ENG.). 80p. 7.95 (978-1-931181-65-5(9), Item # 138) Universal Publishing.

—Second Edition Handwriting: Writing in Cursive. 2006. (ENG.). 80p. 7.95 (978-1-931181-64-8(0), Item # 137) Universal Publishing.

—Second Edition Handwriting: Writing the Manuscript Letters. 2nd ed. 2006. 80p. 7.95 (978-1-931181-58-7(6), Item #131) Universal Publishing.

Watson, Sharon. Jump in, A Workbook for Reluctant Writers: 2-book Set. Wile, Kathleen J., ed. 2006. per. 40.00 (978-1-932012-76-7(1)) Apologia Educational Ministries, Inc.

—Jump in, A Workbook for Reluctant Writers: Student Text. Wile, Kathleen J., ed. 2006. per., wbk. ed. 30.00 (978-1-932012-74-3(5)) Apologia Educational Ministries, Inc.

West, Penelope Pelham. Once upon a Time Nobody Could Read. 2009. pap. 9.00 (978-1-61623-531-4(4)) Independent Pub.

Write on Target for Grade 5. 2006. (J). stu. ed., per., wbk. ed. 16.95 (978-1-59230-159-1(2)) Englefield & Assocs., Inc.

Write on Target Grade 3: Student Workbook. 2005. (J). stu. ed., per. 10.95 (978-1-59230-151-5(7)) Englefield & Assocs., Inc.

Write on Target Grade 4: Student Workbook. 2005. (J). stu. ed., per. 10.95 (978-1-59230-149-2(5)) Englefield & Assocs., Inc.

Write on Target Grade 6: Student Workbook. 2005. (J). pap., stu. ed. 10.95 (978-1-59230-157-7(6)) Englefield & Assocs., Inc.

Write on, Wipe off Writing. 2007. (Early Days: Copy & Learn Ser.). (Illus.). 40p. (978-1-84656-390-1(3)) Top That! Publishing PLC.

WritersCorps, et al. Jump Write In! Creative Writing Exercises for Diverse Communities, Grades 6-12, Grd. 6-12. Tannenbaum, Judith, ed. 2005. (ENG., Illus.). 176p. per. 28.00 (978-0-7879-7777-1(2), Jossey-Bass) Wiley, John & Sons, Inc.

Writing Handbook. (J). 15.00 (978-1-931555-02-9(8)) Our Lady of Victory Schl.

Writing Paragraphs (Gr. 3-4) 2003. (J). (978-1-58232-128-8(0)) ECS Learning Systems, Inc.

Writing Resource Book. (J). (gr. 2-9). (978-0-89688-110-5(5), 88-110) Open Court Publishing Co.

Writing Sentences (Gr. 2-3) 2003. (J). (978-1-58232-127-1(2)) ECS Learning Systems, Inc.

Writing Works with NC Wordcrafter & Joey: Grade 3+ 2004. 28.00 (978-0-9790796-0-3(8)) PJR Assocs., Ltd.

Writing Works with NC Wordcrafter & Joey: Grade 4+ 2004. 28.00 (978-0-9790796-1-0(6)) PJR Assocs., Ltd.

Writing Works with NC Wordcrafter & Joey: Grade 5+ 2004. 28.00 (978-0-9790796-2-7(4)) PJR Assocs., Ltd.

RHINE RIVER AND VALLEY

Leavitt, Amie Jane. The Rhine River. 2012. (J). lib. bdg. 29.95 (978-1-61228-297-8(0)) Mitchell Lane Pubs.

Miller, Gary. The Rhine: Europe's River Highway. 2010. (Rivers Around the World Ser.). (ENG., Illus.). 32p. (J). (gr. 5-8). lib. bdg. (978-0-7787-7446-4(5)) Crabtree Publishing Co.

Miller, Gary G. & Miller, Gary. The Rhine: Europe's River Highway, 1 vol. 2010. (Rivers Around the World Ser.). (ENG., Illus.). 32p. (J). (gr. 5-8). pap. (978-0-7787-7469-3(4)) Crabtree Publishing Co.

The Rhine. 2011. (River Journey Ser.). (ENG.). 48p. (YA). (gr. 5-8). 27.95 (978-1-4488-6013-5(X), Rosen Reference) Rosen Publishing Group, Inc., The.

RHINE RIVER AND VALLEY—FICTION

Brabourne, Edward Hugessen Knatchbull-Hugessen. River Legends of the Thames & Rhine. Doré, Gustave, illus. 2005. (J). pap. (978-0-486-44372-0(8)) Dover Pubns., Inc.

RHINOCEROSES

Adamson, Thomas K. Rhinoceros vs. African Elephant. 2020. (Animal Battles Ser.). (ENG.). 24p. (J). (gr. 3-7). lib. bdg. 26.95 (978-1-64487-160-7(2), Torque Bks.) Bellwether Media.

Arnold, Quinn M. Rhinoceroses. 2016. (Seedlings Ser.). (ENG., Illus.). 24p. (J). (gr. -1-k). (978-1-60818-797-3(7), 20746, Creative Education); pap. 7.99 (978-1-62832-350-4(7), 20744, Creative Paperbacks) Creative Co., The.

Baxter, Bethany. Indian Rhinoceroses. 2013. (Awesome Armored Animals Ser.). 24p. (J). (gr. k-5). pap. 49.50 (978-1-4777-0961-0(4)); (ENG.). (gr. 2-3). pap. 9.25 (978-1-4777-0960-3(6), 322c2964-882e-48df-a356-32047c750814); (ENG.). (gr. 2-3). lib. bdg. 26.27 (978-1-4777-0794-4(8), 268a40ca-b389-48d0-b2c6-40d32320f0d6) Rosen Publishing Group, Inc., The. (PowerKids Pr.).

Bergeron, Alain M. & Quintin, Michel. Do You Know the Rhinoceros?, 1 vol. Messier, Solange, tr. Sampar, illus. 2015. (Do You Know? Ser.). (ENG.). 64p. (J). (gr. 2-4). pap. 9.95 (978-1-55455-354-9(7), 6dd15e9e-bb1f-4fe4-af07-8a66d0438a59) Trifolium Bks., Inc. CAN. Dist: Firefly Bks., Ltd.

Bergeron, Alain M., et al. Les Rhinocéros. 2010. (FRE., Illus.). 64p. (J). pap. 8.95 (978-2-89435-500-8(9)) Quintin Pubs./Editions Michel Quintin CAN. Dist: Crabtree Publishing Co.

Bodden, Valerie. Rhinoceroses. 2013. (Amazing Animals Ser.). (ENG., Illus.). 24p. (J). (gr. 1-4). 25.65 (978-1-60818-090-5(5), 21729, Creative Education) Creative Co., The.

Borgert-Spaniol, Megan. Baby Rhinos. 2017. (Super Cute! Ser.). (ENG., Illus.). 24p. (J). (gr. k-3). lib. bdg. 26.95 (978-1-62617-546-4(2), Blastoff! Readers) Bellwether Media.

Braun, Eric. Tyrannosaurus Rex vs. Rhinoceros. 2018. (Versus! Ser.). (ENG.). 24p. (J). (gr. 4-6). pap. 9.99 (978-1-64466-333-2(3), 12167); (Illus.). lib. bdg. (978-1-68072-350-2(2), 12166) Black Rabbit Bks. (Hi Jinx).

Carr, Aaron. Rhino. 2014. (Illus.). 24p. (J). (978-1-62127-285-4(0)) Weigl Pubs., Inc.

Carson, Mary Kay. Emi & the Rhino Scientist. 2010. (Scientists in the Field Ser.). (ENG., Illus.). 64p. (J). (gr. 5-7). pap. 9.99 (978-0-547-40850-7(1), 1428813, Clarion Bks.) HarperCollins Pubs.

—Emi & the Rhino Scientist. Uhlman, Tom, photos by. 2010. (Scientists in the Field Ser.). (ENG., Illus.). 64p. (J). (gr. 6-8). 26.19 (978-0-618-64639-5(6)) Houghton Mifflin Harcourt Publishing Co.

Ciovacco, Justine. Rhinoceroses, 1 vol. 2010. (Amazing Animals Ser.). (ENG.). 48p. (J). (gr. 3-5). pap. 11.50 (978-1-4339-4023-1(X), 81e23dc4-0783-46ae-a3ab-5ac6e47d92ae); lib. bdg. 30.67 (978-1-4339-4022-4(1), f23ac27f-303f-42f3-8fde-a9cabfd65400) Stevens, Gareth Publishing LLLP. (Gareth Stevens Learning Library).

—Rhinoceroses. 2007. (J). (978-1-59939-122-9(8), Reader's Digest Young Families, Inc.) Studio Fun International.

Czech, Jan M. & Katirgis, Jane. Endangered Rhinos, 1 vol. 2015. (Wildlife at Risk Ser.). (ENG.). 48p. (gr. 6-6). pap. 12.70 (978-0-7660-6900-8(1), fbd60d39-f32a-4b4d-a4a7-2c6f884db1e6); (Illus.). 29.60 (978-0-7660-6902-2(8), d287bb9f-93a9-4637-8a1a-95205c0206a8) Enslow Publishing, LLC.

Firestone, Mary. Top 50 Reasons to Care about Rhinos: Animals in Peril, 1 vol. 2010. (Top 50 Reasons to Care about Endangered Animals Ser.). (ENG., Illus.). 104p. (gr. 5-6). 35.93 (978-0-7660-3457-0(7), b65045df-c016-4239-a1ff-4a79da9bf0c2) Enslow Publishing, LLC.

Gish, Melissa. Living Wild: Rhinoceroses. 2012. (Living Wild Ser.). (ENG., Illus.). 48p. (J). (gr. 4-7). pap. 12.00 (978-0-89812-675-4(4), 22213, Creative Paperbacks) Creative Co., The.

—Rhinoceroses. 2011. (Illus.). 46p. (J). 35.65 (978-1-60818-083-7(2), Creative Education) Creative Co., The.

Goecke, Michael P. Giant Rhino, 1 vol. 2003. (Prehistoric Animals Ser.). (ENG.). 24p. (gr. k-4). 25.65 (978-1-57765-969-3(4), Buddy Bks.) ABDO Publishing Co.

—Woolly Rhinoceros, 1 vol. 2003. (Prehistoric Animals Set II Ser.). (ENG.). 24p. (gr. k-4). 25.65 (978-1-57765-978-5(3), Buddy Bks.) ABDO Publishing Co.

Green, Jen. Rhinoceros. 2009. (Illus.). 52p. (J). (978-0-7172-8034-6(9)) Grolier, Ltd.

Grucella, Ethan. Rhinoceroses, 1 vol. 2010. (Animals That Live in the Grasslands Ser.). (ENG.). 24p. (J). (gr. 1-1). pap. 9.15 (978-1-4339-3882-5(0), 2c7732cb-a192-4cb7-bd98-b9d3a803d63a); lib. bdg. 25.27 (978-1-4339-3881-8(2), f0d76329-fe64-49c6-8f8f-3290b9993029) Stevens, Gareth Publishing LLLP.

Hamilton, Garry. Rhino Rescue: Changing the Future for Endangered Wildlife. 2006. (Firefly Animal Rescue Ser.). (ENG., Illus.). 64p. (J). (gr. 5-12). 19.95 (978-1-55297-912-9(1), 3efa896e-2844-4e37-b806-73507d921231); pap. 9.95 (978-1-55297-910-5(5), 85419e7f-8341-4487-be71-880fe5e24002) Firefly Bks., Ltd.

Hansen, Grace. Help the Black Rhinoceros. 2018. (Little Activists: Endangered Species Ser.). (ENG., Illus.). 24p. (J). (gr. -1-2). lib. bdg. 32.79 (978-1-5321-8198-6(1), 29855, Abdo Kids) ABDO Publishing Co.

—Rhinoceros. 2017. (African Animals (Abdo Kids Jumbo) Ser.). (ENG., Illus.). 24p. (J). (gr. -1-2). lib. bdg. 32.79 (978-1-5321-0421-3(9), 26547, Abdo Kids) ABDO Publishing Co.

—Rinoceronte (Rhinoceros) 2018. (Animales Africanos (African Animals) Ser.). (SPA., Illus.). 24p. (J). (gr. -1-2). lib. bdg. 32.79 (978-1-5321-8032-3(2), 28279, Abdo Kids) ABDO Publishing Co.

Jango-Cohen, Judith. Rhinoceroses, 1 vol. 2006. (Animals, Animals Ser.). (ENG.). 48p. (gr. 5-5). 32.64 (978-0-7614-1753-8(2), 9c313d47-d32e-4b73-991a-554fb947fe76) Cavendish Square Publishing LLC.

Jones, Charles M. Massive Rhinos, 1 vol. 2017. (Great Big Animals Ser.). (ENG.). 24p. (J). (gr. k-k). pap. 9.15 (978-1-5382-0911-0(X), 8e4d478a-facb-43ec-a6ec-cbf9cdb94c2f); lib. bdg. 25.27 (978-1-5382-0913-4(6), 08992079-66a5-4121-aef7-0b9163a65b5e) Stevens, Gareth Publishing LLLP.

Jones, Jack. Chizi's Tale. Taylor, Jacqui, illus. 2nd ed. 2016. (ENG.). 28p. (J). (gr. k-2). pap. 3.99 (978-1-943154-00-5(7)) Peek-A-Boo Publishing.

Kalman, Bobbie. Endangered Rhinoceros. 2004. (Earth's Endangered Animals Ser.). (ENG., Illus.). 32p. (J). pap. (978-0-7787-1898-7(0)) Crabtree Publishing Co.

Kirk, Daniel. Rhino in the House: The Story of Saving Samia. 2017. (ENG., Illus.). 40p. (J). (gr. -1-3). 17.95 (978-1-4197-2316-2(2), 1157201) Abrams, Inc.

Kopp, Megan. Rhinos. 2014. (Illus.). 48p. (J). (978-1-62127-228-1(1)) Weigl Pubs., Inc.

Latta, Jan. Rudy el Rinoceronte (Rudy the Rhinoceros), 1 vol. 2007. (Familias de Animales Salvajes (Wild Animal Families) Ser.). (SPA., Illus.). 24p. (gr. 2-4). lib. bdg. 26.67 (978-0-8368-7970-4(8), abd63d48-0534-4162-bf77-0d9cd9bb2b94, Gareth Stevens Learning Library) Stevens, Gareth Publishing LLLP.

—Rudy the Rhinoceros, 1 vol. 2007. (Wild Animal Families Ser.). (ENG., Illus.). 24p. (gr. 2-4). pap. 9.15 (978-0-8368-7778-6(0), 1454ba3c-e303-4b8d-bdf0-77deda91b59f); lib. bdg. 26.67 (978-0-8368-7771-7(3), a696bfdb-c9f7-401e-80e5-3a5518ebe9d9) Stevens, Gareth Publishing LLLP. (Gareth Stevens Learning Library).

Macheske, Felicia. Hefty Hulks: Rhinoceros. 2017. (Guess What Ser.). (ENG., Illus.). 24p. (J). (gr. k-2). lib. bdg. 30.64 (978-1-63472-169-1(1), 209248) Cherry Lake Publishing.

Markle, Sandra. The Great Rhino Rescue: Saving the Southern White Rhinos. 2018. (Sandra Markle's Science Discoveries Ser.). (ENG., Illus.). 48p. (J). (gr. 4-6). lib. bdg. 33.32 (978-1-5124-4436-0(7), a37400b5-fe18-4c53-b129-3554267faebe, Millbrook Pr.) Lerner Publishing Group.

Meeker, Clare Hodgson. National Geographic Kids Chapters: Rhino Rescue! And More True Stories of Saving Animals. 2016. (NGK Chapters Ser.). (Illus.). 112p. (J). (gr. 3-7). pap. 5.99 (978-1-4263-2311-9(5), National Geographic Kids) Disney Publishing Worldwide.

Nelson, Kristin L. African Rhinos. 2005. (Pull Ahead Bks.). (Illus.). 32p. (J). 22.60 (978-0-8225-2423-6(6), Lerner Pubns.) Lerner Publishing Group.

Orme, Helen. Rhinos in Danger. 2006. (Wildlife Survival Ser.). (Illus.). 32p. (J). (gr. 2-5). lib. bdg. 25.27 (978-1-59716-265-4(5)) Bearport Publishing Co., Inc.

Owen, Ruth. Rhinoceroses, 1 vol. 2012. (Dr. Bob's Amazing World of Animals Ser.). (ENG., Illus.). 32p. (J). (gr. 2-3). pap. 12.75 (978-1-61533-560-2(9), e1835b3a-970a-4f05-8b6c-dde803355417); lib. bdg. 31.27 (978-1-61533-550-3(1), 38785955-352a-4260-bf48-bb6142cadbf6) Rosen Publishing Group, Inc., The. (Windmill Bks.).

Pelusey, Michael & Pelusey, Jane. Rhinoceroses & Hippopotamuses, 1 vol. 2009. (Zoo Animals Ser.). (ENG.). 32p. (gr. 2-2). lib. bdg. 21.27 (978-0-7614-3150-3(0), a49e31d3-2cc9-4284-8ad9-ff4719f536d1) Cavendish Square Publishing LLC.

Pohl, Kathleen. Rhinos, 1 vol. 2007. (Animals I See at the Zoo Ser.). (ENG.). 24p. (gr. k-2). pap. 9.15 (978-0-8368-8229-2(6), 7fbdffc5-f119-4819-a60c-42c3997b0c81); (Illus.). lib. bdg. 24.67 (978-0-8368-8222-3(9), 1573c68f-e599-4068-97a1-897380971b5c) Stevens, Gareth Publishing LLLP. (Weekly Reader Leveled Readers).

Reyes, Gabrielle & Ruelos, Joanne. Odd Animal Helpers. 2011. (Scholastic Reader, Level 3 Ser.). (ENG.). 32p. (J). (gr. 1-3). pap. 3.99 (978-0-545-33147-0(1), Scholastic Paperbacks) Scholastic, Inc.

Schuetz, Kari. Rhinoceroses. 2012. (Animal Safari Ser.). (ENG., Illus.). 24p. (J). (gr. k-3). lib. bdg. 26.95 (978-1-60014-719-7(4), Blastoff! Readers) Bellwether Media.

Scott, Jonathan & Scott, Angela. Africa's Big Three: Band 07/Turquoise (Collins Big Cat) Scott, Jonathan & Scott, Angela, illus. 2006. (Collins Big Cat Ser.). (ENG., Illus.). 24p. (J). (gr. 2-2). pap. 8.99 (978-0-00-718693-8(2)) HarperCollins Pubs. Ltd. GBR. Dist: Independent Pubs. Group.

Snyder, Lydia. Rhinos in Danger, 1 vol. 2013. (Animals at Risk Ser.). 24p. (J). (gr. 2-3). (ENG.). pap. 9.15 (978-1-4339-9160-8(8), b20e25f5-0b75-4563-b20a-94a0ad52b7e8); pap. 48.90 (978-1-4339-9161-5(6)); (ENG., Illus.). lib. bdg. 25.27 (978-1-4339-9159-2(4), 5e8c19ae-5ef2-4666-a759-05fc31e8b40b) Stevens, Gareth Publishing LLLP.

Soundprints, creator. Rhinoceros's Bathtime. 2011. (Let's Go to the Zoo! Ser.). (ENG., Illus.). 16p. (gr. -1). 5.95 (978-1-60727-457-5(4)) Soundprints.

Stone, Tanya Lee. Rhinos. 2003. (Wild Wild World Ser.). 24p. (YA). 24.94 (978-1-56711-821-6(6), Blackbirch Pr., Inc.) Cengage Gale.

Tait, Leia. Emi the Sumatran Rhino. 2008. (Inspiring Animals Ser.). (Illus.). 24p. (J). (gr. 2-4). pap. 8.95 (978-1-59036-857-2(6)); lib. bdg. 24.45 (978-1-59036-856-5(8)) Weigl Pubs., Inc.

Thomas, Isabel. Elephant vs. Rhinoceros. 2017. (Animal Rivals Ser.). (ENG., Illus.). 24p. (J). (gr. k-2). lib. bdg. 25.99 (978-1-4846-4072-2(1), 135683, Heinemann) Capstone.

Walden, Katherine. Rhinoceroses. 2009. (Safari Animals Ser.). 24p. (gr. 1-1). 42.50 (978-1-60852-960-5(6)); (ENG.). (J). lib. bdg. 26.27 (978-1-4358-2687-8(6), 75c59ba2-bdac-4a5f-b7f9-f4073c28273a); (ENG., Illus.). (J). pap. 9.25 (978-1-4358-3061-5(X), 2813280f-247d-4298-ab02-b740b8929639) Rosen Publishing Group, Inc., The. (PowerKids Pr.).

Walker, Sally M. Rhinos. rev. ed. 2007. (Nature Watch Ser.). (ENG., Illus.). 48p. (gr. 4-8). lib. bdg. 27.93 *(978-0-8225-6600-7(1))*, Lerner Pubns.) Lerner Publishing Group.

Zane, Dory. How to Track a Rhinoceros, 1 vol., 1. 2013. (Scatalog: a Kid's Field Guide to Animal Poop Ser.). (ENG.). 24p. (J). (gr. 2-3). 27.27 *(978-1-61533-886-3(1)*, 18be0dac-30c7-4bd3-80e5-e2f87d1eec4d, Windmill Bks.) Rosen Publishing Group, Inc., The.

RHINOCEROSES—FICTION

Blecker, Lisa. The Good in Me from a to Z by Dottie. Blecker, Lisa, illus. 2006. (Illus.). bds. 20.00 *(978-1-931492-21-8(2))* Discover Writing Pr.

Butler, Dori. How the Rhino Got Wrinkly Skin: An Adaptation of a Rudyard Kipling Story. 2006. (J). pap. *(978-1-4108-7162-6(2))* Benchmark Education Co.

Cazet, Denys. Minnie & Moo & the Seven Wonders of the World. Cazet, Denys, illus. 2003. (ENG., Illus.). 144p. (J). (gr. 2-5). 19.99 *(978-0-689-85330-2(0)*, Atheneum/Richard Jackson Bks.) Simon & Schuster Children's Publishing.

Clough, Lisa. Petal & Poppy. Briant, Ed, illus. 2014. (ENG.). 32p. (J). (gr. -1-3). pap. 4.99 *(978-0-544-11380-0(2)*, 1541816, Clarion Bks.) HarperCollins Pubs.

—Petal & Poppy & the Penguin. Briant, Ed, illus. 2014. (ENG.). 32p. (J). (gr. -1-3). pap. 4.99 *(978-0-544-13330-3(7)*, 1544663, Clarion Bks.) HarperCollins Pubs.

Clough, Lisa & Briant, Ed. Petal & Poppy & the Mystery Valentine. 2015. (ENG., Illus.). 32p. (J). (gr. 1-4). pap. 4.99 *(978-0-544-55549-5(X)*, 1610456, Clarion Bks.) HarperCollins Pubs.

Corderoy, Tracey. It's Christmas! Warnes, Tim, illus. 2017. (ENG.). 32p. (J). (gr. -1-2). 16.99 *(978-1-68010-067-9(X))* Tiger Tales.

—More! Warnes, Tim, illus. 2015. (ENG.). 32p. (J). (gr. -1-2). 16.99 *(978-1-58925-193-9(8))* Tiger Tales.

Derrick, Patricia. Riley the Rhinoceros. Martinez, J-P Loppo, illus. 2007. 32p. (J). 18.95 incl. audio compact disk *(978-1-933818-15-3(8))* Animalations.

Ende, Michael. Norberto Nucagorda, Level 5.5. Wittenberg, Stella, illus. 2003. (SPA.). 32p. (J). (gr. 3-5). pap. 8.95 *(978-84-204-3719-4(0)*, AF1328) Santillana USA Publishing Co., Inc.

Eubank, Patti Reeder, illus. Just Where You Belong. 2004. 32p. (J). 8.95 *(978-0-8249-5481-9(5)*, Ideals Pubns.) Worthy Publishing.

Gibbs, Stuart. Big Game. 2015. (FunJungle Ser.). (ENG., Illus.). 352p. (J). (gr. 3-7). 18.99 *(978-1-4814-2333-5(9)*, Simon & Schuster Bks. For Young Readers) Simon & Schuster Bks. For Young Readers.

Gilligan, Alison. Search for the Black Rhino. Semionov, Vladimir, illus. 2011. (ENG.). 144p. (J). (gr. 4-8). pap. 7.99 *(978-1-937133-01-6(X))* Chooseco LLC.

Green, Kim. Rinny Rhino Wants Pink Pearls & a Polka Dotted Penguin. 2013. 46p. pap. 14.99 *(978-1-61863-530-3(1))* Bookstand Publishing.

Grey, Chelsea Gillian. Ema the Rhinoceros. 2004. (African Wildlife Foundation Kids Ser.). (ENG., Illus.). 36p. (J). (gr. -1-2). 8.95 *(978-1-59249-202-2(9)*, SD6500) Soundprints.

Gunaratnam, Tracy. Preposterous Rhinoceros. Costa, Marta, illus. 2019. (Early Bird Readers — Purple (Early Bird Stories (tm)) Ser.). (ENG.). 32p. (J). (gr. k-3). 30.65 *(978-1-5415-4226-6(6)*, 5612a216-a8b2-418f-bb49-ec160f42190a); pap. 9.99 *(978-1-5415-7425-0(7)*, e84ff40a-fd32-471a-95de-aa460bff4171) Lerner Publishing Group. (Lerner Pubns.).

Hanson, Anders. Rhino Horns. Nobens, C. A., illus. 2006. (Fact & Fiction Ser.). 24p. (J). pap. 48.42 *(978-1-59679-964-6(1))* ABDO Publishing Co.

—La Tuba Del Rinoceronte. Nobens, C. A., illus. 2006. (Realidad y Ficción Ser.). (SPA.). 24p. (J). 48.42 *(978-1-59928-666-2(1))* ABDO Publishing Co.

Harrison, Hannah E. Friends Stick Together. 2018. (Illus.). 32p. (J). (gr. -1-3). 17.99 *(978-0-399-18665-3(4)*, Dial Bks) Penguin Young Readers Group.

Harrison, Kevin. I Know a Rhino. Blue, Buster, illus. 2nd rev. ed. 2006. 37p. (J). (gr. -1-3). per. 10.99 *(978-1-59092-223-1(9))* Blue Forge Pr.

Hughes, Fox Carlton. Rainbow Rhino. Hughes, Fox Carlton, illus. 2007. (ENG., Illus.). 36p. (J). (gr. -1-3). 16.95 *(978-0-9790275-3-6(5))* Ovation Bks.

Iadonisi, Carmin & Word, Amanda. Whiny Whiny Rhino. Iadonisi, Carmin & Word, Amanda, illus. 2014. (ENG., Illus.). 32p. (J). 16.99 *(978-0-9903623-0-2(2))* Blue Blanket Publishing.

Jones, Stella J. Glitter. Abbot, Judi, illus. 2017. (ENG.). 32p. (J). (gr. -1-2). 16.99 *(978-1-68010-039-6(4))* Tiger Tales.

Kemp, Anna. Rhinos Don't Eat Pancakes. Ogilvie, Sara, illus. 2015. (ENG.). 32p. (J). (gr. -1-3). 17.99 *(978-1-4814-3845-2(X)*, Simon & Schuster/Paula Wiseman Bks.) Simon & Schuster/Paula Wiseman Bks.

Lester, Helen. A Porcupine Named Fluffy. Munsinger, Lynn, illus. 2013. (Laugh-Along Lessons Ser.). (ENG.). 32p. (J). (gr. -1-3). 8.99 *(978-0-544-00319-4(5)*, 1526352, Clarion Bks.) HarperCollins Pubs.

Low-DuMond, Sabrina. Weakling Willie. 2008. 28p. pap. 24.95 *(978-1-60474-258-9(5))* America Star Bks.

Mammano, Julie. Rhinos Who Play Baseball. Mammano, Julie, illus. 2006. (Illus.). 24p. (J). (gr. k-4). reprint ed. 14.00 *(978-0-7567-9995-3(3))* DIANE Publishing Co.

—Rhinos Who Rescue. 2007. (Rhinos Ser.: RHIN). (ENG., Illus.). 32p. (J). (gr. -1-1). 13.95 *(978-0-8118-5419-1(1))* Chronicle Bks. LLC.

Milgrim, David. See Otto: Ready-To-Read Pre-Level 1. Milgrim, David, illus. 2016. (Adventures of Otto Ser.). (ENG., Illus.). 32p. (J). (gr. -1-k). pap. 4.99 *(978-1-4814-6796-4(4)*, Simon Spotlight) Simon Spotlight.

O'Brien, Timothy J. Rheemer the Rhymer Rhinoceros. 2009. *(978-1-61584-106-6(7))* Independent Pub.

Olsen, Grant Orrin. Rhino Trouble. Carpenter, Mike, illus. 2015. (J). 14.99 *(978-1-4621-1665-2(5))* Cedar Fort, Inc./CFI Distribution.

O'Malley, Kevin. Bruno, You're Late for School! 2012. (ENG.). 32p. (J). (gr. -1-3). 16.95 *(978-1-59687-397-1(3)*, Milk & Cookies) ibooks, Inc.

Pennington, Beverly A. Jonathan's Discovery. Pennington, Beverly A., illus. 2006. (Illus.). 29p. (J). (gr. -1-3). pap. 12.95 *(978-1-56167-920-1(8))* American Literary Pr.

Powers, John. Seymour & the Big Red Rhino. Colavecchio, Alan, illus. 2005. 32p. (J). (gr. -1-3). 14.95 *(978-1-929039-21-0(2))* Ambassador Bks., Inc.

Prose, Francine. Rhino, Rhino, Sweet Potato. Armstrong, Matthew S., illus. 2009. 32p. (J). (gr. -1-1). lib. bdg. 18.89 *(978-0-06-008079-2(5))* HarperCollins Pubs.

Puttock, Simon. Who's the Boss Rhinoceros? (ENG., Illus.). 32p. (J). pap. 8.99 *(978-0-7497-4354-3(9))* Farshore GBR. Dist: Trafalgar Square Publishing.

Rankin, Joan, illus. Goldilocks & the Three Rhinos: A South African Retelling. 2019. (ENG.). 32p. (J). (gr. -1-3). 17.95 *(978-1-62371-916-6(X)*, Crocodile Bks.) Interlink Publishing Group, Inc.

Raúl, III, illus. Otto Es un Rinoceronte. 2003. (SPA.). 102p. (J). (gr. 3-5). pap. 12.95 *(978-958-24-0179-5(6))* Santillana USA Publishing Co., Inc.

Remkiewicz, Frank. Gus Grows a Plant. 2012. (Illus.). (J). pap. *(978-0-545-34052-6(7))* Scholastic, Inc.

Rieback, Milton. The Adventures of Webb Ellis, a Tale from the Heart of Africa: The Return of the Protectors. Crowley, Cheryl, illus. 2006. (J). lib. bdg. 19.95 *(978-0-9777440-0-8(0))* Inyati Press.

Ross, Tony. Rita's Rhino. Ross, Tony, illus. 2015. (ENG., Illus.). 32p. (J). (gr. -1-3). E-Book 27.99 *(978-1-4677-6319-6(5))* Lerner Publishing Group.

Serra, Adolfo. A Different Story. 2019. (ENG., Illus.). 32p. (J). *(978-0-8028-5527-5(X)*, Eerdmans Bks For Young Readers) Eerdmans, William B. Publishing Co.

Shriver, Chelsea & Grey, Chelsea Gillian. Ema the Rhinoceros. Leeper, Christopher, illus. 2005. (African Wildlife Foundation Kids Ser.). (ENG.). 36p. (J). (gr. -1-2). 9.95 *(978-1-59249-180-3(4)*, PS6550) Soundprints.

—Ema the Rhinoceros. 2005. (African Wildlife Foundation Kids Ser.). (ENG., Illus.). 36p. (J). (gr. -1-2). 2.95 *(978-1-59249-179-7(0)*, S6550) Soundprints.

—Ema the Rhinoceros. Leeper, Christopher J., tr. Leeper, Christopher J., illus. 2005. (African Wildlife Foundation Ser.). (ENG.). 36p. (J). (gr. -1-2). 14.95 *(978-1-59249-177-3(4)*, H6500); pap. 6.95 *(978-1-59249-178-0(2)*, S6500) Soundprints.

Summy, Barrie. I So Don't Do Mysteries. 2009. (I So Don't Do... Ser.). (ENG.). 288p. (J). (gr. 3-7). 7.99 *(978-0-385-73603-9(7)*, Yearling) Random Hse. Children's Bks.

Terry, Michael. Rhinos Horns. 2003. (Illus.). (J). *(978-1-58234-796-7(4)*, Bloomsbury USA Childrens) Bloomsbury Publishing USA.

Ulick, Michael Ackerman. Romeo the Rhino's Rocky Romance: A Cautionary Tale about Differences. Guy, Will, illus. 32p. (J). 15.95 *(978-0-9679813-0-7(1))* Footprints Pr.

Van der Merwe, Avril. Once upon a Rhinoceros. Greeff, Heidi-Kate, illus. 2018. (ENG.). 16p. pap. 7.50 *(978-1-4859-0037-5(9))* Penguin Random House South Africa ZAF. Dist: Casemate Pubs. & Bk. Distributors, LLC.

Willis, Jeanne. I'm in Charge! Jarvis, illus. 2018. (ENG.). 32p. (J). (-k). 16.99 *(978-1-5362-0259-5(2))* Candlewick Pr.

You Should Try That with a Rhino: Individual Title Six-Packs. (gr. -1-2). 23.00 *(978-0-7635-8822-9(9))* Rigby Education.

RHODE ISLAND

Allio, Mark R. R Is for Rhode Island Red: A Rhode Island Alphabet. Begin, Mary Jane, illus. 2005. (Discover America State by State Ser.). (ENG.). 40p. (J). (gr. 1-3). 18.99 *(978-1-58536-149-6(6)*, 202009) Sleeping Bear Pr.

Gamble, Adam. Good Night Rhode Island. Rosen, Anne, illus. 2008. (Good Night Our World Ser.). (ENG.). 20p. (J). (gr. -1 — 1). bds. 9.95 *(978-1-60219-024-5(0))* Good Night Bks.

Hallinan, Val. From Sea to Shining Sea: Rhode Island. 2008. (ENG.). 80p. (J). pap. 7.95 *(978-0-531-20812-0(5)*, Children's Pr.) Scholastic Library Publishing.

Heinrichs, Ann. Rhode Island. Kania, Matt, illus. 2017. (U. S. A. Travel Guides). (ENG.). 40p. (J). (gr. 2-5). lib. bdg. 38.50 *(978-1-5038-1979-5(5)*, 211616) Child's World, Inc, The.

Klein, Ted. Rhode Island, 1 vol. 2nd rev. ed. 2008. (Celebrate the States (Second Edition) Ser.). (ENG.). 144p. (gr. 6-6). lib. bdg. 39.79 *(978-0-7614-2560-1(8)*, 69dd7142-6f70-43e4-a302-e5f83652cfdc) Cavendish Square Publishing LLC.

Koontz, Robin Michal. Rhode Island: The Ocean State, 1 vol. 2010. (Our Amazing States Ser.). (ENG., Illus.). 24p. (J). (gr. 3-3). pap. 9.25 *(978-1-4488-0732-1(8)*, 5714f9e3-6972-4a96-a831-69bd4c9f9186, PowerKids Pr.) Rosen Publishing Group, Inc., The.

Labella, Susan. Rhode Island. 2006. (Rookie Read-About Geography Ser.). (ENG., Illus.). 32p. (J). (gr. 1-2). lib. bdg. 20.50 *(978-0-516-25388-6(3))* Scholastic Library Publishing.

Maine, Tyler & Parker, Bridget. Rhode Island. 2016. (States Ser.). (ENG., Illus.). 32p. (J). (gr. 3-6). lib. bdg. 27.99 *(978-1-5157-0427-0(0)*, 132038, Capstone Pr.) Capstone.

Marsh, Carole. Rhode Island Current Events Projects: 30 Cool, Activities, Crafts, Experiments & More for Kids to Do to Learn about Your State! 2003. (Rhode Island Experience Ser.). 32p. (gr. k-8). pap. 5.95 *(978-0-635-02058-1(0)*, Marsh, Carole Bks.) Gallopade International.

—Rhode Island Geography Projects: 30 Cool, Activities, Crafts, Experiments & More for Kids to Do to Learn about Your State! 2003. (Rhode Island Experience Ser.). 32p. (gr. k-5). pap. 5.95 *(978-0-635-01858-8(6)*, Marsh, Carole Bks.) Gallopade International.

—Rhode Island Government Projects: 30 Cool, Activities, Crafts, Experiments & More for Kids to Do to Learn about Your State! 2003. (Rhode Island Experience Ser.). 32p. (gr. k-5). pap. 5.95 *(978-0-635-01958-5(2)*, Marsh, Carole Bks.) Gallopade International.

—Rhode Island History Projects: 30 Cool, Activities, Crafts, Experiments & More for Kids to Do to Learn about Your State! 2003. (Rhode Island Experience Ser.). 32p. (gr. k-5). pap. 5.95 *(978-0-635-01808-3(X)*, Marsh, Carole Bks.) Gallopade International.

—Rhode Island People Projects: 30 Cool, Activities, Crafts, Experiments & More for Kids to Do to Learn about Your State! 2003. (Rhode Island Experience Ser.). 32p. (gr. k-5). pap. 5.95 *(978-0-635-02008-6(4)*, Marsh, Carole Bks.) Gallopade International.

—Rhode Island Symbols & Facts Projects: 30 Cool, Activities, Crafts, Experiments & More for Kids to Do to Learn about Your State! 2003. (Rhode Island Experience Ser.). 32p. (gr. k-5). pap. 5.95 *(978-0-635-01908-0(6)*, Marsh, Carole Bks.) Gallopade International.

Mattern, Joanne. Rhode Island, 1 vol. 2003. (World Almanac(r) Library of the States Ser.). (ENG., Illus.). 48p. (gr. 4-6). pap. 15.05 *(978-0-8368-5330-8(X)*, 209fca14-e5a5-4983-9601-d53bdfab26b4); lib. bdg. 33.67 *(978-0-8368-5159-5(5)*, ba1855f6-f6cf-4478-ab6a-187d495253e6) Stevens, Gareth Publishing LLLP. (Gareth Stevens Learning Library).

Murray, Julie. Rhode Island, 1 vol. 2006. (United States Ser.). (ENG., Illus.). 32p. (gr. 2-4). 27.07 *(978-1-59197-698-1(7)*, Buddy Bks.) ABDO Publishing Co.

Petreycik, Rick. Rhode Island, 1 vol. Santoro, Christopher, illus. 2005. (It's My State! (First Edition)(r) Ser.). (ENG.). 80p. (gr. 4-4). lib. bdg. 34.07 *(978-0-7614-1859-7(8)*, 2d28ca89-1f74-4420-8edc-15875fe7dbd8) Cavendish Square Publishing LLC.

—Rhode Island, 1 vol. 2nd rev. ed. 2013. (It's My State! (Second Edition)(r) Ser.). (ENG.). 80p. (gr. 4-4). pap. 18.64 *(978-1-62712-103-3(X)*, 18a9ed53-7007-4861-b40b-c8508b042dfe) Cavendish Square Publishing LLC.

Severin, Carol. Rhode Island, 1 vol. 2006. (Portraits of the States Ser.). (ENG.). 32p. (gr. 3-5). pap. 11.50 *(978-0-8368-4724-6(5)*, a0a48e8c-6f2d-492c-a2f8-dcf3bf840e2c); (Illus.). lib. bdg. 28.67 *(978-0-8368-4707-9(5)*, 60eae3d6-66c9-443e-8f24-e8eb7b614433) Stevens, Gareth Publishing LLLP. (Gareth Stevens Learning Library).

Warner, J. F. Rhode Island. 2012. lib. bdg. 25.26 *(978-0-7613-4555-8(8)*, Lerner Pubns.) Lerner Publishing Group.

Way, Jennifer. Rhode Island. 2009. (Bilingual Library of the United States of America Ser.). (ENG & SPA.). 32p. (gr. 2-2). 47.90 *(978-1-60853-384-8(0)*, Editorial Buenas Letras) Rosen Publishing Group, Inc., The.

—Rhode Island, 1 vol. Brusca, Maria Cristina, tr. 2005. (Bilingual Library of the United States of America Ser.: Set 2). (ENG & SPA., Illus.). 32p. (J). (gr. 2-2). lib. bdg. 28.93 *(978-1-4042-3105-4(6)*, 28b5e6cc-d856-40d4-ab4a-2e254fabbed4) Rosen Publishing Group, Inc., The.

Weintraub, A. How to Draw Rhode Island's Sights & Symbols. 2009. (Kid's Guide to Drawing America Ser.). 32p. (gr. k-k). 50.50 *(978-1-61511-093-3(3)*, PowerKids Pr.) Rosen Publishing Group, Inc., The.

RHODE ISLAND—FICTION

Ashton, Kenneth. Gale's Gold Ring: The Legend of Lincoln's Lost Gold. Ashton-Briggs, Shelley, illus. 2012. (ENG.). 198p. pap. 14.95 *(978-1-4327-8224-5(X))* Outskirts Pr., Inc.

Asselin, Kristine & Malone, Jen. The Art of the Swap. (ENG., Illus.). 352p. (J). (gr. 3-7). 2019. pap. 8.99 *(978-1-4814-7872-4(9))* 2018. 17.99 *(978-1-4814-7871-7(0))* Simon & Schuster Children's Publishing. (Aladdin).

Avi. The Man Who Was Poe. 2013. (ENG.). 224p. (J). (gr. 6-8). 21.19 *(978-0-545-50523-9(2))* Scholastic, Inc.

Backman, Yvonne. The Adventures of Penny, the Rhode Island. 2006. (ENG.). 88p. pap. 12.99 *(978-1-4303-0951-2(2))* Lulu Pr., Inc.

Bruchac, Joseph. Whisper in the Dark. 2009. (ENG., Illus.). 192p. (J). (gr. 5). pap. 7.99 *(978-0-06-058089-6(5)*, HarperCollins) HarperCollins Pubs.

Callahan, Erin. The Art of Escaping. 2018. (ENG.). 324p. (YA). (gr. 7). pap. 12.99 *(978-1-944995-65-2(X))* Amberjack Publishing Co.

Castlemon, Harry. No Moss; or, the Career of a Rolling Stone, by Harry Castlemon [Pseud.]. 2006. 328p. per. 23.99 *(978-1-4255-3290-1(X))* Michigan Publishing.

Ciocca, Gina. Last Year's Mistake. 2015. (ENG., Illus.). 320p. (YA). (gr. 9). 17.99 *(978-1-4814-3223-8(0)*, Simon Pulse) Simon Pulse.

Cullen, Sean. Hamish X Goes to Providence Rhode Island. 2009. (Hamish X Ser.: 3). (ENG.). 344p. (YA). (gr. 7-18). 9.99 *(978-0-14-316920-8(3)*, Puffin Canada) PRH Canada Young Readers CAN. Dist: Penguin Random Hse. LLC.

Curtis, Alice. Little Maid of Newport. 2006. (Little Maid Ser.). (ENG., Illus.). 212p. (gr. 4-7). pap. 12.95 *(978-1-55709-339-4(3))* Applewood Bks.

Ferrari, Michael. Born to Fly. 2011. 224p. (J). (ENG.). (gr. 4-6). lib. bdg. 21.19 *(978-0-385-90649-4(8)*, Delacorte Pr.); (gr. 3-7). 7.99 *(978-0-375-84607-6(7)*, Yearling) Random Hse. Children's Bks.

Ferris, Aimee. Will Work for Prom Dress. 2011. (ENG.). 272p. (YA). (gr. 7-12). 24.94 *(978-0-60684-141-9(6))* Farshore GBR. Dist: Children's Plus, Inc.

Fine, Sarah. Fractured, 0 vols. 2013. (Guards of the Shadowlands Ser.: 2). (ENG.). 448p. (YA). (gr. 9-12). pap. 9.99 *(978-1-4778-1691-2(7)*, 9781477816912, Skyscape) Amazon Publishing.

Gray, Claudia. Steadfast. 2015. (Spellcaster Ser.: 2). (ENG.). 368p. (YA). (gr. 8). pap. 9.99 *(978-0-06-196123-6(X)*, HarperTeen) HarperCollins Pubs.

Griffin, Adele. Tighter. 2012. (ENG.). 224p. (J). (gr. 8-12). lib. bdg. 24.94 *(978-0-375-96645-3(5))* Random House Publishing Group.

—Tighter. 2012. (ENG.). 240p. (YA). (gr. 7). pap. 8.99 *(978-0-375-85933-5(0)*, Ember) Random Hse. Children's Bks.

—Where I Want to Be. (ENG.). (YA). (gr. 7-12). 2011. 150p. 22.44 *(978-0-399-23783-6(6))* 2007. 176p. 8.99 *(978-0-14-240948-0(0)*, Speak) Penguin Young Readers Group.

Hood, Ann. She Loves You (Yeah, Yeah, Yeah) 2019. 288p. (J). (gr. 5). 8.99 *(978-1-5247-8512-3(1)*, Penguin Workshop) Penguin Young Readers Group.

Jacobs, Lily. The Littlest Bunny in Rhode Island: An Easter Adventure. Dunn, Robert, illus. 2015. (Littlest Bunny Ser.). (ENG.). 32p. (J). (gr. -1-3). 9.99 *(978-1-4926-1189-9(1)*, Hometown World) Sourcebooks, Inc.

James, Eric. Santa's Sleigh Is on Its Way to Rhode Island: A Christmas Adventure. Dunn, Robert, illus. 2016. (Santa's Sleigh Is on Its Way Ser.). (ENG.). 32p. (J). (gr. k-2). 12.99 *(978-1-4926-4353-1(X)*, 9781492643531, Hometown World) Sourcebooks, Inc.

—The Spooky Express Rhode Island. Piwowarski, Marcin, illus. 2017. (Spooky Express Ser.). (ENG.). 32p. (J). (gr. k-6). 9.99 *(978-1-4926-5396-7(9)*, Hometown World) Sourcebooks, Inc.

—Tiny the Rhode Island Easter Bunny. 2018. (Tiny the Easter Bunny Ser.). (ENG.). 40p. (J). (gr. k-3). 9.99 *(978-1-4926-5961-7(4)*, Hometown World) Sourcebooks, Inc.

Johnson, Peter. The Amazing Adventures of John Smith, Jr. AKA Houdini. 2014. (ENG.). 192p. (J). (gr. 3-7). pap. 6.99 *(978-0-06-198891-2(X)*, HarperCollins) HarperCollins Pubs.

Katherine's Story 1848. 2014. (Secrets of the Manor Ser.: 4). (ENG., Illus.). 160p. (J). (gr. 3-7). pap. 6.99 *(978-1-4814-1843-0(2)*, Simon Spotlight) Simon Spotlight.

Licameli, Doris. Rowing to the Rescue: The Story of Ida Lewis, Famous Lighthouse Heroine. 2007. (ENG.). 80p. pap. 13.95 *(978-1-84728-668-0(2))* Lulu Pr., Inc.

Lisle, Janet Taylor. Black Duck. 2007. (ENG.). 256p. (J). (gr. 5-18). 8.99 *(978-0-14-240902-2(2)*, Puffin Books) Penguin Young Readers Group.

—The Crying Rocks. 2005. 281p. (YA). (gr. 7-12). 14.65 *(978-0-7569-5507-6(6))* Perfection Learning Corp.

Livsey, John. '38: The Great Hurricane in Quonochontaug, Rhode Island. 2004. 288p. (YA). per. 15.49 *(978-0-9754979-2-0(8))* Big Wave Bks.

Metz, Melinda. Raven's Point. 2005. pap. *(978-0-06-052373-2(5))* HarperCollins Canada, Ltd.

O'Neill, Elizabeth. Alfred Visits Rhode Island. 2007. (Illus.). 24p. (J). pap. 12.00 *(978-0-9790240-6-1(4))* Funny Bone Bks.

Schumacher, Cassandra, et al. Rhode Island: The Ocean State, 1 vol. 3rd ed. 2019. (It's My State! (Fourth Edition)(r) Ser.). (ENG.). 80p. (gr. 4-4). lib. bdg. 35.93 *(978-1-5026-4244-8(1)*, 26087d4d-3632-4783-9758-7cc4c8a4c778) Cavendish Square Publishing LLC.

Swanberg, Arvon & Spicer, Carolyn. The Big, Blue, Overstuffed Chair. 2013. 46p. pap. 17.99 *(978-1-4808-0432-6(0))* Archway Publishing.

Wilson, J. M. & Zolkowski, Cathy A. Blue: Adventures of a Gymnast. 2004. 150p. (YA). per. 11.95 *(978-0-9667037-5-7(8))* Verona (Bk.) Publishing, Inc.

Zschock, Martha. Hello, Rhode Island! 2011. (Hello Ser.). (ENG., Illus.). 16p. (J). (gr. -1-k). bds. 9.99 *(978-1-933212-62-3(4)*, Commonwealth Editions) Applewood Bks.

RHODE ISLAND—HISTORY

Axelrod-Contrada, Joan. A Primary Source History of the Colony of Rhode Island. (Primary Sources of the Thirteen Colonies & the Lost Colony Ser.). 64p. 2009. (gr. 5-8). 58.50 *(978-1-60851-888-3(4))* 2005. (ENG., Illus.). (gr. 4-6). per. 12.95 *(978-1-4042-0675-5(2)*, 85e783ab-c9fa-46b0-adce-895f258a3951) 2005. (ENG., Illus.). (YA). (gr. 4-6). lib. bdg. 37.13 *(978-1-4042-0434-8(2)*, a6eba2fa-5b70-485b-b662-f3e93f24e0a9) Rosen Publishing Group, Inc., The.

Burgan, Michael. America the Beautiful: Rhode Island (Revised Edition) 2014. (America the Beautiful, Third Ser. (Revised Edition) Ser.). (ENG.). 144p. (J). lib. bdg. 40.00 *(978-0-531-28291-5(0))* Scholastic Library Publishing.

Cunningham, Kevin. The Rhode Island Colony. 2011. (True Bk Ser.). (ENG., Illus.). 48p. (J). pap. 6.95 *(978-0-531-26610-6(9))*; lib. bdg. 29.00 *(978-0-531-25397-7(X))* Scholastic Library Publishing. (Children's Pr.).

Davidson, Tish. Southern New England: Connecticut, Massachusetts, Rhode Island, Vol. 19. 2015. (Let's Explore the States Ser.). (Illus.). 64p. (J). (gr. 5). 23.95 *(978-1-4222-3333-7(2))* Mason Crest.

Everin, Gretchen. Dreaming of Newport: Counting down Around the Town. Chung, Nahyun, illus. 2019. (Dreaming Of Ser.). (ENG.). 16p. (J). bds. 9.99 *(978-1-64194-130-3(8)*, Commonwealth Editions) Applewood Bks.

Felix, Rebecca. What's Great about Rhode Island? 2015. (Our Great States Ser.). (ENG., Illus.). 32p. (J). (gr. 2-5). lib. bdg. 26.65 *(978-1-4677-3856-9(5)*, 4cd90493-39da-4dd1-87c4-af349f5d8585, Lerner Pubns.) Lerner Publishing Group.

Friesen, Helen Lepp. Rhode Island: The Ocean State. 2012. (J). 29.99 *(978-1-61913-399-0(7))*; pap. *(978-1-61913-400-3(4))* Weigl Pubs., Inc.

Furgang, Adam. Rhode Island: Past & Present, 1 vol. 2010. (United States: Past & Present Ser.). (ENG.). 48p. (YA). (gr. 5-5). pap. 12.75 *(978-1-4358-9521-8(5)*, ebe88049-e25b-46cc-813a-68886617f41f); lib. bdg. 34.47 *(978-1-4358-9494-5(4)*, 7a945786-eb2e-4044-8921-fb123898aa32) Rosen Publishing Group, Inc., The. (Rosen Reference).

Hamilton, John. Rhode Island, 1 vol. 2016. (United States of America Ser.). (ENG., Illus.). 48p. (J). (gr. 5-9). 34.21 *(978-1-68078-342-1(4)*, 21669, Abdo & Daughters) ABDO Publishing Co.

Kleinmartin, Hex, et al. Rhode Island. 2015. lib. bdg. *(978-1-62713-219-0(8))* Cavendish Square Publishing LLC.

Koontz, Robin Michal. Rhode Island: The Ocean State, 1 vol. 2010. (Our Amazing States Ser.). (ENG., Illus.). 24p. (J). (gr. 3-3). 26.27 *(978-1-4488-0650-8(X)*, 2ddf2808-101b-4f55-828e-396bca83547f, PowerKids Pr.) Rosen Publishing Group, Inc., The.

Laine, Grannie. Good Night, Block Island. 2010. 24p. 12.00 *(978-1-4520-0753-3(5))* AuthorHouse.

Marsh, Carole. Exploring Rhode Island Through Project-Based Learning: Geography, History, Government, Economics & More. 2016. (Rhode Island Experience Ser.). (ENG.). (J). pap. 9.99 *(978-0-635-12363-3(0))* Gallopade International.

Miller, Jake. The Colony of Rhode Island: A Primary Source History. (Primary Source Library of the Thirteen Colonies & the Lost Colony Ser.). 24p. (gr. 3-4). 2009. 42.50 *(978-1-60854-156-0(8))* 2005. (ENG., Illus.). (J). lib. bdg. 26.27 *(978-1-4042-3032-3(7)*, aaa71c29-490b-499f-a64b-7564d1f38e1a) Rosen Publishing Group, Inc., The. (PowerKids Pr.).

Petreycik, Rick. Rhode Island, 1 vol. 2nd rev. ed. 2013. (It's My State! (Second Edition)(r) Ser.). (ENG.). 80p. (gr. 4-4). 35.93 *(978-0-7614-8002-0(1)*, 9b5868fa-65ba-4193-ba55-619b65c1bfe0) Cavendish Square Publishing LLC.

Wilkins, Ebony Joy. Perron Family Haunting: The Ghost Story That Inspired Horror Movies. 2019. (Real-Life Ghost Stories Ser.). (ENG., Illus.). 32p. (J). (gr. 3-9). pap. 7.95 *(978-1-5435-7480-7(7)*, 140920); lib. bdg. 28.65 *(978-1-5435-7341-1(X)*, 140632) Capstone.

Wilson, James, ed. Rhode Island Treasures. 2003. (Illus.). 112p. per. 15.00 *(978-0-615-12390-5(2))* Narragansett Graphics.

Wimmer, Teresa. Rhode Island. 2009. (This Land Called America Ser.). 32p. (YA). (gr. 3-6). 19.95 *(978-1-58341-792-8(3))* Creative Co., The.

Winans, Jay D. Rhode Island. 2011. (Guide to American States Ser.). (J). (Illus.). 48p. (gr. 3-6). 29.99 *(978-1-61690-812-6(2))*; 29.99 *(978-1-61690-488-3(7))* Weigl Pubs., Inc.

—Rhode Island: The Ocean State. 2016. (J). *(978-1-4896-4935-5(2))* Weigl Pubs., Inc.

Yomtov, Nel. Rhode Island (a True Book: My United States) (Library Edition) 2018. (True Book (Relaunch) Ser.). (ENG., Illus.). 48p. (J). (gr. 3-5). lib. bdg. 31.00 *(978-0-531-23578-2(5)*, Children's Pr.) Scholastic Library Publishing.

RHODES, CECIL, 1853-1902

Phan, Sandy. Cecil Rhodes: The Man Who Expanded an Empire, 1 vol. rev. ed. 2012. (Social Studies: Informational Text Ser.). (ENG.). 32p. (gr. 4-8). pap. 11.99 *(978-1-4333-5016-0(5))* Teacher Created Materials, Inc.

RHODESIA, SOUTHERN

see Zimbabwe

RHYMES

see Limericks; Nonsense Verses; Nursery Rhymes; Poetry—Collections

RHYTHM

see also Versification

Bodden, Valerie. Wording & Tone. (Odysseys in Prose Ser.). (ENG., Illus.). 80p. (J). (gr. 7-11). 2017. pap. 14.99 *(978-1-62832-326-9(4)*, 20689, Creative Paperbacks) 2016. *(978-1-60818-730-0(6)*, 20691, Creative Education) Creative Co., The.

RICE, CONDOLEEZZA, 1954-

Banting, Erinn. Condoleeza Rice. 2007. (Remarkable People Ser.). (Illus.). 24p. (J). (gr. 3-7). lib. bdg. 24.45 *(978-1-59036-639-4(5))* Weigl Pubs., Inc.

—Condoleezza Rice. 2007. (Remarkable People Ser.). (Illus.). 24p. (J). (gr. 3-7). pap. 8.95 *(978-1-59036-640-0(9))* Weigl Pubs., Inc.

Ditchfield, Christin. Condoleezza Rice: America's Leading Stateswoman. 2006. (Great Life Stories Ser.). (ENG., Illus.). 112p. (J). (gr. 6-8). lib. bdg. 30.50 *(978-0-531-13874-8(7)*, Watts, Franklin) Scholastic Library Publishing.

Hubbard-Brown, Janet. Condoleezza Rice: Stateswoman. 2008. (ENG., Illus.). 113p. (gr. 6-12). lib. bdg. 35.00 *(978-0-7910-9715-1(3)*, P145703, Facts On File) Infobase Holdings, Inc.

Marsh, Carole. Condoleezza Rice. 2003. 12p. (gr. k-4). 2.95 *(978-0-635-02385-8(7))* Gallopade International.

Rice, Condoleezza. Condoleezza Rice: a Memoir of My Extraordinary, Ordinary Family & Me. 2012. (ENG.). 336p. (J). (gr. 5). pap. 11.99 *(978-0-385-73880-4(3)*, Ember) Random Hse. Children's Bks.

Wade, Linda R. Condoleezza Rice. 2004. (Illus.). 32p. (J). lib. bdg. 25.70 *(978-1-58415-332-0(6))* Mitchell Lane Pubs.

Wade, Mary Dodson. Condoleezza Rice. rev. ed. 2005. (Gateway Biography Ser.). (Illus.). 48p. (J). (gr. 4-7). pap. 8.95 *(978-0-7613-9549-2(0)*, First Avenue Editions) Lerner Publishing Group.

—Condoleezza Rice: Being the Best. 2003. (Gateway Biography Ser.: 4). 48p. lib. bdg. 23.90 *(978-0-7613-2619-9(7))*; (Illus.). (gr. 2-4). pap. 8.95 *(978-0-7613-1927-6(1))* Lerner Publishing Group. (Millbrook Pr.).

RICE

Brannon, Cecelia H. Rice, 1 vol. 2017. (All about Food Crops Ser.). (ENG.). 24p. (gr. k-1). lib. bdg. 24.27 *(978-0-7660-8583-1(X)*, dad6a9cd-c27b-4c03-a50e-856a1eaa79f3) Enslow Publishing, LLC.

Martineau, Susan & James, Hel. Bread, Rice, & Pasta. 2012. (Healthy Eating Ser.). (Illus.). 32p. (gr. 2-6). pap. 8.95 *(978-1-59920-242-6(5))* Black Rabbit Bks.

Reynolds, Jan. Cycle of Rice, Cycle of Life: A Story of Sustainable Farming. Reynolds, Jan, photos by. 2009. (ENG., Illus.). 48p. (J). (gr. 2-7). 19.95 *(978-1-60060-254-2(1))* Lee & Low Bks., Inc.

Singer, Jane E. Rice. 2013. (Feeding the World Ser.: 8). (Illus.). 48p. (J). (gr. 4-18). 19.95 *(978-1-4222-2747-3(2))* Mason Crest.

Staniford, Linda. Where Do Grains Come From? 2016. (From Farm to Fork: Where Does My Food Come From? Ser.). (ENG., Illus.). 24p. (J). (gr. k-2). lib. bdg. 26.65 *(978-1-4846-3349-6(0)*, 131964, Heinemann) Capstone.

Taylor, Trace. Rice. 2009. (2G Social Studies). (ENG., Illus.). 28p. (J). pap. 8.00 *(978-1-61406-040-6(1))* American Reading Co.

Williams, Nancy Noel. Rice Is Nice. 2010. (J). *(978-1-60617-144-8(5))* Teaching Strategies, LLC.

World Book, Inc. Staff, contrib. by. Rice. 2019. (Illus.). 48p. (J). *(978-0-7166-2863-7(5))* World Bk., Inc.

Zronik, John Paul & Zronik, John. The Biography of Rice. 2005. (How did That Get There? Ser.). (ENG., Illus.). 32p. (J). (gr. 4-5). pap. *(978-0-7787-2518-3(9))*; lib. bdg. *(978-0-7787-2482-7(4))* Crabtree Publishing Co.

RICE—FICTION

Pittman, Helena Clare. A Grain of Rice. 2018. (Illus.). 112p. (J). (gr. 3-7). 14.99 *(978-1-5247-6552-1(X)*, Delacorte Bks. for Young Readers) Random Hse. Children's Bks.

Sherer, Mary (Huston). Ho Fills the Rice Barrel. Greenwood, Marion, illus. 2012. 128p. 40.95 *(978-1-258-25056-0(X))*; pap. 25.95 *(978-1-258-25732-3(7))* Literary Licensing, LLC.

Takayama, Sandi. The Musubi Baby. Hall, Pat, illus. 2007. 32p. (J). (gr. -1-3). 10.95 *(978-1-57306-272-5(3))* Bess Pr., Inc.

RICHARD I, KING OF ENGLAND, 1157-1199

Abbott, Jacob. History of King Richard the First of England. 2003. 336p. 99.00 *(978-0-7950-3593-7(4))* New Library Press LLC.

Crompton, Samuel Willard. The Third Crusade: Richard the Lionhearted vs. Saladin. 2003. (Great Battles Through the Ages Ser.). (Illus.). 112p. (J). (gr. 6-12). 30.00 *(978-0-7910-7437-4(4)*, Facts On File) Infobase Holdings, Inc.

Harkins, Susan Sales & Harkins, William H. The Life & Times of Richard the Lionheart. 2008. (Biography from Ancient Civilizations Ser.). (Illus.). 48p. (J). (gr. 4-8). lib. bdg. 29.95 *(978-1-58415-699-4(6))* Mitchell Lane Pubs.

Hilliam, David. Richard the Lionheart & the Third Crusade: The English King Confronts Saladin in AD 1191. 2009. (Library of the Middle Ages Ser.). 64p. (gr. 5-8). 58.50 *(978-1-60853-902-4(4)*, Rosen Reference) Rosen Publishing Group, Inc., The.

—Richard the Lionhearted & the Third Crusade: The English King Confronts Saladin, AD 1191, 1 vol. 2003. (Library of the Middle Ages Ser.). (ENG., Illus.). 64p. (YA). (gr. 5-8). lib. bdg. 37.13 *(978-0-8239-4213-8(9)*, 9615dcf4-03e8-4f9c-87be-a8d4f0c6c92f, Rosen Reference) Rosen Publishing Group, Inc., The.

West, David. Richard the Lionheart: The Life of a King & Crusader. 2009. (Graphic Nonfiction Biographies Ser.). (Illus.). 48p. (YA). (gr. 4-5). 58.50 *(978-1-61513-025-2(X)*, Rosen Reference) Rosen Publishing Group, Inc., The.

West, David & Gaff, Jackie. Richard the Lionheart: The Life of a King & Crusader, 1 vol. 2005. (Graphic Nonfiction Biographies Ser.). (ENG., Illus.). 48p. (YA). (gr. 4-6). lib. bdg. 37.13 *(978-1-4042-0241-2(2)*, 30cbfce0-287d-4093-988a-3e03ee71d2dc) Rosen Publishing Group, Inc., The.

RICHARD I, KING OF ENGLAND, 1157-1199—FICTION

Harris, Mark W., et al. Ivanhoe. Scott, Walter, ed. (Classics Illustrated Ser.). (Illus.). 52p. (YA). pap. 4.95 *(978-1-57209-023-1(5))* Classics International Entertainment, Inc.

RICHARD II, KING OF ENGLAND, 1367-1400

Abbott, Jacob. History of King Richard the Second of England. 2003. 347p. 99.00 *(978-0-7950-3594-4(2))* New Library Press LLC.

RICHARD III, KING OF ENGLAND, 1452-1485—FICTION

Haddix, Margaret Peterson. Sent. (Missing Ser.: 2). (YA). 2011. 82.75 *(978-1-4407-2678-1(7))* 2009. 218.75 *(978-1-4407-2670-5(1))* 2009. 98.75 *(978-1-4407-2675-0(2))* 2009. 1.25 *(978-1-4407-2679-8(5))* Recorded Bks., Inc.

—Sent. (Missing Ser.: 2). (ENG.). (J). (gr. 3-7). 2010. 336p. pap. 8.99 *(978-1-4169-5423-1(6))* 2009. 320p. 16.99 *(978-1-4169-5422-4(8))* Simon & Schuster Bks. For Young Readers. (Simon & Schuster Bks. For Young Readers).

—Sent. abr. ed. 2009. *(978-1-4424-0767-1(0))* Simon & Schuster Children's Publishing.

—Sent. l.t. ed. 2010. (Missing Ser.: Bk. 2). (ENG.). 345p. 23.99 *(978-1-4104-3245-2(9))* Thorndike Pr.

—Sent. 2010. (Missing Ser.: 2). lib. bdg. 18.40 *(978-0-606-14699-9(7))* Turtleback.

Rose, Simon. The Sorcerer's Letterbox, 1 vol. 2004. (ENG., Illus.). 116p. (J). (gr. 4-7). per. 7.95 *(978-1-896580-52-4(1))* Tradewind Bks. CAN. Dist: Orca Bk. Pubs. USA.

Stevenson, Robert Louis. The Black Arrow. l.t. ed. 2005. 448p. pap. *(978-1-84637-164-6(3))* Echo Library.

RICHTHOFEN, MANFRED ALBRECHT, FREIHERR VON, 1892-1918

Vansant, Wayne. The Red Baron: The Graphic History of Richthofen's Flying Circus & the Air War in WWI. Vansant, Wayne, illus. 2015. (Graphic Histories Ser.). (ENG., Illus.). 104p. (YA). (gr. 8-12). 34.65 *(978-1-939581-80-8(X)*, 0a637c45-08f0-49f9-82e8-d7c7fca3fad3, Zenith Pr.) Quarto Publishing Group USA.

—The Red Baron: The Graphic History of Richthofen's Flying Circus & the Air War in WWI. 2014. (Zenith Graphic Histories Ser.). (ENG., Illus.). 104p. pap. 19.99 *(978-0-7603-4602-0(X)*, 076034602X, Zenith Pr.) Quarto Publishing Group USA.

RICKEY, BRANCH, 1881-1965

Frystak, Timothy D. Jackie Robinson: With Profiles of Satchel Paige & & Branch Rickey. 2006. (Biographical Connections Ser.). (Illus.). 112p. (J). *(978-0-7166-1828-7(1))* World Bk., Inc.

RICOTTA, RICKY (FICTITIOUS CHARACTER)—FICTION

Pilkey, Dav. Ricky Ricotta's Mighty Robot. 2014. (Ricky Ricotta's Mighty Robot Ser.: 1). lib. bdg. 16.00 *(978-0-606-35799-9(8))* Turtleback.

—Ricky Ricotta's Mighty Robot vs. the Jurassic Jackrabbits from Jupiter (Ricky Ricotta's Mighty Robot #5), Vol. 5. Santat, Dan, illus. 2014. (Ricky Ricotta's Mighty Robot Ser.: 5). (ENG.). 128p. (J). (gr. -1-3). pap. 5.99 *(978-0-545-63013-9(4))* Scholastic, Inc.

—Ricky Ricotta's Mighty Robot vs. the Mecha-Monkeys from Mars (Ricky Ricotta's Mighty Robot #4) Santat, Dan, illus. 2014. (Ricky Ricotta's Mighty Robot Ser.: 4). (ENG.). 144p. (J). (gr. -1-3). pap. 5.99 *(978-0-545-63012-2(6))* Scholastic, Inc.

—Ricky Ricotta's Mighty Robot vs. the Mutant Mosquitoes from Mercury (Ricky Ricotta's Mighty Robot #2) Santat, Dan, illus. 2014. (Ricky Ricotta's Mighty Robot Ser.: 2). (ENG.). 128p. (J). (gr. -1-3). pap. 5.99 *(978-0-545-63010-8(X))* Scholastic, Inc.

—Ricky Ricotta's Mighty Robot vs. the Naughty Nightcrawlers from Neptune (Ricky Ricotta's Mighty Robot #8) Santat, Dan, illus. 2016. (Ricky Ricotta's Mighty Robot Ser.: 8). (ENG.). 128p. (J). (gr. -1-3). pap. 5.99 *(978-0-439-37709-6(9))* Scholastic, Inc.

—Ricky Ricotta's Mighty Robot vs. the Uranium Unicorns from Uranus (Ricky Ricotta's Mighty Robot #7), Bk. 7. 2015. (Ricky Ricotta's Mighty Robot Ser.: 7). (ENG., Illus.). 128p. (J). (gr. -1-3). pap. 5.99 *(978-0-545-63015-3(0))* Scholastic, Inc.

—Ricky Ricotta's Mighty Robot vs. the Video Vultures from Venus (Ricky Ricotta's Mighty Robot #3) Santat, Dan, illus. 2014. (Ricky Ricotta's Mighty Robot Ser.: 3). (ENG.). 128p. (J). (gr. -1-3). pap. 5.99 *(978-0-545-63011-5(8))* Scholastic, Inc.

Santat, Dan, illus. Ricky Ricotta's Mighty Robot vs. the Stupid Stinkbugs from Saturn (Ricky Ricotta's Mighty Robot #6) 2015. (Ricky Ricotta's Mighty Robot Ser.: 6). (ENG.). 128p. (J). (gr. -1-3). pap. 5.99 *(978-0-545-63014-6(2))* Scholastic, Inc.

RIDDLES

see also Puzzles

Anholt, Catherine & Anholt, Laurence. Can You Guess? A Lift-the-Flap Birthday Party Book. 2003. (ENG., Illus.). 16p. pap. 7.95 *(978-0-7112-2214-4(2))* Fleming, Randall.

Bathroom Readers' Institute. The Grossest Joke Book Ever! 2016. (ENG., Illus.). 128p. (J). (gr. 3-7). pap. 4.99 *(978-1-62686-585-3(X)*, Portable Pr.) Printers Row Publishing Group.

Beth, Georgia. World's Best (and Worst) Riddles. 2018. (Laugh Your Socks Off! Ser.). (ENG., Illus.). 24p. (J). (gr. 1-4). pap. 6.99 *(978-1-5415-1174-3(3)*, 2fc96074-f036-4170-a5ae-360aa7ce7b72) Lerner Publishing Group.

A Book of Silly Jokes! 2003. (Illus.). (J). *(978-0-439-39056-9(7))* Scholastic, Inc.

Boone, Brian. Uproarious Riddles for Minecrafters: Mobs, Ghasts, Biomes, & More. Brack, Amanda, illus. 2018. (Jokes for Minecrafters Ser.). (ENG.). 184p. (J). (gr. 1-6). pap. 7.99 *(978-1-5107-2717-5(5)*, Sky Pony Pr.) Skyhorse Publishing Co., Inc.

Brennan-Nelson, Denise. Little Colorado. Urban, Helle, illus. 2011. (Little State Ser.). (ENG.). 20p. (J). (gr. -1-1). bds. 9.95 *(978-1-58536-530-2(0)*, 202238) Sleeping Bear Pr.

—Little Michigan. Monroe, Michael Glenn, illus. 2010. (Little State Ser.). (ENG.). 20p. (J). (gr. -1-1). bds. 9.95 *(978-1-58536-479-4(7)*, 202243) Sleeping Bear Pr.

Brett, Jeannie. Little Maine. Brett, Jeannie, illus. 2010. (Little State Ser.). (ENG., Illus.). 20p. (J). (gr. -1-1). bds. 9.95 *(978-1-58536-497-8(5)*, 202242) Sleeping Bear Pr.

Brett, Jeannie & Crane, Carol. Little South Carolina. 2011. (Little State Ser.). (ENG., Illus.). 20p. (J). (gr. -1-1). bds. 9.95 *(978-1-58536-486-2(X)*, 202249) Sleeping Bear Pr.

Bulion, Leslie. Random Body Parts: Gross Anatomy Riddles in Verse. Lowery, Mike, illus. 2019. 48p. (J). (gr. 3-7). pap. 7.95 *(978-1-68263-103-4(6))* Peachtree Publishing Co. Inc.

Burns, Diane L. Horsing Around: Jokes to Make Ewe Smile. Gable, Brian, illus. 2005. (Make Me Laugh! Ser.). 32p. (J). (gr. k-3). lib. bdg. 19.93 *(978-1-57505-662-3(3))* Lerner Publishing Group.

Burns, Diane L. & Scholten, Dan. Horsing Around: Jokes to Make Ewe Smile. Gable, Brian, illus. 2004. (Make Me Laugh! Ser.). 32p. (J). (gr. -1-3). per. 4.95 *(978-1-57505-737-8(9))* Lerner Publishing Group.

Carlson-Berne, Emma. World's Best (and Worst) Animal Jokes. 2018. (Laugh Your Socks Off! Ser.). (ENG., Illus.). 24p. (J). (gr. 1-4). pap. 6.99 *(978-1-5415-1171-2(9)*, 6a1394bf-e82f-44a4-9813-ef2888735c8b); 26.65 *(978-1-5124-8351-2(6)*, fa5d7dff-8024-4668-9546-534e26a71cee, Lerner Pubns.) Lerner Publishing Group.

—World's Best (and Worst) Spooky Jokes. 2018. (Laugh Your Socks Off! Ser.). (ENG., Illus.). 24p. (J). (gr. 1-4). pap. 6.99 *(978-1-5415-1178-1(6)*, e6088a55-3440-46ed-a275-cf23928ace6b); 26.65 *(978-1-5124-8352-9(4)*, c1f5d5fa-3b20-4d50-bbce-afcc64f96dab, Lerner Pubns.) Lerner Publishing Group.

Cerrillo, Pedro César. Adivina qué soy. 2004. (SPA., Illus.). 30p. (J). 6.50 *(978-84-348-7753-5(8))* SM Ediciones ESP. Dist: Lectorum Pubns., Inc.

Charney, Steve. Kids' Kookiest Riddles. Collinet, Rob, illus. 2010. (Jokes & Riddles Ser.). (ENG.). 96p. (J). (gr. k-3). 17.44 *(978-1-4027-7850-6(3))* Sterling Publishing Co., Inc.

—Mr. Potato Head Upside down Joke World. Harpster, Steve, illus. 2008. (Jokes & Riddles Ser.). (ENG.). 96p. (J). (gr. k-3). 17.44 *(978-1-4027-5361-9(6))* Sterling Publishing Co., Inc.

Chirp Magazine, The Editors of. Joking Around with Chirp. Kain, Bob, illus. 2013. (ENG.). 96p. (J). (gr. -1-3). pap. 11.95 *(978-1-926973-65-4(8))* Owlkids Bks. Inc. CAN. Dist: Publishers Group West (PGW).

Christopher, Clara. Animal Jokes, Riddles, & Games. 2016. (ENG., Illus.). 32p. (J). *(978-0-7787-2387-5(9))* Crabtree Publishing Co.

Cliff Road Books Staff & Sweetwater Press Staff, contrib. by. Jokes & Riddles for Kids of All Ages, 3 vols. 2004. (Illus.). *(978-1-58173-312-9(7))*; *(978-1-60261-115-3(7))*; *(978-1-58173-313-6(5))* Cliff Road Bks.

Cole, Joanna & Calmenson, Stephanie, eds. Tons of Fun: Over 300 Action Rhymes, Old & New Riddles, Tongue Twisters, & Play Rhymes. Tiegren, Alan, illus. 2004. 229p. (J). (gr. k-4). reprint ed. pap. 15.00 *(978-0-7567-8222-1(8))* DIANE Publishing Co.

Conley, Erin, ed. Zany Riddles. 2005. (Made You Laugh for Kids). (ENG., Illus.). 96p. pap. 5.95 *(978-1-57528-930-4(X))* Univ. Games.

Connolly, Sean. The Fun on the Farm Joke Book, 1 vol. 2013. (Laugh Out Loud Ser.). (ENG., Illus.). 32p. (J). (gr. 2-3). pap. 12.75 *(978-1-61533-654-8(0)*, 4411dc72-2bec-4eb9-8931-38a229b9c898, Windmill Bks.) Rosen Publishing Group, Inc., The.

—The Hysterical History Joke Book, 1 vol. 2013. (Laugh Out Loud Ser.). (ENG., Illus.). 32p. (gr. 2-3). pap. 12.75 *(978-1-61533-656-2(7)*, 45eff5c7-4c06-4436-b867-26445dc93062, Windmill Bks.) Rosen Publishing Group, Inc., The.

—The Jolly Jungle Joke Book, 1 vol. 2013. (Laugh Out Loud Ser.). (ENG., Illus.). 32p. (J). (gr. 2-3). pap. 12.75 *(978-1-61533-658-6(3)*, 7cc40f00-7f5d-4ef0-9ac6-028f4667ba38, Windmill Bks.) Rosen Publishing Group, Inc., The.

—Laugh Out Loud! The Silly Spells Joke Book, 1 vol. 2013. (Laugh Out Loud Ser.). (ENG., Illus.). 32p. (J). (gr. 2-3). pap. 12.75 *(978-1-61533-662-3(1)*, ac89c5ed-2713-4ee6-9512-aad8f408078d, Windmill Bks.) Rosen Publishing Group, Inc., The.

—The Out to Sea Joke Book, 1 vol. 2013. (Laugh Out Loud Ser.). (ENG., Illus.). 32p. (J). (gr. 2-3). pap. 12.75 *(978-1-61533-660-9(5)*, 11ae99e9-4648-469c-a748-e90815f33218, Windmill Bks.) Rosen Publishing Group, Inc., The.

Connolly, Sean & Harris, Joseph. The Crazy Computers Joke Book, 1 vol. 2013. (Laugh Out Loud Ser.). (ENG., Illus.). 32p. (J). (gr. 2-3). pap. 12.75 *(978-1-61533-652-4(4)*, 282d9131-5620-459a-9f34-8eb2a9695790); lib. bdg. 31.27 *(978-1-61533-643-2(5)*, 187c0a6e-bbc5-4a9c-ac86-69450b8786b2) Rosen Publishing Group, Inc., The. (Windmill Bks.).

Crane, Carol. Little Florida. Monroe, Michael Glenn, illus. 2010. (Little State Ser.). (ENG.). 20p. (J). (gr. -1-1). bds. 9.95 *(978-1-58536-487-9(8)*, 202239) Sleeping Bear Pr.

—Little Georgia. Knorr, Laura, illus. 2013. (Little State Ser.). (ENG.). 20p. (J). (gr. -1-k). bds. 9.95 *(978-1-58536-203-5(4)*, 202355) Sleeping Bear Pr.

—Little North Carolina. Brett, Jeannie, illus. 2011. (Little State Ser.). (ENG.). 20p. (J). (gr. -1-1). bds. 9.95 *(978-1-58536-545-6(9)*, 202245) Sleeping Bear Pr.

—Little Texas. Monroe, Michael Glenn, illus. 2010. (Little State Ser.). (ENG.). 20p. (J). (gr. -1-1). bds. 9.95 *(978-1-58536-488-6(6)*, 202250) Sleeping Bear Pr.

Dahl, Michael. Puzzling Riddles to Stump Your Friends. 2018. (Jokes, Tricks, & Other Funny Stuff Ser.). (ENG., Illus.). 32p. (J). (gr. 3-9). lib. bdg. 27.32 *(978-1-5435-0339-5(X)*, 137191, Capstone Pr.) Capstone.

—Scooby-Doo's Laugh-Out-Loud Jokes! Jeralds, Scott, illus. 2015. (Scooby-Doo Joke Bks.). (ENG.). 224p. (J). (gr. 2-6). pap., pap., pap. 9.95 *(978-1-62370-182-6(1)*, 126993, Capstone Young Readers) Capstone.

Dahl, Michael, et al. Wise Crackers: Riddles & Jokes about Numbers, Names, Letters, & Silly Words, 1 vol. Haugen, Ryan et al, illus. 2010. (Michael Dahl Presents Super Funny Joke Bks.). (ENG.). 80p. (J). (gr. 1-3). 25.32 *(978-1-4048-6102-2(5)*, 103355, Picture Window Bks.) Capstone.

Doering, Jennie Spray. Beach Riddles. Pica, Steve, illus. 2006. (Silly Millies Ser.). 32p. (J). (gr. 2). per. 5.95 *(978-0-8225-6471-3(8)*, First Avenue Editions); (ENG.). (gr. 1-3). lib. bdg. 21.27 *(978-0-7613-2885-8(8)*, Millbrook Pr.) Lerner Publishing Group.

Doolittle, John H. Dr. DooRiddles A2: Associative Reasoning Activities. 2005. (Dr. DooRiddles & Spelling DooRiddles Ser.). 48p. (gr. -1-2). pap. 9.99 *(978-0-89455-877-1(3))* Critical Thinking Co., The.

—Dr. DooRiddles A3: Associative Reasoning Activities. 2012. (Dr. DooRiddles & Spelling DooRiddles Ser.). 48p. (gr. 2-3). pap. 9.99 *(978-0-89455-878-8(1))* Critical Thinking Co., The.

Doolittle, John H. & Doolittle, Tracy A. Dr. DooRiddles B2: Associative Reasoning Activities. 2011. (Dr. DooRiddles & Spelling DooRiddles Ser.). 64p. (gr. 4-7). pap. 9.99 *(978-0-89455-879-5(X))* Critical Thinking Co., The.

Dussling, Jennifer. In a Dark, Dark House. Jones, Davy, illus. Date not set. (All Aboard Reading Ser.). 32p. (J). (gr. -1-k). pap. *(978-0-448-40974-0(7)*, Grosset & Dunlap) Penguin Publishing Group.

Editorial, Equipo. Mis 365 Mejores Adivinanzas. Aubert, Elena G., illus. 2003. (SPA.). *(978-84-7630-904-9(X)*, LA30439) Editorial Libsa, S.A. ESP. Dist: Lectorum Pubns., Inc.

Editors of Portable Press, ed. The Funniest & Grossest Joke Book Ever! 2017. (ENG., Illus.). 256p. (J). (gr. 3-7). pap. 8.99 *(978-1-68412-128-1(0)*, Portable Pr.) Printers Row Publishing Group.

Engelman Berner, Beth. Finding Fairyland: A Picture Riddle Book. Riggs, Jenna, illus. 2005. 12p. (J). 9.95 *(978-1-58117-386-4(5)*, Intervisual/Piggy Toes) Bendon, Inc.

Everest. Adivina, Adivinanza. Quesada, Maria Fe, illus. (SPA.). (J). pap. 5.56 *(978-84-241-8037-9(2))* Everest Editora ESP. Dist: Lectorum Pubns., Inc.

Fabulous PH Riddles Blends/Dig. (J). pap. 18.16 *(978-0-8136-0864-8(3))* Modern Curriculum Pr.

Fontes, Justine. Cheerios Action Park Adventure. 2005. (Picture Clue Math Reader Ser.). (Illus.). 28p. (J). pap. *(978-0-439-70343-7(3))* Scholastic, Inc.

Gagliano, Eugene. Little Wyoming. Urban, Helle, illus. 2010. (Little State Ser.). (ENG.). 20p. (J). (gr. -1-1). bds. 9.95 *(978-1-58536-544-9(0)*, 202251) Sleeping Bear Pr.

Garrett, Ann & Higney, Gene-Michael. Fins & Flippers, Scales & Nippers. 2003. (Illus.). 32p. (J). pap. *(978-1-59034-871-0(0))*; 15.95 *(978-1-59034-869-7(9))* Mondo Publishing.

Gilbert Square Books. The Fun of Rhyme Square Pears. 2005. (Illus.). 40p. (J). 2.50 *(978-0-9745308-3-3(2))* Gilbert Square Bks.

Gómez Yebra, Antonio. ADIVINA ADIVINANZAS: ADIVINANZAS DE HOY PARA NIÑOS. 2003. (SPA.). *(978-84-348-7336-0(2)*, SM31231) SM Ediciones ESP. Dist: Lectorum Pubns., Inc.

Gowan, Barbara. Little Arizona. Urban, Helle, illus. 2012. (Little State Ser.). (ENG.). 20p. (J). (gr. -1-1). bds. 9.95 *(978-1-58536-208-0(5)*, 202274) Sleeping Bear Pr.

Group/McGraw-Hill, Wright. Aunt Victoria's Monster: Level P, 6 vols. (Whispering Pines Ser.). 128p. (gr. 5-18). 36.95 *(978-0-322-05903-0(8))* Wright Group/McGraw-Hill.

Helmer, Marilyn. Funtime Riddles. Kurisu, Jane, illus. 2004. 31p. (J). lib. bdg. 15.38 *(978-1-4242-1184-5(0))* Fitzgerald Bks.

Hentley, Sheila Rose. Nursery Rhymes & Nursery Riddles for All Ages. 2007. 28p. per. 21.99 *(978-1-4257-9011-0(9))* Xlibris Corp.

Hershenhorn, Esther. Little Illinois. Monroe, Michael Glenn, illus. 2011. (Little State Ser.). (ENG.). 20p. (J). (gr. -1-1). bds. 9.95 *(978-1-58536-537-1(8)*, 202240) Sleeping Bear Pr.

Hillert, Margaret. What Am I? 2016. (Beginning-To-Read Ser.). (ENG., Illus.). 32p. (J). (gr. k-2). pap. 13.26 *(978-1-60357-982-7(6))* Norwood Hse. Pr.

—What Am I? Mukuc, Lucy, illus. 2016. (BeginningtoRead Ser.). (ENG.). 32p. (J). (gr. 3-2). 22.60 *(978-1-59953-820-4(2))* Norwood Hse. Pr.

James, Helen Foster. Little America. Brett, Jeannie et al, illus. 2011. (Little Country Ser.). (ENG.). 20p. (J). (gr. -1-1). bds. 8.99 *(978-1-58536-179-3(8)*, 202235) Sleeping Bear Pr.

—Little California. Urban, Helle, illus. 2011. (Little State Ser.). (ENG.). 20p. (J). (gr. -1-1). bds. 9.95 *(978-1-58536-538-8(6)*, 202237) Sleeping Bear Pr.

Klutz Editors, ed. Carabiners: Weird Facts; Random Riddles; Really Dumb Jokes. 2004. (ENG., Illus.). 40p. (J). 3.95 *(978-1-59174-295-1(1))* Klutz.

Kowitt, Holly. Too Funny! 234 Laugh-Out-Loud Jokes. 2008. (Illus.). 63p. (J). pap. *(978-0-439-67172-9(8))* Scholastic, Inc.

Laffin, Ima. Monster Jokes. 2016. (Big Buddy Jokes Ser.). (ENG., Illus.). 32p. (J). (gr. 2-5). lib. bdg. 34.21 *(978-1-68078-513-5(3)*, 23575, Big Buddy Bks.) ABDO Publishing Co.

Lanchais, Aurelie, et al. I Can Fly, What Am I? 2005. (Who Am I? What Am I? Ser.). (Illus.). 16p. (J). (gr. -1-1). (ARA, ENG, URD, CHI & BEN.). 9.95 (978-1-84059-250-4(8)); (URD, ENG, CHI, ARA & BEN., 9.95 (978-1-84059-255-9(9)) Milet Publishing.

—Kto A? 2005. (Who Am I? What Am I? Ser.).Tr. of Who Am I? (RUS, ENG, TUR, VIE & CHI., Illus.). 16p. (J). (gr. -1-1). 9.95 (978-1-84059-232-0(X)) Milet Publishing.

—What Am I? 2005. (Who Am I? What Am I? Ser.). (Illus.). 16p. (J). (gr. -1-1). (URD, ENG, CHI, ARA & BEN.). 9.95 (978-1-84059-248-1(6)); (ARA, ENG, URD, TUR & CHI., 9.95 (978-1-84059-243-6(5)) Milet Publishing.

—Who Am I? 2005. (Who Am I? What Am I? Ser.). (CHI, ENG, VIE, GUJ & RUS., Illus.). 16p. (J). (gr. -1-1). 9.95 (978-1-84059-229-0(X)) Milet Publishing.

LeCompte, David & Padrick, Kendell. Eugene Stillwell Wants to Know!, Pt. 2. 2009. (Eugene Stillwell Wants to Know! Ser.). (ENG.). 96p. (J). (gr. 4-6). pap. 4.95 (978-1-929945-74-0(4)) Big Guy Bks., Inc.

—Eugene Stillwell Wants to Know! Part III. 2009. (Eugene Stillwell Wants to Know! Ser.). (ENG.). 96p. (J). (gr. 4-6). pap. 4.95 (978-1-929945-91-7(4)) Big Guy Bks., Inc.

Lee, Cyl. Really Silly Jokes. 2016. (Big Buddy Jokes Ser.). (ENG., Illus.). 32p. (J). (gr. 2-5). lib. bdg. 34.21 (978-1-68078-514-2(1), 23577, Big Buddy Bks.) ABDO Publishing Co.

—Ridiculous Riddles. 2016. (Big Buddy Jokes Ser.). (ENG., Illus.). 32p. (J). (gr. 2-5). lib. bdg. 34.21 (978-1-68078-515-9(X), 23579, Big Buddy Bks.) ABDO Publishing Co.

Lewis, J. Patrick. National Geographic Kids Just Joking: Animal Riddles. 2015. (Illus.). 208p. (J). (gr. 3-7). pap. 7.99 (978-1-4263-1869-6(3), National Geographic Kids) Disney Publishing Worldwide.

Libal, Autumn. Folk Proverbs & Riddles. 2004. (North American Folklore Ser.). (Illus.). 112p. (YA). (gr. 7-18). lib. bdg. 22.95 (978-1-59084-343-7(6)) Mason Crest.

El Libro de los Acertijos Historicos. (Coleccion Acertijos). (SPA.). (YA). (gr. 5-8). pap. (978-950-724-249-6(X), LMA8235) Lumen ARG. Dist: Lectorum Pubns., Inc.

Lome, Emilio Angel. Lottery of Riddles. Martinez, Enrique, illus. 2011. 46p. (gr. 2-5). pap. 6.95 (978-968-19-0663-4(2)) Aguilar, Altea, Taurus, Alfaguara, S.A. de C.V MEX. Dist: Santillana USA Publishing Co., Inc.

Lupton, Hugh. Riddle Me This! Riddles & Stories to Challenge Your Mind. Fatus, Sophie, illus. 2003. 64p. (J). 19.99 (978-1-84148-169-2(6)) Barefoot Bks., Inc.

—Riddle Me This! Riddles & Stories to Sharpen Your Wits. Fatus, Sophie, illus. 2007. (ENG.). 64p. (J). pap. 12.99 (978-1-905236-92-3(1)) Barefoot Bks., Inc.

Macari, Mario Duilio, ed. & illus. Funny Riddles for Kids: Squeaky Clean Easy Kid Riddles Drawn As Funny Kid's Cartoons in A Cool Comicbook Style. Macari, Mario Duilio, illus. 2007. 104p. (J). per. 10.00 (978-0-9766755-0-1(1)) Cartoonmario.com.

Martin, Norma. Don Martin Brain Games for Kids. 2007. 68p. pap. 3.95 (978-1-4343-2848-9(1)) AuthorHouse.

Marzollo, Jean & Wick, Walter. I Spy a Dinosaur's Eye. 2003. (I Spy — Scholastic Readers Level 1 Ser.). (gr. -1-2). lib. bdg. 13.55 (978-0-613-72243-8(4)) Turtleback.

—School Bus. 2003. (I Spy — Scholastic Readers Level 1 Ser.). (gr. -1-2). lib. bdg. 13.55 (978-0-613-72246-9(9)) Turtleback.

Meachen Rau, Dana. Applesauce, 1 vol. 2009. (What's Cooking? Ser.). (ENG.). 24p. (gr. k-1). pap. 9.23 (978-0-7614-3516-7(6), 5c7d95e0-f6ec-4684-81b7-d0945784e992) Cavendish Square Publishing LLC.

—At the Zoo, 1 vol. 2008. (Fun Time Ser.). (ENG., Illus.). 24p. (gr. k-1). lib. bdg. 25.50 (978-0-7614-2610-3(8), 6d7f5074-b11c-44a6-b918-579799b16eca) Cavendish Square Publishing LLC.

—Baker, 1 vol. 2008. (Jobs in Town Ser.). (ENG., Illus.). 24p. (gr. k-1). lib. bdg. 25.50 (978-0-7614-2623-3(X), c6257c3d-6ea0-434f-bdfa-9c1ede4eaf68) Cavendish Square Publishing LLC.

—Un Bombero (Firefighter), 1 vol. 2009. (Trabajos en Pueblos y Ciudades (Jobs in Town) Ser.). (SPA., Illus.). 24p. (gr. k-1). lib. bdg. 25.50 (978-0-7614-2782-7(1), 32503656-7abe-4dfb-abbf-1d4c0c2d2b91) Cavendish Square Publishing LLC.

—Bread, 1 vol. 2009. (What's Cooking? Ser.). (ENG.). 24p. (gr. k-1). pap. 9.23 (978-0-7614-3517-4(4), f38d2129-d1a3-4324-b0d1-617bd5dd6242) Cavendish Square Publishing LLC.

—Cookies, 1 vol. 2009. (What's Cooking? Ser.). (ENG.). 24p. (gr. k-1). pap. 9.23 (978-0-7614-3520-4(4), 5b2ad2a0-ec27-4c91-903f-dddf870d5349) Cavendish Square Publishing LLC.

—Driving, 1 vol. 2007. (On the Move Ser.). (ENG., Illus.). 24p. (gr. k-1). lib. bdg. 25.50 (978-0-7614-2316-4(8), 8129174d-da44-47b7-8f19-776f6f39a9cd) Cavendish Square Publishing LLC.

—En Movimiento, 6 bks., Set. Incl. ¡a Conducir! (Driving) lib. bdg. 25.50 (978-0-7614-2422-2(9), d562d517-0bcb-4f77-9d9e-55c736a736ce); ¡a Flotar! (Floating) lib. bdg. 25.50 (978-0-7614-2420-8(2), f3c6d2be-3278-48ea-9712-4152559b992e); ¡a Montar! (Riding) lib. bdg. 25.50 (978-0-7614-2423-9(7), 89632a7a-05c8-41c4-88d4-b39adab7ff08); ¡a Rodar! (Rolling) lib. bdg. 25.50 (978-0-7614-2419-2(9), 9332c010-8b6a-4b38-970a-84a3088edc44); ¡a Trepar! (Climbing) lib. bdg. 25.50 (978-0-7614-2424-6(5), 57c869a9-5085-43c9-9d4e-1fdb1a2e78cd); ¡a Volar! (Flying) lib. bdg. 25.50 (978-0-7614-2425-3(3), 3ffa301d-8a07-42c4-985d-0334ceffc052); (Illus.). 32p. (gr. k-1). 2008. (Benchmark Rebus: en Movimiento Ser.). (SPA.). 2006. lib. bdg. (978-0-7614-2417-8(2), Cavendish Square) Cavendish Square Publishing LLC.

—Librarian. 2007. (J). (978-0-7614-2621-9(3)) Marshall Cavendish.

—On a Farm, 1 vol. 2008. (Fun Time Ser.). (ENG., Illus.). 24p. (gr. k-1). lib. bdg. 25.50 (978-0-7614-2605-9(1), 2070f0f7-a0d5-4dcd-80b9-e0d0992c9615) Cavendish Square Publishing LLC.

—Un Panadero (Baker), 1 vol. 2009. (Trabajos en Pueblos y Ciudades (Jobs in Town) Ser.). (SPA., Illus.). 24p. (gr. k-1). lib. bdg. 25.50 (978-0-7614-2781-0(3), 8f35c52e-75fc-4977-b2ed-b6d3b409abbb) Cavendish Square Publishing LLC.

—Riding, 1 vol. 2007. (On the Move Ser.). (ENG., Illus.). 24p. (gr. k-1). lib. bdg. 25.50 (978-0-7614-2317-1(6), fe9446d0-0ac9-46da-8382-235cc6d7db07) Cavendish Square Publishing LLC.

Meachen Rau, Dana & Vargus, Nanci Reginelli. En el Picnic (at the Picnic), 1 vol. 2009. (Tiempo de la Diversión (Fun Time) Ser.). (SPA., Illus.). 24p. (gr. k-1). lib. bdg. 25.50 (978-0-7614-2779-7(1), 13634c26-34be-44d8-880e-acbfb4af0a09) Cavendish Square Publishing LLC.

—Firefighter, 1 vol. 2008. (Jobs in Town Ser.). (ENG., Illus.). 24p. (gr. k-1). lib. bdg. 25.50 (978-0-7614-2617-2(5), 07dd17a3-82fb-445d-a178-8f1def6c4f65) Cavendish Square Publishing LLC.

Menotti, Andrea. How to Tackle Puzzles, Unravel Riddles, Crack Codes, & Other Ways to Bend Your Brain. 2004. (Illus.). 80p. (J). (978-0-439-57905-6(8)) Scholastic, Inc.

Miller, Shane, illus. Riddles, Riddles, Riddles: Enigmas & Anagrams, Puns & Puzzles, Quizzes & Conundrums! 2014. (Dover Kids Activity Bks.). (ENG.). 256p. (J). (gr. 3-8). pap. 9.99 (978-0-486-78186-0(0), 781860) Dover Pubns., Inc.

Morrison, Lillian. Guess Again! Riddle Poems. Hale, Christy, illus. 2006. (ENG.). 48p. (J). (gr. 1-4). 16.95 (978-0-87483-730-8(8)) August Hse. Pubs., Inc.

Napier, Matt. Little Canada. Benoit, Renné, illus. 2012. (Little Country Ser.). (ENG.). 20p. (J). (gr. -1-1). bds. 9.95 (978-1-58536-178-6(X), 202265) Sleeping Bear Pr.

National Geographic Kids. Just Joking: Jumbo: 1,000 Giant Jokes & 1,000 Funny Photos Add up to Big Laughs. 2017. (Just Joking Ser.). (ENG., Illus.). 288p. (J). (gr. 3-7). lib. bdg. 24.90 (978-1-4263-2880-0(X), National Geographic Kids) Disney Publishing Worldwide.

Nature Riddles [Capstone Sole Source]. 2010. (Nature Riddles Ser.). 32p. lib. bdg. 103.96 (978-1-4296-5873-7(8), Capstone Pr.) Capstone.

Nelson, Esther & Hirsch, Davida. Riggeldy Jiggeldy Joggeldy Jam: Can You Guess Who I Am? Ellis, Libby, illus. 2003. (J). bds. 5.95 (978-0-7607-3278-6(7)) Barnes & Noble, Inc.

Noble, Trinka Hakes. Little New Jersey. Brett, Jeannie, illus. 2012. (Little State Ser.). (ENG.). 20p. (J). (gr. -1-1). bds. 9.95 (978-1-58536-786-3(9), 202349) Sleeping Bear Pr.

—Little Pennsylvania. Brett, Jeannie, illus. 2010. (Little State Ser.). (ENG.). 20p. (J). (gr. -1-1). bds. 9.95 (978-1-58536-506-7(8), 202247) Sleeping Bear Pr.

Paletta, Emilio. Squire Dumpty. 2009. 28p. pap. 15.49 (978-1-4389-4533-0(7)) AuthorHouse.

Panec, D. J. Riddle Rhymes (We Both Read - Level Pk-K) 2016. (We Both Read Level Pk-K Ser.). (ENG., Illus.). 42p. (J). 9.95 (978-1-60115-277-0(9)) Treasure Bay, Inc.

Pellowski, Michael J. Mega-Funny Jokes & Riddles. 2019. (Joke Bks.). (ENG., Illus.). 96p. (J). (gr. 2-4). 16.69 (978-1-64310-786-8(0)) Penworthy Co., LLC, The.

Peterson, Scott K. Let the Fun Begin: Nifty Knock-Knocks, Playful Puns, & More. Gable, Brian, illus. 2005. (Make Me Laugh! Ser.). 32p. (J). (gr. k-3). lib. bdg. 19.93 (978-1-57505-661-6(5)) Lerner Publishing Group.

Phillips, Bob. All-Time Awesome Collection of Good Clean Jokes for Kids. 2006. (Illus.). 366p. (J). (gr. 3-12). per. 10.99 (978-0-7369-1777-3(2)) Harvest Hse. Pubs.

Phunny, U. R. Animal Jokes. 2016. (Big Buddy Jokes Ser.). (ENG., Illus.). 32p. (J). (gr. 2-5). lib. bdg. 34.21 (978-1-68078-510-4(9), 23569, Big Buddy Bks.) ABDO Publishing Co.

—Dinosaur Jokes. 2016. (Big Buddy Jokes Ser.). (ENG., Illus.). 32p. (J). (gr. 2-5). lib. bdg. 34.21 (978-1-68078-511-1(7), 23571, Big Buddy Bks.) ABDO Publishing Co.

Prieto, Anita C. Little Louisiana. Knorr, Laura, illus. 2011. (Little State Ser.). (ENG.). 20p. (J). (gr. -1-1). bds. 9.95 (978-1-58536-184-7(4), 202241) Sleeping Bear Pr.

Richards, Kitty. Phineas & Ferb Laughapalooza Joke Book. 2011. (ENG., Illus.). (J). (-3). pap. (978-1-4075-8486-7(3)) Parragon Bk. Service Ltd.

Riddle Me This! 2014. (Riddle Me This! Ser.). 32p. (J). (gr. 1-5). 165.00 (978-1-4777-9181-3(7)) Windmill Bks.

Robleda, Margarita. Quien Soy? Adivinanzas Animales. Gurovich, Natalia, illus. 2003. (SPA.). 32p. (J). 12.95 (978-970-690-805-6(6)) Planeta Mexicana Editorial S. A. de C. V. MEX. Dist: Lectorum Pubns., Inc.

Rodger, Anne-Marie. Sports Jokes, Riddles, & Games. 2016. (ENG., Illus.). 32p. (J). (978-0-7787-2390-5(9)) Crabtree Publishing Co.

Rodger, Ellen. Monster & Creepy-Crawly Jokes, Riddles, & Games. 2016. (ENG., Illus.). 32p. (J). (978-0-7787-2389-9(5)) Crabtree Publishing Co.

Rodger, Marguerite. Around the World in Jokes, Riddles, & Games. 2016. (ENG., Illus.). 32p. (J). (978-0-7787-2388-2(7)) Crabtree Publishing Co.

Sawyers, William. What Am I? Book. 2005. (ENG.). 44p. pap. 8.95 (978-1-4116-2899-1(3)) Lulu Pr., Inc.

—What Am I? Bugs. 2005. (ENG.). 65p. (J). pap. 16.01 (978-1-4116-3402-2(0)) Lulu Pr., Inc.

Scheunemann, Pam. Ape Cape, 1 vol. 2004. (Rhyming Riddles Ser.). (Illus.). 24p. (J). (gr. k-3). lib. bdg. 24.21 (978-1-59197-457-4(7), SandCastle) ABDO Publishing Co.

—Chipper Flipper, 1 vol. 2004. (Rhyming Riddles Ser.). (ENG., Illus.). 24p. (J). (gr. k-3). lib. bdg. 24.21 (978-1-59197-458-1(5), SandCastle) ABDO Publishing Co.

—Cooler Ruler, 1 vol. 2004. (Rhyming Riddles Ser.). (Illus.). 24p. (J). (gr. k-3). lib. bdg. 24.21 (978-1-59197-459-8(3), SandCastle) ABDO Publishing Co.

—Dill Spill, 1 vol. 2004. (Rhyming Riddles Ser.). (Illus.). 24p. (J). (gr. k-3). lib. bdg. 24.21 (978-1-59197-460-4(7), SandCastle) ABDO Publishing Co.

—Loud Crowd, 1 vol. 2004. (Rhyming Riddles Ser.). (Illus.). 24p. (J). (gr. k-3). lib. bdg. 24.21 (978-1-59197-461-1(5), SandCastle) ABDO Publishing Co.

—Overdue Kangaroo, 1 vol. 2004. (Rhyming Riddles Ser.). (ENG., Illus.). 24p. (J). (gr. k-3). lib. bdg. 24.21 (978-1-59197-462-8(3), SandCastle) ABDO Publishing Co.

Scheunemann, Pam & ABDO Publishing Company Staff. Rhyming Riddles. 2004. (Rhyming Riddles Ser.: 6). (J). (gr. k-3). 145.26 (978-1-59197-456-7(9), SandCastle) ABDO Publishing Co.

Scholastic, Inc. Staff. I Spy Fantasy. 2008. 29.99 (978-0-439-82065-3(0)) Scholastic, Inc.

—I Spy Riddle Master. 2008. 29.99 (978-0-439-93519-7(9)) Scholastic, Inc.

Schonberg, Marcia. Little Ohio. Monroe, Michael Glenn, illus. 2011. (Little State Ser.). (ENG.). 20p. (J). (gr. -1-1). bds. 9.95 (978-1-58536-527-2(0), 202246) Sleeping Bear Pr.

Shannon, George. Red All Over. Date not set. (J). (gr. 3-7). pap. 4.99 (978-0-380-80072-8(1)) HarperCollins Pubs.

Shepherd, Rajean Luebs. Little Nebraska. Urban, Helle, illus. 2015. (Little State Ser.). (ENG.). 22p. (J). (gr. -1-k). bds. 9.95 (978-1-58536-928-7(4), 203819) Sleeping Bear Pr.

Shore, Diane Z. & Calvert, Deanna. Riddle Diddle Farm. Bauer, Stephanie, illus. 2018. (ENG.). 10p. (J). (gr. -1-1). bds. 9.99 (978-1-68152-406-1(6), 15465) Amicus.

—Riddle Diddle Ocean. Bauer, Stephanie, illus. 2019. (Riddle Diddle Dumplings Ser.). (ENG.). 10p. (J). (gr. -1-1). bds. 9.99 (978-1-68152-499-3(6), 10867) Amicus.

—Riddle Diddle Rainforest. Bauer, Stephanie, illus. 2019. (Riddle Diddle Dumplings Ser.). (ENG.). 10p. (J). (gr. -1-1). bds. 9.99 (978-1-68152-500-6(3), 10868) Amicus.

Shoulders, Michael. Little Mississippi. Urban, Helle, illus. 2016. (Little State Ser.). (ENG.). 20p. (J). (gr. -1-k). bds. 9.95 (978-1-58536-974-4(8), 204111) Sleeping Bear Pr.

Sky Pony Editors. Belly Laugh Jokes for Kids: 350 Hilarious Jokes. Straker, Bethany, illus. 2015. (ENG.). 144p. (J). (gr. k). 9.99 (978-1-63450-156-9(X), Sky Pony Pr.) Skyhorse Publishing Co., Inc.

Sleeping Bear Press. Little Oklahoma. Urban, Helle, illus. 2015. (Little State Ser.). (ENG.). 22p. (J). (gr. -1-k). bds. 9.95 (978-1-58536-927-0(6), 203817) Sleeping Bear Pr.

Snedeker, Gus. An Apple a Day: Folk Proverbs & Riddles. 2013. (Illus.). 48p. (J). pap. (978-1-4222-2504-2(6)) Mason Crest.

—An Apple a Day: Folk Proverbs & Riddles. Jabbour, Alan, ed. 2012. (North American Folklore for Youth Ser.). (Illus.). 48p. (J). (gr. 4). 19.95 (978-1-4222-2493-9(7)) Mason Crest.

Stemen, Jeffrey, illus. Critter Giggles. 2006. (J). (978-1-58987-035-2(2)) Kindermusik International.

Stewart, Trenton Lee. The Mysterious Benedict Society: Mr. Benedict's Book of Perplexing Puzzles, Elusive Enigmas, & Curious. Sudyka, Diana, illus. 2011. (Mysterious Benedict Society Ser.). (ENG.). 176p. (J). (gr. 3-7). 17.99 (978-0-316-18193-8(5)) Little, Brown Bks. for Young Readers.

Strain Trueit, Trudi. Christmas, 1 vol. 2011. (Holiday Fun Ser.). (ENG.). 24p. (gr. k-1). 25.50 (978-0-7614-4885-3(3), fd1f6190-137b-4113-8f95-0d0c9e647ad7) Cavendish Square Publishing LLC.

—Halloween, 1 vol. 2011. (Holiday Fun Ser.). (ENG.). 24p. (gr. k-1). 25.50 (978-0-7614-4886-0(1), 6f7603ca-42f3-4c7b-b55d-19c5029ca027) Cavendish Square Publishing LLC.

—Hanukkah, 1 vol. 2011. (Holiday Fun Ser.). (ENG.). 24p. (gr. k-1). 25.50 (978-0-7614-4884-6(5), 697abbc3-f63f-4778-86c5-c22b85b53b3d) Cavendish Square Publishing LLC.

—Jellyfish, 1 vol. 2011. (Ocean Life Ser.). (ENG.). 24p. (gr. k-1). 25.50 (978-0-7614-4891-4(8), 1f019af4-b571-4e74-9fd9-6f5245306faa) Cavendish Square Publishing LLC.

—Kwanzaa, 1 vol. 2011. (Holiday Fun Ser.). (ENG.). 24p. (gr. k-1). 25.50 (978-0-7614-4887-7(X), 156d7797-413f-4406-b9b3-88a4ec710a40) Cavendish Square Publishing LLC.

—Octopuses, 1 vol. 2011. (Ocean Life Ser.). (ENG.). 24p. (gr. k-1). 25.50 (978-0-7614-4892-1(6), f1b466d4-f1b6-4c17-b2eb-6ad8d124a56b) Cavendish Square Publishing LLC.

—Thanksgiving, 1 vol. 2011. (Holiday Fun Ser.). (ENG.). 24p. (gr. k-1). 25.50 (978-0-7614-4888-4(8), 0cdaa2d1-798b-4130-bf43-a46ac5e030dd) Cavendish Square Publishing LLC.

—Valentine's Day, 1 vol. 2011. (Holiday Fun Ser.). (ENG.). 24p. (gr. k-1). 25.50 (978-0-7614-4889-1(6), 09316546-9752-4aff-8dae-7559e4fc092c) Cavendish Square Publishing LLC.

Sullivan, Alesha. Funny Tricks & Practical Jokes to Play on Your Friends. 2018. (Jokes, Tricks, & Other Funny Stuff Ser.). (ENG., Illus.). 32p. (J). (gr. 3-9). lib. bdg. 27.32 (978-1-5435-0340-1(3), 137192, Capstone Pr.) Capstone.

Super Giggles: Knock-Knocks, Jokes, & Tongue-Twisters. 2005. (Illus.). 176p. pap. (978-0-7607-6782-5(3)) Barnes & Noble, Inc.

Tait, Chris. Ridiculous Knock-Knocks. Zahnd, Mark, illus. 2010. (Jokes & Riddles Ser.). (ENG.). 96p. (J). (gr. k-3). 17.44 (978-1-4027-7852-0(X)) Sterling Publishing Co., Inc.

Terban, Marvin. Eight Ate: A Feast of Homonym Riddles. Maestro, Giulio, illus. 2007. (ENG.). 64p. (J). (gr. -1-3). pap. 7.99 (978-0-618-76676-5(6), 100537, Clarion Bks.) HarperCollins Pubs.

Terban, Marvin & Huffman, Thomas. The Dove Dove: Funny Homograph Riddles. Huffman, Thomas, illus. 2008. (ENG., Illus.). 64p. (J). (gr. 5-7). pap. 6.95 (978-0-547-03186-6(6), 1033405, Clarion Bks.) HarperCollins Pubs.

Terban, Marvin & Maestro, Giulio. Too Hot to Hoot: Funny Palindrome Riddles. Maestro, Giulio, illus. 2008. (ENG., Illus.). 64p. (J). (gr. 3-7). pap. 8.95 (978-0-618-19165-9(8), 1013224, Clarion Bks.) HarperCollins Pubs.

Vaicikonis, Kris. Puzzle Me-Brain Twisters. 2012. (Illus.). 32p. (J). pap. 4.99 (978-1-62267-006-2(X)) Bright Connections Media.

Vidro, Kenn. Square Pears Three: Hey Diddle Riddle. 2005. (ENG., Illus.). 100p. (J). spiral bd. 9.95 (978-0-9745308-2-6(4)) Gilbert Square Bks.

—Square Pears Two: The Equal Sequel. Vidro, Kenn, illus. 2004. (ENG., Illus.). 100p. (J). spiral bd. 9.95 (978-0-9745308-1-9(6)) Gilbert Square Bks.

Wagner, Kathi & Wagner, Aubrey. The Everything Kids Riddles & Brain Teasers Book: Hours of Challenging Fun. 2004. (Everything(r) Kids Ser.). (ENG., Illus.). 144p. pap. 9.99 (978-1-59337-036-7(9), Everything) Adams Media Corp.

Walton, Rick & Walton, Ann. Foul Play: Sports Jokes That Won't Strike Out. Gable, Brian, illus. 2005. (Make Me Laugh! Ser.). 32p. (J). (gr. k-3). lib. bdg. 19.93 (978-1-57505-666-1(6)) Lerner Publishing Group.

—Magical Mischief: Jokes That Shock & Amaze. Gable, Brian, illus. 2005. (Make Me Laugh! Ser.). 32p. (J). (gr. k-3). lib. bdg. 19.93 (978-1-57505-664-7(X)) Lerner Publishing Group.

Walton, Rick, et al. Real Classy: Silly School Jokes. Gable, Brian, illus. 2005. (Make Me Laugh! Ser.). 32p. (J). (gr. k-3). lib. bdg. 19.93 (978-1-57505-665-4(8)) Lerner Publishing Group.

Wargin, Kathy-jo. Little Minnesota. Urban, Helle, illus. 2011. (Little State Ser.). (ENG.). 20p. (J). (gr. -1-1). bds. 9.95 (978-1-58536-174-8(7), 202263) Sleeping Bear Pr.

—Little Wisconsin. Monroe, Michael Glenn, illus. 2012. (Little State Ser.). (ENG.). 20p. (J). (gr. -1-1). bds. 9.95 (978-1-58536-209-7(3), 202275) Sleeping Bear Pr.

Wee Society. Wee Hee Hee: A Collection of Pretty Funny Jokes & Pictures. 2018. (Wee Society Ser.). (Illus.). 64p. (J). (gr. k-4). 22.00 (978-1-5247-5996-4(1), Clarkson Potter) Potter/Ten Speed/Harmony/Rodale.

Wilbur, Helen L. Little New York. Brett, Jeannie, illus. 2010. (Little State Ser.). (ENG.). 20p. (J). (gr. -1-1). bds. 9.95 (978-1-58536-491-6(6), 202244) Sleeping Bear Pr.

William H. Sadlier Staff. Buggy Riddles, Vol. 2. 2005. (Fluent Library). (gr. 1-3). 29.34 (978-0-8215-8969-4(5)) Sadlier, William H. Inc.

Young, Judy. Little Missouri. Urban, Helle, illus. 2012. (Little State Ser.). (ENG.). 20p. (J). (gr. -1-1). bds. 9.95 (978-1-58536-206-6(9), 202348) Sleeping Bear Pr.

RIDE, SALLY, 1951-2012

Bindi, Paulo. Sally Ride: The Sky's the Limit. 2013. (InfoMax Readers Ser.). (ENG.). 24p. (J). (gr. 2-3). pap. 49.50 (978-1-4777-2452-1(4)); (Illus.). pap. 8.25 (978-1-4777-2451-4(6), d70f7c7b-6573-44ec-b3ae-5dff30a650c8) Rosen Publishing Group, Inc., The. (Rosen Classroom).

Edison, Erin. Sally Ride, 1 vol. 2014. (Great Women in History Ser.). (ENG., Illus.). 24p. (J). (gr. -1-2). lib. bdg. 24.65 (978-1-4765-4215-7(5), 124313, Pebble) Capstone.

Felix, Rebecca. Sally Ride: Trailblazing Astronaut. 2018. (Space Crusaders Ser.). (ENG., Illus.). 32p. (J). (gr. 3-6). lib. bdg. 32.79 (978-1-5321-1704-6(3), 30696, Checkerboard Library) ABDO Publishing Co.

Loh-Hagan, Virginia. Sally Ride. Bane, Jeff, illus. 2018. (Mi Mini Biografía (My Itty-Bitty Bio): My Early Library). (ENG.). 24p. (J). (gr. k-1). pap. 12.79 (978-1-5341-0808-0(4), 210596); lib. bdg. 30.64 (978-1-5341-0709-0(6), 210595) Cherry Lake Publishing.

Murphy, Sage. Sally Ride: Female Astronaut, 1 vol. 2013. (Rosen Readers Ser.). (ENG.). 24p. (J). (gr. 2-2). pap. 8.25 (978-1-4777-2306-7(4), 314cafb2-a62a-41a4-afbf-0d09ace5ca3f); pap. 49.50 (978-1-4777-2307-4(2)) Rosen Publishing Group, Inc., The. (Rosen Classroom).

Nettleton, Pamela Hill. Sally Ride: Astronaut, Scientist, Teacher. Yesh, Jeff & Nichols, Garry, illus. 2003. (Biographies Ser.). (ENG.). 24p. (J). (gr. k-3). 27.32 (978-1-4048-0189-9(8), 90353, Picture Window Bks.) Capstone.

O'Shaughnessy, Tam. Sally Ride: A Photobiography of America's Pioneering Woman in Space. 2015. (ENG., Illus.). 160p. (J). (gr. 5-8). 19.99 (978-1-59643-994-8(7), 900128935) Roaring Brook Pr.

Riddolls, Tom. Sally Ride: The First American Woman in Space. 2010. (Crabtree Groundbreaker Biographies Ser.). (ENG., Illus.). 112p. (J). pap. (978-0-7787-2550-3(2)); (gr. 5-8). lib. bdg. (978-0-7787-2541-1(3)) Crabtree Publishing Co.

Sally Ride: Life on a Mission. 2014. (Real-Life Story Ser.). (ENG., Illus.). 160p. (J). (gr. 3-7). 18.99 (978-1-4424-8854-0(9), Aladdin) Simon & Schuster Children's Publishing.

Smith, Annie Laura. Sally Ride: America's First Woman Astronaut. Gierhart, Steve, ed. 2nd ed. 2015. (ENG., Illus.). 54p. (J). (gr. k-7). pap. 11.95 (978-1-938667-38-1(7)) Ardent Writer Pr., LLC, The.

Stine, Megan. Who Was Sally Ride? 2013. (Who Was... ? Ser.). lib. bdg. 16.00 (978-0-606-31683-5(3)) Turtleback.

Stine, Megan & Who HQ. Who Was Sally Ride? Hammond, Ted, illus. 2013. (Who Was? Ser.). 112p. (J). (gr. 3-7). pap. 6.99 (978-0-448-46687-3(2), Penguin Workshop) Penguin Young Readers Group.

RIDER, ALEX (FICTITIOUS CHARACTER)—FICTION

Anthony, Horowitz. Crocodile Tears, 9 vols. 2010. (Alex Rider Adventure Ser.: 8). (J). 81.75 (978-1-4407-5451-7(9)); 102.75 (978-1-4407-5456-2(X)); 79.75 (978-1-4407-5453-1(5)); 100.75 (978-1-4407-5458-6(6)); 1.25 (978-1-4407-5459-3(4)) Recorded Bks., Inc.

—Crocodile Tears. 2010. (Alex Rider Ser.: 8). lib. bdg. 19.65 (978-0-606-23639-3(2)) Turtleback.

—Point Blanc. 2004. (Alex Rider Ser.: Bk. 2). (SPA.). 264p. 7.95 (978-84-414-1410-5(6)) Editorial Edaf, S.L. ESP. Dist: Spanish Pubs., LLC.

—Scorpia Rising, 9 vols. (J). 2012. 256.75 (978-1-4561-3362-7(4)) 2012. 1.25 (978-1-4640-0577-0(X)) 2012. 90.75 (978-1-4561-3363-4(2)) 2011. 122.75 (978-1-4561-3365-8(9)) 2011. 120.75 (978-1-4561-3367-2(5)) Recorded Bks., Inc.

—Scorpia Rising. 2012. (Alex Rider Ser.: 9). lib. bdg. 19.65 (978-0-606-23638-6(4)) Turtleback.

—Stormbreaker. 2004. (Alex Rider Ser.: Bk. 1). 208p. (J). (gr. 4-7). pap. 38.00 incl. audio (978-0-8072-2277-5(1), Listening Library) Random Hse. Audio Publishing Group.

Horowitz, Anthony. Ark Angel. 2007. (Alex Rider Ser.: 6). (ENG.). 352p. (J). (gr. 5-18). 8.99 (978-0-14-240738-7(0), Puffin Books) Penguin Young Readers Group.

—Crocodile Tears. 2010. (Alex Rider Ser.: 8). (ENG.). 416p. (J). (gr. 5-18). 8.99 (978-0-14-241719-5(X), Puffin Books) Penguin Young Readers Group.

—Eagle Strike. 2006. (Alex Rider Ser.: 4). (ENG.). 368p. (J). (gr. 5-18). 8.99 (978-0-14-240613-7(9), Puffin Books) Penguin Young Readers Group.

—Point Blank. 2006. (Alex Rider Ser.: 2). (ENG.). 320p. (J). (gr. 5-18). 9.99 (978-0-14-240612-0(0), Puffin Books) Penguin Young Readers Group.

—Scorpia. 2006. (Alex Rider Ser.: 5). (ENG.). 416p. (J). (gr. 5-18). pap. 8.99 (978-0-14-240578-9(7), Puffin Books) Penguin Young Readers Group.

—Scorpia Rising. 2012. (Alex Rider Ser.: 9). (ENG.). 432p. (J). (gr. 5-18). 9.99 *(978-0-14-241985-4(0),* Puffin Books) Penguin Young Readers Group.

—Skeleton Key. 2006. (Alex Rider Ser.: 3). (ENG.). 368p. (J). (gr. 5-18). 8.99 *(978-0-14-240614-4(7),* Puffin Books) Penguin Young Readers Group.

—Stormbreaker. 2006. (Alex Rider Ser.: 1). (ENG.). 304p. (J). (gr. 5-18). 9.99 *(978-0-14-240611-3(2),* Puffin Books) Penguin Young Readers Group.

—Stormbreaker: the Graphic Novel. Kanako & Yuzuru, illus. 2006. (Alex Rider Ser.). (ENG.). 144p. (J). (gr. 5-18). pap. 14.99 *(978-0-399-24633-3(9),* Philomel Bks.) Penguin Young Readers Group.

Horowitz, Anthony & Johnston, Antony. Eagle Strike: an Alex Rider Graphic Novel. Kanako & Yuzuru, illus. 2017. (Alex Rider Ser.). (ENG.). 176p. (J). (gr. 4-7). pap. 14.99 *(978-0-7636-9256-8(5))* Candlewick Pr.

RIDING

see Horsemanship

RIEL REBELLION, 1885—FICTION

Bayle, B. J. Battle Cry at Batoche. 2008. (ENG.). 160p. (J). (gr. 7). pap. 11.99 *(978-1-55002-717-4(4))* Dundurn Pr. CAN. Dist: Publishers Group West (PGW).

Scanlan, W. J. Rebellion, 1 vol. 2004. (ENG.). 170p. (J). (gr. 5-7). pap. 9.95 *(978-1-55005-118-6(0),* de733b24-f90b-4a21-8f85-1b07b6f50c90) Fitzhenry & Whiteside, Ltd. CAN. Dist: Firefly Bks., Ltd.

RIFLES

Hemstock, Annie Wendt. Hunting with Rifles, 1 vol. 2014. (Open Season Ser.). (ENG.). 32p. (J). (gr. 4-5). lib. bdg. 28.93 *(978-1-4777-6710-8(X),* 0b337683-ad7d-4822-a378-79fae7af74e6, PowerKids Pr.) Rosen Publishing Group, Inc., The.

Souter, Gerry & Kiland, Taylor Baldwin. Military Rifles: Combat Ready, 1 vol. 2015. (Military Engineering in Action Ser.). (ENG.). 48p. (gr. 6-6). pap. 12.70 *(978-0-7660-7067-7(0),* 9329c181-3d05-4153-85b5-6c3590aa4780); (Illus.). 29.60 *(978-0-7660-6916-9(8),* 11483bf6-1414-4b8a-b260-c11a529f0e15) Enslow Publishing, LLC.

RIGHT (POLITICAL SCIENCE)

see Right and Left (Political Science)

RIGHT AND LEFT (POLITICAL SCIENCE)

see also Conservatism

Cunningham, Jesse G., ed. The McCarthy Hearings. 2003. (At Issue in History Ser.). (Illus.). 144p. (YA). (gr. 7-10). pap. 18.70 *(978-0-7377-1347-3(X),* Greenhaven Pr., Inc.) Cengage Gale.

Doyle, Eamon, ed. Political Extremism in the United States, 1 vol. 2018. (Current Controversies Ser.). (ENG.). 200p. (J). (gr. 10-12). pap. 33.00 *(978-1-5345-0311-3(0),* 314046f5-72c8-4394-8036-1639b077063c, Greenhaven Publishing) Greenhaven Publishing LLC.

RIGHT OF ASSEMBLY

see Assembly, Right of

RIGHT OF PRIVACY

see Privacy, Right of

RIGHT TO DIE

Donnelly, Karen J. Cruzan v. Missouri: The Right to Die, 1 vol. 2003. (Supreme Court Cases Through Primary Sources Ser.). (ENG., Illus.). 64p. (YA). (gr. 5-8). lib. bdg. 37.13 *(978-0-8239-4014-1(4),* 440627a3-2822-4bcd-9cd8-62f407eac8ae) Rosen Publishing Group, Inc., The.

Harris, Nancy. The Right to Die. annot. ed. 2005. (At Issue Ser.). (ENG.). 94p. (YA). (gr. 10-12). pap. 31.80 *(978-0-7377-3439-3(6),* Greenhaven Pr., Inc.) Cengage Gale.

Perl, Lila. Cruzan V. Missouri: The Right to Die, 1 vol. 2008. (Supreme Court Milestones Ser.). (ENG., Illus.). 128p. (YA). (gr. 8-8). lib. bdg. 45.50 *(978-0-7614-2581-6(0),* a2b22d8e-f4bb-4621-87a0-23552342b64f) Cavendish Square Publishing LLC.

Stefoff, Rebecca. The Right to Die, 1 vol. 2009. (Open for Debate Ser.). (ENG.). 144p. (YA). (gr. 8-8). lib. bdg. 45.50 *(978-0-7614-2948-7(4),* bcbd0407-c7ba-4a50-9da6-fe926a35d042) Cavendish Square Publishing LLC.

Thompson, Tamara, ed. The Right to Die, 1 vol. 2014. (At Issue Ser.). (ENG.). 104p. (gr. 10-12). lib. bdg. 41.03 *(978-0-7377-6850-3(9),* 4aa7d9c6-39e0-455f-a508-64f3477e74ce, Greenhaven Publishing) Greenhaven Publishing LLC.

Woodward, John. The Right to Die. annot. ed. 2004. (At Issue Ser.). (ENG.). 94p. (YA). (gr. 10-12). 22.50 *(978-0-7377-3440-9(X),* Greenhaven Pr., Inc.) Cengage Gale.

RIGHT TO WORK

see Discrimination in Employment

RIGHTS, CIVIL

see Civil Rights

RIIS, JACOB A. (JACOB AUGUST), 1849-1914—FICTION

Kroll, Steven. Sweet America: An Immigrant's Story. 2004. 172p. (J). lib. bdg. 16.92 *(978-1-4242-0773-2(8))* Fitzgerald Bks.

RINGLING BROTHERS

Apps, Jerry. Tents, Tigers & the Ringling Brothers. 2006. (Badger Biographies Ser.). (ENG., Illus.). 128p. (J). (gr. 3-7). per. 12.95 *(978-0-87020-374-9(6))* Wisconsin Historical Society.

RIO DE JANEIRO (BRAZIL)

Candlewick Press. Rio de Janeiro: a 3D Keepsake Cityscape. Krauss, Trisha, illus. 2014. (Panorama Pops Ser.). (ENG.). 30p. (J). (gr. k-4). 8.99 *(978-0-7636-7029-0(4))* Candlewick Pr.

Morrison, Marion. Rio de Janeiro, 1 vol. 2004. (Great Cities of the World Ser.). (ENG., Illus.). 48p. (gr. 5-8). lib. bdg. 33.67 *(978-0-8368-5031-4(9),* b55c7c82-7868-4878-a747-fd9f42c255f0, Gareth Stevens Secondary Library) Stevens, Gareth Publishing LLLP.

Scoones, Simon. Rio de Janeiro. 2006. (ENG., Illus.). 61p. (gr. 5-8). 30.00 *(978-0-7910-8857-9(X),* P114468, Facts On File) Infobase Holdings, Inc.

RIO GRANDE RIVER AND VALLEY

Fahey, Kathleen. The Rio Grande River, 1 vol. 2003. (Rivers of North America Ser.). (ENG., Illus.). 32p. (gr. 3-5). lib. bdg. 28.67 *(978-0-8368-3760-5(6),* f228b6f4-75ae-4965-9a63-247809bfe128, Gareth Stevens Learning Library) Stevens, Gareth Publishing LLLP.

Marsico, Katie. The Rio Grande. 2013. (Explorer Library: Social Studies Explorer Ser.). (ENG.). 32p. (gr. 4-8). (J). pap. 14.21 *(978-1-62431-036-2(2),* 202501); (Illus.). 32.07 *(978-1-62431-012-6(5),* 202499) Cherry Lake Publishing.

RIOTS

Archer, Jules. Rage in the Streets: A History of American Riots. 2016. (Jules Archer History for Young Readers Ser.). (ENG., Illus.). 200p. (J). (gr. 6-6). 16.99 *(978-1-63450-186-6(1),* Sky Pony Pr.) Skyhorse Publishing Co., Inc.

Arevalo, Luis Paquime. L. A.'s Riots. 2004. (YA). per. 12.99 *(978-0-9748598-0-4(X))* L. A. Eng Bks.

Brindell Fradin, Dennis. The Stamp Act Of 1765, 1 vol. 2010. (Turning Points in U. S. History Ser.). (ENG., Illus.). 48p. (gr. 4-4). 34.07 *(978-0-7614-4260-8(X),* ebda7934-06c6-4918-bac9-93a066b6efcd) Cavendish Square Publishing LLC.

Gerdes, Louise I., ed. The 1992 Los Angeles Riots, 1 vol. 2014. (Perspectives on Modern World History Ser.). (ENG., Illus.). 200p. (gr. 10-12). lib. bdg. 49.43 *(978-0-7377-7008-7(2),* a74606ef-1de6-48db-b4a3-295274e02a0d, Greenhaven Publishing) Greenhaven Publishing LLC.

McGowen, Tom. The 1968 Democratic Convention. 2003. (Cornerstones of Freedom Ser.). (ENG., Illus.). 48p. (YA). (gr. 4-7). 26.00 *(978-0-516-24220-0(2))* Scholastic Library Publishing.

Stoltman, Joan. Protests & Riots That Changed America, 1 vol. 2018. (American History Ser.). (ENG.). 104p. (gr. 7-7). 41.03 *(978-1-5345-6415-2(2),* 301966b9-2510-40cc-acec-e9abd325953f, Lucent Pr.) Greenhaven Publishing LLC.

Wilson, Sean Michael & Dickson, Benjamin. Fight the Power! A Visual History of Protest among the English Speaking Peoples. Emerson, Hunt et al, illus. 2013. (ENG.). 192p. pap. 19.95 *(978-1-60980-492-3(9))* Seven Stories Pr.

RIOTS—FICTION

Alkaf, Hanna. The Weight of Our Sky. 2019. (ENG., Illus.). 288p. (YA). (gr. 7). 19.99 *(978-1-5344-2608-5(6),* Salaam Reads) Simon & Schuster Bks. For Young Readers.

English, Karen. It All Comes down to This. 2017. (ENG.). 368p. (J). (gr. 5-7). 16.99 *(978-0-544-83957-1(9),* 1646119, Clarion Bks.) HarperCollins Pubs.

Henty, George. At Agincourt: A Tale of the White Hoods of Paris. 2011. 332p. pap. 19.95 *(978-1-61179-111-2(1))* Fireship Pr.

Latham, Jennifer. Dreamland Burning. 2018.Tr. of s. (ENG.). 400p. (YA). (gr. 9-17). pap. 11.99 *(978-0-316-38490-2(9))* Little, Brown Bks. for Young Readers.

Myers, Anna. Tulsa Burning. 2004. (Illus.). 184p. (J). (gr. 3-7). 16.95 *(978-0-8027-8829-0(7))* Walker & Co.

Ostlere, Cathy. Karma: First Edition. 2012. (ENG.). 544p. (YA). (gr. 7-18). 9.99 *(978-1-59514-384-6(X),* Razorbill) Penguin Young Readers Group.

Salkey, Andrew. Riot, 1 vol. 2011. (Caribbean Modern Classics Ser.). (ENG., Illus.). 176p. (J). (gr. 7). pap. 14.95 *(978-1-84523-181-1(3))* Peepal Tree Pr., Ltd. GBR. Dist: Independent Pubs. Group.

Tullson, Diane. Riot Act, 1 vol. 2012. (Orca Soundings Ser.). (ENG.). 128p. (YA). (gr. 8-12). pap. 9.95 *(978-1-4598-0139-4(3))* Orca Bk. Pubs. USA.

RITES AND CEREMONIES

see also Baptism; Fasts and Feasts; Funeral Rites and Ceremonies; Manners and Customs; Marriage Customs and Rites

also classes of people and ethnic groups with the subdivision Rites and Ceremonies, e.g. Jews—Rites and Ceremonies

Barr, J. Bennett. Saying Goodbye. 2009. 20p. pap. 10.49 *(978-1-4490-0000-4(2))* AuthorHouse.

Beker, Jeanne. The Big Night Out. Dion, Nathalie, illus. 2005. 80p. (J). (gr. 4-7). pap. 15.95 *(978-0-88776-719-7(2),* Tundra Bks.) Tundra Bks. CAN. Dist: Penguin Random Hse. LLC.

Harris, Carol & Brown, Mike. Ceremonial Costumes. 2004. (Twentieth-Century Developments in Fashion & Costume Ser.). (Illus.). 64p. (YA). (gr. 7-18). lib. bdg. 19.95 *(978-1-59084-424-3(6))* Mason Crest.

Haywood, John. Through the Ages: Gods, Beliefs & Ceremonies. 2008. (Illus.). 64p. (J). (gr. 4-7). pap. 12.99 *(978-1-84476-601-7(2))* Anness Publishing GBR. Dist: National Bk. Network.

Jenkins, Diana R. Goodness Graces! Ten Short Stories about the Sacraments. 2010. (J). (gr. 3-6). pap. 7.95 *(978-0-8198-3110-1(7))* Pauline Bks. & Media.

MacDonald, Fiona. The Amazing History of Mummies & Tombs: Uncover the Secrets of the Egyptian Pyramids & Other Ancient Burial Sites, Shown in over 350 Exciting Pictures. 2016. (Illus.). 64p. (J). (gr. -1-12). 12.99 *(978-1-86147-735-4(X),* Armadillo) Anness Publishing GBR. Dist: National Bk. Network.

Mahon, Elaine. Preparing for First Reconciliation: A Guide for Families. 2013. (ENG., Illus.). 32p. (J). pap. 8.95 *(978-1-84730-400-1(1))* Veritas Pubns. IRL. Dist: Casemate Pubs. & Bk. Distributors, LLC.

McGahey, Suzanne. Winter Guard. 2009. (Team Spirit! Ser.). 64p. (gr. 6-6). 53.00 *(978-1-60853-274-2(7))* Rosen Publishing Group, Inc., The.

Montillo, Roseanne. Halloween & Commemorations of the Dead. 2009. (ENG., Illus.). 104p. (gr. 5-8). 40.00 *(978-1-60413-097-3(0),* P163114, Facts On File) Infobase Holdings, Inc.

Moore Niver, Heather. Executions & Sacrifices. 2014. (Digging up the Dead Ser.). 32p. (J). (gr. 4-6). pap. 63.00 *(978-1-4824-1230-7(6))* Stevens, Gareth Publishing LLLP.

Murphy, Charles. Celebrations Around the World. 2017. (Adventures in Culture Ser.). (ENG.). 24p. (J). (gr. -1-2). 19.95 *(978-1-5311-8870-2(2))* Perfection Learning Corp.

—Celebrations Around the World, 1 vol. 2016. (Adventures in Culture Ser.). (ENG., Illus.). 24p. (J). (gr. 1-2). pap. 9.15 *(978-1-4824-5575-5(7),* dc2fd717-a633-4afb-97b3-589752ed88dc) Stevens, Gareth Publishing LLLP.

Myers, Jack & Jack Myers Ministries. Flowing in the Anointing: Understanding the Anointing of God. 2004. 90p. pap. 7.95 *(978-0-9720928-1-4(1))* Myers, Jack Ministries, Inc.

Onyefulu, Ifeoma. Welcome Dede! An African Naming Ceremony. 2004. (Illus.). 32p. (J). *(978-1-84507-267-4(7))* ReiseArt Buchhandlung GmbH.

—Your Name is Dede: An African Baby's Naming Ceremony. 2003. (ENG., Illus.). 32p. (J). *(978-0-7112-1938-0(9))* ReiseArt Buchhandlung GmbH.

Post, John R., compiled by. NPKA Book of Biotar Bk. 1: Catalog of Biots & Rituals of Wotanism. num. ed. 2003. (Illus.). 421p. 35.00 *(978-0-9749416-0-8(3))* Himminbjorg Publishing, Inc.

Senker, Cath. Christianity: Signs, Symbols, Stories, 1 vol. 2009. (Religious Signs, Symbols, & Stories Ser.). (ENG., Illus.). 32p. (J). (gr. 3-3). pap. 11.00 *(978-1-4358-3045-5(8),* 3a259bc4-ddcc-4c0c-b85b-92b1e0787dad); lib. bdg. 28.93 *(978-1-4358-3037-0(7),* 2fc509a0-72eb-4c1f-bc82-4ab903b4dfd3) Rosen Publishing Group, Inc., The. (PowerKids Pr.).

Wood, Alix. Human Sacrifice, 1 vol. Wood, Alix, illus. 2013. (Why'd They Do That? Strange Customs of the Past Ser.). (Illus.). 32p. (J). (gr. 4-5). (ENG.). pap. 11.50 *(978-1-4339-9585-9(9),* 119d8337-4b39-4d26-a607-feceaa213bc5); (ENG., lib. bdg. 29.27 *(978-1-4339-9584-2(0),* 85628a83-85b7-4e1b-bda0-e5e00918aa94); pap. 63.00 *(978-1-4339-9586-6(7))* Stevens, Gareth Publishing LLLP.

World Book, Inc. Staff, contrib. by. Birth & Growing up Celebrations. 2009. (Illus.). 46p. (J). *(978-0-7166-5044-7(4))* World Bk., Inc.

—Cumulative Glossary & Index. 46p. (J). 2009. *(978-0-7166-5051-5(7))* 2003. *(978-0-7166-5017-1(7))* World Bk., Inc.

—Everyday Celebrations & Rituals. (Illus.). 46p. (J). 2009. *(978-0-7166-5050-8(9))* 2003. *(978-0-7166-5016-4(9))* World Bk., Inc.

RITUAL

see Rites and Ceremonies

RIVERA, DIEGO, 1886-1957

Bankston, John. Diego Rivera. 2003. (Latinos in American History Ser.). (Illus.). 56p. (J). (gr. 4-8). lib. bdg. 29.95 *(978-1-58415-208-8(7))* Mitchell Lane Pubs.

Bernier-Grand, Carmen T. Diego: Bigger Than Life, 0 vols. Diaz, David, illus. 2012. (ENG.). 64p. (YA). (gr. 9-12). 18.99 *(978-0-7614-5383-3(0),* 9780761453833, Two Lions) Amazon Publishing.

Foard, Sheila Wood. Diego Rivera. 2nd rev. ed. 2010. (Great Hispanic Heritage Ser.). (Illus.). 120p. (gr. 6-12). 35.00 *(978-1-60413-845-0(9),* Facts On File) Infobase Holdings, Inc.

Hillstrom, Kevin. Diego Rivera: Muralist, 1 vol. 2008. (Twentieth Century's Most Influential Hispanics Ser.). (ENG., Illus.). 104p. (gr. 7-10). 41.03 *(978-1-4205-0018-9(X),* 212725d4-e359-4aa5-ae66-34b29c40bd52, Lucent Pr.) Greenhaven Publishing LLC.

Jauregui, Diego. Libros de Arte para Ninos: Diego Rivera.Tr. of Art Books for Children: Diego Rivera. (SPA., Illus.). 73p. (YA). (gr. 5-8). pap. *(978-968-494-026-0(2))* Centro de Informacion y Desarrollo de la Comunicacion y la Literatura.

Marín, Guadalupe Rivera. My Papá Diego & Me (Mi Papa Diego y Yo) Memories of My Father & His Art (Recuerdos de Mi Padre y Su Arte) Rivera, Diego, illus. 2013. (SPA & ENG.). 32p. (J). (gr. k-5). 18.95 *(978-0-89239-228-5(2))* Lee & Low Bks., Inc.

Marsh, Carole. Diego Rivera: Acclaimed Mural Painter: Acclaimed Mural Painter. 2003. 12p. (gr. k-4). 2.95 *(978-0-635-02137-3(4))* Gallopade International.

Reef, Catherine. Frida & Diego: Art, Love, Life. 2014. (ENG., Illus.). 176p. (YA). (gr. 7-12). 18.99 *(978-0-547-82184-9(0),* 1497178, Clarion Bks.) HarperCollins Pubs.

Rubin, Susan Goldman. Diego Rivera: An Artist for the People. 2013. (ENG., Illus.). 56p. (J). (gr. 3-7). 22.95 *(978-0-8109-8411-0(3),* 666701, Abrams Bks. for Young Readers) Abrams, Inc.

Sabbeth, Carol. Frida Kahlo & Diego Rivera: Their Lives & Ideas, 24 Activities. 2005. (For Kids Ser.: 18). (ENG., Illus.). 160p. (J). (gr. 4). pap. 17.95 *(978-1-55652-569-8(9),* 1241061) Chicago Review Pr., Inc.

RIVERS

see also Dams; Floods; Hydraulic Engineering; Water—Pollution; Water Power

also names of rivers

Allman, Barbara. Lakes & Rivers, 1 vol. 2019. (Investigate Earth Science Ser.). (ENG.). 24p. (gr. 2-2). pap. 10.95 *(978-1-9785-0868-2(9),* 83b5dbc1-2ea3-426c-89a8-2a2f617c4718) Enslow Publishing, LLC.

Aloian, Molly. The Yangtze: China's Majestic River, 1 vol. 2010. (Rivers Around the World Ser.). (ENG., Illus.). 32p. (J). (gr. 5-8). pap. *(978-0-7787-7472-3(4));* lib. bdg. *(978-0-7787-7449-5(X))* Crabtree Publishing Co.

Barnes, J. Lou. 101 Facts about Rivers, 1 vol. 2003. (101 Facts about Our World Ser.). (ENG., Illus.). 32p. (gr. 2-4). lib. bdg. 28.67 *(978-0-8368-3711-7(8),* 8dea08c4-9ae8-4270-a46e-718aad8211b7, Gareth Stevens Learning Library) Stevens, Gareth Publishing LLLP.

Bellamy, David & Dow, Jill. Our Changing World: The River. 2004. (Illus.). 32p. (J). pap. *(978-1-84507-218-6(9))* ReiseArt Buchhandlung GmbH.

Benker, Kaily. Great U. S. Rivers, 1 vol. 2013. (Rosen Readers Ser.). (ENG.). 24p. (J). (gr. 3-3). pap. 8.25 *(978-1-4777-2562-7(8),* 9cdea292-f8cc-401f-bfad-89181c1c682d); pap. 49.50 *(978-1-4777-2563-4(6))* Rosen Publishing Group, Inc., The. (Rosen Classroom).

Best, Arthur. Rivers, 1 vol. 2017. (Our World of Water Ser.). (ENG.). 24p. (gr. 1-1). pap. 9.22 *(978-1-5026-3098-8(2),* 2c4a7412-de7d-4b02-be22-fcc2b45baf22) Cavendish Square Publishing LLC.

Best, B. J. How Are Rivers Formed?, 1 vol. 2017. (Nature's Formations Ser.). (ENG., Illus.). 24p. (gr. 1-1). pap. 9.22 *(978-1-5026-2541-0(5),* 60bd7761-db3c-4529-aa67-7cec8dbe8090) Cavendish Square Publishing LLC.

Brocker, Susan. Rivers of the World, 1 vol. 2009. (Our Planet Ser.). (ENG.). 32p. (YA). (gr. 4-4). lib. bdg. 28.93 *(978-1-4358-2816-2(X),* 6ab68fc7-4e87-48e9-bf56-86dbac02ef75) Rosen Publishing Group, Inc., The.

Bulletpoints Oceans & Rivers. 2005. (Illus.). (J). per. 4.99 *(978-1-933581-01-9(8))* Byeway Bks.

La Defensa de los Ríos y Lagos. (Colección Biblioteca Juvenil de Ecología). (SPA., Illus.). (YA). (gr. 5-8). pap. *(978-958-04-2672-1(4),* 80426721) Norma S.A. COL. Dist: Lectorum Pubns., Inc.

Dorling Kindersley Publishing Staff. Rivers & Lakes. 2003. (DK Eye Wonder Ser.). (ENG., Illus.). 48p. (J). (gr. 3-6). lib. bdg. 22.44 *(978-0-7894-9047-6(1))* Dorling Kindersley Publishing, Inc.

Duhig, Holly. Life by the River. 2019. (Human Habitats Ser.). (ENG.). 24p. (J). (gr. 2-2). pap. *(978-0-7787-6485-4(0),* a8f2eb09-69ca-4ab3-bd0c-fe0165d11d87); lib. bdg. *(978-0-7787-6479-3(6),* a4976fad-7133-40a3-8454-036027cf1512) Crabtree Publishing Co.

Early Macken, JoAnn. Ríos (Rivers), 1 vol. 2005. (¿Conoces la Tierra? Geografía Del Mundo (Where on Earth? World Geography) Ser.). (SPA., Illus.). 24p. (gr. 2-4). pap. 9.15 *(978-0-8368-6554-7(5),* 47661db9-c712-4a45-ada4-33a300e998be); lib. bdg. 24.67 *(978-0-8368-6547-9(2),* 13d4c3da-0fb1-4f3f-8fb6-e94f9eb09781) Stevens, Gareth Publishing LLLP. (Weekly Reader Leveled Readers).

—Rivers, 1 vol. 2005. (Water Habitats Ser.). (ENG., Illus.). 24p. (gr. k-2). pap. 9.15 *(978-0-8368-4893-9(4),* 19db1ca6-591e-49cb-bf14-4962fd0f312f); (gr. k-2). lib. bdg. 24.67 *(978-0-8368-4886-1(1),* d75fc27f-8574-425e-b301-287e1b69bd54); (gr. 2-4). pap. 9.15 *(978-0-8368-6404-5(2),* 231c2bc7-444c-4618-9bc3-bfc5cb7a8361) Stevens, Gareth Publishing LLLP. (Weekly Reader Leveled Readers).

—Rivers / Ríos, 1 vol. 2005. (Water Habitats / Hábitats Acuáticos Ser.). 24p. (gr. k-2). (SPA & ENG.). pap. 9.15 *(978-0-8368-6038-2(1),* e1ff114b5-579a-44ca-8032-72b7bf52fd1e); (ENG & SPA., Illus.). lib. bdg. 24.67 *(978-0-8368-6031-3(4),* a9139fda-89f8-4803-a14a-99055cbbb978) Stevens, Gareth Publishing LLLP. (Weekly Reader Leveled Readers).

Frisch, Aaron. Rivers. 2008. (Our World Ser.). (Illus.). 24p. (J). (gr. -1-3). lib. bdg. 24.25 *(978-1-58341-573-3(4),* Creative Education) Creative Co., The.

Gilpin, Daniel. The Snake River, 1 vol. 2003. (Rivers of North America Ser.). (ENG., Illus.). 32p. (gr. 3-5). lib. bdg. 28.67 *(978-0-8368-3761-2(4),* 745f28b3-d49c-4634-aafa-d380bcd7cb57, Gareth Stevens Learning Library) Stevens, Gareth Publishing LLLP.

Goes, Peter. Rivers: A Visual History from River to Sea. Goes, Peter, illus. 2018. (ENG., Illus.). 80p. (J). (gr. 2-6). 29.99 *(978-1-77657-216-8(5),* 64f0c867-7360-4300-a3f8-bccba3ac4c14) Gecko Pr. NZL. Dist: Lerner Publishing Group.

Gray, Leon. The Missouri River, 1 vol. 2003. (Rivers of North America Ser.). (ENG., Illus.). 32p. (gr. 3-5). lib. bdg. 28.67 *(978-0-8368-3758-2(4),* 530384e2-6b95-4e43-bd0f-91626b15463c, Gareth Stevens Learning Library) Stevens, Gareth Publishing LLLP.

—Rivers, 1 vol. 2011. (Geography Wise Ser.). (ENG., Illus.). 32p. (YA). (gr. 2-3). lib. bdg. 30.27 *(978-1-4488-3282-8(9),* 1d85297f-3008-46a4-b5b9-84ccfe071697) Rosen Publishing Group, Inc., The.

—Rivers & Lakes. 2015. (Amazing Biomes Ser.). (ENG., Illus.). 32p. (J). (gr. 3-6). 31.35 *(978-1-78121-244-8(9),* 16392) Brown Bear Bks.

Green, Emily K. Rivers. 2006. (Learning about the Earth Ser.). (ENG., Illus.). 24p. (J). (gr. k-3). lib. bdg. 26.95 *(978-1-60014-040-2(8),* Blastoff! Readers) Bellwether Media.

—Rivers. 2011. (Blastoff! Readers Ser.). 24p. (J). pap. 5.95 *(978-0-531-26036-4(4),* Children's Pr.) Scholastic Library Publishing.

Green, Jen. Mighty Rivers. 2009. (Amazing Planet Earth Ser.). 32p. (gr. 4-7). 31.35 *(978-1-59920-371-3(5))* Black Rabbit Bks.

Green, Mary. Rivers in Action. 2004. (Earth's Changing Landscape Ser.). (Illus.). 46p. (YA). (gr. 7-12). lib. bdg. 28.50 *(978-1-58340-477-5(5))* Black Rabbit Bks.

Group/McGraw-Hill, Wright. Rivers: From Beginning to End, 6 vols. (Book2WebTM Ser.). (gr. 4-8). 36.50 *(978-0-322-04441-8(3))* Wright Group/McGraw-Hill.

—Rivers: Level H, 6 vols. (Take Twostm Ser.). 16p. 29.95 *(978-0-322-08957-0(3))* Wright Group/McGraw-Hill.

Head, Honor. Poisoned Rivers & Lakes, 1 vol. 2018. (Totally Toxic Ser.). (ENG.). 48p. (gr. 4-5). pap. 15.05 *(978-1-5382-3500-3(5),* ab036dd4-0190-431c-a938-f8e84f087c3f) Stevens, Gareth Publishing LLLP.

Hegarty, Patricia. The River. Clulow, Hanako, illus. 2016. (J). 12.99 *(978-1-61067-468-3(5))* Kane Miller.

Hewitt, Sally. Project Geography - Rivers. 2010. (Starting Geography Ser.). 32p. (J). (gr. 2-5). 28.50 *(978-1-60753-128-9(3))* Amicus Learning.

—Project Geography - Rivers. 2012. (Map Smart Ser.). (Illus.). 32p. (gr. 2-6). lib. bdg. 27.10 *(978-1-59920-414-7(2))* Black Rabbit Bks.

Howell, Izzi. River & Coast Geo Facts. 2018. (Geo Facts Ser.). (Illus.). 32p. (J). (gr. 5-5). *(978-0-7787-4393-4(4))* Crabtree Publishing Co.

Jackson, Tom. The Arkansas River, 1 vol. 2003. (Rivers of North America Ser.). (ENG., Illus.). 32p. (gr. 3-5). lib. bdg. 28.67 *(978-0-8368-3752-0(5),* ffb25ba9-1f59-448a-88ae-3916a1022c9a, Gareth Stevens Learning Library) Stevens, Gareth Publishing LLLP.

—The Ohio River, 1 vol. 2003. (Rivers of North America Ser.). (ENG., Illus.). 32p. (gr. 3-5). lib. bdg. 28.67 *(978-0-8368-3759-9(2),* 0fdce26e-5f59-4390-b73b-95cf2c7051c3, Gareth Stevens Learning Library) Stevens, Gareth Publishing LLLP.

Johnson, Rebecca L. A Journey into a River. Saroff, Phyllis V., illus. 2004. (Biomes of North America Ser.). (J). pap. 8.95

(978-0-8225-2044-3(3)); 48p. (gr. 3-6). 23.93 *(978-1-57505-595-4(3))* Lerner Publishing Group.

Junyk, Myra. The 10 Mightiest Rivers. 2008. (J). 14.99 *(978-1-55448-519-2(3))* Scholastic Library Publishing.

Kalman, Bobbie. Earth's Rivers, 1 vol. 2008. (Looking at Earth Ser.). (ENG., Illus.). 32p. (J). (gr. 1-4). pap. *(978-0-7787-3218-1(5))*; lib. bdg. *(978-0-7787-3208-2(8))* Crabtree Publishing Co.

—Los Ríos de la Tierra. 2009. (SPA.). 32p. (J). *(978-0-7787-8239-1(5))*; pap. *(978-0-7787-8256-8(5))* Crabtree Publishing Co.

—Where on Earth Are Rivers? 2014. (Explore the Continents Ser.). (ENG., Illus.). 32p. (J). (gr. 2-3). *(978-0-7787-0502-4(1))* Crabtree Publishing Co.

Keating, Brian. Amazing Animal Adventures in Rivers, 1 vol. 2006. (Going Wild Ser.). (ENG., Illus.). 48p. (J). (gr. 4-7). pap. 5.95 *(978-1-894856-89-8(9)*, 9ee259c3-4018-4b39-8cb7-8f75286e12f1) Fifth Hse. Pubs. CAN. Dist: Firefly Bks., Ltd.

Looye, Juliette, text. I Live near a River. 2004. (Illus.). 16p. (J). pap. *(978-0-7367-1932-2(6))* Zaner-Bloser, Inc.

MacDonald, Margaret. Rivers of the World. 2011. (Learn-Abouts Ser.). (Illus.). 16p. (J). pap. 7.95 *(978-1-59920-646-2(3))* Black Rabbit Bks.

Make It Work Geography, 4 vol. set. 2003. (gr. 4-8). 59.00 *(978-0-7166-5124-6(6))* World Bk., Inc.

Marsico, Katie. The Missouri River. 2013. (Explorer Library: Social Studies Explorer Ser.). (ENG.). 32p. (gr. 4-8). (J). pap. 14.21 *(978-1-62431-034-8(6)*, 202493); (Illus.). 32.07 *(978-1-62431-010-2(9)*, 202491) Cherry Lake Publishing.

McKenzie, Precious. Waterfalls. 2017. (Mother Nature Ser.). (ENG.). 24p. (gr. k-2). pap. 9.95 *(978-1-68342-417-8(4)*, 9781683424178) Rourke Educational Media.

McNeese, Tim, ed. Rivers in World History. 2005. (Rivers in World History Ser.). (Illus.). 120p. (C). (gr. 9-13). 195.00 *(978-0-7910-8473-1(6)*, Facts On File) Infobase Holdings, Inc.

Michele, Tracey. The Life of a River. 2011. (Learn-Abouts Ser.). (Illus.). 16p. (J). pap. 9.95 *(978-1-59920-609-7(9))* Palgrave Macmillan.

Minden, Cecilia. The World Around Us: Rivers. 2010. (21st Century Basic Skills Library: the World Around Us Ser.). (ENG., Illus.). 24p. (gr. k-3). lib. bdg. 26.35 *(978-1-60279-861-8(3)*, 200588) Cherry Lake Publishing.

Morley, Catherine Weyerhaeuser. Where Do Rivers Go, Momma? 2016. (Illus.). (J). *(978-0-87842-656-0(6))* Mountain Pr. Publishing Co., Inc.

Nadeau, Isaac. Water in Rivers & Lakes. 2009. (Water Cycle Ser.). 24p. (gr. 4-4). 42.50 *(978-1-60854-271-0(8)*, PowerKids Pr.) Rosen Publishing Group, Inc., The.

Nardo, Don. Early River Civilizations. 2011. (World History Ser.). (Illus.). 112p. (J). 28.95 *(978-1-59935-140-7(4))* Reynolds, Morgan Inc.

National Geographic Learning. Reading Expeditions (Social Studies: the Land Around Us): Rivers & Lakes. 2007. (Rise & Shine Ser.). (ENG., Illus.). 32p. (J). pap. 18.95 *(978-0-7922-4561-2(X))* CENGAGE Learning.

Nemeth, Jason D. Rivers, Lakes, & Oceans, 1 vol. 2012. (Our Changing Earth Ser.). (ENG.). 24p. (J). (gr. 2-3). pap. 9.25 *(978-1-4488-6300-6(7)*, ce8cfc52-b506-4397-90b6-e5ca09c737b4, PowerKids Pr.); lib. bdg. 26.27 *(978-1-4488-6171-2(3)*, 3cd615a4-4e19-4b57-bc6c-a637bda1fb22) Rosen Publishing Group, Inc., The.

Nestor, John. Rivers. 2009. (21st Century Skills Library: Real World Math Ser.). (ENG.). 32p. (gr. 4-8). lib. bdg. 32.07 *(978-1-60279-497-9(9)*, 200319) Cherry Lake Publishing.

Ostopowich, Melanie. Oceans, Lakes, & Rivers. 2015. (Illus.). 24p. (J). *(978-1-5105-0052-5(9))* SmartBook Media, Inc.

—Oceans, Lakes, & Rivers. 2010. (Water Science Ser.). (Illus.). 24p. (gr. 3-5). (J). pap. 11.95 *(978-1-61690-007-6(5))*; (YA). lib. bdg. 25.70 *(978-1-61690-001-4(6))* Weigl Pubs., Inc.

—Oceans, Rivers, & Lakes. 2005. (Science Matters Ser.). (Illus.). 24p. (J). (gr. 3-7). lib. bdg. 24.45 *(978-1-59036-304-1(3))* Weigl Pubs., Inc.

Oxlade, Chris. Rivers & Lakes, 1 vol. 2003. (Science Files: Earth Ser.). (ENG., Illus.). 32p. (gr. 3-5). lib. bdg. 28.67 *(978-0-8368-3571-7(9)*, 794d79d3-7b15-47ec-afd0-24becb8b5623) Stevens, Gareth Publishing LLLP.

Pollard, Michael. Great Rivers of Britain: The Clyde, Mersey, Severn, Tees, Thames, Trent. (Illus.). 45p. *(978-0-237-51829-5(5))* Evans Brothers, Ltd.

—Rivers of Britain & Ireland: The Avon, Yorkshire Ouse, Tyne, Wye, Forth, Liffey, Lagan. (Illus.). 46p. (J). *(978-0-237-51805-9(8))* Evans Brothers, Ltd.

Puncel, Maria. El Prado del Tio Pedro.Tr. of Uncle Peter's Pasture. (SPA.). 32p. (J). 12.95 *(978-84-348-1226-0(6))* SM Ediciones ESP. Dist: AIMS International Bks., Inc.

Pyers, Greg. Biodiversity of Rivers, 1 vol. 2012. (Biodiversity Ser.). (ENG.). 32p. (gr. 4-4). 31.21 *(978-1-60870-531-3(5)*, d20c2886-2e1f-4892-87ff-72189c16a0be) Cavendish Square Publishing LLC.

Rivers Lakes & Oceans. 2009. (ENG.). 112p. (gr. 5-9). 35.00 *(978-0-7910-9797-7(8)*, P159148, Facts On File) Infobase Holdings, Inc.

Rivers of North America, 14 vols. Incl. Arkansas River. Jackson, Tom. lib. bdg. 28.67 *(978-0-8368-3752-0(5)*, ffb25ba9-1f59-448a-88ae-3916a1022c9a); Columbia River. Jackson, Tom. lib. bdg. 28.67 *(978-0-8368-3754-4(1)*, a183ad6d-d6d4-429b-99bc-8941c637c1e6); Hudson River. Wood, Ira. lib. bdg. 28.67 *(978-0-8368-3755-1(X)*, 86f24afd-76d8-439d-b3fe-7a9279de0f29); Mississippi River. Green, Jen. lib. bdg. 28.67 *(978-0-8368-3757-5(6)*, a37c4e39-d8d7-4725-89ee-2f0ef17d0341); Missouri River. Gray, Leon. lib. bdg. 28.67 *(978-0-8368-3758-2(4)*, 530384e2-6b95-4e43-bd0f-91626b15463c); Ohio River. Jackson, Tom. lib. bdg. 28.67 *(978-0-8368-3759-9(2)*, 0fdce26e-5f59-4390-b73b-95cf2c7051c3); Rio Grande River. Fahey, Kathleen. lib. bdg. 28.67 *(978-0-8368-3760-5(6)*, f228b6f4-75ae-4965-9a63-247809bfe128); Snake River. Gilpin, Daniel. lib. bdg. 28.67 *(978-0-8368-3761-2(4)*, 745f28b3-d49c-4634-aafa-d380bcd7cb57); St. Lawrence River. Cooke, Tim. lib. bdg. 28.67 *(978-0-8368-3762-9(2)*, a9fc3c83-4471-404c-b8d7-7b07af20fc52); (gr. 3-5). (Rivers of North America Ser.). (ENG., Illus.). 32p. 2003. Set lib. bdg. 200.69 *(978-0-8368-3751-3(7)*, 26d1890d-3907-4a65-a45d-5f9f3babf068, Gareth Stevens Learning Library) Stevens, Gareth Publishing LLLP.

Romaine, Claire. Rivers, 1 vol. 2017. (Our Exciting Earth! Ser.). (ENG.). 24p. (J). (gr. k-k). pap. 9.15 *(978-1-5382-0981-3(0)*, ba86d404-c3ca-4dbc-bef5-266f4bd56304) Stevens, Gareth Publishing LLLP.

Rose, Simon. Estuaries. 2017. (J). *(978-1-5105-2171-1(2))* SmartBook Media, Inc.

Ross, Mandy. Rivers. 2004. (Geography Fact Files Ser.). (J). lib. bdg. 28.50 *(978-1-58340-429-4(5))* Black Rabbit Bks.

Siegel, Rebecca. Rivers & Streams! With 25 Science Projects for Kids. Casteel, Tom, illus. 2018. (Explore Your World Ser.). (ENG.). 96p. (J). (gr. 3-4). 19.95 *(978-1-61930-702-5(2)*, 9a151451-487e-4777-8240-a5085ecc0dbc) Nomad Pr.

Sill, Cathryn. About Habitats: Rivers & Streams, 1 vol. Sill, John, illus. 2019. (About Habitats Ser.: 9). 48p. (J). (gr. -1-2). 16.95 *(978-1-68263-091-4(9))* Peachtree Publishing Co. Inc.

Smith, Farhanna. Rivers of the United States. 2013. (InfoMax Readers Ser.). (ENG.). 24p. (J). (gr. 3-4). pap. 49.50 *(978-1-4777-2627-3(6))*; (Illus.). pap. 8.25 *(978-1-4777-2626-6(8)*, 49bcab6d-ad93-4214-8703-0cfc2b4536e8) Rosen Publishing Group, Inc., The. (Rosen Classroom).

Spilsbury, Louise. Surviving the River, 1 vol. 2016. (Sole Survivor Ser.). (ENG.). 48p. (gr. 4-5). pap. 15.05 *(978-1-4824-5075-0(5)*, 15c0e9e1-2ae9-4fc5-a4ce-814cde8c1948) Stevens, Gareth Publishing LLLP.

Spilsbury, Richard & Spilsbury, Louise. At Home in Rivers & Lakes, 1 vol., 1. 2015. (Home in the Biome Ser.). (ENG.). 32p. (J). (gr. 3-4). pap. 11.00 *(978-1-5081-4556-1(3)*, c2296a8c-1aa9-4507-960a-a484d71a29b1, PowerKids Pr.) Rosen Publishing Group, Inc., The.

Stradling, Jan. Ponds & Rivers: Level I, 6 vols. (First Explorers Ser.). 24p. (gr. 1-2). 29.95 *(978-0-7699-1451-0(9))* Shortland Pubns. (U. S. A.) Inc.

Sullivan, Laura. 24 Hours in an Estuary, 1 vol. 2017. (Day in an Ecosystem Ser.). (ENG.). 48p. (J). (gr. 4-4). 33.07 *(978-1-5026-2486-4(9)*, bdac792c-3c26-4c6a-b74b-d4dedb00f04d) Cavendish Square Publishing LLC.

Sundance/Newbridge LLC Staff. Follow the River. 2007. (Early Science Ser.). (gr. k-3). 18.95 *(978-1-4007-6558-4(7))*; pap. 6.10 *(978-1-4007-6554-6(4))* Sundance/Newbridge Educational Publishing.

Sweeney, Alyse. Rivers. 2010. (Natural Wonders Ser.). (ENG.). 24p. (J). (gr. k-1). pap. 44.74 *(978-1-4296-5585-9(2)*, 15466, Capstone Pr.); (Illus.). (gr. -1-2). pap. 7.29 *(978-1-4296-5584-2(4)*, 114098) Capstone.

Taylor, Barbara. Rivers. 2004. (Make It Work! Geography Ser.). (Illus.). 48p. (J). (gr. 3-6). 12.95 *(978-1-58728-256-0(9)*, Two-Can Publishing) T&N Children's Publishing.

Thomson, Ruth. Rivers. 2012. (Geography Corner Ser.). (ENG., Illus.). 24p. (J). (gr. k-3). 21.25 *(978-1-4488-6625-0(1)*, PowerKids Pr.) Rosen Publishing Group, Inc., The.

Troup, Roxanne. Amazing Waterfalls Around the World. 2019. (Passport to Nature Ser.). (ENG., Illus.). 32p. (J). (gr. 4-6). lib. bdg. 28.65 *(978-1-5435-5780-0(5)*, 139736) Capstone.

VaicenaviAiene, Monika. What Is a River? 2021. (Illus.). 48p. (J). 18.95 *(978-1-59270-279-4(1))* Enchanted Lion Bks., LLC.

Van Zandt, Steve & Zecca, Katherine. River Song: With the Banana Slug String Band. 2007. (Illus.). 32p. (J). (gr. k-4). 9.99 *(978-1-58469-094-8(1)*, 1268621, Dawn Pubns.) Sourcebooks, Inc.

—River Song: With the Banana Slug String Band (Includes Music CD) 2007. (Illus.). 32p. (J). (gr. k-4). 17.99 *(978-1-58469-093-1(3)*, 1268621, Dawn Pubns.) Sourcebooks, Inc.

Woods, Michael & Woods, Mary B. Seven Natural Wonders of Central & South America. 2009. (Seven Wonders Ser.). (Illus.). 80p. (YA). (gr. 5-9). lib. bdg. 33.26 *(978-0-8225-9070-5(0))* Twenty First Century Bks.

RIVERS—FICTION

Anthony, Fortuna. Tim Tim the River Crayfish. 2011. 40p. (gr. -1). pap. 19.99 *(978-1-4269-6068-0(9))* Trafford Publishing.

Anthony, Mike. The Adventures of Henry the Patchwork Whale, 1 vol. 2010. 20p. 24.95 *(978-1-60813-076-4(2))* PublishAmerica, Inc.

Arrington, Linda. Ugly Trees. Arrington, Linda, photos by. 2012. (Illus.). 24p. pap. 24.95 *(978-1-4626-8925-5(6))* America Star Bks.

Bickta, Brenda L. Tad's Life in the Lily Pond. 2008. 74p. pap. 19.95 *(978-1-60672-647-1(1))* America Star Bks.

Bingamon-Haller, Mary. The Stillwater River. Burns, Sandra, illus. 2013. 24p. pap. 8.99 *(978-1-938768-30-9(2))* Gypsy Pubns.

Bishop, Michael. By the River Bank, 4 vols. Cloke, Rene, illus. 2012. (ENG.). 30p. (J). 4.95 *(978-1-84135-784-3(7))* Award Pubns. Ltd. GBR. Dist: Parkwest Pubns., Inc.

Boucher, Julie. Small Fry on the Magnetawan. 2009. 24p. pap. 14.95 *(978-0-9819727-4-9(8))* Fiction Publishing, Inc.

Bragg, Lynn. A River Lost. 2009. (Act Ser.). (ENG., Illus.). 32p. (Orig.). (gr. 2-8). pap. 11.95 *(978-0-88839-383-8(0))* Hancock Hse. Pubs.

Byars, Betsy. Trouble River. 158p. (J). (gr. 3-5). pap. 4.99 *(978-0-8072-1388-9(8)*, Listening Library) Random Hse. Audio Publishing Group.

Carlstrom, Nancy White. Raven & River. Van Zyle, Jon, illus. 2011. (ENG.). 32p. pap. 13.95 *(978-1-60223-150-4(8))* Univ. of Alaska Pr.

Cerullo, Jillian. The Danger of the River. 2005. 36p. pap. 14.99 *(978-1-4116-6988-8(6))* Lulu Pr., Inc.

Chapman, Elsie. Along the Indigo. 2018. (ENG.). 392p. (gr. 8-17). 17.99 *(978-1-4197-2531-9(9)*, Amulet Bks.) Abrams, Inc.

Childs, Vicki. Amanda on the River. 2005. (ENG.). 52p. pap. 15.99 *(978-1-4134-8476-2(X))* Xlibris Corp.

Corentin, Philippe. El Ogro, el Lobo, la Niña y el Pastel. 2004. (SPA.). 32p. (J). (gr. k-2). 19.99 *(978-84-8470-157-6(3))* Corimbo, Editorial S.L. ESP. Dist: Lectorum Pubns., Inc.

Corey's Web: Down in the Dumps. 2003. (J). per. *(978-0-9716567-9-6(7))* Book Web Publishing, Limited.

Corwin, Katherine. The River of Glass. Jasuna, Aija, illus. 2009. 24p. (J). 14.95 *(978-1-60131-002-6(1)*, Castlebridge Bks.) Big Tent Bks.

Cowley, Joy. Song of the River. Andrews, Kimberly, illus. 2019. (ENG.). 32p. (J). (gr. k-2). 17.99 *(978-1-77657-253-3(X)*, 79bc1618-5da9-4d6e-bc66-c53f1dc2c0a2) Gecko Pr. NZL. Dist: Lerner Publishing Group.

Dale, Jay. Little Zebra. East, Jacqueline, illus. 2012. (Wonder Words Ser.). (ENG.). 16p. (J). (gr. k-2). pap. 36.94 *(978-1-4296-8907-6(2)*, 18350, Capstone Pr.) Capstone.

Dale, Jay & Scott, Kay. Little Zebra, 1 vol. East, Jacqueline, illus. 2012. (Wonder Words Ser.). (ENG.). 16p. (J). (gr. k-2). pap. 6.99 *(978-1-4296-8906-9(4)*, 119956, Capstone Pr.) Capstone.

Downing, Johnette. Why the Crawfish Lives in the Mud, 1 vol. Downing, Johnette, illus. 2009. (ENG., Illus.). 32p. (J). (gr. k-3). 16.99 *(978-1-58980-678-8(6)*, Pelican Publishing) Arcadia Publishing.

Falk, Elsa. Fire Canoe. Frankenberg, Robert, illus. 2012. 188p. 42.95 *(978-1-258-23680-9(X))*; pap. 27.95 *(978-1-258-24375-3(X))* Literary Licensing, LLC.

Fontenot, Mary Alice. Clovis Crawfish & His Friends, 1 vol. Graves, Keith, illus. 2009. (Clovis Crawfish Ser.). (ENG.). 32p. (J). (gr. k-3). 16.99 *(978-1-58980-762-4(6)*, Pelican Publishing) Arcadia Publishing.

Gonzalez, Maya Christina. Yo Se Que el Rio Me Ama. 2009.Tr. of I Know the River Loves Me. (SPA & ENG., Illus.). 24p. (J). (gr. -1-3). 16.95 *(978-0-89239-233-9(9))* Lee & Low Bks., Inc.

Grahame, Kenneth. The Wind in the Willows. Ingpen, Robert R., illus. 2012. (Union Square Kids Illustrated Classics Ser.). (ENG.). 224p. (J). (gr. 2-8). 24.99 *(978-1-4027-8283-1(7))* Sterling Publishing Co., Inc.

Gray, Grandpa. The Land of the Three Elves Vol. 1: Beginnings. 2012. (ENG.). 317p. pap. 14.95 *(978-1-4327-9551-1(1))* Outskirts Pr., Inc.

Harvey, Roland. On the River. 2016. (ENG.). 32p. (J). (gr. k-3). 17.99 *(978-1-76011-245-5(3))* Allen & Unwin AUS. Dist: Independent Pubs. Group.

Higginson, Sheila Sweeny. Diego rescata al bebé manatí (Diego's Manatee Rescue) McGee, Warner, illus. 2009. (Go, Diego, Go! Ser.). (SPA.). 24p. (J). pap. 3.99 *(978-1-4169-7983-8(2)*, Libros Para Ninos) Libros Para Ninos.

Holman, Doris Anne. Come with Me to the Pond. 2004. (Illus.). 26p. (J). (gr. k-5). pap. 11.00 *(978-0-9667192-8-4(X))* Holman, Doris Anne.

—Oscar, the River Offer. 2003. (gr. 1-5). pap. 11.00 *(978-0-9667192-9-1(8))* Holman, Doris Anne.

Hooper, Meredith. River Story. Willey, Bee, illus. 2015. (ENG.). 32p. (J). (gr. k-3). 8.99 *(978-0-7636-7646-9(2))* Candlewick Pr.

Horton, Jim. The Foot Log Incident. 2008. 30p. pap. 24.95 *(978-1-60610-706-5(2))* America Star Bks.

Johnson, Gwen. The Story of Two-Toed Sam or How the Outer Banks Were Formed. 2006. (J). 8.95 *(978-0-9795860-9-5(7))* Fish Tales Publishing.

Lancaster, Susan. Hell's Gate. 2004. 200p. pap. *(978-0-9730350-2-5(1))* Snosrap Publishing.

Langer Karwoski, Gail. River Beds: Sleeping in the World's Rivers, 1 vol. McLennan, Connie, illus. 2008. (ENG.). 32p. (J). (gr. -1-3). 16.95 *(978-0-9777423-4-9(2))*; pap. 8.95 *(978-1-934359-31-0(9))* Arbordale Publishing.

Lee, WonKyeong. Green River. Yang, HyeWon, illus. 2014. (MySELF Bookshelf Ser.). (ENG.). 32p. (J). (gr. k-2). lib. bdg. 25.27 *(978-1-59953-660-6(9))* Norwood Hse. Pr.

Martin, Marc. A River. 2017. (ENG., Illus.). 44p. (J). 17.99 *(978-1-4521-5423-7(6))* Chronicle Bks. LLC.

Meadows, Daisy. Milly the River Fairy. 2014. (Rainbow Magic — the Earth Fairies Ser.). lib. bdg. 14.75 *(978-0-606-35835-4(8))* Turtleback.

Moore, Wendy Leptien. Eaglet & the River. 2011. 108p. 21.92 *(978-1-4269-5478-8(6))*; pap. 11.92 *(978-1-4269-5477-1(8))* Trafford Publishing.

Morris, Richard T. Bear Came along (Caldecott Honor Book) Pham, LeUyen, illus. 2019. (ENG.). 40p. (J). (gr. -1-3). 18.99 *(978-0-316-46447-5(3))* Little, Brown Bks. for Young Readers.

Newberry, Geoffrey C. The Cape Don Adventure. 2011. 48p. pap. 6.99 *(978-1-61667-262-1(5))* Raider Publishing International.

Nickel, Scott. Race on the River, 1 vol. Harpster, Steve, illus. 2011. (My First Graphic Novel Ser.). (ENG.). 32p. (J). (gr. k-2). pap. 6.25 *(978-1-4342-3061-4(9)*, 114661, Stone Arch Bks.) Capstone.

Niland, Kilmeny. The Gingerbread Man. 2006. (Illus.). 16p. *(978-1-921049-49-1(9))* Little Hare Bks. AUS. Dist: HarperCollins Pubs. Australia.

Novel Units. The River Novel Units Teacher Guide. 2019. (ENG.). (J). pap. 12.99 *(978-1-56137-611-7(6)*, Novel Units, Inc.) Classroom Library Co.

—Trouble River Novel Units Teacher Guide. 2019. (ENG.). (J). pap. 12.99 *(978-1-56137-435-9(0)*, Novel Units, Inc.) Classroom Library Co.

Oguneye, Kunle. Sikulu & Harambe by the Zambezi River: An African Vversion of the Good Samaritan Story. McCorkindale, Bruce & Youtsey, Scott, illus. 2008. 32p. (J). (gr. -1-5). 14.99 *(978-0-9777382-4-3(8))* Blue Brush Media.

O'Neil-Andrews, Milly. Bandolines & Bubbles. 2011. 88p. pap. 11.25 *(978-1-4269-3089-8(5))* Trafford Publishing.

Papp, Robert, illus. The Ghost of the Chattering Bones. 2007. (Boxcar Children Ser.). 120p. 15.00 *(978-0-7569-7611-8(1))* Perfection Learning Corp.

Perkins, R., illus. Earth Whispers. 32p. (J). (gr. 3-18). 16.00 *(978-0-9710860-2-9(8))* Libros, Encouraging Cultural Literacy.

River, Fawn. Sophy & the River. 2012. 24p. pap. 17.99 *(978-1-4772-0272-2(2))* AuthorHouse.

Röder, Marlene & Röder, Marlene. In the River Darkness, 1 vol. 2014. (Scarlet Voyage Ser.). (ENG., Illus.). 224p. (YA). (gr. 9-10). pap. 13.88 *(978-1-62324-011-0(5)*, 91fd001a-28d6-42a3-b57b-2ac27625e82c) Enslow Publishing, LLC.

Sanders, Scott Russell. Floating House. Cogancherry, Helen, illus. 2011. 40p. (J). lib. bdg. 18.00 *(978-1-59098-425-3(0))* Wooster Bk. Co., The.

Sargent, Dave, et al. On the Banks of the Wallowa River: (Nez Perce) Use Your Talent, 20 vols., Vol. 13. Lenoir, Jane, illus. l.t. ed. 2004. (Story Keeper Ser.: 13). 48p. (J). pap. 10.95 *(978-1-56763-928-5(3))* Ozark Publishing.

Schaaf, Ron. BearClaw: Finding Courage Within. 2007. (J). *(978-0-9787555-1-5(0))* Hickory Tales Publishing.

Smith, Steven K. Brother Wars. 2017. (ENG.). 120p. (J). pap. 8.99 *(978-0-9861473-2-6(X))* MyBoys3 Pr.

Susurros de la Tierra. (SPA.). (J). *(978-0-9710860-3-6(6))* Libros, Encouraging Cultural Literacy.

Trimoglie, Mario. The Rivers. Swope, Brenda, illus. 2012. 26p. 24.95 *(978-1-4560-3907-3(5))* America Star Bks.

Warner, Gertrude Chandler, creator. The Ghost of the Chattering Bones. 2005. (Boxcar Children Mysteries Ser.: 102). (ENG., Illus.). 128p. (J). (gr. 2-5). pap. 6.99 *(978-0-8075-0874-9(8)*, 807508748, Random Hse. Bks. for Young Readers) Random Hse. Children's Bks.

Weston Woods Staff, creator. In the Small, Small Pond. 2011. 38.75 *(978-0-439-84578-6(5))* Weston Woods Studios, Inc.

Wiggin, Kate Douglas. Homespun Tales. 2007. 240p. 26.95 *(978-1-60312-668-7(6))*; per. 14.95 *(978-1-60312-410-2(1))* Aegypan.

Williamson, Peggy. Who Was Here First? 2006. (J). per. 12.00 *(978-1-59571-155-7(4))* Word Association Pubs.

Wilsdon, Christina. A New York Sailing Adventure. Hockerman, Dennis, illus. 2006. 26p. (J). 7.99 *(978-1-59939-014-7(0))* Cornerstone Pr.

Wilson, Elaine Moody. Fisherman Jack Meets the River Creatures, 1 vol. Ducker Signs Plus, illus. 2009. 40p. pap. 24.95 *(978-1-60836-967-6(6))* PublishAmerica, Inc.

Wright, Holly. River. 2004. (Illus.). (J). *(978-0-9743690-8-2(X))* Britt Allcroft Productions.

Zackery, Gary D. & Borgstedt, John. Stephen. 2011. 108p. 22.45 *(978-1-4567-2712-3(5))* AuthorHouse.

RIVERS—POLLUTION

see Water—Pollution

RIZAL Y ALONSO, JOSE, 1861-1896

Arruda, Suzanne Middendorf. Freedom's Martyr: The Story of Jose Rizal, National Hero of the Phillipines. 2003. (Avisson Young Adult Ser.). (Illus.). 106p. (J). pap. 19.95 *(978-1-888105-55-1(0))* Avisson Pr., Inc.

ROAD CONSTRUCTION

see Roads

ROAD SIGNS

see Signs and Signboards

ROADRUNNER

Borgert-Spaniol, Megan. Roadrunners. 2014. (Backyard Wildlife Ser.). (ENG., Illus.). 24p. (J). (gr. k-3). lib. bdg. 26.95 *(978-1-62617-061-2(4)*, Blastoff! Readers) Bellwether Media.

Early Macken, JoAnn. Roadrunners, 1 vol. 2nd rev. ed. 2009. (Animals That Live in the Desert (Second Edition) Ser.). (ENG.). 24p. (J). (gr. 1-1). pap. 9.15 *(978-1-4339-2452-1(8)*, 2d8941e9-139f-4812-886e-1636d6b9554c); lib. bdg. 25.27 *(978-1-4339-2391-3(2)*, d949b9b8-3fa9-4d79-9c0a-2b39db57f418) Stevens, Gareth Publishing LLLP. (Weekly Reader Leveled Readers).

—Roadrunners / Correcaminos, 1 vol. 2nd rev. ed. 2009. (Animals That Live in the Desert / Animales Del Desierto (Second Edition) Ser.). (SPA & ENG.). 24p. (J). (gr. 1-1). pap. 9.15 *(978-1-4339-2460-6(9)*, afe3f4df-34ac-4037-8784-62a940020cbe, Weekly Reader Leveled Readers); lib. bdg. 25.27 *(978-1-4339-2423-1(4)*, 04a439ac-3e41-4b32-8f11-ed8f328c0720) Stevens, Gareth Publishing LLLP.

Ganeri, Anita. Roadrunner, 1 vol. 2011. (Day in the Life: Desert Animals Ser.). (ENG., Illus.). 24p. (gr. k-2). pap. 6.49 *(978-1-4329-4784-2(2)*, Heinemann) Capstone.

Macgregor, Eloise. Roadrunner. 2015. (Desert Animals Searchin' for Shade Ser.). (ENG.). 24p. (J). (gr. -1-3). lib. bdg. 26.99 *(978-1-62724-533-3(2))* Bearport Publishing Co., Inc.

Perish, Patrick. Roadrunners. 2019. (Animals of the Desert Ser.). (ENG., Illus.). 24p. (J). (gr. k-3). lib. bdg. 26.95 *(978-1-62617-923-3(9)*, Blastoff! Readers) Bellwether Media.

ROADS

see also Streets

Bernhardt, Carolyn. Engineer It! Road Projects. 2017. (Super Simple Engineering Projects Ser.). (ENG., Illus.). 32p. (J). (gr. k-4). lib. bdg. 34.21 *(978-1-5321-1125-9(8)*, 25826, Super SandCastle) ABDO Publishing Co.

Bowman, Chris. Highways. 2018. (Everyday Engineering Ser.). (ENG., Illus.). 24p. (J). (gr. k-3). lib. bdg. 26.95 *(978-1-62617-823-6(2)*, Blastoff! Readers) Bellwether Media.

Canfield, Michael. Ice Roads, 1 vol. 2016. (Technology Takes on Nature Ser.). (ENG.). 32p. (J). (gr. 3-4). pap. 11.50 *(978-1-4824-5771-1(7)*, 39ed83eb-5af9-4d64-b5a7-c76e1c54a0b3) Stevens, Gareth Publishing LLLP.

Chumin, Nancy. Manjhi Moves a Mountain. Popovici, Danny, illus. 2017. (ENG.). 36p. (J). (gr. k-5). 17.99 *(978-1-939547-34-7(2)*, 0a896958-b1ae-4265-a6a8-dcccf4d81698) Creston Bks.

Furgang, Kathy. Zoom in on Satellite & Street Maps, 1 vol. 2017. (Zoom in on Maps Ser.). (ENG.). 24p. (gr. 2-2). 25.60 *(978-0-7660-9225-9(9)*, 6ff3469e-a0cc-4c24-b5db-da4bfba08ea5) Enslow Publishing, LLC.

—Zoom in on Superhighways, 1 vol. 2017. (Zoom in on Engineering Ser.). (ENG.). 24p. (gr. 2-2). lib. bdg. 25.60 *(978-0-7660-8725-5(5)*, 44d03d84-9626-4cdf-85e5-4e2ca576ed07) Enslow Publishing, LLC.

Die Geschichte einer Strasse. (GER., Illus.). 32p. *(978-3-411-07401-3(9))* Bibliographisches Institut & F. A. Brockhaus AG DEU. Dist: i. b. d., Ltd.

Hennessy, B. G. Road Builders. Taback, Simms, illus. 2018. 32p. (J). (— 1). bds. 7.99 *(978-0-425-29121-4(9)*, Viking Books for Young Readers) Penguin Young Readers Group.

Hinote Lanier, Wendy. Building a Road. 2020. (How It's Done Ser.). (ENG., Illus.). 32p. (J). (gr. 2-3). pap. 9.95 *(978-1-64493-116-5(8)*, 1644931168); lib. bdg. 31.35 *(978-1-64493-037-3(4)*, 1644930374) North Star Editions. (Focus Readers).

Holdren, Annie C. Building a Subway. 2020. (Sequence Amazing Structures Ser.). (ENG.). 32p. (J). (gr. 2-5). pap. 12.00 *(978-1-68152-562-4(3)*, 10759) Amicus.

Krajnik, Elizabeth. Paving Roads & Highways, 1 vol. 2018. (Impacting Earth: How People Change the Land Ser.). (ENG.). 24p. (gr. 2-2). pap. 9.25 *(978-1-5383-4200-8(6)*, b11945cd-105f-440b-a355-ab9f367cb846, PowerKids Pr.) Rosen Publishing Group, Inc., The.

La Bella, Laura. A Career in Paving & Road Surfacing, 1 vol. 2018. (Jobs for Rebuilding America Ser.). (ENG.). 80p. (gr. 6-6). 38.80 *(978-1-5081-8002-9(4)*, d85011e8-1d59-4d88-ac43-3b99e5b2cf29) Rosen Publishing Group, Inc., The.

Linde, Barbara M. All about Road Maps & GPS, 1 vol. 2018. (Map Basics Ser.). (ENG.). 24p. (gr. 2-3). lib. bdg. 24.27 *(978-1-5382-2919-4(6)*, d43eedb6-ccd6-45f6-93af-753d186ab6d2) Stevens, Gareth Publishing LLLP.

Mahaney, Ian F. Road Maps. (Map It! Ser.). 24p. (gr. 3-4). 2009. 42.50 *(978-1-61514-357-3(2)*, PowerKids Pr.) 2006. (ENG., Illus.). (YA). lib. bdg. 26.27 *(978-1-4042-3056-9(4)*, d99cb3f2-dcb2-444a-ab7e-19c8cbe07dc6) Rosen Publishing Group, Inc., The.

Maurer, Tracy Nelson. Using Road Maps & GPS. 2016. (Searchlight Books (tm) — What Do You Know about Maps? Ser.). (ENG., Illus.). 40p. (J). (gr. 3-5). 30.65 *(978-1-5124-0952-9(9)*, 446c684c-5165-4c8f-a3ca-bca4f3c9073b, Lerner Pubns.) Lerner Publishing Group.

Nardo, Don. Roman Roads & Aqueducts. 2014. (History's Great Structures). (ENG., Illus.). 80p. (J). lib. bdg. *(978-1-60152-634-2(2))* ReferencePoint Pr., Inc.

Nittinger, Sharon. How Did They Build That? Road. 2009. (Community Connections: How Did They Build That? Ser.). (ENG.). 24p. (gr. 2-5). lib. bdg. 29.21 *(978-1-60279-482-5(0)*, 200256) Cherry Lake Publishing.

Polinsky, Paige V. Roads. 2017. (Engineering Super Structures Ser.). (ENG., Illus.). 24p. (J). (gr. -1-3). lib. bdg. 29.93 *(978-1-5321-1104-4(5)*, 25784, SandCastle) ABDO Publishing Co.

Rand McNally Staff. Kids' Road Atlas. (Backseat Bks.). 80p. (J). pap. 3.95 *(978-0-528-96544-9(1))* Rand McNally.

Richardson, Gillian. 10 Routes That Crossed the World. Rosen, Kim, illus. 2017. (ENG.). 164p. (J). (gr. 3-7). pap. 12.95 *(978-1-55451-875-3(X))* Annick Pr., Ltd. CAN. Dist: Publishers Group West (PGW).

Roza, Greg. America's First Highway. (American History Milestones Ser.). 32p. (gr. 5-5). 2009. 47.90 *(978-1-61511-372-9(X)*, PowerKids Pr.) 2009. (ENG.). (J). lib. bdg. 28.93 *(978-1-4358-3014-1(8)*, a0364cc5-1ad6-4bf2-85a7-44df8481b980, PowerKids Pr.) 2008. (ENG., Illus.). (J). pap. 10.00 *(978-1-4358-0199-8(7)*, e8e0f04e-c5ba-4325-8de5-e203cb313726, Rosen Classroom) Rosen Publishing Group, Inc., The.

Sikkens, Crystal. A Road Connects Places. 2018. (Be an Engineer! Designing to Solve Problems Ser.). (Illus.). 24p. (J). (gr. 3-3). *(978-0-7787-5161-8(9))* Crabtree Publishing Co.

Snedden, Robert. Roads, 1 vol. 2016. (Engineering Eurekas Ser.). (ENG.). 32p. (J). (gr. 3-4). pap. 11.00 *(978-1-4994-3101-8(5)*, 863f6684-feea-4374-a63b-ef385b8d5967, PowerKids Pr.) Rosen Publishing Group, Inc., The.

Stefoff, Rebecca. Building Roads, 1 vol. 2015. (Great Engineering Ser.). (ENG.). 32p. (gr. 3-3). pap. 11.58 *(978-1-5026-0603-7(8)*, f9c5ea8e-c205-43e2-bc71-7d7d31e40a08) Cavendish Square Publishing LLC.

Sutton, Sally. Roadwork. Lovelock, Brian, illus. 2011. (Construction Crew Ser.). (ENG.). 28p. (J). (gr. k-k). bds. 8.99 *(978-0-7636-4653-0(9))* Candlewick Pr.

Taylor, Charlotte & Bourgeois Molzahn, Arlene. Highways & Roads, 1 vol. 2019. (Exploring Infrastructure Ser.). (ENG.). 48p. (gr. 3-4). 29.60 *(978-1-9785-0335-9(0)*, c7ab3864-7bc7-4103-9055-6873cc7543f3) Enslow Publishing, LLC.

ROADS—FICTION

Barchers, Suzanne I. On the Road with Rose & Bose, 1 vol. rev. ed. 2011. (Phonics Ser.). (ENG.). 16p. (gr. k-2). 6.99 *(978-1-4333-2914-2(X))* Teacher Created Materials, Inc.

Best, Cari. When We Go Walking, 0 vols. Brooker, Kyrsten, illus. 2013. (ENG.). 32p. (J). (gr. -1-3). 17.99 *(978-1-4778-1648-6(8)*, 9781477816486, Two Lions) Amazon Publishing.

Doyle, Brian. Hey Dad!, 1 vol. 3rd ed. 2006. (ENG.). 128p. (J). (gr. 3-7). pap. 6.95 *(978-0-88899-708-1(6))* Groundwood Bks. CAN. Dist: Publishers Group West (PGW).

Eames, Marion. Baner Beca. 2005. (WEL.). 80p. pap. *(978-0-86243-729-9(6))* Y Lolfa.

Educational Adventures, creator. Free Wheelin' Coloring/Activity Book (English) w/ Snipe. 2007. (J). 2.99 *(978-1-933934-52-5(2))* Mighty Kids Media.

—Street Smarts: Coloring/Activity Book (Spanish) w/ Snipe. 2006. (Illus.). (J). 2.99 *(978-1-933934-19-8(0))* Mighty Kids Media.

—Street Smarts: Picture Book (Spanish) 9x9. 2007. (Illus.). (J). per. 5.99 *(978-1-933934-77-8(8))* Mighty Kids Media.

Estes, Eleanor. The Alley. Ardizzone, Edward, illus. 2004. (Odyssey/Harcourt Young Classic Ser.). 283p. 15.95 *(978-0-7569-3475-0(3))* Perfection Learning Corp.

Feiffer, Jules. By the Side of the Road. 2005. (Illus.). 59p. (J). (gr. k-4). reprint ed. 16.00 *(978-0-7567-9371-5(8))* DIANE Publishing Co.

Ford, Robert. Adventures of Hit the Road Jack. l.t. ed. 2003. (Illus.). 40p. per. 10.00 *(978-1-932338-11-9(X))* Lifevest Publishing, Inc.

Free Wheelin' Picture Book (English) NL 9x9 with Snipe. 2007. (J). 5.99 *(978-1-933934-48-8(4))* Mighty Kids Media.

Gerhardt, Barbara. I Am of Scram. 2007. (Illus.). pap. 12.95 *(978-1-934246-15-3(8))* Peppertree Pr., The.

Horvath, James. Work, Dogs, Work: A Highway Tail. 2014. (ENG., Illus.). 40p. (J). (gr. -1-3). 17.99 *(978-0-06-218970-7(0)*, HarperCollins) HarperCollins Pubs.

Miller, Pat Zietlow. Wherever You Go. Wheeler, Eliza, illus. 2019. (ENG.). 26p. (J). (gr. -1 — 1). bds. 7.99 *(978-0-316-48794-8(5))* Little, Brown Bks. for Young Readers.

Rinker, Sherri Duskey. Construction Site: Road Crew, Coming Through! Ford, A. G., illus. 2021. (Goodnight, Goodnight, Construc Ser.). (ENG.). 40p. (J). (gr. -1 — 1). 17.99 *(978-1-7972-0472-7(6))* Chronicle Bks. LLC.

Root, Phyllis. Rattletrap Car Big Book. Barton, Jill, illus. 2009. (ENG.). 40p. (J). (gr. -1-3). pap. 27.99 *(978-0-7636-4139-9(1))* Candlewick Pr.

Sabatino, Nick. Paint Stripes Stop Traffic Dead, 1 vol. 2010. 44p. 24.95 *(978-1-4489-5139-0(9))* PublishAmerica, Inc.

Sargent, Dave & Sargent, David M. Bob White: Use Good Judgement, 20 vols., Vol. 3. Lenoir, Jane, illus. 2003. (Feather Tales Ser.: No. 3). 42p. (J). pap. 10.95 *(978-1-56763-724-3(8))* Ozark Publishing.

Sargent, David M. Bob White: Use Good Judgement, 20 vols., Vol. 3. Lenoir, Jane, illus. 2003. (Feather Tales Ser.: No. 3). 42p. (J). lib. bdg. 20.95 *(978-1-56763-723-6(X))* Ozark Publishing.

Sharp, Euan. Diggedy Dozer in Treetop Troubles. 2008. 34p. 15.95 *(978-1-4357-0982-9(9))* Lulu Pr., Inc.

Shaskan, Stephen. Toad on the Road: Mama & Me. 2018. (ENG., Illus.). 32p. (J). (gr. -1-3). 17.99 *(978-0-06-239349-4(9)*, HarperCollins) HarperCollins Pubs.

Slanina, Anne Maro. Annie Mouse's Route 66 Adventure: A Photo Journal, vols. 6, vol. 5. Collins, Kelsey, illus. 2011. (ENG.). 48p. (J). pap. 14.99 *(978-0-9793379-6-3(8))* Annie Mouse Bks.

Stegall, Kim. Rodney Robbins & the Rainy-Day Pond. Day, Bruce, illus. 2010. 29p. (J). *(978-1-60682-058-2(3))* BJU Pr.

Street Smarts: Coloring/Activity Book (English) Incl. Stickers. 2006. (Illus.). (J). 2.99 *(978-1-933934-18-1(2))* Mighty Kids Media.

Street Smarts: Picture Book 9x9 with Snipe. 2006. (Illus.). (J). 5.99 *(978-1-933934-17-4(4))* Mighty Kids Media.

Street Smarts: Picture Book (English) 8x8. 2006. (Illus.). (J). 5.99 *(978-1-933934-16-7(6))* Mighty Kids Media.

Sutton, Sally. Construction. Lovelock, Brian, illus. 2014. (Construction Crew Ser.). (ENG.). 34p. (J). (gr. -1-2). 17.99 *(978-0-7636-7325-3(0))* Candlewick Pr.

—Dig, Dump, Roll. Lovelock, Brian, illus. (Construction Crew Ser.). (ENG.). (J). 2019. 28p. (-k). bds. 8.99 *(978-1-5362-0902-0(3))* 2018. 32p. (gr. -1-2). 16.99 *(978-1-5362-0391-2(2))* Candlewick Pr.

—Roadwork. Lovelock, Brian, illus. 2017. (Construction Crew Ser.). (ENG.). 32p. (J). (-k). 7.99 *(978-0-7636-9870-6(9))* Candlewick Pr.

ROANOKE ISLAND (N.C.)

Belval, Brian. A Primary Source History of the Lost Colony of Roanoke. (Primary Sources of the Thirteen Colonies & the Lost Colony Ser.). 64p. 2009. (gr. 5-8). 58.50 *(978-1-60851-891-3(4))* 2005. (ENG., Illus.). (gr. 4-6). per. 12.95 *(978-1-4042-0669-4(8)*, a0996c9d-c276-44eb-b574-e346d33f441b) 2005. (ENG., Illus.). (YA). (gr. 4-6). lib. bdg. 37.13 *(978-1-4042-0435-5(0)*, cd3a60fe-371f-4146-8f18-068d68945d1f) Rosen Publishing Group, Inc., The.

Blake, Kevin. Roanoke Island: The Town That Vanished. 2015. (Abandoned: Towns Without People Ser.). (ENG.). 32p. (J). (gr. 2-7). lib. bdg. 26.60 *(978-1-62724-521-0(9))* Bearport Publishing Co., Inc.

Fritz, Jean. The Lost Colony of Roanoke. Talbott, Hudson, illus. 2004. (ENG.). 64p. (J). (gr. 2-5). 18.99 *(978-0-399-24027-0(6)*, G.P. Putnam's Sons Books for Young Readers) Penguin Young Readers Group.

Loh-Hagan, Virginia. Roanoke Colony. 2017. (Urban Legends: Don't Read Alone! Ser.). (ENG., Illus.). 32p. (J). (gr. 4-8). lib. bdg. 32.07 *(978-1-63472-897-3(1)*, 210014, 45th Parallel Press) Cherry Lake Publishing.

McAneney, Caitlin. The Lost Colony of Roanoke, 1 vol. 2015. (Spotlight on the 13 Colonies: Birth of a Nation Ser.). (ENG., Illus.). 24p. (J). (gr. 4-6). pap. 11.00 *(978-1-4994-0596-5(0)*, 0cd92ae6-4c1d-4f53-9d85-4d2e6b510a7f, PowerKids Pr.) Rosen Publishing Group, Inc., The.

Miller, Jake. The Lost Colony of Roanoke: A Primary Source History. 2009. (Primary Source Library of the Thirteen Colonies & the Lost Colony Ser.). 24p. (gr. 3-4). 42.50 *(978-1-60854-163-8(0)*, PowerKids Pr.) Rosen Publishing Group, Inc., The.

Miner Huey, Lois. American Archaeology Uncovers the Earliest English Colonies, 1 vol. 2010. (American Archaeology Ser.). (ENG.). 64p. (gr. 5-5). 34.07 *(978-0-7614-4264-6(2)*, 75bbcf73-c2c4-44e6-b73f-0a8679f9611b) Cavendish Square Publishing LLC.

Schuetz, Kari. Roanoke: The Lost Colony. 2017. (Abandoned Places Ser.). (ENG., Illus.). 24p. (J). (gr. 3-7). lib. bdg. 26.95 *(978-1-62617-698-0(1)*, Torque Bks.) Bellwether Media.

Simmons, Alex. Mysteries of the Past: A Chapter Book. 2005. (True Tales Ser.). (ENG., Illus.). 48p. (J). (gr. 2-4). lib. bdg. 22.50 *(978-0-516-25184-4(8)*, Children's Pr.) Scholastic Library Publishing.

Smith, Andrea P. The Mystery of Roanoke, the Lost Colony. (Illus.). 24p. (J). 2012. 63.60 *(978-1-4488-5209-3(9))* 2011. (ENG., (gr. 2-3). pap. 11.60 *(978-1-4488-5208-6(0)*, 6765d17e-f5f2-4fe1-9a73-dfe289699fcb) 2011. (ENG., (gr. 2-3). lib. bdg. 28.93 *(978-1-4488-5185-0(8)*, d5a35104-4543-4825-863b-f1627e38645d) Rosen Publishing Group, Inc., The. (PowerKids Pr.).

ROBBERS AND OUTLAWS

Bryant, Jill. John Henry Holliday. 2003. (Folk Heroes Ser.). (Illus.). 24p. (J). lib. bdg. 24.45 *(978-1-59036-077-4(X))* Weigl Pubs., Inc.

Callery, Sean. The Dark History of America's Old West, 1 vol. 2011. (Dark Histories Ser.). (ENG.). 64p. (gr. 5-5). 35.50 *(978-1-60870-086-8(0)*, ab883aea-2530-45bd-8ce6-bfe1e124ab05) Cavendish Square Publishing LLC.

Collins, Kathleen. Jesse James: Bank Robber of the American West. (Primary Sources of Famous People in American History Ser.). 32p. (gr. 2-3). 2009. 47.90 *(978-1-60851-690-2(3))* 2003. (ENG & SPA., Illus.). lib. bdg. 29.13 *(978-0-8239-4160-5(4)*, 1e40f58b-78c2-4e1f-911d-e6cd70abd37f, Editorial Buenas Letras) Rosen Publishing Group, Inc., The.

—Jesse James: Bank Robber of the American West / Legendario bandido del oeste Americano. 2009. (Famous People in American History/Grandes personajes en la historia de los Estados Unidos Ser.). (ENG & SPA.). 32p. (gr. 2-3). 47.90 *(978-1-61512-547-0(7)*, Editorial Buenas Letras) Rosen Publishing Group, Inc., The.

—Jesse James: Legendario Bandido del Oeste Americano, 1 vol. 2003. (Grandes Personajes en la Historia de Los Estados Unidos (Famous People in American History) Ser.). (SPA.). 32p. (gr. 3-4). pap. 10.00 *(978-0-8239-4230-5(9)*, 6e7f9fb2-76bb-47aa-a222-9838d6e7e24b, Rosen Classroom); (Illus.). lib. bdg. 29.13 *(978-0-8239-4136-0(1)*, ba04e6c3-aaa3-4019-8265-115cda3cdf68, Editorial Buenas Letras) Rosen Publishing Group, Inc., The.

—Jesse James: Legendario bandido del oeste americano (Jesse James: Bank Robber of the American West) 2009. (Grandes personajes en la historia de los Estados Unidos (Famous People in American History) Ser.). (SPA.). 32p. (gr. 2-3). 47.90 *(978-1-61512-801-3(8)*, Editorial Buenas Letras) Rosen Publishing Group, Inc., The.

—Jesse James: Western Bank Robber, 1 vol. 2003. (Primary Sources of Famous People in American History Ser.). (ENG., Illus.). 32p. (gr. 3-4). lib. bdg. 29.13 *(978-0-8239-4112-4(4)*, 64ea6b9e-e169-4615-8b57-798e12cdd9df, Rosen Reference) Rosen Publishing Group, Inc., The.

Cooke, Tim. Billy the Kid: A Notorious Gunfighter of the Wild West, 1 vol. 2015. (Wanted! Famous Outlaws Ser.). (ENG., Illus.). 48p. (J). (gr. 6-8). pap. 15.05 *(978-1-4824-4243-4(4)*, db263247-1a67-4b89-9656-f6d897eddd3b) Stevens, Gareth Publishing LLLP.

—Butch Cassidy & the Sundance Kid: Notorious Outlaws of the West, 1 vol. 2015. (Wanted! Famous Outlaws Ser.). (ENG., Illus.). 48p. (J). (gr. 6-8). pap. 15.05 *(978-1-4824-4255-7(8)*, e3198923-d01b-44f3-b297-abfabac1b545) Stevens, Gareth Publishing LLLP.

—Jesse James: A Notorious Bank Robber of the Wild West, 1 vol. 2015. (Wanted! Famous Outlaws Ser.). (ENG., Illus.). 48p. (J). (gr. 6-8). pap. 15.05 *(978-1-4824-4259-5(0)*, 5c82e94b-70dd-4a3b-9df6-f4ad8812d3cb) Stevens, Gareth Publishing LLLP.

—Ned Kelly: A Notorious Bandit of the Australian Outback, 1 vol. 2015. (Wanted! Famous Outlaws Ser.). (ENG., Illus.). 48p. (J). (gr. 6-8). 33.60 *(978-1-4824-4262-5(0)*, c629c78e-cbb1-4455-8650-8538147b1301) Stevens, Gareth Publishing LLLP.

DuMont, Brianna. Thrilling Thieves: Thrilling Thieves: Liars, Cheats, & Cons Who Changed History. 2018. (Changed History Ser.). (ENG., Illus.). 192p. (J). (gr. 3-6). 16.99 *(978-1-5107-0169-4(9)*, Sky Pony Pr.) Skyhorse Publishing Co., Inc.

Elborough, Travis. Highwayman, Outlaws & Bandits of London. 2004. (... of London Ser.). (ENG., Illus.). 96p. pap. 8.99 *(978-1-904153-13-9(5))* Watling St., Ltd. GBR. Dist: Trafalgar Square Publishing.

Engsberg Cunningham, Meghan. Jesse James: Outlaw, 1 vol. Lapegüe, Matías, illus. 2016. (American Legends & Folktales Ser.). (ENG.). 32p. (gr. 3-3). 30.21 *(978-1-5026-2197-9(5)*, e7040c0a-5b11-44f5-88ee-79d91f517313) Cavendish Square Publishing LLC.

Fenn, George Manville. Young Robin Hood. 2004. reprint ed. pap. 15.95 *(978-1-4191-9534-1(4))* Kessinger Publishing, LLC.

Finkelstein, Norman H. The Capture of Black Bart: Gentleman Bandit of the Old West. 2018. (ENG., Illus.). 160p. (J). (gr. 5). 17.99 *(978-1-61373-995-2(8))* Chicago Review Pr., Inc.

Frisch, Aaron. Jesse James. 2005. (Legends of the West (Creative Education) Ser.). (Illus.). 48p. (J). (gr. 5-9). lib. bdg. 21.95 *(978-1-58341-338-8(3)*, Creative Education) Creative Co., The.

Green, Carl R. & Sanford, William R. Jesse James, 1 vol. rev. ed. 2008. (Outlaws & Lawmen of the Wild West Ser.). (ENG., Illus.). 48p. (J). (gr. 5-7). lib. bdg. 27.93 *(978-0-7660-3172-2(1)*, 5f7068a6-2645-490d-aac7-944c447c791f) Enslow Publishing, LLC.

Hurley, Trish. The 10 Most Outrageous Outlaws. 2008. 14.99 *(978-1-55448-506-2(1))* Scholastic Library Publishing.

Kovacs, Vic. Outlaws & Sheriffs, 1 vol. 2015. (True History of the Wild West Ser.). (ENG., Illus.). 32p. (J). (gr. 5-5). pap. 11.00 *(978-1-4994-1178-2(2)*, ece130b6-62ea-4bb6-8cce-92b4789aadb4, PowerKids Pr.) Rosen Publishing Group, Inc., The.

McCarthy, Tom. Daring Heists: Real Tales of Sensational Robberies & Robbers. 2017. (Mystery & Mayhem Ser.). (ENG., Illus.). 128p. (J). (gr. 3-7). 19.95 *(978-1-61930-531-1(3)*, e179f086-90d4-4f8c-9c3b-fd70519bf6ec) Nomad Pr.

McDonnell, Julia. The Legend of Robin Hood, 1 vol. 2015. (Famous Legends Ser.). (ENG., Illus.). 32p. (J). (gr. 2-3). pap. 11.50 *(978-1-4824-2748-6(6)*, cdcd0bdb-313f-428a-850d-872557110eb8) Stevens, Gareth Publishing LLLP.

McIntosh, Kenneth. Outlaws & Lawmen: Crime & Punishment in the 1800s. 2009. (Daily Life in America in the 1800s Ser.). 64p. (YA). (gr. 7-18). pap. 9.95 *(978-1-4222-1857-0(0))*; lib. bdg. 22.95 *(978-1-4222-1784-9(1))* Mason Crest.

Moody, Ralph. Wells Fargo. 2005. (ENG., Illus.). 186p. (J). pap. 13.95 *(978-0-8032-8303-9(2)*, MOOWEX, Bison Bks.) Univ. of Nebraska Pr.

Nelson, Vaunda Micheaux. Bad News for Outlaws: The Remarkable Life of Bass Reeves, Deputy U. S. Marshal. Christie, R. Gregory, illus. 2009. (ENG.). 40p. (J). (gr. 3-6). lib. bdg. 19.99 *(978-0-8225-6764-6(4)*, 8c280ef7-9537-47d5-9cb7-1dc0fc1aa019, Carolrhoda Bks.) Lerner Publishing Group.

Nolan, Frederick W. Outlaws & Rebels. 2015. (Wild West Ser.). (Illus.). 64p. (J). (gr. 9-12). 39.95 *(978-1-78404-080-2(0))* Arcturus Publishing GBR. Dist: Black Rabbit Bks.

Outlaws. 2019. (J). *(978-0-7166-3766-0(9))* World Bk., Inc.

Pipe, Jim. Top 10 Worst Vicious Villains, 1 vol. Antram, David, illus. 2012. (Top 10 Worst Ser.). (ENG.). 32p. (J). (gr. 3-5). pap. 11.50 *(978-1-4339-6698-9(0)*, 94b77bbf-585c-4e34-92f7-848385dc5c53); lib. bdg. 29.27 *(978-1-4339-6697-2(2)*, b3aa3e54-61ad-4ee9-9aa4-082165fa4928) Stevens, Gareth Publishing LLLP. (Gareth Stevens Learning Library).

Pipe, Jim & Salariya, David. Top 10 Worst Vicious Villains: You Wouldn't Want to Know! Antram, David, illus. 2013. 32p. (J). *(978-1-4351-5043-0(0))* Barnes & Noble, Inc.

Randolph, Ryan. A Bank Robber's End: The Death of Jesse James. 2009. (Great Moments in American History Ser.). 32p. (gr. 3-3). 47.90 *(978-1-61513-138-9(8))* Rosen Publishing Group, Inc., The.

Randolph, Ryan P. A Bank Robber's End: The Death of Jesse James, 1 vol. 2003. (Great Moments in American History Ser.). (ENG., Illus.). 32p. (J). (gr. 3-3). lib. bdg. 29.13 *(978-0-8239-4359-3(3)*, d0b8bfc2-268f-47e1-8743-de7d5e8bdbd0) Rosen Publishing Group, Inc., The.

—Wild West Lawmen & Outlaws. 2009. (Library of the Westward Expansion Ser.). 24p. (gr. 3-4). 42.50 *(978-1-60853-944-4(X)*, PowerKids Pr.) Rosen Publishing Group, Inc., The.

Rice, Dona Herweck. Bad Guys & Gals of the Wild West, 1 vol. 2nd rev. ed. 2013. (TIME for KIDS(r): Informational Text Ser.). (ENG., Illus.). 64p. (J). (gr. 5-8). lib. bdg. 31.96 *(978-1-4333-7426-5(9))* Teacher Created Materials, Inc.

Sanford, Carl R. & Sanford, William R. Outlaws & Lawmen of the Wild West, 10 bks., Set. (Illus.). (YA). (gr. 4-10). lib. bdg. 169.50 *(978-0-89490-391-5(8))* Enslow Publishing, LLC.

Savage, Jeff. Quick-Draw Gunfighters: True Tales of the Wild West, 1 vol. 2012. (True Tales of the Wild West Ser.). (ENG., Illus.). 48p. (gr. 5-7). pap. 11.53 *(978-1-4644-0029-2(6)*, aac891de-4be3-4d12-acc9-87ad5075d450); lib. bdg. 25.27 *(978-0-7660-4021-2(6)*, c1f8bdce-fe0e-487c-ae9f-9adf9572c8d4) Enslow Publishing, LLC.

Schwartz, Heather E. Outlaws, Gunslingers, & Thieves. 2015. (ShockZone (tm) — Villains Ser.). (ENG., Illus.). 32p. (J). (gr. 5-8). E-Book 46.65 *(978-1-4677-6004-1(8)*, 9781467760041, Lerner Digital) Lerner Publishing Group.

Smith, Neil. Robin Hood, 1 vol. 2014. (Heroes & Legends Ser.). (ENG., Illus.). 88p. (J). (gr. 8-8). 38.80 *(978-1-4777-8139-5(0)*, 80d28836-bff5-4f63-9f0c-c2e8c8ea27c7, Rosen Young Adult) Rosen Publishing Group, Inc., The.

Sullivan, Laura L. Bonnie & Clyde: A Deadly Duo, 1 vol. Abbott, Graham, illus. 2018. (American Legends & Folktales Ser.). (ENG.). 32p. (gr. 3-3). pap. 11.58 *(978-1-5026-3684-3(0)*, aa03a3aa-45d1-4330-af44-fbb85ff186c1); lib. bdg. 30.21 *(978-1-5026-3682-9(4)*, 0c193bf1-f999-4240-8252-a8fcde6fe0c9) Cavendish Square Publishing LLC.

Thompson, Paul B. Billy the Kid: It Was a Game of Two & I Got There First, 1 vol. 2008. (Americans: the Spirit of a Nation Ser.). (ENG., Illus.). 128p. (gr. 5-6). lib. bdg. 35.93 *(978-0-7660-3480-8(1)*, efb3071a-90e0-4603-bfb4-ea376dda4901) Enslow Publishing, LLC.

Waldman, Scott. Gunfight at the O. K. Corral: Wyatt Earp Upholds the Law. 2009. (Great Moments in American History Ser.). 32p. (gr. 3-3). 47.90 *(978-1-61513-143-3(4))* Rosen Publishing Group, Inc., The.

Wommack, Linda. Ann Bassett: Colorado's Cattle Queen. 2018. (Illus.). 247p. *(978-0-87004-619-3(5))* Caxton Pr.

Woog, Adam. Jesse James: The Wild West for Kids. 2014. (ENG., Illus.). 128p. (J). (gr. 2-7). pap. 12.95 *(978-1-62636-160-7(6)*, 263160, Sky Pony Pr.) Skyhorse Publishing Co., Inc.

Yasuda, Anita. Notorious Outlaws, 1 vol. 2016. (Wild West Ser.). (ENG., Illus.). 48p. (J). (gr. 4-8). lib. bdg. 35.64 *(978-1-68078-257-8(6)*, 22115) ABDO Publishing Co.

ROBBERS AND OUTLAWS—FICTION

Adler, David A. Cam Jansen & the Catnapping Mystery. Natti, Susanna, illus. 2005. (Cam Jansen Ser.). 58p. (gr. 2-5). 14.00 *(978-0-7569-5045-3(7))* Perfection Learning Corp.

Ahdieh, Renée. Flame in the Mist. (Flame in the Mist Ser.: 1). (ENG.). (YA). (gr. 7). 2018. 448p. pap. 11.99 *(978-0-14-751387-8(1)*, Penguin Books) 2017. 416p. 17.99 *(978-0-399-17163-5(0)*, G.P. Putnam's Sons Books for Young Readers) Penguin Young Readers Group.

—Flame in the Mist. 2018. lib. bdg. 22.10 *(978-0-606-40878-3(9))* Turtleback.

Alfonsi, Alice. The Almost Invisible Cases. Harrington, Rich, illus. 2007. 96p. (J). *(978-0-545-01585-1(5))* Scholastic, Inc.

—The Code Red Cases. Harrington, Rich, illus. 2006. 96p. (J). *(978-0-439-91447-5(7))* Scholastic, Inc.

—The Playing Card Cases. Harrington, Rich, illus. 2007. 96p. (J). *(978-0-545-01087-0(X))* Scholastic, Inc.

Alger, Horatio. Joe's Luck. 2005. 28.95 *(978-1-4218-1455-1(2))*; 264p. pap. 13.95 *(978-1-4218-1555-8(9))* 1st World Publishing, Inc. (1st World Library - Literary Society).

—Joe's Luck: Or, Always Wide Awake. 2006. (ENG.). 176p. pap. 19.99 *(978-1-4264-0883-0(8))*; 170p. pap. 21.99 *(978-1-4264-0864-9(1))* Creative Media Partners, LLC.

—Joe's Luck: Or, Always Wide Awake. 2006. pap. *(978-1-4065-0713-3(X))* Dodo Pr.

—Struggling Upward: Or, Luke Larkin's Luck. 2006. pap. *(978-1-4065-0723-2(7))* Dodo Pr.

—Struggling Upward; or, Luck Larkin's Luck. 2008. 104p. pap. 7.99 *(978-1-4209-3044-3(3))* Digireads.com Publishing.

Andersen, C. B. The Book of Mormon Sleuth Vol. 3: The Hidden Path. 2003. ix, 214p. (J). pap. *(978-1-57008-988-6(4))* Deseret Bk. Co.

Angleberger, Tom. Fake Mustache: Or, How Jodie o'Rodeo & Her Wonder Horse (and Some Nerdy Kid) Saved the U. S. Presidential Election from a Mad Genius Criminal Mastermind. 2013. (ENG.). 208p. (J). (gr. 3-7). pap. 7.95 *(978-1-4197-1163-3(6)*, 1013303, Amulet Bks.) Abrams, Inc.

Appelt, Kathi. Angel Thieves. (ENG.). 336p. (YA). (gr. 9). 2020. pap. 11.99 *(978-1-4423-3966-8(7)*, Atheneum Bks. for Young Readers) 2019. 18.99 *(978-1-4424-2109-7(6)*, Atheneum/Caitlyn Dlouhy Books) Simon & Schuster Children's Publishing.

Appleton, Victor. Restricted Access. 2019. (Tom Swift Inventors' Academy Ser.: 3). (ENG., Illus.). 160p. (J). (gr. 3-7). 17.99 *(978-1-5344-3637-4(5)*, Simon & Schuster/Paula Wiseman Bks.) Simon & Schuster/Paula Wiseman Bks.

Ausona, Roberto de. Robin Hood. (SPA., Illus.). 156p. (YA). 11.95 *(978-84-7281-110-2(7)*, AF1110) Auriga, Ediciones S.A. ESP. Dist: Continental Bk. Co., Inc.

Auxier, Jonathan. Peter Nimble & His Fantastic Eyes. 2012. (ENG.). 400p. (YA). (gr. 5-17). pap. 9.95 *(978-1-4197-0421-5(4)*, 693403, Amulet Bks.) Abrams, Inc.

Avi. Crispin: the End of Time. 2011. (ENG.). 240p. (J). (gr. 5). pap. 7.99 *(978-0-06-174083-1(7),* Balzer & Bray) HarperCollins Pubs.

Baglio, Ben M. Max Is Missing. 2005. (Pet Finders Club Ser.: Vol. 2). (Illus.). 126p. (J). pap. *(978-0-439-68884-0(1))* Scholastic, Inc.

Balasubramanian, Lalitha. The Twins at the Ancient Villa, 1 vol. 2009. 48p. pap. 16.95 *(978-1-61582-601-8(7))* America Star Bks.

Bardugo, Leigh. Six of Crows. (Illus.). (YA). 2015. 465p. pap. *(978-1-62779-509-8(X))* 2021. (Six of Crows Ser.: 1). (ENG., 496p. pap. 12.99 *(978-1-250-77790-4(9),* 900235404, Holt, Henry & Co. Bks. For Young Readers) 2015. (Six of Crows Ser.: 1). (ENG., 480p. (gr. 7-17). 19.99 *(978-1-62779-212-7(0),* 900141221, Holt, Henry & Co. Bks. For Young Readers) Holt, Henry & Co.

—Six of Crows. 2018. (Six of Crows Ser.: 1). (ENG., Illus.). 496p. (YA). (gr. 9-12). pap. 11.99 *(978-1-250-07696-0(X),* 900152591) Square Fish.

—Six of Crows. 2018. (Six of Crows Ser.: 1). (YA). lib. bdg. 22.10 *(978-0-606-39944-9(5))* Turtleback.

Barnett, Mac. It Happened on a Train. Rex, Adam, illus. 2012. (Brixton Brothers Ser.: 3). (ENG.). 304p. (J). (gr. 3-7). pap. 8.99 *(978-1-4169-7820-6(8),* Simon & Schuster Bks. For Young Readers) Simon & Schuster Bks. For Young Readers.

Barnhill, Kelly. The Witch's Boy. 2014. (ENG.). 400p. (J). (gr. 4-7). 37.99 *(978-1-61620-351-1(X),* 73351) Algonquin Young Readers.

Bell, Hilari. Shield of Stars, No. 1. 2008. (Shield, Sword, & Crown Ser.: 1). (ENG.). 288p. (J). (gr. 3-7). pap. 13.99 *(978-1-4169-0595-0(2),* Simon & Schuster/Paula Wiseman Bks.) Simon & Schuster/Paula Wiseman Bks.

Bell, William. The Blue Helmet. 2009. (ENG.). 224p. mass mkt. 6.99 *(978-0-7704-3002-3(3),* Seal Bks) Random Hse. of Canada CAN. Dist: Random Hse., Inc.

Berlin, Eric. The Puzzler's Mansion: The Puzzling World of Winston Breen. 2013. (Puzzling World of Winston Breen Ser.: 3). 272p. (J). (gr. 3-7). 8.99 *(978-0-14-242643-2(1),* Puffin Books) Penguin Young Readers Group.

Bessen, Luc. Arthur & the Minimoys. Sowchek, Ellen, tr. from FRE. 2005. (ENG.). 240p. (J). 15.99 *(978-0-06-059623-1(6))* HarperCollins Pubs.

Besson, Luc. Arthur & the Minimoys. 2005. (Illus.). 240p. (J). lib. bdg. 16.89 *(978-0-06-059624-8(4))* HarperCollins Pubs.

Bolts, Russ. The Good, the Bad, & the Cowbots. Cooper, Jay, illus. 2019. (Bots Ser.: 2). (ENG.). 128p. (J). (gr. k-4). 16.99 *(978-1-5344-3692-3(8));* pap. 6.99 *(978-1-5344-3691-6(X))* Little Simon. (Little Simon).

Bondor-Stone, Annabeth & White, Connor. Time Tracers: the Stolen Summers. 2018. (ENG.). 256p. (J). (gr. 3-7). 16.99 *(978-0-06-267142-4(1),* HarperCollins) HarperCollins Pubs.

Bonk, John J. Madhattan Mystery. 2012. (ENG., Illus.). 304p. (J). (gr. 4-6). 22.44 *(978-0-8027-2349-9(7),* 9780802723499) Walker & Co.

Bottiglieri, Tim. Robber Raccoon, 1 vol. Bishop, John E., illus. 2009. 16p. pap. 24.95 *(978-1-61546-432-6(8))* America Star Bks.

Bowman, Erin. Retribution Rails. (ENG.). (YA). (gr. 9). 2019. 400p. pap. 9.99 *(978-1-328-60367-8(9),* 1732075) 2017. (Illus.). 384p. 17.99 *(978-0-544-91888-7(6),* 1655796) HarperCollins Pubs. (Clarion Bks.).

Buckley-Archer, Linda. The Time Quake. 2010. (Gideon Trilogy Ser.: 3). (ENG.). 464p. (J). (gr. 5-9). pap. 10.99 *(978-1-4169-1530-0(3),* Simon & Schuster Bks. For Young Readers) Simon & Schuster Bks. For Young Readers.

—The Time Quake, 3. 2009. (Gideon Trilogy Ser.: 3). (ENG.). 464p. (J). (gr. 5-9). 17.99 *(978-1-4169-1529-4(X))* Simon & Schuster, Inc.

—The Time Thief. 2008. (Gideon Trilogy Ser.: 2). (ENG.). 512p. (J). (gr. 5-9). pap. 9.99 *(978-1-4169-1528-7(1),* Simon & Schuster Bks. For Young Readers) Simon & Schuster Bks. For Young Readers.

—The Time Travelers. 2012. (Gideon Trilogy Ser.: 1). (ENG.). 416p. (J). (gr. 5-9). 17.99 *(978-1-4424-6551-0(4),* Simon & Schuster Bks. For Young Readers) Simon & Schuster Bks. For Young Readers.

Bunce, Elizabeth C. Liar's Moon. 2011. (YA). pap. *(978-0-545-13607-5(5),* Levine, Arthur A. Bks.) Scholastic, Inc.

—StarCrossed. 2011. (ENG.). 368p. (YA). pap. 9.99 *(978-0-545-13606-8(7),* Levine, Arthur A. Bks.) Scholastic, Inc.

Burnett, Frances. Editha's Burglar. Sandham, Henry, illus. 2005. reprint ed. pap. 15.95 *(978-1-4179-0135-7(7))* Kessinger Publishing, LLC.

Cajoleas, Jimmy. Goldeline. (ENG.). (J). (gr. 5). 2019. 272p. pap. 6.99 *(978-0-06-249876-2(2))* 2017. 256p. 16.99 *(978-0-06-249875-5(4))* HarperCollins Pubs. (HarperCollins).

Cazet, Denys. Minnie & Moo: Wanted Dead or Alive. Cazet, Denys, illus. 2007. (I Can Read Level 3 Ser.). (ENG., Illus.). 48p. (J). (gr. k-3). pap. 4.99 *(978-0-06-073012-3(9),* HarperCollins) HarperCollins Pubs.

—Wanted Dead or Alive. Cazet, Denys, illus. 2008. (Minnie & Moo Ser.). (Illus.). (J). (gr. -1-3). pap. 16.95 incl. audio *(978-1-4301-0471-1(6))* Live Oak Media.

—Wanted Dead or Alive. 2008. (Minnie & Moo Ser.). (J). (gr. k-2). 25.95 incl. audio *(978-1-4301-0472-8(4))* Live Oak Media.

Chee, Traci. The Reader. (Reader Ser.: 1). 464p. (YA). (gr. 7). 2017. pap. 11.99 *(978-0-14-751805-7(9),* Speak)Bk. 1. 2016. 19.99 *(978-0-399-17677-7(2),* G.P. Putnam's Sons Books for Young Readers) Penguin Young Readers Group.

—The Reader. 2017. (Sea of Ink & Gold Ser.: 1). lib. bdg. 22.10 *(978-0-606-40001-5(X))* Turtleback.

Cherry, Alison. The Classy Crooks Club. 2016. (ENG., Illus.). 336p. (J). (gr. 3-7). 16.99 *(978-1-4814-4637-2(1),* Aladdin) Simon & Schuster Children's Publishing.

Child, Lauren. Ruby Redfort Feel the Fear. Child, Lauren, illus. (Ruby Redfort Ser.: 4). (ENG., Illus.). 528p. (J). (gr. 5-9). 2018. pap. 7.99 *(978-0-7636-9452-4(5))* 2016. 16.99 *(978-0-7636-5470-2(1))* Candlewick Pr.

Choyce, Lesley. Running the Risk, 1 vol. 2009. (Orca Soundings Ser.). (ENG.). (YA). (gr. 8-12). 112p. 16.95 *(978-1-55469-026-8(9));* 144p. pap. 9.95 *(978-1-55469-025-1(0),* 1554690250) Orca Bk. Pubs. USA.

Christopher, Matt. The Mystery under Fugitive House. 2016. (ENG., Illus.). 114p. (J). pap. 9.95 *(978-1-62268-067-2(7))* Bella Rosa Bks.

Cooper, Jay. The Curse of the Mummy's Tummy (the Spy Next Door #2) 2017. (ENG., Illus.). 144p. (J). (gr. 2-5). 9.99 *(978-0-545-93298-1(X),* Scholastic Pr.) Scholastic, Inc.

Coren, Alan. Arthur the Kid. 2004. (Illus.). 64p. *(978-0-903895-76-7(5),* Robson Bks. Ltd.) Pavilion Bks.

—Buffalo Arthur. 2004. (Illus.). 64p. *(978-0-903895-75-0(7),* Robson Bks. Ltd.) Pavilion Bks.

—Railroad Arthur. 2004. (Illus.). 64p. *(978-0-903895-92-7(7),* Robson Bks. Ltd.) Pavilion Bks.

Cornelia, Funke. The Thief Lord. 2004.Tr. of Herr der Diebe. 376p. (J). (gr. 5-18). pap. 44.00 incl. audio *(978-0-8072-2278-2(X),* Listening Library) Random Hse. Audio Publishing Group.

—The Thief Lord. 2003.Tr. of Herr der Diebe. (gr. 3-6). 18.40 *(978-0-613-84572-4(2))* Turtleback.

Cornwell, Betsy. The Forest Queen. (ENG.). (YA). (gr. 7). 2020. 320p. pap. 9.99 *(978-0-358-13361-2(0),* 1749855) 2018. 304p. 17.99 *(978-0-544-88819-7(7),* 1653253) HarperCollins Pubs. (Clarion Bks.).

Couloumbis, Audrey. The Misadventures of Maude March: Or Trouble Rides a Fast Horse. 2007. (Illus.). 295p. (gr. 3-7). 18.00 *(978-0-7569-7770-2(3))* Perfection Learning Corp.

Crain, Kira. SEK Statton. 2009. (GER.). 136p. 29.95 *(978-1-4092-6127-8(1))* Lulu Pr., Inc.

Croall, Marie P. Ali Baba: Fooling the Forty Thieves: an Arabian Tale. 2008. (Graphic Myths & Legends Ser.). (Illus.). 48p. (J). (gr. 3-7). lib. bdg. 26.60 *(978-0-8225-7525-2(6),* Graphic Universe™) Lerner Publishing Group.

Curious George & the Dump Truck (8x8 with Stickers) Curiou. 2010. (Curious George Ser.). (ENG., Illus.). 24p. (J). (gr. -1-3). pap. 4.99 *(978-0-547-50425-4(X),* 1442863, Clarion Bks.) HarperCollins Pubs.

Dahl, Michael. The Sea of Lost Books, 1 vol. Kendall, Bradford, illus. 2010. (Return to the Library of Doom Ser.). (ENG.). 72p. (J). (gr. 4-8). lib. bdg. 23.99 *(978-1-4342-2142-1(3),* 102872, Stone Arch Bks.) Capstone.

—Tome Raider. Evergreen, Nelson, illus. 2015. (Library of Doom: the Final Chapters Ser.). (ENG.). 40p. (J). (gr. 4-8). 23.99 *(978-1-4342-9677-1(6),* 126985, Stone Arch Bks.) Capstone.

Dailey, Reid. Ross the Reader & the Adventure of the Pirate's Treasure. Edgerley, Ross, illus. 2009. 44p. pap. 16.95 *(978-1-59858-900-9(8))* Dog Ear Publishing, LLC.

Dale, Elizabeth. Cara the Cowgirl. Lombardo, Serena, illus. 2021. (Early Bird Readers — Gold (Early Bird Stories (tm)) Ser.). (ENG.). 32p. (J). (gr. k-3). 30.65 *(978-1-5415-9007-6(4),* 2c85c67a-e715-4717-9395-1ee97d95bee3, Lerner Pubns.) Lerner Publishing Group.

—The Detective Club. O'Neill, Kelly, illus. 2021. (Early Bird Readers — Gold (Early Bird Stories (tm)) Ser.). (ENG.). 32p. (J). (gr. k-3). 30.65 *(978-1-5415-9008-3(2),* 3a2c3181-610a-499d-9829-1965afcab114, Lerner Pubns.) Lerner Publishing Group.

Dale, Katie. Shooting Star. Lund, John, illus. 2021. (Early Bird Readers — Gold (Early Bird Stories (tm)) Ser.). (ENG.). 32p. (J). (gr. k-3). 30.65 *(978-1-5415-9002-1(3),* 25b09be9-0db9-4bdc-929c-cbd2c284dbc3, Lerner Pubns.) Lerner Publishing Group.

Daneshvari, Gitty. School of Fear: Class Is Not Dismissed! 2011. (School of Fear Ser.: 2). (ENG.). 336p. (J). (gr. 3-7). pap. 17.99 *(978-0-316-03329-9(4))* Little, Brown Bks. for Young Readers.

Daniels, J. M. The Secret of the Little Dutch Doll. 2009. 68p. pap. 25.49 *(978-1-4343-9356-2(9))* AuthorHouse.

Dare, Will. How to Catch a Dino Thief. Epelbaum, Mariano, illus. 2017. (Dino Riders Ser.: 4). (ENG.). 128p. (J). (gr. 2-5). pap. 7.99 *(978-1-4926-3623-6(1),* Sourcebooks Jabberwocky) Sourcebooks, Inc.

Davis, Kent. A Riddle in Ruby. 2016. (Riddle in Ruby Ser.: 1). (ENG.). 432p. (J). (gr. 3-7). 18.40 *(978-0-606-39257-0(2))* Turtleback.

De Campi, Alex. Kat & Mouse Vol. 1: Teacher Torture, 1 vol. Manfredi, Federica, illus. 2008. (Tokyopop Ser.). (ENG.). 96p. (J). (gr. 2-6). 32.79 *(978-1-59961-564-6(9),* 14807, Graphic Novels) Spotlight.

—Kat & Mouse Vol. 2: Tripped, 1 vol. Manfredi, Federica, illus. 2008. (Tokyopop Ser.). (ENG.). 96p. (J). (gr. 2-6). 32.79 *(978-1-59961-565-3(7),* 14808, Graphic Novels) Spotlight.

—Kat & Mouse Vol. 3: The Ice Storm, 1 vol. Manfredi, Federica, illus. 2008. (Tokyopop Ser.). (ENG.). 96p. (J). (gr. 2-6). 32.79 *(978-1-59961-566-0(5),* 14809, Graphic Novels) Spotlight.

Derby, Sally. Two Fools & a Horse: An Orginal Tale, 1 vol. Rayevsky, Robert, illus. 2003. (ENG.). 32p. (J). (gr. k-3). 16.95 *(978-0-7614-5119-8(6))* Marshall Cavendish Corp.

Deshpande, Shashi. 3 Novels. 2006. 379p. *(978-0-14-333511-5(1),* Puffin) Penguin Publishing Group.

Dickens, Charles. Oliver Twist, 1 vol. McWilliam, Howard, illus. 2011. (Calico Illustrated Classics Ser.: No. 3). (ENG.). 112p. (J). (gr. 2-5). 38.50 *(978-1-61641-106-0(6),* 4019, Calico Chapter Bks.) ABDO Publishing Co.

—Oliver Twist. abr. ed. Date not set. (Nelson Readers Ser.). (J). pap. *(978-0-17-557020-1(5))* Addison-Wesley Longman, Inc.

—Oliver Twist. 2008. (Bring the Classics to Life Ser.). (ENG., Illus.). 72p. (gr. 3-12). pap., act. bk. ed. 10.95 *(978-1-55576-325-1(1),* EDCTR-308B) EDCON Publishing Group.

—Oliver Twist. abr. ed. (J). 9.95 *(978-1-56156-372-2(2))* Kidsbooks, LLC.

—Oliver Twist: With a Discussion of Honesty. 2003. (Values in Action Illustrated Classics Ser.). (J). *(978-1-59203-051-4(3))* Learning Challenge, Inc.

Doane, Pelagie. Riddle of the Double Ring #10, No. 10. Doane, Pelagie, illus. 2008. (Judy Bolton Ser.). (ENG., Illus.). 236p. (J). (gr. 4-7). pap. 14.95 *(978-1-4290-9030-8(8))* Applewood Bks.

Donaldson, Julia. The Highway Rat. Scheffler, Axel, illus. 2013. (ENG.). 32p. (J). (gr. -1-3). 17.99 *(978-0-545-47758-1(1),* Levine, Arthur A. Bks.) Scholastic, Inc.

Dunagan, Ted M. Secret of the Satilfa. 2010. (ENG.). 208p. (J). (gr. 3-18). 21.95 *(978-1-58838-249-8(4),* 8987, NewSouth Bks.) NewSouth, Inc.

Durell, Charles Pend. Lights off Shore or Sam & the Outlaws. 2005. pap. 28.95 *(978-1-4179-9422-9(3))* Kessinger Publishing, LLC.

Erickson, John. The Case of the Monkey Burglar. Holmes, Gerald L., illus. 2011. (Hank the Cowdog Ser.: No. 48). (ENG.). 129p. (J). (gr. 3-6). pap. 5.99 *(978-1-59188-148-3(X))* Maverick Bks., Inc.

Erickson, Mary Ellen. Who Jinxed the CG Ranch? 2009. 196p. 24.95 *(978-1-4401-4218-5(1));* pap. 14.95 *(978-1-4401-4216-1(5))* iUniverse, Inc.

Everett, F. The Burglar's Breakfast. 2004. (Young Reading Ser.: Vol. 1). (Illus.). 48p. (J). (gr. 2-18). pap. 5.95 *(978-0-7945-0221-8(0),* Usborne) EDC Publishing.

Everett-Green, Evelyn. Tom Tufton's Travels. 2007. 196p. per. *(978-1-4065-3395-8(5))* Dodo Pr.

Eves, Rosalyn. Lost Crow Conspiracy (Blood Rose Rebellion, Book 2) (Blood Rose Rebellion Ser.). (ENG.). 464p. (YA). (gr. 7). 2019. pap. 10.99 *(978-1-101-93610-8(X),* Ember) 2018. 18.99 *(978-1-101-93607-8(X),* Knopf Bks. for Young Readers) Random Hse. Children's Bks.

Falls, Kat. Dark Life, 1. 2011. (ENG.). 304p. (J). (gr. 4-7). pap. 9.99 *(978-0-545-17815-0(0))* Scholastic, Inc.

—Rip Tide. 2011. 314p. (J). pap. *(978-0-545-43175-0(1),* Scholastic Pr.) Scholastic, Inc.

Fenn, G. Manville. Young Robin Hood. 2019. (ENG.). 66p. (J). pap. 10.36 *(978-0-368-28235-5(X))* Blurb, Inc.

—Young Robin Hood. 2011. 56p. pap. 7.99 *(978-1-61203-082-1(3))* Bottom of the Hill Publishing.

Feutl, Rita. Bike Thief, 1 vol. 2014. (Orca Soundings Ser.). (ENG.). 136p. (YA). (gr. 8-12). pap. 9.95 *(978-1-4598-0569-9(0))* Orca Bk. Pubs. USA.

Fischel, Ana. The Twelve Quests - Book 5, a Firebird's Feather. 2009. 158p. pap. *(978-1-84923-877-9(4))* YouWriteOn.

Fleischman, Sid. Bandit's Moon. Smith, Jos. A., illus. 2008. (ENG.). 192p. (J). (gr. 3-7). pap. 6.99 *(978-0-06-145096-9(0),* Greenwillow Bks.) HarperCollins Pubs.

—The Whipping Boy. 2011. 7.52 *(978-0-7848-3459-6(8),* Everbind) Marco Bk. Co.

—The Whipping Boy. 2003. (J). 17.20 *(978-0-613-69320-2(5))* Turtleback.

Franquin, André. The Marsupilami Thieves. 2013. (Spirou & Fantasio Ser.: 5). (Illus.). 64p. (J). (gr. 3-12). pap. 15.95 *(978-1-84918-167-9(5))* CineBook GBR. Dist: National Bk. Network.

Frederick, Heather Vogel. Once upon a Toad. 2013. (ENG., Illus.). 288p. (J). (gr. 5-9). pap. 7.99 *(978-1-4169-8479-5(8),* Simon & Schuster Bks. For Young Readers) Simon & Schuster Bks. For Young Readers.

—Once upon a Toad. 2012. (ENG., Illus.). 272p. (J). (gr. 5-9). 16.99 *(978-1-4169-8478-8(X))* Simon & Schuster, Inc.

Funke, Cornelia. The Thief Lord. Birmingham, Christian, illus. 2010.Tr. of Herr der Diebe. (ENG.). 368p. (J). (gr. 4-7). pap. 9.99 *(978-0-545-22770-4(4))* Scholastic, Inc.

Galindo, Renata. The Cherry Thief. Galindo, Renata, illus. 2014. (Child's Play Library). (Illus.). 32p. (J). *(978-1-84643-652-9(4))* Child's Play International Ltd.

Gallo, Tina, adapted by. Hero School. 2017. (Illus.). (J). *(978-1-5182-4737-8(7),* Simon Spotlight) Simon Spotlight.

Garfield, Leon. Smith: the Story of a Pickpocket. 2013. (ENG.). 216p. (J). (gr. 4-7). 15.95 *(978-1-59017-675-7(8),* NYR Children's Collection) New York Review of Bks., Inc., The.

Gilbert, David D. Feodor Fitz: Journey to Harmony Ville. 2012. 40p. pap. 17.57 *(978-1-4772-1983-6(8));* pap. 20.99 *(978-1-4685-8122-5(8))* AuthorHouse.

Gillman, Melanie. Stage Dreams. Gillman, Melanie, illus. 2019. (ENG., Illus.). 104p. (YA). (gr. 8-12). 29.32 *(978-1-5124-4000-3(0),* 3f3783d0-fdab-4aa6-813e-16633529cda8, Graphic Universe™) Lerner Publishing Group.

Goodwin, John. Robin Hood. Date not set. (Nelson Readers Ser.). (Illus.). 36p. (J). pap. *(978-0-17-557050-8(7))* Addison-Wesley Longman, Inc.

Goscinny, René, et al. Lucky Luke: The Dashing White Cowboy. 2008. (ENG.). 48p. (J). (gr. 2-4). pap. *(978-81-8386-014-7(1))* India Research Pr. IND. Dist: Independent Pubs. Group.

—Lucky Luke - Jesse James. 2008. (ENG.). 48p. (J). (gr. 2-4). pap. *(978-81-8386-016-1(8))* India Research Pr. IND. Dist: Independent Pubs. Group.

—Lucky Luke - Ma Dalton. 2008. (ENG.). 48p. (J). (gr. 2-4). pap. *(978-81-8386-015-4(X))* India Research Pr. IND. Dist: Independent Pubs. Group.

—Lucky Luke - the Tender Foot. 2008. (ENG.). 48p. (J). (gr. 2-4). pap. *(978-81-8386-017-8(6))* India Research Pr. IND. Dist: Independent Pubs. Group.

Gosling, Sharon. The Diamond Thief. 2014. (Diamond Thief Ser.). (ENG.). 336p. (J). (gr. 9-12). 16.95 *(978-1-63079-002-8(8),* 126763, Switch Pr.) Capstone.

Grabenstein, Chris. Riley Mack & the Other Known Troublemakers. 2012. (Riley Mack Ser.: 1). (ENG.). 272p. (J). (gr. 3-7). 16.99 *(978-0-06-202620-0(8))* HarperCollins Pubs.

Graceffa, Joey. Children of Eden: A Novel. 2017. (Children of Eden Ser.: 1). (ENG.). 288p. (gr. 7-12). pap. 12.99 *(978-1-5011-4990-0(3),* Atria Bks.) Simon & Schuster.

Graves, Judith. Exposed, 1 vol. 2015. (Orca Soundings Ser.: 2). (ENG.). 144p. (YA). (gr. 8-12). pap. 9.95 *(978-1-4598-0722-8(7))* Orca Bk. Pubs. USA.

Greene, Janice. No Way to Run, 1 vol. unabr. ed. 2010. (Q Reads Ser.). (ENG.). 32p. (YA). (gr. 9-12). pap. 8.50 *(978-1-61651-184-5(2))* Saddleback Educational Publishing, Inc.

Greenfield, A. B. Ra the Mighty: the Great Tomb Robbery. Horne, Sarah, illus. 2019. (Ra the Mighty Ser.: 2). (ENG.). 256p. (J). (gr. 2-5). 16.99 *(978-0-8234-4240-9(3))* Holiday Hse., Inc.

Hahn, Mary Downing. The Gentleman Outlaw & Me — Eli. 2007. (ENG.). 224p. (YA). (gr. 7-7). pap. 6.99 *(978-0-618-83000-8(6),* 100560, Clarion Bks.) HarperCollins Pubs.

Hancock, H. Irving. The Young Engineers in Arizona. rev. ed. 2006. 216p. 27.95 *(978-1-4218-1751-4(9));* pap. 12.95 *(978-1-4218-1851-1(5))* 1st World Publishing, Inc. (1st World Library - Literary Society).

—The Young Engineers in Arizona. 2004. reprint ed. pap. 21.95 *(978-1-4191-8913-5(1))* Kessinger Publishing, LLC.

—The Young Engineers in Colorado. rev. ed. 2006. 212p. 27.95 *(978-1-4218-1744-6(6));* pap. 12.95 *(978-1-4218-1844-3(2))* 1st World Publishing, Inc. (1st World Library - Literary Society).

—The Young Engineers in Mexico. rev. ed. 2006. 208p. 27.95 *(978-1-4218-1738-5(1));* pap. 12.95 *(978-1-4218-1838-2(8))* 1st World Publishing, Inc. (1st World Library - Literary Society).

—The Young Engineers in Nevada. rev. ed. 2006. 220p. 27.95 *(978-1-4218-1754-5(3));* pap. 12.95 *(978-1-4218-1854-2(X))* 1st World Publishing, Inc. (1st World Library - Literary Society).

—The Young Engineers on the Gulf. rev. ed. 2006. 216p. 27.95 *(978-1-4218-1752-1(7));* pap. 12.95 *(978-1-4218-1852-8(3))* 1st World Publishing, Inc. (1st World Library - Literary Society).

Hanzik, Sharon. Raccoons Don't Use Spoons. 2009. 24p. pap. 17.95 *(978-1-4327-2815-1(6))* Outskirts Pr., Inc.

Harris, Neil Patrick. The Magic Misfits. Martin, Lissy & Hilton, Kyle, illus. (Magic Misfits Ser.: 1). (ENG.). (J). (gr. 3-7). 2018. 288p. pap. 8.99 *(978-0-316-35557-5(7))* 2017. 272p. 16.99 *(978-0-316-39182-5(4))* 2017. 336p. 34.99 *(978-0-316-43984-8(3))* Little, Brown Bks. for Young Readers.

Harrison, Charles C. Dick Turpin. 2003. (Historias de Siempre Ser.). (SPA., Illus.). 92p. (J). (gr. 5-8). pap. 12.95 *(978-84-204-5701-7(9))* Santillana USA Publishing Co., Inc.

Heim, Alastair. Hello, Door. Coburn, Alisa, illus. 2018. (ENG.). 32p. (J). (gr. -1-3). 16.99 *(978-1-4998-0536-9(5))* Little Bee Books Inc.

Heimerl, Kristen. Inspector Dewey. 2015. (ENG., Illus.). (J). 19.99 *(978-1-939710-27-7(8))* Orange Frazer Pr.

Hendry, Frances. Quest for a Queen: The Jackdaw. 2006. pap. *(978-1-905665-05-1(9))* Pollinger In Print.

Heneghan, James & Charles, Norma. Bank Job, 1 vol. 2009. (ENG.). 176p. (J). (gr. 4-7). pap. 14.95 *(978-1-55143-855-9(0))* Orca Bk. Pubs. USA.

Higginson, Sheryl. Dilbert's Pets, 1 vol. 2010. 94p. pap. 19.95 *(978-1-4489-5757-6(5))* America Star Bks.

Hillerman, Tony. Buster Mesquite's Cowboy Band. 2006. (J). reprint ed. lib. bdg. 14.95 *(978-0-914001-12-6(4))* Sidewinder Publishing LLC.

Horsfall, S. J. Jodie & Lilly... & the Fake Mansion. 2009. 58p. pap. 7.50 *(978-0-557-12474-9(3))* Lulu Pr., Inc.

Houts, Richard. A Thief's Journey. 2008. (ENG.). 128p. pap. 15.99 *(978-0-557-02192-5(8))* Lulu Pr., Inc.

Howard, Eva. The Stolen Crown. 2017. (League of Archers Ser.: 2). (ENG., Illus.). 304p. (J). (gr. 4-8). 16.99 *(978-1-4814-6040-8(4),* Aladdin) Simon & Schuster Children's Publishing.

Howard, Jeremy. The Countdown: The Adventures of Starforce. 2005. 114p. 23.45 *(978-1-4208-2398-1(1));* pap. 11.95 *(978-1-4208-2397-4(3))* AuthorHouse.

Humphrey, Anna. Quack. 2020. (ENG.). 240p. (J). (gr. 3-7). 16.99 *(978-0-8075-6706-7(X),* 080756706X) Whitman, Albert & Co.

Imbernón, Maite & Dickens, Charles. Oliver Twist. 2003. (Timeless Classics Ser.). (SPA., Illus.). 92p. (J). pap. 10.95 *(978-84-204-5750-5(7))* Santillana USA Publishing Co., Inc.

Jacobson, Rick. The Mona Lisa Caper. Jacobson, Rick & Fernandez, Laura, illus. 2005. 24p. (J). (gr. k-3). 17.99 *(978-0-88776-726-5(5),* Tundra Bks.) Tundra Bks. CAN. Dist: Penguin Random Hse. LLC.

James, Laura. Fabio the World's Greatest Flamingo Detective: Mystery on the Ostrich Express. Fox, Emily, illus. 2020. (ENG.). 128p. (J). 16.99 *(978-1-5476-0459-3(X),* 900223954); pap. 6.99 *(978-1-5476-0458-6(1),* 900223951) Bloomsbury Publishing USA. (Bloomsbury Children's Bks.).

Johnson, Gillian. Thora & the Green Sea-Unicorn. Johnson, Gillian, illus. 2005. (Illus.). 272p. *(978-0-207-20016-8(5))* HarperCollins Pubs. Australia.

Jones, Rob Lloyd. The Story of Robin Hood. Marks, Alan, illus. 2010. (Picture Book Classics Ser.). 24p. (J). 9.99 *(978-0-7945-2859-1(7),* Usborne) EDC Publishing.

Jones, T. Llew. Storïau Cwm-Pen-Llo. 2005. (WEL., Illus.). 100p. pap. *(978-0-86381-750-2(5))* Gwasg Carreg Gwalch.

Jordan, Rosa. Wild Spirits. 2010. (ENG.). 272p. (J). (gr. 6). pap. 12.99 *(978-1-55488-729-3(1))* Dundurn Pr. CAN. Dist: Publishers Group West (PGW).

Keene, Carolyn. The Apple Bandit. Jones, Jan Naimo, illus. 2005. (Nancy Drew Notebooks). 74p. (J). (gr. 1-4). 11.65 *(978-0-7569-6505-1(5))* Perfection Learning Corp.

—The Stolen Show. 2019. (Nancy Drew Diaries: 18). (ENG.). 192p. (J). (gr. 3-7). pap. 6.99 *(978-1-5344-0577-6(1),* Simon & Schuster/Paula Wiseman Bks.) Simon & Schuster/Paula Wiseman Bks.

Kennedy, Robert F., Jr. Robert Smalls: The Boat Thief. Faricy, Patrick, illus. 2008. (Robert F. Kennedy, Jr.'s American Heroes Ser.). (ENG.). 48p. (gr. 5-8). 16.99 *(978-1-4231-0802-3(7))* Hyperion Pr.

King, Trey. Detective Chase McCain: Save That Cargo! 2013. (LEGO City 8X8 Ser.). lib. bdg. 13.55 *(978-0-606-32393-2(7))* Turtleback.

King, Trey & Kiernan, Kenny. Cops, Crocs, & Crooks! 2015. (LEGO City Ser.). (ENG., Illus.). 24p. (J). (gr. -1-3). pap. 3.99 *(978-0-545-78525-9(1))* Scholastic, Inc.

Krawitz, Susan. Viva, Rose! 2017. (ENG.). 240p. (J). (gr. 5). 16.95 *(978-0-8234-3756-6(6))* Holiday Hse., Inc.

Leeuwen, Jean. The Great Cheese Conspiracy, 0 vols. 2012. (ENG.). 96p. (J). (gr. 1-3). 15.99 *(978-0-7614-5972-9(3),* 9780761459729, Two Lions) Amazon Publishing.

Leslie, Emma. For Merrie England: A Tale of the Weavers of Norfolk. Taylor, R., illus. 2010. 168p. 20.95 *(978-1-934671-38-2(X));* pap. 10.95 *(978-1-934671-39-9(8))* Salem Ridge Press LLC.

Lloyd Jones, Rob, retold by. Robin Hood. 2008. (Young Reading Series 2 Gift Bks). 64p. (J). 8.99 *(978-0-7945-2090-8(1),* Usborne) EDC Publishing.

Lynn, Jenna. Archer: Book 4. Cruz, Abigail Dela, illus. 2018. (Robyn Hood Ser.). (ENG.). 48p. (J). (gr. 3-7). lib. bdg. 34.21 *(978-1-5321-3379-4(0),* 31181, Spellbound) Magic Wagon.

P
Q
R

—Hoodnapped: Book 3. Cruz, Abigail Dela, illus. 2018. (Robyn Hood Ser.). (ENG.). 48p. (J). (gr. 3-7). lib. bdg. 34.21 *(978-1-5321-3378-7(2)*, 31179, Spellbound) Magic Wagon.

—Metropolis Orphanage: Book 1. Cruz, Abigail Dela, illus. 2018. (Robyn Hood Ser.). (ENG.). 48p. (J). (gr. 3-7). lib. bdg. 34.21 *(978-1-5321-3376-3(6)*, 31175, Spellbound) Magic Wagon.

—Rivals: Book 2. Cruz, Abigail Dela, illus. 2018. (Robyn Hood Ser.). (ENG.). 48p. (J). (gr. 3-7). lib. bdg. 34.21 *(978-1-5321-3377-0(4)*, 31177, Spellbound) Magic Wagon.

MacAndrewRichard. The Black Pearls Starter/Beginner. 2008. (Cambridge English Readers Ser.). (ENG.). 32p. pap. 14.75 *(978-0-521-73289-5(1))* Cambridge Univ. Pr.

Magoon, Kekla. Rebellion of Thieves. 2017. (Robyn Hoodlum Ser.: 2). (J). lib. bdg. 18.40 *(978-0-606-40596-6(8))* Turtleback.

—Reign of Outlaws. 2017. (Robyn Hoodlum Adventure Ser.). (ENG.). 272p. (J). 16.99 *(978-1-61963-657-6(3)*, 900144923, Bloomsbury USA Childrens) Bloomsbury Publishing USA.

—Shadows of Sherwood. (Robyn Hoodlum Adventure Ser.). (ENG.). 368p. 2016. (J). pap. 8.99 *(978-1-68119-023-5(0)*, 900156154) 2015. (YA). (gr. 3-6). 16.99 *(978-1-61963-634-7(4)*, 900143012) Bloomsbury Publishing USA. (Bloomsbury USA Childrens).

—Shadows of Sherwood. 2016. (Robyn Hoodlum Ser.: 1). (ENG.). 355p. (J). (gr. 3-6). 18.40 *(978-0-606-39281-5(5))* Turtleback.

Manion, Denaé. Sock Stealing Thieves! 2011. 16p. (gr. 1-2). pap. 12.50 *(978-1-4567-5733-5(4))* AuthorHouse.

Manning, Matthew K. Operation Foxhunt. Douglas, Allen, illus. 2018. (Drone Academy Ser.). (ENG.). 112p. (J). (gr. 4-8). lib. bdg. 27.32 *(978-1-4965-6074-2(4)*, 137496, Stone Arch Bks.) Capstone.

Marlow, Susan K. Andrea Carter & the Family Secret, 1 vol. (Circle C Adventures Ser.: 3). 144p. (J). 2018. pap. 8.99 *(978-0-8254-4502-6(7))* 2008. pap. 7.99 *(978-0-8254-3365-8(7))* Kregel Pubns.

—Andrea Carter & the Trouble with Treasure, 1 vol. 2017. (Circle C Adventures Ser.: 5). 144p. (J). pap. 8.99 *(978-0-8254-4504-0(3))* Kregel Pubns.

—Heartbreak Trail: An Andrea Carter Book, 1 vol. 2015. (Circle C Milestones Ser.: 2). 168p. (J). pap. 9.99 *(978-0-8254-4368-8(7))* Kregel Pubns.

—Thick As Thieves: An Andrea Carter Book, 1 vol. 2015. (Circle C Milestones Ser.: 1). 176p. (YA). pap. 9.99 *(978-0-8254-4367-1(9))* Kregel Pubns.

Marsh, Carole. The Mystery of the Ancient Pyramid: Cairo, Egypt. 2006. (Around the World in 80 Mysteries Ser.). (Illus.). 128p. (J). (gr. 4-7). 14.95 *(978-0-635-03473-1(5))* Gallopade International.

Mawter, J. A. Launched! 2007. (ENG.). 258p. *(978-0-207-20073-1(4))* HarperCollins Pubs. Australia.

Mccarthy, Rebecca L. Save This Christmas! 2012. (LEGO City 8X8 Ser.). lib. bdg. 13.55 *(978-0-606-26767-0(0))* Turtleback.

McLean, Hope. Battle of the Brightest. 2013. 140p. (J). *(978-0-545-48292-9(5))* Scholastic, Inc.

—Jewel Society #4: Battle of the Brightest. 2013. (Jewel Society Ser.: 4). (ENG.). 144p. (J). (gr. 3-7). pap. 5.99 *(978-0-545-60765-0(5)*, Scholastic Paperbacks) Scholastic, Inc.

McLelland, Brad & Sylvester, Louis. The Fang of Bonfire Crossing: Legends of the Lost Causes. 2020. (Legends of the Lost Causes Ser.: 2). (ENG.). 400p. (J). pap. 20.99 *(978-1-250-23360-8(7)*, 900174394) Square Fish.

Messner, Kate. Capture the Flag, 1. 2013. (ENG.). 240p. (J). (gr. 3-7). pap. 8.99 *(978-0-545-41974-1(3)*, Scholastic Paperbacks) Scholastic, Inc.

Methods, Bryan. Lessons from Underground. 2018. (Master Diplexito & Mr. Scant Ser.). (ENG., Illus.). 272p. (J). (gr. 5-8). 17.99 *(978-1-5124-0581-1(7)*, 199f9813-c1d3-4053-bc16-93f1f1c16c72, Carolrhoda Bks.) Lerner Publishing Group.

—The Thief's Apprentice. 2016. (Master Diplexito & Mr. Scant Ser.: 1). (ENG.). 272p. (J). (gr. 5-8). 17.99 *(978-1-5124-0579-8(5)*, b528a896-fd8e-4b8d-924a-25ea74a5a790); E-Book 27.99 *(978-1-5124-0891-1(3))* Lerner Publishing Group. (Carolrhoda Bks.).

Meyer, L. A. The Mark of the Golden Dragon: Being an Account of the Further Adventures of Jacky Faber, Jewel of the East, Vexation of the West. 2013. (Bloody Jack Adventures Ser.: 9). (ENG.). 400p. (YA). (gr. 9). pap. 9.99 *(978-0-544-00328-6(4)*, 1526370, Clarion Bks.) HarperCollins Pubs.

—The Mark of the Golden Dragon: Being an Account of the Further Adventures of Jacky Faber, Jewel of the East, Vexation of the West, & Pearl of the South China Sea. 2011. (Bloody Jack Adventures Ser.: 9). (ENG.). 384p. (YA). (gr. 9). 16.99 *(978-0-547-51764-3(5)*, 1444890, Clarion Bks.) HarperCollins Pubs.

Milford, Kate. Bluecrowne: A Greenglass House Story. (Greenglass House Ser.). (ENG., Illus.). (J). (gr. 5-7). 2020. 288p. pap. 9.99 *(978-0-358-09754-9(1)*, 1747616) 2018. 272p. 17.99 *(978-1-328-46688-4(4)*, 1713526) HarperCollins Pubs. (Clarion Bks.).

Miller, Christopher & Miller, Allan. The Legend of Gid the Kid & the Black Bean Bandits, 2 bks., Bk.1. Miller, Christopher & Miller, Allan, illus. 2007. (Heroes of Promise Ser.: Bk. 1). (ENG., Illus.). 32p. (J). (gr. 1-5). 12.99 *(978-1-59317-202-2(8))* Warner Pr., Inc.

Miller, Linsey. Mask of Shadows. 2018. (Mask of Shadows Ser.: 1). lib. bdg. 22.10 *(978-0-606-41234-6(4))* Turtleback.

—Ruin of Stars. 2019. (Mask of Shadows Ser.: 2). 416p. (YA). (gr. 8-12). pap. 12.99 *(978-1-4926-7879-3(1))* Sourcebooks, Inc.

Mills, Charles. The Bandit of Benson Park. 2003. (Honors Club Story Ser.: Vol. 1). 127p. (J). *(978-0-8163-1977-0(4))* Pacific Pr. Pubns.

—The Great Sleepy-Time Stew Rescue. 2004. (Honors Club Story Ser.: Vol. 4). (Illus.). 127p. (J). 7.99 *(978-0-8163-2009-7(8))* Pacific Pr. Publishing Assn.

Mone, Gregory. Dangerous Waters: An Adventure on the Titanic. 2013. (ENG.). 256p. (J). (gr. 4-6). pap. 11.99 *(978-1-250-01671-3(1)*, 900087085) Square Fish.

Morgan, Nicola. The Highwayman's Curse. 2007. 368p. (YA). pap. *(978-1-4063-0312-4(7))* Walker Bks., Ltd.

Morgen, A. M. The Inventors at No. 8. (ENG., Illus.). (J). (gr. 3-7). 2019. 368p. pap. 7.99 *(978-0-316-47151-0(8))* 2018. 352p. 16.99 *(978-0-316-47149-7(6))* Little, Brown Bks. for Young Readers.

Morrison, Megan. Grounded: The Tale of Rapunzel. 2015. (Illus.). 374p. (J). *(978-0-545-75468-2(2))* Scholastic, Inc.

Motayne, Maya. Nocturna. (Nocturna Ser.: 1). (ENG.). (YA). (gr. 8). 2020. 496p. pap. 11.99 *(978-0-06-284274-9(9))* 2019. (Illus.). 480p. 18.99 *(978-0-06-284273-2(0))* HarperCollins Pubs. (Balzer & Bray).

Neil Nugget & the Cow Caper. 2008. (Illus.). 32p. (J). pap. 14.95 *(978-0-9792820-2-7(0))* Toe The Line.

Nesbo, Jo. The Magical Fruit. Chace, Tara F., tr. Lowery, Mike, illus. (Doctor Proctor's Fart Powder Ser.). (ENG.). 320p. (J). (gr. 3-7). 2014. pap. 8.99 *(978-1-4424-9343-8(7))* 2013. 17.99 *(978-1-4424-9342-1(9))* Simon & Schuster Children's Publishing. (Aladdin).

Odgers, Darrel & Odgers, Sally. The Sausage Situation. Dawson, Janine, illus. 2007. (Jack Russell: Dog Detective Ser.: 6). 96p. (J). (gr. 1-6). pap. 4.99 *(978-1-933605-54-8(5))* Kane Miller.

—The Sausage Situation. 2006. (Jack Russell, Dog Detective Ser.: Bk. 6). (Illus.). 78p. (J). pap. *(978-0-439-92197-8(X))* Scholastic, Inc.

Olswanger, Anna. Shlemiel Crooks. Koz, Paula Goodman, illus. 2009. (ENG.). 36p. (J). pap. 11.95 *(978-1-58838-236-8(2)*, 8994, NewSouth Bks.) NewSouth, Inc.

Osborne, Mary Pope. Pirates Past Noon. unabr. ed. 2004. (Magic Tree House Ser.: No. 4). 67p. (J). (gr. k-3). pap. 17.00 incl. audio *(978-0-8072-0333-0(5)*, Listening Library) Random Hse. Audio Publishing Group.

Panckridge, Michael & Harvey, Pam. Into the Fire. 2008. (ENG.). 194p. (J). *(978-0-207-20061-8(0))* HarperCollins Pubs. Australia.

Papp, Robert, illus. The Clue in the Recycling Bin. 2011. (Boxcar Children Mysteries Ser.: 126). (ENG.). 128p. (J). (gr. 2-5). pap. 6.99 *(978-0-8075-1209-8(5)*, 807512095); lib. bdg. 14.99 *(978-0-8075-1208-1(7)*, 807512087) Random Hse. Children's Bks. (Random Hse. Bks. for Young Readers).

—The Dog-Gone Mystery. 2009. (Boxcar Children Mysteries Ser.: 119). (ENG.). 128p. (J). (gr. 2-5). pap. 6.99 *(978-0-8075-1657-7(0)*, 807516570, Random Hse. Bks. for Young Readers) Random Hse. Children's Bks.

Pau Pau. Bird Bandit, 1 vol. 2010. 56p. pap. 16.95 *(978-1-4489-3991-6(7))* America Star Bks.

Paul, Curtis Christopher. Elías de Buxton. 2008. (SPA.). 368p. (gr. 6-12). pap. 12.99 *(978-84-441-4101-5(1))* Everest Editora ESP. Dist: Lectorum Pubns., Inc.

Pearson, Mary E. Dance of Thieves. 2018. (Dance of Thieves Ser.: 1). (ENG.). 512p. (YA). 21.99 *(978-1-250-15901-4(6)*, 900185547, Holt, Henry & Co. Bks. For Young Readers) Holt, Henry & Co.

—Dance of Thieves. 2019. (Dance of Thieves Ser.: 1). (ENG.). 528p. (YA). pap. 12.99 *(978-1-250-30897-9(6)*, 900185548) Square Fish.

Perelman, Helen. Rapunzel: A Day to Remember, 1 vol. Studio IBOIX Staff, illus. 2012. (Disney Princess Ser.). (ENG.). 96p. (J). (gr. 2-6). lib. bdg. 31.36 *(978-1-59961-183-9(X)*, 5184, Chapter Bks.) Spotlight.

Petit, Karen. The Mystery of the Stolen Stallion. 2007. (Illus.). 246p. (J). per. 14.95 *(978-0-9794420-4-9(4))* Red Letter Pr.

Pflugfelder, Bob & Hockensmith, Steve. Nick & Tesla & the High-Voltage Danger Lab: A Mystery with Gadgets You Can Build Yourself Ourself. 2013. (Nick & Tesla Ser.: 1). (ENG., Illus.). 240p. (J). (gr. 4-7). 12.99 *(978-1-59474-648-2(6))* Quirk Bks.

Pindar, Heather. The Great Underwear Robbery. Lombardo, Serena, illus. 2021. (Early Bird Readers — Gold (Early Bird Stories (tm)) Ser.). (ENG.). 32p. (J). (gr. k-3). 30.65 *(978-1-5415-9010-6(4)*, 7079f138-eada-47df-8522-1788b2ee9e10, Lerner Pubns.) Lerner Publishing Group.

Polan, Alex. Catching the Jigglypuff Thief. 2016. (Unofficial Adventures for Pokemon GO Players Ser.: 1). lib. bdg. 18.40 *(978-0-606-39657-8(8))* Turtleback.

Poon, Janice. Claire & the Bakery Thief. Poon, Janice, illus. 2008. (Illus.). 104p. (J). (gr. 2-5). 15.95 *(978-1-55453-286-5(8))*; pap. 7.95 *(978-1-55453-245-2(0))* Kids Can Pr., Ltd. CAN. Dist: Hachette Bk. Group.

Proud, Amy, illus. Izzy the Very Bad Burglar. 2016. (ENG.). 32p. (J). (gr. -1-k). 16.99 *(978-1-63450-174-3(8)*, Sky Pony Pr.) Skyhorse Publishing Co., Inc.

Raffa, Edwina & Rigsby, Annelle. Kidnapped in Key West. (Florida Historical Fiction for Youth Ser.). (ENG.). (J). (gr. -1-12). 2012. 136p. pap. 9.95 *(978-1-56164-537-4(0))* 2008. (Illus.). 127p. 14.95 *(978-1-56164-413-1(7))* Pineapple Pr., Inc.

Rayes, Michael. Bank Robbery! 2007. (J). per. 13.95 *(978-0-9779628-0-8(6))* Rafka Pr. LLC.

Rees, Celia. Sovay. 2010. (ENG.). 432p. (YA). (gr. 7). pap. 9.99 *(978-1-59990-483-2(7)*, 900066312, Bloomsbury USA Childrens) Bloomsbury Publishing USA.

—Sovay. 2009. 1.00 *(978-1-4074-4516-8(2))* Recorded Bks., Inc.

Reeve, Philip. Black Light Express. 2017. (Railhead Ser.). (ENG.). 352p. (YA). (gr. 7-12). 17.95 *(978-1-63079-096-7(6)*, 136360, Switch Pr.) Capstone.

Reilly, Carmel & Ashforth, Kate. The Jewelry Story Robbery. 2008. (Rigby Focus Forward: Level F Ser.). (Illus.). 24p. (J). (gr. 4-7). pap. *(978-1-4190-3685-9(8)*, Rigby) Pearson Education Australia.

Rey, H. A. Curious George's Dump Truck (Mini Movers Shaped Board Books) 2014. (Curious George Ser.). (ENG., Illus.). 12p. (J). (— 1). bds. 8.99 *(978-0-544-14686-0(7)*, 1547360, Clarion Bks.) HarperCollins Pubs.

Reynolds, Aaron. The Dung Beetle Bandits: Tiger Moth. Lervold, Erik, illus. 2007. (Graphic Sparks Ser.). (ENG.). 40p. (J). (gr. 2-5). pap. 5.95 *(978-1-59889-412-7(9)*, 93560, Stone Arch Bks.) Capstone.

The Robber: Individual Title-Six Packs. (Chiquilibros Ser.). (gr. k-1). 23.00 *(978-0-7635-0433-5(5))* Rigby Education.

Roberts, Willo Davis. Hostage. 2016. (ENG., Illus.). 176p. (J). (gr. 3-7). pap. 7.99 *(978-1-4814-5788-0(8)*, Aladdin) Simon & Schuster Children's Publishing.

—Hostage. 2016. (ENG., Illus.). 176p. (J). (gr. 3-7). 17.99 *(978-1-4814-5789-7(6)*, Simon & Schuster/Paula Wiseman Bks.) Simon & Schuster/Paula Wiseman Bks.

Robin Hood. (Coleccion Estrella). (SPA., Illus.). 64p. (J). 14.95 *(978-950-11-0014-3(6)*, SGM014) Sigmar ARG. Dist: Continental Bk. Co., Inc.

Rodman, Sean. Final Crossing, 1 vol. 2014. (Orca Soundings Ser.). (ENG.). 112p. (YA). (gr. 8-12). pap. 9.95 *(978-1-4598-0552-1(6))* Orca Bk. Pubs. USA.

Rowe, W. W. The Robber Chief: A Tale of Vengeance & Compassion. Banigan, Chris, illus. 2003. (ENG.). 48p. (gr. 1-18). 12.95 *(978-1-55939-186-3(3)*, Snow Lion Publications, Inc.) Shambhala Pubns., Inc.

Roy, Pat & Roy, Sandy. Jonathan Park: Return to the Hidden Cave. 2013. (Jonathan Park Adventure Fiction Ser.: Vol. 3). (ENG.). 171p. (J). (gr. 4-7). pap. 10.00 *(978-1-937460-61-7(4))* Vision Forum, Inc., The.

Roy, Ron. A to Z Mysteries Super Edition #5: The New Year Dragon Dilemma. Gurney, John Steven, illus. 5th ed. 2011. (to Z Mysteries Ser.: 5). 144p. (J). (gr. 1-4). 6.99 *(978-0-375-86880-1(1)*, Random Hse. Bks. for Young Readers) Random Hse. Children's Bks.

—Capital Mysteries #12: the Ghost at Camp David. Bush, Timothy, illus. 2010. (Capital Mysteries Ser.: 12). 96p. (J). (gr. 1-4). pap. 5.99 *(978-0-375-85925-0(X)*, Random Hse. Bks. for Young Readers) Random Hse. Children's Bks.

—The Castle Crime. 2014. (to Z Mysteries Ser.: 32). lib. bdg. 16.00 *(978-0-606-35190-4(6))* Turtleback.

—The Ghost at Camp David. 2010. (Capital Mysteries Ser.: 12). lib. bdg. 14.75 *(978-0-606-14010-2(7))* Turtleback.

—Mystery at the Washington Monument. Bush, Timothy, illus. 2007. (Capital Mysteries Ser.: No. 8). 87p. (gr. 1-4). 15.00 *(978-0-7569-7845-7(9))* Perfection Learning Corp.

—Sleepy Hollow Sleepover. 4th ed. 2010. (to Z Mysteries Ser.: 30). lib. bdg. 16.00 *(978-0-606-14007-2(7))* Turtleback.

—A to Z Mysteries: Collection #1, No. 1. Gurney, John Steven, illus. 2010. (to Z Mysteries Ser.: Nos. 1-4). (ENG.). 384p. (J). (gr. 1-4). 9.99 *(978-0-375-85946-5(2)*, Random Hse. Bks. for Young Readers) Random Hse. Children's Bks.

—A to Z Mysteries Super Edition #4: Sleepy Hollow Sleepover. Gurney, John Steven, illus. 4th ed. 2010. (to Z Mysteries Ser.: 4). 144p. (J). (gr. 1-4). pap. 6.99 *(978-0-375-86669-2(8)*, Random Hse. Bks. for Young Readers) Random Hse. Children's Bks.

—A to Z Mysteries: the Talking T. Rex. Gurney, John Steven, illus. 2003. (to Z Mysteries Ser.: 20). 96p. (J). (gr. 1-4). pap. 6.99 *(978-0-375-81369-6(1)*, Random Hse. Bks. for Young Readers) Random Hse. Children's Bks.

—A to Z Mysteries: the White Wolf. Gurney, John Steven, illus. 2004. (to Z Mysteries Ser.: 23). 96p. (J). (gr. 1-4). pap. 6.99 *(978-0-375-82480-7(4)*, Random Hse. Bks. for Young Readers) Random Hse. Children's Bks.

—A to Z Mysteries: the X'ed-Out X-Ray. Gurney, John Steven, illus. 2005. (to Z Mysteries Ser.: 24). 96p. (J). (gr. 1-4). 6.99 *(978-0-375-82481-4(2)*, Random Hse. Bks. for Young Readers) Random Hse. Children's Bks.

Rushford, Patricia H. Secrets of Ghost Island. 2007. (J). *(978-88-02-46255-4(0))* Moody Pubs.

Russell, Christopher & Russell, Christine. The Quest of the Warrior Sheep. 2011. (Warrior Sheep Ser.). (ENG.). 224p. (gr. 4-6). 18.69 *(978-1-4022-5511-3(X))* Sourcebooks, Inc.

Russell, Rachel Renée. The Misadventures of Max Crumbly 3: Masters of Mischief. Russell, Rachel Renée, illus. 2019. (Misadventures of Max Crumbly Ser.: 3). (ENG., Illus.). 272p. (J). (gr. 4-7). 13.99 *(978-1-5344-5349-4(0)*, Aladdin) Simon & Schuster Children's Publishing.

Sander, Sonia. Calling All Cars! 2010. (LEGO City Adventures Scholastic Readers Level 1 Ser.: 3). lib. bdg. 13.55 *(978-0-606-07120-8(2))* Turtleback.

Santillo, LuAnn. Jim & the Thug. Santillo, LuAnn, ed. 2003. (Half-Pint Kids Readers Ser.). (Illus.). 7p. (J). (gr. -1-1). pap. 1.00 *(978-1-59256-078-3(4))* Half-Pint Kids, Inc.

Sargent, Dave & Sargent, Pat. Nick: (Linebacked Claybank Dun) Crime Does Not Pay, 30 vols., Vol. 42. Lenoir, Jane, illus. 2003. (Saddle up Ser.: Vol. 42). 42p. (J). pap. 10.95 *(978-1-56763-702-1(7)*; lib. bdg. 23.60 *(978-1-56763-701-4(9))* Ozark Publishing.

Schachner, Judy. The Great Bean Caper. 2009. (Skippyjon Jones Ser.). (Illus.). 32p. (J). (gr. -1-k). mass mkt. 4.99 *(978-0-448-45167-1(0)*, Grosset & Dunlap) Penguin Young Readers Group.

Schnetzler, Pattie L. Fast 'n Snappy. Manning, Jane K., tr. Manning, Jane K., illus. 2004. (Carolrhoda Picture Books Ser.). 32p. (J). (gr. k-3). 16.95 *(978-1-57505-539-8(2))* Lerner Publishing Group.

Schultz, Jan Neubert. Horse Sense: The Story of Will Sasse, His Horse Star & the Outlaw Jesse James. 2005. (Adventures in Time Ser.). (Illus.). 180p. (J). (gr. 4-8). 15.95 *(978-1-57505-998-3(3))* Lerner Publishing Group.

Scieszka, Jon. Hey Kid, Want to Buy a Bridge? #11. McCauley, Adam, illus. 2004. (Time Warp Trio Ser.: 11). 80p. (J). (gr. 2-4). pap. 5.99 *(978-0-14-240089-0(0)*, Puffin Books) Penguin Young Readers Group.

Shannon, R. J. Rita Rain & the Shadow Apprentice: Book 1. 2012. 472p. 29.95 *(978-1-4626-7390-2(2))* America Star Bks.

Shea, Bob. Kid Sheriff & the Terrible Toads. Smith, Lane, illus. 2014. (ENG.). 32p. (J). (gr. -1-3). 18.99 *(978-1-59643-975-7(0)*, 900127683) Roaring Brook Pr.

Sheth, Kashmira. Feast of Peas. Ebbeler, Jeffrey, illus. 2020. 32p. (J). (gr. -1-3). 17.99 *(978-1-68263-135-5(4))* Peachtree Publishing Co. Inc.

Shire, Poppy. Magic Pony Carousel #4: Jewel the Midnight Pony. Berg, Ron, illus. 2008. (Magic Pony Carousel Ser.: 4). (ENG.). 96p. (J). (gr. 2-5). pap. 4.99 *(978-0-06-083788-4(8)*, HarperCollins) HarperCollins Pubs.

Sid, Fleischman. The Whipping Boy. 2014. (HarperClassics Ser.). (ENG.). 96p. (J). (gr. 3-8). 10.24 *(978-1-63245-335-8(5))* Lectorum Pubns., Inc.

Skelton, Vonda Skinner. Bitsy & the Mystery at Hilton Head Island. 2008. 192p. (J). (gr. 4-7). pap. 8.95 *(978-1-57072-325-4(7))* Overmountain Pr.

Sleiman, Dina L. Dauntless. 2015. (Valiant Hearts Ser.: 1). (ENG.). 368p. (YA). pap. 16.00 *(978-0-7642-1312-0(1))* Bethany Hse. Pubs.

Smith, Alex T. Mr. Penguin & the Lost Treasure. 2019. (Mr. Penguin Ser.: 1). (ENG., Illus.). 208p. (J). (gr. 3-7). 16.95 *(978-1-68263-120-1(6))* Peachtree Publishing Co. Inc.

Song, Amira. Horse Lovers Forever. 2012. 64p. pap. *(978-1-4602-0144-2(2))* FriesenPress.

St. George, Victoria. Barnyard Bandits. 2011. (Illus.). 28p. (J). pap. 12.99 *(978-1-4567-3040-6(1))* AuthorHouse.

Steig, William. The Real Thief. 2007. (SPA.). (J). 1.25 *(978-1-4193-9992-3(6))* Recorded Bks., Inc.

—The Real Thief. Steig, William, illus. 2007. (ENG., Illus.). 64p. (J). (gr. 2-5). per. 9.99 *(978-0-312-37145-6(4)*, 900044683) Square Fish.

Stern, D. G. Disappearing Diamonds: An Upton Charles Adventure. Bartlett, Rebecca, illus. 2008. (ENG.). 126p. (J). pap. 9.99 *(978-0-9754676-9-5(7))* Yeoman Hse.

Stilton, Gerónimo & Schaffer, Andrea. The Invisible Thief. Usai, Luca et al, illus. 2015. 114p. (J). pap. *(978-0-545-92755-0(2))* Scholastic, Inc.

Stilton, Thea. Thea Stilton & the Mystery on the Orient Express. 2012. (Thea Stilton Ser.: 13). lib. bdg. 19.65 *(978-0-606-26757-1(3))* Turtleback.

Stone, David Lee. The Shadewell Shenanigans. 2006. (Illus.). 308p. (J). *(978-1-4156-8147-3(3))* Hyperion Bks. for Children.

Sutcliffe, William. Circus of Thieves on the Rampage. Tazzyman, David, illus. 2017. (ENG.). 288p. (J). pap. 7.99 *(978-1-4711-2025-1(2)*, Simon & Schuster Children's) Simon & Schuster, Ltd. GBR. Dist: Simon & Schuster, Inc.

Sutton, Rosalind, et al. Robin Hood. Rowe, Eric F., tr. 4th ed. (Coleccion Clasicos en Accion). (SPA., Illus.). 80p. (YA). (gr. 5-8). 15.95 *(978-84-241-5782-1(6)*, EV1455) Everest Editora ESP. Dist: Lectorum Pubns., Inc.

Swift, Carolyn. Robbers in the House. (Illus.). 96p. 2.95 *(978-0-900068-59-1(0))* Penguin Publishing Group.

Tanner, Lian. Museum of Thieves. 2011. (Keepers Ser.: Bk. 1). (ENG.). 320p. (J). (gr. 3-7). 8.99 *(978-0-375-85978-6(0)*, Yearling);1. (gr. 4-6). lib. bdg. 22.44 *(978-0-385-90768-2(0)*, Delacorte Pr.) Random Hse. Children's Bks.

—Path of Beasts. 2013. (ENG.). 352p. (J). (gr. 4-7). 8.99 *(978-0-375-85980-9(2)*, Yearling) Random Hse. Children's Bks.

Tenbeth, Kate. Burly & Grum & the Birthday Surprise. Jones, Rob, illus. 2012. 108p. pap. *(978-0-9572119-9-5(6))* Magic Toy Bks.

Thompson, Kate. Highway Robbery. Dress, Robert, illus. 2009. (ENG.). 128p. (J). (gr. 5-18). 15.99 *(978-0-06-173034-4(3)*, Greenwillow Bks.) HarperCollins Pubs.

Trine, Greg. Wyatt Burp Rides Again. Dormer, Frank W., illus. 2014. (Adventures of Jo Schmo Ser.: 2). (ENG.). 112p. (J). (gr. 1-4). pap. 6.99 *(978-0-544-01899-0(0)*, 1528127, Clarion Bks.) HarperCollins Pubs.

Turner, Megan Whalen. The King of Attolia. (Queen's Thief Ser.: 3). (ENG.). (YA). (gr. 8). 2017. 432p. pap. 10.99 *(978-0-06-264298-1(7))* 2007. 432p. pap. 7.99 *(978-0-06-083579-8(6))* 2006. 400p. 17.99 *(978-0-06-083577-4(X))* HarperCollins Pubs. (Greenwillow Bks.).

—The King of Attolia. 2007. (Queen's Thief Ser.: BK.3). 387p. (YA). 18.00 *(978-0-7569-8106-8(9))* Perfection Learning Corp.

—The King of Attolia. (YA). 2008. (Queen's Thief Ser.: BK.3). (ENG.). 84.49 *(978-1-4281-8027-7(3))* 2007. (Attolia Ser.: 3). 119.75 *(978-1-4281-1722-8(9))* 2007. (Queen's Thief Ser.: BK.3). (ENG.). 92.75 *(978-1-4281-1716-7(4))* 2006. (Queen's Thief Ser.: BK.3). (ENG.). 90.75 *(978-1-4281-1718-1(0))* 2006. (Queen's Thief Ser.: BK.3). (ENG.). 122.75 *(978-1-4281-1720-4(2))* 2006. (Queen's Thief Ser.: BK.3). (ENG.). 251.75 *(978-1-4281-1717-4(2))* 2006. (Queen's Thief Ser.: BK.3). 281.75 *(978-1-4281-1721-1(0))* 2006. (Queen's Thief Ser.: BK.3). (ENG.). 1.25 *(978-1-4281-1713-6(X))* Recorded Bks., Inc.

—The Queen of Attolia. (Queen's Thief Ser.: 2). (ENG.). (YA). (gr. 8). 2017. 416p. pap. 12.99 *(978-0-06-264297-4(9))* 2006. 368p. pap. 6.99 *(978-0-06-084182-9(6))* HarperCollins Pubs. (Greenwillow Bks.).

—The Queen of Attolia, 8 vols. (Attolia Ser.: 2). (J). 2013. 188.75 *(978-1-4281-5237-3(7))* 2009. 73.75 *(978-1-4361-6574-7(1))* 2008. 104.75 *(978-1-4281-5236-6(9))* 2008. 75.75 *(978-1-4281-5234-2(2))* 2007. 78.75 *(978-1-4281-5232-8(6))* 2007. 1.25 *(978-1-4281-5229-8(6))* 2007. 162.75 *(978-1-4281-5233-5(4))* 2007. 101.75 *(978-1-4281-5238-0(5))* Recorded Bks., Inc.

—The Queen of Attolia. 2017. (Queen's Thief Ser.: BK.2). (ENG.). (YA). lib. bdg. 20.85 *(978-0-606-40331-3(0))* Turtleback.

—Thick As Thieves. 2018. (Queen's Thief Ser.: 5). (YA). lib. bdg. 20.85 *(978-0-606-41366-4(9))* Turtleback.

—The Thief. 2017. (Queen's Thief Ser.: 1). (ENG.). 320p. (YA). (gr. 8). pap. 12.99 *(978-0-06-264296-7(0)*, Greenwillow Bks.) HarperCollins Pubs.

—The Thief. 2009. (Queen's Thief Ser.: BK.1). (ENG.). (YA). 9.00 *(978-0-7848-3718-4(X))*; 8.32 *(978-0-7848-3065-9(7))* Marco Bk. Co. (Everbind).

—The Thief, 7 vols. (Queen's Thief Ser.: BK.1). (ENG.). (YA). 2005. 169.75 *(978-1-4025-5458-2(3))* 2004. 92.75 *(978-1-4025-5457-5(5))* Recorded Bks., Inc.

—The Thief. (Queen's Thief Ser.: BK.1). (ENG.). 2017. (YA). lib. bdg. 20.85 *(978-0-606-40328-3(0))* 2005. (J). lib. bdg. 17.20 *(978-1-4177-4836-5(2))* Turtleback.

—The Thief: A Newbery Honor Award Winner. 2005. (Queen's Thief Ser.: 1). (ENG.). 304p. (J). (gr. 3-8). reprint ed. pap. 9.99 *(978-0-06-082497-6(2)*, Greenwillow Bks.) HarperCollins Pubs.

Updale, Eleanor. Montmorency's Revenge. 2007. 289p. (J). 25.66 *(978-1-4287-3312-1(4)*, Follettbound) Follett School Solutions.

—Thief, Liar, Gentleman? 2005. (Montmorency Ser.). 232p. (J). (gr. 4-7). 14.65 *(978-0-7569-6316-3(8))* Perfection Learning Corp.

Van Draanen, Wendelin. The Gecko & Sticky: the Greatest Power. Gilpin, Stephen, illus. 2011. (Gecko & Sticky Ser.: 2). (ENG.). 208p. (J). (gr. 3-7). 7.99 *(978-0-440-42243-3(4)*, Yearling) Random Hse. Children's Bks.

—Sammy Keyes & the Hotel Thief. 2008. (Sammy Keyes Ser.: Bk. 1). (J). 54.99 *(978-1-60640-642-7(6))* Findaway World, LLC.

Vande Velde, Vivian. Ghost of a Hanged Man, 1 vol. 2003. (ENG.). 32p. (J). (gr. 5). pap. 5.95 *(978-0-7614-5154-9(4))* Marshall Cavendish Corp.

VanRiper, Gary & VanRiper, Justin. The Great Train Robbery. 2004. (Adirondack Kids Ser.: Vol. 4). (Illus.). 82p. (J). (gr. 2-7). pap. 9.95 *(978-0-9707044-3-6(7))* Adirondack Kids Pr.

Vaught, Susan. Super Max & the Mystery of Thornwood's Revenge. (ENG.). (J). (gr. 3-7). 2018. 368p. pap. 8.99 *(978-1-4814-8684-2(5))* 2017. (Illus.). 352p. 16.99 *(978-1-4814-8683-5(7))* Simon & Schuster/Paula Wiseman Bks. (Simon & Schuster/Paula Wiseman Bks.).

—Super Max & the Mystery of Thornwood's Revenge. 2018. lib. bdg. 19.65 *(978-0-606-41467-8(3))* Turtleback.

Velde, Vivian Vande. 23 Minutes. 2016. (ENG.). 176p. (J). (gr. 7-9). 17.99 *(978-1-62979-441-9(4),* Astra Young Readers) Astra Publishing Hse.

Vern, Jules. The Adventures of a Special Correspondent. 2009. 180p. 25.95 *(978-1-60664-635-9(4));* pap. 13.95 *(978-1-60664-377-8(0))* Rodgers, Alan Bks.

Verral, Charles Spain. Rin Tin Tin & the Outlaw. Crawford, Mel, illus. 2011. 28p. pap. 35.95 *(978-1-258-04034-5(4))* Literary Licensing, LLC.

Vo, Nancy. The Outlaw, 1 vol. 2018. (Crow Stories Trilogy Ser.: 1). (ENG., Illus.). 42p. (J). (gr. k-3). 17.95 *(978-1-77306-016-3(3))* Groundwood Bks. CAN. Dist: Publishers Group West (PGW).

Warner, Gertrude Chandler, creator. The Rock 'n' Roll Mystery. 2006. (Boxcar Children Mysteries Ser.: 109). (ENG., Illus.). 128p. (J). (gr. 2-5). lib. bdg. 14.99 *(978-0-8075-7089-0(3),* 807570893); per. 5.99 *(978-0-8075-7090-6(7),* 807570907) Random Hse. Children's Bks. (Random Hse. Bks. for Young Readers).

Warner, Penny. The Mystery of the Missing Mustangs. 2012. 107p. (J). *(978-0-88166-411-9(1))* Meadowbrook Pr.

Watson, Jude. Loot. 2015. (ENG.). 272p. (J). (gr. 3-7). pap. 8.99 *(978-0-545-46803-9(5),* Scholastic Paperbacks) Scholastic, Inc.

Watson, Tom. Stick Cat: Two Catch a Thief. 2017. (Stick Cat Ser.: 3). (ENG., Illus.). 240p. (J). (gr. 3-7). 15.99 *(978-0-06-241104-4(7),* HarperCollins) HarperCollins Pubs.

Wells, Carolyn & E. C. CASWELL. Two Little Women on a Holiday. l.t. ed. 2006. 178p. pap. 21.99 *(978-1-4264-2807-4(3))* Creative Media Partners, LLC.

Wells, Helen. Cherry Ames, Camp Nurse. 2007. (Cherry Ames Nurse Stories Ser.). 224p. (YA). (gr. 7-12). 14.95 *(978-0-8261-0417-5(7))* Springer Publishing Co., Inc.

—Cherry Ames, Department Store Nurse. 2007. (Cherry Ames Nurse Stories Ser.). 224p. (YA). (gr. 8-12). 14.95 *(978-0-8261-0415-1(0))* Springer Publishing Co., Inc.

West, Tracey. The Audio Files. Harrington, Rich, illus. 2006. 96p. (J). pap. *(978-0-439-90719-4(5))* Scholastic, Inc.

—The Fingerprint Files. Harrington, Rich, illus. 2007. 96p. (J). *(978-0-439-91451-2(5))* Scholastic, Inc.

—The Teeny Tiny Cases. Harrington, Rich, illus. 2007. 96p. (J). *(978-0-439-91450-5(7))* Scholastic, Inc.

White, Lia. Alkis. 2010. (ENG., Illus.). 106p. pap. *(978-1-84748-715-5(7))* Athena Pr.

Wilson, Bob. Stanley Bagshaw & the Mafeking Square Cheese Robbery. 2006. (Stanley Bagshaw Ser.). (Illus.). 32p. (J). (gr. k-2). pap. 6.95 *(978-1-903015-31-5(6))* Barn Owl Bks. London GBR. Dist: Independent Pubs. Group.

Wood, Audrey. Twenty-Four Robbers. 2004. (Child's Play Library). (Illus.). 32p. (J). (gr. 1-1). *(978-1-904550-35-8(5))* Child's Play International Ltd.

Woodfine, Katherine. The Mystery of the Clockwork Sparrow. 2017. (Illus.). 320p. (J). pap. 6.99 *(978-1-61067-437-9(5))* Kane Miller.

Worley, Brandi. Crumb Snatchers, Part I. 2009. 160p. pap. 14.95 *(978-0-557-06521-9(5))* Lulu Pr., Inc.

Wyatt, Ellen. Sheriff Buzzy Bullet & the Bank Robbers. 2009. 28p. pap. 12.25 *(978-1-60860-391-6(1),* Eloquent Bks.) Strategic Book Publishing & Rights Agency (SBPRA).

ROBERT I, KING OF SCOTS, 1274-1329—FICTION

Henty, George. In Freedom's Cause: A Tale of Wallace & Bruce. 2011. 372p. pap. 19.95 *(978-1-61179-152-5(9))* Fireship Pr.

ROBESON, PAUL, 1898-1976

Belton, Sandra. The Tallest Tree. 2008. (Illus.). 160p. (J). (gr. 3-7). 16.99 *(978-0-06-052749-5(8),* Greenwillow Bks.) HarperCollins Pubs.

Mckissack, Patricia & Mckissack, Fredrick. Paul Robeson: A Voice for Change, 1 vol. 2013. (Famous African Americans Ser.). (ENG.). 24p. (gr. k-2). pap. 10.35 *(978-1-4644-0205-0(1),* dc893b8a-0788-4dfc-ad53-35b11b21d047); (Illus.). 25.27 *(978-0-7660-4107-3(7),* 07716234-1468-4642-8459-5686579373a7) Enslow Publishing, LLC. (Enslow Elementary).

Robeson, Susan. Grandpa Stops a War: A Paul Robeson Story. Brown, Rod, illus. 2019. 32p. (J). (gr. k-4). 17.95 *(978-1-60980-882-2(7),* Triangle Square) Seven Stories Pr.

Wright, David K. The Life of Paul Robeson: Actor, Singer, Political Activist, 1 vol. 2014. (Legendary African Americans Ser.). (ENG.). 96p. (gr. 6-7). 31.61 *(978-0-7660-6157-6(4),* 6f8e9895-253b-47ce-b998-cc41b66e00f4); (Illus.). (J). pap. 13.88 *(978-0-7660-6158-3(2),* 616d3255-1d32-439e-928c-494ed21749e3) Enslow Publishing, LLC.

ROBIN HOOD (LEGENDARY CHARACTER)

Calcutt, David. Robin Hood. Baker-Smith, Grahame, illus. 2012. 112p. (J). 24.99 *(978-1-84686-357-8(0))* Barefoot Bks., Inc.

Creswick, Paul. Robin Hood. Wyeth, N. C., illus. 2003. (Scribner Storybook Classics Ser.: Vol. 4). (ENG.). 64p. (J). (gr. 3-7). 19.99 *(978-0-689-85467-5(6),* Atheneum Bks. for Young Readers) Simon & Schuster Children's Publishing.

Fenn, G. Manville. Young Robin Hood. 2007. 52p. per. *(978-1-4065-2352-2(6))* Dodo Pr.

Fenn, George Manville. Young Robin Hood. 2004. reprint ed. pap. 15.95 *(978-1-4191-9534-1(4))* Kessinger Publishing, LLC.

McDonnell, Julia. The Legend of Robin Hood, 1 vol. 2015. (Famous Legends Ser.). (ENG., Illus.). 32p. (J). (gr. 2-3). pap. 11.50 *(978-1-4824-2748-6(6),* cdcd0bdb-313f-428a-850d-872557110eb8) Stevens, Gareth Publishing LLLP.

McSpadden, J. Walker. Robin Hood. 2004. reprint ed. pap. 1.99 *(978-1-4192-4516-9(3));* pap. 22.95 *(978-1-4191-4516-2(9))* Kessinger Publishing, LLC.

Miles, Bernard. Robin Hood: His Life & Legend. Ambrus, Victor G., illus. 128p. (J). (gr. 4-18). 12.95 *(978-1-56288-412-3(3))* Checkerboard Pr., Inc.

Morpurgo, M. Robin of Sherwood. 2018. (ENG., Illus.). 192p. (J). (gr. 4-7). 24.99 *(978-1-78675-046-4(5))* Palazzo Editions, Ltd. GBR. Dist: Independent Pubs. Group.

Pyle, Howard. The Merry Adventures of Robin Hood. (Young Collector's Illustrated Classics Ser.). (Illus.). 192p. (J). (gr. 3-7). 9.95 *(978-1-56156-454-5(0))* Kidsbooks, LLC.

—The Merry Adventures of Robin Hood. l.t. ed. 2004. (Large Print Ser.). 616p. (J). 26.00 *(978-1-58287-684-9(3))* North Bks.

Smith, Neil. Robin Hood, 1 vol. 2014. (Heroes & Legends Ser.). (ENG., Illus.). 88p. (J). (gr. 8-8). 38.80 *(978-1-4777-8139-5(0),* 80d28836-bff5-4f63-9f0c-c2e8c8ea27c7, Rosen Young Adult) Rosen Publishing Group, Inc., The.

Storrie, Paul D. Robin Hood. 2008. pap. 52.95 *(978-0-8225-9463-5(3))* Lerner Publishing Group.

—Robin Hood: Outlaw of Sherwood Forest, an English Legend. Yeates, Thomas, illus. 2008. (Graphic Myths & Legends Ser.). 48p. (J). (gr. 3-7). per. 8.95 *(978-0-8225-6572-7(2))* Lerner Publishing Group.

ROBIN HOOD (LEGENDARY CHARACTER)—FICTION

Ausona, Roberto de. Robin Hood. (SPA., Illus.). 156p. (YA). 11.95 *(978-84-7281-110-2(7),* AF1110) Auriga, Ediciones S.A. ESP. Dist: Continental Bk. Co., Inc.

Bernstein, Nina. Magic by the Book, 4 vols. unabr. ed. 2005. (J). 65.75 *(978-1-4193-3607-2(X),* 42048) Recorded Bks., Inc.

Côté, Denis. La Forêt aux Mille et un Périls, Tome 2. Poulin, Stephane, illus. 2004. (Roman Jeunesse Ser.). (FRE.). 96p. (J). (gr. 4-7). pap. *(978-2-89021-696-9(9))* Diffusion du livre Mirabel (DLM).

Creswick, Paul. Robin Hood: And His Adventures. 2018. (ENG.). 272p. (gr. 3-7). pap. 14.95 *(978-0-486-82429-1(2),* 824292) Dover Pubns., Inc.

Dunkerley, Desmond. Robin Hood. 2016. (Ladybird Classics Ser.). (Illus.). 72p. (J). (gr. k-3). 11.99 *(978-0-7232-9559-4(X))* Penguin Bks., Ltd. GBR. Dist: Independent Pubs. Group.

Fenn, G. Manville. Young Robin Hood. 2019. (ENG.). 66p. (J). pap. 10.36 *(978-0-368-28235-5(X))* Blurb, Inc.

—Young Robin Hood. 2011. 56p. pap. 7.99 *(978-1-61203-082-1(3))* Bottom of the Hill Publishing.

Gaughen, A. C. Lion Heart: A Scarlet Novel. 2017. (Scarlet Ser.). (ENG.). 368p. (YA). pap. 9.99 *(978-1-68119-821-7(5),* 900187603, Bloomsbury USA Childrens) Bloomsbury Publishing USA.

Goodwin, John. Robin Hood. Date not set. (Nelson Readers Ser.). (Illus.). 36p. (J). pap. *(978-0-17-557050-8(7))* Addison-Wesley Longman, Inc.

Green, John. The Story of Robin Hood Coloring Book. 2018. (Dover Classic Stories Coloring Book Ser.). (ENG.). 48p. (J). (gr. 3-5). pap. 5.99 *(978-0-486-82802-2(6),* 828026) Dover Pubns., Inc.

Green, Richard Lancelyn. The Adventures of Robin Hood. Terrazzini, Daniela Jaglenka, illus. 2010. (Puffin Classics Ser.). 336p. (J). (gr. 5-7). 16.99 *(978-0-14-133489-9(4),* Puffin Books) Penguin Young Readers Group.

Green, Roger Lancelyn. The Adventures of Robin Hood. 2010. (Puffin Classics Ser.). (Illus.). 336p. (J). (gr. 5-7). pap. 8.99 *(978-0-14-132938-3(6),* Puffin Books) Penguin Young Readers Group.

Hall, Tim. Shadow of the Wolf. 2016. (ENG.). 480p. (YA). (gr. 9). pap. 9.99 *(978-1-338-03250-5(X))* Scholastic, Inc.

Harvey, Damian & Remphry, Martin. Robin & the Friar. 2009. (Hopscotch Adventures Ser.). (Illus.). 31p. (J). (gr. 1). lib. bdg. 25.65 *(978-1-59771-177-7(2))* Sea-To-Sea Pubns.

—Robin & the Monk. 2009. (Hopscotch Adventures Ser.). (Illus.). 31p. (J). (gr. 1). lib. bdg. 25.65 *(978-1-59771-179-1(9))* Sea-To-Sea Pubns.

Howard, Eva. League of Archers. (League of Archers Ser.: 1). (ENG.). (J). (gr. 4-8). 2017. 304p. pap. 8.99 *(978-1-4814-6038-5(2))* 2016. (Illus.). 288p. 16.99 *(978-1-4814-6037-8(4))* Simon & Schuster Children's Publishing. (Aladdin).

Jackson, Bert, illus. The Adventures of Robin Hood: An English Legend. 2004. (ENG.). 24p. (J). (gr. 3-3). pap. 6.47 net. *(978-0-7685-2125-2(4),* Dominie Elementary) Savvas Learning Co.

Jones, Rob Lloyd. The Story of Robin Hood. Marks, Alan, illus. 2010. (Picture Book Classics Ser.). 24p. (J). 9.99 *(978-0-7945-2859-1(7),* Usborne) EDC Publishing.

Lasky, Kathryn. Hawksmaid: The Untold Story of Robin Hood & Maid Marian. 2011. (ENG.). 320p. (J). (gr. 5). pap. 6.99 *(978-0-06-000072-1(4),* HarperCollins) HarperCollins Pubs.

Lloyd Jones, Rob, retold by. Robin Hood. 2008. (Young Reading Series 2 Gift Bks). 64p. (J). 8.99 *(978-0-7945-2090-8(1),* Usborne) EDC Publishing.

Mattern, Joanne, retold by. The Adventures of Robin Hood. 2018. 137p. (J). *(978-1-338-30378-0(3))* Scholastic, Inc.

Pyle, Howard. The Adventures of Robin Hood. 2014. (ENG.). 416p. 17.50 *(978-1-78270-045-6(5))* Award Pubns. Ltd. GBR. Dist: Parkwest Pubns., Inc.

—The Merry Adventures of Robin Hood. Simon, Ute, illus. 2011. (Calico Illustrated Classics Ser.: No. 3). (ENG.). 112p. (J). (gr. 2-5). 38.50 *(978-1-61641-107-7(4),* 4021, Calico Chapter Bks.) ABDO Publishing Co.

—The Merry Adventures of Robin Hood. (ENG.). 2019. 96p. (YA). (gr. 6). pap. 12.71 *(978-0-368-29050-3(6))* 2018. (Illus.). 372p. (J). 29.99 *(978-1-389-04075-7(5))* Blurb, Inc.

—The Merry Adventures of Robin Hood. 2017. (ENG., Illus.). (J). pap. 16.95 *(978-1-374-89069-5(3))* Capital Communications, Inc.

—The Merry Adventures of Robin Hood. 2019. (ENG.). (YA). (gr. 6). 302p. pap. 13.99 *(978-1-7023-5404-2(0));* 634p. pap. 25.99 *(978-1-6996-5047-9(0));* 634p. pap. 36.99 *(978-1-6899-5447-1(7));* 636p. pap. 36.99 *(978-1-0864-2686-1(X));* 636p. pap. 36.99 *(978-1-6867-2360-5(1));* 634p. pap. 39.99 *(978-1-0801-5233-9(4));* 636p. pap. 31.99 *(978-1-0776-4296-6(2));* 636p. pap. 42.99 *(978-1-0784-6411-6(1));* 634p. pap. 41.99 *(978-1-0825-2707-4(6));* 636p. pap. 36.99 *(978-1-0711-3566-2(X));* 634p. pap. 36.99 *(978-1-0756-9118-8(4));* 636p. pap. 38.99 *(978-1-0959-0218-9(0));* 634p. pap. 37.99 *(978-1-7969-0844-2(4))* Independently Published.

—The Merry Adventures of Robin Hood. Pyle, Howard, illus. 2015. (First Avenue Classics (tm) Ser.). (ENG., Illus.). 342p. (YA). (gr. 5-12). E-Book 19.99 *(978-1-4677-5841-3(8),* First Avenue Editions) Lerner Publishing Group.

—The Merry Adventures of Robin Hood. 2016. (Word Cloud Classics Ser.). (ENG., Illus.). 320p. (gr. 6). pap. 14.99 *(978-1-62686-608-9(2),* Canterbury Classics) Printers Row Publishing Group.

—The Merry Adventures of Robin Hood. 2018. (ENG., Illus.). 254p. (J). 24.99 *(978-1-5154-2933-3(4))* Wilder Pubns., Corp.

Pyle, Robert. The Merry Adventures of Robin Hood. 2009. 284p. (J). pap. 14.99 *(978-1-934941-61-4(1))* Red & Black Pubs.

Raven, Nicky. Robin Hood: The Classic Adventure Tale. Gilbert, Anne Yvonne, illus. 2019. 104p. (J). (gr. 3-7). 14.99 *(978-1-63158-271-4(2),* Racehorse Publishing) Skyhorse Publishing Co., Inc.

Robin Hood. (Coleccion Estrella). (SPA., Illus.). 64p. (J). 14.95 *(978-950-11-0014-3(6),* SGM014) Sigmar ARG. Dist: Continental Bk. Co., Inc.

Sanderson, Jeanette. Robin Hood Shoots for the Queen: A Legend from England. 2006. (J). pap. *(978-1-4108-7167-1(3))* Benchmark Education Co.

Springer, Nancy. Wild Boy. 2005. (Tales of Rowan Hood Ser.). 115p. (J). (gr. 3). 13.65 *(978-0-7569-5490-1(8))* Perfection Learning Corp.

Sutton, Rosalind, et al. Robin Hood. Rowe, Eric F., tr. 4th ed. (Coleccion Clasicos en Accion). (SPA., Illus.). 80p. (YA). (gr. 5-8). 15.95 *(978-84-241-5782-1(6),* EV1455) Everest Editora ESP. Dist: Lectorum Pubns., Inc.

Tanner, Jennifer, illus. Robin Hood. 2010. (Classic Fiction Ser.). 72p. lib. bdg. 4.95 *(978-1-4342-2604-4(2),* Stone Arch Bks.) Capstone.

Tobon, Sara, tr. Robin Hood: Novela Gráfica, 1 vol. Tanner, Jennifer, illus. 2010. (Classic Fiction Ser.). (SPA.). 72p. (J). (gr. 5-9). pap. 7.15 *(978-1-4342-2275-6(6),* 103138, Stone Arch Bks.) Capstone.

ROBINS

Arnold, Quinn M. Robins. 2018. (Seedlings Ser.). (ENG.). 24p. (J). (gr. -1-k). *(978-1-60818-975-5(9),* 19922, Creative Education) Creative Co., The.

—Squirrels. 2018. (Seedlings Ser.). (ENG.). 24p. (J). (gr. -1-k). pap. 8.99 *(978-1-62832-602-4(6),* 19931, Creative Paperbacks) Creative Co., The.

Bechard, Clem. Mrs. Robinson Finds a Home. 2008. 24p. per. 24.95 *(978-1-4241-9692-0(2))* America Star Bks.

Berger, Melvin & Berger, Gilda. A Robin Grows Up. 2008. (Illus.). 32p. (J). *(978-0-439-02525-6(7))* Scholastic, Inc.

Borgert-Spaniol, Megan. American Robins. 2016. (North American Animals Ser.). (ENG., Illus.). 24p. (J). (gr. k-3). 26.95 *(978-1-62617-400-9(8),* Blastoff! Readers) Bellwether Media.

Christelow, Eileen. Robins! How They Grow Up. Christelow, Eileen, illus. 2017. (ENG., Illus.). 48p. (J). (gr. 1-4). 17.99 *(978-0-544-44289-4(X),* 1597294, Clarion Bks.) HarperCollins Pubs.

Gillespie, Katie. Robins. 2017. (Illus.). 24p. (J). *(978-1-4896-4507-4(1))* Weigl Pubs., Inc.

Hudak, Heather C. Robins: Watch Them Grow. 2010. pap. 9.95 *(978-1-60596-923-7(0));* 24p. (J). (gr. 2-4). lib. bdg. 25.70 *(978-1-60596-922-0(2))* Weigl Pubs., Inc.

Jenkins, Priscilla Belz. A Nest Full of Eggs. Rockwell, Lizzy, illus. 2015. (Let's-Read-And-Find-Out Science 1 Ser.). (ENG.). 32p. (J). (gr. -1-3). pap. 6.99 *(978-0-06-238193-4(8),* HarperCollins) HarperCollins Pubs.

Kalz, Jill. Robins. 2003. (Birds Ser.). (Illus.). 24p. (J). lib. bdg. 21.35 *(978-1-58340-131-6(8))* Black Rabbit Bks.

Mara, Wil. Robins, 1 vol. 2014. (Backyard Safari Ser.). (ENG.). 32p. (gr. 3-3). 30.21 *(978-1-62712-825-4(5),* 347b88b6-82e3-4a12-a9e1-f3add7c6d1eb) Cavendish Square Publishing LLC.

Meachen Rau, Dana. El Robin en el Árbol (the Robin in the Tree), 1 vol. 2008. (Naturaleza (Nature) Ser.). (SPA., Illus.). 24p. (gr. k-1). lib. bdg. 25.50 *(978-0-7614-2410-9(5),* 813a8e2f-ae9f-4c4e-80f5-ab3cc4a7aed2) Cavendish Square Publishing LLC.

—The Robin in the Tree, 1 vol. 2007. (Nature Ser.). (ENG., Illus.). 24p. (gr. k-1). lib. bdg. 25.50 *(978-0-7614-2304-1(4),* a3cb6bc7-f261-4b17-b73d-bc6facab0875) Cavendish Square Publishing LLC.

Nelson, Robin. Robins. 2009. pap. 34.95 *(978-0-7613-4113-0(7))* Lerner Publishing Group.

Posada, Mia, tr. & illus. Robins: Songbirds of Spring. Posada, Mia, illus. 2004. (Carolrhoda Picture Books Ser.). 32p. (J). (gr. k-3). 15.95 *(978-1-57505-615-9(1))* Lerner Publishing Group.

Riggs, Kate. Robins. 2016. (In My Backyard Ser.). (ENG., Illus.). 24p. (J). (gr. 1-3). *(978-1-60818-701-0(2),* 20599, Creative Education); pap. 8.99 *(978-1-62832-297-2(7),* 20597, Creative Paperbacks) Creative Co., The.

Schuh, Mari. Robins. 2019. (Spot Backyard Animals Ser.). (ENG.). 16p. (J). (gr. -1-2). lib. bdg. *(978-1-68151-547-2(4),* 14508) Amicus.

ROBINS—FICTION

Bentley, Sue. Double Trouble. 2009. (Magic Kitten Ser.: 4). lib. bdg. 16.00 *(978-0-606-06004-2(9))* Turtleback.

Bonnell, Kris. Robins in the Spring. 2007. (J). pap. 5.95 *(978-1-933727-53-0(5))* Reading Reading Bks., LLC.

Cole, Henry. Nesting. Cole, Henry, illus. 2020. (ENG., Illus.). 40p. (J). (gr. -1-3). 17.99 *(978-0-06-288592-0(8),* Tegen, Katherine Bks) HarperCollins Pubs.

Collins, Stephan. The Chronicles of Timothy Tabbis. 2009. (ENG.). 45p. pap. 8.55 *(978-0-557-09266-6(3))* Lulu Pr., Inc.

Dell, Bella. Rosie the Robin. 2013. 24p. pap. 24.95 *(978-1-63000-892-5(3))* America Star Bks.

Dhade, Sukhdev Kaur. Robin with the Red Hat, 1 vol. 2010. 24p. pap. 24.95 *(978-1-4489-7235-7(3))* PublishAmerica, Inc.

Fleming, Denise. This Is the Nest That Robin Built. Fleming, Denise, illus. 2018. (ENG., Illus.). 32p. (J). (gr. -1-3). 18.99 *(978-1-4814-3083-8(1),* Beach Lane Bks.) Beach Lane Bks.

Hocknell, Barbara. The Robins & the Bell. 2007. (Illus.). 52p. per. *(978-1-84748-132-0(9))* Athena Pr.

Jorgensen, Norman. In Flanders Fields. Harrison-Lever, Brian, illus. 2003. (ENG.). 32p. (J). (gr. -1-3). 16.95 *(978-1-894965-01-9(9))* Simply Read Bks. CAN. Dist: Ingram Publisher Services.

Jorgensen, Norman & Harrison-Lever, Brian. In Flanders Fields. 2004. (Illus.). 32p. pap. 13.50 *(978-1-920731-03-8(2))* Fremantle Pr. AUS. Dist: Independent Pubs. Group.

March, El. Captain Leopold. 2010. 64p. pap. 25.56 *(978-0-557-32169-8(7))* Lulu Pr., Inc.

Morpurgo, Michael. Coming Home. Hyndman, Kerry, illus. 2018. (ENG.). 32p. (J). (gr. -1-2). 17.99 *(978-1-5362-0042-3(5))* Candlewick Pr.

Parish, Herman. Amelia Bedelia Is for the Birds. Avril, Lynne, illus. 2015. (I Can Read Level 1 Ser.). (ENG.). 32p. (J). (gr. -1-3). pap. 4.99 *(978-0-06-233424-4(7),* Greenwillow Bks.) HarperCollins Pubs.

River, Fawn. Sophy & the River. 2012. 24p. pap. 17.99 *(978-1-4772-0272-2(2))* AuthorHouse.

Sawyers, William. The Nest That Could Fly. 2005. 43p. (J). pap. 17.96 *(978-1-4116-5446-4(3))* Lulu Pr., Inc.

Speed, Bryan W. Little Bent Cedar. Todd, Sheri, illus. 2007. (ENG.). 24p. (J). (gr. 2-4). per. *(978-1-933255-38-5(2))* DNA Pr.

Talbott, Shawn M. Springtime Robins. 2006. (J). lib. bdg. 19.95 *(978-1-933732-05-3(9))* Big Ransom Studio.

Wolf, Sallie. The Robin Makes a Laughing Sound: A Birder's Observations. 2010. (ENG., Illus.). 48p. (gr. 4-7). 11.95 *(978-1-58089-318-3(X))* Charlesbridge Publishing, Inc.

Wyss, Johann D. The Swiss Family Robinson (Abridged Edition) Abridged Edition. 2009. (Puffin Classics Ser.). 496p. (J). (gr. 5-7). pap. 8.99 *(978-0-14-132530-9(5),* Puffin Books) Penguin Young Readers Group.

ROBINSON, FRANK, 1935-2019

Skipper, John C. Frank Robinson: A Baseball Biography, 1 vol. 2014. (ENG., Illus.). 220p. pap. 29.95 *(978-0-7864-7561-2(7),* af0d27aa-7fc6-4674-bac0-d054dc597cdf) McFarland & Co., Inc. Pubs.

ROBINSON, JACKIE, 1919-1972

Auster, Michael A. They Led the Way. 2005. (Yellow Umbrella Fluent Level Ser.). (ENG.). 16p. (gr. k-1). pap. 35.70 *(978-0-7368-5315-6(4),* Capstone Pr.) Capstone.

Bailey, Budd. Jackie Robinson: Breaking Baseball's Color Barrier, 1 vol. 2015. (Game-Changing Athletes Ser.). (ENG., Illus.). 112p. (J). (gr. 9-9). lib. bdg. 44.50 *(978-1-5026-1056-0(6),* 1823bdda-1b1f-46da-ab76-1968758f5130) Cavendish Square Publishing LLC.

Bardhan-Quallen, Sudipta. The United States V. Jackie Robinson. Christie, R. Gregory, illus. 2018. (ENG.). 40p. (J). (gr. -1-3). 18.99 *(978-0-06-228784-7(2),* Balzer & Bray) HarperCollins Pubs.

Benjamin, Lisa. Jackie Robinson: Changing the Game. 2005. (Voices Reading Ser.). (Illus.). 32p. (J). *(978-0-7367-2937-6(2))* Zaner-Bloser, Inc.

Bennett, Doraine. Jackie Robinson. 2008. (J). pap. *(978-1-935077-11-4(2));* (ENG., Illus.). 24p. lib. bdg. 19.93 *(978-1-935077-04-6(X))* State Standards Publishing, LLC.

Brown, Jonatha A. Jackie Robinson, 1 vol. 2004. (People We Should Know Ser.). (Illus.). 24p. (gr. 2-4). (ENG.). pap. 9.15 *(978-0-8368-4318-7(5),* 50d58b96-3784-4000-b674-6730cd65194d); (SPA., lib. bdg. 24.67 *(978-0-8368-4353-8(3),* 6c52f439-021b-4f74-ac65-b147509dab46); (ENG., lib. bdg. 24.67 *(978-0-8368-4311-8(8),* e1881212-c531-47a9-8db7-7ecc39010d66) Stevens, Gareth Publishing LLLP. (Weekly Reader Leveled Readers).

Burgan, Michael. Breaking Barriers: The Story of Jackie Robinson. 2018. (Tangled History Ser.). (ENG., Illus.). 112p. (J). (gr. 3-9). lib. bdg. 32.65 *(978-1-5157-7932-2(7),* 136027, Capstone Pr.) Capstone.

Burleigh, Robert. Stealing Home: Jackie Robinson: Against the Odds. Wimmer, Mike, illus. 2007. (ENG.). 32p. (J). (gr. 1-4). 18.99 *(978-0-689-86276-2(8),* Simon & Schuster/Paula Wiseman Bks.) Simon & Schuster/Paula Wiseman Bks.

Christopher, Matt & Stout, Glenn. Jackie Robinson: Legends in Sports. 2006. (ENG., Illus.). 128p. (J). (gr. 5-8). per. 9.99 *(978-0-316-10826-3(X))* Little, Brown Bks. for Young Readers.

Crisp, Victor. Jackie Robinson: Breaking Barriers. 2013. (InfoMax Readers Ser.). (ENG.). 24p. (J). (gr. 3-4). pap. 49.50 *(978-1-4777-2632-7(2));* (Illus.). pap. 8.25 *(978-1-4777-2631-0(4),* 973fa924-0ad5-48cc-acf1-70fb97c7a0f9) Rosen Publishing Group, Inc., The. (Rosen Classroom).

Elish, Dan. Jackie Robinson. 2005. (Cornerstones of Freedom Ser.). (ENG., Illus.). 48p. (YA). (gr. 4-7). lib. bdg. 26.00 *(978-0-516-23635-3(0))* Scholastic Library Publishing.

Frystak, Timothy D. Jackie Robinson: With Profiles of Satchel Paige & & Branch Rickey. 2006. (Biographical Connections Ser.). (Illus.). 112p. (J). *(978-0-7166-1828-7(1))* World Bk., Inc.

Glaser, Jason. Jackie Robinson: Gran Pionero del Béisbol. Lentz, Bob, illus. 2006. (Biografías Gráficas Ser.). (SPA.). 32p. (J). (gr. 3-9). 31.32 *(978-0-7368-6602-6(7),* 86559) Capstone.

Gutman, Dan. Jackie Robinson & the Big Game. Garvin, Elaine, illus. 2006. 32p. (J). lib. bdg. 15.00 *(978-1-4242-0957-6(9))* Fitzgerald Bks.

—Jackie Robinson & the Big Game: Ready-To-Read Level 2. Garvin, Elaine, illus. 2006. (Ready-To-Read Childhood of Famous Americans Ser.). (ENG.). 32p. (J). (gr. k-2). pap. 4.99 *(978-0-689-86239-7(3),* Simon & Schuster/Paula Wiseman Bks.) Simon & Schuster/Paula Wiseman Bks.

Haldy, Emma E. Jackie Robinson. Bane, Jeff, illus. 2016. (My Early Library: My Itty-Bitty Bio Ser.). (ENG.). 24p. (J). (gr. k-1). 30.64 *(978-1-63471-021-3(5),* 208164) Cherry Lake Publishing.

Hanft, Joshua E. Jackie Robinson. Marcos, Pablo, illus. 2005. (Heroes of America Ser.). 238p. (gr. 3-8). lib. bdg. 27.07 *(978-1-59679-259-3(0),* Abdo & Daughters) ABDO Publishing Co.

Hansen, Grace. Jackie Robinson: Baseball Legend, 1 vol. 2015. (History Maker Biographies (Abdo Kids Jumbo) Ser.). (ENG., Illus.). 24p. (J). (gr. -1-2). lib. bdg. 32.79 *(978-1-62970-701-3(5),* 17009, Abdo Kids) ABDO Publishing Co.

Herman, Gail & Who HQ. Who Was Jackie Robinson? O'Brien, John, illus. 2010. (Who Was? Ser.). 112p. (J). (gr. 3-7). pap. 6.99 (978-0-448-45557-0(9), Penguin Workshop) Penguin Young Readers Group.

Hoena, Blake. Jackie Robinson: Athletes Who Made a Difference. Shephard, David, illus. 2020. (Athletes Who Made a Difference Ser.). (ENG.). 32p. (J). (gr. 3-6). 27.99 (978-1-5415-7816-6(3), e9bf1a17-dc86-408b-8073-0bf65bfa25c7); pap. 8.99 (978-1-7284-0294-9(8), 5141cf5c-2f5e-4a37-994b-8c4e9b454c83) Lerner Publishing Group. (Graphic Universe™).

Hurt, Avery Elizabeth. Jackie Robinson: Barrier-Breaking Baseball Legend, 1 vol. 2019. (African American Trailblazers Ser.). (ENG.). 128p. (gr. 9-9). lib. bdg. 47.36 (978-1-5026-4552-4(1), 517c433a-b77b-4b0f-8aa4-c8deb4851f62) Cavendish Square Publishing LLC.

Jd, Duchess Harris & Streissguth, Tom. Jackie Robinson Breaks Barriers. 2018. (Perspectives on American Progress Ser.). (ENG., Illus.). 48p. (J). (gr. 4-8). lib. bdg. 35.64 (978-1-5321-1492-2(3), 29116) ABDO Publishing Co.

Kawa, Katie. Jackie Robinson, 1 vol. 2018. (Heroes of Black History Ser.). (ENG.). 32p. (gr. 3-4). 28.27 (978-1-5382-3018-3(6), 5f73de87-babd-4dc2-8d32-64e934389036) Stevens, Gareth Publishing LLLP.

Lewis, J. Patrick. Always, Jackie. Thompson, John, illus. 2020. (ENG.). 32p. (J). (gr. 1-3). 18.99 (978-1-56846-307-0(3), 18355, Creative Editions) Creative Co., The.

Mara, Wil. Jackie Robinson. 2014. (Rookie Biographies(r) Ser.). (ENG.). 32p. (J). lib. bdg. 23.00 (978-0-531-21062-8(6)) Scholastic Library Publishing.

Martin, Isabel. Jackie Robinson, 1 vol. 2014. (Great African-Americans Ser.). (ENG., Illus.). 24p. (J). (gr. -1-2). pap. 5.95 (978-1-4914-0508-6(2), 125885, Capstone Pr.) Capstone.

McPherson, Stephanie Sammartino. Jackie Robinson. 2010. (J). lib. bdg. 27.93 (978-0-7613-5207-5(4), Lerner Pubns.) Lerner Publishing Group.

Meltzer, Brad. I Am Jackie Robinson. Eliopoulos, Christopher, illus. 2015. (Ordinary People Change the World Ser.). 40p. (J). (gr. k-4). 15.99 (978-0-8037-4086-0(7), Dial Bks) Penguin Young Readers Group.

O'Hern, Kerri & Raatma, Lucia. Jackie Robinson, 1 vol. (Biografías Gráficas (Graphic Biographies) Ser.). (Illus.). 32p. (gr. 3-3). 2007. (SPA.). pap. 11.50 (978-0-8368-7889-9(2), e9c6eb5b-3f15-4fa2-93eb-04bdb46484e8) 2007. (SPA., lib. bdg. 29.67 (978-0-8368-7882-0(5), 1b2744a5-4ce9-4f8f-94d5-4d18365a19a5) 2005. (ENG., pap. 11.50 (978-0-8368-6250-8(3), 368f3a21-8a71-4071-ba9c-9fb2f612048a) 2005. (ENG., lib. bdg. 29.67 (978-0-8368-6198-3(1), 02b39b1a-8e36-46c3-8548-2036b5aca1c8) Stevens, Gareth Publishing LLLP.

Patrick, Denise Lewis. Jackie Robinson Strong Inside & Out. 2005. 44p. (J). lib. bdg. 15.00 (978-1-4242-0850-0(5)) Fitzgerald Bks.

Patrick, Denise Lewis & Time for Kids Editors. Jackie Robinson - Strong Inside & Out. 2005. (Time for Kids Ser.). (ENG., Illus.). 48p. (J). (gr. 2-4). pap. 3.99 (978-0-06-057600-4(6)) HarperCollins Pubs.

Rappaport, Doreen. 42 Is Not Just a Number: The Odyssey of Jackie Robinson, American Hero. 2019. (ENG.). 128p. (J). (gr. 3-7). pap. 6.99 (978-1-5362-0632-6(6)) Candlewick Pr.

Rice, Dona Herweck. Jackie Robinson: Hometown Hero. rev. ed. 2016. (Social Studies: Informational Text Ser.). (ENG., Illus.). 32p. (gr. 2-4). pap. 10.99 (978-1-4938-2560-8(7)) Teacher Created Materials, Inc.

Robinson, Sharon. Child of the Dream (a Memoir Of 1963) 2019. (ENG., Illus.). 240p. (J). (gr. 3-7). 16.99 (978-1-338-28280-1(8), Scholastic Pr.) Scholastic, Inc.

—Jackie Robinson: American Hero. 2013. (ENG.). 48p. (J). (gr. 1-3). pap. 4.99 (978-0-545-54006-3(2), Scholastic Paperbacks) Scholastic, Inc.

—Promises to Keep: How Jackie Robinson Changed America: How Jackie Robinson Changed America. 2004. (ENG., Illus.). 64p. (gr. 4-7). 18.99 (978-0-439-42592-6(1)) Scholastic, Inc.

Rodriguez, Tia. Jackie Robinson: Baseball Legend, 1 vol. 2013. (Rosen Readers Ser.). (ENG.). 24p. (J). (gr. 3-3). pap. 8.25 (978-1-4777-2568-9(7), a1a8a0af-a7db-4118-b4a0-e8782e2556fa); pap. 49.50 (978-1-4777-2569-6(5)) Rosen Publishing Group, Inc., The. (Rosen Classroom).

Saddleback Educational Publishing Staff, ed. Jackie Robinson, 1 vol. unabr. ed. 2007. (Graphic Biographies Ser.). (ENG., Illus.). 25p. (YA). (gr. 4-12). pap. 9.75 (978-1-59905-225-0(3)) Saddleback Educational Publishing, Inc.

Sexton, Colleen. Jackie Robinson: A Life of Determination. 2007. (People of Character Ser.). (ENG., Illus.). 24p. (J). (gr. 2-5). lib. bdg. 26.95 (978-1-60014-089-1(0)) Bellwether Media.

Simmons, Matt J. Jackie Robinson: Breaking the Color Line in Baseball. 2014. (Crabtree Groundbreaker Biographies Ser.). (ENG., Illus.). 112p. (J). (gr. 6-6). (978-0-7787-1242-8(7)) Crabtree Publishing Co.

Strand, Jennifer. Jackie Robinson. 2016. (Trailblazing Athletes Ser.). (ENG.). 24p. (J). (gr. -1-2). 49.94 (978-1-68079-419-9(1), 23040, Abdo Zoom-Launch) ABDO Publishing Co.

Trussell-Cullen, Alan. Jackie Robinson. 2009. pap. 13.25 (978-1-60559-063-9(0)) Hameray Publishing Group, Inc.

Walker, Sally M. Jackie Robinson. Translations.com Staff, tr. Pate, Rodney S., illus. 2005. (Yo Solo: Biografías (on My Own Biographies) Ser.). (SPA & ENG.). 48p. (gr. 2-4). lib. bdg. 25.26 (978-0-8225-3126-5(7), Ediciones Lerner) Lerner Publishing Group.

Wheeler, Jill C. Jackie Robinson. 2003. (Breaking Barriers Ser.). 64p. (gr. 3-8). lib. bdg. 27.07 (978-1-57765-739-2(X), Abdo & Daughters) ABDO Publishing Co.

Williams, Heather. Jackie Robinson. 2018. (21st Century Skills Library: Sports Unite Us Ser.). (ENG., Illus.). 32p. (J). (gr. 3-6). lib. bdg. 32.07 (978-1-5341-2958-0(8), 211876) Cherry Lake Publishing.

Wilmore, Kathy. Jackie Robinson: With a Discussion of Respect. 2004. (Values in Action Ser.). (J). (978-1-59203-071-2(8)) Learning Challenge, Inc.

Wukovits, John F. Jackie Robinson & the Integration of Baseball, 1 vol. 2006. (Lucent Library of Black History Ser.). (ENG., Illus.). 104p. (gr. 7-7). lib. bdg. 35.08 (978-1-59018-913-9(2), 9deb995c-c2eb-447e-9434-112659e16985, Lucent Pr.) Greenhaven Publishing LLC.

ROBINSON, JACKIE, 1919-1972—FICTION

Grossinger, Tania. Jackie & Me: A Very Special Friendship. Esperanza, Charles George, illus. (ENG.). 32p. (J). (gr. -1-k). 2017. 6.99 (978-1-5107-1270-6(4)) 2013. 16.95 (978-1-62087-683-1(3), 620683) Skyhorse Publishing Co., Inc. (Sky Pony Pr.).

Gutman, Dan. Jackie & Me. 2005. (Baseball Card Adventures Ser.). (Illus.). 145p. (YA). (gr. 4-8). reprint ed. 20.00 (978-0-7567-9569-6(9)) DIANE Publishing Co.

Krensky, Stephen. Play Ball, Jackie! Morse, Joe, illus. 2011. (Single Titles Ser.). (ENG.). 32p. (J). (gr. 2-5). lib. bdg. 16.95 (978-0-8225-9030-9(1), Millbrook Pr.) Lerner Publishing Group.

Lorbiecki, Marybeth. Jackie's Bat. Pinkney, Brian, illus. 2006. (ENG.). 40p. (J). (gr. k-3). 19.99 (978-0-689-84102-6(7), Simon & Schuster Bks. For Young Readers) Simon & Schuster Bks. For Young Readers.

Robinson, Sharon. Testing the Ice: a True Story about Jackie Robinson. Nelson, Kadir, illus. 2009. (ENG.). 40p. (J). (gr. 2-5). 18.99 (978-0-545-05251-1(3), Scholastic Pr.) Scholastic, Inc.

Rosenberg, Aaron. 42 - The Official Movie Novel. 2013. (ENG.). 160p. (J). (gr. 4-6). 18.69 (978-0-545-53753-7(3)) Scholastic, Inc.

Russell, Nancy L. M., et al. So Long, Jackie Robinson. rev. ed. 2007. (ENG.). 224p. (J). (gr. 4-7). 7.95 (978-1-55263-863-7(4)) Leaf Storm Pr.

Uhlberg, Myron. Dad, Jackie, & Me, 1 vol. Bootman, Colin, illus. 32p. (J). (gr. -1-3). 2010. pap. 8.99 (978-1-56145-531-7(8)) 2007. 16.95 (978-1-56145-329-0(3)) Peachtree Publishing Co. Inc.

ROBINSON, JOHN ROOSEVELT, 1919-1972

see Robinson, Jackie, 1919-1972

ROBOTS

Abramovitz, Melissa & Alpert, Barbara. Military Machines. 2012. (Military Machines Ser.). (ENG.). 24p. (gr. k-1). pap. 250.20 (978-1-4296-8319-7(8), Capstone Pr.) Capstone.

Alkire, Jessie. Robotics: From Leonardo Da Vinci to Isaac Asimov. 2018. (STEM Stories Ser.). (ENG., Illus.). 32p. (J). (gr. 3-6). lib. bdg. 32.79 (978-1-5321-1548-6(2), 28950, Checkerboard Library) ABDO Publishing Co.

Allen, Kathy. Let's Draw Robots with Crayola (r) ! 2018. (Let's Draw with Crayola (r) ! Ser.). (ENG., Illus.). 32p. (J). (gr. -1-3). pap. 6.99 (978-1-5415-1168-2(9), edc8b195-897b-4b38-8295-af9273256fd2, Lerner Pubns.) Lerner Publishing Group.

Allman, Toney. From Insect Wings to Flying Robots, 1 vol. 2006. (Imitating Nature Ser.). (ENG., Illus.). 32p. (gr. 3-6). lib. bdg. 28.88 (978-0-7377-3488-1(4), e42376ae-77cc-4349-b3e7-d12d3f1726fb, KidHaven Publishing) Greenhaven Publishing LLC.

—Jaws of Life. 2008. (Great Idea Ser.). (Illus.). 48p. (J). (gr. 4-6). lib. bdg. 26.60 (978-1-59953-191-5(7)) Norwood Hse. Pr.

—The Nexi Robot. 2009. (Great Idea Ser.). (Illus.). 48p. (J). (gr. 4-6). lib. bdg. 26.60 (978-1-59953-342-1(1)) Norwood Hse. Pr.

Alpert, Barbara. Military Robots. 2012. (Military Machines Ser.). (ENG.). 24p. (gr. k-1). pap. 41.70 (978-1-4296-8315-9(5), Capstone Pr.) Capstone.

—Military Robots, 1 vol. 2012. (Military Machines Ser.). (ENG.). 24p. (J). (gr. -1-2). lib. bdg. 27.32 (978-1-4296-7573-4(X), 117170, Capstone Pr.) Capstone.

—U. S. Military Robots, 1 vol. 2012. (U. S. Military Technology Ser.). (ENG., Illus.). 32p. (J). (gr. 3-9). lib. bdg. 27.32 (978-1-4296-8438-5(0), 118510, Capstone Pr.) Capstone.

Amazing Robots. 2015. (Amazing Robots Ser.). (ENG.). 48p. (J). (gr. 4-5). pap., pap., pap. 84.30 (978-1-4824-3432-3(6)); pap., pap., pap. 505.80 (978-1-4824-3431-6(8)); lib. bdg. 201.60 (978-1-4824-2556-7(4), 8c074db7-d0cd-45be-b554-ec9e9d3e1c83) Stevens, Gareth Publishing LLLP.

Amstutz, Lisa J. All about Robots. 2017. (Cutting-Edge Technology Ser.). (ENG., Illus.). 32p. (J). (gr. 3-5). lib. bdg. 31.35 (978-1-63517-014-6(1), 1635170141, Focus Readers) North Star Editions.

Andrysek, Jan & Mihailidis, Alex. New Hands, New Life: Robots, Prostheses & Innovation. 2017. (ENG., Illus.). 64p. (J). (gr. 4-7). 19.95 (978-1-77085-969-2(1), 088fb460-e1de-4a59-be35-3beb1e456576); pap. 9.95 (978-1-77085-991-3(8), 88034609-fa56-46cb-818b-9241f613a4a8) Firefly Bks., Ltd.

Bailey, Loren. 30-Minute Robotics Projects. 2019. (30-Minute Makers Ser.). (ENG., Illus.). 32p. (J). (gr. 2-5). 27.99 (978-1-5415-3888-7(9), 9b960eee-814f-4a88-9d13-d177bd528bfc); pap. 8.99 (978-1-5415-5715-4(8), c156119e-ac5f-4942-9690-b4a49298e508) Lerner Publishing Group. (Lerner Pubns.).

Baker, John R. Astonishing Robot Competitions. 2017. (Cool Competitions Ser.). (ENG., Illus.). 32p. (J). (gr. 3-9). lib. bdg. 27.32 (978-1-5157-7352-8(3), 135690, Capstone Pr.) Capstone.

Baum, Margaux & Chaffee, Joel. Engineering & Building Robots for Competitions, 1 vol. 2017. (Hands-On Robotics Ser.). (ENG.). 48p. (J). (gr. 5-5). pap. 12.75 (978-1-4994-3884-0(2), 640db9b5-618f-4932-b312-56c9da0020da) Rosen Publishing Group, Inc., The.

Baum, Margaux & Freedman, Jeri. The History of Robots & Robotics, 1 vol. 2017. (Hands-On Robotics Ser.). (ENG.). 48p. (J). (gr. 5-5). pap. 12.75 (978-1-4994-3892-5(3), 928e0484-e4b1-4f8c-ae52-04a345e323b1) Rosen Publishing Group, Inc., The.

Baum, Margaux & Shea, Therese M. Becoming a Member of a Robotics Club, 1 vol. 2017. (Hands-On Robotics Ser.). (ENG.). 48p. (J). (gr. 5-5). pap. 12.75 (978-1-4994-3876-5(1), 2305fe97-6a20-417a-aa6b-3c330b489158) Rosen Publishing Group, Inc., The.

Becker, Helaine. Zoobots: Wild Robots Inspired by Real Animals, 0 vols. Ries, Alex, illus. 2014. (ENG.). 32p. (J). (gr. 3-7). 17.95 (978-1-55453-971-0(4)) Kids Can Pr., Ltd. CAN. Dist: Hachette Bk. Group.

Bergin, Mark. Robots, 1 vol. 2008. (How to Draw Ser.). (ENG., Illus.). 32p. (J). (gr. 4-5). pap. 12.75 (978-1-4358-2650-2(7), fb3d9055-1990-4eda-8ee8-578c86f4020b); lib. bdg. 30.27 (978-1-4358-2521-5(7), ef5d160b-09d9-4998-92d9-eaae12a13296) Rosen Publishing Group, Inc., The. (PowerKids Pr.).

Besel, Tucker. Build Your Own Bug Bot. Gould, Grant, illus. 2018. (Bot Maker Ser.). (ENG.). 24p. (J). (gr. 4-6). lib. bdg. (978-1-68072-321-2(9), 12068, Hi Jinx) Black Rabbit Bks.

—Build Your Own Bug Bot. 2018. (Bot Maker Ser.). (ENG.). (J). (gr. 3-7). pap. 8.95 (978-1-68072-645-9(5)) Hi Jinx Pr.

—Build Your Own Crazy Car Bot. Gould, Grant, illus. 2018. (Bot Maker Ser.). (ENG.). 24p. (J). (gr. 4-6). lib. bdg. (978-1-68072-322-9(7), 12072, Hi Jinx) Black Rabbit Bks.

—Build Your Own Crazy Car Bot. 2018. (Bot Maker Ser.). (ENG.). (J). (gr. 3-7). pap. 8.95 (978-1-68072-646-6(3)) Hi Jinx Pr.

—Build Your Own Inchworm Bot. Gould, Grant, illus. 2018. (Bot Maker Ser.). (ENG.). 24p. (J). (gr. 4-6). lib. bdg. (978-1-68072-326-7(X), 12088, Hi Jinx) Black Rabbit Bks.

—Build Your Own Inchworm Bot. 2018. (Bot Maker Ser.). (ENG.). (J). (gr. 3-7). pap. 8.95 (978-1-68072-650-3(1)) Hi Jinx Pr.

—Build Your Own Racer Bot. Gould, Grant, illus. 2018. (Bot Maker Ser.). (ENG.). 24p. (J). (gr. 4-6). lib. bdg. (978-1-68072-323-6(5), 12076, Hi Jinx) Black Rabbit Bks.

—Build Your Own Racer Bot. 2018. (Bot Maker Ser.). (ENG.). (J). pap. 8.95 (978-1-68072-647-3(1)) Hi Jinx Pr.

—Build Your Own Scribble Bot. Gould, Grant, illus. 2018. (Bot Maker Ser.). (ENG.). 24p. (J). (gr. 4-6). lib. bdg. (978-1-68072-324-3(3), 12080, Hi Jinx) Black Rabbit Bks.

—Build Your Own Scribble Bot. 2018. (Bot Maker Ser.). (ENG.). (J). (gr. 3-7). pap. 8.95 (978-1-68072-648-0(X)) Hi Jinx Pr.

Biskup, Agnieszka. The Remarkable World of Robots: Max Axiom STEM Adventures. Max, Iman, illus. 2017. (STEM Adventures Ser.). (ENG.). 32p. (J). (gr. 3-9). lib. bdg. 31.32 (978-1-5157-7391-7(4), 135721, Capstone Pr.) Capstone.

Bow, James. Maker Projects for Kids Who Love Robotics. 2016. (Be a Maker! Ser.). (ENG., Illus.). 32p. (J). (978-0-7787-2254-0(6)) Crabtree Publishing Co.

Brasch, Nicolas. Robots of the Future, 1 vol. 2012. (Discovery Education: Technology Ser.). (ENG., Illus.). 32p. (J). (gr. 4-5). 28.93 (978-1-4488-7885-7(3), 0cac1e86-8c11-498a-be7b-d2b6fde7c74b); pap. 11.00 (978-1-4488-7967-0(1), 07c5c39f-566f-4bf1-969d-b3125ef9927f) Rosen Publishing Group, Inc., The. (PowerKids Pr.).

Brown, Don. Machines That Think! Big Ideas That Changed the World #2. 2020. (Big Ideas That Changed the World Ser.). (ENG., Illus.). 128p. (J). (gr. 3-7). 14.99 (978-1-4197-4098-5(9), 1254801, Amulet Bks.) Abrams, Inc.

Brown, Jordan D. Robo World: The Story of Robot Designer Cynthia Breazeal. 2006. (ENG., Illus.). 128p. (gr. 7-9). per. 19.95 (978-0-309-09556-3(5), Joseph Henry Pr.) National Academies Pr.

Cassriel, Betsy R. Robot Builders!, Vol. 10. 2015. (Scientists in Action Ser.). (Illus.). 48p. (J). (gr. 5). 20.95 (978-1-4222-3426-6(6)) Mason Crest.

Chaffee, Joel. How to Build a Prize-Winning Robot, 1 vol. 2011. (Robotics Ser.). (ENG.). 48p. (YA). (gr. 5-5). pap. 12.75 (978-1-4488-2252-2(1), bc1de7bd-e448-4a0a-995c-298b9b11e745); (Illus.). lib. bdg. 34.47 (978-1-4488-1238-7(0), b09cfd69-4655-4b37-a163-36a3317e4c8a) Rosen Publishing Group, Inc., The.

Chow-Miller, Ian. How Robots Work, 1 vol. 2018. (Everyday STEM Ser.). (ENG.). 32p. (J). (gr. 3-3). 30.21 (978-1-5026-3744-4(8), ea117dc6-31cb-4bc4-932c-d45467887e0b) Cavendish Square Publishing LLC.

—Integrated Robotics, 1 vol. 2016. (Robotics Ser.). (ENG., Illus.). 128p. (YA). (gr. 9-9). 47.36 (978-1-5026-1936-5(9), 4cbeb077-0c34-49b5-b3f7-0ceed36af406) Cavendish Square Publishing LLC.

—Sensors & the Environment, 1 vol. 2016. (Robotics Ser.). (ENG., Illus.). 128p. (YA). (gr. 9-9). 47.36 (978-1-5026-1938-9(5), f480463e-3c0d-4ebd-950b-64b49f5bbe8c) Cavendish Square Publishing LLC.

Clay, Kathryn. My First Guide to Robots. 2015. (My First Guides). (ENG., Illus.). 24p. (J). (gr. 1-3). lib. bdg. 27.99 (978-1-4914-2049-2(9), 127527, Capstone Pr.) Capstone.

Clay, Kathryn & Shores, Erika. Cool Robots, 1 vol. 2014. (Cool Robots Ser.). (ENG.). 24p. (J). (gr. -1-2). 117.28 (978-1-4914-0686-1(0), 21493, Capstone Pr.) Capstone.

Cohen, Jacob. Getting the Most Out of Makerspaces to Build Robots, 1 vol. 2014. (Makerspaces Ser.). (ENG.). 64p. (J). (gr. 6-6). 36.13 (978-1-4777-7819-7(5), f7f15b56-ff58-4687-a77e-f64e40fba788) Rosen Publishing Group, Inc., The.

Colins, Luke. Animal Robots. 2020. (World of Robots Ser.). (ENG.). 24p. (J). (gr. k-3). lib. bdg. (978-1-62310-162-6(X), 14418, Bolt Jr.) Black Rabbit Bks.

—Battling Robots. 2020. (World of Robots Ser.). (ENG.). 24p. (J). (gr. k-3). lib. bdg. (978-1-62310-163-3(8), 14422, Bolt Jr.) Black Rabbit Bks.

—Medical Robots. 2020. (World of Robots Ser.). (ENG.). 24p. (J). (gr. k-3). lib. bdg. (978-1-62310-164-0(6), 14426, Bolt Jr.) Black Rabbit Bks.

—Military Robots. 2020. (World of Robots Ser.). (ENG.). 24p. (J). (gr. k-3). pap. 8.99 (978-1-64466-109-3(8), 14431, Bolt Jr.) Black Rabbit Bks.

—Space Robots. 2020. (World of Robots Ser.). (ENG.). 24p. (J). (gr. k-3). lib. bdg. (978-1-62310-166-4(2), 14434, Bolt Jr.) Black Rabbit Bks.

—Underwater Robots. 2020. (World of Robots Ser.). (ENG.). 24p. (J). (gr. k-3). lib. bdg. (978-1-62310-167-1(0), 14438, Bolt Jr.) Black Rabbit Bks.

Cooper, James. Inside Robotics, 1 vol. 2018. (Geek's Guide to Computer Science Ser.). (ENG.). 176p. (gr. 9-9). 41.47 (978-1-5081-8580-2(8), aa1cad08-ff61-40d7-aec4-f60b1e5a3a72, Rosen Young Adult) Rosen Publishing Group, Inc., The.

Crane, Cody. Robots (a True Book: Behind the Scenes) (Library Edition) 2017. (True Book (Relaunch) Ser.). (ENG., Illus.). 48p. (J). (gr. 3-5). lib. bdg. 31.00 (978-0-531-23501-0(7), Children's Pr.) Scholastic Library Publishing.

Cunningham, Kevin. Robot Scientist. 2015. (21st Century Skills Library: Cool STEAM Careers Ser.). (ENG., Illus.). 32p. (J). (gr. 4-7). 32.07 (978-1-63362-562-4(1), 206432) Cherry Lake Publishing.

De La Rosa, Jeff. Robots & People. 2019. (Illus.). 48p. (J). (978-0-7166-4137-7(2)) World Bk.-Childcraft International.

Derrington, Louise. How to Build Robots. 2017. (Technology in Motion Ser.). (Illus.). 32p. (J). (gr. 5-5). (978-0-7787-3394-2(7)) Crabtree Publishing Co.

DK. Robot (Spanish Edition) Descubre Las Máquinas Del Futuro. 2019. Orig. Title: Robot. (SPA., Illus.). 160p. (J). (gr. 4-7). 19.99 (978-1-4654-8282-2(2), DK Children) Dorling Kindersley Publishing, Inc.

Faust, Daniel R. Building Robots: Robotic Engineers, 1 vol., 1. 2015. (Engineers Rule! Ser.). (ENG., Illus.). 32p. (J). (gr. 4-5). pap. 12.75 (978-1-5081-4540-0(7), f7fc73fb-674f-4f36-8814-74578bb544e1, PowerKids Pr.) Rosen Publishing Group, Inc., The.

—Manufacturing Robots, 1 vol. 2016. (Robots & Robotics Ser.). (ENG.). 32p. (J). (gr. 5-5). pap. 12.75 (978-1-4994-2171-2(0), 952af780-a7a4-4d75-90d4-ca53be26b4a3, PowerKids Pr.) Rosen Publishing Group, Inc., The.

—Medical Robots, 1 vol. 2016. (Robots & Robotics Ser.). (ENG.). 32p. (J). (gr. 5-5). pap. 12.75 (978-1-4994-2175-0(3), 990599a1-e9ff-4486-bf00-81365f3a4a13, PowerKids Pr.) Rosen Publishing Group, Inc., The.

—Military & Police Robots, 1 vol. 2016. (Robots & Robotics Ser.). (ENG., Illus.). 32p. (J). (gr. 5-5). pap. 12.75 (978-1-4994-2178-1(8), 451f20f3-ff54-4a6c-b43f-5ecc88c6d81e, PowerKids Pr.) Rosen Publishing Group, Inc., The.

—Underwater Robots, 1 vol. 2016. (Robots & Robotics Ser.). (ENG.). 32p. (J). (gr. 5-5). pap. 12.75 (978-1-4994-2186-6(9), 087a40b7-eb50-4b0c-adeb-63462d08b027, PowerKids Pr.) Rosen Publishing Group, Inc., The.

Fliess, Sue. Robots, Robots Everywhere! Staake, Bob, illus. 2013. (Little Golden Book Ser.). 24p. (J). (-k). 5.99 (978-0-449-81079-8(8), Golden Bks.) Random Hse. Children's Bks.

Freedman, Jeri. Robots Through History, 1 vol. 2011. (Robotics Ser.). (ENG., Illus.). 48p. (YA). (gr. 5-5). 34.47 (978-1-4488-1236-3(4), 57fc2c59-8a01-4a15-baae-ee716ef574bf); pap. 12.75 (978-1-4488-2250-8(5), 94c7ba93-b654-4469-b778-1519c879a9b7, Rosen Reference) Rosen Publishing Group, Inc., The.

Fretland VanVoorst, Jenny. Robots in Space. 2015. (Illus.). 24p. (J). lib. bdg. (978-1-62031-219-3(0)) Jump! Inc.

—Robots in the Factory. 2015. (Illus.). 24p. (J). lib. bdg. (978-1-62031-218-6(2)) Jump! Inc.

Fritz, Sandy. Robotics & Artificial Intelligence. 2003. (Hot Science Ser.). (J). lib. bdg. 28.50 (978-1-58340-364-8(7)) Black Rabbit Bks.

Furstinger, Nancy. Helper Robots. 2014. (Lightning Bolt Books (r) — Robots Everywhere! Ser.). (ENG., Illus.). 32p. (J). (gr. 1-3). pap. 9.99 (978-1-4677-4508-6(1), 31cba0a5-27b7-4963-9558-f4614dd858a2) Lerner Publishing Group.

—Robots in Space. 2014. (Lightning Bolt Books (r) — Robots Everywhere! Ser.). (ENG., Illus.). 32p. (J). (gr. 1-3). pap. 9.99 (978-1-4677-4510-9(3), 865977fb-31b3-4865-a160-1ef1d1c30c35); lib. bdg. 29.32 (978-1-4677-4055-5(1), ea912cc8-ca06-4b2d-a579-a1c46f9dc90f, Lerner Pubns.) Lerner Publishing Group.

Gagne, Tammy. Robots. 2018. (21st Century Inventions Ser.). (ENG.). 24p. (J). (gr. 1-1). pap. 8.95 (978-1-63517-793-0(6), 1635177936) North Star Editions.

—Robots. 2018. (21st Century Inventions Ser.). (ENG., Illus.). 24p. (J). (gr. k-3). lib. bdg. 31.36 (978-1-5321-6042-4(9), 28716, Pop! Cody Koala) Pop!

Galashan, Kathy. Robots. 2005. (ENG., Illus.). 32p. pap. 8.50 (978-0-340-87311-3(6)) Cambridge Univ. Pr.

Gendell, Megan. Rocking & Roving: Everything You Wanted to Know about Rockets, Rovers, & Robots. 2008. (Illus.). 31p. (J). (978-0-545-04460-8(X)) Scholastic, Inc.

Gerdes, Louise I., ed. Robotic Technology, 1 vol. 2014. (Opposing Viewpoints Ser.). (ENG.). 200p. (gr. 10-12). pap. 34.80 (978-0-7377-6339-3(6), a8a25a81-bf19-42cc-96ca-42f82a34d8e3); lib. bdg. 50.43 (978-0-7377-6338-6(8), 3fe70e9b-2710-42f3-af35-3b4bccae2caf) Greenhaven Publishing LLC. (Greenhaven Publishing).

Gifford, Clive. Robots. 2005. (Technology All Around Us Ser.). (Illus.). 32p. (YA). (gr. 4-7). lib. bdg. 27.10 (978-1-58340-752-3(9)) Black Rabbit Bks.

—Robots. 2011. 48p. 11.99 (978-84-96252-41-7(8)) Edilupa Ediciones, S.L. ESP. Dist: Lectorum Pubns., Inc.

—Robots. Picini, Frank, illus. 2008. (ENG.). 32p. (J). (gr. 3-9). 21.99 (978-1-4169-6414-8(2), Atheneum Bks. for Young Readers) Simon & Schuster Children's Publishing.

Giulieri, Anne. Here Is a Robot. 2012. (Engage Literacy Magenta Ser.). (ENG.). 16p. (J). (gr. k-2). pap. 36.94 (978-1-4296-8849-9(1), 18320); (Illus.). pap. 6.99 (978-1-4296-8848-2(3), 119927) Capstone. (Capstone Pr.).

Grack, Rachel. Robots from Then to Now. 2019. (Sequence Developments in Technology Ser.). (ENG.). 32p. (J). (gr. 2-5). pap. 9.99 (978-1-68152-471-9(6), 11056) Amicus.

Graham, Ian. Robot Technology. 2010. (New Technology Ser.). (ENG., Illus.). 48p. (J). 23.99 (978-0-237-54075-3(4)) Evans Brothers, Ltd. GBR. Dist: Independent Pubs. Group.

—You Wouldn't Want to Live Without Robots! (You Wouldn't Want to Live Without...) (Library Edition) Antram, David, illus. 2018. (You Wouldn't Want to Live Without... Ser.). (ENG.).

32p. (J). (gr. 3). lib. bdg. 29.00 *(978-0-531-12813-8(X),* Watts, Franklin) Scholastic Library Publishing.

Gray, Peter C. Robots, 1 vol. 2005. (Drawing Manga Ser.). (ENG., Illus.). 32p. (YA). (gr. 4-4). lib. bdg. 30.27 *(978-1-4042-3332-4(6),* 27e28f22-908e-4ee0-b235-7e285b4f78f1) Rosen Publishing Group, Inc., The.

Gregory, Josh. Robots. 2017. (21st Century Skills Innovation Library: Emerging Tech Ser.). (ENG., Illus.). 32p. (J). (gr. 4-8). lib. bdg. 32.07 *(978-1-63472-701-3(0),* 210130) Cherry Lake Publishing.

Gregory, Joshua. Careers in Robot Technology. 2018. (Bright Futures Press: Emerging Tech Careers Ser.). (ENG., Illus.). 32p. (J). (gr. 4-7). lib. bdg. 32.07 *(978-1-5341-2977-1(4),* 211952) Cherry Lake Publishing.

Hamilton, S. L. Animal Robots. 2018. (Xtreme Robots Ser.). (ENG.). 32p. (J). (gr. 3-9). lib. bdg. 32.79 *(978-1-5321-1822-7(8),* 30562, Abdo & Daughters) ABDO Publishing Co.

—Explorer Robots. 2018. (Xtreme Robots Ser.). (ENG., Illus.). 32p. (J). (gr. 3-9). lib. bdg. 32.79 *(978-1-5321-1823-4(6),* 30564, Abdo & Daughters) ABDO Publishing Co.

—Household Robots. 2018. (Xtreme Robots Ser.). (ENG., Illus.). 32p. (J). (gr. 3-9). lib. bdg. 32.79 *(978-1-5321-1824-1(4),* 30566, Abdo & Daughters) ABDO Publishing Co.

—Humanoid Robots. 2018. (Xtreme Robots Ser.). (ENG., Illus.). 32p. (J). (gr. 3-9). lib. bdg. 32.79 *(978-1-5321-1825-8(2),* 30568, Abdo & Daughters) ABDO Publishing Co.

—Industrial Robots. 2018. (Xtreme Robots Ser.). (ENG., Illus.). 32p. (J). (gr. 3-9). lib. bdg. 32.79 *(978-1-5321-1826-5(0),* 30570, Abdo & Daughters) ABDO Publishing Co.

—Rescue Robots. 2018. (Xtreme Robots Ser.). (ENG., Illus.). 32p. (J). (gr. 3-9). lib. bdg. 32.79 *(978-1-5321-1827-2(9),* 30572, Abdo & Daughters) ABDO Publishing Co.

Hands-On Robotics, 10 vols. 2017. (Hands-On Robotics Ser.). (ENG.). (J). (gr. 5-5). lib. bdg. 167.35 *(978-1-4994-3962-5(8),* aab49c9e-419d-4c21-80ff-6ab04bc6f620, Rosen Reference) Rosen Publishing Group, Inc., The.

Hartman, Ashley Strehle. Entertainment Robots. 2018. (Robot Innovations Ser.). (ENG., Illus.). 48p. (J). (gr. 4-8). lib. bdg. 35.64 *(978-1-5321-1466-3(4),* 29124) ABDO Publishing Co.

Hartson, Tamara. Robots, 1 vol. 2018. (Mega Machines Ser.). (ENG., Illus.). 64p. (J). pap. 6.99 *(978-1-926700-83-0(X),* 953a4bf9-14f4-4773-9a43-cbc0e2e248d9) Blue Bike Bks. CAN. Dist: Lone Pine Publishing USA.

Hayes, Susan & Gordon-Harris, Tory. Really? Robots. 2015. lib. bdg. 19.65 *(978-0-606-37754-6(9))* Turtleback.

Higgins, Nadia. Factory Robots. (Robotics in Our World Ser.). (ENG., Illus.). 32p. (J). (gr. 2-5). 2018. pap. 9.99 *(978-1-68152-172-5(5),* 14803) 2017. 20.95 *(978-1-68151-141-2(X),* 14684) Amicus.

—Medical Robots. (Robotics in Our World Ser.). (ENG., Illus.). 32p. (J). (gr. 2-5). 2018. pap. 9.99 *(978-1-68152-174-9(1),* 14805) 2017. 20.95 *(978-1-68151-143-6(6),* 14686) Amicus.

—Robots at Home. (Robotics in Our World Ser.). (ENG., Illus.). 32p. (J). (gr. 2-5). 2018. pap. 9.99 *(978-1-68152-176-3(8),* 14807) 2017. 20.95 *(978-1-68151-145-0(2),* 14688) Amicus.

—Robots in Fiction. (Robotics in Our World Ser.). (ENG., Illus.). 32p. (J). (gr. 2-5). 2018. pap. 9.99 *(978-1-68152-177-0(6),* 14808) 2017. 20.95 *(978-1-68151-146-7(0),* 14689) Amicus.

Hillman, Emilee. Coding Activities for Coding Robots with LEGO Mindstorms, 1 vol. 2021. (Code Creator Ser.). (ENG., Illus.). 64p. (J). (gr. 7-7). pap. 13.95 *(978-1-7253-4107-4(7),* 4c11b148-721f-48af-a3c1-2fb4840b8b0b) Rosen Publishing Group, Inc., The.

Holmes, Kirsty. Loopy Logic! 2019. (Code Academy Ser.). (ENG.). 24p. (J). (gr. 2-2). pap. *(978-0-7787-6341-3(2),* 54832828-e7a1-41af-8fa6-78cc60a87bf7); lib. bdg. *(978-0-7787-6335-2(8),* 04694e1b-3839-4411-a9ac-9a64929700fb) Crabtree Publishing Co.

Holzweiss, Kristina A. & Barth, Amy. I Can Make Remarkable Robots (Rookie Star: Makerspace Projects) 2017. (Rookie Star Ser.). (ENG., Illus.). 32p. (J). (gr. 2-3). pap. 5.95 *(978-0-531-23879-0(2),* Children's Pr.) Scholastic Library Publishing.

—I Can Make Remarkable Robots (Rookie Star: Makerspace Projects) (Library Edition) 2017. (Rookie Star Ser.). (ENG., Illus.). 32p. (J). (gr. 2-3). lib. bdg. 25.00 *(978-0-531-23410-5(X),* Children's Pr.) Scholastic Library Publishing.

Howard, Ayanna. On the Job with an Engineer. 2003. (Adventures in Science Ser.). (J). pap. *(978-1-58417-122-5(7));* lib. bdg. *(978-1-58417-059-4(X))* Lake Street Pubs.

Howell, Izzi. Robots. 2018. (Adventures in STEAM Ser.). (ENG., Illus.). 48p. (J). (gr. 3-6). lib. bdg. 27.99 *(978-1-5435-3231-9(4),* 138830, Capstone Pr.) Capstone.

Huggins-Cooper, Lynn. DK Readers L4 Robot Universe. 2017. (DK Readers Level 4 Ser.). (ENG., Illus.). 96p. (J). (gr. 4-7). pap. 4.99 *(978-1-4654-6321-0(6),* DK Children) Dorling Kindersley Publishing, Inc.

Hulick, Kathryn. Robotics & Medicine. 2018. (Next-Generation Medical Technology Ser.). (ENG.). 80p. (YA). (gr. 5-12). 39.93 *(978-1-68282-329-3(6))* ReferencePoint Pr., Inc.

—Robotics Engineer. 2017. (ENG.). 64p. (J). (gr. 5-12). *(978-1-68282-186-2(2))* ReferencePoint Pr., Inc.

Hustad, Douglas. Discover Robotics. 2016. (Searchlight Books (tm) — What's Cool about Science? Ser.). (ENG., Illus.). 40p. (J). (gr. 3-5). 30.65 *(978-1-5124-0809-6(3),* e34c83cc-4351-4933-93c8-9fa47e714694, Lerner Pubns.) Lerner Publishing Group.

Incentive Publications by World Book (Firm) Staff, contrib. by. CRISPR & Other Biotech. 2019. (Illus.). 48p. (J). *(978-0-7166-2429-5(X))* World Bk., Inc.

Ithaca, Sciencenter, NY. Is That Robot Real? 2009. 44p. 17.20 *(978-0-578-00196-8(9))* Sciencenter.

Ives, Rob. Build Your Own Robots. 2018. (Makerspace Models Ser.). (ENG., Illus.). 32p. (J). (gr. 3-6). lib. bdg. 27.99 *(978-1-5124-5970-8(4),* d75c299e-4462-4b3f-ba54-f0e209bd5b17, Hungry Tomato (r)) Lerner Publishing Group.

Jefferis, David. Robot Brains. 2006. (Robozones Ser.). (ENG., Illus.). 32p. (J). (gr. 3-7). pap. *(978-0-7787-2900-6(1));* (gr. 4-7). lib. bdg. *(978-0-7787-2886-3(2))* Crabtree Publishing Co.

—Robot Voyagers. 2006. (Robozones Ser.). (ENG., Illus.). 32p. (J). (gr. 4-7). pap. *(978-0-7787-2898-6(6));* lib. bdg. *(978-0-7787-2884-9(6))* Crabtree Publishing Co.

—Robot Warriors. 2006. (Robozones Ser.). (ENG., Illus.). 32p. (J). (gr. 3-7). pap. *(978-0-7787-2901-3(X))* Crabtree Publishing Co.

—Robot Workers. 2006. (Robozones Ser.). (ENG., Illus.). 32p. (J). (gr. 3-7). lib. bdg. *(978-0-7787-2885-6(4))* Crabtree Publishing Co.

Kemmeter, Jennifer. Build It! Robots: Make Supercool Models with Your Favorite LEGO(r) Parts. 2017. (Brick Bks.: 9). (ENG., Illus.). 86p. (J). (gr. -1-2). pap. 16.99 *(978-1-5132-6083-9(9),* Graphic Arts Bks.) West Margin Pr.

Kenney, Karen Latchana. Cutting-Edge Robotics. 2018. (Searchlight Books (tm) — Cutting-Edge STEM Ser.). (ENG., Illus.). 32p. (J). (gr. 3-5). 30.65 *(978-1-5415-2344-9(X),* 8d8f8c7e-e6a8-4d83-9185-d44aba336891, Lerner Pubns.) Lerner Publishing Group.

King, Trey. Training Academy: Sharks & Other Sea Life! (Illus.). 32p. (J). *(978-1-5182-4448-3(3),* Reagan Arthur Bks.) Little Brown & Co.

Kingsley Troupe, Thomas. Animal Robots. 2017. (Mighty Bots Ser.). (ENG.). 32p. (gr. 2-7). 9.95 *(978-1-68072-459-2(2),* Bolt) Black Rabbit Bks.

—Medical Robots. 2017. (Mighty Bots Ser.). (ENG.). 32p. (gr. 2-7). 9.95 *(978-1-68072-461-5(4),* Bolt) Black Rabbit Bks.

—Military Robots. 2017. (Mighty Bots Ser.). (ENG., Illus.). 32p. (J). (gr. 2-7). 9.95 *(978-1-68072-462-2(2),* Bolt) Black Rabbit Bks.

—Space Robots. 2017. (Mighty Bots Ser.). (ENG.). 32p. (gr. 2-7). 9.95 *(978-1-68072-463-9(0),* Bolt) Black Rabbit Bks.

—Underwater Robots. 2017. (Mighty Bots Ser.). (ENG.). 32p. (gr. 2-7). 9.95 *(978-1-68072-464-6(9),* Bolt) Black Rabbit Bks.

Koontz, Robin. Animal-Inspired Robots. 2018. (Nature-Inspired Innovations Ser.). (ENG., Illus.). 48p. (gr. 4-8). pap. 10.95 *(978-1-64156-583-7(7),* 9781641565837) Rourke Educational Media.

Kops, Deborah. Exploring Space Robots. 2011. (Searchlight Books (tm) — What's Amazing about Space? Ser.). (ENG., Illus.). (gr. 3-5). 40p. (J). pap. 9.99 *(978-0-7613-7880-8(4),* 7f33276e-ab87-4aae-ad63-159e4165e1f9); pap. 51.01 *(978-0-7613-8417-5(0))* Lerner Publishing Group.

Kulz, George Anthony. Hobby & Competition Robots. 2018. (Robot Innovations Ser.). (ENG., Illus.). 48p. (J). (gr. 4-8). lib. bdg. 35.64 *(978-1-5321-1467-0(2),* 29126) ABDO Publishing Co.

La Bella, Laura. The Future of Robotics, 1 vol. 2017. (Hands-On Robotics Ser.). (ENG., Illus.). 48p. (J). (gr. 5-5). pap. 12.75 *(978-1-4994-3888-8(5),* 8b299ecb-f669-471e-bc57-bfb4a7f394c0) Rosen Publishing Group, Inc., The.

Lacey, Saskia. STEM Careers. 2nd rev. ed. 2017. (TIME(r): Informational Text Ser.). (ENG., Illus.). 48p. (J). (gr. 6-8). pap. 11.99 *(978-1-4938-3623-9(4))* Teacher Created Materials, Inc.

—STEM Careers: Reinventing Robotics. 2017. (Time for Kids Nonfiction Readers Ser.). lib. bdg. 20.85 *(978-0-606-40279-8(9))* Turtleback.

LaPierre, Yvette. How Do Robots Defuse Bombs? 2018. (How'd They Do That? Ser.). (ENG., Illus.). 32p. (J). (gr. 4-6). lib. bdg. 28.65 *(978-1-5435-4139-7(9),* 139093, Capstone Pr.) Capstone.

Larson, Kirsten W. Hobby Robots. (Robotics in Our World Ser.). (ENG., Illus.). 32p. (J). (gr. 2-5). 2018. pap. 9.99 *(978-1-68152-173-2(3),* 14804) 2017. 20.95 *(978-1-68151-142-9(8),* 14685) Amicus.

—Military Robots. (Robotics in Our World Ser.). (ENG., Illus.). 32p. (J). (gr. 2-5). 2018. pap. 9.99 *(978-1-68152-175-6(X),* 14806) 2017. 20.95 *(978-1-68151-144-3(4),* 14687) Amicus.

—Space Robots. (Robotics in Our World Ser.). (ENG., Illus.). 32p. (J). (gr. 2-5). 2018. pap. 9.99 *(978-1-68152-178-7(4),* 14809) 2017. 20.95 *(978-1-68151-147-4(9),* 14690) Amicus.

Latta, Sara L. Zoom in on Educational Robots, 1 vol. 2017. (Zoom in on Robots Ser.). (ENG.). 24p. (gr. 2-2). pap. 10.95 *(978-0-7660-9446-8(4),* ad8c5b5f-1d26-4071-ab07-285694c473d6); lib. bdg. 25.60 *(978-0-7660-9227-3(5),* 5b5a41c1-3f08-49b0-a00b-281e3b4e5e18) Enslow Publishing, LLC.

—Zoom in on Industrial Robots, 1 vol. 2017. (Zoom in on Robots Ser.). (ENG.). 24p. (gr. 2-2). 25.60 *(978-0-7660-9226-6(7),* 359605f1-921f-48c8-88ae-e0387c565283) Enslow Publishing, LLC.

—Zoom in on Medical Robots, 1 vol. 2017. (Zoom in on Robots Ser.). (ENG.). 24p. (gr. 2-2). 25.60 *(978-0-7660-9228-0(3),* 97670718-0f76-4e52-ab26-d67adfaa89ba) Enslow Publishing, LLC.

—Zoom in on Mining Robots, 1 vol. 2017. (Zoom in on Robots Ser.). (ENG.). 24p. (gr. 2-2). 25.60 *(978-0-7660-9230-3(5),* ca89eb2e-58fe-47a2-9aa1-83037a4ba49c) Enslow Publishing, LLC.

Leider, Rick Allen. Robots: Explore the World of Robots & How They Work for Us. 2015. (Fact Atlas Ser.). (ENG., Illus.). 72p. (J). (gr. 2-7). 14.99 *(978-1-63220-439-4(8),* Sky Pony Pr.) Skyhorse Publishing Co., Inc.

Lepora, Nathan. DKfindout! Robots. 2018. (DK Findout! Ser.). (ENG., Illus.). 64p. (J). (gr. 1-4). 16.99 *(978-1-4654-7319-6(X));* pap. 10.99 *(978-1-4654-6933-5(8))* Dorling Kindersley Publishing, Inc. (DK Children).

Lewis, Katherine. Everyday Robots. 2020. (Lightning Bolt Books (r) — Robotics Ser.). (ENG., Illus.). 24p. (J). (gr. 1-3). 29.32 *(978-1-5415-9693-1(5),* ef0e81f3-0c73-450e-b3e5-52f187baa842, Lerner Pubns.) Lerner Publishing Group.

Lindeen, Mary. Humanoid Robots. 2017. (Cutting-Edge Robotics (Alternator Books (r)) Ser.). (ENG., Illus.). 32p. (J). (gr. 3-6). 29.32 *(978-1-5124-4012-6(4),* 814780a3-cb3b-4325-b8ec-b30164061bb4, Lerner Pubns.) Lerner Publishing Group.

—Law Enforcement Robots. 2017. (Cutting-Edge Robotics (Alternator Books (r)) Ser.). (ENG., Illus.). 32p. (J). (gr. 3-6). 29.32 *(978-1-5124-4011-9(6),* 16cec008-1069-4a09-b7b3-15aef65d0e86, Lerner Pubns.) Lerner Publishing Group.

—Robot Competitions. 2017. (Cutting-Edge Robotics (Alternator Books (r)) Ser.). (ENG., Illus.). 32p. (J). (gr. 3-6). 29.32 *(978-1-5124-4010-2(8),* bd042a0c-e26e-45a8-a05d-7f80c3294e3d, Lerner Pubns.) Lerner Publishing Group.

Littlewood, Peter. Rain Forest Destruction. 2012. (Mapping Global Issues Ser.). 48p. (J). (gr. 7-9). lib. bdg. 34.25 *(978-1-59920-512-0(2))* Black Rabbit Bks.

Lovett, Amber. Controlling an Ozobot. 2017. (21st Century Skills Innovation Library: Makers As Innovators Junior Ser.). (ENG., Illus.). 24p. (J). (gr. 2-5). lib. bdg. 30.64 *(978-1-63472-187-5(X),* 209320) Cherry Lake Publishing.

Manatt, Kathleen. Robot Scientist. 2007. (21st Century Skills Library: Cool Science Careers Ser.). (ENG., Illus.). 32p. (gr. 4-8). lib. bdg. 32.07 *(978-1-60279-051-3(5),* 200016) Cherry Lake Publishing.

Martin, Brett S. Military Robots. 2018. (Robot Innovations Ser.). (ENG., Illus.). 48p. (J). (gr. 4-4). pap. 11.95 *(978-1-64185-277-7(1),* 1641852771, Core Library); lib. bdg. 35.64 *(978-1-5321-1469-4(9),* 29130) ABDO Publishing Co.

—Search-And-Rescue Robots. 2018. (Robot Innovations Ser.). (ENG., Illus.). 48p. (J). (gr. 4-4). pap. 11.95 *(978-1-64185-278-4(X),* 164185278X, Core Library); lib. bdg. 35.64 *(978-1-5321-1470-0(2),* 29132) ABDO Publishing Co.

Masiello, Ralph. Ralph Masiello's Robot Drawing Book. Masiello, Ralph, illus. 2011. (Ralph Masiello's Drawing Bks.). (Illus.). 32p. (J). (gr. 1-4). 16.95 *(978-1-57091-535-2(0))* Charlesbridge Publishing, Inc.

Mason Crest Publishers Staff, contrib. by. Robots, Vol. 6. 2019. (Science & Technology Ser.). 48p. (J). (gr. 8). 27.93 *(978-1-4222-4211-7(0))* Mason Crest.

Mason, Paul. How to Design the World's Best: Robot: In 10 Simple Steps. 2018. (How to Design the World's Best Ser.). (ENG., Illus.). 32p. (J). (gr. 4-6). pap. 12.99 *(978-0-7502-9946-6(0),* Wayland) Hachette Children's Group GBR. Dist: Hachette Bk. Group.

Matteson, Adrienne. Coding with Sphero. 2017. (21st Century Skills Innovation Library: Makers As Innovators Junior Ser.). (ENG., Illus.). 24p. (J). (gr. 2-5). lib. bdg. 30.64 *(978-1-63472-695-5(2),* 210078) Cherry Lake Publishing.

—Sphero. 2017. (21st Century Skills Innovation Library: Makers As Innovators Ser.). (ENG., Illus.). 32p. (J). (gr. 4-8). lib. bdg. 32.07 *(978-1-63472-685-6(5),* 210042) Cherry Lake Publishing.

McCarthy, Cecilia Pinto. Military Robots. 2017. (Tech Bytes Ser.). (ENG.). 48p. (J). (gr. 4-6). pap. 14.60 *(978-1-68404-119-0(8));* (Illus.). 26.60 *(978-1-59953-888-4(1))* Norwood Hse. Pr.

McClintock Miller, Shannon & Hoena, Blake. A Robotics Mission. Brown, Alan, illus. 2018. (Adventures in Makerspace Ser.). (ENG.). 32p. (J). (gr. 3-5). 30.65 *(978-1-4965-7746-7(9),* 138431); pap. 7.95 *(978-1-4965-7750-4(7),* 139048) Capstone. (Stone Arch Bks.).

McClure, Leigh. Rae Builds a Robot: Following Instructions, 1 vol. 2017. (Computer Kids: Powered by Computational Thinking Ser.). (ENG.). 24p. (J). (gr. 4-5). 25.27 *(978-1-5383-2426-4(1),* 5453f3ce-fa17-433a-a415-0023c1514c9a, PowerKids Pr.); pap. *(978-1-5081-3761-0(7),* 41a9c61f-2f53-4143-9f7f-4ccebfdb8f3d, Rosen Classroom) Rosen Publishing Group, Inc., The.

McComb, Gordon. Building Your Own Robots: Design & Build Your First Robot! 2016. (Dummies Junior Ser.). (ENG., Illus.). 128p. (gr. 1-5). pap. 9.99 *(978-1-119-30243-8(9),* For Dummies) Wiley, John & Sons, Inc.

McCombs, Kevin. Locomotion & Mechanics, 1 vol. 2016. (Robotics Ser.). (ENG.). 128p. (YA). (gr. 9-9). 47.36 *(978-1-5026-2026-2(X),* 9defa11e-141b-47d5-ac2b-ffffcafc083f) Cavendish Square Publishing LLC.

Miller, Ron. Robot Explorers. 2007. (Space Innovations Ser.). (ENG., Illus.). 112p. (gr. 6-8). lib. bdg. 31.93 *(978-0-8225-7152-0(8))* Lerner Publishing Group.

Miller, Shannon & Hoena, B. A. A Robotics Mission. 2018. (J). *(978-1-68410-229-7(4))* Cantata Learning.

Morey, Allan. Robonauts. 2017. (Space Tech Ser.). (ENG., Illus.). 24p. (J). (gr. 3-7). lib. bdg. 26.95 *(978-1-62617-704-8(X),* Epic Bks.) Bellwether Media.

Murphy, Maggie. High-Tech DIY Projects with Robotics. 2014. (Maker Kids Ser.). (Illus.). 32p. (J). (gr. 3-6). pap. 70.50 *(978-1-4777-6656-9(1));* (ENG., (gr. 4-5). 29.27 *(978-1-4777-6669-9(3),* bc57e5b1-a468-4c79-a6cc-1a04952850df); (ENG., (gr. 4-5). pap. 12.75 *(978-1-4777-6675-0(8),* a85cbc5e-959c-4c98-84e4-05cb39eb7420) Rosen Publishing Group, Inc., The. (PowerKids Pr.).

Nagelhout, Ryan. Fighting Robots, 1 vol. 2016. (Robots & Robotics Ser.). (ENG., Illus.). 32p. (J). (gr. 5-5). pap. 12.75 *(978-1-4994-2163-7(X),* 23b1cec4-d00a-49b7-bcdb-19eacdf030e1, PowerKids Pr.) Rosen Publishing Group, Inc., The.

Nardo, Don. Robots, 1 vol. 2007. (Monsters Ser.). (ENG., Illus.). 48p. (gr. 4-8). lib. bdg. 31.88 *(978-0-7377-3779-0(4),* dc2b835b-a6d9-4107-b1b3-84a98e835d48, KidHaven Publishing) Greenhaven Publishing LLC.

National Geographic Kids. National Geographic Kids Robots Sticker Activity Book. 2018. 56p. (J). (gr. -1-k). pap. 6.99 *(978-1-4263-3180-0(0),* National Geographic Kids) Disney Publishing Worldwide.

Noll, Elizabeth. Factory Robots. 2017. (World of Robots Ser.). (ENG., Illus.). 32p. (J). (gr. 3-8). 27.95 *(978-1-62617-687-4(6),* Blastoff! Discovery) Bellwether Media.

—Medical Robots. 2017. (World of Robots Ser.). (ENG., Illus.). 32p. (J). (gr. 3-8). lib. bdg. 27.95 *(978-1-62617-689-8(2),* Blastoff! Discovery) Bellwether Media.

—Military Robots. 2017. (World of Robots Ser.). (ENG., Illus.). 32p. (J). (gr. 3-8). lib. bdg. 27.95 *(978-1-62617-690-4(6),* Blastoff! Readers) Bellwether Media.

—Police Robots. 2017. (World of Robots Ser.). (ENG., Illus.). 32p. (J). (gr. 3-8). lib. bdg. 27.95 *(978-1-62617-691-1(4),* Blastoff! Discovery) Bellwether Media.

—Space Robots. 2017. (World of Robots Ser.). (ENG., Illus.). 32p. (J). (gr. 3-8). lib. bdg. 27.95 *(978-1-62617-692-8(2),* Blastoff! Discovery) Bellwether Media.

Olson, Elsie. Robotify It! Robots You Can Make Yourself. 2017. (Cool Makerspace Gadgets & Gizmos Ser.). (ENG., Illus.). 32p. (J). (gr. 3-6). lib. bdg. 34.21 *(978-1-5321-1255-3(6),* 27586, Checkerboard Library) ABDO Publishing Co.

Otterman, Joseph. Stem: Robots: 3-D Shapes (Grade 1) rev. ed. 2018. (Mathematics in the Real World Ser.). (ENG., Illus.). 24p. (J). (gr. 1-2). pap. 9.99 *(978-1-4258-5693-9(4))* Teacher Created Materials, Inc.

Owen, Ruth. Exploring Distant Worlds As a Space Robot Engineer. 2015. (Get to Work with Science & Technology Ser.). (ENG., Illus.). 32p. (J). (gr. 2-7). lib. bdg. 29.32 *(978-1-910549-38-4(X),* 0b72afd5-b4d4-494b-ab6e-73e06e5ac46e) Ruby Tuesday Books Limited GBR. Dist: Lerner Publishing Group.

Owings, Lisa. Robot Uprising. 2019. (It's the End of the World! Ser.). (ENG., Illus.). 24p. (J). (gr. 3-7). lib. bdg. 26.95 *(978-1-64487-083-9(5),* Torque Bks.) Bellwether Media.

Oxlade, Chris. The History of Robots. 2017. (History of Technology Ser.). (ENG., Illus.). 32p. (J). (gr. 2-5). lib. bdg. 29.99 *(978-1-4846-4036-4(5),* 135137, Heinemann) Capstone.

—Readers L3: Robots. 2017. (Kingfisher Readers Ser.). (ENG., Illus.). 32p. (J). 12.99 *(978-0-7534-7343-6(7),* 900174945, Kingfisher) Roaring Brook Pr.

Parker, Andy. Mekanimals: Robotic Reef, Spanish-Language Edition. 2005. (Mekanimals Ser.). (SPA., Illus.). 8p. (J). bds. *(978-970-718-321-6(7),* Silver Dolphin en Español) Advanced Marketing, S. de R. L. de C. V.

Parker, Steve. Build the Robot. 2016. (Build The Ser.). (ENG., Illus.). 32p. (J). (gr. 3-7). pap. 19.95 *(978-1-62686-488-7(8),* Silver Dolphin Bks.) Printers Row Publishing Group.

—Robots for Work & Fun. 2010. (Robot World Ser.). 32p. (J). 28.50 *(978-1-60753-071-8(6))* Amicus Learning.

—Robots in Dangerous Places. 2010. (Robot World Ser.). (ENG.). 32p. (J). (gr. 4-6). lib. bdg. 28.50 *(978-1-60753-072-5(4),* 17227) Amicus.

—Robots in Fiction & Films. 2010. (Robot World Ser.). (ENG.). 32p. (J). (gr. 4-6). lib. bdg. 28.50 *(978-1-60753-073-2(2),* 17228) Amicus.

—Robots in Science & Medicine. 2010. (Robot World Ser.). (ENG., Illus.). 32p. (J). (gr. 4-6). lib. bdg. 28.50 *(978-1-60753-074-9(0),* 17229) Amicus.

—Robots in Space. 2010. (Robot World Ser.). (ENG.). 32p. (J). (gr. 4-6). lib. bdg. 28.50 *(978-1-60753-075-6(9),* 17230) Amicus.

—Robots on the Move. 2010. (Robot World Ser.). (ENG.). 32p. (J). (gr. 4-6). lib. bdg. 28.50 *(978-1-60753-076-3(7),* 17231) Amicus.

Parker, Steve & Bingham, Jane. Robots in Space. 2011. (On the Edge Ser.). 32p. (YA). (gr. 3-6). lib. bdg. 28.50 *(978-1-59920-514-4(9))* Black Rabbit Bks.

Parker, Steve & Pipe, Jim. Robots in Dangerous Places. 2011. (On the Edge Ser.). 32p. (YA). (gr. 3-6). lib. bdg. 28.50 *(978-1-59920-516-8(5))* Black Rabbit Bks.

—Robots in Fiction & Films. 2011. (On the Edge Ser.). 32p. (YA). (gr. 3-6). lib. bdg. 28.50 *(978-1-59920-515-1(7))* Black Rabbit Bks.

—Robots in Science & Medicine. 2011. (On the Edge Ser.). 32p. (YA). (gr. 3-6). lib. bdg. 28.50 *(978-1-59920-513-7(0))* Black Rabbit Bks.

Payment, Simone. Robotics Careers: Preparing for the Future, 1 vol. 2011. (Robotics Ser.). (ENG., Illus.). 48p. (YA). (gr. 5-5). 34.47 *(978-1-4488-1239-4(9),* a7aefcac-e2ff-429c-837a-3901018aee39); pap. 12.75 *(978-1-4488-2253-9(X),* f350d893-f145-4a1c-97ac-dd5833d224cb, Rosen Reference) Rosen Publishing Group, Inc., The.

Peppas, Lynn. Robotics. 2014. (Crabtree Chrome Ser.). (ENG., Illus.). 48p. (J). (gr. 2-2). *(978-0-7787-1369-2(5))* Crabtree Publishing Co.

Porterfield, Jason. Robots, Cyborgs, & Androids, 1 vol. 2018. (Sci-Fi or STEM? Ser.). (ENG.). 64p. (gr. 7-7). 36.13 *(978-1-5081-8043-2(1),* d3f8c22c-e41e-4210-bd41-0f9a20cf8ff0, Rosen Young Adult) Rosen Publishing Group, Inc., The.

—Robots, Jobs, & You, 1 vol. 2019. (Promise & Perils of Technology Ser.). (ENG.). 64p. (gr. 7-7). pap. 13.95 *(978-1-5081-8833-9(5),* 1f7133e3-f658-4a2e-a267-59c9b054dca9) Rosen Publishing Group, Inc., The.

PRESS, Celebration. Remarkable Robots. 2003. (ENG.). (J). (gr. 6-8). pap. 37.95 *(978-0-7652-3243-4(X),* Celebration Pr.) Savvas Learning Co.

Punter, Russell. Robots. Hamilton, Andrew, illus. 2004. 48p. (J). (gr. 2-18). pap. 5.95 *(978-0-7945-0760-2(3),* Usborne) EDC Publishing.

Rakos, Lynnda. Let's Color Together — Robots. 2014. (ENG., Illus.). 64p. (J). (gr. -1-3). pap. 3.99 *(978-0-486-77977-5(7),* 779777) Dover Pubns., Inc.

Rechlin, Ted. Build Your Own Giant Robots Super Sticker Book. 2011. (Dover Sticker Bks.). (ENG., Illus.). 6p. (J). (gr. k-6). 7.99 *(978-0-486-48276-7(6))* Dover Pubns., Inc.

Rechlin, Ted & Stickers. Mecha Robot Stickers. 2011. (Dover Little Activity Books Stickers Ser.). (ENG.). 4p. (J). (gr. k-3). pap. 1.50 *(978-0-486-48275-0(8))* Dover Pubns., Inc.

Reeve, Tim. Action Robots: A Pop-up Book Showing How They Work. MacLeod, Gavin, illus. 2004. 14p. (YA). (gr. 4-10). reprint ed. 17.00 *(978-0-7567-7284-0(2))* DIANE Publishing Co.

Regan, Lisa. Micro Model Battle Bots. 2004. (Illus.). *(978-0-439-68926-7(0))* Scholastic, Inc.

Robotics, 12 vols. 2016. (Robotics Ser.). (ENG.). 128p. (YA). (gr. 9-9). lib. bdg. 284.16 *(978-1-5026-1999-0(7),* 20dd0226-3754-45b4-9a8a-c25df62596e4, Cavendish Square) Cavendish Square Publishing LLC.

Robotics, 6 vols., Set. Incl. How to Build a Prize-Winning Robot. Chaffee, Joel. lib. bdg. 34.47 *(978-1-4488-1238-7(0),* b09cfd69-4655-4b37-a163-36a3317e4c8a); Robotics Careers: Preparing for the Future. Payment, Simone. 34.47 *(978-1-4488-1239-4(9),* a7aefcac-e2ff-429c-837a-3901018aee39); Robotics Club: Teaming up to Build Robots. Shea, Therese. lib. bdg. 34.47 *(978-1-4488-1237-0(2),* 92edb980-c09e-464c-ba7f-18230c20d6fb); Robots Through

History. Freedman, Jeri. 34.47 *(978-1-4488-1236-3(4),* 57fc2c59-8a01-4a15-baae-ee716ef574bf); (YA). (gr. 5-5). 2011. (Robotics Ser.). (ENG., illus.). 48p. 2010. Set lib. bdg. 103.41 *(978-1-4488-1392-6(1),* 6fe1a95a-7713-4a75-b6d6-03e06737be18, Rosen Reference) Rosen Publishing Group, Inc., The.

Robots & Robotics, 14 vols. 2016. (Robots & Robotics Ser.). 32p. (gr. 5-5). (ENG.). 195.51 *(978-1-5081-4903-3(8),* c2f8171e-2b84-45c1-a903-9627747bdf27); pap. 82.25 *(978-1-4994-2456-0(6))* Rosen Publishing Group, Inc., The. (PowerKids Pr.).

Sarma, Kamya. Dash & Dot. 2017. (21st Century Skills Innovation Library: Makers As Innovators Ser.). (ENG., Illus.). 32p. (J). (gr. 4-8). lib. bdg. 32.07 *(978-1-63472-686-3(3),* 210046) Cherry Lake Publishing.

Saunders-Smith, Gail. Robots in Space, 1 vol. 2014. (Cool Robots Ser.). (ENG., Illus.). 24p. (J). (gr. -1-2). 27.32 *(978-1-4914-0585-7(6),* 125923, Capstone Pr.) Capstone.

—Robots on the Job, 1 vol. 2014. (Cool Robots Ser.). (ENG.). 24p. (J). (gr. -1-2). 27.32 *(978-1-4914-0586-4(4),* 125924, Capstone Pr.) Capstone.

Schaefer, Lola. Bot Battles. 2020. (Lightning Bolt Books (r) — Robotics Ser.). (ENG., Illus.). 24p. (J). (gr. 1-3). 29.32 *(978-1-5415-9697-9(8),* 236c380f-e52b-4a0c-9f06-0f5ed82ea3d8, Lerner Pubns.) Lerner Publishing Group.

Scott, Mairghread. Science Comics: Robots & Drones: Past, Present, & Future. Chabot, Jacob, illus. 2018. (Science Comics Ser.). (ENG.). 128p. (J). pap. 12.99 *(978-1-62672-792-2(9),* 900173910, First Second Bks.) Roaring Brook Pr.

Scrace, Carolyn. Drawing Robots. 2016. (Art Works). 32p. (gr. 2-6). 31.35 *(978-1-62588-347-6(1),* Smart Apple Media) Black Rabbit Bks.

Senker, Cath. Poverty & Hunger. 2012. (Mapping Global Issues Ser.). 48p. (J). (gr. 7-9). lib. bdg. 34.25 *(978-1-59920-511-3(4))* Black Rabbit Bks.

Shackleton, Caroline. Robots: the Next Generation? High Intermediate Book with Online Access, 1 vol. 2014. (ENG., Illus.). 28p. pap., E-Book 9.50 *(978-1-107-67762-3(9))* Cambridge Univ. Pr.

Shaw-Russell, Susan. Robots Activity Book. 2009. (Dover Little Activity Bks.). (ENG., Illus.). 64p. (J). (gr. k-3). pap. 2.50 *(978-0-486-47227-0(2),* 472272) Dover Pubns., Inc.

Shea, Therese. Getting to Know Lego Mindstorms. 2014. (Code Power: a Teen Programmer's Guide Ser.). (Illus.). 64p. (J). (gr. 5-8). pap. 77.70 *(978-1-4777-7704-6(0),* Rosen Reference) Rosen Publishing Group, Inc., The.

—The Robotics Club: Teaming up to Build Robots, 1 vol. 2011. (Robotics Ser.). (ENG., Illus.). 48p. (YA). (gr. 5-5). lib. bdg. 34.47 *(978-1-4488-1237-0(2),* 92edb980-c09e-464c-ba7f-18230c20d6fb) Rosen Publishing Group, Inc., The.

Shea, Therese M. Gareth's Guide to Building a Robot, 1 vol. 2018. (Gareth Guides to an Extraordinary Life Ser.). (ENG.). 32p. (gr. 4-5). 29.60 *(978-1-5382-2051-1(2),* 525bbc73-2603-4ab9-84b6-94509595d1fe) Stevens, Gareth Publishing LLLP.

—The Robotics Club: Teaming up to Build Robots, 1 vol. 2011. (Robotics Ser.). (ENG., Illus.). 48p. (YA). (gr. 5-5). pap. 12.75 *(978-1-4488-2251-5(3),* d638fc58-c9ac-4293-b5fa-a2e2e19e5556) Rosen Publishing Group, Inc., The.

Sherman, Jill. Zoom in on Caregiving Robots, 1 vol. 2017. (Zoom in on Robots Ser.). (ENG.). 24p. (gr. 2-2). 25.60 *(978-0-7660-9229-7(1),* 04a57ba7-8a57-4b85-ac60-498555bee3b9) Enslow Publishing, LLC.

—Zoom in on Domestic Robots, 1 vol. 2017. (Zoom in on Robots Ser.). (ENG.). 24p. (gr. 2-2). 25.60 *(978-0-7660-9231-0(3),* 8a42a540-4aae-4888-b363-6c607246196f) Enslow Publishing, LLC.

Shofner, Melissa Raé. The Modern Nerd's Guide to Robot Battles, 1 vol. 2017. (Geek Out! Ser.). (ENG.). 32p. (J). (gr. 3-4). lib. bdg. 28.27 *(978-1-5382-1215-8(3),* 4c697b49-e27d-41f0-88f4-aaea4f111e82) Stevens, Gareth Publishing LLLP.

—The Modern Nerd's Guide to Robot Battles, 1 vol. 2017. (Geek Out! Ser.). (ENG.). 32p. (J). (gr. 3-4). pap. 11.50 *(978-1-5382-1214-1(5),* 5e5e429b-c461-4633-815a-446168a8ac53) Stevens, Gareth Publishing LLLP.

Shores, Erika L. Animal Robots, 1 vol. 2014. (Cool Robots Ser.). (ENG., Illus.). 24p. (J). (gr. -1-2). 27.32 *(978-1-4914-0588-8(0),* 125926, Capstone Pr.) Capstone.

Smibert, Angie. Robots: Designed by Nature. 2018. (Illus.). 32p. (J). *(978-1-4896-9729-5(2),* AV2 by Weigl) Weigl Pubs., Inc.

—Robots Inspired by Nature. 2018. (Technology Inspired by Nature Ser.). (ENG., illus.). 32p. (J). (gr. 3-5). pap. 9.95 *(978-1-64185-045-2(0),* 1641850450); lib. bdg. 31.35 *(978-1-63517-943-9(2),* 1635179432) North Star Editions. (Focus Readers).

—Space Robots. 2018. (Robot Innovations Ser.). (ENG., Illus.). 48p. (J). (gr. 4-4). pap. 11.95 *(978-1-64185-279-1(8),* 1641852798, Core Library); lib. bdg. 35.64 *(978-1-5321-1471-7(0),* 29134) ABDO Publishing Co.

Smith, Aubrey. How to Build a Robot (with Your Dad) 20 Easy-To-build Robotic Projects. 2013. (ENG., Illus.). 160p. (gr. 2-4). pap. 19.99 *(978-1-84317-678-1(8))* O'Mara, Michael Bks., Ltd. GBR. Dist: Independent Pubs. Group.

Sobey, Ed. Build Your Own Robot Science Fair Project, 1 vol. 2015. (Prize-Winning Science Fair Projects Ser.). (ENG.). 128p. (gr. 7-7). lib. bdg. 38.93 *(978-0-7660-7018-9(2),* 666485fa-4c9f-403f-9e1a-804f79e85633) Enslow Publishing, LLC.

—Robot Experiments, 1 vol. 2011. (Cool Science Projects with Technology Ser.). (ENG., Illus.). 128p. (gr. 5-6). lib. bdg. 35.93 *(978-0-7660-3303-0(1),* 90dde4bc-5318-4af9-8c95-1faf71c2cfa8) Enslow Publishing, LLC.

Spilsbury, Louise & Spilsbury, Richard. Robots in Industry, 1 vol. 2015. (Amazing Robots Ser.). (ENG.). 48p. (J). (gr. 4-5). pap. 15.05 *(978-1-4824-3001-1(0),* e468b086-ab64-4237-94d7-473c5ea74673) Stevens, Gareth Publishing LLLP.

—Robots in Law Enforcement, 1 vol. 2015. (Amazing Robots Ser.). (ENG.). 48p. (J). (gr. 4-5). pap. 15.05 *(978-1-4824-3005-9(3),* dbb2a7cd-13b8-4e38-b2ba-c7c169e93ec3) Stevens, Gareth Publishing LLLP.

—Robots in Medicine, 1 vol. 2015. (Amazing Robots Ser.). (ENG.). 48p. (J). (gr. 4-5). pap. 15.05 *(978-1-4824-3009-7(6),* 87a5332c-9b37-4ea8-8c7a-af4e34a82c47) Stevens, Gareth Publishing LLLP.

—Robots in Space, 1 vol. 2015. (Amazing Robots Ser.). (ENG., Illus.). 48p. (J). (gr. 4-5). pap. 15.05 *(978-1-4824-3013-4(4),* 495f3d19-b39e-46da-9960-c2c5bb251110) Stevens, Gareth Publishing LLLP.

—Robots in the Military, 1 vol. 2015. (Amazing Robots Ser.). (ENG.). 48p. (J). (gr. 4-5). pap. 15.05 *(978-1-4824-3017-2(7),* 15e3adf8-8543-4e6b-acb2-d7ae5e22f644) Stevens, Gareth Publishing LLLP.

—Robots Underwater, 1 vol. 2015. (Amazing Robots Ser.). (ENG.). 48p. (J). (gr. 4-5). pap. 15.05 *(978-1-4824-3021-9(5),* 29cb84fc-2d36-444e-939b-1a36ded87f3f) Stevens, Gareth Publishing LLLP.

Squishy, Fishy Robot Explorers: Meet NASA Inventor Mason Peck & His Team's. 2017. (J). *(978-0-7166-6156-6(X))* World Bk., Inc.

Stark, William N. Mighty Military Robots. 2016. (Military Machines on Duty Ser.). (ENG., Illus.). 24p. (J). (gr. 1-3). lib. bdg. 27.99 *(978-1-4914-8847-8(6),* 131474, Capstone Pr.) Capstone.

Stewart, Melissa. National Geographic Readers: Robots. 2014. (Readers Ser.). (Illus.). 48p. (J). (gr. 1-3). pap. 4.99 *(978-1-4263-1344-8(6),* National Geographic Kids) Disney Publishing Worldwide.

—NGR Robots (Level 3) (Special Sales UK Edition) 2014. (Readers Ser.). (ENG., Illus.). 48p. (J). (gr. 1-4). pap. 4.99 *(978-1-4263-1805-4(7))* National Geographic Society.

Stock, Lisa. DK Readers L1: Star Wars: What Is a Droid? 2018. (DK Readers Level 1 Ser.). (ENG., Illus.). 24p. (J). (gr. k-2). pap. 4.99 *(978-1-4654-6753-9(X),* DK Children) Dorling Kindersley Publishing, Inc.

—What Is a Droid? 2018. (Star Wars DK Readers Level 1 Ser.). lib. bdg. 14.75 *(978-0-606-41168-4(2))* Turtleback.

Strom, Laura Layton. Shockwave: from Bugbots to Humanoids. 2007. (Shockwave: Technology & Manufacturing Ser.). (ENG., Illus.). 36p. (J). (gr. 4-6). lib. bdg. 25.00 *(978-0-531-17585-9(5),* Children's Pr.) Scholastic Library Publishing.

Suen, Anastasia. Remarkable Robots. 2003. (ENG., Illus.). 32p. (J). (gr. 6-8). pap. 7.97 net. *(978-0-7652-3263-2(4),* Celebration Pr.) Savvas Learning Co.

Swanson, Jennifer. National Geographic Kids Everything Robotics: All the Photos, Facts, & Fun! 2016. (National Geographic Kids Everything Ser.). (Illus.). 64p. (J). (gr. 3-7). pap. 12.99 *(978-1-4263-2331-7(X),* National Geographic Kids) Disney Publishing Worldwide.

Thai, Chi N. Learning Robotics with Robotis Dream Systems. 2018. (ENG., Illus.). 204p. (J). pap. 17.95 *(978-0-9993918-1-5(X))* CNT Robotics LLC.

Thomas, Rachael L. Make a Robo Pet Your Way! 2018. (Super Simple DIY Ser.). (ENG., Illus.). 32p. (J). (gr. k-4). lib. bdg. 34.21 *(978-1-5321-1719-0(1),* 30726, Super SandCastle) ABDO Publishing Co.

—Revolutionary Robots in Space. 2019. (Cosmos Chronicles (Alternator Books (r)) Ser.). (ENG., Illus.). 32p. (J). (gr. 3-6). pap. 10.99 *(978-1-5415-7370-3(6),* ac8379ce-a411-4aca-bf09-d9827e7dc129, Lerner Pubns.) Lerner Publishing Group.

Troupe, Thomas Kingsley. Animal Robots. 2017. (Mighty Bots Ser.). (ENG.). 32p. (J). (gr. 4-6). pap. 9.99 *(978-1-64466-196-3(9),* 11440); (Illus.). lib. bdg. *(978-1-68072-156-0(9),* 10496) Black Rabbit Bks. (Bolt).

—Battling Robots. 2017. (Mighty Bots Ser.). (ENG.). 32p. (J). (gr. 4-6). pap. 9.99 *(978-1-64466-197-0(7),* 11442); (Illus.). lib. bdg. *(978-1-68072-157-7(7),* 10498) Black Rabbit Bks. (Bolt).

—Medical Robots. 2017. (Mighty Bots Ser.). (ENG.). 32p. (J). (gr. 4-6). pap. 9.99 *(978-1-64466-198-7(5),* 11444); (Illus.). lib. bdg. *(978-1-68072-158-4(5),* 10500) Black Rabbit Bks. (Bolt).

—Military Robots. 2017. (Mighty Bots Ser.). (ENG.). 32p. (J). (gr. 4-6). pap. 9.99 *(978-1-64466-199-4(3),* 11446); (Illus.). lib. bdg. *(978-1-68072-159-1(3),* 10502) Black Rabbit Bks. (Bolt).

—Space Robots. 2017. (Mighty Bots Ser.). (ENG.). 32p. (J). (gr. 4-6). pap. 9.99 *(978-1-64466-200-7(0),* 11448); (Illus.). lib. bdg. *(978-1-68072-160-7(7),* 10504) Black Rabbit Bks. (Bolt).

—Underwater Robots. 2017. (Mighty Bots Ser.). (ENG.). 32p. (J). (gr. 4-6). pap. 9.99 *(978-1-64466-201-4(9),* 11450); (Illus.). lib. bdg. *(978-1-68072-161-4(5),* 10506) Black Rabbit Bks. (Bolt).

Tuchman, Gail. Robots. 2016. (Illus.). 32p. (J). *(978-1-5182-0083-0(4))* Scholastic, Inc.

—Robots (Scholastic Reader, Level 2) 2015. (Scholastic Reader, Level 2 Ser.). (ENG., Illus.). 32p. (J). (gr. 1-3). pap. 3.99 *(978-0-545-89138-7(8))* Scholastic, Inc.

Ventura, Marne. Google Glass & Robotics Innovator Sebastian Thrun. 2014. (STEM Trailblazer Bios Ser.). (ENG., Illus.). 32p. (J). (gr. 2-5). lib. bdg. 26.65 *(978-1-4677-2459-3(9),* 479b5a74-206c-451a-8ef8-301df5fda866, Lerner Pubns.) Lerner Publishing Group.

—The 12 Biggest Breakthroughs in Robot Technology. 2014. (ENG., Illus.). 32p. (J). 32.80 *(978-1-63235-016-9(5),* 12-Story Library) Bookstaves, LLC.

Wainewright, Max. Scratch Code Robots. 2019. (Scratch Code Challenge Ser.). (ENG., Illus.). 32p. (J). (gr. 5-5). pap. *(978-0-7787-6567-7(9),* 12970bee-8ede-4bb7-a5b2-b00bfb0d76f3); lib. bdg. *(978-0-7787-6532-5(6),* 4bba4b11-f0f8-4563-bf3d-793464879734) Crabtree Publishing Co.

Weakland, Mark. Do-4U the Robot Experiences Forces & Motion. Moran, Mike, illus. 2012. (In the Science Lab Ser.). (ENG.). 24p. (J). (gr. k-3). pap. 9.95 *(978-1-4048-7239-4(6),* 118178, Picture Window Bks.) Capstone.

Woog, Adam. SCRATCHbot. 2010. (Great Idea Ser.). 48p. (J). (gr. 4-6). lib. bdg. 26.60 *(978-1-59953-380-3(4))* Norwood Hse. Pr.

World Book, Inc. Staff, contrib. by. Are Robots Aware They're Robots? World Book Answers Your Questions about Technology. 2019. (Illus.). 96p. (J). *(978-0-7166-3829-2(0))* World Bk., Inc.

—Robot Basics. 2019. (Illus.). 48p. (J). *(978-0-7166-4129-2(1))* World Bk., Inc.

—Robot Soldiers & Other Military Tech. 2019. (Illus.). 48p. (J). *(978-0-7166-2431-8(1))* World Bk., Inc.

—Robots at Play. 2019. (Illus.). 48p. (J). *(978-0-7166-4134-6(8))* World Bk., Inc.

—Robots at Work. 2019. (Illus.). 48p. (J). *(978-0-7166-4133-9(X))* World Bk., Inc.

—Robots Helping Out. 2019. (Illus.). 48p. (J). *(978-0-7166-4136-0(4))* World Bk., Inc.

—Robots in Action. 2019. (Illus.). 48p. (J). *(978-0-7166-4135-3(6))* World Bk., Inc.

—Robots on the Move. 2019. (Illus.). 48p. (J). *(978-0-7166-4132-2(1))* World Bk., Inc.

—Robots Sensing & Doing. 2019. (Illus.). 48p. (J). *(978-0-7166-4130-8(5))* World Bk., Inc.

—Robots Thinking & Learning. 2019. (Illus.). 48p. (J). *(978-0-7166-4131-5(3))* World Bk., Inc.

—Weird Robots. 2019. (Illus.). 48p. (J). *(978-0-7166-4138-4(0))* World Bk., Inc.

Zoom in on Robots, 12 vols. 2017. (Zoom in on Robots Ser.). (ENG.). (J). (gr. 2-2). lib. bdg. 153.60 *(978-0-7660-9240-2(2),* 5ce2d777-2cd8-494f-bd89-55a9c5a89f39) Enslow Publishing, LLC.

Zuchora-Walske, Christine. Robots at Home. 2014. (Lightning Bolt Books (r) — Robots Everywhere! Ser.). (ENG., Illus.). 32p. (J). (gr. 1-3). pap. 9.99 *(978-1-4677-4509-3(X),* e1b5e707-78f8-4ea7-a9f3-b207e2560d16); lib. bdg. 29.32 *(978-1-4677-4054-8(3),* 3bc4159b-d1ab-42f9-b144-859ea757a9a1, Lerner Pubns.) Lerner Publishing Group.

—Weather Robots. 2014. (Lightning Bolt Books (r) — Robots Everywhere! Ser.). (ENG., Illus.). 32p. (J). (gr. 1-3). pap. 9.99 *(978-1-4677-4511-6(1),* 433d8598-01ff-4b84-aa23-72ae68fbc476) Lerner Publishing Group.

ROBOTS—FICTION

Ainslie, Claire. Detained. 2019. (AI High Ser.). (ENG.). 104p. (YA). (gr. 6-12). 26.65 *(978-1-5415-5692-8(5),* acbab631-3222-4307-b9a4-4c6567198253, Darby Creek) Lerner Publishing Group.

All Aboard! Softi's Adventures. 2003. (J). mass mkt. *(978-1-932233-36-0(9))* Aurora Libris Corp.

Alpert, Mark. The Siege. 2017. (Six Ser.: 2). 304p. (YA). (gr. 6-12). pap. 12.99 *(978-1-4926-4782-9(9))* Sourcebooks, Inc.

Anderson, J. L. Runaway Robot. Brown, Alan, illus. 2016. (Paisley Atoms Ser.). (ENG.). 64p. (gr. 2-5). 28.50 *(978-1-68191-716-0(5),* 9781681917160) Rourke Educational Media.

Angleberger, Tom. Didi Dodo, Future Spy: Robo-Dodo Rumble (Didi Dodo, Future Spy #2) Chapman, Jared, illus. 2019. (Flytrap Files Ser.). (ENG.). 112p. (J). (gr. 1-4). 12.99 *(978-1-4197-3688-9(4),* 1259401) Abrams, Inc.

Angleberger, Tom & Dellinger, Paul. Fuzzy. (ENG.). (J). (gr. 3-7). 2018. 288p. pap. 9.99 *(978-1-4197-2968-3(3),* 1015003) 2016. 272p. 14.95 *(978-1-4197-2122-9(4),* 1015001, Amulet Bks.) Abrams, Inc.

Appleton, Victor. The Robot Olympics, 2. 2006. (Tom Swift, Young Inventor Ser.: 2). (ENG.). 176p. (J). (gr. 3-7). pap. 7.99 *(978-1-4169-1361-0(0))* Simon & Schuster, Inc.

—The Robot Olympics. 2007. (Tom Swift, Young Inventor Ser.). (ENG.). 160p. (gr. 4-7). 27.07 *(978-1-59961-351-2(4))* Spotlight.

—The Space Hotel. 2007. (Tom Swift, Young Inventor Ser.). (ENG.). 160p. (gr. 4-7). 27.07 *(978-1-59961-353-6(0))* Spotlight.

Ariga, Hitoshi. Mega Man Gigamix, 2 vols., Vol. 3. 2011. (ENG., Illus.). 224p. (J). pap. 13.95 *(978-1-926778-31-0(6),* 0153699d-9923-4f66-bb8d-3b47059957a7) URON Entertainment Corp. CAN. Dist: Diamond Comic Distributors, Inc.

Arnold, Tedd. Fix This Mess! (I Like to Read Ser.). (ENG., Illus.). 24p. (J). (gr. -1-3). 2015. 7.99 *(978-0-8234-3301-8(3))* 2014. 15.99 *(978-0-8234-2942-4(3))* Holiday Hse., Inc.

Artifact Group, The & Shepherd, Jodie. Robot Rampage! 2009. (Backyardigans Ser.). (ENG.). 24p. (J). (gr. -1-1). pap. 3.99 *(978-1-4169-9013-0(5),* Simon Spotlight/Nickelodeon) Simon Spotlight/Nickelodeon.

Atticus, C. J. Stranded in Space: The Stellar Life of Jpeg the Robot Dog. Domschke, Angelika, illus. 2013. 119p. (J). pap. 6.95 *(978-0-9887780-2-3(5))* Atticus, C. J.

Austin, Mike. Junkyard. Austin, Mike, illus. 2014. (ENG., Illus.). 40p. (J). (gr. -1-3). 16.99 *(978-1-4424-5961-8(1),* Beach Lane Bks.) Beach Lane Bks.

Backer, Charles. Fireclaw. 2010. 288p. pap. 15.49 *(978-1-4520-1229-2(6))* AuthorHouse.

Bacon, Lee. The Last Human. 2019. (Last Human Ser.). (ENG., Illus.). 288p. (YA). (gr. 3-7). 16.99 *(978-1-4197-3691-9(4),* 1266301, Amulet Bks.) Abrams, Inc.

Bailey, Loren. Star-Crossed. 2019. (AI High Ser.). (ENG.). 112p. (YA). (gr. 6-12). 26.65 *(978-1-5415-5690-4(9),* ab0a6a2b-9bef-4d5f-af0d-d1d05a0fe21c); pap. 7.99 *(978-1-5415-7293-5(9),* d1461ebf-f2cb-4661-bde4-629992a9e777) Lerner Publishing Group. (Darby Creek).

Baker, Theo. Do Robots Get Space Sick? López, Àlex, illus. 2017. (Galaxy Games Ser.). (ENG.). 48p. (gr. 3-5). pap. 8.95 *(978-1-68342-434-5(4),* 9781683424345) Rourke Educational Media.

Balaban, Mariah. Scooby-Doo & the Rotten Robot, 1 vol. Sur, Duendes Del, illus. 2011. (Scooby-Doo! Ser.: No. 2). (ENG.). 24p. (J). (gr. k-4). lib. bdg. 31.36 *(978-1-59961-868-5(0),* 13246, Picture Bk.) Spotlight.

Barnes, Phil. My Teacher's a Robot! 2015. (ENG.). 63p. (J). (gr. 1-2). mass mkt. 8.95 *(978-1-78455-935-9(0),* 2e43b527-f3de-4545-b9e1-d6f75c93f153) Austin Macauley Pubs. Ltd. GBR. Dist: Baker & Taylor Publisher Services (BTPS).

Barnett, Mac. Oh No! Or How My Science Project Destroyed the World. Santat, Dan, illus. 2010. (ENG.). 40p. (J). (gr. -1-2). 18.99 *(978-1-4231-2312-5(3))* Little, Brown Bks. for Young Readers.

Barr, Lester. Robots Land at Manchester Airport. 2012. (Illus.). 80p. pap. 13.66 *(978-1-4772-2248-5(0))* AuthorHouse.

Bauman, Amy. Everyone Is Special! 2010. 12p. (J). (gr. -1). 9.95 *(978-1-60747-719-8(X),* Pickwick Pr.) Phoenix Bks., Inc.

Beal, Scott, ed. The Chameleon Toothbrush: New Stories from the Neutral Zone. 2008. (Illus.). 100p. (YA). per. 12.00 *(978-0-9779289-4-1(2))* 826michigan.

Bedford, David. Soccer Camp. Brumpton, Keith, illus. 3rd ed. 2004. 80p. *(978-1-877003-45-5(X))* Little Hare Bks. AUS. Dist: HarperCollins Pubs. Australia.

Beecroft, Simon. R2-D2 & Friends. 2008. (Star Wars DK Readers Level 2 Ser.). (Illus.). 32p. lib. bdg. 13.55 *(978-1-4364-5044-7(6))* Turtleback.

Bell, Cece. Rabbit & Robot. 2014. (Candlewick Sparks Ser.). lib. bdg. 13.55 *(978-0-606-35169-0(8))* Turtleback.

—Rabbit & Robot: The Sleepover. Bell, Cece, illus. 2014. (Candlewick Sparks Ser.). (ENG., illus.). 56p. (J). (gr. k-4). pap. 5.99 *(978-0-7636-6875-4(3))* Candlewick Pr.

—Rabbit & Robot & Ribbit. Bell, Cece, illus. 2017. (Candlewick Sparks Ser.). (ENG., Illus.). 48p. (J). (gr. k-4). pap. 5.99 *(978-0-7636-9782-2(6))* Candlewick Pr.

Bellairs, John. The Eyes of the Killer Robot (A Johnny Dixon Mystery: Book Five) 2011. 126p. pap. 14.95 *(978-1-61756-340-9(4))* Open Road Integrated Media, Inc.

Benjamin, A. H. Shamwood. 2006. 140p. pap. 24.95 *(978-1-4137-9193-8(X))* PublishAmerica, Inc.

Bennett, Chris. Robots & Dinosaurs. 2012. (ENG.). 127p. pap. 16.99 *(978-1-926780-26-9(4),* 96a5c842-9432-484c-a7ca-ac79da6f7edd) Key Publishing Hse., Inc., The CAN. Dist: Baker & Taylor Publisher Services (BTPS).

Benton, Jim. The Fran with Four Brains. Benton, Jim, illus. 2011. (Franny K. Stein, Mad Scientist Ser.). (ENG., Illus.). 112p. (J). (gr. 2-6). 31.36 *(978-1-59961-822-7(2),* 7832, Chapter Bks.) Spotlight.

—The Fran with Four Brains. 2007. (Franny K. Stein, Mad Scientist Ser.: 6). lib. bdg. 16.00 *(978-1-4177-9038-8(5))* Turtleback.

—The Invisible Fran. Benton, Jim, illus. 2004. (Franny K. Stein, Mad Scientist Ser.: 3). (ENG., Illus.). 112p. (J). (gr. 2-5). 17.99 *(978-0-689-86293-9(8),* Simon & Schuster Bks. For Young Readers) Simon & Schuster Bks. For Young Readers.

—The Invisible Fran. Benton, Jim, illus. 2011. (Franny K. Stein, Mad Scientist Ser.). (ENG., Illus.). 112p. (J). (gr. 2-6). 31.36 *(978-1-59961-819-7(2),* 7829, Chapter Bks.) Spotlight.

Benz, Derek & Lewis, J. S. Grey Griffins: the Brimstone Key. 2011. (Grey Griffins: the Clockwork Chronicles Ser.: 1). (ENG.). 400p. (J). (gr. 3-7). pap. 19.99 *(978-0-316-04521-6(7))* Little, Brown Bks. for Young Readers.

—Grey Griffins: the Relic Hunters. 2012. (Grey Griffins: the Clockwork Chronicles Ser.: 2). (ENG.). 384p. (J). (gr. 3-7). pap. 19.99 *(978-0-316-04520-9(9))* Little, Brown Bks. for Young Readers.

Black, Jake & Meredith Books Staff. Robo Monster. Stewart, Scott, illus. 2008. 22p. (J). pap. 3.99 *(978-0-696-23957-1(4))* Meredith Bks.

Blackwood, Gary. Curiosity. 2015. 336p. (J). (gr. 4-7). 8.99 *(978-0-14-242448-3(X),* Puffin Books) Penguin Young Readers Group.

Bolts, Russ. The Good, the Bad, & the Cowbots. Cooper, Jay, illus. 2019. (Bots Ser.: 2). (ENG.). 128p. (J). (gr. k-4). 16.99 *(978-1-5344-3692-3(8))*; pap. 6.99 *(978-1-5344-3691-6(X))* Little Simon. (Little Simon).

Bott, Adrian C. Antarctic Attack. Isaac, Andy, illus. 2017. 137p. (J). *(978-1-61067-704-2(8))* Kane Miller.

—Antarctic Attack: Axel & Beast. Isaac, Andy, illus. 2018. (ENG.). 144p. (J). pap. 5.99 *(978-1-61067-634-2(3))* Kane Miller.

—Castle of Cyborgs. Isaac, Andy, illus. 2019. (ENG.). 144p. (J). pap. 5.99 *(978-1-61067-851-3(6))* Kane Miller.

—The Grabbem Getaway. Isaac, Andy, illus. 2017. 134p. (J). *(978-1-61067-703-5(X))* Kane Miller.

—The Grabbem Getaway: Axel & Beast. Isaac, Andy, illus. 2018. (ENG.). 144p. (J). pap. 5.99 *(978-1-61067-633-5(5))* Kane Miller.

—The Omega Operation: Axel & Beast. Isaac, Andy, illus. 2019. (ENG.). 144p. (J). pap. *(978-1-61067-850-6(8))* Kane Miller.

—Robotic Rumble. Isaac, Andy, illus. 2017. 121p. (J). *(978-1-61067-706-6(4))* Kane Miller.

—Robotic Rumble: Axel & Beast. Isaac, Andy, illus. 2018. (ENG.). 144p. (J). pap. 5.99 *(978-1-61067-636-6(X))* Kane Miller.

—Tropical Tangle. Isaac, Andy, illus. 2017. 119p. (J). *(978-1-61067-705-9(6))* Kane Miller.

—Tropical Tangle: Axel & Beast. Isaac, Andy, illus. 2018. (ENG.). 144p. (J). pap. 5.99 *(978-1-61067-635-9(1))* Kane Miller.

Bowen, Carl. Jak & the Magic Nano-Beans: A Graphic Novel. Lozano, Omar, illus. 2016. (Far Out Fairy Tales Ser.). (ENG.). 40p. (J). (gr. 3-6). lib. bdg. 26.65 *(978-1-4965-2510-9(8),* 130480, Stone Arch Bks.) Capstone.

Breach, Jen. Clem Hetherington & the Ironwood Race. Holgate, Douglas, illus. 2018. (Clem Hetherington Ser.: 1). (ENG.). 208p. (J). (gr. 3-7). pap. 14.99 *(978-0-545-81446-1(4),* Graphix) Scholastic, Inc.

Broad, Michael. Zombie Cows!, 2 vols., No. 2. Broad, Michael, illus. 2011. (Agent Amelia Ser.: 2). (ENG., Illus.). 144p. (J). (gr. 2-5). lib. bdg. 22.65 *(978-0-7613-8057-3(4),* 6ab86559-2b7d-4b2e-bf35-1cbee740a7c1, Darby Creek) Lerner Publishing Group.

—#2 Zombie Cows! 2011. (Agent Amelia Ser.). pap. 33.92 *(978-0-7613-8342-0(5),* Darby Creek) Lerner Publishing Group.

Brockington, Drew. CatStronauts: Robot Rescue. 2018. (CatStronauts Ser.: 4). (J). lib. bdg. 19.65 *(978-0-606-40982-7(3))* Turtleback.

—CatStronauts: Robot Rescue. 2018. (CatStronauts Ser.: 4). (ENG., Illus.). 184p. (J). (gr. 1-5). pap. 9.99 *(978-0-316-30756-7(4))* Little, Brown Bks. for Young Readers.

Brouwer, Sigmund. Death Trap. 2009. (Robot Wars Ser.: 1). (ENG.). 288p. (J). pap. 7.99 *(978-1-4143-2309-1(3)*, 4601299, Tyndale Kids) Tyndale Hse. Pubs.

Brown, Heather. The Robot Book. 2010. (ENG., Illus.). 12p. (J). bds. 16.99 *(978-0-7407-9725-5(5))* Andrews McMeel Publishing.

Brown, Jeffrey. My Teacher Is a Robot. 2019. (Illus.). 40p. (J). (gr. -1-2). 17.99 *(978-0-553-53451-1(3))*; (ENG., lib. bdg. 20.99 *(978-0-553-53452-8(1))* Random Hse. Children's Bks. (Crown Books For Young Readers).

Brown, Jennifer. How Lunchbox Jones Saved Me from Robots, Traitors, & Missy the Cruel. (ENG.). 2017. 256p. (J). pap. 8.99 *(978-1-68119-441-7(4)*, 900172653) 2015. 240p. (YA). (gr. 3-6). 16.99 *(978-1-61963-454-1(6)*, 900137050) Bloomsbury Publishing USA. (Bloomsbury USA Childrens).

Brown, Peter. The Wild Robot. (Wild Robot Ser.: 1). (ENG., Illus.). (J). (gr. 3-7). 2020. 320p. pap. 8.99 *(978-0-316-38200-7(0))* 2016. 288p. 17.99 *(978-0-316-38199-4(3))* Little, Brown Bks. for Young Readers.

—The Wild Robot. 2019. (J). lib. bdg. 18.40 *(978-0-606-40825-7(8))* Turtleback.

—The Wild Robot, 1. 2020. (Wild Robot Ser.). (ENG.). 304p. (gr. 3-6). 24.94 *(978-1-5364-3507-8(4))* Little, Brown Bks. for Young Readers.

—The Wild Robot Escapes. (Wild Robot Ser.: 2). (ENG.). 288p. (J). (gr. 3-7). 2020. pap. 8.99 *(978-0-316-47926-4(8))* 2018. (Illus.). 17.99 *(978-0-316-38204-5(3))* Little, Brown Bks. for Young Readers.

—The Wild Robot Escapes, 2. 2020. (Wild Robot Ser.). (ENG.). 288p. (gr. 3-6). 24.94 *(978-1-5364-6223-4(3))* Little, Brown Bks. for Young Readers.

Brown, Peter, illus. The Wild Robot Escapes. 2018. 279p. (J). *(978-0-316-45375-2(7))* Little Brown & Co.

Bunting, Eve. My Robot. Fehlau, Dagmar, illus. 2006. (ENG.). 24p. (J). (gr. -1-3). pap. 4.99 *(978-0-15-205617-9(3)*, 1196894, Clarion Bks.) HarperCollins Pubs.

—My Robot. Fehlau, Dagmar, illus. 2006. (Green Light Readers Level 2 Ser.). (gr. k-2). lib. bdg. 13.95 *(978-0-7569-7211-0(6))* Perfection Learning Corp.

Burns, Dal. The Adventures of Phoo. 2006. 148p. pap. 24.95 *(978-1-4241-1773-4(9))* PublishAmerica, Inc.

Byrne, Bob. Robots Don't Cry. 2006. (Flyers Ser.: 15). (ENG., Illus.). 64p. (J). pap. 11.00 *(978-1-84717-005-7(6))* O'Brien Pr., Ltd., The IRL. Dist: Dufour Editions, Inc.

Capetta, Amy Rose. Entangled. 2013. (ENG.). 336p. (YA). (gr. 9). 17.99 *(978-0-544-08744-6(5)*, 1538242, Clarion Bks.) HarperCollins Pubs.

Carlson, Bryce. Wall- E: Out There. Luthi, Morgan, illus. 2010. (ENG.). 112p. (J). (gr. 3-6). pap. 9.99 *(978-1-60886-568-0(1))* BOOM! Studios.

Carriger, Gail. Curtsies & Conspiracies. 2014. (Finishing School Ser.: 2). (ENG.). 336p. (YA). (gr. 7-17). pap. 10.99 *(978-0-316-19020-6(9))* Little, Brown Bks. for Young Readers.

—Etiquette & Espionage. 2013. (Finishing School Ser.: 1). (ENG.). 336p. (YA). (gr. 7-17). pap. 11.99 *(978-0-316-19010-7(1))* Little, Brown Bks. for Young Readers.

Catalanotto, Peter. Monkey & Robot. Catalanotto, Peter, illus. 2014. (ENG., Illus.). 64p. (J). (gr. 1-4). pap. 8.99 *(978-1-4424-2979-6(8)*, Atheneum Bks. for Young Readers) Simon & Schuster Children's Publishing.

—More of Monkey & Robot. Catalanotto, Peter, illus. 2014. (ENG., Illus.). 64p. (J). (gr. 1-4). 15.99 *(978-1-4424-5251-0(X)*, Atheneum/Richard Jackson Bks.) Simon & Schuster Children's Publishing.

Cawthon, Scott & Breed-Wrisley, Kira. Five Nights at Freddy's Collection: an AFK Series, 1 vol. 2018. (Five Nights at Freddy's Ser.). (ENG.). 2112p. (YA). (gr. 7-7). pap., pap., pap. 29.97 *(978-1-338-32302-3(4))* Scholastic, Inc.

—The Fourth Closet. 2018. 304p. *(978-1-74299-848-0(8))* Scholastic, Inc.

—The Fourth Closet: Five Nights at Freddy's (Original Trilogy Book 3) 3rd ed. 2018. (Five Nights at Freddy's Ser.: 3). (ENG.). 352p. (YA). (gr. 7-7). pap. 9.99 *(978-1-338-13932-7(0))* Scholastic, Inc.

—The Silver Eyes. 2016. 389p. (J). *(978-1-338-14418-5(9))*; *(978-1-5182-3111-7(X))* Scholastic, Inc.

—The Silver Eyes. 2016. (Five Nights at Freddy's Ser.: bk.1). (YA). lib. bdg. 20.85 *(978-0-606-39982-1(8))* Turtleback.

—The Silver Eyes: Five Nights at Freddy's (Original Trilogy Book 1), Vol. 1. 2016. (Five Nights at Freddy's Ser.: 1). (ENG.). 400p. (YA). (gr. 7-7). pap. 9.99 *(978-1-338-13437-7(X))* Scholastic, Inc.

—The Twisted Ones. 2017. (Five Nights at Freddy's Ser.: 2). lib. bdg. 20.85 *(978-0-606-40155-5(5))* Turtleback.

—The Twisted Ones: Five Nights at Freddy's (Original Trilogy Book 2), Vol. 2. Aguirre, Claudia, illus. 2017. (Five Nights at Freddy's Ser.: 2). (ENG.). 304p. (J). (gr. 7-7). pap. 9.99 *(978-1-338-13930-3(4))* Scholastic, Inc.

Chiaramonti, Gregory. Probie: the Space Probe, Mission One: the Ocean of Europa. 2007. 32p. (J). 16.72 *(978-0-615-13848-0(9))* Chiaramonti, Gregory.

Clark, Kent & Snider, Brandon T. Peter Powers & the Rowdy Robot Raiders! Bardin, Dave, illus. 2017. (Peter Powers Ser.: 2). (ENG.). 128p. (J). (gr. 1-5). pap. 5.99 *(978-0-316-35938-2(6))* Little, Brown Bks. for Young Readers.

Clements, Richmond. Turning Tiger Special Edition. Finbow, Alexander, ed. 2012. (Illus.). 56p. pap. 7.99 *(978-1-926914-87-9(2))* Arcana Studio, Inc.

Collicutt, Paul. Rust Attack! Collicutt, Paul, illus. 2009. (Robot City Ser.: 2). (ENG., Illus.). 48p. (J). (gr. 3-7). pap. 8.99 *(978-0-7636-4594-6(X)*, Templar) Candlewick Pr.

Collins, A. L. Tharsis City: The Wonder of Mars. Tikulin, Tomislav, illus. 2017. (Redworld Ser.). (ENG.). 128p. (J). (gr. 3-8). lib. bdg. 25.99 *(978-1-4965-4821-4(3)*, 135343, Stone Arch Bks.) Capstone.

Cornwell, Betsy. Mechanica. 2016. lib. bdg. 19.65 *(978-0-606-37999-1(1))* Turtleback.

Craddock, Erik. Robot Frenzy. 2013. (Stone Rabbit Ser.: 8). lib. bdg. 17.20 *(978-0-606-27004-5(3))* Turtleback.

Craig, Joe. Jimmy Coates: Assassin? 2005. 224p. (J). (gr. 5-18). 15.99 *(978-0-06-077263-5(8))* HarperCollins Pubs.

—Jimmy Coates: Assassin? 2006. 218p. (J). (gr. 5-9). per. 5.99 *(978-0-06-077265-9(4)*, Harper Trophy) HarperCollins Pubs.

Curtis, Simon. Boy Robot. 2016. (ENG., Illus.). 432p. (YA). (gr. 9). 17.99 *(978-1-4814-5929-7(5)*, Simon Pulse) Simon Pulse.

Cushman, Doug. Space Cat. Cushman, Doug, illus. 2006. (I Can Read Level 1 Ser.). (ENG., Illus.). 32p. (J). (gr. -1-3). pap. 4.99 *(978-0-06-008967-2(9)*, HarperCollins) HarperCollins Pubs.

—Space Cat. Cushman, Doug, illus. 2006. (I Can Read Bks.). (Illus.). 32p. (gr. -1-3). 14.00 *(978-0-7569-6977-6(8))* Perfection Learning Corp.

Cusick, John M. Girl Parts. (ENG., Illus.). 240p. (YA). (gr. 9). 2012. pap. 7.99 *(978-0-7636-5644-7(5))* 2010. 16.99 *(978-0-7636-4930-2(9))* Candlewick Pr.

Dahl, Michael. Dino Death-Trap. Vecchio, Luciano, illus. 2016. (Batman Tales of the Batcave Ser.). (ENG.). 40p. (J). (gr. 4-8). lib. bdg. 24.65 *(978-1-4965-4015-7(8)*, 133214, Stone Arch Bks.) Capstone.

—The Robot That Barked. Levins, Tim & Vecchio, Luciano, illus. 2017. (Superman Tales of the Fortress of Solitude Ser.). (ENG.). 40p. (J). (gr. 4-8). lib. bdg. 24.65 *(978-1-4965-4397-4(1)*, 134637, Stone Arch Bks.) Capstone.

Dauber, J. A. Mayhem & Madness: Chronicles of a Teenaged Supervillain. 2019. 304p. (J). (gr. 7). 18.99 *(978-0-8234-4255-3(1))* Holiday Hse., Inc.

Dean, James & Dean, Kimberly. Pete the Cat: Robo-Pete. Dean, James, illus. 2015. (Pete the Cat Ser.). (ENG., Illus.). 24p. (J). (gr. -1-3). pap. 5.99 *(978-0-06-230427-8(5)*, HarperFestival) HarperCollins Pubs.

Derdowski, Chad. All Robots Must Die: Nacho-Geddon. 2013. 187p. (J). pap. 7.99 *(978-1-933925-50-9(7)*, Agent of Danger) Komikwerks, LLC.

Dipucchio, Kelly. Clink. Myers, Matthew, illus. 2011. (ENG.). 32p. (J). (gr. -1-2). 17.99 *(978-0-06-192928-1(X)*, Balzer & Bray) HarperCollins Pubs.

Disney Press Editors. Star Wars: Escape from Darth Vader. 2014. (Star Wars: World of Reading Ser.). (J). lib. bdg. 13.55 *(978-0-606-35924-5(9))* Turtleback.

Dixon, Franklin W. Robot Rumble. 11. Burroughs, Scott, illus. 2013. (Hardy Boys: the Secret Files Ser.: 11). (ENG.). 96p. (J). (gr. 1-4). pap. 5.99 *(978-1-4424-5367-8(2)*, Aladdin) Simon & Schuster Children's Publishing.

Doeden, Matt. Beauty & the Beast: An Interactive Fairy Tale Adventure. Miramon, Sabrina, illus. 2018. (You Choose: Fractured Fairy Tales Ser.). (ENG.). 112p. (J). (gr. 3-7). lib. bdg. 32.65 *(978-1-5435-3007-0(9)*, 138604, Capstone Pr.) Capstone.

Dorling Kindersley Publishing Staff. The Adventures of C-3PO. 2014. (Star Wars DK Readers Level 2 Ser.). lib. bdg. 13.55 *(978-0-606-35324-3(0))* Turtleback.

—The Brain Wars. 2013. (DK Reader Level 3 Ser.). lib. bdg. 13.55 *(978-0-606-32114-3(4))* Turtleback.

Duffett-Smith, James. A Curious Robot on Mars! Straker, Bethany, illus. 2013. (ENG.). 32p. (J). (gr. -1-k). 14.95 *(978-1-62087-994-8(8)*, 620994, Sky Pony Pr.) Skyhorse Publishing Co., Inc.

Dunkle, Clare B. The Walls Have Eyes. 2009. (ENG.). 240p. (YA). (gr. 7). 16.99 *(978-1-4169-5379-1(5)*, Atheneum Bks. for Young Readers) Simon & Schuster Children's Publishing.

Dyckman, Ame. Boy & Bot. Yaccarino, Dan, illus. (J). (-k). 2016. 24p. bds. 7.99 *(978-1-101-93688-7(6))* 2012. 32p. 17.99 *(978-0-375-86756-9(2))* Random Hse. Children's Bks. (Knopf Bks. for Young Readers).

—Girl + Bot. Yaccarino, Dan, illus. 2017. (J). *(978-1-5247-0072-0(X))* Knopf, Alfred A. Inc.

Evans, D. L. & Sinclair, Valerie. How Rolly Robot Saved the Starbabies, 1 vol. 2012. (ENG., Illus.). 32p. (J). *(978-1-55455-201-6(X))* Fitzhenry & Whiteside, Ltd.

Fee, J. M. The Amazing Adventures of Phineas Screwdriver. 2012. 64p. pap. 20.95 *(978-1-4497-7236-9(6)*, WestBow Pr.) Author Solutions, LLC.

Fentiman, David. The Adventures of BB-8. 2016. (Star Wars DK Readers Level 2 Ser.). lib. bdg. 13.55 *(978-0-606-38709-5(9))* Turtleback.

Fickling, Phillip. Fillmore & Geary Take Off! Shulman, Mark, illus. 2003. 40p. (J). lib. bdg. *(978-1-58717-258-8(5)*, SeaStar Bks.) Chronicle Bks. LLC.

Fields, Jan. Lost in Space: An Up2U Action Adventure. Vidal, Oriol, illus. 2017. (Up2U Adventures Set 3 Ser.). (ENG.). 80p. (J). (gr. 2-5). lib. bdg. 35.64 *(978-1-5321-3030-4(9)*, 25508, Calico Chapter Bks.) ABDO Publishing Co.

Fisch, Sholly & Kane, Bob. Manhandled by Manhunters! 2015. (All-New Batman: the Brave & the Bold Ser.). (ENG., Illus.). 32p. (J). (gr. 2-5). lib. bdg. 22.60 *(978-1-4342-9662-7(8)*, 126963, Stone Arch Bks.) Capstone.

Flynn, Ian. Mega Man 8: Redemption. Spaziante, Patrick 'Spaz', illus. 2015. (Mega Man Ser.: 8). (ENG.). 104p. (J). (gr. 4-7). pap. 11.99 *(978-1-61988-944-6(7))* Archie Comic Pubns., Inc.

Foley, James. Brobot. 2018. (S. Tinker Inc Ser.). 112p. (J). (gr. 3-6). 6.99 *(978-1-925163-91-9(1))* Fremantle Pr. AUS. Dist: Independent Pubs. Group.

Fox, Helen. Eager. 2006. (Eager Ser.). (ENG.). 288p. (J). (gr. 3-7). 8.99 *(978-0-553-48795-4(7)*, Yearling) Random Hse. Children's Bks.

Fox, Jennifer. Meet Optimus Prime. 2015. (Transformers Passport to Reading Ser.). (J). lib. bdg. 13.55 *(978-0-606-35938-2(9))* Turtleback.

Foxe, Steve. Decepticon Island! 2017. (Transformers Passport to Reading Ser.). (J). lib. bdg. 14.75 *(978-0-606-39908-1(9))* Turtleback.

Frampton, Otis. Red Riding Hood, Superhero: A Graphic Novel. Frampton, Otis, illus. 2015. (Far Out Fairy Tales Ser.). (ENG., Illus.). 40p. (J). (gr. 3-6). lib. bdg. 25.32 *(978-1-4342-9650-4(4)*, 126941, Stone Arch Bks.) Capstone.

Fruchter, Jason, illus. Space Race. 2017. (J). *(978-1-5182-2283-2(8)*, Golden Bks.) Random Hse. Children's Bks.

Gabolinscy, Jack. Do Not Disturb, 1 vol. Cashmore-Hingley, Michael, illus. 2013. (ENG.). 27p. (gr. 3-4). pap. *(978-1-77654-019-8(0)*, Red Rocket Readers) Flying Start Bks.

Golden Books. Follow the Ninja! (Teenage Mutant Ninja Turtles) Lambe, Steve, illus. 2015. (Little Golden Book Ser.). (ENG.). 24p. (J). (-k). 5.99 *(978-0-553-51204-5(8)*, Golden Bks.) Random Hse. Children's Bks.

—I Am a Droid (Star Wars) Kennett, Chris, illus. 2016. (Little Golden Book Ser.). (ENG.). 24p. (J). (-k). 5.99 *(978-0-7364-3489-8(5)*, Golden Bks.) Random Hse. Children's Bks.

—I Am a Sith (Star Wars) Kennett, Chris, illus. 2016. (Little Golden Book Ser.). (ENG.). 24p. (J). (-k). 5.99 *(978-0-7364-3607-6(3)*, Golden Bks.) Random Hse. Children's Bks.

Grant, Gavin J. & Link, Kelly, eds. Steampunk! an Anthology of Fantastically Rich & Strange Stories. 2013. (ENG.). 432p. (YA). (gr. 9). pap. 19.99 *(978-0-7636-5797-0(2))* Candlewick Pr.

Gray, Claudia. Defy the Fates. 2019. (Defy the Stars Ser.: 3). (ENG.). 480p. (YA). (gr. 9-17). 18.99 *(978-0-316-44075-2(2))* Little, Brown Bks. for Young Readers.

—Defy the Stars. 2018. (Defy the Stars Ser.: 1). (ENG.). 528p. (YA). (gr. 9-17). pap. 23.99 *(978-0-316-39404-8(1))* Little, Brown Bks. for Young Readers.

—Defy the Worlds. 2019. (Defy the Stars Ser.: 2). (ENG.). 496p. (YA). (gr. 9-17). pap. 12.99 *(978-0-316-39407-9(6))* Little, Brown Bks. for Young Readers.

Grecian, Alexander. Rocketbots: Trouble in Time: Trouble in Time. 2010. 48p. (YA). 12.99 *(978-1-60706-183-0(X))* Image Comics.

Greenburg, J. C. Andrew Lost #15: in the Jungle. Gerardi, Jan, illus. 2007. (Andrew Lost Ser.: 15). (ENG.). 96p. (J). (gr. 1-4). 4.99 *(978-0-375-83564-3(4)*, Random Hse. Bks. for Young Readers) Random Hse. Children's Bks.

—Andrew Lost #17: in the Desert. Gerardi, Jan, illus. 2008. (Andrew Lost Ser.: 17). (ENG.). 96p. (J). (gr. 1-4). per. 4.99 *(978-0-375-84667-0(0)*, Random Hse. Bks. for Young Readers) Random Hse. Children's Bks.

Greenwood, Arin. Your Robot Dog Will Die. 2019. 192p. (YA). (gr. 9). pap. 10.99 *(978-1-61695-852-7(9)*, Soho Teen) Soho Pr., Inc.

Gritton, Steve. The Trouble with Sisters & Robots. 2012. (Illus.). 32p. (J). 34.28 *(978-1-61913-150-7(1))* Weigl Pubs., Inc.

Haddix, Margaret Peterson. In over Their Heads. 2017. (Under Their Skin Ser.: 2). (ENG., Illus.). 320p. (J). (gr. 3-7). 18.99 *(978-1-4814-1761-7(4)*, Simon & Schuster Bks. For Young Readers) Simon & Schuster Bks. For Young Readers.

—Under Their Skin. 2016. (Under Their Skin Ser.: 1). (ENG., Illus.). 320p. (J). (gr. 3-7). 18.99 *(978-1-4814-1758-7(4)*, Simon & Schuster Bks. For Young Readers) Simon & Schuster Bks. For Young Readers.

Hale, Bruce. Murder, My Tweet. 2005. (Chet Gecko Mystery Ser.). (Illus.). 117p. (gr. 3-7). 16.00 *(978-0-7569-5248-8(4))* Perfection Learning Corp.

Hale, Nathan. One Trick Pony. 2017. (ENG., Illus.). 128p. (J). (gr. 3-7). 14.95 *(978-1-4197-2128-1(3)*, 1104001, Amulet Bks.) Abrams, Inc.

Hall, Susan, illus. Robot Repairman to the Rescue! 2009. (Backyardigans Ser.). (ENG.). 24p. (J). (gr. -1-2). pap. 3.99 *(978-1-4169-9012-3(7)*, Simon Spotlight/Nickelodeon) Simon Spotlight/Nickelodeon.

Hamilton, Kersten. The Ire of Iron Claw: Gadgets & Gears, Book 2. Hamilton, James, illus. 2016. (Gadgets & Gears Ser.: 2). (ENG.). 192p. (J). (gr. 3-7). pap. 6.99 *(978-0-544-66854-6(5)*, 1625480, Clarion Bks.) HarperCollins Pubs.

Hatke, Ben. Legends of Zita the Spacegirl. 2012. (Zita the Spacegirl Ser.: 2). (ENG., Illus.). 224p. (J). (gr. 3-7). 22.99 *(978-1-59643-806-4(1)*, 900086236); pap. 14.99 *(978-1-59643-447-9(3)*, 900054804) Roaring Brook Pr. (First Second Bks.).

—Legends of Zita the Spacegirl. 2012. (Zita the Spacegirl Ser.: 2). (J). lib. bdg. 24.50 *(978-0-606-26708-3(5))* Turtleback.

Hawking, Lucy. George & the Ship of Time. Parsons, Garry, illus. 2019. (George's Secret Key Ser.). (ENG.). 416p. (J). (gr. 3-7). 18.99 *(978-1-5344-3730-2(4)*, Simon & Schuster Bks. For Young Readers) Simon & Schuster Bks. For Young Readers.

Holmes, Kimberly. Digibots Classroom Adventures. Lawson, Devin, illus. 2004. (J). *(978-0-9755725-0-4(4)*, 1238415) Digibots Corp.

Holsey, Ron. The Great Monkey Show! Cassity, Don, illus. 2018. 24p. (J). *(978-1-5490-4051-1(0))* Random Hse., Inc.

Hopper, Ada. Robots Rule the School. Ricks, Sam, illus. 2016. (DATA Set Ser.: 4). (ENG.). 128p. (J). (gr. k-4). pap. 6.99 *(978-1-4814-6312-6(8)*, Little Simon) Little Simon.

—Robots Rule the School. Ricks, Sam, illus. 2018. 125p. (J). (gr. 1-4). 15.96 *(978-1-64310-199-6(4))* Penworthy Co., LLC, The.

Huddleston, Courtney & Zirkel, Scott. A Bit Haywire. Huddleston, Courtney, illus. 2006. (Illus.). 112p. per. 11.95 *(978-0-9777883-5-4(0))* Viper Comics.

Hughes, Ted. The Iron Man. 2013. (ENG., Illus.). 144p. (J). 8.95 *(978-0-571-30224-6(6)*, Faber & Faber Children's Bks.) Faber & Faber, Inc.

—The Iron Man. Davidson, Andrew, illus. 2nd ed. 2005. (ENG.). 80p. (J). pap. 9.95 *(978-0-571-22612-2(4)*, Faber & Faber Children's Bks.) Faber & Faber, Inc.

Irvine, Alexander C. Have Robot, Will Travel. 2013. (ENG.). 222p. pap. 19.95 *(978-1-59687-959-1(9))* ibooks, Inc.

Ishida, S. E. M. Nick Newton: The Highest Bidder. Thompson, Dana, illus. 2018. 128p. (J). *(978-1-62856-511-9(X))* BJU Pr.

Joyce, William. Sleepy Time Olie. Joyce, William, illus. 2018. (World of William Joyce Ser.). (ENG., Illus.). 40p. (J). (gr. -1-2). 17.99 *(978-1-4814-8963-8(1))* Simon & Schuster Children's Publishing.

—Snowie Rolie. Joyce, William, illus. 2017. (World of William Joyce Ser.). (ENG., Illus.). 40p. (J). (gr. -1-2). 17.99 *(978-1-4814-8967-6(4)*, Atheneum Bks. for Young Readers) Simon & Schuster Children's Publishing.

Jung, Mike. Geeks, Girls, & Secret Identities. Maihack, Mike, illus. 2012. (J). pap. *(978-0-545-33549-2(3)*, Levine, Arthur A. Bks.) Scholastic, Inc.

Kazenbroot, Nelly. Over the Rainbow with Googol & Googolplex, 1 vol. 2006. (Orca Echoes Ser.). (ENG., Illus.). 64p. (J). (gr. 1-3). per. 4.99 *(978-1-55143-469-8(5))* Orca Bk. Pubs. USA.

—Under the Sea with Googol & Googolplex. 2005. 63p. (J). lib. bdg. 20.00 *(978-1-4242-1263-7(4))* Fitzgerald Bks.

—Under the Sea with Googol & Googolplex, 1 vol. 2005. (Orca Echoes Ser.). (ENG., Illus.). 64p. (J). (gr. 1-3). per. 6.95 *(978-1-55143-366-0(4))* Orca Bk. Pubs. USA.

Keats, Israel. Alien Invasion. 2017. (Level Up Ser.). (ENG.). 120p. (YA). (gr. 6-12). pap. 7.99 *(978-1-5124-5356-0(0)*, b9358e54-28d0-4870-96f3-95ea47d4215e); lib. bdg. 26.65 *(978-1-5124-3984-7(3)*, 4bd61854-84ad-4b3c-a63b-159a2525f4ee) Lerner Publishing Group. (Darby Creek).

Kessler, MacKenzie. Murphy the Lonely Robot/Cecil the Lonely Pterodactyl. 2009. (ENG.). 52p. pap. 14.00 *(978-0-557-22226-1(5))* Lulu Pr., Inc.

Kibuishi, Kazu. The Stonekeeper, 1. 2018. (Amulet Ser.). (ENG.). 185p. (J). (gr. 4-5). 23.96 *(978-1-64310-255-9(9))* Penworthy Co., LLC, The.

—The Stonekeeper. 2008. (Amulet Ser.: 1). (Illus.). 185p. lib. bdg. 24.50 *(978-1-4177-9712-7(6))* Turtleback.

—The Stonekeeper: a Graphic Novel (Amulet #1) Kibuishi, Kazu, illus. (Amulet Ser.: 1). (ENG., Illus.). 192p. (J). (gr. 3-7). 2015. 24.99 *(978-0-439-84680-6(3))* Vol. 1. 2008. pap. 12.99 *(978-0-439-84681-3(1))* Scholastic, Inc. (Graphix).

Kingsley Troupe, Thomas. Battling Robots. 2017. (Mighty Bots Ser.). (ENG.). 32p. (gr. 2-7). 9.95 *(978-1-68072-460-8(6)*, Bolt) Black Rabbit Bks.

Korman, Gordon. Ungifted. (ENG.). 288p. (J). (gr. 5). 2014. pap. 9.99 *(978-0-06-174267-5(8))* 2012. 16.99 *(978-0-06-174266-8(X))* 2012. lib. bdg. 17.89 *(978-0-06-174268-2(6))* HarperCollins Pubs. (Balzer & Bray).

Kozlowsky, M. P. Frost. 2016. (ENG.). 352p. (J). (gr. 8). 17.99 *(978-0-545-83191-8(1)*, Scholastic Pr.) Scholastic, Inc.

Kristoff, Jay. Life L1k3. 2018. (Illus.). 402p. (J). *(978-0-525-64459-0(8))* Knopf, Alfred A. Inc.

Krosoczka, Jarrett J. Lunch Lady & the Cyborg Substitute: Lunch Lady #1. 2009. (Lunch Lady Ser.: 1). (ENG.). 96p. (J). (gr. 2-5). pap. 6.99 *(978-0-375-84683-0(2)*, Knopf Bks. for Young Readers) Random Hse. Children's Bks.

Krulik, Nancy & Burwasser, Amanda. Give a 'Bot a Bone. Moran, Mike, illus. 2018. (Project Droid Ser.: 5). (ENG.). 112p. (J). (gr. 1-3). 13.99 *(978-1-5107-2663-5(2))*; pap. 4.99 *(978-1-5107-2655-0(1))* Skyhorse Publishing Co., Inc. (Sky Pony Pr.).

—My Robot Ate My Homework: Project Droid #3. Moran, Mike, illus. 2017. (Project Droid Ser.). (ENG.). 104p. (J). (gr. 1-4). 13.99 *(978-1-5107-1020-7(5)*, Sky Pony Pr.) Skyhorse Publishing Co., Inc.

—Phone-Y Friends. Moran, Mike, illus. 2017. (Project Droid Ser.). (ENG.). 104p. (J). (gr. 1-3). pap. 9.99 *(978-1-5107-2654-3(3)*, Sky Pony Pr.) Skyhorse Publishing Co., Inc.

—Science No Fair! Project Droid #1. Moran, Mike, illus. 2016. (Project Droid Ser.). (ENG.). 112p. (J). (gr. 1-4). 13.99 *(978-1-5107-1018-4(3)*, Sky Pony Pr.) Skyhorse Publishing Co., Inc.

—Soccer Shocker! Project Droid #2. Moran, Mike, illus. 2016. (Project Droid Ser.). (ENG.). 104p. (J). (gr. 1-4). pap. 5.99 *(978-1-5107-1029-0(9)*, Sky Pony Pr.) Skyhorse Publishing Co., Inc.

—Someone's Got a Screw Loose. Moran, Mike, illus. 2018. (Project Droid Ser.: 6). (ENG.). 112p. (J). (gr. 1-3). 13.99 *(978-1-5107-2664-2(0)*, Sky Pony Pr.) Skyhorse Publishing Co., Inc.

Kuhlman, Evan. Brother from a Box. Bruno, Iacopo, illus. 2013. (ENG.). 288p. (J). (gr. 4-7). pap. 6.99 *(978-1-4424-2659-7(4)*, Atheneum Bks. for Young Readers) Simon & Schuster Children's Publishing.

—Brother from a Box. Bruno, Iacopo, illus. 2012. (ENG.). 288p. (J). (gr. 4-7). 16.99 *(978-1-4424-2658-0(6))* Simon & Schuster, Inc.

Kurtz, Rob. Meet the Robots. 2011. 20p. pap. 5.99 *(978-1-60010-512-8(2))* Idea & Design Works, LLC.

—Robots to the Rescue! 2011. 32p. pap. 3.99 *(978-1-60010-513-5(0))* Idea & Design Works, LLC.

Ladybird. Sam & the Robots Activity Book - Ladybird Readers Level 4. 2016. (Ladybird Readers Ser.). (ENG.). 16p. (J). pap., act. bk. ed. 5.99 *(978-0-241-25376-2(4))* Penguin Bks., Ltd. GBR. Dist: Independent Pubs. Group.

Lang, Heidi & Bartkowski, Kati. A Hint of Hydra. (Mystic Cooking Chronicles Ser.). (ENG.). (J). (gr. 3-7). 2019. 336p. pap. 8.99 *(978-1-4814-7796-3(X))* 2018. (Illus.). 320p. 17.99 *(978-1-4814-7795-6(1))* Simon & Schuster Children's Publishing. (Aladdin).

—A Pinch of Phoenix. 2019. (Mystic Cooking Chronicles Ser.). (ENG., Illus.). 384p. (J). (gr. 3-7). 17.99 *(978-1-5344-3709-8(6)*, Aladdin) Simon & Schuster Children's Publishing.

Lawrence, Kay. Robot to the Rescue. De Georgi, Sergio, illus. 2018. (Makers Make It Work Ser.). 32p. (J). (gr. k-3). pap. 5.99 *(978-1-57565-987-9(5)*, 38073f1e-e3ed-498e-8318-e22eee12bc0e, Kane Press) Astra Publishing Hse.

Lefers, Joshie. The Rise of the Bread Baby, Volume 2. 2018. (Hectic Electric Ser.: 2). (ENG., Illus.). 128p. (J). (gr. 2-4). pap. 11.99 *(978-1-76012-801-2(5))* Hardie Grant Children?s Publishing AUS. Dist: Independent Pubs. Group.

Lemke, Donald. Coldfinger: Zinc Alloy. Holgate, Douglas, illus. 2010. (Graphic Sparks Ser.). (ENG.). 40p. (J). (gr. 2-5). pap. 5.95 *(978-1-4342-2314-2(0)*, 103183, Stone Arch Bks.) Capstone.

—Revealed! Zinc Alloy, 1 vol. Holgate, Douglas, illus. 2008. (Graphic Sparks Ser.). (ENG.). 40p. (J). (gr. 2-5). pap. 5.95 *(978-1-4342-0859-0(1)*, 95221, Stone Arch Bks.) Capstone.

—Super Zero, 1 vol. Holgate, Douglas, illus. 2008. (Zinc Alloy Ser.). (ENG.). 40p. (J). (gr. 2-5). 23.99 *(978-1-4342-0762-3(5)*, 95167, Stone Arch Bks.) Capstone.

—Super Zero: Zinc Alloy. Holgate, Douglas, illus. 2008. (Graphic Sparks Ser.). (ENG.). 40p. (J). (gr. 2-5). pap. 5.95 *(978-1-4342-0858-3(3)*, 95219, Stone Arch Bks.) Capstone.

—Zinc Alloy: the Invincible Boy-Bot. 2012. (Zinc Alloy Ser.). (ENG.). 128p. (J). (gr. 2-5). pap., pap., pap. 8.95 *(978-1-4342-4597-7(7)*, 120572, Stone Arch Bks.) Capstone.

—Zinc Alloy vs Frankenstein, 1 vol. Holgate, Douglas, illus. 2010. (Graphic Sparks Ser.). (ENG.). 40p. (J). (gr. 2-5). pap. 5.95 *(978-1-4342-1391-4(9)*, 95681, Stone Arch Bks.) Capstone.

Lerner, Jarrett. EngiNerds. (Max Ser.). (ENG., Illus.). 192p. (J). (gr. 4-8). 2019. pap. 7.99 *(978-1-4814-6871-8(5))* 2017. 17.99 *(978-1-4814-6872-5(3))* Simon & Schuster Children's Publishing. (Aladdin).

Lewis, Axel. Canyon Chaos, 1 vol. 2014. (Robot Racers Ser.). (ENG., Illus.). 160p. (J). (gr. 2-4). pap. 6.95 *(978-1-4342-7936-1(7)*, 124681, Stone Arch Bks.) Capstone.

—Desert Disaster, 1 vol. 2014. (Robot Racers Ser.). (ENG., Illus.). 160p. (J). (gr. 2-4). pap. 6.95 *(978-1-4342-7939-2(1)*, 124684, Stone Arch Bks.) Capstone.

—Rain Forest Rampage, 1 vol. 2014. (Robot Racers Ser.). (ENG.). 160p. (J). (gr. 2-4). 26.65 *(978-1-4342-6571-5(4)*, 124406); (Illus.). pap. 6.95 *(978-1-4342-7937-8(5)*, 124682) Capstone. (Stone Arch Bks.).

Lofficier, Randy & Lofficier, Jean-Marc. Robonocchio. Martiniere, Stephan, illus. 2004. (FRE.). 128p. (YA). per. 14.95 *(978-1-932983-04-3(X)*, Black Coat Pr.) HollywoodComics.com, LLC.

Long, Ethan. Clara & Clem in Outer Space. 2013. (Penguin Young Readers, Level 1 Ser.). (ENG.). 32p. (J). (gr. k-1). pap. 5.99 *(978-0-448-46721-4(6)*, Penguin Young Readers) Penguin Young Readers Group.

Look at the Robot: Individual Title Six-Packs. (Sails Literacy Ser.). 16p. (gr. k-18). 27.00 *(978-0-7635-4421-8(3))* Rigby Education.

Love, Damien. Monstrous Devices. 2019. (ENG., Illus.). 368p. (J). (gr. 3-7). 8.99 *(978-0-451-47859-7(2)*, Puffin Books) Penguin Young Readers Group.

Lucas, David. The Robot & the Bluebird. 2008. (ENG., Illus.). 32p. (J). (-k). pap. 14.99 *(978-1-84270-732-6(9))* Andersen Pr. GBR. Dist: Independent Pubs. Group.

MacLachlan, Patricia & Charest, Emily MacLachlan. Little Robot Alone. Phelan, Matt, illus. 2018. (ENG.). 40p. (J). (gr. -1-3). 17.99 *(978-0-544-44280-1(6)*, 1597246, Clarion Bks.) HarperCollins Pubs.

Maker, Martha. Dream Machine. Yan, Xindi, illus. 2018. (Craftily Ever After Ser.: 4). (ENG.). 128p. (J). (gr. k-4). 17.99 *(978-1-5344-1731-1(1))*; pap. 6.99 *(978-1-5344-1730-4(3))* Little Simon. (Little Simon).

Mass, Wendy. Fast-Forward to the Future!: a Branches Book (Time Jumpers #3), Vol. 3. Vidal, Oriol, illus. 2019. (Time Jumpers Ser.: 3). (ENG.). 96p. (J). (gr. 1-3). pap. 5.99 *(978-1-338-21742-1(9))* Scholastic, Inc.

McCanna, Tim. Bitty Bot. Carpenter, Tad, illus. 2016. (Bitty Bot Ser.). (ENG.). 32p. (J). (gr. -1-3). 16.99 *(978-1-4814-4929-8(X)*, Simon & Schuster Bks. For Young Readers) Simon & Schuster Bks. For Young Readers.

—Bitty Bot's Big Beach Getaway. Carpenter, Tad, illus. 2018. (Bitty Bot Ser.). (ENG.). 32p. (J). (gr. -1-3). 17.99 *(978-1-4814-4931-1(1)*, Simon & Schuster/Paula Wiseman Bks.) Simon & Schuster/Paula Wiseman Bks.

McCLOUD, Scott. Distant Thunder, 1 vol. Burchett, Rick & Austin, Terry, illus. 2012. (Superman Adventures Ser.). (ENG.). 32p. (J). (gr. 2-5). 22.60 *(978-1-4342-4551-9(9)*, 120511, Stone Arch Bks.) Capstone.

McIntosh, Will. Watchdog. 2019. (ENG.). 192p. (J). (gr. 5). 8.99 *(978-1-5247-1387-4(2)*, Yearling) Random Hse. Children's Bks.

McNamara, Margaret. The Three Little Aliens & the Big Bad Robot. Fearing, Mark, illus. 2011. (ENG.). 40p. (J). (gr. -1-3). 18.99 *(978-0-375-86689-0(2))* Random Hse. Children's Bks.

Metz, Melinda. S. M. A. R. T. S. & the Droid of Doom. McKenzie, Heath, illus. 2016. (S. M. A. R. T. S. Ser.). (ENG.). 128p. (J). (gr. 3-6). pap. 9.95 *(978-1-4965-3017-2(9)*, 131904); lib. bdg. 22.65 *(978-1-4965-3015-8(2)*, 131902) Capstone. (Stone Arch Bks.).

Milgrim, David. Go, Otto, Go! Ready-To-Read Pre-Level 1. Milgrim, David, illus. 2016. (Adventures of Otto Ser.). (ENG., Illus.). 32p. (J). (gr. -1-k). pap. 4.99 *(978-1-4814-6723-0(9)*, Simon Spotlight) Simon Spotlight.

—Look Out! a Storm! Ready-To-Read Pre-Level 1. Milgrim, David, illus. 2019. (Adventures of Otto Ser.). (ENG., Illus.). 32p. (J). (gr. -1-k). 17.99 *(978-1-5344-4197-2(2))*; pap. 4.99 *(978-1-5344-4196-5(4))* Simon Spotlight. (Simon Spotlight).

—Poof! a Bot! 2019. (Ready-To-Read Ser.). (ENG.). 32p. (J). (gr. k-1). 13.89 *(978-1-64310-884-1(0))* Penworthy Co., LLC, The.

—Poof! a Bot! Ready-To-Read Ready-to-Go! Milgrim, David, illus. 2019. (Adventures of Zip Ser.). (ENG., Illus.). 32p. (J). (gr. -1-k). pap. 4.99 *(978-1-5344-1102-9(X))* Simon & Schuster, Inc.

—Ride, Otto, Ride! Ready-To-Read Pre-Level 1. Milgrim, David, illus. 2016. (Adventures of Otto Ser.). (ENG., Illus.). 32p. (J). (gr. -1-k). pap. 4.99 *(978-1-4814-6793-3(X)*, Simon Spotlight) Simon Spotlight.

—See Otto: Ready-To-Read Pre-Level 1. Milgrim, David, illus. 2016. (Adventures of Otto Ser.). (ENG., Illus.). 32p. (J). (gr. -1-k). pap. 4.99 *(978-1-4814-6796-4(4)*, Simon Spotlight) Simon Spotlight.

—See Pip Flap. 2019. (Ready-To-Read Ser.). (ENG.). 32p. (J). (gr. k-1). 13.89 *(978-1-64310-885-8(9))* Penworthy Co., LLC, The.

—See Pip Flap: Ready-To-Read Pre-Level 1. Milgrim, David, illus. 2018. (Adventures of Otto Ser.). (ENG., Illus.). 32p. (J). (gr. -1-k). 17.99 *(978-1-5344-1636-9(6))*; pap. 4.99 *(978-1-5344-1635-2(8))* Simon Spotlight. (Simon Spotlight).

—See Pip Point: Ready-To-Read Pre-Level 1. Milgrim, David, illus. 2016. (Adventures of Otto Ser.). (ENG., Illus.). 32p. (J). (gr. -1-k). pap. 4.99 *(978-1-4814-6784-1(0)*, Simon Spotlight) Simon Spotlight.

—See Santa Nap: Ready-To-Read Pre-Level 1. Milgrim, David, illus. 2016. (Adventures of Otto Ser.). (ENG., Illus.). 32p. (J). (gr. -1-k). pap. 4.99 *(978-1-4814-6787-2(5)*, Simon Spotlight) Simon Spotlight.

—Swing Otto Swing! Milgrim, David, illus. 2005. (Ready-to-Read Ser.). (Illus.). (J). (gr. -1-k). 11.65 *(978-0-7569-6497-9(0))* Perfection Learning Corp.

Mohr, L. C. Krumbuckets. Musheno, Erica, illus. 2007. (ENG.). 144p. (J). (gr. 2-7). 13.95 *(978-0-9769417-6-7(7))* Blooming Tree Pr.

Montgomery, R. A. Your Very Own Robot: (Choose Your Own Adventure - Dragonlark) Newton, Keith, illus. 2007. (ENG.). 80p. (J). (gr. 2-2). pap. 8.99 *(978-1-933390-52-9(2))* Chooseco LLC.

—Your Very Own Robot Goes Cuckoo-Bananas! Newton, Keith, illus. 2010. (ENG.). 80p. (J). (gr. 2-2). pap. 7.99 *(978-1-933390-39-0(5))* Chooseco LLC.

Montgomery, R. A. & Gilligan, Shannon. Gus vs. the Robot King. Newton, Keith, illus. 2014. (ENG.). 80p. (J). (gr. 3-3). pap. 7.99 *(978-1-937133-44-3(3))* Chooseco LLC.

Morris, J. S. The Jewel. 2007. (ENG.). 204p. pap. 22.95 *(978-1-4357-0140-3(2))* Lulu Pr., Inc.

Musical Robot. If You're a Robot & You Know It. Carter, David A., illus. 2015. (ENG.). 14p. (J). (gr. -1-k). 16.99 *(978-0-545-81980-0(6)*, Cartwheel Bks.) Scholastic, Inc.

Myklusch, Matt. The Accidental Hero. 2011. (Jack Blank Adventure Ser.: 1). (ENG., Illus.). 496p. (J). (gr. 3-7). pap. 9.99 *(978-1-4169-9562-3(5)*, Aladdin) Simon & Schuster Children's Publishing.

—Jack Blank & the Imagine Nation. 2010. (Jack Blank Adventure Ser.: Bk. 1). (ENG., Illus.). 480p. (J). (gr. 3-7). 19.99 *(978-1-4169-9561-6(7)*, Aladdin) Simon & Schuster Children's Publishing.

National Children's Book and Literacy Alliance Staff, contrib. by. The Exquisite Corpse Adventure. 2011. (ENG., Illus.). 288p. (J). (gr. 4-6). 22.44 *(978-0-7636-5149-7(4))* Candlewick Pr.

Natl Children's Book & Literacy Alliance. The Exquisite Corpse Adventure. 2011. (ENG., Illus.). 288p. (J). (gr. 4-7). pap. 9.99 *(978-0-7636-5773-4(5))* Candlewick Pr.

Nickel, Scott. Robot Rampage: A Buzz Beaker Brainstorm. Smith, Andy J., illus. 2006. (Graphic Sparks Ser.). (ENG.). 40p. (J). (gr. 2-5). per. 5.95 *(978-1-59889-227-7(4)*, 93375, Stone Arch Bks.) Capstone.

—T. Rex vs Robo-Dog 3000. Corts, Enrique, illus. 2008. (Graphic Sparks Ser.). (ENG.). 40p. (J). (gr. 2-5). pap. 5.95 *(978-1-4342-0857-6(5)*, 95218, Stone Arch Bks.) Capstone.

Nolen, Jerdine. Block Party Surprise. Henninger, Michelle, illus. 2015. 41p. (J). *(978-1-4806-8574-1(7))* Harcourt.

—Bradford Street Buddies: Block Party Surprise. Henninger, Michelle, illus. 2015. (ENG.). 48p. (J). (gr. 1-4). pap. 4.99 *(978-0-544-35863-8(5)*, 1587297, Clarion Bks.) HarperCollins Pubs.

North, Laura. The Big Bad Wolf & the Robot Pig. 2014. (Race Ahead with Reading Ser.). (ENG., Illus.). 32p. (J). (gr. 2-2). *(978-0-7787-1291-6(5))* Crabtree Publishing Co.

Nye, Barry. Hannah & the Magic Blanket - Land of the Robots. 2009. (ENG.). 40p. pap. 18.50 *(978-0-557-06602-5(6))* Lulu Pr., Inc.

O'Connor, Grandma. Rodney the Robot: Why Rodney Rebels. 2008. 52p. pap. 8.95 *(978-0-595-51055-9(8))* iUniverse, Inc.

O'Donnell, Liam. Tank & Fizz: the Case of the Battling Bots, 1 vol. Deas, Mike, illus. 2016. (Tank & Fizz Ser.: 2). (ENG.). 176p. (J). (gr. 4-7). pap. 10.95 *(978-1-4598-0813-3(4))* Orca Bk. Pubs. USA.

Onyebuchi, Tochi. War Girls. 2019. (ENG.). 464p. (YA). (gr. 7). 18.99 *(978-0-451-48167-2(4)*, Razorbill) Penguin Young Readers Group.

O'Ryan, Ray. The Annoying Crush. Kraft, Jason, illus. 2014. (Galaxy Zack Ser.: 9). (ENG.). 128p. (J). (gr. k-4). 17.99 *(978-1-4424-9364-3(X))*; pap. 5.99 *(978-1-4424-9363-6(1))* Little Simon. (Little Simon).

—The Annoying Crush. 2014. (Galaxy Zack Ser.: 9). lib. bdg. 16.00 *(978-0-606-36093-7(X))* Turtleback.

Park, Mac. D-Bot Squad Complete Collection (slipcase) Hart, James, illus. 2019. (ENG.). 640p. (J). (gr. k-2). 24.99 *(978-1-76052-860-7(9))* Allen & Unwin AUS. Dist: Independent Pubs. Group.

—Dino Corp: d-Bot Squad 8. Hart, James, illus. 2019. (D-Bot Squad Ser.: 8). (ENG.). 80p. (J). (gr. k-2). pap. 8.99 *(978-1-76029-604-9(X))* Allen & Unwin AUS. Dist: Independent Pubs. Group.

—Dino Hunter: d-Bot Squad 1. Hart, James, illus. 2018. (D-Bot Squad Ser.: 1). (ENG.). 80p. (J). (gr. k-2). pap. 7.99 *(978-1-76029-597-4(3))* Allen & Unwin AUS. Dist: Independent Pubs. Group.

—Double Trouble: d-Bot Squad 3. Hart, James, illus. 2018. (D-Bot Squad Ser.: 3). (ENG.). 80p. (J). (gr. k-2). pap. 8.99 *(978-1-76029-599-8(X))* Allen & Unwin AUS. Dist: Independent Pubs. Group.

—Mega Hatch: d-Bot Squad 7. Hart, James, illus. 2019. (D-Bot Squad Ser.: 7). (ENG.). 80p. (J). (gr. k-2). pap. 8.99 *(978-1-76029-603-2(1))* Allen & Unwin AUS. Dist: Independent Pubs. Group.

—Sky High: d-Bot Squad 2. Hart, James, illus. 2018. (D-Bot Squad Ser.: 2). (ENG.). 80p. (J). (gr. k-2). pap. 7.99 *(978-1-76029-598-1(1))* Allen & Unwin AUS. Dist: Independent Pubs. Group.

—Stack Attack: d-Bot Squad 5. Hart, James, illus. 2018. (D-Bot Squad Ser.: 5). (ENG.). 80p. (J). (gr. k-2). pap. 8.99 *(978-1-76029-601-8(5))* Allen & Unwin AUS. Dist: Independent Pubs. Group.

Parker, Emma. Robot Tim. 2010. (Illus.). 20p. pap. *(978-1-877561-54-2(1))* First Edition Ltd.

Patterson, James. House of Robots: Robot Revolution. Neufeld, Juliana, illus. 2017. (House of Robots Ser.: 3). (ENG.). 336p. (J). (gr. 3-7). 13.99 *(978-0-316-34958-1(5)*, Jimmy Patterson) Little Brown & Co.

Patterson, James & Grabenstein, Chris. House of Robots. Neufeld, Juliana, illus. (House of Robots Ser.: 1). (ENG.). (J). (gr. 3-7). 2015. 336p. pap. 8.99 *(978-0-316-34679-5(9))* 2014. 352p. 13.99 *(978-0-316-40591-1(4))* Little Brown & Co. (Jimmy Patterson).

—House of Robots. 2015. (J). lib. bdg. 18.40 *(978-0-606-37527-6(9))* Turtleback.

—House of Robots: Robots Go Wild! Neufeld, Juliana, illus. 2015. (House of Robots Ser.: 2). (ENG.). 336p. (J). (gr. 3-7). 13.99 *(978-0-316-28479-0(3)*, Jimmy Patterson) Little Brown & Co.

Perry, Fred & Dlin, Doug. Gold Digger Tech Manual. 2011. (ENG.). 352p. (YA). pap., pap. 19.99 *(978-0-9844879-7-4(2)*, d4b0f957-8fe9-4c47-bc07-786055531e90) Antarctic Pr., Inc.

Peschke, Marci. Robot Queen. Mourning, Tuesday, illus. 2018. (Kylie Jean Ser.). (ENG.). 112p. (J). (gr. 1-3). 8.95 *(978-1-5158-2934-8(0)*, 138473); lib. bdg. 22.65 *(978-1-5158-2926-3(X)*, 138469) Capstone. (Picture Window Bks.).

Peters, Stephanie True. The Robo-Battle of Mega Tortoise vs. Hazard Hare: A Graphic Novel. Cano, Fernando, illus. 2017. (Far Out Fables Ser.). (ENG.). 40p. (J). (gr. 3-6). pap. 4.95 *(978-1-4965-5424-6(8)*, 136357); lib. bdg. 25.32 *(978-1-4965-5420-8(5)*, 136353) Capstone. (Stone Arch Bks.).

Pilkey, Dav. Ricky Ricotta's Mighty Robot. 2014. (Ricky Ricotta's Mighty Robot Ser.: 1). lib. bdg. 16.00 *(978-0-606-35799-9(8))* Turtleback.

—Ricky Ricotta's Mighty Robot (Ricky Ricotta's Mighty Robot #1) Santat, Dan, illus. 2014. (Ricky Ricotta's Mighty Robot Ser.: 1). (ENG.). 112p. (J). (gr. -1-3). pap. 5.99 *(978-0-545-63009-2(6))* Scholastic, Inc.

—Ricky Ricotta's Mighty Robot (Ricky Ricotta's Mighty Robot #1) (Library Edition) Santat, Dan, illus. 2014. (Ricky Ricotta's Mighty Robot Ser.: 1). (ENG.). 112p. (J). (gr. -1-3). lib. bdg. 15.99 *(978-0-545-63106-8(8))* Scholastic, Inc.

—Ricky Ricotta's Mighty Robot vs. the Jurassic Jackrabbits from Jupiter (Ricky Ricotta's Mighty Robot #5), Vol. 5. Santat, Dan, illus. 2014. (Ricky Ricotta's Mighty Robot Ser.: 5). (ENG.). 128p. (J). (gr. -1-3). pap. 5.99 *(978-0-545-63013-9(4))* Scholastic, Inc.

—Ricky Ricotta's Mighty Robot vs. the Mecha-Monkeys from Mars (Ricky Ricotta's Mighty Robot #4) Santat, Dan, illus. 2014. (Ricky Ricotta's Mighty Robot Ser.: 4). (ENG.). 144p. (J). (gr. -1-3). pap. 5.99 *(978-0-545-63012-2(6))* Scholastic, Inc.

—Ricky Ricotta's Mighty Robot vs. the Mutant Mosquitoes from Mercury (Ricky Ricotta's Mighty Robot #2) Santat, Dan, illus. 2014. (Ricky Ricotta's Mighty Robot Ser.: 2). (ENG.). 128p. (J). (gr. -1-3). pap. 5.99 *(978-0-545-63010-8(X))* Scholastic, Inc.

—Ricky Ricotta's Mighty Robot vs. the Naughty Nightcrawlers from Neptune (Ricky Ricotta's Mighty Robot #8) Santat, Dan, illus. 2016. (Ricky Ricotta's Mighty Robot Ser.: 8). (ENG.). 128p. (J). (gr. -1-3). pap. 5.99 *(978-0-439-37709-6(9))* Scholastic, Inc.

—Ricky Ricotta's Mighty Robot vs. the Uranium Unicorns from Uranus (Ricky Ricotta's Mighty Robot #7), Bk. 7. 2015. (Ricky Ricotta's Mighty Robot Ser.: 7). (ENG., Illus.). 128p. (J). (gr. -1-3). pap. 5.99 *(978-0-545-63015-3(0))* Scholastic, Inc.

—Ricky Ricotta's Mighty Robot vs. the Video Vultures from Venus (Ricky Ricotta's Mighty Robot #3) Santat, Dan, illus. 2014. (Ricky Ricotta's Mighty Robot Ser.: 3). (ENG.). 128p. (J). (gr. -1-3). pap. 5.99 *(978-0-545-63011-5(8))* Scholastic, Inc.

Platt, Cynthia. Parker Bell & the Science of Friendship. Zhai, Rea, illus. 2019. (ENG.). 160p. (J). (gr. 3-7). 16.99 *(978-1-328-97347-4(6)*, 1708149, Clarion Bks.) HarperCollins Pubs.

Pollack, Pamela. Spy Cats: Revenge of the Robot Rats. 2004. (Illus.). 57p. *(978-0-439-56603-2(7))* Scholastic, Inc.

Pratt, Jeffrey. Team Player. 2019. (AI High Ser.). (ENG.). 112p. (YA). (gr. 6-12). pap. 7.99 *(978-1-5415-7294-2(7)*, 179e9c99-a9e7-43fc-90d3-3828427be6be, Darby Creek) Lerner Publishing Group.

Publications International Ltd. Staff. Wall E Large Sound BK. 2008. 24p. (J). 17.98 *(978-1-4127-8991-2(5)*, PIL Kids) Publications International, Ltd.

Ralph, Brian. Reggie-12. 2013. (ENG., Illus.). 96p. (YA). 21.95 *(978-1-77046-132-1(9)*, 900125200) Drawn & Quarterly Pubns. CAN. Dist: Macmillan.

Random House Staff. I Am Baymax. 2015. (Step into Reading Level 2 Ser.). lib. bdg. 14.75 *(978-0-606-36383-9(1))* Turtleback.

Rau, Dana M. Robot, Go Bot! (Step into Reading Comic Reader) Jung, Wook Jin, illus. 2013. (Step into Reading Ser.). 32p. (J). (gr. -1-1). 5.99 *(978-0-375-87083-5(0)*, Random Hse. Bks. for Young Readers) Random Hse. Children's Bks.

—Robot, Go Bot! (Step into Reading Comic Reader) Read & Listen Edition. Jung, Wook Jin, illus. 2013. (Step into Reading Ser.). (ENG.). 32p. (J). (gr. -1-1). E-Book *(978-0-449-81429-1(7)*, Random Hse. Bks. for Young Readers) Random Hse. Children's Bks.

Rau, Dana Meachen. Robot, Go Bot! 2013. (Step into Reading - Level 1 Ser.). lib. bdg. 13.55 *(978-0-606-31935-5(2))* Turtleback.

Rau, Zachary. Autobots Versus Zombies. 2012. (Transformers 8x8 Ser.). (J). lib. bdg. 13.55 *(978-0-606-26687-1(9))* Turtleback.

Readler, Blaine C. Under the Radar: The Spy Drone Adventure. 2006. (ENG.). 248p. (J). (gr. 7-12). per. *(978-1-933255-18-7(0))* DNA Pr.

Reed, M. K. & Smith, Brian "Smitty". The Castoffs Vol. 3: Rise of the Machines. Yates, Wyeth, illus. 2018. (ENG.). 136p. (YA). pap. 12.99 *(978-1-941302-73-6(4)*, 07e3e1de-d3fd-4b4f-ad0a-9855b730c0ed, Lion Forge) Oni Pr., Inc.

Rex, Michael. Facts vs. Opinions vs. Robots. Rex, Michael, illus. 2020. (Illus.). 32p. (J). (gr. k-3). 18.99 *(978-1-9848-1626-9(8)*, Nancy Paulsen Books) Penguin Young Readers Group.

RH Disney. WALL-E (Disney/Pixar WALL-e) RH Disney, illus. 2008. (Little Golden Book Ser.). (ENG., Illus.). 24p. (J). (gr. -1-2). 5.99 *(978-0-7364-2422-6(9)*, RH/Disney) Random Hse. Children's Bks.

Ricahrdson, Larry. Metal Mike. Ricahrdson, Brittany, illus. 2010. 24p. (J). pap. 9.95 *(978-1-935706-26-7(8))* Wiggles Pr.

Richards, Barnaby. Blip! TOON Level 1. 2016. (Illus.). 40p. (J). (gr. -1-1). 12.95 *(978-1-935179-98-6(5)*, TOON Books) Astra Publishing Hse.

Richards, C. J. Battle of the Bots. 2017. (Robots Rule Ser.: 3). (ENG.). (J). (gr. 2-5). lib. bdg. 17.20 *(978-0-606-39811-4(2))* Turtleback.

—The Junkyard Bot: Robots Rule, Book 1. Fujita, Goro, illus. 2016. (Robots Rule Ser.). (ENG.). 208p. (J). (gr. 5-7). pap. 9.99 *(978-0-544-66843-0(X)*, 1625458, Clarion Bks.) HarperCollins Pubs.

—Lots of Bots. Fujita, Goro, illus. 2016. (Robots Rule Ser.: 2). (ENG.). 224p. (J). (gr. 3-7). pap. 6.99 *(978-0-544-81082-2(1)*, 1641524, Clarion Bks.) HarperCollins Pubs.

Richards, Kitty. Meet the Sparkplugs, Level 3. Simard, Remy, illus. 2006. (ENG.). 24p. (J). (gr. 1-17). per. 3.99 *(978-1-58476-419-9(8)*, IKIDS) Innovative Kids.

Richardson, Larry. Metal Mike. 2010. (Illus.). 32p. (J). pap. 9.95 *(978-1-935706-33-5(0))* Wiggles Pr.

Richman, Sarah. Family Ties. 2019. (AI High Ser.). (ENG.). 112p. (YA). (gr. 6-12). pap. 7.99 *(978-1-5415-7292-8(0)*, 03735ea1-4ab2-4858-880d-9553b52d157c); lib. bdg. 26.65 *(978-1-5415-5691-1(7)*, 1fac8fb4-3f97-4f70-8d02-a23dfb4ececa) Lerner Publishing Group. (Darby Creek).

Roberts, Daniel. Harrison & His Dinosaur Robot. 2009. (Illus.). 32p. pap. 14.95 *(978-1-4389-2846-3(7))* AuthorHouse.

—Harrison & His Dinosaur Robot & the Super-Fast Race Car. 2009. (Illus.). 32p. pap. 14.95 *(978-1-4389-2847-0(5))* AuthorHouse.

Robinson, Michelle. And the Robot Went ... Ruzzier, Sergio, illus. 2017. (ENG.). 32p. (J). (gr. -1-3). 16.99 *(978-0-544-58652-9(2)*, 1614145, Clarion Bks.) HarperCollins Pubs.

The Robot, 6, Pack. (Chiquilibros Ser.). (gr. k-1). 23.00 *(978-0-7635-0442-7(4))* Rigby Education.

Ronan, Amanda. The Decision. Radka, Sara, illus. 2015. (My Brother is a Robot Ser.: 6). (ENG.). 64p. (J). (gr. 3-8). 27.99 *(978-1-62920-509-0(5))* Scobre Pr. Corp.

—The Discovery. Radka, Sara, illus. 2015. (My Brother Is a Robot Ser.: 5). (ENG.). 64p. (J). (gr. 3-8). 27.99 *(978-1-62920-506-9(0))* Scobre Pr. Corp.

—The Experiment. Radka, Sara, illus. 2015. (My Brother Is a Robot Ser.: 1). (ENG.). 64p. (J). (gr. 3-8). 27.99 *(978-1-62920-494-9(3))* Scobre Pr. Corp.

—The Fight. Radka, Sara, illus. 2015. (My Brother Is a Robot Ser.: 4). (ENG.). 64p. (J). (gr. 3-8). 27.99 *(978-1-62920-503-8(6))* Scobre Pr. Corp.

—The Master Plan. Radka, Sara, illus. 2015. (My Brother Is a Robot Ser.: 2). (ENG.). 64p. (J). (gr. 3-8). 27.99 *(978-1-62920-497-0(8))* Scobre Pr. Corp.

—The Switch. Radka, Sara, illus. 2015. (My Brother Is a Robot Ser.: 3). (ENG.). 64p. (J). (gr. 3-8). 27.99 *(978-1-62920-500-7(1))* Scobre Pr. Corp.

Rosen, Lucy. Blast Off! 2015. (Transformers 8x8 Ser.). (J). lib. bdg. 13.55 *(978-0-606-37228-2(8))* Turtleback.

Rosenblum, Gregg. Revolution 19. 2013. (Revolution 19 Ser.: 1). (ENG.). 272p. (YA). (gr. 8). 17.99 *(978-0-06-212595-8(8)*, HarperTeen) HarperCollins Pubs.

Rosenthal, Marc. 1 Robot Lost His Head: a Robot Counting Book. 2015. (ENG., Illus.). 16p. (J). (-k). 17.95 *(978-1-57687-749-4(3)*, powerHouse Bks.) powerHse. Bks.

Rossell, Judith. Sam & the Killer Robot. 2007. 176p. pap. *(978-1-921272-10-3(4))* Little Hare Bks. AUS. Dist: HarperCollins Pubs. Australia.

Roza, Greg. The Messy Robot, 1 vol. 2006. (Neighborhood Readers Ser.). (ENG., Illus.). 16p. (gr. 1-2). pap. 6.50 *(978-1-4042-7184-5(8)*, ab104137-9707-4ea4-b9ca-64861955aa1d, Rosen Classroom) Rosen Publishing Group, Inc., The.

Rubin, Adam. Robo-Sauce. Salmieri, Daniel, illus. 2015. 48p. (J). (gr. -1-3). 18.99 *(978-0-525-42887-9(9)*, Dial Bks) Penguin Young Readers Group.

Rudnick, Elizabeth. Iron Man Is Born, 1 vol. Marvel Artist Staff, illus. 2012. (Avengers: Earth's Mightiest Heroes! Ser.). (ENG.). 24p. (J). (gr. k-5). lib. bdg. 31.36 *(978-1-61479-003-7(5)*, 2887, Marvel Age) Spotlight.

Ruiz, Rachel. The Runaway Robot. May, Steve, illus. 2017. (Superhero Harry Ser.). (ENG.). 48p. (J). (gr. k-2). pap. 8.95 *(978-1-4795-9859-5(3)*, 135316); lib. bdg. 23.32 *(978-1-4795-9855-7(0)*, 135308) Capstone. (Picture Window Bks.).

Santat, Dan, illus. Ricky Ricotta's Mighty Robot vs. the Stupid Stinkbugs from Saturn (Ricky Ricotta's Mighty Robot #6) 2015. (Ricky Ricotta's Mighty Robot Ser.: 6). (ENG.). 128p. (J). (gr. -1-3). pap. 5.99 *(978-0-545-63014-6(2))* Scholastic, Inc.

Santillo, LuAnn. Buzz. Santillo, LuAnn, ed. 2003. (Half-Pint Kids Readers Ser.). (Illus.). 7p. (J). (gr. -1-1). pap. 1.00 *(978-1-59256-046-2(6))* Half-Pint Kids, Inc.

Savage, J. Scott. Fires of Invention. 2015. (Mysteries of Cove Ser.: 1). (ENG., Illus.). 320p. (J). (gr. 5). 17.99 *(978-1-62972-092-0(5)*, 5139121, Shadow Mountain) Shadow Mountain Publishing.

Sazaklis, John. Optimus Prime Versus Predaking. 2013. (Transformers 8x8 Ser.). (J). lib. bdg. 13.55 *(978-0-606-32272-0(8))* Turtleback.

—Salamander Smackdown! Baltazar, Art, illus. 2011. (DC Super-Pets Ser.). (ENG.). 56p. (J). (gr. 1-3). pap. 4.95 *(978-1-4048-6844-1(5)*, 116401); lib. bdg. 25.32 *(978-1-4048-6478-8(4)*, 114159) Capstone. (Stone Arch Bks.).

Schaefer, Elizabeth. Rey's Story. 2016. (Illus.). 138p. (J). *(978-1-5182-1013-6(9)*, Disney Lucasfilm Press) Disney Publishing Worldwide.

Schneider, Josh. Ultrabot's First Playdate. Schneider, Josh, illus. 2019. (ENG., Illus.). 32p. (J). (gr. -1-3). 17.99 *(978-1-328-49013-1(0)*, 1716817, Clarion Bks.) HarperCollins Pubs.

Schorr, Titus. My Robot, 1 vol., 1. 2015. (Rosen REAL Readers: STEM & STEAM Collection). (ENG.). 12p. (J). (gr. 1-2). pap. 6.33 *(978-1-5081-1620-2(2)*, 7c4af020-ee46-44b8-8985-df2f6a264005, Rosen Classroom) Rosen Publishing Group, Inc., The.

Scieszka, Jon. Frank Einstein & the Antimatter Motor. Biggs, Brian, illus. 2014. (Frank Einstein Ser.). 192p. (J). (gr. 3-7). pap. 7.95 *(978-1-4197-1506-8(2))* Abrams, Inc.

—Frank Einstein & the Antimatter Motor. 2017. (Frank Einstein Ser.: 1). (J). lib. bdg. 18.40 *(978-0-606-39683-7(7))* Turtleback.

—Frank Einstein & the Antimatter Motor (Frank Einstein Series #1) Book One. Biggs, Brian, illus. (Frank Einstein Ser.). (ENG.). (J). (gr. 3-7). 2017. 208p. pap. 7.95 *(978-1-4197-2492-3(4)*, 1070006) 2014. 192p. 13.95 *(978-1-4197-1601-0(8)*, Amulet Bks.) Abrams, Inc.

—Frank Einstein & the Bio-Action Gizmo (Frank Einstein #5) Book Five. Biggs, Brian, illus. 2018. (Frank Einstein Ser.: 5). (ENG.). 192p. (J). (gr. 3-7). pap. 7.99 *(978-1-4197-3125-9(4)*, 21) Abrams, Inc.

—Frank Einstein & the BrainTurbo (Frank Einstein Series #3), 3. Biggs, Brian, illus. 2015. (ENG.). 192p. (J). (gr. 3-7). 13.95 *(978-1-4197-1643-0(3)*, 1070201, Amulet Bks.) Abrams, Inc.

—Frank Einstein & the Electro-Finger (Frank Einstein Series #2) Book Two. Biggs, Brian, illus. 2017. (Frank Einstein Ser.). (ENG.). 192p. (J). (gr. 3-7). pap. 7.95 *(978-1-4197-2493-0(2)*, 1070103, Amulet Bks.) Abrams, Inc.

—Frank Einstein & the EvoBlaster Belt (Frank Einstein Series #4) Book Four. Biggs, Brian, illus. (Frank Einstein Ser.).

(ENG.). (J). (gr. 3-7). 2017. 224p. pap. 7.99 *(978-1-4197-2736-8(2)*, 1070303) 2016. 208p. 13.95 *(978-1-4197-1887-8(8)*, 1070301, Amulet Bks.) Abrams, Inc.
—Frank Einstein Book 2. 2015. (Frank Einstein Ser.). (ENG., Illus.). 176p. (YA). (gr. 3-7). pap. 7.95 *(978-1-4197-1666-9(2))* Abrams, Inc.
—Robot Zot! Shannon, David, illus. 2009. (ENG.). 40p. (J). (gr. -1-2). 17.99 *(978-1-4169-6394-3(4)*, Simon & Schuster Bks. For Young Readers) Simon & Schuster Bks. For Young Readers.
—Robot Zot! Shannon, David, illus. 2011. (J). (gr. -1-2). 29.95 *(978-0-545-32739-8(3))* Weston Woods Studios, Inc.
Scieszka, Jon & Brian Biggs. Frank Einstein & the Electro-Finger. 2017. (Frank Einstein Ser.: 2). (J). lib. bdg. 18.40 *(978-0-606-39684-4(5))* Turtleback.
Segal, Andrew. Roberto the Robot. Scott, Peter & JessT, Grant, illus. 2007. 32p. per. *(978-1-905823-26-0(6))* Panoma Pr. Ltd.
Selznick, Brian. The Invention of Hugo Cabret. 2007. (CHI., Illus.). 534p. (J). *(978-957-570-894-8(6))* Eastern Publishing Co., Ltd., The.
—The Invention of Hugo Cabret. 2008. (CHI., Illus.). 465p. (J). pap. *(978-7-5448-0279-6(5))* Jieli Publishing Hse.
—The Invention of Hugo Cabret. Selznick, Brian, illus. 2007. (ENG., Illus.). 544p. (J). (gr. 4-7). 29.99 *(978-0-439-81378-5(6)*, Scholastic Pr.); 534p. *(978-1-4071-0348-8(2))* Scholastic, Inc.
SFX Fantasy. Tween Tales - Robots, Dragons & the Interworld Machine. 2007. (ENG.). 131p. pap. 12.99 *(978-1-4303-2546-8(1))* Lulu Pr., Inc.
Sheehan, Anna. A Long, Long Sleep. 2011. (ENG., Illus.). 352p. (YA). (gr. 9). 16.99 *(978-0-7636-5260-9(1))* Candlewick Pr.
Shelton, C. M. Cosmic Chaos. 2015. (ENG., Illus.). 226p. (J). pap. 8.99 *(978-1-941720-25-7(0))* Ashberry Lane.
Shepard, Aaron. Timothy Tolliver & the Bully Basher. (J). 2017. (ENG., Illus.). (gr. 3-5). pap. 6.00 *(978-1-62035-540-4(X))* 2005. 48p. pap. 2.99 *(978-0-938497-24-0(3))* 2005. 48p. lib. bdg. 15.00 *(978-0-938497-23-3(5))* Shepard Pubns. (Skyhook Pr.).
Shirai, Shiro, illus. Disney Manga: Pixar's Wall-E. 2018. (Disney Manga: Pixar's WALL E Ser.). 144p. (J). (gr. 1-1). pap. 10.99 *(978-1-4278-5771-2(7)*, 2acaa296-e525-4288-8c30-11a544decd87, TOKYOPOP Manga) TOKYOPOP, Inc.
Siems, Thomas F. The Dangerous Pet. Blye, Steven G., illus. 2009. (ENG.). 46p. pap. 21.99 *(978-1-4415-3454-5(7))* Xlibris Corp.
Sima, Jessie. Love, Z. Sima, Jessie, illus. 2018. (ENG., Illus.). 48p. (J). (gr. -1-3). 17.99 *(978-1-4814-9677-3(8)*, Simon & Schuster Bks. For Young Readers) Simon & Schuster Bks. For Young Readers.
Simon, Annette. Robot Zombie Frankenstein! Simon, Annette, illus. 2012. (ENG., Illus.). 40p. (J). (gr. -1-3). 16.99 *(978-0-7636-5124-4(9))* Candlewick Pr.
Simonson, Louise. Snow White & the Seven Robots: A Graphic Novel. Sanchez, Jimena S., illus. 2015. (Far Out Fairy Tales Ser.). (ENG.). 40p. (J). (gr. 3-6). lib. bdg. 25.32 *(978-1-4342-9648-1(2)*, 126939, Stone Arch Bks.) Capstone.
Sisler, Celeste. Robot Power! (Blaze & the Monster Machines) Aikins, Dave, illus. 2018. (Step into Reading Ser.). (ENG.). 24p. (J). (gr. -1-1). pap. 5.99 *(978-0-525-57820-8(X)*, Random Hse. Bks. for Young Readers) Random Hse. Children's Bks.
Smiley, Mark. A Journey Far Away. 2006. 164p. pap. 13.95 *(978-1-59526-494-7(9))* Aeon Publishing Inc.
Smith, Jim. Future Ratboy & the Attack of the Killer Robot Grannies (Future Ratboy) 2015. (Future Ratboy Ser.: 1). (ENG., Illus.). 256p. (J). (gr. 2-4). pap. 5.99 *(978-1-4052-6913-1(8))* Farshore GBR. Dist: HarperCollins Pubs.
Smith, Joseph K. The Substitute Kid. 2008. 54p. pap. 16.95 *(978-1-60672-272-5(7))* America Star Bks.
Snider, Brandon T. Amazo & the Planetary Reboot. Levins, Tim, illus. 2017. (Justice League Ser.). (ENG.). 88p. (J). (gr. 2-6). lib. bdg. 26.65 *(978-1-4965-5156-6(7)*, 136169, Stone Arch Bks.) Capstone.
Snider, Brandon T., adapted by. Ghost in the Machine. 2017. (Illus.). (J). *(978-1-5379-5841-5(0))* Little, Brown Bks. for Young Readers.
—Meet Quickshadow. 2017. (Illus.). 31p. (J). *(978-1-5182-4447-6(5))* Little Brown & Co.
Sonishi, Kenji. Leave It to PET!, Vol. 2. Sonishi, Kenji, illus. 2009. (Leave It to PET! Ser.: 2). (ENG., Illus.). 196p. (J). pap. 7.99 *(978-1-4215-2650-8(6))* Viz Media.
—Leave It to PET!, Vol. 4. Sonishi, Kenji, illus. 2010. (Leave It to PET! Ser.: 4). (ENG., Illus.). 192p. (J). pap. 7.99 *(978-1-4215-2652-2(2))* Viz Media.
Starfall Education. Robot & Mr. Mole. Starfall Education, ed. 2004. (ENG., Illus.). 8p. (J). pap. *(978-1-59577-009-7(7))* Starfall Education.
Steele, Michael Anthony. High-Tech Terror, 1 vol. Schoening, Dan, illus. 2011. (Green Lantern Ser.). (ENG.). 56p. (J). (gr. 3-6). pap. 4.95 *(978-1-4342-3084-3(8)*, 114724); lib. bdg. 26.65 *(978-1-4342-2609-9(3)*, 113654) Capstone. (Stone Arch Bks.).
Stephens, Sarah Hines. Superpowered Pony, 1 vol. Baltazar, Art, illus. 2011. (DC Super-Pets Ser.). (ENG.). 56p. (J). (gr. 1-3). pap. 4.95 *(978-1-4048-6846-5(1)*, 116403, Stone Arch Bks.) Capstone.
Stevenson, Robin. Ben's Robot, 1 vol. Parkins, David, illus. 2010. (Orca Echoes Ser.). (ENG.). 64p. (J). (gr. 1-3). pap. 6.95 *(978-1-55469-153-1(2))* Orca Bk. Pubs. USA.
Stilton, Gerónimo, et al. Robot Attack. Usai, Luca & Verzini, Daniele, illus. 2015. 117p. (J). *(978-0-545-86796-2(7))* Scholastic, Inc.
Stine, R. L. Frankenstein's Dog. 2013. (Goosebumps Most Wanted Ser.: 4). 136p. (J). lib. bdg. 17.20 *(978-0-606-32006-1(7))* Turtleback.
Stohl, Margaret & Peterson, Lewis. Cats vs. Robots #1: This Is War. Peterson, Kay, illus. (ENG.). (J). (gr. 3-7). 2019. 336p. pap. 6.99 *(978-0-06-266571-3(5))* 2018. 320p. 16.99 *(978-0-06-266570-6(7))* HarperCollins Pubs. (Tegen, Katherine Bks).
Stratford, Ann. Tara Toad Meets Roman the Robot Soldier. 2005. (ENG., Illus.). pap. *(978-1-84401-465-1(7))* Athena Pr.
Styles, Walker. Mystery Mountain Getaway. Whitehouse, Ben, illus. 2017. (Rider Woofson Ser.: 9). (ENG.). 128p. (J). (gr. k-4). 16.99 *(978-1-4814-9896-8(7))*; pap. 5.99 *(978-1-4814-9895-1(9))* Little Simon. (Little Simon).
Suen, Anastasia. The Big Catch: A Robot & Rico Story, 1 vol. Laughead, Michael, illus. 2009. (Robot & Rico Ser.). (ENG.). 32p. (J). (gr. 1-2). pap. 6.25 *(978-1-4342-1751-6(5)*, 102223, Stone Arch Bks.) Capstone.
—Dino Hunt: A Robot & Rico Story. Laughead, Michael, illus. 2010. (Robot & Rico Ser.). (ENG.). 32p. (J). (gr. 1-2). pap. 6.25 *(978-1-4342-2300-5(0)*, 103169, Stone Arch Bks.) Capstone.
—La Noche de Terror. Heck, Claudia M., tr. Laughead, Mike, illus. 2012. (Robot y Rico/Robot & Rico Ser.). Tr. of Scary Night. (MUL.). 32p. (J). (gr. 1-2). lib. bdg. 22.65 *(978-1-4342-3779-8(6)*, 117076, Stone Arch Bks.) Capstone.
—The Pirate Map: A Robot & Rico Story. Laughead, Michael, illus. 2010. (Robot & Rico Ser.). (ENG.). 32p. (J). (gr. 1-2). pap. 6.25 *(978-1-4342-2301-2(9)*, 103170, Stone Arch Bks.) Capstone.
—Un Premio Adentro. Heck, Claudia M., tr. Laughead, Mike, illus. 2012. (Robot y Rico/Robot & Rico Ser.). Tr. of Prize Inside. (MUL.). 32p. (J). (gr. 1-2). lib. bdg. 22.65 *(978-1-4342-3780-4(X)*, 117077, Stone Arch Bks.) Capstone.
—A Prize Inside: A Robot & Rico Story, 1 vol. Laughead, Michael, illus. 2009. (Robot & Rico Ser.). (ENG.). 32p. (J). (gr. 1-2). 22.65 *(978-1-4342-1627-4(6)*, 95801, Stone Arch Bks.) Capstone.
—The Scary Night: A Robot & Rico Story, 1 vol. Laughead, Michael, illus. 2009. (Robot & Rico Ser.). (ENG.). 32p. (J). (gr. 1-2). 22.65 *(978-1-4342-1628-1(4)*, 95802); pap. 6.25 *(978-1-4342-1752-3(3)*, 102224) Capstone. (Stone Arch Bks.).
—Snow Games: A Robot & Rico Story. Laughead, Michael, illus. 2010. (Robot & Rico Ser.). (ENG.). 32p. (J). (gr. 1-2). pap. 6.25 *(978-1-4342-2302-9(7)*, 103171); lib. bdg. 22.65 *(978-1-4342-1869-8(4)*, 102326) Capstone. (Stone Arch Bks.).
—Test Drive: A Robot & Rico Story. Laughead, Michael, illus. 2010. (Robot & Rico Ser.). (ENG.). 32p. (J). (gr. 1-2). pap. 6.25 *(978-1-4342-2303-6(5)*, 103172, Stone Arch Bks.) Capstone.
Sutton, Laurie S. Gorilla Warfare, 1 vol. Doescher, Erik & Schoening, Dan, illus. 2011. (Flash Ser.). (ENG.). 56p. (J). (gr. 3-6). pap. 4.95 *(978-1-4342-3087-4(2)*, 114727, Stone Arch Bks.) Capstone.
Thornton, D. S. Scrap City. Bowater, Charlie, illus. 2015. (Middle-Grade Novels Ser.). (ENG.). 352p. (J). (gr. 4-8). lib. bdg. 27.99 *(978-1-4965-0475-3(5)*, 128500, Stone Arch Bks.) Capstone.
Tiger Tales Staff, ed. & compiled by. Stories for Boys. Tiger Tales Staff, compiled by. 2015. (ENG.). 176p. (J). (gr. -1-3). 12.99 *(978-1-58925-535-7(6))* Tiger Tales.
Timmers, Leo. Franky. Timmers, Leo, illus. 2016. (ENG., Illus.). 40p. (J). (gr. -1-2). E-Book 26.65 *(978-1-77657-054-6(5)*, 9781776570546); E-Book 26.65 *(978-1-77657-053-9(7))* Gecko Pr. NZL. Dist: Lerner Publishing Group.
Torres, Mario J. The Incredible Adventures of Kaplan & Dylan: Book One: Present, 1 vol. 2009. 159p. pap. 24.95 *(978-1-4489-9513-4(2))* PublishAmerica, Inc.
Toufexis, George. MONSTER MASH-Up — Robots' Revenge. 2014. (ENG., Illus.). 48p. (J). (gr. 4). pap. 4.99 *(978-0-486-49225-4(7))* Dover Pubns., Inc.
Tougas, Chris. Mechanimals, 1 vol. 2012. (ENG., Illus.). 32p. (J). (gr. -1-k). 14.95 *(978-1-4598-0273-5(X))* Orca Bk. Pubs. USA.
Tra, Frank. Masterpiece Robot: And the Ferocious Valerie Knick Knack!, 1 vol. Evans, Rebecca, illus. 2018. (ENG.). 36p. (J). (gr. 2-6). 17.95 *(978-0-88448-518-6(8)*, 884518) Tilbury Hse. Pubs.
Trimble, Marcia J. Marsby & the Martian Detectives. Hayden, Jennifer H., illus. 2004. 56p. (J). per. 9.95 *(978-1-891577-52-9(2)*, SAN299-4844) Images Pr.
Tucker, Jasmine. Robbie the Robot. 2013. 20p. pap. 24.95 *(978-1-63004-493-0(8))* America Star Bks.
Van Dusen, Chris. Randy Riley's Really Big Hit. Van Dusen, Chris, illus. (ENG., Illus.). 32p. (J). (gr. -1-3). 2016. 8.99 *(978-0-7636-8774-8(X))* 2012. 17.99 *(978-0-7636-4946-3(5))* Candlewick Pr.
Vaughan, M. M. Friendroid. (ENG.). (J). (gr. 3-7). 2020. 400p. pap. 8.99 *(978-1-4814-9066-5(4))* 2019. (Illus.). 384p. 17.99 *(978-1-4814-9065-8(6))* McElderry, Margaret K. Bks. (McElderry, Margaret K. Bks.).
Venditti, Robert. Rise of the Robot Army. Higgins, Dusty, illus. 2016. (Miles Taylor & the Golden Cape Ser.: 2). (ENG.). 304p. (J). (gr. 4-7). 16.99 *(978-1-4814-0557-7(8)*, Simon & Schuster Bks. For Young Readers) Simon & Schuster Bks. For Young Readers.
Villeneuve, Kevin J. The Adventures of Nick the Ecologist & His Robot O-Zone: The Mystery of the Missing Trees. 2007. 96p. per. 9.95 *(978-0-595-42362-0(0))* iUniverse, Inc.
Vlock, Rob. Sven Carter & the Android Army. 2018. (Max Ser.). (ENG.). 368p. (J). (gr. 4-8). 18.99 *(978-1-4814-9017-7(6))*; (Illus.). pap. 7.99 *(978-1-4814-9016-0(8))* Simon & Schuster Children's Publishing. (Aladdin).
—Sven Carter & the Trashmouth Effect. 2017. (Max Ser.). (ENG.). 400p. (J). (gr. 4-8). 17.99 *(978-1-4814-9014-6(1))*; (Illus.). pap. 7.99 *(978-1-4814-9013-9(3))* Simon & Schuster Children's Publishing. (Aladdin).
Weber, Erec-Michael Ollier. Bryce & the Blood Ninjas. Harvey II, Alvin, illus. 2013. 38p. pap. 20.00 *(978-0-9716481-9-7(0))* Kila Springs Pr.
Webster, Christy. Green Team! 2012. (Step into Reading Level 4 Ser.). lib. bdg. 13.55 *(978-0-606-26801-1(4))* Turtleback.
—Robot Rampage! 2013. (Step into Reading Level 4 Ser.). lib. bdg. 13.55 *(978-0-606-26985-8(1))* Turtleback.
—Robot Rampage! (Teenage Mutant Ninja Turtles) Spaziante, Patrick, illus. 2013. (Step into Reading Ser.). (ENG.). 48p. (J). (gr. k-3). pap. 5.99 *(978-0-307-98212-4(2)*, Random Hse. Bks. for Young Readers) Random Hse. Children's Bks.
Wells, Dan. Partials. (ENG.). (YA). 2013. (Partials Sequence Ser.: 1). 528p. (gr. 9). pap. 11.99 *(978-0-06-207105-7(X)*, Balzer & Bray) 2012. (Partials Sequence Ser.: 1). 480p. (gr. 9). 17.99 *(978-0-06-207104-0(1)*, Balzer & Bray) 2012. 496p. pap. 9.99 *(978-0-06-213569-8(4))* HarperCollins Pubs.
Wells, Robison. Feedback. (ENG.). (YA). 2013. (Variant Ser.: 2). 336p. (gr. 8). pap. 10.99 *(978-0-06-202611-8(9))* 2012. 320p. pap. 9.99 *(978-0-06-222830-7(7))* HarperCollins Pubs. (HarperTeen).
West, Tracey. Me & My Robot. Revell, Cindy, illus. 2003. (Penguin Young Readers, Level 2 Ser.). (ENG.). 32p. (J). (gr. 1-2). mass mkt. 5.99 *(978-0-448-42895-6(4)*, Penguin Young Readers) Penguin Young Readers Group.
—Me & My Robot No.2: The Show-and-Tell Show-Off. 2003. (Penguin Young Readers Level 2 Ser.). (gr. k-3). lib. bdg. 13.55 *(978-0-613-64065-7(9))* Turtleback.
West, Tracey, adapted by. Robotic Fish Gone Wild! 2005. (Illus.). 30p. (J). pap. *(978-0-439-76833-7(0))* Scholastic, Inc.
Wheeler, Shannon & Torres, J. Wall E Vol. 1: Recharge. Luthi, Morgan, illus. 2010. (ENG.). 112p. (J). 24.99 *(978-1-60886-554-3(1))* BOOM! Studios.
Wheeler, Shannon, et al. Wall-E Vol. 1: Recharge. Luthi, Morgan & Barks, Carl, illus. 2010. (ENG.). 112p. (J). pap. 9.99 *(978-1-60886-512-3(6))* BOOM! Studios.
Winick, Judd. Hilo Book 1: the Boy Who Crashed to Earth: (a Graphic Novel) 2015. (Hilo Ser.: 1). (ENG., Illus.). 208p. (J). (gr. 3-7). 16.99 *(978-0-385-38618-0(4))* Penguin Random Hse. LLC.
—Hilo Book 2: Saving the Whole Wide World: (a Graphic Novel) 2016. (Hilo Ser.: 2). (ENG., Illus.). 208p. (J). (gr. 3-7). 16.99 *(978-0-385-38624-1(9))*;Bk. 2. 13.99 *(978-0-385-38623-4(0))* Penguin Random Hse. LLC.
—Hilo Book 4: Waking the Monsters: (a Graphic Novel) 2018. (Hilo Ser.: 4). (Illus.). 208p. (J). (gr. 3-7). 13.99 *(978-1-5247-1493-2(3))* Penguin Random Hse. LLC.
—Hilo Book 6: All the Pieces Fit: (a Graphic Novel) 2020. (Hilo Ser.: 6). (Illus.). 224p. (J). (gr. 3-7). 13.99 *(978-0-525-64406-4(7))*; (ENG., 16.99 *(978-0-525-64407-1(5))* Penguin Random Hse. LLC.
Winkler, Henry & Oliver, Lin. Robot on the Loose. 2018. (Here's Hank Ser.: 11). lib. bdg. 16.00 *(978-0-606-40886-8(X))* Turtleback.
Yaccarino, Dan. Doug Unplugged. 2016. (ENG.). 40p. (J). (gr. k-4). 8.99 *(978-0-375-85921-2(7)*, Dragonfly Bks.) Random Hse. Children's Bks.
—Zorgoochi Intergalactic Pizza: Delivery of Doom. Yaccarino, Dan, illus. 2014. (ENG., Illus.). 336p. (J). (gr. 3-7). 16.99 *(978-1-250-00844-2(1)*, 900083572) Feiwel & Friends.
Zafon, Carlos Ruiz. The Watcher in the Shadows. (ENG.). (YA). (gr. 7-17). 2014. 288p. pap. 15.99 *(978-0-316-04475-2(X))* 2013. 272p. 18.00 *(978-0-316-04476-9(8))* Little, Brown Bks. for Young Readers.
Zuchora-Walske, Christine. Weather Robots. 2014. (Lightning Bolt Books (r) — Robots Everywhere! Ser.). (ENG., Illus.). 32p. (J). (gr. 1-3). lib. bdg. 29.32 *(978-1-4677-4057-9(8)*, 62878b01-b114-4a48-bc17-cf0f99a490e3, Lerner Pubns.) Lerner Publishing Group.

ROCK CLIMBING

see Mountaineering

ROCK MUSIC

Aberback, Brian. Black Sabbath: Pioneers of Heavy Metal, 1 vol. 2011. (Rebels of Rock Ser.). (ENG., Illus.). 112p. (gr. 5-6). 35.93 *(978-0-7660-3379-5(1)*, 01aedc0e-5be6-4d2a-9523-2220e98eb30b) Enslow Publishing, LLC.
Alagna, Magdalena. Elvis Presley. 2009. (Rock & Roll Hall of Famers Ser.). 112p. (gr. 5-8). 63.90 *(978-1-60852-474-7(4)*, Rosen Reference) Rosen Publishing Group, Inc., The.
Altmann, Scott. Guitar Rock Star Sticker Activity Book. 2008. (Dover Little Activity Bks.). (ENG.). 4p. (J). (gr. -1-5). pap. 1.50 *(978-0-486-46790-0(2))* Dover Pubns., Inc.
Anderson, Tom. Top 40 Fun Facts: Rock & Roll (Classroom Resource) Ready-To-use Reproducible Activities. 2003. (ENG.). 64p. pap. 27.99 *(978-0-634-06552-1(1)*, 09970424) Leonard, Hal Corp.
Anniss, Matt. Music, Fashion, & Style. 2015. (Music Scene Ser.). (J). lib. bdg. 37.10 *(978-1-59920-912-8(8))* Black Rabbit Bks.
—Performing Live. 2015. (Music Scene Ser.). (J). lib. bdg. 37.10 *(978-1-59920-913-5(6))* Black Rabbit Bks.
—The Story of Punk & Indie. 2013. (Pop Histories Ser.). 32p. (gr. 4-7). 31.35 *(978-1-59920-968-5(3))* Black Rabbit Bks.
—The Story of Rock Music. 2013. (Pop Histories Ser.). 32p. (gr. 4-9). 28.50 *(978-1-59920-969-2(1))* Black Rabbit Bks.
Barbo, Maria S. Doodlemaster: Rock Star! Rock Star! Gonzales, Chuck, illus. 2009. (ENG.). 128p. (J). (gr. 2-6). pap. 16.99 *(978-0-312-59606-4(5)*, 900062987) Feiwel & Friends.
Bowe, Brian J. The Clash: Punk Rock Band, 1 vol. 2011. (Rebels of Rock Ser.). (ENG., Illus.). 112p. (gr. 5-6). 35.93 *(978-0-7660-3232-3(9)*, 602272af-388d-4934-85fe-cc2214e4710f) Enslow Publishing, LLC.
—Judas Priest: Metal Gods, 1 vol. 2009. (Rebels of Rock Ser.). (ENG., Illus.). 112p. (gr. 5-6). lib. bdg. 35.93 *(978-0-7660-3029-9(6)*, 7fa2ddaf-900e-403d-8613-b00a3a04bf1f) Enslow Publishing, LLC.
—The Ramones: American Punk Rock Band, 1 vol. 2011. (Rebels of Rock Ser.). (ENG., Illus.). 128p. (gr. 5-6). 35.93 *(978-0-7660-3233-0(7)*, 0a7ab8f0-3268-4e30-97c4-c655d5bd00c5) Enslow Publishing, LLC.
Breguet, Amy. Yellowcard. 2009. (Contemporary Musicians & Their Music Ser.). 48p. (gr. 6-6). 53.00 *(978-1-61511-948-6(5))* Rosen Publishing Group, Inc., The.
Broadbent, Paul. Rock Stars. 2007. (Trackers-Math Ser.). (gr. 2-5). pap. 5.00 *(978-1-59055-939-0(8))* Pacific Learning, Inc.
Burlingame, Jeff. Aerosmith, 1 vol. 2018. (Bands That Rock! Ser.). (ENG.). 112p. (YA). (gr. 7-7). 38.93 *(978-1-9785-0346-5(6)*, 24e6c9b7-cf87-40e6-b328-7f9f2c651089) Enslow Publishing, LLC.
—Aerosmith: Hard Rock Superstars, 1 vol. 2011. (Rebels of Rock Ser.). (ENG., Illus.). 112p. (gr. 5-6). 35.93 *(978-0-7660-3236-1(1)*, 3e972e34-a73c-4ad8-ac8d-7ba3a9e94d9c) Enslow Publishing, LLC.
Capaccio, George. How Rent Made It to the Stage, 1 vol. 2018. (Getting to Broadway Ser.). (ENG.). 96p. (YA). (gr. 8-8). 45.93 *(978-1-5026-3511-2(9)*, 1ce0e879-6c76-441b-a2cb-5f872d058384) Cavendish Square Publishing LLC.
Carr, Aaron. Rock. 2015. (J). *(978-1-4896-3593-8(9))* Weigl Pubs., Inc.
Clayton, Marie. Elvis Presley: Unseen Archives. (Unseen Archives Ser.). (Illus.). 384p. *(978-0-7525-8335-8(2))* Parragon, Inc.
Cooper, Ilene. This Boy: The Early Lives of John Lennon & Paul Mccartney. 2023. (Illus.). 192p. (J). (gr. 5-9). 17.99 ***(978-0-451-47585-5(2)***, Viking Books for Young Readers) Penguin Young Readers Group.
Corporate Contributor Staff & Perl, Sheri. The Economics of a Rock Concert. 2013. (ENG.). 48p. (J). *(978-0-7787-7969-8(6))*; pap. *(978-0-7787-7974-2(2))* Crabtree Publishing Co.
Dakers, Diane. The Beatles: Leading the British Invasion. 2013. (ENG., Illus.). 112p. (J). *(978-0-7787-1035-6(1))* Crabtree Publishing Co.
Doeden, Matt. Green Day: Keeping Their Edge. 2007. (Gateway Biography Ser.). (Illus.). 48p. (J). (gr. 4-8). pap. 8.95 *(978-0-8225-6429-4(7))* Lerner Publishing Group.
Doll, Susan. Elvis Presley: With Profiles of Muddy Waters & Mick Jagger. 2006. (Biographical Connections Ser.). (Illus.). 112p. (J). *(978-0-7166-1823-2(0))* World Bk., Inc.
Edgers, Geoff. Who Were the Beatles? Tageau, Jerry, illus. 2006. (Who Was... ? Ser.). 106p. (J). *(978-0-448-43907-5(7)*, Grosset & Dunlap) Penguin Publishing Group.
Edgers, Geoff & Who HQ. Who Were the Beatles? Tugeau, Jeremy, illus. 2006. (Who Was? Ser.). 112p. (J). (gr. 3-7). pap. 6.99 *(978-0-448-43906-8(9)*, Penguin Workshop) Penguin Young Readers Group.
Edward, Herman. Pink Floyd. 2007. (Popular Rock Superstars of Yesterday & Today Ser.). (Illus.). 64p. (YA). (gr. 3-7). pap. 7.95 *(978-1-4222-0313-2(1))* Mason Crest.
Faber, Nancy, et al. ShowTime Piano Rock 'n Roll - Level 2A. 2012. (ENG.). 24p. pap. 5.99 *(978-1-61677-632-9(3)*, 00420329) Faber Piano Adventures(r).
Farseth, Erik. American Rock: Guitar Heroes, Punks, & Metalheads. 2012. (American Music Milestones Ser.). (ENG., Illus.). 64p. (J). (gr. 5-12). lib. bdg. 30.65 *(978-0-7613-4503-9(5)*, 869b1f13-0bf3-4c72-a14d-100a04c6b14c, Twenty-First Century Bks.) Lerner Publishing Group.
Flynn, Noa. The Who. 2007. (Popular Rock Superstars of Yesterday & Today Ser.). (Illus.). 64p. (YA). (gr. 3-7). pap. 7.95 *(978-1-4222-0323-1(9))* Mason Crest.
Forget, Thomas. The Rolling Stones. 2009. (Rock & Roll Hall of Famers Ser.). 112p. (gr. 5-8). 63.90 *(978-1-60852-478-5(7)*, Rosen Reference) Rosen Publishing Group, Inc., The.
Gillie, Brian. A Guide to the Best Vocal Harmonies of Rock 'n' Roll: 1955 - 1985. 2004. 225p. 27.00 *(978-0-9760837-1-9(X))*; per. 35.00 *(978-0-9760837-0-2(1))* Keysquake Music.
Golio, Gary. Jimi: Sounds Like a Rainbow: A Story of the Young Jimi Hendrix. Steptoe, Javaka, illus. 2010. (ENG.). 32p. (J). (gr. 1-4). 17.99 *(978-0-618-85279-6(4)*, 100567, Clarion Bks.) HarperCollins Pubs.
Gregory, Peter. The Allman Brothers Band. 2007. (Popular Rock Superstars of Yesterday & Today Ser.). (Illus.). 64p. (YA). (gr. 3-7). pap. 7.95 *(978-1-4222-0310-1(7))* Mason Crest.
—Queen. 2007. (Popular Rock Superstars of Yesterday & Today Ser.). (Illus.). 64p. (YA). (gr. 4-7). pap. 7.95 *(978-1-4222-0318-7(2))* Mason Crest.
Handyside, Chris. A History of Rock & Roll. 2006. (J). *(978-1-4109-1815-4(7))* Steck-Vaughn.
Harmon, Daniel E. How to Start Your Own Band, 1 vol. 2011. (Garage Bands Ser.). (ENG.). 64p. (YA). (gr. 5-5). pap. 13.95 *(978-1-4488-5661-9(2)*, ebf6c50f-1b61-4635-ae07-d5941e3cd499); lib. bdg. 37.13 *(978-1-4488-5657-2(4)*, 4cd33bf9-90a5-4f7c-a0ad-daf21fa5c676) Rosen Publishing Group, Inc., The. (Rosen Reference).
—Managing Your Band, 1 vol. 2011. (Garage Bands Ser.). (ENG.). 64p. (YA). (gr. 5-5). pap. 13.95 *(978-1-4488-5663-3(9)*, 7add6cee-a746-43c1-8bb5-c4e521753e73); lib. bdg. 37.13 *(978-1-4488-5659-6(0)*, 9ee39fc5-90b3-4286-bdf9-087b9c5584ad) Rosen Publishing Group, Inc., The.
Hollow, Michele C. Grateful Dead: What a Long, Strange Trip It's Been, 1 vol. 2009. (Rebels of Rock Ser.). (ENG., Illus.). 104p. (gr. 5-6). lib. bdg. 35.93 *(978-0-7660-3028-2(8)*, 0ab61506-0b7e-4e82-84eb-73d1b93bf997) Enslow Publishing, LLC.
Holub, Joan. What Was Woodstock? Copeland, Gregory, illus. 2016. (What Was-? Chapter Ser.). (ENG.). 112p. (J). (gr. 3-6). 18.69 *(978-1-4844-6936-1(4))* Penguin Publishing Group.
—What Was Woodstock? 2016. (What Was... Ser.). (Illus.). 108p. (J). lib. bdg. 16.00 *(978-0-606-38414-8(6))* Turtleback.
Holub, Joan & Who HQ. What Was Woodstock? Copeland, Gregory, illus. 2016. (What Was? Ser.). 112p. (J). (gr. 3-7). 5.99 *(978-0-448-48696-3(2)*, Penguin Workshop) Penguin Young Readers Group.
Jay, Aye. The Punk Rock Fun Time Activity Book. 2009. (ENG., Illus.). 48p. pap. 9.95 *(978-1-55022-872-4(2)*, 3ab535a3-3663-4173-b1ce-27c6e2be7aee) ECW Pr. CAN. Dist: Baker & Taylor Publisher Services (BTPS).
Johnson, Robin. The Jonas Brothers. 2010. (Superstars! Ser.). (ENG.). 32p. (J). pap. *(978-0-7787-7256-9(X))* Crabtree Publishing Co.
Juzwiak, Rich. Lifehouse. 2009. (Contemporary Musicians & Their Music Ser.). 48p. (gr. 6-6). 53.00 *(978-1-61511-941-7(8))* Rosen Publishing Group, Inc., The.
Juzwiak, Richard. Lifehouse, 1 vol. 2006. (Contemporary Musicians & Their Music Ser.). (ENG., Illus.). 48p. (YA). (gr. 6-6). lib. bdg. 34.47 *(978-1-4042-0710-3(4)*, 2a50c4c6-5c88-4f2e-8cf0-0e761c3800e6) Rosen Publishing Group, Inc., The.
Kallen, Stuart A. Bono. (Role Model Entertainers Ser.). (Illus.). 64p. (YA). 2010. (gr. 7-12). 22.95 *(978-1-4222-0499-3(5))* 2007. pap. 9.95 *(978-1-4222-0786-4(2))* Mason Crest.
—The History of Alternative Rock, 1 vol. 2012. (Music Library). (ENG., Illus.). 120p. (gr. 7-10). lib. bdg. 41.03

(978-1-4205-0738-6(9), 8e263843-1617-460c-8e56-4dd73e3d7b06, Lucent Pr.) Greenhaven Publishing LLC.

—The History of Rock & Roll, 1 vol. 2012. (Music Library). (ENG., Illus.). 128p. (gr. 7-10). lib. bdg. 41.03 *(978-1-4205-0694-5(3),* e2b60ede-194e-4c08-9bf2-938d88b92cad, Lucent Pr.) Greenhaven Publishing LLC.

Kenney, Karen Latchana. Cool Rock Music: Create & Appreciate What Makes Music Great! 2008. (Cool Music Ser.). (ENG., Illus.). 32p. (J). (gr. 3-6). 34.21 *(978-1-59928-974-8(1),* 372, Checkerboard Library) ABDO Publishing Co.

La Bella, Laura. My Chemical Romance, 1 vol. 2008. (Contemporary Musicians & Their Music Ser.). (ENG., Illus.). 48p. (J). (gr. 6-6). lib. bdg. 34.47 *(978-1-4042-1818-5(1),* 4cb39b1a-962b-4483-bb30-876a0e557f8c) Rosen Publishing Group, Inc., The.

Marcovitz, Hal. Rock 'n Roll. 2004. (American Symbols & Their Meanings Ser.). (Illus.). 48p. (J). (gr. 4-18). lib. bdg. 19.95 *(978-1-59084-036-8(4))* Mason Crest.

—Rock 'N' Roll: Voice of American Youth. Moreno, Barry, ed. 2014. (Patriotic Symbols of America Ser.: 20). (Illus.). 48p. (J). (gr. 4-18). lib. bdg. 20.95 *(978-1-4222-3129-6(1))* Mason Crest.

Markel, Rita J. Jimi Hendrix. (Biography Ser.). (Illus.). 112p. (gr. 6-12). 2005. (J). lib. bdg. 27.93 *(978-0-8225-4990-1(5))* 2003. (YA). pap. 7.95 *(978-0-8225-9697-4(0),* Carolrhoda Bks.) Lerner Publishing Group.

Markel, Rita J. & Poole, Rebecca. Jimi Hendrix. 2006. (Just the Facts Biographies Ser.). (ENG., Illus.). 112p. (gr. 5-12). 27.93 *(978-0-8225-3532-4(7),* Lerner Pubns.) Lerner Publishing Group.

Masar, Brendan. The History of Punk Rock, 1 vol. 2006. (Music Library). (ENG., Illus.). 104p. (gr. 7-10). lib. bdg. 35.73 *(978-1-59018-738-8(5),* 0235e321-8c27-4bcf-b0f5-13353301275c, Lucent Pr.) Greenhaven Publishing LLC.

Mattern, Joanne. Jonas Brothers. 2008. (Robbie Reader Ser.). (Illus.). 32p. (YA). (gr. 2-5). lib. bdg. 25.70 *(978-1-58415-721-2(6))* Mitchell Lane Pubs.

McIntosh, Kenneth. The Grateful Dead. 2007. (Popular Rock Superstars of Yesterday & Today Ser.). (Illus.). 64p. (YA). (gr. 4-7). pap. 7.95 *(978-1-4222-0314-9(X))* Mason Crest.

—U2. 2007. (Popular Rock Superstars of Yesterday & Today Ser.). (Illus.). 64p. (YA). (gr. 4-7). pap. 7.95 *(978-1-4222-0322-4(0))* Mason Crest.

Mead, Wendy. The Alternative Rock Scene: The Stars, the Fans, the Music, 1 vol. 2009. (Music Scene Ser.). (ENG., Illus.). 48p. (gr. 5-7). lib. bdg. 27.93 *(978-0-7660-3401-3(1),* 66c09e48-b52d-4d67-af60-6a3ec197125d) Enslow Publishing, LLC.

Merwin, E. Adam Levine. 2018. (Amazing Americans: Pop Music Stars Ser.). (ENG.). 24p. (J). (gr. -1-3). 26.99 *(978-1-68402-680-7(6))* Bearport Publishing Co., Inc.

Miles Kelly Staff. Rock & Pop. 2003. (Flip Quiz Ser.). (Illus.). 152p. (J). spiral bd. 12.95 *(978-1-84236-145-0(7))* Miles Kelly Publishing, Ltd. GBR. Dist: Independent Pubs. Group.

Morse, Eric. What Is Punk? Yi, Anny, illus. 2015. (ENG.). 32p. (J). 15.95 *(978-1-61775-392-3(0),* Black Sheep) Akashic Bks.

Nabais, Rita. The History of Rock: For Big Fans & Little Punks. Raimundo, Joana, illus. 2019. (ENG.). 112p. (J). (gr. 3-6). 19.95 *(978-1-62937-733-9(3))* Triumph Bks.

O'Connor, Jim. What Is Rock & Roll? Copeland, Gregory, illus. 2017. 105p. (J). *(978-1-5379-2401-4(X),* Penguin Workshop) Penguin Young Readers Group.

O'Connor, Jim & Who HQ. What Is Rock & Roll? Copeland, Gregory, illus. 2017. (What Was? Ser.). 112p. (J). (gr. 3-7). 7.99 *(978-0-451-53381-4(X),* Penguin Workshop) Penguin Young Readers Group.

Okun, Milton, ed. Great Rock Ballads. 104p. (YA). pap. 15.95 *(978-0-89524-936-4(7),* 02502173) Cherry Lane Music Co.

—Shawn Colvin - Cover Girl. 32p. (Orig.). (YA). pap. 12.95 *(978-0-89524-867-1(0),* 02506918) Cherry Lane Music Co.

O'Mahony, John. Elton John. 2003. (World Musicmakers Ser.). (Illus.). 64p. (J). 26.20 *(978-1-56711-972-5(7),* Blackbirch Pr., Inc.) Cengage Gale.

Overbey, Theresa. Michael Jackson. l.t. ed. 2003. (Blue Banner Biography Ser.). (Illus.). 32p. (J). (gr. 3-8). lib. bdg. 25.70 *(978-1-58415-216-3(8))* Mitchell Lane Pubs.

Owen, Ruth. I Can Start a Band!, 1 vol. 2017. (Kids Can Do It! Ser.). (ENG.). 32p. (gr. 3-3). 30.27 *(978-1-4994-8347-5(3),* 2488a601-74ef-402d-a139-b94b3a54a15b, Windmill Bks.) Rosen Publishing Group, Inc., The.

Polark, Kelly. Rockabet: Classic Edition. Little, Kelli Ann, illus. 2013. 32p. pap. 10.49 *(978-0-9888462-0-3(9))* Big Smile Pr., LLC.

Pop Rock: Popular Rock Superstars of Yesterday & Today, 17 vols., Set. Incl. AC/DC. Schlesinger, Ethan. (gr. 3-7). lib. bdg. 22.95 *(978-1-4222-0183-1(X));* Aerosmith. Schlesinger, Ethan. (gr. 3-7). lib. bdg. 22.95 *(978-1-4222-0184-8(8));* Allman Brothers. Gregory, Peter. (gr. 3-7). lib. bdg. 22.95 *(978-1-4222-0188-6(0));* Beatles. Gallagher, James. (gr. 4-7). lib. bdg. 22.95 *(978-1-4222-0186-2(4));* Billy Joel. Schlesinger, Ethan. (gr. 3-7). lib. bdg. 22.95 *(978-1-4222-0185-5(6));* Bob Marley & the Wailers. Waters, Rosa. (gr. 7-18). lib. bdg. 22.95 *(978-1-4222-0192-3(9));* Bruce Springsteen. Simons, Rae. (gr. 4-7). lib. bdg. 22.95 *(978-1-4222-0187-9(2));* Doors. Simons, Rae. (gr. 3-7). lib. bdg. 22.95 *(978-1-4222-0190-9(2));* Elton John. Schlesinger, Ethan. (gr. 3-7). lib. bdg. 22.95 *(978-1-4222-0189-3(9));* Grateful Dead. McIntosh, Kenneth. (gr. 4-7). lib. bdg. 22.95 *(978-1-4222-0191-6(0));* Led Zeppelin. Schlesinger, Ethan. (gr. 3-7). lib. bdg. 22.95 *(978-1-4222-0212-8(7));* Lynyrd Skynrd. Walker, Ida. (gr. 4-7). lib. bdg. 22.95 *(978-1-4222-0213-5(5));* Pink Floyd. Edward, Herman. (gr. 3-7). lib. bdg. 22.95 *(978-1-4222-0214-2(3));* Queen. Gregory, Peter. (gr. 4-7). lib. bdg. 22.95 *(978-1-4222-0193-0(7));* Rolling Stones. Schlesinger, Ethan. (gr. 3-7). lib. bdg. 22.95 *(978-1-4222-0194-7(5));* Who. Flynn, Noa. (gr. 3-7). lib. bdg. 22.95 *(978-1-4222-0196-1(1));* (Illus.). 64p. (YA). 2008. 2007. Set lib. bdg. 390.15 *(978-1-4222-0182-4(1))* Mason Crest.

Rau, Dana Meachen. Who Are the Rolling Stones? Thomson, Andrew, illus. 2017. 107p. (J). *(978-1-5182-4233-5(2),* Grosset & Dunlap) Penguin Young Readers Group.

—Who Are the Rolling Stones? 2017. (Who Is... ? Ser.). (Illus.). 107p. (J). lib. bdg. 16.00 *(978-0-606-39778-0(7))* Turtleback.

Reisfeld, Randi. This Is the Sound: The Best of Alternative Rock. 2011. (ENG.). 144p. (YA). (gr. 9). pap. 8.99 *(978-1-4424-3098-3(2),* Simon Pulse) Simon Pulse.

Riggs, Kate. Rock 'n' Roll Music. 2006. (World of Music Ser.). (Illus.). 24p. (J). (gr. -1). lib. bdg. 24.25 *(978-1-58341-569-6(6),* Creative Education) Creative Co., The.

Rivera, Ursula. The Supremes. 2009. (Rock & Roll Hall of Famers Ser.). 112p. (gr. 5-8). 63.90 *(978-1-60852-479-2(5),* Rosen Reference) Rosen Publishing Group, Inc., The.

Roberts, Jeremy. The Beatles. (Biography Ser.). (Illus.). 112p. (J). (gr. 6-12). 2005. lib. bdg. 27.93 *(978-0-8225-4998-7(0))* 2003. pap. 7.95 *(978-0-8225-5002-0(4))* Lerner Publishing Group.

—Bob Dylan: Voice of a Generation. 128p. (J). (gr. 6-18). 18.95 *(978-1-58013-155-1(7),* Kar-Ben Publishing) Lerner Publishing Group.

Robison, Greg. Christian Rock Festivals. (Monster Music Festivals Ser.). 48p. (gr. 5-6). 2009. 53.00 *(978-1-61514-650-5(4),* Rosen Reference) 2008. (ENG., Illus.). (J). lib. bdg. 34.47 *(978-1-4042-1784-3(3),* 9fd40ba8-3226-4e76-9532-00e30d64f22a) 2008. (ENG., Illus.). pap. 12.75 *(978-1-4358-5122-1(6),* a7dca1e3-0654-47df-bb27-1f709830ac45, Rosen Reference) Rosen Publishing Group, Inc., The.

—Coachella, 1 vol. 2008. (Monster Music Festivals Ser.). (ENG., 48p. (gr. 5-6). Illus.). (J). lib. bdg. 34.47 *(978-1-4042-1755-3(X),* 3858f00f-d3d2-499c-96cf-1806bc6a094f); pap. 12.75 *(978-1-4358-5120-7(X),* caf73875-5274-4948-a672-6689494f58e2, Rosen Classroom) Rosen Publishing Group, Inc., The.

—Ozzfest. (Monster Music Festivals Ser.). 48p. (gr. 5-6). 2009. 53.00 *(978-1-61514-656-7(3),* Rosen Reference) 2008. (ENG., Illus.). (J). lib. bdg. 34.47 *(978-1-4042-1756-0(8),* b070d9ac-89b8-421f-8785-b9decde92ee5) Rosen Publishing Group, Inc., The.

—Vans Warped Tour. (Monster Music Festivals Ser.). 48p. (gr. 5-6). 2009. 53.00 *(978-1-61514-659-8(8),* Rosen Reference) 2008. (ENG., Illus.). (J). lib. bdg. 34.47 *(978-1-4042-1754-6(1),* fc4667ca-e0b8-4add-b1f6-ee71e9799885) 2008. (ENG.). pap. 12.75 *(978-1-4358-5119-1(6),* 1539c0f9-3c72-457e-830a-380ce7135e0c, Rosen Classroom) Rosen Publishing Group, Inc., The.

Robson, David. Prince: Singer-Songwriter, Musician, & Record Producer. (Transcending Race in America Ser.). 64p. (YA). 2010. (Illus.). (gr. 4-8). lib. bdg. 22.95 *(978-1-4222-1614-9(4))* 2009. (gr. 5-18). pap. 9.95 *(978-1-4222-1628-6(4))* Mason Crest.

Rosen, Steven & Steventon, John. History of Rock. 2009. (Crabtree Contact Ser.). (ENG., Illus.). 32p. (J). (gr. 6-8). pap. *(978-0-7787-3844-2(2));* lib. bdg. *(978-0-7787-3823-7(X))* Crabtree Publishing Co.

Saulmon, Greg. Linkin Park. 2009. (Contemporary Musicians & Their Music Ser.). 48p. (gr. 6-6). 53.00 *(978-1-61511-942-4(6))* Rosen Publishing Group, Inc., The.

Schaffer, David. Bono. 2003. (Illus.). 112p. (J). 32.45 *(978-1-59018-274-1(X),* Lucent Bks.) Cengage Gale.

Schlesinger, Ethan. AC/DC. 2008. (Pop Rock Ser.). (Illus.). 64p. (YA). (gr. 3-7). lib. bdg. 22.95 *(978-1-4222-0183-1(X))* Mason Crest.

—Aerosmith. (Pop Rock Ser.). (Illus.). 64p. (YA). (gr. 3-7). 2008. lib. bdg. 22.95 *(978-1-4222-0184-8(8))* 2007. pap. 7.95 *(978-1-4222-0309-5(3))* Mason Crest.

—Billy Joel. 2007. (Popular Rock Superstars of Yesterday & Today Ser.). (Illus.). 64p. (YA). (gr. 3-7). pap. 7.95 *(978-1-4222-0315-6(8))* Mason Crest.

—Led Zeppelin. 2008. (Pop Rock Ser.). (Illus.). 64p. (YA). (gr. 3-7). lib. bdg. 22.95 *(978-1-4222-0212-8(7))* Mason Crest.

—The Rolling Stones. 2007. (Popular Rock Superstars of Yesterday & Today Ser.). (Illus.). 64p. (YA). (gr. 3-7). pap. 7.95 *(978-1-4222-0319-4(0))* Mason Crest.

Schuman, Michael A. Bob Dylan: Singer, Songwriter, & Music Icon, 1 vol. 2018. (Influential Lives Ser.). (ENG.). 128p. (gr. 7-7). 40.27 *(978-0-7660-9206-8(2),* 2ae90c4b-9d85-4d39-9b1e-913435f4f042) Enslow Publishing, LLC.

Simons, Rae. The Doors. 2007. (Popular Rock Superstars of Yesterday & Today Ser.). (Illus.). 64p. (YA). (gr. 3-7). pap. 7.95 *(978-1-4222-0312-5(3))* Mason Crest.

Skancke, Jennifer L. The History of Indie Rock, 1 vol. 2007. (Music Library). (ENG., Illus.). 104p. (J). (gr. 7-10). lib. bdg. 41.03 *(978-1-59018-736-4(9),* 4ef7e293-c98b-44e2-ac85-f3b5aaa8e73e, Lucent Pr.) Greenhaven Publishing LLC.

Slavicek, Louise Chipley. Carlos Santana. 2006. (Great Hispanic Heritage Ser.). (ENG., Illus.). 112p. (gr. 6-12). lib. bdg. 35.00 *(978-0-7910-8844-9(8),* P114456, Facts On File) Infobase Holdings, Inc.

Tracy, Kathleen. Chris Daughtry. 2007. (Blue Banner Biography Ser.). (Illus.). 32p. (YA). (gr. 4-7). lib. bdg. 25.70 *(978-1-58415-629-1(5))* Mitchell Lane Pubs.

Vance, Vince. The Vince Vance Rock & Roll Reader: Bedtime Stories, Poems, Songs, Jokes, Pictures & Other Real Cool Stuff for Kids of All Ages. Pennington, Carole, ed. Looney, Bill, illus. Rice, Bob, photos by. 2003. 182p. (J). (gr. 3-8). per. *(978-0-9652918-0-4(4))* Fullerton Bks., Inc.

Wallenfeldt, Jeff, ed. The Birth of Rock & Roll: Music in the 1950s Through the 1960s, 1 vol. 2012. (Popular Music Through the Decades Ser.). (ENG., Illus.). 240p. (J). (gr. 9-9). lib. bdg. 48.59 *(978-1-61530-906-1(3),* cc269c07-99ff-4435-bc80-79ea03a6b91b) Rosen Publishing Group, Inc., The.

—The Birth of Rock & Roll: Music in the 1950S Through The 1960S, 4 vols. 2012. (Popular Music Through the Decades Ser.). (ENG., Illus.). 240p. (YA). (gr. 9-9). 97.18 *(978-1-61530-915-3(2),* 9a381669-fb5b-457e-96c5-932383442833) Rosen Publishing Group, Inc., The.

Watson, Stephanie. Prince: Musical Icon. 2016. (Lives Cut Short Ser.). (ENG., Illus.). 112p. (J). (gr. 6-12). lib. bdg. 41.36 *(978-1-68078-364-3(5),* 23216, Essential Library) ABDO Publishing Co.

Webster, Christine. The Jonas Brothers. 2009. (Remarkable People Ser.). (Illus.). 24p. (J). (gr. 4-6). pap. 8.95 *(978-1-60596-627-4(4));* lib. bdg. 24.45 *(978-1-60596-626-7(6))* Weigl Pubs., Inc.

Weintraub, Aileen. Kiss: I Wanna Rock & Roll All Night, 1 vol. 2009. (Rebels of Rock Ser.). (ENG., Illus.). 112p. (gr. 5-6). lib. bdg. 35.93 *(978-0-7660-3027-5(X),* e5140a54-8143-4870-abd7-f936c142f440) Enslow Publishing, LLC.

Wentzel, Jim. The Beatles. 2009. (Rock & Roll Hall of Famers Ser.). 112p. (gr. 5-8). 63.90 *(978-1-60852-477-8(9),* Rosen Reference) Rosen Publishing Group, Inc., The.

White, Katherine. Elton John. 2009. (Rock & Roll Hall of Famers Ser.). 112p. (gr. 5-8). 63.90 *(978-1-60852-473-0(6),* Rosen Reference) Rosen Publishing Group, Inc., The.

Wilhelm, Peggy Jo. The 10 Most Innovative Bands. 2008. 14.99 *(978-1-55448-554-3(1))* Scholastic Library Publishing.

Wimmer, Teresa. The Beatles' Sgt. Pepper's Lonely Hearts Club Band. 2008. (What in the World? Ser.). 22.95 *(978-1-58341-651-8(X),* Creative Education) Creative Co., The.

Winckelmann, Thom & Abushanab, Lynn. Bono: Rock Star & Humanitarian, 1 vol. 2009. (Essential Lives Set 4 Ser.). (ENG., Illus.). 112p. (YA). (gr. 6-12). lib. bdg. 41.36 *(978-1-60453-698-0(5),* 6687, Essential Library) ABDO Publishing Co.

Winter, Jonah. Elvis Is King! Red Nose Studio, illus. 2019. 40p. (J). (gr. -1-3). 18.99 *(978-0-399-55470-4(X),* Schwartz & Wade Bks.) Random Hse. Children's Bks.

Zimmerman, Robert. Switchfoot. 2009. (Contemporary Musicians & Their Music Ser.). 48p. (gr. 6-6). 53.00 *(978-1-61511-946-2(9))* Rosen Publishing Group, Inc., The.

Zimmerman, Robert K. Switchfoot, 1 vol. 2006. (Contemporary Musicians & Their Music Ser.). (ENG., Illus.). 48p. (YA). (gr. 6-6). lib. bdg. 34.47 *(978-1-4042-0709-7(0),* dad774c2-9a4c-4e0f-b792-3c54d034aeb5) Rosen Publishing Group, Inc., The.

ROCK MUSIC—FICTION

Alvin And The Chipmunks. 2009. 64p. 4.99 *(978-0-06-184568-0(X))* HarperCollins Pubs.

Ambrose, Adrianne. We're with the Band. 2011. (XOXO, Betty & Veronica Ser.). (ENG.). 192p. (J). (gr. 4-7). 17.44 *(978-0-448-45577-8(3),* Grosset & Dunlap) Penguin Publishing Group.

Auerbach, Annie. The Squeakquel: Battle of the Bands. 2009. (Alvin & the Chipmunks Ser.). (ENG., Illus.). 24p. (J). (gr. -1-2). pap. 3.99 *(978-0-06-184565-9(5),* HarperFestival) HarperCollins Pubs.

Auseon, Andrew. Jo-Jo & the Fiendish Lot. 2009. 473p. (YA). lib. bdg. 18.89 *(978-0-06-113924-6(6),* HarperTeen) HarperCollins Pubs.

Blount, Patty. The Way It Hurts. 2017. (ENG., Illus.). 400p. (YA). (gr. 8-12). pap. 10.99 *(978-1-4926-3278-8(3))* Sourcebooks, Inc.

Bradford, Chris. Bodyguard: Target (Book 7) 2018. (Bodyguard Ser.: 7). (ENG.). 288p. (J). (gr. 5). pap. 8.99 *(978-1-5247-3935-5(9),* Philomel Bks.) Penguin Young Readers Group.

—Bodyguard: Traitor (Book 8) 2018. (Bodyguard Ser.: 8). (ENG., Illus.). 224p. (J). (gr. 5). pap. 8.99 *(978-1-5247-3937-9(5),* Philomel Bks.) Penguin Young Readers Group.

Burian, Natalka. Welcome to the Slipstream. 2017. (ENG., Illus.). 272p. (YA). (gr. 9-12). 18.99 *(978-1-5072-0075-9(7),* Simon Pulse) Simon Pulse.

Calame, Don. Beat the Band. 2011. (ENG., Illus.). 400p. (YA). (gr. 9). pap. 11.99 *(978-0-7636-5663-8(1))* Candlewick Pr.

Camp Rock: Second Session: Super Special: under the Mistletoe (Camp Rock: Second Session) 2009. 256p. pap. 6.99 *(978-1-4231-2222-7(4))* Disney Pr.

Carbone, Courtney. Rock Stars! (Sunny Day) Hall, Susan, illus. 2018. (Step into Reading Ser.). (ENG.). 24p. (J). (gr. -1-1). pap. 4.99 *(978-1-5247-6862-1(6),* Random Hse. Bks. for Young Readers) Random Hse. Children's Bks.

Carlisle, Kelly. My Mommy Is A Rocker. 2007. (Illus.). 21p. (J). lib. bdg. *(978-0-9795046-2-4(7))* Kwist, Karla.

Castellucci, Cecil. Beige. (ENG., 320p. (YA). 2009. illus.). (gr. 9). pap. 8.99 *(978-0-7636-4232-7(0))* 2007. 25.66 *(978-1-4287-4767-8(2))* Candlewick Pr.

Chipponeri, Kelli. SpongeBob Rocks! Martinez, Heather, illus. 2006. (SpongeBob SquarePants Ser.: 9). (ENG.). 32p. (J). (gr. -1-3). pap. 3.99 *(978-1-4169-1314-6(9),* Simon Spotlight/Nickelodeon) Simon Spotlight/Nickelodeon.

Cohn, Rachel & Levithan, David. Nick & Norah's Infinite Playlist. 2009. 10.54 *(978-0-7848-2769-7(9),* Everbind) Marco Bk. Co.

—Nick & Norah's Infinite Playlist. 2007. 183p. (gr. 9-12). 19.00 *(978-0-7569-7949-2(8))* Perfection Learning Corp.

—Nick & Norah's Infinite Playlist. 2007. (ENG.). 208p. (YA). (gr. 9-12). pap. 9.99 *(978-0-375-83533-9(4),* Ember) Random Hse. Children's Bks.

Collins, Amberly & Collins, Brandilyn. Final Touch, 1 vol. 2010. (Rayne Tour Ser.). (ENG.). 224p. (YA). (gr. 8-11). pap. 9.99 *(978-0-310-71933-5(X))* Zondervan.

Colman, Michelle Sinclair. Rocker Babies Wear Jeans. Dion, Nathalie, illus. 2009. (Urban Babies Wear Black Book Ser.). (ENG.). 20p. (J). (gr. -1 — 1). bds. 6.99 *(978-1-58246-291-2(7),* Tricycle Pr.) Random Hse. Children's Bks.

Donbavand, Tommy. Scream Street: Flesh of the Zombie, Bk. 4. Cartoon Saloon, Ltd., illus. 2010. (Scream Street Ser.: 4). (ENG.). 128p. (J). (gr. 3-7). pap. 5.99 *(978-0-7636-4637-0(7))* Candlewick Pr.

Edwards, Garth. The Blue Wizard. Stasyuk, Max, illus. 2011. (Adventures of Titch & Mitch Ser.). (J). pap. *(978-0-9567449-9-9(0))* Inside Pocket Publishing, Ltd.

—The King of the Castle. Stasyuk, Max, illus. 2011. (Adventures of Titch & Mitch Ser.). (J). pap. *(978-0-9567449-7-5(4))* Inside Pocket Publishing, Ltd.

—The Magic Boots. Stasyuk, Max, illus. 2011. (Adventures of Titch & Mitch Ser.). (J). pap. *(978-0-9567449-8-2(2))* Inside Pocket Publishing, Ltd.

—The Trolls of Sugar Loaf Wood. Stasyuk, Max, illus. 2011. (Adventures of Titch & Mitch Ser.). (J). pap. *(978-0-9567449-6-8(6))* Inside Pocket Publishing, Ltd.

—The #02 Trolls of Sugar Loaf Wood. Stasyuk, Max, illus. 2011. (Adventures of Titch & Mitch, the Ser.). (J). pap. *(978-0-7613-8422-9(7))* Inside Pocket Publishing, Ltd.

—The #03 King of the Castle. Stasyuk, Max, illus. 2011. (Adventures of Titch & Mitch, the Ser.). (J). pap. *(978-0-7613-8423-6(5))* Inside Pocket Publishing, Ltd.

—The #04 Magic Boots. Stasyuk, Max, illus. 2011. (Adventures of Titch & Mitch, the Ser.). (J). pap. *(978-0-7613-8424-3(3))* Inside Pocket Publishing, Ltd.

—The #05 Blue Wizard. Stasyuk, Max, illus. 2011. (Adventures of Titch & Mitch, the Ser.). (J). pap. *(978-0-7613-8425-0(1))* Inside Pocket Publishing, Ltd.

Forman, Gayle. Sisters in Sanity. (YA). 2016. (ENG.). 304p. (gr. 8). pap. 9.99 *(978-0-06-088749-0(4))* 2007. 290p. (gr. 7-12). lib. bdg. 17.89 *(978-0-06-088748-3(6))* 2007. (ENG.). 304p. (gr. 7-18). 16.99 *(978-0-06-088747-6(8))* HarperCollins Pubs. (HarperTeen).

—Where She Went. l.t. ed. 2015. (If I Stay Ser.: BK.2). (ENG.). 288p. (YA). 23.99 *(978-1-4104-7562-6(X))* Cengage Gale.

—Where She Went. (ENG.). (YA). (gr. 9-18). 2012. 304p. 10.99 *(978-0-14-242089-8(1),* Speak) 2011. 272p. 17.99 *(978-0-525-42294-5(3),* Dutton Books for Young Readers) Penguin Young Readers Group.

—Where She Went. 2012. (If I Stay Ser.: BK.2). (YA). 21.00 *(978-1-61383-394-0(6))* Perfection Learning Corp.

—Where She Went. l.t. ed. 2015. (If I Stay Ser.: BK.2). (ENG.). 286p. (YA). pap. 12.99 *(978-1-59413-855-3(9),* Large Print Pr.) Thorndike Pr.

—Where She Went. 2012. (If I Stay Ser.: BK.2). (YA). lib. bdg. 22.10 *(978-0-606-23644-7(9))* Turtleback.

Garcia, Kami & Stohl, Margaret. Dangerous Creatures. 2014. 327p. (YA). *(978-0-316-37626-6(4))* Little, Brown Bks. for Young Readers.

Garcia, Kami & Stohl, Margaret. Dangerous Creatures. 2015. (ENG.). 400p. (J). (gr. 7-17). pap. 19.99 *(978-0-316-37032-5(0))* Little, Brown Bks. for Young Readers.

Gohmann, Johanna. Pleased to Eat You: Book 3. Zoloti?, Aleksandar, illus. 2018. (Electric Zombie Ser.). (ENG.). 112p. (J). (gr. 2-5). lib. bdg. 38.50 *(978-1-5321-3363-3(4),* 31149, Calico Chapter Bks.) ABDO Publishing Co.

Gonzalez, Gabriela & Triana, Gaby. Backstage Pass. 2004. (Illus.). 224p. (J). (gr. 7-18). 15.99 *(978-0-06-056017-1(7));* lib. bdg. 16.89 *(978-0-06-056018-8(5))* HarperCollins Pubs.

Gownley, Jimmy. Amelia in What Makes You Happy: #6, 1 vol. Gownley, Jimmy, illus. 2010. (Amelia Rules! Ser.). (ENG., Illus.). 36p. (J). (gr. 2-6). 31.36 *(978-1-59961-792-3(7),* 2385, Graphic Novels) Spotlight.

Graham, Hilary Weisman. Reunited. 2012. (ENG.). 336p. (YA). (gr. 7). 16.99 *(978-1-4424-3984-9(X),* Simon & Schuster Bks. For Young Readers) Simon & Schuster Bks. For Young Readers.

Hall, Susan, illus. Rock Stars! 2018. 24p. (J). *(978-1-5444-0161-4(2))* Random Hse., Inc.

Hood, Ann. She Loves You (Yeah, Yeah, Yeah) 2019. 288p. (J). (gr. 5). 8.99 *(978-1-5247-8512-3(1),* Penguin Workshop) Penguin Young Readers Group.

Hopkins, Cathy. The Princess of Pop. 2012. (Truth or Dare Ser.). (ENG.). 224p. (YA). (gr. 7). pap. 10.99 *(978-1-4424-6057-7(1),* Simon Pulse) Simon Pulse.

Huston, Donna. Vincent Rocks. 2006. (Illus.). 30p. (J). spiral bd. 19.99 *(978-0-9771192-0-2(3))* Shayne Publishing.

Jonas. JONAS #5: about Face. 5th ed. 2010. 128p. pap. 4.99 *(978-1-4231-1773-5(5))* Disney Pr.

—Three's a Crowd. 6th ed. 2010. 128p. pap. 4.99 *(978-1-4231-2282-1(8))* Disney Pr.

JONAS #8: Prep School Party. 2010. 128p. pap. 4.99 *(978-1-4231-2673-7(4))* Disney Pr.

Krosoczka, Jarrett J. Punk Farm. 2010. (Punk Farm Bks.). 40p. (J). (gr. -1-2). pap. 8.99 *(978-0-440-41793-4(7),* Dragonfly Bks.) Random Hse. Children's Bks.

Lane, Dakota. Orpheus Obsession. 2005. (Illus.). 288p. (J). lib. bdg. 17.89 *(978-0-06-074174-7(0),* HarperTeen) HarperCollins Pubs.

—The Orpheus Obsession. 2008. (ENG., Illus.). 288p. (YA). (gr. 9). pap. 8.99 *(978-0-06-074175-4(9),* HarperTeen) HarperCollins Pubs.

Ostow, Micol & Ostow, David. So Punk Rock: And Other Ways to Disappoint Your Mother. 2009. (ENG., Illus.). 264p. (YA). (gr. 6-8). 26.19 *(978-0-7387-1471-4(2),* Flux) North Star Editions.

Patterson, James & Tebbetts, Chris. Middle School: Born to Rock. Swaab, Neil, illus. 2019. (Middle School Ser.: 11). (ENG.). 320p. (J). (gr. 3-7). 14.99 *(978-0-316-34952-9(6),* Jimmy Patterson) Little Brown & Co.

Pérez, Celia C. The First Rule of Punk. (Illus.). 336p. (J). (gr. 4-7). 2018. 8.99 *(978-0-425-29042-2(5),* Puffin Books) 2017. 17.99 *(978-0-425-29040-8(9),* Viking Books for Young Readers) Penguin Young Readers Group.

Phillips, Dee. Scout, 1 vol. unabr. ed. 2010. (Right Now! Ser.). (ENG., Illus.). 45p. (YA). (gr. 9-12). pap. 10.75 *(978-1-61651-252-1(0))* Saddleback Educational Publishing, Inc.

Pollock, Hal. Meet the Brittles: In Monstermania. 2009. (ENG., Illus.). 32p. (J). (gr. -1-3). 15.95 *(978-1-59687-858-7(4))* IBks., Inc.

Powell, Randy. Tribute to Another Dead Rock Star. 2003. (ENG.). 224p. (YA). (gr. 7-12). pap. 15.99 *(978-0-374-47968-8(2),* 900021239, Farrar, Straus & Giroux (BYR)) Farrar, Straus & Giroux.

Pratt, Non. Remix. 2017. (ENG.). 320p. (YA). (gr. 9). pap. 10.99 *(978-1-4424-9776-4(9))* Simon & Schuster Children's Publishing.

Prendergast, Gabrielle. The Frail Days, 1 vol. 2015. (Orca Limelights Ser.). (ENG.). 128p. (J). (gr. 4-7). pap. 9.95 *(978-1-4598-0464-7(3))* Orca Bk. Pubs. USA.

Raskin, Joyce. My Misadventures As a Teenage Rock Star. Chu, Carol, illus. 2011. (ENG.). 112p. (YA). (gr. 7-18). pap. 8.99 *(978-0-547-39311-7(3),* 1426898, Clarion Bks.) HarperCollins Pubs.

Rich, Jamie S. Love the Way You Love. Ellerby, Marc, illus. 2006. (J). *(978-1-932664-52-2(1))* Oni Pr., Inc.

Rubens, Michael. The Bad Decisions Playlist. 2017. (ENG.). 304p. (YA). (gr. 9). pap. 9.99 *(978-1-328-74208-7(3),* 1677324, Clarion Bks.) HarperCollins Pubs.

Scarsbrook, Richard. Featherless Bipeds. 2006. (ENG.). 224p. per. 15.95 *(978-1-897235-05-8(4))* Thistledown Pr., Ltd. CAN. Dist: Univ. of Toronto Pr.

Scotton, Rob. Splat the Cat with a Bang & a Clang. 2013. (Splat the Cat: I Can Read Ser.). (J). lib. bdg. 13.55 *(978-0-606-27148-6(1))* Turtleback.

Sedgwick, Chantele. Interlude. 2018. (Love, Lucas Novel Ser.: 3). (ENG.). 284p. (YA). (gr. 7-13). 16.99 *(978-1-5107-1515-8(0),* Sky Pony Pr.) Skyhorse Publishing Co., Inc.

Simon, Francesca. Horrid Henry Rocks. Ross, Tony, illus. 2011. (Horrid Henry Ser.: 0). (ENG.). 112p. (J). (gr. 2-5). pap. 7.99 *(978-1-4022-5674-5(4),* 9781402256745, Sourcebooks Jabberwocky) Sourcebooks, Inc.

Skuse, C. J. Rockoholic. 2012. (YA). *(978-0-545-44251-0(6))* Scholastic, Inc.

Stern, A. J. Rocking Out! Marts, Doreen Mulryan, illus. 2012. (Frankly, Frannie Ser.: 8). 128p. (J). (gr. 1-3). pap. 6.99 *(978-0-448-45750-5(4),* Grosset & Dunlap) Penguin Young Readers Group.

Strand, Jeff. How You Ruined My Life. 2018. 320p. (YA). (gr. 6-12). pap. 11.99 *(978-1-4926-6202-0(X))* Sourcebooks, Inc.

Styles, Walker. Undercover in the Bow-Wow Club. Whitehouse, Ben, illus. 2016. (Rider Woofson Ser.: 3). (ENG.). 128p. (J). (gr. k-4). pap. 5.99 *(978-1-4814-6303-4(9),* Little Simon) Little Simon.

Sutherland, Suzanne. When We Were Good, 1 vol. 2013. (ENG.). 240p. (YA). (gr. 9-12). pap. *(978-1-927513-11-8(1),* Sumach Pr.) Canadian Scholars.

Trine, Greg. The Grateful Fred. Montijo, Rhode, illus. 3rd rev. ed. 2006. (Melvin Beederman, Superhero Ser.: 3). (ENG.). 144p. (J). (gr. 2-5). pap. 9.99 *(978-0-8050-7922-7(X),* 900031581) Square Fish.

Voigt, Cynthia. Orfe. 2009. (ENG.). 162p. (YA). (gr. 7). pap. 8.99 *(978-1-4169-9842-6(X),* Simon Pulse) Simon Pulse.

Warga, Jasmine. Here We Are Now. 2017. (ENG.). 304p. (YA). (gr. 9). 17.99 *(978-0-06-232470-2(5),* Balzer & Bray) HarperCollins Pubs.

Winters, Ben H. The Secret Life of Ms. Finkleman. 2011. (ENG.). 272p. (J). (gr. 3-7). pap. 5.99 *(978-0-06-196543-2(X),* HarperCollins) HarperCollins Pubs.

Yolanda And Reese. The Boy Who Loved to Be Like Michael Jackson. Harrell, Maurice, illus. 2012. 32p. 24.95 *(978-1-4560-8506-3(9))* America Star Bks.

ROCKEFELLER, JOHN D. (JOHN DAVISON), 1839-1937

John D. Rockefeller: Oil Baron & Philanthropist. rev. exp. ed. 2004. (American Business Leaders Ser.). (Illus.). 128p. (YA). (gr. 6-12). 23.95 *(978-1-931798-38-9(9))* Reynolds, Morgan Inc.

Laughlin, Rosemary. John D. Rockefeller: Oil Baron & Philanthropist. 2004. (American Business Leaders Ser.). (Illus.). 128p. (J). (gr. 5-18). 21.95 *(978-1-883846-59-6(5))* Reynolds, Morgan Inc.

Parker, Lewis K. John D. Rockefeller & the Oil Industry. 2009. (American Tycoons Ser.). 24p. (gr. 3-3). 42.50 *(978-1-61511-392-7(4),* PowerKids Pr.) Rosen Publishing Group, Inc., The.

ROCKET FLIGHT

see Space Flight

ROCKETRY

see also Guided Missiles; Rockets (Aeronautics); Space Vehicles

Dahl, Michael. On the Launch Pad: A Counting Book about Rockets, 1 vol. Shea, Denise & Alderman, Derrick, illus. 2004. (Know Your Numbers Ser.). (ENG.). 24p. (J). (gr. -1-2). per. 8.95 *(978-1-4048-1119-5(2),* 92614, Picture Window Bks.) Capstone.

Dartford, Mark. Missiles & Rockets. 2003. (Military Hardware in Action Ser.). (ENG., Illus.). 48p. (gr. 5-9). lib. bdg. 25.26 *(978-0-8225-4709-9(0))* Lerner Publishing Group.

Drozd, Anne & Drozd, Jerzy. Science Comics: Rockets: Defying Gravity. 2018. (Science Comics Ser.). (ENG., Illus.). 128p. (J). pap. 12.99 *(978-1-62672-825-7(9),* 900174979, First Second Bks.) Roaring Brook Pr.

Eason, Sarah. How Does a Rocket Work?, 1 vol. 2010. (How Does It Work? Ser.). (ENG., Illus.). 32p. (J). (gr. 3-4). 28.67 *(978-1-4339-3477-3(9),* 3140ddb7-5970-42d9-8bf6-df5bd9f6b92d, Gareth Stevens Learning Library) Stevens, Gareth Publishing LLLP.

Ferrie, Chris. Rocket Science for Babies. 2017. (Baby University Ser.: 0). (Illus.). 24p. (J). (gr. -1-k). bds. 9.99 *(978-1-4926-5625-8(9))* Sourcebooks, Inc.

Fulton, Kristen. When Sparks Fly: The True Story of Robert Goddard, the Father of US Rocketry. Funck, Diego, illus. 2018. (ENG.). 40p. (J). (gr. -1-3). 18.99 *(978-1-4814-6098-9(6),* McElderry, Margaret K. Bks.) McElderry, Margaret K. Bks.

Gross, Miriam. All about Rockets. 2009. (Blast Off! Ser.). 24p. (gr. 2-3). 42.50 *(978-1-61511-617-1(6));* (ENG.). (J). lib. bdg. 26.27 *(978-1-4358-2735-6(X),* 03aaf6d3-59ed-4f6e-9eca-f0993af09bae) Rosen Publishing Group, Inc., The. (PowerKids Pr.).

Hantula, Richard & Asimov, Isaac. Exploring Outer Space, 1 vol. 2005. (Isaac Asimov's 21st Century Library of the Universe: Past & Present Ser.). (ENG., Illus.). 32p. (gr. 3-5). lib. bdg. 28.67 *(978-0-8368-3981-4(1),* 178ac6e2-ad74-41c4-8f5b-ea4798022921) Stevens, Gareth Publishing LLLP.

Hirschmann, Kris. Blast Off. 2006. (Illus.). 63p. (J). *(978-0-439-55092-5(0))* Scholastic, Inc.

Miller, Ron. Rockets. 2007. (Space Innovations Ser.). (ENG., Illus.). 112p. (gr. 6-8). lib. bdg. 31.93 *(978-0-8225-7153-7(6))* Lerner Publishing Group.

Otfinoski, Steven. Rockets, 1 vol. 2007. (Great Inventions Ser.). (ENG., Illus.). 144p. (YA). (gr. 8-8). lib. bdg. 45.50 *(978-0-7614-2232-7(3),* 6c1b6f58-9052-4e3d-b31e-27e97401193c) Cavendish Square Publishing LLC.

Patchett, Kaye. Robert Goddard: Rocket Pioneer. 2003. (Giants of Science Ser.). (ENG., Illus.). 64p. (J). (gr. 3-7). lib. bdg. 28.35 *(978-1-56711-888-9(7),* Blackbirch Pr., Inc.) Cengage Gale.

Peak, Doris-Jean. Wernher Von Braun: Alabama's Rocket Scientist. 2009. (Alabama Roots Biography Ser.). (Illus.). 112p. (J). *(978-1-59421-044-0(6))* Seacoast Publishing, Inc.

Spilsbury, Louise. Robert Goddard & the Rocket, 1 vol., 1. 2015. (Inventions That Changed the World Ser.). (ENG.). 32p. (J). (gr. 4-5). pap. 11.00 *(978-1-5081-4639-1(X),* 9da15193-9dfc-4c1e-abe8-937be13bebba, PowerKids Pr.) Rosen Publishing Group, Inc., The.

Stoltman, Joan. Shooting for the Stars with a Rocket Scientist, 1 vol. 2018. (Get to Work! Ser.). (ENG.). 24p. (gr. 2-3). 24.27 *(978-1-5382-1674-3(4),* 6282d883-1456-4352-9145-fe9b852fc774) Stevens, Gareth Publishing LLLP.

Thomas, Rachael L. Wernher Von Braun: Revolutionary Rocket Engineer. 2018. (Space Crusaders Ser.). (ENG., Illus.). 32p. (J). (gr. 3-6). lib. bdg. 32.79 *(978-1-5321-1706-0(X),* 30700, Checkerboard Library) ABDO Publishing Co.

Upgrade kit dsm-3 Flight&rocketry. (J). 2004. *(978-1-59242-530-3(5))* 2003. *(978-1-59242-413-9(9))* Delta Education, LLC.

ROCKETS (AERONAUTICS)

see also Guided Missiles

Baker, David. Rockets & Launch Vehicles. 2008. (Exploring Space Ser.). (Illus.). 32p. (J). (gr. 4-6). lib. bdg. 26.00 *(978-1-59036-771-1(5))* Weigl Pubs., Inc.

Baker, David & Kissock, Heather. Rockets. 2016. (Illus.). 32p. (J). *(978-1-4896-5821-0(1),* AV2 by Weigl) Weigl Pubs., Inc.

—Rockets & Launch Vehicles. 2008. (Exploring Space Ser.). (Illus.). 32p. (J). (gr. 4-6). pap. 9.95 *(978-1-59036-772-8(3))* Weigl Pubs., Inc.

Dahl, Michael. On the Launch Pad: A Counting Book about Rockets, 1 vol. Shea, Denise & Alderman, Derrick, illus. 2004. (Know Your Numbers Ser.). (ENG.). 24p. (J). (gr. -1-2). per. 8.95 *(978-1-4048-1119-5(2),* 92614, Picture Window Bks.) Capstone.

Drozd, Anne & Drozd, Jerzy. Science Comics: Rockets: Defying Gravity. 2018. (Science Comics Ser.). (ENG., Illus.). 128p. (J). 21.99 *(978-1-62672-826-4(7),* 900174978); pap. 12.99 *(978-1-62672-825-7(9),* 900174979) Roaring Brook Pr. (First Second Bks.).

Eason, Sarah. How Does a Rocket Work?, 1 vol. 2010. (How Does It Work? Ser.). (ENG., Illus.). 32p. (J). (gr. 3-4). 28.67 *(978-1-4339-3477-3(9),* 3140ddb7-5970-42d9-8bf6-df5bd9f6b92d, Gareth Stevens Learning Library) Stevens, Gareth Publishing LLLP.

Garstecki, Julia & Derkovitz, Stephanie. Make Your Own Stomp Rocket. 2020. (J). pap. *(978-1-62310-130-5(1))* Black Rabbit Bks.

Gendell, Megan. Rocking & Roving: Everything You Wanted to Know about Rockets, Rovers, & Robots. 2008. (Illus.). 31p. (J). *(978-0-545-04460-8(X))* Scholastic, Inc.

Graham, Ian & Salariya, David. Planes, Rockets — And Other — Flying Machines. Hewetson, N. J., illus. 2014. (Time Shift Speed Ser.). 32p. (gr. 3-6). 31.35 *(978-1-908973-95-5(1))* Book Hse. GBR. Dist: Black Rabbit Bks.

Gross, Miriam. All about Rockets, 1 vol. 2009. (Blast Off! Ser.). (ENG., Illus.). 24p. (J). (gr. 2-3). pap. 9.25 *(978-1-4358-3133-9(0),* 1dc2888d-3903-42e3-8472-ce636550e45a, PowerKids Pr.) Rosen Publishing Group, Inc., The.

Latham, Donna. Superfast Rockets. 2005. (Ultimate Speed Ser.). (Illus.). 32p. (YA). (gr. 3-6). lib. bdg. 25.27 *(978-1-59716-083-4(0))* Bearport Publishing Co., Inc.

Linde, Barbara M. Rocket Scientists, 1 vol., 1. 2015. (Out of the Lab: Extreme Jobs in Science Ser.). (ENG., Illus.). 32p. (J). (gr. 4-5). pap. 11.00 *(978-1-4994-1855-2(8),* 5cbe70a5-4786-443f-87c6-fea5ae820431, PowerKids Pr.) Rosen Publishing Group, Inc., The.

Miller, Ron. Rockets. 2007. (Space Innovations Ser.). (ENG., Illus.). 112p. (gr. 6-8). lib. bdg. 31.93 *(978-0-8225-7153-7(6))* Lerner Publishing Group.

Mitton, Tony & Parker, Ant. Roaring Rockets. 2017. (Amazing Machines Ser.). (ENG.). 20p. (J). bds. 6.99 *(978-0-7534-7371-9(2),* 900178401, Kingfisher) Roaring Brook Pr.

Morey, Allan. Rockets. 2017. (Space Tech Ser.). (ENG., Illus.). 24p. (J). (gr. 3-7). lib. bdg. 26.95 *(978-1-62617-705-5(8),* Epic Bks.) Bellwether Media.

Murphy, Maggie. High-Tech DIY Projects with Flying Objects. 2014. (Maker Kids Ser.). (Illus.). 32p. (J). (gr. 3-6). pap. 70.50 *(978-1-4777-6660-6(X),* PowerKids Pr.) Rosen Publishing Group, Inc., The.

My Rocket: KinderWords, 6 Packs. (Kinderstarters Ser.). 8p. (gr. -1-1). 21.00 *(978-0-7635-8693-5(5))* Rigby Education.

Otfinoski, Steven. Rockets, 1 vol. 2007. (Great Inventions Ser.). (ENG., Illus.). 144p. (YA). (gr. 8-8). lib. bdg. 45.50 *(978-0-7614-2232-7(3),* 6c1b6f58-9052-4e3d-b31e-27e97401193c) Cavendish Square Publishing LLC.

Raketen und Raumfahrt. (GER.). 40p. *(978-3-411-08191-2(0))* Bibliographisches Institut & F. A. Brockhaus AG DEU. Dist: i. b. d., Ltd.

Riggs, Kate. NASA X-43a. 2018. (Now That's Fast! Ser.). (ENG.). 24p. (J). (gr. 1-4). pap. 8.99 *(978-1-62832-587-4(9),* 19856, Creative Paperbacks) Creative Co., The.

Ringstad, Arnold. How Do Engineers Reuse Rockets? 2018. (How'd They Do That? Ser.). (ENG., Illus.). 32p. (J). (gr. 4-6). lib. bdg. 28.65 *(978-1-5435-4135-9(6),* 139089, Capstone Pr.) Capstone.

Roby, Cynthia A. Building Aircraft & Spacecraft: Aerospace Engineers, 1 vol., 1. 2015. (Engineers Rule! Ser.). (ENG., Illus.). 32p. (J). (gr. 4-5). pap. 12.75 *(978-1-5081-4528-8(8),* 68cf95a4-db79-43bb-8ce9-d7a6b7f5c885, PowerKids Pr.) Rosen Publishing Group, Inc., The.

Rocket Science. 2004. (Formula Fun Ser.). (Illus.). 48p. (J). *(978-1-84229-586-1(1))* Top That! Publishing PLC.

Rockets: Level O, 6 vols. (Wonder Worldtm Ser.). 48p. 39.95 *(978-0-7802-2958-7(4))* Wright Group/McGraw-Hill.

Rowell, Rebecca. Building Rockets. 2017. (Engineering Challenges Ser.). (ENG., Illus.). 32p. (J). (gr. 3-5). pap. 9.95 *(978-1-63517-320-8(5),* 1635173205); lib. bdg. 31.35 *(978-1-63517-255-3(1),* 1635172551) North Star Editions. (Focus Readers).

Shores, Lori. How to Build a Fizzy Rocket: A 4D Book. rev. ed. 2018. (Hands-On Science Fun Ser.). (ENG., Illus.). 24p. (J). (gr. -1-2). lib. bdg. 29.32 *(978-1-5435-0943-4(6),* 137650, Capstone Pr.) Capstone.

Smibert, Angie. Reusable Rockets. 2019. (Tech Bytes Ser.). (ENG., Illus.). 48p. (J). (gr. 4-6). pap. 14.60 *(978-1-68404-466-5(9))* Norwood Hse. Pr.

Spalding, Maddie. Make a Pop Rocket. 2018. (Make Your Own Ser.). (ENG.). 32p. (J). (gr. 2-4). 26.60 *(978-1-59953-923-2(3))* Norwood Hse. Pr.

Vogt, Gregory. Building Reusable Rockets. 2018. (Illus.). 48p. (J). *(978-1-4896-9826-1(4),* AV2 by Weigl) Weigl Pubs., Inc.

Vogt, Gregory L. Building Reusable Rockets. 2018. (Destination Space Ser.). (ENG., Illus.). 48p. (J). (gr. 5-6). pap. 11.95 *(978-1-63517-566-0(6),* 1635175666); lib. bdg. 34.21 *(978-1-63517-494-6(5),* 1635174945) North Star Editions. (Focus Readers).

Welsh, Clare Helen. Cookie Blast Off! Toulatou, Sophia, illus. 2019. (Early Bird Readers — Purple (Early Bird Stories (tm)) Ser.). (ENG.). 32p. (J). (gr. k-3). 30.65 *(978-1-5415-4230-3(4),* 9e72767a-c14f-4a97-8281-8df31c261978); pap. 9.99 *(978-1-5415-7416-8(8),* 141af35e-9336-4262-86c6-06cc791d5ca4) Lerner Publishing Group. (Lerner Pubns.).

ROCKETS (AERONAUTICS)—FICTION

Achatz, Eric. The Adventures of Ryan Alexander: The Great Space Chase. 2010. 52p. pap. 23.50 *(978-1-4269-3763-7(6))* Trafford Publishing.

Albee, Sarah, et al. To the Center of the Earth! 2008. (Backyardigans Ser.). (ENG.). 24p. (J). pap. 3.99 *(978-1-4169-7094-1(0),* Simon Spotlight/Nickelodeon) Simon Spotlight/Nickelodeon.

Anderson, Lynne. Rocket Ship Shapes: Set Of 6. 2011. (Early Connections Ser.). (J). pap. 37.00 net. *(978-1-4108-1091-5(7))* Benchmark Education Co.

Astrotwins — Project Blastoff. 2015. (Astrotwins Ser.). (ENG., Illus.). 224p. (J). (gr. 3-7). 18.99 *(978-1-4814-1545-3(X),* Simon & Schuster/Paula Wiseman Bks.) Simon & Schuster/Paula Wiseman Bks.

Auerbach, Annie. The Grosse Adventures Vol. 3: Trouble at Twilight Cave, 1 vol. Nicholas, Jamar, illus. 2008. (Tokyopop Ser.). (ENG.). 96p. (J). (gr. 2-6). 32.79 *(978-1-59961-562-2(2),* 14806, Graphic Novels) Spotlight.

Bergman, Mara. Oliver Who Would Not Sleep! Maland, Nick, illus. 2007. (J). *(978-0-439-92827-4(3),* Levine, Arthur A. Bks.) Scholastic, Inc.

Blackburn, Sheila M. Stewie Scraps & the Star Rocket. 2008. 76p. pap. *(978-1-903853-87-0(7))* Brilliant Pubns.

Capucilli, Alyssa Satin. Ralph & the Rocket Ship: Ready-To-Read Level 1. Cole, Henry, illus. 2016. (Ready-To-Read Ser.). (ENG.). 24p. (J). (gr. -1-1). pap. 4.99 *(978-1-4814-5866-5(3),* Simon Spotlight) Simon Spotlight.

Condon, Bill. Race to the Moon, 1 vol. rev. ed. 2013. (Literary Text Ser.). (ENG., Illus.). 28p. (J). (gr. 2-3). pap. 10.99 *(978-1-4333-5605-6(8));* lib. bdg. 19.96 *(978-1-4807-1727-5(4))* Teacher Created Materials, Inc.

Hambrick, Sharon. Tommy's Rocket. Manning, Maurie J., illus. 2003. (Fig Street Kids Ser.). 83p. (J). (gr. 1-2). 7.49 *(978-1-59166-186-3(2))* BJU Pr.

Harmening, Gail. How Did Clancey Get His Color?, 1 vol. 2009. 45p. pap. 24.95 *(978-1-60836-440-4(2))* America Star Bks.

Hillert, Margaret. Up, up & Away. 2016. (BeginningtoRead Ser.). (ENG., Illus.). 32p. (J). (gr. 1-2). 22.60 *(978-1-59953-806-8(7))* Norwood Hse. Pr.

Ishwaran, Wobine. A Journey into Space: Kary to the Moon. 2008. 24p. pap. 11.49 *(978-1-4343-6717-4(7))* AuthorHouse.

Lalley, Kristine. Show & Tell, 1 vol. 2006. (Neighborhood Readers Ser.). (ENG.). 12p. (gr. k-1). pap. 5.90 *(978-1-4042-6465-6(5),* e36681c3-624e-4d88-b629-7e0b96cf87b9, Rosen Classroom) Rosen Publishing Group, Inc., The.

Mai, Lily. Bertie Boom's Trip to the Moon. 2010. (Illus.). 20p. 12.49 *(978-1-4520-1379-4(9))* AuthorHouse.

Milgrim, David. Go, Otto, Go! Ready-To-Read Pre-Level 1. Milgrim, David, illus. 2016. (Adventures of Otto Ser.). (ENG., Illus.). 32p. (J). (gr. -1-k). pap. 4.99 *(978-1-4814-6723-0(9),* Simon Spotlight) Simon Spotlight.

Morrissey, Dean & Krensky, Stephen. The Crimson Comet. Morrissey, Dean, illus. 2006. (Illus.). 32p. (J). (gr. k-4). 17.89 *(978-0-06-008070-9(1))* HarperCollins Pubs.

Oliver, Lin. Revenge of the Itty-Bitty Brothers, 3. Gilpin, Stephen, illus. 2009. (Who Shrunk Daniel Funk? Ser.: 3). (ENG.). 112p. (J). (gr. 2-4). 21.19 *(978-1-4169-0961-3(3))* Simon & Schuster, Inc.

Rosen, Robert. How Do We Get to the Moon? Curzon, Brett, illus. 2017. (My Adventures Ser.). (ENG.). 24p. (gr. -1-2). pap. 9.95 *(978-1-68342-785-8(8),* 9781683427858) Rourke Educational Media.

Santillo, LuAnn. Lift-Off. Santillo, LuAnn, ed. 2003. (Half-Pint Kids Readers Ser.). (Illus.). 7p. (J). (gr. -1-1). pap. 1.00 *(978-1-59256-043-1(1))* Half-Pint Kids, Inc.

Sawler, Kimberly. Rocket & the Magical Cosmic Candies. Walls, Ty, illus. 2006. 32p. (J). (gr. 4-7). 18.95 *(978-1-933285-51-1(6))* Brown Books Publishing Group.

Weston, Greg. The Inventors. 2009. 202p. pap. 13.95 *(978-1-4092-6096-7(8))* Lulu Pr., Inc.

Wilde, Oscar. El Famoso Cohete. Zwerger, Lisbeth, illus. (SPA.). 72p. (J). *(978-84-392-8693-6(7))* Gaviota Ediciones ESP. Dist: Lectorum Pubns., Inc.

Wilson, Zachary. A Circle in the Sky. Adinolfi, JoAnn, illus. (Rookie Ready to Learn Ser.). (ENG.). (J). 2011. 40p. pap. 5.95 *(978-0-531-26746-2(6))* 2006. 32p. lib. bdg. 19.50 *(978-0-531-12570-0(X))* Scholastic Library Publishing. (Children's Pr.).

—Rookie Ready to Learn en Español: un Círculo en el Cielo. Adinolfi, JoAnn, illus. 2011. (Rookie Ready to Learn Español Ser.). Orig. Title: Rookie Ready to Learn: a Circle in the Sky. (SPA.). 40p. (J). pap. 5.95 *(978-0-531-26791-2(1),* Children's Pr.) Scholastic Library Publishing.

Wilson, Zachary & Adinolfi, JoAnn. Un Círculo en el Cielo. Adinolfi, JoAnn, illus. 2011. (Rookie Ready to Learn Español Ser.). (SPA., Illus.). 40p. (J). lib. bdg. 23.00 *(978-0-531-26123-1(9),* Children's Pr.) Scholastic Library Publishing.

ROCKETS (AERONAUTICS)—MODELS

Shores, Lori. Cómo Hacer un Cohete Efervescente. 2010. (Divertirse con la Ciencia/Hands-On Science Fun Ser.).Tr. of How to Build a Fizzy Rocket. (MUL.). 24p. (J). (gr. -1-2). lib. bdg. 27.32 *(978-1-4296-6105-8(4),* 115128) Capstone.

ROCKS

see also Crystallography; Geology; Mineralogy; Stone

Alkire, Jessie. Super Simple Rock Cycle Projects: Science Activities for Future Petrologists. 2017. (Super Simple Earth Investigations Ser.). (ENG.). 32p. (J). (gr. k-4). lib. bdg. 34.21 *(978-1-5321-1239-3(4),* 27626, Super SandCastle) ABDO Publishing Co.

Allen, Nancy Kelly. Earth's Rock Cycle. 2009. (Rock It! Ser.). 24p. (gr. 3-4). 42.50 *(978-1-60852-480-8(9),* PowerKids Pr.); (ENG.). (J). pap. 9.25 *(978-1-4358-3185-8(3),* 7385a9bf-6abc-4a28-be4a-5e1455f6df30); (ENG.). (YA). lib. bdg. 26.27 *(978-1-4358-2762-2(7),* 8166bfbe-6081-45cf-a36b-8a50db088780) Rosen Publishing Group, Inc., The.

—Granite & Other Igneous Rocks. 2009. (Rock It! Ser.). 24p. (gr. 3-4). 42.50 *(978-1-60852-483-9(3),* PowerKids Pr.); (ENG.). (J). lib. bdg. 26.27 *(978-1-4358-2758-5(9),* e8aec20d-857e-4617-bd75-c7c5b01144ce); (ENG., Illus.). (J). pap. 9.25 *(978-1-4358-3181-0(0),* 8812873a-dfbe-48ea-9c1a-f48e2ae0a435, PowerKids Pr.) Rosen Publishing Group, Inc., The.

—Identifying Rocks. 2009. (Rock It! Ser.). 24p. (gr. 3-4). 42.50 *(978-1-60852-486-0(8),* PowerKids Pr.); (ENG.). (YA). lib. bdg. 26.27 *(978-1-4358-2763-9(5),* 070d3a1e-2d19-47d1-8634-0568e1226491); (ENG., Illus.). (J). pap. 9.25 *(978-1-4358-3186-5(1),* e2e56656-b2ee-490f-ae70-3bd2b225bc01) Rosen Publishing Group, Inc., The.

—Limestone & Other Sedimentary Rocks. 2009. (Rock It! Ser.). 24p. (gr. 3-4). 42.50 *(978-1-60852-489-1(2),* PowerKids Pr.); (ENG.). (YA). lib. bdg. 26.27 *(978-1-4358-2759-2(7),* 0820e620-5924-4f3c-becf-41314213812d); (ENG., Illus.). (J). pap. 9.25 *(978-1-4358-3182-7(9),* 8e4c725e-2e2a-4e43-a0c7-4eb5ac1d4788, PowerKids Pr.) Rosen Publishing Group, Inc., The.

—Minerals & Rocks. 2009. (Rock It! Ser.). 24p. (gr. 3-4). 42.50 *(978-1-60852-492-1(2),* PowerKids Pr.); (ENG.). (J). pap. 9.25 *(978-1-4358-3184-1(5),* 366286da-4df6-49cc-9d8b-1583f24cbdbd); (ENG.). (YA). lib. bdg. 26.27 *(978-1-4358-2761-5(9),* cb48fa66-1f83-46a1-b75e-555eadcaad16) Rosen Publishing Group, Inc., The.

—Slate & Other Metamorphic Rocks. 2009. (Rock It! Ser.). 24p. (gr. 3-4). 42.50 *(978-1-60852-495-2(7),* PowerKids Pr.); (ENG.). (YA). lib. bdg. 26.27 *(978-1-4358-2760-8(0),* ca487d26-9700-4af2-b47f-db55ca982bf8); (ENG., Illus.). (J). pap. 9.25 *(978-1-4358-3183-4(7),* 48c9552e-680d-4a13-aa43-c08429b0c411, PowerKids Pr.) Rosen Publishing Group, Inc., The.

Aloian, Molly. What Are Igneous Rocks? 2010. (Let's Rock! Ser.). (ENG., Illus.). 32p. (J). (gr. 4-4). pap. *(978-0-7787-7233-0(0))* Crabtree Publishing Co.

—What Are Metamorphic Rocks? 2010. (ENG.). 32p. (J). lib. bdg. *(978-0-7787-7229-3(2));* (Illus.). (gr. 4-4). pap. *(978-0-7787-7234-7(9))* Crabtree Publishing Co.

Anderson, Michael. Investigating Minerals, Rocks, & Fossils, 1 vol. 2011. (Introduction to Earth Science Ser.). (ENG., Illus.). 88p. (J). (gr. 8-8). lib. bdg. 35.29 *(978-1-61530-500-1(9),* c9677133-40d9-4292-ab20-1c7626071522) Rosen Publishing Group, Inc., The.

Aston, Dianna Hutts. A Rock Is Lively. Long, Sylvia, illus. 2015. (Family Treasure Nature Encylopedias Ser.). (ENG.). 40p. (J). (gr. k-3). pap. 8.99 *(978-1-4521-4555-6(5))* Chronicle Bks. LLC.

—A Rock Is Lively. 2015. (J). lib. bdg. 18.40 *(978-0-606-37444-6(2))* Turtleback.

Atwood, Frederick D. Rocks & Minerals - Pb: A Portrait of the Natural World. 2013. (Portrait of the Natural World Ser.). (Illus.). 72p. pap. 9.95 *(978-1-59764-332-0(7))* New Line Bks.

Barker, Charles Ferguson. Under Ohio: The Story of Ohio's Rocks & Fossils. 2007. (ENG., Illus.). 56p. (J). (gr. 3-7). 34.95 *(978-0-8214-1755-3(X))* Ohio Univ. Pr.

Basher, Simon & Green, Dan. Basher Science: Rocks & Minerals: A Gem of a Book. Basher, Simon, illus. 2009. (Basher Science Ser.). (ENG., Illus.). 128p. (J). (gr. 5-9). pap. 9.99 *(978-0-7534-6314-7(8),* 900059036, Kingfisher) Roaring Brook Pr.

Benchmark Education Company, LLC Staff, compiled by. Rocks & Minerals: Theme Set. 2006. (J). 215.00 *(978-1-4108-7135-0(5))* Benchmark Education Co.

—Rocky Tales & Earth Systems. 2005. spiral bd. 225.00 *(978-1-4108-5819-1(7))* Benchmark Education Co.

Bingham, Caroline & Dorling Kindersley Publishing Staff. Rocks & Minerals. 2004. (DK Eye Wonder Ser.). (ENG., Illus.). 48p. (J). (gr. 3-6). lib. bdg. 22.44 *(978-0-7894-9894-6(4))* Dorling Kindersley Publishing, Inc.

Blevins, Wiley. Rocks & Minerals, 6 vols., Set. 2004. (Phonics Readers Books 37-72 Ser.). (ENG.). 8p. (gr. k-1). pap. 35.70 *(978-0-7368-4083-5(4))* Capstone.

Bowman, Chris. Rocks. 2014. (Earth Science Rocks! Ser.). (ENG., Illus.). 24p. (J). (gr. k-3). lib. bdg. 26.95 *(978-1-60014-981-8(2),* Blastoff! Readers) Bellwether Media.

Bramwell, Martyn. Rocks & Fossils. Bramwell, Martyn, ed. Jackson, Ian & Suttie, Alan, illus. rev. ed. 2007. (Hobby Guides). 31p. (J). pap. 6.99 *(978-0-7945-1526-3(6),* Usborne) EDC Publishing.

Brandt, Daniel & Brandt, Deanna. Rock Log Kids. 2018. (Nature Journals). (ENG., Illus.). 80p. (J). (gr. 1-7). spiral bd. 11.95 *(978-1-59193-777-7(9),* Adventure Pubns.) AdventureKEEN.

Brannon, Cecelia H. A Look at Igneous Rocks, 1 vol. 2015. (Rock Cycle Ser.). (ENG.). 32p. (gr. 3-4). pap. 11.52 *(978-0-7660-7316-6(5),* d8685dc1-38ff-4523-8cad-e990df60112a); (Illus.). 26.93 *(978-0-7660-7318-0(1),* c3ac2ced-f92f-4928-a405-e7d61b6c28a6) Enslow Publishing, LLC.

—A Look at Metamorphic Rocks, 1 vol. 2015. (Rock Cycle Ser.). (ENG.). 32p. (gr. 3-4). pap. 11.52 *(978-0-7660-7320-3(3),* 1c8d4453-3aff-4349-a7f3-51e7dd1c02b1); (Illus.). 26.93 *(978-0-7660-7322-7(X),* dee9ec18-a66b-4dd9-ad2e-c338bcf24247) Enslow Publishing, LLC.

—A Look at Sedimentary Rocks, 1 vol. 2015. (Rock Cycle Ser.). (ENG.). 32p. (gr. 3-4). pap. 11.52 *(978-0-7660-7336-4(X)*, fcbe9522-f4c5-4f09-b159-31643d866672); (Illus.). 26.93 *(978-0-7660-7338-8(6)*, 72619236-0d27-4e26-b48e-73a219733846) Enslow Publishing, LLC.

Brasch, Nicolas. Why Do Volcanoes Erupt?, 1 vol. 2010. (Solving Science Mysteries Ser.). (ENG., Illus.). 24p. (gr. 4-5). (J). pap. 9.25 *(978-1-4488-0401-6(9)*, e91ae71c-260e-4912-85e7-3a331623813e, PowerKids Pr.); (YA). lib. bdg. 26.27 *(978-1-4488-0400-9(0)*, e79e7791-9e42-49ea-81e6-d1191e77d456) Rosen Publishing Group, Inc., The.

—Why Do Volcanoes Erupt? All about Earth Science. 2010. (Illus.). 24p. (J). 49.50 *(978-1-4488-0402-3(7)*, 1307173, PowerKids Pr.) Rosen Publishing Group, Inc., The.

Braun, Eric. Let's Rock! Science Adventures with Rudie the Origami Dinosaur, 1 vol. Christoph, Jamey, illus. 2013. (Origami Science Adventures Ser.). (ENG.). 24p. (J). (gr. -1-3). pap. 6.95 *(978-1-4048-8068-9(2)*, 121840, Picture Window Bks.) Capstone.

Bredeson, Carmen. Weird but True Rocks, 1 vol. 2012. (Weird but True Science Ser.). (ENG., Illus.). 24p. (gr. k-2). pap. 10.35 *(978-1-59845-370-6(X)*, 56f6716a-6ee3-4cc8-bc15-d82d819090ab, Enslow Elementary); lib. bdg. 25.27 *(978-0-7660-3864-6(5)*, ee2b7d8b-ed6c-4143-bda2-eb66712072a9) Enslow Publishing, LLC.

Bredeson, Carmen & Cousins, Lindsey. Can You Find These Rocks?, 1 vol. 2012. (All about Nature Ser.). (ENG.). 24p. (gr. -1-1). 25.27 *(978-0-7660-3979-7(X)*, 4caed6cf-0cce-4e91-b2a9-671216f400c4); (Illus.). pap. 10.35 *(978-1-4644-0066-7(0)*, 259772cd-1ddb-4fa8-b498-5e24cd6da121) Enslow Publishing, LLC. (Enslow Publishing).

Brian, Bethany. How the Rock Cycle Works. 2009. (Science Kaleidoscope Ser.). 32p. (gr. 4-4). 47.90 *(978-1-60853-036-6(1)*, PowerKids Pr.) Rosen Publishing Group, Inc., The.

Brinkman, Patricia. Discover Rock Types. 2006. (J). pap. *(978-1-4108-6497-0(9))* Benchmark Education Co.

—Discover the Rock Cycle. 2006. (J). pap. *(978-1-4108-6496-3(0))* Benchmark Education Co.

—The Rock Cycle. 2006. (J). pap. *(978-1-4108-6493-2(6))* Benchmark Education Co.

—Rock Types. 2006. (J). pap. *(978-1-4108-6494-9(4))* Benchmark Education Co.

Brooke, Samantha. Rock Man vs. Weather Man. 2018. (Scholastic Readers Ser.). (ENG.). 31p. (J). (gr. -1-k). 13.89 *(978-1-64310-248-1(6))* Penworthy Co., LLC, The.

—Rock Man vs. Weather Man (the Magic School Bus Rides Again: Scholastic Reader, Level 2) Artful Doodlers Ltd., illus. 2018. (Scholastic Reader, Level 2 Ser.). (ENG.). 32p. (J). (gr. k-2). pap. 5.99 *(978-1-338-25378-8(6))* Scholastic, Inc.

Bryan, Bethany. How the Rock Cycle Works, 1 vol. (Science Kaleidoscope Ser.). (ENG.). 32p. (gr. 4-4). 2009. (J). lib. bdg. 28.93 *(978-1-4358-2984-8(0)*, 7db329cb-ca2f-4761-9670-93ce4a9b000a, PowerKids Pr.) 2008. pap. 10.00 *(978-1-4358-0151-6(2)*, a00ada8c-cf0a-446b-9ed7-03cfd4baa47a, Rosen Classroom) Rosen Publishing Group, Inc., The.

Burton, Margie, et al. Big & Little. 2011. (Early Connections Ser.). (J). *(978-1-61672-284-5(3))* Benchmark Education Co.

—Rocks. 2011. (Early Connections Ser.). (J). *(978-1-61672-536-5(2))* Benchmark Education Co.

Callery, Sean. Rocks & Minerals. 2010. (Unpredictable Nature Ser.). (Illus.). 48p. (J). (gr. 3-18). lib. bdg. 19.95 *(978-1-4222-2005-4(2))* Mason Crest.

Cardenas, Ernesto & Saavedra, Patricia. Rocas. l.t. ed. 2006. (SPA., Illus.). 16p. pap. 4.95 *(978-1-933668-18-5(0))* Milo Educational Bks. & Resources.

Cardenas, Ernesto A. Rocks. 2009. pap. 4.95 *(978-1-60698-072-9(6))* Milo Educational Bks. & Resources.

Challoner, Jack. Find Out about Rocks & Minerals: With 23 Projects & More Than 350 Pictures. 2013. (Illus.). 64p. (J). (gr. k-8). 9.99 *(978-1-84322-747-2(9)*, Armadillo) Anness Publishing GBR. Dist: National Bk. Network.

Challoner, Jack & Walshaw, Rodney. Rocks & Minerals: Crystals, Erosion, Geology, Fossils: With 19 Easy-To-Do Experiments & 400 Exciting Pictures. 2015. (Illus.). 64p. (J). (gr. -1-12). 12.99 *(978-1-86147-465-0(2)*, Armadillo) Anness Publishing GBR. Dist: National Bk. Network.

Christian, Peggy. If You Find a Rock. 2008. (ENG., Illus.). 32p. (J). (gr. -1-3). pap. 7.99 *(978-0-15-206354-2(4)*, 1199032, Clarion Bks.) HarperCollins Pubs.

Clarke, Phillip & Tudhope, Simon, eds. 100 Rocks & Minerals to Spot. 2009. (Spotter's Cards Ser.). 52p. (J). 9.99 *(978-0-7945-2255-1(6)*, Usborne) EDC Publishing.

Claybourne, Anna. What Do You Know about Rocks & Fossils?, 1 vol. 2017. (Test Your Science Skills Ser.). (ENG.). 32p. (J). (gr. 5-5). 29.27 *(978-1-5383-2217-8(X)*, c9da47aa-dcb1-4017-93e0-4def98dd4b1f); pap. 12.75 *(978-1-5383-2312-0(5)*, 6e52a1b3-7bb3-4fde-b9ee-fe412acle7eb3) Rosen Publishing Group, Inc., The. (PowerKids Pr.).

Close, Edward. Earth's Treasures: Rocks & Minerals: Rocks & Minerals, 1 vol., 1. 2014. (Discovery Education: Earth & Space Science Ser.). (ENG.). 32p. (gr. 4-5). 28.93 *(978-1-4777-6170-0(5)*, c4a4e26d-c7eb-449e-8841-13163d6cb1e9, PowerKids Pr.) Rosen Publishing Group, Inc., The.

Colich, Abby. Rock, 1 vol. 2013. (Exploring Materials Ser.). (ENG.). 24p. (J). (gr. -1-1). pap. 6.95 *(978-1-4329-8026-9(2)*, 123182, Heinemann) Capstone.

Conklin, Wendy. The Rock Cycle. 2015. (Science: Informational Text Ser.). (ENG., Illus.). 32p. (J). (gr. 3-5). pap. 11.99 *(978-1-4807-4688-6(6))* Teacher Created Materials, Inc.

Corriel, Michele. Weird Rocks, 1 vol. Bilyeu, Dan, illus. 2013. (ENG.). 36p. (J). 12.00 *(978-0-87842-597-6(7))* Mountain Pr. Publishing Co., Inc.

Cull, Selby. Rocks & Minerals. 2009. (Restless Earth Ser.). (ENG., Illus.). 112p. (gr. 5-9). 35.00 *(978-0-7910-9702-1(1)*, P159123, Facts On File) Infobase Holdings, Inc.

Culp, Jennifer. What Are Sedimentary Rocks?, 1 vol., 1. 2015. (Junior Geologist Ser.). (ENG., Illus.). 32p. (J). (gr. 2-3). pap. 13.90 *(978-1-5081-0046-1(2)*, 9c3cabeb-f694-4908-83a6-bb1c9442821a, Britannica Educational Publishing) Rosen Publishing Group, Inc., The.

Davidson, Rose. The Big Book of Bling: Ritzy Rocks, Extravagant Animals, Sparkling Science, & More! 2019. (ENG., Illus.). 192p. (J). (gr. 3-7). 19.99 *(978-1-4263-3531-0(8)*, National Geographic Kids) Disney Publishing Worldwide.

Dayton, Connor. Crystals. (Rocks & Minerals Ser.). 24p. (gr. 2-3). 2009. 42.50 *(978-1-60852-498-3(1)*, PowerKids Pr.) 2007. (ENG., Illus.). (YA). lib. bdg. 26.27 *(978-1-4042-3687-5(2)*, 2dae38e0-8527-4208-8824-3f91b3cf2f5a) Rosen Publishing Group, Inc., The.

—Rocks & Minerals, 6 vols., Set. Incl. Crystals. lib. bdg. 26.27 *(978-1-4042-3687-5(2)*, 2dae38e0-8527-4208-8824-3f91b3cf2f5a); Fossils. lib. bdg. 26.27 *(978-1-4042-3689-9(9)*, 80eb0549-38cd-4a93-8ee3-cc6212497920); Gemstones. lib. bdg. 26.27 *(978-1-4042-3686-8(4)*, c20b98f2-57c6-4139-9647-fa661c9e94e6); Minerals. lib. bdg. 26.27 *(978-1-4042-3691-2(0)*, 52a1b0ec-8b2d-4684-9dc0-98772414aaca); Volcanic Rocks. lib. bdg. 26.27 *(978-1-4042-3688-2(0)*, b601e067-75a8-47e3-bb40-10171ded1102); (Illus.). 24p. (YA). (gr. 2-3). 2007. (Rocks & Minerals Ser.). (ENG.). 2006. Set lib. bdg. 78.81 *(978-1-4042-3610-3(4)*, ffbe7174-b5e4-4ab6-a667-cc1ca707c00c, PowerKids Pr.) Rosen Publishing Group, Inc., The.

—Volcanic Rocks. (Rocks & Minerals Ser.). 24p. (gr. 2-3). 2009. 42.50 *(978-1-60852-503-4(1)*, PowerKids Pr.) 2007. (ENG., Illus.). (YA). lib. bdg. 26.27 *(978-1-4042-3688-2(0)*, b601e067-75a8-47e3-bb40-10171ded1102) Rosen Publishing Group, Inc., The.

Dee, Willa. Earth's Rock Cycle, 1 vol., 1. 2014. (Rocks: the Hard Facts Ser.). (ENG.). 24p. (J). (gr. 3-3). 26.27 *(978-1-4777-2903-8(8)*, 087c1be5-1643-4d4a-92ec-ce38499fbb8f, PowerKids Pr.) Rosen Publishing Group, Inc., The.

—Unearthing Igneous Rocks, 1 vol., 1. 2014. (Rocks: the Hard Facts Ser.). (ENG.). 24p. (J). (gr. 3-3). 26.27 *(978-1-4777-2901-4(1)*, d4158853-2fae-4d23-b9c0-73ab4526df71, PowerKids Pr.) Rosen Publishing Group, Inc., The.

—Unearthing Metamorphic Rocks, 1 vol., 1. 2014. (Rocks: the Hard Facts Ser.). (ENG.). 24p. (J). (gr. 3-3). 26.27 *(978-1-4777-2902-1(X)*, 428180ce-9a57-4b2f-a624-f6b438cfd382, PowerKids Pr.) Rosen Publishing Group, Inc., The.

—Unearthing Sedimentary Rocks, 1 vol., 1. 2014. (Rocks: the Hard Facts Ser.). (ENG.). 24p. (J). (gr. 3-3). 26.27 *(978-1-4777-2900-7(3)*, aa67dc47-146e-4301-a58a-05082870c4de, PowerKids Pr.) Rosen Publishing Group, Inc., The.

Delta Education. Sci Res Bk Foss Grade 2 Next Gen Ea. 2014. (Illus.). 251p. (J). lib. bdg. *(978-1-62571-446-6(7))* Delta Education, LLC.

Dennie, Devin. My Book of Rocks & Minerals: Things to Find, Collect, & Treasure. 2017. (My Book Of Ser.). (ENG., Illus.). 96p. (J). (gr. k-4). 14.99 *(978-1-4654-6190-2(6)*, DK Children) Dorling Kindersley Publishing, Inc.

DeWitt, Lockwood. Dig It! Hixson, Bryce, illus. 2003. (J). per. 14.95 *(978-1-931801-02-7(9))* Loose In The Lab.

Dickmann, Nancy. The Rock Cycle, 1 vol. 2015. (Earth Figured Out Ser.). (ENG., Illus.). 32p. (gr. 4-4). pap. 11.58 *(978-1-5026-0870-3(7)*, 5df981a0-8e50-4cb8-8df0-3e3e660c7e7c) Cavendish Square Publishing LLC.

DK. Eye Wonder: Rocks & Minerals: Open Your Eyes to a World of Discovery. 2014. (Eye Wonder Ser.). (ENG.). 56p. (J). (gr. k-4). 10.99 *(978-1-4654-1559-2(9)*, DK Children) Dorling Kindersley Publishing, Inc.

—Pocket Genius: Rocks & Minerals: Facts at Your Fingertips. 2016. (Pocket Genius Ser.: 13). (ENG., Illus.). 160p. (J). (gr. 3-7). pap. 6.99 *(978-1-4654-4590-2(0)*, DK Children) Dorling Kindersley Publishing, Inc.

—The Rock & Gem Book: And Other Treasures of the Natural World. 2016. (DK Our World in Pictures Ser.). (ENG., Illus.). 192p. (J). (gr. 4-7). 24.99 *(978-1-4654-5070-8(X)*, DK Children) Dorling Kindersley Publishing, Inc.

Dunlop, Jenna & Morganelli, Adrianna. Minerals. 2004. (Rocks, Minerals, & Resources Ser.). (ENG., Illus.). 32p. (J). lib. bdg. *(978-0-7787-1415-6(2))* Crabtree Publishing Co.

Earth's Rocky Past. 2015. (Earth's Rocky Past Ser.). (ENG.). 32p. (J). (gr. 4-4). pap., pap., pap. 360.00 *(978-1-4994-1286-4(X)*, PowerKids Pr.) Rosen Publishing Group, Inc., The.

EDC Publishing, creator. Rocks & Fossils Kid Kit. 2009. (Usborne Kid Kits Ser.). (Illus.). (J). (gr. 5). pap. 15.99 *(978-1-60130-025-6(5))* EDC Publishing.

Encyclopaedia Britannica, Inc. Staff, compiled by. Britannica Illustrated Science Library: Rocks & Minerals, 16 vols. 2008. (Illus.). (J). 29.95 *(978-1-59339-396-0(2))* Encyclopaedia Britannica, Inc.

Estigarribia, Diana. Learning about Rocks, Weathering, & Erosion with Graphic Organizers. (Graphic Organizers in Science Ser.). 24p. 2009. (gr. 3-4). 42.50 *(978-1-61513-044-3(6))* 2005. (ENG., Illus.). (gr. 4-5). pap. 8.25 *(978-1-4042-5042-0(5)*, d3a15d23-c906-4ed5-9a8e-b4f566e7c067) Rosen Publishing Group, Inc., The. (PowerKids Pr.).

Farndon, John. Rocks, Minerals & Gems. 2016. (ENG., Illus.). 120p. (J). (gr. 6-10). 24.95 *(978-1-77085-740-7(0)*, d39e1c49-14c0-4156-aa08-850d0f207958); pap. 12.95 *(978-1-77085-868-8(7)*, 2458ce02-8895-4dc3-bb4b-42e8a999fa1c) Firefly Bks., Ltd.

Flood, Nancy Bo. Sand to Stone: And Back Again. 2009. (ENG., Illus.). 32p. (J). (gr. -1-k). pap. 14.95 *(978-1-55591-657-2(0))* Fulcrum Publishing.

Freeman, Marcia S., et al. Let's Look at Rocks. 2003. (Readers for Writers - Early Ser.). (ENG.). 16p. (gr. 1-2). pap. 6.00 *(978-1-59515-258-9(X)*, 9781595152589) Rourke Educational Media.

Fretland VanVoorst, Jenny & VanVoorst, Jenny Fretland. Metamorphic Rocks. 2019. (Rocks & Minerals Ser.). (ENG., Illus.). 32p. (J). (gr. 3-8). lib. bdg. 27.95 *(978-1-64487-076-1(2)*, Blastoff! Discovery) Bellwether Media.

Gallagher, Belinda, et al. Rocks & Minerals: Identify & Record Your Sightings. 2017. (Illus.). 96p. (J). pap. 9.95 *(978-1-78209-572-9(1))* Miles Kelly Publishing, Ltd. GBR. Dist: Parkwest Pubns., Inc.

Gilbert, Sara. Landslides. 2018. (Earth Rocks! Ser.). (ENG.). 24p. (J). (gr. 1-4). *(978-1-60818-895-6(7)*, 19589, Creative Education); pap. 9.99 *(978-1-62832-511-9(9)*, 19587, Creative Paperbacks) Creative Co., The.

Glaser, Rebecca. Rocks. 2012. (ENG., Illus.). 24p. (J). lib. bdg. 25.65 *(978-1-62031-028-1(7))* Jump! Inc.

Goldman, Phyllis B., ed. Monkeyshines on Rocks & Minerals. (Illus.). 148p. (J). (gr. -1-7). reprint ed. pap. 26.95 *(978-1-888325-14-0(3))* Allosaurus Pubs.

Gosman, Gillian. What Do You Know about Rocks?, 1 vol. 2013. (20 Questions: Earth Science Ser.). (J). (ENG.). 24p. (gr. 2-3). pap. 9.25 *(978-1-4488-9850-3(1)*, 605cdd04-75eb-4551-b29a-e39a1facd973); (ENG.). 24p. (gr. 2-3). lib. bdg. 26.27 *(978-1-4488-9696-7(7)*, c05abf7a-7b83-412d-85f7-ee4053963a93); *(978-1-4488-9851-0(X))* Rosen Publishing Group, Inc., The. (PowerKids Pr.).

Graphic Organizers in Science, 8 vols. 2004. (Graphic Organizers in Science Ser.). (ENG., Illus.). (J). (gr. 3-4). 105.08 *(978-1-4042-2955-6(8)*, 7ea88a43-5495-485a-a4dd-4c4826a54526) Rosen Publishing Group, Inc., The.

Green, Jen. Rocks & Soil, 1 vol. 2007. (Our Earth Ser.). (ENG., Illus.). 24p. (YA). (gr. 2-3). lib. bdg. 26.27 *(978-1-4042-4271-5(6)*, 3052c8a7-4172-41d2-b5c1-bc6dfcf217e8) Rosen Publishing Group, Inc., The.

Gregorovna, Anna. Inside Earth: Rocks & Minerals, 1 vol. 2012. (InfoMax Readers Ser.). (ENG., Illus.). 24p. (J). (gr. 1-1). pap. 8.25 *(978-1-4488-9043-9(8)*, 266801ae-a168-4c98-a64d-1604f41cef5d, Rosen Classroom) Rosen Publishing Group, Inc., The.

Guide to Rocks & Minerals, 8 vols. 2007. (Guide to Rocks & Minerals Ser.). (ENG.). 32p. (gr. 3-5). lib. bdg. 114.68 *(978-0-8368-7905-6(8)*, 58071aeb-f6ca-4aba-a00b-dab04fa5b830, Gareth Stevens Learning Library) Stevens, Gareth Publishing LLLP.

Hamilton, John. Landslides, 1 vol. 2006. (Nature's Fury Ser.). (ENG., Illus.). 32p. (gr. 3-8). 27.07 *(978-1-59679-331-6(7)*, Abdo & Daughters) ABDO Publishing Co.

Hand, Carol. Experiments with Rocks & Minerals. 2011. (True Bk Ser.). (ENG., Illus.). 48p. (J). pap. 6.95 *(978-0-531-26648-9(6))*; lib. bdg. 29.00 *(978-0-531-26348-8(7))* Scholastic Library Publishing. (Children's Pr.).

Hansen, Grace. Rocas. 2016. (¡Súper Geología! Ser.). (SPA.). 24p. (J). (gr. -1-2). pap. 7.95 *(978-1-4966-0682-2(5)*, 131734, Capstone Classroom) Capstone.

—Rocks, 1 vol. 2015. (Geology Rocks! (Abdo Kids Jumbo) Ser.). (ENG., Illus.). 24p. (J). (gr. -1-2). 32.79 *(978-1-62970-909-3(3)*, 18276, Abdo Kids) ABDO Publishing Co.

Hantula, Richard. Rocks & Fossils, 1 vol. 2007. (Gareth Stevens Vital Science Library: Earth Science Ser.). (ENG., Illus.). 48p. (gr. 5-8). pap. 15.05 *(978-0-8368-7876-9(0)*, 683f0af3-8c5c-401c-ab7f-adcf0f6b3f7a, Gareth Stevens Secondary Library) Stevens, Gareth Publishing LLLP.

Harkrader, Lisa. What Is a Rock? 2016. (Spring Forward Ser.). (J). (gr. 2). *(978-1-4900-9456-4(3))* Benchmark Education Co.

Harrison, Lorraine. All Kinds of Rocks. 2013. (InfoMax Readers Ser.). (ENG.). 24p. (J). (gr. 2-3). pap. 49.50 *(978-1-4777-2408-8(7))*; (Illus.). pap. 8.25 *(978-1-4777-2407-1(9)*, cfcc71ed-5946-406e-80ad-0ec9a1a0088e) Rosen Publishing Group, Inc., The. (Rosen Classroom).

Hatch Jr., B. J. Butch. Professor Rock Ltd. Chatham, Dennis J., illus. 2003. 32p. (J). 14.95 *(978-1-56167-808-2(2))* American Literary Pr.

Hirsch, Rebecca E. Sedimentary Rocks, 1 vol. 2014. (Rocks & Minerals Ser.). (ENG., Illus.). 48p. (J). (gr. 4-8). lib. bdg. 35.64 *(978-1-62403-390-2(3)*, 1630) ABDO Publishing Co.

Hirschmann, Kris. Rocks & Minerals. 2004. (World Discovery Science Readers Ser.). (Illus.). 31p. (J). pap. 4.95 *(978-0-439-56630-8(4))* Scholastic, Inc.

Hodge, Judith. Riches from Earth & Las riquezas de la Tierra: 6 English, 6 Spanish Adaptations. 2011. (ENG & SPA.). (J). 97.00 net. *(978-1-4108-5716-3(6))* Benchmark Education Co.

Hoffman, Steven M. Rock Study: A Guide to Looking at Rocks, 1 vol. 2011. (Rock It! Ser.). (ENG., Illus.). 24p. (J). (gr. 3-4). pap. 9.25 *(978-1-4488-2713-8(2)*, 6bb46636-3110-4b00-b789-201eef284cef); lib. bdg. 26.27 *(978-1-4488-2562-2(8)*, 5d93d3a4-2b28-4f48-88cb-d8a7037bde18) Rosen Publishing Group, Inc., The. (PowerKids Pr.).

Honovich, Nancy. Ultimate Explorer Field Guide: Rocks & Minerals. 2016. (ENG., Illus.). 160p. (J). (gr. 3-7). lib. bdg. 22.90 *(978-1-4263-2302-7(6)*, National Geographic Kids) Disney Publishing Worldwide.

—Ultimate Explorer Field Guide: Rocks & Minerals. 2016. (Illus.). 160p. (J). (gr. 3-7). pap. 12.99 *(978-1-4263-2301-0(8)*, National Geographic Kids) Disney Publishing Worldwide.

Horning, Nicole. Let's Explore Earth's Rocks!, 1 vol. 2020. (Earth Science Explorers Ser.). (ENG.). 24p. (gr. 1-2). pap. 9.22 *(978-1-5026-5621-6(3)*, 657aa772-649f-4906-8843-8cbe64eed140) Cavendish Square Publishing LLC.

Hosford, William G. Geo the Geode. Hosford, William G., illus. 2006. (Illus.). 32p. (J). lib. bdg. 19.95 *(978-0-9776562-0-2(9)*, CN0601) WGH Arts LLC.

Howell, Sara. The Rock Cycle. 2017. (Let's Find Out! Our Dynamic Earth Ser.). (Illus.). 32p. (J). (gr. 6-10). 77.40 *(978-1-5383-0028-2(1))* Rosen Publishing Group, Inc., The.

Hutmacher, Kimberly. Fossils & Rocks. 2012. (My Science Library). (ENG.). 24p. (gr. 4-5). pap. 8.95 *(978-1-61810-236-2(2)*, 9781618102362) Rourke Educational Media.

Hyde, Natalie. How to Be a Rock Collector. 2012. (Let's Rock! Ser.). (ENG., Illus.). 32p. (J). (gr. 3-6). lib. bdg. *(978-0-7787-7212-5(8))* Crabtree Publishing Co.

—What Are Sedimentary Rocks?, 1 vol. 2010. (Let's Rock! Ser.). (ENG., Illus.). 32p. (J). (gr. 4-4). pap. *(978-0-7787-7235-4(7))* Crabtree Publishing Co.

—What Is the Rock Cycle? 2010. (ENG.). 32p. (J). lib. bdg. *(978-0-7787-7231-6(4))*; (Illus.). (gr. 4-4). pap. *(978-0-7787-7236-1(5))* Crabtree Publishing Co.

Hyler, Nelson W. The How & Why Wonder Book of Rocks & Minerals. Blackwood, Paul E., ed. Shannon, Kenyon, illus. 2011. 52p. 36.95 *(978-1-258-10482-5(2))* Literary Licensing, LLC.

Ipcizade, Catherine. The Rock Cycle: A 4D Book. 2018. (Cycles of Nature Ser.). (ENG., Illus.). 24p. (J). (gr. -1-2). lib. bdg. 29.32 *(978-1-9771-0038-2(4)*, 138180, Capstone Pr.) Capstone.

Jennings, Terry. Rocas y Suelos (Rocks & Soils) (SPA.). 32p. (J). 6.95 *(978-84-348-1912-2(0))* SM Ediciones ESP. Dist: AIMS International Bks., Inc.

Lang, Sheri. I Sort Rocks: Putting Data in Order, 1 vol. 2017. (Computer Science for the Real World Ser.). (ENG.). 8p. (gr. k-1). pap. *(978-1-5383-5020-1(3)*, d0603a54-7817-43af-b1f9-ad81e735a159, Rosen Classroom) Rosen Publishing Group, Inc., The.

Lawrence, Ellen. Baking & Crushing: A Look at Metamorphic Rock. 2015. (Illus.). 24p. (J). lib. bdg. 26.99 *(978-1-62724-300-1(3))* Bearport Publishing Co., Inc.

—Famous Rocks. 2015. (Illus.). 24p. (J). lib. bdg. 26.99 *(978-1-62724-297-4(X))* Bearport Publishing Co., Inc.

—How Do People Use Rocks? 2014. (Science Slam!: Rock-Ology Ser.). (ENG.). 24p. (J). (gr. -1-3). lib. bdg. 26.99 *(978-1-62724-303-2(8))* Bearport Publishing Co., Inc.

—How Do Volcanoes Make Rock? A Look at Igneous Rock. 2015. (Illus.). 24p. (J). lib. bdg. 26.99 *(978-1-62724-298-1(8))* Bearport Publishing Co., Inc.

—How Do Water & Wind Change Rock? A Look at Sedimentary Rock. 2015. (Illus.). 24p. (J). lib. bdg. 26.99 *(978-1-62724-299-8(6))* Bearport Publishing Co., Inc.

—Rocks & Minerals. 2015. (FUN-Damental Experiments Ser.). (ENG.). 24p. (J). (gr. -1-3). lib. bdg. 26.99 *(978-1-62724-540-1(5))* Bearport Publishing Co., Inc.

—What Are Rocks Made Of? 2015. (Illus.). 24p. (J). lib. bdg. 26.99 *(978-1-62724-302-5(X))* Bearport Publishing Co., Inc.

—What Is the Rock Cycle? 2015. (Illus.). 24p. (J). lib. bdg. 26.99 *(978-1-62724-304-9(6))* Bearport Publishing Co., Inc.

Let's Rock, 7 vols., Set. Incl. Igneous Rocks. Oxlade, Chris. pap. 8.29 *(978-1-4329-4687-6(0)*, 114420); Sedimentary Rocks. Oxlade, Chris. pap. 8.29 *(978-1-4329-4689-0(7)*, 114421); Soil. Spilsbury, Richard & Spilsbury, Louise. pap. 8.29 *(978-1-4329-4693-7(5)*, 114425); (J). (gr. 3-6). (Let's Rock Ser.). (ENG.). 32p. 2011. pap., pap., pap. 55.93 o.p. *(978-1-4329-4694-4(3)*, 15642, Heinemann) Capstone.

Lilly, Melinda. Rocks. (Read & Do Science Ser.). (Illus.). (J). 20.64 *(978-1-58952-647-1(3))* Rourke Educational Media.

—Rocks. Thompson, Scott M., photos by. 2005. (Rourke Discovery Library). (Illus.). 24p. (J). (gr. 1-4). lib. bdg. 14.95 *(978-1-59515-404-0(3)*, 1244275) Rourke Educational Media.

Lindeen, Mary. Investigating the Rock Cycle. 2015. (Searchlight Books (tm) — What Are Earth's Cycles? Ser.). (ENG., Illus.). 40p. (J). (gr. 3-5). 30.65 *(978-1-4677-8058-2(8)*, 1d22420e-f1ee-4476-8d7b-56269719199d, Lerner Pubns.) Lerner Publishing Group.

Lockwood, Sophie. Junior Scientists: Experiment with Rocks. 2010. (Explorer Junior Library: Science Explorer Junior Ser.). (ENG., Illus.). 32p. (gr. 3-6). lib. bdg. 32.07 *(978-1-60279-836-6(2)*, 200538) Cherry Lake Publishing.

—Rocks. 2009. (Explorer Library: Science Explorer Ser.). (ENG., Illus.). 32p. (gr. 4-8). lib. bdg. 32.07 *(978-1-60279-523-5(1)*, 200283) Cherry Lake Publishing.

A Look at Earth's Rocks. 2017. (Look at Earth's Rocks Ser.). 32p. (gr. 2-2). pap. 63.00 *(978-1-4824-6283-8(4))*; (ENG.). lib. bdg. 169.62 *(978-1-4824-6281-4(8)*, 4489e588-4bc2-4030-9fcc-8c3105112464) Stevens, Gareth Publishing LLLP.

Lowery, Lawrence F. Spenser & the Rocks. 2013. (I Wonder Why Ser.). (ENG., Illus.). 36p. (J). (gr. k-3). pap. 13.99 *(978-1-938946-11-0(1))* National Science Teachers Assn.

Lugtu, Carol & Lindeen, Carol K. Lo Básico de Las Rocas/Rock Basics. Translations.com, tr. 2010. (Lo Básico de la Naturaleza/Nature Basics Ser.).Tr. of Rock Basics. (MUL.). 24p. (J). (gr. -1-2). lib. bdg. 24.65 *(978-1-4296-5348-0(5)*, 113773) Capstone.

Lynch, Dan R. Rock Collecting for Kids: An Introduction to Geology. 2018. (Simple Introductions to Science Ser.). (Illus.). 144p. (J). (gr. 1-7). pap. 12.95 *(978-1-59193-773-9(6)*, Adventure Pubns.) AdventureKEEN.

Lynch, Dan R. & Lynch, Bob. Rocks & Minerals of the Pacific Coast: Your Way to Easily Identify Rocks & Minerals. 2018. (Adventure Quick Guides). (ENG., Illus.). 22p. spiral bd. 9.95 *(978-1-59193-775-3(2)*, Adventure Pubns.) AdventureKEEN.

MacAulay, Kelley. Why Do We Need Rocks & Minerals? 2014. (Natural Resources Close-Up Ser.). (ENG., Illus.). 24p. (J). (gr. 1-1). *(978-0-7787-0492-8(0))*; pap. *(978-0-7787-0496-6(3))* Crabtree Publishing Co.

Malizia, Diana. A Visual Guide to Rocks & Minerals, 1 vol. 2017. (Visual Exploration of Science Ser.). (ENG.). 104p. (YA). (gr. 8-8). 38.80 *(978-1-5081-7710-4(4)*, 5137ab09-e79c-4934-88e8-e22d50f2276d); pap. 18.65 *(978-1-5081-7886-6(0)*, 4e42db98-1c6f-4537-94b1-4b6ccfa3d72c) Rosen Publishing Group, Inc., The. (Rosen Young Adult).

Maloof, Torrey. Rocks & Minerals, 1 vol. rev. ed. 2014. (Science: Informational Text Ser.). (ENG.). 32p. (gr. 2-3). pap. 10.99 *(978-1-4807-4610-7(X))* Teacher Created Materials, Inc.

Mattern, Joanne. Igneous Rocks & the Rock Cycle. (Shaping & Reshaping of Earth's Surface Ser.). 24p. (gr. 4-4). 2009. 42.50 *(978-1-60854-214-7(9)*, PowerKids Pr.) 2005. (ENG., Illus.). (YA). lib. bdg. 26.27 *(978-1-4042-3196-2(X)*, e5a9cbe6-a91c-45ef-b9bf-cbf51ff16c7f) Rosen Publishing Group, Inc., The.

—Metamorphic Rocks & the Rock Cycle. (Shaping & Reshaping of Earth's Surface Ser.). 24p. (gr. 4-4). 2009. 42.50 (978-1-60854-215-4(7), PowerKids Pr.) 2005. (ENG., Illus.). (YA). lib. bdg. 26.27 (978-1-4042-3194-8(3), db93e260-edd2-44e1-aa99-fdb6bb240a8c) Rosen Publishing Group, Inc., The.

—Minerals & the Rock Cycle. (Shaping & Reshaping of Earth's Surface Ser.). 24p. (gr. 4-4). 2009. 42.50 (978-1-60854-218-5(1), PowerKids Pr.) 2005. (ENG., Illus.). (YA). lib. bdg. 26.27 (978-1-4042-3199-3(4), 1a5c5be0-113a-4da5-b8b7-25c6cbaa5616) Rosen Publishing Group, Inc., The.

—Sedimentary Rocks & the Rock Cycle. (Shaping & Reshaping of Earth's Surface Ser.). 24p. (gr. 4-4). 2009. 42.50 (978-1-60854-224-6(6), PowerKids Pr.) 2005. (ENG., Illus.). (YA). lib. bdg. 26.27 (978-1-4042-3195-5(1), f4ac0854-bed7-4bbe-9371-2b40827bd2d2) Rosen Publishing Group, Inc., The.

McCarthy, Cecilia Pinto. Metamorphic Rocks. 2016. (Geology Rocks! Ser.). (ENG.). 24p. (J). (gr. 3-6). 32.79 (978-1-5038-0802-7(5), 210638) Child's World, Inc, The.

McConnell, William. Rocks & Fossils. (Reading Room Collection 1 Ser.). 16p. (gr. 2-3). 2009. 37.50 (978-1-60851-950-7(3), PowerKids Pr.) 2005. (ENG., Illus.). (J). lib. bdg. 22.27 (978-1-4042-3344-7(X), 62d54fe4-1df2-453a-b6a5-15eb70dcbf90) Rosen Publishing Group, Inc., The.

Meierhenry, Mark, et al. The Mystery of the Round Rocks. 2007. (Mystery Ser.). (ENG., Illus.). 44p. (gr. 2-5). 13.95 (978-0-9777955-3-6(5), P240882, South Dakota State Historical Society Pr.) South Dakota Historical Society Pr.

Melon, Zach. Rocky's Rock Collection, 1 vol. 2013. (Rosen Readers Ser.). (ENG.). 24p. (J). (gr. 2-2). pap. 8.25 (978-1-4777-2243-5(2), 644698da-7167-4ba0-9c08-f2d2b39c7219); pap. 49.50 (978-1-4777-2244-2(0), Rosen Classroom) Rosen Publishing Group, Inc., The.

Meredith, Susan. Las Rocas, los Minerales y el Suelo. 2012. (Let's Explore Science Ser.). (SPA.). 48p. (gr. 4-8). pap. 10.95 (978-1-61810-470-0(5), 9781618104700) Rourke Educational Media.

—Rocks, Minerals, & Soil. 2009. (Let's Explore Science Ser.). (Illus.). 48p. (J). (gr. 4-8). lib. bdg. 32.79 (978-1-60694-411-0(8)) Rourke Educational Media.

Miles, Lisa. Rocks & Minerals. 2003. (Usborne Hotshots Ser.). (ENG., Illus.). 1p. (YA). (gr. 2-18). pap. 2.95 (978-0-7460-2790-5(7)) EDC Publishing.

—Usborne Rocks & Minerals Sticker Book. Khan, Sarah & Armstrong, Carrie, eds. Freeman, Mike & Julings, Emma, photos by. rev. ed. 2006. (Spotter's Guides Sticker Books - New Format Ser.). (Illus.). 16p. (J). (gr. 2-5). pap. 8.99 (978-0-7945-1413-6(8), Usborne) EDC Publishing.

Mills, Nathan & Roza, Greg. Exploring Rocks & Minerals. 2012. (Rosen Readers Ser.). (ENG., Illus.). 24p. (J). (gr. 1-2). pap. 49.50 (978-1-4488-8831-3(X), 1348003); pap. 8.25 (978-1-4488-8830-6(1), cea7c3c6-1c6b-445c-a127-bd820e828bb3) Rosen Publishing Group, Inc., The. (Rosen Classroom).

Moore, Elizabeth. Looking at Rocks, 1 vol. 2011. (Wonder Readers Early Level Ser.). (ENG.). 16p. (gr. -1-1). (J). pap. 6.25 (978-1-4296-7809-4(7), 117981); pap. 35.94 (978-1-4296-8123-0(3)) Capstone. (Capstone Pr.).

Morgan, Sally. Rocks. 2011. (Earth Cycles Ser.). 32p. (YA). (gr. 3-6). lib. bdg. 28.50 (978-1-59920-525-0(4)) Black Rabbit Bks.

Morlock, Theresa. 20 Fun Facts about Rocks & Gems, 1 vol. 2017. (Fun Fact File: Earth Science Ser.). (ENG.). 32p. (J). (gr. 2-3). pap. 11.50 (978-1-5382-1189-2(0), 88cd9cbe-ec6b-49fb-9bb1-04abb719d0ee) Stevens, Gareth Publishing LLLP.

Mortensen, Lori. Salt Rocks! 2016. (Spring Forward Ser.). (J). (gr. 2). (978-1-4900-9436-6(9)) Benchmark Education Co.

Nagle, Frances. What Are Sedimentary Rocks?, 1 vol. 2017. (Look at Earth's Rocks Ser.). (ENG.). 32p. (gr. 2-2). 28.27 (978-1-4824-6240-1(0), 9bbf3178-f7ab-4c39-8f90-4023c3b92d8b) Stevens, Gareth Publishing LLLP.

—What Is the Rock Cycle?, 1 vol. 2017. (Look at Earth's Rocks Ser.). (ENG.). 32p. (J). (gr. 2-2). pap. 11.50 (978-1-4824-6019-3(X), d8e5b8d5-3fd6-42ad-bfa0-4f88c5248a5a) Stevens, Gareth Publishing LLLP.

National Geographic Learning. Reading Expeditions (Science: Earth Science): Rocks & Minerals. 2007. (Nonfiction Reading & Writing Workshops Ser.). (ENG., Illus.). 32p. (J). pap. 18.95 (978-0-7922-4571-1(7)) CENGAGE Learning.

Natural History Museum Collection Staff. Rocks & Minerals Sticker Book. 2013. (ENG.). 14p. (J). (gr. -1-1). pap. 9.99 (978-0-565-09300-6(2)) Natural History Museum Pubns. GBR. Dist: Independent Pubs. Group.

Nelson, Maria. Igneous Rocks, 1 vol. 2013. (That Rocks! Ser.). 24p. (J). (gr. 2-3). (ENG.). 25.27 (978-1-4339-8313-9(3), a665a0e4-a9e8-4965-90b6-558836f58e1d); (ENG.). pap. 9.15 (978-1-4339-8314-6(1), 5d9efcff-745f-4437-b3c6-53efe31520a0); pap. 48.90 (978-1-4339-8315-3(X)) Stevens, Gareth Publishing LLLP.

—Metamorphic Rocks, 1 vol. 2013. (That Rocks! Ser.). 24p. (J). (gr. 2-3). (ENG.). pap. 9.15 (978-1-4339-8318-4(4), 42a6dcec-f385-4547-96d9-d041f5f391a5); (ENG.). lib. bdg. 25.27 (978-1-4339-8317-7(6), 0eb4930a-8e95-46cb-b500-19be5c407e8d); pap. 48.90 (978-1-4339-8319-1(2)) Stevens, Gareth Publishing LLLP.

—The Rock Cycle, 1 vol. 2013. (That Rocks! Ser.). (ENG., Illus.). 24p. (J). (gr. 2-3). pap. 9.15 (978-1-4339-8326-9(5), 4e20a1b5-5c69-489f-8240-7a772b0d361b); lib. bdg. 25.27 (978-1-4339-8325-2(7), 1be59448-1e4d-4938-9b11-77556dc35b35) Stevens, Gareth Publishing LLLP.

—Sedimentary Rocks. 2013. (That Rocks! Ser.). 24p. (J). (gr. 2-5). pap. 48.90 (978-1-4339-8323-8(0)); (ENG., Illus.). pap. 9.15 (978-1-4339-8322-1(2), 2a0a7de4-54a3-4654-8dd9-0122a1f0e9f1); (ENG., Illus.). lib. bdg. 25.27 (978-1-4339-8321-4(4), 40678965-c742-4f41-8e52-4d7675e51211) Stevens, Gareth Publishing LLLP.

—Weathering & Erosion, 1 vol. 2013. (That Rocks! Ser.). (ENG., Illus.). 24p. (J). (gr. 2-3). pap. 9.15 (978-1-4339-8330-6(3), 37a6622d-220a-46f0-972d-dd2e66144852); lib. bdg. 25.27 (978-1-4339-8329-0(X), 404495fd-d351-4b5a-ac65-74083857ef05) Stevens, Gareth Publishing LLLP.

Nelson, Robin. Rocks. 2005. (First Step Nonfiction Ser.). (J). (Illus.). 23p. (gr. -1-3). lib. bdg. 18.60 (978-0-8225-2599-8(2), Lerner Pubns.); pap. 5.95 (978-0-8225-5375-5(9)) Lerner Publishing Group.

Newson, Lesley & Wadsworth, Pamela. Rhagor Am Greigiau, Pridd a Thywydd. 2005. (WEL., Illus.). 24p. pap. (978-1-85596-238-5(1)) Dref Wen.

Nsrc, prod. Science & Technology for Children BOOKS: Rocks & Minerals. 2007. (J). (978-1-933008-40-0(7), Science and Technology Concepts (STC)) Smithsonian Science Education Ctr. (SSEC).

O'Donoghue, Michael. Rocks & Minerals of the World. 2004. (World Book's Science & Nature Guides Ser.). (Illus.). 80p. (J). (978-0-7166-4217-6(4)) World Bk., Inc.

Olson, Elsie. Exploring the Rock Cycle: Petrologists at Work! 2017. (Earth Detectives Ser.). (ENG., Illus.). 24p. (J). (gr. k-4). lib. bdg. 32.79 (978-1-5321-1232-4(7), 27619, Super SandCastle) ABDO Publishing Co.

O'Neal, Claire. A Project Guide to Rocks & Minerals. 2010. (Earth Science Projects for Kids Ser.). (Illus.). 48p. (J). (gr. 4-7). lib. bdg. 29.95 (978-1-58415-866-0(2)) Mitchell Lane Pubs.

Ostopowich, Melanie. The Rock Cycle. (Focus on Earth Science Ser.). (gr. 3-6). 2015. (ENG.). (J). lib. bdg. 27.13 (978-1-4896-4093-2(2), AV2 by Weigl) 2010. (Illus.). 24p. (J). pap. 11.95 (978-1-60596-968-8(0)) 2010. (Illus.). 24p. (YA). lib. bdg. 25.70 (978-1-60596-967-1(2)) 2006. (Illus.). 24p. (J). lib. bdg. 24.45 (978-1-59036-209-9(8)) Weigl Pubs., Inc.

—Rocks. (Focus on Earth Science Ser.). 2015. (ENG.). (J). (gr. 3-6). lib. bdg. 27.13 (978-1-4896-4089-5(4), AV2 by Weigl) 2010. (Illus.). 24p. (J). (gr. 3-5). pap. 11.95 (978-1-60596-962-6(1)) 2010. (Illus.). 24p. (YA). (gr. 3-6). lib. bdg. 25.70 (978-1-60596-961-9(3)) 2004. (Illus.). 24p. (J). lib. bdg. 24.45 (978-1-59036-210-5(1)) Weigl Pubs., Inc.

Owen, Ruth. Science & Craft Projects with Rocks & Soil, 1 vol. 2013. (Get Crafty Outdoors Ser.). (ENG., Illus.). 32p. (J). (gr. 2-3). 30.27 (978-1-4777-0246-8(6), f2a967f2-9843-4ea9-bb1c-19b48ee2cca2); pap. 12.75 (978-1-4777-0255-0(5), d0be45d2-a926-4418-bc9e-b297f565040d) Rosen Publishing Group, Inc., The. (PowerKids Pr.).

Owings, Lisa. Igneous Rocks, 1 vol. 2014. (Rocks & Minerals Ser.). (ENG., Illus.). 48p. (J). (gr. 4-8). lib. bdg. 35.64 (978-1-62403-387-2(3), 1624) ABDO Publishing Co.

Oxlade, Chris. Igneous Rocks, 1 vol. 2011. (Let's Rock Ser.). (ENG.). 32p. (J). (gr. 3-6). pap. 8.29 (978-1-4329-4687-6(0), 114420, Heinemann) Capstone.

—Sedimentary Rocks, 1 vol. 2011. (Let's Rock Ser.). (ENG.). 32p. (J). (gr. 3-6). pap. 8.29 (978-1-4329-4689-0(7), 114421, Heinemann) Capstone.

Pellant, Chris & Pellant, Helen. Granite & Other Igneous Rocks, 1 vol. 2007. (Guide to Rocks & Minerals Ser.). (ENG., Illus.). 32p. (gr. 3-5). lib. bdg. 28.67 (978-0-8368-7906-3(6), dd453a73-3032-4456-aea0-fdb8d2e1c263, Gareth Stevens Learning Library) Stevens, Gareth Publishing LLLP.

—Marble & Other Metamorphic Rocks, 1 vol. 2007. (Guide to Rocks & Minerals Ser.). (ENG., Illus.). 32p. (gr. 3-5). lib. bdg. 28.67 (978-0-8368-7907-0(4), 6095c8ff-a92a-499a-a05f-573f57ebc76f, Gareth Stevens Learning Library) Stevens, Gareth Publishing LLLP.

—Sandstone & Other Sedimentary Rocks, 1 vol. 2007. (Guide to Rocks & Minerals Ser.). (ENG., Illus.). 32p. (gr. 3-5). lib. bdg. 28.67 (978-0-8368-7909-4(0), 91a52fef-630d-4fa3-a0ba-fc054143d02f, Gareth Stevens Learning Library) Stevens, Gareth Publishing LLLP.

Peters, Elisa. What Are Igneous Rocks?, 1 vol., 1. 2015. (Junior Geologist Ser.). (ENG., Illus.). 32p. (J). (gr. 2-3). pap. 13.90 (978-1-5081-0047-8(0), b29d4775-2a76-4122-9366-e92780457bec, Britannica Educational Publishing) Rosen Publishing Group, Inc., The.

Peterson, Judy Monroe. What Are Metamorphic Rocks?, 1 vol., 1. 2015. (Junior Geologist Ser.). (ENG., Illus.). 32p. (J). (gr. 2-3). pap. 13.90 (978-1-5081-0048-5(9), 1c555276-02a9-4355-8618-1c32d42c3e38, Britannica Educational Publishing) Rosen Publishing Group, Inc., The.

Pinet, Michele. Be Your Own Rock & Mineral Expert. Greenbaum, Fay, tr. from FRE. Korkos, Alain, illus. 2003. 40p. (J). (gr. 5-7). 14.95 (978-0-8069-9580-9(7)) Sterling Publishing Co., Inc.

Rafferty, John P. Rocks, 1 vol. 2011. (Geology: Landforms, Minerals, & Rocks Ser.). (ENG., Illus.). 296p. (gr. 10-10). lib. bdg. 55.29 (978-1-61530-492-9(4), d3251e3d-c7cb-49fc-a010-de16b06656d5) Rosen Publishing Group, Inc., The.

Rajczak Nelson, Kristen. What Are Igneous Rocks? 2017. (Look at Earth's Rocks Ser.). (Illus.). 32p. (gr. 2-2). pap. 63.00 (978-1-4824-6252-4(4)) Stevens, Gareth Publishing LLLP.

—What Are Metamorphic Rocks?, 1 vol. 2017. (Look at Earth's Rocks Ser.). (ENG.). 32p. (gr. 2-2). pap. 11.50 (978-1-4824-6248-7(6), 7e605937-d776-411a-acdb-67e212ba4d6b) Stevens, Gareth Publishing LLLP.

Rau, Dana Meachen. Rocks & Minerals. 2009. (21st Century Skills Library: Real World Science Ser.). (ENG., Illus.). 32p. (gr. 4-8). lib. bdg. 32.07 (978-1-60279-463-4(4), 200233) Cherry Lake Publishing.

Red Hot Rocks!, 6 Packs. (Bookweb Ser.). 32p. (gr. 6-18). 34.00 (978-0-7578-0911-8(1)) Rigby Education.

Reid, Struan & McConnell, William. Rocks & Fossils. 2006. (Rosen Real Readers Big Bookstm Ser.). (ENG.). 16p. (gr. 2-3). 37.95 (978-1-4042-6221-8(0)) Rosen Publishing Group, Inc., The.

Reynolds, Shaye. Volcanoes, 1 vol. 2016. (Spotlight on Earth Science Ser.). (ENG.). 24p. (J). (gr. 4-6). pap. 11.00 (978-1-4994-2537-6(6), f8ca81ff-e7e7-439b-ae9a-0d270f3d1cf8, PowerKids Pr.) Rosen Publishing Group, Inc., The.

Riley, Peter. Rocks & Soil, 1 vol. 2016. (Moving up with Science Ser.). (ENG.). 32p. (J). (gr. 3-4). pap. 11.00 (978-1-4994-3153-7(8), 4ba9fcd8-eea1-4dbe-b21a-897f487f00be, PowerKids Pr.) Rosen Publishing Group, Inc., The.

Rissman, Rebecca. Rocks & Soil: Real Size Science. 2013. (Real Size Science Ser.). (ENG., Illus.). 24p. (J). (gr. -1-1). 25.32 (978-1-4329-7882-2(9), 122823); pap. 6.95 (978-1-4329-7889-1(6), 122829) Capstone. (Heinemann).

Rivera, Andrea. Rocks. 2017. (Rocks & Minerals (Launch!) Ser.). (ENG., Illus.). 24p. (J). (gr. -1-2). lib. bdg. 31.36 (978-1-5321-2047-3(8), 25344, Abdo Zoom-Launch) ABDO Publishing Co.

The Rock Cycle. 2013. (That Rocks! Ser.). 24p. (J). (gr. 2-5). pap. 48.90 (978-1-4339-8327-6(3)) Stevens, Gareth Publishing LLLP.

Rocks & Minerals, 5 vols. 2014. (Rocks & Minerals Ser.: 8). (ENG.). 48p. (J). (gr. 4-8). lib. bdg. 213.84 (978-1-62403-383-4(0), 1616) ABDO Publishing Co.

Rocks & Minerals. 2005. 48p. (J). per. 6.99 (978-1-59441-202-8(2), CD-104110) Carson-Dellosa Publishing, LLC.

Rocks & Minerals. 2009. (Hammond Undercover Ser.). 72p. (J). (gr. 3-7). 15.95 (978-0-8437-1932-1(X)) Hammond World Atlas Corp.

Romaine, Garret. Rocking Out with Rocks: Exploring the Wonders of Igneous, Sedimentary, & Metamorphic Rocks. 2018. (Geology Lab for Kids Ser.). (ENG., Illus.). 32p. (J). (gr. 3-6). lib. bdg. 27.99 (978-1-63159-456-4(7), 23bc4fad-8327-42b5-b6ea-0d51fc1ce02a, Quarry Bks.) Quarto Publishing Group USA.

Rosinsky, Natalie M. & Picture Window Books Staff. Las Rocas: Duras, Blandas, Lisas y Ásperas. Robledo, Sol, tr. John, Matthew, illus. 2007. (Ciencia Asombrosa Ser.). (SPA.). 24p. (J). (gr. k-4). 27.32 (978-1-4048-3225-1(4), 93777, Picture Window Bks.) Capstone.

Royston, Angela. Rock: Let's Look at a Pebble. 2005. (J). (978-1-4109-1826-0(2)); (ENG.). 24p. pap. (978-1-4109-1833-8(5)) Steck-Vaughn.

Roza, Greg. Exploring Rocks & Minerals, 1 vol. 2012. (Exploring Earth & Space Ser.). (ENG., Illus.). 24p. (J). (gr. 1-2). 26.27 (978-1-4488-8576-3(0), 21abb025-21f7-4501-b80e-eb3e9c214cbd, PowerKids Pr.) Rosen Publishing Group, Inc., The.

Rupert, Matthews. Visual Factfinder Rocks & Fossils. 2008. 512p. pap. (978-1-84810-080-0(9)) Miles Kelly Publishing, Ltd.

Rupp, Rebecca. Rocks. 2004. (J). (978-1-58017-540-1(6)); pap. (978-1-58017-539-5(2)) Storey Publishing, LLC.

Russell, Carol & Russell, Tally. I Like Rocks! Russell, Fletch, photos by. 2011. (Illus.). 32p. pap. 12.95 (978-1-4634-3271-3(2)) AuthorHouse.

Salas, Laura Purdie. A Rock Can Be ... Dabija, Violeta, illus. 2015. (Can Be ... Bks.). (ENG.). 32p. (J). (gr. k-2). lib. bdg. 18.99 (978-1-4677-2110-3(7), 220a54b5-9250-4c31-9ffc-ae38607e7428, Millbrook Pr.) Lerner Publishing Group.

Salzano, Tammi J. Rocks, Minerals, & Gemstones. Jankowski, Daniel, illus. 2009. 24p. (J). pap. (978-0-545-19868-4(2)) Scholastic, Inc.

Sawyer, Ava. Metamorphic Rocks. 2018. (Rocks Ser.). (ENG., Illus.). 32p. (J). (gr. 3-6). lib. bdg. 27.99 (978-1-5435-2702-5(7), 138138, Capstone Pr.) Capstone.

—Rocks. 2018. (Rocks Ser.). (ENG.). 32p. (J). (gr. 3-6). 119.96 (978-1-5435-2731-5(0), 28211, Capstone Pr.) Capstone.

—Sedimentary Rocks. 2018. (Rocks Ser.). (ENG., Illus.). 32p. (J). (gr. 3-6). lib. bdg. 27.99 (978-1-5435-2703-2(5), 138139, Capstone Pr.) Capstone.

Schuh, Mari. Learning about Rocks. 2011. (Science Builders Ser.). (ENG.). 24p. (J). (gr. k-1). pap. 44.74 (978-1-4296-7114-9(9), 16695, Capstone Pr.) Capstone.

Schuh, Mari C. Learning about Rocks, 1 vol. 2011. (Science Builders Ser.). (ENG.). 24p. (J). (gr. -1-2). lib. bdg. 27.32 (978-1-4296-6072-3(4), 115006); pap. 7.29 (978-1-4296-7108-8(4), 116768) Capstone.

The Shaping & Reshaping of Earth's Surface, 10 vols. 2005. (Shaping & Reshaping of Earth's Surface Ser.). (ENG., Illus.). (J). (gr. 4-4). 131.35 (978-1-4042-3296-9(6), 548acefa-4a4d-43fe-8642-19109429e938) Rosen Publishing Group, Inc., The.

Sian revision rock Origins. 2004. (J). (978-1-59242-063-6(X)) Delta Education, LLC.

Simon, Seymour. Rocks & Minerals. 2017. (ENG., Illus.). 48p. (J). (gr. 1-5). 17.99 (978-0-06-228918-6(7)); pap. 7.99 (978-0-06-228917-9(9)) HarperCollins Pubs. (HarperCollins).

Slade, Suzanne. The Rock Cycle. (Cycles in Nature Ser.). 24p. (gr. 3-3). 2009. 42.50 (978-1-61512-116-8(1), PowerKids Pr.) 2007. (ENG., Illus.). (YA). lib. bdg. 26.27 (978-1-4042-3493-2(4), 3c0fb4ad-ad27-4d3f-8b65-a85f2549d7e7) Rosen Publishing Group, Inc., The.

Smith, Miranda & Callery, Sean. Rocks, Minerals & Gems. 2016. (ENG., Illus.). 224p. (J). (gr. 3-7). 19.99 (978-0-545-94719-0(7), Scholastic Nonfiction) Scholastic, Inc.

Spilsbury, Louise. What Is the Rock Cycle?, 1 vol., 1. 2013. (Let's Find Out! Earth Science Ser.). (ENG., Illus.). 32p. (J). (gr. 2-3). 27.04 (978-1-62275-266-9(X), f8f5bae2-cdea-4a41-9571-520124c7873d) Rosen Publishing Group, Inc., The.

Spilsbury, Richard & Spilsbury, Louise. The Rock Cycle, 1 vol. 2018. (Flowchart Smart Ser.). (ENG.). 48p. (gr. 4-5). pap. 15.05 (978-1-5382-3476-1(9), 4202d731-1413-4e79-9496-b05f9dcf8db7) Stevens, Gareth Publishing LLLP.

Stamper, Judith Bauer. Rocks & Minerals. 2010. (Illus.). 32p. (J). pap. (978-0-545-28544-5(5)) Scholastic, Inc.

Storey, Rita. Rocks & Stones. 2007. (How We Use Materials/Watts Ser.). (Illus.). 30p. (J). (gr. 4-7). lib. bdg. 28.50 (978-1-59920-006-4(6)) Black Rabbit Bks.

Strother, Ruth. Absolute Expert: Rocks & Minerals. 2019. (Absolute Expert Ser.). (Illus.). 112p. (J). (gr. 3-7). 14.99 (978-1-4263-3279-1(3), National Geographic Kids) Disney Publishing Worldwide.

Sundance/Newbridge LLC Staff. Rocks & Soil. 2007. (Early Science Ser.). (gr. k-3). 18.95 (978-1-4007-6441-9(6)); pap. 6.10 (978-1-4007-6437-2(8)) Sundance/Newbridge Educational Publishing.

Swanson, Jennifer. Metamorphic Rocks, 1 vol. 2014. (Rocks & Minerals Ser.). (ENG., Illus.). 48p. (J). (gr. 4-8). lib. bdg. 35.64 (978-1-62403-388-9(1), 1626) ABDO Publishing Co.

That Rocks!, 12 vols. 2013. (That Rocks! Ser.). 24p. (J). (gr. 2-3). (ENG.). 151.62 (978-1-4339-8333-7(8), ddedd381-250e-4877-9401-0deee00d51fa); pap. 48.90 (978-1-4339-9737-2(1)); pap. 293.40 (978-1-4339-9738-9(X)) Stevens, Gareth Publishing LLLP.

Tomecek, Steve. Jump into Science: Rocks & Minerals. 2010. (Jump into Science Ser.). (Illus.). 32p. (J). (gr. -1-k). 16.95 (978-1-4263-0538-2(9), National Geographic Kids) Disney Publishing Worldwide.

—National Geographic Kids Everything Rocks & Minerals: Dazzling Gems of Photos & Info That Will Rock Your World. 2011. (National Geographic Kids Everything Ser.). (ENG., Illus.). 64p. (J). (gr. 3-7). 25.90 (978-1-4263-0801-7(9), National Geographic Kids) Disney Publishing Worldwide.

—National Geographic Kids Everything Rocks & Minerals: Dazzling Gems of Photos & Info That Will Rock Your World! 2011. (National Geographic Kids Everything Ser.). (Illus.). 64p. (J). (gr. 3-7). pap. 12.95 (978-1-4263-0768-3(3), National Geographic Kids) Disney Publishing Worldwide.

Trueit, Trudi Strain. Rocks, Gems, & Minerals. 2003. (Watts Library). (ENG.). 64p. (gr. 5-7). pap. 8.95 (978-0-531-16241-5(9), Watts, Franklin) Scholastic Library Publishing.

Tuchman, Gail. Rocks & Minerals. 2015. (Scholastic Reader Level 2 Ser.). lib. bdg. 13.55 (978-0-606-37757-7(3)) Turtleback.

van Voorst, Jenny Fretland. Metamorphic Rocks. 2019. (Rocks & Minerals Ser.). (ENG., Illus.). 32p. (J). (gr. 3-8). pap. 8.99 (978-1-61891-743-0(9), 12324, Blastoff! Discovery) Bellwether Media.

—Sedimentary Rocks. 2019. (Rocks & Minerals Ser.). (ENG., Illus.). 32p. (J). (gr. 3-8). pap. 8.99 (978-1-61891-744-7(7), 12325, Blastoff! Discovery) Bellwether Media.

van Voorst, Jenny Fretland & VanVoorst, Jenny Fretland. Igneous Rocks. 2019. (Rocks & Minerals Ser.). (ENG., Illus.). 32p. (J). (gr. 3-8). pap. 8.99 (978-1-61891-742-3(0), 12323, Blastoff! Discovery) Bellwether Media.

VanVoorst, Jenny Fretland. Igneous Rocks. 2019. (Rocks & Minerals Ser.). (ENG., Illus.). 32p. (J). (gr. 3-8). lib. bdg. 27.95 (978-1-64487-075-4(4), Blastoff! Discovery) Bellwether Media.

—Sedimentary Rocks. 2019. (Rocks & Minerals Ser.). (ENG., Illus.). 32p. (J). (gr. 3-8). lib. bdg. 27.95 (978-1-64487-077-8(0), Blastoff! Discovery) Bellwether Media.

Vink, Amanda. How Are Rocks Formed? If... Then, 1 vol. 2017. (Computer Kids: Powered by Computational Thinking Ser.). (ENG.). 24p. (J). (gr. 4-5). 25.27 (978-1-5383-2400-4(8), ba0df7cc-062e-4ed7-9dff-c6cf11ac8860, PowerKids Pr.); pap. (978-1-5383-5302-8(4), aba1af58-4abb-4dc0-90cd-ae32a4d48a28, Rosen Classroom) Rosen Publishing Group, Inc., The.

Wadsworth, Pamela. Creigiau, Pridd a Thywydd. 2005. (WEL., Illus.). 24p. pap. (978-1-85596-237-8(3)) Dref Wen.

Wadsworth, Pamela & Tate, Sylvia. Golwg Gyntaf Ar Greigiau, Pridd a Thywydd. 2005. (WEL., Illus.). 24p. pap. (978-1-85596-253-8(5)) Dref Wen.

Walker, Kate. Rocks, 1 vol. 2012. (Investigating Earth Ser.). (ENG.). 32p. (gr. 2-2). 31.21 (978-1-60870-560-3(9), d30ecfd5-a781-4f57-9d41-d82b155a83f3) Cavendish Square Publishing LLC.

Walker, Sally M. Marveling at Minerals. 2013. (Searchlight Books (tm) — Do You Dig Earth Science? Ser.). (ENG., Illus.). 40p. (J). (gr. 3-5). pap. 9.99 (978-1-4677-0792-3(9), 2ce3eac5-2b46-4572-a938-9aa8b1de52d6) Lerner Publishing Group.

—Researching Rocks. 2013. (Searchlight Books (tm) — Do You Dig Earth Science? Ser.). (ENG., Illus.). 40p. (J). (gr. 3-5). pap. 9.99 (978-1-4677-0793-0(7), 97094727-4a7a-4e0d-8721-18f8fc57c9ef) Lerner Publishing Group.

—Rocks. (Illus.). 48p. 2007. (J). pap. 8.95 (978-0-8225-6621-2(4)) 2006. (ENG., (gr. 2-5). lib. bdg. 26.60 (978-0-8225-5947-4(1), Lerner Pubns.) Lerner Publishing Group.

Wallace, Nancy Elizabeth. Rocks! Rocks! Rocks!, 0 vols. Wallace, Nancy Elizabeth, illus. 2012. (ENG., Illus.). 48p. (J). (gr. 1-3). 17.99 (978-0-7614-5528-8(0), 9780761455288, Two Lions) Amazon Publishing.

Watts, Pam. The Rock Cycle. 2016. (Geology Rocks! Ser.). (ENG.). 24p. (J). (gr. 3-6). 32.79 (978-1-5038-0804-1(1), 210642) Child's World, Inc, The.

Weathering & Erosion. 2013. (That Rocks! Ser.). 24p. (J). (gr. 2-5). pap. 48.90 (978-1-4339-8331-3(1)) Stevens, Gareth Publishing LLLP.

Wermund, Jerry. The World According to Rock. Sansevero, Tony, illus. 2005. 48p. (J). pap. (978-0-9726255-1-7(8)) Rockon Publishing.

West, Krista. Hands-On Projects about Rocks, Minerals & Fossils, 1 vol. 2004. (Great Earth Science Projects Ser.). (ENG., Illus.). 24p. (J). (gr. 3-4). lib. bdg. 26.27 (978-0-8239-5842-9(6), c9db3f00-971e-458d-be3b-09eb1599b156, PowerKids Pr.) Rosen Publishing Group, Inc., The.

What Happens to Rock? 6 Each of 1 Student Book, 6 vols. (Sunshinetm Science Ser.). 24p. (gr. 1-2). 41.95 (978-0-7802-2720-0(4)) Wright Group/McGraw-Hill.

What Happens to Rock? Big Book. (Sunshinetm Science Ser.). 24p. (gr. 1-2). 37.50 (978-0-7802-2794-1(8)) Wright Group/McGraw-Hill.

Williams, Zella. Experiments on Rocks & the Rock Cycle. (Do-It-Yourself Science Ser.). 24p. (gr. 2-3). 2009. 47.90 (978-1-61512-187-8(0), PowerKids Pr.) 2007. (ENG., Illus.). (YA). lib. bdg. 28.93 (978-1-4042-3660-8(0), 781c8975-cda2-49cb-beb6-b2ed7849678d) Rosen Publishing Group, Inc., The.

Woolf, Alex. The Science of Rocks & Minerals: the Hard Truth about the Stuff Beneath Our Feet (the Science of the Earth) (Library Edition) Sordo, Paco, illus. 2018. (Science Of... Ser.). (ENG.). 32p. (J). (gr. 3-7). lib. bdg. 29.00 (978-0-531-22768-8(5), Watts, Franklin) Scholastic Library Publishing.

Woolley, A. Rocks & Minerals. 2004. (Spotter's Guides). (Illus.). 64p. (J). lib. bdg. 13.95 *(978-1-58086-309-4(4))* EDC Publishing.

Woolley, Alan. Rocks & Minerals Spotter's Guide: With Internet Links. Freeman, Mike, photos by. rev. ed. 2007. (Spotter's Guides). (Illus.). 64p. (J). pap. 5.99 *(978-0-7945-1304-7(2),* Usborne) EDC Publishing.

Yomtov, Nel. Rocks & the People Who Love Them. Foss, Timothy, illus. 2012. (Adventures in Science Ser.). (ENG.). 32p. (gr. 3-4). pap. 47.70 *(978-1-4296-8466-8(6));* (J). pap. 8.10 *(978-1-4296-7988-6(3),* 118320) Capstone. (Capstone Pr.).

Zemlicka, Shannon. From Rock to Road. 2004. (Start to Finish Ser.). (J). pap. 4.95 *(978-0-8225-2146-4(6));* 18.60 *(978-0-8225-1391-9(9),* Lerner Pubns.) Lerner Publishing Group.

Zoehfeld, Kathleen. National Geographic Readers: Rocks & Minerals. 2012. (Readers Ser.). (Illus.). 32p. (J). (gr. 1-3). pap. 5.99 *(978-1-4263-1038-6(2),* National Geographic Kids); (ENG., lib. bdg. 14.90 *(978-1-4263-1039-3(0),* National Geographic Children's Bks.) Disney Publishing Worldwide.

ROCKS—AGE

see Geology, Stratigraphic

ROCKS—FICTION

Agha-Khan, Aliyar. Cyrus & Kaleo Go Rock Hunting. 2012. 32p. pap. 12.99 *(978-1-4634-1567-9(2))* AuthorHouse.

Backus, Leatha F. Annie & Timmy's Magic Pebbles. 2008. 32p. per. 24.95 *(978-1-4241-9513-8(6))* America Star Bks.

Barker, Charles Ferguson. Under Ohio: The Story of Ohio's Rocks & Fossils. 2016. (ENG.). 56p. (J). (gr. 3-8). pap. 17.95 *(978-0-8214-2195-6(6))* Ohio Univ. Pr.

Bowlby, Linda S. The Rock Garden. Helms, Dana, illus. 2008. 29p. (J). (gr. -1-3). pap. 9.95 *(978-0-9779993-4-7(3))* Red Earth Publishing.

Bradfield, Roger. Hello, Rock. 2012. (ENG., Illus.). 28p. (J). 9.95 *(978-1-930900-64-6(3))* Purple Hse. Pr.

—¡Hola, Piedrita!/Hello, Rock. 2012. (SPA., Illus.). 25p. (J). (gr. -1-3). 9.95 *(978-1-930900-65-3(1))* Purple Hse. Pr.

Briggs, Molly Anne. Momma's Favorite Rock. 2006. (J). pap. 8.00 *(978-0-8059-7070-8(3))* Dorrance Publishing Co., Inc.

Brooke, Samantha. Rock Man vs. Weather Man. 2018. (Illus.). 31p. (J). *(978-1-5444-0658-9(4))* Scholastic, Inc.

Caddy, David. The Reef. 2005. 144p. (Orig.). (J). pap. 13.50 *(978-1-920731-29-8(6))* Fremantle Pr. AUS. Dist: Independent Pubs. Group.

Canavan, Charles Patrick. Rocky's Road to Sunshine. 2013. (ENG., Illus.). 30p. (J). pap. 19.95 *(978-1-4787-1251-0(1))* Outskirts Pr., Inc.

Carney, Charles. A Day Just for Daddies. 2011. (Illus.). 24p. (J). 15.99 *(978-1-60010-439-8(8))* Idea & Design Works, LLC.

Ciraolo, Simona. Hug Me. 2014. (ENG., Illus.). 32p. (J). (gr. -1-k). 17.99 *(978-1-909263-49-9(4))* Flying Eye Bks. GBR. Dist: Penguin Random Hse. LLC.

Cook, Sherry & Johnson, Terri. Ronnie Rock. 26. Kuhn, Jesse, illus. I.t. ed. 2006. (Quirkles — Exploring Phonics through Science Ser.: 18). 32p. (J). 7.99 *(978-1-933815-17-6(5),* Quirkles, The) Creative 3, LLC.

The Coolest Rock. (Early Intervention Levels Ser.). 31.86 *(978-0-7362-0668-6(X))* CENGAGE Learning.

Cornfield, Lynda Ellis. Rocks for Clean Oceans. 2009. 28p. pap. 13.99 *(978-1-4389-8417-9(0))* AuthorHouse.

Dey, Joy M. Agate: What Good Is a Moose? Johnson, Nikki, illus. 2007. 32p. (J). (gr. -1-3). 17.95 *(978-0-942235-73-9(8))* Lake Superior Publishing LLC.

Fagan, Cary. Ella May & the Wishing Stone. Côté, Geneviève, illus. 2011. 32p. (J). (gr. -1-1). 17.95 *(978-1-77049-225-7(9),* Tundra Bks.) Tundra Bks. CAN. Dist: Penguin Random Hse. LLC.

Ferry, Beth. Stick & Stone. 2017. (Stick & Stone Ser.). (ENG., Illus.). 38p. (J). (— 1). bds. 7.99 *(978-1-328-71432-9(2),* 1673785, Clarion Bks.) HarperCollins Pubs.

—Stick & Stone. Lichtenheld, Tom, illus. 2015. (Stick & Stone Ser.). (ENG.). 48p. (J). (gr. -1-3). 19.99 *(978-0-544-03256-9(X),* 1530246, Clarion Bks.) HarperCollins Pubs.

Fitzsimmons, Christy. Krissy & the Indians, 1 vol. Steckler, Megan, illus. 2009. 28p. pap. 24.95 *(978-1-61546-206-3(6))* America Star Bks.

Frazier, Sundee T. Brendan Buckley's Universe & Everything in It. 2008. (ENG.). 208p. (J). (gr. 3-7). 7.99 *(978-0-440-42206-8(X),* Yearling) Random Hse. Children's Bks.

Frazier, Sundee Tucker. Brendan Buckley's Universe & Everything in It, 1. 2008. (Brendan Buckley Ser.). (ENG.). 208p. (J). (gr. 4-6). lib. bdg. 21.19 *(978-0-385-90445-2(2),* Delacorte Pr.) Random Hse. Children's Bks.

Griffin, Molly Beth. Rhoda's Rock Hunt. Bell, Jennifer A., illus. 2014. (ENG.). 32p. (J). (gr. -1-2). 17.95 *(978-0-87351-950-2(7))* Minnesota Historical Society Pr.

Hargis, Alvin. Kingdom of Mystique Series: Book 1. 2007. 25p. pap. 24.95 *(978-1-4241-8635-8(8))* PublishAmerica, Inc.

Hassett, Ann. Bob's Rock. Hassett, John, illus. 2017. (ENG.). 32p. (J). (gr. -1-3). 16.99 *(978-0-8075-0672-1(9),* 807506729) Whitman, Albert & Co.

Herndon, Susen A. Janie's World: Under the Rock. 2013. 40p. (gr. 4-6). pap. 16.46 *(978-1-4669-7472-2(9))* Trafford Publishing.

Hufford, Lottie. God's Talking Child Rocks. 2012. 28p. pap. 13.95 *(978-1-4525-5782-3(9))* Balboa Pr.

Jensen Shaffer, Jody. A Chip off the Old Block. Miyares, Daniel, illus. 2018. 32p. (J). (gr. k-3). 17.99 *(978-0-399-17388-2(9),* Nancy Paulsen Books) Penguin Young Readers Group.

King, Steve. The Stone Dragon. 2005. 80p. pap. 16.95 *(978-1-4137-9628-5(1))* PublishAmerica, Inc.

Klassen, Jon. The Rock from the Sky. Klassen, Jon, illus. 2021. (ENG.). 96p. (J). (gr. -1-3). 18.99 *(978-1-5362-1562-5(7))* Candlewick Pr.

Lukidis, Lydia. The Space Rock Mystery. Ng-Benitez, Shirley, illus. 2018. (Science Solves It! Ser.). 32p. (J). (gr. 1-4). pap. 5.99 *(978-1-63592-005-5(1),* 51229387-47db-44c0-a484-6644dc80d71b, Kane Press) Astra Publishing Hse.

Lyons, Kelly Starling. Rock Star #1. Brantley-Newton, Vanessa, illus. 2017. (Jada Jones Ser.: 1). 96p. (J). (gr. 1-3). 6.99 *(978-0-448-48751-9(9));* (ENG.). lib. bdg. 15.99 *(978-0-448-48752-6(7))* Penguin Young Readers Group. (Penguin Workshop).

Malone, Ladawn. The Master's Garden. 2009. 32p. pap. 14.49 *(978-1-4490-3860-1(3))* AuthorHouse.

Martin, Stephen W. Charlotte & the Rock. Cotterill, Samantha, illus. 2017. (ENG.). 32p. (J). (-k). 18.99 *(978-1-101-99389-7(8),* Dial Bks) Penguin Young Readers Group.

McRary, Janie. The Rock That Became a Friend. 2011. 24p. pap. 12.74 *(978-1-4634-3018-4(3))* AuthorHouse.

Milord, Susan. Pebble: A Story about Belonging. Milord, Susan, illus. 2007. (ENG., Illus.). 32p. (J). (gr. -1-2). 15.99 *(978-0-06-085807-0(9),* HarperCollins) HarperCollins Pubs.

Murray, Andrew. On a Tall, Tall Cliff. Snow, Alan, illus. 2005. (ENG.). 32p. (J). (gr. k-2). 19.99 *(978-0-00-712155-7(5))* HarperCollins Pubs. Ltd. GBR. Dist: Independent Pubs. Group.

Orobosa-Ogbeide, Kathryn. Adam's Magic Pebble. 2012. 20p. pap. 13.77 *(978-1-4669-1896-2(9))* Trafford Publishing.

Pair, Regether. The Little Rock Island & a Little Rock Named Sam Who Doesn't Think He Fits In. 2012. 20p. pap. 24.95 *(978-1-4626-9807-3(7))* America Star Bks.

Parnell, Paul. Talking Rocks. 2009. 52p. pap. 16.95 *(978-1-61546-651-1(7))* America Star Bks.

Perry, Phyllis J. The Secrets of the Rock. Lipking, Ron, illus. 2004. (Fribble Mouse Library Mystery Ser.). 96p. (J). 16.95 *(978-1-932146-22-6(9),* 1237661) Highsmith Inc.

Pilutti, Deb. Old Rock (Is Not Boring) Pilutti, Deb, illus. 2020. (Illus.). 40p. (J). (gr. -1-3). 18.99 *(978-0-525-51818-1(5),* G.P. Putnam's Sons Books for Young Readers) Penguin Young Readers Group.

Viau, Nancy. Samantha Hansen Has Rocks in Her Head, 1 vol. 2019. (ENG.). 192p. (gr. 3-6). 16.99 *(978-0-7643-5692-6(5),* 9887) Schiffer Publishing, Ltd.

Wenzel, Brendan, illus. A Stone Sat Still. 2019. (ENG.). 56p. (J). (gr. -1-k). 17.99 *(978-1-4521-7318-4(4))* Chronicle Bks. LLC.

Weston Woods Staff, creator. Elizabeti's Doll. 2011. 18.95 *(978-0-439-73629-9(3));* 38.75 *(978-0-439-84574-8(2))* Weston Woods Studios, Inc.

Zito, Ann R. Rock, Stream, Tree. Matheny, Melody, illus. 2010. 52p. pap. 11.00 *(978-1-4520-7822-9(X))* AuthorHouse.

ROCKY MOUNTAINS

Aloian, Molly. The Rocky Mountains, 1 vol. 2011. (ENG., Illus.). 48p. (J). pap. *(978-0-7787-7570-6(4));* (gr. 4-7). lib. bdg. *(978-0-7787-7563-8(1))* Crabtree Publishing Co.

Asnong, Jocey, illus. Rocky Mountain ABCs. 2016. 28p. (— 1). bds. 12.00 *(978-1-77160-163-4(9))* Rocky Mountain Bks.

Bauer, Marion Dane. The Rocky Mountains: Ready-To-Read Level 1. Wallace, John, illus. (Wonders of America Ser.). (ENG.). 32p. (J). (gr. -1-1). 2019. 17.99 *(978-1-5344-4539-0(0))* 2006. pap. 4.99 *(978-0-689-86948-8(7))* Simon Spotlight. (Simon Spotlight).

Brucken, Kelli M. Bristlecone Pines. 2005. (Wonders of the World Ser.). (ENG., Illus.). 48p. (J). (gr. 4-8). lib. bdg. 29.15 *(978-0-7377-3061-6(7),* Greenhaven Pr., Inc.) Cengage Gale.

Calvert, Patricia. Zebulon Pike: Lost in the Rockies, 1 vol. 2006. (Great Explorations Ser.). (ENG.). 80p. (gr. 6-6). 36.93 *(978-0-7614-1612-8(9),* 4d70d369-f267-4e75-96e0-c7ced87675ca) Cavendish Square Publishing LLC.

Collard, Sneed B., III. Fire Birds. 2015. (Illus.). 48p. (J). *(978-0-9844460-7-0(9))* Bucking Horse Bks.

Frisch, Nate. Rocky Mountain National Park. 2016. (Preserving America Ser.). (ENG.). 48p. (J). (gr. 4-7). pap. 12.00 *(978-1-62832-182-1(2),* 21008, Creative Paperbacks) Creative Co., The.

Furgang, Kathy. Canyons, 1 vol. 2019. (Investigate Earth Science Ser.). (ENG.). 24p. (gr. 2-2). 25.60 *(978-1-9785-0742-5(9),* 462ead7d-4b2b-4aff-b1d5-1850ece9aa96) Enslow Publishing, LLC.

Goyette, Linda. Rocky Mountain Kids, 1 vol. 2008. (ENG., Illus.). 128p. (J). (gr. 3-7). pap. *(978-1-897142-32-5(3),* Brindle & Glass) TouchWood Editions.

Hansen, Grace. Rocky Mountain National Park. 2018. (National Parks (Abdo Kids Jumbo) Ser.). (ENG., Illus.). 24p. (J). (gr. -1-2). lib. bdg. 32.79 *(978-1-5321-8209-9(0),* 29877, Abdo Kids) ABDO Publishing Co.

Hyde, Natalie. Rocky Mountains Research Journal. 2017. (Ecosystems Research Journal Ser.). (Illus.). 32p. (J). (gr. 4-5). *(978-0-7787-3471-0(4));* pap. *(978-0-7787-3496-3(X))* Crabtree Publishing Co.

Justesen, Kim Williams. Hey Ranger! Kids Ask Questions about Rocky Mountain National Park. Newhouse, Judy, illus. 2005. (Hey Ranger! Ser.). (ENG.). 48p. (J). (gr. 1-5). pap. 9.95 *(978-0-7627-3848-9(0),* Falcon Guides) Globe Pequot Pr., The.

Kathrens, Ginger. Cloud: Wild Stallion of the Rockies, Revised & Updated. 2017. (ENG., Illus.). 160p. (J). pap. 19.99 *(978-1-62008-242-3(X),* 2423, CompanionHouse Bks.) Fox Chapel Publishing Co., Inc.

Kernahan, Maria. R Is for Rocky Mountains. Schafbuch, Michael, illus. 2017. (ENG.). 56p. (J). (gr. -1-k). bds. 9.95 *(978-1-942402-46-6(5),* b4b42ae7-d425-495c-a90b-11ddf96d8ba3) Dry Climate Studios.

Loomis, Jennifer A. Wildlife in the Rocky Mountains. Loomis, Jennifer A., photos by. unabr. ed. 2005. (Illus.). 100p. (J). 24.95 *(978-0-88045-159-8(9))* Stemmer Hse. Pubs.

Maynard, Charles W. The Rocky Mountains. (Great Mountain Ranges of the World Ser.). 2009. 24p. (gr. 3-3). 42.50 *(978-1-61513-171-6(X))* 2004. (J). 21.25 *(978-0-8239-6698-1(4))* Rosen Publishing Group, Inc., The. (PowerKids Pr.).

Peluso, Beth A. The Charcoal Forest: How Fire Helps Animals & Plants. Peluso, Beth A., illus. 2007. (Illus.). 56p. (J). (gr. -1-3). pap. 12.00 *(978-0-87842-532-7(2))* Mountain Pr. Publishing Co., Inc.

Tarbox, A. D. A Mountain Food Chain: Nature's Bounty. 2nd ed. 2015. (Odysseys in Nature Ser.). (ENG., Illus.). 80p. (J). (gr. 7-10). *(978-1-60818-540-5(0),* 20968, Creative Education) Creative Co., The.

Tremblay, Danielle, illus. Rocky Mountains Monsters: A Search & Find Book. 2018. (ENG.). 22p. (J). (gr. -1). bds. 9.99 *(978-2-924734-16-2(9))* City Monsters Bks. CAN. Dist: Publishers Group West (PGW).

Walsh, Steve. Zebulon Montgomery Pike: Explorer & Military Officer. 2011. (ENG & SPA., Illus.). 54p. (J). pap. 8.95 *(978-0-86541-123-4(9))* Filter Pr., LLC.

Zeiger, Jennifer. Rocky Mountain (a True Book: National Parks) (Library Edition) 2017. (True Book (Relaunch) Ser.). (ENG., Illus.). 48p. (J). (gr. 3-5). lib. bdg. 31.00 *(978-0-531-23394-8(4),* Children's Pr.) Scholastic Library Publishing.

ROCKY MOUNTAINS—FICTION

Burchfield, Cindy. Gimme, Gimme Moocher Marmots. Burchfield, Cindy, illus. 2007. (Illus.). 48p. per. 18.95 *(978-1-59858-457-8(X))* Dog Ear Publishing, LLC.

Burns, Emily. Marked Evidence. 2003. (Rocky Mountain Mysteries Ser.: 3). (J). per. 4.95 *(978-0-9723259-2-9(1),* RMM3) Covered Wagon Publishing LLC.

Butler, T. Lee. The Ghost on Tanner's Mountain. 2008. (ENG.). 96p. pap. 11.94 *(978-1-4357-5963-3(X))* Lulu Pr., Inc.

Cangilla-McAdam, Claudia. Maria's Mysterious Mission. Crum, Anna-Maria, illus. 2007. 32p. (J). (gr. 3-7). 12.95 *(978-1-56579-588-4(1))* Fielder, John Publishing.

Carr, Roger Vaughan. The Climb. 2007. 96p. (J). pap. *(978-1-4207-0730-4(2))* Sundance/Newbridge Educational Publishing.

Carson, James. The Saddle Boys of the Rockies. 2007. 104p. per. *(978-1-4068-4406-1(3))* Echo Library.

—Saddle Boys of the Rockies or Lost on Th. 2007. pap. *(978-1-4065-1298-4(2))* Dodo Pr.

Derrick Patricia. Beaser the Bear's Rocky Mountain Christmas. Hoch, Doug, illus. 2007. 32p. (J). (gr. -1-3). 18.95 incl. audio compact disk *(978-1-933818-09-2(3))* Animalations.

Derrick, Patricia. Rickity & Snickity at the Balloon Fiesta. Martinez, J-P Loppo, illus. 2007. 32p. (J). (gr. -1-3). 18.95 incl. audio compact disk *(978-1-933818-11-5(5))* Animalations.

Duffield, J. W. Bert Wilson in the Rockies. 2006. 26.95 *(978-1-4218-2964-7(9));* pap. 11.95 *(978-1-4218-3064-3(7))* 1st World Publishing, Inc.

Farah, Mo & Gray, Kes. Go Mo Go: Monster Mountain Chase! Book 1. Kissi, Marta, illus. 2018. (Go Mo Go Ser.). (ENG.). 96p. (J). (gr. k-2). pap. 9.99 *(978-1-4449-3405-2(8))* Hachette Children's Group GBR. Dist: Hachette Bk. Group.

Freitag, Fred. On Hills & Meadows by the River. 2013. 28p. pap. 24.95 *(978-1-63000-584-9(3))* America Star Bks.

James, Will. Cowboy in the Making. rev. ed. (Illus.). 104p. (J). (gr. 4-6). pap. 15.00 *(978-0-87842-439-9(3),* 811) Mountain Pr. Publishing Co., Inc.

Kingston, W. H. G. In the Rocky Mountains. 2007. (Illus.). 228p. per. *(978-1-4065-2892-3(7))* Dodo Pr.

Marsh, Carole. The Mystery in the Rocky Mountains. 2009. (Real Kids, Real Places Ser.). (Illus.). 145p. (J). lib. bdg. 18.99 *(978-0-635-07000-5(6),* Marsh, Carole Mysteries) Gallopade International.

Nesbit, Troy. Jinx of Payrock Canyon. 2014. (Wilderness Mystery Ser.). (ENG., Illus.). 282p. (J). (gr. 3-7). pap. 12.95 *(978-1-58979-865-6(1))* Taylor Trade Publishing.

Noland, Monica. Slide. 2006. 116p. pap. 19.95 *(978-1-4241-4966-7(5))* PublishAmerica, Inc.

Siamon, Sharon. Brave Horse, 1 vol. 6th ed. 2004. (Mustang Mountain Ser.: 6). (ENG., Illus.). 190p. (J). (gr. 1-7). pap. 6.95 *(978-1-55285-528-7(7),* 8c3dc076-be0d-465e-9a95-be27c8638519) Whitecap Bks., Ltd. CAN. Dist: Firefly Bks., Ltd.

Wolfson, Steve. Monster Cheese. Johnson, Bill, illus. 2013. 34p. pap. 10.95 *(978-0-9798324-3-7(8))* Argami Productions, LLC.

RODENTS

Antill, Sara. Porcupines, 1 vol. 2010. (Unusual Animals Ser.). (ENG., Illus.). 24p. (J). (gr. 2-3). pap. 9.15 *(978-1-61533-005-8(4),* e4cef3d6-4897-4f8f-be99-ec515d841967); lib. bdg. 27.27 *(978-1-60754-995-6(6),* 514b831c-f4ec-4359-b6fe-adaa35fd2762) Rosen Publishing Group, Inc., The. (Windmill Bks.).

Borgert-Spaniol, Megan. Capybaras. 2013. (Animal Safari Ser.). (ENG., Illus.). 24p. (J). (gr. k-3). lib. bdg. 26.95 *(978-1-60014-908-5(1),* Blastoff! Readers) Bellwether Media.

Davidson, Rose. National Geographic Readers: Squeak! (L3) 100 Fun Facts about Hamsters, Mice, Guinea Pigs, & More. 2019. (Readers Ser.). (Illus.). 48p. (J). (gr. 3-7). pap. 5.99 *(978-1-4263-3488-7(5));* (ENG., lib. bdg. 14.90 *(978-1-4263-3489-4(3))* Disney Publishing Worldwide. (National Geographic Kids).

Gagne, Tammy. Backyard Jungle Safari Gray Squirrels: Grey Squirrels. 2015. (ENG., Illus.). 32p. (J). 26.50 *(978-1-62469-104-1(8))* Purple Toad Publishing, Inc.

Grack, Rachel. Capybaras. 2019. (Animals of the Rain Forest Ser.). (ENG., Illus.). 24p. (J). (gr. k-3). lib. bdg. 26.95 *(978-1-62617-948-6(4),* Blastoff! Readers) Bellwether Media.

Graham Gaines, Ann. Kids Top 10 Small Mammal Pets, 1 vol. 2014. (American Humane Association Top 10 Pets for Kids Ser.). (ENG.). 48p. (gr. 3-4). 26.93 *(978-0-7660-6650-2(9),* f9e54a01-448b-4020-a7eb-89e4fc22f5ff) Enslow Publishing, LLC.

Hansen, Grace. Capybaras, 1 vol. 2016. (Super Species Ser.). (ENG., Illus.). 24p. (J). (gr. -1-2). lib. bdg. 32.79 *(978-1-68080-543-7(6),* 21366, Abdo Kids) ABDO Publishing Co.

Kalman, Bobbie. Baby Rodents. 2013. (ENG., Illus.). 24p. (J). *(978-0-7787-1009-7(2));* pap. *(978-0-7787-1014-1(9))* Crabtree Publishing Co.

—Guinea Pigs & Other Rodents. 2005. (What Kind of Animal Is It? Ser.). (ENG., Illus.). 32p. (J). (gr. 1-2). lib. bdg. *(978-0-7787-2163-5(9))* Crabtree Publishing Co.

—Rodent Rap. 2010. (My World Ser.). (ENG., Illus.). 16p. (J). (gr. k-2). *(978-0-7787-9438-7(5));* pap. *(978-0-7787-9482-0(2))* Crabtree Publishing Co.

Kalman, Bobbie & Langille, Jacqueline. Les Rongeurs. 2003. (Petit Monde Vivant Ser.). (FRE., Illus.). 32p. (J). pap. 9.95 *(978-2-89579-005-1(1))* Bayard Canada Livres CAN. Dist: Crabtree Publishing Co.

Kalman, Bobbie & Miller, Reagan. Les Cochons D'Inde et Autres Rongeurs. 2011. (Petit Monde Vivant (Small Living World) Ser.: No. 76). (FRE., Illus.). 32p. (J). pap. 9.95 *(978-2-89579-370-0(0))* Bayard Canada Livres CAN. Dist: Crabtree Publishing Co.

Lunis, Natalie. Capybara: The World's Largest Rodent. 2010. (More SuperSized! Ser.). (Illus.). 24p. (J). (gr. k-3). lib. bdg. 26.99 *(978-1-936087-31-0(6),* 1308043) Bearport Publishing Co., Inc.

Lynette, Rachel. Capybaras. 2013. (Jungle Babies of the Amazon Rain Forest Ser.). 24p. (J). (gr. -1-3). lib. bdg. 25.65 *(978-1-61772-753-5(9))* Bearport Publishing Co., Inc.

Markle, Sandra. Los Puercoespines. 2008. (Animales Presas (Animal Prey) Ser.). (SPA.). (J). (gr. 4-7). 25.26 *(978-0-7613-3897-0(7))* Lerner Publishing Group.

Morey, Allan. Capybaras. (Weird & Unusual Animals Ser.). (ENG.). 24p. (J). (gr. 1-4). 2018. pap. 8.99 *(978-1-68152-186-2(5),* 16098) 2017. 20.95 *(978-1-68151-155-9(X),* 14698) Amicus.

Morgan, Sally. Rodents. 2004. (J). lib. bdg. *(978-1-59389-177-0(6))* Cherrytree Bks.

Munro, Roxie. Rodent Rascals. 2018. (ENG., Illus.). 40p. (J). (gr. 1-4). 17.95 *(978-0-8234-3860-0(0))* Holiday Hse., Inc.

Schafer, Susan. Capybaras, 1 vol. 2014. (Giant Animals Ser.). (ENG.). 48p. (gr. 4-4). lib. bdg. 33.07 *(978-1-62712-969-5(3),* e8ec4eb4-45d2-4ba1-90e4-6e516363ae67) Cavendish Square Publishing LLC.

Sill, Cathryn. About Rodents: A Guide for Children, 1 vol. Sill, John, illus. 2016. (About... Ser.: 11). 48p. (J). (gr. -1-2). pap. 7.95 *(978-1-56145-914-8(3))* Peachtree Publishing Co. Inc.

Statts, Leo. Capybaras. 2016. (Swamp Animals Ser.). (ENG.). 24p. (J). (gr. -1-2). 49.94 *(978-1-68079-375-8(6),* 22996, Abdo Zoom-Launch) ABDO Publishing Co.

Stefoff, Rebecca. The Rodent Order, 1 vol. 2009. (Family Trees Ser.). (ENG.). 96p. (gr. 6-6). lib. bdg. 36.93 *(978-0-7614-3073-5(3),* 17747fc7-f4da-4503-8e15-430370b976b4) Cavendish Square Publishing LLC.

Thatcher, Henry. Capybaras & Pygmy Mice, 1 vol., 1. 2014. (Big Animals, Small Animals Ser.). (ENG.). 32p. (J). (gr. 2-3). 28.93 *(978-1-4777-6114-4(4),* 4e9c2bf6-2f20-4202-848f-7534e775a5f5, PowerKids Pr.) Rosen Publishing Group, Inc., The.

Visca, Kelly. How to Draw Cartoon Rodents. 2009. (Kid's Guide to Drawing Ser.). 24p. (gr. 3-3). 47.90 *(978-1-61511-018-6(6),* PowerKids Pr.) Rosen Publishing Group, Inc., The.

World Book, Inc. Staff, contrib. by. Hamsters & Other Pet Rodents. 2009. (J). *(978-0-7166-1370-1(0))* World Bk., Inc.

Zobel, Derek. Gophers. 2011. (Backyard Wildlife Ser.). (ENG., Illus.). 24p. (J). (gr. k-3). lib. bdg. 26.95 *(978-1-60014-597-1(3),* Blastoff! Readers) Bellwether Media.

RODENTS—FICTION

Aguayo, Sal. The Tiny Detective. 2008. 48p. pap. 16.95 *(978-1-60703-859-7(5))* America Star Bks.

—The Tiny Telepaths: A Continuing Saga, 1 vol. 2010. 62p. pap. 19.95 *(978-1-4489-5212-0(3))* America Star Bks.

Bee, William. Stanley the Mailman, 1 vol. 2016. (Stanley Picture Bks.: 5). (ENG., Illus.). 32p. (J). (gr. -1-2). 14.95 *(978-1-56145-867-7(8))* Peachtree Publishing Co. Inc.

—Stanley's Diner, 1 vol. 2015. (Stanley Picture Bks.: 4). (ENG., Illus.). 32p. (J). (gr. -1-2). 14.99 *(978-1-56145-802-8(3))* Peachtree Publishing Co. Inc.

—Stanley's Opposites, 1 vol. 2017. (Stanley Board Bks.: 4). (ENG., Illus.). 20p. (J). (gr. -1 — 1). bds. 6.95 *(978-1-56145-977-3(1))* Peachtree Publishing Co. Inc.

—Stanley's Shapes, 1 vol. 2016. (Stanley Board Bks.: 2). (ENG., Illus.). 20p. (J). (gr. -1 — 1). bds. 6.95 *(978-1-56145-949-0(6))* Peachtree Publishing Co. Inc.

—Stanley's Train, 1 vol. 2019. (Stanley Picture Bks.: 8). (ENG., Illus.). 32p. (J). (gr. -1-2). 14.95 *(978-1-68263-108-9(7))* Peachtree Publishing Co. Inc.

Bee, William, illus. Stanley the Mailman. 2016. (J). pap. *(978-1-56145-946-9(1),* Peachtree Junior) Peachtree Publishing Co. Inc.

Deeks, Graham. Ratrigues & the Invisible Intelligence. 2011. 264p. 27.08 *(978-1-4269-7019-1(6));* pap. 17.08 *(978-1-4269-7020-7(X))* Trafford Publishing.

Ducharme, P. J. The Adventures of Jungle Foot Rot, 1 vol. 2009. 17p. pap. 24.95 *(978-1-60813-918-7(2))* America Star Bks.

Howe, James. Horace & Morris but Mostly Dolores. Walrod, Amy, illus. 2003. (ENG.). 32p. (J). (gr. -1-3). 7.99 *(978-0-689-85675-4(X),* Atheneum Bks. for Young Readers) Simon & Schuster Children's Publishing.

Hungry Hedgehog, 6 Packs. (Story Steps Ser.). (gr. k-2). 29.00 *(978-0-7635-9583-8(7))* Rigby Education.

Jonell, Lynne. Emmy & the Incredible Shrinking Rat, 1. Bean, Jonathan, illus. 2008. (Emmy & the Rat Ser.: 1). (ENG.). 368p. (J). (gr. 4-6). pap. 8.99 *(978-0-312-38460-9(2),* 900053524) Square Fish.

—Emmy & the Incredible Shrinking Rat. I.t. ed. 2008. 426p. (YA). 23.95 *(978-1-4104-0778-8(0))* Thorndike Pr.

Kraegel, Kenneth. Wild Honey from the Moon. Kraegel, Kenneth, illus. 2019. (ENG., Illus.). 64p. (J). (gr. -1-3). 18.99 *(978-0-7636-8169-2(5))* Candlewick Pr.

Lester, Helen. Hooway for Wodney Wat Book & CD, 1 vol. Munsinger, Lynn, illus. 2011. (ENG.). 32p. (J). (gr. -1-3). audio 10.99 *(978-0-547-55217-0(3),* 1450662, Clarion Bks.) HarperCollins Pubs.

Pevear, Ted F. & Pevear, Linda W. The Date in the Junk Yard. 2012. 28p. 24.95 *(978-1-62709-781-9(3))* America Star Bks.

Rylant, Cynthia. The Storm. McDaniels, Preston, illus. 2003. (Lighthouse Family Ser.: 1). (ENG.). 80p. (J). (gr. 1-5). pap. 5.99 *(978-0-689-84882-7(X),* Simon & Schuster Bks. For Young Readers) Simon & Schuster Bks. For Young Readers.

Who Painted the Porcupine. (J). 23.50 *(978-0-8136-3967-3(0))* Modern Curriculum Pr.

Willems, Mo. Naked Mole Rat Gets Dressed. 2009. (ENG., Illus.). 40p. (J). (gr. -1 — 1). 16.99 *(978-1-4231-1437-6(X),* Hyperion Books for Children) Disney Publishing Worldwide.

Willems, Mo, et al, narrated by. Naked Mole Rat Gets Dressed. 2011. (J). (gr. -1-2). 29.95 *(978-0-545-29678-6(1))* Weston Woods Studios, Inc.

Yee, Wong Herbert. Hammy & Gerbee: Mummies at the Museum. Yee, Wong Herbert, illus. 2018. (ENG., Illus.). 112p. (J). pap. 13.99 *(978-1-62779-462-6(X),* 900151451, Holt, Henry & Co. Bks. For Young Readers) Holt, Henry & Co.

Zuill, Andrea. Sweety. 2019. (Illus.). 32p. (J). (gr. -1-2). 18.99 *(978-0-525-58000-3(X)*, Schwartz & Wade Bks.) Random Hse. Children's Bks.

RODEOS

Abdo, Kenny. Rodeos. 2018. (Arena Events Ser.). (ENG., Illus.). 24p. (J). (gr. 2-8). lib. bdg. 31.36 *(978-1-5321-2538-6(0)*, 30085, Abdo Zoom-Fly) ABDO Publishing Co.

ABDO Publishing Company Staff & Hamilton, John. Xtreme Rodeo, 6 vols. 2013. (Xtreme Rodeo Ser.: 6). (ENG.). 32p. (J). (gr. 3-9). lib. bdg. 196.74 *(978-1-61783-976-4(0)*, 15750, Abdo & Daughters) ABDO Publishing Co.

Ambrosek, Renee. Team Roping. 2009. (World of Rodeo Ser.). 48p. (gr. 6-6). 53.00 *(978-1-60854-311-3(0)*, Rosen Reference) Rosen Publishing Group, Inc., The.

Cohn, Jessica. Rodeo, 1 vol. 2nd ed. 2013. (Incredibly Insane Sports Ser.). (ENG., Illus.). 48p. (J). (gr. 4-5). 34.60 *(978-1-4339-8838-7(0)*, 5e9612d8-1a84-446a-89cf-5fd8e0f11a41); pap. 15.05 *(978-1-4339-8839-4(9)*, ca54ed1b-3844-4883-9e41-e4004972c285) Stevens, Gareth Publishing LLLP. (Gareth Stevens Learning Library).

Fisher, Doris. Jackson Sundown: Native American Bronco Buster, 1 vol. Cotton, Sarah, illus. 2018. (ENG.). 32p. (gr. -1-3). 16.99 *(978-1-4556-2361-7(X)*, Pelican Publishing) Arcadia Publishing.

Hamilton, John. Bareback Riding. 2013. (Xtreme Rodeo Ser.). (ENG., Illus.). 32p. (J). (gr. 3-9). lib. bdg. 32.79 *(978-1-61783-977-1(9)*, 15752, Abdo & Daughters) ABDO Publishing Co.

—Barrel Racing. 2013. (Xtreme Rodeo Ser.). (ENG., Illus.). 32p. (J). (gr. 3-9). lib. bdg. 32.79 *(978-1-61783-978-8(7)*, 15754, Abdo & Daughters) ABDO Publishing Co.

—Bull Riding. 2013. (Xtreme Rodeo Ser.). (ENG., Illus.). 32p. (J). (gr. 3-9). lib. bdg. 32.79 *(978-1-61783-979-5(5)*, 15756, Abdo & Daughters) ABDO Publishing Co.

—Rodeo Clown. 2015. (Xtreme Jobs Ser.). (ENG., Illus.). 32p. (J). (gr. 3-9). 32.79 *(978-1-62403-758-0(5)*, 17750, Abdo & Daughters) ABDO Publishing Co.

—Roping. 2013. (Xtreme Rodeo Ser.). (ENG., Illus.). 32p. (J). (gr. 3-9). lib. bdg. 32.79 *(978-1-61783-982-5(5)*, 15762, Abdo & Daughters) ABDO Publishing Co.

—Saddle Bronc Riding. 2013. (Xtreme Rodeo Ser.). (ENG., Illus.). 32p. (J). (gr. 3-9). lib. bdg. 32.79 *(978-1-61783-980-1(9)*, 15758, Abdo & Daughters) ABDO Publishing Co.

—Steer Wrestling. 2013. (Xtreme Rodeo Ser.). (ENG., Illus.). 32p. (J). (gr. 3-9). lib. bdg. 32.79 *(978-1-61783-981-8(7)*, 15760, Abdo & Daughters) ABDO Publishing Co.

Johnson, Robin. Rodeo. 2009. (ENG., Illus.). 32p. (J). (gr. 3-6). lib. bdg. *(978-0-7787-4977-6(0))*; (gr. 4-5). pap. *(978-0-7787-4993-6(2))* Crabtree Publishing Co.

Kubke, Jane. Bull Riding. 2009. (World of Rodeo Ser.). 48p. (gr. 6-6). 53.00 *(978-1-60854-303-8(X)*, Rosen Reference) Rosen Publishing Group, Inc., The.

Kupperberg, Paul. Rodeo Clowns. 2009. (World of Rodeo Ser.). 48p. (gr. 6-6). 53.00 *(978-1-60854-308-3(0)*, Rosen Reference) Rosen Publishing Group, Inc., The.

Laurryssens, Molly. Intro to Rodeo. 2017. (Saddle Up! Ser.). (ENG., Illus.). 48p. (J). (gr. 3-6). lib. bdg. 34.21 *(978-1-5321-1343-7(9)*, 27641, SportsZone) ABDO Publishing Co.

Murphy, Stuart J. Rodeo Time. Wenzel, David T., illus. 2006. (MathStart 3 Ser.). (ENG.). 40p. (J). (gr. 2-5). pap. 6.99 *(978-0-06-055779-9(6)*, HarperCollins) HarperCollins Pubs.

Nelson, Vaunda Micheaux. Let 'Er Buck! George Fletcher, the People's Champion. James, Gordon C., illus. 2019. (ENG.). 40p. (J). (gr. 3-6). 18.99 *(978-1-5124-9808-0(4)*, 799fe64f-7f88-4d71-96f3-7dbc34d475a7, Carolrhoda Bks.) Lerner Publishing Group.

Otterman, Joseph. Rodeo: Conteo. rev. ed. 2019. (Mathematics in the Real World Ser.). (SPA.). 24p. (J). (gr. 1-2). pap. 9.99 *(978-1-4258-2838-7(8))* Teacher Created Materials, Inc.

—Spectacular Sports: Rodeo: Counting (Grade 1) 2018. (Mathematics in the Real World Ser.). (ENG., Illus.). 24p. (J). (gr. 1-2). pap. 9.99 *(978-1-4258-5676-2(4))* Teacher Created Materials, Inc.

Petruccio, Steven James. Rodeo Coloring Book. 2004. (Dover Kids Coloring Bks.). (ENG., Illus.). 32p. (J). (gr. -1-2). pap. 3.99 *(978-0-486-43330-1(7)*, 433307) Dover Pubns., Inc.

Pirk, Wendy & Radford, Duane. Rodeo Roundup, 1 vol. 2017. (ENG., Illus.). 64p. (J). pap. 6.99 *(978-1-896124-63-6(1)*, c9d2af0a-1071-4f2b-b77c-cb7f261bdbcf) Dragon Hill Publishing CAN. Dist: Lone Pine Publishing USA.

Rodeo, 6 bks., Set. (SPA.). (J). (gr. 1-4). lib. bdg. 115.62 *(978-1-57103-382-6(3))* Rourke Educational Media.

Stone, Lynn M. The Rodeo. 2008. (All about the Rodeo Ser.). (Illus.). 32p. (YA). (gr. 4-7). lib. bdg. 28.50 *(978-1-60472-387-8(4))* Rourke Educational Media.

—Rodeo Bronc Riders. 2008. (All about the Rodeo Ser.). (Illus.). 32p. (YA). (gr. 4-7). lib. bdg. 28.50 *(978-1-60472-388-5(2))* Rourke Educational Media.

The World of Rodeo, 8 vols., Set. Incl. Barrel Racing. Broyles, Janell. lib. bdg. 34.47 *(978-1-4042-0543-7(8)*, cb0bbdc7-5e2f-40c7-b703-4b6cd8692d11); Bull Riding. Kubke, Jane & Kubke, Jessica. lib. bdg. 34.47 *(978-1-4042-0544-4(6)*, c41e2963-c57c-46fa-8ba1-f9e170cc0a5e); Team Roping. Ambrosek, Renee. lib. bdg. 34.47 *(978-1-4042-0548-2(9)*, 4b366613-3186-48d5-b0bd-059662a3a387); (Illus.). 48p. (YA). (gr. 6-6). 2006. (World of Rodeo Ser.). (ENG.). 2005. Set lib. bdg. 137.88 *(978-1-4042-0836-0(4)*, 2a722aea-bac5-4fea-842c-6ba8bab0a8bc) Rosen Publishing Group, Inc., The.

RODEOS—FICTION

Abrams, Kelsey. Heart Horse: A Natalie Story. Tejido, Jomike, illus. 2019. (Second Chance Ranch Set 2 Ser.). (ENG.). 120p. (J). (gr. 3-4). pap. 7.99 *(978-1-63163-260-4(0)*, 1631632604); lib. bdg. 27.13 *(978-1-63163-259-4(0)*, 1631632590) North Star Editions. (Jolly Fish Pr.).

Alene, Catherine. The Sky Between You & Me. 2018. 496p. (YA). (gr. 8-12). pap. 10.99 *(978-1-4926-5276-2(8))* Sourcebooks, Inc.

Beecher, Elizabeth. Roy Rogers & Cowboy Toby. Crawford, Mel, illus. 2011. 30p. 35.95 *(978-1-258-03514-3(6))* Literary Licensing, LLC.

Brett, Jan. Armadillo Rodeo. Brett, Jan, illus. 2004. (Illus.). 32p. (J). (gr. -1-3). pap. 8.99 *(978-0-14-240125-5(0)*, Puffin Books) Penguin Young Readers Group.

Compton, Dawn. Grand Entry. Kollman, Carrie, illus. 2004. 64p. pap. 12.95 *(978-1-932196-45-0(5))* WordWright.biz, Inc.

—Leave 'Em Standing. 2005. (Illus.). pap. 12.95 *(978-1-932196-73-3(0))* WordWright.biz, Inc.

Dixon, Franklin W. Showdown at Widow Creek. 2016. (Hardy Boys Adventures Ser.: 11). (ENG., Illus.). 128p. (J). (gr. 3-7). 17.99 *(978-1-4814-3878-0(6)*, Aladdin) Simon & Schuster Children's Publishing.

Dunlap, Sonya K. Responza the Bull Learns the Ropes. 2008. 24p. pap. 17.95 *(978-0-9815245-5-9(9))* Accelerator Bks.

Garretson, Jerri. Kansas Tall Tales: Tenth Anniversary Anthology. Garretson, Jerri & Dollar, Diane A., illus. 2008. 106p. (J). pap. 19.95 *(978-0-9659712-7-0(9))* Ravenstone Pr.

Halvorson, Marilyn. Monteur de Taureau, 1 vol. 2011. (Orca Soundings en Français Ser.). (FRE.). 128p. (YA). (gr. 7-12). pap. 9.95 *(978-1-55469-859-2(6))* Orca Bk. Pubs. USA.

Krulik, Nancy. Rootin' Tootin' Cow Dog #8. Braun, Sebastien, illus. 2015. (Magic Bone Ser.: 8). 128p. (J). (gr. 1-3). bds. 5.99 *(978-0-448-48097-8(2)*, Grosset & Dunlap) Penguin Young Readers Group.

Leipold, Judith. Destiny's Wild Ride, a Tall Tale of the Legendary Hub Hubbell. White, David, illus. 2013. 32p. 24.95 *(978-1-61493-168-3(2))*; pap. 14.95 *(978-1-61493-167-6(4))* Peppertree Pr., The.

Lewis, Ashley. Roads to Rodeos. 2008. 32p. pap. 24.95 *(978-1-60563-259-9(7))* America Star Bks.

Lockyer, John. Billy Rides the Bull, 1 vol. 2018. (ENG., Illus.). 21p. (J). pap. *(978-1-77654-244-4(4)*, Red Rocket Readers) Flying Start Bks.

Maddox, Jake. Cowgirl Grit. Wood, Katie, illus. 2018. (Jake Maddox Girl Sports Stories Ser.). (ENG.). 72p. (J). (gr. 3-6). lib. bdg. 25.32 *(978-1-4965-5847-3(2)*, 136932, Stone Arch Bks.) Capstone.

—Rodeo Challenge. Aburto, Jesus, illus. 2018. (Jake Maddox Sports Stories Ser.). (ENG.). 72p. (J). (gr. 3-6). lib. bdg. 25.99 *(978-1-4965-5865-7(0)*, 136944, Stone Arch Bks.) Capstone.

Peck, Robert Newton. Horse Thief. 2003. 277p. (YA). (gr. 7). 13.65 *(978-0-7569-1461-5(2))* Perfection Learning Corp.

Peschke, Marci. Rodeo Queen, 1 vol. Mourning, Tuesday & Mourning, Tuesday, illus. 2011. (Kylie Jean Ser.). (ENG.). 112p. (J). (gr. 1-3). pap. 4.95 *(978-1-4048-6618-8(3)*, 114680, Picture Window Bks.) Capstone.

Ransom, Jeanie Franz. Cowboy Car. Nedelcu, Ovi, illus. 2017. (ENG.). 40p. (J). (gr. -1-2). 17.99 *(978-1-5039-5097-9(2)*, 9781503950979, Two Lions) Amazon Publishing.

Rodman, Dennis & Warburton, Dustin. Dennis the Wild Bull. 2013. (ENG.). 32p. (J). (gr. -1-5). pap. 16.00 *(978-0-615-75249-5(7))* Neighborhood Pubs.

Santillo, LuAnn. The Best Tricks. Santillo, LuAnn, ed. 2003. (Half-Pint Kids Readers Ser.). (Illus.). 7p. (J). (gr. -1-1). pap. 1.00 *(978-1-59256-082-0(2))* Half-Pint Kids, Inc.

Sargent, Dave & Sargent, Pat. Rusty: (Red Roan) Be Strong & Brave, 30 vols., Vol. 52. Lenoir, Jane, illus. 2003. (Saddle up Ser.: Vol. 52). 42p. (J). pap. 10.95 *(978-1-56763-804-2(X))*; lib. bdg. 23.60 *(978-1-56763-803-5(1))* Ozark Publishing.

Siamon, Sharon. Rodeo Horse, 1 vol. 5th ed. 2003. (Mustang Mountain Ser.: 5). (ENG., Illus.). 144p. (J). (gr. 4-7). pap. 6.95 *(978-1-55285-467-9(1)*, 5b7417ff-3221-403f-ab0b-f8984dff3d90) Whitecap Bks., Ltd. CAN. Dist: Firefly Bks., Ltd.

Townsend, Tom. The Ballad of Ol' Hook. 2006. (YA). pap. 9.95 *(978-1-932196-91-7(9))* WordWright.biz, Inc.

Williams, Suzanne Morgan. Bull Rider. 2010. (ENG.). 256p. (YA). (gr. 7). pap. 10.99 *(978-1-4424-1252-1(6)*, McElderry, Margaret K. Bks.) McElderry, Margaret K. Bks.

—Bull Rider. 2009. (ENG.). 256p. (YA). (gr. 7-8). 17.99 *(978-1-4169-6130-7(5))* Simon & Schuster, Inc.

RODRIGUEZ, ALEX, 1975-

Bradley, Michael. Alex Rodriguez, 1 vol. 2006. (All-Stars Ser.). (ENG., Illus.). 48p. (J). (gr. 4-4). 34.07 *(978-0-7614-1757-6(5)*, 61105109-198a-41cf-a1d5-b9e174269bc3) Cavendish Square Publishing LLC.

Clark, Travis. Alex Rodriguez. 2010. (Role Model Athletes Ser.). (Illus.). 64p. (YA). (gr. 7-12). 22.95 *(978-1-4222-0488-7(X))* Mason Crest.

Gaspar, Joe. Alex Rodriguez, 1 vol. 2010. (Baseball's MVPs Ser.). (ENG., Illus.). 24p. (J). (gr. 1-2). pap. 9.85 *(978-1-4488-1793-1(5)*, 5d0ca29d-fa6f-4097-8295-4677d37c5fac, PowerKids Pr.); lib. bdg. 26.27 *(978-1-4488-0634-8(8)*, a0913be2-ac8b-4a44-bc69-5959c936d68a) Rosen Publishing Group, Inc., The.

Hoffman, Mary Ann. Alex Rodriguez: Baseball Star. (Sports Superstars Ser.). 24p. (gr. 1-1). 2009. 42.50 *(978-1-60853-173-8(2)*, PowerKids Pr.) 2006. (ENG., Illus.). (J). lib. bdg. 26.27 *(978-1-4042-3533-5(7)*, 86b5a7ad-c3e8-412b-9149-98109184e0f3) Rosen Publishing Group, Inc., The.

—Alex Rodriguez: Baseball Star/Estrella del Beisbol. 2009. (Amazing Athletes/Atletas increíbles Ser.). (SPA.). 24p. (gr. 1-2). 42.50 *(978-1-61511-303-3(7)*, Editorial Buenas Letras) Rosen Publishing Group, Inc., The.

Kappes, Serena. Alex Rodriguez. 2006. (Sports Heroes & Legends Ser.). (Illus.). 106p. (J). (gr. 3-7). lib. bdg. 27.93 *(978-0-8225-5963-4(3)*, Lerner Pubns.) Lerner Publishing Group.

Kjelle, Marylou Morano. Alex Rodriguez: Professional Baseball Player. 2005. (Robbie Reader Ser.). (Illus.). 32p. (J). (gr. 4-8). lib. bdg. 25.70 *(978-1-58415-394-8(6))* Mitchell Lane Pubs.

Rodriguez Gonzalez, Tania. Alex Rodriguez. 2012. (Superstars of Baseball ENGLISH Ser.). 32p. (J). (gr. 4). 19.95 *(978-1-4222-2674-2(3))*; (SPA., Illus.). 19.95 *(978-1-4222-2621-6(2))* Mason Crest.

Torsiello, David P. Read about Alex Rodriguez, 1 vol. 2011. (I Like Sports Stars! Ser.). (ENG., Illus.). 24p. (gr. k-2). pap. 10.35 *(978-1-59845-302-7(5)*, f432749f-9b00-4b0b-9b6c-a11c72297a93, Enslow Elementary); lib. bdg. 25.27 *(978-0-7660-3828-8(9)*, c81877d8-aa90-4b3f-82a7-f5a33590731b) Enslow Publishing, LLC.

Uschan, Michael V. Alex Rodriguez, 1 vol. 2011. (People in the News Ser.). (ENG.). 104p. (gr. 7-7). lib. bdg. 41.03 *(978-1-4205-0350-0(2)*, e5c3a5b3-3f8e-4b4a-89b2-e23eebff4ff6, Lucent Pr.) Greenhaven Publishing LLC.

Weber, Terri Smith. Alex Rodrigues: Improving His Game. 2004. (J). pap. *(978-1-932724-19-6(2)*, Bios for Kids) Panda Publishing, L.L.C.

—Alex Rodriguez: Improving His Game. 2004. (J). lib. bdg. *(978-1-932724-18-9(4)*, Bios for Kids) Panda Publishing, L.L.C.

—Alex Rodriguez: Mejorando Su Juego. 2003. (SPA.). (J). pap. *(978-0-9740180-6-5(6))*; lib. bdg. *(978-0-9740180-5-8(8))* Panda Publishing, L.L.C. (Bios for Kids).

Zuehlke, Jeffrey. Alex Rodriguez. (Amazing Athletes Ser.). 32p. 2005. (Illus.). (J). (gr. 2-5). per. 5.95 *(978-0-8225-2311-6(6))* 2005. (Illus.). (J). (gr. 3-7). lib. bdg. 23.93 *(978-0-8225-2427-4(9))* 2009. (ENG.). (gr. 2-5). 25.26 *(978-0-8225-8871-9(4))* 2009. (ENG.). (gr. 2-5). pap. 7.95 *(978-0-8225-8872-6(2)*, First Avenue Editions) Lerner Publishing Group.

—Alex Rodriguez (Revised Edition) 2009. pap. 40.95 *(978-0-7613-4773-6(9))* Lerner Publishing Group.

ROEBLING, WASHINGTON AUGUSTUS, 1837-1926

Ratliff, Tom. You Wouldn't Want to Work on the Brooklyn Bridge! An Enormous Project That Seemed Impossible. Bergin, Mark, illus. 2009. (You Wouldn't Want to Ser.). (ENG.). 32p. (J). (gr. 3-12). 29.00 *(978-0-531-21328-5(5))* Scholastic Library Publishing.

Tomasi, Peter J. Bridge: How the Roeblings Connected Brooklyn to New York. DuVall, Sara et al, illus. 2019. (ENG.). 208p. (gr. 8-17). pap. 18.99 *(978-1-4197-3616-2(7)*, 1145903) Abrams, Inc.

ROENTGEN RAYS

see X-Rays

ROGERS, BUCK (FICTITIOUS CHARACTER)—FICTION

Lawrence, James. Buck Rogers in the 25th Century - The Gray Morrow Years, 1979-1981, Vol. 1. Herman, Daniel, ed. 2013. (ENG., Illus.). 240p. (YA). 49.99 *(978-1-61345-034-5(6)*, 4dad6690-acd3-4fef-bb98-0bb0b4bfb9d7) Hermes Pr.

ROGERS, ROBERT, 1731-1795

Gauch, Patricia Lee. The Impossible Major Rogers. Parker, Robert Andrew, illus. 2008. (J). *(978-1-59078-334-4(4))* Highlights Pr., c/o Highlights for Children, Inc.

Quasha, Jennifer. Robert Rogers: Rogers' Rangers, & the French & Indian War. 2009. (Library of American Lives & Times Ser.). 112p. (gr. 5-5). 69.20 *(978-1-60853-503-3(7))* Rosen Publishing Group, Inc., The.

ROGERS RANGERS

Quasha, Jennifer. Robert Rogers: Rogers' Rangers, & the French & Indian War. 2009. (Library of American Lives & Times Ser.). 112p. (gr. 5-5). 69.20 *(978-1-60853-503-3(7))* Rosen Publishing Group, Inc., The.

ROLLER SKATING

see also In-Line Skating; Skateboarding

Blomquist, Christopher. Street Luge in the X Games. 2009. (Kid's Guide to the X Games Ser.). 24p. (gr. 3-3). 42.50 *(978-1-61511-211-1(1)*, PowerKids Pr.) Rosen Publishing Group, Inc., The.

Group/McGraw-Hill, Wright. Roma Roller Skater: Level H, 6 vols. (Take Twostm Ser.). 16p. 29.95 *(978-0-322-08965-5(4))* Wright Group/McGraw-Hill.

Jackson, Demi. Roller Derby, 1 vol. 2015. (Daredevil Sports Ser.). (ENG.). 32p. (J). (gr. 1-1). 28.27 *(978-1-4824-2999-2(3)*, ede47f77-9bd4-41e6-98c2-a3e3558a176d) Stevens, Gareth Publishing LLLP.

Loh-Hagan, Virginia. Extreme Street Luging. 2016. (Nailed It! Ser.). (ENG., Illus.). 32p. (J). (gr. 4-8). 32.07 *(978-1-63470-488-5(6)*, 207683) Cherry Lake Publishing.

Macy, Sue. Roller Derby Rivals. Collins, Matt, illus. 2019. 40p. (J). (gr. 1-4). pap. 7.99 *(978-0-8234-4185-3(7))* Holiday Hse., Inc.

Shafran, Michael. Extreme Sports Skate! Your Guide to Blading, Aggressive, Vert, Street, Roller Hockey, Speed & More. 2003. (Extreme Sports Ser.). (ENG., Illus.). 64p. (J). (gr. 4-7). pap. 8.95 *(978-0-7922-5107-1(5)*, National Geographic Children's Bks.) National Geographic Society.

ROLLER SKATING—FICTION

Dougherty, Meghan. Dorothy's Derby Chronicles: Woe of Jade Doe. Birnbach, Alece, illus. 2015. (Dorothy's Derby Chronicles Ser.: 2). 288p. (J). (gr. 4-7). pap. 6.99 *(978-1-4926-0147-0(0))* Sourcebooks, Inc.

—Rise of the Undead Redhead. Birnbach, Alece, illus. 2014. (Dorothy's Derby Chronicles Ser.: 1). 256p. (J). (gr. 3-6). pap. 10.99 *(978-1-4022-9535-5(9))* Sourcebooks, Inc.

Eggers, Jeanette S. Grandmas Don't Rollerskate. 2008. 24p. pap. 12.99 *(978-1-4389-1434-3(2))* AuthorHouse.

Jamieson, Victoria. Roller Girl. 2015. (Illus.). (J). (gr. 4-7). (ENG.). 256p. 22.99 *(978-0-525-42967-8(0))*; 240p. pap. 13.99 *(978-0-8037-4016-7(6))* Penguin Young Readers Group. (Dial Bks).

—Roller Girl. 2015. (J). lib. bdg. 24.50 *(978-0-606-37112-4(5))* Turtleback.

Johnson, Andi. Rollerskate Kate. 2004. (Illus.). 16p. 9.00 *(978-1-84161-115-0(8))* Ravette Publishing, Ltd. GBR. Dist: Parkwest Pubns., Inc.

Nash, Andy. Marcus & His Monkey: For Kids Blessed with Popularity. 2010. (J). *(978-0-8127-0452-5(5))* Autumn Hse. Publishing Co.

Rue, Ginger. Aleca Zamm Is Ahead of Her Time. 2017. (Aleca Zamm Ser.: 2). (ENG., Illus.). 128p. (J). (gr. 2-5). pap. 6.99 *(978-1-4814-7063-6(9)*, Aladdin) Simon & Schuster Children's Publishing.

Scotton, Rob. The Rain Is a Pain. 2012. (Splat the Cat: I Can Read Ser.). (J). lib. bdg. 13.55 *(978-0-606-26861-5(8))* Turtleback.

ROMAN ANTIQUITIES

see Classical Antiquities; Rome—Antiquities

ROMAN ART

see Art, Roman

ROMAN CATHOLIC CHURCH

see Catholic Church

ROMAN LITERATURE

see Latin Literature

ROMAN MYTHOLOGY

see Mythology, Classical

ROMAN PHILOSOPHY

see Philosophy, Ancient

ROMANIA

Benge, Janet & Geoff. Christian Heroes - Then & Now - Richard Wurmbrand: Love Your Enemies. 2017. 208p. (YA). pap. 11.99 *(978-1-57658-987-8(0))* YWAM Publishing.

Brinker, Spencer. Romania. 2018. (Countries We Come From Ser.). (ENG., Illus.). 32p. (J). (gr. k-3). 19.95 *(978-1-68402-691-3(1))* Bearport Publishing Co., Inc.

Burgan, Michael. Dracula's Dark World. 2010. (HorrorScapes Ser.). (Illus.). 32p. (J). (gr. 4-7). lib. bdg. 25.27 *(978-1-936087-96-9(0))* Bearport Publishing Co., Inc.

Goldberg, Enid A. & Itzkowitz, Norman. Vlad the Impaler: the Real Count Dracula (a Wicked History) 2008. (Wicked History Ser.). (ENG.). 128p. (J). (gr. 6-12). pap. 5.95 *(978-0-531-13898-4(4)*, Watts, Franklin) Scholastic Library Publishing.

—Wicked History: Vlad the Impaler: The Real Count Dracula. Goldberg, Enid, illus. 2008. (Wicked History Ser.). (ENG.). 128p. (J). (gr. 8-13). 18.69 *(978-0-531-12599-1(8)*, Watts, Franklin) Scholastic Library Publishing.

Indovino, Shaina Carmel. The European Union: Facts & Figures. 2012. (J). *(978-1-4222-2231-7(4))*; *(978-1-4222-2240-9(3))*; pap. *(978-1-4222-2271-3(3))* Mason Crest.

—Romania. 2012. (J). *(978-1-4222-2256-0(X))*; pap. *(978-1-4222-2287-4(X))* Mason Crest.

Kaplan, Arie. Dracula: The Life of Vlad the Impaler, 1 vol. 2011. (Vampires Ser.). (Illus.). 64p. (J). (ENG.). (gr. 5-5). pap. 13.95 *(978-1-4488-2232-4(7)*, 4bfcfbbb-794b-455d-a512-b24bef640664, Rosen Reference); (ENG., (gr. 5-5). lib. bdg. 37.13 *(978-1-4488-1229-5(1)*, e9db5b59-211d-4fb4-b1f8-1bc704b374c4); 77.70 *(978-1-4488-2233-1(5)*, Rosen Reference) Rosen Publishing Group, Inc., The.

Kerns, Ann. Romania in Pictures. 2006. (Visual Geography Series, Second Ser.). (ENG., Illus.). 80p. (gr. 5-12). lib. bdg. 31.93 *(978-0-8225-2497-7(X))* Lerner Publishing Group.

Knox, Barbara J. Castle Dracula: Romania's Vampire Home. 2005. (Castles, Palaces, & Tombs Ser.). (Illus.). 32p. (J). (gr. 2-5). lib. bdg. 28.50 *(978-1-59716-000-1(8))* Bearport Publishing Co., Inc.

Koestler-Grack, Rachel. Elie Wiesel: Witness for Humanity, 1 vol. 2009. (Life Portraits Ser.). (ENG., Illus.). 112p. (J). (gr. 6-8). lib. bdg. 38.67 *(978-1-4339-0054-9(8)*, 74f0f7fc-d07c-4729-897a-72060673239c) Stevens, Gareth Publishing LLLP.

Molnar, Haya Leah. Under a Red Sky: Memoir of a Childhood in Communist Romania. 2010. (ENG., Illus.). 320p. (YA). (gr. 7-12). 26.99 *(978-0-374-31840-6(9)*, 900054301, Farrar, Straus & Giroux (BYR)) Farrar, Straus & Giroux.

Moore Niver, Heather. Was Count Dracula Real?, 1 vol. 2017. (I Want to Know Ser.). (ENG.). 32p. (gr. 3-3). 26.93 *(978-0-7660-9196-2(1)*, d43836ff-d37f-4d90-99de-228d06ce62b8) Enslow Publishing, LLC.

Oprea, Tiberiu. Romania, 1 vol. 2003. (Countries of the World Ser.). (ENG., Illus.). 96p. (gr. 6-8). lib. bdg. 33.67 *(978-0-8368-2367-7(2)*, 99523813-5d48-4709-a2ee-8936edd2ab3c) Stevens, Gareth Publishing LLLP.

Pundyk, Grace. Welcome to Romania, 1 vol. 2004. (Welcome to My Country Ser.). (ENG., Illus.). 48p. (gr. 2-4). lib. bdg. 29.67 *(978-0-8368-2567-1(5)*, 133f79c2-1464-4b40-ac85-c308e66507b2) Stevens, Gareth Publishing LLLP.

Sabatino, Michael. The Legend of Dracula, 1 vol. 2015. (Famous Legends Ser.). (ENG., Illus.). 32p. (J). (gr. 2-3). 26.93 *(978-1-4824-2734-9(6)*, 26121a94-c404-4f2e-bce2-e72215b454c5) Stevens, Gareth Publishing LLLP.

Sheehan, Sean & Nevins, Debbie. Romania, 1 vol. 3rd rev. ed. 2015. (Cultures of the World (Third Edition)(r) Ser.). (ENG., Illus.). 144p. (gr. 5-5). 48.79 *(978-1-5026-0336-4(5)*, e21c6e37-5234-4363-9fdf-699072f55755) Cavendish Square Publishing LLC.

Sullivan, Laura L. Romania, 1 vol. 2019. (Exploring World Cultures (First Edition) Ser.). (ENG.). 32p. (gr. 3-3). pap. 12.16 *(978-1-5026-5160-0(2)*, 91867147-9258-4e15-9e30-540b4f10bc0f) Cavendish Square Publishing LLC.

Van Cleaf, Kristin. Romania. 2008. (Countries Set 6 Ser.). 40p. (gr. k-6). 27.07 *(978-1-59928-785-0(4)*, Checkerboard Library) ABDO Publishing Co.

Weingarten, Ethan. Transylvania, 1 vol. 2014. (Scariest Places on Earth Ser.). (ENG.). 24p. (J). (gr. 2-3). 24.27 *(978-1-4824-1161-4(X)*, 2aa69228-7c38-446c-bc7d-cf6d272487ad) Stevens, Gareth Publishing LLLP.

ROMANIA—FICTION

Bennett, Jenn. The Lady Rogue. 2019. (ENG., Illus.). 384p. (YA). (gr. 9). 18.99 *(978-1-5344-3199-7(3)*, Simon Pulse) Simon Pulse.

Bush, Suzanne & Takes, Deb. Time Will Tell. 2004. 279p. (YA). lib. bdg. 15.95 *(978-0-9747426-0-1(0))* Imagining Possibilities.

Fantaskey, Beth. Jessica Rules the Dark Side. 2012. (ENG.). 320p. (YA). (gr. 9). 16.99 *(978-0-547-39309-4(1)*, 1426896, Clarion Bks.) HarperCollins Pubs.

Henseleit, Jack. The Vampire Knife, Volume 1. 2017. (Witching Hours Ser.: 1). (ENG., Illus.). 240p. (J). (gr. 3-5). pap. 15.99 *(978-1-76012-925-5(9))* Hardie Grant Children?s Publishing AUS. Dist: Independent Pubs. Group.

Hoena, Blake. Beet Juice Buddies. Bardin, Dave, illus. 2018. (Monster Heroes Ser.). (ENG.). 32p. (J). (gr. k-2). lib. bdg. 21.32 *(978-1-4965-6416-0(2)*, 138263, Stone Arch Bks.) Capstone.

Keeney, Stephen S. Spencer the Adventurer & the Castle of Bran. 2009. (ENG.). 256p. (J). pap. 14.99 *(978-1-934135-31-0(3)*, Zumaya Thresholds) Zumaya Pubns. LLC.

Kramer, J. Kasper. The Story That Cannot Be Told. 2020. (ENG., Illus.). 400p. (J). (gr. 3-7). pap. 8.99 (978-1-5344-3069-3(5), Atheneum Bks. for Young Readers) Simon & Schuster Children's Publishing.

Marsh, Carole. The Mystery at Dracula's Castle: Transylvania, Romania. (Around the World in 80 Mysteries Ser.). 133p. (J). 2009. 18.99 (978-0-635-07039-5(1), Marsh, Carole Mysteries) 2008. (Illus.). (gr. 3-5). 14.95 (978-0-635-06471-4(5))9. 2008. (ENG., Illus.). (gr. 4-6). 18.69 (978-0-635-06469-1(3)) Gallopade International.

Matthews, John. Henry Hunter & the Beast of Snagov: Henry Hunter Series #1. 2016. (Henry Hunter Ser.). (ENG., Illus.). 240p. (J). (gr. 2-7). 15.99 (978-1-5107-1038-2(8), Sky Pony Pr.) Skyhorse Publishing Co., Inc.

Stoker, Bram. Dracula. Gilbert, Anne Yvonne, illus. 2010. (ENG.). 96p. (YA). (gr. 7-18). 19.99 (978-0-7636-4793-3(4), Templar) Candlewick Pr.

—Dracula. Schuler, Susan, tr. Ruiz, Alfonso, illus. 2010. (Classic Fiction Ser.). 72p. pap. 0.90 (978-1-4342-2985-4(8), Stone Arch Bks.) Capstone.

—Dracula. Kliros, Thea, illus. abr. ed. 2011. (Dover Children's Thrift Classics Ser.). (ENG.). 96p. (J). (gr. 3-8). reprint ed. pap. 4.00 (978-0-486-29567-1(2), 295672) Dover Pubns., Inc.

—Drácula: Novela Gráfica. Schuler, Susan, tr. Ruiz, Jose, illus. 2010. (Classic Fiction Ser.). (SPA.). 72p. (J). (gr. 5-9). pap. 7.15 (978-1-4342-2277-0(2), 103140, Stone Arch Bks.) Capstone.

Weber, Lori. Strange Beauty, 1 vol. (SideStreets Ser.). (ENG.). 144p. (YA). (gr. 9-12). 2007. 26.19 (978-1-55028-944-2(6), 944) 2006. 8.99 (978-1-55028-941-1(1), 82271134-f3ec-418d-9ec4-27d241ec0443) James Lorimer & Co. Ltd., Pubs. CAN. Dist: Children's Plus, Inc., Lerner Publishing Group.

White, Kiersten. And I Darken. 2017. (And I Darken Ser.: 1). (ENG.). 528p. (YA). (gr. 7). pap. 10.99 (978-0-553-52234-1(5), Ember) Random Hse. Children's Bks.

—Now I Rise. 2017. (And I Darken Ser.: 2). (ENG.). 480p. (YA). (gr. 7). 18.99 (978-0-553-52235-8(3), Delacorte Pr.) Random Hse. Children's Bks.

ROMANIES—FICTION

Clark, Henry. The Book That Proves Time Travel Happens. 2015. (ENG., Illus.). 416p. (J). (gr. 3-7). 17.00 (978-0-316-40617-8(1)) Little, Brown Bks. for Young Readers.

Cook, Norman. Sam in the Crimea: A Victorian Adventure Based on the Work of Lord Shaftesbury. 2007. (Illus.). 128p. (J). (gr. 4-7). per. 9.00 (978-1-84625-045-3(5)) DayOne Pubns. GBR. Dist: Send The Light Distribution LLC.

Duey, Kathleen. The Sunset Gates. Rayyan, Omar, illus. 2005. 76p. (J). lib. bdg. 15.00 (978-1-59054-918-6(X)) Fitzgerald Bks.

—True Heart. Rayyan, Omar, illus. 2005. 76p. (J). lib. bdg. 15.00 (978-1-59054-920-9(1)) Fitzgerald Bks.

Flood, C. J. Infinite Sky. 2015. (ENG., Illus.). 256p. (YA). (gr. 7). pap. 10.99 (978-1-4814-0659-8(0)) Simon & Schuster Children's Publishing.

Gardner, Sally. The Red Necklace. 2009. (ENG.). 400p. (YA). (gr. 7-18). 8.99 (978-0-14-241488-0(3), Speak) Penguin Young Readers Group.

—The Red Necklace: A Story of the French Revolution. 2009. (ENG.). 378p. (YA). (gr. 7). lib. bdg. 19.80 (978-1-5311-8287-8(9)) Perfection Learning Corp.

—The Red Necklace: A Story of the French Revolution. l.t. ed. 2008. 583p. 23.95 (978-1-4104-1016-0(1)) Thorndike Pr.

—The Silver Blade. 2010. (ENG.). 384p. (YA). (gr. 7-18). 8.99 (978-0-14-241731-7(9), Speak) Penguin Young Readers Group.

Gypsy Kids: The Adventures of Colby Myers & Mark Howard. 2003. 21.95 (978-1-932277-00-5(5)) Crystal Ball Publishing, LLC.

Hartnett, Sonya. The Midnight Zoo. Offermann, Andrea, illus. 2018. (ENG.). 224p. (J). (gr. 5-9). pap. 8.99 (978-0-7636-6462-6(6)) Candlewick Pr.

Kent, Trilby. Medina Hill. 2009. 176p. (YA). (gr. 7-9). 19.95 (978-0-88776-888-0(1), Tundra Bks.) Tundra Bks. CAN. Dist: Penguin Random Hse. LLC.

Lindelauf, Benny. Nine Open Arms. Nieuwenhuizen, John, tr. 2014. (ENG., Illus.). 264p. (J). (gr. 3). 16.95 (978-1-59270-146-9(9)) Enchanted Lion Bks., LLC.

Molesworth, Mary Louisa S. Us. 2008. 116p. 22.95 (978-1-60664-989-3(2)) Aegypan.

Roderman, Anna Marie. Two Tales of Courage. 2004. 116p. (YA). pap. 7.95 (978-0-87714-318-5(8)) i-5 Publishing LLC.

Rutkoski, Marie. The Cabinet of Wonders: The Kronos Chronicles: Book I. 2013. (Kronos Chronicles Ser.: 1). (ENG.). 288p. (J). (gr. 5-9). pap. 21.99 (978-1-250-01804-5(8), 900087537) Square Fish.

—The Celestial Globe: The Kronos Chronicles: Book II. 2013. (Kronos Chronicles Ser.: 2). (ENG.). 320p. (J). (gr. 5-9). pap. 23.99 (978-1-250-02732-0(2), 900093304) Square Fish.

—The Jewel of the Kalderash: The Kronos Chronicles: Book III. 2013. (Kronos Chronicles Ser.: 3). (ENG.). 336p. (J). (gr. 5-9). pap. 18.99 (978-1-250-01025-4(X), 900084763) Square Fish.

Strangway, Melissa. Finding Hope. 2012. 82p. pap. 11.65 (978-1-61933-676-6(6)) FastPrncil, Inc.

Surace, Joan. The Story of Lucia. Rockford, Nancy, illus. 2006. (YA). pap. 8.00 (978-0-8059-7062-3(2)) Dorrance Publishing Co., Inc.

ROMANIES—FOLKLORE

Morden, Daniel. Dark Tales from the Woods. 2006. (ENG., Illus.). 102p. (J). (gr. 4-6). 19.99 (978-1-84323-583-5(8)) Gomer Pr. GBR. Dist: Independent Pubs. Group, Casemate Pubs. & Bk. Distributors, LLC.

ROMANOV, HOUSE OF

Fleming, Candace. The Family Romanov: Murder, Rebellion, & the Fall of Imperial Russia. 2014. (ENG., Illus.). 304p. (YA). (gr. 7). 19.99 (978-0-375-86782-8(1), Schwartz & Wade Bks.) Random Hse. Children's Bks.

ROME

Here are entered works about the Roman Empire. Works only on the modern city of Rome are entered under Rome (Italy).

Ancient Romans. 2009. (J). (978-0-7166-2131-7(2)) World Bk., Inc.

AZ Books Staff. Ancient Rome. Naumovets, Elena & Svistunova, Natalia, eds. 2012. (Mysteries of History Ser.). (ENG.). 18p. (J). (gr. 1-3). bds. 17.95 (978-1-61889-090-0(5)) AZ Bks. LLC.

Barber, Nicola. Ancient Roman Sports & Pastimes, 1 vol. 2010. (Ancient Communities: Roman Life Ser.). (ENG.). 32p. (J). (gr. 4-4). pap. 11.60 (978-1-61532-315-9(5), c9e3a8a9-cf7b-45c5-b1eb-27f5b7275fe5); (Illus.). lib. bdg. 30.27 (978-1-61532-306-7(6), d2bcfc1a-44df-494f-ab3b-ec082266c837) Rosen Publishing Group, Inc., The. (PowerKids Pr.).

Beller, Susan Provost. Roman Legions on the March: Soldiering in the Ancient Roman Army. 2007. (Soldiers on the Battlefront Ser.). (ENG., Illus.). 112p. (gr. 6-8). lib. bdg. 33.26 (978-0-8225-6781-3(4)) Lerner Publishing Group.

Bloom, Harold, ed. Antony & Cleopatra. 2008. (ENG.). 290p. (gr. 9-12). 50.00 (978-0-7910-9630-7(0), P145733, Facts On File) Infobase Holdings, Inc.

Dittmer, Lori. Rome. 2019. (Ancient Times Ser.). (ENG.). 24p. (J). (gr. 1-4). (978-1-64026-115-0(X), 18929, Creative Education) Creative Co., The.

Ganeri, Anita. Gladiators & Ancient Rome. 2009. (History Explorers Ser.). (ENG.). 24p. (J). (gr. k-2). pap. 5.95 (978-1-84696-213-4(7), TickTock Books) Octopus Publishing Group GBR. Dist: Independent Pubs. Group.

—How to Live Like a Roman Gladiator. Epelbaum, Mariano, illus. 2015. (How to Live Like ... Ser.). (ENG.). 32p. (J). (gr. 3-6). lib. bdg. 27.99 (978-1-4677-6355-4(1), 8a922183-854a-4a12-910e-2ab8b32ed04d, Hungry Tomato (r)) Lerner Publishing Group.

Gedacht, Daniel C. Home Life in Ancient Rome, 1 vol. 2003. (Primary Sources of Ancient Civilizations: Egypt, Greece, & Rome Ser.). (ENG., Illus.). 24p. (gr. 3-4). pap. 8.25 (978-0-8239-8945-4(3), fc63046e-a439-40e8-bf71-cf86ac35c917, PowerKids Pr.) Rosen Publishing Group, Inc., The.

—Land & Resources of Ancient Rome, 1 vol. 2003. (Primary Sources of Ancient Civilizations: Egypt, Greece, & Rome Ser.). (ENG., Illus.). 24p. (gr. 3-4). pap. 8.25 (978-0-8239-8943-0(7), 2b3920d1-1dc8-47d0-a34b-f3d8f57c67d4, PowerKids Pr.) Rosen Publishing Group, Inc., The.

—Politics & Government in Ancient Rome, 1 vol. 2003. (Primary Sources of Ancient Civilizations: Egypt, Greece, & Rome Ser.). (ENG., Illus.). 24p. (gr. 3-4). pap. 8.25 (978-0-8239-8948-5(8), 2f915d8e-a5cb-45b8-8850-ae0e836c3139); (J). lib. bdg. 26.27 (978-0-8239-6777-3(8), c8c6a19d-638c-4514-bce6-bb5576627b9f) Rosen Publishing Group, Inc., The. (PowerKids Pr.).

Gifford, Clive. Romans. Scrutton, Ben, illus. 2016. (Reading Ladder Level 3 Ser.). (ENG.). 32p. (gr. 1-4). pap. 4.99 (978-1-4052-8043-3(3), Red Shed) Farshore GBR. Dist: HarperCollins Pubs.

Harrison, Paul. Ancient Roman Clothes, 1 vol. 2010. (Ancient Communities: Roman Life Ser.). (ENG.). 32p. (J). (gr. 4-4). pap. 11.60 (978-1-61532-308-1(2), 689dc9ce-bc35-46e1-93b2-66ad2179693c, PowerKids Pr.) Rosen Publishing Group, Inc., The.

—Ancient Roman Homes, 1 vol. 2010. (Ancient Communities: Roman Life Ser.). (ENG.). 32p. (J). (gr. 4-4). pap. 11.60 (978-1-61532-313-5(9), e05634ef-1f27-45db-b95c-97fcce215cbd); (Illus.). lib. bdg. 30.27 (978-1-61532-305-0(8), e7141177-5891-4925-8347-748a7f452c9a) Rosen Publishing Group, Inc., The. (PowerKids Pr.).

Hinds, Kathryn. Religion, 1 vol. 2006. (Life in the Roman Empire (2006) Ser.). (ENG.). 80p. (gr. 6-6). 36.93 (978-0-7614-1657-9(9), b3d357e0-c1b0-47c1-968d-07590a57fe7e) Cavendish Square Publishing LLC.

Kuntz, Lynn. The Roman Colosseum. 2004. (Great Structures in History Ser.). (ENG., Illus.). 48p. (J). (gr. 4-7). 27.50 (978-0-7377-1561-3(8), Greenhaven Pr., Inc.) Cengage Gale.

Leoni, Cristiana & Pauli, Erika. In Caesar's Rome with Cicero, 1 vol. Cappon, Manuela, illus. 2009. (Come See My City Ser.). (ENG.). 48p. (gr. 4-4). lib. bdg. 31.21 (978-0-7614-4328-5(2), c82c8855-9cfe-44b8-97b2-105ede1c1232) Cavendish Square Publishing LLC.

Life in the Roman Empire, 8 vols. 2016. (Life in the Roman Empire Ser.). (ENG.). 80p. (J) (gr. 6-6). lib. bdg. 149.44 (978-1-5026-2398-0(6), b92c6cb4-efd3-47b2-a9ce-ad9e183c1496, Cavendish Square) Cavendish Square Publishing LLC.

Markel, Rita J. Your Travel Guide to Ancient Rome. 2003. (Passport to History Ser.). (ENG., Illus.). 96p. (gr. 5-9). lib. bdg. 26.60 (978-0-8225-3071-8(6)) Lerner Publishing Group.

Nardo, Don. Cause & Effect: Ancient Rome. 2017. (ENG.). 80p. (J). (gr. 5-12). 39.93 (978-1-68282-160-2(9)) ReferencePoint Pr., Inc.

Riggs, Sandy. Three Ancient Communities: Text Pairs. 2008. (Bridges/Navigators Ser.). (J). (gr. 3). 89.00 (978-1-4108-8374-2(4)) Benchmark Education Co.

Wood, Alix. Gladiators: Fighting to the Death. Wood, Alix, illus. 2013. (Why'd They Do That? Strange Customs of the Past Ser.). (Illus.). 32p. (J). (gr. 4-6). pap. 63.00 (978-1-4339-9582-8(4)) Stevens, Gareth Publishing LLLP.

—Gladiators: Fighting to the Death, 1 vol. Wood, Alix, illus. 2013. (Why'd They Do That? Strange Customs of the Past Ser.). (ENG., Illus.). 32p. (J). (gr. 4-5). 29.27 (978-1-4339-9580-4(8), c4efe634-91b7-4cd1-8c13-1cf25bef1271); pap. 11.50 (978-1-4339-9581-1(6), 22704776-f9d5-41e8-8632-2d6bf2574f84) Stevens, Gareth Publishing LLLP.

ROME—ANTIQUITIES

Dugan, Christine. Rome, 1 vol. rev. ed. 2007. (Social Studies: Informational Text Ser.). (ENG.). 32p. (gr. 4-8). pap. 11.99 (978-0-7439-0432-2(X)) Teacher Created Materials, Inc.

Hanel, Rachael. Ancient Rome: An Interactive History Adventure. 2010. (You Choose: Historical Eras Ser.). (ENG.). 112p. (gr. 3-4). pap. 41.70 (978-1-4296-5101-1(6), Capstone Pr.) Capstone.

Malam, John. The Romans, 1 vol. 2011. (Dig It: History from Objects Ser.). (ENG., Illus.). 32p. (YA). (gr. 3-4). lib. bdg. 30.27 (978-1-4488-3285-9(3), b4fa690b-353e-4a16-b817-936742734368) Rosen Publishing Group, Inc., The.

Nardo, Don. Roman Roads & Aqueducts. 2014. (History's Great Structures). (ENG., Illus.). 80p. (J). lib. bdg. (978-1-60152-634-2(2)) ReferencePoint Pr., Inc.

Spilsbury, Louise. Forensic Investigations of the Romans. 2018. (Forensic Footprints of Ancient Worlds Ser.). (Illus.). 32p. (J). (gr. 5-5). (978-0-7787-4952-3(5)) Crabtree Publishing Co.

ROME—BIOGRAPHY

Abbott, Jacob. Julius Caesar. 2009. 206p. pap. 10.95 (978-1-59915-141-0(3)) Yesterday's Classics.

—Nero. 2009. 202p. (J). pap. 12.00 (978-1-59128-057-6(5)) Canon Pr.

Barter, James. Influential Figures of Ancient Rome. 2003. (Lucent Library of Historical Eras Ser.). (ENG.). 33.45 (978-1-59018-315-1(0), Lucent Bks.) Cengage Gale.

Forsyth, Fiona. Cicero: Defender of the Republic. 2009. (Ancient Leaders Ser.). 112p. (gr. 5-8). 66.50 (978-1-61511-420-7(3), Rosen Reference) Rosen Publishing Group, Inc., The.

Goldberg, Jan. Julius Caesar. 2004. (ZB Reads Trio Books). (Illus.). 106p. (gr. 5-7). pap. 5.50 (978-0-7367-1800-4(1)) Zaner-Bloser, Inc.

Haaren, John. Famous Men of Rome. 2008. 120p. pap. 12.95 (978-1-60459-524-6(8)) Wilder Pubns., Corp.

Haaren, John H. & Poland, A. B. Famous Men of Rome (Yesterday's Classics) 2006. (Illus.). 260p. (J). per. 11.95 (978-1-59915-046-8(8)) Yesterday's Classics.

Mattern, Joanne. Julius Caesar. 2017. (Junior Biography From Ancient Civilization Ser.). (Illus.). 48p. (J). (gr. 4-6). 29.95 (978-1-68020-024-9(0)) Mitchell Lane Pubs.

Medina, Nico & Who HQ. Who Was Julius Caesar? Foley, Tim, illus. 2014. (Who Was? Ser.). 112p. (J). (gr. 3-7). pap. 5.99 (978-0-448-48083-1(2), Penguin Workshop) Penguin Young Readers Group.

Nardo, Don. Influential Figures of Ancient Rome. 2004. (Lucent Library of Historical Eras). (Illus.). 128p. (J). 27.45 (978-1-59018-285-7(5), Lucent Bks.) Cengage Gale.

Orr, Tamra. Marcus Brutus. 2006. (J). lib. bdg. (978-1-58415-511-9(6)) Mitchell Lane Pubs.

Rinaldo, Denise. Julius Caesar: Dictator for Life. (Wicked History Ser.). (ENG.). (J). 2010. 128p. (gr. 6-12). pap. 5.95 (978-0-531-22822-7(3), Watts, Franklin) 2009. 224p. (gr. 5-9). 31.00 (978-0-531-21276-9(9)) Scholastic Library Publishing.

Santillian, Beatriz & Morgan, Julian. Hadrian: Emperor of Rome, 1 vol. 2017. (Leaders of the Ancient World Ser.). (ENG., Illus.). 112p. (J). (gr. 6-6). 38.80 (978-1-5081-7484-4(9), 1ec256a1-3c9d-416c-8596-284ded145c9a, Rosen Young Adult) Rosen Publishing Group, Inc., The.

Saxena, Shalini. Nero: Ruthless Roman Emperor, 1 vol. 2016. (History's Most Murderous Villains Ser.). (ENG., Illus.). 32p. (J). (gr. 4-5). pap. 11.50 (978-1-4824-4799-6(1), b3b131ea-2cca-45bf-ad07-d0fb72992d7d) Stevens, Gareth Publishing LLLP.

Turner, Tracey. Hard As Nails in Ancient Rome. Lenman, Jamie, illus. 2015. (Hard As Nails in History Ser.). (ENG.). 64p. (J). (gr. 4-5). (978-0-7787-1513-9(2)) Crabtree Publishing Co.

White, John S. The Boys' & Girls' Plutarch. 2004. reprint ed. pap. 1.99 (978-1-4192-5511-3(8)); pap. 28.95 (978-1-4191-5511-6(3)) Kessinger Publishing, LLC.

Williams, Rose. The Young Romans. 2003. (Anthem Classics Ser.). (ENG., Illus.). 128p. (J). pap. 26.00 (978-1-84331-047-1(3)) Anthem Pr. GBR. Dist: Bolchazy-Carducci Pubs.

—The Young Romans. 2007. (ENG.). pap. 23.00 (978-0-86516-670-7(6)) Bolchazy-Carducci Pubs.

Wiseman, T. P. Julius Caesar: Roman General, 1 vol. 2017. (History Makers Ser.). (ENG.). 144p. (YA). (gr. 9-9). 47.36 (978-1-5026-3296-8(9), ac73812c-9e80-4d07-8353-252aab53d723) Cavendish Square Publishing LLC.

Yim Bridges, Shirin. Agrippina: "Atrocious & Ferocious" Malone, Peter, illus. 2011. (Thinking Girl's Treasury of Dastardly Dames Ser.). (ENG.). 32p. (J). (gr. 3-8). 18.95 (978-0-9834256-1-8(2)) Goosebottom Bks. LLC.

ROME—FICTION

Angel, Ido. Vipo in Rome: A Trevi Fountain Wish Comes True. 2015. (AV2 Animated Storytime Ser.). (ENG.). (J). lib. bdg. 29.99 (978-1-4896-3920-2(9), AV2 by Weigl) Weigl Pubs., Inc.

Barclay, Katerina & Barclay, Aegea. The Hand of Zeus. Barclay, Katerina, illus. 2004. (Illus.). (J). 29.95 (978-0-9758803-1-9(4), 206 234 2572); 24.95 (978-0-9758803-0-2(6), 206.612.9698) Aegean Design.

Bergvinson, M. E. St. George's Mysterious Cross. 2013. 208p. pap. 23.16 (978-1-300-13979-9(X)) Lulu Pr., Inc.

Downey, Glen. Gladiators. 2007. (Illus.). 48p. (J). lib. bdg. 23.08 (978-1-4242-1627-7(3)) Fitzgerald Bks.

Durkin, Frances. A Roman Adventure. Cooke, Grace, illus. 2019. (Histronauts Ser.). (ENG.). (J). (gr. 3-4). 88p. pap. 10.99 (978-1-63163-244-0(2), 1631632442); 81p. lib. bdg. 29.99 (978-1-63163-243-3(4), 1631632434) North Star Editions. (Jolly Fish Pr.).

Fisher, Meaghan. Giuseppe's Famous Pizza Pies. Barrett, Diana, illus. 2013. 24p. 17.99 (978-1-938768-34-7(5)); pap. 8.99 (978-1-938768-20-0(5)) Gypsy Pubns.

Guthart Strauss, Peggy. Getting the Boot. 2005. (S. A. S. S. Ser.). (Illus.). 224p. (YA). (gr. 7-6). 7.99 (978-0-14-240414-0(4), Speak) Penguin Young Readers Group.

Henty, George. The Young Carthaginian: A Tale of the Times of Hannibal. 2004. pap. 8.95 (978-1-57646-874-6(7)) Quiet Vision Publishing.

Hobbs, Leigh. Mr Chicken Arriva a Roma. 2017. (Mr Chicken Ser.). (ENG., Illus.). 32p. (J). (gr. -1-3). 18.99 (978-1-925266-77-1(X)) Allen & Unwin AUS. Dist: Independent Pubs. Group.

Holm, Kirsten C. Everyday Life in Ancient Rome, 1 vol. 2012. (Jr. Graphic Ancient Civilizations Ser.). (ENG.). 24p. (J). (gr. 2-3). pap. 11.60 (978-1-4488-6389-1(9), b80684de-d9af-4a23-8f43-08d9b4cbe95e); lib. bdg. 28.93 (978-1-4488-6215-3(9), 79bf3ae1-d87e-49c9-a842-4947942e09fe) Rosen Publishing Group, Inc., The. (PowerKids Pr.).

Lawrence, Caroline. The Assassins of Rome. 2003. (ENG., Illus.). 224p. (gr. 2-7). pap. 10.99 (978-1-84255-023-6(3), Orion Children's Bks.) Hachette Children's Group GBR. Dist: Hachette Bk. Group.

—The Colossus of Rhodes. 2005. (ENG., Illus.). 224p. (gr. 4-6). pap. 10.99 (978-1-84255-138-7(8), Orion Children's Bks.) Hachette Children's Group GBR. Dist: Hachette Bk. Group.

—The Enemies of Jupiter. 2004. (ENG., Illus.). 224p. (gr. 4-6). pap. 10.99 (978-1-84255-164-6(7), Orion Children's Bks.) Hachette Children's Group GBR. Dist: Hachette Bk. Group.

Lee, Kathy. Captive in Rome. 2005. pap. (978-1-84427-088-0(2)) Scripture Union.

—A Captive in Rome. 2016. (ENG., Illus.). 160p. (J). pap. 14.99 (978-0-281-07633-8(2), 53bffe0c-1f13-4d3d-a979-2e9d129ad745) SPCK Publishing GBR. Dist: Baker & Taylor Publisher Services (BTPS).

—Rome in Flames. 2016. (ENG., Illus.). 160p. (J). pap. 14.99 (978-0-281-07635-2(9), 0858b034-5f9b-443e-980e-e858b1d1b0c2) SPCK Publishing GBR. Dist: Baker & Taylor Publisher Services (BTPS).

Llorente, Pilar Molina. Aura Gris. (SPA.). 192p. (YA). (gr. 5-8). (978-84-216-0993-4(9), BU3870) Bruño, Editorial ESP. Dist: Lectorum Pubns., Inc.

Marciano, John Bemelmans. Madeline & the Cats of Rome. 2008. (Madeline Ser.). (ENG.). 48p. (J). (gr. 1-3). 19.99 (978-0-670-06297-3(9), Viking Books for Young Readers) Penguin Young Readers Group.

Mitchell, Jack. The Ancient Ocean Blues. 2008. 200p. (J). (gr. 5-8). pap. 9.95 (978-0-88776-832-3(6), Tundra Bks.) Tundra Bks. CAN. Dist: Penguin Random Hse. LLC.

Nicholson, Elizabeth, et al. Cleo & Cornelius: A Tale of Two Cities & Two Kitties. Thies, Michelle, illus. 2018. (ENG.). 32p. (J). (gr. -1-k). 16.99 (978-1-947440-03-6(9), 1323401) Getty Pubns.

Nielsen, Jennifer A. Mark of the Thief. 2015. (Mark of the Thief Ser.: 1). lib. bdg. 18.40 (978-0-606-38064-5(7)) Turtleback.

—Mark of the Thief (Mark of the Thief, Book 1) 2015. (Mark of the Thief Ser.: 1). (ENG.). 352p. (J). (gr. 4-7). pap. 8.99 (978-0-545-56155-6(8), Scholastic Paperbacks) Scholastic, Inc.

Northfield, Gary. Julius Zebra: Rumble with the Romans! Northfield, Gary, illus. (Julius Zebra Ser.: 1). (ENG., Illus.). 288p. (J). (gr. 2-5). 2018. pap. 7.99 (978-0-7636-9846-1(6)) 2016. 15.99 (978-0-7636-7853-1(8)) Candlewick Pr.

Orczy, Emmuska. Unto Caesar. 2008. 260p. 29.95 (978-1-60664-863-6(2)); pap. 15.95 (978-1-60664-110-1(7)) Aegypan.

Parks, Tiffany. Midnight in the Piazza. 2018. (ENG.). 304p. (J). (gr. 3-7). 16.99 (978-0-06-264452-7(1), HarperCollins) HarperCollins Pubs.

Platt, Richard. Roman Diary: The Journal of Iliona, a Young Slave. Parkins, David, illus. 2014. (ENG.). 128p. (J). (gr. 4-7). pap. 7.99 (978-0-7636-7053-5(7)) Candlewick Pr.

Riggs, Sandy. Three Ancient Communities: Set Of 6. 2011. (Navigators Ser.). (J). pap. 44.00 net. (978-1-4108-5093-5(5)) Benchmark Education Co.

Rogers, Terry, illus. Androcles & the Lion: A Roman Legend. 2003. (Dominie Collection of Myths & Legends). (SPA.). 20p. (J). lib. bdg. (978-0-7685-2419-2(9)) Dominie Pr., Inc.

—Androcles & the Lion: A Roman Legend. 2004. (SPA & ENG.). 20p. (J). (gr. 3-3). pap. 6.47 net. (978-0-7685-2122-1(X), Dominie Elementary) Savvas Learning Co.

Scieszka, Jon. See You Later, Gladiator. McCauley, Adam, illus. 2004. (Time Warp Trio Ser.: No. 9). 87p. (J). (gr. 4-7). 12.65 (978-0-7569-5986-9(1)) Perfection Learning Corp.

—See You Later, Gladiator #9. McCauley, Adam, illus. 2004. (Time Warp Trio Ser.: 9). 96p. (J). (gr. 2-4). pap. 5.99 (978-0-14-240117-0(X), Puffin Books) Penguin Young Readers Group.

Seven, John. The Dragon of Rome, 1 vol. Phillips, Craig, illus. 2013. (Time-Tripping Faradays Ser.). (ENG.). 160p. (J). (gr. 4-8). pap. 5.95 (978-1-4342-6439-8(4), 124130, Stone Arch Bks.) Capstone.

Sienkiewicz, Henryk. Quo Vadis: A Narrative of the Time of Nero. (SPA., Illus.). 168p. (YA). 11.95 (978-84-7281-132-4(8), AF1132) Auriga, Ediciones S.A. ESP. Dist: Continental Bk. Co., Inc.

Snedeker, Caroline Dale. A Triumph for Flavius. 2004. (Illus.). 87p. (J). per. 13.95 (978-0-9667067-1-0(4)) American Home-School Publishing, LLC.

ROME—HISTORY

Abbott, Jacob. Hannibal. 2009. (J). pap. 12.00 (978-1-59128-059-0(1)) Canon Pr.

—Julius Caesar. 2009. (J). pap. 12.00 (978-1-59128-060-6(5)) Canon Pr.

Ancient Roman Daily Life: Rome (Spotlight on Ancient Civilizations), 12 vols. 2013. (Spotlight on Ancient Civilizations: Rome Ser.). (ENG.). 24p. (J). (gr. 3-4). 157.62 (978-1-4777-1144-6(9), b4908d56-5a7d-47bf-a6fd-a9243b89da9b, PowerKids Pr.) Rosen Publishing Group, Inc., The.

Ancient Rome. 2003. spiral bd. 16.95 (978-1-56004-154-2(4)); spiral bd. 19.95 (978-1-56004-162-7(5)) Social Studies Schl. Service.

Anderson, Michael. Ancient Rome, 1 vol. 2011. (Ancient Civilizations Ser.). (ENG., Illus.). 88p. (J). (gr. 8-8). lib. bdg. 35.29 (978-1-61530-522-3(X), a85b18f6-2dd2-4907-8335-aa2d9cd743bc) Rosen Publishing Group, Inc., The.

Anderson, Zachary. The Fall of Rome & the Rise of Constantinople, 1 vol. 2015. (Exploring the Ancient & Medieval Worlds Ser.). (ENG., Illus.). 160p. (YA). (gr. 8-8). lib. bdg. 47.36 (978-1-5026-0574-0(0), 2fda55fe-c4a9-405f-bd20-8ff90abfc7a2) Cavendish Square Publishing LLC.

—The Rise of the Roman Empire, 1 vol. 2015. (Exploring the Ancient & Medieval Worlds Ser.). (ENG., Illus.). 160p. (YA). (gr. 8-8). 47.36 (978-1-5026-0572-6(4), 0c19036b-f2e2-4808-933d-312798dfdeec) Cavendish Square Publishing LLC.

Baikie, James. Peeps at Many Lands: Ancient Rome (Yesterday's Classics) 2008. 128p. pap. 8.95 *(978-1-59915-290-5(8))* Yesterday's Classics.

Barnham, Kay. Gory Gladiators, Savage Centurions, & Caesar's Sticky End: A Menacing History of the Unruly Romans!, 1 vol. 2015. (Awfully Ancient Ser.). (ENG., Illus.). 32p. (J). (gr. 5-5). pap. 11.50 *(978-1-4824-3113-1(0),* 42841b57-9e7f-40f0-b222-f81a92bca407) Stevens, Gareth Publishing LLLP.

Baum, Margaux & Morgan, Julian. Constantine, 1 vol. 2016. (Leaders of the Ancient World Ser.). (ENG.). 112p. (J). (gr. 6-6). 38.80 *(978-1-5081-7252-9(8),* 21146d9b-688f-46d2-a2bb-3f62820d7720) Rosen Publishing Group, Inc., The.

Baynard, Kate Holland & Baynard, Holland Callaway. Holland Goes to Rome: A brief look at the ancient city, its history & its Culture. 2010. 16p. 12.50 *(978-1-4490-4604-0(5))* AuthorHouse.

Bedwin, Christa. Romans. 2016. (Illus.). 32p. (J). *(978-1-5105-1104-0(0))* SmartBook Media, Inc.

Beesly. Stories from the History of Rome. 2008. 136p. pap. 8.95 *(978-1-59915-264-6(9))* Yesterday's Classics.

Bell, Samantha S. Ancient Rome. 2019. (Civilizations of the World Ser.). (ENG., Illus.). 32p. (J). (gr. 3-5). pap. 9.95 *(978-1-64185-825-0(7),* 1641858257); lib. bdg. 31.35 *(978-1-64185-756-7(0),* 1641857560) North Star Editions. (Focus Readers).

Benchmark Education Company. Rome Long Ago (Teacher Guide) 2005. *(978-1-4108-4682-2(2))* Benchmark Education Co.

Benduhn, Tea. Ancient Rome, 1 vol. 2007. (Life Long Ago Ser.). (ENG., Illus.). 24p. (gr. 2-4). pap. 9.15 *(978-0-8368-7788-5(8),* 8f45eb0a-0d23-4c3a-a8e9-bdd8699228c1); lib. bdg. 24.67 *(978-0-8368-7783-0(7),* 7db3c6eb-40ef-44be-9cbb-861e2b5a2abd) Stevens, Gareth Publishing LLLP. (Weekly Reader Leveled Readers).

—La Antigua Roma (Ancient Rome), 1 vol. 2007. (Vida en el Pasado (Life Long Ago) Ser.). (SPA., Illus.). 24p. (gr. 2-4). pap. 9.15 *(978-0-8368-8039-7(0),* 0d022ae7-06df-49ee-a950-39e6379114c1); lib. bdg. 24.67 *(978-0-8368-8034-2(X),* fd97f99b-95c2-4a3b-83bf-a6ed18779098) Stevens, Gareth Publishing LLLP. (Weekly Reader Leveled Readers).

Benoit, Peter. Ancient Rome (the Ancient World) 2012. (Ancient World Ser.). (ENG., Illus.). 112p. (J). (gr. 6-9). pap. 9.95 *(978-0-531-25983-2(8),* Children's Pr.) Scholastic Library Publishing.

—The Ancient World: Ancient Rome. 2012. (ENG., Illus.). 112p. (J). lib. bdg. 34.00 *(978-0-531-25183-6(7),* Children's Pr.) Scholastic Library Publishing.

Bingham, Jane. Ancient Rome, 1 vol. 2005. (Ancient Civilizations Ser.). (ENG., Illus.). 48p. (gr. 5-8). lib. bdg. 33.67 *(978-0-8368-6191-4(4),* 811b52f6-34cd-4dd9-b0f3-cc02fe976cfb, Gareth Stevens Secondary Library) Stevens, Gareth Publishing LLLP.

—Classical Myth: A Treasury of Greek & Roman Legends, Art, & History. 2007. (Myth Ser.). (Illus.). 96p. (J). (gr. 4-7). pap. 7.99 *(978-0-7858-2350-6(6))* Book Sales, Inc.

—Classical Myth: a Treasury of Greek & Roman Legends, Art, & History: A Treasury of Greek & Roman Legends, Art, & History. 2007. (ENG., Illus.). 96p. (C). (gr. 6-18). lib. bdg. 165.00 *(978-0-7656-8104-1(8),* Y181755) Routledge.

—How People Lived in Ancient Rome, 1 vol. 2008. (How People Lived Ser.). (ENG., Illus.). 32p. (gr. 4-4). (J). lib. bdg. 30.27 *(978-1-4042-4432-0(8),* 8e03bf97-bb25-40e8-8e2f-6ca8346309b7); pap. 10.60 *(978-1-4358-2622-9(1),* 77c4daa7-76ed-4405-a422-59c0befe4c57, Rosen Classroom) Rosen Publishing Group, Inc., The.

Bingham, Jane, et al. Encyclopedia of the Roman World. 2004. (History Encyclopedias Ser.). (Illus.). 128p. (J). 19.95 *(978-0-7945-0117-4(6),* Usborne) EDC Publishing.

Bodden, Valerie. Gladiators. 2017. (X-Books: Fighters Ser.). (ENG., Illus.). 32p. (J). (gr. 3-6). *(978-1-60818-813-0(2),* 20372, Creative Education) Creative Co., The.

—Rome. 2014. (Ancient Civilizations Ser.). (ENG.). 48p. (J). (gr. 5-8). *(978-1-60818-394-4(7),* 21281, Creative Education); pap. 12.00 *(978-0-89812-981-6(8),* 21282, Creative Paperbacks) Creative Co., The.

Botham, Noel. Did Romans Really Wash Themselves in Wee? 2015. (Dr. Dino's Learnatorium Ser.). (ENG., Illus.). 160p. (J). (gr. 4-7). pap. 8.99 *(978-1-78219-915-1(2))* Blake, John Publishing, Ltd. GBR. Dist: Independent Pubs. Group.

Brannon, Barbara. Discover Ancient Rome. 2005. (J). pap. *(978-1-4108-5164-2(8))* Benchmark Education Co.

Bridges, Shirin Yim. Agrippina: "Atrocious & Ferocious" 2011. 18.95 *(978-0-938425-61-8(7));* 18.95 *(978-0-938425-65-6(X))* Goosebottom Bks. LLC.

Brocklehurst, R. Roman Army. 2004. (Discovery Program Ser.). 48p. (J). lib. bdg. 16.95 *(978-1-58086-609-5(3),* Usborne) EDC Publishing.

Brown Bear Books. The Ancient Romans. 2015. (At Home With ... Ser.). (ENG., Illus.). 32p. (J). (gr. 4-6). lib. bdg. 31.35 *(978-1-78121-082-6(9),* 16438) Brown Bear Bks.

Burgan, Michael. The Empire of Ancient Rome. 2nd rev. ed. 2009. (Great Empires of the Past Ser.). (ENG., Illus.). 160p. (gr. 6-12). 35.00 *(978-1-60413-159-8(4),* P173431, Facts On File) Infobase Holdings, Inc.

Burrell, Carol M. Scavella. Did Greek Soldiers Really Hide Inside the Trojan Horse? And Other Questions about the Ancient World. 2010. (Is That a Fact? Ser.). (ENG.). 40p. (gr. 4-6). lib. bdg. 26.60 *(978-0-7613-4912-9(X))* Lerner Publishing Group.

Butterfield, Moira. Lonely Planet Kids City Trails - Rome 1. Bruff, Alex & Taylor, Matt, illus. 2017. (Lonely Planet Kids Ser.). (ENG.). 104p. (J). (gr. 4-7). pap. 12.99 *(978-1-78657-964-5(2),* 5660) Lonely Planet Global Ltd. IRL. Dist: Hachette Bk. Group.

Callery, Sean. The Dark History of Ancient Rome, 1 vol. 2011. (Dark Histories Ser.). (ENG.). 64p. (gr. 5-5). 35.50 *(978-1-60870-084-4(4),* e3650a71-0ebf-40ef-ac7a-122aaeff3a98) Cavendish Square Publishing LLC.

Church, Alfred J. Stories from Livy. 2008. 212p. pap. 9.95 *(978-1-59915-078-9(6))* Yesterday's Classics.

Cobblestone Publishing. If I Were a Kid in Ancient Rome: Children of the Ancient World. 2007. (If I Were a Kid In... Ser.). (ENG., Illus.). 32p. (J). (gr. 1-5). 17.95 *(978-0-8126-7930-4(X))* Cricket Bks.

Coddington, Andrew. Martyrdom: Christians in the Roman Empire, 1 vol. 2016. (Public Persecutions Ser.). (ENG., Illus.). 128p. (YA). (gr. 9-9). 47.36 *(978-1-5026-2327-0(7),* e83fe10b-9ce1-49cd-9f78-b5ccbb318438) Cavendish Square Publishing LLC.

Cohn, Jessica. The Ancient Romans, 1 vol. 2012. (Crafts from the Past Ser.). (ENG., Illus.). 48p. (J). (gr. 5-5). pap. 15.05 *(978-1-4339-7710-7(9),* b9ce9518-f099-4b75-834b-4a965242da9f); lib. bdg. 34.60 *(978-1-4339-7709-1(5),* 2ac141cf-8ba1-45e1-98f0-5e347e6a8bf2) Stevens, Gareth Publishing LLLP.

Cont Media Staff. Ancient Rome. 2008. (Illus.). 48p. (YA). 12.99 *(978-1-931703-26-0(4))* Creative Publishing Consultants.

Corrick, James A. The Bloody, Rotten Roman Empire: The Disgusting Details about Life in Ancient Rome. 2010. (Disgusting History Ser.). (ENG.). 32p. (J). (gr. 3-4). pap. 49.60 *(978-1-4296-6475-2(4),* 16227); pap. 8.10 *(978-1-4296-6353-3(7),* 115550) Capstone. (Capstone Pr.).

Cottrell, George. Ancient Rome. (Unlocking Ancient Civilizations Ser.). (J). (gr. 4-5). 2017. pap. 63.00 *(978-1-5345-2034-9(1))* 2016. (ENG.). 32p. pap. 11.50 *(978-1-5345-2033-2(3),* 643fcdd3-153d-4896-b85e-1b76f768644c) 2016. (ENG.). 32p. lib. bdg. 28.88 *(978-1-5345-2035-6(X),* 0d17b30f-7b3b-446f-9c19-d1cea502f4c1) Greenhaven Publishing LLC. (KidHaven Publishing).

Croy, Anita. How Did Rome Rise & Fall?, 1 vol. 2017. (Mysteries in History: Solving the Mysteries of the Past Ser.). (ENG.). 48p. (gr. 5-5). lib. bdg. 33.07 *(978-1-5026-2806-0(6),* 75554743-aaaa-4c9b-9dc3-1974c060e8db) Cavendish Square Publishing LLC.

—Myths & Legends of Ancient Rome. 2015. (Illus.). 64p. (J). *(978-0-7166-2635-0(7))* World Bk., Inc.

Daning, Tom. Mitología Romana: Rómulo y Remo, 1 vol. Obregón, José María, illus. 2009. (Historietas Juveniles: Mitologías (Jr. Graphic Mythologies) Ser.). (SPA.). 24p. (J). (gr. 2-3). lib. bdg. 28.93 *(978-1-4358-8570-7(8),* eb4c1f63-3750-40d6-87ee-d6a1fe792f51) Rosen Publishing Group, Inc., The.

—Roman Mythology: Romulus & Remus. 2009. (Jr. Graphic Mythologies Ser.). (ENG.). 24p. (J). (gr. 2-3). 47.90 *(978-1-61513-870-8(6),* PowerKids Pr.) Rosen Publishing Group, Inc., The.

Daning, Tom & Obregón, José María. Mitología Romana: Rómulo y Remo, 1 vol. 2009. (Historietas Juveniles: Mitologías (Jr. Graphic Mythologies) Ser.). (SPA., Illus.). 24p. (gr. 2-3). pap. 10.60 *(978-1-4358-3334-0(1),* b6199b97-3861-4cbd-ba50-bfec01e62f2f) Rosen Publishing Group, Inc., The.

Dargie, Richard. Ancient Rome. 2004. (Picturing the Past Ser.). (Illus.). 32p. (J). 15.95 *(978-1-59270-023-3(3))* Enchanted Lion Bks., LLC.

—Rich & Poor in Ancient Rome. 2005. (Rich & Poor in Ser.). (Illus.). 32p. (YA). (gr. 4-7). lib. bdg. 27.10 *(978-1-58340-722-6(7))* Black Rabbit Bks.

Daynes, Katie. See Inside Ancient Rome. Hancock, David, illus. 2006. (See Inside Board Bks.). 16p. (J). (gr. 2-5). bds. 12.99 *(978-0-7945-1321-4(2),* Usborne) EDC Publishing.

Dickins, Rosie. The Story of Rome. Gower, Teri, illus. 2006. (Usborne Young Reading: Series Two Ser.). 60p. (J). (gr. 2). lib. bdg. 13.99 *(978-1-58086-900-3(9),* Usborne) EDC Publishing.

Dickinson, Rachel. Tools of the Ancient Romans: A Kid's Guide to the History & Science of Life in Ancient Rome. 2006. (Build It Yourself Ser.). (Illus.). 144p. (J). (gr. 3-7). pap. 15.95 *(978-0-9749344-5-7(3),* 844d7743-cc63-4705-bd8e-d3808636d905) Nomad Pr.

DiPrimio, Pete. Ancient Rome. 2009. (How'd They Do That? Ser.). (Illus.). 64p. (J). (gr. 4-8). 33.95 *(978-1-58415-820-2(4))* Mitchell Lane Pubs.

DK. DKfindout! Ancient Rome. 2016. (DK Findout! Ser.). (ENG., Illus.). 64p. (J). (gr. 1-4). pap. 10.99 *(978-1-4654-5427-0(6),* DK Children) Dorling Kindersley Publishing, Inc.

Doeden, Matt. Tools & Treasures of Ancient Rome. 2014. (Searchlight Books (tm) — What Can We Learn from Early Civilizations? Ser.). (ENG., Illus.). 40p. (J). (gr. 3-5). lib. bdg. 30.65 *(978-1-4677-1433-4(X),* f8fc9202-ca30-4a61-bd51-e22ff203106b, Lerner Pubns.) Lerner Publishing Group.

Editors of Kingfisher. Remarkable Romans. 2017. (It's All About... Ser.). (ENG.). 32p. (J). pap. 5.99 *(978-0-7534-7282-8(1),* 9780753472828, Kingfisher) Roaring Brook Pr.

Edwards, Laurie J. Exploring Ancient Rome. 2018. (Exploring Ancient Civilizations Ser.). (ENG., Illus.). 32p. (J). (gr. 3-6). 32.80 *(978-1-63235-466-2(7),* 13889, 12-Story Library) Bookstaves, LLC.

England, Victoria. Top 10 Worst Things about Ancient Rome, 1 vol. Antram, David, illus. 2012. (Top 10 Worst Ser.). (ENG.). 32p. (J). (gr. 3-5). pap. 11.50 *(978-1-4339-6695-8(6),* ba7111a5-aa5f-4e60-8795-d331f62c44c0); lib. bdg. 29.27 *(978-1-4339-6694-1(8),* 56e18f32-c006-49d9-a215-4d5287bf69bd) Stevens, Gareth Publishing LLLP. (Gareth Stevens Learning Library).

Fact Atlas: Ancient Rome. 2009. (FACT ATLAS Ser.). 72p. (J). 14.95 *(978-0-8437-1929-1(X))* Hammond World Atlas Corp.

Fall of Rome/Byzantium DBA. 2003. spiral bd. 16.95 *(978-1-56004-155-9(2))* Social Studies Schl. Service.

Faust, Daniel R. Ancient Rome, 1 vol. 2018. (Look at Ancient Civilizations Ser.). (ENG.). 32p. (gr. 2-2). 28.27 *(978-1-5382-3008-4(9),* d2027f37-a0bc-4e8c-b207-be5de34c116a) Stevens, Gareth Publishing LLLP.

Forsyth, Fiona. Augustus: The First Emperor. 2009. (Ancient Leaders Ser.). 112p. (gr. 5-8). 66.50 *(978-1-61511-419-1(X),* Rosen Reference) Rosen Publishing Group, Inc., The.

—Cicero: Defender of the Republic. 2009. (Ancient Leaders Ser.). 112p. (gr. 5-8). 66.50 *(978-1-61511-420-7(3),* Rosen Reference) Rosen Publishing Group, Inc., The.

Frankel, Karen. Projects about Ancient Rome, 1 vol. 2007. (Hands-On History Ser.). (ENG., Illus.). 48p. (gr. 3-3). lib. bdg. 34.07 *(978-0-7614-2260-0(9),* c50ab922-409b-4a0d-8841-a5a2b9e547c0) Cavendish Square Publishing LLC.

Gallagher, Belinda. Why Why Why... Did Romans Race to the Circus? 2010. (Why Why Why Ser.). (Illus.). 32p. (J). (gr. 1-3). lib. bdg. 18.95 *(978-1-4222-1577-7(6))* Mason Crest.

Ganeri, Anita. How the Ancient Romans Lived, 1 vol. 2010. (Life in Ancient Times Ser.). (ENG.). 32p. (J). (gr. 3-5). lib. bdg. 29.27 *(978-1-4339-4094-1(9),* 4eefb18e-7227-4ccb-8222-b225dc659d17, Gareth Stevens Learning Library) Stevens, Gareth Publishing LLLP.

Gedacht, Daniel C. Economy & Industry in Ancient Rome. 2009. (Primary Sources of Ancient Civilizations Ser.). 24p. (gr. 3-3). 42.50 *(978-1-60851-557-8(5),* PowerKids Pr.) Rosen Publishing Group, Inc., The.

—Land & Resources in Ancient Rome, 1 vol. 2003. (Primary Sources of Ancient Civilizations Ser.). (ENG., Illus.). 24p. (J). (gr. 3-4). lib. bdg. 26.27 *(978-0-8239-6775-9(1),* c797989d-47f6-4af1-ae48-73b4cbd9c209, PowerKids Pr.) Rosen Publishing Group, Inc., The.

—Politics & Government in Ancient Rome. 2009. (Primary Sources of Ancient Civilizations Ser.). 24p. (gr. 3-3). 42.50 *(978-1-60851-563-9(X),* PowerKids Pr.) Rosen Publishing Group, Inc., The.

—Technology of Ancient Rome. 2009. (Primary Sources of Ancient Civilizations Ser.). 24p. (gr. 3-3). 42.50 *(978-1-60851-564-6(8),* PowerKids Pr.) Rosen Publishing Group, Inc., The.

Gould, F. J. The Children's Plutarch: Tales of the Romans. Crane, Walter, illus. 2012. 260p. *(978-1-78139-160-0(2))* Benediction Classics.

Grant, Neil. Every Day Life in Ancient Rome. Cappon, Manuela, tr. Cappon, Manuela, illus. 2003. (Uncovering History Ser.). 46p. (J). lib. bdg. 28.50 *(978-1-58340-249-8(7))* Black Rabbit Bks.

Greenblatt, Miriam. Julius Caesar & the Roman Republic, 1 vol. 2007. (Rulers & Their Times Ser.). (ENG., Illus.). 80p. (gr. 6-6). lib. bdg. 36.93 *(978-0-7614-1836-8(9),* f465e7fb-ce85-4174-90f8-155c5cced41c) Cavendish Square Publishing LLC.

Guerber, H. A. The Story of the Romans (Yesterday's Classics) 2006. (Illus.). 368p. (J). per. 13.95 *(978-1-59915-012-3(3))* Yesterday's Classics.

Haaren, John. Famous Men of Rome. 2008. 120p. pap. 12.95 *(978-1-60459-524-6(8))* Wilder Pubns., Corp.

Hanbury-Murphy, Trudy. Solving the Mysteries of Ancient Rome, 1 vol. 2009. (Digging into History Ser.). (ENG.). 32p. (gr. 3-3). lib. bdg. 32.64 *(978-0-7614-3101-5(2),* 849086a2-b6b6-4f80-8ce8-93e832a7f148) Cavendish Square Publishing LLC.

Hanel, Rachael. Ancient Rome: An Interactive History Adventure. 2010. (You Choose: Historical Eras Ser.). (ENG.). 112p. (gr. 3-4). pap. 41.70 *(978-1-4296-5101-1(6),* Capstone Pr.) Capstone.

Hanel, Rachel. Gladiators. 2007. (Fearsome Fighters Ser.). (ENG., Illus.). 48p. (J). (gr. 5-8). lib. bdg. 31.35 *(978-1-58341-535-1(1),* 22146) Creative Co., The.

Harrison, Paul. Ancient Roman Clothes, 1 vol. 2010. (Ancient Communities: Roman Life Ser.). (ENG., Illus.). 32p. (J). (gr. 4-4). lib. bdg. 30.27 *(978-1-61532-304-3(X),* 1e01ca0a-378c-4439-aaff-e822399c2242, PowerKids Pr.) Rosen Publishing Group, Inc., The.

Hawes, Alison. What the Romans Did for the World. 2010. (Crabtree Connections Ser.). (ENG.). 24p. (J). (gr. 3-6). *(978-0-7787-9943-6(3));* pap. *(978-0-7787-9965-8(4))* Crabtree Publishing Co.

Hinds, Kathryn. The City, 1 vol. 2006. (Life in the Roman Empire (2006) Ser.). (ENG., Illus.). 80p. (gr. 6-6). 36.93 *(978-0-7614-1655-5(2),* 0192091d-dfd0-4bbb-bdd6-164045b6000c) Cavendish Square Publishing LLC.

—Early Germans, 1 vol. 2010. (Barbarians! Ser.). (ENG.). 80p. (gr. 6-6). 38.36 *(978-0-7614-4064-2(X),* 14e45741-532d-41c5-8e2a-625be73fae9d) Cavendish Square Publishing LLC.

—Goths, 1 vol. 2010. (Barbarians! Ser.). (ENG.). 80p. (gr. 6-6). 38.36 *(978-0-7614-4065-9(8),* d096b7e6-3d3d-4b7c-a3b5-44046a7f88e1) Cavendish Square Publishing LLC.

—Lin In The Roman Empire Series, 4 Bks, Set. 2004. (Life in the Roman Empire Ser.). (gr. 6). *(978-0-7614-1653-1(6),* Cavendish Square) Cavendish Square Publishing LLC.

—The Patricians, 1 vol. 2006. (Life in the Roman Empire (2006) Ser.). (ENG., Illus.). 80p. (gr. 6-6). 36.93 *(978-0-7614-1654-8(4),* 528ef3e1-3bb3-4a98-ac95-a0cb893ca44e) Cavendish Square Publishing LLC.

Hirsch, E. D., Jr., ed. Ancient Rome: Level 3. 2003. tchr. ed. 9.95 *(978-0-7690-5057-7(3))* Pearson Learning.

History's Fearless Fighters, 12 vols. 2015. (History's Fearless Fighters Ser.). (ENG.). 48p. (J). (gr. 5-6). lib. bdg. 201.60 *(978-1-4824-2562-8(9),* bd716a05-3fc6-4075-ac59-53c25fadf461) Stevens, Gareth Publishing LLLP.

Hoblin, Paul. Gladiators. 2013. (Great Warriors Ser.). (ENG., Illus.). 48p. (J). (gr. 4-8). pap. 18.50 *(978-1-61783-772-2(5),* 10804) ABDO Publishing Co.

Hurdman, Charlotte, et al. Find Out about Ancient Egypt, Rome & Greece: Exploring the Great Classical Civilizations, with 60 Step-By-Step Projects & 1500 Exciting Images. 2013. (ENG., Illus.). 256p. (J). (gr. 3-7). 17.99 *(978-1-84322-804-2(1),* Armadillo) Anness Publishing GBR. Dist: National Bk. Network.

Hyde, Natalie. Gladiators, 1 vol. 2016. (Crabtree Chrome Ser.). (ENG., Illus.). 48p. (J). (gr. 6-9). pap. *(978-0-7787-2227-4(9))* Crabtree Publishing Co.

Hynson, Colin. Ancient Rome: The Complete Homework Solution. 2010. (Study Buddies Ser.). (ENG.). 32p. (J). (gr. 4-7). pap. 6.95 *(978-1-84898-182-9(1),* TickTock Books) Octopus Publishing Group GBR. Dist: Independent Pubs. Group.

Innes, Brian. Ancient Roman Myths, 1 vol. 2010. (Myths from Around the World Ser.). (ENG.). 48p. (YA). (gr. 6-8). lib. bdg. 33.67 *(978-1-4339-3527-5(9),* 9e91eb08-9824-4bf8-8578-aa4f1cfe7fcc, Gareth Stevens Secondary Library) Stevens, Gareth Publishing LLLP.

Jacobs, Denise. Patricians in the Roman Empire, 1 vol. 2016. (Life in the Roman Empire Ser.). (ENG., Illus.). 80p. (J). (gr. 6-6). 37.36 *(978-1-5026-2257-0(2),* e9332088-2e9b-482b-8de5-d326c39245dc) Cavendish Square Publishing LLC.

Jeffrey, Gary & Petty, Kate. Julius Caesar: The Life of a Roman General, 1 vol. 2005. (Graphic Nonfiction Biographies Ser.). (ENG., Illus.). 48p. (J). (gr. 4-6). lib. bdg. 37.13 *(978-1-4042-0239-9(0),* b0b7de4c-65e7-46fc-bafc-b04ad29f01f4) Rosen Publishing Group, Inc., The.

Jovinelly, Joann. The Crafts & Culture of the Romans. 2009. (Crafts of the Ancient World Ser.). 48p. (gr. 5-8). 58.50 *(978-1-61512-065-9(3),* Rosen Reference) Rosen Publishing Group, Inc., The.

Kemp, Ellwood W. Streams of History: Ancient Rome (Yesterday's Classics) 2008. 104p. per. 7.95 *(978-1-59915-256-1(8))* Yesterday's Classics.

Kerrigan, Michael. Romans, 1 vol. 2011. (Ancients in Their Own Words Ser.). (ENG., Illus.). 64p. (J). (gr. 6-6). 35.50 *(978-1-60870-067-7(4),* 7b54880f-f286-4ed0-909a-1a46e3c457dd) Cavendish Square Publishing LLC.

Klar, Jeremy. The Totally Gross History of Ancient Rome, 1 vol., 1. 2015. (Totally Gross History Ser.). (ENG.). 48p. (J). (gr. 5-5). 33.47 *(978-1-4994-3746-1(3),* 73ae0fba-2f2d-45c8-9f14-bef48d166745); pap. 12.75 *(978-1-4994-3744-7(7),* de799b2e-0d36-4bd1-b089-2f9729603f00) Rosen Publishing Group, Inc., The. (Rosen Central).

Ladybird. Ladybird Histories Romans. 2014. (Ladybird Histories Ser.). (Illus.). 64p. (J). (gr. 2-4). pap. 13.99 *(978-0-7232-7730-9(3))* Penguin Bks., Ltd. GBR. Dist: Independent Pubs. Group.

Leoni, Cristiana & Pauli, Erika. In Caesar's Rome with Cicero, 1 vol. Cappon, Manuela, illus. 2009. (Come See My City Ser.). (ENG.). 48p. (gr. 4-4). lib. bdg. 31.21 *(978-0-7614-4328-5(2),* c82c8855-9cfe-44b8-97b2-105ede1c1232) Cavendish Square Publishing LLC.

Litten, Kristyna. Rome: a 3D Keepsake Cityscape. Litten, Kristyna, illus. 2013. (Panorama Pops Ser.). (ENG., Illus.). 15p. (J). (gr. k-4). 8.99 *(978-0-7636-6415-2(4))* Candlewick Pr.

Lowery, Zoe & Morgan, Julian. Nero, 1 vol. 2016. (Leaders of the Ancient World Ser.). (ENG.). 112p. (J). (gr. 6-6). 38.80 *(978-1-5081-7256-7(0),* 167c953e-c1d8-49b3-986f-90c2c3e781f3) Rosen Publishing Group, Inc., The.

Macaulay, David. City: A Story of Roman Planning & Construction. 2012. 21.00 *(978-1-61383-577-7(9))* Perfection Learning Corp.

Macdonald, Fiona. Ancient Rome. 2013. (Illus.). 48p. (J). *(978-1-4351-5083-6(X))* Barnes & Noble, Inc.

—Do You Want to Be a Roman Soldier? 2015. (Do You Want to Be... Ser.). (Illus.). 32p. (gr. 3-6). 28.50 *(978-1-909645-38-7(9))* Book Hse. GBR. Dist: Black Rabbit Bks.

MacDonald, Fiona. Romans: Dress, Eat, Write & Play Just Like the Romans. 2008. (Hands-on History Ser.). (ENG., Illus.). 32p. (J). (gr. 3-7). pap. *(978-0-7787-4071-1(4))* Crabtree Publishing Co.

Mackley, Daniel. The City in the Roman Empire, 1 vol. 2016. (Life in the Roman Empire Ser.). (ENG., Illus.). 80p. (J). (gr. 6-6). 37.36 *(978-1-5026-2259-4(9),* a59a4860-698c-4051-b32e-289a1b7dffec) Cavendish Square Publishing LLC.

Malam, John. Ancient Rome Inside Out. 2017. (Ancient Worlds Inside Out Ser.). (ENG., Illus.). 32p. (J). (gr. 4-5). *(978-0-7787-2882-5(X));* pap. *(978-0-7787-2896-2(X))* Crabtree Publishing Co.

—Life in Ancient Rome. 2011. (Big Picture: Homes Ser.). (ENG.). 24p. (J). (gr. 1-2). pap. 41.70 *(978-1-4296-6731-9(1),* Capstone Pr.) Capstone.

Mara, Wil. The Romans, 1 vol. 2012. (Technology of the Ancients Ser.). (ENG.). 64p. (gr. 6-6). 35.50 *(978-1-60870-768-3(7),* b291559d-ec79-4731-9cb9-7c154b88abe3) Cavendish Square Publishing LLC.

Marcovitz, Hal. Ancient Rome. 2011. (Understanding World History Ser.). (ENG., Illus.). 80p. (YA). (gr. 7-12). lib. bdg. 43.93 *(978-1-60152-186-6(3))* ReferencePoint Pr., Inc.

Marks, Anthony & Tingay, Graham. Romans. Jackson, Ian & Wood, Gerald, illus. 2005. (Illustrated World History Ser.). 96p. (J). (gr. 6-12). lib. bdg. 20.95 *(978-1-58086-782-5(0),* Usborne) EDC Publishing.

—Romans II. 2010. (Illustrated World History Ser.). 96p. (J). pap. 12.99 *(978-0-7945-2754-9(X),* Usborne) EDC Publishing.

Mason Crest. Rome, Vol. 8. 2016. (Major World Cities Ser.: Vol. 8). (ENG., Illus.). 48p. (J). (gr. 5-8). 20.95 *(978-1-4222-3545-4(9))* Mason Crest.

Mason Crest Publishers Staff. Romans, Vol. 5. 2019. (Untold History of Ancient Civilizations Ser.). (Illus.). 64p. (J). (gr. 8). lib. bdg. 31.93 *(978-1-4222-3521-8(1))* Mason Crest.

Mattern, Joanne. Julius Caesar. 2017. (Junior Biography From Ancient Civilization Ser.). (Illus.). 48p. (J). (gr. 4-6). 29.95 *(978-1-68020-024-9(0))* Mitchell Lane Pubs.

Matthews, Rupert. Gladiators, 1 vol. 2015. (History's Fearless Fighters Ser.). (ENG., Illus.). 48p. (J). (gr. 5-6). pap. 15.05 *(978-1-4824-3165-0(3),* 9b0b869b-bbb8-44f6-8179-df6e165ac7f9) Stevens, Gareth Publishing LLLP.

Maynard, Charles W. The Technology of Ancient Rome. (Technology of the Ancient World Ser.). 48p. (gr. 6-6). 2009. 61.20 *(978-1-60854-242-0(4),* Rosen Reference) 2006. (ENG., Illus.). (J). lib. bdg. 34.47 *(978-1-4042-0556-7(X),* 567ff699-46a1-40b3-9ffd-e7793b6b7c4f) Rosen Publishing Group, Inc., The.

McCullough, Naomi V. The Technology of Ancient Rome, 1 vol. 2016. (Ancient Innovations Ser.). (ENG.). 64p. (gr. 6-6). lib. bdg. 35.93 *(978-1-5026-2233-4(5),* 63ecbfae-03d2-4d65-9f14-408ff385f516) Cavendish Square Publishing LLC.

Mehta-Jones, Shilpa. Life in Ancient Rome. 2004. (Peoples of the Ancient World Ser.). (ENG., Illus.). 32p. (J). lib. bdg. *(978-0-7787-2034-8(9))* Crabtree Publishing Co.

Mincks, Margaret. What We Get from Roman Mythology. 2015. (21st Century Skills Library: Mythology & Culture Ser.). (ENG., Illus.). 32p. (J). (gr. 3-6). pap. 14.21 *(978-1-63188-931-8(1)*, 205985) Cherry Lake Publishing.

Morgan, Julian. Hadrian: Consolidating the Empire. 2009. (Ancient Leaders Ser.). 112p. (gr. 5-8). 66.50 *(978-1-61511-423-8(8)*, Rosen Reference) Rosen Publishing Group, Inc., The.

—Nero: Destroyer of Rome. 2009. (Ancient Leaders Ser.). 112p. (gr. 5-8). 66.50 *(978-1-61511-426-9(2)*, Rosen Reference) Rosen Publishing Group, Inc., The.

Morris, Neil. Everyday Life in Ancient Rome. 2008. (Uncovering History Ser.). (ENG., Illus.). 48p. (J). (gr. 2-7). 19.95 *(978-88-89272-54-1(6))* McRae Bks. Srl ITA. Dist: Independent Pubs. Group.

Murrell, Deborah. The Best Book of Ancient Rome. 2007. (Best Book Of Ser.). (ENG., Illus.). 32p. (J). (gr. k-2). 18.69 *(978-0-7534-6080-1(7)*, 9780753460801) Kingfisher Publications, plc GBR. Dist: Children's Plus, Inc.

Murrell, Deborah Jane & Dennis, Peter. Gladiator. 2012. (ENG., Illus.). 32p. (gr. 3-5). pap. 8.95 *(978-1-926853-52-9(0))* Saunders Bk. Co. CAN. Dist: RiverStream Publishing.

Naden, Corinne J. & Blue, Rose. Ancient Romans & the Colosseum. 2003. (J). *(978-1-58417-316-8(5))*; pap. *(978-1-58417-317-5(3))* Lake Street Pubs.

Nardo, Don. Cause & Effect the Fall of Rome: The Fall of Rome. 2015. (ENG., Illus.). 80p. (J). lib. bdg. *(978-1-60152-794-3(2))* ReferencePoint Pr., Inc.

—The Roman Empire. 2005. (World History Ser.). (ENG., Illus.). 96p. (YA). (gr. 7-10). lib. bdg. 33.45 *(978-1-59018-657-2(5)*, Lucent Bks.) Cengage Gale.

—Rome. 2011. (Classical Civilization Ser.). 128p. (YA). (gr. 7-12). 28.95 *(978-1-59935-174-2(9))* Reynolds, Morgan Inc.

Oachs, Emily Rose. Ancient Rome. 2020. (Ancient Civilizations Ser.). (ENG., Illus.). 32p. (J). (gr. 3-8). pap. 8.99 *(978-1-61891-864-2(8)*, 12593, Blastoff! Discovery) Bellwether Media.

O'Dell, Angela. World's Story 1: Creation to the Roman Empire: the Ancients. 2nd ed. 2018. (World's Story Ser.: 1). (ENG.). 299p. (gr. 6-8). pap. 39.99 *(978-1-68344-077-2(3)*, Master Books) New Leaf Publishing Group.

—World's Story 1 (Teacher Guide) The Ancients: Creation to the Roman Empire. 2nd ed. 2018. (World's Story Ser.: 1). (ENG.). 351p. (gr. 6-8). pap. 29.99 *(978-1-68344-088-8(9)*, Master Books) New Leaf Publishing Group.

Osborne, Mary Pope & Boyce, Natalie Pope. Ancient Rome & Pompeii: A Nonfiction Companion to Magic Tree House #13: Vacation under the Volcano. Murdocca, Sal, illus. 2006. (Magic Tree House (R) Fact Tracker Ser.: 14). 128p. (J). (gr. 2-5). 6.99 *(978-0-375-83220-8(3)*, Random Hse. Bks. for Young Readers) Random Hse. Children's Bks.

Park, Louise & Love, Timothy. The Roman Gladiators, 1 vol. 2010. (Ancient & Medieval People Ser.). (ENG.). 32p. (gr. 5-5). 31.21 *(978-0-7614-4443-5(2)*, 6f2791e8-9240-4ce9-92bc-97c6bbc1ef1d) Cavendish Square Publishing LLC.

Pistone, Nicholas. Art & Culture of Ancient Rome. 2010. (Ancient Art & Cultures Ser.). 40p. (YA). (gr. 5-8). lib. bdg., E-Book 53.00 *(978-1-61532-965-6(X))* Rosen Publishing Group, Inc., The.

Pistone, Nicholas, et al. Art & Culture of Ancient Rome, 1 vol. 2010. (Ancient Art & Cultures Ser.). (ENG., Illus.). 40p. (gr. 6-6). (J). pap. 12.75 *(978-1-61532-885-7(8)*, 43ea857a-ddd9-4c96-982f-89a98f386f4b); (YA). lib. bdg. 31.80 *(978-1-4358-3591-7(3)*, 5ed3d44f-076b-41c3-a109-842270e2e763) Rosen Publishing Group, Inc., The.

Powell, Jillian. The Romans, 1 vol. 2010. (Gruesome Truth About Ser.). (ENG.). 32p. (J). (gr. 5-5). lib. bdg. 29.93 *(978-1-61533-220-5(0)*, b6f11e6a-1c37-47ba-9215-6e7ac4aac097, Windmill Bks.) Rosen Publishing Group, Inc., The.

Rajczak Nelson, Kristen. 20 Fun Facts about Women in Ancient Greece & Rome, 1 vol. 2015. (Fun Fact File: Women in History Ser.). (ENG., Illus.). 32p. (J). (gr. 2-3). 27.93 *(978-1-4824-2818-6(0)*, 4d434707-8ead-41ea-a037-4a8b7544ab7a) Stevens, Gareth Publishing LLLP.

Randolph, Joanne, ed. Living & Working in Ancient Rome, 1 vol. 2017. (Back in Time Ser.). (ENG.). 48p. (gr. 5-6). pap. 12.70 *(978-0-7660-8973-0(8)*, b8d130dc-c8af-4cb9-9dff-58bfbd55d1a5) Enslow Publishing, LLC.

Reece, Katherine E. The Romans: Builders of an Empire. 2005. (Ancient Civilizations Ser.). (Illus.). 48p. (J). (gr. 4-8). lib. bdg. *(978-1-59515-507-8(4)*, 1244352) Rourke Educational Media.

Rice, Rob S. Ancient Roman Warfare, 1 vol. 2009. (Ancient Warfare Ser.). (ENG., Illus.). 32p. (J). (gr. 5-6). lib. bdg. 28.67 *(978-1-4339-1974-9(5)*, 32884157-b843-45aa-a55c-57d6205af466, Gareth Stevens Learning Library) Stevens, Gareth Publishing LLLP.

Ridgley, Sara & Mole, Gavin. Sing It & Say - Ancient Rome. (Illus.). 140p. (J). 10.95 incl. audio *(978-1-85909-390-0(6)*, Warner Bros. Pubns.) Alfred Publishing Co., Inc.

Ridley, Sarah. Life in Roman Times. 2015. (Everyday History Ser.). (Illus.). 32p. (J). 31.35 *(978-1-59920-951-7(9))* Black Rabbit Bks.

Riggs, Kate. Gladiators. 2011. (Great Warriors Ser.). (ENG.). 24p. (J). (gr. 3-6). 16.95 *(978-1-60818-000-4(X)*, 22169, Creative Education) Creative Co., The.

Rinaldo, Denise. Julius Caesar: Dictator for Life. 2010. (Wicked History Ser.). (ENG.). 128p. (J). (gr. 6-12). pap. 5.95 *(978-0-531-22822-7(3)*, Watts, Franklin) Scholastic Library Publishing.

Rogora, Bernardo. Los Romanos. (Coleccion Bravo). (SPA., Illus.). 76p. (YA). (gr. 5-8). *(978-84-7131-907-4(1)*, EDI30259) Editex, Editorial S.A. ESP. Dist: Lectorum Pubns., Inc.

Roxburgh, Ellis. Cleopatra vs. the Roman Empire: Power, Conquest, & Tragedy, 1 vol. 2015. (History's Greatest Rivals Ser.). (ENG., Illus.). 48p. (J). (gr. 6-8). pap. 15.05 *(978-1-4824-4223-6(X)*, 57be58d8-e999-4997-82e7-129fd21b57cd) Stevens, Gareth Publishing LLLP.

Ryall, Michael. Rome Long Ago. 2005. (J). pap. *(978-1-4108-4634-1(2))* Benchmark Education Co.

Samuels, Charlie. Technology in Ancient Rome, 1 vol. 2013. (Technology in the Ancient World Ser.). 48p. (J). (gr. 4-5). (ENG.). pap. 15.05 *(978-1-4339-9637-5(5)*, 944bce43-7d6d-4cf4-9720-0777521616b9); pap. 84.30 *(978-1-4339-9638-2(3))*; (ENG., Illus.). lib. bdg. 34.61 *(978-1-4339-9636-8(7)*, fb1edb51-512e-4f0c-8b4a-f1746913994d) Stevens, Gareth Publishing LLLP.

Santillian, Beatriz & Morgan, Julian. Hadrian: Emperor of Rome, 1 vol. 2017. (Leaders of the Ancient World Ser.). (ENG., Illus.). 112p. (J). (gr. 6-6). 38.80 *(978-1-5081-7484-4(9)*, 1ec256a1-3c9d-416c-8596-284ded145c9a, Rosen Young Adult) Rosen Publishing Group, Inc., The.

Sasek, M. This Is Rome. 2007. (This Is ... Ser.). (ENG., Illus.). 64p. (J). (gr. 2-12). 17.95 *(978-0-7893-1549-6(1))* Universe Publishing.

Saxena, Shalini. Nero: Ruthless Roman Emperor, 1 vol. 2016. (History's Most Murderous Villains Ser.). (ENG., Illus.). 32p. (J). (gr. 4-5). pap. 11.50 *(978-1-4824-4799-6(1)*, b3b131ea-2cca-45bf-ad07-d0fb72992d7d) Stevens, Gareth Publishing LLLP.

Schomp, Virginia. The Ancient Romans, 1 vol. 2009. (Myths of the World Ser.). (ENG., Illus.). 96p. (gr. 6-6). lib. bdg. 36.93 *(978-0-7614-3094-0(6)*, 38280b3a-537a-4619-ae81-62db9178a8d5) Cavendish Square Publishing LLC.

Sewell, E. M. The Child's History of Rome. 2005. reprint ed. pap. 26.95 *(978-1-4179-6641-7(6))* Kessinger Publishing, LLC.

Sheehan, Sean. Ancient Rome, 1 vol. 2010. (Exploring the Ancient World Ser.). (ENG., Illus.). 64p. (YA). (gr. 6-8). lib. bdg. 37.27 *(978-1-4339-4160-3(0)*, 6abdce81-58b0-4dc8-8089-100cee7de438, Gareth Stevens Secondary Library) Stevens, Gareth Publishing LLLP.

Shone, Rob. Spartacus: The Life of a Roman Gladiator. 2009. (Graphic Nonfiction Biographies Ser.). (ENG.). 48p. (YA). (gr. 4-5). 58.50 *(978-1-61513-028-3(4)*, Rosen Reference) Rosen Publishing Group, Inc., The.

Shone, Rob & Ganeri, Anita. Spartacus: The Life of a Roman Gladiator, 1 vol. 2005. (Graphic Nonfiction Biographies Ser.). (ENG., Illus.). 48p. (J). (gr. 4-6). lib. bdg. 37.13 *(978-1-4042-0240-5(4)*, 7bbdd2d7-ef6a-4988-8fb0-1181dbe5671a) Rosen Publishing Group, Inc., The.

Shoulders, Michael & Shoulders, Debbie. G Is for Gladiator: An Ancient Rome Alphabet. Juhasz, Victor, illus. 2010. (Sleeping Bear Alphabets Ser.). (ENG.). 40p. (J). (gr. 1-4). 19.99 *(978-1-58536-457-2(6)*, 202180) Sleeping Bear Pr.

Sims, Lesley. The Roman Soldier's Handbook: Everything a Beginner Soldier Needs to Know. McNee, Ian, illus. 2006. (English Heritage Ser.). 80p. (J). (gr. 4-7). 12.99 *(978-0-7945-0837-1(5)*, Usborne) EDC Publishing.

Snedden, Robert. Ancient Rome. 2009. (Technology in Times Past Ser.). (ENG., Illus.). 48p. (J). (gr. 4-7). pap. *(978-1-897563-63-2(9))* Saunders Bk. Co.

Sonneborn, Liz. The Romans: Life in Ancient Rome. Hiti, Samuel, illus. 2009. (Life in Ancient Civilizations Ser.). (ENG.). 48p. (gr. 3-6). lib. bdg. 29.27 *(978-0-8225-8679-1(7)*, Millbrook Pr.) Lerner Publishing Group.

Spotlight on Ancient Civilizations: Rome. 2013. (Spotlight on Ancient Civilizations: Rome Ser.). 24p. (J). (gr. 3-4). (ENG.). pap. 60.00 *(978-1-4777-2689-1(6))*; pap. 297.00 *(978-1-4777-2690-7(X))* Rosen Publishing Group, Inc., The. (PowerKids Pr.).

Steele, Philip. Ancient Rome: Step into the Time of the Roman Empire, with 15 Step-by-Step Projects & over 370 Exciting Pictures. 2013. (Illus.). 64p. (J). (gr. 3-7). pap. 12.99 *(978-1-84322-692-5(8))* Anness Publishing GBR. Dist: National Bk. Network.

—Hail! Ancient Romans. 2010. (ENG.). 32p. (J). *(978-0-7787-6624-7(1))*; pap. *(978-0-7787-6631-5(4))* Crabtree Publishing Co.

—The Roman Empire. 2007. (Step Into Ser.). (Illus.). 64p. (J). (gr. 4-7). pap. 10.99 *(978-1-84476-348-1(X))* Anness Publishing GBR. Dist: National Bk. Network.

—The Roman Empire, 1 vol. 2009. (Passport to the Past Ser.). (ENG., Illus.). 64p. (J). (gr. 5-6). lib. bdg. 37.13 *(978-1-4358-5176-4(5)*, 63416eb8-27c2-444f-adeb-aa359b405bde) Rosen Publishing Group, Inc., The.

Stewart, David. Inside Ancient Rome. James, John et al, illus. 2005. (Inside... Ser.). 48p. (J). (gr. 5). lib. bdg. 19.95 *(978-1-59270-045-5(4))* Enchanted Lion Bks., LLC.

Stokes, Jonathan W. The Thrifty Guide to Ancient Rome: A Handbook for Time Travelers. Sossella, David, illus. 2019. (Thrifty Guides: 1). 160p. (J). (gr. 3-7). pap. 8.99 *(978-1-101-99810-6(5)*, Puffin Books) Penguin Young Readers Group.

Sullivan, Erin Ash. Ancient Rome: Set Of 6. 2011. (Navigators Ser.). (J). pap. 50.00 net. *(978-1-4108-5115-4(X))* Benchmark Education Co.

—Ancient Rome: Text Pairs. 2008. (Bridges/Navigators Ser.). (J). (gr. 6). 89.00 *(978-1-4108-8429-9(5))* Benchmark Education Co.

Sylvester, Diane. Ancient Rome. Hillam, Corbin, illus. 2006. (Museum Ser.). 64p. (J). (gr. 5-8). pap. 13.99 *(978-0-88160-390-3(2)*, LW445, Learning Works, The) Creative Teaching Pr., Inc.

Tracy, Kathleen. The Life & Times of Constantine. 2005. (Biography from Ancient Civilizations Ser.). (Illus.). 48p. (J). (gr. 4-8). lib. bdg. 29.95 *(978-1-58415-343-6(1))* Mitchell Lane Pubs.

Trajan's Rome Grades 5-9: The Man, the City, the Empire. (J). tchr. ed., spiral bd. 15.00 *(978-0-382-44446-3(9))* Cobblestone Publishing Co.

Turner, Tracey. Hard As Nails in Ancient Rome. Lenman, Jamie, illus. 2015. (Hard As Nails in History Ser.). (ENG.). 64p. (J). (gr. 4-5). *(978-0-7787-1513-9(2))* Crabtree Publishing Co.

Uhl, Xina M. How STEM Built the Roman Empire, 1 vol. 2019. (How STEM Built Empires Ser.). (ENG.). 80p. (gr. 7-7). pap. 16.30 *(978-1-7253-4152-4(2)*, aea2ce53-1be1-444e-b122-08dbb30985d4) Rosen Publishing Group, Inc., The.

Von Zumbusch, Amelie. Ancient Roman Culture, 1 vol. 2013. (Spotlight on Ancient Civilizations: Rome Ser.). (ENG.). 24p. (J). (gr. 3-4). 26.27 *(978-1-4777-0775-3(1)*, c06cdcc1-c94f-4eee-9eb4-dbc2b3f48e50, PowerKids Pr.) Rosen Publishing Group, Inc., The.

—Ancient Roman Daily Life, 1 vol. 2013. (Spotlight on Ancient Civilizations: Rome Ser.). (ENG.). 24p. (J). (gr. 3-4). 26.27 *(978-1-4777-0778-4(6)*, f692502d-88fa-4e51-a9c1-e743d28ad6e7, PowerKids Pr.) Rosen Publishing Group, Inc., The.

Vonne, Mira. Gross Facts about the Roman Empire. 2017. (Gross History Ser.). (ENG., Illus.). 32p. (J). (gr. 3-9). lib. bdg. 27.32 *(978-1-5157-4156-5(7)*, 133956, Capstone Pr.) Capstone.

West, David. The Ancient Romans, 1 vol. 2016. (Discovering Ancient Civilizations Ser.). (ENG.). 32p. (gr. 3-3). pap. 11.50 *(978-1-4824-5059-0(3)*, a3383f85-6a6b-4bde-adde-7511453f007a) Stevens, Gareth Publishing LLLP.

Whiting, Jim. The Life & Times of Julius Caesar. 2005. (Biography from Ancient Civilizations Ser.). (Illus.). 48p. (J). (gr. -1-7). lib. bdg. 29.95 *(978-1-58415-337-5(7))* Mitchell Lane Pubs.

—The Life & Times of Nero. 2005. (Biography from Ancient Civilizations Ser.). (Illus.). 48p. (J). (gr. 5-8). lib. bdg. 29.95 *(978-1-58415-349-8(0))* Mitchell Lane Pubs.

Willard Crompton, Samuel. Discovering Ancient Rome, 4 vols. 2014. (Exploring Ancient Civilizations Ser.). (ENG.). 48p. (YA). (gr. 5-5). 56.82 *(978-1-62275-832-6(3)*, 91124bef-51e2-435f-a1c0-b7aaec7bdd73, Britannica Educational Publishing) Rosen Publishing Group, Inc., The.

Williams, Jane A. A Bluestocking Guide - Ancient Rome: Companion Workbook for Richard J. Maybury's Ancient Rome: How it Affects You Today. Daniels, Kathryn, ed. 2004. (Bluestocking Guide Ser.). 47p. (YA). pap. 9.95 *(978-0-942617-48-1(7))* Bluestocking Pr.

Williams, Marcia. The Romans: Gods, Emperors, & Dormice. Williams, Marcia, illus. 2018. (ENG., Illus.). 40p. (J). (gr. 3-7). 11.99 *(978-0-7636-9978-9(0))* Candlewick Pr.

Williams, Rose. The Young Romans. 2003. (Anthem Classics Ser.). (ENG., Illus.). 128p. (J). pap. 26.00 *(978-1-84331-047-1(3))* Anthem Pr. GBR. Dist: Bolchazy-Carducci Pubs.

—The Young Romans. 2007. (ENG.). pap. 23.00 *(978-0-86516-670-7(6))* Bolchazy-Carducci Pubs.

Woolf, Alex. Meet the Ancient Romans, 1 vol. 2014. (Encounters with the Past Ser.). (ENG.). 32p. (J). (gr. 3-4). 28.27 *(978-1-4824-0886-7(4)*, 53c2f781-2471-4f10-b176-0ef794a3dafd) Stevens, Gareth Publishing LLLP.

Yonge, Charlotte Mary. Aunt Charlotte's Roman History. 2013. 260p. pap. *(978-3-95507-998-7(8))* DOGMA. in Europäischer Hochschulverlag GmbH & Co. KG.

Zumbusch, Amelie von. Ancient Roman Culture, 1 vol. 2013. (Spotlight on Ancient Civilizations: Rome Ser.). (ENG., Illus.). 24p. (J). (gr. 3-4). pap. 11.00 *(978-1-4777-0883-5(9)*, 5ea741b8-9555-4bc5-b7de-c2a6982232bc, PowerKids Pr.) Rosen Publishing Group, Inc., The.

—Ancient Roman Daily Life, 1 vol. 2013. (Spotlight on Ancient Civilizations: Rome Ser.). (ENG., Illus.). 24p. (J). (gr. 3-4). pap. 11.00 *(978-1-4777-0889-7(8)*, a9a78b18-98ac-4535-8152-c488fa47b16e, PowerKids Pr.) Rosen Publishing Group, Inc., The.

—The Ancient Roman Economy, 1 vol. 2013. (Spotlight on Ancient Civilizations: Rome Ser.). (ENG.). 24p. (J). (gr. 3-4). pap. 11.00 *(978-1-4777-0887-3(1)*, 0bd3b5ef-443c-4a91-bd52-f9beb2ea3cf1); lib. bdg. 26.27 *(978-1-4777-0777-7(8)*, a9fecef3-5e2d-4c02-90ee-c4a36866a210) Rosen Publishing Group, Inc., The. (PowerKids Pr.).

—Ancient Roman Geography, 1 vol. 2013. (Spotlight on Ancient Civilizations: Rome Ser.). (ENG., Illus.). 24p. (J). (gr. 3-4). pap. 11.00 *(978-1-4777-0891-0(X)*, 59ddcd6-a422-4286-9189-04aa414c5915, PowerKids Pr.) Rosen Publishing Group, Inc., The.

—Ancient Roman Technology, 1 vol. 2013. (Spotlight on Ancient Civilizations: Rome Ser.). (ENG., Illus.). 24p. (J). (gr. 3-4). pap. 11.00 *(978-1-4777-0893-4(6)*, d6c2dd67-6877-4ff3-b870-972522b18165, PowerKids Pr.) Rosen Publishing Group, Inc., The.

Zumbusch, Amelie Von & Von Zumbusch, Amelie. Ancient Roman Geography, 1 vol. 2013. (Spotlight on Ancient Civilizations: Rome Ser.). (ENG., Illus.). 24p. (J). (gr. 3-4). 26.27 *(978-1-4777-0779-1(4)*, 3c940668-ac2b-4ed6-91b8-6fc49b309a63, PowerKids Pr.) Rosen Publishing Group, Inc., The.

—Ancient Roman Technology, 1 vol. 2013. (Spotlight on Ancient Civilizations: Rome Ser.). (ENG.). 24p. (J). (gr. 3-4). 26.27 *(978-1-4777-0780-7(8)*, 0f5fd559-8cfd-4234-8f30-9e29e8780433, PowerKids Pr.) Rosen Publishing Group, Inc., The.

ROME—HISTORY—FICTION

Banks, Lynne Reid. Tiger, Tiger. 2007. (ENG.). 208p. (YA). (gr. 7-11). mass mkt. 6.99 *(978-0-440-42044-6(X)*, Laurel Leaf) Random Hse. Children's Bks.

Church, Alfred J. The Aeneid for Boys & Girls. 2008. 100p. pap. 9.05 *(978-1-60459-519-2(1))* Wilder Pubns., Corp.

Church, Alfred J. & Virgil. The Aeneid for Boys & Girls. 2017. (ENG., Illus.). (J). pap. 8.95 *(978-1-68422-160-8(9))* Martino Fine Bks.

Dalton, Annie. Fighting Fit (Mel Beeby, Agent Angel, Book 6), Book 6. 2009. (Mel Beeby, Agent Angel Ser.: 6). (ENG.). 192p. (gr. 4-7). pap. 7.99 *(978-0-00-720476-2(0)*, HarperCollins Children's Bks.) HarperCollins Pubs. Ltd. GBR. Dist: HarperCollins Pubs.

Henty, George. The Young Carthaginian: A Story of the Times of Hannibal. 2011. 360p. pap. 19.95 *(978-1-61179-162-4(6))* Fireship Pr.

—The Young Carthaginian: A Tale of the Times of Hannibal. 2004. reprint ed. pap. 27.95 *(978-1-4191-8911-1(5))*; pap. 1.99 *(978-1-4192-8911-8(X))*; pap. 27.95 *(978-1-4191-8911-1(5))* Kessinger Publishing, LLC.

Hulme-Cross, Benjamin. The Gladiator's Victory. Rinaldi, Angelo, illus. 2015. (Warrior Heroes Ser.). (ENG.). 160p. (J). (gr. 6-6). *(978-0-7787-1764-5(X))* Crabtree Publishing Co.

Lawrence, Caroline. The Assassins of Rome. 2005. (Roman Mysteries Ser.). (Illus.). 161p. (J). (gr. 3-7). 14.65 *(978-0-7569-5879-4(2))* Perfection Learning Corp.

—The Beggar of Volubilis. 2008. (ENG., Illus.). 272p. (gr. 4-6). pap. 10.99 *(978-1-84255-604-7(5)*, Orion Children's Bks.) Hachette Children's Group GBR. Dist: Hachette Bk. Group.

—The Charioteer of Delphi. 2007. (ENG., Illus.). 256p. (gr. 4-6). pap. 10.99 *(978-1-84255-544-6(8)*, Orion Children's Bks.) Hachette Children's Group GBR. Dist: Hachette Bk. Group.

—The Dolphins of Laurentum. 2005. (Roman Mysteries Ser.). (Illus.). 161p. (J). (gr. 6-9). 13.65 *(978-0-7569-6538-9(1))* Perfection Learning Corp.

—The Legionary from Londinium & Other Mini Mysteries. 2013. (ENG., Illus.). 192p. (J). (gr. 7-17). 10.99 *(978-1-84255-192-9(2)*, Orion Children's Bks.) Hachette Children's Group GBR. Dist: Hachette Bk. Group.

—The Man from Pomegranate Street, Bk. 17. 2010. (ENG., Illus.). 272p. (YA). (gr. 7-17). 10.99 *(978-1-84255-608-5(8)*, Orion Children's Bks.) Hachette Children's Group GBR. Dist: Hachette Bk. Group.

—The Prophet from Ephesus: The Roman Mysteries 16. 2009. (ENG., Illus.). 224p. (YA). (gr. 7-17). pap. 10.99 *(978-1-84255-606-1(1)*, Orion Children's Bks.) Hachette Children's Group GBR. Dist: Hachette Bk. Group.

—The Scribes from Alexandria. 2008. (ENG., Illus.). 272p. (gr. 4-6). pap. 10.99 *(978-1-84255-605-4(3)*, Orion Children's Bks.) Hachette Children's Group GBR. Dist: Hachette Bk. Group.

—The Sirens of Surrentum. 2006. (ENG., Illus.). 272p. (gr. 4-6). pap. 10.99 *(978-1-84255-506-4(5)*, Orion Children's Bks.) Hachette Children's Group GBR. Dist: Hachette Bk. Group.

—The Sirens of Surrentum. 2007. (Roman Mysteries Ser.: Bk. 11). (ENG., Illus.). 224p. (J). (gr. 6-9). 16.95 *(978-1-59643-084-6(2))* Roaring Brook Pr.

—The Slave-Girl from Jerusalem. 2007. (ENG., Illus.). 240p. (gr. 4-6). pap. 10.99 *(978-1-84255-572-9(3)*, Orion Children's Bks.) Hachette Children's Group GBR. Dist: Hachette Bk. Group.

Lee, Kathy. Rome in Flames. 2005. 144p. pap. *(978-1-84427-089-7(0))* Scripture Union.

Livingston, Lesley. The Valiant. 2018. (Valiant Ser.: 1). (ENG.). 400p. (YA). (gr. 7). pap. 9.99 *(978-0-448-49379-4(9)*, Razorbill) Penguin Young Readers Group.

Nielsen, Jennifer A. Rise of the Wolf. 2016. (Mark of the Thief Ser.: 2). lib. bdg. 18.40 *(978-0-606-39707-0(8))* Turtleback.

—Rise of the Wolf (Mark of the Thief, Book 2) 2016. (Mark of the Thief Ser.: 2). (ENG.). 352p. (J). (gr. 4-7). pap. 8.99 *(978-0-545-56205-8(8)*, Scholastic Pr.) Scholastic, Inc.

Novel Units. The Bronze Bow Novel Units Teacher Guide. 2019. (ENG.). (J). pap. 12.99 *(978-1-56137-726-8(0)*, Novel Units, Inc.) Classroom Library Co.

Rubalcaba, Jill. The Wadjet Eye. 2006. (ENG.). 160p. (J). (gr. 5-7). pap. 7.99 *(978-0-618-68927-9(3)*, 100486, Clarion Bks.) HarperCollins Pubs.

Shakespeare, William. Julius Caesar, 1 vol. Garcia, Eduardo, illus. 2011. (Shakespeare Graphics Ser.). (ENG.). 88p. (J). (gr. 5-9). pap. 7.15 *(978-1-4342-3450-6(9)*, 116471); lib. bdg. 28.65 *(978-1-4342-2631-0(X)*, 113874) Capstone. (Stone Arch Bks.).

—Manga Shakespeare: Julius Caesar. Mahbab, Mustashrik, illus. 2008. (ENG.). 208p. (YA). (gr. 7-11). pap. 16.99 *(978-0-8109-7072-4(4)*, 6553-03, Amulet Bks.) Abrams, Inc.

Surget, Alain & Yeardley, Glynne. Danger at the Circus! Parme, Fabrice, illus. 2014. 95p. (J). *(978-1-4351-5334-9(0))* Barnes & Noble, Inc.

Sutcliff, Rosemary. The Eagle. movie tie-in ed. 2011. (Roman Britain Trilogy Ser.: 1). (ENG.). 240p. (YA). (gr. 5). pap. 10.99 *(978-0-312-56434-6(1)*, 900074782) Square Fish.

—The Eagle of the Ninth. 2010. (Roman Britain Trilogy Ser.: 1). (ENG.). 240p. (YA). (gr. 7). pap. 11.99 *(978-0-312-64429-1(9)*, 900068423) Square Fish.

Trease, Geoffrey, text. Word to Caesar. 2005. (J). per. 14.95 *(978-0-9766386-2-9(2))* Hillside Education.

Wallace, Lew. Ben-Hur. (SPA., Illus.). (YA). 11.95 *(978-84-7281-099-0(2)*, AF1099) Auriga, Ediciones S.A. ESP. Dist: Continental Bk. Co., Inc.

Weatherby, W. J. Chariots of Fire. Morris, Margery, ed. abr. ed. Date not set. (Nelson Readers Ser.: 2). (J). pap. *(978-0-17-557036-2(1))* Addison-Wesley Longman, Inc.

ROME—HISTORY—REPUBLIC, 510-30 B.C.

Ancient Rome II, Grades 5-9: Theater, Sculpture & Painting, Religion, Daily Life, the Roman at Home, Latin Prefixes in English. (Teaching with Primary Sources Ser.). (Illus.). (J). tchr. ed., ring bd. 28.95 *(978-0-382-40865-6(9))* Cobblestone Publishing Co.

Bailey, Gerry & Foster, Karen. Julius Caesar's Sandals. Noyes, Leighton, illus. 2008. (Stories of Great People Ser.). (ENG.). 40p. (J). (gr. 3-6). pap. *(978-0-7787-3717-9(9))*; lib. bdg. *(978-0-7787-3695-0(4))* Crabtree Publishing Co.

Baum, Margaux & Thorne, James. Julius Caesar, 1 vol. 2016. (Leaders of the Ancient World Ser.). (ENG.). 112p. (J). (gr. 6-6). 38.80 *(978-1-5081-7248-2(X)*, b53a547f-12b4-427f-ba2a-deee59e5451e) Rosen Publishing Group, Inc., The.

Brooks, Philip. Hannibal: Rome's Worst Nightmare. 2009. (Wicked History Ser.). (ENG., Illus.). 128p. (J). 18.69 *(978-0-531-18553-7(2)*, Watts, Franklin) Scholastic Library Publishing.

Cox, Phil Roxbee. Who Were the Romans? 2004. (Starting Point History Ser.). (Illus.). 32p. (J). pap. 4.95 *(978-0-7945-0247-8(4)*, Usborne); lib. bdg. 12.95 *(978-1-58086-446-6(5))* EDC Publishing.

Crompton, Samuel Willard. Julius Caesar. 2003. (Ancient World Leaders Ser.). (Illus.). 112p. (J). (gr. 6-12). 30.00 *(978-0-7910-7220-2(7)*, Facts On File) Infobase Holdings, Inc.

Curry, Jane. Brave Cloelia: Retold from the Account in the History of Early Rome by the Roman Historian Titus Livius. Crosby, Jeff, illus. 2004. (ENG.). 34p. 17.95 *(978-0-89236-763-4(6))* Oxford Univ. Pr., Inc.

Firth, Rachel. Julius Caesar. 2007. (Famous Lives Gift Bks). (Illus.). 64p. (J). 8.99 *(978-0-7945-1595-9(9)*, Usborne) EDC Publishing.

Goldberg, Jan. Julius Caesar. 2004. (ZB Reads Trio Books). (Illus.). 16p. (gr. 5-7). pap. 5.50 *(978-0-7367-1800-4(1))* Zaner-Bloser, Inc.

Jeffrey, Gary. Julius Caesar: The Life of a Roman General. 2009. (Graphic Nonfiction Biographies Ser.). (ENG.). 48p. (YA). (gr. 4-5). 58.50 *(978-1-61513-020-7(9),* Rosen Reference) Rosen Publishing Group, Inc., The.

Medina, Nico & Who HQ. Who Was Julius Caesar? Foley, Tim, illus. 2014. (Who Was? Ser.). 112p. (J). (gr. 3-7). pap. 5.99 *(978-0-448-48083-1(2),* Penguin Workshop) Penguin Young Readers Group.

Newsome, Joel. Hannibal, 1 vol. 2017. (Great Military Leaders Ser.). (ENG.). 128p. (YA). (gr. 9-9). 47.36 *(978-1-5026-2869-5(4),* 5a9f24ae-5483-45ea-b2fb-6d1680e49a8f) Cavendish Square Publishing LLC.

Rinaldo, Denise. Julius Caesar (Revised Edition) (a Wicked History) (Library Edition) rev. ed. 2015. (Wicked History Ser.). (ENG., Illus.). 144p. (J). (gr. 6). lib. bdg. 33.00 *(978-0-531-22123-5(7),* Children's Pr.) Scholastic Library Publishing.

Saunders, Nicholas. The Life of Julius Caesar. 2006. (Stories from History Ser.). (ENG., Illus.). 48p. (J). (gr. 3-6). 21.19 *(978-0-7696-4717-3(0))* School Specialty, Incorporated.

Tracy, Kathleen. The Life & Times of Cicero. 2006. (Biography from Ancient Civilizations Ser.). (Illus.). 48p. (J). (gr. 4-8). lib. bdg. 29.95 *(978-1-58415-510-2(8))* Mitchell Lane Pubs.

Zumbusch, Amelie von. Ancient Roman Government, 1 vol. 2013. (Spotlight on Ancient Civilizations: Rome Ser.). (ENG., Illus.). 24p. (J). (gr. 3-4). pap. 11.00 *(978-1-4777-0885-9(5),* 4e151ba3-8952-4b76-9f90-c269daecbb3b, PowerKids Pr.) Rosen Publishing Group, Inc., The.

ROME—HISTORY—EMPIRE, 30 B.C.-476 A.D.

Allan, Tony. Exploring the Life, Myth, & Art of Ancient Rome, 1 vol. 2011. (Civilizations of the World Ser.). (ENG.). 144p. (YA). (gr. 8-8). lib. bdg. 47.80 *(978-1-4488-4831-7(8),* 46841046-c322-44aa-8cf6-b0825a3804bb) Rosen Publishing Group, Inc., The.

Baum, Margaux & Forsyth, Fiona. Augustus, 1 vol. 2016. (Leaders of the Ancient World Ser.). (ENG., Illus.). 112p. (J). (gr. 6-6). 38.80 *(978-1-5081-7242-0(0),* 12038024-1931-4939-b82f-b3acfbb5e4b5) Rosen Publishing Group, Inc., The.

Brocklehurst, R. Roman Army. 2004. (Discovery Program Ser.). (Illus.). 48p. (J). pap. 8.95 *(978-0-7945-0591-2(0))* EDC Publishing.

Cox, Phil Roxbee. Who Were the Romans? 2004. (Starting Point History Ser.). (Illus.). 32p. (J). pap. 4.95 *(978-0-7945-0247-8(4),* Usborne) EDC Publishing.

Hawes, Alison. A Roman Soldier's Handbook. 2010. (Crabtree Connections Ser.). (ENG.). 24p. (J). (gr. 3-6). *(978-0-7787-9952-8(2));* pap. *(978-0-7787-9974-0(3))* Crabtree Publishing Co.

Hinds, Kathryn. Everyday Life in the Roman Empire, 1 vol. 2010. (Everyday Life Ser.). (ENG.). 320p. (gr. 6-7). 45.50 *(978-0-7614-4484-8(X),* 9653d0c2-588b-46fb-a9dd-9bb0146b4e0d) Cavendish Square Publishing LLC.

Lane, Allison. The Countryside in the Roman Empire, 1 vol. 2016. (Life in the Roman Empire Ser.). (ENG., Illus.). 80p. (J). (gr. 6-6). 37.36 *(978-1-5026-2261-7(0),* db830583-64fb-4b17-ab64-56ef09475d95) Cavendish Square Publishing LLC.

Markel, Rita J. The Fall of the Roman Empire. 2007. (Pivotal Moments in History Ser.). (ENG., Illus.). 160p. (J). (gr. 9-12). lib. bdg. 38.60 *(978-0-8225-5919-1(6))* Lerner Publishing Group.

Whiting, Jim. The Life & Times of Augustus Caesar. 2005. (Biography from Ancient Civilizations Ser.). (Illus.). 48p. (J). (gr. -1-7). lib. bdg. 29.95 *(978-1-58415-336-8(9))* Mitchell Lane Pubs.

Yim Bridges, Shirin. Agrippina: "Atrocious & Ferocious" Malone, Peter, illus. 2011. (Thinking Girl's Treasury of Dastardly Dames Ser.). (ENG.). 32p. (J). (gr. 3-8). 18.95 *(978-0-9834256-1-8(2))* Goosebottom Bks. LLC.

ROME (ITALY)

DuTemple, Lesley A. The Pantheon. 2003. (Great Building Feats Ser.). (Illus.). 96p. (J). (gr. 5-9). 27.93 *(978-0-8225-0376-7(X))* Lerner Publishing Group.

In the City of Rome: Individual Title Six-Packs. (Literatura 2000 Ser.). (gr. 2-3). 33.00 *(978-0-7635-0203-4(0))* Rigby Education.

Laidlaw, Jill A. Roman City Guidebook. 2010. (Crabtree Connections Ser.). (ENG.). 24p. (J). (gr. 3-6). *(978-0-7787-9949-8(2));* pap. *(978-0-7787-9971-9(9))* Crabtree Publishing Co.

Lamprell, Klay. Mi primera Lonely Planet. Roma: Grandes secretos para pequeños viajeros, 1 vol. 2012. (Lonely Planet Kids Ser.). (SPA., Illus.). 96p. (J). pap. 14.99 *(978-84-08-10915-0(4),* 103550) Lonely Planet Pubns.

Nelson, Drew. 20 Fun Facts about the Colosseum, 1 vol., Vol. 1. 2013. (Fun Fact File: World Wonders! Ser.). (ENG.). 32p. (J). (gr. 2-3). 27.93 *(978-1-4824-0462-3(1),* e84b4058-1cb3-4dd7-bee7-2b5af6e05c05) Stevens, Gareth Publishing LLLP.

O'Connor, Jim & Who HQ. Where Is the Colosseum? O'Brien, John, illus. 2017. (Where Is? Ser.). 112p. (J). (gr. 3-7). 5.99 *(978-0-399-54190-2(X),* Penguin Workshop) Penguin Young Readers Group.

Rose, Simon. Colosseum. (Structural Wonders of the World Ser.). (J). 2018. (ENG.). 24p. (gr. 2-5). lib. bdg. 28.55 *(978-1-4896-8163-8(9),* AV2 by Weigl) 2012. 27.13 *(978-1-61913-249-8(4))* 2012. pap. 12.95 *(978-1-61913-255-9(9))* Weigl Pubs., Inc.

Rudolph, Jessica. Rome. 2017. (Citified! Ser.). (ENG., Illus.). 24p. (J). (gr. k-3). lib. bdg. 17.95 *(978-1-68402-235-9(5))* Bearport Publishing Co., Inc.

Svagerko, Keith & Svagerko, Sydney. Sydney Travels to Rome: A Guide for Kids - Let's Go to Italy Series! 2013. 128p. pap. 13.95 *(978-1-62646-650-0(5))* Bookiocker.com, Inc.

ROME (ITALY)—FICTION

Baccalario, P. d. Century #1: Ring of Fire. Janeczko, Leah D., tr. 2010. (Century Ser.: 1). (Illus.). 336p. (J). (gr. 3-7). pap. 8.99 *(978-0-375-85795-9(8),* Yearling) Random Hse. Children's Bks.

Baccalario, Pierdomenico. & Janeczko, Leah. The Ring of Fire, 1. Janeczko, Leah D., tr. 2010. (Century Quartet Ser.: No. 1). (ENG., Illus.). 304p. (J). (gr. 6-8). lib. bdg. 24.94 *(978-0-375-95895-3(9))* Random House Publishing Group.

Barnett, Mac. Paolo, Emperor of Rome. 2020. (ENG., Illus.). 48p. (J). (gr. -1-3). 17.99 *(978-1-4197-4109-8(8),* 1182201, Abrams Bks. for Young Readers) Abrams, Inc.

Birchall, Katy. The It Girl in Rome. (It Girl Ser.: 3). (ENG.). (J). (gr. 4-8). 2019. 336p. pap. 8.99 *(978-1-4814-6367-6(5))* 2018. (Illus.). 320p. 16.99 *(978-1-4814-6368-3(3))* Simon & Schuster Children's Publishing. (Aladdin).

Cerulli, Claudia. Ottavia e I Gatti Di Roma - Octavia & the Cats of Rome: A Bilingual Picture Book in Italian & English. Lätti, Leo, illus. 2013. 40p. pap. *(978-1-938712-11-1(0))* Roxby Media Ltd.

Crawford, F. Marion. Cecilia, a Story of Modern Rome. 2011. 172p. pap. 12.99 *(978-1-61203-071-5(8))* Bottom of the Hill Publishing.

Drake, Jennifer & Feltham, Sarah. Scotty's Postcards from Rome. 2012. (ENG., Illus.). 27p. (J). pap. 10.95 *(978-0-578-10548-2(9))* Drake Feltham Publishing.

Gonzalez, Christina Diaz. Moving Target. 2015. (ENG.). 256p. (J). (gr. 3-7). 17.99 *(978-0-545-77318-8(0),* Scholastic Pr.) Scholastic, Inc.

Hobbs, Leigh. Mr Chicken Arriva a Roma. 2019. (Mr Chicken Ser.). (ENG.). 32p. (J). (gr. k-3). pap. 9.99 *(978-1-76052-856-0(0))* Allen & Unwin AUS. Dist: Independent Pubs. Group.

Krulik, Nancy. Follow That Furball. 2013. (Magic Bone Ser.: 3). lib. bdg. 16.00 *(978-0-606-32127-3(6))* Turtleback.

Loccisano, Rina. Baby Dario Is Born. Baker, David, illus. 2012. 36p. pap. 24.95 *(978-1-4560-6099-2(6))* America Star Bks.

Marsh, Carole. The Mystery at the Roman Colosseum. 2006. (Around the World in 80 Mysteries Ser.). (Illus.). 132p. (J). (gr. 4-7). 14.95 *(978-0-635-06157-7(0))* Gallopade International.

Messner, Kate. Danger in Ancient Rome (Ranger in Time #2) McMorris, Kelley, illus. 2015. (Ranger in Time Ser.: 2). (ENG.). 160p. (J). (gr. 2-5). pap. 5.99 *(978-0-545-63917-0(4),* Scholastic Pr.) Scholastic, Inc.

Morris, Paula. The Eternal City. 2015. (ENG.). 304p. (YA). (gr. 7). 17.99 *(978-0-545-25133-4(8))* Scholastic, Inc.

Moss, Marissa. Caravaggio: Painter on the Run. 2016. (ENG., Illus.). 345p. (YA). (gr. 7-12). 16.95 *(978-1-939547-29-3(6),* 1539c575-a382-4f0e-b72d-18c9c2260ca3) Creston Bks.

Stilton, Geronimo. Geronimo Stilton Graphic Novels #3: The Coliseum Con, Vol. 3. 2009. (Geronimo Stilton Graphic Novels Ser.: 3). (ENG., Illus.). 56p. (J). (gr. 2-6). 9.99 *(978-1-59707-172-7(2),* 900063026, Papercutz) Mad Cave Studios.

—The Hunt for the Colosseum Ghost (Geronimo Stilton Special Edition) 2018. (Geronimo Stilton Special Edition Ser.). (ENG., Illus.). 208p. (J). (gr. 2-5). 14.99 *(978-1-338-21522-9(1),* Scholastic Paperbacks) Scholastic, Inc.

Sweeney, Jon M. The Pope's Cat. DeLeon, Roy, illus. 2018. (Pope's Cat Ser.: 1). (ENG.). 64p. (J). (gr. 1). pap. 9.99 *(978-1-61261-935-4(5))* Paraclete Pr., Inc.

ROOMING HOUSES

see Hotels, Motels, etc.

ROOSEVELT, ELEANOR, 1884-1962

Auch, Allison. Women Who Dared & Mujeres que se Atrevieron: 6 English, 6 Spanish Adaptations. 2011. (ENG & SPA.). (J). 97.00 net. *(978-1-4108-5692-0(5))* Benchmark Education Co.

Brown, Jonatha A. Eleanor Roosevelt, 1 vol. 2004. (Gente Que Hay Que Conocer (People We Should Know) Ser.). 24p. (gr. 2-4). (SPA.). pap. 9.15 *(978-0-8368-4591-4(9),* 671df8da-2871-48e5-958d-a951d674cb08); (SPA.). lib. bdg. 24.67 *(978-0-8368-4584-6(6),* 1c0e69f6-59b5-4893-a2b8-cb7079546560); (ENG., Illus.). lib. bdg. 24.67 *(978-0-8368-4468-9(8),* 7d17ffdd-908f-4bd8-81b7-cad97ccbf7c6) Stevens, Gareth Publishing LLLP. (Weekly Reader Leveled Readers).

Cohen, Della. Eleanor Roosevelt: Proud & Tall. 2005. (Illus.). 16p. (J). pap. *(978-0-7367-2879-9(1))* Zaner-Bloser, Inc.

Collard, Sneed B., III. Eleanor Roosevelt: Making the World a Better Place, 1 vol. 2009. (American Heroes Ser.). (ENG.). 48p. (gr. 3-3). lib. bdg. 32.64 *(978-0-7614-3069-8(5),* 1b05b04c-6b03-4112-934f-2eeace2a1983) Cavendish Square Publishing LLC.

Conklin, Wendy. Eleanor Roosevelt, 1 vol. rev. ed. 2007. (Social Studies: Informational Text Ser.). (ENG.). 32p. (gr. 4-8). pap. 11.99 *(978-0-7439-0667-8(5))* Teacher Created Materials, Inc.

Cooper, Ilene. Eleanor Roosevelt, Fighter for Justice: Her Impact on the Civil Rights Movement, the White House, & the World. 2018. (ENG., Illus.). 192p. (J). (gr. 5-9). 17.99 *(978-1-4197-2295-0(6),* 1108501, Abrams Bks. for Young Readers) Abrams, Inc.

Donnelly, Shannon. Eleanor Roosevelt. Wolek, Guy, illus. 2005. (Heroes of America Ser.). 236p. (gr. 3-8). lib. bdg. 27.07 *(978-1-59679-260-9(4),* Abdo & Daughters) ABDO Publishing Co.

Eleanor Roosevelt. 2005. 12p. (gr. k-4). 2.95 *(978-0-635-02622-4(8))* Gallopade International.

Feinberg, Barbara Silberdick. Eleanor Roosevelt: Everything She Could Be. 2003. (Gateway Biography Ser.: 4). (Illus.). 48p. lib. bdg. 23.90 *(978-0-7613-2623-6(5),* Millbrook Pr.) Lerner Publishing Group.

Fleming, Candace. Our Eleanor: A Scrapbook Look at Eleanor Roosevelt's Remarkable Life. 2005. (ENG., Illus.). 192p. (J). (gr. 4-8). 24.99 *(978-0-689-86544-2(9),* Atheneum Bks. for Young Readers) Simon & Schuster Children's Publishing.

Haldy, Emma E. Eleanor Roosevelt. Bane, Jeff, illus. 2016. (My Early Library: My Itty-Bitty Bio Ser.). (ENG.). 24p. (J). (gr. k-1). 30.64 *(978-1-63470-483-0(5),* 207663) Cherry Lake Publishing.

—Eleanor Roosevelt SP. Bane, Jeff, illus. 2018. (My Early Library: Mi Mini Biografía (My Itty-Bitty Bio) Ser.). (SPA.). 24p. (J). (gr. k-1). lib. bdg. 30.64 *(978-1-5341-3002-9(0),* 212056) Cherry Lake Publishing.

Hubbard-Brown, Janet. Eleanor Roosevelt: First Lady. 2009. (Women of Achievement Ser.). (ENG.). 128p. (gr. 6-12). 35.00 *(978-1-60413-076-8(8),* P160529, Facts On File) Infobase Holdings, Inc.

Jd, Duchess Harris & Carser, A. R. Eleanor Roosevelt Champions Women's Rights. 2018. (Perspectives on American Progress Ser.). (ENG., Illus.). 48p. (J). (gr. 4-8). lib. bdg. 35.64 *(978-1-5321-1489-2(3),* 29110) ABDO Publishing Co.

Kimmelman, Leslie. Hot Dog! Eleanor Roosevelt Throws a Picnic. Juhasz, Victor, illus. 2014. (ENG.). 40p. (J). (gr. 3-6). 16.99 *(978-1-58536-830-3(X),* 203013) Sleeping Bear Pr.

Klein, Dvora. Eleanor Roosevelt. 2009. pap. 13.25 *(978-1-60559-059-2(2))* Hameray Publishing Group, Inc.

Kramer, Candice. Eleanor Roosevelt & Marian Anderson. 2005. (J). pap. *(978-1-4108-4537-5(0))* Benchmark Education Co.

Lassieur, Allison. Eleanor Roosevelt: Activist for Social Change. 2006. (Great Life Stories Ser.). (ENG., Illus.). 112p. (J). (gr. 6-8). lib. bdg. 30.50 *(978-0-531-13871-7(2),* Watts, Franklin) Scholastic Library Publishing.

Lee, Sally. Eleanor Roosevelt, 1 vol. 2010. (First Ladies Ser.). (ENG.). 24p. (J). (gr. -1-2). pap. 7.29 *(978-1-4296-5603-0(4),* 114106); (gr. k-1). pap. 43.74 *(978-1-4296-5604-7(2),* 15474, Capstone Pr.) Capstone.

Marsico, Katie. Eleanor Roosevelt: First Lady & Human Rights Advocate, 1 vol. 2008. (Essential Lives Set 2 Ser.). (ENG., Illus.). 112p. (J). (gr. 6-12). lib. bdg. 41.36 *(978-1-60453-040-7(5),* 6661, Essential Library) ABDO Publishing Co.

Massie, Elizabeth. Eleanor Roosevelt. 2016. (Spring Forward Ser.). (J). (gr. 1). *(978-1-4900-9385-7(0))* Benchmark Education Co.

Mattern, Joanne. Eleanor Roosevelt: More Than a First Lady. 2009. (Women Who Shaped History Ser.). 24p. (gr. 2-3). 42.50 *(978-1-60854-817-0(1),* PowerKids Pr.) Rosen Publishing Group, Inc., The.

Nabli, Dina E. L. Eleanor Roosevelt First Lady of the World. 2006. 44p. (J). lib. bdg. 15.00 *(978-1-4242-0847-0(5))* Fitzgerald Bks.

Rappaport, Doreen. Eleanor, Quiet No More: The Life of Eleanor Roosevelt. Kelley, Gary, illus. 2009. (Big Words Book Ser.: 4). (ENG.). 48p. (J). (gr. -1-3). 16.99 *(978-0-7868-5141-6(4))* Little, Brown Bks. for Young Readers.

Rinaldo, Denise. Eleanor Roosevelt: With a Discussion of Respect. 2003. (Values in Action Ser.). (J). *(978-1-59203-063-7(7))* Learning Challenge, Inc.

Shea, John M. Eleanor Roosevelt in Her Own Words, 1 vol. 2015. (Eyewitness to History Ser.). (ENG., Illus.). 32p. (J). (gr. 4-5). pap. 11.50 *(978-1-4824-4062-1(8),* 888c0b4d-7e1e-43d7-9749-856bf6736276) Stevens, Gareth Publishing LLLP.

Stoltman, Joan. Eleanor Roosevelt, 1 vol. 2018. (Little Biographies of Big People Ser.). (ENG.). 24p. (gr. 1-2). 24.27 *(978-1-5382-1832-7(1),* 3e5db8ca-c8eb-442a-baff-08b4749ee825) Stevens, Gareth Publishing LLLP.

Strand, Jennifer. Eleanor Roosevelt. 2017. (First Ladies (Launch!) Ser.). (ENG., Illus.). 24p. (J). (gr. -1-2). lib. bdg. 31.36 *(978-1-5321-2019-0(2),* 25288, Abdo Zoom-Launch) ABDO Publishing Co.

Thompson, Gare. Who Was Eleanor Roosevelt? Wolf, Elizabeth, illus. 2004. (Who Was... ? Ser.). 106p. (gr. 3-7). 15.00 *(978-0-7569-2829-2(X))* Perfection Learning Corp.

—Who Was Eleanor Roosevelt? 2004. (Who Was... ? Ser.). (gr. 3-6). lib. bdg. 16.00 *(978-0-613-72563-7(8))* Turtleback.

Thompson, Gare & Who HQ. Who Was Eleanor Roosevelt? Wolf, Elizabeth, illus. 2004. (Who Was? Ser.). 112p. (J). (gr. 3-7). pap. 5.99 *(978-0-448-43509-1(8),* Penguin Workshop) Penguin Young Readers Group.

Time for Kids Magazine Staff. Time for Kids: Eleanor Roosevelt: First Lady of the World. 2005. (Time for Kids Ser.). (ENG., Illus.). 48p. (J). (gr. 2-4). per. 3.99 *(978-0-06-057613-4(8))* HarperCollins Pubs.

Tor, Regina, et al. Growing Toward Peace. 2011. 90p. 38.95 *(978-1-258-02528-1(0))* Literary Licensing, LLC.

Weakland, Mark. When Eleanor Roosevelt Learned to Jump a Horse. Joseph, John, illus. 2019. (Leaders Doing Headstands Ser.). (ENG.). 32p. (J). (gr. 1-4). pap. 7.95 *(978-1-5158-3050-4(0),* 138685, Picture Window Bks.) Capstone.

Winget, Mary. Eleanor Roosevelt. (Biography Ser.). (Illus.). 2005. 112p. (gr. 6-12). lib. bdg. 27.93 *(978-0-8225-4985-7(9))* 2003. 48p. (J). pap. 8.95 *(978-0-8225-4801-0(1),* Lerner Pubns.) 2003. 48p. (J). (gr. 3-5). lib. bdg. 26.60 *(978-0-8225-4675-7(2))* Lerner Publishing Group.

ROOSEVELT, ELEANOR, 1884-1962—FICTION

Fleming, Candace. Eleanor Roosevelt's in My Garage! Fearing, Mark, illus. 2018. (History Pals Ser.). (J). (gr. 2-5). 272p. 13.99 *(978-1-5247-6786-0(7));* (ENG.). 336p. lib. bdg. 16.99 *(978-1-5247-6787-7(5))* Random Hse. Children's Bks. (Schwartz & Wade Bks.).

Salerni, Dianne K. Eleanor, Alice, & the Roosevelt Ghosts. 2020. (ENG., Illus.). 240p. (J). (gr. 4-7). 17.99 *(978-0-8234-4697-1(2))* Holiday Hse., Inc.

ROOSEVELT, FRANKLIN D. (FRANKLIN DELANO), 1882-1945

Baier, Bret & Whitney, Catherine. Three Days at the Brink: Young Readers' Edition: FDR's Daring Gamble to Win World War II. 2019. (ENG., Illus.). 272p. (J). (gr. 3-7). 17.99 *(978-0-06-291537-5(1),* HarperCollins) HarperCollins Pubs.

Bardhan-Quallen, Sudipta. Franklin Delano Roosevelt: A National Hero. 2007. (Sterling Biographies Ser.). (ENG., Illus.). 124p. (J). (gr. 6-8). 18.69 *(978-1-4027-4747-2(0))* Sterling Publishing Co., Inc.

Brennan, Linda Crotta. Franklin D. Roosevelt's Presidency. 2016. (Presidential Powerhouses Ser.). (ENG., Illus.). 104p. (YA). (gr. 6-12). 35.99 *(978-1-4677-7928-9(8),* ab64e692-1d98-4b8b-ae25-219dbb29d6c0); E-Book 54.65 *(978-1-4677-8549-5(0))* Lerner Publishing Group. (Lerner Pubns.).

Caplan, Jeremy. Franklin D Roosevelt A Leader in Troubled Times. 2006. 44p. (J). lib. bdg. 15.00 *(978-1-4242-0848-7(3))* Fitzgerald Bks.

Cronkite, Walter, frwd. Great American Presidents. (Illus.). (gr. 4-8). pap. *(978-0-7910-8048-1(X),* Facts On File) Infobase Holdings, Inc.

Edison, Erin. Franklin D. Roosevelt, 1 vol. (Presidential Biographies Ser.). (ENG.). 24p. (J). (gr. -1-2). 2014. pap. 6.29 *(978-1-4765-9630-3(1),* 125426, Pebble) 2012. (Illus.). lib. bdg. 27.32 *(978-1-4296-8736-2(3),* 119529, Capstone Pr.) Capstone.

Elish, Dan. Franklin Delano Roosevelt, 1 vol. 2009. (Presidents & Their Times Ser.). (ENG.). 96p. (gr. 6-6). lib. bdg. 36.93 *(978-0-7614-2841-1(0),* 871c231b-419f-45ad-9a9f-f5b6ca2d4cf1) Cavendish Square Publishing LLC.

Fremon, David K. The Great Depression in United States History, 1 vol. 2014. (In United States History Ser.). (ENG.). 96p. (gr. 5-6). 31.61 *(978-0-7660-6087-6(X),* cf88ec4e-8ffd-4534-a38f-8942c4f84d9c); (Illus.). (J). pap. 13.88 *(978-0-7660-6088-3(8),* bbc8ca57-d558-489b-a477-5ecbf2bc2bbc) Enslow Publishing, LLC.

Frith, Margaret & Who HQ. Who Was Franklin Roosevelt? O'Brien, John, illus. 2010. (Who Was? Ser.). 112p. (J). (gr. 3-7). pap. 5.99 *(978-0-448-45346-0(0),* Penguin Workshop) Penguin Young Readers Group.

Gosman, Gillian. Franklin D. Roosevelt, 1 vol. 2011. (Life Stories Ser.). (ENG., Illus.). 24p. (J). (gr. 3-3). pap. 9.25 *(978-1-4488-3182-1(2),* 4c99ad0e-7380-4e41-8192-3dcff322e2bf, PowerKids Pr.); lib. bdg. 26.27 *(978-1-4488-3222-4(5),* 96acf089-22e2-4d2e-a6e6-8a4da767b5e9); lib. bdg. 26.27 *(978-1-4488-3179-1(2),* 3f0b1701-e059-4701-bc74-6783a09d3a80, PowerKids Pr.) Rosen Publishing Group, Inc., The.

Gregory, Josh. Franklin D. Roosevelt: The 32nd President. 2015. (First Look at America's Presidents Ser.). (ENG.). 24p. (J). (gr. -1-3). lib. bdg. 26.99 *(978-1-62724-555-5(3))* Bearport Publishing Co., Inc.

Gunderson, Megan M. Franklin D. Roosevelt, 1 vol. 2016. (United States Presidents *2017 Ser.). (ENG., Illus.). 40p. (J). (gr. 2-5). lib. bdg. 35.64 *(978-1-68078-115-1(4),* 21847, Big Buddy Bks.) ABDO Publishing Co.

Hansen, Grace. Franklin Delano Roosevelt, 1 vol. 2014. (United States President Biographies (Abdo Kids Jumbo) Ser.). (ENG.). 24p. (J). (gr. -1-2). lib. bdg. 32.79 *(978-1-62970-088-5(6),* 1719, Abdo Kids) ABDO Publishing Co.

Kent, Deborah. Franklin Delano Roosevelt: Nothing to Fear! 2006. (Defining Moments Ser.). (Illus.). 32p. (YA). (gr. 2-5). lib. bdg. 28.50 *(978-1-59716-272-2(8))* Bearport Publishing Co., Inc.

Klimo, Kate. Dog Diaries #8: Fala. Jessell, Tim, illus. 2016. (Dog Diaries: 8). 160p. (J). (gr. 2-5). pap. 7.99 *(978-0-553-53490-0(4),* Random Hse. Bks. for Young Readers) Random Hse. Children's Bks.

Krull, Kathleen. A Boy Named FDR: How Franklin D. Roosevelt Grew up to Change America. Johnson, Steve & Fancher, Lou, illus. 2016. 48p. (J). (gr. 1-4). 7.99 *(978-1-101-93251-3(1),* Dragonfly Bks.) Random Hse. Children's Bks.

Kudlinski, Kathleen. Franklin Delano Roosevelt: Champion of Freedom. Henderson, Meryl, illus. 2003. (Childhood of Famous Americans Ser.). (ENG.). 208p. (J). (gr. 3-7). pap. 7.99 *(978-0-689-85745-4(4),* Simon & Schuster/Paula Wiseman Bks.) Simon & Schuster/Paula Wiseman Bks.

Lawson, Barbara Spilman. FDR the Primary Sources. 2016. (Spring Forward Ser.). (J). (gr. 2). *(978-1-4900-9434-2(2))* Benchmark Education Co.

Levine, Michelle & Waxman, Laura Hamilton. Franklin D. Roosevelt. 2005. (History Maker Bios Ser.). (Illus.). 48p. (J). (gr. 3-5). 26.60 *(978-0-8225-1545-6(8))* Lerner Publishing Group.

Mara, Wil. Franklin D. Roosevelt. 2004. (Rookie Biographies Ser.). (ENG.). 32p. (J). (gr. 1-2). pap. 4.95 *(978-0-516-25823-2(0),* Children's Pr.) Scholastic Library Publishing.

—Rookie Biographies: Franklin D. Roosevelt. 2004. (Rookie Biographies Ser.). (ENG., Illus.). 32p. (J). 20.50 *(978-0-516-21844-1(1),* Children's Pr.) Scholastic Library Publishing.

Margaret, Amy. Franklin D. Roosevelt Library & Museum. 2009. (Presidential Libraries Ser.). 24p. (gr. 3-3). 42.50 *(978-1-60851-483-0(8),* PowerKids Pr.) Rosen Publishing Group, Inc., The.

Marrin, Albert. FDR & the American Crisis. (Illus.). 336p. (YA). (gr. 7). 2016. pap. 15.99 *(978-0-385-75362-3(4),* Ember) 2015. 24.99 *(978-0-385-75359-3(4),* Knopf Bks. for Young Readers) Random Hse. Children's Bks.

McKown, Robin. Roosevelt's Americ. 2011. 94p. 38.95 *(978-1-258-10479-5(2))* Literary Licensing, LLC.

Mis, M. S. How to Draw the Life & Times of Franklin Delano Roosevelt. 2009. (Kid's Guide to Drawing the Presidents of the United States of America Ser.). 32p. (gr. 4-4). 50.50 *(978-1-61511-136-7(0),* PowerKids Pr.) Rosen Publishing Group, Inc., The.

Mis, Melody S. How to Draw the Life & Times of Franklin Delano Roosevelt, 1 vol. 2005. (Kid's Guide to Drawing the Presidents of the United States of America Ser.). (ENG., Illus.). 32p. (YA). (gr. 4-4). 30.27 *(978-1-4042-3008-8(4),* 4a6b2a2d-17e9-42d2-bd59-e1e04aa5593e) Rosen Publishing Group, Inc., The.

Panchyk, Richard. Franklin Delano Roosevelt for Kids: His Life & Times with 21 Activities. 2007. (For Kids Ser.: 24). (ENG., Illus.). 160p. (J). (gr. 4-8). pap. 14.95 *(978-1-55652-657-2(1))* Chicago Review Pr., Inc.

Pearson, P. O'Connell. Fighting for the Forest: How FDR's Civilian Conservation Corps Helped Save America. (ENG., Illus.). (J). (gr. 5). 2020. 224p. pap. 7.99 *(978-1-5344-2933-8(6))* 2019. 208p. 17.99 *(978-1-5344-2932-1(8))* Simon & Schuster Bks. For Young Readers. (Simon & Schuster Bks. For Young Readers).

Rajczak, Michael. Before Franklin D. Roosevelt Was President, 1 vol. 2018. (Before They Were President Ser.). (ENG.). 24p. (gr. 2-3). lib. bdg. 24.27 *(978-1-5382-2910-1(2),* 82caad16-4ada-44e5-a486-f28154c27b4a) Stevens, Gareth Publishing LLLP.

Rice, Earle, Jr. How Franklin D. Roosevelt Fought World War II, 1 vol. 2017. (Presidents at War Ser.). (ENG.). 128p. (gr. 8-8). lib. bdg. 38.93 *(978-0-7660-8527-5(9),* 90068e3a-c02b-490c-960b-c2d1bf00735c) Enslow Publishing, LLC.

Rice, Earle. FDR & the New Deal. 2009. (Monumental Milestones Ser.). (Illus.). 48p. (J). (gr. 4-7). lib. bdg. 29.95 *(978-1-58415-828-8(X))* Mitchell Lane Pubs.

Roberts, Jeremy. Franklin D. Roosevelt. 2003. (Presidential Leaders Ser.). (Illus.). 112p. (J). (gr. 6-12). lib. bdg. 29.27 *(978-0-8225-0095-7(7))* Lerner Publishing Group.

Roome, Hugh. Franklin D. Roosevelt: American Hero (Rookie Biographies) 2017. (Rookie Biographies Ser.). (ENG., Illus.). 32p. (J). (gr. 1-2). pap. 5.95 *(978-0-531-23863-9(6)*, Children's Pr.) Scholastic Library Publishing.

—Franklin D. Roosevelt: American Hero (Rookie Biographies) (Library Edition) 2017. (Rookie Biographies Ser.). (ENG., Illus.). 32p. (J). (gr. 1-2). lib. bdg. 25.00 *(978-0-531-23229-3(8)*, Children's Pr.) Scholastic Library Publishing.

Saddleback Educational Publishing Staff, ed. Franklin Roosevelt, 1 vol. unabr. ed. 2007. (Graphic Biographies Ser.). (ENG., Illus.). 25p. (YA). (gr. 4-12). pap. 9.75 *(978-1-59905-222-9(9))* Saddleback Educational Publishing, Inc.

Shea, John M. Franklin D. Roosevelt in His Own Words. 2014. (Eyewitness to History Ser.). (Illus.). 32p. (J). (gr. 4-6). pap. 63.00 *(978-1-4824-1202-4(0))* Stevens, Gareth Publishing LLLP.

Sullivan, Anne Marie. Franklin D. Roosevelt. 2004. (Childhood of the Presidents Ser.). (Illus.). 48p. (J). (gr. 4-18). lib. bdg. 17.95 *(978-1-59084-279-9(0))* Mason Crest.

Time for Kids Magazine Staff. Franklin D. Roosevelt - A Leader in Troubled Times. 2005. (Time for Kids Ser.). (ENG., Illus.). 48p. (J). (gr. 2-4). per. 3.99 *(978-0-06-057615-8(4))* HarperCollins Pubs.

Van Steenwyk, Elizabeth. First Dog Fala, 1 vol. Montgomery, Michael G., illus. 2008. 32p. (J). (gr. -1-3). 16.95 *(978-1-56145-411-2(7))* Peachtree Publishing Co. Inc.

Vander Hook, Sue. Franklin D. Roosevelt: 32nd U. S. President, 1 vol. 2008. (Essential Lives Set 2 Ser.). (ENG., Illus.). 112p. (YA). (gr. 6-12). lib. bdg. 41.36 *(978-1-60453-041-4(3)*, 6663, Essential Library) ABDO Publishing Co.

Venezia, Mike. Franklin D. Roosevelt: Thirty-Second President 1933-1945. 32. Venezia, Mike, illus. 2007. (Getting to Know the U. S. Presidents Ser.). (ENG., Illus.). 32p. (J). (gr. 3-6). 22.44 *(978-0-516-22636-1(3))* Scholastic Library Publishing.

Waxman, Laura Hamilton. Franklin D. Roosevelt. 2004. (History Maker Bios Ser.). (J). pap. 6.95 *(978-0-8225-2539-4(9)*, Lerner Pubns.) Lerner Publishing Group.

Wood, Douglas. Franklin & Winston: A Christmas That Changed the World. Moser, Barry, illus. 2011. (ENG.). 40p. (J). (gr. 1-4). 16.99 *(978-0-7636-3383-7(6))* Candlewick Pr.

ROOSEVELT, FRANKLIN D. (FRANKLIN DELANO), 1882-1945—FICTION

Klimo, Kate. Fala. 2016. (Dog Diaries: 8). lib. bdg. 18.40 *(978-0-606-38448-3(0))* Turtleback.

Kravitz, Danny. Tommy Mcknight & the Great Election. 2016. (Presidential Politics Ser.). (ENG., Illus.). 96p. (J). (gr. 3-6). lib. bdg. 26.65 *(978-1-4965-2585-7(X)*, 130712, Stone Arch Bks.) Capstone.

Winthrop, Elizabeth. Franklin Delano Roosevelt: Letters from a Mill Town Girl. Winthrop, Elizabeth, illus. unabr. ed. 2003. (Illus.). (J). (gr. 4-7). 25.95 incl. audio *(978-1-59112-213-5(9))* Live Oak Media.

ROOSEVELT, THEODORE, 1858-1919

Adler, David A. Colonel Theodore Roosevelt. 2014. (ENG., Illus.). 144p. (J). (gr. 5). 22.99 *(978-0-8234-2950-9(4))* Holiday Hse., Inc.

Baker, Brynn. Roosevelt's Rough Riders: Fearless Cavalry of the Spanish-American War. 2015. (Military Heroes Ser.). (ENG., Illus.). 32p. (J). (gr. 3-6). lib. bdg. 27.99 *(978-1-4914-4840-3(7)*, 128725, Capstone Pr.) Capstone.

Benchmark Education Co. Theodore Roosevelt & the Progressive Era. 2014. (PRIME Ser.). (J). (gr. 6-8). pap. *(978-1-4509-9496-5(2))* Benchmark Education Co.

Benge, Janet & Benge, Geoff. Heroes of History - Theodore Roosevelt: An American Original. 2004. (ENG., Illus.). 224p. (YA). pap. 11.99 *(978-1-932096-10-1(3))* Emerald Bks.

Britton, Tamara L. Theodore Roosevelt, 1 vol. 2016. (United States Presidents *2017 Ser.). (ENG., Illus.). 40p. (J). (gr. 2-5). lib. bdg. 35.64 *(978-1-68078-116-8(2)*, 21849, Big Buddy Bks.) ABDO Publishing Co.

Burgan, Michael. Who Was Theodore Roosevelt? 2014. (Who Was... ? Ser.). lib. bdg. 16.00 *(978-0-606-35691-6(6))* Turtleback.

Burgan, Michael & Who HQ. Who Was Theodore Roosevelt? Hoare, Jerry, illus. 2014. (Who Was? Ser.). 112p. (J). (gr. 3-7). 5.99 *(978-0-448-47945-3(1)*, Penguin Workshop) Penguin Young Readers Group.

Collins, James. Theodore Roosevelt: With Buffalo Bill & Farley's Raiders. Cox, Brian T., illus. 2006. (Time Traveler's Adventure Ser.). 56p. (J). 13.50 incl. audio compact disk *(978-1-932332-60-5(X))* Toy Box Productions.

DeMauro, Lisa & Time for Kids Editors. Theodore Roosevelt: The Adventurous President. 2005. (Time for Kids Ser.). (ENG., Illus.). 48p. (J). (gr. 2-4). 15.99 *(978-0-06-057606-6(5))*; pap. 3.99 *(978-0-06-057604-2(9))* HarperCollins Pubs.

Dodson Wade, Mary. Amazing President Theodore Roosevelt, 1 vol. 2009. (Amazing Americans Ser.). (ENG., Illus.). 24p. (gr. k-2). pap. 10.35 *(978-0-7660-5979-5(0)*, af962ef4-87ed-43ee-a462-c18d93131367, Enslow Elementary); lib. bdg. 25.27 *(978-0-7660-3284-2(1)*, f3d5441f-19f5-4a3c-86f8-68b088cac5ca) Enslow Publishing, LLC.

Elish, Dan. Theodore Roosevelt, 1 vol. 2008. (Presidents & Their Times Ser.). (ENG., Illus.). 96p. (gr. 6-6). lib. bdg. 36.93 *(978-0-7614-2429-1(6)*, e53764ff-c12a-46d7-9a3e-003c63dc9c9d) Cavendish Square Publishing LLC.

Gayle, Sharon. Teddy Roosevelt: The People's President (Ready-To-Read Level 3) Dacey, Bob & Bandelin, Debra, illus. 2004. (Ready-To-Read Stories of Famous Americans Ser.). (ENG.). 32p. (J). (gr. 1-3). pap. 4.99 *(978-0-689-85825-3(6)*, Simon Spotlight) Simon Spotlight.

Gregory, Josh. Theodore Roosevelt: The 26th President. 2015. (First Look at America's Presidents Ser.). (ENG.). 24p. (J). (gr. -1-3). lib. bdg. 26.99 *(978-1-62724-557-9(X))* Bearport Publishing Co., Inc.

Harness, Cheryl. The Remarkable Rough-Riding Life of Theodore Roosevelt & the Rise of Empire America: Wild America Gets a Protector; Panama's Canal; the Big Stick & the Bull Moose; Kids, Pets, & Spitballs in the White House; & Much, Much More. 2007. (Cheryl Harness Histories Ser.). (Illus.). 144p. (J). (gr. 3-7). 16.95 *(978-1-4263-0008-0(5)*, National Geographic Children's Bks.) Disney Publishing Worldwide.

Hollihan, Kerrie Logan. Theodore Roosevelt for Kids: His Life & Times, 21 Activities. 2010. (For Kids Ser.: 33). (ENG., Illus.). 144p. (J). (gr. 4-18). pap. 16.95 *(978-1-55652-955-9(4)*, 1311179) Chicago Review Pr., Inc.

Jackson, Ellen, ed. My Tour of Europe: By Teddy Roosevelt, Age 10. Brighton, Catherine, illus. 2003. 40p. 14.95 *(978-0-7613-1998-6(0)*, Millbrook Pr.) Lerner Publishing Group.

Kay, Helen. The First Teddy Bear. Detwiler, Susan, illus. 2nd enl. ed. 2005. (ENG.). 38p. (J). (gr. -1-3). 18.95 *(978-0-88045-154-3(8))* Stemmer Hse. Pubs.

—First Teddy Bear, 2nd Edition: Enlarged Edition. 2nd rev. enl. ed. 2005. (ENG., Illus.). 38p. (J). (gr. -1-3). per. 11.95 *(978-0-88045-153-6(X))* Stemmer Hse. Pubs.

Keating, Frank. Theodore. Wimmer, Mike, illus. 2006. (Mount Rushmore Presidential Ser.). (ENG.). 32p. (J). (gr. 1-4). 19.99 *(978-0-689-86532-9(5)*, Simon & Schuster/Paula Wiseman Bks.) Simon & Schuster/Paula Wiseman Bks.

Kerley, Barbara. What to Do about Alice? 2011. (J). (gr. 2-5). 29.95 *(978-0-545-29679-3(X))*; 18.95 *(978-0-545-29821-6(0))* Weston Woods Studios, Inc.

Kraft, Betsy Harvey. Theodore Roosevelt: Champion of the American Spirit. 2003. (ENG., Illus.). 192p. (J). (gr. 5-7). tchr. ed. 19.00 *(978-0-618-14264-4(9)*, 111112, Clarion Bks.) HarperCollins Pubs.

Mara, Wil. Theodore Roosevelt. 2007. (Rookie Biographies Ser.). (Illus.). 32p. (J). (gr. 1-2). pap. 4.95 *(978-0-516-27304-4(3)*, Children's Pr.) Scholastic Library Publishing.

Marcovitz, Hal. Theodore Roosevelt. 2004. (Childhood of the Presidents Ser.). (Illus.). 48p. (J). (gr. 4-18). lib. bdg. 17.95 *(978-1-59084-278-2(2))* Mason Crest.

Marsh, Carole. Theodore Roosevelt. 2004. 12p. (gr. k-4). 2.95 *(978-0-635-02362-9(8))* Gallopade International.

McPherson, Stephanie Sammartino. Theodore Roosevelt. 2005. (Presidential Leaders Ser.). (Illus.). 112p. (J). 29.27 *(978-0-8225-0999-8(7)*, Lerner Pubns.) Lerner Publishing Group.

Rappaport, Doreen. To Dare Mighty Things: The Life of Theodore Roosevelt. Payne, C. F., illus. 2013. (Big Words Book Ser.: 7). (ENG.). 48p. (J). (gr. 1-3). 17.99 *(978-1-4231-2488-7(X))* Little, Brown Bks. for Young Readers.

Rice, Dona Herweck. Teedie: The Boy Who Would Be President. rev. ed. 2015. (Reader's Theater Ser.). (ENG., Illus.). 24p. (gr. 1-3). pap. 8.99 *(978-1-4938-1513-5(X))* Teacher Created Materials, Inc.

Rosenstock, Barb. The Camping Trip That Changed America: Theodore Roosevelt, John Muir, & Our National Parks. Gerstein, Mordecai, illus. 2012. 32p. (J). (gr. 1-3). 18.99 *(978-0-8037-3710-5(6)*, Dial Bks) Penguin Young Readers Group.

Ruffin, Frances E. How to Draw the Life & Times of Theodore Roosevelt. 2009. (Kid's Guide to Drawing the Presidents of the United States of America Ser.). 32p. (gr. 4-4). 50.50 *(978-1-61511-160-2(3)*, PowerKids Pr.) Rosen Publishing Group, Inc., The.

Schwartz, Eric. A World Contender. 2006. (How America Became America Ser.). (Illus.). 96p. (YA). lib. bdg. 22.95 *(978-1-59084-911-8(6))* Mason Crest.

Schwartz, Heather E. Theodore Roosevelt's Presidency. 2016. (Presidential Powerhouses Ser.). (ENG., Illus.). 104p. (YA). (gr. 6-12). E-Book 54.65 *(978-1-4677-8601-0(2)*, Lerner Pubns.) Lerner Publishing Group.

Seiple, Samantha. Death on the River of Doubt: Theodore Roosevelt's Amazon Adventure. 2017. (Illus.). 214p. (J). *(978-1-338-12771-3(3)*, Scholastic Pr.) Scholastic, Inc.

Shattuck, Randy. Theodore Roosevelt. 2016. lib. bdg. *(978-1-68048-529-5(6))* Rosen Publishing Group, Inc., The.

Shea, Therese M. Before Teddy Roosevelt Was President, 1 vol. 2017. (Before They Were President Ser.). (ENG.). 24p. (J). (gr. 2-3). pap. 9.15 *(978-1-5382-1076-5(2)*, 53e6b187-3b7b-49f4-a3b2-937901cef493) Stevens, Gareth Publishing LLLP.

Swain, Gwenyth. Theodore Roosevelt. 2004. (History Maker Bios Ser.). (J). pap. 8.95 *(978-0-8225-2542-4(9))*; (ENG., Illus.). 48p. (gr. 3-6). 27.93 *(978-0-8225-1548-7(2))* Lerner Publishing Group. (Lerner Pubns.).

Wadsworth, Ginger. Camping with the President. Dugan, Karen, illus. 2009. (ENG.). 32p. (J). (gr. 2-5). 16.99 *(978-1-59078-497-6(9)*, Calkins Creek) Highlights Pr., c/o Highlights for Children, Inc.

Weston Woods Staff, creator. What to Do about Alice? 2011. 38.75 *(978-0-545-29822-3(9))* Weston Woods Studios, Inc.

ROOSEVELT, THEODORE, 1858-1919—FICTION

Kennedy Center, The. Teddy Roosevelt & the Treasure of Ursa Major. Hoyt, Ard, illus. 2011. (ENG.). 128p. (J). (gr. 2-5). pap. 7.99 *(978-1-4169-4860-5(0)*, Simon & Schuster Bks. For Young Readers) Simon & Schuster Bks. For Young Readers.

Lalicki, Tom. Shots at Sea: A Houdini & Nate Mystery. 2011. (Houdini & Nate Mysteries Ser.). 224p. (J). pap. 6.99 *(978-0-312-65920-2(2))* Square Fish.

Mills, Claudia. Being Teddy Roosevelt: A Boy, a President & a Plan. Alley, R. W., illus. 2012. (ENG.). 112p. (J). (gr. 2-5). pap. 16.99 *(978-0-312-64018-7(8)*, 900077669) Square Fish.

ROOSEVELT FAMILY

Panchyk, Richard. Franklin Delano Roosevelt for Kids: His Life & Times with 21 Activities. 2007. (For Kids Ser.: 24). (ENG., Illus.). 160p. (J). (gr. 4-8). pap. 14.95 *(978-1-55652-657-2(1))* Chicago Review Pr., Inc.

ROOSEVELT FAMILY—FICTION

Buckley, Anne. The Day Mrs. Roosevelt Came to Town. 2003. 186p. (YA). (gr. 9-18). per. 9.99 *(978-0-88092-458-0(6))* Royal Fireworks Publishing Co.

ROOSTERS

Cobb, Amy. Rooster Instructor. Neonakis, Alexandria, illus. 2017. (Libby Wimbley Ser.). (ENG.). 32p. (J). (gr. -1-3). lib. bdg. 32.79 *(978-1-5321-3026-7(0)*, 25530, Calico Chapter Bks) Magic Wagon.

ROOSTERS—FICTION

Anderson, Susan C. Why the Rooster Crowed. 2009. (ENG.). 26p. pap. 15.99 *(978-1-4500-0702-3(3))* Xlibris Corp.

Angelastro, Yvonne. The Four Lost Chicks. Pace, Julie, illus. 2013. (ENG.). 28p. pap. 16.99 *(978-1-4808-0292-6(1))* Archway Publishing.

Black, Michael Ian. Cock-A-Doodle-Doo-Bop! Myers, Matt, illus. 2015. (ENG.). 40p. (J). (gr. -1-3). 17.99 *(978-1-4424-9510-4(3)*, Simon & Schuster Bks. For Young Readers) Simon & Schuster Bks. For Young Readers.

Bobo, W. L. Chickendoodle! Where Are You? 2011. 28p. pap. 21.95 *(978-1-4269-5742-0(4))* Trafford Publishing.

Carle, Eric. Rooster Is off to See the World. 2013. (Eric Carle Ready-To-Read Ser.). lib. bdg. 13.55 *(978-0-606-32063-4(6))* Turtleback.

Caruso, Barbara, reader. Elvis the Rooster Almost Goes to Heaven, 4 bks., Set. unabr. ed. 2006. (Readalongs for Beginning Readers Ser.). (Illus.). (J). (gr. -1-3). pap. 29.95 incl. audio *(978-1-59519-684-2(6))*; pap. 31.95 incl. audio compact disk *(978-1-59519-685-9(4))* Live Oak Media.

Cazet, Denys. Elvis the Rooster & the Magic Words. Cazet, Denys, illus. 2004. (I Can Read Bks.). (ENG., Illus.). 48p. (J). (gr. k-3). 15.99 *(978-0-06-000509-2(2))* HarperCollins Pubs.

—Elvis the Rooster & the Magic Words, 4 bks., Set. unabr. ed. 2006. (Readalongs for Beginning Readers Ser.). (J). (gr. -1-3). pap. 31.95 incl. audio compact disk *(978-1-59519-693-4(5))*; (Illus.). pap. 29.95 incl. audio *(978-1-59519-692-7(7))* Live Oak Media.

Chin, Oliver. The Year of the Rooster: Tales from the Chinese Zodiac. Calle, Juan, illus. 2016. (Tales from the Chinese Zodiac Ser.: 12). (ENG.). 40p. (J). (gr. -1). 15.95 *(978-1-59702-125-8(3))* Immedium.

Davies, Rob. Henhouse High Jinx: Mr. Stevens & Friends. 2013. 176p. pap. 11.99 *(978-1-4669-9491-1(6))*; (Illus.). (J). 21.99 *(978-1-4669-9492-8(4))* Trafford Publishing.

Davis, Peg. After the Storm: A Napoleon & Marigold Adventure. 2009. 40p. pap. 16.50 *(978-1-60860-222-3(2)*, Eloquent Bks.) Strategic Book Publishing & Rights Agency (SBPRA).

—Napoleon & Marigold. 2008. 24p. pap. 13.50 *(978-1-60693-114-1(8)*, Eloquent Bks.) Strategic Book Publishing & Rights Agency (SBPRA).

De Anda, Diane. Kikiriki / Quiquiriquí. Hernández, Karina, tr. from ENG. Lechón, Daniel, illus. 2004. (ENG & SPA.). 32p. 16.95 *(978-1-55885-382-9(0)*, Piñata Books) Arte Publico Pr.

Deedy, Carmen Agra. The Rooster Who Would Not Be Quiet! Yelchin, Eugene, illus. 2017. (ENG.). 48p. (J). (gr. -1-3). 18.99 *(978-0-545-72288-9(8)*, Scholastic Pr.) Scholastic, Inc.

Degman, Lori. Cock-A-Doodle-Oops! Zemke, Deborah, illus. 2014. (ENG.). 36p. (J). (gr. -1-3). 16.99 *(978-1-939547-07-1(5)*, cfe736e0-5259-4a08-984e-aa68e39b4859) Creston Bks.

Doudna, Kelly. Rooster Combs. Haberstroh, Anne, illus. 2006. (Fact & Fiction Ser.). 24p. (J). pap. 48.42 *(978-1-59679-966-0(8))* ABDO Publishing Co.

Edwards, Pamela Duncan. The Mixed-up Rooster. Lloyd, Megan, illus. 2006. 32p. (J). (gr. -1-1). 15.99 *(978-0-06-028999-7(6)*, Tegen, Katherine Bks) HarperCollins Pubs.

—The Wrong Way Rooster. Date not set. 32p. (J). (gr. -1-1). pap. 5.99 *(978-0-06-443689-2(6))* HarperCollins Pubs.

Eggleton, Jill. Rabbit & Rooster's Ride: 3-in-1 Package. Taylor, Clive, illus. (Sails Literacy Ser.). 24p. (gr. k-18). 57.00 *(978-0-7578-8617-1(5))* Rigby Education.

—Rabbit & Rooster's Ride: 6 Small Books. Taylor, Clive, illus. (Sails Literacy Ser.). 24p. (gr. k-18). 25.00 *(978-0-7578-7727-8(3))* Rigby Education.

—Rabbit & Rooster's Ride: Big Book Only. Taylor, Clive, illus. (Sails Literacy Ser.). 24p. (gr. k-18). 27.00 *(978-0-7578-6200-7(4))* Rigby Education.

Ekholm, Jan. The Little Red Rascal. 2011. 88p. pap. 30.28 *(978-1-4567-9501-6(5))* AuthorHouse.

Finch, Mary. The Little Red Hen. Slater, Kate, illus. 2018. (ENG.). 32p. (J). (gr. k-5). pap. 9.99 *(978-1-78285-041-0(4))* Barefoot Bks., Inc.

Finch, Mary & Messing, Debra. The Little Red Hen. Slater, Kate, illus. 2013. 32p. (J). (gr. -1-2). 9.99 *(978-1-84686-751-4(7))*; 16.99 *(978-1-84686-575-6(1))* Barefoot Bks., Inc.

Frazier, Laurence. Cranky the Rooster. 2011. 24p. pap. 12.79 *(978-1-4567-6258-2(3))* AuthorHouse.

Freddie. The Rooster's Story. 2009. 28p. pap. 13.99 *(978-1-4389-8827-6(3))* AuthorHouse.

Garrett, Cindy Crawford. Life's Lessons with the Silly Animals Out on the Ranch: What Is Wrong with Bob the Rooster? 2013. 24p. pap. 17.99 *(978-1-4817-0574-5(1))* AuthorHouse.

Giacomucci, Carol. A New Home. 2006. 23p. pap. 10.95 *(978-0-7414-3498-2(9))* Infinity Publishing.

Giles, Lisa. The Adventures of Sunny the Bunny: The Easter Egg Hunt. 2010. 20p. 10.49 *(978-1-4520-1842-3(1))* AuthorHouse.

Green, Jonathan, illus. Amadeus, the Leghorn Rooster. 2004. (J). 17.95 *(978-0-87844-174-7(3))* Sandlapper Publishing Co., Inc.

GRIMM. The Bremen Town Musicians, 1 vol. Bell, Anthea, ed. Bell, Anthea, tr. Lai, Hsin-Shih, illus. 2007. (ENG.). 32p. (J). (gr. -1-3). 17.95 *(978-0-88010-583-5(6)*, Bell Pond Bks.) SteinerBooks, Inc.

Grimm, Jacob & Grimm, Wilhelm K. Hut in the Forest, 20 vols. Lawson, Polly, tr. Stietencron, Bettina, illus. 2007. (Grimm's Fairy Tales Ser.). (ENG.). 28p. (J). *(978-0-86315-615-1(0))* Floris Bks.

Heisel, Sandra. Pokey & the Rooster. Snyder, Joe, illus. 2009. 28p. pap. 9.95 *(978-0-9818488-1-5(8))* Ajoyin Publishing, Inc.

Hillenbrand, Will. Cock-A-Doodle Christmas!, 0 vols. 2012. (ENG.). 32p. (J). (gr. -1-2). pap. 6.99 *(978-0-7614-5718-3(6)*, 9780761457183, Two Lions) Amazon Publishing.

Jones, Nancy. The Grandpaws. 2005. 57p. pap. 16.95 *(978-1-4137-4778-2(7))* America Star Bks.

Kelly, Thomas E. The Fox & the Young Rooster. Ward, Kelly, illus. 2011. 44p. pap. 24.95 *(978-1-4626-0343-5(2))* America Star Bks.

Kline, Trish & Donev, Mary. Hoops in the Coop: KA Reader 7. 2007. (Illus.). 32p. (J). per. 20.00 *(978-1-934307-00-7(9))* Ghost Hunter Productions.

Krystosek, Richard. Chicken Scratch. 2013. 36p. pap. 24.95 *(978-1-63000-536-8(3))* America Star Bks.

Lambert, Megan Dowd. A Crow of His Own. Costello, David Hyde, illus. 32p. (J). (gr. -1-1). 2019. pap. 7.99 *(978-1-58089-448-7(8))* 2015. lib. bdg. 16.95 *(978-1-58089-447-0(X))* Charlesbridge Publishing, Inc.

—A Kid of Their Own. LANAN, Jessica, illus. 2020. 32p. (J). (gr. -1-3). lib. bdg. 16.99 *(978-1-58089-879-9(3))* Charlesbridge Publishing, Inc.

Landstrom, Lena. Four Hens & a Rooster. Sandin, Joan, tr. from SWE. Landstrom, Olof, illus. 2005. 28p. (J). (gr. -1-3). 16.00 *(978-91-29-66336-5(9))* R & S Bks. SWE. Dist: Macmillan.

Levy, Janice. Gonzalo Grabs the Good Life. Slavin, Bill, illus. 2009. (ENG.). 34p. (J). (gr. k-4). 17.50 *(978-0-8028-5328-8(5)*, Eerdmans Bks For Young Readers) Eerdmans, William B. Publishing Co.

Ocker, Christa Holder. A Rooster Named Lorenz. 2003. (J). per. *(978-1-59196-284-7(6))* Instant Pub.

Okereke, Laurence. Barry & Big Joe. 2007. (ENG., Illus.). 20p. (J). *(978-0-9795739-0-3(4))* Dion's Pubn.

Rebert, Brenda. Rooster Went A' Walkin' 2009. 28p. pap. 13.99 *(978-1-4389-3414-3(9))* AuthorHouse.

Roller, Ellen. Trading Places. Shea, Gary, illus. 2008. (J). pap. 11.95 *(978-0-9792645-0-4(2))* Edgewood Publishing, LLC.

Ruurs, Margriet. Wake up, Henry Rooster!, 1 vol. Cassidy, Sean, illus. 2006. (ENG.). 32p. (J). (gr. k-3). 19.95 *(978-1-55041-952-8(8)*, 45ff6ba8-0ba0-4855-be4a-55990bed8e73) Trifolium Bks., Inc. CAN. Dist: Firefly Bks., Ltd.

Sattler, Jennifer. A Chick 'n' Pug Christmas. 2014. (ENG., Illus.). 32p. (J). E-Book 11.89 *(978-1-61963-463-3(5)*, Bloomsbury USA Childrens) Bloomsbury Publishing USA.

Sommer, Carl. Proud Rooster & Little Hen. Budwine, Greg, illus. 2014. (J). pap. *(978-1-57537-964-7(3))* Advance Publishing, Inc.

—Proud Rooster & Little Hen. 2003. (Another Sommer-Time Story Ser.). (Illus.). 48p. (J). (gr. 1-4). 16.95 incl. audio *(978-1-57537-559-5(1))* Advance Publishing, Inc.

—Proud Rooster & Little Hen. Budwine, Greg, illus. 2003. (Another Sommer-Time Story Ser.). (ENG.). 48p. (J). (gr. 1-4). 16.95 incl. audio compact disk *(978-1-57537-510-6(9))* Advance Publishing, Inc.

—Proud Rooster & Little Hen(Gallito Orgulloso y Gallinita) Budwine, Greg, illus. 2009. (Another Sommer-Time Story Bilingual Ser.). (SPA & ENG.). 48p. (J). 16.95 *(978-1-57537-164-1(2))* Advance Publishing, Inc.

Stevens, Janet & Crummel, Susan Stevens. Cook-A-Doodle-Doo! Stevens, Janet, illus. 2005. (ENG., Illus.). 48p. (J). (gr. -1-3). reprint ed. pap. 7.99 *(978-0-15-205658-2(0)*, 1197013, Clarion Bks.) HarperCollins Pubs.

Stewart, Grandmother. George the Rooster Goes to the Apple Orchard. 2007. (ENG., Illus.). 28p. (J). lib. bdg. 14.95 *(978-0-9792135-0-2(9))* Rooster Pubns.

Stewart, Wilson N. Cock-a-Doodle-Who? 2007. (ENG., Illus.). 6p. (J). 15.99 *(978-0-7868-0826-7(8))* Hyperion Bks. for Children.

Stoeke, Janet Morgan. The Loopy Coop Hens. 2013. (Penguin Young Readers Level 2 Ser.). lib. bdg. 13.55 *(978-0-606-28751-7(5))* Turtleback.

Sutton, Jennifer. Little Dude's Big Day. 2012. 60p. pap. 18.95 *(978-1-60976-835-5(3)*, Strategic Bk. Publishing) Strategic Book Publishing & Rights Agency (SBPRA).

Tillworth, Mary, adapted by. Pua & Heihei. 2017. (Illus.). 21p. (J). *(978-1-5182-3745-4(2))* Random Hse., Inc.

Toepperwein, Emilie & Toepperwein, Fritz A. Chinto, the Chaparral Cock. (J). (gr. 4-7). 2.95 *(978-0-910722-04-9(8))* Highland Pr.

Tullen, Sean. The Not-So-Evil Wizard. Cunyat, Pol, illus. 2016. (Thud & Blunder Ser.). (ENG.). 56p. (J). (gr. 1-3). lib. bdg. 23.99 *(978-1-4965-3221-3(X)*, 132416, Stone Arch Bks.) Capstone.

Underwood, Barbara. Brewster Rooster. DeWitt, Robin & Dewitt Grush, Patricia, illus. 2006.Tr. of Carla's New Glasses. (ENG.). 32p. (gr. 1-2). pap. 9.95 *(978-1-57874-108-3(4)*, Kaeden Bks.) Kaeden Corp.

Valdivia, Rebecca A. The Stepfather Rooster. 2008. (ENG.). 36p. pap. 16.99 *(978-1-4343-9040-0(3))* AuthorHouse.

Vosloo, Isak. Rooster Lost His Crow: Vossie's Children Book Series. 2012. (Illus.). 32p. pap. 21.35 *(978-1-4678-9679-5(9))* AuthorHouse.

—Rooster Verloor Sy Kraai: 'Oom Vossie Vertel ... ' Kinderboekreeks. 2012. 32p. pap. 21.35 *(978-1-4678-9095-3(2))* AuthorHouse.

Ward, Helen, illus. & retold by. The Rooster & the Fox. Ward, Helen, retold by. 2003. 40p. (J). (gr. k-3). 16.95 *(978-0-7613-1846-0(1)*, First Avenue Editions) Lerner Publishing Group.

Ward, Helen & Ward, Helen. The Rooster & the Fox. 2003. (Single Titles Ser.: Vol. 3). 40p. (gr. k-4). lib. bdg. 24.90 *(978-0-7613-2920-6(X)*, Millbrook Pr.) Lerner Publishing Group.

Ziskind, Hélio & Duchesne, Christiane. Le Géant de la Forêt: Un Voyage Musical. Pratt, Pierre, illus. 2014. (ENG.). 48p. (J). (gr. k-2). 16.95 *(978-2-923163-36-9(2))* La Montagne Secrete CAN. Dist: Independent Pubs. Group.

ROOTS (BOTANY)

Aloian, Molly. What Are Bulbs & Roots? 2012. (ENG., Illus.). 24p. (J). *(978-0-7787-4220-3(2))*; pap. *(978-0-7787-4225-8(3))* Crabtree Publishing Co.

Bishop, Celeste. ¿Por Qué Las Plantas Tienen Raíces? / Why Do Plants Have Roots?, 1 vol., 1. 2015. (Partes de la Planta / Plant Parts Ser.). (ENG & SPA., Illus.). 24p. (J). (gr. 1-1). 25.27 *(978-1-5081-4742-8(6)*, 2e452fd1-a274-4896-b638-fe2d5f08cc94, PowerKids Pr.) Rosen Publishing Group, Inc., The.

—Why Do Plants Have Roots?, 1 vol., 1. 2015. (Plant Parts Ser.). (ENG., Illus.). 24p. (J). (gr. 1-1). pap. 9.25 *(978-1-5081-4225-6(4)*,

33292852-f434-4ec9-ae37-d2b1c568b672, PowerKids Pr.) Rosen Publishing Group, Inc., The.

Bodach, Vijaya K. Roots [Scholastic]. 2010. (Plant Parts Ser.). 24p. pap. 0.52 *(978-1-4296-5059-5(1)*, Capstone Pr.) Capstone.

Bodach, Vijaya Khisty. Roots. rev. ed. 2016. (Plant Parts Ser.). (ENG.). 24p. (J). (gr. -1-2). pap. 7.29 *(978-1-5157-4245-6(8)*, 134002, Capstone Pr.) Capstone.

Coldwell, Lamar. The Roots of a Tree, 1 vol. 2016. (Rosen REAL Readers: STEM & STEAM Collection). (ENG.). 8p. (gr. k-1). pap. 5.46 *(978-1-5081-2383-5(7)*, 7b02d85a-3a26-45e8-8a92-a706078ec253, Rosen Classroom) Rosen Publishing Group, Inc., The.

Farndon, John. Roots. 2006. (World of Plants (Blackbirch) Ser.). (ENG., Illus.). 24p. (J). (gr. 2-6). lib. bdg. 26.65 *(978-1-4103-0421-6(3)*, Blackbirch Pr., Inc.) Cengage Gale.

Kirkman, Marissa. Roots. 2019. (Plant Parts Ser.). (ENG., Illus.). 24p. (J). (gr. -1-2). pap. 6.95 *(978-1-9771-1023-7(1)*, 141099, Pebble) Capstone.

Klepeis, Alicia. Roots. 2017. (Closer Look at Plants Ser.). (ENG.). 24p. (gr. 2-4). pap. 8.95 *(978-1-68342-457-4(3)*, 9781683424574) Rourke Educational Media.

Kudlinski, Kathleen V. What Do Roots Do? Schuppert, David, illus. (ENG.). 32p. (J). (gr. k-3). 2007. pap. 7.95 *(978-1-55971-980-3(X))* 2005. 15.95 *(978-1-55971-896-7(X))* Cooper Square Publishing Llc.

Owen, Ruth. What Do Roots, Stems, Leaves, & Flowers Do?, 1 vol. 2014. (World of Plants Ser.). (ENG.). 32p. (J). (gr. 2-3). lib. bdg. 27.93 *(978-1-4777-7137-2(9)*, 73734378-9cc3-4b7c-a6fc-63aba6a08bcd, PowerKids Pr.) Rosen Publishing Group, Inc., The.

Sterling, Kristin. Exploring Roots. 2011. (First Step Nonfiction — Let's Look at Plants Ser.). (gr. k-2). (ENG., Illus.). 24p. (J). pap. 6.99 *(978-0-7613-7834-1(0)*, 56b38d1c-32aa-4c0c-91e0-e90c88fe8809); pap. 33.92 *(978-0-7613-8616-2(5))*; (Illus.). 23p. lib. bdg. 21.27 *(978-0-7613-5781-0(5))* Lerner Publishing Group.

Throp, Claire. All about Roots, 1 vol. (All about Plants Ser.). (ENG.). 24p. (J). (gr. -1-1). 2014. 25.32 *(978-1-4846-0508-0(X)*, 126624) 2016. pap. 5.99 *(978-1-4846-3848-4(4)*, 134789) Capstone. (Heinemann).

ROSES

Jalbert, Brad & Peters, Laura. Roses for British Columbia, 1 vol. rev. ed. 2003. (ENG., Illus.). 272p. (gr. 4). pap. 21.95 *(978-1-55105-261-8(X)*, 23d345fa-c5ef-4a68-bfc4-d88aac77563f) Lone Pine Publishing USA.

Kate, Maggie, ed. Glitter Roses Stickers. 2004. (Dover Stickers Ser.). (ENG., Illus.). 2p. (J). (gr. -1-5). 1.99 *(978-0-486-43534-3(2)*, 435342) Dover Pubns., Inc.

Klose, Elizabeth 'Liz' & Peters, Laura. Roses for Ontario, 1 vol. rev. ed. 2003. (ENG., Illus.). 272p. (gr. 4). pap. 21.95 *(978-1-55105-263-2(6)*, 761e5424-7c48-41a2-983a-482c45066824) Lone Pine Publishing USA.

Lindley, Nancy & Peters, Laura. Roses for Michigan, 1 vol., Vol. 1. rev. ed. 2004. (ENG., Illus.). 272p. (gr. 4). pap. 18.95 *(978-1-55105-367-7(5)*, c2cdef1c-1b30-4b42-b267-35edcca5b467) Lone Pine Publishing USA.

Thomson, Ruth. The Life Cycle of a Rose, 1 vol. 2009. (Learning about Life Cycles Ser.). (ENG.). 24p. (J). (gr. 2-2). pap. 9.25 *(978-1-4358-2887-2(9)*, 5a178fba-e608-42f8-9bad-14f30ca6fde2, PowerKids Pr.); lib. bdg. 26.27 *(978-1-4358-2837-7(2)*, e6dbd973-421d-4383-8360-9a3e39ecb603) Rosen Publishing Group, Inc., The.

ROSES—FICTION

Cohn, Diana. Roses for Isabella, 34 vols. Córdova, Amy, illus. 2011. (ENG.). 32p. (J). 17.95 *(978-0-88010-731-0(6))* SteinerBooks, Inc.

Cook, Cathy T. The Adventures of Rose Bush. 2010. 64p. pap. 10.49 *(978-1-4520-3645-8(4))* AuthorHouse.

de la Ramée, Louise. Bimbi. 2004. reprint ed. pap. 1.99 *(978-1-4192-0998-7(1))*; pap. 19.95 *(978-1-4191-0998-0(7))* Kessinger Publishing, LLC.

Erlich, Bev. Pink Roses Everywhere. gif. ed. 2004. (Illus.). 64p. (J). 14.95 *(978-0-9743913-0-4(1))* Snojoy Publishing.

Fernandez, David R. Lady Godiva & the Legend of the Black Rose. 2008. (Illus.). 32p. (J). pap. 8.99 *(978-0-9817521-4-3(4))* Mirror Publishing.

McKee, Mabel A. The Heart of the Rose. (Illus.). (J). reprint ed. pap. *(978-0-9658838-1-8(7))* Barnes Printing.

My Roses. 2003. (J). per. *(978-1-57657-898-8(4))* Paradise Pr., Inc.

Quattlebaum, Mary. Jackson Jones & the Curse of the Outlaw Rose. 2008. (Jackson Jones Ser.). (ENG.). 112p. (J). (gr. 3-7). 5.99 *(978-0-440-42138-2(1)*, Yearling) Random Hse. Children's Bks.

Randolph, Joanne. Rose: a Flower's Story, 1 vol. 2009. (Nature Stories Ser.). (ENG., Illus.). 24p. (J). (gr. 1-2). pap. 9.15 *(978-1-60754-102-8(5)*, 6e56df0e-d448-45ab-b6f3-befca54da9af); lib. bdg. 27.27 *(978-1-60754-101-1(7)*, 87f4568d-22af-4789-8560-17dcb2322235) Rosen Publishing Group, Inc., The. (Windmill Bks.).

Roses for Renee Set B, 6 vols. 32p. (gr. 1-3). 26.50 *(978-0-7802-8055-7(5))* Wright Group/McGraw-Hill.

Sirotzky, Sara. Red Rose & Blue Butterfly. Weber, Andra, illus. 2012. (ENG.). 32p. (J). (gr. -1-3). 17.95 *(978-1-4507-9594-4(3))* Ampersand, Inc.

Slater, Dashka. Dangerously Ever After. Docampo, Valeria, illus. 2012. 40p. (J). (gr. k-3). 17.99 *(978-0-8037-3374-9(7)*, Dial Bks) Penguin Young Readers Group.

Valentina, Marina. Lost in the Roses. 2008. (Illus.). 24p. (J). pap. 5.95 *(978-1-60108-024-0(7))* Red Cygnet Pr.

—Lost in the Roses. Valentina, Marina, illus. 2007. (Illus.). 24p. (J). (gr. -1-1). 14.95 *(978-1-60108-014-1(X))* Red Cygnet Pr.

Wood, Douglas. Aunt Mary's Rose. Pham, LeUyen, illus. 2010. (ENG.). 32p. (J). (gr. -1-3). 16.99 *(978-0-7636-1090-6(9))* Candlewick Pr.

Yee, Paul. Roses Sing on New Snow: A Delicious Tale. Chan, Harvey, illus. 32p. (J). 16.95 *(978-0-88899-144-7(4))* Groundwood Bks. CAN. Dist: Publishers Group West (PGW).

ROSH HA-SHANAH

Barash, Chris. Is It Rosh Hashanah Yet? Psacharopulo, Alessandra, illus. 2018. (Celebrate Jewish Holidays Ser.). (ENG.). 32p. (J). (gr. -1-3). 16.99 *(978-0-8075-3396-3(3)*, 807533963) Whitman, Albert & Co.

Hashanah, Rosh & Kippur, Yom. Rosh Hashanah & Yom Kippur Coloring Book. 2.99 *(978-1-58330-168-5(2))* Feldheim Pubs.

Kropf, Latifa Berry. It's Shofar Time! Cohen, Tod, photos by. 2006. (ENG., Illus.). 24p. (J). (gr. -1-1). lib. bdg. 12.95 *(978-1-58013-158-2(1)*, Kar-Ben Publishing) Lerner Publishing Group.

Murray, Julie. Rosh Hashanah. 2018. (Holidays (Abdo Kids Junior) Ser.). (ENG., Illus.). 24p. (J). (gr. -1-2). lib. bdg. 31.36 *(978-1-5321-8174-0(4)*, 29821, Abdo Kids) ABDO Publishing Co.

Musleah, Rahel. Apples & Pomegranates: A Rosh Hashanah Seder. Gier, Judy Jarrett, illus. 2004. (ENG.). 64p. (J). (gr. k-5). pap. 7.95 *(978-1-58013-123-0(9)*, b45762af-fdbd-4900-b333-b3b8df81257e, Kar-Ben Publishing) Lerner Publishing Group.

ROSH HA-SHANAH—FICTION

Barash, Chris. Jackie & Jesse & Joni & Jae. Battuz, Christine, illus. 2019. (ENG.). 24p. (J). 17.95 *(978-1-68115-550-0(8)*, c49a0776-fd1b-45cd-90ac-a5a0d78ce718, Apples & Honey Pr.) Behrman Hse., Inc.

Cohen, Deborah Bodin. Engineer Ari & the Rosh Hashanah Ride. 2008. (High Holidays Ser.). (Illus.). 32p. (J). (gr. -1-3). lib. bdg. 17.95 *(978-0-8225-8648-7(7)*, Kar-Ben Publishing) Lerner Publishing Group.

Epstein, Sylvia & Migron, Hagit. How the Rosh Hashanah Challah. 2010. (ENG.). 26p. pap. *(978-965-229-479-1(9))* Gefen Publishing Hse., Ltd.

Jules, Jacqueline. What a Way to Start a New Year! A Rosh Hashanah Story. Stead, Judy, illus. 2013. (ENG.). 24p. (J). (gr. -1-2). 7.95 *(978-0-7613-8117-4(1)*, f7438181-666c-4652-8821-3d6f7f9a904b, Kar-Ben Publishing) Lerner Publishing Group.

Marshall, Linda Elovitz. Talia & the Rude Vegetables. Assirelli, Francesca, illus. 2011. (ENG.). 24p. (J). (gr. k-3). pap. 6.95 *(978-0-7613-5218-1(X)*, 680c74b9-4069-4eeb-aba3-3e3f20cd5862, Kar-Ben Publishing) Lerner Publishing Group.

Newman, Tracy. Rosh Hashanah Is Coming! Garofoli, Viviana, illus. 2016. (ENG.). 12p. (J). (gr. -1 — 1). E-Book 23.99 *(978-1-5124-0945-1(6)*, Kar-Ben Publishing) Lerner Publishing Group.

Ofanansky, Allison. What's the Buzz? Honey for a Sweet New Year. Alpern, Eliyahu, illus. Alpern, Eliyahu, photos by. 2011. (High Holidays Ser.). (J). (gr. -1-k). lib. bdg. 15.95 *(978-0-7613-5640-0(1))* Lerner Publishing Group.

Schnur, Susan. Tashlich at Turtle Rock. Schnur-Fishman, Anna & Steele-Morgan, Alexandra, illus. 2010. (High Holidays Ser.). 32p. (J). (gr. k-4). lib. bdg. 17.95 *(978-0-7613-4509-1(4)*, Kar-Ben Publishing) Lerner Publishing Group.

Sussman, Joni Kibort. Shanah Tovah, Grover! Leigh, Tom, illus. 2019. (ENG.). 12p. (J). (gr. -1 — 1). bds. 6.99 *(978-1-5415-2922-9(7)*, f6a2d4ee-a53f-49a0-8a9c-762d7254701f, Kar-Ben Publishing) Lerner Publishing Group.

Vander Zee, Ruth & Sneider, Marian. Eli Remembers. Farnsworth, Bill, illus. 2007. (ENG.). 32p. (J). (gr. -1-3). 18.00 *(978-0-8028-5309-7(9)*, Eerdmans Bks For Young Readers) Eerdmans, William B. Publishing Co.

Wayland, April Halprin. New Year at the Pier: A Rosh Hashanah Story. Jorisch, Stéphane, illus. 2009. 352p. (J). *(978-0-8037-3110-3(8)*, Dial) Penguin Publishing Group.

ROSS, BETSY, 1752-1836

Buckley, James, Jr. & Who HQ. Who Was Betsy Ross? O'Brien, John, illus. 2014. (Who Was? Ser.). 112p. (J). (gr. 3-7). 6.99 *(978-0-448-48243-9(6)*, Penguin Workshop) Penguin Young Readers Group.

Buckley, James. Who Was Betsy Ross? 2014. (Who Was... ? Ser.). lib. bdg. 16.00 *(978-0-606-36181-1(2))* Turtleback.

Cotton, Jacqueline S. Betsy Ross. 2019. (Illus.). 24p. (J). *(978-1-4896-9554-3(0)*, AV2 by Weigl) Weigl Pubs., Inc.

Cox, Vicki. Betsy Ross: A Flag for a New Nation. 2005. (Leaders of the American Revolution Ser.). (ENG., Illus.). 100p. (gr. 5-8). lib. bdg. 30.00 *(978-0-7910-8618-6(6)*, P114334, Facts On File) Infobase Holdings, Inc.

Harkins, Susan Sales & Harkins, William H. Betsy Ross. 2006. (Profiles in American History Ser.). (Illus.). 48p. (J). (gr. 3-7). lib. bdg. 29.95 *(978-1-58415-446-4(2))* Mitchell Lane Pubs.

Manera, Alexandria. Betsy Ross. 2003. (Women of the Revolution Ser.). (J). pap. *(978-1-58417-085-3(9))*; lib. bdg. *(978-1-58417-022-8(0))* Lake Street Pubs.

Palazzo-Craig, Janet. The Making of the American Flag: Betsy Ross & George Washington. (Great Moments in American History Ser.). 32p. (gr. 3-3). 2009. 47.90 *(978-1-61513-155-6(8))* 2003. (ENG., Illus.). lib. bdg. 29.13 *(978-0-8239-4335-7(6)*, fd35f551-dd6a-40c6-8672-b3c4c53e6e50, Rosen Reference) Rosen Publishing Group, Inc., The.

Randolph, Ryan. Betsy Ross: The American Flag, & Life in a Young America. 2009. (Library of American Lives & Times Ser.). 112p. (gr. 5-5). 69.20 *(978-1-60853-473-9(1))* Rosen Publishing Group, Inc., The.

Silate, Jennifer. Betsy Ross, 1 vol. 2003. (Primary Sources of Famous People in American History Ser.). (ENG., Illus.). 32p. (gr. 3-4). pap. 10.00 *(978-0-8239-4176-6(0)*, b47dfab6-bcb3-478d-8ebd-fb24e811eb35) Rosen Publishing Group, Inc., The.

—Betsy Ross: Creadora de la Bandera Estadounidense, 1 vol. 2003. (Grandes Personajes en la Historia de Los Estados Unidos (Famous People in American History) Ser.). (SPA., Illus.). 32p. (gr. 3-4). lib. bdg. 29.13 *(978-0-8239-4128-5(0)*, 6d1f4398-0ed5-41d6-a0b9-481ee358a5c7, Editorial Buenas Letras) Rosen Publishing Group, Inc., The.

—Betsy Ross: Creadora de la bandera Estadounidense, 1 vol. 2003. (Grandes Personajes en la Historia de Los Estados Unidos (Famous People in American History) Ser.). (SPA.). 32p. (gr. 3-4). pap. 10.00 *(978-0-8239-4222-0(8)*, b34d9aab-1916-4ad0-86a3-3cbffcb1dc18, Rosen Classroom) Rosen Publishing Group, Inc., The.

—Betsy Ross: Creadora de la bandera estadounidense (Betsy Ross: Creator of the American Flag) 2009. (Grandes personajes en la historia de los Estados Unidos (Famous People in American History) Ser.). (SPA.). 32p. (gr. 2-3). 47.90 *(978-1-61512-791-7(7)*, Editorial Buenas Letras) Rosen Publishing Group, Inc., The.

—Betsy Ross: Creator of the American Flag. (Primary Sources of Famous People in American History Ser.). 32p. 2009. (gr. 2-3). 47.90 *(978-1-60851-657-5(1))* 2003. (ENG., Illus.). (J). (gr. 3-4). lib. bdg. 29.13 *(978-0-8239-4104-9(3)*, 89ed74c8-2280-4e97-bcb9-a5df86386585) Rosen Publishing Group, Inc., The.

—Betsy Ross: Creator of the American Flag / Creadora de la bandera Estadounidense. 2009. (Famous People in American History/Grandes personajes en la historia de los Estados Unidos Ser.). (ENG & SPA.). 32p. (gr. 2-3). 47.90 *(978-1-61512-539-5(6)*, Editorial Buenas Letras) Rosen Publishing Group, Inc., The.

Urwin, Kirsten. Betsy Ross & the Creation of the American Flag, 1 vol. 2015. (Spotlight on American History Ser.). (ENG., Illus.). 24p. (J). (gr. 4-6). pap. 11.00 *(978-1-4994-1789-0(6)*, 8ebf0f7d-ef7a-4c92-9bae-8a6cdde1e911, PowerKids Pr.) Rosen Publishing Group, Inc., The.

White, Becky. Betsy Ross. Lloyd, Megan, illus. 2019. (I Like to Read Ser.). 32p. (J). (gr. -1-3). pap. 7.99 *(978-0-8234-4523-3(2))* Holiday Hse., Inc.

ROSSINI, GIOACCHINO, 1792-1868

Balfe, Roberta Rymer, et al. A Young Person's Introduction to the Arts Featuring the Opera La Cenerentola (Cinderella) by Gioachino [sic] Rossini: Music, Drama, Language, Costumes, Games, Puzzles. 2008. (Illus.). 24p. (J). *(978-0-9785364-0-4(1))* Young Patronesses of the Opera, The.

ROUND TABLE

see Arthur, King

ROUSSEAU, HENRI, 1844-1910

de Duve, Catherine. Hello Rousseau: Get to Know Rousseau through Stories, Games & Draw-It-Yourself Fun. 2007. 132p. pap. 9.95 *(978-1-59960-001-7(3))* Birdcage Pr.

Markel, Michelle. The Fantastic Jungles of Henri Rousseau. Hall, Amanda, illus. 40p. (J). 2019. (ENG.). *(978-0-8028-5523-7(7))* 2012. 17.00 *(978-0-8028-5364-6(1))* Eerdmans, William B. Publishing Co. (Eerdmans Bks For Young Readers).

Stephens, Pam. Dropping in on Rousseau. 2003. (ENG., Illus.). 32p. (J). 15.95 *(978-1-56290-303-9(9))* Crystal Productions.

ROUSSEAU, JEAN-JACQUES, 1712-1778

Brezina, Corona. Jean-Jacques Rousseau & the Social Contract. 2016. (J). lib. bdg. *(978-1-5081-0227-4(9))* Rosen Publishing Group, Inc., The.

ROUTES OF TRADE

see Trade Routes

ROWAN (FICTITIOUS CHARACTER)—FICTION

Rodda, Emily. Rowan & the Ice Creepers. 2003. (Rowan of Rin Ser.). 272p. (J). (gr. 3-18). 15.99 *(978-0-06-029780-0(8))* HarperCollins Pubs.

—Rowan & the Zebak. 2003. (Rowan of Rin Ser.). (ENG., Illus.). 208p. (J). (gr. 2-18). pap. 5.99 *(978-0-06-441024-3(2)*, Harper Trophy) HarperCollins Pubs.

—Rowan of Rin #1: Rowan of Rin. 2004. (ENG., Illus.). 176p. (J). (gr. 3-18). pap. 9.99 *(978-0-06-056071-3(1)*, Greenwillow Bks.) HarperCollins Pubs.

—Rowan of Rin #2: Rowan & the Travelers. 2004. (ENG.). 192p. (J). (gr. 3-18). pap. 6.99 *(978-0-06-056072-0(X)*, Greenwillow Bks.) HarperCollins Pubs.

ROWING

Brown, Daniel James. The Boys in the Boat (Young Readers Adaptation) The True Story of an American Team's Epic Journey to Win Gold at the 1936 Olympics. (ENG., Illus.). (J). (gr. 5). 2016. 256p. 11.99 *(978-0-14-751685-5(4)*, Puffin Books) 2015. 240p. 19.99 *(978-0-451-47592-3(5)*, Viking Books for Young Readers) Penguin Young Readers Group.

—The Boys in the Boat (Young Readers Adaptation) The True Story of an American Team's Epic Journey to Win Gold at the 1936 Olympics. 2016. lib. bdg. 22.10 *(978-0-606-39312-6(9))* Turtleback.

ROWING—FICTION

Tetlow, Karin. Harry Goes Rowing. Guze, Tessa, illus. 2013. 32p. pap. 11.95 *(978-0-615-75585-4(2))* Juping Horse Pr.

ROWLING, J. K., 1965-

Bucholz, Dinah. The Unofficial Harry Potter Cookbook: From Cauldron Cakes to Knickerbocker Glory — More Than 150 Magical Recipes for Wizards & Non-Wizards Alike. 2010. (Unofficial Cookbook Ser.). (ENG., Illus.). 256p. 19.95 *(978-1-4405-0325-2(7))* Adams Media Corp.

Burton, Bonnie. J. K. Rowling's Wizarding World: Movie Magic Volume Three: Amazing Artifacts. 2017. (J. K. Rowling's Wizarding World Ser.). (ENG., Illus.). 96p. (J). (gr. 5). 29.99 *(978-0-7636-9584-2(X))* Candlewick Pr.

Gaines, Ann Graham. J. K. Rowling. 2004. (Blue Banner Biography Ser.). (Illus.). 32p. (J). (gr. 3-8). lib. bdg. 25.70 *(978-1-58415-325-2(3))* Mitchell Lane Pubs.

Hallett, Cynthia & Huey, Peggy. J. K. Rowling, 1 vol. 2012. (New Casebooks Ser.: 20). (ENG., Illus.). 224p. (C). 95.00 *(978-0-230-00849-6(6)*, 900264231); pap. 30.95 *(978-0-230-00850-2(X)*, 900260558) Palgrave Macmillan Ltd. GBR. (Red Globe Pr.). Dist: Macmillan.

Harrington, Jamie. The Unofficial Guide to Crafting the World of Harry Potter: 30 Magical Crafts for Witches & Wizards — From Pencil Wands to House Colors Tie-Dye Shirts. 2016. (ENG., Illus.). 192p. pap. 17.99 *(978-1-4405-9504-2(6))* Adams Media Corp.

Hill, Mary. J. K. Rowling. 2003. (Welcome Books: Real People Ser.). (ENG., Illus.). 24p. (J). (gr. k-3). 17.44 *(978-0-516-25866-9(4))* Scholastic Library Publishing.

Hunsicker, Jennifer. J. K. Rowling: Author of the Harry Potter Series. 2016. (Famous Female Authors Ser.). (ENG., Illus.). 32p. (J). (gr. 3-9). lib. bdg. 28.65 *(978-1-5157-1328-9(8)*, 132361, Capstone Pr.) Capstone.

Moore, P.D. About Harry Potter: What Every Kid Should Know... Moore, Rema Harracksingh- & Delande, J., eds. 2003. (Illus.). 170p. (YA). pap. *(978-0-9543596-3-8(1))* Lux-Verbi Bks.

Peterson-Hilleque, Victoria. J. K. Rowling: Extraordinary Author, 1 vol. 2010. (Essential Lives Set 5 Ser.). (ENG.). 112p. (YA). (gr. 6-12). lib. bdg. 41.36 *(978-1-61613-517-1(4)*, 6717, Essential Library) ABDO Publishing Co.

Pezzi, Bryan. J. K. Rowling. (J). 2012. 28.55 *(978-1-61913-057-9(2))* 2012. pap. 13.95 *(978-1-61913-596-3(5))* 2005. (Illus.). 32p. (gr. 5-7). lib. bdg. 26.00 *(978-1-59036-287-7(X))* Weigl Pubs., Inc.

Pollack, Pam, et al. Who Is J. K. Rowling? Marchesi, Stephen, illus. 2012. (Who Was? Ser.). 112p. (J). (gr. 3-7). pap. 5.99 *(978-0-448-45872-4(1)*, Penguin Workshop) Penguin Young Readers Group.

Pollack, Pamela & Belviso, Meg. Who Is J. K. Rowling? 2012. (Who Is... ? Ser.). lib. bdg. 16.00 *(978-0-606-26078-7(1))* Turtleback.

Price, Joan. J. K. Rowling, 1 vol. 2004. (Trailblazers of the Modern World Ser.). (ENG., Illus.). 48p. (gr. 5-8). pap. 15.05 *(978-0-8368-5268-4(0)*, 70983876-d844-4b12-aa22-60b340b12030); lib. bdg. 33.67 *(978-0-8368-5499-2(3)*, 685e19f2-3ac5-4998-bd5f-d3b6e0426510) Stevens, Gareth Publishing LLLP. (Gareth Stevens Secondary Library).

Pyne, Erin A. A Fandom of Magical Proportions: S: an Unauthorized History of the Harry Potter Phenomenon. 2007. (Illus.). 84p. (J). per. 8.36 *(978-0-9788138-8-8(X))* Nimble Bks. LLC.

Rice, Dona Herweck. A Biography of J. K. Rowling, (Grade 8) 2nd rev. ed. 2017. (TIME(r): Informational Text Ser.). (ENG., Illus.). 32p. (J). (gr. 7-8). pap. 10.99 *(978-1-4938-3931-5(4))* Teacher Created Materials, Inc.

—Game Changers: A Biography of J. K. Rowling. 2017. (Time for Kids Nonfiction Readers Ser.). lib. bdg. 19.65 *(978-0-606-40264-4(0))* Turtleback.

Rosenberg, Moshe. Morality for Muggles: Ethics in the Bible & the World of Harry Potter. 2011. (J). *(978-1-60280-183-7(5))* Ktav Publishing Hse., Inc.

Senker, Cath. J. K. Rowling: Creator of Harry Potter, 1 vol. 2011. (Famous Lives Ser.). (ENG., Illus.). 32p. (YA). (gr. 3-4). lib. bdg. 30.27 *(978-1-4488-3288-0(8)*, 898cfb36-976b-437d-a19a-adc2303d6b29) Rosen Publishing Group, Inc., The.

Sexton, Colleen. J. K. Rowling. 2008. pap. 52.95 *(978-1-57505-984-6(3))* Lerner Publishing Group.

Sexton, Colleen A. J. K. Rowling. (Biography Ser.). (Illus.). 112p. (J). 2007. (gr. -1). lib. bdg. 30.60 *(978-0-8225-7949-6(9))* 2007. (gr. -1). per. 7.95 *(978-0-8225-8749-1(1)*, First Avenue Editions) 2005. (gr. 4-7). per. 7.95 *(978-0-8225-3389-4(8))* Lerner Publishing Group.

—J.K. Rowling. 2006. (Just the Facts Biographies Ser.). (Illus.). 112p. (J). 27.93 *(978-0-8225-3423-5(1)*, Lerner Pubns.) Lerner Publishing Group.

Sexton, Colleen A. & Cosgrove, Martha. J. K. Rowling. 2006. (Just the Facts Biographies Ser.). (Illus.). 112p. (J). pap. 9.95 *(978-0-8225-5995-5(1)*, Lerner Pubns.) Lerner Publishing Group.

Shapiro, Marc. J. K. Rowling: the Wizard Behind Harry Potter: The Wizard Behind Harry Potter. 4th ed. 2007. (ENG., Illus.). 288p. pap. 20.99 *(978-0-312-37697-0(9)*, 900049029, St. Martin's Griffin) St. Martin's Pr.

Steffens, Bradley. J. K. Rowling, 1 vol. 2006. (People in the News Ser.). (ENG., Illus.). 104p. (gr. 7-7). lib. bdg. 41.03 *(978-1-59018-963-4(9)*, 15b498e5-655e-4d1d-965d-20b77ee0fd9b, Lucent Pr.) Greenhaven Publishing LLC.

Westerfeld, Scott. Mind-Rain: Your Favorite Authors on Scott Westerfeld's Uglies Series. 2009. (Illus.). 248p. (J). (gr. 7-12). pap. 19.95 *(978-1-933771-34-2(8)*, SmartPop) BenBella Bks.

ROYAL CANADIAN MOUNTED POLICE

Bekkering, Annalise. Mounties: Canadian Icons. 2010. (Illus.). 24p. *(978-1-77071-577-6(0))*; pap. *(978-1-77071-584-4(3))* Weigl Educational Pubs. Ltd.

ROYAL CANADIAN MOUNTED POLICE—FICTION

Bekkering, Annalise. Les Gendarmes: Les Emblèmes Canadiens. McMann, Julie, tr. from ENG. 2011. (FRE.). 24p. (YA). (gr. 2-4). *(978-1-77071-410-6(3))* Weigl Educational Pubs. Ltd.

ROYALTY

see Kings, Queens, Rulers, etc.; Princes; Princesses

RUBBER

Colich, Abby. Rubber, 1 vol. 2013. (Exploring Materials Ser.). (ENG.). 24p. (J). (gr. -1-1). pap. 6.95 *(978-1-4329-8027-6(0)*, 123184, Heinemann) Capstone.

Garry-McCord, Kathleen & Sonsky, Kim. Stamp It! Brush-Free Art Prints & Paint Projects. Sonsky, Kim, illus. 2006. (Illus.). 48p. (J). *(978-0-439-81340-2(9))* Scholastic, Inc.

Gleason, Carrie. The Biography of Rubber. 2005. (How Did That Get There?). (ENG., Illus.). 32p. (J). (gr. 4-5). pap. *(978-0-7787-2522-0(7))*; lib. bdg. *(978-0-7787-2486-5(7))* Crabtree Publishing Co.

Levete, Sarah. Rubber. 2006. (Material Matters Ser.). (J). *(978-1-59389-273-9(X))* Chrysalis Education.

Ridley, Sarah. A Rubber Tire, 1 vol. 2005. (How It's Made Ser.). (ENG., Illus.). 32p. (gr. 2-4). lib. bdg. 28.67 *(978-0-8368-6295-9(3)*, 6576236a-e513-4022-b372-556cc9420e64, Gareth Stevens Learning Library) Stevens, Gareth Publishing LLLP.

SchreyerKarmel. BOUNCE! THE WONDERFUL WORLD OF RUBBER UPPER INTERMEDIATE BOOK WITH ONLINE ACCESS, 1 vol. 2014. (ENG., Illus.). 28p. (J). pap., E-Book 9.50 *(978-1-107-64154-9(3))* Cambridge Univ. Pr.

RUBBER TIRES

see Tires, Rubber

RUDOLPH, WILMA, 1940-1994

Baer, Peter. Wilma Rudolph: Gold-Medal Winner, 1 vol. 2013. (InfoMax Readers Ser.). (ENG.). 24p. (J). (gr. 2-2). pap. 8.25 *(978-1-4777-2381-4(1)*, defcd7f1-a898-47df-9a31-df69535e32f8); pap. 49.50 *(978-1-4777-2383-8(8))* Rosen Publishing Group, Inc., The. (Rosen Classroom).

Baer, Peter & Castle, Grace. Olympic Champion: Wilma Rudolph, 1 vol. 2013. (Rosen Readers Ser.). (ENG.). 24p. (J). (gr. 2-2). pap. 8.25 *(978-1-4777-2385-2(4)*, f1d8f54c-f98a-4788-9c86-4cf49f6347d3); pap. 49.50 *(978-1-4777-2386-9(2))* Rosen Publishing Group, Inc., The. (Rosen Classroom).

Beck, Isabel L., et al. Wilma Rudolph. 2003. (Trophies Ser.). (gr. 6-18). 88.70 *(978-0-15-319349-1(2))* Harcourt Schl. Pubs.

Dodson Wade, Mary. Amazing Olympic Athlete Wilma Rudolph, 1 vol. 2009. (Amazing Americans Ser.). (ENG., Illus.). 24p. (gr. k-2). pap. 10.35 *(978-0-7660-5978-8(2)*, d5d1fbaa-2c64-42f5-ac67-49964d2a9897, Enslow Elementary); lib. bdg. 25.27 *(978-0-7660-3282-8(5)*, 34b5dfbd-0b67-4e34-97fe-24c1037bcaa6) Enslow Publishing, LLC.

Harper, Jo. Wilma Rudolph: Olympic Runner. Henderson, Meryl, illus. 2004. (Childhood of Famous Americans Ser.). (ENG.). 192p. (J). (gr. 3-7). pap. 7.99 *(978-0-689-85873-4(6)*, Simon & Schuster/Paula Wiseman Bks.) Simon & Schuster/Paula Wiseman Bks.

Krull, Kathleen. Wilma Unlimited. Diaz, David, illus. 2015. 44p. pap. 7.00 *(978-1-61003-502-6(X))* Center for the Collaborative Classroom.

Leed, Percy. Wilma Rudolph: Running for Gold. 2020. (Epic Sports Bios (Lerner (tm) Sports) Ser.). (ENG., Illus.). 32p. (J). (gr. 2-5). 30.65 *(978-1-5415-9744-0(3)*, d02fb726-95e7-47ea-aa3b-c085bb381bd2, Lerner Pubns.) Lerner Publishing Group.

Morganelli, Adrianna. Wilma Rudolph: Track & Field Champion. 2016. (Remarkable Lives Revealed Ser.). (ENG.). 32p. (J). (gr. 2-5). *(978-0-7787-2689-0(4))* Crabtree Publishing Co.

Sherrow, Victoria. Wilma Rudolph. Johnson, Larry, illus. 2006. (Yo Solo Biografías Ser.). (ENG & SPA.). 48p. (J). (gr. 2-3). lib. bdg. 23.93 *(978-0-8225-6260-3(X)*, Ediciones Lerner) Lerner Publishing Group.

—Wilma Rudolph. Translations.com Staff, tr. Johnson, Larry, illus. 2006. (Yo Solo: Biografías (on My Own Biographies) Ser.). (SPA.). 48p. (gr. 2-4). pap. 6.95 *(978-0-8225-6623-6(0)*, Ediciones Lerner) Lerner Publishing Group.

Streissguth, Tom. Wilma Rudolph. (Illus.). 2007. 110p. (YA). pap. 9.95 *(978-0-8225-6693-9(1))* 2006. (ENG., 120p. (gr. 5-12). lib. bdg. 30.60 *(978-0-8225-5958-0(7))* Lerner Publishing Group.

Weakland, Mark. When Wilma Rudolph Played Basketball. Duncan, Daniel, illus. 2016. (Leaders Doing Headstands Ser.). (ENG.). 32p. (J). (gr. 1-4). pap. 7.95 *(978-1-5158-0136-8(5)*, 132344); lib. bdg. 28.65 *(978-1-4795-9684-3(1)*, 132340) Capstone. (Picture Window Bks.).

—When Wilma Rudolph Played Basketball. Duncan, Daniel, illus. 2017. 32p. (J). *(978-1-5158-0140-5(3)*, Picture Window Bks.) Capstone.

RUG AND CARPET INDUSTRY

Miller, Raymond H. Jhalak Man Tamang: Slave Labor Whistleblower, 1 vol. 2006. (Young Heroes Ser.). (ENG., Illus.). 48p. (gr. 4-8). lib. bdg. 37.33 *(978-0-7377-3616-8(X)*, 0a9efb6d-233b-47fa-9f49-0d7b3dbac42a, KidHaven Publishing) Greenhaven Publishing LLC.

RUGBY FOOTBALL

Gagne, Tammy. Day by Day with Calvin Johnson. 2014. (Illus.). 32p. (J). (gr. -1-2). 25.70 *(978-1-61228-633-4(X))* Mitchell Lane Pubs.

Gifford, Clive. The Official IRB Rugby World Cup 2015 Fact File. 2015. (Y Ser.). (ENG., Illus.). 64p. (J). (gr. 4-7). 9.95 *(978-1-78312-124-3(6))* Carlton Kids GBR. Dist: Two Rivers Distribution.

Hellebuyck, Adam & Deimel, Laura. Rugby World Cup. 2019. (21st Century Skills Library: Global Citizens: Sports Ser.). (ENG., Illus.). 32p. (J). (gr. 4-7). pap. 14.21 *(978-1-5341-5037-9(4)*, 213455); lib. bdg. 32.07 *(978-1-5341-4751-5(9)*, 213454) Cherry Lake Publishing.

Jones, Emma. Girls Play Rugby, 1 vol. 2016. (Girls Join the Team Ser.). (ENG.). 24p. (J). (gr. 3-3). pap. 9.25 *(978-1-4994-2105-7(2)*, c7cc3f2a-c144-4018-87f4-9e3dee51f4b2, PowerKids Pr.) Rosen Publishing Group, Inc., The.

Jones, Simon. Know the Game: Complete Skills: Rugby. 2015. (Know the Game Ser.). (ENG., Illus.). 64p. (J). pap. 12.00 *(978-1-4729-1960-1(2)*, 900150949, Bloomsbury Sport) Bloomsbury Publishing USA.

Purslow, Frances. For the Love of Rugby. 2006. (For the Love of Sports Ser.). (Illus.). 24p. (J). (gr. 3-7). lib. bdg. 24.45 *(978-1-59036-380-5(9))*; per. 8.95 *(978-1-59036-381-2(7))* Weigl Pubs., Inc.

—Rugby. (For the Love of Sports Ser.). (J). 2019. (ENG., Illus.). 24p. (gr. 3-6). pap. 12.95 *(978-1-7911-0572-3(6))* 2019. (ENG., Illus.). 24p. (gr. 3-6). lib. bdg. 28.55 *(978-1-7911-0017-9(1))* 2013. *(978-1-62127-318-9(0))* 2013. pap. *(978-1-62127-323-3(7))* Weigl Pubs., Inc.

Superstars of Pro Football, 27 vols., Set. Incl. Antonio Gates. Kimmich, Ian. (Illus.). (YA). (gr. 7-12). 2009. lib. bdg. 22.95 *(978-1-4222-0553-2(3))*; Asante Samuel. Mooney, Carla. (Illus.). (YA). (gr. 7-12). 2009. lib. bdg. 22.95 *(978-1-4222-0542-6(8))*; Ben Roethlisberger. Heits, Rudolph T. (YA). (gr. 5-18). 2010. lib. bdg. 22.95 *(978-1-4222-1664-4(0))*; Brett Favre. Lourdes-Pitt, H. H. (YA). (gr. 5-18). 2010. lib. bdg. 22.95 *(978-1-4222-1662-0(4))*; Brian Urlacher. Uschan, Michael V. (Illus.). (YA). (gr. 7-12). 2009. lib. bdg. 22.95 *(978-1-4222-0555-6(X))*; Brian Westbrook. Robson, David W. (Illus.). (J). (gr. 7-12). 2009. lib. bdg. 22.95 *(978-1-4222-0547-1(9))*; Chad Johnson. Angst, Frank. (Illus.). (YA). (gr. 5-18). 2009. lib. bdg. 22.95 *(978-1-4222-0556-3(8))*; Champ Bailey. Snow, D. C. (Illus.). (YA). (gr. 7-12). 2009. lib. bdg. 22.95 *(978-1-4222-0544-0(4))*; DeMarcus Ware. Heits, Rudolph T. (YA). (gr. 5-18). 2010. lib. bdg. 22.95 *(978-1-4222-1665-1(9))*; DeSean Jackson. Pulditor, Seth H. (YA). (gr. 5-18). 2010. lib. bdg. 22.95 *(978-1-4222-1663-7(2))*; Donovan McNabb. Chatlien, Michael. (Illus.). (YA). (gr. 7-12). 2009. lib. bdg. 22.95 *(978-1-4222-0559-4(2))*; Ed Reed. Gitlin, Martin. (Illus.). (YA). (gr. 7-12). 2009. lib. bdg. 22.95 *(978-1-4222-0558-7(4))*; Jason Witten. Heits, Rudolph T. (YA). (gr. 5-18). 2010. lib. bdg. 22.95 *(978-1-4222-1666-8(7))*; LaDanian Tomlinson. Lace, William W. (Illus.). (YA). (gr. 7-12). 2009. lib. bdg. 22.95 *(978-1-4222-0546-4(0))*; Manning Brothers. Marcovitz, Hal. (Illus.). (YA). (gr. 7-12). 2009. lib. bdg. 22.95 *(978-1-4222-0543-3(6)*, 1291172); Plaxico Burress. Grayson, Robert. (Illus.). (YA). (gr. 7-12). 2009. lib. bdg. 22.95 *(978-1-4222-0552-5(5))*; Randy Moss. Robson, David. (Illus.). (YA). (gr. 7-12). 2009. lib. bdg. 22.95 *(978-1-4222-0550-1(9))*; Tony Gonzalez. Hunter, Amy N. (Illus.). (YA). (gr. 7-12). 2009. lib. bdg. 22.95 *(978-1-4222-0541-9(X))*; 64p. 2011. Set lib. bdg. 619.65 *(978-1-4222-1660-6(8))* Mason Crest.

Thaiday, Sam. Rise: The Sam Thaiday Story. 2019. 192p. (J). (gr. 4-6). 17.95 *(978-0-14-379041-9(2)*, Puffin) Penguin Random Hse. AUS. Dist: Independent Pubs. Group.

Woods, Mark & Owen, Ruth. Scrum! 2010. (Top Score Maths Ser.). (Illus.). 32p. pap. *(978-0-237-54281-8(1))* Evans Brothers, Ltd.

RUGBY FOOTBALL—FICTION

BeKa. We'll Win with Big Class & Huge Style. 2008. (Rugger Boys Ser.: 2). (ENG., Illus.). 48p. pap. 11.95 *(978-1-905460-44-1(9))* CineBook GBR. Dist: National Bk. Network.

Dafydd, Myrddin ap. Brwydr y Brodyr. 2005. (WEL.). 68p. pap. *(978-0-86381-906-3(0))* Gwasg Carreg Gwalch.

Folau, Israel & Harding, David. Chance of a Lifetime & Reality Check: Izzy Folau Bindup 1. 2016. (Izzy Folau Ser.). (ENG., Illus.). 352p. (YA). (gr. 7-9). pap. 18.95 *(978-0-14-378092-2(1))* Random Hse. Australia AUS. Dist: Independent Pubs. Group.

Harding, David & Folau, Israel. Pushed to the Limit. 2016. (Izzy Folau Ser.: 3). (Illus.). 176p. (J). (gr. 4-7). pap. 9.99 *(978-0-85798-665-8(1))* Random Hse. Australia AUS. Dist: Independent Pubs. Group.

—Standing Tall. 2016. (Izzy Folau Ser.: 4). (Illus.). 176p. (J). (gr. 4-7). pap. 9.99 *(978-0-85798-667-2(8))* Random Hse. Australia AUS. Dist: Independent Pubs. Group.

Jackson, DeSean & Hoston, William T. No Bullies in the Huddle - Eagles. rev. ed. 2013. (ENG.). 32p. (C). 22.04 *(978-1-4652-4106-1(X)*, P695559) Kendall Hunt Publishing Co.

James, Mike. Bootsie - & the Team. 2012. 136p. pap. *(978-1-922022-14-1(4))* Vivid Publishing.

—Bootsie - Just One More. 2012. 136p. pap. *(978-1-922022-29-5(2))* Vivid Publishing.

Jones, Ceri Wyn. Ruck in the Muck. 2015. (ENG., Illus.). 32p. (J). pap. 8.95 *(978-1-78562-067-6(3))* Gomer Pr. GBR. Dist: Casemate Pubs. & Bk. Distributors, LLC.

K. Hall. The Adventures of Ranald the Rugby Player: The First Game. 2012. (Illus.). 28p. pap. 21.35 *(978-1-4685-8319-9(0))* AuthorHouse.

Oliver, Sarah. Be the Best. 2008. (Illus.). 104p. pap. 25.50 *(978-0-9559820-0-2(6))* Oliver, Sarah GBR. Dist: Lulu Pr., Inc.

Panckridge, Michael & Daley, Laurie. Live Action. 2007. (ENG.). 224p. *(978-0-207-20053-3(X))* HarperCollins Pubs. Australia.

Siggins, Gerard. Rugby Flyer: Haunting History, Thrilling Tries. 2016. (Rugby Spirit Ser.: 4). (ENG.). 176p. (J). 14.00 *(978-1-84717-819-0(7))* O'Brien Pr., Ltd., The IRL. Dist: Casemate Pubs. & Bk. Distributors, LLC.

—Rugby Heroes. 2018. (Rugby Spirit Ser.: 6). (ENG.). 208p. 14.00 *(978-1-84717-997-5(5))* O'Brien Pr., Ltd., The IRL. Dist: Casemate Pubs. & Bk. Distributors, LLC.

—Rugby Rebel. 2015. (Rugby Spirit Ser.: 3). (ENG.). 176p. (J). 14.00 *(978-1-84717-677-6(1))* O'Brien Pr., Ltd., The IRL. Dist: Casemate Pubs. & Bk. Distributors, LLC.

Smith, Andrew. Winger. Bosma, Sam, illus. (ENG.). (YA). (gr. 7). 2014. 464p. pap. 13.99 *(978-1-4424-4493-5(2))* 2013. 448p. 18.99 *(978-1-4424-4492-8(4))* Simon & Schuster Bks. For Young Readers. (Simon & Schuster Bks. For Young Readers).

Spencer, Adam. The Green Zone Kicker. 2011. (ENG.). 32p. pap. 14.99 *(978-1-105-22672-4(7))* Lulu Pr., Inc.

RUINS

see Extinct Cities

RULERS

see Kings, Queens, Rulers, etc.

RUMANIA

see Romania

RUNAWAYS

Bryfonski, Dedria, ed. Street Teens, 1 vol. 2011. (Opposing Viewpoints Ser.). (ENG., Illus.). 224p. (gr. 10-12). 50.43 *(978-0-7377-5761-3(2)*, 586d14ae-665f-4f8c-8012-c378487e5821); pap. 34.80 *(978-0-7377-5762-0(0)*, 0c0a19cb-c896-4850-a471-75c786dce71c) Greenhaven Publishing LLC. (Greenhaven Publishing).

Mills, Charles. Attack of the Angry Legend; Stranger in the Shadows; Planet of Joy. 2016. (J). *(978-0-8163-6158-8(4))* Pacific Pr. Publishing Assn.

RUNAWAYS—FICTION

Adams, W. Royce. Jay. 2005. viii, 115p. (YA). pap. *(978-1-58832-120-6(7))* Unlimited Publishing LLC.

Alcott, Louisa. Under the Lilacs. 2005. 28.95 *(978-1-4218-1487-2(0))*; 280p. pap. 13.95 *(978-1-4218-1587-9(7))* 1st World Publishing, Inc. (1st World Library - Literary Society).

—Under the Lilacs. 2012. (Applewood Bks.). (ENG., Illus.). 328p. (gr. 3-9). pap. 17.95 *(978-1-4290-9311-8(0))* Applewood Bks.

—Under the Lilacs. 2005. pap. *(978-1-4065-0105-6(0))* Dodo Pr.

—Under the Lilacs. 2013. (Works of Louisa May Alcott). 302p. reprint ed. lthr. 79.00 *(978-0-7812-1637-1(0))* Reprint Services Corp.

—Under the Lilacs. 2011. 226p. 26.95 *(978-1-4638-9588-4(7))* Rodgers, Alan Bks.

—Under the Lilacs. 2007. 316p. (gr. 4-7). 32.95 *(978-1-4344-8357-7(6))*; per. 19.95 *(978-1-4344-8356-0(8))* Wildside Pr., LLC.

Alderson, Sarah. Out of Control. 2015. (ENG., Illus.). 320p. (YA). (gr. 9). 17.99 *(978-1-4814-2716-6(4)*, Simon Pulse) Simon Pulse.

Alger, Horatio. Driven from Home: Carl Crawford's Experience. reprint ed. pap. 79.00 *(978-1-4047-3564-4(X))* Classic Textbooks.

—Driven from Home: Carl Crawford's Experience. 2006. pap. *(978-1-4065-0702-7(4))* Dodo Pr.

—Phil the Fiddler. 2006. pap. *(978-1-4068-0667-0(6))* Echo Library.

Allen, Elanna. Itsy Mitsy Runs Away. Allen, Elanna, illus. 2011. (ENG., Illus.). 40p. (J). (gr. -1-2). 16.99 *(978-1-4424-0671-1(2)*, Atheneum Bks. for Young Readers) Simon & Schuster Children's Publishing.

Almond, David. The Boy Who Swam with Piranhas. Jeffers, Oliver, illus. 2015. (ENG.). 256p. (J). (gr. 4-7). pap. 8.99 *(978-0-7636-7680-3(2))* Candlewick Pr.

Anderson, Max Elliot. Reckless Runaway. 2005. 160p. pap. 10.95 *(978-0-9752880-4-7(0))* Baker Trittin Pr.

Anthony, Dan. The Last Big One. 2018. (ENG.). 160p. (J). pap. 13.50 *(978-1-78562-259-5(5))* Gomer Pr. GBR. Dist: Casemate Pubs. & Bk. Distributors, LLC.

Arcos, Carrie. Out of Reach. (ENG., (YA). (gr. 9). 2013. Illus.). 272p. pap. 9.99 *(978-1-4424-4054-8(6))* 2012. 256p. 16.99 *(978-1-4424-4053-1(8))* Simon Pulse. (Simon Pulse).

Armistead, Cal. Being Henry David. (ENG.). 312p. (YA). (gr. 8-12). 2014. pap. 9.99 *(978-0-8075-0616-5(8)*, 807506168) 2013. 16.99 *(978-0-8075-0615-8(X)*, 080750615X) Whitman, Albert & Co.

Babiak, Alexandra Brittany. The Runaway Jacket, 1 vol. 2009. 40p. pap. 24.95 *(978-1-60749-332-7(2))* America Star Bks.

Bailey, Christine. Girl in the Middle. 2013. 236p. pap. 8.99 *(978-0-9890632-0-3(8))* Vinspire Publishing LLC.

Bare, Bart. Girl. 2010. 188p. (YA). pap. 11.95 *(978-0-9825396-4-4(9))* Canterbury Hse. Publishing, Ltd.

Barnholdt, Lauren. Right of Way. (ENG., Illus.). (YA). (gr. 9). 2014. 336p. pap. 9.99 *(978-1-4424-5128-5(9))* 2013. 320p. 16.99 *(978-1-4424-5127-8(0))* Simon Pulse. (Simon Pulse).

Barratt, Mark. The Wild Man. 2010. (ENG.). 352p. (J). (gr. 6-18). pap. 9.00 *(978-0-8028-5377-6(3)*, Eerdmans Bks For Young Readers) Eerdmans, William B. Publishing Co.

Beaufrand, Mary Jane. Primavera. 2009. (ENG.). 272p. (J). (gr. 7-17). pap. 15.99 *(978-0-316-01645-2(4))* Little, Brown Bks. for Young Readers.

Blair, Jamie. Leap of Faith. (ENG.). 240p. (YA). (gr. 9). 2014. pap. 11.99 *(978-1-4424-4716-5(8))* 2013. (Illus.). 16.99 *(978-1-4424-4713-4(3))* Simon & Schuster Bks. For Young Readers. (Simon & Schuster Bks. For Young Readers).

Blair, Katharyn. The Beckoning Shadow. 2019. (ENG.). 480p. (YA). (gr. 9). 17.99 *(978-0-06-265761-9(5)*, Tegen, Katherine Bks) HarperCollins Pubs.

Bledsoe, Lucy Jane. Running Wild. 2019. 224p. (YA). (gr. 4-7). 17.99 *(978-0-8234-4363-5(9)*, Margaret Ferguson Books) Holiday Hse., Inc.

Boyne, John. Noah Barleywater Runs Away. Jeffers, Oliver, illus. 2012. (ENG.). 240p. (J). (gr. 3-7). 7.99 *(978-0-385-75264-0(4)*, Yearling) Random Hse. Children's Bks.

—The Terrible Thing That Happened to Barnaby Brocket. Jeffers, Oliver, illus. 2014. (ENG.). 288p. (J). (gr. 3-7). 7.99 *(978-0-307-97765-6(X)*, Yearling) Random Hse. Children's Bks.

Brett, Jan. Home for Christmas. Brett, Jan, illus. 2011. (Illus.). 32p. (J). (gr. -1-k). 18.99 *(978-0-399-25653-0(9)*, G.P. Putnam's Sons Books for Young Readers) Penguin Young Readers Group.

Brewer, Janey. Mist & Moonlight. 2007. 76p. per. 19.95 *(978-1-4241-9525-1(X))* America Star Bks.

Broach, Elise. The Wolf Keepers. Ratterree, Alice, illus. 2018. (ENG.). 368p. (J). pap. 15.99 *(978-1-250-16501-5(6)*, 900186931) Square Fish.

Brown, Margaret Wise. El Conejito Andarín: The Runaway Bunny (Spanish Edition), 1 vol. Hurd, Clement, illus. 2006. (SPA.). 48p. (J). (gr. -1-3). pap. 8.99 *(978-0-06-077694-7(3))* HarperCollins Español.

—Goodnight Moon Classic Library: Contains Goodnight Moon, the Runaway Bunny, & My World. Hurd, Clement, illus. 2011. (ENG.). 32p. (J). (gr. -1-1). 17.99 *(978-0-06-199823-2(0)*, HarperCollins) HarperCollins Pubs.

—The Runaway Bunny. Hurd, Clement, illus. 2005. (ENG.). 48p. (J). (gr. -1 — 1). lib. bdg. 18.89 *(978-0-06-077583-4(1)*, HarperCollins) HarperCollins Pubs.

—The Runaway Bunny: An Easter & Springtime Book for Kids. Hurd, Clement, illus. 2017. (ENG.). 48p. (J). (gr. -1-3). 21.99 *(978-0-06-077582-7(3)*, HarperCollins) HarperCollins Pubs.

—The Runaway Bunny Padded Board Book: An Easter & Springtime Book for Kids. Hurd, Clement, illus. 2017. (ENG.). 36p. (J). (gr. -1 — 1). bds. 10.99 *(978-0-06-245959-6(7)*, HarperFestival) HarperCollins Pubs.

Brown, Margaret Wise & Marcus, Leonard S. The Runaway Bunny: a 75th Anniversary Retrospective: An Easter & Springtime Book for Kids. Hurd, Clement, illus. 2017. (ENG.). 64p. (J). (gr. -1-3). 19.99 *(978-0-06-248994-4(1)*, HarperCollins) HarperCollins Pubs.

Bruchac, Joseph. The Long Run. 2016. (PathFinders Ser.). (ENG.). 116p. (YA). (gr. 8-12). pap. 9.95 *(978-1-939053-09-1(9)*, 7th Generation) BPC.

Buske, Jody. Wilderness Awakening. 2006. 108p. pap. 19.95 *(978-1-4241-2685-9(1))* PublishAmerica, Inc.

Carbone, Elisa. Jump. 2011. (ENG.). 272p. (YA). (gr. 7-12). 24.94 *(978-0-670-01185-8(1))* Penguin Young Readers Group.

Carter, Alden R. Walkaway. 2008. (ENG.). 192p. (YA). (gr. 7-18). 16.95 *(978-0-8234-2106-0(6))* Holiday Hse., Inc.

Charles, Norma. The Girl in the Backseat. 2008. (ENG., Illus.). 184p. (YA). (gr. 7-18). per. *(978-1-55380-056-9(7))* Ronsdale Pr.

Christie, Ed. The Sweet Smell of Rotten Eggs: Volume Two, the Dude Ranch Rangers. 2009. 108p. pap. 10.95 *(978-1-4401-3764-8(1))* iUniverse, Inc.

Christopher, Matt. Dirt Bike Runaway. 2008. (New Matt Christopher Sports Library). 176p. (J). (gr. 4-6). lib. bdg. 26.60 *(978-1-59953-215-8(8))* Norwood Hse. Pr.

Cleary, Beverly. Runaway Ralph. (Mouse & the Motorcycle Ser.). 175p. (J). (gr. 3-5). pap. 4.50 *(978-0-8072-1394-0(2))*; pap. 4.95 *(978-0-8072-1477-0(9))* Random Hse. Audio Publishing Group. (Listening Library).

Cole, Brock. The Goats. 2003. 20.75 *(978-0-8446-7238-0(6))* Smith, Peter Pub., Inc.

Coley, Patrick. The Chronicles of Maxwell & His Runaways. 2012. 134p. 29.99 *(978-1-4797-0759-1(7))*; pap. 19.99 *(978-1-4797-0758-4(9))* Xlibris Corp.

Collier, James Lincoln. Me & Billy, 0 vols. unabr. ed. 2013. (ENG.). 194p. (J). (gr. 5-7). pap. 9.99 *(978-1-4778-1706-3(9)*, 9781477817063, Two Lions) Amazon Publishing.

Collins, David Paul. Shanghaied. 2011. (ENG.). 320p. 29.95 *(978-1-4620-3184-9(6))*; pap. 19.95 *(978-1-4620-3183-2(8))* iUniverse, Inc.

Collins, Pat Lowery. The Fattening Hut. 2005. (ENG.). 192p. (YA). (gr. 7). pap. 12.95 *(978-0-618-55209-2(X)*, 491911, Clarion Bks.) HarperCollins Pubs.

Conford, Ellen. To All My Fans, with Love, From Sylvie. 2013. (ENG.). 200p. (gr. 4). pap. 12.95 *(978-1-939601-01-8(0))* Ig Publishing, Inc.

Cornelia, Funke. The Thief Lord. 2004.Tr. of Herr der Diebe. 376p. (J). (gr. 5-18). pap. 44.00 incl. audio *(978-0-8072-2278-2(X)*, Listening Library) Random Hse. Audio Publishing Group.

—The Thief Lord. 2003.Tr. of Herr der Diebe. (gr. 3-6). 18.40 *(978-0-613-84572-4(2))* Turtleback.

Coville, Bruce. The Mischief Monster. Coville, Katherine, illus. 2008. (Moongobble & Me Ser.: Bk. 4). (ENG.). 80p. (J). (gr. 1-5). pap. 6.99 *(978-1-4169-0808-1(0)*, Aladdin) Simon & Schuster Children's Publishing.

—The Mischief Monster. Coville, Katherine, illus. 2007. (Moongobble & Me Ser.: Bk. 4). (ENG.). 80p. (J). (gr. 3-6). 16.19 *(978-1-4169-0807-4(2))* Simon & Schuster, Inc.

Curtis, Christopher Paul. Bud, Not Buddy. unabr. ed. 2004. 256p. (J). (gr. 4-7). pap. 36.00 incl. audio *(978-0-8072-8210-6(3)*, LYA 140 S{, Listening Library) Random Hse. Audio Publishing Group.

—Bud, Not Buddy: (Newbery Medal Winner) 2004. (ENG., Illus.). 288p. (J). (gr. 5-7). mass mkt. 8.99 *(978-0-553-49410-5(4)*, Laurel Leaf) Random Hse. Children's Bks.

Curtis, Christopher Paul & Jiménez Rioja, Alberto. Me Llamo Bud, No Buddy. 2016. (SPA.). 240p. (J). (gr. 5-12). pap. 12.99 *(978-1-63245-639-7(7))* Lectorum Pubns., Inc.

Cushman, Karen. Will Sparrow's Road. 2014. (ENG.). 224p. (J). (gr. 5-7). pap. 8.99 *(978-0-544-33632-2(1)*, 1584178, Clarion Bks.) HarperCollins Pubs.

Darrow, Sharon. Trash. 2006. (ENG.). 160p. (YA). (gr. 7-12). 16.99 *(978-0-7636-2624-2(4))* Candlewick Pr.

de Harven, Emile. Suivez la Piste. (FRE.). (YA). (gr. 9-12). pap., tchr.'s training gde. ed. 6.95 *(978-0-88436-342-2(2)*, 40811) EMC/Paradigm Publishing.

De La Peña, Matt. We Were Here. 2010. (ENG.). 368p. (YA). (gr. 8-12). lib. bdg. 26.19 *(978-0-385-90622-7(6))* Random House Publishing Group.

de la Peña, Matt. We Were Here. 2010. (ENG.). 384p. (YA). (gr. 9). pap. 11.99 *(978-0-385-73670-1(3)*, Ember) Random Hse. Children's Bks.

DeFelice, Cynthia. Wild Life. 2013. (ENG.). 208p. (J). (gr. 3-7). pap. 8.99 *(978-1-250-03407-6(8)*, 900120577) Square Fish.

Dembar Greene, Jacqueline. Walk till You Disappear. Sawyer, Odessa, illus. 2019. (ENG.). 208p. (J). (gr. 3-7). 12.99 *(978-1-5415-5722-2(0)*, bff435b6-3586-44fc-908e-e4371282a43d, Kar-Ben Publishing) Lerner Publishing Group.

DiCamillo, Kate. Beverly, Right Here. (ENG.). 256p. 2021. (J). (gr. 5). pap. 7.99 *(978-1-5362-1154-2(0))* 2019. (J). (gr. 5). 16.99 *(978-0-7636-9464-7(9))*3. 2021. (gr. 3-6). 22.44 *(978-1-5364-6764-2(2))* Candlewick Pr.

—Beverly, Right Here. 2019. (ENG.). 256p. lib. bdg. 18.80 *(978-1-6636-3120-6(4))* Perfection Learning Corp.

Dragonwagon, Crescent & Zindel, Paul. To Take a Dare. 2016. (ENG.). (YA). (gr. 7-12). pap. 9.99 *(978-1-63168-028-1(5))* Graymalkin Media.

Duggan, Matt. The Royal Woods. 2018. (ENG., Illus.). 158p. (J). (gr. 4-7). pap. *(978-0-9917115-7-4(2))* Duggan, Matt.

—The Royal Woods. 2010. (ENG., Illus.). 244p. (J). (gr. 4-7). pap. *(978-1-55470-060-8(4))* Me to We.

Duling, Astrid. The Guinea Pigs Twiggy & Molly. 2012. 134p. pap. *(978-3-8423-1287-6(3))* Books on Demand GmbH.

Dunnion, Kristyn. Missing Matthew, 1 vol. 2003. (ENG.). 112p. (J). (gr. 5-7). pap. 9.95 *(978-0-88995-278-2(7)*, c4de4660-fe9f-4547-bfe0-c42f1864668c) Red Deer Pr. CAN. Dist: Firefly Bks., Ltd.

Easton, Kelly. The Outlandish Adventures of Liberty Aimes. Swearingen, Greg, illus. 2011. 224p. (J). (ENG.). (gr. 4-6). lib. bdg. 21.19 *(978-0-375-93771-2(4)*, Lamb, Wendy Bks.); (gr. 3-7). pap. 6.99 *(978-0-375-83772-2(8)*, Yearling) Random Hse. Children's Bks.

Evans, Richard Paul. If Only. 2015. (ENG., Illus.). 288p. (YA). (gr. 9). pap. 12.99 *(978-1-4814-4853-6(6)*, Simon Pulse) Simon Pulse.

Everheart, Chris. Concrete Gallery. 2015. (Tartan House Ser.). (ENG.). 96p. (J). (gr. 3-6). *(978-1-63235-053-4(X)*, 11680, 12-Story Library) Bookstaves, LLC.

Fagan, Cary. Danny, Who Fell in a Hole, 1 vol. 2013. (ENG., Illus.). 96p. (J). 14.95 *(978-1-55498-311-7(8))* Groundwood Bks. CAN. Dist: Publishers Group West (PGW).

—Danny, Who Fell in a Hole. 2013. 84p. pap. *(978-1-4596-6456-2(6))* ReadHowYouWant.com, Ltd.

Fenn, Jennifer. Flight Risk: A Novel. 2017. (ENG.). 384p. (YA). 21.99 *(978-1-62672-760-1(0)*, 900172860) Roaring Brook Pr.

Flinn, Alex. Nothing to Lose. 2004. 288p. (J). 16.99 *(978-0-06-051750-2(6)*, HarperTeen) HarperCollins Pubs.

Foard, Sheila Wood. Harvey Girl. 2006. (ENG., Illus.). 176p. (J). (gr. 7-12). per. 18.95 *(978-0-89672-570-6(7)*, P171685) Texas Tech Univ. Pr.

Funke, Cornelia. The Thief Lord. Birmingham, Christian, illus. 2010.Tr. of Herr der Diebe. (ENG.). 368p. (J). (gr. 4-7). pap. 9.99 *(978-0-545-22770-4(4))* Scholastic, Inc.

Gabriel, Thora. Chessie Bligh & the Scroll of Andelthor. 2006. 284p. (J). 27.95 *(978-0-595-83579-9(1))* iUniverse, Inc.

Gemeinhart, Dan. The Honest Truth. 2015. (ENG.). 240p. (J). (gr. 3-7). pap. 8.99 *(978-0-545-66574-2(4)*, Scholastic Pr.) Scholastic, Inc.

—The Midnight Children. 2022. (ENG.). 352p. (J). 16.99 *(978-1-250-19672-9(8)*, 900194233, Holt, Henry & Co. Bks. For Young Readers) Holt, Henry & Co.

Gillman, Melanie. Stage Dreams. Gillman, Melanie, illus. 2019. (ENG., Illus.). 104p. (YA). (gr. 8-12). 29.32 *(978-1-5124-4000-3(0)*, 3f3783d0-fdab-4aa6-813e-16633529cda8, Graphic Universe™) Lerner Publishing Group.

Gonick, Larry. Kokopelli & Company in Attack of the Smart Pies. 2005. (ENG., Illus.). 192p. (J). 15.95 *(978-0-8126-2740-4(7))* Cricket Bks.

Goodale, E. B. Under the Lilacs. Goodale, E. B., illus. 2020. (ENG., Illus.). 32p. (J). (gr. -1-3). 17.99 *(978-0-358-15393-1(X)*, 1756213, Clarion Bks.) HarperCollins Pubs.

Grainger, A. J. The Sisterhood. 2019. (ENG., Illus.). 304p. (YA). (gr. 7). 18.99 *(978-1-4814-2906-1(X)*, Simon & Schuster Bks. For Young Readers) Simon & Schuster Bks. For Young Readers.

Grant, Vicki. No Te Vayas. 1 vol. 2011. (Spanish Soundings Ser.). (SPA.). 160p. (YA). (gr. 8-12). pap. 9.95 *(978-1-55469-970-4(3))* Orca Bk. Pubs. USA.

Griffin, Paul. Ten Mile River. 2011. (ENG.). 208p. (YA). (gr. 7-18). 7.99 *(978-0-14-241983-0(4)*, Speak) Penguin Young Readers Group.

The Guardians. 2014. (ENG., Illus.). 288p. (J). (gr. 4-8). pap. 7.99 *(978-1-4814-1834-8(3)*, Aladdin) Simon & Schuster Children's Publishing.

Guest, Jacqueline. At Risk. 1 vol. 2004. (Lorimer SideStreets Ser.). (ENG.). 192p. (YA). (gr. 9-12). 8.99 *(978-1-55028-846-9(6)*, a7832d31-abee-469d-a271-d933129b851b); 16.95 *(978-1-55028-847-6(4)*, 847) James Lorimer & Co. Ltd., Pubs. CAN. Dist: Lerner Publishing Group, Formac Lorimer Bks. Ltd.

Gunderson, Jessica. Snow White & the Seven Dwarfs: An Interactive Fairy Tale Adventure. Miramon, Sabrina, illus. 2017. (You Choose: Fractured Fairy Tales Ser.). (ENG.). 112p. (J). (gr. 3-7). pap. 6.95 *(978-1-5157-6951-4(8)*, 135423); lib. bdg. 32.65 *(978-1-5157-6943-9(7)*, 135417) Capstone. (Capstone Pr.).

Hardesty, Ann A. Lucy's Trials in the Black Hills. 2009. 104p. pap. 10.99 *(978-1-4490-5368-0(8))* AuthorHouse.

HardyThomas. The Mayor of Casterbridge Level 5 Upper-Intermediate. 2009. (Cambridge Experience Readers Ser.). (ENG.). 112p. pap. 14.75 *(978-84-8323-560-7(9))* Cambridge Univ. Pr.

Harmon, Michael. Skate. 2008. 256p. (YA). (gr. 9). per. 7.99 *(978-0-553-49510-2(0)*, Laurel Leaf) Random Hse. Children's Bks.

Harrison, Emma. Escaping Perfect. 2016. (ENG., Illus.). 336p. (YA). (gr. 9). 17.99 *(978-1-4814-4212-1(0)*, Simon Pulse) Simon Pulse.

—Finding What's Real. (ENG.). (YA). (gr. 9). 2018. 320p. pap. 11.99 *(978-1-4814-4216-9(3))* 2017. (Illus.). 304p. 17.99 *(978-1-4814-4215-2(5))* Simon Pulse. (Simon Pulse).

Hautman, Pete. Road Tripped. 2019. (ENG., Illus.). 336p. (YA). (gr. 7). 18.99 *(978-1-5344-0590-5(9)*, Simon & Schuster Bks. For Young Readers) Simon & Schuster Bks. For Young Readers.

Hill, Janet Muirhead. Kendall's Storm. Leonhard, Herb, illus. 2011. (J). pap. 12.00 *(978-0-9820893-0-9(9))* Raven Publishing Inc. of Montana.

—Kyleah's Tree. Leonhard, Herb, illus. 2011. (J). pap. 12.00 *(978-0-9827377-9-8(3))* Raven Publishing Inc. of Montana.

Hillert, Margaret. Little Runaway. 21st ed. 2016. (BeginningtoRead Ser.). (ENG., Illus.). 32p. (J). (gr. k-2). 22.60 *(978-1-59953-801-3(6))* Norwood Hse. Pr.

Hoffman, Alice. Indigo. 2003. (ENG.). 96p. (gr. 4-7). pap. 6.99 *(978-0-439-25636-0(4)*, Scholastic Paperbacks) Scholastic, Inc.

Holman, Marilyn Anne. On the Run. 2019. (Lorimer SideStreets Ser.). (ENG.). 192p. (YA). (gr. 9-12). lib. bdg. 27.99 *(978-1-4594-1401-3(2)*, 6020e84d-d0db-4038-b683-4bf4822af892); pap. 8.99 *(978-1-4594-1399-3(7)*, 46cb326b-c02a-44c8-b625-c89471b88c48) James Lorimer & Co. Ltd., Pubs. CAN. Dist: Lerner Publishing Group.

Hopkins, Ellen. Smoke. (ENG., Illus.). (YA). (gr. 9). 2015. 576p. pap. 14.99 *(978-1-4169-8329-3(5))* 2013. 560p. 21.99 *(978-1-4169-8328-6(7))* McElderry, Margaret K. Bks. (McElderry, Margaret K. Bks.).

Hubler, Marsha. Southern Belle's Special Gift. 1 vol., 3. 2009. (Keystone Stables Ser.). (ENG.). 128p. (J). pap. 7.99 *(978-0-310-71794-2(9))* Zonderkidz.

Hughes, Alison. Hit the Ground Running. 1 vol. 2017. (ENG.). 216p. (YA). (gr. 8-12). pap. 14.95 *(978-1-4598-1544-5(0))* Orca Bk. Pubs. USA.

Hughes, Susan. Camp Runaway. 1 vol. 2018. (ENG., Illus.). 21p. (J). pap. *(978-1-77654-245-1(2)*, Red Rocket Readers) Flying Start Bks.

Hutchinson, Shaun David. The Five Stages of Andrew Brawley. Larsen, Christine, illus. 2015. (ENG.). 304p. (YA). (gr. 7). 19.99 *(978-1-4814-0310-8(9)*, Simon Pulse) Simon Pulse.

Jackson, Louise A. Exiled! From Tragedy to Triumph on the Missouri Frontier. 2007. (Illus.). 235p. (YA). (gr. 7-9). per. 16.95 *(978-1-57168-948-1(6)*, Eakin Pr.) Eakin Pr.

Johnson, Angela. Bird. 2006. 133p. (gr. 3-7). 16.00 *(978-0-7569-6660-7(4))* Perfection Learning Corp.

Johnson, Terry Lynn. Falcon Wild. 2017. 176p. (J). (gr. 5). lib. bdg. 16.99 *(978-1-58089-788-4(6))* Charlesbridge Publishing, Inc.

Joyce, Melanie. Goldilocks. 2009. (Fairydust Fairytales Ser.). (ENG.). 5p. (J). (gr. -1-k). bds. 6.95 *(978-1-84696-962-1(X)*, TickTock Books) Octopus Publishing Group GBR. Dist: Independent Pubs. Group.

Juwell & Precious. Runaway. 2006. (Platinum Teen Ser.). 133p. (YA). (gr. 8-12). per. 6.99 *(978-0-9729325-6-1(9))* Precioustymes Entertainment, LLC.

Kapur, Sanjana. Ruckus on the Road. 2017. (ENG., Illus.). 208p. (J). pap. 9.99 *(978-0-14-333431-6(X)*, Puffin) Penguin Bks. India PVT, Ltd IND. Dist: Independent Pubs. Group.

Kaufman, Sashi. The Other Way Around. 2014. (ENG.). 288p. (YA). (gr. 8-12). 17.95 *(978-1-4677-0262-1(5))* Lerner Publishing Group.

Kehret, Peg. Runaway Twin. 2011. (ENG.). 208p. (J). (gr. 5-18). 8.99 *(978-0-14-241849-9(8)*, Puffin Books) Penguin Young Readers Group.

Kelly, Tom. Finn's Going. 2007. 278p. (J). (gr. 8-12). 16.99 *(978-0-06-121453-0(1)*, Greenwillow Bks.) HarperCollins Pubs.

Keplinger, Kody. Run. (ENG.). 304p. (YA). (gr. 9). 2017. pap. 10.99 *(978-0-545-83114-7(8)*, Scholastic Paperbacks) 2016. 17.99 *(978-0-545-83113-0(X)*, Scholastic Pr.) Scholastic, Inc.

Kern, Peggy. Little Peach. 2015. (ENG.). 208p. (YA). (gr. 9). 17.99 *(978-0-06-226695-8(0)*, Balzer & Bray) HarperCollins Pubs.

Keyes, Morgan. Darkbeast. 2012. (ENG.). 288p. (J). (gr. 5-9). 16.99 *(978-1-4424-4205-4(0)*, McElderry, Margaret K. Bks.) McElderry, Margaret K. Bks.

Labatt, Mary. Sam Finds a Monster. Sarrazin, Marisol, illus. 2003. (Kids Can Read Ser.). (ENG.). 32p. (J). (gr. k-1). 11.99 *(978-1-55337-352-0(9))* Kids Can Pr., Ltd. CAN. Dist: Hachette Bk. Group.

LaFleur, Suzanne. Counting to Perfect. 2018. (ENG.). 208p. (J). (gr. 3-7). 16.99 *(978-1-5247-7179-9(1))*; lib. bdg. 19.99 *(978-1-5247-7180-5(5))* Random Hse. Children's Bks. (Lamb, Wendy Bks.).

LaFleur, Suzanne M. Counting to Perfect. 2018. 197p. (J). pap. *(978-1-5247-7182-9(1)*, Delacorte Pr) Random House Publishing Group.

Lawrence, Iain. The Convicts. 2006. 15.10 *(978-0-7569-6901-1(8))* Random House Children's Books GBR. Dist: Perfection Learning Corp.

Lawson, Jessica. Waiting for Augusta. 2016. (ENG., Illus.). 336p. (J). (gr. 3-7). 17.99 *(978-1-4814-4839-0(0)*, Simon & Schuster Bks. For Young Readers) Simon & Schuster Bks. For Young Readers.

Layburn, Joe. Runaways. Williams, John, illus. 2014. (ENG.). 144p. (J). (gr. 4-7). pap. 8.95 *(978-1-84780-080-0(7)*, Frances Lincoln Children's Bks.) Quarto Publishing Group UK GBR. Dist: Hachette Bk. Group.

Lean, Sarah. A Hundred Horses. (ENG.). (J). (gr. 3-7). 2015. 240p. pap. 7.99 *(978-0-06-212230-8(4))* 2014. 224p. 16.99 *(978-0-06-212229-2(0))* HarperCollins Pubs. (Tegen, Katherine Bks).

Lee, Stacey. Under a Painted Sky. 2016. lib. bdg. 22.10 *(978-0-606-38391-2(3))* Turtleback.

Levin, Betty. Shoddy Cove. 2003. 208p. (J). (gr. 5-18). 15.99 *(978-0-06-052271-1(2))* HarperCollins Pubs.

Linka, Catherine. A Girl Called Fearless: A Novel. 2014. (Girl Called Fearless Ser.: 1). (ENG.). 368p. (YA). (gr. 7). 34.99 *(978-1-250-03929-3(0)*, 900123214, St. Martin's Griffin) St. Martin's Pr.

London, Alex. Proxy. 2014. 432p. (YA). (gr. 7). pap. 11.99 *(978-0-14-751133-1(X)*, Speak) Penguin Young Readers Group.

Lowry, Brigid. Guitar Highway Rose: A Novel. 2006. (ENG.). 208p. (YA). (gr. 8-12). reprint ed. pap. 18.99 *(978-0-312-34296-8(9)*, 900030465, St. Martin's Griffin) St. Martin's Pr.

Manning, Matthew K. Operation Runaway. Douglas, Allen, illus. 2018. (Drone Academy Ser.). (ENG.). 112p. (J). (gr. 4-8). lib. bdg. 27.32 *(978-1-4965-6073-5(6)*, 137495, Stone Arch Bks.) Capstone.

Martin, Ann M. & Godwin, Laura. The Runaway Dolls. Selznick, Brian, illus. 2010. (Doll People Ser.: 3). (ENG.). 352p. (J). (gr. 3-7). pap. 7.99 *(978-0-7868-5585-8(1))* Hyperion Pr.

—The Runaway Dolls. Selznick, Brian, illus. 2010. (Doll People Ser.: 3). (J). lib. bdg. 18.40 *(978-0-606-13987-8(7))* Turtleback.

Maruno, Jennifer. Totem. 0 vols. 2014. (ENG.). 168p. (YA). pap. 10.99 *(978-1-4597-1934-7(4)*, 9781459719347) Dundurn Pr. CAN. Dist: Publishers Group West (PGW).

Marvel, Saga, et al. Marvel Saga. 2009. (Astonishing X-Men Ser.). (Illus.). 152p. pap. 14.99 *(978-0-7851-3646-4(3))* Marvel Worldwide, Inc.

Mazer, Harry. Snow Bound. 144p. (YA). (gr. 7-18). pap. 4.99 *(978-0-8072-1367-4(5)*, Listening Library) Random Hse. Audio Publishing Group.

McDowell, Marilyn Taylor. Carolina Harmony. 2010. (ENG.). 336p. (J). (gr. 4-6). 22.44 *(978-0-440-42285-3(X))* Random House Publishing Group.

McKissack, Patricia. Away West. James, Gordon C., illus. 2006. (Scraps of Time Ser.). (ENG.). 144p. (J). (gr. 3-7). 7.99 *(978-0-14-240688-5(0)*, Puffin Books) Penguin Young Readers Group.

McNally, Janet. The Looking Glass. 2018. (ENG., Illus.). 336p. (YA). (gr. 8). 17.99 *(978-0-06-243627-6(9)*, HarperTeen) HarperCollins Pubs.

Michaelis, Antonia. The Secret of the Twelfth Continent. 2013. (ENG., Illus.). 288p. (J). (gr. 2-7). 14.95 *(978-1-62087-539-1(X)*, 620539, Sky Pony Pr.) Skyhorse Publishing Co., Inc.

Michaels, Rune. Fix Me. 2011. (ENG., Illus.). 160p. (YA). (gr. 9). 16.99 *(978-1-4169-5772-0(3)*, Atheneum Bks. for Young Readers) Simon & Schuster Children's Publishing.

Mobley, Jeannie. Bobby Lee Claremont & the Criminal Element. 2017. (ENG., Illus.). 246p. (J). (gr. 3-7). 16.95 *(978-0-8234-3781-8(7))* Holiday Hse., Inc.

Myers, Bill. The Enemy Closes In. 1 vol., 2. 2009. (Elijah Project Ser.). (ENG.). 128p. (J). (gr. 4-7). pap. 6.99 *(978-0-310-71194-0(0))* Zonderkidz.

Niner, Holly L. The Day I Ran Away. Ongaro, Isabella, illus. 2017. (ENG.). 32p. (J). (gr. k-2). 17.95 *(978-1-936261-89-5(8))* Flashlight Pr.

Novak, Ali. Paper Hearts. 2017. (Heartbreak Chronicles Ser.: 2). 400p. (YA). (gr. 8-12). pap. 10.99 *(978-1-4926-5336-3(5))* Sourcebooks, Inc.

Novel Units. Runaway Ralph Novel Units Teacher Guide. 2019. (ENG.). (J). pap. 12.99 *(978-1-56137-174-7(2)*, Novel Units, Inc.) Classroom Library Co.

Olson, Norah. Before Now. 2017. (ENG.). 208p. (YA). (gr. 9). 17.99 *(978-0-06-234707-7(1)*, Tegen, Katherine Bks) HarperCollins Pubs.

Ostow, Micol. Family. 2011. (ENG.). 384p. (YA). (gr. 9-12). 17.99 *(978-1-60684-155-6(6)*, 3cf413e9-28d9-4423-89bd-f642128d3c03, Carolrhoda Lab™) Lerner Publishing Group.

Otis, James. Toby Tyler, or Ten Weeks with a Circus. 2007. 100p. (gr. 4-7). per. *(978-1-4068-4370-5(9))* Echo Library.

Parry, Rosanne. Second Fiddle. 2012. 240p. (J). (gr. 3-7). 6.99 *(978-0-375-86166-6(1)*, Yearling) Random Hse. Children's Bks.

Patron, Susan. The Higher Power of Lucky. 2008. (JPN., Illus.). 215p. (J). *(978-4-7515-2209-7(4))* Asunaro Shobo.

—The Higher Power of Lucky. 2007. (CHI.). 224p. (J). (gr. 4-7). pap. *(978-957-570-888-7(1))* Eastern Publishing Co., Ltd., The.

—The Higher Power of Lucky. 2009. 9.00 *(978-0-7848-2460-3(6)*, Everbind) Marco Bk. Co.

—The Higher Power of Lucky. 2008. 17.00 *(978-1-60686-088-5(7))* Perfection Learning Corp.

—The Higher Power of Lucky. Phelan, Matt, illus. (ENG.). (J). (gr. 4-6). 2008. 160p. pap. 7.99 *(978-1-4169-7557-1(8)*, Atheneum Bks. for Young Readers) 2006. 144p. 19.99 *(978-1-4169-0194-5(9)*, Atheneum/Richard Jackson Bks.) Simon & Schuster Children's Publishing.

—The Higher Power of Lucky. 2008. lib. bdg. 18.40 *(978-0-606-08934-0(9))* Turtleback.

Patterson, James & Raymond, Emily. First Love. (ENG.). 2014. Illus.). 288p. 33.99 *(978-0-316-20704-1(7))* 2015. (Illus.). 336p. (gr. 10-17). pap. 9.99 *(978-0-316-20703-4(9))* 2014. 560p. pap. 16.00 *(978-1-4555-8501-4(7))* Little Brown & Co. (Jimmy Patterson).

—First Love. 2014. (YA). lib. bdg. 28.20 *(978-0-606-35894-1(3))* Turtleback.

Paul, Curtis Christopher. Bud, Not Buddy. 2014. (ENG.). 256p. (J). (gr. 12-12). 11.24 *(978-1-63245-063-0(1))* Lectorum Pubns., Inc.

Paulsen, Gary. The Beet Fields. 2011. (ENG.). 176p. (YA). (gr. 9). pap. 7.99 *(978-0-375-87305-8(8)*, Delacorte Bks. for Young Readers) Random Hse. Children's Bks.

—Tasting the Thunder. 144p. (YA). *(978-0-330-32705-3(4)*, Pan) Pan Macmillan.

Pearson, Maggie. The Pop Star Pirates. 2015. (Race Further with Reading Ser.). (ENG., Illus.). 48p. (J). (gr. 3-3). *(978-0-7787-2089-8(6))* Crabtree Publishing Co.

Peretti, Frank E. Nightmare Academy. 2008. 352p. (YA). mass mkt. 7.99 *(978-1-4003-1017-3(2))* Nelson, Thomas Inc.

Philbrick, Rodman. Freak the Mighty (20th Anniversary Edition) 20th anniv. ed. 2013. (ENG.). 208p. (J). (gr. 3-7). 18.99 *(978-0-545-56645-2(2)*, Blue Sky Pr., The) Scholastic, Inc.

Posesorski, Sherie. Escape Plans. Pearcey, Dawn, illus. 2005. 272p. (J). (gr. 5). 8.95 *(978-1-55050-177-3(1))* Coteau Bks. CAN. Dist: Fitzhenry & Whiteside, Ltd.

Poulsen, David A. Last Sam's Cage. rev. ed. 2004. (ENG.). 224p. (YA). pap. 9.95 *(978-1-55263-611-4(9))* Keyhole Pr.

—Last Sam's Cage. rev. ed. 2008. (ENG.). 222p. (YA). (gr. 9-18). per. *(978-1-55263-953-5(3))* Me to We.

—Last Sam's Cage. 2018. (ENG., Illus.). 232p. (J). pap. 11.99 *(978-0-9959708-0-9(7))* Red Hawk Bks.

Preble, Joy. Finding Paris. 2015. (ENG.). 272p. (YA). (gr. 9). 17.99 *(978-0-06-232130-5(7)*, Balzer & Bray) HarperCollins Pubs.

Ramadurai, Suchitra. The Runaway Peppercorn. Rajagopalan, Ashok, illus. 2005. 28p. (J). *(978-81-8146-119-3(3))* Tulika Pubs.

Rapp, Adam. Punkzilla. (ENG., Illus.). 256p. (YA). (gr. 9). 2010. pap. 7.99 *(978-0-7636-5297-5(0))* 2009. 16.99 *(978-0-7636-3031-7(4))* Candlewick Pr.

Rice, Luanne. The Beautiful Lost. (ENG.). 304p. (YA). (gr. 7-7). 2019. pap. 9.99 *(978-1-338-31631-5(1))* 2017. 18.99 *(978-1-338-11107-1(8))* Scholastic, Inc.

Richtel, Matt. Runaway Booger. Wildish, Lee, illus. 2017. (ENG.). 32p. (J). (gr. -1-3). 14.99 *(978-0-06-234984-2(8)*, HarperCollins) HarperCollins Pubs.

Ripley, T. P. Lily Lovebug & the Unconquered Planet. 2013. 170p. pap. *(978-1-908910-43-1(7))* Crooked Cat Publishing.

Robbins, Trina. The Bark in Space: Book 5, No. 5. Page, Tyler, illus. 2013. (Chicagoland Detective Agency Ser.: 5). (ENG.). 64p. (J). (gr. 4-8). pap. 6.95 *(978-1-4677-0725-1(2)*, 659d0711-80dc-41a4-866d-7c460cfaabf5, Graphic Universe™) Lerner Publishing Group.

Robinson, Anitha. Broken Worlds. 2014. (Broken Worlds Ser.). (ENG.). 200p. (YA). (gr. 7-11). pap. 8.95 *(978-1-933767-37-6(5))* CBAY Bks.

Rose, Caroline Starr. Jasper & the Riddle of Riley's Mine. 2017. (Illus.). 304p. (J). (gr. 5). 16.99 *(978-0-399-16811-6(7)*, G.P. Putnam's Sons Books for Young Readers) Penguin Young Readers Group.

Ross, Elizabeth. Belle Epoque. 2014. (ENG.). 352p. (YA). (gr. 7). pap. 13.99 *(978-0-385-74147-7(2)*, Ember) Random Hse. Children's Bks.

Runaway Pony (revised) 2017. (Sandy Lane Stables Ser.). (ENG.). (J). pap. 5.99 *(978-0-7945-3622-0(0)*, Usborne) EDC Publishing.

Rush, Jennifer. Altered. 2013. (Altered Ser.: 1). (ENG.). 352p. (YA). (gr. 7-17). pap. 10.00 *(978-0-316-19709-0(2))* Little, Brown Bks. for Young Readers.

Saldaña, Jr. A Good Long Way. 2010. 128p. (J). (gr. 6-18). pap. 10.95 *(978-1-55885-607-3(2)*, Piñata Books) Arte Publico Pr.

Sanchez, Priscilla. Champ the Boxing Boxer. 2011. 12p. pap. 8.32 *(978-1-4634-7423-2(7))* AuthorHouse.

Scaletta, Kurtis. The Tanglewood Terror. 2012. (ENG.). 272p. (J). (gr. 4-6). lib. bdg. 18.69 *(978-0-375-96758-0(3)*, Knopf Bks. for Young Readers) Random Hse. Children's Bks.

Scanlon, Liz Garton. The Great Good Summer. 2015. (ENG., Illus.). 224p. (J). (gr. 3-7). 16.99 *(978-1-4814-1147-9(0)*, Beach Lane Bks.) Beach Lane Bks.

Schwabach, Karen. The Storm Before Atlanta. 2011. 320p. (J). (gr. 3-7). pap. 7.99 *(978-0-375-85867-3(9)*, Yearling) Random Hse. Children's Bks.

Seldon, Bonnie Bale. The Adventures of Trevor & the Tiger. 2012. 104p. 21.79 *(978-1-4669-4389-6(0))*; pap. 11.79 *(978-1-4669-4391-9(2))* Trafford Publishing.

Selznick, Brian. Wonderstruck. 1 vol. Selznick, Brian, illus. 2011. (ENG., Illus.). 640p. (J). (gr. 4-7). 29.99 *(978-0-545-02789-2(6)*, Scholastic Pr.) Scholastic, Inc.

Shaw, Tucker. Oh Yeah, Audrey! 2014. (ENG., Illus.). 256p. (YA). (gr. 8-17). 16.95 *(978-1-4197-1223-4(3)*, 1077501, Amulet Bks.) Abrams, Inc.

Shepherd, Lee Walker. Gingerhaus & the Runaway Gingerboy. 2007. (Illus.). 32p. (J). spiral bd. 19.99 *(978-0-9758995-1-9(1))* Indigo, LLC.

Snyder, Zilpha Keatley. William S. & the Great Escape. (ENG.). (J). (gr. 3-7). 2010. 240p. pap. 8.99 *(978-1-4169-6764-4(8))* 2009. 224p. 16.99 *(978-1-4169-6763-7(X))* Simon & Schuster Children's Publishing. (Atheneum Bks. for Young Readers).

Sommer, Carl. Hopeless to Hopeful. Vignolo, Enrique, illus. 2009. (Quest for Success Ser.). (ENG.). 56p. (YA). pap. 4.95 *(978-1-57537-278-5(9))*; lib. bdg. 12.95 *(978-1-57537-253-2(3))* Advance Publishing, Inc.

—Miserable Millie. Vignolo, Enrique, illus. (J). 2014. pap. *(978-1-57537-960-9(0))* 2007. (ENG.). 48p. 16.95 incl. audio compact disk *(978-1-57537-521-2(4))* 2007. (ENG.). 48p. (gr. -1-3). 9.95 *(978-1-57537-022-4(0))* 2007. (ENG.). 48p. (gr. -1-3). lib. bdg. 16.95 *(978-1-57537-071-2(9))* Advance Publishing, Inc.

—Miserable Millie(La Pobrecita Mili) Vignolo, Enrique, illus. 2009. (Another Sommer-Time Story Bilingual Ser.). (SPA & ENG.). 48p. (J). lib. bdg. 16.95 *(978-1-57537-160-3(X))* Advance Publishing, Inc.

—The Runaway(La Escapada) Vignolo, Enrique, illus. 2009. (Quest for Success Bilingual Ser.). (SPA & ENG.). 104p. (YA). lib. bdg. 14.95 *(978-1-57537-234-1(7))* Advance Publishing, Inc.

Stark, Ulf. The Runaways. Crowther, Kitty, illus. 2019. (ENG.). 144p. (J). (gr. k-5). 17.99 *(978-1-77657-233-5(5)*, 3cfe6b1c-e95e-4cff-9856-b32da70acba2) Gecko Pr. NZL. Dist: Lerner Publishing Group.

Steinhöfel, Andreas. If My Moon Was Your Sun: With CD Audiobook & Music. Palmtag, Nele, illus. 2017. (ENG.). 80p. (gr. 8-12). 19.00 *(978-0-87486-079-5(2))* Plough Publishing Hse.

Stokes, K. Lynn. Clouded Visions. 2008. 208p. 24.95 *(978-0-595-51980-4(6))*; pap. 14.95 *(978-0-595-53217-9(9))* iUniverse, Inc.

Stretton, Hesba. Cassy. Hymper, W. & Stacey, W. S., illus. 2006. (Golden Inheritance Ser.: Vol. 9). 117p. (J). pap. *(978-0-921100-94-2(9))* Inheritance Pubns.

Teele, Elinor. The Mechanical Mind of John Coggin. 2016. (ENG., Illus.). 352p. (J). (gr. 3-7). 16.99 *(978-0-06-234510-3(9)*, Walden Pond Pr.) HarperCollins Pubs.

Thomas, Jacquelin. Split Ends. 2010. (ENG.). 231p. pap. 17.99 *(978-1-4165-9879-4(0))* Pocket Books.

Tocher, Timothy. Chief Sunrise, John McGraw, & Me. 2004. (ENG.). 168p. (J). (gr. 4-8). 16.95 *(978-0-8126-2711-4(3))* Cricket Bks.

Tsiang, Sarah Yi-Mei. Breathing Fire. 1 vol. 2014. (Orca Soundings Ser.). (ENG.). 144p. (YA). (gr. 8-12). pap. 9.95 *(978-1-4598-0565-1(8))* Orca Bk. Pubs. USA.

Twain, Mark, pseud. Tom Sawyer. 1 vol. Mullarkey, Lisa & McWilliam, Howard, illus. 2010. (Calico Illustrated Classics Ser.: No. 1). (ENG.). 112p. (J). (gr. 2-5). 38.50 *(978-1-60270-704-7(9)*, 3961, Calico Chapter Bks.) ABDO Publishing Co.

—Tom Sawyer. 2009. 196p. (gr. 4-7). pap. 12.99 *(978-1-934941-63-8(8))* Red & Black Pubs.

Ure, Jean. Gone Missing. 2007. (ENG., Illus.). 192p. (gr. 4-7). pap. 8.99 *(978-0-00-722459-3(1)*, HarperCollins Children's Bks.) HarperCollins Pubs. Ltd. GBR. Dist: HarperCollins Pubs.

VanArsdale, Anthony, illus. Journey on a Runaway Train. 2017. (Boxcar Children Great Adventure Ser.: 1). (ENG.). 160p. (J). (gr. 2-5). 6.99 *(978-0-8075-0696-7(6)*, 807506966); 12.99 *(978-0-8075-0695-0(8)*, 807506958) Random Hse. Children's Bks. (Random Hse. Bks. for Young Readers).

Venkatraman, Padma. The Bridge Home. 2019. 208p. (J). (gr. 5). 17.99 *(978-1-5247-3811-2(5)*, Nancy Paulsen Books) Penguin Young Readers Group.

Voigt, Cynthia. The Tale of Birle. 2015. (Tales of the Kingdom Ser.: 2). (ENG., Illus.). 416p. (YA). (gr. 7). 19.99 *(978-1-4424-8356-9(3)*, Atheneum Bks. for Young Readers) Simon & Schuster Children's Publishing.

Voss, Dawn. Avenging Aja. 2007. (ENG.). 52p. pap. 15.00 *(978-0-615-15324-7(0))* Voss, Dawn L.

Wallace, Brandon. The Journey Home. (Wilder Boys Ser.). (ENG., Illus.). 208p. (J). 2017. (gr. 4-8). pap. 8.99 *(978-1-4814-3266-5(4))* 2016. (gr. 3-7). 17.99 *(978-1-4814-3267-2(2))* Simon & Schuster Children's Publishing. (Aladdin).

—Wilder Boys. 2017. (Wilder Boys Ser.). (ENG.). 256p. (J). (gr. 4-8). pap. 8.99 *(978-1-4814-3263-4(X)*, Simon & Schuster/Paula Wiseman Bks.) Simon & Schuster/Paula Wiseman Bks.

Wang, Jack & Wang, Holman. Cozy Classics: the Adventures of Tom Sawyer: (Classic Literature for Children, Kids Story Books, Mark Twain Books) 2017. (Cozy Classics Ser.). (ENG., Illus.). 24p. (J). bds. 9.95 *(978-1-4521-5250-9(0))* Chronicle Bks. LLC.

Warner, Gertrude Chandler. Journey on a Runaway Train. 2017. (Boxcar Children Great Adventure Ser.: 1). (J). lib. bdg. 17.20 *(978-0-606-40315-3(9))* Turtleback.

Weinbrenner, Darlene. Hannah, Mable, & the Moving Van. 2007. 76p. per. 19.95 *(978-1-4241-6563-6(6))* America Star Bks.

Whelan, Gloria. Chu Ju's House. 2004. 240p. (J). (gr. 5-18). lib. bdg. 17.89 *(978-0-06-050725-1(X))* HarperCollins Pubs.

—Friend on Freedom River. Frankenhuyzen, Gijsbert van, illus. 2004. (Tales of Young Americans Ser.). (ENG.). 48p. (J). (gr. 1-4). 19.99 *(978-1-58536-222-6(0)*, 202052) Sleeping Bear Pr.

Willner-Pardo, Gina. Prettiest Doll. 2012. (ENG.). 240p. (J). (gr. 5-7). 16.99 *(978-0-547-68170-2(4)*, 1476079, Clarion Bks.) HarperCollins Pubs.

Wilson, Jacqueline. Cookie. Sharratt, Nick, illus. 2010. (ENG.). 352p. (J). (gr. 4-7). pap. 17.99 *(978-0-312-64290-7(3)*, 900068061) Square Fish.

Wissing, Caroline. Voiceless. 2012. (ENG.). 240p. (gr. 10-12). pap. 14.95 *(978-1-897235-98-0(4))* Thistledown Pr., Ltd. CAN. Dist: Univ. of Toronto Pr.

Withers, Pam. Camp Wild. 1 vol. 2006. (Orca Currents Ser.). (ENG.). 112p. (J). (gr. 4-7). 14.95 *(978-1-55143-557-2(8))* Orca Bk. Pubs. USA.

—Camp Wild. 2006. (Orca Currents Ser.). 104p. (gr. 5-9). lib. bdg. 19.95 *(978-0-7569-6878-6(X))* Perfection Learning Corp.

Woods, Matilda. The Boy, the Bird & the Coffin Maker. Allepuz, Anuska, illus. 2019. (ENG.). 208p. (J). (gr. 3-7). 7.99 *(978-0-525-51523-4(2)*, Puffin Books) Penguin Young Readers Group.

Woodson, Jacqueline. Beneath a Meth Moon. (ENG.). (YA). (gr. 7). 2013. 240p. pap. 9.99 *(978-0-14-242392-9(0)*, Penguin Books) 2012. 144p. 16.99 *(978-0-399-25250-1(9)*, Nancy Paulsen Books) Penguin Young Readers Group.

—Beneath a Meth Moon: An Elegy. 2013. lib. bdg. 19.65 *(978-0-606-30566-2(1))* Turtleback.

Wright, Richard. Rite of Passage. 2014. (Trophy Bk Ser.). (ENG.). 160p. (J). (gr. 8-12). 13.24 *(978-1-63245-325-9(8))* Lectorum Pubns., Inc.

P Q R

Wynne-Jones, Tim. Blink & Caution. 2012. (ENG., Illus.). 352p. (YA). (gr. 9). pap. 10.99 *(978-0-7636-5697-3(6))* Candlewick Pr.

—The Maestro. l.t. ed. 2013. 304p. pap. *(978-1-4596-6503-3(1))* ReadHowYouWant.com, Ltd.

Yee, Lisa. Absolutely Maybe. 2009. (ENG.). 288p. (J). (gr. 7-7). 16.99 *(978-0-439-83844-3(4),* Levine, Arthur A. Bks.) Scholastic, Inc.

RUNNING

see Track and Field

RURAL ARCHITECTURE

see Architecture, Domestic

RURAL LIFE—FICTION

Bragg, Lynn. A River Lost. 2009. (Act Ser.). (ENG., Illus.). 32p. (Orig.). (gr. 2-8). pap. 11.95 *(978-0-88839-383-8(0))* Hancock Hse. Pubs.

Chambers, Vickie. In the Silence of the Hills. Taylor, LaVonne, ed. (Illus.). (YA). (gr. 9-12). *(978-0-9627735-1-8(4))* Excellence Enterprises.

Fox, Gaines. Go Fly a Kite: A Juvenile Adventure Novel. 2008. 200p. pap. 24.95 *(978-1-60703-573-2(1))* America Star Bks.

Sarja, Jennifer. When Watute Wants Some Water. Phan, Henry et al, illus. 2005. 36p. (J). (gr. -1-3). 20.00 *(978-0-9773451-0-6(6))* Youth Inkwell Publishing.

Wright, Lloyd. Gramp's Variety of Stories. 2007. 200p. 24.95 *(978-0-595-71311-0(4));* per. 14.95 *(978-0-595-47731-9(3))* iUniverse, Inc.

RURAL SOCIOLOGY

see Sociology, Rural

RUSSELL, BILL, 1934-2022

Hayhurst, Chris. Bill Russell. 2009. (Basketball Hall of Famers Ser.). 112p. (gr. 5-8). 63.90 *(978-1-61511-530-3(7),* Rosen Reference) Rosen Publishing Group, Inc., The.

RUSSIA (FEDERATION)

see also Soviet Union, for works discussing the time period before the dissolution of the former Soviet Union; and Former Soviet Republics, for works discussing collecively the independent countries that emerged from the dissolution of the former Soviet Union.

Allen, John. Debates on the Soviet Union's Collapse. 2018. (Debating History Ser.). (ENG.). 80p. (YA). (gr. 6-12). 39.93 *(978-1-68282-375-0(X))* ReferencePoint Pr., Inc.

Beckman, Rosina, ed. The History of Russia from 1801 to the Present, 1 vol. 2018. (Societies & Cultures: Russia Ser.). (ENG.). 128p. (gr. 10-10). pap. 21.60 *(978-1-5383-0387-0(6),* 62826d91-222f-44e0-8762-67afe11af4ef, Britannica Educational Publishing) Rosen Publishing Group, Inc., The.

Beliaev, Edward & Buranbaeva, Oksana. Dagestan, 1 vol. 2006. (Cultures of the World (First Edition)(r) Ser.). (ENG., Illus.). 144p. (gr. 5-5). lib. bdg. 49.79 *(978-0-7614-2015-6(0),* f5b44c63-cdbf-4a5f-8329-445f11034fe1) Cavendish Square Publishing LLC.

Black, Angela, et al. Russia, 1 vol. 3rd rev. ed. 2015. (Cultures of the World (Third Edition)(r) Ser.). (ENG., Illus.). 144p. (gr. 5-5). 48.79 *(978-1-5026-0342-5(X),* bf71bbe4-de25-4222-aa08-5b07588237ab) Cavendish Square Publishing LLC.

Blake, Kevin. Russia. 2016. (Countries We Come From Ser.). (ENG., Illus.). 32p. (J). (gr. -1-3). 28.50 *(978-1-68402-056-0(5))* Bearport Publishing Co., Inc.

Blomquist, Christopher. A Primary Source Guide to Russia. (Countries of the World). 24p. (gr. 2-3). 2009. 42.50 *(978-1-61512-044-4(0))* 2004. (ENG., Illus.). (J). lib. bdg. 26.27 *(978-1-4042-2756-9(3),* 1abede21-a15b-446c-b4b0-dd1baa5f43df) Rosen Publishing Group, Inc., The. (PowerKids Pr.)

Bowden, Rob & Ransome, Galya. Focus on Russia, 1 vol. 2007. (World in Focus Ser.). (ENG.). 64p. (gr. 5-8). pap. 15.05 *(978-0-8368-6756-5(4),* 08099eec-ccc1-44d0-a501-c1edfd5b0ffc); (Illus.). lib. bdg. 36.67 *(978-0-8368-6749-7(1),* 8cbb32e3-b0ad-44c5-9f56-4bf84bd5975f) Stevens, Gareth Publishing LLLP. (Gareth Stevens Secondary Library).

Burton, Jesse. Living in ... Russia: Ready-To-Read Level 2. Woolley, Tom, illus. 2018. (Living In... Ser.). (ENG.). 32p. (J). (gr. k-2). 17.99 *(978-1-5344-1766-3(4));* pap. 4.99 *(978-1-5344-1765-6(6))* Simon Spotlight. (Simon Spotlight).

Centore, Michael. Russia, Vol. 12. 2015. (Major Nations in a Global World: Tradition, Culture, & Daily Life Ser.). 64p. (J). (gr. 7). 23.95 *(978-1-4222-3349-8(9))* Mason Crest.

Charting Russia's Future, 2 bks. 9th ed. 2005. 88p. (YA). pap. *(978-1-891306-81-5(2))* Choices Program, Brown Univ.

Clapper, Nikki Bruno. Let's Look at Russia. 2018. (Let's Look at Countries Ser.). (ENG., Illus.). 24p. (J). (gr. -1-2). lib. bdg. 27.32 *(978-1-5157-9918-4(2),* 136924, Capstone Pr.) Capstone.

De Capua, Sarah. Russia, 1 vol. 2005. (Discovering Cultures Ser.). (ENG., Illus.). 48p. (gr. 3-4). lib. bdg. 31.21 *(978-0-7614-1716-3(8),* efb7f146-8611-4d72-b969-7ca5afec50bd) Cavendish Square Publishing LLC.

Duling, Kaitlyn. Russia, 1 vol. 2018. (Exploring World Cultures (First Edition) Ser.). (ENG.). 32p. (J). (gr. 3-3). 31.64 *(978-1-5026-3810-6(X),* 328f9e76-b07a-4b8f-bb2c-85f623948bbd) Cavendish Square Publishing LLC.

Frederick, Shane. Alexander Ovechkin. 2015. (Hockey Superstars Ser.). (ENG., Illus.). 32p. (J). (gr. 3-9). lib. bdg. 28.65 *(978-1-4914-2141-3(X),* 127624) Capstone.

Ganeri, Anita. Journey Through: Russia. 2017. (Journey Through Ser.). (ENG., Illus.). 32p. (J). (gr. 4-6). 16.99 *(978-1-4451-5620-0(2),* Franklin Watts) Hachette Children's Group GBR. Dist: Hachette Bk. Group.

George, Enzo. Russia's City of the Dead. 2017. (Crypts, Tombs, & Secret Rooms Ser.). 48p. (gr. 4-5). pap. 84.30 *(978-1-5382-0644-7(7))* Stevens, Gareth Publishing LLLP.

Glaser, Jason. Maria Sharapova. 2009. (Sports Idols Ser.). 24p. (gr. 2-3). 42.50 *(978-1-60853-142-4(2),* PowerKids Pr.) Rosen Publishing Group, Inc., The.

Glencoe McGraw-Hill Staff. Exploring Our World - People, Places, & Cultures: Western Hemisphere, Europe, & Russia. 2007. (WORLD & ITS PEOPLE EASTERN Ser.). (ENG., Illus.). 59p. (gr. 6-9). per. 6.48 *(978-0-07-877728-8(3),* 0078777283) McGraw-Hill Higher Education.

Haugen, David M. & Musser, Susan, eds. Russia, 1 vol. 2013. (Opposing Viewpoints Ser.). (ENG.). 272p. (gr. 10-12). pap. 34.80 *(978-0-7377-6970-8(X),* 549ea1c3-1d2e-41ac-9619-dbdc914e5c19); lib. bdg. 50.43 *(978-0-7377-6969-2(6),* ee661011-aaad-4bd7-8c26-e76ba9b103be) Greenhaven Publishing LLC. (Greenhaven Publishing).

Hulick, Kathryn. My Teenage Life in Russia. 2017. (Customs & Cultures of the World Ser.: Vol. 12). (ENG., Illus.). 64p. (J). (gr. 7-12). 23.95 *(978-1-4222-3910-0(1))* Mason Crest.

Johnson, Robin. The Urals, 1 vol. 2011. (ENG., Illus.). 48p. (J). pap. *(978-0-7787-7571-3(2));* (gr. 4-7). lib. bdg. *(978-0-7787-7564-5(X))* Crabtree Publishing Co.

Kalman, Bobbie. Spotlight on Russia. 2010. (ENG.). 32p. (J). pap. *(978-0-7787-3486-4(2))* Crabtree Publishing Co.

Klepeis, Alicia. Explore Russia: 12 Key Facts. 2019. (Country Profiles Ser.). (ENG., Illus.). 32p. (J). (gr. 3-6). 9.95 *(978-1-63235-615-4(5),* 13964); lib. bdg. 32.80 *(978-1-63235-560-7(4),* 13955) Bookstaves, LLC. (12-Story Library).

Litvina, Aleksandra. Istoriia Staroi Kvartiry. 2017. (RUS.). 55p. *(978-5-91759-484-2(8))* Izdatel'skij Dom "Samokat".

Markle, Sandra. The Great Leopard Rescue: Saving the Amur Leopards. 2016. (Sandra Markle's Science Discoveries Ser.). (ENG., Illus.). 48p. (J). (gr. 4-6). 33.32 *(978-1-4677-9247-9(0),* 3561c0d3-eabe-4129-b277-24d7098ea0a8, Millbrook Pr.) Lerner Publishing Group.

Márquez, Herón. Russia in Pictures. 2nd ed. 2003. (Visual Geography Series, Second Ser.). (ENG., Illus.). 80p. (gr. 5-12). 31.93 *(978-0-8225-0937-0(7))* Lerner Publishing Group.

Marsh, Carole. Russia: The Great Bear & Its Dramatic History! 2009. (It's Your World Ser.). 48p. (J). (gr. 2-9). pap. 7.99 *(978-0-635-06809-5(5))* Gallopade International.

Marshall, Deb. Russia. 2017. (Illus.). 32p. (J). *(978-1-5105-0838-5(4))* SmartBook Media, Inc.

Marsico, Katie. It's Cool to Learn about Countries: Russia. 2010. (Explorer Library: Social Studies Explorer Ser.). (ENG., Illus.). 48p. (gr. 4-8). lib. bdg. 34.93 *(978-1-60279-831-1(1),* 200528) Cherry Lake Publishing.

Maynard, Charles W. The Ural Mountains, 1 vol. 2003. (Great Mountain Ranges of the World Ser.). (ENG., Illus.). 24p. (J). (gr. 3-3). lib. bdg. 26.27 *(978-0-8239-6699-8(2),* ff6e7413-7033-41e5-a17f-9e21a8c762d1, PowerKids Pr.) Rosen Publishing Group, Inc., The.

McGraw Hill. Exploring Our World: Western Hemisphere, Europe, & Russia, Europe & Russia, Student Edition. 2nd ed. 2007. (WORLD & ITS PEOPLE EASTERN Ser.). (ENG.). 600p. (gr. 6-9). 57.96 *(978-0-07-874580-5(2),* 0078745802) McGraw-Hill Education.

—Exploring Our World: Western Hemisphere, Europe, & Russia, Interactive Tutor Self-Assessment CD-ROM. 2007. (WORLD & ITS PEOPLE EASTERN Ser.). (ENG.). (gr. 6-9). cd-rom 120.64 *(978-0-07-879068-1(3),* 0078790683) McGraw-Hill Education.

—Exploring Our World: Western Hemisphere, Europe, & Russia, Spanish Reading Essentials & Note-Taking Guide Workbook. 2007. (WORLD & ITS PEOPLE EASTERN Ser.). (SPA., Illus.). 120p. (gr. 6-9). spiral bd. 6.60 *(978-0-07-878172-8(8),* 0078781728) McGraw-Hill Education.

—Exploring Our World, Western Hemisphere with Europe & Russia, Reading Essentials & Note-Taking Guide Workbook. 2007. (WORLD & ITS PEOPLE EASTERN Ser.). (ENG., Illus.). 120p. (gr. 6-9). spiral bd. 7.16 *(978-0-07-878170-4(1),* 0078781701) McGraw-Hill Education.

Mis, Melody S. How to Draw Russia's Sights & Symbols. 2009. (Kid's Guide to Drawing the Countries of the World Ser.). 48p. (gr. 4-4). 53.00 *(978-1-61511-124-4(7),* PowerKids Pr.) Rosen Publishing Group, Inc., The.

Moon, Walt K. Let's Explore Russia. 2017. (Bumba Books (r) — Let's Explore Countries Ser.). (ENG., Illus.). 24p. (J). (gr. -1-1). 26.65 *(978-1-5124-3009-7(9),* 92303b8f-c5ba-4f60-9ca8-8974a1c97b66); E-Book 39.99 *(978-1-5124-3743-0(3),* 9781512437430); E-Book 4.99 *(978-1-5124-3744-7(1),* 9781512437447); E-Book 39.99 *(978-1-5124-3012-7(9))* Lerner Publishing Group. (Lerner Pubns.).

Murdico, Suzanne J. Russia: A Primary Source Cultural Guide. (Primary Sources of World Cultures Ser.). 128p. (gr. 4-5). 2009. 79.90 *(978-1-60851-929-3(5))* 2004. (ENG., Illus.). (J). lib. bdg. 43.60 *(978-1-4042-2913-6(2),* d91eeddf-eafb-4836-881b-28ccf9b4fefe) Rosen Publishing Group, Inc., The.

Murray, Julie. Russia, 1 vol. 2013. (Explore the Countries Ser.). (ENG.). 40p. (J). (gr. 2-5). lib. bdg. 35.64 *(978-1-61783-817-0(9),* 6939, Big Buddy Bks.) ABDO Publishing Co.

National Geographic Learning. Reading Expeditions (World Studies: World Cultures): Europe & Russia: People & Places. 2007. (ENG., Illus.). 64p. (J). pap. 27.95 *(978-0-7922-4375-5(7))* CENGAGE Learning.

—Reading Expeditions (World Studies: World Regions): Europe & Russia: Geography & Environments. 2007. (ENG., Illus.). 64p. pap. 27.95 *(978-0-7922-4374-8(9))* CENGAGE Learning.

Nichols, Susan. Vladimir Putin: Russian Prime Minister & President, 1 vol. 2018. (Influential Lives Ser.). (ENG.). 128p. (gr. 7-7). 40.27 *(978-0-7660-9204-4(6),* b5217e73-6c68-4675-a98f-f5e80d656f48) Enslow Publishing, LLC.

Nickles, Greg. Russia: The Culture. 3rd rev. ed. 2008. (Lands, Peoples & Cultures Ser.). (ENG., Illus.). 32p. (J). (gr. 3-7). pap. *(978-0-7787-9672-5(8))* Crabtree Publishing Co.

—Russia: The Land. 3rd rev. ed. 2008. (Lands, Peoples & Cultures Ser.). (ENG., Illus.). 32p. (J). (gr. 3-7). pap. *(978-0-7787-9670-1(1))* Crabtree Publishing Co.

—Russia - The Land. 3rd rev. ed. 2008. (Lands, Peoples & Cultures Ser.). (ENG., Illus.). 32p. (J). (gr. 3-7). lib. bdg. *(978-0-7787-9302-1(8))* Crabtree Publishing Co.

—Russia - The People. 3rd rev. ed. 2008. (Lands, Peoples & Cultures Ser.). (ENG., Illus.). 32p. (J). (gr. 3-7). pap. *(978-0-7787-9671-8(X))* Crabtree Publishing Co.

Nickles, Greg & Kalman, Bobbie. Russia - The Culture. 3rd rev. ed. 2008. (Lands, Peoples & Cultures Ser.). (ENG., Illus.). 32p. (J). (gr. 3-7). lib. bdg. *(978-0-7787-9304-5(4))* Crabtree Publishing Co.

Nickles, Greg & Nickels, Greg. Russia: The People. 3rd rev. ed. 2008. (Lands, Peoples & Cultures Ser.). (ENG., Illus.). 32p. (J). (gr. 3-7). lib. bdg. *(978-0-7787-9303-8(6))* Crabtree Publishing Co.

Pelleschi, Andrea. Russia, 1 vol. 2013. (Countries of the World Set 2 Ser.). (ENG.). 144p. (YA). (gr. 6-12). lib. bdg. 42.79 *(978-1-61783-635-0(4),* 4894, Essential Library) ABDO Publishing Co.

Powell, Jillian. Descubramos Rusia (Looking at Russia), 1 vol. 2007. (Descubramos Países Del Mundo (Looking at Countries) Ser.). (SPA.). 32p. (gr. 2-4). pap. 11.50 *(978-0-8368-8194-3(X),* bfacb413-a8a8-48dd-8f9d-85b0da2fc51c); (Illus.). lib. bdg. 28.67 *(978-0-8368-8187-5(7),* 32569914-4d46-4a9a-97f7-8d890176c45f) Stevens, Gareth Publishing LLLP. (Gareth Stevens Learning Library).

—Looking at Russia, 1 vol. 2007. (Looking at Countries Ser.). (ENG.). 32p. (gr. 2-4). pap. 11.50 *(978-0-8368-8180-6(X),* 914f093d-fcb3-44ab-8cdc-f300a8050280); (Illus.). lib. bdg. 28.67 *(978-0-8368-8173-8(7),* 1b1c43c1-b323-4421-a9dd-77138aea4843) Stevens, Gareth Publishing LLLP. (Gareth Stevens Learning Library).

Ransome, Galya. Russia in Our World. 2010. (Countries in Our World Ser.). 32p. (gr. 4-7). lib. bdg. 31.35 *(978-1-59920-442-0(8))* Black Rabbit Bks.

Rechner, Amy. Russia. 2017. (Country Profiles Ser.). (ENG., Illus.). 32p. (J). (gr. 3-8). lib. bdg. 27.95 *(978-1-62617-686-7(8),* Blastoff! Discovery) Bellwether Media.

Reid, Sue. Spotlight on Russia: Band 18/Pearl (Collins Big Cat) 2016. (Collins Big Cat Ser.). (ENG.). 80p. (J). (gr. 5-6). pap. 12.99 *(978-0-00-816404-1(5))* HarperCollins Pubs. Ltd. GBR. Dist: Independent Pubs. Group.

Roland, James. Growing up in Russia. 2017. (ENG.). 80p. (YA). (gr. 5-12). *(978-1-68282-223-4(0))* ReferencePoint Pr., Inc.

Rosenberg, Aaron. Vladimir Putin: President of Russia. (Newsmakers Ser.). 112p. (gr. 9-10). 2009. 63.90 *(978-1-60851-136-5(7))* 2007. (ENG., Illus.). (YA). lib. bdg. 39.80 *(978-1-4042-1903-8(X),* 90db8c7b-879e-4e9c-8022-de6cf561dabe) Rosen Publishing Group, Inc., The.

Rothstein, Evelyn. Clara's Great War. Uhlig, Elizabeth, illus. 2011. 88p. (J). pap. 12.95 *(978-0-9815345-9-6(7))* Marble Hse. Editions.

Rozett, Louise. Ice Queen: Catherine the Great Seizes Power in Russia. 2011. (J). pap. *(978-0-545-32946-0(9))* Scholastic, Inc.

Savage, Jeff. Alex Ovechkin. 2011. (Amazing Athletes Set VIII Ser.). pap. 45.32 *(978-0-7613-8601-8(7));* (ENG.). 32p. (gr. 2-5). pap. 7.95 *(978-0-7613-7818-1(9))* Lerner Publishing Group.

—Maria Sharapova. 2008. pap. 40.95 *(978-0-8225-9489-5(7))* Lerner Publishing Group.

Sebastian, Emily, ed. The Culture of Russia, 1 vol. 2018. (Societies & Cultures: Russia Ser.). (ENG., Illus.). 128p. (J). (gr. 10-10). 39.00 *(978-1-5383-0176-0(8),* 4a583c23-ca3f-4428-99ea-1edb7e2be7fd, Britannica Educational Publishing) Rosen Publishing Group, Inc., The.

—The Geography of Russia, 1 vol. 2018. (Societies & Cultures: Russia Ser.). (ENG.). 128p. (gr. 10-10). lib. bdg. 39.00 *(978-1-5383-0179-1(2),* 3f3225c5-46d2-4153-bcfa-c18f0f1f5108, Britannica Educational Publishing) Rosen Publishing Group, Inc., The.

Senker, Cath. Russia, 1 vol. 2016. (Land & the People Ser.). (ENG.). 48p. (gr. 5-5). pap. 15.05 *(978-1-4824-5095-8(X),* 7df33a3a-03bc-4664-ad8d-1db730089976) Stevens, Gareth Publishing LLLP.

Sexton, Colleen & Bartell, Jim. Russia. 2010. (Exploring Countries Ser.). (ENG., Illus.). 32p. (J). (gr. 3-7). lib. bdg. 27.95 *(978-1-60014-488-2(8),* Blastoff! Readers) Bellwether Media.

Sheen, Barbara. Foods of Russia, 1 vol. 2006. (Taste of Culture Ser.). (ENG., Illus.). 64p. (gr. 3-6). lib. bdg. 32.08 *(978-0-7377-3538-3(4),* ea084e40-45d2-4974-8d9b-ee9cab0b26d4, KidHaven Publishing) Greenhaven Publishing LLC.

Snyder, Laurel. Swan: The Life & Dance of Anna Pavlova. Morstad, Julie, illus. 2015. (ENG.). 52p. (J). (gr. 1-4). 17.99 *(978-1-4521-1890-1(6))* Chronicle Bks. LLC.

Steele, Philip. Russia. 2015. (Emerging Nations Ser.). (ENG., Illus.). 48p. (J). (gr. 4-9). 37.10 *(978-1-59920-989-0(6))* Black Rabbit Bks.

Streissguth, Thomas. Russia. 2008. (Country Explorers Ser.). (Illus.). 48p. (J). (gr. 2-5). lib. bdg. 27.93 *(978-0-8225-8664-7(9))* Lerner Publishing Group.

Streissguth, Tom. Russia. 2008. pap. 40.95 *(978-0-8225-9307-2(6))* Lerner Publishing Group.

Suib, Stella. Inside Russia's SVR: The Foreign Intelligence Service. 2009. (Inside the World's Most Famous Intelligence Agencies Ser.). 64p. (gr. 5-5). 58.50 *(978-1-61513-572-1(3))* Rosen Publishing Group, Inc., The.

Thornton, Jeremy. Religious Intolerance: Jewish Immigrants Come to America (1881-1914) 2009. (Primary Sources of Immigration & Migration in America Ser.). 24p. (gr. 3-4). 42.50 *(978-1-60851-783-1(7),* PowerKids Pr.) Rosen Publishing Group, Inc., The.

Torchinskii, O. & Black, Angela. Russia, 1 vol. 2nd rev. ed. 2005. (Cultures of the World (Second Edition)(r) Ser.). (ENG., Illus.). 144p. (gr. 5-5). 49.79 *(978-0-7614-1849-8(0),* f1b3f4d6-2536-4582-bd68-6d8bfae23083) Cavendish Square Publishing LLC.

Trenton, Russell, ed. The Russian Revolution: The Fall of the Tsars & the Rise of Communism, 4 vols. 2015. (Age of Revolution Ser.). (ENG.). 168p. (YA). (gr. 9-10). 75.64 *(978-1-68048-033-7(2),* 2332bf48-1382-4be1-98cb-d7fe141c1cff, Britannica Educational Publishing) Rosen Publishing Group, Inc., The.

Vincent, Zu. Catherine the Great: Empress of Russia (a Wicked History) 2009. (Wicked History Ser.). (ENG.). 128p. (J). (gr. 6-6). pap. 5.95 *(978-0-531-20738-3(2),* Watts, Franklin) Scholastic Library Publishing.

Wiener, Gary. The United States & Russia: A Cold & Complex History, 1 vol. 2017. (World History Ser.). (ENG.). 104p. (YA). (gr. 7-7). 41.53 *(978-1-5345-6245-5(1),* af371576-2aaf-41b0-9a55-1f5f37f01755); pap. 20.99 *(978-1-5345-6311-7(3),* 93f27ef5-9b03-4420-972e-7f197abc7ec0) Greenhaven Publishing LLC. (Lucent Pr.).

Yomtov, Nelson & Rogers, Stillman. Russia. 2012. (ENG., Illus.). 144p. (J). lib. bdg. 40.00 *(978-0-531-27545-0(0))* Scholastic Library Publishing.

Zemlicka, Shannon. Colors of Russia. Reeves, Jeni, illus. (Colors of the World Ser.). 24p. (J). 2005. (gr. 3-6). lib. bdg. 19.93 *(978-1-57505-513-8(9))* 2003. (gr. 1-4). pap. 5.95 *(978-1-57505-564-0(3))* Lerner Publishing Group.

RUSSIA (FEDERATION)—COMMUNISM

see Communism—Soviet Union

RUSSIAN AMERICANS

Behnke, Alison. Russians in America. 2005. (In America Ser.). (ENG., Illus.). 80p. (gr. 5-8). lib. bdg. 27.93 *(978-0-8225-3954-4(3),* Lerner Pubns.) Lerner Publishing Group.

Bryan, Nichol. Russian Americans, 1 vol. 2004. (One Nation Set 2 Ser.). (ENG.). 32p. (gr. k-6). 27.07 *(978-1-59197-533-5(6),* Checkerboard Library) ABDO Publishing Co.

Marcovitz, Hal. Russian Americans. (Major American Immigration Ser.). (Illus.). 64p. (YA). 2010. (gr. 9-12). 22.95 *(978-1-4222-0617-1(3))* 2009. (gr. 9-12). 22.95 *(978-1-4222-0513-6(4))* 2007. (gr. 7-18). pap. 9.95 *(978-1-4222-0868-7(0))* Mason Crest.

Moreno, Barry. The Russian Americans. 2007. (Major American Immigration Ser.). (YA). pap. 9.95 *(978-1-4222-0684-3(X))* Mason Crest.

RUSSIAN AMERICANS—FICTION

Barbara, Cohen. Molly's Pilgrim. 97th rev. ed. 2014. (ENG.). 32p. (J). (gr. 1-5). 8.24 *(978-1-63245-244-3(8))* Lectorum Pubns., Inc.

Blume, Lesley M. M. The Rising Star of Rusty Nail. 2009. (ENG.). 288p. (J). (gr. 3-7). 7.99 *(978-0-440-42111-5(X),* Yearling) Random Hse. Children's Bks.

Brosgol, Vera. Anya's Ghost. Brosgol, Vera, illus. 2011. (ENG., Illus.). 224p. (YA). (gr. 7-12). 24.99 *(978-1-59643-713-5(8),* 900075181, First Second Bks.) Roaring Brook Pr.

Cohen, Barbara. Molly's Pilgrim. Bricking, Jennifer, illus. 2018. (ENG.). 48p. (J). (gr. 1-5). pap. 5.99 *(978-0-06-287094-0(7),* HarperCollins) HarperCollins Pubs.

—Molly's Pilgrim. 97th rev. ed. 2005. (ENG., Illus.). 32p. (J). (gr. 1-5). pap. 3.99 *(978-0-688-16280-1(0),* HarperCollins) HarperCollins Pubs. Ltd. GBR. Dist: HarperCollins Pubs.

—Molly's Pilgrim. (Literature to Go Ser.). pap., tchr. ed. incl. VHS *(978-0-7919-2685-7(0))* Phoenix Films & Video.

Crowder, Melanie. Audacity. 400p. (YA). (gr. 7). 2016. pap. 12.99 *(978-0-14-751249-9(2),* Speak) 2015. bds. 17.99 *(978-0-399-16899-4(0),* Philomel Bks.) Penguin Young Readers Group.

Devlin, Calla. Right Where You Left Me. 2017. (ENG., Illus.). 256p. (YA). (gr. 9). 17.99 *(978-1-4814-8699-6(3),* Atheneum Bks. for Young Readers) Simon & Schuster Children's Publishing.

Greenberger, Tehilla. Gifts to Treasure. Toron, Eli, illus. 2007. (Fun to Read Book). (ENG.). 224p. (J). per. 10.95 *(978-1-929628-32-2(3))* Hachai Publishing.

Hesse, Karen. Brooklyn Bridge: A Novel. Sheban, Chris, illus. 2011. (ENG.). 256p. (J). (gr. 6-8). pap. 11.99 *(978-0-312-67428-1(7),* 900072843) Square Fish.

Hill, Kirkpatrick. Dancing at the Odinochka. 2010. (ENG.). 272p. (J). (gr. 5-9). pap. 12.99 *(978-1-4424-1352-8(2),* McElderry, Margaret K. Bks.) McElderry, Margaret K. Bks.

Hyde, Heidi Smith. Pavel & the Tree Army. Vavouri, Elisa, illus. 2019. (ENG.). 32p. (J). (gr. k-3). 17.99 *(978-1-5124-4446-9(4),* 73217719-2ba5-49a0-995a-fcf9635f5470, Kar-Ben Publishing) Lerner Publishing Group.

Kiem, Elizabeth. Dancer, Daughter, Traitor, Spy. 2014. (Bolshoi Saga Ser.: 1). (Illus.). 304p. (YA). (gr. 9). pap. 10.99 *(978-1-61695-422-2(1),* Soho Teen) Soho Pr., Inc.

Weston Woods Staff, creator. Three Cheers for Catherine the Great. 2011. 18.95 *(978-0-439-80506-3(6))* Weston Woods Studios, Inc.

—Three Cheers for Catherine the Great! 2011. 38.75 *(978-0-439-78620-1(7))* Weston Woods Studios, Inc.

Wolfe, Laura E. Sasha & the Dragon. Malara, Nicholas, illus. l.t. ed. 2017. (ENG.). 32p. (J). 19.95 *(978-1-944967-27-7(3))* Ancient Faith Publishing.

RUSSIAN COMMUNISM

see Communism—Soviet Union

RUSSIAN LANGUAGE

Animals Habitats, 1 vol., 1. 2015. (Our Wonderful World Ser.). 8p. (J). (gr. 2-4). pap. 9.35 *(978-1-5081-1245-7(2),* fad4c3ba-e33b-4ff5-81b2-1f75d16a27ac, Rosen Classroom) Rosen Publishing Group, Inc., The.

Carole Marsh. From Russia with Love! Russian for Kids. 2004. (Little Linguist Ser.). 32p. (gr. 2-6). pap. 5.95 *(978-0-635-02433-6(0))* Gallopade International.

Cartwright, Stephen & Amery, Heather. First Thousand Words in Russian. 2004. (First Thousand Words Ser.). (RUS & ENG., Illus.). 64p. (J). (gr. -1-7). lib. bdg. 20.95 *(978-0-88110-574-2(0))* EDC Publishing.

Fedoruk, Dennis, prod. Bilingual Baby - Flashcard Set - Russian. 2013. (RUS.). (J). 7.99 *(978-1-892703-79-8(3))* Small Fry Beginnings.

Katz, Jill. My First Russian Phrases, 1 vol. TransPerfect, Inc., tr. Fabbri, Daniele, illus. 2012. (Speak Another Language! Ser.). (ENG.). 32p. (J). (gr. k-3). lib. bdg. 27.32 *(978-1-4048-7515-9(8),* 119612, Picture Window Bks.) Capstone.

Kudela, Katy R. My First Book of Russian Words, 1 vol. Translations.com Staff, tr. 2010. (Bilingual Picture Dictionaries Ser.). (MUL.). 32p. (J). (gr. -1-2). pap. 8.10 *(978-1-4296-6336-6(7),* 115536, Capstone Pr.) Capstone.

—My First Book of Russian Words. Translations.com, Inc., tr. 2010. (Bilingual Picture Dictionaries Ser.). (MUL.). 32p. (J). (gr. 1-2). pap. 48.60 *(978-1-4296-6463-9(0),* 16217, Capstone Pr.) Capstone.

Marsh, Carole. False Paw! French for Kids. Beard, Chad, ed. 2004. (Little Linguist Ser.). (Illus.). 32p. lib. bdg. 29.95 *(978-0-635-02438-1(1))* Gallopade International.

—From Russia with Love! Russian for Kids. Beard, Chad, ed. 2004. (Little Linguist Ser.). (Illus.). 32p. 29.95 *(978-0-635-02441-1(1))* Gallopade International.
Milet Publishing Staff. Animals - My First Bilingual Book, 60 vols. 2011. (My First Bilingual Book Ser.). (ENG., Illus.). 24p. (J). (gr. k — 1). bds. 8.99 *(978-1-84059-618-2(X))* Milet Publishing.
—Bilingual Visual Dictionary. 2011. (Milet Multimedia Ser.). (ENG & RUS., Illus.). 1p. (J). (gr. k-2). cd-rom 19.95 *(978-1-84059-590-1(6))* Milet Publishing.
—Fruit - My First Bilingual Book, 60 vols. 2011. (My First Bilingual Book Ser.). (ENG., Illus.). 24p. (J). (gr. k — 1). bds. 8.99 *(978-1-84059-634-2(1))* Milet Publishing.
—My Bilingual Book-Hearing (English-Russian). 1 vol. 2014. (My Bilingual Book Ser.). (ENG & RUS., Illus.). 24p. (J). (gr. -1-k). 9.95 *(978-1-84059-782-0(8))* Milet Publishing.
—My Bilingual Book-Sight (English-Russian), 1 vol. 2014. (My Bilingual Book Ser.). (ENG & RUS., Illus.). 24p. (J). (gr. -1-k). 9.95 *(978-1-84059-798-1(4))* Milet Publishing.
—My Bilingual Book-Smell (English-Russian), 1 vol. 2014. (My Bilingual Book Ser.). (ENG & RUS., Illus.). 24p. (J). (gr. -1-k). 9.95 *(978-1-84059-814-8(X))* Milet Publishing.
—My Bilingual Book-Taste (English-Russian), 1 vol. 2014. (My Bilingual Book Ser.). (ENG & RUS., Illus.). 24p. (J). (gr. -1-k). 9.95 *(978-1-84059-830-8(1))* Milet Publishing.
—My Bilingual Book-Touch (English-Russian), 1 vol. 2014. (My Bilingual Book Ser.). (ENG & RUS., Illus.). 24p. (J). (gr. -1-k). 9.95 *(978-1-84059-846-9(8))* Milet Publishing.
—My First Bilingual Book - Colors, 60 vols. 2011. (My First Bilingual Book Ser.). (ENG.). 24p. (J). (gr. k — 1). bds. 8.99 *(978-1-84059-603-8(1))* Milet Publishing.
—My First Bilingual Book - Vegetables, 1 vol. 2011. (My First Bilingual Book Ser.). (ENG., Illus.). 24p. (J). (gr. k — 1). bds. 8.99 *(978-1-84059-666-3(X))* Milet Publishing.
—My First Bilingual Book-Home (English-Russian), 1 vol. 2011. (My First Bilingual Book Ser.). (ENG., Illus.). 24p. (J). (gr. k — 1). bds. 8.99 *(978-1-84059-650-2(3))* Milet Publishing.
—My First Bilingual Book-Jobs (English-Russian), 1 vol. 2012. (My First Bilingual Book Ser.). (ENG., Illus.). 24p. (J). (gr. k — 1). bds. 7.99 *(978-1-84059-710-3(0))* Milet Publishing.
—My First Bilingual Book-Music (English-Russian), 1 vol. 2012. (My First Bilingual Book Ser.). (ENG., Illus.). 24p. (J). (gr. k — 1). bds. 7.99 *(978-1-84059-726-4(7))* Milet Publishing.
—My First Bilingual Book-Opposites (English-Russian), 1 vol. 2012. (My First Bilingual Book Ser.). (ENG., Illus.). 24p. (J). (gr. k — 1). bds. 7.99 *(978-1-84059-742-4(9))* Milet Publishing.
—My First Bilingual Book-Sports (English-Russian), 1 vol. 2012. (My First Bilingual Book Ser.). (ENG., Illus.). 24p. (J). (gr. k — 1). bds. 7.99 *(978-1-84059-758-5(5))* Milet Publishing.
The Rosetta Stone Language Library: Russian Level 1. 2005. (J). (gr. 1-18). cd-rom 209.00 *(978-1-883972-60-8(4))* Rosetta Stone Ltd.
The Rosetta Stone Language Library: Russian Level 2. 2005. (J). (gr. 1-18). cd-rom 239.00 *(978-1-883972-61-5(2))* Rosetta Stone Ltd.
Tcachenco, Natalya. The Best on the East Mystery & Adventures, Vol. 1. 2006th ed. 2005. Orig. Title: The best on the East. (Illus.). (J). 19.99 *(978-0-9754433-4-7(8))*, Language Transformer Bks.) Velichko, Vera.
Turhan, Sedat. New Bilingual Visual Dictionary (English-Russian), 1 vol. 2nd ed. 2017. (New Bilingual Visual Dictionary Ser.). (ENG., Illus.). 148p. (J). (gr. k-2). 19.95 *(978-1-78508-891-9(2))* Milet Publishing.
York, M. J. Learn Russian Words. Petelinsek, Kathleen, illus. 2014. (Foreign Language Basics Ser.). (ENG & RUS.). 24p. (J). (gr. 2-5). 32.79 *(978-1-62687-378-0(X)*, 207125) Child's World, Inc, The.

RUSSIAN SATELLITES
see Communist Countries

RUSSIANS—UNITED STATES
Parker, Lewis K. Russian Colonies in the Americas. 2009. (European Colonies in the Americas Ser.). 24p. (gr. 2-2). 42.50 *(978-1-61512-319-3(9))*, PowerKids Pr.) Rosen Publishing Group, Inc., The.

RUSSO-TURKISH WAR, 1853-1856
see Crimean War, 1853-1856

RUTH (BIBLICAL FIGURE)
Dorn, Owen A. Ruth: A Love Story. 2003. (God's People Ser.). (Illus.). pap. 6.99 *(978-0-8100-1348-3(7))* Northwestern Publishing Hse.
Frank, Penny. La Nueva Familia de Rut.Tr. of Ruth's New Family. (SPA.). (J). 1.99 *(978-1-56063-785-1(4)*, 490315) Editorial Unilit.
MacKenzie, Carine. Bible Heroes Ruth. 2013. (Bible Art Ser.). (ENG.). 16p. (J). act. bk. ed. 2.50 *(978-1-84550-092-4(X)*, e6255973-e907-4474-9cd1-8dae58e9bf21) Christian Focus Pubns. GBR. Dist: Baker & Taylor Publisher Services (BTPS).
MacLean, Ruth. The Happy Harvest: A Puzzle Book about Ruth. rev. ed. 2008. (Puzzle Ser.). (ENG.). 24p. (J). 4.99 *(978-1-84550-405-2(4)*, 18bf853b-1e68-43cb-8a43-55d487996d45) Christian Focus Pubns. GBR. Dist: Baker & Taylor Publisher Services (BTPS).
Sanders, Karen Nordberg. Ruth & Naomi. Rooney, Ronnie, illus. 2007. 16p. (J). (gr. k-4). 1.99 *(978-0-7586-1283-0(4))* Concordia Publishing Hse.
Schur, Maxine. The Story of Ruth. Connelly, Gwen, illus. 2005. (ENG.). 32p. (J). (gr. 2-4). lib. bdg. 16.95 *(978-1-58013-114-8(X)*, Kar-Ben Publishing) Lerner Publishing Group.
Zondervan, A. Ruth & Naomi, 1 vol. Miles, David, illus. 2015. (I Can Read! / Adventure Bible Ser.). (ENG.). 32p. (J). pap. 4.99 *(978-0-310-74650-8(7))* Zonderkidz.

RUTH (BIBLICAL FIGURE)—FICTION
Lundy, Charlotte. Thank You, Ruth & Naomi. Waldrep, Evelyn L., ed. Sagasti, Miriam, illus. 2004. 32p. (J). (gr. k-4). 15.95 *(978-0-9741817-0-7(6))* Bay Light Publishing.
Silverberg, Selma Kritzer. Naomi's Song. 2009. (ENG.). 142p. (gr. 7-18). pap. 19.95 *(978-0-8276-0886-3(1))* Jewish Pubn. Society.

RUTH, BABE, 1895-1948
Christopher, Matt. Babe Ruth. 2006. (Matt Christopher Legends in Sports Ser.). (Illus.). 91p. (gr. 3-7). 15.00 *(978-0-7569-6922-6(0))* Perfection Learning Corp.
Collins, Tracy Brown. Babe Ruth. (Baseball Superstars Ser.). (gr. 6-12). 2009. 128p. pap. 11.95 *(978-0-7910-9897-4(4))*, Checkmark Bks.) 2008. (ENG., Illus.). 122p. lib. bdg. 30.00 *(978-0-7910-9570-6(3)*, P145705, Facts On File) Infobase Holdings, Inc.
Holub, Joan. Who Was Babe Ruth? 2012. (Who Was... ? Ser.). lib. bdg. 16.00 *(978-0-606-23650-8(3))* Turtleback.
Holub, Joan & Who HQ. Who Was Babe Ruth? Hammond, Ted, illus. 2012. (Who Was? Ser.). 112p. (J). (gr. 3-7). pap. 6.99 *(978-0-448-45586-0(2)*, Penguin Workshop) Penguin Young Readers Group.
Levit, Joe. Babe Ruth: Super Slugger. 2020. (Epic Sports Bios (Lerner (tm) Sports) Ser.). (ENG., Illus.). 32p. (J). (gr. 2-5). 30.65 *(978-1-5415-9747-1(8)*, 356f1bee-8a7f-4e68-a799-9c2fcf7f2802); pap. 9.99 *(978-1-7284-1339-6(7)*, 828c0149-0390-4600-b23e-13a8557c31db) Lerner Publishing Group. (Lerner Pubns.).
Moss, Marissa. Mighty Jackie: The Strike-Out Queen. Payne, C. F., illus. 2004. (ENG.). 32p. (J). (gr. k-3). 18.99 *(978-0-689-86329-5(2)*, Simon & Schuster/Paula Wiseman Bks.) Simon & Schuster/Paula Wiseman Bks.
Murphy, Frank. Babe Ruth Saves Baseball! Walz, Richard, illus. 2005. (Step into Reading Ser.: Vol. 3). 48p. (J). (gr. k-3). pap. 5.99 *(978-0-375-83048-8(0)*, Random Hse. Bks. for Young Readers) Random Hse. Children's Bks.
—Babe Ruth Saves Baseball. Walz, Richard, illus. 2005. (Step into Reading Ser.). 46p. (gr. 1-3). 14.00 *(978-0-7569-5161-0(5))* Perfection Learning Corp.
Patrick, Jean L. S. The Baseball Adventure of Jackie Mitchell, Girl Pitcher vs. Babe Ruth. Hammond, Ted & Carbajal, Richard, illus. 2011. (History's Kid Heroes Ser.). 32p. pap. 51.02 *(978-0-7613-7635-4(6)*, Graphic Universe™) Lerner Publishing Group.
—The Baseball Adventure of Jackie Mitchell, Girl Pitcher vs. Babe Ruth. Carbajal, Richard & Hammond, Ted, illus. 2011. (History's Kid Heroes Ser.). (ENG.). 32p. (J). (gr. 3-5). pap. 8.99 *(978-0-7613-7072-7(2)*, 0eb1f305-1f7c-420f-894e-0428e7d89ce5, Graphic Universe™) Lerner Publishing Group.
—La Nina Que Poncho A Babe Ruth. Reeves, Jeni, illus. 2007. (Yo Solo - Historia (on My Own - History) Ser.). 48p. (J). (gr. 4-7). per. 6.95 *(978-0-8225-7788-1(7))* Lerner Publishing Group.
—La Niña Que Ponchó a Babe Ruth. Translations.com Staff, tr. from ENG. Reeves, Jeni, illus. 2007. (Yo Solo - Historia (on My Own - History) Ser.).Tr. of Girl Who Struck Out Babe Ruth. (SPA.). 48p. (gr. 2-4). lib. bdg. 25.26 *(978-0-8225-7785-0(2))* Lerner Publishing Group.
—La Nina Que Poncho a Babe Ruth; the Girl Who Struck Out Babe Ruth. 2008. pap. 40.95 *(978-0-8225-9725-4(X))* Lerner Publishing Group.
Saddleback Educational Publishing Staff, ed. Babe Ruth, 1 vol. unabr. ed. 2007. (Graphic Biographies Ser.). (ENG., Illus.). 25p. (YA). (gr. 4-12). pap. 9.75 *(978-1-59905-215-1(6))* Saddleback Educational Publishing, Inc.
Shaughnessy, Dan. The Legend of the Curse of the Bambino. Payne, C. F., illus. 2005. (ENG.). 32p. (J). (gr. k-3). 16.95 *(978-0-689-87235-8(6)*, Simon & Schuster/Paula Wiseman Bks.) Simon & Schuster/Paula Wiseman Bks.
Tavares, Matt. Becoming Babe Ruth. Tavares, Matt, illus. 2013. (ENG., Illus.). 40p. (J). (gr. k-3). 17.99 *(978-0-7636-5646-1(1))* Candlewick Pr.
Terrell, Brandon. Calling His Shot: Babe Ruth's Legendary Home Run. Garcia, Eduardo, illus. 2018. (Greatest Sports Moments Ser.). (ENG.). 32p. (J). (gr. 3-9). lib. bdg. 31.32 *(978-1-5435-2868-8(6)*, 138371, Capstone Pr.) Capstone.
Yomtov, Nel. The Bambino: The Story of Babe Ruth's Legendary 1927 Season, 1 vol. Foley, Tim, illus. 2010. (American Graphic Ser.). (ENG.). 32p. (J). (gr. 3-9). pap. 8.10 *(978-1-4296-6265-9(4)*, 115412); lib. bdg. 31.32 *(978-1-4296-5473-9(2)*, 113873) Capstone.
—The Bambino: The Story of Babe Ruth's Legendary 1927 Season. Foley, Tim, illus. 2010. (American Graphic Ser.). (ENG.). 32p. (J). (gr. 3-4). pap. 48.60 *(978-1-4296-6433-2(9)*, 16174, Capstone Pr.) Capstone.

RUTH, GEORGE HERMAN, 1895-1948
see Ruth, Babe, 1895-1948

S

SABBATH
Aroeste, Sarah. Buen Shabat, Shabbat Shalom. Rubio, Ayesha L., illus. 2020. (ENG.). 12p. (J). (gr. -1 — 1). bds. 6.99 *(978-1-5415-4246-4(0)*, 58146829-1d44-44bc-b74e-a1312f1f3b66, Kar-Ben Publishing) Lerner Publishing Group.
Berghard, Durga Yael. Around the World in One Shabbat: Jewish People Celebrate the Sabbath Together. 2011. (ENG., Illus.). 32p. (J). (gr. -1-1). 18.99 *(978-1-58023-433-7(X)*, e778832e-3e84-4c7c-81d1-35545ce7e0dd, Jewish Lights Publishing) LongHill Partners, Inc.
Bird, Rebecca. My Sunday Quiet Book. 2017. (ENG.). (J). pap. 39.99 *(978-1-4621-1936-3(0))* Cedar Fort, Inc./CFI Distribution.
Danis, Naomi. It's Tot Shabbat! Cohen, Tod, photos by. 2011. (ENG., Illus.). 24p. (J). (gr. -1-1). lib. bdg. 14.95 *(978-0-7613-4515-2(9)*, 970b354a-887f-4e69-9398-bfb309d3796f, Kar-Ben Publishing) Lerner Publishing Group.
Duncan, Aubrey. Understanding God's Sabbath: A Decision to Make. 2004. per. 12.95 *(978-0-9749490-0-0(0)*, 500) Advent Truth Ministries.
Ellingson, Jessica B. The Sacrament Is for Me. Jensen, Chase, illus. 2016. (ENG.). (J). (gr. k-3). 14.99 *(978-1-4621-1880-9(1))* Cedar Fort, Inc./CFI Distribution.
Galloway-Blake, Jacqueline. Mommy, Is Today Sabbath? 2012. (ENG., Illus.). 24p. pap. 13.95 *(978-1-57258-544-7(7))* TEACH Services, Inc.
Holdaway, Chelsea. The Sabbath Is a Special Day: A Sacrament Meeting Activity Book. 2017. (ENG.). (J). (gr. -1-k). pap. 5.99 *(978-1-4621-2105-2(5))* Cedar Fort, Inc./CFI Distribution.
Krinsky, Rivkah. Touch of Shabbat: A Touch & Feel Book. Becker, Boruch, illus. 2011. (J). bds. 9.95 *(978-0-8266-0019-6(0))* Kehot Pubn. Society.
Lieberman, Naomi. Shabbos, Shabbos I Love You. Rosenfeld, D. L., ed. Zmora, Avram, illus. 2013. (ENG.). 32p. (J). 11.99 *(978-1-929628-70-4(6))* Hachai Publishing.
Newman, Tracy. Shabbat Is Coming! Garofoli, Viviana, illus. 2014. (ENG.). 12p. (J). (gr. -1 — 1). 5.99 *(978-1-4677-1367-2(8)*, a7e30689-a62e-4613-a1d7-89e32ac57c49, Kar-Ben Publishing) Lerner Publishing Group.
Simon, Norma. Every Friday Night. Weiss, Harvey, illus. (Festival Series of Picture Storybooks). (J). (gr. -1). spiral bd. 4.50 *(978-0-8381-0708-9(7))* United Synagogue of America Bk. Service.
Sofer, Barbara. Ilan Ramon: Israel's First Astronaut. 2004. (General Jewish Interest Ser.). (J). pap. 6.95 *(978-0-929371-49-8(6))* Lerner Publishing Group.
—Shabbat Shalom: Israel's First Astronaut. 2004. (Illus.). 12p. (J). 16.95 *(978-0-930494-91-9(1)*, Kar-Ben Publishing) Lerner Publishing Group.

SABBATH—FICTION
Abramson, Susan & Dvorkin, Aaron. Who Hogged the Hallah? A Shabbat Shabang. 2008. (Illus.). 80p. (J). pap. 9.95 *(978-0-9659546-5-5(X))* Oak Leaf Systems.
Backenroth, Yehudis. More Adventures of PJ Pepperjay, 1 vol. Judowitz, Chani, illus. 2016. (ENG.). 96p. (J). *(978-1-4226-1688-8(6)*, ArtScroll Series) Mesorah Pubns., Ltd.
Barash, Chris. One Fine Shabbat. Mai-Wyss, Tatjana, illus. 2016. (ENG.). 12p. (J). (gr. -1 — 1). E-Book 23.99 *(978-1-4677-9614-9(X)*, Kar-Ben Publishing) Lerner Publishing Group.
—Wait It's Friday. Grove, Christine, illus. 2019. (ENG.). 24p. (J). 17.95 *(978-1-68115-542-5(7)*, 6bc32c17-0b30-46e6-8ae9-a0206e93bcfb, Apples & Honey Pr.) Behrman Hse., Inc.
Ben-Gur, Naomi. The Cricket & the Ant: A Shabbat Story. Kober, Shahar, illus. 2016. (ENG.). 32p. (J). (gr. -1-3). lib. bdg. 9.99 *(978-1-4677-8935-6(6)*, 845b798c-71eb-447a-93f8-674f67360bd4, Kar-Ben Publishing) Lerner Publishing Group.
Berman, Seryl. Around the Shabbos Table. Binus, Ari, illus. 2008. (ENG.). 40p. (J). (gr. -1-k). pap. 11.99 *(978-1-929628-44-5(7))* Hachai Publishing.
Cohen, Deborah Bodin. The Seventh Day. Hall, Melanie, illus. 2005. (ENG.). 24p. (J). (gr. -1-2). 16.95 *(978-0-929371-24-5(0)*, Kar-Ben Publishing) Lerner Publishing Group.
A Dinosaur Goes to Church. 2013. (ENG., Illus.). 32p. (J). 14.99 *(978-1-62108-423-5(X))* Covenant Communications, Inc.
Fabiyi, Jan Goldin. Where Shabbat Lives. Rubinroit, Sue, illus. 2008. (ENG.). 12p. (J). (gr. -1 — 1). bds. 5.95 *(978-0-8225-8946-4(X)*, 461e912a-547a-4d9c-8255-2c823b815bb4, Kar-Ben Publishing) Lerner Publishing Group.
Gehl, Laura. Koala Challah. Mola, Maria, illus. 2017. (ENG.). 24p. (J). (gr. -1-1). pap. 7.99 *(978-1-5124-2088-3(3)*, 26c316b4-e7ec-4d95-9055-b608e472f570, Kar-Ben Publishing) Lerner Publishing Group.
Gellman, Ellie B. Shai's Shabbat Walk. Conger, Holli, illus. 2014. (ENG.). 12p. (J). (gr. -1 — 1). bds. 5.95 *(978-1-4677-4949-7(4)*, 7f8f9e16-92c6-44c5-8d3c-44056cdf0745, Kar-Ben Publishing) Lerner Publishing Group.
Herman, Michael. The Cholent Brigade. Harmer, Sharon, illus. 2017. (ENG.). 24p. (J). (gr. -1-2). 17.99 *(978-1-5124-0844-7(1)*, b722c6c0-cad2-413d-b91b-0dc341c18f8f, Kar-Ben Publishing) Lerner Publishing Group.
—Under the Sabbath Lamp. Massari, Alida, illus. 2017. (ENG.). 32p. (J). (gr. -1-2). 17.99 *(978-1-5124-0841-6(7)*, 9b9c5015-2225-426f-b181-850a9deba823, Kar-Ben Publishing) Lerner Publishing Group.
Kimmelman, Leslie. The Shabbat Puppy, 0 vols. Zollars, Jaime, illus. 2012. (ENG.). 32p. (J). (gr. -1-1). 17.99 *(978-0-7614-6145-6(0)*, 9780761461456, Two Lions) Amazon Publishing.
Koffsky, Ann. Kayla & Kugel. 2015. (ENG., Illus.). 24p. (J). pap. 9.95 *(978-1-68115-502-9(8)*, 6e9b7a61-831d-4a0f-87db-ae2856f1147b) Behrman Hse., Inc.
—Shabbat Shalom, Hey! Koffsky, Ann, illus. 2015. (ENG., Illus.). 24p. (J). (gr. -1-k). lib. bdg. 9.99 *(978-1-4677-4917-6(6)*, d719be77-c753-4940-809e-dd42198c6358); E-Book 23.99 *(978-1-4677-6208-3(3))* Lerner Publishing Group. (Kar-Ben Publishing).
Koffsky, Ann D., illus. Kayla & Kugel. 2015. (J). *(978-0-87441-898-9(4))* Behrman Hse., Inc.
Levine, Anna. Jodie's Shabbat Surprise. Topaz, Ksenia, illus. 2015. (ENG.). 32p. (J). (gr. k-3). lib. bdg. 17.95 *(978-1-4677-3465-3(9)*, 6e98fe25-b7ef-417b-b29e-cbaacfbdc3bf); E-Book 27.99 *(978-1-4677-6204-5(0))* Lerner Publishing Group. (Kar-Ben Publishing).
MacLeod, Jennifer Tzivia. Clarence's Topsy-Turvy Shabbat. Poh, Jennie, illus. 2020. (ENG.). 24p. (J). (gr. -1-2). 17.99 *(978-1-5415-4242-6(8)*, a59457c9-b897-422f-8a06-ed82fd018826, Kar-Ben Publishing) Lerner Publishing Group.
Manushkin, Fran. Many Days, One Shabbat, 0 vols. Monescillo, Maria, illus. 2011. (ENG.). 24p. (J). (gr. -1-3). 12.99 *(978-0-7614-5965-1(0)*, 9780761459651, Two Lions) Amazon Publishing.
Marshall, Linda Elovitz. Shh ... Shh ... Shabbat. Golubeva, Evgenia, illus. 2016. (ENG.). 12p. (J). (gr. -1 — 1). bds. 5.99 *(978-1-4677-5873-4(6)*, 3ba0a891-35f6-4c89-9695-9ac65bea93f1); E-Book 23.99 *(978-1-4677-9615-6(8))* Lerner Publishing Group. (Kar-Ben Publishing).
McClain, Jennie. Monday I Was a Monkey: A "Tale" of Reverence. Eichelberger, Jennifer, illus. 2011. (J). *(978-1-60861-243-7(0))* Covenant Communications.
Meltzer, Amy. The Shabbat Princess. Avilés, Martha Graciela, illus. 2011. (ENG.). 32p. (J). (gr. -1-2). pap. 7.99 *(978-0-7613-5106-1(X)*, ee9de847-6e71-4330-9fe7-ddde39ce88ee, Kar-Ben Publishing) Lerner Publishing Group.
Newman, Tracy. Havdalah Is Coming! Garofoli, Viviana, illus. 2020. (ENG.). 12p. (J). (gr. -1 — 1). bds. 6.99 *(978-1-5415-2163-6(3)*, 701faafe-bdd8-4b76-b195-9290a39c1d77, Kar-Ben Publishing) Lerner Publishing Group.
—Shabbat Hiccups. Exelby, Ilana, illus. 2016. (ENG.). 32p. (J). (gr. -1-3). 16.99 *(978-0-8075-7312-9(4)*, 807573124) Whitman, Albert & Co.
Peer, H. Der Feyerdiger Shabes: An Emese Ertseylung. Kohen, Avigayil, illus. 2018. (YID.). 86p. (J). *(978-1-68091-256-2(9))* Kinder Shpiel USA, Inc.
Press, Judy. Bubbe's Got the Beat. Hall, Mary, illus. 2017. (ENG.). 12p. (J). (gr. -1 — 1). bds. 5.99 *(978-1-5124-4763-7(3)*, d4146f28-8c83-4401-8ded-078b05583b54, Kar-Ben Publishing) Lerner Publishing Group.
Rauchwerger, Diane Levin & Levin, Diane. Dinosaur on Shabbat. Wolff, Jason, illus. 2006. (ENG.). 24p. (J). (gr. -1-1). lib. bdg. 15.95 *(978-1-58013-159-9(X)*, Kar-Ben Publishing) Lerner Publishing Group.
Rosenberg, Madelyn. The Schmutzy Family. Meisel, Paul, illus. 2018. 32p. (J). (gr. -1-3). pap. 8.99 *(978-0-8234-4241-6(1))* Holiday Hse., Inc.
Rouss, Sylvia A. The Littlest Candlesticks. Hannon, Holly, illus. 2005. (Littlest Ser.). 32p. (J). 14.95 *(978-1-930143-48-7(6))*; pap. 9.95 *(978-1-930143-49-4(4))* Simcha Media Group. (Devora Publishing).
Silberman, Shoshana. A Family Haggadah II, Vol. 2. Kahn, Katherine Janus, illus. l.t. ed. 2003. 64p. (J). pap. 6.95 *(978-1-58013-014-1(3)*, Kar-Ben Publishing) Lerner Publishing Group.
Snyder, Laurel. Baxter, the Pig Who Wanted to Be Kosher. 2010. (J). pap. 2.46 *(978-1-58246-373-5(5)*, Tricycle Pr.) Ten Speed Pr.
Swartz, Daniel. Bim & Bom, 2nd Edition: A Shabbat Tale. Iwai, Melissa, illus. 2nd rev. ed. 2011. (ENG.). 24p. (J). (gr. -1-1). pap. 8.95 *(978-0-7613-6717-8(9)*, 17cb14e4-1645-4843-9309-9a4eabea2edc, Kar-Ben Publishing) Lerner Publishing Group.
Walker, Yonette. Soul Soup Sunday. 2012. 24p. pap. 15.99 *(978-1-4691-8226-1(2))* Xlibris Corp.
Wasserman, Mira. Too Much of a Good Thing. Carolan, Christine, illus. 2003. 32p. (J). (gr. -1-3). pap. 6.95 *(978-1-58013-066-0(6))*; (ENG.). 15.95 *(978-1-58013-082-0(8))* Lerner Publishing Group. (Kar-Ben Publishing).

SABOTAGE
Hoose, Phillip. The Boys Who Challenged Hitler: Knud Pedersen & the Churchill Club. 2015. (ENG., Illus.). 208p. (YA). (gr. 7-12). 19.99 *(978-0-374-30022-7(4)*, 900129106, Farrar, Straus & Giroux (BYR)) Farrar, Straus & Giroux.
Seiple, Samantha. Nazi Saboteurs: Hitler's Secret Attack on America. 2019. (Illus.). 206p. (J). pap. *(978-1-338-25919-3(9))* Scholastic, Inc.
—Nazi Saboteurs: Hitler's Secret Attack on America (Scholastic Focus) 2019. (ENG., Illus.). 224p. (YA). (gr. 7-7). 17.99 *(978-1-338-25914-8(8)*, Scholastic Nonfiction) Scholastic, Inc.

SABOTAGE—FICTION
Bailey, Kristin. Rise of the Arcane Fire. 2014. (Secret Order Ser.: 2). (ENG., Illus.). 464p. (YA). (gr. 9). 17.99 *(978-1-4424-6802-3(5)*, Simon Pulse) Simon Pulse.
Baker, Jennifer. The Lying Game. 2014. (ENG., Illus.). 192p. (YA). (gr. 7). pap. 13.99 *(978-1-4814-2878-1(0)*, Simon Pulse) Simon Pulse.
BookSource Staff, compiled by. Sports Sabotage. 2012. (Hardy Boys: Secret Files Ser.: 8). lib. bdg. 16.00 *(978-0-606-23673-7(2))* Turtleback.
Bossley, Michele Martin. Cracked, 1 vol. 2007. (Orca Currents Ser.). (ENG.). 128p. (J). (gr. 4-7). per. 9.95 *(978-1-55143-700-2(7))* Orca Bk. Pubs. USA.
—Tampered, 1 vol. 2013. (Orca Currents Ser.). (ENG.). 136p. (J). (gr. 4-7). pap. 9.95 *(978-1-4598-0356-5(6))* Orca Bk. Pubs. USA.
Brezenoff, Steve. Field Trip Mysteries: the Bowling Lane Without Any Strikes. Calo, Marcos, illus. 2013. (Field Trip Mysteries Ser.). (ENG.). 88p. (J). (gr. 2-3). pap. 35.70 *(978-1-4342-6231-8(6)*, 20036); (gr. 3-6). pap. 5.95 *(978-1-4342-6212-7(X)*, 123510); (gr. 3-6). lib. bdg. 25.32 *(978-1-4342-5979-0(X)*, 122936) Capstone. (Stone Arch Bks.).
Coman, Carolyn. The Memory Bank. Shepperson, Rob, illus. 2010. 263p. (J). pap. *(978-0-545-21067-6(4))*, Levine, Arthur A. Bks.) Scholastic, Inc.
Darlison, Aleesah. Willow's Victory. Brailsford, Jill, illus. 2017. (Unicorn Riders Ser.). (ENG.). 112p. (J). (gr. 3-5). pap. 5.95 *(978-1-4795-6557-3(1)*, 128547, Picture Window Bks.) Capstone.
Dixon, Franklin. Running on Fumes. 2005. 150p. (J). lib. bdg. 16.92 *(978-1-4242-0384-0(8))* Fitzgerald Bks.
Dixon, Franklin W. Peril at Granite Peak. 2014. (Hardy Boys Adventures Ser.: 5). (ENG., Illus.). 160p. (J). (gr. 3-7). pap. 7.99 *(978-1-4424-9395-7(X)*, Aladdin) Simon & Schuster Children's Publishing.
—The Race Is On. Burroughs, Scott, illus. 2015. (Hardy Boys: the Secret Files Ser.: 19). (ENG.). 96p. (J). (gr. 1-4). pap. 5.99 *(978-1-4814-2271-0(5)*, Aladdin) Simon & Schuster Children's Publishing.
—Sports Sabotage, 8. Burroughs, Scott, illus. 2012. (Hardy Boys: the Secret Files Ser.: 8). (ENG.). 112p. (J). (gr. 1-4). pap. 5.99 *(978-1-4424-2316-9(1)*, Aladdin) Simon & Schuster Children's Publishing.
Gurevich, Margaret. Hip-Hop Road Trip. Almon, Claire, illus. 2018. (Academy of Dance Ser.). (ENG.). 72p. (J). (gr. 3-6). lib. bdg. 25.32 *(978-1-4965-6204-3(6)*, 137813, Stone Arch Bks.) Capstone.

S

Hawking, Stephen & Hawking, Lucy. George & the Big Bang. Parsons, Garry, illus. (George's Secret Key Ser.). (ENG.). (J). (gr. 3-7). 2013. 304p. pap. 13.99 *(978-1-4424-4006-7(6))* 2012. 336p. 22.99 *(978-1-4424-4005-0(8))* Simon & Schuster Bks. For Young Readers. (Simon & Schuster Bks. For Young Readers).

Keene, Carolyn. Boo Crew. Francis, Peter, illus. 2018. (Nancy Drew Clue Book Ser.: 10). (ENG.). 112p. (J). (gr. 1-4). 17.99 *(978-1-5344-1389-4(8))*; pap. 5.99 *(978-1-5344-1388-7(X))* Simon & Schuster Children's Publishing. (Aladdin).

—The Clue at Black Creek Farm. 2015. 171p. (J). *(978-1-4806-8613-7(1)*, Simon & Schuster/Paula Wiseman Bks.) Simon & Schuster/Paula Wiseman Bks.

—Designed for Disaster. Pamintuan, Macky, illus. 2011. (Nancy Drew & the Clue Crew Ser.: 29). (ENG.). 96p. (J). (gr. 1-4). pap. 5.99 *(978-1-4169-9439-8(4)*, Aladdin) Simon & Schuster Children's Publishing.

—Famous Mistakes. 2019. (Nancy Drew Diaries: 17). (ENG., Illus.). 176p. (J). (gr. 3-7). pap. 6.99 *(978-1-4814-8549-4(0)*, Simon & Schuster/Paula Wiseman Bks.) Simon & Schuster/Paula Wiseman Bks.

—Once upon a Crime. 2nd ed. 2006. (Nancy Drew: Girl Detective Super Mystery Ser.: 2). (ENG.). 192p. (J). (gr. 3-7). pap. 6.99 *(978-1-4169-1248-4(7)*, Aladdin) Simon & Schuster Children's Publishing.

—Sabotage at Willow Woods. 2014. (Nancy Drew Diaries: 5). (ENG., Illus.). 176p. (J). (gr. 3-7). pap. 7.99 *(978-1-4424-9392-6(5)*, Aladdin) Simon & Schuster Children's Publishing.

—The Stolen Show. 2019. (Nancy Drew Diaries: 18). (ENG.). 192p. (J). (gr. 3-7). pap. 6.99 *(978-1-5344-0577-6(1)*, Simon & Schuster/Paula Wiseman Bks.) Simon & Schuster/Paula Wiseman Bks.

—Trails of Treachery. 2008. (Nancy Drew: Girl Detective Ser.). 136p. (gr. 3-7). 15.00 *(978-0-7569-8295-9(2))* Perfection Learning Corp.

Kelly, David A. Ballpark Mysteries Super Special #4: the World Series Kids. Meyers, Mark, illus. 2019. (Ballpark Mysteries Ser.: 4). (ENG.). 128p. (J). (gr. 1-4). pap. 5.99 *(978-0-525-57895-6(1)*, Random Hse. Bks. for Young Readers) Random Hse. Children's Bks.

Kent, Jaden. Ella & Owen 10: the Dragon Games! Bodnaruk, Iryna, illus. 2018. (Ella & Owen Ser.: 10). (ENG.). 112p. (J). (gr. k-3). 16.99 *(978-1-4998-0617-5(5))*; pap. 5.99 *(978-1-4998-0616-8(7))* Little Bee Books Inc.

Maddox, Jake. Soccer Sabotage. 2018. (Jake Maddox JV Ser.). (ENG., Illus.). 96p. (J). (gr. 4-6). lib. bdg. 26.65 *(978-1-4965-5932-6(0)*, 137134, Stone Arch Bks.) Capstone.

Metz, Melinda. S. M. A. R. T. S. & the Droid of Doom. McKenzie, Heath, illus. 2016. (S. M. A. R. T. S. Ser.). (ENG.). 128p. (J). (gr. 3-6). pap. 9.95 *(978-1-4965-3017-2(9)*, 131904); lib. bdg. 22.65 *(978-1-4965-3015-8(2)*, 131902) Capstone. (Stone Arch Bks.).

—S. M. A. R. T. S. & the Mars Mission Mayhem. McKenzie, Heath, illus. 2016. (S. M. A. R. T. S. Ser.). (ENG.). 128p. (J). (gr. 3-6). lib. bdg. 22.65 *(978-1-4965-3016-5(0)*, 131903, Stone Arch Bks.) Capstone.

Morgan, Alex. Sabotage Season. (Kicks Ser.). (ENG., Illus.). (J). (gr. 3-7). 2014. 192p. pap. 7.99 *(978-1-4424-8576-1(0))* 2013. 176p. 17.99 *(978-1-4424-8574-7(4))* Simon & Schuster Bks. For Young Readers. (Simon & Schuster Bks. For Young Readers).

Ortega, Claribel A. The Golden Frog Games (Witchlings 2) 2023. (Witchlings Ser.). (ENG.). 384p. (J). (gr. 3-7). 17.99 *(978-1-338-74579-5(4)*, Scholastic Pr.) Scholastic, Inc.

Press, Judy. The Case of the Missing Kiddush Cup. 2018. (J). *(978-1-5415-0015-0(6)*, Kar-Ben Publishing) Lerner Publishing Group.

Probst, Jeff & Tebbetts, Chris. The Sabotage. 2015. (Stranded, Shadow Island Ser.: 2). lib. bdg. 17.20 *(978-0-606-36792-9(6))* Turtleback.

Surrisi, C. M. A Side of Sabotage: A Quinnie Boyd Mystery. (Quinnie Boyd Mysteries Ser.). (ENG.). 280p. (J). (gr. 4-8). 2019. pap. 9.99 *(978-1-5415-7758-9(2)*, df48a301-f493-4867-acd0-7099f5d7865c) 2018. 16.99 *(978-1-5124-4836-8(2)*, 2f2233a9-53da-4efc-ba4d-e5c7d38d2937) Lerner Publishing Group. (Carolrhoda Bks.).

Sutherland, Tui T. & Sutherland, Kari H. The Menagerie #3: Krakens & Lies. 2015. (Menagerie Ser.: 3). (ENG., Illus.). 368p. (J). (gr. 3-7). 16.99 *(978-0-06-078067-8(3)*, HarperCollins) HarperCollins Pubs.

Terrell, Brandon. The Undercover Cheerleader. Epelbaum, Mariano, illus. 2017. (Snoops, Inc Ser.). (ENG.). 112p. (J). (gr. 4-8). lib. bdg. 27.32 *(978-1-4965-5061-3(7)*, 135988, Stone Arch Bks.) Capstone.

Wolff, Tracy. Book 2: Sabotage. Kinsella, Pat, illus. 2016. (Mars Bound Ser.). (ENG.). 48p. (J). (gr. 3-7). lib. bdg. 34.21 *(978-1-62402-198-5(0)*, 24575, Spellbound) Magic Wagon.

SABRINA, THE TEENAGE WITCH (FICTITIOUS CHARACTER)—FICTION

Aguirre-Sacasa, Roberto. Chilling Adventures of Sabrina. Hack, Robert, illus. 2016. (Chilling Adventures of Sabrina Ser.: 1). 160p. pap. 17.99 *(978-1-62738-987-7(3))* Archie Comic Pubns., Inc.

Gallagher, Mike. Sabrina Animated. Manak, Dave, illus. 2011. (Archie & Friends All-Stars Ser.: 13). (ENG.). 128p. (J). (gr. 4-7). pap. 9.95 *(978-1-879794-80-1(2))* Archie Comic Pubns., Inc.

SACAGAWEA

Buffalohead, Julie, illus. Sacagawea. 2005. (Libros Ilustrados (Picture Bks.)). (SPA & ENG.). 40p. (J). (gr. 3-6). 16.95 *(978-0-8225-3191-3(7)*, Ediciones Lerner) Lerner Publishing Group.

Byers, Ann. Sacagawea, 1 vol. 2020. (Inside Guide: Famous Native Americans Ser.). (ENG.). 32p. (gr. 4-5). pap. 11.58 *(978-1-5026-5064-1(9)*, 1a6f2658-afa0-4e6b-8867-726a692bb62f) Cavendish Square Publishing LLC.

Collard, Sneed B., III. Sacagawea: Brave Shoshone Girl, 1 vol. 2007. (American Heroes Ser.). (ENG., Illus.). 48p. (gr. 3-3). lib. bdg. 32.64 *(978-0-7614-2166-5(1)*, 8319f4a1-5531-4f32-9e8b-4de0fdedd320) Cavendish Square Publishing LLC.

Cooke, Tim. Sacagawea. 1 vol. 2016. (Meet the Greats Ser.). (ENG.). 48p. (J). (gr. 5-5). pap. 15.65 *(978-1-4824-5960-9(4)*, 65b19569-f3f3-4df9-91be-8c911805294f) Stevens, Gareth Publishing LLLP.

Crosby, Michael T. Sacagawea: Lewis & Clark's Pathfinder. 2007. 144p. (J). (gr. 6-18). 25.95 *(978-1-59556-026-1(2))* OTTN Publishing.

DeFord, Diane. Sacagawea. 2009. pap. 13.25 *(978-1-60559-069-1(X))* Hameray Publishing Group, Inc.

Franklin, Virgil. The Story of Sacagawea. 2009. (Reading Room Collection 2 Ser.). 24p. (gr. 3-4). 42.50 *(978-1-60851-997-2(X)*, PowerKids Pr.) Rosen Publishing Group, Inc., The.

Frazier, Neta. Path to the Pacific: The Story of Sacagawea. 2017. (Great Leaders & Events Ser.). (ENG.). (J). (gr. 4-8). lib. bdg. 35.99 *(978-1-942875-44-4(4))* Quarto Publishing Group USA.

Griffiths, Katie. Sacagawea: Shoshone Guide, Interpreter, & Leading Member of the Corps of Discovery, 1 vol. 2017. (Fearless Female Soldiers, Explorers, & Aviators Ser.). (ENG., Illus.). 128p. (YA). (gr. 9-9). 47.36 *(978-1-5026-2747-6(7)*, 43f581b4-a050-4edd-9ddf-cd88d992402f) Cavendish Square Publishing LLC.

Gunderson, Jessica. Sacagawea: Journey into the West, 1 vol. Martin, Cynthia & Schulz, Barbara, illus. 2006. (Graphic Biographies Ser.). (ENG.). 32p. (J). (gr. 3-9). per. 8.10 *(978-0-7368-9663-4(5)*, 93450) Capstone.

Haldy, Emma E. Sacagawea. Bane, Jeff, illus. 2016. (My Early Library: My Itty-Bitty Bio Ser.). (ENG.). 24p. (J). (gr. k-1). 30.64 *(978-1-63470-482-3(7)*, 207659) Cherry Lake Publishing.

—Sacagawea SP. Bane, Jeff, illus. 2018. (My Early Library: Mi Mini Biografía (My Itty-Bitty Bio) Ser.). (SPA.). 24p. (J). (gr. k-1). lib. bdg. 30.64 *(978-1-5341-3000-5(4)*, 212048) Cherry Lake Publishing.

Jazynka, Kitson. Sacagawea. 2015. (Readers Bios Ser.). (Illus.). 32p. (J). (gr. 1-3). pap. 5.99 *(978-1-4263-1963-1(0)*, National Geographic Kids) Disney Publishing Worldwide.

King, Margaret. The Legacy & Legend of Sacagawea. rev. ed. 2017. (Social Studies: Informational Text Ser.). (ENG., Illus.). 32p. (gr. 4-8). pap. 11.99 *(978-1-4938-3793-9(1))* Teacher Created Materials, Inc.

Krensky, Stephen. Sacagawea. Magnuson, Diana, illus. 2005. 32p. (J). lib. bdg. 15.00 *(978-1-59054-954-4(6))* Fitzgerald Bks.

Lohof, Arle & Jensen, Joyce. My Story as Told by Sacagawea. Little, Gary, illus. 2006. 32p. (J). (gr. 1-2). 3.95 *(978-0-9711667-3-8(0))* Outlook Publishing, Inc.

Lynette, Rachel. Sacagawea, 1 vol. 2013. (Pioneer Spirit: the Westward Expansion Ser.). 24p. (J). (ENG.). (gr. 2-3). 26.27 *(978-1-4777-0782-1(4)*, 27f27716-d062-4a4c-b686-3e1f77b4d591); (gr. 3-6). pap. 49.50 *(978-1-4777-0898-9(7))*; (ENG., Illus.). (gr. 2-3). pap. 9.25 *(978-1-4777-0897-2(9)*, 313c432c-9263-492a-b9c8-e2314cd54659) Rosen Publishing Group, Inc., The. (PowerKids Pr.).

Marcovitz, Hal. Sacagawea: Guide for the Lewis & Clark Expedition. 2007. (Illus.). 63p. (J). pap. 12.00 *(978-1-4223-6712-4(6))* DIANE Publishing Co.

Marsh, Carole. Sacagawea: Native American Heroine: Native American Heroine. 2003. 12p. (gr. k-4). 2.95 *(978-0-635-02143-4(9))* Gallopade International.

McAneney, Caitie. The Life of Sacagawea, 1 vol. 2016. (Native American Biographies Ser.). (ENG., Illus.). 32p. (J). (gr. 4-5). 27.93 *(978-1-5081-4819-7(8)*, 81bd3657-d037-4879-a46c-de5150deaa6f, PowerKids Pr.) Rosen Publishing Group, Inc., The.

Meltzer, Brad. I Am Sacagawea. Eliopoulos, Christopher, illus. (Ordinary People Change the World Ser.). 40p. (J). (gr. k-4). 2023. pap. 9.99 *(978-0-593-61918-6(8)*, Rocky Pond Bks.) 2017. 15.99 *(978-0-525-42853-4(4)*, Dial Bks) Penguin Young Readers Group.

Nelson, Maria. The Life of Sacagawea, 1 vol. 2012. (Famous Lives Ser.). (ENG., Illus.). 24p. (J). (gr. 1-2). pap. 9.15 *(978-1-4339-6359-9(0)*, 7d54f17b-b6a2-43d9-b239-7dc9a194049c); lib. bdg. 25.27 *(978-1-4339-6357-5(4)*, 017bd324-2a9a-4cd4-b51c-3b2ba2208e5f) Stevens, Gareth Publishing LLLP.

Norwich, Grace. I Am Sacagawea (I Am #1) VanArsdale, Anthony, illus. 2012. (I Am Ser.). (ENG.). 128p. (J). (gr. 3-5). pap. 5.99 *(978-0-545-40574-4(2)*, Scholastic Paperbacks) Scholastic, Inc.

Rausch, Monica. Sacagawea, 1 vol. 2007. (Grandes Personajes (Great Americans) Ser.). 24p. (gr. 2-4). (SPA.). pap. 9.15 *(978-0-8368-7991-9(0)*, 867793cb-be46-4835-b2e0-95234bf0f2f2, Weekly Reader Leveled Readers); (ENG., Illus.). pap. 9.15 *(978-0-8368-7692-5(X)*, fca24c8a-5c3c-4f07-9459-871423b2e8e0, Weekly Reader Leveled Readers); (SPA., Illus.). lib. bdg. 24.67 *(978-0-8368-7984-1(8)*, f0398bb5-29a9-4689-829b-5a3f299c15cc); (ENG., Illus.). lib. bdg. 24.67 *(978-0-8368-7685-7(7)*, a6b3bcda-7778-4816-8efa-d05bb06d6d16, Weekly Reader Leveled Readers) Stevens, Gareth Publishing LLLP.

Sanford, William R. & Green, Carl R. Sacagawea: Courageous American Indian Guide, 1 vol. 2013. (Courageous Heroes of the American West Ser.). (ENG., Illus.). 48p. (J). (gr. 5-7). 25.27 *(978-0-7660-4006-9(2)*, 3f6b8c1b-2727-4911-bb11-7579059ee616) Enslow Publishing, LLC.

St. George, Judith. Sacagawea. 2006. pap. 8.75 *(978-0-15-365175-5(X))* Harcourt Schl. Pubs.

Strand, Jennifer. Sacagawea. 2017. (Native American Leaders Ser.). (ENG., Illus.). 24p. (J). (gr. -1-2). lib. bdg. 31.36 *(978-1-5321-2025-1(7)*, 25314, Abdo Zoom-Launch) ABDO Publishing Co.

Sutcliffe, Jane. Sacagawea. 2009. (History Maker Biographies Ser.). (ENG.). 48p. (gr. 3-6). 27.93 *(978-0-7613-4222-9(2)*, Lerner Pubns.) Lerner Publishing Group.

SACCO-VANZETTI TRIAL, DEDHAM, MASS., 1921

Hinton, Kerry. The Trial of Sacco & Vanzetti: A Primary Source Account. 2009. (Great Trials of the Twentieth Century Ser.). 64p. (gr. 5-8). 58.50 *(978-1-61513-220-1(1))* Rosen Publishing Group, Inc., The.

SACRED ART

see Christian Art and Symbolism

SACRED MUSIC

see Church Music

SAFETY EDUCATION

see also Accidents—Prevention

Abramovitz, Melissa. Abc's of Health & Safety. Morris, Alexander, illus. 2018. 16p. pap. 9.95 *(978-1-61633-276-1(X))* Guardian Angel Publishing, Inc.

Acosta, Jamey & Reid, Stephanie. Health & Safety. 2010. (Early Literacy Ser.). (ENG., Illus.). 16p. (gr. k-1). 19.99 *(978-1-4333-1809-2(1))*; 6.99 *(978-1-4333-1808-5(3))* Teacher Created Materials, Inc.

Adams, Jeanne. Tyler's Safe Day, Everyday Safety for Children. 2009. 24p. pap. 13.50 *(978-1-60860-465-4(9)*, Eloquent Bks.) Strategic Book Publishing & Rights Agency (SBPRA).

Adamson, Thomas K. & Lemke, Donald B. Lessons in Science Safety with Max Axiom Super Scientist: 4D an Augmented Reading Science Experience. Smith, Tod, illus. 2018. (Graphic Science 4D Ser.). (ENG.). 32p. (J). (gr. 3-9). pap. 7.95 *(978-1-5435-2959-3(3)*, 138559); lib. bdg. 36.65 *(978-1-5435-2948-7(8)*, 138537) Capstone. (Capstone Pr.).

Adler, Rebecca. Keep Me Safe at Home & in My Community: A handbook on Safety for Young Children & their Families. 2009. (ENG.). 52p. pap. 20.49 *(978-1-4389-0585-3(8))* AuthorHouse.

Adult Guide to Staying Safe. 2003. (YA). *(978-0-88441-663-0(1))* Girl Scouts of the USA.

Amaso, Marcellus Chigbo. 100 Tips for a School Child's Daily Safety Guide. 2013. 120p. 29.99 *(978-1-4797-7243-8(7))*; pap. 19.99 *(978-1-4797-4951-5(6))* Xlibris Corp.

American Academy of Pediatrics, A. A. P. BLAST! Babysitter Lessons & Safety Training (Revised) 3rd rev. ed. 2016. (ENG.). 72p. pap. 14.95 *(978-1-284-13580-0(2))* Jones & Bartlett Learning, LLC.

Bair, Carolyn. Fireman Dave Goes to School. 2012. 16p. pap. 13.99 *(978-1-4685-4194-6(3))* AuthorHouse.

Barr, Linda. The Water Patrol: Saving Surfers' Lives in Big Waves. 2005. (High Five Reading - Blue Ser.). (ENG., Illus.). 48p. (gr. 3-4). per. 9.00 *(978-0-7368-5749-9(4))* Capstone.

Bell, Nasherrall, creator. Child Safety at Home, School & Play l.t. ed. 2004. (Illus.). 32p. (J). pap. *(978-0-9729753-3-9(0))* Really Big Coloring Bks., Inc.

Benchmark Education Company, LLC Staff, compiled by. Safety. 2006. (J). 91.00 *(978-1-4108-7046-9(4))* Benchmark Education Co.

Berry, Joy. Help Me Be Good about Being Careless. 2009. (Help Me Be Good Ser.). 32p. pap. 7.95 *(978-1-60577-103-8(1))* Berry, Joy Enterprises.

Berry, Joy Wilt. A Book about Being Careless. 2005. (Illus.). (J). *(978-0-7172-8582-2(0))* Scholastic, Inc.

Blaine, Victor. Safe in Your Home, 1 vol. 2016. (Safety Smarts Ser.). (ENG.). 24p. (J). (gr. k-1). pap. 9.25 *(978-1-4994-2787-5(5)*, 0f964632-4670-4198-8213-dac92638a267, PowerKids Pr.) Rosen Publishing Group, Inc., The.

—Safe on the Playground, 1 vol. 2016. (Safety Smarts Ser.). (ENG.). 24p. (J). (gr. k-1). pap. 9.25 *(978-1-4994-2785-1(9)*, 08cac96c-773f-47aa-93d1-01bb1cd88248, PowerKids Pr.) Rosen Publishing Group, Inc., The.

Boyer, Richard G. Oddo Safety Series, 4 vols., Set. (Illus.). (J). (gr. -1-6). lib. bdg. 44.60 *(978-0-87783-170-9(X))* Oddo Publishing, Inc.

Brady, Janeen J. Safety Kids Vol. 3: Protect Their Minds. 24p. (J). (gr. k-6). pap. 4.95 *(978-0-944803-82-0(2))* Brite Music, Inc.

Campbell, Maureen & Yoerg, Sharon. Bridges to Safety: A Practical Guide for Adults to Help Teens Teach Conflict Resolution & Character Skills to Children. 2004. (Illus.). 118p. per. 24.94 incl. cd-rom *(978-0-9716772-0-3(4))* Six Seconds.

Candy Cane Press, creator. Safe at Play: Outdoor Safety. 2005. (ENG., Illus.). 14p. (J). (gr. -1-k). bds. 12.95 *(978-0-8249-6593-8(0)*, Ideals Pubns.) Worthy Publishing.

Casanueva, Idilian. You May Touch Here! Puedes Tocar Aqui! Caceres, Marangelie, illus. 2007. 16p. per. 10.95 *(978-1-59858-327-4(1))* Dog Ear Publishing, LLC.

Cavell-Clarke, Steffi. Staying Safe. 2018. (Our Values - Level 2 Ser.). (Illus.). 24p. (J). (gr. 2-3). *(978-0-7787-4730-7(1))* Crabtree Publishing Co.

Cicola, Amanda, et al. Health & Safety 1: Gym Class; Shopping for Lunch; Good for You; My Happy Heart; Just Like Me; Staying Safe; Always Brush Your Teeth; A Visit to the Doctor, 8 bks. Simon, Sue A. et al, illus. 2005. (ENG.). 8p. (J). pap. 120.00 *(978-1-893986-26-8(8))* Keep Bks.

Council Guide to Staying Safe. 2003. (YA). *(978-0-88441-664-7(X))* Girl Scouts of the USA.

Cumberland, Diana. Listen to Your Body: Empowering Children to Be Safe. 2013. 40p. pap. 15.95 *(978-1-4525-8559-8(8)*, Balboa Pr.) Author Solutions, LLC.

Decker, William. Safe at School, 1 vol. 2016. (Safety Smarts Ser.). (ENG., Illus.). 24p. (J). (gr. k-1). pap. 9.25 *(978-1-4994-2764-6(6)*, fb4698a3-ea0f-494a-9f0e-d4bbcbac4aef, PowerKids Pr.) Rosen Publishing Group, Inc., The.

—Safe in the Car, 1 vol. 2016. (Safety Smarts Ser.). (ENG.). 24p. (J). (gr. k-1). pap. 9.25 *(978-1-4994-2788-2(3)*, d71b7a8d-4875-4dc7-ac8c-97765e28d786, PowerKids Pr.) Rosen Publishing Group, Inc., The.

Desalle, Nicole. Safe at Home. 2011. pap. 39.95 *(978-0-7664-3751-7(5))* Abrams & Co. Pubs., Inc.

—Safe at Play. 2011. pap. 39.95 *(978-0-7664-3752-4(3))* Abrams & Co. Pubs., Inc.

—Safe at School. 2011. pap. 39.95 *(978-0-7664-3750-0(7))* Abrams & Co. Pubs., Inc.

Dinmont, Kerry. Emily Goes to the Park: A Book about Healthy Habits. 2017. (My Day Readers Ser.). (ENG.). 24p. (J). (gr. -1-2). lib. bdg. 32.79 *(978-1-5038-2021-0(1)*, 211858) Child's World, Inc, The.

Don't Panic. 2003. (Illus.). pap. 5.60 *(978-0-7398-7505-6(1))* Steck-Vaughn.

Don't Stick Sticks up Your Nose! Don't Stuff Stuff in Your Ears! 2013. (Don't Stick Sticks up Your Nose! Don't Stuff Stuff in Your Ears! Ser.). (ENG.). 22p. bds. 5.99 *(978-0-9888861-0-0(3)*, 9780988886100) Dontstickdontstuff.

Duncan, David A. Dude, Where's Your Helmet?, 1 vol. 2009. (ENG., Illus.). 48p. (J). pap. *(978-1-897522-59-2(2))* RMB Rocky Mountain Bks.

Etingoff, Kim. Navigating Cyberspace. Stephens, Ronald, ed. 2014. (Safety First Ser.: 11). 48p. (J). (gr. 5-18). 20.95 *(978-1-4222-3049-7(X))* Mason Crest.

Eye on the Sky. 2015. (Eye on the Sky Ser.). (ENG.). 32p. (J). (gr. 3-4). pap., pap., pap. 63.00 *(978-1-4824-3461-3(X))* Stevens, Gareth Publishing LLLP.

Feigh, Alison. I Can Play It Safe. Logan, Laura, illus. 2008. (ENG.). 32p. (J). (gr. -1-3). 16.99 *(978-1-57542-285-5(9)*, 1275) Free Spirit Publishing Inc.

First Aid & Home Safety. (YA). (gr. 6-12). pap. 10.95 *(978-0-8224-4366-7(X))* Globe Fearon Educational Publishing.

Ford, Jean. Growth & Development. Forman, Sara, ed. 2013. (Young Adult's Guide to the Science of Health Ser.: 15). 128p. (J). (gr. 7-18). 24.95 *(978-1-4222-2810-4(X))* Mason Crest.

French, Cathy. People Who Keep You Safe. 2011. (Early Connections Ser.). (J). *(978-1-61672-239-5(8))* Benchmark Education Co.

Giles, Sophie & Davies, Kate. The Children's Book of Keeping Safe. 2014. (ENG., Illus.). 320p. (J). pap. 10.00 *(978-1-84135-909-0(2))* Award Pubns. Ltd. GBR. Dist: Parkwest Pubns., Inc.

Gogerly, Liz. Looking after Me. Gordon, Mike, illus. 2008. (ENG.). 32p. (J). (gr. -1-3). *(978-0-7787-4109-1(5))* Crabtree Publishing Co.

—Safety. Gordon, Mike, illus. 2008. (Looking after Me Ser.). (ENG.). 32p. (J). (gr. -1-3). pap. *(978-0-7787-4120-6(6))*; lib. bdg. *(978-0-7787-4113-8(3))* Crabtree Publishing Co.

Goldsmith, Mike & Johnson, Jinny. Being Safe. 2009. (Now We Know About... Ser.). (ENG., Illus.). 24p. (J). (gr. k-3). pap. *(978-0-7787-4734-5(4))*; lib. bdg. *(978-0-7787-4717-8(4))* Crabtree Publishing Co.

Goodbody, Slim. Avoiding Injuries, 1 vol. 2007. (Slim Goodbody's Good Health Guides). (ENG., Illus.). 32p. (J). (gr. 3-5). lib. bdg. 28.67 *(978-0-8368-7739-7(X)*, c358c393-fdbc-46a7-876f-c38e74982b77, Gareth Stevens Learning Library) Stevens, Gareth Publishing LLLP.

—Keeping Safe, 1 vol. 2007. (Slim Goodbody's Good Health Guides). (ENG., Illus.). 32p. (gr. 3-5). lib. bdg. 28.67 *(978-0-8368-7743-4(8)*, 3211a518-e9b4-441a-a8ca-04598647f8c9, Gareth Stevens Learning Library) Stevens, Gareth Publishing LLLP.

Grossblatt, Ben. Keep Out! Door Alarm: Build Your Own Key-Card Security System! 2004. (Illus.). 24p. (J). *(978-0-439-66835-4(2))* Scholastic, Inc.

Guard, Anara. What If a Stranger Approaches You?, 1 vol. Madden, Colleen, illus. 2011. (Danger Zone Ser.). (ENG.). 24p. (J). (gr. k-2). pap. 7.49 *(978-1-4048-7031-4(8)*, 116803, Picture Window Bks.) Capstone.

Hahn, Donna M. Staying Safe When I Go Out. 2009. 24p. pap. 12.00 *(978-1-4389-6498-0(6))* AuthorHouse.

Herrington, Lisa M. Internet Safety. 2012. (Rookie Read-About Safety Ser.). (ENG., Illus.). 32p. (J). (gr. -1-1). pap. 5.95 *(978-0-531-29273-0(8))* Scholastic Library Publishing.

—Rookie Read-About Safety: Stranger Safety. 2012. (Rookie Read-About Safety Ser.). (ENG., Illus.). 32p. (J). pap. 5.95 *(978-0-531-29274-7(6))* Scholastic Library Publishing.

Higgins, Melissa. You're in Charge: Basic Rules Every Babysitter Needs to Know, 1 vol. 2014. (Babysitter's Backpack Ser.). (ENG., Illus.). 32p. (J). (gr. 3-9). lib. bdg. 28.65 *(978-1-4914-0764-6(6)*, 125996) Capstone.

Holmes, Kirsty Louise. My Safety. 2018. (Our Values - Level 1 Ser.). (Illus.). 24p. (J). (gr. 1-1). *(978-0-7787-4728-4(X))* Crabtree Publishing Co.

Holt, Rinehart and Winston Staff. Decisions for Health Blue, Chptr. 13: Preventing Abuse. 4th ed. 2004. pap. 11.20 *(978-0-03-068047-2(6))* Holt McDougal.

—Decisions for Health Blue, Chptr. 19: Safety. 4th ed. 2004. pap. 11.20 *(978-0-03-068054-0(9))* Holt McDougal.

—Decisions for Health Green Chptr. 15: Health & Safety. 4th ed. 2004. pap. 11.20 *(978-0-03-068037-3(9))* Holt McDougal.

—Decisions for Health Red Chptr. 17: Personal Safety. 4th ed. 2004. pap. 11.20 *(978-0-03-068044-1(1))* Holt McDougal.

Hunt, Jilly. Safety, 1 vol. 2010. (Being Healthy, Feeling Great Ser.). (ENG.). 32p. (gr. 3-4). (J). pap. 11.60 *(978-1-61532-383-8(X)*, 5846a690-5c7e-485b-9a79-7c5c48c9f9eb, PowerKids Pr.); (YA). lib. bdg. 30.27 *(978-1-61532-382-1(1)*, 9eb954e6-d3b0-4e54-b265-f10619f116f6) Rosen Publishing Group, Inc., The.

Jackman, Vernon. Bunnies & Butterflies in the Backyard & the Pirates Who Know Where They Live: Stories That Help Children Learn & Remember Their Address & Telephone Number. Theagene, Jeannisse, illus. l.t. ed. 2010. (ENG.). 32p. (J). pap. 6.99 *(978-0-9829371-1-2(3))* New Kid Safety.

Jackson, Joann. Green Light, Red Light, Go! 2008. 20p. per. 24.95 *(978-1-60441-778-4(1))* America Star Bks.

Jakubiak, David J. A Smart Kid's Guide to Avoiding Online Predators, 1 vol. 2009. (Kids Online Ser.). (ENG., Illus.). 24p. (J). (gr. 2-3). pap. 9.25 *(978-1-4358-3354-8(6)*, b04451e0-d6d8-468f-8253-de82a552bf99); lib. bdg. 26.27 *(978-1-4042-8117-2(7)*, 3a0d2fc0-5892-4c0d-b7a5-5b2842dd415b) Rosen Publishing Group, Inc., The. (PowerKids Pr.).

—A Smart Kid's Guide to Social Networking Online, 1 vol. 2009. (Kids Online Ser.). (ENG., Illus.). 24p. (J). (gr. 2-3). pap. 9.25 *(978-1-4358-3358-6(9)*, 85c2ce37-2da7-4b6a-98ec-4da052c7ae60, PowerKids Pr.) Rosen Publishing Group, Inc., The.

James, Cindy. Ten Easy Tips for Staying Safe. 2009. (Reading Room Collection 2 Ser.). 24p. (gr. 3-4). 42.50 *(978-1-60851-991-0(0)*, PowerKids Pr.) Rosen Publishing Group, Inc., The.

James, Sara. Safety. 2013. (Junior Martial Arts Ser.: 9). 32p. (J). (gr. 4-18). 19.95 *(978-1-4222-2737-4(5))* Mason Crest.

Jennings, Rosemary. Safe on Your Bike, 1 vol. 2016. (Safety Smarts Ser.). (ENG.). 24p. (J). (gr. k-1). pap. 9.25 *(978-1-4994-2784-4(0)*, f025559c-3f65-4a61-a0e6-c804fc0cdf0d, PowerKids Pr.) Rosen Publishing Group, Inc., The.

Johnson-Leslie, Natalie & Leslie, H. Steve. Abc's of Surviving School Violence. Allen, Joshua, illus. 2010. (ENG.). 24p. pap. 15.99 (978-1-4490-6397-9(7)) AuthorHouse.

Joyce, Julie. What Should You Do? Safety Tips for Kids. 2004. (J). 3.95 (978-0-9656808-4-4(3), KidBk-1) Dynamic Publishing Co., Inc.

Kallio, Jamie. 12 Tips for Staying Safe. 2017. (Healthy Living Ser.). (ENG., Illus.). 32p. (J). (gr. 3-6). pap. 9.95 (978-1-63235-385-6(7), 11853, 12-Story Library) Bookstaves, LLC.

—12 Tips for Staying Safe. 2017. (Illus.). 32p. (J). (978-1-62143-509-9(1)) Pr. Room Editions LLC.

Keevish, Michele C. When a Stranger Says Hello. 2008. 16p. per. 24.95 (978-1-4241-8669-3(2)) America Star Bks.

Kesselring, Susan. At School. 2018. (J). (978-1-4896-9963-3(5), AV2 by Weigl) Weigl Pubs., Inc.

Knowlton, MaryLee. Safety at Home. Andersen, Gregg, photos by. 2008. (Staying Safe Ser.). (ENG., Illus.). 32p. (J). (gr. -1-3). lib. bdg. (978-0-7787-4316-3(0)) Crabtree Publishing Co.

—Safety at School. Andersen, Gregg, photos by. 2008. (Staying Safe Ser.). (ENG., Illus.). 32p. (J). (gr. -1-3). lib. bdg. (978-0-7787-4317-0(9)) Crabtree Publishing Co.

—Safety at the Playground. Andersen, Gregg, photos by. 2008. (Staying Safe Ser.). (ENG., Illus.). 32p. (J). (gr. -1-3). lib. bdg. (978-0-7787-4318-7(7)) Crabtree Publishing Co.

Knowlton, MaryLee & Dowdy, Penny. Safety at School. Andersen, Gregg, photos by. 2008. (Staying Safe Ser.). (ENG., Illus.). 32p. (J). (gr. -1-3). pap. (978-0-7787-4322-4(5)) Crabtree Publishing Co.

—Safety at the Playground, 1 vol. Andersen, Gregg, photos by. 2008. (Staying Safe Ser.). (ENG., Illus.). 32p. (J). (gr. -1-3). pap. (978-0-7787-4323-1(3)) Crabtree Publishing Co.

Kreiner, Anna. Todo lo que necesitas saber sobre la violencia en la escuela (Everything You Need to Know about Violence in School) 2009. (Todo lo que necesitas (the Need to Know Library) Ser.). (SPA.). 64p. (gr. 6-6). 58.50 (978-1-60854-411-0(7), Editorial Buenas Letras) Rosen Publishing Group, Inc., The.

Kupperstein, Joel. Safety Counts! 2017. (Learn-To-Read Ser.). (ENG., Illus.). (J). (gr. -1-1). pap. 3.49 (978-1-68310-260-1(6)) Pacific Learning, Inc.

LaBerge, Margaret M. Sara Safety, School Safety Pamphlet. Lucas, Stacey L. et al, illus. 2004. (J). pap. (978-0-9755561-0-8(X)) Reading Resc.

Lee, Sally. Staying Safe Online. 2012. (Staying Safe Ser.). (ENG.). 24p. (gr. 1-2). pap. 41.70 (978-1-4296-8389-0(9), Capstone Pr.) Capstone.

Letizia, Kenneth M. Go Ask Ally: Wearing Seat Belts Doesn't Change Lives, Not Wearing Them Does. 2011. 32p. (gr. 1-2). pap. 14.39 (978-1-4567-6326-8(1)) AuthorHouse.

Llewelyn, Claire. Stay Safe! 2006. (Qeb Looking after Me Ser.). (Illus.). 24p. (J). lib. bdg. 16.95 (978-1-59566-195-1(6)) QEB Publishing Inc.

Lombardo, Jennifer & Mooney, Carla. Social Networking: Staying Safe in the Online World, 1 vol. 2016. (Hot Topics Ser.). (ENG.). 120p. (YA). (gr. 7-7). lib. bdg. 41.03 (978-1-5345-6021-5(1), 4db64619-5855-4135-9a55-b2830af01f43, Lucent Pr.) Greenhaven Publishing LLC.

Lyons, Shelly. Safety in My Neighborhood, 1 vol. 2013. (My Neighborhood Ser.). (ENG.). 24p. (J). (gr. -1-2). pap. 7.29 (978-1-62065-887-1(9), 121804); (gr. k-1). pap. 43.74 (978-1-62065-888-8(7), 19443) Capstone. (Capstone Pr.).

Mara, Wil. What Should I Do? If a Stranger Comes Near. 2011. (Community Connections: What Should I Do? Ser.). (ENG., Illus.). 24p. (gr. 2-5). lib. bdg. 29.21 (978-1-61080-049-5(4), 201040) Cherry Lake Publishing.

—What Should I Do? If I See a Stray Animal. 2011. (Community Connections: What Should I Do? Ser.). (ENG., Illus.). 24p. (gr. 2-5). lib. bdg. 29.21 (978-1-61080-050-1(8), 201042) Cherry Lake Publishing.

—What Should I Do? near a Busy Street. 2011. (Community Connections: What Should I Do? Ser.). (ENG., Illus.). 24p. (gr. 2-5). lib. bdg. 29.21 (978-1-61080-051-8(6), 201044) Cherry Lake Publishing.

—What Should I Do? (Set), 8 vols., Set. Incl. What Should I Do? at the Pool. lib. bdg. 29.21 (978-1-61080-056-3(7), 201054); What Should I Do? If a Stranger Comes Near. lib. bdg. 29.21 (978-1-61080-049-5(4), 201040); What Should I Do? If I See a Stray Animal. lib. bdg. 29.21 (978-1-61080-050-1(8), 201042); What Should I Do? If There Is a Fire. lib. bdg. 29.21 (978-1-61080-053-2(2), 201048); What Should I Do? in the Car. lib. bdg. 29.21 (978-1-61080-052-5(4), 201046); What Should I Do? near a Busy Street. lib. bdg. 29.21 (978-1-61080-051-8(6), 201044); What Should I Do? on My Bike. lib. bdg. 29.21 (978-1-61080-055-6(9), 201052); What Should I Do? on the Playground. lib. bdg. 29.21 (978-1-61080-054-9(0), 201050); (gr. 2-5). (Community Connections: What Should I Do? Ser.). (ENG., Illus.). 24p. 2011. 233.68 (978-1-61080-145-4(8), 201000) Cherry Lake Publishing.

Marlowe, Christie. Protecting Your Body: Germs, Super Bugs, Poison & Deadly Diseases. Stephens, Ronald, ed. 2014. (Safety First Ser.: 11). 48p. (J). (gr. 5-18). 20.95 (978-1-4222-3051-0(1)) Mason Crest.

Mattern, Joanne. Staying Safe at Home, 1 vol. 2007. (Safety First Ser.). (ENG., Illus.). 24p. (gr. k-2). pap. 9.15 (978-0-8368-7798-4(5), 266b22ec-fb58-4a47-a908-6b23bb178851); lib. bdg. 24.67 (978-0-8368-7791-5(8), 5713bd1e-f920-4413-a984-203d3bf15a15) Stevens, Gareth Publishing LLLP. (Weekly Reader Leveled Readers).

—Staying Safe at Home / la Seguridad en Casa, 1 vol. 2007. (Safety First / la Seguridad Es lo Primero Ser.). (ENG & SPA., Illus.). 24p. (gr. k-2). pap. 9.15 (978-0-8368-8063-2(3), b2da84ac-ce00-4712-8d85-7e7557ed179a); lib. bdg. 24.67 (978-0-8368-8056-4(0), 71ee7c05-8440-46dc-920f-e9c4ed09b189) Stevens, Gareth Publishing LLLP. (Weekly Reader Leveled Readers).

—Staying Safe at School, 1 vol. 2007. (Safety First Ser.). (ENG., Illus.). 24p. (gr. k-2). pap. 9.15 (978-0-8368-7799-1(3), 82b1bede-75da-44f9-951f-3fa924ff3047); lib. bdg. 24.67 (978-0-8368-7792-2(6), f0372997-8743-41dd-9c06-ce7a163d6861) Stevens, Gareth Publishing LLLP. (Weekly Reader Leveled Readers).

—Staying Safe at School / la Seguridad en la Escuela, 1 vol. 2007. (Safety First / la Seguridad Es lo Primero Ser.). (ENG & SPA., Illus.). 24p. (gr. k-2). lib. bdg. 24.67 (978-0-8368-8057-1(9), 99a23e1d-78ad-4dfc-a2df-90415159f987, Weekly Reader Leveled Readers) Stevens, Gareth Publishing LLLP.

—Staying Safe in the Car, 1 vol. 2007. (Safety First Ser.). (ENG., Illus.). 24p. (gr. k-2). pap. 9.15 (978-0-8368-7800-4(0), 4ff21788-c148-46db-b290-5273f980bfa1); lib. bdg. 24.67 (978-0-8368-7793-9(4), 9b042e38-44fd-4479-9be2-5ab8d55cccc6) Stevens, Gareth Publishing LLLP. (Weekly Reader Leveled Readers).

—Staying Safe in the Car / la Seguridad en el Auto, 1 vol. 2007. (Safety First / la Seguridad Es lo Primero Ser.). (ENG & SPA.). 24p. (gr. k-2). pap. 9.15 (978-0-8368-8065-6(X), 2e9877ca-d766-4a98-814a-27c1650015d8); (Illus.). lib. bdg. 24.67 (978-0-8368-8058-8(7), fe3ec959-a3e3-445d-ac8d-30d68071c0d5) Stevens, Gareth Publishing LLLP. (Weekly Reader Leveled Readers).

—Staying Safe on My Bike, 1 vol. 2007. (Safety First Ser.). (ENG., Illus.). 24p. (gr. k-2). pap. 9.15 (978-0-8368-7801-1(9), 6172f468-320b-490f-93ef-119f79ee8878); lib. bdg. 24.67 (978-0-8368-7794-6(2), 8f1e2c53-4f85-4e83-a93b-809bc1d9289a) Stevens, Gareth Publishing LLLP. (Weekly Reader Leveled Readers).

—Staying Safe on My Bike / la Seguridad en Mi Bicicleta, 1 vol. 2007. (Safety First / la Seguridad Es lo Primero Ser.). (SPA & ENG., Illus.). 24p. (gr. k-2). lib. bdg. 24.67 (978-0-8368-8059-5(5), 00aaf97c-8673-4d88-aaa5-e359bbc56f21, Weekly Reader Leveled Readers) Stevens, Gareth Publishing LLLP.

—Staying Safe on the School Bus, 1 vol. 2007. (Safety First Ser.). (ENG., Illus.). 24p. (gr. k-2). pap. 9.15 (978-0-8368-7802-8(7), 5fc77eb2-13a8-4c82-a43e-eafa6fd68e7a); lib. bdg. 24.67 (978-0-8368-7795-3(0), c1effbba-6977-439b-ba26-9899aa09b12f) Stevens, Gareth Publishing LLLP. (Weekly Reader Leveled Readers).

—Staying Safe on the School Bus / la Seguridad en el Autobús Escolar, 1 vol. 2007. (Safety First / la Seguridad Es lo Primero Ser.). (SPA & ENG., Illus.). 24p. (gr. k-2). lib. bdg. 24.67 (978-0-8368-8060-1(9), 79640e7d-aa8b-48bf-b080-5947e117909d, Weekly Reader Leveled Readers) Stevens, Gareth Publishing LLLP.

—Staying Safe on the Street, 1 vol. 2007. (Safety First Ser.). (ENG., Illus.). 24p. (gr. k-2). pap. 9.15 (978-0-8368-7803-5(5), 827705e1-d543-4fae-a33c-4f12414b3e11); lib. bdg. 24.67 (978-0-8368-7796-0(9), 186398d1-025a-48d4-bcaa-25606efea415) Stevens, Gareth Publishing LLLP. (Weekly Reader Leveled Readers).

—Staying Safe on the Street / la Seguridad en la Calle, 1 vol. 2007. (Safety First / la Seguridad Es lo Primero Ser.). (SPA & ENG., Illus.). 24p. (gr. k-2). lib. bdg. 24.67 (978-0-8368-8061-8(7), 54c42cca-3f75-44ea-b072-72bdab395d5d, Weekly Reader Leveled Readers) Stevens, Gareth Publishing LLLP.

McKay, Sindy. We Both Read-Being Safe. Photodisc-Getty Staff, Images, photos by. 2003. (We Both Read Ser.). (Illus.). 44p. (J). (gr. 1-2). 7.99 (978-1-891327-51-3(8)) Treasure Bay, Inc.

Meachen Rau, Dana. Safety at Home, 1 vol. 2010. (Safe Kids Ser.). (ENG.). 32p. (gr. k-1). 25.50 (978-0-7614-4089-5(5), 64ba899f-afed-4d79-a7d3-b438002886ee) Cavendish Square Publishing LLC.

—Safety on the Go, 1 vol. 2010. (Safe Kids Ser.). (ENG.). 32p. (gr. k-1). 25.50 (978-0-7614-4085-7(2), b72f31f1-6813-4147-9dda-93aaf7c04e6a) Cavendish Square Publishing LLC.

—School Safety, 1 vol. 2010. (Safe Kids Ser.). (ENG.). 32p. (gr. k-1). 25.50 (978-0-7614-4090-1(9), cc66381c-c984-4eb1-85c7-c85855810417) Cavendish Square Publishing LLC.

—Seguridad en la Escuela / School Safety, 1 vol. 2010. (Niños Seguros / Safe Kids Ser.). (ENG & SPA.). 32p. (gr. k-2). lib. bdg. 25.50 (978-0-7614-4782-5(2), 721a7cf0-58fb-4638-88f5-4ef2b4b79ef1) Cavendish Square Publishing LLC.

Meiners, Cheri J. Be Careful & Stay Safe. Johnson, Meredith, illus. 2006. (Learning to Get Along(r) Ser.). (ENG.). 40p. (J). (gr. -1-3). pap. 11.99 (978-1-57542-211-4(5), 1136) Free Spirit Publishing Inc.

Miller, Shannon. Don't Talk to Strangers Online. 2013. (Internet DOs & DON'ts Ser.). (Illus.). 24p. (J). (gr. k-2). pap. 49.50 (978-1-4777-1565-9(7)); (ENG., (gr. 1-2). 26.27 (978-1-4777-0755-5(7), 9abd29e6-a5ed-4771-ac34-9dc357441f9b); (ENG., (gr. 1-2). pap. 9.25 (978-1-4777-1564-2(9), eb3d694b-93f2-4eba-84ad-f8b0f2d8942b) Rosen Publishing Group, Inc., The. (PowerKids Pr.).

Minton, Eric. Smartphone Safety, 1 vol., 1. 2014. (Stay Safe Online Ser.). (ENG.). 32p. (J). (gr. 4-5). 28.93 (978-1-4777-2935-9(6), 598ca0d9-090f-4194-9259-7e6734b50b1e, PowerKids Pr.) Rosen Publishing Group, Inc., The.

Myers, Connie Ellis. Words to Say out Loud: A Safety Book for Children. 2007. (Illus.). 84p. (J). spiral bd. 19.99 (978-0-9799127-0-2(9)) Say Out Loud, LLC.

Nelson, Robin. Staying Safe in Emergencies. 2006. (Pull Ahead Books — Health Ser.). (ENG., Illus.). 32p. (J). (gr. k-3). lib. bdg. 22.65 (978-0-8225-3391-7(X), a2c58950-68ff-4e91-b6a5-8020f83ad9a9, Lerner Pubns.) Lerner Publishing Group.

Nelson, Sara. Stay Safe! How You Can Keep Out of Harm's Way. 2009. pap. 52.95 (978-0-7613-4688-3(0)) Lerner Publishing Group.

Nelson, Sara Kirsten. Stay Safe! How You Can Keep Out of Harm's Way. Desrocher, Jack, illus. 2008. (Health Zone Ser.). (ENG.). 64p. (gr. 4-7). lib. bdg. 30.60 (978-0-8225-7551-1(5)) Lerner Publishing Group.

Newsom, Tony. High School Student Safety Tips. 2007. (ENG., Illus.). 95p. (YA). pap. 8.99 (978-0-9787143-5-2(0)) Carrington Bks.

—Middle School Student Safety Tips. 2007. (ENG., Illus.). 43p. (YA). pap. 8.99 (978-0-9787143-4-5(2)) Carrington Bks.

—Student Safety Tips: 40 that Every 1st - 2nd Grader Must Know!, 2 vols., Vol. 2. 2nd ed. 2007. (ENG., Illus.). 48p. pap. 6.99 (978-0-9787143-1-4(8)) Carrington Bks.

—Student Safety Tips: 45 that Every 3rd - 5th Grader Must Know!, 2 vols., Spanish Edition. 2nd ed. 2007. (ENG., Illus.). 52p. pap. 6.99 (978-0-9787143-2-1(6)) Carrington Bks.

No Way! A Book about Staying Safe for Girls Ages 4-6. 2003. (YA). (978-0-88441-660-9(7)) Girl Scouts of the USA.

Obert, Lois. Help! Willie's Choking! 2006. (ENG., Illus.). (J). 7.95 (978-1-57166-370-2(3)) Quixote Pr.

Olson, Karen W. Living Safe, Playing Safe. Hamelin, Marie-Micheline, illus. 2005. (Caring for Me Ser.). (ENG.). 20p. (J). pap. 10.95 (978-1-894778-33-6(2)) Theytus Bks., Ltd. CAN. Dist: Univ. of Toronto Pr.

—Living Safe, Playing Safe. George, Leonard, Jr. & George, Leonard, illus. 2009. (Caring for Me Ser.). (ENG.). 20p. (J). (gr. -1-k). pap. 9.95 (978-1-894778-51-0(0)) Theytus Bks., Ltd. CAN. Dist: Orca Bk. Pubs. USA.

Oregon Center for Applied Science, creator. Bike Smart. 2006. (J). cd-rom 19.95 (978-1-933898-09-4(7)) Oregon Ctr. for Applied Science, Inc.

—Walk Smart: Children's Pedestrian Safety Program. 2005. (J). cd-rom 19.95 (978-1-933898-10-0(0)) Oregon Ctr. for Applied Science, Inc.

Parker, Helen. Lift Stick & Learn: Emergency. 2006. (Illus.). 12p. (J). (gr. -1-k). (978-1-84610-282-0(0)) Make Believe Ideas.

Pettiford, Rebecca. Crossing Guards. 2015. (J). lib. bdg. 25.65 (978-1-62031-156-1(9), Bullfrog Bks.) Jump! Inc.

Pinnell, Gay Su, et al. Health & Safety 2: Safety First; Don't Be a Couch Potato; Birthday Shots; Just in Case; Time Out; Home Sick; the Eye Doctor; the Big Race, 8 bks., Set. Simon, Sue A. et al, illus. 2005. (ENG.). 8p. (J). pap. 120.00 (978-1-893986-27-5(6)) Keep Bks.

Raatma, Lucia. Staying Safe on the Playground. 2011. (Staying Safe Ser.). (ENG.). 24p. (J). (gr. 1-2). pap. 43.74 (978-1-4296-7198-9(X), 16766, Capstone Pr.) Capstone.

Raatma, Lucia & Lee, Sally. Staying Safe. 2012. (Staying Safe Ser.). (ENG.). 24p. (gr. 1-2). pap. 250.20 (978-1-4296-8391-3(0), Capstone Pr.) Capstone.

Raymer, Dottie. Staying Home Alone. 2015. (Smart Girl's Guide Ser.). lib. bdg. 24.50 (978-0-606-37237-4(7)) Turtleback.

Richardson, Sarah J. What If? The What Ifs of Childhood Safety, 1 bk. 2004. 120p. (J). per. 9.99 (978-0-9752982-0-6(8)) 4 Childrens Sake Pubns.

Rissman, Rebecca. No Running in the House: Safety Tips Every Babysitter Needs to Know, 1 vol. 2014. (Babysitter's Backpack Ser.). (ENG., Illus.). 32p. (J). (gr. 3-9). 28.65 (978-1-4914-0765-3(4), 125997) Capstone.

Rivera, Sheila. Emergencies. 2007. (First Step Nonfiction — Safety Ser.). (ENG., Illus.). 8p. (J). (gr. k-2). pap. 5.99 (978-0-8225-6824-7(1), 9e930d58-665e-4baf-a544-2d8bb564c79a) Lerner Publishing Group.

—School Safety. 2007. (First Step Nonfiction — Safety Ser.). (ENG., Illus.). 8p. (J). (gr. k-2). pap. 5.99 (978-0-8225-6822-3(5), 2d61431a-e43c-4c22-963b-f215e88be4f6) Lerner Publishing Group.

Robinson, Beth. The Safe Touch Book. Green, Noel, illus. 2013. 20p. (J). mass mkt. 8.99 (978-0-9799092-2-1(8)) Robinson, Beth.

Safety Always Matters (SAM), Vol. II. 12p. (J). (gr. k-3). 29.50 (978-1-883994-05-1(5)); 29.50 (978-1-883994-04-4(7)) Safety Always Matters, Inc.

Safety First, 10 vols. 2007. (Safety First Ser.). (ENG.). 24p. (gr. k-2). lib. bdg. 123.35 (978-0-8368-7790-8(X), f2319103-827c-4185-bb9b-64fb6f6ed086, Weekly Reader Leveled Readers) Stevens, Gareth Publishing LLLP.

Safety First/ La Seguridad Es lo Primero, 10 vols. 2007. (Safety First / la Seguridad Es lo Primero Ser.). (SPA & ENG.). 24p. (gr. k-2). lib. bdg. 123.35 (978-0-8368-8055-7(2), 1edd418f-1599-4070-b9a7-cbdbbc5f5a73, Weekly Reader Leveled Readers) Stevens, Gareth Publishing LLLP.

Safety Smarts, 14 vols. 2016. (Safety Smarts Ser.). (ENG.). 00024p. (J). (gr. k-1). 176.89 (978-1-4994-2690-8(9), 59e9d727-a2cb-490f-877e-51f57feb599f, PowerKids Pr.) Rosen Publishing Group, Inc., The.

Scholastic Library Publishing. Rookie Read: About Safety. 2012. (J). 138.00 (978-0-531-24325-1(7), Children's Pr.) Scholastic Library Publishing.

Schuette, Sarah L. Pedestrian Safety. 2019. (Staying Safe! Ser.). (ENG., Illus.). 24p. (J). (gr. -1-2). 24.65 (978-1-9771-0872-2(5), 140483, Pebble) Capstone.

—Stranger Safety. 2019. (Staying Safe! Ser.). (ENG., Illus.). 24p. (J). (gr. -1-2). pap. 6.95 (978-1-9771-1033-6(9), 141109); lib. bdg. 24.65 (978-1-9771-0870-8(9), 140481) Capstone. (Pebble).

Schulz, Kathy. Always Be Safe. 2011. (Rookie Ready to Learn — Out & about: in My Community Ser.). (Illus.). 40p. (J). (gr. -1-k). lib. bdg. 25.00 (978-0-531-27175-9(7), Children's Pr.) Scholastic Library Publishing.

—Always Be Safe. Potter, Katherine, illus. 2003. (Rookie Reader Skill Set Ser.). (ENG.). (J). (gr. k-2). pap. 4.95 (978-0-516-26965-8(8), Children's Pr.) Scholastic Library Publishing.

Senker, Cath. Keeping Safe, 1 vol. 2007. (Healthy Choices Ser.). (ENG., Illus.). 24p. (J). (gr. 1-2). lib. bdg. 26.27 (978-1-4042-4300-2(3), 2c3bb7c7-281a-46c1-8a4d-30357dd30a34, PowerKids Pr.) Rosen Publishing Group, Inc., The.

Simms, Mattie. The (Q) Kids Help Center. 2006. per. 9.99 (978-0-9772077-0-1(6)) Kanlearn, Inc.

Smith, K. Be Safe on the Bus: Learning the B Sound. 2009. (PowerPhonics Ser.). 24p. (gr. 1-1). 39.90 (978-1-60851-434-2(X), PowerKids Pr.) Rosen Publishing Group, Inc., The.

Spikes, James L. Taffey Pop Kids Presents the Adventures of Lemmon Head & Mudd Duck: What to Do if Someone Tries to Grab YOU!!! Spikes, Leon, Jr., illus. 2007. 32p. (J). 14.95 (978-0-9771438-0-1(5)) Taffey Pop Kids Publishing.

Staley, Erin. Improving Community Health & Safety Through Service Learning, 1 vol. 2014. (Service Learning for Teens Ser.). (ENG.). 80p. (YA). (gr. 7-7). 37.80 (978-1-4777-7955-2(8), 5b33c48b-bab4-4dde-982f-726b6cb80c9f, Rosen Young Adult) Rosen Publishing Group, Inc., The.

Stephens, Ronald, ed. Road Safety. 2014. (Safety First Ser.: 11). 48p. (J). (gr. 5-18). 20.95 (978-1-4222-3052-7(X)) Mason Crest.

—Stranger Danger. 2014. (Safety First Ser.: 11). 48p. (J). (gr. 5-18). 20.95 (978-1-4222-3054-1(6)) Mason Crest.

Thomas, Pat. I Can Be Safe: A First Look at Safety. Harker, Lesley, illus. 2003. (First Look At... Ser.). (ENG.). 32p. (J). (gr. -1-2). pap. 8.99 (978-0-7641-2460-0(9)) Sourcebooks, Inc.

Thompson, Gary. What Every Teen Should Know Before Getting Behind the Wheel Alone: A Guide to Increasing Your Child's Safety While Reducing Your Auto Repair Expenses. 2004. 131p. (YA). per. 9.95 (978-0-9749763-1-0(8)) Guiding Horizons.

Torrisi, Cathy. Take a Stand. 2011. pap. 39.95 (978-0-7664-3753-1(1)) Abrams & Co. Pubs., Inc.

—Tell Someone You Trust. 2011. pap. 39.95 (978-0-7664-3754-8(X)) Abrams & Co. Pubs., Inc.

Traveling Wild, 8 vols. 2014. (Traveling Wild Ser.). (ENG.). 32p. (J). (gr. 3-4). 113.08 (978-1-4824-1180-5(6), f4c823c5-d8c9-43b3-aaec-fe2819b4cf23) Stevens, Gareth Publishing LLLP.

Troupe, Thomas Kingsley. Staying Safe at School. Uno, Kat, illus. 2019. (School Rules Ser.). (ENG.). 24p. (J). (gr. k-2). pap. 8.95 (978-1-5158-4065-7(4), 140059, Picture Window Bks.) Capstone.

Unger, Karen. Don't Go There! Staying Safe for Girls Ages 6-8. 2003. (Illus.). 48p. (J). (978-0-88441-661-6(5)) Girl Scouts of the USA.

—I Don't Think So! A Book about Staying Safe for Girls Ages 8-11. 2003. (Illus.). 41p. (J). (978-0-88441-662-3(3)) Girl Scouts of the USA.

van der Zande, Irene. Kidpower Safety Comics: An Introduction to "People Safety" for Young Children Ages 3 to 10 & Their Adults. Golert, Amanda, illus. 2011. 44p. (J). pap. (978-0-9796191-4-4(9)) van der Zande, Irene.

Van Sant, Barb. Kid Sense! Good Answers to Your Child's Tough Questions about Personal Safety. 2010. 39p. pap. 12.95 (978-0-578-06778-0(1)) Boulder Street Bks. LLC.

Walker, Gloria. Stop & Go Safety. 2008. 24p. (J). pap. 14.95 (978-1-883589-91-2(6)) Clark Publishing, Inc.

Weber, Rebecca. Safety Basics, 1 vol. 2012. (Health & Your Body Ser.). (ENG.). 24p. (J). (gr. -1-2). lib. bdg. 27.32 (978-1-4296-7694-6(9), 117291); (gr. k-1). pap. 41.70 (978-1-4296-8346-3(5)) Capstone. (Capstone Pr.).

Weekley, Randy J. Strangers, Bullies, Safety & More (Spanish Version) A How to Guide to Child Safety. 2008. (SPA., Illus.). 54p. (J). pap. 16.99 (978-1-59879-632-2(1), Lifevest) Lifevest Publishing, Inc.

Wood, Ira. How to Stay Safe at Home & On-line. 2009. (Reading Room Collection 2 Ser.). 24p. (gr. 3-4). 42.50 (978-1-60851-972-9(4), PowerKids Pr.) Rosen Publishing Group, Inc., The.

21st Century Safety & Privacy. 2013. (21st Century Safety & Privacy Ser.). 64p. (J). (gr. 5-8). pap. 388.50 (978-1-4777-1678-6(5)); (gr. 5-8). pap. 64.75 (978-1-4777-1677-9(7)); (ENG.). (gr. 6-6). 185.60 (978-1-4488-9579-3(0), 2edb6323-522d-467a-8988-0b1d388fe070) Rosen Publishing Group, Inc., The.

SAFETY EDUCATION—FICTION

Anielski, Angela. My Safe Space: I Don't Know You! 2009. 36p. (J). pap. 19.95 (978-1-4327-3774-0(0)) Outskirts Pr., Inc.

Bernstein, Susan H. N. E. Pominonous Epstein Minds His Mind. (E. Pominonous Epstein Ser.). 18p. (J). (gr. -1-3). pap. 8.95 (978-0-9706596-0-6(1)) Bernstein, Susan.

Blacknall, Sharon. The Abc's & 123's of Child Safety. 2012. 46p. pap. 17.45 (978-1-4624-0437-7(5), Inspiring Voices) Author Solutions, LLC.

Blazin' Hot: Coloring/Activity Book (English) 2005. (Illus.). (J). 2.99 (978-0-9770455-0-1(1)) Mighty Kids Media.

Blazin' Hot: Coloring/Activity Book (English) Incl. Stickers. 2007. (J). 2.99 (978-1-933934-51-8(4)) Mighty Kids Media.

Blazin' Hot: Picture Book (English) NL 9x9 with Snipe. 2007. (J). 5.99 (978-1-933934-46-4(8)) Mighty Kids Media.

Cain, Janan. Roonie B. Moonie: Lost & Alone. 2007. (Illus.). 32p. (J). (gr. -1-3). 15.95 (978-0-9740190-8-6(9)) Illumination Arts Publishing Co., Inc.

Camping Caper: Coloring/Activity Book (English) incl. Stickers. 2007. (Illus.). (J). 2.99 (978-1-933934-65-5(4)) Mighty Kids Media.

Camping Caper: Picture Book (English) 8x8. 2007. (Illus.). (J). 5.99 (978-1-933934-64-8(6)) Mighty Kids Media.

Chatton, Julie. Trains: Safe & Sound. 2008. 24p. pap. 13.50 (978-1-60693-307-7(8), Eloquent Bks.) Strategic Book Publishing & Rights Agency (SBPRA).

Chessen, Sherri. Gorp's Secret: An Empowering Tale in Pumpernickel Park. Bronson, Linda, illus. 2008. (ENG.). 36p. (J). 16.95 (978-0-9724249-3-6(8)) Gorp Group Pr., The.

Chriscoe, Sharon. Scary Weather, Scaredy Cat, 1 vol. 2008. (ENG.). 48p. 24.95 (978-1-60474-143-8(0)) America Star Bks.

Christopher, Matt. The Extreme Team: into Danger Zone. 6th ed. 2004. (Extreme Team Ser.: 6). (ENG., Illus.). 64p. (J). (gr. 1-4). pap. 8.99 (978-0-316-76267-0(9)) Little, Brown Bks. for Young Readers.

—The Extreme Team: Wild Ride. Koelsch, Michael, illus. 7th ed. 2005. (Extreme Team Ser.: 7). (ENG.). 64p. (J). (gr. 1-4). pap. 8.99 (978-0-316-76263-2(6)) Little, Brown Bks. for Young Readers.

Cook, Julia. The Bubble Wrap Queen. Valentine, Allison, illus. 2008. (ENG.). 32p. (J). (gr. k-3). pap. 5.00 (978-1-931636-83-4(4), A411) National Ctr. For Youth Issues.

—Scoop. Ventling, Elisabeth, illus. 2007. 32p. (J). 15.95 (978-1-934073-07-0(5)) National Ctr. For Youth Issues.

Cool by the Pool: Coloring / Activity Book incl Snipe. 2007. (Illus.). (J). 2.99 (978-0-9770455-8-7(7)) Mighty Kids Media.

Cool by the Pool: Picture Book (English) 8x8. 2007. (J). 5.99 (978-1-933934-37-2(9)) Mighty Kids Media.

Cool by the Pool: Picture Book (English) NL 9x9 with Snipe. 2007. (J). 5.99 (978-1-933934-47-1(6)) Mighty Kids Media.

Crowley, Kerry. The Smart Thing to Do. 2006. 60p. pap. 7.61 (978-1-4116-7126-3(0)) Lulu Pr., Inc.

Danger Alert: Coloring/Activity Book (English) Incl. Stickers. 2007. (J). 2.99 *(978-1-933934-54-9(9))* Mighty Kids Media.
Danger Alert: Picture Book (English) 8x8. 2007. (J). 5.99 *(978-1-933934-39-6(5))* Mighty Kids Media.
Danger Alert: Picture Book (English) 9x9 with Snipe. 2007. (J). 5.99 *(978-1-933934-49-5(2))* Mighty Kids Media.
Denice, Sonia. Chow-E-Chowz: Saved by a Whistle. 2011. 44p. pap. 18.46 *(978-1-4567-1020-0(6))* AuthorHouse.
Diggle, David Mark. Douglas: Pays the Price for Not Paying Attention. Preuss, Sarah Louise, illus. 2011. 24p. (J). pap. *(978-0-9871658-5-5(2))* Diggle de Doo Productions Pty, Ltd.
Duracell and the National Center for Missing & Exploited Children (NCMEC), creator. The Great Tomato Adventure: A Story about Smart Safety Choices. 2007. 0.00 *(978-0-9795307-0-8(9))* Duracell & the National Ctr. for Missing & Exploited Children (NCMEC).
Dyan, Penelope. When Touching Is Bad. Dyan, Penelope, illus. 2013. (Illus.). 34p. pap. 11.95 *(978-1-61477-088-6(3))* Bellissima Publishing, LLC.
Educational Adventures, creator. Cool by the Pool: Coloring/Activity Book (Spanish) w/ Snipe. 2007. (Illus.). (J). per. 2.99 *(978-1-933934-73-0(5))* Mighty Kids Media.
—Cool by the Pool: Picture Book (Spanish) 9x9. 2007. (Illus.). (J). per. 5.99 *(978-1-933934-72-3(7))* Mighty Kids Media.
—Danger Alert: Coloring/Activity Book (Spanish) w/ Snipe. 2006. (Illus.). (J). 2.99 *(978-1-933934-06-8(9))* Mighty Kids Media.
—Danger Alert: Picture Book (Spanish) 9x9. 2006. (Illus.). (J). 5.99 *(978-1-933934-04-4(2))* Mighty Kids Media.
—Free Wheelin' Coloring/Activity Book (English) w/ Snipe. 2007. (J). 2.99 *(978-1-933934-52-5(2))* Mighty Kids Media.
—Free Wheelin' Picture Book (Spanish) w/ Snipe. 2006. (Illus.). (J). 5.99 *(978-0-9770455-6-3(0))* Mighty Kids Media.
—Poison Patrol: Coloring/Activity Book (Spanish) w/ Snipe. 2006. (Illus.). (J). 2.99 *(978-1-933934-02-0(6))* Mighty Kids Media.
—Poison Patrol: Picture Book (Spanish) 9x9. 2006. (Illus.). (J). 5.99 *(978-1-933934-00-6(X))* Mighty Kids Media.
—Street Smarts: Coloring/Activity Book (Spanish) w/ Snipe. 2006. (Illus.). (J). 2.99 *(978-1-933934-19-8(0))* Mighty Kids Media.
—Street Smarts: Picture Book (Spanish) 9x9. 2007. (Illus.). (J). per. 5.99 *(978-1-933934-77-8(8))* Mighty Kids Media.
Ennis, Nancy. When Mommy & Daddy Say No, They Still Love You. Meadows, Cynthia, illus. 2014. (ENG.). 24p. (J). 14.95 net. *(978-1-61254-198-3(4))* Brown Books Publishing Group.
Faulk, Terry. Joe the Roadside Crow. 2010. 20p. 12.99 *(978-1-4490-7006-9(X))* AuthorHouse.
Free Wheelin' Picture Book (English) NL 9x9 with Snipe. 2007. (J). 5.99 *(978-1-933934-48-8(4))* Mighty Kids Media.
Glickman, Claudia. Skin Sense. 2007. (Illus.). 16p. (J). *(978-0-615-16242-3(8))* L.G. Publishing.
Goodnight, Craig. Condor the Police K-9 in: Never Talk to Strangers. 2011. 28p. pap. 12.25 *(978-1-4520-7644-7(8))* AuthorHouse.
Gopinath, Karin Ursula. Friends in the Garden. Sutanto, Tommy, illus. 2008. 34p. (J). per. 19.95 *(978-0-9800637-0-7(1))* Lotus Art Works Inc.
Haslett, Katherine A. The Day Amy Met the Prime Minister & Mrs. Blair. 2007. (Illus.). 32p. (J). pap. 8.00 *(978-0-8059-7353-2(2))* Dorrance Publishing Co., Inc.
Health New England, creator. Sammie Sportz My Summer of Sports Safety. 2007. (Illus.). 16p. (J). 9.95 *(978-0-9777159-3-0(0))* Health New England.
Hill, Maree. Nurse Nerid. 2011. 28p. pap. 28.03 *(978-1-4568-5419-5(4))* Xlibris Corp.
Jacobs, Paul DuBois & Swender, Jennifer. Fire Drill. Lee, Huy Voun, illus. 2010. (ENG.). 32p. (J). (gr. -1-2). 19.99 *(978-0-8050-8953-0(5))*, 900055716, Holt, Henry & Co. Bks. For Young Readers) Holt, Henry & Co.
Joyce, Irma. Never Talk to Strangers. Buckett, George, illus. 2009. 32p. (J). (gr. -1-2). 9.99 *(978-0-375-84964-0(5)*, Golden Bks.) Random Hse. Children's Bks.
Judith Mader. I Went to Safety Town! 2009. 40p. pap. 16.99 *(978-1-4389-0129-9(1))* AuthorHouse.
Lane, Kathleen. The Best Worst Thing. 2018. (ENG.). 208p. (J). (gr. 3-7). pap. 12.99 *(978-0-316-25782-4(6))* Little, Brown Bks. for Young Readers.
—The Best Worst Thing. 2018. (J). lib. bdg. 17.20 *(978-0-606-40635-2(2))* Turtleback.
Larson, Jason. Me & My Safety. 2009. 28p. pap. 16.99 *(978-1-4490-4445-9(X))* AuthorHouse.
Marcotte, David A. Be Wary of Strangers. 2005. (ENG., Illus.). 36p. per. 14.95 *(978-1-932672-47-3(3))* Outskirts Pr., Inc.
Matalonis, Anne. The Fox Behind the Chatterbox. McGhee, Chelsea, illus. 2008. 32p. pap. 17.95 *(978-1-59858-783-8(8))* Dog Ear Publishing, LLC.
Mayo, Margaret. Emergency! Ayliffe, Alex, illus. 2003. 32p. (J). (gr. -1-1). 14.95 *(978-0-87614-922-5(0)*, Carolrhoda Bks.) Lerner Publishing Group.
Mishica, Clare. Samantha Stays Safe. Dubin, Jill, illus. 2012. 32p. (J). pap. 8.00 *(978-1-935014-40-9(4))* Hutchings, John Pubs.
Omawumi Kola-Lawal, Constance. We Learn about Road Safety. 2013. 32p. pap. *(978-1-909204-29-4(3))* BookPublishingWorld.
Pace, Anne Marie. Never Ever Talk to Strangers. Francis, Guy, illus. 2010. (J). *(978-0-545-24229-5(0))* Scholastic, Inc.
Pendziwol, Jean E. Once upon a Dragon: Stranger Safety for Kids (and Dragons) Gourbault, Martine, illus. 2006. (ENG.). 32p. (J). (gr. -1-2). 11.99 *(978-1-55337-969-0(1))* Kids Can Pr., Ltd. CAN. Dist: Hachette Bk. Group.
Poison Patrol: Coloring/Activity (English) Incl. Posters, Stickers. 2007. (J). 2.99 *(978-1-933934-53-2(0))* Mighty Kids Media.
Poison Patrol: Picture Book 8x8. 2007. (J). 5.99 *(978-1-933934-40-2(9))* Mighty Kids Media.
Poison Patrol: Picture Book (English) 9x9 with Snipe. 2007. (J). 5.99 *(978-1-933934-50-1(6))* Mighty Kids Media.
Porter, Rhonda. Brody Learns about Strangers, 1 vol. 2009. 29p. pap. 19.95 *(978-1-61546-699-3(1))* PublishAmerica, Inc.
Russell, Pamela L. R. Bee Careful! My Big Kid Safety Manual. 2012. 20p. pap. 17.99 *(978-1-4685-9831-5(7))* AuthorHouse.
Sano, Gina. Traffic Lights. 2017. (ENG., Illus.). (J). pap. 24.14 *(978-1-5434-0348-0(4))* Xlibris Corp.
Sargent, Dave & Sargent, David M. Bob White: Use Good Judgement, 20 vols., Vol. 3. Lenoir, Jane, illus. 2003. (Feather Tales Ser.: No. 3). 42p. (J). pap. 10.95 *(978-1-56763-724-3(8))* Ozark Publishing.
Sargent, David M. Bob White: Use Good Judgement, 20 vols., Vol. 3. Lenoir, Jane, illus. 2003. (Feather Tales Ser.: No. 3). 42p. (J). lib. bdg. 20.95 *(978-1-56763-723-6(X))* Ozark Publishing.
Scoop. 2007. (J). 15.95 *(978-1-934073-00-1(8))* National Ctr. For Youth Issues.
Slater, Teddy. Emergency, Call 911. Lewis, Anthony, illus. 2010. 16p. (J). *(978-0-545-24601-9(6))* Scholastic, Inc.
—Fire Prevention. Lewis, Anthony, illus. 2010. 16p. (J). *(978-0-545-24603-3(2))* Scholastic, Inc.
—Home Safe Home. Smith, Jamie, illus. 2010. 16p. (J). *(978-0-545-24606-4(7))* Scholastic, Inc.
—Safety in the Bus. Smith, Jamie, illus. 2010. 16p. (J). *(978-0-545-24602-6(4))* Scholastic, Inc.
—Stranger Danger. Lewis, Anthony, illus. 2010. 16p. (J). *(978-0-545-24605-7(9))* Scholastic, Inc.
—Street Safety. Smith, Jamie, illus. 2010. 16p. (J). *(978-0-545-24604-0(0))* Scholastic, Inc.
Street Smarts: Coloring/Activity Book (English) Incl. Stickers. 2006. (Illus.). (J). 2.99 *(978-1-933934-18-1(2))* Mighty Kids Media.
Street Smarts: Picture Book 9x9 with Snipe. 2006. (Illus.). (J). 5.99 *(978-1-933934-17-4(4))* Mighty Kids Media.
Street Smarts: Picture Book (English) 8x8. 2006. (Illus.). (J). 5.99 *(978-1-933934-16-7(6))* Mighty Kids Media.
Thomas, Kate. Mother Duck Knows the Way. Larkins, Mona, illus. 2005. 32p. (J). 8.95 *(978-1-58374-122-1(4))* Chicago Spectrum Pr.
Townsend, Peter. Shelly & Muffin's Big Lesson Learned. 2008. 11p. pap. 24.95 *(978-1-60672-379-1(0))* America Star Bks.
Tuchman, Lauryn & Silverhardt, Lauryn. A Visit to the Firehouse. Craig, Karen, illus. 2009. (Blue's Clues Ser.). (ENG.). 24p. (J). (gr. -1-2). pap. 3.99 *(978-1-4169-7193-1(9)*, Simon Spotlight/Nickelodeon) Simon Spotlight/Nickelodeon.
Willis, Jeanne. Cottonball Colin. Ross, Tony, illus. 2008. 26p. (J). (gr. -1-4). 16.00 *(978-0-8028-5331-8(5)*, Eerdmans Bks For Young Readers) Eerdmans, William B. Publishing Co.
Yolen, Jane. How Do Dinosaurs Stay Safe? Teague, Mark, illus. 2015. (ENG.). 40p. (J). (gr. -1-k). 18.99 *(978-0-439-24104-5(9)*, Blue Sky Pr., The) Scholastic, Inc.

SAFETY MEASURES

see Accidents—Prevention

also subjects with the subdivision Safety Measures, e.g. Aeronautics—Safety Measures

SAHARA

Aloian, Molly. The Sahara Desert. 2012. (ENG.). 32p. (J). *(978-0-7787-0714-1(8))*; (Illus.). pap. *(978-0-7787-0722-6(9))* Crabtree Publishing Co.
Chapman, S. I. mon. In the Desert. 2006. (Illus.). 111p. (J). lib. bdg. 20.00 *(978-1-4242-0628-5(6))* Fitzgerald Bks.
Fine, Jil. Sahara: El Desierto Mas Grande del Mundo, 1 vol. 2003. (Maravillas Naturales (Nature's Greatest Hits) Ser.). (SPA.). 24p. (J). (gr. 2-2). lib. bdg. 26.27 *(978-0-8239-6879-4(0)*, 197ee948-2aba-4bce-a299-a21b6ffeb422) Rosen Publishing Group, Inc., The.
—Sahara: El desierto más grande del mundo (the Sahara: World's Largest Desert) 2009. (Maravillas naturales (Natures Greatest Hits) Ser.). (SPA.). 24p. (gr. 2-2). 42.50 *(978-1-61514-365-8(3)*, Editorial Buenas Letras) Rosen Publishing Group, Inc., The.
—The Sahara: World's Largest Desert. 2009. (Nature's Greatest Hits Ser.). 24p. (gr. 2-2). 42.50 *(978-1-61514-842-4(6)*, PowerKids Pr.) Rosen Publishing Group, Inc., The.
Franchino, Vicky. Sahara Desert. 2016. (Community Connections: Getting to Know Our Planet Ser.). (ENG., Illus.). 24p. (J). (gr. 2-5). 29.21 *(978-1-63470-518-9(1)*, 207803) Cherry Lake Publishing.
Heinrichs, Ann. The Sahara, 1 vol. 2008. (Nature's Wonders Ser.). (ENG.). 96p. (gr. 6-6). lib. bdg. 38.36 *(978-0-7614-2855-8(0)*, c67647b4-e723-4c6a-bec5-65e5ead444f1) Cavendish Square Publishing LLC.
Lappi, Megan. The Sahara Desert. 2005. 32p. pap. 9.95 *(978-1-59036-274-7(8))* Weigl Pubs., Inc.
—Sahara Desert. 2013. (J). *(978-1-62127-477-3(2))*; pap. *(978-1-62127-483-4(7))* Weigl Pubs., Inc.
—The Sahara Desert: The Largest Desert in the World. 2006. (Natural Wonders Ser.). (Illus.). 32p. (J). (gr. 3-7). 15.60 *(978-0-7569-6997-4(2))* Perfection Learning Corp.
—The Sahara Desert: The Largest Desert in the World. 2006. (Natural Wonders Ser.). (Illus.). 32p. (J). (gr. 5-6). lib. bdg. 26.00 *(978-1-59036-452-9(X))*; per. 9.95 *(978-1-59036-458-1(9)*, 1266427) Weigl Pubs., Inc.
Reynolds, Jan. Sahara, 1 vol. 2007. (Vanishing Cultures Ser.). (ENG., Illus.). 32p. *(978-1-60060-146-0(4))*; (J). 11.95 *(978-1-60060-131-6(6)*, leelowbooks) Lee & Low Bks., Inc.
Weintraub, Aileen. The Sahara Desert: The Biggest Desert. 2009. (Great Record Breakers in Nature Ser.). 24p. (gr. 3-4). 42.50 *(978-1-61513-186-0(8)*, PowerKids Pr.) Rosen Publishing Group, Inc., The.
Zuravicky, Orli. The Amazon & the Sahara: Using Double Line Graphs & Double Bar Graphs, 1 vol. (Math for the REAL World Ser.). 32p. (gr. 4-5). 2010. (ENG., Illus.). pap. 10.00 *(978-0-8239-8868-6(6)*, 7018b492-5846-494c-b938-36929a7f027b) 2009. 47.90 *(978-1-60851-401-4(3))* Rosen Publishing Group, Inc., The. (PowerKids Pr.).

SAHARA—FICTION

Cunnane, Kelly. Deep in the Sahara. Hadadi, Hoda, illus. 2018. 40p. (J). (gr. -1-3). 8.99 *(978-0-525-64566-5(7)*, Schwartz & Wade Bks.) Random Hse. Children's Bks.
Davies, Stephen. Outlaw. 2011. (ENG.). 304p. (YA). (gr. 7). 16.99 *(978-0-547-39017-8(3))* Houghton Mifflin Harcourt Publishing Co.
Smith, Lisa. Makini, the Impala with a Crooked Horn. 2011. 24p. pap. 24.95 *(978-1-4626-2608-3(4))* America Star Bks.
Terman, D. By Balloon to the Sahara. Millet, Jason, illus. 2015. (ENG.). 144p. (J). (gr. 4-8). pap. 7.99 *(978-1-937133-48-1(6))* Chooseco LLC.
Turner, Tracey. Lost in the Desert of Dread. 2014. (LOST: Can You Survive? Ser.). (ENG., Illus.). 128p. (J). (gr. 6-6). *(978-0-7787-0725-7(3))* Crabtree Publishing Co.

SAILING

see also Boats and Boating; Navigation; Yachts and Yachting

Bruce, Julia. Sail! Can You Command a Sea Voyage?, 1 vol. 2009. (Step into History Ser.). (ENG., Illus.). 32p. (J). (gr. 3-3). lib. bdg. 26.60 *(978-0-7660-3477-8(1)*, 2179b596-e7be-4db3-ad0d-ec836e43f26d) Enslow Publishing, LLC.
Gamble, Adam & Jasper, Mark. Good Night Boats. Veno, Joe, illus. 2016. (Good Night Our World Ser.). (ENG.). 20p. (J). (— 1). bds. 9.95 *(978-1-60219-500-4(5))* Good Night Bks.
Henderson, Richard. First Sail, 1 vol. 2009. (ENG., Illus.). 48p. (gr. 3-6). 15.95 *(978-0-87033-442-9(5)*, 3641, Cornell Maritime Pr./Tidewater Pubs.) Schiffer Publishing, Ltd.
Ives, Burl. Sailing on a Very Fine Day. Myers, Bernice & Myers, Lou, illus. 2011. 32p. pap. 35.95 *(978-1-258-04002-4(6))* Literary Licensing, LLC.
Kibble, Steve & Davison, Tim. Sailing for Kids. 2nd ed. 2015. (ENG., Illus.). 48p. pap. 18.70 *(978-1-909911-26-0(7))* Fernhurst Bks. GBR. Dist: Casemate Pubs. & Bk. Distributors, LLC.
Pelling. Getting Afloat. 2003. (Illus.). 80p. pap. *(978-0-7136-5278-9(0)*, Adlard Coles) Bloomsbury Publishing Plc.
Porter, Suzie. Sailing, 1 vol. 2011. (Get Outdoors Ser.). (ENG., Illus.). 32p. (J). (gr. 5-5). lib. bdg. 28.93 *(978-1-4488-3297-2(7)*, 454e96e7-d687-463b-9118-c0441b978eee, PowerKids Pr.) Rosen Publishing Group, Inc., The.
Sisk, Siobhan. Would You Dare Sail Around the World?, 1 vol. 2016. (Would You Dare? Ser.). (ENG.). 32p. (J). (gr. 1-2). pap. 11.50 *(978-1-4824-5826-8(8)*, 23dc32e8-22bd-42b0-8614-ba74493c4fe9); lib. bdg. 28.27 *(978-1-4824-5828-2(4)*, 5d0d713e-d7d2-4224-bf4c-930c27b46dd8) Stevens, Gareth Publishing LLLP.
Veigele, William J. Sea Bag of Memories: Images, Poems, Thoughts, & Crafts of the small Ship Sailors of World War II. 2003. 320p. (YA). (gr. 10-18). 39.95 *(978-0-9645867-4-1(6))* Astral Publishing Co.

SAILING—FICTION

Appelt, Kathi. Keeper. Hall, August, illus. (ENG.). (J). (gr. 3-7). 2012. 432p. pap. 9.99 *(978-1-4169-5061-5(3))* 2010. 416p. 17.99 *(978-1-4169-5060-8(5))* Simon & Schuster Children's Publishing. (Atheneum Bks. for Young Readers).
Arvidson, Douglas. Brothers of the Fire Star. Scarborough, Rob, illus. 2012. 207p. (YA). pap. 15.95 *(978-1-890109-91-2(6)*, Cross Time) Crossquarter Publishing Group.
Ballantyne, R. M. The Crew of the Water Wagtail. 2011. 146p. pap. 12.95 *(978-1-60664-550-5(1))* Rodgers, Alan Bks.
—Red Rooney: Or, the Last of the Crew. 2007. (R. M. Ballantyne Collection). (Illus.). 408p. 22.00 *(978-1-934554-08-1(1))* Vision Forum, Inc., The.
Basham, Tom. Sailing Home. Calvert, Lissa, illus. 2012. 168p. *(978-1-77097-370-1(2))* FriesenPress.
Basham, Tom & Calvert, Lissa. Sailing Home. 2012. 168p. pap. *(978-1-77097-371-8(0))* FriesenPress.
Beach, John & Lubotsky, Dana, readers. The Wanderer. unabr. ed. 2004. 320p. (J). (gr. 4-7). pap. 36.00 incl. audio *(978-0-8072-0864-9(7)*, LYA 199 SP, Listening Library) Random Hse. Audio Publishing Group.
Bell, Loman. Old Glory. Bell, Loman, illus. 2012. (Illus.). 40p. pap. *(978-0-9866065-8-8(8))* Wood Islands Prints.
Benchmark Education Co., LLC. Sail with Me Big Book. 2014. (Shared Reading Foundations Ser.). (J). (gr. -1). *(978-1-4509-9447-7(4))* Benchmark Education Co.
Blackstone, Stella. Una Isla Bajo el Sol. Ceccoli, Nicoletta, illus. 2003. (SPA.). 24p. (J). pap. 6.99 *(978-1-84148-144-9(0))* Barefoot Bks., Inc.
Blackstone, Stella & Barefoot Books Staff. An Island in the Sun. Ceccoli, Nicoletta, illus. 2005. (ENG.). 24p. (J). pap. 6.99 *(978-1-84148-079-4(7))* Barefoot Bks., Inc.
Borgenicht, David & Lurie, Alexander. Deadly Seas: You Decide How to Survive! 2015. (WorstCase Scenario Ultimate Adventure Ser.). (ENG., Illus.). 204p. (gr. 3-8). 47.10 *(978-1-59920-981-4(0))* Black Rabbit Bks.
Bowman, Crystal. Otter & Owl's Helpful Hike, 1 vol. Zimmer, Kevin J., illus. 2008. (I Can Read! / Otter & Owl Ser.). (ENG.). 32p. (J). pap. 4.99 *(978-0-310-71704-1(3))* Zonderkidz.
Bradford, Arthur. Benny's Brigade. Hanawalt, Lisa, illus. 2012. (ENG.). 48p. (J). 19.95 *(978-1-936365-61-6(8)*, d90f3ed6-666e-4056-88ba-efe956ba2f74) McSweeney's Publishing.
Brown, Jeff. The Flat Stanley Collection Box Set: Flat Stanley, Invisible Stanley, Stanley in Space, & Stanley, Flat Again!, Set. Pamintuan, Macky, illus. 2013. (Flat Stanley Ser.). (ENG.). 400p. (J). (gr. 1-5). pap. 20.96 *(978-0-06-180247-8(6)*, HarperCollins) HarperCollins Pubs.
—Stanley, Flat Again! Pamintuan, Macky, illus. 2009. (Flat Stanley Ser.). (ENG.). 96p. (J). (gr. 2-5). pap. 4.99 *(978-0-06-442173-7(2)*, HarperCollins) HarperCollins Pubs.
Bukiet, Melvin. Undertown. 2013. (ENG.). 304p. (J). (gr. 3-7). 17.95 *(978-1-4197-0589-2(X)*, 1045901, Amulet Bks.) Abrams, Inc.
Burgess, Lisa Maria. Juma's Dhow Race. Gugu, Abdul M., illus. 2013. 32p. 19.95 *(978-1-939604-09-5(5))*; pap. 9.99 *(978-1-939604-05-7(2))* Barranca Pr.
Clements, Andrew. In Harm's Way. Stower, Adam, illus. (Benjamin Pratt & the Keepers of the School Ser.: 4). (ENG.). (J). (gr. 2-5). 2014. 240p. pap. 8.99 *(978-1-4169-3910-8(5))* 2013. 224p. 14.99 *(978-1-4169-3889-7(3))* Simon & Schuster Children's Publishing. (Atheneum Bks. for Young Readers).
—We the Children. 2011. (Benjamin Pratt & the Keepers of the School Ser.: 1). (ENG.). 176p. (J). (gr. 2-5). pap. 8.99 *(978-1-4169-3907-8(5)*, Atheneum Bks. for Young Readers) Simon & Schuster Children's Publishing.
—The Whites of Their Eyes. Stower, Adam, illus. 2013. (Benjamin Pratt & the Keepers of the School Ser.: 3). (ENG.). 240p. (J). (gr. 2-5). pap. 7.99 *(978-1-4169-3909-2(1)*, Atheneum Bks. for Young Readers) Simon & Schuster Children's Publishing.
Coates, Paul. Tim & the Iceberg, 1 vol. Benfold Haywood, Ian P., illus. 2011. (ENG.). 32p. (J). (gr. k-3). 16.95 *(978-1-59572-205-8(X))*; pap. 6.95 *(978-1-59572-206-5(8))* Star Bright Bks., Inc.
Collingwood, Harry. Under the Chilean Flag. 2009. 184p. 26.95 *(978-1-60664-598-7(6))*; pap. 13.95 *(978-1-60664-330-3(4))* Rodgers, Alan Bks.
Costello, David Hyde. Little Pig Saves the Ship. Costello, David Hyde, illus. 2017. (Illus.). 32p. (J). (gr. -1-2). 14.99 *(978-1-58089-715-0(0))* Charlesbridge Publishing, Inc.
Creech, Sharon. The Wanderer: A Newbery Honor Award Winner. Diaz, David, illus. 2011. (ENG.). 304p. (J). (gr. 3-7). pap. 7.99 *(978-0-06-441032-8(3)*, HarperCollins) HarperCollins Pubs.
Daynes, Katie, retold by. Sinbad. 2005. (Young Reading Series 1 Ser.). 48p. (J). (gr. 2-18). pap. 5.95 *(978-0-7945-0825-8(1)*, Usborne) EDC Publishing.
DeGorsky, Gregory J. The Christmas Pirate. DeGorsky, Jon, ed. 2007. (ENG., Illus.). 80p. (J). pap. 4.95 *(978-0-9678542-3-6(7))* Magnetic Image, Inc.
Dogiakis, Helen. Captain Terry the Pirate Cow's Adventure to Italy. 2011. 32p. pap. 14.99 *(978-1-4567-3131-1(9))* AuthorHouse.
Eggleton, Jill. Sailor Sam in Trouble. Storey, Jim, illus. 2004. (Rigby Sails Early Ser.). (ENG.). 16p. (gr. 1-2). pap. 6.95 *(978-0-7578-9295-0(7))* Houghton Mifflin Harcourt Publishing Co.
Ering, Timothy Basil. The Unexpected Love Story of Alfred Fiddleduckling. Ering, Timothy Basil, illus. 2017. (ENG., Illus.). 48p. (J). (-k). 16.99 *(978-0-7636-6432-9(4))* Candlewick Pr.
Espluga, Maria. I Am a Sailor, 1 vol. 2009. (I Am A... Ser.). (ENG., Illus.). 24p. (J). (gr. k-k). pap. 9.15 *(978-1-60754-255-1(2)*, 25f0dec3-1042-4e39-bf1d-73231de471f7); lib. bdg. 27.27 *(978-1-60754-254-4(4)*, 11ceea5b-b1c1-4ef2-89a9-32f4bedc1ab1) Rosen Publishing Group, Inc., The. (Windmill Bks.).
—I, Sailor: Yo, Marinero. 2009. (SPA & ENG.). 28p. (J). 13.95 *(978-1-931398-53-4(4))* Me+Mi Publishing.
Ezirim, E. C. Jet Black & the Ebony Knights. 2010. 40p. 16.99 *(978-1-4520-7567-9(0))* AuthorHouse.
Fan, Terry & Fan, Eric. Ocean Meets Sky. Fan, Terry & Fan, Eric, illus. 2018. (ENG., Illus.). 48p. (J). (gr. -1-3). 17.99 *(978-1-4814-7037-7(X)*, Simon & Schuster Bks. For Young Readers) Simon & Schuster Bks. For Young Readers.
Fleming, Meg. Ready, Set, Sail! Flowers, Luke, illus. 2018. (ENG.). 32p. (J). (gr. -1-3). 16.99 *(978-1-4998-0533-8(0))* Little Bee Books Inc.
Floerchinger, Lori Liddic. Ocean of Dreams. Floerchinger, Jeremy, illus. 2008. 36p. pap. 24.95 *(978-1-60703-003-4(9))* America Star Bks.
Griffin, Paul. Adrift. 2015. 228p. (YA). *(978-0-545-87195-2(6)*, Scholastic Pr.) Scholastic, Inc.
Grylls, Bear. The Sea Challenge. McCann, Emma, illus. 2017. 118p. (J). pap. *(978-1-61067-769-1(2))* Kane Miller.
Gurney, Stella. Sally Sets Sail, 1 vol. Worsley, Belinda, illus. 2009. (Get Ready Readers Ser.). (ENG.). 32p. (J). (gr. k-k). lib. bdg. 27.27 *(978-1-60754-261-2(7)*, 6dfb8530-2dac-464c-8217-c0509b7fe0b1, Windmill Bks.) Rosen Publishing Group, Inc., The.
Hopkinson, Deborah. Sailing for Gold. Farnsworth, Bill, illus. 2005. 76p. (J). lib. bdg. 15.00 *(978-1-59054-915-5(5))* Fitzgerald Bks.
Johnson, Dennis. The Tree That Went Sailing: (Based on a true story - Palm Beach, Florida) 2009. (ENG.). 40p. pap. 21.99 *(978-1-4415-0181-3(9))* Xlibris Corp.
Johnston, James D. The Adventures of Lucas & Celi: Lucas Stows Away. 2009. 32p. pap. 12.99 *(978-1-4343-6372-5(4))* AuthorHouse.
Kisko, Stephen. Sailing the Puddles. 2013. 36p. pap. 12.95 *(978-1-62838-002-6(0))* Page Publishing Inc.
Lumley, Jemima. The Journey Home from Grandpa's. Fatus, Sophie, illus. 2010. 16p. (J). (gr. -1-3). pap. 5.99 *(978-1-84686-277-9(9))* Barefoot Bks., Inc.
Lund, Deb. Dinosailors. Fine, Howard, illus. 2008. (ENG.). 36p. (J). (gr. -1-3). pap. 8.99 *(978-0-15-206124-1(X)*, 1198391, Clarion Bks.) HarperCollins Pubs.
McDougal-Littell Publishing Staff. The True Confessions of Charlotte Doyle. 2004. (McDougal Littell Literature Connections Ser.). (ENG., Illus.). 272p. (gr. 7-7). 18.50 *(978-0-395-87477-6(7)*, 2-70837) Great Source Education Group, Inc.
Meigs, Cornelia. Clearing Weather. 2018. (ENG., Illus.). 320p. (YA). (gr. 2-6). pap. 8.99 *(978-0-486-81742-2(3)*, 817423) Dover Pubns., Inc.
Mercier, Deborah. The Captain's Hat. Mills, Faythe, illus. 2007. 32p. (J). 17.99 *(978-0-9799410-0-9(8))* Minnewaska Pr.
Meyer, L. A. Bloody Jack: Being an Account of the Curious Adventures of Mary 'Jacky' Faber, Ship's Boy. 2nd ed. 2010. (Bloody Jack Adventures Ser.: 1). (ENG., Illus.). 304p. (YA). (gr. 7-12). reprint ed. pap. 9.99 *(978-0-15-205085-6(X)*, 1060807, Clarion Bks.) HarperCollins Pubs.
Miller, Patricia Maida. Carlos the Sailor Visits Atlantic City. 2005. (Illus.). 16p. (J). pap. 12.95 *(978-0-9766889-0-7(5))* ComteQ Publishing.
Mitchen, Scott. Will of the Pirates. 2008. 180p. 22.95 *(978-0-595-70652-5(5))* iUniverse, Inc.
Myers, Byrona. Yo Ho for Strawberry Roam! Jauss, Anne Marie, illus. 2011. 154p. 41.95 *(978-1-258-08204-8(7))* Literary Licensing, LLC.
Neale, Jonathan. Lost at Sea. 2004. (ENG.). 112p. (J). (gr. 5-7). reprint ed. pap. 8.95 *(978-0-618-43236-3(1)*, 491905, Clarion Bks.) HarperCollins Pubs.
Oppenheim, Shulamith. Rescuing Einstein's Compass. Juhasz, George, illus. 2003. (ENG.). 32p. (J). (gr. 1-3). 15.95 *(978-1-56656-507-3(3)*, Crocodile Bks.) Interlink Publishing Group, Inc.
Optic, Oliver, pseud. Sunny Shores; or, Young America in Italy & Austria a Story of Travel & Adventure by William T Adams. 2006. 428p. per. 26.99 *(978-1-4255-4627-4(7))* Michigan Publishing.
Otis, James. Raising the Pearl. 2011. 302p. 48.95 *(978-1-258-10248-7(X))* Literary Licensing, LLC.
Parrish, Fayrene. Pancho Saves the Day: Shipmates Learning Adventures Venture. Parrish, Fayrene, illus. 2010. (Illus.). 42p. (J). 15.95 *(978-0-9826717-8-8(4))* Parrish, Fayrene.

Peters, Stephanie True. The First & Final Voyage: The Sinking of the Titanic, 1 vol. Proctor, Jon, illus. 2008. (Historical Fiction Ser.). (ENG.). 56p. (J). (gr. 3-6). pap. 6.25 *(978-1-4342-0494-3(4)*, 94442, Stone Arch Bks.) Capstone.

Prins, Piet. The Sailing Sleuths. Kramer, Jaap, illus. 2006. 137p. (J). pap. *(978-1-894666-46-6(1))* Inheritance Pubns.

—Stefan Derksen's Polar Adventure. 2004. (Illus.). 237p. (J). pap. *(978-1-894666-67-1(4))* Inheritance Pubns.

Punter, R. Stories of Pirates. 2004. (Young Reading Ser.: Vol. 1). 48p. (J). (gr. 2-18). pap. 5.99 *(978-0-7945-0583-7(X))* EDC Publishing.

Ransome, Arthur. Swallowdale. 2010. (Swallows & Amazons Ser.). (ENG., Illus.). 431p. (J). pap. 15.95 *(978-1-56792-421-3(2))* Godine, David R. Pub.

—We Didn't Mean to Go to Sea: Stage Play. 2010. (ENG., Illus.). 100p. (gr. 2). pap. 17.99 *(978-1-906582-05-0(X))* Aurora Metro Pubns. Ltd. GBR. Dist: Publishers Group West (PGW).

Root, Phyllis. Lilly & the Pirates. Shepperson, Rob, illus. 2013. (ENG.). 180p. (J). (gr. 3-7). pap. 8.95 *(978-1-62091-027-6(6)*, Astra Young Readers) Astra Publishing Hse.

Schaaf, Ron. Tiger's Quest: Rounding Cape Horn. 2007. (J). *(978-0-9787555-0-8(2))* Hickory Tales Publishing.

Smith, Buckley. Moonsailors. Smith, Buckley, illus. 2007. (ENG., Illus.). 40p. (J). (gr. -1-7). 14.95 *(978-0-937822-95-1(7))* WoodenBoat Pubns.

Stevenson, Robin. A Thousand Shades of Blue, 1 vol. 2008. (ENG.). 240p. (YA). (gr. 8-12). pap. 12.95 *(978-1-55143-921-1(2))* Orca Bk. Pubs. USA.

Treasure Island: A Growing Field Adventure. 2011. (Illus.). 64p. (J). 16.95 *(978-0-9770391-4-2(5))* Growing Field Bks.

Wait, Lea. Seaward Born. 2004. (ENG., Illus.). 160p. (J). (gr. 3-7). pap. 8.99 *(978-0-689-84860-5(9)*, McElderry, Margaret K. Bks.) McElderry, Margaret K. Bks.

Winfield, Arthur M. The Rover Boys on the Ocean. 2007. 232p. 26.95 *(978-1-4218-4138-0(X))*; per. 11.95 *(978-1-4218-4236-3(X))* 1st World Publishing, Inc. (1st World Library - Literary Society).

Winkler, Ashley & Winkler, Michael. One Good Quest Deserves Another: A Crown of Amaranth Story. 2009. 292p. 28.95 *(978-0-595-71039-3(5))*; pap. 18.95 *(978-0-595-47365-6(2))* iUniverse, Inc.

Zwingelberg, Wc. The Adventures of Will W. Wilson. 2006. (Illus.). 80p. per. 12.00 *(978-1-4251-0579-2(3))* Trafford Publishing.

SAILING—HISTORY

Brown Bear Books. Land & Water Transportation. 2012. (Invention & Technology Ser.). (ENG.). 64p. (J). (gr. 8-11). lib. bdg. 39.95 *(978-1-936333-42-4(2)*, 16522) Brown Bear Bks.

SAILOR MOON (FICTITIOUS CHARACTER)—FICTION

Takeuchi, Naoko. Sailor Moon 10, Vol. 10. 2013. (Sailor Moon Ser.: 10). (ENG., Illus.). 200p. (gr. 8-12). pap. 10.99 *(978-1-61262-006-0(X))* Kodansha America, Inc.

—Sailor Moon 11, Vol. 11. 2013. (Sailor Moon Ser.: 11). (ENG., Illus.). 200p. (gr. 8-12). pap. 10.99 *(978-1-61262-007-7(8))* Kodansha America, Inc.

—Sailor Moon 12, Vol. 12. 2013. (Sailor Moon Ser.: 12). (ENG., Illus.). 200p. (gr. 8-12). pap. 10.99 *(978-1-61262-008-4(6))* Kodansha America, Inc.

—Sailor Moon 8. 8th ed. 2012. (Sailor Moon Ser.: 8). (ENG., Illus.). 200p. (gr. 8-12). pap. 10.99 *(978-1-61262-004-6(3))* Kodansha America, Inc.

—Sailor Moon 9. 2013. (Sailor Moon Ser.: 9). (ENG., Illus.). 200p. (gr. 8-12). pap. 10.99 *(978-1-61262-005-3(1))* Kodansha America, Inc.

SAILORS

see also Naval Biography

also names of countries with the subhead Navy, e.g. United States—Navy, etc.

Anderson, Dale. Soldiers & Sailors in the American Revolution, 1 vol. 2005. (World Almanac(r) Library of the American Revolution Ser.). (ENG.). 48p. (gr. 5-8). pap. 15.05 *(978-0-8368-5938-6(3)*, fefcb9af-19a9-4101-b561-c76c583fb122); lib. bdg. 33.67 *(978-0-8368-5929-4(4)*, 29863a8e-4cf7-476a-957d-381f6117ed23) Stevens, Gareth Publishing LLLP. (Gareth Stevens Secondary Library).

Brown, Chris. Shiver Me Timbers: A Fun Book of Pirates, Sailors, & Other Sea-Farers. 2006. (ENG., Illus.). 32p. (J). (gr. 4-7). pap. 8.95 *(978-0-7145-3303-2(3))* Consortium Bk. Sales & Distribution.

Burke, John. Granuaile: The Pirate Queen. Burke, Fatti, illus. 2019. (Little Library: 01). (ENG.). 32p. (J). 14.95 *(978-0-7171-8350-0(5))* Gill Bks. IRL. Dist: Casemate Pubs. & Bk. Distributors, LLC.

Duder, Tessa, ed. Down to the Sea Again: True Sea Stories for Young Newzealanders. 2005. 256p. (J). *(978-1-86950-476-2(3))* HarperCollins Pubs. New Zealand NZL. Dist: HarperCollins Pubs. Australia.

Goldish, Meish. Navy: Civilian to Sailor. 2010. (Becoming a Soldier Ser.). 24p. (YA). (gr. 3-6). lib. bdg. 26.99 *(978-1-936088-14-0(2))* Bearport Publishing Co., Inc.

Gunderson, Jessica. Your Life as a Cabin Boy on a Pirate Ship. Burns, Mike, illus. 2012. (Way It Was Ser.). (ENG.). 32p. (J). (gr. 2-5). pap. 8.95 *(978-1-4048-7249-3(3)*, 118192, Picture Window Bks.) Capstone.

Hill, David. Hero of the Sea: Sir Peter Blake's Mighty Ocean Quests. Morris, Phoebe, illus. 2018. (David Hill Kiwi Legends Ser.). 32p. (J). (gr. k-2). 21.99 *(978-0-14-377165-4(5))* Penguin Group New Zealand, Ltd. NZL. Dist: Independent Pubs. Group.

Loh-Hagan, Virginia. Abby Sunderland: Lost at Sea. 2019. (True Survival Ser.). (ENG., Illus.). 32p. (J). (gr. 4-8). pap. 14.21 *(978-1-5341-3988-6(5)*, 212781); lib. bdg. 32.07 *(978-1-5341-4332-6(7)*, 212780) Cherry Lake Publishing. (45th Parallel Press).

Loveless, Antony. Nuclear Submariners. 2009. (World's Most Dangerous Jobs Ser.). (ENG., Illus.). 32p. (J). (gr. 3-6). pap. *(978-0-7787-5111-3(2))*; lib. bdg. *(978-0-7787-5097-0(3))* Crabtree Publishing Co.

Marsico, Katie. Calvin Graham's World War II Story. Hill, Dave, illus. 2018. (Narrative Nonfiction: Kids in War Ser.). (ENG.). 32p. (J). (gr. 2-4). lib. bdg. 27.99 *(978-1-5124-5681-3(0)*, 804aec63-24d9-46d5-80b8-cfeb552b88d1, Lerner Pubns.) Lerner Publishing Group.

Micklos, John & Micklos, John, Jr. Why We Won the American Revolution: Through Primary Sources, 1 vol. 2013. (American Revolution Through Primary Sources Ser.). (ENG.). 48p. (gr. 4-6). pap. 11.53 *(978-1-4644-0192-3(6)*, 5895a7f8-08c5-4a37-9a5e-45c01416fbb5); (Illus.). (J). 27.93 *(978-0-7660-4134-9(4)*, 1427223b-d0b5-47ed-ad69-7c1c441a1350) Enslow Publishing, LLC.

Miller, Adam, et al. Courage under Fire: True Stories of Bravery from the U. S. Army, Navy, Air Force, & Marines, 1 vol. 2014. (Courage under Fire Ser.). (ENG., Illus.). 112p. (J). (gr. 3-9). pap., pap., pap. 9.95 *(978-1-4914-1065-3(5)*, 126702, Capstone Pr.) Capstone.

Miller, Nancy. My Mom Is in the Navy, 1 vol., 1. 2015. (Military Families Ser.). (ENG., Illus.). 24p. (J). (gr. 3-4). pap. 9.25 *(978-1-5081-4438-0(9)*, 45b897c6-e7bd-428e-a515-9a898922be32, PowerKids Pr.) Rosen Publishing Group, Inc., The.

Prentzas, G. S. Lost at Sea. 2015. (Illus.). 32p. (J). lib. bdg. 28.50 *(978-1-62724-290-5(2))* Bearport Publishing Co., Inc.

Raum, Elizabeth. World War II Naval Forces, 1 vol. 2013. (You Choose: World War II Ser.). (ENG., Illus.). 112p. (J). (gr. 3-7). pap. 6.95 *(978-1-62065-720-1(1)*, 121705, Capstone Pr.) Capstone.

—World War II Naval Forces: An Interactive History Adventure. 2013. (You Choose: World War II Ser.). (ENG.). 112p. (J). (gr. 3-4). pap. 41.70 *(978-1-62065-721-8(X)*, 19312); (Illus.). lib. bdg. 32.65 *(978-1-4296-4780-9(9)*, 103305) Capstone. (Capstone Pr.).

Reed, Jennifer. Marineros de la Armada de EE. UU. 2010. (Gente de Las Fuerzas Armadas de EE. UU. /People of the Armed Forces Ser.).Tr. of Sailors of the U. S. Navy. (MUL.). 24p. (J). (gr. -1-2). lib. bdg. 27.32 *(978-1-4296-6117-1(8)*, 115145) Capstone.

—Sailors of the U. S. Navy [Scholastic]. 2010. (People of the U. S. Armed Forces Ser.). (ENG.). 24p. pap. 0.49 *(978-1-4296-5806-5(1)*, Capstone Pr.) Capstone.

Russo, Kristen J. Surprising Facts about Being a Navy Sailor. 2017. (What You Didn't Know about the U. S. Military Life Ser.). (ENG., Illus.). 32p. (J). (gr. 3-9). lib. bdg. 28.65 *(978-1-5157-7430-3(9)*, 135789, Capstone Pr.) Capstone.

Sheinkin, Steve. The Port Chicago 50: Disaster, Mutiny, & the Fight for Civil Rights. 2014. (ENG., Illus.). 208p. (J). (gr. 5-9). 21.99 *(978-1-59643-796-8(0)*, 900083654) Roaring Brook Pr.

Weintraub, Robert. No Better Friend: Young Readers Edition: A Man, a Dog, & Their Incredible True Story of Friendship & Survival in World War II. 2018. (ENG., Illus.). 304p. (J). (gr. 5-17). pap. 9.99 *(978-0-316-34465-4(6))* Little, Brown Bks. for Young Readers.

SAILORS—FICTION

Ballantyne, R. M. The Crew of the Water Wagtail. 2011. 146p. 24.95 *(978-1-4638-9596-9(8))* Rodgers, Alan Bks.

—The Young Trawler. 2011. 250p. 27.95 *(978-1-4638-9496-2(1))* Rodgers, Alan Bks.

Barron, Liz. Salcombe Seaside Fairies: Kevin the Crabshell Fairy. 2010. (Illus.). 24p. pap. 11.49 *(978-1-4490-6142-5(7))* AuthorHouse.

Benchmark Education Co., LLC. Sail with Me Big Book. 2014. (Shared Reading Foundations Ser.). (J). (gr. -1). *(978-1-4509-9447-7(4))* Benchmark Education Co.

Child, Neil. The Creek. 2012. 82p. pap. 19.95 *(978-1-4626-6027-8(4))* America Star Bks.

Collingwood, Harry. The Rover's Secret. 2011. 274p. 29.95 *(978-1-4638-9505-1(4))* Rodgers, Alan Bks.

Cooper, Mark. Fledgling: Jason Steed. 2010. 240p. (J). (gr. 3-7). pap. 10.99 *(978-1-4022-3999-1(8))* Sourcebooks, Inc.

Engle, Margarita. Jazz Owls: A Novel of the Zoot Suit Riots. Gutierrez, Rudy, illus. 2018. (ENG.). 192p. (YA). (gr. 7). 17.99 *(978-1-5344-0943-9(2))* Simon & Schuster Children's Publishing.

Jenkins, Amanda. Mere Moments A Story of Pearl Harbor, the Day the Towers Fell. 2011. (Readers' & Writers' Genre Workshop Ser.). (J). pap. *(978-1-4509-3019-2(0))* Benchmark Education Co.

Mitton, Tony & Parker, Ant. Busy Boats. 2018. (Amazing Machines Ser.). (ENG.). 20p. (J). bds. 6.99 *(978-0-7534-7416-7(6)*, 900187133, Kingfisher) Roaring Brook Pr.

Moore, Jordan. Sinbad the Sailor, 1 vol. rev. ed. 2013. (Literary Text Ser.). (ENG., Illus.). 32p. (gr. 3-4). pap. 11.99 *(978-1-4333-5647-6(3))* Teacher Created Materials, Inc.

Moore, Marcia. Wind & Oyster Jack, 1 vol. Crow, Heather, illus. 2017. (ENG.). 32p. (J). 14.99 *(978-0-7643-5422-9(1)*, 7745) Schiffer Publishing, Ltd.

Russell, Krista. Chasing the Nightbird. 192p. (J). (gr. 5-9). 2018. pap. 7.95 *(978-1-68263-065-5(X))* 2011. 15.95 *(978-1-56145-597-3(0))* Peachtree Publishing Co. Inc.

Sala, George Augustus. Captain Dangerous. 2011. 130p. 24.95 *(978-1-4638-9899-1(1))*; 126p. pap. 10.95 *(978-1-4638-0141-0(6))*; 124p. pap. 10.95 *(978-1-4638-0142-7(4))*; 130p. pap. 10.95 *(978-1-4638-0140-3(8))* Rodgers, Alan Bks.

Schorr, Titus. The Stars & Stripes, 1 vol., 1. 2015. (Rosen REAL Readers: Social Studies Nonfiction / Fiction: Myself, My Community, My World Ser.). (ENG.). 12p. (J). (gr. k-1). pap. 6.33 *(978-1-5081-1958-6(9)*, a1e64b30-83b9-4f31-b695-a5a9db0a19cf, Rosen Classroom) Rosen Publishing Group, Inc., The.

Stanmore, Tony. Tide of Chance: A Holiday Adventure. 2010. (Illus.). 60p. pap. 10.49 *(978-1-4520-0650-5(4))* AuthorHouse.

Tweed, Susan Larned. A Sailor's Adventure: Sailing Stormy Seas. 2012. 24p. pap. 11.50 *(978-1-61897-522-5(6)*, Strategic Bk. Publishing) Strategic Book Publishing & Rights Agency (SBPRA).

SAILORS' LIFE

see Seafaring Life

SAINT LAWRENCE RIVER

Cooke, Tim. The St. Lawrence River, 1 vol. 2003. (Rivers of North America Ser.). (ENG., Illus.). 32p. (gr. 3-5). lib. bdg. 28.67 *(978-0-8368-3792-6(3)*, a9fc3c83-4471-404c-b8d7-7b07af20fc52, Gareth Stevens Learning Library) Stevens, Gareth Publishing LLLP.

Lackey, Jennifer. Jacques Cartier: Exploring the St. Lawrence River, 1 vol. 2006. (In the Footsteps of Explorers Ser.). (ENG., Illus.). 32p. (J). (gr. 4-7). pap. *(978-0-7787-2466-7(2))* Crabtree Publishing Co.

SAINT LAWRENCE RIVER VALLEY

Peppas, Lynn. The St. Lawrence: River Route to the Great Lakes, 1 vol. 2010. (Rivers Around the World Ser.). (ENG., Illus.). 32p. (J). (gr. 5-8). pap. *(978-0-7787-7470-9(8))*; lib. bdg. *(978-0-7787-7447-1(3))* Crabtree Publishing Co.

SAINT LOUIS (MO.)

Dittmer, Lori. The Gateway Arch. 2019. (Landmarks of America Ser.). (ENG.). 24p. (J). (gr. 1-4). *(978-1-64026-124-2(9)*, 18965, Creative Education); pap. 8.99 *(978-1-62832-687-1(5)*, 18966, Creative Paperbacks) Creative Co., The.

Doyle, Amanda E. & Adams, Melanie A. Standing up for Civil Rights in St. Louis. 2017. (ENG., Illus.). 76p. pap. 9.95 *(978-1-883982-91-1(X))* Missouri Historical Society Pr.

Gamble, Adam & Jasper, Mark. Good Night St Louis. Veno, Joe, illus. 2017. (Good Night Our World Ser.). 20p. (J). (— 1). bds. 9.95 *(978-1-60219-467-0(X))* Good Night Bks.

Huddleston, Emma. Exploring the Gateway Arch. 2019. (Travel America's Landmarks Ser.). (ENG., Illus.). 32p. (J). (gr. 2-3). pap. 9.95 *(978-1-64185-855-7(9)*, 1641858559); lib. bdg. 31.35 *(978-1-64185-786-4(2)*, 1641857862) North Star Editions. (Focus Readers).

Klein, Carol Swartout. Painting for Peace in Ferguson. 2nd ed. 2015. (ENG.). 54p. (J). (gr. 2-3). 25.95 *(978-0-9963901-0-1(3))*; pap. 15.95 *(978-0-9892079-9-7(4))* TreeHse. Publishing Group.

Publications International Ltd. Staff. Yesterday & Today St. Louis. 2009. 192p. 24.95 *(978-1-4127-1576-8(8))* Publications International, Ltd.

SAINT LOUIS (MO.)—FICTION

Ingalls, Ann. Fairy Floss: The Sweet Story of Cotton Candy. Blanco, Migy, illus. 2017. (ENG.). 40p. (J). (gr. -1-3). 17.99 *(978-1-4998-0238-2(2))* Little Bee Books Inc.

Jacobs, Lily. The Littlest Bunny in St. Louis: An Easter Adventure. Dunn, Robert, illus. 2015. (Littlest Bunny Ser.). (ENG.). 32p. (J). (gr. -1-3). 9.99 *(978-1-4926-1201-8(4)*, Hometown World) Sourcebooks, Inc.

James, Eric. Santa's Sleigh Is on Its Way to St. Louis: A Christmas Adventure. Dunn, Robert, illus. 2016. (Santa's Sleigh Is on Its Way Ser.). (ENG.). 32p. (J). (gr. k-2). 12.99 *(978-1-4926-4356-2(4)*, 9781492643562, Hometown World) Sourcebooks, Inc.

—The Spooky Express St. Louis. Piwowarski, Marcin, illus. 2017. (Spooky Express Ser.). (ENG.). 32p. (J). (gr. k-6). 9.99 *(978-1-4926-5400-1(0)*, Hometown World) Sourcebooks, Inc.

—Tiny the St. Louis Easter Bunny. 2018. (Tiny the Easter Bunny Ser.). (ENG.). 40p. (J). (gr. k-3). 9.99 *(978-1-4926-5965-5(7)*, Hometown World) Sourcebooks, Inc.

Kelly, David A. Ballpark Mysteries #14: the Cardinals Caper. Meyers, Mark, illus. 2018. (Ballpark Mysteries Ser.: 14). (ENG.). 112p. (J). (gr. 1-4). 5.99 *(978-1-5247-6751-8(4)*, Random Hse. Bks. for Young Readers) Random Hse. Children's Bks.

—The Cardinals Caper. 2018. (Ballpark Mysteries Ser.: 14). lib. bdg. 14.75 *(978-0-606-40921-6(1))* Turtleback.

Maccoll, Michaela & Nichols, Rosemary. Freedom's Price. 2015. (Hidden Histories Ser.). (ENG., Illus.). 288p. (J). (gr. 4-7). 17.95 *(978-1-62091-624-7(X)*, Calkins Creek) Highlights Pr., c/o Highlights for Children, Inc.

Olswanger, Anna. Shlemiel Crooks. Koz, Paula Goodman, illus. (ENG.). 36p. (J). 2009. pap. 11.95 *(978-1-58838-236-8(2)*, 8994) 2005. (gr. 2-4). 15.95 *(978-1-58838-165-1(X)*, 8993) NewSouth, Inc. (NewSouth Bks.).

Sully, Katherine. Night-Night St. Louis. Poole, Helen, illus. 2017. (Night-Night Ser.). (ENG.). 20p. (J). (gr. -1-1). bds. 9.99 *(978-1-4926-5480-3(9)*, Hometown World) Sourcebooks, Inc.

ST. LOUIS CARDINALS (BASEBALL TEAM)

Epstein, Brad. St. Louis Cardinals ABC. 2013. (My First Alphabet Books (Michaelson Entertainment) Ser.). (ENG., Illus.). 28p. (J). bds. *(978-1-60730-211-7(X))* Michaelson Entertainment.

Frisch, Aaron. St. Louis Cardinals. 2009. (World Series Champions Ser.). (Illus.). 23p. (J). (gr. 2-3). 24.25 *(978-1-58341-688-4(9)*, Creative Education) Creative Co., The.

Gilbert, Sara. St. Louis Cardinals. 2013. (World Series Champions Ser.). (ENG.). 24p. (J). (gr. 1-4). pap. 7.99 *(978-0-89812-822-2(6)*, 21864, Creative Paperbacks); (Illus.). 25.65 *(978-1-60818-271-8(1)*, 21863, Creative Education) Creative Co., The.

—The Story of the St. Louis Cardinals. 2011. (Baseball: the Great American Game Ser.). (Illus.). 48p. (J). (gr. 5-8). lib. bdg. 34.25 *(978-1-60818-053-0(0)*, Creative Education) Creative Co., The.

Gitlin, Marty. St. Louis Cardinals, 1 vol. 2015. (Inside MLB Ser.). (ENG., Illus.). 48p. (J). (gr. 3-6). lib. bdg. 34.21 *(978-1-62403-482-4(9)*, 17127, SportsZone) ABDO Publishing Co.

Kelley, K. C. St. Louis Cardinals. 2018. (Illus.). 32p. (J). *(978-1-4896-5952-1(8)*, AV2 by Weigl) Weigl Pubs., Inc.

Kennedy, Mike. Cardinals (St. Louis)-Meet The. 2010. (Smart about Sports Ser.). (ENG.). 24p. (J). (gr. k-3). lib. bdg. *(978-1-59953-373-5(1))* Norwood Hse. Pr.

Lajiness, Katie. St. Louis Cardinals. 2018. (MLB's Greatest Teams Ser.). (ENG., Illus.). 32p. (J). (gr. 2-5). lib. bdg. 34.21 *(978-1-5321-1520-2(2)*, 28876, Big Buddy Bks.) ABDO Publishing Co.

MacRae, Sloan. The St. Louis Cardinals. (Illus.). 24p. (J). 2012. 49.50 *(978-1-4488-5152-2(1))* 2011. (ENG., (gr. 2-3). pap. 9.25 *(978-1-4488-5151-5(3)*, 933b9017-8636-45f0-96e6-8f3c779bacf3) 2011. (ENG., (gr. 2-3). lib. bdg. 26.27 *(978-1-4488-5009-9(6)*, 9cbdd88d-10d4-43d9-8510-92819247636e) Rosen Publishing Group, Inc., The. (PowerKids Pr.).

Mattern, Joanne. Albert Pujols. 2007. (Robbie Reader Ser.). (Illus.). 32p. (J). (gr. 2-5). lib. bdg. 25.70 *(978-1-58415-596-6(5))* Mitchell Lane Pubs.

Needham, Tom. Albert Pujols: MVP on & off the Field, 1 vol. 2008. (Sports Stars with Heart Ser.). (ENG., Illus.). 128p. (J). (gr. 5-6). lib. bdg. 34.93 *(978-0-7660-2866-1(6)*, 18ed61e9-ef79-4830-a8f1-f6530e5f96ca) Enslow Publishing, LLC.

O'Hearn, Michael. The Story of the St. Louis Cardinals. 2007. (Baseball, the Great American Game Ser.). (Illus.). 48p. (YA). (gr. 4-7). lib. bdg. 32.80 *(978-1-58341-551-1(3))* Creative Co., The.

Publications International Ltd. Staff. Yesterday & Today St Louis Cardinals. 2007. 144p. *(978-1-4127-1504-1(0)*, 1412715040, PIL Kids) Publications International, Ltd.

Sandler, Michael. David Eckstein & the St. Louis Cardinals: 2006 World Series. 2008. (World Series Superstars). (Illus.). 24p. (J). (gr. 1-4). lib. bdg. 26.99 *(978-1-59716-636-2(7))* Bearport Publishing Co., Inc.

Stewart, Mark. The St. Louis Cardinals. 2012. (Team Spirit Ser.). 48p. (J). (gr. 3-6). lib. bdg. 29.27 *(978-1-59953-494-7(0))* Norwood Hse. Pr.

SAINT PATRICK'S DAY

Aloian, Molly. Saint Patrick's Day. 2009. (Celebrations in My World Ser.). (ENG., Illus.). 32p. (J). (gr. k-2). pap. *(978-0-7787-4776-5(X)*, 1302581); (gr. 1-3). *(978-0-7787-4758-1(1)*, 1302581) Crabtree Publishing Co.

Balian, Lorna. Leprechauns Never Lie, 1 vol. Balian, Lorna, illus. 2004. (ENG., Illus.). 32p. (J). 16.99 *(978-1-932065-37-4(7))* Star Bright Bks., Inc.

Gnojewski, Carol. Fun St. Patrick's Day Crafts, 1 vol. 2014. (Kid Fun Holiday Crafts! Ser.). (ENG.). 32p. (gr. 3-4). 25.60 *(978-0-7660-6230-6(9)*, 3aed1b06-e12c-486c-a8f2-b0923499b935); pap. 10.35 *(978-0-7660-6231-3(7)*, 76ef0a81-1560-4be5-aef2-9e5d9f2df507, Enslow Elementary) Enslow Publishing, LLC.

Goeller, Dorothy. St. Patrick's Day, 1 vol. 2010. (All about Holidays Ser.). (ENG., Illus.). 24p. (-1). pap. 10.35 *(978-1-59845-177-1(4)*, 1c6aef83-8dc0-4516-a20f-94ab07a141aa); (gr. -1-1). 25.27 *(978-0-7660-3808-0(4)*, 944bb551-3cd7-4328-8b3d-f7cca35ba543) Enslow Publishing, LLC. (Enslow Publishing).

Grack, Rachel. Saint Patrick's Day. 2017. (Celebrating Holidays Ser.). (ENG., Illus.). 24p. (J). (gr. k-3). lib. bdg. 26.95 *(978-1-62617-623-2(X)*, Blastoff! Readers) Bellwether Media.

Haley, Charly. St. Patrick's Day. 2019. (Holidays Ser.). (ENG., Illus.). 24p. (J). (gr. 1-1). pap. 8.95 *(978-1-64185-570-9(3)*, 1641855703) North Star Editions.

—St. Patrick's Day. 2018. (Holidays (Cody Koala) Ser.). (ENG., Illus.). 24p. (J). (gr. k-3). lib. bdg. 31.36 *(978-1-5321-6199-5(9)*, 30181, Pop! Cody Koala) Pop!

Keogh, Josie. St. Patrick's Day, 1 vol. 2013. (PowerKids Readers: Happy Holidays! Ser.). (ENG., Illus.). 24p. (J). (gr. k-k). pap. 9.25 *(978-1-4488-9714-8(9)*, 073a2d4a-efd7-4c13-b5ef-0a325edc44ba); lib. bdg. 26.27 *(978-1-4488-9628-8(2)*, e26f6d76-8f35-42a6-a4fa-4d60017ce5e1) Rosen Publishing Group, Inc., The. (PowerKids Pr.).

—St. Patrick's Day: Dia de San Patricio, 1 vol. Alamán, Eduardo, tr. 2013. (PowerKids Readers: !Felices Fiestas! / Happy Holidays! Ser.). (ENG & SPA., Illus.). 24p. (gr. k-k). lib. bdg. 26.27 *(978-1-4488-9971-5(0)*, 0481f8af-8539-4fa2-8446-f446dceff038, PowerKids Pr.) Rosen Publishing Group, Inc., The.

Landau, Elaine. Celebrating St. Patrick's Day, 1 vol. 2012. (Celebrating Holidays Ser.). (ENG.). 48p. (gr. 3-3). 27.93 *(978-0-7660-4035-9(6)*, 6b099526-2d3e-4bc0-82f5-f2aade72fe22, Enslow Elementary) Enslow Publishing, LLC.

—What Is St. Patrick's Day?, 1 vol. 2012. (I Like Holidays! Ser.). (ENG., Illus.). 24p. (gr. k-2). lib. bdg. 25.27 *(978-0-7660-3704-5(5)*, d21f582f-1189-4b78-bfdc-602d3b83f0a0) Enslow Publishing, LLC.

Lindeen, Mary. St. Patrick's Day. 2015. (BeginningtoRead Ser.). (ENG., Illus.). 32p. (J). (gr. k-2). lib. bdg. 22.60 *(978-1-59953-687-3(0))* Norwood Hse. Pr.

Lynette, Rachel. Let's Throw a St. Patrick's Day Party!, 1 vol. 2011. (Holiday Parties Ser.). (ENG.). 24p. (J). (gr. 2-3). pap. 9.25 *(978-1-4488-2737-4(X)*, b8943a8e-7b50-4656-9e23-ac362a068533); lib. bdg. 26.27 *(978-1-4488-2574-5(1)*, 7fa3539d-531a-461f-87b3-ea7df7d92567) Rosen Publishing Group, Inc., The. (PowerKids Pr.).

McGee, Randel. Paper Crafts for St. Patrick's Day, 1 vol. 2012. (Paper Craft Fun for Holidays Ser.). (ENG., Illus.). 48p. (gr. 3-3). pap. 11.53 *(978-1-59845-337-9(8)*, 4006e828-f509-4acf-a93e-521a20adac48, Enslow Elementary); lib. bdg. 27.93 *(978-0-7660-3725-0(8)*, 9a67da7a-0fad-494d-ad9c-9d553ced7d34) Enslow Publishing, LLC.

McNeil, Niki, et al. HOCPP 1062 Saint Patrick's Day. 2006. spiral bd. 20.00 *(978-1-60308-062-0(7))* In the Hands of a Child.

Mercer, Abbie. Happy St. Patrick's Day. (Holiday Fun Ser.). 24p. (gr. 2-3). 2009. 42.50 *(978-1-61513-377-2(1)*, PowerKids Pr.) 2007. (ENG., Illus.). (J). lib. bdg. 26.27 *(978-1-4042-3811-4(5)*, a780f823-a3be-483d-9010-beb5e7c4cbd5) Rosen Publishing Group, Inc., The.

Murray, Julie. Saint Patrick's Day. 2018. (Holidays (Abdo Kids Junior) Ser.). (ENG., Illus.). 24p. (J). (gr. -1-2). lib. bdg. 31.36 *(978-1-5321-8175-7(2)*, 29823, Abdo Kids) ABDO Publishing Co.

Owen, Ruth. St. Patrick's Day Origami, 1 vol. 2014. (Holiday Origami Ser.). (ENG., Illus.). 32p. (J). (gr. 2-3). 30.27 *(978-1-4777-5718-5(X)*, 62f1622e-cff7-4989-ab7c-dfe7249a03be, PowerKids Pr.) Rosen Publishing Group, Inc., The.

Ponto, Joanna. St. Patrick's Day, 1 vol. 2015. (Story of Our Holidays Ser.). (ENG., Illus.). 32p. (gr. 3-3). 26.93 *(978-0-7660-7461-3(7)*, 5ba8c709-6b45-44e8-8d6a-4e4e9e70d549); pap. 11.52 *(978-0-7660-7473-6(0)*, 9b2fe87e-db5d-4337-8ed3-edfb5c576d82) Enslow Publishing, LLC.

Roop, Peter & Roop, Connie. Let's Celebrate St. Patrick's Day. Connelly, Gwen, illus. 2003. 32p. (J). (gr. 3-6). pap. 6.95 *(978-0-7613-1782-1(1))*; lib. bdg. 22.90

(978-0-7613-2505-5(0)) Lerner Publishing Group. (Millbrook Pr.).

Sebra, Richard. ¡Es el día de San Patricio! (It's St. Patrick's Day!) 2018. (Bumba Books (r) en Español — ¡Es una Fiesta! (It's a Holiday!) Ser.). (SPA., Illus.). 24p. (J). (gr. -1-1). pap. 8.99 *(978-1-5415-2666-2(X)*, 4f627b2e-9806-46ab-bfd9-bdc4a0881ca1, Ediciones Lerner) Lerner Publishing Group.

—It's St. Patrick's Day! 2017. (Bumba Books (r) — It's a Holiday! Ser.). (ENG., Illus.). 24p. (J). (gr. -1-1). E-Book 39.99 *(978-1-5124-2740-0(3))*; E-Book 39.99 *(978-1-5124-3704-1(2)*, 9781512437041); E-Book 4.99 *(978-1-5124-3705-8(0)*, 9781512437058) Lerner Publishing Group. (Lerner Pubns.).

Smith, Mary Lou. Celebrate St. Patrick's Day, 1 vol. 2015. (Our Holidays Ser.). (ENG., Illus.). 24p. (J). (gr. 1-1). pap. 9.23 *(978-1-5026-0418-7(3)*, c856585c-9059-4f93-8a23-d18ca7fb6fad) Cavendish Square Publishing LLC.

Williams, Colleen Madonna Flood. My Adventure on St. Patrick's Day. 2007. 44p. (J). 8.99 *(978-1-59092-556-0(4))* Blue Forge Pr.

York, M. J. Celebrating St. Patrick's Day. 2017. (Welcoming the Seasons Ser.). (ENG.). 24p. (J). (gr. -1-2). lib. bdg. 32.79 *(978-1-5038-1655-8(9)*, 211505) Child's World, Inc, The.

Zocchi, Judy. On Saint Patrick's Day. Wallis, Rebecca, illus. 2005. (Holiday Happenings Ser.). 32p. (J). pap. 10.95 *(978-1-59646-232-8(9))*; per. 10.95 *(978-1-59646-233-5(7))* Dingles & Co.

—On Saint Patrick's Day/el día de San Patricio. Wallis, Rebecca, illus. 2005. (Holiday Happenings Ser.).Tr. of día de San Patricio. (ENG & SPA.). 32p. (J). pap. 10.95 *(978-1-59646-234-2(5))*; lib. bdg. 21.65 *(978-1-891997-40-2(8))*; per. 10.95 *(978-1-59646-235-9(3))* Dingles & Co.

SAINT PATRICK'S DAY—FICTION

Bouthyette, Valerie, illus. The Leprechaun Trap. 2008. 40p. (J). pap. 10.95 *(978-0-9800835-0-7(8))* Clinch Media.

Callahan, Sean. Leprechaun Who Lost His Rainbow, 1 vol. Cote, Nancy, illus. 2010. 32p. (J). (gr. -1-3). pap. 7.99 *(978-0-8075-4455-6(8)*, 807544558) Whitman, Albert & Co.

Diesen, Deborah. Pout-Pout Fish: Lucky Leprechaun. Hanna, Dan, illus. 2019. (Pout-Pout Fish Paperback Adventure Ser.). (ENG.). 24p. (J). 6.99 *(978-0-374-31054-7(8)*, 900193165, Farrar, Straus & Giroux (BYR)) Farrar, Straus & Giroux.

Flor Ada, Alma. Celebra el Dia De3 San Patricio con Samantha y Lola. Lavandeira, Sandra, illus. 2006. (Cuentos para Celebrar / Stories to Celebrate Ser.). (SPA.). 30p. (J). (gr. k-6). per. 11.95 *(978-1-59820-117-8(4)*, Alfaguara) Santillana USA Publishing Co., Inc.

Flor Ada, Alma & Campoy, F. Isabel. Celebrate St. Patrick's Day with Samantha & Lola. Hayes, Joe & Franco, Sharon, trs. from SPA. 2006. (Stories to Celebrate Ser.). (Illus.). 30p. (J). (gr. k-6). per. 11.95 *(978-1-59820-129-1(8)*, Alfaguara) Santillana USA Publishing Co., Inc.

Gorgas, Paula Blais. Little Lost Leprechaun. (Illus.). (J). 2007. 20p. per. 11.99 *(978-0-9797574-5-7(2))* 2006. 24p. lib. bdg. 24.95 *(978-0-9778651-4-7(2))* Dragonfly Publishing, Inc.

Happy St. Patrick's Day, Curious George: Tabbed Board Book. 2014. (Curious George Ser.). (ENG., Illus.). 14p. (J). (— 1). bds. 7.99 *(978-0-544-08888-7(3)*, 1537662, Clarion Bks.) HarperCollins Pubs.

Harimann, Sierra. Puppies on Parade. 2014. (Illus.). 30p. (J). pap. *(978-0-545-59211-6(9))* Scholastic, Inc.

Heling, Kathryn & Hembrook, Deborah. Ten Lucky Leprechauns. Johnson, Jay, illus. 2013. (ENG.). 24p. (J). (gr. -1-k). pap. 3.99 *(978-0-545-43648-9(6)*, Cartwheel Bks.) Scholastic, Inc.

—Ten Lucky Leprechauns. 2013. lib. bdg. 13.55 *(978-0-606-31493-0(8))* Turtleback.

Hillert, Margaret. It's St. Patrick's Day, Dear Dragon. David Schimmell, illus. 2008. (Beginning-To-Read Ser.). (ENG.). 32p. (J). (gr. k-2). pap. 13.26 *(978-1-60357-086-2(1))* Norwood Hse. Pr.

—It's St. Patrick's Day, Dear Dragon. Schimmell, David, illus. 2008. (BeginningtoRead Ser.). 32p. (J). (gr. k-2). lib. bdg. 22.60 *(978-1-59953-161-8(5))* Norwood Hse. Pr.

Holub, Joan. Good Luck! A St. Patrick's Day Story. Terry, Will, illus. 2007. (Ant Hill Ser.). (ENG.). 24p. (J). (gr. -1-k). lib. bdg. 11.89 *(978-1-4169-2560-6(0)*, Aladdin Library) Simon & Schuster Children's Publishing.

—Good Luck! A St. Patrick's Day Story (Ready-To-Read Pre-Level 1) Terry, Will, illus. 2007. (Ant Hill Ser.). (ENG.). 24p. (J). (gr. -1-k). pap. 4.99 *(978-1-4169-0955-2(9)*, Simon Spotlight) Simon Spotlight.

Lee, Quinlan B. & Bridwell, Norman. Happy St. Patrick's Day, Clifford! Haefele, Steve, illus. 2010. (Clifford the Big Red Dog Ser.). (J). *(978-0-545-23401-6(8))* Scholastic, Inc.

McGuirk, Leslie. Lucky Tucker. McGuirk, Leslie, illus. 2008. (ENG., Illus.). 24p. (J). (gr. -1-k). pap. 6.99 *(978-0-7636-3389-9(5))* Candlewick Pr.

—Lucky Tucker. 2008. 14.75 *(978-1-4178-1914-0(6))* Turtleback.

McNamara, Margaret & Gordon, Mike. The Luck of the Irish: Ready-To-Read Level 1. 2007. (Robin Hill School Ser.). (ENG., Illus.). 32p. (J). (gr. -1-1). pap. 4.99 *(978-1-4169-1539-3(7)*, Simon Spotlight) Simon Spotlight.

Meadows, Daisy. Lindsay the Luck Fairy. 2013. (Rainbow Magic — Special Edition Ser.). lib. bdg. 17.20 *(978-0-606-31512-8(8))* Turtleback.

Rockwell, Anne. St. Patrick's Day. Rockwell, Lizzy, illus. 2010. (ENG.). 40p. (J). (gr. -1-3). 14.99 *(978-0-06-050197-6(9))*; lib. bdg. 15.89 *(978-0-06-050198-3(7))* HarperCollins Pubs. (HarperCollins).

Roy, Ron. Calendar Mysteries #3: March Mischief. Gurney, John Steven, illus. 2010. (Calendar Mysteries Ser.: 3). 80p. (J). (gr. 1-4). 6.99 *(978-0-375-85663-1(3)*, Random Hse. Bks. for Young Readers) Random Hse. Children's Bks.

—March Mischief. 2010. (Calendar Mysteries Ser.: 3). lib. bdg. 14.75 *(978-0-606-12460-7(8))* Turtleback.

Sanrio. Happy St. Patrick's Day, Hello Kitty. 2015. (Hello Kitty Ser.). (J). lib. bdg. 17.15 *(978-0-606-37239-8(3))* Turtleback.

Slater, Teddy. The Luckiest St. Patrick's Day Ever! Long, Ethan, illus. 2007. (J). *(978-0-439-86648-4(0))* Scholastic, Inc.

—The Luckiest St. Patrick's Day Ever. Long, Ethan, illus. 2008. (ENG.). 32p. (J). (gr. -1-3). pap. 5.99 *(978-0-545-03943-7(6)*, Cartwheel Bks.) Scholastic, Inc.

Sypolt, Carl W. Fibber Lygood at Christmas, Easter, & St. Patrick's Day. 2006. 108p. (J). pap. 10.95 *(978-0-7414-2982-7(9))* Infinity Publishing.

Thaler, Mike. St. Patrick's Day from the Black Lagoon. Lee, Jared, illus. 2011. 61p. (J). *(978-0-545-27328-2(5))* Scholastic, Inc.

Wallace, Adam. How to Catch a Leprechaun. Elkerton, Andy, illus. 2016. (How to Catch Ser.). (ENG.). 32p. (J). (gr. k-6). 10.99 *(978-1-4926-3291-7(0)*, 9781492632917) Sourcebooks, Inc.

Wing, Natasha. The Night Before St. Patrick's Day. Wummer, Amy, illus. 2009. (Night Before Ser.). (ENG.). 32p. (J). (gr. -1-3). pap. 5.99 *(978-0-448-44852-7(1)*, Grosset & Dunlap) Penguin Young Readers Group.

Wojciechowski, Susan. A Fine St. Patrick's Day. Curry, Tom, illus. 2008. (ENG.). 40p. (J). (gr. -1-2). pap. 7.99 *(978-0-385-73640-4(1)*, Dragonfly Bks.) Random Hse. Children's Bks.

SAINT PETERSBURG (RUSSIA)—HISTORY

Ayo's Awesome Adventures in St. Petersburg: City of Bridges. 2018. (J). *(978-0-7166-3644-1(1))* World Bk., Inc.

Dyan, Penelope. Water & Blood — A Kid's Guide to St Petersburg, Russi. Weigand, John D., photos by. 2011. (Illus.). 34p. pap. 11.95 *(978-1-61477-001-5(8))* Bellissima Publishing, LLC.

SAINT PETERSBURG (RUSSIA)—HISTORY—SIEGE, 1941-1944

Anderson, M. T. Symphony for the City of the Dead: Dmitri Shostakovich & the Siege of Leningrad. 2015. (ENG., Illus.). 464p. (YA). (gr. 9). 25.99 *(978-0-7636-6818-1(4))* Candlewick Pr.

SAINT VALENTINE'S DAY

see Valentine's Day

SAINTS

see also Legends

Amadeo, Diana M. Holy Friends: Thirty Saints & Blesseds of the Americas. Curreli, Augusta & Lombardo, Irina, illus. 2005. 134p. (J). (gr. 3-7). 19.95 *(978-0-8198-3384-6(3))* Pauline Bks. & Media.

Barnes, Kathleen. I Love to See the Temple Reprint. 2009. 32p. pap. 8.95 *(978-1-60641-112-4(8))* Deseret Bk. Co.

—Sacrament Time. 2009. 32p. pap. 9.95 *(978-1-60641-113-1(6))* Deseret Bk. Co.

Baum, Margaux & Morgan, Julian. Constantine, 1 vol. 2016. (Leaders of the Ancient World Ser.). (ENG.). 112p. (J). (gr. 6-6). 38.80 *(978-1-5081-7252-9(8)*, 21146d9b-688f-46d2-a2bb-3f62820d7720) Rosen Publishing Group, Inc., The.

Benson, Robert Hugh. An Alphabet of Saints. Symington, Lindsay, illus. 2013. (ENG.). 32p. (J). (gr. -1-k). reprint ed. 16.95 *(978-1-930873-12-4(3)*, Neumann Pr.) TAN Bks.

Betz, Eva K. Saint Brigid & the Cows. Peterson, Russell, illus. 2013. (ENG.). 48p. (J). (gr. k-3). 12.95 *(978-1-930873-95-7(6)*, NP9155, Neumann Pr.) TAN Bks.

Billington, Rachel. The Life of Saint Francis. (ENG., Illus.). 48p. pap. 11.99 *(978-0-340-71427-0(1))* Hodder & Stoughton GBR. Dist: Trafalgar Square Publishing.

Brassey, Richard. George & the Dragon & Other Saintly Stories. 2003. (ENG., Illus.). 40p. pap. *(978-1-84255-082-3(9)*, Orion Children's Bks.) Hachette Children's Group.

Brassey, Richard, illus. George & the Dragon & Other Saintly Stories. 2003. (ENG.). 40p. *(978-1-84255-019-9(5)*, Orion Children's Bks.) Hachette Children's Group.

Briere, Euphemia. Victor Constantinus, Maximus Augustus: The Life of Saint Constantine, the First Christian Emperor & His Mother, Saint Helena. 2003. (Illus.). (J). 4.00 *(978-0-913026-90-8(5)*, VC) St. Nectarios Pr.

Brown, Don. Across a Dark & Wild Sea. 2004. (Illus.). (J). (gr. k-3). spiral bd. *(978-0-616-14616-3(7))* Canadian National Institute for the Blind/Institut National Canadien pour les Aveugles.

Brown, Laura Rhoderica. Saint John Neumann: Missionary to Immigrants. Esquinaldo, Virginia, illus. 2016. 144p. (J). pap. *(978-0-8198-9066-5(9))* Pauline Bks. & Media.

Buell, Jean. God's Heroes: A Child's Book of Saints. Larkin, Jean, ed. 2006. (Illus.). 32p. (J). (gr. -1-3). pap. 3.95 *(978-1-933178-30-1(2))* Pflaum Publishing Group.

Burnett, Allan. Columba & All That. Anderson, Scoular, illus. 2007. (ENG.). 128p. (J). (gr. 4-8). pap. 5.95 *(978-1-84158-571-0(8))* Birlinn, Ltd. GBR. Dist: Casemate Pubs. & Bk. Distributors, LLC.

Canton, William. Childs Book of Saints. 2006. pap. 27.95 *(978-1-4286-3503-6(3))* Kessinger Publishing, LLC.

—A Child's Book of Saints. Robinson, T. H., illus. 2013. 268p. pap. 12.75 *(978-1-936639-22-9(X))* St. Augustine Academy Pr.

—The Story of Saint Elizabeth of Hungary. 2014. (Illus.). 162p. (J). pap. 11.25 *(978-1-936639-23-6(8))* St. Augustine Academy Pr.

Carr, Simonetta. Augustine of Hippo. Lowe, Wes, illus. 2009. (ENG.). 62p. (J). 18.00 *(978-1-60178-073-7(7))* Reformation Heritage Bks.

Cash, Marie Romero. Santos: A Coloring Book of New Mexican Saints. 2008. 80p. (J). pap. 10.95 *(978-0-86534-701-4(8))* Sunstone Pr.

Celano, Peter, ed. My Year with the Saints: for Kids. 2018. (ENG.). 160p. (J). pap. 14.99 *(978-1-64060-167-3(8))* Paraclete Pr., Inc.

Chryssavgis, John & Rouvelas, Marilyn. Saint Anthony the Great. Brent, Isabelle, illus. 2015. 28p. (J). (gr. k-2). 17.95 *(978-1-937786-46-5(3)*, Wisdom Tales) World Wisdom, Inc.

Daniel-Rops, Henri. Golden Legend of Young Saints. 2009. Orig. Title: Légende Dorée de Mes Filleuls. (J). pap. 15.95 *(978-1-933184-37-1(X))* Sophia Institute Pr.

DeDomenico, Elizabeth Marie. Saint John Vianney: A Priest for All People. Hatke, Ben, illus. 2008. (Encounter the Saints Ser.). 122p. (J). (gr. 4-7). pap. 7.95 *(978-0-8198-7115-2(X))* Pauline Bks. & Media.

Demi. Hildegard of Bingen: Scientist, Composer, Healer, & Saint. 2019. (Illus.). 40p. (J). (gr. k-3). 17.95 *(978-1-937786-77-9(3)*, Wisdom Tales) World Wisdom, Inc.

—Joan of Arc, 0 vols. 2012. (ENG.). 56p. (J). (gr. 4-6). 19.99 *(978-0-7614-5953-8(7)*, 9780761459538, Two Lions) Amazon Publishing.

—Saint Francis of Assisi. 2012. (Illus.). 56p. (J). (gr. -1-3). 19.95 *(978-1-937786-04-5(8))* World Wisdom, Inc.

Denham, Joyce. Saint Francis of Assisi. Temporin, Elena, illus. 2008. (ENG.). 32p. (J). (gr. k-6). pap. 10.00 *(978-1-55725-571-6(7))* Paraclete Pr., Inc.

—Stories of the Saints. Stevens, Judy, illus. 2003. 48p. (J). pap. 11.99 *(978-0-7459-4637-5(2)*, Lion Books) Lion Hudson PLC GBR. Dist: Trafalgar Square Publishing.

dePaola, Tomie. Saint Patrick. 2019. (Illus.). 24p. (J). (— 1). bds. 7.99 *(978-0-8234-4235-5(7))* Holiday Hse., Inc.

Donaghy, Thomas J. My Golden Book of Saints. 2009. (ENG., Illus.). 42p. (J). (gr. k-2). bds. 14.00 *(978-0-89942-363-0(9)*, 455/97) Catholic Bk. Publishing Corp.

Driscoll, Christ. And God Blessed the Irish: The Story of Patrick. Kelley, Patrick, illus. 2007. 59p. (J). (gr. 3-7). 14.95 *(978-1-929039-40-1(9))* Ambassador Bks., Inc.

Elliott, David. Voices: The Final Hours of Joan of Arc. 2019. (ENG., Illus.). 208p. (YA). (gr. 9). 17.99 *(978-1-328-98759-4(0)*, 1709990, Clarion Bks.) HarperCollins Pubs.

Flanagan, Anne. Saints of America Col/Act Bk. 24p. pap. 1.25 *(978-0-8198-7086-5(2)*, 332-382) Pauline Bks. & Media.

Flavin, Pamela. An Alphabet of Saints for Young People. 2009. (Illus.). 64p. pap. *(978-1-84748-533-5(2))* Athena Pr.

Gallery, Philip D. Can You Find Saints? Introducing Your Child to Holy Men & Women. Harlow, Janet L., tr. Harlow, Janet L., illus. 2003. 40p. (J). *(978-2-89507-437-3(2))* Franciscan Media.

Giraldo, Maria Loretta. Saints & Their Stories. Moran, Margaret Edward, tr. Bertelle, Nicoletta, illus. 2010.Tr. of I Santi: i miei primi Amici. 168p. (J). (gr. 2-5). 19.95 *(978-0-8198-7134-3(6))* Pauline Bks. & Media.

Glavich, Mary Kathleen. Saint Therese of Lisieux: The Way of Love. Esquinaldo, Virginia, tr. Esquinaldo, Virginia, illus. 2003. (Encounter the Saints Ser.). 132p. (J). pap. 5.95 *(978-0-8198-7074-2(9)*, 332-370) Pauline Bks. & Media.

Grandgirard, Mélanie. Mary's Story. 2017. (ENG., Illus.). 20p. (J). (gr. -1 — 1). bds. 14.99 *(978-1-61261-916-3(9))* Paraclete Pr., Inc.

Gray, Tricia. The Wondrous Adventures of St. Francis of Assisi. rev. ed. 2003. (Illus.). 164p. (J). pap. 14.95 *(978-0-86716-480-0(8))* Franciscan Media.

Haldy, Emma E. Mother Teresa. Bane, Jeff, illus. 2017. (My Early Library: My Itty-Bitty Bio Ser.). (ENG.). 24p. (J). (gr. k-1). lib. bdg. 30.64 *(978-1-63472-154-7(3)*, 209188) Cherry Lake Publishing.

Heffernan, Anne Eileen. 57 Stories of Saints. Rizzo, Jerry, illus. 3rd ed. 2006. 531p. (J). pap. 16.95 *(978-0-8198-2681-7(2))* Pauline Bks. & Media.

Heffernan, Eileen. Fifty-Seven Stories of Saints. Rizzo, Jerry, illus. 2003. (J). 552p. pap. 16.95 *(978-0-8198-2674-9(X)*, 332-094); 549p. *(978-0-8198-2675-6(8))* Pauline Bks. & Media.

Hilliam, David. Joan of Arc: Heroine of France, 1 vol. 2004. (Leaders of the Middle Ages Ser.). (ENG., Illus.). 112p. (J). (gr. 5-8). lib. bdg. 39.80 *(978-1-4042-0164-4(5)*, 3da45756-c61b-4793-81ad-25b7cecbf6d5) Rosen Publishing Group, Inc., The.

—Thomas Becket: English Saint & Martyr. 2009. (Leaders of the Middle Ages Ser.). 112p. (gr. 5-8). 66.50 *(978-1-61513-902-6(8)*, Rosen Reference) Rosen Publishing Group, Inc., The.

Hodges, Margaret. The Legend of Saint Christopher. Watson, Richard J., illus. 2004. 32p. (J). (gr. 2-6). 18.00 *(978-0-8028-5077-5(4))* Eerdmans, William B. Publishing Co.

—Legend of Saint Christopher. Watson, Richard Jesse, illus. 2009. (ENG.). 32p. (J). (gr. k-5). 9.00 *(978-0-8028-5360-8(9)*, Eerdmans Bks For Young Readers) Eerdmans, William B. Publishing Co.

Hubbard, Margaret Ann. Saint Louis & the Last Crusade. Barton, Harry, illus. 2013. (Vision Bks.). (ENG.). 165p. (J). (gr. 4-10). pap. 12.95 *(978-1-58617-647-1(1))* Ignatius Pr.

Hunt, Jeanne. Celebrating Saints & Seasons: Hundreds of Activities for Catholic Children. 2010. (ENG.). 192p. pap. 15.99 *(978-0-86716-959-1(1))* Franciscan Media.

Hyde, Katherine. Lucia: Saint of Light. Fisher, Daria, illus. 2009. (ENG.). 32p. 19.95 *(978-0-9822770-4-1(0))* Ancient Faith Publishing.

Jablonski, Patricia Edward. Saint Andre Bessette: Miracles in Montreal. Kiwak, Barbara, illus. 2010. (J). (gr. 4-7). pap. 7.95 *(978-0-8198-7140-4(0))* Pauline Bks. & Media.

JOAN of ARC. 2010. (ENG., Illus.). 128p. (gr. 6-12). 35.00 *(978-1-60413-710-1(X)*, P179338, Facts On File) Infobase Holdings, Inc.

Kramer, Barbara. National Geographic Readers: Mother Teresa (L1) 2019. (Readers Bios Ser.). (Illus.). 32p. (J). (gr. -1-k). pap. 4.99 *(978-1-4263-3347-7(1))*; (ENG., lib. bdg. 14.90 *(978-1-4263-3348-4(X))* Disney Publishing Worldwide. (National Geographic Kids).

Lang, Leonora Blanche. The Book of Saints & Heroes. Lang, Andrew, ed. Ford, H. J., illus. 2012. 344p. pap. 13.50 *(978-1-936639-18-2(1))* St. Augustine Academy Pr.

Love, Pamela. The Sword & the Cape: A Tale of Saint Martin of Tours. Sorge, Rebecca, illus. 2018. 29p. (J). pap. *(978-0-8198-7544-0(9))* Pauline Bks. & Media.

Macdonald, Fiona. You Wouldn't Want to Be Joan of Arc! A Mission You Might Want to Miss. Antram, David, illus. 2010. (You Wouldn't Want to Ser.). (ENG.). 32p. (J). 29.00 *(978-0-531-20473-3(1))* Scholastic Library Publishing.

Mardon, May, et al. Early Saints & Other Saintly Stories for Children. 2012. (ENG.). 109p. pap. ***(978-1-897472-44-6(7))*** Golden Meteorite Pr. CAN. Dist: Lulu Pr., Inc.

Marsh, Emily Beata. Saint John Bosco: Champion for the Young. Alfano, Wayne, illus. 2015. 128p. (J). pap. 8.95 *(978-0-8198-9045-0(6))* Pauline Bks. & Media.

Marsh, Emily Beata & Lachuk, Dani, contrib. by. SAINT MARGARET MARY ALACOQUE: AND THE SACRED HEART OF JESUS. 2017. (Illus.). 134p. (J). pap. *(978-0-8198-9092-4(8))* Pauline Bks. & Media.

Matas, Toni. Saint Francis of Assisi, Messenger of Peace. Picanyol, illus. 2013. 64p. (J). 8.95 *(978-0-8198-7297-5(0))* Pauline Bks. & Media.

—St. Ignatius of Loyola, Leading the Way. Picanyol, illus. 2013. (J). 8.95 *(978-0-8198-7298-2(9))* Pauline Bks. & Media.

McGrath, Michael O'Neill, illus. Patrons & Protectors: In Times of Need. 2003. (Patrons & Protectors Ser.: Vol. 3). 58p. (J). 18.95 *(978-1-56854-410-6(3))* Liturgy Training Pubns.

McGrew, Michael. Saint Brendan & the Voyage Before Columbus. Litz, Mamie Saebz, illus. 2005. (ENG.). 32p. (J). pap. 10.95 *(978-0-8091-6705-0(0)*, 6705-0) Paulist Pr.

McKenzie, Janet P. RACE for Heaven's Catholic Study Guides for Mary Fabyan Windeatt's Saint Biographies Grade 5: Saint Rose of Lima, Saint Martin de Porres, King David & His Songs, & Blessed Marie of New France. 2007. 108p. (J). per. 24.95 *(978-1-934185-07-0(8))* Biblio Resource Pubns., Inc.

—RACE for Heaven's Catholic Study Guides for Mary Fabyan Windeatt's Saint Biographies Grade 6: Saint Dominic, the Children of Fatima, Saint John Masias, & Saint Benedict. 2007. 112p. (J). per. 24.95 *(978-1-934185-08-7(6))* Biblio Resource Pubns., Inc.

—RACE for Heaven's Catholic Study Guides for Mary Fabyan Windeatt's Saint Biographies Grade 7: The Curé of Ars (St. John Vianney), the Little Flower (St. Therese of the Child Jesus), Saint Hyacinth of Poland, & Saint Louis de Montfort. 2007. 124p. (J). per. 24.95 *(978-1-934185-09-4(4))* Biblio Resource Pubns., Inc.

—RACE for Heaven's Catholic Study Guides for Mary Fabyan Windeatt's Saint Biographies Grade 8: Saint Margaret Mary, Saint Francis Solano, Pauline Jaricot, & Saint Paul the Apostle. 2007. 156p. (YA). per. 24.95 *(978-1-934185-10-0(8))* Biblio Resource Pubns., Inc.

—RACE for Heaven's Catholic Study Guides for Mary Fabyan Windeatt's Saint Biographies Grades 3 And 4: Saint Thomas Aquinas, the Patron Saint of First Communicants, Saint Catherine of Siena, & the Miraculous Medal. 2007. 108p. (J). per. 24.95 *(978-1-934185-06-3(X))* Biblio Resource Pubns., Inc.

—Reading the Saints: Lists of Catholic Books for Children Plus Book Collecting Tips for the Home & School Library. 2007. 228p. (J). per. 24.95 *(978-1-934185-00-1(0))* 2nd ed. 2013. (ENG.). 278p. pap. 29.95 *(978-1-934185-45-2(0))* Biblio Resource Pubns., Inc.

Mitchell, Patricia. Saints Tell Their Stories. Casco, Maria Cristina Lo, illus. 2009. 62p. (J). (gr. k-5). 12.95 *(978-1-59325-161-1(0))* Word Among Us Pr.

Monahan, Joan. St. Therese of Lisieux: Missionary of Love. 2003. (ENG., Illus.). 144p. (J). pap. 9.95 *(978-0-8091-6710-4(7)*, 6710-7) Paulist Pr.

Moore, Armando. Clare of Assisi. (Illus.). 31p. 7.95 *(978-1-875570-63-8(2))* St Pauls Pubns. AUS. Dist: St Pauls/Alba Hse. Pubs.

Morgan, Julian. Constantine: Ruler of Christian Rome. 2009. (Ancient Leaders Ser.). 112p. (gr. 5-8). 66.50 *(978-1-61511-422-1(X)*, Rosen Reference) Rosen Publishing Group, Inc., The.

Morrow, Thomas G. Who's Who in Heaven: Real Saints for Families in Plain English. 2012. (ENG., Illus.). 176p. (J). pap. 14.95 *(978-1-937155-81-0(1))* Emmaus Road Publishing.

Morse, Letitia M. Yellow Roses on Her Feet. 2008. (J). pap. *(978-0-9815075-0-7(6))* Bienna Bks.

Mortimer, Sheila. St Patrick & the Shamrock. Catchpole, Diana, illus. 2004. (ENG.). 8p. (J). 10.95 *(978-0-7171-3755-8(4))* M.H. Gill & Co. U. C. IRL. Dist: Dufour Editions, Inc.

Muldoon, Kathleen M. Little Book of Saints, 2 bks. Mattozzi, Patricia R., illus. 2005. 24p. (J). Vol. 2. pap. 3.95 *(978-0-8198-4511-5(6)*, 332-187) Vol. I. pap. 3.95 *(978-0-8198-4510-8(8)*, 332-186) Pauline Bks. & Media.

Muldoon, Kathleen M. & Wallace, Susan Helen. My First Book of Saints. Mattozzi, Patricia R. & Kinarney, Tom, illus. 2012. 128p. (J). 12.95 *(978-0-8198-4917-5(0))* Pauline Bks. & Media.

Petras, Julie A. Draw & Tell Saints. 2004. (J). pap. 12.95 *(978-1-59276-048-0(1))* Our Sunday Visitor, Publishing Div.

Plum, Paul S., et al. Teach Me about Saints. 2003. 24p. (J). per. 4.95 *(978-1-931709-84-2(X))* Our Sunday Visitor, Publishing Div.

Pochocki, Ethel. Saints & Heroes. Owens, Mary Beth, illus. 2012. (ENG.). 258p. pap. 15.95 *(978-1-932350-51-7(9))* Ignatius Pr.

—Saints & Heroes for Kids. rev. exp. ed. 2005. (Illus.). 224p. (J). pap. 14.95 *(978-0-86716-554-8(5))* Franciscan Media.

Pollack, Pam, et al. Who Was Joan of Arc? Thomson, Andrew, illus. 2016. (Who Was? Ser.). 112p. (J). (gr. 3-7). pap. 5.99 *(978-0-448-48304-7(1)*, Penguin Workshop) Penguin Young Readers Group.

Pollack, Pamela D. & Belviso, Meg. Who Was Joan of Arc? 2016. (Who Was... ? Ser.). lib. bdg. 16.00 *(978-0-606-38395-0(6))* Turtleback.

Puhalo, Lazar. Lives of Saints for Young People: Twelve Saints. Date not set. (YA). (gr. 7-12). 28p. pap. 4.50 *(978-1-879038-34-9(X)*, 9002); Vol. 1. 28p. pap. 4.50 *(978-1-879038-33-2(1)*, 9001); Vol. 3. 32p. pap. 4.50 *(978-1-879038-35-6(8)*, 9003); Vol. 4. 42p. pap. 4.50 *(978-1-879038-36-3(6)*, 9004); Vol. 5. 32p. pap. 4.50 *(978-1-879038-37-0(4)*, 9005); Vol. 6. 28p. pap. 4.50 *(978-1-879038-38-7(2)*, 9006); Vol. 7. 78p. pap. 6.50 *(978-1-879038-39-4(0)*, 9007); Vol. 8. 32p. pap. *(978-1-879038-40-0(4)*, 9008); Vol. 9. 28p. pap. 4.50 *(978-1-879038-41-7(2)*, 9009); Vol. 10. 28p. pap. *(978-1-879038-42-4(0)*, 9010) Synaxis Pr.

Rodríguez-Ponga, Pedro. Ignatius of Loyola. 2018. (ENG., Illus.). 48p. pap. 12.95 *(978-0-8091-6783-8(2))* Paulist Pr.

Ross, Nancy Wilson. Joan of Arc. 2003. vii, 182p. pap. 29.00 *(978-0-7581-5017-2(2))* Textbook Pubs.

Ross Williamson, Hugh. The Young People's Book of Saints: Sixty-Three Saints of the Western Church from the First to the Twentieth Century. Connelly, Sheila, illus. 2009. (J). 15.95 *(978-1-933184-62-3(0))* Sophia Institute Pr.

Saints: Lives & Illuminations. 2007. (Illus.). 39p. (J). (gr. 3-7). per. 10.00 *(978-0-8028-5332-5(3)*, Eerdmans Bks For Young Readers) Eerdmans, William B. Publishing Co.

Sanderson, Ruth. More Saints: Lives & Illuminations. Sanderson, Ruth, illus. 2007. (Illus.). 40p. (J). (gr. 1). 20.00 *(978-0-8028-5272-4(6)*, Eerdmans Bks For Young Readers) Eerdmans, William B. Publishing Co.

—Saints: Lives & Illuminations. 2010. (ENG., Illus.). 160p. (J). (gr. 3-18). 16.00 *(978-0-8028-5365-3(X),* Eerdmans Bks For Young Readers) Eerdmans, William B. Publishing Co.

—Saints: Lives & Illuminations. Sanderson, Ruth, illus. 2004. (Illus.). 40p. 20.00 *(978-0-8028-5220-5(3))* Eerdmans, William B. Publishing Co.

Schmidt, Gary D. Martin de Porres: The Rose in the Desert. Diaz, David, illus. 2012. (ENG.). 32p. (J). (gr. 1-4). lib. bdg. 19.99 *(978-0-547-61218-8(4),* 1464622, Clarion Bks.) HarperCollins Pubs.

Schroedel, Jenny. The Blackbird's Nest: Saint Kevin of Ireland. Montross, Doug, illus. 2004. 32p. (J). 18.00 *(978-0-88141-258-1(9))* St. Vladimir's Seminary Pr.

Seco, Nina S. & Pilutik, Anastasia D. Saints Adrian & Natalie. Duckworth, Ruth, illus. Date not set. (Cloud of Witnesses Ser.). (Orig.). (J). (gr. -1-1). pap. *(978-0-913026-29-8(8))* St. Nectarios Pr.

Self, David. The Loyola Treasury of Saints: From the Time of Jesus to the Present Day. Hall, Amanda, illus. 2003. (ENG.). 224p. (J). (gr. 2-7). 28.95 *(978-0-8294-1785-2(0))* Loyola Pr.

Spier Weaver, Rachel & Haggard, Anna. An Extraordinary Teacher: A Bible Story about Priscilla. 2018. (Called & Courageous Girls Ser.). (ENG., Illus.). 48p. (J). (gr. -1-2). 14.99 *(978-0-7369-7081-5(9),* 6970815) Harvest Hse. Pubs.

Steedman, Amy. In God's Garden: Stories of the Saints for Children. rev. ed. 2003. (Illus.). 192p. (J). (gr. -1-3). 23.95 *(978-1-929291-32-8(9))* Roman Catholic Bks.

Stewart. Learning Centers: Saints: Saints. 2013. (Illus.). 119p. (J). pap. 16.95 *(978-1-58595-908-2(1))* Twenty-Third Pubns./Bayard.

Stott, Apryl, illus. Brigid & the Butter: A Legend about Saint Brigid of Ireland. 2017. 25p. (J). pap. *(978-0-8198-1233-9(1))* Pauline Bks. & Media.

Streit, Jakob. Brother Francis: The Life of Francis of Assisi, 1 vol. Kuettel, Nina, tr. 2013. (ENG., Illus.). 56p. (J). pap. 10.00 *(978-1-936367-40-5(8))* Waldorf Publications.

Swaim, Colleen. Lleven Su Fuego Al Mundo: Jóvenes Que Alcanzaron la Santidad. 2012. (SPA.). (J). *(978-0-7648-2176-9(8))* Liguori Pubns.

—Radiate: More Stories of Daring Teen Saints. 2012. (J). *(978-0-7648-2147-9(4))* Liguori Pubns.

Thiel, Kristin. Joan of Arc, 1 vol. 2017. (Great Military Leaders Ser.). (ENG.). 128p. (YA). (gr. 9-9). 47.36 *(978-1-5026-2791-9(4),* 61492b8d-dfdd-49d4-9b3c-8b9f9c6129f2) Cavendish Square Publishing LLC.

Trouvé, Marianne Lorraine. Saint Catherine Labouré: And Our Lady of the Miraculous Medal. 2011. (ENG., Illus.). 119p. (J). pap. 7.95 *(978-0-8198-7224-1(5))* Pauline Bks. & Media.

—Saint Clare of Assisi: A Light for the World. Peterson, Mary Joseph, illus. 2009. (J). pap. 7.95 *(978-0-8198-7122-0(2))* Pauline Bks. & Media.

Vazquez, Ana Maria & Dean, Jennings. Blessed Pier Giorgio Frassati: Journey to the Summit. Stewart, Don, illus. 2004. (Encounter Ser.: 18). 144p. (J). pap. 5.95 *(978-0-8198-1165-3(3),* 332-028) Pauline Bks. & Media.

Visconti, Guido. Clare & Francis. Landmann, Bimba, illus. 2004. 40p. 20.00 *(978-0-8028-5269-4(6))* Eerdmans, William B. Publishing Co.

Wallace, Susan F. S. P. & Wright, Melissa. Saints for Young Readers for Every Day, 2 vols., Vol. 1. Aven, Jamie H., illus. 3rd ed. 2005. (J). pap. 15.95 *(978-0-8198-7081-0(1),* 332-377) Pauline Bks. & Media.

Wallace, Susan Helen. Little Book of Saints: Volume 4, 4. Kinarney, Tom, illus. 2009. (J). 4.95 *(978-0-8198-4527-6(2))* Pauline Bks. & Media.

—Saint Bakhita of Sudan: Forever Free. Alfano, Wayne, illus. 2006. (Encounter the Saints Ser.: 21). 102p. (J). pap. 7.95 *(978-0-8198-7094-0(3))* Pauline Bks. & Media.

—Saint Faustina Kowalska: Messenger of Mercy. Waites, Joan, illus. 2007. (Encounter the Saints Ser.: 23). 116p. (J). pap. 7.95 *(978-0-8198-7101-5(X))* Pauline Bks. & Media.

—Saint Gianna Beretta Molla: The Gift of Life. 2012. (ENG., Illus.). 101p. (J). pap. 7.95 *(978-0-8198-7182-4(6))* Pauline Bks. & Media.

—Saint Katharine Drexel: The Total Gift. Kiwak, Barbara, illus. 2003. (Encounter the Saints Ser.: Vol. 15). 144p. (J). pap. 5.95 *(978-0-8198-7068-1(4),* 332-365) Pauline Bks. & Media.

—Saint Teresa of Avila: Joyful in the Lord. Kiwak, Barbara, illus. 2008. (Encounter the Saints Ser.: No. 24). 106p. (J). (gr. 4-7). pap. 7.95 *(978-0-8198-7116-9(8))* Pauline Bks. & Media.

Wilkinson, Philip. Joan of Arc: The Teenager Who Saved Her Nation. 2009. (National Geographic World History Biographies Ser.). (Illus.). 64p. (J). (gr. 3-7). pap. 7.95 *(978-1-4263-0415-6(3),* National Geographic Kids) Disney Publishing Worldwide.

Windeatt, Mary F. Saint Catherine of Siena: The Story of the Girl Who Saw Saints in the Sky. Beccard, Helen L., illus. 2009. (ENG.). 65p. (J). (gr. 3-7). reprint ed. pap. 7.95 *(978-0-89555-421-5(6),* 1201) TAN Bks.

—Saint Hyacinth of Poland: The Story of the Apostle of the North. Mary Jean, illus. 2009. (ENG.). 208p. (J). (gr. 1-8). reprint ed. pap. 13.95 *(978-0-89555-422-2(4),* 1202) TAN Bks.

—Saint John Masias: Marvelous Dominican Gatekeeper of Lima, Peru. Sister Mary of the Compassion, illus. 2009. Orig. Title: Warrior in White. (ENG.). 156p. (J). (gr. 3-9). pap. 11.95 *(978-0-89555-428-4(3),* 1236) TAN Bks.

—Saint Louis de Montfort: The Story of Our Lady's Slave. Grout, Paul A., illus. 2009. Orig. Title: Our Lady's Slave: the Story of St. Louis Mary Grignion de Montfort. (ENG.). 211p. (J). (gr. 2-9). reprint ed. pap. 13.95 *(978-0-89555-414-7(3),* 1142) TAN Bks.

—Saint Maria Goretti. Harmon, Gedge, illus. 2009. (ENG.). 32p. (J). (gr. k-2). reprint ed. pap., stu. ed. 4.50 *(978-0-89555-374-4(0))* TAN Bks.

Windeatt, Mary Fabyan & Ignatz, Marie. Vocabulary Quiz Workbook: Based on 6 Great Saints' Lives by Mary Fabyan Windeatt. Lester, Mary Frances, ed. 2004. (ENG.). 200p. (gr. 2-5). pap., wbk. ed. 21.95 *(978-0-89555-743-8(6),* 1841) TAN Bks.

Windle, Margaret. Assorted Saints & the Virtues. 2006. (Illus.). 64p. (J). 11.99 *(978-0-9798889-1-5(3))* Growing with the Saints, Inc.

Winter, Jonah. The Secret World of Hildegard. Winter, Jeanette, illus. 2007. (J). *(978-0-439-50738-7(3),* Levine, Arthur A. Bks.) Scholastic, Inc.

Wolny, Philip. Joan of Arc: French Soldier & Saint, 1 vol. 2017. (Women Who Changed History Ser.). (ENG., Illus.). 48p. (J). (gr. 6-7). pap. 15.05 *(978-1-68048-645-2(4),* 025bb447-f7cc-45bc-a107-9d8c97a0ee00, Britannica Educational Publishing) Rosen Publishing Group, Inc., The.

Woodfield, Elaine. Stories of the Saints V1, 4 vols. Staggenborg, Kim, illus. 2009. (J). pap. 13.95 *(978-0-9788376-8-6(1))* Catholic Heritage Curricula.

—Stories of the Saints V2, 4 vols. Staggenborg, Kim, illus. 2009. (J). pap. 0.00 *(978-0-9788376-9-3(X))* Catholic Heritage Curricula.

Zarin, Cynthia. Saints among the Animals. Gore, Leonid, illus. 2012. (ENG.). 96p. (J). (gr. 2-7). pap. 6.99 *(978-1-4424-7296-9(0),* Atheneum Bks. for Young Readers) Simon & Schuster Children's Publishing.

SAINTS—FICTION

and Film Studio, Shanghai Animation & Tang, Sanmu. Three Monks. Ying, Wu, tr. from CHI. 2010. (Favorite Childrens Cartoons from China Ser.). (ENG., Illus.). 32p. (gr. -1-3). pap. 5.95 *(978-1-60220-973-2(1))* Shanghai Pr.

Boyce, Frank Cottrell. Millions. 2005. 247p. (gr. 3-7). 19.00 *(978-0-7569-5439-0(8))* Perfection Learning Corp.

Clayden, Julie & Joliffe, Angela. Martha. 2006. (First Word Heroes Ser.). (ENG., Illus.). 14p. bds. 7.99 *(978-1-904637-23-3(X),* 190463723X) Authentic Media GBR. Dist: EMI CMG Distribution.

Davidson, Alice Joyce. St. Therese: the Little Flower. Swanson, Maggie, illus. 2006. 24p. (J). 7.95 *(978-0-88271-214-7(4))* Regina Pr., Malhame & Co.

Evangelista, Susan. Tommy's New Shell, 2nd in series. Coke, Sherrie, illus. 2005. 24p. (J). bds. 19.95 *(978-0-9769602-0-1(6))* Evangelista, Susan.

Everett-Green, Evelyn. A Heroine of France. 2006. (ENG.). 188p. pap. 19.99 *(978-1-4264-7060-8(6))* Creative Media Partners, LLC.

Hemphill, Stephanie. The Language of Fire: Joan of Arc Reimagined. 2019. (ENG.). 512p. (YA). (gr. 8). 17.99 *(978-0-06-249011-7(7),* Balzer & Bray) HarperCollins Pubs.

Hunger, Bill. When Two Saints Meet. Ripley, Jill, ed. Martin, Alice et al, illus. 100p. (Orig.). (YA). (gr. 6-12). pap. 9.95 *(978-0-9625782-0-5(7))* Two Saints Publishing.

Hurley, Tonya. The Blessed. Watkins, Abbey, illus. 2012. (Blessed Ser.). (ENG.). 416p. (YA). (gr. 9). 17.99 *(978-1-4424-2951-2(8),* Simon & Schuster Bks. For Young Readers) Simon & Schuster Bks. For Young Readers.

—Passionaries. (Blessed Ser.). (ENG., Illus.). 368p. (YA). (gr. 9). 2015. pap. 12.99 *(978-1-4424-2955-0(0))* 2014. 17.99 *(978-1-4424-2954-3(2))* Simon & Schuster Bks. For Young Readers. (Simon & Schuster Bks. For Young Readers).

—Precious Blood. Watkins, Abbey, illus. 2013. (Blessed Ser.). (ENG.). 432p. (YA). (gr. 9). pap. 9.99 *(978-1-4424-2952-9(6),* Simon & Schuster Bks. For Young Readers) Simon & Schuster Bks. For Young Readers.

Jackson, Dessi. The Saint & His Bees. Brandenburg, Claire, illus. 2013. (ENG.). 28p. (J). (gr. -1-3). pap. 9.99 *(978-1-62395-487-1(8))* Xist Publishing.

Kuck, Anna. Seven Holy Sleepers: Amazing Saints. 2012. 38p. pap. 15.95 *(978-1-4497-7065-5(7),* WestBow Pr.) Author Solutions, LLC.

Mora, Pat. The Song of Francis & the Animals. Frampton, David, illus. 2005. (ENG.). 32p. (J). (gr. -1-2). 16.00 *(978-0-8028-5253-3(X))* Eerdmans, William B. Publishing Co.

Nobisso, Josephine. Francis Woke up Early. Hyde, Maureen, illus. 2011. (ENG.). 32p. (J). (gr. k-2). 17.95 *(978-0-940112-20-9(5));* pap. 9.95 *(978-0-940112-22-3(1))* Gingerbread Hse.

Roberts, Esyllt Nest, et al. Dwynwen. 2005. (WEL., Illus.). 36p. pap. *(978-0-86381-468-6(9))* Gwasg Carreg Gwalch.

Rupp, Dain Chistopher. The Greatest Saint Stories A-Z: (Book 1 of 2: A-M) 2008. 32p. per. 24.95 *(978-1-60441-067-9(1))* America Star Bks.

Saint Jenni: Chilling Out. 2005. (ENG., Illus.). 96p. (J). (gr. 2-4). per. 6.99 *(978-0-7459-4896-6(0),* 6cf09a65-b48a-4a69-a53d-af315f4c262e, Lion Books) Lion Hudson PLC GBR. Dist: Baker & Taylor Publisher Services (BTPS).

Song-I, Yoon. Saint Teresa of Avila, God's Troublemaker. 2014. (ENG., Illus.). 208p. (J). pap. 14.95 *(978-0-8198-9038-2(3))* Pauline Bks. & Media.

Steedman, Amy. Our Island Saints (Yesterday's Classics) 2006. (J). per. 9.95 *(978-1-59915-031-4(X))* Yesterday's Classics.

Thottam, Meena, adapted by. The Sage's Daughter. 2006. (J). 3.95 *(978-0-9776917-2-2(1),* Curcumin Bks.) Davlaw Press.

Williamson, Denise J. Forbidden Gates. 2008. (J). 8.99 *(978-1-59166-853-4(0))* BJU Pr.

Willoughby, R. Peter Puts His Foot in It! Buckley, Joel, illus. 2004. 64p. pap. *(978-1-85999-765-9(1))* Scripture Union.

Windeatt, Mary F. Saint Teresa of Avila. Harmon, Gedge, illus. 2009. (ENG.). 32p. (J). (gr. k-2). reprint ed. pap., stu. ed. 4.50 *(978-0-89555-372-0(4))* TAN Bks.

SAINTS—LEGENDS

Forest, Jim. Saint Nicholas & the Nine Gold Coins. Andrejev, Vladislav, illus. 2015. (J). *(978-0-88141-511-7(1))* St. Vladimir's Seminary Pr.

Knijpenga, Siegwart. Stories of the Saints: A Collection for Children, 22 vols. 2nd rev. ed. 2012. (Illus.). 224p. (J). (gr. 4-7). pap. 22.95 *(978-0-86315-929-9(X))* Floris Bks. GBR. Dist: Consortium Bk. Sales & Distribution.

McAllister, Margaret. Stories of the Saints, 1 vol. Massari, Alida, illus. 2015. (ENG.). 48p. (J). (gr. 2-4). 12.99 *(978-0-7459-6445-4(1),* 26fe9251-ee92-4d26-90d3-a63c0edea50d, Lion Children's) Lion Hudson PLC GBR. Dist: Baker & Taylor Publisher Services (BTPS).

Rock, Lois. Saintly Tales & Legends. Balit, Christina, illus. 2004. 100p. (J). 15.95 *(978-0-8198-7083-4(8),* 332-379) Pauline Bks. & Media.

SALADS

Beck, Isabel L., et al. Trophies Kindergarten: The Salad. 2003. (Trophies Ser.). (gr. k-6). 13.80 *(978-0-15-329524-9(4))* Harcourt Schl. Pubs.

Dolbear, Emily J. How Did That Get to My Table? Salad. 2009. (Community Connections: How Did That Get to My Table? Ser.). (ENG.). 24p. (gr. 2-5). lib. bdg. 29.21 *(978-1-60279-473-3(1),* 200262) Cherry Lake Publishing.

Head, Honor. Salad. 2010. (J). 24.25 *(978-1-59920-259-4(X))* Black Rabbit Bks.

Kuskowski, Alex. Cool Sides & Salads. 2015. (Cool Home Cooking Ser.). (ENG.). 32p. (J). (gr. 3-6). 34.21 *(978-1-62403-503-6(5),* 16880, Checkerboard Library) ABDO Publishing Co.

SALAMANDERS

Borgert-Spaniol, Megan. Salamanders. 2012. (Backyard Wildlife Ser.). (ENG., Illus.). 24p. (J). (gr. k-3). lib. bdg. 26.95 *(978-1-60014-723-4(2),* Blastoff! Readers) Bellwether Media.

Bredeson, Carmen. Fun Facts about Salamanders!, 1 vol. 2007. (I Like Reptiles & Amphibians! Ser.). (ENG., Illus.). 24p. (gr. k-2). lib. bdg. 25.27 *(978-0-7660-2790-9(2),* e0f652eb-b453-4a85-9150-8c242710c422, Enslow Elementary) Enslow Publishing, LLC.

Carr, Aaron. Salamander. 2014. (J). *(978-1-4896-3106-0(2))* Weigl Pubs., Inc.

Clark, Willow & Rockwood, Leigh. Salamanders Are Gross!, 1 vol. 2010. (Creepy Crawlies Ser.). (ENG., Illus.). 24p. (J). (gr. 2-3). pap. 9.25 *(978-1-4488-1365-0(4),* 36878614-0070-41c5-a7f8-a10fa6db724b, PowerKids Pr.); lib. bdg. 26.27 *(978-1-4488-0702-4(6),* fe9f728b-cd8e-452a-8374-eaed54fff6da) Rosen Publishing Group, Inc., The.

Curtis, Jennifer Keats & Frederick, J. Adam. Temporada de Salamandras. Bersani, Shennen, illus. 2015. (SPA.). 32p. (J). (gr. 2-3). pap. 11.95 *(978-1-62855-574-5(2),* 3792856a-9d8e-469d-a7ec-84f6e8f7b30e) Arbordale Publishing.

Dibble, Traci. Can You See the Salamander? 2017. (1-3Y Animals Ser.). (ENG., Illus.). 12p. (J). pap. 9.60 *(978-1-63437-667-9(6))* American Reading Co.

Gish, Melissa. Salamanders. 2018. (Living Wild Ser.). (ENG.). 48p. (J). (gr. 5-8). pap. 12.00 *(978-1-62832-566-9(6),* 19779, Creative Paperbacks) Creative Co., The.

Goldish, Meish. Slimy Salamanders. 2010. (Amphibiana Ser.). (ENG., Illus.). 24p. (YA). (gr. k-3). lib. bdg. 26.99 *(978-1-936087-37-2(5))* Bearport Publishing Co., Inc.

Hansen, Grace. Becoming a Salamander, 1 vol. 2016. (Changing Animals Ser.). (ENG., Illus.). 24p. (J). (gr. -1-2). lib. bdg. 32.79 *(978-1-68080-512-3(6),* 21304, Abdo Kids) ABDO Publishing Co.

Hibbert, Clare. Salamanders. 2009. (Extreme Pets Ser.). (YA). (gr. 4-7). 28.50 *(978-1-59920-235-8(2))* Black Rabbit Bks.

Keats Curtis, Jennifer & Frederick, J. Adam. Salamander Season, 1 vol. Bersani, Shennen, illus. 2015. (ENG.). 32p. (J). (gr. 1-4). 17.95 *(978-1-62855-556-1(4))* Arbordale Publishing.

Kenney, Karen Latchana. Axolotls. 2018. (Weird & Unusual Animals Ser.). (ENG., Illus.). 24p. (J). (gr. 1-4). pap. 8.99 *(978-1-68152-185-5(7),* 16097) Amicus.

McNab, Chris. Frogs, Toads, & Salamanders, 1 vol. 2005. (Nature's Monsters: Reptiles & Amphibians Ser.). (ENG., Illus.). 32p. (gr. 3-5). lib. bdg. 28.67 *(978-0-8368-6172-3(8),* 89ea3eee-0300-4cd9-8f0b-92c0871522af, Gareth Stevens Learning Library) Stevens, Gareth Publishing LLLP.

Morlock, Rachael. Chinese Salamander: The Largest Amphibian, 1 vol. 2019. (Animal Record Breakers Ser.). (ENG.). 24p. (gr. 2-3). pap. 9.25 *(978-1-7253-0866-4(5),* 9c539dbf-b1c0-4302-8622-6a83bd681477, PowerKids Pr.) Rosen Publishing Group, Inc., The.

Murray, Julie. Salamanders. 2019. (Animal Kingdom Ser.). (ENG.). 32p. (J). (gr. 2-5). lib. bdg. 34.21 *(978-1-5321-1652-0(7),* 32415, Big Buddy Bks.) ABDO Publishing Co.

Nelson, Robin. Salamanders. 2009. pap. 34.95 *(978-0-7613-4109-3(9));* (ENG.). 24p. 23.93 *(978-0-7613-4065-2(3),* Lerner Pubns.) Lerner Publishing Group.

Plattner, Josh. Salamander: Master of Regrowth. 2015. (Animal Superpowers Ser.). (ENG., Illus.). 24p. (J). (gr. k-3). 32.79 *(978-1-62403-740-5(2),* 17986, Super SandCastle) ABDO Publishing Co.

Rudolph, Jessica. Mi Piel Tiene Bultos y Es Babosa. 2015. (Pistas de Animales Ser.). (SPA.). 24p. (J). (gr. -1-3). lib. bdg. 26.99 *(978-1-62724-584-5(7))* Bearport Publishing Co., Inc.

—My Skin Is Bumpy & Slimy (Fire Salamander) 2014. (Zoo Clues Ser.). 24p. (J). (gr. -1-3). lib. bdg. 26.99 *(978-1-62724-115-1(9))* Bearport Publishing Co., Inc.

Schafer, Susan. Chinese Giant Salamanders, 1 vol. 2014. (Giant Animals Ser.). (ENG.). 48p. (gr. 4-4). lib. bdg. 33.07 *(978-1-62712-960-2(X),* b05b9210-6e82-4710-b59e-6112ccaa0d72) Cavendish Square Publishing LLC.

Schuh, Mari. Salamanders. 2019. (Spot Backyard Animals Ser.). (ENG.). 16p. (J). (gr. -1-2). lib. bdg. *(978-1-68151-548-9(2),* 14509) Amicus.

Silverman, Buffy. Can You Tell a Gecko from a Salamander? 2012. (Animal Look-Alikes Ser.). 32p. (gr. k-2). pap. 45.32 *(978-0-7613-9255-2(6))* Lerner Publishing Group.

Squire, Ann O. Chinese Giant Salamander: The World's Biggest Amphibian. 2007. (SuperSized! Ser.). (Illus.). 24p. (J). (gr. k-3). lib. bdg. 26.99 *(978-1-59716-386-6(4),* 1265931) Bearport Publishing Co., Inc.

Statts, Leo. Salamanders. 2016. (Swamp Animals Ser.). (ENG.). 24p. (J). (gr. -1-2). 49.94 *(978-1-68079-379-6(9),* 23000, Abdo Zoom-Launch) ABDO Publishing Co.

Stewart, Melissa. Salamander or Lizard? How Do You Know?, 1 vol. 2011. (Which Animal Is Which? Ser.). (ENG., Illus.). 24p. (gr. k-2). pap. 10.35 *(978-1-59845-238-9(X),* 433dd8df-6264-45e3-8ad7-a4885ef25e17, Enslow Elementary); lib. bdg. 25.27 *(978-0-7660-3679-6(0),* 16dd0931-7ec3-4af2-9f62-3463f9be59b8) Enslow Publishing, LLC.

Tomljanovic, Tatiana. Caring for Your Salamander. 2006. (Caring for Your Pet Ser.). (Illus.). 32p. (J). (gr. 3-7). per. 9.95 *(978-1-59036-477-2(5));* lib. bdg. 26.00 *(978-1-59036-476-5(7))* Weigl Pubs., Inc.

Winnick, Nick. Salamanders. 2009. (Backyard Animals Ser.). (Illus.). 24p. (J). (gr. 3-5). pap. 8.95 *(978-1-60596-085-2(3));* lib. bdg. 24.45 *(978-1-60596-084-5(5))* Weigl Pubs., Inc.

Woodward, John. Salamanders. 2008. (Nature's Children Ser.). (Illus.). 52p. (J). *(978-0-7172-6261-8(8))* Grolier, Ltd.

SALEM (FICTITIOUS CHARACTER)—FICTION

Hemphill, Stephanie. Wicked Girls: A Novel of the Salem Witch Trials. 2013. (ENG.). 432p. (YA). (gr. 8). pap. 10.99 *(978-0-06-185330-2(5),* Balzer & Bray) HarperCollins Pubs.

SALEM (MASS.)—HISTORY

Aronson, Marc. Witch-Hunt: Mysteries of the Salem Witch Trials. 2005. (Illus.). 272p. (YA). (gr. 7-12). 16.65 *(978-0-7569-5659-2(5))* Perfection Learning Corp.

Bloom Fradin, Judith & Brindell Fradin, Dennis. The Salem Witch Trials, 1 vol. 2009. (Turning Points in U. S. History Ser.). (ENG.). 48p. (gr. 4-4). lib. bdg. 34.07 *(978-0-7614-3013-1(X),* b2c5e336-94b8-47b6-be36-ca80b68e06c0) Cavendish Square Publishing LLC.

Crewe, Sabrina & Uschan, Michael V. The Salem Witch Trials, 1 vol. 2004. (Events That Shaped America Ser.). (ENG., Illus.). 32p. (J). (gr. 3-5). lib. bdg. 28.67 *(978-0-8368-3406-2(2),* e3ca2228-b8b1-46d3-a6b0-e7331d447fb7, Gareth Stevens Learning Library) Stevens, Gareth Publishing LLLP.

Doeden, Matt. The Salem Witch Trials: An Interactive History Adventure. 2010. (You Choose: History Ser.). (ENG.). 112p. (J). (gr. 3-4). pap. 41.70 *(978-1-4296-6440-0(1),* 16180); pap. 6.95 *(978-1-4296-6272-7(7),* 115418); (Illus.). 32.65 *(978-1-4296-5478-4(3),* 113878) Capstone. (Capstone Pr.).

Dunn, Joeming W. The Salem Witch Trials, 1 vol. Martin, Cynthia, illus. 2008. (Graphic History Ser.). (ENG.). 32p. (J). (gr. 3-8). 32.79 *(978-1-60270-186-1(5),* 9064, Graphic Planet - Fiction) Magic Wagon.

Forten, Charlotte. Diary of Charlotte Forten: A Free Black Girl Before the Civil War, 1 vol. 2014. (First-Person Histories Ser.). (ENG., Illus.). 32p. (J). (gr. 3-6). lib. bdg. 27.99 *(978-1-4765-4196-9(5),* 124303, Capstone Pr.) Capstone.

Holub, Joan. What Were the Salem Witch Trials? 2015. (What Was... Ser.). lib. bdg. 16.00 *(978-0-606-36761-5(6))* Turtleback.

Holub, Joan & Who HQ. What Were the Salem Witch Trials? Putra, Dede, illus. 2015. (What Was? Ser.). 112p. (J). (gr. 3-7). 7.99 *(978-0-448-47905-7(2),* Penguin Workshop) Penguin Young Readers Group.

Kent, Deborah. Witchcraft Trials: Fear, Betrayal, & Death in Salem, 1 vol. 2008. (America's Living History Ser.). (ENG., Illus.). 128p. (gr. 5-6). lib. bdg. 35.93 *(978-0-7660-2906-4(9),* f48e6595-9950-45a0-840a-3eb1e5d882b5) Enslow Publishing, LLC.

Landau, Elaine. The Salem Witchcraft Trials: Would You Join the Madness?, 1 vol. 2014. (What Would You Do? Ser.). (ENG., Illus.). 48p. (gr. 3-3). lib. bdg. 27.93 *(978-0-7660-4224-7(3),* 44869b5a-9de4-4083-b291-075d1611321f, Enslow Elementary) Enslow Publishing, LLC.

MacBain, Jenny. The Salem Witch Trials: A Primary Source History of the Witchcraft Trials in Salem, Massachusetts. 2009. (Primary Sources in American History Ser.). 64p. (gr. 5-8). 58.50 *(978-1-60851-503-5(6))* Rosen Publishing Group, Inc., The.

Martin, Michael J. The Salem Witch Trials, 1 vol. Bascle, Brian, illus. 2005. (Graphic History Ser.). (ENG.). 32p. (J). (gr. 3-9). per. 8.10 *(978-0-7368-5246-3(8),* 86992, Capstone Pr.) Capstone.

Nardo, Don & Dellaccio, Tanya. The Salem Witch Trials: A Crisis in Puritan New England, 1 vol. 2016. (American History Ser.). (ENG.). 104p. (YA). (gr. 7-7). lib. bdg. 41.03 *(978-1-5345-6039-0(4),* a54bb4c3-1439-472d-bb47-a5595491e3a6, Lucent Pr.) Greenhaven Publishing LLC.

Stern, Steven L. Witchcraft in Salem. (HorrorScapes Ser.). 32p. (gr. 4-9). 2018. (ENG.). (J). 7.99 *(978-1-64280-077-7(5))* 2010. (Illus.). (YA). lib. bdg. 28.50 *(978-1-936088-00-3(2))* Bearport Publishing Co., Inc.

Uschan, Michael V. The Salem Witch Trials, 1 vol. 2004. (Landmark Events in American History Ser.). (ENG., Illus.). 48p. (gr. 5-8). pap. 15.05 *(978-0-8368-5415-2(2),* c80ebd89-e501-4720-8818-457470b372e2); lib. bdg. 33.67 *(978-0-8368-5387-2(3),* ec56240d-e910-4b70-991f-b0a25161bb6b) Stevens, Gareth Publishing LLLP. (Gareth Stevens Secondary Library).

Wallis, Jeffrey. Trials in Salem. 2005. (Houghton Mifflin Social Studies Leveled Readers). (Illus.). 16p. (J). pap. *(978-0-618-56037-0(8))* Houghton Mifflin Harcourt Publishing Co.

SALES PERSONNEL

see also Advertising; Business; Marketing

Blane, Francisco. At theTag Sale: Lap Book. 2009. (My First Reader's Theater Set B Ser.). (J). 28.00 *(978-1-4108-8535-7(6))* Benchmark Education Co.

Carlson Berne, Emma. Run Your Own Bake Sale, 1 vol. 2013. (Young Entrepreneurs Ser.). (ENG., Illus.). 32p. (J). (gr. 4-5). pap. 11.00 *(978-1-4777-3007-2(9),* 973a2ce6-8470-4738-8575-15212c7a9454, PowerKids Pr.) Rosen Publishing Group, Inc., The.

Clark, Betty. Choosing a Career in Real Estate. 2009. (World of Work Ser.). 64p. (gr. 5-5). 58.50 *(978-1-60854-335-9(8))* Rosen Publishing Group, Inc., The.

Ensaff, Najoud, et al. Retail Careers. 2011. (Been There! Ser.). 32p. (gr. 3-6). lib. bdg. 31.35 *(978-1-59920-473-4(8))* Black Rabbit Bks.

Gard, Carolyn. Cool Careers Without College for People Who Love to Sell Things. 2009. (Cool Careers Without College Ser.). 144p. (gr. 6-6). 66.50 *(978-1-61511-979-0(5))* Rosen Publishing Group, Inc., The.

Houghton, Gillian. Goods & Services. 2009. (Invest Kids Ser.). 24p. (gr. 2-3). 42.50 *(978-1-61513-617-9(7));* (ENG., Illus.). (J). pap. 9.25 *(978-1-4358-3210-7(8),* f8895fab-da59-4c48-8d13-f1613b5804f7); (ENG., Illus.). (J). lib. bdg. 26.27 *(978-1-4358-2775-2(9),* b7b07655-5df7-4a23-afdf-0d3cadb35cf5) Rosen Publishing Group, Inc., The. (PowerKids Pr.).

Lewis, Daniel. Sales, Marketing & Finance, Vol. 10. 2018. (Careers in Demand for High School Graduates Ser.). 112p. (J). (gr. 7). 34.60 *(978-1-4222-4142-4(4))* Mason Crest.

Meinking, Mary. Start Your Crafting Business. 2017. (Build Your Business Ser.). (ENG., Illus.). 32p. (J). (gr. 3-9). lib. bdg. 28.65 *(978-1-5157-6690-2(X),* 135252, Capstone Pr.) Capstone.

Mozer, Mindy. Careers As a Commissioned Sales Representative, 1 vol. 2013. (Essential Careers Ser.).

(ENG.). 80p. (YA). (gr. 6-6). 37.47 *(978-1-4777-1794-3(3),* 591954f5-9c30-4825-9ff3-64dfb57ba62a) Rosen Publishing Group, Inc., The.

Reeves, Diane Lindsey. Marketing, Sales & Service. 2017. (Bright Futures Press: World of Work Ser.). (ENG., Illus.). 32p. (J). (gr. 4-7). lib. bdg. 32.07 *(978-1-5341-0177-7(2),* 210178) Cherry Lake Publishing.

Sheen, Barbara. Careers in Sales & Marketing. 2015. (ENG., Illus.). 80p. (YA). lib. bdg. *(978-1-60152-812-4(4))* ReferencePoint Pr., Inc.

Sun-tzu & Gagliardi, Gary. Strategy for Sales Managers: Sun Tzu's the Art of War Plus Book Series. 2005. (Art of War Plus Ser.). (Illus.). 192p. 16.95 *(978-1-929194-33-9(1),* Art of War Plus Bks.) Clearbridge Publishing.

SALES PERSONNEL—FICTION

Andrews, Jan. The Auction. (Illus.). (J). 13.95 *(978-0-88899-110-2(X))*; pap. 5.95 *(978-0-88899-168-3(1))* Groundwood Bks. CAN. Dist: Publishers Group West (PGW).

McOmber, Rachel B., ed. McOmber Phonics Storybooks: The Lemonade Sale. rev. ed. (Illus.). (J). *(978-0-944991-41-1(6))* Swift Learning Resources.

Merrill, Jean. The Elephant Who Liked to Smash Small Cars. Solbert, Ronni, illus. 2015. (ENG.). 40p. (J). (gr. -1-2). 16.95 *(978-1-59017-872-0(6),* NYR Children's Collection) New York Review of Bks., Inc., The.

SALES PERSONNEL—VOCATIONAL GUIDANCE

Endsaff, Najoud & Rooney, Anne. Retail Careers. 2010. (In the Workplace Ser.). 48p. (J). 35.65 *(978-1-60753-093-0(7))* Amicus Learning.

SALESMEN

see Sales Personnel

SALINGER, J. D. (JEROME DAVID), 1919-2010

Novel Units. The Catcher in the Rye Novel Units Student Packet. 2019. (ENG.). (YA). pap. 13.99 *(978-1-56137-450-2(4),* NU4504SP, Novel Units, Inc.) Classroom Library Co.

SALK, JONAS, 1914-1995

Hantula, Richard. Jonas Salk, 1 vol. 2004. (Trailblazers of the Modern World Ser.). (ENG., Illus.). 48p. (J). (gr. 5-8). lib. bdg. 33.67 *(978-0-8368-5100-7(5),* 91b76e1b-e792-41ca-b702-2c41f73c8f78, Gareth Stevens Secondary Library) Stevens, Gareth Publishing LLLP.

Llanas, Sheila. Jonas Salk: Medical Innovator & Polio Vaccine Developer, 1 vol. 2013. (Essential Lives Set 8 Ser.). (ENG., Illus.). 112p. (YA). (gr. 6-12). lib. bdg. 41.36 *(978-1-61783-896-5(9),* 6769, Essential Library) ABDO Publishing Co.

Marsh, Carole. Jonas Salk. 2004. 12p. (gr. k-4). 2.95 *(978-0-635-02377-3(6))* Gallopade International.

McLeese, Don. Jonas Salk. 2005. (Rourke Discovery Library). (Illus.). 24p. (J). (gr. 2-5). lib. bdg. *(978-1-59515-436-1(1))* Rourke Educational Media.

McPherson, Stephanie Sammartino. Jonas Salk: Conquering Polio. 128p. (J). (gr. 6-18). 20.95 *(978-1-58013-207-7(3),* Kar-Ben Publishing) Lerner Publishing Group.

SALMON

Best, B. J. Salmon, 1 vol. 2016. (Migrating Animals Ser.). (ENG., Illus.). 24p. (gr. 1-1). pap. 9.81 *(978-1-5026-2102-3(9),* c6d7c132-5fd5-407a-a38b-63eabc9f6920); lib. bdg. 27.36 *(978-1-5026-2104-7(5),* 6d3b3800-36c5-45b9-8d9f-c64edfe9ad1c) Cavendish Square Publishing LLC.

Catt, Thessaly. Migrating with the Salmon, 1 vol. 2011. (Animal Journeys Ser.). (ENG., Illus.). 24p. (gr. 2-3). (J). pap. 9.25 *(978-1-4488-2674-2(8),* f2d5c753-964c-4ce6-a6e7-dd6448554ba6, PowerKids Pr.); (YA). lib. bdg. 26.27 *(978-1-4488-2545-5(8),* 40be3a5a-a500-4682-a00c-ab5c28af80fc) Rosen Publishing Group, Inc., The.

Cosson, M. J. Salmon: A Journey Home. 2016. (Illus.). 32p. (J). *(978-1-4896-4523-4(3))* Weigl Pubs., Inc.

Fishman, Jon M. The Salmon's Journey. 2018. (Lightning Bolt Books (r) — Amazing Migrators Ser.). (ENG., Illus.). 24p. (J). (gr. 1-3). 29.32 *(978-1-5124-8637-7(X),* 1a120164-4737-47e9-9b0a-094428d97cdd, Lerner Pubns.) Lerner Publishing Group.

Glimmerveen, Ulco. Leaper: The Amazing Life of the Salmon. (Illus.). 32p. (J). pap. *(978-1-86943-042-9(5))* Scholastic New Zealand Ltd.

Hansen, Grace. Salmon Migration. 2017. (Animal Migration Ser.). (ENG., Illus.). 24p. (J). (gr. -1-2). lib. bdg. 32.79 *(978-1-5321-0031-4(0),* 25142, Abdo Kids) ABDO Publishing Co.

Harasymiw, Mark J. The Bizarre Life Cycle of a Salmon, 1 vol. 2012. (Strange Life Cycles Ser.). (ENG., Illus.). 24p. (J). (gr. 2-3). 25.27 *(978-1-4339-7059-7(7),* 5d8b9eb9-c944-4608-aec4-b2774b4924ed); pap. 9.15 *(978-1-4339-7060-3(0),* 618ab6a9-4327-4dec-9d05-e5e95324b203) Stevens, Gareth Publishing LLLP. (Gareth Stevens Learning Library).

Huson, Hetxw'ms Gyetxw Brett D. The Sockeye Mother, 1 vol. Donovan, Natasha, illus. 2017. (Mothers of Xsan Ser.: 1). (ENG.). 32p. (J). (gr. 4-6). *(978-1-55379-739-5(6),* HighWater Pr.) Portage & Main Pr.

Kalman, Bobbie & Sjonger, Rebecca. The Life Cycle of a Salmon, 1 vol. 2006. (Life Cycle Ser.). (ENG., Illus.). 32p. (J). (gr. 2-3). pap. *(978-0-7787-0705-9(9))* Crabtree Publishing Co.

—Les Saumons. Briere, Marie-Josee, tr. from ENG. 2008. (Petit Monde Vivant Ser.). (FRE., Illus.). 32p. (J). (gr. 3-7). pap. 9.95 *(978-2-89579-180-5(5))* Bayard Canada Livres CAN. Dist: Crabtree Publishing Co.

Keefe, Alicia. An Incredible Journey. NOAA Fisheries, West Coast Region (U.S.), ed. Gladnick, Anke, illus. 2018. (ENG.). 47p. (J). (gr. 2). pap. 13.00 *(978-0-16-094604-2(2),* 003-017-0573-9, National Marine Fisheries Service) United States Government Printing Office.

Miller, Debbie S. & Eiler, John H. A King Salmon Journey. 2014. (ENG., Illus.). 44p. 17.95 *(978-1-60223-230-3(X))* Univ. of Alaska Pr.

Reed-jones, Carol. Salmon Stream. Maydak, Michael S., illus. 2004. (Sharing Nature with Children Book Ser.). 32p. (J). (gr. 4-7). 16.95 *(978-1-58469-014-6(3))* Take Heart Pubns.

Ritchie, Scot. P'ésk'a & the First Salmon Ceremony, 1 vol. 2015. (ENG., Illus.). 32p. (J). (gr. -1-1). 16.95 *(978-1-55498-718-4(0))* Groundwood Bks. CAN. Dist: Publishers Group West (PGW).

Royston, Angela. El Salmón, 1 vol. 2010. (Ciclo de Vida Ser.). (SPA & ENG.). 32p. (gr. 1-3). pap. 7.99 *(978-1-4329-4386-8(3))* Heinemann-Raintree.

Schuetz, Kari. Salmon Migration. 2018. (Animals on the Move Ser.). (ENG., Illus.). 24p. (J). (gr. k-3). lib. bdg. 26.95 *(978-1-62617-819-9(4),* Blastoff! Readers) Bellwether Media.

Sexton, Colleen. The Life Cycle of a Salmon. 2010. (Life Cycles Ser.). (ENG., Illus.). 24p. (J). (gr. k-3). lib. bdg. 26.95 *(978-1-60014-311-3(3),* Blastoff! Readers) Bellwether Media.

Thomson, Ruth. The Life Cycle of a Salmon, 1 vol. 2007. (Learning about Life Cycles Ser.). (ENG., Illus.). 24p. (J). (gr. 2-2). lib. bdg. 26.27 *(978-1-4042-3712-4(7),* 0452fc27-b738-47ac-9163-a2b09776e46a, PowerKids Pr.) Rosen Publishing Group, Inc., The.

Winkelman, Barbara Gaines. Sockeye's Journey Home: The Story of a Pacific Salmon. Popeo, Joanie, illus. 2005. (Smithsonian Oceanic Collection: Vol. 19). (ENG.). 32p. (J). (gr. -1-2). 15.95 *(978-1-56899-829-9(5),* B4019) Soundprints.

Winkelman, Barbara Gaines & Thomas, Peter. Sockeye's Journey Home: The Story of a Pacific Salmon. Popeo, Joanie, illus. 2003. (ENG.). 32p. (J). (gr. -1-3). 9.95 *(978-1-56899-834-3(1),* PB4069) Soundprints.

SALOMON, HAYM, 1740-1785

Amler, Jane Frances. Haym Salomon: Patriot Banker of the American Revolution. (Library of American Lives & Times Ser.). 112p. (gr. 5-5). 2009. 69.20 *(978-1-60853-487-6(1))* 2003. (ENG., Illus.). (YA). lib. bdg. 38.27 *(978-0-8239-6629-5(1),* 3a4e1bca-af6e-4a1b-a820-f6c59f1e515f) Rosen Publishing Group, Inc., The.

SALOONS

see Restaurants

SALT

Centore, Michael. Salt. 2017. 64p. (J). *(978-1-4222-3742-7(7))* Mason Crest.

Dunlop, Jenna & Zronik, John. Salt. 2004. (Rocks, Minerals, & Resources Ser.). (ENG., Illus.). 32p. (J). lib. bdg. *(978-0-7787-1411-8(X))* Crabtree Publishing Co.

Furgang, Adam. Salty & Sugary Snacks: The Incredibly Disgusting Story, 1 vol. 2011. (Incredibly Disgusting Food Ser.). (ENG., Illus.). 48p. (YA). (gr. 5-8). pap. 12.75 *(978-1-4488-2283-6(1),* d0080215-01f4-44f5-929a-f81e27126a17, Rosen Reference); lib. bdg. 34.47 *(978-1-4488-1267-7(4),* d5bb4c7d-9142-436e-8f91-6cb697ad4aa8) Rosen Publishing Group, Inc., The.

Kjelle, Marylou Morano. The Properties of Salts. 2009. (Library of Physical Science Ser.). 24p. (gr. 4-4). 42.50 *(978-1-60853-793-8(5),* PowerKids Pr.) Rosen Publishing Group, Inc., The.

Kuhn, Betsy. The Force Born of Truth: Mohandas Gandhi & the Salt March, India 1930. 2010. (Civil Rights Struggles Around the World Ser.). (ENG., Illus.). 160p. (YA). (gr. 6-12). lib. bdg. 38.65 *(978-0-8225-8968-6(0),* deaff85b-8573-436b-a823-e0da6015bbfa, Twenty-First Century Bks.) Lerner Publishing Group.

Kurlansky, Mark. The Story of Salt. Schindler, S. D., illus. 2014. 48p. (J). (gr. -1-3). 8.99 *(978-0-14-751166-9(6),* Puffin Books) Penguin Young Readers Group.

—The Story of Salt. 2014. lib. bdg. 19.65 *(978-0-606-35715-9(7))* Turtleback.

Lawrence, Ellen. Why Is Seawater Salty? 2016. (Drip, Drip, Drop: Earth's Water Ser.). (ENG., Illus.). 24p. (J). (gr. -1-3). 26.99 *(978-1-943553-22-8(X))* Bearport Publishing Co., Inc.

Masters, Nancy Robinson. Salt. 2008. (21st Century Skills Library: Global Products Ser.). (ENG., Illus.). 32p. (gr. 4-8). lib. bdg. 32.07 *(978-1-60279-120-6(1),* 200108) Cherry Lake Publishing.

Nelson, Robin. From Sea to Salt. 2003. (Start to Finish Ser.). (ENG., Illus.). 24p. (gr. k-3). 19.93 *(978-0-8225-0946-2(6),* Lerner Pubns.) Lerner Publishing Group.

Owings, Lisa. From Sea to Salt. 2015. (Start to Finish, Second Ser.). (ENG., Illus.). 24p. (J). (gr. k-3). pap. 7.99 *(978-1-4677-6113-0(3),* cae31365-ff1a-4b0c-879b-aac0913e907a) Lerner Publishing Group.

—The Story of Salt: It Starts with the Sea. 2021. (Step by Step Ser.). (ENG., Illus.). 24p. (J). (gr. -1-2). 26.65 *(978-1-5415-9725-9(7),* a74fc4c5-096c-4fed-93a2-5353d83a0056, Lerner Pubns.) Lerner Publishing Group.

Perritano, John. Salt, Vol. 12. 2015. (North American Natural Resources Ser.). (Illus.). 64p. (J). (gr. 7). 23.95 *(978-1-4222-3388-7(X))* Mason Crest.

Strom, Laura Layton. Shockwave: Rock We Eat: Salt. 2007. (Shockwave: Economics & Geography Ser.). (ENG., Illus.). 36p. (J). (gr. 3-5). 25.00 *(978-0-531-17799-0(8),* Children's Pr.) Scholastic Library Publishing.

World Book, Inc. Staff, contrib. by. Salt & Pepper. 2019. (Illus.). 48p. (J). *(978-0-7166-2864-4(3))* World Bk., Inc.

SALUTATIONS

see Etiquette; Letter Writing

SALVADOR

see El Salvador

SALVAGE

see also Shipwrecks; Skin Diving

Dybvik, Tina. Trendy Jewelry for the Crafty Fashionista, 1 vol. 2011. (Fashion Craft Studio Ser.). (ENG.). 32p. (J). (gr. 3-9). lib. bdg. 28.65 *(978-1-4296-6549-0(1),* 115651) Capstone.

Hewitt, Sally. Reduce & Reuse. 2008. (Rise & Shine Ser.). (ENG., Illus.). 32p. (J). (gr. 3-7). pap. *(978-0-7787-4102-2(8))* Crabtree Publishing Co.

Jones, Jen. Cool Crafts with Newspapers, Magazines, & Junk Mail: Green Projects for Resourceful Kids, 1 vol. 2010. (Green Crafts Ser.). (ENG.). 32p. (J). (gr. 3-9). lib. bdg. 28.65 *(978-1-4296-4764-9(7),* 103295) Capstone.

Kington, Emily. Rad Recycled Art. 2019. (Wild Art Projects Ser.). (ENG., Illus.). 32p. (J). (gr. 3-6). lib. bdg. 27.99 *(978-1-5415-0129-4(2),* 9f22b12e-e1ac-4bea-a898-772041e481bd, Hungry Tomato (r)) Lerner Publishing Group.

Sirrine, Carol. Cool Crafts with Old Jeans: Green Projects for Resourceful Kids. 2010. (Green Crafts Ser.). (ENG.). 32p. (J). (gr. 3-9). lib. bdg. 28.65 *(978-1-4296-4006-0(5),* 102616) Capstone.

Sirrine, Carol & Jones, Jennifer. Re-Craft: Unique Projects That Look Great (and Save the Planet) 2011. (Craft It Yourself Ser.). (ENG.). 112p. (J). (gr. 3-9). 12.95 *(978-1-4296-6637-4(4),* 115769, Capstone Young Readers) Capstone.

Wilcox, Charlotte. Recycling. 2008. pap. 52.95 *(978-0-8225-9329-4(7))* 2007. (ENG., Illus.). 48p. (gr. 4-8). lib. bdg. 27.93 *(978-0-8225-6768-4(7))* Lerner Publishing Group.

SALVAGE—FICTION

Michaels, Craig. Blackbeard's Treasure. 2008. (J). *(978-0-936389-99-8(0))* Tudor Pubs., Inc.

SALVATION ARMY

Marsico, Katie. The Salvation Army. 2014. (Community Connections: How Do They Help? Ser.). (ENG., Illus.). 24p. (J). (gr. 2-5). 29.21 *(978-1-63188-029-2(2),* 205523) Cherry Lake Publishing.

SAMOAN ISLANDS

Burgan, Michael. Puerto Rico y Otras Áreas Periféricas (Puerto Rico & Other Outlying Areas), 1 vol. 2003. (World Almanac(r) Biblioteca de Los Estados (World Almanac(r) Library of the States) Ser.). (SPA.). 48p. (gr. 4-6). lib. bdg. 33.67 *(978-0-8368-5726-9(7),* 143e99dc-fbff-4a14-8c25-211ce284c1ac, Gareth Stevens Learning Library) Stevens, Gareth Publishing LLLP.

SAMOAN ISLANDS—FICTION

Bessey, Siân Ann. Uprising in Samoa: A Novel. 2004. 178p. (J). *(978-1-59156-890-2(0))* Covenant Communications.

Bundschuh, Rick. Burned: A Novel, 1 vol. 2014. (Faithgirlz / Soul Surfer Ser.: 2). (ENG.). 128p. (J). pap. 7.99 *(978-0-310-74555-6(1))* Zonderkidz.

Watson, Leilani. Sina & the Eel: A Tale from Samoa, 1 vol. Cooper, Jenny, illus. 2016. (ENG.). 24p. (J). pap. 9.95 *(978-1-927244-56-2(0))* Flying Start Bks. NZL. Dist: Flying Start Bks.

—Sina & the Eel (Big Book Edition) A Tale from Samoa. Cooper, Jenny, illus. 2016. 24p. (J). pap. *(978-1-927244-66-1(8))* Flying Start Bks.

SAMSON (BIBLICAL JUDGE)

Barberet, Denise-Renée. Samson. (Money at its Best: Millionaires of the Old Testament Ser.). 112p. (YA). (gr. 7-12). 2009. 24.95 *(978-1-4222-0475-7(8))* 2007. pap. 14.95 *(978-1-4222-0850-2(8))* Mason Crest.

SAMSON (BIBLICAL JUDGE)—FICTION

Samson 4 book Set. 2007. (J). mass mkt. *(978-0-9769722-4-2(7))* Leslie, Beverly J.

SAMURAI

Bodden, Valerie. Samurai. 2017. (X-Books: Fighters Ser.). (ENG., Illus.). 32p. (J). (gr. 3-6). *(978-1-60818-815-4(9),* 20378, Creative Education) Creative Co., The.

—X-Books: Samurai. 2017. (X-Bks.). (ENG., Illus.). 32p. (J). (gr. 3-7). pap. 9.99 *(978-1-62832-418-1(X),* 20379, Creative Paperbacks) Creative Co., The.

Dawson, Patricia A. Samurai: Warlords of Japan, 1 vol. 2014. (History's Greatest Warriors Ser.). (ENG., Illus.). 48p. (gr. 4-4). 33.07 *(978-1-5026-0125-4(7),* 6f72efa3-2d16-4b71-9627-c47df6a7625d) Cavendish Square Publishing LLC.

Doeden, Matt. Life as a Samurai. 2010. (You Choose: Warriors Ser.). (ENG.). 112p. (gr. 3-4). pap. 41.70 *(978-1-4296-5726-6(X),* Capstone Pr.) Capstone.

Farndon, John. How to Live Like a Samurai Warrior. Pinelli, Amerigo, illus. 2016. (How to Live Like ... Ser.). (ENG.). 32p. (J). (gr. 3-6). 27.99 *(978-1-5124-0630-6(9),* 39e90686-ac94-477a-bc2a-91d5ac0e3a1c, Hungry Tomato (r)) Lerner Publishing Group.

Green, John. Samurai Stained Glass Coloring Book. 2008. (Dover Fashion Coloring Book Ser.). (ENG., Illus.). 32p. (gr. 3-8). 6.99 *(978-0-486-46558-6(6),* 465586) Dover Pubns., Inc.

—Samurai Warriors. 2008. (Dover History Coloring Book Ser.). (ENG., Illus.). 32p. (gr. 3-8). 3.95 *(978-0-486-46559-3(4),* 465594) Dover Pubns., Inc.

Hanel, Rachel. Samurai. 2007. (Fearsome Fighters Ser.). (ENG., Illus.). 48p. (J). (gr. 5-8). lib. bdg. 31.35 *(978-1-58341-538-2(6),* 22148) Creative Co., The.

Heppermann, Christine. Samurai. 2013. (Great Warriors Ser.). (ENG., Illus.). 48p. (J). (gr. 4-8). pap. 18.50 *(978-1-61783-777-7(6),* 10809) ABDO Publishing Co.

Hoena, Blake. Samurai: Japan's Noble Servant-Warriors. Orban, Jaños, illus. 2019. (Graphic History: Warriors Ser.). (ENG.). 32p. (J). (gr. 3-9). pap. 7.95 *(978-1-5435-5930-9(1),* 139908); lib. bdg. 33.32 *(978-1-5435-5504-2(7),* 139376) Capstone.

Hubbard, Ben. Samurai Warriors, 1 vol. 2016. (Conquerors & Combatants Ser.). (ENG.). 224p. (YA). (gr. 9-9). lib. bdg. 56.71 *(978-1-5026-2459-8(1),* e50fe6b7-017b-4eea-accc-69c43318804b) Cavendish Square Publishing LLC.

Loh-Hagan, Virginia. Samurai vs. Knights. 2019. (Battle Royale: Lethal Warriors Ser.). (ENG., Illus.). 32p. (J). (gr. 4-8). lib. bdg. 32.07 *(978-1-5341-4766-9(7),* 213514, 45th Parallel Press) Cherry Lake Publishing.

—Samurais vs. Knights. 2019. (Battle Royale: Lethal Warriors Ser.). (ENG., Illus.). 32p. (J). (gr. 4-8). pap. 14.21 *(978-1-5341-5052-2(8),* 213515, 45th Parallel Press) Cherry Lake Publishing.

Lusted, Marcia Amidon. Samurai Science: Armor, Weapons, & Battlefield Strategy. 2016. (Warrior Science Ser.). (ENG., Illus.). 32p. (J). (gr. 3-9). 28.65 *(978-1-4914-8124-0(2),* 130615, Capstone Pr.) Capstone.

Macdonald, Fiona. Do You Want to Be a Samurai Warrior? 2015. (Do You Want to Be... Ser.). (Illus.). 32p. (gr. 3-6). 28.50 *(978-1-909645-39-4(7))* Book Hse. GBR. Dist: Black Rabbit Bks.

—You Wouldn't Want to Be a Samurai! A Deadly Career You'd Rather Not Pursue. Antram, David, illus. 2009. (You Wouldn't Want to Ser.). (ENG.). 32p. (J). 29.00 *(978-0-531-21325-4(0))* Scholastic Library Publishing.

Main Idea & Details Spanish Version, Gr. 1-3. 2005. (Spanish Version Ser.). (J). per. *(978-1-58232-147-9(7))* ECS Learning Systems, Inc.

Malam, John. Samurai. 2013. (Illus.). 48p. (J). *(978-1-4351-5097-3(X))* Barnes & Noble, Inc.

—Samurai. 2010. (Remarkable Man & Beast Ser.). (Illus.). 48p. (J). (gr. 3-18). lib. bdg. 19.95 *(978-1-4222-1973-7(9))* Mason Crest.

Matthews, Rupert. Samurai, 1 vol. 2015. (History's Fearless Fighters Ser.). (ENG., Illus.). 48p. (J). (gr. 5-6). pap. 15.05 *(978-1-4824-3177-3(7),* 79589fdd-7178-4c07-91f5-c9df96f824f5) Stevens, Gareth Publishing LLLP.

McLeese, Don. Samurai. 2009. 32p. pap. 7.99 *(978-0-8249-1444-8(9),* Ideals Pubns.) Worthy Publishing.

Murrell, Deborah Jane & Dennis, Peter. Samurai. 2012. (ENG., Illus.). 32p. (gr. 3-5). pap. 8.95 *(978-1-926853-55-0(5))* Saunders Bk. Co. CAN. Dist: RiverStream Publishing.

Olson, Elsie. Samurai! Strong & Steady Warriors. 2017. (History's Hotshots Ser.). (ENG., Illus.). 32p. (J). (gr. 3-6). lib. bdg. 32.79 *(978-1-5321-1274-4(2),* 27598, Checkerboard Library) ABDO Publishing Co.

Osborne, Mary Pope & Boyce, Natalie Pope. Ninjas & Samurai: A Nonfiction Companion to Magic Tree House #5: Night of the Ninjas. Murdocca, Sal, illus. 2014. (Magic Tree House (R) Fact Tracker Ser.: 30). 128p. (J). (gr. 2-5). 6.99 *(978-0-385-38632-6(X),* Random Hse. Bks. for Young Readers) Random Hse. Children's Bks.

—Ninjas & Samurai: A Nonfiction Companion to Magic Tree House #5: Night of the Ninjas. 2014. (Magic Tree House Fact Tracker Ser.: 30). lib. bdg. 16.00 *(978-0-606-36017-3(4))* Turtleback.

Park, Louise & Love, Timothy. Japanese Samurai, 1 vol. 2010. (Ancient & Medieval People Ser.). (ENG.). 32p. (gr. 5-5). 31.21 *(978-0-7614-4448-0(3),* 1a1a6f84-5d32-4503-9bb2-f91e7d521053) Cavendish Square Publishing LLC.

Riggs, Kate. Samurai. 2011. (Great Warriors Ser.). 24p. (J). (gr. k-2). 16.95 *(978-1-60818-003-5(4),* Creative Education) Creative Co., The.

Terp, Gail. Samurai. 2019. (History's Warriors Ser.). (ENG., Illus.). 32p. (J). (gr. 4-6). pap. 9.99 *(978-1-64466-044-7(X),* 12765); lib. bdg. *(978-1-68072-853-8(9),* 12764) Black Rabbit Bks. (Bolt).

Turnbull, Stephen R. The Most Daring Raid of the Samurai, 1 vol. 2011. (Most Daring Raids in History Ser.). (ENG., Illus.). 64p. (YA). (gr. 7-7). lib. bdg. 37.13 *(978-1-4488-1872-3(9),* b7b3e90d-ba10-464d-925e-df4a877d580b) Rosen Publishing Group, Inc., The.

SAMURAI—FICTION

Ahdieh, Renée. Flame in the Mist. (Flame in the Mist Ser.: 1). (ENG.). (YA). (gr. 7). 2018. 448p. pap. 11.99 *(978-0-14-751387-8(1),* Penguin Books) 2017. 416p. 17.99 *(978-0-399-17163-5(0),* G.P. Putnam's Sons Books for Young Readers) Penguin Young Readers Group.

—Flame in the Mist. 2018. lib. bdg. 22.10 *(978-0-606-40878-3(9))* Turtleback.

—Smoke in the Sun. 2018. (Flame in the Mist Ser.: 2). (ENG.). 432p. (YA). (gr. 7). 18.99 *(978-1-5247-3814-3(X),* G.P. Putnam's Sons Books for Young Readers) Penguin Young Readers Group.

Bradford, Chris. The Ring of Earth: Young Samurai. 4th ed. 2010. (Young Samurai Ser.: 4). (Illus.). 336p. (YA). (gr. 7). pap. 12.99 *(978-0-14-133253-6(0),* Penguin Global) Penguin Publishing Group.

—The Ring of Fire: Young Samurai. 6th ed. 2011. (Young Samurai Ser.: 6). (Illus.). 352p. (YA). (gr. 7). pap. 12.99 *(978-0-14-133255-0(7))* Penguin Bks., Ltd. GBR. Dist: Independent Pubs. Group.

—The Ring of Sky. 8th ed. 2012. (Young Samurai Ser.: 8). (Illus.). 384p. (YA). (gr. 7). pap. 12.99 *(978-0-14-133972-6(1))* Penguin Bks., Ltd. GBR. Dist: Independent Pubs. Group.

—The Ring of Water: Young Samurai. 5th ed. 2011. (Young Samurai Ser.: 5). (Illus.). 320p. (YA). (gr. 7). pap. 12.99 *(978-0-14-133254-3(9))* Penguin Bks., Ltd. GBR. Dist: Independent Pubs. Group.

—The Ring of Wind. 7th ed. 2012. (Young Samurai Ser.: 7). (Illus.). 368p. (YA). (gr. 7). 12.99 *(978-0-14-133971-9(3),* Penguin Global) Penguin Publishing Group.

—The Way of the Dragon, 3. 2012. (Young Samurai Ser.). (ENG.). 512p. (J). (gr. 6-8). 22.44 *(978-1-4231-3779-5(5))* Hyperion Bks. for Children.

—The Way of the Dragon. l.t. ed. 2012. (Young Samurai Ser.). (ENG.). 448p. (J). (gr. 9-12). 23.99 *(978-1-4104-4466-0(X))* Thorndike Pr.

—The Way of the Sword. l.t. ed. 2012. (Young Samurai Ser.). (ENG.). 547p. (J). (gr. 6-9). 23.99 *(978-1-4104-4404-2(X))* Thorndike Pr.

—The Way of the Warrior, 1. 2008. (Young Samurai Ser.). (ENG.). 384p. (J). (gr. 6-8). 22.44 *(978-1-4231-1986-9(X))* Hyperion Bks. for Children.

—The Way of the Warrior. l.t. ed. 2011. (Young Samurai Ser.). (ENG.). 328p. (J). 23.99 *(978-1-4104-4329-8(9))* Thorndike Pr.

—Young Samurai: the Way of the Sword, 2. 2011. (Young Samurai Ser.). (ENG.). 448p. (gr. 6-8). 22.44 *(978-1-4231-2937-0(7))* Hyperion Bks. for Children.

—Young Samurai the Way of the Warrior: The Way of the Warrior, Bk. 1. 2008. (Young Samurai Ser.: 1). (Illus.). 352p. (J). (gr. 6-10). pap. 12.99 *(978-0-14-132430-2(9))* Penguin Bks., Ltd. GBR. Dist: Independent Pubs. Group.

Duey, Kathleen. Samurai, 6 vols. 2006. (Time Soldiers Ser.: Bk. 6). (ENG., Illus.). 96p. (J). (gr. k-2). per. 5.95 *(978-1-929945-63-4(9))* Big Guy Bks., Inc.

—Samurai. Epstein, Eugene, illus. l.t. ed. 2006. (Time Soldiers Ser.: Bk. 6). (ENG.). 48p. (J). (gr. k-2). 15.95 *(978-1-929945-62-7(0))* Big Guy Bks., Inc.

Falk, Nick. Curse of the Oni. Flowers, Tony, illus. 2016. (Samurai vs Ninja Ser.: 4). 96p. (J). (gr. 1-3). pap. 7.99 *(978-0-85798-640-5(6))* Random Hse. Australia AUS. Dist: Independent Pubs. Group.

—Day of the Dreadful Undead. Flowers, Tony, illus. 2016. (Samurai vs Ninja Ser.: 3). 96p. (J). (gr. 1-3). pap. 7.99 *(978-0-85798-638-2(4))* Random Hse. Australia AUS. Dist: Independent Pubs. Group.

Fussell, Sandy. Samurai Kids #2: Owl Ninja. James, Rhian Nest, illus. 2011. (Samurai Kids Ser.: 2). (ENG.). 272p. (J). (gr. 4-7). 15.99 *(978-0-7636-5003-2(X))* Candlewick Pr.

—Samurai Kids #4: Monkey Fist. James, Rhian Nest, illus. 2012. (Samurai Kids Ser.: 4). (ENG.). 272p. (J). (gr. 4-7). pap. 6.99 *(978-0-7636-5827-4(8))* Candlewick Pr.

Goto, Scott. The Perfect Sword. Goto, Scott, illus. 2010. (ENG., Illus.). 48p. (J). (gr. 1-4). pap. 8.95 *(978-1-57091-698-4(5))* Charlesbridge Publishing, Inc.

Gratz, Alan. Samurai Shortstop. 2006. (ENG.). 280p. (J). (gr. 9-12). 22.44 *(978-0-8037-3075-5(6)*, Dial) Penguin Publishing Group.

Gratz, Alan M. Samurai Shortstop. 2008. 288p. (YA). (gr. 7-18). 9.99 *(978-0-14-241099-8(3)*, Speak) Penguin Young Readers Group.

Haibara, Yak & Haibara, Yak. Sengoku Basara: Samurai Legends Volume 2: Samurai Legends Volume 2, 2 vols. 2013. (ENG., Illus.). 424p. (YA). pap. 19.99 *(978-1-926778-59-4(6)*, d748e1c6-88c3-40b7-ab2f-84ecedb6a598) URON Entertainment Corp. CAN. Dist: Diamond Comic Distributors, Inc.

Haugaard, Erik C. The Revenge of the Forty-Seven Samurai. 2005. (ENG.). 240p. (J). (gr. 5-7). pap. 14.95 *(978-0-618-54896-5(3)*, 487444, Clarion Bks.) HarperCollins Pubs.

—The Samurai's Tale. 2005. (ENG.). 256p. (J). (gr. 5-7). pap. 7.99 *(978-0-618-61512-4(1)*, 484894, Clarion Bks.) HarperCollins Pubs.

Hoobler, Dorothy & Hoobler, Thomas. The Demon in the Teahouse. 2005. 181p. (J). (gr. 4-7). 13.65 *(978-0-7569-6725-3(2))* Perfection Learning Corp.

—The Ghost in the Tokaido Inn. 2005. 240p. (J). (gr. 3-7). 7.99 *(978-0-14-240541-3(8)*, Puffin Books) Penguin Young Readers Group.

—The Ghost in the Tokaido Inn. 2005. 214p. (J). (gr. 4-7). 14.65 *(978-0-7569-6403-0(2))* Perfection Learning Corp.

—In Darkness, Death. 2005. (Puffin Sleuth Novels Ser.). 195p. (J). (gr. 5-9). 14.65 *(978-0-7569-5457-4(6))* Perfection Learning Corp.

—The Sword That Cut the Burning Grass. 2006. 211p. (gr. 5-9). 17.00 *(978-0-7569-6907-3(7))* Perfection Learning Corp.

Hulme-Cross, Benjamin. The Samurai's Assassin. Rinaldi, Angelo, illus. 2015. (Warrior Heroes Ser.). (ENG.). 160p. (J). (gr. 6-6). *(978-0-7787-1766-9(6))* Crabtree Publishing Co.

Namioka, Lensey. Valley of the Broken Cherry Trees. 2005. (ENG.). 1p. pap. 7.95 *(978-0-8048-3610-4(8))* Tuttle Publishing.

Petrucha, Stefan. Terrible Toys, 2. Henrique, Paulo, illus. 2013. (Papercutz Slices Ser.: 2). (ENG.). 64p. (J). (gr. 6-8). 21.19 *(978-1-59707-339-4(3))* Papercutz.

Phillips, Dee. Samurai: The Story of a Warrior. 2015. (Yesterday's Voices Ser.). (YA). lib. bdg. 19.60 *(978-0-606-36675-5(X))* Turtleback.

Preus, Margi. The Bamboo Sword. 2015. (ENG., Illus.). 335p. (J). (gr. 5-9). 16.95 *(978-1-4197-0807-7(4)*, 1007401, Amulet Bks.) Abrams, Inc.

Richard, Laurent. Ninjas & Knock Outs! Book 2, No. 2. Ryser, Nicolas, illus. 2014. (Tao, the Little Samurai Ser.: 2). (ENG.). 64p. (J). (gr. 2-5). lib. bdg. 29.32 *(978-1-4677-3272-7(9)*, e5d02ec4-9e15-490c-a5e7-a8fd6247b4c7, Graphic Universe™) Lerner Publishing Group.

Sakai, Stan. Usagi Yojimbo Vol. 3: Al Filo de la Vida y la Muerte. 2007. (SPA., Illus.). 200p. reprint ed. pap. 15.95 *(978-1-59497-319-2(9))* Public Square Bks.

—Usagi Yojimbo Vol. 4: Estaciones. 2007. (SPA., Illus.). 200p. reprint ed. pap. 15.95 *(978-1-59497-320-8(2))* Public Square Bks.

—Usagi Yojimbo Vol. 5: Segadora. 2007. (SPA., Illus.). 256p. reprint ed. pap. 17.95 *(978-1-59497-321-5(0))* Public Square Bks.

—Usagi Yojimbo Vol. 6: Primeras Andanzas. 2007. (SPA., Illus.). 128p. reprint ed. pap. 12.95 *(978-1-59497-322-2(9))* Public Square Bks.

—Usagi Yojimbo Vol. 7: Samurai (en Español) 2007. (SPA., Illus.). 144p. reprint ed. pap. 14.95 *(978-1-59497-323-9(7))* Public Square Bks.

Samurai. (Awesome Adventures Ser.). 16p. (J). *(978-2-7643-0167-8(7))* Phidal Publishing, Inc./Editions Phidal, Inc.

Sazaklis, John & Foxe, Steve. Drift's Samurai Showdown. 2015. (ENG.). 144p. (J). E-Book *(978-0-316-30190-9(6))* Little Brown & Co.

Scieszka, Jon. Ay, Samuray!Tr. of Sam Samurai. (SPA.). (J). 7.95 *(978-958-04-6867-7(2))* Norma S.A. COL. Dist: Distribuidora Norma, Inc.

—Sam Samurai. McCauley, Adam, illus. 2006. (Time Warp Trio Ser.: No. 10). 85p. (gr. 4-7). 15.00 *(978-0-7569-6779-6(1))* Perfection Learning Corp.

—Sam Samurai #10. McCauley, Adam, illus. 2004. (Time Warp Trio Ser.: 10). 96p. (J). (gr. 2-4). pap. 5.99 *(978-0-14-240088-3(2)*, Puffin Books) Penguin Young Readers Group.

Snow, Maya. Blade's Edge. 2009. 245p. (J). lib. bdg. 17.89 *(978-0-06-124391-2(4))* HarperCollins Pubs.

—Sisters of the Sword. 2008. (Sisters of the Sword Ser.). (J). (gr. 5-18). 288p. 16.99 *(978-0-06-124387-5(6))*; 275p. lib. bdg. 17.89 *(978-0-06-124388-2(4))* HarperCollins Pubs.

Stilton, Gerónimo. The Way of the Samurai. 2012. (Geronimo Stilton Ser.: 49). lib. bdg. 18.40 *(978-0-606-26094-7(3))* Turtleback.

Sutton, Laurie S. The Time Vortex. Clarey, Patricio, illus. 2018. (Bug Team Alpha Ser.). (ENG.). 112p. (J). (gr. 3-6). lib. bdg. 26.65 *(978-1-4965-5957-9(6)*, 137177, Stone Arch Bks.) Capstone.

SAN (AFRICAN PEOPLE)

Banting, Erinn. Galapagos Islands. 2012. (J). *(978-1-61913-523-9(X))*; pap. *(978-1-61913-436-2(5))* Weigl Pubs., Inc.

Watson, Galadriel. Bushmen of Southern Africa with Code. 2012. (World Cultures Ser.). (ENG., Illus.). 32p. (J). (gr. 4-7). pap. 13.95 *(978-1-61913-529-1(9)*, AV2 by Weigl) Weigl Pubs., Inc.

Watson, Galadriel Findlay. Bushmen of Southern Africa. (J). 2012. *(978-1-61913-094-4(7))* 2005. (Illus.). 32p. (gr. 4-8). lib. bdg. 26.00 *(978-1-59036-222-8(5))* Weigl Pubs., Inc.

SAN ANTONIO (TEX.)

Brindell Fradin, Dennis. The Alamo, 1 vol. 2007. (Turning Points in U. S. History Ser.). (ENG., Illus.). 48p. (gr. 4-4). lib. bdg. 34.07 *(978-0-7614-2127-6(0)*, a890134e-b43a-4bc9-b810-370f9e8fdba1) Cavendish Square Publishing LLC.

Keller, Susanna & Levy, Janey. A Primary Source Investigation of the Alamo, 1 vol. 2015. (Uncovering American History Ser.). (ENG., Illus.). 64p. (J). (gr. 5-6). 36.13 *(978-1-4994-3507-8(X)*, 60d4168b-3fe2-4e52-817d-6f13dffd4862, Rosen Central) Rosen Publishing Group, Inc., The.

Puck. 123 San Antonio: A Cool Counting Book. 2013. (Cool Counting Bks.). (ENG.). 22p. (J). (— 1). bds. 8.95 *(978-1-938093-17-3(8)*, 809317) Duo Pr. LLC.

San Antonio: the River City: Third Grade Guided Reading Level O. (On Our Way to English Ser.). (gr. 3-18). 34.50 *(978-0-7578-7144-3(5))* Rigby Education.

SAN ANTONIO (TEX.)—FICTION

Flor Ada, Alma. Quiero Ayudar! Dominguez, Angela, illus. 2010.Tr. of Let Me Help! (ENG & SPA.). 32p. (J). (gr. -1-3). 16.95 *(978-0-89239-232-2(0))* Lee & Low Bks., Inc.

In the City of San Antonio: Lap Book. (Pebble Soup Explorations Ser.). 16p. (gr. -1-18). 21.00 *(978-0-7578-1659-8(2))* Rigby Education.

In the City of San Antonio: Small Book. (Pebble Soup Explorations Ser.). 16p. (gr. -1-18). 5.00 *(978-0-7578-1699-4(1))* Rigby Education.

Milligan, Bryce. Comanche Captive. 2005. (Illus.). 168p. (YA). (gr. 7). per. *(978-1-57168-849-1(8))* Eakin Pr.

Perelstein, Jennifer. Who Moved the Masterpieces? A Visit to the Mcnay Art Museum. 2010. 30p. pap. 15.99 *(978-1-60844-585-1(2))* Dog Ear Publishing, LLC.

Sheinmel, Courtney & Turetsky, Bianca. Magic on the Map #3: Texas Treasure, 3. Lewis, Stevie, illus. 2020. (Magic on the Map Ser.: 3). 128p. (J). (gr. 2-5). 5.99 *(978-1-9848-9569-1(9)*, Random Hse. Bks. for Young Readers) Random Hse. Children's Bks.

Villareal, Ray. Body Slammed! 2012. (YA). pap. 11.95 *(978-1-55885-749-0(4)*, Piñata Books) Arte Publico Pr.

SAN ANTONIO (TEX.)—HISTORY

Boehm Jerome, Kate. San Antonio & the State of Texas: Cool Stuff Every Kid Should Know. 2011. (Arcadia Kids Ser.). (ENG., Illus.). 48p. (J). (gr. 3-6). pap. 11.99 *(978-1-4396-0089-4(9))* Arcadia Publishing.

Collard, Sneed B., III. David Crockett: Fearless Frontiersman, 1 vol. 2007. (American Heroes Ser.). (ENG., Illus.). 48p. (gr. 3-3). lib. bdg. 32.64 *(978-0-7614-2160-3(2)*, 2038e960-fec3-45e4-bd5d-bcb5eb5fba37) Cavendish Square Publishing LLC.

Erlic, Lily. San Antonio. 2018. (Illus.). 24p. (J). *(978-1-4896-9469-0(2)*, AV2 by Weigl) Weigl Pubs., Inc.

Espinosa, Rod. The Battle of the Alamo, 1 vol. Espinosa, Rod, illus. 2007. (Graphic History Ser.). (ENG., Illus.). 32p. (J). (gr. 3-8). 32.79 *(978-1-60270-073-4(7)*, 9032, Graphic Planet - Fiction) Magic Wagon.

Gibson, Karen. San Antonio. 2009. (Class Trip Ser.). (Illus.). 48p. (J). (gr. 2-5). lib. bdg. 29.95 *(978-1-58415-811-0(5))* Mitchell Lane Pubs.

Huddleston, Emma. Exploring the San Antonio River Walk. 2019. (Travel America's Landmarks Ser.). (ENG., Illus.). 32p. (J). (gr. 2-3). pap. 9.95 *(978-1-64185-856-4(7)*, 1641858567); lib. bdg. 31.35 *(978-1-64185-787-1(0)*, 1641857870) North Star Editions. (Focus Readers).

Koestler-Grack, Rachel A. Daily Life in a Southwestern Settlement: San Antonio. 2003. (J). *(978-1-58417-012-9(3))*; pap. *(978-1-58417-075-4(1))* Lake Street Pubs.

SAN DIEGO CHARGERS (FOOTBALL TEAM)

Epstein, Brad M. San Diego Chargers 101. 2010. (ENG., Illus.). 24p. (J). bds. *(978-1-60730-126-4(1)*, 101 Bk.) Michaelson Entertainment.

Kimmich, Ian. Antonio Gates. 2009. (Superstars of Pro Football Ser.). (Illus.). 64p. (YA). (gr. 7-12). lib. bdg. 22.95 *(978-1-4222-0553-2(3))* Mason Crest.

Lajiness, Katie. San Diego Chargers. 2016. (NFL's Greatest Teams Set 3 Ser.). (ENG., Illus.). 32p. (J). (gr. 2-5). lib. bdg. 34.21 *(978-1-68078-539-5(7)*, 23641, Big Buddy Bks.) ABDO Publishing Co.

Omoth, Tyler. The Story of the San Diego Chargers. 2009. (NFL Today Ser.). (Illus.). 48p. (YA). (gr. 5-9). 22.95 *(978-1-58341-769-0(9))* Creative Co., The.

Scheff, Matt & Kortemeier, Todd. San Diego Chargers, 1 vol. 2016. (NFL up Close Ser.). (ENG., Illus.). 32p. (J). (gr. 3-9). lib. bdg. 32.79 *(978-1-68078-231-8(2)*, 22065, SportsZone) ABDO Publishing Co.

Schmalzbauer, Adam. The History of the San Diego Chargers. 2004. (NFL Today Ser.). (Illus.). 32p. (YA). (gr. 5-9). 18.95 *(978-1-58341-312-8(X))* Creative Co., The.

Whiting, Jim. The Story of the San Diego Chargers. 2013. (J). 35.65 *(978-1-60818-318-0(1)*, Creative Education) Creative Co., The.

Wyner, Zach. San Diego Chargers. (Illus.). 32p. 2015. pap. *(978-1-4896-0883-3(4))* 2014. (ENG., (J). (gr. 4-7). lib. bdg. 28.55 *(978-1-4896-0882-6(6)*, AV2 by Weigl) Weigl Pubs., Inc.

SAN DIEGO PADRES (BASEBALL TEAM)

Goodman, Michael E. The Story of the San Diego Padres. 2011. (J). 35.65 *(978-1-60818-054-7(9)*, Creative Education) Creative Co., The.

Hawkes, Brian. The Story of the San Diego Padres. 2007. (Baseball, the Great American Game Ser.). (Illus.). 48p. (YA). (gr. 4-7). lib. bdg. 32.80 *(978-1-58341-552-8(1))* Creative Co., The.

Stewart, Mark. The San Diego Padres. 2012. (Team Spirit Ser.). 48p. (J). (gr. 3-6). lib. bdg. 29.27 *(978-1-59953-495-4(9))* Norwood Hse. Pr.

SAN FRANCISCO (CALIF.)

Gamble, Adam. Good Night San Francisco. Cohen, Santiago, illus. 2006. (Good Night Our World Ser.). (ENG.). 22p. (J). (gr. k — 1). bds. 9.95 *(978-0-9777979-5-0(3))* Good Night Bks.

Hollander, Barbara Gottfried. Harvey Milk: The First Openly Gay Elected Official in the United States. 2017. (Spotlight on Civic Courage: Heroes of Conscience Ser.). 48p. (J). (gr. 10-15). 70.50 *(978-1-5383-8093-2(5)*, Rosen Young Adult) Rosen Publishing Group, Inc., The.

Luiso, Lisa. What Daddy Sees in San Francisco. 2007. (Illus.). 30p. (J). lib. bdg. 19.95 *(978-1-933732-37-4(7))* Big Ransom Studio.

—What Mommy Sees in San Francisco. abr. ed. 2007. (J). lib. bdg. 19.95 *(978-1-933732-28-2(8))* Big Ransom Studio.

Mackay, Stephanie, illus. San Francisco Monsters: A Search & Find Book. 2017. (ENG.). 22p. (J). (gr. -1). bds. 9.99 *(978-2-924734-03-2(7))* City Monsters Bks. CAN. Dist: Publishers Group West (PGW).

Sasek, M. This Is San Francisco. 2003. (This Is ... Ser.). (ENG., Illus.). 64p. (J). (gr. 2-12). 17.95 *(978-0-7893-0962-4(9))* Universe Publishing.

Segal, Robin. ABC in San Francisco. 2008. (All 'Bout Cities Ser.). (ENG.). 32p. (J). (gr. -1-k). *(978-0-9719697-9-7(5))* Murray Hill Bks., LLC.

Skewes, John & Mullin, Michael. Larry Gets Lost in San Francisco. Skewes, John, illus. 2009. (Larry Gets Lost Ser.). (ENG., Illus.). 32p. (J). (gr. -1-2). 17.99 *(978-1-57061-567-2(5)*, Little Bigfoot) Sasquatch Bks.

Stanborough, Rebecca. Golden Gate Bridge. 2016. (Engineering Wonders Ser.). (ENG., Illus.). 32p. (J). (gr. 3-6). lib. bdg. 27.99 *(978-1-4914-8196-7(X)*, 130669, Capstone Pr.) Capstone.

Turner, Barbara. A Day in San Francisco, Vol. 1. l.t. ed. 2003. (Illus.). 32p. (J). per. 14.95 *(978-0-9747019-0-5(4))* Turner, Barbara.

Wearing, Judy, et al. Golden Gate Bridge. 2014. (Illus.). 24p. (J). *(978-1-62127-463-6(2))* Weigl Pubs., Inc.

Wyner, Zach. Golden State Warriors. 2014. (On the Hardwood Ser.). (ENG.). 48p. (gr. 3-8). pap. 8.95 *(978-1-61570-913-7(4))* Scobre Pr. Corp.

Zschock, Martha Day. Journey Around San Francisco from a to Z. 2003. (Journey Around... Ser.). (ENG., Illus.). 32p. (J). (gr. 1-6). 17.95 *(978-1-889833-49-1(5)*, Commonwealth Editions) Applewood Bks.

SAN FRANCISCO (CALIF.)—BRIDGES

Ashley, Susan. The Golden Gate Bridge, 1 vol. 2004. (Places in American History Ser.). (ENG., Illus.). 24p. (J). (gr. 2-4). lib. bdg. 24.67 *(978-0-8368-4140-4(9)*, e733ea22-5674-401b-8b0a-179de9020aa3, Weekly Reader Leveled Readers) Stevens, Gareth Publishing LLLP.

Eggers, Dave. This Bridge Will Not Be Gray: Revised Edition with Updated Back Matter. rev. ed. 2018. (ENG., Illus.). 112p. (J). (gr. k-3). 22.99 *(978-1-4521-6280-5(8))* Chronicle Bks. LLC.

Wearing, Judy. Golden Gate Bridge. 2009. (Structural Wonders Ser.). (Illus.). 32p. (J). (gr. 4-6). lib. bdg. 26.00 *(978-1-60596-136-1(1))* Weigl Pubs., Inc.

Wearing, Judy & Riddolls, Tom. Golden Gate Bridge. 2009. (Structural Wonders Ser.). (Illus.). 32p. (J). (gr. 4-6). 10.95 *(978-1-60596-137-8(X))* Weigl Pubs., Inc.

SAN FRANCISCO (CALIF.)—EARTHQUAKE AND FIRE, 1906

see San Francisco Earthquake and Fire, Calif., 1906

SAN FRANCISCO (CALIF.)—FICTION

Allen, Skye. The Songbird Thief. (Oaktown Fey Ser.: Vol. 2). (ENG., Illus.). (YA). 2017. 25.99 *(978-1-64080-358-9(0))* 2016. 206p. pap. 14.99 *(978-1-63477-003-3(X))* Dreamspinner Pr. (Harmony Ink Pr.).

Allison, Jennifer. Gilda Joyce, Psychic Investigator. 2006. (Gilda Joyce Ser.: 1). (ENG.). 336p. (J). (gr. 5-18). reprint ed. 9.99 *(978-0-14-240698-4(8)*, Puffin Books) Penguin Young Readers Group.

Applegate, Katherine & Grant, Michael. Eve & Adam. 2013. (ENG.). 304p. (YA). (gr. 8-12). pap. 15.99 *(978-1-250-03419-9(1)*, 900120591) Square Fish.

Argueta, Jorge. Xochitl & the Flowers / Xóchitl, la niña de Las Flores, 1 vol. Angel, Carl, illus. 2013. (ENG.). 32p. (J). (gr. 1-5). pap. 11.95 *(978-0-89239-224-7(X)*, leelowcbp) Lee & Low Bks., Inc.

—Xochitl & the Flowers (Xochitl, la Nina de Las Flores) Angel, Carl, illus. 2003.Tr. of Xochitl, la Nina de Las Flores. (ENG & SPA.). 32p. (J). 16.95 *(978-0-89239-181-3(2))* Lee & Low Bks., Inc.

Averbeck, Jim. A Hitch at the Fairmont. Bertozzi, Nick, illus. (ENG.). 416p. (J). (gr. 3-7). 2015. pap. 9.99 *(978-1-4424-9448-0(4))* 2014. 16.99 *(978-1-4424-9447-3(6)*, Atheneum Bks. for Young Readers) Simon & Schuster Children's Publishing.

Bills, Randall N. Detective Mysteries. 2008. 92p. pap. 6.95 *(978-0-9796392-1-0(2))* Adventure Boys Inc.

Bliss, Bryan. No Parking at the End Times. 2015. (ENG.). 272p. (YA). (gr. 9). 17.99 *(978-0-06-227541-7(0)*, Greenwillow Bks.) HarperCollins Pubs.

Braswell, Liz. The Fallen. movie tie-in ed. 2011. (Nine Lives of Chloe King Ser.: 1). (ENG.). 256p. (YA). (gr. 9). pap. 8.99 *(978-1-4424-4134-7(8)*, Simon Pulse) Simon Pulse.

—The Nine Lives of Chloe King: The Fallen; the Stolen; the Chosen. 2011. (Nine Lives of Chloe King Ser.). (ENG.). 784p. (YA). (gr. 9). pap. 14.99 *(978-1-4424-3570-4(4)*, Simon Pulse) Simon Pulse.

—The Nine Lives of Chloe King: The Fallen; the Stolen; the Chosen. 2011. lib. bdg. 25.75 *(978-0-606-23293-7(1))* Turtleback.

Brenner, Summer. Ivy, Homeless in San Francisco. Bowes, Brian, illus. 2nd ed. 2011. (Reach & Teach Ser.). (ENG.). 176p. (YA). (gr. 4-7). pap. 15.00 *(978-1-60486-317-8(X))* PM Pr.

Brezenoff, Steve. Field Trip Mysteries: the Crook Who Crossed the Golden Gate Bridge. Canga, Chris, illus. 2010. (Field Trip Mysteries Ser.). (ENG.). 88p. (J). (gr. 3-6). 25.32 *(978-1-4342-2138-4(5)*, 102868); pap. 5.95 *(978-1-4342-2770-6(7)*, 114037) Capstone. (Stone Arch Bks.).

Brown, Jeff. Escape to California. 2014. (Flat Stanley's Worldwide Adventures Ser.: 12). (J). lib. bdg. 14.75 *(978-0-606-35951-1(6))* Turtleback.

Bruton, Seth. I'm So Cute, You Can't Be Mad. Hicks, Kaylee, illus. 2012. 24p. pap. 13.97 *(978-1-61204-897-0(8)*, Strategic Bk. Publishing) Strategic Book Publishing & Rights Agency (SBPRA).

Bunting, Eve. Pop's Bridge. Payne, C. F., illus. 2006. (ENG.). 32p. (J). (gr. -1-3). 18.99 *(978-0-15-204773-3(5)*, 1194402, Clarion Bks.) HarperCollins Pubs.

Caletti, Deb. Girl, Unframed. 2020. (ENG.). 368p. (YA). (gr. 9). 18.99 *(978-1-5344-2697-9(3)*, Simon Pulse) Simon Pulse.

Carson, John & Carson, Marlene. Ramblin' Rose: The Chinese Fortune Cookie. 2008. 291p. pap. 8.99 *(978-0-9800034-1-3(5))* Aspirations Media, Inc.

Chambliss Bertman, Jennifer. Book Scavenger. 2016. (Book Scavenger Ser.: 1). (ENG.). 368p. (J). pap. 8.99 *(978-1-250-07980-0(2)*, 900154628) Square Fish.

—The Unbreakable Code. 2018. (Book Scavenger Ser.: 2). (ENG.). 384p. (J). pap. 8.99 *(978-1-250-15839-0(7)*, 900179194) Square Fish.

Childs, Tera Lynn. Sweet Legacy. 2013. (Sweet Venom Ser.: 3). (ENG.). 384p. (YA). (gr. 8). 17.99 *(978-0-06-200185-6(X)*, Tegen, Katherine Bks) HarperCollins Pubs.

—Sweet Shadows. (Sweet Venom Ser.: 2). (ENG.). (YA). (gr. 8). 2013. 352p. pap. 9.99 *(978-0-06-200184-9(1))* 2012. 336p. 17.99 *(978-0-06-200183-2(3))* HarperCollins Pubs. (Tegen, Katherine Bks).

—Sweet Venom. 2012. (Sweet Venom Ser.: 1). (ENG.). 384p. (YA). (gr. 8). pap. 9.99 *(978-0-06-200182-5(5)*, Tegen, Katherine Bks) HarperCollins Pubs.

Clark, Brenda. Spiro & Zinger Rescue the Orphans: Spiro the Shooting Star - Book Three, 1 vol. 2010. 70p. pap. 19.95 *(978-1-4489-3992-3(5))* America Star Bks.

Craft, Elizabeth. Flavor of the Day. 2013. (@cafe Ser.: 4). (ENG., Illus.). 192p. (YA). (gr. 7). pap. 13.99 *(978-1-4814-2113-3(1)*, Simon Pulse) Simon Pulse.

Crowder, Melanie. Three Pennies. 2019. (Penworthy Picks Middle School Ser.). (ENG.). 181p. (J). (gr. 4-5). 19.36 *(978-1-64310-943-5(X))* Penworthy Co., LLC, The.

—Three Pennies. 2017. (ENG., Illus.). 192p. (J). (gr. 3-7). 19.99 *(978-1-4814-7187-9(2)*, Atheneum Bks. for Young Readers) Simon & Schuster Children's Publishing.

de la Cruz, Melissa. The Ashley Project. 2014. (Ashley Project Ser.: 1). (ENG., Illus.). 288p. (J). (gr. 4-8). pap. 6.99 *(978-1-4424-9033-8(0)*, Aladdin) Simon & Schuster Children's Publishing.

—Birthday Vicious. 2014. (Ashley Project Ser.: 3). (ENG., Illus.). 304p. (J). (gr. 4-8). pap. 7.99 *(978-1-4424-9038-3(1)*, Aladdin) Simon & Schuster Children's Publishing.

De la Cruz, Melissa. Jealous? 2008. (Ashleys Ser.: Bk. 2). (ENG.). 256p. (YA). (gr. 4-8). pap. 9.99 *(978-1-4169-3407-3(3)*, Simon & Schuster Bks. For Young Readers) Simon & Schuster Bks. For Young Readers.

de la Cruz, Melissa. Popularity Takeover. 2015. (Ashley Project Ser.: 4). (ENG., Illus.). 272p. (J). (gr. 4-8). 17.99 *(978-1-4814-0974-2(3)*, Aladdin) Simon & Schuster Children's Publishing.

—29 Dates. 2018. (ENG.). 400p. (YA). 18.99 *(978-1-335-54154-3(3))* Harlequin Enterprises ULC CAN. Dist: HarperCollins Pubs.

—29 Dates. 2020. (ENG.). 384p. (YA). pap. 10.99 *(978-1-335-99471-4(8))* Harlequin Enterprises ULC CAN. Dist: HarperCollins Pubs.

Dixon, Franklin W. Comic con Artist. 21st ed. 2008. (Hardy Boys (All New) Undercover Brothers Ser.: 21). (ENG., Illus.). 192p. (J). (gr. 3-7). pap. 6.99 *(978-1-4169-5498-9(8)*, Aladdin) Simon & Schuster Children's Publishing.

Doctorow, Cory. Homeland. 2014. (Little Brother Ser.: 2). (ENG.). 448p. (YA). (gr. 8). pap. 19.99 *(978-0-7653-3370-4(8)*, 900086721, Tor Teen) Doherty, Tom Assocs., LLC.

—Homeland. 2014. (YA). lib. bdg. 24.50 *(978-0-606-38513-8(4))* Turtleback.

—Little Brother. (Little Brother Ser.: 1). (ENG.). (YA). (gr. 8-13). 2010. 432p. pap. 12.99 *(978-0-7653-2311-8(7)*, 900057453) 2008. 384p. 19.99 *(978-0-7653-1985-2(3)*, 900049020) Doherty, Tom Assocs., LLC. (Tor Teen).

—Little Brother. 2010. (YA). lib. bdg. 24.50 *(978-0-606-14347-9(5))* Turtleback.

Dreher, Ruth. Ralph the Red Engine. 2010. 36p. pap. 15.49 *(978-1-4520-2169-0(4))* AuthorHouse.

Duey, K. & Bale, K. A. Salvados! Terremoto. 2003. (Survival Ser.).Tr. of Survival! Earthquake. (SPA.). (J). pap. 9.95 *(978-0-9715256-5-8(X))* Planeta Publishing Corp.

Duey, Kathleen & Bale, Karen A. Earthquake: San Francisco 1906. 2014. (Survivors Ser.). (ENG., Illus.). 160p. (J). (gr. 3-7). pap. 7.99 *(978-1-4814-0079-4(7)*, Aladdin) Simon & Schuster Children's Publishing.

Ee, Susan. Angelfall, 0 vols. 2012. (Penryn & the End of Days Ser.: 1). (ENG.). 288p. (YA). (gr. 9-12). pap. 7.99 *(978-0-7614-6327-6(5)*, 9780761463276, Skyscape) Amazon Publishing.

—Angelfall. 2012. (Penryn & the End of Days Ser.: bk.1). (ENG.). 256p. pap. 12.99 *(978-0-9835970-1-8(4))* Dream, Feral LLC.

—World After, 0 vols. 2013. (Penryn & the End of Days Ser.: 2). (ENG.). 320p. (YA). (gr. 7-12). pap. 7.99 *(978-1-4778-1728-5(X)*, 9781477817285, Skyscape) Amazon Publishing.

Emerson, Scott. The Case of the Cat with the Missing Ear: From the Notebooks of Edward R. Smithfield D. V. M. Mullett, Viv, illus. 2011. (Adventures of Samuel Blackthorne Ser.: 1). (ENG.). 240p. (J). (gr. 3-7). pap. 11.99 *(978-0-689-87615-8(7)*, Simon & Schuster Bks. For Young Readers) Simon & Schuster Bks. For Young Readers.

Finley, Leah. The One & Only Mr C. 2009. 82p. pap. 8.95 *(978-1-935118-75-6(7))* Bellissima Publishing, LLC.

Fox, Janet. Forgiven. 2011. (ENG.). 288p. (YA). (gr. 8-12). 22.44 *(978-0-14-241414-9(X))* Penguin Young Readers Group.

Freeman, Don. Fly High, Fly Low. Freeman, Don, illus. 2007. (Illus.). 56p. (gr. -1-3). 18.00 *(978-0-7569-8001-6(1))* Perfection Learning Corp.

—Fly High, Fly Low (50th Anniversary Ed.) 50th anniv. ed. 2007. (Illus.). 64p. (J). (gr. -1-k). 8.99 *(978-0-14-240817-9(4)*, Puffin Books) Penguin Young Readers Group.

French, Mary B. Bear-Ly There with Compass. Coffey, Kevin, illus. 2012. 122p. pap. 6.00 *(978-0-9852821-0-3(X))* Mary B./French.

Gagnon, Michelle. Unearthly Things. 2018. 228p. (YA). (gr. 9). pap. 10.99 *(978-1-61695-875-6(8)*, Soho Teen) Soho Pr., Inc.

Garis, Howard R. Dick Hamilton's Airship. 2008. 160p. 25.95 *(978-1-60664-781-3(4))*; pap. 13.95 *(978-1-60664-155-2(7))* Aegypan.

Grove, S. E. The Waning Age. 2019. 352p. (YA). (gr. 9). 18.99 *(978-0-451-47985-3(8)*, Viking Books for Young Readers) Penguin Young Readers Group.

Hopkinson, Deborah. Into the Firestorm: a Novel of San Francisco 1906. 2008. (ENG.). 208p. (J). (gr. 3-7). per. 7.99 *(978-0-440-42129-0(2),* Yearling) Random Hse. Children's Bks.

Jacobs, Lily. The Littlest Bunny in San Francisco: An Easter Adventure. Dunn, Robert, illus. 2015. (Littlest Bunny Ser.). (ENG.). 32p. (J). (gr. -1-3). 9.99 *(978-1-4926-1192-9(1),* Hometown World) Sourcebooks, Inc.

James, Brian. The Heights. 2009. (ENG.). 272p. (YA). (gr. 7-12). 22.44 *(978-0-312-60736-4(9))* Square Fish.

James, Eric. Santa's Sleigh Is on Its Way to San Francisco: A Christmas Adventure. Dunn, Robert, illus. 2016. (Santa's Sleigh Is on Its Way Ser.). (ENG.). 32p. (J). (gr. k-2). 12.99 *(978-1-4926-4354-8(8),* 9781492643548, Hometown World) Sourcebooks, Inc.

—The Spooky Express San Francisco. Piwowarski, Marcin, illus. 2017. (Spooky Express Ser.). (ENG.). 32p. (J). (gr. k-6). 9.99 *(978-1-4926-5397-4(7),* Hometown World) Sourcebooks, Inc.

—Tiny the San Francisco Easter Bunny. 2018. (Tiny the Easter Bunny Ser.). (ENG.). 40p. (J). (gr. k-3). 9.99 *(978-1-4926-5962-4(2),* Hometown World) Sourcebooks, Inc.

Jenkins, Ward, illus. San Francisco, Baby! 2012. (ENG.). 24p. (J). (gr. -1 — 1). 12.99 *(978-1-4521-0620-5(7))* Chronicle Bks. LLC.

Jennifer, Chambliss Bertman. The Unbreakable Code. 2017. (Book Scavenger Ser.: 2). (ENG., Illus.). 368p. (J). 16.99 *(978-1-62779-116-8(7),* 900135626, Holt, Henry & Co. Bks. For Young Readers) Holt, Henry & Co.

Keil, Michelle Ruiz. All of Us with Wings. 2019. (ENG., Illus.). 360p. (YA). (gr. 11). 18.99 *(978-1-64129-034-0(X),* Soho Teen) Soho Pr., Inc.

Kleinman, Estelle. Al Capone Does My Shirts. Friedland, Joyce & Kessler, Rikki, eds. 2007. (Al Capone on Alcatraz Ser.: Bk. 1). (Illus.). 38p. pap. 16.95 *(978-0-7675-3758-2(0))* Learning Links Inc.

Kleven, Elisa. The Horribly Hungry Gingerbread Boy: A San Francisco Story. 2016. (ENG., Illus.). 40p. (J). 17.00 *(978-1-59714-352-3(9))* Heyday.

Krueger, Jim. The Argon Deception, 1 vol., 4. Padilla, Ariel, illus. 2008. (Z Graphic Novels / Tomo Ser.). (ENG.). 160p. (J). (gr. 4-7). pap. 6.99 *(978-0-310-71303-6(X))* Zondervan.

Laberje, Reji. Max Explores San Francisco. Fenech, Liza, illus. 2014. (Max Explores Ser.). (ENG.). 20p. (J). (— 1). bds. 9.95 *(978-1-62937-005-7(3))* Triumph Bks.

Larson, Kirby. Hattie Ever After. 2014. (Hattie Ser.: 2). (ENG.). 256p. (YA). (gr. 7). pap. 8.99 *(978-0-375-85090-5(2),* Ember) Random Hse. Children's Bks.

Laurence, Yep. Dragonwings. 25th rev. ed. 2014. (Golden Mountain Chronicles Ser.). (ENG.). 336p. (J). (gr. 12-12). 11.24 *(978-1-63245-143-9(3))* Lectorum Pubns., Inc.

Lavender, William. Aftershocks. 2006. (ENG., Illus.). 352p. (YA). (gr. 7-12). 17.00 *(978-0-15-205882-1(6),* 1197660, Clarion Bks.) HarperCollins Pubs.

Lee, Milly. Landed. Choi, Yangsook, illus. 2006. (ENG.). 40p. (J). (gr. 2-6). 19.99 *(978-0-374-34314-9(4),* 900029288, Farrar, Straus & Giroux (BYR)) Farrar, Straus & Giroux.

Lucido, Aimee. Emmy in the Key of Code. 2019. (ENG.). 416p. (J). (gr. 3-7). 16.99 *(978-0-358-04082-8(5),* 1740459, Versify) HarperCollins Pubs.

Madonia, Kristen-Paige. Fingerprints of You. (ENG., Illus.). 272p. (YA). (gr. 9). 2013. pap. 9.99 *(978-1-4424-2921-5(6))* 2012. 16.99 *(978-1-4424-2920-8(8))* Simon & Schuster Bks. For Young Readers. (Simon & Schuster Bks. For Young Readers).

—Invisible Fault Lines. 2016. (ENG.). 320p. (YA). (gr. 7). 17.99 *(978-1-4814-3071-5(8),* Simon & Schuster Bks. For Young Readers) Simon & Schuster Bks. For Young Readers.

Marsh, Carole. The Ghost of the Golden Gate Bridge. 2009. (Real Kids, Real Places Ser.). (Illus.). 146p. (J). lib. bdg. 18.99 *(978-0-635-07047-0(2),* Marsh, Carole Mysteries) Gallopade International.

Mcallister, Herb West. Doo West to Toadstool. 2011. 44p. pap. 21.99 *(978-1-4628-5530-8(X))* Xlibris Corp.

Mcdonald, Megan. Julie Story Collection. Hunt, Robert, illus. 2007. 472p. pap. 29.95 *(978-1-59369-450-0(4))* American Girl Publishing, Inc.

Messner, Kate. Escape from the Great Earthquake (Ranger in Time #6) McMorris, Kelley, illus. 2017. (Ranger in Time Ser.: 6). (ENG.). 160p. (J). (gr. 2-5). pap. 5.99 *(978-0-545-90983-9(X),* Scholastic Pr.) Scholastic, Inc.

Morris, Paris & Florzak, Douglas. My Twins Are Coming Home. 2010. (ENG., Illus.). 24p. (J). pap. 12.95 *(978-0-9760095-5-9(2))* New Year Publishing.

Morris, Paris & Singer, Thom. I'm Having Twins, 1 vol. 2010. (ENG., Illus.). 24p. (J). pap. 12.95 *(978-0-9760095-4-2(4))* New Year Publishing.

Moss, Marissa. California Dreaming. 2016. (Mira's Diary Ser.). (ENG., Illus.). 190p. (J). (gr. 2-8). 12.99 *(978-1-939547-22-4(9),* 81279f26-461a-4e86-982f-55d09a0047cd) Creston Bks.

Murphy, Pat. The Wild Girls. unabr. ed. 2007. (YA). (gr. 6-9). audio compact disk 45.00 *(978-0-7393-5988-4(6))* Random Hse. Audio Publishing Group.

Myers, Jason. The Mission. 2009. (ENG.). 384p. (YA). (gr. 9-18). pap. 11.99 *(978-1-4169-8455-9(0),* Simon Pulse) Simon Pulse.

Novesky, Amy. Me, Frida. Diaz, David, illus. (ENG.). 32p. (J). 2015. (gr. k-2). pap. 9.95 *(978-1-4197-1516-7(X),* 679403) 2010. (gr. -1-3). 18.99 *(978-0-8109-8969-6(7),* 679401) Abrams, Inc. (Abrams Bks. for Young Readers).

Osborne, Mary Pope. Earthquake in the Early Morning. unabr. ed. 2004. (Magic Tree House Ser.: No. 24). 71p. (J). (gr. k-3). pap. 17.00 incl. audio *(978-0-8072-0933-2(3),* S FTR 256 SP, Listening Library) Random Hse. Audio Publishing Group.

Perkins, Stephanie. Lola & the Boy Next Door. 2013. 368p. (YA). (gr. 9). pap. 12.99 *(978-0-14-242201-4(0),* Speak) Penguin Young Readers Group.

Pollak, Dale. Velocity: From the Front Line to the Bottom Line. 2010. (ENG.). 144p. 29.95 *(978-0-9760095-7-3(9))* New Year Publishing.

Ponti, James. Golden Gate. (City Spies Ser.: 2). (ENG.). 2022. 448p. (J). (gr. 3-7). pap. 8.99 *(978-1-5344-1495-2(9))* 2021. (Illus.). 432p. (J). (gr. 3-7). 18.99 *(978-1-5344-1494-5(0))*2. 2022. 448p. (gr. 4-7). 24.94 *(978-1-5364-7207-3(7))* Simon & Schuster Children's Publishing. (Aladdin).

Rai, Sarbjit. Elfins in San Francisco. 2009. 24p. pap. 11.49 *(978-1-4389-8014-0(0))* AuthorHouse.

Rankin, Cindy. Under the Ashes. (ENG.). 240p. (J). (gr. 3-7). 2018. pap. 7.99 *(978-0-8075-3637-7(7),* 807536377) 2016. 16.99 *(978-0-8075-3635-3(0),* 807536350) Whitman, Albert & Co.

Reich, Susanna. Penelope Bailey Takes the Stage, 1 vol. 2006. (ENG.). 32p. (J). (gr. 3-7). 16.95 *(978-0-7614-5287-4(7))* Marshall Cavendish Corp.

Reiss, Kathryn. The Tangled Web: A Julie Mystery. Tibbles, Jean-Paul, illus. 2009. (ENG.). 168p. (J). (gr. 4-18). 10.95 *(978-1-59369-475-3(X));* pap. 21.19 *(978-1-59369-476-0(8))* American Girl Publishing, Inc.

Resnicoff, Stan. The BIG Parade: San Francisco. 2012. (ENG.). (J). pap. *(978-1-4675-1539-9(6))* Independent Pub.

Robbins, Trina. A Match Made in Heaven: Book 8, No. 8. Ota, Yuko Geneviev & Xian Nu Studio, illus. 2013. (My Boyfriend Is a Monster Ser.: 8). (ENG.). 128p. (YA). (gr. 7-12). pap. 9.95 *(978-1-4677-0732-9(5),* c276bb59-5e33-4667-9435-ffac48deaaac, Graphic Universe™) Lerner Publishing Group.

—A Match Made in Heaven: Book 8. No. 8. Ota, Yuko Geneviev & Xian Nu Studio, Xian Nu, illus. 2013. (My Boyfriend Is a Monster Ser.: 8). (ENG.). 128p. (YA). (gr. 7-12). lib. bdg. 29.32 *(978-0-7613-6857-1(4),* 95f941be-48e3-433b-b670-89a634a7f824, Graphic Universe™) Lerner Publishing Group.

Robles, Anthony D. Lakas & the Manilatown Fish, 1 vol. de Jesus, Eloisa D. & de Guzman, Magdalena, trs. Angel, Carl, illus. 2015. (Lakas Ser.). (ENG.). 32p. (J). (gr. 1-3). pap. 11.95 *(978-0-89239-211-7(8),* leelowcbp, Children's Book Press) Lee & Low Bks., Inc.

Robles, Anthony D. & Children's Book Press Staff. Lakas & the Manilatown Fish (Si Lakas at Ang Isdang Manilatown) de Jesus, Eloisa D. & de Guzman, Magdalena, trs. Angel, Carl, illus. 2003.Tr. of Si Lakas at Ang Isdang Manilatown. (ENG & TAG.). 32p. (J). 16.95 *(978-0-89239-182-0(0))* Lee & Low Bks., Inc.

Roy, Ron. A to Z Mysteries Super Edition #5: The New Year Dragon Dilemma. Gurney, John Steven, illus. 5th ed. 2011. (to Z Mysteries Ser.: 5). 144p. (J). (gr. 1-4). 6.99 *(978-0-375-86880-1(1),* Random Hse. Bks. for Young Readers) Random Hse. Children's Bks.

Sager, Ryan K. The World's Greatest Chocolate-Covered Pork Chops. 2018. (ENG.). 256p. (J). (gr. 3-7). pap. 7.99 *(978-1-4847-6818-1(3))* Hyperion Bks. for Children.

San Francisco Shake-Up, 6 Packs. (Greetings Ser.: Vol. 3). (gr. 3-5). 31.00 *(978-0-7635-2075-5(6))* Rigby Education.

Say, Allen. The Favorite Daughter. 2013. (J). pap. *(978-0-545-17663-7(8),* Levine, Arthur A. Bks.) Scholastic, Inc.

—The Favorite Daughter. Say, Allen, illus. 2013. (ENG., Illus.). 32p. (J). (gr. -1-3). 19.99 *(978-0-545-17662-0(X),* Levine, Arthur A. Bks.) Scholastic, Inc.

Schnell, David. The Night Before Baseball at the Park by the Bay. Pamintuan, Macky, illus. 2013. (ENG.). 32p. 0.00 *(978-0-9891043-0-2(3))* Prospect Palo Alto Publishing.

Schomer-Wendel, Gretchen & Schomer, Adam Anthony. Becka Goes to San Francisco, 1 vol. Renthrope, Damon, illus. 2009. (Becka & the Big Bubble Ser.). (ENG.). 32p. (J). (gr. 1-2). 27.27 *(978-1-60754-107-3(6),* 170513f4-02aa-46b8-9669-835833a908e1); pap. 11.55 *(978-1-60754-108-0(4),* 786c09a2-f35f-4e17-a27d-fb3874f3785c) Rosen Publishing Group, Inc., The. (Windmill Bks.).

Scott, Michael. The Alchemyst. 2009. (ENG., Illus.). 375p. (gr. 6-10). 19.00 *(978-1-60686-514-9(5))* Perfection Learning Corp.

—The Alchemyst. (Secrets of the Immortal Nicholas Flamel Ser.: 1). (ENG.). 400p. (YA). (gr. 7). 2008. pap. 11.99 *(978-0-385-73600-8(2),* Ember) 2007. (Illus.). 18.99 *(978-0-385-73357-1(7),* Delacorte Bks. for Young Readers) Random Hse. Children's Bks.

—The Warlock. l.t. ed. 2011. (Secrets of the Immortal Nicholas Flamel Ser.). (ENG.). 545p. 23.99 *(978-1-4104-4157-7(1))* Thorndike Pr.

Senzai, N. H. Saving Kabul Corner. 2014. (Kabul Chronicles Ser.). (ENG., Illus.). 288p. (J). (gr. 3-7). 16.99 *(978-1-4424-8494-8(2),* Simon & Schuster/Paula Wiseman Bks.) Simon & Schuster/Paula Wiseman Bks.

—Shooting Kabul, 1. 2010. (Kabul Chronicles Ser.). (ENG., Illus.). 272p. (J). (gr. 3-7). 19.99 *(978-1-4424-0194-5(X))* Simon & Schuster, Inc.

—Shooting Kabul. 2011. (Kabul Chronicles Ser.). (ENG., Illus.). 288p. (J). (gr. 3-7). pap. 8.99 *(978-1-4424-0195-2(8),* Simon & Schuster/Paula Wiseman Bks.) Simon & Schuster/Paula Wiseman Bks.

Simmons, Andrew & Averdonz, N. R. I Was an Eighth-Grade Ninja, 1 vol., 1. Padilla, Ariel, illus. 2007. (Z Graphic Novels / Tomo Ser.). (ENG.). 160p. (J). (gr. 3-7). pap. 6.99 *(978-0-310-71300-5(5))* Zondervan.

Sims, Lori. Starvin' Marvin & Skinny Minnie Shake up San Francisco. 2009. 78p. (YA). pap. 9.95 *(978-1-4327-3651-4(5))* Outskirts Pr., Inc.

Smallman, Steve. Santa Is Coming to San Francisco. Dunn, Robert, illus. 2nd ed. 2019. (Santa Is Coming... Ser.). (ENG.). 40p. (J). (gr. -1-3). 12.99 *(978-1-7282-0099-6(7),* Hometown World) Sourcebooks, Inc.

Smith, Roland & Spradlin, Michael P. Alcatraz. 2014. (I, Q Ser.). (ENG.). 272p. (J). (gr. 5-7). 16.99 *(978-1-58536-826-6(1),* 203667);Bk. 6. pap. 9.99 *(978-1-58536-825-9(3),* 203727) Sleeping Bear Pr.

Stone, Tamara Ireland. Time after Time. 2014. (ENG.). 368p. (J). (gr. 7-12). pap. 18.99 *(978-1-4231-5981-0(0))* Hyperion Bks. for Children.

Sully, Katherine. Night-Night San Francisco. Poole, Helen, illus. 2017. (Night-Night Ser.). (ENG.). 20p. (J). (gr. -1-1). bds. 9.99 *(978-1-4926-4765-2(9),* 9781492647652, Hometown World) Sourcebooks, Inc.

Tarshis, Lauren. I Survived the San Francisco Earthquake 1906. 2012. (I Survived Ser.: No. 5). lib. bdg. 14.75 *(978-0-606-23936-3(7))* Turtleback.

—I Survived the San Francisco Earthquake, 1906 (I Survived #5) Dawson, Scott, illus. 2012. (I Survived Ser.: 5). (ENG.). 112p. (J). (gr. 2-5). pap. 5.99 *(978-0-545-20699-0(5),* Scholastic Paperbacks) Scholastic, Inc.

The Calaiacovo Family. The Amazing Adventures of Ruby & Rubette: San Francisco. 2010. 32p. pap. 14.49 *(978-1-4490-6948-3(7))* AuthorHouse.

Thomas, Roger B. The Accidental Marriage. 2014. (ENG.). 219p. 19.95 *(978-1-58617-908-3(X))* Ignatius Pr.

Trine, Greg. Dinos Are Forever. Dormer, Frank W., illus. 2014. (Adventures of Jo Schmo Ser.: 1). (ENG.). 112p. (J). (gr. 1-4). pap. 6.99 *(978-0-544-00325-5(X),* 1526367, Clarion Bks.) HarperCollins Pubs.

—Pinkbeard's Revenge. Dormer, Frank W., illus. 2015. (Adventures of Jo Schmo Ser.: 4). (ENG.). 128p. (J). (gr. 1-4). pap. 7.99 *(978-0-544-45601-3(7),* 1599386, Clarion Bks.) HarperCollins Pubs.

—Wyatt Burp Rides Again. Dormer, Frank W., illus. 2014. (Adventures of Jo Schmo Ser.: 2). (ENG.). 112p. (J). (gr. 1-4). pap. 6.99 *(978-0-544-01899-0(0),* 1528127, Clarion Bks.) HarperCollins Pubs.

Wiggin, Kate Douglas. The Girl & the Kingdom. 2011. 60p. 16.95 *(978-1-4638-9982-0(3))* Rodgers, Alan Bks.

—Polly Oliver's Problem. 2007. 108p. per. 9.95 *(978-1-60312-369-3(5))* Aegypan.

—Polly Oliver's Problem. 2016. (ENG., Illus.). (J). 24.95 *(978-1-357-78791-2(X))* Creative Media Partners, LLC.

Wiggin, Kate Douglas Smith. Polly Oliver's Problem. 2017. (ENG., Illus.). (J). 22.95 *(978-1-374-96499-0(9))* Capital Communications, Inc.

Yang, Belle. Hannah Is My Name. Yang, Belle, illus. 2007. (Illus.). (J). (gr. k-4). 14.65 *(978-0-7569-8124-2(7))* Perfection Learning Corp.

Yep, Laurence. Child of the Owl. (Golden Mountain Chronicles). (J). pap., stu. ed. *(978-0-13-053125-4(1))* Prentice Hall (Schl. Div.).

—The Earth Dragon Awakes: The San Francisco Earthquake Of 1906. 2008. (ENG., Illus.). 128p. (J). (gr. 3-7). pap. 9.99 *(978-0-06-000846-8(6),* HarperCollins) HarperCollins Pubs.

—The Earth Dragon Awakes: The San Francisco Earthquake of 1906. 2006. (ENG., Illus.). 128p. (J). (gr. 3-7). 14.99 *(978-0-06-027524-2(3))* HarperCollins Pubs.

—The Magic Paintbrush. Wang, Suling, illus. 2003. (ENG.). 96p. (J). (gr. 3-7). pap. 6.99 *(978-0-06-440852-3(3),* HarperCollins) HarperCollins Pubs.

—The Magic Paintbrush. Wang, Suling, illus. 2003. 89p. (J). (gr. 3-7). 12.65 *(978-0-7569-1444-8(2))* Perfection Learning Corp.

—The Tiger's Apprentice. 2005. (Tiger's Apprentice Ser.: Bk. 1). 184p. (J). lib. bdg. 24.62 *(978-1-4242-0449-6(6))* Fitzgerald Bks.

—The Tiger's Apprentice. 2005. (Tiger's Apprentice (Tandem Library) Ser.). 184p. (gr. 5-9). 17.00 *(978-0-7569-5074-3(0))* Perfection Learning Corp.

—Tiger's Blood. 2005. (Tiger's Apprentice Ser.: Bk. 2). (ENG.). 240p. (J). (gr. 5-18). 15.99 *(978-0-06-001016-4(9))* HarperCollins Pubs.

Zakatchenko, Lilian. Girls from Brazil, 1 vol. 2010. 16p. 24.95 *(978-1-4489-3834-6(1))* PublishAmerica, Inc.

Zarr, Sara. The Lucy Variations. 2014. (ENG.). 336p. (YA). (gr. 7-17). pap. 17.99 *(978-0-316-20500-9(1))* Little, Brown Bks. for Young Readers.

Zhao, Katie. The Dragon Warrior. 2019. (Dragon Warrior Ser.). (ENG., Illus.). 352p. (J). 16.99 *(978-1-5476-0200-1(7),* 900203292, Bloomsbury Children's Bks.) Bloomsbury Publishing USA.

Zschock, Martha. Hello, San Francisco! 2012. (Hello Ser.). (ENG., Illus.). 16p. (J). (gr. -1-k). bds. 9.99 *(978-1-933212-65-4(9),* Commonwealth Editions) Applewood Bks.

SAN FRANCISCO (CALIF.)—HISTORY

Adams, Jennifer. My Little Cities: San Francisco: (Board Books for Toddlers, Travel Books for Kids, City Children's Books) Pizzoli, Greg, illus. 2017. (My Little Cities Ser.). (ENG.). 22p. (J). (gr. -1 — 1). bds. 9.99 *(978-1-4521-5391-9(4))* Chronicle Bks. LLC.

Andrews McMeel Publishing, Andrews McMeel. San Francisco. 2014. (ENG., Illus.). 12p. (J). bds. 12.99 *(978-1-4494-5583-5(2))* Andrews McMeel Publishing.

Aretha, David. No Compromise: The Story of Harvey Milk. 2009. (Civil Rights Leaders Ser.). 100p. (YA). (gr. 5-9). lib. bdg. 28.95 *(978-1-59935-129-2(3))* Reynolds, Morgan Inc.

Barter, James. San Francisco in the 1960s. 2003. (Travel Guide To Ser.). (ENG., Illus.). 96p. (J). 30.85 *(978-1-59018-359-5(2),* Lucent Bks.) Cengage Gale.

Carr, Aaron. Golden Gate Bridge. 2014. (Illus.). 24p. (J). *(978-1-4896-2894-7(0))* Weigl Pubs., Inc.

Cooke, Tim. 1906 San Francisco Earthquake, 1 vol. 2004. (Disasters Ser.). (ENG., Illus.). 32p. (gr. 3-5). lib. bdg. 28.67 *(978-0-8368-4494-8(7),* d98f342a-dc80-4499-b175-82fc7ca6041f, Gareth Stevens Learning Library) Stevens, Gareth Publishing LLLP.

Dyan, Penelope. Halfway to the Stars! a Kid's Guide to San Francisco. Weigand, John D., photos by. 2009. (Illus.). 44p. pap. 11.95 *(978-1-935118-88-6(9))* Bellissima Publishing, LLC.

Epstein, Brad M. San Francisco 49ers 101. 2010. (ENG., Illus.). 24p. (J). bds. *(978-1-60730-127-1(X),* 101 Bk.) Michaelson Entertainment.

Evanson, Ashley. San Francisco: A Book of Numbers. Evanson, Ashley, illus. 2015. (Hello, World Ser.). (Illus.). 16p. (J). (— 1). bds. 7.99 *(978-0-448-48914-8(7),* Penguin Workshop) Penguin Young Readers Group.

Freedman, Russell. Angel Island: Gateway to Gold Mountain. 2016. (ENG., Illus.). 96p. (J). (gr. 5-7). pap. 10.99 *(978-0-544-81089-1(9),* 1641671, Clarion Bks.) HarperCollins Pubs.

Friesen, Helen Lepp. San Francisco. 2017. (Illus.). 24p. (J). *(978-1-4896-7301-5(6),* AV2 by Weigl) Weigl Pubs., Inc.

Grinapol, Corinne. Harvey Milk: Pioneering Gay Politician, 1 vol. 2014. (Remarkable LGBTQ Lives Ser.). (ENG., Illus.). 112p. (J). (gr. 7-7). 38.80 *(978-1-4777-7899-9(3),* baf68c2c-f448-4cc9-9914-b6fc012920ba, Rosen Young Adult) Rosen Publishing Group, Inc., The.

Herold, Vickey. Discover A Gold Rush Community: San Francisco. 2006. (J). pap. *(978-1-4108-6431-4(6))* Benchmark Education Co.

—A Gold Rush Community: San Francisco. 2006. (J). pap. *(978-1-4108-6428-4(6))* Benchmark Education Co.

Hollander, Barbara Gottfried. Harvey Milk: The First Openly Gay Elected Official in the United States, 1 vol. 2017. (Spotlight on Civic Courage: Heroes of Conscience Ser.). (ENG.). 48p. (J). (gr. 6-6). pap. 12.75 *(978-1-5383-8092-5(7),* 82e9e281-3c17-4b47-ab96-0eb334981d4b, Rosen Young Adult) Rosen Publishing Group, Inc., The.

Jolley, Dan. The Shadow City. 2018. (Five Elements Ser.: 2). (J). lib. bdg. 17.20 *(978-0-606-41026-7(0))* Turtleback.

Krensky, Stephen. Lizzie Newton & the San Francisco Earthquake. 2010. pap. 56.72 *(978-0-7613-6928-8(7))* Lerner Publishing Group.

Kriss, Jane Holton. Next Stop Sausalito. 2016. (ENG., Illus.). (J). 23.95 *(978-1-68418-526-9(2))* Primedia eLaunch LLC.

McDougall, Chros. San Francisco Earthquake & Fire, 1 vol. 2013. (History's Greatest Disasters Ser.). (ENG.). 48p. (J). (gr. 4-8). lib. bdg. 35.64 *(978-1-61783-959-7(0),* 9489) ABDO Publishing Co.

McDougall, Chrs. San Francisco Earthquake & Fire Paperback. 2013. (History's Greatest Disasters Ser.). (ENG.). (J). (gr. 4-8). pap. 18.50 *(978-1-62403-024-6(6),* 10773) ABDO Publishing Co.

Meter, Larry A. Van. Yerba Buena. 2007. (Colonial Settlements in America Ser.). (ENG., Illus.). 100p. (gr. 5-9). lib. bdg. 30.00 *(978-0-7910-9338-2(7),* P124642, Facts On File) Infobase Holdings, Inc.

National Geographic Learning. Content-Based Chapter Books Fiction (Science: Eyewitness): the San Francisco Earthquake. 2007. (Content-Based Chapter Bks.). (ENG., Illus.). 68p. (C). pap. 28.95 *(978-0-7922-5864-3(9))* National Geographic School Publishing, Inc.

O'Connell, Jennifer. The Eye of the Whale: A Rescue Story, 1 vol. 2013. (Tilbury House Nature Book Ser.: 0). (ENG., Illus.). 32p. (J). (gr. 1-7). 17.95 *(978-0-88448-335-9(5),* 884335) Tilbury Hse. Pubs.

Publications International Ltd. Staff. Yesterday & Today San Francisco. 2008. 192p. 24.95 *(978-1-4127-1575-1(X))* Publications International, Ltd.

Shea, Tess & Pohlen, Jerome. San Francisco Baby: An Adorable Book for Babies & Toddlers That Explores the City by the Bay. Features Local Sites & Includes Activities & Reading Tips. Great Gift. 2013. (Local Baby Bks.). (ENG., Illus.). 22p. (J). (— 1). bds. 8.95 *(978-1-938093-16-6(X),* 809316) Duo Pr. LLC.

Skewes, John. Larry Loves San Francisco! A Larry Gets Lost Book. Skewes, John, illus. 2014. (Larry Gets Lost Ser.). (ENG., Illus.). 20p. (J). (— 1). bds. 10.99 *(978-1-57061-912-0(3),* Little Bigfoot) Sasquatch Bks.

Tanaka, Shelley. Earthquake! A Day That Changed America. Craig, David, illus. 2006. 48p. (J). (gr. 4-8). reprint ed. 17.00 *(978-1-4223-5635-7(3))* DIANE Publishing Co.

Walsh, Kenneth C. H. You Are There! San Francisco 1906. 2nd rev. ed. 2017. (TIME(r): Informational Text Ser.). (ENG., Illus.). 32p. (gr. 5-8). pap. 10.99 *(978-1-4938-3617-8(X))* Teacher Created Materials, Inc.

White, Tekla. San Francisco Bay Area Missions. 2007. (Exploring California Missions Ser.). (ENG., Illus.). 64p. (gr. 4-7). lib. bdg. 27.93 *(978-0-8225-0900-4(8),* Lerner Pubns.) Lerner Publishing Group.

SAN FRANCISCO EARTHQUAKE AND FIRE, CALIF., 1906

Cooke, Tim. 1906 San Francisco Earthquake, 1 vol. 2004. (Disasters Ser.). (ENG., Illus.). 32p. (gr. 3-5). lib. bdg. 28.67 *(978-0-8368-4494-8(7),* d98f342a-dc80-4499-b175-82fc7ca6041f, Gareth Stevens Learning Library) Stevens, Gareth Publishing LLLP.

Hoobler, Dorothy & Hoobler, Thomas. What Was the San Francisco Earthquake? Hammond, Ted, illus. 2016. (What Was... Ser.). (ENG.). 112p. (J). (gr. 3-7). 16.00 *(978-0-606-39329-4(3))* Turtleback.

Hoobler, Dorothy, et al. What Was the San Francisco Earthquake? Hammond, Ted, illus. 2016. (What Was? Ser.). 112p. (J). (gr. 3-7). 5.99 *(978-0-399-54159-9(4),* Penguin Workshop) Penguin Young Readers Group.

Krensky, Stephen. Lizzie Newton & the San Francisco Earthquake. 2010. pap. 56.72 *(978-0-7613-6928-8(7))* Lerner Publishing Group.

McDougall, Chros. San Francisco Earthquake & Fire, 1 vol. 2013. (History's Greatest Disasters Ser.). (ENG.). 48p. (J). (gr. 4-8). lib. bdg. 35.64 *(978-1-61783-959-7(0),* 9489) ABDO Publishing Co.

McDougall, Chrs. San Francisco Earthquake & Fire Paperback. 2013. (History's Greatest Disasters Ser.). (ENG.). (J). (gr. 4-8). pap. 18.50 *(978-1-62403-024-6(6),* 10773) ABDO Publishing Co.

Slavicek, Louise Chipley. The San Francisco Earthquake & Fire Of 1906. 2008. (Great Historic Disasters Ser.). (ENG., Illus.). 128p. (gr. 5-8). 35.00 *(978-0-7910-9650-5(5),* P159120, Facts On File) Infobase Holdings, Inc.

Walsh, Kenneth C. H. You Are There! San Francisco 1906. 2nd rev. ed. 2017. (TIME(r): Informational Text Ser.). (ENG., Illus.). 32p. (gr. 5-8). pap. 10.99 *(978-1-4938-3617-8(X))* Teacher Created Materials, Inc.

—You Are There! San Francisco 1906. 2017. (Time for Kids Nonfiction Readers Ser.). lib. bdg. 19.65 *(978-0-606-40271-2(3))* Turtleback.

SAN FRANCISCO GIANTS (BASEBALL TEAM)

Frisch, Aaron. San Francisco Giants. 2009. (World Series Champions Ser.). (Illus.). 23p. (J). (gr. 2-3). 24.25 *(978-1-58341-690-7(0),* Creative Education) Creative Co., The.

Gilbert, Sara. San Francisco Giants. 2013. (World Series Champions Ser.). (ENG.). 24p. (J). (gr. 1-4). pap. 9.99 *(978-0-89812-823-9(4),* 21861, Creative Paperbacks); (Illus.). 25.65 *(978-1-60818-272-5(X),* 21860, Creative Education) Creative Co., The.

Goodman, Michael E. The Story of the San Francisco Giants. 2011. (J). 35.65 *(978-1-60818-055-4(7),* Creative Education) Creative Co., The.

Lajiness, Katie. San Francisco Giants. 2018. (MLB's Greatest Teams Ser.). (ENG., Illus.). 32p. (J). (gr. 2-5). lib. bdg. 34.21 *(978-1-5321-1519-6(9),* 28874, Big Buddy Bks.) ABDO Publishing Co.

Monning, Alex. San Francisco Giants. 2016. (Illus.). 32p. (J). *(978-1-4896-5947-7(1),* AV2 by Weigl) Weigl Pubs., Inc.

Richardson, Adele. The Story of the San Francisco Giants. 2007. (Baseball, the Great American Game Ser.). (Illus.). 48p. (YA). (gr. 4-7). lib. bdg. 32.80 *(978-1-58341-499-6(1))* Creative Co., The.

Stewart, Mark. The San Francisco Giants. 2012. (Team Spirit Ser.). 48p. (J). (gr. 3-6). lib. bdg. 29.27 *(978-1-59953-496-1(7))* Norwood Hse. Pr.

Tometich, Annabelle. Superstars of the San Francisco Giants. 2014. (Pro Sports Superstars - MLB Ser.). (ENG.). 24p. (J). (gr. 1-4). 27.10 *(978-1-60753-596-6(3)*, 16012) Amicus.

SANATORIUMS

see Hospitals

SAND

Brannon, Cecelia H. A Look at Sand, Silt, & Mud, 1 vol. 2015. (Rock Cycle Ser.). (ENG.). 32p. (gr. 3-4). pap. 11.52 *(978-0-7660-7332-6(7)*, 4afb07b6-de1e-4f8d-8ed0-3d44b90dfbb2); (illus.). 26.93 *(978-0-7660-7334-0(3)*, 48410819-1c78-4f74-bc38-1ec527fe7f93) Enslow Publishing, LLC.

dePaola, Tomie. Tomie DePaola's the Quicksand Book. 2019. (ENG., illus.). 32p. (J). (gr. -1-3). 17.99 *(978-0-8234-4237-9(3))* Holiday Hse., Inc.

Gurney, Beth. Sand & Soil. 2004. (Rocks, Minerals, & Resources Ser.). (ENG., illus.). 32p. (J). pap. *(978-0-7787-1449-1(7))* Crabtree Publishing Co.

Lawrence, Ellen. Is Sand a Rock? 2015. (illus.). 24p. (J). lib. bdg. 26.99 *(978-1-62724-301-8(1))* Bearport Publishing Co., Inc.

Rau, Dana Meachen. Building Sandcastles. 2012. (How-To Library). (ENG.). 32p. (gr. 3-6). pap. 14.21 *(978-1-61080-642-8(5)*, 202252); (illus.). 32.07 *(978-1-61080-468-4(6)*, 202078) Cherry Lake Publishing.

TBD. Jump into Science: Sand. 2006. (Jump into Science Ser.). (illus.). 32p. (J). (gr. -1-k). per. 6.95 *(978-0-7922-5583-3(6)*, National Geographic Kids) Disney Publishing Worldwide.

SAND CREEK MASSACRE, COLO., 1864—FICTION

Reeder, Red. Whispering Wind: A Story of the Massacre at Sand Creek. Wilson, Charles Banks, illus. 2011. 216p. 44.95 *(978-1-258-05996-5(7))* Literary Licensing, LLC.

SAND DUNES

Martinez, Clarissa G. & Seagraves, Erin. Sand Dwellers: From Desert to Sea. 2016. (illus.). 18p. (J). pap. *(978-1-60617-723-5(0))* Teaching Strategies, LLC.

Peggy J. Parks. Sand Dunes. 2004. (Wonders of the World Ser.). (ENG.). (J). 29.15 *(978-0-7377-2057-0(3)*, Kidhaven) Cengage Gale.

Robinson, Fay. Sand Dunes. 2016. (Spring Forward Ser.). (J). (gr. 2). *(978-1-4900-9464-9(4))* Benchmark Education Co.

SAND DUNES—FICTION

Barchers, Suzanne I. To the Dunes with Luce, 1 vol. rev. ed. 2011. (Phonics Ser.). (ENG., illus.). 16p. (gr. k-2). 6.99 *(978-1-4333-2918-0(2))* Teacher Created Materials, Inc.

Baumer, Dawn McVay, creator. Dune Daze: Silver Lake. 2004. (illus.). (J). *(978-0-9754960-0-8(X))* Butters Pr.

SANDBURG, CARL, 1878-1967

Murcia, Rebecca Thatcher. Carl Sandburg. 2007. (Poets & Playwrights Ser.). (illus.). 112p. (J). (gr. 3-7). lib. bdg. 37.10 *(978-1-58415-430-3(6))* Mitchell Lane Pubs.

SANDWICHES

Ashley, Susan. I Can Make a Sandwich, 1 vol. 2004. (I Can Do It! Ser.). (ENG., illus.). 24p. (gr. k-2). pap. 9.15 *(978-0-8368-4330-9(4)*, c9d04afb-65c5-47bf-bb76-16661a3d3d17, Weekly Reader Leveled Readers) Stevens, Gareth Publishing LLLP.

Blake, Susannah. Sandwiches & Snacks, 1 vol. 2009. (Make & Eat Ser.). (ENG., illus.). 24p. (J). (gr. 4-4). pap. 10.40 *(978-1-4358-2931-2(X)*, e4e02678-e09d-4953-8b82-07aaa711bab7, PowerKids Pr.) Rosen Publishing Group, Inc., The.

—Sandwiches & Snacks, 1 vol. Crawford, Andy, photos by. 2009. (Make & Eat Ser.). (ENG., illus.). 24p. (J). (gr. 4-4). 28.93 *(978-1-4358-2857-5(7)*, 571f38c4-b3ad-486d-83f9-1b88ceb61677, PowerKids Pr.) Rosen Publishing Group, Inc., The.

Dale, Jay. My Big Sandwich. 2012. (Engage Literacy Red Ser.). (ENG.). 16p. (J). (gr. k-2). pap. 36.94 *(978-1-4296-8842-0(4)*, 18312); (illus.). pap. 6.99 *(978-1-4296-8834-5(3)*, 119890) Capstone. (Capstone Pr.).

Deering, Alison. Fish & Fowl: Easy & Awesome Sandwiches for Kids. Lentz, Bob, illus. 2017. (Between the Bread Ser.). (ENG.). 48p. (J). (gr. 4-8). lib. bdg. 31.99 *(978-1-5157-3920-3(1)*, 133828, Capstone Pr.) Capstone.

—More Meat Please! Delicious Sandwiches for Meat-Eating Kids. Lentz, Bob, illus. 2017. (Between the Bread Ser.). (ENG.). 48p. (J). (gr. 4-8). lib. bdg. 31.99 *(978-1-5157-3921-0(X)*, 133829, Capstone Pr.) Capstone.

—Sandwiches! More Than You've Ever Wanted to Know about Making & Eating America's Favorite Food. Lentz, Bob, illus. 2017. (ENG.). 144p. (J). (gr. 4-8). pap., pap. 15.95 *(978-1-62370-816-0(8)*, 133830, Capstone Young Readers) Capstone.

LaPenta, Marilyn. Super 'Wiches. 2011. (Yummy Tummy Recipes Ser.). 24p. (J). (gr. 1-4). lib. bdg. 26.99 *(978-1-61772-306-3(1))* Bearport Publishing Co., Inc.

Nolan, Janet. PBandJ Hooray! 2016. (J). *(978-1-4896-3870-0(9))* Weigl Pubs., Inc.

—PB&J Hooray! Your Sandwich's Amazing Journey from Farm to Table. Patton, Julia, illus. 2014. (ENG.). 32p. (J). (gr. -1-3). 17.99 *(978-0-8075-6397-7(8)*, 807563978) Whitman, Albert & Co.

Shaw-Russell, Susan. Build Your Own Burger Sticker Activity Book. 2010. (Dover Little Activity Books Stickers Ser.). (ENG., illus.). 4p. (J). (gr. k-3). pap. 2.50 *(978-0-486-47592-9(1)*, 475921) Dover Pubns., Inc.

SANGER, MARGARET, 1883-1966

Archer, Jules. The Feminist Revolution: A Story of the Three Most Inspiring & Empowering Women in American History: Susan B. Anthony, Margaret Sanger, & Betty Friedan. rev. ed. 2015. (Jules Archer History for Young Readers Ser.). (ENG., illus.). 200p. (J). (gr. 6-6). 16.99 *(978-1-63220-603-9(X)*, Sky Pony Pr.) Skyhorse Publishing Co., Inc.

SANITARY AFFAIRS

see Sanitation

SANITATION

see also Cemeteries; Health; Public Health; Refuse and Refuse Disposal; Water—Purification; Water-Supply; World War, 1939-1945—Medical Care

Barnhill, Kelly & Miller, Connie Colwell. The Story of Sanitation. 2018. (Story of Sanitation Ser.). (ENG.). 32p. (J). (gr. 3-6). 119.96 *(978-1-5435-3123-7(7)*, 28575, Capstone Pr.) Capstone.

Boyd, Seren. Loos Save Lives: How Sanitation & Clean Water Help Prevent Poverty, Disease & Death. 2018. (ENG., illus.). 32p. (J). (gr. 4-6). 16.99 *(978-1-5263-0375-2(2)*, Wayland) Hachette Children's Group GBR. Dist: Hachette Bk. Group.

Davies, Monika. The Hidden World of Toilets: Volume (Grade 5) 2018. (Mathematics in the Real World Ser.). (ENG., illus.). 32p. (J). (gr. 4-8). pap. 11.99 *(978-1-4258-5810-0(4))* Teacher Created Materials, Inc.

Forest, Anne. Sanitation Workers, 1 vol., 1. 2015. (Hands-On Jobs Ser.). (ENG., illus.). 24p. (J). (gr. 3-4). pap. 9.25 *(978-1-5081-4371-0(4)*, 62e0da69-1c9f-440d-a266-f2dbd705f58c, PowerKids Pr.) Rosen Publishing Group, Inc., The.

Hand, Carol. Working in Trash & Recycling Collection in Your Community, 1 vol. 2018. (Careers in Your Community Ser.). (ENG.). 80p. (gr. 7-7). 37.47 *(978-1-4994-6734-5(6)*, c59a7435-200e-48ba-8f79-bae42c091ece) Rosen Publishing Group, Inc., The.

Kallen, Stuart A. A Career in Environmental Engineering. 2018. (Careers in Engineering Ser.). (ENG.). 64p. (YA). (gr. 6-12). 39.93 *(978-1-68282-351-4(2))* ReferencePoint Pr., Inc.

Robertson, Charmaine. My Uncle Is a Sanitation Worker, 1 vol. 2016. (Rosen REAL Readers: Social Studies Nonfiction / Fiction: Myself, My Community, My World Ser.). (ENG.). 12p. (gr. k-1). pap. 6.33 *(978-1-5081-2311-8(X)*, b2ea430e-371d-4930-8fe4-2d7a2b6b5c29, Rosen Classroom) Rosen Publishing Group, Inc., The.

Silverstein, Alvin & Silverstein, Virginia. Poop Collectors, Armpit Sniffers, & More: The Yucky Jobs Book, 1 vol. 2010. (Yucky Science Ser.). (ENG., illus.). 48p. (gr. 5-7). 27.93 *(978-0-7660-3316-0(3)*, d5300a86-4d64-4c44-8f4b-d0f08b9ad1fd) Enslow Publishing, LLC.

SANTA CLAUS

Bauchman, 'Delia. The Many Faces of Sant. 2009. 24p. pap. 13.99 *(978-1-4490-4988-1(5))* AuthorHouse.

Bonnice, Sherry. Christmas & Santa Claus Folklore. 2004. (North American Folklore Ser.). (illus.). 112p. (J). (gr. 7-18). lib. bdg. 22.95 *(978-1-59084-330-7(4))* Mason Crest.

Color All About: Santa: A Giant Coloring Book about What Santa Does When It's Not Christmas. 2004. (illus.). (J). *(978-0-9763307-4-5(1))*; (SPA & ENG., *(978-0-9763307-8-3(4))* Food Marketing Consultants, Inc.

Demi. The Legend of Saint Nicholas. 2003. (ENG., illus.). 40p. (J). (gr. k-5). 21.99 *(978-0-689-84681-6(9)*, McElderry, Margaret K. Bks.) McElderry, Margaret K. Bks.

Furman, M. E. A World of Cookies for Santa: Follow Santa's Tasty Trip Around the World: a Christmas Holiday Book for Kids. Gal, Susan, illus. 2017. (ENG.). 48p. (J). (gr. -1-3). 17.99 *(978-0-544-22620-3(8)*, 1563497, Clarion Bks.) HarperCollins Pubs.

Heald, Glenn. Santa Talks! The Life Story of Saint Nicholas. 2013. 96p. pap. 11.95 *(978-1-4759-5069-4(1))* iUniverse, Inc.

Hill, David W. & Hill, Anita R. The Case Of: Is Santa Claus Real? 2012. (ENG.). 63p. pap. 24.95 *(978-1-4327-7713-5(0))* Outskirts Pr., Inc.

Hipple Bob. Jesus Believes in Santa Claus: A Christmas Dream... 2009. 40p. pap. 19.99 *(978-1-4389-7936-6(3))* AuthorHouse.

Jeffers, H. Paul. Legends of Santa Claus. 2005. (Biography Ser.). (illus.). 112p. (J). (gr. 6-12). lib. bdg. 27.93 *(978-0-8225-4983-3(2))* Lerner Publishing Group.

Jones, Bryony. Where's Santa? Whelon, Chuck, illus. 2015. (ENG.). 32p. (J). (gr. k-3). 12.99 *(978-1-4814-0619-2(1)*, Aladdin) Simon & Schuster Children's Publishing.

Jones, Vanessa. Santa's Secret. 2008. (illus.). 24p. pap. 12.99 *(978-1-4389-3333-7(9))* AuthorHouse.

Kalman, Bobbie. Santa Claus. 2010. (ENG., illus.). 16p. (J). *(978-0-7787-9505-6(5))*; pap. *(978-0-7787-9530-8(6))* Crabtree Publishing Co.

Keitz, Roderick K., illus. The North Pole Chronicles, 4 bks., Set. Incl. Christmas Eve Tradition. Thompson, R. W., Jr. (gr. -1-3). 1993. 8.95 *(978-0-9636442-1-3(1))*; Shopping Trip. Thompson, R. W., Jr. (gr. -1-3). 1995. 8.95 *(978-0-9636442-2-0(X))*; Star on the Pole. Thompson, R. W. 1996. 8.95 *(978-0-9636442-3-7(8))*; Wow! I Got to Go to the North Pole. Thompson, R. W., Jr. (gr. -1-3). 1994. 8.95 *(978-0-9636442-0-6(3))*; 16p. (J). (illus.). 29.95 *(978-0-9636442-8-2(9))* North Pole Chronicles.

Keller, Irene. Santa Visits the Thingumajigs. Keller, Dick, illus. 2005. (ENG.). 28p. (J). (gr. -1-k). bds. 7.95 *(978-0-8249-6619-5(8)*, Ideals Pubns.) Worthy Publishing.

Kramer, Mark. Santa Claws: A True Story. 2009. (illus.). 25p. (J). pap. 15.95 *(978-1-4327-4793-0(2))* Outskirts Pr., Inc.

Kurtz, John. Santa Claus Christmas Paper Dolls. 2013. (Dover Paper Dolls Ser.). (ENG.). 32p. (J). (gr. 1-5). 9.99 *(978-0-486-49424-1(1)*, 494241) Dover Pubns., Inc.

Light, Kayte. Nicholas & the Spirit of Love. 2013. 16p. pap. 7.99 *(978-1-4624-0631-9(9)*, Inspiring Voices) Author Solutions, LLC.

Lomax M.Ed., L. E. A Saint Called Nicholas: The Christmas Legends Series, Vol. I. 2012. 52p. pap. 23.99 *(978-1-4582-0584-1(3)*, Abbott Pr.) Author Solutions, LLC.

Mazurkiewicz, Jessica & Dahlen, Noelle. 3-D Coloring Book — Here Comes Santa Claus! 2011. (Dover Christmas Coloring Bks.). (ENG., illus.). 32p. (J). (gr. 2-6). pap. 5.99 *(978-0-486-48413-6(0)*, 484130) Dover Pubns., Inc.

Moritz, Dianne, adapted by. Santa Lives! The Night Before Christmas. 2005. (Charming Petite Ser.). (illus.). 64p. (J). 4.95 *(978-0-88088-467-9(3))* Peter Pauper Pr. Inc.

Publications International Ltd. Staff, ed. Rudolph the Red-Nosed Reindeer (Look & Find) 2010. 24p. (J). 7.98 *(978-1-60553-958-4(9))* Phoenix International Publications, Inc.

Rajczak Nelson, Kristen. All about Santa. 2019. (It's Christmas! Ser.). (ENG.). 24p. (J). (gr. 2-2). 49.50 *(978-1-7253-0085-9(0)*, PowerKids Pr.) Rosen Publishing Group, Inc., The.

Schmidt, Marsha & Schmidt, Matt. The Santa Claus Project: Stories of Discovery about a Man in a Red Suit. 2012. 62p. (J). pap. 11.95 *(978-1-4772-6777-6(8))* AuthorHouse.

Stiegemeyer, Julie. Saint Nicholas: The Real Story of the Christmas Legend. Ellison, Chris, illus. 2003. 32p. (J). 13.49 *(978-0-7586-0376-0(2))* Concordia Publishing Hse.

Taplin, Sam. First Sticker Book Santa. 2011. (First Sticker Bks). 16p. (J). pap. 6.99 *(978-0-7945-3130-0(X)*, Usborne) EDC Publishing.

—Santa Flap Book. Bonnett, Rosalind, illus. 2019. (Flap Bks.). (ENG.). 10ppp. (J). 7.99 *(978-0-7945-3316-8(7)*, Usborne) EDC Publishing.

Walsh, William S. The Story of Santa Klaus: Told for Children of All Ages from Six To. 2007. (ENG.). 216p. per. 24.95 *(978-1-4304-4232-5(8))* Kessinger Publishing, LLC.

Yzermans, Vincent A. Wonderworker: The True Story of How St. Nicholas Became Santa Claus. 2004. (illus.). 64p. pap. 12.95 *(978-0-87946-278-9(7)*, 249) ACTA Pubns.

SANTA CLAUS—FICTION

Aboff, Marcie. Santa's Big Red Helper. Haefele, Steve, illus. 2005. (Clifford Ser.). (ENG.). 80p. (J). (gr. k — 1). 2.99 *(978-0-439-79150-2(2))* Scholastic, Inc.

Agee, Jon. Little Santa. 2013. (ENG., illus.). 40p. (J). (gr. -1-k). 17.99 *(978-0-8037-3906-2(0)*, Dial Bks) Penguin Young Readers Group.

Alexander, Maria. Snowed. 2016. (ENG., illus.). 211p. (YA). pap. 14.95 *(978-1-935738-89-3(5))*; (gr. 7-12). 29.95 *(978-1-935738-91-6(7))* Raw Dog Screaming Pr.

Anderson, Danny. Santa's Spy. 2012. 28p. pap. 15.99 *(978-1-4771-1007-2(0))* Xlibris Corp.

Anderson, Derek. How the Easter Bunny Saved Christmas. Anderson, Derek, illus. 2006. (ENG., illus.). 40p. (J). (gr. -1-3). 19.99 *(978-0-689-87634-9(3)*, Simon & Schuster Bks. For Young Readers) Simon & Schuster Bks. For Young Readers.

Andes, Mary Lou. Santa's Prayer. Mattozzi, Patricia, illus. 2007. (J). (gr. -1-k). bds. 11.95 incl. cd-rom *(978-0-8198-7100-8(1))* Pauline Bks. & Media.

Angel. Santa Claus's Journey to Texusilver. 2009. 28p. pap. 12.49 *(978-1-4490-2432-1(7))* AuthorHouse.

Angel, Bruce. I Believe in Santa Claus. 2006. 121p. pap. 19.95 *(978-1-4241-1486-3(1))* PublishAmerica, Inc.

Anonymous. Rudolph Saves the Day. 2014. (J). lib. bdg. 14.75 *(978-0-606-36126-2(X))* Turtleback.

Antoine, Leon. Santa's Destiny: A Legend Reborn, 1 vol. 2010. 48p. pap. 16.95 *(978-1-4512-9281-7(3))* America Star Bks.

Aoki, Hisako. Santa's Favorite Story: Santa Tells the Story of the First Christmas. Gantschev, Ivan, illus. 2007. (ENG.). 28p. (J). (gr. -1-3). 9.99 *(978-1-4169-5029-5(X)*, Simon & Schuster Bks. For Young Readers) Simon & Schuster Bks. For Young Readers.

Argenta, Joan. Santa Claus Comes to the Thomas Family. 2011. 16p. (gr. -1). pap. 8.43 *(978-1-4567-7846-0(3))* AuthorHouse.

Arnold, Tedd. Fly Guy's Ninja Christmas (Fly Guy #16) Arnold, Tedd, illus. 2016. (Fly Guy Ser.: 16). (ENG., illus.). 32p. (J). (gr. -1-2). 6.99 *(978-0-545-66277-2(X)*, Cartwheel Bks.) Scholastic, Inc.

Aronson, Jeff & Aronson, Miriam. Little Mike & Maddie's Christmas Book. Aronson, Jeff & Zephyr, Jay, illus. 2007. 32p. (J). 16.00 *(978-0-9795302-2-7(9)*, CrumbGobbler Pr.) Downtown Wetmore Pr.

Arrhenius, Ingela P., illus. Where's Santa Claus? 2018. (Where's The Ser.). (ENG.). 10p. (J). (— 1). bds. 9.99 *(978-1-5362-0697-5(0))* Candlewick Pr.

Ashford, Rachel. My First Santa's Coming to Michigan. Dunn, Robert, illus. 2015. (Santa Claus Is on His Way Ser.). (ENG.). 18p. (J). (gr. -1-k). bds. 9.99 *(978-1-4926-2873-6(5)*, Hometown World) Sourcebooks, Inc.

—My First Santa's Coming to Minnesota. Dunn, Robert, illus. 2015. (Santa Claus Is on His Way Ser.). (ENG.). 18p. (J). (gr. -1-k). bds. 9.99 *(978-1-4926-2879-8(4)*, Hometown World) Sourcebooks, Inc.

—My First Santa's Coming to New Jersey. Dunn, Robert, illus. 2015. (Santa Claus Is on His Way Ser.). (ENG.). 18p. (J). (gr. -1-k). bds. 9.99 *(978-1-4926-2882-8(4)*, Hometown World) Sourcebooks, Inc.

—My First Santa's Coming to Ohio. Dunn, Robert, illus. 2015. (Santa Claus Is on His Way Ser.). (ENG.). 18p. (J). (gr. -1-k). bds. 9.99 *(978-1-4926-2876-7(X)*, Hometown World) Sourcebooks, Inc.

—My First Santa's Coming to Texas. Dunn, Robert, illus. 2015. (Santa Claus Is on His Way Ser.). (ENG.). 18p. (J). (gr. -1-k). bds. 9.99 *(978-1-4926-2870-5(0)*, Hometown World) Sourcebooks, Inc.

—My First Santa's Coming to My House. Dunn, Robert, illus. 2015. (Santa Claus Is on His Way Ser.). (ENG.). 18p. (J). (gr. -1-k). bds. 9.99 *(978-1-4926-2885-9(9)*, Hometown World) Sourcebooks, Inc.

Atamer, Bilie. A Christmas Party for Santa. 2013. 36p. pap. 13.95 *(978-1-61244-187-0(4))* Halo Publishing International.

Atamer, Billie. The Magic Sleigh. 2013. 28p. pap. 13.95 *(978-1-61244-213-6(7))* Halo Publishing International.

Attia, Stephan. Other Christmas Stories. 2009. 42p. pap. 19.68 *(978-0-557-11189-3(7))* Lulu Pr., Inc.

Auerbach, Annie. Santa's Sleigh. Pagnoni, Roberta, illus. 2017. 12p. (J). (gr. -1-k). bds. 5.99 *(978-1-4380-5000-3(3))* Sourcebooks, Inc.

Badalamenti, Andrew. Around the World in One Night. Santa's Secrets Unwrapped! 2008. 28p. 14.50 *(978-0-615-25180-6(3))* Badalamenti, Andrew.

Bailey, Linda. When Santa Was a Baby. Godbout, Geneviève, illus. 2015. 32p. (J). (gr. -1-2). 16.99 *(978-1-77049-556-2(8)*, Tundra Bks.) Tundra Bks. CAN. Dist: Penguin Random Hse. LLC.

Bailey, Tressie. The Little Box Kittens meet Santa Claus. 2009. 37p. pap. 24.10 *(978-0-557-03198-6(2))* Lulu Pr., Inc.

Baker, Tommy. Santa Claus, the Fourth Wise Man. 2012. (ENG.). (J). 26p. pap. 13.95 *(978-1-4327-9630-3(5))*; 25p. pap. 18.95 *(978-1-4327-9774-4(3))* Outskirts Pr., Inc.

Baldwin, Sherry. Santa's Tatty Old Boots. 2016. (ENG., illus.). (J). 17.95 *(978-1-937721-37-4(X))* Randall, Peter E. Pub.

Balian, Lorna. Bah! Humbug?, 1 vol. Balian, Lecia, illus. 2006. (ENG.). 32p. (J). (gr. -1-3). 15.95 *(978-1-59572-036-8(7))* Star Bright Bks., Inc.

Banach, Jo-Ann. Sam the First Christmas Pumpkin: Sam Meets Santa Claus. 2006. (ENG., illus.). 28p. per. 19.99 *(978-1-4259-0898-0(5))* AuthorHouse.

Banda, Rey A. The Magical City of Northopolis; a Christmas Story. Patlan, Alyssa A., illus. 2012. 50p. (-18). pap. 16.95 *(978-0-615-69125-1(0))* Northopolis.

Barrett, Judi. Santa from Cincinnati. Hawkes, Kevin, illus. 2012. (ENG.). 48p. (J). (gr. -1-3). 16.99 *(978-1-4424-2993-2(3)*, Atheneum Bks. for Young Readers) Simon & Schuster Children's Publishing.

Bass, William E. A Gift for Sant. Salazar, Vivian Rose, illus. 2012. 36p. pap. 24.95 *(978-1-4626-6731-4(7))* America Star Bks.

—Santa Revisits His Secret Little Helper. Salazar, Vivian, illus. 2012. 26p. 24.95 *(978-1-4626-5396-6(0))* America Star Bks.

Bates, Susan Welch. The Rag Picker's Christmas. 2008. 17p. pap. 24.95 *(978-1-60672-967-0(5))* America Star Bks.

Baugh, Helen. Rudy's Windy Christmas. Mantle, Ben, illus. 2015. (ENG.). 32p. (J). (gr. -1-3). 16.99 *(978-0-8075-7173-6(3)*, 807571733) Whitman, Albert & Co.

Baum, L. Frank. A Kidnapped Santa Claus. 2011. 24p. 12.95 *(978-1-4638-9603-4(4))*; pap. 6.95 *(978-1-4638-0070-3(3))* Rodgers, Alan Bks.

—L Frank Baum's Book of Santa Claus. 2007. 84p. per. 7.99 *(978-1-60459-118-7(8))* Wilder Pubns., Corp.

—The Life & Adventures of Santa Claus. 2007. 112p. 22.95 *(978-1-60312-592-5(2))* Aegypan.

—The Life & Adventures of Santa Claus. Clark, Mary Cowles, illus. 2011. 200p. *(978-1-84902-560-7(6))* Benediction Classics.

—The Life & Adventures of Santa Claus. Clark, Mary, illus. 2007. 156p. (gr. 4-7). 23.95 *(978-1-60206-778-3(3))*; per. 9.95 *(978-1-60206-777-6(5))* Cosimo, Inc.

—The Life & Adventures of Santa Claus. Clark, Mary Cowles, illus. 2015. (Penguin Christmas Classics Ser.: 6). (ENG.). 160p. (gr. 12). 17.00 *(978-0-14-312853-3(1)*, Penguin Classics) Penguin Publishing Group.

—Life & Adventures of Santa Claus. 2008. (Applewood Bks.). (ENG.). 216p. pap. 24.95 *(978-1-55709-180-2(3))* Applewood Bks.

Becker, Curt. The Sad Sant. Fariss, Michelle, illus. 2009. 36p. pap. 14.95 *(978-1-60844-161-7(X))* Dog Ear Publishing, LLC.

Bedford, David. I've Seen Santa! Warnes, Tim, illus. 2006. 32p. (J). (gr. -1-3). 15.95 *(978-1-58925-058-1(3))* Tiger Tales.

Bell, Jonas Fearon, des. Oh! Christmas Tree: A Fun-To-Find Lift-the-Flap Book. 2013. (ENG., illus.). 20p. (gr. -1). bds. 8.99 *(978-1-77093-498-6(7))* Flowerpot Pr.

Bennett, Richard Grant, et al. Secret Santa. 2015. 151p. 17.99 *(978-1-4621-1739-0(2))* Cedar Fort, Inc./CFI Distribution.

Benson, Julian. The Christmas Dog: Lc's Worst Day Ever! 2012. 20p. pap. 24.95 *(978-1-4626-9816-5(6))* America Star Bks.

Bently, Peter. Santa Selfie. Chernyshova, Anna, illus. 2018. (ENG.). 32p. (J). (gr. -1-1). pap. 10.99 *(978-1-5098-3114-2(2))* Pan Macmillan GBR. Dist: Independent Pubs. Group.

—The Tooth Fairy's Christmas. Parsons, Garry, illus. 2014. (J). *(978-1-4351-5739-2(7))* Barnes & Noble, Inc.

Berenstain, Stan & Berenstain, Jan. The Berenstain Bears Meet Santa Bear (Deluxe Edition) 2016. (First Time Books(R) Ser.). (illus.). 32p. (J). (gr. -1-2). pap. 6.99 *(978-0-399-55767-5(9)*, Random Hse. Bks. for Young Readers) Random Hse. Children's Bks.

Berger, Samantha. Santa's Reindeer Games. Manders, John, illus. 2011. (J). *(978-0-545-36866-7(9))* Scholastic, Inc.

Bergeron, Denys. Les Bottes du Pere Noel. 2004. (Arion Pratique Ser.). (FRE., illus.). 92p. (J). *(978-2-921493-88-8(8)*, Spotlight Poets) Arion.

Bernardin, James & Plehal, Christopher J. Yes, Virginia: There Is a Santa Claus. 2010. (ENG., illus.). 32p. (J). (gr. -1-2). 17.99 *(978-0-06-200173-3(6)*, HarperCollins) HarperCollins Pubs.

Berry Byrd, Holly. Jingle & Joy. 2019. (ENG., illus.). 10p. (J). (gr. -1-k). bds. 10.99 *(978-1-68052-128-3(4)*, 1001211) Cottage Door Pr.

—Jingle Bells. Cottage Door Press, ed. Bos, Miriam, illus. 2017. (ENG.). 12p. (J). (gr. -1-k). bds. 10.99 *(978-1-68052-230-3(2)*, 1002160) Cottage Door Pr.

Biedrzycki, David. Santa Retires. Biedrzycki, David, illus. 2012. (illus.). 32p. (J). (gr. -1-3). pap. 7.95 *(978-1-58089-294-0(9))* Charlesbridge Publishing, Inc.

—Santa's New Jet. Biedrzycki, David, illus. 2011. (illus.). 32p. (J). (gr. -1-2). pap. 7.95 *(978-1-58089-292-6(2))* Charlesbridge Publishing, Inc.

—Santa's New Jet. 2007. (illus.). (J). pap. *(978-0-545-00238-7(9))* Scholastic, Inc.

Bigalow, Stephen W. Who Is Santa? And How Did He Get to the North Pole? Megenhardt, Bill, illus. 2013. (ENG.). 144p. (J). (gr. 4-7). 19.95 *(978-0-9773757-3-8(0))* Profit Publishing.

Biggs, Brian. Everything Goes: Santa Goes Everywhere! A Christmas Holiday Book for Kids. Biggs, Brian, illus. 2013. (ENG., illus.). 24p. (J). (gr. -1 — 1). bds. 7.99 *(978-0-06-195817-5(4)*, Balzer & Bray) HarperCollins Pubs.

Bizzarro, Grace. Christmas on the Internet. Bohart, Lisa, illus. 2013. 20p. pap. 12.95 *(978-1-61493-197-3(6))* Peppertree Pr., The.

Blabey, Aaron, illus. Pig the Elf. 2017. 24p. (J). pap. *(978-1-338-23004-8(2)*, Scholastic Pr.) Scholastic, Inc.

Blessing, Victor. Santa Claus Got Sick Because. 2009. 24p. pap. 12.99 *(978-1-4490-1126-0(8))* AuthorHouse.

Blunt, Fred. Santa Claus vs. the Easter Bunny. 2019. (ENG.). 32p. (J). (gr. -1-3). 12.99 *(978-1-4926-9164-8(X)*, Sourcebooks Jabberwocky) Sourcebooks, Inc.

Bolin, Ken & Bolin, Corrine. Santa SP: Santa Clauses of the South Pole. 2003. (J). pap. 9.00 *(978-0-8059-6190-4(9))* Dorrance Publishing Co., Inc.

Booth, Anne. The Christmas Fairy. Beardshaw, Rosalind, illus. 2017. (ENG.). 32p. (J). (gr. -1-2). 15.99 *(978-0-7636-9629-0(3))* Candlewick Pr.

Boyd, Ken. Tinsel Tail Mouse. 2009. 48p. pap. 16.25 *(978-1-60860-403-6(9)*, Eloquent Bks.) Strategic Book Publishing & Rights Agency (SBPRA).

Bradbury, Lynne. Santa Claus Has a Busy Night. (Christmas Titles Ser.: No. S808-6). (illus.). (J). 3.95 *(978-0-7214-5077-3(6)*, Dutton Juvenile) Penguin Publishing Group.

S

Bratun, Katy. Gingerbread Mouse. Bratun, Katy, illus. 2003. (Illus.). 32p. (J). (gr. -1-2). lib. bdg. 13.89 *(978-0-06-009081-4(2))* HarperCollins Pubs.

Brenner, Tom. And Then Comes Christmas. Christy, Jana, illus. 2014. (And Then Comes Ser.). (ENG.). 32p. (J). (gr. -1-3). 15.99 *(978-0-7636-5342-2(X))* Candlewick Pr.

Brett, Jan. The Animals' Santa. Brett, Jan, illus. (Illus.). (J). 2021. 34p. (— 1). bds. 9.99 *(978-1-9848-1680-1(2))* 2014. 40p. (gr. -1-k). 18.99 *(978-0-399-25784-1(5))* Penguin Young Readers Group. (G.P. Putnam's Sons Books for Young Readers).

Bridgman, C. A. Santa's Hawaiian Vacation. (J). 14.95 *(978-0-681-32827-3(4))* Booklines Hawaii, Ltd.

Bridwell, Norman. Clifford's Christmas Treasury. 2005. (Illus.). 96p. (gr. -1-3). pap. 10.99 *(978-0-439-79137-3(5))* Scholastic, Inc.

Brinkley, Lonnie. I Believe: Lost at the North Pole. 2008. (Illus.). 450p. (J). 29.95 *(978-0-9801215-3-7(1))* Big Bear Publishing U.S.

Brown, Jeff. Stanley's Christmas Adventure. 2010. (Flat Stanley Ser.). (J). (gr. k-3). lib. bdg. 14.75 *(978-0-613-68466-8(4))* Turtleback.

—Stanley's Christmas Adventure: A Christmas Holiday Book for Kids. Pamintuan, Macky, illus. 2010. (Flat Stanley Ser.). (ENG.). 96p. (J). (gr. 2-5). pap. 5.99 *(978-0-06-442175-1(9),* HarperCollins) HarperCollins Pubs.

Buckham, Derek. The Santa Stories. 2008. 81p. pap. 34.50 *(978-1-4092-4803-3(8))* Lulu Pr., Inc.

Burgess, Thornton W. The Christmas Reindeer. Chase, Rhoda, illus. 2013. (Dover Children's Classics Ser.). (ENG.). 152p. (J). (gr. k-3). pap. 5.99 *(978-0-486-49153-0(6),* 491536) Dover Pubns., Inc.

Burton, Jeffrey. The Itsy Bitsy Reindeer. Rescek, Sanja, illus. 2016. (Itsy Bitsy Ser.). (ENG.). 16p. (J). (gr. -1 — 1). bds. 5.99 *(978-1-4814-6855-8(3),* Little Simon) Little Simon.

Byrne, Barbara. The Magic Bell On. 2003. 13p. 12.66 *(978-1-4116-1078-1(4))* Lulu Pr., Inc.

Caliri, Matt. The Gnome Exchange Program: North Pole Rescue. 2017. (ENG.). (J). (gr. 3-7). pap. 17.99 *(978-1-4621-2012-3(1),* Sweetwater Bks.) Cedar Fort, Inc./CFI Distribution.

Campbell, H. David. Stanley: The Littlest Elf. 2012. 48p. pap. 21.99 *(978-1-4685-6257-6(6))* AuthorHouse.

Campbell, Suzy. Pennies for Christmas, 1 vol. 2010. 24p. 24.95 *(978-1-4512-0553-4(8))* PublishAmerica, Inc.

Cannon, Sherrill S. Santa's Birthday Gift. 2009. 24p. pap. 11.50 *(978-1-60860-824-9(7),* Eloquent Bks.) Strategic Book Publishing & Rights Agency (SBPRA).

Caro, Joe. Santa's Christmas Train. Shih, Lin, illus. 2005. 32p. pap. *(978-0-9628078-2-4(6))* Cowboy Collector Pubns.

—Santa's Christmas Train Coloring Book. Shih, Lin, illus. 2005. 32p. pap. *(978-0-9628078-5-5(0))* Cowboy Collector Pubns.

Carothers, Nina. Red Ed & the True Meaning of Christmas. Nilsen, Richard J., ed. Padovano, Chris, illus. 2013. 32p. pap. 12.97 *(978-1-937376-27-7(3))* All Star Pr.

Catholic Book Publishing Corp. Merry Christmas! 2015. (ENG., Illus.). 10p. 12.95 *(978-0-88271-393-9(0),* rg10325) Regina Pr., Malhame & Co.

Chand, Emlyn. Courtney Saves Christmas. Giffin, Noelle, illus. 2012. 60p. 21.95 *(978-1-62253-114-1(0))* Evolved Publishing.

Chandler, Jeffery. The Christmas Santa Overslept. 2008. 13p. pap. 24.95 *(978-1-60703-421-6(2))* America Star Bks.

Chichester Clark, Emma. Merry Christmas, Blue Kangaroo! (Blue Kangaroo) Chichester Clark, Emma, illus. 2017. (Blue Kangaroo Ser.). (ENG., Illus.). 32p. 17.99 *(978-0-00-824219-0(4),* HarperCollins Children's Bks.) HarperCollins Pubs. Ltd. GBR. Dist: HarperCollins Pubs.

Christian, Norma. A Christmas Mouse. 2012. 32p. pap. 13.99 *(978-1-4624-0328-8(X),* Inspiring Voices) Author Solutions, LLC.

Christmas Book - Santa Claus. 2005. (J). bds. *(978-1-4194-0074-2(6))* Paradise Pr., Inc.

Christ's Santa. 2004. (YA). 19.95 *(978-0-9747815-0-1(9))* Life's Journey of Hope Pubns.

Clark, Ruth E. Florida Santa: Is He Real? How Do We Know It? Caterisano, Sarah, illus. 2008. (ENG.). 32p. (J). (gr. -1-3). 16.95 *(978-0-9792963-0-7(7))* Hibiscus Publishing.

Clarkson, Kelly. River Rose & the Magical Christmas. Fleming, Lucy, illus. 2017. (J). *(978-0-06-274098-4(9))* Harper & Row Ltd.

Claus, Nancy. Santa's Hat. Ferchaud, Steve, illus. 2006. (J). *(978-0-9746747-6-6(1))* Cypress Bay Publishing.

—Santa's Prize. Ferchaud, Steve, illus. 2006. (J). *(978-0-9746747-5-9(3))* Cypress Bay Publishing.

Claus, Santa. The Santa Legends Present: The Lost Button. 2005. (J). cd-rom 12.00 *(978-1-59971-079-2(X))* Aardvark Global Publishing.

Coffelt, Soraya Diase. It's Not about You Mr. Santa Claus: A Love Letter about the True Meaning of Christmas. 2014. (Love Letters Book Ser.). (ENG., Illus.). 34p. pap. 8.99 *(978-1-63047-261-0(1))* Morgan James Publishing.

Coldon, Christine. Emmalynn: Wondrously Magical Christmas Eve. 2012. 56p. pap. 24.99 *(978-1-4685-8735-7(8))* AuthorHouse.

Collict, Joan E. Robot Horse: A Christmas Tale. 2012. 20p. pap. 13.77 *(978-1-4669-6318-4(2))* Trafford Publishing.

Conners, Lauren. The Stuffed Frog in Santa's Sack. 2009. 28p. pap. 12.49 *(978-1-4490-4623-1(1))* AuthorHouse.

Conteh, Gerald. I Still Believe in Santa. 2007. 188p. per. 14.95 *(978-1-60264-014-6(9))* Virtualbookworm.com Publishing, Inc.

Cooper, Margaret. The Christmas Horse. Bohart, Lisa, illus. 2008. 32p. pap. 12.95 *(978-0-9821654-9-2(8))* Peppertree Pr., The.

Cornell-Castle, Violet R. Santa's Elves. 2008. 32p. pap. 18.65 *(978-1-4363-5899-6(X))* Xlibris Corp.

Craig, Barbara J. Santa's Magical Key. 2010. 20p. 10.49 *(978-1-4520-4399-9(X))* AuthorHouse.

Creamer, Joan Klatil. The Magic Sceptre - the Legend of Blue Santa Claus. Creamer, Joan Klatil, illus. 2006. (Illus.). 32p. (J). 16.95 *(978-0-9778476-3-1(2))* Silver Snowflake Publishing.

Crissey, Brian. The Loneliest Christmas Tree. Crissey, Noah, illus. 2004. 32p. (J). bds. 25.00 *(978-1-893183-35-3(1),* 598) Granite Publishing, LLC.

Crissey, Brian L. The Loneliest Christmas Tree. Crissey, Noah, illus. 2004. (J). *(978-1-930724-12-9(8)); (978-1-930724-13-6(6))* Granite Publishing, LLC.

Crochet, Pat. Randolph Saves Christmas, 1 vol. Gramelspacher, Sarah, illus. 2018. (ENG.). 32p. (J). (gr. -1-3). 16.99 *(978-1-4556-2269-6(9),* Pelican Publishing) Arcadia Publishing.

Crofoot, Nancy. Christmas in the Barn, 1 vol. Rawat, Tania, illus. 2009. 37p. pap. 24.95 *(978-1-61582-585-1(1))* America Star Bks.

Cronin, Doreen. Click, Clack, Ho! Ho! Ho! Lewin, Betsy, illus. 2015. (Click Clack Book Ser.). (ENG.). 40p. (J). (gr. -1-2). 17.99 *(978-1-4424-9673-6(8))* Simon & Schuster Children's Publishing.

Crowley-Ranelli, D. Holiday Island: Santa in a Bathing Suit? 2009. 56p. pap. 9.95 *(978-1-60860-268-1(0),* Eloquent Bks.) Strategic Book Publishing & Rights Agency (SBPRA).

Crowson, Andrew. Flip Flap Christmas. Crowson, Andrew, illus. 2003. (ENG., Illus.). 12p. (J). bds. *(978-1-85602-476-1(8),* Pavilion Children's Books) Pavilion Bks.

Cummings, David W. How Biddikins & Buddikins Made Santa Claus Work Fast! 2005. (J). pap. 15.00 *(978-0-8059-6814-9(8))* Dorrance Publishing Co., Inc.

Curran, John. When I First Saw Santa. 2011. 20p. 10.03 *(978-1-4567-2708-6(7))* AuthorHouse.

Cuyler, Margery. That's Good! That's Bad! on Santa's Journey. 2015. (J). lib. bdg. 17.20 *(978-0-606-37582-5(1))* Turtleback.

Daley-Prado, M. The Super Heroes Save Christmas! 2007. 24p. per. 24.95 *(978-1-4241-9123-9(8))* America Star Bks.

Daly, Jerald James. An Early Snow (the Visions Come) 2008. 180p. pap. 24.95 *(978-1-60703-610-4(X))* America Star Bks.

Daly, Kathleen N. Jingle Bells. Miller, J. P., illus. 2015. (Little Golden Book Ser.). 24p. (J). (-k). 5.99 *(978-0-553-51112-3(2),* Golden Bks.) Random Hse. Children's Bks.

Daniels, Johanna. What About Claus? 2005. (Illus.). 32p. 15.95 *(978-0-9711106-8-7(9))* Mountaintop Pr.

Danowski, Jeffrey K. The Teddy Bear Necklace. 2012. 218p. 29.95 *(978-1-4626-9762-5(3))* America Star Bks.

Davenport, Kathy. Holly's Best Friend. 2010. 36p. 17.49 *(978-1-4520-2065-5(5))* AuthorHouse.

David, Edward. The Soul of Poetry. 2020. (ENG., Illus.). 51p. pap. 15.50 *(978-0-9852501-3-3(5))* Inkwell Books LLC.

Davies, Margo. Do You Believe in Santa Claus? 2003. (J). 6.00 *(978-0-9708959-7-4(6),* Accent Pubns.) Ajoyin Publishing, Inc.

Davies, Valentine. Miracle on 34th Street: [Facsimile Edition]. fac. ed. 2010. (ENG., Illus.). 136p. (J). (gr. 2-4). 22.44 *(978-0-15-216377-8(8))* Houghton Mifflin Harcourt Publishing Co.

Davis, Anne Shirley. No Red Suit for Santa? 2008. 16p. pap. 8.49 *(978-1-4389-2418-2(6))* AuthorHouse.

de Las Casas, Dianne. The House That Santa Built, 1 vol. Stone-Barker, Holly, illus. 2013. (ENG.). 32p. (J). (gr. -1-k). 16.99 *(978-1-4556-1750-0(4),* Pelican Publishing) Arcadia Publishing.

DeLand, M. Maitland. Baby Santa & the Gift of Giving. Wilson, Phil, illus. 2014. (ENG.). 36p. (J). (gr. -1-2). 14.95 *(978-1-62634-086-2(2),* Greenleaf Book Group Pr.) Greenleaf Book Group.

—Baby Santa's Worldwide Christmas Adventure. Wilson, Phil, illus. 2010. 32p. (J). 14.95 *(978-1-60832-062-2(6))* Greenleaf Book Group.

Delrusso, Diana. Pages, the Book-Maker Elf. Schwab, Jordan, illus. 2008. 68p. pap. 23.49 *(978-1-4343-9844-4(7))* AuthorHouse.

Dempster, Al. Santa's Toy Shop (Disney) RH Disney, illus. 2015. (Little Golden Book Ser.). (ENG.). 24p. (J). (-k). 5.99 *(978-0-7364-3401-0(1),* Golden/Disney) Random Hse. Children's Bks.

—Santa's Toy Shop (Disney) Walt Disney Studio, illus. 2015. (Little Golden Book Ser.). (ENG.). 24p. (J). (-k). E-Book *(978-0-7364-3402-7(X),* Golden/Disney) Random Hse. Children's Bks.

DePrisco, Dorothea. Randall Reindeer's Naughty & Nice Report. Reagan, Susan, illus. 2011. (ENG.). (J). (gr. -1-3). 24.95 *(978-1-61524-365-5(8),* Intervisual/Piggy Toes) Bendon, Inc.

Dineen, Kaite. What Santa Wants You to Know: A Story of Santa's Love for Jesus, 1 vol. 2010. 34p. pap. 24.95 *(978-1-4489-7071-1(7))* PublishAmerica, Inc.

Disney Books. Mickey Saves Santa. 2009. (ENG., Illus.). 24p. (J). (gr. -1-k). pap. 5.99 *(978-1-4231-1846-6(4),* Disney Press Books) Disney Publishing Worldwide.

DiTerlizzi, Angela. Seeking a Santa. Smith, Allie, illus. 2016. (ENG.). 30p. (J). (gr. -1 — 1). bds. 7.99 *(978-1-4814-7674-4(2),* Little Simon) Little Simon.

Dodd, Melissa. Santa Sheds, 1 vol. 2009. 17p. pap. 24.95 *(978-1-60749-208-5(3))* America Star Bks.

Dodson, Bert. Helping Santa: My First Christmas Adventure with Grandma. Dodson, Bert, illus. 2011. (ENG., Illus.). 32p. (J). (gr. -1-1). 17.95 *(978-1-59373-093-2(4))* Bunker Hill Publishing, Inc.

Donaldson, Julia. Stick Man. Scheffler, Axel, illus. (ENG.). 32p. (J). (gr. -1-3). 2016. 12.99 *(978-0-545-94789-3(8))* 2009. 18.99 *(978-0-545-15761-2(7))* Scholastic, Inc. (Levine, Arthur A. Bks.).

Donovan, Jane Monroe. Small, Medium & Large. Donovan, Jane Monroe, illus. 2010. (ENG., Illus.). 32p. (J). (gr. 1-4). 15.95 *(978-1-58536-447-3(9),* 202172) Sleeping Bear Pr.

Dove, Karen. A Gift for Santa. 2012. 50p. 23.99 *(978-1-61996-793-9(6));* pap. 12.99 *(978-1-61996-792-2(8))* Salem Author Services.

Drake, Rudy. Dushan, 1 vol. 2010. 20p. 24.95 *(978-1-4489-4875-8(4))* PublishAmerica, Inc.

Driscoll, Colleen. Piper the Elf Trains Santa. Dumm, Brian, illus. 2012. (ENG.). 32p. (J). 16.95 *(978-0-938467-56-4(5))* Headline Bks., Inc.

Dubel, Dorothy. The Magical Shoes of Santa's Elves(c). 2011. 24p. pap. 15.99 *(978-1-4568-7883-2(2))* Xlibris Corp.

Dufresne, Michèle. Apples for Santa: Little Elf Set 1. 2007. (Little Elf Set 1 Ser.). (J). pap. 7.33 *(978-1-932570-73-1(X))* Pioneer Valley Bks.

—Cookies for Santa: Little Elf Set 1. 2006. (Little Elf Set 1 Ser.). (ENG.). (J). pap. 7.33 *(978-1-932570-75-5(6))* Pioneer Valley Bks.

—Help for Santa: Little Elf Set 1. 2006. (Little Elf Set 1 Ser.). (ENG.). (J). pap. 7.33 *(978-1-932570-76-2(4))* Pioneer Valley Bks.

—Santa's Suit: Little Elf Set 1. 2006. (Little Elf Set 1 Ser.). (ENG.). (J). pap. 7.33 *(978-1-932570-71-7(3))* Pioneer Valley Bks.

Dunham, Terri Hoover. The Legend of Papa Noel: A Cajun Christmas Story. Knorr, Laura, illus. 2006. (Myths, Legends, Fairy & Folktales Ser.). (ENG.). 32p. (J). (gr. 2-5). 18.99 *(978-1-58536-256-1(5),* 202072) Sleeping Bear Pr.

Dunrea, Olivier. Merry Christmas, Ollie: A Christmas Holiday Book for Kids. Dunrea, Olivier, illus. 2015. (Gossie & Friends Ser.). (ENG., Illus.). 32p. (J). (gr. -1 — 1). pap. 4.99 *(978-0-544-55394-1(2),* 1610244, Clarion Bks.) HarperCollins Pubs.

—Merry Christmas, Ollie Board Book: A Christmas Holiday Book for Kids. Dunrea, Olivier, illus. 2011. (Gossie & Friends Ser.). (ENG., Illus.). 30p. (J). (gr. k — 1). bds. 7.99 *(978-0-547-37016-3(4),* 1423279, Clarion Bks.) HarperCollins Pubs.

Dunsany, Taylor. The Little Witch Who Lost Her Broom & Other Stories. 2008. 48p. pap. 8.95 *(978-0-595-52506-5(7))* iUniverse, Inc.

Duval, Kathy. The Three Bears' Christmas. Meisel, Paul, illus. 2007. (J). *(978-0-545-05421-8(4))* Scholastic, Inc.

Eight Jolly Reindeer. 2014. (ENG., Illus.). 16p. (J). (gr. -1 — 1). bds. 6.99 *(978-0-545-65145-5(X),* Cartwheel Bks.) Scholastic, Inc.

Eldridge, Les. Santa's Cat. Eldridge, Les & Casey, James, illus. 2003. 24p. (J). *(978-1-877338-03-8(6))* Steele Roberts Aotearoa Ltd.

Elliott, Alan. Willy the Texas Longhorn, 1 vol. Ford, Stephanie, illus. 2013. (ENG.). 32p. (J). (gr. k-3). 16.99 *(978-1-4556-1870-5(5),* Pelican Publishing) Arcadia Publishing.

Emmett, Jonathan. The Santa Trap, 1 vol. Bernatene, Poly, illus. 2012. (ENG.). 32p. (J). (gr. 1-4). 15.95 *(978-1-56145-670-3(5))* Peachtree Publishing Co. Inc.

Evert, Lori. The Christmas Wish. Breiehagen, Per, illus. (Wish Book Ser.). (J). 2022. 32p. (— 1). bds. 10.99 *(978-0-593-56421-9(9))* 2013. 48p. (gr. -1-2). 18.99 *(978-0-449-81681-3(8))* 2013. (ENG.). 48p. (gr. -1-2). E-Book *(978-0-449-81942-5(6))* Random Hse. Children's Bks. (Random Hse. Bks. for Young Readers).

Falk, Barbara Bustetter & Hyman, Helen Kandel. Don't Park on the Roof. 2007. 36p. per. 21.32 *(978-1-4257-7096-9(7))* Xlibris Corp.

Fambro, Sonja Grimsley. Santa Spent the Night with Me! 2011. 52p. pap. 25.06 *(978-1-4634-4626-0(8))* AuthorHouse.

—When Santa Goes to Church. 2011. 84p. pap. 32.26 *(978-1-4634-5983-3(1))* AuthorHouse.

Faulconer, Charlotte. The Green Button Wish. 2010. 28p. pap. 12.49 *(978-1-4490-8003-7(0))* AuthorHouse.

Fearne, Peter. My Week with Father Christmas. 2006. 176p. per. *(978-1-84667-021-3(7))* Derwent Pr., The.

Federici, Diane Marie. The Christmas Stocking. 2006. (J). pap. 8.00 *(978-0-8059-6874-3(1))* Dorrance Publishing Co., Inc.

Felden, Georgia. When Jesus Hired Santa. 2006. (J). pap. *(978-0-9790444-8-9(0))* Dynasty Publishing, Inc.

Figley, Marty Rhodes. Santa's Underwear. Kelley, Marty, illus. 2016. (ENG.). 32p. (J). (gr. k-3). 16.99 *(978-1-58536-954-6(3),* 204109) Sleeping Bear Pr.

Fletcher, Tom. The Christmasaurus. Devries, Shane, illus. 2018. (ENG.). 384p. (J). (gr. 3-7). 13.99 *(978-1-5247-7330-4(1),* Random Hse. Bks. for Young Readers) Random Hse. Children's Bks.

Fouch, Robert L. Christmas Carol & the Defenders of Claus. 2017. (Christmas Carol Adventure Ser.: 1). (ENG.). 256p. (J). 15.99 *(978-1-5107-2452-5(4),* Sky Pony Pr.) Skyhorse Publishing Co., Inc.

Franklin, Kathleen. Uncle Holly saves Christmas. 2010. (Illus.). 32p. 14.89 *(978-1-4520-9689-6(9))* AuthorHouse.

Frazee, Marla. Santa Claus: the World's Number One Toy Expert: A Christmas Holiday Book for Kids. Frazee, Marla, illus. 2010. (ENG., Illus.). 32p. (J). (gr. -1-3). pap. 7.99 *(978-0-547-48074-9(1),* 1439405, Clarion Bks.) HarperCollins Pubs.

—Santa Claus: the World's Number One Toy Expert Board Book: A Christmas Holiday Book for Kids. Frazee, Marla, illus. 2018. (ENG., Illus.). 32p. (J). (— 1). bds. 7.99 *(978-1-328-48542-7(0),* 1715776, Clarion Bks.) HarperCollins Pubs.

Fry, Michael & Jackson, Bradley. The Naughty List: A Christmas Holiday Book for Kids. Fry, Michael, illus. 2015. (ENG., Illus.). 240p. (J). (gr. 3-7). 12.99 *(978-0-06-235475-4(2),* HarperCollins) HarperCollins Pubs.

Fuggle, Debbie. The Two Little Fir Trees. 2012. 28p. pap. 32.70 *(978-1-4691-3253-2(2))* Xlibris Corp.

Garcia, Jeffrey. Santa Claus & the Molokai Mules. 2009. 32p. 17.95 *(978-0-9840942-0-2(2))* Garcia, Jeffrey.

Garis, Howard Roger. Johnnie & Billie Bushytail. 2004. reprint ed. pap. 1.99 *(978-1-4192-2786-8(6));* pap. 15.95 *(978-1-4191-2786-1(1))* Kessinger Publishing, LLC.

Garner, Ellen. Santa's Elves & the Tickets. Street, James, illus. 2012. 56p. pap. 12.99 *(978-0-615-55920-9(4))* EG Bks.

Garza, Xavier. Charro Claus & the Tejas Kid, 1 vol. 2008. (ENG., Illus.). 40p. (J). (gr. k-7). 17.95 *(978-1-933693-24-8(X),* 16d199ce-82b8-4fe3-be9f-43115f4edae3, Cinco Puntos Press) Lee & Low Bks., Inc.

Gausselin, Richard J. How the Grandmas & Grandpas Saved Christmas. 2012. 24p. pap. 17.99 *(978-1-4772-4771-6(8))* AuthorHouse.

George, Joshua. I'm Santa Claus. Green, Barry, illus. 2017. (Googley-Eye Bks.). (ENG.). 12p. (J). (gr. -1-k). bds. 7.99 *(978-1-78700-078-0(8))* Top That! Publishing PLC GBR. Dist: Independent Pubs. Group.

Gerver, Jane E. The Santa Snatcher. Spaziante, Patrick, illus. 2004. 32p. (J). lib. bdg. 15.00 *(978-1-4242-0959-0(5))* Fitzgerald Bks.

Gevry, C. C. A Christmas Kindness. Mabey, Coline, illus. 2012. 24p. pap. 11.99 *(978-0-9852661-4-1(7))* 4RV Pub.

Godley, Marie. The Special Christmas Bear. 2007. (Illus.). 52p. per. *(978-1-84748-005-7(5))* Athena Pr.

Gordon, Peggy T. Santa's Secret. 2009. 24p. pap. 15.99 *(978-1-4415-5330-0(4))* Xlibris Corp.

Goss, Matt. Bear Crimbo. 2010. (ENG., Illus.). 72p. (J). 17.95 *(978-0-9815381-3-6(4))* Hilton Publishing Co.

Graham, Oakley. A Visit from Santa. Gulliver, Amanda, illus. 2017. (In My Bed Bks.). (ENG.). 24p. (J). (gr. -1-k). bds. 9.99 *(978-1-78700-081-0(8))* Top That! Publishing PLC GBR. Dist: Independent Pubs. Group.

Grampa Ralph. Santa's New Boots, 1 vol. 2010. 48p. pap. 16.95 *(978-1-4489-5981-5(0))* America Star Bks.

Grandpa. The Beginning of Meet the Mūsh-Mice: (a Visit to the North Pole) 2012. 34p. 29.95 *(978-1-4626-9377-1(6))* America Star Bks.

Greenberg, Nicki. Naughtiest Reindeer Takes a Bow. 2018. (Naughtiest Reindeer Ser.: 4). (ENG., Illus.). 32p. (J). (gr. -1-1). 15.99 *(978-1-76029-565-3(5))* Allen & Unwin AUS. Dist: Independent Pubs. Group.

Greene, Rhonda. Santa's Stuck. Cole, Henry, illus. 2006. (ENG.). 32p. (J). (gr. -1-3). pap. 8.99 *(978-0-14-240686-1(4),* Puffin Books) Penguin Young Readers Group.

Gregory, Larry. A Christmas Surprise. Woolmer, Nancy, illus. 2004. 24p. pap. 24.95 *(978-1-4137-3014-2(0))* PublishAmerica, Inc.

Grimmer, Constance Marie. Santa's Christmas Dogs: A Legend Begins... 2009. 28p. pap. 15.49 *(978-1-4490-5920-0(1))* AuthorHouse.

Guendelsberger, Erin. Little Red Sleigh. Tretyakova, Elizaveta, illus. 2020. (Little Heroes, Big Hearts Ser.). 40p. (J). (gr. -1-3). 17.99 *(978-1-7282-2355-1(5))* Sourcebooks, Inc.

H M Bricker, et al. The Christmas Santa Had No Beard. Dall, John, illus. 2011.Tr. of Navidad en la Que Santa Claus No Teñia Barba. (ENG & SPA.). 34p. (J). *(978-0-615-42163-6(6))* H M Bricker.

Hagen, Carol. The Night Henry Ford Met Santa. Faulkner, Matt, illus. 2006. (ENG.). 32p. (J). (gr. 1-4). 17.95 *(978-1-58536-132-8(1),* 201994) Sleeping Bear Pr.

Haig, Matt. A Boy Called Christmas. Mould, Chris, illus. (Boy Called Christmas Ser.). (ENG.). (J). (gr. 3-7). 2018. 256p. 8.99 *(978-0-399-55268-7(5),* Yearling) 2016. 240p. 17.99 *(978-0-399-55265-6(0),* Knopf Bks. for Young Readers) Random Hse. Children's Bks.

Hale, Bruce. Santa on the Loose! A Seek & Solve Mystery! a Christmas Holiday Book for Kids. Garbot, Dave, illus. 2012. (ENG.). 32p. (J). (gr. -1-3). 7.99 *(978-0-06-202262-2(8),* HarperCollins) HarperCollins Pubs.

Hall, Annalisa. Tak & Lolly: Santa Clause at Church. 2009. 51p. pap. 6.99 *(978-0-557-04923-3(7))* Lulu Pr., Inc.

Hall, Martha Gamble. A Note from Sant. 2008. 16p. pap. 10.99 *(978-1-4389-2308-6(2))* AuthorHouse.

Hammon, Darrel L. Christmas Beneath the Lake: From the Adventures of Bob the Bullfrog. 2012. (ENG.). (J). (-18). 35p. pap. 17.95 *(978-1-4787-1910-6(9));* 25p. pap. 23.95 *(978-1-4327-7916-0(8))* Outskirts Pr., Inc.

Hansen, Eric. Ian, Ceo, North Pole. 2008. 108p. pap. 9.95 *(978-1-60693-554-5(2),* Eloquent Bks.) Strategic Book Publishing & Rights Agency (SBPRA).

Hardin, Holly. Aurora of the Northern Lights. 2009. 31p. (J). pap. 18.95 *(978-1-4327-2439-9(8))* Outskirts Pr., Inc.

Harley, Bill. Dear Santa: The Letters of James B. Dobbins. Alley, R. W., illus. 2005. 32p. (J). (ENG.). 15.99 *(978-0-06-623778-7(5));* lib. bdg. 16.89 *(978-0-06-623779-4(3))* HarperCollins Pubs.

Harper, Stephan J. One Christmas Story. Steuerwald, Joy, illus. 2003. 32p. (J). lib. bdg. 16.95 *(978-0-9741800-0-7(9))* Inspire Press, Inc.

Harris, Danielle. The Second Chance Sant. 2012. 28p. pap. 24.95 *(978-1-4626-6778-9(3))* America Star Bks.

Harrison, Michael. Cop's Night Before Christmas, 1 vol. Miles, David, illus. 2010. (Night Before Christmas Ser.). (ENG.). 32p. (J). (gr. k-3). 16.99 *(978-1-58980-800-3(2),* Pelican Publishing) Arcadia Publishing.

Hatch, Justina. Charlie the Caterpillar, 1 vol. 2010. 44p. pap. 24.95 *(978-1-4489-9256-0(7))* PublishAmerica, Inc.

Hatfield, Kara. The Real Story of Sant. 2011. 30p. pap. 16.95 *(978-1-4626-1022-8(6))* America Star Bks.

Hazlehurst, Pam. Santa's Dilemma. 2012. (Illus.). 24p. pap. 19.82 *(978-1-4772-5079-2(4))* AuthorHouse.

Head, Jean. Andrew's Christmas Dream. 2012. 28p. pap. 5.00 *(978-1-937260-19-4(4))* Sleepytown Pr.

Healey, Richard (Dick). Holly the Christmas Dove. 2005. 36p. (J). 13.28 *(978-1-4116-5496-9(X))* Lulu Pr., Inc.

Heible, Beverly. A Christmas Party on River Row. 2012. 98p. 22.95 *(978-1-62709-018-6(5));* pap. 17.95 *(978-1-4626-9575-1(2))* America Star Bks.

Heidecker, Samie. Who's Looking at Whom? Christmas, 1 vol. 2010. 38p. 24.95 *(978-1-4489-4855-0(X))* PublishAmerica, Inc.

Heierbacher, Michael. Yo Ho Ho Merry Christmas. 2010. (Illus.). 28p. (J). pap. 15.95 *(978-1-4327-6484-5(5))* Outskirts Pr., Inc.

Helen, Grace. Santa's Way. 2012. 32p. pap. 24.95 *(978-1-4626-7356-8(2))* America Star Bks.

Henderson, Richard. One Christmas Night. Shackelford, David, illus. 2008. 32p. (J). 15.95 *(978-0-615-17629-1(1))* St. Clair Publishing.

Hennessy, B. G. A Christmas Wish for Corduroy. Wheeler, Jody, illus. 2017. (Corduroy Ser.). 34p. (J). (— 1). bds. 8.99 *(978-0-425-28875-7(7),* Viking Books for Young Readers) Penguin Young Readers Group.

Heos, Bridget. A Mustache Baby Christmas: A Christmas Holiday Book for Kids. Ang, Joy, illus. 2019. (Mustache Baby Ser.). (ENG.). 40p. (J). (gr. -1-3). 17.99 *(978-1-328-50653-5(3),* 1718799, Clarion Bks.) HarperCollins Pubs.

Higgins, Tiffany A. We've Seen Sant. Higgins, Clark L., illus. 2011. 26p. pap. 12.27 *(978-1-61204-267-1(8),* Eloquent Bks.) Strategic Book Publishing & Rights Agency (SBPRA).

Hill, Kathi Harper. The Christmas Closet & Other Works. 2012. (ENG.). 48p. 16.99 *(978-1-936815-58-6(3))* Yawn's Bks. & More, Inc.

Hineman, Jonathan. Goodbye, Santa. Cruz, Cheryl, illus. 2013. 26p. (J). 16.95 *(978-1-60131-172-6(9))* Big Tent Bks.

Hodgson, Julie. The Magic of Christmas. 2007. 26p. 18.95 *(978-1-84799-350-2(8))* Lulu Pr., Inc.

Hoffer, Rod. The Strange Christmas Dream. 2012. 64p. pap. 24.99 *(978-1-4772-5949-8(X))* AuthorHouse.

Holm, H. R. Forever Santa. 2009. 14p. (J). pap. 2.99 *(978-1-59955-345-0(7))* Cedar Fort, Inc./CFI Distribution.

Holub, Joan. The Knights Before Christmas. Magoon, Scott, illus. 2015. (ENG.). 32p. (J). (gr. k-3). 16.99 *(978-0-8050-9932-4(8))*, 900126311, Holt, Henry & Co. Bks. For Young Readers) Holt, Henry & Co.

Hooper, Ruth. Santa's Factory. Charbonnel, Olivier & Mostyn, David, illus. 2004. 6p. (J). (gr. k-4). reprint ed. 16.00 *(978-0-7567-7585-8(X))* DIANE Publishing Co.

Hopkins, Charles. Santa's Frost Covered Sleigh Lay Broken in the Snow. 2007. pap. 17.00 *(978-0-8059-8935-9(8))* Dorrance Publishing Co., Inc.

House of Wooden Santas, 1 vol. 2003. (ENG., Illus.). 96p. (J). (gr. 4-6). 22.95 *(978-0-88995-166-2(7),* f1ebd2a2-a16f-4d44-ab93-4ad9394f2bfa) Red Deer Pr. CAN. Dist: Firefly Bks., Ltd.

Howe, James. The Fright Before Christmas: Ready-To-Read Level 3, 5. Mack, Jeff, illus. 2006. (Bunnicula & Friends Ser.: 5). (ENG.). 48p. (J). (gr. 1-3). 17.99 *(978-0-689-86939-6(8),* Simon Spotlight) Simon & Schuster Children's Publishing.

—The Fright Before Christmas: Ready-To-Read Level 3. Mack, Jeff, illus. 2007. (Bunnicula & Friends Ser.: 5). (ENG.). 48p. (J). (gr. 1-3). pap. 4.99 *(978-0-689-86941-9(X),* Simon Spotlight) Simon Spotlight.

Humphrey, Eleanor Cairns. Building Santa's Work Shop from Tales of the Crystal Cave. 2012. 268p. pap. 27.95 *(978-1-4626-7820-4(3))* America Star Bks.

Humphreys, Stephen. Harold Saves Christmas: A Harold & Charlie adventure Story. 2011. (Illus.). 28p. pap. 12.49 *(978-1-4520-9994-1(4))* AuthorHouse.

Hurley, Wes. How the Winter Frog Came to Was: Or, How to Get a Nice Surprise on Thanksgiving! Lee, Susan, illus. 2007. 36p. per. 24.95 *(978-1-4241-8395-1(2))* America Star Bks.

Hurst, Joshua. One Day at the North Pole. Johnson, Jared, illus. 2008. 44p. pap. 24.95 *(978-1-60703-327-1(5))* America Star Bks.

Inches, Alison. Santa Claus Is Green! How to Have an Eco-Friendly Christmas. Kirwan, Wednesday, illus. 2009. (Little Green Book Ser.). (ENG.). 24p. (J). (gr. k-2). 18.69 *(978-1-4169-7223-5(4),* Little Simon) Little Simon.

Iosue, Marilyn. Santa's Busy Day. 2007. pap. 17.00 *(978-0-8059-8761-4(4))* Dorrance Publishing Co., Inc.

Irvine, Patricia McCune. Haunted Pavilion: And Other Short Stories. 2003. 144p. 21.95 *(978-0-595-75249-2(7))* iUniverse, Inc.

It's Santa. 2003. (J). per. *(978-1-57657-909-1(3))* Paradise Pr., Inc.

J. Katyn. Boo & the Halloween Grin. 2011. 36p. pap. *(978-1-4269-7197-6(4))* Trafford Publishing (UK) Ltd.

James, Eric. Santa's Sleigh Is on Its Way to Alabama: A Christmas Adventure. Dunn, Robert, illus. 2015. (Santa's Sleigh Is on Its Way Ser.). (ENG.). 32p. (J). (gr. k-2). 12.99 *(978-1-4926-2763-0(1),* Hometown World) Sourcebooks, Inc.

—Santa's Sleigh Is on Its Way to Arkansas: A Christmas Adventure. Dunn, Robert, illus. 2016. (Santa's Sleigh Is on Its Way Ser.). (ENG.). 32p. (J). (gr. k-2). 12.99 *(978-1-4926-4317-3(3),* 9781492643173, Hometown World) Sourcebooks, Inc.

—Santa's Sleigh Is on Its Way to Boise: A Christmas Adventure. Dunn, Robert, illus. 2016. (Santa's Sleigh Is on Its Way Ser.). (ENG.). 32p. (J). (gr. k-2). 12.99 *(978-1-4926-4318-0(1),* 9781492643180, Hometown World) Sourcebooks, Inc.

—Santa's Sleigh Is on Its Way to Boston: A Christmas Adventure. Dunn, Robert, illus. 2016. (Santa's Sleigh Is on Its Way Ser.). (ENG.). 32p. (J). (gr. k-2). 12.99 *(978-1-4926-4319-7(X),* 9781492643197, Hometown World) Sourcebooks, Inc.

—Santa's Sleigh Is on Its Way to California: A Christmas Adventure. Dunn, Robert, illus. 2015. (Santa's Sleigh Is on Its Way Ser.). (ENG.). 32p. (J). (gr. k-2). 12.99 *(978-1-4926-2747-0(X),* Hometown World) Sourcebooks, Inc.

—Santa's Sleigh Is on Its Way to Canada: A Christmas Adventure. Dunn, Robert, illus. 2016. (Santa's Sleigh Is on Its Way Ser.). (ENG.). 32p. (J). (gr. k-2). 12.99 *(978-1-4926-4321-0(1),* 9781492643210, Hometown World) Sourcebooks, Inc.

—Santa's Sleigh Is on Its Way to Charleston: A Christmas Adventure. Dunn, Robert, illus. 2016. (Santa's Sleigh Is on Its Way Ser.). (ENG.). 32p. (J). (gr. k-2). 12.99 *(978-1-4926-4322-7(X),* 9781492643227, Hometown World) Sourcebooks, Inc.

—Santa's Sleigh Is on Its Way to Cincinnati: A Christmas Adventure. Dunn, Robert, illus. 2016. (Santa's Sleigh Is on Its Way Ser.). (ENG.). 32p. (J). (gr. k-2). 12.99 *(978-1-4926-4324-1(6),* 9781492643241, Hometown World) Sourcebooks, Inc.

—Santa's Sleigh Is on Its Way to Colorado: A Christmas Adventure. Dunn, Robert, illus. 2015. (Santa's Sleigh Is on Its Way Ser.). (ENG.). 32p. (J). (gr. k-2). 12.99 *(978-1-4926-2756-2(9),* Hometown World) Sourcebooks, Inc.

—Santa's Sleigh Is on Its Way to Connecticut: A Christmas Adventure. Dunn, Robert, illus. 2016. (Santa's Sleigh Is on Its Way Ser.). (ENG.). 32p. (J). (gr. k-2). 12.99 *(978-1-4926-4325-8(4),* 9781492643258, Hometown World) Sourcebooks, Inc.

—Santa's Sleigh Is on Its Way to Delaware: A Christmas Adventure. Dunn, Robert, illus. 2016. (Santa's Sleigh Is on Its Way Ser.). (ENG.). 32p. (J). (gr. k-2). 12.99 *(978-1-4926-4326-5(2),* 9781492643265, Hometown World) Sourcebooks, Inc.

—Santa's Sleigh Is on Its Way to Edmonton: A Christmas Adventure. Dunn, Robert, illus. 2016. (Santa's Sleigh Is on Its Way Ser.). (ENG.). 32p. (J). (gr. k-2). 12.99 *(978-1-4926-4327-2(0),* 9781492643272, Hometown World) Sourcebooks, Inc.

—Santa's Sleigh Is on Its Way to Florida: A Christmas Adventure. Dunn, Robert, illus. 2015. (Santa's Sleigh Is on Its Way Ser.). (ENG.). 32p. (J). (gr. k-2). 12.99 *(978-1-4926-2743-2(7),* Hometown World) Sourcebooks, Inc.

—Santa's Sleigh Is on Its Way to Georgia: A Christmas Adventure. Dunn, Robert, illus. 2015. (Santa's Sleigh Is on Its Way Ser.). (ENG.). 32p. (J). (gr. k-2). 12.99 *(978-1-4926-2744-9(5),* Hometown World) Sourcebooks, Inc.

—Santa's Sleigh Is on Its Way to Hawaii: A Christmas Adventure. Dunn, Robert, illus. 2016. (Santa's Sleigh Is on Its Way Ser.). (ENG.). 32p. (J). (gr. k-2). 12.99 *(978-1-4926-4328-9(9),* 9781492643289, Hometown World) Sourcebooks, Inc.

—Santa's Sleigh Is on Its Way to Illinois: A Christmas Adventure. Dunn, Robert, illus. 2015. (Santa's Sleigh Is on Its Way Ser.). (ENG.). 32p. (J). (gr. k-2). 12.99 *(978-1-4926-2746-3(1),* Hometown World) Sourcebooks, Inc.

—Santa's Sleigh Is on Its Way to Indiana: A Christmas Adventure. Dunn, Robert, illus. 2015. (Santa's Sleigh Is on Its Way Ser.). (ENG.). 32p. (J). (gr. k-2). 12.99 *(978-1-4926-2753-1(4),* Hometown World) Sourcebooks, Inc.

—Santa's Sleigh Is on Its Way to Iowa: A Christmas Adventure. Dunn, Robert, illus. 2015. (Santa's Sleigh Is on Its Way Ser.). (ENG.). 32p. (J). (gr. k-2). 12.99 *(978-1-4926-2749-4(6),* Hometown World) Sourcebooks, Inc.

—Santa's Sleigh Is on Its Way to Kansas: A Christmas Adventure. Dunn, Robert, illus. 2016. (Santa's Sleigh Is on Its Way Ser.). (ENG.). 32p. (J). (gr. k-2). 12.99 *(978-1-4926-4330-2(0),* 9781492643302, Hometown World) Sourcebooks, Inc.

—Santa's Sleigh Is on Its Way to Kansas City: A Christmas Adventure. Dunn, Robert, illus. 2016. (Santa's Sleigh Is on Its Way Ser.). (ENG.). 32p. (J). (gr. k-2). 12.99 *(978-1-4926-4331-9(9),* 9781492643319, Hometown World) Sourcebooks, Inc.

—Santa's Sleigh Is on Its Way to Kentucky: A Christmas Adventure. Dunn, Robert, illus. 2015. (Santa's Sleigh Is on Its Way Ser.). (ENG.). 32p. (J). (gr. k-2). 12.99 *(978-1-4926-2761-6(5),* Hometown World) Sourcebooks, Inc.

—Santa's Sleigh Is on Its Way to Las Vegas: A Christmas Adventure. Dunn, Robert, illus. 2016. (Santa's Sleigh Is on Its Way Ser.). (ENG.). 32p. (J). (gr. k-2). 12.99 *(978-1-4926-4332-6(7),* 9781492643326, Hometown World) Sourcebooks, Inc.

—Santa's Sleigh Is on Its Way to Los Angeles: A Christmas Adventure. Dunn, Robert, illus. 2016. (Santa's Sleigh Is on Its Way Ser.). (ENG.). 32p. (J). (gr. k-2). 12.99 *(978-1-4926-4333-3(5),* 9781492643333, Hometown World) Sourcebooks, Inc.

—Santa's Sleigh Is on Its Way to Louisiana: A Christmas Adventure. Dunn, Robert, illus. 2015. (Santa's Sleigh Is on Its Way Ser.). (ENG.). 32p. (J). (gr. k-2). 12.99 *(978-1-4926-2762-3(3),* Hometown World) Sourcebooks, Inc.

—Santa's Sleigh Is on Its Way to Maine: A Christmas Adventure. Dunn, Robert, illus. 2016. (Santa's Sleigh Is on Its Way Ser.). (ENG.). 32p. (J). (gr. k-2). 12.99 *(978-1-4926-4334-0(3),* 9781492643340, Hometown World) Sourcebooks, Inc.

—Santa's Sleigh Is on Its Way to Maryland: A Christmas Adventure. Dunn, Robert, illus. 2016. (Santa's Sleigh Is on Its Way Ser.). (ENG.). 32p. (J). (gr. k-2). 12.99 *(978-1-4926-4335-7(1),* 9781492643357, Hometown World) Sourcebooks, Inc.

—Santa's Sleigh Is on Its Way to Massachusetts: A Christmas Adventure. Dunn, Robert, illus. 2016. (Santa's Sleigh Is on Its Way Ser.). (ENG.). 32p. (J). (gr. k-2). 12.99 *(978-1-4926-4336-4(X),* 9781492643364, Hometown World) Sourcebooks, Inc.

—Santa's Sleigh Is on Its Way to Michigan: A Christmas Adventure. Dunn, Robert, illus. 2015. (Santa's Sleigh Is on Its Way Ser.). (ENG.). 32p. (J). (gr. k-2). 12.99 *(978-1-4926-2741-8(0),* Hometown World) Sourcebooks, Inc.

—Santa's Sleigh Is on Its Way to Minnesota: A Christmas Adventure. Dunn, Robert, illus. 2015. (Santa's Sleigh Is on Its Way Ser.). (ENG.). 32p. (J). (gr. k-2). 12.99 *(978-1-4926-2748-7(8),* Hometown World) Sourcebooks, Inc.

—Santa's Sleigh Is on Its Way to Mississippi: A Christmas Adventure. Dunn, Robert, illus. 2016. (Santa's Sleigh Is on Its Way Ser.). (ENG.). 32p. (J). (gr. k-2). 12.99 *(978-1-4926-4337-1(8),* 9781492643371, Hometown World) Sourcebooks, Inc.

—Santa's Sleigh Is on Its Way to Missouri: A Christmas Adventure. Dunn, Robert, illus. 2015. (Santa's Sleigh Is on Its Way Ser.). (ENG.). 32p. (J). (gr. k-2). 12.99 *(978-1-4926-2759-3(3),* Hometown World) Sourcebooks, Inc.

—Santa's Sleigh Is on Its Way to Montana: A Christmas Adventure. Dunn, Robert, illus. 2016. (Santa's Sleigh Is on Its Way Ser.). (ENG.). 32p. (J). (gr. k-2). 12.99 *(978-1-4926-4338-8(6),* 9781492643388, Hometown World) Sourcebooks, Inc.

—Santa'S Sleigh Is on Its Way to My House: A Christmas Adventure. Dunn, Robert, illus. 2015. (Santa's Sleigh Is on Its Way Ser.). 32p. (J). (gr. k-2). 12.99 *(978-1-4926-2740-1(2),* Hometown World) Sourcebooks, Inc.

—Santa's Sleigh Is on Its Way to Nevada: A Christmas Adventure. Dunn, Robert, illus. 2016. (Santa's Sleigh Is on Its Way Ser.). (ENG.). 32p. (J). (gr. k-2). 12.99 *(978-1-4926-4340-1(8),* 9781492643401, Hometown World) Sourcebooks, Inc.

—Santa's Sleigh Is on Its Way to New England: A Christmas Adventure. Dunn, Robert, illus. 2016. (Santa's Sleigh Is on Its Way Ser.). (ENG.). 32p. (J). (gr. k-2). 12.99 *(978-1-4926-4341-8(6),* 9781492643418, Hometown World) Sourcebooks, Inc.

—Santa's Sleigh Is on Its Way to New Hampshire: A Christmas Adventure. Dunn, Robert, illus. 2016. (Santa's Sleigh Is on Its Way Ser.). (ENG.). 32p. (J). (gr. k-2). 12.99 *(978-1-4926-4342-5(4),* 9781492643425, Hometown World) Sourcebooks, Inc.

—Santa's Sleigh Is on Its Way to New Jersey: A Christmas Adventure. Dunn, Robert, illus. 2015. (Santa's Sleigh Is on Its Way Ser.). (ENG.). 32p. (J). (gr. k-2). 12.99 *(978-1-4926-2758-6(5),* Hometown World) Sourcebooks, Inc.

—Santa's Sleigh Is on Its Way to New Mexico: A Christmas Adventure. Dunn, Robert, illus. 2016. (Santa's Sleigh Is on Its Way Ser.). (ENG.). 32p. (J). (gr. k-2). 12.99 *(978-1-4926-4343-2(2),* 9781492643432, Hometown World) Sourcebooks, Inc.

—Santa's Sleigh Is on Its Way to New York: A Christmas Adventure. Dunn, Robert, illus. 2015. (Santa's Sleigh Is on Its Way Ser.). (ENG.). 32p. (J). (gr. k-2). 12.99 *(978-1-4926-2751-7(8),* Hometown World) Sourcebooks, Inc.

—Santa's Sleigh Is on Its Way to New York City: A Christmas Adventure. Dunn, Robert, illus. 2016. (Santa's Sleigh Is on Its Way Ser.). (ENG.). 32p. (J). (gr. k-2). 12.99 *(978-1-4926-4344-9(0),* 9781492643449, Hometown World) Sourcebooks, Inc.

—Santa's Sleigh Is on It's Way to Newfoundland: A Christmas Adventure. Dunn, Robert, illus. 2016. (Santa's Sleigh Is on Its Way Ser.). (ENG.). 32p. (J). (gr. k-2). 12.99 *(978-1-4926-4505-4(2),* 9781492645054, Hometown World) Sourcebooks, Inc.

—Santa's Sleigh Is on Its Way to North Carolina: A Christmas Adventure. Dunn, Robert, illus. 2015. (Santa's Sleigh Is on Its Way Ser.). (ENG.). 32p. (J). (gr. k-2). 12.99 *(978-1-4926-2750-0(X),* Hometown World) Sourcebooks, Inc.

—Santa's Sleigh Is on Its Way to North Dakota: A Christmas Adventure. Dunn, Robert, illus. 2016. (Santa's Sleigh Is on Its Way Ser.). (ENG.). 32p. (J). (gr. k-2). 12.99 *(978-1-4926-4345-6(9),* 9781492643456, Hometown World) Sourcebooks, Inc.

—Santa's Sleigh Is on It's Way to Nova Scotia: A Christmas Adventure. Dunn, Robert, illus. 2016. (Santa's Sleigh Is on Its Way Ser.). (ENG.). 32p. (J). (gr. k-2). 12.99 *(978-1-4926-4508-5(7),* 9781492645085, Hometown World) Sourcebooks, Inc.

—Santa's Sleigh Is on Its Way to Ohio: A Christmas Adventure. Dunn, Robert, illus. 2015. (Santa's Sleigh Is on Its Way Ser.). (ENG.). 32p. (J). (gr. k-2). 12.99 *(978-1-4926-2742-5(9),* Hometown World) Sourcebooks, Inc.

—Santa's Sleigh Is on Its Way to Oklahoma: A Christmas Adventure. Dunn, Robert, illus. 2016. (Santa's Sleigh Is on Its Way Ser.). (ENG.). 32p. (J). (gr. k-2). 12.99 *(978-1-4926-4346-3(7),* 9781492643463, Hometown World) Sourcebooks, Inc.

—Santa's Sleigh Is on Its Way to Pennsylvania: A Christmas Adventure. Dunn, Robert, illus. 2015. (Santa's Sleigh Is on Its Way Ser.). (ENG.). 32p. (J). (gr. k-2). 12.99 *(978-1-4926-2745-6(3),* Hometown World) Sourcebooks, Inc.

—Santa's Sleigh Is on Its Way to Pittsburgh: A Christmas Adventure. Dunn, Robert, illus. 2016. (Santa's Sleigh Is on Its Way Ser.). (ENG.). 32p. (J). (gr. k-2). 12.99 *(978-1-4926-4351-7(3),* 9781492643517, Hometown World) Sourcebooks, Inc.

—Santa's Sleigh Is on Its Way to Portland: A Christmas Adventure. Dunn, Robert, illus. 2016. (Santa's Sleigh Is on Its Way Ser.). (ENG.). 32p. (J). (gr. k-2). 12.99 *(978-1-4926-4352-4(1),* 9781492643524, Hometown World) Sourcebooks, Inc.

—Santa's Sleigh Is on Its Way to Rhode Island: A Christmas Adventure. Dunn, Robert, illus. 2016. (Santa's Sleigh Is on Its Way Ser.). (ENG.). 32p. (J). (gr. k-2). 12.99 *(978-1-4926-4353-1(X),* 9781492643531, Hometown World) Sourcebooks, Inc.

—Santa's Sleigh Is on Its Way to South Carolina: A Christmas Adventure. Dunn, Robert, illus. 2015. (Santa's Sleigh Is on Its Way Ser.). (ENG.). 32p. (J). (gr. k-2). 12.99 *(978-1-4926-2757-9(7),* Hometown World) Sourcebooks, Inc.

—Santa's Sleigh Is on Its Way to South Dakota: A Christmas Adventure. Dunn, Robert, illus. 2016. (Santa's Sleigh Is on Its Way Ser.). (ENG.). 32p. (J). (gr. k-2). 12.99 *(978-1-4926-4355-5(6),* 9781492643555, Hometown World) Sourcebooks, Inc.

—Santa's Sleigh Is on Its Way to Tampa Bay: A Christmas Adventure. Dunn, Robert, illus. 2016. (Santa's Sleigh Is on Its Way Ser.). (ENG.). 32p. (J). (gr. k-2). 12.99 *(978-1-4926-4357-9(2),* 9781492643579, Hometown World) Sourcebooks, Inc.

—Santa's Sleigh Is on Its Way to Tennessee: A Christmas Adventure. Dunn, Robert, illus. 2015. (Santa's Sleigh Is on Its Way Ser.). (ENG.). 32p. (J). (gr. k-2). 12.99 *(978-1-4926-2752-4(6),* Hometown World) Sourcebooks, Inc.

—Santa's Sleigh Is on Its Way to Texas: A Christmas Adventure. Dunn, Robert, illus. 2015. (Santa's Sleigh Is on Its Way Ser.). (ENG.). 32p. (J). (gr. k-2). 12.99 *(978-1-4926-2739-5(9),* Hometown World) Sourcebooks, Inc.

—Santa's Sleigh Is on Its Way to Tulsa: A Christmas Adventure. Dunn, Robert, illus. 2016. (Santa's Sleigh Is on Its Way Ser.). (ENG.). 32p. (J). (gr. k-2). 12.99 *(978-1-4926-4359-3(9),* 9781492643593, Hometown World) Sourcebooks, Inc.

—Santa's Sleigh Is on Its Way to Utah: A Christmas Adventure. Dunn, Robert, illus. 2016. (Santa's Sleigh Is on Its Way Ser.). (ENG.). 32p. (J). (gr. k-2). 12.99 *(978-1-4926-4360-9(2),* 9781492643609, Hometown World) Sourcebooks, Inc.

—Santa's Sleigh Is on Its Way to Virginia: A Christmas Adventure. Dunn, Robert, illus. 2015. (Santa's Sleigh Is on Its Way Ser.). (ENG.). 32p. (J). (gr. k-2). 12.99 *(978-1-4926-2754-8(2),* Hometown World) Sourcebooks, Inc.

—Santa's Sleigh Is on Its Way to Washington: A Christmas Adventure. Dunn, Robert, illus. 2015. (Santa's Sleigh Is on Its Way Ser.). (ENG.). 32p. (J). (gr. k-2). 12.99 *(978-1-4926-2760-9(7),* Hometown World) Sourcebooks, Inc.

—Santa's Sleigh Is on Its Way to Wisconsin: A Christmas Adventure. Dunn, Robert, illus. 2015. (Santa's Sleigh Is on Its Way Ser.). (ENG.). 32p. (J). (gr. k-2). 12.99 *(978-1-4926-2755-5(0),* Hometown World) Sourcebooks, Inc.

James G. Normand. Santa's Secret Trick. 2009. (Illus.). 52p. pap. 20.49 *(978-1-4389-5788-3(2))* AuthorHouse.

James, Helen Foster. Santa's Christmas Train. Bolton, Bill, illus. 2019. (ENG.). 26p. (J). (gr. -1-1). bds. 7.99 *(978-1-5460-1434-8(9),* Worthy Kids/Ideals) Worthy Publishing.

Jarvis, Cathy. Red Beard Santa's Biker Buddy. 2013. 36p. pap. 15.49 *(978-1-4669-9587-1(4))* Trafford Publishing.

Jeffers, Susan. The Twelve Days of Christmas: A Christmas Holiday Book for Kids. Jeffers, Susan, illus. 2013. (ENG., Illus.). 40p. (J). (gr. -1-3). 17.99 *(978-0-06-206615-2(3),* HarperCollins) HarperCollins Pubs.

Jeffers, Susan, illus. The Twelve Days of Christmas. 2013. (J). *(978-0-06-206616-9(1))* Harper & Row Ltd.

Johansen, Tesia. The Christmas Secret. Johnson, Gary & Johansen, Tesia, illus. 2011. 28p. pap. 24.95 *(978-1-4626-3242-8(4))* America Star Bks.

Johnston, Patches. Mark's Mixed-up Months. 2004. 33p. pap. 24.95 *(978-1-4137-2432-5(9))* PublishAmerica, Inc.

Jones, Carl. Rudy the Rangifer & Why Her Nose Turned Orange. 2007. 64p. pap. 14.99 *(978-0-9748266-3-9(4))* Grampa Jones's Publishing Co.

Jones, Ernest, illus. The Great Mix Up. 2005. (ENG.). 42p. (J). 17.99 *(978-0-9772282-0-1(7))* B. T. Brooks.

Jones, Sandy. Anya's Gift: A Tale of Two Christmases, 1 vol. Yourell, Pam, illus. 2009. 48p. pap. 24.95 *(978-1-61546-129-5(9))* America Star Bks.

Jordan, L. W. Santa Heads South: Casey's Christmas Surprise. Lasson, Matt, illus. 2008. 40p. per. 24.95 *(978-1-60441-374-8(3))* America Star Bks.

Joyce, William & Geringer, Laura. Nicholas St. North & the Battle of the Nightmare King. Joyce, William, illus. 2018. (Guardians Ser.: 1). (ENG., Illus.). 256p. (J). (gr. 2-6). pap. 8.99 *(978-1-4424-3049-5(4),* Atheneum Bks. for Young Readers) Simon & Schuster Children's Publishing.

—Nicholas St. North & the Battle of the Nightmare King, Bk. 1. Joyce, William, illus. 2011. (Guardians Ser.: 1). (ENG., Illus.). 240p. (J). (gr. 2-6). 18.99 *(978-1-4424-3048-8(6),* Atheneum Bks. for Young Readers) Simon & Schuster Children's Publishing.

Karr, Lily. My Santa Claus. Johnson, Jay, illus. 2012. (ENG.). 12p. (J). (gr. -1 — 1). bds. 4.99 *(978-0-545-43649-6(4))* Scholastic, Inc.

Keane, Michael. The Night Santa Got Lost: How NORAD Saved Christmas. Garland, Michael, illus. 2015. (ENG.). 28p. (J). (gr. -1). 16.99 *(978-1-62157-398-2(2),* Regnery Kids) Regnery Publishing.

Kessler, Leonard. That's Not Santa! Kessler, Leonard P., illus. 2018. (ENG.). 32p. (J). (gr. -1-2). pap. 8.99 *(978-1-948959-01-8(1))* Purple Hse. Pr.

—That's Not Santa! (Hello Reader! Ser.). (FRE., Illus.). (J). pap. 5.99 *(978-0-590-24360-5(8))* Scholastic, Inc.

Kibblesmith, Daniel & Quach, A. P. Santa's Husband. 2017. (ENG., Illus.). 32p. 16.99 *(978-0-06-274874-4(2),* Harper) HarperCollins Pubs.

Kilgore, Lee. The Riddle of the Rustled Reindeer: A Christmas Mystery. 2009. 50p. pap. 16.95 *(978-1-61546-863-8(3))* America Star Bks.

Klein, Abby. Ready, Freddy #18: the Perfect Present. McKinley, John, illus. 2009. (Ready, Freddy! Ser.: 18). (ENG.). 96p. (J). (gr. -1-3). 5.99 *(978-0-545-13043-1(3),* Scholastic Paperbacks) Scholastic, Inc.

—Secret Santa Surprise! McKinley, John, illus. 2015. 86p. (J). *(978-0-545-86357-5(0))* Scholastic, Inc.

Klimo, Kate. Dragon Keepers #6: the Dragon at the North Pole. Shroades, John, illus. 2014. (Dragon Keepers Ser.: 6). 176p. (J). (gr. 3-7). 6.99 *(978-0-375-87117-7(9),* Yearling) Random Hse. Children's Bks.

Koontz, Dean. Robot Santa: The Further Adventures of Santa's Twin. Parks, Phil, illus. 2004. (Santa's Twin Ser.: Bk. 2). 72p. (J). 20.89 *(978-0-06-050944-6(9))* HarperCollins Pubs.

—Santa's Twin. Parks, Phil, illus. 2004. (Santa's Twin Ser.: Bk. 1). (ENG.). 64p. pap. 12.95 *(978-0-06-057223-5(X),* William Morrow Paperbacks) HarperCollins Pubs.

Kowitt, Holly & Manis, David. The Elves' Night Before Christmas. Watson, Richard, illus. 2016. (J). pap. *(978-1-338-08903-5(X))* Scholastic, Inc.

Kremer, Kevin. Santa's Our Substitute Teacher. Ely, Dave, illus. 2006. 150p. (gr. 4-7). per. 5.99 *(978-0-9663335-4-1(3),* 703-001) Snow In Sarasota Publishing.

Kulka, Joe. The Christmas Coal Man. Kulka, Joe, illus. 2015. (ENG., Illus.). 32p. (J). (gr. k-3). lib. bdg. 17.99 *(978-1-4677-1607-9(3),* f916800f-8162-44ef-9c4f-8f8d15722894); E-Book 27.99 *(978-1-4677-8808-3(2))* Lerner Publishing Group. (Carolrhoda Bks.).

Kurtz, John. Claus Kids Christmas Coloring Book. 2011. (Dover Holiday Coloring Book Ser.). (ENG.). 32p. (J). (gr. k-5). pap. 3.99 *(978-0-486-48292-7(8))* Dover Pubns., Inc.

—Claus Kids Stickers. 2011. (Dover Little Activity Books Stickers Ser.). (ENG.). 4p. (J). (gr. k-3). 1.50 *(978-0-486-48294-1(4),* 482944) Dover Pubns., Inc.

La Porte, Mary Ellen. The Almost Christmas Story. 2011. 44p. pap. 18.99 *(978-1-4520-9946-0(4))* AuthorHouse.

Lansley, Oliver. Holly & Ivan's Christmas Adventure. 2011. (Oberon Plays for Young People Ser.). (ENG., Illus.). 64p. (J). (gr. k-5). pap. *(978-1-84943-136-1(1),* 513368) Oberon Bks., Ltd.

L.A.S., Alex. Magnificent Sir Johnny & Santa Claus. 2011. 36p. pap. 24.95 *(978-1-4626-3401-9(X))* America Star Bks.

Lee, Chris. Becoming a Sant: A Guidebook for Parents & Santa's Helpers. 2008. 48p. pap. 16.95 *(978-1-60563-449-4(2))* America Star Bks.

Lee, Stan. Stan Lee's Superhero Christmas. Jessell, Tim, illus. 2nd ed. 2016. (ENG.). 32p. (gr. k-2). pap. 27.95 *(978-1-59687-526-5(7),* ipicturebooks) ibooks, Inc.

—Superhero Christmas. Jessell, Tim, illus. 2004. 32p. (J). (gr. -1-2). 16.89 *(978-0-06-056560-2(8))* HarperCollins Pubs.

Lepage, Michaele. A Year at Santa's Workshop. 2009. 32p. pap. 14.55 *(978-1-4343-7989-4(2))* AuthorHouse.

LePage, Michaele L. & Lovass-Nagy, Nicole. A Year at the North Pole. 2009. 31p. 16.95 *(978-0-557-06430-4(9))* Lulu Pr., Inc.

Levine, Whitney Joy. The Tiniest Reindeer. 2008. 24p. pap. 12.99 *(978-1-4389-3102-9(6))* AuthorHouse.

Lewis, Anne Margaret. The Runaway Santa: A Christmas Adventure Story. Zenz, Aaron, illus. 2015. (ENG.). 40p. (J).

S

(gr. -1-k). 15.99 (978-1-63450-589-5(1), Sky Pony Pr.) Skyhorse Publishing Co., Inc.

Lewis, Michael. The Great Pirate Christmas Battle, 1 vol. Jaskiel, Stan, illus. 2014. (ENG.). 32p. (J). (gr. k-3). 16.99 (978-1-4556-1934-4(5), Pelican Publishing) Arcadia Publishing.

Lewis, Norma. Dear Santa, I Know It Looks Bad, but It Wasn't My Fault. Beckman, Olivia, illus. 2018. (ENG.). 40p. (J). 16.99 (978-1-4413-2421-4(6), af65c62f-41d5-4fa2-adec-cc94bc70dba9) Peter Pauper Pr. Inc.

Lincoln, Dallas Ford. The Sawmill Sant. 2011. 36p. pap. 16.95 (978-1-4626-4335-6(3)) America Star Bks.

Lindstrom, Ken. Grandpa, Is There Really a Santa Claus? 2008. 20p. pap. 10.99 (978-1-4389-2127-3(6)) AuthorHouse.

Lippman, Peter. Santa's Workshop. (ENG.). (J). bds. 79.60 (978-0-7611-0489-6(5), 20489) Workman Publishing Co., Inc.

Little, Paul D. The Christmas Chips. 2009. 44p. pap. 15.50 (978-1-60860-578-1(7), Eloquent Bks.) Strategic Book Publishing & Rights Agency (SBPRA).

Litwin, Eric & Dean, Kimberly. Pete the Cat Saves Christmas. Dean, James, illus. 2012. (Pete the Cat Ser.). (ENG.). 40p. (J). (gr. -1-3). lib. bdg. 18.89 (978-0-06-211063-3(2), HarperCollins) HarperCollins Pubs.

—Pete the Cat Saves Christmas: A Christmas Holiday Book for Kids. Dean, James, illus. 2019. (Pete the Cat Ser.). (ENG.). 40p. (J). (gr. -1-3). 10.99 (978-0-06-294516-7(5), HarperCollins) HarperCollins Pubs.

—Pete the Cat Saves Christmas: Includes Sticker Sheet! a Christmas Holiday Book for Kids. Dean, James, illus. 2014. (Pete the Cat Ser.). (ENG.). 40p. (J). (gr. -1-3). 18.99 (978-0-06-211062-6(4), HarperCollins) HarperCollins Pubs.

Lizana, Robert V. Two Weeks Before Christmas. 2012. 24p. pap. 17.99 (978-1-4772-7164-3(3)) AuthorHouse.

Lombardi, Elizabeth L. Jonathan's Journey, 1 vol. 2012. 32p. (J). (978-1-62148-014-3(3)) SteinerBooks, Inc.

Luffman, Alice, et al. Santa Street. Pigott, Louise, illus. 2018. (J). (978-0-312-52889-8(2)) St. Martin's Pr.

Lutz, Nancie Anne. Patsy & Freckles Make Christmas Cookies. Lutz, Nancie Anne, illus. 2005. (Illus.). 25p. (J). (978-0-9760064-1-1(3)) Dollworks.

MacGuire, Maxine. Maddie & the Naughty Elf: Santa Learns a Lesson, 1 vol. 2010. 36p. 24.95 (978-1-4489-8250-9(2)) PublishAmerica, Inc.

MacLennan, David. Santa's Stormy Christmas Eve. Parkinson, Cheryl, tr. Parkinson, Cheryl, illus. 2004. 32p. 7.95 (978-0-9731960-0-9(9)) Full Satchel Pr. CAN. Dist: Gatewood Pr.

Madaras, Diana. Kitty Humbug's Christmas Tail. Madaras, Diana & Nielsen, Ric, illus. 2009. 24p. 17.99 (978-1-892344-56-4(4)) Palomino Publishing.

Mader, Roger. Stowaway in a Sleigh: A Christmas Holiday Book for Kids. Mader, Roger, illus. 2016. (ENG., Illus.). 32p. (J). (gr. -1-3). 17.99 (978-0-544-48174-9(7), 1602693, Clarion Bks.) HarperCollins Pubs.

Major, Kevin. The House of Wooden Santas, 1 vol. Pratt, Ned, photos by. gif. ed. 2004. (ENG., Illus.). 96p. (J). 34.95 (978-0-88995-249-2(3)) Red Deer Pr. CAN. Dist: Fitzhenry & Whiteside, Ltd.

A Manatee Christmas. 2007. (Illus.). 32p. (J). lib. bdg. 15.99 (978-0-9771059-7-7(0)) Thomas Expressions, LLC.

Marsh, Carole. The Story of Santa Claus. 2003. 12p. (J). (gr. k-4). pap. 2.95 (978-0-635-02151-9(X)) Gallopade International.

Martini, T. J. Christmas Lost & Found. Kiejna, Magdalenea, illus. 2022. 80p. (J). 24.95 (978-0-9705018-7-5(0)) Rivertree Media.

Matsuura, Richard & Matsuura, Ruth. Gift from Santa. Chao, Linus, illus. (J). 7.95 (978-1-887916-06-6(7)) Orchid Isle Publishing Co.

McArdle, Donald. Santa's Newest Friend. 2007. 25p. (J). 21.50 (978-0-615-14212-8(5)) McArdle, Donald.

McDade Jr, Bert M. Why Santa Claus Comes at Christmas. Swope, Brenda, illus. 2011. 32p. pap. 24.95 (978-1-4560-0921-2(4)) America Star Bks.

McFarlane, Sheryl. Island Santa, 1 vol. Lott, Sheena, illus. 2012. (ENG.). 32p. (J). (gr. k). 19.95 (978-0-9880536-0-1(8)) Queen Alexandra Foundation for Children CAN. Dist: Orca Bk. Pubs. USA.

McGuirk, Leslie. Ho, Ho, Ho, Tucker!: Candlewick Storybook Animations. McGuirk, Leslie, illus. 2010. (Candlewick Storybook Animations Ser.). (ENG., Illus.). 32p. (J). (-k). 8.99 (978-0-7636-5043-8(9)) Candlewick Pr.

McLean, Michael & McLean, Scott. Fairy Tale Christmas. 2014. (ENG., Illus.). 176p. (J). (gr. 3-9). 15.99 (978-1-60907-930-7(2), 5124315, Shadow Mountain) Shadow Mountain Publishing.

McMahan, Gregg. Christmas Honey. 2012. (ENG.). pap. 10.00 (978-1-4675-5319-3(0)) Independent Pub.

Metzger, Steve. Waiting for Santa. Edgson, Alison, illus. 2015. (J). (978-0-545-89992-5(3)) Scholastic, Inc.

Milgrim, David. See Santa Nap: Ready-To-Read Pre-Level 1. Milgrim, David, illus. 2016. (Adventures of Otto Ser.). (ENG., Illus.). 32p. (J). (gr. -1-k). pap. 4.99 (978-1-4814-6787-2(5), Simon Spotlight) Simon Spotlight.

Mitchell, Laine. We're Going on a Santa Hunt. Shea, Louis, illus. 2017. (J). (978-1-338-25514-0(2)) Scholastic, Inc.

Modugno, Maria. Santa Claus & the Three Bears: A Christmas Holiday Book for Kids. Dyer, Jane & Dyer, Brooke, illus. 2013. (ENG.). 40p. (J). (gr. -1-3). 18.99 (978-0-06-170023-1(1), HarperCollins) HarperCollins Pubs.

Moore, Brian L. The Story Behind Santa Sacks. Mulligan, Todd, illus. 2004. 32p. (978-0-9732651-0-1(8)) Hills-n-Hollows Publishing.

Moore, Clement C. Grumpy Santa. Spiridellis, Gregg & Spiridellis, Evan, illus. 2003. (ENG.). (J). (978-0-439-53039-2(3), Orchard Bks.) Scholastic, Inc.

—My First Night Before Christmas. Newsom, Tom, illus. 2008. (ENG.). 12p. (J). 9.95 (978-1-58117-808-1(5), Intervisual/Piggy Toes) Bendon, Inc.

—The Night Before Christmas. Newsom, Tom, illus. 2007. (ENG.). 18p. (J). (gr. -1-3). 19.95 (978-1-4037-2947-7(6), Intervisual/Piggy Toes) Bendon, Inc.

Moore, Clement Clarke & Goodrich, Carter. A Creature Was Stirring. Goodrich, Carter, illus. 2006. (ENG., Illus.). 40p. (J). (gr. -1-3). 18.99 (978-0-689-86399-8(3), Simon & Schuster Bks. For Young Readers) Simon & Schuster Bks. For Young Readers.

Moore, Joseph. Santa's World: North Pole Series, Volume 1. 2006. (ENG., Illus.). 33p. (J). pap. 12.50 (978-0-9787129-0-7(0)) North Pole Pr.

Morozumi, Atsuko. The Elves' First Christmas. 2009. (Illus.). 32p. (J). (gr. -1-1). 16.95 (978-1-935021-61-2(3)) Price, Mathew Ltd.

Mundt, A. S. The Letter. 2011. 36p. pap. 14.49 (978-1-4634-3936-1(9)) AuthorHouse.

Murphy, T. M. Saving Santa's Seals. Taylor, Adam, illus. 2009. (LeapKids Ser.). (ENG.). 170p. (J). (gr. 1-5). pap. 10.95 (978-0-9815148-8-8(X)) Leapfrog Pr.

Nesbo, Jo. Silent (but Deadly) Night. Lowery, Mike, illus. 2017. (Doctor Proctor's Fart Powder Ser.). (ENG.). 368p. (J). (gr. 3-7). 17.99 (978-1-5344-0999-6(8), Aladdin) Simon & Schuster Children's Publishing.

—Silent (but Deadly) Night. Lowery, Mike, illus. 2018. (Doctor Proctor's Fart Powder Ser.). (ENG.). 368p. (J). (gr. 3-7). pap. 8.99 (978-1-5344-1000-8(7), Simon & Schuster/Paula Wiseman Bks.) Simon & Schuster/Paula Wiseman Bks.

Nguyen, Anthony. Santa with His Reindeer. 2004. pap. 8.00 (978-0-8059-6261-1(1)) Dorrance Publishing Co., Inc.

Nivens, Karen. Benjamin P. Blizzard: Welcome to Christmastown. Grisham, Jason, illus. 2007. 48p. (J). per. (978-0-9798154-1-6(X)) Living Waters Publishing Co.

Norman, Travis D. Christmas Island. Baker, David, illus. 2011. 28p. pap. 24.95 (978-1-4560-9800-1(4)) America Star Bks.

The North Pole Is Sinking! 2005. (J). 9.99 (978-0-9773674-0-5(1)) Blue State Pr.

Nyaradi, J. A. Catching Santa. 2006. 140p. pap. 11.95 (978-0-7414-3462-3(8)) Infinity Publishing.

O., Lila. Lulabelle's Jewels: The Christmas Wish of Mrs. Claus. 2008. 20p. pap. 12.49 (978-1-4389-3189-0(1)) AuthorHouse.

O, Lila & O., Lila. Lula Belle's Jewels: The Christmas Wish of Mrs. Claus. 2011. 28p. pap. 17.50 (978-1-4634-3326-0(3)) AuthorHouse.

O'Dea, Kendra J. Polar Bear Pond. 2007. (Illus.). 62p. (J). per. 11.95 (978-0-9799162-0-5(8)) Shortbread Hill Bk. Co.

O'Donnell, Kevin & Gon, Zang Sung. Stone Age Santa. Kim, Boo Young et al, illus. 2007. (ENG.). 128p. (J). (gr. 4-7). 11.95 (978-1-58818-153-4(7)) Hill Street Pr., LLC.

Pallotta, Jerry. Dinosaur Christmas. McWilliam, Howard, illus. 2013. (ENG.). 32p. (J). (gr. k-2). 16.99 (978-0-545-43360-0(6), Cartwheel Bks.) Scholastic, Inc.

—Santa Pups. Terry, Will, illus. 2016. (ENG.). 32p. (J). (gr. -1-k). 6.99 (978-0-545-48479-4(0)) Scholastic, Inc.

—Santa Pups. Terry, Will, illus. 2016. (ENG.). 32p. (J). (gr. -1-k). 17.20 (978-0-606-39130-5(4)) Turtleback.

Palmer, Slim. Albert & the Christmas Elf. 2005. (ENG.). 88p. pap. 11.55 (978-1-4116-4503-5(0)) Lulu Pr., Inc.

Parsley, Elise. If You Ever Want to Bring a Pirate to Meet Santa, Don't! 2018. (Magnolia Says DON'T! Ser.: 4). (ENG., Illus.). 40p. (J). (gr. -1-3). 17.99 (978-0-316-46677-6(8)) Little, Brown Bks. for Young Readers.

Partridge, Helen L. Blinky: The Bear Who Wouldn't Hibernate. 2008. 32p. per. 24.95 (978-1-4241-9261-8(7)) America Star Bks.

Peet, Amanda & Troyer, Andrea. Dear Santa, Love, Rachel Rosenstein. Davenier, Christine, illus. 2015. 40p. (J). (gr. -1-2). 17.99 (978-0-553-51061-4(4), Doubleday Bks. for Young Readers) Random Hse. Children's Bks.

Perry, Mark. 'Post' Mark — Santa's Misfit Postman. 2013. (ENG., Illus.). 32p. (J). 15.95 (978-0-9838947-0-4(1), 1359686) Delor Francis Pr.

Perry, Rex, illus. 'Twas the Night Before Christmas. 2004. 24p. (J). lib. bdg. 8.00 (978-1-4242-0641-4(3)) Fitzgerald Bks.

Pingk, Rubin. Samurai Santa: A Very Ninja Christmas. Pingk, Rubin, illus. 2015. (Samurai Holiday Ser.). (ENG., Illus.). 40p. (J). (gr. -1-3). 17.99 (978-1-4814-3057-9(2), Simon & Schuster Bks. For Young Readers) Simon & Schuster Bks. For Young Readers.

Ploog, Michael G. L. Frank Baum's the Life & Adventures of Santa Claus. Ploog, Michael G., illus. 2003. (Illus.). 80p. (YA). (gr. 7-12). reprint ed. 25.00 (978-0-7567-6682-5(6)) DIANE Publishing Co.

Powell Zalewski, Amy. Maybe the Truth about Santa. Mugambi, Christina Nkirote, illus. 2005. 32p. (J). (gr. -1-3). 15.00 (978-0-9773608-1-9(4)) Shiny Red Ball Publishing.

Poydar, Nancy. Brave Santa. 2004. (ENG., Illus.). 32p. (J). (gr. k-3). tchr. ed. 16.95 (978-0-8234-1821-3(9)) Holiday Hse., Inc.

Priddy, Roger. Funny Faces Santa Claus: With Lights & Sound. 2012. (Funny Faces Ser.). (ENG., Illus.). 10p. (J). (gr. -1-1). bds. 8.99 (978-0-312-51558-4(8), 900097399) St. Martin's Pr.

Primavera, Elise. Auntie Claus & the Key to Christmas: A Christmas Holiday Book for Kids. Primavera, Elise, illus. 2011. (ENG., Illus.). 40p. (J). (gr. -1-3). pap. 7.99 (978-0-547-57679-4(X), 1458441, Clarion Bks.) HarperCollins Pubs.

—Auntie Claus Deluxe Edition: A Christmas Holiday Book for Kids. Primavera, Elise, illus. 2015. (ENG., Illus.). 40p. (J). (gr. -1-3). 18.99 (978-0-544-53672-6(2), 1608615, Clarion Bks.) HarperCollins Pubs.

Provencio, Marta. The Christmas Dragon. 2013. 24p. pap. 12.99 (978-1-4808-0379-4(0)) Archway Publishing.

Publications International Ltd. Staff, ed. Rudolph the Red-Nosed Reindeer(r): A Flashlight Adventure Sound Book. 2014. 14p. (J). (978-1-4508-9047-2(4), 1450890474) Publications International, Ltd.

Punter, Russell. Stories of Santa. Webb, Philip, illus. 2006. (Young Reading Series 1 Gift Bks.). 48p. (J). 8.99 (978-0-7945-1476-1(6), Usborne) EDC Publishing.

R., Charlie. The Christmas Mama Santa Delivered the Toys. 2012. 36p. 19.95 (978-1-4626-6824-3(0)) PublishAmerica, Inc.

Rae, Jaci. Collista's Search for the True Meaning of Christmas. 2007. (Illus.). 59p. per. 14.95 (978-0-9746229-1-0(5)) North Shore Records, Inc.

Ralph, Grampa. How Santa Knows. 2007. 56p. pap. 16.95 (978-1-4241-2284-4(8)) America Star Bks.

Rasmussen, Liz, illus. Too Fat to Fly. 2007. 32p. (J). 16.95 (978-0-9793517-0-9(7)) Silver Bells Publishing Hse.

Rawlinson, Julia. Fletcher & the Snowflake Christmas: A Christmas Holiday Book for Kids. Beeke, Tiphanie, illus. 2010. (ENG.). 32p. (J). (gr. -1-2). 16.99 (978-0-06-199033-5(7), Greenwillow Bks.) HarperCollins Pubs.

Reagan, Jean. How to Catch Santa. 2020. (How to Pic Bks). (ENG., Illus.). 25p. (J). (gr. k-1). 19.96 (978-1-64697-508-2(1)) Penworthy Co., LLC, The.

—How to Catch Santa. Wildish, Lee, illus. (How to Ser.). (ENG.). (J). 2018. 26p. (— 1). bds. 8.99 (978-0-525-57991-5(5)) 2015. 32p. (gr. -1-3). 17.99 (978-0-553-49839-4(8)) Random Hse. Children's Bks. (Knopf Bks. for Young Readers).

Reagan, Jean & Wildish, Lee. How to Catch Santa. 2020. (How to Ser.). (ENG.). 32p. (J). (gr. -1-3). pap. 7.99 (978-0-593-30190-6(0), Dragonfly Bks.) Random Hse. Children's Bks.

Reasoner, Charles. Inside Santa's Toy Shop. Reasoner, Charles, illus. 2007. (Story Book Ser.). (Illus.). 12p. (J). (gr. k-3). bds. (978-1-84666-151-8(X), Tide Mill Pr.) Top That! Publishing PLC.

Rees, Douglas. Jeannette Claus Saves Christmas. Latyk, Olivier, illus. 2010. (ENG.). 40p. (J). (gr. k-3). 16.99 (978-1-4169-2686-3(0), McElderry, Margaret K. Bks.) McElderry, Margaret K. Bks.

Reindeer. 2003. (Shaped Board Books Ser.). 14p. (J). (gr. -1-k). bds. 9.95 (978-0-7525-8850-6(8)) Parragon, Inc.

Reiss, Mike. Santa's Eleven Months Off, 1 vol. Montgomery, Michael G., illus. 2016. 32p. (J). (gr. -1-3). pap. 7.95 (978-1-56145-962-9(3)) Peachtree Publishing Co. Inc.

Reynolds, Carl. The Turkey Mountain Gang's... . Christmas Adventure! 2010. 44p. pap. 18.49 (978-1-4520-6514-4(4)) AuthorHouse.

Rinker, Sherri Duskey. The 12 Sleighs of Christmas: (Christmas Book for Kids, Toddler Book, Holiday Picture Book & Stocking Stuffer) Parker, Jake, illus. 2017. (ENG.). 40p. (J). (gr. -1-k). 16.99 (978-1-4521-4514-3(8)) Chronicle Bks. LLC.

Rissman, Angelica. Julius & the Lost Letter to Santa. 2003. (J). 7.99 (978-1-59384-019-8(5)) Parklane Publishing.

Ritchie, Joseph R. Where's Santa? Halverson, Lydia, illus. 2006. (ENG.). 14p. (J). (gr. -1-k). bds. 7.95 (978-0-8249-6673-7(2), Ideals Pubns.) Worthy Publishing.

(Robert Thompson), Pau Pau. Santa's Secret Helpers, 1 vol. 2009. 55p. pap. 16.95 (978-1-60836-859-4(9)) America Star Bks.

Robinson, George. Elmer the Elf & the Magical Jingle Bells, 1 vol. Foster, Janet, illus. 2008. (ENG.). 33p. 24.95 (978-1-60610-606-8(6)) America Star Bks.

Robinson, Michelle. Goodnight Santa: The Perfect Bedtime Book. East, Nick, illus. 2015. (Goodnight Ser.). (ENG.). 32p. (J). (gr. -1 — 1). pap. 7.99 (978-1-4380-0660-4(8)) Sourcebooks, Inc.

Rodriguez, Sergio R. Little Santa & Snowboy: The Childhood Adventures of Santa Claus. 2007. (Illus.). 32p. (J). pap. 8.95 (978-0-615-17411-2(6)) Little Santa Bks., Inc.

Rooks, Elizabeth. Where Does Santa Go on Vacation after Christmas? 2012. 24p. pap. 17.99 (978-1-4772-6535-2(X)) AuthorHouse.

—Where Does Santa Work after Christmas? 2012. 24p. pap. 17.99 (978-1-4772-9210-5(1)) AuthorHouse.

Rookstool, Yakiri. A Christmas Star. 2009. 80p. pap. 9.95 (978-1-60693-855-3(X), Eloquent Bks.) Strategic Book Publishing & Rights Agency (SBPRA).

Rosier, Joan. Christmas Stilts. 2008. (ENG.). 24p. 12.99 (978-1-4389-3907-0(8)) AuthorHouse.

Ross, Richard. Arctic Airlift. 2005. (Illus.). 36p. (J). 17.00 (978-0-9763119-0-4(9)) Blue Fox Pr.

Roussos, J. C. A Gift for Santa. 2016. (ENG.). (J). pap. 6.99 (978-1-942840-20-6(9)) Hocus Pocus Publishing, Inc.

Rowland, Teresa. Blusher's First Christmas. 2012. 64p. (-18). pap. 20.95 (978-1-4525-0718-7(X)) Balboa Pr.

Rumbley, Rose-Mary. Dear Santa: Thanks for the Piano. 2004. (Illus.). 46p. (J). pap. 8.95 (978-1-57168-466-0(2)) Eakin Pr.

Russo, Frank M. The Sleigh. Cittadino, Kyle & Cittadino, Kristen, illus. 2012. 24p. 24.95 (978-1-4626-6916-5(6)); pap. 24.95 (978-1-4626-7662-0(6)) America Star Bks.

Russo, Mallory Kate. The Hotel Christmas. 2012. 24p. pap. 24.95 (978-1-4626-8060-3(7)) America Star Bks.

Ryan, Brittney. The Legend of Holly Claus. Long, Laurel, illus. 2004. (Julie Andrews Collection). 544p. (J). (gr. 4-18). 16.99 (978-0-06-058511-2(0)); lib. bdg. 17.89 (978-0-06-058514-3(5)) HarperCollins Pubs. (Julie Andrews Collection).

Sadler, R. D. The Littlest Bell. 2011. 16p. pap. 10.70 (978-1-4567-5364-1(9)) AuthorHouse.

Sammartino, Joseph & Ozimkowski, Edward. The Legend of Kringle. 2009. 48p. pap. 19.95 (978-1-4490-5241-6(X)) AuthorHouse.

Sansone, V. K. The Carpenter & His Wife. 2009. (ENG.). 32p. pap. 14.98 (978-0-557-19204-5(8)) Lulu Pr., Inc.

Santa. 2003. (Shaped Board Books Ser.). 14p. (J). (gr. -1-k). bds. 9.95 (978-0-7525-8851-3(6)) Parragon, Inc.

Santa & the Elves. 2003. (J). per. (978-1-57657-908-4(5)) Paradise Pr., Inc.

Santa Claus & the Kids on the Farm. 2004. (J). per. 15.99 (978-0-9753533-0-1(6)) Golden Eagle Publishing Hse., Inc.

Santa Gets A Haircut. 2005. (J). 5.95 (978-0-9769321-3-0(X)) Steingart, Nathan Publishing.

Santa Gets New Glasses. 2005. (J). 5.95 (978-0-9769321-2-3(1)) Steingart, Nathan Publishing.

Santa Goes to the Dentist. 2005. (J). 5.95 net. (978-0-9769321-5-4(6)) Steingart, Nathan Publishing.

Santa Niclaus. A Letter from Santa: The Original. 2012. 28p. (-18). pap. 16.09 (978-1-4669-6794-6(3)) Trafford Publishing.

Santa Takes A Vacation. 2005. (J). 5.95 (978-0-9769321-4-7(8)) Steingart, Nathan Publishing.

Santa the Chimney Sweep/the Candy Cane That Found a Home: Wee Voices Collection. 2005. (Illus.). 37p. per. 6.95 (978-0-9764444-9-7(6)) E. J. Publishing.

Santa's Birthday. 2005. (J). 5.95 (978-0-9769321-1-6(3)) Steingart, Nathan Publishing.

Santa's Bodyguard. 2005. (J). (978-0-9771639-0-8(3)) Riverview Foundation.

Santa's Busy Christmas Eve. 2003. (J). 4.99 (978-1-59384-011-2(X)) Parklane Publishing.

Santa's Christmas Cookies. 2003. (J). per. (978-1-57657-708-0(2)) Paradise Pr., Inc.

Santa's Elves Alphabet. 2003. (Illus.). (J). per. (978-1-57657-174-3(2)) Paradise Pr., Inc.

Santa's Hat. 2003. (J). per. (978-1-57657-927-5(1)) Paradise Pr., Inc.

Santa's Jolly Belly. 2003. (J). per. (978-1-57657-923-7(9)) Paradise Pr., Inc.

Santa's Little Helpers. 2003. (J). per. (978-1-57657-921-3(2)); per. (978-1-57657-809-4(7)) Paradise Pr., Inc.

Santa's Thanksgiving. 2005. (J). 5.95 (978-0-9769321-0-9(5)) Steingart, Nathan Publishing.

Sargent, Dave & Sargent, Pat. Sweetpea: (Purple Corn Welsh) Be Happy, 30 vols., Vol. 58. Lenoir, Jane, illus. 2003. (Saddle up Ser.: Vol. 58). 42p. (J). pap. 10.95 (978-1-56763-816-5(3)); lib. bdg. 23.60 (978-1-56763-815-8(5)) Ozark Publishing.

Scarry, Richard. Richard Scarry's Christmas Mice. Scarry, Richard, illus. 2014. (Little Golden Book Ser.). (Illus.). 24p. (J). (-k). 5.99 (978-0-385-38421-6(1), Golden Bks.) Random Hse. Children's Bks.

—Richard Scarry's the Night Before the Night Before Christmas! Scarry, Richard, illus. 2014. (ENG., Illus.). 48p. (J). (gr. -1-2). 17.99 (978-0-385-38804-7(7), Golden Bks.) Random Hse. Children's Bks.

Schatzer, Jeffrey L. The Bird in Santa's Beard: How a Christmas Legend Was Forever Changed. 2004. (Illus.). 34p. (J). (978-0-9749554-0-7(X)) Big Belly Bks.

Schick-Jacobowitz, Jeannie, et al. A Bit of Applause for Mrs. Claus. 3rd rev. ed. 2016. (ENG.). 72p. 9.99 (978-1-4926-4123-0(5), 9781492641230) Sourcebooks, Inc.

Schmid, Eleonore. Santa Claus & the Dormouse. 2017. (ENG., Illus.). 32p. (J). (gr. -1-3). 17.95 (978-0-7358-4298-4(1)) North-South Bks., Inc.

Scholastic. Peppa's Christmas Wish (Peppa Pig) 2013. (ENG.). 24p. (J). (gr. -1-k). pap. 4.99 (978-0-545-56511-0(1)) Scholastic, Inc.

Schomer-Wendel, Gretchen & Schomer, Adam Anthony. Becka Goes to the North Pole, 1 vol. Renthrope, Damon, illus. 2009. (Becka & the Big Bubble Ser.). (ENG.). 32p. (J). (gr. 1-2). pap. 11.55 (978-1-60754-117-2(3), c00b48e1-07cf-4ffd-b439-e3a8068d929d, Windmill Bks.) Rosen Publishing Group, Inc., The.

Schonewill, Lisa. Tell Me Mama, Is Santa Claus Real? 2005. (J). pap. 9.00 (978-0-8059-6373-1(1)) Dorrance Publishing Co., Inc.

Schorr, Titus. Secret Santa, 1 vol., 1. 2015. (Rosen REAL Readers: Social Studies Nonfiction / Fiction: Myself, My Community, My World Ser.). (ENG.). 8p. (J). (gr. k-1). pap. 5.46 (978-1-5081-1893-0(0), 7552984f-0e0c-4e53-91a0-8b26fd90a9dc, Rosen Classroom) Rosen Publishing Group, Inc., The.

Scillian, Devin. Memoirs of an Elf. Bowers, Tim, illus. 2014. (ENG.). 32p. (J). (gr. 1-4). 16.99 (978-1-58536-910-2(1), 203676) Sleeping Bear Pr.

Scott, Christina. All in A Night's Work. 2006. (J). lib. bdg. 19.95 (978-1-933732-19-0(9)) Big Ransom Studio.

—The Chimney. 2006. (J). lib. bdg. 19.95 (978-1-933732-18-3(0)) Big Ransom Studio.

—The North Pole. 2006. (J). lib. bdg. 19.95 (978-1-933732-17-6(2)) Big Ransom Studio.

Scott, Eric. Santa & the Cyberspace Plot. 2013. 114p. pap. 7.99 (978-1-78333-397-4(9)) Acorn Bks.

Scotton, Rob. Russell's Christmas Magic. Scotton, Rob, illus. 2007. (Illus.). 32p. (J). (gr. -1-2). lib. bdg. 17.89 (978-0-06-059855-6(7)) HarperCollins Pubs.

Sedrak, Asham. The Santa Claus Fox. 2011. 28p. pap. 13.59 (978-1-4670-2484-6(8)) AuthorHouse.

Sellaro, Brendan. Space Santa Holiday Hero. 2012. (ENG., Illus.). 32p. (J). 16.95 (978-0-938467-60-1(3)) Headline Bks., Inc.

Sesko, Frank & Sesko, Mary Ann. Santa & Sam's Big Secret. 2007. 48p. per. 14.95 (978-1-4327-0769-9(8)) Outskirts Pr., Inc.

Seus. Wie der Grinch Weihnachten. pap. 14.95 (978-3-492-23722-2(3)) Piper Verlag GmbH DEU. Dist: Distribooks, Inc.

Shannon, David. It's Christmas, David! Shannon, David, illus. 2010. (ENG., Illus.). 32p. (J). (gr. -1-3). 18.99 (978-0-545-14311-0(X), Blue Sky Pr., The) Scholastic, Inc.

Sharkey, Niamh. Santasaurus. Sharkey, Niamh, illus. 2005. (ENG., Illus.). 32p. (J). (gr. -1-2). 15.99 (978-0-7636-2671-6(6)) Candlewick Pr.

Sharp, Rhonda Winchell. The Nine Most Famous Reindeer of All. Vandewater, Rena, illus. 2004. 40p. (J). pap. 15.99 (978-0-9748047-8-1(9)) Hickory Bark Productions.

Shaw, Stephanie. A Cookie for Santa. Robert, Bruno, illus. 2014. (ENG.). 32p. (J). (gr. 1-4). 17.99 (978-1-58536-883-9(0), 203675) Sleeping Bear Pr.

Shepherd, Anita. The Santa Genie. 2012. 50p. pap. 7.95 (978-0-9882368-0-6(X)) New Eden Publishing.

Silvano, Wendi. Turkey Claus, 0 vols. Harper, Lee, illus. 2012. (Turkey Trouble Ser.: 2). (ENG.). 40p. (J). (gr. -1-2). 16.99 (978-0-7614-6239-2(2), 9780761462392, Two Lions) Amazon Publishing.

Simon, Tom. El Traje Azul de Papa Noel.Tr. of Santa's Blue Suit. (SPA.). 24p. (J). (gr. k-2). 16.95 (978-84-488-0867-9(3), BS3557) Beascoa, Ediciones S.A. ESP. Dist: Lectorum Pubns., Inc.

Sims, Tom. Repo Elf. Perri, Anthony F., illus. 2008. (ENG.). 104p. (J). 12.95 (978-0-9787213-4-3(9), Cambridge House Pr.) Sterling & Ross Pubs.

Smale, Denise L. Santa I Moved! 2012. 20p. pap. 24.95 (978-1-4626-9241-5(9)) America Star Bks.

Smallman, Steve. Santa Is Coming to Arizona. Dunn, Robert, illus. 2nd ed. 2019. (Santa Is Coming... Ser.). (ENG.). 40p. (J). (gr. -1-3). 12.99 (978-1-7282-0043-9(1), Hometown World) Sourcebooks, Inc.

—Santa Is Coming to Boston. Dunn, Robert, illus. 2nd ed. 2019. (Santa Is Coming... Ser.). (ENG.). 40p. (J). (gr. -1-3). 12.99 (978-1-7282-0045-3(8), Hometown World) Sourcebooks, Inc.

—Santa Is Coming to California. Dunn, Robert, illus. (ENG.). (J). 2012. 32p. (-3). 9.99 (978-1-4022-7515-9(3), Sourcebooks Jabberwocky) 2nd ed. 2019. 40p. (gr. -1-3). 12.99 (978-1-7282-0048-4(2), Hometown World) Sourcebooks, Inc.

—Santa Is Coming to Chicago. Dunn, Robert, illus. 2nd ed. 2019. (Santa Is Coming... Ser.). (ENG.). 40p. (J). (gr. -1-3). 12.99 *(978-1-7282-0050-7(4)*, Hometown World) Sourcebooks, Inc.

—Santa Is Coming to Colorado. Dunn, Robert, illus. 2013. (ENG.). 32p. (J). (-3). 9.99 *(978-1-4022-8815-9(8)*, Sourcebooks Jabberwocky) Sourcebooks, Inc.

—Santa Is Coming to Florida. Dunn, Robert, illus. (ENG.). (J). 2012. 32p. (-3). 9.99 *(978-1-4022-7527-2(7)*, Sourcebooks Jabberwocky) 2nd ed. 2019. 40p. (gr. -1-3). 12.99 *(978-1-7282-0057-6(1)*, Hometown World) Sourcebooks, Inc.

—Santa Is Coming to Georgia. Dunn, Robert, illus. 2013. (ENG.). 32p. (J). (-3). 9.99 *(978-1-4022-8794-7(1)*, Sourcebooks Jabberwocky) Sourcebooks, Inc.

—Santa Is Coming to Hawaii. Dunn, Robert, illus. 2nd ed. 2019. (Santa Is Coming... Ser.). (ENG.). 40p. (J). (gr. -1-3). 12.99 *(978-1-7282-0059-0(8)*, Hometown World) Sourcebooks, Inc.

—Santa Is Coming to Louisiana. Dunn, Robert, illus. 2nd ed. 2019. (Santa Is Coming... Ser.). (ENG.). 40p. (J). (gr. -1-3). 12.99 *(978-1-7282-0067-5(9)*, Hometown World) Sourcebooks, Inc.

—Santa Is Coming to Michigan. Dunn, Robert, illus. (ENG.). (J). 2012. 32p. (-3). 9.99 *(978-1-4022-7539-5(0)*, Sourcebooks Jabberwocky) 2nd ed. 2019. 40p. (gr. -1-3). 12.99 *(978-1-7282-0071-2(7)*, Hometown World) Sourcebooks, Inc.

—Santa Is Coming to Minnesota. Dunn, Robert, illus. (ENG.). (J). 2012. 32p. (-3). 9.99 *(978-1-4022-7530-2(7)*, Sourcebooks Jabberwocky) 2nd ed. 2019. 40p. (gr. -1-3). 12.99 *(978-1-7282-0072-9(5)*, Hometown World) Sourcebooks, Inc.

—Santa Is Coming to My House. Dunn, Robert, illus. 2nd ed. 2019. (Santa Is Coming... Ser.). (ENG.). 40p. (J). (gr. -1-3). 12.99 *(978-1-7282-0076-7(8)*, Hometown World) Sourcebooks, Inc.

—Santa Is Coming to New Jersey. Dunn, Robert, illus. 2013. (ENG.). 32p. (J). (-3). 9.99 *(978-1-4022-8797-8(6)*, Sourcebooks Jabberwocky) Sourcebooks, Inc.

—Santa Is Coming to New York. Dunn, Robert, illus. 2nd ed. 2019. (Santa Is Coming... Ser.). (ENG.). 40p. (J). (gr. -1-3). 12.99 *(978-1-7282-0083-5(0)*, Hometown World) Sourcebooks, Inc.

—Santa Is Coming to New York City. Dunn, Robert, illus. 2nd ed. 2019. (Santa Is Coming... Ser.). (ENG.). 40p. (J). (gr. -1-3). 12.99 *(978-1-7282-0084-2(9)*, Hometown World) Sourcebooks, Inc.

—Santa Is Coming to Newfoundland. Dunn, Robert, illus. 2nd ed. 2019. (Santa Is Coming... Ser.). (ENG.). 40p. (J). (gr. -1-3). 12.99 *(978-1-7282-0085-9(7)*, Hometown World) Sourcebooks, Inc.

—Santa Is Coming to Nova Scotia. Dunn, Robert, illus. 2nd ed. 2019. (Santa Is Coming... Ser.). (ENG.). 40p. (J). (gr. -1-3). 12.99 *(978-1-7282-0088-0(1)*, Hometown World) Sourcebooks, Inc.

—Santa Is Coming to Ohio. Dunn, Robert, illus. 2nd ed. 2019. (Santa Is Coming... Ser.). (ENG.). 40p. (J). (gr. -1-3). 12.99 *(978-1-7282-0089-7(X)*, Hometown World) Sourcebooks, Inc.

—Santa Is Coming to Philadelphia. Dunn, Robert, illus. 2nd ed. 2019. (Santa Is Coming... Ser.). (ENG.). 40p. (J). (gr. -1-3). 12.99 *(978-1-7282-0094-1(6)*, Hometown World) Sourcebooks, Inc.

—Santa Is Coming to Portland. Dunn, Robert, illus. 2nd ed. 2019. (Santa Is Coming... Ser.). (ENG.). 40p. (J). (gr. -1-3). 12.99 *(978-1-7282-0096-5(2)*, Hometown World) Sourcebooks, Inc.

—Santa Is Coming to San Francisco. Dunn, Robert, illus. 2nd ed. 2019. (Santa Is Coming... Ser.). (ENG.). 40p. (J). (gr. -1-3). 12.99 *(978-1-7282-0099-6(7)*, Hometown World) Sourcebooks, Inc.

—Santa Is Coming to Texas. Dunn, Robert, illus. (ENG.). (J). 2012. 32p. (-3). 9.99 *(978-1-4022-7512-8(9)*, Sourcebooks Jabberwocky) 2nd ed. 2019. 40p. (gr. -1-3). 12.99 *(978-1-7282-0104-7(7)*, Hometown World) Sourcebooks, Inc.

—Santa Is Coming to Toronto. Dunn, Robert, illus. 2nd ed. 2019. (Santa Is Coming... Ser.). (ENG.). 40p. (J). (gr. -1-3). 12.99 *(978-1-7282-0105-4(5)*, Hometown World) Sourcebooks, Inc.

—Santa Is Coming to Vancouver. Dunn, Robert, illus. 2nd ed. 2019. (Santa Is Coming... Ser.). (ENG.). 40p. (J). (gr. -1-3). 12.99 *(978-1-7282-0108-5(X)*, Hometown World) Sourcebooks, Inc.

—Santa Is Coming to Virginia. Dunn, Robert, illus. 2013. (ENG.). 32p. (J). (-3). 9.99 *(978-1-4022-8800-5(X)*, Sourcebooks Jabberwocky) Sourcebooks, Inc.

—Santa Is Coming to Washington. Dunn, Robert, illus. (ENG.). (J). 2012. 32p. (-3). 9.99 *(978-1-4022-7524-1(2)*, Sourcebooks Jabberwocky) 2nd ed. 2019. 40p. (gr. -1-3). 12.99 *(978-1-7282-0111-5(X)*, Hometown World) Sourcebooks, Inc.

—Santa Is Coming to Wisconsin. Dunn, Robert, illus. (ENG.). (J). 2012. 32p. (-3). 9.99 *(978-1-4022-7533-3(1)*, Sourcebooks Jabberwocky) 2nd ed. 2019. 40p. (gr. -1-3). 12.99 *(978-1-7282-0114-6(4)*, Hometown World) Sourcebooks, Inc.

Smith, Alex T. Santa Claude. 2017. (J). *(978-1-56145-985-8(2))* Peachtree Publishing Co. Inc.

Smith, Joel D. Santa's Secret Deal: Who Else Signed It, & Where You Can Find Proof of the Deal in Your Room Right Now. 2012. 30p. pap. 14.25 *(978-1-4575-1458-6(3))* Dog Ear Publishing, LLC.

Smith, John A. A Special Christmas for Oscar. 2004. 31p. pap. 24.95 *(978-1-4137-2892-7(8))* PublishAmerica, Inc.

Snow, Alan. How Santa Really Works. Snow, Alan, illus. 2007. (ENG., Illus.). 48p. (J). (gr. -1-3). 9.99 *(978-1-4169-5000-4(1)*, Atheneum Bks. for Young Readers) Simon & Schuster Children's Publishing.

Snyder, Casey. Miss Fit the Dog Saves Christmas. 2013. 20p. pap. 24.95 *(978-1-62709-358-3(3))* America Star Bks.

Sobel, Gerrie. Jacob & His Magical Flying Bears. Torres, Dottie, illus. 2009. 32p. pap. 12.95 *(978-1-936051-16-8(8))* Peppertree Pr., The.

Solheim, James. Santa's Secrets Revealed: All Your Questions Answered about Santa's Super Sleigh, His Flying Reindeer, & Other Wonders. Gott, Barry, illus. 2004. (Carolrhoda Picture Books Ser.). 40p. (J). (gr. k-3). 15.95 *(978-1-57505-600-5(3))* Lerner Publishing Group.

Sonneborn, Scott. The Computer Meltdown. Lozano, Omar, illus. 2015. (North Police Ser.). (ENG.). 32p. (J). (gr. k-2). lib. bdg. 21.32 *(978-1-4795-6485-9(0)*, 128338, Picture Window Bks.) Capstone.

Soper, Stuart A. Milky Saves Christmas. 2011. (Illus.). 290p. pap. 16.00 *(978-1-60976-193-6(6)*, Strategic Bk. Publishing) Strategic Book Publishing & Rights Agency (SBPRA).

Soprano, Sophie, illus. Laughing All the Way. 2008. (J). *(978-1-59811-642-7(8))* Covenant Communications.

Sorenson, E. Randy. The First Reindeer Couldn't Fly. 2007. (Illus.). 32p. (J). 17.99 *(978-0-615-16939-2(2))* Sorenson, E. Randy.

Special Delivery from Santa. 2003. (J). per. *(978-1-57657-922-0(0))*; per. *(978-1-57657-810-0(0))* Paradise Pr., Inc.

Spencer, John Nicholas. Sleigh Ride with Santa. Spencer, Kay Kincannon, illus. 2012. (ENG.). 26p. (J). pap. 14.95 *(978-1-61296-140-8(1))* Black Rose Writing.

Stainton, Sue. Christmas Magic. Melnuish, Eva, illus. 2007. 32p. (J). (gr. -1-1). lib. bdg. 16.89 *(978-0-06-078572-7(1)*, Tegen, Katherine Bks) HarperCollins Pubs.

Stayer, Elizabeth. Santa's Magic Stardust. 2009. 40p. pap. 18.49 *(978-1-4490-2884-8(5))* AuthorHouse.

Stepp, Shirley. Santa Lost His Cell Phone. 2012. 24p. 24.95 *(978-1-4626-5479-6(7))* America Star Bks.

Stoddard, Chad L. Why Is Santa Fat? 2012. 20p. pap. 15.00 *(978-1-4520-0788-5(8))* AuthorHouse.

Sullivan, E. J. How Santa Got His Elves. Eldredge, Ernie, illus. 2006. (J). (gr. -1-3). 9.95 *(978-1-58173-308-2(9))* Sweetwater Pr.

Sykes, Julie. Bless You, Santa! Warnes, Tim, illus. 2004. 32p. (J). tchr. ed. 15.95 *(978-1-58925-041-3(9))* Tiger Tales.

—Shhh! Warnes, Tim, illus. 2006. (Storytime Board Bks.). 18p. (J). (gr. -1-1). bds. 6.95 *(978-1-58925-796-2(0))* Tiger Tales.

Sylvester, Merrill. Ho-Ho Where Did All My Reindeer Go? The Chicken Leg Detective Service. 2011. 72p. pap. 19.95 *(978-1-4626-0794-5(2))* America Star Bks.

Sypolt, Carl W. Fibber Lygood at Christmas, Easter, & St. Patrick's Day. 2006. 108p. (J). pap. 10.95 *(978-0-7414-2982-7(9))* Infinity Publishing.

Tapler, Judy. Santa Horse. Kohler, Michelle, illus. 2008. 36p. pap. 16.99 *(978-1-4389-2290-4(6))* AuthorHouse.

Tavares, Matt. Dasher: How a Brave Little Doe Changed Christmas Forever. Tavares, Matt, illus. 2019. (Dasher Ser.). (ENG., Illus.). (J). E-Book 17.99 *(978-1-5362-1490-1(6)*, 85751); 40p. (gr. -1-3). 17.99 *(978-1-5362-0137-6(5))* Candlewick Pr.

Taylor, Lillian Webb. Santa's Musical Elves. 2009. 28p. pap. 12.25 *(978-1-60860-146-2(3)*, Strategic Bk. Publishing) Strategic Book Publishing & Rights Agency (SBPRA).

Teitelbaum, Michael. Garfield & the Santa Spy. Fentz, Mike, illus. 2004. 92p. (J). *(978-0-439-70543-1(6))* Scholastic, Inc.

Thaler, Mike. The Secret Santa from the Black Lagoon. Lee, Jared D., illus. 2014. 64p. (J). *(978-0-545-78519-8(7))* Scholastic, Inc.

—The Secret Santa from the Black Lagoon. Lee, Jared, illus. 2016. (Black Lagoon Adventures Set 4 Ser.). (ENG.). 64p. (J). (gr. 2-6). lib. bdg. 31.36 *(978-1-61479-607-7(6)*, 24340, Chapter Bks.) Spotlight.

The Bee Guru, Gregg McMahan. Christmas Honey. 2012. (Illus.). 20p. pap. 11.60 *(978-1-4669-5471-7(X))* Trafford Publishing.

Theron Elkins, J. A Christmas Gift for Santa: A Bedtime Book, 1 vol. Jatkowska, Ag, illus. 2019. (ENG.). 32p. (J). 17.99 *(978-0-310-72961-7(0))* Zonderkidz.

Thompson, Emily Weisner & Hussey, Mandy. But What If There's No Chimney? Lampe, Kate, illus. 2016. (ENG.). 24p. (J). (gr. 17). 12.00 *(978-0-253-02392-6(0)*, 978-0-253-02392-6) Indiana Univ. Pr.

Thompson, Lauren. The Christmas Magic. Muth, Jon J., illus. 2009. (ENG.). 40p. (J). (gr. -1-2). 17.99 *(978-0-439-77497-0(7)*, Scholastic Pr.) Scholastic, Inc.

Tolkien, J. R. R. & Tolkien, Baillie. Letters from Father Christmas. 2004. (ENG., Illus.). 128p. pap. 25.00 *(978-0-618-51265-2(9)*, 689483, William Morrow Paperbacks) HarperCollins Pubs.

Tolley, Diane Stringam. Kris Kringle's Magic. 2012. 169p. (J). 14.99 *(978-1-4621-1105-3(X))* Cedar Fort, Inc./CFI Distribution.

Tolley, Diane Stringham & Tolley, Diane Stringam. Carving Angels. 2011. 121p. (J). 12.99 *(978-1-59955-944-5(7)*, Bonneville Bks.) Cedar Fort, Inc./CFI Distribution.

Tonn, Mary Jane. Jolly Old Santa Claus. 2010. 32p. pap. 7.99 *(978-0-8249-5624-0(9)*, Ideals Pubns.) Worthy Publishing.

Trinidad Joe. Santa's Key West Vacation. 2007. (Illus.). 80p. per. 12.95 *(978-0-9799474-0-7(5))* Seastory Pr.

Trivette, Donna K. One Special Christmas. 2012. 44p. pap. 24.95 *(978-1-4626-9363-4(6))* America Star Bks.

Trondheim, Lewis & Robin, Thierry. Happy Halloween, Li'l Santa. Robin, Thierry, illus. 2003. (ENG.). 51p. 14.95 *(978-1-56163-361-6(5))* NBM Publishing Co.

Tullis, Jamie. Rudolph, I Think You Need Glasses! 2012. 24p. pap. 15.99 *(978-1-4797-1624-1(3))* Xlibris Corp.

Tully, Justin. Lost from the Christmas Mansion. 2008. 141p. pap. 16.95 *(978-1-4092-5106-4(3))* Lulu Pr., Inc.

Turner, Christina. Hello Santa! Turner, Christina, illus. 2007. (Illus.). 16p. (J). (gr. -1). bds. 7.95 *(978-0-9790347-0-1(1))* Mackenzie Smiles, LLC.

Turner, Thomas N. Country Music Night Before Christmas, 1 vol. Rice, James, illus. 2003. (Night Before Christmas Ser.). (ENG.). 32p. (J). (gr. k-3). 16.99 *(978-1-58980-148-6(2)*, Pelican Publishing) Arcadia Publishing.

Twenstrup, Norm. A Surprise for Santa. DHP, Inc. Staff, ed. (Illus.). 32p. (J). (gr. -1-3). pap. *(978-1-885531-12-4(5))* Mess Hall Writers.

Vaitonis, Steven. Edison the Christmas Elf & the Imperfect Perfect Toy. Blue, Melissa, illus. 2014. 32p. (J). (gr. -1-1). pap. 12.95 *(978-1-939930-33-0(2)*, Belle Isle Bks.) Brandylane Pubs., Inc.

Van Allsburg, Chris. The Polar Express: Sam's Edition. annot. ed. 2006. (J). (gr. k-3). 35.00 *(978-0-618-83659-8(4))* Houghton Mifflin Harcourt Trade & Reference Pubs.

—Polar Express 30th Anniversary Edition: A Christmas Holiday Book for Kids. Van Allsburg, Chris, illus. 30th anniv. ed. 2015. (ENG., Illus.). 32p. (J). (gr. -1-3). 21.99 *(978-0-544-58014-5(1)*, 1613461, Clarion Bks.) HarperCollins Pubs.

—The Polar Express Big Book: A Caldecott Award Winner. Van Allsburg, Chris, illus. 2014. (ENG., Illus.). 32p. (J). (gr. -1-3). pap. 29.99 *(978-0-544-45798-0(6)*, 1599870, Clarion Bks.) HarperCollins Pubs.

Vanek, Karen & Schmidt, Sharon Vanek. Santa Claus Meets the Tooth Fairy. 2012. 44p. pap. 21.99 *(978-1-4772-4535-4(9))* AuthorHouse.

Velde, Henry. The Night I Became... 2007. (J). per. 16.99 *(978-1-933156-18-7(X)*, Visikid Bks.) GSVQ Publishing.

Vine, Deryth. Fiskers Meets Santa Claus. 2013. (Illus.). 40p. pap. *(978-0-9927157-0-0(9))* Tanglin Publishing.

Waiting for Santa. 2004. (J). per. *(978-1-57657-385-3(0))*; per. *(978-1-57657-451-5(2))* Paradise Pr., Inc.

Walker-Renner, Christa. Santa's Magic. 2009. 20p. pap. 11.00 *(978-1-4389-8206-9(2))* AuthorHouse.

Wallace, R. Mike. Saunter. 2009. 36p. pap. 10.75 *(978-1-60693-994-9(7)*, Strategic Bk. Publishing) Strategic Book Publishing & Rights Agency (SBPRA).

Wallace, William H. Santa's Magic Key. 2010. 20p. (J). 10.49 *(978-1-4490-8924-5(0))* AuthorHouse.

Walters, Eric & Walters, Christina. The True Story of Santa Claus. Gooderham, Andrew, illus. 2005. 38p. (J). 9.95 *(978-1-894601-11-5(4))* Chestnut Publishing Group CAN. Dist: Hushion Hse. Publishing, Ltd.

Wampol, Pam & Woodard, Heather. Oscar's Dreamzz: The Story of Santa's First Elf. 2013. 40p. pap. *(978-1-4602-0414-6(X))* FriesenPress.

Watt, Fiona. Busy Santa Book. 2011. (Pull-Back Bks). 10p. (J). ring bd. 24.99 *(978-0-7945-3178-2(4)*, Usborne) EDC Publishing.

—Santa Claus. 2004. (Sparkly Touchy-Feely Board Bks.). 10p. (J). 15.95 *(978-0-7945-0830-2(8)*, Usborne) EDC Publishing.

—That's Not My Santa. (Touchy-Feely Board Bks). 10p. (J). 2008. bds. 9.99 *(978-0-7945-2390-9(0))* 2012. bds. 8.99 *(978-0-7945-3310-6(8))* EDC Publishing. (Usborne).

Webster, Clare L., retold by. The Elf, 1 vol. 2009. 27p. pap. 24.95 *(978-1-60836-775-7(4))* America Star Bks.

Weiner-Booth, Patsy. The Day Santa Met Jesus: A Christmas story & Play. 2009. 56p. pap. 10.99 *(978-1-4490-1090-4(3))* AuthorHouse.

Wellings, Chris R. Sparkles Goes Home for the Holidays. Kennell, Julie, illus. 2011. 40p. pap. 24.95 *(978-1-4560-4120-5(7))* America Star Bks.

—Sparkles Meets the Easter Bunny: The Adventures of Sparkles. Hammersley, Karen, illus. 2011. 48p. pap. 24.95 *(978-1-4560-7063-2(0))* America Star Bks.

Wells, Rosemary. Max's Christmas. 2013. (Max & Ruby Ser.). (ENG.). 32p. (J). (gr. -1-k). 8.99 *(978-0-14-750947-5(5)*, Puffin Books) Penguin Young Readers Group.

—Max's Christmas. 2013. (Max Ruby Ser.). lib. bdg. 18.40 *(978-0-606-32139-6(X))* Turtleback.

—McDuff's New Friend with Plush Box Set. 2003. (Illus.). 28p. (J). 14.99 *(978-0-7868-1866-2(2)*, Disney Editions) Disney Pr.

Wendel, Gretchen Schomer & Schomer, Adam Anthony. Becka & the Big Bubble: Becka Goes to San Diego. Renthrope, Damon, illus. 2008. 32p. (J). (gr. -1-3). 11.99 *(978-1-933754-51-2(6))* Waterside Pr.

Wendel, Gretchen Schomer & Schomer, Adam Anthony. Becka Goes to Chicago. Renthrope, Damon, illus. 2008. (ENG.). 36p. (J). (gr. -1-3). 11.99 *(978-1-933754-52-9(4))* Waterside Publishing.

Wenger, Brahm. Dewey's Magical Sleigh. 2005. (ENG.). 32p. (J). (gr. -1-2). 15.95 *(978-0-9745143-5-2(7))* RandallFraser Publishing.

—Dewey's Magical Sleigh, from the Dewey Doo-it Series. 2005. (ENG., Illus.). 32p. (J). (gr. -1-2). 15.95 incl. lp *(978-0-9745143-6-9(5))* RandallFraser Publishing.

Werkema, Mark A. The Flight Before Christmas. 2004. (YA). pap. 13.95 *(978-1-58961-306-5(6))* PageFree Publishing, Inc.

Werner, James R. Dave's Christmas Surprise & a Puppy Named Oxley. 2008. 28p. pap. 14.95 *(978-1-4327-3298-1(6))* Outskirts Pr., Inc.

Weston Woods Staff, creator. Fletcher & the Snowflake Christmas. 2011. 29.95 *(978-0-545-42619-0(7))* Weston Woods Studios, Inc.

Wheeler, Lisa. The Christmas Boot. Pinkney, Jerry, illus. 2016. 32p. (J). (gr. -1-3). 18.99 *(978-0-8037-4134-8(0)*, Dial Bks) Penguin Young Readers Group.

White, S.D. Sing along with the Santa Claus That Never Saw a Child. 2008. 20p. pap. 12.89 *(978-1-4389-0305-7(7))* AuthorHouse.

Whitehouse, Anna. The Last Sant. 2012. 118p. pap. *(978-1-78176-289-9(9))* FeedARead.com.

Whybrow, Ian. Miss Wire's Christmas Surprise. Chichester Clark, Emma, illus. 2007. 45p. (J). (gr. -1-3). pap. 3.95 *(978-0-7534-6136-5(6)*, Kingfisher) Roaring Brook Pr.

Wilhite, Cindy. Santa He Sees You When. 2009. (ENG.). 28p. 18.65 *(978-0-557-12852-5(8))* Lulu Pr., Inc.

Wilkins, Nalini. Doby's First Christmas. Robb, Jonathan, illus. 2012. 28p. pap. 12.50 *(978-1-62212-777-1(3)*, Strategic Bk. Publishing) Strategic Book Publishing & Rights Agency (SBPRA).

Wilkinson, Thomas M. Willie-off-the-Pickleboat. 2009. (ENG.). 71p. pap. 12.99 *(978-0-557-06181-5(4))* Lulu Pr., Inc.

Willey, Margaret. A Clever Beatrice Christmas. Solomon, Heather M., illus. 2006. (ENG.). 40p. (J). (gr. -1-2). 19.99 *(978-0-689-87017-0(5)*, Atheneum Bks. for Young Readers) Simon & Schuster Children's Publishing.

Williams, Hap. Henry the Elf. Graves, Michelle, illus. 2012. 28p. pap. 24.95 *(978-1-4626-8999-6(X))* America Star Bks.

Williams, Sam. Santa's Toys. Gill, Tim, illus. 2003. 14p. bds. *(978-1-85602-274-3(9)*, Pavilion Children's Books) Pavilion Bks.

Williamson, K. E. Kayla & the Christmas Monkey. 2010. 28p. pap. 15.49 *(978-1-4520-9749-7(6))* AuthorHouse.

Wilson, Matthew. Scrooge & Santa GN. 2011. (Illus.). 100p. pap. 14.95 *(978-0-897548-98-1(2))* Arcana Studio, Inc.

Witt, Janice. Harold Discovers Santa's Secret: A Very Long Dog with a Very Big Heart. Reznicek, Curtis, illus. 2013. 40p. pap. 11.99 *(978-1-63022-442-4(1))* Speedy Publishing LLC.

Wolf, Carol A. Foggy Dog Discovers Christmas. 2012. (ENG.). 40p. (J). pap. 16.46 *(978-1-4669-6253-8(4))* Trafford Publishing.

Wolfe, Greg. Shmelf the Hanukkah Elf. McWilliam, Howard, illus. 2016. (ENG.). 32p. (J). 17.99 *(978-1-61963-521-0(6)*, 900139020, Bloomsbury USA Childrens) Bloomsbury Publishing USA.

Wolper, Joanna. The Man Who Could Be Santa. 2008. (Illus.). 78p. (J). pap. *(978-0-88092-765-9(8))*; lib. bdg. *(978-0-88092-764-2(X))* Royal Fireworks Publishing Co.

Wood, Francis Eusene. The Christmas Letter. Wood, Christine & Marken, Jon, eds. McDermott, Robert, illus. Wood, Christine, photos by. 2007. pap. 9.95 *(978-0-9746372-6-6(2))* Tip-Of-The-Moon Publishing Co.

Yee, Wong Herbert. A Small Christmas. 2007. (ENG., Illus.). 32p. (J). (gr. -1-3). 6.95 *(978-0-618-91534-7(6)*, 1014889, Clarion Bks.) HarperCollins Pubs.

Young, H. M. (Hal). The huskies & the christmas Fawn. 2007. (ENG.). 56p. pap. 9.95 *(978-1-4357-0070-3(8))* Lulu Pr., Inc.

Zalesny, Michele. The Elves' Surprise. 2008. (ENG., Illus.). 20p. (J). pap. 9.25 *(978-1-935125-06-8(0))* Robertson Publishing.

Zurcher, Corina. Growing up Claus. 2007. 188p. 21.99 *(978-1-60477-046-9(5))*; per. 13.99 *(978-1-60266-917-8(1))* Salem Author Services.

SANTA CLAUS—POETRY

Applewood Books. Visit from Saint Nicholas. 2006. (Applewood Bks.). (ENG., Illus.). 24p. (gr. -1-1). pap. 24.95 *(978-1-55709-592-3(2))* Applewood Bks.

Braller, Christine, illus. The Night Before Christmas. 2013. (ENG.). 32p. (J). 16.99 *(978-0-9789688-2-3(4))* Brownian Bee Pr.

Clement C., Moore. The Night Before Christmas. Cottage Door Press, ed. Fisher, Henry, illus. 2018. (ENG.). 32p. (J). (gr. -1-3). 9.99 *(978-1-68052-456-7(9)*, 2000550) Cottage Door Pr.

Dunn, Chris, illus. The Night Before Christmas. 2021. 32p. (J). 17.95 *(978-1-7364565-0-7(4)*, 8bb24d67-2641-41d8-ba0f-e315966e6a2b) Impossible Dreams Publishing Co.

Kennedy, A. E. & Moore, Clement Clarke. The Night Before Christmas. 2017. (ENG., Illus.). 32p. (J). (gr. -1-5). bds. 9.99 *(978-1-63158-152-6(X)*, Racehorse Publishing) Skyhorse Publishing Co., Inc.

Layne, Steven L. Preacher's Night Before Christmas, 1 vol. Benioff, Carol, illus. 2006. (Night Before Christmas Ser.). (ENG.). 32p. (J). (gr. k-3). 16.99 *(978-1-58980-321-3(3)*, Pelican Publishing) Arcadia Publishing.

Medina, Tony. Just Us. 2004. (Illus.). 48p. (J). (gr. 4-18). pap. 6.95 *(978-0-940975-75-0(0)*, Sankofa Bks.) Just Us Bks., Inc.

Moore, Clemens. The Night Before Christmas. Zwerger, Lisbeth, illus. 2014. 32p. (J). (gr. -1-k). 9.99 *(978-988-8240-88-3(9)*, Minedition) Penguin Young Readers Group.

Moore, Clement. C'etait la Veille de Noel (Twas the Night Before Christmas, French Edition) 2012.Tr. of Twas the Night Before Christmas. (FRE.). 32p. (J). 16.95 *(978-0-9879023-6-8(9)*, 442f7f86-43fa-47fd-ba57-2e2b8cd88c8e) Grafton and Scratch Pubs. CAN. Dist: Baker & Taylor Publisher Services (BTPS).

—The Night Before Christmas. Cottage Door Press, ed. Gianassi, Sara, illus. 2019. (ENG.). 26p. (J). (gr. -1-3). 16.99 *(978-1-68052-703-2(7)*, 1004360) Cottage Door Pr.

—Night Before Christmas. 2011. (ENG.). pap. 9.99 ***(978-1-4585-0069-4(1))*** Applewood Bks.

—Night Before Christmas. 2011. (ENG., Illus.). 26p. (J). (gr. -1-1). bds. 7.99 *(978-0-8249-1884-2(3)*, Ideals Pubns.) Worthy Publishing.

—Night Before Christmas Heirloom Edition: The Classic Edition Hardcover with Audio CD Narrated by Jeff Bridges. 2016. (Classic Edition Ser.). (ENG., Illus.). 48p. (J). (gr. -1). 24.95 *(978-1-60433-677-1(3)*, Applesauce Pr.) Cider Mill Pr. Bk. Pubs., LLC.

—Night Before Christmas Ornament Gift Set: The Classic Edition. gif. ed. 2013. (ENG., Illus.). 48p. (J). (gr. -1). 14.95 *(978-1-60433-437-1(1)*, Applesauce Pr.) Cider Mill Pr. Bk. Pubs., LLC.

Moore, Clement C. Era la Víspera de Navidad (Twas the Night Before Christmas, Spanish Edition) 2012.Tr. of Twas the Night Before Christmas. (SPA., Illus.). 32p. (J). 16.95 *(978-0-9879023-5-1(0)*, be0067cc-c086-4fda-9f64-5a2fafa72ac9) Grafton and Scratch Pubs. CAN. Dist: Baker & Taylor Publisher Services (BTPS).

—The Night Before Christmas. 2006. (J). per. 9.95 *(978-1-4276-0967-0(5))* Aardvark Global Publishing.

—The Night Before Christmas. 2012. 32p. 11.50 *(978-1-84135-796-6(0))* Award Pubns. Ltd. GBR. Dist: Parkwest Pubns., Inc.

—The Night Before Christmas. Basic, Zdenko & Sumberac, Manuel, illus. 2014. (J). *(978-1-4351-6188-7(2))* Barnes & Noble, Inc.

—The Night Before Christmas. Barrett, Angela, illus. 2012. 30p. (J). *(978-1-4351-4416-3(3))* Barnes & Noble, Inc.

—The Night Before Christmas. Adolphe, Joseph, illus. 2013. (J). 19.95 *(978-1-59530-953-2(5))* Hallmark Card, Inc.

—The Night Before Christmas. Kesler, Matt, illus. 2012. 16p. (J). 29.95 *(978-1-59530-407-0(X))* Hallmark Card, Inc.

—The Night Before Christmas. Long, Loren, illus. 2020. (ENG.). 40p. (J). (gr. -1-3). 18.99 *(978-0-06-286946-3(9)*, HarperCollins) HarperCollins Pubs.

—The Night Before Christmas. dePaola, Tomie, illus. 2019. 22p. (J). (— 1). bds. 8.99 *(978-0-8234-4351-2(5))* Holiday Hse., Inc.

—The Night Before Christmas. Price, Margaret Evans, illus. 2020. (J). 11.88 *(978-1-64032-233-2(7))*; pap. 3.48 *(978-1-64032-234-9(5))* Innovative Eggz LLC. (Puppet Theater Bks.).

—The Night Before Christmas. 2008. *(978-1-58865-498-4(2))* Kidsbooks, LLC.

—The Night Before Christmas. Caparo, Antonio Javier, illus. (ENG.). 40p. (J). (gr. -1-2). 2021. 9.99 *(978-1-5344-8445-0(0))* 2017. 17.99 *(978-1-5344-0085-6(0))* Little Simon. (Little Simon).

S

—The Night Before Christmas. 2009. (Illus.). 23p. pap. (978-0-462-09940-8(7)) Marshall Cavendish.

—The Night Before Christmas. 2020. (ENG., Illus.). 48p. (J). 17.95 (978-1-64690-005-3(7)) North-South Bks., Inc.

—The Night Before Christmas. Rand, Ted, illus. 2014. (ENG.). 32p. (J). (gr. -1-2). 17.95 (978-0-7358-4106-2(3)) North-South Bks., Inc.

—The Night Before Christmas. 2019. (ENG.). 16p. (J). 2.99 (978-1-64269-138-2(0), 4012, Sequoia Publishing & Media LLC) Phoenix International Publications, Inc.

—The Night Before Christmas. Lew, Steph, illus. 2021. (ENG.). 48p. (J). (gr. -1-k). 17.99 (978-1-64517-755-5(6), Silver Dolphin Bks.) Printers Row Publishing Group.

—The Night Before Christmas. Newsom, Tom, illus. 2012. (J). (978-1-4508-5375-0(7)) Publications International, Ltd.

—The Night Before Christmas. 2015. (Big Golden Board Book Ser.). (Illus.). 24p. (J). (-k). bds. 10.99 (978-0-553-52226-6(4), Golden Bks.) Random Hse. Children's Bks.

—The Night Before Christmas. Malvern, Corinne, illus. (J). 2014. 26p. (-k). bds. 7.99 (978-0-385-38474-2(2)) 2011. 24p. (gr. -1-k). 5.99 (978-0-375-86359-2(1)) Random Hse. Children's Bks. (Golden Bks.).

—The Night Before Christmas. 2012. 28p. (gr. -1-2). 14.95 (978-1-61382-397-2(5)); (ENG., Illus.). (J). (gr. k-7). pap. 11.99 (978-1-61382-399-6(1)) Simon & Brown.

—The Night Before Christmas. Lobel, Anita, illus. 2020. (ENG.). 32p. (J). (gr. -1-3). 17.99 (978-1-5344-6967-9(2), Simon & Schuster/Paula Wiseman Bks.) Simon & Schuster/Paula Wiseman Bks.

—The Night Before Christmas. Bell, Bill, illus. 2011. (ENG.). 32p. (J). (gr. k-2). 6.95 (978-1-61608-470-7(7), 608470, Sky Pony Pr.) Skyhorse Publishing Co., Inc.

—The Night Before Christmas. Eldredge, Larry, illus. 2006. (Night Before Christmas Ser.). 32p. (J). 9.95 (978-1-58173-306-8(2)); 26p. bds. 9.95 (978-1-58173-300-6(3)) Sweetwater Pr.

—The Night Before Christmas. 2015. (CHI.). 48p. (J). (gr. k-5). (978-7-201-09996-5(5)) Tianjin People's Publishing House.

—The Night Before Christmas. Rackham, Arthur, illus. 2012. 32p. pap. 5.99 (978-1-61720-437-1(4)) Wilder Pubns., Corp.

—The Night Before Christmas. Price, Margaret Evans, illus. 2009. (Dover Children's Classics Ser.). (ENG.). 16p. (J). (gr. k-5). pap. 6.99 (978-0-486-47369-7(4)) Dover Pubns., Inc.

—The Night Before Christmas. Nowakowski, Marcin, illus. 2019. (J). bds. 9.99 (978-1-950416-16-5(X)) Little Hippo Bks.

—The Night Before Christmas. Puybaret, Eric, illus. 2010. (ENG.). 26p. (J). (gr. k-4). 19.95 (978-1-936140-06-0(3)) Charlesbridge Publishing, Inc.

—The Night Before Christmas. Reid, Barbara, illus. adapted ed. 2016. (ENG.). 36p. pap. 6.95 (978-1-945546-47-1(6)) Frederic Thomas USA, Inc.

—The Night Before Christmas. Tudor, Tasha, illus. 10th anniv. ed. 2009. 32p. pap. 6.99 (978-0-316-18947-7(2)) Hachette Bk. Group.

—The Night Before Christmas, Set. Engelbreit, Mary, illus. gif. ed. 2007. (ENG.). 40p. (J). (gr. -1-3). 25.00 (978-0-06-136495-2(9), HarperFestival) HarperCollins Pubs.

—The Night Before Christmas: A Brick Story. Brack, Amanda, illus. 2015. (ENG.). 32p. (J). (gr. -1). 12.99 (978-1-63450-179-8(9), Sky Pony Pr.) Skyhorse Publishing Co., Inc.

—The Night Before Christmas: A Christmas Holiday Book for Kids. Engelbreit, Mary, illus. 2020. (ENG.). 40p. (J). (gr. -1-3). 12.99 (978-0-06-208944-1(7), HarperCollins) HarperCollins Pubs.

—The Night Before Christmas: A Christmas Holiday Book for Kids. Watson, Richard Jesse, illus. 2008. (ENG.). 40p. (J). (gr. -1-3). pap. 6.99 (978-0-06-075744-1(2), HarperCollins) HarperCollins Pubs.

—The Night Before Christmas: A Christmas Holiday Book for Kids. Engelbreit, Mary, illus. rev. ed. 2006. (ENG.). 40p. (J). (gr. -1-3). 18.99 (978-0-06-008160-7(0), HarperCollins) HarperCollins Pubs.

—The Night Before Christmas: A Visit from St. Nicholas. 2008. 48p. 18.99 (978-1-60641-066-0(0)) Deseret Bk. Co.

—The Night Before Christmas: Or, a Visit from St. Nicholas. Santore, Charles, illus. 2011. 41p. (J). (978-1-60464-033-5(2)) Appleseed Pr. Bk. Pub. LLC.

—The Night Before Christmas Board Book: A Christmas Holiday Book for Kids. Whatley, Bruce, illus. 2004. (ENG.). 32p. (J). (gr. -1 — 1). bds. 7.99 (978-0-06-073917-1(7), HarperFestival) HarperCollins Pubs.

—Twas the Night Before Christmas. Whelan, Kat, illus. 2010. (ENG.). 24p. (J). (gr. -1-2). 12.95 (978-1-58925-858-7(4)) Tiger Tales.

—Twas the Night Before Christmas: A Visit from St. Nicholas. Smith, Jessie Willcox, illus. 2015. vi, 29p. (J). pap. (978-1-4677-7805-3(2), First Avenue Editions) Lerner Publishing Group.

—Twas the Night Before Christmas: Edited by Santa Claus for the Benefit of Children of the 21st Century. McColl, Pam, ed. Almazova, Elena & Shvarov, Vitaly, illus. (ENG.). 32p. (J). 2013. pap. 7.95 (978-0-9879023-1-3(8), a006d5d8-1d38-4bd0-9e69-2a58f42c896a) 2012. 16.95 (978-0-9879023-0-6(X), 25500bea-6785-4220-b3e5-77c6145c9e2a) Grafton and Scratch Pubs. CAN. Dist: Baker & Taylor Publisher Services (BTPS).

Moore, Clement C., ed. & illus. The Night Before Christmas. Moore, Clement C., illus. Winget, Susan, illus. 2004. 32p. 18.00 (978-0-7412-1939-8(5)) Lang Graphics, Ltd.

—The Night Before Christmas. Moore, Clement C., illus. Gorsline, Douglas, illus. 32p. (J). Random Hse. Children's Bks.

Moore, Clement C. & Curto Family, The. The Night Before Christmas. Creative Illustrations Studio & Good Times At Home LLC, illus. 2012. (J). pap. 9.99 (978-0-9840338-5-0(8)) Good Times at Home LLC.

Moore, Clement Clarke. The Night Before Christmas. 2013. (ENG., Illus.). 40p. (J). (gr. -1-3). 18.00 (978-0-316-07018-8(1)) Little, Brown Bks. for Young Readers.

—The Night Before Christmas, 0 vols. Spirin, Gennady, illus. ltd. ed. 2012. (ENG.). 32p. (J). (gr. -1-3). 16.99 (978-0-7614-5298-0(2), 9780761452980, Two Lions) Amazon Publishing.

—The Night Before Christmas. Birmingham, Christian, illus. 2005. (ENG.). 48p. (J). (gr. -1-2). 9.95 (978-0-7624-2416-0(8), Running Pr. Kids) Running Pr.

Moore, Clement Clarke. The Night Before Christmas or a Visit from St. Nicholas: A Charming Reproduction of an Antique Christmas Classic. Snow, William Roger, illus. 2021. (ENG.). 24p. (J). 12.99 (978-1-3988-0870-6(9), 602e8280-9184-4f17-a464-603c844de7c6) Arcturus Publishing GBR. Dist: Baker & Taylor Publisher Services (BTPS).

Santore, Charles. Night Before Christmas Hardcover: The Classic Edition (the New York Times Bestseller) 2011. (Charles Santore Children's Classics Ser.). (ENG., Illus.). 48p. (J). (gr. -1). 19.95 (978-1-60433-237-7(9), Applesauce Pr.) Cider Mill Pr. Bk. Pubs., LLC.

Wick, Walter. Can You See What I See? the Night Before Christmas: Picture Puzzles to Search & Solve. Wick, Walter, photos by. 2005. (Can You See What I See? Ser.). (ENG., Illus.). 40p. (J). (gr. k-3). 13.99 (978-0-439-76927-3(2), Cartwheel Bks.) Scholastic, Inc.

SANTA FE (N.M.)

Brown, Rachel K. Santa Fe: Daily Life in a Western Trading Center. 2003. (J). pap. (978-1-58417-074-7(3)); lib. bdg. (978-1-58417-011-2(5)) Lake Street Pubs.

Coll, Ivar Da. Maria Juana. (SPA.). (J). bds. (978-958-04-4908-9(2)) Norma S.A. COL. Dist: Lectorum Pubns., Inc.

Love, Pamela. Staircase for the Sisters: A Story of Prayer & Saint Joseph. 2018. (Illus.). 25p. (J). (978-0-8198-9097-9(9)) Pauline Bks. & Media.

Noble, David Grant, ed. Santa Fe: History of an Ancient City: Revised & Expanded Edition. 2008. (ENG.). 144p. 40.00 (978-1-934691-03-8(8), P181763); (Illus.). pap. 19.95 (978-1-934691-04-5(6), P181764) School for Advanced Research Pr./SAR Pr.

SANTA FE NATIONAL HISTORIC TRAIL

Dean, Arlan. The Santa Fe Trail: From Independence, Missouri to Santa Fe, New Mexico. 2009. (Famous American Trails Ser.). 24p. (gr. 3-3). 42.50 (978-1-61512-492-3(6), PowerKids Pr.) Rosen Publishing Group, Inc., The.

Randolph, Ryan P. The Santa Fe Trail. 2009. (Library of the Westward Expansion Ser.). 24p. (gr. 3-4). 42.50 (978-1-60853-940-6(7), PowerKids Pr.) Rosen Publishing Group, Inc., The.

Thompson, Linda. The Santa Fe Trail. 2005. (Expansion of America Ser.). (Illus.). 48p. (gr. 4-8). 20.95 (978-1-59515-226-8(1)) Rourke Educational Media.

Williams, Jean K. The Perils of the Santa Fe Trail. 2017. (Landmarks in U. S. History Ser.). (ENG., Illus.). 32p. (J). (gr. 3-6). lib. bdg. 27.99 (978-1-5157-7117-3(2), 135518, Capstone Pr.) Capstone.

SANTA FE NATIONAL HISTORIC TRAIL—FICTION

Sperry, Armstrong. Wagons Westward: The Old Trail to Santa Fe. Sperry, Armstrong, illus. 2005. (Illus.). 200p. (YA). (gr. 6-11). reprint ed. pap. 15.00 (978-0-7567-9693-8(8)) DIANE Publishing Co.

SARATOGA CAMPAIGN, 1777

Rushworth, Victoria. Battles of the American Revolution: Saratoga: Text Pairs. 2008. (Bridges/Navigators Ser.). (J). (gr. 5). 81.00 (978-1-4108-8404-6(X)) Benchmark Education Co.

Vierow, Wendy. The Battle of Saratoga. 2009. (Atlas of Famous Battles of the American Revolution Ser.). 24p. (gr. 3-3). 42.50 (978-1-60853-330-5(1), PowerKids Pr.) Rosen Publishing Group, Inc., The.

SARGASSO SEA

Heller, Ruth. A Sea within a Sea: Secrets of the Sargasso. Heller, Ruth, illus. 2006. (Illus.). 29p. (J). (gr. 4-8). reprint ed. 17.00 (978-1-4223-5731-6(7)) DIANE Publishing Co.

SASKATCHEWAN

Aksomitis, Linda. L Is for Land of Living Skies: A Saskatchewan Alphabet. Bennett, Lorna, illus. 2010. (Discover Canada Province by Province Ser.). (ENG.). 32p. (J). (gr. 1-3). 17.95 (978-1-58536-490-9(8), 202194) Sleeping Bear Pr.

Millar, Ruth. Saskatchewan Heroes & Rogues. 2004. (ENG., Illus.). 240p. (gr. 7-18). pap. 17.95 (978-1-55050-289-3(1)) Coteau Bks. CAN. Dist: Fitzhenry & Whiteside, Ltd.

Zintel, James. Saskatchewan a to Z, 1 vol. 2017. (ENG.). 26p. (J). 16.95 (978-1-77276-028-6(5), 97826daa-44fd-4131-9a5f-d795bda69780) MacIntyre Purcell Publishing Inc. CAN. Dist: Baker & Taylor Publisher Services (BTPS).

SASKATCHEWAN—FICTION

Banks, Lynne Reid. Uprooted - a Canadian War Story. 2014. (ENG.). 336p. (J). 8.99 (978-0-00-758943-2(3), HarperCollins Children's Bks.) HarperCollins Pubs. Ltd. GBR. Dist: HarperCollins Pubs.

Croza, Laurel. From There to Here, 1 vol. James, Matt, illus. 2014. (ENG.). 32p. (J). (gr. -1-2). 18.95 (978-1-55498-365-0(7)) Groundwood Bks. CAN. Dist: Publishers Group West (PGW).

Porter, Pamela. The Crazy Man. 2013. 164p. pap. (978-1-4596-6446-3(9)) ReadHowYouWant.com, Ltd.

—I'll Be Watching. 2013. 336p. pap. (978-1-4596-6449-4(3)) ReadHowYouWant.com, Ltd.

Rathborne, St. George. Canoe Mates in Canada; or, Three Boys Afloat on the Saskatchewan. 2007. 100p. per. (978-1-4068-3746-9(6)) Echo Library.

SASQUATCH

Anderson, Jennifer Joline. Bigfoot & Yeti, 1 vol. 2014. (Creatures of Legend Ser.). (ENG., Illus.). 48p. (J). (gr. 4-8). lib. bdg. 35.64 (978-1-62403-150-2(1), 4934) ABDO Publishing Co.

Besel, Jen. Bigfoot. 2020. (Little Bit Spooky Ser.). (ENG.). 24p. (J). (gr. k-3). lib. bdg. (978-1-62310-175-6(1), 14446, Bolt Jr.) Black Rabbit Bks.

Bougie, Matt. Bigfoot, the Loch Ness Monster, & Unexplained Creatures, 1 vol. 2017. (Paranormal Investigations Ser.). (ENG.). 64p. (gr. 6-6). 35.93 (978-1-5026-2847-3(3), 8fb126eb-8bed-4c21-9eef-726c0160d73a) Cavendish Square Publishing LLC.

Cole, Bradley. Bigfoot. 2019. (Monster Histories Ser.). (ENG., Illus.). 32p. (J). (gr. 4-6). pap. 7.95 (978-1-5435-7498-2(X), 141028); lib. bdg. 30.65 (978-1-5435-7121-9(2), 140403) Capstone.

Collins, Terry. Bigfoot & Adaptation. 2011. (Monster Science Ser.). (ENG.). 32p. (J). (gr. 3-4). pap. 49.60 (978-1-4296-7328-0(1), 16832, Capstone Pr.) Capstone.

—Bigfoot & Adaptation, 1 vol. Mallea, Cristian, illus. 2011. (Monster Science Ser.). (ENG.). 32p. (J). (gr. 3-9). pap. 8.10 (978-1-4296-7327-3(3), 116877); lib. bdg. 31.32 (978-1-4296-6579-7(3), 115703) Capstone. (Capstone Pr.).

Colson, Mary. Bigfoot & Yeti: Myth or Reality? 2018. (Investigating Unsolved Mysteries Ser.). (ENG., Illus.). 32p. (J). (gr. 3-9). lib. bdg. 28.65 (978-1-5435-3569-3(0), 138910, Capstone Pr.) Capstone.

Cowley, Stewart & Cox, Greg. Searching for Bigfoot, 1 vol. 2011. (Mystery Explorers Ser.). (ENG.). 64p. (J). (gr. 5-5). pap. 13.95 (978-1-4488-4768-6(0), 6245825c-4d00-48b7-867c-965b5b762ef3); lib. bdg. 37.13 (978-1-4488-4760-0(5), 1cd04fcd-cc1d-4bd8-a622-f52f45372fa4) Rosen Publishing Group, Inc., The. (Rosen Reference).

Cox, Greg. Bigfoot. 2009. (Unsolved Mysteries: the Secret Files Ser.). 48p. (gr. 5-8). 53.00 (978-1-60854-692-3(6), Rosen Reference) Rosen Publishing Group, Inc., The.

DeMolay, Jack. Bigfoot: A North American Legend. (Jr. Graphic Mysteries Ser.). (ENG.). 24p. (gr. 2-3). 2009. (J). 47.90 (978-1-61513-840-1(4), PowerKids Pr.) 2006. (Illus.). (J). lib. bdg. 28.93 (978-1-4042-3405-5(5), 779a8d11-3fc6-43da-8244-b7ff52373540) 2006. (Illus.). pap. 10.60 (978-1-4042-2158-1(1), c7824e03-7004-449e-8142-2dd2e1ec8c4e) Rosen Publishing Group, Inc., The.

—Bigfoot: La Leyenda del Hombre-Monstruo, 1 vol. Obregón, José María, tr. 2008. (Historietas Juveniles: Misterios (Jr. Graphic Mysteries) Ser.). (SPA., Illus.). 24p. (J). (gr. 2-3). lib. bdg. 28.93 (978-1-4358-2536-9(5), bcf2509a-ba14-4737-be3b-a3fc89d306d4) Rosen Publishing Group, Inc., The.

—Bigfoot: La Leyenda del hombre-monstruo (A North American Legend) 2009. (Historietas Juveniles: Misterios (Jr. Graphic Mysteries) Ser.). (SPA.). 24p. (gr. 2-3). 47.90 (978-1-61513-346-8(1), Editorial Buenas Letras) Rosen Publishing Group, Inc., The.

Dennett, Preston. Bigfoot, Yeti, & Other Ape-Men. 2008. (Mysteries, Legends, & Unexplained Phenomena Ser.). (ENG., Illus.). 152p. (gr. 7-12). 29.95 (978-0-7910-9386-3(7), P159098, Facts On File) Infobase Holdings, Inc.

Gish, Ashley. Bigfoot. 2019. (X-Books: Mythical Creatures Ser.). (ENG.). 32p. (J). (gr. 3-5). pap. 9.99 (978-1-62832-757-1(X), 19229, Creative Paperbacks) Creative Co., The.

Hawkins, John. Bigfoot & Other Monsters, 1 vol. 2012. (Mystery Hunters Ser.). (ENG., Illus.). 32p. (J). (gr. 4-5). pap. 11.60 (978-1-4488-6445-4(3), 9a364bfb-b38e-4821-9ae4-2afe083f65e6); lib. bdg. 28.93 (978-1-4488-6431-7(3), 476bb760-6f11-41d1-85b3-d021e27f9b8c) Rosen Publishing Group, Inc., The. (PowerKids Pr.).

Jones, Molly. Bigfoot. 2018. (Mythical Creatures Ser.). (ENG., Illus.). 32p. (J). (gr. 2-3). pap. 9.95 (978-1-64185-001-8(9), 1641850019); lib. bdg. 31.35 (978-1-63517-899-9(1), 1635178991) North Star Editions. (Focus Readers).

—Bigfoot. 2018. (Illus.). 32p. (J). (978-1-4896-9834-6(5), AV2 by Weigl) Weigl Pubs., Inc.

Kallio, Jamie. Investigating Sasquatch. 2018. (Illus.). 24p. (J). pap. (978-1-4896-9988-6(0), AV2 by Weigl) Weigl Pubs., Inc.

Karst, Ken. Bigfoot. 2014. (Enduring Mysteries Ser.). (ENG.). 48p. (J). (gr. 5-8). (978-1-60818-402-6(1), 21328, Creative Education); pap. 12.00 (978-1-62832-073-2(7), 21329, Creative Paperbacks) Creative Co., The.

Kawa, Katie. The Legend of Bigfoot, 1 vol. 2017. (Famous Legends Ser.). (ENG., Illus.). 32p. (J). (gr. 2-3). pap. 11.50 (978-1-5382-0368-2(5), 4b3aec00-43b6-40aa-bc45-eedfbea27159) Stevens, Gareth Publishing LLLP.

Krensky, Stephen. Bigfoot. 2006. (Monster Chronicles Ser.). (Illus.). 48p. (J). (gr. 5-8). lib. bdg. 26.60 (978-0-8225-5925-2(0), Lerner Pubns.) Lerner Publishing Group.

Loh-Hagan, Virginia. Bigfoot. 2016. (Magic, Myth, & Mystery Ser.). (ENG., Illus.). 32p. (J). (gr. 4-8). 32.07 (978-1-63471-116-6(5), 208575, 45th Parallel Press) Cherry Lake Publishing.

McClellan, Ray. Bigfoot. 2014. (Unexplained Mysteries Ser.). (ENG., Illus.). 24p. (J). (gr. 3-7). lib. bdg. 26.95 (978-1-62617-103-9(3), Epic Bks.) Bellwether Media.

Miller, D. L. BigFoot Goes Back in Time: A Spectacular Seek & Find Challenge for All Ages! 2018. (BigFoot Search & Find Ser.). (ENG., Illus.). 48p. (J). 14.99 (978-1-64124-003-1(2), 0031B) Fox Chapel Publishing Co., Inc.

—BigFoot Goes on Big City Adventures: Amazing Facts, Fun Photos, & a Look-And-Find Adventure! 2019. (BigFoot Search & Find Ser.). (ENG., Illus.). 48p. (J). 14.99 (978-1-64124-026-0(1), 0260) Fox Chapel Publishing Co., Inc.

—BigFoot Goes on Great Adventures: Amazing Facts, Fun Photos, & a Look-And-Find Adventure! 2019. (BigFoot Search & Find Ser.). (ENG., Illus.). 48p. (J). 14.99 (978-1-64124-025-3(3), 0253); pap. 9.99 (978-1-64124-043-7(1), 0437) Fox Chapel Publishing Co., Inc.

—BigFoot Goes on Vacation: A Spectacular Seek & Find Challenge for All Ages! (BigFoot Search & Find Ser.). (ENG., Illus.). 48p. (J). 2019. pap. 9.99 (978-1-64124-041-3(5), 0413) 2018. 14.99 (978-1-64124-000-0(8), 0000B) Fox Chapel Publishing Co., Inc.

—BigFoot Spotted at World-Famous Landmarks: A Spectacular Seek & Find Challenge for All Ages! 2018. (BigFoot Search & Find Ser.). (ENG., Illus.). 48p. (J). 14.99 (978-1-64124-002-4(4), 0024B) Fox Chapel Publishing Co., Inc.

—BigFoot Visits the Big Cities of the World: A Spectacular Seek & Find Challenge for All Ages! 2018. (BigFoot Search & Find Ser.). (ENG., Illus.). 48p. (J). (gr. -1-7). 14.99 (978-1-64124-001-7(6), 0017) Fox Chapel Publishing Co., Inc.

Miller, Heather. Bigfoot. 2006. (Monsters Ser.). (ENG., Illus.). 48p. (J). (gr. 4-8). 27.00 (978-0-7377-3161-3(3), Greenhaven Pr., Inc.) Cengage Gale.

Murray, Laura K. Bigfoot. 2017. (Are They Real? Ser.). (ENG.). 24p. (J). (gr. 1-4). pap. 8.99 (978-1-62832-369-6(8), 20057, Creative Paperbacks); (978-1-60818-761-4(6), 20059, Creative Education) Creative Co., The.

Nagle, Frances. Bigfoot, 1 vol. 2016. (Monsters! Ser.). (ENG., Illus.). 32p. (J). (gr. 1-2). pap. 11.50 (978-1-4824-4855-9(6), 0827ba69-e4a1-4f3e-8201-e56ab6eb4969) Stevens, Gareth Publishing LLLP.

Noll, Elizabeth. Bigfoot. 2016. (Strange ... but True? Ser.). (ENG.). 32p. (J). (gr. 4-6). pap. 9.99 (978-1-64466-156-7(X), 10326); (Illus.). 31.35 (978-1-68072-020-4(1), 10325) Black Rabbit Bks. (Bolt).

Oachs, Emily Rose. Bigfoot. 2018. (Investigating the Unexplained Ser.). (ENG., Illus.). 32p. (J). (gr. 3-8). lib. bdg. 27.95 (978-1-62617-852-6(6), Blastoff! Discovery) Bellwether Media.

Olsen, Sylvia. Sebastian Sasquatch, 1 vol. Charko, Kasia, illus. 2013. (ENG.). 32p. (J). (gr. 1-3). 9.95 (978-1-55039-197-8(6)) Sono Nis Pr. CAN. Dist: Orca Bk. Pubs. USA.

Perish, Patrick. Is Bigfoot Real? 2013. (Unexplained: What's the Evidence? Ser.). (ENG.). 32p. (J). (gr. 2-5). lib. bdg. 28.50 (978-1-60753-387-0(1), 16364) Amicus.

Rivkin, Jennifer. Searching for Bigfoot, 1 vol. 2014. (Mysterious Monsters Ser.). (ENG., Illus.). 32p. (J). (gr. 4-5). lib. bdg. 27.93 (978-1-4777-7105-1(0), 9be15831-b38b-4218-ab19-5df79755a317, PowerKids Pr.) Rosen Publishing Group, Inc., The.

Shea, Therese. Bigfoot, 1 vol. 2005. (Content-Area Literacy Collections). (ENG.). 24p. (gr. 3-4). pap. 8.85 (978-1-4042-5675-0(X), 0411d675-8ae8-44eb-94f0-83aac6200627) Rosen Publishing Group, Inc., The.

Shea, Therese M. The Bigfoot Trail, 1 vol. 2014. (Scariest Places on Earth Ser.). (ENG.). 24p. (J). (gr. 2-3). pap. 9.15 (978-1-4824-0928-4(3), ee82e7f7-a47d-4196-9d87-8605f697aca2) Stevens, Gareth Publishing LLLP.

Shone, Rob. Bigfoot & Other Strange Beasts. 2009. (Graphic Mysteries Ser.). (ENG.). 48p. (YA). (gr. 5-5). 58.50 (978-1-61512-961-4(8), Rosen Reference) Rosen Publishing Group, Inc., The.

—Bigfoot & Other Strange Beasts, 1 vol. Spender, Nik, illus. 2006. (Graphic Mysteries Ser.). (ENG.). 48p. (gr. 5-5). pap. 14.05 (978-1-4042-0804-9(6), c20454f9-d03a-4d79-8ded-553c3791d531) Rosen Publishing Group, Inc., The.

—Bigfoot & Other Strange Beasts, 1 vol. Spender, Nick, illus. 2006. (Graphic Mysteries Ser.). (ENG.). 48p. (YA). (gr. 5-5). lib. bdg. 37.13 (978-1-4042-0793-6(7), 63bbb09b-1918-4cff-a780-95b413b15bca) Rosen Publishing Group, Inc., The.

Teitelbaum, Michael. Bigfoot Caught on Film: And Other Monster Sightings! 2008. (24/7: Science Behind the Scenes Ser.). (ENG., Illus.). 64p. (J). (gr. 9-12). 29.00 (978-0-531-12078-1(3), Watts, Franklin) Scholastic Library Publishing.

—Wild Man of the Woods! Following in the Footsteps of Bigfoot. 2011. (J). pap. (978-0-545-32934-7(5)) Scholastic, Inc.

Theisen, Paul. Bigfoot. 2010. (Unexplained Ser.). (ENG., Illus.). 24p. (J). (gr. 3-7). lib. bdg. 26.95 (978-1-60014-498-1(5), Torque Bks.) Bellwether Media.

Walker, Kathryn. Mysteries of Giant Humanlike Creatures. 2008. (ENG., Illus.). 32p. (J). (gr. 3-7). pap. (978-0-7787-4156-5(7)); lib. bdg. (978-0-7787-4143-5(5)) Crabtree Publishing Co.

Woog, Adam. Bigfoot, 1 vol. 2006. (Mysterious Encounters Ser.). (ENG., Illus.). 48p. (gr. 4-8). lib. bdg. 35.23 (978-0-7377-3473-7(6), 65a13121-185c-466a-bb0b-60afadc12948, KidHaven Publishing) Greenhaven Publishing LLC.

Worth, Bonnie. Looking for Bigfoot. Nelson, Jim, illus. 2010. (Step into Reading Ser.). 48p. (J). (gr. 2-4). pap. 4.99 (978-0-375-86331-8(1), Random Hse. Bks. for Young Readers) Random Hse. Children's Bks.

SATAN

see Devil

SATELLITES, ARTIFICIAL

see Artificial Satellites

SATIRE

Doeden, Matt. What Are Satire & Parody? 2019. (Searchlight Books (tm) — Fake News Ser.). (ENG., Illus.). 32p. (J). (gr. 3-5). pap. 9.99 (978-1-5415-7474-8(5), b2f1fbf3-cc2a-4a8b-9800-9ebf14b4e1fe); lib. bdg. 30.65 (978-1-5415-5579-2(1), a53883fb-caaa-40c7-87b2-a3fc89a91eac) Lerner Publishing Group. (Lerner Pubns.).

Johnston, Marianne. Dealing with Insults / Qué hacer con los Insultos. 2009. (Conflict Resolution Library / Biblioteca solución de conflictos Ser.). (ENG & SPA.). 24p. (gr. 2-3). 42.50 (978-1-60853-415-9(4), Editorial Buenas Letras) Rosen Publishing Group, Inc., The.

—Dealing with Insults/Que Hacer con Los Insultos, 1 vol. Velazquez De Leon, Mauricio, tr. 2007. (Conflict Resolution Library / Biblioteca Solución de Conflictos Ser.). (SPA & ENG., Illus.). 24p. (J). (gr. 2-3). lib. bdg. 26.27 (978-1-4042-7661-1(0), 26337065-66d8-40b4-822a-af54f8af1dc9) Rosen Publishing Group, Inc., The.

SATURN (PLANET)

Allyn, Daisy. Saturn, 1 vol. 2010. (Our Solar System Ser.). (ENG.). 24p. (J). (gr. k-2). pap. 9.15 (978-1-4339-3840-5(5), e57bb3b1-c827-46cf-b3d4-949b39f74df0); (Illus.). lib. bdg. 25.27 (978-1-4339-3839-9(1), b4f904d2-0df2-4497-87f9-feac8da648a5) Stevens, Gareth Publishing LLLP.

Austen, Mary. Exploring Saturn. 2017. (Journey Through Our Solar System Ser.). 24p. (gr. 1-2). 49.50 (978-1-5345-2254-1(9), KidHaven Publishing); (ENG.). pap. 9.25 (978-1-5345-2288-6(3), b704a09f-751e-4c69-9602-b5b8898683fa); (ENG.). lib. bdg. 26.23 (978-1-5345-2282-4(4),

c96787f9-edc2-4d91-9479-bd7b716e016e) Greenhaven Publishing LLC.
Beth, Georgia. Discover Saturn. 2018. (Searchlight Books (tm) — Discover Planets Ser.). (ENG., Illus.). 32p. (J). (gr. 3-5). pap. 9.99 *(978-1-5415-2789-8(5),* 4df2f12b-7ddf-4312-9b3b-38c3dbb91e2a); lib. bdg. 30.65 *(978-1-5415-2339-5(3),* e73cebae-e209-456c-b014-890eaa21bebe, Lerner Pubns.) Lerner Publishing Group.
Bloom, J. P. Saturn, 1 vol. 2015. (Planets Ser.). (ENG., Illus.). 24p. (J). (gr. -1-2). lib. bdg. 32.79 *(978-1-62970-720-4(1),* 17239, Abdo Kids) ABDO Publishing Co.
—Saturn. 2017. (Planets Ser.). (ENG.). 24p. (J). (gr. -1-2). pap. 7.95 *(978-1-4966-1285-4(X),* 135017, Capstone Classroom) Capstone.
—Saturno (Saturn), 1 vol. 2016. (Planetas (Planets) Ser.). (SPA., Illus.). 24p. (J). (gr. -1-2). lib. bdg. 32.79 *(978-1-68080-757-8(9),* 22676, Abdo Kids) ABDO Publishing Co.
Bortolotti, Dan. Exploring Saturn. 2003. (ENG., Illus.). 64p. (J). (gr. 4-8). pap. 9.95 *(978-1-55297-765-1(X),* 683d9d3a-7a61-4259-b6c6-f36bd8d9b9ff) Firefly Bks., Ltd.
Carson, Mary Kay. Far-Out Guide to Saturn, 1 vol. 2010. (Far-Out Guide to the Solar System Ser.). (ENG., Illus.). 48p. (gr. 4-6). 27.93 *(978-0-7660-3178-4(0),* f610accb-d855-4c03-8b9b-b0e463631f97); pap. 11.53 *(978-1-59845-187-0(1),* 4f3a3150-9627-4cc0-be5f-ba66b622b612, Enslow Elementary) Enslow Publishing, LLC.
Chiger, Arielle & Elkin, Matthew. 20 Fun Facts about Gas Giants, 1 vol. 2014. (Fun Fact File: Space! Ser.). (ENG.). 32p. (J). (gr. 2-3). 27.93 *(978-1-4824-1001-3(X),* 7ae9a641-b1d0-422a-9dfe-2c66f19a7594); pap. 11.50 *(978-1-4824-1002-0(8),* ed9d7e5f-5dcd-478b-80bf-bb18a853525b) Stevens, Gareth Publishing LLLP.
Geiger, Beth. The Inside Story of Saturn. 2006. (J). 7.80 *(978-1-933798-08-0(4))* Sally Ride Science.
Glaser, Chaya. Saturn: Amazing Rings. 2015. (Out of This World Ser.). (ENG.). 24p. (J). (gr. -1-3). lib. bdg. 26.99 *(978-1-62724-566-1(9))* Bearport Publishing Co., Inc.
—Saturno: Anillos Asombrosos. 2015. (Fuera de Este Mundo Ser.). (SPA., Illus.). 24p. (J). (gr. -1-3). lib. bdg. 26.99 *(978-1-62724-596-8(0))* Bearport Publishing Co., Inc.
Goldstein, Margaret J. Saturn. 2003. (Our Universe Ser.). (ENG., Illus.). 32p. (gr. 2-4). lib. bdg. 22.60 *(978-0-8225-4653-5(1))* Lerner Publishing Group.
Hamilton, John. Cassini: Unlocking the Secrets of Saturn. 2017. (Xtreme Spacecraft Ser.). (ENG., Illus.). 32p. (J). (gr. 3-9). lib. bdg. 32.79 *(978-1-5321-1011-5(1),* 25598, Abdo & Daughters) ABDO Publishing Co.
Hantula, Richard & Asimov, Isaac. Saturno (Saturn), 1 vol. 2003. (Isaac Asimov's Biblioteca Del Universo Del Siglo XXI (Isaac Asimov's 21st Century Library of the Universe) Ser.).Tr. of Saturn: The Ringed Beauty. (SPA., Illus.). 32p. (gr. 3-5). lib. bdg. 28.67 *(978-0-8368-3860-2(2),* 7cabdd3e-00cc-44df-a42c-237e34e0fb1c, Gareth Stevens Learning Library) Stevens, Gareth Publishing LLLP.
Heos, Bridget. Do You Really Want to Visit Saturn? Fabbri, Daniele, illus. 2013. (Do You Really Want to Visit the Solar System? Ser.). (ENG.). 24p. (J). (gr. 1-4). 27.10 *(978-1-60753-200-2(X),* 16268) Amicus.
Hicks, Terry Allan. Saturn, 1 vol. 2010. (Space! Ser.). (ENG.). 64p. (gr. 5-5). lib. bdg. 35.50 *(978-0-7614-4249-3(9),* d15e59fc-e270-4f69-8034-b5bdf0be87f1) Cavendish Square Publishing LLC.
Hofer, Charles. Saturn. (Library of Planets Ser.). 48p. (gr. 5-8). 2009. 55.90 *(978-1-60853-821-8(4),* Rosen Reference) 2008. (ENG.). (J). lib. bdg. 34.47 *(978-1-4358-5075-0(0),* 6df80915-90e5-4494-9811-8ccaf4e70ae4) 2004. (ENG.). (YA). lib. bdg. 34.47 *(978-1-4042-0173-6(4),* fc3b0be7-26f1-44d6-8de4-63254560aaa2) Rosen Publishing Group, Inc., The.
Jefferis, David. Mighty Megaplanets: Jupiter & Saturn. 2008. (Exploring Our Solar System Ser.). (ENG., Illus.). 32p. (J). (gr. 3-7). pap. *(978-0-7787-3753-7(5))* Crabtree Publishing Co.
Miller, Ron. Saturn. 2003. (Worlds Beyond Ser.). (Illus.). 80p. (gr. 7-18). lib. bdg. 27.93 *(978-0-7613-2360-0(0),* Twenty-First Century Bks.) Lerner Publishing Group.
Murray, Julie. Saturn. 2018. (Planets (Dash!) Ser.). (ENG., Illus.). 24p. (J). (gr. k-4). lib. bdg. 31.36 *(978-1-5321-2531-7(3),* 30071, Abdo Zoom-Dash) ABDO Publishing Co.
Nichols, Amie. Journey to Saturn, 1 vol. 2014. (Spotlight on Space Science Ser.). (ENG.). 32p. (J). (gr. 5-5). pap. 12.75 *(978-1-4994-0376-3(3),* 3498b4af-52b0-410f-90f2-0c238659a687, PowerKids Pr.) Rosen Publishing Group, Inc., The.
Orme, Helen & Orme, David. Let's Explore Saturn, 1 vol. 2007. (Space Launch! Ser.). (ENG., Illus.). 24p. (J). (gr. 2-4). lib. bdg. 25.67 *(978-0-8368-7946-9(5),* e119f583-1260-44a0-a4e9-8ab82f51888d, Gareth Stevens Learning Library) Stevens, Gareth Publishing LLLP.
Owen, Ruth. Saturn, 1 vol. 2013. (Explore Outer Space Ser.). (ENG.). 32p. (J). (gr. 2-3). 29.93 *(978-1-61533-727-9(X),* 75a81bac-edb4-4435-a8c9-0744ad268c18); pap. 11.00 *(978-1-61533-771-2(7),* cf637717-e3a9-42ab-956c-336652c3548e) Rosen Publishing Group, Inc., The. (Windmill Bks.).
—Saturn. 2013. (Explore Outer Space Ser.). 32p. (J). (gr. 3-6). pap. 60.00 *(978-1-61533-772-9(5))* Windmill Bks.
Radomski, Kassandra. The Secrets of Saturn. 2015. (Planets Ser.). (ENG., Illus.). 32p. (J). (gr. 2-4). lib. bdg. 32.65 *(978-1-4914-5868-6(2),* 128831) Capstone.
Rathburn, Betsy. Saturn. 2019. (Space Science Ser.). (ENG., Illus.). 24p. (J). (gr. 3-7). lib. bdg. 26.95 *(978-1-62617-978-3(6),* Torque Bks.) Bellwether Media.
Riggs, Kate. Saturn. 2018. (Seedlings Ser.). (ENG., Illus.). 24p. (J). (gr. -1-1). pap. 9.99 *(978-1-62832-534-8(8),* 19640, Creative Paperbacks); *(978-1-60818-918-2(X),* 19642, Creative Education) Creative Co., The.
—Saturne. 2018. (Graines de Savoir Ser.). (FRE., Illus.). 24p. (J). *(978-1-77092-410-9(8),* 19699) Creative Co., The.
Ring, Susan. Saturn. (J). 2013. 27.13 *(978-1-62127-268-7(0))* 2013. pap. 12.95 *(978-1-62127-277-9(X))* 2004. pap. 8.95 *(978-1-59036-227-3(6))* 2004. (Illus.). 24p. (gr. 4-7). lib. bdg. 24.45 *(978-1-59036-100-9(8))* Weigl Pubs., Inc.
Ring, Susan & Roumanis, Alexis. Saturn. 2016. (Illus.). 24p. (J). *(978-1-5105-0989-4(5))* SmartBook Media, Inc.
Roumanis, Alexis. Saturn. 2016. (J). *(978-1-5105-2055-4(4))* SmartBook Media, Inc.
—Saturn. 2015. (J). *(978-1-4896-3300-2(6))* Weigl Pubs., Inc.
Saturn. 2nd rev. ed. 2009. (New Solar System Ser.). (ENG., Illus.). 32p. (gr. 3-6). 23.00 *(978-1-60413-213-7(2),* P166714, Facts On File) Infobase Holdings, Inc.
Slade, Suzanne. A Look at Saturn. 2009. (Astronomy Now! Ser.). 24p. (gr. 2-3). 42.50 *(978-1-61511-473-3(4),* PowerKids Pr.) Rosen Publishing Group, Inc., The.
Sparrow, Giles. Destination Saturn, 1 vol. 2009. (Destination Solar System Ser.). (ENG., Illus.). 32p. (J). (gr. 3-4). 28.93 *(978-1-4358-3447-7(X),* c26fcec7-e2a5-4a6f-83af-c69b029e8758); pap. 11.00 *(978-1-4358-3461-3(5),* 9b0e5f98-0ccf-4620-8015-904ad569d302) Rosen Publishing Group, Inc., The. (PowerKids Pr.).
Taylor-Butler, Christine. Saturn. 2007. (Scholastic News Nonfiction Readers Ser.). (ENG., Illus.). 24p. (J). (gr. 1-2). 22.00 *(978-0-531-14752-8(5))* Scholastic Library Publishing.
Waxman, Laura Hamilton. Saturn. 2009. (Early Bird Astronomy Ser.). (ENG.). 48p. (gr. 2-5). lib. bdg. 26.60 *(978-0-7613-4154-3(4))* Lerner Publishing Group.
Wimmer, Teresa. Saturn. 2007. (My First Look at: Planets Ser.). (Illus.). 24p. (J). (gr. -1-3). lib. bdg. 24.25 *(978-1-58341-522-1(X),* Creative Education) Creative Co., The.
World Book, Inc. Staff, contrib. by. Saturn & Uranus. (J). 2010. *(978-0-7166-9535-6(9))* 2006. (Illus.). 63p. *(978-0-7166-9506-6(5))* 2nd ed. 2006. (Illus.). 64p. *(978-0-7166-9519-6(7))* World Bk., Inc.
Zobel, Derek. Saturn. 2010. (Exploring Space Ser.). (ENG., Illus.). 24p. (J). (gr. k-3). lib. bdg. 26.95 *(978-1-60014-407-3(1),* Blastoff! Readers) Bellwether Media.

SAUDI ARABIA

Anderson, Abby. Saudi Arabia. 2009. pap. 52.95 *(978-0-7613-4734-7(8))* Lerner Publishing Group.
Etheredge, Laura. Saudi Arabia & Yemen, 1 vol. 2011. (Middle East: Region in Transition Ser.). (ENG., Illus.). 176p. (YA). (gr. 10-10). lib. bdg. 43.59 *(978-1-61530-335-9(9),* 86e57c40-80e3-4846-a697-0c5a3ea2c306) Rosen Publishing Group, Inc., The.
Halse Anderson, Laurie & Milivojevic, JoAnn. A Ticket to Saudi Arabia. 2005. (Ticket to Ser.). (Illus.). 48p. (gr. 2-4). 22.60 *(978-1-57505-147-5(8))* Lerner Publishing Group.
Ismail, Vehbi. Muhammad: The Last Prophet. 2011. 190p. 42.95 *(978-1-258-03217-3(1))* Literary Licensing, LLC.
Italia, Bob. Saudi Arabia. 2003. (Countries Set 4 Ser.). 40p. (gr. k-6). 27.07 *(978-1-57765-840-5(X),* Checkerboard Library) ABDO Publishing Co.
Janin, Hunt & Besheer, Margaret. Saudi Arabia, 1 vol. 2nd rev. ed. 2005. (Cultures of the World (Second Edition)(r) Ser.). (ENG., Illus.). 144p. (gr. 5-5). lib. bdg. 49.79 *(978-0-7614-1666-1(8),* d3bf59ef-aa1c-4dcc-b0a2-415bcd01d839) Cavendish Square Publishing LLC.
Keating, Susan Katz. Saudi Arabia. (Major Muslim Nations Ser.). 112p. (gr. 7-18). 2010. (YA). 25.95 *(978-1-4222-1385-8(4))* Vol. 13. 2015. (Illus.). (J). lib. bdg. 25.95 *(978-1-4222-3450-1(9))* Mason Crest.
Kehnemui Donnelly, Susan. Al-Rihlah Al-Mudhishah: Jawlah Fi Al-Mamlakah Wa-Aramku Al-Saudiyah. 2010. (ARA., Illus.). 31p. (J). *(978-1-882771-21-9(4))* History Factory.
Klepeis, Alicia. Understanding Saudi Arabia Today. 2014. (Illus.). 63p. (J). (gr. 3-6). 33.95 *(978-1-61228-651-8(8))* Mitchell Lane Pubs.
Kopp, Megan. Saudi Arabia. 2016. (Illus.). 32p. (J). *(978-1-5105-1905-3(X))* SmartBook Media, Inc.
—Saudi Arabia. 2014. (J). *(978-1-4896-1026-3(X))* Weigl Pubs., Inc.
Mockaitis, Thomas R. Osama Bin Laden: A Biography, 1 vol. 2010. (ENG., Illus.). 188p. 43.00 *(978-0-313-35374-1(3),* 900297497, Bloomsbury Academic) Bloomsbury Publishing Plc GBR. Dist: Macmillan.
Orr, Tamra. Saudi Arabian Heritage. 2018. (21st Century Junior Library: Celebrating Diversity in My Classroom Ser.). (ENG., Illus.). 24p. (J). (gr. 2-4). lib. bdg. 30.64 *(978-1-5341-2903-0(0),* 211656) Cherry Lake Publishing.
Owings, Lisa. Saudi Arabia. 2012. (Exploring Countries Ser.). (ENG., Illus.). 32p. (J). (gr. 3-7). lib. bdg. 27.95 *(978-1-60014-764-7(X),* Blastoff! Readers) Bellwether Media.
Senker, Cath. Costume Around the World: Saudi Arabia. 2008. (Costume Around the World Ser.). (ENG., Illus.). 32p. (gr. 4-6). 28.00 *(978-0-7910-9773-1(0),* P459458, Chelsea Clubhse.) Infobase Holdings, Inc.
Sheen, Barbara, contrib. by. Growing up in Saudi Arabia. 2018. (ENG.). 80p. (YA). (gr. 5-12). lib. bdg. *(978-1-68282-323-1(7))* ReferencePoint Pr., Inc.
Spilling, Michael, et al. Saudi Arabia, 1 vol. 3rd rev. ed. 2014. (Cultures of the World (Third Edition)(r) Ser.). (ENG.). 144p. (gr. 5-5). 48.79 *(978-0-7614-4996-6(5),* b7b63d4b-08f1-4e92-9a22-a7351b8cab8a) Cavendish Square Publishing LLC.
Sullivan, Laura L. Saudi Arabia. 2017. (Exploring World Cultures Ser.). (Illus.). 32p. (J). (gr. 3-3). pap. 63.48 *(978-1-5026-2488-8(5),* Cavendish Square) Cavendish Square Publishing LLC.
Tracy, Kathleen. We Visit Saudi Arabia. 2011. (Your Land & My Land Ser.). (Illus.). 64p. (J). (gr. 4-7). lib. bdg. 33.95 *(978-1-58415-963-6(4))* Mitchell Lane Pubs.
Walsh, Kieran. Saudi Arabia. 2003. (Countries in the News Ser.). (Illus.). 24p. (J). 25.64 *(978-1-58952-681-5(3))* Rourke Educational Media.

SAVINGS BANKS

Lindeen, Mary. Spending & Saving. 2019. (Beginning-To-Read Ser.). (ENG.). 32p. (J). (gr. k-2). pap. 13.26 *(978-1-68404-435-1(9))* Norwood Hse. Pr.

SAWYER, TOM (FICTITIOUS CHARACTER)—FICTION

Barchers, Suzanne I. The Adventures of Tom Sawyer: An Instructional Guide for Literature. rev. ed. 2015. (Great Works). (ENG., Illus.). 72p. (gr. 4-8). pap. 9.99 *(978-1-4258-8973-9(5))* Shell Educational Publishing.
Brook, Henry, retold by. Tom Sawyer. 2008. (Usborne Classics Retold Ser.). 160p. (J). pap. 4.99 *(978-0-7945-2063-2(4),* Usborne) EDC Publishing.
Novel Units. The Adventures of Tom Sawyer Novel Units Student Packet. 2019. (ENG.). (YA). pap., stu. ed. 13.99 *(978-1-56137-528-8(4),* NU5284SP, Novel Units, Inc.) Classroom Library Co.
Rigby Education Staff. Tom Sawyer: Jumbled Tumble. (gr. k-2). 26.00 *(978-0-7635-2424-1(7))* Rigby Education.
Ross, Linda B., adapted by. Tom Sawyer: Read Aloud Classics Edition Big Book. 2014. (Read Aloud Classics Ser.). (J). (gr. -1-2). 9.99 *(978-1-4788-0707-0(5))* Newmark Learning LLC.
Tom Sawyer: 6 Small Books. (gr. k-2). 23.00 *(978-0-7635-8507-5(6))* Rigby Education.
Twain, Mark, pseud. The Adventures of Tom Sawyer - Literary Touchstone Edition. 2005. 216p. (YA). per. 4.99 *(978-1-58049-596-7(6),* PWH5966) Prestwick Hse., Inc.
—The Adventures of Tom Sawyer, Complete. l.t. ed. 2006. 408p. pap. *(978-1-84637-320-6(4))* Echo Library.
—Las Aventuras de Tom Sawyer.Tr. of Adventures of Tom Sawyer. (SPA.). (YA). *(978-84-7525-151-6(X))* Ediciones Generales Anaya SA.
—Las Aventuras de Tom Sawyer. 2003. (Advanced Reading Ser.).Tr. of Adventures of Tom Sawyer. (SPA.). 124p. (J). 11.95 *(978-84-239-9045-0(1))* Espasa Calpe, S.A. ESP. Dist: Planeta Publishing Corp.
—Avventure di Tom Sawyer. pap. 15.95 *(978-88-451-2151-7(8))* Fabbri Editori - RCS Libri ITA. Dist: Distribooks, Inc.
—A Song for Aunt Polly. Bates, Amy, illus. 2004. (Adventures of Tom Sawyer Ser.: Vol. 1). 32p. (J). *(978-0-7607-3963-1(3))* Barnes & Noble, Inc.
—Tom Sawyer. 2005. 264p. 28.95 *(978-1-4218-0768-3(8),* 1st World Library - Literary Society) 1st World Publishing, Inc.
—Tom Sawyer, 1 vol. Mullarkey, Lisa & McWilliam, Howard, illus. 2010. (Calico Illustrated Classics Ser.: No. 1). (ENG.). 112p. (J). (gr. 2-5). 38.50 *(978-1-60270-704-7(9),* 3961, Calico Chapter Bks.) ABDO Publishing Co.
—Tom Sawyer. l.t. ed. 2006. (ENG.). 363p. (J). (gr. 5-8). 22.99 *(978-0-7862-8640-9(7))* Cengage Gale.
—Tom Sawyer. 2006. (Classic Retelling Ser.). (Illus.). 224p. (YA). (gr. 8-12). *(978-0-618-12053-6(X),* 2-00218) Holt McDougal.
—Tom Sawyer. 2004. reprint ed. pap. 1.99 *(978-1-4192-5166-5(X))* Kessinger Publishing, LLC.
—Tom Sawyer. (Young Collector's Illustrated Classics Ser.). (Illus.). 192p. (J). (gr. 3-7). 9.95 *(978-1-56156-453-8(2))* Kidsbooks, LLC.
—Tom Sawyer. (Coleccion Clasicos de la Juventud). (SPA., Illus.). 220p. (J). 12.95 *(978-84-7189-029-0(1),* ORT310) Ortells, Alfredo Editorial S.L. ESP. Dist: Continental Bk. Co., Inc.
—Tom Sawyer. 2009. 196p. (gr. 4-7). pap. 12.99 *(978-1-934941-63-8(8))* Red & Black Pubs.
—Tom Sawyer. 2003. (Timeless Classics Ser.). (SPA., Illus.). 95p. (J). (gr. 5-8). pap. 12.95 *(978-84-372-2235-6(4))* Santillana USA Publishing Co., Inc.
—Tom Sawyer, Detective. (SPA., Illus.). 160p. (YA). 11.95 *(978-84-7281-062-4(3),* AF0623) Auriga, Ediciones S.A. ESP. Dist: Continental Bk. Co., Inc.
Twain, Mark, pseud & Lawson, Jessica. The Tom Sawyer Collection: The Adventures of Tom Sawyer; the Adventures of Huckleberry Finn; the Actual & Truthful Adventures of Becky Thatcher. Bruno, Iacopo, illus. 2014. (ENG.). 944p. (J). (gr. 3-7). 52.99 *(978-1-4814-0536-2(5),* Simon & Schuster Bks. For Young Readers) Simon & Schuster Bks. For Young Readers.

SAXONS

see Anglo-Saxons

SAYINGS

see Proverbs; Quotations

SCANDINAVIA

Crabtree Staff & Williams, Brian. Understanding Norse Myths, 1 vol. 2012. (ENG., Illus.). 48p. (J). pap. *(978-0-7787-4532-7(5))* Crabtree Publishing Co.
Dorling Kindersley Publishing Staff. Vikings: DKFindOut! 2018. (Illus.). 64p. (J). *(978-0-241-32302-1(9))* Dorling Kindersley Publishing, Inc.
Ganeri, Anita. How to Live Like a Viking Warrior. Epelbaum, Mariano, illus. 2015. (How to Live Like ... Ser.). (ENG.). 32p. (J). (gr. 3-6). lib. bdg. 27.99 *(978-1-4677-6354-7(3),* b777eb9b-1d65-475c-8f9c-8cd0579a0a5b, Hungry Tomato (r)) Lerner Publishing Group.
Greenling, Jason. The Technology of the Vikings, 1 vol. 2016. (Ancient Innovations Ser.). (ENG., Illus.). 64p. (gr. 6-6). 35.93 *(978-1-5026-2241-9(6),* 43cd570e-0050-4300-81fa-2dd9c5ee8ed5) Cavendish Square Publishing LLC.
Hopkins, Andrea. Viking Families & Farms. 2009. (Viking Library). 24p. (gr. 3-3). 42.50 *(978-1-60854-257-4(2),* PowerKids Pr.) Rosen Publishing Group, Inc., The.
Park, Louise & Love, Timothy. The Scandinavian Vikings, 1 vol. 2010. (Ancient & Medieval People Ser.). (ENG.). 32p. (gr. 5-5). 31.21 *(978-0-7614-4445-9(9),* 659468e5-be90-4a06-b3a4-4ee7a04c0078) Cavendish Square Publishing LLC.
Steele, Philip & Ljosland, Ragnhild. Vikings. 2018. (Illus.). 64p. (J). *(978-1-5444-1093-7(X))* Dorling Kindersley Publishing, Inc.
Wargin, Kathy-jo. D Is for Dala Horse: A Nordic Countries Alphabet. Graef, Renée, illus. 2010. (Discover the World Ser.). (ENG.). 40p. (J). (gr. 1-3). 17.95 *(978-1-58536-510-4(6),* 202203) Sleeping Bear Pr.
—D Is for Dala Horse: A Nordic Countries Alphabet. 2016. (Av2 Fiction Readalong 2017 Ser.). (ENG.). (J). (gr. k-6). 34.28 *(978-1-4896-5200-3(0),* AV2 by Weigl) Weigl Pubs., Inc.
Williams, Brian. Understanding Norse Myths. 2012. (ENG., Illus.). 48p. (J). *(978-0-7787-4527-3(9))* Crabtree Publishing Co.

SCARECROWS

Wilde, Kim. How to Make a Scarecrow: Band 00/Lilac (Collins Big Cat) 2006. (Collins Big Cat Ser.). (ENG., Illus.). 16p. (J). (gr. -1-k). pap. 6.99 *(978-0-00-718645-7(2))* HarperCollins Pubs. Ltd. GBR. Dist: Independent Pubs. Group.

SCARECROWS—FICTION

Amery, Heather. Scarecrow's Secret. Tyler, Jenny, ed. Cartwright, Stephen, illus. rev. ed. 2004. (Farmyard Tales Readers Ser.). 16p. (J). pap. 5.95 *(978-0-7945-0751-0(4),* Usborne) EDC Publishing.
Awdry, W. Thomas Scares the Crows. 2016. (Thomas & Friends 8X8 Ser.). lib. bdg. 14.75 *(978-0-606-38895-5(8))* Turtleback.
Banks, Rosemary. Moe the Well Dressed Scarecrow. 2013. 20p. pap. 24.95 *(978-1-4626-9683-3(X))* America Star Bks.
Baum, L. Frank. Oz, the Complete Collection, Volume 3: The Patchwork Girl of Oz; Tik-Tok of Oz; the Scarecrow of Oz. 2013. (Oz, the Complete Collection: 3). (ENG.). 720p. (J). (gr. 3-7). 19.99 *(978-1-4424-8892-2(1))*; Vol. 3. pap. 12.99 *(978-1-4424-8549-5(3))* Simon & Schuster Children's Publishing. (Aladdin).
Baum, L. Frank & Thompson, Ruth Plumly. Oz, the Complete Collection, Volume 5 Vol. 5: The Magic of Oz; Glinda of Oz; the Royal Book of Oz. 2013. (Oz, the Complete Collection: 5). (ENG.). 576p. (J). (gr. 3-7). 19.99 *(978-1-4424-8894-6(8),* Aladdin) Simon & Schuster Children's Publishing.
—The Royal Book of Oz. 2011. 160p. (gr. -1-7). 24.95 *(978-1-4638-9602-7(6))*; pap. 13.95 *(978-1-60664-507-9(2))* Rodgers, Alan Bks.
—The Royal Book of Oz. 2009. 112p. pap. 8.99 *(978-1-60459-763-9(1))* Wilder Pubns., Corp.
Blyton, Enid. Ugly Old Scarecrow: And Other Stories. 2013. (Illus.). 192p. (J). 9.95 *(978-1-84135-462-0(7))* Award Pubns. Ltd. GBR. Dist: Parkwest Pubns., Inc.
Broad, Michael. #4 Spooky Ballet! 2011. (Agent Amelia Ser.). pap. 33.92 *(978-0-7613-8344-4(1),* Darby Creek) Lerner Publishing Group.
Brown, Ken. The Scarecrow's Hat, 1 vol. 2011. (ENG., Illus.). 32p. (J). (gr. -1-k). pap. 8.99 *(978-1-56145-570-6(9))* Peachtree Publishing Co. Inc.
Brown, Phillip A. Haywood & Mel: Haywood Wants to Quit, 1 vol. 2010. 24p. pap. 24.95 *(978-1-4489-8371-1(1))* PublishAmerica, Inc.
Chapman, Catherine. The Magical Scarecrows' Garden. 2009. 160p. pap. 35.95 *(978-1-60860-481-4(0),* Strategic Bk. Publishing) Strategic Book Publishing & Rights Agency (SBPRA).
Cunningham, Darrell. The Adventures of Stan: Book One the Awakening. 2011. (Illus.). 80p. (gr. 4-6). pap. 29.00 *(978-1-4567-7918-4(4))* AuthorHouse.
Dillon, Jana. Jeb Scarecrow's Pumpkin Patch, 1 vol. 2016. (ENG., Illus.). 34p. (J). (gr. k-3). pap. 9.95 *(978-1-4556-2181-1(1),* Pelican Publishing) Arcadia Publishing.
Dolan, Penny. At the End of the Garden. 2008. (Tadpoles Ser.). (ENG., Illus.). 24p. (J). (gr. -1-3). pap. *(978-0-7787-3881-7(7))*; lib. bdg. *(978-0-7787-3850-3(7))* Crabtree Publishing Co.
Donaldson, Julia. The Scarecrows' Wedding. Scheffler, Axel, illus. 2014. (ENG.). 32p. (J). (gr. -1-3). 18.99 *(978-0-545-72606-1(9),* Levine, Arthur A. Bks.) Scholastic, Inc.
Gordon, Judy Ann. Grammie's Magical Garden: Beyond the Gate. 2012. 68p. pap. 28.99 *(978-1-4772-7973-1(3))* AuthorHouse.
Hernandez, Christopher. Scaredycrow. 2013. lib. bdg. 14.75 *(978-0-606-31953-9(0))* Turtleback.
Keene, Carolyn. The Secret of the Scarecrow. Pamintuan, Macky, illus. 2013. (Nancy Drew & the Clue Crew Ser.: 36). (ENG.). 96p. (J). (gr. 1-4). pap. 5.99 *(978-1-4424-5353-1(2),* Aladdin) Simon & Schuster Children's Publishing.
Kidwell, Justina. The Enchanted Garden & the Curse of the Evil Witch: The Kent Boys' Adventures. 2009. 68p. pap. 19.95 *(978-1-60749-163-7(X))* America Star Bks.
Knight, Chris. Skaggy the Scarecrow: A Halloween Story. 2010. (Illus.). 40p. pap. 18.49 *(978-1-4520-2473-8(1))* AuthorHouse.
Leday, Linda. Sammy the Scarecrow. 2009. 36p. pap. 16.99 *(978-1-4389-4826-3(3))* AuthorHouse.
Long, Loren. Otis & the Scarecrow. Long, Loren, illus. 2014. (Otis Ser.). (ENG., Illus.). 40p. (J). (gr. -1-2). 19.99 *(978-0-399-16396-8(4),* Philomel Bks.) Penguin Young Readers Group.
Lougher, Jenny. Ted & the Combine Harvester. Lewis, Wayne, illus. 2007. 23p. pap. *(978-1-905553-27-3(7))* BookPublishingWorld.
McFarland, Kim. A Refugee in Oz. 2010. 164p. pap. 11.95 *(978-0-557-48706-6(4))* Lulu Pr., Inc.
Newman, Gerry. Nellie, the Scarecrow: A Dorset Fable. 2003. (Illus.). 188p. pap. 12.50 *(978-1-84426-184-0(0))* Upfront Publishing Ltd. GBR. Dist: Printondemand-worldwide.com.
Norton Kreider, Barbara. Mr Squealy Meets Scarecrow. Dimbylow, Jube, illus. 2013. 24p. pap. *(978-1-921883-53-8(7))* Pick-a-Woo Woo Pubs.
Oblich, Kathleen. Jake & the Scarecrow. 2007. 48p. pap. 16.95 *(978-1-4241-3101-3(4))* PublishAmerica, Inc.
Parker, Emma. The Not So Scary Scarecrow. 2010. (Illus.). pap. *(978-1-877547-88-1(3))* First Edition Ltd.
Pullman, Philip. The Scarecrow & His Servant. Bailey, Peter, illus. 2007. (ENG.). 240p. (J). (gr. 3-7). 7.99 *(978-0-440-42130-6(6),* Yearling) Random Hse. Children's Bks.
Rex, Michael. Scarecrow. Rex, Michael, illus. 2003. (Scholastic Reader: Level 1 Ser.). (ENG., Illus.). 28p. (J). (gr. -1-1). 16.19 *(978-0-439-49311-6(0))* Scholastic, Inc.
Rylant, Cynthia. Scarecrow. Stringer, Lauren, illus. 2014. 32p. pap. 7.00 *(978-1-61003-181-3(4))* Center for the Collaborative Classroom.
Santa Niclaus. Hay Baggins: The Little Scarecrow Boy. 2012. 140p. pap. 39.88 *(978-1-4669-6918-6(0))* Trafford Publishing.
Sillifant, Alec. Farmer Ham. Spoor, Mike, illus. import ed. 2004. 24p. *(978-1-904511-93-9(7))* Meadowside Children's Bks.
Stine, R. L. The Scarecrow Walks at Midnight (Classic Goosebumps #16) 2010. (Classic Goosebumps Ser.: 16). (ENG.). 160p. (J). (gr. 3-7). 7.99 *(978-0-545-17801-3(0),* Scholastic Paperbacks) Scholastic, Inc.
Thompson, Ruth Plumly. The Royal Book of Oz. 2004. reprint ed. pap. 1.99 *(978-1-4192-8123-5(2))*; pap. 20.95 *(978-1-4191-8123-8(8))* Kessinger Publishing, LLC.

S

Whitlock, Matt. Punk 'n Patch. Whitlock, Matt, illus. 2005. (Illus.). 32p. (J). (gr. -1-3). 16.95 *(978-0-9769057-0-7(1))* Little Hero.

Yolen, Jane. The Scarecrow's Dance. Ibatoulline, Bagram, illus. 2009. (ENG.). 32p. (J). (gr. -1-3). 19.99 *(978-1-4169-3770-8(6)*, Simon & Schuster Bks. For Young Readers) Simon & Schuster Bks. For Young Readers.

SCENARIOS

see Motion Picture Plays; Television Plays

SCENERY

see Views

SCENERY (STAGE)

see Theaters—Stage Setting and Scenery

SCHALLENBERGER, MOSES, 1826-1909

Wadsworth, Ginger. Survival in the Snow. Orback, Craig, illus. 2011. 48p. (J). pap. 6.95 *(978-0-7613-3941-0(8)*, First Avenue Editions) Lerner Publishing Group.

SCHLIEMANN, HEINRICH, 1822-1890

Kerns, Ann. Troy. 2008. (Unearthing Ancient Worlds Ser.). (ENG.). 80p. (gr. 5-8). lib. bdg. 30.60 *(978-0-8225-7582-5(5))* Lerner Publishing Group.

Schlitz, Laura Amy. The Hero Schliemann: The Dreamer Who Dug for Troy. Byrd, Robert, illus. 2013. (ENG.). 80p. (J). (gr. 4-7). pap. 8.99 *(978-0-7636-6504-3(5))* Candlewick Pr.

SCHMIDT, KARL PATTERSON, 1890-1957

Knittel, Patty. Red Coats & Scimitars. 2014. (J). pap. *(978-0-8163-5701-7(3))* Pacific Pr. Publishing Assn.

Wright, A. Gilbert. In the Steps of the Great American Herpetologist. Kalmenoff, Matthew, illus. 2014. (ENG.). 128p. (J). (gr. 2-6). pap. 11.95 *(978-1-59077-360-4(8))* Evans, M. & Co., Inc.

SCHOLARSHIP

see Learning and Scholarship

SCHOLARSHIPS

see also Student Loans

Bercik, Mark. America's Complete Sports Scholarship Guide: Giving Back Something to the Game. Wilding, Diane, ed. 2nd rev. ed. 2003. Orig. Title: America's Sports Scholarship Guide. (Illus.). 272p. (YA). (gr. 4-12). per. 19.95 *(978-0-9721199-1-7(4))* America Sports Publishing.

Contagious Community: Living Beyond Yourself: Connect with God, Connect with Others, Connect with Life. 2008. 175p. pap. *(978-1-57494-431-0(2)*, Serendipity Hse.) Lifeway Christian Resources.

Gagne, Tammy. Paying for College. 2020. (ENG.). 80p. (YA). (gr. 6-12). 41.27 *(978-1-68282-805-2(0)*, BrightPoint Pr.) ReferencePoint Pr., Inc.

McCormick, Lisa Wade. Financial Aid Smarts: Getting Money for School, 1 vol. 2012. (Get Smart with Your Money Ser.). (ENG., Illus.). 64p. (J). (gr. 6-6). pap. 13.95 *(978-1-4488-8266-3(4)*, 388641bd-f5c7-4357-b0a0-07e1e7743840); lib. bdg. 37.13 *(978-1-4488-8252-6(4)*, 16f522c3-6840-4cfb-9577-8529dc3a848a) Rosen Publishing Group, Inc., The.

Prentzas, G. S. Smart Strategies for Paying for College, 1 vol. 2014. (Financial Security & Life Success for Teens Ser.). (ENG., Illus.). 80p. (J). (gr. 7-7). 37.47 *(978-1-4777-7614-8(1)*, c9c44a94-2925-495c-bd40-1291a0889075) Rosen Publishing Group, Inc., The.

Rugg, Frederick E. Financial Aid in Less Than 3000 Words. 6p. (YA). 9th rev. ed. 2003. pap. 6.95 *(978-1-883062-51-4(9))* 10th rev. ed. 2004. pap. 6.95 *(978-1-883062-57-6(8))* Rugg's Recommendations.

Tate, Nikki. Better Together: Creating Community in an Uncertain World, 1 vol. 2018. (Orca Footprints Ser.: 13). (ENG., Illus.). 48p. (J). (gr. 4-7). 19.95 *(978-1-4598-1300-7(6))* Orca Bk. Pubs. USA.

SCHOOL ADMINISTRATION

see School Management And Organization

SCHOOL AND HOME

see Home and School

SCHOOL ATTENDANCE

see also Child Labor; Dropouts; First Day of School

Davidson, Tish. Life Balance: School Conflict. 2004. (Life Balance Ser.). (ENG., Illus.). 80p. (YA). (gr. 5-8). pap. 6.95 *(978-0-531-15571-4(4)*, Watts, Franklin) Scholastic Library Publishing.

Go Back to School with Jack & Annie! 2003. *(978-0-375-88495-5(5))* Random Hse. Children's Bks.

Hoffman, Joan. First Grade Basics. 2018. (ENG.). 64p. (J). (gr. 1-1). pap., wbk. ed. 4.49 *(978-1-58947-037-8(0)*, 8fc40707-6730-4473-b079-c3474af265ba) School Zone Publishing Co.

—Second Grade Basics. 2012. (ENG.). 64p. (J). (gr. 2-2). pap., wbk. ed. 4.49 *(978-1-58947-038-5(9)*, bf484597-7a63-43ef-aa9f-7610aa93a535) School Zone Publishing Co.

Machen Pritchard, M. Ann. Phil the Pill & Friends: Making Positive Choices. Machen Pritchard, M. Ann, illus. 2005. (Illus.). 75p. (J). per. 11.99 *(978-0-9772210-0-4(8)*, Phil the Pill & Friends) MAMP Creations.

Ricciuti, Edward R. We Listen, 1 vol. 2008. (Ready for School Ser.). (ENG.). 24p. (gr. k-1). pap. 9.23 *(978-0-7614-3274-6(4)*, 071045d1-073d-4d11-8eb1-15b5887b98a0) Cavendish Square Publishing LLC.

Rosa-Mendoza, Gladys. My School, 1 vol. Murphy, Terri, illus. 2010. (My World Ser.). (ENG.). 24p. (J). (gr. k-1). pap. 9.15 *(978-1-61533-039-3(9)*, 017780f0-76d4-4031-ad5e-6bcc6c282a8b); lib. bdg. 27.27 *(978-1-60754-953-6(0)*, 46760153-2e95-44e0-b3e7-0d6726c802c7) Rosen Publishing Group, Inc., The. (Windmill Bks.).

School Zone Interactive Staff. First Grade. 2003. (On-Track Software Ser.). (ENG.). (J). (gr. 1-18). cd-rom 24.99 *(978-1-58947-547-2(X))* School Zone Publishing Co.

School Zone Publishing. Third Grade. 2003. (Power Packs Ser.). (ENG., Illus.). (J). 24.99 *(978-1-58947-533-5(X))* School Zone Publishing Co.

—Third Grade: Builds Skills & Confidence for Success in School! 2003. (Software Ser.). (ENG.). (J). (gr. 3-18). 24.99 *(978-1-58947-538-0(0))* School Zone Publishing Co.

School Zone Publishing Company Staff. School Time Fun. (Illus.). (J). 19.99 incl. audio compact disk *(978-0-88743-958-2(6))* School Zone Publishing Co.

SCHOOL ATTENDANCE—FICTION

Adler, David A. Young Cam Jansen & the New Girl Mystery. Natti, Susanna, illus. 2005. (Young Cam Jansen Ser.: 10). (ENG.). 32p. (J). (gr. 1-3). mass mkt. 5.99 *(978-0-14-240353-2(9)*, Penguin Young Readers) Penguin Young Readers Group.

Akubue, Chira. Azuka. 2012. (ENG., Illus.). 16p. pap. 18.30 *(978-1-4670-0796-2(X))* AuthorHouse.

Apostolina, M. Hazing Meri Sugarman. 2005. (ENG.). 272p. (YA). pap. 8.99 *(978-1-4169-0610-0(X)*, Simon Pulse) Simon Pulse.

Arden, Richard. Girls' Boarding School. (ENG.). 320p. pap. 6.95 *(978-0-7472-4039-6(6))* Headline Publishing Group GBR. Dist: Trafalgar Square Publishing.

Azuma, Kiyohiko. Azumanga Daioh, Vol. 3. 2004. (Illus.). 172p. (YA). pap. 9.99 *(978-1-4139-0030-9(5))* ADV Manga.

Bentley, Dawn. Fuzzy Bear Goes to School. Nagy, Krisztina, illus. 2005. (Fuzzy Bear Ser.). 10p. (J). 10.95 *(978-1-58117-124-2(2)*, Intervisual/Piggy Toes) Bendon, Inc.

Blance, Ellen & Cook, Tony. Monster Goes to School. Date not set. (Illus.). 24p. pap. 129.15 *(978-0-582-18596-8(3))* Addison-Wesley Longman, Ltd. GBR. Dist: Trans-Atlantic Pubns., Inc.

Blyton, Enid. The Naughtiest Girl Is a Monitor. (Illus.). 160p. (J). pap. 6.95 *(978-0-09-945490-8(4))* Penguin Random Hse. GBR. Dist: Trafalgar Square Publishing.

Brown, Marc. Arthur & the Cootie-Catcher, Vol. 15. unabr. ed. 2004. (Arthur Chapter Bks.: Bk. 15). 60p. (J). (gr. 2-4). pap. 17.00 incl. audio *(978-0-8072-0346-0(7)*, Listening Library) Random Hse. Audio Publishing Group.

—Arthur's off to School. 2004. (ENG., Illus.). 24p. (J). (gr. -1-1). pap. 3.99 *(978-0-316-73378-6(4))* Little, Brown Bks. for Young Readers.

—Arthur's off to School. Brown, Marc, illus. 2019. (ENG., Illus.). 24p. (J). (gr. -1-k). pap. 4.99 *(978-1-338-27761-6(8)*, Cartwheel Bks.) Scholastic, Inc.

Butcher, A. J. Spy High Mission One. 2004. (ENG.). 224p. (YA). (gr. 5-8). pap. 13.99 *(978-0-316-73760-9(7))* Little, Brown Bks. for Young Readers.

—Spy High Mission Two: Chaos Rising. 2004. (ENG., Illus.). 240p. (YA). (gr. 5-8). pap. 14.99 *(978-0-316-73765-4(8))* Little, Brown Bks. for Young Readers.

Capucilli, Alyssa Satin. Biscuit Loves School Giant Lift-The-Flap. Schories, Pat, illus. 2003. (ENG.). 12p. (J). (gr. -1-3). 9.99 *(978-0-06-009454-6(0)*, HarperFestival) HarperCollins Pubs.

Clements, Andrew. Frindle. Selznick, Brian, illus. 105p. (J). (gr. 3-5). pap. 4.50 *(978-0-8072-1522-7(8)*, Listening Library) Random Hse. Audio Publishing Group.

—Frindle. unabr. ed. 2004. (Middle Grade Cassette Librariestm Ser.). 105p. (J). (gr. 3-7). pap. 29.00 incl. audio *(978-0-8072-7994-6(3)*, S YA 961 SP, Listening Library) Random Hse. Audio Publishing Group.

Couric, Katie. The Brand New Kid. 2004. (Illus.). (J). (gr. -1-3). spiral bd. *(978-0-616-07225-7(2))*; spiral bd. *(978-0-616-07226-4(0))* Canadian National Institute for the Blind/Institut National Canadien pour les Aveugles.

Dodd, Christina. Back to School Mom, 18 Copies. 2003. mass mkt. 128.88 *(978-0-06-056267-0(6))* HarperCollins Pubs.

Goldston, Juli-Ette Robin. Bowtie Brownlee Goes to School. 2012. 16p. pap. 14.99 *(978-1-4685-9456-0(7))* AuthorHouse.

Goodman, Jill. Mustang, the Little Dog Who Was Afraid to Go to School. 2004. (Illus.). (J). pap. *(978-1-889636-63-4(0))* Youthlight, Inc.

Hall, Kirsten. First Day of School: All about Shapes & Sizes. Luedecke, Bev, illus. 2004. (Beastieville Ser.). (ENG.). 32p. (J). (gr. k-1). pap. 3.95 *(978-0-516-24654-3(2)*, Children's Pr.) Scholastic Library Publishing.

Harper, Jessica. Lizzy's Ups & Downs: NOT an Ordinary School Day. Dupont, Lindsay Harper, illus. 2004. 32p. (J). (gr. -1-3). 15.99 *(978-0-06-052063-2(9))* HarperCollins Pubs.

Harrison, Lisi. The Revenge of the Wannabes. 2005. (Clique Ser.: 3). (ENG.). 304p. (J). (gr. 7-17). pap. 16.99 *(978-0-316-70133-4(5)*, Poppy) Little, Brown Bks. for Young Readers.

Henson, Dwayne. Mr. Sunny Sunshine "Jump Start!" A special junior toolbox learning edition Featuring: a few valuable lessons & advise to help kids jump start their school Day. 2006. (ENG.). 32p. pap. 14.99 *(978-1-4257-0083-6(7))* Xlibris Corp.

Hurwitz, Johanna. Fourth-Grade Fuss. Hammond, Andy, illus. 2004. 144p. (J). lib. bdg. 16.89 *(978-0-06-052344-2(1))*; (ENG.). (gr. 3-7). 16.99 *(978-0-06-052343-5(3)*, HarperCollins) HarperCollins Pubs.

Kalar, Bonnie. Miss Lane's Class. Spreen, Kathe, illus. Date not set. 12p. (J). (gr. -1-2). pap. *(978-1-891619-38-0(1))* Corona Pr.

Krulik, Nancy. Who's Afraid of Fourth Grade? Super Special. John and Wendy, illus. 2004. (Katie Kazoo, Switcheroo Ser.: No. 1). (ENG.). 160p. (J). (gr. 2-4). mass mkt. 7.99 *(978-0-448-43555-8(1)*, Grosset & Dunlap) Penguin Young Readers Group.

Mazer, Anne. Some Things Never Change. 2004. (Amazing Days of Abby Hayes Ser.: Bk. 13). (Illus.). 101p. (J). (gr. 4-7). 12.65 *(978-0-7569-5302-7(2))* Perfection Learning Corp.

Moss, Marissa. Amelia's Bully Survival Guide. Moss, Marissa, illus. 2006. (Amelia Ser.). (ENG., Illus.). 40p. (J). (gr. 2-5). 14.99 *(978-1-4169-0907-1(9)*, Simon & Schuster/Paula Wiseman Bks.) Simon & Schuster/Paula Wiseman Bks.

Nickelodeon Staff. Hooray for School: Going to School With Nick. 2007. 4.99 *(978-1-4169-5401-9(5)*, Simon Spotlight/Nickelodeon) Simon Spotlight/Nickelodeon.

Novel Units. The Flunking of Joshua T. Bates Novel Units Teacher Guide. 2019. (ENG.). (J). pap. 12.99 *(978-1-56137-612-4(4)*, Novel Units, Inc.) Classroom Library Co.

—Miss Nelson Is Back / Miss Nelson Is Missing Novel Units Teacher Guide. 2019. (Miss Nelson Ser.). (ENG.). (J). (gr. -1-3). pap. 12.99 *(978-1-56137-032-0(0)*, Novel Units, Inc.) Classroom Library Co.

—Slam! Novel Units Student Packet. 2019. (ENG.). (YA). pap. 13.99 *(978-1-58130-641-5(5)*, Novel Units, Inc.) Classroom Library Co.

—Slam! Novel Units Teacher Guide. 2019. (ENG.). (YA). pap. 12.99 *(978-1-58130-640-8(7)*, Novel Units, Inc.) Classroom Library Co.

—Tales of a Fourth Grade Nothing Novel Units Student Packet. 2019. (Fudge Ser.). (ENG.). (J). pap. 13.99 *(978-1-56137-709-1(0)*, Novel Units, Inc.) Classroom Library Co.

—Tales of a Fourth Grade Nothing Novel Units Teacher Guide. 2019. (Fudge Ser.). (ENG.). (J). pap. 12.99 *(978-1-56137-271-3(4)*, Novel Units, Inc.) Classroom Library Co.

—There's a Boy in the Girls' Bathroom Novel Units Teacher Guide. 2019. (ENG.). (J). pap. 12.99 *(978-1-56137-410-6(5)*, Novel Units, Inc.) Classroom Library Co.

Parish, Herman. Amelia Bedelia Goes Back to School. Sweat, Lynn, illus. 2004. (Amelia Bedelia Ser.). (ENG.). 20p. (J). (gr. -1-3). pap. 6.99 *(978-0-06-051873-8(1)*, Greenwillow Bks.) HarperCollins Pubs.

Park, Barbara. Junie B., First Grader - Boss of Lunch. Brunkus, Denise, illus. 2003. (Junie B., First Grader Ser.: No. 2). 96p. (J). (gr. k-3). lib. bdg. 11.99 *(978-0-375-90294-9(5)*, Golden Bks.) Random Hse. Children's Bks.

Rice, David L. Because Brian Hugged His Mother. 2004. (Sharing Nature with Children Book Ser.). (Illus.). 32p. (YA). (gr. -1-3). 16.95 *(978-1-883220-90-7(4))* Take Heart Pubns.

Shepard, Sara. Pretty Little Liars. 2006. (Pretty Little Liars Ser.: No. 1). (ENG.). 304p. (YA). (gr. 9-12). 16.99 *(978-0-06-088730-8(3)*, HarperTeen) HarperCollins Pubs.

Starting First Grade. (Tami & Moishy Ser.: Vol. 4). (J). bds. 6.95 *(978-1-58330-968-1(3))* Feldheim Pubs.

Stolarz, Laurie Faria. Red Is for Remembrance. 2005. (Stolarz Ser.: 4). (ENG.). 336p. (YA). (gr. 9-12). pap. 11.99 *(978-0-7387-0760-0(0)*, 0738707600, Flux) North Star Editions.

Williams, Suzanne. The Leo School Trio No. 1: Here Comes Hilary. 2003. 112p. (J). (gr. 2-5). pap. 3.99 *(978-0-439-32988-0(4))* Scholastic, Inc.

SCHOOL DROPOUTS

see Dropouts

SCHOOL ENROLLMENT

see School Attendance

SCHOOL INSPECTION

see School Management And Organization

SCHOOL INTEGRATION

see Segregation in Education

SCHOOL JOURNALISM

see College and School Journalism

SCHOOL LIBRARIES

see also Children's Literature; Libraries

Austen, Mary. Is It Wrong to Ban Books?, 1 vol. 2017. (Points of View Ser.). (ENG., Illus.). 24p. (J). (gr. 3-3). pap. 9.25 *(978-1-5345-2489-7(4)*, 5b112b10-a401-4c0a-9d67-255f283b5f60); lib. bdg. 26.23 *(978-1-5345-2427-9(4)*, 21e41b58-bb68-4614-af86-35910446c697) Greenhaven Publishing LLC.

Bloom, Paul. Rules in the Library, 1 vol. 2015. (School Rules Ser.). (ENG., Illus.). 24p. (J). (gr. k-k). pap. 9.15 *(978-1-4824-2649-6(8)*, 5fcb3154-6d07-46f7-b5f0-1ee1bf881241) Stevens, Gareth Publishing LLLP.

Buzzeo, Toni. R Is for Research. Wong, Nicole, illus. 2008. (J). (gr. 2-4). 17.95 *(978-1-60213-030-2(2)*, Upstart Bks.) Highsmith Inc.

Lovett, Amber. A Better Library Checkout. 2019. (21st Century Skills Innovation Library: Design a Better World Ser.). (ENG., Illus.). 32p. (J). (gr. 4-7). pap. 14.21 *(978-1-5341-3978-7(8)*, 212741); lib. bdg. 32.07 *(978-1-5341-4322-7(X)*, 212740) Cherry Lake Publishing.

Morris, Ann. That's Our Librarian! Linenthal, Peter, illus. Linenthal, Peter, photos by. 2003. (That's Our School Ser.). (ENG.). 32p. (gr. k-3). lib. bdg. 22.60 *(978-0-7613-2400-3(3)*, Millbrook Pr.) Lerner Publishing Group.

Sue, Grandma. The Best Book in the Library. Cherry, Gale, illus. 2010. 20p. 12.49 *(978-1-4490-9704-2(9))* AuthorHouse.

SCHOOL LIFE

see Students

SCHOOL MANAGEMENT AND ORGANIZATION

see also Teaching

Benchmark Education Co., LLC. Safe at School Big Book. 2014. (Shared Reading Foundations Ser.). (J). (gr. -1). *(978-1-4509-9432-3(6))* Benchmark Education Co.

Coan, Sharon. Rules at School (Foundations) 2nd rev. ed. 2015. (TIME for KIDS(r): Informational Text Ser.). (ENG., Illus.). 12p. (gr. -1-k). 7.99 *(978-1-4938-2065-8(6))* Teacher Created Materials, Inc.

—Trabajadores de Mi Escuela. 2nd rev. ed. 2016. (TIME for KIDS(r): Informational Text Ser.). (SPA., Illus.). 12p. (gr. -1-k). 7.99 *(978-1-4938-3026-8(0))* Teacher Created Materials, Inc.

Coll-Seck, Jayden. Ms. Okafor Is Our Principal, 1 vol., 1. 2015. (Rosen REAL Readers: Social Studies Nonfiction / Fiction: Myself, My Community, My World Ser.). (ENG.). 12p. (J). (gr. k-1). pap. 6.33 *(978-1-5081-1779-7(9)*, cfcc89d7-cdd2-4d7e-87f2-7adf3d2a913e, Rosen Classroom) Rosen Publishing Group, Inc., The.

Devera, Czeena. Principal. Bane, Jeff, illus. 2018. (Mi Mini Biografía (My Itty-Bitty Bio): My Early Library). (ENG.). 24p. (J). (gr. k-1). pap. 12.79 *(978-1-5341-0817-2(3)*, 210632); lib. bdg. 30.64 *(978-1-5341-0718-2(5)*, 210631) Cherry Lake Publishing.

Federico, Julie. The Bad Guys: A Students/Teachers Guide to School Safety & Violence Prevention. 2013. (ENG.). 32p. pap. 16.95 *(978-1-4497-9949-6(3)*, WestBow Pr.) Author Solutions, LLC.

Garrett, Winston. What Does a Library Media Specialist Do?, 1 vol. 2014. (Jobs in My School Ser.). (ENG.). 24p. (J). (gr. 1-2). lib. bdg. 25.27 *(978-1-4777-6546-3(8)*, a1850f21-7494-41d5-a298-ecf37cbf9af0, PowerKids Pr.) Rosen Publishing Group, Inc., The.

—What Does a Library Media Specialist Do? (¿Qué Hace el Especialista de Medios de la Biblioteca Escolar?), 1 vol. de la Vega, Eida, ed. 2014. (Oficios en Mi Escuela / Jobs in My School Ser.). (SPA & ENG.). 24p. (J). (gr. 1-2). lib. bdg. 25.27 *(978-1-4777-6796-2(7)*, 9bf473f5-57bd-4a6a-9303-c0b42f4d9292, PowerKids Pr.) Rosen Publishing Group, Inc., The.

Heitkamp, Kristina Lyn. Gay-Straight Alliances: Networking with Other Teens & Allies, 1 vol. 2017. (LGBTQ+ Guide to Beating Bullying Ser.). (ENG.). 64p. (J). (gr. 6-6). 36.13 *(978-1-5081-7427-1(X)*, d599d0f7-1cb9-43be-9cdb-ca4ded14a3e3, Rosen Young Adult) Rosen Publishing Group, Inc., The.

Hudson, David L. Rights of Students. 2nd rev. ed. 2010. (Point/Counterpoint Ser.). 112p. (C). (gr. 9). 35.00 *(978-1-60413-692-0(8)*, Facts On File) Infobase Holdings, Inc.

Kent, Susan. Learning How to Say Safe at School. 2009. (Violence Prevention Library). 24p. (gr. 2-3). 42.50 *(978-1-60854-266-6(1)*, PowerKids Pr.) Rosen Publishing Group, Inc., The.

Kidde, Rita. What Does a Janitor Do? (¿Qué Hace el Conserje?), 1 vol. de la Vega, Eida, ed. 2014. (Oficios en Mi Escuela / Jobs in My School Ser.). (SPA & ENG.). 24p. (J). (gr. 1-2). lib. bdg. 25.27 *(978-1-4777-6791-7(6)*, 48b380cb-13c3-4bac-8c55-316122b5f2f1, PowerKids Pr.) Rosen Publishing Group, Inc., The.

—What Does the Principal Do? 2014. (Jobs in My School Ser.). (ENG.). 24p. (J). (gr. 1-2). 19.05 *(978-1-5311-7659-4(3))* Perfection Learning Corp.

—What Does the Principal Do?, 1 vol. 2014. (Jobs in My School Ser.). (ENG.). 24p. (J). (gr. 1-2). lib. bdg. 25.27 *(978-1-4777-6477-0(1)*, bb89a253-423f-4404-87fb-e8e841983266, PowerKids Pr.) Rosen Publishing Group, Inc., The.

—What Does the Principal Do? (¿Qué Hace el Director?), 1 vol. de la Vega, Eida, ed. 2014. (Oficios en Mi Escuela / Jobs in My School Ser.). (SPA & ENG.). 24p. (J). (gr. 1-2). lib. bdg. 25.27 *(978-1-4777-6790-0(8)*, 041cc729-0288-441b-9c19-82680d723184, PowerKids Pr.) Rosen Publishing Group, Inc., The.

Kreiner, Anna. Todo lo que necesitas saber sobre la violencia en la escuela (Everything You Need to Know about Violence in School) 2009. (Todo lo que necesitas (the Need to Know Library) Ser.). (SPA.). 64p. (gr. 6-6). 58.50 *(978-1-60854-411-0(7)*, Editorial Buenas Letras) Rosen Publishing Group, Inc., The.

Lawrence, Riley. Should Junk Food Be Banned in Schools?, 1 vol. 2017. (Points of View Ser.). (ENG.). 24p. (J). (gr. 3-3). 26.23 *(978-1-5345-2419-4(3)*, c6343c49-584f-40fd-bf72-8ee079f5d35a, KidHaven Publishing) Greenhaven Publishing LLC.

Liebman, Dan. I Want to Be President. 2009. (I Want to Be Ser.). (ENG., Illus.). 24p. (J). (gr. -1-2). 16.19 *(978-1-55407-562-1(9)*, cb95673d-e9d3-436c-8b37-61d5b91436db); pap. 3.99 *(978-1-55407-563-8(7)*, 744b5193-9d08-442b-a5d3-4b3c75d6e2a8) Firefly Bks., Ltd.

—Quiero Ser Presidente. 2009. (Quiero Ser.). (SPA., Illus.). 24p. (J). (gr. -1-2). 14.95 *(978-1-55407-564-5(5)*, d3b67720-afa5-44a1-8547-83c792d47235); pap. 5.99 *(978-1-55407-565-2(3)*, 98a169f8-0492-4c6a-869d-160f38a861a5) Firefly Bks., Ltd.

Marsico, Katie. Working at a School. 2008. (21st Century Junior Library: Careers Ser.). (ENG., Illus.). 24p. (gr. 2-5). lib. bdg. 29.21 *(978-1-60279-266-1(6)*, 200171) Cherry Lake Publishing.

Marx, Jeff. How to Win a High School Election: Advice & Ideas Collected from over 1,000 High School Seniors. 2003. 180p. (gr. 7-12). pap. 14.95 *(978-0-9667824-0-0(2))* Marx, Jeff.

McCune, Susan. Mr. Morgan Keeps Our School Clean, 1 vol., 1. 2015. (Rosen REAL Readers: Social Studies Nonfiction / Fiction: Myself, My Community, My World Ser.). (ENG.). 12p. (J). (gr. k-1). pap. 6.33 *(978-1-5081-1755-1(1)*, a0ef6f42-3db8-4ea3-a24a-0376beb8c8c7, Rosen Classroom) Rosen Publishing Group, Inc., The.

Mitchell, Melanie. Principals. (Pull Ahead Bks.). (J). 2005. (Illus.). 32p. lib. bdg. 22.60 *(978-0-8225-1694-1(2))* 2004. pap. 6.95 *(978-0-8225-2535-6(6)*, Lerner Pubns.) Lerner Publishing Group.

Murray, Julie. Principals. 2018. (My Community: Jobs Ser.). (ENG., Illus.). 24p. (J). (gr. -1-2). lib. bdg. 31.36 *(978-1-5321-0790-0(0)*, 28141, Abdo Kids) ABDO Publishing Co.

Ogle, Rex. Free Lunch. 2019. (ENG.). 208p. (J). (gr. 6-9). 17.95 *(978-1-324-00360-1(X)*, 340360, Norton Young Readers) Norton, W. W. & Co., Inc.

Olexa, Keith. Working As a School Safety Officer, 1 vol. 2018. (Careers in Your Community Ser.). (ENG.). 80p. (gr. 7-7). 37.47 *(978-1-4994-6728-4(1)*, 956ae4ce-6822-4f8c-9da7-74466ddc4bd6, Rosen Young Adult) Rosen Publishing Group, Inc., The.

Parnell, Declan. Mr. Wilson Is Our Crossing Guard, 1 vol., 1. 2015. (Rosen REAL Readers: Social Studies Nonfiction / Fiction: Myself, My Community, My World Ser.). (ENG.). 8p. (J). (gr. k-1). pap. 5.46 *(978-1-5081-1704-9(7)*, 20bbe29d-2d08-4aeb-b5f1-68b83f790019, Rosen Classroom) Rosen Publishing Group, Inc., The.

Pearl, Melissa Sherman & Sherman, David A. Coat-A-Kid: Charities Started by Kids! 2017. (Community Connections: How Do They Help? Ser.). (ENG., Illus.). 24p. (J). (gr. 2-5). lib. bdg. 29.21 *(978-1-63472-849-2(1)*, 209822) Cherry Lake Publishing.

The School Rules. 2015. (School Rules Ser.). (ENG.). 24p. (gr. k-k). pap., pap., pap. 293.40 *(978-1-4824-3496-5(2))* Stevens, Gareth Publishing LLLP.

Schuh, Mari. Community Helpers at School. 2016. (Community Helpers on the Scene Ser.). (ENG., Illus.). 24p. (J). (gr. -1-2). lib. bdg. 22.65 *(978-1-5157-2400-1(X)*, 132809, Capstone Pr.) Capstone.

Shava, Ryder. Mr. Lagaya Is Our Assistant Principal, 1 vol., 1. 2015. (Rosen REAL Readers: Social Studies Nonfiction / Fiction: Myself, My Community, My World Ser.). (ENG.). 12p. (J). (gr. k-1). pap. 6.33 *(978-1-5081-1782-7(9)*, f4cb136c-dc58-46b3-ab05-5a3778919c52, Rosen Classroom) Rosen Publishing Group, Inc., The.

Verderosa, Laura. At My School. 2010. (Sight Word Readers Ser.). (J). 3.49 *(978-1-60719-606-8(9))* Newmark Learning LLC.

SCHOOL MUSIC

see Music—Study and Teaching; School Songbooks

SCHOOL NEWSPAPERS

see College and School Journalism

SCHOOL NURSING

Garrett, Winston. What Does the School Nurse Do?, 1 vol. 2014. (Jobs in My School Ser.). (ENG., Illus.). 24p. (J). (gr. 1-2). lib. bdg. 25.27 *(978-1-4777-6551-7(4),* 159e2682-adc8-4ea2-bb85-ccd80b5ad90e, PowerKids Pr.) Rosen Publishing Group, Inc., The.

—What Does the School Nurse Do? (¿Qué Hace la Enfermera de la Escuela?), 1 vol. de la Vega, Eida, ed. 2014. (Oficios en Mi Escuela / Jobs in My School Ser.). (SPA & ENG.). 24p. (J). (gr. 1-2). lib. bdg. 25.27 *(978-1-4777-6801-3(7),* 6af04b39-7ce2-42c5-917a-6a30ed97d7bc, PowerKids Pr.) Rosen Publishing Group, Inc., The.

Morris, Ann. That's Our Nurse! Linenthal, Peter, illus. Linenthal, Peter, photos by. 2003. (That's Our School Ser.). (ENG.). 32p. (gr. k-3). lib. bdg. 22.60 *(978-0-7613-2402-7(X),* Millbrook Pr.) Lerner Publishing Group.

Vogel, Elizabeth. Meet the School Nurse. 2009. (My School Ser.). 24p. (gr. 1-2). 37.50 *(978-1-61514-708-3(X),* PowerKids Pr.) Rosen Publishing Group, Inc., The.

SCHOOL ORGANIZATION

see School Management And Organization

SCHOOL PLAYGROUNDS

see Playgrounds

SCHOOL PLAYS

see Plays

SCHOOL SONGBOOKS

Barden, Christine H., et al. Music for Little Mozarts — Little Mozarts Go to Church, Bk 1-2: 10 Favorite Hymns, Spirituals & Sunday School Songs. 2008. (Music for Little Mozarts Ser.: Bk 1-2). (ENG.). 24p. (J). pap. 7.99 *(978-0-7390-5689-9(1))* Alfred Publishing Co., Inc.

—Music for Little Mozarts — Little Mozarts Go to Church, Bk 3-4: 10 Favorite Hymns, Spirituals & Sunday School Songs. 2008. (Music for Little Mozarts Ser.: Bk 3-4). (ENG.). 24p. (J). pap. 6.95 *(978-0-7390-5690-5(5))* Alfred Publishing Co., Inc.

Vogt, Janet. Music Brain Teasers. 2006. pap. 19.95 *(978-0-89328-248-6(0))* Lorenz Corp., The.

SCHOOL SPORTS

see also Coaching (Athletics)

Schwartz, Heather. Sports for All: The Impact of Title IX (Level 5) 2017. (TIME for KIDS(r): Informational Text Ser.). (ENG., Illus.). 48p. (gr. 4-8). pap. 13.99 *(978-1-4258-4987-0(3))* Teacher Created Materials, Inc.

SCHOOL TEACHING

see Teaching

SCHOOL WITHDRAWALS

see Dropouts

SCHOOLS

see also Boarding Schools; Education; Kindergarten; Public Schools; Universities and Colleges

Adamson, Heather. School in Many Cultures. rev. ed. 2016. (Life Around the World Ser.). (ENG.). 24p. (J). (gr. -1-2). pap. 7.29 *(978-1-5157-4239-5(3),* 133998, Capstone Pr.) Capstone.

Aillaud, Cindy Lou. Recess at 20 below, Revised Edition. 2019. (ENG., Illus.). 34p. (J). (gr. k-5). 22.99 *(978-1-5132-6192-8(4));* pap. 12.99 *(978-1-5132-6191-1(6))* West Margin Pr. (Alaska Northwest Bks.).

Ajmera, Maya & Ivanko, John D. Back to School: A Global Journey. 2019. (Illus.). 32p. (J). (gr. -1-3). lib. bdg. 17.99 *(978-1-58089-837-9(8))* Charlesbridge Publishing, Inc.

Allen, John. School Shootings & Violence (Thinking Critically) 2019. (Thinking Critically Ser.). (ENG.). 80p. (J). (gr. 6-12). 41.27 *(978-1-68282-663-8(5))* ReferencePoint Pr., Inc.

Allen, Kenny. My School, 1 vol. 2008. (Real Life Readers Ser.). (ENG.). 8p. (gr. k-1). pap. 5.15 *(978-1-4042-7969-8(5),* 74ce0dbd-de90-4437-ad72-4afedf515922, Rosen Classroom) Rosen Publishing Group, Inc., The.

Ancona, George. Mi Escuela: My School. 2004. (Somos Latino (We Are Latinos) Ser.). 21.00 *(978-0-516-23686-5(5),* Watts, Franklin) Scholastic Library Publishing.

Anderson, Sheila. School. 2008. (J). pap. 3.95 *(978-0-8225-8838-2(2));* pap. 22.95 *(978-0-8225-9374-4(2))* Lerner Publishing Group.

Andrews Henningfeld, Diane, ed. Charter Schools, 1 vol. 2007. (At Issue Ser.). (ENG., Illus.). 120p. (gr. 10-12). pap. 28.80 *(978-0-7377-3915-2(0),* 12df2f8d-af54-457f-90ef-945d58014c46); lib. bdg. 41.03 *(978-0-7377-3914-5(2),* 2e8c69e2-9ae5-4ffa-a3b1-59676dfb000a) Greenhaven Publishing LLC. (Greenhaven Publishing).

Appleby, Alex. Dinosaurs at School. 2013. (Dinosaur School Ser.). 24p. (J). (gr. k-1). pap. 48.90 *(978-1-4339-9043-4(1));* (ENG., Illus.). pap. 9.15 *(978-1-4339-9042-7(3),* c5b7e416-7f2d-4fd5-8b07-710f29ee0710); (ENG., Illus.). lib. bdg. 25.27 *(978-1-4339-9041-0(5),* 8a149547-501b-48af-a86d-28516284b0cb) Stevens, Gareth Publishing LLLP.

Aretha, David. The Story of the Little Rock Nine & School Desegregation in Photographs, 1 vol. 2014. (Story of the Civil Rights Movement in Photographs Ser.). (ENG.). 48p. (gr. 5-6). lib. bdg. 27.93 *(978-0-7660-4235-3(9),* 0ed9ba94-7dcb-4d9d-85ac-d05ae280e19f) Enslow Publishing, LLC.

Barton, Jen. School Shootings. 2019. (In Focus Ser.). (ENG.). 80p. (J). (gr. 6-12). 41.27 *(978-1-68282-721-5(6),* BrightPoint Pr.) ReferencePoint Pr., Inc.

Bell, Cece. El Deafo. 2014. (ENG., Illus.). 248p. (J). (gr. 3-7). pap. 14.99 *(978-1-4197-1217-3(9),* 1048503) Abrams, Inc.

—El Deafo. 2014. (J). lib. bdg. 22.05 *(978-0-606-36148-4(0))* Turtleback.

Bellamy, Adam. This Is My School, 1 vol. 2016. (All about My World Ser.). (ENG., Illus.). 24p. (gr. k-1). pap. 10.35 *(978-0-7660-8083-6(8),* 964e1b30-b55f-433f-a976-2f80ab8ac5ed) Enslow Publishing, LLC.

Bellisario, Gina. Librarians in My Community. Myer, Ed, illus. 2018. (Meet a Community Helper (Early Bird Stories (tm)) Ser.). (ENG.). 24p. (J). (gr. k-2). pap. 9.99 *(978-1-5415-2708-9(9),* 2f2c6f9a-e719-464b-b790-96d3e6a4f9d9) Lerner Publishing Group.

Benjamin, Tina. My Day at School, 1 vol. 2014. (Inside My World Ser.). (ENG.). 24p. (J). (gr. k-k). 24.27 *(978-1-4824-1801-9(0),* b7bd5588-0cd9-4a96-9e06-7f190c6cf4fe) Stevens, Gareth Publishing LLLP.

Berda, Chryste L. Diversion y Juegos: Comprension de la Longitud. rev. ed. 2018. (Mathematics in the Real World Ser.). (SPA., Illus.). 32p. (J). (gr. 2-3). pap. 10.99 *(978-1-4258-2869-1(8))* Teacher Created Materials, Inc.

Bernay, Emma & Berne, Emma Carlson. My School, Your School, Our Schools. Player, Micah, illus. 2018. (How Are We Alike & Different? Ser.). (ENG.). 24p. (J). (gr. -1-2). pap. 7.95 *(978-1-68410-293-8(6),* 139064); lib. bdg. 33.99 *(978-1-68410-241-9(3),* 138445) Cantata Learning.

—100th Day of School. Alder, Charlie, illus. 2018. (Holidays in Rhythm & Rhyme Ser.). (ENG.). 24p. (J). (gr. k-2). lib. bdg. 33.99 *(978-1-68410-396-6(7),* 140356) Cantata Learning.

Berry, Joy. I Love Preschool. Regan, Dana, illus. 2010. (Teach Me About Ser.). (ENG.). 20p. (J). (gr. k — 1). bds. 5.99 *(978-1-60577-015-4(9))* Berry, Joy Enterprises.

Blane, Francisco. People at School: Lap Book. 2009. (My First Reader's Theater Set B Ser.). (J). 28.00 *(978-1-935441-00-7(0))* Benchmark Education Co.

Bloom, Paul. Rules in the Classroom, 1 vol. 2015. (School Rules Ser.). (ENG., Illus.). 24p. (J). (gr. k-k). pap. 9.15 *(978-1-4824-2641-0(2),* 536733b2-bfaf-4efb-96bb-bc254b3a9015) Stevens, Gareth Publishing LLLP.

Boothroyd, Jennifer. From Chalkboards to Computers: How Schools Have Changed. 2011. (Comparing Past & Present Ser.). pap. 45.32 *(978-0-7613-8390-1(5));* pap. 7.95 *(978-0-7613-7840-2(5))* Lerner Publishing Group.

—Schools. 2006. (First Step Nonfiction Ser.). (Illus.). 8p. (J). pap. 3.95 *(978-0-8225-5729-6(0),* Lerner Pubns.) Lerner Publishing Group.

Borene, Mark R. Welcome to the School. 2009. 20p. pap. 10.49 *(978-1-4389-7752-2(2))* AuthorHouse.

Borgenicht, David, et al. The Worst-Case Scenario Survival Handbook: Middle School. 2009. (Worst Case Scenario Ser.). (ENG., Illus.). 128p. (J). (gr. 6-8). pap. 10.99 *(978-0-8118-6864-8(8))* Chronicle Bks. LLC.

Bozzo, Linda. Schools of the Past, Present, & Future, 1 vol. 2010. (Imagining the Future Ser.). (ENG., Illus.). 24p. (gr. k-2). lib. bdg. 25.27 *(978-0-7660-3434-1(8),* 17de1f7c-1433-4825-90cb-f3a6c144d90c, Enslow Elementary) Enslow Publishing, LLC.

Braun, Eric. Awesome, Disgusting, Unusual Facts about School. 2018. (Our Gross, Awesome World Ser.). (ENG.). 24p. (J). (gr. 4-6). pap. 8.99 *(978-1-64466-307-3(4),* 12523); (Illus.). lib. bdg. 28.50 *(978-1-68072-612-1(9),* 12522) Black Rabbit Bks. (Hi Jinx).

—Beurk! le Livre Différent et Fascinant Sur L'école. 2018. (Notre Monde: dégoûtant Mais Génial! Ser.). (FRE.). 24p. (J). (gr. 4-6). *(978-1-77092-450-5(7),* 12585, Hi Jinx) Black Rabbit Bks.

Brezina, Corona. Standing up to Bullying at School, 1 vol. 2017. (LGBTQ+ Guide to Beating Bullying Ser.). (ENG., Illus.). 64p. (J). (gr. 6-6). pap. 13.95 *(978-1-5081-7429-5(6),* e46c582d-4b7d-4c7c-8ccd-ed2e53367afb, Rosen Young Adult) Rosen Publishing Group, Inc., The.

Brinker, Spencer. At School. 2019. (I Spy Ser.). (ENG., Illus.). 16p. (J). (gr. -1-1). 6.99 *(978-1-64280-392-1(8))* Bearport Publishing Co., Inc.

Bullard, Lisa. Who Works at Hannah's School? Becker, Paula J., illus. 2017. (Cloverleaf Books (tm) — off to School Ser.). (ENG.). 24p. (J). (gr. k-2). pap. 8.99 *(978-1-5124-5581-6(4),* ad42b7b5-083b-4e5a-b490-9a462732911b, Millbrook Pr.) Lerner Publishing Group.

—William's 100th Day of School. Byrne, Mike, illus. 2017. (Cloverleaf Books (tm) — off to School Ser.). (ENG.). 24p. (J). (gr. k-2). 25.32 *(978-1-5124-3935-9(5),* cdbdca56-27d4-48d4-a502-86affe7f64c3); pap. 8.99 *(978-1-5124-5582-3(2),* 3d8b2bc0-aa41-4be3-8b27-e2f28070a214) Lerner Publishing Group. (Millbrook Pr.).

Butterfield, Moira. Schools Around the World, 1 vol. 2015. (Children Like Us Ser.). (ENG., Illus.). 32p. (gr. 3-3). pap. 11.58 *(978-1-5026-0846-8(4),* 0ae31151-9fe8-45f3-b1f4-5dcae825631a) Cavendish Square Publishing LLC.

Camisa, Kathryn. Creepy Schools. 2017. (Tiptoe into Scary Places Ser.). (ENG., Illus.). 24p. (J). (gr. k-3). lib. bdg. 26.99 *(978-1-68402-272-4(X))* Bearport Publishing Co., Inc.

—Escuelas Escalofriantes. 2018. (De Puntillas en Lugares Escalofriantes/Tiptoe into Scary Places Ser.). (SPA.). 24p. (J). (gr. k-3). 18.95 *(978-1-68402-611-1(3))* Bearport Publishing Co., Inc.

Canetti, Yanitzia. ABCs of School. 2010. (J). 8.99 *(978-1-59835-277-1(6),* BrickHouse Education) Cambridge BrickHouse, Inc.

—Abecedario Escolar. 2010. (SPA.). 40p. (J). pap. 8.99 *(978-1-59835-275-7(X),* BrickHouse Education) Cambridge BrickHouse, Inc.

—Colores escolares/School Colors: A World of Color. 2010. (ENG & SPA.). 24p. (J). pap. 6.99 *(978-1-59835-272-6(5),* BrickHouse Education) Cambridge BrickHouse, Inc.

Capaccio, George. Schools in Colonial America, 1 vol. 2014. (Life in Colonial America Ser.). (ENG.). 80p. (gr. 6-6). lib. bdg. 37.36 *(978-1-62712-894-0(8),* 2bb6e7ab-cdd0-4e3c-8f79-3c4c3930cfac) Cavendish Square Publishing LLC.

Capucilli, Alyssa Satin. My First Day of School: Ready-To-Read Pre-Level 1. Wachter, Jill, photos by. 2019. (My First Ser.). (ENG., Illus.). 32p. (J). (gr. -1-k). 17.99 *(978-1-5344-2845-4(3));* pap. 4.99 *(978-1-5344-2844-7(5))* Simon Spotlight. (Simon Spotlight).

Capucilli, Alyssa Satine. My First Day of School. 2019. (Ready-To-Read Ser.). (ENG.). 32p. (J). (gr. k-1). 13.96 *(978-0-87617-590-3(6))* Penworthy Co., LLC, The.

Carr, Aaron. The School. 2013. pap. 12.95 *(978-1-62127-353-0(9));* (Illus.). 24p. (J). *(978-1-62127-348-6(2))* Weigl Pubs., Inc.

Cassel, Katrina L. The Middle School Survival Manual. 2010. 128p. (J). (gr. 6-18). pap. 8.99 *(978-0-7586-1790-3(9))* Concordia Publishing Hse.

Catherman, Jonathan. The Manual to Middle School: The Do This, Not That Survival Guide for Guys. 2017. (ENG., Illus.). 224p. pap. 15.99 *(978-0-8007-2847-2(5))* Revell.

Chambers, Catherine. DK Readers L3: School Days Around the World. 2007. (DK Readers Level 3 Ser.). (ENG., Illus.). 48p. (J). (gr. 2-4). pap. 4.99 *(978-0-7566-2548-1(3),* DK Children) Dorling Kindersley Publishing, Inc.

—School Days Around the World. 2007. (DK Readers Level 3 Ser.). (ENG., Illus.). 48p. (J). (gr. 1-3). 16.19 *(978-0-7566-2549-8(1))* Dorling Kindersley Publishing, Inc.

Civardi, Anne. Going to School Sticker Book. 2008. (First Experiences Sticker Bks). (Illus.). 16p. (J). pap. 6.99 *(978-0-7945-2182-0(7),* Usborne) EDC Publishing.

Clark, Veronica, et al. Assembly Packs - Class Assemblies 1, 1 vol. 2010. (and C Black Assembly Packs Ser.). (ENG., Illus.). 64p. (J). pap. 32.95 incl. audio compact disk *(978-1-4081-2456-7(4))* HarperCollins Pubs. Ltd. GBR. Dist: Independent Pubs. Group.

—Assembly Packs - Class Assemblies 2, 1 vol. 2010. (and C Black Assembly Packs Ser.). (ENG., Illus.). 64p. (J). pap. 32.95 incl. audio compact disk *(978-1-4081-2457-4(2))* HarperCollins Pubs. Ltd. GBR. Dist: Independent Pubs. Group.

—Assembly Packs - Class Assemblies 3, 1 vol. 2010. (and C Black Assembly Packs Ser.). (ENG., Illus.). 64p. (J). pap. 32.95 incl. audio compact disk *(978-1-4081-2458-1(0))* HarperCollins Pubs. Ltd. GBR. Dist: Independent Pubs. Group.

Color All About: A Giant Coloring Book about Fun Things to do at School: Back to School. 2004. (Illus.). 36p. (J). *(978-1-59949-005-2(6))* Food Marketing Consultants, Inc.

Connors, Kathleen. We Play School!, 1 vol. 2018. (Ways to Play Ser.). (ENG.). 24p. (gr. k-k). lib. bdg. 24.27 *(978-1-5382-2883-8(1),* 4f17acaa-e86d-4aa3-b8a3-901a6b689c94) Stevens, Gareth Publishing LLLP.

Coughlan, Billy. Not Without My Whale. Karabatzia, Villie, illus. 2019. (Early Bird Readers — Green (Early Bird Stories (tm)) Ser.). (ENG.). 32p. (J). (gr. k-3). 30.65 *(978-1-5415-4204-4(5),* 8f981220-0b58-4e5f-9c0b-823a7ebf46de); pap. 9.99 *(978-1-5415-7409-0(5),* 31c2d9b7-aeb3-47e4-8c7a-058f9da6326c) Lerner Publishing Group. (Lerner Pubns.).

Dale, Jay. Ways We Go to School. 2012. (Engage Literacy Green Ser.). (ENG.). 16p. (J). (gr. k-2). pap. 36.94 *(978-1-4296-9021-8(6),* 18403, Capstone Pr.) Capstone.

Dale, Jay & Scott, Kay. Ways We Go to School, 1 vol. 2012. (Engage Literacy Green Ser.). (ENG.). 16p. (J). (gr. k-2). pap. 6.99 *(978-1-4296-9020-1(8),* 120020, Capstone Pr.) Capstone.

David C. Cook Publishing Company Staff, creator. Action! Cool Theater. 2008. (Bible Fun Stuff for Middle School Ser.). (Illus.). 112p. (J). (gr. 6-8). pap. 16.99 *(978-1-4347-6856-8(2))* Cook, David C.

Desalle, Nicole. Safe at School. 2011. pap. 39.95 *(978-0-7664-3750-0(7))* Abrams & Co. Pubs., Inc.

Devera, Czeena. Lend a Hand at School. 2019. (Helping Out Ser.). (ENG., Illus.). 16p. (J). (gr. -1-2). pap. 11.36 *(978-1-5341-4976-2(7),* 213217, Cherry Blossom Press) Cherry Lake Publishing.

Dinmont, Kerry. Schools Past & Present. 2018. (Bumba Books (r) — Past & Present Ser.). (ENG., Illus.). 24p. (J). (gr. -1-1). 26.65 *(978-1-5415-0329-8(5),* b53d894f-c8cc-432a-a327-075ff19d8574, Lerner Pubns.) Lerner Publishing Group.

Donahue, Jill L., et al. Chuckle Squad: Jokes about Classrooms, Sports, Food, Teachers, & Other School Subjects, 1 vol. Haugen, Ryan et al, illus. 2010. (Michael Dahl Presents Super Funny Joke Bks.). (ENG.). 80p. (J). (gr. 1-3). 25.32 *(978-1-4048-5773-5(7),* 102653, Picture Window Bks.) Capstone.

Dyer, Janice. Designing Positive School Communities. 2018. (Illus.). 48p. (J). *(978-1-4271-2037-3(4))* Crabtree Publishing Co.

Editorial Staff, Gareth. Things at School / Las Cosas de la Escuela, 1 vol. 2006. (Things in My World / Las Cosas de Mi Mundo Ser.). (SPA & ENG., Illus.). 16p. (gr. k-1). pap. 6.30 *(978-0-8368-7227-9(4),* 7db11d9e-f8d9-4eec-968b-fa2d57050701, Weekly Reader Leveled Readers) Stevens, Gareth Publishing LLLP.

Edwards, Rhonda S. A Living Mascot. Owens, Alana, illus. 2013. (ENG.). 38p. (J). pap. 9.99 *(978-0-7443-2013-8(5))* CamCat Publishing.

Elliott, Tommy. I Don't Want To: Go to School. 2009. 24p. pap. 13.49 *(978-1-4389-5123-2(X))* AuthorHouse.

Emmer, Rae. Drama Club. 2009. (School Activities Ser.). 24p. (gr. 1-1). 42.50 *(978-1-60852-998-8(3),* PowerKids Pr.) Rosen Publishing Group, Inc., The.

—Drama Club / Club de Teatro. 2009. (School Activities / Actividades escolares Ser.). (ENG & SPA.). 24p. (gr. 1-2). 42.50 *(978-1-60853-004-5(3),* Editorial Buenas Letras) Rosen Publishing Group, Inc., The.

Emminizer, Theresa. You're Part of a School Community!, 1 vol. 2019. (All Our Communities Ser.). (ENG.). 24p. (gr. 1-2). pap. 9.15 *(978-1-5382-4541-5(8),* f6641aa9-a290-4ffb-bf20-513455004312) Stevens, Gareth Publishing LLLP.

Espejo, Roman, ed. Cell Phones in Schools, 1 vol. 2014. (At Issue Ser.). (ENG.). 88p. (gr. 10-12). pap. 28.80 *(978-0-7377-6156-6(3),* 9a639cc9-50f4-4107-a343-69173d58fc6f); lib. bdg. 41.03 *(978-0-7377-6155-9(5),* 76a56225-8a3f-4a5a-9d7d-c67f7a6f69f3) Greenhaven Publishing LLC. (Greenhaven Publishing).

Falk, Laine. This Is the Way We Go to School. 2009. (Scholastic News Nonfiction Readers: Kids Like Me Ser.). (ENG.). 24p. (J). (gr. k-3). lib. bdg. 21.19 *(978-0-531-21341-4(2),* Children's Pr.) Scholastic Library Publishing.

—This Is the Way We Go to School (Scholastic News Nonfiction Readers: Kids Like Me) 2009. (Scholastic News Nonfiction Readers Ser.). (ENG.). 24p. (J). (gr. 1-2). pap. 6.95 *(978-0-531-21440-4(0),* Children's Pr.) Scholastic Library Publishing.

Fayetteville Elementary, Students & Staf. Memories of Fayetteville Elementary School. 2007. 124p. per. 16.95 *(978-0-9790446-1-8(8))* Pen & Publish, LLC.

Feldman, Ruth Tenzer. Don't Whistle in School: The History of America's Public Schools. 2005. (People's History Ser.). (Illus.). 96p. (gr. 6-12). lib. bdg. 26.60 *(978-0-8225-1745-0(0))* Lerner Publishing Group.

Felix, Rebecca. Patterns at School. 2015. (21st Century Basic Skills Library: Patterns All Around Ser.). (ENG., Illus.). 24p. (J). (gr. k-3). pap. 12.79 *(978-1-63188-934-9(6),* 205997) Cherry Lake Publishing.

Flash Kids Editors, ed. Ready for School: Grade Pre-K-K (Flash Skills) 2010. (Flash Skills Ser.). (ENG.). 64p. (J). pap. 3.95 *(978-1-4114-3466-0(8),* Spark Publishing Group) Sterling Publishing Co., Inc.

Flynn, Brendan. The 100th Day of School. 2019. (Holidays Ser.). (ENG.). 24p. (J). (gr. 1-1). pap. 8.95 *(978-1-64185-566-2(5),* 1641855665) North Star Editions.

—The 100th Day of School. 2018. (Holidays (Cody Koala) Ser.). (ENG.). 24p. (J). (gr. k-3). lib. bdg. 31.36 *(978-1-5321-6195-7(6),* 30173, Pop! Cody Koala) Pop!

Foran, Jill. La Petite école: Le Début de la Colonie. Karvonen, Tanjah, tr. from ENG. 2011. (FRE., Illus.). 24p. (gr. 3-6). *(978-1-77071-421-2(9))* Weigl Educational Pubs. Ltd.

—The School House: Pioneers of Canada. 2011. 24p. (YA). (gr. 2-4). *(978-1-77071-680-3(7));* pap. *(978-1-77071-684-1(X))* Weigl Educational Pubs. Ltd.

Fretland VanVoorst, Jenny. Las Formas en la Escuela. 2015.Tr. of Shapes at School. (SPA., Illus.). 24p. (J). lib. bdg. *(978-1-62031-248-3(4),* Bullfrog Bks.) Jump! Inc.

—Shapes at School. 2015. (Illus.). 24p. (J). lib. bdg. *(978-1-62031-203-2(4),* Bullfrog Bks.) Jump! Inc.

Friedman, Hannah. Everything Sucks: Losing My Mind & Finding Myself in a High School Quest for Cool. 2009. (ENG.). 264p. (YA). (gr. 8-12). pap. 12.95 *(978-0-7573-0775-1(2),* HCI Teens) Health Communications, Inc.

Friedman, Lauri S. School Shootings. 2009. (Writing the Critical Essay Ser.). (ENG., Illus.). 128p. (J). 31.80 *(978-0-7377-4564-1(9),* Greenhaven Pr., Inc.) Cengage Gale.

Fronczak, Blaine. Haley Helps at School, 1 vol. 2013. (Core Math Skills: Numbers & Operations in Base 10 Ser.). (ENG.). 24p. (J). (gr. 1-1). 26.27 *(978-1-4777-2225-1(4),* fe2374ab-7523-47c6-bbb2-7940c865478a); pap. 8.25 *(978-1-4777-2097-4(9),* 4a879267-fd94-431b-85ea-d6ecdafc7033) Rosen Publishing Group, Inc., The. (Rosen Classroom).

—Haley Helps at School: Use Place Value & Properties of Operations to Add. 2013. (Rosen Math Readers Ser.). (ENG.). 24p. (J). (gr. 1-2). pap. 49.50 *(978-1-4777-2098-1(7),* Rosen Classroom) Rosen Publishing Group, Inc., The.

Gaarder-Juntti, Oona. Shapes at School, 1 vol. 2013. (Shapes Everywhere Ser.). (ENG.). 24p. (J). (gr. k-4). lib. bdg. 32.79 *(978-1-61783-412-7(2),* 13328, Super SandCastle) ABDO Publishing Co.

Gaertner, Meg. Henry Goes to School: A Book about School Community. 2018. (My Day Readers Ser.). (ENG.). 24p. (J). (gr. -1-2). lib. bdg. 32.79 *(978-1-5038-2755-4(0),* 212579) Child's World, Inc, The.

Geatches, Hazel, ed. Schools. 2012. (ENG., Illus.). 32p. pap. 11.00 *(978-0-19-464627-7(0))* Oxford Univ. Pr., Inc.

Gosman, Gillian. Simple Machines at School. 2014. (Simple Machines Everywhere Ser.). (Illus.). 24p. (J). (gr. k-3). pap. 49.50 *(978-1-4777-6645-3(6),* PowerKids Pr.) Rosen Publishing Group, Inc., The.

Graves, Karen M. School in Pioneer Times. 2016. (It's Back to School ... Way Back! Ser.). (ENG., Illus.). 32p. (J). (gr. 3-6). lib. bdg. 27.99 *(978-1-5157-2096-6(9),* 132695) Capstone.

Graves, Kerry A. School in the Great Depression. 2016. (It's Back to School ... Way Back! Ser.). (ENG., Illus.). 32p. (J). (gr. 3-6). lib. bdg. 27.99 *(978-1-5157-2098-0(5),* 132703, Capstone Pr.) Capstone.

Greathouse, Lisa. Count Me In! School Carnival, 1 vol. 2nd rev. ed. 2011. (TIME for KIDS(r): Informational Text Ser.). (ENG.). 28p. (gr. 2-3). pap. 10.99 *(978-1-4333-3637-9(5))* Teacher Created Materials, Inc.

Gregoire, Maryellen. Escuelas Viejas y Nuevas. 2012. (Wonder Readers Spanish Emergent Ser.). (SPA.). 16p. (J). (gr. -1-1). pap. 37.50 *(978-1-62065-574-0(8),* 19239) Capstone.

—Old & New Schools, 1 vol. 2012. (Wonder Readers Emergent Level Ser.). (ENG.). 16p. (J). (gr. -1-1). pap. 6.25 *(978-1-4296-9191-8(3),* 120175); pap. 38.50 *(978-1-4296-9201-4(4),* 18490) Capstone. (Capstone Pr.).

Gregory, Cam. When Do I Go to School? 2012. (Level B Ser.). (ENG., Illus.). 16p. (J). (gr. k-2). pap. 7.95 *(978-1-927136-11-9(3),* 19432) RiverStream Publishing.

Greven, Alec. Rules for School. Acedera, Kei, illus. 2010. (ENG.). 48p. (J). (gr. 1-5). 9.99 *(978-0-06-195170-1(6),* HarperCollins) HarperCollins Pubs.

Group/McGraw-Hill, Wright. My School, Your School: Level E, 6 vols. (Take Twostm Ser.). 16p. 29.95 *(978-0-322-08948-8(4))* Wright Group/McGraw-Hill.

Guest, John. Collective Worship Unwrapped: 33 Tried & Tested Story-Based Assemblies for Primary Schools. 2nd ed. 2013. (ENG.). 132p. pap. *(978-1-84101-618-4(7),* Barnabas in Schools) Bible Reading Fellowship.

Hale, Shannon. Real Friends. 2017. (Friends Ser.: 1). (ENG., Illus.). 224p. (J). 22.99 *(978-1-62672-416-7(4),* 900156399, First Second Bks.) Roaring Brook Pr.

Hale, Shannon & Pham, LeUyen. Real Friends. 2017. (J). lib. bdg. 24.50 *(978-0-606-39954-8(2))* Turtleback.

Haley, Charly. Luke Celebrates 100 Days: A Book about the 100th Day of School. 2018. (My Day Readers Ser.). (ENG.). 24p. (J). (gr. -1-2). lib. bdg. 32.79 *(978-1-5038-2490-4(X),* 212358) Child's World, Inc, The.

Hasday, Judy L. Forty-Nine Minutes of Madness: The Columbine High School Shooting, 1 vol. 2013. (Disasters: People in Peril Ser.). (ENG., Illus.). 48p. (gr. 5-7). 27.93 *(978-0-7660-4013-7(5),* ab213889-466c-4cb7-a58b-3a74726c38d3) Enslow Publishing, LLC.

Healy, Nicholas M. If You Were a Period [LTD Commodities]. Gray, Sara, illus. 2010. (Word Fun Ser.). 24p. pap. 3.50 *(978-1-4048-6252-4(8),* Picture Window Bks.) Capstone.

Hely, Patrick. Why Do We Have Rules in School?, 1 vol. 2018. (Common Good Ser.). (ENG.). 24p. (gr. 2-2). 25.27 (978-1-5383-3091-3(1), 5786999b-0364-4773-9f7b-bf6167e6bf73, PowerKids Pr.) Rosen Publishing Group, Inc., The.

Herrington, Lisa M. Rookie Read-About Safety: Back-to-School Safety. 2012. (Rookie Read-About Safety). (ENG., Illus.). 32p. (J). pap. 5.95 (978-0-531-29269-3(X)) Scholastic Library Publishing.

Hinman, Bonnie. The Scoop on School & Work in Colonial America, 1 vol. 2012. (Life in the American Colonies Ser.). (ENG.). 32p. (J). (gr. 3-6). pap. 8.10 (978-1-4296-7986-2(7), 118318) Capstone.

Holmes, Kirsty. My School. 2018. (Our Values - Level 1 Ser.). (Illus.). 24p. (J). (gr. 1-1). (978-0-7787-5424-4(3)); pap. (978-0-7787-5447-3(2)) Crabtree Publishing Co.

Hurt, Avery Elizabeth. Working with Your School to Create a Safe Environment, 1 vol. 2017. (LGBTQ+ Guide to Beating Bullying Ser.). (ENG., Illus.). 64p. (J). (gr. 6-6). 36.13 (978-1-5081-7435-6(0), 24a21c21-2937-4356-adf1-6ab8d0edb145, Rosen Young Adult) Rosen Publishing Group, Inc., The.

Idzikowski, Lisa, ed. School Shootings, 1 vol. 2019. (Introducing Issues with Opposing Viewpoints Ser.). (ENG.). 120p. (gr. 7-10). pap. 29.30 (978-1-5345-0573-5(3), d0cfb1e8-fc80-473c-b7c6-67f48d6c07d3) Greenhaven Publishing LLC.

The Inside Scoop on American Graduate & Professional Schools. 2004. (C). pap. 4.95 net. (978-1-884169-33-5(3)) International Educational Improvement Ctr. Pr.

Jack's Pack: KinderReaders Individual Title Six-Packs. (Kinderstarters Ser.). 8p. (gr. -1-1). 21.00 (978-0-7635-8660-7(9)) Rigby Education.

Jensen, Sean. The Middle School Rules of Brian Urlacher. 2015. (ENG., Illus.). 176p. (J). (gr. 4-8). 14.99 (978-1-4245-4979-5(5)) BroadStreet Publishing.

—The Middle School Rules of Charles Tillman: As Told by Sean Jensen. 2015. (ENG., Illus.). 176p. (J). (gr. 4-8). 14.99 (978-1-4245-5101-9(3)) BroadStreet Publishing.

Jobs in My School, 12 vols. 2014. (Jobs in My School Ser.). (ENG.). 24p. (J). (gr. 1-2). 151.62 (978-1-4777-6561-6(1), 69e52395-2cec-43ee-a82d-a88dbaf47214, PowerKids Pr.) Rosen Publishing Group, Inc., The.

Jones, Tammy. We Go to School. 2009. (Sight Word Readers Set A Ser.). (J). 3.49 net. (978-1-60719-146-9(6)) Newmark Learning LLC.

Kalman, Bobbie. At School. 2010. (ENG.). 16p. (J). (978-0-7787-9497-4(0)); pap. (978-0-7787-9522-3(5)) Crabtree Publishing Co.

—La Comunidad de Mi Escuela. 2010. (SPA.). 24p. (J). pap. (978-0-7787-8590-3(4)); lib. bdg. (978-0-7787-8564-4(5)) Crabtree Publishing Co.

—My School Community. 2010. (My World Ser.). (ENG., Illus.). 24p. (J). (gr. k-2). (978-0-7787-9442-4(3)); pap. (978-0-7787-9486-8(5)) Crabtree Publishing Co.

—School Days Then & Now. 2013. (ENG., Illus.). 24p. (J). (978-0-7787-0127-9(1)); pap. (978-0-7787-0209-2(X)) Crabtree Publishing Co.

Keller, Carolyn & Seaman, Jim. Allegheny College College Prowler off the Record. 2005. (College Prowler off the Record Guides: Vol. 1). 160p. (YA). (gr. 12-18). pap., stu. ed. 14.95 (978-1-59658-000-8(3)) College Prowler, Inc.

Kelly, Sheila M. & Rotner, Shelley. School Days. Rotner, Shelley, photos by. 2020. (ENG., Illus.). 32p. (J). (gr. -1-2). 26.65 (978-1-5415-5776-5(X), 02383e8d-5fe8-4935-9616-e5b47e2a2329, Millbrook Pr.) Lerner Publishing Group.

Kesselring, Susan. At School. 2018. (J). (978-1-4896-9963-3(5), AV2 by Weigl) Weigl Pubs., Inc.

Kimball, Marrae. The Secret Combination to Middle School; Real Advice from Real Kids, Ideas for Success, & Much More! 2013. 200p. (J). pap. 14.95 (978-0-9849322-1-4(6)) Find Your Way Publishing, Inc.

Knowlton, MaryLee. Safety at School. Andersen, Gregg, photos by. 2008. (Staying Safe Ser.). (ENG., Illus.). 32p. (J). (gr. -1-3). lib. bdg. (978-0-7787-4317-0(9)) Crabtree Publishing Co.

Koestler-Grack, Rachel A. School in the Civil Rights Movement. 2016. (It's Back to School ... Way Back! Ser.). (ENG., Illus.). 32p. (J). (gr. 3-6). lib. bdg. 27.99 (978-1-5157-2099-7(3), 132704, Capstone Pr.) Capstone.

Kreiner, Anna. Todo lo que necesitas saber sobre la violencia en la escuela (Everything You Need to Know about Violence in School) 2009. (Todo lo que necesitas (the Need to Know Library) Ser.). (SPA.). 64p. (gr. 6-6). 58.50 (978-1-60854-411-0(7), Editorial Buenas Letras) Rosen Publishing Group, Inc., The.

Kreisman, Rachelle. Places We Go: A Kids' Guide to Community Sites. Haggerty, Tim, illus. 2015. (Start Smart (tm) — Community Ser.). (ENG.). 32p. (J). (gr. 1-3). E-Book 39.99 (978-1-937529-36-9(3)) Red Chair Pr.

Kuskowski, Alex. School. 2014. (Numbers 1-20 Ser.). (ENG.). 24p. (J). (gr. -1-3). lib. bdg. 29.93 (978-1-62403-267-7(2), 1596, SandCastle) ABDO Publishing Co.

A la Escuela: Individual Title Six-Packs. (Chiquilibros Ser.). (SPA.). (gr. k-1). 23.00 (978-0-7635-8594-5(7)) Rigby Education.

Laval, Thierry. Mini Look & Find at School (Mini Look & Find) Laval, Thierry, illus. 2017. (Mini Look & Find Ser.). (ENG., Illus.). 14p. (J). (gr. -1-k). 9.95 (978-0-531-23081-7(3), Children's Pr.) Scholastic Library Publishing.

Lawrence, Riley. Should the School Day Start Later?, 1 vol. 2019. (Points of View Ser.). (ENG.). 24p. (gr. 3-3). 26.23 (978-1-5345-6720-7(8), e874b9e5-ae6a-4499-a4af-a048c7dfe23c, KidHaven Publishing) Greenhaven Publishing LLC.

Layne, Steven L. & Layne, Deborah Dover. T Is for Teachers: A School Alphabet. Ettlinger, Doris, illus. rev. ed. 2005. (ENG.). 52p. (J). (gr. k-6). 14.95 (978-1-58536-266-0(2)) Sleeping Bear Pr.

LeBlanc, Terry. Learning to Recycle with Terry the Trashman. 2004. (J). pap. (978-0-9755913-0-7(4)) LeBlanc, Terry Leonard.

Lee, April. Helping at School, 1 vol. 2012. (InfoMax Readers Ser.). (ENG., Illus.). 16p. (J). (gr. k-k). pap. 7.00 (978-1-4488-8896-2(4), 3ea76b39-1272-4a48-8397-9e0a3deb65a3, Rosen Classroom) Rosen Publishing Group, Inc., The.

Lee, Sally. School Long Ago & Today, 1 vol. 2014. (Long Ago & Today Ser.). (ENG.). 24p. (J). (gr. 1-3). 27.99 (978-1-4914-0296-2(2), 125831) Capstone.

Lerner, Sarah, ed. Parkland Speaks: Survivors from Marjory Stoneman Douglas Share Their Stories. 2019. (Illus.). 192p. (YA). (gr. 9). pap. 17.99 (978-1-9848-4999-1(9), Crown Books For Young Readers) Random Hse. Children's Bks.

Lewis, Jan, illus. At School. 2017. 14p. (J). (gr. -1-12). 11.99 (978-1-86147-726-2(0), Armadillo) Anness Publishing GBR. Dist: National Bk. Network.

Lindeen, Mary. Rules Rule at School! 2019. (BeginningtoRead Ser.). (ENG., Illus.). 32p. (J). (gr. -1-2). 22.60 (978-1-68450-941-6(6)) Norwood Hse. Pr.

Listen & Learn Get Ready for School. 2017. (Listen & Learn First Words Ser.). (ENG.). (J). bds. 19.99 (978-0-7945-3985-6(8), Usborne) EDC Publishing.

Lucas, Eileen. The Little Rock Nine Stand up for Their Rights. Gustavson, Adam, illus. 2011. (History Speaks: Picture Books Plus Reader's Theater Ser.). 48p. pap. 56.72 (978-0-7613-7634-7(8)); pap. 9.95 (978-0-7613-7118-2(4)); (ENG.). (gr. 2-4). lib. bdg. 27.93 (978-0-7613-5874-9(9), Millbrook Pr.) Lerner Publishing Group.

Lunis, Natalie. Spooky Schools. 2013. (Scary Places Ser.). 32p. (J). (gr. 4-8). lib. bdg. 25.27 (978-1-61772-750-4(4)) Bearport Publishing Co., Inc.

Manton, Charlotte. The Community of Lincoln. Stanley, Karen & Bornemeier, Pam, eds. Schellpeper, Kathy, photos by. (Illus.). 116p. (J). (gr. 3-6). pap. 10.50 (978-0-9671920-0-0(5)) Lincoln Public Schls.

Mara, Wil. The Schoolmaster, 1 vol. 2011. (Colonial People Ser.). (ENG.). 48p. (gr. 4-4). 34.07 (978-0-7614-4801-3(2), a4a1cebd-de00-4ad7-8468-880c7ef3dc47) Cavendish Square Publishing LLC.

Marks, Jennifer L. School Times, 1 vol. 2010. (Spot It Ser.). (ENG.). 32p. lib. bdg. 8.99 (978-1-4296-5761-7(8), Pebble) Capstone.

Mattern, Joanne. After School, 1 vol. 2006. (My Day at School Ser.). (ENG., Illus.). 24p. (gr. k-2). pap. 9.15 (978-0-8368-6790-9(4), 07442b10-97e6-4ab1-891c-0c2965d94330); lib. bdg. 24.67 (978-0-8368-6783-1(1), 071bf94d-e6bc-4121-90d9-ffbac818d6d0) Stevens, Gareth Publishing LLLP. (Weekly Reader Leveled Readers).

—Eating Lunch at School, 1 vol. 2006. (My Day at School Ser.). (ENG.). 24p. (gr. k-2). pap. 9.15 (978-0-8368-6791-6(2), c60529cf-2026-48f1-97b7-120788d2ed64); (Illus.). lib. bdg. 24.67 (978-0-8368-6784-8(X), 5fdd0b80-5cab-451d-9c9a-558d72df3068) Stevens, Gareth Publishing LLLP. (Weekly Reader Leveled Readers).

—Getting Ready for School, 1 vol. 2006. (My Day at School Ser.). (ENG., Illus.). 24p. (gr. k-2). pap. 9.15 (978-0-8368-6792-3(0), 333511a4-d275-4480-a273-ac954eb3070a); lib. bdg. 24.67 (978-0-8368-6785-5(8), 6ff17d68-a0ac-4c67-b817-6bfc857315cf) Stevens, Gareth Publishing LLLP. (Weekly Reader Leveled Readers).

—Going to School, 1 vol. 2006. (My Day at School Ser.). (ENG., Illus.). 24p. (gr. k-2). lib. bdg. 24.67 (978-0-8368-6786-2(6), 41b5386e-504e-4c6d-bc19-d88a766ecf3c, Weekly Reader Leveled Readers) Stevens, Gareth Publishing LLLP.

—In the Classroom, 1 vol. 2006. (My Day at School Ser.). (ENG., Illus.). 24p. (gr. k-2). pap. 9.15 (978-0-8368-6794-7(7), 8f232329-13a7-434d-8d75-bf96d01f550f); lib. bdg. 24.67 (978-0-8368-6787-9(4), f61d5b15-3e14-4a97-bf50-4938dd7bc407) Stevens, Gareth Publishing LLLP. (Weekly Reader Leveled Readers).

—In the Classroom / en el Salón de Clases, 1 vol. 2006. (My Day at School / Mi día en la Escuela Ser.). (SPA & ENG., Illus.). 24p. (gr. k-2). lib. bdg. 24.67 (978-0-8368-7361-0(0), da06cb50-feb0-4791-8372-9f89a99faee7, Weekly Reader Leveled Readers) Stevens, Gareth Publishing LLLP.

—Playing at School, 1 vol. 2006. (My Day at School Ser.). (ENG., Illus.). 24p. (gr. k-2). pap. 9.15 (978-0-8368-6795-4(5), f8bb63fa-38be-46ab-89d0-f79319b73465); lib. bdg. 24.67 (978-0-8368-6788-6(2), 10093674-2a48-4727-98d3-92ec508aee8f) Stevens, Gareth Publishing LLLP. (Weekly Reader Leveled Readers).

—Staying Safe at School, 1 vol. 2007. (Safety First Ser.). (ENG., Illus.). 24p. (gr. k-2). pap. 9.15 (978-0-8368-7799-1(3), 82b1bede-75da-44f9-951f-3fa924ff3047); lib. bdg. 24.67 (978-0-8368-7792-2(6), f0372997-8743-41dd-9c06-ce7a163d6861) Stevens, Gareth Publishing LLLP. (Weekly Reader Leveled Readers).

—Staying Safe at School / la Seguridad en la Escuela, 1 vol. 2007. (Safety First / la Seguridad Es lo Primero Ser.). (ENG & SPA., Illus.). 24p. (gr. k-2). lib. bdg. 24.67 (978-0-8368-8057-1(9), 99a23e1d-78ad-4dfc-a2df-90415159f987, Weekly Reader Leveled Readers) Stevens, Gareth Publishing LLLP.

Matteson, Adrienne. A Better Locker. 2019. (21st Century Skills Innovation Library: Design a Better World Ser.). (ENG., Illus.). 32p. (J). (gr. 4-7). pap. 14.21 (978-1-5341-3976-3(1), 212733); lib. bdg. 32.07 (978-1-5341-4320-3(3), 212732) Cherry Lake Publishing.

Meachen Rau, Dana. School Safety, 1 vol. 2010. (Safe Kids Ser.). (ENG.). 32p. (gr. k-1). 25.50 (978-0-7614-4090-1(9), cc66381c-c984-4eb1-85c7-c85855810417) Cavendish Square Publishing LLC.

—Seguridad en la Escuela / School Safety, 1 vol. 2010. (Niños Seguros / Safe Kids Ser.). (ENG & SPA.). 32p. (gr. k-2). lib. bdg. 25.50 (978-0-7614-4782-5(2), 721a7cf0-58fb-4638-88f5-4ef2b4b79ef1) Cavendish Square Publishing LLC.

Meister, Cari. La Biblioteca Pública. 2016. (Los Primeros Viajes Escolares (First Field Trips)).Tr. of Public Library. (SPA., Illus.). 24p. (J). (gr. k-2). lib. bdg. 25.65 (978-1-62031-327-5(8), Bullfrog Bks.) Jump! Inc.

—El Museo de Arte. 2016. (Los Primeros Viajes Escolares (First Field Trips)).Tr. of Art Museum. (SPA.). 24p. (J). (gr. k-2). lib. bdg. 25.65 (978-1-62031-331-2(6), Bullfrog Bks.) Jump! Inc.

—Public Library. Fretland VanVoorst, Jenny, ed. 2016. (First Field Trips). (Illus.). 24p. (J). (gr. k-2). lib. bdg. 25.65 (978-1-62031-296-4(4), Bullfrog Bks.) Jump! Inc.

Meyer, Terry. Navigating a New School, 1 vol. 2012. (Middle School Survival Handbook Ser.). (ENG., Illus.). 64p. (YA). (gr. 6-6). lib. bdg. 37.13 (978-1-4488-8312-7(1), 9b81aa29-13f3-4354-82a9-1482d6f6933c, Rosen Reference) Rosen Publishing Group, Inc., The.

Meyer, Terry Teague. Navigating a New School, 1 vol. 2012. (Middle School Survival Handbook Ser.). (ENG., Illus.). 64p. (YA). (gr. 6-6). pap. 13.95 (978-1-4488-8319-6(9), 675a53a3-9051-45bc-a25a-e8477b4abf5f, Rosen Reference) Rosen Publishing Group, Inc., The.

Michele, Tracey. Map the School. 2011. (ENG., Illus.). 16p. (J). pap. 7.95 (978-1-59920-590-8(4)) Black Rabbit Bks.

—My School, Your School. 2011. (Learn-Abouts Ser.). (ENG., Illus.). 16p. (J). pap. 7.95 (978-1-59920-605-9(6)) Black Rabbit Bks.

Milet Publishing Staff. My First Bilingual Book - School, 1 vol. 2014. (My First Bilingual Book Ser.). (ENG & POR., Illus.). 20p. (J). (— 1). bds. 7.99 (978-1-84059-899-5(9)); bds. 7.99 (978-1-84059-895-7(6)); bds. 7.99 (978-1-84059-892-6(1)); bds. 7.99 (978-1-84059-893-3(X)); bds. 7.99 (978-1-84059-903-9(0)); bds. 8.99 (978-1-84059-905-3(7)); bds. 7.99 (978-1-84059-891-9(3)); bds. 8.99 (978-1-84059-894-0(8)) Milet Publishing.

—My First Bilingual Book - School (English-Korean), 1 vol. 2014. (My First Bilingual Book Ser.). (ENG., Illus.). 20p. (J). (— 1). bds. 7.99 (978-1-84059-897-1(2)) Milet Publishing.

—My First Bilingual Book - School (English-Somali), 1 vol. 2014. (My First Bilingual Book Ser.). (ENG., Illus.). 20p. (J). (— 1). bds. 8.99 (978-1-84059-901-5(4)) Milet Publishing.

—School, 1 vol. 2014. (My First Bilingual Book Ser.). (ENG & ITA., Illus.). 20p. (J). (— 1). bds. 7.99 (978-1-84059-896-4(4)) Milet Publishing.

—School - My First Bilingual Book, 1 vol. 2014. (My First Bilingual Book Ser.). (ENG & SPA., Illus.). 20p. (J). (— 1). bds. 8.99 (978-1-84059-902-2(2)); bds. 7.99 (978-1-84059-890-2(5)); bds. 8.99 (978-1-84059-900-8(6)); bds. 7.99 (978-1-84059-904-6(9)) Milet Publishing.

—School - My First Bilingual Book (Szkola), 1 vol. 2014. (My First Bilingual Book Ser.). (ENG & POR., Illus.). 20p. (J). (— 1). bds. 7.99 (978-1-84059-898-8(0)) Milet Publishing.

Milla Gorilla Goes to School. 2004. pap. 1.50 (978-0-87162-934-0(8)) Warner Pr., Inc.

Miller, Amanda. We Help Out at School. 2009. (Scholastic News Nonfiction Readers Ser.). (ENG.). 24p. (J). (gr. 1-2). lib. bdg. 22.00 (978-0-531-21345-2(5), Children's Pr.) Scholastic Library Publishing.

—We Help Out at School (Scholastic News Nonfiction Readers: We the Kids) 2009. (Scholastic News Nonfiction Readers Ser.). (ENG.). 24p. (J). (gr. 1-2). pap. 6.95 (978-0-531-21449-7(4), Children's Pr.) Scholastic Library Publishing.

Miller, Jake. Who's Who in a School Community, 1 vol. 2004. (Exploring Community Ser.). (ENG., Illus.). 24p. (gr. 2-3). pap. 8.25 (978-1-4042-5030-7(1), df81e871-3fc6-4b7c-947c-7c66a9c31786, PowerKids Pr.) Rosen Publishing Group, Inc., The.

—Who's Who in School Community. (Communities at Work Ser.). 24p. (gr. 2-2). 2009. 42.50 (978-1-61511-902-8(7)) 2004. (ENG., Illus.). (J). lib. bdg. 26.27 (978-1-4042-2788-0(1), 57e4dcff-b4be-43db-9323-6ef723536649) Rosen Publishing Group, Inc., The. (PowerKids Pr.).

Miller, Reagan. 100th Day of School. 2010. (ENG., Illus.). 32p. (J). (978-0-7787-4763-5(8)); pap. (978-0-7787-4781-9(6)) Crabtree Publishing Co.

Mills, Nathan & Rose, Craig. We Help at School, 1 vol. 2012. (Rosen Readers Ser.). (ENG., Illus.). 16p. (J). (gr. k-k). pap. 7.00 (978-1-4488-8661-6(9), 35016a5d-44f9-464c-b3fd-ad1aa8e75ccb, Rosen Classroom) Rosen Publishing Group, Inc., The.

Mills, Nathan & Sotherden, Nora. Our Classroom Rules, 1 vol. 2012. (Rosen Readers Ser.). (ENG., Illus.). 16p. (J). (gr. k-k). pap. 7.00 (978-1-4488-8692-0(9), 0977b2fa-2b0d-4f23-8448-460740219b75, Rosen Classroom) Rosen Publishing Group, Inc., The.

Modoc Press, Inc., ed. Directory of Distance Learning Opportunities: K-12, 1 vol. 2003. (ENG.). 432p. (gr. k-12). 106.00 (978-1-57356-515-8(6), 900318591, Bloomsbury Academic) Bloomsbury Publishing Plc GBR. Dist: Macmillan.

Mortensen, Lori. Manners Matter in the Classroom. Hunt, Lisa, illus. 2011. (First Graphics: Manners Matter Ser.). (ENG.). 24p. (gr. 1-2). pap. 35.70 (978-1-4296-6392-2(8)) Capstone.

—Manners Matter on a Field Trip, 1 vol. Hunt, Lisa, illus. 2010. (First Graphics: Manners Matter Ser.). (ENG.). 24p. (J). (gr. 1-3). lib. bdg. 24.65 (978-1-4296-5331-2(0), 113759) Capstone.

Mortenson, Greg. Listen to the Wind: The Story of Dr. Greg & Three Cups of Tea. Roth, Susan L., illus. 2009. 32p. (J). (gr. 1-3). 18.99 (978-0-8037-3058-8(6), Dial Bks) Penguin Young Readers Group.

—Stones into Schools: Promoting Peace, One School at a Time. 2011. (ENG.). 240p. (J). (gr. 3-18). 16.99 (978-0-8037-3687-0(8), Dial) Penguin Publishing Group.

Moss, Marissa. Amelia's School Survival Guide. Moss, Marissa, illus. 2006. (Amelia Ser.). (ENG., Illus.). 64p. (J). (gr. 2-5). 14.99 (978-1-4169-0915-6(X), Simon & Schuster/Paula Wiseman Bks.) Simon & Schuster/Paula Wiseman Bks.

Mullins, Matt. How Did They Build That? School. 2009. (Community Connections: How Did They Build That? Ser.). (ENG.). 24p. (gr. 2-5). lib. bdg. 29.21 (978-1-60279-487-0(1), 200257) Cherry Lake Publishing.

Murkoff, Heidi. What to Expect at Preschool. Rader, Laura, illus. 2003. (ENG.). 24p. (J). (gr. -1-k). pap. 5.99 (978-0-06-052920-8(2), HarperFestival) HarperCollins Pubs.

Murray, Elizabeth A. The Dozier School for Boys: Forensics, Survivors, & a Painful Past. 2019. (ENG., Illus.). 120p. (YA). (gr. 8-12). lib. bdg. 37.32 (978-1-5415-1978-7(7), 698256b9-e8ed-4069-8a61-1f79ec05c420, Twenty-First Century Bks.) Lerner Publishing Group.

Murray, Julie. The School, 1 vol. 2016. (My Community: Places Ser.). (ENG., Illus.). 24p. (J). (gr. -1-2). lib. bdg. 31.36 (978-1-68080-540-6(1), 21360, Abdo Kids) ABDO Publishing Co.

Myers, Dean. School. 2006. (978-0-06-052311-4(5)); lib. bdg. (978-0-06-052312-1(3)) HarperCollins Canada, Ltd.

Nagle, Jeanne. Reducing Your Carbon Footprint at School. 2009. (Your Carbon Footprint Ser.). 48p. (gr. 5-5). 53.00 (978-1-60854-911-5(9), Rosen Reference) Rosen Publishing Group, Inc., The.

O'Brien, Gretchen. Education in California (California) rev. ed. 2017. (Social Studies: Informational Text Ser.). (ENG., Illus.). 32p. (J). (gr. 3-5). pap. 11.99 (978-1-4258-3246-9(6)) Teacher Created Materials, Inc.

O'Connell, Eleanor. Schools Around the World. 2017. (Adventures in Culture Ser.). (ENG.). 24p. (J). (gr. -1-3). 18.95 (978-1-5311-8643-2(2)) Perfection Learning Corp.

—Schools Around the World, 1 vol. 2016. (Adventures in Culture Ser.). (ENG., Illus.). 24p. (J). (gr. 1-2). pap. 9.15 (978-1-4824-5589-2(7), 1cb4598c-8c16-48eb-b5e7-d847861f39a3) Stevens, Gareth Publishing LLLP.

Orr, Tamra B. & Orr, Tamra. Violence in Our Schools: Halls of Hope, Halls of Fear. 2003. (Single Title: Social Studies Ser.). (ENG., Illus.). 192p. (YA). 30.50 (978-0-531-12268-6(9), Watts, Franklin) Scholastic Library Publishing.

Owenz, Roger. Mr Owenz Goes to School. 2009. 24p. pap. 12.99 (978-1-4490-2655-4(9)) AuthorHouse.

Parramón, José María. Mi Calle. Borday, Irene, illus. (Coleccion Estoy En...).Tr. of My Street. (SPA.). 32p. (J). (gr. k-3). 6.36 (978-84-342-1003-5(7)) Parramon Ediciones S.A. ESP. Dist: Lectorum Pubns., Inc.

—Mi Casa. Borday, Irene, illus. (Coleccion Estoy En...).Tr. of My House. (SPA.). 32p. (J). (gr. k-3). 6.36 (978-84-342-1002-8(9)) Parramon Ediciones S.A. ESP. Dist: Lectorum Pubns., Inc.

—Mi Jardin. Borday, Irene, illus. (Coleccion Estoy En...).Tr. of My Garden. (SPA.). 32p. (J). (gr. k-3). 6.36 (978-84-342-1005-9(3)) Parramon Ediciones S.A. ESP. Dist: Lectorum Pubns., Inc.

Parramón, José María & Borday, Irene. Mi Calle.Tr. of My Street. (SPA., Illus.). (J). (gr. -1-1). 6.95 (978-958-04-1277-9(4)) Norma S.A. COL. Dist: Distribuidora Norma, Inc.

Peirce, Lincoln. Big Nate: Say Good-Bye to Dork City, Volume 12. 2015. (Big Nate Ser.: 12). (ENG., Illus.). 224p. (J). 11.99 (978-1-4494-6225-3(1)) Andrews McMeel Publishing.

Pettiford, Rebecca. El Zoológico. 2016. (Los Primeros Viajes Escolares (First Field Trips)).Tr. of Zoo. (SPA., Illus.). 24p. (J). (gr. k-2). lib. bdg. 25.65 (978-1-62031-333-6(2), Bullfrog Bks.) Jump! Inc.

Phillips, Clifton C. Rabbits Rule at Night School. 2008. 28p. pap. 8.99 (978-1-935105-02-2(7)) Avid Readers Publishing Group.

Pichon, L. Tom Gates Is Absolutely Fantastic (at Some Things) Pichon, L., illus. 2018. (Tom Gates Ser.: 5). (ENG., Illus.). 272p. (J). (gr. 3-7). 12.99 (978-1-5362-0130-7(8)) Candlewick Pr.

Puppet Rescue, creator. Yaker Goes to School. 2007. (Illus.). 10p. (J). 4.95 (978-0-9799958-2-8(5)) Puppet Rescue.

Raatma, Lucia. Staying Safe on the School Bus, 1 vol. 2011. (Staying Safe Ser.). (ENG.). 24p. (J). (gr. 1-3). lib. bdg. 25.99 (978-1-4296-6823-1(7), 116353, Capstone Pr.) Capstone.

Randolph, Ryan P. Frontier Schools & Schoolteachers. 2009. (Library of the Westward Expansion Ser.). 24p. (gr. 3-4). 42.50 (978-1-60853-935-2(0), PowerKids Pr.) Rosen Publishing Group, Inc., The.

Raymer, Dottie. School Smarts Projects. McGuinness, Tracy & McGuinness, Tracey, illus. 2007. (American Girl Library). (ENG.). 96p. (J). (gr. 3-7). pap. 8.95 (978-1-59369-005-2(3), American Girl) American Girl Publishing, Inc.

Rearick, Ben. A Better Lunch Line. 2019. (21st Century Skills Innovation Library: Design a Better World Ser.). (ENG.). 32p. (J). (gr. 4-7). pap. 14.21 (978-1-5341-3977-0(X), 212737); (Illus.). lib. bdg. 32.07 (978-1-5341-4321-0(1), 212736) Cherry Lake Publishing.

Reeves, Diane Lindsey. Making Choices at School. 2018. (21st Century Junior Library: Smart Choices Ser.). (ENG., Illus.). 24p. (J). (gr. k-2). pap. 12.79 (978-1-5341-0884-4(X), 210900); lib. bdg. 30.64 (978-1-5341-0785-4(1), 210899) Cherry Lake Publishing.

—Making Choices at School. 2018. (21st Century Junior Library: Smart Choices Ser.). (ENG.). 24p. (J). (gr. k-2). 19.75 (978-1-5311-8580-0(0)) Perfection Learning Corp.

Reid, Stephanie. School. 2011. (Early Literacy Ser.). (ENG.). 16p. (gr. k-1). 19.99 (978-1-4333-2354-6(0)); 6.99 (978-1-4333-2353-9(2)) Teacher Created Materials, Inc.

Remember: The Journey to School Integration-Display. 2004. (ENG.). 1p. (J). tchr. ed. 162.00 (978-0-618-45334-4(2)) Houghton Mifflin Harcourt Publishing Co.

Rhodes, Corey L. Keep Your Head Up! 2010. 24p. 16.99 (978-1-4490-7580-4(0)) AuthorHouse.

Ricciuti, Edward R. We Share, 1 vol. 2008. (Ready for School Ser.). (ENG.). 24p. (gr. k-1). pap. 9.23 (978-0-7614-3276-0(0), e6d5aeb0-d113-42d9-b070-7e59a7bf1a80) Cavendish Square Publishing LLC.

—We Tell the Truth, 1 vol. 2008. (Ready for School Ser.). (ENG.). 24p. (gr. k-1). pap. 9.23 (978-0-7614-3277-7(9), f76aef0f-a681-48fe-847e-0d0b9b14e5e9) Cavendish Square Publishing LLC.

Rice, Dona Herweck. Big Kid School. 2011. (Early Literacy Ser.). (ENG.). 16p. (gr. k-1). 19.99 (978-1-4333-2356-0(7)); 6.99 (978-1-4333-2355-3(9)) Teacher Created Materials, Inc.

Rice, Dona Herweck & Petersen, Casey Null. School Around the World, 1 vol. 2nd rev. ed. 2011. (TIME for KIDS(r): Informational Text Ser.). (ENG.). 28p. (gr. 3-4). pap. 11.99 (978-1-4333-3654-6(5)) Teacher Created Materials, Inc.

Rigo, Laura, illus. Off to School. 2010. 10p. (J). (gr. -1-1). bds. 7.99 (978-0-7641-6363-0(9)) Sourcebooks, Inc.

Rissman, Rebecca. Going to a Museum, 1 vol. 2012. (World of Field Trips Ser.). (ENG.). 24p. (gr. -1-1). pap. 6.29 (978-1-4329-6076-6(8), 117906, Heinemann) Capstone.

—Going to School: Comparing Past & Present, 1 vol. 2014. (Comparing Past & Present Ser.). (ENG., Illus.). 24p. (J). (gr. -1-1). pap. 6.95 (978-1-4329-9025-1(X), 124794, Heinemann) Capstone.

Rivera, Sheila. School Safety. 2007. (First Step Nonfiction — Safety Ser.). (ENG., Illus.). 8p. (J). (gr. k-2). pap. 5.99

(978-0-8225-6822-3(5), 2d61431a-e43c-4c22-963b-f215e88be4f6) Lerner Publishing Group.

Rogers, Amy B. Do Kids Need Recess?, 1 vol. 2018. (Points of View Ser.). (ENG.). 24p. (gr. 3-3). pap. 9.25 (978-1-5345-2785-0(0), 1e4401bb-5d08-4310-ae78-ba0d094e61d4, KidHaven Publishing) Greenhaven Publishing LLC.

Rookie Preschool, 12 vols., Set. Incl. Piglets Belong to Pigs. Scholastic, Inc. Staff. 23.00 (978-0-531-24408-1(3), Children's Pr.); Rookie Preschool: My First Rookie Reader: It's Circle Time! Shapes. Bolam, Emily. 23.00 (978-0-531-24401-2(6)); Rookie Preschool: My First Rookie Reader: Jack's Room. Woolf, Julia. 23.00 (978-0-531-24400-5(8), Children's Pr.); Rookie Preschool: My First Rookie Reader: Red, Blue, & Yellow Too! lib. bdg. 23.00 (978-0-531-24403-6(2), Children's Pr.); Rookie Preschool: My First Rookie Reader: the Leaves Fall All Around. Mack, Steve. 23.00 (978-0-531-24402-9(4)); Rookie Preschool: Rookie Learn about Nauture: Busy Day, Busy Night. Hendra, Sue. (Illus.). 23.00 (978-0-531-24407-4(5), Children's Pr.); Rookie Preschool: Rookie Learn about Nauture: the Ants Go Marching. 23.00 (978-0-531-24406-7(7), Children's Pr.); Rookie Preschool: Rookie Learn about Nauture: What's the Weather? Cali, Jennifer. Miller, Edward, illus. lib. bdg. 23.00 (978-0-531-24410-4(5)); Rookie Preschool: Rookie Learn about Nauture: Who Is Sleeping? Sapp, Karen. lib. bdg. 23.00 (978-0-531-24411-1(3), Children's Pr.); Three Little Kittens Get Dressed. Scholastic Library Publishing. lib. bdg. 23.00 (978-0-531-24404-3(0), Children's Pr.); 3-2-1 School Is Fun! Haley, Amanda. 23.00 (978-0-531-24405-0(9)); 24p. (J). (gr. -1). 2009. Set lib. bdg. 276.00 (978-0-531-22775-6(8)) Scholastic Library Publishing.

Rosa-Mendoza, Gladys. My School, 1 vol. Murphy, Terri, illus. 2010. (My World Ser.). (ENG.). 24p. (J). (gr. k-1). pap. 9.15 (978-1-61533-039-3(9), 017780f0-76d4-4031-ad5e-6bcc6d282a8b); lib. bdg. 27.27 (978-1-60754-953-6(0), 46760153-2e95-44e0-b3e7-0d6726c802c7) Rosen Publishing Group, Inc., The. (Windmill Bks.).

—My School/Mi Escuela. Murphy, Terri, illus. 2007. (English Spanish Foundations Ser.). (ENG & SPA.). (J). (gr. -1-k). bds. 6.95 (978-1-931398-23-7(2)) Me+Mi Publishing.

Rustad, Martha E. H. Michael Makes Friends at School. Becker, Paula J., illus. 2017. (Cloverleaf Books (tm) — off to School Ser.). (ENG.). 24p. (J). (gr. k-2). pap. 8.99 (978-1-5124-5577-9(6), 648c8b2f-0df2-4053-8957-74269cf84acd); lib. bdg. 25.32 (978-1-5124-3937-3(1), 19226f8c-e0b6-46f1-afa6-45b41bb1dc95) Lerner Publishing Group. (Millbrook Pr.).

Ruurs, Margriet. My School in the Rain Forest: How Children Attend School Around the World. 2009. (ENG., Illus.). 32p. (J). (gr. k-k). 17.99 (978-1-59078-601-7(7), Astra Young Readers) Astra Publishing Hse.

—School Days Around the World. Feagan, Alice, illus. 2015. (Around the World Ser.). (ENG.). 40p. (J). (gr. -1-2). 18.95 (978-1-77138-047-8(0)) Kids Can Pr., Ltd. CAN. Dist: Hachette Bk. Group.

Salzmann, Mary Elizabeth. Money for School, 1 vol. 2010. (Your Piggy Bank: a Guide to Spending & Saving for Kids! Ser.). (ENG.). 24p. (J). (gr. k-4). 31.36 (978-1-61641-031-5(0), 15844, Looking Glass Library) Magic Wagon.

Schauer, Pete, ed. Charter Schools & School Vouchers, 1 vol. 2018. (Introducing Issues with Opposing Viewpoints Ser.). (ENG.). 120p. (gr. 7-10). 43.63 (978-1-5345-0355-7(2), 54b7e27c-d139-42e1-8aae-9ded28fab03e) Greenhaven Publishing LLC.

Scholastic News Nonfiction Readers: Kids Like Me (Global Awareness), 5 vols., Set. Incl. This Is the Way We Dress. Behrens, Janice. lib. bdg. 21.19 (978-0-531-21338-4(2)); This Is the Way We Eat Our Food. Falk, Laine. lib. bdg. 21.19 (978-0-531-21339-1(0)); This Is the Way We Go to School. Falk, Laine. lib. bdg. 21.19 (978-0-531-21341-4(2), Children's Pr.); This Is the Way We Help at Home. Miller, Amanda. lib. bdg. 21.19 (978-0-531-21340-7(4)); This Is the Way We Play. Miller, Amanda. lib. bdg. 21.19 (978-0-531-21342-1(0)); 24p. (J). (gr. k-3). 2009. Set lib. bdg. 110.00 (978-0-531-21035-2(9), Children's Pr.) Scholastic Library Publishing.

Scholl, Elizabeth. New York City. 2009. (Class Trip Ser.). (Illus.). 48p. (J). (gr. 2-5). lib. bdg. 29.95 (978-1-58415-808-0(5)) Mitchell Lane Pubs.

The School Rules. 2015. (School Rules Ser.). (ENG.). 24p. (gr. k-k). pap., pap., pap. 48.90 (978-1-4824-3497-2(0)); lib. bdg. 145.62 (978-1-4824-2541-3(6), c7272df1-39c8-47cb-bfb7-61cf090d3373) Stevens, Gareth Publishing LLLP.

Schuette, Sarah L. School Bus Safety. 2019. (Staying Safe! Ser.). (ENG., Illus.). 24p. (J). (gr. -1-2). 24.65 (978-1-9771-0871-5(7), 140482, Pebble) Capstone.

Scraper, Katherine. Rules at School. 2006. (Early Explorers Ser.). (J). pap. (978-1-4108-6030-9(2)) Benchmark Education Co.

Senge, Peter, et al. Escuelas Que Aprenden: Un Manual de la Quinta Disciplina para Educadores, Padres de Familiar y Todos los Que Se Interesen en la Educacion. Nannetti, Jorge Cardenas, tr. 2006. (Coleccion Vitral Ser.). (SPA., Illus.). 630p. per. (978-958-04-6511-9(8)) Norma S.A. COL. Dist: Distribuidora Norma, Inc.

Sesame Street Staff, creator. Sesame Street: Elmo & Me! Boxed Set. 2011. 40p. (J). bds. 12.99 (978-1-60745-166-2(2)) Flying Frog Pubs.

Sevigny, Eric, illus. Caillou: Preschool Fun - 2 Stories Included. 2018. (ENG.). 32p. (J). (gr. k-2). 7.99 (978-2-89718-484-1(1)) Caillouet, Gerry.

Sévigny, Eric, illus. Caillou Va À l'École. 2017. (Château de Cartes Ser.). (FRE.). 24p. (J). (gr. -1). 4.95 (978-2-89718-314-1(4)) Caillouet, Gerry.

Shava, Ryder. We Come to School to Learn, 1 vol., 1. 2015. (Rosen REAL Readers: Social Studies Nonfiction / Fiction: Myself, My Community, My World Ser.). (ENG.). 8p. (J). (gr. k-1). pap. 5.46 (978-1-5081-1659-2(8), 4ef4f31e-81a5-41c5-a35c-e8554fbf2808, Rosen Classroom) Rosen Publishing Group, Inc., The.

Shofner, Melissa Raé. Why Do We Have to Pay Attention in Class?, 1 vol. 2018. (Common Good Ser.). (ENG.). 24p. (gr. 2-2). 25.27 (978-1-5383-3079-1(2), 5b16a981-3ac3-4a70-94e8-878c67b342ee, PowerKids Pr.) Rosen Publishing Group, Inc., The.

Shoup, Kate. Dealing with School Shootings, 1 vol. 2019. (Helping Yourself, Helping Others Ser.). (ENG.). 112p. (gr. 7-7). lib. bdg. 44.50 (978-1-5026-4630-9(7), bbbc2f24-7c45-4ea2-90d6-d33c0e4668c6) Cavendish Square Publishing LLC.

Silva, Jesselyn. My Corner of the Ring. 2019. (ENG., Illus.). 256p. (J). (gr. 5). 17.99 (978-0-525-51840-2(1), G.P. Putnam's Sons Books for Young Readers) Penguin Young Readers Group.

Silva, Sadie. Finding My School: Sticking to It, 1 vol. 2017. (Computer Science for the Real World Ser.). (ENG.). 8p. (gr. k-1). pap. (978-1-5383-5113-0(7), 51a65192-e81c-49ef-b49b-d87beac1e88d, Rosen Classroom) Rosen Publishing Group, Inc., The.

The Smartest One in Class: Individual Title Six-Packs. (gr. -1-2). 27.00 (978-0-7635-9474-9(1)) Rigby Education.

Smith, Julie. The Magic Pencil: Happy Birthday Kuser Elementary School 1909-2009. 2009. 44p. pap. 19.00 (978-1-4389-7246-6(6)) AuthorHouse.

Smith, Paula. Be the Change in Your School. 2014. (Be the Change! Ser.). (ENG., Illus.). 24p. (J). (gr. 2-3). (978-0-7787-0626-7(5)); pap. (978-0-7787-0638-0(9)) Crabtree Publishing Co.

—Schools in Different Places. 2015. (Learning about Our Global Community Ser.). (ENG., Illus.). 24p. (J). (gr. 2-2). (978-0-7787-2013-3(6)) Crabtree Publishing Co.

Smith, Sarah. School, Vol. 7. 2018. (Etiquette for Success Ser.). 64p. (J). (gr. 7). 31.93 (978-1-4222-3972-8(1)) Mason Crest.

Staff, Gareth Editorial Staff. Things at School, 1 vol. 2006. (Things in My World Ser.). (ENG., Illus.). 16p. (gr. k-1). lib. bdg. 21.67 (978-0-8368-6808-1(0), d1d7f426-9585-42c7-8b02-385a657d40a2, Weekly Reader Leveled Readers) Stevens, Gareth Publishing LLLP.

—Things at School / Las Cosas de la Escuela, 1 vol. 2006. (Things in My World / Las Cosas de Mi Mundo Ser.). (SPA & ENG., Illus.). 16p. (gr. k-1). lib. bdg. 21.67 (978-0-8368-7220-0(7), d517174b-6b0f-4da2-9cc2-f0a77395d117, Weekly Reader Leveled Readers) Stevens, Gareth Publishing LLLP.

Stern, Leonard & Price, Roger. Escape from Detention Mad Libs: World's Greatest Word Game. 2013. (Mad Libs Ser.). 48p. (J). (gr. 3-7). 5.99 (978-0-8431-7379-6(3), Mad Libs) Penguin Young Readers Group.

Stewart, Faith. Teens & Rural Education: Opportunities & Challenges. 2009. (Youth in Rural North America Ser.). (Illus.). 96p. (YA). (gr. 3-7). lib. bdg. 22.95 (978-1-4222-0015-5(9)) Mason Crest.

Stratton, Connor. Working at a School. 2020. (People at Work Ser.). (ENG.). 16p. (J). (gr. k-1). pap. 7.95 (978-1-64493-095-3(1), 1644930951); lib. bdg. 25.64 (978-1-64493-016-8(1), 1644930161) North Star Editions. (Focus Readers).

Swanson Sateren, Shelley. School in Colonial America. 2016. (It's Back to School ... Way Back! Ser.). (ENG., Illus.). 32p. (J). (gr. 3-6). lib. bdg. 27.99 (978-1-5157-2097-3(7), 132702) Capstone.

Taylor-Butler, Christine. Think Like a Scientist in the Gym. 2011. (Explorer Junior Library: Science Explorer Junior Ser.). (ENG., Illus.). 32p. (gr. 4-8). lib. bdg. 32.07 (978-1-61080-163-8(6), 201096) Cherry Lake Publishing.

Telgemeier, Raina. Smile. 2010. 21.00 (978-1-60686-896-6(9)) Perfection Learning Corp.

—Smile. Telgemeier, Raina, illus. 2010. (ENG., Illus.). 224p. (J). (gr. 3-7). pap. 10.99 (978-0-545-13206-0(1), Graphix) Scholastic, Inc.

—Smile. 2010. lib. bdg. 22.10 (978-0-606-14082-9(4)) Turtleback.

—Smile: a Graphic Novel. Telgemeier, Raina, illus. 2010. (ENG.). 224p. (J). (gr. 3-7). 24.99 (978-0-545-13205-3(3), Graphix) Scholastic, Inc.

Thaler, Mike. The Class Trip from the Black Lagoon. Lee, Jared, illus. 2011. (Black Lagoon Adventures Ser.: No. 1). (ENG.). 64p. (J). (gr. 2-6). 31.36 (978-1-59961-811-1(7), 3597, Chapter Bks.) Spotlight.

Top That Publishing Staff, ed. My School Days Yearbook. 2005. (Illus.). 28p. (978-1-84510-657-7(1)) Top That! Publishing PLC.

Troupe, Thomas Kingsley. Schools Have Rules. Zhai, Rea, illus. 2019. (School Rules Ser.). (ENG.). 24p. (J). (gr. k-2). pap. 8.95 (978-1-5158-4064-0(6), 140058, Picture Window Bks.) Capstone.

—Staying Safe at School. Uno, Kat, illus. 2019. (School Rules Ser.). (ENG.). 24p. (J). (gr. k-2). pap. 8.95 (978-1-5158-4065-7(4), 140059, Picture Window Bks.) Capstone.

Vogel, Elizabeth. Meet the Cafeteria Workers. 2009. (My School Ser.). 24p. (gr. 1-2). 37.50 (978-1-61514-705-2(5), PowerKids Pr.) Rosen Publishing Group, Inc., The.

—Meet the Librarian. 2009. (My School Ser.). 24p. (gr. 1-2). 37.50 (978-1-61514-706-9(3), PowerKids Pr.) Rosen Publishing Group, Inc., The.

Wallace Sharp, Anne. Separate but Equal: The Desegregation of American Schools, 1 vol. 2006. (Lucent Library of Black History Ser.). (ENG., Illus.). 104p. (gr. 7-7). lib. bdg. 35.08 (978-1-59018-953-5(1), 67a18b49-effd-4691-9082-a4e2b3d0b328, Lucent Pr.) Greenhaven Publishing LLC.

Watt, Fiona. Sticker Dolly Dressing Back to School. 2012. (Sticker Dolly Dressing Ser.). 34p. (J). pap. 8.99 (978-0-7945-3303-8(5), Usborne) EDC Publishing.

Weakland, Mark. On My Way to School. Zhai, Rea, illus. 2019. (School Rules Ser.). (ENG.). 24p. (J). (gr. k-2). pap. 8.95 (978-1-5158-4063-3(8), 140057, Picture Window Bks.) Capstone.

—This Is My School. de Polonia - Nill, Nina, illus. 2019. (School Rules Ser.). (ENG.). 24p. (J). (gr. k-2). pap. 8.95 (978-1-5158-4066-4(2), 140060, Picture Window Bks.) Capstone.

—Who's Who at School. de Polonia - Nill, Nina, illus. 2019. (School Rules Ser.). (ENG.). 24p. (J). (gr. k-2). lib. bdg. 28.65 (978-1-5158-3852-4(8), 139575, Picture Window Bks.) Capstone.

Whitney, Brooks. How to Master the School Universe: Homework, Teachers, Tests, Bullies, & Other Ways to Survive the Classroom. Kennedy, Kelly, illus. 2004. 80p. (J). pap. (978-0-439-57902-5(3)) Scholastic, Inc.

Williams-Noren, Carolyn. Do Kids Need Year-Round School? 2018. (Shape Your Opinion Ser.). (ENG., Illus.). 48p. (J). (gr. 1-3). 26.60 (978-1-59953-931-7(4)) Norwood Hse. Pr.

Wright, Pamela. Rant Room. 2011. 82p. pap. 19.95 (978-1-4560-9428-7(9)) America Star Bks.

SCHOOLS—ADMINISTRATION

see School Management And Organization

SCHOOLS, COMMERCIAL

see Business Education

SCHOOLS—FICTION

see also Universities and Colleges—Fiction

Abbott, Tony. Firegirl. 2007. (ENG.). 160p. (J). (gr. 3-7). pap. 7.99 (978-0-316-01170-9(3)) Little, Brown Bks. for Young Readers.

—The Mysterious Talent Show Mystery, 4. Madden, Colleen, illus. 2013. (Goofballs Ser.: No. 4). (ENG.). 112p. (J). (gr. 2-4). 17.44 (978-1-60684-167-9(X)) Farshore GBR. Dist: Children's Plus, Inc.

Abdel-Fattah, Randa. Does My Head Look Big in This? 2007. 360p. (YA). 25.66 (978-1-4287-4610-7(2), Follettbound) Follett School Solutions.

—Does My Head Look Big in This? 2008. (ENG.). 368p. (J). (gr. 7). pap. 11.99 (978-0-439-92233-3(X), Scholastic Paperbacks) Scholastic, Inc.

Abdel-Magied, Yassmin. You Must Be Layla. 2019. 288p. (J). 15.99 (978-0-14-378851-5(5)) Penguin Random Hse. AUS. Dist: Independent Pubs. Group.

Aber, Linda Williams. Quien Tiene Manchas; Who's Got Spots? 2008. pap. 34.95 (978-1-58013-759-1(8)) Astra Publishing Hse.

Abercrombie, Barbara. The Show-And-Tell Lion. Avril, Lynne, illus. 2006. (ENG.). 32p. (J). (gr. -1-2). 19.99 (978-0-689-86408-7(6), McElderry, Margaret K. Bks.) McElderry, Margaret K. Bks.

The Abominable Snowman Doesn't Roast Marshmallows, 6 bks., Pack. 2005. 96p. (J). pap. 3.99 (978-0-439-86573-9(5)) Scholastic, Inc.

Abrams, Kelsey. Buddy Blues: An Emily Story. Tejido, Jomike, illus. 2019. (Second Chance Ranch Set 2 Ser.). (ENG.). 120p. (J). (gr. 3-4). pap. 7.99 (978-1-63163-252-5(3), 1631632523); lib. bdg. 27.13 (978-1-63163-251-8(5), 1631632515) North Star Editions. (Jolly Fish Pr.).

—Llama Drama: A Grace Story. Tejido, Jomike, illus. 2019. (Second Chance Ranch Set 2 Ser.). (ENG.). 120p. (J). (gr. 3-4). pap. 7.99 (978-1-63163-264-8(7), 1631632647); lib. bdg. 27.13 (978-1-63163-263-1(9), 1631632639) North Star Editions. (Jolly Fish Pr.).

Abrams, Stacey. Stacey's Extraordinary Words. Thomas, Kitt, illus. 2021. (ENG.). 32p. (J). (gr. -1-3). 19.99 (978-0-06-320947-3(0), Balzer & Bray) HarperCollins Pubs.

Abramsen, Ruth M. Akeelah's Spider. 2008. 36p. per. 13.95 (978-1-59800-440-3(9)) Outskirts Pr., Inc.

Abuhamda, Nasser. A Flower in the Rain. 2009. 40p. pap. 14.95 (978-1-59858-879-8(6)) Dog Ear Publishing, LLC.

Acampora, Paul. Confusion Is Nothing New. 2018. (ENG.). 192p. (J). (gr. 3-7). 16.99 (978-1-338-20999-0(X), Scholastic Pr.) Scholastic, Inc.

Aceves, Fred. The Closest I've Come. (ENG.). (YA). (gr. 9). 2020. 336p. pap. 11.99 (978-0-06-248854-1(6)) 2017. 320p. 17.99 (978-0-06-248853-4(8)) HarperCollins Pubs. (HarperTeen).

Acton, Vanessa. Now You See Me. 2018. (Superhuman Ser.). (ENG.). 104p. (YA). (gr. 6-12). pap. 7.99 (978-1-5415-1049-4(6), fddc9a09-8208-4475-8b21-c7774b643232); 25.32 (978-1-5124-9829-5(7), 3c274272-00b5-4f8c-aa2f-e0b03328c3a3) Lerner Publishing Group. (Darby Creek).

Adams, Colleen. School Is Cool!, 1 vol. 2006. (Neighborhood Readers Ser.). (ENG.). 8p. (gr. k-1). pap. 5.15 (978-1-4042-5676-7(8), 3fac01d4-45f2-4a26-b767-fd8629cbff64, Rosen Classroom) Rosen Publishing Group, Inc., The.

Adams, Keith. The Tales of Henry Tuffin - Henry Goes to School. Hewitt, Geoff, ed. Mawson, Alan, illus. 2013. 20p. pap. (978-1-78222-103-6(4)) Paragon Publishing, Rothersthorpe.

Adams, Michelle Medlock. My First Day of School. 2017. (ENG., Illus.). 20p. (J). (gr. -1-1). bds. 7.99 (978-0-8249-1657-2(3)) Worthy Publishing.

Adams, Sherred Willcox. Five Little Friends. 2006. pap. 15.95 (978-1-4304-4149-6(6)) Kessinger Publishing, LLC.

Adams, W. Royce. The Computer's Nerd. 2011. 154p. (gr. 4-7). 22.99 (978-0-9712206-9-0(7)) Rairarubia Bks.

Adderson, Caroline. Jasper John Dooley: Star of the Week. Clanton, Ben, illus. 2014. (Jasper John Dooley Ser.). (ENG.). 128p. (J). (gr. k-3). pap. 7.99 (978-1-77138-119-2(1)) Kids Can Pr., Ltd. CAN. Dist: Hachette Bk. Group.

Adler, David. Danny's Doodles: The Dog Biscuit Breakfast. 2015. (Danny's Doodles Ser.: 3). (ENG., Illus.). 144p. (J). (gr. 2-5). pap. 8.99 (978-1-4926-1665-8(6), Sourcebooks Jabberwocky) Sourcebooks, Inc.

—Danny's Doodles: The Jelly Bean Experiment. 2013. (Danny's Doodles Ser.: 1). (ENG.). 112p. (J). (gr. 2-5). pap. 8.99 (978-1-4022-8721-3(6), 9781402287213, Sourcebooks Jabberwocky) Sourcebooks, Inc.

—Donut Dilemma: The Squirting Donuts. 2014. (Danny's Doodles Ser.: 2). (ENG., Illus.). 144p. (J). (gr. 2-5). pap. 10.99 (978-1-4022-8728-2(3), 9781402287282, Sourcebooks Jabberwocky) Sourcebooks, Inc.

Adler, David A. Andy & Tamika. Hillenbrand, Will, illus. 2005. (Andy Russell Ser.: 2). (ENG.). 144p. (J). (gr. 1-4). pap. 7.99 (978-0-15-205446-5(4), 1196390, Clarion Bks.) HarperCollins Pubs.

—Andy & Tamika. Hillenbrand, Will, illus. 2005. (Andy Russell Ser.: Bk. 2). 129p. 16.00 (978-0-7569-4898-6(3)) Perfection Learning Corp.

—Andy Russell, Not Wanted by the Police. Franson, Leanne, illus. 2005. (Andy Russell Ser.: Bk. 5). (ENG.). 128p. (J). (gr. 1-4). pap. 7.99 (978-0-15-216719-6(6), 1201719, Clarion Bks.) HarperCollins Pubs.

—Bones & the Cupcake Mystery, No. 3. Johansen Newman, Barbara, illus. 2008. (Bones Ser.: 3). (ENG.). 32p. (J). (gr. 1-3). mass mkt. 4.99 (978-0-14-241147-6(7), Penguin Young Readers) Penguin Young Readers Group.

—Bones & the Math Test. 2010. (Bones Penguin Young Readers Ser.: 6). lib. bdg. 13.55 (978-0-606-10585-9(9)) Turtleback.

—Bones & the Math Test Mystery. Johansen Newman, Barbara, illus. 2010. (Bones Ser.: 6). (ENG.). 32p. (J). (gr. 1-3). mass mkt. 5.99 (978-0-14-241519-1(7), Penguin Young Readers) Penguin Young Readers Group.

—Cam Jansen & the Graduation Day Mystery. 2012. (Cam Jansen Ser.: 31). lib. bdg. 14.75 (978-0-606-26663-5(1)) Turtleback.

—Cam Jansen & the Graduation Day Mystery #31. 2012. (Cam Jansen Ser.: 31). (ENG.). 64p. (J). (gr. 2-5). pap. 4.99 (978-0-14-242208-3(8), Puffin Books) Penguin Young Readers Group.

—Cam Jansen & the Secret Service Mystery #26. Natti, Susanna, illus. 2008. (Cam Jansen Ser.: 26). (ENG.). 64p. (J). (gr. 2-5). 4.99 (978-0-14-241074-5(8), Puffin Books) Penguin Young Readers Group.

—Cam Jansen & the Sports Day Mysteries. Allen, Joy, illus. 2009. (Cam Jansen: A Super Special Ser.). 118p. 16.00 (978-1-60686-431-9(9)) Perfection Learning Corp.

—Cam Jansen & the Sports Day Mysteries: A Super Special. 2009. (Cam Jansen Ser.). lib. bdg. 16.00 (978-0-606-00110-6(7)) Turtleback.

—Cam Jansen: Cam Jansen & the Mystery Writer Mystery #27. Allen, Joy, illus. 27th ed. 2008. (Cam Jansen Ser.: 27). (ENG.). 64p. (J). (gr. 2-5). 5.99 (978-0-14-241194-0(9), Puffin Books) Penguin Young Readers Group.

—Cam Jansen: Cam Jansen & the Sports Day Mysteries: A Super Special. Allen, Joy, illus. 2009. (Cam Jansen Ser.). 128p. (J). (gr. 2-5). 5.99 (978-0-14-241225-1(2), Puffin Books) Penguin Young Readers Group.

—Cam Jansen: the First Day of School Mystery #22, 22 vols. Natti, Susanna, illus. 2005. (Cam Jansen Ser.: 22). (ENG.). 64p. (J). (gr. 2-5). 4.99 (978-0-14-240326-6(1), Puffin Books) Penguin Young Readers Group.

—Cam Jansen: the School Play Mystery #21. Natti, Susanna, illus. 2005. (Cam Jansen Ser.: 21). (ENG.). 64p. (J). (gr. 2-5). 5.99 (978-0-14-240355-6(5), Puffin Books) Penguin Young Readers Group.

—The Day I Lost My Hampster: And Other True School Stories. 2006. 48p. (978-0-439-80289-5(X)) Scholastic, Inc.

—School Trouble for Andy Russell. Hillenbrand, Will, illus. 2005. (Andy Russell Ser.: Bk. 3). (ENG.). 128p. (J). (gr. 1-4). pap. 9.95 (978-0-15-205428-1(6), 1196335, Clarion Bks.) HarperCollins Pubs.

—School Trouble for Andy Russell. Hillenbrand, Will, illus. 2007. (Andy Russell Ser.: Bk. 3). 118p. pap. 6.60 (978-1-4189-5227-3(3)) Houghton Mifflin Harcourt Supplemental Pubs.

—School Trouble for Andy Russell. Hillenbrand, Will, illus. 2008. (Andy Russell Ser.: Bk. 3). (J). (gr. 2-5). pap. 28.95 incl. audio compact disk (978-1-4301-0484-1(8)); pap. 24.95 incl. audio (978-1-4301-0483-4(X)) Live Oak Media.

—The Secret Service Mystery. Natti, Susanna, illus. 2008. (Cam Jansen Ser.: Bk. 26). 57p. (J). (gr. 2-5). 11.65 (978-0-7569-8917-0(5)) Perfection Learning Corp.

—Young Cam Jansen & the 100th Day of School Mystery, 15 vols. Natti, Susanna, illus. 2010. (Young Cam Jansen Ser.: 15). (ENG.). 32p. (J). (gr. 1-3). mass mkt. 4.99 (978-0-14-241685-3(1), Penguin Young Readers) Penguin Young Readers Group.

—Young Cam Jansen & the New Girl Mystery. Natti, Susanna, illus. 2005. (Young Cam Jansen Ser.: Bk. 10). 32p. (gr. k-2). 14.00 (978-0-7569-5522-9(X)) Perfection Learning Corp.

—Young Cam Jansen & the Speedy Car Mystery, 16 vols. Natti, Susanna, illus. 2011. (Young Cam Jansen Ser.: 16). (ENG.). 32p. (J). (gr. 1-3). mass mkt. 4.99 (978-0-14-241868-0(4), Penguin Young Readers) Penguin Young Readers Group.

—Young Cam Jansen & the Spotted Cat Mystery, No. 12. Natti, Susanna, illus. 2007. (Young Cam Jansen Ser.: 12). (ENG.). 32p. (J). (gr. 1-3). pap. 4.99 (978-0-14-241012-7(8), Penguin Young Readers) Penguin Young Readers Group.

—Young Cam Jansen & the Spotted Cat Mystery. Natti, Susanna, illus. 2007. (Young Cam Jansen (prebound) Ser.). 31p. (gr. -1-3). 14.00 (978-0-7569-8155-6(7)) Perfection Learning Corp.

—Young Cam Jansen & the Substitute Mystery, No. 11. Natti, Susanna, illus. 2006. (Young Cam Jansen Ser.: 11). (ENG.). 32p. (J). (gr. 1-3). mass mkt. 4.99 (978-0-14-240660-1(0), Penguin Young Readers) Penguin Young Readers Group.

—Young Cam Jansen & the Zoo Note Mystery. Natti, Susanna, illus. 2013. (Puffin Young Readers, L3 Ser.). (ENG.). 31p. (J). (gr. -1-3). pap. 3.99 (978-0-448-46633-0(3), Puffin) Penguin Publishing Group.

—Young Cam Jansen & the Zoo Note Mystery. Natti, Susanna, illus. 2004. (Young Cam Jansen Ser.: 9). (ENG.). 32p. (J). (gr. 1-3). mass mkt. 4.99 (978-0-14-240204-7(4), Penguin Young Readers) Penguin Young Readers Group.

Adoff, Jaime. Names Will Never Hurt Me. 2005. 192p. (YA). (gr. 7-7). 5.99 (978-0-14-240457-7(8), Speak) Penguin Young Readers Group.

Adornetto, Alexandra. Halo. 2011. (Halo Trilogy Ser.: 1). (ENG.). 512p. (YA). (gr. 7-12). pap. 19.99 (978-0-312-67436-6(8), 900072851) Square Fish.

—HALO. 2010. (SPA.). 416p. (YA). pap. 22.95 (978-84-9918-173-8(2)) Roca Editorial ESP. Dist: Spanish Pubs., LLC.

—Heaven. 2013. (Halo Trilogy Ser.: 3). (ENG.). 448p. (YA). (gr. 7-12). pap. 17.99 (978-1-250-02941-6(4), 900118575) Square Fish.

Aggarwal, Eash. Paradox. 2010. 90p. pap. 8.99 (978-0-557-45261-3(9)) Lulu Pr., Inc.

Agnew, Kate. Shout, Show & Tell! Monks, Lydia, illus. 2005. (Green Bananas Ser.). (ENG.). 48p. (J). (gr. -1-1). (978-0-7787-1040-0(8)) Crabtree Publishing Co.

—Shout, Show, & Tell. Monks, Lydia, illus. 2005. (Green Bananas Ser.). (ENG.). 48p. (J). lib. bdg. (978-0-7787-1024-0(6)) Crabtree Publishing Co.

Agnew, Kate, et al. Gweiddi, Dangos a Dweud. 2005. (WEL., Illus.). 47p. pap. *(978-1-85596-676-5(X))* Dref Wen.

Agro-Melina, Robert Joseph. Joe & the Mysteries of Dream Hall: The Extra Dwarf & the Purloined Parchment. 2012. 152p. pap. 10.99 *(978-1-4575-1239-1(4))* Dog Ear Publishing, LLC.

Aguirre, Ann. Public Enemies. 2015. (ENG.). 384p. (YA). *(978-1-250-07420-1(7))* St. Martin's Pr.

Ahlberg, Allan. Starting School. braille ed. 2004. (J). (gr. k-3). spiral bd. *(978-0-616-01526-1(7))* Canadian National Institute for the Blind/Institut National Canadien pour les Aveugles.

Ahlberg, Allan & Ahlberg, Janet. Starting School. (ENG., Illus.). 32p. (J). pap. 9.95 *(978-0-14-050737-9(X))* Penguin Bks., Ltd. GBR. Dist: Trafalgar Square Publishing.

Ahmed, Samira. Love, Hate & Other Filters. (ENG.). (YA). (gr. 9). 2019. 312p. pap. 10.99 *(978-1-61695-999-9(1))* 2018. 288p. 18.99 *(978-1-61695-847-3(2))* Soho Pr., Inc. (Soho Teen).

Aikawa, Yu. Dark Edge, Vol. 6. Aikawa, Yu, illus. 2006. (Dark Edge Ser.). (ENG., Illus.). 200p. (YA). pap. 9.95 *(978-1-59796-026-7(8))* DrMaster Pubns. Inc.

Ain, Beth. Izzy Kline Has Butterflies. 2018. (ENG.). 192p. (J). (gr. 3-7). pap. 7.99 *(978-0-399-55083-6(6)*, Yearling) Random Hse. Children's Bks.

—Starring Jules (As Herself) 2014. (Starring Jules Ser.: 1). lib. bdg. 16.00 *(978-0-606-35365-6(8))* Turtleback.

Ainslie, Claire. Detained. 2019. (Al High Ser.). (ENG.). 104p. (YA). (gr. 6-12). 26.65 *(978-1-5415-5692-3(5)*, acbab631-3222-4307-b9a4-4c6567198253, Darby Creek) Lerner Publishing Group.

Airgood, Ellen. Prairie Evers. 2014. 224p. (J). (gr. 3-7). pap. 7.99 *(978-0-14-242668-5(7)*, Puffin Books) Penguin Young Readers Group.

Aker, Don. One on One. 2014. (ENG.). 144p. (J). (gr. 3-7). pap. 8.99 *(978-0-06-231353-9(3)*, HarperCollins) HarperCollins Pubs.

Al-Emadi, Hesham. The Savior's Threshold: The Chronicles of Dourren. 2010. 192p. pap. 13.95 *(978-1-4502-1846-7(6))* iUniverse, Inc.

—The Savior's Threshold: The Chronicles of Dourren. 2010. 192p. 23.95 *(978-1-4502-1848-1(2))* iUniverse, Inc.

Al Shaikh, Latifa. I'm Still Waiting for that Chocolate. 2007. 52p. (YA). per. 8.95 *(978-0-595-42982-0(3))* iUniverse, Inc.

Albertalli, Becky. Leah on the off Beat. 2019. (ENG.). (YA). (gr. 9). lib. bdg. 21.80 *(978-1-6636-2843-5(2))* Perfection Learning Corp.

—Leah on the Offbeat. (ENG.). 368p. (YA). (gr. 9). 2019. pap. 10.99 *(978-0-06-264381-0(9))* 2018. 17.99 *(978-0-06-264380-3(0))* HarperCollins Pubs. (Balzer & Bray).

—Simon vs. the Homo Sapiens Agenda. (ENG.). (YA). (gr. 9). 2016. 336p. pap. 15.99 *(978-0-06-234868-5(X))* 2015. 320p. 18.99 *(978-0-06-234867-8(1))* HarperCollins Pubs. (Balzer & Bray).

Alberto, Daisy. Pete for President! Sims, Blanche, illus. 2004. (Social Studies Connects Ser.). 32p. (J). (gr. 1-3). pap. 5.99 *(978-1-57565-142-2(4)*, b2d5eed8-13d1-4a23-936c-a290da5684c3, Kane Press) Astra Publishing Hse.

Albright, Emily. Perfect Harmony. 2018. (ENG.). 304p. (YA). pap. 12.99 *(978-1-944995-82-9(X))* Amberjack Publishing Co.

Alcántara, Ricardo. Huy, Que Miedo! 13th ed. 2003. (SPA., Illus.). 44p. *(978-84-236-2559-8(1)*, ED5263) Edebé ESP. Dist: Lectorum Pubns., Inc.

Alcott, Louisa. Hombrecitos.Tr. of Little Men. (SPA., Illus.). 160p. (YA). 11.95 *(978-84-7281-168-3(9)*, AF1168) Auriga, Ediciones S.A. ESP. Dist: Continental Bk. Co., Inc.

—Jo's Boys. l.t. ed. 2007. (ENG.). 288p. pap. 23.99 *(978-1-4346-0451-4(9))* Creative Media Partners, LLC.

—Jo's Boys. l.t. ed. 2005. 424p. pap. *(978-1-84637-067-0(1))* Echo Library.

—Jo's Boys. 2013. (Works of Louisa May Alcott). 366p. reprint ed. lthr. 79.00 *(978-0-7812-1642-5(7))* Reprint Services Corp.

—Little Men. rev. ed. 2006. 352p. 31.95 *(978-1-4218-1800-9(0))*; pap. 15.95 *(978-1-4218-1900-6(7))* 1st World Publishing, Inc. (1st World Library - Literary Society).

—Little Men. (ENG.). (J). 2020. 300p. pap. 12.98 *(978-1-714-79319-8(2))* 2017. (Illus.). pap. 11.99 *(978-1-366-58954-5(8))* Blurb, Inc.

—Little Men. (ENG.). (J). 2018. 380p. 46.95 *(978-0-343-77916-0(1))* 2018. 380p. pap. 29.95 *(978-0-343-77915-3(3))* 2017. (Illus.). pap. 17.95 *(978-1-375-47932-5(6))* 2015. (Illus.). 27.95 *(978-1-296-65257-9(2))* 2015. (Illus.). 27.95 *(978-1-298-78052-2(7))* Creative Media Partners, LLC.

—Little Men. 2019. (ENG.). (J). (gr. 3-7). 606p. pap. 38.99 *(978-1-6925-3269-7(3))*; 448p. pap. 25.99 *(978-1-0899-8038-4(8))*; 448p. pap. 25.99 *(978-1-0859-0181-9(5))*; 310p. pap. 21.99 *(978-1-0803-8276-7(3))*; 482p. pap. 26.99 *(978-1-0756-8767-9(5))*; 634p. pap. 42.99 *(978-1-0753-6849-3(9))*; 482p. pap. 26.99 *(978-1-0730-0563-5(1))*; 636p. pap. 36.99 *(978-1-0971-3721-3(X))*; 310p. pap. 21.99 *(978-1-0706-0670-5(7))*; 666p. pap. 36.99 *(978-1-0985-5102-5(8))* Independently Published.

—Little Men. 2012. (Signet Classics Ser.). (ENG.). (J). (gr. 12). lib. bdg. 16.55 *(978-1-61383-896-9(4))* Perfection Learning Corp.

—Little Men: Life at Plumfield with Jo's Boys. 2013. (Works of Louisa May Alcott). 292p. reprint ed. lthr. 79.00 *(978-0-7812-1629-6(X))* Reprint Services Corp.

Alcott, Louisa May. Little Men. 2019. (Little Women Series,Virago Modern Classi Ser.). (ENG.). 400p. (J). (gr. 3-7). 15.99 *(978-0-349-01184-4(2)*, Virago Press) Little, Brown Book Group Ltd. GBR. Dist: Hachette Bk. Group.

—Little Men. 2019. (Little Women Collection: 3). (ENG.). 400p. (J). (gr. 3). 17.99 *(978-1-5344-6224-3(4))*; pap. 7.99 *(978-1-5344-6223-6(6))* Simon & Schuster Children's Publishing. (Aladdin).

Alcott, Louisa May & Barbarese, J. T. Little Men. 2012. (Little Women Ser.). 368p. (gr. 12). mass mkt. 5.95 *(978-0-451-53223-7(6)*, Signet) Penguin Publishing Group.

Alegre, Mari. Destiny. 2011. 174p. 29.99 *(978-1-4568-2040-4(0))* Xlibris Corp.

Alegria, Malin. Border Town #2: Quince Clash. 2012. (Border Town Ser.). (ENG.). 192p. (J). (gr. 7). pap. 5.99 *(978-0-545-40241-5(7)*, Scholastic Paperbacks) Scholastic, Inc.

Aleixandre, Marilar & Aleixandre, Marilar. La Branda Sin Futuro. 2003. (SPA.). 156p. *(978-84-348-7193-9(9)*, SM30543) SM Ediciones ESP. Dist: Lectorum Pubns., Inc.

Alender, Katie. As Dead As It Gets. 2013. (Bad Girls Don't Die Ser.: 3). (ENG.). 448p. (J). (gr. 5-9). pap. 9.99 *(978-1-4231-3778-8(7))* Hyperion Pr.

—Bad Girls Don't Die. 2010. (Bad Girls Don't Die Ser.: 1). (ENG.). 352p. (YA). (gr. 9-17). pap. 10.99 *(978-1-4231-0877-1(9))* Little, Brown Bks. for Young Readers.

—From Bad to Cursed. 2012. (Bad Girls Don't Die Ser.: 2). (ENG.). 448p. (YA). (gr. 5-9). pap. 11.99 *(978-1-4231-3777-1(9))* Hyperion Pr.

Alexander, Alma. Spellspam. 2008. (Worldweavers Ser.: Bk. 2). (YA). (gr. 7-18). (ENG.). 448p. 17.99 *(978-0-06-083958-1(9))*; 437p. lib. bdg. 18.89 *(978-0-06-083959-8(7))* HarperCollins Pubs. (Eos).

Alexander, Carol. The Bean Trees. Friedland, Joyce & Kessler, Rikki, eds. 2007. (Novel-Ties Ser.). (Illus.). 35p. pap. 16.95 *(978-0-7675-3554-0(5))* Learning Links Inc.

—Class Clown. Friedland, Joyce & Kessler, Rikki, eds. 2007. (Novel-Ties Ser.). (Illus.). 24p. pap. 16.95 *(978-0-7675-1014-1(3))* Learning Links Inc.

—The Golden Compass: A Study Guide. Friedland, Joyce & Kessler, Rikki, eds. 2008. (Novel-Ties Ser.). 30p. pap. 16.95 *(978-0-7675-4254-8(1))* Learning Links Inc.

—The Planet of Junior Brown. Friedland, Joyce & Kessler, Rikki, eds. 2007. (Novel-Ties Ser.). (Illus.). 30p. pap. 16.95 *(978-0-7675-3561-8(8))* Learning Links Inc.

Alexander, Claire. Back to Front & Upside Down. 2012. (ENG., Illus.). 32p. (J). 16.00 *(978-0-8028-5414-8(1)*, Eerdmans Bks For Young Readers) Eerdmans, William B. Publishing Co.

Alexander, Kwame. He Said, She Said. 2013. 330p. (YA). lib. bdg. *(978-0-06-211897-4(8))* Harper & Row Ltd.

—He Said, She Said. 2013. (ENG.). 336p. (YA). (gr. 9). 17.99 *(978-0-06-211896-7(X)*, Amistad) HarperCollins Pubs.

Alexander, Kwame & Rand Hess, Mary. Swing, 1 vol. 2019. (ENG.). 448p. (YA). (gr. 8). pap. 14.99 *(978-0-310-76194-5(8)*, Clarion Bks.) HarperCollins Pubs.

—Swing ITPE SC, 1 vol. 2018. (ENG., Illus.). 448p. (YA). (gr. 8). pap. 10.99 *(978-0-310-76193-8(X)*, Clarion Bks.) HarperCollins Pubs.

Alexander, Michael. Until Wishes Are Fulfilled II: Alec's Story. 2007. 204p. per. 15.50 *(978-1-84426-468-1(8))* Upfront Publishing Ltd. GBR. Dist: Printondemand-worldwide.com.

Alfonsi, Alice. Lizzie for President. 2004. 149p. (J). lib. bdg. 16.92 *(978-1-4242-0681-0(2))* Fitzgerald Bks.

Alger, Horatio. Making His Way. 2005. 28.95 *(978-1-4218-1456-8(0))*; 260p. pap. 13.95 *(978-1-4218-1556-5(7))* 1st World Publishing, Inc. (1st World Library - Literary Society).

—Strive & Succeed. 2007. 172p. 24.95 *(978-1-4344-8359-1(2))*; per. 14.95 *(978-1-4344-8358-4(4))* Wildside Pr., LLC.

Ali, S. K. Love from a to Z. 2019. (ENG., Illus.). 352p. (YA). (gr. 9). 19.99 *(978-1-5344-4272-6(3)*, Salaam Reads) Simon & Schuster Bks. For Young Readers.

Aliki. Marianthe's Story: Painted Words & Spoken Memories. Aliki, illus. 2019. (ENG., Illus.). 64p. (J). (gr. k-5). pap. 8.99 *(978-0-06-185774-4(2)*, Greenwillow Bks.) HarperCollins Pubs.

—Play's the Thing. Aliki, illus. 2005. (ENG., Illus.). 32p. (J). 16.99 *(978-0-06-074355-0(7))* HarperCollins Pubs.

Allard, Harry & Marshall, James. Miss Nelson Has a Field Day. 2015. 32p. pap. 7.00 *(978-1-61003-506-4(2))* Center for the Collaborative Classroom.

Allard, Harry G., Jr. Miss Nelson Has a Field Day Book & CD, 1 vol. Marshall, James, illus. 2012. (ENG.). 32p. (J). (gr. -1-3). audio 10.99 *(978-0-547-75376-8(4)*, 1487728, Clarion Bks.) HarperCollins Pubs.

—Miss Nelson Is Back Book & CD, 1 vol. Marshall, James, illus. 2011. (ENG.). 32p. (J). (gr. -1-3). audio 10.99 *(978-0-547-57718-0(4)*, 1458493, Clarion Bks.) HarperCollins Pubs.

—Miss Nelson Is Missing! Book & Cd, 1 vol. Marshall, James, illus. 2007. (ENG.). 32p. (J). (gr. -1-3). audio compact disk 12.99 *(978-0-618-85281-9(6)*, 416986, Clarion Bks.) HarperCollins Pubs.

Allard, Harry G., Jr. & Marshall, James. The Miss Nelson Collection: 3 Complete Books In 1! Miss Nelson Is Missing, Miss Nelson Is Back, & Miss Nelson Has a Field Day. 2014. (ENG., Illus.). 112p. (J). (gr. 1-4). 18.99 *(978-0-544-08222-9(2)*, 1537237, Clarion Bks.) HarperCollins Pubs.

Allen, C. William. The African Interior Mission. Lee, Xiongpao, illus. 2006. 232p. (J). pap. 20.00 *(978-0-9653308-5-5(0))* Africana Homestead Legacy Pubs., Inc.

Allen, Crystal. The Laura Line. 2016. (ENG.). 352p. (J). (gr. 3-7). pap. 6.99 *(978-0-06-249021-6(4)*, Balzer & Bray) HarperCollins Pubs.

—The Magnificent Mya Tibbs: Spirit Week Showdown. Kaban, Eda, illus. (ENG.). (J). (gr. 3-7). 2017. 256p. pap. 9.99 *(978-0-06-234234-8(7))* 2016. 240p. 16.99 *(978-0-06-234233-1(9))* HarperCollins Pubs. (Balzer & Bray).

—The Wall of Fame Game. 2018. (Magnificent Mya Tibbs Ser.: 2). (J). lib. bdg. 17.20 *(978-0-606-41018-2(X))* Turtleback.

Allen, Elise & Daryle Connors. Gabby Duran & the Unsittables. 2016. (Gabby Duran Ser.: 1). (J). lib. bdg. 18.40 *(978-0-606-39443-7(5))* Turtleback.

Allen, M. E. Gotta Get Some Bish Bash Bosh. 2005. (Illus.). 208p. (J). 15.99 *(978-0-06-073198-4(2)*, HarperTeen) HarperCollins Pubs.

Allen, Nancy. Amazing Grace: A Kentucky Girl with Gumption During World War II. Shapiro, Meryl R. B., illus. 2014. Orig. Title: Amazing Grace: a Kentucky Girl with Gumption During World War II. (ENG.). 160p. (gr. 4-7). 29.99 *(978-1-62619-405-2(X)*, History Pr., The) Arcadia Publishing.

Allen, Richard L. Cool to Be in School. 2013. 32p. pap. 9.95 *(978-1-60414-674-5(5))* Fideli Publishing, Inc.

Allison, Jennifer. Gilda Joyce: the Ladies of the Lake. 2007. (Gilda Joyce Ser.: 2). (ENG.). 352p. (J). (gr. 5-18). 10.99 *(978-0-14-240907-7(3)*, Puffin Books) Penguin Young Readers Group.

—The Ladies of the Lake. 2006. (Gilda Joyce Ser.). (ENG.). 339p. (J). (gr. 6-8). 22.44 *(978-0-525-47693-1(8))* Penguin Young Readers Group.

Allison, John. Bad Machinery Vol. 3 Vol. 3: The Case of the Simple Soul, Pocket Edition. 2017. (Bad Machinery Ser.: 3). (ENG., Illus.). 136p. pap. 12.99 *(978-1-62010-443-9(1)*, 9781620104439, Lion Forge) Oni Pr., Inc.

Allyson, Libby. Scottie Rides the Bus. 2004. 27p. pap. 24.95 *(978-1-4137-3298-6(4))* PublishAmerica, Inc.

Almond, David. My Name Is Mina. 2012. (Skellig Ser.). (ENG.). 304p. (J). (gr. 5). 7.99 *(978-0-375-87327-0(9)*, Yearling) Random Hse. Children's Bks.

—The Tale of Angelino Brown. Smith, Alex T., illus. 2018. (ENG.). 272p. (J). (gr. 3-7). 16.99 *(978-0-7636-9563-7(7))* Candlewick Pr.

The (Almost) Perfect Guide to Imperfect Boys. 2014. (Mix Ser.). (ENG., Illus.). 304p. (J). (gr. 4-8). pap. 8.99 *(978-1-4814-0563-8(2)*, Aladdin) Simon & Schuster Children's Publishing.

Alonso, Fernando. Sopaboba. 8th ed. 2003. (SPA., Illus.). 136p. *(978-84-239-9025-2(7)*, EC1519) Espasa Calpe, S.A. ESP. Dist: Lectorum Pubns., Inc.

Alphin, Elaine Marie. The Perfect Shot. 2011. (ENG.). 360p. (YA). (gr. 6-12). pap. 9.99 *(978-0-7613-8138-9(4)*, bbde24bb-9d6a-4b93-9b20-9a4a886372a1, Carolrhoda Lab™) Lerner Publishing Group.

—Picture Perfect. 2003. (ENG., Illus.). 256p. (YA). (gr. 5-12). 15.95 *(978-0-8225-0535-8(5)*, c127bed3-b5f7-4f26-be27-1bd20d565a98, Carolrhoda Bks.) Lerner Publishing Group.

—Simon Says. 2005. (ENG.). 264p. (YA). (gr. 9-12). pap. 14.95 *(978-0-15-204678-1(X)*, 1194100, Clarion Bks.) HarperCollins Pubs.

Alpine, Racheie. Operation Pucker Up. 2015. (Mix Ser.). (ENG., Illus.). 256p. (J). (gr. 4-8). 17.99 *(978-1-4814-3236-8(2)*, Aladdin) Simon & Schuster Children's Publishing.

Alpine, Rachele, et al. Best. Night. Ever: A Story Told from Seven Points of View. (Mix Ser.). (ENG., Illus.). 352p. (J). (gr. 4-8). 2018. pap. 8.99 *(978-1-4814-8661-3(6))* 2017. 18.99 *(978-1-4814-8660-6(8))* Simon & Schuster Children's Publishing. (Aladdin).

Alsenas, Linas. Beyond Clueless. 2015. (ENG., Illus.). 256p. (YA). (gr. 7-11). 16.95 *(978-1-4197-1496-2(1)*, 681301, Amulet Bks.) Abrams, Inc.

Altebrando, Tara. The Best Night of Your (Pathetic) Life. 2013. 256p. (YA). (gr. 9). pap. 8.99 *(978-0-14-242640-1(7)*, Speak) Penguin Young Readers Group.

—Take Me with You. 2020. (ENG.). 384p. (YA). 17.99 *(978-1-68119-748-7(0)*, 900184215, Bloomsbury Young Adult) Bloomsbury Publishing USA.

Alter, Anna. Francine's Day. Alter, Anna, illus. 2003. (Illus.). 32p. (J). lib. bdg. 16.89 *(978-0-06-623937-8(0))* HarperCollins Pubs.

Alvarado, Beatriz. Juliana: A girl from the Andes. 2008. 44p. pap. 16.95 *(978-1-4327-0253-3(X))* Outskirts Pr., Inc.

Alvarez, Julia. De Como Tia Lola Aprendio a Ensenar (How Aunt Lola Learned to Teach Spanish Edition) 2011. (Tia Lola Stories Ser.: 2). (SPA.). 160p. (J). (gr. 3-7). 7.99 *(978-0-375-85793-5(1)*, Yearling) Random Hse. Children's Bks.

—How Tia Lola Learned to Teach. 2011. (ENG.). 144p. (J). (Tia Lola Stories Ser.). (gr. 4-6). lib. bdg. 22.44 *(978-0-375-96460-2(6)*, Knopf Bks. for Young Readers); (Tia Lola Stories Ser.: 2). (Illus.). (gr. 3-7). pap. 7.99 *(978-0-375-85792-8(3)*, Yearling) Random Hse. Children's Bks.

Amaker, Anthony D. Makeba's New Adventure. 2009. (ENG.). 26p. pap. 15.99 *(978-1-4415-1438-7(4))* Xlibris Corp.

Amato, Mary. Edgar Allan's Official Crime Investigation Notebook. 2010. (ENG.). 176p. (J). (gr. 4-6). 21.19 *(978-0-8234-2271-5(2))* Holiday Hse., Inc.

—Guitar Notes. 2014. (ENG., Illus.). 320p. (YA). (gr. 7-12). pap. 10.99 *(978-1-60684-503-5(9)*, 012af6c8-2b15-4576-82cf-476ac42f8d26, Carolrhoda Lab™) Lerner Publishing Group.

—Invisible Lines. Caparó, Antonio Javier, illus. 2011. (ENG.). 336p. (gr. 4-8). lib. bdg. 22.44 *(978-1-60684-043-6(6))* Farshore GBR. Dist: Children's Plus, Inc.

—Our Teacher Is a Vampire & Other (Not) True Stories. Long, Ethan, illus. (ENG.). 256p. (J). (gr. 3-7). 2017. pap. 6.99 *(978-0-8234-3769-6(8))* 2016. 16.95 *(978-0-8234-3553-1(9))* Holiday Hse., Inc.

—Please Write in This Book. Brace, Eric, illus. 2008. (ENG.). 97p. (J). (gr. 2-5). pap. 7.99 *(978-0-8234-2138-1(4))* Holiday Hse., Inc.

—Snarf Attack, Underfoodle, & the Secret of Life: The Riot Brothers Tell All. Long, Ethan, illus. (Riot Brothers Ser.: 1). 160p. (J). (gr. 1-4). 2020. pap. 7.99 *(978-0-8234-4526-4(7))* 2017. (ENG.). 12.95 *(978-0-8234-3865-5(1))* Holiday Hse., Inc.

—The Word Eater. Ryniak, Christopher, illus. 2005. (ENG.). 151p. (J). (gr. 3-7). reprint ed. pap. 7.99 *(978-0-8234-1940-1(1))* Holiday Hse., Inc.

Ambrose, Adrianne. What I Learned from Being a Cheerleader. 2010. 202p. pap. 12.95 *(978-1-935661-94-8(9)*, Bell Bridge Bks.) BelleBks., Inc.

Amnesty International, ed. Free? Stories about Human Rights. 2010. (ENG., Illus.). 224p. (J). (gr. 5-18). pap. 9.99 *(978-0-7636-4926-5(0))* Candlewick Pr.

Amos, Angela. 'Twas the Fight Before Christmas. 2013. 34p. pap. 12.95 *(978-1-4327-8204-7(5))* Outskirts Pr., Inc.

Anastasio, Dina. Everyone Clapped for Jason: Set Of 6. 2010. (Early Connections Ser.). (J). pap. 37.00 net. *(978-1-4108-1362-6(2))* Benchmark Education Co.

Andersen, Alan Lance. Wizard Academies - Rumpots, Crackpots, & Pooka-Mazed Halfwits. 2007. (ENG.). 174p. pap. 19.96 *(978-0-615-18594-1(0))* Wizard Academies, LLC.

Anderson, Annette Latva. Alone into Darkness: Was It Fate or an Error in Judgment? 2013. (ENG.). 46p. (J). pap. 9.95 *(978-1-4787-1208-4(2))* Outskirts Pr., Inc.

Anderson, AnnMarie. Attack of the Plants. 2019. (Branches Early Ch Bks). (ENG., Illus.). 96p. (J). (gr. 2-4). 15.96 *(978-1-64310-823-0(9))* Penworthy Co., LLC, The.

—The Attack of the Plants (the Magic School Bus Rides Again #5) 2018. (Magic School Bus Rides Again Ser.: 5). (ENG., Illus.). 96p. (J). (gr. 1-3). pap. 5.99 *(978-1-338-29079-0(7))* Scholastic, Inc.

Anderson, Jennifer. Honey Creek Royalty. 2013. 246p. pap. 12.99 *(978-1-62237-148-8(8))* Turquoise Morning Pr.

Anderson, Jessica. Secret of the School Suitor. 2015. (Rourke's Mystery Chapter Bks.). (ENG.). 64p. (gr. 3-6). 28.50 *(978-1-63430-383-5(0)*, 9781634303835) Rourke Educational Media.

Anderson, Jessica Lee. Trudy. 2005. (Milkweed Prize for Children's Literature Ser.). (ENG.). 192p. (J). (gr. 3-8). per. 6.95 *(978-1-57131-659-2(0))* Milkweed Editions.

Anderson, Jodi Lynn. Loser/Queen. Lee, Brittney, illus. 2010. (ENG.). 272p. (YA). (gr. 7-18). pap. 9.99 *(978-1-4169-9646-0(X)*, Simon & Schuster Bks. For Young Readers) Simon & Schuster Bks. For Young Readers.

Anderson, John David. Insert Coin to Continue. (ENG.). 336p. (J). (gr. 3-7). 2017. pap. 8.99 *(978-1-4814-4705-8(X))* 2016. (Illus.). 17.99 *(978-1-4814-4704-1(1))* Simon & Schuster Children's Publishing. (Aladdin).

—Ms. Bixby's Last Day. (ENG.). (J). (gr. 3-7). 2017. 336p. pap. 7.99 *(978-0-06-233818-1(8))* 2016. 320p. 17.99 *(978-0-06-233817-4(X))* HarperCollins Pubs. (Waldon Pond Pr.).

—Posted. (ENG.). 384p. (J). (gr. 3-7). 2018. pap. 9.99 *(978-0-06-233821-1(8))* 2017. 16.99 *(978-0-06-233820-4(X))* HarperCollins Pubs. (Waldon Pond Pr.).

—Sidekicked. 2013. (ENG.). 384p. (J). (gr. 3-7). 16.99 *(978-0-06-213314-4(4)*, Waldon Pond Pr.) HarperCollins Pubs.

Anderson, Laurie Halse. Catalyst. 2003. (ENG.). 272p. (YA). (gr. 7-18). pap. 10.99 *(978-0-14-240001-2(7)*, Speak) Penguin Young Readers Group.

—The Hair of Zoe Fleefenbacher Goes to School. Hoyt, Ard, illus. 2019. (ENG.). 32p. (J). (gr. -1-3). 7.99 *(978-1-5344-5226-8(5)*, Atheneum Bks. for Young Readers) Simon & Schuster Children's Publishing.

—Hair of Zoe Fleefenbacher Goes to School. Hoyt, Ard, illus. 2009. (ENG.). 32p. (J). (gr. 1-5). 19.99 *(978-0-689-85809-3(4)*, Simon & Schuster Bks. For Young Readers) Simon & Schuster Bks. For Young Readers.

—New Beginnings, 13 vols., 13. 2012. (Vet Volunteers Ser.: 13). (ENG.). 192p. (J). (gr. 3-7). 7.99 *(978-0-14-241675-4(4)*, Puffin) Penguin Young Readers Group.

—Speak. 2011. (ENG.). 224p. (YA). (gr. 7-12). pap. 10.99 *(978-0-312-67439-7(2)*, 900072854) Square Fish.

—Speak: the Graphic Novel. Carroll, Emily, illus. 2nd ed. 2018. (ENG.). 384p. (YA). 21.99 *(978-0-374-30028-9(3)*, 900129381, Farrar, Straus & Giroux (BYR)) Farrar, Straus & Giroux.

—Teacher's Pet. 2009. (Vet Volunteers Ser.: 7). (ENG.). 160p. (J). (gr. 3-7). 7.99 *(978-0-14-241252-7(X)*, Puffin Books) Penguin Young Readers Group.

—Twisted. 2008. (ENG.). 304p. (YA). (gr. 7-18). 10.99 *(978-0-14-241184-1(1)*, Penguin Books) Penguin Young Readers Group.

Anderson, Lynne. Charlie's Championships & Los campeonatos de Charlie: 6 English, 6 Spanish Adaptations. 2011. (ENG & SPA.). (J). 75.00 net. *(978-1-4108-5655-5(0))* Benchmark Education Co.

Anderson, Pamela Dell. My New School: Afro Boy. Lee, Hanlim & WU, Stacie, illus. 2003. 24p. (J). 12.95 *(978-1-932555-01-1(3))* Watch Me Grow Kids.

—My New School: Afro Girl. Lee, Hanlim & WU, Stacie, illus. 2003. 24p. (J). 12.95 *(978-1-932555-00-4(5))* Watch Me Grow Kids.

—My New School: Asian/Latin Boy. Lee, Hanlim & WU, Stacie, illus. 2003. 24p. (J). 12.95 *(978-1-932555-03-5(X))* Watch Me Grow Kids.

—My New School: Latin/Asian Girl. Lee, Hanlim & WU, Stacie, illus. 2003. 24p. (J). 12.95 *(978-1-932555-02-8(1))* Watch Me Grow Kids.

Anderson, Phil. The Thomas Family Values. 2012. 84p. pap. 13.95 *(978-1-4772-2529-5(3))* AuthorHouse.

Anderson, R. J. A Little Taste of Poison. 2016. (ENG., Illus.). 368p. (J). (gr. 4-7). 18.99 *(978-1-4814-3774-5(7)*, Atheneum Bks. for Young Readers) Simon & Schuster Children's Publishing.

Anderson, Salem. Salem Anderson & Her Private Diary. 2011. 24p. pap. 11.32 *(978-1-4490-7115-8(5))* AuthorHouse.

Anderson, William. Hallie's Bad Day, 1 vol. 2009. 48p. pap. 16.95 *(978-1-60836-681-1(2))* America Star Bks.

Andracki, Zenon. Dear Ashley: A Middle Grade Novel. 2006. (ENG.). 84p. per. 19.95 *(978-1-4241-6168-3(1))* America Star Bks.

Andreae, Giles. Captain Flinn & the Pirate Dinosaurs. Ayto, Russell, illus. 2005. (Captain Flinn & the Pirate Dinosaurs Ser.). (ENG.). 32p. (J). (gr. -1-1). 19.99 *(978-1-4169-0713-8(0)*, McElderry, Margaret K. Bks.) McElderry, Margaret K. Bks.

Andrew, Clements. Sin hablar. 2009. (SPA.). 156p. (gr. 4-6). pap. 10.99 *(978-84-441-4100-8(3))* Everest Editora ESP. Dist: Lectorum Pubns., Inc.

Andrews, D. M. The Serpent in the Glass. 2012. 234p. pap. *(978-1-78176-773-3(4))* FeedARead.com.

Andrews, Jesse. Me & Earl & the Dying Girl. 2015. (CHI.). 320p. (YA). (gr. 9-17). pap. *(978-986-344-282-0(8))* Rye Field Publishing, Co.

—Me & Earl & the Dying Girl. 2015. lib. bdg. 20.80 *(978-0-606-37113-1(3))* Turtleback.

—Me & Earl & the Dying Girl (Revised Edition) rev. ed. 2015. (ENG.). 320p. (YA). (gr. 9-17). pap. 11.99 *(978-1-4197-1960-8(2)*, 1003806) Abrams, Inc.

Andrews, Julie & Hamilton, Emma Walton. A Spooky, Sparkly Halloween. 2016. (Very Fairy Princess Ser.). (J). lib. bdg. 16.00 *(978-0-606-38317-2(4))* Turtleback.

—Valentines from the Heart. 2015. (Very Fairy Princess Ser.). (Illus.). (J). lib. bdg. 16.00 *(978-0-606-37466-8(3))* Turtleback.

Andrews, Julie & Hamilton, Emma Walton. The Very Fairy Princess Follows Her Heart. Davenier, Christine, illus. 2013. (Very Fairy Princess Ser.). (ENG.). 32p. (J). (gr. -1-3). 16.99

(978-0-316-18559-2(0)) Little, Brown Bks. for Young Readers.
Andrews, Randall. The Last Guardian of Magic. 2008. 448p. (YA). per. 23.95 (978-0-595-47345-8(8)) iUniverse, Inc.
Angelchild, P. Erotic Memoirs Volume 1. 2007. pap. (978-1-84747-127-7(7)) Chipmunkapublishing.
Angleberger, Tom. Darth Paper Strikes Back. 2011. (Origami Yoda Ser.). (ENG., Illus.). 176p. (J). (gr. 3-7). pap. 7.95 (978-1-4197-0127-6(4)); pap. (978-1-4197-0254-9(8)) Abrams, Inc.
—Darth Paper Strikes Back, 3 vols. 2011. (Origami Yoda Ser.: 2). (J). (978-1-4618-4266-8(2)); 1.25 (978-1-4640-2485-6(5)) Recorded Bks., Inc.
—Darth Paper Strikes Back. (Origami Yoda Files Ser.: 2). (J). 2015. lib. bdg. 18.40 (978-0-606-39395-9(1)) 2011. lib. bdg. 25.70 (978-0-606-33075-6(5)) Turtleback.
—Darth Paper Strikes Back: An Origami Yoda Book. 2011. (Origami Yoda Ser.). (ENG., Illus.). 176p. (J). (gr. 3-7). 13.95 (978-1-4197-0027-9(8), 697401, Amulet Bks.) Abrams, Inc.
—Princess Labelmaker to the Rescue! 2014. (Origami Yoda Files Ser.: 5). (J). lib. bdg. 25.70 (978-0-606-35237-6(6)) Turtleback.
—Princess Labelmaker to the Rescue! (Origami Yoda #5) (Origami Yoda Ser.). (ENG., Illus.). (gr. 3-7). 2016. 224p. (J). pap. 7.95 (978-1-4197-2200-4(X), 1062803) 2014. 208p. (YA). 13.95 (978-1-4197-1052-0(4), 1062801) Abrams, Inc. (Amulet Bks.).
—The Secret of the Fortune Wookiee (Origami Yoda #3), Vol. 3. 2012. (Origami Yoda Ser.: No. 3). (ENG., Illus.). 208p. (J). (gr. 3-7). 13.95 (978-1-4197-0392-8(7), 1013401, Amulet Bks.) Abrams, Inc.
—The Secret of the Fortune Wookiee (Origami Yoda #3) An Origami Yoda Book, Vol. 3. 2015. (Origami Yoda Ser.). (ENG., Illus.). 208p. (J). (gr. 3-7). pap. 7.95 (978-1-4197-1971-4(8), 1013403, Amulet Bks.) Abrams, Inc.
—The Strange Case of Origami Yoda. 2010. pap. (978-0-8109-9650-2(2)) Abrams, Inc.
—The Strange Case of Origami Yoda, 2 vols. 2010. (Origami Yoda Ser.: 1). (J). 48.75 (978-1-4498-4583-4(5)) Recorded Bks., Inc.
—Strange Case of Origami Yoda. 2011. (ENG., Illus.). 160p. pap. (978-0-8109-9877-3(7), Amulet Bks.) Abrams, Inc.
—The Strange Case of Origami Yoda (Origami Yoda #1) 2010. (Origami Yoda Ser.). (ENG., Illus.). 160p. (J). (gr. 3-7). 13.95 (978-0-8109-8425-7(3), 649801) Abrams, Inc.
—Surprise Attack of Jabba the Puppet. 2013. (Origami Yoda Ser.). (ENG., Illus.). 224p. (YA). (gr. 3-7). pap. 7.95 (978-1-4197-1045-2(1)) Abrams, Inc.
—The Surprise Attack of Jabba the Puppett: An Origami Yoda Book. 2013. (Origami Yoda Ser.: 4). (J). 50.75 (978-1-4703-9686-2(6)); 48.75 (978-1-4703-9677-0(7)); 168.75 (978-1-4703-9641-1(6)); 48.75 (978-1-4703-9650-3(5)); 1.25 (978-1-4703-9695-4(5)) Recorded Bks., Inc.
—Surprise Attack of Jabba the Puppett: An Origami Yoda Book. 2013. (Origami Yoda Ser.). (ENG., Illus.). 224p. (YA). (gr. 3-7). 13.95 (978-1-4197-0858-9(9), 1013501, Amulet Bks.) Abrams, Inc.
—The Surprise Attack of Jabba the Puppett: An Origami Yoda Book. 2016. (Origami Yoda Files Ser.: 4). (J). lib. bdg. 18.40 (978-0-606-38208-3(9)) Turtleback.
—The Surprise Attack of Jabba the Puppett (Origami Yoda #4) 2016. (Origami Yoda Ser.). (ENG.). 240p. (YA). (gr. 3-7). pap. 8.99 (978-1-4197-2030-7(9), 1013503) Abrams, Inc.
Angleberger, Tom & Dellinger, Paul. Fuzzy. (ENG.). (J). (gr. 3-7). 2018. 288p. pap. 9.99 (978-1-4197-2968-3(3), 1015003) 2016. 272p. 14.95 (978-1-4197-2122-9(4), 1015001, Amulet Bks.) Abrams, Inc.
Anglin, M. R. Lucas: Guardian of Truth. 2012. 192p. pap. 8.00 (978-1-60039-195-8(8)) Lamp Post Inc.
Anna, Holly. Posey, the Class Pest. Santos, Genevieve, illus. 2018. (Daisy Dreamer Ser.: 7). (ENG.). 128p. (J). (gr. k-4). 16.99 (978-1-5344-1269-9(7)); pap. 6.99 (978-1-5344-1268-2(9)) Little Simon. (Little Simon).
Anselmo, Robert Louis. We're All Different & yet Still the Same. l.t. ed. 2006. (Illus.). 22p. (J). 14.99 (978-1-59879-107-5(9)); per. 9.99 (978-1-59879-088-7(9)) Lifevest Publishing, Inc.
Anstee, Ashlyn. No, No, Gnome! Anstee, Ashlyn, illus. 2016. (ENG., Illus.). 40p. (J). (gr. -1-3). 19.99 (978-1-4814-3091-3(2), Simon & Schuster Bks. For Young Readers) Simon & Schuster Bks. For Young Readers.
Anthony, Horowitz. Point Blanc. 2004. (Alex Rider Ser.: Bk. 2). (SPA.). 264p. 7.95 (978-84-414-1410-5(6)) Editorial Edaf, S.L. ESP. Dist: Spanish Pubs., LLC.
Applegate, Katherine. Don't Swap Your Sweater for a Dog. Biggs, Brian, illus. 2008. (Roscoe Riley Rules Ser.: 3). (ENG.). 96p. (J). (gr. 1-5). pap. 4.99 (978-0-06-114885-9(7)) HarperCollins Pubs.
—Don't Swap Your Sweater for a Dog. 2016. (Roscoe Riley Rules Ser.: 3). (J). lib. bdg. 14.75 (978-0-606-38736-1(6)) Turtleback.
—Don't Tap-Dance on Your Teacher. Biggs, Brian, illus. 2009. (Roscoe Riley Rules Ser.: 5). (ENG.). 96p. (J). (gr. 1-5). pap. 4.99 (978-0-06-114889-7(X)) HarperCollins Pubs.
—Don't Tap-Dance on Your Teacher. Biggs, Brian, illus. 2016. (Roscoe Riley Rules Ser.: 5). (ENG.). 112p. (J). (gr. 1-5). 14.75 (978-0-606-39252-5(1)) Turtleback.
—Don't Tap-Dance on Your Teacher. 2009. (Roscoe Riley Rules Ser.: 5). (J). lib. bdg. 14.75 (978-0-606-05007-4(8)) Turtleback.
—Home of the Brave. 2008. (ENG.). 272p. (J). (gr. 5-9). pap. 8.99 (978-0-312-53563-6(5), 900054740) Square Fish.
—Never Glue Your Friends to Chairs. Biggs, Brian, illus. 2008. (Roscoe Riley Rules Ser.: 1). (ENG.). 96p. (J). (gr. 1-5). pap. 4.99 (978-0-06-114881-1(4)) HarperCollins Pubs.
—Never Race a Runaway Pumpkin. Biggs, Brian, illus. 2009. (Roscoe Riley Rules Ser.: 7). (ENG.). 96p. (J). (gr. 1-5). pap. 4.99 (978-0-06-178370-8(6)) HarperCollins Pubs.
—Never Race a Runaway Pumpkin. 2009. (Roscoe Riley Rules Ser.: 7). (J). lib. bdg. 14.75 (978-0-606-06090-5(1)) Turtleback.
—Never Swim in Applesauce. 2016. (Roscoe Riley Rules Ser.: 4). (J). lib. bdg. 14.75 (978-0-606-38737-8(4)) Turtleback.
—Never Swipe a Bully's Bear. Biggs, Brian, illus. 2008. (Roscoe Riley Rules Ser.: 2). (ENG.). 96p. (J). (gr. 1-5). pap. 4.99 (978-0-06-114883-5(0)) HarperCollins Pubs.
—Never Walk in Shoes That Talk. Biggs, Brian, illus. 2009. (Roscoe Riley Rules Ser.: 6). (ENG.). 96p. (J). (gr. 1-5). pap. 4.99 (978-0-06-114891-0(1)) HarperCollins Pubs.
—Never Walk in Shoes That Talk. 2009. (Roscoe Riley Rules Ser.: 06). lib. bdg. 14.75 (978-0-606-05019-7(1)) Turtleback.
—Roscoe Riley Rules #1: Never Glue Your Friends to Chairs. Biggs, Brian, illus. 2008. (Roscoe Riley Rules Ser.: 1). (ENG.). 96p. (J). (gr. 1-5). 15.99 (978-0-06-114882-8(2), HarperCollins) HarperCollins Pubs.
—Roscoe Riley Rules #3: Don't Swap Your Sweater for a Dog. Biggs, Brian, illus. 2008. (Roscoe Riley Rules Ser.: 3). (ENG.). 96p. (J). (gr. 1-5). 15.99 (978-0-06-114886-6(5), HarperCollins) HarperCollins Pubs.
—Roscoe Riley Rules #6: Never Walk in Shoes That Talk. Biggs, Brian, illus. 2009. (Roscoe Riley Rules Ser.: 6). (ENG.). 96p. (J). (gr. 1-5). 14.99 (978-0-06-114892-7(X), HarperCollins) HarperCollins Pubs.
—Roscoe Riley Rules #7: Never Race a Runaway Pumpkin. Biggs, Brian, illus. 2009. (Roscoe Riley Rules Ser.: 7). (ENG.). 96p. (J). (gr. 1-5). 15.99 (978-0-06-178372-2(2), HarperCollins) HarperCollins Pubs.
Appleton, Victor. The Drone Pursuit. 2019. (Tom Swift Inventors' Academy Ser.: 1). (ENG., Illus.). 144p. (J). (gr. 3-7). pap. 7.99 (978-1-5344-3630-5(8), Simon & Schuster/Paula Wiseman Bks.) Simon & Schuster/Paula Wiseman Bks.
—The Sonic Breach. 2019. (Tom Swift Inventors' Academy Ser.: 2). (ENG., Illus.). 144p. (J). (gr. 3-7). pap. 6.99 (978-1-5344-3633-6(2), Simon & Schuster/Paula Wiseman Bks.) Simon & Schuster/Paula Wiseman Bks.
Arena, Felice & Kettle, Phil. Rotten School Day. Vane, Mitch, illus. 2004. (J). pap. (978-1-59336-364-2(8)) Mondo Publishing.
Arévalo, Josefina. Lo Que Paulito Olvidó. 2006. (SPA.). (J). (978-1-59835-006-7(4)) Cambridge BrickHouse, Inc.
Argueta, Jorge. Moony Luna, 1 vol. Gómez, Elizabeth, illus. 2014.Tr. of Luna, Lunita Lunera. (ENG.). 32p. (J). (gr. 2-4). pap. 11.95 (978-0-89239-306-0(8), leelowcbp, Children's Book Press) Lee & Low Bks., Inc.
Argueta, Jorge & Alvarez, Cecilia Concepcion. Moony Luna: Luna, Lunita Lunera. Gomez, Elizabeth, illus. 2005. (ENG & SPA.). 32p. (J). 16.95 (978-0-89239-205-6(3)) Lee & Low Bks., Inc.
Ariye, Shirley. Our Georgia School: A Wildlife Habitat. 2012. 24p. pap. 11.95 (978-1-60976-608-5(3), Strategic Bk. Publishing) Strategic Book Publishing & Rights Agency (SBPRA).
Armstrong, Kelley. The Gathering. (Darkness Rising Ser.: 1). (ENG.). (YA). (gr. 8). 2012. 384p. pap. 9.99 (978-0-06-179703-3(0)) 2011. 368p. 17.99 (978-0-06-179702-6(2)) HarperCollins Pubs. (HarperCollins).
—The Gathering, 7 vols. (Darkness Rising Ser.: Bk. 1). (YA). 100.75 (978-1-4498-6186-5(5)); 1.25 (978-1-4498-6189-6(X)); 2013. 102.75 (978-1-4498-6184-1(9)) Recorded Bks., Inc.
Arnold, Audrey. Elkin's Tail. 2012. (Illus.). 52p. pap. 27.45 (978-1-4772-2180-8(8)) AuthorHouse.
Arnold, Beth. Elijah Makes New Friends. Arnold, Beth, illus. 2012. (Illus.). 30p. pap. 9.99 (978-0-9860272-3-9(5)) Get Happy Tips, LLC.
Arnold, Louise. Golden & Grey: A Good Day for Haunting. 2008. (Golden & Grey Ser.). (ENG.). 336p. (J). (gr. 4-6). 21.19 (978-1-4169-0863-0(3)) Simon & Schuster, Inc.
—Golden & Grey: a Good Day for Haunting. 2009. (ENG.). 336p. (J). (gr. 3-7). pap. 8.99 (978-1-4169-0864-7(1), McElderry, Margaret K. Bks.) McElderry, Margaret K. Bks.
—Golden & Grey (an Unremarkable Boy & a Rather Remarkable Ghost) 2006. (ENG., Illus.). 272p. (J). (gr. 3-7). reprint ed. pap. 6.99 (978-0-689-87585-4(1), McElderry, Margaret K. Bks.) McElderry, Margaret K. Bks.
Arnold, Tedd. Super Fly Guy! (Fly Guy #2) Arnold, Tedd, illus. 2006. (Fly Guy Ser.: 2). (ENG., Illus.). 32p. (J). (gr. -1-3). 6.99 (978-0-439-63904-0(2), Cartwheel Bks.) Scholastic, Inc.
—Super Fly Guy (Scholastic Reader, Level 2), 1 vol. Arnold, Tedd, illus. 2009. (Scholastic Reader, Level 2 Ser.). (ENG., Illus.). 32p. (J). (gr. -1-3). pap. 3.99 (978-0-439-90374-5(2), Cartwheel Bks.) Scholastic, Inc.
Aronson, Deborah. Dragons from Mars Go to School. Jack, Colin, illus. 2019. (ENG.). 32p. (J). (gr. -1-3). 17.99 (978-0-06-236851-5(6), HarperCollins) HarperCollins Pubs.
Arroyo, Madeline. Callie's Gift. Vavak, S. Dean, illus. 2003. 32p. (gr. 2-5). 16.95 (978-0-9740061-0-9(6), 1234106) Stairway Pubns.
Aryal, Aimee. Hello Herbie Husker! Shrestha, Anuj, illus. 2004. 24p. (J). 14.95 (978-1-932888-43-0(8)) Amplify Publishing Group.
—Hello, Pistol Pete! Craig, Megan, illus. 2007. 24p. (J). lib. bdg. 14.95 (978-1-932888-38-6(1)) Amplify Publishing Group.
Asch, Frank. Battle in a Bottle. Kanzler, John, illus. 2014. (Class Pets Ser.). (ENG.). 96p. (J). (gr. 2-6). pap. 13.99 (978-1-4814-3625-0(2), Simon & Schuster/Paula Wiseman Bks.) Simon & Schuster/Paula Wiseman Bks.
—The Ghost of P. S. 42. Kanzler, John, illus. 2014. (Class Pets Ser.). (ENG.). 96p. (J). (gr. 2-5). pap. 13.99 (978-1-4814-3624-3(4), Simon & Schuster/Paula Wiseman Bks.) Simon & Schuster/Paula Wiseman Bks.
Ashburn, Boni. The Class. Gee, Kimberly, illus. 2016. (ENG.). 40p. (J). (gr. -1-3). 17.99 (978-1-4424-2248-3(3), Beach Lane Bks.) Beach Lane Bks.
Ashby, Amanda. Fairy Bad Day. 2011. (ENG.). 352p. (YA). (gr. 7-12). 22.44 (978-0-14-241259-6(7)) Penguin Young Readers Group.
Ashcraft, Carolyn. Hamlet Goes to School. 2004. (Illus.). 108p. (J). per. 5.99 net. (978-0-9755232-0-9(1)) Word Seed Publishing.
Asher, Diana Harmon. Sidetracked. (ENG.). (J). (gr. 3-7). 2018. 256p. pap. 8.99 (978-1-4197-3139-6(4), 1153303) 2017. 240p. 16.99 (978-1-4197-2601-9(3), 1153301) Abrams, Inc. (Amulet Bks.).
Asher, Jay. Thirteen Reasons Why. 2014. (ENG.). 336p. (YA). 15.24 (978-1-63245-099-9(2)) Lectorum Pubns., Inc.
—Thirteen Reasons Why. 2009. 11.72 (978-0-7848-3782-5(1), Everbind) Marco Bk. Co.
—Thirteen Reasons Why. (ENG.). (YA). (gr. 7-18). 2011. 336p. pap. 11.99 (978-1-59514-188-0(X)) 2007. 320p. 18.99 (978-1-59514-171-2(5)) Penguin Young Readers Group. (Razorbill).
—Thirteen Reasons Why. 2011. (ENG.). (YA). (gr. 7-12). lib. bdg. 21.60 (978-1-60686-991-8(4)) Perfection Learning Corp.
—Thirteen Reasons Why. 2011. (CHI & ENG.). 304p. (YA). (gr. 7-12). pap. (978-986-6345-81-4(5)) Spring International Pubs.
—Thirteen Reasons Why. 2011. lib. bdg. 22.10 (978-0-606-15085-9(4)) Turtleback.
—Thirteen Reasons Why 10th Anniversary Edition. 10th anniv. ed. 2016. (ENG.). 352p. (YA). (gr. 7). 18.99 (978-1-59514-788-2(8), Razorbill) Penguin Young Readers Group.
—13 Reasons Why. 2017. (ENG., Illus.). 320p. (YA). (gr. 7). pap. 11.99 (978-0-451-47829-0(0), Razorbill) Penguin Young Readers Group.
Asher, Jay & Mackler, Carolyn. The Future of Us. 2012. (ENG., Illus.). 384p. (YA). (gr. 7). pap. 11.99 (978-1-59514-516-1(8), Razorbill) Penguin Young Readers Group.
Ashes to Ashes. 2014. (Burn for Burn Trilogy Ser.). (ENG., Illus.). 400p. (YA). (gr. 9). 19.99 (978-1-4424-4081-4(3), Simon & Schuster Bks. For Young Readers) Simon & Schuster Bks. For Young Readers.
Ashman, Linda. Take Your Pet to School Day. Kaufman, Suzanne, illus. 2019. 40p. (J). (gr. -1-2). 17.99 (978-1-5247-6559-0(7)); (ENG.). 20.99 (978-1-5247-6560-6(0)) Random Hse. Children's Bks. (Random Hse. Bks. for Young Readers).
Ashton, Brodi. Diplomatic Immunity. 2016. (ENG.). 368p. (YA). (gr. 8). 17.99 (978-0-06-236856-0(7), Balzer & Bray) HarperCollins Pubs.
Ashton, Victoria. Juicy Secrets. 2006. (Confessions of a Teen Nanny Ser.). 208p. (J). lib. bdg. 16.89 (978-0-06-077526-1(2)); (ENG.). (gr. 9-12). 15.99 (978-0-06-073181-6(8)) HarperCollins Pubs. (HarperTeen).
—Rich Girls. 2006. (Confessions of a Teen Nanny Ser.). (ENG.). 224p. (YA). (gr. 9-12). 15.99 (978-0-06-073179-3(6)) HarperCollins Pubs.
Asquith, Ros. Letters from an Alien Schoolboy. 2013. (ENG., Illus.). 192p. (J). (gr. 1-5). 12.95 (978-1-62087-536-0(5), 620536, Sky Pony Pr.) Skyhorse Publishing Co., Inc.
—Trixie Ace Ghost Buster. 2008. (Trixie Ser.). (ENG., Illus.). 176p. (J). (gr. 3-6). pap. 7.99 (978-0-00-725909-0(3)) HarperCollins Pubs. Ltd. GBR. Dist: Independent Pubs. Group.
—Trixie Gets the Witch Factor. 2007. (Trixie Ser.). (ENG., Illus.). 176p. (J). (gr. 3-6). pap. 13.95 (978-0-00-725910-6(7)) HarperCollins Pubs. Ltd. GBR. Dist: Independent Pubs. Group.
Astro, Ian. Moon School, 1 vol. 2006. (Neighborhood Readers Ser.). (ENG.). 16p. (gr. 1-2). pap. 6.50 (978-1-4042-7196-8(1), 5462beef-9025-4a84-b0cd-78c50d2a7eb8, Rosen Classroom) Rosen Publishing Group, Inc., The.
Atkins, Catherine. Alt Ed. 2004. (ENG.). 208p. (YA). (gr. 7-12). reprint ed. 6.99 (978-0-14-240235-1(4), Speak) Penguin Young Readers Group.
Atkins, Eddie. McCool School: If I ran the School. 2006. 32p. per. 19.95 (978-1-59858-155-3(4)) Dog Ear Publishing, LLC.
Atkinson, Elizabeth. From Alice to Zen & Everyone in Between. 2008. (Exceptional Reading & Language Arts Titles for Intermediate Grades Ser.). 247p. (YA). (gr. 4-7). 16.95 (978-0-8225-7271-8(0)) Lerner Publishing Group.
Attack of the Tagger. unabr. ed. 2006. (Shredderman Ser.: Bk. 2). (Illus.). (J). (gr. 3-6). audio compact disk 28.95 (978-1-59519-759-7(1)) Live Oak Media.
Atwood, D. E. If We Shadows. 2016. (ENG., Illus.). (J). 24.99 (978-1-63533-033-5(5), Harmony Ink Pr.) Dreamspinner Pr.
Atwood, Megan. Molly Meets Trouble (Whose Real Name Is Jenna) Fleming, Lucy, illus. 2016. (Dear Molly, Dear Olive Ser.). (ENG.). 96p. (J). (gr. 1-3). lib. bdg. 21.99 (978-1-4795-8696-7(X), 130933, Picture Window Bks.) Capstone.
—Once upon a Winter. Andrewson, Natalie, illus. 2017. (Orchard Novel Ser.: 2). (ENG.). 240p. (J). (gr. 2-6). 12.99 (978-1-4814-9049-8(4), Aladdin) Simon & Schuster Children's Publishing.
Auch, M. J. One Plus One Equals Blue. 2014. (ENG.). 288p. (J). (gr. 5-9). pap. 15.99 (978-1-250-03992-7(4), 900123695) Square Fish.
Auch, Mary Jane. I Was a Third Grade Spy. Auch, Herm, illus. 2004. 86p. (gr. 2-5). 16.00 (978-0-7569-4138-3(5)) Perfection Learning Corp.
—I Was a Third Grade Spy. 2003. (ENG., Illus.). 96p. (J). (gr. 3-7). 7.99 (978-0-440-41871-9(2), Yearling) Random Hse. Children's Bks.
Auerbach, Annie. The Grosse Adventures: The Good, the Bad, & the Gassy, Vol. 1. Norton, Mike, illus. 2006. (Grosse Adventures Manga Ser.: 1). (ENG.). 96p. (J). (gr. 4-1). pap. 9.99 (978-1-59816-049-9(4)) TOKYOPOP, Inc.
Auseon, Andrew. Alienated. 2010. (ENG.). 352p. (J). (gr. 3-7). pap. 5.99 (978-1-4169-8299-9(X), Aladdin) Simon & Schuster Children's Publishing.
Avi. Don't You Know There's a War On? 2nd ed. 2003. 208p. (J). pap. (978-0-439-53096-5(2), HarperCollins) HarperCollins Pubs.
—Don't You Know There's a War On? 2003. 193p. (gr. 3-7). 18.00 (978-0-7569-1383-0(7)) Perfection Learning Corp.
—Nothing but the Truth. 2010. lib. bdg. 17.20 (978-0-606-12300-6(8)) Turtleback.
—Nothing but the Truth (Scholastic Gold), 1 vol. 2010. (ENG.). 208p. (J). (gr. 4-7). pap. 9.99 (978-0-545-17415-2(5), Scholastic Paperbacks) Scholastic, Inc.
—School of the Dead. 2017. (ENG.). 288p. (J). (gr. 3-7). pap. 6.99 (978-0-06-174086-2(1), HarperCollins) HarperCollins Pubs.
—School of the Dead. 2017. (ENG.). (J). (gr. 3-7). lib. bdg. 17.20 (978-0-606-40053-4(2)) Turtleback.
—The Secret School. 2003. (ENG., Illus.). 176p. (J). (gr. 3-7). pap. 7.99 (978-0-15-204699-6(2), 1194153, Clarion Bks.) HarperCollins Pubs.
—The Secret School. 2003. 157p. (J). (gr. 3-7). 13.60 (978-0-7569-1625-1(9)) Perfection Learning Corp.
Avi & Vail, Rachel. Never Mind! 2005. (Twin Novels Ser.). 200p. (gr. 5-9). 16.00 (978-0-7569-5667-7(6)) Perfection Learning Corp.
—Never Mind! A Twin Novel. 2005. (ENG.). 208p. (J). (gr. 5-18). reprint ed. pap. 6.99 (978-0-06-054316-7(7), HarperCollins) HarperCollins Pubs.
Ayoub, Sarah. The Yearbook Committee. 2020. 336p. 9.99 (978-0-7322-9685-8(4), HarperCollins) HarperCollins Pubs.
Ayres, Katherine. Family Tree. 2012. 116p. pap. 7.99 (978-1-936495-21-4(X)) BookPartners, LLC.
—Macaroni Boy. 2004. 192p. (J). (gr. 3-7). per. 7.99 (978-0-440-41884-9(4), Yearling) Random Hse. Children's Bks.
Ayton, Shalanna. The Adventures of Missy the Moose. 2009. 68p. pap. 26.99 (978-1-4389-7827-7(8)) AuthorHouse.
Babiak, Alexandra Brittany. The Runaway Jacket, 1 vol. 2009. 40p. pap. 24.95 (978-1-60749-332-7(2)) America Star Bks.
Babich, Elaine. You Never Called Me Princess. 2012. 210p. pap. 14.00 (978-1-105-70209-9(X)) Lulu.com GBR. Dist: Lulu Pr., Inc.
Baccellia, Kim. No More Goddesses. 2013. (ENG.). 252p. (J). (gr. 3-7). pap. 14.99 (978-1-61271-012-9(3), Zumaya Thresholds) Zumaya Pubns. LLC.
Backenroth, Yehudis. More Adventures of PJ Pepperjay, 1 vol. Judowitz, Chani, illus. 2016. (ENG.). 96p. (J). (978-1-4226-1688-8(6), ArtScroll Series) Mesorah Pubns., Ltd.
Backes, M. Molly. The Princesses of Iowa. (ENG.). 464p. (YA). (gr. 9). 2014. pap. 9.99 (978-0-7636-7161-7(4)) 2012. (Illus.). 16.99 (978-0-7636-5312-5(8)) Candlewick Pr.
Bacon, C. G. Mean Mandy. 2009. 103p. pap. 11.00 (978-0-557-05740-5(X)) Lulu Pr., Inc.
Bacon, Lee. Joshua Dread. 2013. (Joshua Dread Ser.: 1). (ENG.). 272p. (J). (gr. 4-7). 7.99 (978-0-307-92998-3(1), Yearling) Random Hse. Children's Bks.
—Joshua Dread: the Dominion Key. 2015. (Joshua Dread Ser.: 3). (ENG.). 256p. (J). (gr. 4-7). 7.99 (978-0-385-37126-1(8), Yearling) Random Hse. Children's Bks.
Bacon, S. N. & Cunningham, Susan. Crow Flight. 2018. (ENG.). 352p. (YA). pap. 12.99 (978-1-948705-16-5(8)) Amberjack Publishing Co.
Badeaux, Dewey. Sam & Skully. Ball, Lauren, illus. 2013. 126p. pap. 12.99 (978-0-9884057-4-5(1)) Alligator Pr.
Bader, Bonnie. 100 Monsters in My School. Hendrix, Bryan, illus. 2003. (All Aboard Math Reader Ser.). 48p. (gr. -1-3). 14.00 (978-0-7569-1648-0(8)) Perfection Learning Corp.
Badger, Meredith. Fairy School Dropout Undercover. 2011. (Fairy School Ser.: 2). (ENG., Illus.). 160p. (J). (gr. 2-4). pap. 15.99 (978-0-312-61951-0(0), 900065967) Square Fish.
Baier, Jeanne M. The Twins Jeffrey & Jeanne. 2012. 28p. pap. 16.00 (978-1-4669-5194-5(X)) Trafford Publishing.
Bailey, Charles. Slick Glickman, Unlikely Hero. 2008. 164p. 22.95 (978-0-595-49014-1(X)); pap. 12.95 (978-0-595-48014-2(4)) iUniverse, Inc.
Bailey, Christine. Girl in the Middle. 2013. 236p. pap. 8.99 (978-0-9890632-0-3(8)) Vinspire Publishing LLC.
Bailey, Em. Shift. 2016. (ENG.). 320p. (YA). (gr. 9). pap. 18.99 (978-1-76012-698-8(5)) Hardie Grant Children?s Publishing AUS. Dist: Independent Pubs. Group.
Bailey, Linda. Stanley at School. Slavin, Bill, illus. 2015. (ENG.). 32p. (J). (gr. -1-2). 17.95 (978-1-77138-096-6(9)) Kids Can Pr., Ltd. CAN. Dist: Hachette Bk. Group.
Bailey, Loren. Star-Crossed. 2019. (Al High Ser.). (ENG.). 112p. (YA). (gr. 6-12). 26.65 (978-1-5415-5690-4(9), ab0a6a2b-9bef-4d5f-af0d-d1d05a0fe21c); pap. 7.99 (978-1-5415-7293-5(9), d1461ebf-f2cb-4661-bde4-629992a9e777) Lerner Publishing Group. (Darby Creek).
Baker, Kim. Pickle: The (Formerly) Anonymous Prank Club of Fountain Point Middle School. Probert, Tim, illus. 2014. (ENG.). 256p. (J). (gr. 3-7). pap. 7.99 (978-1-250-04427-3(8), 900128319) Square Fish.
Baker, Theo. Hank Zipzer: the Cow Poop Treasure Hunt. 2018. (Hank Zipzer Ser.). (ENG.). 144p. (J). (gr. 2-5). pap. 6.99 (978-1-5362-0333-2(5), Candlewick Entertainment) Candlewick Pr.
Balan, Judy. Tweenache in the Time of Hashtags. 2016. (Nina the Philosopher Ser.: 1). 192p. 6.99 (978-93-5177-550-8(X), Harper) HarperCollins Pubs.
Baldwin, Rich & Jones, Sandie. The Detective Company. Dawn, Baumer, illus. 2004. 183p. (YA). pap. 9.95 (978-0-9742920-0-7(1), 2001) Buttonwood Pr.
Balen, Katya. The Space We're In. 2019. (ENG., Illus.). 208p. (J). (gr. 3-7). 17.99 (978-0-8234-4289-8(6), Margaret Ferguson Books) Holiday Hse., Inc.
Ball, Nate. Alien in My Pocket: Blast Off! 2014. (Alien in My Pocket Ser.: 1). (ENG., Illus.). 160p. (J). (gr. 1-5). pap. 6.99 (978-0-06-221623-6(6), HarperCollins) HarperCollins Pubs.
—Alien in My Pocket: On Impact! 2014. (Alien in My Pocket Ser.: 4). (ENG., Illus.). 128p. (J). (gr. 1-5). pap. 5.99 (978-0-06-221629-8(5), HarperCollins) HarperCollins Pubs.
—Alien in My Pocket: The Science Unfair. 2014. (Alien in My Pocket Ser.: 2). (ENG., Illus.). 144p. (J). (gr. 1-5). pap. 4.99 (978-0-06-221625-0(2), HarperCollins) HarperCollins Pubs.
—Radio Active. 2014. (Alien in My Pocket Ser.: 3). (J). lib. bdg. 14.75 (978-0-606-35349-6(6)) Turtleback.
—The Science Unfair. 2014. (Alien in My Pocket Ser.: 2). (J). lib. bdg. 14.75 (978-0-606-35182-9(5)) Turtleback.
Ball, S. N. Daddies Don't Get Snow Days. Howard, Ellie Nothaus, illus. 2013. (ENG.). 28p. (J). pap. 13.95 (978-1-4787-1188-9(4)) Outskirts Pr., Inc.
Ballarini, Joe. A Babysitter's Guide to Monster Hunting #2: Beasts & Geeks. To, Vivienne, illus. 2018. (Babysitter's Guide to Monsters Ser.: 2). (ENG.). 320p. (J). (gr. 3-7). 13.99 (978-0-06-243787-7(9), Tegen, Katherine Bks) HarperCollins Pubs.
Balliett, Blue. The Wright 3. Helquist, Brett, illus. 2008. 318p. (gr. 4-7). 18.00 (978-0-7569-8942-2(6)) Perfection Learning Corp.
—The Wright 3. Helquist, Brett, illus. 2007. (ENG.). 352p. (J). (gr. 4-7). pap. 8.99 (978-0-439-69368-4(3), Scholastic Paperbacks) Scholastic, Inc.
Bancks, Tristan. Mac Slater Hunts the Cool. (Mac Slater Hunts the Cool Ser.). (ENG.). 224p. (J). (gr. 3-7). 2011. pap. 6.99 (978-1-4169-8575-4(1)) 2010. 15.99 (978-1-4169-8574-7(3)) Simon & Schuster Bks. For Young Readers. (Simon & Schuster Bks. For Young Readers).
—My Life & Other Massive Mistakes. Gordon, Gus, illus. 2018. (Tom Weekly Ser.: 3). 240p. (J). (gr. 4-7). 9.99

S

(978-0-14-379010-5(2)) Random Hse. Australia AUS. Dist: Independent Pubs. Group.
Bang, Molly. When Sophie's Feelings Are Really, Really Hurt. Bang, Molly, illus. 2015. (ENG., Illus.). 40p. (J). (gr. -1-3). 18.99 (978-0-545-78831-1(5), Blue Sky Pr., The) Scholastic, Inc.
Banim, Lisa. In the Doghouse. 2005. 124p. (J). lib. bdg. 16.92 (978-1-4242-0685-8(5)) Fitzgerald Bks.
Banim, Lisa & Minsky, Terri. The Case of the Kate Haters. 2005. (Illus.). 124p. (J). (978-1-4156-3927-6(2)) Disney Pr.
Banks, Jacqueline Turner. A Day for Vincent Chin & Me. 2005. (ENG.). 128p. (J). (gr. 5-7). pap. 11.95 (978-0-618-54879-8(3), 481194, Clarion Bks.) HarperCollins Pubs.
—Egg-Drop Blues. 2003. (ENG.). 128p. (J). (gr. 5-7). pap. 10.95 (978-0-618-25080-6(8), 481193, Clarion Bks.) HarperCollins Pubs.
Banks, Piper. Geek Abroad, 2 vols. 2008. (Geek High Ser.: 2). (ENG.). 256p. (YA). (gr. 9-18). 9.99 (978-0-451-22393-7(4), Berkley) Penguin Publishing Group.
—Geek High. 2007. (Geek High Ser.: 1). (ENG.). 256p. (YA). (gr. 9-18). 9.99 (978-0-451-22225-1(3), Berkley) Penguin Publishing Group.
—Revenge of the Geek. 2010. (Geek High Ser.: 4). (ENG.). 256p. (gr. 12-18). 9.99 (978-0-451-23134-5(1), Berkley) Penguin Publishing Group.
Banks, Steven. Middle School Bites. Fearing, Mark, illus. 2020. (Middle School Bites Ser.: 1). 304p. (J). (gr. 3-7). 13.99 (978-0-8234-4543-1(7)) Holiday Hse., Inc.
Banks, Tyra. Modelland. 2011. 569p. (YA). (gr. 7). 17.99 (978-0-375-97259-1(5), Delacorte Pr) Random House Publishing Group.
Banville, Vincent. Hennessy. 180p. pap. (978-0-7022-2505-5(3)) Univ. of Queensland Pr.
Baratz-Logsted, Lauren. Angel's Choice. 2006. (ENG.). 256p. (YA). (gr. 9-12). pap. 6.99 (978-1-4169-2524-8(4), Simon Pulse) Simon Pulse.
—Crazy Beautiful. 2011. (ENG.). 204p. (YA). (gr. 7). pap. 12.95 (978-0-547-40310-6(0), 1428146, Clarion Bks.) HarperCollins Pubs.
—The Education of Bet. 2011. (ENG.). 192p. (YA). (gr. 7). pap. 11.99 (978-0-547-55024-4(3), 1450234, Clarion Bks.) HarperCollins Pubs.
Barbara, Cohen. Molly's Pilgrim. 97th rev. ed. 2014. (ENG.). 32p. (J). (gr. 1-5). 8.24 (978-1-63245-244-3(8)) Lectorum Pubns., Inc.
Barber, Tiki & Barber, Ronde. Red Zone. (Barber Game Time Bks.). (ENG., 176p. (J). (gr. 3-7). 2013. Illus.). pap. 7.99 (978-1-4169-6861-0(X)) 2010. 15.99 (978-1-4169-6860-3(1)) Simon & Schuster/Paula Wiseman Bks. (Simon & Schuster/Paula Wiseman Bks.).
Barbour, Ralph Henry. The Half-Back. 2005. 27.95 (978-1-4218-1494-0(3)); 220p. pap. 12.95 (978-1-4218-1594-7(X)) 1st World Publishing, Inc. (1st World Library - Literary Society).
—The Half-Back. 2007. 132p. per. (978-1-4068-3665-3(6)) Echo Library.
—The New Boy at Hilltop & Other Stories. 2006. pap. (978-1-4065-0779-9(2)) Dodo Pr.
Barden, Stephanie. Cinderella Smith. Goode, Diane, illus. (Cinderella Smith Ser.: 1). (ENG.). (J). (gr. 3-7). 2012. 176p. pap. 6.99 (978-0-06-196425-1(5)) 2011. 160p. 16.99 (978-0-06-196423-7(9)) HarperCollins Pubs. (HarperCollins).
—Cinderella Smith: the Super Secret Mystery, Vol. 3. Goode, Diane, illus. 2013. (Cinderella Smith Ser.: 3). (ENG.). 144p. (J). (gr. 1-5). 16.99 (978-0-06-200443-7(3), HarperCollins) HarperCollins Pubs.
Bare, Bart. Girl. 2010. 188p. (YA). pap. 11.95 (978-0-9825396-4-4(9)) Canterbury Hse. Publishing, Ltd.
Bargiel, Nina G. & Amsterdam, Shane. Fintastic Friends Forever. 2016. (Illus.). 32p. (J). (978-1-5182-1661-9(7)) Little Brown & Co.
Barham, Paul Richard. The Adventures of Damen the Duck. 2012. 72p. pap. 41.99 (978-1-4691-5476-3(5)) Xlibris Corp.
Barkley, Callie. Amy Is a Little Bit Chicken. Bishop, Tracy, illus. 2015. (Critter Club Ser.: 13). (ENG.). 128p. (J). (gr. k-4). pap. 6.99 (978-1-4814-5174-1(X), Little Simon) Little Simon.
—Liz Learns a Lesson. Riti, Marsha, illus. 2013. (Critter Club Ser.: 3). (ENG.). 128p. (J). (gr. -1-2). 17.99 (978-1-4424-6770-5(3)); pap. 6.99 (978-1-4424-6768-2(1)) Little Simon. (Little Simon).
—Liz Learns a Lesson. 2013. (Critter Club Ser.: 3). lib. bdg. 16.00 (978-0-606-32032-0(6)) Turtleback.
—Marion & the Secret Letter. Bishop, Tracy, illus. 2017. (Critter Club Ser.: 16). (ENG.). 128p. (J). (gr. k-4). pap. 6.99 (978-1-4814-8702-3(7), Little Simon) Little Simon.
Barkow, Henriette. The Giant Turnip. Johnson, Richard, illus. 2004. 32p. (J). (POL & ENG.). pap. (978-1-85269-743-3(1)); (ENG & POR.). pap. (978-1-85269-744-0(X)) Mantra Lingua.
Barlow, Andrew. Jellytoes Misses the Bus. Barlow, Andrew, illus. 2005. (Jellytoes Ser.). (ENG., Illus.). 32p. (J). per. 8.95 (978-0-9764336-0-6(5)) MJS Publishing Group LLC.
Barlow, Cassie & Norrod, Sue. Journey Through the Unified Field, 1 vol. Gantt, Amy, illus. 2019. (ENG.). 128p. (J). (gr. 3-7). pap. 9.95 (978-1-4556-2478-2(0), Pelican Publishing) Arcadia Publishing.
Barnes, Bobbie Jo. The Message. 2012. 24p. pap. 24.95 (978-1-4626-9047-3(5)) America Star Bks.
Barnes, Derrick. The King of Kindergarten. Brantley-Newton, Vanessa, illus. 2019. 32p. (J). (-k). 17.99 (978-1-5247-4074-0(8), Nancy Paulsen Books) Penguin Young Readers Group.
—The Queen of Kindergarten. Brantley-Newton, Vanessa, illus. 2022. (ENG.). 32p. (J). (-k). 17.99 (978-0-593-11142-0(7), Nancy Paulsen Books) Penguin Young Readers Group.
—We Could Be Brothers. 2010. (Illus.). 164p. (J). (978-0-545-13574-0(5), Scholastic Pr.) Scholastic, Inc.
Barnes, Derrick D. Brand New School, Brave New Ruby (Ruby & the Booker Boys #1) Newton, Vanessa Brantley, illus. 2008. (Ruby & the Booker Boys Ser.: 1). (ENG.). 144p. (J). (gr. 2-5). pap. 5.99 (978-0-545-01760-2(2), Scholastic Paperbacks) Scholastic, Inc.
—Ruby Flips for Attention (Ruby & the Booker Boys #4) Newton, Vanessa Brantley, illus. 2009. (Ruby & the Booker Boys Ser.: 4). (ENG.). 144p. (J). (gr. 2-5). pap. 5.99 (978-0-545-01763-3(7), Scholastic Paperbacks) Scholastic, Inc.
—The Slumber Party Payback (Ruby & the Booker Boys #3). 3. Newton, Vanessa Brantley, illus. 2008. (Ruby & the Booker Boys Ser.: 3). (ENG.). 176p. (J). (gr. 2-5). pap. 5.99 (978-0-545-01762-6(9)) Scholastic, Inc.
—Trivia Queen, Third Grade Supreme (Ruby & the Booker Boys #2) Newton, Vanessa Brantley, illus. 2008. (Ruby & the Booker Boys Ser.: 2). (ENG.). 144p. (J). (gr. 2-5). pap. 5.99 (978-0-545-01761-9(0)) Scholastic, Inc.
Barnes, Jennifer Lynn. The Long Game: A Fixer Novel. 2017. (ENG.). 368p. (YA). pap. 12.99 (978-1-61963-599-9(2), 900141878, Bloomsbury USA Childrens) Bloomsbury Publishing USA.
—The Squad: Perfect Cover. 2008. (Squad Ser.). (ENG.). 288p. (YA). (gr. 7). mass mkt. 7.99 (978-0-385-73454-7(9), Laurel Leaf) Random Hse. Children's Bks.
Barnes, John. Tales of the Madman Underground. 2011. (ENG.). 544p. (YA). (gr. 9-18). pap. 9.99 (978-0-14-241702-7(5), Speak) Penguin Young Readers Group.
Barnes, Phil. My Teacher's a Robot! 2015. (ENG.). 63p. (J). (gr. 1-2). mass mkt. 8.95 (978-1-78455-935-9(0), 2e43b527-f3de-4545-b9e1-d6f75c93f153) Austin Macauley Pubs. Ltd. GBR. Dist: Baker & Taylor Publisher Services (BTPS).
Barnett, Mac. Billy Twitters & His Blue Whale Problem. Rex, Adam, illus. 2009. (ENG.). 48p. (J). (gr. -1-3). 18.99 (978-0-7868-4958-1(4)) Little, Brown Bks. for Young Readers.
—Terrible Two Get Worse (UK Edition) 2016. (Terrible Two Ser.). (ENG., Illus.). 224p. (J). (gr. 3-7). pap. 7.95 (978-1-4197-1925-7(4)) Abrams, Inc.
—Terrible Two Go Wild (UK Edition) 2018. (Terrible Two Ser.). (ENG., Illus.). 224p. (J). (gr. 3-7). pap. 7.99 (978-1-4197-2341-4(3)) Abrams, Inc.
Barnett, Mac & John, Jory. The Terrible Two. Cornell, Kevin, illus. 2017. (Terrible Two Ser.). (ENG.). 240p. (J). (gr. 3-7). pap. 8.99 (978-1-4197-2737-5(0), 1196503, Amulet Bks.) Abrams, Inc.
—The Terrible Two. 2017. (Terrible Two Ser.: 1). (J). lib. bdg. 18.40 (978-0-606-40723-6(5)); lib. bdg. 18.40 (978-0-606-40724-3(3)) Turtleback.
—The Terrible Two Get Worse. Cornell, Kevin, illus. (Terrible Two Ser.). (ENG.). (J). (gr. 3-7). 2017. 240p. pap. 8.99 (978-1-4197-2738-2(9), 1196403) 2016. 224p. 15.99 (978-1-4197-1680-5(8), 1093701, Amulet Bks.) Abrams, Inc.
—The Terrible Two Go Wild. Cornell, Kevin, illus. 2018. (Terrible Two Ser.). (ENG.). 240p. (J). (gr. 3-7). pap. 8.99 (978-1-4197-3205-8(6), 1093803) Abrams, Inc.
—Terrible Two Go Wild. Cornell, Kevin, illus. 2018. (Terrible Two Ser.). (ENG.). 224p. (J). (gr. 3-7). 13.99 (978-1-4197-2185-4(2), 1093801, Amulet Bks.) Abrams, Inc.
Barnholdt, Lauren. Devon Delaney Should Totally Know Better. 2009. (Mix Ser.). (ENG.). 288p. (J). (gr. 4-8). pap. 6.99 (978-1-4169-8019-3(9), Aladdin) Simon & Schuster Children's Publishing.
—Fake Me a Match. 2012. (Mix Ser.). (ENG.). 304p. (J). (gr. 4-8). pap. 6.99 (978-1-4424-2259-9(9), Aladdin) Simon & Schuster Children's Publishing.
—Girl Meets Ghost. 2013. (Girl Meets Ghost Ser.: 1). (ENG.). (J). (gr. 4-9). 240p. pap. 7.99 (978-1-4424-2146-2(0)); 224p. 15.99 (978-1-4424-4246-7(8)) Simon & Schuster Children's Publishing. (Aladdin).
—The Harder the Fall. 2014. (Girl Meets Ghost Ser.: 2). (ENG., Illus.). 256p. (J). (gr. 4-9). pap. 7.99 (978-1-4424-2147-9(9), Aladdin) Simon & Schuster Children's Publishing.
—Rules for Secret Keeping. 2011. (Mix Ser.). (ENG.). 304p. (J). (gr. 4-8). pap. 7.99 (978-1-4169-8021-6(0), Aladdin) Simon & Schuster Children's Publishing.
—Sometimes It Happens. (ENG.). (YA). (gr. 9). 2012. 336p. pap. 9.99 (978-1-4424-1315-3(8)) 2011. 320p. 16.99 (978-1-4424-1314-6(X)) Simon Pulse. (Simon Pulse).
—The Thing about the Truth. (ENG.). (YA). (gr. 9). 2013. 320p. pap. 9.99 (978-1-4424-3461-5(9)) 2012. 304p. 16.99 (978-1-4424-3460-8(0)) Simon Pulse. (Simon Pulse).
Barnholdt, Lauren & Beaky, Suzanne. Hailey Twitch Is Not a Snitch. 2010. (Hailey Twitch Ser.: 1). (Illus.). 160p. (J). (gr. 2-4). pap. 6.99 (978-1-4022-2444-7(3), Sourcebooks Jabberwocky) Sourcebooks, Inc.
Barns, Crosby H. Who Programmed the Species? The Theory of Scientific Coincidence. 2008. 36p. pap. 16.99 (978-1-4389-0727-7(3)) AuthorHouse.
Baron, Jeff. Sean Rosen Is Not for Sale. 2015. (ENG.). 384p. (J). (gr. 3-7). pap. 6.99 (978-0-06-218751-2(1), Greenwillow Bks.) HarperCollins Pubs.
Barreintez, Elsa. I'm Only Eight, by Reynaldo: I Survived Being Eight. 2010. 46p. pap. 14.95 (978-1-4327-5489-1(0)) Outskirts Pr., Inc.
Barrett, Jennifer. Lethal Delivery, Postage Prepaid. (Thumbprint Mysteries Ser.). 32.86 (978-0-8092-0425-0(8)) McGraw-Hill/Contemporary.
Barrett, Kendra J., et al. Yes I Can! A Girl & Her Wheelchair. Lemay, Violet, illus. 2018. 32p. (J). (978-1-4338-2869-0(3), Magination Pr.) American Psychological Assn.
Barrows, Annie. Nothing. 2018. (ENG.). 240p. (YA). (gr. 9). pap. 9.99 (978-0-06-266824-0(2), Greenwillow Bks.) HarperCollins Pubs.
Barrows, Annie & Blackall, Sophie. Ivy + Bean & the Ghost That Had to Go. 2011. (Ivy & Bean Ser.). (ENG., Illus.). 136p. (J). (gr. 2-5). 31.36 (978-1-59961-929-3(6), 10109, Chapter Bks.) Spotlight.
—Ivy & Bean What's the Big Idea?, 7. 2011. (Ivy & Bean Ser.). (ENG., Illus.). 132p. (J). (gr. 2-5). 31.36 (978-1-59961-934-7(2), 10114, Chapter Bks.) Spotlight.
Barrows, Annie, et al. Ivy & Bean What's the Big Idea? (Book 7) Blackall, Sophie, illus. 2010. (ENG.). 128p. (J). (gr. 1-5). 14.99 (978-0-8118-6692-7(0)) Chronicle Bks. LLC.
Barry, Cotter. The Adventures of Morgan Morgan the Rhymester. 2010. 16p. 12.99 (978-1-4520-0116-6(2)) AuthorHouse.
Barry, Dave. The Worst Night Ever. Cannell, Jon, illus. 2016. (Class Trip Ser.: 2). (ENG.). 256p. (J). (gr. 3-7). 13.99 (978-1-4847-0850-7(4)) Hyperion Bks. for Children.
Barshaw, Ruth McNally. The Ellie Mcdoodle Diaries: Ellie for President. 2014. (Ellie Mcdoodle Ser.). (ENG., Illus.). 176p. (YA). (gr. 3-6). 13.99 (978-1-61963-061-1(3), 900118520, Bloomsbury USA Childrens) Bloomsbury Publishing USA.
—The Ellie Mcdoodle Diaries: New Kid in School. 2013. (Ellie Mcdoodle Diaries). (ENG., Illus.). 192p. (YA). (gr. 3-6). 13.99 (978-1-61963-174-8(1), 900123470, Bloomsbury USA Childrens) Bloomsbury Publishing USA.
—The Ellie Mcdoodle Diaries: the Show Must Go On. 2013. (Ellie Mcdoodle Diaries). (ENG., Illus.). 176p. (YA). (gr. 3-6). 13.99 (978-1-61963-059-8(1), 900118518, Bloomsbury USA Childrens) Bloomsbury Publishing USA.
Barthelmess, Nikki. The Quiet You Carry. 2019. (Quiet You Carry Ser.). (ENG.). 352p. (YA). (gr. 9-12). pap. 14.99 (978-1-63583-028-6(1), 1635830281, Flux) North Star Editions.
Bartlett, Roberta. How I Met an Alien. 2011. 74p. pap. 19.95 (978-1-4560-7818-8(6)) America Star Bks.
Barton, Chris. Book or Bell? Spires, Ashley, illus. 2017. (ENG.). 40p. (J). 16.99 (978-1-68119-729-6(4), 900182504, Bloomsbury USA Childrens) Bloomsbury Publishing USA.
Bashline, Trent. How Jake & Daisy Stopped Bullying at Dogwood Elementary. 2011. 32p. pap. 12.79 (978-1-4634-2895-2(2)) AuthorHouse.
Baskin, Nora Raleigh. Anything but Typical. (ENG.). 208p. (J). (gr. 5-9). 2010. pap. 8.99 (978-1-4169-9500-5(5)) 2009. (Illus.). 18.99 (978-1-4169-6378-3(2)) Simon & Schuster Bks. For Young Readers. (Simon & Schuster Bks. For Young Readers).
—Runt. (ENG., Illus.). 208p. (J). (gr. 3-7). 2014. pap. 7.99 (978-1-4424-5808-6(9)) 2013. 15.99 (978-1-4424-5807-9(0)) Simon & Schuster Bks. For Young Readers. (Simon & Schuster Bks. For Young Readers).
Bass, Alexis. Love & Other Theories. 2014. (ENG.). 384p. (YA). (gr. 9). 17.99 (978-0-06-227532-5(1), HarperTeen) HarperCollins Pubs.
—What's Broken Between Us. 2015. (ENG.). 304p. (YA). (gr. 9). 17.99 (978-0-06-227535-6(6), HarperTeen) HarperCollins Pubs.
Bass, Patrik Henry. The Zero Degree Zombie Zone. Craft, Jerry, illus. 2014. (ENG.). 144p. (J). (gr. 3-7). 16.99 (978-0-545-13210-7(X), Scholastic Pr.) Scholastic, Inc.
Bast, Michael. Death's Academy. 2014. (J). pap. 14.99 (978-1-4621-1380-4(X), Horizon Pubs.) Cedar Fort, Inc./CFI Distribution.
Basye, Dale E. Blimpo Vol. 3: The Third Circle of Heck. Dob, Bob, illus. 2011. (Heck Ser.: 3). 464p. (J). (gr. 3-7). pap. 9.99 (978-0-375-85677-8(3), Yearling) Random Hse. Children's Bks.
—Fibble: the Fourth Circle of Heck. Dob, Bob, illus. 2012. (Heck Ser.: 4). 384p. (J). (gr. 4-7). pap. 7.99 (978-0-375-85679-2(X), Yearling) Random Hse. Children's Bks.
—Heck: Where the Bad Kids Go. Dob, Bob, illus. 2009. (Heck Ser.: 1). 304p. (J). (gr. 3-7). 6.99 (978-0-375-84076-0(1), Yearling) Random Hse. Children's Bks.
—Precocia: the Sixth Circle of Heck. Dob, Bob, illus. 2013. (Heck Ser.: 6). 432p. (J). (gr. 3-7). 7.99 (978-0-375-86807-8(0), Yearling) Random Hse. Children's Bks.
—Rapacia: the Second Circle of Heck. Dob, Bob, illus. 2010. (Heck Ser.: 2). 384p. (J). (gr. 3-7). pap. 7.99 (978-0-375-84078-4(8), Yearling) Random Hse. Children's Bks.
Bateman, Anya. I Just Got a Letter from Allyson Pringle. 2008. 256p. (YA). pap. 15.95 (978-1-60641-028-8(8)) Deseret Bk. Co.
—The Makeover of James Orville Wickenbee. 2007. 262p. (J). pap. (978-1-59038-707-8(4)) Deseret Bk. Co.
Bateman, Teresa. The Bully Blockers Club. Urbanovic, Jackie, illus. 2004. (ENG.). 32p. (J). (gr. -1-3). 8.99 (978-0-8075-0919-7(1), 807509191) Whitman, Albert & Co.
Bates, Melinda. Nick Pricer: An American Heir. 2012. 88p. 19.95 (978-1-4697-8478-6(5)); pap. 9.95 (978-1-4697-8476-2(9)) iUniverse, Inc.
Bates, Michelle. Horse in Danger. (Sandy Lane Stables Ser.). 2017. (ENG.). 128p. (YA). pap. 5.99 (978-0-7945-3915-3(7)) 2009. (Illus.). 114p. (J). (gr. 5). pap. 4.99 (978-0-7945-2530-9(X)) EDC Publishing. (Usborne).
—Midnight Horse. rev. ed. 2011. (Sandy Lane Stables Ser.). 128p. (J). pap. 4.99 (978-0-7945-2529-3(6), Usborne) EDC Publishing.
Bauer, A. C. E. Come Fall. 2011. 240p. (J). (gr. 3-7). pap. 7.99 (978-0-375-85826-0(1), Yearling) Random Hse. Children's Bks.
Bauer, Joan. Peeled. 2009. (ENG.). 256p. (YA). (gr. 7-18). 10.99 (978-0-14-241430-9(1), Speak) Penguin Young Readers Group.
—Stand Tall. 2005. (ENG.). 192p. (YA). (gr. 7-7). pap. 9.99 (978-0-14-240427-0(6), Speak) Penguin Young Readers Group.
Bauer, Michael Gerard. Don't Call Me Ishmael. 2007. 255p. (J). (gr. 9-12). lib. bdg. 17.89 (978-0-06-134835-8(X), HarperTeen) HarperCollins Pubs.
Baumgartner, John Robert. Like Losing Your Left Hand. 2011. 244p. pap. 24.95 (978-1-4560-4043-7(X)) America Star Bks.
Baxter, Alice L. Adam's Atomic Adventures. 2007. 76p. per. 8.95 (978-0-595-45616-1(2)) iUniverse, Inc.
Beamer, Cheryl & Beamer, Frank. Yea, It's Hokie Game Day! De Angel, Miguel, illus. 2006. 24p. (J). lib. bdg. 17.95 (978-1-932888-44-7(6)) Amplify Publishing Group.
Beamish, Diane. Gentle Jack. 2006. 25p. (J). 10.25 (978-1-4116-5553-9(2)) Lulu Pr., Inc.
Bean, Raymond. Sweet Farts #1, 0 vols. unabr. ed. 2012. (Sweet Farts Ser.: 1). (ENG.). 138p. (J). (gr. 2-6). pap. 9.95 (978-1-61218-250-6(X), 9781612182506, Two Lions) Amazon Publishing.
Beasley, Kate. Gertie's Leap to Greatness. 2018. (ENG., Illus.). 272p. (J). pap. 12.99 (978-1-250-14374-7(8), 900180551) Square Fish.
Beaty, Andrea. Artist Ted. Lemaitre, Pascal, illus. 2012. (ENG.). 32p. (J). (gr. -1-3). 19.99 (978-1-4169-5374-6(4), McElderry, Margaret K. Bks.) McElderry, Margaret K. Bks.
—Firefighter Ted. Lemaitre, Pascal, illus. 2009. (ENG.). 32p. (J). (gr. -1-3). 18.99 (978-1-4169-2821-8(9), McElderry, Margaret K. Bks.) McElderry, Margaret K. Bks.
—Iggy Peck, Architect. 2007. (Questioneers Ser.). (ENG., Illus.). 32p. (J). (gr. k-17). 19.99 (978-0-8109-1106-2(X), 05326) Abrams, Inc.
—Iggy Peck, Architect. Roberts, David, illus. 2010. (ENG.). 32p. (J). (gr. k-17). pap. 7.95 (978-0-8109-8928-3(X)) UK Abrams Bks. for Young Readers.
Beaudoin, Sean. Fade to Blue. 2011. (ENG., Illus.). 208p. (YA). (gr. 6-8). 24.94 (978-0-316-01417-5(6)) Little Brown & Co.
Beaumier, Randy P. Snapshot Billy: I Remember. 2012. 36p. pap. 24.95 (978-1-4626-1787-6(5)) America Star Bks.
Becher, Susan. Silly Friend. 2010. 28p. pap. 12.50 (978-1-4520-0244-6(4)) AuthorHouse.
Beck, Sharon. The Fish in Our Class. 2011. (Randy's Corner Ser.). (Illus.). 32p. (J). (gr. -1-2). lib. bdg. 25.70 (978-1-58415-978-0(2)) Mitchell Lane Pubs.
Beck, W. H. Malcolm at Midnight. Lies, Brian, illus. 2015. (ENG.). 272p. (J). (gr. 3-7). pap. 7.99 (978-0-544-33666-7(6), 1584188, Clarion Bks.) HarperCollins Pubs.
Becker, Bonny. The Magical Ms. Plum. Portnoy, Amy, illus. 2011. (ENG.). 112p. (J). (gr. 1-4). 7.99 (978-0-375-84760-8(X), Yearling) Random Hse. Children's Bks.
Becker, Helaine. Dirk Daring, Secret Agent, 1 vol. 2014. (Dirk Daring, Secret Agent Ser.: 1). (ENG., Illus.). 208p. (J). (gr. 4-7). pap. 9.95 (978-1-4598-0683-2(2)) Orca Bk. Pubs. USA.
—Let Sleeping Dogs Lie, 1 vol. 2016. (Dirk Daring, Secret Agent Ser.: 2). (ENG., Illus.). 240p. (J). (gr. 4-7). pap. 9.95 (978-1-4598-1038-9(4)) Orca Bk. Pubs. USA.
Beckford, Lois. The Interesting Pen Pal. 2010. 44p. pap. 21.99 (978-1-4415-0878-2(3)) Xlibris Corp.
Beckham, David. Charlie Barker & the Secret of the Deep Dark Woods. 2006. 570p. pap. 33.20 (978-1-4120-9264-7(7)) Trafford Publishing.
Beckley, N. K. The Three-Some: Book 2. 2012. 66p. 24.99 (978-1-4771-2938-8(3)) Xlibris Corp.
—The Writer's Corner: Book 3. 2012. 90p. 24.99 (978-1-4797-1241-0(8)); pap. 15.99 (978-1-4797-1240-3(X)) Xlibris Corp.
Beckwith, Kathy. Critical Mass: I Never Thought It Would Be Like This. . 2003. (ENG.). 192p. (J). pap. 9.95 (978-1-930572-25-6(5)) Educational Media Corp.
Bedford, David A. Angela. 2009. 190p. 25.50 (978-1-60860-755-6(0), Eloquent Bks.) Strategic Book Publishing & Rights Agency (SBPRA).
Bee, Clair. Pitcher's Duel: A Chip Hilton Sports Story. 2011. 224p. (gr. 4-7). 44.95 (978-1-258-09630-4(7)) Literary Licensing, LLC.
BEEBE, Diane. School's Out. 2006. (J). (978-1-4276-0238-1(7)) Aardvark Global Publishing.
Beil, Michael D. The Red Blazer Girls: the Mistaken Masterpiece. 2012. (Red Blazer Girls Ser.: 3). (ENG.). 336p. (J). (gr. 5). 8.99 (978-0-375-86494-0(6), Yearling) Random Hse. Children's Bks.
—The Red Blazer Girls: the Ring of Rocamadour. 2010. (Red Blazer Girls Ser.: 1). (ENG.). 320p. (J). (gr. 3-7). 7.99 (978-0-375-84303-7(5), Yearling) Random Hse. Children's Bks.
—The Red Blazer Girls: the Secret Cellar. 2013. (Red Blazer Girls Ser.: 4). (ENG., Illus.). 288p. (J). (gr. 5). pap. 8.99 (978-0-375-86495-7(4), Yearling) Random Hse. Children's Bks.
—The Red Blazer Girls: the Vanishing Violin. 2011. (Red Blazer Girls Ser.: 2). (ENG.). 336p. (J). (gr. 3-7). 8.99 (978-0-375-85454-5(1), Yearling) Random Hse. Children's Bks.
—The Ring of Rocamadour, 1. 2009. (Red Blazer Girls Ser.). (ENG.). 304p. (J). (gr. 6-8). lib. bdg. 21.19 (978-0-375-94814-5(7), Knopf Bks. for Young Readers) Random Hse. Children's Bks.
Beitler, Stacey Ann. Willy Goes to School. 2011. 28p. pap. 14.50 (978-1-61204-397-5(6), Strategic Bk. Publishing) Strategic Book Publishing & Rights Agency (SBPRA).
Bell, Braden. The Kindling. 2012. (YA). (978-1-4621-1027-8(4)) Cedar Fort, Inc./CFI Distribution.
—Luminescence. 2014. pap. 14.99 (978-1-4621-1405-4(9), Horizon Pubs.) Cedar Fort, Inc./CFI Distribution.
—Penumbras. 2013. (Middle School Magic Ser.). (ENG.). 305p. (J). (gr. 3-7). 14.99 (978-1-4621-1220-3(X), Sweetwater Bks.) Cedar Fort, Inc./CFI Distribution.
Bell, Cece. Chuck & Woodchuck. Bell, Cece, illus. 2016. (ENG., Illus.). 32p. (J). (gr. -1-3). 15.99 (978-0-7636-7524-0(5)) Candlewick Pr.
Bell, Eric. Alan Cole Doesn't Dance. 2018. (ENG.). 288p. (J). (gr. 3-7). 16.99 (978-0-06-256706-2(3), Tegen, Katherine Bks) HarperCollins Pubs.
—Alan Cole Is Not a Coward. (ENG.). (J). (gr. 3-7). 2018. 288p. pap. 9.99 (978-0-06-256704-8(7)) 2017. 272p. 16.99 (978-0-06-256702-4(0)) HarperCollins Pubs. (Tegen, Katherine Bks).
Bell, Kristen & Hart, Benjamin. The World Needs More Purple Schools. Wiseman, Daniel, illus. 2022. (My Purple World Ser.). 40p. (J). (gr. -1-2). 18.99 (978-0-593-43490-1(0)); (ENG.). lib. bdg. 21.99 (978-0-593-43491-8(9)) Random Hse. Children's Bks. (Random Hse. Bks. for Young Readers).
Bell, Rebecca. Capitano Ricco. Bell, Rebecca, illus. 2005. (Illus.). 36p. (J). 9.95 (978-1-934138-06-9(1)) Bouncing Ball Bks., Inc.
Bell, Shelia. The Life of Payne: Book II Fairley High Series. 2014. (ENG.). (YA). (gr. 7-18). pap. 9.95 (978-0-9838935-7-8(8), Seraphina) Bonita and Hodge Publishing Group.
Bellisario, Gina. An Extra-Ordinary Girl. Von Innerebner, Jessika, illus. 2016. (Ellie Ultra Ser.). (ENG.). 128p. (J). (gr. 1-3). lib. bdg. 25.99 (978-1-4965-3139-1(6), 132194, Stone Arch Bks.) Capstone.
—Queen of the Spelling Bee. Von Innerebner, Jessika, illus. 2016. (Ellie Ultra Ser.). (ENG.). 128p. (J). (gr. 1-3). lib. bdg. 25.99 (978-1-4965-3141-4(8), 132195, Stone Arch Bks.) Capstone.
—Superhero for President. von Innerebner, Jessika, illus. 2018. (Ellie Ultra Ser.). (ENG.). 128p. (J). (gr. 1-3). lib. bdg. 25.99 (978-1-4965-5239-6(3), 136264, Stone Arch Bks.) Capstone.
—Team Earth Takeover. von Innerebner, Jessika, illus. 2017. (Ellie Ultra Ser.). (ENG.). 128p. (J). (gr. 1-3). pap. 6.95 (978-1-4965-3147-6(7), 132201, Stone Arch Bks.) Capstone.

Benchmark Education. Bienvenido a nuestra escuela y el primer día de escuela de Katy: Teacher's Guide. 2004. (Fiction-To-Fact Ser.). (SPA.). instr.'s gde. ed. 2.00 net. *(978-1-4108-2370-0(9))* Benchmark Education Co.

Benchmark Education Co., LLC. At My School Big Book. 2014. (Shared Reading Foundations Ser.). (J). (gr. -1). *(978-1-4509-9427-9(X))* Benchmark Education Co.

Benjamin, Ali. The Next Great Paulie Fink. 2019. (ENG., illus.). 368p. (J). (gr. 3-7). 16.99 *(978-0-316-38088-1(1))* Little, Brown Bks. for Young Readers.

Benn, Iris H. Penelope's New Friends: Early Childhood Life Lesson. 2013. 32p. 29.95 *(978-1-4787-1210-7(4))* Outskirts Pr., Inc.

Bennett, Anna Elizabeth. Little Witch: 60th Anniversary Edition. Stone, Helen, illus. 60th anniv. ed. 2013. 128p. (J). (gr. k-3). pap. 12.95 *(978-1-61608-964-1(4)*, 608964, Sky Pony Pr.) Skyhorse Publishing Co., Inc.

Bennett, Cindy C. Geek Girl. 2011. 280p. (YA). pap. 15.99 *(978-1-59955-925-4(0))* Bonneville B.V. NLD. Dist: Cedar Fort, Inc./CFI Distribution.

Bennett, Olivia. The Allegra Biscotti Collection. 2010. (Allegra Biscotti Ser.: 1). (ENG., illus.). 256p. (J). (gr. 6-8). pap. 11.99 *(978-1-4022-4391-2(X))* Sourcebooks, Inc.

—Who What Wear: The Allegra Biscotti Collection. 2011. (Allegra Biscotti Ser.: 0). (ENG., illus.). 240p. (J). (gr. 5-7). pap. 12.99 *(978-1-4022-4392-9(8))* Sourcebooks, Inc.

Bennett, Sandra. Gingerbread Aliens. Welsh, Hayley, illus. 2012. (ENG.). 56p. (J). pap. *(978-0-9872356-4-0(8))* Australian Self Publishing Group/ Inspiring Pubs.

Benoit, Charles. Cold Calls. 2016. (ENG.). 304p. (YA). (gr. 7). pap. 8.99 *(978-0-544-54121-4(9)*, 1608880, Clarion Bks.) HarperCollins Pubs.

Benson, Amber. Among the Ghosts. Grace, Sina, illus. 2011. (ENG.). 256p. (J). (gr. 3-7). pap. 6.99 *(978-1-4169-9426-8(2)*, Aladdin) Simon & Schuster Children's Publishing.

Benson, Cindy. Chloe & Hairy Go to School. 2012. 32p. pap. 12.99 *(978-0-9855202-9-8(9))* Kids At Heart Publishing, LLC.

Benson, Donna. Spotlight on the Cupcakes: The Cupcakes Club #3. 2008. (ENG.). 115p. (J). pap. 7.95 *(978-0-9799159-2-5(9))* Pink Lemonade, LLC.

Bentley, Catherine & Bentley, Dawn. Hoppy Goes to School. Huerta, Catherine, illus. 2006. (Pet Tales Ser.). (ENG.). 32p. (J). 2.95 *(978-1-59249-558-0(3))* Soundprints.

Bentley, Dawn. Hoppy Goes to School. Huerta, Catherine, illus. 2006. (ENG.). 32p. (J). pap. 9.95 *(978-1-59249-559-7(1))*; (gr. -1-3). 4.95 *(978-1-59249-556-6(7))* Soundprints.

Bentley, Sue. Chocolate Wishes #1. Swan, Angela, illus. 2013. (Magic Bunny Ser.: 1). (ENG.). 128p. (J). (gr. 1-3). pap. 6.99 *(978-0-448-46727-6(5)*, Grosset & Dunlap) Penguin Young Readers Group.

—Classroom Chaos #2, 2 vols. Swan, Angela, illus. 2008. (Magic Kitten Ser.: 2). (ENG.). 128p. (J). (gr. 1-3). pap. 6.99 *(978-0-448-44999-9(4)*, Grosset & Dunlap) Penguin Young Readers Group.

Bently, Peter. Casketball Capers, 1. Harrison, Chris, illus. 2011. (Vampire School Ser.: 1). (ENG.). 96p. (J). (gr. 1-4). 17.44 *(978-0-8075-8462-0(2))* Whitman, Albert & Co.

Benton, Jim. Attack of the 50-Ft. Cupid. Benton, Jim, illus. 2004. (Franny K. Stein, Mad Scientist Ser.: 2). (ENG., illus.). 112p. (J). (gr. 2-5). 17.99 *(978-0-689-86292-2(X)*, Simon & Schuster Bks. For Young Readers) Simon & Schuster Bks. For Young Readers.

—Attack of the 50-Ft. Cupid. Benton, Jim, illus. 2011. (Franny K. Stein, Mad Scientist Ser.). (ENG., illus.). 112p. (J). (gr. 2-6). 31.36 *(978-1-59961-818-0(4)*, 7828, Chapter Bks.) Spotlight.

—The Fran with Four Brains. Benton, Jim, illus. 2011. (Franny K. Stein, Mad Scientist Ser.). (ENG., illus.). 112p. (J). (gr. 2-6). 31.36 *(978-1-59961-822-7(2)*, 7832, Chapter Bks.) Spotlight.

—The Fran with Four Brains. 2007. (Franny K. Stein, Mad Scientist Ser.: 6). lib. bdg. 16.00 *(978-1-4177-9038-8(5))* Turtleback.

—The Frandidate. Benton, Jim, illus. 2011. (Franny K. Stein, Mad Scientist Ser.). (ENG., illus.). 128p. (J). (gr. 2-6). 31.36 *(978-1-59961-823-4(0)*, 7833, Chapter Bks.) Spotlight.

—Franny K. Stein, Mad Scientist, 5 vols., Set. Benton, Jim, illus. Incl. Attack of the 50-Ft. Cupid. 112p. 31.36 *(978-1-59961-818-0(4)*, 7828); Fran with Four Brains. 112p. 31.36 *(978-1-59961-822-7(2)*, 7832); Frandidate. 128p. 31.36 *(978-1-59961-823-4(0)*, 7833); Invisible Fran. 112p. 31.36 *(978-1-59961-819-7(2)*, 7829); Lunch Walks among Us. 112p. 31.36 *(978-1-59961-817-3(6)*, 7827); (J). (gr. 2-6). (Franny K. Stein, Mad Scientist Ser.). (ENG., illus.). 2011. Set lib. bdg. 188.16 *(978-1-59961-816-6(8)*, 7826, Chapter Bks.) Spotlight.

—The Invisible Fran. Benton, Jim, illus. 2004. (Franny K. Stein, Mad Scientist Ser.: 3). (ENG., illus.). 112p. (J). (gr. 2-5). 17.99 *(978-0-689-86293-9(8)*, Simon & Schuster Bks. For Young Readers) Simon & Schuster Bks. For Young Readers.

—The Invisible Fran. Benton, Jim, illus. 2011. (Franny K. Stein, Mad Scientist Ser.). (ENG., illus.). 112p. (J). (gr. 2-6). 31.36 *(978-1-59961-819-7(2)*, 7829, Chapter Bks.) Spotlight.

—It's Not My Fault I Know Everything. 2009. (Dear Dumb Diary Ser.: 8). lib. bdg. 17.20 *(978-0-606-00142-7(5))* Turtleback.

—It's Not My Fault I Know Everything (Dear Dumb Diary #8) Benton, Jim, illus. 2009. (Dear Dumb Diary Ser.: 8). (ENG., illus.). 144p. (J). (gr. 4-7). 7.99 *(978-0-439-82597-9(0)*, Scholastic Paperbacks) Scholastic, Inc.

—Let's Pretend This Never Happened. Benton, Jim, illus. 2004. (Dear Dumb Diary Ser.: 1). (illus.). 95p. (gr. -1-2). 17.20 *(978-1-4176-3050-9(7))* Turtleback.

—Lunch Walks among Us. Benton, Jim, illus. (Franny K. Stein, Mad Scientist Ser.: 1). (ENG., illus.). 112p. (J). (gr. 2-5). 2004. mass mkt. 6.99 *(978-0-689-86295-3(4))* 2003. 17.99 *(978-0-689-86291-5(1))* Simon & Schuster Bks. For Young Readers. (Simon & Schuster Bks. For Young Readers).

—Lunch Walks among Us. Benton, Jim, illus. 2011. (Franny K. Stein, Mad Scientist Ser.). (ENG., illus.). 112p. (J). (gr. 2-6). 31.36 *(978-1-59961-817-3(6)*, 7827, Chapter Bks.) Spotlight.

—Lunch Walks among Us. Benton, Jim, illus. 2004. (Franny K. Stein, Mad Scientist Ser.: 1). (illus.). 102p. (gr. 2-5). lib. bdg. 16.00 *(978-1-4176-4054-6(5))* Turtleback.

—Never Do Anything, Ever (Dear Dumb Diary #4) Benton, Jim, illus. 2005. (Dear Dumb Diary Ser.: 4). (ENG., illus.). 144p. (J). (gr. 4-7). pap. 7.99 *(978-0-439-62908-9(X)*, Scholastic Paperbacks) Scholastic, Inc.

—Never Underestimate Your Dumbness (Dear Dumb Diary #7) Benton, Jim, illus. 2008. (Dear Dumb Diary Ser.: 7). (ENG., illus.). 160p. (J). (gr. 4-7). 7.99 *(978-0-439-82596-2(2))* Scholastic, Inc.

—Nobody's Perfect. I'm As Close As It Gets. 2013. (Dear Dumb Diary: Year Two Ser.: 3). lib. bdg. 16.00 *(978-0-606-31535-7(7))* Turtleback.

—The Problem with Here Is That It's Where I'm From. 2007. (Dear Dumb Diary Ser.: 6). 17.20 *(978-1-4177-8231-4(5))* Turtleback.

—School. Hasn't This Gone on Long Enough? 2012. (Dear Dumb Diary: Year Two Ser.: 1). lib. bdg. 16.00 *(978-0-606-23731-4(3))* Turtleback.

—The Super-Nice Are Super-Annoying. 2012. (Dear Dumb Diary: Year Two Ser.: 2). lib. bdg. 16.00 *(978-0-606-26188-3(5))* Turtleback.

—That's What Friends Aren't For. 2010. (Dear Dumb Diary Ser.: 09). lib. bdg. 17.20 *(978-0-606-06876-5(7))* Turtleback.

—The Worst Things in Life Are Also Free (Dear Dumb Diary #10) Benton, Jim, illus. 2010. (Dear Dumb Diary Ser.: 10). (ENG., illus.). 160p. (J). (gr. 4-7). pap. 7.99 *(978-0-545-11614-5(7)*, Scholastic Paperbacks) Scholastic, Inc.

Bentz, Lindsay. Really Good Friends. 2007. (ENG.). 182p. pap. 12.95 *(978-1-59526-720-7(4)*, Llumina Pr.) Aeon Publishing Inc.

Benz, Derek & Lewis, J. S. Grey Griffins: the Brimstone Key. 2011. (Grey Griffins: the Clockwork Chronicles Ser.: 1). (ENG.). 400p. (J). (gr. 3-7). pap. 19.99 *(978-0-316-04521-6(7))* Little, Brown Bks. for Young Readers.

—Grey Griffins: the Relic Hunters. 2012. (Grey Griffins: the Clockwork Chronicles Ser.: 2). (ENG.). 384p. (J). (gr. 3-7). pap. 19.99 *(978-0-316-04520-9(9))* Little, Brown Bks. for Young Readers.

Berenstain, Jan & Berenstain, Mike. The Berenstain Bears Come Clean for School. Berenstain, Jan & Berenstain, Mike, illus. 2011. (Berenstain Bears Ser.). (ENG., illus.). 32p. (J). (gr. -1-3). pap. 3.99 *(978-0-06-057395-9(3)*, HarperFestival) HarperCollins Pubs.

Berenstain, Jan, et al. The Berenstain Bears Go Back to School. Berenstain, Mike, illus. 2009. (Berenstain Bears Ser.). (ENG.). 32p. (J). (gr. -1-3). pap. 7.99 *(978-0-06-052675-7(0)*, HarperFestival) HarperCollins Pubs.

Berenstain, Mike. The Berenstain Bears Blessed Are the Peacemakers, 1 vol. 2014. (Berenstain Bears/Living Lights: a Faith Story Ser.). (ENG.). 24p. (J). pap. 5.99 *(978-0-310-73481-9(9))* Zonderkidz.

—The Berenstain Bears' Show-And-Tell. Berenstain, Mike, illus. 2017. (Berenstain Bears Ser.). (ENG., illus.). 24p. (J). (gr. -1-3). pap. 3.99 *(978-0-06-235031-2(5)*, HarperFestival) HarperCollins Pubs.

Berenstain, Mike, et al. The Berenstain Bears & the Golden Rule, 1 vol. 2008. (Berenstain Bears/Living Lights: a Faith Story Ser.). (ENG., illus.). 32p. (J). (gr. -1-2). pap. 4.99 *(978-0-310-71247-3(5))* Zonderkidz.

Berenzy, Alix. Sammy: The Classroom Guinea Pig. Berenzy, Alix, illus. 2008. (ENG., illus.). 32p. (J). (gr. k-3). pap. 9.99 *(978-0-312-37964-3(1)*, 900050314) Square Fish.

Berg, Dorlisa H. Fat Freddy Gets Fit. 2012. 158p. pap. 19.99 *(978-1-4797-6309-2(8))* Xlibris Corp.

Bergen, Lara. Drama Queen. 2007. 164p. (J). pap. *(978-0-545-03702-0(6))* Scholastic, Inc.

—Sophie the Awesome. Tallardy, Laura, illus. 2010. 99p. (J). *(978-0-545-24231-8(2))* Scholastic, Inc.

—Stand up & Cheer. 2013. 134p. (J). pap. *(978-0-545-56280-5(5))* Scholastic, Inc.

Berk, Josh. The Dark Days of Hamburger Halpin. 2011. 256p. (YA). (gr. 7). pap. 8.99 *(978-0-375-84625-0(5)*, Ember) Random Hse. Children's Bks.

Berk, Sheryl & Berk, Carrie. Ask Emma (Ask Emma Book 1) 2018. (Ask Emma Ser.: 1). (ENG.). 192p. (J). (gr. 3-7). 16.99 *(978-1-4998-0647-2(7)*, Yellow Jacket) Bonnier Publishing USA.

—Cupcakes Are Forever. 2017. (Cupcake Club Ser.: 12). 144p. (J). (gr. 3-7). pap. 7.99 *(978-1-4926-3748-6(3))* Sourcebooks, Inc.

—Designer Drama. 2016. (Fashion Academy Ser.: 3). 192p. (J). (gr. 5-8). pap. 10.99 *(978-1-4926-1353-4(3)*, 9781492613534) Sourcebooks, Inc.

—Fashion Academy. 2015. (Fashion Academy Ser.: 1). 160p. (J). (gr. 5-8). pap. 10.99 *(978-1-4926-0162-3(4))* Sourcebooks, Inc.

—Fashion Academy: Model Madness. 2017. (Fashion Academy Ser.: 4). 192p. (J). (gr. 5-8). pap. 10.99 *(978-1-4926-4496-5(X)*, 9781492644965) Sourcebooks, Inc.

Berke, Lindsey Jensen. Am I Pretty? 2013. 28p. 22.99 *(978-1-4808-0106-6(2))*; pap. 16.99 *(978-1-4808-0108-0(9))* Archway Publishing.

Berkowitz, Barbara. The Talent Show. 2009. 108p. 21.49 *(978-1-4389-9826-8(0))*; pap. 10.99 *(978-1-4389-9825-1(2))* AuthorHouse.

Berman, Ali. Misdirected: A Novel. 2014. (illus.). 288p. (YA). (gr. 7). 18.95 *(978-1-60980-573-9(9)*, Triangle Square) Seven Stories Pr.

Bernard, Norah S. CLIVE & BRIE. 2007. (ENG.). 176p. (YA). per. *(978-0-615-15932-4(X))* HELORO Publishing Group.

Bernstein, Ariel. Warren & Dragon 100 Friends. Malbrough, Mike, illus. 2018. (Warren & Dragon Ser.: 1). 96p. (J). (gr. k-3). 5.99 *(978-0-425-28846-7(3)*, Puffin Books); 14.99 *(978-0-425-28844-3(7)*, Viking Books for Young Readers) Penguin Young Readers Group.

Berry, Eileen M. Haiku on Your Shoes. Regan, Dana, illus. 2005. 56p. (J). (gr. -1-3). per. 7.49 *(978-1-59166-374-4(1))* BJU Pr.

Berry, Julie & Gardner, Sally Faye. The Rat Brain Fiasco. 2010. (Splurch Academy for Disruptive Boys Ser.: 1). (ENG.). 187p. (J). (gr. 4-6). 21.19 *(978-0-448-45359-0(2))* Penguin Young Readers Group.

Bertram, Debbie & Bloom, Susan. The Best Book to Read. Garland, Michael, illus. 2011. 32p. (J). (gr. -1-2). pap. 7.99 *(978-0-375-87300-3(7)*, Dragonfly Bks.) Random Hse. Children's Bks.

Bertrand, Diane Gonzales. The F Factor. 2010. 256p. (J). (gr. 6-18). pap. 12.95 *(978-1-55885-598-4(X)*, Piñata Books) Arte Publico Pr.

—El Momento de Trino. Sanmiguel, Rosario, tr. from ENG. 2006. (SPA.). 181p. (J). (gr. 3-7). per. 9.95 *(978-1-55885-473-4(8)*, Piñata Books) Arte Publico Pr.

Bertrand, Diane Gonzales, et al. Adelita & the Veggie Cousins / Adelita y las primas Verduritas. Rodriguez, Tina, illus. 2011. (SPA.). (J). 16.95 *(978-1-55885-699-8(4)*, Piñata Books) Arte Publico Pr.

Besser, Kenneth/R. Arnie Carver & the Plague of Demeverde. 2007. (illus.). x, 338p. (J). *(978-1-934316-02-3(4))* RTMC Organization, LLC.

Bessler, edward. A Smile for Billy. 2008. 175p. pap. 13.95 *(978-1-4357-4439-4(X))* Lulu Pr., Inc.

Best, Cari. My Three Best Friends & Me, Zulay. Brantley-Newton, Vanessa, illus. 2015. (ENG.). 40p. (J). (gr. -1-3). 19.99 *(978-0-374-38819-5(9)*, 900031513, Farrar, Straus & Giroux (BYR)) Farrar, Straus & Giroux.

Bethune, Helen. Way Back When, 1 vol. rev. ed. 2013. (Literary Text Ser.). (ENG., illus.). 28p. (gr. 2-3). pap. 9.99 *(978-1-4333-5570-7(1))* Teacher Created Materials, Inc.

Bette, Grandma. The Excellent Adventures of Max & Madison: Bedtime stories for Youngsters. 2012. 116p. pap. 42.95 *(978-1-4525-0432-2(6))* Balboa Pr.

Beverly, Cleary. Dear Mr. Henshaw. 2014. (Cleary Reissue Ser.). (ENG.). 160p. (J). (gr. 7-12). 10.24 *(978-1-63245-195-8(6))* Lectorum Pubns., Inc.

Bhathena, Tanaz. The Beauty of the Moment. 2020. (ENG.). 400p. (YA). pap. 10.99 *(978-1-250-23383-7(6)*, 900186335) Square Fish.

Bianchi, John. Bird at School. 2015. (1-3Y Bird, Bunny & Bear Ser.). (ENG., illus.). 16p. (J). pap. 8.00 *(978-1-63437-438-5(X))* American Reading Co.

—Snowed in at Pokeweed Public School. (illus.). 24p. (J). (gr. 1-5). *(978-1-894323-34-5(3))* Pokeweed Pr.

Biggs, Brian. Time for School! (a Tinyville Town Book) 2017. (Tinyville Town Ser.). (ENG., illus.). 32p. (J). (gr. -1-k). 16.95 *(978-1-4197-2566-1(1)*, 1119301, Abrams Appleseed) Abrams, Inc.

Bildner, Phil. Busted. 2013. (ENG., illus.). 256p. (YA). (gr. 9). pap. 16.99 *(978-1-4814-2171-3(9)*, Simon & Schuster Bks. For Young Readers) Simon & Schuster Bks. For Young Readers.

—A High Five for Glenn Burke. 2020. (ENG.). 288p. (J). 17.99 *(978-0-374-31273-2(7)*, 900201599, Farrar, Straus & Giroux (BYR)) Farrar, Straus & Giroux.

—A High Five for Glenn Burke. 2021. (ENG.). 304p. (J). pap. 7.99 *(978-1-250-76328-0(2)*, 900201600) Square Fish.

—A Whole New Ballgame. 2016. (Rip & Red Ser.: 1). (J). lib. bdg. 17.20 *(978-0-606-38553-4(3))* Turtleback.

Biller, Maxim. Poppy's Biggest Wish. 2006. (illus.). 32p. (J). (gr. -1-k). 17.99 *(978-0-7475-8236-6(X)*, Bloomsbury Children's Bks.) Bloomsbury Publishing Plc GBR. Dist: Independent Pubs. Group.

Billingsley, ReShonda Tate. Friends 'til the End. 2009. (Good Girlz Ser.: 6). (ENG., illus.). 174p. pap. 14.99 *(978-1-4165-5877-4(2)*, Gallery Bks.) Gallery Bks.

Bingham, Mark Jay. Woolie & the Bully. 2013. 52p. 30.95 *(978-1-4582-0843-9(5))*; pap. 23.95 *(978-1-4582-0844-6(3))* Author Solutions, LLC. (Abbott Pr.).

Binns, B. A. Pull. 2010. 310p. (YA). (gr. 9-18). 16.95 *(978-1-934813-43-0(5))* Westside Bks.

Binns, B. A. & McKenzie, C. Lee. The Princess of Las Pulgas. 2010. 334p. (YA). (gr. 8-18). 16.95 *(978-1-934813-44-7(3))* Westside Bks.

Birchall, Katy. The It Girl. 2016. (It Girl Ser.: 1). (ENG., illus.). 352p. (J). (gr. 4-8). 16.99 *(978-1-4814-6362-1(4)*, Aladdin) Simon & Schuster Children's Publishing.

—Team Awkward. 2018. (It Girl Ser.: 2). (ENG.). 320p. (J). (gr. 4-8). pap. 7.99 *(978-1-4814-6364-5(0)*, Aladdin) Simon & Schuster Children's Publishing.

—Team Awkward. 2017. (It Girl Ser.: 2). (ENG., illus.). 304p. (YA). (gr. 4-8). 16.99 *(978-1-4814-6365-2(9)*, Simon & Schuster/Paula Wiseman Bks.) Simon & Schuster/Paula Wiseman Bks.

Birdseye, Tom. Attack of the Mutant Underwear. 2006. (ENG., illus.). 208p. (J). (gr. 3-7). 7.99 *(978-0-14-240734-9(8)*, Puffin Books) Penguin Young Readers Group.

Birney, Betty G. Friendship According to Humphrey. 2006. (Humphrey Ser.: 2). (ENG.). 176p. (J). (gr. 3-7). 7.99 *(978-0-14-240633-5(3)*, Puffin Books) Penguin Young Readers Group.

—Friendship According to Humphrey. 2007. (Humphrey Ser.). 150p. (gr. 4-7). 16.00 *(978-0-7569-8277-5(4))* Perfection Learning Corp.

—Humphrey's Big Birthday Bash. Burris, Priscilla, illus. 2018. (Humphrey's Tiny Tales Ser.: 8). (ENG.). 96p. (J). (gr. k-3). 5.99 *(978-1-5247-3721-4(6)*, Puffin Books) Penguin Young Readers Group.

—Humphrey's Mixed-Up Magic Trick. Burris, Priscilla, illus. 2016. (Humphrey's Tiny Tales Ser.: 5). (ENG.). 96p. (J). (gr. k-3). 6.99 *(978-0-14-751461-5(4)*, Puffin Books) Penguin Young Readers Group.

—Humphrey's Playful Puppy Problem. Burris, Priscilla, illus. 2014. (Humphrey's Tiny Tales Ser.: 2). (ENG.). 96p. (J). (gr. k-3). pap. 6.99 *(978-0-14-751484-4(3)*, Puffin Books) Penguin Young Readers Group.

—Humphrey's Really Wheely Racing Day. Burris, Priscilla, illus. 2014. (Humphrey's Tiny Tales Ser.: 1). (ENG.). 96p. (J). (gr. k-3). pap. 6.99 *(978-0-14-751485-1(1)*, Puffin Books) Penguin Young Readers Group.

—Humphrey's School Fair Surprise. 2016. (Humphrey's Tiny Tales Ser.: 04). lib. bdg. 14.75 *(978-0-606-38423-0(5))* Turtleback.

—Life According to Og the Frog. 2019. (Og the Frog Ser.: 1). (ENG.). 192p. (J). (gr. 3-7). 7.99 *(978-1-5247-3996-6(0)*, Puffin Books) Penguin Young Readers Group.

—Mysteries According to Humphrey. 2013. (According to Humphrey Ser.: 8). lib. bdg. 16.00 *(978-0-606-31699-6(X))* Turtleback.

—The Princess & the Peabodys. 2007. (ENG.). 256p. (J). (gr. 5-9). 15.99 *(978-0-06-084720-3(4))* HarperCollins Pubs.

—School Days According to Humphrey. 2012. (Humphrey Ser.: 7). (ENG.). 176p. (J). (gr. 3-7). pap. 7.99 *(978-0-14-242106-2(5)*, Puffin Books) Penguin Young Readers Group.

—School Days According to Humphrey. 2012. (According to Humphrey Ser.: 7). lib. bdg. 16.00 *(978-0-606-26085-5(4))* Turtleback.

—Secrets According to Humphrey. 2015. (Humphrey Ser.: 10). (ENG.). 160p. (J). (gr. 3-7). 6.99 *(978-0-14-751431-8(2)*, Puffin Books) Penguin Young Readers Group.

—Surprises According to Humphrey. 2009. (Humphrey Ser.: 4). (ENG.). 160p. (J). (gr. 3-7). 6.99 *(978-0-14-241296-1(1)*, Puffin Books) Penguin Young Readers Group.

—Surprises According to Humphrey. 2009. (According to Humphrey Ser.: 4). lib. bdg. 16.00 *(978-0-606-00906-5(X))* Turtleback.

—Trouble According to Humphrey. 2008. (Humphrey Ser.: 3). (ENG.). 192p. (J). (gr. 3-7). 6.99 *(978-0-14-241089-9(6)*, Puffin Books) Penguin Young Readers Group.

—Winter According to Humphrey. 2013. (Humphrey Ser.: 9). (ENG.). 176p. (J). (gr. 3-7). pap. 7.99 *(978-0-14-242759-0(4)*, Puffin Books) Penguin Young Readers Group.

—Winter According to Humphrey. 2013. (According to Humphrey Ser.: 9). lib. bdg. 16.00 *(978-0-606-32138-9(1))* Turtleback.

—The World According to Humphrey. (Humphrey Ser.: 1). (ENG.). (J). (gr. 3-7). 2005. 144p. pap. 7.99 *(978-0-14-240352-5(0)*, Puffin Books) 2004. 128p. 16.99 *(978-0-399-24198-7(1)*, G.P. Putnam's Sons Books for Young Readers) Penguin Young Readers Group.

—The World According to Humphrey. 2005. (According to Humphrey Ser.: 1). lib. bdg. 16.00 *(978-1-4176-7532-6(2))* Turtleback.

Black, Holly. The Iron Trial. 2014. (Magisterium Ser.: Bk. 1). pap. *(978-0-545-84067-5(8)*, Scholastic Pr.) Scholastic, Inc.

Black, Holly & Clare, Cassandra. The Bronze Key (Magisterium #3), 1 vol. 2017. (Magisterium Ser.: 3). (ENG., illus.). 256p. (J). (gr. 3-7). pap. 8.99 *(978-0-545-52232-8(3)*, Scholastic Pr.) Scholastic, Inc.

—The Golden Tower (Magisterium #5) 2018. (Magisterium Ser.: 5). (ENG., illus.). 256p. (J). (gr. 3-7). 17.99 *(978-0-545-52240-3(4)*, Scholastic Pr.) Scholastic, Inc.

—The Iron Trial. 2014. (ENG., illus.). 320p. (J). *(978-0-85753-250-3(2)*, Scholastic Pr.) Scholastic, Inc.

—The Iron Trial. 2015. (Magisterium Ser.: 1). lib. bdg. 18.40 *(978-0-606-37028-8(5))* Turtleback.

—The Iron Trial (Magisterium #1), 1 vol. 2015. (Magisterium Ser.: 1). (ENG.). 304p. (J). (gr. 3-7). pap. 8.99 *(978-0-545-52226-7(9)*, Scholastic Pr.) Scholastic, Inc.

Black, Yelena. Dance of Shadows. 2014. (Dance of Shadows Ser.). (ENG., illus.). 384p. (YA). (gr. 7). pap. 9.99 *(978-1-61963-185-4(7)*, 900125810, Bloomsbury USA Childrens) Bloomsbury Publishing USA.

Blackburn, Sheila M. Stewie Scraps & the Super Sleigh. 2008. 72p. pap. *(978-1-903853-89-4(3))* Brilliant Pubns.

Blackwood, Sage. Miss Ellicott's School for the Magically Minded. (ENG.). 368p. (J). (gr. 3-7). 2019. pap. 6.99 *(978-0-06-240264-6(1))* 2017. (illus.). 16.99 *(978-0-06-240263-9(3))* HarperCollins Pubs. (Tegen, Katherine Bks).

Blade, Adam. Team Hero: Falcon of Fury: Series 2 Book 3, Bk. 3. 2020. (Team Hero Ser.). (ENG., illus.). 144p. (J). (gr. 2-4). 7.99 *(978-1-4083-4363-0(0)*, Orchard Bks.) Hachette Children's Group GBR. Dist: Hachette Bk. Group.

—Team Hero: Fight for the Hidden City: Series 2 Book 1 with Bonus Extra Content!, Bk. 1. 2020. (Team Hero Ser.). (ENG., illus.). 176p. (J). (gr. 2-4). 7.99 *(978-1-4083-4359-3(2)*, Orchard Bks.) Hachette Children's Group GBR. Dist: Hachette Bk. Group.

Blagden, Scott. Dear Life, You Suck. 2015. (ENG.). 320p. (YA). (gr. 9). pap. 9.99 *(978-0-544-33621-6(6)*, 1584167, Clarion Bks.) HarperCollins Pubs.

Blake, Jillian. Antisocial. 2018. (ENG.). 256p. (YA). (gr. 9). pap. 9.99 *(978-1-101-93899-7(4)*, Ember) Random Hse. Children's Bks.

Blake, Stéphanie. No Quiero Ir a la Escuela. 2007. (SPA., illus.). 40p. (gr. k-2). 17.99 *(978-84-8470-268-9(5))* Corimbo, Editorial S.L. ESP. Dist: Lectorum Pubns., Inc.

Blanc, Katherine. Melvin the Mouth. Ebbeler, Jeffrey, illus. 2017. 32p. (J). (gr. -1-3). lib. bdg. 16.99 *(978-1-58089-714-3(2))* Charlesbridge Publishing, Inc.

Bland, Anita D. Matilda's Apple. 2011. 24p. pap. 15.99 *(978-1-4653-4329-1(6))* Xlibris Corp.

Blanda, Dominick. The Super Duper Kid Fantastic. 2009. 32p. pap. 14.99 *(978-1-4389-4566-8(3))* AuthorHouse.

Blankenship, Paula. We Both Read-Lulu's Lost Shoes. Reinhart, Larry, illus. (We Both Read Ser.). (J). (gr. k-3). 2011. (ENG.). 48p. 17.44 *(978-1-891327-55-1(0))* 2005. 44p. pap. 5.99 *(978-1-891327-56-8(9))* Treasure Bay, Inc.

Bledsoe Jr, Reuben Booo. Bullybuster. 2013. (ENG.). 98p. (J). pap. 14.95 *(978-1-4787-1215-2(5))* Outskirts Pr., Inc.

Blejwas, Emily. Like Nothing Amazing Ever Happened. 2020. (ENG.). 224p. (J). (gr. 4-7). 19.99 *(978-1-9848-4849-9(6)*, Delacorte Bks. for Young Readers) Random Hse. Children's Bks.

Bliss, Bryan. We'll Fly Away. (ENG.). 416p. (YA). (gr. 9). 2019. pap. 10.99 *(978-0-06-249428-3(7))* 2018. 18.99 *(978-0-06-249427-6(9))* HarperCollins Pubs. (Greenwillow Bks.).

Bitt, Natalie. The Truth about Leaving. 2019. (ENG.). 304p. (YA). pap. 12.99 *(978-1-948705-09-7(5))* Amberjack Publishing Co.

Bloom, Steve. The Stand-In. (ENG.). 360p. (YA). (gr. 8-12). 2018. pap. 9.99 *(978-1-5415-1484-3(X)*, ef16da22-6bda-4a9a-b3cc-fb51cb52fdb1) 2016. 18.99 *(978-1-5124-1023-5(3)*, ad1a2cb5-3967-4d9a-95c9-732e41848b05) 2016. E-Book 29.32 *(978-1-5124-1121-8(3))* Lerner Publishing Group. (Carolrhoda Lab™).

Bloom, Suzanne. The Bus for Us. 2013. (ENG., illus.). 32p. (J). (gr. k-2). pap. 8.99 *(978-1-62091-441-0(7)*, Astra Young Readers) Astra Publishing Hse.

Bloor, Edward. London Calling. 2008. (illus.). 304p. (YA). (gr. 7-9). per. 8.99 *(978-0-375-84363-1(9)*, Ember) Random Hse. Children's Bks.

S

—Story Time. 2005. (ENG., Illus.). 444p. (YA). (gr. 7-12). reprint ed. pap. 8.99 *(978-0-15-205222-5(4),* 1195738, Clarion Bks.) HarperCollins Pubs.
Blount, Patty. Send. 2012. (ENG.). 304p. (YA). (gr. 7-12). pap. 12.99 *(978-1-4022-7337-7(1))* Sourcebooks, Inc.
—Someone I Used to Know. 2018. (ENG.). 384p. (YA). (gr. 8-12). pap. 10.99 *(978-1-4926-3281-8(3))* Sourcebooks, Inc.
Blume-D'Ausilio, Carole Ed. D. The Bronx Bully. 2011. 28p. pap. 15.99 *(978-1-4628-5235-2(1))* Xlibris Corp.
Blume, Judy. Cool Zone with the Pain & the Great One. Stevenson, James, illus. 2009. (Pain & the Great One Ser.: 2). (ENG.). 128p. (J). (gr. 3-7). 5.99 *(978-0-440-42093-4(8),* Yearling) Random Hse. Children's Bks.
—Friend or Fiend? with the Pain & the Great One. Stevenson, James, illus. 2010. (Pain & the Great One Ser.: 4). (ENG.). 128p. (J). (gr. 3-7). 5.99 *(978-0-440-42095-8(4),* Yearling) Random Hse. Children's Bks.
—Going, Going, Gone! with the Pain & the Great One. Stevenson, James, illus. 2010. (Pain & the Great One Ser.: 3). (ENG.). 128p. (J). (gr. 3-7). 5.99 *(978-0-440-42094-1(6),* Yearling) Random Hse. Children's Bks.
—Just As Long As We're Together. 2010. (ENG.). 288p. (YA). (gr. 7). pap. 10.99 *(978-0-385-73988-7(5),* Delacorte Bks. for Young Readers) Random Hse. Children's Bks.
—The One in the Middle Is the Green Kangaroo. Ohi, Debbie Ridpath, illus. 2014. (ENG.). 48p. (J). (gr. 1-5). pap. 5.99 *(978-1-4814-1131-8(4),* Atheneum Bks. for Young Readers) Simon & Schuster Children's Publishing.
BMI Staff, compiled by. Fear Street Collection - Set, 98 vols. 2009. (YA). 114.81 *(978-1-60884-415-9(3))* BMI Educational Services.
Boatwright-Cook, Jane. The Skeleton Leaf Stories: Behind the Shutters. 2012. 124p. 23.99 *(978-1-4772-1346-9(5));* pap. 14.95 *(978-1-4772-1347-6(3))* AuthorHouse.
Boelts, Maribeth. Those Shoes. Jones, Noah Z., illus. 2009. (ENG.). 40p. (J). (gr. k-3). pap. 8.99 *(978-0-7636-4284-6(3))* Candlewick Pr.
Bogaerts, Jorge. El Dia Que Hizo Mucho Viento. (SPA.). 112p. (J). *(978-84-207-3535-1(3))* Grupo Anaya, S.A.
Boggess, Eileen. Mia the Meek. 2006. (ENG.). 166p. (J). (gr. 6-9). per. 14.95 *(978-1-890862-47-3(9),* 19189455-bd03-4ce0-bb2b-b2fc6ec8ccd7) Bancroft Pr.
Boggs, Garnett Reed. Totally Katy: Katy Is Always Planning, but Just How Well do Her Plans Work Out? 2011. 108p. (gr. 4-6). pap. 10.95 *(978-1-4634-3233-1(X))* AuthorHouse.
Bolger, Kevin. Zombiekins 2. Blecha, Aaron, illus. 2011. (J). 10.99 *(978-1-59514-432-4(3),* Razorbill) Penguin Publishing Group.
Bond, Felicia. The Halloween Play. Bond, Felicia, illus. 2008. Orig. Title: The Halloween Performance. (ENG., Illus.). 32p. (J). (gr. -1-1). pap. 7.99 *(978-0-06-135796-1(0),* HarperCollins) HarperCollins Pubs.
Bond, Gwenda. Double Down. 2016. (Lois Lane Ser.). (ENG.). 384p. (YA). (gr. 9-12). 16.95 *(978-1-63079-038-7(9),* 130898, Switch Pr.) Capstone.
—Fallout. (Lois Lane Ser.). (ENG.). 304p. (YA). (gr. 9-12). 2016. pap. 9.95 *(978-1-63079-006-6(0),* 127340) 2015. 16.95 *(978-1-63079-005-9(2),* 127326) Capstone. (Switch Pr.).
Bond, Roland. Harvey Plumstead & the Dinnertime Dog. 2012. (Illus.). 96p. (gr. 4-18). pap. 13.66 *(978-1-4772-4317-6(8))* AuthorHouse.
Bondor-Stone, Annabeth & White, Connor. Jaclyn Hyde. 2019. (ENG.). 240p. (J). (gr. 3-7). 16.99 *(978-0-06-267145-5(6),* HarperCollins) HarperCollins Pubs.
Bonnett-Rampersaud, Louise. The Great Sleep-Under, 0 vols. McHeffey, Adam, illus. 2016. (Secret Knock Club Ser.: 4). (ENG.). 112p. (J). (gr. 1-4). pap. 9.99 *(978-1-5039-5063-4(8),* 9781503950634, Two Lions) Amazon Publishing.
BookSource Staff, compiled by. Robot Rumble. 2013. (Hardy Boys: Secret Files Ser.: 11). lib. bdg. 16.00 *(978-0-606-27027-4(2))* Turtleback.
Booth, Anne. The Christmas Fairy. Beardshaw, Rosalind, illus. 2017. (ENG.). 32p. (J). (gr. -1-2). 15.99 *(978-0-7636-9629-0(3))* Candlewick Pr.
Borden, Louise. The a+ Custodian. Gustavson, Adam, illus. 2004. (ENG.). 40p. (J). (gr. 2-5). 19.99 *(978-0-689-84995-4(8),* McElderry, Margaret K. Bks.) McElderry, Margaret K. Bks.
—The Last Day of School. Gustavson, Adam, illus. 2006. (ENG.). 40p. (J). (gr. 2-5). 19.99 *(978-0-689-86869-6(3),* McElderry, Margaret K. Bks.) McElderry, Margaret K. Bks.
—The Lost-And-Found Tooth. Gustavson, Adam, illus. 2008. (ENG.). 40p. (J). (gr. 2-5). 16.99 *(978-1-4169-1814-1(0),* McElderry, Margaret K. Bks.) McElderry, Margaret K. Bks.
—Off to First Grade. Rankin, Joan, illus. 2008. (ENG.). 40p. (J). (gr. -1-3). 19.99 *(978-0-689-87395-9(6),* McElderry, Margaret K. Bks.) McElderry, Margaret K. Bks.
Bossley, Michele Martin. Swiped, 1 vol. 2011. (Orca Currents Ser.). (ENG.). 109p. (J). (gr. 6-8). 26.19 *(978-1-55143-652-4(3))* Orca Bk. Pubs. USA.
Bost, Richard. Taekwon Tales. 2012. 120p. pap. 9.99 *(978-0-9848626-1-0(7))* ImBost Inc.
Bottner, Barbara. Miss Brooks Loves Books (and I Don't) 2016. (CHI.). 32p. (J). (gr. k-3). *(978-7-5552-3723-5(7))* Qingdao Publishing Hse.
—Miss Brooks Loves Books (and I Don't) Emberley, Michael, illus. 2018. (ENG.). 32p. (J). (gr. -1-2). 8.99 *(978-1-9848-5210-6(8),* Dragonfly Bks.) Random Hse. Children's Bks.
—Priscilla Gorilla. Emberley, Michael, illus. 2017. (ENG.). 40p. (J). (gr. -1-2). 17.99 *(978-1-4814-5897-9(3),* Atheneum/Caitlyn Dlouhy Books) Simon & Schuster Children's Publishing.
Bouchard, John L. A Taste of Soda. 2006. 92p. pap. 16.95 *(978-1-4241-2482-4(4))* PublishAmerica, Inc.
Boudreau, Helene. Real Mermaids Don't Need High Heels. 2013. (ENG.). 240p. (J). (gr. 4-8). pap. 10.99 *(978-1-4022-6458-0(5))* Sourcebooks, Inc.
Bowe, Julie. Dance Fever. 2017. (Victoria Torres, Unfortunately Average Ser.). (ENG.). 160p. (J). (gr. 4-8). lib. bdg. 27.99 *(978-1-4965-3819-2(6),* 133118, Stone Arch Bks.) Capstone.
—Face the Music. 2015. (Victoria Torres, Unfortunately Average Ser.). (ENG., Illus.). 160p. (J). (gr. 4-8). pap. 5.95 *(978-1-4965-0538-5(7),* 128610, Stone Arch Bks.) Capstone.
—Formula for Friends. 2015. (Victoria Torres, Unfortunately Average Ser.). (ENG., Illus.). 160p. (J). (gr. 4-8). pap. 5.95 *(978-1-4965-0539-2(5),* 128611, Stone Arch Bks.) Capstone.
—Friends for Keeps: My Forever Friends. 2012. (Friends for Keeps Ser.: 4). (ENG.). 240p. (J). (gr. 3-7). pap. 6.99 *(978-0-14-242104-8(9),* Puffin Books) Penguin Young Readers Group.
—My Last Best Friend. 2008. (Friends for Keeps Ser.). (ENG., Illus.). 160p. (J). (gr. 3-7). pap. 6.99 *(978-0-15-206197-5(5),* 1198599, Clarion Bks.) HarperCollins Pubs.
—My New Best Friend. 2010. (Friends for Keeps Ser.). (ENG.). 192p. (J). (gr. 3-7). pap. 7.99 *(978-0-547-32869-0(9),* 1416982, Clarion Bks.) HarperCollins Pubs.
—Pompom Problems. 2015. (Victoria Torres, Unfortunately Average Ser.). (ENG., Illus.). 160p. (J). (gr. 4-8). lib. bdg. 27.99 *(978-1-4965-0532-3(8),* 128604, Stone Arch Bks.) Capstone.
—So Much Drama. 2016. (Victoria Torres, Unfortunately Average Ser.). (ENG., Illus.). 160p. (J). (gr. 4-8). pap. 5.95 *(978-1-4965-3807-9(2),* 133115); lib. bdg. 27.99 *(978-1-4965-3799-7(8),* 133112) Capstone. (Stone Arch Bks.).
—Vicka for President! 2016. (Victoria Torres, Unfortunately Average Ser.). (ENG., Illus.). 160p. (J). (gr. 4-8). lib. bdg. 27.99 *(978-1-4965-3800-0(5),* 133113, Stone Arch Bks.) Capstone.
Bowen, Fred. Speed Demon, 1 vol. 2019. (Fred Bowen Sports Story Ser.: 23). (Illus.). 144p. (J). (gr. 2-6). 14.95 *(978-1-68263-076-1(5))* Peachtree Publishing Co. Inc.
—Throwing Heat, 1 vol. 2010. (Fred Bowen Sports Story Ser.: 12). 128p. (J). (gr. 2-6). pap. 6.99 *(978-1-56145-540-9(7))* Peachtree Publishing Co. Inc.
Bowie, Barbara Kay. Ready for School: An Activity & Story Book for Parents & Children Entering Kindergarten. 2004. (J). 7.95 *(978-0-9713450-1-0(5))* Educational Expertise, LLC.
Bowyer, Clifford B. The Darkness Within: The Imperium Saga: the Adventures of Kyria, 12 vols., Vol. 9. Brigman, June, illus. 2009. (Imperium Saga: 9). (ENG.). (J). 5.99 *(978-0-9787782-4-8(3))* Silver Leaf Bks., LLC.
Bracken, Beth. The Little Bully, 1 vol. Bell, Jennifer A., illus. 2012. (Little Boost Ser.). (ENG.). 32p. (J). (gr. -1-1). lib. bdg. 23.99 *(978-1-4048-6795-6(3),* 116233, Picture Window Bks.) Capstone.
—The Social Butterfly. Cardoso, Sofia, illus. 2018. (Little Boost Ser.). (ENG.). 32p. (J). (gr. -1-2). lib. bdg. 23.99 *(978-1-5158-1696-6(6),* 136371, Picture Window Bks.) Capstone.
—Too Shy for Show-And-Tell, 1 vol. Bell, Jennifer A., illus. (Little Boost Ser.). (ENG.). 32p. (J). (gr. -1-1). 2012. 7.95 *(978-1-4048-7418-3(6),* 119306) 2011. lib. bdg. 23.99 *(978-1-4048-6654-6(X),* 114891) Capstone. (Picture Window Bks.).
Braden, Ann. The Benefits of Being an Octopus. 2018. 256p. (J). (gr. 3-7). 16.99 *(978-1-5107-3748-8(0),* Sky Pony Pr.) Skyhorse Publishing Co., Inc.
Bradley, Timothy J. Infestation. Bradley, Timothy J., illus. 2013. (ENG., Illus.). 192p. (J). (gr. 3-7). pap. 5.99 *(978-0-545-45904-4(4))* Scholastic, Inc.
Bradman, Tony. Flora the Fairy's Magic Spells: Green Banana (Reading Ladder Level 1) Carlow, Emma, illus. 2nd ed. 2016. (Reading Ladder Level 1 Ser.). (ENG.). 48p. (gr. k-2). 4.99 *(978-1-4052-8227-7(4),* Reading Ladder) Farshore GBR. Dist: HarperCollins Pubs.
—Goldilocks & the Just Right Club. Warburton, Sarah, illus. 2014. (After Happily Ever After Ser.). (ENG.). 56p. (J). (gr. 3-6). pap. 4.95 *(978-1-4342-7963-7(4),* 124712, Stone Arch Bks.) Capstone.
Bradshaw, Jennifer. No School Today, My Son. 2009. 24p. pap. 11.49 *(978-1-4490-4174-8(4))* AuthorHouse.
Brady, Bill. A Charm for Jo. Brady, Laurie, illus. l.t. ed. 2005. (Turtle Books). 32p. (J). (gr. 2-5). lib. bdg. 15.95 *(978-0-944727-48-5(4))* Jason & Nordic Pubs.
Brady, Bill & Brady, Laurie. A Charm for Jo. Fargo, Todd, illus. l.t. ed. 2005. (Turtle Bks.). (ENG.). 32p. (J). (gr. 2-5). pap. 9.95 *(978-0-944727-47-8(6))* Jason & Nordic Pubs.
Braem, Viola Brunette. Woodside: A Novel about the Years from 1930 to 1943. A Fictionalized Autobiography & Funny Events in a One-room School. 2005. (YA). per. 14.95 *(978-0-9772315-0-8(X))* EPS Digital.
Brager, Allison. Off-Colored Rainbows. 2005. 64p. pap. 16.95 *(978-1-4241-0267-9(7))* PublishAmerica, Inc.
Braidich, Victoria. Monday with Meg, 1 vol. 2006. (Neighborhood Readers Ser.). (ENG.). 12p. (gr. k-1). pap. 5.90 *(978-1-4042-6459-5(0),* e3e562d3-16d5-408a-8351-792ecb72cfe9, Rosen Classroom) Rosen Publishing Group, Inc., The.
Bramwell, Wendie & Normand, Bridgid. Rhymitis. Kim, Julie J., tr. Kim, Julie J., illus. 2003. 32p. (J). pap. *(978-0-9741388-8-6(6))* Committee for Children.
Brande, Robin. Fat Cat. 2011.Tr. of Fat Cat. (ENG.). 336p. (YA). (gr. 8-12). lib. bdg. 26.19 *(978-0-375-94449-9(4),* Knopf Bks. for Young Readers) Random Hse. Children's Bks.
Brandt, Courney. A Fine Line. 2008. 164p. pap. 12.95 *(978-0-595-52500-3(8))* iUniverse, Inc.
Brannon, Pat. Filthy Farley O'Charlie Mcbarley. 2007. 48p. per. 16.95 *(978-1-4241-8904-5(7))* PublishAmerica, Inc.
Brashares, Ann. The Here & Now. 2014. 242p. (YA). *(978-0-385-39008-8(4),* Delacorte Pr) Random House Publishing Group.
—The Here & Now. 2015. (ENG.). 256p. (YA). (gr. 7). pap. 10.99 *(978-0-385-73683-1(5),* Ember) Random Hse. Children's Bks.
Braun, Eric. Rumpelstiltskin: An Interactive Fairy Tale Adventure. Brown, Alan, illus. 2017. (You Choose: Fractured Fairy Tales Ser.). (ENG.). 112p. (J). (gr. 3-7). pap. 6.95 *(978-1-5157-8777-8(X),* 136328); lib. bdg. 32.65 *(978-1-5157-8775-4(3),* 136326) Capstone. (Capstone Pr.).
Braver, Vanita. Madison & the Two Wheeler, 1 vol. DiRocco, Carl, illus. 2007. (ENG.). 32p. (J). (gr. -1-3). 14.95 *(978-1-59572-109-9(6))* Star Bright Bks., Inc.
Bray, Libba. A Great & Terrible Beauty. 2005. (Gemma Doyle Trilogy Ser.: 1). (ENG.). 432p. (YA). (gr. 7). reprint ed. pap. 10.99 *(978-0-385-73231-4(7),* Ember) Random Hse. Children's Bks.
Brazil, Angela. The Jolliest School of All. 2017. (ENG., Illus.). (J). 24.95 *(978-1-374-85154-2(X));* pap. 14.95 *(978-1-374-85153-5(1))* Capital Communications, Inc.
Breisacher, Cathy. Petunia Pepper's Picture Day. Elden, Christian, illus. 2010. 32p. (J). 14.99 *(978-1-59317-397-5(0))* Warner Pr., Inc.
Bremauntz, M. The Adventures of Marcela & Little Joey: Little Joey Loves Bugs. 2010. 32p. 17.25 *(978-1-4269-4417-8(9))* Trafford Publishing.
Brenner, Emily. On the First Day of Grade School. Whatley, Bruce, illus. 2004. 32p. (J). (gr. -1-1). lib. bdg. 16.89 *(978-0-06-051041-1(2))* HarperCollins Pubs.
Brent-Dyer, Elinor M. Bride Leads the Chalet School. 2011. (ENG., Illus.). 287p. (YA). (gr. 8-12). pap. *(978-1-84745-103-3(9))* Girls Gone By.
Brewer, Elly. Jerry & the Jannans. 2006. 320p. (J). (gr. 4-7). pap. 11.99 *(978-0-7475-8213-7(0))* Bloomsbury Publishing Plc GBR. Dist: Independent Pubs. Group.
Brewer, Heather. Eighth Grade Bites #1: The Chronicles of Vladimir Tod. 2008. (Chronicles of Vladimir Tod Ser.: 1). (ENG.). 192p. (YA). (gr. 7). 10.99 *(978-0-14-241187-2(6),* Speak) Penguin Young Readers Group.
—Eleventh Grade Burns, 4. 4th ed. 2010. (Chronicles of Vladimir Tod Ser.: 4). (ENG.). 208p. (J). (gr. 7-12). 24.94 *(978-0-525-42243-3(9))* Penguin Young Readers Group.
—Eleventh Grade Burns #4: The Chronicles of Vladimir Tod, 4 vols. 2010. (Chronicles of Vladimir Tod Ser.: 4). (ENG.). 320p. (YA). (gr. 7-18). 10.99 *(978-0-14-241647-1(9),* Speak) Penguin Young Readers Group.
—Ninth Grade Slays #2: The Chronicles of Vladimir Tod, 2 vols. 2009. (Chronicles of Vladimir Tod Ser.: 2). (ENG.). 288p. (YA). (gr. 7-18). 10.99 *(978-0-14-241342-5(9),* Speak) Penguin Young Readers Group.
—Tenth Grade Bleeds. 2010. (Chronicles of Vladimir Tod Ser.: 03). lib. bdg. 19.65 *(978-0-606-10594-1(8))* Turtleback.
—Tenth Grade Bleeds #3: The Chronicles of Vladimir Tod. 2010. (Chronicles of Vladimir Tod Ser.: 3). (ENG.). 304p. (YA). (gr. 7-18). pap. 10.99 *(978-0-14-241560-3(X),* Speak) Penguin Young Readers Group.
—Twelfth Grade Kills #5: The Chronicles of Vladimir Tod. 2011. (Chronicles of Vladimir Tod Ser.: 5). (ENG.). 336p. (YA). (gr. 7-18). 9.99 *(978-0-14-241752-2(1),* Speak) Penguin Young Readers Group.
Brewis, Alan. Boris Returns A Hero! 2008. 72p. pap. 12.50 *(978-1-4357-4377-9(6))* Lulu Pr., Inc.
Brezenoff, Steve. The Absolute Value of -1. 2010. (Carolrhoda YA Ser.). (ENG.). 296p. (YA). (gr. 9-12). lib. bdg. 16.95 *(978-0-7613-5417-8(4),* Carolrhoda Bks.) Lerner Publishing Group.
—Cheaters. 2013. (Ravens Pass Ser.). (ENG.). 96p. (J). (gr. 2-3). pap. 36.90 *(978-1-4342-6291-2(X),* 20262, Stone Arch Bks.) Capstone.
—Cheaters, 1 vol. Pinelli, Amerigo, illus. 2013. (Ravens Pass Ser.). (ENG.). 96p. (J). (gr. 3-6). lib. bdg. 25.32 *(978-1-4342-4616-5(7),* 120605, Stone Arch Bks.) Capstone.
—Field Trip Mysteries: the Burglar Who Bit the Big Apple. Canga, Chris, illus. 2010. (Field Trip Mysteries Ser.). (ENG.). 88p. (J). (gr. 3-6). 25.32 *(978-1-4342-2139-1(3),* 102869, Stone Arch Bks.) Capstone.
—Field Trip Mysteries: the Crook Who Crossed the Golden Gate Bridge. Canga, Chris, illus. 2010. (Field Trip Mysteries Ser.). (ENG.). 88p. (J). (gr. 3-6). 25.32 *(978-1-4342-2138-4(5),* 102868); pap. 5.95 *(978-1-4342-2770-6(7),* 114037) Capstone. (Stone Arch Bks.).
—Field Trip Mysteries: the Ghost Who Haunted the Capitol. Canga, Chris, illus. 2010. (Field Trip Mysteries Ser.). (ENG.). 88p. (J). (gr. 3-6). 25.32 *(978-1-4342-2140-7(7),* 102870); pap. 5.95 *(978-1-4342-2772-0(3),* 114039) Capstone. (Stone Arch Bks.).
—Field Trip Mysteries: the Ride That Was Really Haunted. Calo, Marcos, illus. 2011. (Field Trip Mysteries Ser.). (ENG.). 88p. (J). (gr. 3-6). pap. 5.95 *(978-1-4342-3427-8(4),* 116448, Stone Arch Bks.) Capstone.
—Field Trip Mysteries: the Teacher Who Forgot Too Much. Canga, Chris, illus. 2009. (Field Trip Mysteries Ser.). (ENG.). 88p. (J). (gr. 3-6). lib. bdg. 25.32 *(978-1-4342-1609-0(8),* 95782, Stone Arch Bks.) Capstone.
—Field Trip Mysteries: the Village That Almost Vanished. Canga, Chris, illus. 2009. (Field Trip Mysteries Ser.). (ENG.). 88p. (J). (gr. 3-6). lib. bdg. 25.32 *(978-1-4342-1611-3(X),* 95785, Stone Arch Bks.) Capstone.
—Field Trip Mysteries: the Zoo with the Empty Cage. Canga, Chris, illus. 2009. (Field Trip Mysteries Ser.). (ENG.). 88p. (J). (gr. 3-6). lib. bdg. 25.32 *(978-1-4342-1610-6(1),* 95784, Stone Arch Bks.) Capstone.
—Guitarist Wanted. 2017. (Boy Seeking Band Ser.). (ENG., Illus.). 96p. (J). (gr. 5-8). lib. bdg. 25.99 *(978-1-4965-4448-3(X),* 134762, Stone Arch Bks.) Capstone.
—The Library Shelves: An Interactive Mystery Adventure. Calo, Marcos, illus. 2019. (You Choose Stories: Field Trip Mysteries Ser.). (ENG.). 112p. (J). (gr. 3-7). lib. bdg. 32.65 *(978-1-4965-4860-3(4),* 135459, Stone Arch Bks.) Capstone.
—The Messed-Up Museum: An Interactive Mystery Adventure. Calo, Marcos, illus. 2019. (You Choose Stories: Field Trip Mysteries Ser.). (ENG.). 112p. (J). (gr. 3-7). lib. bdg. 32.65 *(978-1-4965-4859-7(0),* 135458, Stone Arch Bks.) Capstone.
—The Zombie Who Visited New Orleans, 1 vol. Canga, Chris, illus. 2010. (Field Trip Mysteries Ser.). (ENG.). 88p. (J). (gr. 3-6). 25.32 *(978-1-4342-2141-4(5),* 102871); pap. 5.95 *(978-1-4342-2773-7(1),* 114040) Capstone. (Stone Arch Bks.).
Brian, Kate, pseud. Confessions. 2009. (Private Ser.: No. 4). (ENG.). 240p. (YA). pap. 9.99 *(978-1-4169-9949-2(3),* Simon & Schuster Bks. For Young Readers) Simon & Schuster Bks. For Young Readers.
—Cruel Love. 2011. (Privilege Ser.). (ENG.). 224p. (YA). (gr. 9). pap. 9.99 *(978-1-4424-0788-6(3),* Simon & Schuster Bks. For Young Readers) Simon & Schuster Bks. For Young Readers.
—Fake Boyfriend. 2009. (ENG.). 288p. (YA). (gr. 9). pap. 8.99 *(978-1-4169-1368-9(8),* Simon & Schuster Bks. For Young Readers) Simon & Schuster Bks. For Young Readers.
—Invitation Only. 2009. (Private Ser.: No. 2). (ENG.). 272p. (YA). pap. 9.99 *(978-1-4169-9947-8(7),* Simon & Schuster Bks. For Young Readers) Simon & Schuster Bks. For Young Readers.
—Megan Meade's Guide to the Mcgowan Boys. 2006. (ENG.). 288p. (YA). (gr. 7-12). pap. 11.99 *(978-1-4169-0031-3(4),* Simon & Schuster Bks. For Young Readers) Simon & Schuster Bks. For Young Readers.
—Ominous. 2011. (Private Ser.). (ENG.). 224p. (YA). (gr. 9-18). pap. 9.99 *(978-1-4169-8472-6(0),* Simon & Schuster Bks. For Young Readers) Simon & Schuster Bks. For Young Readers.
Bridges, Eunice. A Day Like Mine. Goodwin, Adrienne Annette, illus. 2011. 32p. pap. 24.95 *(978-1-4560-5766-4(9))* America Star Bks.
Briggs, Meredith. Polka-Dot Parade. 2007. 52p. per. 16.95 *(978-1-4241-8366-1(9))* America Star Bks.
Britt, Fanny. Jane, the Fox & Me, 1 vol. Ouriou, Susan & Morelli, Christelle, trs. Arsenault, Isabelle, illus. 2013. (ENG.). 104p. (J). (gr. 5-8). 21.99 *(978-1-55498-360-5(6))* Groundwood Bks. CAN. Dist: Publishers Group West (PGW).
Brix, Liz. Josephine Prairie Dog. 2009. 28p. pap. 12.70 *(978-1-4389-4448-7(9))* AuthorHouse.
Broach, Elise. Trouble at School for Marvin & James. Murphy, Kelly, illus. 2018. (Masterpiece Adventures Ser.: 3). (ENG.). 112p. (J). pap. 8.99 *(978-1-250-18338-5(3),* 900190818) Square Fish.
—Trouble at School for Marvin & James. 2018. (Masterpiece Adventures Ser.: 3). (J). lib. bdg. 16.00 *(978-0-606-41106-6(2))* Turtleback.
Broaddus, Maurice. The Usual Suspects. 2019. (ENG., Illus.). 288p. (J). (gr. 3-7). 17.99 *(978-0-06-279631-8(3),* Tegen, Katherine Bks) HarperCollins Pubs.
Brockway, Stephanie. The Mystic Phyles: Beasts. Masiello, Ralph, illus. 2011. 144p. (J). (gr. 4-7). 15.95 *(978-1-57091-718-9(3))* Charlesbridge Publishing, Inc.
Brody, Jessica. Ally's Mad Mystery. 2017. 185p. (J). pap. *(978-1-4847-9931-4(3))* Disney Publishing Worldwide.
—In Some Other Life. 2018. (ENG.). 480p. (YA). pap. 10.99 *(978-1-250-15860-4(5),* 900185518) Square Fish.
—The Karma Club. 2011. (ENG.). 288p. (YA). (gr. 7-12). pap. 14.99 *(978-0-312-67473-1(2,* 900072884) Square Fish.
Bromley, Peter David. Aunty Liz the Lollipop Lady. 2004. 48p. pap. *(978-0-7552-1013-8(1))* Authors OnLine, Ltd.
Brooke, Samantha. Deep-Sea Dive. 2019. (Scholastic Readers Ser.). (ENG.). 32p. (J). (gr. 2-3). 13.89 *(978-0-87617-309-1(1))* Penworthy Co., LLC, The.
—Deep-Sea Dive. Artful Doodlers Ltd., illus. 2019. (Scholastic Reader, Level 2 Ser.). (ENG.). 32p. (J). (gr. k-2). pap. 4.99 *(978-1-338-25382-5(4))* Scholastic, Inc.
—Magic School Bus Rides Again: Meet the Class. 2018. lib. bdg. 13.55 *(978-0-606-41173-8(9))* Turtleback.
Brooks, Amy. Dorothy Dainty's Gay Times. 2017. (ENG., Illus.). (J). 22.95 *(978-1-374-91772-9(9))* Capital Communications, Inc.
Brooks, Mel & Reiner, Carl. The 2000 Year Old Man Goes to School. Bennett, James, illus. 2006. 32p. (J). (gr. 4-8). reprint ed. 18.00 *(978-1-4223-5622-7(1))* DIANE Publishing Co.
—The 2000 Year Old Man Goes to School. Bennett, James, illus. 2005. (ENG.). 40p. (J). (gr. -1-3). 17.99 *(978-0-06-076676-4(X))* HarperCollins Pubs.
Brosgol, Vera. Anya's Ghost. Brosgol, Vera, illus. 2011. (ENG., Illus.). 224p. (YA). (gr. 7-12). 24.99 *(978-1-59643-713-5(8),* 900075181, First Second Bks.) Roaring Brook Pr.
Brothers, Marilee. Moonstone. 2008. 236p. (YA). pap. 14.95 *(978-0-9802453-4-9(6),* Bell Bridge Bks.) BelleBks., Inc.
Broutin & Stehr. Baldomero Va A la Escuela. (SPA.). 26p. *(978-84-95150-47-9(6))* Corimbo, Editorial S.L.
Brouwer, Sigmund. Justine Mckeen, Pooper Scooper, 1 vol. Whamond, Dave, illus. 2012. (Orca Echoes Ser.). (ENG.). 64p. (J). (gr. 1-3). pap. 6.95 *(978-1-55469-931-5(2))* Orca Bk. Pubs. USA.
—Justine Mckeen vs. the Queen of Mean, 1 vol. Whamond, Dave, illus. 2014. (Orca Echoes Ser.). (ENG.). 64p. (J). (gr. 1-3). pap. 6.95 *(978-1-4598-0397-8(3))* Orca Bk. Pubs. USA.
—Justine Mckeen, Walk the Talk, 1 vol. Whamond, Dave, illus. 2012. (Orca Echoes Ser.). (ENG.). 64p. (J). (gr. 1-3). pap. 6.95 *(978-1-55469-929-2(0))* Orca Bk. Pubs. USA.
Brown, Devin. Not Exactly Normal. 2006. (ENG.). 238p. (J). (gr. 4). per. 8.00 *(978-0-8028-5287-8(4),* Eerdmans Bks For Young Readers) Eerdmans, William B. Publishing Co.
Brown, Gavin. Josh Baxter Levels Up. 2016. (ENG., Illus.). 192p. (J). (gr. 3-7). 12.99 *(978-0-545-77294-5(X),* Scholastic Pr.) Scholastic, Inc.
Brown, Herman. A Cut Too Far. 2015. (Suspended Ser.). (ENG.). 96p. (YA). (gr. 6-12). 27.99 *(978-1-4677-5709-6(8),* c5ec2a3b-580e-4371-aff2-b61368f8c5d2, Darby Creek) Lerner Publishing Group.
Brown, Jaye Robin. The Meaning of Birds. (ENG.). (YA). (gr. 9). 2020. 384p. pap. 10.99 *(978-0-06-282456-1(2))* 2019. (Illus.). 368p. 17.99 *(978-0-06-282444-8(9))* HarperCollins Pubs. (HarperTeen).
Brown, Jeff. Flat Stanley: Show-And-Tell, Flat Stanley! Pamintuan, Macky, illus. 2014. (I Can Read Level 2 Ser.). (ENG.). 32p. (J). (gr. -1-3). pap. 4.99 *(978-0-06-218975-2(1),* HarperCollins) HarperCollins Pubs.
—Show & Tell, Flat Stanley! 2014. (Flat Stanley: I Can Read Ser.). (J). lib. bdg. 13.55 *(978-0-606-35493-6(X))* Turtleback.
Brown, Jeffrey. My Teacher Is a Robot. 2019. (Illus.). 40p. (J). (gr. -1-2). 17.99 *(978-0-553-53451-1(3));* (ENG., lib. bdg. 20.99 *(978-0-553-53452-8(1))* Random Hse. Children's Bks. (Crown Books For Young Readers).
Brown, Jennifer. Hate List. 2017. (ENG.). 528p. (YA). (gr. 9-17). pap. 11.99 *(978-0-316-55678-1(5))* Little, Brown Bks. for Young Readers.
—Hate List. 2011. 10.36 *(978-0-7848-3563-0(2),* Everbind) Marco Bk. Co.
—How Lunchbox Jones Saved Me from Robots, Traitors, & Missy the Cruel. 2015. (ENG.). 240p. (YA). (gr. 3-6). 16.99 *(978-1-61963-454-1(6),* 900137050, Bloomsbury USA Childrens) Bloomsbury Publishing USA.
—Pennybaker School Is Headed for Disaster. 2018. (J). lib. bdg. 18.40 *(978-0-606-41073-1(2))* Turtleback.
Brown Lcsw, Jennifer. Star's Unexpected News. 2011. 32p. pap. 13.49 *(978-1-4389-3567-6(6))* AuthorHouse.

Brown, Liz. The Bully. 2012. (HIP Sr Ser.). (ENG., Illus.). 90p. (gr. 7-12). 26.19 *(978-1-897039-08-3(5))* High Interest Publishing (HIP) CAN. Dist: Children's Plus, Inc.

Brown, Marc. Arthur Turns Green. 2014. (ENG., Illus.). 32p. (J). (gr. 1-4). 7.99 *(978-0-316-12923-7(2))* Little, Brown Bks. for Young Readers.

—Arthur Turns Green. 2014. (Arthur Adventures Ser.). (J). lib. bdg. 17.20 *(978-0-606-34069-4(6))* Turtleback.

—Arthur's Classroom Fib. 2007. (Arthur Step into Reading Ser.). lib. bdg. 13.55 *(978-1-4177-7281-0(6))* Turtleback.

—Arthur's Teacher Trouble. 2004. (Arthur Adventure Ser.). (J). (gr. k-3). spiral bd. *(978-0-616-00406-7(0))*; spiral bd. *(978-0-616-01603-9(4))* Canadian National Institute for the Blind/Institut National Canadien pour les Aveugles.

—Arturo y el Misterioso Sobre. Sarfatti, Esther, tr. from ENG. 2006. (Libro de Capitulos de Arturo Ser.). (Illus.). 58p. (J). (gr. 6-8). per. 4.99 *(978-1-930332-93-5(9))* Lectorum Pubns., Inc.

—Buster Makes the Grade. 2005. (Arthur Chapter Bks.: No. 16). (Illus.). 55p. (J). lib. bdg. 15.00 *(978-1-59054-737-3(3))* Fitzgerald Bks.

—La Visita del Senor Rataquemada. Sarfatti, Esther, tr. from ENG. 2003.Tr. of Arthur's Teacher Moves In. (SPA.). (J). (gr. k-2). pap. 6.95 *(978-1-930332-41-6(6))* Lectorum Pubns., Inc.

Brown, Monica. Drama Queen. 2016. (Lola Levine Ser.: 2). (J). lib. bdg. 16.00 *(978-0-606-38329-5(8))* Turtleback.

—Lola Levine: Drama Queen. 2016. (Lola Levine Ser.: 2). (ENG., Illus.). (J). (gr. 1-5). 112p. pap. 5.99 *(978-0-316-25842-5(3))*; 96p. 15.99 *(978-0-316-25843-2(1))* Little, Brown Bks. for Young Readers.

Brown, Peter. My Teacher Is a Monster! (No, I Am Not.) 2014. (ENG., Illus.). 40p. (J). (gr. -1-3). 18.99 *(978-0-316-07029-4(7))* Little, Brown Bks. for Young Readers.

Brown, Roberta Simpson. Scared in School. 2005. (ENG.). 141p. (J). (gr. 6-9). pap. 8.95 *(978-0-87483-496-3(1))* August Hse. Pubs., Inc.

Brown Sr., David F. Tabby Goes to School: The First in the Tabatha Adventures Series, 1 vol. Brown Jr., David F., illus. 2009. 20p. pap. 24.95 *(978-1-60836-181-6(0))* America Star Bks.

Brown, Tiffany M. Gallery Eleven Twenty-Two. Sefcik, Wendy, illus. 2013. 30p. 17.99 *(978-0-9854423-0-9(1))*; pap. 9.99 *(978-0-9854423-1-6(X))* Brewster Moon.

Brownlee, Browne. Bad Breath. 2007. 108p. 19.95 *(978-1-4241-5487-6(1))* America Star Bks.

Bruchac, Joseph. Bearwalker. 2010. (ENG., Illus.). 240p. (J). (gr. 5). pap. 7.99 *(978-0-06-112315-3(3)*, HarperCollins) HarperCollins Pubs.

Bruna, Dick. The School. 2013. (ENG., Illus.). 28p. (J). (gr. -1-1). 7.95 *(978-1-84976-215-1(5))* Tate Publishing, Ltd. GBR. Dist: Hachette Bk. Group.

Bruno, Yvonne. Lisa Finds a New Friend. 2011. 24p. 12.79 *(978-1-4567-1780-3(4))* AuthorHouse.

Bryant, Jen. Pieces of Georgia. 2007. (ENG., Illus.). 176p. (J). (gr. 5-9). per. 8.99 *(978-0-440-42055-2(5)*, Yearling) Random Hse. Children's Bks.

Bryant, Mary. Sped Spud: He May Be a Tater, but He's No Dud. 2008. 28p. pap. 24.95 *(978-1-60563-436-4(0))* America Star Bks.

—Sped Spud: He May Be a Tater, but He's No Dud, 1 vol. 2010. 28p. 24.95 *(978-1-4512-1075-0(2))* PublishAmerica, Inc.

Bryant, Megan E. Set the Stage! (Tiny Geniuses #2) 2018. (Tiny Geniuses Ser.: 2). (ENG.). 128p. (J). (gr. 2-5). pap. 5.99 *(978-0-545-90957-0(0)*, Scholastic Paperbacks) Scholastic, Inc.

Buchanan, Paul & Buchanan, P. The Last Place I Want to Be, 1 vol. 2009. 176p. (J). pap. 7.99 *(978-0-8254-2408-3(9))* Kregel Pubns.

Buchanan, Selena. Sunday Chimes, 1 vol. 2009. 51p. pap. 16.95 *(978-1-4489-2208-6(9))* America Star Bks.

Buckley, Michael. The Fairy-Tale Detectives: And the Unusual Suspects. Ferguson, Peter, illus. 2012. 580p. (J). *(978-1-4351-4487-3(2)*, Amulet Bks.) Abrams, Inc.

—M Is for Mama's Boy. Beavers, Ethen, illus. 2010. (ENG.). 288p. (J). (gr. 3-7). pap. 6.95 *(978-0-8109-9674-8(X)*, Amulet Bks.) Abrams, Inc.

—Nerds: Book Two: M Is for Mama's Boy, Bk. 2. 2011. (ENG., Illus.). 288p. (J). (gr. 3-7). pap. 9.99 *(978-1-4197-0023-1(5)*, Amulet Bks.) Abrams, Inc.

—NERDS: National Espionage, Rescue, & Defense Society, 5 vols. 2009. (N. E. R. D. S. Ser.: 1). (J). 190.75 *(978-1-4407-4234-7(0))*; 71.75 *(978-1-4407-4235-4(9))*; 88.75 *(978-1-4407-4237-8(5))*; 73.75 *(978-1-4407-4233-0(2))*; 86.75 *(978-1-4407-4239-2(1))*; 1.25 *(978-1-4407-4243-9(X))* Recorded Bks., Inc.

—Nerds: National Espionage, Rescue, & Defense Society (Book One), Bk. 1. 2010. (ENG., Illus.). 352p. (J). (gr. 3-7). pap. 9.99 *(978-0-8109-8985-6(9)*, 660103, Amulet Bks.) Abrams, Inc.

—NERDS - National Espionage, Rescue, & Defense Society. 2010. (Nerds Ser.: 1). (J). lib. bdg. 18.40 *(978-0-606-15084-2(6))* Turtleback.

—NERDS 2: M für Muttersöhnchen. 2011. (SPA.). 260p. (J). (gr. 6-8). pap. 10.99 *(978-987-612-335-8(1))* V&R Editoras.

—The Unusual Suspects. 2006. (Sisters Grimm Ser.: Bk. 2). 1.00 *(978-1-4237-8623-8(8))* Recorded Bks., Inc.

—The Unusual Suspects. (Sisters Grimm Ser.: 2). (J). 2017. lib. bdg. 19.60 *(978-0-606-39686-8(1))* 2007. lib. bdg. 18.40 *(978-1-4178-0732-1(6))* Turtleback.

—A Very Grimm Guide. Ferguson, Peter, illus. 2012. (Sisters Grimm Ser.). (ENG.). 128p. (J). (gr. 3-7). 17.99 *(978-1-4197-0201-3(7)*, 1019601, Amulet Bks.) Abrams, Inc.

Buckner, Chuck. The Death of Arkie Baker. 2008. 84p. pap. 8.86 *(978-1-4357-4105-8(6))* Lulu Pr., Inc.

Budhos, Marina. Ask Me No Questions. 2007. 159p. (gr. 7-12). 20.00 *(978-0-7569-8114-3(X))* Perfection Learning Corp.

—Ask Me No Questions. 2007. (ENG.). 192p. (YA). (gr. 7-12). pap. 11.99 *(978-1-4169-4920-6(8)*, Atheneum Bks. for Young Readers) Simon & Schuster Children's Publishing.

—The Long Ride. 2019. (Illus.). 208p. (J). (gr. 5). 16.99 *(978-0-553-53422-1(X)*, Lamb, Wendy Bks.) Random Hse. Children's Bks.

Buffington, Cecil. High School Super-Star: The Junior Year. 2008. 244p. pap. 16.95 *(978-0-595-51914-9(8))* iUniverse, Inc.

Bui-Quang, Phuong-Mai. Tea Club. 2006. (YA). per. 10.95 *(978-1-59971-581-0(3))* Aardvark Global Publishing.

Bulion, Leslie. The Trouble with Rules, 1 vol. 2011. (Illus.). 160p. (J). (gr. 3-7). pap. 6.95 *(978-1-56145-576-8(8))* Peachtree Publishing Co. Inc.

Bunker, Lisa. Felix Yz. (ENG.). 288p. (J). (gr. 5-9). 2018. 8.99 *(978-0-425-28851-1(X)*, Puffin Books) 2017. 16.99 *(978-0-425-28850-4(1)*, Viking Books for Young Readers) Penguin Young Readers Group.

Bunting, Eve. My Special Day at Third Street School. Bloom, Suzanne, illus. 2009. (ENG.). 32p. (J). (gr. k-2). pap. 10.95 *(978-1-59078-745-8(5)*, Astra Young Readers) Astra Publishing Hse.

Burch, Robert. Queenie Peavey. l.t. ed. 2003. (LRS Large Print Cornerstone Ser.). 166p. (J). lib. bdg. 29.95 *(978-1-58118-115-9(9))* LRS.

Burchette, Ruby J. The Dog Went to School, 1 vol. 2010. 48p. pap. 16.95 *(978-1-4489-4962-5(9))* America Star Bks.

Burchill, Julie. Sugar Rush. 2005. 288p. (J). lib. bdg. 17.89 *(978-0-06-077620-6(X)*, HarperTeen) HarperCollins Pubs.

Burke, Morgan. Get It Started. 2010. (Party Room Ser.: 1). (ENG.). 272p. (J). (gr. 11). pap. 12.99 *(978-1-4424-1420-4(0)*, Simon Pulse) Simon Pulse.

Burkhart, Alma J. If You Could See Her Smile. Burns, Sandra, illus. 2013. 24p. pap. 8.99 *(978-1-938768-32-3(9))* Gypsy Pubns.

Burkhart, Jessica. Chasing Blue, 2. 2009. (Canterwood Crest Ser.: 2). (ENG.). 272p. (J). (gr. 4-8). pap. 7.99 *(978-1-4169-5841-3(X))* Simon & Schuster, Inc.

—Chosen: Super Special, 1. 2011. (Canterwood Crest Ser.). (ENG.). 304p. (J). (gr. 5-8). pap. 8.99 *(978-1-4424-1946-9(6))* Simon & Schuster, Inc.

—Comeback. 2012. (Canterwood Crest Ser.: 15). lib. bdg. 18.40 *(978-0-606-26312-2(8))* Turtleback.

—Famous, 18. 2013. (Canterwood Crest Ser.: 18). (ENG.). 240p. (J). (gr. 4-7). pap. 7.99 *(978-1-4424-3659-6(X))* Simon & Schuster, Inc.

—Jealousy. 2013. (Canterwood Crest Ser.: 17). (ENG.). 208p. (J). (gr. 4-7). pap. 7.99 *(978-1-4424-3657-2(3)*, Aladdin) Simon & Schuster Children's Publishing.

—Masquerade. 2012. (Canterwood Crest Ser.: 16). lib. bdg. 18.40 *(978-0-606-26887-5(1))* Turtleback.

—Popular. 2012. (Canterwood Crest Ser.: 14). lib. bdg. 18.40 *(978-0-606-26311-5(X))* Turtleback.

—Unfriendly Competition, 12. 2011. (Canterwood Crest Ser.: 12). (ENG.). 192p. (J). (gr. 4-8). pap. 7.99 *(978-1-4424-0386-4(1))* Simon & Schuster, Inc.

Burkhart, Kiersi. Honor Code. 2018. (ENG.). 320p. (YA). (gr. 8-12). 17.99 *(978-1-5124-2996-1(1)*, 442fa84d-2e5f-4312-a94f-11968ae42c11, Carolrhoda Lab™) Lerner Publishing Group.

Burkholder, Sheila M. Elsie Waits Patiently. 2004. (Illus.). 32p. (gr. -1-5). 2.70 *(978-0-7399-2339-9(0)*, 2778) Rod & Staff Pubs., Inc.

Burks, Megan. Sally the Circle. 2012. 28p. pap. 21.99 *(978-1-4771-3343-9(7))* Xlibris Corp.

Burnett, Eric. Gymnastics Jenny Stands on Her Own. 2003. 108p. pap. 9.95 *(978-0-595-27919-7(8))* iUniverse, Inc.

Burnett, Frances. A Little Princess. 2008. 156p. 25.95 *(978-1-60664-768-4(7))*; pap. 13.95 *(978-1-60664-141-5(7))* Aegypan.

—A Little Princess. 2008. 212p. (gr. 2-4). 27.99 *(978-0-554-29155-0(X))* Creative Media Partners, LLC.

—A Little Princess. Aldous, Kate, illus. 2005. 62p. (J). (gr. 4-7). 8.95 *(978-0-7945-1123-4(6)*, Usborne) EDC Publishing.

—A Little Princess. 188p. 2009. pap. 13.95 *(978-1-4385-0876-4(X))* 2008. pap. 13.45 *(978-1-4385-0194-9(3))* Standard Publications, Inc. (Bk. Jungle).

—A Little Princess. Engelbreit, Mary, illus. 2007. (Mary Engelbreit's Classic Library). (ENG.). 304p. (J). (gr. 3-7). 9.99 *(978-0-06-008137-9(6)*, HarperFestival) HarperCollins Pubs.

—A Little Princess. 2012. (Children's Classics Ser.). (ENG.). 186p. pap. 19.99 *(978-1-909438-52-1(9)*, Sovereign) Bollinger, Max GBR. Dist: Lightning Source UK, Ltd.

—A Little Princess: Being the whole story of Sara Crewe now told for T. 2007. 196p. per. 19.99 *(978-1-4346-7028-1(7))*; (ENG.). 210p. per. 22.99 *(978-1-4346-7029-8(5))* Creative Media Partners, LLC.

—A Little Princess: The Story of Sara Crewe. (J). 16.95 *(978-0-8488-1253-9(0))* Amereon Ltd.

—A Little Princess: The Story of Sara Crewe. Warren, Eliza, ed. Marcos, Pablo, illus. 2006. 239p. (YA). reprint ed. 10.00 *(978-0-7567-9835-2(3))* DIANE Publishing Co.

—A Little Princess: The Story of Sara Crewe. 2005. 112p. per. 4.95 *(978-1-4209-2529-6(6))* Digireads.com Publishing.

—A Little Princess: The Story of Sara Crewe. 2006. pap. *(978-1-4065-0559-7(5))* Dodo Pr.

—A Little Princess: The Story of Sara Crewe. l.t. ed. 2005. 376p. pap. *(978-1-84637-117-2(1))* Echo Library.

—A Little Princess: The Story of Sara Crewe. 2004. reprint ed. pap. 1.99 *(978-1-4192-0213-1(8))*; pap. 22.95 *(978-1-4191-0213-4(3))* Kessinger Publishing, LLC.

—A Little Princess: The Story of Sara Crewe. 2006. 204p. (YA). 19.95 *(978-1-934169-20-9(X))*; pap. 7.95 *(978-1-934169-21-6(8))* Norilana Bks.

—A Little Princess: The Story of Sara Crewe. 2005. (Twelve-Point Ser.). lib. bdg. 25.00 *(978-1-58287-320-6(8))*; lib. bdg. 26.00 *(978-1-58287-814-0(5))* North Bks.

—A Little Princess: The Story of Sara Crewe. Rust, Graham, illus. (J). pap. 22.95 *(978-0-590-24079-6(X))* Scholastic, Inc.

—A Little Princess: The Story of Sara Crewe. l.t. ed. 2003. 342p. pap. 10.95 *(978-0-7862-6247-2(8))* Thorndike Pr.

—A Little Princess: With a Discussion of Generosity. Gribbon, Sean & Jael, trs. Gribbon, Sean & Jael, illus. 2003. (Values in Action Illustrated Classics Ser.). (J). *(978-1-59203-050-7(5))* Learning Challenge, Inc.

—Sara Crewe. l.t. ed. 2006. 92p. pap. *(978-1-84637-263-6(1))* Echo Library.

—Sara Crewe. 2009. 68p. pap. 7.95 *(978-1-60664-388-4(6))* Rodgers, Alan Bks.

—Sara Crewe or What Happened at Miss Minc. 2005. pap. 20.95 *(978-0-7661-9708-4(5))* Kessinger Publishing, LLC.

Burnett, Frances Hodgson. Classic Starts(r): a Little Princess. Corvino, Lucy, illus. 2005. (Classic Starts(r) Ser.). 160p. (J). (gr. 2-4). 6.95 *(978-1-4027-1275-3(8))* Sterling Publishing Co., Inc.

—A Little Princess. Rust, Graham, illus. 2019. (ENG.). 192p. (J). (gr. 4-7). reprint ed. 18.95 *(978-0-87923-784-4(8))* Godine, David R. Pub.

—A Little Princess. 2012. (ENG., Illus.). 280p. *(978-1-905716-04-3(4)*, Collector's Library, The) Pan Macmillan.

—A Little Princess. 2008. (Puffin Classics Ser.). (ENG., Illus.). 320p. (J). (gr. 5-7). 8.99 *(978-0-14-132112-7(1)*, Puffin Books) Penguin Young Readers Group.

Burns, A. M. Hunters. 2016. (ENG., Illus.). (J). 24.99 *(978-1-63533-031-1(9)*, Harmony Ink Pr.) Dreamspinner Pr.

Burns, Catherine Lloyd. The Half-True Lies of Cricket Cohen. 2018. (J). lib. bdg. 18.40 *(978-0-606-41096-0(1))* Turtleback.

Burns, Ellen Flanagan. The Tallest Bridge in the World: A Story for Children about Social Anxiety. Lewis, Anthony, illus. 2017. 64p. (J). *(978-1-4338-2760-0(3)*, Magination Pr.) American Psychological Assn.

Burns, T. R. The Bad Apple. (Merits of Mischief Ser.: 1). (ENG.). (J). (gr. 3-7). 2013. 368p. pap. 7.99 *(978-1-4424-4030-2(9))*1. 2012. 352p. 16.99 *(978-1-4424-4029-6(5))* Simon & Schuster Children's Publishing. (Aladdin).

—Watch Your Step. 2015. (Merits of Mischief Ser.: 3). (ENG., Illus.). 464p. (J). (gr. 3-7). pap. 7.99 *(978-1-4424-4036-4(8)*, Aladdin) Simon & Schuster Children's Publishing.

—A World of Trouble. (Merits of Mischief Ser.: 2). (ENG., Illus.). (J). (gr. 3-7). 2014. 400p. pap. 7.99 *(978-1-4424-4033-3(3))* 2013. 384p. 16.99 *(978-1-4424-4032-6(5))* Simon & Schuster Children's Publishing. (Aladdin).

Burris, Priscilla. Hello School! Burris, Priscilla, illus. 2018. (Illus.). 32p. (J). (-k). 16.99 *(978-0-399-17202-1(5)*, Nancy Paulsen Books) Penguin Young Readers Group.

Burt, Jake. The Right Hook of Devin Velma. 2019. (ENG.). 256p. (J). pap. 14.99 *(978-1-250-21141-5(7)*, 900187725) Square Fish.

Burt, Steve. Even Odder: More Stories to Chill the Heart. Hagerman, Jessica, illus. 2003. 144p. pap. 14.95 *(978-0-9741407-0-4(8))* Burt, Steven E.

Burton, Rebecca. Leaving Jetty Road. 2004. (ENG.). 274p. *(978-0-207-20015-1(7))* HarperCollins Pubs. Australia.

Burton, Shovon. Banton Hits A Homerun. 2010. (ENG.). 46p. pap. 21.99 *(978-1-4500-7165-9(1))* Xlibris Corp.

Bush Hager, Jenna. Read All about It! 2010. (ENG., Illus.). 32p. (J). (gr. -1-3). pap. 7.99 *(978-0-06-156077-4(4)*, HarperCollins) HarperCollins Pubs.

Bushnell, Candace. The Carrie Diaries. (Carrie Diaries: 1). (ENG.). (YA). (gr. 9). 2011. 416p. pap. 11.99 *(978-0-06-172892-1(6))* 2010. 400p. 18.99 *(978-0-06-172891-4(8))* HarperCollins Pubs. (Balzer & Bray).

Bushweller, Ellie. The Tree with A Hundred Hands. 2008. 40p. 18.50 *(978-0-615-24478-5(5))* Bushweller, Ellie.

Bustard, Anne. Anywhere but Paradise. (ENG., Illus.). 288p. (J). (gr. 5-12). 2018. pap. 9.99 *(978-1-5415-1481-2(5)*, 8e45d442-59ae-45b4-b23c-96b160e2e472) 2015. E-Book 27.99 *(978-1-5124-0110-3(2))* Lerner Publishing Group. (Carolrhoda Bks.).

Butler, Dori. Late Again! 2005. (J). pap. *(978-1-4108-4209-1(6))* Benchmark Education Co.

Butler, Dori Hillestad. Alexandra Hopewell, Labor Coach. 2005. 136p. (J). (gr. 3-6). 15.99 *(978-0-8075-0242-6(1))* Whitman, Albert & Co.

—The Case of the Fire Alarm, 4. Tugeau, Jeremy, illus. 2011. (Buddy Files Ser.: 4). (ENG.). 128p. (J). (gr. 1-3). 17.44 *(978-0-8075-0913-5(2))* Whitman, Albert & Co.

—The Case of the Fire Alarm Bk. 4. Tugeau, Jeremy, illus. 2011. (Buddy Files Ser.: 4). (ENG.). 144p. (J). (gr. 1-5). pap. 5.99 *(978-0-8075-0935-7(3)*, 807509353) Whitman, Albert & Co.

—The Case of the Library Monster. Tugeau, Jeremy, illus. 2012. (Buddy Files Ser.: 5). (J). lib. bdg. 16.00 *(978-0-606-23839-7(5))* Turtleback.

—The Case of the School Ghost. 2013. (Buddy Files Ser.: 6). lib. bdg. 16.00 *(978-0-606-31843-3(7))* Turtleback.

—The Truth about Truman School, 1 vol. 2009. (ENG.). 176p. (J). (gr. 3-7). pap. 8.99 *(978-0-8075-8096-7(1)*, 807580961) Whitman, Albert & Co.

Butler, Shirley. The First-Class Adventure of Flat Freddie. 2008. 60p. pap. 19.95 *(978-1-60672-882-6(2))* America Star Bks.

Butterfield, MaryAnn Milton. You Are Too a Bully! 2013. 126p. (gr. 4-6). 28.99 *(978-1-4582-0968-9(7))*; pap. 11.99 *(978-1-4582-0969-6(5))* Author Solutions, LLC. (Abbott Pr.).

Button, Lana. Willow's Whispers, 0 vols. Howells, Tania, illus. 2014. (Willow Ser.). (ENG.). 32p. (J). (gr. -1-2). pap. 15.99 *(978-1-55453-744-0(4))* Kids Can Pr., Ltd. CAN. Dist: Hachette Bk. Group.

Buxbaum, Julie. Tell Me Three Things. 2017. (ENG.). 352p. (YA). (gr. 7). pap. 11.99 *(978-0-553-53567-9(6)*, Ember) Random Hse. Children's Bks.

—What to Say Next. (ENG.). (YA). (gr. 7). 2018. 320p. pap. 9.99 *(978-0-553-53571-6(4)*, Ember) 2017. 304p. 18.99 *(978-0-553-53568-6(4)*, Delacorte Pr.) Random Hse. Children's Bks.

Buyea, Rob. Because of Mr. Terupt. (J). (gr. 3-7). 2011. (Mr. Terupt Ser.: 1). 336p. 8.99 *(978-0-375-85824-6(5)*, Yearling) 2010. 288p. 17.99 *(978-0-385-73882-8(X)*, Delacorte Bks. for Young Readers) Random Hse. Children's Bks.

—The Perfect Score. (Perfect Score Ser.: 1). (J). (gr. 4-7). 2018. 384p. 8.99 *(978-1-101-93828-7(5)*, Yearling) 2017. 368p. 16.99 *(978-1-101-93825-6(0)*, Delacorte Bks. for Young Readers) Random Hse. Children's Bks.

—The Perfect Star. 2019. (Perfect Score Ser.: 3). (ENG.). 384p. (J). (gr. 4-7). lib. bdg. 19.99 *(978-1-5247-6464-7(7)*, Delacorte Bks. for Young Readers) Random Hse. Children's Bks.

Buzzeo, Toni. Adventure Annie Goes to Kindergarten. Wummer, Amy, illus. 2013. 32p. (J). (gr. -1-k). mass mkt. 8.99 *(978-0-14-242695-1(4)*, Puffin Books) Penguin Young Readers Group.

—Fire up with Reading! Yoshikawa, Sachiko, illus. 2007. (Mrs. Skorupski Story Ser.). 32p. (J). (gr. -1-3). 17.95 *(978-1-932146-91-2(1)*, Upstart Bks.) Highsmith Inc.

—The Great Dewey Hunt. Yoshikawa, Sachiko, illus. 2009. (Mrs. Skorupski Story Ser.). (J). 36p. (gr. -1-3). 17.95 *(978-1-60213-041-8(8))*; *(978-1-60213-029-6(9))* Highsmith Inc. (Upstart Bks.).

—Our Librarian Won't Tell Us Anything! Yoshikawa, Sachiko, illus. 2006. 32p. (J). (gr. -1-k). lib. bdg. 17.95 *(978-1-932146-73-8(3)*, Upstart Bks.) Highsmith Inc.

Bykowski, Christy. Gluten-Free Me Beckman Goes to School. Thompson, Chad, illus. 2013. 24p. pap. 11.95 *(978-1-61244-228-0(5))* Halo Publishing International.

Bylsma, Dan & Bylsma, Jay M. Slam Dunks Not Allowed! 2003. (Illus.). 238p. (YA). *(978-0-938682-72-1(5))*; pap. *(978-0-938682-77-6(6))* River Road Pubns., Inc.

C., Cindy. Return to the Wilds. 2019. 218p. (gr. 7-12). pap. 10.95 *(978-1-64279-170-9(9))* Morgan James Publishing.

Cabot, Meg. All-American Girl. 2008. (All-American Girl Ser.: 1). (ENG.). 416p. (YA). (gr. 8). pap. 10.99 *(978-0-06-147989-2(6)*, HarperTeen) HarperCollins Pubs.

—All-American Girl. 2008. (All-American Girl Ser.: Vol. 1). 398p. (YA). (gr. 7-12). 19.65 *(978-1-4178-2386-4(0))* Turtleback.

—Avalon High. (ENG., (YA). (gr. 8-12). 2007. Illus.). 320p. pap. 10.99 *(978-0-06-075588-1(1))* 2005. 304p. lib. bdg. 17.89 *(978-0-06-075587-4(3))* HarperCollins Pubs. (HarperTeen).

—Avalon High: Coronation #2: Homecoming, 2. Coronado, Jinky, illus. 2008. (ENG.). 192p. (J). (gr. 8-12). pap. 9.99 *(978-0-06-117709-5(1)*, HarperCollins) HarperCollins Pubs.

—Avalon High: Coronation #3: Hunter's Moon. Coronado, Jinky, illus. 2009. (ENG.). 160p. (J). (gr. 8-18). pap. 9.99 *(978-0-06-117710-1(5)*, HarperCollins) HarperCollins Pubs.

—From the Notebooks of a Middle-School Princess. 2016. (From the Notebooks of a Middle School Princess Ser.: 1). (J). lib. bdg. 18.40 *(978-0-606-38554-1(1))* Turtleback.

—From the Notebooks of a Middle School Princess: Meg Cabot; Read by Kathleen Mcinerney. 2015. (From the Notebooks of a Middle School Princess Ser.: 1). (ENG., Illus.). 192p. (J). (gr. 3-7). 16.99 *(978-1-250-06602-2(6)*, 900145229) Feiwel & Friends.

—Haunted. 2007. (Mediator Ser.: No. 5). 263p. 18.00 *(978-0-7569-7831-0(9))* Perfection Learning Corp.

—How to Be Popular. 2008. (ENG.). 320p. (YA). (gr. 8-12). pap. 8.99 *(978-0-06-088014-9(7)*, HarperTeen) HarperCollins Pubs.

—How to Be Popular: When You're a Social Reject Like Me, Steph L. 2006. (ENG.). 304p. (YA). (gr. 7-12). 16.99 *(978-0-06-088012-5(0)*, HarperTeen) HarperCollins Pubs.

—Jinx. 2007. (gr. 7-12). 262p. (YA). lib. bdg. 17.89 *(978-0-06-083765-5(9))*; (ENG.). 272p. (J). 16.99 *(978-0-06-083764-8(0))* HarperCollins Pubs. (HarperTeen).

—The Mediator: Shadowland & Ninth Key. 2010. (Mediator Ser.). (ENG.). 544p. (YA). (gr. 8). pap. 9.99 *(978-0-06-204020-6(0)*, HarperTeen) HarperCollins Pubs.

—The Merlin Prophecy. 2006. (Avalon High Coronation Ser.: Bk. 1). (ENG.). 304p. (YA). (gr. 7-12). 16.99 *(978-0-06-075586-7(5))* HarperCollins Pubs.

—Moving Day. 2009. (Allie Finkle's Rules for Girls Ser.: 1). lib. bdg. 17.20 *(978-0-606-06818-5(X))* Turtleback.

—Party Princess. 2006. (Princess Diaries: Vol. 7). (ENG., Illus.). 304p. (YA). (gr. 7-12). 16.99 *(978-0-06-072453-5(6))* HarperCollins Pubs.

—The Princess Diaries, Volume II: Princess in the Spotlight Vol. 2. 2008. (Princess Diaries: 2). (ENG.). 256p. (YA). (gr. 8-12). pap. 11.99 *(978-0-06-147994-6(2)*, HarperTeen) HarperCollins Pubs.

—The Princess Diaries, Volume IX: Princess Mia, Vol. 9. 2009. (Princess Diaries: 9). (ENG.). 304p. (YA). (gr. 8). pap. 10.99 *(978-0-06-072463-4(3)*, HarperTeen) HarperCollins Pubs.

—The Princess Diaries, Volume V: Princess in Pink. 2008. (Princess Diaries: 5). (ENG.). 288p. (YA). (gr. 8). pap. 10.99 *(978-0-06-154363-0(2)*, HarperTeen) HarperCollins Pubs.

—The Princess Diaries, Volume VI: Princess in Training, Vol. VI. 2008. (Princess Diaries: 6). (ENG.). 304p. (YA). (gr. 8). pap. 10.99 *(978-0-06-154365-4(9)*, HarperTeen) HarperCollins Pubs.

—The Princess Diaries, Volume VII: Party Princess, Vol. VII. 2008. (Princess Diaries: 7). (ENG.). 320p. (YA). (gr. 8). pap. 9.99 *(978-0-06-154374-6(8)*, HarperTeen) HarperCollins Pubs.

—The Princess Diaries, Volume VIII: Princess on the Brink. 2007. (Princess Diaries: 8). (ENG.). 272p. (YA). (gr. 8). pap. 10.99 *(978-0-06-072460-3(9)*, HarperTeen) HarperCollins Pubs.

—The Princess Diaries, Volume X: Forever Princess, Vol. X. 2009. (Princess Diaries: 10). (ENG.). 416p. (YA). (gr. 8). pap. 10.99 *(978-0-06-123294-7(7)*, HarperTeen) HarperCollins Pubs.

—Princess in Love. 2004. (Princess Diaries: Vol. 3). 288p. (J). (gr. 7-18). pap. 38.00 incl. audio *(978-0-8072-2284-3(4)*, Listening Library) Random Hse. Audio Publishing Group.

—Princess in Pink. 2004. (Princess Diaries: Vol. 5). (ENG., Illus.). 272p. (J). (gr. 7-18). 15.99 *(978-0-06-009610-6(1))* HarperCollins Pubs.

—Princess in Pink. 2008. (Princess Diaries: 5). 256p. (YA). (gr. 7-12). 20.85 *(978-1-4178-2563-9(4))* Turtleback.

—Princess in the Spotlight. 2008. (Princess Diaries). 222p. (gr. 7-12). 19.00 *(978-0-7569-8794-7(6))* Perfection Learning Corp.

—Princess in the Spotlight, unabr. ed. 2004. (Princess Diaries: Vol. 2). 272p. (J). (gr. 7-18). pap. 38.00 incl. audio *(978-0-8072-1197-7(4)*, S YA 332 SP, Listening Library) Random Hse. Audio Publishing Group.

—Princess in Training. 2005. (Princess Diaries: Vol. 6). (ENG., Illus.). 288p. (J). (gr. 7-18). 16.99 *(978-0-06-009613-7(6))* HarperCollins Pubs.

—Princess Mia. 2008. (Princess Diaries: Vol. 9). (ENG.). 256p. (J). (gr. 7-18). 16.99 *(978-0-06-072461-0(7))* HarperCollins Pubs.

—Princess Mia. 2009. (Princess Diaries: 9). (YA). lib. bdg. 20.85 *(978-0-606-02178-4(7))* Turtleback.

—Ready or Not. (All-American Girl Ser.: 2). 2008. (ENG.). 336p. (YA). (gr. 8). pap. 10.99 *(978-0-06-147996-0(9)*, HarperTeen) 2005. (ENG.). 256p. (J). (gr. 7-18). 16.99 *(978-0-06-072450-4(1))* 2nd ed. 2005. 256p. (J). (gr. 7-18). lib. bdg. 16.89 *(978-0-06-072451-1(X))* HarperCollins Pubs.

—Royal Crown: from the Notebooks of a Middle School Princess. Cabot, Meg, illus. 2019. (From the Notebooks of a Middle School Princess Ser.: 4). (ENG., Illus.). 224p. (J). pap. 10.99 *(978-1-250-30868-9(2)*, 900170016) Square Fish.

—Royal Crush. 2018. (From the Notebooks of a Middle School Princess Ser.: 3). (J). lib. bdg. 18.40 *(978-0-606-41094-6(5))* Turtleback.

—Teen Idol. 2005. (ENG., Illus.). 320p. (YA). (gr. 8-18). reprint ed. pap. 9.99 *(978-0-06-009618-2(7)*, HarperTeen) HarperCollins Pubs.

—Teen Idol. 2005. 291p. (YA). 16.65 *(978-0-7569-5735-3(4))* Perfection Learning Corp.

—Twilight. 2005. (Mediator Ser.: No. 6). (ENG.). 256p. (J). 15.99 *(978-0-06-072467-2(6))* HarperCollins Pubs.

—Vanished Books One & Two: When Lightning Strikes; Code Name Cassandra. 2010. (Vanished Ser.: Bks. 1 & 2). (ENG., Illus.). 560p. (YA). (gr. 7). pap. 15.99 *(978-1-4424-0629-2(1)*, Simon Pulse) Simon Pulse.

Cabral, Jeane. All Aboard the Yellow School Bus: Follow the Bus Through the Pages on a Counting Adventure! Top That Publishing Staff, ed. Petrlik, Andrea, illus. 2008. (Story Book Ser.). 20p. (J). (gr. -1). *(978-1-84666-543-1(4)*, Tide Mill Pr.) Top That! Publishing PLC.

Cach, Lisa. Wake unto Me. 2011. 320p. (YA). (gr. 7-18). 8.99 *(978-0-14-241436-1(0)*, Speak) Penguin Young Readers Group.

Cadenhead, MacKenzie. Sleeper. 2017. (ENG.). 272p. (YA). (gr. 6-12). pap. 10.99 *(978-1-4926-3614-4(2))* Sourcebooks, Inc.

Calame, Don. Beat the Band. 2011. (ENG., Illus.). 400p. (YA). (gr. 9). pap. 11.99 *(978-0-7636-5663-8(1))* Candlewick Pr.

Calandrelli, Emily. Ada Lace & the Impossible Mission. Kurilla, Renée, illus. 2018. (Ada Lace Adventure Ser.: 4). (ENG.). 112p. (J). (gr. 1-5). pap. 6.99 *(978-1-5344-1684-0(6)*, Simon & Schuster Bks. For Young Readers) Simon & Schuster Bks. For Young Readers.

Caletti, Deb. A Heart in a Body in the World. 2018. (ENG., Illus.). 368p. (YA). (gr. 9). 18.99 *(978-1-4814-1520-0(4)*, Simon Pulse) Simon Pulse.

—The Last Forever. 2016. (ENG., Illus.). 352p. (YA). (gr. 7-7). pap. 11.99 *(978-1-4424-5002-8(9)*, Simon & Schuster Bks. For Young Readers) Simon & Schuster Bks. For Young Readers.

—The Six Rules of Maybe. 2011. (ENG.). 352p. (YA). (gr. 7). pap. 12.99 *(978-1-4169-7971-5(9)*, Simon Pulse) Simon Pulse.

Cali, Davide & Chaud, Benjamin. The Truth about My Unbelievable School ... 2018. (Funny Thing Happened Ser.). (ENG., Illus.). 44p. (J). (gr. 1-4). 12.99 *(978-1-4521-5594-4(1))* Chronicle Bks. LLC.

Callahan, Erin. The Art of Escaping. 2018. (ENG.). 324p. (YA). (gr. 7). pap. 12.99 *(978-1-944995-65-2(X))* Amberjack Publishing Co.

Callen, Sharon. Ms. Wilde & Oscar, 1 vol. rev. ed. 2013. (Literary Text Ser.). (ENG., Illus.). 32p. (J). (gr. 2-3). pap. 10.99 *(978-1-4333-5611-7(2))*; lib. bdg. 19.96 *(978-1-4807-1733-6(9))* Teacher Created Materials, Inc.

Callender, Kacen. This Is Kind of an Epic Love Story. 2019. (ENG.). 304p. (YA). (gr. 9). pap. 10.99 *(978-0-06-282023-5(0)*, Balzer & Bray) HarperCollins Pubs.

Callender, Kheryn. This Is Kind of an Epic Love Story. 2018. (ENG.). 304p. (YA). (gr. 9). 17.99 *(978-0-06-282022-8(2)*, Balzer & Bray) HarperCollins Pubs.

Calmenson, Stephanie. The Frog Principal. Brunkus, Denise, illus. 2006. (ENG.). 32p. (J). pap. 5.99 *(978-0-439-81217-7(8)*, Scholastic Paperbacks) Scholastic, Inc.

—Our Principal Is a Frog! A QUIX Book. Blecha, Aaron, illus. 2018. (Our Principal Ser.). (ENG.). 64p. (J). (gr. k-3). 17.99 *(978-1-4814-6667-7(4))*; pap. 5.99 *(978-1-4814-6665-3(8))* Simon & Schuster Children's Publishing. (Aladdin).

Calmenson, Stephanie & Cole, Joanna. Teacher's Pets. Ross, Heather, illus. 2015. (Ready, Set, Dogs! Ser.: 2). (ENG.). 144p. (J). (gr. 1-4). pap. 11.99 *(978-1-250-05705-1(1)*, 900139115) Square Fish.

Calonita, Jen. Belles. 2012. (Belles Ser.: 1). (ENG.). 384p. (YA). (gr. 7-17). pap. 19.99 *(978-0-316-09112-1(X)*, Poppy) Little, Brown Bks. for Young Readers.

—Misfits: Royal Academy Rebels, Book 1. (Royal Academy Rebels Ser.: 1). 288p. (J). (gr. 3-7). 2019. pap. 7.99 *(978-1-4926-9390-1(1))* 2018. 16.99 *(978-1-4926-5128-4(1))* Sourcebooks, Inc.

—Secrets of My Hollywood Life. 2007. (Secrets of My Hollywood Life Ser.: 1). (ENG.). 256p. (YA). (gr. 7-17). per. 15.99 *(978-0-316-15443-7(1)*, Poppy) Little, Brown Bks. for Young Readers.

—Switched. 2018. (Fairy Tale Reform School Ser.: 4). (ENG.). 304p. (J). (gr. 5-8). 15.99 *(978-1-4926-5164-2(8))* Sourcebooks, Inc.

—Switched: Fairy Tale Reform School #4. 2019. (Fairy Tale Reform School Ser.: 4). 320p. (J). (gr. 5-8). pap. 7.99 *(978-1-4926-6912-8(1))* Sourcebooks, Inc.

—Tricked. 2018. (Fairy Tale Reform School Ser.: 3). lib. bdg. 18.40 *(978-0-606-40515-7(1))* Turtleback.

—Tricked: Fairy Tale Reform School. 2017. (Fairy Tale Reform School Ser.: 3). (ENG.). 272p. (J). (gr. 5-8). 15.99 *(978-1-4926-3795-0(5)*, 9781492637950) Sourcebooks, Inc.

—Tricked: Fairy Tale Reform School #3. 2018. (Fairy Tale Reform School Ser.: 3). 320p. (J). (gr. 5-8). pap. 8.99 *(978-1-4926-5237-3(7))* Sourcebooks, Inc.

—Winter White. 2013. (Belles Ser.: 2). (ENG.). 384p. (YA). (gr. 7-17). pap. 19.99 *(978-0-316-09118-3(9)*, Poppy) Little, Brown Bks. for Young Readers.

Caloyeras, Jennifer. Strays: A Novel. 2015. (ENG.). 219p. (J). pap. 17.95 *(978-1-61822-037-0(3)*, Ashland Creek Pr.) Byte Level Research.

Cameron, Anne. The Storm Tower Thief. Jamieson, Victoria, illus. 2014. (Lightning Catcher Ser.: 2). (ENG.). 432p. (J). (gr. 3-7). 16.99 *(978-0-06-211279-8(1)*, Greenwillow Bks.) HarperCollins Pubs.

Cammuso, Frank. The Dodgeball Chronicles: a Graphic Novel (Knights of the Lunch Table #1), Vol. 1. Cammuso, Frank, illus. 2008. (Knights of the Lunch Table Ser.: 1). (ENG., Illus.). 144p. (J). (gr. 3-5). pap. 10.99 *(978-0-439-90322-6(X)*, Graphix) Scholastic, Inc.

—The Misadventures of Salem Hyde: Spelling Trouble. 2013. (Misadventures of Salem Hyde Ser.: 1). (J). lib. bdg. 17.15 *(978-0-606-33440-2(8))* Turtleback.

Campbell, K. G. Dylan the Villain. Campbell, K. G., illus. 2016. (Illus.). 32p. (J). (gr. -1-1). 17.99 *(978-0-451-47642-5(5)*, Viking Books for Young Readers) Penguin Young Readers Group.

Campbell, K. G., illus. Dylan the Villain. 2016. (J). *(978-0-698-40517-2(X))* Penguin Bks., Ltd.

Campbell, Marcy. Adrian Simcox Does NOT Have a Horse. Luyken, Corinna, illus. 2018. 40p. (J). (-k). 18.99 *(978-0-7352-3037-8(4)*, Dial Bks) Penguin Young Readers Group.

Campbell, S. E. Tasting Silver. 2013. 178p. pap. 10.99 *(978-1-62237-220-1(4))* Turquoise Morning Pr.

Candlewick Press. Peppa Pig & the Busy Day at School. Candlewick Press, illus. 2013. (Peppa Pig Ser.). (ENG., Illus.). 32p. (J). (-k). 12.99 *(978-0-7636-6525-8(8)*, Candlewick Entertainment) Candlewick Pr.

—Peppa Pig & the Career Day. 2018. (Peppa Pig Ser.). (ENG., Illus.). 32p. (J). (-k). 12.99 *(978-1-5362-0344-8(0)*, Candlewick Entertainment) Candlewick Pr.

Capin, Hannah. Foul Is Fair: A Novel. 2020. (ENG.). 336p. (YA). 18.99 *(978-1-250-23954-9(0)*, 900211181, Wednesday Bks.) St. Martin's Pr.

Caprara, Rebecca. The Magic of Melwick Orchard. 2018. (ENG.). 376p. (J). (gr. 4-8). 17.99 *(978-1-5124-6687-4(5)*, cbdf4843-d3d6-457a-9fa0-9e412f2c3008, Carolrhoda Bks.) Lerner Publishing Group.

Capucilli, Alyssa Satin. Biscuit Goes to School Book & CD. abr. ed. 2005. (My First I Can Read Ser.). (ENG., Illus.). 32p. (J). (gr. -1 — 1). audio compact disk 9.99 *(978-0-06-078686-1(8)*, HarperCollins) HarperCollins Pubs.

—Biscuit's 100th Day of School. Schories, Pat, illus. 2006. (Biscuit Ser.). (ENG.). 20p. (J). (gr. -1-1). pap. 6.99 *(978-0-06-079467-5(4)*, HarperFestival) HarperCollins Pubs.

Carbone, Courtney. Butterfly Battle! Ørum, Pernille, illus. 2018. 29p. (J). *(978-1-5444-0226-0(0))* Random Hse., Inc.

—Showdown in Space! Ørum, Pernille, illus. 2017. 32p. (J). *(978-1-5182-5211-2(7))* Random Hse., Inc.

—Showdown in Space! (DC Super Hero Girls) Orum, Pernille, illus. 2017. (Step into Reading Ser.). 32p. (J). (gr. k-3). pap. 5.99 *(978-1-5247-6606-1(2)*, Random Hse. Bks. for Young Readers) Random Hse. Children's Bks.

—This Makes Me Jealous: Dealing with Feelings. Kushnir, Hilli, illus. 2019. (Rodale Kids Curious Readers/Level 2 Ser.: 6). 32p. (J). (gr. -1-1). pap. 4.99 *(978-1-63565-077-8(1)*, 9781635650778, Rodale Kids) Random Hse. Children's Bks.

—Welcome to Super Hero High! 2017. (Step into Reading Level 3 Ser.). (Illus.). 30p. (J). lib. bdg. 14.75 *(978-0-606-40233-0(0))* Turtleback.

—Welcome to Super Hero High! (DC Super Hero Girls) Brizuela, Dario, illus. 2017. (Step into Reading Ser.). 32p. (J). (gr. k-3). pap. 4.99 *(978-1-5247-6611-5(9)*, Random Hse. Bks. for Young Readers) Random Hse. Children's Bks.

Cardi, Annie. The Chance You Won't Return. 2014. (ENG.). 352p. (YA). (gr. 7). 16.99 *(978-0-7636-6292-9(5))* Candlewick Pr.

Carleson, J. C. The Tyrant's Daughter. 2015. (ENG.). 304p. (YA). (gr. 7). pap. 10.99 *(978-0-449-80999-0(4)*, Ember) Random Hse. Children's Bks.

Carlson, Melody. Beyond Reach. 2007. (Secret Life of Samantha Mcgregor Ser.: 2). 256p. (J). (gr. 7-12). per. 15.99 *(978-1-59052-693-4(7)*, Multnomah Bks.) Crown Publishing Group, The.

—Homecoming Queen, 1 vol. 2014. (Carter House Girls Ser.: 3). (ENG.). 224p. (YA). pap. 9.99 *(978-0-310-74725-3(2))* Zondervan.

—Last Dance, 1 vol. 2014. (Carter House Girls Ser.: 8). (ENG.). 208p. (YA). pap. 9.99 *(978-0-310-74900-4(X))* Zondervan.

—My Name Is Chloe. 2005. (Diary of a Teenage Girl: Bk. 5). 288p. (YA). mass mkt. 7.99 *(978-1-59052-736-8(4)*, Multnomah) Doubleday Religious Publishing Group, The.

—Payback. 2008. (Secret Life of Samantha Mcgregor Ser.: 4). 240p. (gr. 8-12). pap. 14.99 *(978-1-59052-934-8(0)*, Multnomah Bks.) Crown Publishing Group, The.

—Playing with Fire. 2007. (Secret Life of Samantha Mcgregor Ser.: 3). (ENG.). 256p. (YA). (gr. 7-12). per. 12.99 *(978-1-59052-694-1(5)*, Multnomah Bks.) Crown Publishing Group, The.

—Stealing Bradford, 1 vol. 2014. (Carter House Girls Ser.: 2). (ENG.). 224p. (YA). pap. 9.99 *(978-0-310-74654-6(X))* Zondervan.

Carlson, Nancy. First Grade, Here I Come! 2006. (Illus.). (J). *(978-1-4156-8114-5(7)*, Viking Adult) Penguin Publishing Group.

—Henry & the Bully. 2012. (ENG., Illus.). 32p. (J). (gr. -1-1). 21.19 *(978-0-670-01148-3(7)*, Viking) Penguin Publishing Group.

—Henry's 100 Days of Kindergarten. Carlson, Nancy, illus. 2004. (ENG., Illus.). 32p. (J). (gr. -1-1). 18.69 *(978-0-670-05977-5(3)*, Viking) Penguin Publishing Group.

—Henry's 100 Days of Kindergarten. 2007. 16.00 *(978-1-4177-5983-5(6))* Turtleback.

—Henry's Amazing Imagination. 2010. (ENG.). 32p. (J). (gr. k-2). 18.69 *(978-0-670-06296-6(0))* Penguin Young Readers Group.

—Henry's Show & Tell. Carlson, Nancy, illus. 2012. (Nancy Carlson Picture Bks). (Illus.). 32p. (J). (gr. k-2). 56.72 *(978-0-7613-9308-5(0)*, Carolrhoda Bks.) Lerner Publishing Group.

—I Don't Like to Read! Carlson, Nancy, illus. 2009. (ENG., Illus.). 32p. (J). (gr. k-2). pap. 8.99 *(978-0-14-241451-4(4)*, Puffin Books) Penguin Young Readers Group.

—It's Not My Fault! Carlson, Nancy, illus. 2003. (Illus.). 32p. (J). (gr. k-2). 15.95 *(978-1-57505-598-5(8))* Lerner Publishing Group.

—¡Piensa en Grande! 2005. (Libros ilustrados (Picture Bks.)). (SPA., Illus.). 32p. (J). (gr. k-2). lib. bdg. 15.95 *(978-0-8225-3192-0(5)*, Ediciones Lerner) Lerner Publishing Group.

—Think Big! 2005. (Illus.). 28p. (J). (gr. -1-3). 15.95 *(978-1-57505-622-7(4)*, Carolrhoda Bks.) Lerner Publishing Group.

Carlson, Sarah. Everything's Not Fine. 2020. 304p. (YA). (ENG.). 31.99 *(978-1-68442-411-5(9))*; pap. 17.99 *(978-1-68442-410-8(0))* Turner Publishing Co.

Carman, Patrick. Pulse. 2013. (Pulse Ser.: 1). (ENG.). 384p. (YA). (gr. 8). 17.99 *(978-0-06-208576-4(X)*, Tegen, Katherine Bks) HarperCollins Pubs.

Carmen, Martín Anguita. Marta y su dragón. 2008. (SPA., Illus.). 32p. (J). 10.99 *(978-84-241-5444-8(4))* Everest Editora ESP. Dist: Lectorum Pubns., Inc.

—El primer día de colegio de David. 2008. (SPA., Illus.). 32p. (J). 10.99 *(978-84-241-5790-6(7))* Everest Editora ESP. Dist: Lectorum Pubns., Inc.

Carmi, Rebecca. Amazing Magnetism. Speirs, John, illus. 2003. (Magic School Bus Science Chapter Bks.). 76p. (gr. 2-4). 15.00 *(978-0-7569-1576-6(7))* Perfection Learning Corp.

Carmichael, Jodi & Ackerley, Sarah. Spaghetti Is Not a Finger Food: And Other Life Lessons. Ponce, Sarah, illus. 2013. (ENG.). 152p. (J). (gr. 1-5). pap. 6.95 *(978-1-939775-03-0(5)*, Little Pickle Pr.) Sourcebooks, Inc.

Carminati, Chiara. Smile, Breathe, & Go Slowly: Slumby the Sloth Goes to School. Angaramo, Roberta, illus. 2020. 40p. (J). (gr. -1-2). 18.99 *(978-0-8234-4246-1(2))* Holiday Hse., Inc.

Carmona, Adela. The Boy Who Could See. Chapman, Robert E., illus. 2008. 32p. pap. 24.95 *(978-1-60672-697-6(8))* PublishAmerica, Inc.

Carolan, Jill. Sadie's Bargain. 2008. 148p. pap. 10.94 *(978-0-615-26231-4(7))* Never Quit Productions, Inc.

Carr, Annie Roe. Nan Sherwood at Pine Camp or the Old Lum. 2007. pap. *(978-1-4065-1294-6(X))* Dodo Pr.

—Nan Sherwood at Rose Ranch. 2007. 124p. per. *(978-1-4068-4396-5(2))* Echo Library.

—Nan Sherwood at Rose Ranch or the Old Me. 2007. pap. *(978-1-4065-1295-3(8))* Dodo Pr.

Carr, Patrick W. The Legend's Granddaughter: Not Quite Super, Book 1. Dabbs, Douglas, illus. 2007. 281p. (J). pap. *(978-0-9793168-0-7(4))* NQSBks.

Carrier, Therese & Carrier, Stephen. Josiah's School Fun Day. Hatfield, Tommy, illus. 2007. 29p. (J). 16.95 *(978-0-9797648-0-6(7))* Carrier, Therese.

Carriger, Gail. Curtsies & Conspiracies. 2014. (Finishing School Ser.: 2). (ENG.). 336p. (YA). (gr. 7-17). pap. 10.99 *(978-0-316-19020-6(9))* Little, Brown Bks. for Young Readers.

—Etiquette & Espionage. 2013. (Finishing School Ser.: 1). (ENG.). 336p. (YA). (gr. 7-17). pap. 11.99 *(978-0-316-19010-7(1))* Little, Brown Bks. for Young Readers.

—Waistcoats & Weaponry. 2015. (Finishing School Ser.: 3). (ENG.). 320p. (YA). (gr. 7-17). pap. 18.99 *(978-0-316-19025-1(X))* Little, Brown Bks. for Young Readers.

Carroll, Jonathan. Meet Julius Carmichael: First Day Blues. Koltun, Amy, illus. 2003. 96p. (J). (gr. 3-6). pap. 6.95 *(978-0-9724935-0-5(6))* Striking Presence Pubns.

Carson, Jana. We Both Read-The New Tribe. Treatner, Meryl, illus. 2013. 44p. (J). pap. 5.99 *(978-1-60115-264-0(7))* Treasure Bay, Inc.

Cartaya, Pablo. Each Tiny Spark. 2019. (ENG.). 336p. (J). (gr. 5). 17.99 *(978-0-451-47972-3(6)*, Kokila) Penguin Young Readers Group.

—Marcus Vega Doesn't Speak Spanish. 2018. (ENG.). 272p. (J). (gr. 5). 17.99 *(978-1-101-99726-0(5)*, Viking Books for Young Readers) Penguin Young Readers Group.

Carter, Alden R. Wart, Son of Toad, 0 vols. unabr. ed. 2013. (ENG.). 224p. (YA). (gr. 8-10). pap. 9.99 *(978-1-4778-1698-1(4)*, 9781477816981, Skyscape) Amazon Publishing.

Carter, Ally. I'd Tell You I Love You, but Then I'd Have to Kill You. 2016. (Gallagher Girls Ser.: 1). (ENG.). 304p. (YA). (gr. 7-17). pap. 11.99 *(978-1-4847-8505-8(3))* Hyperion Bks. for Children.

—I'd Tell You I Love You, but Then I'd Have to Kill You. 2016. (Gallagher Girls Ser.: 1). (J). lib. bdg. 20.85 *(978-0-606-39572-4(5))* Turtleback.

—Only the Good Spy Young. 10th anniv. ed. 2016. (Gallagher Girls Ser.: 4). (ENG.). 288p. (YA). (gr. 7-17). pap. 9.99 *(978-1-4847-8506-5(1))* Little, Brown Bks. for Young Readers.

—Out of Sight, Out of Time. 10th anniv. ed. 2016. (Gallagher Girls Ser.: 5). (ENG.). 320p. (YA). (gr. 7-17). pap. 9.99 *(978-1-4847-8507-2(X))* Hyperion Bks. for Children.

—Out of Sight, Out of Time. 2016. (Gallagher Girls Ser.: 5). (YA). lib. bdg. 20.85 *(978-0-606-38299-1(2))* Turtleback.

—United We Spy. 2016. (Gallagher Girls Ser.: 6). (ENG.). 320p. (YA). (gr. 7-17). pap. 10.99 *(978-1-4847-8508-9(8))* Hyperion Bks. for Children.

Carter, David A. School Bugs: An Elementary Pop-Up Book by David A. Carter. Carter, David A., illus. 2009. (David Carter's Bugs Ser.). (ENG., Illus.). 20p. (J). (gr. -1-2). 14.99 *(978-1-4169-5056-1(7)*, Little Simon) Little Simon.

Casanova, Mary. Chrissa, Bk. 1. England, Tamara, ed. Jones, Richard, illus. 2009. (American Girl: Chrissa Ser.). (ENG.). 130p. (J). (gr. 2-4). pap. 21.19 *(978-1-59369-566-8(7))* American Girl Publishing, Inc.

Casella, Jody. Thin Space. 2013. (ENG.). 256p. (YA). (gr. 7). 16.99 *(978-1-58270-435-7(X))*; pap. 10.99 *(978-1-58270-392-3(2))* Simon Pulse. (Simon Pulse).

Cassidy, Cathy. Indigo Blue. 2006. (ENG.). 240p. (J). (gr. 5-18). 7.99 *(978-0-14-240703-5(8)*, Puffin Books) Penguin Young Readers Group.

Castellucci, Cecil. Boy Proof, 4 vols. 2005. (YA). 62.75 *(978-1-4193-5131-0(1))* Recorded Bks., Inc.

—The PLAIN Janes. 2020. (ENG., Illus.). 496p. (YA). (gr. 7-17). pap. 18.99 *(978-0-316-52281-6(3))* Little, Brown Bks. for Young Readers.

Castle, M. E. Cloneward Bound. 2013. (Clone Chronicles Ser.: No. 2). (ENG., Illus.). 272p. (J). (gr. 3-6). pap. 6.99 *(978-1-60684-473-1(3)*, c69c9afc-d454-47fc-abf1-3de157a7bd9d, Darby Creek) Lerner Publishing Group.

—Game of Clones, No. 3. 2014. (Clone Chronicles Ser.: No. 3). (ENG., Illus.). 256p. (J). (gr. 3-6). pap. 6.99 *(978-1-60684-538-7(1)*, ba3c56fd-6d94-42af-be8a-35582221b366, Darby Creek) Lerner Publishing Group.

Catalanotto, Peter & Schembri, Pamela. The Veterans Day Visitor. Catalanotto, Peter, illus. 2008. (Second Grade Friends Ser.). (ENG., Illus.). 64p. (J). (gr. 2-5). 17.99 *(978-0-8050-7840-4(1)*, 900030187, Holt, Henry & Co. Bks. For Young Readers) Holt, Henry & Co.

Catling, Patrick Skene. The Chocolate Touch. Apple, Margo, illus. 2006. (ENG.). 128p. (J). (gr. 3-7). pap. 9.99 *(978-0-688-16133-0(2)*, HarperCollins) HarperCollins Pubs.

—The Chocolate Touch. 2014. (ENG.). 128p. (J). (gr. 3-7). 10.24 *(978-1-63245-319-8(3))* Lectorum Pubns., Inc.

—The Chocolate Touch. 2009. 8.32 *(978-1-55744-369-4(6)*, Everbind) Marco Bk. Co.

—The Chocolate Touch. 2006. 16.00 *(978-0-7569-6383-5(4))* Perfection Learning Corp.

—The Chocolate Touch. 87p. (J). (gr. 3-5). pap. 4.99 *(978-0-8072-1454-1(X)*, Listening Library) Random Hse. Audio Publishing Group.

Catling, Patrick Skene & Catling, P. The Chocolate Touch. Apple, Margot, illus. 2006. 126p. (J). (gr. 3-7). 17.20 *(978-1-4177-3437-5(X))* Turtleback.

Caudill, Rebecca. Did You Carry the Flag Today, Charley. Grossman, Nancy, illus. 2007. 96p. (J). pap. 7.95 *(978-0-8050-8141-1(0)*, Holt, Henry & Co. Bks. For Young Readers) Holt, Henry & Co.

—Schoolroom in the Parlor. Merwin, Decie, illus. l.t. ed. 2005. (ENG.). 145p. (J). (gr. 2-3). pap. 11.95 *(978-1-883937-82-9(5))* Ignatius Pr.

Caudill, Rebecca & Merwin, Decie. Schoolhouse in the Woods. l.t. ed. 2004. (ENG., Illus.). 130p. (J). (gr. 3-4). pap. 11.95 *(978-1-883937-80-5(9))* Ignatius Pr.

Cazet, Denys. Rumors. 2017. (ENG., Illus.). 212p. (J). (gr. 1-5). 16.99 *(978-1-939547-32-3(6)*, 091db7fb-6140-480f-b98d-5e831ea61f79) Creston Bks.

Cervantes, Angela. Allie, First at Last: a Wish Novel. 2016. (ENG.). 208p. (J). (gr. 3-7). 16.99 *(978-0-545-81223-8(2)*, Scholastic Pr.) Scholastic, Inc.

Cervantes, Gerard. Hilda Bee's Special Home. 2012. 48p. pap. 17.45 *(978-1-4497-3140-3(6)*, WestBow Pr.) Author Solutions, LLC.

Chabert, Jack. The Art Show Attacks!: a Branches Book (Eerie Elementary #9), Vol. 9. Loveridge, Matt, illus. 2018. (Eerie Elementary Ser.: 9). (ENG.). 96p. (J). (gr. 1-3). pap. 5.99 *(978-1-338-18197-5(1))* Scholastic, Inc.

—The Art Show Attacks!: a Branches Book (Eerie Elementary #9) (Library Edition), Vol. 9. Loveridge, Matt, illus. 2018. (Eerie Elementary Ser.: 9). (ENG.). 96p. (J). (gr. 1-3). lib. bdg. 24.99 *(978-1-338-18198-2(X))* Scholastic, Inc.

—Classes Are Canceled! 2017. (Eerie Elementary — Branches Ser.: 7). (J). lib. bdg. 14.75 *(978-0-606-40669-7(7))* Turtleback.

—Classes Are Canceled!: a Branches Book (Eerie Elementary #7) Loveridge, Matt, illus. 2017. (Eerie Elementary Ser.: 7). (ENG.). 96p. (J). (gr. 1-3). pap. 5.99 *(978-1-338-18180-7(7))* Scholastic, Inc.

—The End of Orson Eerie? a Branches Book (Eerie Elementary #10) Loveridge, Matt, illus. 2019. (Eerie Elementary Ser.: 10). (ENG.). 96p. (J). (gr. 1-3). pap. 5.99 *(978-1-338-31856-2(X))* Scholastic, Inc.

—The Hall Monitors Are Fired!: a Branches Book (Eerie Elementary #8) Loveridge, Matt, illus. 2018. (Eerie Elementary Ser.: 8). (ENG.). 96p. (J). (gr. 1-3). pap. 5.99 *(978-1-338-18188-3(2))* Scholastic, Inc.

—The Locker Ate Lucy! 2014. (Eerie Elementary — Branches Ser.: bk.2). (ENG.). (J). lib. bdg. 14.75 *(978-0-606-36052-4(2))* Turtleback.

—The Locker Ate Lucy!: a Branches Book (Eerie Elementary #2) Ricks, Sam, illus. 2014. (Eerie Elementary Ser.: 2). (ENG.). 96p. (J). (gr. 1-3). pap. 5.99 *(978-0-545-62395-7(2))* Scholastic, Inc.

—Recess Is a Jungle!: a Branches Book (Eerie Elementary #3) (Library Edition), Vol. 3. Ricks, Sam, illus. 2016. (Eerie Elementary Ser.: 3). (ENG.). 96p. (J). (gr. 1-3). 24.99 *(978-0-545-87353-6(3))* Scholastic, Inc.

—Sam Battles the Machine! 2017. (Eerie Elementary — Branches Ser.: bk.6). (ENG.). (J). lib. bdg. 14.75 *(978-0-606-40191-3(1))* Turtleback.

—Sam Battles the Machine!: a Branches Book (Eerie Elementary #6) Ricks, Sam, illus. 2017. (Eerie Elementary Ser.: 6). (ENG.). 96p. (J). (gr. 1-3). pap. 5.99 *(978-0-545-87378-9(9))* Scholastic, Inc.

—School Freezes over!: a Branches Book (Eerie Elementary #5) Ricks, Sam, illus. 2016. (Eerie Elementary Ser.: 5). (ENG.). 96p. (J). (gr. 1-3). pap. 5.99 *(978-0-545-87373-4(8))* Scholastic, Inc.

—The School Is Alive! 2014. (Eerie Elementary — Branches Ser.: bk.1). (ENG.). (J). lib. bdg. 14.75 *(978-0-606-35822-4(6))* Turtleback.

—The School Is Alive!: a Branches Book (Eerie Elementary #1) Ricks, Sam, illus. 2014. (Eerie Elementary Ser.: 1). (ENG.). 96p. (J). (gr. 1-3). pap. 5.99 *(978-0-545-62392-6(8))* Scholastic, Inc.

—The Science Fair Is Freaky! 2016. (Eerie Elementary — Branches Ser.: bk.4). (ENG.). (J). lib. bdg. 14.75 *(978-0-606-38806-1(0))* Turtleback.

—The Science Fair Is Freaky!: a Branches Book (Eerie Elementary #4) Ricks, Sam, illus. 2016. (Eerie Elementary Ser.: 4). (ENG.). 96p. (J). (gr. 1-3). pap. 5.99 *(978-0-545-87368-0(1))* Scholastic, Inc.

Chachas, George & Wojtak, James. Doolittle's Very, Very Bad Day. De Soto, Ben, illus. 2011. 26p. (J). pap. 9.95 *(978-0-9793144-2-1(9))* Doolittle Edutainment Corp.

Chainani, Soman. The Last Ever After. Bruno, Iacopo, illus. 2015. 655p. (J). *(978-0-06-241756-5(8))* Harper & Row Ltd.

—The Last Ever After. 2015. (School for Good & Evil Ser.: No. 3). 672p. (J). (gr. 3-7). pap. 9.99 *(978-0-06-239625-9(0))* HarperCollins Pubs.

—The Last Ever After. 2016. (School for Good & Evil Ser.: 3). (J). lib. bdg. 18.40 *(978-0-606-38761-3(7))* Turtleback.

—Quests for Glory. 2018. (School for Good & Evil Ser.: 4). (J). lib. bdg. 19.65 *(978-0-606-41379-4(0))* Turtleback.

—The School for Good & Evil. Bruno, Iacopo, illus. 2014. (School for Good & Evil Ser.: 1). 496p. (J). lib. bdg. 17.20 *(978-0-606-36513-0(3))* Turtleback.

—The School for Good & Evil: Now a Netflix Originals Movie. Bruno, Iacopo, illus. (School for Good & Evil Ser.: 1). (ENG.). (J). (gr. 3-7). 2018. 544p. pap. 8.99 *(978-0-06-210490-8(X))* 2013. 496p. 18.99 *(978-0-06-210489-2(6))* HarperCollins Pubs. (HarperCollins).

—The School for Good & Evil #2: a World Without Princes: Now a Netflix Originals Movie. Bruno, Iacopo, illus. (School for Good & Evil Ser.: 2). (ENG.). (J). (gr. 3-7). 2018. 512p.

pap. 8.99 (978-0-06-210493-9(4)) 2014. 448p. 18.99 (978-0-06-210492-2(6)) HarperCollins Pubs. (HarperCollins).

—The School for Good & Evil #3: the Last Ever After: Now a Netflix Originals Movie. (School for Good & Evil Ser.: 3). (ENG.). (J). (gr. 3-7). 2018. 704p. pap. 8.99 (978-0-06-210496-0(9)) 2015. (Illus.). 672p. 17.99 (978-0-06-210495-3(0)) HarperCollins Pubs. (HarperCollins).

—The School for Good & Evil #4: Quests for Glory: Now a Netflix Originals Movie. (School for Good & Evil Ser.: 4). (ENG.). (J). (gr. 3-7). 2018. 672p. pap. 11.99 (978-0-06-265848-7(4)) 2017. (Illus.). 576p. 17.99 (978-0-06-265847-0(6)) HarperCollins Pubs. (HarperCollins).

—The School for Good & Evil Books 1-4 Paperback Box Set: Now a Netflix Originals Movie. 2018. (School for Good & Evil Ser.). (ENG.). 2432p. (J). (gr. 3-7). pap. 35.96 (978-0-06-285557-2(3), HarperCollins) HarperCollins Pubs.

—The School for Good & Evil Series 3-Book Paperback Box Set: Books 1-3. 2022. (School for Good & Evil Ser.). (ENG.). 1760p. (J). (gr. 3). pap. 26.97 (978-0-06-245624-3(5), HarperCollins) HarperCollins Pubs.

—The School for Good & Evil Series Box Set: Books 1-3. 2015. (School for Good & Evil Ser.: Nos. 1-3). (ENG.). 1334p. (J). (gr. 3). 53.97 (978-0-06-243497-5(7), HarperCollins) HarperCollins Pubs.

—The School for Good & Evil: the Ever Never Handbook. Blank, Michael, illus. 2016. (School for Good & Evil Ser.). (ENG.). 304p. (J). (gr. 3-7). 17.99 (978-0-06-242305-4(3), HarperCollins) HarperCollins Pubs.

—A World Without Princes. 2014. (School for Good & Evil Trilogy: No. 2). (Illus.). 448p. (J). pap. (978-0-06-233135-9(3)) Harper & Row Ltd.

—A World Without Princes. Bruno, Iacopo, illus. 2014. (School for Good & Evil Trilogy: No. 2). (ENG.). 400p. (J). (978-0-06-234072-6(7)) Harper & Row Ltd.

—A World Without Princes. 2015. (School for Good & Evil Ser.: 2). (J). lib. bdg. 17.20 (978-0-606-36514-7(1)) Turtleback.

Chaltas, Thalia. Because I Am Furniture. 2010. (ENG.). 368p. (YA). (gr. 7-18). 8.99 (978-0-14-241510-8(3), Speak) Penguin Young Readers Group.

Champion, Dionne N., et al. The Spirit of the Baobab Tree. Champion, Dionne N. & Champion, Daryl, illus. 2008. 37p. (J). 31.99 (978-1-4363-7842-0(7)) Xlibris Corp.

Chang, Hae-Kyung. Oh No, School! Bisaillon, Josée, illus. 2014. 32p. (J). (978-1-4338-1333-7(5), Magination Pr.) American Psychological Assn.

Changing Schools: Individual Title Six-Packs. (gr. -1-2). 27.00 (978-0-7635-9440-4(7)) Rigby Education.

Chapman, Lara. Accidentally Evil. 2015. (Mix Ser.). (ENG., Illus.). 240p. (J). (gr. 4-8). pap. 7.99 (978-1-4814-0110-4(6), Aladdin) Simon & Schuster Children's Publishing.

—The XYZs of Being Wicked. 2014. (Mix Ser.). (ENG., Illus.). 272p. (J). (gr. 4-8). pap. 6.99 (978-1-4814-0107-4(6), Aladdin) Simon & Schuster Children's Publishing.

CHaracter Ed & the Magical Lesson of the Bully. 2004. (J). pap. 15.95 (978-1-59526-181-6(8)) Aeon Publishing Inc.

Charbonneau, Joelle. The Testing. 2015. (Testing Ser.: 1). (ENG.). 352p. (YA). (gr. 7). pap. 15.99 (978-0-544-33623-0(2), 1584169, Clarion Bks.) HarperCollins Pubs.

—Time Bomb. (ENG.). 352p. (YA). (gr. 7). 2020. pap. 9.99 (978-0-358-10805-4(5), 1748877) 2018. 17.99 (978-0-544-41670-3(8), 1594757) HarperCollins Pubs. (Clarion Bks.).

Charisse, April. Say Hello to Me: A Story about a Little Girl on the Autism Spectrum. 2012. 16p. pap. 15.99 (978-1-4685-9475-1(3)) AuthorHouse.

Charles L. Wilson. The Search Is On: The Wild Adventures of Lester & Dora. 2009. 200p. 24.99 (978-1-4269-1813-1(5)); pap. 14.99 (978-1-4269-1812-4(7)) Trafford Publishing.

Charles, Tami. Daphne Definitely Doesn't Do Dances. Calo, Marcos, illus. 2018. (Daphne, Secret Vlogger Ser.). (ENG.). 96p. (J). (gr. 4-7). pap. 4.95 (978-1-4965-6301-9(8), 138030); lib. bdg. 24.65 (978-1-4965-6297-5(6), 138024) Capstone. (Stone Arch Bks.).

—Daphne Definitely Doesn't Do Drama. Calo, Marcos, illus. 2018. (Daphne, Secret Vlogger Ser.). (ENG.). 96p. (J). (gr. 4-7). pap. 4.95 (978-1-4965-6299-9(2), 138029); lib. bdg. 24.65 (978-1-4965-6295-1(X), 138021) Capstone. (Stone Arch Bks.).

—Daphne Definitely Doesn't Do Fashion. Calo, Marcos, illus. 2018. (Daphne, Secret Vlogger Ser.). (ENG.). 96p. (J). (gr. 4-7). pap. 4.95 (978-1-4965-6300-2(X), 138031, Stone Arch Bks.) Capstone.

—Daphne Definitely Doesn't Do Sports. Calo, Marcos, illus. 2018. (Daphne, Secret Vlogger Ser.). (ENG.). 96p. (J). (gr. 4-7). lib. bdg. 24.65 (978-1-4965-6294-4(1), 138020, Stone Arch Bks.) Capstone.

—Daphne, Secret Vlogger, 4 vols. Calo, Marcos, illus. 2018. (Daphne, Secret Vlogger Ser.). (ENG.). 96p. (J). (gr. 4-7). 101.28 (978-1-4965-6306-4(9), 28113, Stone Arch Bks.) Capstone.

—Like Vanessa. Brantley-Newton, Vanessa, illus. (J). (gr. 5). 2019. 304p. pap. 8.99 (978-1-58089-899-7(8)) 2018. 288p. 16.99 (978-1-58089-777-8(0)) Charlesbridge Publishing, Inc.

Charlesworth, Liza. Fish School: An Animal Friends Reader. Smith, Ian, illus. 2015. 16p. (J). pap. (978-0-545-85963-9(8)) Scholastic, Inc.

Charlton-Trujillo, E. E. Fat Angie. 2013. (ENG.). 272p. (YA). (gr. 9). 16.99 (978-0-7636-6119-9(8)) Candlewick Pr.

Chartier, Brent & Jones, Patrick. Collateral Damage. 2015. (Support & Defend Ser.). (ENG.). 128p. (YA). (gr. 6-12). pap. 7.99 (978-1-4677-8091-9(X), aa18a38c-207a-4040-b2b0-3605af3fe712, Darby Creek) Lerner Publishing Group.

Chast, Roz. Marco Goes to School. Chast, Roz, illus. 2012. (ENG., Illus.). 32p. (J). (gr. -1-3). 16.99 (978-1-4169-8475-7(5), Atheneum Bks. for Young Readers) Simon & Schuster Children's Publishing.

Chastain, Emma. Confessions of a High School Disaster. 2017. (Chloe Snow's Diary Ser.). (ENG., Illus.). 352p. (YA). (gr. 7). 18.99 (978-1-4814-8875-4(9), Simon Pulse) Simon Pulse.

—Confessions of a High School Disaster: Freshman Year. 2018. (ENG.). 368p. (YA). (gr. 7). pap. 11.99 (978-1-4814-8876-1(7), Simon Pulse) Simon Pulse.

—Notes from a Former Virgin: Junior Year. 2019. (ENG., Illus.). 448p. (YA). (gr. 9). 18.99 (978-1-5344-2110-3(6), Simon Pulse) Simon Pulse.

—The Year of Living Awkwardly: Sophomore Year. 2018. (ENG., Illus.). 384p. (YA). (gr. 7). 18.99 (978-1-4814-8878-5(3), Simon Pulse) Simon Pulse.

Chbosky, Stephen. The Perks of Being a Wallflower. 2014. (ENG.). 224p. (gr. 7-12). 18.25 (978-1-63245-042-5(9)) Lectorum Pubns., Inc.

—The Perks of Being a Wallflower. movie tie-in ed. 2012. (ENG.). 224p. (YA). (gr. 7). pap. 15.99 (978-1-4516-9619-6(1), MTV Bks.) MTV Books.

—The Perks of Being a Wallflower. 2009. 13.77 (978-0-7848-1530-4(5), Everbind) Marco Bk. Co.

—The Perks of Being a Wallflower. 2008. (ENG.). 24.30 (978-1-60686-308-4(8), Covercraft) Perfection Learning Corp.

—The Perks of Being a Wallflower. 2007. 1.25 (978-1-4281-3271-9(6)) Recorded Bks., Inc.

Cheeseboro, Tyrese. Why Did Ronald Break the Rules? Rules at Home & Rules at School! 2010. 28p. 12.49 (978-1-4490-8871-2(6)) AuthorHouse.

Chen, Bill. The Musical. Sun, Jun, illus. 2013. (J). (978-0-9845523-1-3(6)) Heryin Publishing Corp.

Cheng, Andrea. The Year of the Baby. Barton, Patrice, illus. 2014. (Anna Wang Novel Ser.: 2). (ENG.). 176p. (J). (gr. 1-4). pap. 6.99 (978-0-544-22525-1(2), 1563367, Clarion Bks.) HarperCollins Pubs.

—The Year of the Book. Halpin, Abigail, illus. (Anna Wang Novel Ser.: 1). (ENG.). 160p. (J). (gr. 1-4). 2013. pap. 7.99 (978-0-544-02263-8(7), 1528485) 2012. 16.99 (978-0-547-68463-5(0), 1476526) HarperCollins Pubs. (Clarion Bks.).

Child, Lauren. Clarice Bean Spells Trouble. Child, Lauren, illus. 2006. (Clarice Bean Ser.: 2). (ENG., Illus.). 192p. (J). (gr. 3-7). pap. 7.99 (978-0-7636-2903-8(0)) Candlewick Pr.

—Clarice Bean Spells Trouble. Child, Lauren, illus. 2006. (Clarice Bean Ser.). (Illus.). 189p. (J). (gr. 3-6). 13.65 (978-0-7569-7919-5(6)) Perfection Learning Corp.

—I Am Going to Save a Panda! 2010. (Charlie & Lola Ser.). lib. bdg. 13.55 (978-0-606-10628-3(6)) Turtleback.

—I Am Too Absolutely Small for School. Child, Lauren, illus. (Charlie & Lola Ser.). (ENG., Illus.). 32p. (J). (gr. -1-2). 2004. 16.99 (978-0-7636-2403-3(9)) 2005. reprint ed. per. 9.99 (978-0-7636-2887-1(5)) Candlewick Pr.

—I Am Too Absolutely Small for School. 2007. (Charlie & Lola (Shang Yi Publishing) Ser.). (CHI., Illus.). (J). (978-957-762-437-6(5)) Hsin Yi Pubns.

—I Am Too Absolutely Small for School. Child, Lauren, illus. 2005. (ENG., Illus.). (J). (gr. -1-1). lib. bdg. 14.65 (978-0-7569-6495-5(4)) Perfection Learning Corp.

—I Can't Stop Hiccuping! 2010. (Charlie & Lola Ser.). lib. bdg. 13.55 (978-0-606-10629-0(4)) Turtleback.

—Utterly Me, Clarice Bean. Child, Lauren, illus. 2005. (Clarice Bean Ser.). (ENG., Illus.). (J). 190p. (gr. 4-6). 18.69 (978-0-7636-2186-5(2)); 208p. (gr. 3-7). reprint ed. pap. 7.99 (978-0-7636-2788-1(7)) Candlewick Pr.

—Utterly Me, Clarice Bean. Child, Lauren, illus. 2006. (Clarice Bean Ser.). (Illus.). 16.00 (978-0-7569-6567-9(5)) Perfection Learning Corp.

Child, Lauren, et al. Fi'n Hollol, Carys Blodyn. 2005. (WEL., Illus.). 192p. pap. (978-1-85596-675-8(1)) Dref Wen.

Childrens Books Staff. Smell You Later! Childrens Books Staff & Lambe, Steve, illus. 2012. (Fanboy & Chum Chum Ser.). (ENG.). 96p. (J). (gr. 2-4). 21.19 (978-1-4424-2834-8(1), Simon Spotlight) Simon & Schuster Children's Publishing.

Childs, Tera Lynn. Fins Are Forever. 2012. (Forgive My Fins Ser.: 2). (ENG.). 288p. (YA). (gr. 8). pap. 8.99 (978-0-06-191470-6(3), Tegen, Katherine Bks) HarperCollins Pubs.

Chima, Cinda Williams. The Wizard Heir. 2008. (Heir Chronicles Ser.: 2). (ENG.). 480p. (YA). (gr. 7-17). pap. 12.99 (978-1-4231-0488-9(9)) Little, Brown Bks. for Young Readers.

Chisolm, Melinda. Remembering to Breathe. Cross, Jo Ellen, illus. 2009. 31p. pap. 24.95 (978-1-60703-914-3(1)) America Star Bks.

Chmakova, Svetlana. Awkward. 2015. (J). lib. bdg. 22.10 (978-0-606-38218-2(6)) Turtleback.

Choi, Yangsook. The Name Jar. Choi, Yangsook, illus. 2003. (ENG., Illus.). 40p. (J). (gr. -1-2). pap. 8.99 (978-0-440-41799-6(6), Dragonfly Bks.) Random Hse. Children's Bks.

Choldenko, Gennifer. If a Tree Falls at Lunch Period. 2007. (ENG., Illus.). 224p. (YA). (gr. 9-12). 18.69 (978-0-15-205753-4(6)) Harcourt Children's Bks.

—If a Tree Falls at Lunch Period. 2009. (ENG., Illus.). 224p. (J). (gr. 5-7). pap. 7.99 (978-0-15-206644-4(6), 1099003, Clarion Bks.) HarperCollins Pubs.

Choyce, Lesley. Carrie Loses Her Nerve, 1 vol. Thurman, Mark, illus. 2003. (Formac First Novels Ser.: 26). (ENG.). 64p. (J). (gr. 1-5). 4.95 (978-0-88780-591-2(4), 591); 14.95 (978-0-88780-592-9(2), 592) Formac Publishing Co., Ltd. CAN. Dist: Formac Lorimer Bks. Ltd.

—The End of the World As We Know It, 1 vol. 2007. (ENG.). 224p. (YA). (gr. 6-11). per. 9.95 (978-0-88995-379-6(1), f1834eb8-5fae-4c43-bf6f-b102526ce72c) Red Deer Pr. CAN. Dist: Firefly Bks., Ltd.

—Rat, 1 vol. 2012. (Orca Soundings Ser.). (ENG.). 128p. (YA). (gr. 8-12). pap. 9.95 (978-1-4598-0300-8(0)) Orca Bk. Pubs. USA.

Chriscoe, Sharon. Scary Weather, Scaredy Cat, 1 vol. 2008. (ENG.). 48p. 24.95 (978-1-60474-143-8(0)) America Star Bks.

Christie, Tory. Curious Mccarthy's Electric Ideas. Price, Mina, illus. 2017. (Curious Mccarthy Ser.). (ENG.). 112p. (J). (gr. 2-4). pap. 6.95 (978-1-5158-1648-5(6), 136303); lib. bdg. 25.32 (978-1-5158-1644-7(3), 136299) Capstone. (Picture Window Bks.).

—Curious Mccarthy's Not-So-Perfect Pitch. Price, Mina, illus. 2017. (Curious Mccarthy Ser.). (ENG.). 112p. (J). (gr. 2-4). pap. 6.95 (978-1-5158-1647-8(8), 136302, Picture Window Bks.) Capstone.

—Curious Mccarthy's Power of Observation. Price, Mina, illus. 2017. (Curious Mccarthy Ser.). (ENG.). 112p. (J). (gr. 2-4). pap. 6.95 (978-1-5158-1650-8(8), 136305); lib. bdg. 25.32 (978-1-5158-1646-1(X), 136301) Capstone. (Picture Window Bks.).

Christopher, Lawrence. The Tickle Fingers: Where Is Pinky? Christopher, Lawrence, illus. 2006. (ENG., Illus.). 24p. (J). (gr. -1-18). 9.95 (978-0-9712278-3-5(7)) MF Unlimited.

Christopher, Matt. Football Double Threat. 2008. (ENG.). 128p. (J). (gr. 3-7). pap. 9.99 (978-0-316-01632-2(2)) Little, Brown Bks. for Young Readers.

—QB Blitz. 2011. (ENG.). 144p. (J). (gr. 3-7). pap. 10.99 (978-0-316-17682-8(6)) Little, Brown Bks. for Young Readers.

—Soccer Scoop. 2007. (New Matt Christopher Sports Library). 133p. (J). (gr. 4-6). lib. bdg. 26.60 (978-1-59953-117-5(8)) Norwood Hse. Pr.

—Stealing Home. 2004. (ENG.). 144p. (J). (gr. 3-7). pap. 6.99 (978-0-316-60742-1(8)) Little, Brown Bks. for Young Readers.

Chung, Helena. Jennifer, the Special One. 2004. (J). pap. 8.00 (978-0-8059-6395-3(2)) Dorrance Publishing Co., Inc.

Ciencin, Scott. Attack of the Cling-Ons, 1 vol. Crowther, Jeff, illus. 2011. (Graphic Sparks Ser.). (ENG.). 40p. (J). (gr. 2-4). pap. 5.95 (978-1-4342-3067-6(8), 114683); lib. bdg. 23.99 (978-1-4342-2637-2(9), 113961) Capstone. (Stone Arch Bks.).

Cinema, Bobby. Princess School. 2012. 68p. 18.66 (978-1-4669-3968-4(0)); 18p. pap. 8.66 (978-1-4669-3967-7(2)) Trafford Publishing.

Ciocca, Donna. Harley & Homer. 2004. (YA). per. 9.95 (978-0-9747361-2-9(0)) Oak Manor Publishing, Inc.

—Harley & Homer for Hire. 2006. (YA). per. 11.95 (978-0-9747361-9-8(8)) Oak Manor Publishing, Inc.

Ciocca, Gina. A Kiss in the Dark. 2018. (ENG., Illus.). 352p. (YA). (gr. 9). 17.99 (978-1-4814-3226-9(5), Simon Pulse) Simon Pulse.

—Last Year's Mistake. 2015. (ENG., Illus.). 320p. (YA). (gr. 9). 17.99 (978-1-4814-3223-8(0), Simon Pulse) Simon Pulse.

Cirrone, Dorian. Prom Kings & Drama Queens. 2008. 200p. (YA). (gr. 7). lib. bdg. 17.89 (978-0-06-114373-1(1), HarperTeen) HarperCollins Pubs.

Clampitt, Ed & Fortier, Robert. Team Dawg Trevor's Bully Problem. 2007. (J). per. 14.99 (978-0-9749378-2-3(7)) Team Dawg Productions, Inc.

Clark, Brenda. Spiro & Zinger Rescue the Orphans: Spiro the Shooting Star - Book Three, 1 vol. 2010. 70p. pap. 19.95 (978-1-4489-3992-3(5)) America Star Bks.

Clark, Bridie. Maybe Tonight? 2013. (Snap Decision Ser.: 1). (ENG.). 224p. (YA). (gr. 7). pap. 18.99 (978-1-59643-816-3(9), 900087053) Roaring Brook Pr.

—You Only Live Once: Every Decision You Make Has Consequences. 2014. (Snap Decision Ser.: 2). (ENG.). 224p. (YA). (gr. 7). pap. 16.99 (978-1-59643-817-0(7), 900087054) Roaring Brook Pr.

Clark, Catherine. Frozen Rodeo. 2003. (ENG.). 304p. (YA). (gr. 8-18). 15.99 (978-0-06-009070-8(7)) HarperCollins Pubs.

Clark, Clara Gillow. Secrets of Greymoor. 2009. (Trials of Hattie Belle Basket Ser.). (Illus.). 176p. (J). (gr. 5). 15.99 (978-0-7636-3249-6(X)) Candlewick Pr.

Clark, Eleanor. Victoria Grace: Courageous Patriot. 2007. (Eleanor Ser.: Bk. 2). 209p. (J). (gr. 4-7). 14.99 (978-0-9753036-8-9(6)) HonorNet.

Clark, Jay. The Edumacation of Jay Baker. 2012. (ENG.). 288p. (YA). (gr. 9-12). pap. 9.99 (978-1-250-01675-1(4), 900087089) Square Fish.

Clark, Kristin Elizabeth. Freakboy. 2016. (ENG.). 448p. (YA). (gr. 7-13). 22.10 (978-0-606-39285-3(8)) Turtleback.

Clark, Lillian. Immoral Code. 2019. 320p. (YA). (gr. 7). 17.99 (978-0-525-58046-1(8), Knopf Bks. for Young Readers) Random Hse. Children's Bks.

Clark, Sherryl & Perry, Ellyse. Ellyse Perry: Double Time. 2017. (Ellyse Perry Ser.: 4). 160p. (J). (gr. 4-7). 13.99 (978-0-14-378130-1(8)) Random Hse. Australia AUS. Dist: Independent Pubs. Group.

—Magic Feet. 2017. (Ellyse Perry Ser.: 2). 160p. (J). (gr. 4-7). 14.99 (978-0-14-378126-4(X)) Random Hse. Australia AUS. Dist: Independent Pubs. Group.

—Pocket Rocket. 2017. (Ellyse Perry Ser.: 1). 160p. (J). (gr. 4-7). 13.99 (978-0-14-378124-0(3)) Random Hse. Australia AUS. Dist: Independent Pubs. Group.

Clark, Todd. The Ice Cream Kid: Brain Freeze! 2014. (ENG.). 176p. (J). 13.99 (978-1-4494-4424-2(5)) Andrews McMeel Publishing.

Clarke, David. Snake Bite: A Novel. 2009. 188p. 23.95 (978-0-595-71833-7(7)); pap. 13.95 (978-0-595-48406-5(9)) iUniverse, Inc.

Clarke, Judith. Al Capsella & Watchdogs. 164p. pap. (978-0-7022-2294-8(1)) Univ. of Queensland Pr.

Clarke, Kevin & Dutton, Demi. Jenny Can't Read: A Story about Dyslexia & Its Effect on Self-Esteem. 2012. 90p. pap. 13.66 (978-1-4772-1909-6(9)) AuthorHouse.

Clawson, David. My Fairy Godmother Is a Drag Queen. 2017. (ENG.). 336p. (J). (gr. 8-8). 17.99 (978-1-5107-1411-3(1), Sky Pony Pr.) Skyhorse Publishing Co., Inc.

Cleary, Beverly. Ellen Tebbits. Dockray, Tracy, illus. 2008. (ENG.). 192p. (J). (gr. 3-7). 16.99 (978-0-688-21264-3(6), HarperCollins) HarperCollins Pubs.

—Henry & Beezus. Darling, Louis, illus. 2017. (Henry Huggins Ser.: 2). (ENG.). 176p. (J). (gr. 3-7). 16.99 (978-0-06-265236-2(2), HarperCollins) HarperCollins Pubs.

—Muggie Maggie. Dockray, Tracy, illus. 2015. (ENG.). 96p. (J). (gr. 3-7). reprint ed. pap. 8.99 (978-0-380-71087-4(0), HarperCollins) HarperCollins Pubs.

—Ramona Empieza el Curso: A Newbery Honor Award Winner, 1 vol. Rogers, Jacqueline, illus. 2006.Tr. of Ramona Quimby, Age 8. (SPA.). 224p. (J). (gr. 3-7). pap. 7.99 (978-0-688-15487-5(5), MR7554) HarperCollins Español.

—Ramona la Chinche. Palacios, Argentina, tr. Darling, Louis, illus. 2006. (Ramona Quimby Spanish Ser.: 2).Tr. of Ramona the Pest. (SPA.). 181p. (J). (gr. 4-7). lib. bdg. 16.00 (978-0-613-00464-0(7)) Turtleback.

—Ramona la Chinche: Ramona the Pest (Spanish Edition), 1 vol. Rogers, Jacqueline, illus. 2006.Tr. of Ramona the Pest. (SPA.). 192p. (J). (gr. 3-7). pap. 7.99 (978-0-688-14888-1(3), MR2295) HarperCollins Español.

—Ramona Quimby, Age 8. Rogers, Jacqueline, illus. 2016. (Ramona Ser.: 6). (ENG.). 208p. (J). (gr. 3-7). 12.99 (978-0-06-246454-5(X), HarperCollins) HarperCollins Pubs.

—Ramona Quimby, Age 8. (Ramona Quimby Ser.). (J). (gr. 3-5). Random House Publishing Group.

—Ramona Quimby, Age 8. (Ramona Quimby Ser.). 190p. (J). (gr. 3-5). pap. 4.99 (978-0-8072-1436-7(1), Listening Library) Random Hse. Audio Publishing Group.

—Ramona Quimby, Age 8: A Newbery Honor Award Winner. Rogers, Jacqueline, illus. 2020. (Ramona Ser.: 6). (ENG.). 208p. (J). (gr. 3-7). 18.99 (978-0-688-00477-4(6)); pap. 7.99 (978-0-380-70956-4(2)) HarperCollins Pubs. (HarperCollins).

—Ramona Quimby, Age 8 Read-Aloud Edition. Rogers, Jacqueline, illus. 2016. (Ramona Ser.: 6). (ENG.). 208p. (J). (gr. 3-7). 17.99 (978-0-06-245327-3(0), HarperCollins) HarperCollins Pubs.

—Ramona the Brave. Rogers, Jacqueline, illus. 2020. (Ramona Ser.: 3). (ENG.). 208p. (J). (gr. 3-7). 16.99 (978-0-688-22015-0(0)); pap. 9.99 (978-0-380-70959-5(7)) HarperCollins Pubs. (HarperCollins).

—Ramona the Brave. (Ramona Quimby Ser.). 190p. (J). (gr. 3-5). pap. 4.99 (978-0-8072-1440-4(X), Listening Library) Random Hse. Audio Publishing Group.

—Ramona the Pest. Rogers, Jacqueline, illus. 2020. (Ramona Ser.: 2). (ENG.). 240p. (J). (gr. 3-7). 16.99 (978-0-688-21721-1(4)); pap. 7.99 (978-0-380-70954-0(6)) HarperCollins Pubs. (HarperCollins).

—Ramona the Pest. (Ramona Quimby Ser.). (J). (gr. 3-5). Random House Publishing Group.

—Ramona the Pest. (Ramona Quimby Ser.). 192p. (J). (gr. 3-5). pap. 4.99 (978-0-8072-1438-1(8), Listening Library) Random Hse. Audio Publishing Group.

—Ramona's World. Rogers, Jacqueline, illus. 2020. (Ramona Ser.: 8). (ENG.). 240p. (J). (gr. 3-7). 17.99 (978-0-688-16816-2(7)); pap. 7.99 (978-0-380-73272-2(6)) HarperCollins Pubs. (HarperCollins).

—Ramona's World. unabr. ed. 2004. (Ramona Quimby Ser.). 194p. (J). (gr. 3-7). pap. 29.00 incl. audio (978-0-8072-8169-7(7), Listening Library) Random Hse. Audio Publishing Group.

—Ramona's World. 2013. (Ramona Quimby Ser.: 8). (J). (gr. 3-6). lib. bdg. 17.20 (978-0-613-35794-4(9)) Turtleback.

Cleary, Brian P. Crunch & Crack, Oink & Whack! An Onomatopoeia Story. Pino, Pablo, illus. 2019. (ENG.). 32p. (J). (gr. 2-5). 26.65 (978-1-4677-8799-4(X), fe74533a-b23b-4109-88d5-d9414ab7877c, Millbrook Pr.) Lerner Publishing Group.

Clements, Andrew. About Average. Elliott, Mark, illus. (ENG.). (J). (gr. 3-7). 2014. 144p. pap. 7.99 (978-1-4169-9725-2(3)) 2012. 128p. 18.99 (978-1-4169-9724-5(5)) Simon & Schuster Children's Publishing. (Atheneum Bks. for Young Readers).

—Andrew Clements' School Stories (Boxed Set) Frindle; Landry News; the Janitor's Boy; the School Story; a Week in the Woods; Lunch Money; Room One; No Talking; Lost & Found; Extra Credit. 2013. (ENG., Illus.). 1856p. (J). (gr. 3-7). pap. 79.99 (978-1-4424-9386-5(0), Atheneum Bks. for Young Readers) Simon & Schuster Children's Publishing.

—Bully Buster. 2014. (Jake Drake Ser. Bk. 1 Ser.). (ENG.). 80p. (J). (gr. 2-5). 9.24 (978-1-63245-290-0(1)) Lectorum Pubns., Inc.

—Bully Buster. Frazee, Marla & Pedersen, Janet, illus. 2008. (Jake Drake Ser.: Bk. 1). 67p. (gr. 2-5). 15.00 (978-0-7569-9001-5(7)) Perfection Learning Corp.

—Fear Itself. Stower, Adam, illus. 2011. (Benjamin Pratt & the Keepers of the School Ser.: 2). (ENG.). (J). (gr. 2-5). 240p. pap. 8.99 (978-1-4169-3908-5(3)); 224p. 16.99 (978-1-4169-3887-3(7)) Simon & Schuster Children's Publishing. (Atheneum Bks. for Young Readers).

—The Friendship War. 2020. 208p. (J). (gr. 3-7). pap. 7.99 (978-0-399-55762-0(8), Yearling) Random Hse. Children's Bks.

—Frindle. 2014. (ENG.). 112p. (J). 11.24 (978-1-63245-158-3(1)) Lectorum Pubns., Inc.

—Head of the Class (Boxed Set) Frindle; the Landry News; the Janitor's Boy. Selznick, Brian, illus. 2007. (ENG.). 416p. (J). (gr. 3-7). pap. 23.99 (978-1-4169-4974-9(7), Atheneum Bks. for Young Readers) Simon & Schuster Children's Publishing.

—In Harm's Way. Stower, Adam, illus. (Benjamin Pratt & the Keepers of the School Ser.: 4). (ENG.). (J). (gr. 2-5). 2014. 240p. pap. 8.99 (978-1-4169-3910-8(5)) 2013. 224p. 14.99 (978-1-4169-3889-7(3)) Simon & Schuster Children's Publishing. (Atheneum Bks. for Young Readers).

—The Jacket. 2014. (ENG.). 96p. (J). (gr. 3-7). 10.24 (978-1-63245-301-3(0)) Lectorum Pubns., Inc.

—The Jacket. Henderson, McDavid, illus. 2003. (ENG.). 96p. (J). (gr. 3-7). pap. 6.99 (978-0-689-86010-2(2), Atheneum Bks. for Young Readers) Simon & Schuster Children's Publishing.

—Jake Drake, Bully Buster. Pedersen, Janet, illus. 2007. (Jake Drake Ser.: Bk. 1). (ENG.). 80p. (J). (gr. 2-5). pap. 5.99 (978-1-4169-3933-7(4), Atheneum Bks. for Young Readers) Simon & Schuster Children's Publishing.

—Jake Drake, Class Clown. Pedersen, Janet, illus. 2007. (Jake Drake Ser.: Bk. 4). (ENG.). 96p. (J). (gr. 2-5). pap. 5.99 (978-1-4169-4912-1(7), Atheneum Bks. for Young Readers) Simon & Schuster Children's Publishing.

—Jake Drake, Know-It-All. Frazee, Marla & Pedersen, Janet, illus. 2007. (Jake Drake Ser.: Bk. 2). 88p. (gr. 2-5). 15.00 (978-0-7569-8212-6(X)) Perfection Learning Corp.

—Jake Drake, Know-It-All. Pedersen, Janet, illus. 2007. (Jake Drake Ser.: Bk. 2). (ENG.). 112p. (J). (gr. 2-5). pap. 6.99 (978-1-4169-3931-3(8), Atheneum Bks. for Young Readers) Simon & Schuster Children's Publishing.

—Jake Drake, Teacher's Pet. Pedersen, Janet, illus. 2007. (Jake Drake Ser.: 3). (ENG.). 96p. (J). (gr. 2-5). pap. 5.99 (978-1-4169-3932-0(6), Atheneum Bks. for Young Readers) Simon & Schuster Children's Publishing.

—Jake Drake, Teacher's Pet. 2007. (Jake Drake Ser.: 3). lib. bdg. 16.00 (978-1-4177-9035-7(0)) Turtleback.

—The Last Holiday Concert. (ENG., Illus.). 176p. (J). (gr. 3-7). 2006. pap. 7.99 (978-0-689-84525-3(1)) 2004. 19.99 (978-0-689-84516-1(2)) Simon & Schuster Children's Publishing. (Atheneum Bks. for Young Readers).

—The Last Holiday Concert. rev. l.t. ed. 2007. (Literacy Bridge Middle Reader Ser.). 165p. (J). (gr. 3-7). 22.95 (978-0-7862-9374-2(8)) Thorndike Pr.

—The Losers Club. 2017. 240p. (J). (gr. 3-7). 16.99 (978-0-399-55755-2(5), Random Hse. Bks. for Young Readers) Random Hse. Children's Bks.

S

—Lost & Found. Elliott, Mark, illus. (ENG.). (J). (gr. 3-7). 2010. 192p. pap. 7.99 (978-1-4169-0986-6(9)) 2008. 176p. 18.99 (978-1-4169-0985-9(0)) Simon & Schuster Children's Publishing. (Atheneum Bks. for Young Readers).

—Lunch Money. Selznick, Brian, illus. (ENG.). (J). (gr. 3-7). 2007. 240p. pap. 7.99 (978-0-689-86685-2(2)) 2005. 224p. 19.99 (978-0-689-86683-8(6)) Simon & Schuster Children's Publishing. (Atheneum Bks. for Young Readers).

—Lunch Money. 2007. 17.20 (978-1-4177-8116-4(5)) Turtleback.

—The Map Trap. Andreasen, Dan, illus. 2016. (ENG.). 160p. (J). (gr. 3-7). pap. 7.99 (978-1-4169-9728-3(8)) Simon & Schuster Children's Publishing.

—The Map Trap. 2016. lib. bdg. 18.40 (978-0-606-38977-8(6)) Turtleback.

—No Talking. 2014. (ENG.). 160p. (J). (gr. 3-7). 11.24 (978-1-63245-298-6(7)) Lectorum Pubns., Inc.

—No Talking. (J). 2008. 78.75 (978-1-4361-5835-0(4)) 2007. 54.75 (978-1-4281-5418-6(3)) 2007. 52.75 (978-1-4281-5420-9(5)) 2007. 209.75 (978-1-4281-5419-3(1)) 2007. 1.25 (978-1-4281-5415-5(9)) 2007. 51.75 (978-1-4281-5424-7(8)) 2007. (SPA.). 54.75 (978-1-4281-5422-3(1)) Recorded Bks., Inc.

—No Talking. Elliott, Mark, illus. (ENG.). 160p. (J). (gr. 3-7). 2009. pap. 7.99 (978-1-4169-0984-2(2)) 2007. 19.99 (978-1-4169-0983-5(4)) Simon & Schuster Children's Publishing. (Atheneum Bks. for Young Readers).

—No Talking. Elliott, Mark, illus. l.t. ed. 2007. (Literacy Bridge Middle Reader Ser.). 155p. (J). (gr. 3-7). 23.95 (978-1-4104-0294-3(0)) Thorndike Pr.

—No Talking. 2009. (CHI., Illus.). 180p. (J). pap. 14.95 (978-7-5309-5645-8(0)) Tianjin Education Pr.

—No Talking. 2009. lib. bdg. 18.40 (978-0-606-14508-4(7)) Turtleback.

—El Periodico Landry. Selznick, Brian, illus. 2004.Tr. of Landry News. (SPA.). (YA). pap. 9.99 (978-84-241-7886-4(6)) Everest Editora ESP. Dist: Lectorum Pubns., Inc.

—The Report Card. (ENG., Illus.). (J). (gr. 3-7). 2004. 176p. 19.99 (978-0-689-84515-4(4)) 2006. 192p. reprint ed. pap. 7.99 (978-0-689-84524-6(3)) Simon & Schuster Children's Publishing. (Atheneum Bks. for Young Readers).

—Room One: A Mystery or Two. Elliott, Mark, illus. (ENG.). (J). (gr. 3-7). 2008. 192p. pap. 7.99 (978-0-689-86687-6(9)) 2006. 176p. 19.99 (978-0-689-86686-9(0)) Simon & Schuster Children's Publishing. (Atheneum Bks. for Young Readers).

—Troublemaker. Elliott, Mark, illus. (ENG.). (J). (gr. 3-7). 2013. 176p. pap. 7.99 (978-1-4169-4932-9(1)) 2011. 160p. lib. bdg. 18.99 (978-1-4169-4930-5(5)) Simon & Schuster Children's Publishing. (Atheneum Bks. for Young Readers).

—We Hold These Truths. Stower, Adam, illus. 2013. (Benjamin Pratt & the Keepers of the School Ser.: 5). (ENG.). 272p. (J). (gr. 2-5). 14.99 (978-1-4169-3890-3(7), Atheneum Bks. for Young Readers) Simon & Schuster Children's Publishing.

—We the Children. 2011. (Benjamin Pratt & the Keepers of the School Ser.: 1). (ENG.). 176p. (J). (gr. 2-5). pap. 8.99 (978-1-4169-3907-8(5), Atheneum Bks. for Young Readers) Simon & Schuster Children's Publishing.

—We the Children, 1. Stower, Adam, illus. 2010. (Benjamin Pratt & the Keepers of the School Ser.: 1). (ENG.). 160p. (J). (gr. 2-5). 16.99 (978-1-4169-3886-6(9)) Simon & Schuster, Inc.

—The Whites of Their Eyes. Stower, Adam, illus. 2013. (Benjamin Pratt & the Keepers of the School Ser.: 3). (ENG.). 240p. (J). (gr. 2-5). pap. 7.99 (978-1-4169-3909-2(1), Atheneum Bks. for Young Readers) Simon & Schuster Children's Publishing.

Clewarth, John. Firestorm Rising. 2012. (Illus.). 200p. pap. (978-1-4710-3681-1(2)) Lulu.com.

—Firestorm Rising. 2018. (ENG., Illus.). 216p. (J). (gr. 4-6). pap. (978-1-912513-70-3(6)) Silver Quill Publishing.

Cline-Ransome, Lesa. Freedom's School. Ransome, James E., illus. 2015. (ENG.). 32p. (J). (gr. -1-3). 18.99 (978-1-4231-6103-5(3)) Little, Brown Bks. for Young Readers.

Clough, Lisa. Me, Penelope. 2009. (ENG.). 208p. (YA). (gr. 9). pap. 12.99 (978-0-547-07632-4(0), 1042010, Clarion Bks.) HarperCollins Pubs.

Coats, J. Anderson. R Is for Rebel. 2018. (ENG., Illus.). 256p. (J). (gr. 5). 16.99 (978-1-4814-9667-4(0), Atheneum Bks. for Young Readers) Simon & Schuster Children's Publishing.

Cobb, Daryl K. Do Pirates Go to School. 2010. pap. 11.99 (978-0-578-05535-0(X)) 10 To 2 Children's Bks.

Coben, Harlan. Seconds Away. l.t. ed. 2012. (Mickey Bolitar Ser.: 2). (ENG.). 396p. 23.99 (978-1-4104-5348-8(0)) Thorndike Pr.

—Seconds Away. 2013. (Mickey Bolitar Ser.: 2). lib. bdg. 20.85 (978-0-606-32141-9(1)) Turtleback.

—Seconds Away (Book Two) A Mickey Bolitar Novel, Bk. 2. 2013. (Mickey Bolitar Novel Ser.: 2). (ENG.). 368p. (YA). (gr. 7). pap. 11.99 (978-0-14-242635-7(0), Speak) Penguin Young Readers Group.

—Shelter. l.t. ed. 2011. (Mickey Bolitar Ser.: Bk. 1). (ENG.). 354p. (J). (gr. 9-12). 23.99 (978-1-4104-4365-6(5)) Thorndike Pr.

—Shelter. 2012. (Mickey Bolitar Ser.: 1). lib. bdg. 20.85 (978-0-606-26669-7(0)) Turtleback.

—Shelter (Book One) A Mickey Bolitar Novel, Bk. 1. 2012. (Mickey Bolitar Novel Ser.: 1). (ENG.). 336p. (YA). (gr. 7). pap. 11.99 (978-0-14-242203-8(7), Speak) Penguin Young Readers Group.

Cobot, Meg. All-American Girl. 2004. 416p. (J). (gr. 7-18). pap. 44.00 incl. audio (978-0-8072-2281-2(X), Listening Library) Random Hse. Audio Publishing Group.

Cocca-Leffler, Maryann. Mr. Tanen's Ties. Cocca-Leffler, Maryann, illus. 2004. (ENG., Illus.). 32p. (J). (gr. k-2). pap. 6.95 (978-0-8075-5302-2(6)) Whitman, Albert & Co.

—Princess Kim & Too Much Truth. 2012. (J). 34.28 (978-1-61913-121-7(8)) Weigl Pubs., Inc.

—Theo's Mood: A Book of Feelings. Cocca-Leffler, Maryann, illus. 2013. (ENG., Illus.). 24p. (J). (gr. -1-3). 17.99 (978-0-8075-7778-3(2), 807577782) Whitman, Albert & Co.

Cochran, Molly. Legacy, 1. 2011. (Legacy Ser.). (ENG.). 432p. (YA). (gr. 9-12). 17.99 (978-1-4424-1739-7(0)) Simon & Schuster, Inc.

—Poison. 2012. (Legacy Ser.). (ENG.). 368p. (YA). (gr. 9). 17.99 (978-1-4424-5050-9(9), Simon & Schuster/Paula Wiseman Bks.) Simon & Schuster/Paula Wiseman Bks.

Cockroft, Kimberly. Reading Beauty, 1 vol. Corpus, Mary, illus. 2018. (ENG.). 32p. (J). (gr. -1-3). 16.99 (978-1-4556-2359-4(8), Pelican Publishing) Arcadia Publishing.

Cocks, Heather & Morgan, Jessica. Spoiled. 2012. (ENG.). 384p. (YA). (gr. 10-17). pap. 19.99 (978-0-316-09827-4(2), Poppy) Little, Brown Bks. for Young Readers.

Codell, Esmé Raji. Vive la Paris. 2006. (ENG.). 224p. (J). (gr. 4-7). 15.99 (978-0-7868-5124-9(4)) Hyperion Pr.

Codell, Esmé Raji & Codell, Esmé Raji. Sahara Special. 2004. (ENG.). 192p. (J). (gr. 3-7). pap. 7.99 (978-0-7868-1611-8(2)) Little, Brown Bks. for Young Readers.

Cody, Matthew. Powerless. 2011. 288p. (J). (Supers of Noble's Green Ser.: 1). (gr. 3-7). 8.99 (978-0-375-84489-8(9), Yearling);1. (Supers of Noble Green Ser.). (ENG.). (gr. 4-6). lib. bdg. 18.69 (978-0-375-95595-2(X), Knopf Bks. for Young Readers) Random Hse. Children's Bks.

Cohen, Barbara. Molly's Pilgrim. Bricking, Jennifer, illus. 2018. (ENG.). 48p. (J). (gr. 1-5). pap. 5.99 (978-0-06-287094-0(7), HarperCollins) HarperCollins Pubs.

—Molly's Pilgrim. 97th rev. ed. 2005. (ENG., Illus.). 32p. (J). (gr. 1-5). pap. 3.99 (978-0-688-16280-1(0), HarperCollins) HarperCollins Pubs. Ltd. GBR. Dist: HarperCollins Pubs.

—Molly's Pilgrim. (Literature to Go Ser.). pap., tchr. ed. incl. VHS (978-0-7919-2685-7(0)) Phoenix Films & Video.

Cohen, Joshua C. Leverage. 2012. (ENG.). 432p. (YA). (gr. 9). pap. 8.99 (978-0-14-242086-7(7), Speak) Penguin Young Readers Group.

Cohen, Miriam. Bee My Valentine, 1 vol. Himler, Ronald, illus. (ENG.). 32p. (J). (gr. k-3). 2009. pap. 5.95 (978-1-59572-086-3(3)) 2008. 15.95 (978-1-59572-085-6(5)) Star Bright Bks., Inc.

—First Grade Takes a Test. 2008. (J). (gr. k-2). 29.95 incl. audio compact disk (978-0-8045-4187-9(6)); 27.95 incl. audio (978-0-8045-6964-4(9)) Spoken Arts, Inc.

—First Grade Takes a Test, 1 vol. Himler, Ronald, illus. 2006. (ENG.). 32p. (J). (gr. -1-3). 15.95 (978-1-59572-054-2(5)); (gr. k-3). pap. 5.95 (978-1-59572-055-9(3)) Star Bright Bks., Inc.

—First Grade Takes a Test: Spanish, 1 vol. Himler, Ronald, illus. 2006.Tr. of First Grade Takes a Test. (SPA.). 32p. (J). (gr. k-3). 15.95 (978-1-59572-153-2(3)); pap. 5.95 (978-1-59572-152-5(5)) Star Bright Bks., Inc.

—First Grade Takes a Test (Spanish/English), 1 vol. Himler, Ronald, illus. 2008. (ENG.). 32p. (J). (gr. k-3). 15.95 (978-1-59572-150-1(9)); pap. 5.95 (978-1-59572-151-8(7)) Star Bright Bks., Inc.

—Jim's Dog Muffins. 2008. (ENG., Illus.). 32p. (J). (gr. -1-3). pap. 5.95 (978-1-59572-100-6(2)) Star Bright Bks., Inc.

—Jim's Dog, Muffins, 1 vol. Himler, Ronald, illus. 2008. (ENG.). 32p. (J). 15.95 (978-1-59572-099-3(5)) Star Bright Bks., Inc.

—Layla's Head Scarf, 1 vol. Himler, Ronald, illus. 2009. (ENG.). 32p. (J). (gr. -1-3). 15.95 (978-1-59572-177-8(0)); pap. 5.95 (978-1-59572-178-5(9)) Star Bright Bks., Inc.

—Tough Jim, 1 vol. Himler, Ronald, illus. (ENG.). 32p. (J). (gr. -1-3). 2008. 15.95 (978-1-59572-071-9(5)) 2007. pap. 5.95 (978-1-59572-072-6(3)) Star Bright Bks., Inc.

Cohen, Paula Marantz. Beatrice Bunson's Guide to Romeo & Juliet. 2016. (ENG.). 223p. (YA). (gr. 4-9). pap. 11.95 (978-1-58988-105-1(2)) Dry, Paul Bks., Inc.

Cohn, Rachel. Shrimp, 7 vols. 2005. (YA). 171.75 (978-1-4193-5253-9(9)) Recorded Bks., Inc.

Colasanti, Susane. Take Me There. 2009. 320p. (YA). (gr. 7-18). 9.99 (978-0-14-241435-4(2), Speak) Penguin Young Readers Group.

Colbert, Brandy. Pointe. 2015. 352p. (YA). (gr. 9). pap. 10.99 (978-0-14-751441-7(X), Speak) Penguin Young Readers Group.

Cole, Anjennetta. Cory's Classroom Rules. 2012. 28p. pap. 15.99 (978-1-4685-3652-2(4)) AuthorHouse.

Cole, Barbara H. Anna & Natalie, 1 vol. Himler, Ronald, illus. (ENG.). 32p. (J). 2010. pap. 6.95 (978-1-59572-211-9(4)) 2007. 16.95 (978-1-59572-105-1(3)) Star Bright Bks., Inc.

Cole, Diedra. The Adventures of Chris & Abby: First Day of School. 2012. (ENG.). 34p. (J). pap. 14.95 (978-1-4327-8170-5(7)) Outskirts Pr., Inc.

Cole, Frank. The Adventures of Hashbrown Winters. 2009. (Illus.). xi, 100p. (J). pap. 7.99 (978-1-59955-303-0(1)) Cedar Fort, Inc./CFI Distribution.

—Hashbrown Winters & the Mashimoto Madness. 2010. 128p. (J). pap. 8.99 (978-1-59955-378-8(3)) Cedar Fort, Inc./CFI Distribution.

—Hashbrown Winters & the Phantom of Pordunce. 2010. 128p. (J). pap. 7.99 (978-1-59955-398-6(8)) Cedar Fort, Inc./CFI Distribution.

Cole, Frank L. Hashbrown Winters & Whiz-Tastrophe. 2013. pap. 14.99 (978-1-4621-1056-8(8), Bonneville Bks.) Cedar Fort, Inc./CFI Distribution.

Cole, Henry. Eddie the Bully. 2016. (ENG., Illus.). 40p. (J). (gr. -1-3). 17.99 (978-1-4998-0181-1(5)) Little Bee Books Inc.

Cole, Kenneth. Friends & Neighbors: We Love to Learn. Ruebartsch, John, photos by. 2005. (Illus.). (J). pap. 9.95 (978-0-9770816-1-5(3)) SHARP Literacy, Inc.

—Friends & Neighbors: We Love to Learn. Ruebartsch, John, photos by. 2005. (Illus.). (J). 16.95 (978-0-9770816-0-8(5)) SHARP Literacy, Inc.

Cole, Myke. The Wildsidhe Chronicles Bk. 6: Car Trouble. 2003. (J). pap. 7.99 (978-1-890096-18-2(0)) Padwolf Publishing Inc.

Coleman, Evelyn. Freedom Train. 2012. (ENG.). 160p. (J). (gr. 3-7). pap. 7.99 (978-1-4424-3652-7(2), McElderry, Margaret K. Bks.) McElderry, Margaret K. Bks.

—Freedom Train. Riley, David, illus. 2008. (ENG.). 160p. (J). (gr. 3-7). 17.99 (978-0-689-84716-5(5)) Simon & Schuster, Inc.

Coleman, K. R. The Late Hit. 2017. (Gridiron Ser.). (ENG.). 128p. (YA). (gr. 6-12). pap. 7.99 (978-1-5124-5352-2(8), debde038-672d-404d-9650-c1cadaea5fe6); 26.65 (978-1-5124-3982-3(7), c8c09ee2-a0f1-433e-9a15-2f49c3097e12) Lerner Publishing Group. (Darby Creek).

—Showdown. 2017. (Gridiron Ser.). (ENG.). 112p. (YA). (gr. 6-12). lib. bdg. 26.65 (978-1-5124-3978-6(9), 5cdc41d2-2c25-47db-8298-ba63d0ce53e8, Darby Creek) Lerner Publishing Group.

—Signing Day. 2017. (Gridiron Ser.). (ENG.). 120p. (YA). (gr. 6-12). pap. 7.99 (978-1-5124-5355-3(2), fc3c473a-2f65-43a2-a364-aaf71dc95b2a); lib. bdg. 26.65 (978-1-5124-3983-0(5), b1ba131c-ad53-47ae-b1d9-ecd5d3177206) Lerner Publishing Group. (Darby Creek).

Coleman, Rowan. Ruby Parker: Musical Star. 2011. (ENG., Illus.). 256p. (gr. 6-9). pap. 9.99 (978-0-00-724434-8(7), HarperCollins Children's Bks.) HarperCollins Pubs. Ltd. GBR. Dist: HarperCollins Pubs.

Colfer, Chris. Struck by Lightning: The Carson Phillips Journal. (Land of Stories Ser.). (ENG., Illus.). 272p. (YA). (gr. 10-17). 2013. pap. 10.99 (978-0-316-23293-7(9)) 2012. 17.99 (978-0-316-23295-1(5)) Little, Brown Bks. for Young Readers.

—A Tale of Witchcraft... Dorman, Brandon, illus. 2020. 432p. (J). (978-0-316-59120-1(3)) Little Brown & Co.

—A Tale of Witchcraft... (Tale of Magic... Ser.: 2). (ENG.). (J). (gr. 3-7). 2021. 464p. pap. 9.99 (978-0-316-52354-7(2)) 2020. (Illus.). 448p. 18.99 (978-0-316-52356-1(9)) 2020. 528p. pap. 26.99 (978-0-316-54175-6(3)) Little, Brown Bks. for Young Readers.

Collicott, Sharleen. Mildred & Sam & Their Babies. Collicott, Sharleen, illus. 2005. (I Can Read Bks.). (Illus.). 48p. (J). (gr. -1-2). 15.99 (978-0-06-058111-4(5), Geringer, Laura Book) HarperCollins Pubs.

Collins, Amanda E. Bff!!! or Not??? 2007. 168p. 30.99 (978-1-4257-3371-1(9)) Xlibris Corp.

Collins, Charles. Hover for a Day. Seltzer, Jerry, illus. 2006. (ENG.). 56p. (J). 19.95 (978-1-60131-004-0(8), Castlebridge Bks.) Big Tent Bks.

Collins, Christina. After Zero. 2018. (ENG.). 256p. (J). (gr. 3-7). 16.99 (978-1-4926-5532-9(5)) Sourcebooks, Inc.

Collins, Nancy A. Vamps. 2008. (Vamps Ser.: 1). (ENG.). 256p. (YA). (gr. 9-18). pap. 8.99 (978-0-06-134917-1(8), HarperTeen) HarperCollins Pubs.

Collins, P. J. Sarah. Sam & Nate. Jin, Katherine, illus. 2005. 60p. (J). lib. bdg. 20.00 (978-1-4242-1261-3(8)) Fitzgerald Bks.

Collins, Rudy. Vanessa Owens & the Bond of Sisterhood. 2011. 106p. pap. 19.95 (978-1-4560-7873-7(9)) America Star Bks.

Collins, Tim. Fangs a Lot: Final Notes from a Totally Lame Vampire. Pinder, Andrew, illus. 2014. (ENG.). 320p. (J). (gr. 5-9). 13.99 (978-1-4814-2134-8(4), Aladdin) Simon & Schuster Children's Publishing.

—Notes from a Hairy-Not-Scary Werewolf. Pinder, Andrew, illus. 2013. (ENG.). 288p. (J). (gr. 5-9). 12.99 (978-1-4424-8207-4(9), Aladdin) Simon & Schuster Children's Publishing.

—Notes from a Totally Lame Vampire: Because the Undead Have Feelings Too! Pinder, Andrew, illus. 2010. (ENG.). 336p. (J). (gr. 5-9). 12.99 (978-1-4424-1183-8(X), Aladdin) Simon & Schuster Children's Publishing.

—Prince of Dorkness: More Notes from a Totally Lame Vampire. Pinder, Andrew, illus. 2011. (ENG.). 336p. (J). (gr. 5-9). 12.99 (978-1-4424-3388-5(4), Aladdin) Simon & Schuster Children's Publishing.

Compestine, Ying Chang. The Story of Paper: Amazing Chinese Inventions. Xuan, YongSheng, illus. 2016. (Amazing Chinese Inventions Ser.). (ENG.). 40p. (J). (gr. -1-3). 15.95 (978-1-59702-123-4(7)) Immedium.

Complete Nothing. 2014. (True Love Ser.: 2). (ENG., Illus.). 336p. (YA). (gr. 7). pap. 9.99 (978-1-4424-7720-9(2), Simon & Schuster Bks. For Young Readers) Simon & Schuster Bks. For Young Readers.

Condie, Ally. Being Sixteen. 2010. 249p. (YA). (978-1-60641-233-6(7)) Deseret Bk. Co.

—Reunion. 2008. 288p. (YA). pap. 15.95 (978-1-59038-989-8(1)) Deseret Bk. Co.

—Yearbook. 2006. 208p. (YA). pap. 14.95 (978-1-59038-690-3(6)) Deseret Bk. Co.

Conford, Ellen. Jenny Archer, Author. 2006. (ENG., Illus.). 64p. (J). (gr. 1-4). per. 5.99 (978-0-316-01487-8(7)) Little, Brown Bks. for Young Readers.

Conforto, Lisa. The Very Compromising Adventures of Thumby Blackstone, 1 vol. 2010. 34p. 24.95 (978-1-4512-0270-0(9)) PublishAmerica, Inc.

Conklin, Jennie Maria. Miss Prudence A Story of Two Girls' Lives. 2004. reprint ed. pap. 1.99 (978-1-4192-3464-4(1)) Kessinger Publishing, LLC.

Connatser, Scott. Excited about Pre-School. 2011. 32p. pap. 12.77 (978-1-4567-6564-4(7)) AuthorHouse.

Connye, Aunt. Club House: Stories That Teach. Greg, Uncle, illus. 2012. (ENG.). 74p. pap. 28.99 (978-1-4670-4413-4(X)) AuthorHouse.

The Contagious Colors of Mumpley Middle School. 2014. (ENG., Illus.). 288p. (J). (gr. 2-5). pap. 8.99 (978-1-4424-7830-5(6), Atheneum Bks. for Young Readers) Simon & Schuster Children's Publishing.

Conway, Celeste. The Goodbye Time. 2011. (ENG.). 112p. (J). (gr. 2-4). lib. bdg. 18.69 (978-0-385-90540-4(8), Delacorte Pr.) Random Hse. Children's Bks.

Cook, Eileen. Fourth Grade Fairy, 1. 2011. (Fourth Grade Fairy Ser.: 1). (ENG.). 176p. (J). (gr. 3-7). pap. 7.99 (978-1-4169-9811-2(X), Aladdin) Simon & Schuster Children's Publishing.

—Getting Revenge on Lauren Wood. 2010. (ENG.). (YA). (gr. 9). 288p. pap. 9.99 (978-1-4424-0976-7(2)); 272p. 15.99 (978-1-4169-7433-8(4)) Simon Pulse. (Simon Pulse).

—Gnome Invasion, 3. 2011. (Fourth Grade Fairy Ser.: 3). (ENG.). 160p. (J). (gr. 3-7). pap. 6.99 (978-1-4169-9813-6(6)) Simon & Schuster, Inc.

—Wishes for Beginners. 2011. (Fourth Grade Fairy Ser.: 2). (ENG.). 160p. (J). (gr. 3-7). pap. 6.99 (978-1-4169-9812-9(8), Aladdin) Simon & Schuster Children's Publishing.

Cook, Jacqueline. On to Nationals. 2008. 296p. per. 12.95 (978-1-4327-1681-3(6)) Outskirts Pr., Inc.

Cook, Kristi. Eternal. 2014. (ENG., Illus.). 432p. (YA). (gr. 9). pap. 9.99 (978-1-4424-8531-0(0), Simon Pulse) Simon Pulse.

—Magnolia. 2014. (ENG., Illus.). 336p. (YA). (gr. 9). 17.99 (978-1-4424-8535-8(3)); pap. 10.99 (978-1-4424-8534-1(5)) Simon Pulse. (Simon Pulse).

—Mirage. 2012. (ENG.). 384p. (YA). (gr. 9). 16.99 (978-1-4424-4299-3(9), Simon Pulse) Simon Pulse.

Cooke, Stephanie. Oh My Gods! Graphic Novel. Moon, Juliana, illus. 2021. (OMGs Ser.). (ENG.). 208p. (J). (gr. 3-7). 24.99 (978-0-358-29951-6(9), 1776006); pap. 12.99 (978-0-358-29952-3(7), 1776007) HarperCollins Pubs. (Clarion Bks.).

Cooke, Tobias. The Secret of the Lost Soul: A Ben Street Mystery. 2011. 272p. pap. (978-1-907499-80-7(6)) Pen Pr. Pubs., Ltd.

A Cool School: Individual Title Six-Packs. (gr. -1-2). 27.00 (978-0-7635-9442-8(3)) Rigby Education.

Coolidge, Susan. What Katy Did at School. 2016. (ENG., Illus.). (J). 26.95 (978-1-358-88715-4(2)) Creative Media Partners, LLC.

Cooling, Wendy, ed. Ten of the Best: School Stories with a Difference. 2009. (ENG., Illus.). 192p. pap. 7.99 (978-0-00-713339-0(1), HarperCollins Children's Bks.) HarperCollins Pubs. Ltd. GBR. Dist: HarperCollins Pubs.

Cooney, Caroline B. Code Orange. 2007. 200p. (gr. 7-12). 17.00 (978-0-7569-8210-2(3)) Perfection Learning Corp.

—Code Orange. 2007. (ENG.). 224p. (YA). (gr. 7-12). mass mkt. 8.99 (978-0-385-73260-4(0), Laurel Leaf) Random Hse. Children's Bks.

—Code Orange. 2007. lib. bdg. 17.20 (978-1-4177-7788-4(5)) Turtleback.

—The Lost Songs. 2013. (ENG.). 256p. (YA). (gr. 7). pap. 8.99 (978-0-385-73967-2(2), Ember) Random Hse. Children's Bks.

Cooney, Doug. I Know Who Likes You. Bernardin, James, illus. 2005. (ENG.). 224p. (J). (gr. 3-7). pap. 10.99 (978-1-4169-0261-4(9), Simon & Schuster Bks. For Young Readers) Simon & Schuster Bks. For Young Readers.

Coons, Timothy A. School of Chaos, 1 vol. 2010. 74p. pap. 19.95 (978-1-4512-9345-6(3)) America Star Bks.

Cooper, Abby. Sticks & Stones. 2017. (J). lib. bdg. 18.40 (978-0-606-39950-0(X)) Turtleback.

Cooper, Ilene. Absolutely Lucy #3: Look at Lucy! Merrell, David, illus. 2009. (Lucy Ser.: 3). (ENG.). 112p. (J). (gr. 1-4). 5.99 (978-0-375-85558-0(0), Random Hse. Bks. for Young Readers) Random Hse. Children's Bks.

—Absolutely Lucy #5: Lucy's Tricks & Treats. Merrell, David, illus. 2012. (Lucy Ser.: 5). 112p. (J). (gr. 1-4). 5.99 (978-0-375-86997-6(2), Random Hse. Bks. for Young Readers) Random Hse. Children's Bks.

Cooper, Jay. The Curse of the Mummy's Tummy (the Spy Next Door #2) 2017. (ENG., Illus.). 144p. (J). (gr. 2-5). 9.99 (978-0-545-93298-1(X), Scholastic Pr.) Scholastic, Inc.

Copeland, Cynthia L. Dilly for President. 2005. (Illus.). 64p. (J). (gr. -1-k). pap. 6.95 (978-0-7613-2442-3(9), First Avenue Editions) Lerner Publishing Group.

—The 15 Best Things about Being the New Kid. Vargo, Sharon, illus. 2006. (Silly Millies Ser.). 32p. (J). (gr. -1-3). lib. bdg. 21.27 (978-0-7613-2889-6(0), Millbrook Pr.); (gr. 2). per. 5.95 (978-0-8225-6473-7(4), First Avenue Editions) Lerner Publishing Group.

Coppock, Phil & Bower's 2008-2009 4th Grade Class. Rubber Tuesday. 2010. 70p. pap. 12.95 (978-1-4327-5751-9(2)) Outskirts Pr., Inc.

Corbett Sampson, Natalie. Game Plan. 2013. 362p. pap. (978-1-927746-09-7(4)) Fierce ink Pr. Co-Op, Ltd.

Cordone Warner, Debra. A Busy Day for Baby Duck & Little Boy Blue. 2010. 34p. pap. 19.99 (978-0-557-59587-7(8)) Lulu Pr., Inc.

Coriell, Shelley. Welcome, Caller, This Is Chloe. 2013. (ENG.). 320p. (YA). (gr. 8-17). pap. 7.95 (978-1-4197-0545-8(8), 1003903, Amulet Bks.) Abrams, Inc.

Cormier, Robert. The Chocolate War. 191p. (YA). (gr. 7-18). pap. 4.99 (978-0-8072-1428-2(0), Listening Library) Random Hse. Audio Publishing Group.

—The Chocolate War. 30th ed. 2004. (Chocolate War Ser.: 1). (ENG.). 272p. (YA). (gr. 7-12). pap. 10.99 (978-0-375-82987-1(3), Ember) Random Hse. Children's Bks.

Corp, Carey & Langdon, Lorie. Doon, 1 vol. 2014. (Doon Novel Ser.: 1). (ENG.). 416p. (YA). pap. 12.99 (978-0-310-74239-5(0)) Blink.

Cosgrove, Stephen. Flynn "Flea" Flicker: Sticking to the Truth. Arroyo, Fian, illus. 2004. (J). (978-1-58804-353-5(3)) P C I Education.

—Mizz Buggly: Doing Your Best. Arroyo, Fian, illus. 2004. (J). (978-1-58804-380-1(0)) P C I Education.

Costain, Meredith. Double Dare You. McDonald, Danielle, illus. 2017. (Ella Diaries Ser.: 1). 144p. (J). pap. 5.99 (978-1-61067-520-8(7)) Kane Miller.

Costner, Arianne. My Life As a Potato. 2020. (ENG., Illus.). 272p. (J). (gr. 3-7). lib. bdg. 19.99 (978-0-593-11867-2(7), Random Hse. Bks. for Young Readers) Random Hse. Children's Bks.

Cotler, Steve. Cheesie Mack Is Running Like Crazy! Holgate, Douglas, illus. 2014. (Cheesie Mack Ser.: 3). 256p. (J). (gr. 3-7). pap. 7.99 (978-0-307-97716-8(1), Yearling) Random Hse. Children's Bks.

Cottle Street: Individual Title Six-Packs. (Action Packs Ser.). 120p. (gr. 3-5). 44.00 (978-0-7635-8423-8(1)) Rigby Education.

Cotton, Peter B. When Jungle Jim Comes to Visit Fred the Snake. Lemaire, Bonnie, illus. 2013. 48p. 24.95 (978-0-9883370-4-6(5)) Fig & The Vine, LLC, The.

Couloumbis, Audrey. Not Exactly a Love Story. 2014. (ENG.). 288p. (YA). (gr. 7). pap. 9.99 (978-0-375-86606-7(X), Ember) Random Hse. Children's Bks.

CourseCrafters Staff, des. Interactive Storybooks - Let's Go to School! 2003. (J). spiral bd. 14.95 (978-1-58605-961-3(0)) LeapFrog Enterprises, Inc.

—Interactive Storybooks - School Time. 2003. (J). spiral bd. 14.95 (978-1-58605-960-6(2)) LeapFrog Enterprises, Inc.

Courtin, Thierry. T choupi rentre a l Ecole. 13.95 (978-2-09-202041-8(2)) Nathan, Fernand FRA. Dist: Distribooks, Inc.

Coven, Wanda. Heidi Heckelbeck 3 Books In 1! Heidi Heckelbeck Has a Secret; Heidi Heckelbeck Casts a Spell; Heidi Heckelbeck & the Cookie Contest. Burris, Priscilla, illus. 2014. (Heidi Heckelbeck Ser.). (ENG.). 384p. (J). (gr. k-4). pap. 8.99 (978-1-4814-2771-5(7), Little Simon) Little Simon.

—Heidi Heckelbeck & the Big Mix-Up. Burris, Priscilla, illus. 2016. (Heidi Heckelbeck Ser.: 18). (ENG.). 128p. (J). (gr.

k-4). pap. 5.99 *(978-1-4814-7169-5(4),* Little Simon) Little Simon.
—Heidi Heckelbeck & the Cookie Contest. Burris, Priscilla, illus. 2012. (Heidi Heckelbeck Ser.: 3). (ENG.). 128p. (J). (gr. k-4). 17.99 *(978-1-4424-4166-8(6))*; pap. 6.99 *(978-1-4424-4165-1(8))* Little Simon. (Little Simon).
—Heidi Heckelbeck & the Cookie Contest. 2012. (Heidi Heckelbeck Ser.: 3). lib. bdg. 16.00 *(978-0-606-26328-3(4))* Turtleback.
—Heidi Heckelbeck & the Secret Admirer. Burris, Priscilla, illus. 2012. (Heidi Heckelbeck Ser.: 6). (ENG.). 128p. (J). (gr. k-4). 17.99 *(978-1-4424-4175-0(5))*; pap. 6.99 *(978-1-4424-4174-3(7))* Little Simon. (Little Simon).
—Heidi Heckelbeck & the Secret Admirer. 2012. (Heidi Heckelbeck Ser.: 6). lib. bdg. 16.00 *(978-0-606-26905-6(3))* Turtleback.
—Heidi Heckelbeck & the Wacky Tacky Spirit Week. Burris, Priscilla, illus. 2019. (Heidi Heckelbeck Ser.: 27). (ENG.). 128p. (J). (gr. k-4). 16.99 *(978-1-5344-4636-6(2),* Little Simon) Little Simon.
—Heidi Heckelbeck Casts a Spell. Burris, Priscilla, illus. 2012. (Heidi Heckelbeck Ser.: 2). (ENG.). 128p. (J). (gr. k-4). 17.99 *(978-1-4424-4088-3(0))*; pap. 6.99 *(978-1-4424-3567-4(4))* Little Simon. (Little Simon).
—Heidi Heckelbeck Casts a Spell. 2012. (Heidi Heckelbeck Ser.: 2). lib. bdg. 16.00 *(978-0-606-26327-6(6))* Turtleback.
—Heidi Heckelbeck Gets Glasses. Burris, Priscilla, illus. 2012. (Heidi Heckelbeck Ser.: 5). (ENG.). 128p. (J). (gr. k-4). 17.99 *(978-1-4424-4172-9(0))*; pap. 6.99 *(978-1-4424-4171-2(2))* Little Simon. (Little Simon).
—Heidi Heckelbeck Gets Glasses. 2012. (Heidi Heckelbeck Ser.: 5). lib. bdg. 16.00 *(978-0-606-26888-2(X))* Turtleback.
—Heidi Heckelbeck Has a Secret. Burris, Priscilla, illus. 2012. (Heidi Heckelbeck Ser.: 1). (ENG.). 128p. (J). (gr. k-4). 17.99 *(978-1-4424-4087-6(2))*; pap. 6.99 *(978-1-4424-3565-0(8))* Little Simon. (Little Simon).
—Heidi Heckelbeck Makes a Wish. 2016. (Heidi Heckelbeck Ser.: 17). lib. bdg. 16.00 *(978-0-606-38962-4(8))* Turtleback.
—Heidi Heckelbeck Makes a Wish: Super Special! Burris, Priscilla, illus. 2016. (Heidi Heckelbeck Ser.: 17). (ENG.). 160p. (J). (gr. k-4). pap. 6.99 *(978-1-4814-6613-4(5),* Little Simon) Little Simon.
—Heidi Heckelbeck Tries Out for the Team. Burris, Priscilla, illus. 2017. (Heidi Heckelbeck Ser.: 19). (ENG.). 128p. (J). (gr. k-4). pap. 6.99 *(978-1-4814-7172-5(4),* Little Simon) Little Simon.
Covey, Sean. Just the Way I Am: Habit 1. Curtis, Stacy, illus. 2018. (7 Habits of Happy Kids Ser.: 1). (ENG.). 32p. (J). (gr. -1-1). 6.99 *(978-1-5344-1577-5(7),* Simon & Schuster Bks. For Young Readers) Simon & Schuster Bks. For Young Readers.
—Just the Way I Am: Habit 1 (Ready-To-Read Level 2) Curtis, Stacy, illus. 2019. (7 Habits of Happy Kids Ser.: 1). (ENG.). 32p. (J). (gr. k-2). 17.99 *(978-1-5344-4445-4(9))*; pap. 4.99 *(978-1-5344-4444-7(0))* Simon Spotlight. (Simon Spotlight).
—Sophie & the Perfect Poem: Habit 6. Curtis, Stacy, illus. (7 Habits of Happy Kids Ser.: 6). (ENG.). 32p. (J). (gr. -1-1). 2018. 6.99 *(978-1-5344-1583-6(1))* 2013. 7.99 *(978-1-4424-7651-6(6))* Simon & Schuster Bks. For Young Readers. (Simon & Schuster Bks. For Young Readers).
—Sophie & the Perfect Poem: Habit 6 (Ready-To-Read Level 2) Curtis, Stacy, illus. 2020. (7 Habits of Happy Kids Ser.: 6). (ENG.). 32p. (J). (gr. k-2). 17.99 *(978-1-5344-4460-7(2))*; pap. 4.99 *(978-1-5344-4459-1(9))* Simon Spotlight. (Simon Spotlight).
Coville, Bruce. The Monster's Ring: A Magic Shop Book. Coville, Katherine, illus. 2008. (Magic Shop Book Ser.: 1). (ENG.). 128p. (J). (gr. 5-7). pap. 7.99 *(978-0-15-206442-6(7),* 1199254, Clarion Bks.) HarperCollins Pubs.
—My Teacher Fried My Brains. 2014. (My Teacher Bks.: 2). (ENG., Illus.). 176p. (J). (gr. 3-7). 17.99 *(978-1-4814-0431-0(8),* Aladdin) Simon & Schuster Children's Publishing.
—My Teacher Is an Alien. 2014. (My Teacher Bks.: 1). (ENG., Illus.). 160p. (J). (gr. 3-7). 17.99 *(978-1-4814-0430-3(X),* Simon & Schuster/Paula Wiseman Bks.) Simon & Schuster/Paula Wiseman Bks.
—The Skull of Truth: A Magic Shop Book. Lippincott, Gary A., illus. 2007. (Magic Shop Book Ser.: 4). (ENG.). 208p. (J). (gr. 5-7). pap. 7.99 *(978-0-15-206084-8(7),* 1198275, Clarion Bks.) HarperCollins Pubs.
—There's an Alien in My Classroom! (ENG., Illus.). 201p. (J). pap. 8.95 *(978-0-340-73634-0(8))* Hodder & Stoughton GBR. Dist: Trafalgar Square Publishing.
Cowling, Chani. Cookie Baker, Sweet & Sour. 2008. 24p. pap. 24.95 *(978-1-60703-021-8(7))* America Star Bks.
Cox, Amy. Odetta the Octopus Teacher. 2013. 28p. pap. 24.95 *(978-1-63000-491-0(X))* America Star Bks.
Cox, Judy. Carmen Learns English. Dominguez, Angela N., illus. 2010. (ENG.). 32p. (J). (gr. -1-3). 16.95 *(978-0-8234-2174-9(0))* Holiday Hse., Inc.
—Don't Be Silly, Mrs. Millie!, 0 vols. Mathieu, Joe, illus. 2012. (ENG.). 34p. (J). (gr. -1-2). pap. 6.99 *(978-0-7614-5727-5(5),* 9780761457275, Two Lions) Amazon Publishing.
—Happy Birthday, Mrs. Millie!, 0 vols. Mathieu, Joe, illus. 2012. (ENG.). 32p. (J). (gr. -1-2). 16.99 *(978-0-7614-6126-5(4),* 9780761461265, Two Lions) Amazon Publishing.
Cox, Steven. Justin's Very Own Drum. Saavedra, Anthony, illus. 2009. 24p. pap. 24.95 *(978-1-60749-553-6(8))* America Star Bks.
Coy, John. Box Out. 2010. (ENG.). 304p. (J). (gr. 7-12). 24.94 *(978-0-545-17416-9(3))* Scholastic, Inc.
—Crackback. 2007. 201p. (gr. 7-12). 17.00 *(978-0-7569-8274-4(X))* Perfection Learning Corp.
—Love of the Game. 2011. (4 For 4 Ser.: 3). (ENG.). 192p. (J). (gr. 3-7). pap. 9.99 *(978-1-250-00637-0(6),* 900081964) Square Fish.
—Top of the Order: The 4 for 4 Series. 2010. (4 For 4 Ser.: 1). (ENG.). 208p. (J). (gr. 3-6). pap. 14.99 *(978-0-312-61111-8(0),* 900065447) Square Fish.
Cozzo, Karole. How to Say I Love You Out Loud. 2015. (ENG.). 240p. (YA). (gr. 7). pap. 17.99 *(978-1-250-06359-5(0),* 900142824) Feiwel & Friends.
Crabtree, Julie. Discovering Pig Magic. 2008. (ENG.). 144p. (J). (gr. 2-8). 16.95 *(978-1-57131-683-7(3))*; pap. 6.95 *(978-1-57131-684-4(1))* Milkweed Editions.

Craft, Jerry. New Kid: A Newbery Award Winner. Craft, Jerry, illus. 2019. (ENG., Illus.). 256p. (J). (gr. 3-7). 22.99 *(978-0-06-269120-0(1))*; pap. 12.99 *(978-0-06-269119-4(8))* HarperCollins Pubs. (Quill Tree Bks.).
Crane, Caprice. Confessions of a Hater. 2014. (ENG.). 384p. (YA). (gr. 8). pap. 14.99 *(978-1-250-04433-4(2),* 900128328) Square Fish.
Crane, Carol. Handkerchief Quilt. Palmer, Gary, illus. 2010. (ENG.). 32p. (J). (gr. 1-4). 15.95 *(978-1-58536-344-5(8),* 202134) Sleeping Bear Pr.
Crane, Cheri J. Moment of Truth: A Novel. 2005. 238p. (YA). *(978-1-59156-727-1(0))* Covenant Communications.
Crayton, Tina Anderson. Sniffles: Each Season Brings New Sniffles. 2012. 12p. pap. 15.99 *(978-1-4772-8454-4(0))* AuthorHouse.
Creagh, Kelly. Enshadowed: A Nevermore Book. (ENG., Illus.). (YA). (gr. 7). 2013. 464p. pap. 9.99 *(978-1-4424-0206-5(7))* 2012. 448p. 17.99 *(978-1-4424-0204-1(0),* Atheneum Bks. for Young Readers) Simon & Schuster Children's Publishing.
—Nevermore. 2011. (ENG., Illus.). 576p. (YA). (gr. 9). pap. 16.99 *(978-1-4424-0201-0(6),* Atheneum Bks. for Young Readers) Simon & Schuster Children's Publishing.
Creech, Sharon. Absolutely Normal Chaos. 2012. 230p. (J). (gr. 4-7). lib. bdg. 18.40 *(978-0-613-02936-0(4))* Turtleback.
—Bloomability. 2012. (ENG., Illus.). 272p. (J). (gr. 3-7). pap. 7.99 *(978-0-06-440823-3(X),* HarperCollins) HarperCollins Pubs.
—Bloomability. unabr. ed. 2004. 273p. (J). (gr. 4-7). pap. 38.00 incl. audio *(978-0-8072-8754-5(7),* YA257SP, Listening Library) Random Hse. Audio Publishing Group.
—Bloomability. 2012. (J). (gr. 3-6). 17.20 *(978-0-613-22826-8(X))* Turtleback.
—A Fine, Fine School. 2004. (Illus.). (J). (gr. k-3). spiral bd. *(978-0-616-11107-9(X))* Canadian National Institute for the Blind/Institut National Canadien pour les Aveugles.
—A Fine, Fine School. Bliss, Harry, illus. 2004. (J). (gr. k-3). spiral bd. *(978-0-616-11106-2(1))* Canadian National Institute for the Blind/Institut National Canadien pour les Aveugles.
—A Fine, Fine School. Bliss, Harry, illus. 2003. (ENG.). 32p. (J). (gr. -1-3). pap. 8.99 *(978-0-06-000728-7(1),* HarperCollins) HarperCollins Pubs.
—A Fine, Fine School. 2003. (Illus.). 25.95 incl. audio *(978-1-59112-221-0(X))* Live Oak Media.
—A Fine, Fine School. Bliss, Harry, illus. 2003. pap. 39.95 incl. audio compact disk *(978-1-59112-555-6(3))*; pap. 37.95 incl. audio *(978-1-59112-222-7(8))* Live Oak Media.
—A Fine, Fine School. 2003. (Illus.). (J). (gr. -1-2). 28.95 incl. audio compact disk *(978-1-59112-496-2(4))* Live Oak Media.
—A Fine, Fine School. Bliss, Harry, illus. 2004. (J). (gr. -1-3). 14.65 *(978-0-7569-3179-7(7))* Perfection Learning Corp.
—Hate That Cat: A Novel. (ENG.). (J). (gr. 3-7). 2010. 176p. pap. 7.99 *(978-0-06-143094-7(3))* 2008. 160p. 16.99 *(978-0-06-143092-3(7))* HarperCollins Pubs. (HarperCollins).
—Replay. (J). (gr. 3-7). 2013. (ENG.). 224p. pap. 9.99 *(978-0-06-054021-0(4),* HarperCollins) 2005. 240p. lib. bdg. 16.89 *(978-0-06-054020-3(6),* Cotler, Joanna Books) HarperCollins Pubs.
Crews, G. S. The Adventures of Mercy Saint. 2011. 258p. pap. 15.00 *(978-0-9795236-5-6(6))* Crews Pubns., LLC.
Cribbs, Gia. The Disappearance of Sloane Sullivan. 2018. (ENG.). 400p. (YA). 18.99 *(978-1-335-01537-2(X),* Harlequin Teen) Harlequin Enterprises ULC CAN. Dist: HarperCollins Pubs.
Crichton, L. D. All Our Broken Pieces. 2019. (ENG.). 416p. (YA). (gr. 9-17). 17.99 *(978-1-368-02396-2(7))* Hyperion Pr.
Crockett, Mary. How She Died, How I Lived. 2019. (ENG.). 416p. (YA). (gr. 9-17). pap. 10.99 *(978-0-316-52382-0(8))* Little, Brown Bks. for Young Readers.
Cronin, Doreen. Click, Clack, Quack to School! Lewin, Betsy, illus. 2018. (Click Clack Book Ser.). (ENG.). 40p. (J). (gr. -1-3). 17.99 *(978-1-5344-1449-5(5),* Atheneum/Caitlyn Dlouhy Books) Simon & Schuster Children's Publishing.
Cronn-Mills, Kirstin. Beautiful Music for Ugly Children. 2012. (ENG.). 288p. (YA). (gr. 9-12). pap. 14.99 *(978-0-7387-3251-0(6),* 0738732516, Flux) North Star Editions.
Cross, P. C. Summer Job: A Virgil & Cy Mystery. 2008. 260p. pap. 16.95 *(978-0-595-50921-8(5))* iUniverse, Inc.
Crossan, Sarah. One. 2015. (ENG.). 400p. (YA). (gr. 8). 17.99 *(978-0-06-211875-2(7),* Greenwillow Bks.) HarperCollins Pubs.
Crosshill, Tom. The Cat King of Havana. 2016. (ENG.). 368p. (YA). (gr. 8). 17.99 *(978-0-06-242283-5(9),* Tegen, Katherine Bks) HarperCollins Pubs.
Crow, Kristyn. Zombelina. Idle, Molly, illus. 2013. (ENG.). 32p. (J). (gr. -1-3). 16.99 *(978-0-8027-2803-6(0),* 900081980, Bloomsbury USA Childrens) Bloomsbury Publishing USA.
Crow, Marilee. A Pocketful of Manners. Snider, K. C., illus. 2011. 16p. pap. 9.95 *(978-1-61633-176-4(3))* Guardian Angel Publishing, Inc.
Crow, Melinda Melton. Field Trip for School Bus, 1 vol. Thompson, Chad, illus. 2012. (Wonder Wheels Ser.). (ENG.). 32p. (J). (gr. -1-1). pap. 6.25 *(978-1-4342-4237-2(4),* 120295, Stone Arch Bks.) Capstone.
—Helpful Tractor, 1 vol. Thompson, Chad, illus. 2011. (Wonder Wheels Ser.). (ENG.). 32p. (J). (gr. -1-1). lib. bdg. 22.65 *(978-1-4342-3027-0(9),* 114521, Stone Arch Bks.) Capstone.
—Lucky School Bus, 1 vol. Thompson, Chad, illus. 2011. (Wonder Wheels Ser.). (ENG.). 32p. (J). (gr. -1-1). pap. 6.25 *(978-1-4342-3381-3(2),* 116388); lib. bdg. 22.65 *(978-1-4342-3026-3(0),* 114520) Capstone. (Stone Arch Bks.).
Crowley, Suzanne. The Very Ordered Existence of Merilee Marvelous. 2007. 380p. (J). (gr. 5-9). 16.99 *(978-0-06-123197-1(5),* Greenwillow Bks.) HarperCollins Pubs.
Crutcher, Chris. Deadline. (ENG.). (YA). (gr. 9). 2009. 336p. pap. 10.99 *(978-0-06-085091-3(4))* 2007. 320p. 17.99 *(978-0-06-085089-0(2))* HarperCollins Pubs. (Greenwillow Bks.).
—Deadline. 2011. 10.36 *(978-0-7848-3487-9(3),* Everbind) Marco Bk. Co.
—Losers Bracket. (ENG.). 256p. (YA). (gr. 9). 2019. pap. 10.99 *(978-0-06-222008-0(X))* 2018. 17.99 *(978-0-06-222006-6(3))* HarperCollins Pubs. (Greenwillow Bks.).

—Period 8. 2013. (ENG.). 288p. (YA). (gr. 9). 17.99 *(978-0-06-191480-5(0),* Greenwillow Bks.) HarperCollins Pubs.
—The Sledding Hill. 2006. (ENG.). 256p. (YA). (gr. 8-12). pap. 9.99 *(978-0-06-050245-4(2),* Greenwillow Bks.) HarperCollins Pubs.
—Staying Fat for Sarah Byrnes. 2003. (ENG.). 304p. (YA). (gr. 8). pap. 9.99 *(978-0-06-009489-8(3),* Greenwillow Bks.) HarperCollins Pubs.
—Whale Talk. (ENG.). (YA). 2018. 352p. (gr. 9). pap. 11.99 *(978-0-06-268775-3(1))* 2009. 304p. (gr. 8). pap. 9.99 *(978-0-06-177131-6(7))* HarperCollins Pubs. (Greenwillow Bks.).
—Whale Talk. 2004. 224p. (J). (gr. 7-18). pap. 38.00 incl. audio *(978-0-8072-2289-8(5),* Listening Library) Random Hse. Audio Publishing Group.
Cuate, Melodie A. Journey to Goliad. 2009. (Mr. Barrington's Mysterious Trunk Ser.). (ENG., Illus.). 176p. (J). (gr. 4-6). 18.95 *(978-0-89672-649-9(5),* P171404) Texas Tech Univ. Pr.
—Journey to Gonzales. 2008. (Mr. Barrington's Mysterious Trunk Ser.). (ENG., Illus.). 174p. (J). (gr. 4-6). 18.95 *(978-0-89672-624-6(X),* P171712) Texas Tech Univ. Pr.
—Journey to la Salle's Settlement. 2010. (Mr. Barrington's Mysterious Trunk Ser.). (ENG., Illus.). 184p. (J). (gr. 4-6). lib. bdg. 18.95 *(978-0-89672-704-5(1),* P176357) Texas Tech Univ. Pr.
—Journey to San Jacinto. 2007. (Mr. Barrington's Mysterious Trunk Ser.). (ENG., Illus.). 160p. (J). (gr. 4-6). 18.95 *(978-0-89672-602-4(9),* P171713) Texas Tech Univ. Pr.
—Journey to the Alamo. 2006. (Mr. Barrington's Mysterious Trunk Ser.). (ENG., Illus.). 144p. (J). (gr. 4-6). 18.95 *(978-0-89672-592-8(8),* P171714) Texas Tech Univ. Pr.
Cube Kid. Path of the Diamond. Saboten, illus. 2017. 249p. (J). *(978-1-5182-4674-6(5))* Andrews McMeel Publishing.
Culbertson, Kim. Songs for a Teenage Nomad. 2010. (ENG.). 256p. (YA). (gr. 7-12). pap. 12.99 *(978-1-4022-4301-1(4))* Sourcebooks, Inc.
The Culverdale School Tales. 2005. (J). per. *(978-1-59872-011-2(2))* Instant Pub.
Cummings, Pat. Trace. 2019. (ENG., Illus.). 320p. (J). (gr. 3-7). 16.99 *(978-0-06-269884-1(2),* HarperCollins) HarperCollins Pubs.
Cummings, Troy. Attack of the Shadow Smashers. 2013. (Notebook of Doom Ser.: 3). lib. bdg. 14.75 *(978-0-606-32369-7(4))* Turtleback.
—Attack of the Shadow Smashers: a Branches Book (the Notebook of Doom #3) Cummings, Troy, illus. 2013. (Notebook of Doom Ser.: 3). (ENG.). 96p. (J). (gr. 1-3). pap. 5.99 *(978-0-545-55297-4(4))* Scholastic, Inc.
—Battle of the Boss-Monster. Cummings, Troy, illus. 2017. (Notebook of Doom Ser.: 13). (ENG.). 96p. (J). (gr. 1-3). lib. bdg. 15.99 *(978-1-338-03457-8(X))* Scholastic, Inc.
—Battle of the Boss-Monster: a Branches Book (the Notebook of Doom #13) Cummings, Troy, illus. 2017. (Notebook of Doom Ser.: 13). (ENG., Illus.). 96p. (J). (gr. 1-3). pap. 5.99 *(978-1-338-03456-1(1))* Scholastic, Inc.
—Charge of the Lightning Bugs: a Branches Book (the Notebook of Doom #8) Cummings, Troy, illus. 2015. (Notebook of Doom Ser.: 8). (ENG., Illus.). 96p. (J). (gr. 1-3). pap. 5.99 *(978-0-545-79555-5(9))*; 8th ed. 15.99 *(978-0-545-79554-8(0))* Scholastic, Inc.
—Chomp of the Meat-Eating Vegetables. 2014. (Notebook of Doom Ser.: 4). lib. bdg. 14.75 *(978-0-606-35362-5(3))* Turtleback.
—Chomp of the Meat-Eating Vegetables: a Branches Book (the Notebook of Doom #4) Cummings, Troy, illus. 2014. (Notebook of Doom Ser.: 4). (ENG., Illus.). 96p. (J). (gr. 1-3). pap. 5.99 *(978-0-545-55299-8(0))* Scholastic, Inc.
—Day of the Night Crawlers. 2013. (Notebook of Doom Ser.: 2). (ENG.). 96p. (J). (gr. 1-3). 15.99 *(978-0-545-49324-6(2))* Scholastic, Inc.
—Day of the Night Crawlers. 2013. (Notebook of Doom Ser.: 2). lib. bdg. 14.75 *(978-0-606-32368-0(6))* Turtleback.
—Day of the Night Crawlers: a Branches Book (the Notebook of Doom #2) Cummings, Troy, illus. 2013. (Notebook of Doom Ser.: 2). (ENG.). 96p. (J). (gr. 1-3). pap. 6.99 *(978-0-545-49325-3(0))* Scholastic, Inc.
—Day of the Night Crawlers: a Branches Book (the Notebook of Doom #2) A Branches Book. Cummings, Troy, illus. 2013. (Notebook of Doom Ser.: 2). (ENG.). 96p. (J). (gr. 1-3). E-Book *(978-0-545-49327-7(7))* Scholastic, Inc.
—March of the Vanderpants. 2017. (Notebook of Doom — Branches Ser.: 12). lib. bdg. 14.75 *(978-0-606-40192-0(X))* Turtleback.
—March of the Vanderpants: a Branches Book (the Notebook of Doom #12) Cummings, Troy, illus. 2017. (Notebook of Doom Ser.: 12). (ENG., Illus.). 96p. (J). (gr. 1-3). pap. 5.99 *(978-1-338-03452-3(9))* Scholastic, Inc.
—The Notebook of Doom #6: Pop of the Bumpy Mummy (a Branches Book) - Library Edition. 2014. (Notebook of Doom Ser.: 6). (ENG.). 96p. (J). (gr. 1-3). 15.99 *(978-0-545-69899-3(5))* Scholastic, Inc.
—The Notebook of Doom (Books 1-3): a Branches Box Set, 1 vol. Cummings, Troy, illus. 2016. (Notebook of Doom Ser.). (ENG., Illus.). 288p. (J). (gr. 1-3). pap., pap., pap. 9.99 *(978-1-338-10199-7(4))* Scholastic, Inc.
—Pop of the Bumpy Mummy: a Branches Book (the Notebook of Doom #6) Cummings, Troy, illus. 2014. (Notebook of Doom Ser.: 6). (ENG., Illus.). 96p. (J). (gr. 1-3). pap. 5.99 *(978-0-545-69898-6(7))* Scholastic, Inc.
—Rise of the Balloon Goons: a Branches Book (the Notebook of Doom #1) Cummings, Troy, illus. 2013. (Notebook of Doom Ser.: 1). (ENG., Illus.). 96p. (J). (gr. 1-3). pap. 5.99 *(978-0-545-49323-9(4))* Scholastic, Inc.
—Rumble of the Coaster Ghost: a Branches Book (the Notebook of Doom #9) Cummings, Troy, illus. 2016. (Notebook of Doom Ser.: 9). (ENG., Illus.). 96p. (J). (gr. 1-3). pap. 5.99 *(978-0-545-86497-8(6))* Scholastic, Inc.
—Snap of the Super-Goop: A Branches Book , Vol. 10. Cummings, Troy, illus. 2016. (Notebook of Doom Ser.: 10). (ENG., Illus.). 96p. (J). (gr. 1-3). 24.99 *(978-0-545-86500-5(X))* Scholastic, Inc.
—Snap of the Super-Goop: a Branches Book (the Notebook of Doom #10) Cummings, Troy, illus. 2016. (Notebook of Doom Ser.: 1). (ENG., Illus.). 96p. (J). (gr. 1-3). pap. 5.99 *(978-0-545-86499-2(2))* Scholastic, Inc.

—Sneeze of the Octo-Schnozz: a Branches Book (the Notebook of Doom #11) Cummings, Troy, illus. 2016. (Notebook of Doom Ser.: 11). (ENG.). 96p. (J). (gr. 1-3). pap. 5.99 *(978-1-338-03448-6(0))* Scholastic, Inc.
—The Notebook of Doom: Rise of the Balloon Goons, Vol. 1. Cummings, Troy, illus. 2013. (Notebook of Doom Ser.: 1). (ENG., Illus.). 96p. (J). (gr. 1-3). 15.99 *(978-0-545-49322-2(6))* Scholastic, Inc.
—Whack of the P-Rex: a Branches Book (the Notebook of Doom #5) Cummings, Troy, illus. 2014. (Notebook of Doom Ser.: 5). (ENG.). 96p. (J). (gr. 1-3). pap. 5.99 *(978-0-545-69895-5(2))* Scholastic, Inc.
Curtin, Ann. Dreamcatcher. 2015. 201p. (YA). *(978-1-61271-246-8(0))* Zumaya Pubns. LLC.
Curtis, Manley. Shawn Loves Sharks. 2017. (ENG., Illus.). 32p. (J). 17.99 *(978-1-62672-134-0(3),* 900139956) Roaring Brook Pr.
Cusack, Geraldine O'Connell. Wrecker's Cove. 2013. 100p. pap. *(978-1-78407-081-6(5))* FeedARead.com.
Cushman, Karen. The Loud Silence of Francine Green. 2019. (ENG.). 240p. (J). (gr. 5-7). pap. 9.99 *(978-1-328-49799-4(2),* 1717855, Clarion Bks.) HarperCollins Pubs.
—The Loud Silence of Francine Green. 2008. (ENG.). 240p. (YA). (gr. 6-8). 21.19 *(978-0-375-84117-0(2))* Random House Publishing Group.
Cuyler, Margery. Hooray for Reading Day! Howard, Arthur, illus. 2008. (Jessica Worries Ser.). (ENG.). 32p. (J). (gr. k-3). 17.99 *(978-0-689-86188-8(5),* Simon & Schuster Bks. For Young Readers) Simon & Schuster Bks. For Young Readers.
—I Repeat, Don't Cheat! Howard, Arthur, illus. 2010. (ENG.). 32p. (J). (gr. k-3). 19.99 *(978-1-4169-7167-2(X),* Simon & Schuster Bks. For Young Readers) Simon & Schuster Bks. For Young Readers.
—Kindness Is Cooler, Mrs. Ruler. Yoshikawa, Sachiko, illus. 2007. (ENG.). 48p. (J). (gr. k-5). 19.99 *(978-0-689-87344-7(1),* Simon & Schuster Bks. For Young Readers) Simon & Schuster Bks. For Young Readers.
—100th Day Worries. Howard, Arthur, illus. 2006. (ENG.). 32p. (J). (gr. k-3). reprint ed. 7.99 *(978-1-4169-0789-3(0),* Simon & Schuster Bks. For Young Readers) Simon & Schuster Bks. For Young Readers.
Dadey, Debbie. Dream of the Blue Turtle. Avakyan, Tatevik, illus. 2014. (Mermaid Tales Ser.: 7). (ENG.). 128p. (J). (gr. 1-4). 17.99 *(978-1-4424-8264-7(8),* Aladdin) Simon & Schuster Children's Publishing.
—Flower Girl Dreams. Avakyan, Tatevik, illus. 2017. (Mermaid Tales Ser.: 16). (ENG.). 128p. (J). (gr. 1-4). pap. 5.99 *(978-1-4814-4084-4(5),* Simon & Schuster/Paula Wiseman Bks.) Simon & Schuster/Paula Wiseman Bks.
—Great Green Gator Graduation. Lucas, Margeaux, illus. 2006. (Swamp Monster in Third Grade Ser.). 58p. (J). pap. *(978-0-439-79401-5(3))* Scholastic, Inc.
—The Lost Princess. Avakyan, Tatevik, illus. 2013. (Mermaid Tales Ser.: 5). (ENG.). 128p. (J). (gr. 1-4). 17.99 *(978-1-4424-8258-6(3))*; pap. 6.99 *(978-1-4424-8257-9(5))* Simon & Schuster Children's Publishing. (Aladdin).
—The Narwhal Problem. Avakyan, Tatevik, illus. 2019. (Mermaid Tales Ser.: 19). (ENG.). 112p. (J). (gr. 1-4). 18.99 *(978-1-4814-8715-3(9))*; pap. 6.99 *(978-1-4814-8714-6(0))* Simon & Schuster Children's Publishing. (Aladdin).
—Treasure in Trident City. Avakyan, Tatevik, illus. 2014. (Mermaid Tales Ser.: 8). (ENG.). 128p. (J). (gr. 1-4). pap. 6.99 *(978-1-4424-8266-1(4),* Aladdin) Simon & Schuster Children's Publishing.
—Trouble at Trident Academy. Avakyan, Tatevik, illus. 2012. (Mermaid Tales Ser.: 1). (ENG.). 112p. (J). (gr. 1-4). 17.99 *(978-1-4424-4978-7(0))*; pap. 6.99 *(978-1-4424-2980-2(1))* Simon & Schuster Children's Publishing. (Aladdin).
Dadey, Debby & Dadey, Debbie. Danger in the Deep Blue Sea, Bk. 4. Avakyan, Tatevik, illus. 2015. (Mermaid Tales Ser.). (ENG.). 104p. (J). (gr. 1-4). 31.36 *(978-1-61479-325-0(5),* 17147, Chapter Bks.) Spotlight.
—Treasure in Trident City, Bk. 8. Avakyan, Tatevik, illus. 2015. (Mermaid Tales Ser.). (ENG.). 120p. (J). (gr. 1-4). 31.36 *(978-1-61479-329-8(8),* 17151, Chapter Bks.) Spotlight.
—Trouble at Trident Academy, Bk. 1. Avakyan, Tatevik, illus. 2015. (Mermaid Tales Ser.). (ENG.). 104p. (J). (gr. 1-4). 31.36 *(978-1-61479-322-9(0),* 17144, Chapter Bks.) Spotlight.
Daffern, Brian. Prince Albert Bk. 2: The Beast School. 2005. 160p. (YA). per. 10.95 *(978-0-9709104-6-2(0))* Hickory Tales Publishing.
Dahl, Michael. Be a Star, Wonder Woman! Lozano, Omar, illus. 2017. (DC Super Heroes Ser.). (ENG.). 32p. (J). (gr. -1-2). lib. bdg. 23.99 *(978-1-5158-1402-3(5),* 135195, Stone Arch Bks.) Capstone.
—Crush Hour: A 4D Book. Cook, Euan, illus. 2018. (School Bus of Horrors Ser.). (ENG.). 40p. (J). (gr. 4-8). pap. 4.95 *(978-1-4965-6275-3(5),* 138006, Stone Arch Bks.) Capstone.
—Dead End: A 4D Book. Cook, Euan, illus. 2018. (School Bus of Horrors Ser.). (ENG.). 40p. (J). (gr. 4-8). pap. 4.95 *(978-1-4965-6274-6(7),* 138005, Stone Arch Bks.) Capstone.
—Destruction Zone: A 4D Book. Cook, Euan, illus. 2018. (School Bus of Horrors Ser.). (ENG.). 40p. (J). (gr. 4-8). pap. 4.95 *(978-1-4965-6273-9(9),* 138004); lib. bdg. 24.65 *(978-1-4965-6267-8(4),* 137994) Capstone. (Stone Arch Bks.).
—Friday Night Headlights: A 4D Book. Cook, Euan, illus. 2018. (School Bus of Horrors Ser.). (ENG.). 40p. (J). (gr. 4-8). pap. 4.95 *(978-1-4965-6277-7(1),* 138008, Stone Arch Bks.) Capstone.
—The Marshmallow Mermaid. Crowther, Jeff, illus. 2010. (Princess Candy Ser.). (ENG.). 40p. (J). (gr. 2-5). pap. 5.95 *(978-1-4342-2802-4(9),* 114069, Stone Arch Bks.) Capstone.
—Sugar Hero. Crowther, Jeff, illus. (Princess Candy Ser.). (ENG.). 40p. (J). (gr. 2-5). 2010. pap. 5.95 *(978-1-4342-2801-7(0),* 114068) 2009. lib. bdg. 23.99 *(978-1-4342-1587-1(3),* 95761) Capstone. (Stone Arch Bks.).
Dahl, Michael & Nickel, Scott. The Evil Echo, 1 vol. Crowther, Jeff, illus. 2010. (Princess Candy Ser.). (ENG.). 40p. (J). (gr. 2-5). 23.99 *(978-1-4342-1977-0(1),* 102739); pap. 5.95

S

(978-1-4342-2804-8(5), 114071) Capstone. (Stone Arch Bks.).
—The Green Queen of Mean. Crowther, Jeff, illus. 2010. (Princess Candy Ser.). (ENG.). 40p. (J). (gr. 2-5). pap. 5.95 *(978-1-4342-2803-1(7)*, 114070, Stone Arch Bks.) Capstone.
Dahl, Roald. Matilda. 2012.Tr. of Matilda. (CHI & ENG.). 320p. (J). (gr. 2). pap. *(978-986-320-015-4(8))* Commonwealth Publishing Co., Ltd.
—Matilda.Tr. of Matilda. (FRE.). (J). pap. 19.95 *(978-2-07-051254-6(1))* Gallimard, Editions FRA. Dist: Distribooks, Inc.
—Matilda. Walsh, Sarah, illus. 2020.Tr. of Matilda. (ENG.). 192p. (J). (gr. 1-4). 25.00 *(978-1-9848-3610-6(2)*, Viking Books for Young Readers) Penguin Young Readers Group.
—Matilda. Blake, Quentin & Terrazzini, Daniela Jaglenka, illus. 2013.Tr. of Matilda. (ENG.). 240p. (J). (gr. 3-7). 17.99 *(978-0-14-242427-8(7)*, Puffin Books) Penguin Young Readers Group.
—Matilda. Blake, Quentin, illus. 2007.Tr. of Matilda. (ENG.). 256p. (J). (gr. 3-7). 8.99 *(978-0-14-241037-0(3)*, Puffin Books) Penguin Young Readers Group.
—Matilda. 2018.Tr. of Matilda. (KOR.). (J). (gr. 3-7). pap. *(978-89-527-8733-0(1))* Sigongsa Co., Ltd.
—Matilda. 2007.Tr. of Matilda. 18.40 *(978-1-4177-8613-8(2))* Turtleback.
—MATILDA. 46th ed. 2006. (Alfaguara Juvenil Ser.). (SPA., Illus.). 230p. (J). (gr. 5-8). pap. 12.95 *(978-84-204-6454-1(6))* Ediciones Alfaguara ESP. Dist: Santillana USA Publishing Co., Inc.
—Matilda: Broadway Tie-In. Blake, Quentin, illus. 2013.Tr. of Matilda. (ENG.). 256p. (J). (gr. 3-7). pap. 8.99 *(978-0-14-242538-1(9)*, Puffin Books) Penguin Young Readers Group.
—Matilda: The Chocolate Cake Edition. Blake, Quentin, illus. 2019.Tr. of Matilda. (ENG.). 256p. (J). (gr. 3-7). 8.99 *(978-1-9848-3620-5(X)*, Puffin Books) Penguin Young Readers Group.
—Matilda (Puffin Modern Classics) Blake, Quentin, illus. 2004. (Puffin Modern Classics Ser.).Tr. of Matilda. (ENG.). 240p. (J). (gr. 3-7). pap. 8.99 *(978-0-14-240253-5(2)*, Puffin Books) Penguin Young Readers Group.
Dail, Maggie. Getting to First Base - Chris Struggles to Read. 2006. 157p. pap. 13.95 *(978-1-4116-8125-5(8))* Lulu Pr., Inc.
Daiman, Tara. Stars So Sweet: An All Four Stars Book. 2016. (All Four Stars Ser.: 3). 288p. (J). (gr. 3-7). 17.99 *(978-1-101-99648-5(X)*, G.P. Putnam's Sons Books for Young Readers) Penguin Young Readers Group.
Dajani, Suad Farsakh. Grandma's Stories: A Collection of Six Children's Stories. 2013. 40p. 25.99 *(978-1-4808-0051-9(1))*; pap. 16.99 *(978-1-4808-0049-6(X))* Archway Publishing.
Dakos, Kalli. Our Principal Promised to Kiss a Pig. 2018. (2019 Av2 Fiction Ser.). (ENG.). 32p. (J). lib. bdg. 34.28 *(978-1-4896-8275-8(9)*, AV2 by Weigl) Weigl Pubs., Inc.
Dakos, Kalli & DesMarteau, Alicia. Our Principal Promised to Kiss a Pig. DiRocco, Carl, illus. (ENG.). 32p. (J). 2017. (gr. -1-3). pap. 7.99 *(978-0-8075-6635-0(7)*, 807566357) 2004. (gr. 2-5). 16.99 *(978-0-8075-6629-9(2))* Whitman, Albert & Co.
Dale, Jay. Captain Ross & the Old Sea Ferry. Smith, Graham, illus. 2012. (Engage Literacy Green Ser.). (ENG.). 16p. (J). (gr. k-2). pap. 36.94 *(978-1-4296-9018-6(6)*, 18402, Capstone Pr.) Capstone.
Dale, Jay & Scott, Kay. Captain Ross & the Old Sea Ferry, 1 vol. Smith, Graham, illus. 2012. (Engage Literacy Green Ser.). (ENG.). 16p. (J). (gr. k-2). pap. 6.99 *(978-1-4296-9016-4(X)*, 120017, Capstone Pr.) Capstone.
D'Allessandro, Alan. Growing Out of Fear. 2005. 62p. pap. 16.95 *(978-1-4137-8547-0(6))* PublishAmerica, Inc.
D'Amico, Carmela. Ella Sets the Stage. D'Amico, Steven, illus. 2006. 41p. (J). pap. 16.99 *(978-0-439-83153-6(9)*, Levine, Arthur A. Bks.) Scholastic, Inc.
D'Amico, Carmela & D'Amica, Steve. Ella the Elegant Elephant. 2005. (J). (gr. k-3). 29.95 incl. audio compact disk *(978-0-8045-4128-2(0)*, SACD4128) Spoken Arts, Inc.
D'Amico, Carmela & D'Amico, Steven. Ella the Elegant Elephant. 2004. (Illus.). (J). *(978-0-439-62793-1(1)*, Levine, Arthur A. Bks.) Scholastic, Inc.
—Ella the Elegant Elephant. 2005. (J). (gr. k-3). 27.95 incl. audio *(978-0-8045-6933-0(9)*, SAC6933) Spoken Arts, Inc.
D'Amico, Christine. Higgledy-Piggledy: Mabel's World. Bell-Myers, Darcy, illus. 2005. (ENG.). 32p. (J). 16.95 *(978-0-9716631-1-4(4))* Attitude Pr. Inc.
Dammier, Patti. Got Carrots? Rescued Horse: The Winter Vacation. 2012. 142p. 21.95 *(978-1-4759-2842-6(4))* iUniverse, Inc.
Dana, Kimberly. Lucy & Cecee's How to Survive (and Thrive) in Middle School. 2012. 278p. (gr. 4-6). 27.95 *(978-1-4620-3967-8(7))*; pap. 17.95 *(978-1-4620-3966-1(9))* iUniverse, Inc.
Daneshvari, Gitty. School of Fear. 2010. (School of Fear Ser.: 1). (ENG., Illus.). 368p. (J). (gr. 3-7). pap. 8.99 *(978-0-316-03327-5(8))* Little, Brown Bks. for Young Readers.
—School of Fear: Class Is Not Dismissed! 2011. (School of Fear Ser.: 2). (ENG.). 336p. (J). (gr. 3-7). pap. 17.99 *(978-0-316-03329-9(4))* Little, Brown Bks. for Young Readers.
—The School of Fear: the Final Exam. (School of Fear Ser.: 3). (ENG.). (J). (gr. 3-7). 2012. 352p. pap. 18.99 *(978-0-316-18285-0(0))* 2011. (Illus.). 336p. 16.99 *(978-0-316-18287-4(7))* Little, Brown Bks. for Young Readers.
Daniel: Individual Title Six-Packs. (Literatura 2000 Ser.). (gr. 1-2). 28.00 *(978-0-7635-0129-7(8))* Rigby Education.
Danneberg, Julie. Field-Trip Fiasco. Love, Judy, illus. 2015. (Jitters Ser.: 5). 32p. (J). (gr. k-3). 16.95 *(978-1-58089-671-9(5))* Charlesbridge Publishing, Inc.
—First Year Letters. Love, Judy, illus. 2014. 32p. pap. 7.00 *(978-1-61003-320-6(5))* Center for the Collaborative Classroom.
—Last Day Blues. Love, Judy, illus. 2006. (Jitters Ser.: 2). (ENG.). 32p. (J). (gr. k-3). 7.99 *(978-1-58089-104-2(7))* Charlesbridge Publishing, Inc.
—Que Nervios! el Primer Dia de Escuela. Love, Judy, illus. 2006. (Jitters Ser.). (SPA.). 32p. (J). (gr. k-3). pap. 7.99 *(978-1-58089-126-4(8))* Charlesbridge Publishing, Inc.
Danziger, Paula. Amber Brown Goes Fourth. 2007. (Amber Brown Ser.: 3). (ENG., Illus.). 128p. (J). (gr. 2-5). 6.99 *(978-0-14-240901-5(4)*, Puffin Books) Penguin Young Readers Group.
—Amber Brown Goes Fourth. Ross, Tony, illus. 2007. (Amber Brown Ser.: No. 3). 101p. (gr. 2-5). 15.00 *(978-0-7569-8197-6(2))* Perfection Learning Corp.
—Amber Brown Goes Fourth. (Amber Brown Ser.: No. 3). 112p. (J). (gr. 3-6). pap. 3.99 *(978-0-8072-1291-2(1)*, Listening Library) Random Hse. Audio Publishing Group.
—Amber Brown Is Not a Crayon. Ross, Tony, illus. 2006. (Amber Brown Ser.: 1). (ENG.). 96p. (J). (gr. 2-5). 6.99 *(978-0-14-240619-9(8)*, Puffin Books) Penguin Young Readers Group.
—Amber Brown Is Not a Crayon. (Amber Brown Ser.: No. 1). 80p. (J). (gr. 3-6). pap. 3.50 *(978-0-8072-1289-9(X)*, Listening Library) Random Hse. Audio Publishing Group.
—Amber Brown Sees Red. 2011. (Amber Brown Ser.: No. 6). 7.64 *(978-0-7848-3448-0(2)*, Everbind) Marco Bk. Co.
—Amber Brown Sees Red. 2009. (Amber Brown Ser.: 6). (ENG.). 144p. (J). (gr. 2-5). 6.99 *(978-0-14-241261-9(9)*, Puffin Books) Penguin Young Readers Group.
—Amber Brown Sees Red. (Amber Brown Ser.: No. 6). 116p. (J). (gr. 3-6). pap. 3.99 *(978-0-8072-1294-3(6)*, Listening Library) Random Hse. Audio Publishing Group.
—Amber Brown Sees Red. 2009. (Amber Brown Ser.: 6). (gr. 3-6). lib. bdg. 16.00 *(978-0-613-09442-9(5))* Turtleback.
—Amber Brown Wants Extra Credit. Ross, Tony, illus. 2008. (Amber Brown Ser.: 4). (ENG.). 144p. (J). (gr. 2-5). 6.99 *(978-0-14-241049-3(7)*, Puffin Books) Penguin Young Readers Group.
—Amber Brown Wants Extra Credit. (Amber Brown Ser.: No. 4). 120p. (J). (gr. 3-6). pap. 3.99 *(978-0-8072-1292-9(X)*, Listening Library) Random Hse. Audio Publishing Group.
—Forever Amber Brown. 2008. (Amber Brown Ser.: 5). (ENG.). 128p. (J). (gr. 2-5). 6.99 *(978-0-14-241201-5(5)*, Puffin Books) Penguin Young Readers Group.
—Get Ready for Second Grade, Amber Brown. Ross, Tony, illus. 2003. (Is for Amber Ser.: 4). (ENG.). 48p. (J). (gr. -1-3). mass mkt. 4.99 *(978-0-14-250081-1(X)*, Penguin Young Readers) Penguin Young Readers Group.
—Get Ready for Second Grade, Amber Brown. Ross, Tony, illus. 2004. (A Is for Amber Ser.). 48p. (J). (gr. k-2). 14.00 *(978-0-7569-2177-4(5))* Perfection Learning Corp.
—Get Ready for Second Grade, Amber Brown. 2003. (Young Amber Brown Easy-To-Read Ser.: 3). (gr. k-3). lib. bdg. 13.55 *(978-0-613-67547-5(9))* Turtleback.
—Orange You Glad It's Halloween, Amber Brown?, 4 bks., Set. Ross, Tony, illus. 2007. (Amber Brown Ser.). (J). (gr. 1-3). pap. 29.95 incl. audio *(978-1-4301-0080-5(X))* Live Oak Media.
—Orange You Glad It's Halloween, Amber Brown? Ross, Tony, illus. 2007. (Amber Brown Ser.). 48p. (J). (gr. k-3). 11.65 *(978-0-7569-8154-9(9))* Perfection Learning Corp.
—Second Grade Rules, Amber Brown. Ross, Tony, illus. 2005. (Is for Amber Ser.: 5). (ENG.). 48p. (J). (gr. -1-3). mass mkt. 5.99 *(978-0-14-240421-8(7)*, Penguin Young Readers) Penguin Young Readers Group.
—Second Grade Rules, Amber Brown. Ross, Tony, illus. 2005. (Amber Brown Ser.). 48p. (gr. k-2). 14.00 *(978-0-7569-5521-2(1))* Perfection Learning Corp.
—¿Seguiremos Siendo Amigos? 97th ed. 2003.Tr. of Amber Brown is Not a Crayon. (SPA., Illus.). 106p. (gr. 3-5). 24.60 *(978-84-204-4857-2(5)*, SAN8575) Harcourt Schl. Pubs.
—Segundo Grado Es Increible, Ambar Dorado. Ross, Tony, illus. 2007. (de Ambar / a Is for Amber Easy-To-Read Ser.).Tr. of Second Grade Rules, Amber Brown. (SPA.). 48p. (gr. k-3). pap. 8.95 *(978-1-59820-594-7(3))* Santillana USA Publishing Co., Inc.
Danziger, Paula, et al. Amber Brown Is on the Move. Lewis, Anthony, illus. 2014. (Amber Brown Ser.: 11). (ENG.). 192p. (J). (gr. 2-5). pap. 7.99 *(978-0-14-751223-9(9)*, Puffin Books) Penguin Young Readers Group.
Danzinger, Paula. Get Ready for Second Grade, Amber Brown. Ross, Tony, illus. 2003. pap. 31.95 incl. audio compact disk *(978-1-59112-562-4(6))* Live Oak Media.
Dara Cicciarelli. Sam Loses His Sneaker. Hoke, Jason, illus. 2011. 20p. pap. 24.95 *(978-1-4560-9178-1(6))* America Star Bks.
Darling, Angela. Lindsay's Surprise Crush. 2013. (Crush Ser.: 3). (ENG., Illus.). 144p. (J). (gr. 3-7). 15.99 *(978-1-4424-8045-2(9)*, Simon Spotlight) Simon Spotlight.
Daudet, Alphonse. The Siege of Berlin & Other Stories. 2004. reprint ed. pap. 15.95 *(978-1-4191-8248-8(X))*; pap. 1.99 *(978-1-4192-8248-5(4))* Kessinger Publishing, LLC.
Davick, Linda. It's Not Easy Being Mimi. Davick, Linda, illus. (Mimi's World Ser.: 1). (ENG., Illus.). (J). (gr. 1-4). 2019. 192p. pap. 7.99 *(978-1-4424-5890-1(9))* 2018. 176p. 13.99 *(978-1-4424-5889-5(5))* Beach Lane Bks. (Beach Lane Bks.).
David, Stuart. My Brilliant Idea (and How It Caused My Downfall) 2017. (ENG.). 240p. (YA). (gr. 7). pap. 9.99 *(978-0-544-93886-1(0)*, 1658465, Clarion Bks.) HarperCollins Pubs.
Davidson, Danica. Escape from the Overworld: An Unofficial Overworld Adventure, Book One. 2015. (Unofficial Overworld Adventure Ser.). (ENG.). 112p. (J). (gr. 1-7). pap. 7.99 *(978-1-63450-103-3(9)*, Sky Pony Pr.) Skyhorse Publishing Co., Inc.
Davidson, Jenny. The Explosionist. 2008. 464p. (YA). (gr. 7-18). lib. bdg. 18.89 *(978-0-06-123976-2(3)*, HarperTeen) HarperCollins Pubs.
Davies, Jacqueline. The Candy Smash. 2022. (Lemonade War Ser.: 4). (ENG., Illus.). 240p. (J). (gr. 3-7). pap. 9.99 *(978-0-544-22500-8(7)*, 1563385, Clarion Bks.) HarperCollins Pubs.
—The Lemonade Crime. 2011. (Lemonade War Ser.: 2). (ENG., Illus.). 160p. (J). (gr. 3-7). 16.99 *(978-0-547-27967-1(1)*, 1411007, Clarion Bks.) HarperCollins Pubs.
—The Lemonade Crime. 2012. (Lemonade War Ser.: 2). lib. bdg. 18.40 *(978-0-606-24518-0(9))* Turtleback.
—Nothing but Trouble. (ENG.). 320p. (J). (gr. 3-7). 2018. pap. 6.99 *(978-0-06-236989-5(X))* 2016. 16.99 *(978-0-06-236988-8(1))* HarperCollins Pubs. (Tegen, Katherine Bks).
—Nothing but Trouble. 2018. (J). lib. bdg. 17.20 *(978-0-606-41032-8(5))* Turtleback.
Davies, Kate, illus. Little Squeak School. 2014. (J). *(978-1-4351-5582-4(3))* Barnes & Noble, Inc.
—Welcome to the Mouse House. 2014. (J). *(978-1-4351-5583-1(1))* Barnes & Noble, Inc.
Davies, Mike. Lousy Thinking: Hitching a Ride on a Schoolboy's Mind. 2012. 162p. pap. *(978-1-906954-53-6(4))* Live It Publishing.
Davies, Peter. Molly's Magic Pencil: The Blue Genie. 2011. 28p. (gr. 1-2). 14.99 *(978-1-4567-3018-5(5))* AuthorHouse.
Davis, Angela. Prinsetta. 2006. (ENG., Illus.). 32p. per. 19.99 *(978-1-4208-9174-4(X))* AuthorHouse.
Davis, Diane. Something Is Wrong at My House: A Book about Parents' Fighting. Neely, Keith R., illus. 2010.Tr. of Algo anda mal en mi Casa. 32p. (J). (gr. -1-3). pap. 9.95 *(978-1-884734-65-6(0))* Parenting Pr., Inc.
Davis, Eleanor. Secret Science Alliance. 2010. (J). *(978-1-59990-143-5(9))* Bloomsbury Publishing USA.
—The Secret Science Alliance & the Copycat Crook. Davis, Eleanor, illus. 2009. (ENG., Illus.). 160p. (YA). (gr. 3-6). pap. 17.99 *(978-1-59990-396-5(2)*, 900062420, Bloomsbury USA Childrens) Bloomsbury Publishing USA.
Davis, Graeme. Re-Read Harry Potter & the Chamber of Secrets Today! an Unauthorized Guide. 2008. 112p. pap. 15.49 *(978-1-934840-72-6(6))* Nimble Bks. LLC.
Davis, Heather. The Clearing. 2010. (ENG., Illus.). 224p. (YA). (gr. 9). pap. 13.99 *(978-0-547-26367-0(8)*, 1406284, Clarion Bks.) HarperCollins Pubs.
Davis Jones, Melanie, et al. The School Box: Field Day - 100th Da of School - One Happy Classroom. Molnar, Albert & McKillip Thornburgh, Rebecca, illus. 2004. (Rookie Reader Ser.). (ENG.). 96p. (J). (gr. k-2). pap. 9.95 *(978-0-516-24554-6(6)*, Children's Pr.) Scholastic Library Publishing.
Davis, Katie. Kindergarten Rocks! A Kindergarten Readiness Book for Kids. Davis, Katie, illus. 2008. (ENG., Illus.). 32p. (J). (gr. -1-3). pap. 7.99 *(978-0-15-206468-6(0)*, 1199319, Clarion Bks.) HarperCollins Pubs.
Davis, Lois. Happy to Be Me. 2013. 20p. pap. 24.95 *(978-1-63000-789-8(7))* America Star Bks.
Davis, Milton J. Amber & the Hidden City. 2013. 220p. pap. 16.95 *(978-0-9800842-7-6(X))* MVmedia.
Davis, Rebecca. Jake Riley: Irreparably Damaged. 2003. 240p. (J). 16.89 *(978-0-06-051838-7(3))* HarperCollins Pubs.
Davis, Rhonda L. Faces of Darkness: The Daredevil Friends. 2008. 284p. pap. 14.95 *(978-1-934925-75-1(6)*, Eloquent Bks.) Strategic Book Publishing & Rights Agency (SBPRA).
Davis, Samira And Edwina. Nikko & Sierra's Adventures: I Hate Knuckle Sandwiches. 2011. 24p. pap. 11.32 *(978-1-4634-0408-6(5))* AuthorHouse.
DAVIS, Tamika. If i knew back then what i know Now. 2010. (ENG.). 119p. pap. 15.00 *(978-0-557-37544-8(4))* Lulu Pr., Inc.
Dawe, Ted. Into the River. 2016. (ENG.). 304p. (J). (gr. 7). 17.99 *(978-1-943818-19-8(3))* Polis Bks.
Dawson, Jennifer. Silly Sally Sue. 2013. 24p. pap. 24.95 *(978-1-62709-938-7(7))* America Star Bks.
Dawson, Stephanie Mara. The best recess Ever. 2nd ed. 2004. (Illus.). 28p. (J). per. 15.95 *(978-0-9748990-0-8(3))* Bk. Nook Productions.
Daywalt, Drew. The Crayons Go Back to School. Jeffers, Oliver, illus. 2023. (ENG.). 32p. (J). (gr. -1-3). 9.99 *(978-0-593-62111-0(5)*, Philomel Bks.) Penguin Young Readers Group.
De Baun, Hillary Hall. The Last Stop Before Heaven. Cooper, Floyd, illus. 2012. (ENG.). 236p. (J). pap. 9.00 *(978-0-8028-5398-1(6)*, Eerdmans Bks For Young Readers) Eerdmans, William B. Publishing Co.
De Bode, Ann & Broere, Rien. Leave Me Alone! 2011. (Side by Side Ser.). (Illus.). 32p. (J). (gr. k-3). lib. bdg. 28.50 *(978-1-60753-182-1(8))* Amicus Learning.
de Brunhoff, Laurent. Babar et ses Amis a L'Ecole. (Babar Ser.). (FRE., Illus.). 48p. (J). (gr. -1-3). 19.95 *(978-0-7859-8802-1(5))* French & European Pubns., Inc.
—Babar et ses Amis Font les Courses. (Babar Ser.). (FRE., Illus.). 48p. (J). (gr. -1-3). 19.95 *(978-0-7859-8810-6(6))* French & European Pubns., Inc.
de Campi, Alex. Kat & Mouse: The Ice Storm, Vol. 3. Manfredi, Federica, illus. 2007. (Kat & Mouse Manga Ser.: 3). (ENG.). 96p. (J). (gr. 4-1). pap. 5.99 *(978-1-59816-550-0(X)*, 16378622-17e1-44c2-93b0-5762be9e3952, TOKYOPOP Manga) TOKYOPOP, Inc.
De Campi, Alex. Kat & Mouse Vol. 1: Teacher Torture, 1 vol. Manfredi, Federica, illus. 2008. (Tokyopop Ser.). (ENG.). 96p. (J). (gr. 2-6). 32.79 *(978-1-59961-564-6(9)*, 14807, Graphic Novels) Spotlight.
—Kat & Mouse Vol. 2: Tripped, 1 vol. Manfredi, Federica, illus. 2008. (Tokyopop Ser.). (ENG.). 96p. (J). (gr. 2-6). 32.79 *(978-1-59961-565-3(7)*, 14808, Graphic Novels) Spotlight.
—Kat & Mouse Vol. 3: The Ice Storm, 1 vol. Manfredi, Federica, illus. 2008. (Tokyopop Ser.). (ENG.). 96p. (J). (gr. 2-6). 32.79 *(978-1-59961-566-0(5)*, 14809, Graphic Novels) Spotlight.
De Fonté, Desiree. Jazzy: A Story of Love. 2012. 26p. 24.95 *(978-1-4626-5106-1(2))* America Star Bks.
De Kinder, Jan. Red. 2015. (ENG., Illus.). 32p. (J). 16.00 *(978-0-8028-5446-9(X)*, Eerdmans Bks For Young Readers) Eerdmans, William B. Publishing Co.
de la Cruz, Melissa. The Ashley Project. 2014. (Ashley Project Ser.: 1). (ENG., Illus.). 288p. (J). (gr. 4-8). pap. 6.99 *(978-1-4424-9033-8(0)*, Aladdin) Simon & Schuster Children's Publishing.
De la Cruz, Melissa. The Ashleys. 2008. (Ashleys Ser.: Bk. 1). (ENG.). 272p. (J). (gr. 4-8). 9.99 *(978-1-4169-3406-6(5)*, Simon & Schuster Bks. For Young Readers) Simon & Schuster Bks. For Young Readers.
—Jealous? 2008. (Ashleys Ser.: Bk. 2). (ENG.). 256p. (YA). (gr. 4-8). pap. 9.99 *(978-1-4169-3407-3(3)*, Simon & Schuster Bks. For Young Readers) Simon & Schuster Bks. For Young Readers.
de la Cruz, Melissa. Popularity Takeover. 2015. (Ashley Project Ser.: 4). (ENG., Illus.). 272p. (J). (gr. 4-8). 17.99 *(978-1-4814-0974-2(3)*, Aladdin) Simon & Schuster Children's Publishing.
—Social Order. 2014. (Ashley Project Ser.: 2). (ENG., Illus.). 288p. (J). (gr. 4-8). 16.99 *(978-1-4814-0667-3(1)*, Simon & Schuster/Paula Wiseman Bks.) Simon & Schuster/Paula Wiseman Bks.
—29 Dates. 2018. (ENG.). 400p. (YA). 18.99 *(978-1-335-54154-3(3))* Harlequin Enterprises ULC CAN. Dist: HarperCollins Pubs.
—29 Dates. 2020. (ENG.). 384p. (YA). pap. 10.99 *(978-1-335-99471-4(8))* Harlequin Enterprises ULC CAN. Dist: HarperCollins Pubs.
de, Paola Tomie. Oliver Button es una nena. 2003. (SPA.). 48p. (J). (gr. k-1). 14.99 *(978-84-241-8108-6(5))* Everest Editora ESP. Dist: Lectorum Pubns., Inc.
De Valera, Sinead. The Magic Gifts: Classic Irish Fairytales. (Illus.). 224p. 16.95 *(978-0-86327-822-8(1))* Wolfhound Pr. IRL. Dist: Irish Bks. & Media, Inc.
Dean, Carolee. Comfort. 2004. (ENG.). 256p. (YA). (gr. 7-18). pap. 14.95 *(978-0-618-43912-6(9)*, 410118, Clarion Bks.) HarperCollins Pubs.
—Forget Me Not. (ENG.). (YA). (gr. 9). 2013. 400p. pap. 11.99 *(978-1-4424-3255-0(1))* 2012. 384p. 16.99 *(978-1-4424-3254-3(3))* Simon Pulse. (Simon Pulse).
Dean, James. Too Cool for School. 2014. (Pete the Cat I Can Read Ser.). (J). lib. bdg. 13.55 *(978-0-606-35062-4(4))* Turtleback.
Dean, James, illus. Pete the Cat & the Surprise Teacher. 2017. 32p. (J). *(978-1-5182-3399-9(6))* Harper & Row Ltd.
Dean, James & Dean, Kimberly. Pete the Cat: Too Cool for School. Dean, James, illus. 2014. (My First I Can Read Ser.). (ENG., Illus.). 32p. (J). (gr. -1-3). 16.99 *(978-0-06-211076-3(4))*; pap. 4.99 *(978-0-06-211075-6(6))* HarperCollins Pubs. (HarperCollins).
Dean, James, et al. Pete the Cat: Three Bite Rule. 2018. (Pete the Cat Ser.). (ENG., Illus.). 32p. (J). (gr. -1-3). 12.99 *(978-0-06-287260-9(5)*, HarperFestival) HarperCollins Pubs.
Dean, Kimberly. I Can Read Pete the Cat: Too Cool for School. 2017. (ENG.). pap. *(978-0-545-86457-2(7))* Scholastic Canada, Ltd.
Dean, Zoey. Blonde Ambition. 2004. (A-List Ser.: 3). (ENG.). 240p. (YA). (gr. 10-17). pap. 13.99 *(978-0-316-73474-5(8)*, Poppy) Little, Brown Bks. for Young Readers.
DeAngelo, Jeremy. The Out Crowd. 2006. (J). pap. *(978-0-88092-613-3(9))*; lib. bdg. *(978-0-88092-612-6(0))* Royal Fireworks Publishing Co.
Deb, Capone. Dumplings are Delicious Learning & Activity Guide. Stan, Jaskiel, illus. 2007. 20p. (J). 9.95 *(978-0-9728666-9-9(8))* As Simple As That Publishing.
Decker-Ahmed, Stasia. The Weirder the Better. 2011. (ENG.). 175p. (J). (gr. 4-11). pap. 8.99 *(978-0-930773-97-7(7))* Black Heron Pr.
DeClements, Barthe. Fourth Grade Wizards. 2008. 128p. (J). (gr. 3-7). 5.99 *(978-0-14-241348-7(8)*, Puffin Books) Penguin Young Readers Group.
—Nothing's Fair in Fifth Grade. 2008. (ENG.). 144p. (J). (gr. 3-7). 7.99 *(978-0-14-241349-4(6)*, Puffin Books) Penguin Young Readers Group.
—Sixth Grade Can Really Kill You. 2008. 160p. (J). (gr. 3-7). 5.99 *(978-0-14-241380-7(1)*, Puffin Books); (ENG.). (gr. 4-6). 18.69 *(978-0-670-80656-0(0))* Penguin Young Readers Group.
Dee, Barbara. Halfway Normal. 2017. (ENG., Illus.). 256p. (J). (gr. 4-8). 16.99 *(978-1-4814-7851-9(6)*, Aladdin) Simon & Schuster Children's Publishing.
—Just Another Day in My Insanely Real Life. 2007. (Mix Ser.). (ENG.). 256p. (J). (gr. 4-8). pap. 8.99 *(978-1-4169-4739-4(6)*, Aladdin) Simon & Schuster Children's Publishing.
—Maybe He Just Likes You. 2019. (ENG., Illus.). 304p. (J). (gr. 4-8). 19.99 *(978-1-5344-3237-6(X)*, Simon & Schuster/Paula Wiseman Bks.) Simon & Schuster/Paula Wiseman Bks.
—Solving Zoe. 2010. (Mix Ser.). (ENG.). 256p. (J). (gr. 4-8). pap. 7.99 *(978-1-4169-9159-5(X)*, Aladdin) Simon & Schuster Children's Publishing.
—Star-Crossed. 2017. (ENG., Illus.). 288p. (J). (gr. 4-8). 18.99 *(978-1-4814-7848-9(6)*, Simon & Schuster/Paula Wiseman Bks.) Simon & Schuster/Paula Wiseman Bks.
—This Is Me from Now On. 2010. (Mix Ser.). (ENG.). 272p. (J). (gr. 4-8). pap. 7.99 *(978-1-4169-9414-5(9))* Simon & Schuster, Inc.
—Trauma Queen. 2011. (Mix Ser.). (ENG.). 272p. (J). (gr. 4-8). pap. 8.99 *(978-1-4424-0923-1(1)*, Aladdin) Simon & Schuster Children's Publishing.
Dee, Carole. The Bully Returns to Margaret. 2012. 36p. pap. 10.95 *(978-1-4626-7766-5(5))* America Star Bks.
Deedy, Carmen Agra. The Library Dragon, 1 vol. White, Michael P., illus. 2012. (ENG.). 32p. (J). (gr. 1-4). 16.95 *(978-1-56145-091-6(X)*, Q06826) Peachtree Publishing Co. Inc.
—Return of the Library Dragon, 1 vol. White, Michael P., illus. 2012. (ENG.). 32p. (J). (gr. -1-3). 16.95 *(978-1-56145-621-5(7))* Peachtree Publishing Co. Inc.
DeFelice, Cynthia. The Ghost & Mrs. Hobbs. 2010. (Ghost Mysteries Ser.: 2). (ENG.). 208p. (J). (gr. 3-7). pap. 14.99 *(978-0-312-62909-0(5)*, 900066873) Square Fish.
Degen, Bruce. I Gotta Draw. Degen, Bruce, illus. 2012. (ENG., Illus.). 40p. (J). (gr. k-4). 16.99 *(978-0-06-028417-6(X)*, HarperCollins) HarperCollins Pubs.
Degroat, Diane. Ants in Your Pants, Worms in Your Plants! 2011. (Gilbert Ser.). (ENG., Illus.). 32p. (J). (gr. -1-3). 17.99 *(978-0-06-176511-7(2)*, HarperCollins) HarperCollins Pubs.
deGroat, Diane. April Fool! Watch Out at School! deGroat, Diane, illus. 2009. (Gilbert Ser.). (Illus.). 32p. (J). (gr. -1-3). lib. bdg. 18.89 *(978-0-06-143043-5(9))* HarperCollins Pubs.
—April Fool! Watch Out at School! A Springtime Book for Kids. deGroat, Diane, illus. 2009. (Gilbert Ser.). (ENG., Illus.). 32p. (J). (gr. -1-3). 17.99 *(978-0-06-143042-8(0)*, HarperCollins) HarperCollins Pubs.
—Brand-New Pencils, Brand-New Books. deGroat, Diane, illus. 2005. (ENG., Illus.). 32p. (J). (gr. -1-3). 15.99 *(978-0-06-072613-3(X))* HarperCollins Pubs.
—Brand-New Pencils, Brand-New Books. deGroat, Diane, illus. 2007. (Gilbert & Friends Ser.). (Illus.). (J). (gr. -1-3). 14.65 *(978-0-7569-8087-0(9))* Perfection Learning Corp.
—Brand-New Pencils, Brand-new Books. deGroat, Diane, illus. 2007. (ENG., Illus.). 32p. (J). (gr. -1-3). pap. 7.99 *(978-0-06-072616-4(4)*, HarperCollins) HarperCollins Pubs.
—Happy Birthday to You, You Belong in a Zoo. deGroat, Diane, illus. 2007. (ENG., Illus.). 32p. (J). (gr. -1-3). pap. 7.99 *(978-0-06-001029-4(0)*, HarperCollins) HarperCollins Pubs.

—Happy Birthday to You, You Belong in a Zoo. deGroat, Diane, illus. 2007. (Gilbert & Friends Ser.). (Illus.). (gr. -1-3). 17.00 (978-0-7569-8108-2(5)) Perfection Learning Corp.

—Jingle Bells, Homework Smells. deGroat, Diane, illus. 2008. (Illus.). (J). (gr. -1-3). pap. 16.95 incl. audio (978-1-4301-0419-3(8)) Live Oak Media.

—Jingle Bells, Homework Smells: A Christmas Holiday Book for Kids. deGroat, Diane, illus. 2003. (ENG., Illus.). 32p. (J). (gr. -1-3). pap. 7.99 (978-0-688-17545-0(7), HarperCollins) HarperCollins Pubs.

—No More Pencils, No More Books, No More Teacher's Dirty Looks! deGroat, Diane, illus. (Gilbert Ser.). (Illus.). 32p. (J). (gr. -1-3). 2009. (ENG.). pap. 7.99 (978-0-06-079116-2(0), HarperCollins) 2006. 15.99 (978-0-06-079114-8(4)) 2006. (ENG., lib. bdg. 18.89 (978-0-06-079115-5(2), HarperCollins) HarperCollins Pubs.

—Trick or Treat, Smell My Feet, 4 bks., Set. 2008. (J). (gr. -1-2). pap. 37.95 incl. audio (978-1-4301-0426-1(0)); pap. 39.95 incl. audio compact disk (978-1-4301-0428-5(7)) Live Oak Media.

DeGross, Monalisa. Donavan's Double Trouble. Bates, Amy, illus. 192p. (J). (gr. 2-5). 2008. lib. bdg. 16.89 (978-0-06-077294-9(8)) 2007. (ENG.). 16.99 (978-0-06-077293-2(X)) HarperCollins Pubs. (Amistad).

DeJong, Meindert. The Wheel on the School. 82p. (J). pap. 5.95 (978-0-8072-1539-5(2), Listening Library) Random Hse. Audio Publishing Group.

del Rosario, Juleah. 500 Words or Less. 2018. (ENG., Illus.). 384p. (YA). (gr. 9). 18.99 (978-1-5344-1044-2(9), Simon Pulse) Simon Pulse.

Delacruz, Z. Me & My Big Mouth. 2016. (Zack Delacruz Ser.: 1). (ENG., Illus.). 176p. (J). (gr. 5-8). pap. 7.95 (978-1-4549-2127-1(7)) Sterling Publishing Co., Inc.

Delgado, Alvin. Spirit of the Gang. 2007. (ENG.). 192p. pap. 12.95 (978-1-4303-1334-2(X)) Lulu Pr., Inc.

Delios, Louis & Sharma, Vicky. Tomorrow Will Be a New Day. 2011. 20p. pap. (978-1-4269-7318-5(7)) Trafford Publishing (UK) Ltd.

Dellasega, Cheryl. Nugrl90 (Sadie), 0 vols. LaPierre, Karina, illus. 2012. (Bloggrls Ser.: 1). (ENG.). 192p. (YA). (gr. 7-12). pap. 9.99 (978-0-7614-5396-3(2), 9780761453963, Skyscape) Amazon Publishing.

Delle Donne, Elena. Digging Deep. 2019. (Hoops Ser.: 4). (ENG., Illus.). 144p. (J). (gr. 3-7). 16.99 (978-1-5344-4124-8(7), Simon & Schuster Bks. For Young Readers) Simon & Schuster Bks. For Young Readers.

—Elle of the Ball. (Hoops Ser.: 1). (ENG., Illus.). (J). (gr. 3-7). 2019. 176p. pap. 7.99 (978-1-5344-1232-3(8)) 2018. 160p. 17.99 (978-1-5344-1231-6(X)) Simon & Schuster Bks. For Young Readers. (Simon & Schuster Bks. For Young Readers).

—Full-Court Press. (Hoops Ser.: 2). (ENG.). (J). (gr. 3-7). 2019. 176p. pap. 7.99 (978-1-5344-1235-4(2)) 2018. (Illus.). 160p. 17.99 (978-1-5344-1234-7(4)) Simon & Schuster Bks. For Young Readers. (Simon & Schuster Bks. For Young Readers).

—Out of Bounds. 2018. (Hoops Ser.: 3). (ENG., Illus.). 176p. (J). (gr. 3-7). 16.99 (978-1-5344-1237-8(9), Simon & Schuster Bks. For Young Readers) Simon & Schuster Bks. For Young Readers.

DelleCava, Karen. A Closer Look. 2011. 304p. (YA). (gr. 9-18). 16.95 (978-1-934813-49-2(4)) Westside Bks.

Dellicurti, Dana. Joey's First Day at School. 2008. 24p. per. 14.95 (978-1-4327-1408-6(2)) Outskirts Pr., Inc.

Delsol, Wendy. Flock. 2013. (ENG.). 400p. (YA). (gr. 7). pap. 8.99 (978-0-7636-6467-1(7)) Candlewick Pr.

—Frost. (ENG., Illus.). 384p. (YA). (gr. 7). 2012. pap. 8.99 (978-0-7636-6249-3(6)) 2011. 15.99 (978-0-7636-5386-6(1)) Candlewick Pr.

—Stork. (ENG., Illus.). 368p. (YA). (gr. 7). 2011. pap. 8.99 (978-0-7636-5687-4(9)) 2010. 15.99 (978-0-7636-4844-2(2)) Candlewick Pr.

Deluca, Laura. Demon. 2013. 298p. pap. 12.95 (978-1-938397-46-2(0), Pagan Writers Pr.) Mroczka Media.

Delval, Marie-Hélène. L 'Ecole des Geants. pap. 18.95 (978-2-227-72802-8(7)) Bayard Editions FRA. Dist: Distribooks, Inc.

Demas, Corinne. Middle Grade Novel. Date not set. 196p. (J). (gr. 3-7). 4.99 (978-0-06-440845-5(0)); 15.99 (978-0-06-028725-2(X)) HarperCollins Pubs.

Demcak, Andrew. Ghost Songs. (ENG., 2016. Illus.). (J). 24.99 (978-1-63533-019-9(X)) 2014. 210p. (YA). pap. 14.99 (978-1-62798-795-0(9)) Dreamspinner Pr. (Harmony Ink Pr.).

Demetrios, Heather. Bad Romance. 2018. (ENG.). 384p. (YA). pap. 16.99 (978-1-250-15877-2(X), 900159573) Square Fish.

Denice, Sonia. Chow-E-Chowz: Saved by a Whistle. 2011. 44p. pap. 18.46 (978-1-4567-1020-0(6)) AuthorHouse.

Denman, K. L. La Cache, 1 vol. 2012. (Orca Currents en Français Ser.). (FRE.). 128p. (J). (gr. 4-7). pap. 9.95 (978-1-4598-0314-5(0)) Orca Bk. Pubs. USA.

Denou, Violeta. Teo en la Escuela (Teo at School) (SPA.). 32p. (J). 12.95 (978-84-7176-311-2(7)) Timun Mas, Editorial S.A. ESP. Dist: AIMS International Bks., Inc.

Dent, Grace & Dent, Grace. Diva Without a Cause. 2009. (ENG.). 240p. (YA). (gr. 10-17). pap. 14.99 (978-0-316-03482-1(7), Poppy) Little, Brown Bks. for Young Readers.

dePaola, Tomie. Meet the Barkers. dePaola, Tomie, illus. 2003. (Barker Twins Ser.). (Illus.). 32p. (J). (gr. -1-3). 7.99 (978-0-14-250083-5(6), Puffin Books) Penguin Young Readers Group.

—Meet the Barkers: Morgan & Moffat Go to School. 2005. (J). (gr. k-3). pap. 17.95 incl. audio (978-0-8045-6934-7(7), SAC6934) Spoken Arts, Inc.

—Stagestruck. 2007. (Illus.). 32p. (J). (gr. -1-3). pap. 6.99 (978-0-14-240899-5(9), Puffin Books) Penguin Young Readers Group.

—Stagestruck. dePaola, Tomie, illus. 2005. (ENG., Illus.). 32p. (J). (gr. -1-1). 21.19 (978-0-399-24338-7(0)) Penguin Young Readers Group.

—Stagestruck. dePaola, Tomie, illus. 2007. (Illus.). (gr. -1-3). 17.00 (978-0-7569-8159-4(X)) Perfection Learning Corp.

Derby, Kenneth. The Top Ten Ways to Ruin the First Day of 5th Grade. 2004. (ENG.). 176p. (J). (gr. 4-6). tchr. ed. 16.95 (978-0-8234-1851-0(0)) Holiday Hse., Inc.

Deriso, C. H. Elisabeth & the Unwanted Advice. 2016. (Babysitter Chronicles Ser.). (ENG., Illus.). 160p. (J). (gr. 4-7). lib. bdg. 26.65 (978-1-4965-2757-8(7), 131485, Stone Arch Bks.) Capstone.

Deriso, Christine Hurley. Talia Talk. 2009. 184p. (J). pap. (978-0-375-84496-6(1), Delacorte Pr) Random House Publishing Group.

Dernavich, Drew. Elvin Link, Please Report to the Principal's Office! Dernavich, Drew, illus. 2021. (ENG., Illus.). 224p. (J). pap. 7.99 (978-1-250-79170-2(7), 900238557) Square Fish.

Derting, Kimberly. The Body Finder. 2011. (Body Finder Ser.: 1). (ENG.). 352p. (YA). (gr. 9). pap. 10.99 (978-0-06-177983-1(0), HarperCollins) HarperCollins Pubs.

—Desires of the Dead. 2012. (Body Finder Ser.: 2). (ENG.). 384p. (YA). (gr. 9). pap. 8.99 (978-0-06-177986-2(5), HarperCollins) HarperCollins Pubs.

deRubertis, Barbara. Una Coleccion para Kate (A Collection for Kate) Fiammenghi, Gioia, illus. 2007. (Math Matters Ser.). (SPA.). 29p. (J). (gr. -1-3). pap. 5.95 (978-1-57565-240-5(4)) Astra Publishing Hse.

—Lana Llama's Little Lamb. Alley, R. W., illus. 2011. (Animal Antics A to Z Ser.). 32p. (J). pap. 45.32 (978-0-7613-7658-3(5)); (ENG.). lib. bdg. 22.60 (978-1-57565-333-4(8)) Astra Publishing Hse.

—Nina Nandu's Nervous Noggin. Alley, R. W., illus. 2011. (Animal Antics A to Z Ser.). 32p. (J). pap. 45.32 (978-0-7613-7660-6(7)); (ENG.). lib. bdg. 22.60 (978-1-57565-335-8(4)) Astra Publishing Hse.

—Quentin Quokka's Quick Questions. Alley, R. W., illus. 2011. (Animal Antics A to Z Ser.). 32p. (J). pap. 45.32 (978-0-7613-7663-7(1)); (gr. -1-3). pap. 7.95 (978-1-57565-329-7(X), 9c55e9d4-7175-44c4-b744-82d723862abb, Kane Press) Astra Publishing Hse.

Derubertis, Barbara. Xavier Ox's Xylophone Experiment. Alley, R. W., illus. 2011. (Animal Antics A to Z Set III Ser.). pap. 45.32 (978-0-7613-8433-5(2)) Astra Publishing Hse.

deRubertis, Barbara. Xavier Ox's Xylophone Experiment. Alley, R. W., illus. 2011. (Animal Antics a to Z Ser.). 32p. (J). (gr. -1-3). pap. 7.95 (978-1-57565-349-5(4), 65fbdd96-a532-4d2d-bc28-c31fd51103d9, Kane Press) Astra Publishing Hse.

deRubertis, Barbara & DeRubertis, Barbara. Bobby Baboon's Banana Be-Bop. Alley, R. W., illus. 2012. (Animal Antics A to Z Ser.). 32p. (J). (gr. -1-2). cd-rom 7.95 (978-1-57565-395-2(8)) Astra Publishing Hse.

—Lana Llama's Little Lamb. Alley, R. W., illus. 2012. (Animal Antics A to Z Ser.). 32p. (J). (gr. 2 — 1). cd-rom 7.95 (978-1-57565-405-8(9)) Astra Publishing Hse.

—Nina Nandu's Nervous Noggin. Alley, R. W., illus. 2012. (Animal Antics A to Z Ser.). 32p. (J). (gr. 2 — 1). cd-rom 7.95 (978-1-57565-407-2(5)) Astra Publishing Hse.

—Quentin Quokka's Quick Questions. Alley, R. W., illus. 2012. (Animal Antics A to Z Ser.). 32p. (J). (gr. 2 — 1). cd-rom 7.95 (978-1-57565-410-2(5)) Astra Publishing Hse.

—Xavier Ox's Xylophone Experiment. Alley, R. W., illus. 2012. (Animal Antics A to Z Ser.). 32p. (J). (gr. 2 — 1). cd-rom 7.95 (978-1-57565-417-1(2)) Astra Publishing Hse.

—Yoko Yak's Yakety Yakking. Alley, R. W., illus. 2012. (Animal Antics A to Z Ser.). 32p. (J). (gr. 2 — 1). cd-rom 7.95 (978-1-57565-418-8(0)) Astra Publishing Hse.

Desir, C. Fault Line. 2013. (ENG.). 240p. (YA). (gr. 10). 16.99 (978-1-4424-6072-0(5), Simon Pulse) Simon Pulse.

Dessen, Sarah. Just Listen. 2008. (ENG.). 400p. (YA). (gr. 7-18). 12.99 (978-0-14-241097-4(7), Speak) Penguin Young Readers Group.

—Just Listen. 2007. 20.00 (978-0-7569-8270-6(7)) Perfection Learning Corp.

—Just Listen. 2008. 22.10 (978-1-4178-2016-0(0)) Turtleback.

—What Happened to Goodbye. (ENG.). 432p. (YA). (gr. 7). 2023. pap. 6.99 (978-0-593-62349-7(5), Viking Books for Young Readers) 2013. pap. 12.99 (978-0-14-242383-7(1), Speak) Penguin Young Readers Group.

—What Happened to Goodbye. 2013. lib. bdg. 20.85 (978-0-606-30864-9(4)) Turtleback.

DeStefano, Lauren. Dreaming Dangerous. 2018. (ENG.). 208p. (J). 16.99 (978-1-68119-447-9(3), 900172801, Bloomsbury Children's Bks.) Bloomsbury Publishing USA.

Destiny, A. & Helms, Rhonda. Never Too Late. 2015. (Flirt Ser.). (ENG., Illus.). 224p. (YA). (gr. 7). pap. 9.99 (978-1-4814-5188-8(X), Simon Pulse) Simon Pulse.

Deuker, Carl. Gutless. 2017. (ENG.). 336p. (YA). (gr. 7). pap. 11.99 (978-1-328-74206-3(7), 1677320, Clarion Bks.) HarperCollins Pubs.

—Gym Candy. 2008. (ENG., Illus.). 320p. (YA). (gr. 7). pap. 11.99 (978-0-547-07631-7(2), 1042009, Clarion Bks.) HarperCollins Pubs.

—Gym Candy. 2008. 313p. 19.00 (978-1-60686-376-3(2)) Perfection Learning Corp.

—High Heat. 2005. (ENG.). 352p. (J). (gr. 8-18). pap. 8.99 (978-0-06-057248-8(5), HarperTeen) HarperCollins Pubs.

Deutsch, Stacia. The Friendship Code. 2017. 137p. (J). (978-0-605-97742-6(9)); (978-1-5182-5263-1(X)) Penguin Young Readers Group. (Penguin Workshop).

—The Friendship Code #1. 2017. (Girls Who Code Ser.: 1). (Illus.). 144p. (J). (gr. 3-7). 13.99 (978-0-399-54251-0(5), Penguin Workshop) Penguin Young Readers Group.

—Team BFF: Race to the Finish! #2. 2017. (Girls Who Code Ser.: 2). (Illus.). 144p. (J). (gr. 3-7). 13.99 (978-0-399-54252-7(3), Penguin Workshop) Penguin Young Readers Group.

DeVillers, Julia. Lynn Visible. 2011. (ENG.). 160p. (gr. 6-8). 18.69 (978-0-525-47691-7(1)) Penguin Young Readers Group.

—New Girl in Town, 2. Pooler, Paige, illus. 2010. (Liberty Porter, First Daughter Ser.: 2). (ENG.). 208p. (J). (gr. 3-7). 17.99 (978-1-4169-9128-1(X)) Simon & Schuster, Inc.

—New Girl in Town. Pooler, Paige, illus. 2011. (Liberty Porter, First Daughter Ser.: 2). (ENG.). 224p. (J). (gr. 3-7). pap. 7.99 (978-1-4169-9129-8(8), Simon & Schuster/Paula Wiseman Bks.) Simon & Schuster/Paula Wiseman Bks.

DeVillers, Julia & Roy, Jennifer. Double Feature. 2012. (Mix Ser.). (ENG.). (J). (gr. 4-8). 288p. pap. 7.99 (978-1-4424-3403-5(1)); 272p. 16.99 (978-1-4424-3402-8(3)) Simon & Schuster Children's Publishing. (Aladdin).

—Take Two. 2010. (Mix Ser.). (ENG.). 304p. (J). (gr. 4-8). pap. 8.99 (978-1-4169-6731-6(1), Aladdin) Simon & Schuster Children's Publishing.

—Times Squared. 2011. (Mix Ser.). (ENG.). (J). (gr. 4-8). 272p. pap. 8.99 (978-1-4169-6732-3(X)); 240p. 16.99 (978-1-4169-7532-8(2)) Simon & Schuster Children's Publishing. (Aladdin).

—Trading Faces. 2008. (Mix Ser.). (ENG.). 304p. (J). (gr. 4-8). 16.99 (978-1-4169-7531-1(4), Simon & Schuster/Paula Wiseman Bks.) Simon & Schuster/Paula Wiseman Bks.

—Triple Trouble. 2014. (Mix Ser.). (ENG., Illus.). 240p. (J). (gr. 4-8). pap. 7.99 (978-1-4424-3406-6(6), Aladdin) Simon & Schuster Children's Publishing.

Dewdney, Anna. Llama Llama & the Bully Goat. 2013. (Llama Llama Ser.). (Illus.). 40p. (J). (gr. -1-k). 18.99 (978-0-670-01395-1(1), Viking Books for Young Readers) Penguin Young Readers Group.

—Llama Llama Misses Mama. (Llama Llama Ser.). (Illus.). (J). 2019. (ENG.). 36p. (— 1). bds. 9.99 (978-0-593-11671-5(2)) 2009. 40p. (gr. -1-k). 18.99 (978-0-670-06198-3(0)) Penguin Young Readers Group. (Viking Books for Young Readers).

DeWitt, Fowler. The Contagious Colors of Mumpley Middle School. Montalvo, Rodolfo, illus. 2013. (ENG.). 272p. (J). (gr. 2-5). 16.99 (978-1-4424-7829-9(2), Atheneum Bks. for Young Readers) Simon & Schuster Children's Publishing.

DeWoskin, Rachel. Blind. 2014. 416p. (YA). (gr. 7). 17.99 (978-0-670-78522-3(9), Viking Books for Young Readers) Penguin Young Readers Group.

Dhami, Narinder & Dhami, Narinder. Bhangra Babes. 2006. (Bindi Babes Ser.). (ENG.). 185p. (J). (gr. 4-6). 18.69 (978-0-440-42106-1(3)) Random House Publishing Group.

Un Día de Escuela de Oso. 2014. (SPA., Illus.). (J). (978-1-78285-087-8(2)) Barefoot Bks., Inc.

Diaz, Alexandra. The Crossroads. (ENG.). (J). (gr. 3-7). 2019. 352p. pap. 8.99 (978-1-5344-1456-3(8)) 2018. (Illus.). 336p. 18.99 (978-1-5344-1455-6(X)) Simon & Schuster/Paula Wiseman Bks. (Simon & Schuster/Paula Wiseman Bks.).

Díaz, Junot. Islandborn. 2019. (CHI.). (J). (gr. k-3). (978-957-13-7696-7(5)) China Times Publishing Co.

—Islandborn. Espinosa, Leo, illus. 2018. (ENG.). 48p. (J). (gr. k-3). 17.99 (978-0-7352-2986-0(4), Dial Bks) Penguin Young Readers Group.

Dickson, Darnell G. Small Town, Big Dreams: A Dane Jordan Sports Novel. 2008. pap. 14.99 (978-1-59955-229-3(9)) Cedar Fort, Inc./CFI Distribution.

Diesen, Deborah. Pout-Pout Fish: Back to School. Hanna, Dan, illus. 2019. (Pout-Pout Fish Paperback Adventure Ser.). (ENG.). 24p. (J). 5.99 (978-0-374-31047-9(5), 900193159, Farrar, Straus & Giroux (BYR)) Farrar, Straus & Giroux.

—The Pout-Pout Fish Goes to School. Hanna, Dan, illus. (Pout-Pout Fish Adventure Ser.). (ENG.). 32p. (J). 2018. bds. 7.99 (978-0-374-30852-0(7), 900187130) 2014. (gr. -1-k). 18.99 (978-0-374-36095-5(2), 900085614) Farrar, Straus & Giroux. (Farrar, Straus & Giroux (BYR)).

DiGerolamo, Tony. The Wildsidhe Chronicles Bk. 5: The Undercover Dragon. 2003. (J). pap. 7.99 (978-1-890096-17-5(2)) Padwolf Publishing Inc.

Diggins, Matthew. Andrew & the Secret Gallery. Diggins, Matthew, illus. (Illus.). (J). 2008. 32p. pap. 6.95 (978-1-60108-026-4(3)) 2007. 30p. (gr. 1-5). 15.95 (978-1-60108-016-5(6)) Red Cygnet Pr.

Dillard, Sarah. First Day at Zoo School. Dillard, Sarah, illus. 2014. (ENG., Illus.). 40p. (J). (gr. k-2). 14.99 (978-1-58536-890-7(3), 203670) Sleeping Bear Pr.

Dillon, James. Okay Kevin: A Story to Help Children Discover How Everyone Learns Differently. 2017. (Illus.). 36p. (J). 19.95 (978-1-78592-732-4(9), 696347) Kingsley, Jessica Pubs. GBR. Dist: Hachette UK Distribution.

DiLorenzo, Barbara. Quincy: The Chameleon Who Couldn't Blend In. 2018. (ENG., Illus.). 40p. (J). (gr. -1-3). 17.99 (978-1-4998-0542-0(X)) Little Bee Books Inc.

Dinan, Kurt. Don't Get Caught. 2016. (ENG.). 336p. (YA). (gr. 8-12). pap. 18.99 (978-1-4926-3014-2(4), 9781492630142) Sourcebooks, Inc.

Dinosaur School: Set 5. 2016. (Dinosaur School Ser.). 24p. (gr. k-k). pap. 48.90 (978-1-4824-5337-9(1)); (ENG.). lib. bdg. 151.62 (978-1-4824-4517-6(4), 284e432c-f455-47d9-b1bf-2984727a9fba) Stevens, Gareth Publishing LLLP.

Dionne, Erin. Lights, Camera, Disaster. 2018. (ENG.). 272p. (J). (gr. 3-7). 16.99 (978-1-338-13408-7(6), Levine, Arthur A. Bks.) Scholastic, Inc.

DiPucchio, Kelly. Dog Days of School. 2017. (J). lib. bdg. 16.00 (978-0-606-39971-5(2)) Turtleback.

—The Sandwich Swap. Tusa, Tricia, illus. 2010. (ENG.). 32p. (J). (gr. -1-2). 18.99 (978-1-4231-2484-9(7)) Little, Brown Bks. for Young Readers.

Diroma, Joseph. Pinuccio. Jones, Bob, illus. 2009. 24p. pap. 14.99 (978-1-60844-036-8(2)) Dog Ear Publishing, LLC.

DiSalvo-Ryan, DyAnne. The Sloppy Copy Slipup. 2006. (ENG., Illus.). 103p. (J). (gr. 2-4). 22.44 (978-0-8234-1947-0(9)) Holiday Hse., Inc.

Disney Press Staff. School's Out. 2010. 128p. pap. 4.99 (978-1-4231-2677-5(7)) Disney Pr.

Diver, Lucienne. Faultlines. 2016. (ENG., Illus.). 254p. (YA). (gr. 7-12). pap. 14.95 (978-1-62268-100-6(2)) Bella Rosa Bks.

—Vamped. 2017. (ENG., Illus.). (YA). pap. 14.95 (978-1-62268-115-0(0)) Bella Rosa Bks.

Divine, Jill. Wicked Rabbit. 2011. (Illus.). 86p. pap. 12.95 (978-1-4457-3797-3(3)) Lulu Pr., Inc.

Divine, L. Drama High: Second Chance. 2006. (Drama High Ser.: 2). (ENG., Illus.). 208p. (YA). (gr. 9-12). pap. 9.95 (978-0-7582-1635-9(1), K-Teen/Dafina) Kensington Publishing Corp.

—Frenemies. 2008. (Drama High Ser.: Vol. 4). 218p. (gr. 8-12). 19.95 (978-0-7569-8832-6(2)) Perfection Learning Corp.

—Hustlin' 2009. (Drama High Ser.: 7). lib. bdg. 26.95 (978-0-606-00156-4(5)) Turtleback.

—Lady J. 2008. (Drama High Ser.: Vol. 5). 214p. (gr. 8-12). 19.95 (978-0-7569-8833-3(0)) Perfection Learning Corp.

Dixon, Franklin. Water-Ski Wipeout. David, Matt, illus. 2016. (Hardy Boys Clue Book Ser.: 3). (ENG.). 96p. (J). (gr. 1-4). 16.99 (978-1-4814-5056-0(5), Simon & Schuster/Paula Wiseman Bks.) Simon & Schuster/Paula Wiseman Bks.

Dixon, Franklin W. Bound for Danger. 2016. (Hardy Boys Adventures Ser.: 13). (ENG., Illus.). 144p. (J). (gr. 3-7). pap. 6.99 (978-1-4814-6831-2(6), Aladdin) Simon & Schuster Children's Publishing.

—Bound for Danger. 2016. (Hardy Boys Adventures Ser.: 13). (ENG., Illus.). 144p. (J). (gr. 3-7). 17.99 (978-1-4814-6832-9(4), Simon & Schuster/Paula Wiseman Bks.) Simon & Schuster/Paula Wiseman Bks.

—The Great Escape. Burroughs, Scott, illus. 2015. (Hardy Boys: the Secret Files Ser.: 17). (ENG.). 112p. (J). (gr. 1-4). pap. 5.99 (978-1-4814-2267-3(7), Aladdin) Simon & Schuster Children's Publishing.

—The Race Is On. Burroughs, Scott, illus. 2015. (Hardy Boys: the Secret Files Ser.: 19). (ENG.). 96p. (J). (gr. 1-4). pap. 5.99 (978-1-4814-2271-0(5), Aladdin) Simon & Schuster Children's Publishing.

—Robot Rumble, 11. Burroughs, Scott, illus. 2013. (Hardy Boys: the Secret Files Ser.: 11). (ENG.). 96p. (J). (gr. 1-4). pap. 5.99 (978-1-4424-5367-8(2), Aladdin) Simon & Schuster Children's Publishing.

DK. How to Be a Big Kid. 2018. (ENG., Illus.). 48p. (J). (-k). 12.99 (978-1-4654-6858-1(7), DK Children) Dorling Kindersley Publishing, Inc.

Do, Anh. Super Weird! (WeirDo #4) 2019. (WeirDo Ser.: 4). (ENG., Illus.). 160p. (J). (gr. 2-5). pap. 5.99 (978-1-338-30565-4(4)) Scholastic, Inc.

Doan, Lisa. Chadwick's Epic Revenge. Andrewson, Natalie, illus. 2018. (ENG.). 288p. (J). 27.99 (978-1-250-15409-5(X), 900184346) Roaring Brook Pr.

Doerrfeld, Cori. Truth in Sight: Book 2, No. 2. Doerrfeld, Cori & Page, Tyler, illus. 2016. (Cici: a Fairy's Tale Ser.: 2). (ENG.). 48p. (J). (gr. 2-5). lib. bdg. 26.65 (978-1-4677-6153-6(2), e6bba0b4-2fa7-4a1e-9099-fe73b146e422, Graphic Universe™) Lerner Publishing Group.

Doherty, Berlie. Coconut Comes to School. Bates, Ivan, illus. 2004. (ENG.). 32p. (J). (gr. k-2). 18.00 (978-0-00-710433-8(2), HarperCollins Children's Bks.) HarperCollins Pubs. Ltd. GBR. Dist: Independent Pubs. Group.

Doleski, Shannon. Mary Underwater. 2020. (ENG., Illus.). 240p. (J). (gr. 5-9). 16.99 (978-1-4197-4080-0(6), 1276901, Amulet Bks.) Abrams, Inc.

Dominguez, Angela. Stella Diaz Has Something to Say. 2018. (Stella Diaz Ser.: 1). (ENG., Illus.). 208p. (J). 18.99 (978-1-62672-858-5(5), 900175839) Roaring Brook Pr.

—Stella díaz Has Something to Say. Dominguez, Angela, illus. 2019. (Stella Diaz Ser.: 1). (ENG., Illus.). 224p. (J). pap. 6.99 (978-1-250-29410-4(X), 900175840) Square Fish.

Donaldson, Julia. A Gold Star for Zog. Scheffler, Axel, illus. 2012. (ENG.). 32p. (J). (gr. -1-3). 18.99 (978-0-545-41724-2(4), Levine, Arthur A. Bks.) Scholastic, Inc.

—The Wrong Kind of Bark. Parsons, Garry, illus. 2005. (Red Bananas Ser.). (ENG.). 48p. (J). lib. bdg. (978-0-7787-1073-8(4)); (gr. 1-3). (978-0-7787-1089-9(0)) Crabtree Publishing Co.

Dong, Haidan. Of Trouble & Trickery. 2004. 58p. pap. 8.95 (978-0-595-31170-5(9)) iUniverse, Inc.

Donley, Jan. The Side Door. 2010. (ENG.). 288p. (J). (gr. 9). pap. 14.95 (978-1-935226-12-3(6)) Spinsters Ink Bks.

Donovan, Gail. 100th Day Fun. Clar, David Austin, illus. 2003. (Rainbow Fish & Friends Ser.). 24p. (J). lib. bdg. 9.95 (978-1-59014-141-0(5)) Night Sky Bks.

Donovan, Rebecca. Barely Breathing, 0 vols. unabr. ed. 2013. (Breathing Ser.: 2). (ENG.). 512p. (YA). (gr. 7-12). pap. 9.99 (978-1-4778-1717-9(4), 9781477817179, Skyscape) Amazon Publishing.

—The Breathing Series: Books 1 And 2, 0 vols. 2013. (Breathing Ser.). (ENG.). 978p. (YA). (gr. 7-12). pap. 12.99 (978-1-4778-1695-0(X), 9781477816950, Skyscape) Amazon Publishing.

—Reason to Breathe, 0 vols. 2013. (Breathing Ser.: 1). (ENG.). 466p. (YA). (gr. 7-12). pap. 9.99 (978-1-4778-1714-8(X), 9781477817148, Skyscape) Amazon Publishing.

Doodler, Todd H. Super Rawr! Doodler, Todd H., illus. 2016. (ENG., Illus.). 40p. (J). (gr. -1-k). 12.99 (978-0-545-79969-0(4), Scholastic Pr.) Scholastic, Inc.

Dorfman, Joaquin. The Long Wait for Tomorrow. 2009. (YA). (978-0-375-84696-0(4)) Random Hse., Inc.

Doti, James. Jimmy Finds His Voice. Mertins, Lisa, illus. 2013. (J). 14.95 (978-1-935204-47-3(5)) Salem Author Services.

Doty, M. Surviving High School. 2012. (Surviving High School Ser.: 1). (ENG.). 224p. (YA). (gr. 7-17). pap. 13.99 (978-0-316-22015-6(9), Poppy) Little, Brown Bks. for Young Readers.

Double or Nothing. 2014. (It Takes Two Ser.: 3). (ENG., Illus.). 160p. (J). (gr. 3-7). pap. 6.99 (978-1-4814-1652-8(9), Simon Spotlight) Simon Spotlight.

Doudna, Kelly. Goat Cheese. Haberstroh, Anne, illus. 2006. (Fact & Fiction Ser.). 24p. (J). pap. 48.42 (978-1-59679-938-7(2)) ABDO Publishing Co.

Dougherty, Brandi. The Friendship Experiment. 2009. 147p. (J). pap. (978-0-545-07929-7(2)) Scholastic, Inc.

—The Valentine's Day Disaster. 2008. 204p. (J). pap. (978-0-545-03168-4(0)) Scholastic, Inc.

Dougherty, Meghan. Rise of the Undead Redhead. Birnbach, Alece, illus. 2014. (Dorothy's Derby Chronicles Ser.: 1). 256p. (J). (gr. 3-6). pap. 10.99 (978-1-4022-9535-5(9)) Sourcebooks, Inc.

Douglas, Babette. Kiss a Me Goes to School. Rockwell, Barry, illus. 2006. (Kiss a Me Teacher Creature Stories Ser.). (J). (gr. -1-3). 9.99 (978-1-890343-09-5(9)) Kiss A Me Productions, Inc.

Dowding, Philippa. The Gargoyle at the Gates. 2012. (Lost Gargoyle Ser.: 3). (ENG.). 192p. (J). pap. 10.99 (978-1-4597-0394-0(4), 9781459703940) Dundurn Pr. CAN. Dist: Publishers Group West (PGW).

Dowell, Frances O'Roark. Chicken Boy. 2007. (ENG., Illus.). 224p. (J). (gr. 5-9). pap. 7.99 (978-1-4169-3482-0(0), Atheneum Bks. for Young Readers) Simon & Schuster Children's Publishing.

—The Class. 2019. (ENG., Illus.). 320p. (J). (gr. 4-8). 18.99 (978-1-4814-8179-3(7)) Simon & Schuster Children's Publishing.

—The Kind of Friends We Used to Be. (Secret Language of Girls Trilogy Ser.). (ENG., Illus.). (J). (gr. 3-7). 2010. 256p. pap. 7.99 (978-1-4169-9779-5(2)) 2009. 240p. 16.99 (978-1-4169-5031-8(1)) Simon & Schuster Children's Publishing. (Atheneum Bks. for Young Readers).

—Phineas L. MacGuire ... Blasts Off! McDaniels, Preston, illus. 2011. (From the Highly Scientific Notebooks of Phineas L. MacGuire Ser.). (ENG.). 224p. (J). (gr. 3-7). pap. 7.99 *(978-1-4424-2204-9(1),* Atheneum Bks. for Young Readers) Simon & Schuster Children's Publishing.
—Phineas L. MacGuire ... Erupts! The First Experiment. McDaniels, Preston, illus. (From the Highly Scientific Notebooks of Phineas L. MacGuire Ser.). (ENG.). 176p. (J). (gr. 3-7). 2007. pap. 7.99 *(978-1-4169-4734-9(5))* 2006. 18.99 *(978-1-4169-0195-2(7))* Simon & Schuster Children's Publishing. (Atheneum Bks. for Young Readers).
—Phineas L. MacGuire ... Gets Cooking! McDaniels, Preston, illus. (From the Highly Scientific Notebooks of Phineas L. MacGuire Ser.). (ENG.). (J). (gr. 3-7). 2015. 224p. pap. 6.99 *(978-1-4814-0100-5(9))* 2014. 208p. 16.99 *(978-1-4814-0099-2(1),* Atheneum Bks. for Young Readers) Simon & Schuster Children's Publishing.
—Phineas L. MacGuire ... Gets Slimed! McDaniels, Preston, illus. 2010. (From the Highly Scientific Notebooks of Phineas L. MacGuire Ser.). (ENG.). 224p. (J). (gr. 3-7). pap. 7.99 *(978-1-4169-9775-7(X),* Atheneum Bks. for Young Readers) Simon & Schuster Children's Publishing.
—Phineas L. MacGuire... Gets Slimed! McDaniels, Preston, illus. l.t. ed. 2008. (From the Highly Scientific Notebooks of Phineas L. MacGuire Ser.). 159p. (J). (gr. 3-7). 22.95 *(978-1-4104-0440-4(4))* Thorndike Pr.
—Sam the Man & the Secret Detective Club Plan. Bates, Amy June, illus. 2018. (Sam the Man Ser.: 4). (ENG.). 192p. (J). (gr. 1-4). 16.99 *(978-1-5344-1258-3(1),* Atheneum/Caitlyn Dlouhy Books) Simon & Schuster Children's Publishing.
—The Secret Language of Girls. 2005. 247p. (gr. 3-7). 17.00 *(978-0-7569-5463-5(0))* Perfection Learning Corp.
—The Secret Language of Girls. (Secret Language of Girls Trilogy Ser.). (ENG., Illus.). 256p. (J). (gr. 3-7). 2005. pap. 8.99 *(978-1-4169-0717-6(3))* 2004. 19.99 *(978-0-689-84421-8(2))* Simon & Schuster Children's Publishing. (Atheneum Bks. for Young Readers).
—The Sound of Your Voice, Only Really Far Away. (Secret Language of Girls Trilogy Ser.). (ENG., Illus.). (J). (gr. 5-9). 2014. 256p. pap. 7.99 *(978-1-4424-3290-1(X),* Atheneum Bks. for Young Readers) 2013. 240p. 16.99 *(978-1-4424-3289-5(6))* Simon & Schuster Children's Publishing.
—Ten Miles Past Normal. (ENG., 224p. (YA). (gr. 7). 2012. Illus.). pap. 10.99 *(978-1-4169-9586-9(2))* 2011. 16.99 *(978-1-4169-9585-2(4))* Simon & Schuster Children's Publishing. (Atheneum Bks. for Young Readers).
Dower, Laura. Gabi & the Great Big Bakeover. Lazuli, Lilly, illus. 2016. (Dessert Diaries). (ENG.). 160p. (J). (gr. 4-8). lib. bdg. 26.65 *(978-1-4965-3119-3(1),* 132190, Stone Arch Bks.) Capstone.
—Gabi & the Great Big Bakeover. Lazuli, Lilly, illus. 2017. (ENG.). 160p. (J). pap. *(978-1-4747-2213-1(X),* Stone Arch Bks.) Capstone.
—On the Case. 2004. 170p. (J). lib. bdg. 16.92 *(978-1-4242-0648-3(0))* Fitzgerald Bks.
—The Slime That Would Not Die. 1. Schlafman, Dave, illus. 2009. (Monster Squad Ser.: 1). (ENG.). 144p. (J). (gr. 4-6). 17.44 *(978-0-448-44912-8(9))* Penguin Young Readers Group.
Downer, Denise. Tombstone Twins: Soul Mates, 1 vol. Frampton, Otis, illus. 2013. (Tombstone Twins Ser.). (ENG.). 48p. (J). (gr. 3-5). pap. 5.95 *(978-1-4342-3873-3(3),* 118054); lib. bdg. 23.99 *(978-1-4342-2248-0(9),* 103111) Capstone. (Stone Arch Bks.).
—Tombstone Twins Package: Soul Mates. Frampton, Otis, illus. 2013. (ENG.). 41p. (J). (gr. 2-4). pap. 35.70 *(978-1-4342-3955-6(1),* Stone Arch Bks.) Capstone.
Doxey, Heidi. The Jane Journals at Pemberley Prep: Liam Darcy, I Loathe You. 2015. 215p. (YA). pap. 14.99 *(978-1-4621-1682-9(5))* Cedar Fort, Inc./CFI Distribution.
DPWW, ed. High School Musical Actors' Biography. 2007. (J). (gr. 2-7). pap. 6.99 *(978-1-4231-0827-6(2))* Disney Pr.
Drake, Paula. How to Make a Snow Day: The Official Rules & Regulations. 2011. 28p. (gr. -1). pap. 15.00 *(978-1-4567-1830-5(4))* AuthorHouse.
Drake, Raelyn. Lockdown. 2018. (Attack on Earth Ser.). (ENG.). 104p. (YA). (gr. 6-12). 26.65 *(978-1-5415-2576-4(0),* d024674c-99ad-49a8-84f7-ac4c4ad7c6bb, Darby Creek) Lerner Publishing Group.
—Picking up Speed. 2018. (Superhuman Ser.). (ENG.). 104p. (YA). (gr. 6-12). pap. 7.99 *(978-1-5415-1050-0(X),* a3c8eb1b-eecb-4d50-a140-ef741d3cd510); 25.32 *(978-1-5124-9831-8(9),* 0d62eed7-3333-4987-81f2-288feafcf1dd) Lerner Publishing Group. (Darby Creek).
Draper, Sharon. Fire from the Rock. 2008. (ENG.). 240p. (YA). (gr. 7-18). 11.99 *(978-0-14-241199-5(X),* Speak) Penguin Young Readers Group.
Draper, Sharon M. The Battle of Jericho. (Jericho Trilogy Ser.: 1). (ENG., Illus.). (YA). (gr. 7). 2017. 320p. pap. 11.99 *(978-1-4814-9029-0(X),* Atheneum/Caitlyn Dlouhy Books) 2003. 304p. 19.99 *(978-0-689-84232-0(5),* Atheneum Bks. for Young Readers) Simon & Schuster Children's Publishing.
—The Battle of Jericho. 2005. (Jericho Trilogy Ser.). (ENG., Illus.). 352p. (YA). (gr. 7). mass mkt. 8.99 *(978-0-689-84233-7(3),* Simon Pulse) Simon Pulse.
—Darkness Before Dawn. 2014. (Hazelwood High Trilogy Ser. 3 Ser.). (ENG.). 288p. (YA). (gr. k-k). 11.24 *(978-1-63245-162-0(X))* Lectorum Pubns., Inc.
—Darkness Before Dawn. 2013. (Hazelwood High Trilogy Ser.: 3). (ENG., Illus.). 256p. (YA). (gr. 7). pap. 10.99 *(978-1-4424-8915-8(4),* Atheneum Bks. for Young Readers) Simon & Schuster Children's Publishing.
—Darkness Before Dawn. 2013. (Hazelwood High Trilogy Ser.: 3). lib. bdg. 20.85 *(978-0-606-32334-5(1))* Turtleback.
—Double Dutch. 2004. 183p. (gr. 6-9). 17.00 *(978-0-7569-2934-3(2))* Perfection Learning Corp.
—Double Dutch. 2004. (ENG.). 192p. (J). (gr. 5-9). pap. 7.99 *(978-0-689-84231-3(7),* Atheneum Bks. for Young Readers) Simon & Schuster Children's Publishing.
—Fire from the Rock. 2014. (ENG.). 240p. (YA). (gr. 7-12). 12.24 *(978-1-63245-286-3(3))* Lectorum Pubns., Inc.
—Just Another Hero. (Jericho Trilogy Ser.: 3). (ENG., (YA). (gr. 7). 2017. Illus.). 304p. pap. 12.99 *(978-1-4814-9030-6(3),* Atheneum/Caitlyn Dlouhy Books) 2009. 288p. 19.99 *(978-1-4169-0700-8(9),* Atheneum Bks. for Young Readers) Simon & Schuster Children's Publishing.
—Just Another Hero. 2010. (Jericho Trilogy Ser.). (ENG., Illus.). 352p. (YA). (gr. 7). mass mkt. 7.99 *(978-1-4169-0701-5(7),* Simon Pulse) Simon Pulse.
—Just Another Hero. 2010. (Jericho Trilogy Ser.: 3). lib. bdg. 18.40 *(978-0-606-14725-5(X))* Turtleback.
—Lost in the Tunnel of Time. Watson, Jesse Joshua, illus. 2011. (Clubhouse Mysteries Ser.: 2). (ENG.). 112p. (J). (gr. 3-7). pap. 6.99 *(978-1-4424-2704-4(3),* Aladdin) Simon & Schuster Children's Publishing.
—Lost in the Tunnel of Time. Watson, Jesse Joshua, illus. 2011. (Clubhouse Mysteries Ser.: 2). (ENG.). 112p. (J). (gr. 3-7). lib. bdg. 16.99 *(978-1-4424-2703-7(5),* Simon & Schuster/Paula Wiseman Bks.) Simon & Schuster/Paula Wiseman Bks.
—November Blues. 2011. 9.00 *(978-0-7848-3495-4(4),* Everbind) Marco Bk. Co.
—November Blues. (Jericho Trilogy Ser.: 2). (ENG., Illus.). (YA). (gr. 7). 2017. 336p. pap. 11.99 *(978-1-4814-9031-3(1),* Atheneum/Caitlyn Dlouhy Books) 2007. 320p. 19.99 *(978-1-4169-0698-8(3),* Atheneum Bks. for Young Readers) Simon & Schuster Children's Publishing.
—Tears of a Tiger. 2014. (Hazelwood High Trilogy Ser. 1 Ser.). (ENG.). 192p. (YA). (gr. 12-12). 12.24 *(978-1-63245-075-3(5))* Lectorum Pubns., Inc.
—Tears of a Tiger. 2007. (Hazelwood High Trilogy: Bk. 1). 45p. ring bd. 54.95 *(978-1-60843-737-5(X))* Prestwick Hse., Inc.
—Tears of a Tiger. 2013. (Hazelwood High Trilogy Ser.: 1). (ENG., Illus.). 192p. (J). (gr. 7). pap. 11.99 *(978-1-4424-8913-4(8),* Atheneum Bks. for Young Readers) Simon & Schuster Children's Publishing.
—Tears of a Tiger. l.t. ed. 2006. (Hazelwood High Trilogy: Bk. 1). 207p. (YA). (gr. 8-12). per. 10.95 *(978-0-7862-8361-3(0))* Thorndike Pr.
—Tears of a Tiger. 2013. (Hazelwood High Trilogy Ser.: 1). lib. bdg. 20.85 *(978-0-606-32332-1(5))* Turtleback.
Dream Pony (revised) 2017. (Sandy Lane Stables Ser.). (ENG.). (J). pap. 5.99 *(978-0-7945-3624-4(7),* Usborne) EDC Publishing.
Dreissigacker Martin, Susan. Princess Stephanie Stories: The Road Trip & the New School. 2009. 32p. pap. 18.79 *(978-1-4389-1836-5(4))* AuthorHouse.
Driving Mom Crazy 6 Packs: Individual Title. (gr. -1-2). 27.00 *(978-0-7635-9446-6(6))* Rigby Education.
Drown, Merle. Lighting the World. 2015. (ENG.). 278p. pap. 18.00 *(978-0-9898971-4-3(1))* Whitepoint Pr.
Drummond, Ree. Charlie Goes to School. deGroat, Diane, illus. 2013. (Charlie the Ranch Dog Ser.). (ENG.). 40p. (J). (gr. -1-3). 18.99 *(978-0-06-221920-6(0),* HarperCollins) HarperCollins Pubs.
Du Jardin, Rosamond. A Man for Marcy. 2003. (YA). pap. 12.95 *(978-1-930009-76-9(3),* 800-691-7779) Image Cascade Publishing.
Dubosarsky, Ursula. The Golden Day. 2013. (ENG.). 160p. (YA). (gr. 7). 15.99 *(978-0-7636-6399-5(9))* Candlewick Pr.
Duey, Kathleen. Skin Hunger. 2008. (Resurrection of Magic Ser.: 1). (ENG.). 368p. (YA). (gr. 7-7). pap. 12.99 *(978-0-689-84094-4(2),* Atheneum Bks. for Young Readers) Simon & Schuster Children's Publishing.
Dufresne, Michèle. Dad Goes to School. 2003. (Mom & Dad Ser.). (J). pap. 7.33 *(978-1-58453-252-1(1))* Pioneer Valley Bks.
—Recess. 2004. (At School Ser.). (J). pap. 7.33 *(978-1-58453-268-2(8))* Pioneer Valley Bks.
DuJardin, Rosamond. Boy Trouble. 2003. (YA). pap. 12.95 *(978-1-930009-70-7(4),* 800-691-7779) Image Cascade Publishing.
—One of the Crowd. 2003. (YA). pap. 12.95 *(978-1-930009-73-8(9),* 800-691-7779) Image Cascade Publishing.
—Senior Prom. 2003. (YA). pap. 12.95 *(978-1-930009-77-6(1),* 800-691-7779) Image Cascade Publishing.
Dumble, Carol. R U My Friend? 2011. 20p. pap. 11.99 *(978-1-4567-1825-1(8))* AuthorHouse.
Duncan, Randy. Miranda & Her Pand. 2009. 28p. pap. 12.49 *(978-1-4389-6132-3(4))* AuthorHouse.
Dungy, Tony. You Can Do It! Bates, Amy June, illus. 2008. (ENG.). 32p. (J). (gr. -1-2). 19.99 *(978-1-4169-5461-3(9),* Little Simon Inspirations) Little Simon Inspirations.
Dunlop, Ed. Sherlock Jones: The Assassination Plot. 2004. 116p. (J). 8.99 *(978-1-59166-315-7(6))* BJU Pr.
Dunsany, Taylor. The Little Witch Who Lost Her Broom & Other Stories. 2008. 48p. pap. 8.95 *(978-0-595-52506-5(7))* iUniverse, Inc.
Dupuis, Jenny Kay & Kacer, Kathy. I Am Not a Number, 1 vol. Newland, Gillian, illus. 2016. (ENG.). 32p. (J). (gr. 3-6). 19.95 *(978-1-927583-94-4(2))* Second Story Pr. CAN. Dist: Orca Bk. Pubs. USA.
Durand, Hallie. Catch That Cookie! 2014. *(978-0-8037-3960-4(5),* Dial) Penguin Publishing Group.
—Catch That Cookie! Small, David, illus. 2014. 32p. (J). (gr. -1-k). 17.99 *(978-0-525-42835-6(0),* Dial Bks) Penguin Young Readers Group.
—Dessert First. Davenier, Christine, illus. 2010. (ENG.). 176p. (J). (gr. 2-5). pap. 5.99 *(978-1-4169-6386-8(3),* Atheneum Bks. for Young Readers) Simon & Schuster Children's Publishing.
—Dessert First, 1. Davenier, Christine, illus. 2009. (ENG.). 160p. (J). (gr. 2-5). 14.99 *(978-1-4169-6385-1(5))* Simon & Schuster, Inc.
—Just Desserts. Davenier, Christine, illus. 2011. (ENG.). 224p. (J). (gr. 2-5). pap. 5.99 *(978-1-4169-6388-2(X),* Atheneum Bks. for Young Readers) Simon & Schuster Children's Publishing.
—No Room for Dessert. Davenier, Christine, illus. 2012. (ENG.). 192p. (J). (gr. 2-5). pap. 6.99 *(978-1-4424-0361-1(6),* Atheneum Bks. for Young Readers) Simon & Schuster Children's Publishing.
Durst, Sarah Beth. Drink, Slay, Love. (ENG., Illus.). 400p. (YA). (gr. 9). 2012. pap. 10.99 *(978-1-4424-2374-9(9))* 2011. 17.99 *(978-1-4424-2373-2(0))* McElderry, Margaret K. Bks. (McElderry, Margaret K. Bks.).
—Into the Wild. 2007. (ENG.). 278p. (J). (gr. 6-8). 22.44 *(978-1-59514-156-9(1),* Razorbill) Penguin Young Readers Group.
Dwyer, Cynthia. Four-Eyed Philip. Schuepbach, Lynnette, illus. 2007. (J). 14.95 *(978-0-9793296-0-9(4))* Grannie Annie Family Story Celebration, The.
E. S. Townsend. The Secrets of Marsh House. 2013. 208p. pap. *(978-1-907011-44-3(7))* Esteemworld Pubns.
Eaddy, Susan. Poppy's Best Paper. Bonnet, Rosalinde, illus. 2015. 40p. (J). (gr. k-3). lib. bdg. 15.95 *(978-1-58089-614-6(6))* Charlesbridge Publishing, Inc.
—Poppy's Best Paper (1 Hardcover/1 CD) Bonnet, Rosalinde, illus. 2016. (ENG.). (J). (gr. 1-4). audio compact disk 29.95 *(978-1-4301-2187-9(4))* Live Oak Media.
Eagle, Rita. Sniffy the Beagle. Rasmussen, Gerry, illus. 2007. (ENG.). 44p. per. 13.95 *(978-1-59800-537-0(5))* Outskirts Pr., Inc.
Easley, Maryann. Warriors Daughter. 2007. 150p. pap. 24.95 *(978-1-4241-4875-2(8))* PublishAmerica, Inc.
East, Bob. Tommy Cat & the Haunted Well, 1 vol. 2009. 42p. pap. 24.95 *(978-1-60703-754-5(8))* America Star Bks.
Easton, Kelly. To Be Mona. (ENG.). 224p. (YA). (gr. 7). 2009. pap. 7.99 *(978-1-4169-0055-9(1))* 2008. 16.99 *(978-1-4169-0054-2(3))* McElderry, Margaret K. Bks. (McElderry, Margaret K. Bks.).
Eaton, Kelly Toole. Kellina Makes Her Dreams Come True. 2011. 40p. pap. 21.99 *(978-1-4568-8824-4(2))* Xlibris Corp.
Eaves, Victor Caleb. Vee's the Chapters of Expudict: Book One. 2008. 128p. pap. 12.00 *(978-1-4389-3385-6(1))* AuthorHouse.
Echols, Jennifer. Biggest Flirts. 2014. (Superlatives Ser.). (ENG., Illus.). 336p. (YA). (gr. 9). pap. 9.99 *(978-1-4424-7445-1(9),* Simon Pulse) Simon Pulse.
—Most Likely to Succeed. 2015. (Superlatives Ser.). (ENG., Illus.). 352p. (YA). (gr. 9). 17.99 *(978-1-4424-7452-9(1),* Simon Pulse) Simon Pulse.
—The One That I Want. 2012. (ENG., Illus.). 288p. (YA). (gr. 7). pap. 9.99 *(978-1-4424-5236-7(6),* Simon Pulse) Simon Pulse.
—Perfect Couple. 2015. (Superlatives Ser.). (ENG., Illus.). 336p. (YA). (gr. 9). pap. 12.99 *(978-1-4424-7448-2(3),* Simon Pulse) Simon Pulse.
Eckelberg, Aimie. Walk the Walk. 2010. (Illus.). 32p. (J). 15.00 *(978-1-4520-3644-1(6))* AuthorHouse.
Ecker, Rebecca. Miss Emmalou Strain & the Hunt for Hermie. 2008. 32p. pap. 12.95 *(978-1-4327-0182-6(7))* Outskirts Pr., Inc.
Ecton, Anne Massey. Passing Through Camelot. 2006. (J). *(978-0-88092-620-1(1))* Royal Fireworks Publishing Co.
Edelman, Lana. School Friends. 2012. (Penguin Young Readers Level 2 Ser.). lib. bdg. 13.55 *(978-0-606-26023-7(4))* Turtleback.
Edward, Judy. Calvin Can - Be Happy. Edward, Aaron, illus. 2012. 32p. pap. *(978-1-4602-0097-1(7))* FriesenPress.
Edwards, Michelle. Pa Lia's First Day. 2005. (Jackson Friends Bks.). (Illus.). 55p. (gr. 1-4). 15.95 *(978-0-7569-5773-5(7))* Perfection Learning Corp.
—Pa Lia's First Day: A Jackson Friends Book. Edwards, Michelle, illus. 2005. (Jackson Friends Ser.: 1). (ENG., Illus.). 64p. (J). (gr. -1-3). pap. 5.99 *(978-0-15-205748-0(X),* 1197275, Clarion Bks.) HarperCollins Pubs.
—Stinky Stern Forever. 2007. (Jackson Friends Bks.). (Illus.). 49p. (gr. 1-4). 15.95 *(978-0-7569-8198-3(0))* Perfection Learning Corp.
—Stinky Stern Forever: A Jackson Friends Book. Edwards, Michelle, illus. 2007. (Jackson Friends Ser.). (ENG., Illus.). 56p. (J). (gr. 1-4). pap. 6.95 *(978-0-15-206101-2(0),* 1198326, Clarion Bks.) HarperCollins Pubs.
—Zero Grandparents. 2005. (Jackson Friends Bks.). (Illus.). 59p. (gr. 1-4). 15.95 *(978-0-7569-5774-2(5))* Perfection Learning Corp.
Edwards, Nancy. Mom for Mayor. Chesworth, Michael, illus. 2006. (ENG.). (J). (gr. 1-5). 16.95 *(978-0-8126-2743-5(1))* Cricket Bks.
Edwards, Pamela Duncan. Gigi & Lulu's Gigantic Fight. Cole, Henry, tr. Cole, Henry, illus. 2004. 40p. (J). (gr. -1-2). lib. bdg. 15.89 *(978-0-06-050753-4(5))* HarperCollins Pubs.
Edwards, Pat & Edwards, LaVell. Hello, Cosmo! De Angel, Miguel, illus. 2006. 24p. (J). lib. bdg. 17.95 *(978-1-932888-45-4(4))* Amplify Publishing Group.
Edwardson, Debby Dahl. My Name Is Not Easy, 0 vols. 2013. (ENG.). 256p. (YA). (gr. 7-9). pap. 9.99 *(978-1-4778-1629-5(1),* 9781477816295, Skyscape) Amazon Publishing.
Ehrenberg, Pamela. Ethan, Suspended. 2009. (ENG.). 272p. (J). (gr. 6-9). pap. 8.50 *(978-0-8028-5317-2(X))* 2007. 266p. (YA). (gr. 7-18). 16.00 *(978-0-8028-5324-0(2),* Eerdmans Bks For Young Readers) Eerdmans, William B. Publishing Co.
Ehrlich, Esther. Nest. 2016. (ENG.). 336p. (J). (gr. 5). pap. 9.99 *(978-0-385-38610-4(9),* Yearling) Random Hse. Children's Bks.
Ehrlich, Nikki. Twindergarten. Wagner, Zoey Abbott, illus. 2017. (ENG.). 32p. (J). (gr. -1-3). 16.99 *(978-0-06-256423-8(4),* HarperCollins) HarperCollins Pubs.
Eisenson, Adam. Hope. 2005. (Illus.). 35p. (J). 14.95 *(978-0-9766157-0-5(3))* Lone Star Pubns.
Eland, Lindsay. Five Times Revenge. 2016. (ENG.). 384p. (J). (gr. 3-7). 16.99 *(978-0-06-239730-0(3),* Greenwillow Bks.) HarperCollins Pubs.
Elder, Joshua. Mail Order Ninja, 1 vol., Vol. 1. Owen, Erich, illus. 2008. (Tokyopop Ser.). (ENG.). 96p. (J). (gr. 2-6). 32.79 *(978-1-59961-568-4(1),* 14810, Graphic Novels) Spotlight.
—Mail Order Ninja Vol. 2: Timmy Strikes Back, 1 vol. Owen, Erich, illus. 2008. (Tokyopop Ser.). (ENG.). 104p. (J). (gr. 2-6). 32.79 *(978-1-59961-569-1(X),* 14811, Graphic Novels) Spotlight.
Eldridge, Courtney. Ghost Time. 2016. (ENG.). 418p. (YA). (gr. 7-12). pap. 9.99 *(978-1-4778-1697-4(6),* 9781477816974, Skyscape) Amazon Publishing.
Elish, Dan. The School for the Insanely Gifted. 2011. (ENG.). 304p. (J). (gr. 3-7). 15.99 *(978-0-06-113873-7(8),* Balzer & Bray) HarperCollins Pubs.
Elkeles, Simone. How to Ruin a Summer Vacation. 2006. (How to Ruin a Summer Vacation Novel Ser.: 1). (ENG.). 240p. (YA). (gr. 9-12). pap. 11.99 *(978-0-7387-0961-1(1),* 0738709611, Flux) North Star Editions.
—How to Ruin My Teenage Life. 2007. (How to Ruin a Summer Vacation Novel Ser.: 2). (ENG.). 288p. (YA). (gr. 9-12). per. 11.99 *(978-0-7387-1019-8(9),* 0738710199, Flux) North Star Editions.
—Leaving Paradise. 2007. 23.30 *(978-1-4177-8393-9(1))* Turtleback.
—Rules of Attraction. 2015. (Perfect Chemistry Novel Ser.). (ENG.). 352p. (YA). (gr. 9). pap. 10.99 *(978-1-61963-702-3(2),* 900146045, Bloomsbury USA Childrens) Bloomsbury Publishing USA.
Ella, Peter Leo. Class Party on the Big Yellow School Bus. Ella, Peter Leo, illus. 2013. (Illus.). 28p. pap. *(978-9980-86-513-7(X))* Univ. of Papua New Guinea Pr.
Ellen, Connie. Marvel Mansion Gang. 2012. 114p. pap. 12.19 *(978-1-4269-5968-4(0))* Trafford Publishing.
Elliott, Laura Malone. Hunter's Best Friend at School. Munsinger, Lynn, illus. 2005. (ENG.). 32p. (J). (gr. -1-2). reprint ed. pap. 7.99 *(978-0-06-075319-1(6),* Tegen, Katherine Bks) HarperCollins Pubs.
—Hunter's Best Friend at School. Munsinger, Lynn, illus. 2005. (gr. -1-2). 17.00 *(978-0-7569-5786-5(9))* Perfection Learning Corp.
—Thanksgiving Day Thanks. Munsinger, Lynn, illus. 2013. (ENG.). 32p. (J). (gr. -1-3). 17.99 *(978-0-06-000236-7(0),* Tegen, Katherine Bks) HarperCollins Pubs.
Elliott, Rebecca. Eva & the New Owl: a Branches Book (Owl Diaries #4) Elliott, Rebecca, illus. 2016. (Owl Diaries: 4). (ENG., Illus.). 80p. (J). (gr. k-2). pap. 5.99 *(978-0-545-82559-7(8))* Scholastic, Inc.
—Eva in the Spotlight: a Branches Book (Owl Diaries #13) Elliott, Rebecca, illus. 2020. (Owl Diaries: 13). (ENG., Illus.). 80p. (J). (gr. k-2). pap. 4.99 *(978-1-338-29875-8(5))* Scholastic, Inc.
—Eva in the Spotlight: a Branches Book (Owl Diaries #13) (Library Edition) Elliott, Rebecca, illus. 2020. (Owl Diaries: 13). (ENG., Illus.). 80p. (J). (gr. k-2). lib. bdg. 24.99 *(978-1-338-29876-5(3))* Scholastic, Inc.
—Eva Sees a Ghost. 2015. (Owl Diaries: 2). lib. bdg. 14.75 *(978-0-606-37038-7(2))* Turtleback.
—Eva Sees a Ghost: a Branches Book (Owl Diaries #2) Elliott, Rebecca, illus. 2015. (Owl Diaries: 2). (ENG., Illus.). 80p. (J). (gr. k-2). pap. 5.99 *(978-0-545-78783-3(1))* Scholastic, Inc.
—Eva Sees a Ghost: a Branches Book (Owl Diaries #2) (Library Edition) Elliott, Rebecca, illus. 2015. (Owl Diaries: 2). (ENG., Illus.). 80p. (J). (gr. k-2). 24.99 *(978-0-545-78784-0(X))* Scholastic, Inc.
—Eva's Treetop Festival. 2015. (Owl Diaries: 1). lib. bdg. 14.75 *(978-0-606-36337-2(8))* Turtleback.
—Eva's Treetop Festival: a Branches Book (Owl Diaries #1), 1 vol., Bk. 1. Elliott, Rebecca, illus. 2015. (Owl Diaries: 1). (ENG., Illus.). 80p. (J). (gr. k-2). pap. 5.99 *(978-0-545-68362-3(9),* b705f388-0996-4860-8f27-1a68fd6e0f94) Scholastic, Inc.
—The Wildwood Bakery, 7. 2019. (Branches Early Ch Bks). (ENG.). 72p. (J). (gr. 2-3). 15.36 *(978-0-87617-988-8(X))* Penworthy Co., LLC, The.
—The Wildwood Bakery. 2017. (Owl Diaries — Branches Ser.: 7). lib. bdg. 14.75 *(978-0-606-40660-4(3))* Turtleback.
—The Wildwood Bakery: a Branches Book (Owl Diaries #7) Elliott, Rebecca, illus. 2017. (Owl Diaries: 7). (ENG., Illus.). 80p. (J). (gr. k-2). pap. 4.99 *(978-1-338-16300-1(0))* Scholastic, Inc.
—The Wildwood Bakery: a Branches Book (Owl Diaries #7) (Library Edition) Elliott, Rebecca, illus. 2017. (Owl Diaries: 7). (ENG., Illus.). 80p. (J). (gr. k-2). lib. bdg. 15.99 *(978-1-338-16301-8(9))* Scholastic, Inc.
—A Woodland Wedding. 2016. (Owl Diaries: 3). (ENG.). 80p. (J). (gr. k-2). lib. bdg. 14.75 *(978-0-606-38068-3(X))* Turtleback.
—A Woodland Wedding: a Branches Book (Owl Diaries #3) (Library Edition), Vol. 3. Elliott, Rebecca, illus. 2016. (Owl Diaries: 3). (ENG., Illus.). 80p. (J). (gr. k-2). 24.99 *(978-0-545-82558-0(X))* Scholastic, Inc.
Ellis, Ann Dee. This Is What I Did. 2011. 9.68 *(978-0-7848-3387-2(7),* Everbind) Marco Bk. Co.
Ellis, Deborah & Walters, Eric. Bifocal, 1 vol. 2007. (ENG.). 280p. (YA). (gr. 7-12). per. 12.95 *(978-1-55455-062-3(9),* 40c1a241-5a17-43bc-857e-e8bb6cabba4f) Fitzhenry & Whiteside, Ltd. CAN. Dist: Firefly Bks., Ltd.
—Bifocal, 1 vol. 2007. (ENG.). 240p. (YA). (gr. 7-12). 17.95 *(978-1-55455-036-4(X),* 81472636-fc44-4218-a9bb-bdaa0b47264c) Trifolium Bks., Inc. CAN. Dist: Firefly Bks., Ltd.
Ellis, Leanne Statland. Tree Huggers. 2010. (J). pap. *(978-0-88092-521-1(3))* Royal Fireworks Publishing Co.
Elwell, Sharon. Caught in the Middle: Reflections of a Middle School Teacher. 2007. 112p. per. 10.95 *(978-1-4327-0621-0(7))* Outskirts Pr., Inc.
Emerson, Kevin. Carlos Is Gonna Get It. 2008. (J). pap. *(978-0-439-93526-5(1),* Levine, Arthur A. Bks.) Scholastic, Inc.
Emery, Anne. Dinny Gordon Senior. 2004. (J). per. 9.95 *(978-1-59511-000-8(3))* Image Cascade Publishing.
—Senior Year. Krush, Beth, illus. 2006. (YA). per. 11.95 *(978-1-59511-005-3(4))* Image Cascade Publishing.
—Sorority Girl. 2006. (YA). per. 11.95 *(978-1-59511-007-7(0))* Image Cascade Publishing.
Emond, Stephen. Happyface. 2011. (ENG., Illus.). 336p. (YA). (gr. 7-17). pap. 17.99 *(978-0-316-04099-0(1))* Little, Brown Bks. for Young Readers.
Emzer, Counselor. The Day Before Summer Vacation. 2004. 31p. pap. 24.95 *(978-1-4137-2680-0(1))* PublishAmerica, Inc.
Endacott, C. R. Afflatus. 2008. 232p. pap. 15.95 *(978-0-595-52418-1(4))* iUniverse, Inc.
Enderle, Dotti. Tell No One!, 1 vol. McWilliam, Howard, illus. 2009. (Ghost Detectors Ser.: No. 1). (ENG.). 80p. (J). (gr. 2-5). 35.64 *(978-1-60270-692-7(1),* 8804, Calico Chapter Bks.) ABDO Publishing Co.
English, Karen. Dog Days: The Carver Chronicles, Book One, 1 vol. Humaran, Aurora & Monge, Leticia, trs. Freeman, Laura, illus. 2014. (Carver Chronicles Ser.). (ENG.). 128p. (J). (gr. 1-4). pap. 6.99 *(978-0-544-33912-5(6),* eeece7c5-4442-418b-a3f1-08e1410d9daf, Clarion Bks.) HarperCollins Pubs.
—Don't Feed the Geckos! The Carver Chronicles, Book 3. Freeman, Laura, illus. 2016. (Carver Chronicles Ser.). (ENG.). 144p. (J). (gr. 1-4). pap. 6.99

(978-0-544-81083-9(X), 1641525, Clarion Bks.) HarperCollins Pubs.
—Francie. 2007. (ENG.). 208p. (J). (gr. 4-8). per. 14.99 (978-0-312-37383-2(X), 900045529) Square Fish.
—The New Kid: The Carver Chronicles, Book Five. Freeman, Laura, illus. 2018. (Carver Chronicles Ser.: 5). (ENG.). 128p. (J). (gr. 1-4). pap. 6.99 (978-1-328-49797-0(6), 1717851, Clarion Bks.) HarperCollins Pubs.
—Nikki & Deja. Freeman, Laura, illus. 2007. (Nikki & Deja Ser.). (ENG.). 80p. (J). (gr. 2-4). 16.19 (978-0-618-75238-6(2), Clarion Bks.) HarperCollins Pubs.
—Nikki & Deja: Nikki & Deja, Book One. Freeman, Laura, illus. 2009. (Nikki & Deja Ser.: 1). (ENG.). 80p. (J). (gr. -1-3). pap. 9.99 (978-0-547-13362-1(6), 1048763, Clarion Bks.) HarperCollins Pubs.
—Nikki & Deja: Birthday Blues: Nikki & Deja, Book Two, Bk. 2. Freeman, Laura, illus. 2010. (Nikki & Deja Ser.: 2). (ENG.). 96p. (J). (gr. 1-4). pap. 9.99 (978-0-547-24893-6(8), 1100905, Clarion Bks.) HarperCollins Pubs.
—Nikki & Deja: Substitute Trouble. Freeman, Laura, illus. 2014. (Nikki & Deja Ser.). (ENG.). 112p. (J). (gr. 1-4). pap. 6.99 (978-0-544-22388-2(8), 1563368, Clarion Bks.) HarperCollins Pubs.
—Nikki & Deja: the Newsy News Newsletter: Nikki & Deja, Book Three, Bk. 3. Freeman, Laura, illus. 2011. (Nikki & Deja Ser.: 3). (ENG.). 96p. (J). (gr. 1-4). pap. 6.99 (978-0-547-40626-8(6), 1428504, Clarion Bks.) HarperCollins Pubs.
—Nikki & Deja: Wedding Drama. Freeman, Laura, illus. 2013. (Nikki & Deja Ser.). (ENG.). 112p. (J). (gr. 1-4). pap. 6.99 (978-0-544-00324-8(1), 1526366, Clarion Bks.) HarperCollins Pubs.
—Pizza Party: The Carver Chronicles, Book Six. Freeman, Laura, illus. 2019. (Carver Chronicles Ser.: 6). (ENG.). 128p. (J). (gr. 1-4). pap. 7.99 (978-0-358-09747-1(9), 1747602, Clarion Bks.) HarperCollins Pubs.
Ennis-Hill, Jessica. The Clocktower Charm, Bk. 5. Caldecott, Elen, illus. 2022. (Evie's Magic Bracelet Ser.). (ENG.). 144p. (J). (gr. 2-4). pap. 9.99 (978-1-4449-3443-4(0)) Hachette Children's Group GBR. Dist: Hachette Bk. Group.
Enright, Elizabeth. The Four-Story Mistake. Enright, Elizabeth, illus. 3rd ed. 2008. (Melendy Quartet Ser.: 2). (ENG., Illus.). 208p. (J). (gr. 3-7). per. 9.99 (978-0-312-37599-7(9), 900048318) Square Fish.
Ensor, Rod. Getting It. 2007. 216p. per. 14.95 (978-0-595-44800-5(3)) iUniverse, Inc.
Erikson, Harvey. Basketball Fever... Bring It On! 2014. 206p. pap. 11.95 (978-1-62652-583-2(8), Mill City Press, Inc) Salem Author Services.
Erlbaum, Janice. Let Me Fix That for You. 2020. (ENG.). 304p. (J). pap. 12.99 (978-1-250-25030-8(7), 900184341) Square Fish.
Erskine, Kathryn. Mockingbird. (ENG.). (J). (gr. 5-18). 2011. 256p. 8.99 (978-0-14-241775-1(0), Puffin Books) 2010. 240p. 17.99 (978-0-399-25264-8(9), Philomel Bks.) Penguin Young Readers Group.
—Mockingbird. (J). 2012. 1.25 (978-1-4407-4671-0(0)) 2010. 74.75 (978-1-4407-4665-9(6)) 2010. 72.75 (978-1-4407-4667-3(2)) 2010. (SPA.). 62.75 (978-1-4407-4663-5(X)) 2010. 64.75 (978-1-4407-4661-1(3)) 2010. 210.75 (978-1-4407-4662-8(1)) Recorded Bks., Inc.
—Mockingbird. 2011. lib. bdg. 18.40 (978-0-606-15356-0(X)) Turtleback.
—Quaking. 2007. (ENG.). 240p. (YA). (gr. 7-12). 22.44 (978-0-399-24774-3(2)) Penguin Young Readers Group.
Erway, Chad Lee. An Appointment with Fear. 2019. (ENG., Illus.). 184p. (J). (gr. 2-7). pap. 9.99 (978-1-7335610-1-3(3)) Parallel Vortex.
Esckilsen, Erik E. Offsides. 2004. (ENG.). 176p. (J). (gr. 5-7). tchr. ed. 15.00 (978-0-618-46284-1(8), 543211, Clarion Bks.) HarperCollins Pubs.
Esham, Barbara. Last to Finish: A Story about the Smartest Boy in Math Class. Gordon, Mike, illus. 2008. 32p. (J). (gr. k-18). 16.95 (978-1-60336-456-0(0), Adventures of Everyday Geniuses, The) Mainstream Connections Publishing.
—Stacey Coolidge's Fancy Smancy Cursive Handwriting. Gordon, Mike, illus. 2008. 32p. (J). (gr. k-18). 16.95 (978-1-60336-462-1(5), Adventures of Everyday Geniuses, The) Mainstream Connections Publishing.
Esola, Mike. Diary of a Dinosaur: The Attack of Benny. 2013. (ENG.). 154p. pap. 10.95 (978-1-4787-1363-0(1)) Outskirts Pr., Inc.
Esprit, Keisha. Serena Goes to School. 2013. 24p. pap. 24.95 (978-1-62709-460-3(1)) America Star Bks.
Esquivel, Rosaura. It's Time for School, 1 vol. 2017. (Let's Tell Time Ser.). (ENG.). 24p. (J). (gr. 1-1). 25.27 (978-1-5081-5725-0(1), 6176e84c-af4d-4851-8416-254ee45f3d8e, PowerKids Pr.) Rosen Publishing Group, Inc., The.
Ethington, Rebecca. Through Glass Omni 1: Omnibus Books 1-3. 2013. 324p. (YA). pap. 13.59 (978-0-9884837-6-7(9)) Imdalind Pr.
Eulberg, Elizabeth. The Great Shelby Holmes Meets Her Match. (ENG., Illus.). (J). 2018. 256p. pap. 8.99 (978-1-68119-056-3(7), 900157442, Bloomsbury Children's Bks.) 2017. 240p. 16.99 (978-1-68119-054-9(0), 900157431, Bloomsbury USA Childrens) Bloomsbury Publishing USA.
—The Lonely Hearts Club. 2011. (ENG.). 304p. (J). (gr. 3-7). pap. 10.99 (978-0-545-14032-4(3)) Scholastic, Inc.
—Past Perfect Life. 2019. (ENG.). 336p. (YA). 18.99 (978-1-5476-0092-2(6), 900198456, Bloomsbury Young Adult) Bloomsbury Publishing USA.
—Take a Bow. 2012. 280p. (YA). pap. (978-0-545-43982-4(5)) Scholastic, Inc.
Evans, Ann. Cry Danger. 2012. 114p. pap. (978-1-907670-27-5(0)) Greenstream Publishing.
Evans, John D. The Cut. 2003. (ENG.). 262p. (YA). per. 18.95 (978-1-888725-82-7(6), BeachHouse Bks.) Science & Humanities Pr.
Evans, Leslie, illus. You Have to Be Smart If You're Going to Be Tall/Tienes Que Ser Inteligente Si Vas a Ser Alta. 2006. 46p. (J). (gr. -1-3). per. 16.99 (978-1-59879-217-1(2)) Lifevest Publishing, Inc.
Evans, Mari. Trusting Love. 2014. (ENG., Illus.). 200p. (YA). pap. 14.99 (978-1-62798-955-8(2)) Dreamspinner Pr.
Evans, Rhonda Boone. Johnny Lumpkin Wants a Friend. Evans, Chadrick Michael, illus. 2007. 32p. per. 24.95 (978-1-4241-8614-3(5)) America Star Bks.
Evans, Rose-Marie. The Unexpected Adventure at East Haddam High. 2009. 80p. pap. 10.75 (978-1-60860-182-0(X), Strategic Bk. Publishing) Strategic Book Publishing & Rights Agency (SBPRA).
Evans, Sandra. This Is Not a Werewolf Story. 2016. (ENG., Illus.). 352p. (J). (gr. 4-7). 18.99 (978-1-4814-4480-4(8), Atheneum Bks. for Young Readers) Simon & Schuster Children's Publishing.
Fabian, Cynthia. Orchestra in Our Brain: The Story of a Child with Epilepsy. Stevens, Daniel, illus. 2011. 20p. pap. 10.95 (978-1-60976-783-9(7), Eloquent Bks.) Strategic Book Publishing & Rights Agency (SBPRA).
Fabrikant, Amy. When Kayla Was Kyle. Levine, Jennifer, illus. 2013. 32p. pap. 8.95 (978-1-61286-154-8(7)) Avid Readers Publishing Group.
Facey, La-Toya S. Brielle-Elaine Tries to Fit In! Yamyamin, Floyd, illus. 2011. (ENG.). 24p. pap. 14.99 (978-1-4634-2353-7(5)) AuthorHouse.
Fagan, Cary. Banjo of Destiny, 1 vol. Demirel, Selcuk, illus. 2011. (ENG.). 128p. (J). (gr. 3-4). pap. 8.95 (978-1-55498-086-4(0)) Groundwood Bks. CAN. Dist: Publishers Group West (PGW).
Fairlie, Emily. The Magician's Bird. Caparo, Antonio Javier, illus. 2014. (Tuckernuck Mysteries Ser.: 2). (ENG.). 288p. (J). (gr. 3-7). pap. 6.99 (978-0-06-211894-3(3), Tegen, Katherine Bks) HarperCollins Pubs.
Falatko, Julie. Two Dogs in a Trench Coat Start a Club by Accident (Two Dogs in a Trench Coat #2) Jack, Colin, illus. 2019. (Two Dogs in a Trench Coat Ser.: 2). (ENG.). 208p. (J). (gr. 3-7). 9.99 (978-1-338-18953-7(0)) Scholastic, Inc.
Falconer, Ian. Olivia Saves the Circus. 2004. (Olivia Ser.). (J). (gr. k-2). spiral bd. (978-0-616-11110-9(X)); spiral bd. (978-0-616-11111-6(8)) Canadian National Institute for the Blind/Institut National Canadien pour les Aveugles.
—Olivia Saves the Circus. Falconer, Ian, illus. 2010. (Classic Board Bks.). (ENG., Illus.). 36p. (J). (gr. -1-2). bds. 8.99 (978-1-4424-1287-3(9), Atheneum Bks. for Young Readers) Simon & Schuster Children's Publishing.
Fallin, Rachel. Little Blessings. 2012. 24p. pap. 17.99 (978-1-4685-6209-5(6)) AuthorHouse.
Falzon, Adrienne. What Is an Angel? Salzberg, Helen, illus. 2012. (ENG.). 32p. 18.99 (978-0-9855562-2-8(6)) Blue Note Pubns.
Faris, Stephanie. Piper Morgan in Charge! Fleming, Lucy, illus. 2016. (Piper Morgan Ser.: 2). (ENG.). 112p. (J). (gr. 1-4). 16.99 (978-1-4814-5712-5(8), Simon & Schuster/Paula Wiseman Bks.) Simon & Schuster/Paula Wiseman Bks.
—Piper Morgan Plans a Party. 5. Fleming, Lucy, illus. 2017. (Piper Morgan Ser.). (ENG.). 96p. (J). (gr. 1-3). 18.69 (978-1-5364-2740-0(3), Aladdin) Simon & Schuster Children's Publishing.
—25 Roses. 2015. (Mix Ser.). (ENG., Illus.). 224p. (J). (gr. 4-8). pap. 7.99 (978-1-4814-2420-2(3), Aladdin) Simon & Schuster Children's Publishing.
—30 Days of No Gossip. 2014. (Mix Ser.). (ENG., Illus.). 208p. (J). (gr. 4-8). 17.99 (978-1-4424-8282-1(6), Aladdin) Simon & Schuster Children's Publishing.
Farizan, Sara. Here to Stay. 2018. (ENG.). 272p. (YA). (gr. 8-12). 17.95 (978-1-61620-700-7(0), 73700) Algonquin Young Readers.
Farley, Camille. Emma Just Wants to be Cool!, 1 vol. 2010. 34p. 24.95 (978-1-4489-4529-0(1)) PublishAmerica, Inc.
Farley, Robin. Mia & the Girl with a Twirl. Ivanov, Olga & Ivanov, Aleksey, illus. 2013. (My First I Can Read Ser.). (ENG.). 32p. (J). (gr. -1-3). 16.99 (978-0-06-208689-1(8)); pap. 4.99 (978-0-06-208688-4(X)) HarperCollins Pubs. (HarperCollins).
—Mia Dances Back to School! 2013. (Mia Ser.). (ENG., Illus.). 24p. (J). (gr. -1-3). 4.99 (978-0-06-210014-6(9), HarperFestival) HarperCollins Pubs.
—Mia Sets the Stage. 2013. (My First I Can Read Ser.). (ENG., Illus.). 32p. (J). (gr. -1-3). pap. 4.99 (978-0-06-208685-3(5), HarperCollins) HarperCollins Pubs.
Farquhar, Polly. Itch. 2020. (ENG.). 256p. (J). (gr. 3-7). 17.99 (978-0-8234-4552-3(6)) Holiday Hse., Inc.
Farrant, Natasha. A Talent for Trouble. 2019. (ENG.). 272p. (J). (gr. 5-7). 16.99 (978-1-328-58078-8(4), 1728482, Clarion Bks.) HarperCollins Pubs.
Farrar, F. W. Eric, or, Little by Little. 2007. 276p. per. (978-1-4065-1686-9(4)) Dodo Pr.
Farrar, Frederic William. Eric; or, Little by Little. 2006. 372p. per. 26.99 (978-1-4255-3870-5(3)) Michigan Publishing.
Farruggia, M. E. Lost Memories. 2013. 352p. pap. 21.99 (978-1-4582-1247-4(5), Abbott Pr.) Author Solutions, LLC.
Faruqi, Reem. Lailah's Lunchbox: A Ramadan Story, 1 vol. Lyon, Lea, illus. 2015. (ENG.). 32p. (J). (gr. 1-7). 16.95 (978-0-88448-431-8(9), 884431) Tilbury Hse. Pubs.
Faruqi, Saadia. Meet Yasmin! Aly, Hatem, illus. 2018. (Yasmin Ser.). (ENG.). 96p. (J). (gr. k-2). pap., pap., pap. 5.95 (978-1-68436-022-2(6), 137937, Picture Window Bks.) Capstone.
—Yasmin la Maestra. Aparicio Publishing LLC, Aparicio Publishing, tr. from ENG. Aly, Hatem, illus. 2020. (Yasmin en Español Ser.).Tr. of Yasmin the Teacher. (SPA.). 32p. (J). (gr. k-2). pap. 5.95 (978-1-5158-5732-7(8), 142097); lib. bdg. 20.65 (978-1-5158-5728-0(X), 142092) Capstone. (Picture Window Bks.).
—Yasmin the Builder. Aly, Hatem, illus. 2018. (Yasmin Ser.). (ENG.). 32p. (J). (gr. k-2). 22.65 (978-1-5158-2727-6(5), 137931, Picture Window Bks.) Capstone.
—Yasmin the Teacher. Aly, Hatem, illus. 2019. (Yasmin Ser.). (ENG.). 32p. (J). (gr. k-2). pap. 5.95 (978-1-5158-4580-5(X), 141180); lib. bdg. 22.65 (978-1-5158-3782-4(3), 139364) Capstone. (Picture Window Bks.).
Favole, Robert. Monday Redux. 2003. 200p. (YA). 15.99 (978-1-930826-11-3(7)) Flywheel Publishing Co.
Feder, Aliza & Sofer, Rochel. We Need to Talk. 2008. 250p. 18.95 (978-1-934440-30-8(2), Devora Publishing) Simcha Media Group.
Federle, Tim. Nate Expectations. (Nate Ser.). (ENG.). (J). (gr. 5). 2019. 272p. pap. 8.99 (978-1-4814-0413-6(X)) 2018. (Illus.). 256p. 17.99 (978-1-4814-0412-9(1)) Simon & Schuster Bks. For Young Readers. (Simon & Schuster Bks. For Young Readers).
Fehlbaum, Beth. Big Fat Disaster. (ENG.). (YA). 2015. 286p. pap. 9.99 (978-1-4405-9267-6(5)) 2014. 288p. 17.99 (978-1-4405-7048-3(5)) Simon Pulse. (Simon Pulse).
—Hope in Patience. 2010. 312p. (YA). (gr. 8-18). 16.95 (978-1-934813-41-6(9)) Westside Bks.
Fehler, Gene. Beanball. 2011. (ENG.). 144p. (YA). (gr. 7). pap. 15.99 (978-0-547-55001-5(4), 1450202, Clarion Bks.) HarperCollins Pubs.
Feinstein, John. Backfield Boys: A Football Mystery in Black & White. 2018. (ENG.). 384p. (YA). pap. 12.99 (978-1-250-18064-3(3), 900172809) Square Fish.
—Benchwarmers. 2019. (Benchwarmers Ser.: 1). (ENG.). 320p. (J). 16.99 (978-0-374-31203-9(6), 900198272, Farrar, Straus & Giroux (BYR)) Farrar, Straus & Giroux.
—The DH (the Triple Threat, 3) 2017. (Triple Threat Ser.: 3). 304p. (J). (gr. 5). 8.99 (978-0-553-53585-3(4), Yearling) Random Hse. Children's Bks.
—The Sixth Man. 2016. (Triple Threat Ser.: 2). (ENG.). 304p. (J). (gr. 5). 18.40 (978-0-606-39342-3(0)) Turtleback.
—The Walk On. 2015. (Triple Threat Ser.: 1). lib. bdg. 18.40 (978-0-606-37704-1(2)) Turtleback.
—The Walk on (the Triple Threat, 1) 2015. (Triple Threat Ser.: 1). 384p. (J). (gr. 5). pap. 8.99 (978-0-385-75349-4(7), Yearling) Random Hse. Children's Bks.
Feldman, Jody. The Seventh Level. 2011. (ENG.). 320p. (J). (gr. 5). pap. 6.99 (978-0-06-195107-7(2), Greenwillow Bks.) HarperCollins Pubs.
Fergus, Maureen. Buddy & Earl Go to School, 1 vol. Sookocheff, Carey, illus. 2017. (Buddy & Earl Ser.: 4). (ENG.). 32p. (J). (gr. k-2). 16.95 (978-1-55498-927-0(2)) Groundwood Bks. CAN. Dist: Publishers Group West (PGW).
Ferguson, Donald. Chums of Scranton High. 2006. 25.95 (978-1-4218-2935-7(5)); pap. 10.95 (978-1-4218-3035-3(3)) 1st World Publishing, Inc.
—The Chums of Scranton High at Ice Hockey. 2007. 124p. per. (978-1-4065-2361-4(5)) Dodo Pr.
—The Chums of Scranton High on the Cinder Path. 2007. 124p. per. (978-1-4065-2363-8(1)) Dodo Pr.
—The Chums of Scranton High, or, Hugh Morgan's Uphill Fight. 2007. 136p. per. (978-1-4065-2362-1(3)) Dodo Pr.
—The Chums of Scranton High Out for the Pennant, or, in the Three Town League. 2007. 124p. per. (978-1-4065-2364-5(X)) Dodo Pr.
Ferguson, Terrence. Stuttering Sammie: I'm Just Like You, I Just Repeat Some Letters or Words When I Talk. 2012. 24p. 24.95 (978-1-4626-6267-8(6)); pap. 24.95 (978-1-4626-8326-0(6)) America Star Bks.
Ferreira, Ninha. The Breakthrough: All Star Cheer Articles - Book 1. 2008. (ENG.). 194p. (YA). per. 13.95 (978-0-9815202-0-9(0)) Higgins Publishing.
Ferris, Aimee. Will Work for Prom Dress. 2011. (ENG.). 272p. (YA). (gr. 7-12). 24.94 (978-1-60684-141-9(6)) Farshore GBR. Dist: Children's Plus, Inc.
Ferruolo, Jeanne Zulick. Ruby in the Sky. 2020. (ENG.). 320p. (J). pap. 9.99 (978-1-250-23329-5(1), 900188386) Square Fish.
Field, C. D. & Duffield, Christine. The Medicine Tree. 2015. (ENG.). 108p. (YA). (gr. 3-4). mass mkt. 11.95 (978-1-78554-535-1(3), 6f8fee73-c3f4-4327-9282-68fce3c2c0c0) Austin Macauley Pubs. Ltd. GBR. Dist: Baker & Taylor Publisher Services (BTPS).
Fielding, Sarah. The Governess, or, the Little Female Academy. 2007. 140p. (gr. 4-7). per. (978-1-4065-2397-3(6)) Dodo Pr.
Fields, Jan. Really New School: An Up2U Action Adventure, 1 vol. To, Vivienne, illus. 2013. (Up2U Adventures Ser.). (ENG.). 80p. (J). (gr. 2-5). lib. bdg. 35.64 (978-1-61641-969-1(5), 15221, Calico Chapter Bks.) ABDO Publishing Co.
Figley, Marty Rhodes. The Prairie Adventure of Sarah & Annie, Blizzard Survivors. Hammond, Ted & Carbajal, Richard Pimentel, illus. 2011. (History's Kid Heroes Set III Ser.). pap. 51.02 (978-0-7613-8621-6(1), Graphic Universe™) Lerner Publishing Group.
—The Prairie Adventure of Sarah & Annie, Blizzard Survivors. Carbajal, Richard & Hammond, Ted, illus. 2011. (History's Kid Heroes Ser.). (ENG.). 32p. (J). (gr. 3-5). pap. 9.99 (978-0-7613-7808-2(1), d4c7e7ff-1ce6-47c5-8250-3453ef99ba72, Graphic Universe™) Lerner Publishing Group.
Finch, Michelle & Finch, Phoenix. Phoenix Goes to School: A Story to Support Transgender & Gender Diverse Children. 2018. (Illus.). 40p. (C). 18.95 (978-1-78592-821-5(X), 696833) Kingsley, Jessica Pubs. GBR. Dist: Hachette UK Distribution.
Finchler, Judy. Testing Miss Malarkey. O'Malley, Kevin, illus. 2003. (Miss Malarkey Ser.). (ENG.). 32p. (J). (gr. k-4). pap. 8.99 (978-0-8027-7624-2(8), 900033137, Bloomsbury USA Childrens) Bloomsbury Publishing USA.
—Testing Miss Malarkey. 2004. (J). (gr. 1-5). 17.95 incl. audio (978-0-8045-6897-5(9)) Spoken Arts, Inc.
Finchler, Judy & O'Malley, Kevin. Congratulations, Miss Malarkey! O'Malley, Kevin, illus. 2011. (Miss Malarkey Ser.). (ENG., Illus.). 32p. (J). (gr. k-2). 21.19 (978-0-8027-9836-7(5), 9780802798367) Walker & Co.
—Miss Malarkey's Field Trip. O'Malley, Kevin, illus. 2004. (Miss Malarkey Ser.). (ENG., Illus.). 32p. (J). (gr. k-2). 21.19 (978-0-8027-8913-6(7), 9780802789136) Walker & Co.
Fine, Anne. Friday Surprise (Reading Ladder Level 3) Flook, Helen, illus. 2nd ed. 2016. (Reading Ladder Level 3 Ser.). (ENG.). 48p. (gr. k-2). pap. 10.99 (978-1-4052-8246-8(0), Reading Ladder) Farshore GBR. Dist: HarperCollins Pubs.
Finley, Ucal P. A Proper Place for Boogers. Stroud, Brenda D., illus. 2011. 54p. pap. 12.95 (978-0-9834307-0-4(5)) G Publishing LLC.
Finn, Caitlin. Harold the Misfit. 2012. 24p. pap. 14.93 (978-1-4669-5131-0(1)) Trafford Publishing.
Finn, Perdita. Crashing the Party. Dorman, Brandon, illus. 2007. 109p. (J). (978-0-439-74436-2(9)) Scholastic, Inc.
—Going for the Gold. 2007. 118p. (J). (978-0-439-89208-7(2)) Scholastic, Inc.
Finn, Perdita, adapted by. Meet Crystal Winter. 2016. (Illus.). 31p. (J). (978-1-5182-2557-4(8)) Little Brown & Co.
Finney, Jasson. The Adventures of Captain Pump: The World's First Fitness Superhero! 2018. (Illus.). 59p. (gr. 4-8). pap. 10.95 (978-1-939096-05-0(7), Xeno Bks.) Red Hen Pr.
Finney, Ruth. A Prayer for Momma. 2007. 38p. pap. 8.00 (978-0-8059-7483-6(0)) Dorrance Publishing Co., Inc.
Fiorella, Christina. Timothy's New School Worries. 2008. 24p. pap. 14.49 (978-1-4343-6364-0(3)) AuthorHouse.
Firestone, Carrie. Dress Coded. 2020. (ENG.). 320p. (J). (gr. 5). 17.99 (978-1-9848-1643-6(8), G.P. Putnam's Sons Books for Young Readers) Penguin Young Readers Group.
Fisch, Sarah & Bridwell, Norman. Backpack Puppy. Durk, Jim, illus. 2005. (J). pap. (978-0-439-73379-3(0)) Scholastic, Inc.
Fischer, Ellen. If an Elephant Went to School. Wood, Laura, illus. 2015. (ENG.). 32p. (J). (-2). 14.95 (978-1-938063-61-9(9), Mighty Media Kids) Mighty Media Pr.
Fischer, JoAnn. Our Teacher Is A Fish! 2008. (ENG.). 34p. pap. 10.00 (978-1-4196-7477-8(3)) CreateSpace Independent Publishing Platform.
Fishbone, Greg. The Penguins of Doom. 2007. (From the Desk of Septina Nash Ser.). (ENG., Illus.). 182p. (J). (gr. 2-7). 13.95 (978-1-933831-03-9(0)) Blooming Tree Pr.
Fisher, Doris & Sneed, Dani. One Odd Day, 1 vol. Lee, Karen, illus. 2006. (Basic Math Numbers Ser.). (ENG.). 32p. (J). (gr. -1-3). 15.95 (978-0-9768823-3-6(7)) Arbordale Publishing.
Fisher, Jane Smith. On the Air!, Vol. 1. 2003. (Illus.). 96p. (gr. 4-8). pap. 11.95 (978-0-9744235-0-0(5)) Wilson Place Comics.
Fisk, Katie. Flying with the Angels. 2008. 62p. pap. 19.95 (978-1-60563-608-5(8)) America Star Bks.
FitzGerald, Dawn. Getting in the Game. 2007. (ENG.). 144p. (J). (gr. 4-8). pap. 16.99 (978-0-312-37753-3(3), 900049148) Square Fish.
—Soccer Chick Rules. 2007. (ENG.). 160p. (J). (gr. 5-9). per. 16.99 (978-0-312-37662-8(6), 900048593) Square Fish.
Fitzgerald, Mary. Jodie Has Jagged Edges. 2012. (ENG.). 21p. (J). pap. 22.95 (978-1-4327-8839-1(6)) Outskirts Pr., Inc.
Fitzhugh, Louise. Harriet the Spy. 298p. (J). (gr. 3-5). pap. 5.95 (978-0-8072-1535-7(X), Listening Library) Random Hse. Audio Publishing Group.
—Harriet the Spy: 50th Anniversary Edition. 50th anniv. ed. 2014. (Harriet the Spy Ser.). (ENG., Illus.). 336p. (J). (gr. 3-7). 18.99 (978-0-385-37610-5(3), Delacorte Bks. for Young Readers) Random Hse. Children's Bks.
Fitzhugh, Louise & Gold, Maya. Harriet the Spy, Double Agent. 2007. (ENG.). 160p. (J). (gr. 3-7). 6.99 (978-0-440-41691-3(4), Yearling) Random Hse. Children's Bks.
Fitzpatrick, Becca. The Complete Hush, Hush Saga (Boxed Set) Hush, Hush; Crescendo; Silence; Finale. 2012. (Hush, Hush Saga Ser.: Bks. 1-4). (ENG.). 1744p. (YA). (gr. 9). 87.99 (978-1-4424-7372-0(X), Simon & Schuster Bks. For Young Readers) Simon & Schuster Bks. For Young Readers.
—Hush, Hush. 2010. (Hush, Hush Saga: Bk. 1). (SPA.). 368p. (YA). pap. 20.95 (978-84-666-4417-4(2)) Ediciones B ESP. Dist: Spanish Pubs., LLC.
—Hush, Hush, 3 vols. Ruiz, Derek, ed. 2012. (Hush, Hush Saga: Bk. 1). (Illus.). 120p. (YA). 19.95 (978-0-9836131-1-4(7)) Sea Lion Bks.
—Hush, Hush. (Hush, Hush Saga Ser.: Bk. 1). (ENG.). (YA). (gr. 9-18). 2010. 432p. pap. 13.99 (978-1-4169-8942-4(0)) 2009. 400p. 21.99 (978-1-4169-8941-7(2)) Simon & Schuster Bks. For Young Readers. (Simon & Schuster Bks. For Young Readers).
Flake, Sharon G. Pinned. 2014. (ENG.). 240p. (YA). (gr. 9-9). pap. 10.99 (978-0-545-05733-2(7), Scholastic Pr.) Scholastic, Inc.
—The Skin I'm In. 2007. (J). lib. bdg. 19.65 (978-1-4178-0860-1(8)) Turtleback.
Fleischman, Paul. The Dunderheads. Roberts, David, illus. 2012. (ENG.). 56p. (J). (gr. 1-4). pap. 8.99 (978-0-7636-5239-5(3)) Candlewick Pr.
Fleming, Candace. The Fabled Fifth Graders of Aesop Elementary School. 2012. (Aesop Elementary School Ser.: 2). 176p. (J). (gr. 2-5). 8.99 (978-0-375-87187-0(X), Yearling) Random Hse. Children's Bks.
—The Fabled Fourth Graders of Aesop Elementary School. (Aesop Elementary School Ser.: 1). 192p. (J). 2009. (gr. 2-5). 7.99 (978-0-440-42229-7(9))1. 2007. (ENG.). (gr. 4-6). lib. bdg. 18.69 (978-0-375-93672-2(6)) Random Hse. Children's Bks. (Yearling).
Fletcher, Brenden. Yearbook. 2016. (Gotham Academy Ser.: 3). lib. bdg. 29.40 (978-0-606-39222-8(X)) Turtleback.
Fletcher, Ralph. Flying Solo. 2008. (ENG.). 144p. (J). (gr. 5-7). pap. 7.99 (978-0-547-07652-2(5), 1042026, Clarion Bks.) HarperCollins Pubs.
—Spider Boy. 2009. (ENG.). 192p. (J). (gr. 5-7). pap. 7.99 (978-0-547-24820-2(2), 1100710, Clarion Bks.) HarperCollins Pubs.
Flinn, Alex. Diva. 2013. (ENG.). 304p. (YA). (gr. 9). pap. 9.99 (978-0-06-212434-0(X)) 2007. (ENG.). 304p. (J). (gr. 9-12). pap. 8.99 (978-0-06-056846-7(1)) 2006. 263p. (YA). (gr. 7-12). 16.99 (978-0-06-056843-6(7)) 2006. 263p. (YA). (gr. 7-12). lib. bdg. 18.89 (978-0-06-056845-0(3)) HarperCollins Pubs. (HarperTeen).
—Fade to Black. 2006. (ENG.). 208p. (YA). (gr. 9-12). pap. 9.99 (978-0-06-056842-9(9), HarperTeen) HarperCollins Pubs.
—Mirrored. 2015. (Kendra Chronicles Ser.: 3). (ENG.). 384p. (YA). (gr. 8). 17.99 (978-0-06-213451-6(5), HarperTeen) HarperCollins Pubs.
Flint, Shamini. Game Changer! the Susie K Files 2. Heinrich, Sally, illus. 2018. (Susie K Files Ser.: 2). (ENG.). 112p. (J). (gr. 2-7). pap. 8.99 (978-1-76029-669-8(4)) Allen & Unwin AUS. Dist: Independent Pubs. Group.
Flood, Pansie Hart. It's Test Day, Tiger Turcotte. Wummer, Amy, tr. Wummer, Amy, illus. 2004. (Young Reader Fiction Ser.). 72p. (J). (gr. 1-4). pap. 6.95 (978-1-57505-670-8(4)); lib. bdg. 19.93 (978-1-57505-056-0(0), Carolrhoda Bks.) Lerner Publishing Group.
—Sometimey Friend. Marshall, Felicia, illus. 2005. 124p. (J). (gr. 3-7). 15.95 (978-1-57505-866-5(9)) Lerner Publishing Group.
—Tiger's Trouble with Donut Head. Wummer, Amy, illus. 2005. 71p. (J). lib. bdg. 19.93 (978-1-57505-814-6(6), Carolrhoda Bks.) Lerner Publishing Group.

S

Flor Ada, Alma. Celebra el Cinco de Mayo con un Jarabe Tapatío. Gomez, Marcela & Silva, David, illus. 2006. (Cuentos para Celebrar / Stories to Celebrate Ser.). 30p. (gr. k-6). per. 11.95 *(978-1-59820-118-5(2))* Ediciones Alfaguara ESP. Dist: Santillana USA Publishing Co., Inc.

—Celebrate Martin Luther King, Jr. Day with Mrs. Park's Class. Weiss, Monica, illus. 2006. (Stories to Celebrate Ser.). 30p. (J). (gr. k-6). per. 11.95 *(978-1-59820-125-3(5),* Alfaguara) Santillana USA Publishing Co., Inc.

Flor, Ada Alma. My Name Is Maria Isabel. 2014. (ENG.). 64p. (J). (gr. 12-12). 9.24 *(978-1-63245-189-7(1))* Lectorum Pubns., Inc.

Flores-Scott, Patrick. Jumped In. 2014. (ENG., Illus.). 304p. (YA). (gr. 7). pap. 15.99 *(978-1-250-05398-5(6),* 900137223) Square Fish.

Florido, Lorraine. Hugo the Punk. Shami, Susan, ed. Ewing, John, illus. 2013. 108p. (YA). pap. 9.98 *(978-0-9818449-6-1(0))* Thinkus Pubs.

Flower, Graham Jessie. Grace Harlowe's Senior Year at High School. 2006. 156p. pap. 19.99 *(978-1-4264-1912-6(0))* Creative Media Partners, LLC.

—Grace Harlowe's Senior Year at High School. 2004. reprint ed. pap. 21.95 *(978-1-4191-2224-8(X))* Kessinger Publishing, LLC.

Floyd, Kara. Olivia West vs. Middle School: Round One. 2013. 164p. pap. 11.99 *(978-1-937165-34-5(5))* Orange Hat Publishing.

Floyd, Lucy. Rabbit & Turtle Go to School/Conejo y Tortuga Van a la Escuela: Bilingual English-Spanish. Ada, Alma Flor & Campoy, F. Isabel, trs. Denise, Christopher, illus. 2010. (Green Light Readers Level 1 Ser.).Tr. of Rabbit & Turtle Go to School. (ENG.). 28p. (J). (gr. -1-3). pap. 5.99 *(978-0-547-33898-9(8),* 1418429, Clarion Bks.) HarperCollins Pubs.

Flying Solo. 2011. 8.32 *(978-0-7848-3634-7(5),* Everbind) Marco Bk. Co.

Flynn, Pat. Alex Jackson: Dropping In. 2004. (Illus.). 80p. (Orig.). (J). pap. *(978-0-7022-3433-0(8))* Univ. of Queensland Pr.

Flynn, Warren. Return Ticket. 2003. (Illus.). 272p. pap. 13.50 *(978-1-920731-90-8(3))* Fremantle Pr. AUS. Dist: Independent Pubs. Group.

Fogelin, Adrian. The Big Nothing. 2006. (Neighborhood Novels Ser.: 4). 224p. (J). (gr. 3-7). pap. 7.99 *(978-1-56145-388-7(9))* Peachtree Publishing Co. Inc.

—The Real Question, 1 vol. 2009. 256p. (YA). (gr. 7-9). pap. 7.95 *(978-1-56145-501-0(6))* Peachtree Publishing Co. Inc.

Fogleman, Laurie. Jimmy, What Are You Eating?! 2011. 64p. (gr. -1). pap. 9.99 *(978-1-4634-1206-7(1))* AuthorHouse.

Fontes, Justine. Deadly Drive. 2013. (Surviving Southside Ser.). (ENG.). 104p. (YA). (gr. 6-12). pap. 7.95 *(978-1-4677-0704-6(X),* 5c48578d-899a-4c8e-8346-cd1eb212b284); lib. bdg. 27.99 *(978-1-4677-0310-9(9),* c9a0bca8-bd5f-4333-a2d8-4acb9e86b077) Lerner Publishing Group. (Darby Creek).

Ford, Carrie Elizabeth. Anonymous. 2012. 150p. 24.95 *(978-1-4626-6158-9(0))* America Star Bks.

Forester, Victoria. The Girl Who Could Fly. 2015. (Piper Mccloud Ser.: 1). (ENG.). 352p. (J). (gr. 4-7). pap. 8.99 *(978-1-250-07246-7(8),* 900150204) Square Fish.

Forgetful Fred: 6 Small Books. (gr. k-3). 24.00 *(978-0-7635-6237-3(8))* Rigby Education.

Formento, Alison. This Tree Counts! Snow, Sarah, illus. 2013. (AV2 Fiction Readalong Ser.: Vol. 72). (ENG.). (J). (gr. k-3). 34.28 *(978-1-62127-902-0(2),* AV2 by Weigl) Weigl Pubs., Inc.

—This Tree Counts! Snow, Sarah, illus. 2019. (These Things Count! Ser.). (ENG.). 32p. (J). (gr. -1-3). pap. 7.99 *(978-0-8075-7897-1(5),* 807578975) Whitman, Albert & Co.

Forney, Lane. The Super Power Teens 2: A Blast from the Past. 2009. (ENG.). 137p. pap. 14.99 *(978-0-557-09707-4(X))* Lulu Pr., Inc.

Forte, Lauren. Simon in Charge! 2018. (Simon & Schuster Ready-To-Read Level 2 Ser.). lib. bdg. 14.75 *(978-0-606-41414-2(2))* Turtleback.

Forte, Lauren, adapted by. Simon in Charge! 2018. (ENG., Illus.). 32p. (J). pap. *(978-1-5344-2451-7(2),* Simon Spotlight) Simon Spotlight.

Foster, Stewart. All the Things That Could Go Wrong. 2018. (ENG.). 336p. (J). (gr. 3-7). 29.00 *(978-0-316-41685-6(1))* Little, Brown Bks. for Young Readers.

Fox, Kir & Coats, M. Shelley. A Friendly Town That's Almost Always by the Ocean! 2018. (Secrets of Topsea Ser.: 1). (ENG.). 208p. (J). (gr. 3-7). E-Book 45.00 *(978-1-368-00051-2(7))* Little, Brown Bks. for Young Readers.

Foxe, Steve. Mr. Kazarian, Alien Librarian. Boller, Gary, illus. 2019. (Mr. Kazarian, Alien Librarian Ser.). (ENG.). 64p. (J). (gr. 3-5). 21.99 *(978-1-4965-8366-6(3),* 140650, Stone Arch Bks.) Capstone.

Frampton, David. Beastie ABC. Frampton, David, illus. Date not set. (Illus.). 32p. (J). (gr. -1-1). pap. 5.99 *(978-0-06-443653-3(5))* HarperCollins Pubs.

France, Richard. Joshua Stories: Book 1 - New School, New Friends. 2011. (Illus.). 104p. (gr. 4-6). pap. 14.09 *(978-1-4567-7732-6(7))* AuthorHouse.

Franco, Betsy. Metamorphosis: Junior Year. Franco, Tom, illus. 2009. (ENG.). 128p. (YA). (gr. 9-18). 16.99 *(978-0-7636-3765-1(3))* Candlewick Pr.

Frank, Lucy. Lucky Stars. 2014. (ENG.). 304p. (J). (gr. 5-9). pap. 14.99 *(978-1-4814-2901-6(9),* Atheneum Bks. for Young Readers) Simon & Schuster Children's Publishing.

Frank, Steven B. Armstrong & Charlie. (ENG.). (J). (gr. 5-7). 2018. 320p. pap. 7.99 *(978-1-328-94166-4(3),* 1705033) 2017. 304p. 16.99 *(978-0-544-82608-3(6),* 1644260) HarperCollins Pubs. (Clarion Bks.)

—Class Action. (ENG.). (J). (gr. 5-7). 2019. 288p. pap. 7.99 *(978-0-358-11802-2(6),* 1750753) 2018. 272p. 16.99 *(978-1-328-79920-3(4),* 1685687) HarperCollins Pubs. (Clarion Bks.)

Franklin, Miriam Spitzer. Call Me Sunflower. (ENG.). (J). (gr. 2-7). 2019. 256p. pap. 8.99 *(978-1-5107-3914-7(9))* 2017. 272p. 15.99 *(978-1-5107-1179-2(1))* Skyhorse Publishing Co., Inc. (Sky Pony Pr.).

Frasier, Debra. Miss Alaineus: A Vocabulary Disaster. Frasier, Debra, illus. 2007. (ENG., Illus.). 40p. (J). (gr. -1-3). pap. 7.99 *(978-0-15-206053-4(7),* 1198181, Clarion Bks.) HarperCollins Pubs.

Frazier, Sundee T. Brendan Buckley's Sixth-Grade Experiment. 2013. (ENG.). 288p. (J). (gr. 4-7). 7.99 *(978-0-385-74051-7(4),* Yearling) Random Hse. Children's Bks.

Fredericks, Mariah. Crunch Time. 2007. (ENG.). 336p. (YA). (gr. 7-12). pap. 15.99 *(978-1-4169-3973-3(3),* Atheneum Bks. for Young Readers) Simon & Schuster Children's Publishing.

—The Girl in the Park. 2013. (ENG.). 224p. (YA). (gr. 9). pap. 8.99 *(978-0-449-81591-5(9),* Ember) Random Hse. Children's Bks.

—Head Games. 2006. (ENG., Illus.). 272p. (YA). (gr. 7). pap. 6.99 *(978-1-4169-1335-1(1),* Atheneum Bks. for Young Readers) Simon & Schuster Children's Publishing.

Freeman, Martha. Fourth-Grade Weirdo. 2004. (Illus.). 147p. (gr. 4-7). 15.50 *(978-0-7569-4117-8(2))* Perfection Learning Corp.

—The Secret Cookie Club. 2015. (Secret Cookie Club Ser.). (ENG., Illus.). 304p. (J). (gr. 3-7). 16.99 *(978-1-4814-1046-5(6),* Simon & Schuster Bks. For Young Readers) Simon & Schuster Bks. For Young Readers.

Freeman, Shannon. High School High, 1 vol. 2013. (Port City High Ser.). (ENG.). 199p. (YA). (gr. 9-12). pap. 11.95 *(978-1-62250-037-6(7))* Saddleback Educational Publishing, Inc.

—High School High. 2013. (Port City High Ser.: 1). (YA). lib. bdg. 20.80 *(978-0-606-31773-3(2))* Turtleback.

—Taken, 1 vol. 2013. (Port City High Ser.). (ENG.). 199p. (YA). (gr. 9-12). pap. 11.95 *(978-1-62250-038-3(5))* Saddleback Educational Publishing, Inc.

—Traumatized. 2014. (Port City High Ser.: 7). (YA). lib. bdg. 20.80 *(978-0-606-36619-9(9))* Turtleback.

Frelinghuysen Eighth Grade Storytellers Staff. Flash Before My Eyes. 2008. 52p. pap. 8.95 *(978-0-595-52714-4(0))* iUniverse, Inc.

French, Felicity, illus. Gift Boxes to Decorate & Make: Easter. 2018. (ENG.). 50p. (J). (gr. 3-7). pap. 15.99 *(978-0-7636-9638-2(2))* Candlewick Pr.

French, Jackie. My Dad the Dragon. King, Stephen Michael, illus. 2018. (Wacky Families Ser.: 03). (ENG.). 128p. 5.99 *(978-0-207-19950-9(7),* HarperCollins) HarperCollins Pubs.

French, Moira. The Swingewood Stories. 2009. 36p. pap. 16.99 *(978-1-4490-4777-1(7))* AuthorHouse.

French, Vivian. Princess Charlotte & the Enchanted Rose. Gibb, Sarah, illus. 2007. (Tiara Club Ser.: No. 7). 80p. (J). (gr. 1-4). pap. 3.99 *(978-0-06-112441-9(9),* Tegen, Katherine Bks) HarperCollins Pubs.

—Princess Katie & the Silver Pony. Gibb, Sarah, illus. 2007. (Tiara Club Ser.: No.2). 80p. (J). (gr. 1-4). 15.99 *(978-0-06-112432-7(X),* Tegen, Katherine Bks) HarperCollins Pubs.

—The Tiara Club at Ruby Mansions No. 5: Princess Lauren & the Diamond Necklace. 2008. (Tiara Club Ser.). (ENG., Illus.). 80p. (J). (gr. 1-4). pap. 3.99 *(978-0-06-143488-4(4),* Tegen, Katherine Bks) HarperCollins Pubs.

Frey, Hildegard G. The Camp Fire Girls at School or the Wohelo Weavers. 2004. reprint ed. pap. 21.95 *(978-1-4191-5575-8(X));* pap. 1.99 *(978-1-4192-5575-5(4))* Kessinger Publishing, LLC.

Fridolfs, Derek. Secret Hero Society- Study Hall of Justice. Nguyen, Dustin, illus. 2016. 176p. (J). pap. *(978-1-76027-653-9(7))* Scholastic, Inc.

Friedland, Joyce, ed. Cool Zone with Pain & the Great One: Novel-Ties Study Guide. 2011. 29p. pap. 16.95 *(978-0-7675-4471-9(4))* Learning Links Inc.

Friedman, Becky. Daniel Goes to School. 2014. (Daniel Tiger's Neighborhood 8X8 Ser.). lib. bdg. 13.55 *(978-0-606-35756-2(4))* Turtleback.

—Munch Your Lunch! 2018. (Daniel Tiger's Neighborhood 8X8 Ser.). (Illus.). (J). lib. bdg. 16.00 *(978-0-606-41413-5(4))* Turtleback.

Friedman, Darlene. Star of the Week: A Story of Love, Adoption, & Brownies with Sprinkles. 2009. (ENG., Illus.). 32p. (J). (gr. k-3). 17.99 *(978-0-06-114136-2(4),* HarperCollins) HarperCollins Pubs.

Friedman, Laurie. Back to School, Mallory. Schmitz, Tamara, illus. 2005. (Mallory Ser.: 2). (ENG.). 176p. (J). (gr. 2-5). per. 7.99 *(978-1-57505-865-8(0),* bb96daab-2d2d-475e-94ad-0d7331a6e756, Darby Creek) Lerner Publishing Group.

—Back-To-School Rules. Murfin, Teresa, illus. 2011. (ENG.). 32p. (J). (gr. k-3). lib. bdg. 17.99 *(978-0-7613-6070-4(0),* 232a5142-f743-4756-8b4d-39d5020b27e4, Carolrhoda Bks.) Lerner Publishing Group.

—High Five, Mallory! Kalis, Jennifer, illus. (Mallory Ser.: 26). (ENG.). 160p. (J). (gr. 2-5). 2016. E-Book 23.99 *(978-1-5124-0898-0(0),* 9781512408980)No. 26. 2017. pap. 6.99 *(978-1-5124-5867-1(8),* e77b2c75-4827-4a72-b6c0-96702204305a) Lerner Publishing Group. (Darby Creek).

—Honestly, Mallory! 2009. pap. 34.95 *(978-0-7613-4788-0(7))* Lerner Publishing Group.

—Honestly, Mallory! Pollak, Barbara, illus. (Mallory Ser.: 8). (ENG.). 160p. (J). (gr. 2-5). 2008. pap. 7.99 *(978-1-58013-840-6(3),* cbae7cde-0701-4e69-b123-1da3c7067db3, Darby Creek) 2007. 15.95 *(978-0-8225-6193-4(X),* Carolrhoda Bks.) Lerner Publishing Group.

—Mallory Goes Green! Kalis, Jennifer, illus. (Mallory Ser.: 13). (ENG.). 160p. (J). (gr. 2-5). 2011. pap. 6.99 *(978-0-7613-3949-6(3),* 078f7fbd-a3be-4605-b3fc-3859d04c2443, Darby Creek) 2010. 15.95 *(978-0-8225-8885-6(4),* Carolrhoda Bks.) Lerner Publishing Group.

—Mallory in the Spotlight. Kalis, Jennifer, illus. (Mallory Ser.). 2011. pap. 33.92 *(978-0-7613-8359-8(X))* 2011. (ENG.). 160p. (J). (gr. 2-5). pap. 6.99 *(978-0-7613-3948-9(5),* b60d9d35-7f73-4915-b0b6-80f3cbac5d25) 2010. (ENG.). 160p. (J). (gr. 2-5). 15.95 *(978-0-8225-8884-9(6),* d124d3d1-c47a-4c88-a381-c43b43796758) Lerner Publishing Group. (Darby Creek).

—Mallory Makes a Difference. Kalis, Jennifer, illus. 2018. (Mallory Ser.). (ENG.). 152p. (J). (gr. 2-5). pap. 6.99 *(978-1-5415-2816-1(6),* a33b0439-34ff-42da-8e72-ae42a5d91648, Darby Creek) Lerner Publishing Group.

—Mallory's Guide to Boys, Brothers, Dads, & Dogs. Kalis, Jennifer, illus. 2012. (Mallory Ser.). 160p. (J). (gr. 2-5). pap. 33.92 *(978-0-7613-9206-4(8));* (ENG.). pap. 6.99 *(978-0-7613-5250-1(3),* 507439dc-473a-473f-bff1-a237c1bcf67b) Lerner Publishing Group. (Darby Creek).

—Not What I Expected. Shaloshvili, Natasha, illus. 2015. (Mostly Miserable Life of April Sinclair Ser.: 5). (ENG.). 176p. (J). (gr. 5-9). E-Book 27.99 *(978-1-4677-8829-8(5));*No. 5. 17.95 *(978-1-4677-8588-4(1),* 637bd166-d785-4299-98b0-52ee10dc4672) Lerner Publishing Group. (Darby Creek).

—Play It Again, Mallory, No. 20. Kalis, Jennifer, illus. 2014. (Mallory Ser.: 20). (ENG.). 160p. (J). (gr. 2-5). pap. 6.99 *(978-1-4677-0936-1(0),* e50c9a1a-fc58-4ee9-a0cb-4db612cc14d2, Darby Creek) Lerner Publishing Group.

—Red, White & True Blue Mallory. Kalis, Jennifer, illus. 2009. (Mallory Ser.: 11). (ENG.). 184p. (J). (gr. 2-5). 15.95 *(978-0-8225-8882-5(X),* 25f4d989-183f-4ef3-89d8-84c63c627d23, Darby Creek) Lerner Publishing Group.

—Step Fourth, Mallory! Kalis, Jennifer, illus. (Mallory Ser.: 10). (ENG.). 176p. (J). (gr. 2-5). 2009. pap. 7.99 *(978-1-58013-842-0(X),* d23322a6-c883-4212-88ef-12fdb29c04c7, Darby Creek) 2008. 15.95 *(978-0-8225-8881-8(1),* Carolrhoda Bks.) Lerner Publishing Group.

—Too Much Drama. Shaloshvili, Natasha, illus. 2016. (Mostly Miserable Life of April Sinclair Ser.: 6). (ENG.). 184p. (J). (gr. 5-9). E-Book 27.99 *(978-1-4677-9570-8(4),* Darby Creek) Lerner Publishing Group.

Friend, Natasha. For Keeps. 2011. (YA). (ENG.). 256p. (gr. 8-12). 22.44 *(978-0-670-01190-2(8));* 272p. (gr. 7-18). 7.99 *(978-0-14-241846-8(3),* Speak) Penguin Young Readers Group.

—Where You'll Find Me. 2017. (YA). lib. bdg. 20.85 *(978-0-606-39591-5(1))* Turtleback.

Frino, Michael G. Welcome to Waycool School: Where Learning Is Fun & Lessons are Learned by Everyone! 2010. 32p. pap. 17.25 *(978-1-4269-4048-4(3))* Trafford Publishing.

Frino Ph. D., Michael G. Waycool School Takes the Bus. 2011. 40p. pap. *(978-1-4269-9003-8(0))* Trafford Publishing (UK) Ltd.

Frizzell, Colin. Chill, 1 vol. 2006. (Orca Soundings Ser.). (ENG.). 128p. (YA). (gr. 8-12). per. 9.95 *(978-1-55143-507-7(1))* Orca Bk. Pubs. USA.

Frost, Helen. Diamond Willow. 2011. (ENG.). 144p. (J). (gr. 5-9). pap. 8.99 *(978-0-312-60383-0(5),* 900076343) Square Fish.

—Room 214: a Year in Poems. 2014. (ENG., Illus.). 128p. (J). (gr. 5-9). pap. 8.99 *(978-1-250-04009-1(4),* 900123712) Square Fish.

Fruchter, Jason, illus. Daniel Goes to School. 2014. (Daniel Tiger's Neighborhood Ser.). (ENG.). 24p. (J). (gr. -1-2). pap. 4.99 *(978-1-4814-0318-4(4),* Simon Spotlight) Simon Spotlight.

—Daniel Plays at School: Ready-To-Read Pre-Level 1. 2016. (Daniel Tiger's Neighborhood Ser.). (ENG.). 32p. (J). (gr. -1-k). pap. 4.99 *(978-1-4814-6102-3(8),* Simon Spotlight) Simon Spotlight.

—Munch Your Lunch! 2018. (Daniel Tiger's Neighborhood Ser.). (ENG.). 16p. (J). (gr. -1-2). pap. 5.99 *(978-1-5344-1778-6(8),* Simon Spotlight) Simon Spotlight.

Fry, Michael & Jackson, Bradley. Bobbie Mendoza Saves the World (Again) Fry, Michael, illus. 2018. (ENG., Illus.). 272p. (J). (gr. 3-7). 12.99 *(978-0-06-265193-8(5),* HarperCollins) HarperCollins Pubs.

Fujieda, Toru, creator. Dragon Girl, Vol. 1. 2010. (Dragon Girl Ser.: 1). (ENG., Illus.). 496p. (gr. 8-17). pap. 20.99 *(978-0-7595-3166-6(8))* Yen Pr. LLC.

Fuller, Kimberly. H a Carter. 2012. 138p. 28.99 *(978-1-105-83103-4(5))* Lulu Pr., Inc.

Fulton-Vengco, Aletha. Felicidad & Her Pen Pal Kamar. 2009. 33p. 13.90 *(978-0-578-02728-9(3))* Vengco, Aletha Fulton.

Funk, J. Albie Newton. 2018. (ENG., Illus.). 32p. (J). (gr. k-4). 16.95 *(978-1-4549-2258-2(3))* Sterling Publishing Co., Inc.

Funke, Cornelia. Ghost Knight. 2013.Tr. of Geisterritter. (ENG., Illus.). 352p. (J). (gr. 3-7). pap. 18.99 *(978-0-316-05616-8(2))* Little, Brown Bks. for Young Readers.

Funny School Stories: Learning to Read Box Set. 2016. (I Can Read Level 1 Ser.). (ENG.). 192p. (J). (gr. -1-3). 19.99 *(978-0-06-231336-2(3),* HarperCollins) HarperCollins Pubs.

Fuqua, Jonathon Scott. The Reappearance of Sam Webber. 2010. (ENG.). 250p. (J). pap. 12.95 *(978-1-890862-60-2(6),* cb4b7efc-fa7c-4a12-9a81-b27771d1d626) Bancroft Pr.

Fuss, Kevin. The Brothers Geek. 2010. 180p. 24.99 *(978-1-4490-7366-4(2))* AuthorHouse.

Fussell, Sandy. Samurai Kids #2: Owl Ninja. James, Rhian Nest, illus. 2011. (Samurai Kids Ser.: 2). (ENG.). 272p. (J). (gr. 4-7). 15.99 *(978-0-7636-5003-2(X))* Candlewick Pr.

Gailey, Sarah. When We Were Magic. 2020. (ENG.). 352p. (YA). (gr. 9). 18.99 *(978-1-5344-3287-1(6),* Simon Pulse) Simon Pulse.

Galante, Cecilia. Little Wings #4: the One & Only Willa Bean. Valiant, Kristi, illus. 2012. (Little Wings Ser.: 4). 112p. (J). (gr. 1-4). pap. 4.99 *(978-0-375-86950-1(6),* Random Hse. Bks. for Young Readers) Random Hse. Children's Bks.

—The One & Only Willa Bean, 4. Valiant, Kristi, illus. 2013. (Little Wings Ser.: No. 4). (ENG.). 112p. (J). (gr. 1-3). lib. bdg. 17.44 *(978-0-375-96950-8(0))* Random House Publishing Group.

—Willowood. 2011. (ENG.). 288p. (J). (gr. 4-8). pap. 6.99 *(978-1-4169-8303-3(1),* Aladdin) Simon & Schuster Children's Publishing.

—Willowood. 2010. (ENG.). 272p. (J). (gr. 4-8). 16.99 *(978-1-4169-8022-3(9),* Simon & Schuster/Paula Wiseman Bks.) Simon & Schuster/Paula Wiseman Bks.

Galbraith, Kathryn O. Sparky & Tidbit: Ready-To-Read Level 3. Kelley, Gerald, illus. 2015. (Ready-To-Read Ser.). (ENG.). 40p. (J). (gr. 1-3). pap. 4.99 *(978-1-4814-0424-2(5),* Simon Spotlight) Simon Spotlight.

Gale, Eric Kahn. The Bully Book: A Novel. 2013. (ENG.). 256p. (J). (gr. 3-7). pap. 6.99 *(978-0-06-212513-2(3),* HarperCollins) HarperCollins Pubs.

Gall, Chris. Substitute Creacher. 2011. (ENG., Illus.). 40p. (J). (gr. -1-3). 18.99 *(978-0-316-08915-9(X))* Little, Brown Bks. for Young Readers.

Gallagher, Diana G. Advice about School: Claudia Cristina Cortez Uncomplicates Your Life. Garvey, Brann, illus. 2010. (Claudia Cristina Cortez Ser.). (ENG.). 80p. (J). (gr. 4-8). pap. 6.10 *(978-1-4342-2252-7(7),* 103115, Stone Arch Bks.) Capstone.

—Dance Trap: The Complicated Life of Claudia Cristina Cortez, 1 vol. Garvey, Brann, illus. 2007. (Claudia Cristina Cortez Ser.). (ENG.). 88p. (J). (gr. 4-8). per. 6.10 *(978-1-59889-879-8(5),* 94315, Stone Arch Bks.) Capstone.

—Friends Forever? The Complicated Life of Claudia Cristina Cortez, 1 vol. Garvey, Brann, illus. 2008. (Claudia Cristina Cortez Ser.). (ENG.). 88p. (J). (gr. 4-8). pap. 6.10 *(978-1-4342-0868-2(0),* 95229, Stone Arch Bks.) Capstone.

—Guilty! The Complicated Life of Claudia Cristina Cortez, 1 vol. Garvey, Brann, illus. 2007. (Claudia Cristina Cortez Ser.). (ENG.). 88p. (J). (gr. 4-8). per. 6.10 *(978-1-59889-881-1(7),* 94317, Stone Arch Bks.) Capstone.

—Haunted Love, 1 vol. 2013. (Claudia & Monica: Freshman Girls Ser.). (ENG.). 144p. (J). (gr. 4-8). 9.95 *(978-1-4342-6286-8(3),* 123730, Stone Arch Bks.) Capstone.

—Homecoming, 1 vol. 2013. (Claudia & Monica: Freshman Girls Ser.). (ENG.). 144p. (J). (gr. 4-8). 9.95 *(978-1-4342-4887-9(9),* 121888, Stone Arch Bks.) Capstone.

—Mice Capades, 1 vol. Puglisi, Adriana & Puglisi, Adriana, illus. 2013. (Pet Friends Forever Ser.). (ENG.). 88p. (J). (gr. 1-3). pap. 5.95 *(978-1-4795-1863-0(8),* 123501, Picture Window Bks.) Capstone.

—Monica & the School Spirit Meltdown, 1 vol. 2010. (Monica Ser.). (ENG.). 88p. (J). (gr. 4-8). 27.32 *(978-1-4342-1983-1(6),* 102745, Stone Arch Bks.) Capstone.

—New Firsts, 1 vol. 2012. (Claudia & Monica: Freshman Girls Ser.). (ENG.). 144p. (J). (gr. 4-8). lib. bdg. 26.65 *(978-1-4342-3275-5(1),* 116220, Stone Arch Bks.) Capstone.

—Party! The Complicated Life of Claudia Cristina Cortez, 1 vol. Garvey, Brann, illus. 2008. (Claudia Cristina Cortez Ser.). (ENG.). 88p. (J). (gr. 4-8). pap. 6.10 *(978-1-4342-0867-5(2),* 95228); lib. bdg. 27.32 *(978-1-4342-0771-5(4),* 95176) Capstone. (Stone Arch Bks.).

—Tested, 1 vol. 2012. (Claudia & Monica: Freshman Girls Ser.). (ENG.). 144p. (J). (gr. 4-8). lib. bdg. 26.65 *(978-1-4342-3278-6(6),* 116223, Stone Arch Bks.) Capstone.

—Vote! The Complicated Life of Claudia Cristina Cortez, 1 vol. Garvey, Brann, illus. 2008. (Claudia Cristina Cortez Ser.). (ENG.). 88p. (J). (gr. 4-8). pap. 6.10 *(978-1-4342-0866-8(4),* 95227); lib. bdg. 27.32 *(978-1-4342-0770-8(6),* 95175) Capstone. (Stone Arch Bks.).

—Whatever! The Complicated Life of Claudia Cristina Cortez, 1 vol. Garvey, Brann, illus. 2007. (Claudia Cristina Cortez Ser.). (ENG.). 88p. (J). (gr. 4-8). pap. 6.10 *(978-1-59889-880-4(9),* 94316, Stone Arch Bks.) Capstone.

Gallagher, Mary C. Ginny Morris & Dad's New Girlfriend. Martin, Whitney, illus. 2006. (Ginny Morris Ser.). 64p. (J). (gr. 3-7). 14.95 *(978-1-59147-386-2(1),* Magination Pr.) American Psychological Assn.

—Ginny Morris & Mom's House, Dad's House. Martin, Whitney, illus. 2005. (ENG.). 48p. (J). 14.95 *(978-1-59147-157-8(5),* Magination Pr.) American Psychological Assn.

Gallagher, Mary Collins. Ginny Morris & Dads New Girlfriend. Martin, Whitney, illus. 2006. 64p. (J). (gr. 3-7). per. 9.95 *(978-1-59147-387-9(X),* Magination Pr.) American Psychological Assn.

—Nine Is Not an Even Number. Martin, Whitney, illus. 2005. 48p. (J). pap. 9.95 *(978-1-59147-158-5(3),* Magination Pr.) American Psychological Assn.

Gallier, Laura. The Delusion: We All Have Our Demons. 2017. (Delusion Ser.: 1). (ENG.). 336p. (YA). 22.99 *(978-1-4964-2236-1(8),* 20_29568, Wander) Tyndale Hse. Pubs.

Gallo, Tina & S. I. International Staff. Let's Go, Go, Go! 2010. (Playskool Ser.). (ENG.). 32p. (J). 4.99 *(978-1-4424-0181-5(8),* Simon Scribbles) Simon Scribbles.

Gamblin, Rose Tooley & Hernández, Oscar. Bill's Lunch: El Almuerzo de Bill. 2010. (ENG & SPA., Illus.). 32p. (J). *(978-0-8127-0472-3(X))* Review & Herald Publishing Assn.

Gantos, Jack. Jack Adrift: Fourth Grade Without a Clue: A Jack Henry Adventure. 2005. (Jack Henry Ser.: 1). (ENG.). 208p. (J). (gr. 4-8). pap. 9.99 *(978-0-374-43718-3(1),* 900029883) Square Fish.

—Joey Pigza Swallowed the Key. 2009. 8.30 *(978-0-7848-3764-1(3));* 8.32 *(978-0-7848-1771-1(5))* Marco Bk. Co. (Everbind).

—Joey Pigza Swallowed the Key. unabr. ed. 2004. (Joey Pigza Ser.: Bk. 1). 154p. (J). (gr. 5-9). pap. 29.00 incl. audio *(978-0-8072-8166-6(2),* YA120SP, Listening Library) Random Hse. Audio Publishing Group.

—Joey Pigza Swallowed the Key. 2007. (Joey Pigza Ser.: 1). (J). 1.25 *(978-1-4193-6006-0(X))* Recorded Bks., Inc.

—Joey Pigza Swallowed the Key. 2014. (Joey Pigza Ser.: 1). (ENG.). 176p. (J). (gr. 5-9). pap. 7.99 *(978-1-250-06168-3(7),* 900142030) Square Fish.

—Joey Pigza Swallowed the Key. 2014. (Joey Pigza Ser.: 1). (J). lib. bdg. 18.40 *(978-0-606-23019-3(X))* Turtleback.

—Rotten Ralph Helps Out. Rubel, Nicole, illus. unabr. ed. 2006. (Readalongs for Beginning Readers Ser.). (J). (gr. -1-3). 28.95 incl. audio compact disk *(978-1-59519-679-8(X));* 24.95 incl. audio *(978-1-59519-678-1(1))* Live Oak Media.

—Rotten Ralph Helps Out, 4 bks., Set. unabr. ed. 2006. (Readalongs for Beginning Readers Ser.). (Illus.). (J). (gr. -1-3). pap. 31.95 incl. audio compact disk *(978-1-59519-677-4(3));* pap. 29.95 incl. audio *(978-1-59519-676-7(5))* Live Oak Media.

—What Would Joey Do? 2004. (Joey Pigza Ser.: Bk. 3). 240p. (J). (gr. 5-9). pap. 36.00 incl. audio *(978-1-4000-9020-4(2),* Listening Library) Random Hse. Audio Publishing Group.

Ganz-Schmitt, Sue. Planet Kindergarten. Prigmore, Shane, illus. 2016. (ENG.). 36p. (J). (gr. -1-k). 7.99 *(978-1-4521-5644-6(1))* Chronicle Bks. LLC.

Ganz, Yaffa. The Adventures of Jeremy & Heddy Levi. Katz, Avi, illus. 2005. 204p. (J). 16.95 *(978-1-930143-50-0(8),*

3508); pap. 12.95 *(978-1-930143-51-7(6)*, 3516) Simcha Media Group. (Devora Publishing).

Ganzer, Diane. Summer School Blues. 2008. 124p. pap. 9.99 *(978-1-935105-19-0(1))* Avid Readers Publishing Group.

Garant, Andre J. The Circus Kids. 2008. 140p. pap. 11.99 *(978-1-4389-2833-3(5))* AuthorHouse.

Garcia, Cristina. Dreams of Significant Girls. (ENG.). 256p. (YA). (gr. 9). 2012. pap. 8.99 *(978-1-4169-7930-2(1))* 2011. 16.99 *(978-1-4169-7920-3(4))* Simon & Schuster Bks. For Young Readers. (Simon & Schuster Bks. For Young Readers).

Garcia, Kami & Stohl, Margaret. Beautiful Creatures. 2010. (Beautiful Creatures Ser.: 1). (ENG.). 592p. (YA). (gr. 7-17). pap. 16.99 *(978-0-316-07703-3(8))* Little, Brown Bks. for Young Readers.

García, Kami & Stohl, Margaret. Beautiful Creatures. 2010. (Beautiful Creatures Ser.: 1). (YA). lib. bdg. 23.30 *(978-0-606-26699-4(2))* Turtleback.

Garden, Nancy. Endgame. (ENG., Illus.). 304p. (YA). (gr. 7-12). 2012. pap. 9.99 *(978-0-15-206377-1(3)*, 1199096) 2006. 17.00 *(978-0-15-205416-8(2)*, 1196302) HarperCollins Pubs. (Clarion Bks.).

Gardner, (Grandpa). Starting School. 2011. 32p. pap. 24.95 *(978-1-4560-0903-8(6))* America Star Bks.

Gardner, Graham. Inventing Elliot. 2005. (ENG.). 192p. (YA). (gr. 7-7). 5.99 *(978-0-14-240344-0(X)*, Speak) Penguin Young Readers Group.

—Inventing Elliot. 2005. 181p. (YA). 13.65 *(978-0-7569-5704-9(4))* Perfection Learning Corp.

Gardner, Whitney. Fake Blood. Gardner, Whitney, illus. 2018. (ENG., Illus.). 336p. (J). (gr. 5). 21.99 *(978-1-4814-9556-1(9))*; pap. 14.99 *(978-1-4814-9557-8(7))* Simon & Schuster Bks. For Young Readers. (Simon & Schuster Bks. For Young Readers).

Garfinkle, D. L. Stuck in the 70's. 2007. 182p. (YA). *(978-1-4287-4661-9(7))* Penguin Publishing Group.

Garland, Michael. Miss Smith Reads Again! 2006. (Illus.). (J). *(978-1-4156-8098-8(1)*, Dutton Juvenile) Penguin Publishing Group.

—Miss Smith's Incredible Storybook. Garland, Michael, illus. 2005. (Illus.). 32p. (J). (gr. -1-2). pap. 8.99 *(978-0-14-240282-5(6)*, Puffin Books) Penguin Young Readers Group.

—Miss Smith's Incredible Storybook. 2007. 27.95 incl. audio *(978-0-8045-6945-3(2))*; 29.95 incl. audio compact disk *(978-0-8045-4159-6(0))* Spoken Arts, Inc.

Garland, Taylor. Celebrate the Season: Secret Snowflake. 2017. (Celebrate the Season Ser.: 1). (ENG.). 176p. (J). (gr. 3-7). pap. 6.99 *(978-0-316-47248-7(4))* Little, Brown Bks. for Young Readers.

Garrett, Nicole. The Cupid Factor. 2007. (ENG.). 203p. pap. 14.50 *(978-1-4357-0276-9(X))* Lulu Pr., Inc.

Garrett, Troy. Kramer's World. 2010. 204p. pap. 12.50 *(978-1-60693-155-4(5)*, Eloquent Bks.) Strategic Book Publishing & Rights Agency (SBPRA).

Garsee, Jeannine. Before, after, & Somebody in Between. 2008. (ENG., Illus.). 368p. (YA). (gr. 9-12). pap. 8.99 *(978-1-59990-292-0(3)*, 900053610, Bloomsbury USA Childrens) Bloomsbury Publishing USA.

Garton, Sam. Otter: Hello, Sea Friends! 2016. (My First I Can Read Ser.). (ENG., Illus.). 32p. (J). (gr. -1-3). pap. 4.99 *(978-0-06-236660-3(2)*, Balzer & Bray) HarperCollins Pubs.

—Otter Goes to School. Garton, Sam, illus. 2016. (ENG., Illus.). 32p. (J). (gr. -1-3). 17.99 *(978-0-06-235225-5(3)*, Balzer & Bray) HarperCollins Pubs.

Garvin, Jeff. Symptoms of Being Human. 2016. (ENG.). 352p. (YA). (gr. 9). 17.99 *(978-0-06-238286-3(1)*, Balzer & Bray) HarperCollins Pubs.

Gary, Meredith. Sometimes You Get What You Want. Brown, Lisa, illus. 2008. (ENG.). 32p. (J). (gr. -1 — 1). 17.99 *(978-0-06-114015-0(5)*, HarperCollins) HarperCollins Pubs.

Garza, Xavier. Rooster Joe & the Bully / el Gallo Joe y el Abusón. 2016. (ENG & SPA., Illus.). 128p. (J). (gr. 5-8). pap. 9.95 *(978-1-55885-835-0(0)*, Piñata Books) Arte Publico Pr.

Gassman, Julie. Do Not Bring Your Dragon to Recess. Elkerton, Andy, illus. 2018. (ENG.). 32p. (J). (gr. -1-2). lib. bdg. 22.65 *(978-1-5158-2843-3(3)*, 138276, Picture Window Bks.) Capstone.

—Do Not Take Your Dragon on a Field Trip. Elkerton, Andy, illus. 2019. (ENG.). 32p. (J). (gr. -1-2). lib. bdg. 16.95 *(978-1-68446-059-5(X)*, 140409, Capstone Editions) Capstone.

Gateley, Edwina, illus. & text. God Goes to School. Gateley, Edwina, text. 2009. (ENG.). 32p. (J). pap. 9.95 *(978-0-8091-6748-7(4))* Paulist Pr.

Gates, J. Gabriel & Keel, Charlene. Ghost Crown. 2012. (Tracks Ser.). (ENG.). 456p. (YA). (gr. 6-12). pap. 9.95 *(978-0-7573-1594-7(1)*, HCI Teens) Health Communications, Inc.

Gatou, Shouji. Full Metal Panic - Overload!, Vol. 5. Nagai, Tomohiro, illus. 2006. (Full Metal Panic: Overload! Ser.). 200p. (YA). pap. 9.99 *(978-1-4139-0342-3(8))* ADV Manga.

Gaulkin, Marianne Quigley. Playdance Studio. Baker, David, illus. 2011. 28p. pap. 24.95 *(978-1-4560-2163-4(X))* America Star Bks.

Gay, Delmas Levi. The Ears at the Top of the Stairs. 2008. 56p. per. 15.99 *(978-1-4363-0273-9(0))* Xlibris Corp.

Gaydos, Nora. Now I'm Growing! - First Day of School. Gutierrez, Akemi, illus. 2011. (ENG.). 30p. (J). (gr. -1-17). 8.99 *(978-1-60169-152-1(1))* Innovative Kids.

Gee, T. S. Dress up for When I Grow Up. 2013. 28p. pap. 24.95 *(978-1-62709-078-0(9))* America Star Bks.

Geesey, Kathleen. Black Fog. 2011. 200p. pap. 24.95 *(978-1-4560-7000-7(2))* America Star Bks.

Gelenius, Deb. My Mom, My Teacher. 2013. 28p. pap. 11.95 *(978-1-61244-135-1(1))* Halo Publishing International.

Gene, Barbara. Lamar Montgomery & the Freaky Faces Club. 2006. (J). per. 14.95 *(978-1-889743-50-9(X))* Robbie Dean Pr.

Gensler, Sonia. The Revenant. 2011. (ENG.). 336p. (J). (gr. 7-12). lib. bdg. 26.19 *(978-0-375-96701-6(X)*, Knopf Bks. for Young Readers) Random Hse. Children's Bks.

George, Bobby & George, June. Montessori: Letter Work. Nassner, Alyssa, illus. 2012. (Montessori Ser.). (ENG.). 24p. (J). (gr. -1-k). bds. 10.99 *(978-1-4197-0411-6(7)*, 1040410, Abrams Appleseed) Abrams, Inc.

—Montessori: Number Work. Nassner, Alyssa, illus. 2012. (Montessori Ser.). (ENG.). 24p. (J). (gr. -1-k). bds. 10.99 *(978-1-4197-0412-3(5)*, 1040310) Abrams, Inc.

Georgiana, Vanessa. Lulu: And the Garden of Life. 2013. 104p. (gr. 4-6). pap. 8.99 *(978-1-4582-0936-8(9)*, Abbott Pr.) Author Solutions, LLC.

Gephart, Donna. How to Survive Middle School. 2011. (ENG.). 256p. (J). (gr. 3-7). 8.99 *(978-0-375-85411-8(8)*, Yearling) Random Hse. Children's Bks.

—Lily & Dunkin. (ENG.). 352p. (J). (gr. 5). 2018. 8.99 *(978-0-553-53677-5(X)*, Yearling) 2016. 16.99 *(978-0-553-53674-4(5)*, Delacorte Bks. for Young Readers) Random Hse. Children's Bks.

Geraldi, Michele J. Pennies at Piper Park. 2009. 24p. pap. 12.99 *(978-1-4389-2829-6(7))* AuthorHouse.

Geras, Adèle. The Tower Room. 2005. (ENG.). 204p. (YA). (gr. 7-12). pap. 12.95 *(978-0-15-205537-0(1))* Houghton Mifflin Harcourt Publishing Co.

Geras, Adèle & Geras, Adèle. Pictures of the Night: The Egerton Hall Novels, Volume Three. 2005. (ENG.). 192p. (YA). (gr. 7-12). pap. 11.95 *(978-0-15-205543-1(6)*, 1196670, Clarion Bks.) HarperCollins Pubs.

Gerbay, Susanne. I Am Jack. 2013. (ENG., Illus.). 144p. (J). pap. 5.99 *(978-1-61067-128-6(7))* Kane Miller.

Gerber, Carole. Jessica Mcbean, Tap Dance Queen. Barton, Patrice, illus. 2006. 144p. (J). 13.95 *(978-0-9718348-7-3(3))* Blooming Tree Pr.

—Jessica McBean, Tap Dance Queen. Barton, Patrice, illus. 2007. (ENG.). 144p. (J). (gr. 1-5). pap. 6.95 *(978-0-9718348-9-7(X))* Blooming Tree Pr.

Gerber, Linda. Now & Zen. 2006. (S. A. S. S. Ser.). (Illus.). 224p. (YA). (gr. 7-18). 7.99 *(978-0-14-240657-1(0)*, Speak) Penguin Young Readers Group.

Gerrity, Arlene. The Tale of Chicken Noodle & Rabbit Stew Number Two. 2010. 24p. 10.99 *(978-1-4251-6258-0(4))* Trafford Publishing.

Gervay, Susanne. Being Jack. Wilcox, Cathy, illus. (J). 2016. (ENG.). 192p. pap. 5.99 *(978-1-61067-379-2(4))* 2015. 167p. *(978-1-61067-455-3(3))* Kane Miller.

Ghani, Samna. The Tooth Fairy Goes to School. Williams, Nancy E., ed. Cappoen, Jennifer Tipton, illus. 2013. 44p. (J). pap. 10.98 *(978-1-938526-31-2(7))* Laurus Co., Inc., The.

Ghost, Derek The. Scary School. Fischer, Scott M., illus. (Scary School Ser.: 1). (ENG.). (J). (gr. 3-7). 2012. 272p. pap. 6.99 *(978-0-06-196094-9(2))* 2011. 256p. 16.99 *(978-0-06-196092-5(6))* HarperCollins Pubs. (HarperCollins).

—Scary School #2: Monsters on the March. Fischer, Scott M., illus. 2013. (Scary School Ser.: 2). (ENG.). 272p. (J). (gr. 3-7). pap. 6.99 *(978-0-06-196097-0(7)*, HarperCollins) HarperCollins Pubs.

—Scary School #3: the Northern Frights. Fischer, Scott M., illus. 2013. (Scary School Ser.: 3). (ENG.). 272p. (J). (gr. 3-7). 16.99 *(978-0-06-196098-7(5)*, HarperCollins) HarperCollins Pubs.

Gianferrari, Maria. Hello Goodbye Dog. 2017. (ENG., Illus.). 40p. (J). 18.99 *(978-1-62672-177-7(7)*, 900141433) Roaring Brook Pr.

Gibbs, Stuart. Evil Spy School. 2015. (Spy School Ser.). (ENG., Illus.). 336p. (J). (gr. 3-7). 18.99 *(978-1-4424-9489-3(1)*, Simon & Schuster Bks. For Young Readers) Simon & Schuster Bks. For Young Readers.

—Spy School. (Spy School Ser.). (ENG., (J). (gr. 3-7). 2013. Illus.). 320p. pap. 8.99 *(978-1-4424-2183-7(5))* 2012. 304p. 18.99 *(978-1-4424-2182-0(7))* Simon & Schuster Bks. For Young Readers. (Simon & Schuster Bks. For Young Readers).

—Spy School British Invasion. 2019. (Spy School Ser.). (ENG., Illus.). 320p. (J). (gr. 3-7). 17.99 *(978-1-5344-2470-8(9)*, Simon & Schuster Bks. For Young Readers) Simon & Schuster Bks. For Young Readers.

—Spy School Goes South. 2018. (Spy School Ser.). (ENG., Illus.). 352p. (J). (gr. 3-7). 17.99 *(978-1-4814-7785-7(4)*, Simon & Schuster Bks. For Young Readers) Simon & Schuster Bks. For Young Readers.

—Spy School Secret Service. (Spy School Ser.). (ENG.). (J). (gr. 3-7). 2018. 368p. pap. 8.99 *(978-1-4814-7783-3(8))* 2017. (Illus.). 352p. 18.99 *(978-1-4814-7782-6(X))* Simon & Schuster Bks. For Young Readers. (Simon & Schuster Bks. For Young Readers).

—Spy Ski School. (Spy School Ser.). (ENG.). (J). (gr. 3-7). 2017. 384p. pap. 8.99 *(978-1-4814-4563-4(4))* 2016. (Illus.). 368p. 18.99 *(978-1-4814-4562-7(6))* Simon & Schuster Bks. For Young Readers. (Simon & Schuster Bks. For Young Readers).

Gibson, Marley. Radiate. 2012. (ENG.). 416p. (YA). (gr. 7). pap. 21.99 *(978-0-547-61728-2(3)*, 1465511, Clarion Bks.) HarperCollins Pubs.

Gideon, John. The Little Soup Spoon. 2010. 32p. pap. 12.99 *(978-1-4520-3001-2(4))* AuthorHouse.

Gidney, Craig Laurance. Bereft. 2013. (ENG.). 170p. (J). (gr. 7). pap. 9.95 *(978-0-9849146-4-7(1))* Tiny Stachel Pr.

Gifaldi, David. Toby Scudder, King of the School. 2005. (ENG.). 208p. (J). (gr. 5-7). pap. 12.95 *(978-0-618-55158-3(1)*, 100824, Clarion Bks.) HarperCollins Pubs.

Giff, Patricia Reilly. Bears Beware. 2012. (Zigzag Kids Ser.: 5). (ENG., Illus.). 80p. (J). (gr. 1-4). pap. 4.99 *(978-0-375-85913-7(6)*, Yearling) Random Hse. Children's Bks.

—Big Whopper. Bright, Alasdair, illus. 2010. (Zigzag Kids Ser.: 2). (ENG.). 80p. (J). (gr. 1-4). pap. 4.99 *(978-0-553-49469-3(4)*, Yearling) Random Hse. Children's Bks.

—The Big Whopper, 2. Bright, Alasdair, illus. 2010. (Zigzag Kids Ser.). (ENG.). 80p. (gr. 1-4). lib. bdg. 17.44 *(978-0-385-90926-6(8)*, Lamb, Wendy Bks.) Random Hse. Children's Bks.

—Eleven. (ENG.). (J). 2009. 176p. (gr. 3-7). 7.99 *(978-0-440-23802-7(1)*, Yearling) 2008. 164p. (gr. 4-6). lib. bdg. 21.19 *(978-0-385-90098-0(8)*, Lamb, Wendy Bks.) Random Hse. Children's Bks.

—Flying Feet. Bright, Alasdair, illus. 2011. (Zigzag Kids Ser.: 3). (ENG.). 80p. (J). (gr. 1-4). 4.99 *(978-0-375-85911-3(X)*, Yearling);3. lib. bdg. 17.44 *(978-0-385-90754-5(0)*, Lamb, Wendy Bks.) Random Hse. Children's Bks.

—Jubilee. 2017. (ENG.). 160p. (J). (gr. 3-7). 6.99 *(978-0-385-74489-8(7)*, Yearling) Random Hse. Children's Bks.

—Number One Kid. Bright, Alasdair, illus. 2010. (Zigzag Kids Ser.: 1). (ENG.). 80p. (J). (gr. 1-4). pap. 4.99 *(978-0-553-49468-6(6)*, Yearling) Random Hse. Children's Bks.

—The Secret at the Polk Street School. (J). (gr. 1-2). pap. 3.99 *(978-0-8072-1274-5(1)*, Listening Library) Random Hse. Audio Publishing Group.

—Star Time. Bright, Alasdair, illus. 2011. (Zigzag Kids Ser.: 4). (ENG.). 80p. (J). (gr. 1-4). 4.99 *(978-0-375-85912-0(8)*, Yearling) Random Hse. Children's Bks.

—Super Surprise. 2012. (Zigzag Kids Ser.: 6). (ENG., Illus.). 80p. (J). (gr. 1-4). pap. 4.99 *(978-0-375-85914-4(4)*, Yearling) Random Hse. Children's Bks.

—Zigzag Zoom. 2013. (Zigzag Kids Ser.: 8). (ENG., Illus.). 80p. (J). (gr. 1-4). pap. 4.99 *(978-0-307-97703-8(X)*, Yearling) Random Hse. Children's Bks.

Gilden, Mel. M Is for Monster. Pierard, John & Fastner, Steve, illus. 2018. (ENG.). 104p. (J). (gr. 4-7). pap. 11.95 *(978-1-59687-778-8(2))* ibooks, Inc.

Giles, Gail. Right Behind You. 2008. (ENG.). 320p. (J). (gr. 10-17). pap. 17.99 *(978-0-316-16637-9(5))* Little, Brown Bks. for Young Readers.

—Shattering Glass. 2004. 215p. (J). (gr. 7-18). pap. 37.00 incl. audio *(978-1-4000-9013-6(X)*, Listening Library) Random Hse. Audio Publishing Group.

Gill, Timothy. Flip & Fin: We Rule the School! 2014. (ENG., Illus.). 32p. (J). (gr. -1-3). 14.99 *(978-0-06-224300-3(4)*, Greenwillow Bks.) HarperCollins Pubs.

Gilles, Almira Astudillo. Willie Wins, 1 vol. Angel, Carl, illus. 2013. (ENG.). 32p. (J). (gr. -1-3). 16.95 *(978-1-58430-023-6(X))* Lee & Low Bks., Inc.

Gilley, Jane. Thibault Goes Missing - Book Two of the Troglodyte Trilogy. 2008. 16p. pap. *(978-1-906210-73-1(X))* Grosvenor Hse. Publishing Ltd.

Gilman, Grace. Dixie. McConnell, Sarah, illus. 2011. (I Can Read Level 1 Ser.). (ENG.). 32p. (J). (gr. -1-3). 16.99 *(978-0-06-171914-1(5))*; pap. 4.99 *(978-0-06-171913-4(7))* HarperCollins Pubs. (HarperCollins).

—Dixie & the Best Day Ever. 2014. (I Can Read Level 1 Ser.). (ENG., Illus.). 32p. (J). (gr. -1-3). pap. 4.99 *(978-0-06-208659-4(6)*, HarperCollins) HarperCollins Pubs.

—Dixie & the Big Bully. McConnell, Sarah, illus. 2013. (I Can Read Level 1 Ser.). (ENG.). 32p. (J). (gr. -1-3). 16.99 *(978-0-06-208637-2(5)*, HarperCollins) HarperCollins Pubs.

—Dixie & the Big Bully. 2013. (Dixie: I Can Read Ser.). (J). lib. bdg. 13.55 *(978-0-606-27136-3(8))* Turtleback.

—Dixie & the Class Treat. Rogers, Jacqueline, illus. 2012. (I Can Read Level 1 Ser.). (ENG.). 32p. (J). (gr. -1-3). pap. 4.99 *(978-0-06-208605-1(7)*, HarperCollins) HarperCollins Pubs.

—Dixie & the School Trip. 2012. (Dixie: I Can Read Ser.). (J). lib. bdg. 13.55 *(978-0-606-26284-2(9))* Turtleback.

—Dixie Loves School Pet Day. 2011. (I Can Read Level 1 Ser.). (ENG., Illus.). 32p. (J). (gr. -1-3). 16.99 *(978-0-06-171912-7(9)*, HarperCollins) HarperCollins Pubs.

—Dixie Loves School Pet Day. McConnell, Sarah, illus. 2011. (I Can Read Level 1 Ser.). (ENG.). 32p. (J). (gr. -1-3). pap. 5.99 *(978-0-06-171911-0(0)*, HarperCollins) HarperCollins Pubs.

Gilmore, Grace. The New Kid. Brown, Petra, illus. 2016. (Tales from Maple Ridge Ser.: 6). (ENG.). 128p. (J). (gr. k-4). pap. 6.99 *(978-1-4814-4746-1(7)*, Little Simon) Little Simon.

Gilmore, Rachna. A Group of One, 1 vol. 2005. (ENG.). 184p. (YA). (gr. 6-11). pap. 12.95 *(978-1-55041-925-2(0)*, e4efbebf-1b4d-45dd-b868-3ff0947c418d) Trifolium Bks., Inc. CAN. Dist: Firefly Bks., Ltd.

Gilson, Jamie. Bug in a Rug. 2003. (ENG., Illus.). 80p. (J). pap. 7.95 *(978-0-618-31670-0(1)*, 150103, Clarion Bks.) HarperCollins Pubs.

—Gotcha! Wummer, Amy, illus. 2006. (ENG.). 80p. (J). (gr. -1-3). 15.00 *(978-0-618-54356-4(2)*, 100819, Clarion Bks.) HarperCollins Pubs.

Gingold, Janet. Danger, Long Division. 2006. 188p. per. 14.99 *(978-1-59092-122-7(4))* Blue Forge Pr.

—Finch Goes Wild. 2007. 280p. (YA). pap. 14.99 *(978-1-59092-385-6(5))* Blue Forge Pr.

Giordano, Anthony. Another Boring Summer... Again! 2009. 154p. (YA). pap. 11.25 *(978-1-60695-077-7(0))* Cacoethes Publishing Hse., LLC.

Giris, B. J. Kahmal's Big Day! 2012. 40p. pap. 16.50 *(978-1-4669-3548-8(0))* Trafford Publishing.

Glaser, Linda. Hannah's Way. Gustavson, Adam, illus. 2012. 32p. (J). (gr. k-3). (ENG.). pap. 7.95 *(978-0-7613-5138-2(8)*, 59392402-0f00-41e2-b7cf-f8230b7c8ebc); lib. bdg. 17.95 *(978-0-7613-5137-5(X))* Lerner Publishing Group. (Kar-Ben Publishing).

Glass, Alberta. My Seeing Eye Glasses. Buehrle, Jacquelyn, illus. 2011. 28p. pap. 24.95 *(978-1-4560-2829-9(4))* PublishAmerica, Inc.

Glennon, Michelle. My Big Green Teacher: Please Turn off the Lights. Glennon, Michelle, illus. 2008. (ENG., Illus.). 32p. (J). 19.95 *(978-0-9796625-3-9(2))* GDG Publishing.

—My Big Green Teacher: Seven Generations from Now. Glennon, Michelle, illus. 2008. (Illus.). (J). 19.95 *(978-0-9797952-1-3(4))* GDG Publishing.

—My Big Green Teacher: Take a Deep Breath: Saving Our Rainforests. Glennon, Michelle, illus. 2008. (ENG., Illus.). 32p. (J). 19.95 *(978-0-9797952-0-6(6))* GDG Publishing.

—My Big Green Teacher: Recycling: It's Easy Being Green. Glennon, Michelle, illus. 2007. (Illus.). 32p. (J). 19.95 *(978-0-9796625-6-0(7))* GDG Publishing.

Glickman, Susan. Bernadette & the Lunch Bunch, 1 vol. 2008. (Lunch Bunch Ser.: 1). (ENG., Illus.). 124p. (J). (gr. 1-4). pap. 6.95 *(978-1-897187-51-7(3))* Second Story Pr. CAN. Dist: Orca Bk. Pubs. USA.

Glines, Abbi. Losing the Field. 2018. (Field Party Ser.). (ENG., Illus.). 336p. (YA). (gr. 9). 19.99 *(978-1-5344-0389-5(2)*, Simon Pulse) Simon Pulse.

—Under the Lights. 2016. (Field Party Ser.: 2). (ENG., Illus.). 336p. (YA). (gr. 9). 18.99 *(978-1-4814-3889-6(1)*, Simon Pulse) Simon Pulse.

Glynn, Connie. The Rosewood Chronicles #1: Undercover Princess. (Rosewood Chronicles Ser.: 1). (ENG.). (J). (gr. 3-7). 2019. 464p. pap. 9.99 *(978-0-06-284782-9(1))* 2018. 448p. 16.99 *(978-0-06-284780-5(5))* HarperCollins Pubs. (HarperCollins).

Go! Fight! Twin! 2014. (It Takes Two Ser.: 4). (ENG., Illus.). 160p. (J). (gr. 3-7). 17.99 *(978-1-4814-1656-6(1))*; pap. 6.99 *(978-1-4814-1655-9(3))* Simon Spotlight. (Simon Spotlight).

Goddard, D. L. Agondray: The Guardian of the Clouds. 2012. (Illus.). 100p. pap. 10.67 *(978-1-4678-8516-4(9))* AuthorHouse.

Goff, John. The Take Over. Evans, Patricia, ed. 2012. 196p. (J). pap. 18.99 *(978-0-9841934-8-6(0))* Bryson Taylor Publishing.

Gohmann, Johanna. A Bad Day at Pirate School. Innerebner, Jessika von, illus. 2017. (Pirate Kids Ser.). (ENG.). 32p. (J). (gr. -1-3). lib. bdg. 32.79 *(978-1-5321-3038-0(4)*, 27040, Calico Chapter Bks) Magic Wagon.

Going to School: Individual Title Six-Packs. (Chiquilibros Ser.). (gr. k-1). 23.00 *(978-0-7635-0408-3(4))* Rigby Education.

Gold, Rachel. Just Girls. 2014. (ENG.). 254p. (J). pap. 16.95 *(978-1-59493-419-3(3))* Bella Bks., Inc.

Goldblatt, Mark. Finding the Worm (Twerp Sequel) 2016. (Twerp Ser.: 2). 368p. (J). (gr. 4-7). 7.99 *(978-0-385-39111-5(0)*, Yearling) Random Hse. Children's Bks.

Goldfinger, Jennifer P. Hello, My Name Is Tiger. Goldfinger, Jennifer P., illus. 2016. (ENG., Illus.). 40p. (J). (gr. -1-3). 17.99 *(978-0-06-239951-9(9)*, HarperCollins) HarperCollins Pubs.

Golightly, Holly. School Bites: Blood Drinking 101, 2. 2005. (Illus.). 64p. (YA). per. *(978-0-9745367-3-6(3))* BroadSword Comics/ Jim Balent Studios.

Golightly, Holly, creator. School Bites. 2004. 64p. (YA). per. *(978-0-9745367-2-9(5)*, SB1A) BroadSword Comics/ Jim Balent Studios.

Gómez, Rebecca. Boo la la: School for Ghost Girls. 2017. (ENG., Illus.). 112p. (J). (gr. 1-3). pap. 4.99 *(978-0-545-91798-8(0)*, Scholastic Paperbacks) Scholastic, Inc.

Gomez, Rebecca. Spooktacular! 2016. (Illus.). 107p. (J). *(978-0-545-91799-5(9))* Scholastic, Inc.

Gomez, Sally. Too Many Freckles! Mitchell, Hazel, illus. 2008. (ENG.). 32p. (J). pap. *(978-1-934363-32-4(4))* Zoe Life Christian Communications.

Gonzales Betrand, Diane. The Story Circle / el Circulo de Cuentos. Martin, Wendy, illus. 2016. (ENG, MUL & SPA.). 32p. (J). (gr. k-3). 17.95 *(978-1-55885-826-8(1)*, Piñata Books) Arte Publico Pr.

Gonzales, Rave And Linda. Saved: A Short Story. 2012. 60p. pap. 19.95 *(978-1-4626-7625-5(1))* America Star Bks.

Gonzales, Sophie. Only Mostly Devastated: A Novel. 2020. (ENG.). 288p. (YA). 17.99 *(978-1-250-31589-2(1)*, 900199396, Wednesday Bks.) St. Martin's Pr.

González, Rigoberto & Alvarez, Cecilia Concepcion. Antonio's Card/la Tarjeta de Antonio. 2013. (ENG & SPA., Illus.). 32p. (J). 17.95 *(978-0-89239-204-9(5))* Lee & Low Bks., Inc.

Goo, Maurene. Since You Asked... 2013. (YA). 262p. pap. *(978-0-545-44822-2(0))*; (ENG.). 272p. (gr. 7). 17.99 *(978-0-545-44821-5(2))* Scholastic, Inc. (Scholastic Pr.).

Goobie, Beth. Jason's Why, 1 vol. 2012. (ENG.). 80p. (J). (gr. 4-6). pap. 8.95 *(978-0-88995-484-7(4)*, 9c7bbc8b-0448-4e1b-911b-a87fc6d00ec2) Red Deer Pr. CAN. Dist: Firefly Bks., Ltd.

—The Throne: A Novel, 1 vol. 2013. (ENG., Illus.). 282p. (YA). (gr. 8-10). pap. 4.95 *(978-0-88995-496-0(8)*, 5418f614-aaa5-45f1-9516-0fb7add7ba90) Trifolium Bks., Inc. CAN. Dist: Firefly Bks., Ltd.

Goode, John. Going the Distance. (YA). 2016. (ENG., Illus.). (gr. 8-12). 24.99 *(978-1-63533-020-5(3)*, Harmony Ink Pr.) 2015. 190p. lib. bdg. *(978-1-63216-620-3(8))* Dreamspinner Pr.

—151 Days. 2016. (ENG., Illus.). (J). 32.99 *(978-1-63477-925-8(8)*, Harmony Ink Pr.) Dreamspinner Pr.

Goode, Laura. Sister Mischief. 2011. (ENG., Illus.). 384p. (YA). (gr. 9-18). 16.99 *(978-0-7636-4640-0(7))* Candlewick Pr.

Goodman, Gabriel. The Alliance. 2013. (Surviving Southside Ser.). (ENG.). 104p. (YA). (gr. 6-12). pap. 7.95 *(978-1-4677-0708-4(2)*, e5cb9cdc-9b00-47a5-ad22-bf04c49ba93a, Darby Creek) Lerner Publishing Group.

Gooney Bird Is So Absurd. 2013. (Gooney Bird Greene Ser.: 4). (ENG., Illus.). 112p. (J). (gr. 1-4). pap. 7.99 *(978-0-547-87559-0(2)*, 1505831, Clarion Bks.) HarperCollins Pubs.

Gorgas, Paula Blais. Little Lost Leprechaun. 2007. (Illus.). 20p. (J). per. 11.99 *(978-0-9797574-5-7(2))* Dragonfly Publishing, Inc.

Gorman, Carol. A Midsummer Night's Dork. 2004. (ENG.). 224p. (J). 15.99 *(978-0-06-050718-3(7))* HarperCollins Pubs.

Gorrell, Nancy. Corey's Story. 2007. (ENG., Illus.). 96p. (J). (gr. 2-5). per. 6.99 *(978-1-84550-258-4(2)*, 16889563-d370-49af-98d4-d01b97170712) Christian Focus Pubns. GBR. Dist: Baker & Taylor Publisher Services (BTPS).

Goscinny, René & Sempé, Jean-Jacques. Nicholas. Bell, Anthea, tr. 2011. (ENG., Illus.). 136p. (gr. 7-17). pap. 9.95 *(978-0-7148-6115-9(4))* Phaidon Pr., Inc.

Gosselin, Kim. Sportsercise: A School Story about Exercise-Induced Asthma. Ravanelli, Terry, illus. 2nd ed. 2004. (Children's Asthma Ser.). (J). per. 9.95 *(978-1-891383-25-0(6))* JayJo Bks., LLC.

Gough, Erin. Amelia Westlake Was Never Here. 2019. (ENG., Illus.). 368p. (YA). (gr. 9-17). 17.99 *(978-0-316-45066-9(9)*, Poppy) Little, Brown Bks. for Young Readers.

Gould, M. & Gould, R. About Gossip: What Would Jesus Do, 1 vol. Hurst, Debbie, illus. 2009. 28p. pap. 24.95 *(978-1-60749-680-9(1))* America Star Bks.

Gownley, Jimmy. Amelia & the Gym Class System: #2, 1 vol. Gownley, Jimmy, illus. 2010. (Amelia Rules! Ser.). (ENG., Illus.). 36p. (J). (gr. 2-6). 31.36 *(978-1-59961-788-6(9)*, 2381, Graphic Novels) Spotlight.

—The Dumbest Idea Ever! Gownley, Jimmy, illus. 2014. (ENG., Illus.). 240p. (J). (gr. 4-7). 24.99 *(978-0-545-45346-2(1)*, Graphix) Scholastic, Inc.

—Her Permanent Record. Gownley, Jimmy, illus. 2012. (Amelia Rules! Ser.). (ENG., Illus.). 160p. (J). (gr. 2-7). 24.99 *(978-1-4169-8615-7(4))*; pap. 12.99 *(978-1-4169-8614-0(6))* Simon & Schuster Children's Publishing. (Atheneum Bks. for Young Readers).

—Her Permanent Record. 2012. (Amelia Rules! Ser.: 8). lib. bdg. 23.30 *(978-0-606-26885-1(5))* Turtleback.

—True Things (Adults Don't Want Kids to Know) Gownley, Jimmy, illus. 2010. (Amelia Rules! Ser.). (ENG., Illus.). 176p. (J). (gr. 2-7). 19.99 *(978-1-4169-8611-9(1))*; pap. 12.99 *(978-1-4169-8609-6(X))* Simon & Schuster Children's Publishing. (Atheneum Bks. for Young Readers).

—The Tweenage Guide to Not Being Unpopular. Gownley, Jimmy, illus. 2010. (Amelia Rules! Ser.). (ENG., Illus.). 192p. (J). (gr. 2-7). pap. 12.99 *(978-1-4169-8608-9(1))*, Atheneum Bks. for Young Readers) Simon & Schuster Children's Publishing.

—The Whole World's Crazy. Gownley, Jimmy, illus. 2011. (Amelia Rules! Ser.). (ENG., Illus.). 176p. (J). (gr. 2-7). 21.99 *(978-1-4424-4538-3(6))*, Atheneum Bks. for Young Readers) Simon & Schuster Children's Publishing.

Grab, Daphne. Alive & Well in Prague, New York. 2008. (Laura Geringer Bks.). 247p. (YA). (gr. 7-18). lib. bdg. 17.89 *(978-0-06-125671-4(4))*, Geringer, Laura Book) HarperCollins Pubs.

—Halftime. 2010. (J). *(978-0-385-73783-8(1))*; *(978-0-385-90693-7(5))* Random House Publishing Group. (Delacorte Pr).

Grabenstein, Chris. Riley Mack & the Other Known Troublemakers. 2012. (Riley Mack Ser.: 1). (ENG.). 272p. (J). (gr. 3-7). 16.99 *(978-0-06-202620-0(8))* HarperCollins Pubs.

—Riley Mack Stirs up More Trouble. 2013. (Riley Mack Ser.: 2). (ENG.). 336p. (J). (gr. 3-7). 16.99 *(978-0-06-202622-4(4))* HarperCollins Pubs.

—The Smartest Kid in the Universe. 2020. (Smartest Kid in the Universe Ser.: 1). 304p. (J). (gr. 3-7). 17.99 *(978-0-525-64778-2(3))*, Random Hse. Bks. for Young Readers) Random Hse. Children's Bks.

Grabenstein, J. J. & Grabenstein, Chris. Shine! 2019. (Illus.). 224p. (J). (gr. 3-7). 16.99 *(978-1-5247-1766-7(5))*, Random Hse. Bks. for Young Readers) Random Hse. Children's Bks.

Grace, Amanda. But I Love Him. 2011. (ENG.). 264p. (YA). (gr. 9-12). pap. 9.95 *(978-0-7387-2594-9(3))*, 0738725943, Flux) North Star Editions.

—In Too Deep. 2012. (ENG.). 240p. (YA). (gr. 9-12). pap. 9.95 *(978-0-7387-2600-7(1))*, 0738726001, Flux) North Star Editions.

Grace, N. B. Battle of the Bands. 2007. (High School Musical Stories from East High Ser.). 142p. (J). (gr. 3-7). 12.65 *(978-0-7569-8337-6(1))* Perfection Learning Corp.

Graff, Lisa. Double Dog Dare. 2013. (ENG.). (J). 320p. (gr. 3-7). pap. 8.99 *(978-0-14-242412-4(9))*, Puffin Books); 304p. (gr. 4-6). 22.44 *(978-0-399-25516-8(8))* Penguin Young Readers Group.

—The Life & Crimes of Bernetta Wallflower. 2015. (ENG.). 288p. (J). (gr. 3-7). 9.99 *(978-0-14-751675-6(7))*, Puffin Books) Penguin Young Readers Group.

—Sophie Simon Solves Them All. Beene, Jason, illus. 2012. (ENG.). 112p. (J). (gr. 3-5). pap. 7.99 *(978-1-250-02898-3(1))*, 900118313) Square Fish.

—The Thing about Georgie. 2008. (ENG.). 224p. (J). (gr. 3-7). pap. 9.99 *(978-0-06-087591-6(7))*, HarperCollins) HarperCollins Pubs.

—The Thing about Georgie: A Novel. 2006. 220p. (J). *(978-0-06-087589-3(5))*, Geringer, Laura Book) HarperCollins Pubs.

Grambling, Lois G. Can I Bring My Pterodactyl to School, Ms. Johnson? Love, Judy, illus. 2006. (Prehistoric Pets Ser.: 1). 32p. (J). (gr. k-3). 7.95 *(978-1-58089-141-7(1))* Charlesbridge Publishing, Inc.

Grandits, John. Seven Rules You Absolutely Must Not Break If You Want to Survive the Cafeteria. Austin, Michael Allen, illus. 2017. (ENG.). 32p. (J). (gr. 1-4). 16.99 *(978-0-544-69951-9(3))*, 1627721, Clarion Bks.) HarperCollins Pubs.

Grandma, Sue. Rocky the Rocking Horse. 2010. 24p. 12.99 *(978-1-4520-7333-0(3))* AuthorHouse.

Grant, Myrna. Ivan & the Hidden Bible. rev. ed. 2006. (Flamingo Fiction 9-13s Ser.). (ENG., Illus.). 144p. (J). (gr. 4-7). per. 6.99 *(978-1-84550-133-4(0))*, a73bcfb0-1d15-46e7-ad2b-7adb1c86a432) Christian Focus Pubns. GBR. Dist: Baker & Taylor Publisher Services (BTPS).

Grant, Vicki. Cochonnet, 1 vol. 2011. (Orca Currents en Français Ser.). (FRE.). 112p. (J). (gr. 4-7). pap. 9.95 *(978-1-4598-0006-9(0))* Orca Bk. Pubs. USA.

—Pigboy. 2007. (Orca Currents Ser.). 101p. (gr. 5). 19.95 *(978-0-7569-8067-2(4))* Perfection Learning Corp.

Gratz, Alan. Code of Honor. 2018. lib. bdg. 20.85 *(978-0-606-41139-4(9))* Turtleback.

Grau, Sheila. Polar Distress: Dr. Critchlore's School for Minions #3. Sutphin, Joe, illus. 2017. (Dr. Critchlore's School for Minions Ser.). (ENG.). 288p. (J). (gr. 3-7). 14.95 *(978-1-4197-2294-3(8))*, 1132101) Abrams, Inc.

—Twice Cursed (Dr. Critchlore's School for Minions #4) Sutphin, Joe, illus. 2018. (Dr. Critchlore's School for Minions Ser.). (ENG.). 304p. (J). (gr. 3-7). 14.99 *(978-1-4197-2863-1(6))*, 1132201, Amulet Bks.) Abrams, Inc.

Grau, Sheila & Sutphin, Joe. Dr. Critchlore's School for Minions: Book Two: Gorilla Tactics. 2016. (Dr. Critchlore's School for Minions Ser.). (ENG., Illus.). 304p. (J). (gr. 3-7). 14.95 *(978-1-4197-1371-2(X))*, 1091701, Amulet Bks.) Abrams, Inc.

Graves, Damien. The Deadly Catch. 2006. (Midnight Library: 8). (ENG., Illus.). 170p. (J). (gr. 6-8). 18.69 *(978-0-439-89395-4(X))* Scholastic, Inc.

Graves, Emma T. OMG, Zombie! Boo, Binny, illus. 2018. (My Undead Life Ser.). (ENG.). 112p. (J). (gr. 3-6). pap. 7.95 *(978-1-4965-6448-1(0))*, 138360); lib. bdg. 25.99 *(978-1-4965-6444-3(8))*, 138356) Capstone. (Stone Arch Bks.).

—Really Rotten Drama. Boo, Binny, illus. 2018. (My Undead Life Ser.). (ENG.). 112p. (J). (gr. 3-6). lib. bdg. 25.99 *(978-1-4965-6445-0(6))*, 138357, Stone Arch Bks.) Capstone.

—Total FREAK-Out. Boo, Binny, illus. 2018. (My Undead Life Ser.). (ENG.). 112p. (J). (gr. 3-6). pap. 7.95 *(978-1-4965-6450-4(2))*, 138362); lib. bdg. 25.99 *(978-1-4965-6446-7(4))*, 138358) Capstone. (Stone Arch Bks.).

Gray, Bianca. Back to School: Adventures of Alex & Joey. 2013. 20p. pap. 17.99 *(978-1-4817-0425-0(7))* AuthorHouse.

Gray, Claudia. Steadfast. 2015. (Spellcaster Ser.: 2). (ENG.). 368p. (YA). (gr. 8). pap. 9.99 *(978-0-06-196123-6(X))*, HarperTeen) HarperCollins Pubs.

Green, Corey. Managing Stan: Buckley School Books #1. 2007. (ENG.). 162p. (J). 16.95 *(978-1-934437-01-8(8))*; pap. 7.99 *(978-1-934437-02-5(6))* Abligio Bks.

Green, D. L. Being a Punch Line Is No Joke: A 4D Book. Rosa, Leandra La, illus. 2018. (Funny Girl Ser.). (ENG.). 112p. (J). (gr. 3-5). lib. bdg. 26.65 *(978-1-4965-6469-6(3))*, 138378, Stone Arch Bks.) Capstone.

—Good Deeds & Other Laughing Matters: A 4D Book. Rosa, Leandra La, illus. 2018. (Funny Girl Ser.). (ENG.). 112p. (J). (gr. 3-5). pap. 7.95 *(978-1-4965-6474-0(X))*, 138383, Stone Arch Bks.) Capstone.

—Kaitlyn & the Competition. 2016. (Babysitter Chronicles Ser.). (ENG.). 160p. (J). (gr. 4-7). pap. 6.95 *(978-1-4914-8861-4(1))*, 131486, Stone Arch Bks.) Capstone.

—Making Friends & Horsing Around: A 4D Book. Rosa, Leandra La, illus. 2018. (Funny Girl Ser.). (ENG.). 112p. (J). (gr. 3-5). lib. bdg. 26.65 *(978-1-4965-6467-2(7))*, 138376, Stone Arch Bks.) Capstone.

—Something Smells Funny at the Talent Show: A 4D Book. Rosa, Leandra La, illus. 2018. (Funny Girl Ser.). (ENG.). 112p. (J). (gr. 3-5). pap. 7.95 *(978-1-4965-6472-6(3))*, 138381, Stone Arch Bks.) Capstone.

—Zeke Meeks vs the Gruesome Girls, 1 vol. Alves, Josh, illus. 2012. (Zeke Meeks Ser.). (ENG.). 128p. (J). (gr. 2-4). pap. 5.95 *(978-1-4048-7221-9(3))*, 118073, Picture Window Bks.) Capstone.

—Zeke Meeks vs the Horrifying TV-Turnoff Week, 1 vol. Alves, Josh, illus. 2012. (Zeke Meeks Ser.). (ENG.). 128p. (J). (gr. 2-4). pap. 5.95 *(978-1-4048-7220-2(5))*, 118072, Picture Window Bks.) Capstone.

—Zeke Meeks vs the No-Fun Fund-Raiser, 1 vol. Alves, Josh, illus. 2013. (Zeke Meeks Ser.). (ENG.). 128p. (J). (gr. 2-4). lib. bdg. 22.65 *(978-1-4048-7640-8(5))*, 120159, Picture Window Bks.) Capstone.

—Zeke Meeks vs the Pain-In-the-Neck Pets, 1 vol. Alves, Josh, illus. 2014. (Zeke Meeks Ser.). (ENG.). 128p. (J). (gr. 2-4). 22.65 *(978-1-4795-2166-1(3))*, 123881, Picture Window Bks.) Capstone.

—Zeke Meeks vs the Stinkin' Science Fair, 1 vol. Alves, Josh, illus. 2012. (Zeke Meeks Ser.). (ENG.). 128p. (J). (gr. 2-4). pap. 5.95 *(978-1-4048-7222-6(1))*, 118074); lib. bdg. 22.65 *(978-1-4048-6802-1(X))*, 116247) Capstone. (Picture Window Bks.).

—Zeke Meeks vs the Super Stressful Talent Show, 1 vol. Alves, Josh, illus. 2013. (Zeke Meeks Ser.). (ENG.). 128p. (J). (gr. 2-4). 8.95 *(978-1-4048-8106-8(9))*, 121878, Picture Window Bks.) Capstone.

Green, Jessica. Diary of a Would-Be Princess: The Journal of Jillian Jones, 5b. 2007. (Illus.). 236p. (J). (gr. 4-7). 15.95 *(978-1-58089-166-0(7))* Charlesbridge Publishing, Inc.

Green, Margaret, adapted by. Let the Dragon Games Begin! 2016. (Illus.). 32p. (J). *(978-0-316-39412-3(2))* Little Brown & Co.

Green, Poppy. A New Friend. Bell, Jennifer A., illus. 2015. (Adventures of Sophie Mouse Ser.: 1). (ENG.). 128p. (J). (gr. k-4). pap. 6.99 *(978-1-4814-2832-3(2))*, Little Simon) Little Simon.

Green, S. E. Killer Instinct. 2014. (ENG., Illus.). 272p. (YA). (gr. 9). 17.99 *(978-1-4814-0285-9(4))*, Simon Pulse) Simon Pulse.

Green, Tim. Baseball Great. (Baseball Great Ser.: 1). (ENG.). (J). (gr. 3-7). 2010. 272p. 7.99 *(978-0-06-162688-3(0))* 2009. 256p. 16.99 *(978-0-06-162686-9(4))* HarperCollins Pubs. (HarperCollins).

—Baseball Great. 2010. (Baseball Great Ser.: 1). (J). lib. bdg. 17.20 *(978-0-606-10356-5(2))* Turtleback.

—The Big Game. (ENG.). (J). (gr. 3-7). 2019. 336p. pap. 9.99 *(978-0-06-248561-8(X))* 2018. 320p. 16.99 *(978-0-06-248504-5(0))* HarperCollins Pubs. (HarperCollins).

—First Team. 2015. (ENG.). 352p. (J). (gr. 3-7). pap. 7.99 *(978-0-06-220876-7(4))*, HarperCollins) HarperCollins Pubs.

—First Team. 2014. (ENG.). 336p. (J). (gr. 3-7). 16.99 *(978-0-06-220875-0(6))*, HarperCollins) HarperCollins Pubs.

—First Team. 2015. (J). lib. bdg. 17.20 *(978-0-606-37616-7(X))* Turtleback.

—New Kid. 2014. (ENG.). 320p. (J). (gr. 3-7). 16.99 *(978-0-06-220872-9(1))*, HarperCollins) HarperCollins Pubs.

Greene, Stephanie. Owen Foote, Mighty Scientist. Smith, Catharine Bowman, illus. 2004. (ENG.). 96p. (J). (gr. 1-4). tchr. ed. 15.00 *(978-0-618-43016-1(4))*, 100349, Clarion Bks.) HarperCollins Pubs.

—Princess Posey & the First Grade Ballet. Roth Sisson, Stephanie, illus. 2014. (Princess Posey, First Grader Ser.: 9). 96p. (J). (gr. k-3). pap. 6.99 *(978-0-14-751292-5(1))*, Puffin Books) Penguin Young Readers Group.

—Princess Posey & the First Grade Parade: Book 1, Bk. 1. Roth Sisson, Stephanie, illus. 2011. (Princess Posey, First Grader Ser.: 1). 96p. (J). (gr. k-3). 6.99 *(978-0-14-241827-7(7))*, Puffin Books) Penguin Young Readers Group.

—Princess Posey & the First Grade Play. Roth Sisson, Stephanie, illus. 2017. (Princess Posey, First Grader Ser.: 11). 96p. (J). (gr. k-3). 5.99 *(978-0-14-751719-7(2))*, Puffin Books) Penguin Young Readers Group.

—Princess Posey & the Monster Stew, 4 vols. Roth Sisson, Stephanie, illus. 2012. (Princess Posey, First Grader Ser.: 4). 96p. (J). (gr. k-3). pap. 5.99 *(978-0-14-242105-5(7))*, Puffin Books) Penguin Young Readers Group.

—Princess Posey & the New First Grader. Roth Sisson, Stephanie, illus. 2013. (Princess Posey, First Grader Ser.: 6). 96p. (J). (gr. k-3). pap. 5.99 *(978-0-14-242763-7(2))*, Puffin Books) Penguin Young Readers Group.

—Princess Posey & the Perfect Present: Book 2, Bk. 2. Roth Sisson, Stephanie, illus. 2011. (Princess Posey, First Grader Ser.: 2). 96p. (J). (gr. k-3). 6.99 *(978-0-14-241828-4(5))*, Puffin Books) Penguin Young Readers Group.

—Princess Posey & the Tiny Treasure. Roth Sisson, Stephanie, illus. 2013. (Princess Posey, First Grader Ser.: 5). 96p. (J). (gr. k-3). pap. 5.99 *(978-0-14-242415-5(3))*, Puffin Books) Penguin Young Readers Group.

Greensill, Rowina Anne. James Goes to Play School. 2010. (Illus.). 28p. pap. 12.49 *(978-1-4490-7039-7(6))* AuthorHouse.

Greenwald, Lisa. Friendship List #1: 11 Before 12. (Friendship List Ser.: 1). (ENG.). 416p. (J). (gr. 3-7). 2018. pap. 9.99 *(978-0-06-241775-4(6))* 2017. 16.99 *(978-0-06-241774-7(8))* HarperCollins Pubs. (Tegen, Katherine Bks).

—Friendship List #2: 12 Before 13. 2018. (Friendship List Ser.: 2). (ENG., Illus.). 368p. (J). (gr. 3-7). 16.99 *(978-0-06-241177-8(2))*, Tegen, Katherine Bks) HarperCollins Pubs.

—Pink & Green Is the New Black. 2014. (ENG.). 272p. (J). (gr. 5-9). 16.95 *(978-1-4197-1225-8(X))*, 1072101, Amulet Bks.) Abrams, Inc.

—Pink & Green Is the New Black: Pink & Green Book Three. 2015. (Pink & Green Ser.). (ENG.). 280p. (J). (gr. 3-7). pap. 9.99 *(978-1-4197-1679-9(4))*, 1072103, Amulet Bks.) Abrams, Inc.

—TBH #1: TBH, This Is So Awkward. 2018. (Tbh Ser.: 1). (ENG., Illus.). 224p. (J). (gr. 3-7). 12.99 *(978-0-06-268990-0(8))*, Tegen, Katherine Bks) HarperCollins Pubs.

—TBH #3: TBH, Too Much Drama. 2019. (Tbh Ser.: 3). (ENG., Illus.). 224p. (J). (gr. 3-7). pap. 9.99 *(978-0-06-268997-9(5))*; 12.99 *(978-0-06-268996-2(7))* HarperCollins Pubs. (Tegen, Katherine Bks).

Greenwald, Tommy. Charlie Joe Jackson's Guide to Extra Credit. Coovert, J. P., illus. 2013. (Charlie Joe Jackson Ser.: 2). (ENG.). 288p. (J). (gr. 4-7). pap. 10.99 *(978-1-250-01670-6(3))*, 900087084) Square Fish.

—Charlie Joe Jackson's Guide to Extra Credit. 2013. (Charlie Joe Jackson's Guide Ser.: 2). (J). lib. bdg. 18.40 *(978-0-606-28461-5(3))* Turtleback.

—Charlie Joe Jackson's Guide to Not Growing Up. Coovert, J. P., illus. 2018. (Charlie Joe Jackson Ser.: 6). (ENG.). 208p. (J). pap. 12.99 *(978-1-250-15835-2(4))*, 900185487) Square Fish.

—Charlie Joe Jackson's Guide to Not Reading. 2012. (Charlie Joe Jackson's Guide Ser.: 1). (J). lib. bdg. 17.20 *(978-0-606-26127-2(3))* Turtleback.

Greenway, Glen. Ant Cook & the Giant Sangom. 2008. 144p. pap. 12.95 *(978-1-4327-1898-5(3))* Outskirts Pr., Inc.

Gregg, Stacy. The Auditions, Book 1. 2010. (Pony Club Rivals Ser.: 1). (ENG.). 288p. (J). (gr. 4-7). 7.99 *(978-0-00-733343-1(9))*, HarperCollins Children's Bks.) HarperCollins Pubs. Ltd. GBR. Dist: HarperCollins Pubs.

—Riding Star, Book 3. 2011. (Pony Club Rivals Ser.: 3). (ENG.). 304p. (J). (gr. 4-7). pap. 7.99 *(978-0-00-733345-5(5))*, HarperCollins Children's Bks.) HarperCollins Pubs. Ltd. GBR. Dist: HarperCollins Pubs.

Greig, Allison. Stacey's Adventures. 2006. (Illus.). 64p. pap. *(978-1-84401-035-6(X))* Athena Pr.

—Stacey's Adventures. 2017. (ENG., Illus.). (J). (gr. k-2). pap. *(978-1-78719-400-7(0))* Authors OnLine, Ltd.

Grennan, Conor. The Hadley Academy for the Improbably Gifted, 1 vol. Valdrighi, Alessandro, illus. 2019. (ENG.). 368p. (J). 16.99 *(978-1-4002-1534-8(X))*, Tommy Nelson) Nelson, Thomas Inc.

Gresh, Dannah. Danika's Totally Terrible Toss. 2008. (True Girl Fiction Ser.). (ENG., Illus.). 112p. pap. 7.99 *(978-0-8024-8702-5(5))* Moody Pubs.

Gresh, Dannah & Anderson, Chizuruoke. Yuzi's False Alarm. 2008. (True Girl Fiction Ser.). (ENG., Illus.). 96p. pap. 7.99 *(978-0-8024-8704-9(1))* Moody Pubs.

Gresh, Dannah & Mylin, Janet. Just Call Me Kate. 2008. (True Girl Fiction Ser.). (ENG., Illus.). 112p. pap. 7.99 *(978-0-8024-8703-2(3))* Moody Pubs.

Gresh, Dannah K. & Weibel, Suzy. T Is for AnTONia. 2008. (True Girl Fiction Ser.). (ENG.). 96p. pap. 7.99 *(978-0-8024-8705-6(X))* Moody Pubs.

Griffin, Adele. Amandine. 2003. (ENG.). 208p. (gr. 5-9). pap. 6.99 *(978-0-7868-1441-1(1))* Disney Pr.

—The Julian Game. 2011. (ENG.). 208p. (YA). (gr. 7-18). 7.99 *(978-0-14-241973-1(7))*, Speak) Penguin Young Readers Group.

—The Knaveheart's Curse: A Vampire Island Book. 2009. (Vampire Island Ser.: 2). (ENG.). 160p. (J). (gr. 3-7). 6.99 *(978-0-14-241407-1(7))*, Puffin Books) Penguin Young Readers Group.

Griffin, Molly Beth. Field Day Fun. Deas, Mike, illus. 2019. (School Sidekicks Ser.). (ENG.). 32p. (J). (gr. -1-2). lib. bdg. 21.32 *(978-1-5158-4418-1(8))*, 140513, Picture Window Bks.) Capstone.

—Field Trip Trouble. Deas, Mike, illus. 2019. (School Sidekicks Ser.). (ENG.). 32p. (J). (gr. -1-2). lib. bdg. 21.32 *(978-1-5158-4416-7(1))*, 140510, Picture Window Bks.) Capstone.

—Hard Hat Heroes. Deas, Mike, illus. 2019. (School Sidekicks Ser.). (ENG.). 32p. (J). (gr. -1-2). lib. bdg. 21.32 *(978-1-5158-4417-4(X))*, 140511, Picture Window Bks.) Capstone.

—Plans Gone Wrong. Jack, Colin, illus. 2019. (ENG.). 32p. (J). pap. *(978-1-4747-7178-8(5))*, Picture Window Bks.) Capstone.

—Test Trouble. Deas, Mike, illus. 2019. (School Sidekicks Ser.). (ENG.). 32p. (J). (gr. -1-2). lib. bdg. 21.32 *(978-1-5158-4419-8(6))*, 140512, Picture Window Bks.) Capstone.

Griffin, N. Just Wreck It All. 2018. (ENG., Illus.). 336p. (YA). (gr. 7). 18.99 *(978-1-4814-6518-2(X))*, Atheneum/Caitlyn Dlouhy Books) Simon & Schuster Children's Publishing.

—Smashie Mcperter & the Mystery of Room 11. Hindley, Kate, illus. 2015. (Smashie Mcperter Investigates Ser.: 1). (ENG.). 256p. (J). (gr. 2-5). 15.99 *(978-0-7636-6145-8(7))* Candlewick Pr.

Griffin, Paul. When Friendship Followed Me Home. 2016. (ENG.). 256p. (J). (gr. 5-9). 16.99 *(978-0-8037-3816-4(1))*, Dial Bks) Penguin Young Readers Group.

Griffis, Molly Levite. The Rachel Resistance. 224p. 8.95 *(978-1-57168-553-7(7))* Eakin Pr.

Griffiths, Andy. Treasure Fever! 2008. (Schooling Around Ser.: No. 1). 198p. (J). pap. *(978-0-545-09222-7(1))* Scholastic, Inc.

Grigsby, Susan. First Peas to the Table: How Thomas Jefferson Inspired a School Garden. Tadgell, Nicole, illus. 2012. (ENG.). 32p. (J). (gr. -1-3). 16.99 *(978-0-8075-2452-7(2))*, 807524522) Whitman, Albert & Co.

—In the Garden with Dr. Carver. Tadgell, Nicole, illus. 2012. (J). *(978-1-61913-157-6(9))* Weigl Pubs., Inc.

—In the Garden with Dr. Carver. Tadgell, Nicole, illus. 2010. (ENG.). 32p. (J). (gr. -1-3). 16.99 *(978-0-8075-3630-8(X))*, 080753630X) Whitman, Albert & Co.

—Wisteria's Show & Tell Spectacular: Older Than the Dinosaurs. Miller, Alexandra, illus. 2012. (J). *(978-1-934860-12-0(3))* Shenanigan Bks.

Grimes, Nikki. Almost Zero: A Dyamonde Daniel Book. Christie, R. Gregory, illus. 2010. (Dyamonde Daniel Book Ser.: 3). (ENG.). 128p. (J). (gr. 2-4). 12.99 *(978-0-399-25177-1(4))*, G.P. Putnam's Sons Books for Young Readers) Penguin Young Readers Group.

—Bronx Masquerade. 2017. (ENG.). 192p. (YA). (gr. 7). pap. 10.99 *(978-0-425-28976-1(1))*, Speak) Penguin Young Readers Group.

—Bronx Masquerade. 2003. (gr. 7-12). lib. bdg. 17.20 *(978-0-613-81701-1(X))* Turtleback.

—Danitra Brown, Class Clown. Lewis, E. B., illus. 2005. 32p. (J). lib. bdg. 17.89 *(978-0-688-17291-6(1))*; (ENG.). (gr. 3). 16.99 *(978-0-688-17290-9(3))*, HarperCollins) HarperCollins Pubs.

—Halfway to Perfect: A Dyamonde Daniel Book. Christie, R. Gregory, illus. (Dyamonde Daniel Book Ser.: 4). (ENG.). 128p. (J). (gr. 2-4). 2018. 6.99 *(978-0-425-29175-7(8))*, Puffin Books) 2012. 12.99 *(978-0-399-25178-8(2))*, G.P. Putnam's Sons Books for Young Readers) Penguin Young Readers Group.

—Planet Middle School. (ENG., 160p. (J). 2018. Illus.). (gr. 3-6). pap. 7.99 *(978-1-61963-012-3(5))*, 900098195) 2011. 16.99 *(978-1-59990-284-5(2))*, 900051865) Bloomsbury Publishing USA. (Bloomsbury USA Childrens).

—Planet Middle School. 2019. (Penworthy Picks Middle School Ser.). (ENG.). 154p. (J). (gr. 6-8). 18.96 *(978-1-64310-917-6(0))* Penworthy Co., LLC, The.

Grisham, John. The Scandal. 2017. (Theodore Boone Ser.: 6). lib. bdg. 19.65 *(978-0-606-40086-2(9))* Turtleback.

Griswell, Kim T. Rufus Goes to School. Valeri, Gorbachev, illus. 2013. 32p. (J). (gr. -1-1). 16.95 *(978-1-4549-0416-8(X))* Sterling Publishing Co., Inc.

Grogan, John. Marley Goes to School. Cowdrey, Richard, illus. 2012. (Marley Ser.). (ENG.). 40p. (J). (gr. -1-3). bds. 9.99 *(978-0-06-211366-5(6))*, HarperCollins) HarperCollins Pubs.

Gross, S. D. Freddie, Fireman Mike. 2007. (Illus.). 24p. (J). (gr. -1-3). per. 12.99 *(978-1-59879-343-7(8))* Lifevest Publishing, Inc.

Grosso, Mike. I Am Drums. (ENG.). 256p. (J). (gr. 5-7). 2019. pap. 7.99 *(978-1-328-90013-5(4))*, 1700043) 2016. 17.99 *(978-0-544-70710-8(9))*, 1628642) HarperCollins Pubs. (Clarion Bks.).

Group/McGraw-Hill, Wright. Secrets & Strays, 6 vols. (D-Man Beans Ser.). 47p. (gr. 4-6). 42.50 *(978-0-322-06258-0(6))* Wright Group/McGraw-Hill.

Grover, Lorie Ann. Hold Me Tight. 2007. (ENG.). 352p. (J). (gr. 5-9). pap. 16.95 *(978-1-4169-6753-8(2))*, McElderry, Margaret K. Bks.) McElderry, Margaret K. Bks.

Groves. Back to School, Bk. 15. Date not set. (Illus.). 32p. (J). pap. 129.15 *(978-0-582-18058-1(9))* Addison-Wesley Longman, Ltd. GBR. Dist: Trans-Atlantic Pubns., Inc.

Grund, Carol A. Anna Mei, Blessing in Disguise. 2011. 181p. (J). pap. *(978-0-8198-0796-0(6))* Pauline Bks. & Media.

—Anna Mei, Cartoon Girl. 2010. 140p. (J). (gr. 4-7). pap. 8.95 *(978-0-8198-0788-5(5))* Pauline Bks. & Media.

Grunwell, Jeanne Marie. Mind Games. 2006. (ENG., Illus.). 144p. (J). (gr. 5-7). pap. 10.95 *(978-0-618-68947-7(8))*, 410165, Clarion Bks.) HarperCollins Pubs.

Guarente, Gabe. Satan's Prep: A Graphic Novel. 2014. (ENG., Illus.). 112p. (J). (gr. 6-6). 17.95 *(978-1-62873-592-5(9))*, Sky Pony Pr.) Skyhorse Publishing Co., Inc.

Guatemala, Anne. The Story of Señor Pico. Frazao, Catia, illus. 2007.Tr. of Historia del Señor Pico. (ENG & SPA.). 32p. (J). pap. 17.00 *(978-0-8059-7818-6(6))* Dorrance Publishing Co., Inc.

Gudsnuk, Kristen. Making Friends: a Graphic Novel (Making Friends #1) Gudsnuk, Kristen, illus. 2018. (Making Friends Ser.: 1). (ENG., Illus.). 272p. (J). (gr. 3-7). pap. 12.99 *(978-1-338-13921-1(5))*; Vol. 1. 24.99 *(978-1-338-13922-8(3))* Scholastic, Inc. (Graphix).

Guerin, F. A. The Witch at NO46: Verbroia. 2011. (Illus.). 140p. pap. 14.69 *(978-1-4567-7118-8(3))* AuthorHouse.

Guerra, Stephanie. Betting Blind, 0 vols. 2014. (Betting Blind Ser.: 1). (ENG.). 256p. (YA). (gr. 9-12). pap. 9.99 *(978-1-4778-4785-5(5))*, 9781477847855, Skyscape) Amazon Publishing.

Guest, Elissa Haden. Iris & Walter - The School Play. Davenier, Christine, illus. 2006. (Iris & Walter Ser.). 44p. (gr. 1-4). 15.95 *(978-0-7569-6679-9(5))* Perfection Learning Corp.

—Iris & Walter & the Substitute Teacher. Davenier, Christine, illus. 2006. (Iris & Walter Ser.). 44p. (gr. 1-4). 15.95 *(978-0-7569-7122-9(5))* Perfection Learning Corp.

Guignard, Lars. The Yogi's Curse. 2013. 342p. pap. *(978-0-9877753-9-9(1))* Guignard, Lars.

Gumfounded. 2004. (J). 13.95 *(978-0-9759866-0-8(0))* Garr, Sherry B.

Gunderson, Jessica. Desastre en el Musical. Aparicio Publishing LLC, Aparicio Publishing, tr. Cho, Sumin, illus. 2020. (Drama en la Secundaria Ser.). (SPA.). 64p. (J). (gr. 3-6). pap. 6.95 *(978-1-4965-9318-4(9))*, 142348); lib. bdg. 25.99 *(978-1-4965-9163-0(1))*, 142080) Capstone. (Stone Arch Bks.).

—The School Musical Meltdown. Cho, Sumin, illus. 2018. (Junior High Drama Ser.). (ENG.). 64p. (J). (gr. 3-6). 25.99 *(978-1-4965-4711-8(X))*, 135225, Stone Arch Bks.) Capstone.

Gunter, Tina. Monday. 2012. 30p. 24.95 *(978-1-4626-5164-1(X))* America Star Bks.

Gurevich, Margaret. All or Nothing. Hagel, Brooke, illus. 2016. (Chloe by Design Ser.). (ENG.). 96p. (J). (gr. 5-8). lib. bdg. 25.32 *(978-1-4965-3263-3(5))*, 132431, Stone Arch Bks.) Capstone.

—Back to Basics. Hagel, Brooke, illus. 2016. (Chloe by Design Ser.). (ENG.). 96p. (J). (gr. 5-8). lib. bdg. 25.32 *(978-1-4965-3261-9(9))*, 132429, Stone Arch Bks.) Capstone.

—Ballet Breakdown. Almon, Claire, illus. 2018. (Academy of Dance Ser.). (ENG.). 72p. (J). (gr. 3-6). lib. bdg. 25.32

(978-1-4965-6206-7(2), 137815, Stone Arch Bks.) Capstone.

—BFF Breakup. Almon, Claire, illus. 2018. (Academy of Dance Ser.). (ENG.). 72p. (J). (gr. 3-6). lib. bdg. 25.32 (978-1-4965-6205-0(4), 137814, Stone Arch Bks.) Capstone.

—Dance Team Bully. Almon, Claire, illus. 2018. (Academy of Dance Ser.). (ENG.). 72p. (J). (gr. 3-6). lib. bdg. 25.32 (978-1-4965-6203-6(8), 137812, Stone Arch Bks.) Capstone.

—The Final Cut. Hagel, Brooke, illus. 2016. (Chloe by Design Ser.). (ENG.). 96p. (J). (gr. 5-8). lib. bdg. 25.32 (978-1-4965-3264-0(3), 132432, Stone Arch Bks.) Capstone.

Gutknecht, Allison. The Bling Queen. 2016. (Mix Ser.). (ENG., Illus.). 208p. (J). (gr. 4-8). 17.99 (978-1-4814-5309-7(2), Simon & Schuster/Paula Wiseman Bks.) Simon & Schuster/Paula Wiseman Bks.

—A Cast Is the Perfect Accessory: (and Other Lessons I've Learned) Lewis, Stevie, illus. 2014. (ENG.). 160p. (J). (gr. 2-5). 16.99 (978-1-4424-8396-5(2)); pap. 6.99 (978-1-4424-8395-8(4)) Simon & Schuster Children's Publishing. (Aladdin).

—Don't Wear Polka-Dot Underwear with White Pants: (and Other Lessons I've Learned) Lewis, Stevie, illus. 2013. (ENG.). 160p. (J). (gr. 2-5). pap. 6.99 (978-1-4424-8392-7(X), Aladdin) Simon & Schuster Children's Publishing.

—Don't Wear Polka-Dot Underwear with White Pants: (and Other Lessons I've Learned) Lewis, Stevie, illus. 2013. (ENG.). 160p. (J). (gr. 2-5). 15.99 (978-1-4424-8393-4(8), Simon & Schuster/Paula Wiseman Bks.) Simon & Schuster/Paula Wiseman Bks.

—Never Wear Red Lipstick on Picture Day: (and Other Lessons I've Learned) Lewis, Stevie, illus. 2014. (ENG.). 176p. (J). (gr. 2-5). 16.99 (978-1-4814-2959-7(0)); pap. 6.99 (978-1-4814-2958-0(2)) Simon & Schuster Children's Publishing. (Aladdin).

—Sing Like Nobody's Listening. 2018. (Mix Ser.). (ENG.). 256p. (J). (gr. 4-8). 18.99 (978-1-4814-7157-2(0)); (Illus.). pap. 7.99 (978-1-4814-7156-5(2)) Simon & Schuster Children's Publishing. (Aladdin).

—Spring Break Mistake. 2017. (Mix Ser.). (ENG., Illus.). 240p. (J). (gr. 4-8). pap. 7.99 (978-1-4814-7153-4(8), Simon & Schuster/Paula Wiseman Bks.) Simon & Schuster/Paula Wiseman Bks.

Gutman, Dan. Bunny Double, We're in Trouble! 2014. (My Weird School Ser.). (J). lib. bdg. 16.00 (978-0-606-35055-6(1)) Turtleback.

—The Christmas Genie. Santat, Dan, illus. 2010. (ENG.). 176p. (J). (gr. 3-7). pap. 7.99 (978-1-4169-9002-4(X), Simon & Schuster Bks. For Young Readers) Simon & Schuster Bks. For Young Readers.

—Dr. Brad Has Gone Mad! 2009. (My Weird School Daze Ser.: 7). (J). lib. bdg. 14.75 (978-0-606-06969-4(0)) Turtleback.

—Dr. Carbles Is Losing His Marbles! Paillot, Jim, illus. 2007. (My Weird School Ser.: No. 19). 112p. (J). (gr. 2-5). lib. bdg. 15.89 (978-0-06-123478-1(8)) HarperCollins Pubs.

—Dr. Carbles Is Losing His Marbles! Paillot, Jim, illus. 2007. (My Weird School Ser.: No. 19). 99p. (J). (gr. 2-5). 11.65 (978-0-7569-8810-4(1)) Perfection Learning Corp.

—Dr. Nicholas Is Ridiculous! 2013. (My Weirder School Ser.: 8). (J). lib. bdg. 14.75 (978-0-606-31820-4(8)) Turtleback.

—The Homework Machine. 2014. (ENG.). 176p. (J). (gr. 3-7). 11.24 (978-1-63245-274-0(X)) Lectorum Pubns., Inc.

—The Homework Machine. 2006. (ENG., Illus.). 160p. (J). (gr. 3-7). 18.99 (978-0-689-87678-3(5), Simon & Schuster Bks. For Young Readers) Simon & Schuster Bks. For Young Readers.

—Mayor Hubble Is in Trouble! 2012. (My Weirder School Ser.: 6). (J). lib. bdg. 14.75 (978-0-606-26525-6(2)) Turtleback.

—The Million Dollar Putt. 2007. 69p. (J). (gr. 3-7). 13.65 (978-0-7569-8281-2(2)) Perfection Learning Corp.

—Miss Klute Is a Hoot! 2014. (My Weirder School Ser.: 11). (J). lib. bdg. 14.75 (978-0-606-35503-2(0)) Turtleback.

—Miss Kraft Is Daft! Paillot, Jim, illus. 2012. (My Weirder School Ser.: 7). (J). lib. bdg. 14.75 (978-0-606-27125-7(2)) Turtleback.

—Miss Laney Is Zany! 2010. (My Weird School Daze Ser.: 8). (J). lib. bdg. 14.75 (978-0-606-10112-7(8)) Turtleback.

—Miss Newman Isn't Human! Paillot, Jim, illus. 2018. 105p. (J). (978-1-5182-5371-3(7)) Harper & Row Ltd.

—Miss Newman Isn't Human! 2018. (My Weirdest School Ser.: 10). (Illus.). 105p. (J). lib. bdg. 14.75 (978-0-606-41046-5(5)) Turtleback.

—Miss Suki Is Kooky! Paillot, Jim, illus. 2007. (My Weird School Ser.: 17). (J). 14.75 (978-1-4177-7430-2(4)) Turtleback.

—Mr. Burke Is Berserk! 2012. (My Weirder School Ser.: 4). (J). lib. bdg. 14.75 (978-0-606-23571-6(X)) Turtleback.

—Mr. Cooper Is Super! Paillot, Jim, illus. 2015. (My Weirdest School Ser.: 1). (J). lib. bdg. 14.75 (978-0-606-36482-9(X)) Turtleback.

—Mr. Hynde Is Out of His Mind! Paillot, Jim, illus. 2005. (My Weird School Ser.: No. 6). 112p. (J). (gr. 2-5). lib. bdg. 15.89 (978-0-06-074521-9(5)) HarperCollins Pubs.

—Mr. Jack Is a Maniac! 2014. (My Weirder School Ser.: 10). (J). lib. bdg. 13.55 (978-0-606-35066-2(7)) Turtleback.

—Mr. Macky Is Wacky! Paillot, Jim, illus. 2006. (My Weird School Ser.: 15). (J). lib. bdg. 14.75 (978-1-4177-7429-6(0)) Turtleback.

—Mr. Will Needs to Chill. 2018. (My Weirdest School Ser.: 11). (J). lib. bdg. 14.75 (978-0-606-41378-7(2)) Turtleback.

—Mr. Will Needs to Chill!, 11. 2019. (My Weirdest School Ser.). (ENG.). 105p. (J). (gr. 2-3). 15.36 (978-1-64310-846-9(8)) Penworthy Co., LLC, The.

—Mrs. Jafee Is Daffy! 2009. (My Weird School Daze Ser.: 6). (J). lib. bdg. 14.75 (978-0-606-05035-7(3)) Turtleback.

—Mrs. Lane Is a Pain! 2014. (My Weirder School Ser.: 12). (J). lib. bdg. 14.75 (978-0-606-35964-1(8)) Turtleback.

—Mrs. Lizzy Is Dizzy! 2010. (My Weird School Daze Ser.: 9). (J). lib. bdg. 14.75 (978-0-606-10113-4(6)) Turtleback.

—Mrs. Master Is a Disaster! 2017. (My Weirdest School Ser.: 8). (Illus.). 105p. (J). lib. bdg. 14.75 (978-0-606-40078-7(8)) Turtleback.

—Mrs. Meyer Is on Fire! Paillot, Jim, illus. 2016. 105p. (J). (978-1-4806-9926-7(8)) Harper & Row Ltd.

—Mrs. Yonkers Is Bonkers! Paillot, Jim, illus. 2007. (My Weird School Ser.: 18). (J). 14.75 (978-1-4177-8222-2(6)) Turtleback.

—Ms. Beard Is Weird! 2012. (My Weirder School Ser.: 5). (J). lib. bdg. 14.75 (978-0-606-26295-8(4)) Turtleback.

—Ms. Coco Is Loco! Paillot, Jim, illus. 2007. (My Weird School Ser.: 16). (J). 14.75 (978-1-4177-7428-9(2)) Turtleback.

—Ms. Cuddy Is Nutty! Paillot, Jim, illus. 2015. 106p. (J). (978-1-4242-6518-3(5)) Harper & Row Ltd.

—Ms. Joni Is a Phony! Paillot, Jim, illus. 2017. 105p. (J). (978-1-5182-3403-3(8)) Harper & Row Ltd.

—Ms. Sue Has No Clue! 2013. (My Weirder School Ser.: 9). (J). lib. bdg. 14.75 (978-0-606-32173-0(X)) Turtleback.

—My Weird Reading Tips: Tips, Tricks & Secrets by the Author of My Weird School. 2019. (My Weird School Ser.). (ENG., Illus.). 224p. (J). (gr. 1-5). 16.99 (978-0-06-288240-0(6), HarperCollins) HarperCollins Pubs.

—My Weird Reading Tips: Tips, Tricks & Secrets from the Author of My Weird School. 2019. (My Weird School Ser.). (ENG., Illus.). 224p. (J). (gr. 1-5). pap. 6.99 (978-0-06-288239-4(2), HarperCollins) HarperCollins Pubs.

—My Weird School. 2017. (My Weird School - I Can Read Ser.). (J). lib. bdg. 13.55 (978-0-606-40067-1(2)) Turtleback.

—My Weird School: Talent Show Mix-Up. Paillot, Jim, illus. 2016. (My Weird School - I Can Read Ser.). (ENG.). 32p. (J). (gr. -1-3). 13.55 (978-0-606-39276-1(9)) Turtleback.

—My Weird School #1: Miss Daisy Is Crazy!, 1 vol. Paillot, Jim, illus. 2004. (My Weird School Ser.: 1). (ENG.). 96p. (J). (gr. 1-5). pap. 5.99 (978-0-06-050700-8(4), cd7f67f8-4d4e-4aec-9bc9-50817b6dc3f9, HarperCollins) HarperCollins Pubs.

—My Weird School #10: Mr. Docker Is off His Rocker! Paillot, Jim, illus. 2006. (My Weird School Ser.: 10). (ENG.). 112p. (J). (gr. 1-5). pap. 5.99 (978-0-06-082227-9(9), HarperCollins) HarperCollins Pubs.

—My Weird School #11: Mrs. Kormel Is Not Normal! Paillot, Jim, illus. 2006. (My Weird School Ser.: 11). (ENG.). 96p. (J). (gr. 1-5). pap. 5.99 (978-0-06-082229-3(5), HarperCollins) HarperCollins Pubs.

—My Weird School #13: Mrs. Patty Is Batty! Paillot, Jim, illus. 2006. (My Weird School Ser.: 13). (ENG.). 112p. (J). (gr. 1-5). pap. 5.99 (978-0-06-085380-8(8), HarperCollins) HarperCollins Pubs.

—My Weird School #14: Miss Holly Is Too Jolly! A Christmas Holiday Book for Kids. Paillot, Jim, illus. 2006. (My Weird School Ser.: 14). (ENG.). 112p. (J). (gr. 1-5). pap. 5.99 (978-0-06-085382-2(4), HarperCollins) HarperCollins Pubs.

—My Weird School #15: Mr. Macky Is Wacky! Paillot, Jim, illus. 2006. (My Weird School Ser.: 15). (ENG.). 112p. (J). (gr. 1-5). pap. 5.99 (978-0-06-114151-5(8), HarperCollins) HarperCollins Pubs.

—My Weird School #16: Ms. Coco Is Loco! Paillot, Jim, illus. 2007. (My Weird School Ser.: 16). (ENG.). 112p. (J). (gr. 1-5). pap. 5.99 (978-0-06-114153-9(4), HarperCollins) HarperCollins Pubs.

—My Weird School #17: Miss Suki Is Kooky! Paillot, Jim, illus. 2007. (My Weird School Ser.: 17). (ENG.). 112p. (J). (gr. 1-5). pap. 5.99 (978-0-06-123473-6(7), HarperCollins) HarperCollins Pubs.

—My Weird School #18: Mrs. Yonkers Is Bonkers! Paillot, Jim, illus. 2007. (My Weird School Ser.: 18). (ENG.). 112p. (J). (gr. 1-5). pap. 4.99 (978-0-06-123475-0(3), HarperCollins) HarperCollins Pubs.

—My Weird School #19: Dr. Carbles Is Losing His Marbles! Paillot, Jim, illus. 2007. (My Weird School Ser.: 19). (ENG.). 112p. (J). (gr. 1-5). pap. 5.99 (978-0-06-123477-4(X), HarperCollins) HarperCollins Pubs.

—My Weird School #2: Mr. Klutz Is Nuts!, No. 2. Paillot, Jim, illus. 2004. (My Weird School Ser.: 2). (ENG.). 112p. (J). (gr. 1-5). pap. 5.99 (978-0-06-050702-2(0), HarperCollins) HarperCollins Pubs.

—My Weird School #20: Mr. Louie Is Screwy! Paillot, Jim, illus. 2007. (My Weird School Ser.: 20). (ENG.). 112p. (J). (gr. 1-5). pap. 5.99 (978-0-06-123479-8(6), HarperCollins) HarperCollins Pubs.

—My Weird School #21: Ms. Krup Cracks Me Up! Paillot, Jim, illus. 2008. (My Weird School Ser.: 21). (ENG.). 112p. (J). (gr. 1-5). pap. 4.99 (978-0-06-134605-7(5), HarperCollins) HarperCollins Pubs.

—My Weird School #3: Mrs. Roopy Is Loopy! Paillot, Jim, illus. 2004. (My Weird School Ser.: 3). (ENG.). 96p. (J). (gr. 1-5). pap. 4.99 (978-0-06-050704-6(7), HarperCollins) HarperCollins Pubs.

—My Weird School 4 Books in 1! Books 1-4, 4 bks. in 1. Paillot, Jim, illus. 2016. (My Weird School Ser.). (ENG.). 384p. (J). (gr. 1-5). 16.99 (978-0-06-249668-3(9), HarperCollins) HarperCollins Pubs.

—My Weird School #4: Ms. Hannah Is Bananas! Paillot, Jim, illus. 2004. (My Weird School Ser.: 4). (ENG.). 96p. (J). (gr. 1-5). pap. 4.99 (978-0-06-050706-0(3), HarperCollins) HarperCollins Pubs.

—My Weird School #5: Miss Small Is off the Wall! Paillot, Jim, illus. 2005. (My Weird School Ser.: 5). (ENG.). 112p. (J). (gr. 1-5). pap. 4.99 (978-0-06-074518-9(5), HarperCollins) HarperCollins Pubs.

—My Weird School #6: Mr. Hynde Is Out of His Mind! Paillot, Jim, illus. 2005. (My Weird School Ser.: 6). (ENG.). 112p. (J). (gr. 1-5). pap. 5.99 (978-0-06-074520-2(7), HarperCollins) HarperCollins Pubs.

—My Weird School #7: Mrs. Cooney Is Loony! Paillot, Jim, illus. 2005. (My Weird School Ser.: 7). (ENG.). 112p. (J). (gr. 1-5). pap. 5.99 (978-0-06-074522-6(3), HarperCollins) HarperCollins Pubs.

—My Weird School #8: Ms. Lagrange Is Strange! Paillot, Jim, illus. 2005. (My Weird School Ser.: 8). (ENG.). 112p. (J). (gr. 1-5). pap. 5.99 (978-0-06-082223-1(6), HarperCollins) HarperCollins Pubs.

—My Weird School #9: Miss Lazar Is Bizarre! Paillot, Jim, illus. 2005. (My Weird School Ser.: 9). (ENG.). 96p. (J). (gr. 1-5). pap. 5.99 (978-0-06-082225-5(2), HarperCollins) HarperCollins Pubs.

—My Weird School: Class Pet Mess! Paillot, Jim, illus. 2017. (I Can Read Level 2 Ser.). (ENG.). 32p. (J). (gr. -1-3). pap. 4.99 (978-0-06-236746-4(3), HarperCollins) HarperCollins Pubs.

—My Weird School Collection: Books 1 To 4, Bks. 1-4. Paillot, Jim, illus. 2010. (My Weird School Ser.). (ENG.). (J). (gr. 1-5). pap. 16.99 (978-0-06-189489-3(3), HarperCollins) HarperCollins Pubs.

—My Weird School Daze! Paillot, Jim, illus. 2007. (J). (978-1-4287-4814-9(8)) HarperCollins Pubs.

—My Weird School Daze #1: Mrs. Dole Is Out of Control! Paillot, Jim, illus. 2008. (My Weird School Daze Ser.: 1). (ENG.). 112p. (J). (gr. 1-5). pap. 4.99 (978-0-06-134607-1(1), HarperCollins) HarperCollins Pubs.

—My Weird School Daze #10: Miss Mary Is Scary! Paillot, Jim, illus. 2010. (My Weird School Daze Ser.: 10). (ENG.). 112p. (J). (gr. 1-5). pap. 4.99 (978-0-06-170397-3(4), HarperCollins) HarperCollins Pubs.

—My Weird School Daze #11: Mr. Tony Is Full of Baloney! Paillot, Jim, illus. 2010. (My Weird School Daze Ser.: 11). (ENG.). 112p. (J). (gr. 1-5). pap. 4.99 (978-0-06-170399-7(0)); lib. bdg. 15.89 (978-0-06-170400-0(8)) HarperCollins Pubs. (HarperCollins).

—My Weird School Daze #12: Ms. Leakey Is Freaky! Paillot, Jim, illus. 2011. (My Weird School Daze Ser.: 12). (ENG.). 112p. (J). (gr. 1-5). lib. bdg. 15.89 (978-0-06-170403-1(2), HarperCollins) HarperCollins Pubs.

—My Weird School Daze #12: Ms. Leakey Is Freaky! No. 12. Paillot, Jim, illus. 2011. (My Weird School Daze Ser.: 12). (ENG.). 112p. (J). (gr. 1-5). pap. 4.99 (978-0-06-170402-4(4), HarperCollins) HarperCollins Pubs.

—My Weird School Daze #2: Mr. Sunny Is Funny! Paillot, Jim, illus. 2008. (My Weird School Daze Ser.: 2). (ENG.). 112p. (J). (gr. 1-5). pap. 4.99 (978-0-06-134609-5(8));No. 2. lib. bdg. 15.89 (978-0-06-134610-1(1)) HarperCollins Pubs. (HarperCollins).

—My Weird School Daze #3: Mr. Granite Is from Another Planet!, No. 3. Paillot, Jim, illus. 2008. (My Weird School Daze Ser.: 3). (ENG.). 112p. (J). (gr. 1-5). pap. 4.99 (978-0-06-134611-8(X), HarperCollins) HarperCollins Pubs.

—My Weird School Daze #4: Coach Hyatt Is a Riot! Paillot, Jim, illus. 2008. (My Weird School Daze Ser.: 4). (ENG.). 112p. (J). (gr. 1-5). lib. bdg. 15.89 (978-0-06-155408-7(1)); 4th ed. pap. 4.99 (978-0-06-155406-3(5)) HarperCollins Pubs. (HarperCollins).

—My Weird School Daze #5: Officer Spence Makes No Sense! Paillot, Jim, illus. 2009. (My Weird School Daze Ser.: 5). (ENG.). 112p. (J). (gr. 1-5). pap. 4.99 (978-0-06-155409-4(X), HarperCollins) HarperCollins Pubs.

—My Weird School Daze #6: Mrs. Jafee Is Daffy! Paillot, Jim, illus. 2009. (My Weird School Daze Ser.: 6). (ENG.). 128p. (J). (gr. 1-5). pap. 4.99 (978-0-06-155411-7(1), HarperCollins) HarperCollins Pubs.

—My Weird School Daze #8: Miss Laney Is Zany! Paillot, Jim, illus. 2010. (My Weird School Daze Ser.: 8). (ENG.). 112p. (J). (gr. 1-5). pap. 4.99 (978-0-06-155415-5(4), HarperCollins) HarperCollins Pubs.

—My Weird School Daze #9: Mrs. Lizzy Is Dizzy! Paillot, Jim, illus. 2010. (My Weird School Daze Ser.: 9). (ENG.). 112p. (J). (gr. 1-5). pap. 4.99 (978-0-06-155416-2(2)); lib. bdg. 15.89 (978-0-06-155418-6(9)) HarperCollins Pubs. (HarperCollins).

—My Weird School Goes to the Museum. Paillot, Jim, illus. 2016. 30p. (J). (978-1-5182-2157-6(2)) Harper & Row Ltd.

—My Weird School Goes to the Museum. Paillot, Jim, illus. 2016. (I Can Read Level 2 Ser.). (ENG.). 32p. (J). (gr. -1-3). pap. 5.99 (978-0-06-236742-6(0), HarperCollins) HarperCollins Pubs.

—My Weird School Special: Back to School, Weird Kids Rule! Paillot, Jim, illus. 2014. (My Weird School Special Ser.). (ENG.). 144p. (J). (gr. 1-5). lib. bdg. 16.89 (978-0-06-220686-2(9), HarperCollins) HarperCollins Pubs.

—My Weird School Special: Bummer in the Summer! Paillot, Jim, illus. 2019. (My Weird School Special Ser.). (ENG.). 144p. (J). (gr. 1-5). pap. 5.99 (978-0-06-279681-3(X)); lib. bdg. 16.89 (978-0-06-279682-0(8)) HarperCollins Pubs. (HarperCollins).

—My Weird School Special: Deck the Halls, We're off the Walls! Paillot, Jim, illus. 2013. (My Weird School Special Ser.). (ENG.). 144p. (J). (gr. 1-5). lib. bdg. 16.89 (978-0-06-220683-1(4), HarperCollins) HarperCollins Pubs.

—My Weird School Special: Deck the Halls, We're off the Walls! A Christmas Holiday Book for Kids. Paillot, Jim, illus. 2013. (My Weird School Special Ser.). (ENG.). 144p. (J). (gr. 1-5). pap. 5.99 (978-0-06-220682-4(6), HarperCollins) HarperCollins Pubs.

—My Weird School Special: It's Halloween, I'm Turning Green! Paillot, Jim, illus. 2013. (My Weird School Special Ser.). (ENG.). 144p. (J). (gr. 1-5). pap. 5.99 (978-0-06-220679-4(6), HarperCollins) HarperCollins Pubs.

—My Weird School Special: Oh, Valentine, We've Lost Our Minds! Paillot, Jim, illus. 2014. (My Weird School Special Ser.). (ENG.). 144p. (J). (gr. 1-5). pap. 6.99 (978-0-06-228403-7(7), HarperCollins) HarperCollins Pubs.

—My Weird School: Teamwork Trouble. Paillot, Jim, illus. 2018. (I Can Read Level 2 Ser.). (ENG.). 32p. (J). (gr. -1-3). 16.99 (978-0-06-236750-1(1)); pap. 5.99 (978-0-06-236749-5(8)) HarperCollins Pubs. (HarperCollins).

—My Weirder-Est School #1: Dr. Snow Has Got to Go! Paillot, Jim, illus. 2019. (My Weirder-Est School Ser.: 1). (ENG.). 112p. (J). (gr. 1-5). pap. 4.99 (978-0-06-269101-9(5)); lib. bdg. 16.89 (978-0-06-269102-6(3)) HarperCollins Pubs. (HarperCollins).

—My Weirder-Est School #2: Miss Porter Is Out of Order! Paillot, Jim, illus. 2019. (My Weirder-Est School Ser.: 2). (ENG.). 112p. (J). (gr. 1-5). pap. 6.99 (978-0-06-269104-0(X)); lib. bdg. 16.89 (978-0-06-269105-7(8)) HarperCollins Pubs. (HarperCollins).

—My Weirder School #10: Mr. Jack Is a Maniac! Paillot, Jim, illus. 2014. (My Weirder School Ser.: 10). (ENG.). 112p. (J). (gr. 1-5). pap. 4.99 (978-0-06-219841-9(6), HarperCollins) HarperCollins Pubs.

—My Weirder School #11: Miss Klute Is a Hoot! Paillot, Jim, illus. 2014. (My Weirder School Ser.: 11). (ENG.). 112p. (J). (gr. 1-5). 15.89 (978-0-06-219845-7(9)); pap. 6.99 (978-0-06-219844-0(0)) HarperCollins Pubs. (HarperCollins).

—My Weirder School #12: Mrs. Lane Is a Pain! Paillot, Jim, illus. 2014. (My Weirder School Ser.: 12). (ENG.). 112p. (J). (gr. 1-5). pap. 6.99 (978-0-06-219847-1(5), HarperCollins) HarperCollins Pubs.

—My Weirder School #2: Mr. Harrison Is Embarrassin'! 2. Paillot, Jim, illus. 2011. (My Weirder School Ser.: 2). (ENG.). 112p. (J). (gr. 1-5). pap. 4.99 (978-0-06-196918-8(4), HarperCollins) HarperCollins Pubs.

—My Weirder School #4: Mr. Burke Is Berserk! Paillot, Jim, illus. 2012. (My Weirder School Ser.: 4). (ENG.). 112p. (J). (gr. 1-5). pap. 6.99 (978-0-06-196922-5(2)); lib. bdg. 15.89 (978-0-06-196923-2(0)) HarperCollins Pubs. (HarperCollins).

—My Weirder School #6: Mayor Hubble Is in Trouble! Paillot, Jim, illus. 2012. (My Weirder School Ser.: 6). (ENG.). 112p. (J). (gr. 1-5). pap. 6.99 (978-0-06-204212-5(2)); lib. bdg. 15.89 (978-0-06-204213-2(0)) HarperCollins Pubs. (HarperCollins).

—My Weirder School #7: Miss Kraft Is Daft! Paillot, Jim, illus. 2012. (My Weirder School Ser.: 7). (ENG.). 112p. (J). (gr. 1-5). lib. bdg. 15.89 (978-0-06-204216-3(5));7. pap. 4.99 (978-0-06-204215-6(7)) HarperCollins Pubs. (HarperCollins).

—My Weirder School #8: Dr. Nicholas Is Ridiculous! Paillot, Jim, illus. 2013. (My Weirder School Ser.: 8). (ENG.). 112p. (J). (gr. 1-5). 15.89 (978-0-06-204219-4(X)); pap. 6.99 (978-0-06-204218-7(1)) HarperCollins Pubs. (HarperCollins).

—My Weirder School #9: Ms. Sue Has No Clue! Paillot, Jim, illus. 2013. (My Weirder School Ser.: 9). (ENG.). 112p. (J). (gr. 1-5). pap. 6.99 (978-0-06-219838-9(6)); lib. bdg. 15.89 (978-0-06-219839-6(4)) HarperCollins Pubs. (HarperCollins).

—My Weirdest School #1: Mr. Cooper Is Super! Paillot, Jim, illus. 2015. (My Weirdest School Ser.: 1). (ENG.). 112p. (J). (gr. 1-5). pap. 4.99 (978-0-06-228421-1(5), HarperCollins) HarperCollins Pubs.

—My Weirdest School #10: Miss Newman Isn't Human! Paillot, Jim, illus. 2018. (My Weirdest School Ser.: 10). (ENG.). 112p. (J). (gr. 1-5). pap. 4.99 (978-0-06-242939-1(6)); lib. bdg. 16.89 (978-0-06-242940-7(X)) HarperCollins Pubs. (HarperCollins).

—My Weirdest School #11: Mr. Will Needs to Chill! Paillot, Jim, illus. 2018. (My Weirdest School Ser.: 11). (ENG.). 112p. (J). (gr. 1-5). pap. 6.99 (978-0-06-242942-1(6), HarperCollins) HarperCollins Pubs.

—My Weirdest School #2: Ms. Cuddy Is Nutty! Paillot, Jim, illus. 2015. (My Weirdest School Ser.: 2). (ENG.). 112p. (J). (gr. 1-5). pap. 5.99 (978-0-06-228424-2(X)); lib. bdg. 15.89 (978-0-06-228425-9(8)) HarperCollins Pubs. (HarperCollins).

—My Weirdest School #3: Miss Brown Is Upside Down! Paillot, Jim, illus. 2015. (My Weirdest School Ser.: 3). (ENG.). 112p. (J). (gr. 1-5). pap. 5.99 (978-0-06-228427-3(4), HarperCollins) HarperCollins Pubs.

—My Weirdest School #4: Mrs. Meyer Is on Fire! Paillot, Jim, illus. 2016. (My Weirdest School Ser.: 4). (ENG.). 112p. (J). (gr. 1-5). pap. 5.99 (978-0-06-228430-3(4), HarperCollins) HarperCollins Pubs.

—My Weirdest School #5: Miss Daisy Is Still Crazy! Paillot, Jim, illus. 2016. (My Weirdest School Ser.: 5). (ENG.). 112p. (J). (gr. 1-5). lib. bdg. 15.89 (978-0-06-228433-4(9), HarperCollins) HarperCollins Pubs.

—My Weirdest School #6: Mr. Nick Is a Lunatic! Paillot, Jim, illus. 2016. (My Weirdest School Ser.: 6). (ENG.). 112p. (J). (gr. 1-5). pap. 5.99 (978-0-06-228436-5(3), HarperCollins) HarperCollins Pubs.

—My Weirdest School #7: Ms. Joni Is a Phony! Paillot, Jim, illus. 2017. (My Weirdest School Ser.: 7). (ENG.). 112p. (J). (gr. 1-5). pap. 4.99 (978-0-06-242929-2(9), HarperCollins) HarperCollins Pubs.

—My Weirdest School #8: Mrs. Master Is a Disaster! Paillot, Jim, illus. 2017. (My Weirdest School Ser.: 8). (ENG.). 112p. (J). (gr. 1-5). pap. 5.99 (978-0-06-242933-9(7), HarperCollins) HarperCollins Pubs.

—My Weirdest School #9: Miss Tracy Is Spacey! Paillot, Jim, illus. 2017. (My Weirdest School Ser.: 9). (ENG.). 112p. (J). (gr. 1-5). pap. 4.99 (978-0-06-242936-0(1)); lib. bdg. 16.89 (978-0-06-242937-7(X)) HarperCollins Pubs. (HarperCollins).

—Oh, Valentine, We've Lost Our Minds! 2014. (My Weird School Ser.). (J). lib. bdg. 16.00 (978-0-606-36460-7(9)) Turtleback.

—Rappy Goes to School. Bowers, Tim, illus. 2016. (ENG.). 40p. (J). (gr. -1-3). 17.99 (978-0-06-229181-3(5), HarperCollins) HarperCollins Pubs.

—Return of the Homework Machine. (ENG.). (J). (gr. 3-7). 2011. 192p. pap. 7.99 (978-1-4169-5459-0(7)) 2009. 176p. 18.99 (978-1-4169-5416-3(3)) Simon & Schuster Bks. For Young Readers. (Simon & Schuster Bks. For Young Readers).

—Teamwork Trouble. Paillot, Jim, illus. 2018. 30p. (J). (978-1-5444-0102-7(7)) Harper & Row Ltd.

—Teamwork Trouble. 2018. (My Weird School - I Can Read Ser.). (J). lib. bdg. 13.55 (978-0-606-41040-3(6)) Turtleback.

Guzzardi, Mary. The Magical Ice Skates. 2011. 50p. pap. 24.95 (978-1-4560-3246-3(1)) PublishAmerica, Inc.

Haas, Jessie. Saige Paints the Sky. Davis, Sarah, illus. 2012. (American Girl Today Ser.: Bk. 2). lib. bdg. 17.15 (978-0-606-31569-2(1)) Turtleback.

Haberdasher, Violet. Knightley Academy. 2011. (ENG.). 512p. (J). (gr. 3-7). pap. 5.99 (978-1-4169-9144-1(1), Aladdin) Simon & Schuster Children's Publishing.

—The Secret Prince: A Knightley Academy Book. (ENG.). 512p. (J). (gr. 3-7). 2012. pap. 7.99 (978-1-4169-9146-5(8)) 2011. 16.99 (978-1-4169-9145-8(X)) Simon & Schuster/Paula Wiseman Bks. (Simon & Schuster/Paula Wiseman Bks.).

Haddix, Margaret Peterson. Because of Anya. 2005. 114p. 16.00 (978-0-7569-4922-8(X)) Perfection Learning Corp.

—Children of Refuge. (Children of Exile Ser.: 2). (ENG.). (J). (gr. 5). 2018. 288p. pap. 7.99 (978-1-4424-5007-3(X)) 2017. (Illus.). 272p. 18.99 (978-1-4424-5006-6(1)) Simon & Schuster Bks. For Young Readers. (Simon & Schuster Bks. For Young Readers).

—Dexter the Tough. Elliott, Mark, illus. 2008. (ENG.). 144p. (J). (gr. 2-5). pap. 6.99 (978-1-4169-1170-8(7)) 2007. 141p. pap. 7.99 (978-0-15-377020-3(1)) Simon & Schuster Bks. For Young Readers. (Simon & Schuster Bks. For Young Readers).

—Full Ride. 2014. (ENG.). 368p. (YA). (gr. 7). pap. 12.99 (978-1-4424-4279-5(4), Simon & Schuster Bks. For Young Readers) Simon & Schuster Bks. For Young Readers.

Hahn, Mary Downing. Daphne's Book. 2008. (ENG., Illus.). 192p. (J). (gr. 5-7). pap. 7.99 *(978-0-547-01641-2(7),* 1031471, Clarion Bks.) HarperCollins Pubs.

—Janey & the Famous Author. Bush, Timothy, illus. 2005. (ENG.). 48p. (J). (gr. -1-3). 15.00 *(978-0-618-35408-5(5),* 100317, Clarion Bks.) HarperCollins Pubs.

Haig, Matt. To Be a Cat. Curtis, Stacy, illus. (ENG.). 304p. (J). (gr. 3-7). 2014. pap. 8.99 *(978-1-4424-5406-4(7))* 2013. 16.99 *(978-1-4424-5405-7(9))* Simon & Schuster Children's Publishing.

Halahmy, Miriam. Hidden. 2018. (ENG.). 224p. (YA). (gr. 7). pap. 9.99 *(978-0-8234-4026-9(5))* Holiday Hse., Inc.

Hale, Bruce. The Big Nap. unabr. ed. 2004. (Chet Gecko Mystery Ser.: No. 4). 128p. (J). (gr. 3-6). pap. 17.00 incl. audio *(978-0-8072-1707-8(7),* S FTR 272 SP, Listening Library) Random Hse. Audio Publishing Group.

—Clark the Shark. Francis, Guy, illus. 2013. (Clark the Shark Ser.). (ENG.). 32p. (J). (gr. -1-3). 18.99 *(978-0-06-219226-4(4),* HarperCollins) HarperCollins Pubs.

—Clark the Shark & the Big Book Report. Francis, Guy, illus. 2017. 32p. (J). *(978-1-5182-4609-8(5))* HarperCollins Pubs.

—Dial M for Mongoose: A Chet Gecko Mystery. 2010. (Chet Gecko Ser.: 15). (ENG., Illus.). 128p. (J). (gr. 3-7). pap. 6.99 *(978-0-547-48079-4(2),* 1439406, Clarion Bks.) HarperCollins Pubs.

—Farewell, My Lunchbag: A Chet Gecko Mystery. Hale, Bruce, illus. 2009. (Chet Gecko Ser.: 3). (ENG., Illus.). 128p. (J). (gr. 3-7). pap. 6.99 *(978-0-15-202629-5(0),* 1193357, Clarion Bks.) HarperCollins Pubs.

—From Russia with Lunch: A Chet Gecko Mystery. Hale, Bruce, illus. 2010. (Chet Gecko Ser.: 14). (ENG., Illus.). 128p. (J). (gr. 3-7). pap. 6.99 *(978-0-547-32882-9(6),* 1416990, Clarion Bks.) HarperCollins Pubs.

—Give My Regrets to Broadway. 2005. (Chet Gecko Mystery Ser.). (Illus.). 115p. (gr. 3-7). 16.00 *(978-0-7569-5247-1(6))* Perfection Learning Corp.

—Give My Regrets to Broadway: A Chet Gecko Mystery. Hale, Bruce, illus. 2005. (Chet Gecko Ser.: 9). (ENG., Illus.). 144p. (J). (gr. 3-7). pap. 6.99 *(978-0-15-216730-1(7),* 1201742, Clarion Bks.) HarperCollins Pubs.

—The Hamster of the Baskervilles: A Chet Gecko Mystery. Hale, Bruce, illus. 2003. (Chet Gecko Ser.: 5). (ENG., Illus.). 144p. (J). (gr. 3-7). pap. 6.99 *(978-0-15-202509-0(X),* 1063329, Clarion Bks.) HarperCollins Pubs.

—Hiss Me Deadly: A Chet Gecko Mystery. Hale, Bruce, illus. 2009. (Chet Gecko Ser.: 13). (ENG., Illus.). 128p. (J). (gr. 3-7). pap. 6.99 *(978-0-15-206424-2(9),* 1063327, Clarion Bks.) HarperCollins Pubs.

—Key Lardo: A Chet Gecko Mystery. Hale, Bruce, illus. 2007. (Chet Gecko Ser.: 12). (ENG., Illus.). 128p. (J). (gr. 3-7). pap. 7.99 *(978-0-15-205235-5(6),* 1195772, Clarion Bks.) HarperCollins Pubs.

—The Malted Falcon. 2004. (Chet Gecko Mystery Ser.: 7). (ENG., Illus.). 128p. (J). (gr. 4-6). 17.44 *(978-0-15-216706-6(4))* Harcourt Children's Bks.

—The Malted Falcon. 2007. (Chet Gecko Mystery Ser.). (Illus.). 107p. (J). (gr. 4-7). pap. 6.60 *(978-1-4189-5239-6(7))* Harcourt Trade Pubs.

—The Malted Falcon: A Chet Gecko Mystery. Hale, Bruce, illus. 2008. (Chet Gecko Ser.: 7). (ENG., Illus.). 128p. (J). (gr. 3-7). pap. 9.99 *(978-0-15-216712-7(9),* 1201705, Clarion Bks.) HarperCollins Pubs.

—Murder, My Tweet. 2005. (Chet Gecko Mystery Ser.). (Illus.). 117p. (gr. 3-7). 16.00 *(978-0-7569-5248-8(4))* Perfection Learning Corp.

—The Possum Always Rings Twice. Hale, Bruce, illus. 2007. (Chet Gecko Ser.: 11). (ENG., Illus.). 128p. (J). (gr. 3-7). pap. 7.99 *(978-0-15-205233-1(X),* 1195769, Clarion Bks.) HarperCollins Pubs.

—This Gum for Hire. 2007. (Chet Gecko Mystery Ser.). (Illus.). 115p. (J). (gr. 4-7). pap. 6.60 *(978-1-4189-5216-7(8))* Houghton Mifflin Harcourt Supplemental Pubs.

—This Gum for Hire: A Chet Gecko Mystery. Hale, Bruce, illus. 2003. (Chet Gecko Ser.: 6). (ENG., Illus.). 144p. (J). (gr. 3-7). pap. 6.99 *(978-0-15-202497-0(2),* 1192976, Clarion Bks.) HarperCollins Pubs.

—Trouble Is My Beeswax. Weinman, Brad, illus. 2003. (Chet Gecko Mystery Ser.: 8). (ENG.). 128p. (J). (gr. 4-6). 17.44 *(978-0-15-216718-9(8))* Houghton Mifflin Harcourt Publishing Co.

—Trouble Is My Beeswax. 2004. (Chet Gecko Mystery Ser.). (Illus.). 111p. (gr. 3-7). 16.00 *(978-0-7569-3488-0(5))* Perfection Learning Corp.

—Trouble Is My Beeswax: A Chet Gecko Mystery. Hale, Bruce, illus. 2004. (Chet Gecko Ser.: 8). (ENG., Illus.). 144p. (J). (gr. 3-7). pap. 6.99 *(978-0-15-216724-0(2),* 1099020, Clarion Bks.) HarperCollins Pubs.

Hale, Shannon. Palace of Stone. 2015. (Princess Academy Ser.: 2). (YA). lib. bdg. 18.40 *(978-0-606-36439-3(0))* Turtleback.

—Princess Academy. (Princess Academy Ser.: 1). (ENG.). (gr. 5-8). 2005. 320p. (YA). 17.99 *(978-1-58234-993-0(2),* 900031142) 2nd ed. 2015. 336p. (J). pap. 9.99 *(978-1-61963-613-2(1),* 900142415) Bloomsbury Publishing USA. (Bloomsbury USA Childrens).

—Princess Academy. 2009. (Princess Academy Ser.: No. 1). 8.86 *(978-0-7848-2867-0(9),* Everbind) Marco Bk. Co.

—Princess Academy. 2007. (Princess Academy Ser.: No. 1). 314p. (gr. 5-9). 18.00 *(978-0-7569-8180-8(8))* Perfection Learning Corp.

—Princess Academy. (Princess Academy Ser.: No. 1). *(978-0-439-88811-0(5),* Scholastic) Scholastic, Inc.

—Princess Academy. I.t. ed. 2006. (Princess Academy Ser.: No. 1). 339p. (J). (gr. 5-9). 23.95 *(978-0-7862-8733-8(0))* Thorndike Pr.

—Princess Academy. 2015. (Princess Academy Ser.: 1). (YA). lib. bdg. 18.40 *(978-0-606-36438-6(2))* Turtleback.

—Princess Academy: Palace of Stone. (Princess Academy Ser.: 2). (ENG.). (gr. 5-8). 2015. 352p. (J). pap. 8.99 *(978-1-61963-257-8(8),* 900131475) 2012. 336p. (YA). 17.99 *(978-1-59990-873-1(5),* 900082614) Bloomsbury Publishing USA. (Bloomsbury USA Childrens).

—Princess Academy: the Forgotten Sisters. 2015. (Princess Academy Ser.: 3). (ENG.). 336p. (YA). (gr. 5-8). 18.99 *(978-1-61963-485-5(6),* 900138574, Bloomsbury USA Childrens) Bloomsbury Publishing USA.

—The Storybook of Legends. 2017. (Ever after High Ser.: 1). (J). lib. bdg. 18.40 *(978-0-606-40630-7(1))* Turtleback.

—The Unfairest of Them All. 2018. (Ever after High Ser.: 2). (J). lib. bdg. 18.40 *(978-0-606-40986-5(6))* Turtleback.

—A Wonderlandiful World. 2018. (Ever after High Ser.: 3). (J). lib. bdg. 18.40 *(978-0-606-40985-8(8))* Turtleback.

Hale, Shannon, et al. Real Friends. 1. 2017. (Real Friends Ser.). (ENG., Illus.). 224p. (J). (gr. 4-6). lib. bdg. 31.19 *(978-1-5364-0968-0(5),* First Second Bks.) Roaring Brook Pr.

Hall, Hannah. God Bless My School. 1 vol. Whitlow, Steve, illus. 2017. (God Bless Book Ser.). (ENG.). 20p. (J). bds. 9.99 *(978-0-7180-1109-3(0),* Tommy Nelson) Nelson, Thomas Inc.

Hall, Kirsten. My New School (My First Reader) Gott, Barry, illus. 2004. (My First Reader (Reissue) Ser.). (ENG.). 32p. (J). (gr. k-1). pap. 4.95 *(978-0-516-25505-7(3),* Children's Pr.) Scholastic Library Publishing.

Hall, Rosemary. The Kids Knee Garden from the Adventures with Lamb E. Boy Series. 2008. (ENG.). 30p. pap. 9.13 *(978-1-4196-8967-3(3))* CreateSpace Independent Publishing Platform.

Hall, Sandy. A Prom to Remember. 2018. (ENG.). 320p. (YA). 27.99 *(978-1-250-11914-8(6),* 900172684) Feiwel & Friends.

—A Prom to Remember. 2019. (ENG.). 336p. (YA). pap. 10.99 *(978-1-250-30920-4(4),* 900198433) Square Fish.

Halliday, Gemma. Social Suicide. 2012. (Deadly Cool Ser.: 2). (ENG.). 288p. (YA). (gr. 8). pap. 8.99 *(978-0-06-200332-4(1),* HarperTeen) HarperCollins Pubs.

Hallinan, P. K. Let's Learn All We Can! (ENG., Illus.). 24p. (J). pap. 6.55 *(978-0-8249-5449-9(1),* Ideals Pubns.) Worthy Publishing.

Halpern, Julie. Into the Wild Nerd Yonder. 2011. (ENG.). 272p. (YA). (gr. 8-12). 17.99 *(978-0-312-65307-1(7),* 900069445) Square Fish.

Halse Anderson, Laurie. Prom. 2006. (YA). 1.25 *(978-1-4193-5096-2(X))* Recorded Bks., Inc.

—Speak. 2010. (CHI.). (YA). (gr. 7-12). pap. *(978-986-6488-66-5(7))* Ecus Publishing Hse.

—Speak. 2006. 24.50 *(978-0-8446-7292-2(0))* Smith, Peter Pub., Inc.

—Twisted. 2014. (ENG.). 288p. (YA). (gr. 7-12). 14.24 *(978-1-63245-343-3(6))* Lectorum Pubns., Inc.

—Twisted. 2011. 11.04 *(978-0-7848-3388-9(5),* Everbind) Marco Bk. Co.

—Twisted. I.t. ed. 2007. (Literacy Bridge Young Adult Ser.). 299p. (YA). (gr. 7-12). 23.95 *(978-0-7862-9885-3(5))* Thorndike Pr.

Hambrick, Sharon. Brain Games. 2009. (J). 8.99 *(978-1-59166-954-8(5))* BJU Pr.

—Tommy's Rocket. Manning, Maurie J., illus. 2003. (Fig Street Kids Ser.). 83p. (J). (gr. 1-2). 7.49 *(978-1-59166-186-3(2))* BJU Pr.

Hamburg, Jennifer. Hazy Bloom & the Tomorrow Power. Harney, Jenn, illus. 2018. (Hazy Bloom Ser.: 1). (ENG.). 192p. (J). pap. 9.99 *(978-1-250-14355-6(1),* 900162027) Square Fish.

Hamilton, Laura, reader. Vera's First Day of School. unabr. ed. 2006. (Picture Book Readalong Ser.). (Illus.). (J). (gr. -1-3). 25.95 incl. audio *(978-1-59519-662-0(5));* pap. 39.95 incl. audio compact disk *(978-1-59519-661-3(7));*Set. pap. 37.95 incl. audio *(978-1-59519-660-6(9))* Live Oak Media.

Hamilton, Pamela Greenhalgh. Snow Day. 2011. 34p. (J). pap. 18.95 *(978-1-4327-5743-4(1))* Outskirts Pr., Inc.

Hamlyn, Jean. Clumsy Daisy Goes to School. 2009. (Illus.). 36p. pap. 16.99 *(978-1-4490-3517-4(5))* AuthorHouse.

Hammonds Reed, Christina. The Black Kids. (ENG.). (YA). (gr. 9). 2022. 400p. pap. 12.99 *(978-1-5344-6273-1(2))* 2020. (Illus.). 368p. 19.99 *(978-1-5344-6272-4(4))* Simon & Schuster Bks. For Young Readers. (Simon & Schuster Bks. For Young Readers).

Han, Jenny. Clara Lee & the Apple Pie Dream. 2014. (ENG.). 160p. (J). (gr. 3-7). pap. 10.99 *(978-0-316-07037-9(8))* Little, Brown Bks. for Young Readers.

Han, Jenny & Vivian, Siobhan. Burn for Burn. (Burn for Burn Trilogy Ser.). (ENG.). (YA). (gr. 9). 2013. Illus.). 400p. pap. 12.99 *(978-1-4424-4076-0(7))* 2012. 368p. 19.99 *(978-1-4424-4075-3(9))* Simon & Schuster Bks. For Young Readers. (Simon & Schuster Bks. For Young Readers).

—Fire with Fire. 2013. (Burn for Burn Trilogy Ser.). (ENG., Illus.). 528p. (YA). (gr. 9). 17.99 *(978-1-4424-4078-4(3),* Simon & Schuster Bks. For Young Readers) Simon & Schuster Bks. For Young Readers.

Hancock, H. Irving. The High School Freshmen: Or, Dick & Co. 's First Year Pranks & Sports. 2017. (ENG., Illus.). (J). 23.95 *(978-1-374-93030-8(X));* pap. 13.95 *(978-1-374-93029-2(6))* Capital Communications, Inc.

—The High School Freshmen: Or, Dick & Co. 's First Year Pranks & Sports. 2017. (ENG., Illus.). (J). pap. *(978-0-649-60244-5(7))* Trieste Publishing Pty Ltd.

—The High School Freshmen; or, Dick & Co. 's First Year Pranks & Sports. 2017. (ENG., Illus.). (J). pap. *(978-0-649-14431-0(7))* Trieste Publishing Pty Ltd.

—The High School Pitcher. 2007. 176p. per. *(978-1-4065-1990-7(1))* Dodo Pr.

Hand, Cynthia. Boundless. 2013. (Unearthly Ser.: 3). (ENG.). 448p. (YA). (gr. 8). pap. 9.99 *(978-0-06-199621-4(1),* HarperTeen) HarperCollins Pubs.

—Hallowed: An Unearthly Novel. 2012. (Unearthly Ser.: 2). (ENG.). 432p. (YA). (gr. 8). pap. 10.99 *(978-0-06-199619-1(X),* HarperTeen) HarperCollins Pubs.

—Unearthly. 2011. (Unearthly Ser.: 1). (ENG.). 464p. (YA). (gr. 8). pap. 9.99 *(978-0-06-199617-7(3),* HarperTeen) HarperCollins Pubs.

Hanks, Larry R. Stickboy. 1 vol. 2010. 28p. 24.95 *(978-1-4489-5141-3(0))* PublishAmerica, Inc.

Hanlon, Abby. Dory & the Real True Friend. 2016. (Dory Ser.: 2). lib. bdg. 18.40 *(978-0-606-38846-7(X))* Turtleback.

—Dory Fantasmagory: the Real True Friend. 2015. (Dory Fantasmagory Ser.: 2). (ENG., Illus.). 160p. (J). (gr. 1-3). 16.99 *(978-0-525-42866-4(6),* Dial Bks) Penguin Young Readers Group.

—Ralph Tells a Story. 0 vols. Hanlon, Abby, illus. 2012. (ENG.). 40p. (J). (gr. 1-3). 16.99 *(978-0-7614-6180-7(9),* 9780761461807, Two Lions) Amazon Publishing.

Hannigan, Katherine. Ida B: ... & Her Plans to Maximize Fun, Avoid Disaster, & (Possibly) Save the World. 2004. (ENG.). 256p. (J). (gr. 4-18). 17.99 *(978-0-06-073024-6(2),* Greenwillow Bks.) HarperCollins Pubs.

—Ida B: ... And Her Plans to Maximize Fun, Avoid Disaster, & (Possibly) Save the World. 2004. 256p. (gr. 4-18). lib. bdg. 16.89 *(978-0-06-073025-3(0))* HarperCollins Pubs.

—Ida B: ... & Her Plans to Maximize Fun, Avoid Disaster, & (Possibly) Save the World. 2011. (ENG.). 272p. (J). (gr. 5-9). reprint ed. pap. 7.99 *(978-0-06-073026-0(9),* Greenwillow Bks.) HarperCollins Pubs.

Hanover, Rebecca. The Similars. 2019. (Similars Ser.). (ENG.). (YA). (gr. 8-12). 416p. pap. 10.99 *(978-1-4926-9180-8(1));* 400p. 17.99 *(978-1-4926-6510-6(X))* Sourcebooks, Inc.

Hansen, Joyce. Yellow Bird & Me. 2005. (ENG.). 160p. (J). (gr. 5-7). pap. 7.99 *(978-0-618-61116-4(9),* 100446, Clarion Bks.) HarperCollins Pubs.

—Yellow Bird & Me. 2005. (163rd Street Ser.). 155p. (gr. 5-9). 16.95 *(978-0-7569-6228-9(5))* Perfection Learning Corp.

Hanson, Bonnie Compton. Meet the Ponytail Girls. 2004. (Ponytail Girls Ser.). (Illus.). 208p. (J). pap. 7.99 *(978-1-58411-029-3(5),* Legacy Pr.) Rainbow Pubs. & Legacy Pr.

Hapka, Catherine A., et al. How to Start Kindergarten: A Book for Kindergarteners. Palen, Debbie, illus. 2018. (Step into Reading Ser.). 32p. (J). (gr. -1-1). pap. 5.99 *(978-1-5247-1551-9(4),* Random Hse. Bks. for Young Readers) Random Hse. Children's Bks.

Hapka, Catherine, pseud. Dolphin School: Echo's New Pet. 2017. (ENG., Illus.). 107p. (J). pap. 4.99 *(978-1-338-05374-6(4))* Scholastic, Inc.

—Friends 4 Ever? 2008. (High School Musical Stories from East High Ser.). 124p. (J). (gr. 3-7). 12.65 *(978-0-7569-8820-3(9))* Perfection Learning Corp.

Hapka, Cathy, pseud & Titlebaum, Ellen. How Not to Start Third Grade. Palen, Debbie, illus. 2007. (Step into Reading Ser.). 48p. (J). (gr. 2-4). pap. 5.99 *(978-0-375-83904-7(6),* Random Hse. Bks. for Young Readers) Random Hse. Children's Bks.

Hara, Yui. Kiniro Mosaic, Vol. 1. 2016. (Kiniro Mosaic Ser.: 1). (ENG., Illus.). 128p. (J). (gr. 8-17). pap. 17.00 *(978-0-316-50146-0(8))* Yen Pr. LLC.

Harcourt School Publishers Staff. Going to School, Unit 1. 3rd ed. 2003. (Horizons Ser.). (Illus.). (gr. 1). pap. 166.70 *(978-0-15-340220-3(2))* Harcourt Schl. Pubs.

Hardy, LeAnne. Between Two Worlds: A Novel. 2003. 160p. (J). pap. 7.99 *(978-0-8254-2793-0(2))* Kregel Pubns.

Hare, Eric B. Curse Proof. 2007. (Illus.). 95p. (J). 10.99 *(978-0-8163-2208-4(2))* Pacific Pr. Publishing Assn.

Harewood, Sean C. It's Only the First Day. 2008. 48p. pap. 19.49 *(978-1-4343-7367-0(3))* AuthorHouse.

Harimann, Sierra. Caring Classmates. Aparicio, Núria, illus. 2016. 32p. (J). *(978-1-338-03340-3(9))* Scholastic, Inc.

—Diploma Day. 2011. (Illus.). 30p. (J). pap. *(978-0-545-28143-0(1))* Scholastic, Inc.

Harkrader, Lisa. A Fishy Mystery. Pillo, Cary, illus. 2017. (Math Matters Ser.). 32p. (J). (gr. k-4). 5.99 *(978-1-57565-866-7(6),* 6d95be58-8319-4d28-9b99-9a327899b7ae, Kane Press) Astra Publishing Hse.

—A Fishy Mystery: Venn Diagrams. Pillo, Cary, illus. 2017. (Math Matters (r) Ser.). (ENG.). 32p. (J). (gr. k-3). E-Book 23.99 *(978-1-57565-869-8(0))* Astra Publishing Hse.

—Librarians of the Galaxy (Book 11) Warrick, Jessica, illus. 2018. (How to Be an Earthling Ser.). 64p. (J). (gr. 1-4). pap. 6.99 *(978-1-63592-024-6(8),* a1e9e1da-a4fc-4072-a75d-e437b7560403, Kane Press) Astra Publishing Hse.

—Planet of the Eggs (Book 9) Warrick, Jessica, illus. 2018. (How to Be an Earthling Ser.). 64p. (J). (gr. 1-4). pap. 6.99 *(978-1-63592-018-5(3),* ca37f429-326f-4c6e-981a-791228884feb, Kane Press) Astra Publishing Hse.

Harley, Bill. Charlie Bumpers vs. His Big Blabby Mouth. Gustavson, Adam, illus. 2018. (Charlie Bumpers Ser.: 6). 192p. (J). (gr. 2-5). pap. 7.99 *(978-1-68263-064-8(1))* Peachtree Publishing Co. Inc.

—Charlie Bumpers vs. the End of the Year. 1 vol. Gustavson, Adam, illus. 2019. (Charlie Bumpers Ser.: 7). 208p. (J). (gr. 2-5). 14.95 *(978-1-68263-042-6(0))* Peachtree Publishing Co. Inc.

—Charlie Bumpers vs. the Really Nice Gnome. 1 vol. Gustavson, Adam, illus. (Charlie Bumpers Ser.: 2). 160p. (J). (gr. 2-5). 2015. pap. 7.99 *(978-1-56145-831-8(7))* 2014. 13.95 *(978-1-56145-740-3(X))* Peachtree Publishing Co. Inc.

—Charlie Bumpers vs. the Squeaking Skull. 1 vol. Gustavson, Adam, illus. 2015. (Charlie Bumpers Ser.: 3). 176p. (J). (gr. 2-5). pap. 7.99 *(978-1-56145-888-2(0))* Peachtree Publishing Co. Inc.

—Charlie Bumpers vs. the Teacher of the Year. 1 vol. Gustavson, Adam, illus. (Charlie Bumpers Ser.: 1). 160p. (J). (gr. 2-5). 2014. pap. 7.99 *(978-1-56145-824-0(4))* 2013. 14.95 *(978-1-56145-732-8(9))* Peachtree Publishing Co. Inc.

—Lost & Found. 1 vol. Gustavson, Adam, illus. 2012. 32p. (J). (gr. -1-3). 16.95 *(978-1-56145-628-4(4))* Peachtree Publishing Co. Inc.

Harmer, Wendy. I Lost My Mobile at the Mall. 2011. (ENG.). 272p. (YA). (gr. 7-18). 10.99 *(978-1-935279-97-6(1))* Kane Miller.

Harmon, Michael. Brutal. 2011. 240p. (YA). (gr. 9). pap. 8.99 *(978-0-440-23995-6(8),* Knopf Bks. for Young Readers) Random Hse. Children's Bks.

—Skate. 2008. 256p. (YA). (gr. 9). per. 7.99 *(978-0-553-49510-2(0),* Laurel Leaf) Random Hse. Children's Bks.

Harney, D. G. Meet Mr. Ugly. 1 vol. 2010. 133p. pap. 24.95 *(978-1-4489-5191-8(7))* America Star Bks.

Harper, Charise Mericle. Crafty Cat & the Great Butterfly Battle. 2018. (Crafty Cat Ser.: 3). (ENG., Illus.). 128p. (J). 13.99 *(978-1-62672-487-7(3),* 900158674, First Second Bks.) Roaring Brook Pr.

—Just Grace. 2008. (Just Grace Ser.: 1). (ENG., Illus.). 144p. (J). (gr. 1-4). pap. 7.99 *(978-0-547-01440-1(6),* 1030987, Clarion Bks.) HarperCollins Pubs.

—Just Grace & the Snack Attack. 2010. (Just Grace Ser.: 5). (ENG., Illus.). 176p. (J). (gr. 1-4). pap. 7.99 *(978-0-547-40629-9(0),* 1428507, Clarion Bks.) HarperCollins Pubs.

—Just Grace & the Trouble with Cupcakes. 2014. (Just Grace Ser.: 10). (ENG., Illus.). 208p. (J). (gr. 1-4). pap. 7.99 *(978-0-544-33910-1(X),* 1584481, Clarion Bks.) HarperCollins Pubs.

—Just Grace, Star on Stage. 2014. (Just Grace Ser.: 9). (ENG., Illus.). 208p. (J). (gr. 1-4). pap. 7.99 *(978-0-544-22533-6(3),* 1563387, Clarion Bks.) HarperCollins Pubs.

—Just Grace Walks the Dog. 2009. (Just Grace Ser.: 3). (ENG., Illus.). 176p. (J). (gr. 1-4). pap. 7.99 *(978-0-547-23753-4(7),* 1083855, Clarion Bks.) HarperCollins Pubs.

—Still Just Grace. 2009. (Just Grace Ser.: 2). (ENG., Illus.). 160p. (J). (gr. 1-4). pap. 7.99 *(978-0-618-93482-9(0),* 1018125, Clarion Bks.) HarperCollins Pubs.

Harper, Jamie. Miss Mingo & the Fire Drill. Harper, Jamie, illus. 2012. (Miss Mingo Ser.). (ENG., Illus.). 40p. (J). (gr. -1-3). pap. 7.99 *(978-0-7636-6086-4(8))* Candlewick Pr.

—Miss Mingo & the First Day of School. Harper, Jamie, illus. 2009. (Miss Mingo Ser.). (ENG., Illus.). 32p. (J). (gr. -1-3). pap. 7.99 *(978-0-7636-4134-4(0))* Candlewick Pr.

—Miss Mingo & the First Day of School. 2006. (Illus.). 26p. (J). *(978-1-4156-9174-8(6))* Candlewick Pr.

—Miss Mingo Weathers the Storm. Harper, Jamie, illus. (Miss Mingo Ser.). (ENG., Illus.). 40p. (J). (gr. -1-3). 2017. 6.99 *(978-0-7636-9514-9(9))* 2012. 15.99 *(978-0-7636-4931-9(7))* Candlewick Pr.

Harper, Jessica. A Place Called Kindergarten. Karas, G. Brian, illus. 2008. 32p. (J). (gr. -1-k). pap. 7.99 *(978-0-14-241174-2(4),* Puffin Books) Penguin Young Readers Group.

Harper, Meg. No More School. 2006. 184p. per. *(978-1-904529-28-6(3),* Back to Front) Solidus.

Harrar, George. Not As Crazy As I Seem. 2004. (ENG.). 240p. (YA). (gr. 7). pap. 6.99 *(978-0-618-49480-4(4),* 487272, Clarion Bks.) HarperCollins Pubs.

Harrell, Rob. Wink. 2020. (ENG.). 320p. (J). (gr. 4-7). 17.99 *(978-1-9848-1514-9(8),* Dial Bks) Penguin Young Readers Group.

Harrington, Dylan, et al. The Harrington Five & the Case of the School Sandals Err Vandals. 2006. 144p. pap. 11.25 *(978-1-4116-7883-5(4))* Lulu Pr., Inc.

Harrington, Kim. Revenge of the Red Club. 2020. (ENG., Illus.). 256p. (J). (gr. 4-8). pap. 8.99 *(978-1-5344-3573-5(5),* Simon & Schuster/Paula Wiseman Bks.) Simon & Schuster/Paula Wiseman Bks.

Harris, Lee. Carla & the Great Talent Show. 2009. 80p. pap. 10.00 *(978-1-60860-515-6(9),* Strategic Bk. Publishing) Strategic Book Publishing & Rights Agency (SBPRA).

Harris, Michael. Teenagers. 2010. 131p. pap. 13.97 *(978-0-557-31733-2(9))* Lulu Pr., Inc.

—TEENAGERS II: High School Blowout!!! 2010. 153p. pap. 16.50 *(978-0-557-61163-8(6))* Lulu Pr., Inc.

Harris, Patrice. Grandma Asks: Were You Good at School Today? Harrison, Nicholas, illus. 2013. 26p. pap. 10.00 *(978-0-9892358-5-3(8))* CLF Publishing.

Harris, Robie H. I Am NOT Going to School Today! Omerod, Jan, illus. 2003. (ENG.). 32p. (J). (gr. -1-3). 19.99 *(978-0-689-83913-9(8),* McElderry, Margaret K. Bks.) McElderry, Margaret K. Bks.

Harris, Teresa E. Gabriela Speaks Out. 2017. 176p. (J). *(978-1-338-16733-7(2))* Scholastic, Inc.

Harrison, Emma. Sacked: A Rival High Novel. 2008. (YA). *(978-1-4114-0525-7(0),* Spark Publishing Group) Sterling Publishing Co., Inc.

—S.C.A.M. 170p. (YA). pap. *(978-1-4114-0441-0(6),* SparkNotes) Barnes & Noble, Inc.

—That's a Wrap: A Rival High Novel. 2008. (YA). *(978-1-4114-0527-1(7),* Spark Publishing Group) Sterling Publishing Co., Inc.

—Toe the Line: A Rival High Novel. 2008. (YA). *(978-1-4114-0526-4(9),* Spark Publishing Group) Sterling Publishing Co., Inc.

Harrison, Lisi. Alphas. 2009. (Alphas Ser.: 1). (ENG.). 272p. (YA). (gr. 7-17). pap. 9.99 *(978-0-316-03579-8(3),* Poppy) Little, Brown Bks. for Young Readers.

—Best Friends for Never: A Clique Novel. 2004. (Clique Ser.: 2). (ENG.). 208p. (J). (gr. 7-17). pap. 13.99 *(978-0-316-70131-0(9),* Poppy) Little, Brown Bks. for Young Readers.

—Bratfest at Tiffany's, No. 9. 2008. (Clique Ser.: 9). (ENG., Illus.). 256p. (J). (gr. 7-17). per. 9.99 *(978-0-316-00680-4(7),* Poppy) Little, Brown Bks. for Young Readers.

—Charmed & Dangerous: The Clique Prequel. 2012. (Clique Ser.). (ENG.). 208p. (YA). (gr. 7-17). pap. 8.99 *(978-0-316-05536-9(0),* Poppy) Little, Brown Bks. for Young Readers.

—Dial L for Loser. 2008. (Clique Novels Ser.). 268p. 20.00 *(978-1-60686-291-9(X))* Perfection Learning Corp.

—Dial l for Loser. 2006. (Clique Ser.: 6). (ENG.). 272p. (J). (gr. 7-17). per. 9.99 *(978-0-316-11504-9(5),* Poppy) Little, Brown Bks. for Young Readers.

—It's Not Easy Being Mean, No. 7. rev. ed. 2007. (Clique Ser.: 7). (ENG.). 224p. (YA). (gr. 7-17). per. 13.99 *(978-0-316-11505-6(3),* Poppy) Little, Brown Bks. for Young Readers.

—It's Not Easy Being Mean. 2008. (Clique Ser.). 193p. 20.00 *(978-1-60686-330-5(4))* Perfection Learning Corp.

—Monster High. 2011. (Monster High Ser.: 1). (YA). lib. bdg. 19.65 *(978-0-606-23459-7(4))* Turtleback.

—Sealed with a Diss. 2008. (Clique Novels Ser.). 248p. 20.00 *(978-1-60686-345-9(2))* Perfection Learning Corp.

—Sealed with a Diss: A Clique Novel. 2007. (Clique Ser.: 8). (ENG.). 272p. (YA). (gr. 7-17). pap. 15.99 *(978-0-316-11506-3(1),* Poppy) Little, Brown Bks. for Young Readers.

—A Tale of Two Pretties. 2011. (Clique Ser.: 14). (ENG.). 224p. (J). (gr. 7-17). pap. 13.99 *(978-0-316-08442-0(5),* Poppy) Little, Brown Bks. for Young Readers.

—These Boots Are Made for Stalking. 12th ed. 2010. (Clique Ser.: 12). (ENG.). 256p. (J). (gr. 7-17). pap. 9.99 *(978-0-316-00683-5(1),* Poppy) Little, Brown Bks. for Young Readers.

—Top of the Feud Chain. 4. 2011. (Alphas Ser.: 4). (ENG.). 240p. (YA). (gr. 7-17). pap. 9.99 *(978-0-316-03582-8(3),* Poppy) Little, Brown Bks. for Young Readers.

Harrison, Zac. Frozen Enemies. 1 vol. 2013. (Hyperspace High Ser.). (ENG.). 288p. (J). (gr. 4-8). 27.32

(978-1-4342-6307-0(X), 123753, Stone Arch Bks.) Capstone.

—Robot Warriors, 1 vol. 2013. (Hyperspace High Ser.). (ENG., Illus.). 288p. (J). (gr. 4-8). pap. 8.95 (978-1-4342-6312-4(6), 123758, Stone Arch Bks.) Capstone.

—Warlord's Revenge, 1 vol. 2013. (Hyperspace High Ser.). (ENG.). 288p. (J). (gr. 4-8). pap. 8.95 (978-1-4342-6313-1(4), 123759, Stone Arch Bks.) Capstone.

Hart, Alison. Anna's Blizzard, 1 vol. Bachem, Paul, illus. 2017. 176p. (J). (gr. 2-5). pap. 7.95 (978-1-68263-002-0(1)) Peachtree Publishing Co. Inc.

Hart, Carla. A Kid Named Cancer: A Story about a Bully & How He Got Treated. 2009. 50p. pap. 16.50 (978-1-60693-659-7(X), Eloquent Bks.) Strategic Book Publishing & Rights Agency (SBPRA).

Hart, Kevin. Marcus Makes a Movie, 1. 2022. (Marcus Ser.). (ENG.). 202p. (J). (gr. 3-7). 19.96 **(978-1-68505-541-7(9))** Penworthy Co., LLC, The.

—Marcus Makes a Movie. Cooper, David, illus. (Marcus Ser.). (J). (gr. 3-7). 2022. 224p. pap. 8.99 (978-0-593-17917-8(X), Yearling) 2021. 208p. 16.99 (978-0-593-17914-7(5), Crown Books For Young Readers) 2021. (ENG.). 208p. lib. bdg. 19.99 (978-0-593-17915-4(3), Crown Books For Young Readers) Random Hse. Children's Bks.

Hart, Louise. Rosie's Rule. 2004. 96p. pap. 19.95 (978-1-4137-0546-1(4)) America Star Bks.

Hartinger, Brent. Geography Club. (ENG.). 240p. 2003. (J). 17.99 (978-0-06-001221-2(8)) 2004. (YA). (gr. 9). reprint ed. pap. 10.99 (978-0-06-001223-6(4), HarperTeen) HarperCollins Pubs.

Hartley, Susan. Bienvenido a nuestra Escuela: Fiction-to-Fact Big Book. enl. ed. 2004. (SPA.). (J). pap. 26.00 (978-1-4108-2364-9(4), 23644) Benchmark Education Co.

Harvey, Jacqueline. Alice-Miranda at School. 2012. (Alice-Miranda Ser.). (ENG.). 272p. (J). (gr. 2-5). 7.99 (978-0-385-73994-8(X), Yearling) Random Hse. Children's Bks.

—Alice-Miranda Keeps the Beat. 2020. (Alice-Miranda Ser.: 18). (Illus.). 384p. (J). (gr. 3-7). 9.99 (978-0-14-378603-0(2), Puffin) Penguin Random Hse. AUS. Dist: Independent Pubs. Group.

Harvey, Kate. Tiberius Goes to School, 1 vol. Brown, Kelli, illus. 2009. (Tiberius Tales Ser.). (ENG.). 24p. (J). (gr. 1-1). pap. 9.15 (978-1-60754-837-9(2), 537bd707-9b7a-45c4-94fb-3635a32c62ee); lib. bdg. 27.27 (978-1-60754-833-1(X), 32c9f65e-77ca-462e-a74f-80baf37214e2) Rosen Publishing Group, Inc., The. (Windmill Bks.).

Harvey, Keith. Tiberius Goes to School. Brown, Kate & Hickman, Paula, illus. 2014. (ENG.). 24p. pap. 8.95 (978-1-84135-919-9(X)) Award Pubns. Ltd. GBR. Dist: Parkwest Pubns., Inc.

Hassan, Michael. Crash & Burn. 2014. (ENG.). 544p. (YA). (gr. 9). pap. 9.99 (978-0-06-211291-0(0), Balzer & Bray) HarperCollins Pubs.

Haston, Meg. How to Rock Best Friends & Frenemies. 2013. (How to Rock Ser.: 2). (ENG.). 352p. (J). (gr. 3-7). pap. 18.99 (978-0-316-06827-7(6), Poppy) Little, Brown Bks. for Young Readers.

—How to Rock Braces & Glasses. (How to Rock Ser.: 1). (ENG.). (J). (gr. 3-7). 2012. 352p. pap. 18.99 (978-0-316-06824-6(1)) 2011. 336p. 16.99 (978-0-316-06825-3(X)) Little, Brown Bks. for Young Readers. (Poppy).

Hathaway, Jill. Impostor. 2013. (Slide Ser.: 2). (ENG.). 272p. (YA). (gr. 9). 17.99 (978-0-06-207798-1(8), Balzer & Bray) HarperCollins Pubs.

—Slide, 1. 2013. (Slide Ser.: 1). (ENG.). 272p. (YA). (gr. 9-12). pap. 9.99 (978-0-06-207796-7(1), Balzer & Bray) HarperCollins Pubs.

Hattemer, Kate. The Feminist Agenda of Jemima Kincaid. 2020. (ENG.). 304p. (YA). (gr. 9). lib. bdg. 20.99 (978-1-9848-4913-7(1), Knopf Bks. for Young Readers) Random Hse. Children's Bks.

Hattle, Jay. The Boy Who Didn't Try. 2011. 16p. pap. 9.00 (978-1-4634-1634-8(2)) AuthorHouse.

Hautman, Pete. The Big Crunch. 2011. (ENG.). 288p. (J). (gr. 9-8). 17.99 (978-0-545-24075-8(1), Scholastic Pr.) Scholastic, Inc.

—Blank Confession. (ENG.). 176p. (YA). (gr. 7). 2011. pap. 10.99 (978-1-4169-1328-3(9)) 2010. 16.99 (978-1-4169-1327-6(0)) Simon & Schuster Bks. For Young Readers. (Simon & Schuster Bks. For Young Readers).

—Invisible. Hautman, Pete, illus. 2006. (ENG., Illus.). 160p. (YA). (gr. 7-12). reprint ed. pap. 10.99 (978-0-689-86903-7(7), Simon & Schuster Bks. For Young Readers) Simon & Schuster Bks. For Young Readers.

—Sweetblood. 2010. (ENG.). 208p. (YA). (gr. 7). pap. 8.99 (978-1-4424-0755-8(7), Simon & Schuster Bks. For Young Readers) Simon & Schuster Bks. For Young Readers.

Hautzig, Deborah. Little Witch Learns to Read. Wickstrom, Sylvie, illus. 2003. (Step into Reading Ser.). 48p. (J). (gr. k-3). pap. 5.99 (978-0-375-82179-0(1), Random Hse. Bks. for Young Readers) Random Hse. Children's Bks.

Havill, Juanita. Jamaica's Blue Marker. O'Brien, Anne Sibley, illus. 2003. (ENG.). 32p. (J). (gr. -1-3). pap. 8.99 (978-0-618-36917-1(1), 487457, Clarion Bks.) HarperCollins Pubs.

Hawes, Adrienne Hill. Moving Danielle. 2008. 22p. pap. 24.95 (978-1-4241-4977-3(0)) America Star Bks.

Hawkins, A. D. The Time Princess. 2013. 208p. pap. (978-1-78299-661-3(3)) FeedARead.com.

Hawkins-Rodgers, Donzella. No Bulley Destroys Chloe's Hairdo. 2003. (Illus.). 32p. (J). (gr. 3-18). pap. 10.95 (978-1-884242-58-8(8)) Multicultural Pubns.

—No Bulley Destroy's Chloe's Hairdo. Hewins, Shirley, illus. 2003. 32p. (J). (gr. 3-18). lib. bdg. 16.95 (978-1-884242-56-4(1)) Multicultural Pubns.

Hawkins, Wendy. Binky Goes to School. 2009. 20p. pap. 13.99 (978-1-4389-6990-9(2)) AuthorHouse.

Hayes, Angela. The Mop Heads, 1 vol. Polly Jr., Jimmy Wayne, illus. 2009. 14p. pap. 24.95 (978-1-61546-006-9(3)) America Star Bks.

Hayes, Daniel. Flyers. 2013. (ENG.). 208p. (YA). (gr. 7). pap. 10.99 (978-1-4424-8881-6(6), Simon & Schuster Bks. For Young Readers) Simon & Schuster Bks. For Young Readers.

Hayes, Gwen. Dreaming Awake. 2012. (Falling under Novel Ser.). (ENG.). 336p. (YA). (gr. 7-18). 9.99 (978-0-451-23554-1(1), Berkley) Penguin Publishing Group.

—Falling Under. 2011. (Falling under Novel Ser.: 1). (ENG.). 336p. (YA). (gr. 7-18). 9.99 (978-0-451-23268-7(2), Berkley) Penguin Publishing Group.

Hayes, Sonia. Urban Goddess. 2007. 224p. (YA). per. 9.95 (978-0-9777573-1-2(5)) NUA Multimedia.

Haynes, Marilee. A. K. A. Genius. 2013. (ENG.). 208p. (J). 9.95 (978-0-8198-0830-1(X)) Pauline Bks. & Media.

—Genius under Construction. 2014. (ENG.). (YA). pap. (978-0-8198-3126-2(3)) Pauline Bks. & Media.

—Pictures of Me. 2016. 149p. (J). pap. (978-0-8198-6019-4(0)) Pauline Bks. & Media.

Hays, Anna Jane. Kindergarten Countdown: A Book for Kindergarteners. Davick, Linda, illus. 2013. 24p. (J). (gr. -1-2). 8.99 (978-0-385-75371-5(3), Dragonfly Bks.) Random Hse. Children's Bks.

Haywood, Carolyn. B is for Betsy. Haywood, Carolyn, illus. 2004. (ENG., Illus.). 144p. (J). (gr. 1-4). pap. 7.99 (978-0-15-205099-3(X), 1195397, Clarion Bks.) HarperCollins Pubs.

—Back to School with Betsy. Haywood, Carolyn, illus. 2004. (ENG., Illus.). 160p. (J). (gr. 1-4). pap. 11.95 (978-0-15-205101-3(5), 1195403, Clarion Bks.) HarperCollins Pubs.

—Betsy & Billy. Haywood, Carolyn, illus. 2004. (ENG., Illus.). 144p. (J). (gr. 1-4). pap. 7.99 (978-0-15-205100-6(7), 1195400, Clarion Bks.) HarperCollins Pubs.

Hazelton, Tanya & Bonanni, Constance. Ian's Golden Passage. 2009. 168p. pap. 9.99 (978-1-935105-33-6(7)) Avid Readers Publishing Group.

HB Staff. Today Is Monday. 97th ed. 2003. (Signatures Ser.). (gr. 1-18). pap. 16.50 (978-0-15-308169-9(4)) Harcourt Schl. Pubs.

Headley, Justina Chen. The Patch. Vane, Mitch, illus. 2007. (ENG.). 32p. (J). (gr. k-3). pap. 7.95 (978-1-58089-170-7(5)) Charlesbridge Publishing, Inc.

Hearst, Allyson. White Pajamas: A Karate Story. 2011. 68p. pap. 19.95 (978-1-4626-3871-0(6)) America Star Bks.

Heasley, Gwendolyn. Where I Belong. 2011. (Where I Belong Ser.: 1). (ENG.). 304p. (YA). (gr. 8-18). pap. 9.99 (978-0-06-197884-5(1), HarperTeen) HarperCollins Pubs.

Heiligman, Deborah. Cool Dog, School Dog, 0 vols. Bowers, Tim, illus. 2013. (ENG.). 32p. (J). (gr. -1-2). pap. 9.99 (978-1-4778-1670-7(4), 9781477816707, Two Lions) Amazon Publishing.

Heldring, Thatcher. Roy Morelli Steps up to the Plate. 2011. (ENG.). 240p. (J). (gr. 4-6). lib. bdg. 18.69 (978-0-385-90406-3(1), Delacorte Pr.) Random Hse. Children's Bks.

Helgeson, Kat. Say No to the Bro. 2017. (ENG., Illus.). 272p. (YA). (gr. 9). 17.99 (978-1-4814-7193-0(7), Simon & Schuster Bks. For Young Readers) Simon & Schuster Bks. For Young Readers.

Helget, Nicole. The End of the Wild. 2018. (ENG., Illus.). 288p. (J). (gr. 3-7). pap. 7.99 (978-0-316-24513-5(5)) Little, Brown Bks. for Young Readers.

The Hell House Experience. 2008. (ENG.). 70p. 14.99 (978-0-9817520-8-2(X)) Torch Legacy Pubns.

Heller, Alyson. After-School Sports Club Adventures. Björkman, Steve, illus. 2016. (J). (978-1-4814-7741-3(2)) Simon & Schuster Children's Publishing.

—Soccer Day: Ready-To-Read Level 1. Björkman, Steve, illus. 2009. (After-School Sports Club Ser.). (ENG.). 32p. (J). (gr. -1-1). pap. 4.99 (978-1-4169-9410-7(6), Simon Spotlight) Simon Spotlight.

Helms, Rhonda. Promposal. 2015. (ENG., Illus.). 224p. (YA). (gr. 7). pap. 9.99 (978-1-4814-2231-4(6), Simon Pulse) Simon Pulse.

Helmso, Candy Grant. Cakewalk. Taylor, Stephen, illus. 2003. (Books for Young Learners). (ENG.). 16p. (J). pap. 5.75 net. (978-1-57274-250-5(X), 2727, Bks. for Young Learners) Owen, Richard C. Pubs., Inc.

Henderson, Lauren. Kiss Me Kill Me. 2009. (Scarlett Wakefield Ser.). 272p. (YA). (gr. 9). pap. 10.99 (978-0-385-73488-2(3), Delacorte Pr.) Random Hse. Children's Bks.

—Kisses & Lies, 2. 2009. (Scarlett Wakefield Novels Ser.). (ENG.). 320p. (J). (gr. 9-12). lib. bdg. 26.19 (978-0-385-90486-5(X), Delacorte Pr.) Random Hse. Children's Bks.

Hendrickson, David H. Cracking the Ice. 2018. (ENG., Illus.). 256p. (YA). 24.99 (978-1-948134-02-6(0)); pap. 12.99 (978-1-948134-07-1(1)) Pentucket Publishing.

—Cracking the Ice. 2011. (YA). 365p. (gr. 9-18). 16.95 (978-1-934813-55-3(9)); 366p. (978-1-934813-56-0(7)) Westside Bks.

Heneghan, James. Hit Squad, 1 vol. 2003. (Orca Soundings Ser.). (ENG.). 128p. (YA). (gr. 8-12). pap. 9.95 (978-1-55143-269-4(2), 1551432692) Orca Bk. Pubs. USA.

—Hit Squad. 2004. (Orca Soundings Ser.). 106p. 19.95 (978-0-7569-4300-4(0)) Perfection Learning Corp.

Hengel, Katherine. No Easy Race, 1 vol. unabr. ed. 2010. (District 13 Ser.). (ENG.). 47p. (YA). (gr. 9-12). 9.75 (978-1-61651-277-4(6)) Saddleback Educational Publishing, Inc.

—Wings, 1 vol. unabr. ed. 2010. (District 13 Ser.). (ENG.). 48p. (YA). (gr. 9-12). pap. 9.75 (978-1-61651-280-4(6)) Saddleback Educational Publishing, Inc.

Henkes, Kevin. Chrysanthemum. 2004. (Illus.). (J). (gr. k-3). spiral bd. (978-0-616-14575-3(6)) Canadian National Institute for the Blind/Institut National Canadien pour les Aveugles.

—Chrysanthemum. 2008. (J). (gr. -1-2). lib. bdg. 17.20 (978-0-613-00459-6(0)) Turtleback.

—Chrysanthemum Big Book: A First Day of School Book for Kids. Henkes, Kevin, illus. 2007. (ENG., Illus.). 32p. (J). (gr. -1-3). pap. 24.99 (978-0-06-111974-3(1), Greenwillow Bks.) HarperCollins Pubs.

—Crisantemo. 2017.Tr. of Chrysanthemum. (SPA., Illus.). 32p. (J). pap. 9.99 (978-1-63245-664-9(8)) Lectorum Pubns., Inc.

—Crisantemo. Mlawer, Teresa, tr. from ENG. 2006.Tr. of Chrysanthemum. (Illus.). 31p. (gr. 4-7). 19.00 (978-0-7569-7316-2(3)) Perfection Learning Corp.

—Lilly Adore l'École! pap. 16.95 (978-2-07-054873-6(2)) Gallimard, Editions FRA. Dist: Distribooks, Inc.

—Lilly's Purple Plastic Purse. Henkes, Kevin, illus. 10th anniv. ed. 2006. (ENG., Illus.). 40p. (J). (gr. -1-4). 19.99 (978-0-688-12897-5(1), Greenwillow Bks.) HarperCollins Pubs.

—Lilly's Purple Plastic Purse. Henkes, Kevin, illus. (Illus.). pap. incl. audio (978-0-87499-688-3(0)); pap. 16.95 incl. audio (978-0-87499-686-9(4)); pap. incl. audio compact disk (978-1-59112-557-0(X)); pap. 18.95 incl. audio compact disk (978-1-59112-347-7(X)) Live Oak Media.

—Lilly's Purple Plastic Purse 20th Anniversary Edition. Henkes, Kevin, illus. 20th ed. 2016. (ENG., Illus.). 40p. (J). (gr. -1-3). 17.99 (978-0-06-242419-8(X), Greenwillow Bks.) HarperCollins Pubs.

—Lily y Su Bolso de Plastico Morado. 2017.Tr. of Lilly's Purple Plastic Purse. (SPA.). (J). pap. 9.99 (978-1-63245-667-0(2)) Lectorum Pubns., Inc.

—Prudencia Se Preocupa. 2017.Tr. of Wemberly Worried. (SPA.). (J). pap. 9.99 (978-1-63245-666-3(4)) Lectorum Pubns., Inc.

—Wemberly Worried. Henkes, Kevin, illus. (Illus.). pap. 39.95 incl. audio compact disk (978-1-59112-561-7(8)); pap. 18.95 incl. audio compact disk (978-1-59112-359-0(3)); pap. incl. audio (978-0-87499-808-5(5)); pap. 16.95 incl. audio (978-0-87499-806-1(9)) Live Oak Media.

—The Year of Billy Miller. Henkes, Kevin, illus. 2015. (ENG., Illus.). (J). (gr. 3-7). lib. bdg. 17.60 (978-1-62765-762-4(2)) Perfection Learning Corp.

—The Year of Billy Miller. 2015. (J). lib. bdg. 18.40 (978-0-606-36977-0(5)) Turtleback.

—The Year of Billy Miller: A Newbery Honor Award Winner. Henkes, Kevin, illus. 2013. (ENG., Illus.). 240p. (J). (gr. 3-7). 17.99 (978-0-06-226812-9(0)); lib. bdg. 17.89 (978-0-06-226813-6(9)) HarperCollins Pubs. (Greenwillow Bks.).

Hennessy, Claire. Afterwards. 2005. 188p. (YA). pap. (978-1-84223-207-1(X)) Poolbeg Pr.

Henry in Love. 2009. (ENG., Illus.). 48p. (J). (gr. -1-1). 16.99 (978-0-06-114288-8(3), Balzer & Bray) HarperCollins Pubs.

Henry, Isabelle. The Hundred-Penny Rub. 2008. 36p. pap. 16.99 (978-1-4343-4912-5(8)) AuthorHouse.

Henry, Katie. Heretics Anonymous. 2018. (ENG.). 336p. (YA). (gr. 8). 17.99 (978-0-06-269887-2(7), Tegen, Katherine Bks) HarperCollins Pubs.

Henshon, Suzanna E. Spiders on the Ceiling. 2006. (J). (978-0-88092-614-0(7)) Royal Fireworks Publishing Co.

Hensley, Judith Victoria. Terrible Tin. 2008. 136p. pap. 14.95 (978-0-9795103-3-5(3)) Ascended Ideas.

Henson, S. F. Devils Within. 2017. (ENG.). 404p. (J). (gr. 8-8). 17.99 (978-1-5107-1456-4(1), Sky Pony Pr.) Skyhorse Publishing Co., Inc.

Heos, Bridget. Fairy's First Day of School. Not, Sara, illus. 2018. (ENG.). 32p. (J). (gr. -1-3). 17.99 (978-1-328-71559-3(0), 1674034, Clarion Bks.) HarperCollins Pubs.

Hepler, Linda McGhee. How to Survive Seventh Grade (If You're Lucky) 2008. 146p. pap. 24.95 (978-1-60563-610-8(X)) America Star Bks.

Herbach, Geoff. Fat Boy vs. the Cheerleaders. 2014. 320p. (YA). (gr. 7-12). 16.99 (978-1-4022-9141-8(8), 9781402291418) Sourcebooks, Inc.

—Gabe Johnson Takes Over. 2015. 352p. (YA). (gr. 6-12). pap. 13.99 (978-1-4926-0865-3(3)) Sourcebooks, Inc.

—Stupid Fast. 2011. (Felton Reinstein Trilogy Ser.: 1). (ENG.). 320p. (YA). (gr. 7-12). pap. 11.99 (978-1-4022-5630-1(2), 9781402256301) Sourcebooks, Inc.

Herman, Charlotte. My Chocolate Year: A Novel with 12 Recipes. Pham, LeUyen, illus. 2008. (ENG.). 176p. (J). (gr. 3-7). 15.99 (978-1-4169-3341-0(7), Simon & Schuster Bks. For Young Readers) Simon & Schuster Bks. For Young Readers.

Herman, Gail. The Color Day Coach. Lewis, Anthony, illus. 2018. (Makers Make It Work Ser.). 32p. (J). (gr. k-3). pap. 5.99 (978-1-57565-993-0(X), 5ed95eba-7a9f-4377-b99b-a02b58719962, Kane Press) Astra Publishing Hse.

—Time for School, Little Dinosaur. Fleming, Michael, illus. 2017. (Step into Reading Ser.). 32p. (J). (gr. -1-1). pap. 5.99 (978-0-399-55645-6(1), Random Hse. Bks. for Young Readers) Random Hse. Children's Bks.

Hermes, Patricia. The Wild Year Bk. 3: Joshua's Oregon Trail Diary. 2003. (My America Ser.). (ENG., Illus.). 112p. (J). 12.95 (978-0-439-37055-4(8)) Scholastic, Inc.

Hernandez, David. No More Us for You. 2009. 281p. (YA). lib. bdg. 17.89 (978-0-06-117334-9(7), HarperTeen) HarperCollins Pubs.

Hershey, Mary. My Big Sister Is So Bossy She Says You Can't Read This Book. 2006. (Illus.). 176p. (J). (gr. 3-7). per. 6.99 (978-0-553-48797-8(3), Yearling) Random Hse. Children's Bks.

Heyliger, William. Quarterback Hothead. Grubb, W. B., illus. 2011. 262p. 47.95 (978-1-258-09738-7(9)) Literary Licensing, LLC.

Hickey, Joshalyn M. Good Morning Lovey! Chaveevah, Banks Ferguson, illus. 2005. (ENG.). 28p. (J). 12.00 (978-0-9718939-3-1(4)) BaHar Publishing, L.C.

Hicks, John Bryant. The Day Charlie Lost His Weirdiness. 2nd ed. 2007. (J). per. 5.99 (978-0-9742829-4-7(4)) Quiet Man Publishing.

Higgins, Chris. The Secrets Club: No Match for Dani. 3rd ed. 2016. (Secrets Club Ser.: 3). 176p. (J). (gr. 2-4). pap. 10.99 (978-0-14-133524-7(6)) Penguin Bks., Ltd. GBR. Dist: Independent Pubs. Group.

Higgins, M. G. Bi-Normal, 1 vol. 2013. (Gravel Road Ser.). (ENG.). 144p. (YA). (gr. 9-12). pap. 11.95 (978-1-62250-004-8(0)) Saddleback Educational Publishing, Inc.

—Falling Out of Place, 1 vol. 2012. (Gravel Road Ser.). (ENG.). 144p. (YA). (gr. 9-12). pap. 11.95 (978-1-62250-021-5(0)) Saddleback Educational Publishing, Inc.

—Falling Out of Place. 2013. (Gravel Road Ser.). (YA). lib. bdg. 20.80 (978-0-606-26963-6(0)) Turtleback.

—I'm Just Me. 2014. (Gravel Road Ser.). (YA). lib. bdg. 20.80 (978-0-606-35220-8(1)) Turtleback.

Higgins, Nadia. Zombie Field Day: Zombie Zappers Book 2, 1 vol. 2014. (Zombie Zappers Ser.). (ENG.). 64p. (J). (gr. 5-7). pap. 12.71 (978-1-62285-006-8(8), 9aad20e2-c587-4658-a366-bbcdea9eced7); (Illus.). 30.60 (978-1-62285-005-1(X), fe324f99-324c-4e5e-8143-36ca3f62ec23) Enslow Publishing, LLC.

Higgins, Ryan T. We Don't Eat Our Classmates: A Penelope Rex Book. 2018. (Penelope Rex Book Ser.). (Illus.). 48p. (J). (-k). 17.99 **(978-1-368-00355-1(9)**, Disney-Hyperion) Disney Publishing Worldwide.

Hileman, Linda L. Dawn's Secret. 2006. (J). per. 9.95 (978-1-59571-117-5(1)) Word Association Pubs.

Hill, Andrew G. The Song of the Seraphim. 2009. 196p. pap. 13.95 (978-1-60860-194-3(3), Strategic Bk. Publishing) Strategic Book Publishing & Rights Agency (SBPRA).

Hill, Eric. Spot Goes to School (color) Hill, Eric, illus. 2004. (Spot Ser.). (ENG., Illus.). 24p. (J). (gr. -1-k). 7.99 (978-0-14-240167-5(6), Warne) Penguin Young Readers Group.

Hill, Grace Brooks. The Corner House Girls at School. 2018. (ENG., Illus.). 176p. (YA). (gr. 7-12). pap. (978-93-5297-326-2(7)) Alpha Editions.

Hill, Joyce. A Penny in My Pocket. 2007. 220p. 27.95 (978-0-9795818-0-9(X)); pap. 14.95 (978-0-9795818-1-6(8)) Mushgush Pr.

Hill, Kirkpatrick. The Year of Miss Agnes. 2003. (Aladdin Historical Fiction Ser.). 115p. (gr. 3-7). 17.00 (978-0-7569-1407-3(8)) Perfection Learning Corp.

Hillenbrand, Will. Mighty Reader & the Big Freeze. 2019. (ENG., Illus.). 32p. (J). (gr. -1-3). pap. 7.99 (978-0-8234-4733-6(2)) Holiday Hse., Inc.

Hillert, Margaret. Come to School, Dear Dragon. Pullan, Jack, illus. 2016. (BeginningtoRead Ser.). (ENG.). 32p. (J). (-2). lib. bdg. 22.60 (978-1-59953-764-1(8)) Norwood Hse. Pr.

—Ven a la Escuela, Querido Dragón. Pullan, Jack, illus. 2017. (BeginningtoRead Ser.).Tr. of Come to School, Dear Dragon. (ENG & SPA.). 32p. (J). (-2). 22.60 (978-1-59953-827-3(X)) Norwood Hse. Pr.

—Who Goes to School? Woodworth, Viki, illus. 2016. (BeginningtoRead Ser.). (ENG.). 32p. (J). (gr. k-2). 22.60 (978-1-59953-808-2(3)) Norwood Hse. Pr.

—Who Goes to School? Viki Woodworth, illus. 2016. (Beginning-To-Read Ser.). (ENG.). 32p. (J). (gr. k-2). pap. 13.26 (978-1-60357-949-0(4)) Norwood Hse. Pr.

Hillner, Brenda. The Invisible Girl. 2012. 86p. 19.10 (978-1-4669-5398-7(5)); pap. 9.10 (978-1-4669-5396-3(9)) Trafford Publishing.

Hills, Tad. Rocket's 100th Day of School (Step into Reading, Step 1) 2014. (Rocket Ser.). 32p. (J). (gr. -1-1). pap. 5.99 (978-0-385-39097-2(1), Random Hse. Bks. for Young Readers) Random Hse. Children's Bks.

Hilton, Charlotte. Adventure of the Pen Pot Pals. 2009. 36p. pap. 16.99 (978-1-4389-4434-0(9)) AuthorHouse.

Hilton, Nette. Sprite Downberry. 2008. (ENG.). 288p. (978-0-7322-8548-7(8)) HarperCollins Pubs. Australia.

Himle, Lisa. Hands as Warm as Toast. Langton, Bruce, illus. 2006. 32p. (J). (gr. -1-3). 17.95 (978-1-58726-298-2(3), Mitten Pr.) Ann Arbor Editions LLC.

Hiranandani, Veera. The Whole Story of Half a Girl. 2013. (ENG.). 224p. (J). (gr. 4-6). lib. bdg. 21.19 (978-0-375-98995-7(1), Delacorte Pr.); 8.99 (978-0-375-87167-2(5), Yearling) Random Hse. Children's Bks.

Hirschmann, Kris. A Serious Case of the Sillies. Jennings, C. S., illus. 2013. 32p. (J). pap. (978-0-545-56765-7(3)) Scholastic, Inc.

Ho, Jannie, illus. Violet Rose & the Little School. 2016. (Violet Rose Ser.). (ENG.). 52p. (J). (gr. -1-3). 8.99 (978-0-7636-9002-1(3)) Candlewick Pr.

Hobbs, Leigh. Freaks on the Loose: The Whole Scary Story. 2018. (ENG., Illus.). 240p. (J). (gr. 2-6). pap. 13.99 (978-1-76029-431-1(4)) Allen & Unwin AUS. Dist: Independent Pubs. Group.

Hobbs, Valerie. Minnie Mcclary Speaks Her Mind. 2013. (ENG.). 240p. (J). (gr. 4-8). pap. 17.99 (978-1-250-03408-3(6), 900120578) Square Fish.

Hoblin, Paul. False Start. 2017. (Gridiron Ser.). (ENG.). 128p. (YA). (gr. 6-12). pap. 7.99 (978-1-5124-5351-5(X), 3dcdd02d-4ddd-450a-a9c5-5aff913be20a); 26.65 (978-1-5124-3979-3(7), 01c7661e-c94b-4ba3-8660-24f6cb39cdcf) Lerner Publishing Group. (Darby Creek).

Hodge, Merle. For the Life of Laetitia. 2003. 21.25 (978-0-8446-7246-5(7)) Smith, Peter Pub., Inc.

Hodkin, Michelle. The Unbecoming of Mara Dyer. (Mara Dyer Trilogy Ser.: 1). (ENG., Illus.). (YA). (gr. 9). 2012. 480p. pap. 14.99 (978-1-4424-2177-6(0)) 2011. 464p. 24.99 (978-1-4424-2176-9(2)) Simon & Schuster Bks. For Young Readers. (Simon & Schuster Bks. For Young Readers).

Hoeffner, Karol Ann. Surf Ed. 2010. (ENG.). 288p. (YA). (gr. 9). pap. 13.99 (978-1-4424-1418-1(9), Simon Pulse) Simon Pulse.

Hoena, Blake. The Werewolf Bully. Bardin, Dave, illus. 2018. (Monster Heroes Ser.). (ENG.). 32p. (J). (gr. k-2). lib. bdg. 21.32 (978-1-4965-6415-3(4), 138262, Stone Arch Bks.) Capstone.

Hoena, Blake A. Swamp Sting!, 1 vol. Facio, Sebastian, illus. 2011. (Graphic Sparks Ser.). (ENG.). 40p. (J). (gr. 2-4). pap. 5.95 (978-1-4342-3065-2(1), 114681, Stone Arch Bks.) Capstone.

Hoestlandt, Jo. Robin del Bosque. (SPA.). (J). 7.95 (978-958-04-5041-2(2)) Norma S.A. COL. Dist: Distribuidora Norma, Inc.

Hoff, Syd. Danny & the Dinosaur. 2017. (Danny & the Dinosaur — I Can Read Ser.). (J). lib. bdg. 13.55 (978-0-606-40063-3(X)) Turtleback.

—Danny & the Dinosaur: School Days. Hoff, Syd, illus. 2017. (I Can Read Level 1 Ser.). (ENG., Illus.). 32p. (J). (gr. -1-3). pap. 4.99 (978-0-06-228161-6(5), HarperCollins) HarperCollins Pubs.

Hoffman, Mary. Bravo, Grace! 2011. (ENG.). 112p. (J). (gr. 3-7). 5.99 (978-0-14-241850-5(1), Puffin Books) Penguin Young Readers Group.

—Encore, Grace! 2011. (ENG.). 112p. (J). (gr. 3-7). 5.99 (978-0-14-241854-3(4), Puffin Books) Penguin Young Readers Group.

S

Hoffman, Sarah & Hoffman, Ian. Jacob's Room to Choose. Case, Chris, illus. 2019. 32p. (J). *(978-1-4338-3073-0(6),* Magination Pr.) American Psychological Assn.

Hoffmann, Kerry Cohen. It's Not You, It's Me. 2011. (ENG.). 192p. (YA). (gr. 8-12). lib. bdg. 22.44 *(978-0-385-90638-8(2))* Random House Publishing Group.

Holder, Amy. The Lipstick Laws. 2011. (ENG.). 240p. (YA). (gr. 7-18). pap. 13.99 *(978-0-547-36306-6(0),* 1421941, Clarion Bks.) HarperCollins Pubs.

Holder, Nancy & Viguie, Debbie. Unleashed. 2012. (Wolf Spring Chronicles Ser.: 1). (ENG.). 400p. (YA). (gr. 7). pap. 9.99 *(978-0-385-74099-9(9),* Ember) Random Hse. Children's Bks.

Holland, Frances. Ryan's Praying Mantis, 1 vol. 2009. 19p. pap. 24.95 *(978-1-60749-432-4(9))* PublishAmerica, Inc.

Holland, L. Tam. The Counterfeit Family Tree of Vee Crawford-Wong. (ENG.). 368p. (YA). (gr. 9). 2014. pap. 12.99 *(978-1-4424-1265-1(8))* 2013. 17.99 *(978-1-4424-1264-4(X))* Simon & Schuster Children's Publishing.

Holliday, S. L. My Identity Christ-Is: Stay in the Game. 2012. (ENG.). 166p. (J). pap. 12.95 *(978-1-4787-1827-7(7))* Outskirts Pr., Inc.

Holm, Jennifer L. Eighth Grade Is Making Me Sick. 2015. (Ginny Davis Year in Stuff Ser.: 2). lib. bdg. 18.40 *(978-0-606-37710-2(7))* Turtleback.

—Lights, Camera, Middle School! Holm, Matthew, illus. 2017. (Babymouse Tales from the Locker Ser.: 1). (ENG.). 208p. (J). (gr. 3-7). 13.99 *(978-0-399-55438-4(6),* Random Hse. Bks. for Young Readers) Random Hse. Children's Bks.

—Middle School Is Worse Than Meatloaf: A Year Told Through Stuff. Castaldi, Elicia, illus. (ENG.). 128p. (J). (gr. 3-7). 2011. pap. 9.99 *(978-1-4424-3663-3(8))* 2007. 14.99 *(978-0-689-85281-7(9))* Simon & Schuster Children's Publishing. (Atheneum Bks. for Young Readers).

—Miss Communication. Holm, Matthew, illus. 2018. (Babymouse Tales from the Locker Ser.: 2). (ENG.). 208p. (J). (gr. 3-7). 13.99 *(978-0-399-55441-4(6),* Random Hse. Bks. for Young Readers) Random Hse. Children's Bks.

—School-Tripped. Holm, Matthew, illus. 2019. (Babymouse Tales from the Locker Ser.: 3). (ENG.). 208p. (J). (gr. 3-7). 13.99 *(978-0-399-55444-5(0),* Random Hse. Bks. for Young Readers) Random Hse. Children's Bks.

—Swing It, Sunny: a Graphic Novel (Sunny #2) Holm, Matthew, illus. 2017. (Sunny Ser.: 2). (ENG.). 224p. (J). (gr. 3-7). 24.99 *(978-0-545-74170-5(X));* pap. 12.99 *(978-0-545-74172-9(6))* Scholastic, Inc. (Graphix).

—The Third Mushroom. 2018. (ENG., Illus.). 240p. (J). (gr. 3-7). 16.99 *(978-1-5247-1980-7(3),* Random Hse. Bks. for Young Readers) Random Hse. Children's Bks.

Holm, Jennifer L. & Holm, Matthew. Babymouse #10: the Musical. Holm, Jennifer L. & Holm, Matthew, illus. 2009. (Babymouse Ser.: 10). (ENG., Illus.). 96p. (J). (gr. 2-5). pap. 6.99 *(978-0-375-84388-4(4));* lib. bdg. 12.99 *(978-0-375-93791-0(9))* Penguin Random Hse. LLC.

—Babymouse #11: Dragonslayer. Holm, Jennifer L. & Holm, Matthew, illus. 2009. (Babymouse Ser.: 11). (ENG., Illus.). 96p. (J). (gr. 2-5). pap. 6.99 *(978-0-375-85712-6(5))* Penguin Random Hse. LLC.

—Babymouse #14: Mad Scientist. Holm, Jennifer L. & Holm, Matthew, illus. 2011. (Babymouse Ser.: 14). (ENG., Illus.). 96p. (J). (gr. 2-5). pap. 7.99 *(978-0-375-86574-9(8));* lib. bdg. 12.99 *(978-0-375-96574-6(2))* Penguin Random Hse. LLC.

—Babymouse #16: Babymouse for President. Holm, Jennifer L. & Holm, Matthew, illus. 2012. (Babymouse Ser.: 16). (ENG., Illus.). 96p. (J). (gr. 2-5). pap. 7.99 *(978-0-375-86780-4(5))* Penguin Random Hse. LLC.

—Babymouse #17: Extreme Babymouse. Holm, Jennifer L. & Holm, Matthew, illus. 2013. (Babymouse Ser.: 17). (ENG., Illus.). 96p. (J). (gr. 2-5). pap. 6.99 *(978-0-307-93160-3(9))* Penguin Random Hse. LLC.

—Babymouse #2: Our Hero. 2005. (Babymouse Ser.: 2). (ENG., Illus.). 96p. (J). (gr. 2-5). pap. 6.99 *(978-0-375-83230-7(0))* Penguin Random Hse. LLC.

—Extreme Babymouse. 2013. (Babymouse Ser.: 17). lib. bdg. 17.20 *(978-0-606-26999-5(1))* Turtleback.

—Squish #1: Super Amoeba. Holm, Jennifer L. & Holm, Matthew, illus. 2011. (Squish Ser.: 1). (Illus.). 96p. (J). (gr. 3-7). pap. 6.99 *(978-0-375-84389-1(2))* Penguin Random Hse. LLC.

—Squish #2: Brave New Pond. Holm, Jennifer L. & Holm, Matthew, illus. 2011. (Squish Ser.: 2). (Illus.). 96p. (J). (gr. 3-7). (ENG.). 12.99 *(978-0-375-93784-2(6));* pap. 6.99 *(978-0-375-84390-7(6))* Penguin Random Hse. LLC.

Holm, Jennifer L., et al. Comics Squad: Recess! 2014. (Comics Squad Ser.: 1). (ENG., Illus.). 144p. (J). (gr. 2-5). pap. 7.99 *(978-0-385-37003-5(2))* Penguin Random Hse. LLC.

Holm, Matthew & Holm, Jennifer L. Lunch! 2016. (Comics Squad Ser.: 2). lib. bdg. 18.40 *(978-0-606-38446-9(4))* Turtleback.

Holmes, Kimberly. Digibots Classroom Adventures. Lawson, Devin, illus. 2004. (J). *(978-0-9755725-0-4(4),* 1238415) Digibots Corp.

Holmes, Lynda. Spring Cleaning. 2006. 55p. pap. 16.95 *(978-1-4241-4324-5(1))* PublishAmerica, Inc.

Holmes, Sara Lewis. Letters from Rapunzel. 2007. 184p. (J). (gr. 3-7). lib. bdg. 16.89 *(978-0-06-078074-6(6))* HarperCollins Pubs.

Holmes, Stephanie. Grady Goes to Puppy School. 2011. 20p. (gr. 1-2). pap. 11.99 *(978-1-4634-1000-1(X))* AuthorHouse.

Holmqvist, Carin. African Tales. 2009. (ENG.). 64p. pap. 28.70 *(978-0-557-18184-1(4))* Lulu Pr., Inc.

Holt, Catherine. Midnight Reynolds & the Spectral Transformer. 2017. (Midnight Reynolds Ser.: 1). 272p. (J). (gr. 3-7). (ENG.). 14.99 *(978-0-8075-5125-7(2),* 807551252); pap. 9.99 *(978-0-8075-5126-4(0),* 807551260) Whitman, Albert & Co.

Holt, K. A. Brains for Lunch: A Zombie Novel in Haiku?! Wilson, Gahan, illus. 2010. (ENG.). 96p. (J). (gr. 4-9). 22.99 *(978-1-59643-629-9(8),* 900068270) Roaring Brook Pr.

—Redwood & Ponytail: (Novels for Preteen Girls, Children's Fiction on Social Situations, Fiction Books for Young Adults, LGBTQ Books, Stories in Verse) 2019. (ENG., Illus.). 424p. (J). (gr. 5-9). 18.99 *(978-1-4521-7288-0(9))* Chronicle Bks. LLC.

Holt, Kimberly Willis. Piper Reed, Clubhouse Queen. Davenier, Christine, illus. 2011. (Piper Reed Ser.: 2). (ENG.). 160p. (J). (gr. 3-6). 15.99 *(978-0-8050-9431-2(8),* 900076845, Holt, Henry & Co. Bks. For Young Readers) Holt, Henry & Co.

—Piper Reed, Clubhouse Queen. Davenier, Christine, illus. 2011. (Piper Reed Ser.: 2). (ENG.). 176p. (J). (gr. 3-6). pap. 9.99 *(978-0-312-61676-2(7),* 900076846) Square Fish.

—Piper Reed, Navy Brat. Davenier, Christine, illus. 2011. (Piper Reed Ser.: 1). (ENG.). 176p. (J). (gr. 3-6). pap. 9.99 *(978-0-312-62548-1(0),* 900077153) Square Fish.

Holt, Theresa. What If I Wet My Pants. 2011. 28p. pap. 15.99 *(978-1-4628-5319-9(6))* Xlibris Corp.

Holub, Joan. Apple Countdown. Smith, Jan, illus. 2009. (ENG.). 32p. (J). (gr. -1-3). 16.99 *(978-0-8075-0398-0(3),* 807503983) Whitman, Albert & Co.

—Big Heart! A Valentine's Day Tale. Terry, Will, illus. 2007. (Ant Hill Ser.). (ENG.). 24p. (J). (gr. -1-k). lib. bdg. 13.89 *(978-1-4169-2562-0(7),* Simon & Schuster/Paula Wiseman Bks.) Simon & Schuster/Paula Wiseman Bks.

—Big Heart! A Valentine's Day Tale (Ready-To-Read Pre-Level 1) Terry, Will, illus. 2007. (Ant Hill Ser.). (ENG.). 24p. (J). (gr. -1-k). pap. 4.99 *(978-1-4169-0957-6(5),* Simon Spotlight) Simon Spotlight.

—Twinkle, Star of the Week. Nicholls, Paul, illus. 2012. (J). *(978-1-61913-137-8(4))* Weigl Pubs., Inc.

Holub, Joan & Williams, Suzanne. Aphrodite the Beauty. (Goddess Girls Ser.: 3). (ENG.). 176p. (J). (gr. 3-7). 2013. 17.99 *(978-1-4424-5751-5(1))* 2010. pap. 7.99 *(978-1-4169-8273-9(6))* Simon & Schuster Children's Publishing. (Aladdin).

—Aphrodite the Diva. 2013. (Goddess Girls Ser.: 6). (ENG., Illus.). 288p. (J). (gr. 3-7). 17.99 *(978-1-4424-7478-9(5),* Aladdin) Simon & Schuster Children's Publishing.

—Artemis the Brave. (Goddess Girls Ser.: 4). (ENG.). 240p. (J). (gr. 3-7). 2013. 17.99 *(978-1-4424-6139-0(X))* 2010. pap. 7.99 *(978-1-4169-8274-6(4))* Simon & Schuster Children's Publishing. (Aladdin).

—Artemis the Loyal. 2013. (Goddess Girls Ser.: 7). (ENG., Illus.). 288p. (J). (gr. 3-7). 16.99 *(978-1-4424-8594-5(9),* Aladdin) Simon & Schuster Children's Publishing.

—Athena the Brain. (Goddess Girls Ser.: 1). (ENG.). 176p. (J). (gr. 3-7). 2012. 17.99 *(978-1-4424-5765-2(1))* 2010. pap. 7.99 *(978-1-4169-8271-5(X))* Simon & Schuster Children's Publishing. (Aladdin).

—Athena the Wise. (Goddess Girls Ser.: 5). (ENG., 256p. (J). (gr. 3-7). 2013. Illus.). 17.99 *(978-1-4424-7477-2(7))* 2011. pap. 8.99 *(978-1-4424-2097-7(9))* Simon & Schuster Children's Publishing. (Aladdin)

—Calliope the Muse. 2016. (Goddess Girls Ser.: 20). (ENG., Illus.). 256p. (J). (gr. 3-7). 17.99 *(978-1-4814-5005-8(0),* Simon & Schuster/Paula Wiseman Bks.) Simon & Schuster/Paula Wiseman Bks.

—Freya & the Magic Jewel. 2018. (Thunder Girls Ser.: 1). (ENG., Illus.). 272p. (J). (gr. 3-7). 16.99 *(978-1-4814-9640-7(9),* Aladdin) Simon & Schuster Children's Publishing.

—Freya & the Magic Jewel. 2019. (Thunder Girls Ser.: 1). (ENG.). 288p. (J). (gr. 3-7). pap. 7.99 *(978-1-4814-9639-1(5),* Simon & Schuster/Paula Wiseman Bks.) Simon & Schuster/Paula Wiseman Bks.

—Medusa the Mean. (Goddess Girls Ser.: 8). (ENG., 256p. (J). (gr. 3-7). 2013. Illus.). 17.99 *(978-1-4424-8595-2(7))* 2012. pap. 8.99 *(978-1-4424-3379-3(5))* Simon & Schuster Children's Publishing. (Aladdin).

—Medusa the Mean. 2012. (Goddess Girls Ser.: 8). lib. bdg. 18.40 *(978-0-606-26348-1(9))* Turtleback.

—Pandora the Curious. 2012. (Goddess Girls Ser.: 9). (ENG.). 256p. (J). (gr. 3-7). 17.99 *(978-1-4424-5975-5(1));* pap. 8.99 *(978-1-4424-4935-0(7))* Simon & Schuster Children's Publishing. (Aladdin).

—Pandora the Curious. 2012. (Goddess Girls Ser.: 9). lib. bdg. 18.40 *(978-0-606-26903-2(7))* Turtleback.

—Persephone the Daring. 2013. (Goddess Girls Ser.: 11). lib. bdg. 18.40 *(978-0-606-32050-4(4))* Turtleback.

—Persephone the Phony. (Goddess Girls Ser.: 2). (ENG.). 160p. (J). (gr. 3-7). 2012. 17.99 *(978-1-4424-5752-2(X))* 2010. (Illus.). pap. 7.99 *(978-1-4169-8272-2(8))* Simon & Schuster Children's Publishing. (Aladdin).

—Rapunzel Cuts Loose. 2014. (Grimmtastic Girls Ser.: 4). lib. bdg. 16.00 *(978-0-606-36064-7(6))* Turtleback.

—Snow White Lucks Out. 2014. (Grimmtastic Girls Ser.: 3). lib. bdg. 16.00 *(978-0-606-35852-1(8))* Turtleback.

Homework, 6 Packs. (gr. -1-2). 27.00 *(978-0-7635-9453-4(9))* Rigby Education.

Homzie, Hillary. Ellie May on April Fools' Day: An Ellie May Adventure. Ebbeler, Jeffrey, illus. 2018. (Ellie May Ser.: 2). (ENG.). 112p. (J). (gr. 1-4). lib. bdg. 14.99 *(978-1-58089-820-1(3))* Charlesbridge Publishing, Inc.

—Ellie May on Presidents' Day: An Ellie May Adventure. Ebbeler, Jeffrey, illus. 2018. (Ellie May Ser.: 1). (ENG.). 112p. (J). (gr. 1-4). lib. bdg. 14.99 *(978-1-58089-819-5(X))* Charlesbridge Publishing, Inc.

—Pumpkin Spice Secrets: A Swirl Novel. 2017. (Swirl Ser.: 1). (ENG.). 248p. (J). (gr. 3-7). 7.99 *(978-1-5107-3007-6(9));* 16.99 *(978-1-5107-3045-8(1))* Skyhorse Publishing Co., Inc. (Sky Pony Pr.).

Honeycutt, Natalie. The Best-Laid Plans of Jonah Twist. 2014. (ENG.). 128p. (J). (gr. 2-5). pap. 13.99 *(978-1-4814-3107-1(2),* Simon & Schuster Bks. For Young Readers) Simon & Schuster Bks. For Young Readers.

Hood, Ann. She Loves You (Yeah, Yeah, Yeah) 2019. 288p. (J). (gr. 5). 8.99 *(978-1-5247-8512-3(1),* Penguin Workshop) Penguin Young Readers Group.

Hood-Caddy, Karen. Howl: The Wild Place Adventure Series. 2011. (Wild Place Adventure Ser.: 1). (ENG.). 256p. (J). (gr. 6-8). pap. 9.99 *(978-1-926607-25-2(2))* Dundurn Pr. CAN. Dist: Publishers Group West (PGW).

Hooks, Gwendolyn. The Best Trick: A Pet Club Story, 1 vol. Byrne, Mike, illus. 2010. (Pet Club Ser.). (ENG.). 32p. (J). (gr. 1-2). 22.65 *(978-1-4342-2052-3(4),* 102782, Stone Arch Bks.) Capstone.

—Buddy Bench, 1 vol. Ng-Benitez, Shirley, illus. 2019. (Confetti Kids Ser.: 8). (ENG.). 32p. (J). (gr. k-2). 14.95 *(978-1-62014-571-5(5),* leelowbooks); pap. 10.95 *(978-1-62014-572-2(3),* leelowbooks) Lee & Low Bks., Inc.

Hooper, Mary. Down to Earth. Harker, Lesley, illus. 2008. (Two Naughty Angels Ser.). 96p. (J). (gr. 2-4). pap. 11.95 *(978-0-7475-9061-3(3))* Bloomsbury Publishing Plc GBR. Dist: Independent Pubs. Group.

—The Ghoul at School. Harker, Lesley, illus. 2008. (Two Naughty Angels Ser.). 96p. (J). (gr. 2-4). pap. 11.95 *(978-0-7475-9060-6(5))* Bloomsbury Publishing Plc GBR. Dist: Independent Pubs. Group.

—Round the Rainbow. Harker, Lesley, illus. 2008. (Two Naughty Angels Ser.). 96p. (J). (gr. 2-4). pap. 11.95 *(978-0-7475-9062-0(1))* Bloomsbury Publishing Plc GBR. Dist: Independent Pubs. Group.

Hoover, P. J. Tut. 2016. (J). lib. bdg. 20.85 *(978-0-606-38442-1(1))* Turtleback.

Hopkins, Cathy. Mates, Dates, & Inflatable Bras. 2011. (Mates, Dates Ser.). (ENG.). 176p. (YA). (gr. 7). pap. 9.99 *(978-1-4424-3113-3(X),* Simon Pulse) Simon Pulse.

—Teen Queens & Has-Beens. 2010. (Truth or Dare Ser.). (ENG.). 192p. (YA). (gr. 7). pap. 9.99 *(978-1-4424-1416-7(2),* Simon Pulse) Simon Pulse.

Hopkins, Ellen. Crank. (Crank Trilogy Ser.). (ENG., (YA). (gr. 9). 2013. Illus.). 576p. pap. 14.99 *(978-1-4424-7181-8(6))* 2010. 544p. 24.99 *(978-1-4169-9513-5(7))* McElderry, Margaret K. Bks. (McElderry, Margaret K. Bks.).

—Crank. 2013. lib. bdg. 24.50 *(978-0-606-35118-8(3))* Turtleback.

—The Crank Trilogy: Crank; Glass; Fallout. 2013. (Crank Trilogy Ser.). (ENG., Illus.). 1952p. (YA). (gr. 9). pap. 38.99 *(978-1-4424-9959-1(1),* McElderry, Margaret K. Bks.) McElderry, Margaret K. Bks.

—Rumble. 2016. (ENG., Illus.). 576p. (YA). (gr. 9). pap. 14.99 *(978-1-4424-8285-2(0),* McElderry, Margaret K. Bks.) McElderry, Margaret K. Bks.

Hopkinson, Deborah. A Letter to My Teacher: A Teacher Appreciation Gift. Carpenter, Nancy, illus. 2017. 40p. (J). (gr. -1-3). 18.99 *(978-0-375-86845-0(3),* Schwartz & Wade Bks.) Random Hse. Children's Bks.

Hopper, Laura. I Never. 2019. (ENG.). 304p. (YA). (gr. 9). pap. 9.99 *(978-1-328-59587-4(0),* 1730762, Clarion Bks.) HarperCollins Pubs.

Horn, Lorri. Dewey Fairchild, Sibling Problem Solver. 2019. (Dewey Fairchild Ser.: 3). (ENG.). 256p. (J). (gr. 4-7). 13.99 *(978-1-948705-41-7(9))* Amberjack Publishing Co.

—Dewey Fairchild, Teacher Problem Solver. 2018. (Dewey Fairchild Ser.: 2). (ENG., Illus.). 286p. (J). (gr. 4-7). 13.99 *(978-1-944995-85-0(4))* Amberjack Publishing Co.

Horowitz, Anthony. Point Blank. 2006. (Alex Rider Ser.: 2). (ENG.). 320p. (J). (gr. 5-18). 9.99 *(978-0-14-240612-0(0),* Puffin Books) Penguin Young Readers Group.

—Return to Groosham Grange: The Unholy Grail. 2010. (ENG.). 224p. (J). (gr. 5-18). 7.99 *(978-0-14-241571-9(5),* Puffin Books) Penguin Young Readers Group.

Horowitz, Lauren Bird. Shattered Blue, 0 vols. 2015. (Light Trilogy Ser.: 1). (ENG.). 336p. (YA). (gr. 9-12). pap. 9.99 *(978-1-5039-4997-3(4),* 9781503949973, Skyscape) Amazon Publishing.

Hosford, Kate. Infinity & Me. Swiatkowska, Gabi, illus. 2012. (ENG.). 32p. (J). (gr. k-4). lib. bdg. 19.99 *(978-0-7613-6726-0(8),* b5831ad3-c96a-45d4-b1c4-f4aa9e049398, Carolrhoda Bks.) Lerner Publishing Group.

Houran, Lori Haskins. Alien in the Outfield (Book 6) Warrick, Jessica, illus. 2017. (How to Be an Earthling Ser.: 6). 64p. (J). (gr. 1-4). 6.99 *(978-1-57565-848-3(8),* 6b5c279a-7e30-4bcd-be2d-055ec8834290, Kane Press) Astra Publishing Hse.

—Earth's Got Talent! (Book 4) Courage. Warrick, Jessica, illus. 2016. (How to Be an Earthling (r) Ser.: 4). (ENG.). 64p. (J). (gr. 1-3). E-Book 34.65 *(978-1-57565-829-2(1))* Astra Publishing Hse.

—Parks & Wrecks (Book 10) Warrick, Jessica, illus. 2018. (How to Be an Earthling Ser.). 64p. (J). (gr. 1-4). pap. 6.99 *(978-1-63592-021-5(3),* 7d90ddd2-a724-4d48-a707-23a7f6533ea1, Kane Press) Astra Publishing Hse.

Houtman, Jacqueline. Reinvention of Edison Thomas. 2012. (ENG.). 192p. (J). (gr. 3-7). pap. 8.95 *(978-1-59078-951-3(2),* Astra Young Readers) Astra Publishing Hse.

Houts, Michelle. Nuts about Science: Lucy's Lab #1. Zechel, Elizabeth, illus. 2017. (Lucy's Lab Ser.: 1). (ENG.). 112p. (J). (gr. 1-4). 13.99 *(978-1-5107-1064-1(7),* Sky Pony Pr.) Skyhorse Publishing Co., Inc.

—Solids, Liquids, Guess Who's Got Gas? Lucy's Lab #2. Zechel, Elizabeth, illus. 2017. (Lucy's Lab Ser.: 2). (ENG.). 104p. (J). (gr. 1-4). 13.99 *(978-1-5107-1067-2(1),* Sky Pony Pr.) Skyhorse Publishing Co., Inc.

Howard, Denise. Greentown Elementary: The Seafood Nightmare. 2012. (ENG.). pap. *(978-1-4675-3556-4(7))* Independent Pub.

Howard, Elizabeth Fitzgerald. Virgie Goes to School with Us Boys. Lewis, E. B., illus. 2005. (gr. k-3). 18.00 *(978-0-7569-5088-0(0))* Perfection Learning Corp.

—Virgie Goes to School with Us Boys. Lewis, E. B., illus. 2005. (ENG.). 32p. (J). (gr. k-3). reprint ed. 8.99 *(978-0-689-87793-3(5),* Aladdin) Simon & Schuster Children's Publishing.

Howard, Greg. Social Intercourse. 2018. (ENG., Illus.). 320p. (YA). (gr. 9). 18.99 *(978-1-4814-9781-7(2),* Simon & Schuster Bks. For Young Readers) Simon & Schuster Bks. For Young Readers.

Howard, Kate, illus. On Our Way to First Grade. 2015. 32p. (J). *(978-0-545-82340-1(4))* Scholastic, Inc.

Howard, Victoria. The Adventures of Max: The Bolognese Dog. 2012. 72p. pap. 28.99 *(978-1-4772-6560-4(0))* AuthorHouse.

Howe, James. Addie on the Inside. 2012. (Misfits Ser.). (ENG., Illus.). 240p. (J). (gr. 5-9). pap. 8.99 *(978-1-4169-1385-6(8),* Atheneum Bks. for Young Readers) Simon & Schuster Children's Publishing.

—The Complete Misfits Collection: The Misfits; Totally Joe; Addie on the Inside; Also Known As Elvis. 2015. (Misfits Ser.). (ENG., Illus.). 1072p. (J). (gr. 5-9). pap. 27.99 *(978-1-4814-2898-9(5),* Atheneum Bks. for Young Readers) Simon & Schuster Children's Publishing.

—The Misfits. 2003. (Misfits Ser.). (ENG.). 304p. (J). (gr. 5-9). mass mkt. 8.99 *(978-0-689-83956-6(1),* Atheneum Bks. for Young Readers) Simon & Schuster Children's Publishing.

—Totally Joe. (Misfits Ser.). (ENG.). (J). 2007. 224p. (gr. 4-8). pap. 8.99 *(978-0-689-83958-0(8))* 2005. (Illus.). 208p. (gr. 5-9). 19.99 *(978-0-689-83957-3(X))* Simon & Schuster Children's Publishing. (Atheneum Bks. for Young Readers).

Howe, Katherine. Conversion. 2015. (ENG.). 432p. (YA). (gr. 7). pap. 11.99 *(978-0-14-751155-3(0),* Speak) Penguin Young Readers Group.

Howland, Ashley. The Homework Goblin. 2013. 24p. pap. 13.97 *(978-1-62516-301-1(0),* Strategic Bk. Publishing) Strategic Book Publishing & Rights Agency (SBPRA).

Hruza, Rachel. Dear Isaac Newton, You're Ruining My Life. 2018. (ENG.). 356p. (J). (gr. 3-7). 16.99 *(978-1-5107-2526-3(1),* Sky Pony Pr.) Skyhorse Publishing Co., Inc.

Hubbard, Jenny. Paper Covers Rock. 2012. (ENG.). 192p. (YA). (gr. 9). pap. 7.99 *(978-0-385-74056-2(5),* Ember) Random Hse. Children's Bks.

Hubert, Adrian & the Tree of Secrets. Caillou, Marie, illus. 2014. 128p. (gr. 6). pap. 18.95 *(978-1-55152-556-3(9))* Arsenal Pulp Pr. CAN. Dist: Consortium Bk. Sales & Distribution.

Hudson, Wade. The Two Tyrones. Page, Mark, illus. 2004. 32p. (J). lib. bdg. 15.00 *(978-1-4242-0239-3(6))* Fitzgerald Bks.

Hue, Wendy. Tópé Arrives. 2011. (Illus.). 100p. pap. 12.10 *(978-1-4567-7640-4(1))* AuthorHouse.

Huelin, Jodi. Alvin & the Big Art Show. 2013. (I Can Read! Level 2 Ser.). (J). lib. bdg. 13.55 *(978-0-606-35040-2(3))* Turtleback.

—Alvin & the Substitute Teacher. 2013. (I Can Read! Level 2 Ser.). (J). lib. bdg. 13.55 *(978-0-606-32462-5(3))* Turtleback.

Hueller, Andy. Skipping Stones at the Center of the Earth: A Middle Grade Novel. 2011. 241p. (J). pap. 8.99 *(978-1-59955-488-4(7),* Bonneville Bks.) Cedar Fort, Inc./CFI Distribution.

Hueller, P. W. Wolf High. 2015. (Tartan House Ser.). (ENG.). 96p. (J). (gr. 3-6). *(978-1-63235-055-8(6),* 11682, 12-Story Library) Bookstaves, LLC.

Hugelmeyer, Michele. Alex King, Famous Fourth Grader. 2007. 78p. pap. 8.99 *(978-1-4303-0821-8(4))* Lulu Pr., Inc.

Hughes, Alison. Kings of the Court, 1 vol. 2017. (ENG.). 192p. (J). (gr. 4-7). pap. 9.95 *(978-1-4598-1219-2(0))* Orca Bk. Pubs. USA.

—On a Scale from Idiot to Complete Jerk, 1 vol. 2014. (ENG., Illus.). 144p. (J). (gr. 4-7). pap. 9.95 *(978-1-4598-0484-5(8))* Orca Bk. Pubs. USA.

Hughes, Dawn Marie. Deadwood: Haunted Stories. 2006. 94p. pap. 16.95 *(978-1-4241-2600-2(2))* PublishAmerica, Inc.

Hughes, Diane. Wilbur Goes to School. 2011. 20p. pap. 11.99 *(978-1-4670-3964-2(0))* AuthorHouse.

Hughes, Mark Peter. Lemonade Mouth: Adapted Movie Tie-In Edition. movie tie-in ed. 2011. (ENG.). 352p. (YA). (gr. 7-7). pap. 8.99 *(978-0-385-74208-5(8),* Ember) Random Hse. Children's Bks.

—Lemonade Mouth Puckers Up. 2013. (ENG.). 304p. (YA). (gr. 7). pap. 11.99 *(978-0-385-73713-5(0),* Ember) Random Hse. Children's Bks.

Hughes, Shirley. Bobbo Goes to School. Hughes, Shirley, illus. 2013. (ENG., Illus.). 32p. (J). (gr. -1-2). 16.99 *(978-0-7636-6524-1(X))* Candlewick Pr.

—Lucy & Tom at School. 2018. (Lucy & Tom Ser.). (Illus.). 32p. (J). (gr. -1-k). pap. 12.99 *(978-1-78295-659-4(X),* Red Fox) Random House Children's Books GBR. Dist: Independent Pubs. Group.

Hughes, Thomas. Tom Brown's School Days by an Old Boy. 2004. reprint ed. pap. 1.99 *(978-1-4192-9039-8(8))* Kessinger Publishing, LLC.

—Tom Browns Schooldays. 2006. pap. *(978-1-4068-1407-1(5))* Echo Library.

Hulme, Joy N. Climbing the Rainbow. 2004. 224p. (J). 15.99 *(978-0-380-81572-2(9))* HarperCollins Pubs.

Hulst, W. G. van de & Hulst, Willem G. van de, illus. The Secret in the Box. 2014. (J). *(978-1-928136-17-0(6))* Inheritance Pubns.

Hunt, Lynda Mullaly. Fish in a Tree. l.t. ed. 2019. (ENG.). 296p. (J). (gr. 5). pap. 12.99 *(978-1-4328-6397-5(5),* Large Print Pr.) Thorndike Pr.

—Fish in a Tree. 2017. lib. bdg. 19.65 *(978-0-606-39991-3(7))* Turtleback.

Huntley, Amy. The Everafter. 2010. (ENG.). 272p. (YA). (gr. 8). pap. 9.99 *(978-0-06-177681-6(5),* Balzer & Bray) HarperCollins Pubs.

Hurley Deriso, Christine. Things I'd Rather Do Than Die. 2018. (ENG.). 304p. (YA). (gr. 9-12). pap. 14.99 *(978-1-63583-022-4(2),* 1635830222, Flux) North Star Editions.

Hurley, Tonya. Ghostgirl. 2010. (Ghostgirl Ser.: 1). (ENG., Illus.). 336p. (YA). (gr. 7-17). pap. 17.99 *(978-0-316-03635-1(8))* Little, Brown Bks. for Young Readers.

—Ghostgirl: Homecoming. 2010. (Ghostgirl Ser.: 2). (ENG.). 304p. (YA). (gr. 7-17). pap. 16.99 *(978-0-316-08943-2(5))* Little, Brown Bks. for Young Readers.

Hurwitz, Johanna. Amazing Monty. McGrory, Anik, illus. 2013. (Monty Ser.: 3). (ENG.). 112p. (J). (gr. k-4). pap. 5.99 *(978-0-7636-6561-6(4))* Candlewick Pr.

—Class Clown. Hamanaka, Sheila, illus. 2011. (ENG.). 112p. (J). (gr. 1-4). 16.19 *(978-0-590-41821-8(1))* Scholastic, Inc.

—Mostly Monty, 1. McGrory, Anik, illus. 2008. (Monty Ser.: 1). (ENG.). 86p. (J). (gr. k-3). 18.69 *(978-0-7636-2831-4(X))* Candlewick Pr.

—Mostly Monty: First Grader. McGrory, Anik, illus. 2008. (Monty Ser.: 1). (ENG.). 96p. (J). (gr. 1-4). pap. 5.99 *(978-0-7636-4062-0(X))* Candlewick Pr.

Hurwitz, Kathleen A. Timothy's Tic. McKelvey, Shawn, illus. 2008. 40p. (gr. -1 — 1). 16.99 *(978-1-4389-1924-9(7))* AuthorHouse.

Hurwitz, Michele Weber. Calli Be Gold. 2012. 208p. (J). (gr. 3-7). 7.99 *(978-0-375-86528-2(4),* Yearling) Random Hse. Children's Bks.

—Ethan Marcus Stands Up. (ENG.). (J). (gr. 3-7). 2018. 288p. pap. 7.99 *(978-1-4814-8926-3(7))* 2017. (Illus.). 272p. 17.99 *(978-1-4814-8925-6(9))* Simon & Schuster Children's Publishing. (Aladdin).

Huser, Glen. Skinnybones & the Wrinkle Queen, 1 vol. 2006. (ENG.). 192p. (J). (gr. 7-10). pap. 8.95

(978-0-88899-733-3(7)) Groundwood Bks. CAN. Dist: Publishers Group West (PGW).

—The Snuggly, 1 vol. Pavlović, Milan, illus. 2018. (ENG.). 32p. (J). (gr. k-2). 16.95 (978-1-55498-901-0(9)) Groundwood Bks. CAN. Dist: Publishers Group West (PGW).

Hutchinson, Shaun David, et al. Violent Ends. (ENG., Illus.). (YA). (gr. 9). 2016. 368p. pap. 10.99 (978-1-4814-3746-2(1)) 2015. 352p. 19.99 (978-1-4814-3745-5(3)) Simon Pulse. (Simon Pulse).

Hyde, Catherine Ryan. Jumpstart the World. 2011. 192p. (YA). (gr. 9). pap. 7.99 (978-0-375-86626-5(4), Ember) Random Hse. Children's Bks.

Hyde, Noreen. The Adventures of Miss Chief: Miss Chief Goes to School. Pushee, Marisa, illus. 2007. 28p. per. 9.95 (978-1-59858-368-7(9)) Dog Ear Publishing, LLC.

Hymas, Allison K. Under Locker & Key. 2017. (Max Ser.). (ENG., Illus.). 256p. (J). (gr. 4-8). pap. 7.99 (978-1-4814-6342-3(X), Simon & Schuster/Paula Wiseman Bks.) Simon & Schuster/Paula Wiseman Bks.

Iannantuano, Theresa. Who Took My Lunch? 2012. 24p. pap. 15.99 (978-1-4771-1582-4(X)) Xlibris Corp.

Ide, Laurie S. & Langcaon, Jeff. Super Puffy. 2004. (Illus.). 32p. (J). 12.95 (978-1-56647-686-7(0)) Mutual Publishing LLC.

Ignatow, Amy. The Popularity Papers: Book Five: the Awesomely Awful Melodies of Lydia Goldblatt & Julie Graham-Chang, Bk. 5. 2014. (Popularity Papers). (ENG., Illus.). 208p. (J). (gr. 3-7). pap. 9.95 (978-1-4197-1308-8(6), 1046603, Amulet Bks.) Abrams, Inc.

—The Popularity Papers: Research for the Social Improvement & General Betterment of Lydia Goldblatt & Julie Graham-Chang. 2011. (Popularity Papers). (ENG., Illus.). 208p. (J). (gr. 3-7). pap. 10.99 (978-0-8109-9723-3(1), 675503, Amulet Bks.) Abrams, Inc.

—The Popularity Papers: Book Three: Words of (Questionable) Wisdom from Lydia Goldblatt & Julie Graham-Chang. 2013. (ENG., Illus.). 208p. (J). (gr. 3-7). pap. 10.99 (978-1-4197-0535-9(0), 1003603, Amulet Bks.) Abrams, Inc.

Igneri, David S. The Boy & Girl Who Hated History. Wigley, Audrey Watson, illus. 2009. 44p. pap. 24.95 (978-1-61546-828-7(5)) America Star Bks.

Ikegami, Aiko. Friends. Ikegami, Aiko, illus. 2016. (ENG., Illus.). 32p. (J). (gr. -1-3). 16.99 (978-0-8075-2550-0(2), 807525502) Whitman, Albert & Co.

Imam, Seema & Imam, Ibrahim. I am Listening. 2007. (I Am Good Ser.). (Illus.). 32p. (J). mass mkt. (978-0-9787849-8-0(7)) Lucent Interpretations, LLC.

Immenschuh, Marilyn Y. Samantha & the Kids of Room 220. 2007. 148p. per. 11.95 (978-0-595-46842-3(X)) iUniverse, Inc.

Imperato, Teresa. Fiona's Fairy Magic. Huang, Benrei, illus. 2005. 14p. (J). 10.95 (978-1-58117-322-2(9), Intervisual/Piggy Toes) Bendon, Inc.

In a World Just Right. 2015. (ENG., Illus.). 432p. (YA). (gr. 7). 18.99 (978-1-4814-1660-3(X)) Simon & Schuster Children's Publishing.

Inagaki, Riichiro. Eyeshield 21, Vol. 8, Vol. 8. 2006. (Eyeshield 21 Ser.: 8). (ENG., Illus.). 216p. pap. 9.99 (978-1-4215-0637-1(8)) Viz Media.

—Eyeshield 21, Vol. 9. 2006. (Eyeshield 21 Ser.: 9). (ENG., Illus.). 208p. (gr. 11). pap. 9.99 (978-1-4215-0638-8(6)) Viz Media.

Ingold, Jeanette. Mountain Solo. 2005. (ENG.). 320p. (YA). (gr. 7-12). pap. 15.95 (978-0-15-205358-1(1), 1062824, Clarion Bks.) HarperCollins Pubs.

Ingram, Laura. Stand Up. 2018. 120p. (J). pap. (978-1-937849-95-5(3), Nesting Tree Bks.) Raven Publishing Inc. of Montana.

Irbinskas, Heather. The Lost Kachina. Albert, Robert & Anthis, Brian, illus. 2004. 32p. (J). 15.95 (978-1-885772-33-6(5)) Kiva Publishing, Inc.

Ireland, Justina. Evie Allen vs. the Quiz Bowl Zombies. Champion, Tyler, illus. 2017. (Devils' Pass Ser.). (ENG.). 128p. (J). (gr. 4-8). lib. bdg. 25.99 (978-1-4965-4988-4(0), 135880, Stone Arch Bks.) Capstone.

—Tiffany Donovan vs. the Cookie Elves of Destruction. Champion, Tyler, illus. 2017. (Devils' Pass Ser.). (ENG.). 128p. (J). (gr. 4-8). lib. bdg. 25.99 (978-1-4965-4987-7(2), 135879, Stone Arch Bks.) Capstone.

—Vengeance Bound. (ENG., (YA). (gr. 9). 2014. Illus.). 336p. pap. 12.99 (978-1-4424-4463-8(0)) 2013. 320p. 17.99 (978-1-4424-4462-1(2)) Simon & Schuster Bks. For Young Readers. (Simon & Schuster Bks. For Young Readers).

—Zach Lopez vs. the Unicorns of Doom. Champion, Tyler, illus. 2017. (Devils' Pass Ser.). (ENG.). 128p. (J). (gr. 4-8). lib. bdg. 25.99 (978-1-4965-4989-1(9), 135881, Stone Arch Bks.) Capstone.

Irwin, Ms. Judy. We're Done. 2012. 104p. pap. (978-0-9877088-4-7(8)) Irwin, Judy.

Ius, Dawn. Anne & Henry. 2015. (ENG., Illus.). 304p. (YA). (gr. 9). 18.99 (978-1-4814-3941-1(3), Simon Pulse) Simon Pulse.

Iyengar, Malathi Michelle. Romina's Rangoli. 2007. (Romina's Rangoli Ser.). (ENG., Illus.). 32p. (J). (gr. -1-3). 16.95 (978-1-885008-32-9(5), Shen's Bks.) Lee & Low Bks., Inc.

Izakson, Meron H. & Raday, Leanne. The Essential List: A Letter to the Teacher. 2017. (ENG., Illus.). 59p. (J). pap. (978-965-229-919-2(7)) Gefen Publishing Hse., Ltd.

Jackson, Al, Jr. Adventures of Middle School: The Handbook. 2013. (ENG.). 60p. (YA). pap. 12.95 (978-1-4787-0892-6(1)) Outskirts Pr., Inc.

Jackson, Ellen. The Cupcake Thief. 2008. pap. 34.95 (978-1-58013-765-2(2)) Astra Publishing Hse.

—The Cupcake Thief. Sims, Blanche, illus. 2007. (Social Studies Connects Ser.). 32p. (J). (gr. 1-3). pap. 5.95 (978-1-57565-247-4(1), 081b7736-fccb-4c97-afb0-316316c1edd1, Kane Press) Astra Publishing Hse.

Jackson, Kyle. Back on Track. Rumble, Simon, illus. 2018. (Mac's Sports Report). (ENG.). 128p. (J). (gr. 3-4). pap. 7.99 (978-1-63163-224-2(8), 1631632248); lib. bdg. 27.13 (978-1-63163-223-5(X), 163163223X) North Star Editions. (Jolly Fish Pr.).

—Concussion Comeback. Rumble, Simon, illus. 2018. (Mac's Sports Report). (ENG.). 128p. (J). (gr. 3-4). pap. 7.99 (978-1-63163-228-0(0), 1631632280); lib. bdg. 27.13 (978-1-63163-227-3(2), 1631632272) North Star Editions. (Jolly Fish Pr.).

—Racket Rumors. Rumble, Simon, illus. 2018. (Mac's Sports Report). (ENG.). 128p. (J). (gr. 3-4). pap. 7.99 (978-1-63163-232-7(9), 1631632329); lib. bdg. 27.13 (978-1-63163-231-0(0), 1631632310) North Star Editions. (Jolly Fish Pr.).

—Sideline Pressure. 2018. (Mac's Sports Report). (ENG., Illus.). 128p. (J). (gr. 3-4). lib. bdg. 27.13 (978-1-63163-235-8(3), 1631632353, Jolly Fish Pr.) North Star Editions.

—Sideline Pressure. Rumble, Simon, illus. 2018. (Mac's Sports Report). (ENG.). 128p. (J). (gr. 3-4). pap. 7.99 (978-1-63163-236-5(1), 1631632361, Jolly Fish Pr.) North Star Editions.

Jackson, Ladain. Rare Vision. 2013. 100p. pap. 8.99 (978-1-937165-35-2(3)) Orange Hat Publishing.

Jackson, Marcus. Because My Teacher Said I Can. 2011. 24p. pap. 13.86 (978-1-4567-6492-0(6)) AuthorHouse.

Jacobs, Evan. Screaming Quietly, 1 vol. 2013. (Gravel Road Ser.). (ENG.). 224p. (YA). (gr. 9-12). pap. 11.95 (978-1-62250-003-1(2)) Saddleback Educational Publishing, Inc.

—Varsity 170, 1 vol., Bk. 10. 2015. (Gravel Road Ser.). (ENG.). 184p. (YA). (gr. 9-12). pap. 11.95 (978-1-62250-889-1(0)) Saddleback Educational Publishing, Inc.

Jacobs, John. I Wanna Be. 2006. (Illus.). 144p. 9.95 (978-0-9774659-6-5(9)) Cameo Pubns., LLC.

Jacobs, Lana. Show-And-Tell. 2013. (Penguin Young Readers Level 2 Ser.). (Illus.). 31p. (J). lib. bdg. 13.55 (978-0-606-31694-1(9)) Turtleback.

Jacobs, Paul DuBois & Swender, Jennifer. The Bow-Wow Bus. Laberis, Stephanie, illus. 2017. (Animal Inn Ser.: 3). (ENG.). 112p. (J). (gr. 2-5). pap. 5.99 (978-1-4814-6229-7(6), Simon & Schuster/Paula Wiseman Bks.) Simon & Schuster/Paula Wiseman Bks.

—Fire Drill. Lee, Huy Voun, illus. 2010. (ENG.). 32p. (J). (gr. -1-2). 19.99 (978-0-8050-8953-0(5), 900055716, Holt, Henry & Co. Bks. For Young Readers) Holt, Henry & Co.

Jacobson, Jennifer Richard. Andy Shane & the Queen of Egypt. Carter, Abby, illus. 2009. (Andy Shane Ser.: 3). (ENG.). 64p. (J). (gr. k-3). 5.99 (978-0-7636-4404-8(8)) Candlewick Pr.

—Andy Shane & the Queen of Egypt. 2009. (Andy Shane Ser.: 3). lib. bdg. 14.75 (978-0-606-06592-4(X)) Turtleback.

—Andy Shane & the Very Bossy Dolores Starbuckle. Carter, Abby, illus. 2006. (Andy Shane Ser.: 1). (ENG.). 64p. (J). (gr. k-3). 5.99 (978-0-7636-3044-7(6)) Candlewick Pr.

—Andy Shane & the Very Bossy Dolores Starbuckle. Carter, Abby, illus. 2008. (Andy Shane Ser.). (J). (gr. -1-3). 25.95 incl. audio (978-1-4301-0321-9(3)); pap. 16.95 incl. audio (978-1-4301-0320-2(5)) Live Oak Media.

—Andy Shane Is Not in Love. 2009. (Andy Shane Ser.: 4). lib. bdg. 14.75 (978-0-606-06618-1(7)) Turtleback.

Jacques, Taryn Elise. What's Wrong with the New Girl? Reilly, Meghan M., illus. 2004. 33p. pap. 24.95 (978-1-4137-1999-4(6)) PublishAmerica, Inc.

Jaden, Denise. Losing Faith. 2010. (ENG.). 400p. (YA). (gr. 9-18). pap. 9.99 (978-1-4169-9609-5(5), Simon Pulse) Simon Pulse.

Jager, Hartmut. The Secret of the Green Paint: Annette Vetter Adventure #2. 2007. (Illus.). 196p. (YA). pap. 9.95 (978-0-944851-28-9(2)) Earth Star Pubns.

Jaimet, Kate. Dunces Rock, 1 vol. 2014. (ENG.). 224p. (J). (gr. 4-7). pap. 9.95 (978-1-4598-0585-9(2)) Orca Bk. Pubs. USA.

Jake. 2004. (ENG.). 224p. (J). (gr. 8-12). 19.95 (978-1-890862-31-2(2), 7908bdb9-87ec-4d1d-aea2-f649f8397701) Bancroft Pr.

Jakubowski, Michele. Dodgeball, Drama, & Other Dilemmas. Montalto, Luisa, illus. (Sidney & Sydney Ser.). (ENG.). 128p. (J). (gr. 1-3). 2016. pap. 6.95 (978-1-4795-6755-3(8), 128798) 2013. 8.95 (978-1-4795-2116-6(7), 123811) 2013. lib. bdg. 25.32 (978-1-4048-8061-0(5), 121784) Capstone. (Picture Window Bks.).

—Third Grade Mix-Up, 1 vol. Montalto, Luisa, illus. 2013. (Sidney & Sydney Ser.). (ENG.). 128p. (J). (gr. 1-3). 8.95 (978-1-4048-8104-4(2), 121876, Picture Window Bks.) Capstone.

James, Brian. Ahoy, Ghost Ship Ahead! #2. Zivoin, Jennifer, illus. 2007. (Pirate School Ser.: 2). 64p. (J). (gr. 1-3). pap. 4.99 (978-0-448-44625-7(1), Grosset & Dunlap) Penguin Young Readers Group.

James, Cheryl D. Leah's Treasure Book. 2012. 36p. pap. 16.99 (978-1-4624-0422-3(7), Inspiring Voices) Author Solutions, LLC.

James, Howe. The Misfits. 2014. (Misfits Ser.). (ENG.). 304p. (J). 11.24 (978-1-63245-171-2(9)) Lectorum Pubns., Inc.

James, Mike. Bootsie - & the Team. 2012. 136p. pap. (978-1-922022-14-1(4)) Vivid Publishing.

—Bootsie - Just One More. 2012. 136p. pap. (978-1-922022-29-5(2)) Vivid Publishing.

James, Syrie & James, Ryan M. Forbidden. 2012. (Forbidden Ser.: 1). (ENG.). 416p. (YA). (gr. 8). pap. 9.99 (978-0-06-202789-4(1), HarperTeen) HarperCollins Pubs.

Jamieson, Victoria. All's Faire in Middle School. 2017. (Illus.). 264p. (J). (gr. 4-7). 22.99 (978-0-525-42998-2(0)); pap. 12.99 (978-0-525-42999-9(9)) Penguin Young Readers Group. (Dial Bks).

—All's Faire in Middle School. 2017. lib. bdg. 24.50 (978-0-606-40484-6(8)) Turtleback.

Jamison, Jo Lynn & Elliott, Lela Mae. Siren's Call of the Caves, 1 vol. 2009. 55p. pap. 16.95 (978-1-4489-8627-9(3)) PublishAmerica, Inc.

Janovitz, Marilyn. Nos Encanta la Escuela / We Love School. 2009. (SPA., Illus.). 32p. (J). (gr. -1-1). 7.95 (978-0-7358-2246-7(8)) North-South Bks., Inc.

Jansen, Karen. The Coming of an Astronaut. 2009. 68p. pap. 9.99 (978-1-60911-076-5(5), Eloquent Bks.) Strategic Book Publishing & Rights Agency (SBPRA).

Jardine, Kathy & Jardine, Ashley. The Durples: Go to School. 2010. 28p. pap. 17.99 (978-1-4490-3405-4(5)) AuthorHouse.

Jarek, Janice. Emma & Her Angels. 2012. 24p. 24.95 (978-1-4626-6255-5(2)) America Star Bks.

Jarman, Benjamin. Tony's Last Touchdown, 1 vol. 2012. (Champion Sports Story Ser.). (ENG.). 104p. (J). (gr. 3-5). 30.60 (978-0-7660-3885-1(8), 88dd6ebb-4e5a-4e51-a3e0-3bbed8fd734f); pap. 13.88 (978-1-4644-0004-9(0), f04c313c-3386-4d8c-802d-e318174c0684) Enslow Publishing, LLC.

Jarman, Julia. Harry the Clever Spider at School: Band 07/Turquoise (Collins Big Cat) Fowkes, Charlie, illus. 2007. (Collins Big Cat Ser.). (ENG.). 24p. (J). (gr. 1-2). pap. 6.99 (978-0-00-718670-9(3)) HarperCollins Pubs. Ltd. GBR. Dist: Independent Pubs. Group.

—The Magic Backpack. Gon, Adriano, illus. 2003. (Flying Foxes Ser.). (ENG.). 48p. (J). lib. bdg. (978-0-7787-1487-3(X)) Crabtree Publishing Co.

Jayne, Hannah. Copycat. 2018. (ENG.). 272p. (YA). (gr. 8-12). pap. 10.99 (978-1-4926-4739-3(X)) Sourcebooks, Inc.

Jeffs, Dixie. Pokey's Chance. 2013. 24p. pap. 24.95 (978-1-62709-292-0(7)) America Star Bks.

Jempsa, Alice B. Why Does Everything Happen to Me? 2011. 28p. (gr. -1). pap. 13.54 (978-1-4269-5005-6(5)) Trafford Publishing.

Jenkins, A. M. Out of Order. 2003. 256p. (J). lib. bdg. 16.89 (978-0-06-623969-9(9)) HarperCollins Pubs.

—Repossessed. 2008. (ENG.). 240p. (YA). (gr. 8). pap. 9.99 (978-0-06-083570-5(2), HarperTeen) HarperCollins Pubs.

Jenkins, Amanda. Mere Moments A Story of Pearl Harbor, the Day the Towers Fell. 2011. (Readers' & Writers' Genre Workshop Ser.). (J). pap. (978-1-4509-3019-2(0)) Benchmark Education Co.

Jennings, Patrick. Guinea Dog. 2011. (Guinea Dog Ser.). (ENG.). 208p. (J). (gr. 3-6). 7.99 (978-1-60684-153-2(X), 6f45a8b7-97af-4a08-9755-6539ef205dfb, Darby Creek) Lerner Publishing Group.

—Wish Riders. 2006. (ENG.). 288p. (gr. 5-9). 15.99 (978-1-4231-0010-2(7)) Hyperion Pr.

Jennings, Rashad. Arcade & the Triple T Token, 1 vol. 2019. (Coin Slot Chronicles Ser.). (ENG., Illus.). 256p. (J). 16.99 (978-0-310-76741-1(5)) Zonderkidz.

Jensen, Olivia. Thomas & the Bully. 2009. 16p. pap. 8.49 (978-1-4389-1848-8(8)) AuthorHouse.

Jeremiah, Omari. Paper Boy Four: L. O. E. P. S. Worst Nightmare. Rollins, Berni, illus. 2007. 96p. (YA). (gr. 7-12). pap. 12.99 (978-1-929188-15-4(3)) Morton Bks.

—Paperboy 3: The School of Doom. Rollins, Bernie, illus. 2006. 75p. pap. 12.99 (978-1-929188-13-0(7)) Morton Bks.

Jerry, Spinelli. Loser. 2014. (ENG.). 224p. (J). (gr. 7-7). 11.24 (978-1-63245-207-8(3)) Lectorum Pubns., Inc.

—Stargirl. 2014. (ENG.). 208p. (YA). 11.24 (978-1-63245-152-1(2)) Lectorum Pubns., Inc.

Jette, Sarah Marie. What the Wind Can Tell You, 1 vol. 2018. (ENG.). 200p. (J). pap. 14.95 (978-1-944762-41-4(8), fc663e39-efc7-4487-a1c0-96325ef48495) Islandport Pr., Inc.

Jiménez, Francisco. La Mariposa. Silva, Simon, illus. 2004. 38p. (J). (gr. k-4). reprint ed. pap. 14.00 (978-0-7567-8433-1(6)) DIANE Publishing Co.

Jinks, Catherine. Evil Genius. 2007. 486p. (J). (978-1-4287-3510-1(0)) Harcourt Trade Pubs.

—Evil Genius. 2011. (ENG., Illus.). 496p. (YA). (gr. 7). pap. 11.99 (978-0-15-206185-2(1), 1198564, Clarion Bks.) HarperCollins Pubs.

Jocelyn, Marthe. Mable Riley: A Reliable Record of Humdrum, Peril, & Romance. 2007. 279p. (gr. 4-7). 17.00 (978-0-7569-8183-9(2)) Perfection Learning Corp.

Johannes, Shelley. Beatrice Zinker, Upside down Thinker. Johannes, Shelley, illus. 2017. (Beatrice Zinker, Upside down Thinker Ser.: 1). (ENG., Illus.). 160p. (J). (gr. 2-5). 14.99 (978-1-4847-6738-2(1)) Hyperion Bks. for Children.

—Beatrice Zinker, Upside down Thinker. Johannes, Shelley, illus. 2018. (Beatrice Zinker, Upside down Thinker Ser.: 1). (ENG., Illus.). 160p. (J). (gr. 2-5). pap. 5.99 (978-1-4847-6814-3(0)) Little, Brown Bks. for Young Readers.

—Beatrice Zinker, Upside down Thinker. 2018. (Beatrice Zinker, Upside down Thinker Ser.: 1). (J). lib. bdg. 16.00 (978-0-606-40960-5(2)) Turtleback.

—Incognito. Johannes, Shelley, illus. 2018. (Beatrice Zinker, Upside down Thinker Ser.: 2). (ENG., Illus.). 224p. (J). (gr. 1-5). 14.99 (978-1-4847-6739-9(X)); (gr. 2-5). pap. 5.99 (978-1-4847-6815-0(9)) Hyperion Bks. for Children.

Johns, Eric. Mindreaders. 2007. 184p. pap. 16.95 (978-1-4357-0121-2(6)) Lulu Pr., Inc.

Johnson, Angela. A Certain October. (ENG.). 176p. (YA). (gr. 9). 2013. pap. 10.99 (978-0-689-87065-1(5)) 2012. 16.99 (978-0-689-86505-3(8)) Simon & Schuster Bks. For Young Readers. (Simon & Schuster Bks. For Young Readers).

—Sweet, Hereafter. 2011. (ENG.). 128p. (YA). (gr. 7). pap. 9.99 (978-0-689-87386-7(7), Simon & Schuster Bks. For Young Readers) Simon & Schuster Bks. For Young Readers.

—Sweet, Hereafter, Bk. 3. 2010. 128p. (YA). (gr. 9-18). pap. 16.99 (978-1-4169-9995-9(7)) Simon & Schuster Children's Publishing.

Johnson-Choong, Shelly. The Jewelry Box. 2nd ed. 2004. (YA). reprint ed. pap. 10.95 (978-1-932280-40-1(5), 80405) Granite Publishing & Distribution.

Johnson, Christine. Nocturne. 2011. (ENG.). 368p. (YA). (gr. 7). 16.99 (978-1-4424-0776-3(X), Simon Pulse) Simon Pulse.

—Nocturne: A Claire de Lune Novel. 2012. (ENG.). 384p. (YA). (gr. 7). pap. 9.99 (978-1-4424-0777-0(8), Simon Pulse) Simon Pulse.

Johnson, Donna. The Story of the Little Red Leaf. Johnson, Emily, illus. l.t. ed. 2006. (ENG.). 22p. (J). 25.00 (978-0-9778774-0-9(X)) Choice Point Editions.

Johnson, Kristel. Even When We Are Apart. 2008. 20p. pap. 24.95 (978-1-60610-435-4(7)) America Star Bks.

Johnson, Kristin. Enough to Go Around: A Story of Generosity. Wood, Hannah, illus. 2018. (Cloverleaf Books (tm) — Stories with Character Ser.). (ENG.). 24p. (J). (gr. k-2). pap. 8.99 (978-1-5415-1067-8(4), b11a2eb6-d3de-4c4e-b031-b886dd34886c, Millbrook Pr.) Lerner Publishing Group.

—In It Together: A Story of Fairness. Byrne, Mike, illus. 2018. (Cloverleaf Books (tm) — Stories with Character Ser.). (ENG.). 24p. (J). (gr. k-2). pap. 8.99 (978-1-5415-1068-5(2), 832e11af-cbe0-4049-9bde-ea470b9ad403); lib. bdg. 25.32 (978-1-5124-8649-0(3), 0bbe6ba7-5b99-480d-800a-bc7633614f91) Lerner Publishing Group. (Millbrook Pr.).

Johnson, LouAnne. Muchacho: a Novel. 2011. (ENG.). 208p. (YA). (gr. 7). pap. 9.99 (978-0-375-85903-8(9), Ember) Random Hse. Children's Bks.

Johnson, Margaret. Ask Alice, 1 vol. 2011. (ENG.). 64p. pap. 14.25 incl. audio compact disk (978-84-8323-958-2(2)) Cambridge Univ. Pr.

Johnson, Maureen. The Madness Underneath: Book 2. 2013. (Shades of London Ser.: 2). (ENG.). 304p. (YA). (gr. 7). pap. 10.99 (978-0-14-242754-5(3), Speak) Penguin Young Readers Group.

—The Name of the Star. 2012. (Shades of London Ser.: 1). (ENG.). 400p. (YA). (gr. 7). pap. 12.99 (978-0-14-242205-2(3), Speak) Penguin Young Readers Group.

—The Vanishing Stair. 2019. (Truly Devious Ser.: 2). (ENG.). (YA). (gr. 9). 400p. pap. 12.99 (978-0-06-233809-9(9)); 384p. 17.99 (978-0-06-233808-2(0)); 400p. E-Book (978-0-06-233810-5(2), 9780062338105) HarperCollins Pubs. (Tegen, Katherine Bks).

Johnson, Patricia. Make Your Own Magic Soil: Life's Lessons on Sustainable Living. 2013. 60p. 24.99 (978-1-4797-0525-2(X)); pap. 15.99 (978-1-4797-0524-5(1)) Xlibris Corp.

Johnson, Peter. The Life & Times of Benny Alvarez. 2014. (ENG.). 224p. (J). (gr. 3-7). 16.99 (978-0-06-221596-3(5), HarperCollins) HarperCollins Pubs.

Johnson, Richard, illus. The Giant Turnip. 2004. 24p. (J). (978-1-85269-748-8(2)); (978-1-85269-747-1(4)); (978-1-85269-745-7(8)); (978-1-85269-741-9(5)); (978-1-85269-736-5(9)) Mantra Lingua.

Johnson, Sandi. My Teacher Is an Alien. Durant, Sybrina, ed. Sturgen, Bobbi, illus. 2014. (ENG.). 30p. (J). (gr. k-5). pap. 12.99 (978-1-929063-75-8(X), 285) Moons & Stars Publishing For Children.

Johnson, Temeka & Phillips, Quency. Decisions, Decisions, Decisions. 2010. 32p. 19.99 (978-1-4520-5758-3(3)) AuthorHouse.

Johnson, Varian. Gabriela: Time for Change, 3. 2018. (American Girl Contemporary Ser.). (ENG.). 182p. (J). (gr. 3-5). 19.36 (978-1-64310-683-0(X)) Penworthy Co., LLC, The.

JohnsonMargaret. Ask Alice Level 2 Elementary/Lower-Intermediate. 2011. (Cambridge Experience Readers Ser.). (ENG., Illus.). 64p. pap. 14.75 (978-84-8323-616-1(8)) Cambridge Univ. Pr.

Johnston, E. K. Prairie Fire. 2015. (ENG.). 304p. (YA). (gr. 6-12). 18.99 (978-1-4677-3909-2(X), fa11c482-3c24-4845-82cc-25c4039fa640); E-Book 29.32 (978-1-4677-6181-9(8)) Lerner Publishing Group. (Carolrhoda Lab™).

—The Story of Owen: Dragon Slayer of Trondheim. 2019. 320p. (YA). (gr. 7). pap. 10.99 (978-0-8234-4502-8(X)) Holiday Hse., Inc.

—The Story of Owen: Dragon Slayer of Trondheim. 2014. (ENG.). 312p. (YA). (gr. 6-12). 18.99 (978-1-4677-1066-4(0), f669e0ce-8a16-433a-8fa4-f4875da6de4d, Carolrhoda Lab™) Lerner Publishing Group.

Johnston, Tony. The Spoon in the Bathroom Wall. 2006. (ENG., Illus.). 144p. (J). (gr. 3-7). pap. 10.95 (978-0-15-205625-4(4), 1196920, Clarion Bks.) HarperCollins Pubs.

Jonas. JONAS #5: about Face. 5th ed. 2010. 128p. pap. 4.99 (978-1-4231-1773-5(5)) Disney Pr.

—Three's a Crowd. 6th ed. 2010. 128p. pap. 4.99 (978-1-4231-2282-1(8)) Disney Pr.

JONAS #8: Prep School Party. 2010. 128p. pap. 4.99 (978-1-4231-2673-7(4)) Disney Pr.

Jones, Andrea. The Spitting Twins. Kulka, Joe, illus. 2004. 32p. (J). (978-1-58394-095-2(2), Frog Ltd.) North Atlantic Bks.

Jones, Darynda. Death & the Girl He Loves. 2013. (Darklight Ser.: 3). (ENG.). 272p. (YA). (gr. 8-12). pap. 18.99 (978-0-312-62522-1(7), 900076867, St. Martin's Griffin) St. Martin's Pr.

Jones, Janey Louise. Cloudberry Castle, 56 vols. 2010. (ENG., Illus.). 176p. (J). (gr. 2-5). 11.95 (978-0-86315-765-3(3)) Floris Bks. GBR. Dist: SteinerBooks, Inc.

Jones, Jasmine, adapted by. Lizzie Loves Ethan. 2003. (Lizzie Mcguire Ser.). (Illus.). 152p. (J). 12.65 (978-0-7569-2721-9(8)) Perfection Learning Corp.

Jones, Jasmine & Alfonsi, Alice. My Second Way Cool, Set. 2nd gif. novel rev. ed. 2004. (ENG.). 144p. (gr. 3-7). 12.99 (978-0-7868-4678-8(X)) Disney Pr.

Jones, Jen. Brooke's Quest for Captain: #2, 1 vol. (Team Cheer Ser.). (ENG.). 112p. (J). (gr. 4-6). 2012. pap. 7.19 (978-1-4342-4250-1(1), 120308)No. 2. 2011. (Illus.). lib. bdg. 25.32 (978-1-4342-2995-3(5), 114388) Capstone. (Stone Arch Bks.).

—The Competition for Gaby: #4, 1 vol. (Team Cheer Ser.). (ENG.). 112p. (J). (gr. 4-6). 2012. pap. 7.19 (978-1-4342-4252-5(8), 120310)No. 4. 2011. (Illus.). lib. bdg. 25.32 (978-1-4342-2997-7(1), 114390) Capstone. (Stone Arch Bks.).

—Faith & the Camp Snob: #1, 1 vol. (Team Cheer Ser.). (ENG.). 112p. (J). (gr. 4-6). 2012. pap. 7.19 (978-1-4342-4249-5(8), 120307)No. 1. 2011. lib. bdg. 25.32 (978-1-4342-2994-6(7), 114387) Capstone. (Stone Arch Bks.).

—Lissa & the Fund-Raising Funk: #3, 1 vol. (Team Cheer Ser.). (ENG.). 112p. (J). (gr. 4-6). 2012. pap. 7.19 (978-1-4342-4251-8(X), 120309)No. 3. 2011. lib. bdg. 25.32 (978-1-4342-2996-0(3), 114389) Capstone. (Stone Arch Bks.).

—The New Ashley. Franco, Paula, illus. 2014. (Sleepover Girls Ser.). (ENG.). 128p. (J). (gr. 3-5). lib. bdg. 22.65 (978-1-4342-9758-7(6), 127106, Stone Arch Bks.) Capstone.

—Save Our Squad, Gaby, No. 7. Adams, Liz, illus. 2012. (Team Cheer Ser.). (ENG.). 112p. (J). (gr. 4-8). lib. bdg. 25.32 (978-1-4342-4035-4(5), 118420, Stone Arch Bks.) Capstone.

—Save Our Squad, Gaby: #7, 1 vol. 2013. (Team Cheer Ser.). (ENG.). 112p. (J). (gr. 4-8). pap. 7.19 (978-1-4342-4265-5(X), 120329, Stone Arch Bks.) Capstone.

—Team Cheer. 2013. (Team Cheer Ser.). (ENG.). 112p. (J). (gr. 4-8). pap., pap., pap. 55.60 (978-1-4342-6326-1(6), 20349, Stone Arch Bks.) Capstone.

Jones, Lori M. Riley's Heart MacHine. Hammond, Julie, illus. 2012. 16p. pap. 9.95 *(978-1-61633-312-6(X))* Guardian Angel Publishing, Inc.

Jones, Marcia. A Very Haunted Holiday. 2006. (Ghostville Elementary Ser.: Bk. 15). (Illus.). 67p. (J). pap. *(978-0-439-88361-0(X))* Scholastic, Inc.

Jones, Marcia & Dadey, Debbie. Dragons Do Eat Homework. Dreidemy, Joëlle, illus. 2007. 64p. (J). *(978-0-545-00234-9(6))* Scholastic, Inc.

—Guys & Ghouls. Francis, Guy, illus. 2006. (Ghostville Elementary Ser.: Bk. 13). 81p. *(978-0-439-79402-2(1))* Scholastic, Inc.

Jones, Melanie Davis. Field Day (Rookie Ready to Learn - Out & about: in My Community) Molnar, Albert, illus. 2011. (Rookie Ready to Learn Ser.). (ENG.). 40p. (J). (gr. -1-k). pap. 5.95 *(978-0-531-26826-1(8),* Children's Pr.) Scholastic Library Publishing.

Jones, Nicky. Toby Fletcher's Fly-Away Tree. 2013. 182p. pap. *(978-1-78299-798-6(9))* FeedARead.com.

Jones, Patrick. Always Faithful. 2015. (Support & Defend Ser.). (ENG.). 112p. (YA). (gr. 6-12). E-Book 6.99 *(978-1-4677-9014-7(1),* 9781467790147, Darby Creek) Lerner Publishing Group.

—Barrier. 2014. (Alternative Ser.). (ENG.). 104p. (YA). (gr. 6-12). pap. 7.95 *(978-1-4677-4481-2(6),* 8735726f-8fde-40f2-b04a-ba121c0d9533, Darby Creek) Lerner Publishing Group.

—Combat Zone. 2015. (Support & Defend Ser.). (ENG.). 96p. (YA). (gr. 6-12). pap. 7.99 *(978-1-4677-8094-0(4),* 7fcd07df-4780-48e5-8547-63a22f685b50, Darby Creek) Lerner Publishing Group.

—Heart or Mind. 2016. (Unbarred Ser.). (ENG., Illus.). 120p. (YA). (gr. 6-12). pap. 7.99 *(978-1-5124-0091-5(2),* 5fb7039d-e377-4665-92a9-0f19e5db448c, Darby Creek) Lerner Publishing Group.

—Heart or Mind. 2016. (Unbarred Ser.). (ENG.). 120p. (YA). (gr. 6-12). E-Book 42.65 *(978-1-5124-0092-2(0),* Darby Creek) Lerner Publishing Group.

—Out of the Tunnel, No. 1. 2014. (Red Zone Ser.: 1). (ENG.). 104p. (YA). (gr. 6-12). lib. bdg. 27.99 *(978-1-4677-2126-4(3),* 4476b74e-4129-497a-8de3-332d949ef3ba, Darby Creek) Lerner Publishing Group.

—Outburst. 2014. (Alternative Ser.). (ENG.). 104p. (YA). (gr. 6-12). pap. 7.95 *(978-1-4677-4484-3(0),* 19373d2e-a571-4166-b228-9cdb9f563141, Darby Creek) Lerner Publishing Group.

—Target. 2014. (Alternative Ser.). (ENG.). 128p. (YA). (gr. 6-12). pap. 7.95 *(978-1-4677-4485-0(9),* 815eac86-fe78-4694-a1af-f5c35ba24a5b, Darby Creek) Lerner Publishing Group.

—To the Point. 2016. (Bounce Ser.). (ENG.). 96p. (YA). (gr. 6-12). lib. bdg. 26.65 *(978-1-5124-1124-9(8),* 16e843e6-0a11-44fb-b27c-7d3418899160, Darby Creek) Lerner Publishing Group.

Jones, Pixy. Teen Dumb Come. 2008. 285p. pap. 17.50 *(978-0-557-00089-0(0))* Lulu Pr., Inc.

Jones, Traci L. Standing Against the Wind. 2010. (ENG.). 208p. (YA). (gr. 7-12). pap. 11.99 *(978-0-312-62293-0(7),* 900066262) Square Fish.

Jordan, Rosa. The Goatnappers. 2007. 224p. (J). (gr. 3-7). 14.95 *(978-1-56145-400-6(1))* Peachtree Publishing Co. Inc.

Jordan, Sophie. Firelight. (Firelight Ser.: 1). (ENG.). (YA). (gr. 8). 2011. 352p. pap. 9.99 *(978-0-06-193509-1(3))* 2010. 336p. 16.99 *(978-0-06-193508-4(5))* HarperCollins Pubs. (HarperCollins).

Joseph, Bruchac. Eagle Song. 2014. (ENG.). 80p. (J). (gr. 12-12). 9.24 *(978-1-63245-103-3(4))* Lectorum Pubns., Inc.

Joshi, Bhabika. Mortals: Hayden Roux Chronicles. 2009. 208p. 24.95 *(978-1-4401-5014-2(1));* pap. 14.95 *(978-1-4401-5016-6(8))* iUniverse, Inc.

Joyal, Lisa. Swahili for Beginners, 1 vol. 2008. (ENG., Illus.). 176p. (YA). (gr. 5-9). pap. *(978-1-894549-69-1(4),* Sumach Pr.) Canadian Scholars.

Joyce, Carol. Just Friends. 2011. 228p. (gr. 10-12). 33.95 *(978-1-4497-2972-1(X));* pap. 17.95 *(978-1-4497-2971-4(1))* Author Solutions, LLC. (WestBow Pr.).

Joyce, Jan. The Wizard Visits Magic School. 2018. (ENG., Illus.). 50p. (J). *(978-1-5289-2388-0(X));* pap. *(978-1-5289-2389-7(8))* Austin Macauley Pubs. Ltd.

Joyce, Sandie May. Aunt Sandie Goes to School - the Comics. 2008. 55p. pap. 22.50 *(978-0-557-02295-3(9))* Lulu Pr., Inc.

Joyce, William & Moonbot. Billy's Booger. Joyce, William, illus. 2015. (ENG., Illus.). 40p. (J). (gr. -1-3). 19.99 *(978-1-4424-7351-5(7))* Simon & Schuster Children's Publishing.

Joyner, Andrew. Boris for the Win. 2013. (Boris Ser.: 3). lib. bdg. 14.75 *(978-0-606-31976-8(X))* Turtleback.

—Boris for the Win: a Branches Book (Boris #3) Joyner, Andrew, illus. 2013. (Boris Ser.: 3). (ENG., Illus.). 80p. (J). (gr. k-2). pap. 5.99 *(978-0-545-48449-7(9))* Scholastic, Inc.

Ju-Yeon, Rhim. President Dad, 7 vols., Vol. 5. Ju-Yeon, Rhim, illus. 5th rev. ed. 2006. (President Dad Ser.). (Illus.). 208p. per. 9.99 *(978-1-59532-238-8(8))* TOKYOPOP, Inc.

Juby, Susan. Getting the Girl: A Guide to Private Investigation, Surveillance, & Co Okery. 2010. (ENG.). 352p. (YA). (gr. 8). pap. 8.99 *(978-0-06-076528-6(3),* HarperTeen) HarperCollins Pubs.

Judd, Merlynne. Circle of Friendship. 2010. 76p. pap. 24.99 *(978-1-4520-6783-4(X))* AuthorHouse.

Judge, Malcolm. Jonny Jakes Investigates the Old School Ghoul. Brown, Alan, illus. 2016. (Middle-Grade Novels Ser.). (ENG.). 240p. (J). (gr. 4-7). lib. bdg. 25.99 *(978-1-4965-2829-2(8),* 131698, Stone Arch Bks.) Capstone.

Jukes, Mavis. The New Kid. (ENG.). 288p. (J). (gr. 4-6). 2013. lib. bdg. 21.19 *(978-0-375-95879-3(7),* Knopf Bks. for Young Readers) 2012. 7.99 *(978-0-375-85367-8(7),* Yearling) Random Hse. Children's Bks.

Jules, Jacqueline. Duck for Turkey Day. 2018. (ENG.). 32p. (J). (gr. -1-1). 19.49 *(978-1-64310-547-5(7))* Penworthy Co., LLC, The.

—Duck for Turkey Day. 2018. (2019 Av2 Fiction Ser.). (ENG.). 32p. (J). (gr. 1-3). lib. bdg. 34.28 *(978-1-4896-8259-8(7),* AV2 by Weigl) Weigl Pubs., Inc.

—Duck for Turkey Day. Mitter, Kathryn, illus. 2017. (ENG.). 32p. (J). (gr. -1-3). pap. 8.99 *(978-0-8075-1735-2(6),* 807517356) Whitman, Albert & Co.

—Freddie Ramos Adds It All Up. Benítez, Miguel, illus. 2019. (Zapato Power Ser.: 8). (ENG.). 96p. (J). (gr. 1-5). 14.99 *(978-0-8075-9539-8(X),* 080759539X) Whitman, Albert & Co.

Julie, Aunt. Paddleduck! Julie, A Little Girl from Texas. 2011. 56p. (gr. 2-4). pap. 8.95 *(978-1-4269-2584-9(0))* Trafford Publishing.

Jung, Mike. Geeks, Girls, & Secret Identities. Maihack, Mike, illus. 2012. (J). pap. *(978-0-545-33549-2(3),* Levine, Arthur A. Bks.) Scholastic, Inc.

—Unidentified Suburban Object. 2019. (Penworthy Picks Middle School Ser.). (ENG.). 265p. (J). (gr. 4-5). 17.96 *(978-1-64310-936-7(7))* Penworthy Co., LLC, The.

—Unidentified Suburban Object. 2017. (ENG.). 272p. (J). (gr. 3-7). pap. 7.99 *(978-0-545-78227-2(9))* Scholastic, Inc.

K., J. Harry Potter e Il Prigioniero Di Azkaban. (Harry Potter Ser.: Year 3). (ITA.). pap. 32.95 *(978-88-7782-852-1(8))* Salani ITA. Dist: Distribooks, Inc.

Kahler, A. R. Echoes of Memory. 2017. (Ravenborn Ser.: 2). (ENG.). 336p. (YA). (gr. 9). pap. 11.99 *(978-1-4814-3261-0(3));* (Illus.). 17.99 *(978-1-4814-3260-3(5))* Simon Pulse. (Simon Pulse).

—Shades of Darkness. 2016. (Ravenborn Ser.: 1). (ENG., Illus.). 304p. (YA). (gr. 9). 17.99 *(978-1-4814-3257-3(5),* Simon Pulse) Simon Pulse.

Kain, P. G. The Social Experiments of Dorie Dilts: The School for Cool. 2008. (Mix Ser.). (ENG.). 288p. (J). (gr. 4-8). pap. 13.99 *(978-1-4169-3520-9(7),* Simon & Schuster/Paula Wiseman Bks.) Simon & Schuster/Paula Wiseman Bks.

Kalman, Maira. Smartypants: Pete in School. 2005. (J). 27.95 incl. audio *(978-0-8045-6929-3(0),* SAC6929); 29.95 incl. audio compact disk *(978-0-8045-4105-3(1),* SACD4105) Spoken Arts, Inc.

Kalomas, Alice & Kerr, Lenora. Sir Wrinkles Goes to School. Utomo, Gabhor, illus. 2005. (J). 16.95 *(978-0-9766639-1-0(0))* Sir Wrinkles Pr.

Kamateros, Litsa & Morfonios, Nia. Sarah's Socks: My World of Autism. 2010. 24p. pap. 10.95 *(978-1-61633-023-1(6))* Guardian Angel Publishing, Inc.

Kammer, Gina. Dream Monsters: A 4D Book. Chalik, Chris, illus. 2018. (Mind Drifter Ser.). (ENG.). 128p. (J). (gr. 3-8). lib. bdg. 27.32 *(978-1-4965-5896-1(0),* 137057, Stone Arch Bks.) Capstone.

—Reject Rebound: A 4D Book. Chalik, Chris, illus. 2018. (Mind Drifter Ser.). (ENG.). 128p. (J). (gr. 3-8). lib. bdg. 27.32 *(978-1-4965-5899-2(5),* 137061, Stone Arch Bks.) Capstone.

Kann, Victoria. Pinkalicious: School Lunch. Kann, Victoria, illus. 2015. (Pinkalicious Ser.). (ENG., Illus.). 24p. (J). (gr. -1-3). pap. 4.99 *(978-0-06-224590-8(2),* HarperFestival) HarperCollins Pubs.

—Pinkalicious: School Rules! Kann, Victoria, illus. 2010. (I Can Read Level 1 Ser.). (ENG., Illus.). 32p. (J). (gr. -1-3). 16.99 *(978-0-06-192886-4(0));* pap. 4.99 *(978-0-06-192885-7(2))* HarperCollins Pubs. (HarperCollins).

Kann, Victoria, illus. Pinkalicious & the Sick Day. 2015. 30p. (J). *(978-1-4806-8664-9(6))* Harper & Row Ltd.

Kann, Victoria & Kann, Elizabeth. Purplicious. Kann, Victoria, illus. 2007. (ENG., Illus.). 40p. (J). (gr. -1-3). 19.99 *(978-0-06-124405-6(8));* lib. bdg. 19.89 *(978-0-06-124406-3(6))* HarperCollins Pubs. (HarperCollins).

Kantar, Andrew. Game Face. Keleher, Fran, illus. 2013. 160p. pap. 12.95 *(978-1-61160-566-2(0))* Whiskey Creek Restorations.

Kantor, Melissa. The Amanda Project. 2011. 287p. (J). 8.99 *(978-0-06-202706-1(9),* HarperTeen) HarperCollins Pubs.

—If I Have a Wicked Stepmother, Where's My Prince? 2005. 283p. (YA). *(978-1-4156-2763-1(0))* Hyperion Pr.

Kaplan, Arie. The New Kid from Planet Glorf, 1 vol. Bradley, Jess, illus. 2013. (Comics Land Ser.). (ENG.). 32p. (J). (gr. k-2). lib. bdg. 25.32 *(978-1-4342-4032-3(0),* 118417, Stone Arch Bks.) Capstone.

Kaplan, Ariel. We Regret to Inform You. 2018. (ENG.). 352p. (YA). (gr. 7). lib. bdg. 20.99 *(978-1-5247-7371-7(9),* Knopf Bks. for Young Readers) Random Hse. Children's Bks.

Kaplan, Isabel. Hancock Park. 2010. (ENG.). 272p. (YA). (gr. 9). pap. 8.99 *(978-0-06-137370-1(2),* HarperTeen) HarperCollins Pubs.

Kappier, Kathleen. Whitney's School Morning. 2004. 38p. pap. 24.95 *(978-1-4137-3711-0(0))* PublishAmerica, Inc.

Karas, Phyllis. The Hate Crime. 2004. 190p. (YA). pap. 13.95 *(978-0-595-33138-3(6),* Authors Choice Pr.) iUniverse, Inc.

Kares, P. S. The Prairie Orphans' Journey. 2008. 32p. per. 24.95 *(978-1-4241-8396-8(0))* America Star Bks.

Kargman, Jill & Karasyov, Carrie. Bittersweet Sixteen. 2006. (YA). (gr. 7-12). (ENG.). 240p. 15.99 *(978-0-06-077844-6(X));* 230p. lib. bdg. 16.89 *(978-0-06-077845-3(8))* HarperCollins Pubs.

Karo, Aaron. Me You Us (Previously Published As Galgorithm) 2016. lib. bdg. 22.10 *(978-0-606-39928-9(3))* Turtleback.

Karre, Elizabeth. Calling the Shots. 2014. (Gift Ser.). (ENG.). 104p. (YA). (gr. 6-12). pap. 7.95 *(978-1-4677-4478-2(6),* 68c8e6c9-1a13-4766-b31b-ace90ffa7513); lib. bdg. 27.99 *(978-1-4677-3514-8(0),* 38d6efef-08fe-471f-a72e-188edb389e4b) Lerner Publishing Group. (Darby Creek).

—Certain Signals. 2014. (Gift Ser.). (ENG.). 112p. (YA). (gr. 6-12). pap. 7.95 *(978-1-4677-4479-9(4),* c7e0be5a-2e55-4339-9db4-7405e8913c8c); lib. bdg. 27.99 *(978-1-4677-3511-7(6),* eb702a74-7dbd-4cb2-9b02-79165c604231) Lerner Publishing Group. (Darby Creek).

—The Fight. 2013. (Surviving Southside Ser.). (ENG.). 128p. (YA). (gr. 6-12). pap. 7.95 *(978-1-4677-0709-1(0),* 554aa69c-e617-40b7-bf91-a64fd0acb6c7, Darby Creek) Lerner Publishing Group.

Kasper, Kathy. Mary Jean Learns to Shine. 2008. 51p. pap. 16.95 *(978-1-60441-680-0(7))* America Star Bks.

Katar, Al. Captain Scratch: Island of Simanj. 2007. (J). 21.99 *(978-1-934035-31-3(9))* Trent's Prints.

Katcher, Brian. Almost Perfect. 2010. 368p. (YA). (gr. 9). pap. 10.99 *(978-0-385-73665-7(7),* Delacorte Bks. for Young Readers) Random Hse. Children's Bks.

—Playing with Matches. 2009. 304p. (YA). (gr. 9). mass mkt. 8.99 *(978-0-385-73545-2(6),* Laurel Leaf) Random Hse. Children's Bks.

Kate, Lauren. Fallen. (Fallen Ser.: 1). (ENG.). (YA). (gr. 7). 2010. 480p. pap. 12.99 *(978-0-385-73913-9(3),* Ember) 2009. 464p. 18.99 *(978-0-385-73893-4(5),* Delacorte Pr.) Random Hse. Children's Bks.

—Fallen. 2010. (Fallen Ser.: 1). lib. bdg. 22.10 *(978-0-606-15168-9(0))* Turtleback.

—Passion. (Fallen Ser.: 3). (ENG.). (YA). (gr. 7). 2012. 448p. pap. 13.99 *(978-0-385-73917-7(6),* Ember) 2011. 432p. 18.99 *(978-0-385-73916-0(8),* Delacorte Pr.) Random Hse. Children's Bks.

—Passion. 2012. (Fallen Ser.: 3). lib. bdg. 22.10 *(978-0-606-26410-5(8))* Turtleback.

—Torment. (Fallen Ser.: 2). (ENG.). (YA). (gr. 7). 2011. 480p. pap. 10.99 *(978-0-385-73915-3(X),* Ember) 2010. 464p. 17.99 *(978-0-385-73914-6(1),* Delacorte Pr.) Random Hse. Children's Bks.

—Torment. 2011. (Fallen Ser.: 2). lib. bdg. 22.10 *(978-0-606-22247-1(2))* Turtleback.

—Unforgiven. 2016. (Fallen Ser.). (ENG.). 368p. (YA). (gr. 7). pap. 10.99 *(978-0-385-74264-1(9),* Ember) Random Hse. Children's Bks.

Kats, Jewel. Miss Popular Steals the Show: Girls in Wheelchairs Rule! Stenton, Murray, illus. 2014. 37p. (J). pap. 14.95 *(978-1-61599-236-2(7))* Loving Healing Pr., Inc.

Katschke, Judy. First Grade Feast!/By Judy Katschke; Illustrated by Clare Elsom. Elsom, Clare, illus. 2014. 32p. (J). pap. *(978-0-545-75844-4(0))* Scholastic, Inc.

—Hooray for the 100th Day! Elsom, Clare, illus. 2015. 32p. (J). *(978-0-545-77607-3(4))* Scholastic, Inc.

—Second Grade Rocks! Elsom, Clare, illus. 2015. 32p. (J). *(978-0-545-82338-8(2))* Scholastic, Inc.

Katschke, Judy, adapted by. Z-O-M-B-I-E-S: The Junior Novelization. 2018. (Illus.). 138p. (J). *(978-1-5444-1848-3(5))* Random Hse., Inc.

Katz, Alan. Don't Say That Word! Catrow, David, illus. 2007. (ENG.). 32p. (J). (gr. -1-3). 19.99 *(978-0-689-86971-6(1),* McElderry, Margaret K. Bks.) McElderry, Margaret K. Bks.

—Ricky Vargas: The Funniest Kid in the World. Curtis, Stacy, illus. 2011. 57p. (J). pap. *(978-0-545-24583-8(4),* Cartwheel Bks.) Scholastic, Inc.

—That Stinks! A Punny Show-And-Tell. Gilpin, Stephen, illus. 2016. (ENG.). 32p. (J). (gr. -1-3). 19.99 *(978-1-4169-7880-0(1),* Simon & Schuster Bks. For Young Readers) Simon & Schuster Bks. For Young Readers.

Katz, Danny. Little Lunch Four. Vane, Mitch, illus. 2005. (Little Lunch Ser.). 64p. (J). pap. *(978-1-876372-84-2(2),* Black Dog Books) Walker Bks. Australia Pty. Ltd.

Katz, Karen. Rosie Goes to Preschool. Katz, Karen, illus. 2019. (Illus.). 34p. (J). (-k). bds. 8.99 *(978-1-9848-3052-4(X),* Schwartz & Wade Bks.) Random Hse. Children's Bks.

Katz, Nikki. The Midnight Dance. 2018. (ENG.). 336p. (YA). pap. 16.99 *(978-1-250-18812-0(1),* 900192048) Square Fish.

Kaufman, Sashi. Wired Man & Other Freaks of Nature. 2016. (ENG.). 264p. (YA). (gr. 9-12). 17.99 *(978-1-4677-8563-1(6),* 993090f4-4dbe-49de-98b1-080d77fec992); E-Book 27.99 *(978-1-4677-9564-7(X))* Lerner Publishing Group. (Carolrhoda Lab™).

Kaufman, Seufert. Wee Wilhelmina & Her Magic Marbles. 2012. (ENG.). pap. *(978-1-4675-4364-4(0))* Independent Pub.

Keane, Dave. Monster School: First Day Frights. Keane, Dave, illus. 2012. (I Can Read Level 2 Ser.). (ENG., Illus.). 32p. (J). (gr. -1-3). 16.99 *(978-0-06-085476-8(6));* pap. 4.99 *(978-0-06-085475-1(8))* HarperCollins Pubs. (HarperCollins).

Kear, Nicole C. The Fix-It Friends: Eyes on the Prize. Dockray, Tracy, illus. 2018. (Fix-It Friends Ser.: 5). (ENG.). 160p. (J). pap. 7.99 *(978-1-250-08672-3(8),* 900157583) Imprint IND. Dist: Macmillan.

—The Fix-It Friends: Sticks & Stones. Dockray, Tracy, illus. 2017. (Fix-It Friends Ser.: 2). (ENG.). 144p. (J). pap. 7.99 *(978-1-250-08586-3(1),* 900157366) Imprint IND. Dist: Macmillan.

—The Fix-It Friends: the Show Must Go On. Dockray, Tracy, illus. 2017. (Fix-It Friends Ser.: 3). (ENG.). 160p. (J). pap. 7.99 *(978-1-250-08668-6(X),* 900157576) Imprint IND. Dist: Macmillan.

—The Fix-It Friends: Wish You Were Here. Dockray, Tracy, illus. 2017. (Fix-It Friends Ser.: 4). (ENG.). 160p. (J). pap. 7.99 *(978-1-250-08670-9(1),* 900157581) Imprint IND. Dist: Macmillan.

Keating, Jess. How to Outrun a Crocodile When Your Shoes Are Untied. 2014. (My Life is a Zoo Ser.: 1). 288p. (J). (gr. 4-7). pap. 11.99 *(978-1-4022-9755-7(6),* 9781402297557) Sourcebooks, Inc.

—How to Outswim a Shark Without a Snorkel. 2015. (My Life is a Zoo Ser.: 2). 304p. (J). (gr. 4-7). pap. 11.99 *(978-1-4022-9758-8(0),* 9781402297588) Sourcebooks, Inc.

Keats, Israel. The Heir. 2018. (Kick! Ser.). (ENG.). 104p. (YA). (gr. 6-12). pap. 7.99 *(978-1-5415-0031-0(8),* 77235fd9-4dc6-471c-ae90-65c49b54210a); 25.32 *(978-1-5415-0021-1(0),* 4cf8e1b1-c047-4866-b372-67240732d868) Lerner Publishing Group. (Darby Creek).

Keeling, Evan. CrumbSnatchers. 2008. 60p. (J). per. 5.95 *(978-0-9796902-4-2(2))* Silent Devil Productions.

Keenan-Bolger, Andrew & Wetherhead, Kate. Act 3. 2018. (Jack & Louisa Ser.: 3). (Illus.). 256p. (J). (gr. 3-7). 8.99 *(978-1-5247-8497-3(4),* Penguin Workshop) Penguin Young Readers Group.

Keene, Carolyn. Double Take. Pamintuan, Macky, illus. 2009. (Nancy Drew & the Clue Crew Ser.: 21). (ENG.). 112p. (J). (gr. 1-4). pap. 5.99 *(978-1-4169-7812-1(7),* Aladdin) Simon & Schuster Children's Publishing.

—Earth Day Escapade. Pamintuan, Macky, illus. 2009. (Nancy Drew & the Clue Crew Ser.: 18). (ENG.). 96p. (J). (gr. 1-4). pap. 5.99 *(978-1-4169-7218-1(8),* Aladdin) Simon & Schuster Children's Publishing.

Keil, Melissa. Life in Outer Space, 1 vol. 2016. (ENG.). 320p. (YA). (gr. 7-11). pap. 9.95 *(978-1-56145-975-9(5))* Peachtree Publishing Co. Inc.

—The Secret Science of Magic, 1 vol. 2018. (ENG.). 320p. (YA). (gr. 7-12). 17.95 *(978-1-68263-014-3(5))* Peachtree Publishing Co. Inc.

Keller, Tae. The Science of Breakable Things. (J). (gr. 3-7). 2019. (ENG.). 320p. 8.99 *(978-1-5247-1569-4(7),* Yearling) 2018. 304p. 17.99 *(978-1-5247-1566-3(2),* Random Hse. Bks. for Young Readers) Random Hse. Children's Bks.

Kellerman, Faye & Kellerman, Aliza. Prism. 2009. 272p. (YA). (gr. 7-18). lib. bdg. 17.89 *(978-0-06-168722-8(7),* HarperTeen) HarperCollins Pubs.

Kelley, Jane. Sol-Ray Man & the Freaky Flood. 2017. (Escapades of Clint Mccool Ser.: 2). lib. bdg. 16.00 *(978-0-606-40112-8(1))* Turtleback.

Kelley, Marty. Lucky Break. Kelley, Marty, illus. 2017. (Molly Mac Ser.). (ENG., Illus.). 56p. (J). (gr. k-2). lib. bdg. 22.65 *(978-1-5158-0837-4(8),* 134387, Picture Window Bks.) Capstone.

—Magic Molly. 2018. (Molly Mac Ser.). (ENG., Illus.). 56p. (J). (gr. k-2). pap. 4.95 *(978-1-5158-2388-9(1),* 137203); lib. bdg. 22.65 *(978-1-5158-2384-1(9),* 137198) Capstone. (Picture Window Bks.).

—The Messiest Desk. 2009. (J). *(978-1-55933-319-1(7))* Zino Pr. Children's Bks.

—Three . . . Two . . . one . . . Blastoff! Kelley, Marty, illus. 2018. (Molly Mac Ser.). (ENG., Illus.). 56p. (J). (gr. k-2). pap. 4.95 *(978-1-5158-2391-9(1),* 137206, Picture Window Bks.) Capstone.

—Three ... Two ... One ... Blastoff! Kelley, Marty, illus. 2018. (Molly Mac Ser.). (ENG., Illus.). 56p. (J). (gr. k-2). lib. bdg. 22.65 *(978-1-5158-2387-2(3),* 137202, Picture Window Bks.) Capstone.

—Top Secret Author Visit. Kelley, Marty, illus. 2018. (Molly Mac Ser.). (ENG., Illus.). 56p. (J). (gr. k-2). lib. bdg. 22.65 *(978-1-5158-2386-5(5),* 137201, Picture Window Bks.) Capstone.

Kelly, Brynn. Welcome To 4B, 1 vol. 2018. (Bad Kids In 4B Ser.). (ENG.). 88p. (YA). (gr. 2-3). 24.55 *(978-1-5383-8222-6(9),* f3e17516-c6d4-4b23-9a93-59ad366ac71a); pap. 14.85 *(978-1-5383-8221-9(0),* c8eed664-cd81-41bb-8df0-d03b9b7085bd) Enslow Publishing, LLC.

Kelly, Claire. Nellie in the News. Hicks, Faith, illus. 2007. 48p. (J). lib. bdg. 23.08 *(978-1-4242-1631-4(1))* Fitzgerald Bks.

Kelly, David A. MVP #1: the Gold Medal Mess. Brundage, Scott, illus. 2016. (Most Valuable Players Ser.: 1). 128p. (J). (gr. 1-4). 5.99 *(978-0-553-51319-6(2),* Random Hse. Bks. for Young Readers) Random Hse. Children's Bks.

Kelly, Erin Entrada. Blackbird Fly. Peterschmidt, Betsy, illus. 2015. (ENG.). 304p. (J). (gr. 3-7). 16.99 *(978-0-06-223861-0(2),* Greenwillow Bks.) HarperCollins Pubs.

—You Go First. (ENG.). (J). (gr. 3-7). 2019. 320p. pap. 7.99 *(978-0-06-241419-9(4))* 2018. 304p. 17.99 *(978-0-06-241418-2(6))* HarperCollins Pubs. (Greenwillow Bks.).

Kelly, Jamie & Benton, Jim. Never Underestimate Your Dumbness. 2008. (Dear Dumb Diary Ser.). (Illus.). 150p. (gr. 4-7). 16.00 *(978-0-7569-8814-2(4))* Perfection Learning Corp.

Kelly, Joan L. The Dna Connection: Tannenhauser's Theory. 2013. 198p. pap. 9.99 *(978-1-936453-25-2(8))* Bezalel Bks.

Kelly, Katy. Lucy Rose: Here's the Thing about Me. Rex, Adam, illus. 2006. (Lucy Rose Ser.: 1). 160p. (J). (gr. 3-7). reprint ed. per. 7.99 *(978-0-440-42026-2(1),* Yearling) Random Hse. Children's Bks.

Kelly, Liam. Worried William. 2018. (ENG., Illus.). 114p. (J). (gr. -1-3). *(978-1-5289-2497-9(5));* pap. *(978-1-5289-2498-6(3))* Austin Macauley Pubs. Ltd.

—Worried William. 2017. (ENG., Illus.). 114p. (J). 19.95 *(978-1-78629-421-0(4),* 6c0b758c-e15d-47c9-984a-5c01224b1389); pap. 13.95 *(978-1-78629-420-3(6),* 4b555159-806c-4019-b3f4-0fec1fe71393) Austin Macauley Pubs. Ltd. GBR. Dist: Baker & Taylor Publisher Services (BTPS).

Kelm, Tracy Martin. Light. 2011. 116p. pap. 11.95 *(978-1-4327-6308-4(3))* Outskirts Pr., Inc.

Kelsey, Annie. Love & Chicken Nuggets. Larsen, Kate, illus. 2017. (Pippa Morgan's Diary Ser.: 2). (ENG.). 176p. (J). (gr. 3-7). pap. 9.99 *(978-1-4926-4794-2(2))* Sourcebooks, Inc.

Kemmerer, Brigid. Call It What You Want. (ENG.). 384p. (YA). 2020. pap. 10.99 *(978-1-68119-812-5(6),* 900187431) 2019. 18.99 *(978-1-68119-809-5(6),* 900187438) Bloomsbury Publishing USA. (Bloomsbury Young Adult).

Kemnitz, Dianna. Another Lesson for Jack. 2012. 42p. 24.95 *(978-1-4626-6897-7(6))* America Star Bks.

Kenah, Katharine. The Best Chef in Second Grade. Carter, Abby, illus. (I Can Read Level 2 Ser.). 48p. (J). 2008. (ENG.). (gr. k-3). pap. 4.99 *(978-0-06-053563-6(6),* HarperCollins) 2007. (gr. -1-3). lib. bdg. 16.89 *(978-0-06-053562-9(8))* HarperCollins Pubs.

—The Best Teacher in Second Grade. Carter, Abby, illus. 2007. (I Can Read Level 2 Ser.). (ENG.). 48p. (J). (gr. k-3). pap. 4.99 *(978-0-06-053566-7(0),* HarperCollins) HarperCollins Pubs.

—The Best Teacher in Second Grade. Carter, Abby, illus. 2007. (I Can Read Bks.). 48p. (gr. -1-3). 14.00 *(978-0-7569-8105-1(0))* Perfection Learning Corp.

Kendall, Jane. Horse Diaries #4: Maestoso Petra. Sanderson, Ruth, illus. 2010. (Horse Diaries: 4). 160p. (J). (gr. 3-7). pap. 7.99 *(978-0-375-85842-0(3),* Random Hse. Bks. for Young Readers) Random Hse. Children's Bks.

Kenley, Holli. Another Way: A Novel. 2015. 155p. (YA). pap. *(978-1-61599-259-1(6))* Loving Healing Pr., Inc.

Kenneally, Miranda. Defending Taylor. 2016. (Hundred Oaks Ser.: 7). 304p. (YA). (gr. 8-12). pap. 12.99 *(978-1-4926-3008-1(X),* 9781492630081) Sourcebooks, Inc.

—Stealing Parker. 2012. (Hundred Oaks Ser.: 2). 256p. (YA). (gr. 7-12). pap. 10.99 *(978-1-4022-7187-8(5))* Sourcebooks, Inc.

Kenney, Rebecca. The Silent. 2009. (YA). 8.99 *(978-1-60682-054-4(0),* JourneyForth) BJU Pr.

Kent, Renee Holmes. Robyn Flies Home, Vol. 4. 2004. (Adventures in Misty Falls Ser.: Vol. 4). (Illus.). 100p. (gr. 4-7). pap. 4.99 *(978-1-56309-764-5(8),* N007106, New Hope Pubs.) Iron Stream Media.

—Tell the Truth, Cassie, Vol. 6. 2004. (Adventures in Misty Falls Ser.: Vol. 6). (Illus.). 100p. (J). (gr. 4-7). pap. 4.99 *(978-1-56309-452-1(5),* N007110, New Hope Pubs.) Iron Stream Media.

Kenyon, Sherrilyn. The Dark-Hunters: Infinity, Vol. 1, Vol. 1. 2013. (Dark-Hunters Ser.: 1). (ENG., Illus.). 240p. (gr. 11-17). 13.00 *(978-0-316-19053-4(5)*, Yen Pr.) Yen Pr. LLC.

—Inferno: Chronicles of Nick. 2014. (Chronicles of Nick Ser.: 4). (ENG.). 464p. (YA). (gr. 7). pap. 14.99 *(978-1-250-00286-0(9)*, 900079522, St. Martin's Griffin) St. Martin's Pr.

—Infinity: Chronicles of Nick. 2011. (Chronicles of Nick Ser.: 1). (ENG.). 480p. (YA). (gr. 7-18). pap. 14.00 *(978-0-312-60304-5(5)*, 900064303, St. Martin's Griffin) St. Martin's Pr.

—Invincible: The Chronicles of Nick. (Chronicles of Nick Ser.: 2). (ENG.). 432p. (YA). (gr. 7). 2012. pap. 15.00 *(978-0-312-60327-4(4)*, 900064304) 2011. 27.99 *(978-0-312-59906-5(4)*, 900063529) St. Martin's Pr. (St. Martin's Griffin).

Keplinger, Kody. The DUFF: (Designated Ugly Fat Friend) (ENG.). (YA). (gr. 10-17). 2011. 304p. pap., pap. 10.99 *(978-0-316-08424-6(7))* 2015. 320p. pap. 10.00 *(978-0-316-38180-2(2))* Little, Brown Bks. for Young Readers. (Poppy).

—Shut Out. 2012. (ENG.). 288p. (YA). (gr. 10-17). pap. 15.99 *(978-0-316-17555-5(2)*, Poppy) Little, Brown Bks. for Young Readers.

—That's Not What Happened, 1 vol. (ENG.). 336p. (YA). (gr. 7). 2020. pap. 10.99 *(978-1-338-18653-6(1))* 2018. 18.99 *(978-1-338-18652-9(3)*, Scholastic Pr.) Scholastic, Inc.

Kerascoët & Kerascoët. I Walk with Vanessa: A Picture Book Story about a Simple Act of Kindness. 2018. (Illus.). 40p. (J). (gr. -1-3). 17.99 *(978-1-5247-6955-0(X))* Random Hse. Children's Bks.

Kerick, Mia. Us Three. (ENG., 2016. Illus.). (J). 24.99 *(978-1-63477-989-0(4))* 2014. (One Voice Ser.: 1). 180p. (YA). pap. 14.99 *(978-1-62798-908-4(0))* Dreamspinner Pr. (Harmony Ink Pr.).

Kerns, Ann. I Date Dead People: Book 5, No. 5. Görrissen, Janina, illus. 2012. (My Boyfriend Is a Monster Ser.: 5). (ENG.). 128p. (YA). (gr. 7-12). lib. bdg. 29.32 *(978-0-7613-6007-0(7)*, 9d507722-2da6-4d7e-920d-92005f529790, Graphic Universe™) Lerner Publishing Group.

Kerr, B. Modern Persona: Valhalla High School. 2007. 296p. (YA). per. 18.95 *(978-0-595-44412-0(1))* iUniverse, Inc.

Kerr, M. E., pseud. If I Love You, Am I Trapped Forever?, 0 vols. 2012. (ENG.). 192p. (YA). (gr. 7-12). pap. 9.99 *(978-0-7614-5839-5(5)*, 9780761458395, Skyscape) Amazon Publishing.

Kessler, Jackie Morse. Loss. 2012. (Riders of the Apocalypse Ser.: 3). (ENG.). 272p. (YA). (gr. 7-12). pap. 8.99 *(978-0-547-71215-4(4)*, 1480762, Clarion Bks.) HarperCollins Pubs.

—Loss. 2012. (Riders of the Apocalypse Ser.: 3). lib. bdg. 19.65 *(978-0-606-24742-9(4))* Turtleback.

Kevin, Henkes. Chrysanthemum. 2014. (ENG.). 32p. (J). (gr. k-3). 11.24 *(978-1-63245-281-8(2))* Lectorum Pubns., Inc.

Kew, Trevor. Trading Goals, 1 vol. 2009. (Lorimer Sports Stories Ser.). (ENG.). 144p. (J). (gr. 3-7). 26.19 *(978-1-55277-425-0(2)*, 425) James Lorimer & Co. Ltd., Pubs. CAN. Dist: Children's Plus, Inc.

Khan, Hena. Bounce Back. 2018. (Zayd Saleem, Chasing the Dream Ser.: 3). (ENG., Illus.). 144p. (J). (gr. 2-5). 16.99 *(978-1-5344-1205-7(0))*; pap. 6.99 *(978-1-5344-1204-0(2))* Simon & Schuster Bks. For Young Readers. (Salaam Reads).

—More to the Story. 2019. (ENG., Illus.). 272p. (J). (gr. 3-7). 17.99 *(978-1-4814-9209-6(8)*, Salaam Reads) Simon & Schuster Bks. For Young Readers.

—On Point. Comport, Sally Wern, illus. 2018. (Zayd Saleem, Chasing the Dream Ser.: 2). (ENG.). 144p. (J). (gr. 2-5). 17.99 *(978-1-5344-1202-6(6))*; pap. 6.99 *(978-1-5344-1201-9(8))* Simon & Schuster Bks. For Young Readers. (Salaam Reads).

—On Point. 2018. (Zayd Saleem, Chasing the Dream Ser.: 2). lib. bdg. 17.20 *(978-0-606-41417-3(7))* Turtleback.

—Power Forward. Comport, Sally Wern, illus. 2018. (Zayd Saleem, Chasing the Dream Ser.: 1). (ENG.). 144p. (J). (gr. 2-5). 16.99 *(978-1-5344-1198-2(4))*; pap. 6.99 *(978-1-5344-1199-9(2))* Simon & Schuster Bks. For Young Readers. (Salaam Reads).

Khoury, Jessica. The Mystwick School of Musicraft. 2020. (ENG., Illus.). 368p. (J). (gr. 5-7). 16.99 *(978-1-328-62563-2(X)*, 1734231, Clarion Bks.) HarperCollins Pubs.

Kids Can Learn Franklin Staff, ed. Ready for School. 2004. 32p. pap. *(978-1-55337-605-7(6))* Kids Can Pr., Ltd.

Kidwell, Leigh-Anne. The Year I Lost My Popularity! 2005. 115p. pap. 19.95 *(978-1-4137-8376-6(7))* PublishAmerica, Inc.

Kiely, Brendan. Tradition. 2018. (ENG., Illus.). 352p. (YA). (gr. 9). 18.99 *(978-1-4814-8034-5(0)*, McElderry, Margaret K. Bks.) McElderry, Margaret K. Bks.

Kieza, Grantlee. Mrs Kelly: the Astonishing Life of Ned Kelly's Mother. 2019. 496p. 19.99 *(978-0-7333-3871-7(2))* ABC Bks. AUS. Dist: HarperCollins Pubs.

Kim, Sagwa. B, Book, & Me. Jeong, Sunhee, tr. 2020. (ENG.). 160p. (YA). pap. 16.95 *(978-1-931883-96-2(3))* Two Lines Pr.

Kimmel, E. Cody. In the Eye of the Storm. Snow, Scott, illus. 2003. (Adventures of Young Buffalo Bill Ser.). (ENG.). 144p. (J). (gr. 3-7). 15.99 *(978-0-06-029115-0(X))* HarperCollins Pubs.

Kimmel, Elizabeth Cody. In the Eye of the Storm. Snow, Scott, illus. 2003. (Adventures of Young Buffalo Bill Ser.). 144p. (J). (gr. 3-7). lib. bdg. 16.89 *(978-0-06-029116-7(8))* HarperCollins Pubs.

—Leading Ladies #2. Mingus, Cathi, illus. 2012. (Forever Four Ser.: 2). 224p. (J). (gr. 3-7). pap. 6.99 *(978-0-448-45549-5(8)*, Grosset & Dunlap) Penguin Young Readers Group.

—Lily B. on the Brink of Love. 2005. (ENG.). 192p. (J). 15.99 *(978-0-06-075541-6(5))* HarperCollins Pubs.

—Mary Ingalls on Her Own. 2007. (Little House Sequel Ser.). (ENG.). 192p. (J). (gr. 3-7). 17.99 *(978-0-06-000905-2(5)*, HarperCollins) HarperCollins Pubs.

—The Reinvention of Moxie Roosevelt. 2011. (ENG.). 256p. (J). (gr. 5-18). 6.99 *(978-0-14-241870-3(6)*, Puffin Books) Penguin Young Readers Group.

—Suddenly Supernatural: Scaredy Kat. 2010. (Suddenly Supernatural Ser.: 2). (ENG.). 272p. (J). (gr. 3-7). pap. 15.99 *(978-0-316-08745-2(9))* Little, Brown Bks. for Young Readers.

—Suddenly Supernatural: School Spirit. 2010. (Suddenly Supernatural Ser.: 1). (ENG.). 336p. (J). (gr. 3-7). pap. 17.99 *(978-0-316-07821-4(2))* Little, Brown Bks. for Young Readers.

Kimmel, Haven. Kaline Klattermaster's Tree House. Brown, Peter, illus. 2008. (ENG.). 152p. (J). (gr. 4-6). 18.69 *(978-0-689-87402-4(2))* Simon & Schuster, Inc.

Kinard, Kami. The Boy Project: a Wish Novel: Notes & Observations of Kara Mcallister. 2016. (Wish Ser.). (ENG.). 272p. (J). (gr. 4-7). pap. 6.99 *(978-0-545-34516-3(2)*, Scholastic Paperbacks) Scholastic, Inc.

Kindig, Tess. Luv @ First Site. 2004. 128p. (J). pap. 5.99 *(978-1-4003-0325-0(7))* Nelson, Thomas Inc.

King, A. S. Ask the Passengers. 2013. (ENG.). 336p. (YA). (gr. 10-17). pap. 18.99 *(978-0-316-19467-9(0))* Little, Brown Bks. for Young Readers.

King, J. Eric & Graham, Greg. Byron Carmichael Book One: The Human Corpse Trade. Mizer, Lindsay, ed. Warner, Michael, illus. 2008. (ENG.). 408p. (gr. 8-12). 18.95 *(978-0-615-15770-2(X))* G & K Publishing.

King, Jane. Welcome to Chillsville Elementary. 2013. (Ghoul School Ser.: 1). (ENG.). 80p. (J). (gr. 1-4). pap. 13.99 *(978-1-4814-2162-1(X)*, Simon & Schuster/Paula Wiseman Bks.) Simon & Schuster/Paula Wiseman Bks.

King, Zach. Zach King: The Magical Mix-Up. Arce, Beverly, illus. 2018. 192p. (J). *(978-0-241-32188-1(3))* Harper & Row Ltd.

—Zach King: the Magical Mix-Up. 2018. (ENG., Illus.). 192p. (J). (gr. 3-7). 18.99 *(978-0-06-267721-1(7)*, HarperCollins) HarperCollins Pubs.

King, Zelda. The Class Surprise, 1 vol. 2006. (Neighborhood Readers Ser.). (ENG.). 16p. (gr. 1-2). pap. 6.50 *(978-1-4042-6994-1(0)*, ce91d7dc-161e-4b30-94f8-41fcf95a8609, Rosen Classroom) Rosen Publishing Group, Inc., The.

Kinney, Jeff. Cabin Fever, 2 vols. 2011. (Diary of a Wimpy Kid Ser.: 6). (J). 44.75 *(978-1-4640-2152-7(X))*; 44.75 *(978-1-4640-2151-0(1))*; 1.25 *(978-1-4640-4524-0(0))*; *(978-1-4640-2149-7(X))*; 46.75 *(978-1-4640-2148-0(1))* Recorded Bks., Inc.

—Cabin Fever. 2011. (Diary of a Wimpy Kid Ser.: 6). (J). lib. bdg. 25.70 *(978-0-606-23667-6(8))* Turtleback.

—Carnet de Bord de Greg Heffley. 2012. (Journal d'un Degonfle Ser.: Vol. 1). (FRE., Illus.). 223p. (J). (gr. 4-8). pap. *(978-2-02-101196-8(8))* Editions du Seuil.

—El Diario de Greg, un Renacuajo. Morán, Esteban, tr. 2008. (SPA.). 218p. (J). (gr. 3-6). 16.99 *(978-1-933032-52-8(9))* Lectorum Pubns., Inc.

—Diary o a Wimpy Wean: Diary of a Wimpy Kid in Scots. Clark, Thomas, tr. 2019. (Diary o a Wimpy Wean Ser.). (SCO., Illus.). 226p. (J). (gr. 4-7). pap. 12.99 *(978-1-78530-214-5(0))* Black and White Publishing Ltd. GBR. Dist: Independent Pubs. Group.

—Diary of a Wimpy Kid. 2014. pap. *(978-1-4197-1499-3(6))* 2013. pap. *(978-1-4197-1176-3(8))* 2009. pap. *(978-0-8109-8888-0(7))* 2007. pap. *(978-0-8109-8893-4(3))* 2007. pap. *(978-0-8109-8292-5(7))* 2007. (Diary of a Wimpy Kid Ser.: Bk. 1). 217p. pap. *(978-0-8109-9455-3(0))* Abrams, Inc. (Amulet Bks.).

—Diary of a Wimpy Kid. (Diary of a Wimpy Kid Ser.). (CHI., Illus.). (J). 2009. (gr. 4-8). *(978-986-84847-4-0(X))* 2008. (gr. 3-7). *(978-986-84847-0-2(7))* DaskoviK, Izdatel'sko-torgovaja korporacija.

—Diary of a Wimpy Kid. 2013. (Diary of a Wimpy Kid Ser.: 16). (CHI.). (J). pap. 13.95 *(978-7-5405-7891-6(2))* Guangdong New Era Publishing Hse. CHN. Dist: Chinasprout, Inc.

—Diary of a Wimpy Kid. 2009. (Diary of a Wimpy Kid Ser.: Bk. 1). 1.00 *(978-1-4074-4434-5(4))* 2008. (Diary of a Wimpy Kid Ser.: 1). (J). 75.75 *(978-1-4361-3290-9(8))* 2008. (Diary of a Wimpy Kid Ser.: 1). (J). 44.75 *(978-1-4281-8196-0(2))* 2008. (Diary of a Wimpy Kid Ser.: 1). (J). 46.75 *(978-1-4281-8194-6(6))* 2008. (Diary of a Wimpy Kid Ser.: 1). (J). 1.25 *(978-1-4281-8191-5(1))* 2008. (Diary of a Wimpy Kid Ser.: 1). (J). 173.75 *(978-1-4281-8195-3(4))* 2008. (Diary of a Wimpy Kid Ser.: 1). (J). 46.75 *(978-1-4281-8198-4(9))* 2008. (Diary of a Wimpy Kid Ser.: 1). (J). 44.75 *(978-1-4281-8200-4(4))* Recorded Bks., Inc.

—Diary of a Wimpy Kid. 2007. (Diary of a Wimpy Kid Ser.: 1). (Illus.). 217p. (J). lib. bdg. 25.70 *(978-0-606-23662-1(7))* Turtleback.

—Diary of a Wimpy Kid Box of Books 1-4 Revised, Bks. 1-4. rev. ed. 2007. (Diary of a Wimpy Kid Ser.). (ENG.). 896p. (J). (gr. 3-7). 56.00 *(978-1-4197-1669-0(7))* Abrams, Inc.

—Hard Luck. 2013. (Diary of a Wimpy Kid Ser.: 8). (J). lib. bdg. 25.70 *(978-0-606-32062-7(8))* Turtleback.

—The Last Straw. 2009. (Diary of a Wimpy Kid Ser.: 3). (Illus.). 218p. (J). (gr. 3-7). pap. *(978-0-8109-7108-0(9))* Abrams, Inc.

—The Last Straw. 2009. (Diary of a Wimpy Kid Ser.: 3). (ENG.). 224p. (J). (gr. 4-6). pap. 17.95 *(978-1-4395-8262-6(9)*, 0008062297, Paw Prints) Baker & Taylor, CATS.

—The Last Straw. 2012. (ENG., Illus.). 240p. pap. *(978-0-14-132492-0(9)*, Puffin) Penguin Bks., Ltd.

—The Last Straw. 2009. (Diary of a Wimpy Kid Ser.: Bk. 3). (JPN., Illus.). 221p. (J). *(978-4-591-10910-6(0))* Poplar Publishing.

—The Last Straw. (Diary of a Wimpy Kid Ser.: 3). (J). 2010. 1.25 *(978-1-4407-2984-3(0))* 2010. 46.75 *(978-1-4407-2976-8(X))* 2009. 75.75 *(978-1-4407-2986-7(7))* 2009. 44.75 *(978-1-4407-2982-9(4))* 2009. 173.75 *(978-1-4407-2977-5(8))* 2009. 45.75 *(978-1-4407-2980-5(8))* 2009. 44.75 *(978-1-4407-2978-2(6))* Recorded Bks., Inc.

—The Last Straw. 2009. (Diary of a Wimpy Kid Ser.: 3). (Illus.). 217p. (J). lib. bdg. 25.70 *(978-0-606-23664-5(3))* Turtleback.

—Rodrick Rules. 2008. (Diary of a Wimpy Kid Ser.: No. 2). (Illus.). 216p. (J). pap. 4.99 *(978-0-8109-9552-9(2))* Abrams, Inc.

—Rodrick Rules. 2008. (Diary of a Wimpy Kid Ser.: Bk. 2). (JPN., Illus.). 220p. (J). *(978-4-591-10464-4(8))* Poplar Publishing.

—Rodrick Rules, 2 vols. (Diary of a Wimpy Kid Ser.: 2). (J). 2010. 173.75 *(978-1-4361-3864-2(7))* 2010. 75.75 *(978-1-4407-0420-8(1))* 2009. 1.25 *(978-1-4361-3860-4(4))* 2009. 46.75 *(978-1-4361-3863-5(9))* 2009. 44.75 *(978-1-4361-3865-9(5))* 2009. 44.75 *(978-1-4361-3869-7(8))* 2009. (gr. 4-8). 46.75 *(978-1-4361-3867-3(1))* Recorded Bks., Inc.

—Rodrick Rules. 2008. (Diary of a Wimpy Kid Ser.: 2). (Illus.). 216p. (J). lib. bdg. 25.70 *(978-0-606-23663-8(5))* Turtleback.

—The Third Wheel. 2012. (ENG.). (J). (gr. 3-7). pap. 8.49 *(978-1-4197-0729-2(9))* Abrams, Inc.

Kirby, Lee. Super Turbo & the Fire-Breathing Dragon. O'Connor, George, illus. 2017. (Super Turbo Ser.: 5). (ENG.). 128p. (J). (gr. k-4). 16.99 *(978-1-4814-9997-2(1))*; pap. 5.99 *(978-1-4814-9996-5(3))* Little Simon. (Little Simon).

—Super Turbo vs. Wonder Pig. O'Connor, George, illus. 2018. (Super Turbo Ser.: 6). (ENG.). 128p. (J). (gr. k-4). 16.99 *(978-1-5344-1182-1(8))*; pap. 6.99 *(978-1-5344-1181-4(X))* Little Simon. (Little Simon).

Kirby, Stan. Captain Awesome & the Easter Egg Bandit. O'Connor, George, illus. 2015. (Captain Awesome Ser.: 13). (ENG.). 128p. (J). (gr. k-4). pap. 5.99 *(978-1-4814-2558-2(7)*, Little Simon) Little Simon.

—Captain Awesome & the Missing Elephants. O'Connor, George, illus. 2014. (Captain Awesome Ser.: 10). (ENG.). 128p. (J). (gr. k-4). 17.99 *(978-1-4424-8995-0(2))*; pap. 6.99 *(978-1-4424-8994-3(4))* Little Simon. (Little Simon).

—Captain Awesome & the New Kid. O'Connor, George, illus. 2012. (Captain Awesome Ser.: 3). (ENG.). 128p. (J). (gr. k-4). 17.99 *(978-1-4424-4200-9(X))*; pap. 6.99 *(978-1-4424-4199-6(2))* Little Simon. (Little Simon).

—Captain Awesome & the New Kid. 2012. (Captain Awesome Ser.: 3). (Illus.). 112p. (J). lib. bdg. 16.00 *(978-0-606-26324-5(1))* Turtleback.

—Captain Awesome & the Ultimate Spelling Bee. O'Connor, George, illus. 2013. (Captain Awesome Ser.: 7). (ENG.). 128p. (J). (gr. k-4). 17.99 *(978-1-4424-5156-8(4))*; pap. 6.99 *(978-1-4424-5158-2(0))* Little Simon. (Little Simon).

—Captain Awesome & the Ultimate Spelling Bee. 2013. (Captain Awesome Ser.: 7). lib. bdg. 16.00 *(978-0-606-27035-9(3))* Turtleback.

—Captain Awesome for President. O'Connor, George, illus. 2018. (Captain Awesome Ser.: 20). (ENG.). 128p. (J). (gr. k-4). 17.99 *(978-1-5344-2084-7(3))*; pap. 5.99 *(978-1-5344-2083-0(5))* Little Simon. (Little Simon).

—Captain Awesome Gets Crushed. O'Connor, George, illus. 2013. (Captain Awesome Ser.: 9). (ENG.). 128p. (J). (gr. k-2). pap. 6.99 *(978-1-4424-8212-8(5))*; 17.99 *(978-1-4424-8213-5(3))* Little Simon. (Little Simon).

—Captain Awesome Gets Crushed. 2013. (Captain Awesome Ser.: 9). lib. bdg. 16.00 *(978-0-606-32331-4(7))* Turtleback.

—Captain Awesome Saves the Winter Wonderland. O'Connor, George, illus. 2012. (Captain Awesome Ser.: 6). (ENG.). 128p. (J). (gr. k-4). 17.99 *(978-1-4424-4335-8(9))*; pap. 6.99 *(978-1-4424-4334-1(0))* Little Simon. (Little Simon).

—Captain Awesome Saves the Winter Wonderland. 2012. (Captain Awesome Ser.: 6). lib. bdg. 16.00 *(978-0-606-26894-3(4))* Turtleback.

—Captain Awesome Saves the Winter Wonderland: #6. O'Connor, George, illus. 2018. (Captain Awesome Ser.). (ENG.). 128p. (J). (gr. k-4). lib. bdg. 31.36 *(978-1-5321-4204-8(8)*, 28548, Chapter Bks.) Spotlight.

—Captain Awesome to the Rescue! O'Connor, George, illus. 2012. (Captain Awesome Ser.: 1). (ENG.). 128p. (J). (gr. k-2). 17.99 *(978-1-4424-4090-6(2))*; pap. 5.99 *(978-1-4424-3561-2(5))* Little Simon. (Little Simon).

—Captain Awesome to the Rescue! 2012. (Captain Awesome Ser.: 1). lib. bdg. 16.00 *(978-0-606-26322-1(5))* Turtleback.

—Captain Awesome vs. the Sinister Substitute Teacher. O'Connor, George, illus. 2016. (Captain Awesome Ser.: 16). (ENG.). 128p. (J). (gr. k-4). pap. 5.99 *(978-1-4814-5858-0(2)*, Little Simon) Little Simon.

—Captain Awesome vs. the Spooky, Scary House. O'Connor, George, illus. 2013. (Captain Awesome Ser.: 8). (ENG.). 128p. (J). (gr. k-2). 17.99 *(978-1-4424-7255-6(3))*; pap. 6.99 *(978-1-4424-7254-9(5))* Little Simon. (Little Simon).

—Captain Awesome vs. the Spooky, Scary House. 2013. (Captain Awesome Ser.: 8). lib. bdg. 16.00 *(978-0-606-32048-1(2))* Turtleback.

Kishimoto, Masashi. Naruto: Chapter Book, Vol. 8: Intruders. 2009. (Naruto: Chapter Bks.: 8). (ENG., Illus.). 80p. (J). pap. 4.99 *(978-1-4215-2318-7(3))* Viz Media.

Kisner, Adrienne. Dear Rachel Maddow. 2019. (ENG.). 288p. (YA). pap. 12.99 *(978-1-250-30883-2(6)*, 900181147) Square Fish.

Kittle, Katrina. Reasons to Be Happy. 2011. 288p. (J). (gr. 6-8). pap. 10.99 *(978-1-4022-6020-9(2))* Sourcebooks, Inc.

Kittscher, Kristen. The Wig in the Window. 2016. (ENG.). 384p. (J). (gr. 3-7). pap. 6.99 *(978-0-06-211051-0(9)*, HarperCollins) HarperCollins Pubs.

Klass, David. Home of the Braves. 2004. 355p. (YA). (gr. 7-12). 17.65 *(978-0-7569-2805-6(2))* Perfection Learning Corp.

—Losers Take All. 2016. (YA). lib. bdg. 20.85 *(978-0-606-39480-2(X))* Turtleback.

—You Don't Know Me. 2010. (ENG.). 288p. (YA). (gr. 9-12). pap. 12.99 *(978-0-312-65302-6(6)*, 900069443) Square Fish.

Klass, David & Klass, Perri. Second Impact: Making the Hardest Call of All. 2014. (ENG.). 304p. (YA). (gr. 7). pap. 16.99 *(978-1-250-04436-5(7)*, 900128331) Square Fish.

Klein, Abby. Don't Sit on My Lunch! (Ready, Freddy! #4), Vol. 4. McKinley, John, illus. 2005. (Ready, Freddy! Ser.: 4). (ENG.). 96p. (J). (gr. -1-3). 5.99 *(978-0-439-55602-6(3)*, Blue Sky Pr., The) Scholastic, Inc.

—The One Hundredth Day of School! McKinley, John, illus. 2008. (Ready, Freddy! Ser.: Bk. 13). 94p. (J). (gr. -1-3). 11.65 *(978-0-7569-8836-4(5))* Perfection Learning Corp.

—Ready, Freddy! #5: Talent Show Scardey-Pants: Talent Show Scardey-Pants. McKinley, John, illus. 5th ed. 2005. (Ready, Freddy! Ser.: 5). (ENG.). 96p. (J). (gr. -1-3). 5.99 *(978-0-439-55604-0(X))* Scholastic, Inc.

—Ready, Set, Snow! (Ready, Freddy! #16), Vol. 16. McKinley, John, illus. 2009. (Ready, Freddy! Ser.: 16). (ENG.). 96p. (J). (gr. -1-3). pap. 5.99 *(978-0-439-89596-5(0))* Scholastic, Inc.

—Second Grade Rules! McKinley, John, illus. 2014. 85p. (J). pap. *(978-0-545-69031-7(5))* Scholastic, Inc.

—Secret Santa Surprise! McKinley, John, illus. 2015. 86p. (J). *(978-0-545-86357-5(0))* Scholastic, Inc.

—Thanks for Giving. McKinley, John, illus. 2009. (Ready, Freddy! Reader List: No. 4). 32p. (J). pap. *(978-0-545-14176-5(1))* Scholastic, Inc.

—Thanksgiving Turkey Trouble. McKinley, John, illus. 2008. (Ready, Freddy! Ser.: Bk. 15). 95p. (gr. -1-3). 16.00 *(978-0-7569-8838-8(1))* Perfection Learning Corp.

—Tooth Trouble. 2011. (Ready, Freddy Ser.: Bk. 1). 8.32 *(978-0-7848-3613-2(2)*, Everbind) Marco Bk. Co.

Klein, Adria F. Max Goes to School. Gallagher-Cole, Mernie, illus. 2007. (Read-It! Readers: the Life of Max Ser.). (ENG.). 24p. (J). (gr. -1-2). per. 3.95 *(978-1-4048-3059-2(6)*, 94335, Picture Window Bks.) Capstone.

—Max Va a la Escuela, 1 vol. Lozano, Clara, tr. Gallagher-Cole, Mernie, illus. 2007. (Read-It! Readers en Español: la Vida de Max Ser.). (SPA.). 24p. (J). (gr. -1-3). per. 3.95 *(978-1-4048-3037-0(5)*, 94375, Picture Window Bks.) Capstone.

—Tool School. Rowland, Andrew, illus. 2013. (Tool School Ser.). (ENG.). 32p. (J). (gr. -1-1). 181.20 *(978-1-4342-8842-4(0)*, 21114, Stone Arch Bks.) Capstone.

Klein, Glasko. The Lie. 2019. (Do-Over Ser.). (ENG.). 104p. (YA). (gr. 6-12). pap. 7.99 *(978-1-5415-4551-9(6)*, f87bd7c0-6122-44e1-bfa1-d95fa8232e26); 26.65 *(978-1-5415-4032-3(8)*, 8ccda28b-d533-4941-9e47-a18f7789bd8a) Lerner Publishing Group. (Darby Creek).

Klein, J. M. New School, New Me!, 1 vol. 2018. (Totally Secret Diary of Dani D. Ser.). (ENG.). 64p. (YA). (gr. 2-3). 23.25 *(978-1-5383-8196-0(6)*, 765fbfc3-1486-4ed4-94b5-27d0895051d1); pap. 13.35 *(978-1-5383-8195-3(8)*, ca0db874-610c-4d21-a737-ad4327ae802c) Enslow Publishing, LLC.

Klein, Jen. Hearts Made for Breaking. 2019. 320p. (YA). (gr. 7). pap. 9.99 *(978-1-5247-0008-9(8)*, Random Hse. Bks. for Young Readers) Random Hse. Children's Bks.

—Shuffle, Repeat. 2017. 352p. (YA). (gr. 7). pap. 9.99 *(978-0-553-50985-4(3)*, Ember) Random Hse. Children's Bks.

Kleinman, Estelle. The City of Ember. Friedland, Joyce & Kessler, Rikki, eds. 2007. (Novel-Ties Ser.). (Illus.). 31p. pap. 16.95 *(978-0-7675-3754-4(8))* Learning Links Inc.

—Tears of a Tiger. Friedland, Joyce & Kessler, Rikki, eds. 2008. (Novel-Ties Ser.). (Illus.). 31p. pap. 16.95 *(978-0-7675-4259-3(2))* Learning Links Inc.

Kleinman, Liza & Gideon, Brook. Azalea, Unschooled, 1 vol. 2015. (ENG., Illus.). 140p. 16.95 *(978-1-939017-58-1(0)*, 2947f8ca-087f-436e-933d-f002ceed8103) Islandport Pr., Inc.

Klimpton, Diana. Amy Wild, Animal Talker - the Musical Mouse. 2013. pap. 4.99 *(978-0-7945-3145-4(8)*, Usborne) EDC Publishing.

Kline, Lisa Williams. Write Before Your Eyes. 2010. (ENG.). 192p. (J). (gr. 3-7). 6.99 *(978-0-440-42251-8(5)*, Yearling) Random Hse. Children's Bks.

Kline, Suzy. Horrible Harry & the Dragon War. Remkiewicz, Frank, illus. 2003. (Horrible Harry Ser.: 14). 64p. (J). (gr. 2-4). 4.99 *(978-0-14-250166-5(2)*, Puffin Books) Penguin Young Readers Group.

—Horrible Harry & the Dragon War. 2003. (Horrible Harry Ser.: 14). lib. bdg. 14.75 *(978-0-613-92539-6(4))* Turtleback.

—Horrible Harry & the Goog. Remkiewicz, Frank, illus. 2006. (Horrible Harry Ser.: 18). 64p. (J). (gr. 2-4). pap. 4.99 *(978-0-14-240728-8(3)*, Puffin Books) Penguin Young Readers Group.

—Horrible Harry & the Goog. Remkiewicz, Frank, illus. 2006. (Horrible Harry Ser.). 56p. (gr. 2-5). 14.00 *(978-0-7569-6948-6(4))* Perfection Learning Corp.

—Horrible Harry & the Hallway Bully. Wummer, Amy, illus. 2015. (Horrible Harry Ser.: 31). 80p. (J). (gr. 1-3). 5.99 *(978-0-14-750967-3(X)*, Puffin Books) Penguin Young Readers Group.

—Horrible Harry & the Holidaze. Remkiewicz, Frank, illus. 2004. (Horrible Harry Ser.: 16). 80p. (J). (gr. 2-4). 4.99 *(978-0-14-240205-4(2)*, Puffin Books) Penguin Young Readers Group.

—Horrible Harry & the June Box. Wummer, Amy, illus. 2012. (Horrible Harry Ser.: 27). 80p. (J). (gr. 2-4). pap. 4.99 *(978-0-14-242185-7(5)*, Puffin Books) Penguin Young Readers Group.

—Horrible Harry & the Locked Closet. Remkiewicz, Frank, illus. 2005. (Horrible Harry Ser.). 68p. (gr. 2-5). 14.00 *(978-0-7569-5825-1(3))* Perfection Learning Corp.

—Horrible Harry & the Missing Diamond. Wummer, Amy, illus. 2014. (Horrible Harry Ser.: 30). 80p. (J). (gr. 2-4). pap. 4.99 *(978-0-14-242228-1(2)*, Puffin Books) Penguin Young Readers Group.

—Horrible Harry & the Mud Gremlins. Remkiewicz, Frank, illus. 2004. (Horrible Harry Ser.). 50p. (gr. 2). 14.00 *(978-0-7569-2815-5(X))* Perfection Learning Corp.

—Horrible Harry & the Secret Treasure. Wummer, Amy, illus. 2012. (Horrible Harry Ser.: 26). 80p. (J). (gr. 2-4). 5.99 *(978-0-14-242021-8(2)*, Puffin Books) Penguin Young Readers Group.

—Horrible Harry & the Wedding Spies. 2016. (Horrible Harry Ser.: 32). lib. bdg. 14.75 *(978-0-606-38389-9(1))* Turtleback.

—Horrible Harry Bugs the Three Bears. Remkiewicz, Frank, illus. 2009. (Horrible Harry Ser.: 22). 80p. (J). (gr. 2-4). 4.99 *(978-0-14-241295-4(3)*, Puffin Books) Penguin Young Readers Group.

—Horrible Harry Cracks the Code. Remkiewicz, Frank, illus. 2008. (Horrible Harry Ser.: 21). 80p. (J). (gr. 2-4). 5.99 *(978-0-14-241247-3(3)*, Puffin Books) Penguin Young Readers Group.

—Horrible Harry Goes Cuckoo. Wummer, Amy, illus. 2011. (Horrible Harry Ser.: 25). 80p. (J). (gr. 2-4). 4.99 *(978-0-14-241876-5(5)*, Puffin Books) Penguin Young Readers Group.

—Horrible Harry Goes to Sea. Remkiewicz, Frank, illus. 2003. (Horrible Harry Ser.: 13). 64p. (J). (gr. 2-4). 5.99 *(978-0-14-250002-6(X)*, Puffin Books) Penguin Young Readers Group.

—Horrible Harry Goes to Sea: Puffine Chapters. 2003. (Horrible Harry Ser.: 13). (gr. 3-6). lib. bdg. 14.75 *(978-0-613-61629-4(4))* Turtleback.

—Horrible Harry on the Ropes. Remkiewicz, Frank, illus. 2011. (Horrible Harry Ser.: 24). 80p. (J). (gr. 2-4). 4.99 *(978-0-14-241695-2(9),* Puffin Books) Penguin Young Readers Group.
—Horrible Harry Takes the Cake. Remkiewicz, Frank, illus. 2007. (Horrible Harry Ser.: 19). 64p. (J). (gr. 2-4). 4.99 *(978-0-14-240939-8(1),* Puffin Books) Penguin Young Readers Group.
—Horrible Harry Takes the Cake. Remkiewicz, Frank, illus. 2007. (Horrible Harry Ser.). 45p. (gr. 2-5). 14.00 *(978-0-7569-8158-7(1))* Perfection Learning Corp.
Klise, James. Love Drugged. 2010. (ENG.). 312p. (YA). (gr. 9-12). pap. 9.95 *(978-0-7387-2175-0(1),* 0738721751, Flux) North Star Editions.
Klise, Kate. Regarding the Bathrooms: A Privy to the Past. Klise, M. Sarah, illus. 2008. (Regarding The ... Ser.: Bk. 4). (ENG.). 160p. (J). (gr. 3-7). pap. 7.99 *(978-0-15-206261-3(0),* 1198771, Clarion Bks.) HarperCollins Pubs.
—Regarding the Bathrooms: A Privy to the Past. Klise, Kate & Klise, M. Sarah, illus. 2008. (Regarding the Fountain Ser.: Bk. 4). (ENG.). 160p. (J). (gr. 4-6). 21.19 *(978-0-15-205164-8(3))* Houghton Mifflin Harcourt Publishing Co.
Klise, Kate & Klise, Kate. Regarding the Bees: A Lesson, in Letters, on Honey, Dating, & Other Sticky Subjects. Klise, M. Sarah, illus. 2009. (Regarding The ... Ser.: Bk. 5). (ENG.). 144p. (J). (gr. 3-7). pap. 6.99 *(978-0-15-206668-0(3),* 1099002, Clarion Bks.) HarperCollins Pubs.
Klise, Kate & Klise, M. Sarah. Regarding the Trees: A Splintered Saga Rooted in Secrets. Klise, Kate & Klise, M. Sarah, illus. 2007. (Regarding The ... Ser.: Bk. 3). (ENG., Illus.). 160p. (J). (gr. 3-7). pap. 7.99 *(978-0-15-206090-9(1),* 1198293, Clarion Bks.) HarperCollins Pubs.
Kluck, Ted. The Outstanding Life of an Awkward Theater Kid: God, I'll Do Anything — Just Don't Let Me Fail. 2020. (Adventures with Flex Ser.). (ENG., Illus.). 192p. (J). (gr. 2-7). 12.99 *(978-0-7369-7886-6(0),* 6978866) Harvest Hse. Pubs.
Knife, Ivan M. Uses the. Black Thursday. 2010. 108p. pap. 15.99 *(978-1-4500-6311-1(X))* Xlibris Corp.
Knight, Chris. Karen Bighead: The Story of a Little Girl with a Big Head. 2011. (Illus.). 24p. 12.12 *(978-1-4520-7730-7(4))* AuthorHouse.
Knight, Karsten. Wildefire. 2011. (ENG.). 400p. (YA). (gr. 9-18). 16.99 *(978-1-4424-2117-2(7),* Simon & Schuster Bks. For Young Readers) Simon & Schuster Bks. For Young Readers.
Knowles, Jo. Read Between the Lines. 2015. (ENG.). 336p. (YA). (gr. 9). 16.99 *(978-0-7636-6387-2(5))* Candlewick Pr.
Knowlton, Laurie. N 2 Deep. 2004. 128p. (J). pap. 5.99 *(978-1-4003-0327-4(3))* Nelson, Thomas Inc.
Knudsen, Michelle. Argus. Wesson, Andrea, illus. 2011. (ENG.). 32p. (J). (gr. -1-3). 17.99 *(978-0-7636-3790-3(4))* Candlewick Pr.
—The Case of Vampire Vivian. Wummer, Amy, illus. 2003. (Science Solves It! Ser.). (ENG.). 32p. (J). (gr. 1-3). pap. 5.99 *(978-1-57565-127-9(0),* 2c9530f1-72fd-49cf-9a9e-9544a676ab37, Kane Press) Astra Publishing Hse.
—El Caso de Vivian la Vampira. Wummer, Amy, illus. 2008. (Science Solves It! en Espanol Ser.). (SPA.). 32p. (J). (gr. -1-3). pap. 5.95 *(978-1-57565-277-1(3))* Astra Publishing Hse.
—El Caso de Vivian la Vampira (the Case of Vampire Vivian) Wummer, Amy, illus. 2009. (Science Solves It! (r) en Espanol Ser.). (SPA.). (gr. 1-3). pap. 33.92 *(978-0-7613-4800-9(X))* Lerner Publishing Group.
—A Slimy Story. Billin-Frye, Paige, illus. 2004. 32p. (J). lib. bdg. 20.00 *(978-1-4242-1150-0(6))* Fitzgerald Bks.
Knudson, Mike. Raymond & Graham: Dancing Dudes. 2010. (Raymond & Graham Ser.: 2). (Illus.). 144p. (J). (gr. 3-7). 6.99 *(978-0-14-241508-5(1),* Puffin Books) Penguin Young Readers Group.
Knudson, Mike & Wilkinson, Steve. Raymond & Graham: Bases Loaded. Curtis, Stacy, illus. 2011. (Raymond & Graham Ser.: 3). 160p. (J). (gr. 3-7). 6.99 *(978-0-14-241751-5(3),* Puffin Books) Penguin Young Readers Group.
Kobayashi, Jin. School Rumble. (JPN., Illus.). (YA). Vol. 1. pap. *(978-4-06-363244-6(X))* Vol. 2. 162p. pap. *(978-4-06-363290-3(3))* Vol. 3. 158p. pap. *(978-4-06-363321-4(7))* Vol. 4. 154p. pap. *(978-4-06-363346-7(2))* Kodansha, Ltd.
Koch, Edward R. Relay. 2009. 188p. pap. 12.95 *(978-1-59858-989-4(X))* Dog Ear Publishing, LLC.
Kochalka, James. Mechaboys. 2018. (Illus.). 192p. pap. 19.99 *(978-1-60309-423-8(7))* Top Shelf Productions.
Koertge, Ron. Where the Kissing Never Stops. 2005. (ENG.). 256p. (YA). (gr. 9-18). per. 6.99 *(978-0-7636-2696-9(1))* Candlewick Pr.
Kogler, Jennifer. The Otherworldlies. 2008. 400p. (J). lib. bdg. 17.89 *(978-0-06-073960-7(6));* (ENG.). (gr. 5-18). 16.99 *(978-0-06-073959-1(2))* HarperCollins Pubs. (Eos).
Koja, Kathe. Buddha Boy. 2004. (ENG.). 128p. (YA). (gr. 7-11). reprint ed. 7.99 *(978-0-14-240209-2(5),* Speak) Penguin Young Readers Group.
—Buddha Boy. 2004. 117p. (gr. 3-7). 16.00 *(978-0-7569-3117-9(7))* Perfection Learning Corp.
—Straydog. 2004. (ENG.). 128p. (YA). (gr. 7-18). reprint ed. 7.99 *(978-0-14-240071-5(8),* Speak) Penguin Young Readers Group.
—Talk. 2008. (ENG.). 144p. (YA). (gr. 7-12). per. 16.99 *(978-0-312-37605-5(7),* 900048334) Square Fish.
Kolb, Joseph J. Reservation Dreams. 2004. 185p. pap. 24.95 *(978-1-4137-3054-8(X))* America Star Bks.
Kolczynski, Sean. The Night Before Middle School! 2012. 28p. pap. 21.99 *(978-1-4771-4794-8(2))* Xlibris Corp.
Konigsberg, Bill. Openly Straight. (ENG.). (YA). (gr. 9). 2015. 352p. pap. 10.99 *(978-0-545-79865-5(5))* 2013. 336p. 17.99 *(978-0-545-50989-3(0))* Scholastic, Inc. (Levine, Arthur A. Bks.).
Konigsburg, E. L. The View from Saturday. 280p. (YA). (gr. 5-18). pap. 4.95 *(978-0-8072-1511-1(2),* Listening Library) Random Hse. Audio Publishing Group.
Kopley, Richard. The Remarkable David Wordsworth. Fazio, Michael, illus. 2013. 30p. (J). pap. *(978-1-936172-67-2(4))* Eifrig Publishing.
Korelitz, Jean Hanff. Interference Powder, 0 vols. 2006. (ENG.). 146p. (J). (gr. 4-6). pap. 7.99 *(978-0-7614-5275-1(3),* 9780761452751, Two Lions) Amazon Publishing.
—Interference Powder, 1 vol. 2003. (ENG.). 300p. (J). 15.95 *(978-0-7614-5139-6(0))* Marshall Cavendish Corp.
Korman, Gordon. Framed. (J). 2010. *(978-0-545-27081-6(2),* Scholastic Pr.)Bk. 3. 2011. (Swindle Ser.: 3). (ENG.). 240p. (gr. 3-7). pap. 7.99 *(978-0-545-19763-2(5),* Scholastic Paperbacks) Scholastic, Inc.
—Jake, Reinvented. rev. ed. 2017. (ENG.). 192p. (J). (gr. 5-9). pap. 8.99 *(978-1-4847-9842-3(2))* Little, Brown Bks. for Young Readers.
—Macdonald Hall #1: This Can't Be Happening at Macdonald Hall! (Reissue) 2011. (ENG.). 136p. (J). (gr. 4-6). pap. 18.69 *(978-0-545-28924-5(6))* Scholastic, Inc.
—No More Dead Dogs. rev. ed. 2017. Orig. Title: Touchdown Stage Left. (ENG.). 240p. (J). (gr. 5-9). pap. 8.99 *(978-1-4847-9844-7(9))* Little, Brown Bks. for Young Readers.
—No More Dead Dogs. 2017. Orig. Title: Touchdown Stage Left. (J). lib. bdg. 17.20 *(978-0-606-40570-6(4))* Turtleback.
—Pop. (ENG.). 272p. (YA). (gr. 8). 2019. pap. 9.99 *(978-0-06-174261-3(9))* 2009. 16.99 *(978-0-06-174228-6(7))* HarperCollins Pubs. (Balzer & Bray).
—Restart. 2019. (Penworthy Picks Middle School Ser.). (ENG.). 243p. (J). (gr. 4-5). 18.36 *(978-1-64310-935-0(9))* Penworthy Co., LLC, The.
—Restart. 2017. (ENG.). 256p. (J). (gr. 3-7). 17.99 *(978-1-338-05377-7(9),* Scholastic Pr.) Scholastic, Inc.
—Schooled. 2008. (ENG.). 224p. (J). (gr. 3-7). pap. 8.99 *(978-1-4231-0516-9(8))* Little, Brown Bks. for Young Readers.
—Schooled. 2010. 17.00 *(978-1-60686-894-2(2))* Perfection Learning Corp.
—Schooled. (J). 2012. 1.25 *(978-1-4281-7185-5(1))* 2008. 70.75 *(978-1-4361-1568-1(X))* 2008. 69.75 *(978-1-4281-7190-9(8))* 2007. 90.75 *(978-1-4281-7194-7(0))* 2007. 147.75 *(978-1-4281-7189-3(4))* 2007. 71.75 *(978-1-4281-7188-6(6))* 2007. 92.75 *(978-1-4281-7192-3(4))* Recorded Bks., Inc.
—Schooled. 2008. (J). lib. bdg. 17.20 *(978-1-4178-2839-5(0))* Turtleback.
—Supergifted. (ENG.). (J). (gr. 3-7). 2019. 320p. pap. 8.99 *(978-0-06-256386-6(6))* 2018. 304p. 16.99 *(978-0-06-256384-2(X))* 2018. 304p. lib. bdg. 17.89 *(978-0-06-256385-9(8))* HarperCollins Pubs. (Balzer & Bray).
—Ungifted. (ENG.). 288p. (J). (gr. 5). 2014. pap. 9.99 *(978-0-06-174267-5(8))* 2012. 16.99 *(978-0-06-174266-8(X))* 2012. lib. bdg. 17.89 *(978-0-06-174268-2(6))* HarperCollins Pubs. (Balzer & Bray).
—The Unteachables. 2019. (ENG.). (J). (gr. 3-7). 304p. pap. 9.99 *(978-0-06-256390-3(4));* 288p. 18.99 *(978-0-06-256388-0(2));* 288p. lib. bdg. 17.89 *(978-0-06-256389-7(0))* HarperCollins Pubs. (Balzer & Bray).
—Whatshisface. 2019. (ENG.). 240p. (J). (gr. 3-7). pap. 8.99 *(978-1-338-20018-8(6))* Scholastic, Inc.
—The 6th Grade Nickname Game. rev. ed. 2017. (ENG.). 160p. (J). (gr. 3-7). pap. 7.99 *(978-1-4847-9840-9(6))* Hyperion Bks. for Children.
Korman, Susan J. Bad Deal. 2015. (Surviving Southside Ser.). (ENG.). 104p. (YA). (gr. 6-12). E-Book 53.32 *(978-1-4677-6006-5(4),* 9781467760065, Lerner Digital) Lerner Publishing Group.
—Overexposed. 2013. (Surviving Southside Ser.). (ENG.). 104p. (YA). (gr. 6-12). pap. 7.95 *(978-1-4677-0706-0(6),* 091b163c-8f58-4068-b967-aef626809667, Darby Creek) Lerner Publishing Group.
Kosara, Victoria. Graduation Party. Durk, Jim, illus. 2010. (J). pap. *(978-0-545-23400-9(X))* Scholastic, Inc.
Kosgei, William. The Talented & Gifted: African Writers Series. 2013. 106p. pap. 10.95 *(978-1-62516-165-9(4),* Strategic Bk. Publishing) Strategic Book Publishing & Rights Agency (SBPRA).
Koss, Amy Goldman. Poison Ivy. 2008. (ENG.). 192p. (J). (gr. 5-9). pap. 9.99 *(978-0-312-38453-1(X),* 900053458) Square Fish.
Kotecki, Nathan. The Suburban Strange. (Suburban Strange Ser.). (ENG.). (YA). (gr. 9). 2013. 384p. pap. 8.99 *(978-0-544-10479-2(X),* 1540788) 2012. 368p. 16.99 *(978-0-547-72996-1(0),* 1483969) HarperCollins Pubs. (Clarion Bks.).
Kovalski, Maryann. Omar on Board, 1 vol. (ENG., Illus.). 32p. (J). (gr. k-2). 2007. 6.95 *(978-1-55455-033-3(5),* 3004aa42-52a5-46f1-8a96-10ede06c1961) 2005. 9.95 *(978-1-55041-918-4(8),* 7d9c1192-3556-42ca-98d3-6d2aa997bf2f) Trifolium Bks., Inc. CAN. Dist: Firefly Bks., Ltd.
Kowitt, Holly. The Principal's Underwear Is Missing. Kowitt, Holly, illus. 2018. (ENG., Illus.). 224p. (J). pap. 16.99 *(978-1-250-15862-8(1),* 900185519) Square Fish.
—The Principal's Underwear Is Missing. 2018. (J). lib. bdg. 18.40 *(978-0-606-41102-8(X))* Turtleback.
Kraft, Erik P. Lenny & Mel. Kraft, Erik P., illus. 2012. (Ready-For-Chapters Ser.). (ENG., Illus.). 64p. (J). (gr. 2-5). pap. 6.99 *(978-0-689-85891-8(4),* Aladdin) Simon & Schuster Children's Publishing.
—Lenny & Mel after-School Confidential. Kraft, Erik P., illus. 2012. (Lenny & Mel Ser.). (ENG., Illus.). 64p. (J). (gr. 2-5). pap. 6.99 *(978-1-4424-6314-1(7),* Simon & Schuster/Paula Wiseman Bks.) Simon & Schuster/Paula Wiseman Bks.
Kramer, Stacy & Thomas, Valerie. Karma Bites. 2010. (ENG.). 348p. (J). (gr. 5-7). pap. 18.99 *(978-0-547-36301-1(X),* 1422027, Clarion Bks.) HarperCollins Pubs.
Kraus, Daniel. Rotters. 2012. (ENG.). 464p. (YA). (gr. 9). pap. 10.99 *(978-0-385-73858-3(7),* Ember) Random Hse. Children's Bks.
Kraus, Jeanne. Get Ready for Jetty! My Journal about ADHD & Me. 2012. 96p. (J). pap. 9.95 *(978-1-4338-1197-5(9));* (Illus.). 14.95 *(978-1-4338-1196-8(0))* American Psychological Assn. (Magination Pr.).
Kraus, Jeanne R. Annie's Plan: Taking Charge of Schoolwork & Homework. Beyl, Charles, illus. 2006. 48p. (J). (gr. 2-5). 14.95 *(978-1-59147-481-4(7));* pap. 9.95 *(978-1-59147-482-1(5))* American Psychological Assn. (Magination Pr.).
Kreidler, Shannon. The Adventures of Sally the Squirrel: Interactive... Educational & Earn Gold Stars. 2013. 28p. pap. 15.99 *(978-1-4797-7674-0(2))* Xlibris Corp.
Kreie, Chris. The Natural. 2018. (Kick! Ser.). (ENG.). 104p. (YA). (gr. 6-12). pap. 7.99 *(978-1-5415-0025-9(3),* 5c37029c-2df8-4087-a189-198db8ede35b); lib. bdg. 25.32 *(978-1-5415-0019-8(9),* 291afa5b-95d7-4b8b-ba09-32948c4c1298) Lerner Publishing Group. (Darby Creek).
—The Superstar. 2018. (Kick! Ser.). (ENG.). 104p. (YA). (gr. 6-12). 25.32 *(978-1-5415-0024-2(5),* 1b86e765-43e2-4a01-aaa5-a2d1cf2da395, Darby Creek) Lerner Publishing Group.
Krensky, Stephen. Big Bad Wolves at School. Sneed, Brad, illus. 2007. (ENG.). 32p. (J). (gr. -1-3). 18.99 *(978-0-689-83799-9(2),* Simon & Schuster Bks. For Young Readers) Simon & Schuster Bks. For Young Readers.
Kristina Takes the Stage. 2008. (Illus.). 56p. (J). mass mkt. 10.95 *(978-0-9792361-3-6(4))* Inspire U., LLC.
Kroll, Steven. Patches Lost & Found, 0 vols. Gott, Barry, illus. 2012. (ENG.). 32p. (J). (gr. 1-3). pap. 7.95 *(978-0-7614-5217-1(6),* 9780761452171, Two Lions) Amazon Publishing.
Kropp, Alex. Hacker! (Illus.). 93p. *(978-1-897039-09-0(3))* High Interest Publishing (HIP).
Krosoczka, Jarrett J. Lunch Lady & the Author Visit Vendetta: Lunch Lady #3. 2009. (Lunch Lady Ser.: 3). (ENG.). 96p. (J). (gr. 2-5). pap. 6.99 *(978-0-375-86094-2(0),* Knopf Bks. for Young Readers) Random Hse. Children's Bks.
—Lunch Lady & the Cyborg Substitute: Lunch Lady #1. 2009. (Lunch Lady Ser.: 1). (ENG.). 96p. (J). (gr. 2-5). pap. 6.99 *(978-0-375-84683-0(2),* Knopf Bks. for Young Readers) Random Hse. Children's Bks.
—Lunch Lady & the Mutant Mathletes. 2012. (Lunch Lady Ser.: 7). lib. bdg. 17.20 *(978-0-606-23871-7(9))* Turtleback.
—Lunch Lady & the Mutant Mathletes: Lunch Lady #7. 2012. (Lunch Lady Ser.: 7). (ENG., Illus.). 96p. (J). (gr. 2-5). pap. 6.99 *(978-0-375-87028-6(8),* Knopf Bks. for Young Readers) Random Hse. Children's Bks.
—Lunch Lady & the Picture Day Peril. 2012. (Lunch Lady Ser.: 8). lib. bdg. 17.20 *(978-0-606-26811-0(1))* Turtleback.
—Lunch Lady & the Picture Day Peril: Lunch Lady #8. 2012. (Lunch Lady Ser.: 8). (ENG., Illus.). 96p. (J). (gr. 2-5). pap. 6.99 *(978-0-375-87035-4(0),* Knopf Bks. for Young Readers) Random Hse. Children's Bks.
—Lunch Lady & the Schoolwide Scuffle. 2014. (Lunch Lady Ser.: 10). lib. bdg. 17.20 *(978-0-606-32235-5(3))* Turtleback.
—Lunch Lady & the Schoolwide Scuffle: Lunch Lady & the Schoolwide Scuffle. 2014. (Lunch Lady Ser.: 10). (ENG., Illus.). 96p. (J). (gr. 2-5). pap. 6.99 *(978-0-385-75279-4(2),* Knopf Bks. for Young Readers) Random Hse. Children's Bks.
—Lunch Lady & the Video Game Villain. 2013. (Lunch Lady Ser.: 9). lib. bdg. 17.20 *(978-0-606-27003-8(5))* Turtleback.
—Lunch Lady & the Video Game Villain: Lunch Lady #9. 2013. (Lunch Lady Ser.: 9). (ENG.). 96p. (J). (gr. 2-5). pap. 7.99 *(978-0-307-98079-3(0),* Knopf Bks. for Young Readers) Random Hse. Children's Bks.
—The Principal Strikes Back. 2018. (Illus.). 176p. (J). *(978-1-76066-157-1(0))* Scholastic, Inc.
Krosoczka, Jarrett J., illus. The Force Oversleeps. 2017. 172p. (J). *(978-1-338-20871-9(3))* Scholastic, Inc.
Krueger, Kathryn L. Road to Grandma's House. 2005. 128p. pap. 13.95 *(978-1-59800-366-6(6))* Outskirts Pr., Inc.
Krulik, Nancy. Attack of the Tighty Whities! 2012. (George Brown, Class Clown Ser.: 7). lib. bdg. 14.75 *(978-0-606-23651-5(1))* Turtleback.
—Attack of the Tighty Whities! #7. Blecha, Aaron, illus. 2012. (George Brown, Class Clown Ser.: 7). 128p. (J). (gr. 2-4). pap. 6.99 *(978-0-448-45575-4(7),* Grosset & Dunlap) Penguin Young Readers Group.
—Crash! #1. Thomas, Louis, illus. 2017. (Kid from Planet Z Ser.: 1). 96p. (J). (gr. 1-3). 6.99 *(978-0-448-49012-0(9),* Grosset & Dunlap) Penguin Young Readers Group.
—Dance Your Pants Off! 2013. (George Brown, Class Clown Ser.: 9). lib. bdg. 14.75 *(978-0-606-29802-5(9))* Turtleback.
—Dance Your Pants Off! #9, No. 9. Blecha, Aaron, illus. 2013. (George Brown, Class Clown Ser.: 9). 128p. (J). (gr. 2-4). pap. 6.99 *(978-0-448-45679-9(6),* Grosset & Dunlap) Penguin Young Readers Group.
—Don't Be Such a Turkey! John and Wendy, illus. 2010. (Katie Kazoo, Switcheroo Ser.). 160p. (J). (gr. 2-4). pap. 6.99 *(978-0-448-45448-1(3),* Grosset & Dunlap) Penguin Young Readers Group.
—Don't Sneeze! 2017. (Kid from Planet Z Ser.: 2). lib. bdg. 16.00 *(978-0-606-40108-1(3))* Turtleback.
—Don't Sneeze! #2. Thomas, Louis, illus. 2017. (Kid from Planet Z Ser.: 2). 96p. (J). (gr. 1-3). 5.99 *(978-0-451-53343-2(7),* Grosset & Dunlap) Penguin Young Readers Group.
—Eww! What's on My Shoe? 2013. (George Brown, Class Clown Ser.: 11). lib. bdg. 14.75 *(978-0-606-32126-6(8))* Turtleback.
—Flower Power. John and Wendy Staff, illus. 2008. (Katie Kazoo, Switcheroo Ser.). 78p. (gr. 2-5). 14.00 *(978-0-7569-8806-7(3))* Perfection Learning Corp.
—Free the Worms! John & Wendy, illus. 2008. (Katie Kazoo, Switcheroo Ser.). 78p. (J). 11.65 *(978-0-7569-8807-4(1))* Perfection Learning Corp.
—Friends for Never #14, 14 vols., 14. John and Wendy, illus. 2004. (Katie Kazoo, Switcheroo Ser.: 14). 80p. (J). (gr. 2-4). 6.99 *(978-0-448-43606-7(X),* Grosset & Dunlap) Penguin Young Readers Group.
—How Do You Pee in Space? 2014. (George Brown, Class Clown Ser.: 13). lib. bdg. 14.75 *(978-0-606-36163-7(4))* Turtleback.
—How I Survived Middle School: Madame President. 2006. 104p. pap. *(978-0-439-90090-4(5))* Scholastic, Inc.
—I Hate Rules! #5. John and Wendy, illus. 5th ed. 2006. (Katie Kazoo, Switcheroo Ser.: 5). 80p. (J). (gr. 2-4). pap. 6.99 *(978-0-448-43100-0(9),* Grosset & Dunlap) Penguin Young Readers Group.
—I Heard a Rumor. Martini, Angela, illus. 2007. (How I Survived Middle School Ser.: No. 3). 105p. (J). *(978-0-439-90091-1(3))* Scholastic, Inc.
—Lice Check. 2014. (George Brown, Class Clown Ser.: 12). (Illus.). 121p. (J). lib. bdg. 14.75 *(978-0-606-34144-8(7))* Turtleback.
—Lice Check #12, No. 12. Blecha, Aaron, illus. 2014. (George Brown, Class Clown Ser.: 12). 128p. (J). (gr. 2-4). 6.99 *(978-0-448-46112-0(9),* Grosset & Dunlap) Penguin Young Readers Group.
—Major League Mess-Up #29. John and Wendy, illus. 2008. (Katie Kazoo, Switcheroo Ser.: 29). 80p. (J). (gr. 2-4). pap. 6.99 *(978-0-448-44676-9(6),* Grosset & Dunlap) Penguin Young Readers Group.
—No Bones about It #12. John and Wendy, illus. 12th ed. 2004. (Katie Kazoo, Switcheroo Ser.: 12). 80p. (J). (gr. 2-4). pap. 5.99 *(978-0-448-43358-5(3),* Grosset & Dunlap) Penguin Young Readers Group.
—Return to the Scene of the Burp #19. Blecha, Aaron, illus. 2017. (George Brown, Class Clown Ser.: 19). 128p. (J). (gr. 1-3). 5.99 *(978-0-448-48287-3(8),* Grosset & Dunlap) Penguin Young Readers Group.
—A Royal Pain in the Burp #15, No. 15A. Blecha, Aaron, illus. 2015. (George Brown, Class Clown Ser.: 15). 128p. (J). (gr. 1-3). bds. 6.99 *(978-0-448-48283-5(5),* Grosset & Dunlap) Penguin Young Readers Group.
—Super Burp! #1, No. 1. Blecha, Aaron, illus. 2010. (George Brown, Class Clown Ser.: 1). 128p. (J). (gr. 2-4). pap. 6.99 *(978-0-448-45367-5(3),* Grosset & Dunlap) Penguin Young Readers Group.
—Three Cheers For... Who? #35. John and Wendy, illus. 2011. (Katie Kazoo, Switcheroo Ser.: 35). (ENG.). 80p. (J). (gr. 2-4). pap. 5.99 *(978-0-448-45449-8(1),* Grosset & Dunlap) Penguin Young Readers Group.
—Trouble Magnet #2. Blecha, Aaron, illus. 2010. (George Brown, Class Clown Ser.: 2). 128p. (J). (gr. 2-4). pap. 6.99 *(978-0-448-45368-2(1),* Grosset & Dunlap) Penguin Young Readers Group.
—What's Black & White & Stinks All Over? #4. Blecha, Aaron, illus. 2011. (George Brown, Class Clown Ser.: 4). (ENG.). 128p. (J). (gr. 2-4). pap. 6.99 *(978-0-448-45370-5(3),* Grosset & Dunlap) Penguin Young Readers Group.
Krulik, Nancy & Burwasser, Amanda. Science No Fair! Project Droid #1. Moran, Mike, illus. 2016. (Project Droid Ser.). (ENG.). 112p. (J). (gr. 1-4). 13.99 *(978-1-5107-1018-4(3),* Sky Pony Pr.) Skyhorse Publishing Co., Inc.
Krulik, Nancy E. Lice Check, 12. Blecha, Aaron, illus. 2014. (George Brown, Class Clown Ser.). (ENG.). 128p. (J). (gr. 2-4). 21.19 *(978-1-4844-2140-6(X))* Penguin Young Readers Group.
Kuhlman, Evan. Brother from a Box. Bruno, Iacopo, illus. 2013. (ENG.). 288p. (J). (gr. 4-7). pap. 6.99 *(978-1-4424-2659-7(4),* Atheneum Bks. for Young Readers) Simon & Schuster Children's Publishing.
—Brother from a Box. Bruno, Iacopo, illus. 2012. (ENG.). 288p. (J). (gr. 4-7). 16.99 *(978-1-4424-2658-0(6))* Simon & Schuster, Inc.
—The Last Invisible Boy. Coovert, J. P., illus. (ENG.). 240p. (J). (gr. 5-9). 2010. pap. 7.99 *(978-1-4169-6089-8(9))* 2008. 16.99 *(978-1-4169-5797-3(9))* Simon & Schuster Children's Publishing. (Atheneum Bks. for Young Readers).
Kuhn, Douglas Wolcik. The Summer of the Monarch Butterflies. 2012. 28p. pap. 24.95 *(978-1-4626-9302-3(4))* America Star Bks.
Kuipers, Alice. Polly Diamond & the Super Stunning Spectacular School Fair: Book 2 (Book Series for Kids, Polly Diamond Book Series, Books for Elementary School Kids) Book 2, Bk. 2. Toledano, Diana, illus. 2019. (Polly Diamond Ser.). (ENG.). 112p. (J). (gr. 2-5). 14.99 *(978-1-4521-5233-2(0))* Chronicle Bks. LLC.
Kurkosky, Tina. Bunny Brothers. 2011. 24p. pap. 24.95 *(978-1-4626-3608-2(X))* America Star Bks.
Kuroda, Yosuke & Hayashiya, Shizuru. Onegai Teacher, No. 2. 2003. 120p. pap. 9.95 *(978-1-58899-179-9(2))* ComicsOne Corp./Dr. Masters.
Kurzweil, Allen. Leon & the Spitting Image. Bertholf, Bret, illus. (ENG.). 320p. (J). (gr. 3-18). 2005. pap. 7.99 *(978-0-06-053932-0(1),* Greenwillow Bks.) 2003. 16.99 *(978-0-06-053930-6(5))* HarperCollins Pubs.
Kuskowski, Alex. Line Up, 1 vol. unabr. ed. 2010. (District 13 Ser.). (ENG.). 48p. (YA). (gr. 9-12). pap. 9.75 *(978-1-61651-279-8(2))* Saddleback Educational Publishing, Inc.
Kyi, Tanya Lloyd. My Time As Caz Hazard, 1 vol. 2004. (Orca Soundings Ser.). (ENG.). 128p. (YA). (gr. 8-12). pap. 9.95 *(978-1-55143-319-6(2),* 1234557) Orca Bk. Pubs. USA.
—Truth. 2003. (YA). (gr. 7-18). pap. 7.95 *(978-1-55143-235-9(8))* Orca Bk. Pubs. USA.
—Truth. 2004. (Orca Soundings Ser.). 108p. 19.95 *(978-0-7569-4346-2(9))* Perfection Learning Corp.
Kyle, Tracey. A Paintbrush for Paco. Heinsz, Joshua, illus. 2018. (ENG.). 40p. (J). (gr. -1-3). 17.99 *(978-1-4998-0544-4(6))* Little Bee Books Inc.
La Clair, Claire. School Crossing Guard. 2012. 24p. pap. 24.95 *(978-1-4626-7541-8(7))* PublishAmerica, Inc.
Laban, Elizabeth. The Tragedy Paper. 2014. (ENG.). 320p. (YA). (gr. 7). pap. 10.99 *(978-0-307-93048-4(3),* Ember) Random Hse. Children's Bks.
Labatt, Mary. Sam Gets Lost. Sarrazin, Marisol, illus. 2004. (Kids Can Read Ser.: Vol. 1). (ENG.). 32p. (J). (gr. k-1). 11.99 *(978-1-55337-563-0(7))* Kids Can Pr., Ltd. CAN. Dist: Hachette Bk. Group.
—Sam Goes to School. Sarrazin, Marisol, illus. 2004. (Kids Can Read Ser.: Vol. 1). (ENG.). 32p. (J). (gr. k-1). 4.95 *(978-1-55337-565-4(3))* Kids Can Pr., Ltd. CAN. Dist: Hachette Bk. Group.
LaBree Stute, Lela. Freedom Pugs! 2010. 38p. pap. 19.99 *(978-0-557-42621-8(9))* Lulu Pr., Inc.
Lach, Will. Norman Rockwell's a Day in the Life of a Boy. Rockwell, Norman, illus. 2017. (ENG.). 60p. (J). (gr. -1-3). 16.95 *(978-0-7892-1289-4(7),* 791289, Abbeville Kids) Abbeville Pr., Inc.
Lachtman, Ofelia Dumas. Pepita & the Bully: Pepita y la Peleonera. Baeza Ventura, Gabriela, tr. Pardo DeLange, Alex, illus. 2011. (SPA & ENG.). 32p. (J). (gr. -1-3). 16.95 *(978-1-55885-689-9(7),* Piñata Books) Arte Publico Pr.
Lackey, Mercedes & Edghill, Rosemary. Shadow Grail #2: Conspiracies: Conspiracies. 2011. (Shadow Grail Ser.: 2). (ENG.). 352p. (YA). (gr. 8-12). pap. 18.99

(978-0-7653-1762-9(1), 900041774, Tor Teen) Doherty, Tom Assocs., LLC.
LaCour, Nina. Hold Still. 2019. (ENG.). 272p. (YA). (gr. 7). pap. 11.99 *(978-0-525-55608-4(7)*, Penguin Books) Penguin Young Readers Group.
LaFaye, A. No Frogs in School. Ceulemans, Eglantine, illus. 2018. 32p. (J). (gr. -1-2). 16.95 *(978-1-4549-2698-6(8))* Sterling Publishing Co., Inc.
LaFleur, John. The Misadventures of Dreary & Naughty, 1 vol. 2013. (ENG., Illus.). 64p. (YA). (gr. 8-12). 14.99 *(978-0-7643-4494-7(3)*, 4928) Schiffer Publishing, Ltd.
LaFleur, Suzanne. Eight Keys. 2012. (ENG.). 224p. (J). (gr. 4-7). 7.99 *(978-0-375-87213-6(2)*, Yearling) Random Hse. Children's Bks.
—Love, Aubrey. 2011. (ENG.). 272p. (J). (gr. 3-7). pap. 7.99 *(978-0-375-85159-9(3)*, Yearling) Random Hse. Children's Bks.
Lagercrantz, Rose. My Happy Life. Eriksson, Eva, illus. 2013. (My Happy Life Ser.). (ENG.). 136p. (J). (gr. k-3). 17.99 *(978-1-877579-35-6(1)*, 2895400f-2a72-4054-be64-a2dc480a5f30) Gecko Pr. NZL. Dist: Lerner Publishing Group.
Lai, Remy. Pie in the Sky. Lai, Remy, illus. 2019. (ENG., Illus.). 384p. (J). 21.99 *(978-1-250-31409-3(7)*, 900199487); pap. 14.99 *(978-1-250-31410-9(0)*, 900199488) Holt, Henry & Co. (Holt, Henry & Co. Bks. For Young Readers).
Laínez, René Colato. I Am Rene, the Boy. Graullera, Fabiola, illus. 2005.Tr. of Yo Soy Rene, el Nino. (ENG & SPA.). 32p. (J). (gr. -1-2). 16.95 *(978-1-55885-378-2(2)*, Piñata Books) Arte Publico Pr.
—René Has Two Last Names/René Tiene Dos Apellidos. Laínez, René Colato & Graullera Ramírez, Fabiola, illus. 2009. (SPA & ENG.). 32p. (J). (gr. -1-3). 16.95 *(978-1-55885-530-4(0))* Arte Publico Pr.
Laird, Elizabeth & Davison, Roz. Jungle School. Sim, David, illus. 2006. (Green Bananas Ser.). (ENG.). 48p. (J). (gr. -1-3). *(978-0-7787-1042-4(4))*; lib. bdg. *(978-0-7787-1026-4(2))* Crabtree Publishing Co.
Lakes, Lofton & Metu, illus. The Dream Team. 2007. 48p. (YA). pap. *(978-0-9799320-0-7(9))* Pinkney, Gail.
Lakin, Patricia. Max & Mo Go Apple Picking: Ready-To-Read Level 1. Floca, Brian, illus. 2007. (Max & Mo Ser.). (ENG.). 32p. (J). (gr. -1-1). pap. 4.99 *(978-1-4169-2535-4(X)*, Simon Spotlight) Simon Spotlight.
—Max & Mo Make a Snowman: Ready-To-Read Level 1. Floca, Brian, illus. 2007. (Max & Mo Ser.). (ENG.). 32p. (J). (gr. -1-1). pap. 4.99 *(978-1-4169-2537-8(6)*, Simon Spotlight) Simon Spotlight.
—Max & Mo's First Day at School: Ready-To-Read Level 1. Floca, Brian, illus. 2007. (Max & Mo Ser.). (ENG.). 32p. (J). (gr. -1-1). pap. 4.99 *(978-1-4169-2533-0(3)*, Simon Spotlight) Simon Spotlight.
Lambert, Janet. Hi Neighbor: A Sugar Bradley Story. 2003. (J). pap. 9.95 *(978-1-930009-82-0(8)*, 800-691-7779) Image Cascade Publishing.
—Sweet As Sugar: A Sugar Bradley Story. 2003. (YA). pap. 9.95 *(978-1-930009-81-3(X)*, 800-691-7779) Image Cascade Publishing.
Laminack, Lester L. Jake's 100th Day of School, 1 vol. Love, Judy, illus. 32p. (J). (gr. -1-3). 2008. pap. 8.95 *(978-1-56145-463-1(X))* 2006. 16.95 *(978-1-56145-355-9(2))* Peachtree Publishing Co. Inc.
—Snow Day!, 1 vol. Gustavson, Adam, illus. 2007. 32p. (J). (gr. -1-3). 17.99 *(978-1-56145-418-1(4))* Peachtree Publishing Co. Inc.
Lancett, Peter. Seeing Red. 2008. (Cutting Edge Ser.). (ENG.). 224p. pap. *(978-1-84167-696-8(9))* Ransom Publishing Ltd.
Landis, Matthew. The Not So Boring Letters of Private Nobody. 2019. (ENG.). 320p. (J). (gr. 5-9). 8.99 *(978-0-7352-2799-6(3)*, Puffin Books) Penguin Young Readers Group.
Landon, Kristen. Life in the Pit. 2008. (ENG., Illus.). 248p. (YA). (gr. 5-13). pap. 8.95 *(978-1-933831-08-4(1))* Blooming Tree Pr.
Lane, Melaina. Chubs. . Another Day at School. 2011. 20p. 9.14 *(978-1-4251-7330-2(6))* Trafford Publishing.
Lang, Diane & Buchanan, Michael. The Fat Boy Chronicles. 2010. (Fat Boy Chronicles Ser.). (ENG.). 224p. (J). (gr. 7-11). pap. 9.95 *(978-1-58536-543-2(2)*, 202220) Sleeping Bear Pr.
Langan, Paul. The Fallen. 2008. (Bluford Ser.: No. 11). (ENG.). 144p. (gr. 7-18). 5.50 *(978-1-59194-066-1(4))* Perfection Learning Corp.
Langcaon, Jeff, illus. My Grandpa's Battleship Missouri Tour. 2007. (J). 14.95 *(978-1-56647-831-1(6))* Mutual Publishing LLC.
Lange, Erin Jade. The Chaos of Now. 2018. (ENG.). 352p. (YA). 17.99 *(978-1-61963-502-9(X)*, 900138604, Bloomsbury Young Adult) Bloomsbury Publishing USA.
—Dead Ends. 2013. (ENG.). 304p. E-Book 7.99 *(978-1-61963-081-9(8)*, Bloomsbury USA Childrens) Bloomsbury Publishing USA.
Langston, Laura. The Trouble with Cupid, 1 vol. 2008. (ENG.). 240p. (J). (gr. 4-8). per. 11.95 *(978-1-55455-059-3(9)*, 52e238a2-2250-4c67-9459-8fec96827b71) éditeur, Annika Parance CAN. Dist: Firefly Bks., Ltd.
LaPorte, Tom. Hembree Hopefuls: A Hembree Elementary Story. 2003. 164p. (gr. 2-13). pap. 11.95 *(978-0-595-27537-3(0)*, Weekly Reader Teacher's Pr) iUniverse, Inc.
Larbalestier, Justine & Brennan, Sarah Rees. Team Human. 2012. (ENG.). 352p. (YA). (gr. 8). 17.99 *(978-0-06-208964-9(1)*, HarperTeen) HarperCollins Pubs.
Larkin, Jim & Rambo, Lee Elliot. Books for Oliver. Brown, Dan, illus. 2006. (J). *(978-1-59336-336-9(2))*; pap. *(978-1-59336-337-6(0))* Mondo Publishing.
Larsen, C. S. The Chronicles of Marvin Archibald Trekker: Boy Magician Book 1 - Penguins of Choice. Lt. ed. 2006. (Illus.). 163p. (YA). per. 5.99 *(978-0-9779844-1-9(9))* KnowledgeGain.
Larsen, Elizabeth. Open House at Buster's New School: Season 1, Book 2: Buster Hardings, 1 vol. 2010. 85p. pap. 19.95 *(978-1-60749-559-8(7))* America Star Bks.
Larson, Kirsten. The Ghost Town Mystery. 2008. pap. 34.95 *(978-1-58013-773-7(3))* Astra Publishing Hse.
Lascarso, Laura. Counting Backwards. 2013. (ENG., Illus.). 288p. (YA). (gr. 9). pap. 9.99 *(978-1-4424-0691-9(7))* Simon & Schuster Children's Publishing.
Lathan, Betty Jean. Are You Sure That's My Child? 2011. 48p. pap. 31.99 *(978-1-4628-5759-3(0))* Xlibris Corp.
Latimer, Brenda. I See God. 2008. (Illus.). 28p. 12.95 *(978-0-9797429-2-7(7))* Halo Publishing International.
Laubach, Melody. Words & Thoughts. 2008. (Illus.). 28p. (J). pap. 17.95 *(978-1-4327-2596-9(3))* Outskirts Pr., Inc.
Lauren, Christina. Autoboyography. 2017. (ENG., Illus.). 416p. (YA). (gr. 9). 19.99 *(978-1-4814-8168-7(1)*, Simon & Schuster Bks. For Young Readers) Simon & Schuster Bks. For Young Readers.
Laurens, Jennifer. Falling for Romeo. 2007. (YA). per. 12.95 *(978-1-933963-94-5(8))* Grove Creek Publishing, LLC.
Laurie Douglas, Inez. No One Heard His Cry. 2008. 185p. pap. 11.95 *(978-1-4327-2870-0(9))* Outskirts Pr., Inc.
Lawler, Janet. Fright School. Galletti, Chiara, illus. 2018. (ENG.). 32p. (J). (gr. -1-3). 16.99 *(978-0-8075-2553-1(7)*, 807525537) Whitman, Albert & Co.
Lawrence, Lisa J. Rodent, 1 vol. 2016. (ENG.). 288p. (YA). (gr. 8-12). pap. 14.95 *(978-1-4598-0976-5(9))* Orca Bk. Pubs. USA.
Lawson, Barbara. Three Little Pigs Go to School. 2012. 28p. pap. 24.95 *(978-1-4626-8185-3(9))* America Star Bks.
Lay, Kathryn. The Substitutes: An Up2U Action Adventure, 1 vol. Calo, Marcos, illus. 2015. (Up2U Adventures Ser.). (ENG.). 80p. (J). (gr. 2-5). 35.64 *(978-1-62402-095-7(X)*, 17359, Calico Chapter Bks.) ABDO Publishing Co.
Layton, Neal. The Mammoth Academy. Layton, Neal, illus. 2010. (ENG., Illus.). 176p. (J). (gr. 4-6). 21.19 *(978-0-312-60882-8(9))* Square Fish.
LaZebnik, Claire. Epic Fail. 2011. (ENG.). 304p. (YA). (gr. 8-18). pap. 9.99 *(978-0-06-192126-1(2)*, HarperTeen) HarperCollins Pubs.
Lcg. The Pencil Monster! 2011. 28p. pap. 14.95 *(978-0-557-94993-9(9))* Lulu Pr., Inc.
Leader, Jessica. Nice & Mean. 2010. (Mix Ser.). (ENG.). 272p. (J). (gr. 4-8). pap. 6.99 *(978-1-4169-9160-1(3))* Simon & Schuster, Inc.
LeapFrog Staff. Ozzie & Mack. 2008. (J). pap. 39.99 *(978-1-59319-976-0(7))*; pap. 49.99 *(978-1-59319-924-1(4))* LeapFrog Enterprises, Inc.
Leblanc, Louise. Maddie Stands Tall. Cummins, Sarah, tr. Gay, Marie-Louise, illus. 2005. (Formac First Novels Ser.: 54). (ENG.). 64p. (J). (gr. 2-5). 14.95 *(978-0-88780-683-4(X)*, 683); 4.95 *(978-0-88780-682-7(1)*, 682) Formac Publishing Co., Ltd. CAN. Dist: Formac Lorimer Bks. Ltd.
—Maddie's Big Test. Cummins, Sarah, tr. Gay, Marie-Louise, illus. 2006. (Formac First Novels Ser.: 58). (ENG.). 64p. (J). (gr. 2-5). 14.95 *(978-0-88780-718-3(6)*, 718); 4.95 *(978-0-88780-714-5(3)*, 714) Formac Publishing Co., Ltd. CAN. Dist: Formac Lorimer Bks. Ltd.
Lee, Honest & Gilbert, Matthew J. The Disastrous Magical Wishes of Classroom 13. Dreidemy, Joëlle, illus. 2017. (Classroom 13 Ser.: 2). (ENG.). 128p. (J). (gr. 1-5). pap. 5.99 *(978-0-316-46456-7(2))* Little, Brown Bks. for Young Readers.
—The Disastrous Magical Wishes of Classroom 13. 2017. (Classroom 13 Ser.: 2). (J). lib. bdg. 16.00 *(978-0-606-40638-3(7))* Turtleback.
—The Fantastic & Terrible Fame of Classroom 13. Dreidemy, Joëlle, illus. 2017. (Classroom 13 Ser.: 3). (ENG.). 128p. (J). (gr. 1-5). pap. 5.99 *(978-0-316-46458-1(9))* Little, Brown Bks. for Young Readers.
—The Fantastic & Terrible Fame of Classroom 13. 2018. (Classroom 13 Ser.: 3). (J). lib. bdg. 16.00 *(978-0-606-40639-0(5))* Turtleback.
—The Happy & Heinous Halloween of Classroom 13. Dreidemy, Joëlle, illus. 2018. (Classroom 13 Ser.: 5). (ENG.). 128p. (J). (gr. 1-5). pap. 9.99 *(978-0-316-50115-6(8))* Little, Brown Bks. for Young Readers.
—The Rude & Ridiculous Royals of Classroom 13. 2018. (Classroom 13 Ser.: 6). (ENG., Illus.). 128p. (J). (gr. 1-5). pap. 5.99 *(978-0-316-43786-8(7))* Little, Brown Bks. for Young Readers.
—The Super Awful Superheroes of Classroom 13. Dreidemy, Joëlle, illus. 2018. (Classroom 13 Ser.: 4). (ENG.). 128p. (J). (gr. 1-5). 27.99 *(978-0-316-50109-5(3))*; pap. 5.99 *(978-0-316-50112-5(3))* Little, Brown Bks. for Young Readers.
—The Unlucky Lottery Winners of Classroom 13. Dreidemy, Joëlle, illus. 2017. (Classroom 13 Ser.: 1). (ENG.). 128p. (J). (gr. 1-5). pap. 5.99 *(978-0-316-46462-8(7))* Little, Brown Bks. for Young Readers.
Lee, Howard. Jamshid & the Lost Mountain of Light. 2008. (ENG.). 248p. pap. 14.99 *(978-1-4196-8958-1(4))* CreateSpace Independent Publishing Platform.
Lee, Jenny. Elvis & the Underdogs. Light, Kelly, illus. 2013. (Elvis & the Underdogs Ser.: 1). (ENG.). 304p. (J). (gr. 3-7). 16.99 *(978-0-06-223554-1(0)*, Balzer & Bray) HarperCollins Pubs.
Lee, Kathy. Space Invaders. 2011. 144p. pap. *(978-1-84427-507-6(8))* Scripture Union.
Lee, Penny. Schoolio: Pets, Projects & Pandemonium. 2013. 72p. pap. *(978-1-4602-0568-6(5))* FriesenPress.
Lee, Quinlan B. & Bridwell, Norman. Clifford's Best School Day. Haefele, Steve, illus. 2007. (J). *(978-0-545-02844-8(2))* Scholastic, Inc.
Lee, Stacey. The Secret of a Heart Note. 2016. (ENG.). 384p. (YA). (gr. 8). 17.99 *(978-0-06-242832-5(2)*, Tegen, Katherine Bks) HarperCollins Pubs.
Lee, Vanessa. The Beauty Queen & the School Nerd. 2007. 78p. (YA). (gr. 4-6). per. 8.95 *(978-0-595-45936-0(6))* iUniverse, Inc.
Lee Wardlaw. Seventh-Grade Weirdo. 2010. 160p. pap. 11.95 *(978-1-4401-8263-1(9))* iUniverse, Inc.
Lefebvre, Jason. Too Much Glue. Retz, Zac, illus. 2013. (ENG.). 32p. (J). (gr. k-2). 17.95 *(978-1-936261-27-7(8))* Flashlight Pr.
LeFlore, Lyah B. The World Is Mine. Warfield, D. L., illus. 2009. (Come Up Ser.). (ENG.). 304p. (YA). (gr. 9-18). pap. 8.99 *(978-1-4169-7963-0(8)*, Simon Pulse) Simon Pulse.
Lehrhaupt, Adam. Chicken in School. Kober, Shahar, illus. 2017. (ENG.). 40p. (J). (gr. -1-3). 17.99 *(978-0-06-236413-5(8)*, HarperCollins) HarperCollins Pubs.
Lemieux, Jean. Toby & the Mysterious Creature. Cummins, Sarah, tr. Casson, Sophie, illus. 2008. (Formac First Novels Ser.). (ENG.). 64p. (J). (gr. 2-5). 14.95 *(978-0-88780-761-9(5)*, 761); 5.95 *(978-0-88780-759-6(3)*, 759) Formac Publishing Co., Ltd. CAN. Dist: Formac Lorimer Bks. Ltd.
Leonard, Elise. Monday Morning Blitz. 2007. (Al's World Ser.: 1). (ENG.). 144p. (J). (gr. 5-9). pap. 8.99 *(978-1-4169-3464-6(2)*, Simon & Schuster/Paula Wiseman Bks.) Simon & Schuster/Paula Wiseman Bks.
Leslie, Robyn. Rinny & the Trail of Clues. 2003. Orig. Title: Miss President & the Trail of Clues. (Illus.). 192p. (J). pap. 7.95 *(978-0-9727388-8-0(6))* Sugar Ducky Bks., Inc.
Lester, Helen. Hooway for Wodney Wat Book & CD, 1 vol. Munsinger, Lynn, illus. 2011. (ENG.). 32p. (J). (gr. -1-3). audio 10.99 *(978-0-547-55217-0(3)*, 1450662, Clarion Bks.) HarperCollins Pubs.
—Tackylocks & the Three Bears. Munsinger, Lynn, illus. 2004. (Tacky the Penguin Ser.). (ENG.). 32p. (J). (gr. -1-3). pap. 7.99 *(978-0-618-43953-9(6)*, 439862, Clarion Bks.) HarperCollins Pubs.
Lettera, Janine Hamel. My First Day of School. 2012. 16p. pap. 7.31 *(978-1-4251-1614-9(0))* Trafford Publishing.
Leuck, Laura. My Creature Teacher. Nash, Scott, illus. 2004. (ENG.). 32p. (J). (gr. -1-1). 15.99 *(978-0-06-029694-0(1))* HarperCollins Pubs.
Leveen, Tom. Mercy Rule. 2018. (ENG.). 456p. (YA). (gr. 9-9). 17.99 *(978-1-5107-2698-7(5)*, Sky Pony Pr.) Skyhorse Publishing Co., Inc.
—Random. 2014. (ENG., Illus.). 224p. (YA). (gr. 9). 17.99 *(978-1-4424-9956-0(7)*, Simon Pulse) Simon Pulse.
Levine, Gail Carson. The Wish. 2005. (ENG.). 256p. (J). (gr. 3-7). pap. 6.99 *(978-0-06-075911-7(9)*, HarperCollins) HarperCollins Pubs.
—The Wish. 2004. 197p. (gr. 3-7). 16.00 *(978-0-7569-4272-4(1))* Perfection Learning Corp.
Levine, Kristin. The Lions of Little Rock. 2013. 320p. (J). (gr. 5-9). pap. 8.99 *(978-0-14-242435-3(8)*, Puffin Books) Penguin Young Readers Group.
Levithan, David. Another Day. 2015. (ENG.). 336p. (YA). (gr. 7-12). 18.99 *(978-0-385-75620-4(8)*, Knopf Bks. for Young Readers) Random Hse. Children's Bks.
—Every You, Every Me. Farmer, Jonathan, photos by. 2012. (Illus.). 256p. (YA). (gr. 7). pap. 9.99 *(978-0-375-85451-4(7)*, Ember) Random Hse. Children's Bks.
—Every You, Every Me. Farmer, Jonathan, photos by. 2012. (Illus.). lib. bdg. 20.85 *(978-0-606-26816-5(2))* Turtleback.
—The Realm of Possibility. 2006. (ENG.). 224p. (YA). (gr. 7-12). reprint ed. pap. 9.99 *(978-0-375-83657-2(8)*, Ember) Random Hse. Children's Bks.
Levithan, David & Ehrenhaft, Daniel. 21 Proms. Lt. ed. 2007. (YA). 22.95 *(978-0-7862-9866-2(9))* Thorndike Pr.
Levy, Elizabeth. A Hare-Raising Tale. Gerstein, Mordicai, illus. unabr. ed. 2006. (First Chapter Bks.). (J). (gr. 2-4). pap. 17.95 incl. audio *(978-1-59519-704-7(4))*; pap. 20.95 incl. audio compact disk *(978-1-59519-705-4(2))* Live Oak Media.
Levy, Janice. School Rules for Diva Duck, 1 vol. Madden, Colleen M., illus. 2012. (Diva Duck Ser.). (ENG.). 32p. (J). (gr. -1-4). 32.79 *(978-1-61641-889-2(3)*, 5197, Looking Glass Library) Magic Wagon.
—Showtime for Flip-Flop, 1 vol. Madden, Colleen M., illus. 2011. (Flip-Flop Adventure Ser.). (ENG.). 32p. (J). (gr. -1-4). 32.79 *(978-1-61641-654-6(8)*, 7774, Looking Glass Library) Magic Wagon.
Levy, Joanne. Crushing It. 2017. (Mix Ser.). (ENG., Illus.). 240p. (J). (gr. 4-8). pap. 8.99 *(978-1-4814-6473-4(6)*, Aladdin) Simon & Schuster Children's Publishing.
Lewis, Doreen. The Bubblegum Babes' Guide to Sixth Grade. 2005. (J). per. 9.95 *(978-0-9769193-0-8(3))* Helm Publishing.
Lewis, Fiona. Dreaming in Color. 2011. (ENG.). 304p. (J). (gr. 7). pap. 16.95 *(978-0-9845318-5-1(8))* Tiny Stachel Pr.
Lewis, Jan, illus. School. 2012. (First Time Ser.). (ENG.). 24p. (J). *(978-1-84643-491-2(2))* Child's Play International Ltd.
Lewis, Jill. A Mom in a Million. Gulbis, Stephen, illus. 2005. 32p. (J). *(978-1-84458-368-3(6)*, Pavilion Children's Books) Pavilion Bks.
Lewis, Judith. Not Like Any Bird I've Ever Heard. 2011. 24p. pap. 24.95 *(978-1-4626-2730-1(7))* America Star Bks.
Lewis, Kelly. What Do We Do at School? Peattie, Cindy; Lewis, ed. 2016. (Spring Forward Ser.). (ENG.). (J). (gr. k). 6.84 net. *(978-1-4900-6021-7(9))* Benchmark Education Co.
Libenson, Terri. Just Jaime. Libenson, Terri, illus. 2019. (Emmie & Friends Ser.). (ENG., Illus.). 256p. (J). (gr. 3-7). 24.99 *(978-0-06-285107-9(1))*; pap. 15.99 *(978-0-06-285106-2(3))* HarperCollins Pubs. (Balzer & Bray).
—Positively Izzy. Libenson, Terri, illus. 2018. (Emmie & Friends Ser.). (ENG., Illus.). 224p. (J). (gr. 3-7). 22.99 *(978-0-06-248497-0(4))*; pap. 13.99 *(978-0-06-248496-3(6))* HarperCollins Pubs. (Balzer & Bray).
—Positively Izzy. 2018. (J). lib. bdg. 22.10 *(978-0-606-41363-3(4))* Turtleback.
Liberto, Lorenzo. Matt the Rat & His Magic Cloud / Raton Mateo y Su Nube Magica: A Day at School / un Dia de Escuela. Gomez, Rocio, ed. Torres, Irving, illus. 2003. (Matt the Rat Ser. / La Serie de Ratón Mateo). (ENG & SPA.). 32p. (J). lib. bdg. 20.00 *(978-0-9743668-0-7(3))* Harvest Sun Pr., LLC.
Lichtman, Wendy. Do the Math #2: the Writing on the Wall. 2008. (Do the Math Ser.: 2). (ENG.). 224p. (YA). (gr. 8-9). 16.99 *(978-0-06-122958-9(X)*, Greenwillow Bks.) HarperCollins Pubs.
—Do the Math: Secrets, Lies, & Algebra. 2008. (Do the Math Ser.: 1). (ENG., Illus.). 208p. (YA). (gr. 8-8). pap. 15.99 *(978-0-06-122957-2(1)*, Greenwillow Bks.) HarperCollins Pubs.
Lieb, Josh. I Am a Genius of Unspeakable Evil & I Want to Be Your Class President. 2010. (J). (ENG.). 272p. (gr. 7-12). 24.94 *(978-1-59514-240-5(1))*; 304p. (gr. 5-7). 9.99 *(978-1-59514-354-9(8))* Penguin Young Readers Group. (Razorbill).
Lien, Henry. Peasprout Chen, Future Legend of Skate & Sword. 2019. (Peasprout Chen Ser.: 1). (ENG., Illus.). 352p. (J). pap. 12.99 *(978-1-250-29436-4(3)*, 900187110) Square Fish.
Light, Steve. Have You Seen My Lunch Box? Light, Steve, illus. 2017. (ENG., Illus.). 18p. (J). (-k). bds. 6.99 *(978-0-7636-9068-7(6))* Candlewick Pr.
Limbaugh, Rush. Rush Revere & the Brave Pilgrims: Time-Travel Adventures with Exceptional Americans. 2013. (Rush Revere Ser.: 1). (ENG., Illus.). 224p. 21.00 *(978-1-4767-5586-1(8)*, Threshold Editions) Threshold Editions.
—Rush Revere & the First Patriots: Time-Travel Adventures with Exceptional Americans. 2014. (Rush Revere Ser.: 2). (ENG., Illus.). 256p. 21.00 *(978-1-4767-5588-5(4)*, Threshold Editions) Threshold Editions.
Limbaugh, Rush & Adams Limbaugh, Kathryn. Rush Revere & the American Revolution: Time-Travel Adventures with Exceptional Americans. 2014. (Rush Revere Ser.: 3). (ENG.). 256p. 21.00 *(978-1-4767-8987-3(8)*, Threshold Editions) Threshold Editions.
Limbaugh, Rush H., III & Limbaugh, Kathryn Adams. Rush Revere & the American Revolution. Hiers, Christopher, illus. 2014. 244p. (J). pap. *(978-1-4767-8989-7(4))*, Threshold Editions) Threshold Editions.
Lin, Grace. The Year of the Dog. 2007. (Pacy Lin Novel Ser.: 1). (ENG., Illus.). 160p. (J). (gr. 3-7). per. 8.99 *(978-0-316-06002-8(X))* Little, Brown Bks. for Young Readers.
—The Year of the Dog. 2007. (Illus.). 134p. (gr. 3-7). 16.00 *(978-0-7569-8143-3(3))* Perfection Learning Corp.
Lindner, Brooke. Hooray for School! Going to School with Nick Jr. Hall, Susan & Hall, Susan, illus. 2008. (ENG.). 16p. (J). (gr. -1-2). pap. 6.99 *(978-1-4169-5861-1(4)*, Simon Spotlight/Nickelodeon) Simon Spotlight/Nickelodeon.
Lindo, Elvira. Manolito Four-Eyes: The 1st Volume of the Great Encyclopedia of My Life, 0 vols. Moriarty, Joanne, tr. Urberuaga, Emilio, illus. 2010. (Manolito Four-Eyes Ser.: 1). (ENG.). 155p. (J). (gr. 4-6). pap. 9.99 *(978-0-7614-5729-9(1)*, 9780761457299, Two Lions) Amazon Publishing.
—Manolito Gafotas, 0 vols. Urberuaga, Emilio, illus. 2012. (SPA.). 192p. (J). (gr. 4-6). pap. 9.99 *(978-0-7614-5730-5(5)*, 9780761457305, Two Lions) Amazon Publishing.
Lindquist, N. J. The Best of Friends. 2016. (Circle of Friends Ser.: Vol. 1). (ENG., Illus.). (YA). pap. *(978-1-927692-03-5(2))* That's Life! Communications.
Lindsay, Elizabeth. Bugs & Butterflies. 2012. (Silverlake Fairy School Ser.). 100p. (J). pap. 4.99 *(978-0-7945-3066-2(4)*, Usborne) EDC Publishing.
—Dancing Magic. 2012. (Silverlake Fairy School Ser.). 100p. (J). pap. 4.99 *(978-0-7945-3067-9(2)*, Usborne) EDC Publishing.
—Ready to Fly, 3. 2011. (Silverlake Fairy School Ser.). (ENG.). 123p. (J). (gr. 3-6). 17.44 *(978-0-7945-3064-8(8))* EDC Publishing.
—Stardust Surprise. 2012. (Silverlake Fairy School Ser.). 100p. (J). pap. 4.99 *(978-0-7945-3065-5(6)*, Usborne) EDC Publishing.
—Wands & Charms (Book 2), 2. 2011. (Silverlake Fairy School Ser.). (ENG.). 117p. (J). (gr. 3-6). 17.44 *(978-0-7945-3063-1(X))* EDC Publishing.
Linke, Glenn Colin. The Gargantuan Boy. 2011. 102p. pap. 30.50 *(978-1-60976-079-3(4)*, Eloquent Bks.) Strategic Book Publishing & Rights Agency (SBPRA).
Linn, Laurent. Draw the Line. Linn, Laurent, illus. 2016. (ENG., Illus.). 528p. (YA). (gr. 7). 17.99 *(978-1-4814-5280-9(0)*, McElderry, Margaret K. Bks.) McElderry, Margaret K. Bks.
Lipp, Frederick. Fatima. Lindmark, Margaret, illus. 2006. 32p. (J). pap. *(978-1-59336-302-4(8))* Mondo Publishing.
Lippert, Tonya. Goodbye, School. Bishop, Tracy, illus. 2019. 32p. (J). *(978-1-4338-3029-7(9)*, Magination Pr.) American Psychological Assn.
Lippmann, Wilfried. The Gift of Eye. 2008. 140p. (gr. 7-12). pap. 11.95 *(978-0-595-52251-4(3))* iUniverse, Inc.
Lipsey, Shelia E. House of Cars: Book 1 Fairley High Series. 2013. (ENG.). 158p. (YA). pap. 6.99 *(978-0-9838935-4-7(3)*, Seraphina) Bonita and Hodge Publishing Group.
Lipsyte, Robert. Center Field. 2010. (ENG.). 288p. (YA). (gr. 8-18). 17.99 *(978-0-06-055704-1(4)*, HarperTeen) HarperCollins Pubs.
—The Twinning Project. 2014. (ENG.). 288p. (J). (gr. 5-7). pap. 16.99 *(978-0-544-22522-0(8)*, 1563389, Clarion Bks.) HarperCollins Pubs.
Little Airplane Productions & Scanlon, Michael, illus. Off to School! 2009. (Wonder Pets! Ser.). (ENG.). 24p. (J). (gr. -1-1). 16.19 *(978-1-4169-7197-9(1))* Simon & Schuster, Inc.
Little, Robert. Fun Day in Mrs. Walker's Class. Galey, Chuck, illus. 2005. 32p. (J). *(978-0-9701863-6-2(3))* Relde Publishing.
Littman, Sarah Darer. Life, After. 2010. (ENG.). 288p. (J). (gr. 7-18). 17.99 *(978-0-545-15144-3(9)*, Scholastic Pr.) Scholastic, Inc.
—Taming of the Shoe. 2019. (ENG.). 240p. (J). (gr. 3-7). 17.99 *(978-1-5344-3157-7(8))*; (Illus.). pap. 7.99 *(978-1-5344-3156-0(X))* Simon & Schuster Children's Publishing. (Aladdin).
—Want to Go Private? (ENG.). 336p. (YA). (gr. 9-9). 2019. pap. 10.99 *(978-0-545-15147-4(3))* 2011. 17.99 *(978-0-545-15146-7(5)*, Scholastic Pr.) Scholastic, Inc.
Litwin, Eric, ed. Rocking in My School Shoes. 2011. *(978-0-545-50106-4(7))* Scholastic, Inc.
Litwin, Eric & Dean, Kimberly. Pete the Cat: Rocking in My School Shoes: A Back to School Book for Kids. Dean, James, illus. 2011. (Pete the Cat Ser.). (ENG.). 40p. (J). (gr. -1-3). 19.99 *(978-0-06-191024-1(4))*; lib. bdg. 17.89 *(978-0-06-191025-8(2))* HarperCollins Pubs. (HarperCollins).
Liu, Carol & Caldarone, Marybeth Sidoti. Arlene on the Scene. 2010. 206p. (J). (gr. 3-5). pap. 7.95 *(978-1-934572-54-2(3))* Emerald Bk. Co.
Llewellyn, Claire. Late for School Yellow Band. Pérez, Moni, illus. 2016. (Cambridge Reading Adventures Ser.). (ENG.). 16p. pap. 7.95 *(978-1-107-57679-7(2))* Cambridge Univ. Pr.
Lloyd-Jones, Emily. The Hearts We Sold. 2019. (ENG., Illus.). 416p. (YA). (gr. 9-17). pap. 10.99 *(978-0-316-31455-8(2))* Little, Brown Bks. for Young Readers.
Lobo, Chris. Brand New Day: (of School) 2008. 36p. pap. 24.95 *(978-1-60441-973-3(3))* America Star Bks.
Lockard, Lynn. Gone Batty!!! 2009. 40p. pap. 16.99 *(978-1-4389-8516-9(9))* AuthorHouse.
Locke, Thomas, pseud. Renegades. 2017. (Recruits Ser.). (ENG.). 288p. pap. 16.00 *(978-0-8007-2790-1(8))* Revell.
Lockhart, E. The Boy Book: A Study of Habits & Behaviors, Plus Techniques for Taming Them. 2008. (Ruby Oliver Quartet Ser.: 2). (ENG.). 224p. (YA). (gr. 7). pap. 9.99 *(978-0-385-73209-3(0)*, Delacorte Pr.) Random Hse. Children's Bks.

S

—The Boyfriend List: 15 Guys, 11 Shrink Appointments, 4 Ceramic Frogs & Me, Ruby Oliver, 1. 2006. (Ruby Oliver Quartet Ser.: 1). (ENG.). 256p. (YA). (gr. 7-12). reprint ed. pap. 9.99 *(978-0-385-73207-9(4)*, Delacorte Pr.) Random Hse. Children's Bks.

—Dramarama. 2007. (ENG.). 320p. (YA). 24.80 *(978-1-4287-4612-1(9))* Hyperion Pr.

—Fly on the Wall. 2007. (ENG., Illus.). 192p. (YA). (gr. 7-12). pap. 8.99 *(978-0-385-73282-6(1)*, Delacorte Pr.) Random Hse. Children's Bks.

—Real Live Boyfriends: Yes. Boyfriends, Plural. If My Life Weren't Complicated, I Wouldn't Be Ruby Oliver. 2011. (Ruby Oliver Quartet Ser.: 4). (ENG.). 240p. (YA). (gr. 7). pap. 9.99 *(978-0-385-73429-5(8)*, Ember) Random Hse. Children's Bks.

—The Treasure Map of Boys: Noel, Jackson, Finn, Hutch, Gideon — And Me, Ruby Oliver. 2010. (Ruby Oliver Quartet Ser.: 3). (ENG.). 256p. (YA). (gr. 7). pap. 8.99 *(978-0-385-73427-1(1)*, Delacorte Pr.) Random Hse. Children's Bks.

Lodding, Linda Ravin. The Busy Life of Ernestine Buckmeister. Beaky, Suzanne, illus. 2011. (ENG.). 32p. (J). (gr. -1-1). 16.95 *(978-0-9799746-9-4(0))* Flashlight Pr.

Loewen, Nancy. The Last Day of Kindergarten, 0 vols. Yoshikawa, Sachiko, illus. 2012. (ENG.). 32p. (J). (gr. -1-k). 16.99 *(978-0-7614-5807-4(7)*, 9780761458074, Two Lions) Amazon Publishing.

Lois, Lowry. The Birthday Ball. Feiffer, Jules, illus. 2011. (ENG.). 192p. (J). (gr. 4-6). 21.19 *(978-0-547-23869-2(X))* Houghton Mifflin Harcourt Publishing Co.

—Gooney Bird Greene. Middy Chilman, Thomas, illus. 2004. (Gooney Bird Ser.: No. 1). 88p. (gr. 2-5). 16.00 *(978-0-7569-2583-3(5))* Perfection Learning Corp.

Lombard, Jenny. Drita, My Homegirl. 2008. 144p. (J). (gr. 3-7). 6.99 *(978-0-14-240905-3(7)*, Puffin Books) Penguin Young Readers Group.

—Drita, My Homegirl. 2008. 135p. (J). (gr. 4-6). 13.65 *(978-0-7569-8919-4(1))* Perfection Learning Corp.

Lon Rogers. The Between Season. 2009. 280p. pap. 17.95 *(978-1-4401-8368-3(6))* iUniverse, Inc.

Lonczak, Heather. Mookey the Monkey Gets over Being Teased. Ramsey, Marcy, illus. 2006. 32p. (J). (gr. -1-3). 14.95 *(978-1-59147-479-1(5)*, Magination Pr.) American Psychological Assn.

Lonczak, Heather Suzanne. Mookey the Monkey Gets over Being Teased. Ramsey, Marcy Dunn, illus. 2006. 32p. (J). (gr. -1-3). 9.95 *(978-1-59147-480-7(9)*, Magination Pr.) American Psychological Assn.

London, Jonathan. Froggy Goes to School. Remkiewicz, Frank, illus. 2006. (Froggy Ser.). 28p. (gr. -1-1). 16.00 *(978-0-7569-6986-8(7))* Perfection Learning Corp.

Long, Ethan. Superhero vs. School. 2020. (ENG., Illus.). 32p. (J). 17.99 *(978-1-68119-828-6(2)*, 900188266, Bloomsbury Children's Bks.) Bloomsbury Publishing USA.

Longmeyer, C. M. My Life As a Third Grade Werewolf. Blanding, Dexter, illus. 2014. (ENG.). (J). (gr. 2-3). pap. 7.99 *(978-0-635-11144-9(6))* Gallopade International.

—My Life As a Third Grade Zombie. Blanding, Dexter, illus. 2013. (My Life As a Third Grade... Ser.). (ENG.). (J). (gr. -1-3). pap. 7.99 *(978-0-635-11131-9(4))* Gallopade International.

Longstreet, Barbara, et al. Woodsey School Kids Thanksgiving Feast. 2004. 28p. pap. 24.95 *(978-1-4137-1992-5(9))* PublishAmerica, Inc.

Look, Lenore. Alvin Ho: Allergic to Babies, Burglars, & Other Bumps in the Night. Pham, LeUyen, illus. 2014. (Alvin Ho Ser.: 5). 192p. (J). (gr. 1-4). 7.99 *(978-0-385-38600-5(1)*, Yearling) Random Hse. Children's Bks.

—Alvin Ho: Allergic to Birthday Parties, Science Projects, & Other Man-Made Catastrophes. Pham, LeUyen, illus. 2011. (Alvin Ho Ser.: 3). 192p. (J). (gr. 1-4). 7.99 *(978-0-375-87369-0(4)*, Yearling) Random Hse. Children's Bks.

—Alvin Ho: Allergic to Girls, School, & Other Scary Things. Pham, LeUyen, illus. 2009. (Alvin Ho Ser.: 1). (ENG.). 192p. (J). (gr. 1-4). 7.99 *(978-0-375-84930-5(0)*, Yearling) Random Hse. Children's Bks.

—Ruby Lu, Brave & True. 2004. (Illus.). 104p. (J). lib. bdg. 15.00 *(978-1-4242-0914-9(5))* Fitzgerald Bks.

—Ruby Lu, Brave & True. Wilsdorf, Anne, illus. 2006. (Ruby Lu Ser.). 105p. (J). (gr. 1-5). 11.65 *(978-0-7569-6553-2(5))* Perfection Learning Corp.

—Ruby Lu, Brave & True. Wilsdorf, Anne, illus. 2006. (Ruby Lu Ser.). (ENG.). 112p. (J). (gr. 1-5). pap. 6.99 *(978-1-4169-1389-4(0)*, Atheneum Bks. for Young Readers) Simon & Schuster Children's Publishing.

—Ruby Lu, Star of the Show. Choi, Stef, illus. (Ruby Lu Ser.). (ENG.). 144p. (J). (gr. 1-5). 2012. pap. 6.99 *(978-1-4169-1776-2(4))* 2011. 17.99 *(978-1-4169-1775-5(6))* Simon & Schuster Children's Publishing. (Atheneum Bks. for Young Readers).

López, Lorraine. Call Me Henri. 2012. (ENG.). 242p. (gr. 9-17). pap. 19.95 *(978-0-8101-2893-4(4))* Curbstone Pr.

Lord, Bette Bao. In the Year of the Boar & Jackie Robinson. Simont, Marc, illus. 2019. (ENG.). 176p. (J). (gr. 3-7). pap. 7.99 *(978-0-06-440175-3(8)*, HarperCollins) HarperCollins Pubs.

—In the Year of the Boar & Jackie Robinson. 2009. 8.32 *(978-0-7848-0826-9(0)*, Everbind) Marco Bk. Co.

—In the Year of the Boar & Jackie Robinson. (J). 2008. 67.75 *(978-1-4281-8016-1(8))* 2004. 46.75 *(978-1-4025-9147-1(0))* Recorded Bks., Inc.

—In the Year of the Boar & Jackie Robinson. 2003. (J). (gr. 3-6). 16.00 *(978-0-8085-7599-3(6))* Turtleback.

Lord, Cynthia. Because of the Rabbit (Scholastic Gold) 2019. (ENG.). 192p. (J). (gr. 3-7). 17.99 *(978-0-545-91424-6(8)*, Scholastic Pr.) Scholastic, Inc.

Lord, Emery. The Map from Here to There. 2020. (ENG.). 368p. (YA). 17.99 *(978-1-68119-938-2(6)*, 900194066, Bloomsbury Young Adult) Bloomsbury Publishing USA.

Lore, Pittacus. I Am Number Four. (Lorien Legacies Ser.: 1). (ENG.). (YA). (gr. 9). 2011. 496p. pap. 15.99 *(978-0-06-196957-7(5))* 2010. 448p. 18.99 *(978-0-06-196955-3(9))* HarperCollins Pubs. (HarperCollins).

—I Am Number Four. 2009. (Lorien Legacies Ser.: Bk. 1). 11.04 *(978-0-7848-3715-3(5)*, Everbind) Marco Bk. Co.

—I Am Number Four. 2011. (I Am Number Four Ser.: Vol. 1). (ENG.). 440p. (gr. 9-12). 20.00 *(978-1-61383-207-3(9))* Perfection Learning Corp.

—I Am Number Four. 2011. (Lorien Legacies Ser.: 1). (YA). lib. bdg. 20.85 *(978-0-606-23545-7(0))* Turtleback.

—I Am Number Four Movie Tie-In Edition. movie tie-in ed. 2011. (Lorien Legacies Ser.: 1). (ENG.). (YA). (gr. 9). 496p. pap. 9.99 *(978-0-06-211655-0(X))*; 480p. 17.99 *(978-0-06-202624-8(0))* HarperCollins Pubs. (HarperCollins).

—I Am Number Four: the Lost Files: Rebel Allies. 2015. (Lorien Legacies: the Lost Files Ser.). (ENG.). 416p. (YA). (gr. 9). pap. 10.99 *(978-0-06-236404-3(9)*, HarperCollins) HarperCollins Pubs.

—I Am Number Four: the Lost Files: Secret Histories. 2013. (Lorien Legacies: the Lost Files Ser.). (ENG.). 416p. (YA). (gr. 9). pap. 10.99 *(978-0-06-222367-8(4)*, HarperCollins) HarperCollins Pubs.

—I Am Number Four: the Lost Files: Zero Hour. 2016. (Lorien Legacies: the Lost Files Ser.). (ENG.). 416p. (YA). (gr. 9). pap. 11.99 *(978-0-06-238771-4(5)*, HarperCollins) HarperCollins Pubs.

—Secret Histories. 2013. (Lorien Legacies: the Lost Files Ser.). (YA). lib. bdg. 20.85 *(978-0-606-31823-5(2))* Turtleback.

Lorenz, Albert. The Exceptionally, Extraordinarily Ordinary First Day of School. 2010. (ENG., Illus.). 32p. (J). (gr. 1-4). 16.95 *(978-0-8109-8960-3(3)*, 649501, Abrams Bks. for Young Readers) Abrams, Inc.

Lorenzi, Natalie Dias. Flying the Dragon. 240p. (J). (gr. 4-7). 2014. (ENG.). pap. 8.95 *(978-1-58089-435-7(6))* 2012. 16.95 *(978-1-58089-434-0(8))* Charlesbridge Publishing, Inc.

Lorey, Dean. Monster Law. 2009. 304p. 10.99 *(978-0-06-134048-2(0))* HarperCollins Pubs.

Lorimer, Janet. The Bad Luck Play, 1 vol. unabr. ed. 2010. (Q Reads Ser.). (ENG.). 32p. (YA). (gr. 9-12). pap. 8.50 *(978-1-61651-198-2(2))* Saddleback Educational Publishing, Inc.

—Student Bodies, 1 vol. unabr. ed. 2010. (Q Reads Ser.). (ENG.). 32p. (YA). (gr. 9-12). pap. 8.50 *(978-1-61651-219-4(9))* Saddleback Educational Publishing, Inc.

Lottridge, Celia Barker. Wings to Fly, 1 vol. 3rd ed. 2007. (ENG.). 168p. (J). (gr. 3-7). pap. 8.95 *(978-0-88899-844-6(9))* Groundwood Bks. CAN. Dist: Publishers Group West (PGW).

Loughead, Deb. Sidetracked, 1 vol. 2012. (Orca Sports Ser.). (ENG.). 136p. (J). (gr. 4-7). pap. 9.95 *(978-1-4598-0250-6(0))* Orca Bk. Pubs. USA.

Louis, Sachar. There's a Boy in the Girls' Bathroom. 2014. (ENG.). 208p. (J). (gr. 7-12). 11.24 *(978-1-63245-256-6(1))* Lectorum Pubns., Inc.

Love, D. Anne. Defying the Diva. 2008. (ENG., Illus.). 272p. (YA). (gr. 7-12). 17.99 *(978-1-4169-3481-3(2)*, McElderry, Margaret K. Bks.) McElderry, Margaret K. Bks.

—Semiprecious. (ENG.). 304p. (J). (gr. 5-9). 2009. pap. 6.99 *(978-0-689-87389-8(1))* 2006. (Illus.). 17.99 *(978-0-689-85638-9(5))* McElderry, Margaret K. Bks. (McElderry, Margaret K. Bks.).

Lovelady, W. f. The Adventures of Johnny Saturday: Back to the Drawing Board. 2012. 76p. pap. 12.95 *(978-1-4685-5286-7(4))* AuthorHouse.

Lovell, Brandy. Crazy Colours. Mitchell, Tina, illus. 2011. 42p. pap. *(978-0-9867761-0-6(6))* Bing Long Bks.

Lowe, E. Van. Never Slow Dance with a Zombie. 2009. (ENG.). 256p. (YA). (gr. 8-12). pap. 16.99 *(978-0-7653-2040-7(1)*, 900050608, Tor Teen) Doherty, Tom Assocs., LLC.

Lowe, Natasha. The Marvelous Magic of Miss Mabel. (Poppy Pendle Ser.). (ENG.). (J). (gr. 3-7). 2017. 304p. pap. 8.99 *(978-1-4814-6534-2(1))* 2016. (Illus.). 288p. 16.99 *(978-1-4814-6533-5(3))* Simon & Schuster/Paula Wiseman Bks. (Simon & Schuster/Paula Wiseman Bks.).

—The Power of Poppy Pendle. (Poppy Pendle Ser.). (ENG., 272p. (J). (gr. 3-7). 2013. Illus.). pap. 8.99 *(978-1-4424-4926-8(8))* 2012. 16.99 *(978-1-4424-4679-3(X))* Simon & Schuster/Paula Wiseman Bks. (Simon & Schuster/Paula Wiseman Bks.).

Lowry, Lois. The Birthday Ball. Feiffer, Jules, illus. 2011. (ENG.). 192p. (J). (gr. 5-7). pap. 8.99 *(978-0-547-57710-4(9)*, 1458458, Clarion Bks.) HarperCollins Pubs.

—Gooney Bird & the Room Mother. 2006. (Gooney Bird Ser.: No. 2). (ENG., Illus.). 80p. (J). (gr. 3-7). 5.99 *(978-0-440-42133-7(0)*, Yearling) Random Hse. Children's Bks.

—Gooney Bird on the Map. Thomas, Middy, illus. (Gooney Bird Greene Ser.: 5). (ENG.). 128p. (J). (gr. 1-4). 2013. pap. 7.99 *(978-0-547-85088-7(3)*, 1501066) 2011. 16.99 *(978-0-547-55622-2(5)*, 1452833) HarperCollins Pubs. (Clarion Bks.).

Loye, Scott. Moon Ring. 2011. 160p. (gr. 10-12). 22.95 *(978-1-4502-9682-3(3))*; pap. 12.95 *(978-1-4502-9680-9(7))* iUniverse, Inc.

Lubar, David. The Big Stink. 2010. (Nathan Abercrombie, Accidental Zombie Ser.: 4). (ENG.). 176p. (J). (gr. 3-7). pap. 13.99 *(978-0-7653-2510-5(1)*, 900063903, Starscape) Doherty, Tom Assocs., LLC.

—The Bully Bug: A Monsterrific Tale. 2014. (Monsterrific Tales Ser.). (ENG., Illus.). 144p. (J). (gr. 3-7). 24.99 *(978-0-7653-3082-6(2)*, 900078525, Starscape) Doherty, Tom Assocs., LLC.

—Enter the Zombie. 2011. (Nathan Abercrombie, Accidental Zombie Ser.: 5). (ENG.). 192p. (J). (gr. 4-8). 18.69 *(978-0-7653-2344-6(3)*, Starscape) Doherty, Tom Assocs., LLC.

—My Rotten Life. 2009. (Nathan Abercrombie, Accidental Zombie Ser.: 1). (ENG., Illus.). 160p. (J). (gr. 3-7). pap. 13.99 *(978-0-7653-1634-9(X)*, 900038898, Starscape) Doherty, Tom Assocs., LLC.

—Sleeping Freshmen Never Lie. 2007. (ENG.). 288p. (YA). (gr. 7-18). 11.99 *(978-0-14-240780-6(1)*, Speak) Penguin Young Readers Group.

—Strikeout of the Bleacher Weenies. 2017. (Weenies Stories Ser.). (J). lib. bdg. 18.40 *(978-0-606-40600-0(X))* Turtleback.

Lucan, Dawn. My Challenge Memories. 2011. (ENG.). 106p. pap. 8.95 *(978-1-4583-4714-5(1))* Lulu Pr., Inc.

Lucas, Sally. Dancing Dinos Go to School. Lucas, Margeaux, illus. 2006. (Step into Reading Ser.: Vol. 1). 32p. (J). (gr. -1-1). pap. 5.99 *(978-0-375-83241-3(6)*, Random Hse. Bks. for Young Readers) Random Hse. Children's Bks.

Lucido, Aimee. Emmy in the Key of Code. 2019. (ENG.). 416p. (J). (gr. 3-7). 16.99 *(978-0-358-04082-8(5)*, 1740459, Versify) HarperCollins Pubs.

Luck, Gail. Bumduggle Davis Beats the Boobrats or the Inauguration of the Motherless Club. 2011. 146p. pap. 12.50 *(978-1-61204-727-0(0)*, Strategic Bk. Publishing) Strategic Book Publishing & Rights Agency (SBPRA).

—Bumduggle Davis Joins the Dots: Or It's All There in Black & White. 2012. 166p. pap. 13.50 *(978-1-62212-379-7(4)*, Strategic Bk. Publishing) Strategic Book Publishing & Rights Agency (SBPRA).

Luddy, Karon. Spelldown: The Big-Time Dreams of a Small-Town Word Whiz. 2008. (Mix Ser.). (ENG.). 224p. (J). (gr. 4-8). pap. 10.99 *(978-1-4169-5452-1(X)*, Simon & Schuster/Paula Wiseman Bks.) Simon & Schuster/Paula Wiseman Bks.

Ludwig, Trudy. Confessions of a Former Bully. Adams, Beth, illus. 2012. 48p. (J). (gr. 3-7). pap. 8.99 *(978-0-307-93113-9(7)*, Dragonfly Bks.) Random Hse. Children's Bks.

—Confessions of a Former Bully. 2012. lib. bdg. 18.40 *(978-0-606-26382-5(9))* Turtleback.

—The Invisible Boy. Barton, Patrice, illus. 2013. (ENG.). 40p. (J). (gr. 1-4). 18.99 *(978-1-58246-450-3(2)*, Knopf Bks. for Young Readers) Random Hse. Children's Bks.

—Just Kidding. Gustavson, Adam, illus. 2006. 32p. (J). (gr. 1-4). 18.99 *(978-1-58246-163-2(5)*, Tricycle Pr.) Random Hse. Children's Bks.

—Trouble Talk. Prevost, Mikela, illus. 2008. 32p. (J). (gr. 1-4). 18.99 *(978-1-58246-240-0(2)*, Tricycle Pr.) Random Hse. Children's Bks.

Ludwig, Trudy & Barton, Patrice. Quiet Please, Owen Mcphee! 2018. (Illus.). 40p. (J). (gr. k-3). 17.99 *(978-0-399-55713-2(X)*, Knopf Bks. for Young Readers) Random Hse. Children's Bks.

Luedeke, Lisa. Smashed. 2012. (ENG.). 336p. (YA). (gr. 9). 16.99 *(978-1-4424-2779-2(5)*, McElderry, Margaret K. Bks.) McElderry, Margaret K. Bks.

Luen Yang, Gene. American Born Chinese. Luen Yang, Gene, illus. rev. ed. 2006. (ENG., Illus.). 240p. (YA). (gr. 7-12). pap. 18.99 *(978-1-59643-152-2(0)*, 900037739, First Second Bks.) Roaring Brook Pr.

—Secret Coders. 2015. (Secret Coders Ser.: 1). (ENG., Illus.). 96p. (J). (gr. 3-7). pap. 10.99 *(978-1-62672-075-6(4)*, 900134876, First Second Bks.) Roaring Brook Pr.

—Secret Coders: Robots & Repeats. 2017. (Secret Coders Ser.: 4). (ENG., Illus.). 96p. (J). pap. 10.99 *(978-1-62672-606-2(X)*, 900162979, First Second Bks.) Roaring Brook Pr.

Luna, James. Growing up on the Playground / Nuestro Patio de Recreo. Barela-Di Bisceglie, Monica, illus. 2018. (ENG & SPA.). 32p. (J). (gr. -1-3). 17.95 *(978-1-55885-871-8(7)*, Piñata Books) Arte Publico Pr.

Lundquist, Jenny. The Charming Life of Izzy Malone. 2017. (ENG., Illus.). 304p. (J). (gr. 3-7). pap. 8.99 *(978-1-4814-6031-6(5)*, Aladdin) Simon & Schuster Children's Publishing.

—The Charming Life of Izzy Malone. 2016. (ENG., Illus.). 288p. (J). (gr. 3-7). 17.99 *(978-1-4814-6032-3(3)*, Simon & Schuster/Paula Wiseman Bks.) Simon & Schuster/Paula Wiseman Bks.

Lunsford, Susie. The Magical Wishing Well Forest Series. 2006. pap. 25.32 *(978-1-4134-9491-4(9))* Xlibris Corp.

Lupa, Mary R. Stacy Takes the Train to School. Andriyevskaya, Yevgeniya, illus. 2009. 20p. (J). pap. 10.95 *(978-1-4327-1609-7(3))* Outskirts Pr., Inc.

Lupica, Mike. The Football Fiasco. 2018. (Zach & Zoe Mysteries Ser.: 3). (ENG., Illus.). 80p. (J). (gr. 1-4). 6.99 *(978-0-425-28943-3(5)*, Puffin Books); 14.99 *(978-0-425-28942-6(7)*, Philomel Bks.) Penguin Young Readers Group.

—The Missing Baseball. 2018. (Zach & Zoe Mysteries Ser.: 1). (ENG., Illus.). 80p. (J). (gr. 1-4). 6.99 *(978-0-425-28937-2(0)*, Puffin Books) Penguin Young Readers Group.

—Qb 1. 2014. (ENG.). 288p. (J). (gr. 5). pap. 8.99 *(978-0-14-751152-2(6)*, Puffin Books) Penguin Young Readers Group.

—Travel Team. l.t. ed. 2005. (Thorndike Literacy Bridge Ser.). 400p. (J). (gr. 4-7). lib. bdg. 23.95 *(978-0-7862-7415-4(8))* Thorndike Pr.

—True Legend. 2013. (ENG.). 320p. (J). (gr. 5). pap. 8.99 *(978-0-14-242650-0(4)*, Puffin Books) Penguin Young Readers Group.

Lutz, Nancie Anne. Patsy Ann Back Again. Lutz, Nancie Anne, illus. 2005. (Illus.). 25p. (J). pap. 14.50 *(978-0-9760064-0-4(5))* Dollworks.

Lux, Josephine Kei & Doerflinger, Marion. Daydreaming Daisy Part of the Daydreamer's Club Series. 2009. 40p. pap. 17.50 *(978-1-60860-252-0(4)*, Eloquent Bks.) Strategic Book Publishing & Rights Agency (SBPRA).

Luzzatto, Caroline. Interplanetary Avenger. 2005. (ENG., Illus.). 128p. (J). (gr. 3-7). 16.95 *(978-0-8234-1933-3(9))* Holiday Hse., Inc.

Lyga, Barry. The Astonishing Adventures of Fanboy & Goth Girl. 2007. (ENG.). 320p. (YA). (gr. 7-12). pap. 9.99 *(978-0-618-91652-8(0)*, 1015005, Clarion Bks.) HarperCollins Pubs.

—Boy Toy. 2007. (ENG.). 416p. (YA). (gr. 7-12). 22.44 *(978-0-618-72393-5(5))* Houghton Mifflin Harcourt Publishing Co.

—Hero-Type. 2009. (ENG.). 312p. (YA). (gr. 7). pap. 17.99 *(978-0-547-24877-6(6)*, 1100781, Clarion Bks.) HarperCollins Pubs.

Lyle, Patrice. The Case of the Invisible Witch. 2013. 194p. pap. 9.99 *(978-1-61603-034-6(8))* Leap Bks.

Lynch, Brian. Ready for Action (Toy Academy #2) Taylor, Edwardian, illus. 2019. (ENG.). 192p. (J). (gr. 2-5). 14.99 *(978-1-338-14916-6(4)*, Scholastic Pr.) Scholastic, Inc.

Lynch, Chris. Inexcusable. 2005. (ENG., Illus.). 176p. (YA). (gr. 7-18). 19.99 *(978-0-689-84789-9(0)*, Atheneum Bks. for Young Readers) Simon & Schuster Children's Publishing.

—Inexcusable: 10th Anniversary Edition. 10th ed. 2015. (ENG., Illus.). 192p. (YA). (gr. 8). pap. 11.99 *(978-1-4814-3202-3(8)*, Simon & Schuster Bks. For Young Readers) Simon & Schuster Bks. For Young Readers.

—Sins of the Fathers. 2006. 232p. (YA). (gr. 9-12). lib. bdg. 17.89 *(978-0-06-074038-2(8)*, HarperTeen) HarperCollins Pubs.

Lynch, F. Michael. I Will Always Need You. 2008. 24p. pap. 14.50 *(978-1-60693-141-7(5)*, Eloquent Bks.) Strategic Book Publishing & Rights Agency (SBPRA).

Lynch, Janet Nichols. Addicted to Her. 2010. (ENG.). 256p. (YA). (gr. 7-18). pap. 17.95 *(978-0-8234-2186-2(4))* Holiday Hse., Inc.

—Messed Up. 2009. (ENG.). 320p. (YA). (gr. 7-18). 17.95 *(978-0-8234-2185-5(6))* Holiday Hse., Inc.

—Peace Is a Four-Letter Word. 2005. 158p. (YA). (gr. 8-12). per. 9.95 *(978-1-59714-014-0(7)*, Great Valley Bks.) Heyday.

Lynellen Sullivan & Bryan Castle. Poppers to the Rescue: Book 1 of the Popcorn Series. 2010. 72p. pap. 8.95 *(978-1-4401-9764-2(4))* iUniverse, Inc.

Lyon, George Ella. The Pirate of Kindergarten. Avril, Lynne, illus. 2010. (ENG.). 40p. (J). (gr. -1-3). 19.99 *(978-1-4169-5024-0(9)*, Atheneum/Richard Jackson Bks.) Simon & Schuster Children's Publishing.

Lyons, Kelly Starling. Class Act #2. Brantley-Newton, Vanessa, illus. 2017. (Jada Jones Ser.: 2). 96p. (J). (gr. 1-3). (ENG.). 6.99 *(978-0-451-53427-9(1))*; lib. bdg. 15.99 *(978-0-451-53428-6(X))* Penguin Young Readers Group. (Penguin Workshop).

—Rock Star #1. Brantley-Newton, Vanessa, illus. 2017. (Jada Jones Ser.: 1). 96p. (J). (gr. 1-3). 6.99 *(978-0-448-48751-9(9))*; (ENG.). lib. bdg. 15.99 *(978-0-448-48752-6(7))* Penguin Young Readers Group. (Penguin Workshop).

Lytton, Deborah. The Fantastic Library Rescue & Other Major Plot Twists. 2018. (Ruby Starr Ser.: 2). (ENG., Illus.). 224p. (J). (gr. 3-7). pap. 10.99 *(978-1-4926-4580-1(X))* Sourcebooks, Inc.

—Ruby Starr. 2017. (Ruby Starr Ser.: 1). (ENG., Illus.). 272p. (J). (gr. 3-7). pap. 7.99 *(978-1-4926-4577-1(X))* Sourcebooks, Inc.

M. Alvarado. We Are Different, but the Same. 2012. 16p. pap. 15.99 *(978-1-4685-4425-1(X))* AuthorHouse.

MacCarthy, Mariah. Squad. 2020. (ENG.). 256p. (YA). pap. 16.99 *(978-1-250-23384-4(4)*, 900180241) Square Fish.

MacDonald, Maryann. Starring Francie O'Leary. Richards, Virginia Helen, illus. 2010. 64p. (J). (gr. 1-3). pap. 6.95 *(978-0-8198-7132-9(X))* Pauline Bks. & Media.

MacDowell, Diane. Adventures of Timkin: The Early Years. 2012. 28p. pap. 19.99 *(978-1-4772-7101-8(5))* AuthorHouse.

MacDowell, Maureen. Tomorrow Is the First Day of School. Hergenrother, Max, illus. 2007. 32p. (J). 15.95 *(978-0-9791463-0-5(5))* Wading River Bks., LLC.

MacGregor, Joanne. Fault Lines. 2016. (ENG.). 272p. pap. 11.25 *(978-1-4853-0422-7(9))* Protea Boekhuis ZAF. Dist: Casemate Pubs. & Bk. Distributors, LLC.

MacHale, D. J. Black Moon Rising (the Library Book 2) (Library: 2). 304p. (J). (gr. 3-7). 2018. pap. 7.99 *(978-1-101-93260-5(0)*, Yearling) 2017. 16.99 *(978-1-101-93257-5(0)*, Random Hse. Bks. for Young Readers) Random Hse. Children's Bks.

Machon, Daphne E. Charlee's New Glasses. 2013. (ENG., Illus.). 16p. pap. 8.50 *(978-1-78035-736-2(2)*, Fastprint Publishing) Upfront Publishing Ltd. GBR. Dist: Printondemand-worldwide.com.

Maciejewski, Mark. Electric Boogerloo: I Am Fartacus. 2018. (Max Ser.). (ENG.). 352p. (J). (gr. 4-8). 17.99 *(978-1-4814-6423-9(X))*; (Illus.). pap. 7.99 *(978-1-4814-6422-2(1))* Simon & Schuster Children's Publishing. (Aladdin).

—I Am Fartacus. 2017. (Max Ser.). (ENG., Illus.). 336p. (J). (gr. 4-8). pap. 8.99 *(978-1-4814-6419-2(1)*, Simon & Schuster/Paula Wiseman Bks.) Simon & Schuster/Paula Wiseman Bks.

Maciel, Amanda. Tease. 2015. (ENG.). 336p. (YA). (gr. 9). pap. 9.99 *(978-0-06-230531-2(X)*, Balzer & Bray) HarperCollins Pubs.

Mack, Jeff. Mr. Monkey Visits a School. Mack, Jeff, illus. 2018. (Mr. Monkey Ser.: 2). (ENG., Illus.). 64p. (J). (gr. -1-3). 9.99 *(978-1-5344-0429-8(5)*, Simon & Schuster Bks. For Young Readers) Simon & Schuster Bks. For Young Readers.

Mack, W. C. Athlete vs. Mathlete. 2013. (ENG., 208p. (YA). Illus.). (gr. 3-6). pap. 8.99 *(978-1-59990-858-8(1)*, 900081981);1. (gr. 4-6). 16.99 *(978-1-59990-915-8(4)*, 900084829) Bloomsbury Publishing USA. (Bloomsbury USA Childrens).

Mackall, Dandi Daley. Larger-Than-Life Lara. 2016. (ENG., Illus.). 176p. (J). 14.99 *(978-1-4964-1429-8(2)*, 20_11896) Tyndale Hse. Pubs.

—Natalie: School's First Day of Me, 1 vol. Blakeslee, Lys, illus. 2009. (That's Nat! Ser.: 3). (ENG.). 96p. (J). (gr. 1-4). pap. 4.99 *(978-0-310-71568-9(7))* Zonderkidz.

—Natalie & the Downside-Up Birthday, 1 vol. Blakeslee, Lys, illus. 2009. (That's Nat! Ser.: 4). (ENG.). 96p. (J). (gr. 1-4). pap. 4.99 *(978-0-310-71569-6(5))* Zonderkidz.

—Natalie Really Very Much Wants to Be a Star, 1 vol. Blakeslee, Lys, illus. 2009. (That's Nat! Ser.: 2). (ENG.). 96p. (J). (gr. 1-4). pap. 4.99 *(978-0-310-71567-2(9))* Zonderkidz.

Mackey, Weezie Kerr. Throwing Like a Girl, 0 vols. 2013. (ENG.). 272p. (YA). (gr. 7-12). pap. 9.99 *(978-0-7614-5606-3(6)*, 9780761456063, Skyscape) Amazon Publishing.

Mackintosh, David. The Frank Show. 2012. (ENG., Illus.). 32p. (J). (gr. k-2). 16.95 *(978-1-4197-0393-5(5)*, 1003401, Abrams Bks. for Young Readers) Abrams, Inc.

Mackler, Carolyn. The Earth, My Butt, & Other Big Round Things. 2018. (ENG.). 288p. (YA). pap. 11.99 *(978-1-68119-798-2(7)*, 900187324, Bloomsbury USA Childrens) Bloomsbury Publishing USA.

—The Earth, My Butt, & Other Big Round Things, 1. 2012. (Earth, My Butt, & Other Big Round Things Ser.). (ENG., Illus.). 246p. (YA). (gr. 9). 24.94 *(978-0-7636-1958-9(2))* Candlewick Pr.

—The Future of Us. 2012. lib. bdg. 20.85 *(978-0-606-26498-3(1))* Turtleback.

—The Universe Is Expanding & So Am I. 2019. (ENG.). 304p. (YA). pap. 10.99 *(978-1-68119-982-5(3)*, 900194721, Bloomsbury Young Adult) Bloomsbury Publishing USA.

—Vegan Virgin Valentine. 2004. (ENG., Illus.). 240p. (YA). (gr. 9-18). 16.99 *(978-0-7636-2155-1(2))* Candlewick Pr.

MacLachlan, Patricia. Word after Word after Word. 2010. (ENG.). 128p. (J). (gr. 1-5). 17.99 *(978-0-06-027971-4(0),* Tegen, Katherine Bks) HarperCollins Pubs.

Maclean, Jill. The Hidden Agenda of Sigrid Sugden, 1 vol. 2013. (ENG.). 240p. (J). (gr. 6-8). pap. 11.95 *(978-1-55455-279-5(6),* 24392fb9-84ba-4d89-a341-ac677d0ddcc8) Trifolium Bks., Inc. CAN. Dist: Firefly Bks., Ltd.

MacLellan, Erin. Run from the Nun! 2003. (ENG.). 128p. (J). (gr. 4-6). tchr. ed. 16.95 *(978-0-8234-1796-4(4))* Holiday Hse., Inc.

MacTire, Norwyn. The Ghost Runner. 2019. (League of the Paranormal Ser.). (ENG.). 104p. (YA). (gr. 6-12). 26.65 *(978-1-5415-5681-2(X),* 2c58b643-cdbb-4eeb-8d51-9c888ec41e0c, Darby Creek) Lerner Publishing Group.

Macvie, Meagan. The Ocean in My Ears. 2017. (ENG.). 300p. (YA). pap. 16.00 *(978-1-932010-94-7(7))* Ooligan Pr.

Maddox, Jake. Dance Team Dilemma, 1 vol. Wood, Katie, illus. 2013. (Jake Maddox Girl Sports Stories Ser.). (ENG.). 72p. (J). (gr. 3-6). pap. 5.95 *(978-1-4342-4201-3(3),* 120259); lib. bdg. 25.32 *(978-1-4342-4014-9(2),* 118395) Capstone. (Stone Arch Bks.).

—Dance Team Drama. 2016. (Jake Maddox JV Girls Ser.). (ENG., Illus.). 96p. (J). (gr. 4-8). pap. 5.95 *(978-1-4965-3678-5(9),* 132929); lib. bdg. 26.65 *(978-1-4965-3674-7(6),* 132925) Capstone. (Stone Arch Bks.).

—Heavyweight Takedown. 2015. (Jake Maddox JV Ser.). (ENG., Illus.). 96p. (J). (gr. 4-6). lib. bdg. 26.65 *(978-1-4342-9638-2(5),* 126917, Stone Arch Bks.) Capstone.

—Home-Field Football, 1 vol. Tiffany, Sean, illus. 2012. (Jake Maddox Sports Stories Ser.). (ENG.). 72p. (J). (gr. 3-6). 25.99 *(978-1-4342-4008-8(8),* 118389); pap. 5.95 *(978-1-4342-4206-8(4),* 120264) Capstone. (Stone Arch Bks.).

—Hoop Hustle. Aburto, Jesus, illus. 2015. (Jake Maddox Sports Stories Ser.). (ENG.). 72p. (J). (gr. 3-6). lib. bdg. 25.99 *(978-1-4965-0494-4(1),* 128566, Stone Arch Bks.) Capstone.

—Second-Chance Soccer, 1 vol. Ray, Michael, illus. 2014. (Jake Maddox JV Ser.). (ENG.). 96p. (J). (gr. 4-6). 26.65 *(978-1-4342-9154-7(5),* 125604, Stone Arch Bks.) Capstone.

—Slap-Shot Slump. 2015. (Jake Maddox JV Ser.). (ENG., Illus.). 96p. (J). (gr. 4-6). lib. bdg. 26.65 *(978-1-4342-9635-1(0),* 126914, Stone Arch Bks.) Capstone.

—Touchdown Triumph. Aburto, Jesus, illus. 2015. (Jake Maddox Sports Stories Ser.). (ENG.). 72p. (J). (gr. 3-6). lib. bdg. 25.99 *(978-1-4965-0492-0(5),* 128564, Stone Arch Bks.) Capstone.

Maddox, Jake & Maddox, Jake. Track & Field Takedown, 1 vol. Garcia, Eduardo, illus. 2012. (Jake Maddox Sports Stories Ser.). (ENG.). 72p. (J). (gr. 3-6). pap. 5.95 *(978-1-4342-3901-3(2),* 118086); lib. bdg. 25.99 *(978-1-4342-3287-8(5),* 116250) Capstone. (Stone Arch Bks.).

Madge, Amy. The Adventures of Kwun-Gee & Uba Dooba Boy. 2012. 24p. 29.95 *(978-1-4626-9270-5(2))* America Star Bks.

Madison, Alan. Velma Gratch & the Way Cool Butterfly. Hawkes, Kevin, illus. 2012. 40p. (J). (gr. -1-3). pap. 8.99 *(978-0-307-97804-2(4),* Schwartz & Wade Bks.) Random Hse. Children's Bks.

Mae, Jamie. Isle of Misfits 1: First Class. Hartas, Freya, illus. 2019. (Isle of Misfits Ser.: 1). (ENG.). 112p. (J). (gr. k-3). 16.99 *(978-1-4998-0822-3(4))*; pap. 5.99 *(978-1-4998-0821-6(6))* Little Bee Books Inc.

—Isle of Misfits 2: the Missing Pot of Gold. Hartas, Freya, illus. 2019. (Isle of Misfits Ser.: 2). (ENG.). 112p. (J). (gr. k-3). 16.99 *(978-1-4998-0825-4(9))*; pap. 5.99 *(978-1-4998-0824-7(0))* Little Bee Books Inc.

—Isle of Misfits 3: Prank Wars! Hartas, Freya, illus. 2019. (Isle of Misfits Ser.: 3). (ENG.). 112p. (J). (gr. k-3). 16.99 *(978-1-4998-0853-7(4))*; pap. 5.99 *(978-1-4998-0852-0(6))* Little Bee Books Inc.

Magnus, Kellie. Little Lion Goes to School. Robinson, Michael, illus. l.t. ed. 2003. 16p. (J). 9.99 *(978-0-9744211-0-0(3))* Media Magic New York.

Magoon, Kekla. Camo Girl. 2012. (ENG.). 224p. (J). (gr. 3-9). pap. 8.99 *(978-1-4169-7805-3(4),* Aladdin) Simon & Schuster Children's Publishing.

—Camo Girl. 2011. (ENG., Illus.). 224p. (J). (gr. 3-9). 19.99 *(978-1-4169-7804-6(6),* Simon & Schuster/Paula Wiseman Bks.) Simon & Schuster/Paula Wiseman Bks.

—37 Things I Love (in No Particular Order) 2013. (ENG.). 240p. (YA). (gr. 9-13). pap. 14.99 *(978-1-250-03430-4(2),* 900120604) Square Fish.

Mahony, Mary. Harry Scores A Hat Trick, Pawns, Pucks, & Scoliosis: The Sequel to Stand Tall, Harry. Pasternack, Susan, ed. Larkin, Catherine, illus. 2003. 130p. (YA). (gr. 5-8). per. 14.95 *(978-0-9658879-3-9(6))* Redding Pr.

—School is Not for Me, Jeremy James Conor McGee. Frederick, Sarah, illus. 2009. (J). pap. 7.95 *(978-0-9658879-4-6(4))* Redding Pr.

Maihack, Mike. Secret of the Time Tablets: a Graphic Novel (Cleopatra in Space #3) 2016. (Cleopatra in Space Ser.: 3). (ENG., Illus.). 192p. (J). (gr. 3-7). pap. 14.99 *(978-0-545-83867-2(3),* Graphix) Scholastic, Inc.

Mainwaring, Anna. Rebel with a Cupcake. 2018. (ENG., Illus.). 216p. (J). (gr. 9-12). pap. 10.99 *(978-1-5253-0033-2(4))* Kids Can Pr., Ltd. CAN. Dist: Hachette Bk. Group.

Maizel, Rebecca. Infinite Days: A Vampire Queen Novel. 2010. (Vampire Queen Ser.: 1). (ENG.). 336p. (YA). (gr. 7-18). pap. 16.99 *(978-0-312-64991-3(6),* 900069066, St. Martin's Griffin) St. Martin's Pr.

Maldonado, Torrey. Secret Saturdays. 2012. (ENG.). 208p. (YA). (gr. 5-18). 7.99 *(978-0-14-241747-8(5),* Puffin Books) Penguin Young Readers Group.

—Secret Saturdays. 2012. lib. bdg. 18.40 *(978-0-606-23645-4(7))* Turtleback.

Mallery, Sydra. A Most Unusual Day. Goodale, E. B., illus. 2018. (ENG.). 40p. (J). (gr. -1-3). 18.99 *(978-0-06-236430-2(8),* Greenwillow Bks.) HarperCollins Pubs.

Malone, Lee Gjertsen. The Last Boy at St. Edith's. 2016. (Max Ser.). (ENG., Illus.). 272p. (J). (gr. 3-7). 16.99 *(978-1-4814-4435-4(2),* Aladdin) Simon & Schuster Children's Publishing.

—The Last Boy at St. Edith's. 2017. lib. bdg. 18.40 *(978-0-606-40157-9(1))* Turtleback.

Malone, Marianne. The Sixty-Eight Rooms, 1. Triplett, Gina & Call, Greg, illus. 2011. (Sixty-Eight Rooms Adventures Ser.). (ENG.). 288p. (J). (gr. 4-6). lib. bdg. 22.44 *(978-0-375-95710-9(3))* Random House Publishing Group.

Maloney, Peter. A Bump on the Head. 2003. (Just Schoolin' Around Ser.). (Illus.). 32p. (J). pap. *(978-0-439-39520-5(8))* Scholastic, Inc.

Maloney, Peter & Zekauskas, Felicia. Thanks for Nothing! 2003. (Illus.). 31p. (J). *(978-0-439-55360-5(1))* Scholastic, Inc.

Maltby, Robert I. Diquan & the Book Monster, 1 vol. 2009. 39p. pap. 24.95 *(978-1-61546-964-2(8))* America Star Bks.

Mammay, Judith. It's Time. Fargo, Todd, illus. l.t. ed. 2007. 32p. (J). pap. 9.95 *(978-0-944727-20-1(4))*; lib. bdg. 15.95 *(978-0-944727-21-8(2))* Jason & Nordic Pubs. (Turtle Bks.).

—Knowing Joseph. (ENG., Illus.). 256p. (J). (gr. 2-7). 2009. pap. 8.95 *(978-1-933831-06-0(5))* 2008. 13.95 *(978-1-933831-05-3(7))* Blooming Tree Pr.

Mancusi, Mari. Gamer Girl. 2010. 256p. (YA). (gr. 7-18). 7.99 *(978-0-14-241509-2(X),* Speak) Penguin Young Readers Group.

Mandel, Lee. Barf for Lunch. 2012. 184p. pap. 8.99 *(978-0-9831996-4-9(7))* Blast Off to Learning, LLC.

Mangum, Kay Lynn. When the Bough Breaks. 2007. 352p. (YA). pap. 15.95 *(978-1-59038-748-1(1))* Deseret Bk. Co.

Mangum, Lisa. The Hourglass Door. (Hourglass Door Trilogy: Bk. 1). (YA). 2010. 408p. mass mkt. 7.99 *(978-1-60641-679-2(0))* 2009. 432p. (gr. 9-18). 18.95 *(978-1-60641-093-6(8))* Shadow Mountain Publishing. (Shadow Mountain).

Mann, Elizabeth. Little Man: A Novel. 2014. (ENG., Illus.). 208p. (J). (gr. 5-7). 18.95 *(978-1-931414-49-4(1),* 38f69c8a-89d2-4d48-aaba-c6ec00ff1c92) Mikaya Pr.

Mann, J. Albert. What Every Girl Should Know: Margaret Sanger's Journey. (ENG.). (YA). (gr. 9). 2020. 256p. pap. 11.99 *(978-1-5344-1933-9(0))* 2019. (Illus.). 240p. 18.99 *(978-1-5344-1932-2(2))* Simon & Schuster Children's Publishing. (Atheneum Bks. for Young Readers).

Mann, Jennifer K. I Will Never Get a Star on Mrs. Benson's Blackboard. Mann, Jennifer K., illus. 2017. (ENG., Illus.). 40p. (J). (gr. k-3). 7.99 *(978-0-7636-9299-5(9))* Candlewick Pr.

Manny goes to Preschool. 2010. 32p. pap. 3.99 *(978-1-4231-3403-9(6))* Disney Pr.

Mantell, Paul & Christopher, Matt. Mountain Bike Mania. l.t. ed. 2007. (New Matt Christopher Sports Library). 160p. (J). (gr. 4-6). lib. bdg. 26.60 *(978-1-59953-108-3(9))* Norwood Hse. Pr.

Manternach, Karla. Meena Meets Her Match. Alencar, Rayner, illus. 2019. (Meena Zee Bks.). (ENG.). 192p. (J). (gr. 3-7). 17.99 *(978-1-5344-2817-1(8),* Simon & Schuster Bks. For Young Readers) Simon & Schuster Bks. For Young Readers.

Manushkin, Fran. The Big Lie, 1 vol. Lyon, Tammie, illus. 2009. (Katie Woo Ser.). (ENG.). 32p. (J). (gr. k-2). 21.32 *(978-1-4048-5497-0(5),* 95720, Picture Window Bks.) Capstone.

—The Big Stink. Lyon, Tammie, illus. 2018. (Pedro Ser.). (ENG.). 32p. (J). (gr. k-2). lib. bdg. 21.32 *(978-1-5158-2820-4(4),* 137985, Picture Window Bks.) Capstone.

—La Gran Mentira, 1 vol. Lyon, Tammie & Lyon, Tammie, illus. 2012. (Katie Woo en Español Ser.). (SPA.). 32p. (J). (gr. k-2). pap. 6.95 *(978-1-4048-7678-1(2),* 120354); lib. bdg. 21.32 *(978-1-4048-7522-7(0),* 119824) Capstone. (Picture Window Bks.).

—Katie & the Class Pet, 1 vol. Lyon, Tammie, illus. 2011. (Katie Woo Ser.). (ENG.). 32p. (J). (gr. k-2). pap. 5.95 *(978-1-4048-6856-4(9),* 116437); lib. bdg. 21.32 *(978-1-4048-6520-4(9),* 114216) Capstone. (Picture Window Bks.).

—Katie & the Fancy Substitute, 1 vol. Lyon, Tammie, illus. 2014. (Katie Woo Ser.). (ENG.). 32p. (J). (gr. k-2). 21.32 *(978-1-4795-5188-0(0),* 125542, Picture Window Bks.) Capstone.

—Katie Blows Her Top. Lyon, Tammie, illus. 2018. (Katie Woo Ser.). (ENG.). 32p. (J). (gr. k-2). lib. bdg. 22.65 *(978-1-5158-2265-3(6),* 136884, Picture Window Bks.) Capstone.

—Katie Finds a Job, 1 vol. Lyon, Tammie, illus. 2011. (Katie Woo Ser.). (ENG.). 32p. (J). (gr. k-2). pap. 5.95 *(978-1-4048-6614-0(0),* 114675); lib. bdg. 21.32 *(978-1-4048-6513-6(6),* 114209) Capstone. (Picture Window Bks.).

—Katie Woo Loves School, 1 vol. Lyon, Tammie, illus. 2013. (Katie Woo Ser.). (ENG.). 96p. (J). (gr. k-2). pap., pap., pap. 4.95 *(978-1-4795-2027-5(6),* 123733, Picture Window Bks.) Capstone.

—Katie Woo Rules the School, 1 vol. Lyon, Tammie, illus. 2012. (Katie Woo Ser.). (ENG.). 96p. (J). (gr. k-2). pap., pap., pap. 4.95 *(978-1-4048-7908-9(0),* 120563, Picture Window Bks.) Capstone.

—Katie's Lucky Birthday, 1 vol. Lyon, Tammie, illus. 2011. (Katie Woo Ser.). (ENG.). 32p. (J). (gr. k-2). pap. 5.95 *(978-1-4048-6612-6(4),* 114671); lib. bdg. 21.32 *(978-1-4048-6514-3(4),* 114210) Capstone. (Picture Window Bks.).

—Make-Believe Class, 1 vol. Lyon, Tammie, illus. 2010. (Katie Woo Ser.). (ENG.). 32p. (J). (gr. k-2). lib. bdg. 21.32 *(978-1-4048-5732-2(X),* 102311, Picture Window Bks.) Capstone.

—Moo, Katie Woo! Lyon, Tammie, illus. 2013. (Katie Woo Ser.). (ENG.). 32p. (J). pap. 35.70 *(978-1-4048-8093-1(3),* 19501); lib. bdg. 21.32 *(978-1-4048-7653-8(7),* 120170) Capstone. (Picture Window Bks.).

—No Valentines for Katie, 1 vol. Lyon, Tammie, illus. 2010. (Katie Woo Ser.). (ENG.). 32p. (J). (gr. k-2). pap. 5.95 *(978-1-4048-6365-1(6),* 114017); lib. bdg. 21.32 *(978-1-4048-5986-9(1),* 102854) Capstone. (Picture Window Bks.).

—Pedro, Candidato a Presidente. Trusted Translations, Trusted, tr. Lyon, Tammie, illus. 2018. (Pedro en Español Ser.). (SPA.). 32p. (J). (gr. k-2). lib. bdg. 21.32 *(978-1-5158-2508-1(6),* 137567, Picture Window Bks.) Capstone.

—Pedro, First-Grade Hero. Lyon, Tammie, illus. 2016. (Pedro Ser.). (ENG.). 96p. (J). (gr. k-2). pap., pap., pap. 4.95 *(978-1-5158-0112-2(8),* 133199, Picture Window Bks.) Capstone.

—Pedro for President. Lyon, Tammie, illus. 2016. (Pedro Ser.). (ENG.). 32p. (J). (gr. k-2). lib. bdg. 21.32 *(978-1-5158-0087-3(3),* 132126, Picture Window Bks.) Capstone.

—Pedro's Tricky Tower. Lyon, Tammie, illus. 2017. (Pedro Ser.). (ENG.). 32p. (J). (gr. k-2). lib. bdg. 21.32 *(978-1-5158-1903-5(5),* 136537, Picture Window Bks.) Capstone.

—La Torre Embromada de Pedro. Trusted Translations, Trusted, tr. Lyon, Tammie, illus. 2018. (Pedro en Español Ser.). (SPA.). 32p. (J). (gr. k-2). lib. bdg. 21.32 *(978-1-5158-2513-5(2),* 137572, Picture Window Bks.) Capstone.

—Who Needs Glasses?, 1 vol. Lyon, Tammie, illus. 2013. (Katie Woo Ser.). (ENG.). 32p. (J). (gr. k-2). pap. 5.95 *(978-1-4048-8049-8(6),* 121724); lib. bdg. 21.32 *(978-1-4048-7655-2(3),* 120172) Capstone. (Picture Window Bks.).

Manushkin, Fran & Lyon, Tammie. Basta de Burlas, 1 vol. Lyon, Tammie, illus. 2012. (Katie Woo en Español Ser.). (SPA., Illus.). 32p. (J). (gr. k-2). pap. 6.95 *(978-1-4048-7677-4(4),* 120351, Picture Window Bks.) Capstone.

Manzak, Bonnie. The Big Red Cat. 2011. 32p. pap. 21.99 *(978-1-4568-6607-5(9))* Xlibris Corp.

Marchetta, Melina. Looking for Alibrandi. 2006. (ENG.). 320p. (YA). (gr. 7-12). reprint ed. per. 9.99 *(978-0-375-83694-7(2),* Knopf Bks. for Young Readers) Random Hse. Children's Bks.

—Saving Francesca. 2006. (ENG.). 256p. (YA). (gr. 7-12). reprint ed. per. 8.99 *(978-0-375-82983-3(0),* Knopf Bks. for Young Readers) Random Hse. Children's Bks.

Marciniak, Christine. Always Ali. 2015. 258p. (YA). *(978-1-61271-279-6(7))* Zumaya Pubns. LLC.

—Honestly, Ali! 2014. 223p. (YA). *(978-1-61271-249-9(5))* Zumaya Pubns. LLC.

—Reality Ali. 2012. (J). *(978-1-61271-076-1(X))*; *(978-1-61271-075-4(1))*; pap. 13.99 *(978-1-61271-074-7(3))* Zumaya Pubns. LLC.

Margaret I. Pascuzzo. Anton Finds a Treasure. Bicking, Judith, illus. 2008. (ENG.). 18p. pap. 12.00 *(978-1-4251-8683-8(1))* Trafford Publishing.

Margolis, Leslie. Ghosted. 2019. (ENG.). 256p. (J). pap. 7.99 *(978-1-250-21116-3(6),* 900181421) Square Fish.

—Girl's Best Friend. 2011. (Maggie Brooklyn Mystery Ser.). (ENG.). 288p. (J). (gr. 3-12). pap. 7.99 *(978-1-59990-690-4(2),* 900076050, Bloomsbury USA Childrens) Bloomsbury Publishing USA.

—Secrets at the Chocolate Mansion. 2014. (Maggie Brooklyn Mystery Ser.). (ENG.). 272p. (J). (gr. 3-6). pap. 7.99 *(978-1-61963-493-0(7),* 900138595, Bloomsbury USA Childrens) Bloomsbury Publishing USA.

—Vanishing Acts. 2013. (Maggie Brooklyn Mystery Ser.). (ENG.). 256p. (J). (gr. 3-6). pap. 7.99 *(978-1-59990-981-3(2),* 900096404, Bloomsbury USA Childrens) Bloomsbury Publishing USA.

Marin, Victoria. Aiden's Waltz. 2012. 24p. pap. 15.99 *(978-1-4691-6271-3(7))* Xlibris Corp.

MariNaomi. Distant Stars: Book 3. MariNaomi, illus. 2020. (Life on Earth Ser.). (ENG., Illus.). 272p. (YA). (gr. 9-12). 29.32 *(978-1-5124-4912-9(1),* 719fa10c-28dc-4369-8938-1705d46ad2ad, Graphic Universe™) Lerner Publishing Group.

—Gravity's Pull: Book 2. MariNaomi, illus. 2019. (Life on Earth Ser.). (ENG., Illus.). 224p. (YA). (gr. 9-12). 29.32 *(978-1-5124-4911-2(3),* 548a8fb2-504e-4895-9420-fca6c9b02ba8, Graphic Universe™) Lerner Publishing Group.

Marineau, Michele. Lean Mean Machines, 1 vol. 2003. (ENG., Illus.). 128p. (J). (gr. 7-9). pap. 6.95 *(978-0-88995-230-0(2),* 78bf4573-3ccf-457b-8c3e-fc1f2ee4d79f) Red Deer Pr. CAN. Dist: Firefly Bks., Ltd.

Marino, Peter. Dough Boy. 2005. (ENG.). 176p. (J). (gr. 7-12). 17.95 *(978-0-8234-1873-2(1))* Holiday Hse., Inc.

Mariolle, Mathieu. Changing Moon. rev. ed. 2010. pap. 56.72 *(978-0-7613-6953-0(8))* Lerner Publishing Group.

Mariz, Rae. The Unidentified. 2012. (ENG.). 304p. (YA). (gr. 8). pap. 8.99 *(978-0-06-180209-6(3),* Balzer & Bray) HarperCollins Pubs.

Markey, Kevin. Wall Ball. 2011. (ENG.). 208p. (J). (gr. 3-7). pap. 7.99 *(978-0-06-115223-8(4),* HarperCollins) HarperCollins Pubs.

Markus, Deborah. The Letting Go. 2018. (ENG.). 360p. (YA). (gr. 9-9). 16.99 *(978-1-5107-3405-0(8),* Sky Pony Pr.) Skyhorse Publishing Co., Inc.

Marlow, Herb. The Classroom Vandal. 2003. (J). 19.95 *(978-1-893595-36-1(6))* Four Seasons Bks., Inc.

Marmon, Jim. Alexander Barnaby Meadowlark. 2007. 132p. per. 19.95 *(978-1-4241-7662-5(X))* America Star Bks.

Marr Osb, Andrew. From Beyond to Here: Merendael's Gift & Other Stories. 2012. 320p. (gr. 4-6). 29.95 *(978-1-4759-3460-1(2))*; pap. 19.95 *(978-1-4759-3458-8(0))* iUniverse, Inc.

Marsden, Carolyn. The Quail Club. 2006. (ENG.). 138p. (J). (gr. 2-4). 18.69 *(978-0-7636-2635-8(X))* Candlewick Pr.

Marsh, Carole. Adventure to the Eight Wonders of the World. 2009. (Carole Marsh's Fantasy Field Trips Ser.). (ENG., Illus.). 118p. (J). (gr. 2-4). 18.69 *(978-0-635-06335-9(2))* Gallopade International.

—Adventure to the Planet Mars! 2007. (Field Trips (Gallopade International) Ser.). (Illus.). 114p. (J). (gr. 4-9). per. 5.99 *(978-0-635-06336-6(0))* Gallopade International.

Marsh, Robert. Monster & Me, Set. Percival, Tom, illus. Incl. Monster Moneymaker. (ENG., Illus.). 40p. (J). (gr. 2-5). 2010. lib. bdg. 23.99 *(978-1-4342-1891-9(0),* 102350, Stone Arch Bks.); (Monster & Me Ser.). (ENG.). Illus.). 40p. 2010. 71.97 o.p. *(978-1-4342-2671-6(9),* 15368, Stone Arch Bks.) Capstone.

—Monster Moneymaker, 1 vol. Percival, Tom, illus. 2010. (Monster & Me Ser.). (ENG.). 40p. (J). (gr. 2-5). lib. bdg. 23.99 *(978-1-4342-1891-9(0),* 102350, Stone Arch Bks.) Capstone.

Marsh, Sarah Glenn. Diabetes Doesn't Stop Maddie! Di Gravio, Maria Luisa, illus. 2020. (ENG.). 32p. (J). (gr. -1-3). 16.99 *(978-0-8075-4703-8(4),* 807547034) Whitman, Albert & Co.

Marshall, Jane Garrett. The Christmas Tree That Cried. Tomasek, Dean, illus. 2013. 106p. pap. 24.99 *(978-0-9896247-0-1(6))* WRB Pub.

Marshall, Rita. I Still Hate to Read! Delessert, Etienne, illus. 2008. (ENG.). 32p. (J). (gr. 1-3). 19.95 *(978-1-56846-174-8(7),* 22048, Creative Editions) Creative Co., The.

Marshall, Stacey A. Captain Courage & the Fear-Squishing Shoes. Morse, Michelle, illus. 2012. 16p. pap. 9.95 *(978-1-61633-319-5(7))* Guardian Angel Publishing, Inc.

Marston, Carrie. Catch Me If You Can. 2012. 82p. (gr. 10-12). pap. 9.95 *(978-1-4497-6706-8(0),* WestBow Pr.) Author Solutions, LLC.

Martin, Ann M. Abby's un-Valentine (the Baby-Sitters Club #127) A Geronimo Stilton Adventure. 2011. (Thea Stilton Ser.: 127). (ENG.). 160p. (J). (gr. 2-5). E-Book 8.99 *(978-0-545-87475-5(0),* Scholastic Paperbacks) Scholastic, Inc.

—Belle Teal. 2004. (Illus.). 214p. (gr. 4-7). 17.00 *(978-0-7569-2929-9(6))* Perfection Learning Corp.

—Here Today. 2005. 308p. (gr. 5-9). 18.00 *(978-0-7569-5104-7(6))* Perfection Learning Corp.

—Mallory & the Dream Horse (the Baby-Sitters Club #54) 2022. (Hombre Mosca Presenta Ser.: 54). (ENG.). 160p. (J). (gr. k-2). E-Book 4.99 *(978-0-545-69047-8(1))* Scholastic, Inc.

—The Secret Book Club, 5. 2008. (Main Street Ser.: 5). (ENG., Illus.). 212p. (J). (gr. 4-6). 21.19 *(978-0-439-86883-9(1))* Scholastic, Inc.

—September Surprises, 6. 2008. (Main Street Ser.: 6). (ENG.). 208p. (J). (gr. 4-6). pap. 21.19 *(978-0-439-86884-6(X))* Scholastic, Inc.

Martin, Bill, Jr., et al. Kitty Cat, Kitty Cat, Are You Going to School?, 0 vols. Bryant, Laura J., illus. 2013. (ENG.). 24p. (J). (gr. -1-2). 16.99 *(978-1-4778-1722-3(0),* 9781477817223, Two Lions) Amazon Publishing.

Martin, C. K. Kelly. The Lighter Side of Life & Death. 2010. (YA). pap. *(978-0-375-84590-1(9))* Random Hse. Children's Bks.

Martin Ed.D., Pamela. Include Me. 2013. 48p. pap. *(978-1-4602-2643-8(7))* FriesenPress.

Martin, R. T. Mind over Matter. 2018. (Superhuman Ser.). (ENG.). 112p. (YA). (gr. 6-12). pap. 7.99 *(978-1-5415-1048-7(8),* 331f58f1-f78d-4f1c-a9b5-5e35e012222a); lib. bdg. 25.32 *(978-1-5124-9832-5(7),* ea451f11-ccb2-4291-8564-1427489277a9) Lerner Publishing Group. (Darby Creek).

—Stronghold. 2018. (Superhuman Ser.). (ENG.). 104p. (YA). (gr. 6-12). 25.32 *(978-1-5124-9830-1(0),* e6c75144-c1fd-4055-a108-e7b63de78922, Darby Creek) Lerner Publishing Group.

—Take to the Skies. 2018. (Superhuman Ser.). (ENG.). 104p. (YA). (gr. 6-12). pap. 7.99 *(978-1-5415-1053-1(4),* 2afc049f-c6c5-45da-99dd-b716f130bb24); lib. bdg. 25.32 *(978-1-5124-9827-1(0),* 2c13bd57-4f4d-4fb8-99a4-42417aef6a3e) Lerner Publishing Group. (Darby Creek).

—The Turnaround. 2018. (Mason Falls Mysteries Ser.). (ENG.). 104p. (YA). (gr. 6-12). pap. 7.99 *(978-1-5415-0119-5(5),* 9d659811-f39e-4341-9e00-79462b3015ea); 25.32 *(978-1-5415-0111-9(X),* 2b1e3214-da27-43ce-875f-e57fa7bb3dbd) Lerner Publishing Group. (Darby Creek).

Martin, Sheila. Muddy Water. 2005. pap. 16.95 *(978-1-4137-8551-7(4))* PublishAmerica, Inc.

Martinez, Angel. The Story of Natalie: Natalie gets prepare for a day of School. 2011. 28p. pap. 13.95 *(978-1-4633-0761-5(6))* Palibrio.

Martínez, Arturo O. & Martínez, Arturo O. Pedrito's World. 2007. (ENG., Illus.). 160p. (J). (gr. 4-6). pap. 16.95 *(978-0-89672-600-0(2),* P171756) Texas Tech Univ. Pr.

Martinez, Claudia Guadalupe. The Smell of Old Lady Perfume, 1 vol. 2011. (ENG., Illus.). 256p. (J). (gr. 6-8). pap. 9.95 *(978-1-933693-88-0(6),* 23353382, Cinco Puntos Press) Lee & Low Bks., Inc.

Martinez, Jessica. The Space Between Us. (ENG., (YA). (gr. 9). 2013. Illus.). 416p. pap. 9.99 *(978-1-4424-2056-4(1))* 2012. 400p. 16.99 *(978-1-4424-2055-7(3))* Simon Pulse. (Simon Pulse).

Marty, Joyce D. I Was in School When...,Dane's Great Day. 2004. (J). 17.00 *(978-0-9753992-0-0(9))* Martin Publishing.

Mary-Todd, Jonathan. Lock-In. 2011. (Night Fall (tm) Ser.). (ENG.). 112p. (YA). (gr. 6-12). lib. bdg. 27.99 *(978-0-7613-7743-6(3),* 428ca348-d51c-42f6-9130-f956c338417f, Darby Creek) Lerner Publishing Group.

Marzullo, Re. Sped. 2013. 214p. pap. 9.99 *(978-0-9889618-0-7(6))* Sauvignon Pr.

Masciola, Carol. The Yearbook. 2015. (ENG.). 224p. (YA). 17.99 *(978-1-4405-8897-6(X),* Simon Pulse) Simon Pulse.

Mason, Charlene. William's First Day of Preschool. 2012. 24p. pap. 24.95 *(978-1-4626-7471-8(2))* America Star Bks.

Mason, Jane B. & Hines-Stephens, Sarah. Let Sleeping Dogs Spy. Phillips, Craig, illus. 2012. 91p. (J). pap. *(978-0-545-37470-5(7))* Scholastic, Inc.

Mason, Richard. The Red Scarf: A Country Boy's Christmas Story. 2011. (ENG.). 155p. (J). (gr. 3-7). pap. 11.95 *(978-0-87483-954-8(8))* August Hse. Pubs., Inc.

Mason, Simon. Kid Alone: a Garvie Smith Mystery: A Garvie Smith Mystery. 2017. (ENG.). 384p. (YA). (gr. 9). 18.99 *(978-1-338-03649-7(1))* Scholastic, Inc.

Mass, Wendy. Heaven Looks a Lot Like the Mall. 2008. (ENG.). 256p. (J). (gr. 7-17). pap. 14.99 *(978-0-316-05850-6(5))* Little, Brown Bks. for Young Readers.

S

—Leap Day. 2006. (ENG.). 208p. (YA). (gr. 7-17). per. 13.99 *(978-0-316-05828-5(9))* Little, Brown Bks. for Young Readers.

—A Mango-Shaped Space. 2005. (ENG.). 240p. (YA). (gr. 5-8). per. 8.99 *(978-0-316-05825-4(4))* Little, Brown Bks. for Young Readers.

Massaro, Michael. Tony Towne & the Amazing Brain. 2011. (ENG.). 248p. pap. 9.55 *(978-1-4565-2044-1(X))* CreateSpace Independent Publishing Platform.

Massey, Carol. Not a Friend. 2005. 79p. pap. 9.95 *(978-0-7414-2319-1(7))* Infinity Publishing.

Masterson, Josephine. Henry's Hamster Goes to School, 1 vol. 2015. (Rosen REAL Readers: STEM & STEAM Collection). (ENG.). 8p. (gr. k-1). pap. 5.46 *(978-1-4994-9595-9(1),* c240ff1d-ae5b-4a64-b0f3-8fb9a8362bc2, Rosen Classroom) Rosen Publishing Group, Inc., The.

Matharu, Taran. The Novice. 2016. (Summoner Trilogy: Bk. 1). (ENG.). (YA). (gr. 7-12). lib. bdg. 22.10 *(978-0-606-39884-8(8))* Turtleback.

—The Novice: Summoner: Book One. 2015. (Summoner Trilogy Ser.: 1). (ENG.). 368p. (YA). (gr. 7). 19.99 *(978-1-250-06712-8(X),* 900146166) Feiwel & Friends.

—The Novice: Summoner: Book One. 2016. (Summoner Trilogy Ser.: 1). (ENG.). 384p. (YA). pap. 11.99 *(978-1-250-08005-9(3),* 900154654) Square Fish.

Matheis, Mickie. Save the School Bus! (PAW Patrol) Petrossi, Fabrizio, illus. 2017. (Little Golden Book Ser.). (ENG.). 24p. (J). (-k). 5.99 *(978-1-5247-1665-3(0),* Golden Bks.) Random Hse. Children's Bks.

Mathieu, Jennifer. Moxie: A Novel. 2018. (ENG.). 352p. (YA). pap. 10.99 *(978-1-250-10426-7(2),* 900163699) Square Fish.

Matranga, Cindy. It Never Rains in Sunny California. 2010. 32p. pap. 12.99 *(978-1-4389-4816-4(6))* AuthorHouse.

Matthews, Ian. Albert the Big Eyed Squirrel. 2011. 25p. (J). pap. 15.95 *(978-1-4327-5904-9(3))* Outskirts Pr., Inc.

Maurer, Shari. Change of Heart. 2010. 290p. (YA). 16.95 *(978-1-934813-36-2(2))* Westside Bks.

May, Eleanor. Albert Starts School. 2018. (Mouse Math Ser.). (ENG.). 32p. (J). (gr. -1-1). lib. bdg. 34.28 *(978-1-4896-8311-3(9),* AV2 by Weigl) Weigl Pubs., Inc.

—The Bay School Blogger. 2008. pap. 34.95 *(978-1-58013-772-0(5))* Astra Publishing Hse.

—Mac & Cheese, Pleeeeeeze! 2008. pap. 34.95 *(978-1-58013-780-5(6))* Astra Publishing Hse.

May, J. E. Louis' School Days. 2007. 252p. 97.99 *(978-1-4280-7719-5(7));* per. 90.99 *(978-1-4280-7714-0(6))* IndyPublish.com.

May, Kyla. Coco: My Delicious Life. 2013. (Lotus Lane Ser.: 2). lib. bdg. 14.75 *(978-0-606-31978-2(6))* Turtleback.

—Kiki: My Stylish Life. 2013. (Lotus Lane Ser.: 1). lib. bdg. 14.75 *(978-0-606-31977-5(8))* Turtleback.

—Mika: My New Life. 2013. (Lotus Lane Ser.: 4). lib. bdg. 14.75 *(978-0-606-32365-9(1))* Turtleback.

Mayer, Mercer. Little Critter: Exploring the Great Outdoors. Mayer, Mercer, illus. 2019. (My First I Can Read Ser.). (ENG., Illus.). 32p. (J). (gr. -1-3). 16.99 *(978-0-06-243145-5(5));* pap. 4.99 *(978-0-06-243144-8(7))* HarperCollins Pubs. (HarperCollins).

—Little Critter: Just Pick Us, Please! Mayer, Mercer, illus. 2017. (My First I Can Read Ser.). (ENG., Illus.). 32p. (J). (gr. -1-3). 16.99 *(978-0-06-243143-1(9));* pap. 4.99 *(978-0-06-243142-4(0))* HarperCollins Pubs. (HarperCollins).

Mayer, Shannon & Breene, K. F. Shadowspell Academy: the Culling Trials. 2019. 576p. (YA). (gr. 9-12). 16.99 *(978-1-5107-5510-9(1),* Sky Pony Pr.) Skyhorse Publishing Co., Inc.

Mayhall, Robin. He Loves Me, He Loves Me Not: Book 7, No. 7. Irwin, Jane Elizabeth et al, illus. 2013. (My Boyfriend Is a Monster Ser.: 7). (ENG.). 128p. (YA). (gr. 7-12). lib. bdg. 29.32 *(978-0-7613-6005-6(0),* ae79c15f-787b-43fa-9d0a-94255bbea1be, Graphic Universe™) Lerner Publishing Group.

Maynard, Joyce. The Cloud Chamber. 2006. (ENG.). 288p. (YA). (gr. 7-7). pap. 13.99 *(978-1-4169-2699-3(2),* Simon Pulse) Simon Pulse.

Mazer, Anne. Good Things Come in Small Packages. 2003. (Amazing Days of Abby Hayes Ser.: Bk. 12). (Illus.). 101p. (J). (gr. 4-7). 12.65 *(978-0-7569-3935-9(6))* Perfection Learning Corp.

—It's Music to My Ears. 2005. (Amazing Days of Abby Hayes Ser.). (Illus.). 110p. (J). (gr. 3-7). 12.65 *(978-0-7569-5910-4(1))* Perfection Learning Corp.

—Now You See It, Now You Don't. 2005. (Amazing Days of Abby Hayes Ser.: Bk. 15). (Illus.). 126p. (J). (gr. 4-7). 12.65 *(978-0-7569-5932-6(2))* Perfection Learning Corp.

—Some Things Never Change. 2004. (Amazing Days of Abby Hayes Ser.: Bk. 13). (Illus.). 101p. (J). (gr. 4-7). 12.65 *(978-0-7569-5302-7(2))* Perfection Learning Corp.

—That's the Way the Cookie Crumbles. 2005. (Amazing Days of Abby Hayes Ser.: Bk. 16). (Illus.). 119p. (J). (gr. 3-7). 12.65 *(978-0-7569-6480-1(6))* Perfection Learning Corp.

Mazer, Norma Fox. Crazy Fish. 2007. (ENG., Illus.). 160p. (J). (gr. 3-7). pap. 11.95 *(978-0-15-206373-3(0),* 1199084, Clarion Bks.) HarperCollins Pubs.

—Ten Ways to Make My Sister Disappear. (ENG.). 160p. (J). (gr. 4-6). 2012. 21.19 *(978-0-439-83984-6(X))* 2007. 16.99 *(978-0-439-83983-9(1))* Scholastic, Inc. (Levine, Arthur A. Bks.).

—Ten Ways to Make My Sister Disappear. l.t. ed. 2008. (Thorndike Literacy Bridge Ser.). 207p. (J). (gr. 4-7). 22.95 *(978-1-4104-0510-4(9))* Thorndike Pr.

McAnulty, Stacy. Goldie Blox Rules the School! 2017. (Goldie Blox Ser.). lib. bdg. 17.20 *(978-0-606-40256-9(X))* Turtleback.

—The Miscalculations of Lightning Girl. 2018. (Illus.). 304p. (J). (gr. 3-7). 17.99 *(978-1-5247-6757-0(3),* Random Hse. Bks. for Young Readers) Random Hse. Children's Bks.

McBrier, Page. Beatrice's Goat. Lohstoeter, Lori, illus. 2004. (ENG.). 40p. (J). (gr. -1-3). reprint ed. 8.99 *(978-0-689-86990-7(8),* Aladdin) Simon & Schuster Children's Publishing.

McCafferty, Megan. Jessica Darling's It List: The (Totally Not) Guaranteed Guide to Popularity, Prettiness & Perfection. 2014. (Jessica Darling's It List Ser.: 1). (ENG.). 240p. (J). (gr. 3-7). pap. 14.99 *(978-0-316-24498-5(8),* Poppy) Little, Brown Bks. for Young Readers.

—Jessica Darling's It List 2: The (Totally Not) Guaranteed Guide to Friends, Foes & Faux Friends. 2015. (Jessica Darling's It List Ser.: 2). (ENG.). 208p. (J). (gr. 3-7). pap. 12.99 *(978-0-316-24503-6(8),* Poppy) Little, Brown Bks. for Young Readers.

—Jessica Darling's It List 3: The (Totally Not) Guaranteed Guide to Stressing, Obsessing & Second-Guessing. 2015. (Jessica Darling's It List Ser.: 3). (ENG.). 224p. (J). (gr. 3-7). 30.99 *(978-0-316-33324-5(7),* Poppy) Little, Brown Bks. for Young Readers.

McCarthy, Jenna & Evans, Carolyn. Maggie Malone Makes a Splash. 2015. (Maggie Malone Ser.: 3). (ENG.). 192p. (J). (gr. 4-7). pap. 8.99 *(978-1-4022-9312-2(7))* Sourcebooks, Inc.

McClintock, Norah. Dooley Takes the Fall, 1 vol. 2007. (Dooley Ser.). (ENG.). 256p. (YA). (gr. 7-12). per. 12.95 *(978-0-88995-403-8(8),* 4f86ceaa-f9c8-4d68-a820-8fb4039fda28) Trifolium Bks., Inc. CAN. Dist: Firefly Bks., Ltd.

—From Above, 1 vol. 2016. (Riley Donovan Ser.: 2). (ENG.). 240p. (YA). (gr. 8-12). pap. 10.95 *(978-1-4598-0933-8(5))* Orca Bk. Pubs. USA.

—My Side, 1 vol. 2013. (Orca Soundings Ser.). (ENG.). 128p. (YA). (gr. 8-12). pap. 9.95 *(978-1-4598-0511-8(9))* Orca Bk. Pubs. USA.

—Out of Tune, 1 vol. 2017. (Riley Donovan Ser.: 3). (ENG.). 240p. (YA). (gr. 8-12). pap. 10.95 *(978-1-4598-1465-3(7))* Orca Bk. Pubs. USA.

McCombie, Karen. My Big (Strange) Happy Family. Monks, Lydia, illus. 2009. (J). pap. *(978-0-385-73597-1(9),* Yearling) Random Hse. Children's Bks.

McConnell, Edith J. Their Times. 2004. 44p. (J). per. 11.66 *(978-1-4116-1370-6(8))* Lulu Pr., Inc.

McConville, Alexandra. The Adventures of Sass-O-Frask: A Tale of Kindness. 2012. 32p. pap. 19.99 *(978-1-4772-6006-7(4))* AuthorHouse.

McCormick, Wilfred. The Three-Two Pitch: A Bronc Burnett Story. 2011. 192p. 42.95 *(978-1-258-10008-7(8))* Literary Licensing, LLC.

McCourt, Lisa. Ready for Kindergarten, Stinky Face? Moore, Cyd, illus. 2010. (Scholastic Reader: Level 1 Ser.). (ENG.). 32p. (J). (gr. -1-1). 16.19 *(978-0-545-11518-6(3))* Scholastic, Inc.

McCoy, Mary. I, Claudia. 2018. (ENG.). 424p. (YA). (gr. 8-12). 18.99 *(978-1-5124-4846-7(X),* b20fa032-6e7b-4832-b19e-6ba725ea062f, Carolrhoda Lab™) Lerner Publishing Group.

McCranie, Stephen. Mal & Chad: the Biggest, Bestest Time Ever! McCranie, Stephen, illus. 2011. (Mal & Chad Ser.: 1). (Illus.). 224p. (J). (gr. 3-7). 12.99 *(978-0-399-25221-1(5),* Philomel Bks.) Penguin Young Readers Group.

Mccroary, Greg. Mia. 2008. (ENG., Illus.). 1p. (J). 6.95 *(978-1-74110-636-7(2))* New Holland Pubs. Pty. Ltd. AUS. Dist: Tuttle Publishing.

McCullough, Dicy. Tired of School. 2011. 28p. pap. 15.99 *(978-1-4628-9229-7(9))* Xlibris Corp.

McCully, Emily Arnold. My Heart Glow: Alice Cogswell, Thomas Gallaudet, & the Birth of American Sign Language. McCully, Emily Arnold, illus. 2008. (ENG., Illus.). 40p. (gr. 1-4). 15.99 *(978-1-4231-0028-7(X))* Hyperion Pr.

—School. McCully, Emily Arnold, illus. 2005. (Illus.). 32p. (J). lib. bdg. 16.89 *(978-0-06-623857-9(9))* HarperCollins Pubs.

McCune, Susan. Mr. Morgan Saves the Day, 1 vol., 1. 2015. (Rosen REAL Readers: Social Studies Nonfiction / Fiction: Myself, My Community, My World Ser.). (ENG.). 12p. (J). (gr. k-1). pap. 6.33 *(978-1-5081-1940-1(6),* 4a21a5b9-9a93-4494-94f3-08feb03edad3, Rosen Classroom) Rosen Publishing Group, Inc., The.

McDaniel, Lurlene. Hit & Run. 2013. (ENG.). 192p. (YA). (gr. 7). pap. 8.99 *(978-0-385-74381-5(5),* Ember) Random Hse. Children's Bks.

—Letting Go of Lisa. 2007. (ENG.). 192p. (YA). (gr. 7-12). mass mkt. 6.99 *(978-0-440-23868-3(4),* Laurel Leaf) Random Hse. Children's Bks.

—Prey. (ENG.). 208p. (YA). 2010. (gr. 7). mass mkt. 7.99 *(978-0-440-24015-0(8),* Laurel Leaf) 2008. (gr. 9-12). lib. bdg. 21.19 *(978-0-385-90457-5(6),* Delacorte Pr.) Random Hse. Children's Bks.

—Red Heart Tattoo. 2013. (ENG.). 224p. (YA). (gr. 7). pap. 8.99 *(978-0-440-24019-8(0),* Ember) Random Hse. Children's Bks.

McDonald, Abby. The Anti-Prom. (ENG., Illus.). 288p. (YA). (gr. 9). 2012. pap. 7.99 *(978-0-7636-5847-2(2))* 2011. 16.99 *(978-0-7636-4956-2(2))* Candlewick Pr.

—Sophomore Switch. 2010. (ENG., Illus.). 304p. (YA). (gr. 9). pap. 8.99 *(978-0-7636-4774-2(8))* Candlewick Pr.

Mcdonald, Megan. Around the World in 8 1/2 Days. 2007. (Judy Moody Ser.: 7). (SPA.). (J). 1.25 *(978-1-4281-3376-1(3))* Recorded Bks., Inc.

McDonald, Megan. Beetle Mcgrady Eats Bugs! Manning, Jane, illus. 2005. (ENG.). 32p. (J). (gr. k-5). 17.99 *(978-0-06-001354-7(0),* Greenwillow Bks.) HarperCollins Pubs.

Mcdonald, Megan. The Doctor Is In! 2010. (Judy Moody Ser.: 5). lib. bdg. 16.00 *(978-0-606-12343-3(1))* Turtleback.

McDonald, Megan. It's Picture Day Today! Tillotson, Katherine, illus. 2009. (ENG.). 36p. (J). (gr. -1-3). 16.99 *(978-1-4169-2434-0(5),* Atheneum/Richard Jackson Bks.) Simon & Schuster Children's Publishing.

—Judy Moody. Reynolds, Peter H., illus. 2010. (Judy Moody Ser.: 1). (ENG.). 160p. (J). (gr. 1-4). 16.99 *(978-0-7636-4850-3(7))* Candlewick Pr.

Mcdonald, Megan. Judy Moody. 2010. (Judy Moody Ser.: 1). lib. bdg. 16.00 *(978-0-606-12330-3(X))* Turtleback.

McDonald, Megan. Judy Moody & Friends: Judy Moody, Tooth Fairy. Madrid, Erwin, illus. 2017. (Judy Moody & Friends Ser.: 9). (ENG.). 64p. (J). (gr. -1-1). pap. 5.99 *(978-0-7636-9168-4(2))* Candlewick Pr.

—Judy Moody & Stink: the Holly Joliday. Reynolds, Peter H., illus. 2008. (Judy Moody & Stink Ser.: 1). (ENG.). 96p. (J). (gr. k-3). pap. 7.99 *(978-0-7636-4113-9(8))* Candlewick Pr.

—Judy Moody & the Bad Luck Charm. Reynolds, Peter H., illus. 2018. (Judy Moody Ser.: 11). (ENG.). 176p. (J). (gr. 1-4). pap. 5.99 *(978-1-5362-0080-5(8))* Candlewick Pr.

Mcdonald, Megan. Judy Moody & the Bad Luck Charm. 2018. (Judy Moody Ser.: 11). lib. bdg. 16.00 *(978-0-606-41201-8(8))* Turtleback.

McDonald, Megan. Judy Moody: Around the World in 8 1/2 Days. Reynolds, Peter H., illus. 2010. (Judy Moody Ser.: 7). (ENG.). 176p. (J). (gr. 1-4). 15.99 *(978-0-7636-4864-0(7))* Candlewick Pr.

—The Judy Moody Double-Rare Collection: Books 4-6, 3 vols. Reynolds, Peter H., illus. 2019. (Judy Moody Ser.). (ENG.). 496p. (J). (gr. 1-4). pap. 17.97 *(978-1-5362-0951-8(1))* Candlewick Pr.

Mcdonald, Megan. Judy Moody, M. D. Reynolds, Peter H., illus. 2010. (Judy Moody Ser.: 5). (ENG.). 176p. (J). (gr. 1-4). 15.99 *(978-0-7636-4862-6(0))* Candlewick Pr.

—Judy Moody Saves the World! Reynolds, Peter H., illus. 2004. (Judy Moody Ser.: Bk. 3). 144p. (J). (gr. 1-5). 13.65 *(978-0-7569-2588-8(6))* Perfection Learning Corp.

McDonald, Megan. Judy Moody Saves the World! Reynolds, Peter H., illus. 2010. (Judy Moody Ser.: 3). (ENG.). 160p. (J). (gr. 1-4). 16.99 *(978-0-7636-4860-2(4))* Candlewick Pr.

Mcdonald, Megan. Judy Moody Saves the World! 2010. (Judy Moody Ser.: 3). 144p. lib. bdg. 16.00 *(978-0-606-12340-2(7))* Turtleback.

—Solar System Superhero. Reynolds, Peter H., illus. 2012. (Stink Ser.: No. 2). (ENG.). 144p. (J). (gr. 1-5). 31.36 *(978-1-59961-197-6(X),* 13838, Chapter Bks.) Spotlight.

—Solar System Superhero. 2013. (Stink Ser.: 5). lib. bdg. 14.75 *(978-0-606-31591-3(8))* Turtleback.

—Stink. 2013. (Stink Ser.: 1). lib. bdg. 14.75 *(978-0-606-31587-6(X))* Turtleback.

—Stink: The Incredible Shrinking Kid. Reynolds, Peter H., illus. 2010. (Stink Ser.: No. 1). (ENG.). 112p. (J). (gr. 1-5). 31.36 *(978-1-59961-686-5(6),* 13833, Chapter Bks.) Spotlight.

McDonald, Megan. Stink: The Incredible Shrinking Kid. Reynolds, Peter H., illus. 2013. (Stink Ser.: 1). (ENG.). 112p. (J). (gr. 1-4). 14.99 *(978-0-7636-6388-9(3))* Candlewick Pr.

Mcdonald, Megan. Stink & the Attack of the Slime Mold. Reynolds, Peter H., illus. 2019. (Stink Ser.). (ENG.). 136p. (J). (gr. 1-5). lib. bdg. 31.36 *(978-1-5321-4330-4(3),* 31860, Chapter Bks.) Spotlight.

McDonald, Megan. Stink & the Attack of the Slime Mold. Reynolds, Peter H., illus. 2016. (Stink Ser.: 10). (ENG.). 144p. (J). (gr. 1-4). 12.99 *(978-0-7636-5554-9(6))* Candlewick Pr.

Mcdonald, Megan. Stink & the Attack of the Slime Mold. Reynolds, Peter H., illus. 2017. (Stink Ser.: 10). (ENG.). (J). (gr. 1-4). lib. bdg. 14.75 *(978-0-606-39836-7(8))* Turtleback.

—Stink & the Incredible Super-Galactic Jawbreaker. Reynolds, Peter H., illus. 2010. (Stink Ser.: No. 2). (ENG.). 128p. (J). (gr. 1-5). 31.36 *(978-1-59961-684-1(X),* 13831, Chapter Bks.) Spotlight.

—Stink & the Incredible Super-Galactic Jawbreaker. 2013. (Stink Ser.: 2). lib. bdg. 14.75 *(978-0-606-31588-3(8))* Turtleback.

McDonald, Megan. Stink & the Incredible Super-Galactic Jawbreaker, Bk. 2. Reynolds, Peter H., illus. 2013. (Stink Ser.: 2). (ENG.). 128p. (J). (gr. 1-4). 14.99 *(978-0-7636-6389-6(1))* Candlewick Pr.

Mcdonald, Megan. Stink & the Ultimate Thumb-Wrestling Smackdown, 1 vol. Reynolds, Peter H., illus. 2012. (Stink Ser.: No. 2). (ENG.). 144p. (J). (gr. 1-5). 31.36 *(978-1-59961-194-5(5),* 13835, Chapter Bks.) Spotlight.

McDonald, Megan. Stink: Solar System Superhero, Bk. 5. Reynolds, Peter H., illus. 2013. (Stink Ser.: 5). (ENG.). 128p. (J). (gr. 1-4). 14.99 *(978-0-7636-6392-6(1))* Candlewick Pr.

—Stink: the Ultimate Thumb-Wrestling Smackdown, Bk. 6. Reynolds, Peter H., illus. 2013. (Stink Ser.: 6). (ENG.). 144p. (J). (gr. 1-4). 15.99 *(978-0-7636-6393-3(X))* Candlewick Pr.

McElligott, Matthew & Tuxbury, Larry David. Benjamin Franklinstein Lives!, 1. McElligott, Matthew, illus. 2011. (Benjamin Franklinstein Ser.: 1). (ENG., Illus.). 128p. (J). (gr. 4-6). 22.44 *(978-0-399-25229-7(0))* Penguin Young Readers Group.

Mcgee, Ken. Forever. 2013. 224p. pap. 15.49 *(978-1-62509-504-6(X))* Salem Author Services.

Mcghee, Alison. Countdown to Kindergarten. Bliss, Harry, illus. pap. incl. audio compact disk *(978-1-59112-469-6(7));* pap. 39.95 incl. audio *(978-1-59112-929-5(X));* 2004. (J). 28.95 incl. audio compact disk *(978-1-59112-928-8(1))* Live Oak Media.

McGhee, Alison. Countdown to Kindergarten: A Kindergarten Readiness Book for Kids. Bliss, Harry, illus. 2006. (ENG.). 32p. (J). (gr. -1-3). reprint ed. pap. 8.99 *(978-0-15-205586-8(X),* 1196800, Clarion Bks.) HarperCollins Pubs.

Mcghee, Alison. Mrs. Watson Wants Your Teeth. Bliss, Harry, illus. 2007. 32p. (J). reprint ed. 16.00 *(978-1-4223-6777-3(0))* DIANE Publishing Co.

—Mrs. Watson Wants Your Teeth. Bliss, Harry, illus. unabr. ed. 2007. (Picture Book Readalong Ser.). (J). (gr. -1-2). 28.95 incl. audio compact disk *(978-1-59519-902-7(0))* Live Oak Media.

McGhee, Katie Mariah. The Case of the Missing Chimpanzee from Classroom C2. McGhee, Katie Mariah & Herrera, Aaron Jeremiah, illus. 2012. 28p. 24.95 *(978-1-4560-0039-4(X))* America Star Bks.

McGinnis, Bsn. Call My Mom!! 2013. 24p. pap. 14.99 *(978-1-4669-5595-0(3))* Trafford Publishing.

McGinty, Alice B. Eliza's Kindergarten Pet, 0 vols. Speir, Nancy, illus. 2012. (ENG.). 32p. (J). (gr. -1-1). 15.99 *(978-0-7614-5702-2(X),* 9780761457022, Two Lions) Amazon Publishing.

—Eliza's Kindergarten Surprise, 0 vols. Speir, Nancy, illus. 2013. (ENG.). 34p. (J). (gr. -1-1). pap. 9.99 *(978-1-4778-1683-7(6),* 9781477816837, Two Lions) Amazon Publishing.

McGovern, DeeDee. Zachary, the Adventure Boy!, 1 vol. 2009. 88p. pap. 19.95 *(978-1-4489-8249-3(9))* America Star Bks.

McGowan, Angel. Stomp Out the Bullying! 2011. (ENG.). 28p. (J). pap. 14.95 *(978-1-4327-7994-8(X))* Outskirts Pr., Inc.

McGowan, Anthony. The Knife That Killed Me. 2011. (ENG.). 224p. (YA). (gr. 9). pap. 8.99 *(978-0-375-85516-0(5),* Ember) Random Hse. Children's Bks.

McGowan, Joby. Bossy Blanc. 2011. 20p. pap. 24.95 *(978-1-4626-2908-4(3))* America Star Bks.

McGroary, Mary Beth. My Teacher Hates Me. 2012. 24p. 24.95 *(978-1-4626-6012-4(6))* America Star Bks.

McGugan, Jim. Josepha: A Prairie Boy's Story, 1 vol. Kimber, Murray, illus. 2012. (ENG.). 32p. (J). (gr. 2-5). pap. 9.95 *(978-0-88995-461-8(5),* 0c9fb147-13e3-4ba8-84bb-e00e50287726) Trifolium Bks., Inc. CAN. Dist: Firefly Bks., Ltd.

McKay, Hilary. Cold Enough for Snow. Melling, David, tr. Melling, David, illus. 2003. (Pudding Bag School Ser.: Bk. 2). (ENG.). 144p. (J). pap. *(978-0-340-87750-0(2),* Hodder Children's Books) Hachette Children's Group.

—Lulu & the Duck in the Park. 2014. (Lulu Ser.: 1). (J). lib. bdg. 16.00 *(978-0-606-41564-4(5))* Turtleback.

McKee, Rosie. Tara Takes a Vote: Gathering Data, 1 vol. 2017. (Computer Science for the Real World Ser.). (ENG.). 8p. (gr. k-1). pap. *(978-1-5383-5000-3(9),* 305fb66c-92e6-462d-b651-ef2cc0346f72, Rosen Classroom) Rosen Publishing Group, Inc., The.

McKenna, K. J. Take Three Girls. 2005. 96p. pap. 10.00 *(978-1-4116-6290-2(3))* Lulu Pr., Inc.

McKenney, M. W. Roosevelt Junior High. 2008. 73p. pap. 19.95 *(978-1-60672-157-5(7))* America Star Bks.

McKenzie, C. Lee. The Princess of Las Pulgas. 2010. (ENG.). 348p. (YA). *(978-1-934813-46-1(X))* Westside Bks.

McKenzie, Sophie. In a Split Second. 2015. (ENG., Illus.). 368p. (YA). (gr. 7). 17.99 *(978-1-4814-1394-7(5))* Simon & Schuster Children's Publishing.

McKinlay, Meg. Duck for a Day. Rudge, Leila, illus. 2012. (ENG.). 96p. (J). (gr. 2-4). 12.99 *(978-0-7636-5784-0(0))* Candlewick Pr.

McKissack, Fredrick L. & McKissack, Fredrick L., Jr. Shooting Star. 2009. (ENG., Illus.). 288p. (YA). (gr. 7-18). 16.99 *(978-1-4169-4745-5(0),* Atheneum Bks. for Young Readers) Simon & Schuster Children's Publishing.

McKissack, Robert. Try Your Best. Cepeda, Joe, illus. 2004. (ENG.). 24p. (J). (gr. -1-3). pap. 4.99 *(978-0-15-205090-0(6),* 1195368, Clarion Bks.) HarperCollins Pubs.

McKissack, Robert L. Try Your Best. Cepeda, Joe, illus. 2005. (Green Light Readers Level 2 Ser.). (gr. k-2). 13.95 *(978-0-7569-5630-1(7))* Perfection Learning Corp.

McKnight, Marty. Jim Nasium Is a Basket Case. Jones, Chris B., illus. 2015. (Jim Nasium Ser.). (ENG.). 88p. (J). (gr. 2-3). pap. 5.95 *(978-1-4965-0526-2(3),* 128598, Stone Arch Bks.) Capstone.

—Jim Nasium Is a Hockey Hazard. Jones, Chris B., illus. 2015. (Jim Nasium Ser.). (ENG.). 88p. (J). (gr. 2-3). pap. 5.95 *(978-1-4965-0524-8(7),* 128596, Stone Arch Bks.) Capstone.

—Jim Nasium Is a Soccer Goofball. Jones, Chris B., illus. 2015. (Jim Nasium Ser.). (ENG.). 88p. (J). (gr. 2-3). pap. 5.95 *(978-1-4965-0525-5(5),* 128597, Stone Arch Bks.) Capstone.

McLean, Hope. Catch Us If You Can, 1. 2013. (Jewel Society Ser.: 1). (ENG.). 144p. (J). (gr. 4-6). 18.69 *(978-0-545-60762-9(0))* Scholastic, Inc.

McLellan, Gretchen Brandenburg. Mrs. Mcbee Leaves Room 3, 1 vol. Zong, Grace, illus. 2017. 32p. (J). (gr. -1-3). 16.95 *(978-1-56145-944-5(5))* Peachtree Publishing Co. Inc.

McMahon, P. J. Case of the Psychic Hamster. Manders, John, illus. 2005. 153p. (J). lib. bdg. 15.38 *(978-1-4242-0404-5(6))* Fitzgerald Bks.

McMahon, Susan. Wee Mary from Derry. 2008. 12p. pap. 24.95 *(978-1-60610-876-5(X))* America Star Bks.

McMann, Lisa. Bang. (Visions Ser.: 2). (ENG.). (YA). (gr. 9). 2014. Illus.). 272p. pap. 9.99 *(978-1-4424-6628-9(6))* 2013. 256p. 16.99 *(978-1-4424-6625-8(1))* Simon Pulse. (Simon Pulse).

—Fade. (Wake Ser.: Bk. 2). (ENG., (YA). (gr. 9-18). 2010. Illus.). 304p. pap. 11.99 *(978-1-4169-7448-2(2))* 2009. 256p. 17.99 *(978-1-4169-5358-6(2))* Simon Pulse. (Simon Pulse).

—Wake. 2008. (Wake Ser.: Bk. 1). (ENG.). 224p. (YA). (gr. 9). pap. 12.99 *(978-1-4169-7447-5(4));* 1. 17.99 *(978-1-4169-5357-9(4))* Simon Pulse. (Simon Pulse).

McMillan, Bruce. Mouse Views. 2014. 32p. pap. 7.00 *(978-1-61003-308-4(6))* Center for the Collaborative Classroom.

McMillan, Melody DeFields. Addison Addley & the Things That Aren't There, 1 vol. 2008. (Orca Young Readers Ser.). (ENG.). 96p. (J). (gr. 4-7). pap. 7.95 *(978-1-55143-949-5(2))* Orca Bk. Pubs. USA.

McMullan, Kate. Class Trip to the Cave of Doom #3, 3 vols. Basso, Bill, illus. 2003. (Dragon Slayers' Academy Ser.: 3). (ENG.). 112p. (J). (gr. 2-5). pap. 6.99 *(978-0-448-43110-9(6),* Grosset & Dunlap) Penguin Young Readers Group.

—Countdown to the Year 1000 #8. Basso, Bill, illus. 2003. (Dragon Slayers' Academy Ser.: 8). 112p. (J). (gr. 2-5). pap. 6.99 *(978-0-448-43508-4(X),* Grosset & Dunlap) Penguin Young Readers Group.

—A Fine Start Bk. 3: Meg's Prairie Diary. 2003. (My America Ser.). (ENG.). 112p. (J). 12.95 *(978-0-439-37061-5(2))* Scholastic, Inc.

—Fluffy's Happy Halloween. Smith, Mavis, illus. 2004. (Fluffy, the Classroom Guinea Pig Ser.). 40p. (J). lib. bdg. 15.00 *(978-1-59054-464-8(1))* Fitzgerald Bks.

—Help! It's Parents at DSA: Dragon Slayer's Academy 10. Basso, Bill, illus. 2004. (Dragon Slayers' Academy Ser.: 10). 112p. (J). (gr. 2-5). pap. 5.99 *(978-0-448-43220-5(X),* Grosset & Dunlap) Penguin Young Readers Group.

—The New Kid at School #1. Basso, Bill, illus. 2003. (Dragon Slayers' Academy Ser.: 1). (ENG.). 112p. (J). (gr. 2-5). mass mkt. 6.99 *(978-0-448-43108-6(4),* Grosset & Dunlap) Penguin Young Readers Group.

—One Funny Day. Alley, R. W., illus. 2012. (Pearl & Wagner Ser.: 1). 48p. (J). (gr. 1-3). pap. 4.99 *(978-0-448-45866-3(7),* Penguin Young Readers) Penguin Young Readers Group.

—Pearl & Wagner: Five Days till Summer. 2014. (Penguin Young Readers: Level 3 Ser.). lib. bdg. 13.55 *(978-0-606-35727-2(0))* Turtleback.

—Pearl & Wagner: Five Days till Summer. Alley, R. W., illus. 2014. (Pearl & Wagner Ser.: 5). 48p. (J). (gr. 1-3). pap. 4.99 *(978-0-448-48137-1(5),* Penguin Young Readers) Penguin Young Readers Group.

—Pearl & Wagner: Four Eyes. Alley, R. W., illus. 2013. (Pearl & Wagner Ser.: 4). 48p. (J). (gr. 1-3). pap. 4.99 *(978-0-448-47781-7(5),* Penguin Young Readers) Penguin Young Readers Group.

—Pearl & Wagner: Two Good Friends. Alley, R. W., illus. 2011. (Pearl & Wagner Ser.: 2). 48p. (J). (gr. 1-3). pap. 4.99 *(978-0-448-45690-4(7),* Penguin Young Readers) Penguin Young Readers Group.

—Pig Latin — Not Just for Pigs! Dragon Slayer's Academy 14. Basso, Bill, illus. 2005. (Dragon Slayers' Academy Ser.: 14).

112p. (J). (gr. 2-5). pap. 5.99 (978-0-448-43820-7(8), Grosset & Dunlap) Penguin Young Readers Group.
—Revenge of the Dragon Lady. 2005. (Dragon Slayers Academy Ser.: No. 2). (J). 28.75 (978-1-4193-1910-5(8)) Recorded Bks., Inc.
—School! Adventures at the Harvey N. Trouble Elementary School. Booth, George, illus. 2012. (ENG.). 176p. (J). (gr. 1-4). pap. 18.99 (978-0-312-55595-5(4), 900074611) Square Fish.
—Wheel of Misfortune #7. Basso, Bill, illus. 2003. (Dragon Slayers' Academy Ser.: 7). 112p. (J). (gr. 2-5). pap. 6.99 (978-0-448-43507-7(1), Grosset & Dunlap) Penguin Young Readers Group.
—97 Ways to Train a Dragon: Dragon Slayer's Academy 9. Basso, Bill, illus. 2003. (Dragon Slayers' Academy Ser.: 9). 112p. (J). (gr. 2-5). pap. 6.99 (978-0-448-43177-2(7), Grosset & Dunlap) Penguin Young Readers Group.
McMullen, Beth. Mrs. Smith's Spy School for Girls. 2018. (Mrs. Smith's Spy School for Girls Ser.: 1). (ENG., Illus.). 320p. (J). (gr. 4-8). pap. 8.99 (978-1-4814-9021-4(4), Simon & Schuster/Paula Wiseman Bks.) Simon & Schuster/Paula Wiseman Bks.
McMullen, Judy. Stephanie & the Excellent E's. 2012. (ENG.). pap. (978-1-4675-4211-1(3)) Independent Pub.
McNamara, Margaret. Butterfly Garden. 2012. (Robin Hill School Ready-To-Read Ser.). lib. bdg. 13.55 (978-0-606-23694-2(5)) Turtleback.
—Butterfly Garden: Ready-To-Read Level 1. Gordon, Mike, illus. 2012. (Robin Hill School Ser.). (ENG.). 32p. (J). (gr. -1-1). 17.99 (978-1-4424-3643-5(3)); pap. 4.99 (978-1-4424-3642-8(5)) Simon Spotlight. (Simon Spotlight).
—Class Mom: Ready-To-Read Level 1. Gordon, Mike, illus. 2009. (Robin Hill School Ser.). (ENG.). 32p. (J). (gr. -1-1). pap. 4.99 (978-1-4169-5537-5(2), Simon Spotlight) Simon Spotlight.
—Class Picture Day: Ready-To-Read Level 1. Gordon, Mike, illus. 2011. (Robin Hill School Ser.). (ENG.). 32p. (J). (gr. -1-1). 17.99 (978-1-4424-3611-4(5)); pap. 4.99 (978-1-4169-9173-1(5)) Simon Spotlight. (Simon Spotlight).
—Counting Race: Ready-To-Read Level 1. Gordon, Mike, illus. 2003. (Robin Hill School Ser.). (ENG.). 32p. (J). (gr. -1-1). pap. 4.99 (978-0-689-85539-9(7), Simon Spotlight) Simon Spotlight.
—Dad Goes to School: Ready-To-Read Level 1. Gordon, Mike, illus. 2007. (Robin Hill School Ser.). (ENG.). 32p. (J). (gr. -1-1). pap. 4.99 (978-1-4169-1541-6(9), Simon Spotlight) Simon Spotlight.
—Earth Day: Ready-To-Read Level 1. Gordon, Mike, illus. 2009. (Robin Hill School Ser.). (ENG.). 32p. (J). (gr. -1-1). pap. 4.99 (978-1-4169-5535-1(6), Simon Spotlight) Simon Spotlight.
—Election Day. Gordon, Mike, illus. 2008. (Robin Hill School Ser.). (J). (gr. -1-1). pap. 16.95 (978-1-4301-0598-5(4)) Live Oak Media.
—Fall Leaf Project: Ready-To-Read Level 1. Gordon, Mike, illus. 2006. (Robin Hill School Ser.). (ENG.). 32p. (J). (gr. -1-1). pap. 4.99 (978-1-4169-1537-9(0), Simon Spotlight) Simon Spotlight.
—The First Day of School. Gordon, Mike, illus. 2008. (Robin Hill School Ser.). (J). (gr. -1-3). pap. 16.95 (978-1-4301-0604-3(2)) Live Oak Media.
—The First Day of School: Ready-To-Read Level 1. Gordon, Mike, illus. 2005. (Robin Hill School Ser.). (ENG.). 32p. (J). (gr. -1-1). pap. 4.99 (978-0-689-86914-3(2), Simon Spotlight) Simon Spotlight.
—First-Grade Bunny. Gordon, Mike, illus. 2005. (Ready-To-Read Level 1 Ser.). (ENG.). 32p. (J). (gr. -1-1). lib. bdg. 16.19 (978-0-689-86428-5(0)) Simon & Schuster, Inc.
—First-Grade Bunny: Ready-To-Read Level 1. Gordon, Mike, illus. 2005. (Robin Hill School Ser.). (ENG.). 32p. (J). (gr. -1-1). pap. 4.99 (978-0-689-86427-8(2), Simon Spotlight) Simon Spotlight.
—The Garden Project: Ready-To-Read Level 1. Gordon, Mike, illus. 2010. (Robin Hill School Ser.). (ENG.). 32p. (J). (gr. -1-1). pap. 4.99 (978-1-4169-9171-7(9), Simon Spotlight) Simon Spotlight.
—Groundhog Day. Gordon, Mike, illus. 2005. (Robin Hill School Ser.). 32p. (J). (gr. -1-3). 11.65 (978-0-7569-7146-5(2)) Perfection Learning Corp.
—Groundhog Day: Ready-To-Read Level 1. Gordon, Mike, illus. 2006. (Robin Hill School Ser.). (ENG.). 32p. (J). (gr. -1-1). pap. 4.99 (978-1-4169-0507-3(3), Simon Spotlight) Simon Spotlight.
—Happy Graduation! Gordon, Mike, illus. 2008. (Robin Hill School Ser.). (J). (gr. -1-1). pap. 16.95 (978-1-4301-0610-4(7)) Live Oak Media.
—Happy Graduation! Ready-To-Read Level 1. Gordon, Mike, illus. 2006. (Robin Hill School Ser.). (ENG.). 32p. (J). (gr. -1-1). pap. 4.99 (978-1-4169-0509-7(X), Simon Spotlight) Simon Spotlight.
—How Many Seeds in a Pumpkin? (Mr. Tiffin's Classroom Series) Karas, G. Brian, illus. 2007. (Mr. Tiffin's Classroom Ser.). (ENG.). 40p. (J). (gr. -1-2). 17.99 (978-0-375-84014-2(1), Schwartz & Wade Bks.) Random Hse. Children's Bks.
—Martin Luther King Jr. Day. Gordon, Mike, illus. 2007. (Ready-To-Read Level 1 Ser.). (ENG.). 32p. (J). (gr. -1-1). lib. bdg. 17.44 (978-1-4169-3495-0(2)) Simon & Schuster, Inc.
—Martin Luther King Jr. Day: Ready-To-Read Level 1. Gordon, Mike, illus. 2007. (Robin Hill School Ser.). (ENG.). 32p. (J). (gr. -1-1). pap. 4.99 (978-1-4169-3494-3(4), Simon Spotlight) Simon Spotlight.
—One Hundred Days (Plus One) Gordon, Mike, illus. 2008. (Robin Hill School Ser.). (J). (gr. -1-3). pap. 16.95 (978-1-4301-0616-6(6)) Live Oak Media.
—One Hundred Days (Plus One) Gordon, Mike, illus. 2003. (Ready-to-Read Robin Hill School Ser.). 32p. (J). (gr. -1-3). 11.65 (978-0-7569-1805-7(7)) Perfection Learning Corp.
—One Hundred Days (Plus One) Ready-To-Read Level 1. Gordon, Mike, illus. 2003. (Robin Hill School Ser.). (ENG.). 32p. (J). (gr. -1-1). pap. 4.99 (978-0-689-85535-1(4), Simon Spotlight) Simon Spotlight.
—Picking Apples: Ready-To-Read Level 1. Gordon, Mike, illus. 2009. (Robin Hill School Ser.). (ENG.). 32p. (J). (gr. -1-1). pap. 4.99 (978-1-4169-5539-9(9), Simon Spotlight) Simon Spotlight.
—Playground Problem: Ready-To-Read Level 1. Gordon, Mike, illus. 2004. (Robin Hill School Ser.). (ENG.). 32p. (J). (gr. -1-1). pap. 4.99 (978-0-689-85876-5(0), Simon Spotlight) Simon Spotlight.
—A Poem in Your Pocket (Mr. Tiffin's Classroom Series) Karas, G. Brian, illus. 2015. (Mr. Tiffin's Classroom Ser.). 40p. (J). (gr. -1-3). 17.99 (978-0-307-97947-6(4), Schwartz & Wade Bks.) Random Hse. Children's Bks.
—Presidents' Day: Ready-To-Read Level 1. Gordon, Mike, illus. 2010. (Robin Hill School Ser.). (ENG.). 32p. (J). (gr. -1-1). pap. 4.99 (978-1-4169-9170-0(0), Simon Spotlight) Simon Spotlight.
—The Pumpkin Patch. Gordon, Mike, illus. 2005. (Ready-to-Read Ser.). 32p. (J). lib. bdg. 15.00 (978-1-59054-932-2(5)) Fitzgerald Bks.
—Secret Santa: Ready-To-Read Level 1. Gordon, Mike, illus. 2012. (Robin Hill School Ser.). (ENG.). 32p. (J). (gr. -1-1). 15.99 (978-1-4424-3649-7(2)); pap. 4.99 (978-1-4424-3648-0(4)) Simon Spotlight. (Simon Spotlight).
—Too Many Valentines: Ready-To-Read Level 1. Gordon, Mike, illus. 2003. (Robin Hill School Ser.). (ENG.). 32p. (J). (gr. -1-1). pap. 4.99 (978-0-689-85537-5(0), Simon Spotlight) Simon Spotlight.
—A Tooth Story: Ready-To-Read Level 1. Gordon, Mike, illus. 2004. (Robin Hill School Ser.). (ENG.). 32p. (J). (gr. -1-1). pap. 4.99 (978-0-689-86423-0(X), Simon Spotlight) Simon Spotlight.
—Wash Your Hands! Ready-To-Read Level 1. Gordon, Mike, illus. 2010. (Robin Hill School Ser.). (ENG.). 32p. (J). (gr. -1-1). pap. 4.99 (978-1-4169-9172-4(7), Simon Spotlight) Simon Spotlight.
McNamara, Margaret & Gordon, Mike. The Luck of the Irish: Ready-To-Read Level 1. 2007. (Robin Hill School Ser.). (ENG., Illus.). 32p. (J). (gr. -1-1). pap. 4.99 (978-1-4169-1539-3(7), Simon Spotlight) Simon Spotlight.
McNaughton, Colin. Once upon an Ordinary School Day. Kitamura, Satoshi, illus. 2005. (ENG.). 32p. (J). (-k). pap. 14.99 (978-1-84270-469-1(9)) Andersen Pr. GBR. Dist: Independent Pubs. Group.
McNeal, Laura & McNeal, Tom. Crooked. 2007. (ENG.). 368p. (YA). (gr. 7-11). pap. 9.99 (978-0-375-84191-0(1), Ember) Random Hse. Children's Bks.
McNish, Cliff. Angel. (Exceptional Reading & Language Arts Titles for Intermediate Grades Ser.). (YA). 2012. (ENG.). 312p. (gr. 7-12). pap. 9.95 (978-0-7613-8501-1(0), Carolrhoda Lab™) 2008. 311p. (gr. 8-12). 16.95 (978-0-8225-8900-6(1)) Lerner Publishing Group.
McOmber, Rachel B., ed. McOmber Phonics Storybooks: The Wizz Kid. rev. ed. (Illus.). (J). (978-0-944991-23-7(8)) Swift Learning Resources.
McPhail, J. A. Dawn of Day. Battis, Gwen, illus. 2012. 200p. 17.99 (978-0-9851196-2-1(4)) Rowe Publishing.
McPhee, Peter. New Blood, 1 vol. 2007. (Lorimer SideStreets Ser.). (ENG.). 168p. (YA). (gr. 9-12). 8.99 (978-1-55028-996-1(9), d77672f0-a096-41fa-ae87-84d4752432e8) James Lorimer & Co. Ltd., Pubs. CAN. Dist: Lerner Publishing Group.
McQuestion, Karen. Life on Hold, 0 vols. unabr. ed. 2011. (ENG.). 196p. (YA). (gr. 3-6). pap. 9.95 (978-1-935597-27-8(2), 9781935597278, Skyscape) Amazon Publishing.
McQuinn, Anna. Lola Goes to School. Beardshaw, Rosalind, illus. 2019. (Lola Reads Ser.: 6). (ENG.). 32p. (J). (-k). lib. bdg. 16.99 (978-1-58089-938-3(2)) Charlesbridge Publishing, Inc.
McTrustry, Chris. Cleopatra's Report, 1 vol. rev. ed. 2013. (Literary Text Ser.). (ENG., Illus.). 32p. (J). (gr. 2-4). pap. 11.99 (978-1-4333-5639-1(2)) Teacher Created Materials, Inc.
McVoy, Terra Elan. After the Kiss. 2011. (ENG.). 416p. (YA). (gr. 9). pap. 10.99 (978-1-4424-0216-4(4), Simon Pulse) Simon Pulse.
Mcwherter, Barbara. Little Pumpkin & Sally: It's O. K. to Be Different. 2008. 26p. pap. 24.95 (978-1-60563-199-8(X)) America Star Bks.
Mead, Richelle. Blood Promise. 2010. (Vampire Academy Ser.: 4). lib. bdg. 20.85 (978-0-606-14565-7(6)) Turtleback.
—Blood Promise: A Vampire Academy Novel. 2010. (Vampire Academy Ser.: 4). (ENG.). 528p. (YA). (gr. 7-18). pap. 13.99 (978-1-59514-310-5(6), Razorbill) Penguin Young Readers Group.
—Frostbite: A Vampire Academy Novel. 2008. (Vampire Academy Ser.: 2). 336p. (YA). (gr. 7-18). pap. 12.99 (978-1-59514-175-0(8), Razorbill) Penguin Young Readers Group.
—Shadow Kiss. 2013. (Vampire Academy (Graphic Novels) Ser.: 3). lib. bdg. 24.50 (978-0-606-34129-5(3)) Turtleback.
—Spirit Bound: A Vampire Academy Novel. 2011. (Vampire Academy Ser.: 5). (ENG.). 512p. (YA). (gr. 7-18). 13.99 (978-1-59514-366-2(1), Razorbill) Penguin Young Readers Group.
—Vampire Academy. 2007. (Vampire Academy Ser.: 1). 336p. (YA). (gr. 7-18). 11.99 (978-1-59514-174-3(X), Razorbill) Penguin Young Readers Group.
—Vampire Academy: A Graphic Novel. Viecell, Emma, illus. 2011. (Vampire Academy Ser.: 1). 144p. (YA). (gr. 7-18). pap. 12.99 (978-1-59514-429-4(3), Razorbill) Penguin Young Readers Group.
—Vampire Academy 10th Anniversary Edition. 10th ed. 2016. (Vampire Academy Ser.). 512p. (YA). (gr. 7). pap. 11.99 (978-0-448-49429-6(9), Razorbill) Penguin Young Readers Group.
—Vampire Academy Box Set 1-6, 6 vols. 2013. (Vampire Academy Ser.). (ENG.). 2784p. (YA). (gr. 7). pap., pap., pap. 77.94 (978-1-59514-758-5(6), Razorbill) Penguin Young Readers Group.
Meade, L. T. The Rebel of the School. 2007. (ENG.). 272p. pap. 21.99 (978-1-4346-4869-3(9)) Creative Media Partners, LLC.
—Red Rose & Tiger Lily or in a Wider Wo. 2004. reprint ed. pap. 28.95 (978-0-7661-8345-2(9)) Kessinger Publishing, LLC.
Meadowbrook Press. Meadowbrook Kids Three Book Back to School Set. 2005. 250p. pap. 26.85 (978-0-689-05307-8(X)) Meadowbrook Pr.
Meadows, Daisy. Alison the Art Fairy. 2018. 65p. (J). (gr. 1-4). 15.36 (978-1-64310-182-8(X)) Penworthy Co., LLC, The.
—Alison the Art Fairy. 2016. (Illus.). 65p. (J). (978-0-545-95523-2(8)) Scholastic, Inc.
—Carly the School Fairy. 2015. (Illus.). 155p. (J). (978-1-4806-8807-0(X)) Scholastic, Inc.
—Kathryn the Gym Fairy. 2018. 65p. (J). (gr. 1-4). 15.36 (978-1-64310-186-6(2)) Penworthy Co., LLC, The.
—Kathryn the Gym Fairy. 2016. (Rainbow Magic — the School Day Fairies Ser.: 4). lib. bdg. 14.75 (978-0-606-38792-7(7)) Turtleback.
Meaney, Flynn. The Boy Recession. 2012. (ENG.). 256p. (YA). (gr. 10-17). 32.99 (978-0-316-10213-1(X), Poppy) Little, Brown Bks. for Young Readers.
Mechling, Lauren & Moser, Laura. All Q, No A: More Tales of a 10th-Grade Social Climber. 2006. (ENG.). 288p. (YA). (gr. 7-12). pap. 15.95 (978-0-618-66378-1(9), 419818, Clarion Bks.) HarperCollins Pubs.
Mechling, Lauren, et al. The Rise & Fall of a 10th Grade Social Climber. 2005. (ENG.). 304p. (YA). (gr. 7). pap. 16.99 (978-0-618-55519-2(6), 491380, Clarion Bks.) HarperCollins Pubs.
Meddaugh, Susan. The Show Must Go On. 2012. (Martha Speaks: Chapter Bks.). (ENG., Illus.). 96p. (J). (gr. 1-4). 18.69 (978-0-547-69145-9(9)); pap. 5.99 (978-0-547-69147-3(5)) Houghton Mifflin Harcourt Publishing Co.
Medina, Juana. Juana & Lucas. Medina, Juana, illus. (Juana & Lucas Ser.: 1). (ENG., Illus.). 96p. (J). (gr. k-3). 2019. pap. 8.99 (978-1-5362-0639-5(3)) 2016. 15.99 (978-0-7636-7208-9(4)) Candlewick Pr.
Medina, Kathleen. Born into Greyworld. 2008. 220p. 29.99 (978-1-4363-2619-3(2)); pap. 19.99 (978-1-4363-2618-6(4)) Xlibris Corp.
Medina, Meg. Merci Suárez Changes Gears. (Merci Suárez Ser.: 1). (ENG.). 368p. (J). (gr. 4-7). 2020. pap. 8.99 (978-1-5362-1258-7(X)) 2018. 18.99 (978-0-7636-9049-6(X)) Candlewick Pr.
—Yaqui Delgado Wants to Kick Your Ass. 2014. (ENG., Illus.). 272p. (YA). (gr. 9). pap. 12.99 (978-0-7636-7164-8(9)) Candlewick Pr.
Meek, Carol. Believer Boy's Power. 2007. 32p. (J). pap. 9.00 (978-0-8059-7249-8(8)) Dorrance Publishing Co., Inc.
Meens, Estelle & Mijade Publications (Belgium). Boss No More. Meens, Estelle, illus. 2014. (Illus.). 32p. (J). (978-1-4338-1641-3(5), Magination Pr.) American Psychological Assn.
Meister, Cari. Buzz Beaker & the Race to School, 1 vol. McGuire, Bill, illus. 2011. (Buzz Beaker Bks.). (ENG.). 32p. (J). (gr. 2-3). pap. 6.25 (978-1-4342-3057-7(0), 114657, Stone Arch Bks.) Capstone.
—Tiny Goes Back to School. Davis, Rich, illus. 2014. (Tiny Ser.). 32p. (J). (gr. k-1). pap. 4.99 (978-0-448-48134-0(0), Penguin Young Readers) Penguin Young Readers Group.
Mele, Dana. People Like Us. 2018. 384p. (YA). (gr. 7). 18.99 (978-1-5247-4170-9(1), G.P. Putnam's Sons Books for Young Readers) Penguin Young Readers Group.
_Meli, Ayani & D., Jessie. God Says I've Changed Your Dna: Walk As Children of the Light. Mallette, Dania, illus. 2013. 24p. pap. 12.00 (978-0-9846315-7-5(7)) JWD Publishing.
Mellom, Robin. Ditched: A Love Story. 2013. (ENG.). 288p. (YA). (gr. 7-17). pap. 8.99 (978-1-4231-4351-2(5)) Disney Pr.
Meminger, Neesha. Shine, Coconut Moon. 2010. (ENG.). 256p. (YA). (gr. 9). pap. 11.99 (978-1-4424-0305-5(5), McElderry, Margaret K. Bks.) McElderry, Margaret K. Bks.
Menard, Lucille. The Top of the Bottom: Inky to the Rescue, Volume 1. 2013. 38p. pap. 12.50 (978-0-9887969-6-6(1)) Four Menards, The.
Menard, Michele Rose. The Ghoul in Our School. Menard, Adrienne, illus. 2013. 36p. pap. 11.95 (978-0-9887969-9-7(6)) Four Menards, The.
Mendelsohn, Martha. Bromley Girls. 2015. (ENG.). 192p. (YA). pap. 14.95 (978-0-89672-922-3(2)) Texas Tech Univ. Pr.
Mendle, Jane. My Ultimate Sister Disaster: A Novel. 2010. (ENG.). 208p. (YA). (gr. 7-18). pap. 18.99 (978-0-312-36904-0(2), 900042729, St. Martin's Griffin) St. Martin's Pr.
Menon, Sandhya. There's Something about Sweetie. (ENG.). (YA). (gr. 7). 2020. 400p. pap. 12.99 (978-1-5344-1679-6(X)) 2019. (Illus.). 384p. 18.99 (978-1-5344-1678-9(1)) Simon Pulse. (Simon Pulse).
Mercer, Sienna. My Sister the Vampire #2: Fangtastic! 2007. (My Sister the Vampire Ser.: 2). (ENG.). 208p. (J). (gr. 3-7). per. 6.99 (978-0-06-087115-4(6), HarperCollins) HarperCollins Pubs.
Merkel, Ruth Vitrano. Ann: 1833-1897. 2006. (Hannah's Girls Ser.). (Illus.). 112p. (J). (gr. 4-7). per. 9.99 (978-0-8280-1951-4(7)) Review & Herald Publishing Assn.
—Grace: 1890-1973, 6. 2006. (Hannah's Girls Ser.). (Illus.). 128p. (J). (gr. 4-7). per. 9.99 (978-0-8280-1953-8(3)) Review & Herald Publishing Assn.
—Marilla 1851-1916, 6 bks. 2006. (Hannah's Girls Ser.). (Illus.). 144p. (J). (gr. 4-7). per. 9.99 (978-0-8280-1952-1(5)) Review & Herald Publishing Assn.
—Ruthie: Born 1931. 2007. (Hannah's Girls Ser.). (Illus.). 144p. (J). (gr. 4-7). per. 9.99 (978-0-8280-1954-5(1)) Review & Herald Publishing Assn.
Merschel, Michael. Revenge of the Star Survivors. 2018. (ENG.). 320p. (J). (gr. 5). pap. 8.99 (978-0-8234-4041-2(9)) Holiday Hse., Inc.
Messer, Celeste M. The Broken Wing: The Adventures of Andi O'Malley. Hoeffner, Deb, illus. 2004. (Adventures of Andi O'Malley Ser.). 82-92p. (J). (gr. 4-7). 4.95 (978-0-9702171-1-0(0)) AshleyAlan Enterprises.
Messner, Kate. All the Answers. 2016. (ENG.). 272p. (J). pap. 8.99 (978-1-68119-020-4(6), 900156128, Bloomsbury USA Childrens) Bloomsbury Publishing USA.
—Breakout. (ENG.). 448p. (J). 2019. pap. 9.99 (978-1-68119-538-4(0), 900176499) 2018. (Illus.). 17.99 (978-1-68119-536-0(4), 900176497) Bloomsbury Publishing USA. (Bloomsbury Children's Bks.).
—The Brilliant Fall of Gianna Z. 2017. (ENG.). 224p. (J). pap. 8.99 (978-1-68119-547-6(X), 900177249, Bloomsbury USA Childrens) Bloomsbury Publishing USA.
—The Brilliant Fall of Gianna Z. 2017. (J). lib. bdg. 19.65 (978-0-606-40595-9(X)) Turtleback.
—The Brilliant Fall of Gianna Z. 2010. (ENG.). 208p. (YA). (gr. 4-6). 24.94 (978-0-8027-9842-8(X), 9780802798428) Walker & Co.
—Marty Mcguire, 1. Floca, Brian, illus. 2011. (ENG.). 144p. (J). (gr. 1-4). pap. 6.99 (978-0-545-14246-5(6), Scholastic Paperbacks) Scholastic, Inc.
—Marty McGuire Digs Worms! Floca, Brian, illus. 2012. (ENG.). 176p. (J). (gr. -1-3). pap. 5.99 (978-0-545-14247-2(4), Scholastic Pr.) Scholastic, Inc.
Metz, Melinda. Bri's Big Crush. 2016. (Babysitter Chronicles Ser.). (ENG.). 160p. (J). (gr. 4-7). lib. bdg. 26.65 (978-1-4965-2756-1(9), 1400591, Stone Arch Bks.) Capstone.
—S. M. A. R. T. S. & the 3-D Danger. McKenzie, Heath, illus. 2015. (S. M. A. R. T. S. Ser.). (ENG.). 128p. (J). (gr. 3-6). 22.65 (978-1-4965-0465-4(8), 128490, Stone Arch Bks.) Capstone.
—S. M. A. R. T. S. & the Droid of Doom. McKenzie, Heath, illus. 2016. (S. M. A. R. T. S. Ser.). (ENG.). 128p. (J). (gr. 3-6). pap. 9.95 (978-1-4965-3017-2(9), 131904); lib. bdg. 22.65 (978-1-4965-3015-8(2), 131902) Capstone. (Stone Arch Bks.).
—S. M. A. R. T. S. & the Mars Mission Mayhem. McKenzie, Heath, illus. 2016. (S. M. A. R. T. S. Ser.). (ENG.). 128p. (J). (gr. 3-6). pap. 9.95 (978-1-4965-3018-9(7), 131905); lib. bdg. 22.65 (978-1-4965-3016-5(0), 131903) Capstone. (Stone Arch Bks.).
—S. M. A. R. T. S. & the Poison Plates. McKenzie, Heath, illus. 2015. (S. M. A. R. T. S. Ser.). (ENG.). 128p. (J). (gr. 3-6). 22.65 (978-1-4965-0464-7(X), 128489, Stone Arch Bks.) Capstone.
Metzger, Joanna. The Space Program. Elizalde, Marcelo, illus. 2006. 142p. (J). (978-1-59336-695-7(7)) Mondo Publishing.
Metzger, Lois. A Trick of the Light. (ENG.). 208p. (YA). (gr. 9). 2014. pap. 10.99 (978-0-06-213309-0(8)) 2013. 17.99 (978-0-06-213308-3(X)) HarperCollins Pubs. (Balzer & Bray).
Metzger, Steve. Five Spooky Ghosts Playing Tricks at School. Harrald-Pilz, Marilee, illus. 2005. (J). (978-0-439-80381-6(0)) Scholastic, Inc.
Meunier, Sylvain. Ma Premiere de Classe. Eudes-Pascal, Elisabeth, tr. 2003. (Roman Jeunesse Ser.). (FRE., Illus.). 96p. (J). (gr. 4-7). pap. (978-2-89021-634-1(9)) Diffusion du livre Mirabel (DLM).
Meyer, Stephenie. Amanecer / Breaking Dawn. 2008. (Saga Crepusculo / the Twilight Saga Ser.: 4).Tr. of Breaking Dawn. (SPA.). 832p. (YA). (gr. 9-12). pap. 23.95 (978-607-11-0033-7(X), Alfaguara) Penguin Random House Grupo Editorial ESP. Dist: Penguin Random Hse. LLC.
—Eclipse. 2007. (Twilight Saga Ser.: 3). (ENG.). 640p. (YA). (gr. 7-17). 22.99 (978-0-316-16020-9(2)) Little, Brown Bks. for Young Readers.
—Eclipse. 2008. 576p. (978-1-904233-91-6(0), Atom Books) Little, Brown Book Group Ltd.
—Eclipse. 2011. (Twilight Saga: Bk. 3). 13.08 (978-0-7848-3531-9(4), Everbind) Marco Bk. Co.
—Eclipse. 2010. (Twilight Saga: Bk. 3). 629p. (YA). (gr. 9-12). 22.10 (978-1-60686-303-9(7)) Perfection Learning Corp.
—Eclipse. 2007. (Twilight Saga Spanish Ser.: 3). (SPA.). 637p. (gr. 7-12). lib. bdg. 28.15 (978-1-4177-9862-9(9)) Turtleback.
—New Moon. 2008. (Twilight Saga: Bk. 2). 563p. (gr. 9-12). 21.00 (978-1-60686-336-7(3)) Perfection Learning Corp.
—New Moon. 2006. (Twilight Saga Ser.: 2). (ENG.). 608p. (J). (gr. 7-17). 24.99 (978-0-316-16019-3(9)) Little, Brown Bks. for Young Readers.
—New Moon. 2011. (Twilight Saga: Bk. 2). 11.72 (978-0-7848-3535-7(7), Everbind) Marco Bk. Co.
—Twilight. 2008. (Twilight Saga: Bk. 1). (CHI.). 375p. (YA). pap. (978-7-5448-0333-5(3)) Jieli Publishing Hse.
—Twilight. 2005. (Twilight Saga Ser.: 1). (ENG.). 544p. (YA). (gr. 7-17). 24.99 (978-0-316-16017-9(2)) Little, Brown Bks. for Young Readers.
—Twilight. 2008. 480p. pap. (978-1-905654-34-5(0), Atom Books) Little, Brown Book Group Ltd.
—Twilight. 2009. (Twilight Saga: Bk. 1). 11.72 (978-0-7848-1934-0(3), Everbind) Marco Bk. Co.
—Twilight. (Twilight Saga: Bk. 1). 2010. 498p. (YA). (gr. 9-12). 20.10 (978-1-60686-352-7(5)) 2006. 21.00 (978-0-7569-6825-0(9)) Perfection Learning Corp.
—Twilight. (Twilight Ser.: 1). (YA). 2007. 1.25 (978-1-4193-9974-9(8)) 2006. 87.75 (978-1-4193-9975-6(6)) Recorded Bks., Inc.
—Twilight. 2006. (Twilight Saga Ser.: 1). (Illus.). 498p. (YA). (gr. 9-12). lib. bdg. 28.15 (978-1-4177-5591-2(1)) Turtleback.
—The Twilight Saga Collection Set, 4 vols. 2008. (ENG.). 2560p. (YA). (gr. 7-17). 92.00 (978-0-316-03184-4(4)) Little, Brown Bks. for Young Readers.
Meyerhoff, Jenny. Green Thumbs-Up! Chatelain, Éva & Chatelain, Éva, illus. 2015. (Friendship Garden Ser.: 1). (ENG.). 176p. (J). (gr. 2-5). pap. 6.99 (978-1-4814-3904-6(9), Aladdin) Simon & Schuster Children's Publishing.
MIA the Meek. 2006. (ENG.). 166p. (J). (gr. 6-11). 16.95 (978-1-890862-46-6(0), 008ac6fb-e1b7-42f2-948d-8297dcf6bc97) Bancroft Pr.
Mia the Melodramatic. 2008. (ENG.). 168p. (J). (gr. 6-13). 19.95 (978-1-890862-56-5(8), e9f019f6-b51f-4b2e-bccf-94b27b92cc3e) Bancroft Pr.
Mian, Zanib. Planet Omar: Accidental Trouble Magnet. Mafaridik, Nasaya, illus. 2020. (Planet Omar Ser.: 1). (ENG.). 224p. (J). (gr. 2-5). 13.99 (978-0-593-10921-2(X), G.P. Putnam's Sons Books for Young Readers) Penguin Young Readers Group.
Michael-Angelo Goes to School. 2012. (Illus.). 34p. pap. 9.99 (978-1-937107-10-9(8)) Morning Joy Media.
Michelle, Sara. The Beginning: Book 5, 1 vol., 5. unabr. ed. 2012. (My New Normal Ser.: 5). (ENG.). 97p. (YA). (gr. 9-12). pap. 10.75 (978-1-61651-785-4(9)) Saddleback Educational Publishing, Inc.
Michener, Tara. Summer Camp Survival. 2010. (ENG.). 76p. pap. 10.99 (978-1-4520-6297-6(8)) AuthorHouse.
Michiko Florence, Debbi. Jasmine Toguchi, Drummer Girl. Vukovic, Elizabet, illus. 2018. (Jasmine Toguchi Ser.: 3). (ENG.). 128p. (J). pap. 5.99 (978-0-374-30836-0(5), 900185579, Farrar, Straus & Giroux (BYR)) Farrar, Straus & Giroux.
Mickelson, Marcia. The Huaca. 2013. (J). pap. 16.99 (978-1-4621-1190-9(4), Horizon Pubs.) Cedar Fort, Inc./CFI Distribution.

Mientus, Andy. The Backstagers & the Ghost Light (Backstagers #1) Sygh, Rian, illus. 2018. (Backstagers Ser.). (ENG.). 208p. (J). (gr. 5-9). 14.99 *(978-1-4197-3120-4(3),* 1220801, Amulet Bks.) Abrams, Inc.
—The Backstagers & the Theater of the Ancients (Backstagers #2) Sygh, Rian & BOOM! Studios, illus. 2019. (Backstagers Ser.). (ENG.). 192p. (YA). (gr. 5-9). 14.99 *(978-1-4197-3365-9(6),* 1262501, Amulet Bks.) Abrams, Inc.
Mikaelsen, Ben. Ghost of Spirit Bear. (Spirit Bear Ser.: 2). (ENG.). (J). (gr. 3-7). 2010. 176p. pap. 7.99 *(978-0-06-009009-8(X))* 2008. 160p. 16.99 *(978-0-06-009007-4(3))* HarperCollins Pubs. (HarperCollins).
Milanes, Janelle. Analee, in Real Life. (ENG.). (YA). (gr. 7). 2019. 432p. pap. 12.99 *(978-1-5344-1030-5(9))* 2018. (Illus.). 416p. 18.99 *(978-1-5344-1029-9(5))* Simon Pulse. (Simon Pulse).
—The Victoria in My Head. (ENG.). (YA). (gr. 7). 2018. 416p. pap. 12.99 *(978-1-4814-8090-1(1))* 2017. (Illus.). 400p. 17.99 *(978-1-4814-8089-5(8))* Simon Pulse. (Simon Pulse).
Miles, Chris. Spurt. 2017. (ENG., Illus.). 272p. (J). (gr. 6-9). 16.99 *(978-1-4814-7972-1(5),* Simon & Schuster Bks. For Young Readers) Simon & Schuster Bks. For Young Readers.
Miles, Elizabeth. Envy. 2013. (Fury Ser.: 2). (ENG., Illus.). 416p. (YA). (gr. 9). pap. 9.99 *(978-1-4424-2222-3(X),* Simon Pulse) Simon Pulse.
—Eternity. 2013. (Fury Ser.: 3). (ENG., Illus.). 336p. (YA). (gr. 9). 17.99 *(978-1-4424-2227-8(0));* pap. 9.99 *(978-1-4424-2228-5(9))* Simon Pulse. (Simon Pulse).
—Fury. 11 vols. 2012. (YA). 126.75 *(978-1-4640-3958-4(5));* 271.75 *(978-1-4640-3955-3(0));* 110.75 *(978-1-4640-3957-7(7));* 112.75 *(978-1-4640-3954-6(2))* Recorded Bks., Inc.
—Fury. 2012. (Fury Ser.: 1). (ENG.). 400p. (YA). (gr. 9). pap. 9.99 *(978-1-4424-2225-4(4),* Simon Pulse) Simon Pulse.
Miller, Amanda E. Pete the Pencil. 2008. 20p. pap. 24.95 *(978-1-60610-814-7(X))* America Star Bks.
Miller, Andrew. Arthur Dudley Dunstan. 2009. (ENG.). 47p. pap. 12.03 *(978-0-557-07115-9(1))* Lulu Pr., Inc.
Miller, Kristine Elizabeth. Albert's Lunch Box. 2008. 24p. pap. 24.95 *(978-1-60672-096-7(1))* America Star Bks.
Miller, Lee. Ete: (Extraterrestrial Elements) 2006. 80p. pap. 16.95 *(978-1-4241-3498-4(6))* PublishAmerica, Inc.
Miller, Robin Caroll. Samantha Sanderson at the Movies, 1 vol. 2014. (FaithGirlz / Samantha Sanderson Ser.: 1). (ENG.). 272p. (J). pap. 8.99 *(978-0-310-74245-6(5))* Zonderkidz.
—Samantha Sanderson on the Scene, 1 vol. 2014. (FaithGirlz / Samantha Sanderson Ser.: 2). (ENG.). 256p. (J). pap. 8.99 *(978-0-310-74247-0(1))* Zonderkidz.
Milliken, Lyndsay Nicole. Blossom Plays Possum: (Because She's Shy) McDonnell, Janet, illus. 2017. (ENG.). 32p. (J). 15.95 *(978-1-4338-2735-8(2),* Magination Pr.) American Psychological Assn.
Millman, M. C. Always Something Else: The whimsical adventures of Elisheva Raskin. 2005. (Illus.). 160p. (J). 14.95 *(978-1-932443-23-3(1),* ASEH) Judaica Pr., Inc., The.
—Always Something Else 2. 2006. (Illus.). 160p. (J). 14.95 *(978-1-932443-43-1(6),* ASE2H) Judaica Pr., Inc., The.
Millner, Denene & Miller, Mitzi. If Only You Knew, Bk. 2. 2008. (Hotlanta Ser.: 2). (ENG.). 254p. (J). (gr. 7-18). 24.94 *(978-0-545-00309-4(1))* Scholastic, Inc.
Mills, Arthur. The Crawl Space. Mills, Arthur, ed. Bochgeri, Ghanshyam, illus. 2012. (ENG.). 254p. (J). pap. 9.99 *(978-0-9860166-0-8(8))* Branching Plot Bks.
Mills, Claudia. Being Teddy Roosevelt: A Boy, a President & a Plan. Alley, R. W., illus. 2012. (ENG.). 112p. (J). (gr. 2-5). pap. 16.99 *(978-0-312-64018-7(8),* 900077669) Square Fish.
—How Oliver Olson Changed the World. Malone, Heather, illus. 2011. (ENG.). 128p. (J). (gr. 2-5). pap. 8.99 *(978-0-312-67282-9(9),* 900072371) Square Fish.
—Kelsey Green, Reading Queen. Shepperson, Rob, illus. 2014. (Franklin School Friends Ser.: 1). (ENG.). 144p. (J). (gr. 2-5). pap. 6.99 *(978-1-250-03405-2(1),* 900120575) Square Fish.
—Lucy Lopez: Coding Star. Zong, Grace, illus. 2020. (After-School Superstars Ser.: 3). 128p. (J). (gr. 2-5). 15.99 *(978-0-8234-4628-5(X),* Margaret Ferguson Books) Holiday Hse., Inc.
—Mason Dixon: Basketball Disasters. Francis, Guy, illus. 2013. (Mason Dixon Ser.: 3). 176p. (J). (gr. 2-5). pap. 6.99 *(978-0-375-87276-1(0),* Yearling) Random Hse. Children's Bks.
—Nixie Ness: Cooking Star. Zong, Grace, illus. 2019. (After-School Superstars Ser.: 1). 144p. (J). (gr. 2-5). 15.99 *(978-0-8234-4093-1(1),* Margaret Ferguson Books) Holiday Hse., Inc.
—The Nora Notebooks, Book 1: the Trouble with Ants. Kath, Katie, illus. 2016. (Nora Notebooks Ser.: 1). 176p. (J). (gr. 2-5). 7.99 *(978-0-385-39163-4(3),* Yearling) Random Hse. Children's Bks.
—The Nora Notebooks, Book 2: the Trouble with Babies. Kath, Katie, illus. 2016. (Nora Notebooks Ser.: 2). 192p. (J). (gr. 2-5). 12.99 *(978-0-385-39165-8(X),* Knopf Bks. for Young Readers) Random Hse. Children's Bks.
—Zero Tolerance. 2014. (ENG.). 256p. (J). (gr. 3-7). pap. 13.99 *(978-1-250-04422-8(7),* 900128310) Square Fish.
—7 X 9 = Trouble! Karas, G. Brian, illus. 2004. 103p. (J). (gr. 2-5). 13.60 *(978-0-7569-3397-5(8))* Perfection Learning Corp.
Mills, David. Sam's First Day. Finlay, Lizzie, illus. 2004. 24p. (J). *(978-1-85269-637-5(0)); (978-1-85269-631-3(1));* (TUR & ENG.). *(978-1-85269-630-6(3)); (978-1-85269-644-3(3)); (978-1-85269-702-0(4)); (978-1-85269-646-7(X)); (978-1-85269-645-0(1)); (978-1-85269-643-6(5)); (978-1-85269-642-9(7));* (ENG.). *(978-1-85269-640-5(0)); (978-1-85269-635-1(4)); (978-1-85269-636-8(2)); (978-1-85269-639-9(7));* 2nd ed. (PER & ENG.). *(978-1-85269-634-4(6))* Mantra Lingua.
Mills, David & Finlay, Lizzie. Sam's First Day. 2004. (Illus.). 24p. (J). *(978-1-85269-641-2(9))* Mantra Lingua.
Mills, Lauren A. Minna's Patchwork Coat. 2015. (ENG., Illus.). 288p. (J). (gr. 3-7). 17.00 *(978-0-316-40621-5(X))* Little, Brown Bks. for Young Readers.
Mills, Nathan & Holtz, Mary Elizabeth. Sabrina's School, 1 vol. 2012. (Rosen Readers Ser.). (ENG., Illus.). 16p. (J). (gr. k-k). pap. 7.00 *(978-1-4488-8719-4(4),* d4d5cd12-8a8c-4e3a-9b68-87c958c15dea, Rosen Classroom) Rosen Publishing Group, Inc., The.
Mills, Wendy. Positively Beautiful. 2016. (ENG.). 368p. (YA). pap. 9.99 *(978-1-68119-025-9(7),* 9781681190259, Bloomsbury USA Childrens) Bloomsbury Publishing USA.
Mills, Wynette. Nana's Backyard Alphabet. 2012. 36p. pap. 15.99 *(978-1-4771-4061-1(1))* Xlibris Corp.
Millsap, Ella. A Portrait of a Church in Stone: The Keeper of the Honeybees. 2013. 62p. (J). pap. 12.00 *(978-0-9891960-3-1(8))* Professional Publishing Hse. LLC.
Minami, Natsuki, illus. Disney Manga: Descendants - Rotten to the Core, Book 2: The Rotten to the Core Trilogy, Bk. 2. 2017. (Disney Manga: Descendants - the Rotten to the Core Trilogy Ser.: 2). (ENG.). 80p. (J). (gr. 3-1). pap. 10.99 *(978-1-4278-5689-0(3),* 793adea8-abae-4a59-91c8-7d530cde05b3, TOKYOPOP Manga) TOKYOPOP, Inc.
Mincks, Margaret. President of Poplar Lane. 2019. 288p. (J). (gr. 3-7). 16.99 *(978-0-425-29093-4(X),* Viking Books for Young Readers) Penguin Young Readers Group.
Minsky, Terri. All over It! 2005. (Illus.). 138p. (J). *(978-1-4156-0271-3(9))* Disney Pr.
Miranda, Megan. Hysteria. 2014. (ENG.). 352p. (YA). (gr. 9). pap. 10.99 *(978-0-8027-3592-8(4),* 900123271, Bloomsbury USA Childrens) Bloomsbury Publishing USA.
Misra, Michelle. Birthday Surprise. Chaffey, Samantha, illus. 2016. (Angel Wings Ser.: 2). (ENG.). 128p. (J). (gr. 1-4). pap. 5.99 *(978-1-4814-5800-9(0),* Aladdin) Simon & Schuster Children's Publishing.
—Rainbows & Halos. Chaffey, Samantha, illus. 2017. (Angel Wings Ser.: 4). (ENG.). 112p. (J). (gr. 1-4). pap. 5.99 *(978-1-4814-5806-1(X),* Simon & Schuster/Paula Wiseman Bks.) Simon & Schuster/Paula Wiseman Bks.
—Secrets & Sapphires. Chaffey, Samantha, illus. 2016. (Angel Wings Ser.: 3). (ENG.). 128p. (J). (gr. 1-4). pap. 6.99 *(978-1-4814-5803-0(5),* Aladdin) Simon & Schuster Children's Publishing.
—Secrets & Sapphires. Chaffey, Samantha, illus. 2016. (Angel Wings Ser.: 3). (ENG.). 128p. (J). (gr. 1-4). 16.99 *(978-1-4814-5804-7(3),* Simon & Schuster/Paula Wiseman Bks.) Simon & Schuster/Paula Wiseman Bks.
Miss Gomez's Third Grade Class Staff. Wacky Stories from Wisdom Academy for Young Scientists. 2013. (ENG.). 63p. (YA). pap. 16.95 *(978-1-4787-1103-2(5))* Outskirts Pr., Inc.
Mistretta, T. P. C. Jay Francis. The Parkour Code. 2010. (ENG.). 114p. pap. 13.95 *(978-0-557-38476-1(1))* Lulu Pr., Inc.
Mitchard, Jacquelyn. All We Know of Heaven. 2008. (ENG.). 320p. (YA). (gr. 8-18). 16.99 *(978-0-06-134578-4(4),* HarperTeen) HarperCollins Pubs.
Mitchell, Devon L. The Candy Dragon: Torchy's Adventures of Starting School. 2009. 40p. pap. 16.99 *(978-1-4389-4626-9(0))* AuthorHouse.
Mitchell, Ed. You Never Can Tell What's Least Expected Most. 2009. 232p. pap. 18.95 *(978-1-4092-5434-8(8))* Lulu Pr., Inc.
Mitchell, Julie & Chambers, Mal. Bertha. 2008. (Rigby Focus Forward: Level G Ser.). (Illus.). 24p. (J). (gr. 4-7). pap. *(978-1-4190-3703-0(X),* Rigby) Pearson Education Australia.
Mitchell, Julie & Konye, Paul. The Bully. 2008. (Rigby Focus Forward: Level K Ser.). (Illus.). 24p. (J). (gr. 4-7). pap. *(978-1-4190-3784-9(6),* Rigby) Pearson Education Australia.
Mittal, Anjali. The Convent Rules. 2009. (Illus.). 80p. pap. 10.49 *(978-1-4389-8575-6(4))* AuthorHouse.
Miyares, Daniel. Night Out. 2018. (Illus.). 40p. (J). (gr. -1-3). 17.99 *(978-1-5247-6572-9(4),* Schwartz & Wade Bks.) Random Hse. Children's Bks.
Mlynowski, Sarah. Frogs & French Kisses. 2007. (Magic in Manhattan Ser.: 2). (ENG.). 304p. (YA). (gr. 7). pap. 8.99 *(978-0-385-73185-0(X),* Delacorte Pr.) Random Hse. Children's Bks.
—Gimme a Call. 2011. (ENG.). 320p. (YA). (gr. 7). pap. 9.99 *(978-0-385-73589-6(8),* Ember) Random Hse. Children's Bks.
—Parties & Potions. 2010. (Magic in Manhattan Ser.: 4). (ENG., Illus.). 368p. (YA). (gr. 7). pap. 10.99 *(978-0-385-73646-6(0),* Ember) Random Hse. Children's Bks.
Mlynowski, Sarah, et al. Dragon Overnight (Upside-Down Magic #4), 1 vol. (Upside-Down Magic Ser.: 4). (ENG.). 192p. (J). (gr. 3-7). 2019. pap. 5.99 *(978-1-338-11116-3(7))* 2018. 14.99 *(978-1-338-11115-6(9),* Scholastic Pr.) Scholastic, Inc.
—Dragon Overnight (Upside-Down Magic #4) (Unabridged Edition), 1 vol. unabr. ed. 2018. (Upside-Down Magic Ser.: 4). (ENG.). 1p. (J). (gr. 3-7). audio compact disk 24.99 *(978-1-338-22741-3(6))* Scholastic, Inc.
—Showing off (Upside-Down Magic #3), 1 vol. (Upside-Down Magic Ser.: 3). (ENG.). 208p. (J). (gr. 3-7). 2018. pap. 5.99 *(978-0-545-80054-9(4))* 2016. 14.99 *(978-0-545-80053-2(6),* Scholastic Pr.) Scholastic, Inc.
—Sticks & Stones (Upside-Down Magic #2), 1 vol. (Upside-Down Magic Ser.: 2). (ENG.). 208p. (J). (gr. 3-7). 2017. pap. 5.99 *(978-0-545-80050-1(1))* 2016. 14.99 *(978-0-545-80049-5(8),* Scholastic Pr.) Scholastic, Inc.
—Upside-Down Magic. 2015. 196p. (J). pap. *(978-0-545-90822-1(1),* Scholastic Pr.) Scholastic, Inc.
—Upside-Down Magic (Upside-down Magic #1), 1 vol. 2016. (Upside-Down Magic Ser.: 1). (ENG.). 208p. (J). (gr. 3-7). pap. 5.99 *(978-0-545-80046-4(3))* Scholastic, Inc.
—Weather or Not (Upside-Down Magic #5), 1 vol. (Upside-Down Magic Ser.: 5). (ENG.). 192p. (J). (gr. 3-7). 2019. pap. 5.99 *(978-1-338-22148-0(5))* 2018. 14.99 *(978-1-338-22147-3(7),* Scholastic Pr.) Scholastic, Inc.
Mobin-Uddin, Asma. My Name Is Bilal. Kiwak, Barbara, illus. 2005. (ENG.). 32p. (J). (gr. 1-4). 17.99 *(978-1-59078-175-3(9),* Astra Young Readers) Astra Publishing Hse.
Moffitt, Debra. Best Kept Secret. 2011. (Pink Locker Society Novels Ser.: 2). (ENG.). 128p. (J). (gr. 6-8). pap. 17.99 *(978-0-312-64503-8(1),* 900068658, St. Martin's Griffin) St. Martin's Pr.
—Girls in Charge. 2011. (Pink Locker Society Novels Ser.: 4). (ENG.). 208p. (J). (gr. 3-7). pap. 18.99 *(978-0-312-64506-9(6),* 900068660, St. Martin's Griffin) St. Martin's Pr.
Mohr, L. C. Krumbuckets. Musheno, Erica, illus. 2007. (ENG.). 144p. (J). (gr. 2-7). 13.95 *(978-0-9769417-6-7(7))* Blooming Tree Pr.
Mohsenian, Javad. 9/11 Children. 2006. (ENG.). 128p. per. 10.95 *(978-0-7414-3218-6(8))* Infinity Publishing.
Moiser, Liam. Moore Field School & the Mystery. 2013. 118p. pap. 10.95 *(978-1-62516-787-3(3),* Strategic Bk. Publishing) Strategic Book Publishing & Rights Agency (SBPRA).
Moisher, Phil. Long Before I Knew Better. 2011. 70p. pap. 19.95 *(978-1-4560-4007-9(3))* America Star Bks.
Moldover, Joseph. Every Moment After. 2019. (ENG.). 368p. (YA). (gr. 9). 17.99 *(978-1-328-54727-9(2),* 1724070, Clarion Bks.) HarperCollins Pubs.
Molinari, Laurice Elehwany. The Ether: Vero Rising, 1 vol. 2014. (Ether Novel Ser.: 1). (ENG.). 368p. (J). pap. 8.99 *(978-0-310-73561-8(0))* Zonderkidz.
—Pillars of Fire, 1 vol. 2016. (Ether Novel Ser.: 2). (ENG.). 368p. (J). pap. 8.99 *(978-0-310-73562-5(9))* Zonderkidz.
Money, Mo. Fashionistas, 1. 2010. (School Gyrls Ser.). (ENG.). 112p. (J). (gr. 2-4). 18.69 *(978-1-4424-0876-0(6))* Simon & Schuster, Inc.
Mongredien, Sue. Oliver Moon's Fangtastic Sleepover. 2011. (Oliver Moon, Junior Wizard Ser.). (ENG.). 92p. (J). (gr. 2-5). 17.44 *(978-0-7945-3094-5(X))* EDC Publishing.
Monir, Alexandra. The Girl in the Picture. 2016. 272p. (YA). (gr. 7). 17.99 *(978-0-385-74390-7(4),* Delacorte Pr.) Random Hse. Children's Bks.
A Monkey Ate My Homework. 2007. 32p. pap. 4.50 *(978-0-8341-2287-1(1),* 083-412-2871) Beacon Hill Pr. of Kansas City.
Monninger, Joseph. Game Change. 2019. (ENG.). 240p. (YA). (gr. 9). pap. 15.99 *(978-1-328-59586-7(2),* 1730760, Clarion Bks.) HarperCollins Pubs.
Monroe, Mary. Milagro en la Escuela Monty. 2010. (SPA.). 188p. pap. 13.95 *(978-1-61764-099-5(9))* AuthorHouse.
Monroe, Mary A. Tagger: Graffiti Was His Life - & Soul. 2011. 176p. 29.99 *(978-1-4567-5028-2(3));* pap. 19.99 *(978-1-4567-5029-9(1))* AuthorHouse.
Montes, Marisa. A Crazy Mixed-Up Spanglish Day. Cepeda, Joe, illus. 2004. (Get Ready for Gabi Ser.). 120p. (gr. 2-5). 14.00 *(978-0-7569-3403-3(6))* Perfection Learning Corp.
—A Crazy Mixed-Up Spanglish Day. Cepeda, Joe, illus. 2003. (Get Ready for Gabi Ser.). 128p. (J). 12.95 *(978-0-439-51710-2(9),* Scholastic Paperbacks) Scholastic, Inc.
Montgomery, L. M. Anne of Avonlea. 2011. 214p. (gr. 4-7). pap. 15.95 *(978-1-4638-0054-3(1))* Rodgers, Alan Bks.
—Emily Climbs: Emily of New Moon Series. 2014. (Emily Ser.: 2). (ENG.). 368p. (YA). (gr. 5-12). pap. 13.99 *(978-1-4022-8915-6(4))* Sourcebooks, Inc.
Montgomery, Lewis B. The Case of the Crooked Campaign. Wummer, Amy, illus. 2012. (Milo & Jazz Mysteries (r) Ser.: 9). (ENG.). 112p. (J). (gr. 2-5). lib. bdg. 22.60 *(978-1-57565-435-5(0))* Astra Publishing Hse.
—The Case of the Crooked Campaign (Book 9), No. 9. Wummer, Amy, illus. 2012. (Milo & Jazz Mysteries Ser.: 9). 112p. (J). (gr. 2-6). pap. 6.99 *(978-1-57565-436-2(9),* ba48c164-9388-4a16-9fbf-8e780216d18e, Kane Press) Astra Publishing Hse.
—The Case of the Diamonds in the Desk. Wummer, Amy, illus. 2012. (Milo & Jazz Mysteries Ser.). 96p. (J). (gr. 2-5). pap. 39.62 *(978-0-7613-9207-1(6));* lib. bdg. 22.60 *(978-1-57565-392-1(3))* Astra Publishing Hse.
—The Case of the Diamonds in the Desk (Book 8), No. 8. Wummer, Amy, illus. 2012. (Milo & Jazz Mysteries Ser.: 8). 96p. (J). (gr. 2-6). pap. 6.99 *(978-1-57565-391-4(5),* f97daf45-42da-4bca-ba88-456280d60669, Kane Press) Astra Publishing Hse.
—The Case of the Haunted Haunted House, Vol. 3. Wummer, Amy, illus. 2009. (Milo & Jazz Mysteries Ser.). 96p. (J). (gr. k-3). 22.60 *(978-1-57565-297-9(8))* Astra Publishing Hse.
—The Case of the Haunted Haunted House. Wummer, Amy, illus. 2012. (Milo & Jazz Mysteries Ser.: Vol. 3). (ENG.). (J). (gr. 2-4). pap. 20.95 incl. audio compact disk *(978-1-4301-1206-8(9))* Live Oak Media.
—The Case of the Haunted Haunted House (Book 3), Vol. 3. Wummer, Amy, illus. 2009. (Milo & Jazz Mysteries Ser.). 96p. (J). (gr. 2-6). pap. 6.99 *(978-1-57565-295-5(1),* 9cc65eec-16ba-4a80-b83c-15a3d4b1b5d2, Kane Press) Astra Publishing Hse.
—The Case of the Locked Box. Wummer, Amy, illus. 2013. (Milo & Jazz Mysteries Ser.: Vol. 11). (ENG.). 106p. (J). (gr. 2-4). lib. bdg. 22.60 *(978-1-57565-625-0(6))* Astra Publishing Hse.
—The Case of the Locked Box (Book 11), No. 11. Wummer, Amy, illus. 2013. (Milo & Jazz Mysteries Ser.: 11). 112p. (J). (gr. 2-6). pap. 6.99 *(978-1-57565-626-7(4),* 4eb267cb-73d0-4237-8cdc-45a0c519fde1, Kane Press) Astra Publishing Hse.
Montgomery, Ross. Christmas Dinner of Souls. 2017. (ENG., Illus.). 240p. (J). 12.50 *(978-0-571-31797-4(9),* Faber & Faber Children's Bks.) Faber & Faber, Inc.
—Max & the Millions. 2018. 265p. (J). pap. *(978-1-5247-1887-9(4))* Earthscan Canada.
—Max & the Millions. 2018. (ENG.). 272p. (J). (gr. 3-7). 16.99 *(978-1-5247-1884-8(X),* Lamb, Wendy Bks.) Random Hse. Children's Bks.
Moore, Stephanie Perry. Better Than Picture Perfect, No. 2. 2014. (Sharp Sisters Ser.: 2). (ENG.). 160p. (YA). (gr. 6-12). pap. 7.95 *(978-1-4677-4486-7(7),* add2aaa3-7821-4781-9f47-582ec3843188, Darby Creek) Lerner Publishing Group.
—Forever Hot/Truly Fine. 2013. (Grovehill Giants Ser.). (YA). lib. bdg. 26.90 *(978-0-606-31877-8(1))* Turtleback.
—Give It Up, No. 1. 2015. (Swoop List Ser.: 1). (ENG., Illus.). 128p. (YA). (gr. 6-12). lib. bdg. 27.99 *(978-1-4677-5804-8(3),* 03890806-974c-4ceb-8661-7ba91c6d43ae, Darby Creek) Lerner Publishing Group.
—Yell Out/Do You. 2012. (Lockwood Lions Ser.). (YA). lib. bdg. 26.90 *(978-0-606-26493-8(0))* Turtleback.
Moore, Stephanie Perry & Moore, Derrick. Forever Hot/Truly Fine, 1 vol. 2013. (Grovehill Giants Ser.: Bk. 1). (ENG.). 318p. (YA). (gr. 9-12). pap. 16.95 *(978-1-62250-683-5(9))* Saddleback Educational Publishing, Inc.
—Golden Heart - Deep Soul, 1 vol. 2013. (Grovehill Giants Ser.: Bk. 2). (ENG.). 320p. (YA). (gr. 9-12). pap. 16.95 *(978-1-62250-684-2(7))* Saddleback Educational Publishing, Inc.
—Golden Heart/Deep Soul. 2013. (Grovehill Giants Ser.). (YA). lib. bdg. 26.90 *(978-0-606-31878-5(X))* Turtleback.
Mora, Pat. The Rainbow Tulip. Sayles, Elizabeth, illus. 2003. 32p. (J). (gr. k-3). 7.99 *(978-0-14-250009-5(7),* Puffin Books) Penguin Young Readers Group.
—Rainbow Tulip. 2014. 17.00 *(978-1-63419-680-2(5))* Perfection Learning Corp.
Moradian, Afsaneh. Jamie Is Jamie: A Book about Being Yourself & Playing Your Way. Bogade, Maria, illus. 2018. (Jamie Is Jamie Ser.). (ENG.). 32p. (J). (gr. -1-3). 15.99 *(978-1-63198-139-5(0),* 81395) Free Spirit Publishing Inc.
Morait, Tracey. Goalden Girl. 2007. (ENG.). 160p. pap. 13.95 *(978-1-84799-758-6(9))* Lulu Pr., Inc.
Moreillon, Judi. Ready & Waiting for You. Stock, Catherine, illus. 2013. (ENG.). 32p. (J). 17.00 *(978-0-8028-5355-4(2),* Eerdmans Bks For Young Readers) Eerdmans, William B. Publishing Co.
Morgan, Alex. Choosing Sides. 2018. (Kicks Ser.). (ENG., Illus.). 112p. (J). (gr. 3-7). 17.99 *(978-1-4814-8156-4(8),* Simon & Schuster Bks. For Young Readers) Simon & Schuster Bks. For Young Readers.
—Hat Trick. 2015. (Kicks Ser.). (ENG., Illus.). 128p. (J). (gr. 3-7). 17.99 *(978-1-4814-5096-6(4),* Simon & Schuster Bks. For Young Readers) Simon & Schuster Bks. For Young Readers.
—In the Zone. 2018. (Kicks Ser.). (ENG., Illus.). 128p. (J). (gr. 3-7). 17.99 *(978-1-4814-8153-3(3),* Simon & Schuster Bks. For Young Readers) Simon & Schuster Bks. For Young Readers.
—Switching Goals. (Kicks Ser.). (ENG.). (J). (gr. 3-7). 2020. 144p. pap. 7.99 *(978-1-5344-2796-9(1))* 2019. 128p. 17.99 *(978-1-5344-2795-2(3))* Simon & Schuster Bks. For Young Readers. (Simon & Schuster Bks. For Young Readers).
Morgan, Amanda K. Secrets, Lies, & Scandals. (ENG.). (YA). (gr. 9). 2017. 368p. pap. 10.99 *(978-1-4814-4955-7(9))* 2016. (Illus.). 352p. 17.99 *(978-1-4814-4954-0(0))* Simon Pulse. (Simon Pulse).
—Such a Good Girl. (ENG.). (YA). (gr. 9). 2018. 304p. pap. 11.99 *(978-1-4814-4958-8(3))* 2017. (Illus.). 288p. 17.99 *(978-1-4814-4957-1(5))* Simon Pulse. (Simon Pulse).
Morgan, Kass. Light Years. 2018. (ENG.). 384p. (YA). E-Book *(978-0-316-51046-2(7))* Little Brown & Co.
—Light Years. (Light Years Ser.: 1). (ENG.). (YA). (gr. 9-17). 2019. 416p. pap. 10.99 *(978-0-316-51043-1(2))* 2018. 384p. 17.99 *(978-0-316-51044-8(0))* Little, Brown Bks. for Young Readers.
—Supernova. 2019. (ENG.). 368p. (YA). (gr. 9-17). 18.99 *(978-0-316-51051-6(3))* Little, Brown Bks. for Young Readers.
Morgan, Melissa J. Freaky Tuesday #17, 17 vols. 2007. (Camp Confidential Ser.: 17). 160p. (J). (gr. 3-7). pap. 4.99 *(978-0-448-44651-5(0),* Grosset & Dunlap) Penguin Young Readers Group.
Morgan, Michaela. Mouse with No Name. Mikhail, Jess, illus. 2004. (ENG.). 24p. (J). lib. bdg. 23.65 *(978-1-59646-682-1(0))* Dingles & Co.
Morgan, Nicolette, illus. All about Me: Briana's Neighborhood. 2007. 24p. (J). 15.99 *(978-0-9793904-0-1(0))* It's Me Briana, LLC.
Morgan, Ruth. Batter Splatter! Mikhail, Jess, illus. 2005. (ENG.). 24p. (J). lib. bdg. 23.65 *(978-1-59646-704-0(5))* Dingles & Co.
Morgan, Winter. Hidden in the Chest. 2017. (Unofficial Minecrafters Academy Ser.: 5). lib. bdg. 18.40 *(978-0-606-40310-8(8))* Turtleback.
—Skeleton Battle: The Unofficial Minecrafters Academy Series, Book Two. 2016. (Unofficial Minecrafters Academy Seri Ser.). (ENG.). 112p. (J). (gr. 1-7). pap. 7.99 *(978-1-5107-0595-1(3),* Sky Pony Pr.) Skyhorse Publishing Co., Inc.
Morimoto, Diana. Max, He Likes it that Way, 1 vol. 2010. 24p. pap. 24.95 *(978-1-4489-6851-0(8))* PublishAmerica, Inc.
Morin, James F. Rothshield Chasing Shadows. 2006. pap. 14.95 *(978-1-59330-422-5(6))* Aventine Pr.
Moritzky, Kayla. The Great I Don't Know. 2009. 28p. pap. 15.49 *(978-1-4389-8651-7(3))* AuthorHouse.
Moritzky, Sager. The Super Bad Slime Ball from Outer Space. 2011. 28p. pap. 14.99 *(978-1-4389-8652-4(1))* AuthorHouse.
Morpurgo, Michael. Snakes & Ladders. Wilson, Anne, illus. 2006. (Yellow Bananas Ser.). (ENG.). 48p. (J). (gr. -1-3). lib. bdg. *(978-0-7787-0952-7(3))* Crabtree Publishing Co.
—Snakes & Ladders. Kober, Shahar, illus. 2013. (Red Bananas Ser.). (ENG.). 48p. (J). (gr. -1-2). pap. 17.44 *(978-1-4052-6081-7(5))* Farshore GBR. Dist: Children's Plus, Inc.
Morris, Brittney. Slay. 2019. (ENG., Illus.). 336p. (YA). (gr. 7). 19.99 *(978-1-5344-4542-0(0),* Simon Pulse) Simon Pulse.
Morris, Chad. Cragbridge Hall, Book 2: The Avatar Battle. 2014. (Cragbridge Hall Ser.: 2). (ENG., Illus.). 360p. (J). (gr. 3-9). 17.99 *(978-1-60907-809-6(8),* Shadow Mountain) Shadow Mountain Publishing.
—Cragbridge Hall, Book 3: The Impossible Race. 2015. (Cragbridge Hall Ser.: 3). (ENG., Illus.). 432p. (J). (gr. 3-9). 18.99 *(978-1-60907-979-6(5),* 5127575, Shadow Mountain) Shadow Mountain Publishing.
Morris, Chad & Brown, Shelly. Squint. 2018. (ENG., Illus.). 256p. (J). (gr. 3-6). 16.99 *(978-1-62972-485-0(8),* 5206075) Shadow Mountain Publishing.
Morris, Kimberly. Take Me to Your Weeder (Book 3) Responsibility. Warrick, Jessica, illus. 2016. (How to Be an Earthling (r) Ser.: 3). (ENG.). 64p. (J). (gr. 1-3). E-Book 34.65 *(978-1-57565-826-1(7))* Astra Publishing Hse.
Morris, Taylor. BFF Breakup. 2011. (Mix Ser.). (ENG.). 288p. (J). (gr. 4-8). pap. 6.99 *(978-1-4424-0758-9(1),* Aladdin) Simon & Schuster Children's Publishing.
—Blowout, 1. Higgins, Anne Keenan, illus. 2011. (Hello, Gorgeous! Ser.: 1). (ENG.). 224p. (J). (gr. 6-8). 18.69 *(978-0-448-45526-6(9),* Grosset & Dunlap) Penguin Publishing Group.
—Do's & Don'ts, 5 vols., 5. Higgins, Anne Keenan, illus. 2012. (Hello, Gorgeous! Ser.: 5). (ENG.). 224p. (J). (gr. 6-8). 21.19 *(978-0-448-45861-8(6))* Penguin Young Readers Group.
Morrison, Julia. Wishes. Fabian, Gabriella, illus. 2013. 42p. pap. 10.00 *(978-1-883651-65-7(4))* Winters Publishing.

Morrissey, Lynda I. Monsters in My Class. 2013. 32p. pap. *(978-1-4602-2017-7(X))* FriesenPress.

Morse, Scott. Magic Pickle: a Graphic Novel. Morse, Scott, illus. 2008. (ENG., Illus.). 112p. (J). (gr. 2-5). pap. 9.99 *(978-0-439-87995-8(7)*, Graphix) Scholastic, Inc.

Mortensen, Lori. The Lost Lunch, 1 vol. Simard, Rémy, illus. 2011. (My First Graphic Novel Ser.). (ENG.). 32p. (J). (gr. k-2). pap. 6.25 *(978-1-4342-3103-1(8)*, 114743, Stone Arch Bks.) Capstone.

Mortenson, Greg & Husain, Farzana. Listen to the Children: The Story of Dr. Greg & Stones into Schools. Roth, Susan L., illus. 2011. (ENG.). 32p. (J). (gr. 1-3). 17.99 *(978-0-8037-3593-4(6)*, Dial) Penguin Publishing Group.

Morton, Carlene. The Library Pages. Docampo, Valeria, illus. 2010. 32p. (J). (gr. k-4). 17.95 *(978-1-60213-045-6(0)*, Upstart Bks.) Highsmith Inc.

Moser, Lisa. The Monster in the Backpack: Candlewick Sparks. Jones, Noah Z., illus. 2013. (Candlewick Sparks Ser.). (ENG.). 40p. (J). (gr. k-4). pap. 5.99 *(978-0-7636-6643-9(2))* Candlewick Pr.

Mosher, Jennifer. Who Caught the Yawn? & Where Did the Sneeze Go? Sharp, Todd, illus. 2013. 38p. pap. *(978-0-9874832-3-2(4))* MoshPit Publishing.

Mosier, Paul. Echo's Sister. 2018. (ENG., Illus.). 240p. (J). (gr. 3-7). 16.99 *(978-0-06-245567-3(2)*, HarperCollins) HarperCollins Pubs.

Mosley, Walter. When the Thrill Is Gone: A Leonid Mcgill Mystery, 3 vols. 2012. (Leonid Mcgill Mystery Ser.: 3). (ENG.). 384p. (gr. 12). 16.00 *(978-0-451-23565-7(7)*, Berkley) Penguin Publishing Group.

Moss, Marissa. The All-New Amelia. Moss, Marissa, illus. (ENG., Illus.). (J). 2013. 5.99 *(978-1-4169-1289-7(4))* 2007. 40p. (gr. 2-5). 14.99 *(978-1-4169-0908-8(7))* Simon & Schuster/Paula Wiseman Bks. (Simon & Schuster/Paula Wiseman Bks.).

—Amelia Writes Again. Moss, Marissa, illus. (Amelia Ser.). (ENG., Illus.). (J). (gr. 2-5). 2012. 32p. pap. 8.99 *(978-1-4169-1285-9(1))* 2006. 40p. 14.99 *(978-1-4169-0904-0(4))* Simon & Schuster/Paula Wiseman Bks. (Simon & Schuster/Paula Wiseman Bks.).

—Amelia's 5th-Grade Notebook. Moss, Marissa, illus. 2006. (Amelia Ser.). (ENG., Illus.). 40p. (J). (gr. 2-5). 14.99 *(978-1-4169-0912-5(5)*, Simon & Schuster/Paula Wiseman Bks.) Simon & Schuster/Paula Wiseman Bks.

—Amelia's 6th-Grade Notebook. Moss, Marissa, illus. 2005. (Amelia Ser.). (ENG., Illus.). 80p. (J). (gr. 4-7). 14.99 *(978-0-689-87040-8(X)*, Simon & Schuster/Paula Wiseman Bks.) Simon & Schuster/Paula Wiseman Bks.

—Amelia's BFF. Moss, Marissa, illus. 2011. (Amelia Ser.). (ENG., Illus.). 64p. (J). (gr. 5-8). 9.99 *(978-1-4424-0376-5(4)*, Simon & Schuster/Paula Wiseman Bks.) Simon & Schuster/Paula Wiseman Bks.

—Amelia's Boy Survival Guide. Moss, Marissa, illus. 2012. (Amelia Ser.). (ENG., Illus.). 80p. (J). (gr. 4-8). 9.99 *(978-1-4424-4084-5(8)*, Simon & Schuster/Paula Wiseman Bks.) Simon & Schuster/Paula Wiseman Bks.

—Amelia's Middle-School Graduation Yearbook. 2015. (ENG., Illus.). 80p. (J). (gr. 4-6). 12.95 *(978-1-939547-09-5(1)*, cc1703b1-73b5-4d09-abf9-7ef376bb0cb7) Creston Bks.

—Amelia's Middle School Survival Guide: Amelia's Most Unforgettable Embarrassing Moments, Amelia's Guide to Gossip. Moss, Marissa, illus. 2009. (Amelia Ser.). (ENG., Illus.). 160p. (J). (gr. 5-8). 14.99 *(978-1-4169-7987-6(5)*, Simon & Schuster/Paula Wiseman Bks.) Simon & Schuster/Paula Wiseman Bks.

—Blood Diaries: Tales of a 6th-Grade Vampire. 2014. (ENG., Illus.). 136p. (J). (gr. 4-6). 13.00 *(978-1-939547-05-7(9)*, 443b9f74-42dd-4a5c-a10d-c918bb9b0e82) Creston Bks.

—The Fake Friend! Moss, Marissa, illus. 2012. (Daphne's Diary of Daily Disasters Ser.). (ENG., Illus.). 96p. (J). (gr. 2-5). 9.99 *(978-1-4424-4014-2(7))*; pap. 5.99 *(978-1-4424-4015-9(5))* Simon & Schuster/Paula Wiseman Bks. (Simon & Schuster/Paula Wiseman Bks.).

—The Name Game! Moss, Marissa, illus. 2011. (Daphne's Diary of Daily Disasters Ser.). (ENG., Illus.). 80p. (J). (gr. 2-5). lib. bdg. 9.99 *(978-1-4424-2676-4(4)*, Simon & Schuster/Paula Wiseman Bks.) Simon & Schuster/Paula Wiseman Bks.

—The Vampire Dare! Moss, Marissa, illus. 2011. (Daphne's Diary of Daily Disasters Ser.). (ENG., Illus.). 80p. (J). (gr. 2-5). pap. 5.99 *(978-1-4424-1737-3(4))*; lib. bdg. 9.99 *(978-1-4424-2677-1(2))* Simon & Schuster/Paula Wiseman Bks. (Simon & Schuster/Paula Wiseman Bks.).

—Vote 4 Amelia. Moss, Marissa, illus. 2007. (Amelia Ser.). (ENG., Illus.). 80p. (J). (gr. 4-7). 14.99 *(978-1-4169-2789-1(1)*, Simon & Schuster/Paula Wiseman Bks.) Simon & Schuster/Paula Wiseman Bks.

Moss, Peggy. One of Us, 1 vol. 2010. (ENG., Illus.). 32p. (J). (gr. 1-7). 16.95 *(978-0-88448-322-9(3)*, 884322) Tilbury Hse. Pubs.

—Say Something: 10th-Anniversary Edition, 1 vol. Lyon, Lea, illus. 2013. (ENG.). 32p. (J). (gr. 2-7). pap. 9.95 *(978-0-88448-360-1(6)*, 884360) Tilbury Hse. Pubs.

Moss, Peggy & Lyon, Lea. Say Something, 1 vol. 2008. (ENG., Illus.). 32p. (J). (gr. 1-7). pap. 7.95 *(978-0-88448-310-6(X))* Tilbury Hse. Pubs.

Mostoller, Marcia. Emma's Dilemm. 2011. 42p. pap. 16.95 *(978-1-4560-9859-9(4))* America Star Bks.

Mounts, Samia. Frunk the Skunk. Matricardi, Luca, illus. 2008. (ENG.). 150p. (J). (gr. 4-6). pap. 9.95 *(978-0-9798841-0-8(1))* 4N Publishing LLC.

Moverley, Richard. The Reluctant Rajput. Dean, David, illus. 2005. (Yellow Go Bananas Ser.). (ENG.). 48p. (J). (gr. 3-4). lib. bdg. *(978-0-7787-2723-1(8))* Crabtree Publishing Co.

Muhammad, Ibtihaj. The Proudest Blue: A Story of Hijab & Family. Aly, Hatem, illus. 2019. (ENG.). 40p. (J). (gr. -1-3). 17.99 *(978-0-316-51900-7(6))* Little, Brown Bks. for Young Readers.

Mulford, Carolyn. The Feedsack Dress. 2007. 227p. (J). per. 7.95 *(978-0-9713497-4-2(6))* Cave Hollow Pr.

Mullaly Hunt, Lynda. Fish in a Tree. (J). (gr. 5). 2017. (Illus.). 320p. 8.99 *(978-0-14-242642-5(3)*, Puffin Books) 2015. 288p. 17.99 *(978-0-399-16259-6(3)*, Nancy Paulsen Books) Penguin Young Readers Group.

Mullarkey, Lisa. Carly. Franco, Paula, illus. 2016. (Chicas Poni (Pony Girls) Ser.).Tr. of Carly. (SPA.). 112p. (J). (gr. 1-4). lib. bdg. 38.50 *(978-1-61479-621-3(1)*, 25052, Calico Chapter Bks.) ABDO Publishing Co.

—Gabriela. Franco, Paula, illus. 2016. (Chicas Poni (Pony Girls) Ser.).Tr. of Gabriela. (SPA.). 112p. (J). (gr. 1-4). lib. bdg. 38.50 *(978-1-61479-623-7(8)*, 25056, Calico Chapter Bks.) ABDO Publishing Co.

—Kianna. Franco, Paula, illus. 2016. (Chicas Poni (Pony Girls) Ser.).Tr. of Kianna. (SPA.). 112p. (J). (gr. 1-4). lib. bdg. 38.50 *(978-1-61479-624-4(6)*, 25058, Calico Chapter Bks.) ABDO Publishing Co.

Mullican, Judy. Jonah Starts School. Cress, Michelle H., illus. l.t. ed. 2003. (HRL Little Book Ser.). 8p. (J). (gr. -1-1). pap. 10.95 *(978-1-57332-269-0(5))*; pap. 10.95 *(978-1-57332-268-3(7))* Carson-Dellosa Publishing, LLC. (HighReach Learning, Incorporated).

Mulligan, Andy. Ribblestrop. (Ribblestrop Ser.). (ENG., Illus.). (J). (gr. 3-7). 2016. 400p. pap. 7.99 *(978-1-4424-9905-8(2))* 2014. 384p. 16.99 *(978-1-4424-9904-1(4))* Beach Lane Bks. (Beach Lane Bks.).

—Ribblestrop Forever! 2016. (Ribblestrop Ser.). (ENG., Illus.). 320p. (J). (gr. 3-7). 16.99 *(978-1-4424-9910-2(9)*, Beach Lane Bks.) Beach Lane Bks.

Mullins, Julie. School Play Stars. Maddock, Monika, illus. 2005. (Girlz Rock! Ser.). (J). pap. *(978-1-59336-706-0(6))* Mondo Publishing.

Muluka, B. Kandu & the Lake. 2004. (Illus.). 44p. pap. *(978-9966-25-165-7(0))* Heinemann Kenya, Limited (East African Educational Publishers Ltd E.A.E.P.) KEN. Dist: Michigan State Univ. Pr.

Munday, Evan. Loyalist to a Fault: The Dead Kid Detective Agency #3. 2015. (ENG., Illus.). 304p. (J). (gr. 2-7). pap. 11.95 *(978-1-77041-074-9(0)*, 66f4ad47-f8c6-47ec-af19-682ae5eedb9c) ECW Pr. CAN. Dist: Baker & Taylor Publisher Services (BTPS).

Munsch, Robert. Class Clown. Martchenko, Michael, illus. 2019. (ENG.). 32p. (J). pap. 7.99 *(978-0-439-93594-4(6))* Scholastic Canada, Ltd. CAN. Dist: Publishers Group West (PGW).

—Get Out of Bed! 2004. (Illus.). (J). (gr. k-3). spiral bd. *(978-0-616-04557-2(3))*; spiral bd. *(978-0-616-03049-3(5))* Canadian National Institute for the Blind/Institut National Canadien pour les Aveugles.

—Kiss Me, I'm Perfect! Martchenko, Michael, illus. 2008. (J). (gr. -1-3). 11.65 *(978-0-7569-9007-7(6))* Perfection Learning Corp.

—Pyjama Day! Martchenko, Michael, illus. 2019. (ENG.). 32p. (J). pap. 8.99 *(978-1-4431-3917-5(3))* Scholastic Canada, Ltd. CAN. Dist: Publishers Group West (PGW).

—El Traje de Nieve de Tomás. Martchenko, Michael, illus. 2004. (Munsch for Kids Ser.). (ENG.). 24p. (J). (gr. -1-2). pap. 7.95 *(978-1-55037-854-2(6)*, 9781550378542) Annick Pr., Ltd. CAN. Dist: Publishers Group West (PGW).

Murail, Marie-aude. Sin Azúcar, Gracias. 2003. (la Orilla Del Viento Ser.). (SPA.). 101p. (J). pap. 8.50 *(978-968-16-6725-2(5))* Fondo de Cultura Economica USA.

Murdoch, Patricia. Exposure, 1 vol. 2006. (Orca Soundings Ser.). (ENG.). 128p. (YA). (gr. 8-12). pap. 9.95 *(978-1-55143-493-3(8))* Orca Bk. Pubs. USA.

—Revelación, 1 vol. 2008. (Spanish Soundings Ser.). (SPA.). 112p. (YA). (gr. 8-12). pap. 9.95 *(978-1-55469-053-4(6))* Orca Bk. Pubs. USA.

Murdock, Kita Helmetag. Future Flash. 2014. (ENG.). 208p. (J). (gr. 2-7). 12.95 *(978-1-62873-822-3(7)*, Sky Pony Pr.) Skyhorse Publishing Co., Inc.

Mureddu, R. The Laundromat. 2011. 96p. pap. 19.95 *(978-1-4560-8389-2(9))* America Star Bks.

Murozumi, Hikaru & Inokuma, Shinobu. The School of Water Business. (Illus.). (YA). 206p. pap. *(978-4-09-153102-5(4))*; Vol. 4. 2005. (JPN., 205p. mass mkt. *(978-4-09-153104-9(0))*; Vol. 5. (JPN., 205p. mass mkt. *(978-4-09-153105-6(9))* Shogakukan.

Murphy, Eileen. 3 Big Steps. Montgomery, Violet, illus. 2008. 25p. pap. 24.95 *(978-1-60563-310-7(0))* America Star Bks.

Murphy, Jill. A Bad Spell for the Worst Witch. Murphy, Jill, illus. 2014. (Worst Witch Ser.: 2). (ENG., Illus.). 128p. (J). (gr. 3-7). pap. 6.99 *(978-0-7636-7252-2(1))* Candlewick Pr.

—The Worst Witch Saves the Day. Murphy, Jill, illus. 2014. (Worst Witch Ser.: 5). (ENG., Illus.). 160p. (J). (gr. 3-7). pap. 6.99 *(978-0-7636-7255-3(6))* Candlewick Pr.

—The Worst Witch to the Rescue. Murphy, Jill, illus. 2014. (Worst Witch Ser.: 6). (ENG., Illus.). 176p. (J). (gr. 3-7). 14.99 *(978-0-7636-6999-7(7))* Candlewick Pr.

Murphy, Pat. The Wild Girls. unabr. ed. 2007. (YA). (gr. 6-9). audio compact disk 45.00 *(978-0-7393-5988-4(6))* Random Hse. Audio Publishing Group.

Murphy, Sally. Pearl Verses the World. Potter, Heather, illus. 2011. (ENG.). 80p. (J). (gr. 3-7). 14.99 *(978-0-7636-4821-3(3))* Candlewick Pr.

Murphy, Stuart J. Freda Is Found. 2011. (I See I Learn Ser.: 7). (Illus.). 32p. (J). (-k). 14.95 *(978-1-58089-462-3(3))*; pap. 6.95 *(978-1-58089-463-0(1))* Charlesbridge Publishing, Inc.

—Freda Stops a Bully. 2012. (I See I Learn Ser.: 11). (ENG., Illus.). 32p. (J). (-k). pap. 6.95 *(978-1-58089-467-8(4))* Charlesbridge Publishing, Inc.

—Great Choice, Camille! 2013. (I See I Learn Ser.: 14). (Illus.). 32p. (J). (-k). pap. 6.95 *(978-1-58089-477-7(1))*; (gr. -1-k). lib. bdg. 14.95 *(978-1-58089-476-0(3))* Charlesbridge Publishing, Inc.

Murray, Alison. Hickory Dickory Dog. Murray, Alison, illus. 2014. (ENG., Illus.). 32p. (J). (-k). 16.99 *(978-0-7636-6826-6(5))* Candlewick Pr.

Murray, C. J. Shayna Gladstone: In Search of the Scientist. 2011. 148p. 22.95 *(978-1-4502-8992-4(4))*; pap. 12.95 *(978-1-4502-8990-0(8))* iUniverse, Inc.

Murray, Fisher C & Murray, Colleen O. One & Only Bernadette P. McMull. 2009. (ENG.). 32p. pap. 10.95 *(978-1-933916-52-1(4)*, Ferne Pr.) Nelson Publishing & Marketing.

Murray, Jaye. Bottled Up. 2004. 224p. (YA). (gr. 7-12). reprint ed. 8.99 *(978-0-14-240240-5(0)*, Speak) Penguin Young Readers Group.

Murray, Laura. The Gingerbread Man & the Leprechaun Loose at School. Lowery, Mike, illus. 2018. (Gingerbread Man Is Loose Ser.: 5). 32p. (J). (-k). 18.99 *(978-1-101-99694-2(3)*, G.P. Putnam's Sons Books for Young Readers) Penguin Young Readers Group.

—The Gingerbread Man Loose at Christmas. Lowery, Mike, illus. 2015. (Gingerbread Man Is Loose Ser.: 3). 32p. (J). (gr. k-k). bds. 18.99 *(978-0-399-16866-6(4)*, G.P. Putnam's Sons Books for Young Readers) Penguin Young Readers Group.

—The Gingerbread Man Loose in the School. Lowery, Mike, illus. 2011. (Gingerbread Man Is Loose Ser.: 1). 32p. (J). (gr. k-3). 18.99 *(978-0-399-25052-1(2)*, G.P. Putnam's Sons Books for Young Readers) Penguin Young Readers Group.

Murray, Stuart A. P. Todd Goes for the Goal, 1 vol. 2012. (Champion Sports Story Ser.). (ENG.). 104p. (J). (gr. 3-5). pap. 13.88 *(978-1-4644-0000-1(8)*, 87b16cab-bcf9-4436-b487-a5de5c41931f); lib. bdg. 30.60 *(978-0-7660-3887-5(4)*, 08a03198-79a7-4c86-82be-341a28864a30) Enslow Publishing, LLC.

Murtagh, Ciaran. Megastar: the Fincredible Diary of Fin Spencer. Wesson, Tim, illus. 2016. (Fincredible Diary of Fin Spencer Ser.: 2). (ENG.). 224p. (J). (gr. 4-7). pap. 7.99 *(978-1-84812-447-9(3))* Bonnier Publishing GBR. Dist: Independent Pubs. Group.

Musolf, Nell. Jessica James. 2003. (J). per. *(978-0-9740833-0-8(5))* Port Town Publishing.

My First Day at School. 2005. (J). 16.95 *(978-0-9769004-0-5(8))* Sinanan, Cindy.

My Teacher Glows in the Dark. 2014. (My Teacher Bks.: 3). (ENG., Illus.). 192p. (J). (gr. 3-7). 17.99 *(978-1-4814-0432-7(6)*, Simon & Schuster/Paula Wiseman Bks.) Simon & Schuster/Paula Wiseman Bks.

Myers, Edward. Duck & Cover. 2004. 200p. (J). per. 11.95 *(978-0-9674477-8-0(X))* Montemayor Pr.

—Ice. 2005. 222p. (J). per. 12.95 net. *(978-0-9674477-9-7(8))* Montemayor Pr.

Myers, Jean Emily. Mickey's Mini Farm. Tanner Voyles, illus. 2009. 32p. pap. 21.99 *(978-1-4389-5544-5(8))* AuthorHouse.

Myers, Lily. This Impossible Light. 2017. 352p. (YA). (gr. 7). 17.99 *(978-0-399-17372-1(2)*, Philomel Bks.) Penguin Young Readers Group.

Myers, Suzanne. I'm from Nowhere. 2017. 304p. (YA). (gr. 9). pap. 10.99 *(978-1-61695-706-3(9)*, Soho Teen) Soho Pr., Inc.

Myers, Walter Dean. The Beast. 2005. 17.00 *(978-0-7569-5107-8(0))* Perfection Learning Corp.

—Game. (ENG.). (YA). (gr. 8). 2009. 240p. pap. 15.99 *(978-0-06-058296-8(0))* 2008. 224p. 17.99 *(978-0-06-058294-4(4))* HarperCollins Pubs. (HarperTeen).

—Game. 2011. 10.36 *(978-0-7848-3476-3(8)*, Everbind) Marco Bk. Co.

—Shooter. (ENG.). 2004. 224p. (J). 15.99 *(978-0-06-029519-6(8)*, HarperTeen) 2005. 256p. (YA). (gr. 9-17). reprint ed. pap. 11.99 *(978-0-06-447290-6(6)*, Amistad) HarperCollins Pubs.

—Slam! 2008. (ENG.). 288p. (J). (gr. 7). pap. 12.99 *(978-0-545-05574-1(1)*, Scholastic Paperbacks) Scholastic, Inc.

—Slam! 2008. (Point Signature Ser.). 266p. (gr. 7-12). lib. bdg. 19.65 *(978-0-613-12111-8(2))* Turtleback.

—A Star Is Born. 2012. (Cruisers Ser.: Bk. 3). 160p. (J). *(978-0-439-91631-8(3))* Scholastic, Inc.

Myracle, Lauren. Awesome Blossom: A Flower Power Book. 2013. (Flower Power Ser.). (ENG.). 272p. (J). (gr. 3-7). pap. 7.95 *(978-1-4197-0791-9(4)*, 694403); (YA). (gr. 4-8). 17.95 *(978-1-4197-0405-5(2)*, 694401) Abrams, Inc. (Amulet Bks.).

—Eleven. 2005. (Winnie Years Ser.: 2). 224p. (J). (gr. 3-7). reprint ed. pap. 7.99 *(978-0-14-240346-4(6)*, Puffin Books) Penguin Young Readers Group.

—The Fashion Disaster That Changed My Life. 2008. 160p. (J). (gr. 5-18). 6.99 *(978-0-14-240717-2(8)*, Puffin Books) Penguin Young Readers Group.

—Friends of a Feather. Henry, Jed, illus. 2015. (Life of Ty Ser.: 3). (ENG.). 144p. (J). (gr. 1-4). 7.99 *(978-0-14-242320-2(3)*, Puffin Books) Penguin Young Readers Group.

—Luv Ya Bunches: A Flower Power Book. 2010. (ENG.). 352p. (YA). (gr. 4-8). pap. 8.95 *(978-0-8109-8982-5(4)*, 629503, Amulet Bks.) Abrams, Inc.

—Luv Ya Bunches: Book One, Bk. 1. 2009. (ENG., Illus.). 340p. (J). (gr. 4-8). 16.95 *(978-0-8109-4211-0(9)*, 629501, Amulet Bks.) Abrams, Inc.

—Non-Random Acts of Kindness. Henry, Jed, illus. 2015. (Life of Ty Ser.: 2). (ENG.). 128p. (J). (gr. 1-4). 5.99 *(978-0-14-242319-6(X)*, Puffin Books) Penguin Young Readers Group.

—Oopsy Daisy: A Flower Power Book. 2012. (Flower Power Ser.). (ENG.). 368p. (YA). (gr. 4-8). pap. 8.95 *(978-1-4197-0418-5(4)*, 694303, Amulet Bks.) Abrams, Inc.

—Penguin Problems. 2014. (Life of Ty Ser.: 1). lib. bdg. 16.00 *(978-0-606-34213-1(3))* Turtleback.

—Rhymes with Witches. (ENG.). (YA). (gr. 8-17). 2006. 272p. pap. 7.95 *(978-0-8109-9215-3(9))* 2005. 224p. 16.95 *(978-0-8109-5859-3(7)*, Amulet Bks.) Abrams, Inc.

—Ten. 2012. (Winnie Years Ser.: 1). (ENG.). 240p. (J). (gr. 3-7). pap. 9.99 *(978-0-14-242134-5(0)*, Puffin Books) Penguin Young Readers Group.

—Thirteen. (ENG.). (J). 2009. (Winnie Years Ser.: 4). 272p. (gr. 3-7). 9.99 *(978-0-14-241370-8(4)*, Puffin Books)3. 2008. (Winnie Years Ser.). 244p. (gr. 6-8). 18.69 *(978-0-525-47896-6(5))* Penguin Young Readers Group.

Naitanui, Nic. Little Nic's Big Day. Anaya, Fatima, illus. 2019. (ENG.). 32p. (J). (gr. -1-k). 15.99 *(978-1-76087-687-6(9)*, Albert Street Bks.) Allen & Unwin AUS. Dist: Independent Pubs. Group.

Nakakuma, Chie. Whazzup, Wolly Ayaka? 2007. 128p. per. 10.95 *(978-0-595-44646-9(9))* iUniverse, Inc.

Nana, Auntie. I Can't Go to School Today. 2012. pap. 12.95 *(978-0-7414-8105-4(7))* Infinity Publishing.

—I Can't Go to School Today with CD. 2012. pap. 16.95 *(978-0-7414-7756-9(4))* Infinity Publishing.

Napoli, Linda. Sailing Away on a Windy Day. 2012. 24p. pap. 17.32 *(978-1-4797-2962-3(0))* Xlibris Corp.

Nash, Andy. Melinda & Her Mule: For Kids Blessed with a Strong Will. 2008. (J). *(978-0-8127-0453-2(3))* Autumn Hse. Publishing Co.

Na'Shae. The Magic Chronicles: Ice. 2008. 80p. pap. 9.99 *(978-0-9814650-6-7(4))* G Publishing LLC.

Nathoo, Aalaynah. The World above Us!!! 2012. 16p. pap. 15.99 *(978-1-4772-3222-4(2))* AuthorHouse.

National Geographic Learning. Windows on Literacy Emergent (Social Studies: History/Culture): My Friend & I. 2007. (ENG., Illus.). 12p. (J). pap. 11.95 *(978-0-7922-8949-4(8))* CENGAGE Learning.

Nawrocki, Mike. Boy Meets Squirrels. Séguin-Magee, Luke, illus. 2019. (Dead Sea Squirrels Ser.: 2). (ENG.). 128p. (J). pap. 6.99 *(978-1-4964-3502-6(8)*, 20_32041, Tyndale Kids) Tyndale Hse. Pubs.

Nayeri, Daniel & Nayeri, Dina. Another Jekyll, Another Hyde. 2012. (ENG., Illus.). 400p. (YA). (gr. 9). 17.99 *(978-0-7636-5261-6(X))* Candlewick Pr.

Naylor, Phyllis Reynolds. Eating Enchiladas, 0 vols. Ramsey, Marcy, illus. 2013. (Simply Sarah Ser.: 4). (ENG.). 80p. (J). (gr. 1-4). pap. 9.99 *(978-0-7614-5885-2(9)*, 9780761458852, Two Lions) Amazon Publishing.

Neal-Bailey, Ashley L. I Don't Want To. 2007. 20p. per. 24.95 *(978-1-4241-8928-1(4))* America Star Bks.

Neal, Elizabeth. The Game. 2019. (Do-Over Ser.). (ENG.). 104p. (YA). (gr. 6-12). pap. 7.99 *(978-1-5415-4550-2(8)*, 753d5a92-d328-441e-a1eb-15f1319548eb); 26.65 *(978-1-5415-4031-6(X)*, 776a0bbc-83fa-422f-a2a2-262e3925a662) Lerner Publishing Group. (Darby Creek).

Neely, Wilma F. Aaron & Abbey Go to School: Trevor Tutors His Friends. 2009. 28p. pap. 12.49 *(978-1-4389-5420-2(4))* AuthorHouse.

Neenan, Colin. Idiot! A Love Story with Drama, Betrayal & E-mail. 2004. (Illus.). 152p. (YA). (gr. 7-13). per. 8.95 *(978-0-9746481-1-8(6))* Brown Barn Bks.

—Thick. 2006. 126p. (YA). (gr. 7-16). per. 6.95 *(978-0-9746481-9-4(1))* Brown Barn Bks.

Nees, Susan. Class Pets. 2013. (Missy's Super Duper Royal Deluxe Ser.: 2). (ENG., Illus.). 80p. (J). (gr. k-2). pap. 4.99 *(978-0-545-43852-0(7))* Scholastic, Inc.

—Class Pets. 2013. (Missy's Super Duper Royal Deluxe Ser.: 2). lib. bdg. 14.75 *(978-0-606-31980-5(8))* Turtleback.

—Missy's Super Duper Royal Deluxe: Picture Day. 2013. (Missy's Super Duper Royal Deluxe Ser.: 1). (ENG., Illus.). 80p. (J). (gr. k-2). pap. 4.99 *(978-0-545-43851-3(9))* Scholastic, Inc.

—Picture Day. 2013. (Missy's Super Duper Royal Deluxe Ser.: 1). lib. bdg. 14.75 *(978-0-606-31979-9(4))* Turtleback.

—School Play. 2013. (Missy's Super Duper Royal Deluxe Ser.: 3). (ENG., Illus.). 80p. (J). (gr. k-2). pap. 4.99 *(978-0-545-43853-7(5))* Scholastic, Inc.

Neff, Henry H. The Fiend & the Forge: Book Three of the Tapestry. 2011. (Tapestry Ser.: 3). (ENG., Illus.). 560p. (J). (gr. 3-7). 9.99 *(978-0-375-83899-6(6)*, Yearling) Random Hse. Children's Bks.

—The Hound of Rowan, 1. Neff, Henry H., illus. 2007. (Tapestry Ser.: Bk. 1). (ENG., Illus.). 432p. (J). (gr. 4-6). lib. bdg. 24.94 *(978-0-375-93894-8(X))* Random House Publishing Group.

—The Hound of Rowan: Book One of the Tapestry. 2008. (Tapestry Ser.: 1). (ENG., Illus.). 448p. (J). (gr. 3-7). 9.99 *(978-0-375-83895-8(3)*, Yearling) Random Hse. Children's Bks.

—The Maelstrom: Book Four of the Tapestry, Bk. 4. Neff, Henry H., illus. 2013. (Tapestry Ser.: 4). (Illus.). 480p. (J). (gr. 3-7). 8.99 *(978-0-375-87148-1(9)*, Yearling) Random Hse. Children's Bks.

—The Second Siege: Book Two of the Tapestry. 2010. (Tapestry Ser.: 2). (ENG., Illus.). 512p. (J). (gr. 3-7). 9.99 *(978-0-375-83897-2(X)*, Yearling) Random Hse. Children's Bks.

Neill, Chloe. Charmfall: A Novel of the Dark Elite. 2012. (Dark Elite Ser.: 3). (ENG.). 288p. (YA). (gr. 9). 9.99 *(978-0-451-23080-5(9)*, Berkley) Penguin Publishing Group.

Nelid, Piper. At the School Store, 1 vol., 1. 2015. (Rosen REAL Readers: STEM & STEAM Collection). (ENG.). 8p. (J). (gr. k-1). pap. 5.46 *(978-1-5081-1511-3(7)*, 0a897907-21d4-46c6-8a79-14a0110ceabf, Rosen Classroom) Rosen Publishing Group, Inc., The.

Nelson, Blake. Boy. (ENG.). (YA). (gr. 9). 2018. 384p. pap. 12.99 *(978-1-4814-8814-3(7))* 2017. (Illus.). 368p. 18.99 *(978-1-4814-8813-6(9))* Simon Pulse. (Simon Pulse).

—The New Rules of High School. 2004. (ENG.). 240p. (YA). (gr. 7-18). reprint ed. 7.99 *(978-0-14-240242-9(7)*, Speak) Penguin Young Readers Group.

—Paranoid Park. 2008. (ENG.). 192p. (YA). (gr. 7-18). 6.99 *(978-0-14-241156-8(6)*, Puffin Books) Penguin Young Readers Group.

Nelson, James Gary. Dientecito y la Placa Peligros. Bumstead, Debbie, illus. 2011. 16p. pap. 9.95 *(978-1-61633-132-0(1))* Guardian Angel Publishing, Inc.

Nelson, Jim. Crosstown Crush. 2005. 82p. Vol. 1, Bk. 1. (YA). pap. 9.00 *(978-1-4116-5266-8(5))* Vol. 1,Bk. 2. (ENG.). pap. 9.00 *(978-1-4116-6654-2(2))* Lulu Pr., Inc.

Nelson, Katie A. The Duke of Bannerman Prep. 2017. (ENG.). 320p. (J). (gr. 8-8). 17.99 *(978-1-5107-1040-5(X)*, Sky Pony Pr.) Skyhorse Publishing Co., Inc.

Nelson, Shareese. The Me Inside. 2009. 20p. 10.99 *(978-1-4389-4937-6(5))* AuthorHouse.

Nelson, Sheila K. The Backpack Bears' Adventure: Friendship. 2009. 24p. pap. 16.50 *(978-1-4490-0554-2(3))* AuthorHouse.

Nelson, Suzanne. You're Bacon Me Crazy. 2014. 248p. (J). pap. *(978-0-545-65268-1(5))* Scholastic, Inc.

Nemeth, Sally. The Heights, the Depths, & Everything in Between. 2008. (ENG.). 262p. (J). (gr. 6-8). lib. bdg. 21.19 *(978-0-375-93458-2(8)*, Yearling) Random Hse. Children's Bks.

Neri, G. Chess Rumble. Watson, Jesse Joshua, illus. 2007. (ENG.). 64p. (J). (gr. 3-7). 18.95 *(978-1-58430-279-7(8))* Lee & Low Bks., Inc.

Nero, Molly. Smarty Pig & the Test Taking Terror. Turchan, Monique, illus. 2012. 28p. pap. 12.95 *(978-1-61244-055-2(X))* Halo Publishing International.

Ness, Berthetta. Originals: Short Stories for Children. 2007. (YA). pap. *(978-1-57579-351-1(2))* Pine Hill Pr.

Ness, Patrick. A Monster Calls: Inspired by an Idea from Siobhan Dowd. Kay, Jim, illus. (ENG.). 224p. (YA). (gr. 7). 2013. pap. 12.00 *(978-0-7636-6065-9(5))* 2011. 22.99 *(978-0-7636-5559-4(7))* Candlewick Pr.

—A Monster Calls: Inspired by an Idea from Siobhan Dowd. 2011. (Playaway Children Ser.). (YA). (gr. 7-12). 54.99 *(978-1-4558-4499-9(3))* Findaway World, LLC.

—A Monster Calls: Inspired by an Idea from Siobhan Dowd. 2013. lib. bdg. 23.30 *(978-0-606-31603-3(5))* Turtleback.

—A Monster Calls: a Novel (Movie Tie-In) Inspired by an Idea from Siobhan Dowd. 2016. (ENG.). 240p. (YA). (gr. 7). pap. 9.99 *(978-0-7636-9215-5(8))* Candlewick Pr.

—The Rest of Us Just Live Here. (YA). 2016. (ENG.). 336p. (gr. 9). pap. 12.99 *(978-0-06-240317-9(6),* Quill Tree Bks.) 2015. (ENG.). 336p. (gr. 9-12). 17.99 *(978-0-06-240316-2(8),* Quill Tree Bks.) 2015. 317p. *(978-0-06-241563-9(8))* 2015. 352p. *(978-1-4063-3116-5(3))* HarperCollins Pubs.

Neubecker, Robert. Fall Is for School. Neubecker, Robert, illus. 2017. (ENG., Illus.). 32p. (J). (gr. -1-k). 17.99 *(978-1-4847-3254-0(5))* Disney Pr.

New York Hall of Science, The. Charlie & Kiwi: An Evolutionary Adventure. FableVision & Reynolds, Peter H., illus. 2011. (ENG.). 48p. (J). (gr. -1-3). 19.99 *(978-1-4424-2112-7(6),* Atheneum Bks. for Young Readers) Simon & Schuster Children's Publishing.

Newman, Yvette. Missy's Day with Butterflies. 2007. 84p. pap. 11.96 *(978-1-4357-0172-4(0))* Lulu Pr., Inc.

Newton, A. I. The Alien Next Door 1: the New Kid. Sarkar, Anjan, illus. 2018. (Alien Next Door Ser.: 1). (ENG.). 112p. (J). (gr. k-3). 16.99 *(978-1-4998-0559-8(4));* pap. 5.99 *(978-1-4998-0558-1(6))* Little Bee Books Inc.

—The Alien Next Door 6: the Mystery Valentine. Sarkar, Anjan, illus. 2018. (Alien Next Door Ser.: 6). (ENG.). 112p. (J). (gr. k-3). 16.99 *(978-1-4998-0726-4(0));* pap. 5.99 *(978-1-4998-0725-7(2))* Little Bee Books Inc.

—The Mystery Valentine, 6. 2019. (Alien Next Door Ch Bks). (ENG.). 95p. (J). (gr. 2-3). 15.59 *(978-0-87617-272-8(9))* Penworthy Co., LLC, The.

—The New Kid, 1. 2019. (Alien Next Door Ch Bks). (ENG.). 95p. (J). (gr. 2-3). 15.59 *(978-0-87617-273-5(7))* Penworthy Co., LLC, The.

Nichols, C. D. Kids Courageous. 2010. 66p. pap. 9.99 *(978-1-60911-809-9(X),* Eloquent Bks.) Strategic Book Publishing & Rights Agency (SBPRA).

Nichols, Travis. Matthew Meets the Man. 2012. (ENG., Illus.). 176p. (YA). (gr. 6-9). 24.99 *(978-1-59643-545-2(3),* 900061886) Roaring Brook Pr.

Nickel, Scott. Attack of the Mutant Lunch Lady: A Buzz Beaker Brainstorm. Smith, Andy, illus. 2008. (Graphic Sparks Ser.). (ENG.). 40p. (J). (gr. 2-5). per. 5.95 *(978-1-4342-0501-8(0),* 94449, Stone Arch Bks.) Capstone.

—Invasion of the Gym Class Zombies. Luxich, Matt, illus. 2008. (Graphic Sparks Ser.). (ENG.). 40p. (J). (gr. 2-5). pap. 5.95 *(978-1-4342-0503-2(7),* 94451, Stone Arch Bks.) Capstone.

—Secret of the Summer School Zombies. Luxich, Matt, illus. 2008. (Graphic Sparks Ser.). (ENG.). 40p. (J). (gr. 2-5). pap. 5.95 *(978-1-4342-0856-9(7),* 95217, Stone Arch Bks.) Capstone.

Nickelodeon Staff & LeapForg Staff/Nickelodeon. Dora the Explorer: Dora Goes to School. 2008. (J). 13.99 *(978-1-59319-985-2(6))* LeapFrog Enterprises, Inc.

Nielson, Laney. Peppermint Cocoa Crushes: A Swirl Novel. 2017. (Swirl Ser.: 2). (ENG.). 256p. (J). (gr. 3-7). 7.99 *(978-1-5107-3008-3(7));* 16.99 *(978-1-5107-3046-5(X))* Skyhorse Publishing Co., Inc. (Sky Pony Pr.).

The Night Before Kindergarten. 2014. (Night Before Ser.). (ENG.). 32p. (J). (gr. 7-12). 8.24 *(978-1-63245-263-4(4))* Lectorum Pubns., Inc.

Night, P. J. The Show Must Go On! (You're Invited to a Creepover Ser.: 4). (ENG.). 160p. (J). (gr. 3-7). 2018. 17.99 *(978-1-5344-2108-0(4))* 2011. pap. 6.99 *(978-1-4424-2905-5(4))* Simon Spotlight. (Simon Spotlight).

—The Show Must Go On! 2011. (Creepover Ser.: 4). lib. bdg. 16.00 *(978-0-606-23748-2(8))* Turtleback.

—Truth or Dare ..., 1. 2011. (You're Invited to a Creepover Ser.: 1). (ENG., Illus.). 160p. (J). (gr. 3-7). pap. 7.99 *(978-1-4424-2096-0(0),* Simon Spotlight) Simon & Schuster Children's Publishing.

—Truth or Dare ... 2018. (You're Invited to a Creepover Ser.: 1). (ENG.). 160p. (J). (gr. 3-7). 17.99 *(978-1-5344-1657-4(9),* Simon Spotlight) Simon Spotlight.

—You're Invited to a Creep over: The Show Must Go On!, 1 vol. 2013. (You're Invited to a Creepover Ser.). (ENG.). 160p. (J). (gr. 3-6). lib. bdg. 31.36 *(978-1-61479-063-1(9),* 15851, Chapter Bks.) Spotlight.

Nigro, D. M. The Wolfman, the Shrink & the Eighth-Grade Election. 2006. 116p. (J). pap. 13.50 *(978-1-931201-66-7(8))* Twilight Times Bks.

Nijkamp, Marieke. This Is Where It Ends. (YA). (gr. 8-12). 2019. 336p. pap. 10.99 *(978-1-4926-7111-4(8))* 2016. (ENG.). 288p. 17.99 *(978-1-4926-2246-8(X),* 9781492622468) Sourcebooks, Inc.

—This Is Where It Ends. 2016. lib. bdg. 22.10 *(978-0-606-39479-6(6))* 2017. lib. bdg. 22.10 *(978-0-606-39992-0(5))* Turtleback.

Nikki, Grimes. Bronx Masquerade. 2014. (ENG.). 176p. (YA). 11.24 *(978-1-63245-077-7(1))* Lectorum Pubns., Inc.

Nimble, Jacque. Copy Cat, 2. 2010. (School Gyrls Ser.). (ENG.). 128p. (J). (gr. 2-4). 18.69 *(978-1-4424-0877-7(4))* Simon & Schuster, Inc.

—Prank Wars. 2011. (School Gyrls Ser.). (ENG.). 144p. (J). (gr. 3-7). pap. 5.99 *(978-1-4424-0880-7(4),* Simon & Schuster/Paula Wiseman Bks.) Simon & Schuster/Paula Wiseman Bks.

Nimmo, Jenny. Midnight for Charlie Bone. 2003. (Children of the Red King Ser.: Bk. 1). (J). (gr. 2-6). per. 4.99 *(978-0-439-48839-6(7))* Scholastic, Inc.

Nishimori, Hiroyuki. Cheeky Angel, Vol. 13. Nishimori, Hiroyuki, illus. 2006. (Cheeky Angel Ser.). (ENG., Illus.). 208p. pap. 9.99 *(978-1-4215-0447-6(2))* Viz Media.

Nixon, Kareh. The Little Woman in My House. 2012. 24p. pap. 14.93 *(978-1-4669-6302-3(6))* Trafford Publishing.

Nobel, Julia. The Mystery of Black Hollow Lane. 2020. (Black Hollow Lane Ser.: 1). 320p. (J). (gr. 3-7). pap. 8.99 *(978-1-4926-9154-9(2))* Sourcebooks, Inc.

Nobisso, Josephine. En Ingles, por Supuesto. Ziborova, Dasha, illus. 2003. Orig. Title: In English, of Course. (SPA.). 32p. (J). (gr. k-2). 16.95 *(978-0-940112-14-8(0))* Gingerbread Hse.

—En ingles, por Supuesto. Ziborova, Dasha, illus. 2003. Orig. Title: In English, of Course. (SPA.). 32p. (J). (gr. k-2). pap. 8.95 *(978-0-940112-16-2(7))* Gingerbread Hse.

—In English, of Course. Ziborova, Dasha, illus. 2003.Tr. of En Ingles, Por Supuesto. (ENG.). 32p. (J). (gr. -1). 16.95 *(978-0-940112-07-0(8));* pap. 8.95 *(978-0-940112-08-7(6))* Gingerbread Hse.

Noble, Trinka Hakes. Jimmy's Boa & the Bungee Jump Slam Dunk. Kellogg, Steven, illus. 2005. 28p. (gr. -1-3). 16.00 *(978-0-7569-5765-0(6))* Perfection Learning Corp.

—Lizzie & the Last Day of School. McLeod, Kris Aro, illus. 2015. (ENG.). 32p. (J). (gr. k-2). 17.99 *(978-1-58536-895-2(4),* 203811) Sleeping Bear Pr.

—The Orange Shoes. Ettlinger, Doris, illus. rev. ed. 2007. (ENG.). 40p. (J). (gr. 1-4). 16.95 *(978-1-58536-277-6(8),* 202088) Sleeping Bear Pr.

Noel, Alyson. Shadowland: The Immortals. 2010. (Immortals Ser.: 3). (ENG.). 368p. (YA). (gr. 7-12). pap. 15.00 *(978-0-312-65005-6(1),* 900069209, St. Martin's Griffin) St. Martin's Pr.

Nolan, Lea. Illusion. 2015. (ENG., Illus.). 370p. (YA). (gr. 7). pap. 19.99 *(978-1-943892-53-2(9))* Entangled Publishing, LLC.

Nolen, Gale. Johnny, My Favorite Mouse. Cain, Doreyl Ammons, illus. 2007. 32p. (J). per. 18.95 *(978-0-9753023-7-8(X))* Ammons Communications, Ltd.

Nordling, Lee. Belinda the Unbeatable. Roberts, Scott, illus. 2017. (Game for Adventure Ser.). (ENG.). 40p. (J). (gr. k-3). pap. 7.99 *(978-1-5124-5413-0(3),* 7a9a22e0-0436-4379-a428-63687de7d873, Graphic Universe™) Lerner Publishing Group.

Norris, Elizabeth. Unraveling. 2013. (Unraveling Ser.: 1). (ENG.). 480p. (YA). (gr. 8). pap. 9.99 *(978-0-06-210374-1(1),* Balzer & Bray) HarperCollins Pubs.

Norris, Shana. Something to Blog About. 2008. (ENG.). 256p. (J). (gr. 2-7). 16.95 *(978-0-8109-9474-4(7),* 6308, Amulet Bks.) Abrams, Inc.

—Troy High. 2009. (ENG.). 208p. (YA). (gr. 8-17). 16.95 *(978-0-8109-4647-7(5),* 630901, Amulet Bks.) Abrams, Inc.

Northrop, Michael. Trapped. 2011. (ENG.). 240p. (J). (gr. 7-10). 17.99 *(978-0-545-21012-6(7),* Scholastic Pr.) Scholastic, Inc.

Norton, Preston. Neanderthal Opens the Door to the Universe. 2018. (ENG.). 416p. (YA). (gr. 9-12). E-Book 45.00 *(978-1-4847-9839-3(2))* Little, Brown Bks. for Young Readers.

Norton, Tamra. Molly Mormon? Myth or Me? 2011. (Illus.). 170p. (YA). pap. 11.99 *(978-1-55517-606-8(2),* Bonneville Bks.) Cedar Fort, Inc./CFI Distribution.

—Shayla Witherwood: A Half-Faerie Tale. 2012. pap. 16.99 *(978-1-59955-963-6(3))* Cedar Fort, Inc./CFI Distribution.

Nöstlinger, Christine. Nuevas Historias de Franz en la Escuela. (Torre de Papel Ser.). (SPA.). (J). (gr. 2). 7.95 *(978-958-04-1013-3(5))* Norma S.A. COL. Dist: Distribuidora Norma, Inc.

Noth, Paul. How to Properly Dispose of Planet Earth. 2019. (ENG., Illus.). 192p. (J). 13.99 *(978-1-68119-659-6(X),* 900179851, Bloomsbury Children's Bks.) Bloomsbury Publishing USA.

Nothing Ever Happens 6 Packs. Individual Title. (gr. -1-2). 27.00 *(978-0-7635-9467-1(9))* Rigby Education.

Novel Units. The Best (Worst) School Year Ever Novel Units Student Packet. 2019. (ENG.). (J). pap., stu. ed. 13.99 *(978-1-58130-647-7(4),* Novel Units, Inc.) Classroom Library Co.

—The Best (Worst) School Year Ever Novel Units Teacher Guide. 2019. (ENG.). (J). pap., tchr. ed. 12.99 *(978-1-58130-646-0(6),* Novel Units, Inc.) Classroom Library Co.

—Harry Potter & the Prisoner of Azkaban Novel Units Student Packet. 2019. (Harry Potter Ser.: Year 3). (ENG.). (J). pap., stu. ed. 13.99 *(978-1-58130-657-6(1),* Novel Units, Inc.) Classroom Library Co.

—Harry Potter & the Prisoner of Azkaban Novel Units Teacher Guide. 2019. (Harry Potter Ser.: Year 3). (ENG.). (J). pap., tchr. ed. 12.99 *(978-1-58130-656-9(3),* Novel Units, Inc.) Classroom Library Co.

—A Ramona Quimby, Age 8 Novel Units Student Packet. 2019. (Ramona Quimby Ser.). (ENG.). (J). (gr. 3-5). pap. 13.99 *(978-1-56137-708-4(2),* NU7082SP, Novel Units, Inc.) Classroom Library Co.

—A Ramona Quimby, Age 8 Novel Units Teacher Guide. 2019. (ENG.). (J). (gr. 3-5). pap. 12.99 *(978-1-56137-448-9(2),* Novel Units, Inc.) Classroom Library Co.

—Ramona the Brave Novel Units Teacher Guide. 2019. (Ramona Quimby Ser.). (ENG.). (J). (gr. 3-5). pap. 12.99 *(978-1-56137-444-1(X),* Novel Units, Inc.) Classroom Library Co.

—Surviving the Applewhites Novel Units Student Packet. 2019. (ENG.). (J). (gr. 7-8). pap., stu. ed. 13.99 *(978-1-58130-868-6(X),* Novel Units, Inc.) Classroom Library Co.

—Surviving the Applewhites Novel Units Teacher Guide. 2019. (ENG.). (J). (gr. 7-8). pap., tchr. ed. 12.99 *(978-1-58130-867-9(1),* Novel Units, Inc.) Classroom Library Co.

—The View from Saturday Novel Units Student Packet. 2019. (ENG.). (J). pap. 13.99 *(978-1-56137-936-1(0),* Novel Units, Inc.) Classroom Library Co.

Novik, Naomi. Will Supervillains Be on the Final? Liberty Vocational Volume 1. Li, Yishan, illus. 2011. 192p. pap. 12.99 *(978-0-345-51656-5(7),* Del Rey) Random Hse. Worlds.

Nowlin, Laura. This Song Is (Not) for You. 2016. 240p. (YA). (gr. 8-12). pap. 12.99 *(978-1-4926-0290-3(6),* 9781492602903) Sourcebooks, Inc.

Ntihemuka, Patty Froese. Hyacinth Doesn't Go to Jail: And, Hyacinth Doesn't Miss Christmas. 2009. (Illus.). 157p. (J). pap. 10.99 *(978-0-8163-2372-2(0))* Pacific Pr. Publishing Assn.

—Hyacinth Doesn't Grow Up: And Hyacinth Doesn't Drown. 2010. (J). pap. 10.99 *(978-0-8163-2386-9(0))* Pacific Pr. Publishing Assn.

Numeroff, Laura. Si Llevas un Ratón a la Escuela: If You Take a Mouse to School (Spanish Edition), 1 vol. Bond, Felicia, illus. 2003. (If You Give... Ser.).Tr. of If You Take a Mouse to School. (SPA.). 32p. (J). (gr. -1-3). 17.99 *(978-0-06-052340-4(9),* HarperCollins) HarperCollins Pubs.

—Time for School, Mouse! Bond, Felicia, illus. 2019. (If You Give... Ser.). (ENG.). 24p. (J). (gr. -1 — 1). bds. 7.99 *(978-0-06-143307-8(1),* HarperFestival) HarperCollins Pubs.

—Time for School, Mouse! Lap Edition. Bond, Felicia, illus. 2016. (If You Give... Ser.). (ENG.). 24p. (J). (gr. -1-3). bds. 12.99 *(978-0-06-242741-0(5),* HarperFestival) HarperCollins Pubs.

Numeroff, Laura Joffe. If You Take a Mouse to School. 2004. (Illus.). (J). (gr. k-3). spiral bd. *(978-0-616-14593-7(4));* spiral bd. *(978-0-616-14594-4(2))* Canadian National Institute for the Blind/Institut National Canadien pour les Aveugles.

Nunez, Alonso & Brasil, Bruna Assis. No! I Won't Go to School, 1 vol. Morrison, Dave, illus. 2018. (ENG.). 32p. (J). (gr. -1-1). 16.95 *(978-0-88448-646-6(X),* 884646) Tilbury Hse. Pubs.

Nunn, Malla. When the Ground Is Hard. 2019. (ENG.). 272p. (YA). (gr. 7). 17.99 *(978-0-525-51557-9(7),* G.P. Putnam's Sons Books for Young Readers) Penguin Young Readers Group.

Nuurali, Siman. Sadiq & the Desert Star. Sarkar, Anjan, illus. 2019. (Sadiq Ser.). (ENG.). 64p. (J). (gr. 1-3). 23.32 *(978-1-5158-3878-4(1),* 139596, Picture Window Bks.) Capstone.

—Sadiq & the Pet Problem. Sarkar, Anjan, illus. 2019. (Sadiq Ser.). (ENG.). 64p. (J). (gr. 1-3). pap. 6.95 *(978-1-5158-4568-3(0),* 141156, Picture Window Bks.) Capstone.

Nydam, Anne. The Bad Advice of Grandma Hasenfuss. 2010. 112p. pap. 14.00 *(978-0-557-26037-9(X))* Lulu Pr., Inc.

Oakes, Colleen. The Black Coats. 2020. (ENG.). 416p. (YA). (gr. 9). pap. 10.99 *(978-0-06-267964-2(3),* HarperTeen) HarperCollins Pubs.

—Blood of Wonderland. 2017. (Queen of Hearts Ser.: 2). (ENG.). (YA). (gr. 8). 352p. pap. 9.99 *(978-0-06-240977-5(8));* 336p. 17.99 *(978-0-06-240976-8(X))* HarperCollins Pubs. (HarperTeen).

Oakes, Cory Putman. Dinosaur Boy Saves Mars. 2016. (Dinosaur Boy Ser.: 2). (ENG.). 224p. (J). (gr. 3-7). 18.40 *(978-0-606-39306-5(4))* Turtleback.

Oates, Joyce Carol. Sexy. 2005. 272p. (J). (gr. 7-18). 16.99 *(978-0-06-054149-1(0),* HarperTeen) HarperCollins Pubs.

—Two or Three Things I Forgot to Tell You. (ENG.). (YA). (gr. 9). 2013. 304p. pap. 9.99 *(978-0-06-211048-0(9))* 2012. 288p. 17.99 *(978-0-06-211047-3(0))* HarperCollins Pubs. (HarperTeen).

Oberne, Sharon. Kelsey. 2006. 88p. (YA). pap. 13.95 *(978-1-58909-340-9(2))* Bookstand Publishing.

Obioha, Natalie O. Emotions. 2010. 120p. pap. 19.99 *(978-1-4500-2791-5(1))* Xlibris Corp.

Obstacles in Our Way: Individual Title Six-Packs. (gr. k-1). 23.00 *(978-0-7635-9067-3(3))* Rigby Education.

Ocean, Davy. Deep-Sea Disaster. Blecha, Aaron, illus. 2014. (Shark School Ser.: 1). (ENG.). 128p. (J). (gr. 1-4). 17.99 *(978-1-4814-0679-6(5),* Aladdin) Simon & Schuster Children's Publishing.

—Deep-Sea Treasury: Deep-Sea Disaster; Lights! Camera! Hammerhead!; Squid-Napped; the Boy Who Cried Shark. Blecha, Aaron, illus. 2015. (Shark School Ser.). (ENG.). 528p. (J). (gr. 1-4). 14.99 *(978-1-4814-5115-4(4),* Aladdin) Simon & Schuster Children's Publishing.

—Fishin' Impossible, 8. Blecha, Aaron, illus. 2017. (Shark School Ser.). (ENG.). 144p. (J). (gr. 1-3). 21.19 *(978-1-5364-1675-6(4),* Aladdin) Simon & Schuster Children's Publishing.

—Fishin': Impossible. Blecha, Aaron, illus. 2017. (Shark School Ser.: 8). (ENG.). 144p. (J). (gr. 1-4). pap. 6.99 *(978-1-4814-6549-6(X),* Aladdin) Simon & Schuster Children's Publishing.

—Long Fin Silver. Blecha, Aaron, illus. 2018. (Shark School Ser.: 9). (ENG.). 144p. (J). (gr. 1-4). 16.99 *(978-1-4814-6553-3(8));* pap. 6.99 *(978-1-4814-6552-6(X))* Simon & Schuster Children's Publishing. (Aladdin).

—Splash Dance. Blecha, Aaron, illus. 2015. (Shark School Ser.: 6). (ENG.). 128p. (J). (gr. 1-4). pap. 5.99 *(978-1-4814-0694-9(9),* Aladdin) Simon & Schuster Children's Publishing.

Oceanak, Karla. Dumbstruck. Spanjer, Kendra, illus. 2011. (Aldo Zelnick Comic Novel Ser.: 4). (ENG.). 160p. (J). (gr. 3-7). 12.95 *(978-1-934649-16-9(3))* Bailiwick Pr.

Ockler, Sarah. #scandal. 2014. (ENG., Illus.). 416p. (YA). (gr. 9). 17.99 *(978-1-4814-0124-1(6),* Simon Pulse) Simon Pulse.

O'Connell, Jenny. The Book of Luke. 2007. (ENG.). 304p. (YA). (gr. 7). pap. 11.00 *(978-1-4165-2040-5(6),* MTV Bks.) MTV Books.

O'Connell, Rebecca. Penina Levine Is a Hard-Boiled Egg. Lue Sue, Majella, illus. 2009. (ENG.). 192p. (J). (gr. 3-7). pap. 18.99 *(978-0-312-55026-4(X),* 900055956) Square Fish.

O'Connell, Tyne. A Royal Match. 2011. (Calypso Chronicles Ser.). (ENG.). 512p. (YA). pap. 9.99 *(978-1-59990-751-2(8),* 9781599907512, Bloomsbury USA Childrens) Bloomsbury Publishing USA.

O'Connor, Barbara. Fame & Glory in Freedom, Georgia. 2008. (ENG.). 112p. (J). (gr. 2-4). pap. 8.99 *(978-0-374-40018-7(0),* 900050869) Square Fish.

O'connor, Jane. Best Reading Buddies. 2016. (Fancy Nancy - I Can Read! Ser.). (J). lib. bdg. 13.55 *(978-0-606-39273-0(4))* Turtleback.

O'Connor, Jane. Fancy Day in Room 1-A. 2012. (Fancy Nancy - I Can Read! Ser.). (J). lib. bdg. 13.55 *(978-0-606-26259-0(8))* Turtleback.

—Fancy Nancy: Fancy Day in Room 1-A. 2012. (I Can Read Level 1 Ser.). (ENG., Illus.). 32p. (J). (gr. -1-3). 16.99 *(978-0-06-208305-0(8),* HarperCollins) HarperCollins Pubs.

—Fancy Nancy: Fancy Day in Room 1A. 2012. (I Can Read Level 1 Ser.). (ENG., Illus.). 32p. (J). (gr. -1-3). pap. 4.99 *(978-0-06-208304-3(X),* HarperCollins) HarperCollins Pubs.

—Fancy Nancy: My Family History. 2010. (I Can Read Level 1 Ser.). (ENG., Illus.). 32p. (J). (gr. -1-3). pap. 5.99 *(978-0-06-188271-5(2),* HarperCollins) HarperCollins Pubs.

—Fancy Nancy: Nancy Clancy Seeks a Fortune. Glasser, Robin Preiss, illus. 2016. (Nancy Clancy Ser.: 7). (ENG.). 144p. (J). (gr. 1-5). 9.99 *(978-0-06-226969-0(0),* HarperCollins) HarperCollins Pubs.

—Fancy Nancy: Nancy Clancy, Soccer Mania. Glasser, Robin Preiss, illus. 2016. (Nancy Clancy Ser.: 6). (ENG.). 144p. (J). (gr. 1-5). pap. 4.99 *(978-0-06-226966-9(6),* HarperCollins) HarperCollins Pubs.

—Fancy Nancy: Nancy Clancy, Super Sleuth. 2013. (Nancy Clancy Ser.: 1). (J). lib. bdg. 14.75 *(978-0-606-31795-5(3))* Turtleback.

—Fancy Nancy: Splendid Speller. Glasser, Robin Preiss, illus. 2011. (I Can Read Level 1 Ser.). (ENG.). 32p. (J). (gr. -1-3). 17.99 *(978-0-06-200176-4(0),* HarperCollins) HarperCollins Pubs.

—Fancy Nancy: The Dazzling Book Report. 2009. (I Can Read Level 1 Ser.). (ENG., Illus.). 32p. (J). (gr. -1-3). pap. 4.99 *(978-0-06-170368-3(0),* HarperCollins) HarperCollins Pubs.

—Fancy Nancy: The Dazzling Book Report. Glasser, Robin Preiss & Enik, Ted, illus. 2009. (Fancy Nancy Ser.). 32p. lib. bdg. 14.00 *(978-1-60686-531-6(5))* Perfection Learning Corp.

—Fancy Nancy: The Show Must Go On. 2009. (I Can Read Level 1 Ser.). (ENG., Illus.). 32p. (J). (gr. -1-3). pap. 5.99 *(978-0-06-170372-0(9),* HarperCollins) HarperCollins Pubs.

—Fancy Nancy: Time for Puppy School. Glasser, Robin Preiss, illus. 2017. (I Can Read Level 1 Ser.). (ENG.). 32p. (J). (gr. -1-3). pap. 4.99 *(978-0-06-237786-9(8),* HarperCollins) HarperCollins Pubs.

—Fancy Nancy & the Boy from Paris. Glasser, Robin Preiss, illus. 2008. (I Can Read Level 1 Ser.). (ENG.). 32p. (J). (gr. -1-3). 16.99 *(978-0-06-123610-5(1));* pap. 4.99 *(978-0-06-123609-9(8))* HarperCollins Pubs. (HarperCollins).

—Fancy Nancy & the Too-Loose Tooth. Glasser, Robin Preiss, illus. 2012. (I Can Read Level 1 Ser.). (ENG.). 32p. (J). (gr. -1-3). 17.99 *(978-0-06-208301-2(5));* pap. 4.99 *(978-0-06-208302-9(3))* HarperCollins Pubs. (HarperCollins).

—Fancy Nancy & the Too-Loose Tooth. 2012. (Fancy Nancy - I Can Read! Ser.). (J). lib. bdg. 13.55 *(978-0-606-23551-8(5))* Turtleback.

—Fancy Nancy Collector's Quintet. 2009. (I Can Read Level 1 Ser.). (ENG., Illus.). (J). (gr. k-3). 19.99 *(978-0-06-171905-9(6),* HarperCollins) HarperCollins Pubs.

—Fancy Nancy: Every Day Is Earth Day: A Springtime Book for Kids. Glasser, Robin Preiss et al, illus. 2010. (I Can Read Level 1 Ser.). (ENG.). 32p. (J). (gr. -1-3). 16.99 *(978-0-06-187327-0(6));* pap. 5.99 *(978-0-06-187326-3(8))* HarperCollins Pubs. (HarperCollins).

—Fancy Nancy: Nancy Clancy, Secret Admirer. Glasser, Robin Preiss, illus. 2013. (Nancy Clancy Ser.: 2). (ENG.). (J). (gr. 1-5). 144p. pap. 5.99 *(978-0-06-208420-0(8));* 128p. 9.99 *(978-0-06-208295-4(7))* HarperCollins Pubs. (HarperCollins).

—Fancy Nancy: Nancy Clancy, Soccer Mania. Glasser, Robin Preiss, illus. 2015. (Nancy Clancy Ser.: 6). (ENG.). 128p. (J). (gr. 1-5). 9.99 *(978-0-06-226967-6(4),* HarperCollins) HarperCollins Pubs.

—Fancy Nancy: Nancy Clancy, Super Sleuth. Glasser, Robin Preiss, illus. (Nancy Clancy Ser.: 1). (ENG.). (J). (gr. 1-5). 2013. 144p. pap. 5.99 *(978-0-06-208419-4(4))* 2012. 128p. 9.99 *(978-0-06-208293-0(0))* HarperCollins Pubs. (HarperCollins).

—Fancy Nancy: Nancy Clancy's Tres Charming Chapter Book Box Set: Books 1-3, 3 vols., Set. Glasser, Robin Preiss, illus. 2013. (Nancy Clancy Ser.). (ENG.). 384p. (J). (gr. 1-5). 24.99 *(978-0-06-227793-0(6),* HarperCollins) HarperCollins Pubs.

—Fancy Nancy: Pajama Day. Glasser, Robin Preiss et al, illus. 2009. (I Can Read Level 1 Ser.). (ENG.). 32p. (J). (gr. -1-3). 16.99 *(978-0-06-170371-3(0),* HarperCollins) HarperCollins Pubs.

—Fancy Nancy Pajama Day. 2009. (I Can Read Level 1 Ser.). (ENG., Illus.). 32p. (J). (gr. -1-3). pap. 4.99 *(978-0-06-170370-6(2),* HarperCollins) HarperCollins Pubs.

—Fancy Nancy: Poet Extraordinaire! Glasser, Robin Preiss, illus. 2010. (Fancy Nancy Ser.). (ENG.). 32p. (J). (gr. -1-2). 12.99 *(978-0-06-189643-9(8),* HarperCollins) HarperCollins Pubs.

—Fancy Nancy Sees Stars. 2008. (I Can Read Level 1 Ser.). (ENG., Illus.). 32p. (J). (gr. -1-3). pap. 4.99 *(978-0-06-123611-2(X),* HarperCollins) HarperCollins Pubs.

—Fancy Nancy Sees Stars. Glasser, Robin Preiss, illus. 2008. (I Can Read Level 1 Ser.). (ENG.). 32p. (J). (gr. -1-3). 17.99 *(978-0-06-123612-9(8),* HarperCollins) HarperCollins Pubs.

—Fancy Nancy: Splendid Speller. Glasser, Robin Preiss, illus. 2011. (I Can Read Level 1 Ser.). (ENG.). 32p. (J). (gr. -1-3). pap. 4.99 *(978-0-06-200175-7(2),* HarperCollins) HarperCollins Pubs.

—Fancy Nancy: the 100th Day of School. Glasser, Robin Preiss, illus. 2009. (I Can Read Level 1 Ser.). (ENG.). 32p. (J). (gr. -1-3). 16.99 *(978-0-06-170375-1(3));* pap. 4.99 *(978-0-06-170374-4(5))* HarperCollins Pubs. (HarperCollins).

—Fancy Nancy: the Dazzling Book Report. Glasser, Robin Preiss, illus. 2009. (I Can Read Level 1 Ser.). (ENG.). 32p. (J). (gr. -1-3). 16.99 *(978-0-06-170369-0(9),* HarperCollins) HarperCollins Pubs.

—Fancy Nancy: the Show Must Go On. Glasser, Robin Preiss, illus. 2009. (I Can Read Level 1 Ser.). (ENG.). 32p. (J). (gr. -1-3). 16.99 *(978-0-06-170373-7(7),* HarperCollins) HarperCollins Pubs.

—Lulu Goes to Witch School. 2013. (I Can Read Level 2 Ser.). (ENG., Illus.). 48p. (J). (gr. -1-3). 16.99 *(978-0-06-223351-6(3),* HarperCollins) HarperCollins Pubs.

—Lulu Goes to Witch School: A Halloween Book for Kids. Sinclair, Bella, illus. 2013. (I Can Read Level 2 Ser.). (ENG.). 48p. (J). (gr. -1-3). pap. 4.99 *(978-0-06-223350-9(5),* HarperCollins) HarperCollins Pubs.

—My Family History. 2010. (Fancy Nancy - I Can Read! Ser.). (J). lib. bdg. 13.55 *(978-0-606-14988-4(0))* Turtleback.

—Nancy Clancy, Secret Admirer. 2013. (Nancy Clancy Ser.: 2). (J). lib. bdg. 14.75 *(978-0-606-35045-7(4))* Turtleback.

—Nancy Clancy, Soccer Mania. Glasser, Robin Preiss, illus. 2016. (Nancy Clancy Ser.: 6). (ENG.). 144p. (J). (gr. 1-5). 14.75 *(978-0-606-39270-9(X))* Turtleback.

—Nancy Clancy, Star of Stage & Screen. 2016. (Nancy Clancy Ser.: 5). (J). lib. bdg. 14.75 *(978-0-606-38153-6(8))* Turtleback.

O'connor, Jane. Time for Puppy School. 2017. (Fancy Nancy - I Can Read! Ser.). (Illus.). 32p. (J). lib. bdg. 13.55 *(978-0-606-40059-6(1))* Turtleback.

O'Connor, Jane & Glasser, Robin Preiss. Fancy Nancy: My Family History. 2010. (I Can Read Level 1 Ser.). (ENG., Illus.). 32p. (J). (gr. -1-3). 16.99 *(978-0-06-188270-8(4),* HarperCollins) HarperCollins Pubs.

—It's Backward Day! Enik, Ted, illus. 2016. 32p. (J). (978-1-4806-9929-8(2)) Harper & Row Ltd.

O'Dell, Kathleen. Agnes Parker ... Girl in Progress. 2004. (ENG.). 176p. (J). (gr. 2-5). reprint ed. 6.99 (978-0-14-240228-3(1), Puffin Books) Penguin Young Readers Group.

O'Doherty, David. Danger Is Totally Everywhere: School of Danger. 2017. (Danger Is Everywhere Ser.: 3). (ENG., Illus.). 240p. (J). (gr. 3-7). 13.99 (978-0-316-50202-3(2)) Little, Brown Bks. for Young Readers.

O'Donnell, Tom. Hamstersaurus Rex Gets Crushed. Miller, Tim, illus. 2018. (Hamstersaurus Rex Ser.: 3). (ENG.). 304p. (J). (gr. 3-7). 13.99 (978-0-06-237758-6(2), HarperCollins) HarperCollins Pubs.

—Hamstersaurus Rex vs. the Cutepocalypse. Miller, Tim J., illus. 2018. (Hamstersaurus Rex Ser.: 4). (ENG.). 368p. (J). (gr. 3-7). 13.99 (978-0-06-237760-9(4), HarperCollins) HarperCollins Pubs.

Ofanansky, Allison. What's the Buzz? Honey for a Sweet New Year. Alpern, Eliyahu, illus. Alpern, Eliyahu, photos by. 2011. (High Holidays Ser.). (J). (gr. -1-k). lib. bdg. 15.95 (978-0-7613-5640-0(1)) Lerner Publishing Group.

Off to School: Individual Title Six-Packs. (Story Steps Ser.). (gr. k-2). 29.00 (978-0-7635-9577-7(2)) Rigby Education.

Oh, Jiwon. Mr. Monkey's Classroom. Oh, Jiwon, illus. 2005. (Illus.). 32p. (J). (gr. -1-2). lib. bdg. 15.89 (978-0-06-055722-5(2)) HarperCollins Pubs.

O'Hara, Mo. Jurassic Carp: My Big Fat Zombie Goldfish. Jagucki, Marek, illus. 2017. (My Big Fat Zombie Goldfish Ser.: 6). (ENG.). 224p. (J). pap. 6.99 (978-1-250-10260-7(X), 900163247) Square Fish.

Ohlin, Nancy. Consent. 2015. (ENG., Illus.). 288p. (YA). (gr. 9). 17.99 (978-1-4424-6490-2(9), Simon Pulse) Simon Pulse.

—Thorn Abbey. 2013. (ENG.). 304p. (YA). (gr. 9). 16.99 (978-1-4424-6486-5(0), Simon Pulse) Simon Pulse.

O'Keefe, Susan Heyboer. My Life & Death by Alexandra Canarsie, 1 vol. 2006. 224p. (J). (gr. 7-9). pap. 7.95 (978-1-56145-387-0(0)) Peachtree Publishing Co. Inc.

Okugas, Juanaiga. The tales of Mew the Cat. 2011. 92p. pap. 35.30 (978-1-4567-3480-0(6)) AuthorHouse.

Oliver, Carmen. Bears Make the Best Math Buddies. Claude, Jean, illus. 2019. (ENG.). 32p. (J). (gr. k-2). lib. bdg. 17.95 (978-1-68446-079-3(4), 140866, Capstone Editions) Capstone.

—Bears Make the Best Reading Buddies. Claude, Jean, illus. 2016. (Fiction Picture Bks.). (ENG.). 32p. (J). (gr. -1-1). lib. bdg. 21.27 (978-1-4795-9181-7(5), 131444, Picture Window Bks.) Capstone.

—No Hay Nada Más Chistoso Que Leer con un Oso. Aparicio Publishing LLC, Aparicio Publishing, tr. Claude, Jean, illus. (Cuentos Ilustrados de Ficción Ser.).Tr. of Bears Make the Best Reading Buddies. (SPA.). 32p. (J). (gr. -1-1). 2020. pap. 7.95 (978-1-5158-6081-5(7), 142360) 2019. lib. bdg. 21.27 (978-1-5158-4665-9(2), 141302) Capstone. (Picture Window Bks.).

Oliver, Ilanit. Olivia & the Best Teacher Ever. 2012. (Olivia 8x8 Ser.). lib. bdg. 13.55 (978-0-606-26367-2(5)) Turtleback.

Oliver, Lauren. Before I Fall. (ENG.). (YA). (gr. 9). 2021. 544p. pap. 11.99 (978-0-06-172681-1(8)) 2010. 480p. 17.99 (978-0-06-172680-4(X)) HarperCollins Pubs. (HarperCollins).

—Before I Fall. 2010. 368p. pap. (978-0-340-98090-3(7), Hodder Paperbacks) Hodder & Stoughton.

—Before I Fall. 2016. (YA). lib. bdg. 22.10 (978-0-606-23576-1(0)) Turtleback.

Olker, Constance. The Punctuation Pals Meet at School. 2005. (Illus.). 40p. (J). per. 18.95 (978-1-933449-07-4(1)) Nightengale Pr.

—The Punctuation Pals Meet at School. Guzman, Minerva, illus. 2004. (Punctuation Pals Ser.). 24p. (J). (gr. 1-18). 19.95 (978-0-9743348-6-8(3)) Nightengale Pr.

—The Punctuation Pals Meet at School. l.t. ed. 2005. (Illus.). 18p. (J). per. 16.95 (978-0-9761289-4-6(2)) Nightengale Pr.

Olsen EdS, Marci. Lessons to Live by: Character Building Books for School-Age Children. 2008. 52p. pap. 24.95 (978-1-60474-501-6(0)) America Star Bks.

Olson, Justin. Earth to Charlie. 2019. (ENG., Illus.). 288p. (YA). (gr. 7). 18.99 (978-1-5344-1952-0(7), Simon & Schuster Bks. For Young Readers) Simon & Schuster Bks. For Young Readers.

Olswanger, Anna. Greenhorn. Nerlove, Miriam, illus. 2012. (ENG.). (J). 48p. 17.95 (978-1-58838-235-1(4), 8806); E-Book 9.99 (978-1-60306-159-9(2), 8807) NewSouth, Inc. (NewSouth Bks.).

O'Malley, Kevin & Finchler, Judy. Miss Malarkey Leaves No Reader Behind. O'Malley, Kevin, illus. 2010. (Miss Malarkey Ser.). (ENG., Illus.). 32p. (J). (gr. k-3). pap. 8.99 (978-0-8027-2098-6(6), 900066992, Bloomsbury USA Childrens) Bloomsbury Publishing USA.

Onwusilikam, Ify Chinedum. The Drama Queen. 2009. 56p. pap. 10.00 (978-1-60860-126-4(9), Strategic Bk. Publishing) Strategic Book Publishing & Rights Agency (SBPRA).

Opio, Leoncio. The Adventures of Mr. Nimbus & the School House Bullies. 2012. 98p. pap. 19.95 (978-1-4626-9442-6(X)) America Star Bks.

Oram, Hiawyn. Filbert, the Good Little Fiend. Liao, Jimmy, illus. 2013. (ENG.). 32p. (J). (gr. -1-2). 15.99 (978-0-7636-5870-0(7)) Candlewick Pr.

Oramas, Jennifer. Peter's Purpose. Huseman, Ryan, illus. 2012. 34p. 24.95 (978-1-4626-6585-3(3)) America Star Bks.

O'Reilly, Sean. The Missing Mummy, 1 vol. 2011. (Mighty Mighty Monsters Ser.). (ENG., Illus.). 48p. (J). (gr. 2-4). lib. bdg. 23.99 (978-1-4342-3218-2(2), 116190, Stone Arch Bks.) Capstone.

Orme, David & Orme, Helen. Up for It? 2008. (Backstreet Ser.). (ENG., Illus.). 36p. pap. (978-1-84167-769-9(8)) Ransom Publishing Ltd.

Orme, Helen. Moving. 2008. (Siti's Sisters Ser.). (ENG., Illus.). 36p. pap. (978-1-84167-689-0(6)) Ransom Publishing Ltd.

—Rats! 2008. (Backstreet Ser.). (ENG., Illus.). 36p. pap. (978-1-84167-772-9(8)) Ransom Publishing Ltd.

—Taken for a Ride. Brett, Cathy, illus. 2007. (Siti's Sisters Ser.). (ENG.). 36p. (J). per. (978-1-84167-596-1(2)) Ransom Publishing Ltd.

—Trouble with Teachers. Brett, Cathy, illus. 2007. (Siti's Sisters Ser.). (ENG.). 36p. (J). per. (978-1-84167-599-2(7)) Ransom Publishing Ltd.

—Who's Who?, 2 vols., Set. 2008. (Siti's Sisters Ser.). (ENG., Illus.). 36p. pap. (978-1-84167-687-6(X)) Ransom Publishing Ltd.

—Won't Talk, Can't Talk. 2008. (Backstreet Ser.). (ENG., Illus.). 36p. pap. (978-1-84167-777-4(9)) Ransom Publishing Ltd.

Ormerod, Jan. Molly & Her Dad. Thompson, Carol, illus. 2008. 32p. (978-1-921272-55-4(4)) Little Hare Bks. AUS. Dist: HarperCollins Pubs. Australia.

Ormerod, Nicola. Roxy May, Help My Boyfriend Is a Fairy. 2012. 224p. pap. (978-1-909402-03-4(6)) Vamptasy Publishing.

Osa, Nancy. Cuba 15. 2011. 10.54 (978-0-7848-3376-6(1), Everbind) Marco Bk. Co.

Osborne, Mary Pope, et al. The Fun Starts Here! Four Favorite Chapter Books in One: Junie B. Jones, Magic Tree House, Purrmaids, & a to Z Mysteries. Murdocca, Sal, illus. 2018. (ENG.). 336p. (J). (gr. 1-4). 9.99 (978-1-9848-3059-3(7), Random Hse. Bks. for Young Readers) Random Hse. Children's Bks.

Oshima, Towa. High School Girls, Vol. 5. 2005. (High School Girls Ser.). (ENG., Illus.). 200p. (YA). pap. 9.95 (978-1-59796-058-8(6)) DrMaster Pubns. Inc.

—High School Girls Volume 1-6 Set. 2007. (ENG., Illus.). 200p. pap. 44.95 (978-1-59796-072-4(1)) DrMaster Pubns. Inc.

Osterlund, Anne. Academy 7. 2009. 272p. (YA). (gr. 7-18). pap. 8.99 (978-0-14-241437-8(9), Speak) Penguin Young Readers Group.

Ostler, Heather. The Siren's Secret. 2013. 16.99 (978-1-4621-1223-4(4), Horizon Pubs.) Cedar Fort, Inc./CFI Distribution.

Ostow, Micol. GoldenGirl. 2009. (Bradford Ser.). (ENG.). 224p. (YA). (gr. 9-18). pap. 9.99 (978-1-4169-6118-5(6), Simon Pulse) Simon Pulse.

Ostrovski, Emil. Away We Go. 2016. (ENG.). 272p. (YA). (gr. 9). 17.99 (978-0-06-223855-9(8), Greenwillow Bks.) HarperCollins Pubs.

Owens, L. L. The New Girl. Tolson, Scott, illus. 2004. 27p. (978-1-57021-029-7(2)) Comprehensive Health Education Foundation.

Oxenbury, Helen. Primer Dia de Escuela (First Day of School) 4th ed. (SPA., Illus.). 24p. (J). 7.50 (978-84-261-2002-1(4)) Juventud, Editorial ESP. Dist: AIMS International Bks., Inc.

Oz, Galia & Kahn-Hoffman, Gilah. Dog Trouble! 2017. 135p. (J). pap. (978-0-399-55023-2(2)) Bantam Doubleday Dell Large Print Group, Inc.

P. Cotton & Clyde & the Chameleons. 2011. 28p. (gr. -1 — 1). pap. 13.99 (978-1-4520-9675-9(9)) AuthorHouse.

Pace, Anne Marie. A Teacher for Bear. Wohnoutka, Mike, illus. 2011. (J). (978-0-545-37776-8(5)) Scholastic, Inc.

Pace, Marisa. Gina Goes to School: Over & over Again, 1 vol. 2017. (Computer Science for the Real World Ser.). (ENG.). 8p. (gr. k-1). pap. (978-1-5383-5086-7(6), 6ed6faa9-34c7-4869-8a78-92663d7e90a5, Rosen Classroom) Rosen Publishing Group, Inc., The.

Pacolet Elementary School Bookroom. 2018. (ENG.). pap. 5210.93 (978-1-4966-1798-9(3), Capstone Classroom) Capstone.

Padian, Maria. Brett McCarthy: Work in Progress. 2008. (ENG.). 288p. (J). (gr. 7-12). lib. bdg. 24.94 (978-0-375-94675-2(6), Knopf Bks. for Young Readers) Random Hse. Children's Bks.

—Brett Mccarthy: Work in Progress. 2009. (ENG.). 288p. (YA). (gr. 7). pap. 8.99 (978-0-440-24055-6(7), Knopf Bks. for Young Readers) Random Hse. Children's Bks.

Padula, Stacy A. Montgomery Lake High #2-When Darkness Tries to Hide. 2011. 146p. pap. 11.50 (978-1-60976-857-7(4), Eloquent Bks.) Strategic Book Publishing & Rights Agency (SBPRA).

Page, Winter. Breaking Free. (ENG., 2016. Illus.). (J). 24.99 (978-1-63477-943-2(6)) 2014. 180p. (YA). pap. 14.99 (978-1-62798-914-5(5)) Dreamspinner Pr. (Harmony Ink Pr.).

Palacio, R. J. Auggie & Me: Three Wonder Stories. 2015. (Wonder Ser.). (ENG.). 320p. (J). (gr. 3-7). 16.99 (978-1-101-93485-2(9)); lib. bdg. 19.99 (978-1-101-93486-9(7)) Random Hse. Children's Bks. (Knopf Bks. for Young Readers).

—Wonder. 2015. (JPN.). 420p. (J). (978-4-593-53495-1(X)) Holp Shuppan, Publishing.

—Wonder. 2017. (Illus.). 341p. (J). (978-1-5247-6446-3(9)) Knopf, Alfred A. Inc.

—Wonder. 2012. (Wonder Ser.). (ENG.). 320p. (J). (gr. 3-7). 17.99 (978-0-375-86902-0(6)); lib. bdg. 19.99 (978-0-375-96902-7(0)) Random Hse. Children's Bks. (Knopf Bks. for Young Readers).

—Wonder. l.t. ed. 2013. (ENG.). 482p. 23.99 (978-1-4104-5741-7(9)) Thorndike Pr.

—Wonder. 2012. lib. bdg. 29.40 (978-0-606-36646-5(6)) Turtleback.

—The Wonder Journal. 2015. (Wonder Ser.). (ENG.). 176p. (J). (gr. 3-7). 12.99 (978-0-553-49907-0(6), Knopf Bks. for Young Readers) Random Hse. Children's Bks.

—Wonder: la Historia de Julián / the Julian Chapter: a Wonder Story. 2015. (SPA.). 160p. (J). (gr. 3-7). pap. 9.95 (978-607-31-3242-8(5), Nube De Tinta) Penguin Random House Grupo Editorial ESP. Dist: Penguin Random Hse. LLC.

Palatini, Margie. Geek Chic: the Zoey Zone. Palatini, Margie, illus. 2010. (ENG., Illus.). 192p. (J). (gr. 3-6). pap. 6.99 (978-0-06-113900-0(9), Tegen, Katherine Bks) HarperCollins Pubs.

Pallotta, Jerry. How Will I Get to School This Year? Biedrzycki, David, illus. 2011. (J). (978-0-545-26659-8(9)) Scholastic, Inc.

—What I Saw in the Teachers' Lounge. McWilliam, Howard, illus. 2012. (J). (978-0-545-38472-8(9)) Scholastic, Inc.

Palmer, Iva-Marie. Gabby Garcia's Ultimate Playbook. Kissi, Marta, illus. 2017. (Gabby Garcia's Ultimate Playbook Ser.: 1). (ENG.). 304p. (J). (gr. 3-7). 13.99 (978-0-06-239180-3(1), Tegen, Katherine Bks) HarperCollins Pubs.

—Gabby Garcia's Ultimate Playbook #2: MVP Summer. Kissi, Marta, illus. 2018. (Gabby Garcia's Ultimate Playbook Ser.: 2). (ENG.). 304p. (J). (gr. 3-7). 12.99 (978-0-06-239183-4(6), Tegen, Katherine Bks) HarperCollins Pubs.

—Gabby Garcia's Ultimate Playbook #3: Sidelined. Kissi, Marta, illus. 2019. (Gabby Garcia's Ultimate Playbook Ser.: 3). (ENG.). 288p. (J). (gr. 3-7). 12.99 (978-0-06-239186-5(0), Tegen, Katherine Bks) HarperCollins Pubs.

Palmer, Robin. Geek Charming. 2009. 368p. (YA). (gr. 7-12). 9.99 (978-0-14-241122-3(1), Speak) Penguin Young Readers Group.

Pam, Miss. Never Never Be a Bully. Stutz, Chris, illus. 2011. 24p. pap. 24.95 (978-1-4626-4325-7(6)) America Star Bks.

Panckridge, Michael & Harvey, Pam. In the Deep End. 2007. (ENG.). 220p. (978-0-207-20064-9(5)) HarperCollins Pubs. Australia.

Papell, David. Harlem Awakenings. 2007. (ENG.). 48p. pap. 12.95 (978-0-615-17531-7(7)) Papell, David.

—Harlem Awakenings Color Edition. 2007. (ENG.). 50p. pap. (978-0-615-17931-5(2)) Papell, David.

Paratore, Coleen Murtagh. Sunny Holiday. 2008. (Sunny Holiday Ser.: 1). (ENG.). 176p. (J). (gr. 2-4). 18.69 (978-0-545-07588-6(2)) Scholastic, Inc.

Pardoe, David. Jasper Tippett's Amazing Journey to Page 42. 2006. (Illus.). 132p. pap. (978-1-84401-785-0(0)) Athena Pr.

Parente, Peter. Boomer to the Rescue. Ivanov, Aleksey, illus. l.t. ed. 2005. 28p. 15.95 (978-0-9745052-3-7(4), Peeper & Friends) Tree Of Life Publishing.

Parish, Herman. Amelia Bedelia Chapter Book #5. Avril, Lynne, illus. 2014. (Amelia Bedelia Ser.). (ENG.). 160p. (J). (gr. 1-5). 9.99 (978-0-06-233399-5(2), Greenwillow Bks.) HarperCollins Pubs.

—Amelia Bedelia Chapter Book #5: Amelia Bedelia Shapes Up. 2014. (Amelia Bedelia Ser.). (ENG., Illus.). 160p. (J). (gr. 1-5). pap. 5.99 (978-0-06-233396-4(8), Greenwillow Bks.) HarperCollins Pubs.

—Amelia Bedelia Chapter Book #9: Amelia Bedelia on the Job. Avril, Lynne, illus. 2016. (Amelia Bedelia Ser.). (ENG.). 160p. (J). (gr. 1-5). pap. 6.99 (978-0-06-233412-1(3), Greenwillow Bks.) HarperCollins Pubs.

—Amelia Bedelia, Cub Reporter. 2012. (I Can Read Level 2 Ser.). (ENG., Illus.). 64p. (J). (gr. -1-3). pap. 4.99 (978-0-06-209509-1(9), Greenwillow Bks.) HarperCollins Pubs.

—Amelia Bedelia Hits the Trail. Avril, Lynne, illus. 2013. (I Can Read Level 1 Ser.). (ENG.). 32p. (J). (gr. -1-3). 16.99 (978-0-06-209527-5(7), Greenwillow Bks.) HarperCollins Pubs.

—Amelia Bedelia Joins the Club. 2014. (I Can Read Level 1 Ser.). (ENG., Illus.). 32p. (J). (gr. -1-3). 16.99 (978-0-06-222131-5(0), Greenwillow Bks.) HarperCollins Pubs.

—Amelia Bedelia Joins the Club. Avril, Lynne, illus. 2014. (I Can Read Level 1 Ser.). (ENG.). 32p. (J). (gr. -1-3). pap. 4.99 (978-0-06-222130-8(2), Greenwillow Bks.) HarperCollins Pubs.

—Amelia Bedelia, Rocket Scientist? Sweat, Lynn, illus. (I Can Read Level 2 Ser.). 64p. (J). 2007. (ENG.). (gr. k-3). pap. 4.99 (978-0-06-051889-9(8), Greenwillow Bks.) 2005. (gr. 1-18). 15.99 (978-0-06-051887-5(1)) 2005. (ENG.). (gr. k-4). lib. bdg. 17.89 (978-0-06-051888-2(X), Greenwillow Bks.) HarperCollins Pubs.

—Amelia Bedelia, Rocket Scientist? Sweat, Lynn, illus. 2007. (I Can Read Ser.). 64p. 14.00 (978-0-7569-8058-0(5)) Perfection Learning Corp.

—Amelia Bedelia, Rocket Scientist? Sweat, Lynn, illus. 2007. (Amelia Bedelia: I Can Read! Ser.: 19). (J). lib. bdg. 13.55 (978-1-4177-8068-6(1)) Turtleback.

—Amelia Bedelia Talks Turkey. 2009. (I Can Read Level 2 Ser.). (ENG., Illus.). 64p. (J). (gr. k-3). pap. 4.99 (978-0-06-084354-0(3), Greenwillow Bks.) HarperCollins Pubs.

—Amelia Bedelia Talks Turkey. Sweat, Lynn, illus. 2008. (Amelia Bedelia Ser.). (ENG.). 64p. (J). (gr. k-4). 16.99 (978-0-06-084352-6(7), Greenwillow Bks.) HarperCollins Pubs.

—Amelia Bedelia Talks Turkey. 2009. (Amelia Bedelia: I Can Read! Ser.). (J). lib. bdg. 13.55 (978-0-606-06937-3(2)) Turtleback.

—Amelia Bedelia's Backpack Bundle. Sweat, Lynn, illus. 2012. 192p. (J). (978-1-4351-4392-0(2), Greenwillow Bks.) HarperCollins Pubs.

—Amelia Bedelia's First Day of School. Avril, Lynne, illus. (Amelia Bedelia Ser.). (ENG.). 32p. (J). (gr. -1-3). 2015. pap. 7.99 (978-0-06-154457-6(4)) 2011. 9.99 (978-0-06-203274-4(7)) 2009. 16.99 (978-0-06-154455-2(8)) HarperCollins Pubs. (Greenwillow Bks.).

—Amelia Bedelia's First Field Trip. 2013. (Amelia Bedelia Picture Bks.). (J). lib. bdg. 17.20 (978-0-606-31818-1(6)) Turtleback.

—Amelia Bedelia's First Valentine. Avril, Lynne, illus. (Amelia Bedelia Ser.). (ENG.). 32p. (J). (gr. -1-3). 2014. pap. 7.99 (978-0-06-154460-6(4)) 2011. 9.99 (978-0-06-203275-1(5)) 2009. 16.99 (978-0-06-154458-3(2)) HarperCollins Pubs. (Greenwillow Bks.).

—Amelia Bedelia's First Valentine. 2014. (Amelia Bedelia Picture Bks.). (J). lib. bdg. 17.20 (978-0-606-35971-9(0)) Turtleback.

—Amelia Bedelia's First Vote. Avril, Lynne, illus. 2012. (Amelia Bedelia Ser.). (ENG.). 32p. (J). (gr. -1-3). 16.99 (978-0-06-209405-6(X), Greenwillow Bks.) HarperCollins Pubs.

Parish, Peggy. Teach Us, Amelia Bedelia. Sweat, Lynn, illus. 2005. (Amelia Bedelia Ser.). 58p. (gr. -1-3). 14.00 (978-0-7569-4804-7(5)) Perfection Learning Corp.

Parisi, Mark. Marty Pants #1: Do Not Open! 2017. (Marty Pants Ser.: 1). (ENG., Illus.). 256p. (J). (gr. 3-7). 15.99 (978-0-06-242776-2(8), HarperCollins) HarperCollins Pubs.

Park, Barbara. Junie B., First Grader - Aloha-Ha-Ha! Brunkus, Denise, illus. 2007. (Junie B. Jones Ser.). 119p. (gr. 1-4). 15.00 (978-0-7569-8085-6(2)) Perfection Learning Corp.

—Junie B. First Grader - Aloha-Ha-Ha! 2007. (Junie B. Jones Ser.: 26). lib. bdg. 14.75 (978-1-4177-8157-7(2)) Turtleback.

—Junie B. Jones: Boss of Lunch. 2003. (Junie B. Jones Ser.: 19). (gr. k-3). lib. bdg. 14.75 (978-0-613-63168-6(4)) Turtleback.

—Junie B. Jones #19: Boss of Lunch. Brunkus, Denise, illus. 2003. (Junie B. Jones Ser.: 19). 96p. (J). (gr. 1-4). 4.99 (978-0-375-80294-2(0), Random Hse. Bks. for Young Readers) Random Hse. Children's Bks.

—Junie B. Jones #21: Cheater Pants. Brunkus, Denise, illus. 2004. (Junie B. Jones Ser.: 21). 96p. (J). (gr. 1-4). 5.99 (978-0-375-82302-2(6), Random Hse. Bks. for Young Readers) Random Hse. Children's Bks.

—Junie B. Jones #22: One-Man Band. Brunkus, Denise, illus. 2004. (Junie B. Jones Ser.: 22). 96p. (J). (gr. 1-4). 5.99 (978-0-375-82536-1(3), Random Hse. Bks. for Young Readers) Random Hse. Children's Bks.

—Junie B. Jones #23: Shipwrecked, No. 23. Brunkus, Denise, illus. 2005. (Junie B. Jones Ser.: 23). (ENG.). 96p. (J). (gr. 1-4). mass mkt. 5.99 (978-0-375-82805-8(2), Random Hse. Bks. for Young Readers) Random Hse. Children's Bks.

—Junie B. Jones #25: Jingle Bells, Batman Smells! (P. S. So Does May.) Brunkus, Denise, illus. 2009. (Junie B. Jones Ser.: 25). (ENG.). 128p. (J). (gr. 1-4). 5.99 (978-0-375-82809-6(5), Random Hse. Bks. for Young Readers) Random Hse. Children's Bks.

—Junie B. Jones #26: Aloha-Ha-ha! Brunkus, Denise, illus. 2007. (Junie B. Jones Ser.: 26). (ENG.). 128p. (J). (gr. 1-4). per. 5.99 (978-0-375-83404-2(4), Random Hse. Bks. for Young Readers) Random Hse. Children's Bks.

—Junie B. Jones & Her Big Fat Mouth. unabr. ed. 2004. (Junie B. Jones Ser.: No. 3). 69p. (J). (gr. k-3). pap. 17.00 incl. audio (978-0-8072-0780-2(2), LFTR 239 SP, Listening Library) Random Hse. Audio Publishing Group.

—Junie B. Jones & Some Sneaky Peeky Spying. unabr. ed. 2004. (Junie B. Jones Ser.: No. 4). 66p. (J). (gr. k-3). pap. 17.00 incl. audio (978-0-8072-0781-9(0), LFTR 240 SP, Listening Library) Random Hse. Audio Publishing Group.

—Junie B. Jones Third Boxed Set Ever! Books 9-12, 4 vols., Bks. 9-12. Brunkus, Denise, illus. 2003. (Junie B. Jones Ser.). (ENG.). (J). (gr. 1-4). 19.96 (978-0-375-82552-1(5), Random Hse. Bks. for Young Readers) Random Hse. Children's Bks.

—Toothless Wonder. Brunkus, Denise, illus. 2003. (Junie B. Jones Ser.: Bk. 3). 80p. (gr. 1-4). 15.00 (978-0-7569-1621-3(6)) Perfection Learning Corp.

Park, Linda Sue. The One Thing You'd Save. Sae-Heng, Robert, illus. 2021. (ENG.). 72p. (J). (gr. 3-7). 16.99 (978-1-328-51513-1(3), 1719818, Clarion Bks.) HarperCollins Pubs.

Parker Ma Csac, Nacole A. A Day in the Life of Ruby. 2011. 28p. pap. 16.25 (978-1-4634-1152-7(9)) AuthorHouse.

Parker, S. M. The Girl Who Fell. (ENG., Illus.). (YA). (gr. 11). 2017. 384p. pap. 12.99 (978-1-4814-3724-0(0)) 2016. 368p. 17.99 (978-1-4814-3725-7(9)) Simon Pulse. (Simon Pulse).

Parkhurst, Johanna. Here's to You, Zeb Pike [Library Edition]. 2014. 180p. pap. 14.99 (978-1-62798-526-0(3), Harmony Ink Pr.) Dreamspinner Pr.

Parks, Marquin. Wrinkles Wallace: Knights of Night School. 2012. 174p. pap. 12.00 (978-0-9832330-5-3(5)) Meridia Pubs. LLC.

Parnell, Declan. Mom Comes to School, 1 vol., 1. 2015. (Rosen REAL Readers: STEM & STEAM Collection). (ENG.). 12p. (J). (gr. 1-2). pap. 6.33 (978-1-5081-1611-0(3), 48727dc8-9405-4e22-9ef3-f933c692ba6f, Rosen Classroom) Rosen Publishing Group, Inc., The.

—School Rules!, 1 vol., 1. 2015. (Rosen REAL Readers: Social Studies Nonfiction / Fiction: Myself, My Community, My World Ser.). (ENG.). 8p. (J). (gr. k-1). pap. 5.46 (978-1-5081-1848-0(5), d65b30a8-0832-4dfd-b929-c4ac82da914f, Rosen Classroom) Rosen Publishing Group, Inc., The.

Parnell, Robyn. The Mighty Quinn. DeYoe, Katie & Aaron, illus. 2013. (ENG.). 272p. (J). (gr. 2-7). pap. 10.95 (978-1-938063-10-7(4), Mighty Media Junior Readers) Mighty Media Pr.

Parr, todd. Otto Goes to School. 2013. (Passport to Reading Level 1 Ser.). (J). lib. bdg. 14.75 (978-0-606-31740-5(6)) Turtleback.

—The School Book. 2019. (ENG., Illus.). 32p. (J). (gr. -1-3). 17.99 (978-0-316-42380-9(7)) Little, Brown Bks. for Young Readers.

—Teachers Rock! 2016. (ENG., Illus.). 32p. (J). (gr. -1-1). 18.99 (978-0-316-26512-6(8)) Little, Brown Bks. for Young Readers.

Parsley, Elise. If You Ever Want to Bring an Alligator to School, Don't! 2015. (Magnolia Says DON'T! Ser.: 1). (ENG., Illus.). 40p. (J). (gr. -1-3). 18.99 (978-0-316-37657-0(4)) Little, Brown Bks. for Young Readers.

Pascal, Francine. The Ruling Class. 2010. (ENG.). 208p. (YA). (gr. 9). pap. 10.99 (978-1-4424-1423-5(5), Simon Pulse) Simon Pulse.

—Terror de la Escuela. Orig. Title: The Bully. (SPA.). 120p. (J). 6.95 (978-84-272-3789-6(8)) Molino, Editorial ESP. Dist: AIMS International Bks., Inc.

Passen, Lisa. The Attack of the 50-Foot Teacher. 2005. (Illus.). 28p. (J). (gr. k-4). reprint ed. 16.00 (978-0-7567-9665-5(2)) DIANE Publishing Co.

Pastis, Stephan. Now Look What You've Done. 2016. (Timmy Failure Ser.: 2). lib. bdg. 18.40 (978-0-606-37947-2(9)) Turtleback.

—Timmy Failure: Now Look What You've Done! 2014. (Timmy Failure Ser.: 2). (J). 184.75 (978-1-4906-0682-8(3)) Recorded Bks., Inc.

—Timmy Failure: Now Look What You've Done. Pastis, Stephan, illus. 2016. (Timmy Failure Ser.: 2). (ENG., Illus.). 304p. (J). (gr. 3-7). pap. 7.99 (978-0-7636-8014-5(1)) Candlewick Pr.

—Timmy Failure: the Book You're Not Supposed to Have. Pastis, Stephan, illus. (Timmy Failure Ser.: 5). (ENG., Illus.). 304p. (J). (gr. 3-7). 2019. pap. 7.99 (978-1-5362-0908-2(2)) 2016. 15.99 (978-0-7636-9004-5(X)) Candlewick Pr.

Paterson, Katherine. Marvin One Too Many. Clark Brown, Jane, illus. 2003. 25.95 incl. audio (978-1-59112-254-8(6)); 28.95 incl. audio compact disk (978-1-59112-635-5(5)); pap. 31.95 incl. audio compact disk (978-1-59112-636-2(3)) Live Oak Media.

Patneaude, David. Colder Than Ice. 2003. (ENG.). 168p. (J). (gr. 4-6). 18.69 (978-0-8075-8135-3(6)) Whitman, Albert & Co.

Patricelli, Leslie. The Rizzlerunk Club: Best Buds under Frogs. Patricelli, Leslie, illus. 2018. (ENG., Illus.). 288p. (J). (gr. 2-5). 15.99 (978-0-7636-5104-6(4)) Candlewick Pr.

Patrick, Cat. Forgotten. 2012. (ENG.). 320p. (YA). (gr. 7-17). pap. 17.99 (978-0-316-09460-3(9)) Little, Brown Bks. for Young Readers.

—Revived. 2013. (ENG.). 368p. (YA). (gr. 7-17). pap. 18.99 (978-0-316-09463-4(3)) Little, Brown Bks. for Young Readers.
Patterson, C. Marie. Little Dinky's Love for Basketball. 2009. 24p. pap. 15.99 (978-1-4415-1255-0(1)) Xlibris Corp.
Patterson, Eric. Nature Boy Nature Strikes Back. Wright, Chris, illus. 2008. 108p. pap. 6.95 (978-1-935105-15-2(9)) Avid Readers Publishing Group.
Patterson, James. Ali Cross: the Secret Detective. 2022. (Ali Cross Ser.: 3). (ENG.). 272p. (J). (gr. 5-9). 16.99 (978-0-316-40991-9(X), Jimmy Patterson) Little Brown & Co.
—Expelled. 2017. (ENG.). 304p. (YA). (gr. 10-17). 17.99 (978-0-316-44039-4(6), Jimmy Patterson) Little Brown & Co.
—The Injustice. 2018. (ENG.). 336p. (YA). (gr. 10-17). pap. 9.99 (978-0-316-47883-0(0), Jimmy Patterson) Little Brown & Co.
—Middle School: Escape to Australia. Griffo, Daniel, illus. 2017. (Middle School Ser.: 9). (ENG.). 288p. (J). (gr. 3-7). 14.99 (978-0-316-27262-9(0), Jimmy Patterson) Little Brown & Co.
—Pottymouth & Stoopid. Gilpin, Stephen, illus. (ENG.). 336p. (J). (gr. 3-7). 2019. pap. 7.99 (978-0-316-51498-9(5)) 2017. 13.99 (978-0-316-34963-5(1)) Little Brown & Co. (Jimmy Patterson).
—Public School Superhero. 2015. (ENG., Illus.). 304p. (J). (gr. 3-7). 13.99 (978-0-316-32214-0(8), Jimmy Patterson) Little Brown & Co.
—School's Out - Forever. 2008. (Maximum Ride Ser.: Bk. 2). 418p. (gr. 4-7). 18.00 (978-0-7569-8349-9(5)) Perfection Learning Corp.
—School's Out - Forever. 2007. (Maximum Ride Ser.: 2). (YA). lib. bdg. 20.85 (978-1-4177-7493-7(2)) Turtleback.
—School's Out — Forever: A Maximum Ride Novel. 2nd ed. 2006. (Maximum Ride Ser.: 2). (ENG.). 416p. (J). (gr. 5-17). 38.99 (978-0-316-15559-5(4), Jimmy Patterson) Little Brown & Co.
—Unbelievably Boring Bart. Bonet, Xavier, illus. 2018. (ENG.). 272p. (J). (gr. 3-7). 13.99 (978-0-316-41153-0(1), Jimmy Patterson) Little Brown & Co.
—The Worst Years of My Life. 2014. lthr. 79.00 (978-1-62715-524-3(4)) Leatherbound Bestsellers.
—The Worst Years of My Life. 2012. 18.00 (978-1-61383-331-5(8)) Perfection Learning Corp.
Patterson, James & Bergen, Julia. Middle School: Ultimate Showdown. 2014. (Middle School Ser.: 5). (ENG., Illus.). 256p. (J). (gr. 3-7). 13.99 (978-0-316-32211-9(3), Jimmy Patterson) Little Brown & Co.
Patterson, James & Grabenstein, Chris. Best Nerds Forever. (ENG.). (J). (gr. 5-9). 2022. 272p. pap. 7.99 (978-0-316-50067-8(4)) 2021. (Illus.). 256p. 13.99 (978-0-316-50024-1(0)) Little Brown & Co. (Jimmy Patterson).
—House of Robots. Neufeld, Juliana, illus. (House of Robots Ser.: 1). (ENG.). (J). (gr. 3-7). 2015. 336p. pap. 8.99 (978-0-316-34679-5(9)) 2014. 352p. 13.99 (978-0-316-40591-1(4)) Little Brown & Co. (Jimmy Patterson).
—House of Robots. 2015. (J). lib. bdg. 18.40 (978-0-606-37527-6(9)) Turtleback.
—House of Robots: Robots Go Wild! Neufeld, Juliana, illus. 2015. (House of Robots Ser.: 2). (ENG.). 336p. (J). (gr. 3-7). 13.99 (978-0-316-28479-0(3), Jimmy Patterson) Little Brown & Co.
—I Even Funnier: A Middle School Story. Park, Laura, illus. (I Funny Ser.: 2). (ENG.). 368p. (J). (gr. 3-7). 2017. pap. 8.99 (978-0-316-20695-2(4)) 2013. 13.99 (978-0-316-20697-6(0)) Little Brown & Co. (Jimmy Patterson).
—I Funny: School of Laughs. Tejido, Jomike, illus. 2017. 299p. (J). (978-0-316-50853-7(5)) Little Brown & Co.
—I Funny TV: A Middle School Story. Park, Laura, illus. 2015. (I Funny Ser.: 4). (ENG.). 336p. (J). (gr. 3-7). 13.99 (978-0-316-30109-1(4), Jimmy Patterson) Little Brown & Co.
—Jacky Ha-Ha. Kerascoët, illus. (Jacky Ha-Ha Ser.: 1). (ENG.). 384p. (J). (gr. 3-7). 2017. pap. 7.99 (978-0-316-43253-5(9)) 2016. 36.99 (978-0-316-26249-1(8)) Little Brown & Co. (Jimmy Patterson).
—Jacky Ha-Ha. Kerascoët, illus. 2023. (Jacky Ha-Ha Ser.: 1). (ENG.). 384p. (J). (gr. 3-7). pap. 7.99 (978-0-316-50834-6(9), Jimmy Patterson) Little Brown & Co.
—Jacky Ha-Ha. 2017. (Jacky Ha-Ha Ser.: 1). (J). lib. bdg. 18.40 (978-0-606-40732-8(4)) Turtleback.
Patterson, James & Papademetriou, Lisa. Homeroom Diaries. Keino, illus. 2014. (ENG.). 272p. (YA). (gr. 7-17). 32.99 (978-0-316-20762-1(4), Jimmy Patterson) Little Brown & Co.
—Middle School: Big Fat Liar. Swaab, Neil, illus. 2014. (Middle School Ser.: 3). (ENG.). 304p. (J). (gr. 3-7). 13.99 (978-0-316-32203-4(2), Jimmy Patterson) Little Brown & Co.
—Middle School: My Brother Is a Big, Fat Liar. Swaab, Neil, illus. 2013. (Middle School Ser.: 3). (ENG.). 304p. (J). (gr. 3-7). 33.99 (978-0-316-20754-6(3), Jimmy Patterson) Little Brown & Co.
Patterson, James & Tebbetts, Chris. Middle School: Born to Rock. Swaab, Neil, illus. 2019. (Middle School Ser.: 11). (ENG.). 320p. (J). (gr. 3-7). 14.99 (978-0-316-34952-9(6), Jimmy Patterson) Little Brown & Co.
—Middle School: Dog's Best Friend. Tejido, Jomike, illus. 2016. (Middle School Ser.: 8). (ENG.). 256p. (J). (gr. 3-7). 13.99 (978-0-316-34954-3(2), Jimmy Patterson) Little Brown & Co.
—Middle School: from Hero to Zero. Park, Laura, illus. 2018. (Middle School Ser.: 10). (ENG.). 288p. (J). (gr. 3-7). 13.99 (978-0-316-34690-0(X), Jimmy Patterson) Little Brown & Co.
—Middle School: Get Me Out of Here! Park, Laura, illus. (Middle School Ser.: 2). (ENG.). 288p. (J). (gr. 3-7). 2018. pap. 9.99 (978-0-316-20669-3(5)) 2014. 13.99 (978-0-316-32201-0(6)) 2012. 32.99 (978-0-316-20671-6(7)) Little Brown & Co. (Jimmy Patterson).
—Middle School: Just My Rotten Luck. Park, Laura, illus. 2015. (Middle School Ser.: 7). (ENG.). 320p. (J). (gr. 3-7). 14.99 (978-0-316-28477-6(7), Jimmy Patterson) Little Brown & Co.
—Middle School, the Worst Years of My Life. Park, Laura, illus. (Middle School Ser.: 1). (ENG.). (J). (gr. 3-7). 2014. 320p. 13.99 (978-0-316-32202-7(4)) 2012. 336p. pap. 9.99 (978-0-316-10169-1(9)) 2011. 288p. 33.99 (978-0-316-10187-5(7)) Little Brown & Co. (Jimmy Patterson).
—Public School Superhero. Thomas, Cory, illus. 2016. (ENG.). 304p. (J). (gr. 3-7). pap. 8.99 (978-0-316-26598-0(5), Jimmy Patterson) Little Brown & Co.
—The Worst Years of My Life. Park, Laura, illus. 2013. (Middle School Ser.: Bk. 1). (ENG.). (J). (gr. 3-7). pap. 0.01 (978-0-316-25251-5(4)) Little Brown & Co.
—The Worst Years of My Life. Park, Laura, illus. 2012. (Middle School Ser.: 1). (J). lib. bdg. 18.45 (978-0-606-26164-7(8)) Turtleback.
Patterson, James & Tebbetts, Christopher. From Hero to Zero. Park, Laura, illus. 2017. 268p. (J). pap. (978-0-316-35756-2(1)) Little Brown & Co.
Patterson, James, et al. Public School Superhero. 2015. (978-0-316-34231-5(9)) Little, Brown Bks. for Young Readers.
Pattou, Edith. Mrs. Spitzer's Garden. [Gift Edition]. Tusa, Tricia, illus. gif. ed. 2007. (ENG.). 32p. (J). (gr. -1-3). 12.99 (978-0-15-205802-9(8), 1197433, Clarion Bks.) HarperCollins Pubs.
Paul, Ann Whitford. If Animals Went to School. Walker, David, illus. 2019. (If Animals Kissed Good Night Ser.). (ENG.). 32p. (J). 16.99 (978-0-374-30902-2(7), 900188210, Farrar, Straus & Giroux (BYR)) Farrar, Straus & Giroux.
Paul, Marcy Beller. Underneath Everything. 2015. (ENG., Illus.). 304p. (YA). (gr. 9). 17.99 (978-0-06-232721-5(6), Balzer & Bray) HarperCollins Pubs.
Paul, Volponi. Black & White. 2014. (ENG.). 208p. (YA). 11.24 (978-1-63245-196-5(4)) Lectorum Pubns., Inc.
Pauley, Kimberly. Cat Girl's Day Off, 1 vol. (ENG.). (YA). 2018. 352p. (gr. 6-12). pap. 13.95 (978-1-64379-050-3(1), leelowtu) 2012. 336p. 17.95 (978-1-60060-883-4(3)) Lee & Low Bks., Inc. (Tu Bks.).
—Sucks to Be Me: The All-True Confessions of Mina Hamilton, Teen Vampire. 2008. (ENG.). 293p. (YA). (gr. 6-8). 24.94 (978-0-7869-5028-7(5)) Wizards of the Coast.
Paulsen, Gary. Liar, Liar: The Theory, Practice & Destructive Properties of Deception. 2012. (Liar Liar Ser.). (ENG.). 128p. (J). (gr. 3-7). 7.99 (978-0-375-86611-1(6), Yearling) Random Hse. Children's Bks.
—Molly Mcginty Has a Really Good Day. 2006. (Illus.). 105p. (J). (gr. 3-7). 13.15 (978-0-7569-6621-8(3)) Perfection Learning Corp.
—Mudshark. 2010. (ENG.). 96p. (J). (gr. 3-7). 6.99 (978-0-553-49464-8(3), Yearling) Random Hse. Children's Bks.
—Six Kids & a Stuffed Cat. 2016. (ENG., Illus.). 144p. (J). (gr. 3-7). 18.99 (978-1-4814-5223-6(1), Simon & Schuster Bks. For Young Readers) Simon & Schuster Bks. For Young Readers.
—Vote. 2014. (Liar Liar Ser.). (ENG.). 144p. (J). (gr. 4-7). pap. 7.99 (978-0-385-74229-0(0), Yearling) Random Hse. Children's Bks.
Payne, C. C. Lula Bell on Geekdom, Freakdom, & the Challenges of Bad Hair, 0 vols. 2012. (ENG.). 276p. (J). (gr. 4-6). 16.99 (978-0-7614-6225-5(2), 9780761462255, Two Lions) Amazon Publishing.
Payne, Gregory. Chase to the Brazen Head. 2010. (ENG.). 228p. (YA). (gr. 4-7). pap. 11.95 (978-988-18094-6-9(0)) Haven Bks.
Payne, Jody. Miss Spellin' Helen. Payne, Rachel & Song, Danielle, illus. 2012. 148p. pap. 6.99 (978-0-9846687-0-0(5)) Absalon Pr.
Payne, K. E. Another 365 Days. 2013. (ENG.). 264p. (J). (gr. 7). pap. 11.95 (978-1-60282-775-2(3)) Bold Strokes Bks.
—365 Days. 2011. (ENG.). 280p. (YA). (gr. 7). pap. 13.95 (978-1-60282-540-6(8)) Bold Strokes Bks.
Payton, Belle. Even the Score. 2015. (It Takes Two Ser.: 5). (ENG., Illus.). 160p. (J). (gr. 3-7). pap. 6.99 (978-1-4814-1951-2(X), Simon Spotlight) Simon Spotlight.
—May the Best Twin Win. 2015. (It Takes Two Ser.: 7). (ENG., Illus.). 160p. (J). (gr. 3-7). pap. 6.99 (978-1-4814-3134-7(X), Simon Spotlight) Simon Spotlight.
—'Tis the Off-Season. 2015. (It Takes Two Ser.: 10). (ENG., Illus.). 160p. (J). (gr. 3-7). pap. 6.99 (978-1-4814-4205-3(8), Simon Spotlight) Simon Spotlight.
—Twice the Talent. 2016. (It Takes Two Ser.: 11). (ENG., Illus.). 160p. (J). (gr. 3-7). pap. 6.99 (978-1-4814-5263-2(0), Simon Spotlight) Simon Spotlight.
—Two Cool for School. 2014. (It Takes Two Ser.: 2). (ENG., Illus.). 160p. (J). (gr. 3-7). 16.99 (978-1-4814-0645-1(0), Simon Spotlight) Simon Spotlight.
—Two Steps Back. 2015. (It Takes Two Ser.: 6). (ENG., Illus.). 160p. (J). (gr. 3-7). 17.99 (978-1-4814-2519-3(6), Simon Spotlight) Simon Spotlight.
PeachMoon Publishing. The Adventures of Lucky the Lizard Las aventuras del lagarto Lucky. 2008. (ENG & SPA., Illus.). 100p. (J). pap. 19.95 (978-0-9795831-4-8(4)) PeachMoon Publishing.
—Lucky Goes to School. 2007. (J). pap. 9.95 (978-0-9795831-1-7(X)) PeachMoon Publishing.
Pearce, Jackson. The Doublecross: (And Other Skills I Learned As a Superspy) 2015. (ENG.). 304p. (YA). (gr. 3-6). 16.99 (978-1-61963-414-5(7), 9781619634145, Bloomsbury USA Childrens) Bloomsbury Publishing USA.
—The Doublecross: (and Other Skills I Learned As a Superspy) 2016. (ENG.). 304p. (J). pap. 8.99 (978-1-61963-939-3(4), 900152561, Bloomsbury USA Childrens) Bloomsbury Publishing USA.
Pearce, Richard & Story, Ken. Dorkman. 2006. (YA). mass mkt. 8.50 (978-0-9753367-8-6(9)) Onstage Publishing, LLC.
Pearlman, Robb. The Office: a Day at Dunder Mifflin Elementary. Demmer, Melanie, illus. 2020. (ENG.). 40p. (J). (gr. -1-3). 17.99 (978-0-316-42838-5(8)) Little, Brown Bks. for Young Readers.
—Parks & Recreation: Leslie for Class President! Demmer, Melanie, illus. 2021. (ENG.). 40p. (J). (gr. -1-3). 17.99 (978-0-316-42865-1(5)) Little, Brown Bks. for Young Readers.
Pearsall, Shelley. All of the Above. 2008. (ENG., Illus.). 256p. (J). (gr. 3-7). per. 8.00 (978-0-316-11526-1(6)) Little, Brown Bks. for Young Readers.
—All Shook Up. 2009. 272p. (J). (gr. 3-7). 7.99 (978-0-440-42139-9(X), Yearling) Random Hse. Children's Bks.
Pearson, Joanna. The Rites & Wrongs of Janice Wills. 2011. (YA). pap. (978-0-545-19774-8(0), Levine, Arthur A. Bks.) Scholastic, Inc.
Peck, Richard. The Best Man. 2017. (ENG.). 256p. (J). (gr. 4-7). 8.99 (978-0-14-751579-7(3), Puffin Books) Penguin Young Readers Group.
Peers, Bobbie. William Wenton & the Impossible Puzzle. Chace, Tara F., tr. (William Wenton Ser.: 1). (ENG.). (J). (gr. 3-7). 2018. 288p. pap. 7.99 (978-1-4814-7826-7(5)) 2017. (Illus.). 272p. 16.99 (978-1-4814-7825-0(7)) Simon & Schuster Children's Publishing. (Aladdin).
Peets, Risa. It's OK to Be Different: An Amazing School Day. 2013. (ENG., Illus.). 76p. (J). pap. 7.99 (978-1-937008-17-8(7)) Heart to Heart Publishing, Inc.
Peirce, Lincoln. Big Nate. 2012. (ENG.). 224p. pap. 12.99 (978-1-4494-1144-2(4)) Andrews McMeel Publishing.
—Big Nate: A Good Old-Fashioned Wedgie. 2017. (Big Nate Ser.: Vol. 17). (ENG., Illus.). 174p. (J). (gr. 3-6). 35.99 (978-1-4494-9402-5(1)) Andrews McMeel Publishing.
—Big Nate: Thunka, Thunka, Thunka. 2016. (Big Nate Ser.: Vol. 14). (ENG., Illus.). (J). (gr. 3-6). 29.99 (978-1-4494-7581-9(7)) Andrews McMeel Publishing.
—Big Nate — Genius Mode. 2013. (Big Nate Graphic Novels Ser.). (Illus.). 211p. (J). lib. bdg. 20.85 (978-0-606-31802-0(X)) Turtleback.
—Big Nate — Here Goes Nothing. 2012. (Big Nate Graphic Novels Ser.: 6). (J). lib. bdg. 20.85 (978-0-606-26526-3(0)) Turtleback.
—Big Nate — In a Class by Himself. 2010. pap. (978-0-06-199287-2(9)) HarperCollins Pubs.
—Big Nate — In a Class by Himself. 2015. (Big Nate Ser.: 1). (J). lib. bdg. 17.20 (978-0-606-36505-5(2)) Turtleback.
—Big Nate — Mr. Popularity. 2014. (Big Nate Graphic Novels Ser.: 4). (J). lib. bdg. 20.85 (978-0-606-35482-0(4)) Turtleback.
—Big Nate - The Crowd Goes Wild! 2014. (Big Nate Graphic Novels Ser.). lib. bdg. 20.85 (978-0-606-36143-9(X)) Turtleback.
—Big Nate & Friends. 2011. (Illus.). 224p. (J). (Big Nate Ser.: 3). (ENG.). pap. 11.99 (978-1-4494-2043-7(5)); (978-0-545-46801-5(9)); (978-1-60744-837-2(8)) Andrews McMeel Publishing.
—Big Nate Blasts Off. Peirce, Lincoln, illus. 2016. (Big Nate Ser.: 8). (ENG., Illus.). 224p. (J). (gr. 3-7). 13.99 (978-0-06-211111-1(6), Balzer & Bray) HarperCollins Pubs.
—Big Nate Doodlepalooza. Peirce, Lincoln, illus. (Big Nate Activity Book Ser.: 3). (ENG., Illus.). 224p. (J). (gr. 3-7). 2016. pap. 6.99 (978-0-06-234952-1(X)) 2013. 10.99 (978-0-06-211114-2(0)) HarperCollins Pubs. (HarperCollins).
—Big Nate: Double Trouble: In a Class by Himself & Strikes Again. 2018. (Big Nate Ser.). (ENG.). 448p. (J). (gr. 3-7). pap. 9.99 (978-0-06-283946-6(2), Balzer & Bray) HarperCollins Pubs.
—Big Nate Goes for Broke. Peirce, Lincoln, illus. (Big Nate Ser.: 4). (ENG., Illus.). 224p. (J). (gr. 3-7). 2016. pap. 7.99 (978-0-06-236753-2(6)) 2012. 15.99 (978-0-06-199661-0(0)) 2012. lib. bdg. 14.89 (978-0-06-199662-7(9)) HarperCollins Pubs. (HarperCollins).
—Big Nate Goes for Broke. 2016. (Big Nate Ser.: 4). 224p. (J). lib. bdg. 17.20 (978-0-606-38137-6(6)) Turtleback.
—Big Nate: Great Minds Think Alike. 2014. (Big Nate Ser.: 8). (ENG., Illus.). 224p. (J). 12.99 (978-1-4494-3635-3(8)) Andrews McMeel Publishing.
—Big Nate: in a Class by Himself. Peirce, Lincoln, illus. (Big Nate Ser.: 1). (ENG., Illus.). 224p. (J). (gr. 3-7). 2015. pap. 7.99 (978-0-06-228359-7(6)) 2010. 15.99 (978-0-06-194434-5(3)) 2010. lib. bdg. 14.89 (978-0-06-194435-2(1)) HarperCollins Pubs. (HarperCollins).
—Big Nate: in a Class by Himself. Peirce, Lincoln, illus. 2021. (Big Nate Ser.). (ENG.). 224p. (J). (gr. 3-7). lib. bdg. 32.79 (978-1-5321-4528-5(4), 36964, Chapter Bks.) Spotlight.
—Big Nate: in a Class by Himself Special Edition: Includes 16 Extra Pages of Fun! Peirce, Lincoln, illus. 2012. (Big Nate Ser.: 1). (ENG., Illus.). 240p. (J). (gr. 3-7). 12.99 (978-0-06-220773-9(3), HarperCollins) HarperCollins Pubs.
—Big Nate Lives It Up. Peirce, Lincoln, illus. 2015. (Big Nate Ser.: 7). (ENG., Illus.). 224p. (J). (gr. 3-7). lib. bdg. 14.89 (978-0-06-211109-8(4), Balzer & Bray) HarperCollins Pubs.
—Big Nate Makes the Grade. 2012. (Big Nate Ser.: 4). (ENG., Illus.). 224p. (J). 12.99 (978-1-4494-2566-1(6)) Andrews McMeel Publishing.
—Big Nate Makes the Grade. 2012. (Big Nate Graphic Novels Ser.). (Illus.). 224p. lib. bdg. 20.85 (978-0-606-26308-5(X)) Turtleback.
—Big Nate: Mr. Popularity. Peirce, Lincoln, illus. 2014. (Big Nate Comix Ser.: 4). (ENG., Illus.). 224p. (J). (gr. 3-7). pap. 9.99 (978-0-06-208700-3(2), HarperCollins) HarperCollins Pubs.
—Big Nate on a Roll. Peirce, Lincoln, illus. 2011. (Big Nate Ser.: 3). (ENG., Illus.). 224p. (J). (gr. 3-7). 13.99 (978-0-06-194438-3(6)); lib. bdg. 14.89 (978-0-06-194439-0(4)) HarperCollins Pubs. (HarperCollins).
—Big Nate Out Loud. 2011. (Big Nate Ser.: 2). (ENG., Illus.). 224p. (J). pap. 11.99 (978-1-4494-0718-6(8)) Andrews McMeel Publishing.
—Big Nate: Revenge of the Cream Puffs, Volume 15. 2016. (Big Nate Ser.: 15). (ENG., Illus.). 184p. (J). (gr. 3-7). pap. 12.99 (978-1-4494-6228-4(6)) Andrews McMeel Publishing.
—Big Nate Strikes Again. Peirce, Lincoln, illus. 2010. (Big Nate Ser.: 2). (ENG., Illus.). 224p. (J). (gr. 3-7). 13.99 (978-0-06-194436-9(X)); lib. bdg. 14.89 (978-0-06-194437-6(8)) HarperCollins Pubs. (HarperCollins).
—Big Nate: the Crowd Goes Wild!, Volume 9. 2014. (Big Nate Ser.: 9). (ENG., Illus.). 224p. (J). 9.99 (978-1-4494-3634-6(X)) Andrews McMeel Publishing.
—Big Nate: Thunka, Thunka, Thunka, Volume 14. 2016. (Big Nate Ser.: 14). (ENG., Illus.). 176p. (J). (gr. 3-6). pap. 12.99 (978-1-4494-6227-7(8)) Andrews McMeel Publishing.
—Big Nate: Welcome to My World, Volume 13. 2015. (Big Nate Ser.: 13). (ENG., Illus.). 176p. (J). pap. 12.99 (978-1-4494-6226-0(X)) Andrews McMeel Publishing.
—Big Nate: What Could Possibly Go Wrong? Peirce, Lincoln, illus. 2012. (Big Nate Comix Ser.: 1). (ENG., Illus.). 224p. (J). (gr. 3-7). pap. 9.99 (978-0-06-208694-5(4), HarperCollins) HarperCollins Pubs.
—Big Nate's Greatest Hits, Volume 11. 2015. (Big Nate Ser.: 11). (ENG., Illus.). 376p. (J). pap. 16.99 (978-1-4494-6489-9(0)) Andrews McMeel Publishing.
—Nate el Grande Ataca de Nuevo. 2012.Tr. of Big Nate Strikes Again. (SPA.). 216p. (gr. 3-5). 17.99 (978-1-933032-79-5(0)) Lectorum Pubns., Inc.
—Thunka, Thunka, Thunka. 2016. (Big Nate Graphic Novels Ser.). lib. bdg. 20.85 (978-0-606-38234-2(8)) Turtleback.
—Welcome to My World. 2015. (Big Nate Graphic Novels Ser.). lib. bdg. 20.85 (978-0-606-37391-3(8)) Turtleback.
Peirce, Lincoln, illus. Big Nate Flips Out. 2013. 216p. (J). (978-0-06-224637-0(2)) Harper & Row Ltd.
Pemberton, Teresa. Trissy's New Shoes. 2013. 32p. pap. 13.95 (978-1-4497-9337-1(1), WestBow Pr.) Author Solutions, LLC.
Pendergrass, Daphne. Daniel Plays at School. 2016. (Daniel Tiger's Neighborhood Ready-To-Read Ser.). lib. bdg. 13.55 (978-0-606-38991-4(1)) Turtleback.
Penfold, Alexandra. All Are Welcome. Kaufman, Suzanne, illus. 2018. (ENG.). 44p. (J). (gr. -1-3). 17.99 (978-0-525-57964-9(8), Knopf Bks. for Young Readers) Random Hse. Children's Bks.
Penn, Audrey. A. D. D. Not B. A. D. Wyrick, Monica, illus. 2003. (New Child & Family Press Titles Ser.). 32p. pap. 9.95 (978-0-87868-849-4(8), 8498, Child & Family Pr.) Child Welfare League of America, Inc.
—Un Beso en Mi Mano (the Kissing Hand) Harper, Ruth, illus. 2006. (ENG.). 32p. (J). (gr. -1-3). 18.99 (978-1-933718-01-9(3)) Tanglewood Pr.
—Chester Raccoon & the Big Bad Bully. Gibson, Barbara, illus. 2008. (Kissing Hand Ser.). (ENG.). 32p. (J). (gr. -1-3). 16.99 (978-1-933718-15-6(3)) Tanglewood Pr.
—The Kissing Hand. Harper, Ruth, illus. 2007. (ENG.). 32p. (J). (gr. -1-3). 28.95 (978-1-933718-07-1(2)) Tanglewood Pr.
—A Kissing Hand for Chester Raccoon. Gibson, Barbara, illus. 2014. (Kissing Hand Ser.). (ENG.). 14p. (J). (gr. -1-2). bds. 8.99 (978-1-933718-77-4(3)) Tanglewood Pr.
Penn, Audrey, et al, illus. The Kissing Hand. 2010. 23.05 (978-0-7569-9299-6(0)) Natl Bk. Network.
Penn, Farrah. Twelve Steps to Normal. 2018. (ENG.). 384p. (YA). (gr. 8-17). 17.99 (978-0-316-47160-2(7), Jimmy Patterson) Little Brown & Co.
Penn, Linda M. Clayton's Birding Adventure: A Young Boy Learns the Secret Ways of Birds. 2013. 46p. pap. 10.95 (978-0-9852488-5-7(8)) Linda M. Penn Author.
Pennels, Geraldine. The School Shenanigans of Amy & Nontand. 2009. 152p. pap. 33.50 (978-1-60860-496-8(9), Strategic Bk. Publishing) Strategic Book Publishing & Rights Agency (SBPRA).
Penner, Evelyn. The Kid Who Ate Dog Food. Chullabrahm, T. M., illus. 2008. 32p. (J). 15.99 (978-0-9796500-0-0(3)) Peppernut Publishing.
Pennypacker, Sara. Clementine. Frazee, Marla, illus. 2006. (Clementine Ser.: 1). (ENG.). 144p. (J). (gr. 1-5). 14.99 (978-0-7868-3882-0(5)) Hyperion Pr.
—Clementine. Frazee, Marla, illus. 2008. (Clementine Ser.: 1). (ENG.). 160p. (J). (gr. 1-5). pap. 5.99 (978-0-7868-3883-7(3)) Little, Brown Bks. for Young Readers.
—Clementine Friend of the Week. Frazee, Marla, illus. (Clementine Ser.: 4). (ENG.). 176p. (J). (gr. 1-3). 2011. pap. 5.99 (978-1-4231-1560-1(0)) 2010. 14.99 (978-1-4231-1355-3(1)) Little, Brown Bks. for Young Readers.
—Clementine's Letter. Frazee, Marla, illus. 2009. (Clementine Ser.: 3). (ENG.). 160p. (J). (gr. 1-5). pap. 5.99 (978-0-7868-3885-1(X)) Little, Brown Bks. for Young Readers.
—The Talented Clementine. Frazee, Marla, illus. (Clementine Ser.: 2). (ENG.). (J). (gr. 1-5). 2008. 160p. pap. 5.99 (978-0-7868-3871-4(X)) 2007. 144p. 28.99 (978-0-7868-3870-7(1)) Little, Brown Bks. for Young Readers.
Perelman, Helen. A Royal Rescue: A QUIX Book. Chin Mueller, Olivia, illus. 2018. (Royal Sweets Ser.: 1). (ENG.). 80p. (J). (gr. k-3). 16.99 (978-1-4814-9478-6(3)); pap. 5.99 (978-1-4814-9477-9(5)) Simon & Schuster Children's Publishing. (Aladdin).
—Sugar Secrets: A QUIX Book. Chin Mueller, Olivia, illus. 2018. (Royal Sweets Ser.: 2). (ENG.). 80p. (J). (gr. k-3). 16.99 (978-1-4814-9481-6(3)); pap. 5.99 (978-1-4814-9480-9(5)) Simon & Schuster Children's Publishing. (Aladdin).
Peretti, Frank E. Hangman's Curse. 2008. 352p. (YA). mass mkt. 7.99 (978-1-4003-1016-6(4)) Nelson, Thomas Inc.
—Nightmare Academy. 2008. 352p. (YA). mass mkt. 7.99 (978-1-4003-1017-3(2)) Nelson, Thomas Inc.
Pérez, Ashley Hope. Out of Darkness. 2019. 400p. (YA). (gr. 9). pap. 12.99 (978-0-8234-4503-5(8)) Holiday Hse., Inc.
—Out of Darkness. 2015. (ENG., Illus.). 408p. (YA). (gr. 8-12). 20.99 (978-1-4677-4202-3(3), ba661708-6e62-4586-8cfb-a9177c8dc6e3, Carolrhoda Lab™) Lerner Publishing Group.
Pérez, Celia C. The First Rule of Punk. (Illus.). 336p. (J). (gr. 4-7). 2018. 8.99 (978-0-425-29042-2(5), Puffin Books) 2017. 17.99 (978-0-425-29040-8(9), Viking Books for Young Readers) Penguin Young Readers Group.
Perez, L. King. First Day in Grapes, 1 vol. Casilla, Robert, illus. 2004. (ENG.). 32p. (J). pap. 9.95 (978-1-55041-340-3(6), a920fac5-51e0-4465-9963-9c60eb81b190) Fitzhenry & Whiteside, Ltd. CAN. Dist: Firefly Bks., Ltd.
Perez, Marlene. The Comeback. 2009. (ENG.). 208p. (J). (gr. 7). pap. 8.99 (978-0-545-08807-7(0)) Scholastic, Inc.
—Dead Is a Battlefield. 2012. (Dead Is Ser.: 6). (ENG.). 240p. (YA). (gr. 7). pap. 7.99 (978-0-547-60734-4(2), 1463411, Clarion Bks.) HarperCollins Pubs.
—Dead Is a Battlefield. 2012. (Dead Is Ser.: 6). lib. bdg. 18.40 (978-0-606-24759-7(9)) Turtleback.
—Dead Is a Killer Tune. 2012. (Dead Is Ser.: 7). lib. bdg. 18.40 (978-0-606-26623-9(2)) Turtleback.
—Dead Is a State of Mind. 2009. (Dead Is Ser.: 2). (ENG., Illus.). 192p. (YA). (gr. 7-18). pap. 7.99 (978-0-15-206210-1(6), 1063350, Clarion Bks.) HarperCollins Pubs.
—Dead Is Just a Dream. 2014. (Dead Is Ser.: 8). lib. bdg. 18.40 (978-0-606-35990-0(7)) Turtleback.
—Dead Is Not an Option. 2011. (Dead Is Ser.: 5). (ENG.). 256p. (YA). (gr. 7-18). pap. 7.99 (978-0-547-34593-2(3), 1419607, Clarion Bks.) HarperCollins Pubs.

—Dead Is the New Black. 2008. (Dead is Ser.: 1). (ENG., Illus.). 208p. (YA). (gr. 7-18). pap. 8.99 *(978-0-15-206408-2(7)*, 1199183, Clarion Bks.) HarperCollins Pubs.

Perez-Martinez, Irella. Suyensita & Her Adventures. 2011. 48p. pap. 21.99 *(978-1-4568-5767-7(3))* Xlibris Corp.

Perkins, Stephanie. There's Someone Inside Your House. (ENG.). (YA). (gr. 9). 2018. 320p. pap. 10.99 *(978-0-14-242498-8(6)*, Speak) 2017. 304p. 18.99 *(978-0-525-42601-1(9)*, Dutton Books for Young Readers) Penguin Young Readers Group.

Perry, Chrissie. Lucky Jars & Broken Promises. Egmont, Hardie Grant, illus. 2017. (Penelope Perfect Ser.: 3). (ENG.). 144p. (J). (gr. 2-5). 16.99 *(978-1-4814-9088-7(5))*; pap. 5.99 *(978-1-4814-9087-0(7))* Simon & Schuster Children's Publishing. (Aladdin).

—Private List for Camp Success. 2017. (Penelope Perfect Ser.: 2). lib. bdg. 16.00 *(978-0-606-40211-8(X))* Turtleback.

—Project Best Friend. Egmont, Hardie Grant, illus. 2017. (Penelope Perfect Ser.: 1). (ENG.). 144p. (J). (gr. 2-5). 16.99 *(978-1-4814-6602-8(X)*, Simon & Schuster/Paula Wiseman Bks.) Simon & Schuster/Paula Wiseman Bks.

—The Truly Terrible Mistake. Egmont, Hardie Grant, illus. 2018. (Penelope Perfect Ser.: 4). (ENG.). 144p. (J). (gr. 2-5). 16.99 *(978-1-4814-9085-6(0))*; pap. 5.99 *(978-1-4814-9084-9(2))* Simon & Schuster Children's Publishing. (Aladdin).

Perry, Fred. Gold Digger - Platinum, Vol. 2. 2011. (ENG., Illus.). 132p. (YA). pap., pap. 14.99 *(978-0-9831823-4-4(5)*, ed7bb848-5af9-46b5-b053-3704c30ed543) Antarctic Pr., Inc.

Perry, Jolene. Has to Be Love. 2015. (ENG.). 272p. (YA). (gr. 8-12). 16.99 *(978-0-8075-6557-5(1)*, 807565571) Whitman, Albert & Co.

—Stronger Than You Know. 2014. (ENG.). 256p. (YA). (gr. 8-12). 16.99 *(978-0-8075-3155-6(3)*, 807531553) Whitman, Albert & Co.

Perry, Laurie. Kaycee's New School, 1 vol. 2009. 48p. pap. 16.95 *(978-1-61582-638-4(6))* America Star Bks.

Perry, M. LaVora. Taneesha Never Disparaging. Cooper, Floyd, illus. 2008. (ENG.). 216p. (J). (gr. 2-7). pap. 8.95 *(978-0-86171-550-3(0))* Wisdom Pubns.

Peschke, Marci. Pirate Queen, 1 vol. Mourning, Tuesday, illus. 2013. (Kylie Jean Ser.). (ENG.). 112p. (J). (gr. 1-3). lib. bdg. 22.65 *(978-1-4048-7581-4(6)*, 119873, Picture Window Bks.) Capstone.

—Robot Queen. Mourning, Tuesday, illus. 2018. (Kylie Jean Ser.). (ENG.). 112p. (J). (gr. 1-3). 8.95 *(978-1-5158-2934-8(0)*, 138473); lib. bdg. 22.65 *(978-1-5158-2926-3(X)*, 138469) Capstone. (Picture Window Bks.).

Peters, Julie Anne. Keeping You a Secret. 2005. (ENG., Illus.). 272p. (J). (gr. 10-17). pap. 10.99 *(978-0-316-00985-0(7))* Little, Brown Bks. for Young Readers.

Peterson, Donna. The Misadventures of Phillip Isaac Penn. 2011. 96p. pap. 7.99 *(978-1-59955-893-6(9))* Cedar Fort, Inc./CFI Distribution.

Peterson, Shelley. Sundancer. Drake, Marybeth, illus. rev. ed. 2007. (ENG.). 264p. (YA). (gr. 7-12). pap. 7.95 *(978-1-55263-842-2(1))* Leaf Storm Pr.

Petert, Joetakecarer. 2012. 12p. (-18). pap. 10.67 *(978-1-4669-6739-7(0))* Trafford Publishing.

Petrillo, Genevieve. Keep Your Ear on the Ball, 1 vol. Lyon, Lea, illus. 2007. (ENG.). 32p. (J). (gr. -1-3). 16.95 *(978-0-88448-296-3(0))* Tilbury Hse. Pubs.

Petruck, Rebecca. Boy Bites Bug. 2019. (ENG.). 272p. (J). (gr. 3-17). pap. 9.99 *(978-1-4197-3481-6(4)*, 1136803, Amulet Bks.) Abrams, Inc.

Pett, Mark & Rubinstein, Gary. The Girl Who Never Made Mistakes. 2011. (ENG., Illus.). 32p. (J). (gr. -1-3). 16.99 *(978-1-4022-5544-1(6)*, Sourcebooks Jabberwocky) Sourcebooks, Inc.

Philbin, Joanna. The Daughters. 2010. (Daughters Ser.: 1). (ENG.). 304p. (YA). (gr. 7-17). pap. 16.99 *(978-0-316-04901-6(8)*, Poppy) Little, Brown Bks. for Young Readers.

—The Daughters Break the Rules. 2011. (Daughters Ser.: 2). (ENG.). 304p. (YA). (gr. 7-17). pap., pap. 16.99 *(978-0-316-04905-4(0)*, Poppy) Little, Brown Bks. for Young Readers.

—The Daughters Take the Stage. 2011. (Daughters Ser.: 3). (ENG.). 304p. (YA). (gr. 7-17). pap. 16.99 *(978-0-316-04908-5(5)*, Poppy) Little, Brown Bks. for Young Readers.

Philippe, Ben. The Field Guide to the North American Teenager. (ENG.). 384p. (YA). (gr. 8). 2020. pap. 11.99 *(978-0-06-282412-7(0))* 2019. 18.99 *(978-0-06-282411-0(2))* HarperCollins Pubs. (Balzer & Bray).

Phillips, Barry. Cave Express. 2010. 84p. pap. 12.61 *(978-0-557-25038-7(2))* Lulu Pr., Inc.

Phillips, Dee. The Ghostly Secret of Lakeside School. 2016. (Cold Whispers II Ser.). (ENG., Illus.). 32p. (J). (gr. 2-6). 28.50 *(978-1-944102-33-3(7))* Bearport Publishing Co., Inc.

Phillips, Lyda. Mr Touchdown. 2008. 184p. 23.95 *(978-1-4401-0976-8(1))*; pap. 13.95 *(978-1-60528-029-5(1))* iUniverse, Inc. (iUniverse Star).

Phillips-Poovey, Lisa. Lucy Wants to Go to School. 2013. 32p. pap. 10.95 *(978-1-936912-71-1(6))* Parsons Porch Bks.

Picano, Jaime Gianna. The Mood Ring Adventure. 2008. 128p. pap. 11.95 *(978-0-595-47958-0(8))* iUniverse, Inc.

Pichon, L. Tom Gates: Everything's Amazing (Sort Of) Pichon, L., illus. 2015. (Tom Gates Ser.: 3). (ENG., Illus.). 416p. (J). (gr. 3-7). 12.99 *(978-0-7636-7473-1(7))* Candlewick Pr.

—Tom Gates: Excellent Excuses (and Other Good Stuff) Pichon, L., illus. 2015. (Tom Gates Ser.: 2). (ENG., Illus.). 352p. (J). (gr. 3-7). 12.99 *(978-0-7636-7474-8(5))* Candlewick Pr.

—Tom Gates: Genius Ideas (Mostly) Pichon, L., illus. (Tom Gates Ser.: 4). (ENG., Illus.). 320p. (J). (gr. 3-7). 2019. pap. 8.99 *(978-1-5362-0867-2(1))* 2018. 12.99 *(978-1-5362-0129-1(4))* Candlewick Pr.

Pichon, Liz. Excellent Excuses (and Other Good Stuff) 2016. (Brilliant World of Tom Gates Ser.: 2). lib. bdg. 18.40 *(978-0-606-37941-0(X))* Turtleback.

—TOM GATES: FESTIVAL DE GENIALIDADES (MÁS O MENOS) 2013. (SPA.). 410p. (J). pap. 21.99 *(978-84-216-8814-4(6))* Lectorum Pubns., Inc.

Picoult, Jodi & van Leer, Samantha. Between the Lines. (ENG., Illus.). 368p. (YA). (gr. 7). 2013. pap. 15.99 *(978-1-4516-3581-2(8))* 2012. 19.99 *(978-1-4516-3575-1(3))* Atria/Emily Bestler Bks. (Atria/Emily Bestler Bks.).

Pierce, Seth J. The Day the School Blew Up. 2009. (J). pap. 12.99 *(978-0-8163-2329-6(1))* Pacific Pr. Publishing Assn.

Pike, Aprilynne. Hechizos. 2012.Tr. of Spells. (UND & SPA.). 352p. (YA). pap. 18.95 *(978-84-96886-27-8(1))* Ediciones Urano S. A. ESP. Dist: Spanish Pubs., LLC.

—Illusions. 2012. (Wings Ser.: 3). (ENG.). 400p. (YA). (gr. 8). pap. 9.99 *(978-0-06-166811-1(7)*, HarperTeen) HarperCollins Pubs.

—Spells. 2011. (Wings Ser.: 2). (ENG.). 384p. (YA). (gr. 8). pap. 9.99 *(978-0-06-166808-1(7)*, HarperTeen) HarperCollins Pubs.

—Spells, 7 vols. 2010. (YA). 78.75 *(978-1-4407-8375-3(6))* Recorded Bks., Inc.

Pike, Tabitha R. Dragon Tears: The Legacy. 2011. 232p. pap. 24.95 *(978-1-4560-6664-2(1))* America Star Bks.

Pilger, Seamus. Fart Squad. Gilpin, Stephen, illus. 2015. (Fart Squad Ser.: 1). (ENG.). 112p. (J). (gr. 1-5). pap. 4.99 *(978-0-06-229045-8(2)*, HarperCollins) HarperCollins Pubs.

—Fart Squad #3: Unidentified Farting Objects. Gilpin, Stephen, illus. 2016. (Fart Squad Ser.: 3). (ENG.). 112p. (J). (gr. 1-5). pap. 4.99 *(978-0-06-229049-6(5)*, HarperCollins) HarperCollins Pubs.

Pilkey, Dav. Big, Bad Battle of the Bionic Booger Boy: The Night of the Nasty Nostril Nuggets. 2003. (Captain Underpants Ser.: 6). 173p. (gr. 3-6). lib. bdg. 16.00 *(978-0-613-68836-9(8))* Turtleback.

—El Capitán Calzoncillos y la Furia de la Supermujer Macroelástica (Captain Underpants #5) (Spanish Language Edition of Captain Underpants & the Wrath of the Wicked Wedgie Women) Azaola, Miguel, tr. Pilkey, Dav, illus. 2003. (Capitán Calzoncillos Ser.: 5). (SPA., Illus.). 176p. (gr. 2-5). pap. 7.99 *(978-0-439-53820-6(3)*, Scholastic en Espanol) Scholastic, Inc.

—El Capitan Calzoncillos y la Ridicula Historia de los Seres del Inodoro Morado. Pilkey, Dav, illus. 2008. (Capitán Calzoncillos Ser.: 8). (SPA., Illus.). 176p. (gr. 2-5). pap. 5.99 *(978-0-545-02583-6(4)*, Scholastic en Espanol) Scholastic, Inc.

—Captain Underpants & the Attack of the Talking Toilets. 2004. (Captain Underpants Ser.: No. 2). (J). lib. bdg. 19.95 *(978-0-439-68436-1(6)*, Scholastic, Inc.) Scholastic, Inc.

—Captain Underpants & the Big, Bad Battle of the Bionic Booger Boy Part 1: The Night of the Nasty Nostril Nuggets. 2004. (Captain Underpants Ser.: Bk. 6). (J). lib. bdg. 19.95 *(978-0-439-68438-5(2)*, Scholastic, Inc.) Scholastic, Inc.

—Captain Underpants & the Big, Bad Battle of the Bionic Booger Boy Part 2: The Revenge of the Ridiculous Robo-Boogers. 2004. (Captain Underpants Ser.: Bk. 7). (J). lib. bdg. 19.95 *(978-0-439-68437-8(4)*, Scholastic, Inc.) Scholastic, Inc.

—Captain Underpants & the Big, Bad Battle of the Bionic Booger Boy Part 2: The Revenge of the Ridiculous Robo-Boogers. 2003. (Captain Underpants Ser.: 7). (Illus.). 173p. lib. bdg. 16.00 *(978-0-613-68837-6(6))* Turtleback.

—Captain Underpants & the Invasion of the Incredibly Naughty Cafeteria Ladies from Outer Space: (and the Subsequent Assault of the Equally Evil Lunchroom Zombie Nerds) 2004. (Captain Underpants Ser.: No. 3). (J). lib. bdg. 19.95 *(978-0-439-68439-2(0)*, Scholastic, Inc.) Scholastic, Inc.

—Captain Underpants & the Perilous Plot of Professor Poopypants. 2004. (Captain Underpants Ser.: No. 4). (J). lib. bdg. 19.95 *(978-0-439-68440-8(4)*, Scholastic, Inc.) Scholastic, Inc.

—Captain Underpants & the Sensational Saga of Sir Stinks-a-Lot. Pilkey, Dav, illus. 2015. (Captain Underpants Ser.: 12). (ENG., Illus.). 208p. (J). (gr. 2). lib. bdg. 20.85 *(978-0-606-37924-3(X))* Turtleback.

—Captain Underpants & the Wrath of the Wicked Wedgie Woman. 2004. (Captain Underpants Ser.: No. 5). (J). lib. bdg. 19.95 *(978-0-439-68441-5(2)*, Scholastic, Inc.) Scholastic, Inc.

—Captain Underpants & the Wrath of the Wicked Wedgie Woman (Color Edition) 2018. (Captain Underpants Color Edition Ser.: 5). lib. bdg. 20.85 *(978-0-606-41140-0(2))* Turtleback.

Pilkey, Dav & Garibaldi, Jose. Captain Underpants & the Wrath of the Wicked Wedgie Woman. Pilkey, Dav, illus. 2018. (Illus.). 165p. (J). *(978-1-5444-0229-1(5))* Scholastic, Inc.

Pilkons, Alyssa. Confessions of a Teenage Lima Bean. 2009. 232p. pap. 14.98 *(978-1-4303-1132-4(0))* Lulu Pr., Inc.

Pin, Isabel. Bumblebee Blues. James, J. Alison, tr. from GER. 2003. (Illus.). 32p. (J). (gr. k-3). 15.95 *(978-0-7358-1813-2(4))*; lib. bdg. 16.50 *(978-0-7358-1814-9(2))* North-South Bks., Inc. (Michael Neugebauer Bks.).

Pincus, Greg. The Homework Strike. 2017. (ENG., Illus.). 272p. (J). (gr. 3-7). 16.99 *(978-0-439-91301-0(2))* Scholastic, Inc.

—The 14 Fibs of Gregory K. 2013. (ENG.). 240p. (J). (gr. 3-7). 17.99 *(978-0-439-91299-0(7)*, Levine, Arthur A. Bks.) Scholastic, Inc.

Pincus, Gregory K. The 14 Fibs of Gregory K. 2013. 226p. (J). pap. *(978-0-439-91300-3(4)*, Levine, Arthur A. Bks.) Scholastic, Inc.

Pinder, Eric. I'd Rather Be Riding My Bike. Cardinal, John, illus. I.t. ed. 2013. 42p. (gr. k-1). pap. 10.95 *(978-1-62253-401-2(8))* Evolved Publishing.

Piner, Huston. My Life As a Myth. 2017. (ENG., Illus.). (YA). pap. 11.99 *(978-1-947139-73-2(8))* NineStar Pr.

Pinkwater, Daniel M. The Education of Robert Nifkin. 2005. (ENG.). 192p. (YA). (gr. 7). pap. 12.95 *(978-0-618-55208-5(1)*, 493402, Clarion Bks.) HarperCollins Pubs.

—Yo-Yo Man. Davis, Jack E., illus. 2007. (ENG.). 32p. (J). (gr. -1-3). 16.99 *(978-0-06-055502-3(5))* HarperCollins Pubs.

Pinto, Amy B. Sophie's Perfume. 2012. 100p. 19.95 *(978-1-4759-2715-3(0))* iUniverse, Inc.

Piper, Deb. From A — to Zulinski. 2008. (J). pap. *(978-0-88092-713-0(5))*; lib. bdg. *(978-0-88092-712-3(7))* Royal Fireworks Publishing Co.

Pippenger, Jack G. The Young Rebel. 2007. 292p. 27.95 *(978-0-595-86314-3(0))*; per. 17.95 *(978-0-595-41077-4(4))* iUniverse, Inc.

Pitcher, Chelsea. The S-Word. 2013. (ENG.). 320p. pap. 19.99 *(978-1-4516-9516-8(0)*, Gallery Bks.) Gallery Bks.

Pitcock, Tiffany. Just Friends. 2017. (ENG.). 320p. (YA). pap. 11.99 *(978-1-250-08405-7(9)*, 900156550) Feiwel & Friends.

Pittar, Gill. Milly, Molly & Henry (book W/dolls) 2006. 28p. pap. *(978-1-86972-103-9(9))* Milly Molly Bks.

—Milly, Molly & Jimmy's Seeds (book W/dolls) 2006. 28p. pap. *(978-1-86972-091-9(1))* Milly Molly Bks.

—Milly, Molly & the Stowaways (book W/dolls) 2006. 28p. pap. *(978-1-86972-106-0(3))* Milly Molly Bks.

Piven, Hanoch. My Best Friend Is As Sharp As a Pencil: & Other Funny Classroom Portraits. Piven, Hanoch, illus. 2010. (Illus.). 40p. (J). (gr. -1-3). 17.99 *(978-0-375-85338-8(3))* Random Hse. Children's Bks.

Pixley, Marcella. Freak: A Novel. 2013. (ENG.). 160p. (YA). (gr. 7-10). pap. 14.99 *(978-1-250-02742-9(X)*, 900098314) Square Fish.

The Place Between Breaths. (ENG., Illus.). (YA). (gr. 7). 2019. 208p. pap. 10.99 *(978-1-4814-2226-0(X)*, Atheneum Bks. for Young Readers) 2018. 192p. 17.99 *(978-1-4814-2225-3(1)*, Atheneum/Caitlyn Dlouhy Books) Simon & Schuster Children's Publishing.

Plata, Sebastian J. Freak 'N' Gorgeous. 2018. (ENG.). 288p. (YA). (gr. 8-12). 16.99 *(978-1-5107-3210-0(1)*, Sky Pony Pr.) Skyhorse Publishing Co., Inc.

Platt, Cynthia. Parker Bell & the Science of Friendship. Zhai, Rea, illus. 2019. (ENG.). 160p. (J). (gr. 3-7). 16.99 *(978-1-328-97347-4(6)*, 1708149, Clarion Bks.) HarperCollins Pubs.

Platt, Jason. Middle School Misadventures. 2019. (Middle School Misadventures Ser.: 1). (ENG., Illus.). 232p. (J). (gr. 3-7). pap. 12.99 *(978-0-316-41688-7(6))* Little, Brown Bks. for Young Readers.

Plourde, Lynn. Book Fair Day. Wickstrom, Thor, illus. 2006. (J). *(978-1-4156-8095-7(7)*, Dutton Juvenile) Penguin Publishing Group.

—Maxi's Secrets: (or, What You Can Learn from a Dog) 2017. 272p. (J). (gr. 5). 8.99 *(978-0-399-54568-9(9)*, Puffin Books) Penguin Young Readers Group.

Plum-Ucci, Carol. The Body of Christopher Creed: A Printz Honor Winner. 2008. (ENG., Illus.). 272p. (YA). (gr. 7). pap. 7.99 *(978-0-15-206386-3(2)*, 1199120, Clarion Bks.) HarperCollins Pubs.

Poblocki, Dan. The Nightmarys. 2011. 336p. (J). (gr. 3-7). pap. 8.99 *(978-0-375-84257-3(8)*, Yearling) Random Hse. Children's Bks.

Poindexter, Stephanie. Octavious & His Busy Tentacles. 2010. 21p. 13.50 *(978-0-557-30136-2(X))* Lulu Pr., Inc.

Pointon, Janet. A Matter of Choice. 2008. 82p. pap. 11.51 *(978-1-4092-3108-0(9))* Lulu Pr., Inc.

Polacco, Patricia. The Art of Miss Chew. Polacco, Patricia, illus. 2012. (Illus.). 40p. (J). (gr. k-3). 18.99 *(978-0-399-25703-2(9)*, G.P. Putnam's Sons Books for Young Readers) Penguin Young Readers Group.

—Bully. Polacco, Patricia, illus. 2012. (ENG., Illus.). 48p. (J). (gr. 2-5). 18.99 *(978-0-399-25704-9(7)*, G.P. Putnam's Sons Books for Young Readers) Penguin Young Readers Group.

—The Junkyard Wonders. Polacco, Patricia, illus. 2010. (ENG., Illus.). 48p. (J). (gr. 1-4). 18.99 *(978-0-399-25078-1(6)*, Philomel Bks.) Penguin Young Readers Group.

—The Lemonade Club. Polacco, Patricia, illus. 2007. (Illus.). 48p. (J). (gr. 1-4). 18.99 *(978-0-399-24540-4(5)*, Philomel Bks.) Penguin Young Readers Group.

—Mr. Wayne's Masterpiece. Polacco, Patricia, illus. 2014. (Illus.). 40p. (J). (gr. k-3). 18.99 *(978-0-399-16095-0(7)*, G.P. Putnam's Sons Books for Young Readers) Penguin Young Readers Group.

Polak, Monique. Leggings Revolt. 2016. (Orca Currents Ser.). lib. bdg. 20.80 *(978-0-606-38696-8(3))* Turtleback.

Polatin, Daria. Devil in Ohio. 2018. (ENG.). 336p. (YA). pap. 12.99 *(978-1-250-18077-3(5)*, 900170879) Square Fish.

Polsky, Sara. This Is How I Find Her. 2015. (ENG.). 272p. (YA). (gr. 8-12). pap. 9.99 *(978-0-8075-7880-3(0)*, 807578800) Whitman, Albert & Co.

Pons, Lele & de la Cruz, Melissa. Surviving High School: A Novel. 2017. (ENG.). 272p. (gr. 8). pap. 16.00 *(978-1-5011-2054-1(9)*, Gallery Bks.) Gallery Bks.

Ponti, James. Vanished! (Framed! Ser.: 2). (ENG.). (J). (gr. 3-7). 2018. 400p. pap. 8.99 *(978-1-4814-3634-2(1))* 2017. (Illus.). 384p. 19.99 *(978-1-4814-3633-5(3))* Simon & Schuster Children's Publishing. (Aladdin).

Popescu, Petru. Weregirls: Birth of the Pack: Birth of the Pack. rev. ed. 2007. (ENG.). 352p. (YA). (gr. 8-12). pap. 18.99 *(978-0-7653-1641-7(2)*, 900039012, Tor Teen) Doherty, Tom Assocs., LLC.

Porter, Rhonda. Brody Meets a Bully. 2008. 16p. pap. 24.95 *(978-1-60610-311-1(3))* America Star Bks.

Porter, Sarah. Tentacle & Wing. 2017. (ENG.). 272p. (J). (gr. 5-7). 16.99 *(978-1-328-70733-8(4)*, 1672696, Clarion Bks.) HarperCollins Pubs.

Portis, Antoinette. Kindergarten Diary. Portis, Antoinette, illus. 2010. (ENG., Illus.). 32p. (J). (gr. -1-3). 12.99 *(978-0-06-145691-6(8)*, HarperCollins) HarperCollins Pubs.

Portman, Frank. King Dork. 2007. 344p. 19.00 *(978-0-7569-7950-8(1))* Perfection Learning Corp.

Poskitt, Kjartan. Agatha Parrot & the Odd Street School Ghost. Hargis, Wes, illus. 2017. (Agatha Parrot Ser.). (ENG.). 160p. (J). (gr. 3-7). pap. 6.99 *(978-0-544-93530-3(6)*, 1658369, Clarion Bks.) HarperCollins Pubs.

Posner, Richard. Goodnight Cinderella. 2014. (ENG.). 248p. (J). (gr. 8-11). pap. 15.95 *(978-1-59077-314-7(4))* Evans, M. & Co., Inc.

Posner-Sanchez, Andrea. Peeps at School. Massironi, Daniela, illus. 2018. 24p. (J). *(978-1-5490-4055-9(3))* Random Hse., Inc.

Potter, Dave. Storm Clouds over Mountain View Middle School. 2009. 60p. pap. 9.99 *(978-1-60860-665-8(1)*, Strategic Bk. Publishing) Strategic Book Publishing & Rights Agency (SBPRA).

Potter, Ellen. The Monster Detector (Big Foot & Little Foot #2) Sala, Felicita, illus. 2018. (Big Foot & Little Foot Ser.). (ENG.). 128p. (J). (gr. 1-4). 13.99 *(978-1-4197-3122-8(X)*, 1201501, Amulet Bks.) Abrams, Inc.

—Olivia Kidney Secret Beneath City. 2009. (ENG.). 336p. (J). (gr. 3-7). 9.99 *(978-0-14-241263-3(5)*, Puffin Books) Penguin Young Readers Group.

—Piper Green & the Fairy Tree, 1 vol. Leng, Qin, illus. 2015. (Piper Green & the Fairy Tree Ser.: 1). 112p. (J). (gr. 2-4). pap. 6.99 *(978-0-553-49926-1(2)*, dba7eb01-1f52-4f48-bc93-b0465825d4b4, Rosen Classroom) Random Hse. Children's Bks.

—Piper Green & the Fairy Tree: Going Places. Leng, Qin, illus. 2017. (Piper Green & the Fairy Tree Ser.). (ENG.). (J). (gr. 2-4). 20.95 *(978-1-4301-2680-5(9))* Live Oak Media.

—Piper Green & the Fairy Tree: Going Places. Leng, Qin, illus. 2017. (Piper Green & the Fairy Tree Ser.: 4). (ENG.). 128p. (J). (gr. 2-4). lib. bdg. 17.99 *(978-1-101-93962-8(1)*, Knopf Bks. for Young Readers) Random Hse. Children's Bks.

Powell, Jillian. Sam's Sunflower. Boccardo, Johanna, illus. 2008. (Tadpoles Ser.). (ENG.). 24p. (J). (gr. -1-3). pap. *(978-0-7787-3895-4(7))*; lib. bdg. *(978-0-7787-3864-0(7))* Crabtree Publishing Co.

Powell Zalewski, Amy. Summer School in the City. 2006. (Illus.). 32p. (J). (gr. 1-8). 15.00 *(978-0-9773608-2-6(2))* Shiny Red Ball Publishing.

Poydar, Nancy. The Bad-News Report Card. Poydar, Nancy, illus. 2006. (ENG., Illus.). 32p. (J). (gr. -1-3). 16.95 *(978-0-8234-1992-0(4))* Holiday Hse., Inc.

—The Biggest Test in the Universe. Poydar, Nancy, illus. 2005. (ENG., Illus.). 32p. (J). (gr. -1-3). 16.95 *(978-0-8234-1944-9(4))* Holiday Hse., Inc.

—Bunny Business. 2003. (ENG., Illus.). 32p. (J). (gr. k-3). tchr. ed. 16.95 *(978-0-8234-1771-1(9))* Holiday Hse., Inc.

—Fish School. 2009. (ENG., Illus.). 32p. (J). (gr. -1-3). 16.95 *(978-0-8234-2140-4(6))* Holiday Hse., Inc.

—The Perfectly Horrible Halloween. Poydar, Nancy, illus. 2005. (ENG., Illus.). 32p. (J). (gr. k-3). pap. 6.95 *(978-0-8234-1769-8(7))* Holiday Hse., Inc.

Pratt, Jeffrey. The Prank. 2019. (Do-Over Ser.). (ENG.). 112p. (YA). (gr. 6-12). 26.65 *(978-1-5415-4030-9(1)*, 31ac7147-b85c-4abb-b1a5-205ab7b7fc80, Darby Creek) Lerner Publishing Group.

—Team Player. 2019. (Al High Ser.). (ENG.). 112p. (YA). (gr. 6-12). pap. 7.99 *(978-1-5415-7294-2(7)*, 179e9c99-a9e7-43fc-90d3-3828427be6be, Darby Creek) Lerner Publishing Group.

Pratts, Christine. Tabby Wise for School Secretary. 2005. 61p. pap. 8.99 *(978-1-4116-4935-4(4))* Lulu Pr., Inc.

Preller, James. Bee the Change. 2019. (Big Idea Gang Ser.). (ENG., Illus.). 96p. (J). (gr. 1-4). pap. 6.99 *(978-1-328-97339-9(5)*, 1708133, Clarion Bks.) HarperCollins Pubs.

—Better off Undead. 2018. (ENG.). 304p. (J). pap. 18.99 *(978-1-250-17905-0(X)*, 900189919) Square Fish.

—Better off Undead. 2018. (J). lib. bdg. 18.40 *(978-0-606-41113-4(5))* Turtleback.

—Bystander. 2011. (ENG.). 256p. (YA). (gr. 5-9). pap. 8.99 *(978-0-312-54796-7(X)*, 900074323) Square Fish.

—Everybody Needs a Buddy. 2019. (Big Idea Gang Ser.). (ENG., Illus.). 96p. (J). (gr. 1-4). pap. 6.99 *(978-1-328-97340-5(9)*, 1708135, Clarion Bks.) HarperCollins Pubs.

—Jigsaw Jones: the Case from Outer Space. 2017. (Jigsaw Jones Mysteries Ser.). (ENG., Illus.). 96p. (J). pap. 6.99 *(978-1-250-11017-6(3)*, 900165779) Feiwel & Friends.

—Jigsaw Jones: the Case of the Bicycle Bandit. 2017. (Jigsaw Jones Mysteries Ser.). (ENG., Illus.). 96p. (J). pap. 6.99 *(978-1-250-11084-8(X)*, 900169772) Feiwel & Friends.

—Jigsaw Jones: the Case of the Buried Treasure. 2017. (Jigsaw Jones Mysteries Ser.). (ENG., Illus.). 112p. (J). pap. 6.99 *(978-1-250-11086-2(6)*, 900169774) Feiwel & Friends.

—Jigsaw Jones: the Case of the Glow-In-the-Dark Ghost. 2017. (Jigsaw Jones Mysteries Ser.). (ENG., Illus.). 96p. (J). pap. 6.99 *(978-1-250-11020-6(3)*, 900165781) Feiwel & Friends.

—Jigsaw Jones: the Case of the Hat Burglar. Alley, R. W., illus. 2019. (Jigsaw Jones Mysteries Ser.). (ENG.). 96p. (J). pap. 6.99 *(978-1-250-20768-5(1)*, 900201639) Feiwel & Friends.

—Jigsaw Jones: the Case of the Million-Dollar Mystery. 2017. (Jigsaw Jones Mysteries Ser.). (ENG., Illus.). 112p. (J). pap. 6.99 *(978-1-250-11095-4(5)*, 900169793) Feiwel & Friends.

—Jigsaw Jones: the Case of the Mummy Mystery. 2017. (Jigsaw Jones Mysteries Ser.). (ENG., Illus.). 96p. (J). pap. 6.99 *(978-1-250-11082-4(3)*, 900169770) Feiwel & Friends.

—Jigsaw Jones: the Case of the Smelly Sneaker. 2017. (Jigsaw Jones Mysteries Ser.). (ENG., Illus.). 96p. (J). pap. 6.99 *(978-1-250-11080-0(7)*, 900169768) Feiwel & Friends.

—A Pirate's Guide to First Grade. 2013. (J). lib. bdg. 18.40 *(978-0-606-31896-9(8))* Turtleback.

—The Worst Mascot Ever. 2019. (Big Idea Gang Ser.). (ENG., Illus.). 96p. (J). (gr. 1-4). pap. 6.99 *(978-1-328-91511-5(5)*, 1702126, Clarion Bks.) HarperCollins Pubs.

Prendergast, Gabrielle. Audacious, 1 vol. 2015. (ENG.). 336p. (YA). (gr. 8-12). pap. 12.95 *(978-1-4598-0264-3(0))* Orca Bk. Pubs. USA.

—Pandas on the Eastside, 1 vol. 2016. (ENG., Illus.). 192p. (J). (gr. 4-7). pap. 9.95 *(978-1-4598-1143-0(7))* Orca Bk. Pubs. USA.

—Pinch Me, 1 vol. 2017. (Orca Soundings Ser.). (ENG.). 144p. (YA). (gr. 8-12). pap. 9.95 *(978-1-4598-1364-9(2))* Orca Bk. Pubs. USA.

Press, J. Abra-Ca-Doodle! 2013. (Doodles of Sam Dibble Ser.: 4). lib. bdg. 14.75 *(978-0-606-32125-9(X))* Turtleback.

—The Doodles of Sam Dibble. 2013. (Doodles of Sam Dibble Ser.: 1). lib. bdg. 14.75 *(978-0-606-29777-6(4))* Turtleback.

—Double Trouble #2, 2. Kline, Michael, illus. 2013. (Doodles of Sam Dibble Ser.: 2). (ENG.). 128p. (J). (gr. 1-3). 17.44 *(978-0-448-46108-3(0))* Penguin Young Readers Group.

Preston, Mary Lou. Do You Know What Wildcats Do at School in P. E. Class? Wildcat's First Day in Class. 2006. (J). pap. 8.00 *(978-0-8059-7013-5(4))* Dorrance Publishing Co., Inc.

Prévert, Jacques. En Sortant de l'Ecole. (FRE.). (J). pap. *(978-2-07-050633-0(9))* Gallimard, Editions FRA. Dist: Distribooks, Inc.

Price, Allison W. A. The Dragons & the Words of Knowledge. 2009. 112p. pap. 14.98 *(978-0-557-05766-5(3))* Lulu Pr., Inc.

Primavera, Elise. Louise the Big Cheese & the Back-To-School Smarty-Pants. Goode, Diane, illus. 2011. (ENG.). 40p. (J). (gr. k-3). 16.99 *(978-1-4424-0600-1(3)*, Simon &

Schuster/Paula Wiseman Bks.) Simon & Schuster/Paula Wiseman Bks.

Prime, Derek. Sarah & Paul Go Back to School Bk. 1. 2006. (Sarah & Paul Ser.). (ENG., Illus.). 128p. (J). (gr. 2-5). per. 6.99 (978-1-84550-157-0(8), 607ff22b-e8f5-4688-a389-9c7f700cd974) Christian Focus Pubns. GBR. Dist: Baker & Taylor Publisher Services (BTPS).

Prinz, Yvonne. Still There, Clare. 2005. (ENG.). 4p. (J). pap., tchr. ed. (978-1-55192-821-0(3)) Raincoast Bk. Distribution CAN. Dist: Publishers Group West (PGW).

Prisant, Guillermo Murray. Que Miedo! rev. ed. 2006. (Castillo del Terror Ser.). (SPA & ENG.). 112p. (J). (gr. 6-9). pap. 6.95 (978-970-20-0338-0(5)) Castillo, Ediciones, S. A. de C. V. MEX. Dist: Macmillan.

Prom Crashers. 2014. (Romantic Comedies Ser.). (ENG., Illus.). 256p. (YA). (gr. 9). pap. 12.99 (978-1-4814-2747-0(4), Simon Pulse) Simon Pulse.

Prom Etiquette Scrapbook. 2011. 128p. 8.99 (978-1-4231-4566-0(6)) Disney Pr.

Prom: He Said/She Said. 2011. 256p. (J). 12.99 (978-1-4231-4565-3(8)) Disney Pr.

Prose, Francine. After. 2003. 336p. (J). (gr. 5-18). lib. bdg. 17.89 (978-0-06-008082-2(5), Cotler, Joanna Books) 2004. (ENG.). 352p. (YA). (gr. 8). reprint ed. pap. 9.99 (978-0-06-008083-9(3), HarperTeen) HarperCollins Pubs.

—Bullyville. 2007. 260p. (YA). (gr. 7-12). 16.99 (978-0-06-057497-0(6)); lib. bdg. 17.89 (978-0-06-057498-7(4)) HarperCollins Pubs. (HarperTeen).

—Bullyville. 2011. 10.36 (978-0-7848-3625-5(6), Everbind) Marco Bk. Co.

Publications International Ltd. Staff. Little Lift & Listen Sound Dora Go to School. 2007. 12p. (J). 10.98 (978-1-4127-8575-4(8), PIL Kids) Publications International, Ltd.

Publications International Ltd. Staff, ed. Finding Nemo - Let's Go to School. 2011. 12p. (J). bds. (978-1-4508-0510-0(8)) Publications International, Ltd.

—Record-A-Memory School Years. 2011. 16p. (J). 25.98 (978-1-4508-1341-9(0)) Publications International, Ltd.

Puffin. The Otterbury Incident. 2017. (Puffin Book Ser.). (Illus.). 240p. (J). (gr. 3-7). mass mkt. 15.99 (978-0-14-137988-3(X)) Penguin Bks., Ltd. GBR. Dist: Independent Pubs. Group.

Pugh, Tracey D. A Show & Tell Lesson. McCracken, Jaime, photos by. l.t. ed. 2006. (Illus.). 32p. (J). 12.95 (978-1-59879-105-1(2)) Lifevest Publishing, Inc.

Pugin-Rodas, M. C. The Eight Ball Club: Ocean of Fire. 2007. (ENG., Illus.). 144p. pap. 15.95 (978-0-9793761-2-2(2)) ESOL Publishing.

Pugliano-Martin, Carol. My Little Red Lunchbox Book. Ottinger, Jon, illus. 2004. (Sparkle Shape Bks.). 10p. (J). (gr. -1-18). bds. 6.99 (978-1-57151-716-6(2)) Playhouse Publishing.

Pulver, Robin. Happy Endings: A Story about Suffixes. Reed, Lynn Rowe, illus. 2012. (ENG.). 32p. (J). (gr. -1-3). pap. 8.99 (978-0-8234-2434-4(0)) Holiday Hse., Inc.

—Happy Endings: A Story about Suffixes. Reed, Lynn Rowe, illus. 2013. (ENG.). (J). (gr. 1-3). pap. 44.95 (978-1-4301-1435-2(5)) Live Oak Media.

—Happy Endings: A Story about Suffixes. 2013. 18.95 (978-1-4301-1433-8(9)) Live Oak Media.

—Nouns & Verbs Have a Field Day. Reed, Lynn Rowe, illus. 2007. (ENG.). 32p. (J). (gr. k-3). 8.99 (978-0-8234-2097-1(3)) Holiday Hse., Inc.

—Nouns & Verbs Have a Field Day. Reed, Lynn Rowe, illus. 2013. pap. 18.95 incl. audio compact disk (978-1-4301-1115-3(1)) Live Oak Media.

—Persuading Miss Doover. Sisson, Stephanie Roth, illus. 2018. 32p. (J). (gr. 1-4). 17.99 (978-0-8234-3426-8(5)) Holiday Hse., Inc.

—Punctuation Takes a Vacation. Reed, Lynn Rowe, illus. 2004. (ENG.). 32p. (J). (gr. k-3). reprint ed. pap. 7.99 (978-0-8234-1820-6(0)) Holiday Hse., Inc.

—Punctuation Takes a Vacation. Reed, Lynn Rowe, illus. 2009. (J). (gr. 1-3). 29.95 incl. audio compact disk (978-1-4301-0708-8(1)) Live Oak Media.

—Silent Letters Loud & Clear. Reed, Lynn Rowe, illus. 2010. (ENG.). 32p. (J). (gr. 1-4). pap. 8.99 (978-0-8234-2309-5(3)) Holiday Hse., Inc.

Pung, Alice. Lucy & Linh. 2018. (ENG.). 352p. (YA). (gr. 7). pap. 9.99 (978-0-399-55051-5(8), Ember) Random Hse. Children's Bks.

—Marly Walks on the Moon: Marly: Book 4. 2016. (Our Australian Girl Ser.: 4). 144p. (J). (gr. 3-7). 14.99 (978-0-14-330852-2(1)) Penguin Random Hse. AUS. Dist: Independent Pubs. Group.

—Marly's Business: Marly: Book 2. 2016. (Our Australian Girl Ser.: 2). (Illus.). 144p. (J). (gr. 3-7). 7.99 (978-0-14-330850-8(5)) Penguin Random Hse. AUS. Dist: Independent Pubs. Group.

Punter, Russell. Hyena Ballerina IR. 2018. (Phonics Readers Ser.). (ENG.). 24p. (J). pap. 6.99 (978-0-7945-4040-1(6), Usborne) EDC Publishing.

Purves, William C. Fairmont Forever. 2011. 180p. pap. 13.95 (978-1-4502-3878-6(5)) iUniverse, Inc.

Puttock, Simon. Mouse's First Night at Moonlight School. Pye, Ali, illus. 2015. (ENG.). 32p. (J). (gr. -1-2). 16.99 (978-0-7636-7607-0(1)) Candlewick Pr.

Pyros, Andrea. Pink Hair & Other Terrible Ideas. 2019. (ENG.). 256p. (J). (gr. 4-7). lib. bdg. 15.95 (978-1-68446-028-1(X), 139700, Capstone Editions) Capstone.

Quackenbush, Robert. First Grade Jitters. Nascimbene, Yan, illus. 2010. (ENG.). 32p. (J). (gr. k-2). 17.99 (978-0-06-077632-9(3), HarperCollins) HarperCollins Pubs.

Qualey, Marsha. Gracie Laroo Goes to School. Litten, Kristyna, illus. 2017. (Gracie Laroo Ser.). (ENG.). 40p. (J). (gr. k-2). lib. bdg. 21.32 (978-1-5158-1440-5(8), 135710, Picture Window Bks.) Capstone.

Qualls, Shirley. Marigold Duck Comes to Our School. 2009. 28p. pap. 12.49 (978-1-4389-8386-8(7)) AuthorHouse.

Quick, Matthew. Boy21. 2013. (ENG.). 272p. (YA). (gr. 7-17). pap. 11.99 (978-0-316-12796-7(5)) Little, Brown Bks. for Young Readers.

—Sorta Like a Rock Star. 2011. (ENG.). 384p. (YA). (gr. 7-17). pap., pap. 19.99 (978-0-316-04353-3(2)) Little, Brown Bks. for Young Readers.

Quintanilla, Billie. Never Again a Homeless Christmas! 2012. 28p. pap. 24.95 (978-1-4626-5197-9(6)) America Star Bks.

Quintero, Isabel. Gabi, a Girl in Pieces, 1 vol. 2014. (ENG.). 208p. (YA). (gr. 9-12). pap. 16.95 (978-1-935955-95-5(0), 23353382, Cinco Puntos Press) Lee & Low Bks., Inc.

Quintero, Sofia. Efrain's Secret. 2011. (ENG.). 272p. (YA). (gr. 9). pap. 8.99 (978-0-440-24062-4(X), Ember) Random Hse. Children's Bks.

Quitzel, Ivey. Out of Control. 2009. (ENG.). 132p. pap. 11.00 (978-0-557-08762-4(7)) Lulu Pr., Inc.

Rabe, Tish. On the First Day of First Grade. Jennings, Sarah, illus. 2018. (ENG.). 32p. (J). (gr. -1-3). 10.99 (978-0-06-266851-6(X), HarperCollins) HarperCollins Pubs.

Rach, W. Dennis. The Goofy Principal at Silly School. 2007. (J). per. (978-0-9792579-0-2(5)) Rach, W. Dennis.

Rad, Charles J. The Boy they called a Snowball. 2007. (ENG.). 140p. pap. 20.95 (978-1-84753-461-3(9)) Lulu Pr., Inc.

Rae, Angela. All of Us. 2009. 81p. pap. 12.99 (978-0-557-05491-6(5)) Lulu Pr., Inc.

—The Choices Witch Make Us. 2008. 113p. pap. 15.95 (978-1-4357-4287-1(7)) Lulu Pr., Inc.

Raiku, Makoto, contrib. by. Zatchbell!, Vol. 3. 2005. 200p. 9.99 (978-1-4215-0208-3(9)) Viz Media.

Raines, Jennifer. Alex & Andrew Swap Places. 2008. 32p. per. 24.95 (978-1-4241-8938-0(1)) America Star Bks.

Rainey. School Is Cool. Huggens, Karin, illus. 2004. (J). (978-0-9666199-9-7(4)) DreamDog Pr.

Rallison, Janette. It's a Mall World after All. 2006. (ENG.). 230p. (YA). (gr. 6-8). 22.44 (978-0-8027-8853-5(X), 9780802788535) Walker & Co.

Rameaka, Thomas. Bee Haven. 2006. (ENG.). 188p. per. 24.95 (978-1-4241-5646-7(7)) America Star Bks.

Ramesh, Serita. Jason & the Ingenious Number Trick: A Story about Patterns. 2010. 28p. pap. 15.49 (978-1-4490-4740-5(8)) AuthorHouse.

Ramirez, Terry. Growing up with Olivi: The Beguiling Blue-Haired Beauty of Boysenberry Lane. 2009. 96p. pap. 9.95 (978-0-595-47668-8(6)) iUniverse, Inc.

Ramona Quimby, Age 8. 2005. (J). (978-1-59564-976-8(X)) Steps To Literacy, LLC.

Ramos, Juan Antonio. El Principe de Blancanieves. (Torre de Papel Ser.). (SPA.). (J). (gr. 4-18). 8.95 (978-958-04-3943-1(5)) Norma S.A. COL. Dist: Distribuidora Norma, Inc.

Ramos, Pilar. UN LARGO DIA. (SPA.). 32p. (J). 10.00 (978-84-342-2518-3(2)) Parramon Ediciones S.A. ESP. Dist: Distribuidora Norma, Inc.

Ramthun, Bonnie. The White Gates. 2008. (ENG.). 256p. (J). (gr. 6-8). lib. bdg. 22.44 (978-0-375-94554-0(7)) Random House Publishing Group.

Randall, Thomas. The Waking: A Winter of Ghosts. 2011. (YA). pap. 9.99 (978-1-59990-252-4(4), Bloomsbury USA Childrens) Bloomsbury Publishing USA.

Randle, Kristen. The Only Alien on the Planet. 2009. 240p. (YA). (gr. 7-12). pap. 11.99 (978-1-4022-2669-4(1), 9781402226694) Sourcebooks, Inc.

Randle, Kristen D. Slumming. 2003. (Illus.). 240p. (J). lib. bdg. 16.89 (978-0-06-001023-2(1), HarperTeen) HarperCollins Pubs.

Rankin, Laura. Ruthie & the (Not So) Teeny Tiny Lie. Rankin, Laura, illus. 2007. (ENG., Illus.). 32p. (J). (gr. -1-3). 18.99 (978-1-59990-010-0(6), 900041434, Bloomsbury USA Childrens) Bloomsbury Publishing USA.

Ransom, Jeanie Franz. Don't Squeal Unless It's a Big Deal: A Tale of Tattletales. Urbanovic, Jackie, illus. 2005. 32p. (J). (ENG.). 14.95 (978-1-59147-239-1(3)); (gr. -1-3). pap. 9.95 (978-1-59147-240-7(7)) American Psychological Assn. (Magination Pr.).

—There's a Cat in Our Class! A Tale about Getting Along. Langdo, Bryan, illus. 2016. 32p. (J). (978-1-4338-2262-9(8), Magination Pr.) American Psychological Assn.

Rapson, Helen. Reggie Did It!, 1 vol. 2009. 49p. pap. 16.95 (978-1-60813-161-7(0)) America Star Bks.

Rasheed, Leila. Socks, Shocks & Secrets. 2013. (Fantastic Diary of Bathsheba Claric de Trop Ser.). 293p. (J). pap. 5.99 (978-0-7945-3029-7(X), Usborne) EDC Publishing.

Rateau, Loy. David's Prayers: A Boy's Perseverance of Conquering the Enemy. 2005. 17.00 (978-0-8059-9834-4(9)) Dorrance Publishing Co., Inc.

Rather, Sherri. Upside down Danny, 1 vol. Rather, Sherri, illus. 2009. (Illus.). 27p. pap. 24.95 (978-1-61582-924-8(5)) America Star Bks.

Rathmann, Peggy. Ruby the Copycat. Rathmann, Peggy, illus. 2006. (Scholastic Bookshelf Ser.). (ENG., Illus.). 32p. (J). (gr. -1-3). per. 7.99 (978-0-439-47228-9(8), Teaching Resources) Scholastic, Inc.

Ray, Delia. Here Lies Linc. 2012. 320p. (J). (gr. 3-7). 7.99 (978-0-375-86538-1(1), Yearling) Random Hse. Children's Bks.

Ray, Gracie. Falling Slowly. 2012. 270p. (978-1-105-59084-9(4)) Lulu.com.

Reagan, Jean. How to Get Your Teacher Ready. Wildish, Lee, illus. 2017. (How to Ser.). (ENG.). 32p. (J). (gr. -1-3). 18.99 (978-0-553-53825-0(X), Knopf Bks. for Young Readers) Random Hse. Children's Bks.

Real Bout High School, Vol. 6. 2005. (YA). pap. 9.99 (978-1-59182-523-4(7)) TOKYOPOP, Inc.

RealBuzz Studios Staff. Hits & Misses. 2007. 128p. (YA). No. 1. pap. 4.97 (978-1-59789-569-9(5))No. 3. pap. 4.97 (978-1-59789-571-2(7))No. 4. pap. 4.97 (978-1-59789-572-9(5)) Barbour Publishing, Inc. (Barbour Bks.).

Reasoner, Charles. A Day at School. 2009. (Inside Outside Board Bks.). (Illus.). (J). bds. 10.99 (978-1-934650-56-1(0)) Just For Kids Pr., LLC.

Reavis, Vicky 'A' Blevins. The Night Before Christmas. 2013. 72p. pap. 17.95 (978-1-4241-2838-9(2)) America Star Bks.

Rech, Lindsay Faith. It Started with a Dare. 2010. (ENG.). 312p. (YA). (gr. 7-18). pap. 17.99 (978-0-547-23558-5(5), 1083194, Clarion Bks.) HarperCollins Pubs.

Reck, Jared. A Short History of the Girl Next Door. 2018. 272p. (YA). (gr. 7). pap. 9.99 (978-1-5247-1610-3(3), Ember) Random Hse. Children's Bks.

Recorvits, Helen. My Name Is Yoon. Swiatkowska, Gabi, illus. 2003. (ENG.). 32p. (J). (gr. -1-3). 18.99 (978-0-374-35114-4(7), 900020207, Farrar, Straus & Giroux (BYR)) Farrar, Straus & Giroux.

—My Name Is Yoon. Swiatkowska, Gabi, illus. 2014. (ENG.). 32p. (J). (gr. -1-3). 8.99 (978-1-250-05711-2(6), 900139124) Square Fish.

Red & Green Choices by Green Irene: Niki's Next Grade. 2003. (J). per. 14.50 (978-0-9742280-1-3(X)) Green Irene.

Redgate, Riley. Noteworthy. 2017. (ENG.). 400p. (YA). (gr. 8-17). 17.95 (978-1-4197-2373-5(1), 1164601, Amulet Bks.) Abrams, Inc.

—Seven Ways We Lie. 2017. (ENG.). 368p. (YA). (gr. 8-17). pap. 9.95 (978-1-4197-2348-3(0), 1132503, Amulet Bks.) Abrams, Inc.

Reece, Colleen L. Wilderness Warriors. 2012. 114p. 18.95 (978-1-61633-309-6(X)); pap. 8.95 (978-1-61633-310-2(3)) Guardian Angel Publishing, Inc.

Reed, Amy. Nowhere Girls. 2017. (ENG.). (YA). (gr. 9). pap. 12.99 (978-1-5344-1555-3(6)) Simon & Schuster.

—The Nowhere Girls. (ENG., Illus.). (YA). (gr. 9). 2019. 432p. pap. 12.99 (978-1-4814-8174-8(6)) 2017. 416p. 19.99 (978-1-4814-8173-1(8)) Simon Pulse. (Simon Pulse).

Reed, Melody. The Major Eights 3: the Goo Disaster! Pépin, Émilie, illus. 2018. (Major Eights Ser.: 3). (ENG.). 112p. (J). (gr. k-3). 16.99 (978-1-4998-0587-1(X)); pap. 5.99 (978-1-4998-0586-4(1)) Little Bee Books Inc.

Rees, Douglas. Uncle Pirate. Auth, Tony, illus. (ENG.). 112p. (J). (gr. 2-5). 2009. pap. 6.99 (978-1-4169-4763-9(9)) 2008. 15.99 (978-1-4169-4762-2(0)) McElderry, Margaret K. Bks. (McElderry, Margaret K. Bks.).

—Uncle Pirate to the Rescue. Auth, Tony, illus. 2010. (ENG.). 112p. (J). (gr. 2-5). pap. 6.99 (978-1-4169-7505-2(5), McElderry, Margaret K. Bks.) McElderry, Margaret K. Bks.

—Vampire High. 2010. (ENG.). 240p. (YA). (gr. 6-8). lib. bdg. 24.94 (978-0-385-90143-7(7)) Random House Publishing Group.

—Vampire High. 2010. (Vampire High Ser.). 240p. (YA). (gr. 7-18). pap. 9.99 (978-0-385-73920-7(6), Delacorte Bks. for Young Readers) Random Hse. Children's Bks.

Reeves, Pamela. United We Stand, a Story about Two Bullies. LaGrange, Tiffany, illus. 2009. 24p. pap. 12.95 (978-1-936051-36-6(2)) Peppertree Pr., The.

Regan, Peter. Riverside: Spring Fever. 2007. (ENG.). 112p. (J). pap. (978-1-901737-56-1(X), Anvil Bks.) Mercier Pr., Ltd., The.

Reid, David. The Shade Girls Were Right. 2012. (ENG.). 23p. (J). pap. 14.95 (978-1-4327-8179-8(0)) Outskirts Pr., Inc.

Reid, Isabelle. Serafina Moon. 2009. 48p. pap. (978-1-84923-771-0(9)) YouWriteOn.

Reid, Kimberly. Prettyboy Must Die: A Novel. 2019. (ENG.). 288p. (YA). pap. 16.99 (978-0-7653-9088-2(4), 900169701, Tor Teen) Doherty, Tom Assocs., LLC.

Reilly, Carmel & Young, Karen. Buzz & Zip Get Lost. 2008. (Rigby Focus Forward: Level G Ser.). (Illus.). 24p. (J). (gr. 4-7). pap. (978-1-4190-3704-7(8), Rigby) Pearson Education Australia.

Reilly, K. J. Words We Don't Say. 2019. (ENG.). 288p. (YA). (gr. 7-17). pap. 9.99 (978-1-368-01860-9(2)) Hyperion Bks. for Children.

—Words We Don't Say. 2018. (ENG.). 288p. (YA). (gr. 7-12). 17.99 (978-1-368-01633-9(2)) Little, Brown Bks. for Young Readers.

Reindeer Flight School. 2003. (J). per. (978-1-57657-808-7(9)); per. (978-1-57657-920-6(4)) Paradise Pr., Inc.

Reinhardt, Dana. A Brief Chapter in My Impossible Life. 2007. (ENG.). 256p. (YA). (gr. 9-12). pap. 8.99 (978-0-375-84691-5(3), Ember) Random Hse. Children's Bks.

Reisz, Kristopher. Unleashed. 2010. (ENG.). 352p. (YA). (gr. 9). pap. 9.99 (978-1-4424-0637-7(2), Simon Pulse) Simon Pulse.

Reiter, Douglas. Back to School in Cedar Heights. 2006. 79p. pap. 19.95 (978-1-4137-9058-0(5)) America Star Bks.

Remington, Laurel. Cake & Confessions. 2019. (Secret Recipe Book Ser.: 2). (ENG.). 304p. (J). (gr. 3-7). pap. 7.99 (978-1-4926-6967-8(9)) Sourcebooks, Inc.

—Secrets & Scones. 2018. (Secret Recipe Book Ser.: 1). (ENG.). 288p. (J). (gr. 3-7). pap. 7.99 (978-1-4926-6964-7(4)) Sourcebooks, Inc.

Rempel, Leah. Hey, Hmong Girl, Whassup? The Journal of Choua Vang. 2004. (Illus.). v, 138p. (YA). pap. (978-0-9723721-5-2(6)) Hamline Univ. Pr.

Remza, Freddie. Ride the Wave. 2011. 272p. pap. 16.95 (978-1-4327-6642-9(2)) Outskirts Pr., Inc.

Renee Daeumler Thompson. I Made a Bad Choice. 2009. 16p. pap. 8.49 (978-1-4389-7561-0(9)) AuthorHouse.

Rennert, Laura Joy. Emma, the Extra Ordinary Princess. Florian, Melanie, illus. 2009. (J). (978-0-525-42152-8(1), Dutton Juvenile) Penguin Publishing Group.

—Royal Princess Academy: Dragon Dreams. Florian, Melanie, illus. 2012. (Royal Princess Academy Ser.). (ENG.). 112p. (J). (gr. 1-4). 18.69 (978-0-8037-3750-1(5)) Penguin Young Readers Group.

Rennison, Louise. A Midsummer Tights Dream. 2013. (Misadventures of Tallulah Casey Ser.: 2). (ENG.). 272p. (YA). (gr. 8). pap. 9.99 (978-0-06-179938-9(6), HarperTeen) HarperCollins Pubs.

Rentala, Sita Kanaka Valli. Ocean Flows: In Prose: Zcumby's Judo (on Global Warming) 2010. 44p. (J). pap. 19.99 (978-1-4490-8780-7(9)) AuthorHouse.

Rentas, Donna. Leticia Goes to School. 2008. 16p. pap. 24.95 (978-1-4241-8966-3(7)) America Star Bks.

Repka, Janice. The Clueless Girl's Guide to Being a Genius. 2011. (ENG.). 176p. (J). (gr. 4-6). 21.19 (978-0-525-42333-1(8)) Penguin Young Readers Group.

Revenge of the Bully. 2014. (How to Beat the Bully Ser.). (ENG., Illus.). 288p. (J). (gr. 3-7). 17.99 (978-1-4424-5677-8(9), Simon & Schuster/Paula Wiseman Bks.) Simon & Schuster/Paula Wiseman Bks.

Rex, Adam. Fat Vampire: A Never Coming of Age Story. 2011. (ENG.). 336p. (YA). (gr. 9). pap. 8.99 (978-0-06-192092-9(4), Balzer & Bray) HarperCollins Pubs.

—School's First Day of School. 2016. (ENG., Illus.). 40p. (J). (gr. -1-3). 17.99 (978-1-59643-964-1(5), 900126201) Roaring Brook Pr.

Rex, Michael. The Egg of Misery: Fangbone, Third Grade Barbarian. Rex, Michael, illus. 2012. (Fangbone! Third Grade Barbarian Ser.: 2). (Illus.). 128p. (J). (gr. 2-4). 9.99 (978-0-399-25522-9(2), G.P. Putnam's Sons Books for Young Readers) Penguin Young Readers Group.

—Fangbone! Third-Grade Barbarian. 2012. (Illus.). 120p. (J). (978-0-545-44042-4(4), Putnam Juvenile) Penguin Publishing Group.

Rey, H. A. Curious George: Time for School Lift-The-Flaps (CGTV) 2011. (Curious George Ser.). (ENG., Illus.). 16p. (J). (gr. -1-3). 6.99 (978-0-547-42230-5(X), 1431226, Clarion Bks.) HarperCollins Pubs.

—Curious George's First Day of School. 2005. (Curious George Ser.). (ENG., Illus.). 24p. (J). (gr. -1-3). pap. 5.99 (978-0-618-60564-4(9), 448941, Clarion Bks.) HarperCollins Pubs.

—Curious George's First Day of School Book & Cd. 2005. (Curious George Ser.). (ENG., Illus.). 24p. (J). (gr. -1-3). audio compact disk 10.99 (978-0-618-60565-1(7), 448943, Clarion Bks.) HarperCollins Pubs.

Rey, H. A. & Hines, Anna Grossnickle. Curious George & the Firefighters Board Book: Lap Edition. 2007. (Curious George Ser.). (ENG., Illus.). 24p. (J). (gr. -1-3). bds. 11.99 (978-0-618-89194-8(3), 569981, Clarion Bks.) HarperCollins Pubs.

Reynolds, Aaron. Superhero School. Rash, Andy, illus. 2009. (ENG.). 32p. (J). (gr. k-2). 18.99 (978-1-59990-166-4(8), 900048407, Bloomsbury USA Childrens) Bloomsbury Publishing USA.

—Tiger Moth: Adventures of an Insect Ninja, 1 vol. Lervold, Erik, illus. 2011. (Tiger Moth Ser.). (ENG.). 128p. (J). (gr. 2-5). 7.95 (978-1-4342-3032-4(5), 114568, Stone Arch Bks.) Capstone.

Reynolds, Jason. Look Both Ways: A Tale Told in Ten Blocks. 2020. (ENG.). 240p. (gr. 7-12). 24.94 (978-1-5364-6605-8(0), Atheneum Bks. for Young Readers) Simon & Schuster Children's Publishing.

—Look Both Ways: A Tale Told in Ten Blocks. Nabaum, Alexander, illus. (ENG.). (J). (gr. 5-9). 2020. 240p. pap. 8.99 (978-1-4814-3829-2(8)) 2019. 208p. 17.99 (978-1-4814-3828-5(X)) Simon & Schuster Children's Publishing. (Atheneum/Caitlyn Dlouhy Books).

Reynolds Naylor, Phyllis. Alice in April. 2011. (Alice Ser.: 5). (ENG.). 192p. (J). (gr. 5-9). pap. 7.99 (978-1-4424-2757-0(4), Atheneum Bks. for Young Readers) Simon & Schuster Children's Publishing.

—Alice in Blunderland. 2005. 200p. (J). (gr. 2-7). 13.65 (978-0-7569-5075-0(9)) Perfection Learning Corp.

—Alice in Blunderland. 2012. (Alice Ser.). (ENG., Illus.). 240p. (J). (gr. 2-7). pap. 7.99 (978-1-4424-4643-4(9), Atheneum Bks. for Young Readers) Simon & Schuster Children's Publishing.

—Alice in Charge. (Alice Ser.: 22). (ENG., (YA). (gr. 9). 2011. Illus.). 304p. pap. 8.99 (978-1-4169-7555-7(1)) 2010. 336p. 16.99 (978-1-4169-7552-6(7)) Simon & Schuster Children's Publishing. (Atheneum Bks. for Young Readers).

—Alice in Lace. 2009. (Alice McKinley Ser.: No. 8). (ENG.). 160p. (J). pap. 7.99 (978-1-4169-7543-4(8), Simon & Schuster/Paula Wiseman Bks.) Simon & Schuster/Paula Wiseman Bks.

—Alice on Her Way. 2006. (Alice McKinley Ser.: No. 17). 322p. (gr. 9-12). 17.00 (978-0-7569-6909-7(3)) Perfection Learning Corp.

—Alice on Her Way. 2006. (Alice Ser.: No. 17). (ENG.). 352p. (YA). (gr. 9-12). mass mkt. 6.99 (978-0-689-87091-0(4), Simon Pulse) Simon Pulse.

—Alice on the Outside. 2012. (Alice Ser.: 11). (ENG., Illus.). 208p. (J). (gr. 5-9). pap. 7.99 (978-1-4424-3495-0(3), Atheneum Bks. for Young Readers) Simon & Schuster Children's Publishing.

—All but Alice. 2011. (Alice Ser.: 4). (ENG.). 192p. (J). (gr. 5-9). pap. 7.99 (978-1-4424-2756-3(6), Atheneum Bks. for Young Readers) Simon & Schuster Children's Publishing.

—Dangerously Alice. 2007. (Alice Ser.: 19). (ENG.). 304p. (YA). (gr. 9-12). 15.99 (978-0-689-87094-1(9), Atheneum Bks. for Young Readers) Simon & Schuster Children's Publishing.

—Dangerously Alice. 2008. (Alice Ser.: No. 19). (ENG.). 320p. (YA). mass mkt. 6.99 (978-0-689-87095-8(7), Simon Pulse) Simon Pulse.

—I Like Him, He Likes Her: Alice Alone; Simply Alice; Patiently Alice. 2010. (Alice Ser.). (ENG.). 640p. (J). (gr. 7). pap. 12.99 (978-1-4424-0978-1(9), Atheneum Bks. for Young Readers) Simon & Schuster Children's Publishing.

—Including Alice. 2005. (Alice McKinley Ser.: No. 16). 277p. (J). (gr. 4-7). 13.65 (978-0-7569-5460-4(6)) Perfection Learning Corp.

—Incredibly Alice. (Alice Ser.: 23). (ENG., (YA). (gr. 9). 2012. Illus.). 304p. pap. 8.99 (978-1-4169-7556-4(X)) 2011. 288p. 16.99 (978-1-4169-7553-3(5)) Simon & Schuster Children's Publishing. (Atheneum Bks. for Young Readers).

—Lovingly Alice. 2004. (Alice Bks.). 166p. (J). (gr. 4-6). 13.65 (978-0-7569-6604-1(3)) Perfection Learning Corp.

—Lovingly Alice. 2006. (Alice Ser.). (ENG., Illus.). 176p. (J). (gr. 4-7). pap. 5.99 (978-0-689-84400-3(X), Atheneum Bks. for Young Readers) Simon & Schuster Children's Publishing.

—Outrageously Alice. 2011. (Alice Ser.: 9). (ENG., Illus.). 176p. (J). (gr. 5-9). pap. 7.99 (978-1-4424-2853-9(8), Atheneum Bks. for Young Readers) Simon & Schuster Children's Publishing.

—Please Don't Be True: Dangerously Alice; Almost Alice; Intensely Alice. 2011. (Alice Ser.). (ENG., Illus.). 768p. (YA). (gr. 9). pap. 12.99 (978-1-4424-1721-2(8), Atheneum Bks. for Young Readers) Simon & Schuster Children's Publishing.

—Reluctantly Alice. 2011. (Alice Ser.: 3). (ENG.). 240p. (J). (gr. 5-9). pap. 7.99 (978-1-4424-2361-9(7), Atheneum Bks. for Young Readers) Simon & Schuster Children's Publishing.

—Reluctantly Alice. 2008. (Alice McKinley Ser.: No. 3). (ENG.). 208p. (J). pap. 5.99 (978-1-4169-5876-5(2), Simon & Schuster/Paula Wiseman Bks.) Simon & Schuster/Paula Wiseman Bks.

—Starting with Alice. 2004. (Alice Bks.). 181p. (J). (gr. 4-7). 12.65 (978-0-7569-2940-4(7)) Perfection Learning Corp.

—Starting with Alice. 2012. (Alice Ser.). (ENG., Illus.). 224p. (J). (gr. 2-7). pap. 7.99 (978-1-4424-4642-7(0), Atheneum Bks. for Young Readers) Simon & Schuster Children's Publishing.

—You & Me & the Space in Between: Alice in Charge; Incredibly Alice; Alice on Board. 2013. (Alice Ser.). (ENG., Illus.). 880p. (YA). (gr. 9). pap. 10.99 (978-1-4424-8664-5(3), Atheneum Bks. for Young Readers) Simon & Schuster Children's Publishing.

Reynolds, Paul A. Sydney & Simon: to the Moon! Reynolds, Peter H., illus. 2017. (Sydney & Simon Ser.: 3). 48p. (J). (gr. 1-4). lib. bdg. 12.99 (978-1-58089-679-5(0)) Charlesbridge Publishing, Inc.

Reynolds, Peter H. The Dot. Reynolds, Peter H., illus. 2003. (Creatrilogy Ser.). (ENG., Illus.). 32p. (J). (gr. k-4). 15.00 (978-0-7636-1961-9(2), 53509533) Candlewick Pr.

Reynolds, Wendy. Moby for Justice. 2006. 17.00 (978-0-8059-8861-1(0)) Dorrance Publishing Co., Inc.

Rhae, Sympne. My Name Is Johnson? l.t. ed. 2006. (Illus.). 53p. (J). per. 13.75 (978-0-9770043-9-3(2)) New Global Publishing.

Rhodes, Jewell Parker. Towers Falling. 2016. (ENG., Illus.). 240p. (J). (gr. 3-7). 16.99 (978-0-316-26222-4(6)) Little, Brown Bks. for Young Readers.

—Towers Falling. 2018. (J). lib. bdg. 18.40 (978-0-606-39916-6(X)) Turtleback.

Rhude, Steven. Natalie's Glasses, 1 vol. 2011. (ENG.). 80p. (J). (gr. k-2). pap. 19.95 (978-1-926916-16-3(6), d3d6b267-df59-4a31-bab4-e011658962e6) MacIntyre Purcell Publishing Inc. CAN. Dist: Baker & Taylor Publisher Services (BTPS).

Rice, Morgan. Before Dawn (Vampire, Fallen-Book 1) 2016. (ENG., Illus.). 118p. (J). pap. 6.99 (978-1-63291-611-2(8)) Morgan Rice Bks.

Richard, Laurent. Ninjas & Knock Outs! Book 2, No. 2. Ryser, Nicolas, illus. 2014. (Tao, the Little Samurai Ser.: 2). (ENG.). 64p. (J). (gr. 2-5). lib. bdg. 29.32 (978-1-4677-3272-7(9), e5d02ec4-9e15-490c-a5e7-a8fd6247b4c7, Graphic Universe™) Lerner Publishing Group.

Richards, Anthony Lee. The Golden Bird, 1 vol. 2009. 56p. pap. 16.95 (978-1-60703-712-5(2)) America Star Bks.

Richards, Dan. Stu Truly. (Stu Truly Ser.). (ENG.). 304p. (J). (gr. 3-7). 2019. pap. 7.99 (978-1-4998-0866-7(6)) 2018. 16.99 (978-1-4998-0646-5(9)) Bonnier Publishing USA. (Yellow Jacket).

Richards, Justin. Licence to Fish, Book 3. 2011. (Agent Alfie Ser.). (ENG., Illus.). 176p. (J). (gr. 2-4). 6.99 (978-0-00-727359-1(2)) HarperCollins Pubs. Ltd. GBR. Dist: Independent Pubs. Group.

—Thunder Raker (Agent Alfie, Book 1), Book 1. 2008. (Agent Alfie Ser.: 1). (ENG., Illus.). 144p. (J). (gr. 2-4). pap. 6.99 (978-0-00-727357-7(6), HarperCollins Children's Bks.) HarperCollins Pubs. Ltd. GBR. Dist: HarperCollins Pubs.

Richards, Natalie D. Gone Too Far. 2015. (ENG.). 320p. (YA). (gr. 7-12). pap. 9.99 (978-1-4022-8554-7(X), 9781402285547) Sourcebooks, Inc.

Richardson, S. Lee. The Backyard Series Volume Two: The Baby Bear Scare Story. 2012. 28p. pap. 24.95 (978-1-4626-9615-4(5)) America Star Bks.

Richardson, Sharde. Watched. 2011. (ENG.). 290p. (YA). pap. 12.99 (978-0-9831498-0-4(1)) Jolt.

Richler, Mordecai. Jacob Two-Two-'s First Spy Case. Eyolfson, Norman, illus. 2003. (Jacob Two-Two Ser.). (ENG.). 144p. (J). (gr. 3-7). pap. 6.95 (978-0-88776-694-7(3)) Tundra Bks. CAN. Dist: Random Hse., Inc.

—Jacob Two-Two's First Spy Case. Petricic, Dusan, illus. 2009. (Jacob Two-Two Ser.). (ENG.). 176p. (J). (gr. 4-7). 10.95 (978-0-88776-927-6(6)) Tundra Bks. CAN. Dist: Random Hse., Inc.

Richman, Sarah. The Cheat. 2019. (Do-Over Ser.). (ENG.). 104p. (YA). (gr. 6-12). pap. 7.99 (978-1-5415-4548-9(6), 454f3086-d325-4e5f-997e-dc9eae8bf025); 26.65 (978-1-5415-4034-7(4), 97b36653-876d-44d0-b498-83efc9981311) Lerner Publishing Group. (Darby Creek).

—Family Ties. 2019. (Al High Ser.). (ENG.). 112p. (YA). (gr. 6-12). pap. 7.99 (978-1-5415-7292-8(0), 03735ea1-4ab2-4858-880d-9553b52d157c); lib. bdg. 26.65 (978-1-5415-5691-1(7), 1fac8fb4-3f97-4f70-8d02-a23dfb4ececa) Lerner Publishing Group. (Darby Creek).

Richter, Jutta. The Cat: Or, How I Lost Eternity. Brailovsky, Anna, tr. Berner, Rotraut Susanne, illus. 2007. (ENG.). 80p. (J). (gr. 1-6). 14.00 (978-1-57131-676-9(0)) Milkweed Editions.

Riddell, Chris. Ottoline va al Colegio. 2008. (SPA.). 172p. (J). 13.95 (978-84-263-6833-1(6)) Vives, Luis Editorial (Edelvives) ESP. Dist: Baker & Taylor Bks.

Rigby Education Staff. When I Go to School. (Illus.). (J). 20.00 (978-0-7635-6441-4(9), 764419C99) Rigby Education.

Rigby, Jill. I Put It Right There! I Swear! The story of one boy's master plan to overcome executive functioning Difficulties! 2011. 28p. pap. 12.77 (978-1-4634-3710-7(2)) AuthorHouse.

Riggs, Shannon. Not in Room 204: Breaking the Silence of Abuse. Zollars, Jaime, illus. 2017. (ENG.). 32p. (J). (gr. -1-3). pap. 7.99 (978-0-8075-5766-2(8), 807557668) Whitman, Albert & Co.

Riker, Richard K. School Days Daze. l.t. ed. 2005. (Illus.). 168p. (J). 15.95 (978-0-9760416-0-3(X)) Family Christian Ctr.

Rinaldi, Ann. The Education of Mary: A Little Miss of Color, 1832. 2005. 176p. (J). pap. (978-0-7868-1377-3(6)) Hyperion Pr.

Riordan, Rick. Daughter of the Deep. Naidu, Lavanya, illus. 2021. xii, 336p. (J). **(978-1-368-08084-2(7))** Disney Pr.

—Daughter of the Deep. (ENG.). 2023. 368p. (J). (gr. 5-9). pap. 9.99 (978-1-368-07793-4(5), Disney-Hyperion) 2023. 368p. (gr. 6-8). 26.19 **(978-1-5364-7874-7(1))** 2021. (Illus.). 352p. (J). (gr. 5-9). 19.99 (978-1-368-07792-7(7), Disney-Hyperion) Disney Publishing Worldwide.

Ripken Jr., Cal. Cal Ripken Jr. 's All-Stars Super-Sized Slugger. Cowherd, Kevin, illus. 2013. (Cal Ripken Jr. 's All Stars Ser.: 2). (ENG.). 208p. (J). (gr. 3-7). pap. 6.99 (978-1-4231-4004-7(4)) Hyperion Pr.

Rippin, Sally. The Copycat Kid. Fukuoka, Aki, illus. 2015. (Billie B. Brown Ser.). (ENG.). 42p. (J). (978-1-61067-449-2(9)) Kane Miller.

—The Little Lie. Fukuoka, Aki, illus. 2014. (Billie B. Brown Ser.). (ENG.). 43p. (J). (978-1-61067-291-7(7)) Kane Miller.

—Treasure Hunt: A Billie B. Mystery. Fukuoka, Aki, illus. 2016. (ENG.). 96p. (J). pap. 4.99 (978-1-61067-464-5(2)) Kane Miller.

Rise Above, No. 6. 2014. (Red Zone Ser.: 6). (ENG.). 104p. (YA). (gr. 6-12). lib. bdg. 27.99 (978-1-4677-2127-1(1), 1c8854f0-2c2c-43cc-9ba5-e6d29b06b126, Darby Creek) Lerner Publishing Group.

Rissi, Anica Mrose. Anna, Banana, & the Friendship Split. Park, Meg, illus. 2015. (Anna, Banana Ser.: 1). (ENG.). 128p. (J). (gr. 1-5). 17.99 (978-1-4814-1605-4(7), Simon & Schuster Bks. For Young Readers) Simon & Schuster Bks. For Young Readers.

Ritter, Joshua & Ellis-Ritter, Karen. Be It Every Day! 2012. 40p. pap. 20.99 (978-1-4634-5231-5(4)) AuthorHouse.

Rivera, Raquel. Show Mode, 1 vol. 2017. (Orca Limelights Ser.). (ENG.). 144p. (J). (gr. 4-7). pap. 9.95 (978-1-4598-1204-8(2)) Orca Bk. Pubs. USA.

Rivers, Phoebe. Mischief Night. 2012. (Saranormal Ser.: 3). (ENG.). 160p. (J). (gr. 3-7). 15.99 (978-1-4424-5380-7(X)); pap. 5.99 (978-1-4424-5221-3(8)) Simon Spotlight. (Simon Spotlight).

Roache, Kiley. Frat Girl: a novel. 2018. (ENG., Illus.). 448p. (YA). 18.99 (978-0-373-21234-7(8), Harlequin Teen) Harlequin Enterprises ULC CAN. Dist: HarperCollins Pubs.

Roat, Sharon Huss. Between the Notes. 2015. (ENG.). 400p. (YA). (gr. 9). 17.99 (978-0-06-229172-1(6), HarperTeen) HarperCollins Pubs.

—How to Disappear. (ENG.). (YA). (gr. 8). 2019. 400p. pap. 9.99 (978-0-06-229176-9(9)) 2017. 384p. 17.99 (978-0-06-229175-2(0)) HarperCollins Pubs. (HarperTeen).

Robaard, Jedda. Silly Lily & the First Day of Kindergarten. 2018. (Silly Lily Ser.). (ENG.). 16p. (J). (gr. -1). bds. 13.99 (978-1-76040-560-1(4)) Little Hare Bks. AUS. Dist: Independent Pubs. Group.

Robberecht, Thierry. Sam's New Friend. Goossens, Philippe, illus. 2008. (ENG.). 32p. (J). (gr. -1-3). 12.00 (978-0-618-91448-7(X), 1014548, Clarion Bks.) HarperCollins Pubs.

—Superhero School. Goossens, Philippe, illus. 2012. (ENG.). 30p. (J). (gr. -1-k). 16.95 (978-1-60537-140-5(8)) Clavis Publishing.

Robbins, Jacqui. The New Girl ... & Me. Phelan, Matt, illus. 2006. (ENG.). 32p. (J). (gr. -1-2). 19.99 (978-0-689-86468-1(X), Atheneum/Richard Jackson Bks.) Simon & Schuster Children's Publishing.

—Two of a Kind. Phelan, Matt, illus. 2009. (ENG.). 32p. (J). (gr. -1-2). 19.99 (978-1-4169-2437-1(X), Atheneum Bks. for Young Readers) Simon & Schuster Children's Publishing.

Robbins, Trina. The Drained Brains Caper: Book 1, No. 1. Page, Tyler, illus. 2010. (Chicagoland Detective Agency Ser.: 1). (ENG.). 64p. (J). (gr. 4-8). pap. 8.99 (978-0-7613-5635-6(5), 3b3c032d-e980-466a-9075-55d5ee724833, Graphic Universe™) Lerner Publishing Group.

—A Match Made in Heaven: Book 8, No. 8. Ota, Yuko Geneviev & Xian Nu Studio, illus. 2013. (My Boyfriend Is a Monster Ser.: 8). (ENG.). 128p. (YA). (gr. 7-12). pap. 9.95 (978-1-4677-0732-9(5), c276bb59-5e33-4667-9435-ffac48deaaac, Graphic Universe™) Lerner Publishing Group.

—A Match Made in Heaven: Book 8, No. 8. Ota, Yuko Geneviev & Xian Nu Studio, Xian Nu, illus. 2013. (My Boyfriend Is a Monster Ser.: 8). (ENG.). 128p. (YA). (gr. 7-12). lib. bdg. 29.32 (978-0-7613-6857-1(4), 95f941be-48e3-433b-b670-89a634a7f824, Graphic Universe™) Lerner Publishing Group.

Robert, Cormier. The Chocolate War. 2014. (ENG.). 272p. (J). 12.24 (978-1-63245-138-5(7)) Lectorum Pubns., Inc.

Roberts, Barbara. The Adventures of Phoebe Flower: Stories of a Girl with ADHD. 2010. (ENG.). 176p. (J). (gr. 2-6). pap. 14.95 (978-0-9714609-6-6(5)) Advantage Bks., LLC.

Roberts, Barbara Carroll. Nikki on the Line. 2019. (ENG.). 336p. (J). (gr. 3-7). 16.99 (978-0-316-52190-1(6)) Little, Brown Bks. for Young Readers.

Roberts, D. W. Pep Squad Mysteries Book 2:the Haunting of Townsand Hall. 2008. (ENG.). 101p. pap. 8.95 (978-0-557-05289-9(0)) Lulu Pr., Inc.

Roberts, Justin. The Smallest Girl in the Smallest Grade. Robinson, Christian, illus. 2014. 32p. (J). (gr. -1-k). 18.99 (978-0-399-25743-8(8), G.P. Putnam's Sons Books for Young Readers) Penguin Young Readers Group.

Roberts, LaDawna. The Haunted Birthday Party. 2007. 48p. per. 16.95 (978-1-4241-8723-2(0)) America Star Bks.

Roberts, Lisa Brown. Playing the Player. 2015. (ENG., Illus.). 316p. (J). pap. 17.99 (978-1-943892-56-3(3)) Entangled Publishing, LLC.

Robertson, Elysia Hill. Tool of Life My Pink School Books. Robertson, Elysia Hill, illus. 2005. (Illus.). 112p. (J). per. 12.95 (978-0-9764444-3-5(7), EJWV-004) E. J. Publishing.

Robertson, Kathy & Hooker, Jennifer. Jasmine & Chad Make New Friends. 2012. 28p. pap. 15.99 (978-1-4797-1656-2(1)) Xlibris Corp.

Robico. My Little Monster 3. 2014. (My Little Monster Ser.: 3). (Illus.). 168p. (gr. 8-12). pap. 10.99 (978-1-61262-599-7(1)) Kodansha America, Inc.

—My Little Monster 4. 2014. (My Little Monster Ser.: 4). (Illus.). 176p. (gr. 8-12). pap. 10.99 (978-1-61262-600-0(9)) Kodansha America, Inc.

Robins, Eleanor. Be Fair, 1 vol. unabr. ed. 2010. (Carter High Senior Year Ser.). (ENG.). 52p. (YA). (gr. 9-12). pap. 9.75 (978-1-61651-323-8(3)) Saddleback Educational Publishing, Inc.

—Boy of Their Dreams, 1 vol. unabr. ed. 2010. (Carter High Chronicles Ser.). (ENG.). 52p. (YA). (gr. 9-12). pap. 9.75 (978-1-61651-305-4(5)) Saddleback Educational Publishing, Inc.

—Drama Club Mystery, 1 vol. unabr. ed. 2011. (Carter High Mysteries Ser.). (ENG.). 48p. (YA). (gr. 9-12). 9.75 (978-1-61651-562-1(7)) Saddleback Educational Publishing, Inc.

—Easy Pass, 1 vol. unabr. ed. 2011. (Choices Ser.). (ENG.). 52p. (YA). (gr. 5-12). 9.75 (978-1-61651-596-6(1)) Saddleback Educational Publishing, Inc.

—The Easy Way, 1 vol. unabr. ed. 2010. (Carter High Chronicles Ser.). (ENG.). 52p. (YA). (gr. 9-12). pap. 9.75 (978-1-61651-307-8(1)) Saddleback Educational Publishing, Inc.

—The Fastest Runner, 1 vol. unabr. ed. 2010. (Carter High Chronicles Ser.). (ENG.). 52p. (YA). (gr. 9-12). pap. 9.75 (978-1-61651-308-5(X)) Saddleback Educational Publishing, Inc.

—The Field Trip Mystery, 1 vol. unabr. ed. 2011. (Carter High Mysteries Ser.). (ENG.). 48p. (YA). (gr. 9-12). 9.75 (978-1-61651-563-8(5)) Saddleback Educational Publishing, Inc.

—It Does Matter, 1 vol. unabr. ed. 2010. (Carter High Senior Year Ser.). (ENG.). 52p. (YA). (gr. 9-12). pap. 9.75 (978-1-61651-324-5(1)) Saddleback Educational Publishing, Inc.

—It Is Not a Date, 1 vol. unabr. ed. 2010. (Carter High Chronicles Ser.). (ENG.). 52p. (YA). (gr. 9-12). pap. 9.75 (978-1-61651-309-2(8)) Saddleback Educational Publishing, Inc.

—Just Be Yourself, 1 vol. unabr. ed. 2010. (Carter High Senior Year Ser.). (ENG.). 52p. (YA). (gr. 9-12). pap. 9.75 (978-1-61651-325-2(X)) Saddleback Educational Publishing, Inc.

—The Last Time, 1 vol. unabr. ed. 2010. (Carter High Senior Year Ser.). (ENG.). 52p. (YA). (gr. 9-12). pap. 9.75 (978-1-61651-326-9(8)) Saddleback Educational Publishing, Inc.

—Lucky Falcon Mystery, 1 vol. unabr. ed. 2011. (Carter High Mysteries Ser.). (ENG.). 48p. (YA). (gr. 9-12). 9.75 (978-1-61651-565-2(1)) Saddleback Educational Publishing, Inc.

—No Exceptions, 1 vol. unabr. ed. 2011. (Choices Ser.). (ENG.). 52p. (YA). (gr. 5-12). 9.75 (978-1-61651-597-3(X)) Saddleback Educational Publishing, Inc.

—One Date Too Many, 1 vol. unabr. ed. 2010. (Carter High Chronicles Ser.). (ENG.). 52p. (YA). (gr. 9-12). pap. 9.75 (978-1-61651-310-8(1)) Saddleback Educational Publishing, Inc.

—One More Chance, 1 vol. unabr. ed. 2010. (Carter High Senior Year Ser.). (ENG.). 52p. (YA). (gr. 9-12). pap. 9.75 (978-1-61651-327-6(6)) Saddleback Educational Publishing, Inc.

—The Secret Admirer Mystery, 1 vol. unabr. ed. 2011. (Carter High Mysteries Ser.). (ENG.). 48p. (YA). (gr. 9-12). 9.75 (978-1-61651-567-6(8)) Saddleback Educational Publishing, Inc.

—Someone to Count, 1 vol. unabr. ed. 2010. (Carter High Senior Year Ser.). (ENG.). 52p. (YA). (gr. 9-12). pap. 9.75 (978-1-61651-328-3(4)) Saddleback Educational Publishing, Inc.

—Time to Move On, 1 vol. unabr. ed. 2010. (Carter High Senior Year Ser.). (ENG.). 52p. (YA). (gr. 9-12). pap. 9.75 (978-1-61651-329-0(2)) Saddleback Educational Publishing, Inc.

—Too Late, 1 vol. unabr. ed. 2010. (Carter High Chronicles Ser.). (ENG.). 52p. (YA). (gr. 9-12). pap. 9.75 (978-1-61651-312-2(8)) Saddleback Educational Publishing, Inc.

—Trust Me, 1 vol. unabr. ed. 2011. (Choices Ser.). (ENG.). 52p. (YA). (gr. 5-12). 9.75 (978-1-61651-599-7(6)) Saddleback Educational Publishing, Inc.

—The Worst Year Ever, 1 vol. unabr. ed. 2010. (Carter High Senior Year Ser.). (ENG.). 52p. (YA). (gr. 9-12). pap. 9.75 (978-1-61651-330-6(6)) Saddleback Educational Publishing, Inc.

Robinson, A. M. Vampire Crush. 2010. (ENG.). 416p. (YA). (gr. 8-18). pap. 8.99 (978-0-06-198971-1(1), HarperTeen) HarperCollins Pubs.

Robinson, Barbara. The Best Halloween Ever. 2006. (Illus.). 117p. (J). (gr. 3-7). 13.65 (978-0-7569-6985-1(9)) Perfection Learning Corp.

—The Best School Year Ever. 2005. (Best Ever Ser.). (ENG.). 176p. (J). (gr. 3-18). pap. 7.99 (978-0-06-440492-1(7), HarperCollins) HarperCollins Pubs.

Robinson, Craig & Mansbach, Adam. Jake the Fake Keeps It Real. Knight, Keith, illus. 2018. (Jake the Fake Ser.: 1). 160p. (J). (gr. 3-7). 7.99 (978-0-553-52354-6(6), Yearling) Random Hse. Children's Bks.

Robley Blake, Colleen. I Can't Wait till I'm Five. 2006. (J). 9.95 (978-0-9767342-0-8(6)) Imaajinn This.

Rocha, Ruth. Lines, Squiggles, Letters, Words. Matoso, Madalena, illus. 2016. 40p. (J). (gr. -1-k). 16.95 (978-1-59270-208-4(2)) Enchanted Lion Bks., LLC.

Roche, Denis. The Best Class Picture Ever! 2003. (Illus.). (J). pap. (978-0-439-57819-6(1), Scholastic Pr.) Scholastic, Inc.

Rockwell, Anne. Father's Day. Rockwell, Lizzy, illus. 2005. 40p. (J). (gr. -1-1). lib. bdg. 15.89 (978-0-06-051378-8(0)) HarperCollins Pubs.

—First Day of School. 2006. (978-0-06-050192-1(8)) HarperCollins Canada, Ltd.

—First Day of School. Rockwell, Lizzy, illus. (ENG.). 40p. (J). (gr. -1-3). 2013. pap. 7.99 (978-0-06-050193-8(6)) 2011. 16.99 (978-0-06-050191-4(X)) HarperCollins Pubs. (HarperCollins).

—Presidents' Day. Rockwell, Lizzy, illus. (ENG.). 40p. (J). (gr. -1-1). 2009. pap. 8.99 (978-0-06-050196-9(0)) 2007. 16.99 (978-0-06-050194-5(4)) HarperCollins Pubs. (HarperCollins).

—St. Patrick's Day. Rockwell, Lizzy, illus. 2010. (ENG.). 40p. (J). (gr. -1-3). 14.99 (978-0-06-050197-6(9)); lib. bdg. 15.89 (978-0-06-050198-3(7)) HarperCollins Pubs. (HarperCollins).

—Welcome to Kindergarten. Rockwell, Anne, illus. 2004. (ENG., Illus.). 32p. (J). (gr. -1-1). pap. 7.99 (978-0-8027-7664-8(7), 900032897, Bloomsbury USA Childrens) Bloomsbury Publishing USA.

Rockwell, Anne F. 100 School Days. 2004. (ENG., Illus.). 40p. (J). (gr. -1-3). pap. 8.99 (978-0-06-443727-1(2), HarperCollins) HarperCollins Pubs.

Roddie, Shen. Baby Goes Too. Stojic, Manya, illus. 2003. 32p. (YA). (978-1-85602-460-0(1), Pavilion Children's Books) Pavilion Bks.

Rodkey, Geoff. The Tapper Twins Go to War (with Each Other) 2016. (Tapper Twins Ser.: 1). (ENG., Illus.). 240p. (J). (gr. 3-7). pap. 7.99 (978-0-316-31597-5(4)) Little, Brown Bks. for Young Readers.

—The Tapper Twins Run for President. 2016. (Tapper Twins Ser.: 3). (ENG., Illus.). 304p. (J). (gr. 3-7). 13.99 (978-0-316-29785-1(2)) Little, Brown Bks. for Young Readers.

—The Tapper Twins Tear up New York. 2016. (Tapper Twins Ser.: 2). (ENG., Illus.). 288p. (J). (gr. 3-7). pap. 8.99 (978-0-316-31601-9(6)) Little, Brown Bks. for Young Readers.

Rodman, Mary Ann. Yankee Girl. 2008. (ENG.). 240p. (J). (gr. 4-6). pap. 19.99 (978-0-312-53576-6(7), 900054756) Square Fish.

Rodman, Sean. Infiltration, 1 vol. 2011. (Orca Soundings Ser.). (ENG.). 144p. (YA). (gr. 8-12). pap. 9.95 (978-1-55469-985-8(1)) Orca Bk. Pubs. USA.

Rodriguez, Cindy L. When Reason Breaks. 2015. (ENG.). 304p. (YA). (gr. 7-12). 17.99 (978-1-61963-412-1(0), 900135717, Bloomsbury USA Childrens) Bloomsbury Publishing USA.

Rodriguez Ferrer, Janel. The Arts-Angels Track 1: Drawn to You. 2012. 252p. pap. 8.99 (978-1-936214-91-4(1)) Wyatt-MacKenzie Publishing.

Roesti, Delores. Mareena Maree Mulligan & the Flying Wheelchair: Book 2: The Busybodies. 2008. 102p. pap. 10.95 (978-0-7414-4477-6(1)) Infinity Publishing.

Rogers, Kelly. Buyer Beware, 1 vol. Peterschmidt, Betsy, illus. 2016. (Rm. 201 Ser.). (ENG.). 48p. (J). (gr. 3-7). lib. bdg. 34.21 (978-1-62402-167-1(0), 21581, Spellbound) Magic Wagon.

—The Key, 1 vol. Peterschmidt, Betsy, illus. 2016. (Rm. 201 Ser.). (ENG.). 48p. (J). (gr. 3-7). lib. bdg. 34.21 (978-1-62402-169-5(7), 21585, Spellbound) Magic Wagon.

—Study Group. Peterschmidt, Betsy, illus. 2016. (Rm. 201 Ser.). (ENG.). 48p. (J). (gr. 3-7). lib. bdg. 34.21 (978-1-62402-170-1(0), 21587, Spellbound) Magic Wagon.

Rogers, Lon. The Between Season. 2009. 280p. 27.95 (978-1-4401-8370-6(8)) iUniverse, Inc.

Rogers, Suzanne. Pawsitive Tails. 2012. 40p. (978-1-77097-298-8(6)) FriesenPress.

Rogers Yaeger, Nancy. Constantine Goes to School. Grace, Bill, illus. 2006. 60p. (J). (gr. 2-5). (978-1-4050-5714-1(9)) Macmillan Caribbean.

Roland, Timothy. Monkey Me & the Pet Show. 2014. (Monkey Me Ser.: 2). lib. bdg. 14.75 (978-0-606-35359-5(3)) Turtleback.

—Monkey Me & the Pet Show: a Branches Book (Monkey Me #2) Roland, Timothy, illus. 2014. (Monkey Me Ser.: 2). (ENG., Illus.). 96p. (J). (gr. 1-3). pap. 4.99 (978-0-545-55980-5(4)) Scholastic, Inc.

—Monkey Me & the School Ghost. 2014. (Monkey Me Ser.: 4). lib. bdg. 14.75 (978-0-606-36053-1(0)) Turtleback.

—Our Crazy Class Election. 2007. (Illus.). 90p. (J). (978-0-545-00401-5(2)) Scholastic, Inc.

Roller, Pat Kellogg. Pink Hat's Adventure with Kites. Salazar, Riana, illus. Roller, John, photos by. 2009. 36p. pap. 10.95 (978-1-59858-957-3(1)) Dog Ear Publishing, LLC.

Romanek, Trudee. Raising the Stakes, 1 vol. 2015. (Orca Limelights Ser.). (ENG.). 160p. (J). (gr. 4-7). pap. 9.95 (978-1-4598-0779-2(0)) Orca Bk. Pubs. USA.

Romito, Dee. No Place Like Home. 2017. (Mix Ser.). (ENG.). 256p. (J). (gr. 4-8). 17.99 (978-1-4814-9109-9(1)); (Illus.). pap. 7.99 (978-1-4814-9108-2(3)) Simon & Schuster Children's Publishing. (Aladdin).

—No Place Like Home. 2017. 234p. (J). (978-965-278-469-8(9), Simon & Schuster/Paula Wiseman Bks.) Simon & Schuster/Paula Wiseman Bks.

Rompella, Natalie. Cookie Cutters & Sled Runners. 2017. (ENG.). 272p. (J). (gr. 4-8). 15.99 (978-1-5107-1771-8(4), Sky Pony Pr.) Skyhorse Publishing Co., Inc.

Rone, Trenton. Once upon a Hamster 2003. (YA). spiral bd. 14.95 (978-0-9744437-3-7(5)) Imagination Workshop, The.

Rooks, Jo. Sophie's Shell. 2019. (Illus.). 32p. (J). (978-1-4338-3089-1(2), Magination Pr.) American Psychological Assn.

Roos, Stephen. The Gypsies Never Came. 2010. (ENG., Illus.). 128p. (J). (gr. 3-7). pap. 7.99 (978-1-4424-2940-6(2), Simon & Schuster Bks. For Young Readers) Simon & Schuster Bks. For Young Readers.

—Recycling George. 2010. (ENG.). 144p. (J). (gr. 3-7). pap. 8.99 (978-1-4424-2941-3(0), Simon & Schuster Bks. For Young Readers) Simon & Schuster Bks. For Young Readers.

Roper, Robert, illus. Dora Goes to School. 2004. (Dora the Explorer Ser.: Vol. 8). (ENG.). 24p. (J). pap. 3.99 (978-0-689-86494-0(9), Simon Spotlight/Nickelodeon) Simon Spotlight/Nickelodeon.

Rosario, Joann. Secret Swan King. 2004. 27p. (J). pap. 10.00 (978-0-9758746-0-8(8), 1246169) J.G.R. Enterprises.

Rose, Jasmine. The Last Caterpillar Princess. 2011. 16p. pap. 8.64 (978-1-4634-1953-0(8)) AuthorHouse.

Rose, Nancy. The Secret Life of Squirrels: Back to School! 2018. (ENG., Illus.). 32p. (J). (gr. -1-3). 17.99 (978-0-316-50621-2(4)) Little, Brown Bks. for Young Readers.

Rose, Sandra. My Mom Has Wheels. Talbott, Sherri, illus. 2009. 28p. pap. 24.95 (978-1-60836-889-1(0)) America Star Bks.

Rose, Sue. Jinxed! 2006. (Unfabulous! Ser.). (Illus.). 118p. (J). (978-1-4156-5170-4(1)) Scholastic, Inc.

Rosen, Michael J. A School for Pompey Walker. 2012. (ENG.). (J). pap. (978-1-4675-1412-5(8)) Independent Pub.

Rosen, Robert. Where Is My Eraser? Piworski, Marcin, illus. 2017. (School Days Ser.). (ENG.). 24p. (gr. -1-2). 28.50 (978-1-68342-710-0(6), 9781683427100) Rourke Educational Media.

—Where Is My Eraser? Piwowarski, Marcin, illus. 2017. (School Days Ser.). (ENG.). 24p. (gr. -1-2). pap. 9.95 (978-1-68342-762-9(9), 9781683427629) Rourke Educational Media.

Rosenberg, Madelyn & Crockett, Mary. Dream Boy. 2014. 336p. (YA). (gr. 7-12). pap. 9.99 (978-1-4022-9583-6(9), 9781402295836) Sourcebooks, Inc.

Rosensweig, Jay B. & Repka, Janice. The Stupendous Dodgeball Fiasco. Dibley, Glin, illus. 2012. 181p. (J). (gr. 4-6). 21.19 (978-0-525-47346-6(7)) Penguin Young Readers Group.

Roske, Melissa. Kat Greene Comes Clean. 2017. 192p. (J). (gr. 4-7). lib. bdg. 16.99 (978-1-58089-776-1(2)) Charlesbridge Publishing, Inc.

Ross, Jay. Bungalow 29. Klimko, Andrew, illus. 2015. 92p. pap. 5.99 (978-0-9771994-0-2(1)) Visor Bks.

Roth, Carol. Five Little Ducklings Go to School. Julian, Sean, illus. 2019. (ENG.). 32p. (J). (gr. -1-2). pap. 8.95 (978-0-7358-4346-2(5)) North-South Bks., Inc.

Roth, Jonathan. Take Us to Your Sugar, 3. 2019. (Beep & Bob Ser.). (ENG.). 128p. (J). (gr. 2-4). 15.59 (978-1-64310-828-5(X)) Penworthy Co., LLC, The.

—Take Us to Your Sugar. Roth, Jonathan, illus. 2018. (Beep & Bob Ser.: 3). (ENG., Illus.). 128p. (J). (gr. 1-4). 16.99

(978-1-4814-8859-4(7)); pap. 5.99 *(978-1-4814-8858-7(9))* Simon & Schuster Children's Publishing. (Aladdin).

—Too Much Space!, 1. 2019. (Beep & Bob Ser.). (ENG.). 128p. (J). (gr. 2-4). 15.59 *(978-1-64310-829-2(8))* Penworthy Co., LLC, The.

—Too Much Space! Roth, Jonathan, illus. 2018. (Beep & Bob Ser.: 1). (ENG., Illus.). 128p. (J). (gr. 1-4). 17.99 *(978-1-4814-8853-2(8))*; pap. 5.99 *(978-1-4814-8852-5(X))* Simon & Schuster Children's Publishing. (Aladdin).

Rothberg, Abraham. Pinocchio's Sister: A Feminist Fable. 2005. 159p. pap. 11.95 *(978-1-4116-4347-5(X))* Lulu Pr., Inc.

Rothstein, Evelyn. Evelyn & the Two Evas. Uhlig, Elizabeth, illus. 2013. 63p. (YA). pap. 12.95 *(978-0-9834030-5-0(8))* Marble Hse. Editions.

—My Great Grandpa Dave. 2007. (J). per. 12.95 *(978-0-9786745-1-9(0))* Marble Hse. Editions.

Rountree, Wendy. Lost Soul. 2003. 87p. (J). pap. 19.95 *(978-1-59129-975-2(6))* America Star Bks.

Rouss, Shannan & Rouss, Sylvia A. A Watermelon in the Sukkah. Iosa, Ann, illus. 2013. (ENG.). 24p. (J). (gr. -1-2). E-Book 23.99 *(978-1-4677-1642-0(1)*, Kar-Ben Publishing) Lerner Publishing Group.

Rouss, Sylvia A. No Rules for Michael. Simon, Susan, illus. 2004. (ENG.). 24p. (J). (gr. -1-1). pap. 6.99 *(978-1-58013-044-8(5)*, 5623322b-f279-47d0-93f4-f63811ef709f, Kar-Ben Publishing) Lerner Publishing Group.

—Sammy Spider's First Day of School. Kahn, Katherine Janus, illus. 2009. (Kar-Ben Favorites Ser.). (ENG.). 32p. (J). (gr. -1-2). 16.95 *(978-0-8225-8583-1(9)*, Kar-Ben Publishing) Lerner Publishing Group.

Rowling, J. K. Hare Pota Me Te Whatu Manapou [Harry Potter & the Philosopher's Stone]. Blake, Leon Heketu, tr. 2021. (Kotahi Rau Pukapuka Ser.: 1). 328p. pap. 24.99 *(978-1-86940-914-2(0))* Auckland Univ. Pr. NZL. Dist: Independent Pubs. Group.

—Harrius Potter et Philosophi Lapis: (Harry Potter & the Philosopher's Stone) 2003. (Harry Potter Ser.).Tr. of Harry Potter & the Philosopher's Stone. (LAT., Illus.). 256p. (YA). (gr. 7). 29.99 *(978-1-58234-825-4(1)*, 900020066, Bloomsbury USA Childrens) Bloomsbury Publishing USA.

—Harry Potter à l'École des Sorciers. Menard, Jean-François, tr. from ENG. 2007. (Harry Potter Ser.: Year 1).Tr. of Harry Potter & the Sorcerer's Stone. 311p. (J). per. 14.95 *(978-2-07-061236-9(8))* Gallimard, Editions FRA. Dist: Distribooks, Inc.

—Harry Potter & the Chamber of Secrets. 2009. 9.64 *(978-0-7848-1444-4(9)*, Everbind) Marco Bk. Co.

—Harry Potter & the Chamber of Secrets. unabr. ed. 2004. (Harry Potter Ser.: Year 2). 352p. (J). (gr. 3-18). pap. 46.00 incl. audio *(978-0-8072-8207-6(3)*, S YA 137 SP, Listening Library) Random Hse. Audio Publishing Group.

—Harry Potter & the Chamber of Secrets. (Harry Potter Ser.: 2). (J). 2006. 1.25 *(978-1-4193-8079-2(6))* 2003. 78.75 *(978-1-4025-6698-1(0))* Recorded Bks., Inc.

—Harry Potter & the Chamber of Secrets. (Harry Potter Ser.: Year 2). (RUS., Illus.). 28.95 *(978-5-8451-0947-7(7))* Rosmen-Izdat RUS. Dist: Distribooks, Inc.

—Harry Potter & the Chamber of Secrets, Bk. 2. Selznick, Brian & GrandPré, Mary, illus. 2018. (Harry Potter Ser.: 2). (ENG.). 368p. (J). (gr. 3). pap. 12.99 *(978-1-338-29915-1(8)*, Levine, Arthur A. Bks.) Scholastic, Inc.

—Harry Potter & the Chamber of Secrets, Bk. 2. Kay, Jim, illus. 2016. (Harry Potter Ser.: 2). (ENG.). 272p. (J). (gr. 3). 39.99 *(978-0-545-79132-8(4)*, Levine, Arthur A. Bks.) Scholastic, Inc.

—Harry Potter & the Chamber of Secrets. l.t. ed. 2003. (Harry Potter Ser.: Year 2). (ENG.). 466p. pap. 13.95 *(978-1-59413-001-4(9))* Thorndike Pr.

—Harry Potter & the Deathly Hallows. (illus.). 2008. 832p. pap. *(978-0-7475-9586-1(0))* 2007. (ENG., 608p. *(978-0-7475-9106-1(7))* Bloomsbury Publishing Plc.

—Harry Potter & the Deathly Hallows. Menard, Jean-François, tr. 2017. (FRE.). 896p. (J). (gr. 4-10). pap. *(978-2-07-058523-6(9))* Gallimard, Editions.

—Harry Potter & the Deathly Hallows. braille ed. 2007. (Harry Potter Ser.: Year 7). (J). (gr. 4-7). 34.99 *(978-0-939173-57-0(3))* National Braille Pr.

—Harry Potter & the Deathly Hallows. 2010. 25.00 *(978-1-60686-882-9(9))* Perfection Learning Corp.

—Harry Potter & the Deathly Hallows, 17 vols. 2007. (Harry Potter Ser.: 7). (YA). 129.79 *(978-1-4281-6654-7(8))*; 131.75 *(978-1-4281-6652-3(1))* Recorded Bks., Inc.

—Harry Potter & the Deathly Hallows, Bk. 7. Selznick, Brian & GrandPré, Mary, illus. 2018. (Harry Potter Ser.: 7). (ENG.). 784p. (J). (gr. 3). pap. 16.99 *(978-1-338-29920-5(4)*, Levine, Arthur A. Bks.) Scholastic, Inc.

—Harry Potter & the Deathly Hallows, 7 vols., Bk. 7. GrandPré, Mary, illus. 2007. (Harry Potter Ser.: 7). (ENG.). 784p. (J). (gr. 3-9). 37.99 *(978-0-545-01022-1(5)*, Levine, Arthur A. Bks.) Scholastic, Inc.

—Harry Potter & the Deathly Hallows. l.t. ed. 2009. (ENG.). 970p. pap. 14.95 *(978-1-59413-355-8(7)*, Large Print Pr.) 2007. (Harry Potter Ser.: Year 7). (Illus.). 969p. (J). (gr. 4-7). 34.95 *(978-0-7862-9665-1(8))* Thorndike Pr.

—Harry Potter & the Deathly Hallows. (Harry Potter (Kazu Kibuishi Illustrations) Ser.: 7). 2013. lib. bdg. 29.40 *(978-0-606-32351-2(1))* 2009. lib. bdg. 26.95 *(978-0-606-00420-6(3))* Turtleback.

—Harry Potter & the Deathly Hallows. Bar-hillel, Gili, tr. from ENG. 2007. (Harry Potter Ser.: Year 7). (HEB., Illus.). 568p. (J). (gr. 4-7). pap. *(978-965-482-635-8(6))* Yediot Aharonot Bks., Miscal.

—Harry Potter & the Goblet of Fire. 2009. 10.24 *(978-0-7848-1587-8(9)*, Everbind) Marco Bk. Co.

—Harry Potter & the Goblet of Fire. (Harry Potter Ser.: 4). (J). 2006. 1.25 *(978-1-4193-8531-5(3))* 2003. 101.75 *(978-1-4025-6702-5(2))* Recorded Bks., Inc.

—Harry Potter & the Goblet of Fire, Bk. 4. Selznick, Brian & GrandPré, Mary, illus. 2018. (Harry Potter Ser.: 4). (ENG.). 768p. (J). (gr. 3). pap. 14.99 *(978-1-338-29917-5(4)*, Levine, Arthur A. Bks.) Scholastic, Inc.

—Harry Potter & the Goblet of Fire. GrandPré, Mary, illus. l.t. ed. 2003. (Harry Potter Ser.: Vol. 4). (ENG.). 936p. pap. 11.66 *(978-1-59413-003-8(5))* Thorndike Pr.

—Harry Potter & the Half-Blood Prince. 2005. audio compact disk *(978-0-7475-8258-8(0))* Bloomsbury Publishing Plc.

—Harry Potter & the Half-Blood Prince, 9 vols. braille ed. 2005. (Harry Potter Ser.: Year 6). (J). (gr. 4-8). 29.99 *(978-0-939173-39-6(5)*, HALF) National Braille Pr.

—Harry Potter & the Half-Blood Prince. GrandPré, Mary, illus. 2006. (Harry Potter Ser.: Year 6). 652p. (gr. 4-8). 23.00 *(978-0-7569-6765-9(1))* Perfection Learning Corp.

—Harry Potter & the Half-Blood Prince. (Harry Potter Ser.: 6). (J). 2007. 1.25 *(978-1-4193-5430-4(2))* 2006. 110.75 *(978-1-4193-5436-6(1))* 2006. 193.75 *(978-1-4193-5432-8(9))* 2005. 113.75 *(978-1-4193-5434-2(5))* Recorded Bks., Inc.

—Harry Potter & the Half-Blood Prince, Bk. 6. Selznick, Brian & GrandPré, Mary, illus. 2018. (Harry Potter Ser.: 6). (ENG.). 688p. (J). (gr. 3). pap. 14.99 *(978-1-338-29919-9(0)*, Levine, Arthur A. Bks.) Scholastic, Inc.

—Harry Potter & the Half-Blood Prince, Bk. 6. GrandPré, Mary, illus. 2005. (Harry Potter Ser.: 6). (ENG.). 672p. (J). (gr. 3-8). 32.99 *(978-0-439-78454-2(9)*, Levine, Arthur A. Bks.) Scholastic, Inc.

—Harry Potter & the Half-Blood Prince. l.t. ed. (Illus.). (J). (gr. 4-7). 2007. (ENG.). 832p. per. 14.95 *(978-1-59413-221-6(6))* 2005. (Harry Potter Ser.: Year 6). 831p. 29.95 *(978-0-7862-7745-2(9))* Thorndike Pr. (Large Print Pr.).

—Harry Potter & the Half-Blood Prince. 2013. (Harry Potter (Kazu Kibuishi Illustrations) Ser.: 6). lib. bdg. 26.95 *(978-0-606-32350-5(3))* Turtleback.

—Harry Potter & the Half Blood Prince - Chinese Language. 2005. (Harry Potter Ser.: Year 6). (CHI.). 496p. (YA). (gr. 4-8). pap. 28.95 *(978-7-02-005323-0(8)*, HAP06) People's Literature Publishing Hse. CHN. Dist: Chinasprout, Inc.

—Harry Potter & the Order of the Phoenix. 768p. (J). (gr. 6-10). pap. *(978-0-7475-6107-1(9))* Bloomsbury Publishing Plc.

—Harry Potter & the Order of the Phoenix. 2008. *(978-977-14-2697-4(4))* Nahdat Misr Bkshop for Printing and Pubs.

—Harry Potter & the Order of the Phoenix, 13 vols. braille ed. 2003. (Harry Potter Ser.: Year 5). (YA). 29.99 *(978-0-939173-38-9(7))* National Braille Pr.

—Harry Potter & the Order of the Phoenix. 2003. (Harry Potter Ser.: Year 5). (CHI.). 575p. (YA). pap. 26.95 *(978-7-02-004327-9(5)*, HAP05) People's Literature Publishing Hse. CHN. Dist: Chinasprout, Inc.

—Harry Potter & the Order of the Phoenix. 2004. (Harry Potter Ser.). 870p. (gr. 4-6). 16.49 *(978-0-7569-4163-5(6))* Perfection Learning Corp.

—Harry Potter & the Order of the Phoenix. 2003. (ENG.). 768p. *(978-1-55192-570-7(2))* Raincoast Bk. Distribution.

—Harry Potter & the Order of the Phoenix. 2004. (JPN.). (J). (gr. 6-10). *(978-4-915512-51-3(7))* Sayzansha.

—Harry Potter & the Order of the Phoenix, Bk. 5. Selznick, Brian & GrandPré, Mary, illus. 2018. (Harry Potter Ser.: 5). (ENG.). 912p. (J). (gr. 3). pap. 14.99 *(978-1-338-29918-2(2)*, Levine, Arthur A. Bks.) Scholastic, Inc.

—Harry Potter & the Order of the Phoenix, Bk. 5. GrandPré, Mary, illus. 2003. (Harry Potter Ser.: 5). (ENG.). 896p. (gr. 3-7). 32.99 *(978-0-439-35806-4(X)*, Levine, Arthur A. Bks.) Scholastic, Inc.

—Harry Potter & the Order of the Phoenix. l.t. ed. 2003. (Harry Potter Ser.: Year 5). 1093p. 29.95 *(978-0-7862-5778-2(4)*, Large Print Pr.) Thorndike Pr.

—Harry Potter & the Order of the Phoenix. GrandPré, Mary, illus. l.t. ed. 2003. (Thorndike Young Adult Ser.). (ENG.). 1232p. (J). (gr. 4-7). per. 14.95 *(978-1-59413-112-7(0)*, Large Print Pr.) Thorndike Pr.

—Harry Potter & the Order of the Phoenix. 2004. (Harry Potter Ser.: 5). lib. bdg. 24.50 *(978-0-613-99916-8(9))* Turtleback.

—Harry Potter & the Philosopher's Stone. 2014. (ENG., Illus.). 352p. *(978-1-4088-5589-8(5))* Bloomsbury Publishing Plc.

—Harry Potter & the Philosopher's Stone (Irish) 2015. (ENG.). 272p. (J). *(978-1-4088-6619-1(6)*, 283017, Bloomsbury Children's Bks.) Bloomsbury Publishing Plc.

—Harry Potter & the Philosopher's Stone (Latin) Harrius Potter et Philosophi Lapis (Latin) Needham, Peter, tr. 2015. (LAT.). 256p. (J). *(978-1-4088-6618-4(8)*, 283019, Bloomsbury Children's Bks.) Bloomsbury Publishing Plc.

—Harry Potter & the Prisoner of Azkaban. 2009. 9.64 *(978-0-7848-1542-7(9)*, Everbind) Marco Bk. Co.

—Harry Potter & the Prisoner of Azkaban. 2005. (Harry Potter Ser.: Year 3). (CHI.). 260p. (YA). pap. 16.95 *(978-7-02-003345-4(8)*, HAP03) People's Literature Publishing Hse. CHN. Dist: Chinasprout, Inc.

—Harry Potter & the Prisoner of Azkaban, 10 vols. 2003. (Harry Potter Ser.: 3). (J). 84.75 *(978-1-4025-6700-1(6))* Recorded Bks., Inc.

—Harry Potter & the Prisoner of Azkaban, Bk. 3. Selznick, Brian & GrandPré, Mary, illus. 2018. (Harry Potter Ser.: 3). (ENG.). 464p. (J). (gr. 3). pap. 12.99 *(978-1-338-29916-8(6)*, Levine, Arthur A. Bks.) Scholastic, Inc.

—Harry Potter & the Prisoner of Azkaban. l.t. ed. 2003. (Harry Potter Ser.: Year 3). (ENG.). 592p. pap. 13.95 *(978-1-59413-002-1(7)*, Large Print Pr.) Thorndike Pr.

—Harry Potter & the Prisoner of Azkaban. 2013. (Harry Potter (Kazu Kibuishi Illustrations) Ser.: 3). lib. bdg. 24.50 *(978-0-606-32347-5(3))* Turtleback.

—Harry Potter & the Sorcerer's Stone. 2014. (ENG.). lthr. 79.00 *(978-1-62715-772-8(7))* Leatherbound Bestsellers.

—Harry Potter & the Sorcerer's Stone. 2009. 8.44 *(978-0-7848-2438-2(X))*; 10.84 *(978-0-7848-1357-7(4))* Marco Bk. Co. (Everbind).

—Harry Potter & the Sorcerer's Stone. 2003. (Harry Potter Ser.: Year 1). (CHI.). 191p. (YA). pap. 14.95 *(978-7-02-003343-0(1)*, HAP01) People's Literature Publishing Hse. CHN. Dist: Chinasprout, Inc.

—Harry Potter & the Sorcerer's Stone. (Harry Potter Ser.: 1). (J). 2004. 1.25 *(978-1-4025-6757-5(X))* 2003. 80.75 *(978-1-4025-6696-7(4))* Recorded Bks., Inc.

—Harry Potter & the Sorcerer's Stone, Bk. 1. Selznick, Brian & GrandPré, Mary, illus. 2018. (Harry Potter Ser.: 1). (ENG.). 336p. (J). (gr. 3). pap. 12.99 *(978-1-338-29914-4(X)*, Levine, Arthur A. Bks.) Scholastic, Inc.

—Harry Potter & the Sorcerer's Stone, Bk. 1. Kay, Jim, illus. 2015. (Harry Potter Ser.: 1). (ENG.). 256p. (J). (gr. 3). 39.99 *(978-0-545-79035-2(2)*, Levine, Arthur A. Bks.) Scholastic, Inc.

—Harry Potter & the Sorcerer's Stone. 2013. (Harry Potter (Kazu Kibuishi Illustrations) Ser.: 1). lib. bdg. 24.50 *(978-0-606-32345-1(7))* Turtleback.

—Harry Potter e a Camara Secreta. (Harry Potter Ser.: Year 2).Tr. of Harry Potter & the Chamber of Secrets. (POR.). pap. 28.95 *(978-85-325-1166-9(X))* Rocco, Editora, Ltda BRA. Dist: Distribooks, Inc.

—Harry Potter e a Pedra Filosofal. (Harry Potter Ser.: Year 1).Tr. of Harry Potter & the Philospher's Stone. (POR.). pap. 28.95 *(978-85-325-1101-0(5))* Rocco, Editora, Ltda BRA. Dist: Distribooks, Inc.

—Harry Potter e a Prisioneiro de Azkaban. (Harry Potter Ser.: Year 3).Tr. of Harry Potter & the Prisioner of Azkaban. (POR.). pap. 29.95 *(978-85-325-1206-2(2))* Rocco, Editora, Ltda BRA. Dist: Distribooks, Inc.

—Harry Potter e o Cálice de Fogo. (Harry Potter Ser.: Year 4).Tr. of Harry Potter & the Goblet of Fire. (POR.). pap. 38.95 *(978-85-325-1252-9(6))* Rocco, Editora, Ltda BRA. Dist: Distribooks, Inc.

—Harry Potter Signature Hardback Boxed Set X 7, 7 vols., Set. 2011. (ENG.). 7p. *(978-1-4088-2594-5(5))* Bloomsbury Publishing Plc.

—Harry Potter y el Prisionero de Azkaban. 2015. (Harry Potter Spanish Ser.: 3).Tr. of Harry Potter & the Prisoner of Azkaban. (SPA.). (gr. 3-6). lib. bdg. 28.10 *(978-0-613-35958-0(5))* Turtleback.

Rowling, J.k. Harry Potter y el prisionero de Azkaban (Harry Potter 3) 2004. (Harry Potter Ser.: Year 3). (SPA., Illus.). 360p. (gr. 3-18). 17.95 *(978-84-7888-519-0(6)*, SAL1889) Emece Editores ESP. Dist: Lectorum Pubns., Inc.

—Harry Potter y la cámara secreta (Harry Potter 2) 2004. (Harry Potter Ser.: Year 2). (SPA., Illus.). 288p. (YA). (gr. 3-18). 15.95 *(978-84-7888-495-7(5)*, SAL4595) Emece Editores ESP. Dist: Lectorum Pubns., Inc.

—Harry Potter y la piedra filosofal (Harry Potter 1) 2004. (Harry Potter Ser.: Year 1). (SPA., Illus.). 256p. (YA). (gr. 7-18). 15.95 *(978-84-7888-445-2(9)*, SAL2819) Emece Editores ESP. Dist: Lectorum Pubns., Inc.

Roy, Ron. The School Skeleton. Gurney, John, illus. 2003. (to Z Mysteries Ser.: 19). (gr. k-3). lib. bdg. 14.75 *(978-0-613-62405-3(X))* Turtleback.

—A to Z Mysteries: the School Skeleton. Gurney, John Steven, illus. 2003. (to Z Mysteries Ser.: 19). 96p. (J). (gr. 1-4). pap. 6.99 *(978-0-375-81368-9(3)*, Random Hse. Bks. for Young Readers) Random Hse. Children's Bks.

Royce, Brenda Scott. The Date. 2019. (Do-Over Ser.). (ENG.). 112p. (YA). (gr. 6-12). pap. 7.99 *(978-1-5415-4549-6(4)*, ac56717e-2154-4887-acea-801399c2e744); 26.65 *(978-1-5415-4033-0(6)*, 35f7f76c-2c31-43a9-8dcd-ebd463897d40) Lerner Publishing Group. (Darby Creek).

Rubens, Michael. Sons of The 613. 2012. (ENG.). 320p. (YA). (gr. 7). 16.99 *(978-0-547-61216-4(8)*, 1464621, Clarion Bks.) HarperCollins Pubs.

Ruby, Laura. Bad Apple. 2011. (ENG.). 272p. (YA). (gr. 8). pap. 10.99 *(978-0-06-124333-2(7)*, HarperTeen) HarperCollins Pubs.

—Good Girls. 2008. (ENG.). 304p. (YA). (gr. 9-12). pap. 8.99 *(978-0-06-088225-9(5))* 2006. 288p. (J). lib. bdg. 17.89 *(978-0-06-088224-2(7))* 2006. (ENG.). 288p. (YA). (gr. 9-12). 16.99 *(978-0-06-088223-5(9))* HarperCollins Pubs. (HarperTeen).

Ruckdeschel, Liz & James, Sara. What If ... All Your Friends Turned on You. 2009. (What If... Ser.). (ENG.). 320p. (YA). (gr. 7-12). 26.19 *(978-0-385-73818-7(8)*, Delacorte Pr.) Random Hse. Children's Bks.

Rud, Jeff. Centerville, 1 vol. 2016. (Orca Sports Ser.). (ENG.). 176p. (J). (gr. 4-7). pap. 10.95 *(978-1-4598-1031-0(7))* Orca Bk. Pubs. USA.

—Centerville. 2016. (Orca Sports Ser.). lib. bdg. 20.80 *(978-0-606-38688-3(2))* Turtleback.

Rudetsky, Seth. My Awesome/Awful Popularity Plan. 2013. 224p. (YA). (gr. 7). pap. 8.99 *(978-0-375-89997-3(9)*, Ember) Random Hse. Children's Bks.

Rudolph, Shaina & Royer, Danielle. All My Stripes: A Story for Children with Autism. Zivoin, Jennifer, illus. 2014. (J). pap. *(978-1-4338-1917-9(1)*, Magination Pr.) American Psychological Assn.

Rue, Ginger. Aleca Zamm Is a Wonder. 2017. (Aleca Zamm Ser.: 1). (ENG., Illus.). 160p. (J). (gr. 2-5). 16.99 *(978-1-4814-7061-2(2)*, Aladdin) Simon & Schuster Children's Publishing.

—Hard Rock. 2017. (Tig Ripley Ser.). (ENG.). 368p. (YA). (gr. 4-7). 16.99 *(978-1-58536-947-8(0)*, 204223) Sleeping Bear Pr.

—Rock 'n' Roll Rebel. 2016. (Tig Ripley Ser.). (ENG.). 349p. (J). (gr. 4-7). 16.99 *(978-1-58536-945-4(4)*, 204106) Sleeping Bear Pr.

Rue, Nancy. So Not Okay: Mean Girl Makeover Series, 1 vol. 2014. (Mean Girl Makeover Ser.: 1). (ENG.). 304p. (J). pap. 9.99 *(978-1-4003-2370-8(3)*, Tommy Nelson) Nelson, Thomas Inc.

—You Can't Sit with Us, 1 vol. 2014. (Mean Girl Makeover Ser.: 2). (ENG.). 224p. (J). pap. 9.99 *(978-1-4003-2371-5(1)*, Tommy Nelson) Nelson, Thomas Inc.

Rue, Nancy N. Faithgirlz Sophies Drama, 1 vol. 2009. (Faithgirlz! Ser.: No. 11). (ENG.). 178p. (J). pap. 6.99 *(978-0-310-71844-4(9))* Zonderkidz.

—Sophie Steps Up, 1 vol. 2009. (Faithgirlz! Ser.: No. 4). (ENG.). 128p. (J). pap. 6.99 *(978-0-310-71841-3(4))* Zonderkidz.

—Sophie's Friendship Fiasco. 2009. (Faithgirlz! Ser.: No. 7). (ENG.). 128p. (J). pap. 6.99 *(978-0-310-71842-0(2))* Zonderkidz.

—Totally Unfair, 1 vol., 4. 2005. (Nama Beach High Ser.). (ENG.). 160p. (YA). pap. 6.99 *(978-0-310-25183-5(4))* Zondervan.

Ruiz, Rachel. The Superhero Project. May, Steve, illus. 2017. (Superhero Harry Ser.). (ENG.). 48p. (J). (gr. k-2). pap. 8.95 *(978-1-4795-9862-5(3)*, 135319); lib. bdg. 23.32 *(978-1-4795-9858-8(5)*, 135311) Capstone. (Picture Window Bks.).

Rumble. 2014. (ENG., Illus.). 560p. (YA). (gr. 9). 21.99 *(978-1-4424-8284-5(2)*, McElderry, Margaret K. Bks.) McElderry, Margaret K. Bks.

Rumford, James. Rain School. 2010. (ENG., Illus.). 32p. (J). (gr. -1-3). 17.99 *(978-0-547-24307-8(3)*, 1099430, Clarion Bks.) HarperCollins Pubs.

Rummel, Verna. My School, 1 vol. 2010. 16p. 24.95 *(978-1-4489-6214-3(5))* PublishAmerica, Inc.

Rundell, Katherine. Cartwheeling in Thunderstorms. Castrillón, Melissa & Castrillón, Melissa, illus. 2014. (ENG.). 256p. (J). (gr. 3-7). 18.99 *(978-1-4424-9061-1(6)*, Simon & Schuster Bks. For Young Readers) Simon & Schuster Bks. For Young Readers.

Rupert Goes to School: Level M, 6 vols. 128p. (gr. 2-3). 49.95 *(978-0-7699-1028-4(9))* Shortland Pubns. (U. S. A.) Inc.

Rusackas, Francesca. I Love You All Day Long. Burris, Priscilla, illus. 2004. (ENG.). 32p. (J). (gr. -1-k). reprint ed. pap. 7.99 *(978-0-06-050278-2(9)*, HarperCollins) HarperCollins Pubs.

Russell Brown, Eleanor. A C Robat Goes to Circus School. 2009. 32p. pap. 14.49 *(978-1-4389-3939-1(6))* AuthorHouse.

Russell, Rachel Renee. Dork Diaries: Tales from a Not-So-Fabulous Life. 2009. (Illus.). 282p. (J). *(978-0-85707-475-1(X)*, Simon & Schuster/Paula Wiseman Bks.) Simon & Schuster/Paula Wiseman Bks.

Russell, Rachel Renée. Dork Diaries 1: Tales from a Not-So-Fabulous Life. Russell, Rachel Renée, illus. 2009. (Dork Diaries: 1). (ENG., Illus.). 352p. (J). (gr. 4-8). 14.99 *(978-1-4169-8006-3(7)*, Aladdin) Simon & Schuster Children's Publishing.

—Dork Diaries 10: Tales from a Not-So-Perfect Pet Sitter. Russell, Rachel Renée, illus. 2015. (Dork Diaries: 10). (ENG., Illus.). 320p. (J). (gr. 4-8). 13.99 *(978-1-4814-5704-0(7)*, Aladdin) Simon & Schuster Children's Publishing.

—Dork Diaries 11: Tales from a Not-So-Friendly Frenemy. Russell, Rachel Renée, illus. 2016. (Dork Diaries: 11). (ENG., Illus.). 288p. (J). (gr. 4-8). 13.99 *(978-1-4814-7920-2(2)*, Aladdin) Simon & Schuster Children's Publishing.

—Dork Diaries 2: Tales from a Not-So-Popular Party Girl. Russell, Rachel Renée, illus. 2010. (Dork Diaries: 2). (ENG., Illus.). 288p. (J). (gr. 4-8). 14.99 *(978-1-4169-8008-7(3)*, Aladdin) Simon & Schuster Children's Publishing.

—Dork Diaries 3: Tales from a Not-So-Talented Pop Star. Russell, Rachel Renée, illus. 2011. (Dork Diaries: 3). (ENG., Illus.). 336p. (J). (gr. 4-8). 14.99 *(978-1-4424-1190-6(2)*, Aladdin) Simon & Schuster Children's Publishing.

—Dork Diaries 3 1/2: How to Dork Your Diary. Russell, Rachel Renée, illus. 2011. (Dork Diaries: No. 3.5). (ENG., Illus.). 288p. (J). (gr. 4-8). 14.99 *(978-1-4424-2233-9(5)*, Aladdin) Simon & Schuster Children's Publishing.

—Dork Diaries 4: Tales from a Not-So-Graceful Ice Princess. Russell, Rachel Renée, illus. 2012. (Dork Diaries: 4). (ENG., Illus.). 368p. (J). (gr. 4-8). 14.99 *(978-1-4424-1192-0(9)*, Aladdin) Simon & Schuster Children's Publishing.

—Dork Diaries 5: Tales from a Not-So-Smart Miss Know-It-All. Russell, Rachel Renée, illus. 2012. (Dork Diaries: 5). (ENG., Illus.). 368p. (J). (gr. 4-8). 14.99 *(978-1-4424-4961-9(6)*, Aladdin) Simon & Schuster Children's Publishing.

—Dork Diaries 6: Tales from a Not-So-Happy Heartbreaker. Russell, Rachel Renée, illus. 2013. (Dork Diaries: 6). (ENG., Illus.). 368p. (J). (gr. 4-8). 14.99 *(978-1-4424-4963-3(2)*, Aladdin) Simon & Schuster Children's Publishing.

—Dork Diaries 9, 3 vols. unabr. ed. 2015. (Dork Diaries: 8). (ENG.). 320p. (J). (gr. 4-8). audio compact disk 14.99 *(978-1-4423-7023-4(8))* Simon & Schuster Audio.

—Dork Diaries 9: Tales from a Not-So-Dorky Drama Queen. Russell, Rachel Renée, illus. 2015. (Dork Diaries: 9). (ENG., Illus.). 352p. (J). (gr. 4-8). 14.99 *(978-1-4424-8769-7(0)*, Aladdin Paperbacks) Simon & Schuster Children's Publishing.

—Dork Diaries Boxed Set (Books 1-3) Set: Dork Diaries; Dork Diaries 2; Dork Diaries 3, Set. Russell, Rachel Renée, illus. 2011. (Dork Diaries: Nos. 1-3). (ENG., Illus.). 928p. (J). (gr. 4-8). 41.99 *(978-1-4424-2662-7(4)*, Aladdin) Simon & Schuster Children's Publishing.

—The Misadventures of Max Crumbly 1: Locker Hero. Russell, Rachel Renée, illus. 2016. (Misadventures of Max Crumbly Ser.: 1). (ENG., Illus.). 320p. (J). (gr. 4-8). 13.99 *(978-1-4814-6001-9(3)*, Aladdin) Simon & Schuster Children's Publishing.

—The Misadventures of Max Crumbly 2: Middle School Mayhem. Russell, Rachel Renée, illus. 2017. (Misadventures of Max Crumbly Ser.: 2). (ENG., Illus.). 240p. (J). (gr. 4-8). 13.99 *(978-1-4814-6003-3(X)*, Aladdin) Simon & Schuster Children's Publishing.

—The Misadventures of Max Crumbly 3: Masters of Mischief. Russell, Rachel Renée, illus. 2019. (Misadventures of Max Crumbly Ser.: 3). (ENG., Illus.). 272p. (J). (gr. 4-7). 13.99 *(978-1-5344-5349-4(0)*, Aladdin) Simon & Schuster Children's Publishing.

—The Misadventures of Max Crumbly Books 1-3 (Boxed Set) The Misadventures of Max Crumbly 1; the Misadventures of Max Crumbly 2; the Misadventures of Max Crumbly 3. Russell, Rachel Renée, illus. 2019. (Misadventures of Max Crumbly Ser.). (ENG.). 832p. (J). (gr. 4-7). 41.99 *(978-1-5344-5351-7(2)*, Aladdin) Simon & Schuster Children's Publishing.

—Tales from a Not-So-Fabulous Life. 2009. (Dork Diaries: 1). lib. bdg. 25.75 *(978-0-606-32419-9(4))* Turtleback.

—Tales from a Not-So-Happily Ever After. 2014. (Dork Diaries: 8). lib. bdg. 25.75 *(978-0-606-36241-2(X))* Turtleback.

Russell, Rachel Renee. Tales from a Not-So-Happy Birthday. 2018. (Dork Diaries: 13). lib. bdg. 25.75 *(978-0-606-41455-5(X))* Turtleback.

Russell, Rachel Renée. Tales from a Not-So-Happy Heartbreaker. 2013. (Dork Diaries: 6). lib. bdg. 25.75 *(978-0-606-32424-3(0))* Turtleback.

—Tales from a Not-So-Perfect Pet Sitter. Russell, Rachel Renée, illus. 2015. (Dork Diaries: 10). (ENG., Illus.). 320p. (J). (gr. 4-8). lib. bdg. 25.75 *(978-0-606-37923-6(1))* Turtleback.

—Tales from a Not-So-Popular Party Girl. 2010. (Dork Diaries: 2). lib. bdg. 25.75 *(978-0-606-32420-5(8))* Turtleback.

Russell, Rachel Renée, et al. Tales from a Not-So-Friendly Frenemy. 2016. (Illus.). 243p. (J). *(978-1-5182-1819-4(9)*, Aladdin) Simon & Schuster Children's Publishing.

—Tales from a Not-So-Popular Party Girl. 2010. (ENG.). pap. *(978-1-4424-4042-5(2)*, Aladdin Paperbacks) Simon & Schuster Children's Publishing.

Russell, Randy. Dead Rules. 2011. (ENG.). 384p. (YA). (gr. 8-18). 16.99 *(978-0-06-198670-3(4)*, HarperTeen) HarperCollins Pubs.

Rusu, Meredith. School for Crooks (LEGO Ninjago: Brick Adventures) 2018. (LEGO Ninjago: Brick Adventures Ser.). (ENG.). 64p. (J). (gr. 1-3). pap. 4.99 (978-1-338-26249-0(1)) Scholastic, Inc.

Rutkoski, Marie. The Shadow Society. 2013. (ENG.). 448p. (YA). (gr. 7-12). pap. 17.99 (978-1-250-03424-3(8), 900120597) Square Fish.

Rutland, Mirium. Miss Pistachios Big Day. 2007. (Illus.). 48p. pap. (978-1-58690-063-2(3)) Mould, Paul Publishing.

Ruzima, Keza. Girl Power: The Adventures of a Teenage Circle. 2009. 112p. pap. 23.75 (978-1-60860-647-4(3), Eloquent Bks.) Strategic Book Publishing & Rights Agency (SBPRA).

Ryan, Amy Kathleen. Vibes. 2010. (ENG.). 264p. (YA). (gr. 9). pap. 14.95 (978-0-547-24889-9(X), 1100901, Clarion Bks.) HarperCollins Pubs.

Ryan, Carol. A Bridge Through Time, 1 vol. 2010. 276p. pap. 27.95 (978-1-4489-4254-1(3)) PublishAmerica, Inc.

Ryan, Darlene. Responsible, 1 vol. 2007. (Orca Soundings Ser.). (ENG.). (YA). (gr. 8-12). 128p. pap. 9.95 (978-1-55143-685-2(X)); 112p. lib. bdg. 14.95 (978-1-55143-687-6(6)) Orca Bk. Pubs. USA.

Ryan, Hugh. The Hunt. 2012. 90p. (J). (978-0-545-46306-5(8)) Scholastic, Inc.

Ryan, Pam Muñoz. Tony Baloney: Pen Pal. Fotheringham, Ed, illus. 2014. 39p. (J). pap. (978-0-545-69227-4(X), Scholastic Pr.) Scholastic, Inc.

Ryan, Sara. Empress of the World. 2003. 304p. (YA). (gr. 9-18). 8.99 (978-0-14-250059-0(3), Speak) Penguin Young Readers Group.

Ryan, Tom. Big Time, 1 vol. 2014. (Orca Limelights Ser.). (ENG.). 144p. (J). (gr. 4-7). pap. 9.95 (978-1-4598-0461-6(9)) Orca Bk. Pubs. USA.

Rylander, Chris. Codename Zero. 2014. (Codename Conspiracy Ser.: 1). (ENG.). 368p. (J). (gr. 3-7). 16.99 (978-0-06-212008-3(5), Waldon Pond Pr.) HarperCollins Pubs.

—Countdown Zero. 2015. (Codename Conspiracy Ser.: 2). (ENG.). 368p. (J). (gr. 3-7). 16.99 (978-0-06-212011-3(5), Waldon Pond Pr.) HarperCollins Pubs.

—The Fourth Stall. 2011. (Fourth Stall Ser.: 1). (ENG.). 320p. (J). (gr. 3-7). 16.99 (978-0-06-199496-8(0), Waldon Pond Pr.) HarperCollins Pubs.

—The Fourth Stall Part III. (Fourth Stall Ser.: 3). (ENG.). (J). (gr. 3-7). Pt. 3. 2014. 320p. pap. 7.99 (978-0-06-212006-9(9))Pt. III. 2013. 304p. 16.99 (978-0-06-212005-2(0)) HarperCollins Pubs. (Waldon Pond Pr.).

Rylant, Cynthia. Mr. Putter & Tabby Ring the Bell. Howard, Arthur, illus. 2012. (Mr. Putter & Tabby Ser.). (ENG.). 44p. (J). (gr. 1-4). pap. 5.99 (978-0-547-85075-7(1), 1501053, Clarion Bks.) HarperCollins Pubs.

—Mr. Putter & Tabby Ring the Bell. Howard, Arthur, illus. 2012. (Mr. Putter & Tabby Ser.). lib. bdg. 16.00 (978-0-606-26614-7(3)) Turtleback.

Sachar, Louis. Fuzzy Mud. 2015. (KOR.). 228p. (J). (gr. 5). pap. (978-89-364-5671-9(7)) Chang-jag and Bipyeong Co.

—Fuzzy Mud. 2015. (CHI.). 240p. (J). pap. (978-986-211-551-0(3)) Hsaio Lu Publishing Co., Ltd.

—Fuzzy Mud. 2018. (Penworthy Picks Middle School Ser.). (ENG.). 181p. (J). (gr. 5-7). 19.96 (978-1-64310-305-1(9)) Penworthy Co., LLC, The.

—Fuzzy Mud. 2017. (ENG.). 208p. (J). (gr. 5). 8.99 (978-0-385-37022-6(9), Yearling) Random Hse. Children's Bks.

—Fuzzy Mud. 2017. lib. bdg. 18.40 (978-0-606-39871-8(6)) Turtleback.

—Gets a Little Stranger. 150p. (J). (gr. 3-5). pap. 4.99 (978-0-8072-1543-2(0)); 2004. pap. 29.00 incl. audio (978-0-8072-8141-3(7), S YA 116 SP) Random Hse. Audio Publishing Group. (Listening Library).

—Gets a Little Stranger. 2003. (Wayside School Ser.). (J). (gr. 3-6). lib. bdg. 16.00 (978-0-613-86690-3(8)) Turtleback.

—Sideways Stories from Wayside School. McCauley, Adam, illus. 2019. (Wayside School Ser.). (ENG.). 176p. (J). (gr. 3-7). pap. 9.99 (978-0-380-69871-4(4), HarperCollins) HarperCollins Pubs.

—Sideways Stories from Wayside School. 124p. (J). (gr. 3-5). pap. 4.99 (978-0-8072-1458-9(2), Listening Library) Random Hse. Audio Publishing Group.

—Sideways Stories from Wayside School. 2003. (Wayside School Ser.). (J). (gr. 3-6). lib. bdg. 17.20 (978-0-613-87805-0(1)) Turtleback.

—Someday Angeline. 2005. (ENG., Illus.). 192p. (J). (gr. 3-7). pap. 9.99 (978-0-380-83444-0(8), HarperCollins) HarperCollins Pubs.

—The Wayside School 3-Book Box Set: Sideways Stories from Wayside School, Wayside School Is Falling down, Wayside School Gets a Little Stranger, 3 vols., Set. McCauley, Adam, illus. 2019. (Wayside School Ser.). (ENG.). 608p. (J). (gr. 3-7). pap. 23.97 (978-0-380-79171-2(4), HarperCollins) HarperCollins Pubs.

—Wayside School Beneath the Cloud of Doom. Heitz, Tim, illus. 2020. (Wayside School Ser.: 4). (ENG.). 192p. (J). (gr. 3-7). 17.99 (978-0-06-296538-7(7)); 18.89 (978-0-06-296540-0(9)) HarperCollins Pubs. (HarperCollins).

—Wayside School Gets a Little Stranger. McCauley, Adam, illus. (Wayside School Ser.). (ENG.). (J). (gr. 3-7). 2019. 208p. pap. 9.99 (978-0-380-72381-2(6), HarperCollins) 2004. 160p. pap. 6.99 (978-0-380-73149-7(5)) HarperCollins Pubs.

—Wayside School Is Falling Down. McCauley, Adam, illus. (Wayside School Ser.). (ENG.). (J). (gr. 3-7). 2019. 224p. pap. 9.99 (978-0-380-75484-7(3), HarperCollins) 2004. 160p. pap. 6.99 (978-0-380-73150-3(9)) HarperCollins Pubs.

—Wayside School Is Falling Down. 179p. (J). (gr. 3-5). pap. 4.99 (978-0-8072-1461-9(2), Listening Library) Random Hse. Audio Publishing Group.

—Wayside School Is Falling Down. 2003. (Wayside School Ser.). (J). (gr. 3-6). lib. bdg. 17.20 (978-0-613-89269-8(0)) Turtleback.

Sachs, Marilyn. The Bears' House. 2008. 80p. (gr. 4-7). pap. 8.95 (978-0-595-53553-8(4)) iUniverse, Inc.

—The Fat Girl. 2nd ed. 2007. (ENG.). 240p. (YA). (gr. 9-12). per. 8.95 (978-0-7387-1000-6(8), 0738710008, Flux) North Star Editions.

Sackier, Shelley. Dear OPL. 2015. (ENG.). 240p. (J). (gr. 5-8). pap. 12.99 (978-1-4926-0859-2(9), 9781492608592) Sourcebooks, Inc.

Sadd, Kenn. Crazy Cracked Pots. 2009. 144p. pap. 24.95 (978-1-61546-673-3(8)) America Star Bks.

Saddlewick, A. B. Monstrous Maud: Big Fright. 2017. (ENG., Illus.). 128p. (J). (gr. 1-5). pap. 7.99 (978-1-5107-1698-8(X), Sky Pony Pr.) Skyhorse Publishing Co., Inc.

Sadler, Marilyn. Honey Bunny's Honey Bear. Bollen, Roger, illus. 2007. (Step into Reading Ser.). (ENG.). 32p. (J). (gr. -1-1). per. 4.99 (978-0-375-84326-6(4), Random Hse. Bks. for Young Readers) Random Hse. Children's Bks.

Saft, Lauren. Those Girls. 2016. (ENG.). 336p. (YA). (gr. 10-17). pap. 9.99 (978-0-316-26016-9(9), Poppy) Little, Brown Bks. for Young Readers.

Sagner, Sibel. The Show & Tell Day Blue Band. Perez, Moni, illus. 2017. (Cambridge Reading Adventures Ser.). (ENG.). 16p. pap. 6.15 (978-1-108-40191-3(0)) Cambridge Univ. Pr.

Said, Taunya D. Smart Alec- Alex: The 5th Grade Schedule Change. 2009. 53p. (YA). pap. 10.95 (978-1-4327-4187-7(X)) Outskirts Pr., Inc.

Salane, Jeffrey. Lawless. 2013. 277p. (J). (978-0-545-54882-3(9), Scholastic Pr.) Scholastic, Inc.

Saldaña, Jr. A Good Long Way. 2010. 128p. (J). (gr. 6-18). pap. 10.95 (978-1-55885-607-3(2), Piñata Books) Arte Publico Pr.

Saldana, Rene. Case of Pen Gone Missing/El Caso de la Pluma Perdida. Villarroel, Carolina, tr. from ENG. Mora, Giovanni, illus. 2009. (SPA & ENG.). 80p. (J). (gr. 3-7). pap. 9.95 (978-1-55885-555-7(6), Piñata Books) Arte Publico Pr.

Saldana, Rene, Jr. A Mystery Bigger Than Big / un Misterio Mas Grande Que Grandisimo: A Mickey Rangel Mystery / Colección Mickey Rangel, Detective Privado. 2016. (Mickey Rangel Mystery / Coleccion Mickey Rangel, Detective P Ser.). (MUL, ENG & SPA., Illus.). 64p. (J). (gr. 3-6). pap. 9.95 (978-1-55885-824-4(5), Piñata Books) Arte Publico Pr.

Saldin, Erin. The Girls of No Return. 2012. (YA). pap. (978-0-545-31027-7(X), Levine, Arthur A. Bks.) Scholastic, Inc.

Saldivar, Jose A. The Adventures of Oskar: Oskar's New School. Nilsson, Janet Busbey, ed. Jasnoch, Dorothy, illus. 2013. (ENG.). 32p. pap. 13.99 (978-1-937752-07-1(0)) Owl About Bks. Pubs.

Sales, Leila. Mostly Good Girls. (ENG.). 368p. (YA). (gr. 9). 2011. pap. 9.99 (978-1-4424-0680-3(1)) 2010. 17.99 (978-1-4424-0679-7(8)) Simon Pulse. (Simon Pulse).

Salisbury, Graham. Calvin Coconut: Dog Heaven. Rogers, Jacqueline, illus. 2011. (Calvin Coconut Ser.: 3). (ENG.). 160p. (J). (gr. 3-7). 7.99 (978-0-375-84602-1(6), Yearling) Random Hse. Children's Bks.

—Calvin Coconut: Kung Fooey. Rogers, Jacqueline, illus. 2012. (Calvin Coconut Ser.: 6). 144p. (J). (gr. 2-5). 7.99 (978-0-375-86506-0(3), Yearling) Random Hse. Children's Bks.

—Calvin Coconut: Rocket Ride. Rogers, Jacqueline, illus. 2013. (Calvin Coconut Ser.: 8). 160p. (J). (gr. 2-5). pap. 6.99 (978-0-375-86508-4(X), Yearling) Random Hse. Children's Bks.

—Calvin Coconut: Trouble Magnet. 2010. (Calvin Coconut Ser.: 1). (ENG., Illus.). 160p. (J). (gr. 3-7). pap. 7.99 (978-0-375-84600-7(X), Yearling) Random Hse. Children's Bks.

—Calvin Coconut: Zoo Breath. Rogers, Jacqueline, illus. 2011. (Calvin Coconut Ser.: 4). (ENG.). 160p. (J). (gr. 3-7). 6.99 (978-0-375-84603-8(4), Yearling) Random Hse. Children's Bks.

—Dog Heaven. Rogers, Jacqueline, illus. 2011. (Calvin Coconut Ser.). (ENG.). 160p. (J). (gr. 3-6). lib. bdg. 21.19 (978-0-385-90641-8(2), Lamb, Wendy Bks.) Random Hse. Children's Bks.

—Trouble Magnet. Rogers, Jacqueline, illus. 2009. (Calvin Coconut Ser.). (ENG.). 160p. (J). (gr. 4-6). lib. bdg. 21.19 (978-0-385-90639-5(0), Lamb, Wendy Bks.) Random Hse. Children's Bks.

Salom, Susie. Kyle Finds Her Way. 2016. (ENG.). 256p. (J). (gr. 5-9). 16.99 (978-0-545-85266-1(8), Levine, Arthur A. Bks.) Scholastic, Inc.

Saltzberg, Barney. Crazy Hair Day. Saltzberg, Barney, illus. 2008. (ENG., Illus.). 32p. (J). (gr. k-3). pap. 7.99 (978-0-7636-2464-4(0)) Candlewick Pr.

—Crazy Hair Day. Saltzberg, Barney, illus. 2011. (Illus.). (J). (gr. k-3). 29.95 (978-0-545-13450-7(1)) Weston Woods Studios, Inc.

—Crazy Hair Day, 5 bks., Set. 2011. (J). (gr. k-3). 38.75 (978-0-545-15157-3(0)) Weston Woods Studios, Inc.

—Crazy Hair Day Big Book. Saltzberg, Barney, illus. 2008. (ENG., Illus.). 32p. (J). (gr. k-3). pap. 27.99 (978-0-7636-3969-3(9)) Candlewick Pr.

—Star of the Week. Saltzberg, Barney, illus. 2010. (ENG., Illus.). 32p. (J). (gr. k-3). pap. 7.99 (978-0-7636-3076-8(4)) Candlewick Pr.

Salvatierra, Dante. Latchkey Kids & the Fight for A Free F. 2006. (ENG.). 236p. pap. 13.95 (978-1-4303-0969-7(5)) Lulu Pr., Inc.

Sampson, Jeff. Vesper. 2011. (Deviants Ser.: 1). (ENG.). 304p. (YA). (gr. 8-18). 16.99 (978-0-06-199276-6(3), Balzer & Bray) HarperCollins Pubs.

Sanchez, Alex. Getting It. 2007. (ENG., Illus.). 232p. (YA). (gr. 7-12). pap. 8.99 (978-1-4169-0898-2(6), Simon & Schuster Bks. For Young Readers) Simon & Schuster Bks. For Young Readers.

—The God Box. 2009. (ENG., Illus.). 264p. (YA). (gr. 7). pap. 12.99 (978-1-4169-0900-2(1), Simon & Schuster Bks. For Young Readers) Simon & Schuster Bks. For Young Readers.

—Rainbow Boys. 2003. (ENG., Illus.). 262p. (YA). (gr. 7). pap. 12.99 (978-0-689-85770-6(5), Simon & Schuster Bks. For Young Readers) Simon & Schuster Bks. For Young Readers.

—So Hard to Say. 2006. (ENG., Illus.). 232p. (YA). (gr. 7-12). reprint ed. pap. 12.99 (978-1-4169-1189-0(8), Simon & Schuster Bks. For Young Readers) Simon & Schuster Bks. For Young Readers.

Sanchez, Jenny Torres. Death, Dickinson, & the Demented Life of Frenchie Garcia. 2013. (ENG.). 272p. (YA). (gr. 7-17). pap. 15.99 (978-0-7624-4680-3(3), Running Pr. Kids) Running Pr.

Sanchez, Lorrie Christel & Blank, Carol. Virgil: The Bully from Cyberspace. Margolis, Al, illus. 2013. 54p. (J). 20.99 (978-0-9891338-0-7(X)) Utterly Global.

—Virgil: The Bully from Cyberspace Teacher Edition. Margolis, Al, illus. 2013. 88p. 99.00 (978-0-9891338-1-4(8)) Utterly Global.

Sanchez, Pete. A Friend for Petro. 2008. 73p. pap. 19.95 (978-1-60474-902-1(4)) America Star Bks.

Sand-Eveland, Cyndi. Dear Toni. 2008. (Illus.). 136p. (J). (gr. 3-7). 14.95 (978-0-88776-876-7(8), Tundra Bks.) Tundra Bks. CAN. Dist: Penguin Random Hse. LLC.

Sandberg, Winter. Private Display of Affection. 2016. (ENG., Illus.). (YA). (gr. 8-12). 24.99 (978-1-63533-065-6(3), Harmony Ink Pr.) Dreamspinner Pr.

—Private Display of Affection [Library Edition]. 2014. 210p. pap. 14.99 (978-1-62798-537-6(9), Harmony Ink Pr.) Dreamspinner Pr.

Sanders, Rob. Ruby Rose: off to School She Goes. Ohi, Debbie Ridpath, illus. 2016. (ENG.). 32p. (J). (gr. -1-3). 15.99 (978-0-06-223569-5(9), HarperCollins) HarperCollins Pubs.

Sandoval, Alex. Zack Goes to School. 2009. 20p. pap. 10.50 (978-1-4389-5537-7(5)) AuthorHouse.

Sandoval, Melba. Our Class Wants Perfect Attendance! Mousey, Where Are You? Moreno, Eli, illus. 2010. (ENG.). 28p. pap. 15.99 (978-1-4568-1398-7(6)) Xlibris Corp.

Sansone, V. K. Katie Bear: Fun Days at School. WillowRaven, Aidana, illus. 2007. 84p. pap. 16.95 (978-0-9798154-7-8(9)) Living Waters Publishing Co.

—Katie Bear & Friends (Book One) 2009. 36p. pap. 16.97 (978-0-557-09358-8(9)) Lulu Pr., Inc.

—A Strange Day at the Zoo. 2009. 32p. pap. 14.98 (978-0-557-06519-6(4)) Lulu Pr., Inc.

Santomero, Angela C., adapted by. You Are Special, Daniel Tiger! 2014. (Daniel Tiger's Neighborhood Ser.). (ENG., Illus.). 26p. (J). (gr. -1-2). 12.99 (978-1-4814-1915-4(3), Simon Spotlight) Simon Spotlight.

Santopolo, Jill. Nina, the Pinta, & the Vanishing Treasure (an Alec Flint Mystery #1), 1. 2009. (ENG.). 192p. (J). (gr. 2-5). mass mkt. 6.99 (978-0-439-90353-0(X), Scholastic Paperbacks) Scholastic, Inc.

—Sparkle Spa Spa-Tacular Collection Books 1-10 (Boxed Set) All That Glitters; Purple Nails & Puppy Tails; Makeover Magic; True Colors; Bad News Nails; a Picture-Perfect Mess; Bling It on!; Wedding Bell Blues; Fashion Disaster; Glam Opening! 2017. (Sparkle Spa Ser.). (ENG., Illus.). 1184p. (J). (gr. 2-5). pap. 59.99 (978-1-4814-9981-1(5), Aladdin) Simon & Schuster Children's Publishing.

Santoro, Scott. Which Way to Witch School? Santoro, Scott, illus. (ENG., Illus.). 32p. (J). (gr. -1-2). 2012. pap. 5.99 (978-0-06-078183-5(1)) 2010. 16.99 (978-0-06-078181-1(5)) HarperCollins Pubs. (HarperCollins).

Sarfatti, Esther, tr. from ENG. Berto Da la Talla. 2006. (Libro de Capitulos de Arturo Ser.). (Illus.). 55p. (J). (gr. 6-8). per. 4.99 (978-1-930332-94-2(7)) Lectorum Pubns., Inc.

Sargent, Dave. Sammy Goes to School #8, 10 vols. 2007. (Little Stinker Ser.: 8). (J). lib. bdg. 23.60 (978-1-59381-294-2(9)) Ozark Publishing.

—Sammy Goes to School #8 (PB), 10 vols. 2007. (Little Stinker Ser.: 8). (J). pap. 10.95 (978-1-59381-295-9(7)) Ozark Publishing.

Sargent, Dave & Sargent, Pat. Zeb: (Zebra Dun) Be Prepared, 30 vols., Vol. 60. Lenoir, Jane, illus. 2003. (Saddle up Ser.: Vol. 60). 42p. (J). pap. 10.95 (978-1-56763-718-2(3)); lib. bdg. 23.60 (978-1-56763-717-5(5)) Ozark Publishing.

Sarn, Amélie & Trouillot, Virgile. Looking for Trouble, 1 vol. 2009. (Groove High Ser.). (ENG., Illus.). 112p. (YA). (gr. 5-5). 16.93 (978-1-60754-206-3(4), 0e875d69-2bd0-4669-9b7d-04fd4b6f2834, Windmill Bks.) Rosen Publishing Group, Inc., The.

—Love Is in the Air, 1 vol. 2009. (Groove High Ser.). (ENG., Illus.). 112p. (YA). (gr. 5-5). 16.93 (978-1-60754-212-4(9), 96c07ce5-b8a3-40f6-9b24-585dd67efe6c); pap. 8.95 (978-1-60754-213-1(7), 412be38f-e2f3-4675-8501-8a1be8c4b484) Rosen Publishing Group, Inc., The. (Windmill Bks.).

Sarno, Melissa. Just under the Clouds. 2019. (ENG.). 256p. (J). (gr. 3-7). pap. 8.99 (978-1-5247-2011-7(9), Yearling) Random Hse. Children's Bks.

Sarratt, Carla. Freshman Focus Carter G Woodson High Sc. 2006. 292p. pap. 14.95 (978-1-4327-0109-3(6)) Outskirts Pr., Inc.

Sarratt, Carla R. Just Be. 2008. 312p. pap. 14.95 (978-1-4327-2212-8(3)) Outskirts Pr., Inc.

Sauer, Tammi. Mostly Monsterly. Magoon, Scott, illus. 2010. (ENG.). 40p. (J). (gr. -1-3). 18.99 (978-1-4169-6110-9(0), Simon & Schuster/Paula Wiseman Bks.) Simon & Schuster/Paula Wiseman Bks.

Saunders, Brianna. The Magic Marble. 2013. 32p. pap. 24.95 (978-1-63004-598-2(5)) America Star Bks.

Saunders, Kate. Beswitched. 2012. (ENG.). 272p. (J). (gr. 4-7). 7.99 (978-0-375-87329-4(5), Yearling) Random Hse. Children's Bks.

—The Land of Neverendings. 2017. (ENG.). 336p. (J). 14.50 (978-0-571-31084-5(2), Faber & Faber Children's Bks.) Faber & Faber, Inc.

Sawyer, Kim Vogel. Katy's New World, 1 vol., 1. 2010. (Katy Lambright Ser.: No. 1). (ENG.). 208p. (YA). (gr. 9-12). pap. 9.99 (978-0-310-71924-3(0)) Zondervan.

Say, Allen. The Favorite Daughter. 2013. (J). pap. (978-0-545-17663-7(8), Levine, Arthur A. Bks.) Scholastic, Inc.

—The Favorite Daughter. Say, Allen, illus. 2013. (ENG., Illus.). 32p. (J). (gr. -1-3). 19.99 (978-0-545-17662-0(X), Levine, Arthur A. Bks.) Scholastic, Inc.

Sazaklis, John. The Ferret Fiasco. Robinson, Lee, illus. 2016. (Billy Burger, Model Citizen Ser.). (ENG.). 96p. (J). (gr. 2-4). lib. bdg. 22.65 (978-1-4965-2589-5(2), 130718, Stone Arch Bks.) Capstone.

—Jumping for Junk Food. Robinson, Lee, illus. 2016. (Billy Burger, Model Citizen Ser.). (ENG.). 96p. (J). (gr. 2-4). lib. bdg. 22.65 (978-1-4965-2586-4(8), 130715, Stone Arch Bks.) Capstone.

—Recess Is Ruined. Robinson, Lee, illus. 2016. (Billy Burger, Model Citizen Ser.). (ENG.). 96p. (J). (gr. 2-4). lib. bdg. 22.65 (978-1-4965-2588-8(4), 130717, Stone Arch Bks.) Capstone.

Schachner, Judy. Class Action. 2017. (Skippyjon Jones Ser.). lib. bdg. 19.65 (978-0-606-40104-3(0)) Turtleback.

—Sarabella's Thinking Cap. 2017. (Illus.). 32p. (J). (gr. k-3). 17.99 (978-0-525-42918-0(2), Dial Bks) Penguin Young Readers Group.

—Skippyjon Jones, Class Action. (Skippyjon Jones Ser.). 32p. (J). 2017. (-k). pap. 8.99 (978-0-425-28892-4(7), Puffin Books) 2011. (Illus.). (gr. -1-k). 17.99 (978-0-525-42228-0(5), Dutton Books for Young Readers) Penguin Young Readers Group.

Schaefer, Lola M. Mittens at School. Hartung, Susan Kathleen, illus. 2012. (My First I Can Read Ser.). (ENG.). 32p. (J). (gr. -1-3). 16.99 (978-0-06-170224-2(2)); pap. 5.99 (978-0-06-170223-5(4)) HarperCollins Pubs. (HarperCollins).

—Mittens at School. 2012. (My First I Can Read Ser.). (J). lib. bdg. 13.55 (978-0-606-26292-7(X)) Turtleback.

Schantz, Sarah Elizabeth. Fig. 2016. (ENG.). 352p. (YA). (gr. 9). pap. 11.99 (978-1-4814-2359-5(2), McElderry, Margaret K. Bks.) McElderry, Margaret K. Bks.

Schechter, Lynn R. My Big Fat Secret: How Jenna Takes Control of Her Emotions & Eating. Chin, Jason, illus. 2009. 64p. (J). (gr. 3-7). 14.95 (978-1-4338-0540-0(5)); pap. 9.95 (978-1-4338-0541-7(3)) American Psychological Assn. (Magination Pr.).

Scheerger, Sarah. Operation Frog Effect. 2020. 320p. (J). (gr. 3-7). pap. 8.99 (978-0-525-64415-6(6), Yearling) Random Hse. Children's Bks.

Scheerger, Sarah Lynn. Are You Still There. 2015. (ENG.). 288p. (YA). (gr. 8-12). 16.99 (978-0-8075-4557-7(0), 807545570) Whitman, Albert & Co.

Scheier, Leah. Your Voice Is All I Hear. 2015. 336p. (YA). (gr. 8-12). pap. 9.99 (978-1-4926-1441-8(6)) Sourcebooks, Inc.

Schindler, Holly. Feral. 2014. (ENG.). 432p. (YA). (gr. 8). 17.99 (978-0-06-222020-2(9), HarperTeen) HarperCollins Pubs.

Schizas, Lea. Bubba & Giganto: Odds Against Us. 2008. 68p. (J). pap. (978-0-9797513-6-3(5)) 4RV Pub.

Schleuning, Todd & Schleuning, Cheryl. The Misphits: Story of Snake. Vene, Alessandro, illus. 2013. (ENG.). (J). (gr. -1-3). 15.95 (978-1-62086-302-2(2)) Amplify Publishing Group.

Schlick Noe, Katherine. Something to Hold. 2011. (ENG., Illus.). 256p. (J). (gr. 5-7). 17.99 (978-0-547-55813-4(9), 1453477, Clarion Bks.) HarperCollins Pubs.

Schmatz, Pat. Bluefish. (ENG.). 240p. (YA). (gr. 7). 2013. pap. 9.99 (978-0-7636-6341-4(7)) 2011. (Illus.). 15.99 (978-0-7636-5334-7(9)) Candlewick Pr.

—Mousetraps. Hauser, Bill, illus. 2008. (ENG.). 192p. (YA). (gr. 7-12). 17.95 (978-0-8225-8657-9(6), Carolrhoda Bks.) Lerner Publishing Group.

Schmid, Paul. Hugs from Pearl. Schmid, Paul, illus. 2011. (ENG., Illus.). 40p. (J). (gr. -1-2). 14.99 (978-0-06-180434-2(7), HarperCollins) HarperCollins Pubs.

Schmidt, Gary D. Okay for Now. 2011. (Playaway Children Ser.). (J). (gr. 5-9). 54.99 (978-1-61707-313-7(X)) Random Hse., Inc.

—Okay for Now. 2013. lib. bdg. 18.40 (978-0-606-31670-5(1)) Turtleback.

—Okay for Now: A National Book Award Winner. (ENG.). (J). (gr. 5-7). 2013. 384p. pap. 9.99 (978-0-544-02280-5(7), 1528501) 2011. (Illus.). 368p. 17.99 (978-0-547-15260-8(4), 1051989) HarperCollins Pubs. (Clarion Bks.).

—Pay Attention, Carter Jones. 2019. (ENG.). 224p. (J). (gr. 5-7). 16.99 (978-0-544-79085-8(5), 1639146, Clarion Bks.) HarperCollins Pubs.

—The Wednesday Wars. 2008. (978-0-545-10562-0(5)) Scholastic, Inc.

—The Wednesday Wars. 2009. lib. bdg. 18.40 (978-0-606-10573-6(5)) Turtleback.

—The Wednesday Wars: A Newbery Honor Award Winner. (ENG.). (J). (gr. 5-7). 2009. 288p. pap. 9.99 (978-0-547-23760-2(X), 1083872) 2007. 272p. 18.99 (978-0-618-72483-3(4), 100515) HarperCollins Pubs. (Clarion Bks.).

Schmidt, Tiffany. Bookish Boyfriends. 2018. (ENG.). 272p. (gr. 8-17). pap. 9.99 (978-1-4197-2860-0(1), 1199603, Amulet Bks.) Abrams, Inc.

—Boy Next Story: A Bookish Boyfriends Novel. 2019. (ENG., Illus.). 272p. (gr. 7-17). pap. 9.99 (978-1-4197-3436-6(9), 1210203, Amulet Bks.) Abrams, Inc.

—Talk Nerdy to Me: A Bookish Boyfriends Novel. 2020. (Bookish Boyfriends Ser.). (ENG.). 336p. (J). (gr. 7-17). pap. 9.99 (978-1-4197-4010-7(5), 1295903, Amulet Bks.) Abrams, Inc.

Schmitt, Gary. R. O. Dents in the School. 2009. 73p. pap. 19.95 (978-1-60813-737-4(6)) America Star Bks.

Schmitt, H. D. Pee Wee Pickle Goes to Kinder-Garden. Spears, Sheri, illus. 2008. 20p. pap. 24.95 (978-1-60672-731-7(1)) America Star Bks.

Schnee-Bosch, Penny. Mommy Always Comes Back. Bosch, David, illus. 2013. 40p. pap. 13.95 (978-0-9727993-6-2(2)) Athanata Arts, Ltd.

Schnee, Silke. Prince Noah & the School Pirates. Sistig, Heike, illus. 2016. (Prince Noah Book Ser.). (ENG.). 32p. (J). 16.00 (978-0-87486-765-7(7)) Plough Publishing Hse.

Schneider, Robyn. The Beginning of Everything. (ENG.). 352p. (YA). (gr. 8). 2014. pap. 11.99 (978-0-06-221714-1(3)) 2013. 17.99 (978-0-06-221713-4(5)) HarperCollins Pubs. (Tegen, Katherine Bks).

Schnell, Selynn. The Backpack Jungle. 2011. 48p. pap. 16.95 (978-1-4560-3332-3(8)) America Star Bks.

Schofield-Morrison, Connie. I Got the School Spirit. Morrison, Frank, illus. 2020. (ENG.). 32p. (J). 17.99 (978-1-5476-0261-2(9), 900208429, Bloomsbury Children's Bks.) Bloomsbury Publishing USA.

Scholz, Susie. I'm Not Going to School Today. 2008. 32p. pap. 12.50 (978-1-60693-109-7(1), Eloquent Bks.) Strategic Book Publishing & Rights Agency (SBPRA).

School-Days. collector's gif. ed. 2003. (J). bds., act. bk. ed. (978-0-9744302-0-1(X)) School Days.

School Days, Cool Days! Level J, 6 vols. 128p. (gr. 2-3). 41.95 (978-0-7699-0989-9(2)) Shortland Pubns. (U. S. A.) Inc.

The School Play: Individual Title Six-Packs. (gr. -1-2). 27.00 (978-0-7635-9473-2(3)) Rigby Education.

School Time. 2003. (J). per. (978-1-57657-892-6(5)) Paradise Pr., Inc.

Schories, Pat, illus. Biscuit's Graduation Day. 2005. (J). (978-1-4155-9660-9(3), HarperFestival) HarperCollins Pubs.

S

Schorr, Bill & Smith, Ralph. Tucker Grizzwell's Worst Week Ever. 2017. (Illus.). (J). (ENG.). 248p. pap. 9.99 *(978-1-4494-6910-8(8))*; 242p. *(978-1-5182-4664-7(8))* Andrews McMeel Publishing.

Schotter, Roni. Doo-Wop Pop. Collier, Bryan, illus. 2008. 40p. (J). (gr. -1-3). lib. bdg. 17.89 *(978-0-06-057974-6(9),* Amistad) HarperCollins Pubs.

Schraff, Anne. The Accuser, 1 vol. unabr. ed. 2010. (Q Reads Ser.). (ENG.). 32p. (YA). (gr. 9-12). pap. 8.50 *(978-1-61651-188-3(5))* Saddleback Educational Publishing, Inc.

—A Boy Called Twister, 1 vol. unabr. ed. 2010. (Urban Underground Ser.). (ENG.). 180p. (YA). (gr. 9-12). pap. 11.95 *(978-1-61651-002-2(1))* Saddleback Educational Publishing, Inc.

—A Boy Called Twister. 2010. (Urban Underground — Harriet Tubman High School Ser.). (YA). lib. bdg. 20.80 *(978-0-606-14271-7(1))* Turtleback.

—The Fairest, 1 vol. unabr. ed. 2010. (Urban Underground Ser.). (ENG.). 179p. (YA). (gr. 9-12). pap. 11.95 *(978-1-61651-007-7(2))* Saddleback Educational Publishing, Inc.

—Going for Gold. 2008. 124p. lib. bdg. 13.95 *(978-0-7569-8403-8(3))* Perfection Learning Corp.

—The Haunting of Hawthorne. 2008. (Passages Ser.). 125p. (YA). (gr. 7-9). lib. bdg. 13.95 *(978-0-7569-8379-6(7))* Perfection Learning Corp.

—Like a Broken Doll, 1 vol. unabr. ed. 2010. (Urban Underground Ser.). (ENG.). 182p. (YA). (gr. 9-12). pap. 11.95 *(978-1-61651-005-3(6))* Saddleback Educational Publishing, Inc.

—Lost & Found. Langan, Paul, ed. 2007. (Bluford High Ser.). 133p. (gr. 8-12). 16.00 *(978-0-7569-8076-4(3))* Perfection Learning Corp.

—Lost & Found. 2007. (Bluford High — Scholastic Ser.: 1). lib. bdg. 16.00 *(978-1-4177-7141-7(0))* Turtleback.

—A Matter of Trust. 2007. (Bluford High — Scholastic Ser.: 2). lib. bdg. 16.00 *(978-1-4177-7142-4(9))* Turtleback.

—No Fear, 1 vol. unabr. ed. 2010. (Urban Underground Ser.). (ENG.). 198p. (YA). (gr. 9-12). pap. 11.95 *(978-1-61651-268-2(7))* Saddleback Educational Publishing, Inc.

—Outrunning the Darkness, 1 vol. unabr. ed. 2010. (Urban Underground Ser.). (ENG.). 191p. (YA). (gr. 9-12). pap. 11.95 *(978-1-61651-000-8(5))* Saddleback Educational Publishing, Inc.

—The Power of the Rose. 2008. (Passages Ser.). 94p. (YA). (gr. 7-12). pap. 8.50 *(978-0-7891-7541-0(X))*; (J). lib. bdg. 13.95 *(978-0-7569-8381-9(9))* Perfection Learning Corp.

—The Price of Friendship. 2008. (Passages Ser.). 138p. (J). (gr. 4-6). lib. bdg. 13.95 *(978-0-7569-8373-4(8))* Perfection Learning Corp.

—The Quality of Mercy. 2011. (Urban Underground — Harriet Tubman High School Ser.). (YA). lib. bdg. 20.80 *(978-0-606-14800-9(0))* Turtleback.

—Secrets in the Shadows. Langan, Paul, ed. 2007. (Bluford High Ser.). 126p. (gr. 8-12). 16.00 *(978-0-7569-8078-8(X))* Perfection Learning Corp.

—Secrets in the Shadows. 2007. (Bluford High — Scholastic Ser.: 3). lib. bdg. 16.00 *(978-1-4177-7149-3(6))* Turtleback.

—Shadows of Guilt, 1 vol. unabr. ed. 2010. (Urban Underground Ser.). (ENG.). 179p. (YA). (gr. 9-12). pap. 11.95 *(978-1-61651-001-5(3))* Saddleback Educational Publishing, Inc.

—Someone to Love Me. 2007. (Bluford High — Scholastic Ser.: 4). lib. bdg. 16.00 *(978-1-4177-7151-6(8))* Turtleback.

—Sounds of Terror, 1 vol. unabr. ed. 2010. (Q Reads Ser.). (ENG.). 32p. (YA). (gr. 9-12). pap. 8.50 *(978-1-61651-206-4(7))* Saddleback Educational Publishing, Inc.

—The Stranger, 1 vol. unabr. ed. 2010. (Urban Underground Ser.). (ENG.). 200p. (YA). (gr. 9-12). pap. 11.95 *(978-1-61651-266-8(0))* Saddleback Educational Publishing, Inc.

—To Be Somebody. 2008. (Passages Ser.). 120p. (J). (gr. 4-6). lib. bdg. 13.95 *(978-0-7569-8390-1(8))* Perfection Learning Corp.

—The Water's Edge. unabr. ed. 2011. (Urban Underground Ser.). (ENG.). 197p. (YA). (gr. 9-12). pap. 11.95 *(978-1-61651-589-8(9))* Saddleback Educational Publishing, Inc.

—Wildflower, 1 vol. unabr. ed. 2010. (Urban Underground Ser.). (ENG.). 183p. (YA). (gr. 9-12). pap. 11.95 *(978-1-61651-009-1(9))* Saddleback Educational Publishing, Inc.

—Winners & Losers, 1 vol. unabr. ed. 2012. (Urban Underground Ser.). (ENG.). 204p. (YA). (gr. 9-12). pap. 11.95 *(978-1-61651-962-9(2))* Saddleback Educational Publishing, Inc.

Schraff, Anne E. The Outcasts. 2012. (Urban Underground — Harriet Tubman High School Ser.: 21). (YA). lib. bdg. 20.80 *(978-0-606-23794-9(1))* Turtleback.

—The Rescuers. 2012. (Urban Underground — Harriet Tubman High School Ser.: 25). (YA). lib. bdg. 20.80 *(978-0-606-23798-7(4))* Turtleback.

—Second Chances. 2013. (Urban Underground — Harriet Tubman High School Ser.). (YA). lib. bdg. 20.80 *(978-0-606-31584-5(5))* Turtleback.

—Someone to Love Me. 2007. (Bluford High Ser.). 162p. (gr. 8-12). 16.00 *(978-0-7569-8079-5(8))* Perfection Learning Corp.

—Vengeance. 2012. (Urban Underground — Cesar Chavez High School Ser.: 29). (YA). lib. bdg. 20.80 *(978-0-606-26599-7(6))* Turtleback.

—Winners & Losers. 2012. (Urban Underground — Cesar Chavez High School Ser.: 30). (YA). lib. bdg. 20.80 *(978-0-606-26600-0(3))* Turtleback.

Schreiber, Ellen. Full Moon Kisses. 2013. (Full Moon Ser.: 3). (ENG.). 224p. (YA). (gr. 8). pap. 9.99 *(978-0-06-198654-3(2),* Tegen, Katherine Bks) HarperCollins Pubs.

—Magic of the Moonlight, 2. 2012. (Full Moon Ser.: 2). (ENG.). 256p. (YA). (gr. 8-12). pap. 9.99 *(978-0-06-198656-7(9),* Tegen, Katherine Bks) HarperCollins Pubs.

—Once in a Full Moon. 2011. (Full Moon Ser.: 1). (ENG.). 320p. (YA). (gr. 8). pap. 9.99 *(978-0-06-198652-9(6),* Tegen, Katherine Bks) HarperCollins Pubs.

—Vampire Kisses 7: Love Bites. 2011. (Vampire Kisses Ser.: 7). (ENG.). 208p. (YA). (gr. 8). pap. 9.99 *(978-0-06-168944-4(0),* Tegen, Katherine Bks) HarperCollins Pubs.

—Vampire Kisses 8: Cryptic Cravings. 2012. (Vampire Kisses Ser.: 8). (ENG.). 240p. (YA). (gr. 8). pap. 11.99 *(978-0-06-168947-5(5),* Tegen, Katherine Bks) HarperCollins Pubs.

—Vampire Kisses Boxed Set: Vampire Kisses; Kissing Coffins; Vampireville. 2008. (Vampire Kisses Ser.: Nos. 1-3). (J). pap. 15.99 *(978-0-06-169160-7(7),* HarperTeen) HarperCollins Pubs.

Schreiber, Joe. Con Academy. 2016. (ENG.). 240p. (YA). (gr. 9). pap. 9.99 *(978-0-544-81355-7(3),* 1641955, Clarion Bks.) HarperCollins Pubs.

—Lenny Cyrus, School Virus. Smith, Matt, illus. 2014. (ENG.). 288p. (J). (gr. 5-7). pap. 16.99 *(978-0-544-33628-5(3),* 1584174, Clarion Bks.) HarperCollins Pubs.

Schreiber, Sam. Raise Your Voice. 2004. (Illus.). 187p. (J). pap. *(978-0-439-73083-9(X))* Scholastic, Inc.

Schroeder, Lisa. Falling for You. 2013. (ENG., (YA). (gr. 9). Illus.). 384p. pap. 9.99 *(978-1-4424-4400-3(2))*; 368p. 16.99 *(978-1-4424-4399-0(5))* Simon Pulse. (Simon Pulse).

Schumacher, Julie. Black Box. 2010. (ENG.). 176p. (YA). (gr. 7-18). pap. 7.99 *(978-0-440-24064-8(6),* Delacorte Bks. for Young Readers) Random Hse. Children's Bks.

Schusterman, Michelle. Spotlight on Coding Club! #4. 2018. (Girls Who Code Ser.: 4). (Illus.). 144p. (J). (gr. 3-7). 13.99 *(978-0-399-54254-1(X),* Penguin Workshop) Penguin Young Readers Group.

Schwartz, Amy & Marcus, Leonard S. Oscar: The Big Adventure of a Little Sock Monkey. Schwartz, Amy, illus. 2006. (Illus.). 32p. (J). (gr. -1-2). 16.99 *(978-0-06-072622-5(9),* Tegen, Katherine Bks) HarperCollins Pubs.

Scieszka, Jon. The All-Purpose SPHDZ Boxed Set: SPHDZ Book #1!; SPHDZ Book #2!; SPHDZ Book #3!; SPHDZ 4 Life!, Set. Prigmore, Shane, illus. 2013. (Spaceheadz Ser.). (ENG.). 864p. (J). (gr. 2-5). pap. 23.99 *(978-1-4424-9858-7(7),* Simon & Schuster Bks. For Young Readers) Simon & Schuster Bks. For Young Readers.

—Baloney (Henry P.) Smith, Lane, illus. 2005. (gr. -1-3). 17.00 *(978-0-7569-5494-9(0))* Perfection Learning Corp.

—Math Curse. 2004. (Illus.). (J). (gr. k-4). spiral bd. *(978-0-616-01778-4(2))* Canadian National Institute for the Blind/Institut National Canadien pour les Aveugles.

—Science Verse. Smith, Lane, illus. 2004. 40p. (J). (gr. 2-5). 18.99 *(978-0-670-91057-1(0),* Viking Books for Young Readers) Penguin Young Readers Group.

—SPHDZ 4 Life! Prigmore, Shane, illus. 2013. (Spaceheadz Ser.: 4). (ENG.). 192p. (J). (gr. 2-5). pap. 5.99 *(978-1-4169-7958-6(1))*;Bk. 4. 16.99 *(978-1-4169-7957-9(3))* Simon & Schuster Bks. For Young Readers. (Simon & Schuster Bks. For Young Readers).

—SPHDZ Book #1! Prigmore, Shane, illus. (Spaceheadz Ser.: 1). (ENG.). (J). (gr. 2-5). 2011. 192p. pap. 7.99 *(978-1-4424-1986-5(5))* 2010. 176p. 14.99 *(978-1-4169-7951-7(4))* Simon & Schuster Bks. For Young Readers. (Simon & Schuster Bks. For Young Readers).

—SPHDZ Book #2! Prigmore, Shane, illus. 2011. (Spaceheadz Ser.: 2). (ENG.). 256p. (J). (gr. 2-5). pap. 7.99 *(978-1-4169-7954-8(9),* Simon & Schuster Bks. For Young Readers) Simon & Schuster Bks. For Young Readers.

—SPHDZ Book #3! Prigmore, Shane, illus. (Spaceheadz Ser.: 3). (ENG.). 224p. (J). (gr. 2-5). 2012. pap. 8.99 *(978-1-4169-7956-2(5))* 2011. 15.99 *(978-1-4169-7955-5(7))* Simon & Schuster Bks. For Young Readers. (Simon & Schuster Bks. For Young Readers).

—2095. Smith, Lane, illus. 2005. (Time Warp Trio Ser.: No. 5). 72p. (gr. 4-7). 15.00 *(978-0-7569-5989-0(6))* Perfection Learning Corp.

Scott B, Bryon. The School by Blue Lake. 2010. 60p. pap. 27.99 *(978-1-4520-1658-0(5))* AuthorHouse.

Scott, Elizabeth. Love You Hate You Miss You. 2010. (ENG.). 304p. (YA). (gr. 8). pap. 9.99 *(978-0-06-112285-9(8),* HarperTeen) HarperCollins Pubs.

—Miracle. 2013. (ENG., Illus.). 240p. (YA). (gr. 9). pap. 9.99 *(978-1-4424-1707-6(2),* Simon Pulse) Simon Pulse.

—Perfect You. 2008. (ENG.). 304p. (YA). (gr. 9-12). pap. 9.99 *(978-1-4169-5355-5(8),* Simon Pulse) Simon Pulse.

Scott, Jordan. I Talk Like a River. Smith, Sydney, illus. 2020. (ENG.). 40p. (J). (gr. -1-3). 18.99 *(978-0-8234-4559-2(3),* Neal Porter Bks) Holiday Hse., Inc.

Scott, Kieran. Brunettes Strike Back. 2007. (ENG.). 272p. (YA). (gr. 7-18). 8.99 *(978-0-14-240778-3(X),* Speak) Penguin Young Readers Group.

—I Was a Non-Blonde Cheerleader. 2007. (ENG.). 272p. (YA). (gr. 7-18). 8.99 *(978-0-14-240910-7(3),* Speak) Penguin Young Readers Group.

—Only Everything. 2014. (True Love Ser.: 1). (ENG., Illus.). 352p. (YA). (gr. 7). pap. 9.99 *(978-1-4424-7716-2(4),* Simon & Schuster Bks. For Young Readers) Simon & Schuster Bks. For Young Readers.

—She's So Dead to Us. (He's So/She's So Trilogy Ser.). (ENG.). (YA). (gr. 7). 2011. 304p. pap. 11.99 *(978-1-4169-9952-2(3))* 2010. 288p. 16.99 *(978-1-4169-9951-5(5))* Simon & Schuster Bks. For Young Readers. (Simon & Schuster Bks. For Young Readers).

—Something True. 2015. (True Love Ser.: 3). (ENG., Illus.). 288p. (YA). (gr. 7). pap. 9.99 *(978-1-4424-7723-0(7))* Simon & Schuster Children's Publishing.

—This Is So Not Happening. (He's So/She's So Trilogy Ser.). (ENG., 320p. (YA). (gr. 7). 2013. Illus.). pap. 9.99 *(978-1-4169-9956-0(6))* 2012. 16.99 *(978-1-4169-9955-3(8))* Simon & Schuster Bks. For Young Readers. (Simon & Schuster Bks. For Young Readers).

Scott, Ladena Mae. Bossy Rossy. 2013. 36p. pap. 18.41 *(978-1-4669-8965-8(3))* Trafford Publishing.

Scott, Lisa Ann. All That Glitters. Burns, Heather, illus. 2017. 117p. (J). pap. *(978-1-338-13559-6(7))* Scholastic, Inc.

—Dreams That Sparkle, 4. Burns, Heather, illus. 2017. (Enchanted Pony Academy Ser.). (ENG.). 128p. (J). (gr. 1-4). 17.44 *(978-1-5364-0219-3(2))* Scholastic, Inc.

—Let It Glow, 3. Burns, Heather, illus. 2017. (Enchanted Pony Academy Ser.). (ENG.). 128p. (J). (gr. 1-4). 17.44 *(978-1-5364-0218-6(4))* Scholastic, Inc.

Scott, Mary Ann. New Girl, 1 vol. 2003. (ENG.). 208p. (YA). *(978-1-55041-725-8(8))* Fitzhenry & Whiteside, Ltd.

—New Girl, 1 vol. 2004. (ENG.). 208p. (YA). (gr. 8-9). pap. 5.95 *(978-1-55041-727-2(4),* f5198467-0f01-464f-93b4-acbac286a983) Fitzhenry & Whiteside, Ltd. CAN. Dist: Firefly Bks., Ltd.

Scott, Michele. Dark Harmony: A Vivienne Taylor Horse Lover's Mystery, 0 vols. 2014. (Fairmont Riding Academy Ser.: 2). (ENG.). 384p. (YA). (gr. 7-12). pap. 9.99 *(978-1-4778-4726-8(X),* 9781477847268, Skyscape) Amazon Publishing.

—Perfect Harmony: A Vivienne Taylor Horse Lover's Mystery, 0 vols. 2014. (Fairmont Riding Academy Ser.: 3). (ENG.). 274p. (YA). (gr. 7-9). pap. 9.99 *(978-1-4778-4779-4(0),* 9781477847794, Skyscape) Amazon Publishing.

—Silent Harmony: A Vivienne Taylor Horse Lover's Mystery, 0 vols. unabr. ed. 2013. (Fairmont Riding Academy Ser.: 1). (ENG.). 256p. (YA). (gr. 7-12). pap. 9.99 *(978-1-4778-1713-1(1),* 9781477817131, Skyscape) Amazon Publishing.

Scotton, Rob. Love, Splat. Scotton, Rob, illus. (Splat the Cat Ser.). (ENG., Illus.). 40p. (J). (gr. -1-2). 2011. 9.99 *(978-0-06-207776-9(7))* 2008. 17.99 *(978-0-06-083157-8(X))* HarperCollins Pubs. (HarperCollins).

—On with the Snow. 2013. (Splat the Cat 8X8 Ser.). (J). lib. bdg. 13.55 *(978-0-606-27152-3(X))* Turtleback.

—Splat & the Cool School Trip. Scotton, Rob, illus. 2013. (Splat the Cat Ser.). (ENG., Illus.). 40p. (J). (gr. -1-3). 17.99 *(978-0-06-213386-1(1),* HarperCollins) HarperCollins Pubs.

—Splat the Cat. Scotton, Rob, illus. 2008. (Splat the Cat Ser.). (ENG., Illus.). 40p. (J). (gr. -1-3). 17.99 *(978-0-06-083154-7(5))*; lib. bdg. 17.89 *(978-0-06-083155-4(3))* HarperCollins Pubs. (HarperCollins).

—Splat the Cat. 2011. (J). (gr. -1-2). 29.95 *(978-0-545-23794-9(7))* Weston Woods Studios, Inc.

—Splat the Cat: Splat the Cat Sings Flat. 2011. (I Can Read Level 1 Ser.). (ENG., Illus.). 32p. (J). (gr. -1-3). 16.99 *(978-0-06-197854-8(X),* HarperCollins) HarperCollins Pubs.

—Splat the Cat: The Name of the Game. 2012. (I Can Read Level 1 Ser.). (ENG., Illus.). 32p. (J). (gr. -1-3). 16.99 *(978-0-06-209015-7(1),* HarperCollins) HarperCollins Pubs.

—Splat the Cat: Back to School, Splat! Scotton, Rob, illus. 2011. (Splat the Cat Ser.). (ENG., Illus.). 24p. (J). (gr. -1-3). pap. 3.99 *(978-0-06-197851-7(5),* HarperFestival) HarperCollins Pubs.

—Splat the Cat: Big Reading Collection. Scotton, Rob, illus. 2012. (I Can Read Level 1 Ser.). (ENG., Illus.). 100p. (J). (gr. k-3). pap. 19.99 *(978-0-06-209029-4(1),* HarperCollins) HarperCollins Pubs.

—Splat the Cat: Splat the Cat Sings Flat. Scotton, Rob, illus. 2011. (I Can Read Level 1 Ser.). (ENG., Illus.). 32p. (J). (gr. -1-3). pap. 4.99 *(978-0-06-197853-1(1),* HarperCollins) HarperCollins Pubs.

—Up in the Air at the Fair. 2014. (Splat the Cat: I Can Read Ser.). (J). lib. bdg. 13.55 *(978-0-606-35059-4(4))* Turtleback.

Scotton, Rob & Driscoll, Laura. I Scream for Ice Cream. 2015. (Splat the Cat: I Can Read Ser.). (J). lib. bdg. 13.55 *(978-0-606-36948-0(1))* Turtleback.

Scruggs, Sheldon. Tyler: The Strongest Boy on the Block. 2012. 140p. pap. 12.95 *(978-1-4575-1355-8(2))* Dog Ear Publishing, LLC.

Seals, Hollie. When You Can't Find the Words. 2007. 144p. per. 11.95 *(978-0-595-45023-7(7))* iUniverse, Inc.

Searl, Duncan. Ellen Tebbits. Friedland, Joyce & Kessler, Rikki, eds. 2007. (Novel-Ties Ser.). (Illus.). 26p. pap. 16.95 *(978-0-7675-3531-1(6))* Learning Links Inc.

Searl, Duncan, et al. Keep the Lights Burning, Abbie. Friedland, Joyce & Kessler, Rikki, eds. 2007. (Novel-Ties Ser.). (Illus.). 25p. pap. 16.95 *(978-0-7675-1456-9(4))* Learning Links Inc.

Second and Fourth Grade Franklin Elementary. The Cat Has Class! 2007. (Illus.). 32p. (J). (gr. k-10). 16.95 *(978-0-929915-71-5(2))* Headline Bks., Inc.

Sedell, Kirsten J. Remembering Sarah: A Child's Story. 2007. (J). *(978-0-9800838-0-4(X))* Sedell, Kirsten.

Sedoti, Chelsea. Hundred Lies of Lizzie Lovett. 2017. (ENG.). 400p. (YA). (gr. 8-12). 17.99 *(978-1-4926-3608-3(8),* 9781492636083) Sourcebooks, Inc.

Seeberger, Beverley, illus. Razzle Dazzler. 2007. (J). per. 15.00 *(978-0-9713589-8-0(2))* Ubaviel's Gifts.

Seegert, Scott & Martin, John. Sci-Fi Junior High: Crash Landing. 2018. (Sci-Fi Junior High Ser.: 2). (ENG., Illus.). 336p. (J). (gr. 3-7). 13.99 *(978-0-316-31521-0(4),* Jimmy Patterson) Little Brown & Co.

Segal, Douglas. I Can Go to School: An I-Can-Do-It Book. Widdowson, Kay, illus. 2007. (ENG.). 10p. (J). (gr. -1-k). bds. 10.95 *(978-1-58117-594-3(9),* Intervisual/Piggy Toes) Bendon, Inc.

Segal, Zoe. Confessions of a Tenth-Grade Social Climber. 2005. 290p. (YA). *(978-0-618-44981-1(7))* Houghton Mifflin Harcourt Publishing Co.

Selfors, Suzanne. Coffeehouse Angel. 2010. (ENG.). 288p. (YA). (gr. 7-12). 24.94 *(978-0-8027-9812-1(8),* 9780802798121) Walker & Co.

—A Semi-Charming Kind of Life. 2015. (Ever after High Ser.: Bk. 3). (ENG., Illus.). 224p. (J). E-Book *(978-0-316-40135-7(8))* Little Brown & Co.

Sellers, Sandra. Gran's Story II: A Shy Maiden Finds Her Voice in the Tune of an Old Fiddle. 2010. 28p. pap. 16.99 *(978-1-4269-2776-8(2))* Trafford Publishing.

—Gran's Story IV: Gathering Wild Violets. 2011. 24p. (gr. -1). pap. 15.99 *(978-1-4269-5707-9(6))* Trafford Publishing.

Sempe & Goscinny. Los Recreos del Pequeno Nicolas. 2003. (SPA., Illus.). 116p. (J). (gr. 3-5). pap. 9.95 *(978-84-204-4814-5(1))* Santillana USA Publishing Co., Inc.

Serafin, Jordan. Bella: The Crooked Hat Witch. Rubino, Alisa A., illus. 2004. (J). *(978-0-932991-57-7(2))* Place In The Woods, The.

Serwacki, Kevin & Pallace, Chris. Joey & Johnny, the Ninjas: Get Mooned. Serwacki, Kevin & Pallace, Chris, illus. 2015. (Joey & Johnny, the Ninjas Ser.: 1). (ENG., Illus.). 320p. (J). (gr. 3-7). 12.99 *(978-0-06-229933-8(6),* Balzer & Bray) HarperCollins Pubs.

Seuling, Barbara. Robert & the Great Escape. Brewer, Paul, illus. 2003. (Robert Bks.). (ENG.). 120p. (J). 15.95 *(978-0-8126-2700-8(8))* Cricket Bks.

—Robert & the Happy Endings. Brewer, Paul, illus. 2007. (Robert Bks.). (ENG.). 160p. (J). (gr. 1-4). 16.95 *(978-0-8126-2748-0(2))* Cricket Bks.

—Robert & the Lemming Problem. Brewer, Paul, illus. 2003. (Robert Bks.). (ENG.). 120p. (J). 15.95 *(978-0-8126-2686-5(9))* Cricket Bks.

—Robert & the Practical Jokes. Brewer, Paul, illus. 2006. (Robert Bks.). (ENG.). 150p. (J). (gr. k-4). 16.95 *(978-0-8126-2741-1(5))* Cricket Bks.

—Robert Finds a Way. 2005. (Robert Bks.). (ENG., Illus.). 150p. (J). 15.95 *(978-0-8126-2734-3(2))* Cricket Bks.

—Robert Takes a Stand. Brewer, Paul, illus. 2004. (Robert Bks.). (ENG.). 120p. (J). 15.95 *(978-0-8126-2712-1(1))* Cricket Bks.

S.E.W. The Year at Widows' Creek: The Beginning. 2009. 44p. pap. 17.49 *(978-1-4389-5546-9(4))* AuthorHouse.

Sewell, Kristin. A Collection of Seven Children's Stories. 2012. 80p. pap. 28.99 *(978-1-4685-3770-3(9))* AuthorHouse.

Sewer, Anecia. Why Transfer Day, Anyway? Samuel, Karen, illus. 2007. 16p. (J). 15.99 *(978-0-9752986-0-2(7))* Research Institute Pr., The.

Seyforth, Edward L. A Horribly Frightening Deception, 1 vol. 2009. 75p. pap. 19.95 *(978-1-61546-260-5(0))* America Star Bks.

Shade, Jeff. An Unusual Education. 2010. (J). pap. *(978-0-88092-317-0(2))* Royal Fireworks Publishing Co.

Sham And Geri Mahabir. Freddie Learns Responsibility. 2009. 24p. pap. 13.99 *(978-1-4389-5573-5(1))* AuthorHouse.

Shane, Rachel. Alice in Wonderland High. 2015. (ENG.). 300p. (YA). 17.99 *(978-1-4405-8466-4(4),* Simon Pulse) Simon Pulse.

Shang, Wendy Wan-Long. The Great Wall of Lucy Wu. 2013. (ENG.). 320p. (J). (gr. 3-7). pap. 8.99 *(978-0-545-16216-6(5),* Scholastic Paperbacks) Scholastic, Inc.

Shank, Marilyn Sue. Child of the Mountains. 2013. 272p. (J). (gr. 4-7). 7.99 *(978-0-375-87331-7(5),* Yearling) Random Hse. Children's Bks.

Shann, Taylor. Strange Day. 2003. (J). 13.00 *(978-0-9679552-4-7(6))* Mushroom Cloud Pr. of Orlando.

Sharkey, Niamh. I'm a Happy Hugglewug: Laugh & Play the Hugglewug Way. Sharkey, Niamh, illus. 2008. (ENG., Illus.). 34p. (J). (gr. k-k). bds. 6.99 *(978-0-7636-3981-5(8))* Candlewick Pr.

Sharma, Nick. Shalu, Holi: The Festival of Colors. 2015. (ENG., Illus.). 38p. (J). (gr. -1-3). 9.00 *(978-0-9914804-3-2(0))* Penman Productions.

Sharmat, Marjorie Weinman & Sharmat, Mitchell. The Princess of the Fillmore Street School. Brunkus, Denise, illus. 2005. (Olivia Sharp: Agent for Secrets Ser.). 80p. (J). (gr. 3-7). 5.99 *(978-0-440-42060-6(1),* Yearling) Random Hse. Children's Bks.

Sharp, N. L. Effie's Image. 2008. (ENG., Illus.). 29p. pap. 8.95 *(978-0-9759829-2-1(3))* Prairieland Pr.

Sharpe, Luke. Billy Sure Kid Entrepreneur & the Attack of the Mysterious Lunch Meat. Ross, Graham, illus. 2017. (Billy Sure Kid Entrepreneur Ser.: 12). (ENG.). 160p. (J). (gr. 3-7). pap. 6.99 *(978-1-4814-7909-7(1),* Simon Spotlight) Simon Spotlight.

—Billy Sure Kid Entrepreneur & the Everything Locator. Ross, Graham, illus. 2016. (Billy Sure Kid Entrepreneur Ser.: 10). (ENG.). 160p. (J). (gr. 3-7). pap. 6.99 *(978-1-4814-6898-5(7),* Simon Spotlight) Simon Spotlight.

Shaw, LaVerne. Mesa Magic. 2006. 184p. per. 19.95 *(978-1-59879-238-6(5))* Lifevest Publishing, Inc.

Shaw, Susan. One of the Survivors. (ENG.). 208p. (J). (gr. 5-9). 2011. pap. 6.99 *(978-1-4169-6389-9(8))* 2009. 15.99 *(978-1-4169-6129-1(1))* McElderry, Margaret K. Bks. (McElderry, Margaret K. Bks.).

Shea, Bob. Dinosaur vs. School. Shea, Bob, illus. 2016. (Dinosaur vs. Book Ser.: 5). (ENG., Illus.). 32p. (J). (gr. -1-k). bds. 7.99 *(978-1-4231-6094-6(0))* Hyperion Bks. for Children.

Shea, John & Harmon, Michael B. A Kid from Southie. 2011. 240p. (YA). (gr. 9-18). 16.95 *(978-1-934813-53-9(2))* Westside Bks.

Shefelman, Janice. Anna Maria's Gift. Papp, Robert, illus. 2011. (Stepping Stone Book(TM) Ser.). 112p. (J). (gr. 2-5). pap. 4.99 *(978-0-375-85882-6(2),* Random Hse. Bks. for Young Readers) Random Hse. Children's Bks.

Shefelman, Janice Jordan. Anna Maria's Gift. Papp, Robert, illus. 2010. (Stepping Stones Chapter Book: History Ser.). (ENG.). 112p. (J). (gr. 1-4). lib. bdg. 17.44 *(978-0-375-95881-9(9))* Random House Publishing Group.

Sheinkin, Steve. Abraham Lincoln, Pro Wrestler. Swaab, Neil, illus. 2019. (Time Twisters Ser.). (ENG.). 176p. (J). pap. 8.99 *(978-1-250-20787-6(8),* 900201775) Roaring Brook Pr.

Sheinmel, Alyssa. R. I. P. Eliza Hart. 2017. (ENG.). 336p. (YA). (gr. 7). 18.99 *(978-1-338-08762-8(2),* Scholastic Pr.) Scholastic, Inc.

Sheinmel, Courtney. The Kindness Club: Chloe on the Bright Side. 2016. (Kindness Club Ser.). (ENG.). 224p. (J). 15.99 *(978-1-68119-091-4(5),* 900158417, Bloomsbury USA Childrens) Bloomsbury Publishing USA.

—The Kindness Club: Designed by Lucy. (Kindness Club Ser.). (ENG.). 224p. (J). 2018. pap. 7.99 *(978-1-68119-899-6(1),* 900191667, Bloomsbury Children's Bks.) 2017. 15.99 *(978-1-68119-117-1(2),* 900159227, Bloomsbury USA Childrens) Bloomsbury Publishing USA.

—Sincerely: Sincerely, Sophie; Sincerely, Katie. 2010. (ENG.). 400p. (J). (gr. 3-7). 15.99 *(978-1-4169-4010-4(3),* Simon & Schuster Bks. For Young Readers) Simon & Schuster Bks. For Young Readers.

—Sincerely: Sincerely, Sophie, Sincerely, Katie. 2011. (ENG.). 416p. (J). (gr. 3-7). pap. 8.99 *(978-1-4169-4022-7(7),* Simon & Schuster Bks. For Young Readers) Simon & Schuster Bks. For Young Readers.

—Stella Batts: None of Your Beeswax. Bell, Jennifer A., illus. 2014. (Stella Batts Ser.). (ENG.). 184p. (J). (gr. 1-3). 9.99 *(978-1-58536-853-2(9),* 203677) Sleeping Bear Pr.

—Stella Batts Needs a New Name. Bell, Jennifer A., illus. 2012. (Stella Batts Ser.). (ENG.). 160p. (J). (gr. 1-3). pap. 7.99 *(978-1-58536-183-0(6),* 202266);1. lib. bdg. 9.99 *(978-1-58536-185-4(2),* 202267) Sleeping Bear Pr.

—Stella Batts Scaredy Cat. Bell, Jennifer A., illus. 2016. (Stella Batts Ser.). (ENG.). 160p. (J). (gr. 1-3). 9.99 *(978-1-58536-919-5(5),* 204026) Sleeping Bear Pr.

—Superstar. Bell, Jennifer A., illus. 2015. (Stella Batts Ser.). (ENG.). 184p. (J). (gr. 1-3). pap. 5.99 *(978-1-58536-856-3(3)*, 203956) Sleeping Bear Pr.

Sheldon, Dyan. The Crazy Things Girls Do for Love. 2011. (ENG., Illus.). 352p. (YA). (gr. 7-9). 16.99 *(978-0-7636-5018-6(8))* Candlewick Pr.

Sheldon, Kaylene Kauwila. A Day with Makana. 2007.Tr. of I Kekahi la me Makana. (ENG & HAW., Illus.). 19p. (J). lib. bdg. *(978-0-9773495-2-4(7))* Na Kamalei Koolauloa Early Education Program.

Shelton, Crystal G. Theodore's Rings. 2013. 24p. pap. 24.95 *(978-1-62709-378-1(8))* America Star Bks.

Shen, E. L. The Comeback: A Figure Skating Novel. 2021. (ENG., Illus.). 272p. (J). 16.99 *(978-0-374-31379-1(2)*, 900221649, Farrar, Straus & Giroux (BYR)) Farrar, Straus & Giroux.

Shepard, Sara. Burned. 2013. (Pretty Little Liars Ser.: 12). (YA). lib. bdg. 20.85 *(978-0-606-32177-8(2))* Turtleback.

—Deadly. 2014. (Pretty Little Liars Ser.: 14). (YA). lib. bdg. 20.85 *(978-0-606-35972-6(9))* Turtleback.

—Flawless. 2007. (Pretty Little Liars Ser.: No. 2). (ENG.). 352p. (YA). (gr. 9-12). 16.99 *(978-0-06-088733-9(8)*, HarperTeen) HarperCollins Pubs.

—Flawless. 2008. (Pretty Little Liars Ser.: 2). (YA). lib. bdg. 20.85 *(978-0-606-12267-2(2))* Turtleback.

—The Good Girls. 2015. (Perfectionists Ser.: 2). (ENG.). 368p. (YA). (gr. 9). 17.99 *(978-0-06-207452-2(0)*, HarperTeen) HarperCollins Pubs.

—Perfect. 2007. (Pretty Little Liars Ser.: No. 3). (ENG.). 320p. (YA). (gr. 9-12). 16.99 *(978-0-06-088736-0(2)*, HarperTeen) HarperCollins Pubs.

—The Perfectionists. 2014. (Perfectionists Ser.: 1). (ENG.). 336p. (YA). (gr. 9). 17.99 *(978-0-06-207469-0(5)*, HarperTeen) HarperCollins Pubs.

—The Perfectionists TV Tie-In Edition. 2019. (ENG.). 352p. (YA). (gr. 9). pap. 10.99 *(978-0-06-296756-5(8)*, HarperTeen) HarperCollins Pubs.

—Pretty Little Liars. 2007. (Pretty Little Liars Ser.: 1). (ENG.). 304p. (YA). (gr. 9-12). pap. 10.99 *(978-0-06-088732-2(X)*, HarperTeen) HarperCollins Pubs.

—Pretty Little Liars #10: Ruthless. (Pretty Little Liars Ser.: 10). (ENG.). (YA). (gr. 9). 2012. 368p. pap. 10.99 *(978-0-06-208187-2(X))* 2011. 352p. 17.99 *(978-0-06-208186-5(1))* HarperCollins Pubs. (HarperTeen).

—Pretty Little Liars #11: Stunning. 2013. (Pretty Little Liars Ser.: 11). (ENG.). 336p. (YA). (gr. 9). pap. 10.99 *(978-0-06-208190-2(X)*, HarperTeen) HarperCollins Pubs.

—Pretty Little Liars #12: Burned. 2013. (Pretty Little Liars Ser.: 12). (ENG.). 352p. (YA). (gr. 9). pap. 10.99 *(978-0-06-208193-3(4)*, HarperTeen) HarperCollins Pubs.

—Pretty Little Liars #14: Deadly. (Pretty Little Liars Ser.: 14). (ENG.). (YA). (gr. 9). 2014. 336p. pap. 11.99 *(978-0-06-219975-1(7))* 2013. 320p. 17.99 *(978-0-06-219974-4(9))* HarperCollins Pubs. (HarperTeen).

—Pretty Little Liars #15: Toxic. 2014. (Pretty Little Liars Ser.: 15). (ENG.). 336p. (YA). (gr. 9). 17.99 *(978-0-06-228701-4(X)*, HarperTeen) HarperCollins Pubs.

—Pretty Little Liars #2: Flawless. 2008. (Pretty Little Liars Ser.: 2). (ENG.). 352p. (YA). (gr. 9-12). pap. 10.99 *(978-0-06-088735-3(4)*, HarperTeen) HarperCollins Pubs.

—Pretty Little Liars #3: Perfect, No. 3. 2008. (Pretty Little Liars Ser.: 3). (ENG.). 336p. (YA). (gr. 9-12). pap. 11.99 *(978-0-06-088738-4(9)*, HarperTeen) HarperCollins Pubs.

—Pretty Little Liars #5: Wicked. 2009. (Pretty Little Liars Ser.: 5). (ENG.). 336p. (YA). (gr. 9). pap. 12.99 *(978-0-06-156610-3(1)*, HarperTeen) HarperCollins Pubs.

—Pretty Little Liars #7: Heartless. 2010. (Pretty Little Liars Ser.: 7). (ENG.). 304p. (YA). (gr. 9-18). pap. 10.99 *(978-0-06-156616-5(0)*, HarperTeen) HarperCollins Pubs.

—Pretty Little Liars #8: Wanted. (Pretty Little Liars Ser.: 8). (ENG.). (YA). (gr. 9). 2011. 288p. pap. 10.99 *(978-0-06-156619-6(5))* 2010. 272p. 16.99 *(978-0-06-156617-2(9))* HarperCollins Pubs. (HarperTeen).

—Pretty Little Liars #9: Twisted. (Pretty Little Liars Ser.: 9). (ENG.). (YA). (gr. 9). 2012. 336p. pap. 11.99 *(978-0-06-208102-5(0))* 2011. 320p. 16.99 *(978-0-06-208101-8(2))* HarperCollins Pubs. (HarperTeen).

—Pretty Little Liars Bind-Up #2: Perfect & Unbelievable. 2014. (Pretty Little Liars Ser.). (ENG.). 672p. (YA). (gr. 9). pap. 10.99 *(978-0-06-232293-7(1)*, HarperTeen) HarperCollins Pubs.

—Pretty Little Liars Box Set: Books 1 To 4, 4 vols., Set, Bks. 1-4. 2009. (Pretty Little Liars Ser.: Bks. 1-4). (ENG.). (YA). (gr. 9). pap. 39.99 *(978-0-06-180131-0(3)*, HarperTeen) HarperCollins Pubs.

—Pretty Little Liars: Pretty Little Secrets. (Pretty Little Liars Companion Novel Ser.). (ENG.). (YA). (gr. 9). 2013. 480p. pap. 9.99 *(978-0-06-212592-7(3))* 2012. 464p. 17.99 *(978-0-06-212591-0(5))* HarperCollins Pubs. (HarperTeen).

—Ruthless. 2012. (Pretty Little Liars Ser.: 10). (YA). lib. bdg. 20.85 *(978-0-606-26873-8(1))* Turtleback.

—Stunning. 2013. (Pretty Little Liars Ser.: 11). (YA). lib. bdg. 20.85 *(978-0-606-31813-6(5))* Turtleback.

—Twisted. 2012. (Pretty Little Liars Ser.: 9). (YA). lib. bdg. 20.85 *(978-0-606-26288-0(1))* Turtleback.

—Unbelievable. 2008. (Pretty Little Liars Ser.: No. 4). (ENG.). 352p. (J). (gr. 9-18). 16.99 *(978-0-06-088739-1(7)*, HarperTeen) HarperCollins Pubs.

Sher, Abby. Miss You Love You Hate You Bye. 2021. (ENG.). 304p. (YA). pap. 10.99 *(978-1-250-76285-6(5)*, 900178886) Square Fish.

Sherrard, Valerie. Speechless. 2007. (ENG.). 176p. (YA). (gr. 6). pap. 12.99 *(978-1-55002-701-3(8))* Dundurn Pr. CAN. Dist: Publishers Group West (PGW).

Shields, Gillian. Eternal. 2012. (Immortal Ser.: 3). (ENG.). 384p. (YA). (gr. 8). pap. 9.99 *(978-0-06-200040-8(3)*, Tegen, Katherine Bks) HarperCollins Pubs.

Shinkai, Makoto & Kanoh, Arata. Your Name. Another Side:Earthbound (light Novel) 2017. (ENG., Illus.). 192p. (gr. 8-17). 20.00 *(978-0-316-47311-8(1)*, Yen Pr.) Yen Pr. LLC.

Shmuel, Naomi. Too Far from Home. Katz, Avi, illus. 2020. (ENG.). 96p. (J). (gr. 3-7). 15.99 *(978-1-5415-4671-4(7)*, 15d83bab-1d1f-4e49-9c2f-6edeed30b6ae, Kar-Ben Publishing) Lerner Publishing Group.

Shortt, Yvonne. A New York City Public School Goes Green. 2009. 44p. pap. 19.95 *(978-0-557-07182-1(8))* Lulu Pr., Inc.

Shreve, Steve. Stan & the Toilet Monster. Shreve, Steve, illus. 2019. (ENG., Illus.). 160p. (J). (gr. 2-6). pap. 9.99 *(978-1-4778-4744-2(8)*, 9781477847442, Two Lions) Amazon Publishing.

Shreve, Susan Richards. Kiss Me Tomorrow. 2006. 220p. (J). *(978-1-4156-5592-4(8)*, Levine, Arthur A. Bks.) Scholastic, Inc.

Shubert's Choice. 2004. (YA). 9.00 *(978-1-889609-26-3(9))* Loving Guidance, Inc.

Shull, Megan. The Swap. (ENG.). 400p. (J). (gr. 5-9). 2016. pap. 7.99 *(978-0-06-231170-2(0))* 2014. 16.99 *(978-0-06-231169-6(7))* HarperCollins Pubs. (Tegen, Katherine Bks).

Shulman, Polly. Enthusiasm. 2007. 224p. (YA). (gr. 7-18). pap. 8.99 *(978-0-14-240935-0(9)*, Speak) Penguin Young Readers Group.

Shusterman, Neal. Antsy Does Time. 256p. 2010. (J). (gr. 5-18). pap. 6.99 *(978-0-14-241487-3(5)*, Puffin Books)2. 2008. (ENG.). (YA). (gr. 6-8). 21.19 *(978-0-525-47825-6(6))* Penguin Young Readers Group.

—Dread Locks #1. 2006. (Dark Fusion Ser.: 1). 176p. (YA). (gr. 7-18). 7.99 *(978-0-14-240599-4(X)*, Speak) Penguin Young Readers Group.

—The Shadow Club Rising. 2003. 208p. (YA). (gr. 7-7). 7.99 *(978-0-14-250089-7(5)*, Speak) Penguin Young Readers Group.

Siddoway, Richard M. The Cottage Park Puzzle. 2015. 200p. (YA). pap. 14.99 *(978-1-4621-1562-4(4))* Cedar Fort, Inc./CFI Distribution.

Sidney, Margaret. Five Little Peppers at School. 2011. 208p. 26.95 *(978-1-4638-9924-0(6))* Rodgers, Alan Bks.

Siggins, Gerard. Rugby Warrior: Back in School. Back in Sport. Back in Time. 2014. (Rugby Spirit Ser.: 2). (ENG., Illus.). 176p. (J). pap. 14.00 *(978-1-84717-591-5(0))* O'Brien Pr., Ltd., The IRL. Dist: Casemate Pubs. & Bk. Distributors, LLC.

Siggs, Sarah. Mud Boy: A Story about Bullying. Crosby, Amy, illus. 2019. 48p. 17.95 *(978-1-78592-870-3(8)*, 697073) Kingsley, Jessica Pubs. GBR. Dist: Hachette UK Distribution.

Sigmon-Heck, Christina. The Birthday Wish. 2012. 24p. pap. 24.95 *(978-1-4626-6207-4(2))* America Star Bks.

Silberberg, Alan. The Awesome, Almost 100% True Adventures of Matt & Craz. Silberberg, Alan, illus. 2014. (ENG., Illus.). 336p. (J). (gr. 4-8). pap. 8.99 *(978-1-4169-9433-6(5)*, Aladdin) Simon & Schuster Children's Publishing.

Silva, Kenny. The Card. 2007. 84p. per. 19.95 *(978-1-60441-320-5(4))* America Star Bks.

Silverman, Erica. Cowgirl Kate & Cocoa: School Days. Lewin, Betsy, illus. 2008. (Cowgirl Kate & Cocoa Ser.). (ENG.). 48p. (J). (gr. 1-4). pap. 5.95 *(978-0-15-206130-2(4)*, 1198404, Clarion Bks.) HarperCollins Pubs.

Silverman, Laura. You Asked for Perfect. 2019. (ENG.). 288p. (YA). (gr. 8-12). pap. 11.99 *(978-1-4926-5827-6(8))* Sourcebooks, Inc.

Silverstein, Karol Ruth. Cursed. 2019. (Illus.). 336p. (YA). (gr. 7). lib. bdg. 17.99 *(978-1-58089-940-6(4)*, Charlesbridge Teen) Charlesbridge Publishing, Inc.

Silvestro, Annie. Bunny's Book Club Goes to School. Mai-Wyss, Tatjana, illus. 2019. 40p. (J). (gr. -1-2). 17.99 *(978-0-525-64464-4(4)*, Doubleday Bks. for Young Readers) Random Hse. Children's Bks.

Simeton, Julia. Mom, Why Can't I Catch Up? 2009. 20p. pap. 12.95 *(978-1-4389-7620-4(8))* AuthorHouse.

Simmons, Andrew & Averdonz, N. R. I Was an Eighth-Grade Ninja, 1 vol., 1. Padilla, Ariel, illus. 2007. (Z Graphic Novels / Tomo Ser.). (ENG.). 160p. (J). (gr. 3-7). pap. 6.99 *(978-0-310-71300-5(5))* Zondervan.

Simmons, Cari. Picture Perfect #2: You First. 2015. (Picture Perfect Ser.: 2). (ENG.). 256p. (J). (gr. 3-7). pap. 6.99 *(978-0-06-231058-3(5)*, HarperCollins) HarperCollins Pubs.

Simmons, Cari & Alexander, Heather. Picture Perfect #1: Bending over Backwards. 2015. (Picture Perfect Ser.: 1). (ENG.). 224p. (J). (gr. 3-7). pap. 6.99 *(978-0-06-231022-4(4)*, HarperCollins) HarperCollins Pubs.

Simmons, Cari & Zulkey, Claire. Picture Perfect #3: Best Frenemies. 2015. (Picture Perfect Ser.: 3). (ENG., Illus.). 224p. (J). (gr. 3-7). pap. 6.99 *(978-0-06-231845-9(4)*, HarperCollins) HarperCollins Pubs.

Simmons, Steven J. Alice & Greta: A Tale of Two Witches. Moore, Cyd, illus. 2019. 32p. (J). (gr. -1-2). 16.99 *(978-1-62354-110-1(7))* Charlesbridge Publishing, Inc.

Simon, Charnan. Dance Team. 2013. (Surviving Southside Ser.). (ENG.). 104p. (YA). (gr. 6-12). pap. 7.95 *(978-1-4677-0707-7(4)*, c991b57f-bb73-44cf-945f-fc054f105600, Darby Creek) Lerner Publishing Group.

—Shattered Star. (Surviving Southside Ser.). (ENG.). 104p. (YA). (gr. 6-12). 2011. pap. 7.95 *(978-0-7613-6168-8(5)*, 1ed5f678-1d5d-404f-8a8f-49150e157d71, Darby Creek) 2011. lib. bdg. 27.99 *(978-0-7613-6154-1(5)*, 1a8163e0-50cc-490f-9aa9-787901e7c8fd, Darby Creek) 2015. E-Book 53.32 *(978-1-4677-6011-9(0)*, 9781467760119, Lerner Digital) Lerner Publishing Group.

Simon, Coco. Alexis Cool As a Cupcake. 2013. (Cupcake Diaries: 8). (ENG., Illus.). 160p. (J). (gr. 3-7). 17.99 *(978-1-4424-8569-3(8)*, Simon Spotlight) Simon Spotlight.

—Alexis Cool as a Cupcake. 2012. (Cupcake Diaries: 8). lib. bdg. 16.00 *(978-0-606-26334-4(9))* Turtleback.

—Alexis Gets Frosted. (Cupcake Diaries: 12). (ENG., Illus.). 160p. (J). (gr. 3-7). 2014. 17.99 *(978-1-4424-9612-5(6))* 2013. pap. 7.99 *(978-1-4424-6867-2(X))* Simon Spotlight. (Simon Spotlight).

—Alexis Gets Frosted. 2013. (Cupcake Diaries: 12). lib. bdg. 17.20 *(978-0-606-27026-7(4))* Turtleback.

—Alexis the Icing on the Cupcake. 2014. (Cupcake Diaries: 20). (ENG., Illus.). 160p. (J). (gr. 3-7). pap. 7.99 *(978-1-4814-0468-6(7)*, Simon Spotlight) Simon Spotlight.

—The Cupcake Diaries Collection (Boxed Set) Katie & the Cupcake Cure; Mia in the Mix; Emma on Thin Icing; Alexis & the Perfect Recipe. 2012. (Cupcake Diaries). (ENG.). 640p. (J). (gr. 3-7). pap. 27.99 *(978-1-4424-8445-0(4)*, Simon Spotlight) Simon Spotlight.

—Emma: Sugar & Spice & Everything Nice. 2013. (Cupcake Diaries: 15). lib. bdg. 16.00 *(978-0-606-32052-8(0))* Turtleback.

—Emma, Smile & Say "Cupcake!" 2014. (Cupcake Diaries: 11). (ENG., Illus.). 160p. (J). (gr. 3-7). 17.99 *(978-1-4424-9611-8(8)*, Simon Spotlight) Simon Spotlight.

—Katie & the Cupcake Cure. (Cupcake Diaries: 1). (ENG., 160p. (J). (gr. 3-7). 2013. Illus.). 17.99 *(978-1-4424-7490-1(4))* 2011. pap. 7.99 *(978-1-4424-2275-9(0))* Simon Spotlight. (Simon Spotlight).

—Katie & the Cupcake War. 2014. (Cupcake Diaries: 9). (ENG., Illus.). 160p. (J). (gr. 3-7). 17.99 *(978-1-4424-9609-5(6)*, Simon Spotlight) Simon Spotlight.

—Katie, Batter Up! 2013. (Cupcake Diaries: 5). (ENG., Illus.). 160p. (J). (gr. 3-7). 17.99 *(978-1-4424-8564-8(7)*, Simon Spotlight) Simon Spotlight.

—Katie Sprinkles & Surprises. 2013. (Cupcake Diaries: 17). (ENG., Illus.). 160p. (J). (gr. 3-7). 18.99 *(978-1-4424-8591-4(4))*; pap. 6.99 *(978-1-4424-8590-7(6))* Simon Spotlight. (Simon Spotlight).

—Katie Sprinkles & Surprises. 2013. (Cupcake Diaries: 17). lib. bdg. 17.20 *(978-0-606-32327-7(9))* Turtleback.

—Katie's New Recipe. (Cupcake Diaries: 13). (ENG., Illus.). 160p. (J). (gr. 3-7). 2014. 17.99 *(978-1-4814-0379-5(6))* 2013. pap. 7.99 *(978-1-4424-7168-9(9))* Simon Spotlight. (Simon Spotlight).

—Katie's New Recipe. 2013. (Cupcake Diaries: 13). lib. bdg. 16.00 *(978-0-606-27034-2(5))* Turtleback.

—Mia: A Matter of Taste. 2013. (Cupcake Diaries: 14). lib. bdg. 16.00 *(978-0-606-32042-9(3))* Turtleback.

—Mia: Fashion Plates & Cupcakes. 2014. (Cupcake Diaries: 18). lib. bdg. 16.00 *(978-0-606-35436-3(0))* Turtleback.

—Mia a Matter of Taste. 2013. (Cupcake Diaries: 14). (ENG., Illus.). 160p. (J). (gr. 3-7). 17.99 *(978-1-4424-7480-2(7))*; pap. 6.99 *(978-1-4424-7435-2(1))* Simon Spotlight. (Simon Spotlight).

—Mia Fashion Plates & Cupcakes. 2014. (Cupcake Diaries: 18). (ENG., Illus.). 160p. (J). (gr. 3-7). pap. 6.99 *(978-1-4424-9790-0(4)*, Simon Spotlight) Simon Spotlight.

—Mia in the Mix. (Cupcake Diaries: 2). (ENG., 160p. (J). (gr. 3-7). 2013. Illus.). 17.99 *(978-1-4424-7491-8(2))* 2011. pap. 7.99 *(978-1-4424-2277-3(7))* Simon Spotlight. (Simon Spotlight).

—Mia the Way the Cupcake Crumbles. 2015. (Cupcake Diaries: 26). (ENG., Illus.). 160p. (J). (gr. 3-7). pap. 6.99 *(978-1-4814-4167-4(1)*, Simon Spotlight) Simon Spotlight.

—Mia's Baker's Dozen, 6. 2012. (Cupcake Diaries: 6). (ENG.). 160p. (J). (gr. 3-7). pap. 6.99 *(978-1-4424-4613-7(7)*, Simon Spotlight) Simon & Schuster Children's Publishing.

—Mia's Baker's Dozen. 2013. (Cupcake Diaries: 6). (ENG., Illus.). 160p. (J). (gr. 3-7). 17.99 *(978-1-4424-8566-2(3)*, Simon Spotlight) Simon Spotlight.

—Mia's Baker's Dozen. 2012. (Cupcake Diaries: 6). lib. bdg. 17.20 *(978-0-606-26570-6(8))* Turtleback.

—Mia's Boiling Point. 2014. (Cupcake Diaries: 10). (ENG., Illus.). 160p. (J). (gr. 3-7). 17.99 *(978-1-4424-9610-1(X)*, Simon Spotlight) Simon Spotlight.

—Mia's Boiling Point. 2012. (Cupcake Diaries: 10). lib. bdg. 16.00 *(978-0-606-26895-0(2))* Turtleback.

Simon, Coco & West, Tracey. MIA, the Way the Cupcake Crumbles. 2015. 127p. (J). *(978-1-4806-9834-5(2)*, Simon Spotlight) Simon Spotlight.

Simon, Kitty. Preschool Here I Come! 2011. 20p. 11.99 *(978-1-4567-5779-3(2))* AuthorHouse.

Simon, Norma. All Families Are Special. Flavin, Teresa, illus. 2013. (AV2 Fiction Readalong Ser.: Vol. 59). (ENG.). 32p. (J). (gr. k-3). 34.28 *(978-1-62127-867-2(0)*, AV2 by Weigl) Weigl Pubs., Inc.

—All Families Are Special. Flavin, Teresa, illus. 2003. (ENG.). 32p. (J). (gr. -1-3). 16.99 *(978-0-8075-2175-5(2)*, 807521752) Whitman, Albert & Co.

Simone, Kriss. Fairy Forest. 2007. (ENG.). 106p. pap. 7.78 *(978-1-84799-156-0(4))* Lulu Pr., Inc.

Simone, Ni-Ni. No Boyz Allowed. 2012. lib. bdg. 20.80 *(978-0-606-26377-1(2))* Turtleback.

Simonet, Andrew. Wilder. 2021. (ENG.). 320p. (YA). pap. 10.99 *(978-1-250-21159-0(X)*, 900189992) Square Fish.

Simonson, Louise. Las Malvadas de la Escuela Secundaria. Aparicio Publishing LLC, Aparicio Publishing, tr. from ENG. Cho, Sumin, illus. 2020. (Drama en la Secundaria Ser.).Tr. of Middle School Mean Queens. (SPA.). 64p. (J). (gr. 3-6). pap. 6.95 *(978-1-4965-9317-7(0)*, 142347); lib. bdg. 25.99 *(978-1-4965-9162-3(3)*, 142079) Capstone. (Stone Arch Bks.).

Simpson, N. J. Not So Random. 2011. 200p. pap. 13.67 *(978-0-557-83059-6(1))* Lulu Pr., Inc.

Simpson, Rodney. Frannie Fern Goes to Kindergarten. 2011. 52p. pap. 20.26 *(978-1-4490-5455-7(2))* AuthorHouse.

Sinclair, Gardine. Keira at Stageschool. 2013. 186p. (J). pap. *(978-1-78299-387-2(8))* FeedARead.com.

—Stageschool by the Sea. 2013. 176p. (J). pap. *(978-1-78299-389-6(4))* FeedARead.com.

Singleton, Linda Joy. Don't Die, Dragonfly. Karre, Andrew, ed. 2004. (Seer Ser.: 1). (ENG.). 288p. (YA). pap. 9.95 *(978-0-7387-0526-2(8))* Llewellyn Pubns.

Sirod, G. p. & Sirod, G. P. Scabs. 2010. 190p. pap. *(978-1-84923-457-3(4))* YouWriteOn.

Sirowy, Alexandra. First We Were IV. (ENG.). (YA). (gr. 7). 2018. 464p. pap. 12.99 *(978-1-4814-7843-4(5))* 2017. (Illus.). 448p. 21.99 *(978-1-4814-7842-7(7))* Simon & Schuster Bks. For Young Readers. (Simon & Schuster Bks. For Young Readers).

Skármeta, Antonio. The Composition, 1 vol. Ruano, Alfonso, illus. 2003. (ENG.). 36p. (J). (gr. 3-3). pap. 8.95 *(978-0-88899-550-6(4))* Groundwood Bks. CAN. Dist: Publishers Group West (PGW).

Skead, Robert & Simmel, Mike. Mighty Mike Bounces Back: A Boy's Life with Epilepsy. 2011. 80p. (J). pap. 9.95 *(978-1-4338-1042-8(5)*, Magination Pr.) American Psychological Assn.

Skead, Robert, et al. Mighty Mike Bounces Back: A Boy's Life with Epilepsy. 2011. (ENG.). 80p. (J). 14.95 *(978-1-4338-1043-5(3)*, Magination Pr.) American Psychological Assn.

Skeers, Linda. The Impossible Patriotism Project. 2009. (Illus.). 32p. (J). (gr. -1-1). pap. 7.99 *(978-0-14-241391-3(7)*, Puffin Books) Penguin Young Readers Group.

Skipper, Angelic. Launching Out into the Deep. 2006. 14p. 9.81 *(978-1-4116-7345-8(X))* Lulu Pr., Inc.

Skye, Obert. Wonkenstein. Skye, Obert, illus. 2015. (Creature from My Closet Ser.: 1). (ENG., Illus.). 256p. (J). (gr. 4-7). pap. 9.99 *(978-1-250-01022-3(5)*, 900084759) Square Fish.

Slate, Joseph. Miss Bindergarten & the Very Wet Day. Wolff, Ashley, illus. 2015. (Penguin Young Readers, Level 2 Ser.). 32p. (J). (gr. 1-2). 4.99 *(978-0-448-48700-7(4)*, Penguin Young Readers) Penguin Young Readers Group.

—Miss Bindergarten Celebrates the Last Day of Kindergarten. Wolff, Ashley, illus. 2008. 40p. (J). (gr. -1-k). pap. 8.99 *(978-0-14-241060-8(8)*, Puffin Books) Penguin Young Readers Group.

—Miss Bindergarten Has a Wild Day in Kindergarten. Wolff, Ashley, illus. 2006. 40p. (J). (gr. -1-k). reprint ed. pap. 8.99 *(978-0-14-240709-7(7)*, Puffin Books) Penguin Young Readers Group.

—Miss Bindergarten Takes a Field Trip with Kindergarten. Wolff, Ashley, illus. 2004. 40p. (J). (gr. -1-k). pap. 8.99 *(978-0-14-240139-2(0)*, Puffin Books) Penguin Young Readers Group.

Sloan, Holly Goldberg. Counting by 7s. 2015. (CHI.). 392p. (J). pap. *(978-986-6104-68-8(0))* DaskoviK, Izdatel'sko-torgovaja korporacija.

—Counting by 7s. 2014. (ENG.). (J). (gr. 5). lib. bdg. 19.60 *(978-1-62765-616-0(2))* Perfection Learning Corp.

—Counting by 7s. 2014. (gr. 5-8). lib. bdg. 19.65 *(978-0-606-36583-3(4))* Turtleback.

—Counting By 7s. (ENG.). (J). (gr. 5-9). 2014. 416p. 9.99 *(978-0-14-242286-1(X)*, Puffin Books) 2013. 384p. 18.99 *(978-0-8037-3855-3(2)*, Dial Bks) Penguin Young Readers Group.

Slocombe, Megan. A Trip to Italy. 2013. 34p. pap. *(978-3-7103-0389-0(3))* united p.c. Verlag.

Smadja, Brigitte. Tarte aux Escargots. pap. 17.95 *(978-2-211-03633-7(3))* Archimede Editions FRA. Dist: Distribooks, Inc.

Small, Wylie J. The Great Prune Caper. 2009. 94p. pap. 9.98 *(978-1-84728-350-4(0))* Lulu Pr., Inc.

Smiley, Jane. Pie in the Sky: Book Four of the Horses of Oak Valley Ranch. 2013. (Horses of Oak Valley Ranch Ser.: 4). (ENG.). 272p. (J). (gr. 5). 7.99 *(978-0-375-87131-3(4)*, Yearling) Random Hse. Children's Bks.

Smith, Alexander Gordon. The Devil's Engine: Hellraisers: (Book 1) 2015. (Devil's Engine Ser.: 1). (ENG.). 352p. (YA). (gr. 7). 29.99 *(978-0-374-30169-9(7)*, 900140530, Farrar, Straus & Giroux (BYR)) Farrar, Straus & Giroux.

Smith, Andrew. The Size of the Truth. 2019. (Sam Abernathy Bks.). (ENG., Illus.). 272p. (J). (gr. 3-7). 17.99 *(978-1-5344-1955-1(1)*, Simon & Schuster Bks. For Young Readers) Simon & Schuster Bks. For Young Readers.

—Stand-Off. Bosma, Sam, illus. 2016. (ENG.). 432p. (YA). (gr. 7). pap. 12.99 *(978-1-4814-1830-0(0)*, Simon & Schuster Bks. For Young Readers) Simon & Schuster Bks. For Young Readers.

—Winger. Bosma, Sam, illus. (ENG.). (YA). (gr. 7). 2014. 464p. pap. 13.99 *(978-1-4424-4493-5(2))* 2013. 448p. 18.99 *(978-1-4424-4492-8(4))* Simon & Schuster Bks. For Young Readers. (Simon & Schuster Bks. For Young Readers).

Smith, Carrie. Mary's Lamb Goes to School: Lap Book Edition. Corbalán, Begoña, illus. 2016. (My First Reader's Theater Tales Ser.). (J). (gr. k). *(978-1-5021-5506-1(0))* Benchmark Education Co.

—Mary's Lamb Goes to School: Small Book Edition. Corbalán, Begoña, illus. 2016. (My First Reader's Theater Tales Ser.). (J). (gr. k). *(978-1-5021-5511-5(7))* Benchmark Education Co.

Smith, Cynthia Leitich. Diabolical. 2012. (Tantalize Ser.: 4). (ENG., Illus.). 368p. (YA). (gr. 9-12). 17.99 *(978-0-7636-5118-3(4))* Candlewick Pr.

Smith, Emma Bland. Crafting for a Cause. Marlin, Lissy, illus. 2018. (Maddy Mcguire, CEO Ser.). (ENG.). 112p. (J). (gr. 2-5). lib. bdg. 38.50 *(978-1-5321-3184-4(4)*, 28463, Calico Chapter Bks.) ABDO Publishing Co.

Smith, Evelyn. The First Fifth Form. Wiles, Frank, illus. 2013. 176p. pap. *(978-1-909423-05-3(X))* Bks. to Treasure.

—The Small Sixth Form. Wiles, Frank, illus. 2013. 200p. pap. *(978-1-909423-08-4(4))* Bks. to Treasure.

Smith, Heather. Baygirl, 1 vol. 2013. (ENG.). 288p. (YA). (gr. 8-12). pap. 12.95 *(978-1-4598-0274-2(8))* Orca Bk. Pubs. USA.

Smith, James. The Wonderer of Time. 2006. 52p. pap. 16.95 *(978-1-4241-3316-1(5))* PublishAmerica, Inc.

Smith, Jane. It's the First Day of Preschool, Chloe Zoe! Smith, Jane, illus. 2016. (Chloe Zoe Ser.). (ENG., Illus.). 32p. (J). (gr. -1-3). 12.99 *(978-0-8075-2456-5(5)*, 807524565) Whitman, Albert & Co.

Smith, Julie. Hearts for the Homeless. 2012. 28p. pap. 19.99 *(978-1-4685-5602-5(9))* AuthorHouse.

Smith, Kirsten. Trinkets. 2019. (ENG.). 288p. (YA). (gr. 9-17). pap. 10.99 *(978-0-316-45762-0(0))* Little, Brown Bks. for Young Readers.

Smith, Kourtney. The Adventures of Stanley the Staple. 2013. 28p. pap. 24.95 *(978-1-63004-276-9(5))* America Star Bks.

Smith, L. J. Dark Visions: The Strange Power; the Possessed; the Passion. 2009. (Dark Visions Ser.: Bks 1-3). (ENG.). 752p. (YA). (gr. 7). pap. 15.99 *(978-1-4169-8956-1(0)*, Simon Pulse) Simon Pulse.

Smith, Matthew Ross. Lizzy Legend. 2019. (ENG., Illus.). 240p. (J). (gr. 3-7). 17.99 *(978-1-5344-2024-3(X)*, Aladdin) Simon & Schuster Children's Publishing.

Smith-Ready, Jeri. This Side of Salvation. 2014. (ENG., Illus.). 384p. (YA). (gr. 9). 17.99 *(978-1-4424-3948-1(3)*, Simon Pulse) Simon Pulse.

Smith, Stuart. My School's a Zoo! Catrow, David, illus. 2004. 40p. (J). (gr. k-3). lib. bdg. 16.89 *(978-0-06-028511-1(7))* HarperCollins Pubs.

Smith, Yeardley. I, Lorelei. 2009. 352p. (J). (gr. 3-7). lib. bdg. 17.89 *(978-0-06-149345-4(7)*, Geringer, Laura Book) HarperCollins Pubs.

Snader, Elisa Linovitz. The Wheelchair. Robb, Kimberly Gewerth, illus. 2008. (ENG.). 24p. pap. 12.50 *(978-1-4343-6234-6(5))* AuthorHouse.

Snadowsky, Daria. Anatomy of a Boyfriend. 2008. (Anatomy of A... Ser.). (ENG.). 272p. (YA). (gr. 9). pap. 10.99 *(978-0-440-23944-4(3)*, Ember) Random Hse. Children's Bks.

S

Snicket, Lemony, pseud. Cauchemar a la Scierie. pap. 24.95 *(978-2-09-282357-6(4))* Nathan, Fernand FRA. Dist: Distribooks, Inc.

Snodgrass, Lady Cecily. The Really Rotten Princess & the Cupcake Catastrophe: Ready-To-Read Level 2. Lester, Mike, illus. 2013. (Really Rotten Princess Ser.). (ENG.). 32p. (J). (gr. k-2). 17.99 *(978-1-4424-8974-5(X))*; pap. 4.99 *(978-1-4424-8973-8(1))* Simon Spotlight. (Simon Spotlight).

Snyder, Susan E. Shivers & Shakes. 2006. (Illus.). 31p. (J). (gr. k-2). 9.95 *(978-0-9767163-5-8(6))* Kotzig Publishing, Inc.

Snyder, Zilpha Keatley. The Unseen. 2005. 199p. 16.00 *(978-0-7569-5670-7(6))* Perfection Learning Corp.

Soderberg, Erin. Puppy Pirates Super Special #2: Best in Class. 2017. (Puppy Pirates Ser.: 2). (Illus.). 128p. (J). (gr. 1-4). 5.99 *(978-1-5247-1328-7(7)*, Random Hse. Bks. for Young Readers) Random Hse. Children's Bks.

—The Quirks in Circus Quirkus. 2014. (Quirks Ser.). (ENG., Illus.). 240p. (YA). (gr. 3-6). 13.99 *(978-1-59990-790-1(9)*, 900080308, Bloomsbury USA Childrens) Bloomsbury Publishing USA.

Solomon, Michelle & Pereira, Lavinia. Too Big! Faust, Laurie A., illus. 2009. 24p. pap. 10.96 *(978-1-4251-8949-5(0))* Trafford Publishing.

Sones, Sonya. What My Girlfriend Doesn't Know. 2011. 9.68 *(978-0-7848-3389-6(3)*, Everbind) Marco Bk. Co.

—What My Girlfriend Doesn't Know. 2013. (ENG., Illus.). 320p. (YA). (gr. 7). pap. 12.99 *(978-1-4424-9384-1(4)*, Simon & Schuster Bks. For Young Readers) Simon & Schuster Bks. For Young Readers.

Sonnebom, Scott. Pete Bogg: King of the Frogs. Aburto, Jesus, illus. 2013. (Pete Bogg Ser.). (ENG.). 48p. (J). (gr. 3-5). lib. bdg. 23.99 *(978-1-4342-3284-7(0)*, 123900, Stone Arch Bks.) Capstone.

Sonnenblick, Jordan. After Ever After. 2014. (ENG.). 272p. (YA). (gr. 7-7). pap. 10.99 *(978-0-545-72287-2(X))* Scholastic, Inc.

—Curveball: the Year I Lost My Grip. (ENG.). 304p. 2014. (J). (gr. 7). pap. 10.99 *(978-0-545-32070-2(4)*, Scholastic Paperbacks) 2012. E-Book 17.99 *(978-0-545-39311-9(6))* Scholastic, Inc.

—Falling over Sideways. (ENG.). 272p. (YA). (gr. 7). 2017. pap. 10.99 *(978-0-545-86325-4(2))* 2016. 17.99 *(978-0-545-86324-7(4)*, Scholastic Pr.) Scholastic, Inc.

—The Secret Sheriff of Sixth Grade. 2017. (ENG.). 208p. (J). (gr. 5-9). 16.99 *(978-0-545-86320-9(1)*, Scholastic Pr.) Scholastic, Inc.

—Zen & the Art of Faking It. 2010. (ENG.). 272p. (J). (gr. 7-12). 9.99 *(978-0-439-83709-5(X)*, Scholastic Paperbacks) Scholastic, Inc.

Soto, Gary. Accidental Love. 2008. (ENG., Illus.). 192p. (YA). (gr. 7). pap. 9.99 *(978-0-15-206113-5(4)*, 1198363, Clarion Bks.) HarperCollins Pubs.

Souliere, Lisa. Toasters Are Easy, School Not So Much. Rockwell, Joanna, illus. 2012. 20p. pap. 10.95 *(978-1-60976-654-2(7)*, Strategic Bk. Publishing) Strategic Book Publishing & Rights Agency (SBPRA).

Sovern, Megan Jean. The Meaning of Maggie. 2015. (ENG.). 232p. (J). (gr. 3-7). pap. 7.99 *(978-1-4521-2876-4(6))* Chronicle Bks. LLC.

Sowunmi, Lakeysha. Apple Leaves. 2009. (ENG.). 48p. pap. 17.49 *(978-1-4490-2055-2(0))* AuthorHouse.

Spalding, Amy. We Used to Be Friends. 2020. (ENG., Illus.). 368p. (YA). (gr. 9-17). 17.99 *(978-1-4197-3866-1(6)*, 1269101) Abrams, Inc.

Spanabel, H. A. Skyler & the Skunks. 2009. 48p. pap. *(978-1-84923-954-7(1))* YouWriteOn.

Sparks, Kerry. Frost Bites. 2009. 92p. pap. 11.49 *(978-1-4389-5414-1(X))* AuthorHouse.

Sparks, Megan. Falling Hard, 1 vol. 2013. (Roller Girls Ser.). (ENG.). 256p. (YA). (gr. 8-10). 12.95 *(978-1-62370-023-2(X)*, 123788, Capstone Young Readers) Capstone.

—Hell's Belles, 1 vol. 2013. (Roller Girls Ser.). (ENG.). 256p. (YA). (gr. 8-10). 12.95 *(978-1-62370-024-9(8)*, 123789, Capstone Young Readers) Capstone.

—Hell's Belles/By Megan Sparks. 2013. 255p. (YA). *(978-1-62370-022-5(1)*, Capstone Young Readers) Capstone.

Spencer, James. Sally Small & the Judith-Situation. 2011. 86p. pap. *(978-1-908147-61-5(X))* YouWriteOn.

Spiegelman, Nadja. Zig & Wikki in Something Ate My Homework: Toon Books Level 3. Loeffler, Trade, illus. 2013. (Toon Ser.). (ENG.). 40p. (J). (gr. -1-3). pap. 7.99 *(978-1-935179-38-2(1)*, Toon Books) Astra Publishing Hse.

Spiegelman, Nadja & Loeffler, Trade. Zig & Wikki in Something Ate My Homework. 2013. (Toon Books Level 3 Ser.). lib. bdg. 14.75 *(978-0-606-32252-2(3))* Turtleback.

Spindler, Rebecca Williams & Spindler, Madelyn. Life According to Liz. 2012. 204p. pap. 12.95 *(978-0-9848050-5-1(2)*, Little Creek Bks.) Jan-Carol Publishing, INC.

Spinelli, Eileen. Miss Fox's Class Earns a Field Trip. Kennedy, Anne, illus. 2012. (J). *(978-1-61913-122-4(6))* Weigl Pubs., Inc.

—Miss Fox's Class Gets It Wrong. Kennedy, Anne, illus. 2018. (Miss Fox's Class Ser.). (ENG.). 32p. (J). (gr. -1-3). 7.99 *(978-0-8075-5173-8(2)*, 807551732) Whitman, Albert & Co.

—Miss Fox's Class Goes Green. Kennedy, Anne, illus. 2012. (J). 34.28 *(978-1-61913-123-1(4))* Weigl Pubs., Inc.

—Miss Fox's Class Goes Green. Kennedy, Anne, illus. 2011. (Miss Fox's Class Ser.). (ENG.). 32p. (J). (gr. -1-3). 7.99 *(978-0-8075-5167-7(8)*, 807551678) Whitman, Albert & Co.

—Peace Week in Miss Fox's Class. Kennedy, Anne, illus. 2012. (J). *(978-1-61913-155-2(2))* Weigl Pubs., Inc.

Spinelli, Jerry. Fourth Grade Rats. 2012. (ENG.). 160p. (J). (gr. 2-5). pap. 6.99 *(978-0-545-46478-9(1)*, Levine, Arthur A. Bks.) Scholastic, Inc.

—Fourth Grade Rats. 2012. lib. bdg. 16.00 *(978-0-606-26731-1(X))* Turtleback.

—Loser. 2018. (ENG.). 240p. (J). (gr. 3-7). pap. 9.99 *(978-0-06-054074-6(5)*, HarperCollins) HarperCollins Pubs.

—Loser. 2003. (J). (gr. 3-6). lib. bdg. 17.20 *(978-0-613-66899-6(5))* Turtleback.

—Smiles to Go. 2009. (ENG.). 272p. (J). (gr. 5-8). pap. 7.99 *(978-0-06-447197-8(7)*, HarperCollins) HarperCollins Pubs.

—Stargirl. 2003. (EMC Masterpiece Series Access Editions). xiv, 199p. (YA). 12.99 *(978-0-8219-2504-1(0)*, 35378) EMC/Paradigm Publishing.

—Stargirl. unabr. ed. 2004. 192p. (J). (gr. 7-18). pap. 40.00 incl. audio *(978-0-8072-0855-7(8)*, LYA 323 SP, Listening Library) Random Hse. Audio Publishing Group.

—Stargirl. 2004. (Stargirl Ser.: 1). (ENG.). 208p. (YA). (gr. 7). mass mkt. 9.99 *(978-0-440-41677-7(9)*, Laurel Leaf) Random Hse. Children's Bks.

—There's a Girl in My Hammerlock. 2008. 199p. (gr. 4-8). 16.00 *(978-0-7569-8465-6(3))* Perfection Learning Corp.

—Third Grade Angels. Bell, Jennifer A., illus. 2014. (ENG.). 160p. (J). (gr. 2-5). pap. 6.99 *(978-0-545-38773-6(6)*, Levine, Arthur A. Bks.) Scholastic, Inc.

Spirn, Michele Sobel. I Am the Turkey. Allen, Joy, illus. 2006. (I Can Read Level 2 Ser.). (ENG.). 48p. (J). (gr. k-3). pap. 4.99 *(978-0-06-053232-1(7)*, HarperCollins) HarperCollins Pubs.

—I Am the Turkey. Allen, Joy, illus. 2007. (I Can Read Bks.). 48p. (gr. -1-3). 14.00 *(978-0-7569-8055-9(0))* Perfection Learning Corp.

Spirn, Michele Sobel & Spirn, Michele S. I Am the Turkey. Allen, Joy, illus. 2004. (I Can Read Bks.). 48p. (J). (gr. k-3). 15.99 *(978-0-06-053230-7(0))* HarperCollins Pubs.

Spradlin, Michael P. Live & Let Shop. 2005. (Spy Goddess Ser.: Bk. 1). (ENG., Illus.). 224p. (gr. 7-18). 15.99 *(978-0-06-059407-7(1))* HarperCollins Pubs.

Spring, Melanie. Practice Makes Perfect. 2014. (Varsity Novel Ser.: 3). (ENG.). 192p. (YA). (gr. 7-17). pap. 12.99 *(978-0-316-22733-9(1)*, Poppy) Little, Brown Bks. for Young Readers.

—Turn It Up. 2014. (Varsity Novel Ser.: 2). (ENG.). 208p. (YA). (gr. 7-17). pap. 12.99 *(978-0-316-22724-7(2)*, Poppy) Little, Brown Bks. for Young Readers.

Springer, Nancy. Possessing Jessie. 2010. (ENG.). 128p. (YA). (gr. 7-18). pap. 16.95 *(978-0-8234-2259-3(3))* Holiday Hse., Inc.

Springstubb, Tricia. Cody & the Mysteries of the Universe. Wheeler, Eliza, illus. 2016. (Cody Ser.). (ENG.). 144p. (J). (gr. 2-5). 14.99 *(978-0-7636-5858-8(8))* Candlewick Pr.

—Cody & the Rules of Life. Wheeler, Eliza, illus. (Cody Ser.). (ENG.). 176p. (J). (gr. 2-5). 2018. pap. 7.99 *(978-1-5362-0054-6(9))* 2017. 14.99 *(978-0-7636-7920-0(8))* Candlewick Pr.

Sproule, Acquanetta M. Scamp. 2010. 40p. pap. 18.00 *(978-0-557-37187-7(2))* Lulu Pr., Inc.

Spurling, Wesley. Books for Jacob. 2009. 24p. pap. 14.79 *(978-1-4389-2231-7(0))* AuthorHouse.

—Gerry the Giraffe. 2009. 36p. pap. 16.99 *(978-1-4389-4223-0(0))* AuthorHouse.

Spurr, Judy. Trapped. 2007. 84p. per. 8.95 *(978-0-595-43915-7(2))* iUniverse, Inc.

Spyri, Johanna. How Wiseli Was Provided For. 2006. 108p. per. 9.95 *(978-1-59818-473-0(3))* Aegypan.

—Rico & Stineli. 2006. 148p. (gr. 4-7). per. 11.95 *(978-1-59818-873-8(9))* Aegypan.

St. Claire, Roxanne. They All Fall Down. 2016. (ENG.). 352p. (YA). (gr. 7). pap. 10.99 *(978-0-385-74272-6(X)*, Ember) Random Hse. Children's Bks.

St. Crow, Lili. Betrayals, 10 vols. 2010. (Strange Angels Ser.: 2). (YA). 95.75 *(978-1-4407-7156-9(1))* Recorded Bks., Inc.

—Betrayals. 2009. (Strange Angels Ser.: 2). lib. bdg. 20.85 *(978-0-606-09020-9(7))* Turtleback.

—Betrayals: A Strange Angels Novel, 2. 2009. (Strange Angels Ser.: 2). (ENG., Illus.). 304p. (YA). (gr. 7-18). pap. 26.19 *(978-1-59514-252-8(5)*, Razorbill) Penguin Young Readers Group.

—Defiance, 4. 2011. (Strange Angels Ser.: 4). (ENG.). 304p. (YA). (gr. 7-18). 26.19 *(978-1-59514-392-1(0)*, Razorbill) Penguin Young Readers Group.

St. James, James. Freak Show. 2008. (ENG.). 304p. (YA). (gr. 9-18). 8.99 *(978-0-14-241231-2(7)*, Puffin Books) Penguin Young Readers Group.

Stadelmann, Amy Marie. Olive & Beatrix: The Super-Smelly Moldy Blob, Vol. 2. Stadelmann, Amy Marie, illus. 2016. (Olive & Beatrix Ser.: 2). (ENG., Illus.). 80p. (J). (gr. k-2). 15.99 *(978-0-545-81485-0(5))* Scholastic, Inc.

Stadler, Alexander. Beverly Billingsly Takes a Bow. 2003. (ENG., Illus.). 32p. (J). (gr. -1-3). 16.00 *(978-0-15-216816-2(8)*, 1201940, Clarion Bks.) HarperCollins Pubs.

Stahler, David, Jr. Spinning Out. 2011. (ENG.). 288p. (YA). (gr. 7-17). 16.99 *(978-0-8118-7780-0(9))* Chronicle Bks. LLC.

Stalling-Patton, Deborah. Shypoodle: Getting to Know You. 2009. 40p. pap. 17.99 *(978-1-4389-3899-8(3))* AuthorHouse.

Stamper, Judith Bauer. Rocky Road Trip. Gangloff, Hope, illus. 2004. (Magic School Bus Science Chapter Bks.). 89p. (gr. 2-5). lib. bdg. 15.00 *(978-0-7569-3093-6(6))* Perfection Learning Corp.

Stampler, Ann Redisch. Afterparty. 2013. (ENG., Illus.). 416p. (YA). (gr. 9). 17.99 *(978-1-4424-2324-4(2)*, Simon Pulse) Simon Pulse.

—Where It Began. 2013. (ENG.). 384p. (YA). (gr. 7-12). 26.19 *(978-1-4424-2321-3(8))*; (gr. 9). pap. 9.99 *(978-1-4424-2322-0(6))* Simon Pulse. (Simon Pulse).

Standiford, Natalie. Breaking up Is Really, Really Hard to Do. 2005. (Dating Game Ser.: 2). (ENG.). 224p. (YA). (gr. 7-17). pap. 13.99 *(978-0-316-11041-9(8))* Little, Brown Bks. for Young Readers.

—The Dating Game, No. 1. 2005. (Dating Game Ser.: 1). (ENG.). 224p. (J). (gr. 7-17). pap. 13.99 *(978-0-316-11040-2(X))* Little, Brown Bks. for Young Readers.

—Ex-Rating. 4th rev. ed. 2006. (Dating Game Ser.: 4). (ENG.). 224p. (YA). (gr. 7-17). per. 13.99 *(978-0-316-15876-3(3))* Little, Brown Bks. for Young Readers.

—Speed Dating. 5th ed. 2006. (Dating Game Ser.: 5). (ENG.). 224p. (YA). (gr. 8-17). per. 13.99 *(978-0-316-11530-8(4))* Little, Brown Bks. for Young Readers.

Standish, Burt L. Frank Merriwell in Camp. Rudman, Jack, ed. 2003. (Frank Merriwell Ser.). (YA). (gr. 9-18). 29.95 *(978-0-8373-9324-7(8))*; pap. 9.95 *(978-0-8373-9024-6(9)*, FM-024) Merriwell, Frank Inc.

Stanek, Robert, pseud. The Bugville Critters Go to School. 2007. (ENG.). 28p. (J). per. 9.99 *(978-1-57545-145-9(X))* RP Media.

—The Bugville Critters Have a Sleepover. 2008. (ENG.). 28p. (J). per. 9.99 *(978-1-57545-146-6(8))* RP Media.

—The Bugville Critters Make New Friends: Buster Bee's School Days #2. 2008. (ENG., Illus.). 60p. (J). per. 18.95 *(978-1-57545-168-8(9))* RP Media.

—The Bugville Critters So Many Lessons to Learn. 2009. (Illus.). 68p. (J). pap. 18.95 *(978-1-57545-237-1(5)*, Reagent Pr. Bks. for Young Readers) RP Media.

—Go to School. 2008. (ENG., Illus.). 28p. (J). pap. 5.29 *(978-1-57545-188-6(3))* RP Media.

—Have Trouble at School. 2009. (Illus.). 24p. pap. 9.99 *(978-1-57545-212-8(X))*; 52p. (J). pap. 14.95 *(978-1-57545-204-3(9))* RP Media. (Reagent Pr. Bks. for Young Readers).

—Robert Stanek's Bugville Critters Storybook Treasury. 2008. (ENG., Illus.). 132p. (J). per. 24.95 *(978-1-57545-171-8(9))* RP Media.

—Robert Stanek's Bugville Critters Storybook Treasury Volume 2 (the Bugville Critters Storybook Collection, Volume 2), 4 vols., Vol. 2. 2008. (ENG., Illus.). 124p. (J). per. 24.95 *(978-1-57545-173-2(5))* RP Media.

—Stay after School. 2009. (Bugville Critters Ser.: No. 10). (ENG., Illus.). 52p. (J). 14.95 *(978-1-57545-206-7(5)*, Reagent Pr. Bks. for Young Readers) RP Media.

—Visit City Hall. 2009. (Bugville Critters Ser.: No. 12). (ENG., Illus.). 52p. (J). 14.95 *(978-1-57545-208-1(1)*, Reagent Pr. Bks. for Young Readers) RP Media.

Staniszewski, Anna. Dirt Diary. 2014. (Dirt Diary Ser.: 1). 256p. (J). (gr. 5-9). pap. 11.99 *(978-1-4022-8636-0(8)*, 9781402286360) Sourcebooks, Inc.

—The Wonder of Wildflowers. 2020. (ENG.). 192p. (J). (gr. 3-7). 17.99 *(978-1-5344-4278-8(2)*, Simon & Schuster Bks. For Young Readers) Simon & Schuster Bks. For Young Readers.

Stanton, Matt. Funny Kid Stand up (Funny Kid, #2) The Hilarious, Laugh-Out-loud Children's Series for 2023 from Million-copy Mega-bestselling Author Matt Stanton. 2017. (ENG., Illus.). 272p. (J). *(978-0-7333-3598-3(5))* Harper & Row Ltd.

Stapleton, Rhonda. Flirting with Disaster. 2010. (ENG.). 256p. (YA). (gr. 7-18). pap. 9.99 *(978-1-4169-7465-9(2)*, Simon Pulse) Simon Pulse.

Star, Danielle. The Surprise Visit (Melowy #5) 2018. (Melowy Ser.: 5). (ENG., Illus.). 96p. (J). (gr. 2-5). pap. 6.99 *(978-1-338-28176-7(3)*, Scholastic Paperbacks) Scholastic, Inc.

Stark, Henry. Heart Lessons. 2008. (ENG.). 502p. pap. 19.99 *(978-1-4196-4881-6(0))* CreateSpace Independent Publishing Platform.

Starkey, Scott. How to Beat the Bully Without Really Trying. (How to Beat the Bully Ser.). (ENG.). 272p. (J). (gr. 3-7). 2013. pap. 8.99 *(978-1-4424-8473-3(X))* 2012. 15.99 *(978-1-4424-1685-7(8))* Simon & Schuster/Paula Wiseman Bks. (Simon & Schuster/Paula Wiseman Bks.).

Starmer, Aaron. Dweeb: Burgers, Beasts, & Brainwashed Bullies. Rash, Andy, illus. 2011. (ENG.). 240p. (J). (gr. 4-6). 21.19 *(978-0-385-73705-0(X)*, Delacorte Pr.) Random Hse. Children's Bks.

Staunton, Ted. Morgan & the Money. Slavin, Bill, illus. 2008. (First Novel Ser.). (ENG.). 64p. (J). (gr. 1-5). *(978-0-88780-776-3(3))* Formac Publishing Co., Ltd.

—Morgan & the Money, 1 vol. 2008. (Formac First Novels Ser.). (ENG., Illus.). 64p. (J). (gr. 1-5). 4.95 *(978-0-88780-774-9(7)*, 774) Formac Publishing Co., Ltd. CAN. Dist: Formac Lorimer Bks. Ltd.

—Pucker up, Morgan, 1 vol. Slavin, Bill, illus. 2008. (Formac First Novels Ser.). (ENG.). 64p. (J). (gr. 1-5). 5.95 *(978-0-88780-744-2(5)*, e71cb825-7b16-4801-85e4-653b908033f6); (gr. 2-5). 14.95 *(978-0-88780-746-6(1)*, 746) Formac Publishing Co., Ltd. CAN. Dist: Lerner Publishing Group, Formac Lorimer Bks. Ltd.

Stavans, Ilan. Golemito. Villegas, Teresa, illus. 2013. (ENG.). 32p. (J). 16.95 *(978-1-58838-292-4(3)*, 8804, NewSouth Bks.) NewSouth, Inc.

Stead, Rebecca. Goodbye Stranger. 2017. (ENG.). 320p. (J). (gr. 5). 8.99 *(978-0-307-98086-1(3)*, Yearling) Random Hse. Children's Bks.

—Liar & Spy. 2013. (ENG.). 208p. (J). (gr. 3-7). 8.99 *(978-0-375-85087-5(2)*, Yearling) Random Hse. Children's Bks.

Steinberg, D. J. Kindergarten, Here I Come! Chambers, Mark, illus. 2012. (Here I Come! Ser.). 32p. (J). (gr. -1-k). pap. 5.99 *(978-0-448-45624-9(9)*, Grosset & Dunlap) Penguin Young Readers Group.

—Second Grade, Here I Come! Wood, Laura, illus. 2017. (Here I Come! Ser.). 32p. (J). (gr. k-2). pap. 5.99 *(978-0-515-15808-3(9)*, Grosset & Dunlap) Penguin Young Readers Group.

Steiner, Hartley. This Is Gabriel: Making Sense of School - 2nd Edition: A Book about Sensory Processing Disorder. 2nd rev. ed. 2012. (ENG., Illus.). 32p. pap. 12.95 *(978-1-935567-34-9(9)*, P217127) Future Horizons, Inc.

Steinke, Aron Nels. Mr. Wolf's Class: a Graphic Novel (Mr. Wolf's Class #1) 2018. (Mr. Wolf's Class Ser.: 1). (ENG., Illus.). 160p. (J). (gr. 2-5). pap. 9.99 *(978-1-338-04768-4(X))*; Vol. 1. 18.99 *(978-1-338-04769-1(8))* Scholastic, Inc. (Graphix).

Steinkellner, Teddy. Two Roads from Here. 2017. (ENG., Illus.). 448p. (YA). (gr. 9). 17.99 *(978-1-4814-3061-6(0)*, Simon & Schuster Bks. For Young Readers) Simon & Schuster Bks. For Young Readers.

Stenger, D. L. Pumpkin's Secret. 2006. (ENG.). 44p. per. 18.49 *(978-1-4259-5055-2(8))* AuthorHouse.

Step Up 2 - The Streets. 2008. 160p. pap. 4.99 *(978-1-4231-1319-5(5))* Disney Pr.

Stephenson, Lynda. Dancing with Elvis. (YA). (gr. 7). 2006. (ENG.). 331p. per. 8.00 *(978-0-8028-5300-4(5))* 2005. 323p. 17.00 *(978-0-8028-5293-9(9))* Eerdmans, William B. Publishing Co. (Eerdmans Bks For Young Readers).

Stern, A. J. Check, Please!, 3 vols. Marts, Doreen Mulryan, illus. 2010. (Frankly, Frannie Ser.: 3). 128p. (J). (gr. 1-3). pap. 5.99 *(978-0-448-45352-1(5)*, Grosset & Dunlap) Penguin Young Readers Group.

—Fashion Frenzy. Marts, Doreen Mulryan, illus. 2011. (Frankly, Frannie Ser.: 6). 128p. (J). (gr. 1-3). pap. 6.99 *(978-0-448-45544-0(7)*, Grosset & Dunlap) Penguin Young Readers Group.

—Frankly, Frannie, 1 vol. Marts, Doreen Mulryan, illus. 2010. (Frankly, Frannie Ser.: 1). 128p. (J). (gr. 1-3). pap. 6.99 *(978-0-448-45348-4(7)*, Grosset & Dunlap);1. (ENG.). (gr. 2-5). 18.69 *(978-0-448-45349-1(5))* Penguin Young Readers Group.

—Miss Fortune, 7 vols. Marts, Doreen Mulryan, illus. 2012. (Frankly, Frannie Ser.: 7). 128p. (J). (gr. 1-3). pap. 6.99 *(978-0-448-45748-2(2)*, Grosset & Dunlap) Penguin Young Readers Group.

—Principal for the Day. Marts, Doreen Mulryan, illus. 2011. (Frankly, Frannie Ser.: 5). 128p. (J). (gr. 1-3). pap. 5.99 *(978-0-448-45542-6(0)*, Grosset & Dunlap);5. (ENG.). (gr. 2-5). 18.69 *(978-0-448-45543-3(9))* Penguin Young Readers Group.

Stern, Ricki & Worcester, Heidi P. Adventure: Lonely Leader. Bates, Amy, illus. 2003. (Beryl E. Bean Ser.: No. 3). 64p. (J). lib. bdg. 16.89 *(978-0-06-028774-0(8))* HarperCollins Pubs.

Sternberg, Julie. Everything's Changed. Wright, Johanna, illus. 2017. (Top-Secret Diary of Celie Valentine Ser.). (ENG.). 176p. (J). (gr. 3-7). 16.95 *(978-1-62979-672-7(7)*, Astra Young Readers) Astra Publishing Hse.

Stevens, Cara J. Creepers Crashed My Party. 2018. (Redstone Jr. High Ser.: 2). lib. bdg. 23.30 *(978-0-606-41299-5(9))* Turtleback.

Stevens, Eric. Finn Reeder, Flu Fighter: How I Survived a Worldwide Pandemic, the School Bully, & the Craziest Game of Dodge Ball Ever. Fraser, Kay, illus. 2009. (Finn Reeder Ser.). (ENG.). 80p. (J). (gr. 3-8). 9.99 *(978-1-4342-2562-7(3)*, 158476); lib. bdg. 27.32 *(978-1-4342-2450-7(3)*, 112917) Capstone. (Stone Arch Bks.).

Stevens, Janet & Crummel, Susan Stevens. The Little Red Pen. Stevens, Janet, illus. (ENG.). 56p. (J). (gr. 1-4). 2019. pap. 8.99 *(978-0-358-13730-6(6)*, 1754882) 2011. (Illus.). 17.99 *(978-0-15-206432-7(X)*, 1199238) HarperCollins Pubs. (Clarion Bks.).

Stevens, Robin. Jolly Foul Play. (Murder Most Unladylike Mystery Ser.). (ENG.). (J). (gr. 5). 2019. 384p. pap. 8.99 *(978-1-4814-8910-2(0))* 2018. (Illus.). 368p. 19.99 *(978-1-4814-8909-6(7))* Simon & Schuster Bks. For Young Readers. (Simon & Schuster Bks. For Young Readers).

—Murder Is Bad Manners. 2015. (Murder Most Unladylike Mystery Ser.). (ENG., Illus.). 320p. (J). (gr. 5). 19.99 *(978-1-4814-2212-3(X)*, Simon & Schuster Bks. For Young Readers) Simon & Schuster Bks. For Young Readers.

Stevenson, Peggy. Meet the Spencers & the Smart Knots. 2009. 48p. pap. 16.95 *(978-1-60813-517-2(9))* America Star Bks.

Stevenson, Robin. Attitude, 1 vol. 2013. (Orca Limelights Ser.). (ENG.). 144p. (J). (gr. 4-7). pap. 9.95 *(978-1-4598-0382-4(5))* Orca Bk. Pubs. USA.

Stevenson, Sarah Jamila. The Latte Rebellion. 2011. (ENG., Illus.). 336p. (YA). (gr. 9-12). pap. 9.95 *(978-0-7387-2278-8(2)*, 0738722782, Flux) North Star Editions.

Stewart, Dianne C. Quimbaya. 2008. (ENG.). 200p. (gr. 1-18). pap. 8.95 *(978-0-9667359-8-7(6)*, BeanPole Bks.) OH Industries.

Stewart, Kenneth. The Kickball Kid. 2012. 24p. pap. 24.95 *(978-1-4626-7683-5(9))* America Star Bks.

Stewart, Kiera. Fetching. 2012. (ENG.). 304p. (J). (gr. 5-9). pap. 7.99 *(978-1-4231-4245-4(4))* Little, Brown Bks. for Young Readers.

Stewart, Mark R. Malcolm's Cubby House. Swope, Brenda, illus. 2011. 28p. pap. 24.95 *(978-1-4560-0958-8(3))* America Star Bks.

Stewart, Trenton Lee. The Mysterious Benedict Society. Ellis, Carson, illus. (Mysterious Benedict Society Ser.: 1). (ENG.). (J). (gr. 3-7). 2008. 512p. pap. 9.99 *(978-0-316-00395-7(6))* 2007. 496p. 19.99 *(978-0-316-05777-6(0))* Little, Brown Bks. for Young Readers.

—The Mysterious Benedict Society. 2021. (Mysterious Benedict Society Ser.). (ENG., Illus.). 496p. (J). (gr. 3-7). pap. 9.99 *(978-0-316-29760-8(7))* Little, Brown Bks. for Young Readers.

—The Mysterious Benedict Society. 2009. 17.45 *(978-1-60686-527-9(7))* Perfection Learning Corp.

—The Mysterious Benedict Society. 2010. (Mysterious Benedict Society Ser.: 3). (J). lib. bdg. 19.65 *(978-0-606-15117-7(6))* Turtleback.

—The Mysterious Benedict Society. Ellis, Carson, illus. 2008. (Mysterious Benedict Society Ser.: 1). 485p. (J). (gr. 3-7). lib. bdg. 19.65 *(978-1-4178-1817-4(4))* Turtleback.

—The Mysterious Benedict Society & the Prisoner's Dilemma. Sudyka, Diana, illus. (Mysterious Benedict Society Ser.: 3). (ENG.). 400p. (J). (gr. 3-7). 2010. pap. 9.99 *(978-0-316-04550-6(0))* 2009. 36.99 *(978-0-316-04552-0(7))* Little, Brown Bks. for Young Readers.

Stier, Catherine. Bugs in My Hair?! Lyon, Tammie, illus. 2012. (J). 34.28 *(978-1-61913-111-8(0))* Weigl Pubs., Inc.

—Bugs in My Hair?!, 1 vol. Lyon, Tammie, illus. 2010. (ENG.). 32p. (J). (gr. -1-3). pap. 7.99 *(978-0-8075-0909-8(4)*, 807509094) Whitman, Albert & Co.

—The Terrible Secrets of the Tell-All Club. 2011. (ENG.). 128p. (J). (gr. 4-6). lib. bdg. 18.69 *(978-0-8075-7798-1(7))* Whitman, Albert & Co.

—What's Bugging Nurse Penny? A Story about Lice. Beaky, Suzanne, illus. 2013. (ENG.). 32p. (J). (gr. -1-3). 16.99 *(978-0-8075-8803-1(2)*, 807588032) Whitman, Albert & Co.

Stiles, Norman. On My Very First School Day I Met... Mayer, Bill, illus. 2005. 32p. (J). (gr. -1). 9.95 *(978-0-689-03924-9(7)*, Milk & Cookies) ibooks, Inc.

Stillman, Josh. The Chinese Finger Trap. 2012. 116p. pap. 11.50 *(978-1-59330-803-2(5))* Aventine Pr.

Stilton, Gerónimo. A Fabumouse School Adventure. 2009. (Geronimo Stilton Ser.: 38). lib. bdg. 18.40 *(978-0-606-00229-5(4))* Turtleback.

—Thea Stilton & the Dragon's Code. 2009. (Geronimo Stilton Special Edition Ser.: No. 1). (Illus.). 158p. 18.00 *(978-1-60686-420-3(3))* Perfection Learning Corp.

—Thea Stilton & the Dragon's Code. 2009. (Thea Stilton Ser.: 1). lib. bdg. 19.65 *(978-0-606-00231-8(6))* Turtleback.

Stilton, Gerónimo & Stilton, Thea. Thea Stilton & the Ghost of the Shipwreck. 2010. (Thea Stilton Ser.: 3). lib. bdg. 19.65 *(978-0-606-06843-7(0))* Turtleback.

Stilton, Thea. A Fashionable Mystery (Thea Stilton Mouseford Academy #8) Stilton, Thea, illus. 2019. (Thea Stilton Mouseford Academy Ser.: 8). (ENG., Illus.). 128p. (J). (gr.

2-5). pap. 7.99 (978-0-545-87096-2(8), Scholastic Paperbacks) Scholastic, Inc.

—A Mouseford Musical (Mouseford Academy #6) Stilton, Thea, illus. 2018. (Thea Stilton Mouseford Academy Ser.: 6). (ENG., Illus.). 128p. (J). (gr. 2-5). pap. 7.99 (978-0-545-78905-9(2), Scholastic Paperbacks) Scholastic, Inc.

Stilton, Thea & Dami, Elisabetta. The Secret Invention. 2015. (Illus.). 112p. (J). (978-0-545-80899-6(5)) Scholastic, Inc.

Stine, R. L. Battle of the Dum Diddys, 12. Park, Trip, illus. 2011. (Rotten School Ser.: No. 12). (ENG.). 128p. (J). (gr. 2-6). 31.36 (978-1-59961-836-4(2), 13139, Chapter Bks.) Spotlight.

—The Big Blueberry Barf-Off! Park, Trip, illus. 2005. (Rotten School Ser.: No. 1). 128p. (J). (ENG.). 6.99 (978-0-06-078586-4(1)); lib. bdg. 14.89 (978-0-06-078587-1(X)) HarperCollins Pubs.

—The Big Blueberry Barf-Off! Park, Trip, illus. 2011. (Rotten School Ser.: No. 1). (ENG.). 128p. (J). (gr. 2-6). 31.36 (978-1-59961-825-8(7), 13128, Chapter Bks.) Spotlight.

—Drop Dead Gorgeous. 2019. (Return to Fear Street Ser.: 3). (ENG.). 336p. (YA). (gr. 8). pap. 10.99 (978-0-06-269429-4(4), HarperTeen) HarperCollins Pubs.

—Dudes, the School Is Haunted! Park, Trip, illus. 2011. (Rotten School Ser.: No. 7). (ENG.). 128p. (J). (gr. 2-6). 31.36 (978-1-59961-831-9(1), 13134, Chapter Bks.) Spotlight.

—The Ghost of Slappy, 6. 2019. (Goosebumps SlappyWorld Ser.). (ENG.). 133p. (J). (gr. 4-5). 16.49 (978-0-87617-664-1(3)) Penworthy Co., LLC, The.

—The Ghost of Slappy (Goosebumps SlappyWorld #6) 2018. (Goosebumps SlappyWorld Ser.: 6). (ENG.). 160p. (J). (gr. 3-7). pap. 7.99 (978-1-338-22301-9(1), Scholastic Paperbacks) Scholastic, Inc.

—The Good, the Bad & the Very Slimy. Park, Trip, illus. 2011. (Rotten School Ser.: No. 3). (ENG.). 128p. (J). (gr. 2-6). 31.36 (978-1-59961-827-2(3), 13130, Chapter Bks.) Spotlight.

—The Great Smelling Bee, 2. Park, Trip, illus. 2011. (Rotten School Ser.: No. 2). (ENG.). 128p. (J). (gr. 2-6). 31.36 (978-1-59961-826-5(5), 13129, Chapter Bks.) Spotlight.

—The Heinie Prize, 1 vol. Park, Trip, illus. 2011. (Rotten School Ser.: No. 6). (ENG.). 128p. (J). (gr. 2-6). 31.36 (978-1-59961-830-2(3), 13133, Chapter Bks.) Spotlight.

—How I Met My Monster. 2013. (Goosebumps Most Wanted Ser.: 3). lib. bdg. 17.20 (978-0-606-31534-0(9)) Turtleback.

—How I Met My Monster (Goosebumps Most Wanted #3) 2013. (Goosebumps Most Wanted Ser.: 3). (ENG.). 160p. (J). (gr. 3-7). pap. 7.99 (978-0-545-41800-3(3), Scholastic Paperbacks) Scholastic, Inc.

—Lose, Team, Lose!, 4. Park, Trip, illus. 2011. (Rotten School Ser.: No. 4). (ENG.). 128p. (J). (gr. 2-6). 31.36 (978-1-59961-828-9(1), 13131, Chapter Bks.) Spotlight.

—The New Girl. 2006. (Fear Street Ser.: Bk. 1). (ENG., Illus.). 176p. (YA). (gr. 7-12). mass mkt. 7.99 (978-1-4169-1810-3(8), Simon Pulse) Simon Pulse.

—Night of the Creepy Things. Park, Trip, illus. (Rotten School Ser.: Bk. 14). 4.99 (978-0-06-123274-9(2)) HarperCollins Pubs.

—Party Poopers. Park, Trip, illus. (Rotten School Ser.: Bk. 9). 4.99 (978-0-06-078826-1(7)) HarperCollins Pubs.

—Party Poopers. Park, Trip, illus. 2011. (Rotten School Ser.: No. 9). (ENG.). 128p. (J). (gr. 2-6). 31.36 (978-1-59961-833-3(8), 13136, Chapter Bks.) Spotlight.

—Punk'd & Skunked, 1 vol. Park, Trip, illus. 2011. (Rotten School Ser.: No. 11). (ENG.). 128p. (J). (gr. 2-6). 31.36 (978-1-59961-835-7(4), 13138, Chapter Bks.) Spotlight.

—Rotten School, 11 vols., Set. Park, Trip, illus. Incl. Big Blueberry Barf-Off! 31.36 (978-1-59961-825-8(7), 13128); Dudes, the School Is Haunted! 31.36 (978-1-59961-831-9(1), 13134); Good, the Bad & the Very Slimy. 31.36 (978-1-59961-827-2(3), 13130); Heinie Prize. 31.36 (978-1-59961-830-2(3), 13133); Party Poopers. 31.36 (978-1-59961-833-3(8), 13136); Punk'd & Skunked. 31.36 (978-1-59961-835-7(4), 13138); Shake, Rattle, & Hurl! 31.36 (978-1-59961-829-6(X), 13132); 2. Great Smelling Bee. 31.36 (978-1-59961-826-5(5), 13129); 4. Lose, Team, Lose! 31.36 (978-1-59961-828-9(1), 13131); 12. Battle of the Dum Diddys. 31.36 (978-1-59961-836-4(2), 13139); Set. Rottenest Angel. 31.36 (978-1-59961-834-0(6), 13137); (J). (gr. 2-6). (Rotten School Ser.). (ENG., Illus.). 128p. 2011. Set lib. bdg. 344.96 (978-1-59961-824-1(9), 13127, Chapter Bks.) Spotlight.

—Rotten School #11: Punk'd & Skunked. Park, Trip, illus. 2007. (Rotten School Ser.: 11). (ENG.). 128p. (J). (gr. 3-7). 6.99 (978-0-06-078830-8(5), HarperCollins) HarperCollins Pubs.

—Rotten School #12: Battle of the Dum Diddys. Park, Trip, illus. 4.99 (978-0-06-078835-3(6)) HarperCollins Pubs.

—Rotten School #15: Calling All Birdbrains. Park, Trip, illus. 4.99 (978-0-06-123277-0(7)) HarperCollins Pubs.

—Rotten School #16: Dumb Clucks. Park, Trip, illus. 4.99 (978-0-06-123280-0(7)) HarperCollins Pubs.

—The Rottenest Angel, Set. Park, Trip, illus. 2011. (Rotten School Ser.: No. 10). (ENG.). 128p. (J). (gr. 2-6). 31.36 (978-1-59961-834-0(6), 13137, Chapter Bks.) Spotlight.

—Shake, Rattle, & Hurl! Park, Trip, illus. 2006. (Rotten School Ser.: No. 5). (ENG.). 128p. (J). (gr. 3-7). 6.99 (978-0-06-078811-7(9)) HarperCollins Pubs.

—Shake, Rattle, & Hurl! Park, Trip, illus. 2011. (Rotten School Ser.: No. 5). (ENG.). 128p. (J). (gr. 2-6). 31.36 (978-1-59961-829-6(X), 13132, Chapter Bks.) Spotlight.

Stoddard, Lindsey. Just Like Jackie. 2018. (ENG.). (J). (gr. 3-7). 272p. pap. 6.99 (978-0-06-265292-8(3)); 256p. 16.99 (978-0-06-265291-1(5)) HarperCollins Pubs. (HarperCollins).

Stokes, Maura Ellen. Fadeaway. 2018. (ENG.). 304p. (J). (gr. 4-9). 16.99 (978-1-4998-0674-8(4), Yellow Jacket) Bonnier Publishing USA.

Stolarz, Laurie Faria. White Is for Magic. 2004. (Stolarz Ser.: 2). (ENG.). 312p. (YA). (gr. 9-12). pap. 11.99 (978-0-7387-0443-2(1), 0738704431, Flux) North Star Editions.

Stone, Kate. Mouse Goes to School. 2012. (ENG.). 16p. (J). bds. 10.99 (978-1-4494-1788-8(4)) Andrews McMeel Publishing.

Stone, Nic. Odd One Out. 2018. (ENG.). 320p. (YA). (gr. 9). 17.99 (978-1-101-93953-6(2), Crown Books For Young Readers) Random Hse. Children's Bks.

Stone, Phoebe. The Boy on Cinnamon Street. 2012. 234p. (J). (978-0-545-43368-6(1), Levine, Arthur A. Bks.) Scholastic, Inc.

Stone, Sonja. Desert Dark: A Desert Dark Novel. 2016. (Desert Dark Novel Ser.: 1). (ENG.). 336p. (YA). (gr. 7). 17.95 (978-0-8234-3562-3(8)) Holiday Hse., Inc.

Stone, Tamara Ireland. Every Last Word. 2017. (ENG.). (YA). (gr. 7-12). lib. bdg. 20.85 (978-0-606-39885-5(6)) Turtleback.

—Time after Time. 2014. (ENG.). 368p. (J). (gr. 7-12). pap. 18.99 (978-1-4231-5981-0(0)) Hyperion Bks. for Children.

—Time Between Us. 2013. (ENG.). 384p. (J). (gr. 7-12). pap. 19.99 (978-1-4231-5977-3(2)) Hyperion Pr.

Stone, Tanya Lee. A Bad Boy Can Be Good for a Girl. 2007. (ENG.). 240p. (YA). (gr. 7-11). per. 8.99 (978-0-553-49509-6(7), Lamb, Wendy Bks.) Random Hse. Children's Bks.

Storrie, Paul D. #02 Made for Each Other. Cowgur, Eldon, illus. 2011. (My Boyfriend Is a Monster Ser.). 128p. (YA). pap. 56.72 (978-0-7613-7604-0(6), Graphic Universe™) Lerner Publishing Group.

Stoudemire, Amar'e. Home Court. 2012. (STAT: Standing Tall & Talented Ser.: 1). lib. bdg. 16.00 (978-0-606-26169-2(9)) Turtleback.

—Home Court (STAT: Standing Tall & Talented #1) Jessell, Tim, illus. 2012. (Stat Ser.: 1). (ENG.). 144p. (J). (gr. 3-7). pap. 5.99 (978-0-545-38759-0(0), Scholastic Pr.) Scholastic, Inc.

Stout, Katie M. Hello, I Love You. 2015. (ENG.). 304p. (YA). pap. (978-1-250-08195-7(5), St. Martin's Griffin) St. Martin's Pr.

Stout, Shawn K. Don't Chicken Out. Ying, Victoria, illus. 2013. (Not-So-Ordinary Girl Ser.: 3). (ENG.). 176p. (J). (gr. 1-5). pap. 5.99 (978-1-4169-7111-5(4), Aladdin) Simon & Schuster Children's Publishing.

—Don't Chicken Out. Ying, Victoria, illus. 2013. (Not-So-Ordinary Girl Ser.: 3). (ENG.). 176p. (J). (gr. 1-5). 15.99 (978-1-4169-7929-6(8), Simon & Schuster/Paula Wiseman Bks.) Simon & Schuster/Paula Wiseman Bks.

—Miss Matched. Martini, Angela, illus. 2013. (Not-So-Ordinary Girl Ser.: 2). (ENG.). 176p. (J). (gr. 1-5). pap. 5.99 (978-1-4424-7404-8(1), Aladdin) Simon & Schuster Children's Publishing.

—Miss Matched. Martini, Angela, illus. 2013. (Not-So-Ordinary Girl Ser.: 2). (ENG.). 160p. (J). (gr. 1-5). 15.99 (978-1-4424-7405-5(X), Simon & Schuster/Paula Wiseman Bks.) Simon & Schuster/Paula Wiseman Bks.

Strand, Jeff. Elrod McBugle on the Loose. 2006. (ENG.). 136p. (YA). per. 9.25 (978-0-7599-4325-4(7)) Hard Shell Word Factory.

Strange, Jason. Basement of the Undead, 1 vol. Parks, Phil, illus. 2011. (Jason Strange Ser.). (ENG.). 72p. (J). (gr. 3-6). pap. 6.25 (978-1-4342-3433-9(9), 116454, Stone Arch Bks.) Capstone.

—Faceless Friend, 1 vol. Parks, Phil, illus. 2011. (Jason Strange Ser.). (ENG.). 72p. (J). (gr. 3-6). pap. 6.25 (978-1-4342-3431-5(2), 116452); lib. bdg. 25.32 (978-1-4342-3232-8(8), 116204) Capstone. (Stone Arch Bks.).

Strasnick, Lauren. Nothing Like You. 2010. (ENG.). 240p. (YA). (gr. 9). pap. 8.99 (978-1-4169-8265-4(5), Simon Pulse) Simon Pulse.

—Then You Were Gone. 2013. (ENG.). 272p. (YA). (gr. 9). 16.99 (978-1-4424-2715-0(9), Simon Pulse) Simon Pulse.

Strasser, Todd. Is That an Angry Penguin in Your Gym Bag? 2009. (Is That... ? Ser.). (ENG.). 208p. (J). (gr. 4-6). 18.69 (978-0-439-77697-4(X)) Scholastic, Inc.

—The Wave. 2013. (ENG.). 144p. (YA). (gr. 7). pap. 10.99 (978-0-307-97912-4(1), Ember) Random Hse. Children's Bks.

—Wish You Were Dead. (ENG.). 240p. (gr. 9-12). 2010. (YA). pap. 9.99 (978-1-60684-138-9(6), 83351663-102d-409d-ba04-349ec33baab2) 2009. 16.99 (978-1-60684-007-8(X)) Lerner Publishing Group. (Carolrhoda Lab™).

Strickland, Sharon. Even Though: A Story about Being Different, 1 vol. 2009. 15p. pap. 24.95 (978-1-60813-821-0(6)) PublishAmerica, Inc.

Strickler, Ashley. Once upon A Time. 2007. 212p. pap. 12.95 (978-1-4327-0207-6(6)) Outskirts Pr., Inc.

Stringam, Jean. How Not to Cry in Public. 2013. 390p. pap. 16.99 (978-0-9855540-1-9(0)) Dollison Road Bks.

Strohm, Stephanie Kate. The Date to Save. 2017. (ENG.). 288p. (YA). (gr. 7-7). 17.99 (978-1-338-14906-7(7)) Scholastic, Inc.

—That's Not What I Heard. 2019. (ENG.). 368p. (YA). (gr. 7-7). 18.99 (978-1-338-28181-1(X), Scholastic Pr.) Scholastic, Inc.

Strohmeyer, Sarah. Smart Girls Get What They Want. 2013. (ENG.). 368p. (YA). (gr. 8). pap. 9.99 (978-0-06-195341-5(5), Balzer & Bray) HarperCollins Pubs.

Stromberg, Ronica. Living It up to Live It Down. 2009. (J). lib. bdg. (978-0-88092-752-9(6)) Royal Fireworks Publishing Co.

Stroud, Scott. Grumpy Mr. Grady. Hunt, Jim, illus. 2007. 24p. (J). 8.95 (978-1-60131-008-8(0), Castlebridge Bks.) Big Tent Bks.

Struyk-Bonn, Chris. Nice Girls Endure. 2016. (ENG.). 256p. (YA). (gr. 9-12). 16.95 (978-1-63079-047-9(8), 131502, Switch Pr.) Capstone.

Stryker, Robin. Goldie, the Homeless Calico Cat. Rubino, Alisa A., illus. 2005. (J). pap. (978-0-932991-35-5(1)) Place In The Woods, The.

Sturges, Philemon. I Love School! Halpern, Shari, illus. 2014. 32p. pap. 7.00 (978-1-61003-329-9(9)) Center for the Collaborative Classroom.

—I Love School! Halpern, Shari, illus. 32p. (J). (gr. -1-1). 2004. lib. bdg. 14.89 (978-0-06-009285-6(8)) 2006. (ENG.). reprint ed. pap. 9.99 (978-0-06-009286-3(6), HarperCollins) HarperCollins Pubs.

Stuve-Bodeen, Stephanie. Babu's Song. Boyd, Aaron, illus. 2003. (ENG.). 32p. (J). 16.95 (978-1-58430-058-8(2)) Lee & Low Bks., Inc.

Suen, Anastasia. Girls Can, Too! A Tolerence Story, 1 vol. Ebbeler, Jeff, illus. 2008. (Main Street School~ Kids with Character Ser.). (ENG.). 32p. (J). (gr. k-4). 32.79 (978-1-60270-271-4(3), 11277, Looking Glass Library) Magic Wagon.

—A Great Idea? An Up2U Character Education Adventure, 1 vol. Dippold, Jane, illus. 2015. (Up2U Adventures Ser.). (ENG.). 80p. (J). (gr. 2-5). 35.64 (978-1-62402-093-3(3), 17355, Calico Chapter Bks.) ABDO Publishing Co.

—Helping Sophia, 1 vol. Ebbeler, Jeffrey, illus. 2007. (Main Street School~ Kids with Character Ser.). (ENG.). 32p. (J). (gr. -1-4). 32.79 (978-1-60270-030-7(3), 11261, Looking Glass Library) Magic Wagon.

—New Girl: An Up2U Character Education Adventure, 1 vol. Dippold, Jane, illus. 2013. (Up2U Adventures Ser.). (ENG.). 80p. (J). (gr. 2-5). lib. bdg. 35.64 (978-1-61641-968-4(7), 15219, Calico Chapter Bks.) ABDO Publishing Co.

—Vote for Isaiah! A Citizenship Story, 1 vol. Ebbeler, Jeff, illus. 2008. (Main Street School~ Kids with Character Ser.). (ENG.). 32p. (J). (gr. k-4). 32.79 (978-1-60270-274-5(8), 11283, Looking Glass Library) Magic Wagon.

Sugg, Zoe. Girl Online: Going Solo: The Third Novel by Zoella. 2017. (Girl Online Book Ser.: 3). (ENG.). 336p. (gr. 7). pap. 17.99 (978-1-5011-6212-1(8), Atria Bks.) Simon & Schuster.

Sullivan, Dana. Ozzie & the Art Contest. Sullivan, Dana, illus. 2013. (ENG., Illus.). 32p. (J). (gr. -1-1). 15.99 (978-1-58536-820-4(2), 202885) Sleeping Bear Pr.

Sullivan, Deirdre. Ming Goes to School. Löfdahl, Maja, illus. 2016. (ENG.). 32p. (J). (gr. -1-k). 16.99 (978-1-5107-0050-5(1), Sky Pony Pr.) Skyhorse Publishing Co., Inc.

Sullivan, Derek E. Biggie. 2015. (ENG.). 272p. (YA). (gr. 8-12). 16.99 (978-0-8075-0727-8(X), 080750727X) Whitman, Albert & Co.

Sullivan, Jenny. A Guardian What? 2006. (ENG.). 84p. (J). pap. 7.50 (978-1-84323-646-7(X)) Gomer Pr. GBR. Dist: Casemate Pubs. & Bk. Distributors, LLC.

—The Magic Apostrophe. 2003. (ENG.). 216p. pap. 19.95 (978-1-85902-116-3(6)) Beekman Bks., Inc.

Sullivan, Maureen. Cabbages & Queens. Ferrando, Carol, illus. 2010. 57p. (J). pap. (978-0-9820381-3-0(5)) MoJo InkWorks.

Sullivan, Michael. Escapade Johnson & the Witches of Belknap County. Kolitsky, Joy, illus. 2008. (Escapade Johnson Ser.). (ENG.). 99p. (J). (gr. 2-4). pap. 3.95 (978-1-929945-90-0(6)) Big Guy Bks., Inc.

Summers, Courtney. Cracked up to Be: A Novel. 2020. (ENG.). 240p. (YA). pap. 10.99 (978-1-250-25697-3(6), 900219321, Wednesday Bks.) St. Martin's Pr.

—Some Girls Are. 2010. (ENG.). 256p. (YA). (gr. 8-12). 11.99 (978-0-312-57380-5(4), 900060851, St. Martin's Griffin) St. Martin's Pr.

—This Is Not a Test. 2012. (ENG.). 336p. (YA). (gr. 8). pap. 14.00 (978-0-312-65674-4(2), 900069754, St. Martin's Griffin) St. Martin's Pr.

—What Goes Around. 2013. (ENG.). 480p. (YA). (gr. 9-12). pap. 29.99 (978-1-250-03844-9(8), 900122299, St. Martin's Griffin) St. Martin's Pr.

Sundquist, Josh. Love & First Sight. 2017. (ENG.). 288p. (YA). (gr. 7-17). 17.99 (978-0-316-30535-8(9)) Little, Brown Bks. for Young Readers.

Supplee, Suzanne. Artichoke's Heart. 2009. 288p. (YA). (gr. 7-18). 8.99 (978-0-14-241427-9(1), Speak) Penguin Young Readers Group.

—When Irish Guys Are Smiling. 2008. (S. A. S. S. Ser.). 224p. (YA). (gr. 7-18). 6.99 (978-0-14-241016-5(0), Speak) Penguin Young Readers Group.

Sutcliffe, Kathy. When Romeo Kissed Mercutio. 2012. (ENG.). 242p. pap. (978-1-922120-28-1(6), IP Digital) Interactive Pubns. Pty, Ltd.

Sutherland, Krystal. A Semi-Definitive List of Worst Nightmares. 2018. (ENG.). 416p. (YA). (gr. 9). pap. 11.99 (978-0-399-54660-0(X), Speak) Penguin Young Readers Group.

Sutherland, Suzanne. Something Wiki. 2015. (ENG.). 160p. (J). pap. 12.99 (978-1-4597-2821-9(1)) Dundurn Pr. CAN. Dist: Publishers Group West (PGW).

Sutherland, Tui T. Moon Rising (Wings of Fire #6), Vol. 6. 2016. (Wings of Fire Ser.: 6). (ENG.). 336p. (J). (gr. 3-7). pap. 8.99 (978-0-545-68536-8(2)) Scholastic, Inc.

—This Must Be Love. 256p. (J). 2005. pap. 7.99 (978-0-06-056477-3(6), Harper Trophy) 2004. (gr. 7-18). lib. bdg. 16.89 (978-0-06-056476-6(8)) HarperCollins Pubs.

Suzy, Kline. Horrible Harry in Room 2B. 2014. (Horrible Harry Ser. No. 1 Ser.). (ENG.). 64p. (J). (gr. 3-7). 8.24 (978-1-63245-257-3(X)) Lectorum Pubns., Inc.

Swaab, Neil. Secrets to Ruling School (Without Even Trying) (Secrets to Ruling School #1) 2015. (Secrets to Ruling School Ser.). (ENG., Illus.). 232p. (J). (gr. 5-9). 13.95 (978-1-4197-1221-0(7), 1076001, Amulet Bks.) Abrams, Inc.

Swain, Cynthia. Sorting at the Nature Center. 2006. (Early Explorers Ser.). (J). pap. (978-1-4108-6039-2(6)) Benchmark Education Co.

Swallow, Pamela. It Only Looks Easy. 2009. (ENG.). 192p. (J). (gr. 3-7). pap. 18.99 (978-0-312-56114-7(8), 900058844) Square Fish.

Swan, Bill. Mud Happens, 1 vol. 2005. (Lorimer Sports Stories Ser.: 82). (ENG.). 112p. (J). (gr. 4-8). 16.95 (978-1-55028-899-5(7), 899); 8.95 (978-1-55028-898-8(9), 898) James Lorimer & Co. Ltd., Pubs. CAN. Dist: Formac Lorimer Bks. Ltd.

Swanson, Matthew. The Real Mccoys. Behr, Robbi, illus. 2018. (Real Mccoys Ser.: 1). (ENG.). 352p. (J). pap. 7.99 (978-1-250-09853-5(X), 900161849) Square Fish.

—The Real Mccoys: Wonder Undercover. Behr, Robbi, illus. 2019. (Real Mccoys Ser.: 3). (ENG.). 352p. (J). 16.99 (978-1-250-30782-8(1), 900198140) Imprint IND. Dist: Macmillan.

Swanson Sateren, Shelley. Max & Zoe at School, 1 vol. Sullivan, Mary, illus. 2013. (Max & Zoe Ser.). (ENG.). 32p. (J). (gr. k-2). pap. 5.19 (978-1-4048-8059-7(3), 121735, Picture Window Bks.) Capstone.

—Max & Zoe: the Lunchroom Fight, 1 vol. Sullivan, Mary, illus. 2013. (Max & Zoe Ser.). (ENG.). 32p. (J). (gr. k-2). pap. 5.19 (978-1-4795-2328-3(3), 124365, Picture Window Bks.) Capstone.

—Max & Zoe: Too Many Tricks, 1 vol. Sullivan, Mary, illus. 2013. (Max & Zoe Ser.). (ENG.). 32p. (J). (gr. k-2). pap. 5.19 (978-1-4795-2327-6(5), 124366); lib. bdg. 21.32 (978-1-4048-7197-7(7), 117657) Capstone. (Picture Window Bks.).

Swanson Sateren, Shelley & Swanson Sateren, Shelley. Max & Zoe at Recess, 1 vol. Sullivan, Mary, illus. 2012. (Max & Zoe Ser.). (ENG.). 32p. (J). (gr. k-2). lib. bdg. 21.32 (978-1-4048-7200-4(0), 117698, Picture Window Bks.) Capstone.

Sweeney, Joyce. Players, 1 vol. 2013. (ENG.). 226p. (YA). (gr. 7-12). reprint ed. pap. 9.99 (978-0-7614-5236-2(2), 9780761452362, Skyscape) Amazon Publishing.

—Waiting for June, 0 vols. 2012. (ENG.). 158p. (YA). (gr. 7-12). pap. 7.99 (978-0-7614-5329-1(6), 9780761453291, Skyscape) Amazon Publishing.

Sykes, Julie. Unicorn Academy #1: Sophia & Rainbow. Truman, Lucy, illus. 2019. (Unicorn Academy Ser.: 1). (ENG.). 128p. (J). (gr. 1-4). 5.99 (978-1-9848-5082-9(2), Random Hse. Bks. for Young Readers) Random Hse. Children's Bks.

—Unicorn Academy #2: Scarlett & Blaze. Truman, Lucy, illus. 2019. (Unicorn Academy Ser.: 2). (ENG.). 128p. (J). (gr. 1-4). 5.99 (978-1-9848-5085-0(7), Random Hse. Bks. for Young Readers) Random Hse. Children's Bks.

—Unicorn Academy #3: Ava & Star. Truman, Lucy, illus. 2019. (Unicorn Academy Ser.: 3). (ENG.). 128p. (J). (gr. 1-4). pap. 5.99 (978-1-9848-5088-1(1), Random Hse. Bks. for Young Readers) Random Hse. Children's Bks.

—Unicorn Academy #4: Isabel & Cloud. Truman, Lucy, illus. 2019. (Unicorn Academy Ser.: 4). (ENG.). 128p. (J). (gr. 1-4). pap. 5.99 (978-1-9848-5091-1(1), Random Hse. Bks. for Young Readers) Random Hse. Children's Bks.

—Unicorn Academy #5: Layla & Dancer. Truman, Lucy, illus. 2019. (Unicorn Academy Ser.: 5). (ENG.). 128p. (J). (gr. 1-4). 12.99 (978-1-9848-5168-0(3), Random Hse. Bks. for Young Readers) Random Hse. Children's Bks.

—Unicorn Academy #6: Olivia & Snowflake. Truman, Lucy, illus. 2019. (Unicorn Academy Ser.: 6). (ENG.). 128p. (J). (gr. 1-4). 12.99 (978-1-9848-5171-0(3), Random Hse. Bks. for Young Readers) Random Hse. Children's Bks.

Szish, Jill Henry. TJ & the Good Luck Cricket. Perry, Jennifer A., illus. 2007. 32p. per. 24.95 (978-1-4241-8502-3(5)) America Star Bks.

Szpirglas, Jeff. Wild Cards, 1 vol. Whamond, Dave, illus. 2017. (Orca Echoes Ser.). (ENG.). 88p. (J). (gr. 1-3). pap. 7.95 (978-1-4598-1211-6(5)) Orca Bk. Pubs. USA.

Tackett, Wendy. The Snow Wish. 2011. 100p. (gr. 4-6). 19.95 (978-1-4620-2608-1(7)); pap. 9.95 (978-1-4620-2606-7(0)) iUniverse, Inc.

Tada, Joni Eareckson & Jensen, Steve. The Meanest Teacher. 2005. (Darcy & Friends Ser.). 144p. (gr. 3-6). pap. 5.99 (978-1-58134-256-7(X), Crossway Bibles) Crossway.

Taddonio, Lea. The Curse of Deadwood Hill: Book 2. Trunfio, Alessia, illus. 2017. (Lucky 8 Ser.). (ENG.). 48p. (J). (gr. 3-7). lib. bdg. 34.21 (978-1-5321-3054-0(6), 27061, Spellbound) Magic Wagon.

—Frankensteve. 2019. (Shiverwood Academy Ser.). (ENG., Illus.). 48p. (J). (gr. 3-7). lib. bdg. 34.21 (978-1-5321-3501-9(7), 31921, Spellbound) Magic Wagon.

Taekema, Sylvia. Ripple Effect, 1 vol. 2015. (ENG.). 144p. (J). (gr. 4-7). pap. 9.95 (978-1-4598-0872-0(X)) Orca Bk. Pubs. USA.

Talbot, Rose. The Adventures of Peanut, the Sugar Glider. 2007. 80p. per. 15.99 (978-1-4257-9629-7(X)) Xlibris Corp.

Tan, Valerie Genevivie. Hello! I'm Sha Sha: Join Sha Sha in Her New School. 2009. (Illus.). 50p. (J). pap. 14.95 (978-1-4327-4195-2(0)) Outskirts Pr., Inc.

Tanigawa, Nagaru. The Boredom of Haruhi Suzumiya (light Novel) 2010. (Haruhi Suzumiya Ser.: 3). (ENG., Illus.). 224p. (YA). (gr. 10-17). 24.00 (978-0-316-03886-7(5), Yen Pr.) Yen Pr. LLC.

—The Melancholy of Suzumiya Haruhi-Chan, Vol. 6. 2012. (Melancholy of Suzumiya Haruhi-Chan Ser.: 6). (ENG., Illus.). 160p. (gr. 11-17). pap. 11.99 (978-0-316-22914-2(8)) Yen Pr. LLC.

—The Sigh of Haruhi Suzumiya. 2009. (Haruhi Suzumiya Ser.: Bk. 1). (ENG., Illus.). 208p. (YA). (gr. 10-18). 14.99 (978-0-316-03881-2(4)) Hachette Bk. Group.

Tarkington, Booth. Ramsey Milholland. 2009. 108p. 22.95 (978-1-60664-679-3(6)); 104p. pap. 9.95 (978-1-60664-308-2(8)) Rodgers, Alan Bks.

Tarshis, Lauren. Emma-Jean Lazarus Fell in Love. 2009. (Emma-Jean Lazarus Ser.). (ENG.). 176p. (J). (gr. 6-8). 21.19 (978-0-8037-3321-3(6)) Penguin Young Readers Group.

Taschek, Karen. The the Risen Horse. 2010. (ENG.). 248p. (YA). (gr. 7-18). pap. 15.95 (978-0-8263-4837-1(8), P198426) Univ. of New Mexico Pr.

Tashjian, Janet. My Life As a Gamer. Tashjian, Jake, illus. 2018. (My Life Ser.: 5). (ENG.). 288p. (J). pap. 8.99 (978-1-250-14368-6(3), 900180543) Square Fish.

—My Life As a Joke. Tashjian, Jake, illus. 2014. (My Life Ser.: 4). (ENG.). 272p. (J). (gr. 4-7). 15.99 (978-0-8050-9850-1(X), 900122324, Holt, Henry & Co. Bks. For Young Readers) Holt, Henry & Co.

—My Life As a Meme. Tashjian, Jake, illus. 2019. (My Life Ser.: 8). (ENG.). 256p. (J). 13.99 (978-1-250-19657-6(4), 900194128, Holt, Henry & Co. Bks. For Young Readers) Holt, Henry & Co.

—My Life As a Stuntboy. Tashjian, Jake, illus. 2015. (My Life Ser.: 2). (ENG.). 288p. (J). (gr. 4-7). pap. 8.99 (978-1-250-01038-4(1), 900084784) Square Fish.

—My Life As a Youtuber. Tashjian, Jake, illus. 2018. (My Life Ser.: 7). (ENG.). 272p. (J). 13.99 (978-1-62779-892-1(7), 900161978, Holt, Henry & Co. Bks. For Young Readers) Holt, Henry & Co.

—My Life As a Youtuber. Tashjian, Jake, illus. 2020. (My Life Ser.: 7). (ENG.). 288p. (J). pap. 7.99 (978-1-250-23367-7(4), 900161979) Square Fish.

Tatulli, Mark. Desmond Pucket & the Cloverfield Junior High Carnival of Horrors. 2016. (Desmond Pucket Ser.: 3). (ENG., Illus.). 240p. (J). 13.99 (978-1-4494-6628-2(1)) Andrews McMeel Publishing.

—Desmond Pucket & the Mountain Full of Monsters. 2014. (Desmond Pucket Ser.: 2). (ENG.). 240p. (J). 13.99 (978-1-4494-3549-3(1)) Andrews McMeel Publishing.

—Desmond Pucket & the Mountain Full of Monsters. 2015. (Desmond Pucket Ser.: 2). lib. bdg. 20.85 (978-0-606-38232-8(1)) Turtleback.

—Desmond Pucket Makes Monster Magic. 2015. (Desmond Pucket Ser.: 1). lib. bdg. 20.85 (978-0-606-38231-1(3)) Turtleback.

Tayleur, Karen. Promises! Vote for David Mortimore Baxter. Garvey, Brann, illus. 2007. (David Mortimore Baxter Ser.). (ENG.). 96p. (J). (gr. 4-8). per. 6.05 (978-1-59889-208-6(8), 91168, Stone Arch Bks.) Capstone.

Taylor, Chet. Last, but Not Least. 2007. (Illus.). 20p. (J). per. 11.99 (978-0-9797574-8-8(7)) Dragonfly Publishing, Inc.

Taylor, Chloë. A Change of Lace. Zhang, Nancy, illus. 2014. (Sew Zoey Ser.: 9). (ENG.). 176p. (J). (gr. 3-7). pap. 6.99 (978-1-4814-1961-1(7), Simon Spotlight) Simon Spotlight.

Taylor, Chloe. Knot Too Shabby! Zhang, Nancy, illus. 2014. (Sew Zoey Ser.: 7). (ENG.). 176p. (J). (gr. 3-7). pap. 5.99 (978-1-4814-1398-5(8), Simon Spotlight) Simon Spotlight.

—Lights, Camera, Fashion! Zhang, Nancy, illus. 2013. (Sew Zoey Ser.: 3). (ENG.). 176p. (J). (gr. 3-7). pap. 6.99 (978-1-4424-8979-0(0), Simon Spotlight) Simon Spotlight.

—Stitches & Stones. Zhang, Nancy, illus. 2013. (Sew Zoey Ser.: 4). (ENG.). 176p. (J). (gr. 3-7). 16.99 (978-1-4424-9803-7(X));Bk. 4. pap. 7.99 (978-1-4424-9802-0(1)) Simon Spotlight. (Simon Spotlight).

Taylor, Chloë. A Tangled Thread. Zhang, Nancy, illus. 2014. (Sew Zoey Ser.: 6). (ENG.). 176p. (J). (gr. 3-7). 16.99 (978-1-4814-0444-0(X), Simon Spotlight) Simon Spotlight.

Taylor, Chloe. A Tangled Thread. Zhang, Nancy, illus. 2014. (Sew Zoey Ser.: 6). (ENG.). 176p. (J). (gr. 3-7). pap. 5.99 (978-1-4814-0443-3(1), Simon Spotlight) Simon Spotlight.

Taylor, Kara. Deadly Little Sins: A Prep School Confidential Novel. 2014. (Prep School Confidential Novel Ser.: 3). (ENG.). 288p. (YA). (gr. 7). pap. 19.99 (978-1-250-03363-5(2), 900120137, St. Martin's Griffin) St. Martin's Pr.

Taylor, Laini. Daughter of Smoke & Bone. 2023. (YA). 75.00 (978-1-955876-21-6(5)) LitJoy Crate.

—Daughter of Smoke & Bone. (Daughter of Smoke & Bone Ser.: 1). (ENG.). (YA). (gr. 10-17). 2020. 448p. pap. 12.99 (978-0-316-45918-1(6)) 2012. 624p. pap. 26.99 (978-0-316-22435-2(9)) Little, Brown Bks. for Young Readers.

—Daughter of Smoke & Bone. 2012. (Daughter of Smoke & Bone Ser.: 1). (YA). lib. bdg. 24.50 (978-0-606-26704-5(2)) Turtleback.

—Days of Blood & Starlight. l.t. ed. 2012. (Daughter of Smoke & Bone Ser.: 2). (ENG.). 688p. (YA). (gr. 10-17). 47.99 (978-0-316-22433-8(2)) Little, Brown Bks. for Young Readers.

Taylor, Mari Jo. Not One of the Robot Children. 2005. 11.00 (978-0-8059-9791-0(1)) Dorrance Publishing Co., Inc.

Taylor Sr., Anthony. I Pray. 2012. 20p. pap. 24.95 (978-1-4626-8113-6(1)) America Star Bks.

Teagan, Erin. The Friendship Experiment. (ENG.). 256p. (J). (gr. 5-7). 2019. pap. 7.99 (978-1-328-91125-4(X), 1701810) 2016. 16.99 (978-0-544-63622-4(8), 1619956) HarperCollins Pubs. (Clarion Bks.).

Teague, Monica. Diary of a Teenager in Junior High. 2011. 32p. pap. 16.95 (978-1-4560-8552-0(2)) America Star Bks.

Telgemeier, Raina. Drama. 2012. lib. bdg. 22.10 (978-0-606-26738-0(7)) Turtleback.

—Drama (Spanish Edition) Telgemeier, Raina, illus. 2018. (SPA., Illus.). 240p. (J). (gr. 4-7). pap. 12.99 (978-1-338-26916-1(X), Scholastic en Espanol) Scholastic, Inc.

Teller, Janne. Nothing. Aitken, Martin, tr. 2012. (ENG., Illus.). 240p. (YA). (gr. 7). pap. 11.99 (978-1-4424-4116-3(X), Atheneum Bks. for Young Readers) Simon & Schuster Children's Publishing.

Terheyden, Jerry, reader. Crow Boy. 2004. (Illus.). (J). (gr. -1-2). 28.95 incl. audio compact disk (978-1-59112-802-1(1)) Live Oak Media.

Terrell, Brandon. The Cursed Stage. Epelbaum, Mariano, illus. 2017. (Snoops, Inc Ser.). (ENG.). 112p. (J). (gr. 4-8). lib. bdg. 27.32 (978-1-4965-4346-2(7), 134263, Stone Arch Bks.) Capstone.

—Dive for the Goal Line. 2015. (Game On! Ser.). (ENG.). 80p. (J). (gr. 3-6). (978-1-63235-046-6(7), 11657, 12-Story Library) Bookstaves, LLC.

—High Drama. 2015. (Suspended Ser.). (ENG.). 112p. (YA). (gr. 6-12). 27.99 (978-1-4677-5710-2(1), 69b6a1cf-f764-4c60-ab45-5f974b79e897, Darby Creek) Lerner Publishing Group.

Terrian, Michael W. Chalie's Brand New Coat. 2011. 24p. pap. 12.50 (978-1-4670-3858-4(X)) AuthorHouse.

Terry, Teri. Fractured: Book Two in the Slated Trilogy. 2014. (Slated Ser.: 2). (ENG.). 352p. (YA). (gr. 7). pap. 10.99 (978-0-14-242504-6(4), Speak) Penguin Young Readers Group.

—Shattered: Book Three in the Slated Trilogy. 2015. (Slated Ser.: 3). (ENG.). 336p. (YA). (gr. 7). pap. 9.99 (978-0-14-242507-7(9), Speak) Penguin Young Readers Group.

—Slated: Book One in the Slated Trilogy. 2013. (Slated Ser.: 1). (ENG.). 368p. (YA). (gr. 7). pap. 10.99 (978-0-14-242503-9(6), Speak) Penguin Young Readers Group.

Tewkesbury, Alexa. Paul's Potty Pages. 2008. (ENG., Illus.). 128p. (J). (978-1-85345-456-1(7)) Crusade for World Revival.

Thaler, Mike. The Art Teacher from the Black Lagoon, 1 vol. Lee, Jared, illus. 2012. (Black Lagoon Ser.: No. 2). (ENG.). 32p. (J). (gr. k-4). lib. bdg. 31.36 (978-1-59961-952-1(0), 3627, Picture Bk.) Spotlight.

—The Author Visit from the Black Lagoon. Lee, Jared D., illus. 2010. 61p. (J). (978-0-545-27327-5(7)) Scholastic, Inc.

—The Author Visit from the Black Lagoon, 1 vol. Lee, Jared, illus. 2012. (Black Lagoon Adventures Ser.: No. 2). (ENG.). 64p. (J). (gr. 2-6). 31.36 (978-1-59961-960-6(1), 3604, Chapter Bks.) Spotlight.

—Back-to-School Fright from the Black Lagoon. Lee, Jared, illus. 2012. (Black Lagoon Adventures Ser.: No. 2). (ENG.). 64p. (J). (gr. 2-6). 31.36 (978-1-59961-961-3(X), 3605, Chapter Bks.) Spotlight.

—The Big Game from the Black Lagoon. Lee, Jared D., illus. 2013. 63p. (J). pap. (978-0-545-61639-3(5)) Scholastic, Inc.

—The Big Game from the Black Lagoon. Lee, Jared, illus. 2016. (Black Lagoon Adventures Set 4 Ser.). (ENG.). 64p. (J). (gr. 2-6). lib. bdg. 31.36 (978-1-61479-601-5(7), 24334, Chapter Bks.) Spotlight.

—Black Lagoon, 6 vols., Set. Lee, Jared, illus. Incl. Gym Teacher from the Black Lagoon. lib. bdg. 31.36 (978-1-59961-794-7(3), 3620); Librarian from the Black Lagoon. lib. bdg. 31.36 (978-1-59961-795-4(1), 3621); Music Teacher from the Black Lagoon. lib. bdg. 31.36 (978-1-59961-796-1(X), 3622); Principal from the Black Lagoon. lib. bdg. 31.36 (978-1-59961-797-8(8), 3623); School Nurse from the Black Lagoon. lib. bdg. 31.36 (978-1-59961-798-5(6), 3624); Teacher from the Black Lagoon. lib. bdg. 31.36 (978-1-59961-799-2(4), 3625); (J). (gr. k-4). (Black Lagoon Ser.: 6). (ENG., Illus.). 32p. 2011. Set lib. bdg. 188.16 (978-1-59961-793-0(5), 3619, Picture Bk.) Spotlight.

—Black Lagoon Adventures, 6 vols., Set. Lee, Jared, illus. Incl. Class Election from the Black Lagoon. 31.36 (978-1-59961-810-4(9), 3596); Class Trip from the Black Lagoon. 31.36 (978-1-59961-811-1(7), 3597); Field Day from the Black Lagoon. 31.36 (978-1-59961-812-8(5), 3598); Little League Team from the Black Lagoon. 31.36 (978-1-59961-813-5(3), 3599); Science Fair from the Black Lagoon. 31.36 (978-1-59961-814-2(1), 3600); Talent Show from the Black Lagoon. 31.36 (978-1-59961-815-9(X), 3601); (J). (gr. 2-6). (Black Lagoon Adventures Ser.: 6). (ENG., Illus.). 64p. 2011. Set lib. bdg. 188.16 (978-1-59961-809-8(5), 3595, Chapter Bks.) Spotlight.

—The Book Fair from the Black Lagoon. Lee, Jared, illus. 2006. pap. (978-0-439-88348-1(2)) Scholastic, Inc.

—The Bully from the Black Lagoon. Lee, Jared, illus. 2008. (From the Black Lagoon Ser.). (gr. -1-3). 14.00 (978-0-7569-8834-0(9)) Perfection Learning Corp.

—The Bully from the Black Lagoon. Lee, Jared, illus. (Black Lagoon Adventures Ser.). (J). 2008. (ENG.). 32p. (gr. -1-3). pap. 3.99 (978-0-545-06521-4(6), Cartwheel Bks.) 2004. (978-0-439-68072-1(7)) Scholastic, Inc.

—The Bully from the Black Lagoon, 1 vol. Lee, Jared, illus. 2012. (Black Lagoon Ser.: No. 2). (ENG.). 32p. (J). (gr. k-4). lib. bdg. 31.36 (978-1-59961-953-8(9), 3628, Picture Bk.) Spotlight.

—The Christmas Party from the Black Lagoon. Lee, Jared, illus. 2006. 64p. (J). pap. (978-0-439-87160-0(3)) Scholastic, Inc.

—The Class Election from the Black Lagoon. Lee, Jared, illus. 2011. (Black Lagoon Adventures Ser.: No. 1). (ENG.). 64p. (J). (gr. 2-6). 31.36 (978-1-59961-810-4(9), 3596, Chapter Bks.) Spotlight.

—The Class Picture Day from the Black Lagoon. Lee, Jared D., illus. 2012. 64p. (J). pap. (978-0-545-47666-9(6)) Scholastic, Inc.

—The Class Picture Day from the Black Lagoon. Lee, Jared, illus. 2016. (Black Lagoon Adventures Set 4 Ser.). (ENG.). 64p. (J). (gr. 2-6). lib. bdg. 31.36 (978-1-61479-602-2(5), 24335, Chapter Bks.) Spotlight.

—The Computer Teacher from the Black Lagoon. Lee, Jared, illus. 2007. (J). (978-0-439-87133-4(6)) Scholastic, Inc.

—The Computer Teacher from the Black Lagoon, 1 vol. Lee, Jared, illus. 2012. (Black Lagoon Ser.: No. 2). (ENG.). 32p. (J). (gr. k-4). lib. bdg. 31.36 (978-1-59961-955-2(5), 3630, Picture Bk.) Spotlight.

—The Custodian from the Black Lagoon. Lee, Jared, illus. 2014. (Black Lagoon Ser.). (ENG.). 32p. (J). (gr. -1-4). lib. bdg. 31.36 (978-1-61479-196-6(1), 3636, Picture Bk.) Spotlight.

—The Dentist from the Black Lagoon. Lee, Jared D., illus. 2014. (Black Lagoon Ser.). (ENG.). 32p. (J). (gr. -1-4). 31.36 (978-1-61479-197-3(X), 3637, Picture Bk.) Spotlight.

—Earth Day from the Black Lagoon. Lee, Jared D., illus. 2013. 64p. (J). (978-0-545-47669-0(0)) Scholastic, Inc.

—Earth Day from the Black Lagoon. Lee, Jared, illus. 2016. (Black Lagoon Adventures Set 4 Ser.). (ENG.). 64p. (J). (gr. 2-6). lib. bdg. 31.36 (978-1-61479-603-9(3), 24336, Chapter Bks.) Spotlight.

—The Field Day from the Black Lagoon. Lee, Jared, illus. 2008. (From the Black Lagoon Ser.). 64p. (gr. 2-5). 14.00 (978-0-7569-8801-2(2)) Perfection Learning Corp.

—The Field Day from the Black Lagoon. Lee, Jared, illus. 2011. (Black Lagoon Adventures Ser.: No. 1). (ENG.). 64p. (J). (gr. 2-6). 31.36 (978-1-59961-812-8(5), 3598, Chapter Bks.) Spotlight.

—The Field Day from the Black Lagoon (Black Lagoon Adventures #6) Lee, Jared, illus. 2008. (Black Lagoon Adventures Ser.: 6). (ENG.). 64p. (J). (gr. 2-5). pap. 4.99 (978-0-439-68076-9(X), Scholastic Paperbacks) Scholastic, Inc.

—Friday the 13th from the Black Lagoon. Lee, Jared D., illus. 2017. 64p. (J). (978-0-545-61638-6(7)) Scholastic, Inc.

—Friday the 13th from the Black Lagoon. Lee, Jared, illus. 2016. (Black Lagoon Adventures Set 4 Ser.). (ENG.). 64p. (J). (gr. 2-6). lib. bdg. 31.36 (978-1-61479-604-6(1), 24337, Chapter Bks.) Spotlight.

—The Gym Teacher from the Black Lagoon. Lee, Jared, illus. 2008. (Black Lagoon Adventures Ser.). (ENG.). 32p. (J). (gr. -1-3). pap. 3.99 (978-0-545-06931-1(9), Cartwheel Bks.) Scholastic, Inc.

—The Gym Teacher from the Black Lagoon, 1 vol. Lee, Jared, illus. 2011. (Black Lagoon Ser.: No. 1). (ENG.). 32p. (J). (gr. k-4). lib. bdg. 31.36 (978-1-59961-794-7(3), 3620, Picture Bk.) Spotlight.

—The Gym Teacher from the Black Lagoon. Lee, Jared, illus. 2009. (J). (gr. -1-3). pap. 18.95 incl. audio compact disk (978-0-545-19706-9(6)) Weston Woods Studios, Inc.

—Hubie Cool: Super Spy. Lee, Jared D., illus. 2016. 64p. (J). (978-0-545-85076-6(2)) Scholastic, Inc.

—Hubie Cool: Vampire Hunter. Lee, Jared D., illus. 2015. 64p. (J). pap. (978-0-545-85075-9(4)) Scholastic, Inc.

—The Librarian from the Black Lagoon, 1 vol. Lee, Jared, illus. 2011. (Black Lagoon Ser.: No. 1). (ENG.). 32p. (J). (gr. k-4). lib. bdg. 31.36 (978-1-59961-795-4(1), 3621, Picture Bk.) Spotlight.

—The Little League Team from the Black Lagoon. Lee, Jared, illus. 2011. (Black Lagoon Adventures Ser.: No. 1). (ENG.). 64p. (J). (gr. 2-6). 31.36 (978-1-59961-813-5(3), 3599, Chapter Bks.) Spotlight.

—Meatloaf Monster from the School Cafeteria. Lee, Jared D., illus. 2012. (J). pap. (978-0-545-48570-8(3)) Scholastic, Inc.

—The Music Teacher from the Black Lagoon, 1 vol. Lee, Jared, illus. 2011. (Black Lagoon Ser.: No. 1). (ENG.). 32p. (J). (gr. k-4). lib. bdg. 31.36 (978-1-59961-796-1(X), 3622, Picture Bk.) Spotlight.

—The New Kid from the Black Lagoon. 2004. (Black Lagoon Ser.). (Illus.). 32p. (978-0-439-55719-1(4)) Scholastic, Inc.

—The New Kid from the Black Lagoon, 1 vol. Lee, Jared, illus. 2012. (Black Lagoon Ser.: No. 2). (ENG.). 32p. (J). (gr. k-4). lib. bdg. 31.36 (978-1-59961-956-9(3), 3631, Picture Bk.) Spotlight.

—The Principal from the Black Lagoon. Lee, Jared, illus. 2009. (From the Black Lagoon Ser.). 14.00 (978-1-60686-507-1(2)) Perfection Learning Corp.

—The Principal from the Black Lagoon. Lee, Jared, illus. 2008. (Black Lagoon Adventures Ser.). (ENG.). 32p. (J). (gr. -1-3). pap. 3.99 (978-0-545-06932-8(7), Cartwheel Bks.) Scholastic, Inc.

—The Principal from the Black Lagoon, 1 vol. Lee, Jared, illus. 2011. (Black Lagoon Ser.: No. 1). (ENG.). 32p. (J). (gr. k-4). lib. bdg. 31.36 (978-1-59961-797-8(8), 3623, Picture Bk.) Spotlight.

—The Reading Challenge from the Black Lagoon. Lee, Jared D., illus. 2015. 64p. (J). pap. (978-0-545-78521-1(9)) Scholastic, Inc.

—The Reading Challenge from the Black Lagoon. Lee, Jared, illus. 2016. (Black Lagoon Adventures Set 4 Ser.). (ENG.). 64p. (J). (gr. 2-6). lib. bdg. 31.36 (978-1-61479-606-0(8), 24339, Chapter Bks.) Spotlight.

—The School Carnival from the Black Lagoon. Lee, Jared, illus. 2005. 64p. (J). pap. (978-0-439-80075-4(7)) Scholastic, Inc.

—The School Carnival from the Black Lagoon, 1 vol. Lee, Jared, illus. 2012. (Black Lagoon Adventures Ser.: No. 2). (ENG.). 64p. (J). (gr. 2-6). 31.36 (978-1-59961-962-0(8), 3606, Chapter Bks.) Spotlight.

—The School Nurse from the Black Lagoon, 1 vol. Lee, Jared, illus. 2011. (Black Lagoon Ser.: No. 1). (ENG.). 32p. (J). (gr. k-4). lib. bdg. 31.36 (978-1-59961-798-5(6), 3624, Picture Bk.) Spotlight.

—School Play from the Black Lagoon, 1 vol. Lee, Jared, illus. 2014. (Black Lagoon Adventures Ser.). (ENG.). 64p. (J). (gr. 2-6). lib. bdg. 31.36 (978-1-61479-205-5(4), 3614, Chapter Bks.) Spotlight.

—The School Secretary from the Black Lagoon. Lee, Jared, illus. 2006. (J). (978-0-439-80077-8(3)) Scholastic, Inc.

—The Science Fair from the Black Lagoon. Lee, Jared, illus. 2011. (Black Lagoon Adventures Ser.: No. 1). (ENG.). 64p. (J). (gr. 2-6). 31.36 (978-1-59961-814-2(1), 3600, Chapter Bks.) Spotlight.

—The Secret Santa from the Black Lagoon. Lee, Jared D., illus. 2014. 64p. (J). (978-0-545-78519-8(7)) Scholastic, Inc.

—The Secret Santa from the Black Lagoon. Lee, Jared, illus. 2016. (Black Lagoon Adventures Set 4 Ser.). (ENG.). 64p. (J). (gr. 2-6). lib. bdg. 31.36 (978-1-61479-607-7(6), 24340, Chapter Bks.) Spotlight.

—The Substitute Teacher from the Black Lagoon. Lee, Jared, illus. 2014. (Black Lagoon Ser.). (ENG.). 32p. (J). (gr. -1-4). 31.36 (978-1-61479-199-7(6), 3639, Picture Bk.) Spotlight.

—The Talent Show from the Black Lagoon. Lee, Jared, illus. 2011. (Black Lagoon Adventures Ser.: No. 1). (ENG.). 64p. (J). (gr. 2-6). 31.36 (978-1-59961-815-9(X), 3601, Chapter Bks.) Spotlight.

—The Teacher from the Black Lagoon. Lee, Jared, illus. 2008. (From the Black Lagoon Ser.). (gr. -1-3). 14.00 (978-0-7569-8779-4(2)) Perfection Learning Corp.

—The Teacher from the Black Lagoon. Lee, Jared, illus. 2008. (Black Lagoon Adventures Ser.). (ENG.). 32p. (J). (gr. -1-3). pap. 5.99 (978-0-545-06522-1(4), Cartwheel Bks.) Scholastic, Inc.

—The Teacher from the Black Lagoon, 1 vol. Lee, Jared, illus. 2011. (Black Lagoon Ser.: No. 1). (ENG.). 32p. (J). (gr. k-4). lib. bdg. 31.36 (978-1-59961-799-2(4), 3625, Picture Bk.) Spotlight.

—The Teacher from the Black Lagoon. Lee, Jared, illus. 2004. (J). (gr. k-3). 18.95 (978-1-55592-495-9(6)) Weston Woods Studios, Inc.

—The Vice Principal from the Black Lagoon. Lee, Jared, illus. 2007. (J). pap. (978-0-439-87132-7(8)) Scholastic, Inc.

—The 100th Day of School from the Black Lagoon. Lee, Jared, illus. 2012. 64p. (J). pap. (978-0-545-37325-8(5)) Scholastic, Inc.

Thame, Val. Witches in Deed. l.t. ed. 2007. 100p. per. (978-1-905665-25-9(3)) Pollinger In Print.

Tharp, Jason & Rose, J. B. A School Tail (Peachy & Keen) 2018. (Peachy & Keen Ser.: 1). (ENG., Illus.). 96p. (J). (gr. 2-5). pap. 4.99 (978-1-338-11043-2(8)) Scholastic, Inc.

Tharp, Tim. Knights of the Hill Country. 2013. (ENG.). 240p. (YA). (gr. 7). pap. 8.99 (978-0-449-81287-7(1), Ember) Random Hse. Children's Bks.

—Mojo. 2014. (ENG.). 288p. (YA). (gr. 7). pap. 8.99 (978-0-375-86402-5(4), Ember) Random Hse. Children's Bks.

—The Spectacular Now. 2010. (ENG.). 304p. (YA). (gr. 9). pap. 9.99 (978-0-375-86502-2(0), Knopf Bks. for Young Readers) Random Hse. Children's Bks.

The Book Company, ed. School. (Sparkle Bks.). (ENG.). (J). bds. 4.99 (978-1-74047-331-6(0)) Book Co. Publishing Pty, Ltd., The AUS. Dist: Penton Overseas, Inc.

The Equality Of Genders Project. Billy Conquers the Bully. 2009. (ENG.). 24p. pap. 8.49 (978-1-4389-5376-2(3)) AuthorHouse.

Thiel, Annie. Danny Is Moving. Edwards, William M., illus. 2006. (Playdate Kids Ser.). 32p. (J). (gr. -1-3). 14.95 (978-1-933721-02-6(2)) Playdate Kids Publishing.

Thielbar, Melinda. The Ancient Formula: A Mystery with Fractions. Pantoja, Maria Kristina Sb., illus. 2011. (Manga Math Mysteries Ser.: 5). (ENG.). 48p. (J). (gr. 3-5). pap. 6.95 (978-0-7613-8134-1(1), 1c74d365-5757-4fe3-8be4-721e1b06585d, Graphic Universe™) Lerner Publishing Group.

—The Fishy Fountain: A Mystery with Multiplication & Division. Lin, Yali, illus. 2011. (Manga Math Mysteries Ser.: 6). (ENG.). 48p. (J). (gr. 3-5). pap. 7.99 (978-0-7613-8135-8(X), 86863ee0-c152-4a00-ae62-5a6fc9a6ebe3, Graphic Universe™) Lerner Publishing Group.

—The Hundred-Dollar Robber. 2nd rev. ed. 2010. pap. 39.62 (978-0-7613-6943-1(0)) Lerner Publishing Group.

—The Hundred-Dollar Robber: A Mystery with Money. Pantoja, Maria Kristina Sb., illus. 2010. (Manga Math Mysteries Ser.: 2). (ENG.). 48p. (J). (gr. 3-5). pap. 6.99 (978-0-7613-5243-3(0), eb5149e7-387a-4f32-8264-1a6ba34243fa, Graphic Universe™) Lerner Publishing Group.

—The Hundred-Dollar Robber: A Mystery with Money. Pantoja, Maria Kristina, illus. 2009. (Manga Math Mysteries Ser.: 2). (ENG.). 48p. (gr. 3-5). 29.27 (978-0-7613-3854-3(3)) Lerner Publishing Group.

—The Kung Fu Puzzle. 4th rev. ed. 2010. pap. 39.62 (978-0-7613-6945-5(7)) Lerner Publishing Group.

—The Kung Fu Puzzle: A Mystery with Time & Temperature. Helmer, Der-shing, illus. 2010. (Manga Math Mysteries Ser.: 4). (ENG.). 48p. (J). (gr. 3-5). pap. 7.99 (978-0-7613-5246-4(5), 95692add-0fab-4091-b7e1-e284d00dadc2, Graphic Universe™) Lerner Publishing Group.

—The Kung Fu Puzzle: A Mystery with Time & Temperature. Ota, Yuko & Helmer, Der-shing, illus. 2009. (Manga Math Mysteries Ser.: No. 4). 48p. (J). (gr. 2-5). 29.27 (978-0-7613-3856-7(X)) Lerner Publishing Group.

—The Lost Key. rev. ed. 2010. pap. 39.62 (978-0-7613-6942-4(2)) Lerner Publishing Group.

—The Lost Key: A Mystery with Whole Numbers. Pantoja, Maria Kristina Sb., illus. 2010. (Manga Math Mysteries Ser.: 1). (ENG.). 48p. (J). (gr. 3-5). pap. 6.99 (978-0-7613-5244-0(9), db9985c2-e8b5-4556-bfe1-78181351eb7d, Graphic Universe™) Lerner Publishing Group.

—#5 the Ancient Formula: A Mystery with Fractions. Pantoja, Tintin, illus. 2011. (Manga Math Mysteries Set II Ser.). pap. 39.62 (978-0-7613-8362-8(X), Graphic Universe™) Lerner Publishing Group.

—#6 the Fishy Fountain: A Mystery with Multiplication & Division. Lin, Yali, illus. 2011. (Manga Math Mysteries Set II Ser.). pap. 39.62 (978-0-7613-8363-5(8), Graphic Universe™) Lerner Publishing Group.

Thomas, G. D. Keep Your Head Down. 2012. (ENG.). 160p. pap. 11.00 (978-1-78035-281-7(6), Fastprint Publishing) Upfront Publishing Ltd. GBR. Dist: Printondemand-worldwide.com.

Thomas, Jatavius. Weird Things Happening at Southside Middle School: And Other Stories. 2010. 52p. pap. 8.95 (978-1-4502-4049-9(6)) iUniverse, Inc.

Thomas, Kara. The Cheerleaders. 2019. (ENG.). 400p. (YA). (gr. 9). pap. 12.99 (978-1-5247-1835-0(1), Ember) Random Hse. Children's Bks.

Thomas, Lex. The Burnouts. 2016. (Quarantine Ser.: 3). (ENG.). 296p. (YA). (gr. 9-12). pap. 9.99 (978-1-5124-0419-7(5), e71b4da5-69dd-42c0-af43-1a1b573637a4, Carolrhoda Lab™) Lerner Publishing Group.

—The Loners. (Quarantine Ser.: No. 1). (ENG.). 416p. (gr. 9). 2012. 17.99 (978-1-60684-329-1(X))Bk. 1. 2013. (YA). pap. 9.99 (978-1-60684-438-0(5), a4290b32-f23c-40fb-9b34-385c9b02c589) Lerner Publishing Group. (Carolrhoda Lab™).

Thomas, Peggy. Snow Dance, 1 vol. Facklam, Paul, illus. 2008. (ENG.). 32p. (J). (gr. 1-3). 16.99 (978-1-58980-478-4(3), Pelican Publishing) Arcadia Publishing.

Thomas, Rob. Rats Saw God. 2009. 9.00 (978-0-7848-2881-6(4), Everbind) Marco Bk. Co.

—Rats Saw God. 2010. (ENG.). 202p. 17.10 (978-0-7569-8366-6(5)) Perfection Learning Corp.

—Rats Saw God. 2013. (ENG., Illus.). 224p. (YA). (gr. 7). pap. 12.99 (978-1-4424-5738-6(4), Simon & Schuster Bks. For Young Readers) Simon & Schuster Bks. For Young Readers.

—Rats Saw God. 2013. (ENG.). 224p. (YA). (gr. 7-12). 16.99 (978-1-4424-5976-2(X)) Simon & Schuster, Inc.

—Slave Day. 2018. (ENG.). 256p. (YA). (gr. 7). pap. 10.99 (978-1-5344-2966-6(2), Simon & Schuster Bks. For Young Readers) Simon & Schuster Bks. For Young Readers.

Thomas, Rob & Macaya, Leopoldo. Doing Time: Notes from the Undergrad. 2018. (ENG.). 176p. (YA). (gr. 7). pap. 10.99 (978-1-5344-3009-9(1), Simon & Schuster Bks. For Young Readers) Simon & Schuster Bks. For Young Readers.

Thomas, Terri. J Mac Is the Freestyle King! Sefcik, Wendy, illus. 2010. 38p. pap. 20.00 (978-1-60844-453-3(8)) Dog Ear Publishing, LLC.

Thompson, Anne. Arrow Sparrow. 2009. (Illus.). 32p. pap. (978-1-84549-369-1(9), Swirl) arima publishing.

Thompson, Brian. Reject High. 2013. 270p. pap. 11.95 (978-0-9891056-0-6(1)) Great Nation Publishing.

Thompson, C. Michael. Twinsational. 2009. 120p. (YA). pap. 14.95 (978-1-4327-3033-8(9)) Outskirts Pr., Inc.

Thompson, Colin. The Floods #2: School Plot. Scrambly, Crab, illus. 2008. (Floods Ser.). (J). (ENG.). 224p. 15.99 (978-0-06-113861-4(4)); 256p. lib. bdg. 16.89 (978-0-06-113855-3(X)) HarperCollins Pubs.

Thompson, Dorothy. Dewey Does Adding & Subtractions Bk. 2: Activity Sports Book. 2004. (Dewey Does Ser.). (Illus.). 44p. (J). (gr. -1-3). pap., act. bk. ed. 4.95 (978-0-9711474-2-3(6)) Dewey Does Corp, A.

Thompson, Holly. Orchards. 2012. 336p. (YA). (gr. 7). pap. 10.99 (978-0-385-73978-8(8), Ember) Random Hse. Children's Bks.

Thompson, Kelly. Lasting. 2005. 120p. pap. 19.95 (978-1-4137-9653-7(2)) PublishAmerica, Inc.

Thompson, Lauren. Mouse Loves School: Ready-To-Read Pre-Level 1. Erdogan, Buket, illus. 2011. (Mouse Ser.). (ENG.). 24p. (J). (gr. -1-k). pap. 4.99 (978-1-4424-2898-0(8)); lib. bdg. 17.99 (978-1-4424-2899-7(6)) Simon Spotlight. (Simon Spotlight).

—Mouse's First Day of School. Erdogan, Buket, illus. 2010. (Mouse Ser.). (ENG.). 34p. (J). (gr. -1 — 1). bds. 8.99 (978-1-4169-9476-3(9), Little Simon) Little Simon.

—Mouse's First Day of School. Erdogan, Buket, illus. 2003. (Mouse Ser.). (ENG.). 32p. (J). (gr. -1-3). 19.99 (978-0-689-84727-1(0), Simon & Schuster Bks. For Young Readers) Simon & Schuster Bks. For Young Readers.

Thompson, Shannon Raines. Mad about Miller. Stone, Kathrine Thompson, ed. Shehan, Terece, illus. 2006. 24p. (YA). 12.95 (978-1-59971-853-8(7)) Aardvark Global Publishing.

—Nuts about Neal. Stone, Kathrine Thompson, ed. Shehan, Terece, illus. 2006. 24p. (YA). 12.95 (978-1-59971-852-1(9)) Aardvark Global Publishing.

Thompson, Tate. Senioritis. 2nd ed. 2003. (YA). per. 13.50 (978-0-943864-47-1(X)) Davenport, May Pubs.

Thompson, Tolya L. Catchin' Cooties Consuelo. Harrold, Brian, illus. 2004. (Smarties Ser.: 3). (SPA.). (J). 16.00 (978-0-9708296-3-4(9)) Savor Publishing Hse., Inc.

Thompson, Vivian L. Neat! Said Jeremy. 2003. 33p. (J). pap. 8.95 (978-0-7414-1579-0(8)) Infinity Publishing.

Thomson, Melissa. Keena Ford & the Field Trip Mix-Up. 2010. (Keena Ford Ser.: 2). 112p. (J). (gr. 1-3). 6.99 (978-0-14-241572-6(3), Puffin Books) Penguin Young Readers Group.

—Keena Ford & the Secret Journal Mix-Up. Morrison, Frank, illus. 2011. (Keena Ford Ser.: 3). 128p. (J). (gr. 1-3). 6.99 (978-0-14-241937-3(0), Puffin Books) Penguin Young Readers Group.

Thor, Annika. The Lily Pond. Schenck, Linda, tr. (Faraway Island Ser.). 224p. (J). (gr. 4-7). 2012. 7.99 (978-0-385-74040-1(9), Yearling)2. 2013. (ENG.). lib. bdg. 21.19 (978-0-385-90838-2(5), Delacorte Pr.) Random Hse. Children's Bks.

Thorne, Bella. Autumn's Wish. 2017. (Autumn Falls Ser.: 3). (ENG.). 320p. (YA). (gr. 7). pap. 10.99 (978-0-385-74438-6(2), Ember) Random Hse. Children's Bks.

Thorpe, Kiki. Never Girls #9: Before the Bell (Disney: the Never Girls) Christy, Jana, illus. 2015. (Never Girls Ser.: 9). (ENG.). 128p. (J). (gr. 1-4). lib. bdg. 12.99 (978-0-7364-8167-0(2), RH/Disney) Random Hse. Children's Bks.

Thrash, Maggie. Strange Lies. (Strange Ser.: 2). (ENG.). 336p. (YA). (gr. 9). 2018. pap. 11.99 (978-1-4814-6204-4(0)) 2017. (Illus.). 17.99 (978-1-4814-6203-7(2)) Simon Pulse. (Simon Pulse).

—We Know It Was You. 2016. (Strange Ser.). (ENG., Illus.). 352p. (YA). (gr. 9). 17.99 (978-1-4814-6200-6(8), Simon Pulse) Simon Pulse.

Tidd, Louise Vitellaro. Lo Haré Después. Translations.com Staff, tr. from ENG. Handelman, Dorothy, photos by. 2007. (Lecturas para niños de verdad - Nivel 2 (Real Kids Readers - Level 2) Ser.).Tr. of I'll Do It Later. (SPA., Illus.). 32p. (gr. k-3). per. 5.95 (978-0-8225-7805-5(0)) Lerner Publishing Group.

—Ya Te Enteraste? Handelman, Dorothy, photos by. 2007. (Lecturas para niños de verdad - Nivel 2 (Real Kids Readers - Level 2) Ser.).Tr. of Did You Hear About Jake? (SPA., Illus.). 32p. (J). (gr. -1-3). per. 5.95 (978-0-8225-7802-4(6), Ediciones Lerner) Lerner Publishing Group.

Tidwell, Deborah Swayne. Magic Eraser: And the Substitute Teacher. 2008. 24p. pap. 12.99 (978-1-4343-8107-1(2)) AuthorHouse.

Tilley. Damaged. 2011. (ENG.). 260p. (gr. 9-13). pap. 11.95 (978-988-18967-0-4(3)) Haven Bks.

Time, Nicholas O. Going, Going, Gone. 2016. (In Due Time Ser.: 1). (ENG., Illus.). 160p. (J). (gr. 3-7). pap. 6.99 (978-1-4814-6729-2(8), Simon Spotlight) Simon Spotlight.

—Going, Going, Gone. 2016. (In Due Time Ser.: 1). lib. bdg. 17.20 (978-0-606-38985-3(7)) Turtleback.

—Houston, We Have a Klutz! 2016. (In Due Time Ser.: 4). (ENG., Illus.). 160p. (J). (gr. 3-7). 17.99 (978-1-4814-7237-1(2), Simon Spotlight) Simon Spotlight.

—Stay a Spell. 2016. (In Due Time Ser.: 2). (ENG., Illus.). 160p. (J). (gr. 3-7). pap. 6.99 (978-1-4814-6726-1(3), Simon Spotlight) Simon Spotlight.

Tinti, Natalie. Magic in Us. the Power of Imagination: The Power of Imagination, bks. 1, vol. 2. T, N., illus. ed. 2013. (Sewing a Friendship Ser.). (ENG.). 116p. (J). pap. 12.95 (978-0-9842625-3-3(9)) Tintinatie Publishing Hse.

Titherington, Karen M. Gavin Goes to Kindergarten! Prepare Your Child for the First Day of School. 2011. (Illus.). 80p. (J). 19.99 (978-0-9795741-6-0(1)) Bloated Toe Publishing.

Toader, Alex. Max's Journal: The Adventures of Shark Boy & Lava Girl. Rodriguez, Robert, illus. 2005. 128p. (J). (978-1-933104-03-4(1)) Troublemaker Publishing, LP.

Tobias, Anne B. Harry's Problem First Loose Tooth. Tobias, Tom, illus. 2008. 16p. pap. 9.95 (978-0-9818683-9-4(8)) Peppertree Pr., The.

Todd, Strasser. Give a Boy a Gun. 2014. (ENG.). 208p. (YA). 11.24 (978-1-63245-176-7(X)) Lectorum Pubns., Inc.

Toews, Rita. The Bully: A Discussion & Activity Story. Ljungberg, Jon, illus. 2011. 40p. (J). pap. 11.95 (978-1-59850-102-5(X)) Youthlight, Inc.

Toki, Sela Tuita. Pati Loves to Walk Barefoot to School. 2009. 44p. pap. 24.95 (978-1-60749-433-1(7)) America Star Bks.

Tokio, Marnelle. Room 207. Hendry, Linda, illus. 2006. 120p. (J). (gr. 4-7). pap. 8.95 (978-0-88776-695-4(1), Tundra Bks.) Tundra Bks. CAN. Dist: Penguin Random Hse. LLC.

Tolan, Stephanie S. Surviving the Applewhites. l.t. ed. 2005. pap. 10.95 (978-0-7862-7259-4(7), Large Print Pr.) Thorndike Pr.

—Surviving the Applewhites: A Newbery Honor Award Winner. 2012. (Applewhites Ser.: 1). (ENG.). 240p. (J). (gr. 5-18). pap. 9.99 (978-0-06-441044-1(7), HarperCollins) HarperCollins Pubs.

Toliver, K. S. Pam Brown Is Picture Perfect!! 2008. 28p. pap. 12.95 (978-1-4327-2058-2(9)) Outskirts Pr., Inc.

Toliver, Wendy. The Secret Life of a Teenage Siren. 2012. (Romantic Comedies Ser.). (ENG.). 304p. (YA). (gr. 7). pap. 14.99 (978-1-4424-7494-9(7), Simon Pulse) Simon Pulse.

Tolman, Stacia. The Spaces Between Us. 2020. (ENG.). 304p. (YA). pap. 10.99 (978-1-250-25091-9(9), 900189272) Square Fish.

Tomsic, Kim. The 11:11 Wish. (ENG.). 368p. (J). (gr. 3-7). 2019. pap. 6.99 (978-0-06-265495-3(0)) 2018. 16.99 (978-0-06-265494-6(2)) HarperCollins Pubs. (Tegen, Katherine Bks).

Toriyama, Akira. Dragon Ball Z, Vol. 22. 2005. (Dragon Ball Z Ser.: 22). (ENG., Illus.). 192p. pap. 9.99 (978-1-4215-0051-5(5)) Viz Media.

—Dragon Ball Z, Vol. 24. 2006. (Dragon Ball Z Ser.: 24). (ENG., Illus.). 192p. pap. 9.99 (978-1-4215-0273-1(9)) Viz Media.

—Dragon Ball Z, Vol. 25. 2006. (Dragon Ball Z Ser.: 25). (ENG., Illus.). 240p. pap. 9.99 (978-1-4215-0404-9(9)) Viz Media.

Torres, Jose A. Joey Kanga Roo: First Day of School. 2009. 36p. pap. 15.99 (978-1-4389-3964-3(7)) AuthorHouse.

Tosten, S. Kennedy. Troy's Amazing Universe Bk. 1: M for Mall. 2003. (Illus.). 116p. (YA). (gr. 2-18). pap. 13.95 (978-1-59113-318-6(1)) Booklocker.com, Inc.

Toten, Teresa. The Unlikely Hero of Room 13B. 2018. (ENG.). 304p. (YA). (gr. 7). pap. 9.99 (978-0-553-50789-8(3), Ember) Random Hse. Children's Bks.

Touchell, Dianne. A Small Madness, 1 vol. 2016. (ENG.). 192p. (YA). (gr. 9). 16.95 (978-1-55498-837-2(3)) Groundwood Bks. CAN. Dist: Publishers Group West (PGW).

Tougas, Chris. Dojo Surprise. 2016. (Dojo Ser.: 3). (ENG., Illus.). 32p. (J). (gr. -1-3). 16.95 (978-1-77147-143-5(3), Owlkids) Owlkids Bks. Inc. CAN. Dist: Publishers Group West (PGW).

Towell, Katy. Skary Childrin & the Carousel of Sorrow. 2013. (ENG.). 272p. (J). (gr. 8-12). lib. bdg. 24.94 (978-0-375-96860-0(1), Knopf Bks. for Young Readers) Random Hse. Children's Bks.

Townley, Roderick. Sky. 2010. (ENG.). 272p. (YA). (gr. 7). pap. 12.99 (978-1-4423-3973-6(X), Atheneum Bks. for Young Readers) Simon & Schuster Children's Publishing.

Townsend, Jessica. Wundersmith: The Calling of Morrigan Crow. (Nevermoor Ser.: 2). (ENG.). (J). (gr. 3-7). 2019. 560p. pap. 8.99 (978-0-316-50892-6(6)) 2018. 544p. 17.99 (978-0-316-50891-9(8)) 2018. 720p. 48.99 (978-0-316-41990-1(7)) Little, Brown Bks. for Young Readers.

Townsend, John. Never Odd or Even: US Edition. 2018. (ENG.). 100p. (J). (gr. 4-13). pap. 8.99 (978-1-944589-31-8(7), Incorgnito Publishing Pr.) Incorgnito Publishing Pr. LLC.

Tracy, Judith. The Wildsidhe Chronicles Bk. 3: Dark Proposal. 2003. (J). pap. 7.99 (978-1-890096-15-1(6)) Padwolf Publishing Inc.

Tracy, Kathleen. The Hamster in Our Class. 2011. (Randy's Corner Ser.). (Illus.). 32p. (J). (gr. -1-2). lib. bdg. 25.70 (978-1-58415-980-3(4)) Mitchell Lane Pubs.

—The Turtle in Our Class. 2011. (Randy's Corner Ser.). (Illus.). 32p. (J). (gr. -1-2). lib. bdg. 25.70 (978-1-58415-979-7(0)) Mitchell Lane Pubs.

Tracy, Kristen. Bessica Lefter Bites Back. 2013. (Bessica Lefter Ser.). (ENG.). 272p. (J). (gr. 5). 7.99 (978-0-375-87295-2(7), Yearling) Random Hse. Children's Bks.

—Camille Mcphee Fell under the Bus. 2010. (ENG.). 304p. (J). (gr. 3-7). 7.99 (978-0-375-84546-8(1), Yearling) Random Hse. Children's Bks.

—Project (un)Popular Book #1. 2017. (Project (un)Popular Ser.: 1). (ENG.). 336p. (J). (gr. 5). 8.99 (978-0-553-51051-5(7), Yearling) Random Hse. Children's Bks.

—Project (un)Popular Book #2: Totally Crushed. 2017. (Project (un)Popular Ser.: 2). (ENG.). 224p. (J). (gr. 5). 16.99 (978-0-553-51052-2(5), Delacorte Bks. for Young Readers) Random Hse. Children's Bks.

—The Reinvention of Bessica Lefter. 2012. (Bessica Lefter Ser.). (ENG.). 320p. (J). (gr. 5). 7.99 (978-0-375-84547-5(X), Yearling) Random Hse. Children's Bks.

—Totally Crushed. 2017. 211p. (J). (978-0-553-51053-9(3), Delacorte Pr) Random House Publishing Group.

Trailblazers! Individual Title Six-Packs. (Action Packs Ser.). 104p. (gr. 3-5). 44.00 (978-0-7635-2992-5(3)) Rigby Education.

Trapped by a Teacher: Individual Title Six-Packs. (Action Packs Ser.). 128p. (gr. 3-5). 44.00 (978-0-7635-3309-0(2)) Rigby Education.

Traylor, Javier. A Day at School with Sally Sue. 2012. 40p. pap. 24.95 (978-1-4137-8929-4(3)) America Star Bks.

Traylor, Marci. What Will I Be? 2008. 40p. pap. 19.50 (978-1-4389-0247-0(6)) AuthorHouse.

Tregay, Sarah. Fan Art. DeJesus, Melissa, illus. 2014. (ENG.). 368p. (YA). (gr. 8). 17.99 (978-0-06-224315-7(2), Tegen, Katherine Bks) HarperCollins Pubs.

Trevino, David. A Colorful Carnival of Kids in the Kingdom of Marbles: Mission #1 the Cemetery Ghost. 2011. 126p. pap. 19.95 (978-1-4626-1087-7(0)) America Star Bks.

Trice, Linda. Kenya's Song. Johnson, Pamela, illus. 2013. 32p. (J). (gr. -1-3). pap. 7.95 (978-1-57091-847-6(3)); lib. bdg. 17.95 (978-1-57091-846-9(5)) Charlesbridge Publishing, Inc.

Trine, Greg. Dinos Are Forever. Dormer, Frank W., illus. 2014. (Adventures of Jo Schmo Ser.: 1). (ENG.). 112p. (J). (gr. 1-4). pap. 6.99 (978-0-544-00325-5(X), 1526367, Clarion Bks.) HarperCollins Pubs.

Trionfo, Nikki. Shatter. 2017. 346p. (YA). pap. 18.99 (978-1-4621-2013-0(X), Horizon Pubs.) Cedar Fort, Inc./CFI Distribution.

Trivas, Tracy. The Wish Stealers. 2011. (ENG.). 288p. (J). (gr. 3-7). pap. 8.99 (978-1-4169-8726-0(6), Aladdin) Simon & Schuster Children's Publishing.

Tromly, Stephanie. Trouble Never Sleeps. 2019. (ENG.). 304p. (YA). (gr. 7). pap. 10.99 (978-0-14-751545-2(9), Penguin Books) Penguin Young Readers Group.

Trouble in the Barkers' Class. 2005. (J). 29.95 incl. audio compact disk (978-0-8045-4134-3(5)); 27.95 incl. audio (978-0-8045-6935-4(5)) Spoken Arts, Inc.

Trueit, Trudi. Explorer Academy: the Falcon's Feather (Book 2) 2019. (Explorer Academy Ser.: 2). (Illus.). 208p. (J). (gr. 3-7). 16.99 (978-1-4263-3304-0(8)); (ENG., lib. bdg. 26.90 (978-1-4263-3305-7(6)) Disney Publishing Worldwide. (Under the Stars).

—No Girls Allowed (Dogs Okay) Paillot, Jim, illus. 2010. (Secrets of a Lab Rat Ser.). (ENG.). 144p. (J). (gr. 3-7). pap. 5.99 (978-1-4169-6111-6(9), Aladdin) Simon & Schuster Children's Publishing.

—No Girls Allowed (Dogs Okay) Paillot, Jim, illus. 2009. (Secrets of a Lab Rat Ser.). (ENG.). 128p. (J). (gr. 3-7). 14.99 (978-1-4169-7592-2(6), Simon & Schuster/Paula Wiseman Bks.) Simon & Schuster/Paula Wiseman Bks.

—Scab for Treasurer? Paillot, Jim, illus. 2011. (Secrets of a Lab Rat Ser.). (ENG.). 160p. (J). (gr. 3-7). pap. 5.99 (978-1-4169-6113-0(5), Aladdin) Simon & Schuster Children's Publishing.

—Scab for Treasurer?, 3. Paillot, Jim, illus. 2011. (Secrets of a Lab Rat Ser.). (ENG.). 160p. (J). (gr. 3-7). 15.99 (978-1-4169-7594-6(2)) Simon & Schuster, Inc.

—The Sister Solution. 2015. (Mix Ser.). (ENG., Illus.). 240p. (J). (gr. 4-8). pap. 7.99 (978-1-4814-3239-9(7), Aladdin) Simon & Schuster Children's Publishing.

—Stealing Popular. 2012. (Mix Ser.). (ENG.). 240p. (J). (gr. 4-8). pap. 6.99 (978-1-4424-4154-5(2), Aladdin) Simon & Schuster Children's Publishing.

Trufant, Robert & Mullins, Tinnesha. Angel Fingers Series: Na'dyd Goes to School. 2004. (Angel Fingers Ser.). (Illus.). 19p. (J). (gr. -1-2). 14.95 (978-0-9760160-0-7(1)) Mullins Pubns. & Apparel, LLC.

Trumbo, Stephen. Friends of the Forest. 2008. 39p. pap. 24.95 (978-1-60563-781-5(5)) America Star Bks.

Tsang, Evonne. #01 I Love Him to Pieces. Görrissen, Janina, illus. 2011. (My Boyfriend Is a Monster Ser.). 128p. (YA). pap. 56.72 (978-0-7613-7602-6(X), Graphic Universe™) Lerner Publishing Group.

Tuck, Pamela M. As Fast As Words Could Fly?, 1 vol. Velasquez, Eric, illus. 2013. (ENG.). 40p. (J). 18.95 (978-1-60060-348-8(3)) Lee & Low Bks., Inc.

Tucker, Jasmin. Robot School. 2010. 28p. 12.49 (978-1-4520-5011-9(2)) AuthorHouse.

Tullson, Diane. Edge, 1 vol. 2009. (ENG.). 214p. (YA). (gr. 6-10). pap. 11.95 (978-1-55005-142-1(3), 31aaba7e-4ef1-425e-9483-2fe49ffe6534) Trifolium Bks., Inc. CAN. Dist: Firefly Bks., Ltd.

—Lockdown, 1 vol. 2008. (Orca Soundings Ser.). (ENG.). 128p. (YA). (gr. 8-12). pap. 9.95 (978-1-55143-916-7(6)) Orca Bk. Pubs. USA.

Tuma, Refe & Tuma, Susan. What the Dinosaurs Did at School. 2017. (What the Dinosaurs Did Ser.: 2). (ENG., Illus.). 40p. (J). (gr. -1-3). 18.99 (978-0-316-55289-9(5)) Little, Brown Bks. for Young Readers.

Turgeon, Carolyn. The Next Full Moon. 2012. (ENG.). 192p. (J). (gr. 4-7). pap. 6.99 (978-1-935703-34-1(X)) Downtown Bookworks.

Turley, Beth. If This Were a Story. 2018. (ENG., Illus.). 256p. (J). (gr. 3-7). 16.99 (978-1-5344-2061-8(4), Simon & Schuster Bks. For Young Readers) Simon & Schuster Bks. For Young Readers.

Turnbull, Ann. Deep Water. 3rd ed. 2013. 102p. pap. (978-1-78132-160-7(4)) SilverWood Bks.

Turnbull-Kennedy, Tiffany. No School for Evil Eraser! 2011. (Illus.). 48p. pap. 16.59 (978-1-4634-3965-1(2)) AuthorHouse.

Turpin, Nick. Molly Is New. Raga, Silvia, illus. 2010. 32p. pap. (978-1-84089-650-3(7)) Zero to Ten, Ltd.

Uegaki, Chieri. Suki's Kimono. Jorisch, Stéphane, illus. 2005. (ENG.). 32p. (J). (gr. -1-3). pap. 8.99 (978-1-55337-752-8(4)) Kids Can Pr., Ltd. CAN. Dist: Hachette Bk. Group.

Ugezene, Esther I. KiKi, the School Truant. 2005. per. 10.00 (978-0-9767678-1-7(3)) Professional Publishing Hse. LLC.

Umezz, Kazuo. The Drifting Classroom, Vol. 9. 2007. (Drifting Classroom Ser.: 9). (ENG., Illus.). 192p. pap. 9.99 (978-1-4215-0961-7(X)) Viz Media.

Underwood, Deborah. Here Comes Teacher Cat. Rueda, Claudia, illus. 2017. 88p. (J). (-k). 17.99 (978-0-399-53905-3(0), Dial Bks) Penguin Young Readers Group.

Underwood, Deborah K. A Balloon for Isabel. Rankin, Laura, illus. 2010. (ENG.). 32p. (J). (gr. -1-2). 16.99 (978-0-06-177987-9(3), Greenwillow Bks.) HarperCollins Pubs.

Unsworth, Anne. Danny Is Dyslexic. 2011. 68p. (gr. 4-6). pap. 12.10 (978-1-4567-8417-1(X)) AuthorHouse.

Urban, Linda. A Crooked Kind of Perfect. 2009. (ENG., Illus.). 224p. (J). (gr. 5-7). pap. 7.99 (978-0-15-206608-6(X), 1099010, Clarion Bks.) HarperCollins Pubs.

Urdahl, Catherine. Polka-Dot Fixes Kindergarten. Kemble, Mai S., illus. 2011. 32p. (J). (gr. -1-3). 16.95 (978-1-57091-737-0(X)); pap. 7.95 (978-1-57091-738-7(8)) Charlesbridge Publishing, Inc.

Ure, Jean. Dazzling Danny. Donnelly, Karen, illus. 2011. (ENG.). 96p. pap. 5.99 (978-0-00-713370-3(7), HarperCollins Children's Bks.) HarperCollins Pubs. Ltd. GBR. Dist: HarperCollins Pubs.

—Hunky Dory. 2011. (ENG., Illus.). 192p. pap. 7.99 (978-0-00-722460-9(5), HarperCollins Children's Bks.) HarperCollins Pubs. Ltd. GBR. Dist: HarperCollins Pubs.

—Sugar & Spice. 2005. (ENG., Illus.). 224p. (gr. 4-7). per. 11.95 (978-0-00-716137-9(9), HarperCollins Children's Bks.) HarperCollins Pubs. Ltd. GBR. Dist: HarperCollins Pubs.

Urey, Gary. Super Schnoz & the Gates of Smell. Long, Ethan, illus. (Super Schnoz Ser.: 1). (ENG.). 160p. (J). (gr. 3-7). 2015. pap. 6.99 (978-0-8075-7560-4(7), 807575607) 2013. 14.99 (978-0-8075-7555-0(0), 807575550) Whitman, Albert & Co.

Ursu, Anne. Breadcrumbs. McGuire, Erin, illus. 2013. (ENG.). 336p. (J). (gr. 3-7). pap. 7.99 (978-0-06-201506-8(0), Waldon Pond Pr.) HarperCollins Pubs.

—Breadcrumbs. McGuire, Erin, illus. 2012. 320p. 55.00 (978-0-449-01400-4(2)) Random Hse., Inc.

—Breadcrumbs. 2013. (J). lib. bdg. 17.20 (978-0-606-27130-1(9)) Turtleback.

Usher, Carolyn. Chip Takes Off. 2013. (ENG.). 167p. (YA). pap. 8.95 (978-1-4787-1637-2(1)) Outskirts Pr., Inc.

Uvezian, Verne. The Day Benny Stuck His Neck Out. 2011. 12p. (gr. 1-2). 9.95 (978-1-4567-3119-9(X)) AuthorHouse.

Vail, Rachel. If We Kiss. 2005. (If We Kiss Ser.: Bk. 1). (ENG.). 272p. (J). 15.99 (978-0-06-056914-3(X)) HarperCollins Pubs.

—Unfriended. 2015. 304p. (J). (gr. 5). 8.99 (978-0-14-751154-6(2), Puffin Books) Penguin Young Readers Group.

—Well, That Was Awkward. 2018. 336p. (J). (gr. 5). 8.99 (978-0-14-751398-4(7), Puffin Books) Penguin Young Readers Group.

—Well, That Was Awkward. 2018. lib. bdg. 19.65 (978-0-606-40876-9(2)) Turtleback.

—You, Maybe: The Profound Asymmetry of Love in High School. 2006. (YA). (gr. 7-12). (ENG.). 208p. 15.99 (978-0-06-056917-4(4)); 199p. lib. bdg. 16.89 (978-0-06-056918-1(2)) HarperCollins Pubs.

Vaizey, George de Horne. Etheldreda the Ready. Horrell, Charles, illus. 2007. 200p. per. (978-1-4065-4688-0(7)) Dodo Pr.

—Tom & Some Other Girls. Tarrant, Percy, illus. 2007. 208p. per. (978-1-4065-4698-9(4)) Dodo Pr.

Valdes, Leslie. Dora Goes to School. Roper, Robert, illus. 2005. (Dora the Explorer Ser.: 8). 22p. (J). lib. bdg. 15.00 (978-1-59054-791-5(8)) Fitzgerald Bks.

Valdes-Rodriguez, Alisa. Haters, 8 vols. (YA). 2008. 198.75 (978-1-4281-2205-5(2)) 2007. 79.75 (978-1-4281-2200-0(1)) 2007. 105.75 (978-1-4281-2204-8(4)) 2006. 76.75 (978-1-4281-2202-4(8)) 2006. 1.25 (978-1-4281-2197-3(8)) 2006. 172.75 (978-1-4281-2201-7(X)) 2006. 102.75 (978-1-4281-2206-2(0)) Recorded Bks., Inc.

Valentine, Sally. The Ghost of the Charlotte Lighthouse. 2006. (ENG.). (J). pap. (978-1-59531-013-2(4)) North Country Bks., Inc.

van Diepen, Allison. Snitch. 2013. (ENG., Illus.). 320p. (YA). (gr. 9). pap. 13.99 (978-1-4424-8165-7(X), Simon Pulse) Simon Pulse.

Van Dolzer, Krista. Don't Vote for Me. 2016. (ENG.). 240p. (J). (gr. 5-8). pap. 10.99 (978-1-4926-3184-2(1), 9781492631842) Sourcebooks, Inc.

Van Draanen, Wendelin. Attack of the Tagger. Biggs, Brian, illus. unabr. ed. 2006. (Shredderman Ser.: Bk. 2). (J). (gr. 3-6). audio 24.95 (978-1-59519-758-0(3)) Live Oak Media.

—Confessions of a Serial Kisser. 2009. (ENG.). 304p. (YA). (gr. 7-18). pap. 10.99 (978-0-375-84249-8(7), Ember) Random Hse. Children's Bks.

—The Running Dream. 2011. (ENG.). 352p. (YA). (gr. 7-18). 18.99 (978-0-375-86667-8(1), Knopf Bks. for Young Readers) Random Hse. Children's Bks.

—Sammy Keyes & the Dead Giveaway. 2008. (Sammy Keyes Ser.: Bk. 10). (J). 64.99 (978-1-60640-639-7(6)) Findaway World, LLC.

—Sammy Keyes & the Dead Giveaway. unabr. ed. 2006. (Sammy Keyes Ser.: Bk. 10). (J). (gr. 5-7). pap. 54.95 incl. audio compact disk (978-1-59519-771-9(0)); pap. 36.95 incl. audio (978-1-59519-770-2(2)) Live Oak Media.

—Sammy Keyes & the Dead Giveaway. 2007. (Sammy Keyes Ser.: 10). (ENG., Illus.). 304p. (J). (gr. 5-7). per. 7.99 (978-0-440-41911-2(5), Yearling) Random Hse. Children's Bks.

—Sammy Keyes & the Night of Skulls. 2012. (Sammy Keyes Ser.: 14). (ENG.). 336p. (J). (gr. 5-7). 10.99 (978-0-375-85457-6(6), Yearling) Random Hse. Children's Bks.

—Sammy Keyes & the Wedding Crasher. 2011. (Sammy Keyes Ser.: 13). (ENG.). 320p. (J). (gr. 5). 8.99 (978-0-375-85456-9(8), Yearling) Random Hse. Children's Bks.

—Shredderman: Secret Identity. Biggs, Brian, illus. unabr. ed. 2006. (Shredderman Ser.: Bk. 1).Tr. of Shredderman - Al Haqiqa Wara ¿Al Fatak¿. (J). (gr. 2-4). audio 24.95 (978-1-59519-762-7(1)) Live Oak Media.

—Shredderman: Secret Identity. unabr. ed. 2006. (Shredderman Ser.: Bk. 1).Tr. of Shredderman - Al Haqiqa Wara ¿Al Fatak¿. (Illus.). (J). (gr. 2-4). pap. 28.95 incl. audio compact disk (978-1-59519-763-4(X)) Live Oak Media.

—Shredderman: Attack of the Tagger. 2006. (Shredderman Ser.: 2). (ENG., Illus.). 176p. (J). (gr. 1-4). 7.99 (978-0-440-41913-6(1), Yearling) Random Hse. Children's Bks.

—Shredderman: Enemy Spy. 2006. (Shredderman Ser.: 4). (ENG., Illus.). 192p. (J). (gr. 1-4). 7.99 (978-0-440-41915-0(8), Yearling) Random Hse. Children's Bks.

—Shredderman: Meet the Gecko, 3. 2006. (Shredderman Ser.: 3). (ENG., Illus.). 176p. (J). (gr. 1-4). 6.99 (978-0-440-41914-3(X), Yearling) Random Hse. Children's Bks.

—Shredderman: Secret Identity, 1. Biggs, Brian, illus. 2006. (Shredderman Ser.: 1). (ENG.). 144p. (J). (gr. 1-4). reprint ed. 6.99 (978-0-440-41912-9(3), Yearling) Random Hse. Children's Bks.

Van Dusen, Chris. If I Built a School. Van Dusen, Chris, illus. 2019. (If I Built Ser.). (Illus.). 32p. (J). (gr. k-3). 18.99 (978-0-525-55291-8(X), Dial Bks) Penguin Young Readers Group.

Van Kersen, Elizabeth. Who's Riley. 2005. (Illus.). 50p. (J). per. 8.99 (978-1-932338-90-4(X)) Lifevest Publishing, Inc.

Van Leeuwen, Jean. Amanda Pig, First Grader. Schweninger, Ann, illus. 2007. (Oliver & Amanda Ser.). 40p. (J). (978-1-4287-4781-4(8), Dial) Penguin Publishing Group.

—Amanda Pig, First Grader. Schweninger, Ann, illus. 2009. (Oliver & Amanda Ser.). (ENG.). 48p. (J). (gr. 1-3). mass mkt. 4.99 (978-0-14-241276-3(7), Penguin Young Readers) Penguin Young Readers Group.

Van Stockum, Hilda. A Day on Skates: The Story of a Dutch Picnic. Van Stockum, Hilda, illus. 2007. (Illus.). 40p. (J). (gr. 1). 19.95 (978-1-932350-18-0(7)) Bethlehem Bks.

Van Tol, Alex. Food Freak. 2017. (Orca Currents Ser.). lib. bdg. 20.80 (978-0-606-40452-5(X)) Turtleback.

Van Vleet, Carmella. Eliza Bing Is (Not) a Star. (Eliza Bing Ser.). (ENG.). 256p. (J). (gr. 3-7). 2019. pap. 7.99 (978-0-8234-4430-4(9)) 2018. 16.99 (978-0-8234-4024-5(9)) Holiday Hse., Inc.

Vande Velde, Vivian. 8 Class Pets + 1 Squirrel ÷ 1 Dog = Chaos. Björkman, Steve & Björkman, Steve, illus. 2012. (Twitch the Squirrel Ser.: 1). (ENG.). 80p. (J). (gr. 1-4). pap. 6.99 (978-0-8234-2594-5(0)) Holiday Hse., Inc.

Vandever, Daniel W. Fall in Line, Holden. Frank, LaFrenda, ed. Vandever, Daniel W., illus. 2017. (Illus.). 32p. (J). (978-1-893354-50-0(4)) Salina Bookshelf Inc.

Varian, H. K. The Changer War. 2017. (Hidden World of Changers Ser.: 8). (ENG.). 176p. (J). (gr. 3-7). 17.99 (978-1-5344-0146-4(6)); (Illus.). pap. 6.99 (978-1-5344-0145-7(8)) Simon Spotlight. (Simon Spotlight).

—The Gathering Storm. 2016. (Hidden World of Changers Ser.: 1). (ENG., Illus.). 176p. (J). (gr. 3-7). pap. 6.99 (978-1-4814-6616-5(X), Simon Spotlight) Simon Spotlight.

Varnes, Allison. Property of the Rebel Librarian. 2019. (Illus.). 288p. (J). (gr. 3-7). 7.99 (978-1-5247-7150-8(3), Yearling) Random Hse. Children's Bks.

Vaughan, M. M. The Ability. Bruno, Iacopo, illus. (Ability Ser.). (ENG.). (YA). (gr. 3-7). 2014. 352p. pap. 8.99 (978-1-4424-5201-5(3)) 2013. 336p. 15.99 (978-1-4424-5200-8(5)) McElderry, Margaret K. Bks. (McElderry, Margaret K. Bks.).

—Mindscape. Bruno, Iacopo, illus. 2015. (Ability Ser.). (ENG.). 336p. (YA). (gr. 3-7). pap. 7.99 (978-1-4424-5205-3(6), McElderry, Margaret K. Bks.) McElderry, Margaret K. Bks.

S

Vega, Danielle. The Merciless. 2014. (Merciless Ser.: 1). (ENG.). 288p. (YA). (gr. 9). 17.99 (978-1-59514-722-6(5), Razorbill) Penguin Young Readers Group.

—The Merciless IV: Last Rites. 2019. (Merciless Ser.). (ENG.). 320p. (YA). (gr. 9). pap. 10.99 (978-0-425-29219-8(3), Razorbill) Penguin Young Readers Group.

Vega, Denise. Click Here (to Find Out How I Survived Seventh Grade) 2006. (ENG., Illus.). 224p. (J). (gr. 5-17). reprint ed. pap. 14.99 (978-0-316-98559-8(7)) Little, Brown Bks. for Young Readers.

—Rock On: A Story of Guitars, Gigs, Girls, & a Brother (not Necessarily in That Order) 2013. (ENG., Illus.). 304p. (YA). (gr. 7-17). pap. 8.99 (978-0-316-13309-8(4)) Little, Brown Bks. for Young Readers.

Velásquez, Gloria. Forgiving Moses. 2018. (Roosevelt High School Ser.). (ENG.). 160p. (YA). (gr. 8-12). pap. 10.95 (978-1-55885-864-0(4), Piñata Books) Arte Publico Pr.

Velasquez, Gloria. Tyrone's Betrayal. 2006. (Roosevelt High School Series Bks.). 135p. (J). (gr. 3-7). per. 9.95 (978-1-55885-465-9(7), Piñata Books) Arte Publico Pr.

Venditti, Robert. Attack of the Alien Horde. Higgins, Dusty, illus. 2015. (Miles Taylor & the Golden Cape Ser.: 1). (ENG.). 304p. (J). (gr. 4-7). 16.99 (978-1-4814-0542-3(X)) Simon & Schuster, Inc.

—Rise of the Robot Army. Higgins, Dusty, illus. 2016. (Miles Taylor & the Golden Cape Ser.: 2). (ENG.). 304p. (J). (gr. 4-7). 16.99 (978-1-4814-0557-7(8), Simon & Schuster Bks. For Young Readers) Simon & Schuster Bks. For Young Readers.

Ventura, Marne. Anxious Adam Braves the Test. Trinidad, Leo, illus. 2016. (Worry Warriors Ser.). (ENG.). 96p. (J). (gr. 2-4). lib. bdg. 25.99 (978-1-4965-3611-2(8), 132817, Stone Arch Bks.) Capstone.

—Jittery Jake Conquers Stage Fright. Trinidad, Leo, illus. 2016. (Worry Warriors Ser.). (ENG.). 96p. (J). (gr. 2-4). lib. bdg. 25.99 (978-1-4965-3612-9(6), 132818, Stone Arch Bks.) Capstone.

—Nervous Nellie Fights First-Day Frenzy. Trinidad, Leo, illus. 2016. (Worry Warriors Ser.). (ENG.). 96p. (J). (gr. 2-4). lib. bdg. 25.99 (978-1-4965-3613-6(4), 132819, Stone Arch Bks.) Capstone.

Venturini, Fred. The Escape of Light. 2019. (ENG.). 240p. (YA). pap. 16.99 (978-1-68442-392-7(9)) Turner Publishing Co.

Verday, Jessica. The Haunted. (ENG.). (YA). (gr. 9). 2011. 496p. pap. 14.99 (978-1-4169-7896-1(8)) 2010. 480p. 17.99 (978-1-4169-7895-4(X)) Simon Pulse. (Simon Pulse).

—The Hidden. (ENG.). 400p. (YA). (gr. 9). 2012. pap. 14.99 (978-1-4169-7898-5(4)) 2011. 17.99 (978-1-4169-7897-8(6)) Simon Pulse. (Simon Pulse).

—The Hollow. (ENG.). (YA). (gr. 7). 2010. 528p. pap. 14.99 (978-1-4169-7894-7(1))No. 1. 2009. 544p. 17.99 (978-1-4169-7893-0(3)) Simon Pulse. (Simon Pulse).

Verde, Susan. Rock 'n' Roll Soul. Cordell, Matthew, illus. 2018. (ENG.). 32p. (J). (gr. k-2). 16.99 (978-1-4197-2849-5(0), 697701, Abrams Bks. for Young Readers) Abrams, Inc.

Verdi, Jessica. My Life after Now. 2013. (ENG.). 304p. (YA). (gr. 7-12). pap. 9.99 (978-1-4022-7785-6(7), 9781402277856) Sourcebooks, Inc.

Vergo, Franny. Jonathan Ray & His Superhero Pack: Respect. 2012. 42p. pap. 16.50 (978-1-4685-7602-3(X)) AuthorHouse.

Vernick, Audrey. First Grade Dropout. Cordell, Matthew, illus. 2015. (ENG.). 32p. (J). (gr. -1-3). 17.99 (978-0-544-12985-6(7), 1544741, Clarion Bks.) HarperCollins Pubs.

—Is Your Buffalo Ready for Kindergarten? Jennewein, Daniel, illus. 2010. (ENG.). 32p. (J). (gr. -1-3). 16.99 (978-0-06-176275-8(X), Balzer & Bray) HarperCollins Pubs.

—Second Grade Holdout. Cordell, Matthew, illus. 2017. (ENG.). 32p. (J). (gr. -1-3). 18.99 (978-0-544-87681-1(4), 1649576, Clarion Bks.) HarperCollins Pubs.

Vernon, Ursula. Curse of the Were-Wiener. 2014. (Dragonbreath Ser.: 3). lib. bdg. 17.20 (978-0-606-35710-4(6)) Turtleback.

—Dragonbreath. 2009. (Dragonbreath Ser.: 1). (Illus.). 160p. (J). (gr. 3-7). 14.99 (978-0-8037-3363-3(1), Dial Bks) Penguin Young Readers Group.

—Dragonbreath. 2012. (Dragonbreath Ser.: 1). lib. bdg. 17.20 (978-0-606-26665-9(8)) Turtleback.

—Dragonbreath #1. 2012. (Dragonbreath Ser.: 1). (Illus.). 160p. (J). (gr. 3-7). pap. 8.99 (978-0-14-242095-9(6), Puffin Books) Penguin Young Readers Group.

—Dragonbreath #3: Curse of the Were-Wiener. 3rd ed. (Dragonbreath Ser.: 3). 208p. (J). (gr. 3-7). 2014. pap. 8.99 (978-0-14-751321-2(9), Puffin Books) 2010. (ENG.). 14.99 (978-0-8037-3469-2(7), Dial Bks) Penguin Young Readers Group.

Vic Visits Ground Zero. 2004. (J). (978-0-9761102-0-0(2)) Adams, Evelyn.

Vicente, Alidis. The Shameless Shenanigans of Mister Malo / Las Terribles Travesuras de Mister Malo: The Mister Malo Series / Serie Mister Malo. 2017. (ENG & SPA., Illus.). 115p. (J). (gr. 4-8). pap. 9.95 (978-1-55885-853-4(9), Piñata Books) Arte Publico Pr.

Villareal, Ray. Alamo Wars. 2008. 187p. (J). (gr. 6-18). pap. 10.95 (978-1-55885-513-7(0), Piñata Books) Arte Publico Pr.

—Body Slammed! 2012. (YA). pap. 11.95 (978-1-55885-749-0(4), Piñata Books) Arte Publico Pr.

Villoro, Juan. El Profesor Ziper y la Fabulosa Guitarra Electrica. El Fisgsn, illus. 2005. (Infantil Ser.). (SPA.). 96p. (J). (gr. 5-8). pap. 9.95 (978-968-19-0206-3(8)) Santillana USA Publishing Co., Inc.

Vincent, Rachel. With All My Soul, 7. 2013. (Soul Screamers Ser.: 7). (ENG.). 384p. (YA). (gr. 7-12). pap. 9.99 (978-0-373-21066-4(3), Harlequin Teen) Harlequin Enterprises ULC CAN. Dist: HarperCollins Pubs.

Viorst, Judith. Alexander, Who's Trying His Best to Be the Best Boy Ever. 2014. (ENG., Illus.). 40p. (J). (gr. -1-3). 17.99 (978-1-4814-2353-3(3), Atheneum Bks. for Young Readers) Simon & Schuster Children's Publishing.

A Visit to the Schoolhouse. 2003. (J). per. (978-1-57657-903-9(4)) Paradise Pr., Inc.

Vivat, Booki. Frazzled: Everyday Disasters & Impending Doom. Vivat, Booki, illus. 2016. (ENG., Illus.). 240p. (J). (gr. 3-7). 13.99 (978-0-06-239879-6(2), HarperCollins) HarperCollins Pubs.

—Frazzled #3: Minor Incidents & Absolute Uncertainties. Vivat, Booki, illus. 2019. (ENG., Illus.). 224p. (J). (gr. 3-7). 13.99 (978-0-06-239883-3(0), HarperCollins) HarperCollins Pubs.

Vivian, Siobhan. The List. 2014. (ENG.). 336p. (YA). (gr. 9). pap. 10.99 (978-0-545-16918-9(6), Scholastic Paperbacks) Scholastic, Inc.

—Same Difference. 2014. (ENG.). 304p. (YA). (gr. 7-7). pap. 10.99 (978-0-545-75802-4(5)) Scholastic, Inc.

Vizzini, Med. Be More Chill. 2011. 9.68 (978-0-7848-3414-5(8), Everbind) Marco Bk. Co.

Vizzini, Ned. Be More Chill. 2005. (ENG.). 320p. (YA). (gr. 7-12). per. 8.99 (978-0-7868-0996-7(5), Disney-Hyperion) Disney Publishing Worldwide.

Voake, Steve. Daisy Dawson & the Secret Pond. Meserve, Jessica, illus. 2010. (Daisy Dawson Ser.: 2). (ENG.). 96p. (J). (gr. 1-4). pap. 6.99 (978-0-7636-4730-8(6)) Candlewick Pr.

—Daisy Dawson & the Secret Pond. 2. Meserve, Jessica, illus. 2009. (Daisy Dawson Ser.: 2). (ENG.). 96p. (J). (gr. 1-4). 18.69 (978-0-7636-4009-5(3)) Candlewick Pr.

Vogiel, Eva. Facing the Music. 2003. 284p. 19.95 (978-1-880582-94-7(5)) Judaica Pr., Inc., The.

Voigt, Cynthia. Bad Girls in Love. 2004. (ENG., Illus.). 240p. (J). (gr. 4-8). pap. 11.99 (978-0-689-86620-3(8), Atheneum Bks. for Young Readers) Simon & Schuster Children's Publishing.

Volponi, Paul. The Hand You're Dealt. 2010. (ENG.). 192p. (YA). (gr. 7). pap. 12.99 (978-1-4169-3990-0(3), Atheneum Bks. for Young Readers) Simon & Schuster Children's Publishing.

—The Hand You're Dealt. 2008. (ENG.). 168p. (YA). (gr. 7-12). 24.94 (978-1-4169-3989-4(X)) Simon & Schuster, Inc.

—Top Prospect. 2016. (ENG.). 280p. (J). (gr. 4-9). 17.99 (978-1-4677-9433-6(3), 562bcb0c-1250-4c82-a79e-6b1e36ad4d0f); E-Book 27.99 (978-1-5124-0887-4(5)) Lerner Publishing Group. (Carolrhoda Bks.).

von Ziegesar, Cecily. Adored. 2009. (It Girl Ser.: 8). (ENG.). 240p. (YA). (gr. 10-17). pap. 14.99 (978-0-316-02509-6(7), Poppy) Little, Brown Bks. for Young Readers.

—Gossip Girl #10: Would I Lie to You: A Gossip Girl Novel. 2006. (Gossip Girl Ser.: 10). (ENG.). 224p. (YA). (gr. 10-17). per. 13.99 (978-0-316-01183-9(5), Poppy) Little, Brown Bks. for Young Readers.

—Gossip Girl: Don't You Forget about Me: A Gossip Girl Novel. 2007. (Gossip Girl Ser.: 11). (ENG.). 304p. (YA). (gr. 10-17). per. 16.99 (978-0-316-01184-6(3), Poppy) Little, Brown Bks. for Young Readers.

—Gossip Girl: I Like It Like That: A Gossip Girl Novel, 5. 2004. (Gossip Girl Ser.: 5). (ENG.). 224p. (YA). (gr. 10-17). pap. 12.99 (978-0-316-73518-6(3), Poppy) Little, Brown Bks. for Young Readers.

—Gossip Girl: Nobody Does It Better: A Gossip Girl Novel, 7. 7th ed. 2005. (Gossip Girl Ser.: 7). (ENG.). 256p. (YA). (gr. 10-17). pap. 13.99 (978-0-316-73512-4(4), Poppy) Little, Brown Bks. for Young Readers.

—Gossip Girl: Only in Your Dreams: A Gossip Girl Novel. 2006. (Gossip Girl Ser.: 9). (ENG.). 256p. (YA). (gr. 10-17). per. 14.99 (978-0-316-01182-2(7), Poppy) Little, Brown Bks. for Young Readers.

—Gossip Girl: You're the One That I Want: A Gossip Girl Novel, 6. 2004. (Gossip Girl Ser.: 6). (ENG.). 256p. (YA). (gr. 10-17). pap. 14.99 (978-0-316-73516-2(7), Poppy) Little, Brown Bks. for Young Readers.

—The It Girl. 2005. (It Girl Ser.: 1). (ENG.). 272p. (YA). (gr. 10-17). per. 15.99 (978-0-316-01185-3(1), Poppy) Little, Brown Bks. for Young Readers.

Voorhees, Coert. The Brothers Torres. 2009. (ENG.). 336p. (J). (gr. 7-12). 24.94 (978-1-4231-0306-6(8)) Hyperion Bks. for Children.

Vosailagi, Jo, illus. Pentapus. 2006. 120p. per. 12.56 (978-1-4120-9272-2(8)) Trafford Publishing.

Votruba, Erik C. The Cowboy Mile. 2009. 231p. pap. 14.99 (978-0-557-09002-0(4)) Lulu Pr., Inc.

Vrabel, Beth. A Blind Guide to Normal. (ENG.). (J). (gr. 3-7). 2018. 304p. pap. 7.99 (978-1-5107-2733-5(7)) 2016. 272p. 16.99 (978-1-5107-0228-8(8)) Skyhorse Publishing Co., Inc. (Sky Pony Pr.).

—Bringing Me Back. 2018. (ENG.). 256p. (J). (gr. 3-7). 16.99 (978-1-5107-2527-0(X), Sky Pony Pr.) Skyhorse Publishing Co., Inc.

—Pack of Dorks. (Pack of Dorks Ser.: 1). (ENG.). 240p. (J). (gr. 2-7). 2015. pap. 7.99 (978-1-5107-0179-3(6)) 2014. 15.95 (978-1-62914-623-2(4)) Skyhorse Publishing Co., Inc. (Sky Pony Pr.).

—Super Dorks. 2018. (Pack of Dorks Ser.: 3). (ENG.). 304p. (J). (gr. 3-7). 16.99 (978-1-5107-3144-8(X), Sky Pony Pr.) Skyhorse Publishing Co., Inc.

Vrettos, Adrienne Maria. Best Friends for Never. 2016. (ENG.). 240p. (J). (gr. 3-7). 16.99 (978-0-545-56149-5(3), Scholastic Pr.) Scholastic, Inc.

—The Exile of Gigi Lane. 2011. (ENG.). 368p. (YA). (gr. 7). pap. 8.99 (978-1-4424-2121-9(5), McElderry, Margaret K. Bks.) McElderry, Margaret K. Bks.

—Sight. 2008. (ENG.). 272p. (YA). (gr. 7). pap. 8.99 (978-1-4169-0658-2(4), McElderry, Margaret K. Bks.) McElderry, Margaret K. Bks.

—Sight. 2007. (ENG., Illus.). 254p. (YA). (gr. 7-12). 21.19 (978-1-4169-0657-5(6)) Simon & Schuster, Inc.

Vulliamy, Clara. Bear with Sticky Paws Goes to School. Vulliamy, Clara, illus. 2010. (ENG., Illus.). 32p. pap. 7.95 (978-1-58925-424-4(4)) Tiger Tales.

Wagman, Diana. Extraordinary October. 2016. (ENG.). 264p. (J). (gr. 6). 18.95 (978-1-63246-036-3(X)) Ig Publishing, Inc.

Wagstaff, Janiel. Stella Writes an Opinion. 2015. (ENG.). (J). (gr. -1-3). pap. 7.95 (978-1-63133-022-3(5)) Staff Development for Educators.

Walde, Christine. The Candy Darlings. 2006. (ENG.). 310p. (YA). (gr. 9-12). per. 18.95 (978-0-618-58969-2(4), 497559, Clarion Bks.) HarperCollins Pubs.

Walden, Mark. Dreadnought. (H. I. V. E. Ser.: 4). (ENG.). (J). (gr. 3-7). 2012. 320p. pap. 8.99 (978-1-4424-1368-9(9)) 2011. 304p. 18.99 (978-1-4424-2186-8(X)) Simon & Schuster Bks. For Young Readers. (Simon & Schuster Bks. For Young Readers).

—Escape Velocity. (H. I. V. E. Ser.: 3). (ENG.). (J). (gr. 3-7). 2012. 368p. pap. 8.99 (978-1-4424-1367-2(0)) 2011. 352p. 18.99 (978-1-4424-2185-1(1)) Simon & Schuster Bks. For Young Readers. (Simon & Schuster Bks. For Young Readers).

—H. I. V. E. Higher Institute of Villainous Education. (H. I. V. E. Ser.: 1). (ENG.). 320p. (J). (gr. 3-7). 2008. pap. 8.99 (978-1-4169-3572-8(X)) 2007. (Illus.). 19.99 (978-1-4169-3571-1(1)) Simon & Schuster Bks. For Young Readers. (Simon & Schuster Bks. For Young Readers).

—The Overlord Protocol. (H. I. V. E. Ser.: 2). (ENG.). 384p. (J). (gr. 3-7). 2009. pap. 8.99 (978-1-4169-3574-2(6)) 2008. 18.99 (978-1-4169-3573-5(8)) Simon & Schuster Bks. For Young Readers. (Simon & Schuster Bks. For Young Readers).

—Rogue. (H. I. V. E. Ser.: 5). (ENG.). (J). (gr. 3-7). 2012. 320p. pap. 8.99 (978-1-4424-1369-6(7)) 2011. 304p. 18.99 (978-1-4424-2187-5(8)) Simon & Schuster Bks. For Young Readers. (Simon & Schuster Bks. For Young Readers).

Wales, Sid. Freddie & Mee. Bryant, Kerry, illus. 2013. 28p. pap. (978-1-78222-097-8(6)) Paragon Publishing, Rothersthorpe.

Walker, Brian F. Black Boy White School. 2012. (ENG.). 256p. (YA). (gr. 9). 17.99 (978-0-06-191483-6(5), HarperTeen) HarperCollins Pubs.

Walker, Kate. I Hate Books! Cox, David, illus. 2007. 88p. (J). (gr. 1-4). 16.95 (978-0-8126-2745-9(8)) Cricket Bks.

Walker, Kristin. 7 Clues to Winning You. 2012. (ENG.). 240p. (YA). (gr. 7-12). 26.19 (978-1-59514-414-0(5)) Penguin Young Readers Group.

Walker, Landry Q. Super Hero School: #3, 1 vol. Jones, Eric, illus. 2013. (Supergirl: Cosmic Adventures in the 8th Grade Ser.). (ENG.). 32p. (J). (gr. 3-6). 22.60 (978-1-4342-4719-3(8), 120850, Stone Arch Bks.) Capstone.

—Supergirl: Cosmic Adventures in the 8th Grade. Jones, Eric, illus. 2013. (Supergirl: Cosmic Adventures in the 8th Grade Ser.). (ENG.). 32p. (J). (gr. 3-6). 143.94 (978-1-4342-8830-1(7), 21103, Stone Arch Bks.) Capstone.

Walker, Landry Q. & Mason, Joey. Evil in a Skirt! #5, 1 vol. Jones, Eric, illus. 2013. (Supergirl: Cosmic Adventures in the 8th Grade Ser.). (ENG.). 32p. (J). (gr. 3-6). 22.60 (978-1-4342-6045-1(3), 123199, Stone Arch Bks.) Capstone.

Walker, Nan. Spork Out of Orbit (Book 1) Respect. Warrick, Jessica, illus. 2016. (How to Be an Earthling (r) Ser.: 1). (ENG.). 64p. (J). (gr. 1-3). E-Book 34.65 (978-1-57565-820-9(8)) Astra Publishing Hse.

Walker-Renner, Christa. Santa's Magic. 2009. 20p. pap. 11.00 (978-1-4389-8206-9(2)) AuthorHouse.

Wall, Laura. Goose Goes to School. Wall, Laura, illus. 2015. (ENG., Illus.). 48p. (J). (gr. -1-3). 12.99 (978-0-06-232437-5(3), HarperCollins) HarperCollins Pubs.

Wallace, Barbara Brooks. The Perils of Peppermints. 2005. (ENG., Illus.). 272p. (J). (gr. 3-7). pap. 12.99 (978-0-689-85045-5(X), Simon & Schuster/Paula Wiseman Bks.) Simon & Schuster/Paula Wiseman Bks.

Wallace, Kim. Erik & Isabelle Senior Year at Foresthill High. 2008. (Foresthill High Ser.). 220p. (YA). (gr. 8-12). per. 12.00 (978-0-9755848-3-5(9)) Foglight Pr.

Wallace, Nancy Elizabeth. The Kindness Quilt, 0 vols. 2012. (ENG., Illus.). 48p. (J). (gr. -1-3). 16.99 (978-0-7614-5313-0(X), 9780761453130, Two Lions) Amazon Publishing.

—Recycle Every Day!, 0 vols. Wallace, Nancy Elizabeth, illus. 2012. (ENG., Illus.). 41p. (J). (gr. 1-3). pap. 9.99 (978-0-7614-5290-4(7), 9780761452904, Two Lions) Amazon Publishing.

Wallace, Rich. Backcourt Battle: An Up2U Character Education Adventure. King, Chris, illus. 2017. (Up2U Adventures Set 3 Ser.). (ENG.). 80p. (J). (gr. 2-5). lib. bdg. 35.64 (978-1-5321-3028-1(7), 25504, Calico Chapter Bks.) ABDO Publishing Co.

—Pressure Point, 1 vol. Heitz, Tim, illus. 2015. (Game Face Ser.). (ENG.). 112p. (J). (gr. 2-5). 38.50 (978-1-62402-135-0(2), 19198, Calico Chapter Bks.) ABDO Publishing Co.

—Shots on Goal. 2005. 160p. (YA). (gr. 7-11). per. 5.99 (978-0-679-88671-6(0), Laurel Leaf) Random Hse. Children's Bks.

—Southpaw. 2006. 105p. (J). lib. bdg. 15.38 (978-1-4242-2166-0(8)) Fitzgerald Bks.

—Southpaw. 2006. (Winning Season Ser.). (ENG.). 112p. (J). (gr. 3-6). 17.44 (978-0-670-06053-5(4)) Penguin Young Readers Group.

—Southpaw: Winning Season. 6th ed. 2007. (Winning Season Ser.: 6). 128p. (J). (gr. 3-7). 5.99 (978-0-14-240785-1(2), Puffin Books) Penguin Young Readers Group.

Wallach, Tommy. We All Looked Up. 2015. (ENG., Illus.). 384p. (YA). (gr. 9). 17.99 (978-1-4814-1877-5(7), Simon & Schuster Bks. For Young Readers) Simon & Schuster Bks. For Young Readers.

Wallis, Quvenzhané. Shai & Emmie Star in Break an Egg! Miller, Sharee, illus. 2017. (Shai & Emmie Story Ser.: 1). (ENG.). 128p. (J). (gr. 1-5). 17.99 (978-1-4814-5882-5(5), Simon & Schuster Bks. For Young Readers) Simon & Schuster Bks. For Young Readers.

Wallis, Quvenzhané & Wallis, Quvenzhané. Shai & Emmie Star in Dancy Pants! Miller, Sharee, illus. 2018. (Shai & Emmie Story Ser.: 2). (ENG.). 128p. (J). (gr. 1-5). 17.99 (978-1-4814-5885-6(X), Simon & Schuster Bks. For Young Readers) Simon & Schuster Bks. For Young Readers.

Walsh, Jean. Gaffer Samson's Luck. 2003. (J). (gr. 3-18). 20.25 (978-0-8446-7252-6(1)) Smith, Peter Pub., Inc.

Walters, Abby. Growing Up. de Polonia, Nina, illus. 2017. (School Days Ser.). (ENG.). 24p. (gr. -1-2). pap. 9.95 (978-1-68342-799-5(8), 9781683427995) Rourke Educational Media.

Walters, Eric. Ricky. 2011. (ENG.). 238p. (J). (gr. 5-7). pap. 9.95 (978-1-55455-121-7(8), 5ab2257a-79a4-4920-8a0c-2f3a783d7c18) Fitzhenry & Whiteside, Ltd. CAN. Dist: Firefly Bks., Ltd.

—Special Edward, 1 vol. 2009. (Orca Currents Ser.). (ENG.). 136p. (J). (gr. 4-7). pap. 9.95 (978-1-55469-092-3(7)) Orca Bk. Pubs. USA.

Waltman, Kevin. Quicks, 1 vol. 2016. (D-Bow High School Hoops Ser.). (ENG.). 304p. (J). (gr. 9-12). 16.95 (978-1-941026-61-8(3), 23353382, Cinco Puntos Press) Lee & Low Bks., Inc.

Walton, Evangeline. The Misadventures of Rufus & Misha: Two Dogs Who Are Smart Enough to Go to School. 2013. 24p. pap. 14.93 (978-1-4669-9970-1(5)) Trafford Publishing.

Walton, K. M. Cracked. 2012. (ENG.). (YA). (gr. 9). 336p. pap. 13.99 (978-1-4424-2917-8(8)); 320p. 16.99 (978-1-4424-2916-1(X)) Simon Pulse. (Simon Pulse).

—Empty. 2013. (ENG., Illus.). 272p. (YA). (gr. 9). pap. 12.99 (978-1-4424-5358-6(3), Simon Pulse) Simon Pulse.

Walvoord, Linda. Rosetta, Rosetta, Sit by Me!, 0 vols. Velasquez, Eric, illus. 2012. (ENG.). 98p. (J). (gr. 1-3). 14.95 (978-0-7614-5171-6(4), 9780761451716, Two Lions) Amazon Publishing.

Wamsley, Jody. What Am I Gonna Do? Turchan, Monique, illus. 2013. 24p. pap. 11.95 (978-1-61244-070-5(3)) Halo Publishing International.

Ward, Dan. Meet the Boomer Sisters. 2006. 131p. pap. 13.95 (978-1-4116-6927-7(4)) Lulu Pr., Inc.

Warden, Andrew J. Grecko the Gecko Starts School. 2010. 24p. 17.93 (978-1-4269-0375-5(8)) Trafford Publishing.

Warner, Gertrude Chandler, creator. Hidden in the Haunted School. 2016. (Boxcar Children Mysteries Ser.: 144). (ENG., Illus.). 128p. (J). (gr. 2-5). 15.99 (978-0-8075-0718-6(0), 807507180, Random Hse. Bks. for Young Readers) Random Hse. Children's Bks.

Warner, Sally. Absolutely Alfie & the First Week Friends. Malone, Shearry, illus. 2017. (Absolutely Alfie Ser.: 2). (ENG.). 144p. (J). (gr. 1-3). 14.99 (978-1-101-99989-9(6), Viking Books for Young Readers) Penguin Young Readers Group.

—Absolutely Alfie & the Princess Wars, 4. Malone, Shearry, illus. 2018. (Absolutely Alfie Ser.). (ENG.). 142p. (J). (gr. 1-3). 21.19 (978-1-5364-4646-3(7), Puffin) Penguin Publishing Group.

—Absolutely Alfie & the Princess Wars. Malone, Shearry, illus. 2018. (Absolutely Alfie Ser.: 4). (ENG.). 144p. (J). (gr. 1-3). 6.99 (978-1-101-99997-4(7), Puffin Books) Penguin Young Readers Group.

—EllRay Jakes Is a Rock Star, 2 vols. Harper, Jamie, illus. 2012. (EllRay Jakes Ser.: 2). (ENG.). 128p. (J). (gr. 1-3). 6.99 (978-0-14-241989-2(3), Puffin Books) Penguin Young Readers Group.

—Ellray Jakes Is a Rock Star! 2012. (EllRay Jakes Ser.: 2). lib. bdg. 16.00 (978-0-606-23633-1(3)) Turtleback.

—EllRay Jakes Is Magic. Biggs, Brian, illus. 2014. (EllRay Jakes Ser.: 6). (ENG.). 176p. (J). (gr. 1-3). pap. 6.99 (978-0-14-242360-8(2), Puffin Books) Penguin Young Readers Group.

—Ellray Jakes Is Magic. 2014. (EllRay Jakes Ser.: 6). lib. bdg. 16.00 (978-0-606-34215-5(X)) Turtleback.

—EllRay Jakes Is Not a Chicken, 1 vol. Harper, Jamie, illus. 2012. (EllRay Jakes Ser.: 1). (ENG.). 128p. (J). (gr. 1-3). 6.99 (978-0-14-241988-5(5), 3eaeef4a-fcff-4b73-8510-6c3963df92b4, Rosen Classroom) Penguin Young Readers Group.

—EllRay Jakes Is Not a Chicken! 2012. (EllRay Jakes Ser.: 1). lib. bdg. 16.00 (978-0-606-23632-4(5)) Turtleback.

—Ellray Jakes Rocks the Holidays! 2014. (EllRay Jakes Ser.: 7). lib. bdg. 16.00 (978-0-606-36188-0(X)) Turtleback.

—EllRay Jakes Stands Tall. Biggs, Brian, illus. 2016. (EllRay Jakes Ser.: 9). (ENG.). 176p. (J). (gr. 1-3). 6.99 (978-0-14-751253-6(0), Puffin Books) Penguin Young Readers Group.

—EllRay Jakes the Dragon Slayer. 2013. (EllRay Jakes Ser.: 4). lib. bdg. 16.00 (978-0-606-32136-5(5)) Turtleback.

—Ellray Jakes the Dragon Slayer, No. 4. Biggs, Brian, illus. 2013. (EllRay Jakes Ser.: 4). (ENG.). 144p. (J). (gr. 1-3). pap. 6.99 (978-0-14-242358-5(0), Puffin Books) Penguin Young Readers Group.

—EllRay Jakes the Recess King! Biggs, Brian, illus. 2015. (EllRay Jakes Ser.: 8). (ENG.). 176p. (J). (gr. 1-3). 6.99 (978-0-14-751252-9(2), Puffin Books) Penguin Young Readers Group.

—Ellray Jakes Walks the Plank. Harper, Jamie, illus. 2013. (EllRay Jakes Ser.: 3). (ENG.). 128p. (J). (gr. 1-3). pap. 6.99 (978-0-14-242409-4(9), Puffin Books) Penguin Young Readers Group.

—EllRay Jakes Walks the Plank! 2013. (EllRay Jakes Ser.: 3). lib. bdg. 16.00 (978-0-606-30188-6(7)) Turtleback.

—Super Emma. Harper, Jamie, illus. 2008. (Emma Ser.: 3). (ENG.). 112p. (J). (gr. 3-7). 5.99 (978-0-14-241088-2(8), Puffin Books) Penguin Young Readers Group.

Washington, Kathleen. The School Bully. 2006. 9.00 (978-0-8059-8201-5(9)) Dorrance Publishing Co., Inc.

Wasserman, Robin. Life, Starring Me! 2009. (Candy Apple Ser.). 182p. (J). (978-0-545-19777-9(5)) Scholastic, Inc.

—Lust. 2005. (Seven Deadly Sins Ser.: 1). (ENG.). 256p. (YA). (gr. 9-12). pap. 9.99 (978-0-689-87782-7(X), Simon Pulse) Simon Pulse.

—Pride. 2006. (Seven Deadly Sins Ser.: 3). (ENG.). 256p. (YA). (gr. 9-12). pap. 8.99 (978-0-689-87784-1(6), Simon Pulse) Simon Pulse.

—Seven Deadly Sins Vol. 3 Vol. 3: Sloth; Gluttony; Greed. 2013. (ENG., Illus.). 880p. (YA). (gr. 9). pap. 10.99 (978-1-4424-7508-3(0), Simon Pulse) Simon Pulse.

—Sloth. 2006. (Seven Deadly Sins Ser.: 5). (ENG.). 256p. (YA). (gr. 9). pap. 9.99 (978-1-4169-0718-3(1), Simon Pulse) Simon Pulse.

—Wrath. 2006. (Seven Deadly Sins Ser.: 4). (ENG., Illus.). 256p. (YA). (gr. 9-12). pap. 9.99 (978-0-689-87785-8(4), Simon Pulse) Simon Pulse.

Wassner, Gary. The Mystery of the Jubilee Emerald. 2006. (J). pap. (978-1-59336-712-1(0)) Mondo Publishing.

Watase, Yuu. Absolute Boyfriend, Vol. 3, 6 vols. 2007. (Absolute Boyfriend Ser.: 3). (ENG., Illus.). 200p. pap. 9.99 (978-1-4215-1003-3(0)) Viz Media.

Waters, Cassie. Dive In! 2012. (Pool Girls Ser.: 1). (ENG.). 160p. (J). (gr. 3-7). 15.99 (978-1-4424-5375-3(3)); pap. 5.99 (978-1-4424-4144-6(5)) Simon Spotlight. (Simon Spotlight).

Waters, Daniel. Break My Heart 1,000 Times. 2013. (ENG., Illus.). 352p. (J). (gr. 7-17). pap. 9.99 (978-1-4231-2228-9(3)) Hyperion Pr.

—Kiss of Life. 2009. (Generation Dead Ser.: Bk. 2). (ENG.). 432p. (J). (gr. 7-12). 22.44 (978-1-4231-0924-2(4)) Hyperion Bks. for Children.

Waters, Erica-Jane. Penny for Your Thoughts. Waters, Erica-Jane, illus. 2020. (Miss Bunsen's School for Brilliant

Girls Ser.: 3). (ENG., Illus.). 128p. (J). (gr. 1-5). 14.99 *(978-0-8075-5159-2(7)*, 807551597) Whitman, Albert & Co.
Watkins, Sam. Creature Teacher. O'Connell, David, illus. 2017. (Creature Teacher Ser.). (ENG.). 176p. (J). (gr. 2-4). pap. 6.95 *(978-1-4965-5681-3(X)*, 136595); pap., pap., pap. 27.80 *(978-1-4965-5682-0(8)*, 27297); lib. bdg. 24.65 *(978-1-4965-5702-5(6)*, 136591) Capstone. (Stone Arch Bks.).
—Creature Teacher Out to Win. O'Connell, David, illus. 2017. (Creature Teacher Ser.). (ENG.). 176p. (J). (gr. 2-4). pap. 6.95 *(978-1-4965-5687-5(9)*, 136598, Stone Arch Bks.) Capstone.
Watkins, Steve. Down Sand Mountain. (ENG., Illus.). 336p. (YA). (gr. 7). 2011. pap. 7.99 *(978-0-7636-4835-0(3))* 2008. 16.99 *(978-0-7636-3839-9(0))* Candlewick Pr.
Watson, Cristy. Living Rough, 1 vol. 2011. (Orca Currents Ser.). (ENG.). 128p. (J). (gr. 4-7). 9.95 *(978-1-55469-434-1(5))* Orca Bk. Pubs. USA.
Watson, J. A. Monarch Mystery: A Butterfly Researcher's Journal. 2018. (Science Squad Ser.). (ENG., Illus.). 192p. (J). (gr. 3-4). lib. bdg. 28.50 *(978-1-63163-183-2(7)*, 1631631837, Jolly Fish Pr.) North Star Editions.
—Monarch Mystery: A Butterfly Researcher's Journal. Olbey, Arpad, illus. 2018. (Science Squad Ser.). (ENG.). 192p. (J). (gr. 3-4). pap. 9.99 *(978-1-63163-184-9(5)*, 1631631845, Jolly Fish Pr.) North Star Editions.
—Pigeon Problems: An Urban Bird Researcher's Journal. 2018. (Science Squad Ser.). (ENG., Illus.). 192p. (J). (gr. 3-4). lib. bdg. 28.50 *(978-1-63163-187-0(X)*, 163163187X, Jolly Fish Pr.) North Star Editions.
—Pigeon Problems: An Urban Bird Researcher's Journal. Olbey, Arpad, illus. 2018. (Science Squad Ser.). (ENG.). 192p. (J). (gr. 3-4). pap. 9.99 *(978-1-63163-188-7(8)*, 1631631888, Jolly Fish Pr.) North Star Editions.
Watson, Kate. Shoot the Moon. 2018. lib. bdg. 26.95 *(978-0-606-41245-2(X))* Turtleback.
Watson, Renee. Piecing Me Together. (ENG.). (YA). 2018. 288p. pap. 10.99 *(978-1-68119-107-2(5)*, 900159236, Bloomsbury Young Adult) 2017. 272p. 18.99 *(978-1-68119-105-8(9)*, 900159235, Bloomsbury USA Childrens) Bloomsbury Publishing USA.
—Piecing Me Together. 2018. (YA). lib. bdg. 20.85 *(978-0-606-41081-6(3))* Turtleback.
—Ways to Make Sunshine. Mata, Nina, illus. (Ryan Hart Story Ser.). (ENG.). (J). 2021. 208p. pap. 7.99 *(978-1-5476-0665-8(7)*, 900237158) 2020. 192p. 16.99 *(978-1-5476-0056-4(X)*, 900196518) Bloomsbury Publishing USA. (Bloomsbury Children's Bks.).
Watson, Renee & Hagan, Ellen. Watch Us Rise. (ENG.). 368p. (YA). 2020. pap. 11.99 *(978-1-5476-0311-4(9)*, 900211274) 2019. 18.99 *(978-1-5476-0008-3(X)*, 900194808) Bloomsbury Publishing USA. (Bloomsbury Young Adult).
Watson, Stephanie. The Club. 2010. (Night Fall (tm) Ser.). (ENG.). 112p. (YA). (gr. 6-12). pap. 7.95 *(978-0-7613-6162-6(6)*, aa5df9a4-b2bc-4430-b15a-6286b036d1d5, Darby Creek) Lerner Publishing Group.
Watts, Jeri. Kizzy Ann Stamps. (ENG., Illus.). 192p. (J). (gr. 4-7). 2013. pap. 8.99 *(978-0-7636-6976-8(8))* 2012. 15.99 *(978-0-7636-5895-3(2))* Candlewick Pr.
Watts, Leander. Beautiful City of the Dead. 2007. (ENG.). 256p. (YA). (gr. 7-12). pap. 14.99 *(978-0-618-59499-3(X)*, 474084, Clarion Bks.) HarperCollins Pubs.
We Hold These Truths. 2014. (Benjamin Pratt & the Keepers of the School Ser.: 5). (ENG., Illus.). 288p. (J). (gr. 2-5). pap. 8.99 *(978-1-4169-3911-5(3)*, Atheneum Bks. for Young Readers) Simon & Schuster Children's Publishing.
Weatherly, L. A. Them. 2013. (ENG.). 80p. (YA). (gr. 6-12). pap. 6.95 *(978-1-78112-185-6(0))*; lib. bdg. 22.60 *(978-1-78112-184-9(2))* Lerner Publishing Group.
Weaver, Verity. Lab Mice Heist. Huddleston, Courtney, illus. 2019. (What Happened? Ser.). (ENG.). 120p. (J). (gr. 3-4). pap. 7.99 *(978-1-63163-308-9(2)*, 1631633082); lib. bdg. 27.13 *(978-1-63163-307-2(4)*, 1631633074) North Star Editions. (Jolly Fish Pr.).
—Math Test Mischief. Huddleston, Courtney, illus. 2019. (What Happened? Ser.). (ENG.). 120p. (J). (gr. 3-4). pap. 7.99 *(978-1-63163-312-6(0)*, 1631633120); lib. bdg. 27.13 *(978-1-63163-311-9(2)*, 1631633112) North Star Editions. (Jolly Fish Pr.).
—Sandwich Shenanigans. Huddleston, Courtney, illus. 2019. (What Happened? Ser.). (ENG.). 120p. (J). (gr. 3-4). pap. 7.99 *(978-1-63163-316-4(3)*, 1631633163); lib. bdg. 27.13 *(978-1-63163-315-7(5)*, 1631633155) North Star Editions. (Jolly Fish Pr.).
Weaver, Will. Clay. 2004. 232p. (YA). (gr. 8-12). 14.65 *(978-0-7569-4594-7(1))* Perfection Learning Corp.
Webb, Dave. Barkley Rules. 2011. 148p. pap. 9.99 *(978-1-4575-0607-9(6))* Dog Ear Publishing, LLC.
Webb, Derek & Webb, Arthur. Is. 2011. (ENG., Illus.). 182p. (J). (gr. 7). pap. 11.95 *(978-1-906998-11-0(6))* Parthian Bks. GBR. Dist: Independent Pubs. Group.
Webb, Holly. Dog Magic. 2009. (Animal Magic Ser.). (ENG.). 144p. (J). (gr. 2-4). 18.69 *(978-0-545-12415-7(8))* Scholastic, Inc.
—A Little Princess Finds Her Voice. 2018. (ENG.). 208p. (J). (gr. 3-7). pap. 7.99 *(978-1-4926-3912-1(5))* Sourcebooks, Inc.
Webb, Mack H., Jr. Danny & the Detention Demons. Espinola, Nicole & Nealon, Eve, illus. l.t. ed. 2007. 52p. (J). per. 15.95 *(978-0-9779576-2-0(4))* Piiinut Pr., Inc.
Weber, Penny, illus. On My Way to School. 2009. (J). pap. 13.95 *(978-0-9842146-0-0(7))* Concinnity Initiatives.
Webster, Frank V. The Boys of Bellwood School. 2004. reprint ed. pap. 20.95 *(978-1-4191-5509-3(1))*; pap. 1.99 *(978-1-4192-5509-0(6))* Kessinger Publishing, LLC.
Weeks, Sarah. Cheese: a Combo of Oggie Cooder & Oggie Cooder, Party Animal, 1 vol. 2016. (ENG.). 352p. (J). (gr. 2-5). pap. 9.99 *(978-0-545-93957-7(7)*, Scholastic Pr.) Scholastic, Inc.
—Oggie Cooder, Party Animal. 2, 2011. (ENG.). 176p. (J). (gr. 2-5). pap. 6.99 *(978-0-439-92796-3(X)*, Scholastic Paperbacks) Scholastic, Inc.
Weeks, Sarah & Varadarajan, Gita. Save Me a Seat (Scholastic Gold) (ENG.). (J). (gr. 3-7). 2018. 256p. pap. 8.99 *(978-0-545-84661-5(7))* 2016. 240p. 17.99 *(978-0-545-84660-8(9)*, Scholastic Pr.) Scholastic, Inc.
Weil, Zoe. Claude & Medea: The Hellburn Dogs. 2007. (ENG., Illus.). 112p. (J). (gr. 2-7). per. 12.00 *(978-1-59056-105-8(8))* Lantern Publishing & Media.
Weingarten, Lynn. The Secret Sisterhood of Heartbreakers. 2011. (ENG.). 352p. (YA). (gr. 8). 17.99 *(978-0-06-192618-1(3)*, HarperTeen) HarperCollins Pubs.
Weir, Arabella. The Rise & Rise of Tabitha Baird. 2014. (Tabitha Baird Ser.). (ENG., Illus.). 224p. (YA). (gr. 7). pap. 13.95 *(978-1-84812-419-6(8))* Bonnier Publishing GBR. Dist: Independent Pubs. Group.
—Testing Times for Tabitha Baird. 2017. (Tabitha Baird Ser.: 2). (ENG., Illus.). 208p. (YA). (gr. 4-6). pap. 12.99 *(978-1-84812-465-3(1))* Bonnier Publishing GBR. Dist: Independent Pubs. Group.
Weisenberg, Marit. Select. (Select Ser.: 1). (YA). (gr. 9). 2018. 384p. pap. 10.99 *(978-1-58089-895-9(5))* 2017. 352p. lib. bdg. 17.99 *(978-1-58089-806-5(8))* Charlesbridge Publishing, Inc. (Charlesbridge Teen).
Weissman, Elissa Brent. Standing for Socks. 2010. (ENG., Illus.). 224p. (J). (gr. 3-7). pap. 6.99 *(978-1-4169-9777-1(6)*, Atheneum Bks. for Young Readers) Simon & Schuster Children's Publishing.
—Standing for Socks. Sonkin, Jessica, illus. 2009. (ENG.). 224p. (J). (gr. 3-7). 15.99 *(978-1-4169-4801-8(5)*, Atheneum Bks. for Young Readers) Simon & Schuster Children's Publishing.
Welch, Ginger. The Dream Reader. 2012. 76p. 19.95 *(978-1-4626-7276-9(0))*; pap. 19.95 *(978-1-4626-8291-1(X))* America Star Bks.
Welch, Willy. Grumbly Bunnies. Lyon, Tammie Speer, illus. 2004. 32p. (J). 15.95 *(978-1-58089-086-1(5))* Charlesbridge Publishing, Inc.
Wellings, Chris R. How Sparkles Came About: The Adventures of Sparkles. Nunnally, Carson, illus. 2011. 32p. pap. 24.95 *(978-1-4560-4119-9(3))* America Star Bks.
Wells, Carolyn. Patty at Home. 2011. 182p. 26.95 *(978-1-4638-9971-4(8))* Rodgers, Alan Bks.
Wells, Naomi. Sophie Helps at School: Taking Civic Action, 1 vol. 2018. (Civics for the Real World Ser.). (ENG.). 8p. (gr. k-1). pap. *(978-1-5383-6379-9(8)*, f6f336ac-1d32-4b19-b01b-0a24ce77f3a1, Rosen Classroom) Rosen Publishing Group, Inc., The.
Wells, Robin. Sarah's Day in Kindergarten. Grott, Isabella, illus. 2017. (School Days Ser.). (ENG.). 24p. (gr. -1-2). pap. 9.95 *(978-1-68342-775-9(0)*, 9781683427759) Rourke Educational Media.
Wells, Robison. Variant. (Variant Ser.: 1). (ENG.). (YA). (gr. 8-18). 2011. 384p. 17.99 *(978-0-06-202608-8(9))* 1. 2012. 400p. pap. 10.99 *(978-0-06-202609-5(7))* HarperCollins Pubs. (HarperTeen).
Wells, Rosemary. Eduardo: El Primer Dia de Colegio. 2003. Orig. Title: Edward's First Day at School. (SPA., Illus.). 22p. (J). (gr. -1-k). 12.95 *(978-1-56014-620-9(6))* Santillana USA Publishing Co., Inc.
—Emily's First 100 Days of School. Wells, Rosemary, illus. 2005. (ENG., Illus.). 64p. (J). (gr. -1-1). pap. 9.99 *(978-0-7868-1354-4(7))* Little, Brown Bks. for Young Readers.
—Emily's First 100 Days of School. 2006. (Illus.). (J). (gr. -1-4). 18.95 *(978-0-439-84903-6(9)*, WPCD654) Weston Woods Studios, Inc.
—Fiona's Little Accident. Wells, Rosemary, illus. (Felix & Fiona Ser.). (ENG., Illus.). 32p. (J). (gr. k-3). 2019. 5.99 *(978-1-5362-0895-5(7))* 2018. 14.99 *(978-0-7636-8982-7(3))* Candlewick Pr.
—Kindergators: Hands off, Harry! Wells, Rosemary, illus. 2011. (ENG., Illus.). 40p. (J). (gr. -1-1). 16.99 *(978-0-06-192112-4(2)*, Tegen, Katherine Bks) HarperCollins Pubs.
—Max at School. Grey, Andrew, illus. 2017. (Max & Ruby Ser.). 32p. (J). (gr. 1-2). pap. 4.99 *(978-0-515-15743-7(0)*, Penguin Young Readers) Penguin Young Readers Group.
—Otto Runs for President. Wells, Rosemary, illus. 2011. (Illus.). (J). (gr. -1-4). 29.95 *(978-0-545-10690-0(7))* Weston Woods Studios, Inc.
—Yoko. Wells, Rosemary, illus. 2009. (Yoko Book Ser.: 1). (ENG., Illus.). 32p. (J). (gr. -1-3). pap. 8.99 *(978-1-4231-1983-8(5))* Little, Brown Bks. for Young Readers.
Wells, Rosemary & Rosemary, Wells. Yoko. Varela, Sandra Lopez, tr. Wells, Rosemary, illus. 2003. (SPA., Illus.). 34p. (J). (gr. k-2). pap. 8.50 *(978-84-241-8034-8(8))* Everest Editora ESP. Dist: Lectorum Pubns., Inc.
Wells, Tina. Mackenzie Blue, 1. 2013. (Mackenzie Blue Ser.: 1). (ENG.). 224p. (J). (gr. 3-7). pap. 6.99 *(978-0-06-158310-0(3)*, HarperCollins) HarperCollins Pubs.
—Mackenzie Blue: The Secret Crush. 2013. (Mackenzie Blue Ser.: 2). (ENG.). 240p. (J). (gr. 3-7). pap. 6.99 *(978-0-06-158313-1(8)*, HarperCollins) HarperCollins Pubs.
—Mackenzie Blue Vol. 5: Double Trouble. 2014. (Mackenzie Blue Ser.: 5). (ENG., Illus.). 224p. (J). (gr. 3-7). pap. 6.99 *(978-0-06-224412-3(4)*, HarperCollins) HarperCollins Pubs.
—Mackenzie Blue #4 Mixed Messages. 2013. (Mackenzie Blue Ser.: 4). (ENG.). 224p. (J). (gr. 3-7). pap. 6.99 *(978-0-06-158319-3(7)*, HarperCollins) HarperCollins Pubs.
Wells, Tom. Strange Seasons: Summer. 2008. 212p. 24.95 *(978-0-595-50888-4(X))*; pap. 14.95 *(978-0-595-52016-9(2))* iUniverse, Inc.
Welton, Jude. Adam's Alternative Sports Day: An Asperger Story. 2004. (Illus.). 112p. (J). pap. 22.95 *(978-1-84310-300-4(1)*, 695769) Kingsley, Jessica Pubs. GBR. Dist: Hachette UK Distribution.
Wenberg, Michael. Stringz. 2010. 216p. (YA). (gr. 6-10). 16.95 *(978-1-934813-33-1(8))* Westside Bks.
Wendig, Chuck. The Hunt, 0 vols. 2016. (Atlanta Burns Ser.: 2). (ENG.). 329p. (YA). (gr. 9-13). pap. 9.99 *(978-1-5039-5339-0(4)*, 9781503953390, Skyscape) Amazon Publishing.
Wenger, Brahm. Dewey Doo-It at the Jingle Jangle Jamboree: A Musical Storybook Inspired by Arnold Schwarzenegger to Benefit Inner-City Games. 2006. (ENG.). 32p. (J). (gr. -1-3). 18.95 *(978-0-9745143-4-5(9))* RandallFraser Publishing.
Wertheim, L. Jon & Moskowitz, Tobias J. The Rookie Bookie. 2015. (ENG., Illus.). 272p. (J). (gr. 3-7). pap. 15.99 *(978-0-316-24979-9(3))* Little, Brown Bks. for Young Readers.
West, Kasie. Fame, Fate, & the First Kiss. 2019. (ENG.). (YA). (gr. 8). 400p. pap. 11.99 *(978-0-06-285100-0(4))*; 384p. 17.99 *(978-0-06-267579-8(6))* HarperCollins Pubs. (HarperTeen).
—Listen to Your Heart. (ENG.). 336p. (YA). (gr. 7-7). 2019. pap. 9.99 *(978-1-338-21006-4(8))* 2018. 17.99 *(978-1-338-21005-7(X))* Scholastic, Inc.
—P. S. I Like You. 2016. (ENG.). 336p. (YA). (gr. 7). 17.99 *(978-0-545-85097-1(5))* Scholastic, Inc.
—Pivot Point. 2013. (Pivot Point Ser.: 1). (ENG.). 384p. (YA). (gr. 8). pap. 9.99 *(978-0-06-211736-6(X)*, HarperTeen) HarperCollins Pubs.
West, Tracey. Masquerade Brawl. 2009. (Bakugan Battle Brawlers Ser.). (ENG.). 32p. (J). (gr. 2-4). 16.19 *(978-0-545-13121-6(9))* Scholastic, Inc.
Westem, Colleen. Why Elephants Don't Ride School Buses. 2011. 16p. (gr. 1-2). pap. 10.67 *(978-1-4269-6865-5(5))* Trafford Publishing.
Westlund, Emmaline. Fatim. 2012. 42p. pap. 16.95 *(978-1-4626-9660-4(0))* America Star Bks.
Weston Woods Staff, creator. Crazy Hair Day. 2011. 18.95 *(978-0-545-15156-6(2))* Weston Woods Studios, Inc.
—Emily's First 100 Days of School. 2011. 38.75 *(978-0-439-84892-3(X))* Weston Woods Studios, Inc.
—The Gym Teacher from the Black Lagoon. 2011. 38.75 *(978-0-545-19711-3(2))* Weston Woods Studios, Inc.
—How Do Dinosaurs Go to School? 2011. 38.75 *(978-0-545-19712-0(0))* Weston Woods Studios, Inc.
—Miss Nelson Is Missing. 2011. 18.95 *(978-0-439-72847-8(9))*; 29.95 *(978-0-439-73499-8(1))*; 38.75 *(978-0-439-72853-9(3))* Weston Woods Studios, Inc.
—Otto Runs for President. 2011. 18.95 *(978-0-545-31400-8(3))*; 38.75 *(978-0-545-31401-5(1))* Weston Woods Studios, Inc.
—Ready, Freddy! #1: Tooth Trouble. 2011. 20.95 *(978-0-545-05008-1(1))* Weston Woods Studios, Inc.
—Ready, Freddy! #3: Homework Hassles. 2011. 20.95 *(978-0-545-05007-4(3))* Weston Woods Studios, Inc.
—Ready, Freddy! #4: Don't Sit on My Lunch! 2011. 20.95 *(978-0-545-05006-7(5))* Weston Woods Studios, Inc.
—Will I Have a Friend? 2011. 38.75 *(978-0-439-72970-3(X))* Weston Woods Studios, Inc.
Wetzel, JoAnne Stewart. Mermaid School. Swaney, Julianna, illus. 2018. (ENG.). 32p. (J). (gr. -1-2). 18.99 *(978-0-399-55716-3(4)*, Knopf Bks. for Young Readers) Random Hse. Children's Bks.
Weyn, Suzanne. The Bar Code Tattoo (the Bar Code Trilogy, Book 1) 2012. (Bar Code Ser.: 1). (ENG.). 256p. (YA). (gr. 7). pap. 12.99 *(978-0-545-47054-4(4)*, Scholastic Paperbacks) Scholastic, Inc.
—Beaten. (Surviving Southside Ser.). (ENG.). 104p. (YA). (gr. 6-12). 2011. pap. 7.95 *(978-0-7613-6164-0(2)*, 29d7dc43-a6ae-41bd-a65d-1bbc498763a0, Darby Creek) 2015. E-Book 53.32 *(978-1-4677-6007-2(2)*, 9781467760072, Lerner Digital) Lerner Publishing Group.
—Full Impact. 2013. (Surviving Southside Ser.). (ENG.). 104p. (YA). (gr. 6-12). pap. 7.95 *(978-1-4677-0705-3(8)*, 34230826-a7ac-4da4-b4d9-0a88c1b46d70, Darby Creek) Lerner Publishing Group.
—Snapstreak: How My Friends Saved My (Social) Life. 2018. (ENG., Illus.). 192p. (J). (gr. 5-7). 14.99 *(978-1-328-71346-9(6)*, 1673599, Clarion Bks.) HarperCollins Pubs.
Whamond, Dave. Oddrey. 2012. 32p. *(978-1-926973-52-4(6))* Owlkids Bks. Inc.
—Oddrey & the New Kid. 2018. (Oddrey Ser.: 2). (ENG., Illus.). 32p. (J). (gr. -1-3). pap. 8.95 *(978-1-77147-246-3(4))* Owlkids Bks. Inc. CAN. Dist: Publishers Group West (PGW).
—Oddrey & the New Kid. 2018. lib. bdg. 19.60 *(978-0-606-41226-1(3))* Turtleback.
Wheeler, Lisa. Even Monsters Go to School. Van Dusen, Chris, illus. 2019. (ENG.). 32p. (J). (gr. -1-3). 17.99 *(978-0-06-236642-9(4)*, Balzer & Bray) HarperCollins Pubs.
—New Pig in Town: Ready-To-Read Level 3. Ansley, Frank, illus. 2003. (Fitch & Chip Ser.: 1). (ENG.). 48p. (J). (gr. 1-3). 16.99 *(978-0-689-84950-3(8)*, Atheneum/Richard Jackson Bks.) Simon & Schuster Children's Publishing.
—When Pigs Fly. Ansley, Frank, illus. 2005. 48p. (J). lib. bdg. 15.00 *(978-1-59054-996-4(1))* Fitzgerald Bks.
—When Pigs Fly. Ansley, Frank, illus. 2005. (Fitch & Chip Ser.). 48p. (gr. 1-3). 14.00 *(978-0-7569-5472-7(X))* Perfection Learning Corp.
—When Pigs Fly: Ready-To-Read Level 3. Ansley, Frank, illus. 2003. (Fitch & Chip Ser.: 2). (ENG.). 48p. (J). (gr. 1-3). 16.99 *(978-0-689-84951-0(6)*, Atheneum/Richard Jackson Bks.) Simon & Schuster Children's Publishing.
Whelan, Gloria. The Hedge School. 2015. (ENG.). 184p. (J). pap. 14.95 *(978-1-932350-52-4(7))* Bethlehem Bks.
Whitaker, Alecia. The Queen of Kentucky. 2013. (ENG.). 384p. (J). (gr. 7-17). pap. 19.99 *(978-0-316-12494-2(X)*, Poppy) Little, Brown Bks. for Young Readers.
Whitaker, Nathan. Snap Decision, 1 vol. 2015. (Game Face Ser.). (ENG.). 272p. (J). pap. 8.99 *(978-0-310-73703-2(6))* Zonderkidz.
White, Andrea. Windows on the World. 2011. 238p. (J). 18.95 *(978-1-60898-105-2(3))*; pap. 9.95 *(978-1-60898-106-9(1))* namelos llc.
White, Dorine. The Emerald Ring (Cleopatra's Legacy) 2013. 183p. (YA). pap. 13.99 *(978-1-4621-1133-6(5)*, Horizon Pubs.) Cedar Fort, Inc./CFI Distribution.
White, J. A. Shadow School #1: Archimancy. 2019. (Shadow School Ser.: 1). (ENG.). 304p. (J). (gr. 3-7). 16.99 *(978-0-06-283828-5(8)*, Tegen, Katherine Bks) HarperCollins Pubs.
White, Kathryn. Ruby's School Walk. Latimer, Miriam, illus. 2012. (ENG.). 29p. (J). (gr. -1-1). pap. 22.44 *(978-1-84686-786-6(X))* Barefoot Bks., Ltd. GBR. Dist: Children's Plus, Inc.
White, Michelle A. Anthony with an A. 2011. 16p. pap. 9.50 *(978-1-4634-1641-6(5))* AuthorHouse.
White, Russ. Cat Got Your Tongue? A Book of Idioms. Cornelison, Reuel, illus. l.t. ed. 2004. 44p. (J). per. *(978-0-9742865-0-5(0)*, 00) White, Russ.
White, Toni. Ridge Street Prom. 2008. 182p. pap. 12.96 *(978-1-4357-1966-8(2))* Lulu Pr., Inc.
Whitesides, Tyler. Curse of the Broomstaff. 2013. (Janitors Ser.: 3). (ENG., Illus.). 384p. (J). (gr. 5). 18.99 *(978-1-60907-605-4(2)*, 5107237, Shadow Mountain) Shadow Mountain Publishing.
—Heroes of the Dustbin. 2015. (Janitors Ser.: 5). (ENG., Illus.). 416p. (J). (gr. 5). 18.99 *(978-1-62972-065-4(8)*, 5136476, Shadow Mountain) Shadow Mountain Publishing.
—Janitors. 2011. (Janitors Ser.: Bk. 1). pap. 34.99 *(978-1-60908-075-4(0))* Deseret Bk. Co.
—Janitors. (Janitors Ser.: 1). (ENG., Illus.). (J). (gr. 5). 2012. 320p. pap. 9.99 *(978-1-60907-065-6(8)*, 5078581) 2011. 312p. 17.99 *(978-1-60908-056-3(4)*, 5057487) Shadow Mountain Publishing. (Shadow Mountain).
—Secrets of New Forest Academy. 2013. (Janitors Ser.: 2). (ENG., Illus.). 368p. (J). (gr. 5). pap. 8.99 *(978-1-60907-546-0(3)*, 5105035, Shadow Mountain) Shadow Mountain Publishing.
—Strike of the Sweepers. 2014. (Janitors Ser.: 4). (ENG., Illus.). 400p. (J). (gr. 5). 18.99 *(978-1-60907-907-9(8)*, 5121465, Shadow Mountain) Shadow Mountain Publishing.
Whitmore, Hugh. The Three Madelines. Wilson, Raylene Jenee & Gibbons, Deanna, illus. 2012. 124p. pap. 15.95 *(978-0-9848314-4-9(4))* Sincerity Publishing.
Whittemore, Jo. Brooke's Bad Luck, 5. 2017. (Confidentially Yours Ser.). (ENG.). 288p. (J). (gr. 4-7). 21.19 *(978-1-5364-0247-6(8))* HarperCollins Pubs.
—Confidentially Yours #1: Brooke's Not-So-Perfect Plan. 2016. (Confidentially Yours Ser.: 1). (ENG., Illus.). 320p. (J). (gr. 3-7). pap. 6.99 *(978-0-06-235893-6(6)*, HarperCollins) HarperCollins Pubs.
—Confidentially Yours #3: Heather's Crush Catastrophe. 2016. (Confidentially Yours Ser.: 3). (ENG.). 288p. (J). (gr. 3-7). 6.99 *(978-0-06-235897-4(9)*, HarperCollins) HarperCollins Pubs.
—D Is for Drama. 2012. (Mix Ser.). (ENG.). 272p. (J). (gr. 4-8). pap. 6.99 *(978-1-4424-4152-1(6)*, Aladdin) Simon & Schuster Children's Publishing.
—Front Page Face-Off. 2010. (ENG.). 240p. (J). (gr. 4-8). pap. 5.99 *(978-1-4169-9169-4(7))* Simon & Schuster, Inc.
—Odd Girl In. 2011. (Mix Ser.). (ENG.). 240p. (J). (gr. 4-8). pap. 8.99 *(978-1-4424-1284-2(4)*, Aladdin) Simon & Schuster Children's Publishing.
Whitten, A. J. The Cellar. 2011. (ENG.). 288p. (YA). (gr. 7-18). pap. 16.99 *(978-0-547-23253-9(5)*, 1082798, Clarion Bks.) HarperCollins Pubs.
—The Well. 2009. (ENG., Illus.). 336p. (YA). (gr. 7-18). pap. 18.95 *(978-0-547-23229-4(2)*, 1082742, Clarion Bks.) HarperCollins Pubs.
Who Will Look Out for Danny? Individual Title Six-Packs. (Action Packs Ser.). 120p. (gr. 3-5). 44.00 *(978-0-7635-8420-7(7))* Rigby Education.
Whybrow, Ian. Little Wolf's Haunted Hall for Small Horrors. Ross, Tony, illus. (Middle Grade Fiction Ser.). (J). 2005. 132p. (gr. 3-6). 14.95 *(978-1-57505-412-4(4))* 2004. 125p. (gr. 4-7). per. 6.95 *(978-1-57505-794-1(8))* Lerner Publishing Group.
Whytock, Cherry. My Cup Runneth Over: The Life of Angelica Cookson Potts. Whytock, Cherry, illus. 2012. (ENG., Illus.). 192p. (YA). (gr. 7). pap. 9.99 *(978-1-4424-6055-3(5)*, Simon Pulse) Simon Pulse.
Wicke, Ed. Bullies. 2nd rev. ed. 2003. 212p. (J). per. 9.99 *(978-0-9677652-2-8(6)*, BlacknBlue Pr. UK) Blacknblue Pr.
Wientge, Kristi. Karma Khullar's Mustache. (ENG., Illus.). (J). (gr. 3-7). 2018. 288p. pap. 8.99 *(978-1-4814-7771-0(4))* 2017. 272p. 16.99 *(978-1-4814-7770-3(6))* Simon & Schuster Bks. For Young Readers. (Simon & Schuster Bks. For Young Readers).
—Karma Khullar's Mustache. 2018. lib. bdg. 18.40 *(978-0-606-41410-4(X))* Turtleback.
Wiggins, Rosie. Adventures at a Ray of Hope Preschool. 2007. 32p. per. 12.95 *(978-1-4327-1657-8(3))* Outskirts Pr., Inc.
Wight, Eric. Frankie Pickle & the Mathematical Menace. Wight, Eric, illus. 2011. (Frankie Pickle Ser.). (ENG., Illus.). 96p. (J). (gr. 2-5). 10.99 *(978-1-4169-8972-1(2)*, Simon & Schuster Bks. For Young Readers) Simon & Schuster Bks. For Young Readers.
Wilcut-Bledsoe, Robin. The Imagination of Hollie Mason. 2008. 88p. pap. 19.95 *(978-1-60703-804-7(8))* America Star Bks.
Wilde, Jerry. Peace in the Halls: Stories & Activities to Manage Anger & Prevent School Violence. 2003. 112p. (YA). (gr. 4-12). pap. 9.95 *(978-0-9657610-4-8(5))* LGR Publishing, Inc.
Wilhelm, Doug. The Revealers. 2011. (ENG.). 240p. (YA). (gr. 5-9). pap. 11.99 *(978-0-312-56374-5(4)*, 900074765) Square Fish.
Wilhelm, Hans. Noodles: I Love School (Scholastic Reader, Level 1) Wilhelm, Hans, illus. 2010. (Scholastic Reader, Level 1 Ser.). (ENG., Illus.). 32p. (J). (gr. -1-1). pap. 3.99 *(978-0-545-13474-3(9)*, Cartwheel Bks.) Scholastic, Inc.
Wilkerson, Dana. Mustang Macy. 2017. (ENG.). 122p. (J). (gr. 2-5). pap. 7.99 *(978-1-948148-00-9(5))* Dana Wilkerson, LLC.
Wilkinson, Brenda. Ludell. 2014. (ENG., Illus.). 228p. (J). (-9). pap. 12.95 *(978-1-939601-16-2(9))* Ig Publishing, Inc.
Wilkinson, Lili. Pink. 2012. (ENG.). 320p. (YA). (gr. 8). pap. 9.99 *(978-0-06-192654-9(X)*, HarperTeen) HarperCollins Pubs.
Willems, Mo. Knuffle Bunny Too: A Case of Mistaken Identity. rev. ed. 2007. (Knuffle Bunny Ser.). (ENG., Illus.). 48p. (J). (gr. -1-k). 17.99 *(978-1-4231-0299-1(1)*, Hyperion Books for Children) Disney Publishing Worldwide.
—The Pigeon HAS to Go to School! 2019. (Pigeon Ser.). (ENG.). 40p. (J). (gr. -1-k). 17.99 *(978-1-368-04645-9(2)*, Hyperion Books for Children) Disney Publishing Worldwide.
Willems, Mo & Willems, Trixie, narrated by. Knuffle Bunny Too: A Case of Mistaken Identity. 2011. (J). (gr. -1-2). 29.95 *(978-0-545-13456-9(0))* Weston Woods Studios, Inc.
Williams, Bonnie. Meet Teddy Rex! Ready-To-Read Level 1. Gordon, John, illus. 2012. (Dino School Ser.). (ENG.). 24p. (J). (gr. -1-1). 17.99 *(978-1-4424-4996-1(9))*; pap. 4.99 *(978-1-4424-4995-4(0))* Simon Spotlight. (Simon Spotlight).
—Say Cheese, Teddy Rex! Gordon, John, illus. 2016. (J). *(978-1-5182-1896-5(2)*, Simon Spotlight) Simon Spotlight.
—Say Cheese, Teddy Rex! Ready-To-Read Level 1. Gordon, John, illus. 2016. (Dino School Ser.). (ENG.). 24p. (J). (gr. -1-1). pap. 4.99 *(978-1-4814-6609-7(7)*, Simon Spotlight) Simon Spotlight.

S

Williams, C. E. Cj's World: My First Day of Second Grade. 2012. 28p. pap. 24.95 *(978-1-4626-6249-4(8))* America Star Bks.

Williams, Felisha. I'm No Bully, Am I? 2012. 24p. (-18). pap. 15.99 *(978-1-4797-0973-1(5))* Xlibris Corp.

—The Milk Chocolate Kid. 2012. 24p. (-18). pap. 15.99 *(978-1-4797-0971-7(9))* Xlibris Corp.

Williams, Heather. Nellie Oleson Meets Laura Ingalls. 2007. (Little House Ser.). 234p. (J). (gr. 3-7). lib. bdg. 16.89 *(978-0-06-124249-6(7))* HarperCollins Pubs.

Williams, Jared T. Rabbit Ninja. Williams, Jared T., illus. 2019. (Illus.). 32p. (J). 17.95 *(978-1-56792-628-6(2))* Godine, David R. Pub.

Williams, Lori. Being Me. 2003. (Summit Books Ser.). 268p. (J). (gr. 3-6). lib. bdg. 13.95 *(978-0-7569-1372-4(1))*; pap. 6.95 *(978-0-7891-6024-9(2))* Perfection Learning Corp.

Williams, Maggy. Celia & the Glue Man: A Girl's Journey to Becoming Gluten-Free & Happy. Agresta, Elizabeth, illus. 2018. (J). pap. *(978-1-61599-390-1(8))* Loving Healing Pr., Inc.

Williams, Rozanne. Five Little Monsters Went to School. 2017. (Learn-To-Read Ser.). (ENG., Illus.). (J). pap. 3.49 *(978-1-68310-244-1(4))* Pacific Learning, Inc.

Williams, Rozanne Lanczak. The Author with the Fancy Purple Pen. Richard, Ilene, illus. (Learn to Write Ser.). 16p. (J). 2007. (gr. -1-3). pap. 8.99 *(978-1-59198-346-0(0))* 2006. (gr. k-2). pap. 2.99 *(978-1-59198-299-9(5)*, 6189) Creative Teaching Pr., Inc.

—Emily Santos, Star of the Week. Burris, Priscilla, illus. 2006. (Learn to Write Ser.). 16p. (J). (gr. k-2). pap. 2.99 *(978-1-59198-298-2(7)*, 6194) Creative Teaching Pr., Inc.

—Emily Santos, Star of the Week. Maio, Barbara, ed. Burris, Priscilla, illus. 2006. (J). per. 8.99 *(978-1-59198-358-3(4))* Creative Teaching Pr., Inc.

—Room 9 Writes a Report. Lucas, Margeaux, illus. 2006. (Learn to Write Ser.). 16p. (J). (gr. k-2). pap. 3.49 *(978-1-59198-297-5(9)*, 6193) Creative Teaching Pr., Inc.

—Room 9 Writes a Report. Maio, Barbara, ed. Lucas, Margeaux, illus. 2006. (J). per. 8.99 *(978-1-59198-357-6(6))* Creative Teaching Pr., Inc.

—Tess Builds a Snowman. Harris, Jenny B., illus. 2006. (Learn to Write Ser.). 8p. (J). (gr. k-2). pap. 3.49 *(978-1-59198-286-9(3)*, 6180) Creative Teaching Pr., Inc.

—Tess Builds a Snowman. Maio, Barbara & Faulkner, Stacey, eds. Harris, Jenny B., illus. 2006. (J). per. 6.99 *(978-1-59198-337-8(1))* Creative Teaching Pr., Inc.

—When You Go Walking. Briles, Patty, illus. 2006. (Learn to Write Ser.). 16p. (J). (gr. k-2). pap. 3.49 *(978-1-59198-292-0(8)*, 6188) Creative Teaching Pr., Inc.

Williams, Sam. School Bus Bunny Bus. Trotter, Stuart, illus. 2006. (ENG.). 10p. (J). (gr. -1-1). 12.95 *(978-1-905417-17-9(9))* Boxer Bks., Ltd. GBR. Dist: Sterling Publishing Co., Inc.

Williams-Sanchez, Valerie. Eddie & the Hot Cocoa Hot Rod. Russell, Brooklyn, illus. 2015. 37p. (J). pap. *(978-1-4834-4173-3(3))* Lulu Pr., Inc.

—Isaiah & the Chocolate Mountain. 2015. (ENG., Illus.). 36p. (J). pap. 16.95 *(978-1-4834-3820-7(1))* Lulu Pr., Inc.

Williams, Shanica. Amy Goes Shopping for School. 2012. 16p. pap. 15.99 *(978-1-4772-1360-5(0))* AuthorHouse.

Williams, Shannon. School Rules! Nelson, Anndria, illus. 2010. 36p. pap. 16.99 *(978-1-4520-3924-4(0))* AuthorHouse.

Williams, Stanley R. Not Me. 2008. 47p. pap. 24.95 *(978-1-4241-9577-0(2))* America Star Bks.

Williams, Suzanne. Master of Minds? Carter, Abby, illus. 2004. 58p. (J). lib. bdg. 15.00 *(978-1-4242-0911-8(0))* Fitzgerald Bks.

—Master of Minds? Carter, Abby, illus. 2004. (Marvelous Mind of Matthew Mcghee Age 8 Ser.). 58p. (J). 11.65 *(978-0-7569-5530-4(0))* Perfection Learning Corp.

Williams, T. E. Fluffy!! 2011. 24p. 16.25 *(978-1-4520-3743-1(4))* AuthorHouse.

Williamson, Greg. Why Do I Have to Wear Glasses? Popko, Wendy, illus. 2005. (J). 12.99 *(978-0-9666076-5-9(1))* Peerless Publishing, L.L.C.

—Why Do I Have to Wear Glasses? Popkp, Wendy, illus. 2005. (J). pap. 7.99 *(978-0-9666076-3-5(5))* Peerless Publishing, L.L.C.

Williamson, Lisa. The Art of Being Normal: A Novel. 2018. (ENG.). 352p. (YA). pap. 11.99 *(978-1-250-14427-0(2)*, 900180627) Square Fish.

Willink, Jocko. Marc's Mission: Way of the Warrior Kid. Bozak, Jon, illus. 2018. (Way of the Warrior Kid Ser.: 2). (ENG.). 224p. (J). 14.99 *(978-1-250-15679-2(3)*, 900185103) Feiwel & Friends.

—Way of the Warrior Kid: From Wimpy to Warrior the Navy SEAL Way. Bozak, Jon, illus. 2017. (Way of the Warrior Kid Ser.: 1). (ENG.). 192p. (J). 14.99 *(978-1-250-15107-0(4)*, 900182685) Feiwel & Friends.

Willis, Jeanne. Be Gentle, Python! Birchall, Mark, illus. 2005. (Picture Bks.). 28p. (J). (gr. k-2). 7.95 *(978-1-57505-508-4(2))* Lerner Publishing Group.

—I Hate School. Ross, Tony, illus. 2005. (ENG.). 32p. (J). (gr. -1-k). pap. 12.99 *(978-1-84270-463-9(X))* Andersen Pr. GBR. Dist: Independent Pubs. Group.

—Lucinda Belinda Melinda Mccool. Ross, Tony, illus. 2016. (ENG.). 32p. (J). (-k). 23.99 *(978-1-78344-202-7(6))* Andersen Pr. GBR. Dist: Independent Pubs. Group.

—No Biting, Puma! Birchall, Mark, illus. 2005. (Picture Bks.). 28p. (J). (gr. k-2). 7.25 *(978-1-57505-509-1(0))* Lerner Publishing Group.

Willis, Meredith Sue. Meli's Way. 2015. 178p. (YA). *(978-1-932727-15-9(9))* Montemayor Pr.

Willis, S. J. The Wishwasher. 2011. 128p. (gr. 4-6). pap. 13.32 *(978-1-4567-8751-6(9))* AuthorHouse.

Willner-Pardo, Gina. The Hard Kind of Promise. 2011. (ENG.). 204p. (J). (gr. 5-7). pap. 12.99 *(978-0-547-55017-6(0)*, 1450220, Clarion Bks.) HarperCollins Pubs.

Willsea, Hedley. The Heath of the Graves. 2009. (ENG.). 371p. pap. 31.50 *(978-1-4092-2226-2(8))* Lulu Pr., Inc.

Wilson, Sarah. Cookie Crisis! Ross, Sharon & Bergman, Shannon, illus. 2005. 32p. (J). lib. bdg. 15.00 *(978-1-59054-981-0(3))* Fitzgerald Bks.

Wilson, Bob, illus. Football Fred, Vol. 4. 2003. (ENG.). 80p. (J). pap. *(978-0-330-37091-2(X)*, Pan) Pan Macmillan.

Wilson, Bryan M. Benjamin's Report Card Blues. 2011. 28p. pap. 12.95 *(978-1-4567-3530-2(6))* AuthorHouse.

Wilson, Debra. 65 Mustang: A Novel. 2011. 300p. pap. *(978-1-934922-47-7(1))* IBJ Custom Publishing.

Wilson, Jacqueline. Candyfloss. Sharratt, Nick, illus. 2008. (ENG.). 352p. (J). (gr. 4-7). pap. 13.99 *(978-0-312-38418-0(1)*, 900053319) Square Fish.

—Cookie. Sharratt, Nick, illus. 2010. (ENG.). 352p. (J). (gr. 4-7). pap. 17.99 *(978-0-312-64290-7(3)*, 900068061) Square Fish.

Wilson, Martin. What They Always Tell Us. 2010. (ENG.). 304p. (YA). (gr. 9). pap. 8.99 *(978-0-385-73508-7(1)*, Delacorte Bks. for Young Readers) Random Hse. Children's Bks.

Wilson, Troy. Perfect Man, 1 vol. Griffiths, Dean, illus. 2005. (ENG.). 32p. (J). (gr. 1-3). per. 9.95 *(978-1-55143-435-3(0))* Orca Bk. Pubs. USA.

Winerip, Michael. Adam Canfield of the Slash. (Adam Canfield of the Slash Ser.: 1). (ENG., Illus.). 336p. (J). (gr. 3-7). 2007. per. 8.99 *(978-0-7636-2794-2(1))* 2005. 15.99 *(978-0-7636-2340-1(7))* Candlewick Pr.

—Adam Canfield: the Last Reporter. 2010. (Adam Canfield of the Slash Ser.: 3). (ENG., Illus.). 384p. (J). (gr. 3-7). 7.99 *(978-0-7636-4838-1(8))* Candlewick Pr.

—Adam Canfield, Watch Your Back! 2009. (Adam Canfield of the Slash Ser.: 2). (ENG., Illus.). 352p. (J). (gr. 3-7). 8.99 *(978-0-7636-4412-3(9))* Candlewick Pr.

Winfield, Arthur M. The Rover Boys at School. 2007. 236p. 27.95 *(978-1-4218-4132-8(0))*; per. 12.95 *(978-1-4218-4230-1(0))* 1st World Publishing, Inc. (1st World Library - Literary Society).

—The Rover Boys at School. 2004. reprint ed. pap. 1.99 *(978-1-4192-8115-0(1))* Kessinger Publishing, LLC.

Winfrey, Kerry. Love & Other Alien Experiences. 2017. (ENG.). 272p. (YA). pap. 19.99 *(978-1-250-11952-0(9)*, 900172820) Feiwel & Friends.

Wing, Natasha. The Night Before Class Picture Day. 2016. (Night Before Ser.). lib. bdg. 14.75 *(978-0-606-38834-4(6))* Turtleback.

—The Night Before First Grade. Zemke, Deborah, illus. 2005. (Night Before Ser.). 32p. (J). (gr. k-1). pap. 4.99 *(978-0-448-43747-7(3)*, Grosset & Dunlap) Penguin Young Readers Group.

—The Night Before Kindergarten Graduation. Wummer, Amy, illus. 2019. (Night Before Ser.). 32p. (J). (gr. -1-1). pap. 5.99 *(978-1-5247-9001-1(X)*, Grosset & Dunlap) Penguin Young Readers Group.

—The Night Before Preschool. Wummer, Amy, illus. 2011. (Night Before Ser.). 32p. (J). (gr. -1-k). pap. 4.99 *(978-0-448-45451-1(3)*, Grosset & Dunlap) Penguin Young Readers Group.

—The Night Before the 100th Day of School. Pierce, Mindy, illus. 2005. (Night Before Ser.). 32p. (J). (gr. -1-3). pap. 5.99 *(978-0-448-43923-5(9)*, Grosset & Dunlap) Penguin Young Readers Group.

Winget, Susan. Tucker's Four-Carrot School Day. Winget, Susan, illus. 2005. (ENG., Illus.). 40p. (J). (gr. -1-k). 12.99 *(978-0-06-054642-7(5))* HarperCollins Pubs.

Winkler, Henry & Oliver, Lin. Bookmarks Are People Too! 2014. (Here's Hank Ser.: 1). lib. bdg. 16.00 *(978-0-606-34142-4(0))* Turtleback.

—Bookmarks Are People Too! #1, No. 1. Garrett, Scott, illus. 2014. (Here's Hank Ser.: 1). (ENG.). 128p. (J). (gr. 1-3). 6.99 *(978-0-448-47997-2(4)*, Penguin Workshop) Penguin Young Readers Group.

—A Brand-New Me! #17. 2010. (Hank Zipzer Ser.: 17). (ENG., Illus.). 160p. (J). (gr. 3-7). pap. 6.99 *(978-0-448-45210-4(3)*, Grosset & Dunlap) Penguin Young Readers Group.

—The Curtain Went up, My Pants Fell Down #11. 2007. (Hank Zipzer Ser.: 11). (ENG., Illus.). 160p. (J). (gr. 3-7). pap. 6.99 *(978-0-448-44267-9(1)*, Grosset & Dunlap) Penguin Young Readers Group.

—Help! Somebody Get Me Out of Fourth Grade #7. 2004. (Hank Zipzer Ser.: 7). (ENG., Illus.). 160p. (J). (gr. 3-7). mass mkt. 6.99 *(978-0-448-43619-7(1)*, Grosset & Dunlap) Penguin Young Readers Group.

—Holy Enchilada! #6. 2004. (Hank Zipzer Ser.: 6). (ENG., Illus.). 160p. (J). (gr. 3-7). pap. 6.99 *(978-0-448-43353-0(2)*, Grosset & Dunlap) Penguin Young Readers Group.

—How to Scare the Pants off Your Pets, 3. 2013. (Ghost Buddy Ser.: 3). (ENG.). 176p. (J). (gr. 4-6). 18.69 *(978-0-545-29884-1(9))* Scholastic, Inc.

—I Got a D in Salami. 2004. (Hank Zipzer Ser.: No. 2). 128p. (J). (gr. 2-6). pap. 29.00 incl. audio *(978-1-4000-9007-5(5)*, Listening Library) Random Hse. Audio Publishing Group.

—I Got a d in Salami #2. 2004. (Hank Zipzer Ser.: 2). (ENG., Illus.). 176p. (J). (gr. 3-7). mass mkt. 7.99 *(978-0-448-43163-5(7)*, Grosset & Dunlap) Penguin Young Readers Group.

—The Life of Me (Enter at Your Own Risk) 2008. (Hank Zipzer Ser.: No. 14). (Illus.). 186p. (gr. 3-7). 16.00 *(978-0-7569-8819-7(5))* Perfection Learning Corp.

—Life of Me, The #14: Enter at Your Own Risk. 2008. (Hank Zipzer Ser.: 14). (ENG., Illus.). 256p. (J). (gr. 3-7). pap. 7.99 *(978-0-448-44376-8(7)*, Grosset & Dunlap) Penguin Young Readers Group.

—Niagara Falls, or Does It? 2004. (Hank Zipzer Ser.: No. 1). 128p. (J). (gr. 2-6). pap. 29.00 incl. audio *(978-1-4000-9006-8(7)*, Listening Library) Random Hse. Audio Publishing Group.

—Niagara Falls, or Does It? #1. 2004. (Hank Zipzer Ser.: 1). (ENG., Illus.). 144p. (J). (gr. 3-7). pap. 7.99 *(978-0-448-43162-8(9)*, Grosset & Dunlap) Penguin Young Readers Group.

—Summer School! What Genius Thought That Up? 2006. (Hank Zipzer Ser.: No. 8). (Illus.). 157p. (J). (gr. 3-9). lib. bdg. 24.21 *(978-1-59961-107-5(4))* Spotlight.

—A Tale of Two Tails #15. 2008. (Hank Zipzer Ser.: 15). (ENG., Illus.). 160p. (J). (gr. 3-7). pap. 6.99 *(978-0-448-44378-2(3)*, Grosset & Dunlap) Penguin Young Readers Group.

—The Zippity Zinger. 2004. (Hank Zipzer Ser.: No. 4). 160p. (J). (gr. 2-6). pap. 29.00 incl. audio *(978-1-4000-9009-9(1)*, Listening Library) Random Hse. Audio Publishing Group.

—The Zippity Zinger. 2006. (Hank Zipzer Ser.: No. 4). 154p. (J). (gr. 3-9). lib. bdg. 24.21 *(978-1-59961-103-7(1))* Spotlight.

—The Zippity Zinger #4: The Zippity Zinger the Mostly True Confessions of the World's Best Underachiever, 4 vols. 2004. (Hank Zipzer Ser.: 4). (ENG., Illus.). 160p. (J). (gr. 3-7). mass mkt. 6.99 *(978-0-448-43193-2(9)*, Grosset & Dunlap) Penguin Young Readers Group.

Winn, Sheridan. The Sprite Sisters: Magic at Drysdale's School (Vol 7) Winn, Christopher, illus. 2017. 256p. pap. *(978-0-9574231-2-1(8))* Winn, Sheridan.

Winner, Ramona Moreno. It's Okay to Be Different! (Esta Bien Ser Diferente!) Velasquez, Nicole, illus. Date not set. (ENG & SPA.). 40p. (J). (gr. k-3). 9.95 *(978-0-9651174-0-1(5))* BrainStorm 3000.

Winston, Sherri. President of the Whole Fifth Grade. 2012. (President Ser.: 1). (ENG.). 288p. (J). (gr. 3-7). pap. 8.99 *(978-0-316-11433-2(2))* Little, Brown Bks. for Young Readers.

—President of the Whole Sixth Grade: Girl Code. (President Ser.: 3). (ENG.). (J). (gr. 3-7). 2019. 288p. pap. 8.99 *(978-0-316-50529-1(3))* 2018. 272p. 16.99 *(978-0-316-50528-4(5))* Little, Brown Bks. for Young Readers.

Winter, Ariel S. One of a Kind. Hitch, David, illus. 2012. (ENG.). 32p. (J). (gr. -1-2). 15.99 *(978-1-4424-2016-8(2)*, Aladdin) Simon & Schuster Children's Publishing.

Winters, Ben H. The Mystery of the Missing Everything. 2012. (ENG.). 272p. (J). (gr. 3-7). pap. 6.99 *(978-0-06-196546-3(4)*, HarperCollins) HarperCollins Pubs.

—The Secret Life of Ms. Finkleman. 2011. (ENG.). 272p. (J). (gr. 3-7). pap. 5.99 *(978-0-06-196543-2(X)*, HarperCollins) HarperCollins Pubs.

Winters, Kay. My Teacher for President. Brunkus, Denise, illus. 2008. (ENG.). 32p. (J). (gr. k-3). pap. 7.99 *(978-0-14-241170-4(1)*, Puffin Books) Penguin Young Readers Group.

—My Teacher for President. Brunkus, Denise, illus. 2008. (gr. -1-k). 17.00 *(978-0-7569-8925-5(6))* Perfection Learning Corp.

—The Teeny Tiny Ghost & the Monster, Vol. 3. Munsinger, Lynn, illus. 2004. (ENG.). 32p. (J). (gr. -1-3). 14.99 *(978-0-06-028884-6(1))* HarperCollins Pubs.

—This School Year Will Be the BEST! Andriani, Renee, illus. 32p. (J). (gr. 1-3). 2013. mass mkt. 6.99 *(978-0-14-242696-8(2)*, Puffin Books) 2010. 17.99 *(978-0-525-42275-4(7)*, Dutton Books for Young Readers) Penguin Young Readers Group.

Wise, Anna. The Vala of Trinity: Book One Norse Series, 1 vol. 2009. 195p. pap. 24.95 *(978-1-61582-763-3(3))* America Star Bks.

Wise, Rachel. Cast Your Ballot! 2013. (Dear Know-It-All Ser.: 9). (ENG., Illus.). 160p. (J). (gr. 3-7). 15.99 *(978-1-4424-8793-2(3))*; pap. 5.99 *(978-1-4424-8792-5(5))* Simon Spotlight. (Simon Spotlight).

—Everyone's a Critic, 5. 2013. (Dear Know-It-All Ser.: 5). (ENG.). 160p. (J). (gr. 3-7). 15.99 *(978-1-4424-6821-4(1)*, Simon Spotlight) Simon & Schuster Children's Publishing.

—Late Edition. 2014. (Dear Know-It-All Ser.: 11). (ENG., Illus.). 160p. (J). (gr. 3-7). pap. 5.99 *(978-1-4424-9724-5(6)*, Simon Spotlight) Simon Spotlight.

—A Level Playing Field, 3. 2012. (Dear Know-It-All Ser.: 3). (ENG.). 160p. (J). (gr. 3-7). 15.99 *(978-1-4424-5384-5(2)*, Simon Spotlight) Simon & Schuster Children's Publishing.

—A Level Playing Field. 2012. (Dear Know-It-All Ser.: 3). (ENG.). 160p. (J). (gr. 3-7). pap. 5.99 *(978-1-4424-5326-5(5)*, Simon Spotlight) Simon Spotlight.

—Old Story, New Twist, 4. 2012. (Dear Know-It-All Ser.: 4). (ENG.). 160p. (J). (gr. 3-7). 15.99 *(978-1-4424-5385-2(0)*, Simon Spotlight) Simon & Schuster Children's Publishing.

—Old Story, New Twist. 2012. (Dear Know-It-All Ser.: 4). (ENG.). 160p. (J). (gr. 3-7). pap. 5.99 *(978-1-4424-5328-9(1)*, Simon Spotlight) Simon Spotlight.

—Read All about It! 2012. (Dear Know-It-All Ser.: 1). (ENG.). 176p. (J). (gr. 3-7). 15.99 *(978-1-4424-5382-1(6))*; pap. 5.99 *(978-1-4424-4402-7(9))* Simon Spotlight. (Simon Spotlight).

—Set the Record Straight! 2012. (Dear Know-It-All Ser.: 2). (ENG.). 160p. (J). (gr. 3-7). 15.99 *(978-1-4424-5383-8(4))*; pap. 5.99 *(978-1-4424-4445-4(2))* Simon Spotlight. (Simon Spotlight).

Wiseman, Rosalind. Boys, Girls, & Other Hazardous Materials. 2011. 304p. (YA). (gr. 7-18). 8.99 *(978-0-14-241819-2(6)*, Speak) Penguin Young Readers Group.

Wishinsky, Frieda. Give Maggie a Chance, 1 vol. Griffiths, Dean, illus. 2004. (ENG.). 32p. (J). (gr. -1-2). pap. 7.95 *(978-1-55041-704-3(5)*, eb81180e-3dfe-4e48-b712-508c885f886a) Trifolium Bks., Inc. CAN. Dist: Firefly Bks., Ltd.

—Jennifer Jones Won't Leave Me Alone. Layton, Neal, illus. 2005. (Carolrhoda Picture Bks.). 32p. (J). (gr. -1-3). per. 6.95 *(978-1-57505-921-1(5))*; (gr. k-2). 15.95 *(978-0-87614-921-8(2))* Lerner Publishing Group.

—Queen of the Toilet Bowl, 1 vol. 2005. (Orca Currents Ser.). (ENG., Illus.). 128p. (J). (gr. 4-7). per. 9.95 *(978-1-55143-364-6(8))* Orca Bk. Pubs. USA.

Witschen, Kay. Johnny Coalboy. Luckemeyer, Norma, illus. 2003. (J). per. 5.95 *(978-0-9741352-0-5(8))* Dwitt Publishing.

Wittlinger, Ellen. Sandpiper. 2007. (ENG.). 288p. (YA). (gr. 7-12). pap. 6.99 *(978-1-4169-3651-0(3)*, Simon & Schuster Bks. For Young Readers) Simon & Schuster Bks. For Young Readers.

Wizner, Jake. Spanking Shakespeare. Ewing, Richard, illus. 2008. (ENG.). 304p. (YA). (gr. 9). pap. 8.99 *(978-0-375-85594-8(7)*, Ember) Random Hse. Children's Bks.

—Spanking Shakespeare. 2007. (YA). *(978-0-375-84086-9(9))* Random Hse. Children's Bks.

Wodehouse, Pelham Grenville. Mike at Wrykyn. 2013. 189p. reprint ed. lthr. 69.00 *(978-0-7426-3265-3(2))* Classic Bks.

Wohnoutka, Mike. So Big! 2019. (ENG., Illus.). 32p. (J). 17.99 *(978-1-5476-0079-3(9)*, 900197955, Bloomsbury Children's Bks.) Bloomsbury Publishing USA.

Wojciechowski, Susan. Beany & the Magic Crystal. Natti, Susanna, illus. 2005. (Beany Adventures Ser.). 87p. (J). lib. bdg. 13.65 *(978-0-7569-5836-7(9))* Perfection Learning Corp.

—Beany (Not Beanhead) Natti, Susanna, illus. 2005. (Beany Adventures Ser.). 68p. (J). lib. bdg. 12.65 *(978-0-7569-5835-0(0))* Perfection Learning Corp.

Wojtowicz, Jen. The Boy Who Grew Flowers. Adams, Steve, illus. 2012. (ENG.). 32p. (J). (gr. k-5). pap. 9.99 *(978-1-84686-749-1(5))* Barefoot Bks., Inc.

Wojtowicz, Jen & Wojzowitz, Jen. The Boy Who Grew Flowers. Adams, Steve, illus. 2005. (ENG.). 32p. (J). (gr. -1-3). 16.99 *(978-1-84148-686-4(8))* Barefoot Bks., Inc.

Wolf, Aline D. Our Peaceful Classroom. 2017. (ENG.). (Orig.). (J). 19.95 *(978-0-939195-54-1(2))* Parent Child Pr., Inc.

Wolf, Joan M. Runs with Courage. 2017. (ENG.). 224p. (J). (gr. 4-7). pap. 9.99 *(978-1-58536-985-0(3)*, 204116) Sleeping Bear Pr.

—Someone Named Eva. 2009. (ENG., Illus.). 208p. (J). (gr. 5-7). pap. 7.99 *(978-0-547-23766-4(9)*, 1083877, Clarion Bks.) HarperCollins Pubs.

Wolff, Virginia Euwer. This Full House. 2011. (ENG.). 496p. (YA). (gr. 9). pap. 9.99 *(978-0-06-158306-3(5)*, HarperTeen) HarperCollins Pubs.

Wolfgang, Jane. Art Today. 2013. (ENG., Illus.). 32p. (J). 14.95 *(978-1-56290-706-8(9))* Crystal Productions.

Wolitzer, Meg. Belzhar. 2015. (ENG.). 272p. (YA). (gr. 9). 10.99 *(978-0-14-242629-6(6)*, Speak) Penguin Young Readers Group.

Wonder/365 Days of Wonder Boxed Set, 2 vols., Set. 2014. (Wonder Ser.). (ENG.). 432p. (J). (gr. 3-7). 31.98 *(978-0-553-49906-3(8)*, Knopf Bks. for Young Readers) Random Hse. Children's Bks.

Wonderley, Stanley. A Boy & His Horse. 2012. 19.95 *(978-0-7414-7806-1(4))*; pap. 11.95 *(978-0-7414-7805-4(6))* Infinity Publishing.

Wood, Fiona. Six Impossible Things. 2016. (ENG.). 304p. (YA). (gr. 7-17). pap. 16.99 *(978-0-316-29941-1(3)*, Poppy) Little, Brown Bks. for Young Readers.

—Wildlife. 2016. (ENG.). 416p. (YA). (gr. 10-17). pap. 19.99 *(978-0-316-24208-0(X)*, Poppy) Little, Brown Bks. for Young Readers.

Wood, Kristen. Find Masked Rider. 2008. 19.95 *(978-1-935159-06-3(2))* My Campus Adventure, Inc.

Woodard, Amy. The Day the Teacher Rode a Horse to School. 2008. 24p. pap. 24.95 *(978-1-60441-736-4(6))* America Star Bks.

Woodberry, Gareth. Gakeva Gluntok's New School. 2005. 65p. pap. 16.95 *(978-1-4137-9894-4(2))* PublishAmerica, Inc.

Woodlan Jr. Sr. High Students. Devon Makes a Promise. 2008. 36p. pap. 14.00 *(978-0-9817264-2-7(9))* Pen & Publish, LLC.

Woodrow, Allan. Class Dismissed. 2017. (ENG.). 272p. (J). (gr. 3-7). pap. 6.99 *(978-0-545-80072-3(2)*, Scholastic Paperbacks) Scholastic, Inc.

—Unschooled. 2018. (ENG.). 288p. (J). (gr. 3-7). pap. 7.99 *(978-1-338-11689-2(4))* Scholastic, Inc.

Woods, Brenda. Emako Blue. 2005. 128p. (YA). (gr. 7-18). 7.99 *(978-0-14-240418-8(7)*, Speak) Penguin Young Readers Group.

—Emako Blue. 2005. 124p. (gr. 7). 16.00 *(978-0-7569-5495-6(9))* Perfection Learning Corp.

Woods, Elizabeth. Choker. 2012. (ENG.). 240p. (YA). (gr. 9). pap. 12.99 *(978-1-4424-1234-7(8)*, Simon & Schuster Bks. For Young Readers) Simon & Schuster Bks. For Young Readers.

Woodson, Jacqueline. The Day You Begin. López, Rafael & López, Rafael, illus. 2018. (ENG.). 32p. (J). (gr. k-3). 18.99 *(978-0-399-24653-1(3)*, Nancy Paulsen Books) Penguin Young Readers Group.

—El día en Que Descubres Quién Eres. Mlawer, Teresa, tr. López, Rafael, illus. 2018. 32p. (J). (gr. k-3). 18.99 *(978-1-9848-1207-0(6)*, Nancy Paulsen Books) Penguin Young Readers Group.

—Each Kindness. Lewis, E. B., illus. 2012. 32p. (J). (gr. k-3). 18.99 *(978-0-399-24652-4(5)*, Nancy Paulsen Books) Penguin Young Readers Group.

—Feathers. (ENG.). (J). (gr. 5-18). 2010. 160p. 8.99 *(978-0-14-241550-4(2)*, Puffin Books) 2007. 128p. 17.99 *(978-0-399-23989-2(8)*, G.P. Putnam's Sons Books for Young Readers) Penguin Young Readers Group.

—Harbor Me. (ENG.). 192p. (J). (gr. 5). 2020. 8.99 *(978-0-525-51514-2(3)*, Puffin Books) 2018. 17.99 *(978-0-399-25252-5(5)*, Nancy Paulsen Books) Penguin Young Readers Group.

—If You Come Softly: Twentieth Anniversary Edition. 20th ed. 2018. (ENG.). 192p. (YA). (gr. 7). 17.99 *(978-0-525-51548-7(8)*, Nancy Paulsen Books) Penguin Young Readers Group.

Wray, Patricia. Sasha, the Dreamer, 1 vol. 2009. 192p. pap. 24.95 *(978-1-60672-885-7(7))* PublishAmerica, Inc.

Wright, Bil. Putting Makeup on the Fat Boy. (ENG., 240p. (YA). (gr. 7). 2012. Illus.). pap. 12.99 *(978-1-4169-4004-3(9))* 2011. 19.99 *(978-1-4169-3996-2(2))* Simon & Schuster Bks. For Young Readers. (Simon & Schuster Bks. For Young Readers).

Wright, Gail R. The Adventures of Alfred in the Greatest Fruit of All: Conflicts & Resolutions. 2011. 112p. (gr. 1-2). 28.95 *(978-1-4497-1586-1(9))*; pap. 11.95 *(978-1-4497-1585-4(0))* Author Solutions, LLC. (WestBow Pr.).

Wright, Lanikka. The Fab Four 2: Eva's Obsession. 2012. (ENG.). 244p. pap. 13.95 *(978-1-4327-9846-8(4))* Outskirts Pr., Inc.

Wright, Lloyd. Gramp's Variety of Stories. 2007. 200p. 24.95 *(978-0-595-71311-0(4))*; per. 14.95 *(978-0-595-47731-9(3))* iUniverse, Inc.

Wright, Michael. Jake Starts School. Wright, Michael, illus. 2010. (ENG., Illus.). 48p. (J). (gr. -1-1). 21.19 *(978-0-312-60884-2(5)*, 900065180) Square Fish.

Wright, Pauline. Why Did My Dad Go to War? 2008. 48p. pap. 19.49 *(978-1-4343-4677-3(3))* AuthorHouse.

Wunsch, Emma. Banana Pants! (Miranda & Maude #2) von Innerebner, Jessika, illus. 2019. (ENG.). 144p. (J). (gr. 2-5). 12.99 *(978-1-4197-3180-8(7)*, 1247401, Amulet Bks.) Abrams, Inc.

—The Princess & the Absolutely Not a Princess (Miranda & Maude #1) von Innerebner, Jessika, illus. 2018. (ENG.). 144p. (J). (gr. 2-5). 12.99 *(978-1-4197-3179-2(3)*, 1247301, Amulet Bks.) Abrams, Inc.

—The Princess & the Absolutely Not a Princess (Miranda & Maude #1), Vol. 1. von Innerebner, Jessika, illus. 2019. (Miranda & Maude Ser.). (ENG.). 160p. (J). (gr. 1-4). pap. 6.99 *(978-1-4197-3374-1(5)*, 1247303) Abrams, Inc.

—Recess Rebels (Miranda & Maude #3) von Innerebner, Jessika, illus. 2019. (Miranda & Maude Ser.). (ENG.). 144p. (J). (gr. 2-5). 12.99 *(978-1-4197-3737-4(6)*, 1278601, Amulet Bks.) Abrams, Inc.

Wyatt, Cherokee. The Adventures of Margaret Mouse: School Days. Redmon, Angela M., illus. l.t. ed. 2004. 32p. (J). 6.95 *(978-0-9761326-0-8(5))* www.margaretmouse.com publishing co.

Wymer, Tracy Edward. Soar. (ENG., Illus.). 288p. (J). (gr. 3-7). 2017. pap. 7.99 *(978-1-4814-4712-6(2))* 2016. 17.99 *(978-1-4814-4711-9(4))* Simon & Schuster Children's Publishing. (Aladdin).

Wynne-Jones, Tim. Rex Zero & the End of the World. 2013. (ENG.). 208p. (J). (gr. 3-7). pap. 14.99 *(978-0-312-64460-4(4)*, 900068529) Square Fish.

—Rex Zero, the Great Pretender. 2013. (Rex Zero Ser.). (ENG.). 240p. (J). (gr. 4-6). 21.19 *(978-1-250-01673-7(8))* Square Fish.

Yagmin, Daniel, Jr., illus. Norton B. Nice. 2009. (J). *(978-1-60108-018-9(2))* Red Cygnet Pr.

Yang, Gene Luen. American Born Chinese. 2011. 10.04 *(978-0-7848-3435-0(0)*, Everbind) Marco Bk. Co.

—American Born Chinese. 2011. 20.00 *(978-1-60686-920-8(5))* 2007. 29.00 *(978-0-7569-7745-0(2))* Perfection Learning Corp.

—American Born Chinese. Yang, Gene Luen, illus. 2007. (ENG., Illus.). 240p. (YA). (gr. 7-18). 24.99 *(978-1-59643-373-1(6)*, 900050139, First Second Bks.) Roaring Brook Pr.

—American Born Chinese. 2008. (YA). lib. bdg. 22.10 *(978-0-606-14484-1(6))* Turtleback.

—Robots & Repeats. 2017. (Secret Coders Ser.: 4). (J). lib. bdg. 22.10 *(978-0-606-40541-6(0))* Turtleback.

—Secret Coders: Secrets & Sequences. 2017. (Secret Coders Ser.: 3). (ENG., Illus.). 112p. (J). pap. 10.99 *(978-1-62672-077-0(0)*, 900134878, First Second Bks.) Roaring Brook Pr.

—Secrets & Sequences. 2017. (Secret Coders Ser.: 3). (J). lib. bdg. 22.10 *(978-0-606-40345-0(0))* Turtleback.

Yang, Kelly. Finally Seen. 2023. (ENG., Illus.). 304p. (J). (gr. 3-7). 17.99 *(978-1-5344-8833-5(2)*, Simon & Schuster Bks. For Young Readers) Simon & Schuster Bks. For Young Readers.

Yangsook, Choi. The Name Jar. 2014. (ENG.). 40p. (J). (gr. k-2). 11.24 *(978-1-63245-313-6(4))* Lectorum Pubns., Inc.

Yankovic, Al, pseud. My New Teacher & Me! Hargis, Wes, illus. 2013. (ENG.). 40p. (J). (gr. -1-3). 18.99 *(978-0-06-219203-5(5)*, HarperCollins) HarperCollins Pubs.

—When I Grow Up. Hargis, Wes, illus. 2011. (ENG.). 32p. (J). (gr. -1-3). 19.99 *(978-0-06-192691-4(4)*, HarperCollins) HarperCollins Pubs.

Yarnell, Duane. The Winning Basket. 2005. pap. 26.95 *(978-1-4191-5930-5(5))* Kessinger Publishing, LLC.

Yashima, Taro. Crow Boy. Yashima, Taro, illus. 2004. (Illus.). 34p. (J). (gr. k-3). reprint ed. pap. 14.00 *(978-0-7567-7102-7(1))* DIANE Publishing Co.

—Crow Boy. Yashima, Taro, illus. (Illus.). pap. 35.95 incl. audio compact disk *(978-1-59112-803-8(X))* Live Oak Media.

Yates, Alma J. Sammy's Song: A Novel. 2005. 272p. (J). *(978-1-59156-945-9(1))* Covenant Communications.

Yatscoff, Edward R. Archie's Gold. 2013. 200p. pap. *(978-0-9869678-7-0(4))* Yatscoff, Edward R.

Yee, Lisa. Bobby the Brave (Sometimes) Santat, Dan, illus. 2012. (ENG.). 160p. (J). (gr. 2-5). pap. 5.99 *(978-0-545-05595-6(4)*, Scholastic Paperbacks) Scholastic, Inc.

—Bobby vs. Girls (Accidentally) Santat, Dan, illus. 2010. (ENG.). 176p. (J). (gr. 2-5). pap. 5.99 *(978-0-545-05593-2(8)*, Scholastic Paperbacks) Scholastic, Inc.

—Stanford Wong Flunks Big-Time (the Millicent Min Trilogy, Book 2) 2007. (Millicent Min Trilogy Ser.). (ENG., Illus.). 320p. (J). (gr. 4-7). per. 6.99 *(978-0-439-62248-6(4)*, Levine, Arthur A. Bks.) Scholastic, Inc.

—Supergirl at Super Hero High (DC Super Hero Girls) Random House, illus. 2016. (ENG.). 240p. (J). (gr. 3-7). 13.99 *(978-1-101-94062-4(X)*, Random Hse. Bks. for Young Readers) Random Hse. Children's Bks.

—Warp Speed. 2011. (ENG.). 320p. (J). (gr. 4-7). 16.99 *(978-0-545-12276-4(7)*, Levine, Arthur A. Bks.) Scholastic, Inc.

Yeh, Kat. The Way to Bea. 2018. (ENG.). 368p. (J). (gr. 3-7). pap. 7.99 *(978-0-316-23669-0(1))* Little, Brown Bks. for Young Readers.

Yeh, Shao-Min. What Do You See? 2011. 28p. pap. 15.99 *(978-1-4628-5030-3(8))* Xlibris Corp.

Yelchin, Eugene. Spy Runner. Yelchin, Eugene, illus. 2019. (ENG., Illus.). 352p. (J). 21.99 *(978-1-250-12081-6(0)*, 900173090, Holt, Henry & Co. Bks. For Young Readers) Holt, Henry & Co.

Yochum, Nikki. Shy Cheyenne & the Substitute Teacher. 2010. 36p. pap. 13.95 *(978-1-60911-140-3(0)*, Eloquent Bks.) Strategic Book Publishing & Rights Agency (SBPRA).

Yolen, Jane. Friendship on the High Seas: Ready-To-Read Level 1. Moran, Mike, illus. 2019. (School of Fish Ser.). (ENG.). 32p. (J). (gr. -1-1). pap. 4.99 *(978-1-5344-3891-0(2)*, Simon Spotlight) Simon Spotlight.

—How Do Dinosaurs Go to School? Teague, Mark, illus. 2007. (ENG.). 40p. (J). (gr. -1-k). 18.99 *(978-0-439-02081-7(6)*, Blue Sky Pr., The) Scholastic, Inc.

—How Do Dinosaurs Go to School? Teague, Mark, illus. 2011. (J). (gr. -1-3). 29.95 *(978-0-545-19700-7(7))*; 18.95 *(978-0-545-19707-6(4))* Weston Woods Studios, Inc.

—A Plague of Unicorns. 2014. (ENG.). 192p. (J). E-Book 4.19 *(978-0-310-74610-2(8)*, 9780310746102) Zonderkidz.

—School of Fish: Ready-To-Read Level 1. Moran, Mike, illus. 2019. (School of Fish Ser.). (ENG.). 32p. (J). (gr. -1-1). 17.99 *(978-1-5344-3889-7(0))*; pap. 4.99 *(978-1-5344-3888-0(2))* Simon Spotlight. (Simon Spotlight).

Yoo, David. The Detention Club. 2012. (ENG.). 304p. (J). (gr. 5). pap. 6.99 *(978-0-06-178380-7(3)*, Balzer & Bray) HarperCollins Pubs.

Yoon, David. Frankly in Love. (ENG.). (YA). (gr. 9). 2020. 448p. pap. 12.99 *(978-1-9848-1222-3(X)*, Penguin Books) 2019. 432p. 18.99 *(978-1-9848-1220-9(3)*, G.P. Putnam's Sons Books for Young Readers) Penguin Young Readers Group.

Yoon, Salina. Bear's Big Day. (ENG., Illus.). (J). 2017. 32p. bds. 7.99 *(978-1-68119-436-3(8)*, 900172658) 2016. 40p. 14.99 *(978-0-8027-3832-5(X)*, 900141994) Bloomsbury Publishing USA. (Bloomsbury USA Childrens).

Yoshino, Genzaburo. How Do You Live? Navasky, Bruno, tr. (ENG.). 288p. (J). (gr. 5-9). 2023. pap. 9.99 ***(978-1-64375-307-2(X))*** 2021. (Illus.). 17.95 *(978-1-61620-977-3(1)*, 73977) Algonquin Young Readers.

Young, Janet Ruth. The Babysitter Murders. 2011. (ENG., Illus.). 336p. (YA). (gr. 9-18). 16.99 *(978-1-4169-5944-1(0)*, Atheneum Bks. for Young Readers) Simon & Schuster Children's Publishing.

Young, Jessica. Fin-Tastic Fashion. Sécheret, Jessica, illus. 2017. (Finley Flowers Ser.). (ENG.). 128p. (J). (gr. 1-3). lib. bdg. 25.32 *(978-1-4795-9804-5(6)*, 133579, Picture Window Bks.) Capstone.

—Original Recipe. Sécheret, Jessica, illus. 2015. (Finley Flowers Ser.). (ENG.). 128p. (J). (gr. 1-3). 8.95 *(978-1-4795-5878-0(8)*, 126922, Picture Window Bks.) Capstone.

—Room to Bloom. Sécheret, Jessica, illus. 2017. (Finley Flowers Ser.). (ENG.). 128p. (J). (gr. 1-3). lib. bdg. 25.32 *(978-1-4795-9806-9(2)*, 133581, Picture Window Bks.) Capstone.

—Super Spooktacular. Sécheret, Jessica, illus. 2017. (Finley Flowers Ser.). (ENG.). 128p. (J). (gr. 1-3). lib. bdg. 25.32 *(978-1-4795-9807-6(0)*, 133582, Picture Window Bks.) Capstone.

Young, Jessica & Spark, Sylvie. Finley Flowers Collection. Secheret, Jessica, illus. 2016. (Finley Flowers Ser.). (ENG.). 256p. (J). (gr. 1-3). 9.99 *(978-1-4795-9850-2(X)*, 135049, Picture Window Bks.) Capstone.

Young, Judy. Promise. 2016. (ENG.). 368p. (J). (gr. 4-6). pap. 8.99 *(978-1-58536-915-7(2)*, 204079) Sleeping Bear Pr.

Young, Karen Romano. Stuck in the Middle (of Middle School) A Novel in Doodles. 2014. (ENG., Illus.). 128p. (J). (gr. 3-7). pap. 12.99 *(978-1-250-03997-2(5)*, 900123700) Square Fish.

Young, Paige. The Homework Dilemm. 2011. 26p. pap. 16.95 *(978-1-4626-2366-2(2))* America Star Bks.

Young, Samantha. The Fragile Ordinary. 2018. (ENG.). 384p. (YA). 18.99 *(978-1-335-01674-4(0)*, Harlequin Teen) Harlequin Enterprises ULC CAN. Dist: HarperCollins Pubs.

Young, Suzanne. Girls with Sharp Sticks. 2019. (Girls with Sharp Sticks Ser.: 1). (ENG., Illus.). 400p. (YA). (gr. 9). 19.99 *(978-1-5344-2613-9(2)*, Simon Pulse) Simon Pulse.

Yoyo. Ready for School. 2005. 40p. bds. *(978-90-5843-890-4(2))* YoYo Bks.

Yum, Hyewon. Mom, It's My First Day of Kindergarten!, 1 vol. Yum, Hyewon, illus. 2012. (ENG., Illus.). 40p. (J). (gr. -1-2). 19.99 *(978-0-374-35004-8(3)*, 900077454, Farrar, Straus & Giroux (BYR)) Farrar, Straus & Giroux.

Yunisa. Schoolaholic Princess 1: the Miracle Boys. 2008. 242p. pap. 15.88 *(978-1-4357-6026-4(3))* Lulu Pr., Inc.

—Schoolaholic Princess 2: Romansa Singapura. 2008. 232p. pap. 14.88 *(978-1-4357-6044-8(1))* Lulu Pr., Inc.

—Schoolaholic Princess 3: Simfoni Cinta. 2008. 220p. pap. 14.88 *(978-1-4357-6045-5(X))* Lulu Pr., Inc.

Yusuf, Hanna S. & Day, Cansarra. Katie Mcchoir. 2010. 80p. pap. 10.49 *(978-1-4490-7378-7(6))* AuthorHouse.

Zadoff, Allen. Food, Girls, & Other Things I Can't Have. 2011. (ENG., Illus.). 320p. (gr. 9). pap. 9.99 *(978-1-60684-151-8(3)*, Carolrhoda Lab™) Lerner Publishing Group.

Zamolo, Rebecca & Slays, Matt. The Game Master: Summer Schooled. (Game Master Ser.). (ENG.). 176p. (J). (gr. 3-7). 2023. pap. 9.99 *(978-0-06-302509-7(4))* 2021. 16.99 *(978-0-06-302507-3(8))* HarperCollins Pubs. (HarperCollins).

Zann, Tara. Wild Child: Forest's First Bully. Otto, Nicole, ed. Widdowson, Dan, illus. 2017. (Wild Child Ser.: 4). (ENG.). 128p. (J). pap. 16.99 *(978-1-250-10393-2(2)*, 900163653) Imprint IND. Dist: Macmillan.

Zappa, Shana Muldoon, et al. Astra's Mixed-Up Mission, 8. 2016. (Star Darlings Ser.). (ENG.). 176p. (J). (gr. 3-6). 21.19 *(978-1-4844-8084-7(8))* Disney Pr.

—Cassie Comes Through. 2016. 147p. (J). *(978-1-4806-9840-6(7))* Disney Publishing Worldwide.

—Leona's Unlucky Mission, 3. 2016. (Star Darlings Ser.). (ENG., Illus.). 176p. (J). (gr. 3-6). 21.19 *(978-1-4844-7387-0(6))* Disney Pr.

—Libby & the Class Election. 2015. (Illus.). 158p. (J). *(978-1-4242-6608-1(4))* Disney Publishing Worldwide.

—Piper's Perfect Dream. 2016. 156p. (J). *(978-1-4806-9807-9(5))* Disney Publishing Worldwide.

—Scarlet Discovers True Strength, 5. 2016. (Star Darlings Ser.). (ENG., Illus.). 176p. (J). (gr. 3-6). 21.19 *(978-1-4844-7390-0(6))* Disney Pr.

—Vega & the Fashion Disaster, 4. 2016. (Star Darlings Ser.). (ENG., Illus.). 176p. (J). (gr. 3-6). lib. bdg. 21.19 *(978-1-4844-7389-4(2))* Disney Pr.

Zappia, Francesca. Eliza & Her Monsters. (ENG.). (YA). (gr. 9). 2019. 432p. pap. 11.99 *(978-0-06-229014-4(2))* 2017. (Illus.). 400p. 17.99 *(978-0-06-229013-7(4))* HarperCollins Pubs. (Greenwillow Bks.).

Zarins, Kim. Sometimes We Tell the Truth. 2016. *(978-1-4814-7554-9(1))* Simon & Schuster, Inc.

—Sometimes We Tell the Truth. 2017. (ENG.). 448p. (YA). (gr. 9). pap. 12.99 *(978-1-4814-6500-7(7)*, Simon Pulse) Simon Pulse.

Zarr, Sara. Sweethearts. 2009. (ENG.). 224p. (YA). (gr. 7-17). pap. 13.99 *(978-0-316-01456-4(7))* Little, Brown Bks. for Young Readers.

Zatch Bell 1: The Lightning Boy From Another World. 2005. 24.98 *(978-1-4215-0215-1(1))* Viz Media.

Zemach, Kaethe. Ms. McCaw Learns to Draw. 2006. (J). *(978-0-439-82915-1(1)*, Levine, Arthur A. Bks.) Scholastic, Inc.

Zepeda, Frank. A Wad of Gum. 2012. (ENG.). 39p. pap. 19.99 *(978-1-105-73944-6(9))* Lulu Pr., Inc.

Zevin, Gabrielle. Memoirs of a Teenage Amnesiac. 2011. 9.46 *(978-0-7848-3492-3(X)*, Everbind) Marco Bk. Co.

—Memoirs of a Teenage Amnesiac: A Novel. 2009. (ENG.). 304p. (YA). (gr. 9-13). pap. 15.99 *(978-0-312-56128-4(8)*, 900058863) Square Fish.

Zia, Farhana. The Garden of My Imaan, 1 vol. 2016. 192p. (J). (gr. 3-7). pap. 8.99 *(978-1-56145-921-6(6))* Peachtree Publishing Co. Inc.

Zidrou. Ducoboo: In the Corner! Godi, illus. 2007. (Ducoboo Ser.: 2). 48p. (J). (gr. 4-7). pap. 9.99 *(978-1-905460-26-7(0))* CineBook GBR. Dist: National Bk. Network.

—Ducoboo: The Class Struggle. Spear, Luke, tr. Godi & Grobet, Veronique, illus. 2010. (Ducoboo Ser.: 4). 46p. (J). (gr. 3-17). pap. 11.95 *(978-1-84918-031-3(8))* CineBook GBR. Dist: National Bk. Network.

—Ducoboo No. 3: Your Answers or Your Life! Godi, illus. 2008. (Ducoboo Ser.: 3). 48p. pap. 11.95 *(978-1-905460-28-1(7))* CineBook GBR. Dist: National Bk. Network.

Ziegler, Jennifer. How Not to Be Popular. 2010. 352p. (YA). (gr. 7). mass mkt. 8.99 *(978-0-440-24024-2(7)*, Delacorte Bks. for Young Readers) Random Hse. Children's Bks.

—Revenge of the Teacher's Pets. 2018. (ENG.). 256p. (J). (gr. 3-7). 16.99 *(978-1-338-09123-6(9)*, Scholastic Pr.) Scholastic, Inc.

—Sass & Serendipity. 2012. 384p. (YA). (gr. 7-12). (ENG.). lib. bdg. 26.19 *(978-0-385-90762-0(1)*, Delacorte Pr.); pap. 9.99 *(978-0-375-85964-9(0)*, Ember) Random Hse. Children's Bks.

Zielinski, Valerie & Skaletski, Roslyn. The Adventures of Bella. 2011. 48p. pap. 14.00 *(978-1-4634-2018-5(8))* AuthorHouse.

Zimelman, Nathan. How the Second Grade Got $8,205. 50 to Visit the Statue of Liberty. Slavin, Bill, illus. 2017. (ENG.). 32p. (J). (gr. -1-3). pap. 7.99 *(978-0-8075-3435-9(8)*, 807534358) Whitman, Albert & Co.

Zimmer, Tracie Vaughn. 42 Miles. 2008. (ENG., Illus.). 80p. (J). (gr. 5-7). 16.00 *(978-0-618-61867-5(8)*, 100453, Clarion Bks.) HarperCollins Pubs.

Zoellick, Todd. Daniel Harrington Fairbanks the Third & the Dog That Wouldn't Bark. 2009. 52p. pap. 20.49 *(978-1-4490-1047-8(4))* AuthorHouse.

Zumo. An Awesome Run: Selected Works, 1978-2008. 2008. 284p. 31.99 *(978-1-4389-2394-9(5))* AuthorHouse.

Zuravicky, Orli. Drama. 2017. 181p. (J). *(978-1-338-19299-5(X))* Scholastic, Inc.

—School Spirit. 2017. 177p. (J). *(978-1-338-19300-8(7))* Scholastic, Inc.

Zurchin, Cynthia, et al. The Whale Done School: Transforming a School's Culture by Catching Students Doing Things Right. 2012. 124p. pap. 14.95 *(978-1-4685-9536-9(9))* AuthorHouse.

50 Cent, 50. Playground. Akana, Lizzi, illus. 2012. (ENG.). 320p. (YA). (gr. 7). pap. 10.99 *(978-1-59514-478-2(1)*, Razorbill) Penguin Young Readers Group.

SCHOOLS—MANAGEMENT AND ORGANIZATION

see School Management And Organization

SCHOOLS, MILITARY

see Military Education

SCHUBERT, FRANZ, 1797-1828

Summerer, Eric Michael. Franz Peter Schubert. (Primary Source Library of Famous Composers Ser.). 32p. (gr. 4-4). 2009. 42.50 *(978-1-60854-107-2(X)*, PowerKids Pr.) 2005. (ENG., Illus.). (J). lib. bdg. 27.60 *(978-1-4042-2768-2(7)*, 83bb78a5-66ab-45c6-9e38-b8cef4bbcc84) Rosen Publishing Group, Inc., The.

Wheeler, Opal & Deucher, Sybil. Franz Schubert & his Merry Friends. Greenwalt, Mary, illus. 2008. 128p. (J). pap. 13.95 *(978-1-933573-13-7(9))* Zeezok Publishing, LLC.

SCHULZ, CHARLES M. (CHARLES MONROE), 1922-2000

Marvis, Barbara J. Charles Schulz. 2004. (Robbie Reader Ser.). (Illus.). 32p. (J). (gr. 1-4). lib. bdg. 25.70 *(978-1-58415-289-7(3))* Mitchell Lane Pubs.

Perkins, Chloe. The Great American Story of Charlie Brown, Snoopy, & the Peanuts Gang! Ready-To-Read Level 3. Burroughs, Scott, illus. 2017. (History of Fun Stuff Ser.). (ENG.). 48p. (J). (gr. 1-3). pap. 4.99 *(978-1-4814-9553-0(4)*, Simon Spotlight) Simon Spotlight.

Schuman, Michael A. Charles Schulz: Cartoonist & Writer, 1 vol. 2018. (Influential Lives Ser.). (ENG.). 128p. (gr. 7-7). 40.27 *(978-0-7660-9209-9(7)*, 1dd0314c-bf50-45f0-9e54-9dfca036eaed) Enslow Publishing, LLC.

Strand, Jennifer. Charles Schulz. 2016. (Amazing Authors Ser.). (ENG.). 24p. (J). (gr. -1-2). 49.94 *(978-1-68079-381-9(0)*, 23002, Abdo Zoom-Launch) ABDO Publishing Co.

SCHUMANN, CLARA, 1819-1896

Shichtman, Sandra H. & Indenbaum, Dorothy. The Joy of Creation: The Story of Clara Schumann. 2011. (Classical Composers Ser.). (Illus.). 159p. lib. bdg. 28.95 *(978-1-59935-123-0(4))* Reynolds, Morgan Inc.

SCIENCE

see also Astronomy; Bacteriology; Biology; Botany; Chemistry; Crystallography; Ethnology; Forensic Sciences; Fossils; Geology; Mathematics; Meteorology; Metrology; Mineralogy; Natural History; Physics; Physiology; Space Sciences; Zoology

also headings beginning with the word Scientific

A Visual Exploration of Science: Set 1, 8 vols. 2017. (Visual Exploration of Science Ser.). (ENG.). 96p. (gr. 8-8). 155.20 *(978-1-4994-6657-7(9)*, ddbd742a-6be1-4a77-a1da-93403ab7d338, Rosen Young Adult) Rosen Publishing Group, Inc., The.

ABDO Publishing Company Staff & Doudna, Kelly. Science Made Simple. 2007. (Science Made Simple Ser.: 24). 24p. (J). (gr. k-3). 581.04 *(978-1-59928-578-8(9)*, SandCastle) ABDO Publishing Co.

Accelerated Curriculum for Science Grade 11 Exit Taks Student Edition. 2005. (Region IV ESC Resources for Science Ser.). spiral bd. *(978-1-932797-27-5(0))* Region 4 Education Service Ctr.

ACT Science Reasoning Victory Student Textbook. 2nd ed. 2005. per. *(978-1-58894-034-6(9))* Cambridge Educational Services, Inc.

Action Science. 2010. (Action Science Ser.). (ENG.). 32p. (gr. 3-4). pap. 190.80 *(978-1-4296-5134-9(2)*, Capstone Pr.) Capstone.

Action Science [Capstone Sole Source]. 2010. (Action Science Ser.). 32p. lib. bdg. 103.96 *(978-1-4296-5836-2(3)*, Capstone Pr.) Capstone.

¿Adonde Van los Residuos? (Coleccion Primeros Pasos en la Ciencia). (SPA., Illus.). (J). (gr. 1-3). pap. *(978-950-724-216-8(3)*, LMA8222) Lumen ARG. Dist: Lectorum Pubns., Inc.

A.H.Hashmi. Children's Science Encyclopedia. 2009. 518p. pap. *(978-81-223-1061-0(3))* Mahal, Pustak Pubs., Booksellers & Order Suppliers.

Aire. (Coleccion Jugando Con la Ciencia). (SPA., Illus.). 39p. (J). pap. 9.95 *(978-950-11-0681-7(0)*, SGM341) Sigmar ARG. Dist: Continental Bk. Co., Inc.

Al-Greene, Bob, illus. Ghost in the Water. Al-Greene, Bob, . 2014. (League of Scientists Ser.). (ENG.). 192p. (J). (gr. 5-9). pap. 12.95 *(978-0-9700106-2-9(1))* Platypus Media, L.L.C.

Amazing World of Science & Math. 2016. (Amazing World of Science & Math Ser.). 48p. (gr. 5-5). pap. 56.20 *(978-1-4824-5335-5(5))*; (ENG.). lib. bdg. 134.40 *(978-1-4824-4970-9(6)*, 9d4e086f-e589-40ba-ae53-e2fd73bdddf3) Stevens, Gareth Publishing LLLP.

Anderson, James. The Science of Magic (Grade 6) 2nd rev. ed. 2016. (TIME(r): Informational Text Ser.). (ENG., Illus.). 64p. (gr. 5-8). pap. 13.99 *(978-1-4938-3606-2(4))* Teacher Created Materials, Inc.

Anderson, James D. The Science of Magic. 2016. (Time for Kids Nonfiction Readers Ser.). (ENG.). (J). (gr. 5-8). lib. bdg. 22.10 *(978-0-606-39542-7(3))* Turtleback.

Anderson, Kelli. This Book Is a Planetarium: And Other Extraordinary Pop-Up Contraptions. 2017. (ENG., Illus.). 5p. 40.00 *(978-1-4521-3621-9(1))* Chronicle Bks. LLC.

Animal Eaters of the Pond: 6 Each of 1 Student Book, 6 vols. (Sunshinetm Science Ser.). 24p. (gr. 1-2). 41.95 *(978-0-7802-2696-8(8))* Wright Group/McGraw-Hill.

Animal Eaters of the Pond: Big Book. (Sunshinetm Science Ser.). 24p. (gr. 1-2). 37.50 *(978-0-7802-2782-8(4))* Wright Group/McGraw-Hill.

Animal Fibers: 6 Each of 1 Student Book, 6 vols. (Sunshinetm Science Ser.). 24p. (gr. 1-2). 41.95 *(978-0-7802-1434-7(X))* Wright Group/McGraw-Hill.

Animal Fibers: Big Book. (Sunshinetm Science Ser.). 24p. (gr. 1-2). 37.50 *(978-0-7802-1435-4(8))* Wright Group/McGraw-Hill.

Animales Nocturnos de la Selva. (Colección Ventana Transparente). (SPA., Illus.). (J). (gr. 3-5). *(978-950-11-1280-1(2)*, SG5231) Sigmar ARG. Dist: Lectorum Pubns., Inc.

Animals & Their Teeth, 6 vols. (Sunshinetm Science Ser.). 24p. (gr. 1-2). 41.95 *(978-0-7802-1443-9(9))* Wright Group/McGraw-Hill.

Animals & Their Teeth: Big Book. (Sunshinetm Science Ser.). 24p. (gr. 1-2). 37.50 *(978-0-7802-1444-6(7))* Wright Group/McGraw-Hill.

Applied Science, Set. 2010. (Extreme! Ser.). (ENG.). 32p. (gr. 3-4). pap. 429.30 *(978-1-4296-5136-3(9)*, Capstone Pr.) Capstone.

Applin, D. G., et al. AQA Modular Science for GCSE. 2003. (ENG., Illus.). 336p. pap. *(978-0-7487-7286-5(3))* Nelson Thornes Ltd.

Arnold, Brian. Quick Revision KS3 Science. 2007. (ENG., Illus.). 46p. pap. 9.95 *(978-0-340-94308-3(4)*, Hodder Education) Hodder Education Group GBR. Dist: Trans-Atlantic Pubns., Inc.

Arnold, Nick. Esa Fascinante Arqueologia. 2003. (Coleccion Esa Gran Cultura).Tr. of Awesome Archaeology. (SPA., Illus.). 160p. (YA). (gr. 5-8). 7.96 *(978-84-272-2139-0(8))* Molino, Editorial ESP. Dist: Lectorum Pubns., Inc.

Arnold, Nick & De Saulles, Tony. Ese Voluminoso Cerebro. De Saulles, Tony, tr. 2003. (Coleccion Esa Horrible Cienca). (SPA., Illus.). 158p. (YA). *(978-84-272-2065-2(0)*, ML31376) Molino, Editorial ESP. Dist: Lectorum Pubns., Inc.

ART & ARCHITECTURE. 2010. (Experimenting with Everyday Science Ser.). (ENG., Illus.). 176p. (gr. 6-12). 35.00 *(978-1-60413-168-0(3)*, P179238, Facts On File) Infobase Holdings, Inc.

Atlas de la Prehistoria. (Coleccion Atlas del Saber). (SPA., Illus.). (YA). (gr. 4-18). 20.95 *(978-950-11-0889-7(9)*, SGM74) Sigmar ARG. Dist: Continental Bk. Co., Inc.

Atlas de la Tierra. (Coleccion Atlas del Saber). (SPA., Illus.). (YA). (gr. 4-18). 20.95 *(978-950-11-0916-0(X)*, SGM16) Sigmar ARG. Dist: Continental Bk. Co., Inc.

Atlas de los Pueblos. (Coleccion Atlas del Saber). (SPA., Illus.). (YA). (gr. 4-18). 20.95 *(978-950-11-0917-7(8)*, SGM73) Sigmar ARG. Dist: Continental Bk. Co., Inc.

Atlas del Espacio. (Coleccion Atlas del Saber). (SPA., Illus.). (YA). (gr. 4-18). 20.95 *(978-950-11-0887-3(2)*, SGM72) Sigmar ARG. Dist: Continental Bk. Co., Inc.

Baeuerle, Patrick A. & Landa, Norbert. Microexplorers - Physical Science Series, 4 bks. (Illus.). (J). (gr. k-6). lib. bdg. 75.80 *(978-1-56674-946-6(8))* Forest Hse. Publishing Co., Inc.

Baker, Lawrence W. Space Exploration - Primary Sources, 4.0. 2004. (Space Exploration Reference Library). (ENG.). 800p. 372.00 *(978-0-7876-9208-7(5)*, Greenhaven Pr., Inc.) Cengage Gale.

Bakowski, Barbara & Brent Sandvold, Lynnette. Superhero Science: Kapow! Comic Book Crime Fighters Put Physics to the Test, 1 vol. 2009. (Current Science Ser.). (ENG.). 48p. (YA). (gr. 4-6). lib. bdg. 33.67 *(978-1-4339-2243-5(6)*, 8d91c020-b1c8-4630-a920-11cc55c995ed) Stevens, Gareth Publishing LLLP.

Baldwin, Comingore. Access to Science for Infants & Toddlers. 2012. 21p. (J). pap. 19.99 *(978-1-4691-9785-2(5))* Xlibris Corp.

Balice, Mary Lee, ed. Information Science, 4 vols. 2016. (Study of Science Ser.). (ENG.). 144p. (gr. 8-8). 75.64 *(978-1-68048-231-7(9)*, 2adbb13a-9b79-4f4a-b6df-c10064946e87, Britannica Educational Publishing) Rosen Publishing Group, Inc., The.

Bardley, Kimberly Brubaker. POP! a Book about Bubbles. Miller, Margaret, photos by. 2015. (Illus.). 40p. pap. 6.00 *(978-1-61003-614-6(X))* Center for the Collaborative Classroom.

Baredes, Carla & Lotersztain, Ileana. Preguntas que Ponen los Pelos de Punta: Sobre el Aqua y el Fuego. Basile, Javier, illus. 2004. (SPA.). pap. *(978-987-98042-1-6(X))* Iamique, Ediciones.

—Preguntas que Ponen los Pelos de Punta: Sobre la Tierra y el Sol. Basile, Javier, illus. 2004. (SPA.). pap. *(978-987-98042-0-9(1))* Iamique, Ediciones.

Barnes, John, et al. Science, Maths & Technology. 2003. (ENG., Illus.). 184p. pap. *(978-0-7487-7121-9(2))* Nelson Thornes Ltd.

Barr, George. Sports Science for Young People. 2011. (Dover Science for Kids Ser.). (ENG., Illus.). 176p. (J). (gr. 3-8). pap. 11.95 *(978-0-486-26527-8(7)*, 265277) Dover Pubns., Inc.

Basher, Simon & Budzik, Mary. Basher Basics: Creative Writing. Basher, Simon, illus. 2013. (Basher Basics Ser.). (ENG., Illus.). 64p. (J). (gr. 3-7). pap. 8.99

S

(978-0-7534-7055-8(1), 900118685, Kingfisher) Roaring Brook Pr.

Basic Science Mysteries: Activities, Quizzes & Tests. 2003. Vol. 1. spiral bd. *(978-1-928629-92-4(X))* Vol. 2. spiral bd. *(978-1-928629-93-1(8))* Paradigm Accelerated Curriculum.

Basic Science Mysteries: Text. 2003. Vol. 1. spiral bd. *(978-1-928629-90-0(3))* Vol. 2. spiral bd. *(978-1-928629-91-7(1))* Paradigm Accelerated Curriculum.

Basic Science Mysteries Full Kit (with TRK) 2005. (Illus.). 796p. (YA). 75.00 *(978-1-59476-096-9(9))* Paradigm Accelerated Curriculum.

Bauer, David. Everything Is Matter!, 6 vols., Set. 2003. (Yellow Umbrella Early Level Ser.). (ENG.). 16p. (gr. k-1). pap. 35.70 *(978-0-7368-3019-5(7)*, Capstone Pr.) Capstone.

Be a Plant Scientist: Level L, 6 vols. (Take-Twostm Ser.). 16p. 36.95 *(978-0-322-03403-7(5))* Wright Group/McGraw-Hill.

Beacon Science. 2004. per. *(978-1-932948-04-2(X))* Student Pr. Initiative.

Beccia, Carlyn. Monstrous: The Lore, Gore, & Science Behind Your Favorite Monsters. Beccia, Carlyn, illus. 2019. (ENG., Illus.). 148p. (J). (gr. 4-8). lib. bdg. 24.99 *(978-1-5124-4916-7(4)*, 1c9e5fb1-af4a-4f21-bff0-9f7f6f19a85d, Carolrhoda Bks.) Lerner Publishing Group.

Benchmark Education Company, LLC Staff, compiled by. Bloom & Grow & Simple Systems. 2005. spiral bd. 225.00 *(978-1-4108-5804-7(9))* Benchmark Education Co.

—English Explorers Science Set. 2007. (English Explorers Ser.). (J). spiral bd. 4595.00 *(978-1-4108-9740-4(0))* Benchmark Education Co.

—My First Reader's Theater Lap Books. 2009. (My First Reader's Theater Ser.). (J). (gr. k-1). 575.00 *(978-1-4108-8455-8(4))* Benchmark Education Co.

—Science & Technology. 2006. spiral bd. 105.00 *(978-1-4108-6935-7(0))* 2006. spiral bd. 115.00 *(978-1-4108-6923-4(7))* 2005. spiral bd. 170.00 *(978-1-4108-5855-9(3))* 2005. spiral bd. 60.00 *(978-1-4108-3843-8(9))* 2005. spiral bd. 115.00 *(978-1-4108-3854-4(4))* 2005. spiral bd. 55.00 *(978-1-4108-3855-1(2))* 2005. spiral bd. 110.00 *(978-1-4108-3866-7(8))* 2005. spiral bd. 42.00 *(978-1-4108-3880-3(3))* 2005. spiral bd. 125.00 *(978-1-4108-3842-1(0))* 2005. spiral bd. 130.00 *(978-1-4108-5856-6(1))* 2005. spiral bd. 235.00 *(978-1-4108-4520-7(6))* 2005. spiral bd. 145.00 *(978-1-4108-5445-2(0))* 2005. spiral bd. 255.00 *(978-1-4108-5444-5(2))* Benchmark Education Co.

—Science As Inquiry. 2005. spiral bd. 85.00 *(978-1-4108-5848-1(0))*; spiral bd. 80.00 *(978-1-4108-3918-3(4))*; spiral bd. 55.00 *(978-1-4108-3919-0(2))* Benchmark Education Co.

—Science as Inquiry. 2005. spiral bd. 145.00 *(978-1-4108-5435-3(3))*; spiral bd. 85.00 *(978-1-4108-4516-0(8))* Benchmark Education Co.

—Science Classroom Library. 2005. spiral bd. 390.00 *(978-1-4108-6019-4(1))* Benchmark Education Co.

—Science in Personal & Social Perspectives. 2006. spiral bd. 185.00 *(978-1-4108-6948-7(2))* 2006. spiral bd. 295.00 *(978-1-4108-6944-9(X))* 2006. spiral bd. 205.00 *(978-1-4108-6929-6(6))* 2005. spiral bd. 185.00 *(978-1-4108-5854-2(5))* 2005. spiral bd. 245.00 *(978-1-4108-5853-5(7))* 2005. spiral bd. 335.00 *(978-1-4108-5443-8(4))* 2005. spiral bd. 375.00 *(978-1-4108-5442-1(6))* 2005. spiral bd. 300.00 *(978-1-4108-4519-1(2))* 2005. spiral bd. 35.00 *(978-1-4108-3877-3(3))* 2005. spiral bd. 75.00 *(978-1-4108-3863-6(3))* 2005. spiral bd. 225.00 *(978-1-4108-3862-9(5))* 2005. spiral bd. 80.00 *(978-1-4108-3857-5(9))* 2005. spiral bd. 140.00 *(978-1-4108-3856-8(0))* Benchmark Education Co.

—Science in Personal Social Perspectives. 2005. spiral bd. 90.00 *(978-1-4108-3847-6(1))*; spiral bd. 125.00 *(978-1-4108-3846-9(3))* Benchmark Education Co.

—Science Standards Set. 2006. pap. 350.00 *(978-1-4108-6952-4(0))* 2006. pap. 215.00 *(978-1-4108-6953-1(9))* 2006. spiral bd. 1195.00 *(978-1-4108-6951-7(2))* 2006. spiral bd. 2065.00 *(978-1-4108-6950-0(4))* 2006. spiral bd. 195.00 *(978-1-4108-6941-8(5))* 2006. spiral bd. 785.00 *(978-1-4108-6937-1(7))* 2006. spiral bd. 1075.00 *(978-1-4108-6940-1(7))* 2005. spiral bd. 6110.00 *(978-1-4108-5446-9(9))* Benchmark Education Co.

—Science Strands Set. 2005. spiral bd. 2580.00 *(978-1-4108-5459-9(0))*; spiral bd. 695.00 *(978-1-4108-5562-6(7))* Benchmark Education Co.

—Science, Technology & Society. 2005. spiral bd. 185.00 *(978-1-4108-3753-0(X))* Benchmark Education Co.

—Science, Technology, & Society. 2005. spiral bd. 70.00 *(978-1-4108-3954-1(0))*; spiral bd. 80.00 *(978-1-4108-3961-9(3))*; spiral bd. 80.00 *(978-1-4108-3962-6(1))*; spiral bd. 145.00 *(978-1-4108-4499-6(4))*; spiral bd. 110.00 *(978-1-4108-5425-4(6))*; spiral bd. 115.00 *(978-1-4108-5841-2(3))*; spiral bd. 74.00 *(978-1-4108-5842-9(1))* Benchmark Education Co.

—Science Text Set. 2005. spiral bd. 715.00 *(978-1-4108-3818-6(8))*; spiral bd. 4475.00 *(978-1-4108-3820-9(X))*; spiral bd. 1025.00 *(978-1-4108-3822-3(6))*; spiral bd. 315.00 *(978-1-4108-3824-7(2))*; spiral bd. 175.00 *(978-1-4108-3839-1(0))*; spiral bd. 200.00 *(978-1-4108-3840-7(4))* Benchmark Education Co.

—Science Texts Set. 2005. (Navigators Ser.). (J). spiral bd. 875.00 *(978-1-4108-5309-7(8))* Benchmark Education Co.

—Science Theme: Science in Personal & Social Perspectives. 2005. spiral bd. 115.00 *(978-1-4108-5313-4(6))* Benchmark Education Co.

—Science Themes. 2006. spiral bd. 2460.00 *(978-1-4108-7022-3(7))* Benchmark Education Co.

—Science Themes: Levels N-P Grade 3. 2006. (J). 1050.00 *(978-1-4108-7109-1(6))* Benchmark Education Co.

—Science Themes: Levels Q-R Grade 4. 2006. (J). 1025.00 *(978-1-4108-7123-7(1))* Benchmark Education Co.

—Science Themes: Levels S-U Grade 5. 2006. (J). 1080.00 *(978-1-4108-7138-1(X))* Benchmark Education Co.

—Science Themes: Levels V-X Grade 6. 2006. (J). 765.00 *(978-1-4108-7150-3(9))* Benchmark Education Co.

—Spanish Science Standard Set. 2005. spiral bd. 3455.00 *(978-1-4108-5857-3(X))* Benchmark Education Co.

Bennett, Andrea T. & Kessler, James H. Sunlight, Skyscrapers, & Soda-Pop: The Wherever-You-Look Science Book. Sarecky, Melody, illus. 2003. (J). 12.95 *(978-0-8412-3870-1(7))* American Chemical Society.

Berenstain, Stan, et al. The Berenstain Bears' Big Book of Science & Nature. 2013. (Dover Science for Kids Ser.). (ENG.). 192p. (J). (gr. k-3). pap. 15.99 *(978-0-486-49834-8(4)*, 498344) Dover Pubns., Inc.

Bergethon, Peter R. Marty's Miraculous Monday: The Student Reader. Bacon, Edith Noble, illus. 2022. 89p. (J). (gr. k-3). pap. *(978-1-58447-011-3(9))* Symmetry Learning Pr.

—Measuring My World: Student Science Journal. Date not set. (Illus.). (J). pap. *(978-1-58447-006-9(2))* Symmetry Learning Pr.

—Understanding My World: Student Science Journal. Date not set. (Illus.). (J). pap. *(978-1-58447-008-3(9))* Symmetry Learning Pr.

Bernardy, Catherine J., et al. Let's Investigate, 12 Vol., Set. (Illus.). 384p. (J). 167.40 *(978-0-88682-667-3(5))* Creative Co., The.

Big Book Collection. 2003. (Scott Foresman Science Ser.). (gr. 1-18). 138.60 *(978-0-328-00684-7(X))*; (gr. 3-18). 138.60 *(978-0-328-00686-1(6))* Addison-Wesley Educational Pubs., Inc.

BJU Staff. Science Activity Manual St Gr6. 2004. pap. 15.00 *(978-1-59166-008-8(4))* BJU Pr.

—Science Student Notebook Grd 1. 2004. pap. 7.50 *(978-1-57924-927-4(2))* BJU Pr.

—Science Student Notebook Grd 3. 2004. pap. 7.50 *(978-1-57924-929-8(9))* BJU Pr.

—Science Student Text Grd 1. 2004. 23.50 *(978-1-57924-908-3(6))* BJU Pr.

—Science Student Text Grd 3. 2004. 23.50 *(978-1-57924-914-4(0))* BJU Pr.

—Science Student Text Grd 6. 2004. pap. 17.00 *(978-1-59166-006-4(8))* BJU Pr.

Blake, Carly, et al. 1000+ Science Facts. Kelly, Richard, ed. 2017. (ENG., Illus.). 512p. (J). 39.95 *(978-1-78209-939-0(5))* Miles Kelly Publishing, Ltd. GBR. Dist: Parkwest Pubns., Inc.

Blane, Francisco. Up & Down: Lap Book. 2009. (My First Reader's Theater Set B Ser.). (J). 28.00 *(978-1-60634-989-2(9))* Benchmark Education Co.

Blastoff! (Group 2), 10 vols., Set. 2003. (Blastoff! Ser.). (ENG.). (gr. 5-5). 170.35 *(978-0-7614-1400-1(2)*, e61f5d1a-5d29-49c3-ac47-d4edcf27afd2, Cavendish Square) Cavendish Square Publishing LLC.

Block, Cheryl. The Rainbow Web. 2005. (Illus.). 32p. (J). 19.95 *(978-0-9761625-0-6(4))* Block Publishing.

Board, Joan. Cambridge Primary Science. Stage 4. Per la Scuola Media. Con Espansione Online. Con Libro: Activity Book. 2014. (Cambridge Primary Science Ser.). (ENG., Illus.). 52p. pap. 6.90 *(978-1-107-65665-9(6))* Cambridge Univ. Pr.

—Cambridge Primary Science. Stage 4. Per la Scuola Media. Con Espansione Online. Con Libro: Learner's Book. 2014. (Cambridge Primary Science Ser.). (ENG., Illus.). 104p. pap. 24.40 *(978-1-107-67450-9(6))* Cambridge Univ. Pr.

Board, Jon & Cross, Alan. Cambridge Primary Science Stage 1 Learner's Book. 2014. (Cambridge Primary Science Ser.). (ENG., Illus.). 68p. pap. 21.45 *(978-1-107-61138-2(5))* Cambridge Univ. Pr.

—Cambridge Primary Science. Stage 2. Learner's Book. Per le Scuole Superiori. 2014. (Cambridge Primary Science Ser.). (ENG., Illus.). 78p. pap. 21.45 *(978-1-107-61139-9(3))* Cambridge Univ. Pr.

—Cambridge Primary Science. Stage 3. Learner's Book. Per le Scuole Superiori. 2014. (Cambridge Primary Science Ser.). (ENG., Illus.). 80p. pap. 21.45 *(978-1-107-61141-2(5))* Cambridge Univ. Pr.

Bodach, Vijaya Khisty. Sink or Float? 2008. (Discovering & Exploring Science Ser.). (Illus.). 16p. (J). (gr. -1-3). lib. bdg. 12.95 *(978-0-7569-8414-4(9))* Perfection Learning Corp.

—What Is Missing? 2008. (Discovering & Exploring Science Ser.). (Illus.). 16p. (J). (gr. -1-3). lib. bdg. 12.95 *(978-0-7569-8253-9(7))* Perfection Learning Corp.

Body Numbers, 6 pack. (Discovery World Ser.). 16p. (gr. 1-2). 28.00 *(978-0-7635-8467-2(3))* Rigby Education.

Body Parts: KinderFacts Individual Title Six-Packs. (Kinderstarters Ser.). 8p. (gr. -1-1). 21.00 *(978-0-7635-8741-3(9))* Rigby Education.

Body Talk: Individual Title Six-Packs. (Story Steps Ser.). (gr. k-2). 32.00 *(978-0-7635-9815-0(1))* Rigby Education.

Bones Sets: 1 Each of 3 Big Books. (Sunshinetm Science Ser.). (gr. 1-2). 93.95 *(978-0-7802-0530-7(8))* Wright Group/McGraw-Hill.

Bones Sets: 1 Each of 3 Student Books. (Sunshinetm Science Ser.). (gr. 1-2). 17.95 *(978-0-7802-0271-9(6))* Wright Group/McGraw-Hill.

Books Are Fun Exclusive Let's Start Science 5 Set. 2005. (J). lib. bdg. *(978-1-59566-165-4(4))* QEB Publishing Inc.

Bow, James. Impossible Science. 2012. (ENG.). 32p. (J). *(978-0-7787-8009-0(0))*; pap. *(978-0-7787-8014-4(7))* Crabtree Publishing Co.

Bradley, Timothy. The Science of Monsters (Grade 6) 2nd rev. ed. 2016. (TIME(r): Informational Text Ser.). (ENG., Illus.). 64p. (gr. 5-8). pap. 13.99 *(978-1-4938-3607-9(2))* Teacher Created Materials, Inc.

Branigan, Carrie. First Steps in Science: Big Story Book. 2003. (ENG., Illus.). 24p. (J). 75.00 *(978-0-7487-6865-3(3))* Nelson Thornes Ltd. GBR. Dist: Trans-Atlantic Pubns., Inc.

—Image Bank. 2003. (ENG., Illus.). 96p. (J). 150.00 *(978-0-7487-6866-0(1))* Nelson Thornes Ltd. GBR. Dist: Trans-Atlantic Pubns., Inc.

Brasch, Nicolas. Theme Parks, Playgrounds, & Toys. 2010. (Science Behind Ser.). (Illus.). 32p. (J). lib. bdg. 28.50 *(978-1-59920-562-5(9))* Black Rabbit Bks.

Brewer, Ebenezer Cobham. A Guide to the Scientific Knowledge of Things Familiar by Rev Dr Brewer Carefully Revised, & Adapted for Use in Families & Schools of the U. 2006. 504p. per. 29.99 *(978-1-4255-5648-8(5))* Michigan Publishing.

Britannica, Learning Library. Science & Nature. 2003. (Illus.). 64p. 14.95 *(978-1-59339-033-4(5))* Encyclopaedia Britannica, Inc.

Brocker, Susan & Furgang, Kathy. Pioneers in Medicine: Set Of 6. 2011. (Navigators Ser.). (J). pap. 48.00 net. *(978-1-4108-0422-8(4))* Benchmark Education Co.

Bronson, Cary. I am Not a Flying Elephant Fish! A Children's Science Book on the Butterfly. Gomer, William, illus. l.t. ed. 2004. 32p. (J). lib. bdg. 14.95 *(978-0-9746094-0-9(4))* Connect With Your Kid Bks.

Brown Bag Science Set Gr. 1-2. 2004. (J). *(978-1-57022-470-6(6))* ECS Learning Systems, Inc.

Brown Bag Science Set Gr. 3-4. 2004. (J). *(978-1-57022-471-3(4))* ECS Learning Systems, Inc.

Brown Bear Books. Life Sciences. 2009. (Great Scientists Ser.). (ENG.). 64p. (J). (gr. 8-11). 39.95 *(978-1-933834-45-0(5)*, 16493) Brown Bear Bks.

—Prehistory & the Classical Period. 2010. (Technology Through the Ages Ser.). (ENG.). 112p. (J). (gr. 9-12). 42.80 *(978-1-933834-83-2(8)*, 16804) Brown Bear Bks.

Brown, Jordan D. Unmasking the Science of Superpowers! Ready-To-Read Level 3. Burroughs, Scott, illus. 2016. (Science of Fun Stuff Ser.). (ENG.). 48p. (J). (gr. 1-3). pap. 4.99 *(978-1-4814-6778-0(6)*, Simon Spotlight) Simon Spotlight.

Brown, Laaren. Volcanoes: Run for Your Life! 2013. (Illus.). 32p. (J). *(978-0-545-62413-8(4))* Scholastic, Inc.

Buckley, Arabella. The Fairy-Land of Science. 2007. 204p. 19.99 *(978-1-59986-737-3(0))*; per. 9.99 *(978-1-59986-823-3(7))* Filiquarian Publishing, LLC.

—The Fairy-Land of Science (Yesterday's Classics) 2006. (Illus.). 244p. (J). per. 10.95 *(978-1-59915-024-6(7))* Yesterday's Classics.

Buckley, Arabella Burton. The Fairy Land of Science. 2004. reprint ed. pap. 20.95 *(978-1-4191-6179-7(2))* Kessinger Publishing, LLC.

Bulging Brains. (YA). (gr. 5-8). pap. *(978-0-439-14976-1(2))* Scholastic GBR. Dist: Lectorum Pubns., Inc.

Burncrot, Curt & Dunlap, Shiree. Testing Targets: For Science of the Physical Creation. Zyp, Nicole & Robinson, Heldi, eds. 2004. 19p. (YA). (gr. 9-12). pap. 5.00 *(978-1-888786-44-6(2))* Basic Skills Assessment & Educational Services.

Calhoun, Yael, ed. Science News Flash Set. 2007. (Science News Flash Ser.). (ENG.). (gr. 6-12). 127.80 *(978-0-7910-9660-4(2)*, P179175, Facts On File) Infobase Holdings, Inc.

Cambridge Studios. Interactive World Issues, Set. 2nd ed. 2003. (C). (gr. 6-12). cd-rom 55.31 *(978-0-07-255648-3(X)*, 9780072556483) Glencoe/McGraw-Hill.

Canavan, Thomas. Why Do Ice Cubes Float? Questions & Answers about the Science of Everyday Materials. 2013. (Science F. A. Q. Ser.). (Illus.). 32p. (gr. 3-6). 31.35 *(978-1-78212-396-5(2))* Arcturus Publishing GBR. Dist: Black Rabbit Bks.

Canetti, Yanitzia. Rhyming Tongue Twisters Science: Science. 2010. 32p. (J). pap. 6.99 *(978-1-59835-265-8(2)*, BrickHouse Education) Cambridge BrickHouse, Inc.

—Trabalenguas Científicos. 2010. 32p. (J). pap. 6.99 *(978-1-59835-264-1(4)*, BrickHouse Education) Cambridge BrickHouse, Inc.

Capstone Press. Nasty (But Useful!) Science. 2010. (Nasty (but Useful!) Science Ser.). (ENG.). 32p. lib. bdg. 103.96 *(978-1-4296-5921-5(1)*, Capstone Pr.) Capstone.

Carangelo, Audrey & Hess, Debra. Radiation, Rats, & Mutant Monsters! 2007. (Read on! Special Edition: Level RA Ser.). (Illus.). 23p. (J). (gr. 4-7). pap. 18.51 *(978-1-4190-3506-7(1))* Steck-Vaughn.

Carey, Bjorn. Answers to the World's Greatest Questions, 1 vol. 2017. (Popular Science Fact Book for Inquiring Minds Ser.). (ENG.). 224p. (YA). (gr. 8-8). lib. bdg. 49.50 *(978-1-5026-3290-6(X)*, e4165398-d00f-41f0-bd2a-5ad106fa14ae) Cavendish Square Publishing LLC.

Cells & Things. 2004. (Illus.). lib. bdg. 7.95 *(978-0-8225-4371-8(0))* Lerner Publishing Group.

Challoner, Jack. Start-Up Science, 8 bks., Set. Incl. Big & Small. lib. bdg. 24.26 *(978-0-8172-4319-7(4))*; Fast & Slow. lib. bdg. 24.26 *(978-0-8172-4320-3(8))*; Floating & Sinking. lib. bdg. 16.98 *(978-0-8172-4317-3(8))*; Hot & Cold. lib. bdg. 24.76 *(978-0-8172-4323-4(2))*; Light & Dark. lib. bdg. 24.76 *(978-0-8172-4321-0(6))*; Loud & Quiet. lib. bdg. 24.26 *(978-0-8172-4318-0(6))*; Push & Pull. lib. bdg. 24.26 *(978-0-8172-4316-6(X))*; Wet & Dry. lib. bdg. 24.26 *(978-0-8172-4322-7(4))*; 32p. (J). (gr. 1-4). 1996. (Illus.). Set lib. bdg. 135.84 *(978-0-8172-4324-1(0))* Heinemann-Raintree.

Chasse, Betsy. The Little Book of Bleeps: Quotations from the Movie... What the Bleep Do We Know? 2005. (ENG., Illus.). 160p. pap. 14.95 *(978-0-9761074-0-8(6)*, Beyond Words) Simon & Schuster.

Chelsea Clubhouse Science Exploration. (Illus.). (J). 418.50 *(978-0-7910-7274-5(6)*, Facts On File) Infobase Holdings, Inc.

Christopher, Garrett. Look at These Animals: A Content Area Reader-science. 2005. (Sadlier Phonics Reading Program). (Illus.). 16p. (gr. k-2). 25.20 *(978-0-8215-7812-4(X))* Sadlier, William H. Inc.

Churchill, E. Richard. Amazing Science Experiments. Garbot, Dave & Gallagher, Jack, illus. 2005. (No-Sweat Science Ser.). (ENG.). 128p. (J). (gr. 3-6). 18.69 *(978-1-4027-2331-5(8))* Sterling Publishing Co., Inc.

Ciencias. (Enciclopedias Everest Internacional Ser.). (SPA., Illus.). (YA). (gr. 5-8). 41.95 *(978-84-241-9405-5(5)*, EV7495) Everest Editora ESP. Dist: Lectorum Pubns., Inc.

Ciencias Naturales. (Coleccion Ciencas Naturales Ser.). (SPA., Illus.). (J). Bk. 1. (gr. 1). pap. 8.95 *(978-968-416-500-7(5)*, FN5005)Bk. 2. (gr. 2). pap. 10.95 *(978-968-416-489-5(0)*, FN4890)Bk. 3. (gr. 3). pap. 10.95 *(978-968-416-490-1(4)*, FN4904)Bk. 4. (gr. 4). pap. 10.95 *(978-968-416-491-8(2)*, FN4912)Bk. 5. (gr. 5). pap. 11.95 *(978-968-416-492-5(0)*, FN4920)Bk. 6. (gr. 6). pap. 12.95 *(978-968-416-493-2(9)*, FN4939) Fernandez USA Publishing.

Cientificos! (SPA.). (J). Vol. 7. wbk. ed. 15.00 *(978-958-04-6435-8(9))* Vol. 8. wbk. ed. 15.00 *(978-958-04-6436-5(7))* Vol. 9. wbk. ed. 15.00 *(978-958-04-6437-2(5))* Norma S.A. COL. Dist: Distribuidora Norma, Inc.

Cientificos! Ciencia Integrada 1. (SPA.). (J). 30.00 *(978-958-04-5245-4(8))* Norma S.A. COL. Dist: Distribuidora Norma, Inc.

Cientificos! Ciencia Integrada 2. (SPA.). (J). 30.00 *(978-958-04-5246-1(6))* Norma S.A. COL. Dist: Distribuidora Norma, Inc.

Cientificos! Ciencia Integrada 3. (SPA.). (J). 30.00 *(978-958-04-5247-8(4))* Norma S.A. COL. Dist: Distribuidora Norma, Inc.

Cientificos! Ciencia Integrada 4. 35.00 *(978-958-04-5248-5(2))* Norma S.A. COL. Dist: Distribuidora Norma, Inc.

Cientificos! Ciencia Integrada 5. (SPA.). (J). 40.00 *(978-958-04-5249-2(0))* Norma S.A. COL. Dist: Distribuidora Norma, Inc.

Cientificos! Ciencia Integrada 6. (SPA.). (J). 45.00 *(978-958-04-5250-8(4))* Norma S.A. COL. Dist: Distribuidora Norma, Inc.

Cipriano, Jeri S. Let's Look at Rocks, 6 vols., Set. 2003. (Yellow Umbrella Early Level Ser.). (ENG.). 16p. (gr. k-1). pap. 35.70 *(978-0-7368-3015-7(4)*, Capstone Pr.) Capstone.

Clarke, Phillip. Mysteries & Marvels of Science - Internet Linked. rev. ed. 2008. (Mysteries & Marvels of Science Ser.). 96p. (J). pap. 16.99 *(978-0-7945-1985-8(7)*, Usborne) EDC Publishing.

Clarke, Phillip, et al. The Usborne Internet-Linked Mysteries & Marvels of Science. Furnival, Keith, illus. 2005. 96p. (J). *(978-0-439-81568-0(1))* Scholastic, Inc.

Claybourne, Anna. Whiz Kid Science, 1 vol. Scott, Kimberly & Dean, Venetia, illus. 2014. (Whiz Kid Science Ser.). (ENG.). 32p. (gr. 2-4). 183.90 *(978-1-4109-6751-0(4)*, Raintree) Capstone.

Cleary, Brian P. Mrs. Riley Bought Five Itchy Aardvarks & Other Painless Tricks for Memorizing Science Facts. Sandy, J. P., illus. 2008. (Adventures in Memory Ser.). (ENG.). 48p. (gr. 4-6). 26.60 *(978-0-8225-7819-2(0))* Lerner Publishing Group.

Cleveland, Don. How Do We Know How the Brain Works, 1 vol. 2004. (Great Scientific Questions & the Scientists Who Answered Them Ser.). (ENG., Illus.). 112p. (J). (gr. 7-12). lib. bdg. 39.80 *(978-1-4042-0078-4(9)*, 568b474b-da88-4669-b05f-245bc6e90bdc) Rosen Publishing Group, Inc., The.

Climatologists & Meteorologists: Out of the Lab: Extreme Jobs in Science, 12 vols. 2013. (Out of the Lab: Extreme Jobs in Science Ser.). (ENG.). 32p. (J). (gr. 4-5). 173.58 *(978-1-4777-1540-6(1)*, fa9d08f6-255d-40c0-9085-761b07bb0abc, PowerKids Pr.) Rosen Publishing Group, Inc., The.

Clouds, Rain, & Fog: Big Book. (Sunshinetm Science Ser.). 24p. (gr. 1-2). 37.50 *(978-0-7802-1374-6(2))* Wright Group/McGraw-Hill.

Cloyd, J. B. Rocks We Use: A Content Area Reader. 2005. (Emergent/Early (Prek-2) Science Package Ser.). 12p. (gr. k-2). 25.20 *(978-0-8215-7813-1(8))* Sadlier, William H. Inc.

Cobb, Vicki. What's the Big Idea? Amazing Science Questions for the Curious Kid. 2010. (ENG., Illus.). 208p. (J). (gr. 3-6). pap. 19.95 *(978-1-61608-013-6(2)*, 1310418) Skyhorse Publishing Co., Inc.

—What's the BIG Idea? Amazing Science Questions for the Curious Kid. 2013. (ENG., Illus.). 208p. (J). (gr. 2-5). pap. 12.95 *(978-1-62087-685-5(X)*, 620685, Sky Pony Pr.) Skyhorse Publishing Co., Inc.

—Where's the Science Here? Classroom Library. 2008. pap. 34.95 *(978-0-8225-8979-2(6))* Lerner Publishing Group.

—Where's the Science Here? Complete Library. 2008. pap. 210.95 *(978-0-8225-9379-9(3))* Lerner Publishing Group.

Collard, Sneed B., III. Science Adventures, 8 vols., Set. Incl. In the Deep Sea. lib. bdg. 32.64 *(978-0-7614-1952-5(7)*, 51a1271b-3391-4430-aee9-cd04cde8adbb); In the Rain Forest Canopy. lib. bdg. 32.64 *(978-0-7614-1954-9(3)*, bc7e6cf1-bc45-4030-b1ad-9735ea8337cc); In the Wild. lib. bdg. 32.64 *(978-0-7614-1955-6(1)*, f6a29e18-2839-462e-97d0-11e8759beac6); On the Coral Reefs. lib. bdg. 32.64 *(978-0-7614-1953-2(5)*, 1835758b-57a9-4fe7-93d6-a5287c1d13aa); (Illus.). 48p. (gr. 4-4). (Science Adventures Ser.). (ENG.). 2007. 130.56 *(978-0-7614-1951-8(9)*, 135734b4-2f5a-45d5-b44b-727df55abccb, Cavendish Square) Cavendish Square Publishing LLC.

Collins Kids. Science (Collins Fascinating Facts) rev. ed. 2016. (Collins Fascinating Facts Ser.). (ENG., Illus.). 72p. (J). (gr. 1-3). pap. 10.99 *(978-0-00-816918-3(7))* HarperCollins Pubs. Ltd. GBR. Dist: Independent Pubs. Group.

Collins KS3. KS3 Science All-In-One Complete Revision & Practice: Ideal for Years 7, 8 And 9. 2014. (ENG.). 216p. (YA). (gr. 6-9). pap. 17.95 *(978-0-00-756283-1(7))* HarperCollins Pubs. Ltd. GBR. Dist: Independent Pubs. Group.

—KS3 Science Year 7 Workbook: Ideal for Year 7. 2014. (ENG.). 80p. (J). (gr. 6-7). pap., wbk. ed. 8.95 *(978-0-00-756273-2(X))* HarperCollins Pubs. Ltd. GBR. Dist: Independent Pubs. Group.

—KS3 Science Year 9 Workbook: Ideal for Year 9. 2014. (ENG.). 80p. (YA). (gr. 8-9). pap., wbk. ed. 8.95 *(978-0-00-756275-6(6))* HarperCollins Pubs. Ltd. GBR. Dist: Independent Pubs. Group.

Collins KS3, Collins. KS3 Science Revision Guide: Ideal for Years 7, 8 And 9. 2014. (ENG., Illus.). 144p. (YA). (gr. 6-9). pap. 12.95 *(978-0-00-756282-4(9))* HarperCollins Pubs. Ltd. GBR. Dist: Independent Pubs. Group.

Collison, Paul, et al. Nelson Modular Science, Bk. 1. 2nd rev. ed. 2005. (ENG., Illus.). 296p. (YA). pap. 36.50 *(978-0-7487-6856-1(4))* Nelson Thornes Ltd. GBR. Dist: Trans-Atlantic Pubns., Inc.

Cook, Sherry & Johnson, Terri. Andy Acid, 26 vols. Kuhn, Jesse, illus. l.t. ed. 2006. (Quirkles — Exploring Phonics through Science Ser.: 1). 32p. (J). 7.99 *(978-1-933815-00-8(0)*, Quirkles, The) Creative 3, LLC.

—Botanist Bert, 26 vols. Kuhn, Jesse, illus. l.t. ed. 2006. (Quirkles — Exploring Phonics through Science Ser.: 2). 32p. (J). 7.99 *(978-1-933815-01-5(9)*, Quirkles, The) Creative 3, LLC.

—Colorful Caroline, 26 vols. Kuhn, Jesse, illus. l.t. ed. 2006. (Quirkles — Exploring Phonics through Science Ser.: 3). 32p. (J). 7.99 *(978-1-933815-02-2(7)*, Quirkles, The) Creative 3, LLC.

—Density Dan, 26 vols. Kuhn, Jesse, illus. l.t. ed. 2006. (Quirkles — Exploring Phonics through Science Ser.: 4). 32p. (J). 7.99 (978-1-933815-03-9(5), Quirkles, The) Creative 3, LLC.

—Friction Fred, 26 vols. Kuhn, Jesse, illus. l.t. ed. 2006. (Quirkles — Exploring Phonics through Science Ser.: 6). 32p. (J). 7.99 (978-1-933815-05-3(1), Quirkles, The) Creative 3, LLC.

Cooke, Andy, et al. Spectrum 8. 2003. (Spectrum Key Stage 3 Science Ser.). (ENG., Illus.). 168p. pap. 12.95 (978-0-521-75007-3(5)) Cambridge Univ. Pr.

—Spectrum Year 9. 2003. (Spectrum Key Stage 3 Science Ser.). (ENG., Illus.). 184p. pap. 13.50 (978-0-521-75010-3(5)) Cambridge Univ. Pr.

Cooper, Bob. Little Leonardo's Fascinating World of Science, 1 vol. Paprocki, Greg, illus. 2018. 24p. (J). (gr. -1-3). 12.99 (978-1-4236-4874-1(9)) Gibbs Smith, Publisher.

Core Concepts: Set 2, 20 vols. 2013. (Core Concepts Ser.). (ENG.). 96p. (YA). (gr. 7-7). 397.70 (978-1-4777-2727-0(2), 42c06b90-f8b0-4217-883c-dc16033dd5a0) Rosen Publishing Group, Inc., The.

Core Concepts: Sets 1 - 3, 60 vols. 2014. (Core Concepts Ser.). (ENG.). 96p. (YA). (gr. 7-7). 1193.10 (978-1-4777-8100-5(5), b71034cd-bc41-4f53-8eee-83ebc1b0d7d1) Rosen Publishing Group, Inc., The.

Corliss, William R. Scientific Anomalies & other Provocative Phenomena. 2003. (Illus.). 300p. (Orig.). (YA). (gr. 9-12). pap. 17.95 (978-0-915554-45-4(3)) Sourcebook Project, The.

Cornsweet, Tom. Why Is Everything! Doing Science. 2009. 260p. 29.95 (978-0-595-51834-0(6)); pap. 19.95 (978-0-595-52871-4(6)) iUniverse, Inc.

Corrigan, Patricia. Bringing Science to Life: A Guide from the St. Louis Science Center. 2007. 128p. (J). pap. 16.00 (978-1-933370-16-3(5)) Reedy Pr.

Cover Your Bases. 2004. (YA). ring bd. (978-0-9747576-0-5(8)) Event-Based Science Institute, Inc.

Crews, G. Ellen G Goes Fishing. marion, designs & proctor, brian, illus. 2007. 28p. pap. 4.99 (978-0-9795236-0-1(5)) Crews Pubns., LLC.

Cuaderno Cientificos! 4, Vol. 4. (SPA.). (J). wbk. ed. 15.00 (978-958-04-5346-8(2)) Norma S.A. COL. Dist: Distribuidora Norma, Inc.

Cuaderno Cientificos! 5, Vol. 5. (SPA.). (J). wbk. ed. 15.00 (978-958-04-5347-5(0)) Norma S.A. COL. Dist: Distribuidora Norma, Inc.

Cuaderno Cientificos! 6, Vol. 6. (SPA.). (J). wbk. ed. 15.00 (978-958-04-5348-2(9)) Norma S.A. COL. Dist: Distribuidora Norma, Inc.

Cullen, Dave. Big Book of Science. Leeks, David, illus. 2004. 48p. (J). 7.99 (978-1-85854-532-5(3)) Brimax Books Ltd. GBR. Dist: Byeway Bks.

Culp, Jennifer. Ancient Chinese Technology, 1 vol. 2016. (Spotlight on the Rise & Fall of Ancient Civilizations Ser.). (ENG., Illus.). 48p. (J). (gr. 6-6). pap. 12.75 (978-1-4777-8897-4(2), dd3b59dd-ac62-494b-8cd3-d0bafe1e9aa7) Rosen Publishing Group, Inc., The.

Curious Jane, Curious. Curious Jane: Science + Design + Engineering for Inquisitive Girls. 2017. (Illus.). 128p. (J). (gr. 1-6). pap. 16.95 (978-1-4549-2235-3(4)) Sterling Publishing Co., Inc.

Current Science, 12 vols. 2009. (Current Science Ser.). (ENG.). 48p. (J). (gr. 4-6). lib. bdg. 202.02 (978-1-4339-2063-9(8), e259cd0d-b1de-4a9b-a9d9-d3c972303f2a, Gareth Stevens Learning Library) Stevens, Gareth Publishing LLLP.

Cutting-Edge Science & Technology, 8 vols. 2015. (Cutting-Edge Science & Technology Ser.: 8). (ENG.). 112p. (J). (gr. 6-12). lib. bdg. 330.88 (978-1-62403-911-9(1), 19112, Essential Library) ABDO Publishing Co.

Cutting-Edge STEM Careers. 2014. (Cutting-Edge STEM Careers Ser.). 128p. (J). pap. 75.40 (978-1-4777-8106-7(4), Rosen Classroom) Rosen Publishing Group, Inc., The.

Cutting Machines, 6 vols. (Sunshinetm Science Ser.). 24p. (gr. 1-2). 31.50 (978-0-7802-0302-0(X)); 36.95 (978-0-7802-0553-6(7)) Wright Group/McGraw-Hill.

Dalgleish, Sharon. It's a Mystery. 2003. (Real Deal Ser.). (Illus.). 32p. (J). pap. (978-0-7608-6692-4(9)) Sundance/Newbridge Educational Publishing.

Davidson, Avelyn. Shockwave: Dollars & Sense. 2007. (Shockwave: Economics & Geography Ser.). (ENG., Illus.). 36p. (J). (gr. 3-5). 25.00 (978-0-531-17750-1(5), Children's Pr.) Scholastic Library Publishing.

Davidson, Gary, des. Mesozoic & Cenozoic, 2 vols. 2004. (Time Line Companion Bks.). (Illus.). (J). per. 8.50 (978-0-9745560-1-7(7)) Azoka Co., The.

—Paleozoic Era, 2 vols. 2004. (Time Line Companion Bks.). (Illus.). 65p. (J). per. (978-0-9745560-0-0(9)) Azoka Co., The.

Davies, Kate. What's Science All About? 2010. (Science Stories Ser.). 283p. (YA). (gr. 3-18). pap. 15.99 (978-0-7945-2120-2(7), Usborne) EDC Publishing.

Day Two PSAE Student Textbook. 3rd ed. 2005. per. (978-1-58894-035-3(7)) Cambridge Educational Services, Inc.

Days We Celebrate, 6 vols. (Book2WebTM Ser.). (gr. 4-8). 36.50 (978-0-322-02846-3(9)) Wright Group/McGraw-Hill.

De Long, Ron, et al. Dream-Makers Science: Art & Science. De Long, Ron et al, eds. 2007. (Illus.). 104p. spiral bd. 9.99 (978-0-86696-328-2(6)) Binney & Smith, Inc.

De Waard, Nancy & De Waard, E. John. Science Challenge Level 2: 190 Fun & Creative Brainteasers for Kids, Level 2. 2005. (Challenge Ser.). (Illus.). 192p. (J). per. 9.95 (978-1-59647-068-2(2), EAS002) Good Year Bks.

Delta Education. Sci Res Bk Foss Grade 1 Next Gen Ea. 2015. (Illus.). 244p. (J). lib. bdg. (978-1-62571-445-9(9)) Delta Education, LLC.

—Sci Res Bk Foss Grade 2 Next Gen Ea. 2014. (Illus.). 251p. (J). lib. bdg. (978-1-62571-446-6(7)) Delta Education, LLC.

—Sci Res Bk Foss Grade 3 Next Gen Ea. 2014. (Illus.). 274p. (J). lib. bdg. (978-1-62571-375-9(4)) Delta Education, LLC.

—Sci Res Bk Foss Grade 4 Next Gen Ea. 2015. (Illus.). 322p. (J). lib. bdg. (978-1-62571-447-3(5)) Delta Education, LLC.

—Sci Res Bk Foss Grade 5 Next Gen Ea. 2015. (Illus.). 336p. (J). lib. bdg. (978-1-62571-448-0(3)) Delta Education, LLC.

—Sci Res Bk Foss Grade K Next Gen Ea. 2015. (Illus.). 231p. (J). lib. bdg. (978-1-62571-444-2(0)) Delta Education, LLC.

dePaola, Tomie. Tomie DePaola's the Quicksand Book. 2019. (ENG., Illus.). 32p. (J). (gr. -1-3). 17.99 (978-0-8234-4237-9(3)) Holiday Hse., Inc.

Dichter, Paul & Heiman, Larry. The Magic of Our World: From the Night Sky to the Pacific Islands with Favorite Disney Characters. 2018. (ENG., Illus.). 176p. (J). (gr. 2-5). pap. 14.99 (978-1-5415-4250-1(9), Lerner Pubns.) Lerner Publishing Group.

Dickmann, Nancy. Math in Science. 2018. (Amazing World of Math Ser.). (ENG., Illus.). 32p. (J). (gr. 3-6). 27.99 (978-1-5415-0098-3(9), 107634eb-aaa6-4d65-9088-50fdb7b09ca8, Hungry Tomato (r)) Lerner Publishing Group.

Different Kinds of Bread: 6 Each of 1 Student Book, 6 vols. (Sunshinetm Science Ser.). 24p. (gr. 1-2). 41.95 (978-0-7802-2726-2(3)) Wright Group/McGraw-Hill.

Different Kinds of Bread: Big Book. (Sunshinetm Science Ser.). 24p. (gr. 1-2). 37.50 (978-0-7802-2797-2(2)) Wright Group/McGraw-Hill.

Discover Series: Science, Nature, Wildlife, 11 bks. (Illus.). (J). (gr. 3-6). lib. bdg. 175.45 (978-1-56674-935-0(2)) Forest Hse. Publishing Co., Inc.

Discovery!, 13 vols., Set. Incl. Circulating Life: Blood Transfusion from Ancient Superstition to Modern Medicine. Winner, Cherie. (Illus.). 112p. 2007. lib. bdg. 31.93 (978-0-8225-6606-9(0)); Dinosaur Eggs Discovered! Unscrambling the Clues. Dingus, Lowell. (Illus.). 112p. 2007. lib. bdg. 31.93 (978-0-8225-6791-2(1)); Investigating Climate Change: Scientists' Search for Answers in a Warming World. Johnson, Rebecca L. (Illus.). 112p. 2008. lib. bdg. 31.93 (978-0-8225-6792-9(X)); Invisible Invaders: Dangerous Infectious Diseases. Goldsmith, Connie. (Illus.). 112p. 2006. 31.93 (978-0-8225-3416-7(9)); Killer Rocks from Outer Space: Asteroids, Comets, & Meteorites. Koppes, Steven N. (Illus.). 112p. 2003. lib. bdg. 31.93 (978-0-8225-2861-6(4)); Little People & a Lost World: An Anthropological Mystery. Goldenberg, Linda. (Illus.). 112p. 2006. lib. bdg. 31.93 (978-0-8225-5983-2(8)); Mass Extinction: Examining the Current Crisis. Andryszewski, Tricia. (Illus.). 112p. 2008. lib. bdg. 31.93 (978-0-8225-7523-8(X)); Mutants, Clones, & Killer Corn: Unlocking the Secrets of Biotechnology. Seiple, Todd & Seiple, Samantha. (Illus.). 112p. 2005. lib. bdg. 31.93 (978-0-8225-4860-7(7)); Neandertals: A Prehistoric Puzzle. La Pierre, Yvette. (Illus.). 112p. 2008. lib. bdg. 31.93 (978-0-8225-7524-5(8)); Outbreak: Disease Detectives at Work. 2nd rev. ed. Friedlander, Mark P. 128p. 2009. 31.93 (978-0-8225-9039-2(5)); Parasites: Latching on to a Free Lunch. Fleisher, Paul. (Illus.). 112p. (J). 2006. lib. bdg. 31.93 (978-0-8225-3415-0(0)); Superbugs Strike Back: When Antibiotics Fail. Goldsmith, Connie. (Illus.). 112p. 2007. lib. bdg. 31.93 (978-0-8225-6607-6(9)); (gr. 6-12). 2010. Set lib. bdg. 415.09 (978-0-8225-8203-8(1), Twenty-First Century Bks.) Lerner Publishing Group.

Discovery Channel School Science: Our Planet Earth Set 4, 12 vols. 2004. (Discovery Channel School Science: Our Planet Earth Ser.). (ENG., Illus.). 32p. (gr. 5-7). lib. bdg. 172.02 (978-0-8368-3376-8(7), 34536607-b557-4bde-93a9-96b0b0249650, Gareth Stevens Learning Library) Stevens, Gareth Publishing LLLP.

Dise, Molly. Fun at the Zoo! 2011. (Wonder Readers Ser.). (ENG.). 16p. (J). (gr. -1-1). 25.95 (978-1-4296-8672-3(3), 195213, Capstone Pr.) Capstone.

DiSiena, Laura Lyn & Eliot, Hannah. Rainbows Never End: And Other Fun Facts. Oswald, Pete, illus. 2014. (Did You Know? Ser.). (ENG.). 32p. (J). (gr. -1-3). 17.99 (978-1-4814-0277-4(3)); pap. 7.99 (978-1-4814-0275-0(7)) Little Simon. (Little Simon).

DK. Big Book of Knowledge. 2019. (ENG., Illus.). 480p. (J). (gr. 4-7). pap. 17.99 (978-1-4654-8041-5(2), DK Children) Dorling Kindersley Publishing, Inc.

—DK Workbooks: Science, First Grade: Learn & Explore. 2013. (DK Workbooks Ser.). (ENG.). 60p. (J). (gr. 1-2). pap. 6.99 (978-1-4654-1728-2(1), DK Children) Dorling Kindersley Publishing, Inc.

—DK Workbooks: Science, Kindergarten: Learn & Explore. 2013. (DK Workbooks Ser.). (ENG.). 60p. (J). (gr. -1-1). pap. 6.99 (978-1-4654-1727-5(3), DK Children) Dorling Kindersley Publishing, Inc.

—DK Workbooks: Science, Pre-K: Learn & Explore. 2013. (DK Workbooks Ser.). (ENG.). 60p. (J). (gr. -1-k). pap. 6.99 (978-1-4654-1726-8(5), DK Children) Dorling Kindersley Publishing, Inc.

—DK Workbooks: Science, Second Grade: Learn & Explore. 2013. (DK Workbooks Ser.). (ENG.). 60p. (J). (gr. 1-3). pap. 6.99 (978-1-4654-1729-9(X), DK Children) Dorling Kindersley Publishing, Inc.

—DK Workbooks: Science, Third Grade: Learn & Explore. 2013. (DK Workbooks Ser.). (ENG.). 60p. (J). (gr. 3-4). pap. 6.99 (978-1-4654-1730-5(3), DK Children) Dorling Kindersley Publishing, Inc.

—How to Be Good at Science, Technology, & Engineering. 2018. (DK How to Be Good At Ser.). (ENG., Illus.). 320p. (J). (gr. 4-7). pap. 19.99 (978-1-4654-7359-2(9), DK Children) Dorling Kindersley Publishing, Inc.

—Pocket Genius: Science: Facts at Your Fingertips. 2016. (Pocket Genius Ser.: 14). (ENG., Illus.). 160p. (J). (gr. 3-7). pap. 6.99 (978-1-4654-4591-9(9), DK Children) Dorling Kindersley Publishing, Inc.

—Science: a Visual Encyclopedia. 2018. (DK Children's Visual Encyclopedias Ser.). (ENG., Illus.). 304p. (J). (gr. 3-7). 29.99 (978-1-4654-7322-6(X), DK Children) Dorling Kindersley Publishing, Inc.

Dobson. Holt Science Spectacular: Physical Science. 6th ed. 2006. stu. ed. 79.33 (978-0-03-039093-7(1)) Harcourt Schl. Pubs.

Doudna, Kelly. It's My Mission to Make a Definition!, 1 vol. 2007. (Science Made Simple Ser.). (Illus.). 24p. (J). (gr. k-3). lib. bdg. 24.21 (978-1-59928-600-6(9), SandCastle) ABDO Publishing Co.

Doyle, Eamon, ed. The Role of Science in Public Policy, 1 vol. 2018. (At Issue Ser.). (ENG.). 128p. (gr. 10-12). 41.03 (978-1-5345-0334-2(X), 76285a4b-fb66-45d0-8f2a-8383105de819) Greenhaven Publishing LLC.

Doyle, James. Why Can't I Feel the Earth Spinning? And Other Vital Questions about Science. 2018. (ENG., Illus.). 96p. (J). (gr. 2-4). 19.95 (978-0-500-65118-6(3), 565118) Thames & Hudson.

—A Young Scientist's Guide to Faulty Freaks of Nature: Including 20 Experiments for the Sink, Bathtub & Backyard (Large Print 16pt) 2013. 200p. pap. (978-1-4596-5848-6(5)) ReadHowYouWant.com, Ltd.

Driver, Stephanie Schwartz & Garcia, Rachel. I Wish I Knew That Science: Cool Stuff You Need to Know. 2012. (J). (978-1-60652-387-2(2)) Reader's Digest Assn., Inc., The.

Duke, Shirley. Animal Science. 2012. (Let's Explore Science Ser.). (ENG., Illus.). 48p. (gr. 4-6). pap. 10.95 (978-1-61810-257-7(5), 9781618102577) Rourke Educational Media.

—Enterprise Stem. 2011. (Let's Explore Science Ser.). (ENG., Illus.). 48p. (gr. 4-6). pap. 10.95 (978-1-61741-983-6(4), 9781617419836) Rourke Educational Media.

Dunn, Justine. Hey! There's Science in My Literature! Grades 1-2. Radtke, Becky, illus. 2007. (Rigby Best Teachers Press Ser.). 96p. per. 13.99 (978-1-4190-2848-9(0)) Houghton Mifflin Harcourt Supplemental Pubs.

Dunn, Karen Lewit. What's the Solution? 2008. (Discovering & Exploring Science Ser.). (Illus.). 16p. (J). (gr. -1-3). lib. bdg. 12.95 (978-0-7569-8433-5(5)) Perfection Learning Corp.

Dunne, Abbie. Life Science. 2016. (Life Science Ser.). (ENG., Illus.). 24p. (J). (gr. -1-2). pap., pap., pap. 41.70 (978-1-5157-1384-5(9), 24889, Capstone Pr.) Capstone.

—Physical Science. 2016. (Physical Science Ser.). (ENG., Illus.). 24p. (J). (gr. -1-2). pap., pap., pap. 41.70 (978-1-5157-1386-9(5), 24891, Capstone Pr.) Capstone.

DynaNotes Grade 8 Science TAKS Review Guide. 2006. (YA). pap. (978-1-933854-28-1(6)) DynaStudy, Inc.

DynaNotes Grade 8 Science TAKS Review Guide Transparency Set. 2006. (YA). trans. (978-1-933854-32-8(4)) DynaStudy, Inc.

DynaNotes Laboratory Review Guide. 2007. (J). pap. (978-1-933854-61-8(8)) DynaStudy, Inc.

DynaNotes Laboratory Review Guide Transparency Set. 2007. (J). trans. (978-1-933854-69-4(3)) DynaStudy, Inc.

DynaNotes Mass Transparency Set. 2007. (J). trans. (978-1-933854-53-3(7)) DynaStudy, Inc.

Early Fluency Set 2: 1 Each of 8 Big Books. (Sunshinetm Science Ser.). (gr. 1-2). 296.50 (978-0-7802-1764-5(0)) Wright Group/McGraw-Hill.

Early Fluency Set 2: 1 Each of 8 Big Books, 1 Each of 8 Student Books, 1 Teacher Guide, & 1 Duplicate Masters Book. (Sunshinetm Science Ser.). (gr. 1-2). 391.50 (978-0-7802-1763-8(2)) Wright Group/McGraw-Hill.

Early Fluency Set 2: 1 Each of 8 Student Books. (Sunshinetm Science Ser.). (gr. 1-2). 55.95 (978-0-7802-1765-2(9)) Wright Group/McGraw-Hill.

Early Fluency Set 3. (Sunshinetm Science Ser.). (gr. 1-2). 296.50 (978-0-7802-1767-6(5)) Wright Group/McGraw-Hill.

Early Fluency Set 3: 1 Each of Student Books. (Sunshinetm Science Ser.). (gr. 1-2). 55.95 (978-0-7802-1768-3(3)) Wright Group/McGraw-Hill.

Early Fluency Set 4: 1 Each of 8 Big Books. (Sunshinetm Science Ser.). (gr. 1-2). 296.50 (978-0-7802-2800-9(6)) Wright Group/McGraw-Hill.

Early Fluency Set 4: 1 Each of 8 Student Books. (Sunshinetm Science Ser.). (gr. 1-2). 55.96 (978-0-7802-2801-6(4)) Wright Group/McGraw-Hill.

Early Fluency Set 5: 1 Each of 8 Big Books. (Sunshinetm Science Ser.). (gr. 1-2). 296.50 (978-0-7802-2803-0(0)) Wright Group/McGraw-Hill.

Early Fluency Set 5: 1 Each of 8 Student Books. (Sunshinetm Science Ser.). (gr. 1-2). 55.95 (978-0-7802-2804-7(9)) Wright Group/McGraw-Hill.

Early Fluency Set 6: 1 Each of 8 Big Books. (Sunshinetm Science Ser.). (gr. 1-2). 296.50 (978-0-7802-2806-1(5)) Wright Group/McGraw-Hill.

Early Fluency Set 6: 1 Each of 8 Big Books, 1 Each of 8 Student Books, 1 Teacher Guide, & 1 Duplicate Master Book. (Sunshinetm Science Ser.). (gr. 1-2). 391.50 (978-0-7802-2805-4(7)) Wright Group/McGraw-Hill.

Early Fluency Set 6: 1 Each of 8 Student Books. (Sunshinetm Science Ser.). (gr. 1-2). 55.95 (978-0-7802-2807-8(3)) Wright Group/McGraw-Hill.

Earth & Space Classroom Library. (gr. k-2). lib. bdg. 54.95 (978-0-7368-3284-7(X), Red Brick Learning) Capstone.

Eboch, Christine Elizabeth. Sweet Eats with a Side of Science 4D. 2018. (Sweet Eats with a Side of Science 4D Ser.). (ENG.). 32p. (J). (gr. 3-9). 133.28 (978-1-5435-1087-4(6), 27837, Capstone Pr.) Capstone.

Edelman, Brad, et al. Science Brain Builders, 4 vols. 2017. (Science Brain Builders Ser.). (ENG.). 48p. (J). (gr. 4-9). 138.60 (978-1-5157-6462-5(1), 26492); pap., pap., pap. 36.40 (978-1-5157-6463-2(X), 26493) Capstone. (Capstone Classroom).

Education.com. All Sorts of Science: A Workbook Full of Science Fun Facts. 2015. (ENG.). 128p. (J). (gr. 5-5). pap. 7.99 (978-0-486-80273-2(6), 802736) Dover Pubns., Inc.

—Creatures & Counting: A Workbook of Counting, Sorting, & Discovery. 2015. (ENG.). 128p. (J). (gr. -1-k). pap. 7.99 (978-0-486-80274-9(4)) Dover Pubns., Inc.

—Earth & Sky: A Workbook of Science Facts & Math Practice. 2015. (Dover Science for Kids Ser.). (ENG.). 112p. (J). (gr. 3-3). pap. 7.99 (978-0-486-80269-5(8), 802698) Dover Pubns., Inc.

Edwards, Mark, et al. Connecting Science. 2008. (ENG., Illus.). 228p. (gr. 12-13). pap., stu. ed. 39.50 (978-0-340-94598-8(2)) Hodder Education Group GBR. Dist: Trans-Atlantic Pubns., Inc.

Ehlke, Paul. Clouds: Science Information in American Sign Language: A Paws Science Adventure. 2003. (J). cd-rom 29.95 (978-0-9752933-2-4(X)) Institute for Disabilities Research & Training, Inc.

Eikum, John. The 4th Dimension & Beyond: Imagining Worlds with 0, 1, 2, 3, 4 Dimensions & More. 2007. 120p. (J). per. 16.95 (978-1-59298-172-4(0)) Beaver's Pond Pr., Inc.

Elementary Science 2000: Big Book Collection. 2003. (gr. k-18). 138.60 (978-0-328-00683-0(1)) Addison-Wesley Educational Pubs., Inc.

Elkin, Susan, ed. The 100 Greatest Unsolved Mysteries, 1 vol. 2017. (Popular Science Fact Book for Inquiring Minds Ser.). (ENG.). 176p. (YA). (gr. 8-8). lib. bdg. 49.50 (978-1-5026-3288-3(8), aaf5fe79-1a0e-499d-b35d-ce320ae45ad5) Cavendish Square Publishing LLC.

Elliott, Cathy. Can You Guess What It Is? 2008. (Discovering & Exploring Science Ser.). (Illus.). 16p. (J). (gr. -1-3). lib. bdg. 12.95 (978-0-7569-8418-2(1)) Perfection Learning Corp.

Emergent Set: 1 Each of 8 Student Books. (Sunshinetm Science Ser.). (gr. 1-2). 48.95 (978-0-7802-0568-0(5)) Wright Group/McGraw-Hill.

Emergent Set: 1 Each of Student Books, Vol. 2. (Sunshinetm Science Ser.). (gr. 1-2). 48.95 (978-0-7802-0570-3(7)) Wright Group/McGraw-Hill.

Enciclopedia Ilustrada de Ciencia Naturaleza (Understanding Science & Nature), 16 bks. Incl. Comportamiento de los Animales (Animal Behavior) 17.95 (978-0-7835-3358-2(6)); Cuerpo Humano (Human Body) 17.95 (978-0-7835-3350-6(0)); Era de la Computadora. 17.95 (978-0-7835-3375-9(6)); Espacio y Planetas. 17.95 (978-0-7835-3370-4(5)); Estructura de la Materia (Structure of Matter) 17.95 (978-0-7835-3383-4(7)); Evolucion de la Vida. 17.95 (978-0-7835-3354-4(3)); Fuerzas Fisicas (Physical Forces) 17.95 (978-0-7835-3395-7(0)); Geografia. 17.95 (978-0-7835-3387-2(X)); Insectos y Aranas. 17.95 (978-0-7835-3398-8(5)); Maquinas e Inventos (Machines & Inventions) 17.95 (978-0-7835-3400-8(0)); Mundo Submarino (Underwater World) 17.95 (978-0-7835-3397-1(7)); Planeta Tierra (Planet Earth) 17.95 (978-0-7835-3396-4(9)); Plantas (Plant Life) 17.95 (978-0-7835-3399-5(3)); Tiempo y Clima (Weather & Climate) 17.95 (978-0-7835-3366-7(7)); Transporte y la Navegacion (Transportation) 17.95 (978-0-7835-3379-7(9)); 152p. (YA). (gr. 6-18). 1996. (Illus.). Set lib. bdg. 319.20 (978-0-7835-3391-9(8)) Time-Life, Inc.

Encyclopaedia Britannica Publishers, Inc. Staff. Britannica Illustrated Science Library, 16 vols., Set. 2008. (Illus.). 1664p. (YA). (gr. 5-8). 425.00 (978-1-59339-382-3(2)) Encyclopaedia Britannica, Inc.

Endres, Hollie J. What Computers Do, 6 vols., Set. 2003. (Yellow Umbrella Early Level Ser.). (ENG.). 16p. (gr. k-1). pap. 35.70 (978-0-7368-3018-8(9), Capstone Pr.) Capstone.

Enz, Tammy & Biskup, Agnieszka. Superman Science. 2016. (Superman Science Ser.). (ENG.). 32p. (J). (gr. 3-9). 119.96 (978-1-5157-0932-9(9), 24825, Stone Arch Bks.) Capstone.

Enz, Tammy, et al. Graphic Science & Engineering in Action. Baez, Marcelo, illus. 2013. (Graphic Science & Engineering in Action Ser.). (ENG.). 32p. (J). (gr. 3-9). pap., pap., pap. 31.80 (978-1-62065-707-2(4), 19303, Capstone Pr.) Capstone.

—Graphic Science & Engineering in Action Classroom Collection. Baez, Marcelo, illus. 2013. (Graphic Science & Engineering in Action Ser.). (ENG.). 32p. (J). (gr. 3-4). 198.40 (978-1-62065-708-9(2), 19304, Capstone Pr.) Capstone.

Esbaum, Jill. National Geographic Little Kids First Big Book of How. 2016. (National Geographic Little Kids First Big Bks.). (Illus.). 128p. (J). (gr. -1-k). 14.99 (978-1-4263-2329-4(8), National Geographic Kids) Disney Publishing Worldwide.

Essential Words Science(Intermediate) Intermediate/Middle School. 2005. (Illus.). 37p. (J). 8.95 (978-0-9764217-2-6(0)) New Leaf Educ., Inc.

Evan-Moor. English / Spanish Science Activities, Grades 1-3. 2005. (ENG & SPA.). 304p. (gr. 1-3). pap. 26.99 (978-1-55799-860-6(4), EMC 5306) Evan-Moor Educational Pubs.

—Spanish / English Read & nderstand Science Grades 4-6. 2007. (Spanish/English Read & Understand Ser.). (ENG., Illus.). 304p. (J). (gr. 4-6). pap. 29.99 (978-1-59673-077-9(3), EMC 5312) Evan-Moor Educational Pubs.

Evan-Moor Educational Publishers. Hands-On Science Themes. 2003. (ENG., Illus.). 208p. (J). (gr. 1-3). pap., tchr. ed. 24.99 (978-1-55799-935-1(X), EMC 5000) Evan-Moor Educational Pubs.

—Science Centers. 2005. (Take It to Your Seat: Science Centers Ser.). (ENG., Illus.). 192p. (J). (gr. -1-k). pap., tchr. ed. 24.99 (978-1-59673-090-8(0), EMC 5004) Evan-Moor Educational Pubs.

—Science Centers Grades 1-2. 2004. (Take It to Your Seat: Science Centers Ser.). (ENG., Illus.). 192p. (J). (gr. 1-2). pap., tchr. ed. 24.99 (978-1-55799-961-0(9), EMC 5002) Evan-Moor Educational Pubs.

—Science Centers Grades 3-4. 2004. (Take It to Your Seat: Science Centers Ser.). (ENG., Illus.). 192p. (J). (gr. 3-4). pap., tchr. ed. 23.99 (978-1-55799-962-7(7), EMC 5003) Evan-Moor Educational Pubs.

Evans, David & Williams, Claudette. Make It Change. (Let's Explore Science Ser.). (Illus.). (J). 12.95 (978-0-590-74511-6(5)) Scholastic, Inc.

Explore-a-Science Series. (J). (gr. k-6). 300.00 (978-0-669-19316-9(X)) Houghton Mifflin Harcourt School Pubs.

Exploring Physical Science, 6 vols. 2007. (Exploring Physical Science Ser.). (ENG.). (J). (gr. 6-6). lib. bdg. 103.41 (978-1-4042-1105-6(5), b660738b-510e-4345-91ee-62f9064e9c6c, Rosen Reference) Rosen Publishing Group, Inc., The.

Fabre, Jean-Henri. The Secret of Everyday Things. Bicknell, Florence Constable, tr. 2008. 404p. pap. 14.95 (978-1-59915-252-3(5)) Yesterday's Classics.

Facts on File, Inc. Staff, ed. Science in Focus, 6 Vols., Set. 2006. (Science in Focus Ser.). 48p. (gr. 4-6). 135.00 (978-0-7910-9444-0(8), Chelsea Clubhse.) Infobase Holdings, Inc.

Fantastic Science Journeys, 12 vols. 2014. (Fantastic Science Journeys Ser.). (ENG.). 32p. (J). (gr. 2-3). lib. bdg. 161.58 (978-1-4824-1637-4(9), 6c563eea-e072-48df-aec2-197a062ef1b1) Stevens, Gareth Publishing LLLP.

Farndon, John. Stickmen's Guide to Science. Matthews, Joe, illus. 2018. (Stickmen's Guides to STEM Ser.). (ENG.). 32p. (J). (gr. 3-6). lib. bdg. 27.99 (978-1-5415-0059-4(8), 99e95b9e-886e-47c0-88d3-0d509a4bd28a, Hungry Tomato (r)) Lerner Publishing Group.

Farndon, John & Beattie, Rob. Stuff You Need to Know! 2015. (ENG., Illus.). 80p. (J). (gr. 4-7). 19.95 (978-1-77085-656-1(0), 05bc71b6-bf30-49a9-af58-ab078a3845f2) Firefly Bks., Ltd.

Farndon, John & Graham, Ian. Discovering Science. 2010. (Science Library). 40p. (J). (gr. 3-18). lib. bdg. 19.95 *(978-1-4222-1548-7(2))* Mason Crest.

Farndon, John & Neave, Rosie. The Science Book. Kelly, Richard, ed. 2017. (ENG., Illus.). 160p. (J). 22.95 *(978-1-78209-841-6(0))* Miles Kelly Publishing, Ltd. GBR. Dist: Parkwest Pubns., Inc.

Farndon, John, et al. Stuff You Need to Know! 2015. (ENG., Illus.). 80p. (J). (gr. 4-7). pap. 12.95 *(978-1-77085-494-9(0),* b1c76cec-77bd-4fcd-9fcd-fd677c74e60a) Firefly Bks., Ltd.

Faucets & Water Sets: 1 Each of 3 Student Books. (Sunshinetm Science Ser.). (gr. 1-2). 20.95 *(978-0-7802-2815-3(4))* Wright Group/McGraw-Hill.

Ferrie, Chris. ABCs of Science. 2017. (Baby University Ser.: 0). (Illus.). 26p. (J). (gr. -1-k). bds. 9.99 *(978-1-4926-5631-9(3))* Sourcebooks, Inc.

Ferrie, Chris & Florance, Cara. Nuclear Physics for Babies. 2018. (Baby University Ser.: 0). (Illus.). 24p. (J). (gr. -1-k). bds. 9.99 *(978-1-4926-7117-6(7))* Sourcebooks, Inc.

Film Ideas Staff, creator. The Little Scientist: Here I Am! Camouflage. 2013. 89.00 *(978-1-60572-707-3(5))* Film Ideas, Inc.

Fischer, Stephen David & Caroll, Joseph. Science Detective Beginning: Higher-Order Thinking Reading Writing in Science. 2005. (Science Detective Ser.). 112p. (gr. 3-4). pap. 19.99 *(978-0-89455-834-4(X))* Critical Thinking Co., The.

Fleming, Christine. Art As Science. 2007. (Shockwave: Science in Practice Ser.). 36p. (J). lib. bdg. 6.95 *(978-0-531-15461-8(0),* Children's Pr.) Scholastic Library Publishing.

Flip Chart. 2003. (Scott Foresman Science Ser.). (gr. 3-18). suppl. ed. 262.50 *(978-0-673-59353-5(3))* Addison-Wesley Educational Pubs., Inc.

Floating & Sinking, 6 vols. (Sunshinetm Science Ser.). 24p. (gr. 1-2). 31.50 *(978-0-7802-0296-2(1));* 36.95 *(978-0-7802-0547-5(2))* Wright Group/McGraw-Hill.

Flynn, Riley. Finding Information & Making Arguments. 2016. (Science & Engineering Practices Ser.). (ENG., Illus.). 24p. (J). (gr. -1-2). lib. bdg. 27.32 *(978-1-5157-0948-0(5),* 132268, Capstone Pr.) Capstone.

—Science & Engineering Practices. 2016. (Science & Engineering Practices Ser.). (ENG., Illus.). 24p. (J). (gr. -1-2). pap., pap., pap. 27.80 *(978-1-5157-1388-3(1),* 24893, Capstone Pr.) Capstone.

—Using Facts & Investigating. 2016. (Science & Engineering Practices Ser.). (ENG., Illus.). 24p. (J). (gr. -1-2). lib. bdg. 27.32 *(978-1-5157-0949-7(3),* 132269, Capstone Pr.) Capstone.

—Using Models & Math in Science. 2016. (Science & Engineering Practices Ser.). (ENG., Illus.). 24p. (J). (gr. -1-2). lib. bdg. 27.32 *(978-1-5157-0950-3(7),* 132270, Capstone Pr.) Capstone.

Focus on Science Practice Test Book. 2005. (Focus on Science Ser.). 32p. pap. 30.60 *(978-1-4042-5212-7(6),* Rosen Classroom) Rosen Publishing Group, Inc., The.

Focus on Science Transparencies. 2005. (Focus on Science Ser.). 44.00 *(978-1-4042-5213-4(4),* Rosen Classroom) Rosen Publishing Group, Inc., The.

Forest Service (U.S.), ed. NSI: Nature Science Investigator: Nature Science Investigator Is a Natural Inquirer Publication. Pfeiffer, Stephanie, illus. 2017. (ENG.). 24p. (J). pap. 4.00 *(978-0-16-093869-6(4),* Forest Service) United States Government Printing Office.

Forte, Imogene. Ready to Learn Beginning Science. 2003. (Illus.). 64p. per. 7.95 *(978-0-86530-593-4(6))* Incentive Pubns., Inc.

—Ready to Learn Following Directions. 2003. (Illus.). 64p. per. 7.95 *(978-0-86530-596-0(X))* Incentive Pubns., Inc.

—Science Fun. 2004. (Fun Things to Make & Do Ser.). (Illus.). (J). per. 9.95 *(978-0-86530-620-2(6))* Incentive Pubns., Inc.

Forte, Imogene & Schurr, Sandra. Standards-Based Science Graphic Organizers & Rubrics. 2004. 128p. (J). per. 13.95 *(978-0-86530-628-8(1))* Incentive Pubns., Inc.

Foster, Patience. Pocket Scientist. 2004. (ENG.). 1p. (J). 8.95 *(978-0-7945-0209-6(1))* EDC Publishing.

Foster, Ruth. Nonfiction Reading Comprehension - Science. 2006. (ENG.). 144p. pap. 16.99 *(978-1-4206-8026-3(9))* Teacher Created Resources, Inc.

—Nonfiction Reading Comprehension - Science, Grade 3. 2006. (ENG.). 144p. pap. 16.99 *(978-1-4206-8021-8(8))* Teacher Created Resources, Inc.

Freaky True Science. 2015. (Freaky True Science Ser.). (ENG.). 32p. (J). (gr. 4-5). pap., pap., pap. 63.00 *(978-1-4824-3470-5(9));* pap., pap., pap. 378.00 *(978-1-4824-3469-9(5));* lib. bdg. 169.62 *(978-1-4824-2554-3(8),* c2ce9237-884a-45ac-b6a6-36d32bbc9e07) Stevens, Gareth Publishing LLLP.

Freaky True Science: Set 2, 12 vols. 2016. (Freaky True Science Ser.). 32p. (ENG.). (gr. 4-5). lib. bdg. 169.62 *(978-1-4824-4608-1(1),* 486b71eb-4fa0-4572-b13f-f0e16a6fa013); (gr. 5-4). pap. 63.00 *(978-1-4824-5396-6(7))* Stevens, Gareth Publishing LLLP.

Frith, Alex. See Inside Science. 2007. 16p. (J). bds. 12.99 *(978-0-7945-1549-2(5),* Usborne) EDC Publishing.

—100 Things to Know about Science. 2015. (Illustrated Dictionaries Ser.). (ENG.). 128p. (J). (gr. k-5). pap. 12.99 *(978-0-7945-3502-5(X),* Usborne) EDC Publishing.

From Flowers to Fruit: 6 Each of 1 Student Book, 6 vols. (Sunshinetm Science Ser.). 24p. (gr. 1-2). 41.95 *(978-0-7802-2686-9(0))* Wright Group/McGraw-Hill.

From Flowers to Fruit: Big Book. (Sunshinetm Science Ser.). 24p. (gr. 1-2). 37.50 *(978-0-7802-2777-4(8))* Wright Group/McGraw-Hill.

Fry, Jenny & Award, Anna. The Ultimate Book of Questions & Answers. 2012. (Illus.). 48p. (J). 24.95 *(978-1-899762-93-4(0))* Award Pubns. Ltd. GBR. Dist: Parkwest Pubns., Inc.

Fuerst, Jeffrey B. Look at it Go! Lap Book. 2009. (My First Reader's Theater Set B Ser.). (J). 28.00 *(978-1-935441-02-1(7))* Benchmark Education Co.

Furgang, Kathy. Working with Electricity & Magnetism: Set Of 6. 2011. (Navigators Ser.). (J). pap. 48.00 net. *(978-1-4108-0438-9(0))* Benchmark Education Co.

Ganeri, Anita. Fearsome Forces of Nature, 1 vol. 2012. (Extreme Nature Ser.). (ENG.). 32p. (gr. 3-5). pap. 8.29 *(978-1-4109-4701-7(7),* 119202, Raintree) Capstone.

Gardner, Jane. Black Achievement in Science: Environmental Science, Vol. 10. Pouson, Mel, ed. 2016. (Black Achievement in Science Ser.: Vol. 10). (ENG., Illus.). 64p. (J). (gr. 7-12). 23.95 *(978-1-4222-3559-1(9))* Mason Crest.

Georgia Striving Readers Science K-5. 2012. (CAP-Marketing Ser.). (ENG.). (gr. k-5). pap. 1782.84 *(978-1-62065-957-1(3))* Capstone.

Getting Cold! Getting Hot!, 6 vols. (Sunshinetm Science Ser.). 24p. (gr. 1-2). 37.50 *(978-0-7802-1405-7(6));* 41.95 *(978-0-7802-1404-0(8))* Wright Group/McGraw-Hill.

Getting Rid of Waste Water: 6 Each of 1 Student Book, 6 vols. (Sunshinetm Science Ser.). 24p. (gr. 1-2). 41.95 *(978-0-7802-2692-0(5))* Wright Group/McGraw-Hill.

Getting Rid of Waste Water: Big Book. (Sunshinetm Science Ser.). 24p. (gr. 1-2). 37.50 *(978-0-7802-2780-4(8))* Wright Group/McGraw-Hill.

Getting the Water We Need: 6 Each of 1 Student Book, 6 vols. (Sunshinetm Science Ser.). 24p. (gr. 1-2). 41.95 *(978-0-7802-2690-6(9))* Wright Group/McGraw-Hill.

Getting the Water We Need: Big Book. (Sunshinetm Science Ser.). 24p. (gr. 1-2). 37.50 *(978-0-7802-2779-8(4))* Wright Group/McGraw-Hill.

Gifford, Clive. Science of Computers. 2015. (Get Connected to Digital Literacy Ser.). (ENG.). 32p. (J). (gr. 3-6). 19.75 *(978-1-5311-8488-9(X))* Perfection Learning Corp.

Gilpin, Rebecca & Pratt, Leonie. Big Book of Science Things to Make & Do. Thompson, Josephine, illus. 2008. (Big Book of Science Things to Make & Do Ser.). 95p. (J). (gr. 1). pap. 14.99 *(978-0-7945-1923-0(7),* Usborne) EDC Publishing.

Glencoe McGraw-Hill Staff, creator. Glencoe Science Level Blue, Level Blue. 2003. (Illus.). 818p. (J). lib. bdg., stu. ed. 74.64 *(978-0-07-828242-3(X))* Glencoe/McGraw-Hill.

Gottlieb. Matter, Motion & Machines. 2004. (Wonders of Science Ser.). (ENG.). (gr. 7-12). 176p. pap., tchr. ed. 27.70 *(978-0-7398-9185-8(5));* (Illus.). 144p. pap. 24.55 *(978-0-7398-9179-7(0))* Houghton Mifflin Harcourt Publishing Co.

Graham, Amy. Astonishing Ancient World Scientists: Eight Great Brains, 1 vol. 2009. (Great Scientists & Famous Inventors Ser.). (ENG., Illus.). 128p. (gr. 6-7). lib. bdg. 37.27 *(978-1-59845-079-8(4),* 4e5b556f-9694-404a-a25e-3fa0eafcb78a) Enslow Publishing, LLC.

Grant, R. G. Superstars of Science. Basher, Simon, illus. 2015. (ENG.). 96p. (J). (gr. 3-7). pap. 7.99 *(978-0-545-82627-3(6),* Scholastic Paperbacks) Scholastic, Inc.

—Superstars of Science: The Brave, the Bold, & the Brainy. 2015. lib. bdg. 18.40 *(978-0-606-37753-9(0))* Turtleback.

Graphic Science Collection. 2010. (Graphic Science Ser.). (ENG.). 32p. (gr. 3-4). pap. 174.90 *(978-1-4296-5148-6(2),* Capstone Pr.) Capstone.

Great Minds of Science, 19 bks., Set. (Illus.). (J). (gr. 4-10). lib. bdg. 398.05 *(978-0-89490-566-7(X))* Enslow Publishing, LLC.

Greenling, Jason. The Technology of Ancient China, 1 vol. 2016. (Ancient Innovations Ser.). (ENG., Illus.). 64p. (gr. 6-6). 35.93 *(978-1-5026-2235-8(1),* c72737ab-45b0-4f71-aee0-91b356953737) Cavendish Square Publishing LLC.

Groessen und Masse. (Duden-Schuelerhilfen Ser.). (GER.). 96p. (J). (gr. 4-5). *(978-3-411-02610-4(3))* Bibliographisches Institut & F. A. Brockhaus AG DEU. Dist: International Bk. Import Service, Inc.

Group/McGraw-Hill, Wright. Cold Facts about Ice Ages, 6 vols. (Book2WebTM Ser.). (gr. 4-8). 36.50 *(978-0-322-04434-0(0))* Wright Group/McGraw-Hill.

—Dreams of Flight, 6 vols. (Book2WebTM Ser.). (gr. 4-8). 36.50 *(978-0-322-04433-3(2))* Wright Group/McGraw-Hill.

—Earth & Physical Science: Color & Light, 6 vols. (Book2WebTM Ser.). (gr. 4-8). 36.50 *(978-0-322-04429-6(4))* Wright Group/McGraw-Hill.

—Earth & Physical Science: Exploring Electricity, 6 vols. (Book2WebTM Ser.). (gr. 4-8). 36.50 *(978-0-322-04428-9(6))* Wright Group/McGraw-Hill.

—Famous Shipwrecks, 6 vols. (Book2WebTM Ser.). (gr. 4-8). 36.50 *(978-0-322-04458-6(8))* Wright Group/McGraw-Hill.

—Inventors Create Tomorrow, 6 vols. (Book2WebTM Ser.). (gr. 4-8). 36.50 *(978-0-322-04469-2(3))* Wright Group/McGraw-Hill.

—Mountain Majesty, 6 vols. (Book2WebTM Ser.). (gr. 4-8). 36.50 *(978-0-322-04440-1(5))* Wright Group/McGraw-Hill.

—People on the Path Toward Human Rights, 6 vols. (Book2WebTM Ser.). (gr. 4-8). 36.50 *(978-0-322-04466-1(9))* Wright Group/McGraw-Hill.

—Wonder World Complete Sets: Science Set - 1 Each of 97 Titles. (Wonder Worldtm Ser.). (gr. k-6). 501.95 *(978-0-322-06714-1(6))* Wright Group/McGraw-Hill.

—Wonder World Early & Upper Emergent Sets: Science Set - 1 Each of 49 Titles. (Wonder Worldtm Ser.). (gr. k-6). 229.50 *(978-0-322-06721-9(9))* Wright Group/McGraw-Hill.

—Wonder World Early Fluency & Fluency: Science Set - 1 Each of 48 Titles. (Wonder Worldtm Ser.). (gr. k-6). 299.50 *(978-0-322-06717-2(0))* Wright Group/McGraw-Hill.

Groves, Marcia, et al. Science & Technology in the Middle Ages, 1 vol. 2004. (Medieval World Ser.). (ENG., Illus.). 32p. (J). pap. *(978-0-7787-1386-9(5))* Crabtree Publishing Co.

Gutman, Dan. My Weird School Fast Facts: Space, Humans, & Farts. Paillot, Jim, illus. 2017. (My Weird School Fast Facts Ser.). (ENG.). 192p. (J). (gr. 1-5). pap. 5.99 *(978-0-06-230626-5(X),* HarperCollins) HarperCollins Pubs.

Hagler, Gina. The Technology of Ancient India, 1 vol. 2016. (Spotlight on the Rise & Fall of Ancient Civilizations Ser.). (ENG.). 48p. (YA). (gr. 6-6). pap. 12.75 *(978-1-4777-8942-1(1),* 570bb2ec-28dd-4ef7-9e72-bb28cd2f9b45) Rosen Publishing Group, Inc., The.

Hall, Kirsten. Glow-in-The-Dark Zombie Science. Myers, Lawrence E., illus. 2009. 32p. (J). pap. *(978-0-545-22626-4(0))* Scholastic, Inc.

Hands: Level B, 6 vols. 8p. 24.95 *(978-0-7802-8915-4(3))* Wright Group/McGraw-Hill.

Hands-On Science, 12 vols. 2016. (Hands-On Science Ser.). (ENG.). 48p. (J). (gr. 4-4). lib. bdg. 177.60 *(978-0-7660-8392-9(6),* 53c71e7d-3bc8-4976-b861-4fcc7c4322d1) Enslow Publishing, LLC.

Hansen, Grace. Beginning Science, 6 vols., Set. 2018. (Beginning Science: Body Systems Ser.). (ENG.). 24p. (J). (gr. -1-2). lib. bdg. 196.74 *(978-1-5321-8183-2(3),* 29839, Abdo Kids) ABDO Publishing Co.

—Curiosidades Científicas Increíbles! (Science Facts to Surprise You!) 2016. (Ver para Creer (Seeing Is Believing) Ser.). (SPA., Illus.). 24p. (J). (gr. -1-2). lib. bdg. 32.79 *(978-1-68080-771-4(4),* 22704, Abdo Kids) ABDO Publishing Co.

—Science Facts to Surprise You!, 1 vol. 2015. (Seeing Is Believing Ser.). (ENG.). 24p. (J). (gr. -1-2). lib. bdg. 32.79 *(978-1-62970-734-1(1),* 17285, Abdo Kids) ABDO Publishing Co.

Hansen, Merrily P. A Close-Up Look at Plants: A Content Area Reader-Science. 2005. (Sadlier Phonics Reading Program). (Illus.). 16p. (gr. k-2). 25.20 *(978-0-8215-7811-7(1))* Sadlier, William H. Inc.

Hantula, Richard & Asimov, Isaac. Science Fiction: Vision of Tomorrow?, 1 vol. 2004. (Isaac Asimov's 21st Century Library of the Universe: Fact & Fantasy Ser.). (ENG., Illus.). 32p. (gr. 3-5). lib. bdg. 28.67 *(978-0-8368-3952-4(8),* 88ba2be3-3e6c-46e6-9149-e224d6fb5b51) Stevens, Gareth Publishing LLLP.

Harbo, Christopher L. Monster Science. Aón, Carlos, illus. 2013. (Monster Science Ser.). (ENG.). 32p. (J). (gr. 3-9). pap., pap., pap. 81.00 *(978-1-4765-3674-3(0),* 20166, Capstone Pr.) Capstone.

Harcourt School Publishers, creator. Energy Transfer & Weather: Lessons 2-3. 2006. (ENG.). pap. 27.00 *(978-0-15-354814-7(2))* Harcourt Schl. Pubs.

—Matter Matters! 2006. (ENG.). pap. 27.00 *(978-0-15-354738-6(3))* Harcourt Schl. Pubs.

Harcourt School Publishers Staff. Harcourt Science: Physical Science Instant Reader CD-ROM Teacher's Guide. 2nd ed. 2003. (Harcourt Science Ser.). (gr. k-18). tchr. ed. 8.00 incl. cd-rom *(978-0-15-324957-0(9))* Harcourt Schl. Pubs.

Harris, Tim. Life Science, 1 vol. 2015. (Science Q & A Ser.). (ENG.). 32p. (gr. 3-3). pap. 11.58 *(978-1-5026-0621-1(6),* d4b44eb0-90db-4c25-a2fc-3134e6e96e67) Cavendish Square Publishing LLC.

Hassard, Jack. Science As Inquiry. 2004. (Illus.). 280p. pap. 19.95 *(978-0-673-57731-3(7))* Good Year Bks.

Hawkins, Jay. Really Horrible Science Facts, 1 vol. 2013. (Really Horrible Facts Ser.). (ENG.). 32p. (J). (gr. 4-5). pap. 11.00 *(978-1-61533-807-8(1),* 65ff4f6c-5b2b-4395-ba50-28bc0f020edd, Windmill Bks.) Rosen Publishing Group, Inc., The.

—Really Horrible Science Facts. 2013. (Really Horrible Facts Ser.). 32p. (J). (gr. k-3). pap. 60.00 *(978-1-61533-808-5(X))* Windmill Bks.

Hessel-Mial, Michael. How STEM Built the Chinese Dynasties, 1 vol. 2019. (How STEM Built Empires Ser.). (ENG.). 80p. (gr. 7-7). pap. 16.30 *(978-1-7253-4137-1(9),* 52c40482-3afd-4b12-b46b-eb95bffaa821) Rosen Publishing Group, Inc., The.

—How STEM Built the Incan Empire, 1 vol. 2019. (How STEM Built Empires Ser.). (ENG.). 80p. (gr. 7-7). pap. 16.30 *(978-1-7253-4146-3(8),* 8e00ab78-4c0f-4950-9a94-e3ae4af76b2e) Rosen Publishing Group, Inc., The.

Hestermann, Bethanie & Hestermann, Josh. Marine Science for Kids: Exploring & Protecting Our Watery World, Includes Cool Careers & 21 Activities. 2017. (For Kids Ser.: 66). (Illus.). 144p. (J). (gr. 4). pap. 18.99 *(978-1-61373-536-7(7))* Chicago Review Pr., Inc.

Hewitt, Sally. Listen Up!, 5 vols. 2005. (QEB Let's Start! Science Ser.). (Illus.). 24p. (J). (gr. 1-4). lib. bdg. 15.95 *(978-1-59566-086-2(0))* QEB Publishing Inc.

—Look Here!, 5 vols. 2005. (QEB Let's Start! Science Ser.). (Illus.). 24p. (J). (gr. 1-4). lib. bdg. 15.95 *(978-1-59566-087-9(9))* QEB Publishing Inc.

—Smell That!, 5 vols. 2005. (QEB Let's Start! Science Ser.). (Illus.). 24p. (J). (gr. 1-4). lib. bdg. 15.95 *(978-1-59566-088-6(7))* QEB Publishing Inc.

—Tastes Good!, 5 vols. 2005. (QEB Let's Start! Science Ser.). (Illus.). 24p. (J). (gr. 1-4). lib. bdg. 15.95 *(978-1-59566-089-3(5))* QEB Publishing Inc.

—Touch That!, 5 vols. 2005. (QEB Let's Start! Science Ser.). (Illus.). 24p. (J). (gr. 1-4). lib. bdg. 15.95 *(978-1-59566-090-9(9))* QEB Publishing Inc.

Hibbert, Clare. The Story of Life, 1 vol. 2018. (Science Explorers Ser.). (ENG.). 32p. (gr. 3-3). lib. bdg. 26.93 *(978-1-9785-0646-6(5),* 7c91984f-62f3-40cb-a4fd-a018f08715ed) Enslow Publishing, LLC.

Hicks, Kelli. Analyze This: Testing Ingredients. 2012. (My Science Library). (ENG., Illus.). 24p. (gr. 4-5). pap. 8.95 *(978-1-61810-243-0(5),* 9781618102430) Rourke Educational Media.

—I Can Prove It! Investigating Science. 2012. (My Science Library). (ENG.). 24p. (gr. 4-5). pap. 8.95 *(978-1-61810-244-7(3),* 9781618102447) Rourke Educational Media.

Hilltree, Angela. ABC Coloring Book: Creation Science & Geology. 2004. (Illus.). 26p. (J). 6.50 *(978-1-931941-10-5(6))* Media Angels, Inc.

Hirschfeld, Pam, ed. Under the Sea with Jacques Cousteau. Urbanovic, Jackie; Hirschfeld, illus. 2004. (Reader's Theater Content-Area Concepts Ser.). (ENG.). (J). (gr. 1-2). 5.00 net. *(978-1-4108-0801-1(7))* Benchmark Education Co.

—Welcome to Waterworld. Porte, Carolyn La; Hirschfeld, illus. 2004. (Reader's Theater Content-Area Concepts Ser.). (ENG.). (J). (gr. 2). 5.00 net. *(978-1-4108-0796-0(7))* Benchmark Education Co.

Hirschmann, Kris. The Science of Super Powers: An Incredibles Discovery Book. 2019. (Disney Learning Discovery Bks.). (ENG., Illus.). 48p. (J). (gr. 2-5). pap. 8.99 *(978-1-5415-7390-1(0),* 9781541573901); lib. bdg. 31.99 *(978-1-5415-5489-4(2),* 9781541554894) Lerner Publishing Group. (Lerner Pubns.).

Hirschmann, Kris & Herndon, Ryan. Test Your Smarts! Science. 2009. (Illus.). 80p. (J). pap. *(978-0-545-12041-8(1))* Scholastic, Inc.

Hixson, Bryce. Newton Take 3. Hixson, Bryce, illus. 2003. (Illus.). (J). per. 14.95 *(978-0-9660965-3-8(3))* Loose In The Lab.

—What's Up? Hixson, Bryce, illus. 2003. (Illus.). (J). per. 14.95 *(978-1-931801-05-8(3))* Loose In The Lab.

Holden, Arianne. It's Fun to Learn about Science: A Busy Picture Book Full of Fabulous Facts & Things to Do! 2016. (Illus.). 32p. (J). (gr. -1-12). 9.99 *(978-1-86147-742-2(2),* Armadillo) Anness Publishing GBR. Dist: National Bk. Network.

Holden, Edward S. The Sciences. 2009. (Illus.). 254p. pap. 11.95 *(978-1-59915-338-4(6))* Yesterday's Classics.

Holmes. Gateway Science. 5th ed. (J). Level 3. 349.98 *(978-0-07-030003-3(8))*Level K. 23.61 *(978-0-07-029942-9(0))* Macmillan/McGraw-Hill Schl. Div.

Holt, Rinehart and Winston Staff. Environmental Science Chptr. 8: Population & Communities. 4th ed. Date not set. pap. 11.20 *(978-0-03-068067-0(0))* Holt McDougal.

—Environmental Science Chptr. 9: The Human Population. 4th ed. Date not set. pap. 11.20 *(978-0-03-068068-7(9))* Holt McDougal.

—Harcourt Science & Technology: Strategies & Practice Answer Key. 4th ed. 2004. (Illus.). pap. 6.00 *(978-0-03-019863-2(1))* Holt McDougal.

—Holt Science & Technology. 4th annot. ed. 2004. tchr. ed. 128.80 *(978-0-03-073174-7(7))* Holt McDougal.

—Holt Science & Technology: Chapter Resources. 5th ed. 2005. pap. 87.36 *(978-0-03-030632-7(9))* Holt McDougal.

—Holt Science & Technology: Directed Reading Answer Key. 4th ed. 2004. (Illus.). pap. 11.20 *(978-0-03-037018-2(3))* Holt McDougal.

—Holt Science & Technology: Directed Reading Worksheets. 4th ed. 2004. pap. 15.00 *(978-0-03-036994-0(0));* pap. 15.00 *(978-0-03-036993-3(2));* pap. 15.00 *(978-0-03-036992-6(4))* Holt McDougal.

—Holt Science & Technology: Enhanced Online Edition - Short Course. 5th ed. 2004. (J). (gr. k). 18.60 *(978-0-03-030493-4(8));* (gr. 1). 18.60 *(978-0-03-030496-5(2));* (gr. 2). 18.60 *(978-0-03-030501-6(2))* Holt McDougal.

—Holt Science & Technology: Physical Science. 5th ed. 2004. (Holt Science & Technology Ser.). (Illus.). pap., stu. ed. 17.13 *(978-0-03-030161-2(0))* Holt McDougal.

—Holt Science & Technology: Physical Science: Reading & Comprehension Guide. 5th ed. 2004. (Holt Science & Technology Ser.). pap. 17.13 *(978-0-03-036063-3(3))* Holt McDougal.

—Holt Science & Technology: Physical Science: Special Needs Workbook. 5th ed. 2004. (Holt Science & Technology Ser.). pap., wbk. ed. 17.13 *(978-0-03-036056-5(0))* Holt McDougal.

—Holt Science & Technology: Program Introduction Booklet. 5th ed. 2004. (Illus.). 4.33 *(978-0-03-030162-9(9))* Holt McDougal.

—Life Science: Directed Reading & Vocabulary Workbook. 5th ed. 2004. (Holt Science & Technology Ser.). (SPA., Illus.). pap., wbk. ed. 17.13 *(978-0-03-036057-2(9))* Holt McDougal.

—Life Science: Study Guide. 5th ed. 2004. (Holt Science & Technology Ser.). (SPA., Illus.). pap., stu. ed. 17.13 *(978-0-03-030151-3(3))* Holt McDougal.

—Life Science 2005. 5th ed. 2004. (Holt Ciencias y Technologia Ser.). (SPA & ENG., Illus.). 912p. (gr. 6-6). stu. ed. 110.60 *(978-0-03-021179-9(4))* Houghton Mifflin Harcourt Publishing Co.

—Physical Science: Chapter Resources. 5th ed. 2004. (Holt Science & Technology Ser.). (Illus.). pap. 290.13 *(978-0-03-030126-1(2))* Holt McDougal.

—Physical Science: Directed Reading & Vocabulary Workbook. 5th ed. 2004. (Holt Science & Technology Ser.). (SPA., Illus.). pap., wbk. ed. 17.13 *(978-0-03-036059-6(5))* Holt McDougal.

—Physical Science 2005. 5th ed. 2004. (Holt Ciencias y Technologia Ser.). (SPA & ENG., Illus.). 848p. (gr. 8-8). stu. ed. 110.60 *(978-0-03-021272-7(3))* Houghton Mifflin Harcourt Publishing Co.

—Science Skills Workshop. 2nd ed. 2009. (Holt Biology Ser.). (ENG.). 192p. (gr. 6-12). pap. 34.25 *(978-0-03-064424-5(0))* Houghton Mifflin Harcourt Publishing Co.

Hopper, Whitney. Time to Go to the Science Museum! Work with Time, 1 vol. 2014. (Math Masters: Measurement & Data Ser.). (ENG.). 24p. (J). (gr. 2-2). 25.27 *(978-1-4777-6406-0(2),* 0b60b671-2de3-4651-839b-bef3c3dceaf8); pap. 8.25 *(978-1-4777-4819-0(9),* 3d4f306a-11c5-4baf-9205-f39ebd8c3f6b) Rosen Publishing Group, Inc., The. (Rosen Classroom).

How Are They Built?, 6 bks., Set. (J). (gr. 4-8). lib. bdg. 179.57 *(978-1-58952-133-9(1))* Rourke Educational Media.

How Bread Is Made: 6 Each of 1 Student Book, 6 vols. (Sunshinetm Science Ser.). 24p. (gr. 1-2). 41.95 *(978-0-7802-2724-8(7))* Wright Group/McGraw-Hill.

How Bread Is Made: Big Book. (Sunshinetm Science Ser.). 24p. (gr. 1-2). 37.50 *(978-0-7802-2796-5(4))* Wright Group/McGraw-Hill.

How Can We See in the Dark?, 6 vols. (Sunshinetm Science Ser.). 24p. (gr. 1-2). 36.95 *(978-0-7802-0556-7(1));* 31.50 *(978-0-7802-0305-1(4))* Wright Group/McGraw-Hill.

Hubble Science Cards. 2003. (Illus.). 44p. 7.99 *(978-0-9741147-0-5(7))* Phlare, Inc.

Huffman, Julie. 101 Ways to Gross Out Your Friends. 2017. (101 Ser.). (ENG., Illus.). 144p. (J). (gr. 3-5). 33.32 *(978-1-942875-16-1(9),* 1fe51a52-d2f5-4da2-ba13-15dffcad564b, Walter Foster Jr) Quarto Publishing Group USA.

Hughes, Colin & Wade, Winnie. How to Be a Wizard at Science Investigations. (J). (gr. 3-6). pap. *(978-1-876367-30-5(X))* Wizard Bks.

—How to Be Brilliant at Living Things. 2004. (Illus.). 48p. pap. 30.00 *(978-1-897675-66-3(6))* Brilliant Pubns. GBR. Dist: Parkwest Pubns., Inc.

Hunter, Dru. How Do We Apply Science? 2016. (Think Like a Scientist Ser.). (ENG.). 48p. (J). (gr. 4-7). pap. 12.00 *(978-1-62832-197-5(0),* 21061, Creative Paperbacks) Creative Co., The.

Hurd. Physical Science. 3rd ed. (J). 59.47 *(978-0-13-982158-5(9))* Prentice Hall (Schl. Div.).

Ignotofsky, Rachel. I Love Science: A Journal for Self-Discovery & Big Ideas. 2017. (Women in Science Ser.). (Illus.). 192p. 14.99 (978-1-60774-980-6(7), Ten Speed Pr.) Potter/Ten Speed/Harmony/Rodale.

The Impact of Science & Technology, 12 vols. 2009. (Pros & Cons Ser.). (ENG.). 64p. (J). (gr. 5-8). lib. bdg. 226.02 (978-1-4339-2004-2(2), 3adbae23-5f06-44dc-8c90-bb05fca799f9, Gareth Stevens Secondary Library) Stevens, Gareth Publishing LLLP.

Innes, Brian. Forensic Science. 2004. (Crime & Detection Ser.). (Illus.). 96p. (YA). (gr. 7-18). lib. bdg. 22.95 (978-1-59084-373-4(8)) Mason Crest.

Instructional Resources. 2003. (Scott Foresman Science Ser.). (gr. 6-18). suppl. ed. 47.95 (978-0-673-59337-5(1)) Addison-Wesley Educational Pubs., Inc.

Interactive Transparency Package. 2003. (gr. k-18). suppl. ed. 109.15 (978-0-673-59454-9(8)); (gr. 1-18). suppl. ed. 109.15 (978-0-673-59455-6(6)); (gr. 2-18). suppl. ed. 109.15 (978-0-673-59456-3(4)); (gr. 3-18). suppl. ed. 109.15 (978-0-673-59457-0(2)); (gr. 4-18). suppl. ed. 109.15 (978-0-673-59458-7(0)); (gr. 5-18). suppl. ed. 109.15 (978-0-673-59459-4(9)); (gr. 6-18). suppl. ed. 109.15 (978-0-673-59460-0(2)) Addison-Wesley Educational Pubs., Inc.

Inventions. 2017. (J). (978-0-7166-7948-6(5)) World Bk., Inc.

Iopeners: Big Book Collection, 20 vols. 2005. (J). (gr. k-18). 525.95 (978-0-7652-4972-2(3)); (gr. 1-18). 587.50 (978-0-7652-4976-0(6)) Modern Curriculum Pr.

Iopeners: Classroom Library. 2005. (J). (gr. k-18). 440.50 (978-0-7652-4969-2(3)); (gr. 1-18). 518.50 (978-0-7652-4973-9(1)); (gr. 2-18). 518.50 (978-0-7652-4977-7(4)); (gr. 3-18). 616.50 (978-0-7652-4980-7(4)); (gr. 4-18). 616.50 (978-0-7652-4983-8(9)); (gr. 5-18). 694.50 (978-0-7652-4986-9(3)); (gr. 6-18). 694.50 (978-0-7652-4989-0(8)) Modern Curriculum Pr.

Is it Floating?, 6 vols. (Sunshinetm Science Ser.). 24p. (gr. 1-2). 31.50 (978-0-7802-0295-5(3)); 36.95 (978-0-7802-0546-8(4)) Wright Group/McGraw-Hill.

Issues, Evidence & You Complete Materials Package. 2003. (Illus.). (YA). tchr. ed., ring bd. (978-1-887725-71-2(7)) Lab-Aids, Inc.

Issues, Evidence & You Complete Materials Package: Includes Teacher's Guide & Student Books. 2003. (Illus.). (YA). (978-1-887725-72-9(5)) Lab-Aids, Inc.

Issues, Evidence & You Complete Materials Package for Chicago Public Schools. 2003. (Illus.). (YA). ring bd. (978-1-887725-84-2(9)) Lab-Aids, Inc.

Ivanoff, George. How to Make a Fake Death Ray into a Real Laser. 2007. 96p. (J). (978-1-4207-0735-9(3)) Sundance/Newbridge Educational Publishing.

Iyer, Rani. The Science of Super Strength & Super Speed, 1 vol. 2018. (Science of Superpowers Ser.). (ENG.). 48p. (J). (gr. 4-4). 33.07 (978-1-5026-3793-2(6), 4f749d7c-9328-4125-bd3c-ce66be4d0999) Cavendish Square Publishing LLC.

Jacobs, Daniel. For Your Information. Date not set. (Early Science Big Bks.). (Illus.). 16p. (J). (gr. -1-2). pap. 16.95 (978-1-58273-123-0(3)) Sundance/Newbridge Educational Publishing.

James, Frank A. J. L., ed. Christmas at the Royal Institution: An Anthology of Lectures by M Faraday, J Tyndall, R S Ball, S P Thompson, E R Lankester, W H Bragg, W L Bragg, R L Gregory, & I Stewart. 2008. (ENG., Illus.). 366p. (978-981-277-108-7(5)) World Scientific Publishing Co. Pte Ltd.

James, Frank A. L., ed. Christmas at the Royal Institution: An Anthology of Lectures by M Faraday, J Tyndall, R S Ball, S P Thompson, E R Lankester, W H Bragg, W L Bragg, R L Gregory, & I Stewart. 2008. (ENG., Illus.). 366p. pap. (978-981-277-109-4(3)) World Scientific Publishing Co. Pte Ltd.

Jason Science Adventure: Aquatic Field Study. 2004. (J). (978-0-9763809-0-0(0)) JASON Project, The.

Jo, Eun-sook. Ah, I Am Full! Food Chain. Kwon, Yeong-mook, illus. 2015. (Science Storybooks Ser.). (ENG.). 32p. (J). (gr. k-4). 27.99 (978-1-925233-59-9(6), 9446d666-8835-45fb-913d-d4bdf5a2a861, Big and SMALL) ChoiceMaker Pty. Ltd., The AUS. Dist: Lerner Publishing Group.

Johnson, Rose. Discoveries in Life Science That Changed the World, 1 vol. 2014. (Scientific Breakthroughs Ser.). (ENG.). 48p. (YA). (gr. 6-6). 33.47 (978-1-4777-8607-9(4), a4c7da51-2568-4813-b30a-a10d2a1245d9, Rosen Reference) Rosen Publishing Group, Inc., The.

Jones, Mary. Cambridge Checkpoint Science Coursebook 7. 2012. (ENG., Illus.). 191p. pap. 41.30 (978-1-107-61333-1(7)) Cambridge Univ. Pr.

—Cambridge Checkpoint Science Workbook 7. 2012. (ENG., Illus.). 96p. pap. 19.60 (978-1-107-62285-2(9)) Cambridge Univ. Pr.

—Cambridge IGCSE(r) Combined & Co-Ordinated Sciences Coursebook with CD-ROM, 1 vol. 2017. (Cambridge International IGCSE Ser.). (ENG., Illus.). 680p. pap. 61.20 incl. cd-rom (978-1-316-63101-0(X)) Cambridge Univ. Pr.

Jones, Mary, et al. Cambridge Checkpoint Science. Coursebook. Per la Scuola Media. 2013. (ENG., Illus.). 188p. pap. 41.30 (978-1-107-62606-5(4)) Cambridge Univ. Pr.

—Cambridge Checkpoint Science. Workbook. Per la Scuola Media. 2013. (ENG., Illus.). 120p. pap. 19.60 (978-1-107-69574-0(0)) Cambridge Univ. Pr.

Juliano, Larissa. How to Build a Leprechaun Trap. 2018. 96p. (J). (gr. k-5). pap. 10.99 (978-1-4926-6388-1(3)) Sourcebooks, Inc.

Kalam, A. P. J. Reignited. 2015. (ENG., Illus.). 272p. (J). pap. 8.99 (978-0-14-333354-8(2), Puffin) Penguin Bks. India PVT, Ltd IND. Dist: Independent Pubs. Group.

Kalman, Bobbie. El Ciclo de Vida de la Abeja. 2005. (Serie Ciclos de Vida Ser.). (SPA., Illus.). 32p. (J). lib. bdg. (978-0-7787-8666-5(8)); (gr. 1-4). pap. (978-0-7787-8712-9(5)) Crabtree Publishing Co.

Kalman, Bobbie & Langille, Jacqueline. ¿Qué Es el Ciclo de Vida? 2005. (Ciencia de los Seres Vivos Ser.). (SPA., Illus.). 32p. (J). (gr. 2-4). pap. (978-0-7787-8800-3(8)) Crabtree Publishing Co.

Karapetian, Marjam. Bilingual Content Dictionary: English to Spanish. 2004. (SPA & ENG.). 13.95 (978-0-9764829-4-9(0)); 15.95 (978-0-9764829-5-6(9)) WizdomInc.

Kassnoff, David. What Degree Do I Need to Pursue a Career in Information Technology & Information Systems?, 1 vol. 2014. (Right Degree for Me Ser.). (ENG., Illus.). 80p. (J). (gr. 7-7). 37.80 (978-1-4777-7865-4(9), 7b6dc337-1c5f-48aa-9cf5-71badf3f1c07, Rosen Young Adult) Rosen Publishing Group, Inc., The.

Kean, Sam. The Disappearing Spoon: And Other True Tales of Rivalry, Adventure, & the History of the World from the Periodic Table of the Elements (Young Readers Edition) 2018. (ENG., Illus.). 240p. (J). E-Book (978-0-316-38824-5(6)) Little Brown & Co.

—The Disappearing Spoon: And Other True Tales of Rivalry, Adventure, & the History of the World from the Periodic Table of the Elements (Young Readers Edition) 2019. (ENG., Illus.). 240p. (J). (gr. 5-17). pap. 9.99 (978-0-316-38827-6(0)) Little, Brown Bks. for Young Readers.

Kimmelman, Leslie. What Is It? 2004. (ENG., Illus.). 8p. (J). (gr. k-k). pap. 6.97 net. (978-0-7652-5140-4(X), Celebration Pr.) Savvas Learning Co.

Kinser, Kathy. Doomed to Disappear? Endangered Species: Set Of 6. 2011. (Navigators Ser.). (J). pap. 48.00 net. (978-1-4108-0418-1(6)) Benchmark Education Co.

Koellhoffer, Tara. Science News for Kids, 6-Volume Set. 2006. (Science News for Kids Ser.). 144p. (gr. 4-6). 180.00 (978-0-7910-9292-7(5), Chelsea Clubhse.) Infobase Holdings, Inc.

Kops, Deborah. Were Early Computers Really the Size of a School Bus? And Other Questions about Inventions. 2011. (Is That a Fact? Ser.). (ENG.). 40p. (gr. 4-6). 26.60 (978-0-7613-6098-8(0)) Lerner Publishing Group.

Kramer, Alan; Leon. The Wright Brothers at Kitty Hawk. Leon, Karen, illus. 2004. (Reader's Theater Content-Area Concepts Ser.). (ENG.). (J). (gr. 1-2). 5.00 net. (978-1-4108-0794-6(0)) Benchmark Education Co.

Kramer, Candice. Farflings from Farflung. Hanner, Albert; Kramer, illus. 2004. (Reader's Theater Content-Area Concepts Ser.). (ENG.). (J). (gr. 2). 5.00 net. (978-1-4108-0797-7(5)) Benchmark Education Co.

Kroll, Jennifer. The Science of Superpowers (Grade 6) 2nd rev. ed. 2016. (TIME(r): Informational Text Ser.). (ENG., Illus.). 64p. (gr. 5-8). pap. 13.99 (978-1-4938-3608-6(0)) Teacher Created Materials, Inc.

Kroutil Artists, creator. The Elements: A Fun, Easy to Learn, Introduction to the Elements in Character! 2004. (YA). per. 24.95 (978-1-932689-00-6(1)) EDGEucation Publishing.

Lacey, Minna. Look Inside Science. 2011. (Look Inside Board Bks). 13p. (J). ring bd. 15.99 (978-0-7945-2946-8(1), Usborne) EDC Publishing.

LaCompte, Angie. I Am a Scientist. 2011. (Wonder Readers Ser.). (ENG.). 16p. (J). (gr. -1-1). 25.95 (978-1-4296-8535-1(2), 195205, Capstone Pr.) Capstone.

Ladybird, Ladybird. I'm Ready ... for Science! 2016. (Illus.). 48p. (J). (gr. k-2). 11.99 (978-0-241-23835-6(8)) Penguin Bks., Ltd. GBR. Dist: Independent Pubs. Group.

Language Arts Explorer (Set), 26 vols., Set. Incl. Save the Planet: Compost It. Barker, David M. 2010. lib. bdg. 32.07 (978-1-60279-656-0(4), 200349); Save the Planet: Growing Your Own Garden. Hirsch, Rebecca. 2010. lib. bdg. 32.07 (978-1-60279-657-7(2), 200350); Save the Planet: Helping Endangered Animals. Hirsch, Rebecca. 2010. lib. bdg. 32.07 (978-1-60279-658-4(0), 200351); Save the Planet: Keeping Water Clean. Farrell, Courtney. 2010. lib. bdg. 32.07 (978-1-60279-659-1(9), 200352); Save the Planet: Local Farms & Sustainable Foods. Vogel, Julia. 2010. lib. bdg. 32.07 (978-1-60279-660-7(2), 200353); Save the Planet: Protecting Our Natural Resources. Hirsch, Rebecca. 2010. lib. bdg. 32.07 (978-1-60279-661-4(0), 200354); Save the Planet: Reduce, Reuse, & Recycle. Minden, Cecilia. 2010. lib. bdg. 32.07 (978-1-60279-662-1(9), 200355); Save the Planet: Using Alternative Energies. Farrell, Courtney. 2010. lib. bdg. 32.07 (978-1-60279-663-8(7), 200356); Set. History Digs (Set) 2011. 320.70 (978-1-61080-243-7(8), 201030); Set. Science Lab (Set) 2011. 256.56 (978-1-61080-245-1(4), 201032); 32p. (gr. 4-8). (Explorer Library: Language Arts Explorer Ser.). (ENG., Illus.). 2011. 741.00 (978-1-61080-239-0(X), 201026) Cherry Lake Publishing.

Lassieur, Allison & Lusted, Marcia. Warrior Science. 2016. (Warrior Science Ser.). (ENG., Illus.). 32p. (J). (gr. 3-9). 122.60 (978-1-4914-8147-9(1), 23977, Capstone Pr.) Capstone.

Leavitt, Amie Jane. How STEM Built the Mayan Empire, 1 vol. 2019. (How STEM Built Empires Ser.). (ENG.). 80p. (gr. 7-7). pap. 16.30 (978-1-7253-4149-4(2), ccee7b83-7ab1-4a52-8605-764ba3b58500) Rosen Publishing Group, Inc., The.

Leavitt, Amie Jane & Garbe, Suzanne. The Science Behind Natural Phenomena. 2016. (Science Behind Natural Phenomena Ser.). (ENG.). 32p. (J). (gr. 3-9). 122.60 (978-1-5157-0809-4(8), 24786, Capstone Pr.) Capstone.

Leber, Nancy. What Plants & Animals Need, 6 vols., Set. 2003. (Phonics Readers 1-36 Ser.). (ENG.). 8p. (gr. k-1). pap. 29.70 (978-0-7368-3215-1(7)) Capstone.

Lemonick, Michael D. Science Alive, No. 1. 2005. 48p. (J). (978-0-7868-2106-8(X)) Hyperion Bks. for Children.

—Science Alive, No. 2. 2005. (J). (978-0-7868-0134-3(4)) Hyperion Pr.

Lerner, K. Lee, et al. U-X-L Doomed: The Science Behind Disasters. 2015. (Illus.). (J). (978-1-4103-1777-3(3)) Cengage Gale.

LernerClassroom Editors, ed. Cool Science Set III: Classroom Library. 2008. pap. 34.95 (978-0-8225-9175-7(8)) Lerner Publishing Group.

—Cool Science Set III: Complete Library. 2008. pap. 210.95 (978-0-8225-9281-5(9)) Lerner Publishing Group.

Let's Explore Science, 33 vols., Set. Incl. MP3 Players. Sturm, Jeanne. 2008. lib. bdg. 31.36 (978-1-60472-332-8(7)); Rocks, Minerals, & Soil. Meredith, Susan. 2009. lib. bdg. 32.79 (978-1-60694-411-0(8)); (Illus.). 48p. (J). (gr. 4-8). 2011. lib. bdg. o.p. (978-1-61590-875-2(7)) Rourke Educational Media.

Let's Find Out! 2014. (Let's Find Out! Ser.). 32p. (J). (gr. 3-6). 562.80 (978-1-62275-539-4(1)); pap. 309.60 (978-1-62275-771-8(8)) Rosen Publishing Group, Inc., The.

Let's Find Out! Complete Set. 2016. (Let's Find Out! Ser.). 32p. (gr. 3-2). 1858.20 (978-1-5081-0232-8(5), Britannica Educational Publishing) Rosen Publishing Group, Inc., The.

Let's Find Out! Physical Science, 24 vols. 2014. (Let's Find Out! Physical Science Ser.). (ENG.). 32p. (J). (gr. 2-3). 312.72 (978-1-62275-756-5(4), 3ded3b5c-f5d3-4a2f-b4c1-96211d62e14e); 156.36 (978-1-62275-517-2(0), f200ac91-d2ab-45ba-97a0-28a9745a0459) Rosen Publishing Group, Inc., The.

Letts KS3, Letts. KS3 Science Complete Coursebook (Letts KS3 Revision Success) 2019. (Letts KS3 Revision Success Ser.). (ENG., Illus.). 240p. (J). (gr. 6-9). pap. 23.95 (978-0-00-831624-2(4), Letts & Londsale) HarperCollins Pubs. Ltd. GBR. Dist: Independent Pubs. Group.

Leveled Reader Collection. 2003. (Scott Foresman Science Ser.). (gr. k-18). 198.00 (978-0-673-65126-6(6)); (gr. 1-18). 198.00 (978-0-673-65127-3(4)); (gr. 2-18). 198.00 (978-0-673-65128-0(2)); (gr. 3-18). 231.00 (978-0-673-65129-7(0)); (gr. 4-18). 231.00 (978-0-673-65130-3(4)); (gr. 5-18). 231.00 (978-0-673-65131-0(2)); (gr. 6-18). 231.00 (978-0-673-65132-7(0)) Addison-Wesley Educational Pubs., Inc.

Levete, Sarah. Science Fact or Fiction? You Decide! 2010. (ENG.). 32p. (J). pap. (978-0-7787-9916-0(6)); (Illus.). (978-0-7787-9895-8(X), 1325460) Crabtree Publishing Co.

Levit, Joe. Let's Explore Science. 2018. (Bumba Books (r) — a First Look at STEM Ser.). (ENG., Illus.). 24p. (J). (gr. -1-1). pap. 8.99 (978-1-5415-2701-0(1), 129407c9-853a-4bc9-bb0c-095d0018ed81) Lerner Publishing Group.

Levy, Joel. The Universe Explained, 1 vol., 1. 2013. (Guide for Curious Minds Ser.). (ENG.). 150p. (YA). (gr. 8-8). 42.41 (978-1-4777-2958-8(5), a531c7ef-f867-444f-ba60-1017e0824937) Rosen Publishing Group, Inc., The.

Life Science, Set. 2010. (Extreme! Ser.). (ENG.). 32p. (gr. 3-4). pap. 429.30 (978-1-4296-5138-7(5), Capstone Pr.) Capstone.

Life Science (Reading Room Collection 1), 10 vols. 2005. (Reading Room Collection 1 Ser.). (ENG.). (J). (gr. 2-3). 111.65 (978-1-4042-3384-3(9), d9c7fd32-1d50-44a1-8313-d6a6cfd00722) Rosen Publishing Group, Inc., The.

Lift-The-Flap Questions & Answers about Science IR. 2017. (Lift-The-Flap Questions & Answers Ser.). (ENG.). (J). bds. 14.99 (978-0-7945-3940-5(8), Usborne) EDC Publishing.

Literature Library. 2003. (Literature Library). (gr. k-18). 105.85 (978-0-673-59585-0(4)); (gr. 1-18). 105.85 (978-0-673-59586-7(2)); (gr. 2-18). 105.85 (978-0-673-59587-4(0)); (gr. 3-18). 105.85 (978-0-673-59588-1(9)); (gr. 4-18). 35.30 (978-0-673-59589-8(7)); (gr. 5-18). 35.30 (978-0-673-59590-4(0)); (gr. 6-18). 35.30 (978-0-673-59591-1(9)) Addison-Wesley Educational Pubs., Inc.

Littlefield, Cindy A. Awesome Ocean Science. 2006. (ENG., Illus.). 120p. (J). (gr. 2-7). pap. 14.99 (978-0-8249-6796-3(8), Ideals Pubns.) Worthy Publishing.

Living on the Edge Series, 8 vols., Set. 2003. (Living on the Edge Ser.). (ENG.). (gr. 3-4). 113.44 (978-0-7614-1436-0(3), 70f353a2-1491-4e4d-9048-83f003963ab8, Cavendish Square) Cavendish Square Publishing LLC.

Llewellyn, Claire. Caliente y Frio. (Coleccion de Lado a Lado Ser.). (SPA., Illus.). (J). (gr. k-3). 11.16 (978-970-656-279-1(6), CM30003) Publicaciones Citem, S.A. de C.V. MEX. Dist: Lectorum Pubns., Inc.

—Dia y Noche. (Coleccion de Lado a Lado Ser.). (SPA., Illus.). 11.16 (978-970-656-281-4(8), CM30004) Publicaciones Citem, S.A. de C.V. MEX. Dist: Lectorum Pubns., Inc.

—Diminuto y Enorme. (Coleccion de Lado a Lado Ser.). (SPA., Illus.). 11.16 (978-970-656-280-7(X), CM30005) Publicaciones Citem, S.A. de C.V. MEX. Dist: Lectorum Pubns., Inc.

—Tierra y Mar. (Coleccion de Lado a Lado Ser.). (SPA., Illus.). (J). (gr. k-3). 11.16 (978-970-656-282-1(6), CM30006) Publicaciones Citem, S.A. de C.V. MEX. Dist: Lectorum Pubns., Inc.

Lo Bosco, Maryellen. Famous Immigrant Scientists, 1 vol. 2017. (Making America Great: Immigrant Success Stories Ser.). (ENG.). 112p. (gr. 7-7). 38.93 (978-0-7660-9244-0(5), ae4ecab6-755a-4647-b5f3-8a4a24233a23) Enslow Publishing, LLC.

Londt, Claire, et al. English Matters for Zambia Basic Education Grade 3 Pupil's Book. 2nd ed. 2007. (ENG., Illus.). 64p. pap., stu. ed. 5.75 (978-0-521-68755-3(1)) Cambridge Univ. Pr.

A Look into Space: Individual Title Six-Packs. (Discovery World Ser.). 12p. (gr. k-1). 28.00 (978-0-7635-8452-8(5)) Rigby Education.

Ludeke, Kenneth L. & Ludeke, Amalia H. A Day with Anion, an Ion Science. 2013. 28p. (J). pap. 24.95 (978-1-63000-636-5(X)) America Star Bks.

Lunis, Natalie. Backyard Scientist. Date not set. (Thinking Like a Scientist Ser.). (Illus.). 20p. (J). pap. 16.95 (978-1-58273-107-0(1)) Sundance/Newbridge Educational Publishing.

Lunis, Natalie & White, Nancy. Being a Scientist. Date not set. (Thinking Like a Scientist Ser.). (Illus.). 20p. (J). pap. 16.95 (978-1-58273-085-1(7)) Sundance/Newbridge Educational Publishing.

—Exploring Everyday Wonders. Date not set. (Thinking Like a Scientist Ser.). (Illus.). 20p. (J). pap. 16.95 (978-1-58273-368-5(6)) Sundance/Newbridge Educational Publishing.

—Popcorn Science. Date not set. (Thinking Like a Scientist Ser.). (Illus.). 20p. (J). pap. 16.95 (978-1-58273-370-8(8)) Sundance/Newbridge Educational Publishing.

—A World of Change. Date not set. (Thinking Like a Scientist Ser.). (Illus.). 20p. (J). pap. 16.95 (978-1-58273-077-6(6)) Sundance/Newbridge Educational Publishing.

Luz. (Coleccion Jugando Con la Ciencia). (SPA., Illus.). 39p. (J). pap. 9.95 (978-950-11-0683-1(7), SGM35X) Sigmar ARG. Dist: Continental Bk. Co., Inc.

MacGregor, Fiona, et al. International Primary Science Student's Book 3. Miller, Jonathan & Pilling, Anne, eds. Robinson, Pete, tr. Hannigan, Pauline et al, illus. 2015. (Collins International Primary Science Ser.). (ENG.). 96p. (J). (gr. 2). pap. 12.95 (978-0-00-758616-5(7)) HarperCollins Pubs. Ltd. GBR. Dist: Independent Pubs. Group.

Maclaine, James. Lift-The-Flap General Knowledge IR. 2015. (Lift-The-Flap Board Bks.). (ENG.). 16p. (J). (gr. k-5). 14.99 (978-0-7945-3418-9(X), Usborne) EDC Publishing.

Mara, Wil. The Mesopotamians, 1 vol. 2012. (Technology of the Ancients Ser.). (ENG., Illus.). 64p. (gr. 6-6). 35.50 (978-1-60870-767-6(9), 00958fae-07f7-4813-87b7-d738e5fb4a87) Cavendish Square Publishing LLC.

—The Romans, 1 vol. 2012. (Technology of the Ancients Ser.). (ENG.). 64p. (gr. 6-6). 35.50 (978-1-60870-768-3(7), b291559d-ec79-4731-9cb9-7c154b88abe3) Cavendish Square Publishing LLC.

Mast, Steven. God's Wonderful World: Science 5. 2004. (God's World Science Ser.). (Illus.). 272p. (gr. 5-18). 15.10 (978-0-7399-0614-9(3), 14501) Rod & Staff Pubs., Inc.

—God's Wonderful World: Science 5 Tests. 2004. (God's World Science Ser.). 31p. (gr. 5-18). 1.95 (978-0-7399-0615-6(1), 14511) Rod & Staff Pubs., Inc.

Math Attack: Exploring Life Science with Math, 12 vols. 2016. (Math Attack: Exploring Life Science with Math Ser.). (ENG.). 00032p. (J). (gr. 3-4). 167.58 (978-1-4994-3195-7(3), ca14f1bc-9508-4dda-848c-708e874aea8c, PowerKids Pr.) Rosen Publishing Group, Inc., The.

Mattern, Joanne. Can Lightning Strike the Same Place Twice? And Other Questions about Earth, Weather, & the Environment. 2010. (Is That a Fact? Ser.). 40p. (YA). (gr. 3-6). lib. bdg. 26.60 (978-0-8225-9081-1(6)) Lerner Publishing Group.

Mayes, Susan. Starting Point Science: What Makes It Rain? / What Makes a Flower Grow? / Where Does Electricity Come from? / What's under the Ground? Amery, Heather, ed. rev. ed. 2007. (Starting Point Science Ser.). (Illus.). 98p. (J). (gr. 4-7). 13.99 (978-0-7945-1626-0(2), Usborne) EDC Publishing.

McDougal-Littell Publishing Staff. Integrated Course. I.t. ed. 2004. (McDougal Littell Middle School Science Ser.). (ENG.). 128p. (gr. 7-7). 86.05 (978-0-618-42301-9(X), 2-01159) Great Source Education Group, Inc.

—Integrated Course 3. I.t. ed. 2004. (McDougal Littell Middle School Science Ser.). (ENG.). 128p. (gr. 8-8). 86.05 (978-0-618-42303-3(6), 2-01161) Great Source Education Group, Inc.

—Modules: Physical Science - Diversity of Living Things. 2004. (McDougal Littell Science Ser.). (ENG.). 64p. (gr. 6-8). pap., lab manual ed. 15.30 (978-0-618-43724-5(X), 2-01217) Great Source Education Group, Inc.

—Modules: Physical Science; Ecology Unit. 2004. (McDougal Littell Science Ser.). (ENG.). 40p. (gr. 6-8). pap., lab manual ed. 15.30 (978-0-618-43728-3(2), 2-01221) Great Source Education Group, Inc.

—Modules: Physical Science; Life over Time. 2004. (McDougal Littell Science Ser.). (ENG.). 40p. (gr. 6-8). pap., lab manual ed. 15.30 (978-0-618-43731-3(2), 2-01224) Great Source Education Group, Inc.

—Modules: Physical Science; Visual Glossary. 2004. (McDougal Littell Science Ser.). (ENG.). 48p. (gr. 6-8). pap. 28.65 (978-0-618-41587-8(4), 2-01136) Great Source Education Group, Inc.

—Physical Science. 2004. (McDougal Littell Middle School Science Ser.). (ENG.). 112p. (gr. 6-8). 84.85 (978-0-618-30369-4(3), 2-01004) Great Source Education Group, Inc.

—Science: Integrated Course 1. I.t. ed. 2004. (McDougal Littell Middle School Science Ser.). (ENG.). 128p. (gr. 6-6). 86.05 (978-0-618-42299-9(4), 2-01157) Great Source Education Group, Inc.

McFall, Sally, ed. Pro/Con 2, 6 vols. 2003. (Illus.). 1392p. (YA). 339.00 (978-0-7172-5753-9(3)) Scholastic Library Publishing.

—Pro/Con 3, 12 vols. 2004. (Illus.). (YA). 339.00 (978-0-7172-5927-4(7), Grolier) Scholastic Library Publishing.

McGill, Jordan. Life Science Fair Projects. 2011. (J). (978-1-61690-330-5(9)); (gr. 3-5). pap. 12.95 (978-1-61690-658-0(8), AV2 by Weigl); (Illus.). 24p. (gr. 3-6). 27.13 (978-1-61690-654-2(5)) Weigl Pubs., Inc.

McGraw Hill. Glencoe IScience: Level Blue, Grade 8, Reinforcement & Study Guide, Student Edition. 2004. (Integrated Science Ser.). (ENG., Illus.). 96p. (gr. 8-8). stu. ed., spiral bd., pupil's gde. ed. 8.92 (978-0-07-867169-2(8), 0078671698) McGraw-Hill Education.

—Glencoe IScience, Level Green, Grade 7, Reinforcement & Study Guide, Student Edition. 2004. (Integrated Science Ser.). (ENG., Illus.). 96p. (gr. 7-7). stu. ed., spiral bd., pupil's gde. ed. 8.92 (978-0-07-867188-3(4), 0078671884) McGraw-Hill Education.

—Glencoe IScience, Level Red, Grade 6, Reinforcement & Study Guide, Student Edition. 2004. (Integrated Science Ser.). (ENG., Illus.). 80p. (gr. 6-6). stu. ed., spiral bd., pupil's gde. ed. 9.36 (978-0-07-867216-3(3), 0078672163) McGraw-Hill Education.

—Glencoe IScience: the Air Around You, Student Edition. 2nd ed. 2004. (Glen Sci: the Air above Us Ser.). (ENG., Illus.). 192p. (gr. 6-8). lib. bdg., stu. ed. 34.40 (978-0-07-861758-4(8), 0078617588) McGraw-Hill Education.

—Glencoe Science: the Nature of Matter, Student Edition. 2nd ed. 2004. (Glen Sci: the Nature of Matter Ser.). (ENG., Illus.). 192p. (gr. 6-8). stu. ed. 38.36 (978-0-07-861765-2(0), 0078617650) McGraw-Hill Education.

—The Outer Edge Cool Science. 2005. (Jt: Non-Fiction Reading Ser.). (ENG., Illus.). 120p. (gr. 6-12). per. 30.28 (978-0-07-869053-2(6), 0078690536) McGraw-Hill Education.

McGraw-Hill Staff. Life Science Animations. 2nd ed. 2004. (gr. 6-12). cd-rom (978-0-07-248438-0(1)) Glencoe/McGraw-Hill.

McGraw-Hill Staff, creator. Science. 2004. (Integrated Science Ser.). (ENG., Illus.). 346p. (gr. 6-6). stu. ed., per. 21.32 (978-0-07-867214-9(7), 0078672147) McGraw-Hill Education.

McKinney, Donna Bowen. How STEM Built the Greek Empire, 1 vol. 2019. (How STEM Built Empires Ser.). (ENG.). 80p. (gr. 7-7). pap. 16.30 (978-1-7253-4143-2(3),

4b7c4e01-adb4-4aa2-9f8e-2ada50a64347) Rosen Publishing Group, Inc., The.

Meissner, David. Habitat Rescue: Set Of 6. 2010. (Navigators Ser.). (J). pap. 44.00 net. (978-1-4108-0411-2(9)) Benchmark Education Co.

Michels, Michael, et al. Cooperative Learning & Science High School Activities. 2005. per. (978-1-879097-74-2(5)) Kagan Publishing.

Miles Kelly Staff. Science: Family Flip Quiz. 2003. (Family Flip Quiz Ser.). (Illus.). 152p. (J). spiral bd. 12.95 (978-1-84236-073-6(6)) Miles Kelly Publishing, Ltd. GBR. Dist: Independent Pubs. Group.

Miller, John & Scott, Chris Fornell. Unofficial Minecraft STEM Lab for Kids: Family-Friendly Projects for Exploring Concepts in Science, Technology, Engineering, & Math, Volume 16. 2018. (Lab for Kids Ser.: 16). (ENG., Illus.). 144p. (J). (gr. 2-5). pap. 24.99 (978-1-63159-483-0(4), 301354, Quarry Bks.) Quarto Publishing Group USA.

Mills, Nathan & Ludlow, Susan. From Ice to Steam, 1 vol. 2012. (Rosen Readers Ser.). (ENG., Illus.). 24p. (J). (gr. 1-1). pap. 8.25 (978-1-4488-8812-2(3), fad63b32-b88e-4731-9e9c-6972bacbb900, Rosen Classroom) Rosen Publishing Group, Inc., The.

Mills, Nathan & Worthy, Shanya. Ana's Community Helpers, 1 vol. 2012. (Rosen Readers Ser.). (ENG., Illus.). 16p. (J). (gr. k-k). pap. 7.00 (978-1-4488-8698-2(8), 37289a23-be39-42d9-8ba3-cde0ddec457d, Rosen Classroom) Rosen Publishing Group, Inc., The.

Mitchell, Ainslie. Collecting Seashells. Walker, Anna, illus. 2005. (Science (Harcourt) Ser.). 14p. pap. 6.00 (978-0-15-349999-9(0)) Harcourt Schl. Pubs.

Mitchell Lane Publishers Inc. Staff. A Robbie Reader-Science Biography, 5 vols., Set. 2005. (Robbie Reader Ser.). (Illus.). 32p. (gr. 1-4). lib. bdg. 128.50 (978-1-58415-351-1(2)) Mitchell Lane Pubs.

MoCasins: Level A. 8p. 20.95 (978-0-322-00624-9(4)) Wright Group/McGraw-Hill.

Modern Staff. Apple Tree. 2003. 38.95 (978-0-8136-4107-2(1)) Modern Curriculum Pr.

Modules: Physical Science; English Learners Package. 2005. (gr. 6-12). (978-0-618-41579-3(3), 2-01131) Holt McDougal.

Modules: Physical Science; How Stuff Works Express Magazine. 2005. (gr. 6-12). (978-0-618-41615-8(3), 2-01137) Holt McDougal.

Modules: Physical Science; Lab Generator. 2005. (gr. 6-12). cd-rom (978-0-618-42033-9(9), 2-01147) Holt McDougal.

Modules: Physical Science; Process & Lab Skills PE. 2005. (Module: Physical Science Ser.). (gr. 6-18). (978-0-618-41364-5(2), 2-01113); (gr. 7-18). (978-0-618-41365-2(0), 2-01114); (gr. 8-18). (978-0-618-41366-9(9), 2-01115) Holt McDougal.

Modules: Physical Science; Science Toolkit. 2005. (gr. 6-12). (978-0-618-41583-0(1), 2-01134) Holt McDougal.

Modules: Physical Science; Standardized Test Practice PE. 2005. (gr. 6-12). cd-rom (978-0-618-41372-0(3), 2-01121); (gr. 7-18). (978-0-618-41371-3(5), 2-01120) Holt McDougal.

Moehlenpah, Arlo. Creation Versus Evolution: Scientific & Religious Considerations. 2003. 36p. (YA). (978-0-9667054-6-1(7)) Doing Good Ministries.

Monroe, Elliot. Interdependence of Species, 1 vol. 2016. (Spotlight on Ecology & Life Science Ser.). (ENG.). 24p. (J). (gr. 4-6). pap. 11.00 (978-1-4994-2595-6(3), 602b79a3-25fd-4560-a112-daf3e8fdbfa2, PowerKids Pr.) Rosen Publishing Group, Inc., The.

Morris, Paul & Deo, Patricia. Sciences for IB MYP 1. 2016. (ENG.). 160p. (gr. 6-6). pap. 26.00 (978-1-4718-8037-7(0)) Hodder Education Group GBR. Dist: Ingram Publisher Services.

Morrison, Karen, et al. International Primary Science Student's Book 4. Pilling, Anne & Robinson, Pete, eds. Loughrey, Anita et al, illus. 2015. (Collins International Primary Science Ser.). (ENG.). 96p. (gr. 3). pap., stu. ed. 12.95 (978-0-00-758620-2(5)) HarperCollins Pubs. Ltd. GBR. Dist: Independent Pubs. Group.

—International Primary Science Student's Book 6. Pilling, Anne & Robinson, Pete, eds. Loughrey, Anita et al, illus. 2015. (Collins International Primary Science Ser.). (ENG.). 96p. (J). (gr. 5). pap. 12.95 (978-0-00-758627-1(2)) HarperCollins Pubs. Ltd. GBR. Dist: Independent Pubs. Group.

Morter, Peter. Atlas Visual de los Descubrimientos. (SPA., Illus.). 412p. (YA). (gr. 5-8). (978-84-216-1814-1(8), BU4892) Bruño, Editorial ESP. Dist: Lectorum Pubns., Inc.

Mother Goose Cares about Math & Science: Professional Development Manual. 2004. (978-0-9753985-2-4(0)) Mother Goose Programs.

Mother Goose Programs, prod. What's the BIG Idea? Shapes & Spaces Librarian Manual. 2008. 70p. pap. (978-0-9753985-9-3(8)) Mother Goose Programs.

El Motin del Amistad: Libros Aventuras (Adventure Books) 2003. (MacMillan/McGraw-Hill. Estudios Sociales Ser.). (ENG & SPA.). (gr. 5-18). (978-0-02-150125-0(4)) Macmillan/McGraw-Hill Schl. Div.

Movimiento. (Coleccion Jugando Con la Ciencia). (SPA., Illus.). 39p. (J). pap. 9.95 (978-950-11-0684-8(5), SGM325) Sigmar ARG. Dist: Continental Bk. Co., Inc.

Moving up with Science, 12 vols. 2016. (Moving up with Science Ser.). (ENG.). 00032p. (J). (gr. 3-4). 167.58 (978-1-4994-3192-6(9), d7975891-f044-4163-af0b-71b01447bb08, PowerKids Pr.) Rosen Publishing Group, Inc., The.

Mullins, Lisa & Smith, Elizabeth. Science in the Renaissance, 1 vol. 2009. (Renaissance World Ser.). (ENG., Illus.). 32p. (J). (gr. 5-8). pap. (978-0-7787-4614-0(3)) Crabtree Publishing Co.

El Mundo de la Ciencia. (Coleccion Lo Sabias?). (SPA., Illus.). 44p. (J). 12.95 (978-950-11-0940-5(2), SGM9402) Sigmar ARG. Dist: Continental Bk. Co., Inc.

Murphy, Glenn. Why Is Snot Green? And Other Extremely Important Questions (and Answers) 2009. (ENG., Illus.). 240p. (J). (gr. 3-6). pap. 13.99 (978-1-59643-500-1(3), 900057452) Square Fish.

Museums: Collections to Share, 6 vols. (Book2WebTM Ser.). (gr. 4-8). 36.50 (978-0-322-02986-6(4)) Wright Group/McGraw-Hill.

My Big Book of Science. 2004. (Illus.). 48p. (J). pap. 5.99 (978-1-85854-843-2(8)) Brimax Books Ltd. GBR. Dist: Byeway Bks.

My Body Does Strange Stuff!, 12 vols. 2013. (My Body Does Strange Stuff! Ser.). 24p. (J). (gr. 1-2). (ENG.). 151.62 (978-1-4339-9673-3(1), 865b90b3-4674-43e8-ad3c-ab72732d4f97); pap. 48.90 (978-1-4339-9763-1(0)); pap. 293.40 (978-1-4339-9764-8(9)) Stevens, Gareth Publishing LLLP.

My Feet: Big Book: Level C. 8p. 20.95 (978-0-322-00364-4(4)) Wright Group/McGraw-Hill.

My World of Science: Set 1, 8 vols. 2005. (My World of Science Ser.). (ENG., Illus.). (J). (gr. 2-2). 89.08 (978-1-4042-3379-9(2), 608daec7-c895-4684-8baf-c373eb02737a); 66.81 (978-1-4042-7568-3(1), 08d2861c-cd9d-4332-8ff5-77a816041d7b, Editorial Buenas Letras) Rosen Publishing Group, Inc., The.

My World of Science: Set 2, 6 vols. 2005. (My World of Science Ser.). (ENG., Illus.). (J). (gr. 2-2). 66.81 (978-1-4042-3289-1(3), cf7568b3-00ff-4f3f-91c1-b167b3d21271) Rosen Publishing Group, Inc., The.

National Geographic Kids. Science Encyclopedia: Atom Smashing, Food Chemistry, Animals, Space, & More! 2016. (Illus.). 304p. (J). (gr. 3-7). 24.99 (978-1-4263-2542-7(8), National Geographic Kids) Disney Publishing Worldwide.

National Geographic Learning. Language, Literacy & Vocabulary - Reading Expeditions (Physical Science): Machines: Simple & Compound. 2007. (ENG., Illus.). 36p. (J). pap. 20.95 (978-0-7922-5439-3(2)) CENGAGE Learning.

—Reading Expeditions (Science: Everyday Science): Science at the Grocery. 2007. (ENG., Illus.). 24p. (J). pap. 15.95 (978-0-7922-4567-4(9)) CENGAGE Learning.

—Reading Expeditions (Science: Everyday Science): Science at the Mall. 2007. (ENG., Illus.). 24p. (J). pap. 15.95 (978-0-7922-4569-8(5)) CENGAGE Learning.

National Science Resources Center, creator. Science & Technology for Children Books: Animal Studies. 2004. (J). (978-1-933008-00-4(8)) Smithsonian Science Education Ctr. (SSEC).

Natural Science Mysteries Full Kit. 2005. (Illus.). 856p. (YA). 75.00 (978-1-59476-097-6(7)) Paradigm Accelerated Curriculum.

Nature's Fury: Lightning!, Killer Quake! & Hurricane!, 3 cass.; set. gif. ed. 2004. (NOVA Ser.). (gr. 7-18). 49.95 incl. VHS (978-1-884738-68-5(0), WG027) WGBH Boston Video.

NCPTA Staff, et al. SATs Practice in Science Age 11. (ENG., Illus.). 32p. pap. 6.99 (978-0-340-71046-3(2), Coronet) Hodder & Stoughton GBR. Dist: Trafalgar Square Publishing.

Nelson, Robin. Float & Sink. 2004. (Illus.). 22p. 5.95 (978-0-8225-5296-3(5)); 24p. (J). lib. bdg. 18.60 (978-0-8225-5135-5(7)) Lerner Publishing Group.

—Magnets. 2005. (Forces & Motion Ser.). (Illus.). 22p. (J). pap. 5.95 (978-0-8225-5298-7(1), Lerner Pubns.) Lerner Publishing Group.

—Push & Pull. 2005. (Forces & Motion Ser.). (Illus.). 22p. (J). pap. 5.95 (978-0-8225-5299-4(X)) Lerner Publishing Group.

—Se Congela y Se Derrite. Castañer, Mercedes & Fitzpatrick, Julia, trs. 2003. (Mi Primer Paso Al Mundo Real - el Agua (First Step Nonfiction - Water) Ser.). (SPA., Illus.). 24p. (gr. k-2). lib. bdg. 23.93 (978-0-8225-4865-2(8)) Lerner Publishing Group.

Nichols, Susan. Al-Karaji: Tenth Century Mathematician & Engineer, 1 vol. 2016. (Physicians, Scientists, & Mathematicians of the Islamic World Ser.). (ENG.). 112p. (J). (gr. 6-6). lib. bdg. 38.80 (978-1-5081-7143-0(2), feec6450-8f3f-4ba8-81fe-9722e950492a) Rosen Publishing Group, Inc., The.

Nick, Arnold. Esas funestas fuerzas. 2003. (Coleccion Esa Horrible Cienca). (SPA., Illus.). 160p. (YA). (978-84-272-2054-6(5), ML8313) Molino, Editorial ESP. Dist: Lectorum Pubns., Inc.

Nsrc. Science & Technology for Children Books: Microworlds. 2004. (Illus.). 64p. (J). (978-1-933008-04-2(0)) Smithsonian Science Education Ctr. (SSEC).

Nuevo Investiguemos 1: Ciencias Naturales y de la Salud. (SPA.). (J). (gr. 1). (978-958-02-1575-2(8)) Editorial Voluntad S.A. COL. Dist: Distribuidora Norma, Inc.

Nuevo Investiguemos 2: Ciencias Naturales y de la Salud. (SPA.). (J). (gr. 2). (978-958-02-1576-9(6)) Editorial Voluntad S.A. COL. Dist: Distribuidora Norma, Inc.

Nuevo Investiguemos 3: Ciencias Naturales y de la Salud. (SPA.). (J). (gr. 3). (978-958-02-1577-6(4)) Editorial Voluntad S.A. COL. Dist: Distribuidora Norma, Inc.

Nuevo Investiguemos 4: Ciencias Naturales y de la Salud. (SPA.). (J). (gr. 4). (978-958-02-1578-3(2)) Editorial Voluntad S.A. COL. Dist: Distribuidora Norma, Inc.

Nuevo Investiguemos 5: Ciencias Naturales y de la Salud. (SPA.). (J). (gr. 5). (978-958-02-1579-0(0)) Editorial Voluntad S.A. COL. Dist: Distribuidora Norma, Inc.

Nuevo Investiguemos 6: Ciencias Naturales y de la Salud. (SPA.). (978-958-02-1534-9(0)) Editorial Voluntad S.A. COL. Dist: Distribuidora Norma, Inc.

Nuevo Investiguemos 8: Ciencias Naturales y de la Salud. (SPA.). (YA). (gr. 8). (978-958-02-1536-3(7)) Editorial Voluntad S.A. COL. Dist: Distribuidora Norma, Inc.

Nye, Bill & Mone, Gregory. Bill Nye's Great Big World of Science. 2020. (ENG., Illus.). 264p. (J). (gr. 5-9). 29.99 (978-1-4197-4676-5(6), 1214501, Abrams Bks. for Young Readers) Abrams, Inc.

of, The Editors of Popular Science. The Popular Science Hacker's Manual, 1 vol. 2018. (Popular Science Guide for Hackers & Inventors Ser.). (ENG.). 248p. (gr. 8-8). lib. bdg. 56.71 (978-1-5026-4468-8(1), 79a35a54-ef00-4797-b56e-9a41fe43bfcc) Cavendish Square Publishing LLC.

Ohio 8th Gr Science. 2007. 52p. pap. 8.95 (978-0-9769459-5-6(9)) Hollandays Publishing Corp.

Olien, Rebecca & Hansen, Amy S. First Graphics: Science Mysteries: A Science Mystery. Scott, Korey & McDermed, Kathryn, illus. 2011. (First Graphics: Science Mysteries Ser.). (ENG.). 24p. (J). (gr. k-3). pap., pap., pap. 25.16 (978-1-4296-7181-1(5), 16735) Capstone.

—First Graphics: Science Mysteries Classroom Collection: A Science Mystery. Scott, Korey & McDermed, Kathryn, illus. 2011. (First Graphics: Science Mysteries Ser.). (ENG.). 24p. (J). (gr. 1-2). 146.80 (978-1-4296-7182-8(3), 16736) Capstone.

Oliver, Clare. Tell Me Who Lives in Space? And More about Space. 2004. (Illus.). 32p. (J). pap. (978-1-84458-057-6(1), Pavilion Children's Books) Pavilion Bks.

One Each of 8 Big Books. (Sunshinetm Science Ser.). (gr. 1-2). 250.50 (978-0-7802-0567-3(7)) Wright Group/McGraw-Hill.

Operation: Top Secret. 2005. (J). per. (978-1-932855-33-3(5)) becker&mayer! books.

Orme, David. Extreme Science. 2008. (Trailblazers Ser.). (ENG., Illus.). 36p. pap. (978-1-84167-648-7(9)) Ransom Publishing Ltd.

—Extreme Science. 2009. (Fact to Fiction Ser.). (Illus.). 36p. (J). lib. bdg. 16.95 (978-0-7569-9279-8(6)) Perfection Learning Corp.

Orme, Helen. What Things Are Made Of. 2010. (Science Everywhere! Ser.). 24p. 24.25 (978-1-84898-298-7(4)) Black Rabbit Bks.

Orr, Tamra B. Planet Earth Discoveries. 2018. (Marvelous Discoveries Ser.). (ENG., Illus.). 32p. (J). (gr. 2-5). lib. bdg. 28.65 (978-1-5435-2618-9(7), 138089, Capstone Pr.) Capstone.

Out of the Lab: Extreme Jobs in Science. 2013. (Out of the Lab: Extreme Jobs in Science Ser.). 32p. (J). (gr. 3-6). pap. 60.00 (978-1-4777-2734-8(5)); pap. 360.00 (978-1-4777-2735-5(3)) Rosen Publishing Group, Inc., The. (PowerKids Pr.).

Oxford, ed. Graphic Library - Science Complete Program. 2013. (Graphic Science Ser.). (ENG.). 32p. (gr. 3-4). pap. 1535.55 (978-1-4765-3740-5(2), Capstone Pr.) Capstone.

Oxlade, Chris. Why Why Why... Do Magnets Push & Pull? 2010. (Why Why Why Ser.). 32p. (J). (gr. 1-3). lib. bdg. 18.95 (978-1-4222-1583-8(0)) Mason Crest.

Oxlade, Chris, et al. Science: Practical Projects, 8 vols. 2012. (Illus.). 64p. (J). (gr. 3-7). pap. 20.00 (978-1-84322-796-0(7)) Anness Publishing GBR. Dist: National Bk. Network.

Padilla, Michael J., et al. Adventures in Life, Earth, & Physical Science, 3 vols. 2003. (ENG.). 866p. (YA). (gr. 6-8). stu. ed. 433.00 (978-0-13-115416-2(8)) Prentice Hall Pr.

—Discoveries in Life, Earth, & Physical Science, 3 vols. 2003. (ENG.). 858p. (YA). (gr. 6-8). 429.00 (978-0-13-115415-5(X), Prentice Hall) Savvas Learning Co.

—Investigations in Life, Earth, & Physical Science, 3 vols. 2003. (ENG.). 890p. (YA). (gr. 6-8). 445.00 (978-0-13-115414-8(1), Prentice Hall) Savvas Learning Co.

Paizee, Daphne, et al. International Primary Science Student's Book 5. Miller, Jonathan & Pilling, Anne, eds. Robinson, Pete, tr. Hannigan, Pauline et al, illus. 2015. (Collins International Primary Science Ser.). (ENG.). 96p. (gr. 4). pap., stu. ed. 12.95 (978-0-00-758623-3(X)) HarperCollins Pubs. Ltd. GBR. Dist: Independent Pubs. Group.

Paris, John Ayrton. Philosophy in Sport Made Science in Earnest: Being an Attempt to Illustrate the First Principles of Natural Philosophy by the Aid of the Popular Toys & Sports. Cruikshank, George, illus. 2013. (Cambridge Library Collection - Education Ser.: Volume 1). (ENG.). Volume 1. 340p. pap. 44.99 (978-1-108-05739-4(X))Volume 2. 328p. pap. 44.99 (978-1-108-05740-0(3))Volume 3. 220p. pap. 33.99 (978-1-108-05741-7(1)) Cambridge Univ. Pr.

Parker, Steve. Complete Guides Our World. 2012. (ENG.). 144p. (J). (978-1-4351-4406-4(6)) Barnes & Noble, Inc.

—Science. 2014. (100 Facts You Should Know Ser.). 48p. (J). (gr. 4-6). pap. 84.95 (978-1-4824-1189-8(X)) Stevens, Gareth Publishing LLLP.

Pauli, Gunter. La Bruja del Desierto. 2007. (Zeri Fables Ser.).Tr. of Desert Witch. (ENG & SPA., Illus.). 32p. (J). (gr. k-3). pap. 9.95 (978-958-692-844-1(6)) Fondo Editorial Grania, Fundacion Hogares Juveniles Campesinos COL. Dist: Chelsea Green Publishing.

—Can Apples Fly? 2007. (Zeri Fables Ser.). (ENG & SPA., Illus.). 32p. (J). (gr. k-3). pap. 9.95 (978-958-692-854-0(3)) Fondo Editorial Grania, Fundacion Hogares Juveniles Campesinos COL. Dist: Chelsea Green Publishing.

—Cold Feet (Pies Frios) 2007. (Zeri Fables Ser.). (ENG & SPA., Illus.). 32p. (J). (gr. k-3). pap. 9.95 (978-958-692-861-8(6)) Fondo Editorial Grania, Fundacion Hogares Juveniles Campesinos COL. Dist: Chelsea Green Publishing.

—El Oso y el Zorro. 2007. (Zeri Fables Ser.). (ENG & SPA., Illus.). 32p. (J). (gr. k-3). pap. 9.95 (978-958-692-840-3(3)) Fondo Editorial Grania, Fundacion Hogares Juveniles Campesinos COL. Dist: Chelsea Green Publishing.

—Red Rice (Arroces Rojos) 2007. (Zeri Fables Ser.). (ENG & SPA., Illus.). 32p. (J). (gr. k-3). pap. 9.95 (978-958-692-831-1(4)) Fondo Editorial Grania, Fundacion Hogares Juveniles Campesinos COL. Dist: Chelsea Green Publishing.

—Tree Candy. 2007. (Zeri Fables Ser.). (ENG & SPA., Illus.). 32p. (J). (gr. k-3). pap. 9.95 (978-958-692-836-6(5)) Fondo Editorial Grania, Fundacion Hogares Juveniles Campesinos COL. Dist: Chelsea Green Publishing.

Pemberton, Rose. Inheritance & Variation of Traits, 1 vol. 2016. (Spotlight on Ecology & Life Science Ser.). (ENG.). 24p. (J). (gr. 4-6). pap. 11.00 (978-1-4994-2569-7(4), 1e005ee3-7806-4dee-b803-12ca50939062, PowerKids Pr.) Rosen Publishing Group, Inc., The.

Petersen, Christine. Plants Need Sunlight. 2008. (21st Century Junior Library: Plants Ser.). (ENG., Illus.). 24p. (gr. 2-5). lib. bdg. 29.21 (978-1-60279-273-9(9), 200178) Cherry Lake Publishing.

Peterson, R. E. (Robert Evans). Peterson's Familiar Science; 2006. 600p. per. 32.99 (978-1-4255-6416-2(X)) Michigan Publishing.

Petheram, Louise, et al. Ascent! 2003. (ENG.). Bk. 2. 200p. pap. (978-0-7487-6795-3(9))Bk. 3. 240p. pap. (978-0-7487-6796-0(7)) Nelson Thornes Ltd.

PH Inc. Staff. Parade of Life: Animals. 2nd ed. (J). pap., act. bk. ed. (978-0-13-225616-2(9)) Prentice Hall (Schl. Div.).

—PH Science Ecology Earth. (J). pap., act. bk. ed. (978-0-13-225582-0(0)) Prentice Hall (Schl. Div.).

—PH Science Evolution. 2nd ed. (J). pap., act. bk. ed. (978-0-13-225541-7(3)) Prentice Hall (Schl. Div.).

Physical, Module B. 2003. (Scott Foresman Science Ser.). (gr. 3-18). suppl. ed. 15.50 (978-0-328-03436-9(3)); (gr. 4-18). suppl. ed. 15.50 (978-0-328-03440-6(1)); (gr. 5-18). suppl. ed. 16.00 (978-0-328-03444-4(4)); (gr. 6-18). suppl. ed. 16.00 (978-0-328-03448-2(7)) Addison-Wesley Educational Pubs., Inc.

Physical Science, Set. 2010. (Extreme! Ser.). (ENG.). 32p. (gr. 3-4). pap. 286.20 (978-1-4296-5139-4(3), Capstone Pr.) Capstone.

Physical Science, 10 vols. 2013. (Physical Science Ser.). 48p. (J). (gr. 4-5). (ENG.). 191.70 (978-1-4339-9681-8(2), 26ceafab-e581-4f1e-a287-4afb5ad54d6b); pap. 505.80 (978-1-4339-9810-2(6)) Stevens, Gareth Publishing LLLP.

Physical Science: Physical Science Unit Resource Materials. 2005. (gr. 6-12). (978-0-618-41242-6(5), 2-01097) Holt McDougal.

Plant Eaters of the Pond: 6 Each of 1 Student Book, 6 vols. (Sunshinetm Science Ser.). 24p. (gr. 1-2). 41.95 (978-0-7802-2698-2(4)) Wright Group/McGraw-Hill.

Plant Eaters of the Pond: Big Book. (Sunshinetm Science Ser.). 24p. (gr. 1-2). 37.50 (978-0-7802-2783-5(2)) Wright Group/McGraw-Hill.

Platt, Richard & Biesty, Stephen. Stephen Biesty's Incredible Cross-Sections Book. (Illus.). (J). pap. 24.95 (978-0-590-73870-5(4)) Scholastic, Inc.

Plummer, Todd. Superhero Science: Kapow! Comic Book Crime Fighters Put Physics to the Test. 2009. (Current Science Ser.). (ENG.). 48p. (J). (gr. 4-6). pap. 8.95 (978-1-4339-2247-3(9), Gareth Stevens Learning Library) Stevens, Gareth Publishing LLLP.

Pocket Scientist: The Blue Book. 2004. (Illus.). 290p. (J). 8.99 (978-0-7945-0148-8(6), Usborne) EDC Publishing.

Podesto, Martine. My Science Notebook, 6 vols., Set. Incl. Body. (YA). lib. bdg. 33.67 (978-0-8368-9212-3(7), 63c0610b-0e9e-45b9-8329-89604dfbf439); Dinosaurs. (J). lib. bdg. 33.67 (978-0-8368-9213-0(5), ccd84418-d861-46e4-b5cf-66ababc8b0c6); Inventions. (J). lib. bdg. 33.67 (978-0-8368-9214-7(3), 19591178-09ac-489a-bf12-e5d9174ae650); Moon. (YA). lib. bdg. 33.67 (978-0-8368-9215-4(1), e794d5c4-8de1-4366-8914-50d2eebe66b7); (Illus.). (gr. 4-5). (My Science Notebook Ser.). (ENG.). 104p. 2008. Set lib. bdg. 101.01 (978-0-8368-9306-9(9), 54a52ee6-7e8c-4a29-8834-9896c3a7d359, Gareth Stevens Learning Library) Stevens, Gareth Publishing LLLP.

The Pond: 6 Each of 1 Student Book, 6 vols. (Sunshinetm Science Ser.). 24p. (gr. 1-2). 41.95 (978-0-7802-2694-4(1)) Wright Group/McGraw-Hill.

The Pond: Big Book. (Sunshinetm Science Ser.). 24p. (gr. 1-2). 37.50 (978-0-7802-2781-1(6)) Wright Group/McGraw-Hill.

Pond Life Sets: 1 Each of 3 Big Books. (Sunshinetm Science Ser.). (gr. 1-2). 111.50 (978-0-7802-2820-7(0)) Wright Group/McGraw-Hill.

Pond Life Sets: 1 Each of 3 Student Books. (Sunshinetm Science Ser.). (gr. 1-2). 20.95 (978-0-7802-2821-4(9)) Wright Group/McGraw-Hill.

The Popular Science Fact Book for Inquiring Minds, 8 vols. 2017. (Popular Science Fact Book for Inquiring Minds Ser.). (ENG.). (J). (gr. 8-8). lib. bdg. 198.00 (978-1-5026-3332-3(9), ff42a32c-6a5b-4312-ac7b-4f843e3c41c6) Cavendish Square Publishing LLC.

Prentice-Hall Staff. Building Block. (J). pap., act. bk. ed. (978-0-13-402140-9(1)) Prentice Hall (Schl. Div.).

—Learning System Integrated Science, Bk. 1. (J). pap., act. bk. ed. 21.97 (978-0-13-402199-7(1)) Prentice Hall (Schl. Div.).

—Things Fall Apart. 2nd ed. (J). stu. ed. (978-0-13-716846-0(2)) Prentice Hall (Schl. Div.).

PRESS, Celebration. Iopeners: Science Library, 10 vols. 2004. (ENG.). (J). (gr. k-k). 220.95 (978-0-7652-4970-8(7), Celebration Pr.) Savvas Learning Co.

Pressberg, Dava. Producers, Consumers, & Decomposers, 1 vol. 2016. (Spotlight on Ecology & Life Science Ser.). (ENG.). 24p. (J). (gr. 4-6). 27.93 (978-1-4994-2594-9(5), e644a378-34d7-4df6-adea-9cfdf812e47a, PowerKids Pr.) Rosen Publishing Group, Inc., The.

Primary Sources of Revolutionary Scientific Discoveries & Theories, 6 vols. 2004. (Primary Sources of Revolutionary Scientific Discoveries & Theories Ser.). (ENG.). (YA). (gr. 5-5). lib. bdg. 111.39 (978-1-4042-0373-0(7), 23c21d00-972c-41fb-b334-1fb4d98d8378) Rosen Publishing Group, Inc., The.

Prism the Rainbow Pony. 2004. (Region IV ESC Resources for Science Ser.). per. (978-1-932797-90-9(4)) Region 4 Education Service Ctr.

Profiles in Science, bks. 14, vol. 14. Incl. Curious Bones: Mary Anning & the Birth of Paleontology. Goodhue, Thomas W. (Illus.). 112p. (YA). (gr. 6-12). 2004. lib. bdg. 23.95 (978-1-883846-93-0(5), First Biographies); Double Stars: The Story of Caroline Herschel. Venkatraman, Padma. (Illus.). 176p. (gr. 6-12). 2007. lib. bdg. 27.95 (978-1-59935-042-4(4)); Fire, Water, & Air: The Story of Antoine Lavoisier. Baxter, Roberta. (J). 2009. 28.95 (978-1-59935-087-5(4)); Galileo Galilei & the Science of Motion. Boerst, William J. (Illus.). 144p. (YA). (gr. 6-12). 2004. lib. bdg. 26.95 (978-1-931798-00-6(1)); Great Explainer: The Story of Richard Feynman. LeVine, Harry, III. (Illus.). 144p. (J). (gr. 7-10). 2009. 28.95 (978-1-59935-113-1(7), 1309604); Ibn Al-Haytham: First Scientist. Steffens, Bradley. (Illus.). 128p. (J). (gr. 4-7). 2007. lib. bdg. 27.95 (978-1-59935-024-0(6)); Johannes Kepler: Discovering the Laws of Celestial Motion. Boerst, William J. (Illus.). 144p. (YA). (gr. 6-12). 2004. lib. bdg. 26.95 (978-1-883846-98-5(6), First Biographies); Lise Meitner: Discoverer of Nuclear Fission. Barron, Rachel Stiffler. (Illus.). 112p. (YA). (gr. 6-12). 2004. lib. bdg. 23.95 (978-1-883846-52-7(8), First Biographies); Louis Pasteur & the Founding of Microbiology. Ackerman, Jane. (Illus.). 144p. (YA). (gr. 6-12). 2004. 26.95 (978-1-931798-13-6(3)); New Elements: The Story of Marie Curie. (Illus.). 144p. (J). (gr. 4-7). 2006. lib. bdg. 27.95 (978-1-59935-023-3(8)); Nicholas Copernicus & the Founding of Modern Astronomy. Boerst, William J. (Illus.). 144p. (YA). (gr. 6-12). 2004. lib. bdg. 26.95 (978-1-883846-99-2(4), First Biographies); Nikola Tesla & the Taming of Electricity. Aldrich, Lisa J. (Illus.). 160p. (J). (gr. 3-7). 2005. lib. bdg. 26.95 (978-1-931798-46-4(X)); Rosalind Franklin & the Structure of Life. Polcovar, Jane. (Illus.). 144p. (J). (gr. 3-7). 2006. lib. bdg. 27.95 (978-1-59935-022-6(X)); Scheduling the Heavens: The Story of Edmond Halley. Fox,

Mary Virginia. (Illus.). 128p. (gr. 6-12). 2007. lib. bdg. 27.95 (978-1-59935-021-9(1)); Skeptical Chemist: The Story of Robert Boyle. Baxter, Roberta. (Illus.). 128p. (gr. 6-12). 2006. lib. bdg. 27.95 (978-1-59935-025-7(4)); Tycho Brahe: Mapping the Heavens. Boerst, William J. (Illus.). 144p. (YA). (gr. 6-12). 2004. 26.95 (978-1-883846-97-8(8), First Biographies); 2007. Set lib. bdg. 405.30 (978-1-59935-033-2(5)) Reynolds, Morgan Inc.

Publishers, Chelsea House, creator. Scientific American Set. 2007. (Scientific American Ser.). (ENG.). (gr. 5-8). 240.00 (978-0-7910-9811-0(7), P179192, Facts On File) Infobase Holdings, Inc.

QEB Start Reading & Writing National Book Stores Edition: What's in the Sky? 2006. (J). per. (978-1-59566-266-8(9)) QEB Publishing Inc.

Ragan, Sean Michael. The Popular Science Inventor's Manual, 1 vol. 2018. (Popular Science Guide for Hackers & Inventors Ser.). (ENG.). 248p. (gr. 8-8). lib. bdg. 56.71 (978-1-5026-4469-5(X), a86c6636-b773-4b5b-a56a-7e06443e1e09) Cavendish Square Publishing LLC.

Raintree. Itlp 2004 Grade 4 Science Stat. 2004. pap. (978-1-4109-1570-2(0)); pap. (978-1-4109-1619-8(7)) Harcourt Schl. Pubs.

—Itlp 2004 Grades 2-4 Science S. 2004. pap. (978-1-4109-1571-9(9)); pap. (978-1-4109-1567-2(0)); pap. (978-1-4109-1569-6(7)) Harcourt Schl. Pubs.

Reader dsm-3 sink or float Ea. 2004. (J). (978-1-59242-525-9(9)) Delta Education, LLC.

Reading First Through Science Grade 1. 2005. (ENG.). 10.95 (978-0-9766802-8-4(9)) Educational Tools, Inc.

Reading First Through Science Grade 2. 2008. 10.95 (978-0-9766802-7-7(0)) Educational Tools, Inc.

Reading First Through Science Grade 4. 2005. (ENG., Illus.). (978-0-9766802-6-0(2)) Educational Tools, Inc.

Resler, T. J. Nerd a to Z: Your Reference to Literally Figuratively Everything You've Always Wanted to Know. 2019. (Illus.). 176p. (J). (gr. 3-7). 14.99 (978-1-4263-3474-0(5), National Geographic Kids) Disney Publishing Worldwide.

Rice, Dona Herweck. All in the Family, 1 vol. rev. ed. 2014. (Science: Informational Text Ser.). (ENG., Illus.). 24p. (gr. 1-2). lib. bdg. 22.96 (978-1-4938-1150-2(9)) Teacher Created Materials, Inc.

—Science Detectives, 1 vol. rev. ed. 2014. (Science: Informational Text Ser.). (ENG., Illus.). 24p. (gr. 1-2). pap. 9.99 (978-1-4807-4574-2(X)) Teacher Created Materials, Inc.

Rice, William B. The World of Rocks & Minerals, 1 vol. rev. ed. 2007. (Science: Informational Text Ser.). (ENG., Illus.). 32p. (gr. 4-6). pap. 12.99 (978-0-7439-0553-4(9)) Teacher Created Materials, Inc.

Ring, Susan. Design It! Build It! Date not set. (Early Science Big Bks.). (Illus.). 16p. (J). (gr. -1-2). pap. 16.95 (978-1-58273-121-6(7)) Sundance/Newbridge Educational Publishing.

—The Ocean, 6 vols., Set. 2003. (Yellow Umbrella Early Level Ser.). (ENG.). 16p. (gr. k-1). pap. 35.70 (978-0-7368-2997-7(0), Capstone Pr.) Capstone.

—Show Us Your Wings, 6 vols., Set. 2003. (Yellow Umbrella Early Level Ser.). (ENG.). 16p. (gr. k-1). pap. 35.70 (978-0-7368-2999-1(7), Capstone Pr.) Capstone.

Ripley, Catherine. Why? The Best Ever Question & Answer Book about Nature, Science & the World Around You. Ritchie, Scot, illus. 2018. (ENG.). 192p. (J). (gr. -1-4). pap. 19.95 (978-1-77147-321-7(5)) Owlkids Bks. Inc. CAN. Dist: Publishers Group West (PGW).

Roberts, Don & Roberts, Susan. Things That Scratch: The Story of Abrasives. (Illus.). 60p. (YA). (gr. 8-18). pap. 14.95 (978-1-57555-170-8(5)); pap. 24.95 (978-1-57555-169-2(1)) Cedar Bay Pr., L.L.C.

Rohrig, Brian. Pure Slime: 50 Incredible Ways to Make Slime Using Household Substances. 2004. (Illus.). 232p. (YA). per. 12.95 (978-0-9718480-5-4(X)) FizzBang Science.

Roman, Nora. Using a Ruler, 1 vol. 2017. (Super Science Tools Ser.). (ENG.). 24p. (gr. 1-2). pap. 9.15 (978-1-4824-6401-6(2), a55da0b6-dc13-4032-99b8-99e29eb59181) Stevens, Gareth Publishing LLLP.

Rookie Read-About(r) Science. 2013. (Rookie Read-About(r) Science Ser.). (J). 92.00 (978-0-531-21404-6(4), Children's Pr.) Scholastic Library Publishing.

Rookie Read-About(r) Science: How Things Work (Set Of 7) 2015. (Rookie Read-About(r) Science: How Things Work Ser.). (J). lib. bdg. 161.00 (978-0-531-22376-5(0), Children's Pr.) Scholastic Library Publishing.

Rookie Read-About(r) Science — It's a Good Thing..., 7, Set. 2014. (Rookie Read-About(r) Science — It's a Good Thing... Ser.). (J). (978-0-531-24359-6(1)) Scholastic Library Publishing.

Rookie Read-About Science: Life Science, 6 bks., Set. Incl. Tiny Life in a Puddle. Early, Bobbi. lib. bdg. 20.50 (978-0-516-25272-8(0)); Tiny Life in the Air. Taylor-Butler, Christine. lib. bdg. 20.50 (978-0-516-25273-5(9)); Tiny Life in Your Home. Trumbauer, Lisa. lib. bdg. 20.50 (978-0-516-25274-2(7)); Tiny Life on Plants. Lindström, Karin. lib. bdg. 20.50 (978-0-516-25297-1(6)); Tiny Life on the Ground. Wade, Mary Dodson. 20.50 (978-0-516-25298-8(4)); Tiny Life on Your Body. Taylor-Butler, Christine. lib. bdg. 20.50 (978-0-516-25299-5(2)); (Illus.). 32p. (J). (gr. 1-2). 2005. 2005. 117.00 o.p. (978-0-516-25395-4(6), Children's Pr.) Scholastic Library Publishing.

Rookie Read-About(r) Science: What's the Difference? (Set Of 6) 2015. (Rookie Read-About(r) Science: What's the Difference? Ser.). (J). lib. bdg. 138.00 (978-0-531-22420-5(1), Children's Pr.) Scholastic Library Publishing.

Roselli, Stephanie, ed. The Budding Scientist. 2012. (Budding Ser.). (ENG., Illus.). 72p. pap. 9.95 (978-0-87659-385-1(6), Gryphon House Inc) Gryphon Hse., Inc.

Ryles, Briony & Hall, Derek. Medieval Period & the Renaissance. 2010. (CC: Technology Through the Ages Ser.). 112p. (gr. 6-12). 42.80 (978-1-933834-84-9(6)) Brown Bear Bks.

—The Scientific Revolution. 2010. (Curriculum Connections: Technology Through the Ages Ser.). 112p. 39.95 (978-1-933834-85-6(4)) Brown Bear Bks.

Sandler, Michael & Hess, Debra. Checkered Flag! 2007. (Read on! Special Edition: Level AA Ser.). (Illus.). 23p. (J). (gr. 4-7). pap. 4.84 (978-1-4190-3516-6(9)) Steck-Vaughn.

Schaefer, Lola M. & Endres, Hollie J. Push & Pull, 6 vols., Set. 2003. (Yellow Umbrella Early Level Ser.). (ENG.). 16p. (gr. k-1). pap. 35.70 (978-0-7368-2998-4(9), Capstone Pr.) Capstone.

Scheppler, Bill. Al-Biruni: Master Astronomer & Muslim Scholar of the Eleventh Century. 2009. (Great Muslim Philosophers & Scientists of the Middle Ages Ser.). 112p. (gr. 6-6). 66.50 (978-1-61513-177-8(9), Rosen Reference) Rosen Publishing Group, Inc., The.

Scholastic. Superscience Mysteries Kit. 2018. (ENG.). (gr. 3-6). pap. 59.99 (978-1-338-25522-5(3)) Scholastic, Inc.

Scholastic, Inc. Staff. Brain Play 1st-3rd. 2008. (J). 29.99 (978-0-545-05207-8(6)) Scholastic, Inc.

—Brain Play Preschool-1st. 2008. (J). 29.99 (978-0-439-81350-1(6)) Scholastic, Inc.

Scholastic Library Publishing. A True Book-Physical Science. 2011. (True Book-Physical Science Ser.). (J). 174.00 (978-0-531-25935-1(8), Children's Pr.) Scholastic Library Publishing.

School Zone Staff. Big Science: Hours of Fun! 2006. (ENG.). 320p. (J). (gr. 2-3). pap. 9.99 (978-1-58947-317-1(5)) School Zone Publishing Co.

Schuh, Mari & Alpert, Barbara. Science Builders. 2011. (Science Builders Ser.). (ENG.). 24p. (J). (gr. -1-2). 136.60 (978-1-4296-6074-7(0), 15928); pap., pap., pap. 36.45 (978-1-4296-7117-0(3), 16698) Capstone. (Capstone Pr.).

—Science Builders Classroom Collection. 2011. (Science Builders Ser.). (ENG.). 24p. (J). (gr. k-1). 221.70 (978-1-4296-7118-7(1), 16699, Capstone Pr.) Capstone.

Schwartz, Heather E. Incredible Science Trivia: Fun Facts & Quizzes. 2018. (Trivia Time! (Alternator Books (r)) Ser.). (ENG., Illus.). 32p. (J). (gr. 3-6). 29.32 (978-1-5124-8334-5(6), 311c19a1-6932-4844-bcbf-28b8b1916cd3, Lerner Pubns.) Lerner Publishing Group.

Schwartz, Linda. Primary Science Quiz Whiz, Vol. 429. VanBlaricum, Pam, ed. Mason, Mark, illus. 2004. 128p. (J). (gr. 1-3). pap. 14.99 (978-0-88160-372-9(4), LW-429) Creative Teaching Pr., Inc.

—Social Studies & Science Quiz Whiz 3-5, Vol. 432. VanBlaricum, Pam, ed. Armstrong, Beverly, illus. 2004. 128p. (J). (gr. 3-5). pap. 10.99 (978-0-88160-375-0(9), LW-432) Creative Teaching Pr., Inc.

Science, Set. 2004. (gr. 6). tchr. ed., stu. ed. 47.95 (978-1-58095-765-6(X), SCI0615); (Illus.). (gr. 5). tchr. ed., stu. ed. 47.95 (978-1-58095-762-5(5), SCI0515) Alpha Omega Pubns., Inc. (Lifepac).

Science. 2011. (New Discovering Careers for Your Future Ser.). (Illus.). 128p. (gr. 4-9). 24.95 (978-0-8160-8053-3(4), Ferguson Publishing Company) Infobase Holdings, Inc.

Science: Chemistry, 11 vols., Set. 2004. (Illus.). (gr. 11). tchr. ed., stu. ed. 47.95 (978-1-58095-780-9(3), SCI1115, Lifepac) Alpha Omega Pubns., Inc.

Science: Physics, 11 vols., Set. 2004. (Illus.). (gr. 12). tchr. ed., stu. ed. 47.95 (978-1-58095-783-0(8), SCI1215, Lifepac) Alpha Omega Pubns., Inc.

Science: Student Testing Kit. 2004. (Illus.). (J). (gr. 1-8). stu. ed. 5.00 (978-0-7403-0045-5(8), SD001); (YA). (gr. 7-12). pap., stu. ed. 5.00 (978-0-7403-0046-2(6), SD002) Alpha Omega Pubns., Inc.

Science & Technology for Children Books, MicroWorlds Set, 8 vols. 2004. (Illus.). 64p. (J). (978-1-933008-16-5(4)) Smithsonian Science Education Ctr. (SSEC).

Science & Technology for Children Books, Physical Sciences & Technology Library Set, 6 vols. 2004. (Illus.). 64p. (J). (978-1-933008-26-4(1)) Smithsonian Science Education Ctr. (SSEC).

Science & Technology for Children Books, Science Library Set, 12 vols. 2004. (Illus.). 64p. (J). (978-1-933008-24-0(5)) Smithsonian Science Education Ctr. (SSEC).

Science & You. (Illus.). (J). 502.60 (978-0-7910-7275-2(4), Facts On File) Infobase Holdings, Inc.

Science Explorer (Set), 24 vols., Set. Incl. Bugs. Gray, Susan H. lib. bdg. 32.07 (978-1-60279-521-1(5), 200281); Cells. Mullins, Matt. lib. bdg. 32.07 (978-1-60279-517-4(7), 200287); Circulation. Orr, Tamra B. lib. bdg. 32.07 (978-1-60279-520-4(7), 200304); Compounds & Mixtures. Simon, Charnan. lib. bdg. 32.07 (978-1-60279-536-5(3), 200288); Digestion. Orr, Tamra B. lib. bdg. 32.07 (978-1-60279-518-1(5), 200303); Ecosystems. Mullins, Matt. lib. bdg. 32.07 (978-1-60279-516-7(9), 200300); Electricity. Lockwood, Sophie. lib. bdg. 32.07 (978-1-60279-533-4(9), 200289); Erosion. Simon, Charnan. lib. bdg. 32.07 (978-1-60279-525-9(8), 200284); Heat. Lockwood, Sophie. lib. bdg. 32.07 (978-1-60279-534-1(7), 200290); Levers & Pulleys. Rau, Dana Meachen. lib. bdg. 32.07 (978-1-60279-537-2(1), 200282); Light. Rau, Dana Meachen. lib. bdg. 32.07 (978-1-60279-531-0(2), 200285); Magnets. Taylor-Butler, Christine. lib. bdg. 32.07 (978-1-60279-530-3(4), 200296); Minerals. Lockwood, Sophie. lib. bdg. 32.07 (978-1-60279-524-2(X), 200291); Planet Earth. Mullins, Matt. lib. bdg. 32.07 (978-1-60279-515-0(0), 200302); Plants. Gray, Susan H. lib. bdg. 32.07 (978-1-60279-522-8(3), 200286); Respiration. Orr, Tamra B. lib. bdg. 32.07 (978-1-60279-519-8(3), 200292); Rocks. Lockwood, Sophie. lib. bdg. 32.07 (978-1-60279-523-5(1), 200283); Seeds. Gray, Susan H. lib. bdg. 32.07 (978-1-60279-514-3(2), 200293); Soil. Franchino, Vicky. lib. bdg. 32.07 (978-1-60279-526-6(6), 200297); Solar Energy. Taylor-Butler, Christine. lib. bdg. 32.07 (978-1-60279-527-3(4), 200295); Sound. Taylor-Butler, Christine. lib. bdg. 32.07 (978-1-60279-532-7(0), 200301); States of Matter. Mullins, Matt. lib. bdg. 32.07 (978-1-60279-535-8(5), 200299); Water. Simon, Charnan. lib. bdg. 32.07 (978-1-60279-529-7(0), 200298); Weather. Orr, Tamra B. lib. bdg. 32.07 (978-1-60279-528-0(2), 200294); (Illus.). (gr. 4-8). (Explorer Library: Science Explorer Ser.). (ENG.). 32p. 2009. 769.68 (978-1-60279-588-4(6), 200243) Cherry Lake Publishing.

Science Factory, 8 vols., Set. 2007. (Science Factory Ser.). (ENG.). (J). (gr. 4-5). lib. bdg. 121.08 (978-1-4042-4251-7(1), fecba1d6-49d9-4f53-ab7b-36bdbe3ecaac) Rosen Publishing Group, Inc., The.

Science Fun. 2005. (Little Celebrations Thematic Packages Ser.). (J). (gr. k-3). 133.50 (978-0-673-75382-3(4)) Celebration Pr.

Science in Action, 6 vols. 2015. (Science in Action Ser.: 6). (ENG.). 32p. (J). (gr. 3-6). lib. bdg. 196.74 (978-1-62403-959-1(6), 19415, Checkerboard Library) ABDO Publishing Co.

Science Links. 2005. (Science Links Ser.). (Illus.). 32p. (gr. 4-6). 345.00 (978-0-7910-7415-2(3), Facts On File) Infobase Holdings, Inc.

Science Made Simple, 12 vols., Set. Incl. Atomic & Molecular Structure. Chaffee, Joel. lib. bdg. 37.13 (978-1-4488-1230-1(5), 3a12e7b0-7abb-4f22-ab48-7c987f52f35d, Rosen Reference); Cell Biology. Stimola, Aubrey. lib. bdg. 37.13 (978-1-4488-1234-9(8), ef84f849-97f3-4e5b-8542-8a9787ffbd18); Chemical Reactions. Wolny, Philip. lib. bdg. 37.13 (978-1-4488-1235-6(6), edbe731d-130e-4bdb-b011-de2eeb7de3b1, Rosen Reference); Electric & Magnetic Phenomena. Galiano, Dean. lib. bdg. 37.13 (978-1-4488-1231-8(3), 14ef026a-ff3a-4419-bbf8-2246e2a92de5, Rosen Reference); Gases & Their Properties. Meyer, Susan. lib. bdg. 37.13 (978-1-4488-1233-2(X), fa7247f2-bf7d-4898-b36f-329da90224f4, Rosen Reference); Motion & Forces. Orr, Tamra. lib. bdg. 37.13 (978-1-4488-1232-5(1), 3a451b7e-074f-47f0-9ea0-ec37351d9324); (YA). (gr. 7-7). 2011. (Science Made Simple Ser.). (ENG., Illus.). 64p. 2010. Set lib. bdg. 222.78 (978-1-4488-1393-3(X), f335c142-383e-4fd0-8399-1eeb4f562d7d, Rosen Reference) Rosen Publishing Group, Inc., The.

The Science Of..., 10 vols., Set. Incl. Science of a Bicycle. Graham, Ian. lib. bdg. 28.67 (978-1-4339-0040-2(8), caf12869-a1da-4245-9545-4af4f51f5a11); Science of a Glass of Water. Claybourne, Anna. (Illus.). lib. bdg. 28.67 (978-1-4339-0041-9(6), eb7e775e-10e9-4845-ae67-41feea29c034); Science of a Guitar. Claybourne, Anna. (Illus.). lib. bdg. 28.67 (978-1-4339-0042-6(4), 9837157f-1dfb-45cd-86ed-976f05989798); Science of a Pair of Glasses. Williams, Brian. (Illus.). lib. bdg. 28.67 (978-1-4339-0044-0(0), 31f40d75-9525-4c30-8af8-0b5b56cd1ff5); Science of a Piece of Paper. De La Bédoyère, Camilla. lib. bdg. 28.67 (978-1-4339-0045-7(9), 2c7729a0-0344-4cd2-b1ab-a6ffe146ada0); (YA). (gr. 4-5). (Science Of... Ser.). (ENG.). 32p. 2009. Set lib. bdg. 143.35 (978-1-4339-0046-4(7), 49220dcc-74fa-4515-bb97-18e3378d7128, Gareth Stevens Learning Library) Stevens, Gareth Publishing LLLP.

Science on Patrol, 12 vols. 2016. (Science on Patrol Ser.). (ENG.). 00048p. (J). (gr. 4-5). lib. bdg. 201.60 (978-1-4824-5860-2(8), 55e47415-7cab-4120-9c2a-e08212c90b8d) Stevens, Gareth Publishing LLLP.

Science Program, Early Level. 2003. (Yellow Umbrella Early Level Ser.). (ENG.). 16p. (gr. k-1). pap. 428.40 (978-0-7368-3068-3(5), Capstone Pr.) Capstone.

Science Q & A, 12 vols. 2015. (Science Q & A Ser.). (ENG.). 32p. (J). (gr. 3-3). lib. bdg. 181.26 (978-1-5026-0380-7(2), 3a1a67d4-d70d-45a9-87cb-1af80c3dbef8); (gr. 5-5). pap., pap., pap. 63.48 (978-1-5026-0697-6(6)) Cavendish Square Publishing LLC. (Cavendish Square).

Science Reading Stories. (J). (gr. 2). (978-0-8374-0622-0(6), 656); (gr. 3). (978-0-8374-0623-7(4), 657); (gr. 4). (978-0-8374-0624-4(2), 658); (gr. 5). (978-0-8374-0625-1(0), 659) Weekly Reader Corp.

Science Rocks! Set 2 Site CD+Book. 2010. (Science Rocks! Set 2 Site CD+Book Ser.). (Illus.). 32p. lib. bdg. 504.84 incl. cd-rom (978-1-61641-007-0(8)) ABDO Publishing Co.

Science Set, 8 vols. (Content Collections). (gr. k-2). 276.08 (978-0-7362-2269-3(3)) CENGAGE Learning.

Science Spanish Content Area Standard Set. 2005. spiral bd. 2500.00 (978-1-4108-4530-6(3)) Benchmark Education Co.

Science Stories, 4 bks. (J). (gr. 2-4). lib. bdg. 59.80 (978-1-56674-934-3(4)) Forest Hse. Publishing Co., Inc.

Science stories foss spanish models & designs ea Cr05. 2005. (J). (978-1-59242-592-1(5)) Delta Education, LLC.

Scientific American Cutting-Edge Science: Set 1, 10 vols. Incl. Extreme Engineering. Rosen Publishing Group, creator. (Illus.). 120p. lib. bdg. 39.80 (978-1-4042-0986-2(7), 276477d9-7f91-4bc2-9f5a-6e73f109ffef); Fighting Infectious Diseases. Rosen Editors. (Illus.). 144p. lib. bdg. 39.80 (978-1-4042-0988-6(3), f312c5ae-078e-4b4f-a98a-9539ad9c69b3); Future of the Web. Rosen Publishing Group, creator. (Illus.). 118p. lib. bdg. 39.80 (978-1-4042-0989-3(1), c72a47ba-6f13-4e59-8bd6-bcc7cae17540); Nanotech Revolution. Rosen Publishing Group, creator. (Illus.). 136p. lib. bdg. 39.80 (978-1-4042-0990-9(5), d08a8d66-3faa-4a10-aff9-9e9f68a4adce); Tackling Cancer. Rosen Editors. 120p. lib. bdg. 38.80 (978-1-4042-0987-9(5), 536e35a0-ef07-4279-bade-72943b8f35cd); 21st-Century Robotics. Rosen Publishing Group, creator. (Illus.). 104p. lib. bdg. 39.80 (978-1-4042-0985-5(9), 9ee2646a-f786-43e1-9809-d34258b953de); (YA). (gr. 9-9). (Scientific American Cutting-Edge Science Ser.). (ENG.). 2006. Set lib. bdg. 199.00 (978-1-4042-0939-8(5), 7ba597cd-0988-4303-9b85-df8e65f253cd) Rosen Publishing Group, Inc., The.

Scientific American Staff. 21st Century Robotics. 2009. (Scientific American Cutting-Edge Science Ser.). 101p. (gr. 9-9). 63.90 (978-1-60853-072-4(8)) Rosen Publishing Group, Inc., The.

Scientific Breakthroughs, 10 vols. 2014. (Scientific Breakthroughs Ser.). (ENG.). 48p. (YA). (gr. 6-6). lib. bdg. 167.35 (978-1-4777-8613-0(9), e6246205-15e2-4c99-9a39-efb5d8e190c9, Rosen Central) Rosen Publishing Group, Inc., The.

Scirri, Kaitlin. The Science of Invisibility & X-Ray Vision, 1 vol. 2018. (Science of Superpowers Ser.). (ENG.). 48p. (gr. 4-4). 33.07 (978-1-5026-3790-1(1), 55b850c3-c1f1-4248-89dd-6134f201f18d) Cavendish Square Publishing LLC.

Scott, Foresman and Company Staff. Discover Science. (J). (gr. 1). pap. 12.34 (978-0-673-42490-7(1)); (gr. 2). pap. 12.90 (978-0-673-42491-4(X)); (gr. 3). pap. 14.59 (978-0-673-42492-1(8)); (gr. 4). pap. 16.06 (978-0-673-42493-8(6)); (gr. 5). pap. 17.00 (978-0-673-42494-5(4)); (gr. 6). pap. 17.62 (978-0-673-42495-2(2)) Addison Wesley Schl. (Scott Foresman).

Scotti, Alberto Douglas. Cocina y Ciencia. 2012. 44p. (J). (gr. 3-5). pap. 23.99 (978-958-30-3715-3(X)) Juventud, Editorial ESP. Dist: Lectorum Pubns., Inc.

Seeds Grow, 6 vols. (Sunshinetm Science Ser.). 24p. (gr. 1-2). 31.50 (978-0-7802-0290-0(2)); 36.95 (978-0-7802-0541-3(3)) Wright Group/McGraw-Hill.

Shannon, Terry Miller. Forces That Shape Earth. 2016. (Spring Forward Ser.). (J). (gr. 2). (978-1-4900-9438-0(5)) Benchmark Education Co.

Sharkawy, Azza. Share It! 2014. (Science Sleuths Ser.). (ENG., Illus.). 24p. (J). (gr. 2-2). (978-0-7787-0781-3(4)) Crabtree Publishing Co.

Shevick, Ed. Great Scientists in Action. Wheeler, Ron, illus. 2004. (Science Action Labs Ser.). 64p. (J). pap. 9.95 (978-1-57310-436-4(1), 1238118) Teaching & Learning Co.

Shoup, Kate. The Technology of Ancient Greece, 1 vol. 2016. (Ancient Innovations Ser.). (ENG.). 64p. (gr. 6-6). 35.93 (978-1-5026-2231-0(9), b89700dd-0c36-4559-8cc3-9d8c4d20dffd) Cavendish Square Publishing LLC.

Show What You Know on the OGT, Science Student Self Study Workbook. 2007. (YA). per. 18.95 (978-1-59230-274-1(2)) Englefield & Assocs., Inc.

Showers, Paul. Where Does the Garbage Go? 2015. (Let's-Read-And-Find-Out Science: Stage 2 Ser.). (J). (gr. k-3). lib. bdg. 17.20 (978-0-613-01320-8(4)) Turtleback.

Sian Revision Work: Plane & Simple. 2004. (Science in A Nutshell Ser.). (J). (978-1-59242-089-6(3)) Delta Education, LLC.

Silva Lee, Alfonso. Mi Isla y Yo: La Naturaleza de Cuba. Hayskar, Bonnie J., ed. Lago, Alexis, illus. 2010. (SPA.). 32p. (J). pap. 9.95 (978-1-929165-22-3(6)) PANGAEA.

Simply Science, 16 vols., Set. Incl. Body & Health. Bailey, Gerry. (J). lib. bdg. 28.67 (978-1-4339-0030-3(0), 5c843853-9c63-44c6-964e-ba0cd95c9e23); Electricity. Law, Felicia. (YA). lib. bdg. 28.67 (978-1-4339-0031-0(9), 4a726896-0822-469c-8cf9-c21305e1d85d); Flight. Bailey, Gerry. (YA). lib. bdg. 28.67 (978-1-4339-0032-7(7), a2162e64-63b2-45f3-b562-4dc36668830b); Materials. Way, Steve. (YA). lib. bdg. 28.67 (978-1-4339-0033-4(5), a8705e69-5c1b-4ae8-80eb-7c27fc292ae4); Powerful Machines. Bailey, Gerry. (YA). lib. bdg. 28.67 (978-1-4339-0035-8(1), 690398c4-ebd0-45df-971d-ecec03844ea5); Structures. Bailey, Gerry. (YA). lib. bdg. 28.67 (978-1-4339-0036-5(X), ae30ed5c-1b6b-49f5-86c0-4bb45c3b97e4); Technology. Bailey, Gerry. (YA). lib. bdg. 28.67 (978-1-4339-0034-1(3), 41fecaf2-f9dd-41d3-b0d6-0cb4a013b4fd); Water. Bailey, Gerry. (YA). lib. bdg. 28.67 (978-1-4339-0037-2(8), bd8d8f6d-887b-45d8-96cb-6f274e57d44a); (Illus.). (gr. 3-5). (Simply Science Ser.). (ENG.). 32p. 2009. Set lib. bdg. 229.36 (978-1-4339-0038-9(6), 487e0e4a-c5b1-4340-9d88-ec57cdab0a16); Set lib. bdg. 200.69 (978-0-8368-9312-0(3), 66eb4849-2b30-431f-8201-c3f19dccb564) Stevens, Gareth Publishing LLLP. (Gareth Stevens Learning Library).

Singh, Simon. The Code Book: the Secrets Behind Codebreaking. 2003. (ENG.). 272p. (YA). (gr. 7). pap. 9.99 (978-0-385-73062-4(4), Ember) Random Hse. Children's Bks.

Sitarski, Anita. Cold Light: Creatures, Discoveries, & Inventions That Glow. 2007. (ENG., Illus.). 48p. (J). (gr. 4-7). 16.95 (978-1-59078-468-6(5), Astra Young Readers) Astra Publishing Hse.

Skillicorn, Phillipa, et al. International Primary Science Student's Book 1, Bk. 1. Miller, Jonathan & Pilling, Anne, eds. Robinson, Pete, tr. Hannigan, Pauline et al, illus. 2014. (Collins International Primary Science Ser.). (ENG.). 96p. (J). (gr. -1-k). pap., stu. ed. 12.95 (978-0-00-758609-7(4)) HarperCollins Pubs. Ltd. GBR. Dist: Independent Pubs. Group.

Smibert, Angie. Dramatic Discoveries. 2018. (Unbelievable Ser.). (ENG., Illus.). 32p. (J). (gr. 3-6). 32.80 (978-1-63235-419-8(5), 13767, 12-Story Library) Bookstaves, LLC.

—Mind-Blowing Physical Science Activities. 2017. (Curious Scientists Ser.). (ENG., Illus.). 24p. (J). (gr. 1-3). pap. 7.95 (978-1-5157-6893-7(7), 135386, Capstone Pr.) Capstone.

Smith, Carrie. We See with Our Eyes: Lap Book. 2009. (My First Reader's Theater Set B Ser.). (J). 28.00 (978-1-60634-992-2(9)) Benchmark Education Co.

Smith, Jodene. Cut & Paste - Science. 2003. (ENG.). 96p. pap. 12.99 (978-0-7439-3706-1(6)) Teacher Created Resources, Inc.

Snedden, Robert. The Medieval World. 2009. (Technology in Times Past Ser.). (ENG., Illus.). 48p. (J). (gr. 4-7). pap. (978-1-897563-65-6(5)) Saunders Bk. Co.

Sobey, Ed. Rocket-Powered Science: Invent to Learn! Create, Build & Test Rocket Designs. 2006. (Illus.). 106p. (J). (gr. 4-7). per. 14.95 (978-1-59647-055-2(0)) Good Year Bks.

Solving Science Mysteries, 22 vols., Set. Incl. Why Do Airplanes Fly? Moore, Rob. lib. bdg. 26.27 (978-1-61531-890-2(9), d1d2cfd5-8e9c-4aa1-802f-8b4bb90cd0ee); Why Do Balls Bounce? Moore, Rob. lib. bdg. 26.27 (978-1-61531-889-6(5), 3efae534-857c-4e61-b464-5310dbb9e276); Why Do Diamonds Sparkle? All about Earth's Resources. Bethune, Helen. lib. bdg. 26.27 (978-1-61531-894-0(1), 1d6dbd02-d336-4098-b0db-27d583de7b90); Why Do Glaciers Grind? Bethune, Helen. lib. bdg. 26.27 (978-1-4488-0391-0(8), de2e39fb-2cea-4860-a61e-1f2cd1d46861); Why Do Monkeys Chatter? Bethune, Helen. lib. bdg. 26.27 (978-1-4488-0394-1(2), a14bb143-2381-4778-a413-571c4712fcff); Why Do Shadows Lengthen? Brasch, Nicolas. lib. bdg. 26.27

S

(978-1-61531-891-9(7), 82df3909-363c-42ec-9e66-87d93386a3b0); Why Do Spiders Live in Webs? Brasch, Nicolas. lib. bdg. 26.27 *(978-1-4488-0397-2(7),* 1a2a5133-05d6-46f9-8f28-8b0ff7651e99); Why Do Stars Twinkle? McMahon, Michael. lib. bdg. 26.27 *(978-1-61531-895-7(X),* 5cb41215-5515-48d4-961e-8de23820e0e3); Why Does Electricity Flow? Moore, Rob. lib. bdg. 26.27 *(978-1-61531-893-3(3),* 5aa95371-ba5f-435a-ade2-3d05f7a5004b); Why Does Water Evaporate? Moore, Rob. lib. bdg. 26.27 *(978-1-61531-892-6(5),* a61ea7af-15fc-4977-80d6-6c83a0a62c8d); Why Is It So Loud? Brasch, Nicolas. lib. bdg. 26.27 *(978-1-61531-888-9(7),* be0e23e3-0ff9-4975-91cf-320daa17e939); (YA). (gr. 4-5). (Solving Science Mysteries Ser.). (ENG., Illus.). 24p. 2010. Set lib. bdg. 216.70 *(978-1-61531-924-4(7),* cfec4bf3-f4ce-42c5-b111-e9d48c547a1a, PowerKids Pr.) Rosen Publishing Group, Inc., The.

Sonido. (Coleccion Jugando Con la Ciencia). (SPA., Illus.). 39p. (J). pap. 9.95 *(978-950-11-0831-6(7),* SGM317) Sigmar ARG. Dist: Continental Bk. Co., Inc.

Sparrow, Giles. Children's Encyclopedia of Science. 2018. (Arcturus Children's Reference Library: 4). (ENG.). 128p. (J). 14.99 *(978-1-78828-507-0(7),* 0fa8bdfd-84ef-4bcd-8710-3c5900791d31) Arcturus Publishing GBR. Dist: Baker & Taylor Publisher Services (BTPS).

Spear, Michael J. Life Science Catholic Heritage Edition Textbook. 2014. (Illus.). 275p. (J). pap. 0.00 *(978-0-9913264-0-2(7))* Catholic Heritage Curricula.

Spilsbury, Richard & Louise. Future World. 2013. (Zap! Ser.). (ENG., Illus.). 32p. (J). *(978-1-911242-71-0(7))* Book Hse.

—How to Be a Science Superhero. 2013. (Zap! Ser.). (ENG., Illus.). 32p. (J). *(978-1-911242-72-7(5))* Book Hse.

Stanbury, Jean. How to Dazzle at Being a Scientist. 2004. (Illus.). 48p. pap. 30.00 *(978-1-897675-52-6(6))* Brilliant Pubns. GBR. Dist: Parkwest Pubns., Inc.

Staton, Hilarie N. & McCarthy, Tara. Science & Stories Grade K-3: Integrating Science & Literature. 2005. (Illus.). 129p. (gr. k-3). per. 15.95 *(978-1-59647-082-8(8))* Good Year Bks.

Steck-Vaughn Staff. Creepy Creatures. 2003. pap. 4.10 *(978-0-7398-7629-9(5))* Steck-Vaughn.

—Focus on Science. 2004. (Focus on Science Ser.). (ENG.). 96p. (gr. 1-1). pap. 21.20 *(978-0-7398-9144-5(8));* (Illus.). 128p. (gr. 4-4). pap. 24.00 *(978-0-7398-9147-6(2));*Level C. 64p. (gr. 3-3). pap., tchr. ed. 21.95 *(978-0-7398-9152-0(9));*Level C. (Illus.). 128p. (gr. 3-3). pap., stu. ed. 24.00 *(978-0-7398-9146-9(4));*Level D. 64p. (gr. 4-4). pap., tchr. ed. 21.95 *(978-0-7398-9153-7(7));*Level A. 64p. (gr. 1-1). pap., tchr. ed. 21.95 *(978-0-7398-9150-6(2));*Level B. 64p. (gr. 2-2). pap., tchr. ed. 21.95 *(978-0-7398-9151-3(0));*Level B. (Illus.). 96p. (gr. 2-2). pap. 21.20 *(978-0-7398-9145-2(6));*Level E. (Illus.). 144p. (gr. 5-5). pap. 25.15 *(978-0-7398-9148-3(0));*Level F. 64p. (gr. 6-6). pap., tchr. ed. 21.95 *(978-0-7398-9155-1(3));*Level F. (Illus.). 144p. (gr. 6-6). pap. 25.15 *(978-0-7398-9149-0(9))* Houghton Mifflin Harcourt Publishing Co.

—Focus on Science 2004, Level E. 2004. (Focus on Science Ser.). (ENG.). 64p. (gr. 5-5). pap., tchr. ed. 21.95 *(978-0-7398-9154-4(5))* Houghton Mifflin Harcourt Publishing Co.

—Science: Earth & Space Life, Physical. 2003. (Science Ser.). (ENG.). 176p. (gr. 3-3). pap. 16.99 *(978-0-7398-7935-1(9))* Houghton Mifflin Harcourt Publishing Co.

—Science: Life, Physical, Earth & Spac. 2003. (Science Ser.). (ENG.). 176p. (gr. 1-1). pap. 16.99 *(978-0-7398-7933-7(2));* (gr. 4-4). pap. 16.99 *(978-0-7398-7936-8(7))* Houghton Mifflin Harcourt Publishing Co.

—Science: Life, Physical, Earth & Space. 2003. (Science Ser.). (ENG.). 176p. (gr. 2-2). pap. 16.99 *(978-0-7398-7934-4(0));* (gr. 5-5). pap. 16.99 *(978-0-7398-7937-5(5))* Houghton Mifflin Harcourt Publishing Co.

—Science Level H-J: Hello, Hello! 2003. (Illus.). pap. *(978-0-7398-7635-0(X))* Steck-Vaughn.

—Science - Earth & Space Life - Physical. 2003. (Science Ser.). (ENG.). 176p. (gr. 6-6). pap. 16.99 *(978-0-7398-7938-2(3))* Houghton Mifflin Harcourt Publishing Co.

—What Goes up Must Come Down. 2003. pap. 4.10 *(978-0-7398-7632-9(5))* Steck-Vaughn.

The STEM Guide to the Universe, 12 vols. 2016. (STEM Guide to the Universe Ser.). (ENG.). 192p. (gr. 9-9). 286.80 *(978-1-5081-7165-2(3),* 7af8e022-a887-4fcc-aeee-deef6cf98ff4, Rosen Young Adult) Rosen Publishing Group, Inc., The.

STEM in the Real World, 6 vols. 2015. (STEM in the Real World Ser.: 6). (ENG.). 48p. (J). (gr. 4-8). lib. bdg. 213.84 *(978-1-68078-037-6(9),* 19513) ABDO Publishing Co.

STEM in the Real World. 2015. (STEM in the Real World Ser.). (ENG.). 24p. (gr. 2-3). pap., pap., pap. 297.00 *(978-1-4994-1315-1(7),* PowerKids Pr.) Rosen Publishing Group, Inc., The.

Steve, Parker. What about Science & Technology. 2008. 40p. pap. *(978-1-84810-074-9(4))* Miles Kelly Publishing, Ltd.

Stille, Darlene R. Amazing Science, 12 bks. Boyd, Sheree, illus. Incl. Electricity: Bulbs, Batteries, & Sparks. (ENG., Illus.). 24p. (J). (gr. k-4). 2004. 27.32 *(978-1-4048-0245-2(2),* 90443, Picture Window Bks.); (Amazing Science Ser.). (ENG.). Illus.). 24p. 2004. 319.80 o.p. *(978-1-4048-0244-5(4),* Picture Window Bks.) Capstone.

The Story of Science (Group 3), 8 vols., Set. 2003. (Story of Science Ser.). (ENG.). (gr. 6-6). 147.72 *(978-0-7614-1424-7(X),* 11a29d81-af33-4b06-a01a-371997a300fc, Cavendish Square) Cavendish Square Publishing LLC.

Stosch, Dawn. Science Math, 1 vol. 2009. (Math Alive! Ser.). (ENG.). 32p. (gr. 4-4). lib. bdg. 31.21 *(978-0-7614-3213-5(2),* 1bc024e4-895e-47f2-b8a6-27b25f284992) Cavendish Square Publishing LLC.

Stuart, Colin. Why Space Matters to Me. 2015. (ENG., Illus.). 48p. (J). (gr. 3-6). E-Book 19.99 *(978-1-5124-0201-8(X),* Millbrook Pr.) Lerner Publishing Group.

Sundance/Newbridge LLC Staff. Animal Life Cycles. 2004. (Reading PowerWorks Ser.). (gr. 1-3). pap. 6.10 *(978-0-7608-9234-3(2))* Sundance/Newbridge Educational Publishing.

Sunshine Science Early Fluency Sets 1-3: 1 Each of 24 Big Books from Sets 1-3. (Sunshine Ser.). (gr. 1-2). 845.95 *(978-0-7802-1370-8(X))* Wright Group/McGraw-Hill.

Sunshine Science Early Fluency Sets 1-3: 1 Each of 24 Student Books from Sets 1-3. (gr. 1-2). 167.95 *(978-0-7802-1371-5(8))* Wright Group/McGraw-Hill.

Sunshine Science Early Fluency Sets 4-6: 1 Each of 24 Big Books from Sets 4-6. (gr. 1-2). 845.95 *(978-0-7802-2924-2(X))* Wright Group/McGraw-Hill.

Sunshine Science Early Fluency Sets 4-6: 1 Each of 24 Student Books from Sets 4-6. (gr. 1-2). 167.95 *(978-0-7802-3189-4(9))* Wright Group/McGraw-Hill.

Sunshine Science Emergent Sets: 1 Each of 24 Big Books from Sets 1-3. (gr. 1-2). 750.50 *(978-0-7802-2751-4(4))* Wright Group/McGraw-Hill.

Sunshine Science Emergent Sets: 1 Each of 24 Student Books from Sets 1-3. (gr. 1-2). 146.50 *(978-0-7802-1944-1(9))* Wright Group/McGraw-Hill.

Super-Awesome Science, 8 vols. 2016. (Super-Awesome Science Ser.). (ENG.). 48p. (J). (gr. 4-8). lib. bdg. 285.12 *(978-1-68078-245-5(2),* 22091) ABDO Publishing Co.

Superheroes of Science, 12 vols. 2015. (Superheroes of Science Ser.). (ENG.). 48p. (J). (gr. 6-6). lib. bdg. 201.60 *(978-1-4824-2561-1(0),* 16c5f325-c2d0-4d65-912c-c1125d7eb9ec) Stevens, Gareth Publishing LLLP.

Susaeta, Equipo. 1000 PREGUNTAS Y RESPUESTAS. (SPA., Illus.). 96p. (J). (gr. 3-5). *(978-84-305-8671-4(7),* SU2565) Susaeta Ediciones, S.A. ESP. Dist: Lectorum Pubns., Inc.

Suzuki, David T. & Hehner, Barbara. Descubre el Cuerpo Humano. 2004. (Juego de la Ciencia Ser.). (SPA., Illus.). 96p. 14.99 *(978-84-9754-033-9(6),* 87813) Ediciones Oniro S.A. ESP. Dist: Lectorum Pubns., Inc.

Swain, Cynthia. What Do You Think? 2003. (BuildUp Ser.). (J). pap. 22.00 *(978-1-4108-0758-8(4))* Benchmark Education Co.

Syverson, Carolyn. Places to Go! 2011. (Wonder Readers Ser.). (ENG.). 16p. (J). (gr. -1-1). 25.95 *(978-1-4296-8667-9(7),* 195208, Capstone Pr.) Capstone.

TAKS Science Preparation Elementary - Student Edition. 2003. (Region IV ESC Resources for Science Ser.). stu. ed., per., wbk. ed. *(978-1-932524-62-8(2))* Region 4 Education Service Ctr.

TAKS Science Preparation Elementary - Student Edition - Spanish. 2004. (SPA.). stu. ed., per., wbk. ed. *(978-1-932524-87-1(8))* Region 4 Education Service Ctr.

TAKS Science Preparation Grade 11 Exit. 2004. (Region IV ESC Resources for Science Ser.). stu. ed., per., wbk. ed. *(978-1-932524-64-2(9))* Region 4 Education Service Ctr.

Taylor, Kim. Action. (Illus.). 32p. (YA). (gr. 3-18). lib. bdg. 27.10 *(978-1-931983-72-3(0))* Chrysalis Education.

—Cold. (Illus.). 32p. (YA). (gr. 3-18). lib. bdg. 27.10 *(978-1-931983-73-0(9))* Chrysalis Education.

—Pattern. (Illus.). 32p. (YA). (gr. 3-18). lib. bdg. 27.10 *(978-1-931983-76-1(3))* Chrysalis Education.

—Structure. (Illus.). 32p. (YA). (gr. 3-18). lib. bdg. 27.10 *(978-1-931983-78-5(X))* Chrysalis Education.

Teacher Created Materials Staff, ed. Physical Science: Add-on Pack. 2007. (Science Readers Ser.). 89.99 *(978-1-4333-0068-4(0))* Teacher Created Materials, Inc.

—Physical Science: Themed Classroom Reader Set. 2007. (Themed Reader Sets Ser.). pap. 249.99 *(978-1-4333-0154-4(7))* Teacher Created Materials, Inc.

Teeth, 6 vols. (Sunshinetm Science Ser.). 24p. (gr. 1-2). 41.95 *(978-0-7802-1401-9(3));* 37.50 *(978-0-7802-1402-6(1))* Wright Group/McGraw-Hill.

Teeth Sets: 1 Each of 3 Student Books. (Sunshinetm Science Ser.). (gr. 1-2). 20.95 *(978-0-7802-1751-5(9))* Wright Group/McGraw-Hill.

Test Your Science Skills, 12 vols. 2017. (Test Your Science Skills Ser.). (ENG., Illus.). (J). (gr. 5-5). lib. bdg. 175.62 *(978-1-5081-6262-9(X),* 80edef16-9721-4eaa-91fa-47061bb45e6b, PowerKids Pr.) Rosen Publishing Group, Inc., The.

The Basics of Biology, 20 vols. 2013. (Core Concepts Ser.). (ENG.). 96p. (YA). (gr. 7-7). 397.70 *(978-1-4777-0568-1(6),* ed674dc1-666e-4d62-a24f-1972e25b4c81) Rosen Publishing Group, Inc., The.

Thimmesh, Catherine. The Sky's the Limit: Stories of Discovery by Women & Girls. Sweet, Melissa, illus. 2005. 73p. (J). (gr. 4-8). reprint ed. 16.00 *(978-0-7567-9631-0(8))* DIANE Publishing Co.

Thompson, Gene. Kitchen Science. Date not set. (Thinking Like a Scientist Ser.). (Illus.). 20p. (J). pap. 16.95 *(978-1-58273-097-4(0))* Sundance/Newbridge Educational Publishing.

Tilden, Thomasine E. Lewis. Mind Readers (24/7: Science Behind the Scenes: Mystery Files) 2008. (24/7: Science Behind the Scenes Ser.). (ENG., Illus.). 64p. (J). (gr. 8-12). pap. 7.95 *(978-0-531-17532-3(4),* Watts, Franklin) Scholastic Library Publishing.

TIME for Kids Science Guide. (J). *(978-0-06-079271-8(X))* HarperCollins Pubs.

Top That Publishing Staff, ed. Electric Science. 2004. (Top That! Labs Ser.). (Illus.). 24p. (J). *(978-1-84510-152-7(9))* Top That! Publishing PLC.

—Lets Go Bubbletastic. 2005. (Illus.). 48p. *(978-1-84510-548-8(6))* Top That! Publishing PLC.

—Mirror Science. 2004. (Top That! Labs Ser.). (Illus.). 24p. (J). *(978-1-84510-155-8(3))* Top That! Publishing PLC.

Trefil, James. (WCS)Sciences. 4th ed. 2004. pap., stu. ed. 71.95 *(978-0-471-72701-9(6))* Wiley, John & Sons, Inc.

—(WCS)Sciences: With eGrade Set. 4th ed. 2004. pap., stu. ed. 71.95 *(978-0-471-72702-6(4))* Wiley, John & Sons, Inc.

Trefil, James, et al. Life Science 2005. I.t. ed. 2004. (McDougal Littell Middle School Science Ser.). (ENG., Illus.). 128p. (gr. 6-8). 84.85 *(978-0-618-30367-0(7),* 2-01002) Great Source Education Group, Inc.

A True Book(tm) — Extreme Science (Set Of 5) 2014. (True Book — Extreme Science Ser.). (J). lib. bdg. 145.00 *(978-0-531-24355-8(9))* Scholastic Library Publishing.

Trumbauer, Lisa. Eating Well, 6 vols., Set. 2003. (Yellow Umbrella Early Level Ser.). (ENG.). 16p. (gr. k-1). pap. 35.70 *(978-0-7368-3014-0(6),* Capstone Pr.) Capstone.

—Trees Are Terrific!, 6 vols., Set. 2003. (Yellow Umbrella Early Level Ser.). (ENG.). 16p. (gr. k-1). pap. 35.70 *(978-0-7368-3000-3(6),* Capstone Pr.) Capstone.

U X L, ed. UXL Man-Made Disasters, 3 vols. 2015. (U-X-L Man-Made Disasters Ser.). (ENG., Illus.). 348.00 *(978-1-4103-1774-2(9),* UXL) Cengage Gale.

Uhl, Xina M. How STEM Built the Roman Empire, 1 vol. 2019. (How STEM Built Empires Ser.). (ENG.). 80p. (gr. 7-7). pap. 16.30 *(978-1-7253-4152-4(2),* aea2ce53-1be1-444e-b122-08dbb30985d4) Rosen Publishing Group, Inc., The.

Uncharted, Unexplored, & Unexplained: Scienctific Advancements of the 19th Century, 16 Bks, Set. 2004. (Illus.). (gr. 4-8). lib. bdg. 319.20 *(978-1-58415-322-1(9))* Mitchell Lane Pubs.

Uncharted, Unexplored, & Unexplained: Scientific Advancements of the 19th Century, 26 vols., Set. Incl. Alexander Graham Bell & the Story of the Telephone. Bankston, John. (gr. 4-8). 2004. lib. bdg. 29.95 *(978-1-58415-243-9(5));* Antoine Lavoisier: Father of Modern Chemistry. Kjelle, Marylou. (gr. 4-8). 2004. lib. bdg. 29.95 *(978-1-58415-309-2(1));* Auguste & Louis Lumiere: And the Rise of Motion Pictures. Whiting, Jim. (gr. 3-8). 2005. lib. bdg. 29.95 *(978-1-58415-365-8(2));* Charles Babbage & the Story of the First Computer. Sherman, Josepha. (gr. 4-8). 2005. lib. bdg. 29.95 *(978-1-58415-372-6(5));* Charles Darwin & the Origin of the Species. Whiting, Jim. (gr. 3-8). 2005. lib. bdg. 29.95 *(978-1-58415-364-1(4));* Dmitri Mendeleyev & the Periodic Table. Zannos, Susan. (gr. 4-8). 2004. lib. bdg. 29.95 *(978-1-58415-267-5(2));* Florence Nightingale & the Advancement of Nursing. Hinman, Bonnie. (gr. 4-8). 2004. lib. bdg. 29.95 *(978-1-58415-257-6(5));* Friedrich Miescher & the Story of Nucleic Acid. Tracy, Kathleen. (gr. 4-8). 2005. lib. bdg. 29.95 *(978-1-58415-369-6(5));* George Eastman & Photographic Film. Mattern, Joanne. (gr. 4-8). 2004. lib. bdg. 29.95 *(978-1-58415-258-3(3));* Gregor Mendel & the Discovery of the Gene. Bankston, John. (gr. 4-8). 2004. lib. bdg. 29.95 *(978-1-58415-266-8(4));* Guglielmo Marconi & Radio Waves. Zannos, Susan. (gr. 4-8). 2004. lib. bdg. 29.95 *(978-1-58415-265-1(6));* Henry Bessemer: Making Steel from Iron. Tracy, Kathleen. (gr. 4-8). 2005. lib. bdg. 29.95 *(978-1-58415-366-5(0));* Henry Cavendish & the Discovery of Hydrogen. Sherman, Josepha. (gr. 4-8). 2005. lib. bdg. 29.95 *(978-1-58415-368-9(7));* J. J. Thomson & the Discovery of Electrons. Sherman, Josepha. (gr. 4-8). 2005. lib. bdg. 29.95 *(978-1-58415-370-2(9));* James Watt & the Steam Engine. Whiting, Jim. (gr. 4-8). 2005. lib. bdg. 29.95 *(978-1-58415-371-9(7));* John Dalton & the Atomic Theory. Kjelle, Marylou. (gr. 4-8). 2004. lib. bdg. 29.95 *(978-1-58415-308-5(3));* Joseph Lister & the Story of Antiseptics. Bankston, John. (gr. 4-8). 2004. lib. bdg. 29.95 *(978-1-58415-262-0(1));* Joseph Priestly & the Discovery of Oxygen. Conley, Kate A. (gr. 4-8). 2005. lib. bdg. 29.95 *(978-1-58415-367-2(9));* Karl Benz & the Single Cylinder Engine. Bankston, John. (gr. 4-8). 2004. lib. bdg. 29.95 *(978-1-58415-244-6(3));* Louis Daguerre & the Story of the Daguerreotype. Bankston, John. (gr. 4-8). 2004. lib. bdg. 29.95 *(978-1-58415-247-7(8));* Louis Pasteur: Fighter Against Contagious Disease. Kjelle, Marylou Morano. (gr. 4-8). 2005. lib. bdg. 29.95 *(978-1-58415-363-4(6),* 1244912); Michael Faraday & the Discovery of Electromagnetism. Zannos, Susan. (gr. 4-8). 2004. lib. bdg. 29.95 *(978-1-58415-307-8(5));* Pierre & Marie Curie & the Discovery of Radium. Tracy, Kathleen. (gr. 4-8). 2004. lib. bdg. 29.95 *(978-1-58415-310-8(5));* Robert Koch & the Study of Anthrax. Tracy, Kathleen. (gr. 4-8). 2004. lib. bdg. 29.95 *(978-1-58415-261-3(3));* Samuel Morse & the Telegraph. Zannos, Susan. (gr. 4-8). 2004. lib. bdg. 29.95 *(978-1-58415-269-9(9));* Thomas Edison: Great Inventor. Thatcher Murcia, Rebecca. (gr. 4-8). 2004. lib. bdg. 29.95 *(978-1-58415-306-1(7));* (Illus.). 48p. (J). 2005. Set lib. bdg. 778.70 *(978-1-58415-410-5(1))* Mitchell Lane Pubs.

Unlocking the Secrets of Science: Profiling 20th Century Achievers in Science, Medicine, & Technology, 30 vols., set. (Illus.). 56p. (J). (gr. 5-6). 718.00 *(978-1-58415-163-0(3))* Mitchell Publishing, Inc.

Up in the Air: 6 Each of 1 Anthology, 6 vols. (Wildcats Ser.). 32p. (gr. 2-8). *(978-0-322-00596-9(5))* Wright Group/McGraw-Hill.

VanVoorst, Jennifer. Make It Move!, 6 vols., Set. 2003. (Yellow Umbrella Early Level Ser.). (ENG.). 16p. (gr. k-1). pap. 35.70 *(978-0-7368-3016-4(2),* Capstone Pr.) Capstone.

—Who Builds?, 6 vols., Set. 2003. (Yellow Umbrella Early Level Ser.). (ENG.). 16p. (gr. k-1). pap. 35.70 *(978-0-7368-3001-0(4),* Capstone Pr.) Capstone.

A Visual Exploration of Science: Set 3, 10 vols. 2018. (Visual Exploration of Science Ser.). (ENG., Illus.). 104p. (gr. 8-8). lib. bdg. 194.00 *(978-1-5081-8285-6(X),* 5a45ba13-43b3-4a0f-a00c-d3a7b97f6758) Rosen Publishing Group, Inc., The.

Voege, Debra & Science Applications, inc Staff. Science in the Real World Set, 10-Volumes. 2009. (Science in the Real World Ser.). (gr. 4-6). 280.00 *(978-1-60413-829-0(7),* Chelsea Clubhse.) Infobase Holdings, Inc.

Walch Publishing Staff. Assessment Strategies for Science. 2004. 54p. 24.99 *(978-0-8251-5174-3(0));* 80p. (J). pap. 24.99 *(978-0-8251-5175-0(9))* Walch Education.

Walch Publishing Staff, creator. Math & Science. 2007. (Daily Warm-Ups Ser.). 204p. (gr. 5-6). tchr. ed., spiral bd. 24.99 *(978-0-8251-6447-7(8))* Walch Education.

Walker, Colin, et al. Los Seres Vivos. (Coleccion Conceptos de Ciencia en Big Books). (SPA., Illus.). (J). (gr. k-3). 12.00 net. *(978-0-8136-6704-1(6),* MD7209) Modern Curriculum Pr.

—La Superficie de la Tierra. (Coleccion Conceptos de Ciencia en Big Books). (SPA., Illus.). (J). (gr. k-3). 12.00 *(978-0-8136-6754-6(2),* MD7212) Modern Curriculum Pr.

Walker, Kathryn. Mysteries of the Cosmic Joker. 2009. (Unsolved! Ser.). (ENG., Illus.). 32p. (J). (gr. 3-5). pap. *(978-0-7787-4161-9(3));* (gr. 4-6). *(978-0-7787-4148-0(6))* Crabtree Publishing Co.

Walking, Walking: Big Book: Level D. 8p. 20.95 *(978-0-322-00626-3(0))* Wright Group/McGraw-Hill.

Wall Chart. 2003. (Scott Foresman Science Ser.). (gr. 3-18). suppl. ed. 81.90 *(978-0-673-65118-1(5))* Addison-Wesley Educational Pubs., Inc.

Warm up to Science for Grade 5. 2005. spiral bd. *(978-1-933049-16-8(2))* Region 4 Education Service Ctr.

Warming up! Cooling Off! 6 Each of 1 Student Book, 6 vols. (Sunshinetm Science Ser.). 24p. (gr. 1-2). 41.95 *(978-0-7802-1407-1(2))* Wright Group/McGraw-Hill.

Warming up! Cooling Off! Big Book. (Sunshinetm Science Ser.). 24p. (gr. 1-2). 37.50 *(978-0-7802-1408-8(0))* Wright Group/McGraw-Hill.

Weakland, Mark. Science Starts. 2010. (Science Starts Ser.). (ENG.). 32p. (J). (gr. -1-2). pap., pap., pap. 32.40 *(978-1-4296-6180-5(1),* 16058, Capstone Pr.) Capstone.

—Science Starts Classroom Collection. 2010. (Science Starts Ser.). (ENG.). 32p. (J). (gr. 1-2). pap., pap. 195.40 *(978-1-4296-6179-9(8),* 16057, Capstone Pr.) Capstone.

Weakland, Mark & Bros., Warner. Clang! Wile E. Coyote Experiments with Magnetism. Billiau, Loic & Sordo, Paco, illus. 2017. (Wile E. Coyote, Physical Science Genius Ser.). (ENG.). 32p. (J). (gr. 3-5). lib. bdg. 31.32 *(978-1-5157-3731-5(4),* 133675, Capstone Pr.) Capstone.

Weakland, Mark, et al. LOL Physical Science Classroom Collection. Lum, Bernice, illus. 2012. (LOL Physical Science Ser.). (ENG.). 32p. (J). (gr. 3-4). 198.40 *(978-1-4296-9305-9(3),* 18537, Capstone Pr.) Capstone.

Weird & Wacky Science, 6 bks., Set. (Illus.). (YA). (gr. 4-10). lib. bdg. 113.70 *(978-0-89490-662-6(3))* Enslow Publishing, LLC.

Weird Careers in Science. 2005. (Weird Careers in Science Ser.). (Illus.). 64p. (gr. 5-8). 175.00 *(978-0-7910-9088-6(4),* Facts On File) Infobase Holdings, Inc.

Weird Science. (Eyes on Adventure Ser.). 32p. (J). (gr. 1). pap. *(978-1-882210-82-4(4))* Action Publishing, Inc.

Wells, Robert E. What's Older Than a Giant Tortoise? Wells, Robert E., illus. 2004. (Wells of Knowledge Science Ser.). (ENG., Illus.). 32p. (J). (gr. -1-3). 7.99 *(978-0-8075-8832-1(6),* 807588326) Whitman, Albert & Co.

Wells, Robert E. & Wells, Robert. Como Se Mide el Tiempo? 2003. (SPA.). 176p. (J). (gr. 2-3). 15.99 *(978-84-261-3287-1(1))* Juventud, Editorial ESP. Dist: Lectorum Pubns., Inc.

Welsh, Anne Marie & Fenly, Leigh. Wow! Wonders of Water. Garcia, Helena, illus. 2009. 112p. (J). pap. *(978-0-88441-732-3(8))* Girl Scouts of the USA.

Westrup, Hugh & Barchers, Suzanne I. Let's Explore Physical Science Grades 4-5, 10 bks., Set. 2015. (Book Collection). (ENG., Illus.). 32p. (gr. 4-5). 89.90 *(978-1-4938-1429-9(X))* Teacher Created Materials, Inc.

What About..., 10 vols., Set. Incl. Dinosaurs. Matthews, Rupert. lib. bdg. 19.95 *(978-1-4222-1558-6(X));* History. Williams, Brian. lib. bdg. 19.95 *(978-1-4222-1559-3(8));* How We Live. Williams, Brian. lib. bdg. 19.95 *(978-1-4222-1560-9(1));* Human Body. Parker, Steve. lib. bdg. 19.95 *(978-1-4222-1561-6(X));* Natural World. Williams, Brian. lib. bdg. 19.95 *(978-1-4222-1562-3(8));* People & Places. Williams, Brian. lib. bdg. 19.95 *(978-1-4222-1563-0(6));* Planet Earth. Williams, Brian. lib. bdg. 19.95 *(978-1-4222-1564-7(4));* Science & Technology. Parker, Steve. lib. bdg. 19.95 *(978-1-4222-1565-4(2));* Universe. Williams, Brian. lib. bdg. 19.95 *(978-1-4222-1566-1(0));* World Wonders. Williams, Brian. lib. bdg. 19.95 *(978-1-4222-1567-8(9));* (J). (gr. 6-8). 2010. (Question & Answer Book Ser.). (Illus.). 40p. 2009. Set lib. bdg. 199.50 *(978-1-4222-1557-9(1))* Mason Crest.

What Goes into Bread? 6 Each of 1 Student Book, 6 vols. (Sunshinetm Science Ser.). 24p. (gr. 1-2). 41.95 *(978-0-7802-2728-6(X))* Wright Group/McGraw-Hill.

What Goes into Bread? Big Book. (Sunshinetm Science Ser.). 24p. (gr. 1-2). 37.50 *(978-0-7802-2798-9(0))* Wright Group/McGraw-Hill.

What Is Rock? 6 Each of 1 Student Book, 6 vols. (Sunshinetm Science Ser.). 24p. (gr. 1-2). 41.95 *(978-0-7802-2718-7(2))* Wright Group/McGraw-Hill.

What Is Rock? Big Book. (Sunshinetm Science Ser.). 24p. (gr. 1-2). 37.50 *(978-0-7802-2793-4(X))* Wright Group/McGraw-Hill.

What Is Soil? 6 Each of 1 Student Book, 6 vols. (Sunshinetm Science Ser.). 24p. (gr. 1-2). 41.95 *(978-0-7802-2722-4(0))* Wright Group/McGraw-Hill.

What Is Soil? Big Book. (Sunshinetm Science Ser.). 24p. (gr. 1-2). 37.50 *(978-0-7802-2795-8(6))* Wright Group/McGraw-Hill.

What Is this Skeleton?, 6 vols. (Sunshinetm Science Ser.). 24p. (gr. 1-2). 31.50 *(978-0-7802-0298-6(8));* 36.95 *(978-0-7802-0550-5(2))* Wright Group/McGraw-Hill.

What Makes Light?, 6 vols. (Sunshinetm Science Ser.). 24p. (gr. 1-2). 36.95 *(978-0-7802-0555-0(3));* 31.50 *(978-0-7802-0304-4(6))* Wright Group/McGraw-Hill.

What will Float?, 6 vols. (Sunshinetm Science Ser.). 24p. (gr. 1-2). 31.50 *(978-0-7802-0297-9(X))* Wright Group/McGraw-Hill.

White, Nancy. Push, Pull, Play the Game: A Content Area Reader-science. 2005. (Sadlier Phonics Reading Program). (Illus.). 20p. (gr. k-2). 25.20 *(978-0-8215-7815-5(4))* Sadlier, William H. Inc.

William H. Sadlier Staff. Float or Sink? 2005. (Emergent/Early (Prek-2) Science Package Ser.). 12p. (gr. -1-2). 25.20 *(978-0-8215-7840-7(5))* Sadlier, William H. Inc.

—Splish, Splash! 2005. (Emergent/Early (Prek-2) Science Package Ser.). 12p. (gr. -1-1). 25.20 *(978-0-8215-7838-4(3))* Sadlier, William H. Inc.

—What Is the Weather Today? 2005. (Emergent/Early (Prek-2) Science Package Ser.). 12p. (gr. k-2). 25.20 *(978-0-8215-7839-1(1))* Sadlier, William H. Inc.

Wolf, Cathrine, ed. Inside Space Jam. Date not set. 64p. (Orig.). (J). (gr. 4-8). pap. 3.95 *(978-1-886749-19-1(1))* Sports Illustrated For Kids.

Wollard, Kathy & Solomon, Debra. El Libro de Los Porqués 2: Las Preguntas Más Difíciles y Las Respuestas Más Fáciles Sobre Las Personas, Los Animales y Las Cosas. Solomon, Debra, tr. 2004. (SPA., Illus.). 208p. 28.99 *(978-84-9754-047-6(6),* 87432) Ediciones Oniro S.A. ESP. Dist: Lectorum Pubns., Inc.

Wonderful Ears: 6 Each of 1 Student Book, 6 vols. (Sunshinetm Science Ser.). 24p. (gr. 1-2). 41.95 *(978-0-7802-1416-3(1))* Wright Group/McGraw-Hill.

Wonderful Ears: Big Book. (Sunshinetm Science Ser.). 24p. (gr. 1-2). 37.50 *(978-0-7802-1417-0(X))* Wright Group/McGraw-Hill.

Wonderful Eyes, 6 vols. (Sunshinetm Science Ser.). 24p. (gr. 1-2). 37.50 *(978-0-7802-1414-9(5))*; 42.95 *(978-0-7802-1413-2(7))* Wright Group/McGraw-Hill.

Wonders of the World. (Eyes on Adventure Ser.). 32p. (J). (gr. 1). pap. *(978-1-882210-65-7(4))* Action Publishing, Inc.

Wood, Matthew Brenden. The Science of Science Fiction. Casteel, Tom, illus. 2017. (Inquire & Investigate Ser.). 128p. (J). (gr. 6-10). 22.95 *(978-1-61930-466-6(X)*, ce54db0d-b489-48ba-91ae-3dc881aeaf52); pap. 17.95 *(978-1-61930-470-3(8)*, 352b91a6-0bfa-4535-acf7-e01e8b0f38e8) Nomad Pr.

World Almanac Puzzler Deck for Kids: Science (BoMC) World Almanac Deck: Science, 9-11. 2007. 9.95 *(978-0-8118-6242-4(9))* Chronicle Bks. LLC.

World Book, Inc. Staff. World Book's Young Scientist, 10 vols., Vol. 10. 2004. (Illus.). 1,280p. (gr. 3-8). pap., tchr. ed. 249.00 *(978-0-7166-2750-0(7)*, 60031) World Bk., Inc.

World Book, Inc. Staff, contrib. by. Earth & Space. 2008. (J). *(978-0-7166-3017-3(6))*; *(978-0-7166-3016-6(8))* World Bk., Inc.

—If the World Is Round, Then Why Is the Ground Flat? World Book Answers Your Questions about Science. 2019. (Illus.). 96p. (J). *(978-0-7166-3827-8(4))* World Bk., Inc.

—Science & Technology. 2008. (J). *(978-0-7166-3018-0(4))* World Bk., Inc.

—World Book's Science & Nature Guides, 12 vols. 2004. (World Book's Science & Nature Guides Ser.). (Illus.). 80p. (gr. 5-9). 319.00 *(978-0-7166-4208-4(5)*, SKU 30119) World Bk., Inc.

World of Science. Date not set. (Children's Reference Ser.). (Illus.). 256p. (J). *(978-1-4054-1635-1(1))* Parragon, Inc.

You & Your Teeth. (Sunshinetm Science Ser.). 24p. (gr. 1-2). 37.50 *(978-0-7802-1441-5(2))*;Set. 41.95 *(978-0-7802-1440-8(4))* Wright Group/McGraw-Hill.

You Wouldn't Want to Live Without... (Set Of 6) 2014. (You Wouldn't Want to Live Without... Ser.). (J). lib. bdg. 174.00 *(978-0-531-24362-6(1)*, Watts, Franklin) Scholastic Library Publishing.

Young Explorers in Science. (J). 105.00 *(978-0-8136-4363-2(5))* Modern Curriculum Pr.

Zev, Marc, et al. 101 Things Everyone Should Know about Math. 2010. (101 Things You Should Know about Ser.). (Illus.). 128p. (J). (gr. 5-9). pap. 12.95 *(978-0-9678020-3-9(2))* Science, Naturally!

5-book Set, 10 vols. 2005. (Great Inventions Ser.). (ENG., Illus.). 128-144p. (gr. 8-8). lib. bdg. 227.50 *(978-0-7614-1535-0(1)*, 3077d7c6-d8c5-4207-a6be-86f0afe1101e, Cavendish Square) Cavendish Square Publishing LLC.

100 Things You Should Know About, 15 vols., Set. (Illus.). 48p. (gr. 3-18). lib. bdg. *(978-1-59084-444-1(0))* Mason Crest.

1000 Things You Should Know About, 13 vols., Set. (Illus.). 64p. (gr. 3-18). lib. bdg. *(978-1-59084-460-1(2))* Mason Crest.

SCIENCE—DATA PROCESSING

Allen-Conn, B. J. & Rose, Kim. Powerful Ideas in the Classroom Using Squeak to Enhance Math & Science Learning. 2003. (Illus.). 86p. per. *(978-0-9743131-0-8(6))* Viewpoints Research Institute, Inc.

Group/McGraw-Hill, Wright. Caretakers of the Earth, 6 vols. (Book2WebTM Ser.). (gr. 4-8). 36.50 incl. 5.25 hd *(978-0-322-04470-8(7))* Wright Group/McGraw-Hill.

SCIENCE—DICTIONARIES

Brooks, F. First Encyclopedia of Science II. rev. ed. 2011. (First Encyclopedias Ser.). 64p. (J). pap. 9.99 *(978-0-7945-3043-3(5)*, Usborne) EDC Publishing.

, Chambers, Chambers. School Science Dictionary. 2003. (ENG., Illus.). 400p. *(978-0-550-10070-2(9)*, Chambers) Hodder & Stoughton.

Craig, A. & Rosney, C. Science Encyclopedia. 2004. (Encyclopedias Ser.). (Illus.). 128p. (J). 7.95 *(978-0-7945-0007-8(2))* EDC Publishing.

Delta science dictionary gr3-4 single Title. 2003. 64p. (J). (gr. 3-4). *(978-1-59242-297-5(7))* Delta Education, LLC.

Delta science dictionary gr5-6 single Title. 2003. 80p. (J). (gr. 5-6). *(978-1-59242-299-9(3))* Delta Education, LLC.

Dictionary of Science Words: Individual Title Six-Packs. (Discovery World Ser.). 24p. (gr. 1-2). 33.00 *(978-0-7635-8482-5(7))* Rigby Education.

DK. First Science Encyclopedia. 2017. (DK First Reference Ser.). (ENG., Illus.). 136p. (J). (gr. 2-5). 16.99 *(978-1-4654-4344-1(4)*, DK Children) Dorling Kindersley Publishing, Inc.

—Knowledge Encyclopedia Science! 2018. (DK Knowledge Encyclopedias Ser.). (ENG.). 208p. (J). (gr. 4-7). 24.99 *(978-1-4654-7363-9(7)*, DK Children) Dorling Kindersley Publishing, Inc.

—Science: a Visual Encyclopedia. 2018. (DK Children's Visual Encyclopedias Ser.). (ENG., Illus.). 304p. (J). (gr. 3-7). pap. 19.99 *(978-1-4654-7323-3(8)*, DK Children) Dorling Kindersley Publishing, Inc.

Encyclopaedia Britannica, Inc. Staff. Britannica Illustrated Science Library Series (18 Title Series), 18 vols. 2010. 599.00 *(978-1-61535-423-8(9))* Encyclopaedia Britannica, Inc.

The Encyclopedia of Junior Science, 10 Vol Set, 10 vols., Set. 2009. (ENG.). (gr. 4-9). 230.00 *(978-1-60413-554-1(9)*, P166828, Facts On File) Infobase Holdings, Inc.

Firth, Rachel. First Encyclopedia of Science. 2004. (First Encyclopedias Ser.). (ENG., Illus.). 64p. (J). (gr. 3-18). pap. 9.99 *(978-0-7945-0273-7(3)*, Usborne) EDC Publishing.

—The Usborne Little Encyclopedia of Science: Internet-Linked. Hancock, David, illus. 2006. 64p. (J). 6.99 *(978-0-7945-1095-4(7)*, Usborne) EDC Publishing.

Hackney Blackwell, Amy & Manar, Elizabeth P. UXL Encyclopedia of Science. 2015. (Illus.). 10p. (YA). *(978-1-4144-3085-0(X))* Cengage Gale.

Holt, Rinehart and Winston Staff. Earth Science. 5th ed. 2003. (Holt Science & Technology Ser.). (ENG., Illus.). 880p. (gr. 7-7). 103.35 *(978-0-03-066478-6(0))* Houghton Mifflin Harcourt Publishing Co.

—Holt Science & Technology: Online Edition Upgrade. 2nd ed. 2003. Level A. 2.60 *(978-0-03-037236-0(4))*Level K. 2.60 *(978-0-03-037248-3(8))* Holt McDougal.

—Life Science. 5th ed. 2003. (Holt Science & Technology Ser.). (ENG., Illus.). 912p. (gr. 6-6). 103.35 *(978-0-03-066476-2(4))* Houghton Mifflin Harcourt Publishing Co.

—Physical Science. 5th ed. 2003. (Holt Science & Technology Ser.). (ENG., Illus.). 848p. (gr. 8-8). 103.35 *(978-0-03-066481-6(0))* Houghton Mifflin Harcourt Publishing Co.

Jugendhandbuch Naturwissen: Bausteine des Lebens, 6 vols., Vol. 1. (GER.). 144p. (J). pap. 750.00 *(978-3-499-16203-9(2)*, M-7486) French & European Pubns., Inc.

Khan, Sarah. First Illustrated Science Dictionary. Robson, Kirsteen, ed. Whatmore, Candice, illus. 2013. (ENG.). 104p. (J). (gr. -1-3). 9.99 *(978-0-7945-3383-0(3)*, Usborne) EDC Publishing.

Oxlade, Chris. Illustrated Dictionary of Science. 2004. (Illustrated Dictionaries Ser.). (Illus.). 382p. (J). lib. bdg. 37.95 *(978-1-58086-363-6(9))* EDC Publishing.

Rigby Education Staff. Discovery World Red Dictionary. (Discovery World Ser.). (Illus.). 12p. (gr. 1-2). 31.00 *(978-0-7635-2707-5(6))* Rigby Education.

Rogers, Kirsteen. Illustrated Elementary Science Dictionary IR. 2012. (Illustrated Dictionaries Ser.). 136p. (J). pap. 12.99 *(978-0-7945-3255-0(1)*, Usborne) EDC Publishing.

Science Encyclopedia. 2004. (Library of Science Ser.). (ENG., Illus.). 1p. (J). (gr. 4-18). 39.95 *(978-0-7460-3833-8(X))* EDC Publishing.

Simon, Seymour. Science Dictionary. 2012. (Dover Children's Science Bks.). (ENG., Illus.). 272p. (J). (gr. 3-8). pap. 19.99 *(978-0-486-48865-3(9)*, 488659) Dover Pubns., Inc.

Stockley, Corinne, et al. The Usborne Illustrated Dictionary of Science. Rogers, Kirsteen, ed. Chen, Kuo Kang & Smith, Guy, illus. rev. ed. 2007. (Illustrated Dictionaries Ser.). 382p. (J). (gr. 4-7). pap. 29.99 *(978-0-7945-1847-9(8)*, Usborne) EDC Publishing.

—The Usborne Illustrated Dictionary of Science: A Complete Reference Guide to Physics, Chemistry & Biology. Rogers, Kirsteen, ed. Smith, G. & Chen, Kuo Kang, trs. 2004. (Illustrated Dictionaries Ser.). (ENG., Illus.). 1p. (J). pap. 29.95 *(978-0-7945-0064-1(1)*, Usborne) EDC Publishing.

Tatchell, Judy. Science Encyclopedia. 2004. (Library of Science Ser.). (Illus.). 448p. (J). (gr. 4-18). lib. bdg. 47.95 *(978-1-58086-337-7(X))* EDC Publishing.

Taylor, Charles & Editors of Kingfisher. The Kingfisher Science Encyclopedia. 4th ed. 2017. (Kingfisher Encyclopedias Ser.). (ENG., Illus.). 496p. (J). 34.99 *(978-0-7534-7384-9(4)*, 900183785, Kingfisher) Roaring Brook Pr.

U X L, ed. UXL Encyclopedia of Science, 10 vols. 3rd ed. 2015. (U-X-L Encyclopedia of Science Ser.). (ENG., Illus.). 10p. 995.00 *(978-1-4144-3075-1(2)*, UXL) Cengage Gale.

Wilkes, Angela. Science Encyclopedia. Bhachu, Verindr, illus. 2009. (Library of Science Ser Ser.). 448p. (J). 39.99 *(978-0-7945-2527-9(X)*, Usborne) EDC Publishing.

SCIENCE—EXPERIMENTS

see also Science Projects

see also particular branches of science with the subdivision Experiments, e.g. Chemistry—Experiments, etc.

Adamick, Mike. Dad's Book of Awesome Science Experiments: From Boiling Ice & Exploding Soap to Erupting Volcanoes & Launching Rockets, 30 Inventive Experiments to Excite the Whole Family! 2014. (ENG., Illus.). 192p. pap. 18.99 *(978-1-4405-7077-3(9))* Adams Media Corp.

Adamson, Thomas K. & Lemke, Donald B. Lessons in Science Safety with Max Axiom, Super Scientist, 1 vol. Smith, Tod, illus. 2007. (Graphic Science Ser.). (ENG.). 32p. (J). (gr. 3-9). per. 8.10 *(978-0-7368-7887-6(4)*, 93884) Capstone.

—Lessons in Science Safety with Max Axiom Super Scientist: 4D an Augmented Reading Science Experience. Smith, Tod, illus. 2018. (Graphic Science 4D Ser.). (ENG.). 32p. (J). (gr. 3-9). pap. 7.95 *(978-1-5435-2959-3(3)*, 138559); lib. bdg. 36.65 *(978-1-5435-2948-7(8)*, 138537) Capstone. (Capstone Pr.).

Adolph, Jonathan. Mason Jar Science: 40 Slimy, Squishy, Super-Cool Experiments; Capture Big Discoveries in a Jar, from the Magic of Chemistry & Physics to the Amazing Worlds of Earth Science & Biology. 2018. (ENG., Illus.). 136p. (J). (gr. 3-7). 14.95 *(978-1-61212-986-0(2)*, 622986) Storey Publishing, LLC.

AIMS Education Foundation. Ray's Reflections. 2007. (ENG.). 200p. (gr. 4-8). pap., wbk. ed. 21.95 *(978-1-881431-84-8(3)*, 1316) AIMS Education Foundation.

Akass, Susan. Bubbles & Balloons: 35 Amazing Science Experiments. 2018. (ENG., Illus.). 128p. (J). pap. 14.95 *(978-1-78249-577-2(0)*, 1782495770, CICO Books) Ryland Peters & Small GBR. Dist: WIPRO.

Alexander, Alison, et al. Science Interact 7. 2008. (ENG., Illus.). 108p. 36.50 *(978-0-340-94897-2(3))* Hodder Education Group GBR. Dist: Trans-Atlantic Pubns., Inc.

Alkire, Jessie. Chemistry You Can Chomp. 2018. (Super Simple Science You Can Snack On Ser.). (ENG., Illus.). 32p. (J). (gr. k-4). lib. bdg. 34.21 *(978-1-5321-1723-7(X)*, 30734, Super SandCastle) ABDO Publishing Co.

—Geology You Can Gobble. 2018. (Super Simple Science You Can Snack On Ser.). (ENG., Illus.). 32p. (J). (gr. k-4). lib. bdg. 34.21 *(978-1-5321-1725-1(6)*, 30738, Super SandCastle) ABDO Publishing Co.

—Super Gross Germ Projects. 2018. (Super Simple Super Gross Science Ser.). (ENG., Illus.). 32p. (J). (gr. k-4). lib. bdg. 34.21 *(978-1-5321-1731-2(0)*, 30750, Super SandCastle) ABDO Publishing Co.

—Super Simple Fossil Projects: Science Activities for Future Paleontologists. 2017. (Super Simple Earth Investigations Ser.). (ENG., Illus.). 32p. (J). (gr. k-4). lib. bdg. 34.21 *(978-1-5321-1237-9(8)*, 27624, Super SandCastle) ABDO Publishing Co.

—Technology You Can Taste. 2018. (Super Simple Science You Can Snack On Ser.). (ENG., Illus.). 32p. (J). (gr. k-4). lib. bdg. 34.21 *(978-1-5321-1727-5(2)*, 30742, Super SandCastle) ABDO Publishing Co.

Allegra, Mike. Scampers Thinks Like a Scientist. Zechel, Elizabeth, illus. 2019. 32p. (J). (gr. k-3). 16.95 *(978-1-58469-642-1(7)*, Dawn Pubns.) Sourcebooks, Inc.

Amery, Heather, et al. The Usborne Book of KnowHow. King, Colin, illus. 2008. (Usborne Book Of... Ser.). 127p. (J). (gr. 4-7). 19.99 *(978-0-7945-2040-3(5)*, Usborne) EDC Publishing.

Andrews, Georgina & Knighton, Kate. Usborne 100 Science Experiments: Internet-Linked. Chisholm, Jane, ed. Baggott, Stella, illus. Allman, Howard, photos by. 2006. 96p. (J). (gr. 4-7). 15.99 *(978-0-7945-1076-3(0))* EDC Publishing.

—100 Science Experiments. 2006. (Illus.). 96p. (J). (gr. 5). lib. bdg. 23.99 *(978-1-58086-879-2(7)*, Usborne) EDC Publishing.

Ardley, Neil. 101 Great Science Experiments: A Step-By-Step Guide. rev. ed. 2014. (ENG., Illus.). 120p. (J). (gr. 3-7). pap. 9.99 *(978-1-4654-2826-4(7)*, DK Children) Dorling Kindersley Publishing, Inc.

Arner, Elizabeth. Weather Detectives. 2004. (Illus.). (J). (gr. 4-6). 40.00 *(978-1-57336-404-1(5)*, I2065) Interaction Pubs., Inc.

Arnold, Nick. Tools, Robotics, & Gadgets Galore. 2018. (STEM Quest Ser.). lib. bdg. 22.10 *(978-0-606-41260-5(3))* Turtleback.

Austin, John. Labcraft Wizards: Magical Projects & Experiments. 2016. (ENG., Illus.). 256p. (J). (gr. 4). pap. 16.99 *(978-1-61373-621-0(5))* Chicago Review Pr., Inc.

Baker, Amber. The Ice Cube Experiment, 1 vol. 2008. (Real Life Readers Ser.). (ENG.). 12p. (gr. 1-2). pap. 5.90 *(978-1-4042-7901-8(6)*, dc50a7ff-527b-4e24-bce4-91c2c3a68aef, Rosen Classroom) Rosen Publishing Group, Inc., The.

Bell-Rehwoldt, Sheri. Science Experiments That Surprise & Delight: Fun Projects for Curious Kids. 2011. (Kitchen Science Ser.). (ENG.). 32p. (gr. 3-4). pap. 47.70 *(978-1-4296-6421-9(5)*, Capstone Pr.) Capstone.

Bennett, Andrea T. & Kessler, James H. Apples, Bubbles, & Crystals: Your Science ABCs. Sarecky, Melody, illus. 2004. (J). *(978-0-8412-3944-9(4))* American Chemical Society.

Bingham, Jane. El Libro de los Experimentos Cientificos. (SPA., Illus.). (YA). (gr. 5-8). pap. *(978-950-724-263-2(5)*, LMA8241) Lumen ARG. Dist: Lectorum Pubns., Inc.

Biskup, Agnieszka & Enz, Tammy. Max Axiom Science & Engineering Activities. Baez, Marcelo, illus. 2015. (Max Axiom Science & Engineering Activities Ser.). (ENG.). 32p. (J). (gr. 3-9). pap., pap., pap. 31.80 *(978-1-4914-2536-7(9)*, 22516, Capstone Pr.) Capstone.

—Super Cool Science & Engineering Activities: With Max Axiom Super Scientist. 2015. (ENG., Illus.). 128p. (J). (gr. 3-9). pap., pap., pap. 14.95 *(978-1-62370-232-8(1)*, 127870, Capstone Young Readers) Capstone.

Blevins, Wiley. You Can Use a Magnifying Glass. 2004. (Rookie Read-About Science Ser.). (ENG., Illus.). 32p. (J). (gr. 1-2). pap. 4.95 *(978-0-516-27328-0(0)*, Children's Pr.) Scholastic Library Publishing.

Brandolini, Anita. Fizz, Bubble, & Flash. 2004. (ENG., Illus.). 128p. (gr. 4-7). pap. 12.99 *(978-1-885593-83-2(X)*, Ideals Pubns.) Worthy Publishing.

Braun, Eric. Mad Margaret Experiments with the Scientific Method, 1 vol. Boyden, Robin Oliver, illus. 2012. (In the Science Lab Ser.). (ENG.). 24p. (J). (gr. k-3). pap. 9.95 *(978-1-4048-7710-8(X)*, 120445, Picture Window Bks.) Capstone.

Brown, Jordan D. Science Stunts: Fun Feats of Physics. Owsley, Anthony, illus. 2016. 80p. (J). (gr. 3-7). 16.95 *(978-1-62354-064-7(X))* Charlesbridge Publishing, Inc.

Brunelle, Lynn. Big Science for Little People: 52 Activities to Help You & Your Child Discover the Wonders of Science. 2016. (ENG., Illus.). 144p. (gr. -1-3). pap. 16.95 *(978-1-61180-350-1(0)*, Roost Books) Shambhala Pubns., Inc.

—Pop Bottle Science. 2004. (ENG., Illus.). 128p. (gr. 3-7). pap. 17.95 *(978-0-7611-2980-6(4)*, 12980) Workman Publishing Co., Inc.

Brynie, Faith Hickman. Six-Minute Nature Experiments. Whittingham, Kim, illus. 2006. 80p. (J). (gr. 4-8). reprint ed. pap. 11.00 *(978-1-4223-5105-5(X))* DIANE Publishing Co.

Butterfield, M. & Edom, H. Science with Air. rev. ed. 2008. (Science Activities Ser.). 24p. (J). pap. 5.99 *(978-0-7945-2331-2(5)*, Usborne) EDC Publishing.

Canavan, Thomas. Awesome Experiments with Living Things. Linley, Adam, illus. 2017. (Mind-Blowing Science Experiments Ser.). 32p. (gr. 4-5). pap. 63.00 *(978-1-5382-0728-4(1))* Stevens, Gareth Publishing LLLP.

—Fantastic Experiments with Forces. Linley, Adam, illus. 2017. (Mind-Blowing Science Experiments Ser.). 32p. (gr. 4-5). pap. 63.00 *(978-1-5382-0731-4(1))* Stevens, Gareth Publishing LLLP.

Candlewick Press. FETCH! with Ruff Ruffman: Ruff Ruffman's 44 Favorite Science Activities. WGBH, illus. 2015. (Fetch! with Ruff Ruffman Ser.). (ENG.). 132p. (J). (gr. 3-7). pap. 12.99 *(978-0-7636-7432-8(X)*, Candlewick Entertainment) Candlewick Pr.

Cardenas, Ernesto A. The Science Lab. 2009. pap. 4.95 *(978-1-60698-094-1(7))* Milo Educational Bks. & Resources.

Carlson Berne, Emma. Answer! Analyze Your Data, 1 vol. 2014. (Scientific Method in Action Ser.). (Illus.). 24p. (J). (gr. 3-3). (ENG.). 25.27 *(978-1-4777-2930-4(5)*, 65980130-6256-493a-9f85-c51e66a8c715); (ENG., pap. 9.25 *(978-1-4777-3017-1(6)*, 8875c218-bafb-4b73-b1e0-ac0d026636fb); pap. 49.50 *(978-1-4777-3088-1(5))* Rosen Publishing Group, Inc., The. (PowerKids Pr.).

—Share! Present Your Findings. 2014. (Scientific Method in Action Ser.). (Illus.). 24p. (J). (gr. 3-6). pap. 49.50 *(978-1-4777-3089-8(3)*, PowerKids Pr.) Rosen Publishing Group, Inc., The.

Challoner, Jack. Maker Lab: 28 Super Cool Projects. 2016. (DK Activity Lab Ser.). (ENG., Illus.). 160p. (J). (gr. 3-7). 19.99 *(978-1-4654-5135-4(8)*, DK Children) Dorling Kindersley Publishing, Inc.

—Maker Lab Outdoors: 25 Super Cool Projects: Build, Invent, Create, Discover. 2018. (Illus.). 160p. (J). *(978-1-4654-7392-9(0))* Dorling Kindersley Publishing, Inc.

—STEM Lab. 2019. (DK Activity Lab Ser.). (ENG., Illus.). 160p. (J). (gr. 4-7). 19.99 *(978-1-4654-7561-9(3)*, DK Children) Dorling Kindersley Publishing, Inc.

Ciencia con Todo: Experimentos Simples con las Cosas Que Nos Rodean. (Coleccion Pura Ciencia).Tr. of Everyday Science. (SPA.). (YA). (gr. 5-8). pap. 9.56 *(978-950-24-0746-3(6))* Albatros ARG. Dist: Lectorum Pubns., Inc.

Ciencia en Segundos: Experimentos Que Puedes Hacer en 10 Minutos o Menos.Tr. of Science in Seconds. (SPA.). (YA). (gr. 5-8). pap. 9.56 *(978-950-24-0748-7(2))* Albatros ARG. Dist: Lectorum Pubns., Inc.

Ciencia Magica: Experimentos Extranos y Asombrosos. (SPA.). (YA). (gr. 5-8). pap. *(978-950-24-0747-0(4))* Albatros ARG. Dist: Lectorum Pubns., Inc.

Citro, Asia. The Curious Kid's Science Book: 100+ Creative Hands-On Activities for Ages 4-8. 2015. (Illus.). 224p. (J). (gr. -1-3). pap. 21.95 *(978-1-943147-00-7(0)*, 4ccc7376-d0b5-481b-a2a9-01b540ed54cd) Innovation Pr., The.

Clark, Jennifer. The Wizard's Workshop. 2018. (ENG.). (J). pap. 13.99 *(978-1-4621-2167-0(5))* Cedar Fort, Inc./CFI Distribution.

Clark, Michael. Evil Ecosystems, 1 vol. 2017. (Strange Science & Explosive Experiments Ser.). (ENG.). 32p. (J). (gr. 4-5). 29.27 *(978-1-5383-2264-2(1)*, c818c1fd-340c-4b02-b997-cc4b0f8ecd16); pap. 12.75 *(978-1-5383-2360-1(5)*, 6b3850bd-3790-42fe-a427-f38603ae54a7) Rosen Publishing Group, Inc., The. (PowerKids Pr.).

—Fearsome Forces, 1 vol. 2017. (Strange Science & Explosive Experiments Ser.). (ENG.). 32p. (J). (gr. 4-5). 29.27 *(978-1-5383-2266-6(8)*, 455ce758-cd59-42cd-bc8a-2822c82dc562); pap. 12.75 *(978-1-5383-2362-5(1)*, 0b9e761b-c232-42cb-917d-6102962ea3b0) Rosen Publishing Group, Inc., The. (PowerKids Pr.).

—Ghastly Gases, 1 vol. 2017. (Strange Science & Explosive Experiments Ser.). (ENG.). 32p. (J). (gr. 4-5). 29.27 *(978-1-5383-2268-0(4)*, 0e697e89-cdeb-4602-8baa-b07592b0d6cf); pap. 12.75 *(978-1-5383-2364-9(8)*, 0928f486-684c-4768-9b85-270d1b3ced51) Rosen Publishing Group, Inc., The. (PowerKids Pr.).

—Ludicrous Light, 1 vol. 2017. (Strange Science & Explosive Experiments Ser.). (ENG.). 32p. (J). (gr. 4-5). 29.27 *(978-1-5383-2270-3(6)*, 707ecc47-17ca-4673-a102-3bdf8196f097); pap. 12.75 *(978-1-5383-2366-3(4)*, 3a173671-9fd2-4c89-8692-d388a53be0c5) Rosen Publishing Group, Inc., The. (PowerKids Pr.).

—Shattering Sounds, 1 vol. 2017. (Strange Science & Explosive Experiments Ser.). (ENG.). 32p. (J). (gr. 4-5). 29.27 *(978-1-5383-2272-7(2)*, f5928782-15e4-4e34-a4d7-5b9ca4364559); pap. 12.75 *(978-1-5383-2368-7(0)*, 8e911f69-b383-41fe-b9d9-e6d75c7cab6b) Rosen Publishing Group, Inc., The. (PowerKids Pr.).

Claybourne, Anna. Experiments with Heat & Cold, 1 vol. 2018. (Ultimate Science Lab Ser.). (ENG.). 32p. (gr. 4-5). pap. 11.50 *(978-1-5382-3546-1(3)*, 0c9feb38-b689-4533-8e7f-4babd0b78b33) Stevens, Gareth Publishing LLLP.

—Experiments with Movement, 1 vol. 2018. (Ultimate Science Lab Ser.). (ENG.). 32p. (gr. 4-5). pap. 11.50 *(978-1-5382-3542-3(0)*, 3f5ff22b-7b01-4ab9-8e64-ea40a03b83e3) Stevens, Gareth Publishing LLLP.

—Messy Experiments, 1 vol. 2018. (Ultimate Science Lab Ser.). (ENG.). 32p. (gr. 4-5). pap. 11.50 *(978-1-5382-3534-8(X)*, 10f201ef-257d-40d9-90a0-9f079a06bcdb) Stevens, Gareth Publishing LLLP.

—Mysterious Experiments, 1 vol. 2018. (Ultimate Science Lab Ser.). (ENG.). 32p. (gr. 4-5). pap. 11.50 *(978-1-5382-3538-6(2)*, 3a441006-4688-456e-aa46-4448fd4f1354) Stevens, Gareth Publishing LLLP.

—Recreate Discoveries about Living Things. 2018. (Recreate Scientific Discoveries Ser.). (Illus.). 32p. (J). (gr. 4-5). *(978-0-7787-5053-6(1))* Crabtree Publishing Co.

—Recreate Discoveries about States of Matter. 2018. (Recreate Scientific Discoveries Ser.). (Illus.). 32p. (J). (gr. 4-5). *(978-0-7787-5062-8(0))* Crabtree Publishing Co.

—The Science of a Glass of Water, 1 vol. 2009. (Science Of... Ser.). (ENG., Illus.). 32p. (YA). (gr. 4-5). lib. bdg. 28.67 *(978-1-4339-0041-9(6)*, eb7e775e-10e9-4845-ae67-41feea29c034) Stevens, Gareth Publishing LLLP.

Cleland, Jo. I Can Make Colors. 2006. (Science about Me Ser.). (Illus.). 8p. (J). (gr. 3-7). pap. 5.95 *(978-1-59515-925-0(8))* Rourke Educational Media.

Cobb, Vicki. I Face the Wind. Gorton, Julia, illus. 2003. (ENG.). 40p. (J). (gr. -1-3). 17.99 *(978-0-688-17840-6(5)*, HarperCollins) HarperCollins Pubs.

—Science Experiments You Can Eat. Carpenter, Tad, illus. 2016. (ENG.). 256p. (J). (gr. 3-7). pap. 9.99 *(978-0-06-237729-6(9)*, HarperCollins) HarperCollins Pubs.

—Science Surprises: More Than 100 Amazing Experiments. 2015. (Illus.). 192p. (J). (gr. 3-7). pap. 14.99 *(978-1-63220-316-8(2)*, Sky Pony Pr.) Skyhorse Publishing Co., Inc.

—See for Yourself! More Than 100 Amazing Experiments for Science Fairs & School Projects. 2nd ed. 2010. (ENG., Illus.). 192p. (J). (gr. 1-3). pap. 14.95 *(978-1-61608-083-9(3)*, 608083) Skyhorse Publishing Co., Inc.

—We Dare You: Hundreds of Fun Science Bets, Challenges, & Experiments You Can Do at Home. 2009. (ENG., Illus.). 336p. (J). (gr. 2-7). pap. 14.95 *(978-1-60239-775-0(9)*, 239775) Skyhorse Publishing Co., Inc.

—We Dare You! Hundreds of Fun Science Bets, Challenges, & Experiments You Can Do at Home. rev. ed. 2015. (ENG., Illus.). 336p. (J). (gr. 2-7). pap. 12.95 *(978-1-62914-631-7(5)*, Sky Pony Pr.) Skyhorse Publishing Co., Inc.

Connolly, Sean. The Book of Potentially Catastrophic Science: 50 Experiments for Daring Young Scientists. 2010. (Irresponsible Science Ser.). (ENG., Illus.). 306p. (J). (gr. 3-9). 14.95 *(978-0-7611-5687-1(9)*, 15687) Workman Publishing Co., Inc.

—The Book of Totally Irresponsible Science: 64 Daring Experiments for Young Scientists. 2008. (Irresponsible Science Ser.). (ENG., Illus.). 205p. (J). (gr. 3-9). 14.95 *(978-0-7611-5020-6(X)*, 15020) Workman Publishing Co., Inc.

Crabtree Publishing Co. Staff & Burns, Kylie. What's Going On? Collecting & Recording Your Data, 1 vol. 2009. (Step into Science Ser.). (ENG., Illus.). 32p. (J). (gr. 3-6). pap.

(978-0-7787-5170-0(8)); lib. bdg. (978-0-7787-5155-7(4)) Crabtree Publishing Co.

—What's the Problem? How to Start Your Scientific Investigation, 1 vol. 2009. (Step into Science Ser.). (ENG., Illus.). 32p. (J). (gr. 3-6). pap. (978-0-7787-5173-1(2)); lib. bdg. (978-0-7787-5158-8(9)) Crabtree Publishing Co.

Crabtree Publishing Co. Staff & Challen, Paul. What Just Happened? Reading Results & Making Inferences. 2009. (Step into Science Ser.). (ENG., Illus.). 32p. (J). (gr. 3-6). pap. (978-0-7787-5171-7(6)); lib. bdg. (978-0-7787-5156-4(2)) Crabtree Publishing Co.

—What's Going to Happen? Making Your Hypothesis. 2009. (Step into Science Ser.). (ENG., Illus.). 32p. (J). (gr. 3-6). pap. (978-0-7787-5172-4(4)); lib. bdg. (978-0-7787-5157-1(0)) Crabtree Publishing Co.

Crabtree Publishing Co. Staff & Hyde, Natalie. What's the Plan? Designing Your Experiment, 1 vol. 2009. (Step into Science Ser.). (ENG., Illus.). 32p. (J). (gr. 3-6). pap. (978-0-7787-5169-4(4)); lib. bdg. (978-0-7787-5154-0(6)) Crabtree Publishing Co.

Crabtree Publishing Co. Staff & Johnson, Robin. What Do We Know Now? Drawing Conclusions & Answering the Question. 2009. (Step into Science Ser.). (ENG., Illus.). 32p. (J). (gr. 3-6). pap. (978-0-7787-5168-7(6)); lib. bdg. (978-0-7787-5153-3(8)) Crabtree Publishing Co.

Crane, Cody. Amazing Makerspace DIY Slippery Slime (a True Book: Makerspace Projects) (Library Edition) 2018. (True Book (Relaunch) Ser.). (ENG., Illus.). 48p. (J). (gr. 3-5). lib. bdg. 31.00 (978-0-531-12735-3(4), Children's Pr.) Scholastic Library Publishing.

—I Can Make Slippery Slime (Rookie Star: Makerspace Projects) (Library Edition) 2018. (Rookie Star Ser.). (ENG., Illus.). 32p. (J). (gr. 2-3). lib. bdg. 25.00 (978-0-531-13849-6(6), Children's Pr.) Scholastic Library Publishing.

—The Moon (Rookie Read-About Science: the Universe) 2018. (Rookie Read-About Science Ser.). (ENG., Illus.). 32p. (J). (gr. 1-2). pap. 5.95 (978-0-531-22862-3(2), Children's Pr.) Scholastic Library Publishing.

—Phineas & Ferb Big Book of Science Experiments. 2013. (Illus.). 136p. (J). pap. (978-0-545-48195-3(3)) Scholastic, Inc.

David C. Cook Publishing Company Staff, creator. Fun Science That Teaches God's Word for Tweeners. 2008. (BFS Ser.). (Illus.). 120p. (gr. 4-6). per. 19.99 (978-0-7814-4558-0(2)) Cook, David C.

Discovery Channel (Firm) Staff, contrib. by. Mythbusters. 2013. (Illus.). 48p. (J). (978-1-935442-24-0(4), Beckon Bks.) Southwestern Publishing Hse., Inc.

Dorling Kindersley Publishing Staff. Look I'm a Scientist. 2017. (Illus.). 48p. (J). (978-0-241-23107-4(8)) Dorling Kindersley Publishing, Inc.

Doudna, Kelly. I'll Use a Hand Lens with My Friends!, 1 vol. 2007. (Science Made Simple Ser.). (Illus.). 24p. (J). (gr. k-3). lib. bdg. 24.21 (978-1-59928-586-3(X), SandCastle) ABDO Publishing Co.

—Im on a Roll with Variable Control!, 1 vol. 2007. (Science Made Simple Ser.). (Illus.). 24p. (J). (gr. k-3). lib. bdg. 24.21 (978-1-59928-590-0(8), SandCastle) ABDO Publishing Co.

—It's a Date, Let's Investigate!, 1 vol. 2007. (Science Made Simple Ser.). (Illus.). 24p. (J). (gr. k-3). lib. bdg. 24.21 (978-1-59928-596-2(7), SandCastle) ABDO Publishing Co.

—It's an Event When We Experiment!, 1 vol. 2007. (Science Made Simple Ser.). (Illus.). 24p. (J). (gr. k-3). lib. bdg. 24.21 (978-1-59928-598-6(3), SandCastle) ABDO Publishing Co.

—The Kid's Book of Simple Everyday Science. 2013. (ENG., Illus.). 112p. (J). (gr. k-4). pap. 13.95 (978-1-938063-34-3(1), Mighty Media Kids) Mighty Media Pr.

Doyle, James. A Young Scientist's Guide to Defying Disasters with Skill & Daring: Includes 20 Experiments for the Sink, Bathtub & Backyard, 1 vol. 2012. (ENG., Illus.). 160p. (J). (gr. 5-6). 14.99 (978-1-4236-2440-0(8)) Gibbs Smith, Publisher.

Dragotta, Nick, et al. Howtoons: Tools of Mass Construction. 2014. (ENG., Illus.). 360p. (J). pap. 17.99 (978-1-63215-101-8(4), 4de65120-4aec-4e27-863d-b7cb0baecc8b) Image Comics.

Duncan, Terri Kaye. Eerie Science Experiments, 1 vol. 2019. (Creepy, Kooky Science Ser.). (ENG.). 48p. (gr. 5-5). pap. 12.70 (978-1-9785-1374-7(7), c9a17a9a-634e-40ae-9589-56ad57c4b4b7) Enslow Publishing, LLC.

Dyer, Janice. Get into Wow-Factor Science. 2017. (Get-Into-It Guides). (Illus.). 32p. (J). (gr. 4-5). (978-0-7787-3643-1(1)) Crabtree Publishing Co.

Dziengel, Ana. STEAM Play & Learn: 20 Fun Step-By-step Preschool Projects about Science, Technology, Engineering, Art, & Math! 2018. (ENG., Illus.). 80p. (J). (gr. -1-k). pap. 15.95 (978-1-63322-526-8(7), 301714, Walter Foster Jr) Quarto Publishing Group USA.

—STEAM Play & Learn: Fun Step-By-step Projects to Teach Kids about STEAM. 2019. (Little Engineers Ser.). (ENG., Illus.). 32p. (J). (gr. -1-2). 26.65 (978-1-942875-77-2(0), 9a5a584b-10ee-45cb-a76e-7f2c88302c0c, Walter Foster Jr) Quarto Publishing Group USA.

—STEAM Projects 101: Fun Step-By-step Projects to Teach Kids about STEAM. 2019. (Little Engineers Ser.). (ENG., Illus.). 32p. (J). (gr. -1-2). 26.65 (978-1-942875-80-2(0), 907d93e9-c566-4283-8e00-2ec337e53e59, Walter Foster Jr) Quarto Publishing Group USA.

Ecociencia: Experimentos Ecologicos para Chicos.Tr. of Projects for a Healthy Planet. (SPA.). (YA). (gr. 5-8). pap. 9.56 (978-950-24-0745-6(8)) Albatros ARG. Dist: Lectorum Pubns., Inc.

Editors of Klutz & Murphy, Pat. LEGO(r) Chain Reactions: Design & Build Amazing Moving Machines, 1 vol. 2015. (ENG.). 80p. (J). (gr. 3). 21.99 (978-0-545-70330-7(1)) Klutz.

Edom, H. Science Activities, Vol. 1. 2010. (Science Activities Ser.). 72p. (J). 13.99 (978-0-7945-2752-5(3), Usborne) EDC Publishing.

Edom, Helen. Science with Plants. Abel, Simone, illus. rev. ed. 2007. (Science Activities Ser.). 24p. (J). (gr. 3-7). pap. 5.99 (978-0-7945-1485-3(5), Usborne) EDC Publishing.

Enz, Tammy & Wheeler-Toppen, Jodi. Recycled Science. 2016. (Recycled Science Ser.). (ENG.). 32p. (J). (gr. 3-9). 122.60 (978-1-5157-0876-6(4), 24806, Capstone Pr.) Capstone.

Excellent Science Experiments, 8 vols. 2014. (Excellent Science Experiments Ser.). (ENG.). 32p. (J). (gr. 4-5). lib. bdg. 117.08 (978-1-4777-5723-9(6), 960db95b-bf2f-4270-960b-e1a15840b697, PowerKids Pr.) Rosen Publishing Group, Inc., The.

Experiments for Future STEM Professionals: Set 1, 8 vols. 2016. (Experiments for Future STEM Professionals Ser.). (ENG.). 128p. (gr. 6-6). lib. bdg. 155.72 (978-0-7660-7502-3(8), ac0cc2cc-137f-4ffc-85be-17c04a36fb91) Enslow Publishing, LLC.

Experiments for Future STEM Professionals: Set 2, 8 vols. 2016. (Experiments for Future STEM Professionals Ser.). (ENG.). 128p. (J). (gr. 6-6). lib. bdg. 155.72 (978-0-7660-8391-2(8), 7eaaf6ba-1eda-4e2c-9ad4-eb163130af11) Enslow Publishing, LLC.

Experiments for Future STEM Professionals: Sets 1 - 2, 16 vols. 2016. (Experiments for Future STEM Professionals Ser.). (ENG.). 128p. (J). (gr. 6-6). lib. bdg. 311.44 (978-0-7660-8471-1(X), 2e047b01-2445-4010-9da1-4bcd90d248a8) Enslow Publishing, LLC.

Factastic Challenge, Grades 1-2. 2005. (J). spiral bd. 15.95 (978-1-932855-17-3(3)) becker&mayer! books.

Factastic Challenge, Grades 3-4. 2005. (J). spiral bd. 15.95 (978-1-932855-18-0(1)) becker&mayer! books.

Factastic Challenge, Grades 5-6. 2005. (J). spiral bd. 15.95 (978-1-932855-19-7(X)) becker&mayer! books.

Falk, John H., et al. Bubble Monster: And Other Science Fun. 2003. (Illus.). 176p. (J). (gr. -1-3). pap. 17.95 (978-1-55652-301-4(7)) Chicago Review Pr., Inc.

Farndon, John. Buoyancy, 1 vol. 2003. (Science Experiments Ser.). (ENG.). 32p. (gr. 4-4). 32.64 (978-0-7614-1467-4(3), 693b0f08-f824-44fd-9a45-128cd947eeca) Cavendish Square Publishing LLC.

—Experimenting with Science, 2 bks., Set. Incl. Experimenting with Chemistry. lib. bdg. 38.36 (978-0-7614-3928-8(5), 456e5545-1948-4209-817a-08539f6c61a5); Experimenting with Physics. lib. bdg. 38.36 (978-0-7614-3929-5(3), bdfadb4c-4e0d-4c1e-82ef-7f54c8eb74ab); 104p. (gr. 5-5). 2009. 2008. Set lib. bdg. 49.90 net. (978-0-7614-3967-7(6), Cavendish Square) Cavendish Square Publishing LLC.

—Rocks & Minerals, 1 vol. 2003. (Science Experiments Ser.). (ENG.). 32p. (gr. 4-4). 32.64 (978-0-7614-1468-1(1), c912a925-68bb-4bcf-91d3-938acd968a7b) Cavendish Square Publishing LLC.

Felix, Rebecca. Body Oddity Projects: Floating Arms, Balancing Challenges, & More. 2019. (Unplug with Science Buddies (r) Ser.). (ENG., Illus.). 32p. (J). (gr. 2-5). pap. 8.99 (978-1-5415-7488-5(5), 571badf3-6eb5-41b8-a5e9-ea2da9f8ca97); lib. bdg. 27.99 (978-1-5415-5494-8(9), 5bf4e718-ae24-40f2-acf1-cfdfc7208d30) Lerner Publishing Group. (Lerner Pubns.).

—Mini Science Fun. 2017. (Mini Makers Ser.). (ENG., Illus.). 32p. (J). (gr. 2-5). 26.65 (978-1-5124-2634-2(2), 1e9c8c64-ddb8-4778-9acd-443c8077a880); E-Book 39.99 (978-1-5124-3839-0(1), 9781512438390); E-Book 39.99 (978-1-5124-2812-4(4)); E-Book 6.99 (978-1-5124-3840-6(5), 9781512438406) Lerner Publishing Group. (Lerner Pubns.).

—Movin' & Shakin' Projects: Balloon Rockets, Dancing Pepper, & More. 2019. (Unplug with Science Buddies (r) Ser.). (ENG., Illus.). 32p. (J). (gr. 2-5). pap. 8.99 (978-1-5415-7490-8(7), fd155c10-e936-43fc-8c82-258cb61b660c); lib. bdg. 27.99 (978-1-5415-5495-5(7), 32d283fe-b84b-4cb4-910b-0cfecc6ffeec) Lerner Publishing Group. (Lerner Pubns.).

First Science Experiments, 8 vols. 2016. (First Science Experiments Ser.). (ENG.). 32p. (J). (gr. 2-3). 121.08 (978-1-4994-8098-6(9), c594ad2b-6c3f-4987-ba39-1cbb8f3ee142, Windmill Bks.) Rosen Publishing Group, Inc., The.

Fredericks, Anthony D. Simple Nature Experiments with Everyday Materials. Zweifel, Frances, illus. 2004. 128p. (J). (gr. 4-8). reprint ed. pap. 6.00 (978-0-7567-7727-2(5)) DIANE Publishing Co.

Frederickson, A. Experimentos Sencillos con la Naturaleza. 2004. (Juego de la Ciencia Ser.). (SPA., Illus.). 128p. (978-84-95456-48-9(6), 87801) Ediciones Oniro S.A.

Freedman, Claire. Monstersaurus. Cort, Ben, illus. 2013. (J). (978-1-4351-4952-6(1)) Barnes & Noble, Inc.

Gadd, Ken. Applied Science. 2003. (ENG., Illus.). 352p. (YA). pap. 47.50 (978-0-7487-7044-1(5)) Nelson Thornes Ltd. GBR. Dist: Trans-Atlantic Pubns., Inc.

Galat, Joan Marie. Solve This! Wild & Wacky Challenges for the Genius Engineer in You. 2018. (Illus.). 160p. (J). (gr. 3-7). pap. 16.99 (978-1-4263-2732-2(3)); (ENG., lib. bdg. 26.90 (978-1-4263-2733-9(1)) Disney Publishing Worldwide. (National Geographic Kids).

Gardner, Martin. Martin Gardner's Science Magic: Tricks & Puzzles. 2011. (Dover Magic Bks.). (ENG., Illus.). 96p. (gr. 4). pap. 4.99 (978-0-486-47657-5(X), 47657X) Dover Pubns., Inc.

Gardner, Robert. Energy Experiments Using Ice Cubes, Springs, Magnets, & More: One Hour or Less Science Experiments, 1 vol. 2012. (Last-Minute Science Projects Ser.). (ENG., Illus.). 48p. (gr. 5-6). 27.93 (978-0-7660-3959-9(5), 009ef01c-8442-4113-a49d-24705a03c42f) Enslow Publishing, LLC.

—Experiments with Electricity & Magnetism, 1 vol. 2017. (Science Whiz Experiments Ser.). (ENG.). 128p. (gr. 5-5). 38.93 (978-0-7660-8678-4(X), 8673fc7d-bb50-4e2b-a503-cdf5a8fcbe1a) Enslow Publishing, LLC.

—How Big Is Big? Science Projects with Volume, 1 vol. 2014. (Hot Science Experiments Ser.). (ENG.). 48p. (gr. 3-4). 26.93 (978-0-7660-6620-5(7), 59e2ffbd-3dfa-44d1-a217-89a1d798828c) Enslow Publishing, LLC.

—Solids, Liquids, & Gases Experiments Using Water, Air, Marbles, & More: One Hour or Less Science Experiments, 1 vol. 2012. (Last-Minute Science Projects Ser.). (ENG., Illus.). 48p. (gr. 5-6). 27.93 (978-0-7660-3962-9(5), 3c0ba31a-d01e-4f25-9776-287319b424eb) Enslow Publishing, LLC.

Gardner, Robert & Conklin, Joshua. Experiments for Future Chemists, 1 vol. 2016. (Experiments for Future STEM Professionals Ser.). (ENG.). 128p. (gr. 6-6). lib. bdg. 38.93 (978-0-7660-7856-7(6), ea68f0f5-6b5a-465c-a7b7-a7431ea3b20c) Enslow Publishing, LLC.

—Experiments for Future Doctors, 1 vol. 2016. (Experiments for Future STEM Professionals Ser.). (ENG.). 128p. (gr. 6-6). 38.93 (978-0-7660-7854-3(X), c6f55851-73a1-475c-88dc-399004716d1c) Enslow Publishing, LLC.

—A Kid's Book of Experiments with Light, 1 vol. 2015. (Surprising Science Experiments Ser.). (ENG., Illus.). 48p. (gr. 4-4). 29.60 (978-0-7660-7205-3(3), 415607dd-2f50-4b02-999e-94bc995993f7) Enslow Publishing, LLC.

—A Kid's Book of Experiments with Sound, 1 vol. 2015. (Surprising Science Experiments Ser.). (ENG., Illus.). 48p. (gr. 4-4). 29.60 (978-0-7660-7209-1(6), 7844d024-d3f5-421c-a5f1-7b20dd35cc1d) Enslow Publishing, LLC.

—A Kid's Book of Experiments with Stars, 1 vol. 2015. (Surprising Science Experiments Ser.). (ENG., Illus.). 48p. (gr. 4-4). lib. bdg. 29.60 (978-0-7660-7270-1(3), b6ef8515-d5c9-441a-ac77-e0dbc2001334) Enslow Publishing, LLC.

Gardner, Robert & Shortelle, Dennis. Slam Dunk! Science Projects with Basketball, 1 vol. 2009. (Score! Sports Science Projects Ser.). (ENG., Illus.). 104p. (gr. 5-6). lib. bdg. 35.93 (978-0-7660-3366-5(X), 3a1ecb7c-3db4-4917-9411-3322e74f5780) Enslow Publishing, LLC.

Garrett, Ginger. Scientists Ask Questions (Rookie Read-About Science: Physical Science: Previous Editions) 2005. (Rookie Read-About Science Ser.). (ENG., Illus.). 32p. (J). (gr. 1-2). pap. 4.95 (978-0-516-24662-8(3), Children's Pr.) Scholastic Library Publishing.

Gates, Stefan. Science You Can Eat: 20 Activities That Put Food under the Microscope. 2019. (ENG., Illus.). 96p. (J). (gr. 2-4). 16.99 (978-1-4654-6843-7(9), DK Children) Dorling Kindersley Publishing, Inc.

Getting Creative with Fab Lab, 12 vols. 2016. (Getting Creative with Fab Lab Ser.). (ENG.). 00064p. (J). (gr. 6-6). 216.78 (978-1-5081-7366-3(4), aecafc58-7636-4ee8-80a2-77e2813e2f0c, Rosen Central) Rosen Publishing Group, Inc., The.

Gingold, Janet. My Adventure as a Scientist: Advanced My Adventure. 2009. (ENG.). 44p. (J). pap. 8.99 (978-1-59092-408-2(8)) Blue Forge Pr.

Gould, Alan. Hot Water & Warm Homes from Sunlight. Gould, Alan et al, illus. Sneider, Cary I., photos by. rev. ed. 2005. (Great Explorations in Math & Science Ser.). 80p. 13.50 (978-1-931542-04-3(X), GEMS) Univ. of California, Berkeley, Lawrence Hall of Science.

Graham, Ian. The Science of a Bicycle, 1 vol. 2009. (Science Of... Ser.). (ENG.). 32p. (YA). (gr. 4-5). lib. bdg. 28.67 (978-1-4339-0040-2(8), caf12869-a1da-4245-9545-4af4f51f5a11) Stevens, Gareth Publishing LLLP.

Grandin, Temple. Calling All Minds: How to Think & Create Like an Inventor. 2019. (ENG.). 240p. (J). (gr. 3-7). pap. 10.99 (978-1-5247-3822-8(0), Puffin Books) Penguin Young Readers Group.

Gray, Susan H. Seeds. 2009. (Explorer Library: Science Explorer Ser.). (ENG., Illus.). 32p. (gr. 4-8). lib. bdg. 32.07 (978-1-60279-514-3(2), 200293) Cherry Lake Publishing.

Green, Joey. The Electric Pickle: 50 Experiments from the Periodic Table, from Aluminum to Zinc. 2017. (ENG., Illus.). 272p. pap. 19.99 (978-1-61373-959-4(1)) Chicago Review Pr., Inc.

Haas, Trisha & Haas, Charlotte. Slime! Do-It-Yourself Projects to Make at Home. 2017. (ENG., Illus.). 64p. (J). pap. 7.99 (978-1-63158-216-5(X), Racehorse Publishing) Skyhorse Publishing Co., Inc.

Haggis-On-Whey, Doris & Haggis-On-Whey, Benny. Cold Fusion. 2009. (How Ser.). (ENG., Illus.). 64p. (gr. 3). 20.00 (978-1-934781-21-0(5), d0db239a-ab92-4596-99d4-2d0ed57e5154) McSweeney's Publishing.

Halls, Kelly. Goo Makers. 2018. (Project: STEAM Ser.). (ENG., Illus.). 48p. (gr. 4-8). pap. 10.95 (978-1-64156-591-2(8), 9781641565912) Rourke Educational Media.

Harris, Elizabeth Snoke. Weird & Wonderful Science Experiments Volume 2: Cool Creations: Make Slime, Crystals, Invisible Ink, & More! 2018. (Weird & Wonderful Science Ser.). (ENG., Illus.). 64p. (J). (gr. 5-8). 33.32 (978-1-942875-58-1(4), 9e2901ee-5a08-4fb8-b2e6-354e47cc7b19, Moondance) Quarto Publishing Group USA.

—Weird & Wonderful Science Experiments Volume 3: Build It: Build Rockets & Racers & Test Energy & Forces! 2018. (Weird & Wonderful Science Ser.). (ENG., Illus.). 64p. (J). (gr. 5-8). 33.32 (978-1-942875-59-8(2), 98e32b7d-afef-4f38-b331-65715ff981e4, Moondance) Quarto Publishing Group USA.

—Weird & Wonderful Science Experiments Volume 4: the World Around Us: Get Dirty Outdoors, Test Your Brain, & More! 2018. (Weird & Wonderful Science Ser.). (ENG., Illus.). 64p. (J). (gr. 5-8). 33.32 (978-1-942875-60-4(6), fa626b50-5e58-4d98-b3f9-2d39a98fb0db, Moondance) Quarto Publishing Group USA.

Harrison, Paul. Collins Big Cat Phonics for Letters & Sounds - This Is My Kit: Band 02A/Red A, Bd. 2A. 2018. (Collins Big Cat Phonics Ser.). (ENG., Illus.). 16p. (J). (gr. -1-k). pap. 6.99 (978-0-00-825146-8(0)) HarperCollins Pubs. Ltd. GBR. Dist: Independent Pubs. Group.

Haslam, Andrew. Earth. 2004. (Make It Work! Science Ser.). (Illus.). 48p. (J). (gr. 3-6). 12.95 (978-1-58728-376-5(X), Two-Can Publishing) T&N Children's Publishing.

Haslam, Andrew, et al. Building. (Make It Work! Ser.). (Illus.). 48p. (J). pap. 15.95 (978-0-590-24332-2(2)) Scholastic, Inc.

Hawbaker, Emily. Energy Lab for Kids: 40 Exciting Experiments to Explore, Create, Harness, & Unleash Energy, Volume 11. 2017. (Lab for Kids Ser.: 11). (ENG., Illus.). 144p. (J). (gr. 5-9). pap. 22.99 (978-1-63159-250-8(5), 223698, Quarry Bks.) Quarto Publishing Group USA.

Hawkins, Jay. Material World: The Science of Matter, 1 vol. 2013. (Big Bang Science Experiments Ser.). (ENG., Illus.). 32p. (gr. 4-5). pap. 12.75 (978-1-4777-0367-0(5), 545b97cc-ccc4-4059-a600-fc75349632d7, Windmill Bks.) Rosen Publishing Group, Inc., The.

Haysom, John. Science Fair Warm-Up: Learning the Practice of Scientists. (ENG., Illus.). 2013. 55p. (J). pap. (978-1-936959-20-4(8)) 2012. 65p. pap. 19.99 (978-1-936959-21-1(6), P218227) 2012. 75p. pap. 19.99 (978-1-936959-22-8(4), P218651) National Science Teachers Assn.

Hedde, Rebecca. Science with Magnets. rev. ed. 2008. (Science Activities Ser.). 24p. (J). pap. 5.99 (978-0-7945-1406-8(5), Usborne) EDC Publishing.

Heddle, Rebecca. Science in the Kitchen. Edom, Helen, ed. Davies, Kate, illus. rev. ed. 2007. (Usborne Science Activities Ser.). 24p. (J). (gr. 3-7). pap. 5.99 (978-0-7945-1405-1(7), Usborne) EDC Publishing.

Heinecke, Liz Lee. Kitchen Science Lab for Kids: 52 Family Friendly Experiments from Around the House, Volume 4. 2014. (Lab for Kids Ser.: 4). (ENG., Illus.). 144p. (J). (gr. 2-5). pap. 24.99 (978-1-59253-925-3(4), 213626, Quarry Bks.) Quarto Publishing Group USA.

—Little Learning Labs: Kitchen Science for Kids, Abridged Paperback Edition: 26 Fun, Family-Friendly Experiments for Fun Around the House; Activities for STEAM Learners, Volume 3. abr. ed. 2018. (Little Learning Labs Ser.: 3). (ENG., Illus.). 80p. (J). (gr. k-4). pap. 12.99 (978-1-63159-562-2(8), 305729, Quarry Bks.) Quarto Publishing Group USA.

—STEAM Lab for Kids: 52 Creative Hands-On Projects for Exploring Science, Technology, Engineering, Art, & Math, Volume 17. 2018. (Lab for Kids Ser.: 17). (ENG., Illus.). 144p. (J). (gr. 3-7). pap. 23.99 (978-1-63159-419-9(2), 301162, Quarry Bks.) Quarto Publishing Group USA.

Henry, Sally & Cook, Trevor. Cool Stuff to Do: Jam-Packed with Brilliant Things to Make & Do! 2012. (ENG.). 128p. (J). pap. 9.95 (978-1-84858-084-8(3), 6f095c41-4bc3-4028-a78b-35cee7a278c1) Arcturus Publishing GBR. Dist: Baker & Taylor Publisher Services (BTPS).

Heuer, Steve. Spectacular Experiments & Mad Science Kids Love: Science That Dazzles @ Home, School or on the Go! 2010. 204p. pap. 19.99 (978-1-4490-7041-0(8)) AuthorHouse.

Hewitt, Sally. Plants. (Illus.). 32p. (YA). (gr. 2-18). lib. bdg. 27.10 (978-1-932333-30-5(4)) Chrysalis Education.

Hindman, Susan. Think Like a Scientist in the Classroom. 2011. (Explorer Junior Library: Science Explorer Junior Ser.). (ENG., Illus.). 32p. (J). (gr. 4-8). lib. bdg. 32.07 (978-1-61080-170-6(9), 201110) Cherry Lake Publishing.

Hirschmann, Kris, et al. Slimy, Sticky, Stinky Science. 2012. (Illus.). 32p. (J). (978-0-545-51540-5(8), Tangerine Pr.) Scholastic, Inc.

Hoffman, Jane. Backyard Scientist A Science Wonderland for the Very Young: Simple, fun-to-do Science Experiments Ages 2 To 7. 2005. (Illus.). 56p. (J). pap. 8.95 (978-0-9618663-8-9(1)) Backyard Scientist, Inc.

Holt, Rinehart and Winston Staff. Holt Science & Technology: Inquiry Labs. 5th ed. 2004. (Illus.). pap. 14.60 (978-0-03-035184-6(7)) Holt McDougal.

—Holt Science & Technology: Labs You Can Eat. 5th ed. 2004. (Illus.). pap. 14.60 (978-0-03-035183-9(9)) Holt McDougal.

Holzweiss, Kristina A. & Barth, Amy. I Can Make Exciting Electronics (Rookie Star: Makerspace Projects) (Library Edition) 2017. (Rookie Star Ser.). (ENG., Illus.). 32p. (J). (gr. 2-3). lib. bdg. 25.00 (978-0-531-23411-2(8), Children's Pr.) Scholastic Library Publishing.

—I Can Make Marvelous Movers (Rookie Star: Makerspace Projects) (Library Edition) 2017. (Rookie Star Ser.). (ENG., Illus.). 32p. (J). (gr. 2-3). lib. bdg. 25.00 (978-0-531-23413-6(4), Children's Pr.) Scholastic Library Publishing.

Homer, Holly, et al. The 101 Coolest Simple Science Experiments: Awesome Things to Do with Your Parents, Babysitters & Other Adults. 2016. (ENG., Illus.). 192p. pap. 19.99 (978-1-62414-133-1(1), 900149516) Page Street Publishing Co.

Inventions in Land Vehicles. 2005. (Illus.). 28p. (J). pap. 19.99 incl. audio (978-0-9724983-0-2(3)) Jazwares Distribution, Inc.

Ives, Rob. Fun Experiments with Matter: Invisible Ink, Giant Bubbles, & More. Sassin, Eva, illus. 2017. (Amazing Science Experiments Ser.). (ENG.). 32p. (J). (gr. 3-6). lib. bdg. 27.99 (978-1-5124-3216-9(4), a8503d73-4445-434c-bf6d-2da4ebd9590f, Hungry Tomato (r)) Lerner Publishing Group.

Iyer, Rani. Amazing Life Science Activities. 2017. (Curious Scientists Ser.). (ENG., Illus.). 24p. (J). (gr. 1-3). pap. 7.95 (978-1-5157-6892-0(9), 135385); lib. bdg. 25.99 (978-1-5157-6886-9(4), 135381) Capstone. (Capstone Pr.).

—Eye-Opening Earth Science Activities. 2017. (Curious Scientists Ser.). (ENG., Illus.). 24p. (J). (gr. 1-3). lib. bdg. 25.99 (978-1-5157-6885-2(6), 135380, Capstone Pr.) Capstone.

Janice VanCleave's Wild, Wacky, & Weird Science Experiments: Set 1, 10 vols. 2016. (Janice VanCleave's Wild, Wacky, & Weird Science Experiments Ser.). 64p. (gr. 5-5). (ENG.). 192.35 (978-1-4777-8960-5(X), 5b8eece7-503b-4a81-9ada-570f2ee82d79); pap. 64.75 (978-1-4994-3841-3(9)) Rosen Publishing Group, Inc., The. (Rosen Central).

Janice VanCleave's Wild, Wacky, & Weird Science Experiments: Set 2. 2016. (Janice VanCleave's Wild, Wacky, & Weird Science Experiments Ser.). 00064p. (J). (gr. 5-5). pap. 64.75 (978-1-4994-6560-0(2), Rosen Young Adult) Rosen Publishing Group, Inc., The.

Janice VanCleave's Wild, Wacky, & Weird Science Experiments: Set 3. 2017. (Janice VanCleave's Wild, Wacky, & Weird Science Experiments Ser.). 64p. (gr. 10-10). pap. 64.75 (978-1-4994-6701-7(X)); (ENG.). (gr. 5-5). 192.35 (978-1-4994-6662-1(5), 479f9562-4389-4ffd-9253-54c5ea16ca24) Rosen Publishing Group, Inc., The. (Rosen Central).

Janice VanCleave's Wild, Wacky, & Weird Science Experiments: Set 4, 10 vols. 2017. (Janice VanCleave's Wild, Wacky, & Weird Science Experiments Ser.). (ENG., Illus.). (J). (gr. 5-5). lib. bdg. 192.35 *(978-1-4994-3961-8(X),* 9d9eed13-aa90-4aae-a704-31d5717b754c, Rosen Reference) Rosen Publishing Group, Inc., The.

Der Jugend Brockhaus: Natur und Technik. (GER., Illus.). 640p. (YA). (gr. 5-11). *(978-3-7653-1851-1(5))* Brockhaus, F. A., GmbH DEU. Dist: International Bk. Import Service, Inc.

Kellett, Sarah, et al, eds. Hands-On Science: 50 Kids' Activities from CSIRO. 2017. (Illus.). 128p. (gr. 7-14). pap. 16.50 *(978-1-4863-0614-5(4))* CSIRO Publishing AUS. Dist: Stylus Publishing, LLC.

Kessler, Colleen. A Project Guide to the Solar System. 2010. (Earth Science Projects for Kids Ser.). (Illus.). 48p. (J). (gr. 4-7). lib. bdg. 29.95 *(978-1-58415-867-7(0))* Mitchell Lane Pubs.

Kitchen Science. 2011. (Kitchen Science Ser.). (ENG.). 32p. (gr. 3-4). pap. 190.80 *(978-1-4296-6422-6(3),* Capstone Pr.) Capstone.

Kneidel, Sally. Creepy Crawlies & the Scientific Method: More Than 100 Hands-On Science Experiments for Children. 2nd ed. 2015. (ENG., Illus.). 240p. (gr. 4-9). pap. 24.95 *(978-1-938486-32-6(3))* Fulcrum Publishing.

Knighton, Kate. 50 Science Things to Make & Do. (50 Things to Make & Do Ser.). (J). 2009. 104p. spiral bd. 9.99 *(978-0-7945-2379-4(X))* 2007. (Illus.). 50p. (gr. 4-7). 9.99 *(978-0-7945-1698-7(X))* EDC Publishing. (Usborne).

Korman, Gordon. Criminal Destiny. 2017. (Masterminds Ser.: 2). (J). lib. bdg. 18.40 *(978-0-606-39612-7(8))* Turtleback.

Krautwurst, Terry, et al. Science Smart: Cool Projects for Exploring the Marvels of the Planet Earth. 2004. (ENG., Illus.). 400p. (J). pap. 12.98 *(978-1-4027-1436-8(X))* Sterling Publishing Co., Inc.

Kurzweil, Allen. Potato Chip Science: 29 Incredible Experiments. 2010. (ENG., Illus.). 96p. (J). (gr. 3-7). 22.95 *(978-0-7611-4825-8(6),* 14825) Workman Publishing Co., Inc.

Ladd, Karol. The Glad Scientist Explores the Human Body. 2004. (Glad Scientist Ser.). pap., act. bk. ed. 6.99 *(978-0-8054-0829-4(0))* B&H Publishing Group.

LaFosse, Michael. Making Origami Science Experiments Step by Step, 1 vol. 2003. (Kid's Guide to Origami Ser.). (ENG., Illus.). 24p. (J). (gr. 3-4). lib. bdg. 28.93 *(978-0-8239-6705-6(0),* 3febf6e4-92a7-4741-934b-29290f9b05ea, PowerKids Pr.) Rosen Publishing Group, Inc., The.

LaFosse, Michael G. Making Origami Science Experiments Step by Step. 2009. (Kid's Guide to Origami Ser.). 24p. (gr. 3-4). 47.90 *(978-1-61511-195-4(6),* PowerKids Pr.) Rosen Publishing Group, Inc., The.

Leavitt, Loralee. Candy Experiments. 2013. (Candy Experiments Ser.: 1). (ENG., Illus.). 160p. (J). pap. 14.99 *(978-1-4494-1836-6(8))* Andrews McMeel Publishing.

—Candy Experiments 2. 2014. (Candy Experiments Ser.: 2). (ENG.). 160p. (J). pap. 14.99 *(978-1-4494-6103-4(4))* Andrews McMeel Publishing.

Leigh, Anna. 30-Minute Outdoor Science Projects. 2019. (30-Minute Makers Ser.). (ENG., Illus.). 32p. (J). (gr. 2-5). 27.99 *(978-1-5415-3889-4(7),* dd4c77ec-de4f-4ded-af5b-0026f9e9f813); pap. 8.99 *(978-1-5415-5713-0(1),* 7eaba67d-e59c-416b-b5bb-abd70681eb55) Lerner Publishing Group. (Lerner Pubns.).

Leonard, Sue, ed. Kitchen Science: With over 50 Fantastic Experiments. 2004. (Illus.). 48p. (J). (gr. k-8). reprint ed. 13.00 *(978-0-7567-7265-7(0))* DIANE Publishing Co.

Let's Go! Elementary Science. 2004. spiral bd. 30.00 *(978-1-929075-38-6(3))* Vernier Software & Technology.

Let's Investigate, 6 bks. (J). (gr. 2-6). lib. bdg. 86.70 *(978-1-56674-929-9(8))* Forest Hse. Publishing Co., Inc.

Levine, Shar. Bathtub Science. 2003. (Illus.). 80p. pap. 10.95 *(978-0-8069-7243-5(2))* Sterling Publishing Co., Inc.

Levine, Shar & Johnstone, Leslie. Wonderful Weather. Harpster, Steve, illus. 2005. (First Science Experiments Ser.). (ENG.). 48p. (J). (gr. 2-4). 17.44 *(978-0-8069-7249-7(1))* Sterling Publishing Co., Inc.

Lew, Kristi. Kitchen Science, 4 vols., Set. Incl. Science Experiments That Fly & Move: Fun Projects for Curious Kids. (ENG.). 32p. (J). (gr. 3-9). 2010. lib. bdg. 28.65 *(978-1-4296-5426-5(0),* 113839, Capstone Pr.); (Kitchen Science Ser.). (ENG.). 32p. 2010. 85.95 o.p. *(978-1-4296-5429-6(5),* 170564, Capstone Pr.) Capstone.

—Science Experiments That Fly & Move: Fun Projects for Curious Kids. (Kitchen Science Ser.). (ENG.). 32p. (gr. 3-4). 2011. pap. 47.70 *(978-1-4296-6420-2(7))* 2010. (J). lib. bdg. 28.65 *(978-1-4296-5426-5(0),* 113839) Capstone. (Capstone Pr.).

Lindsey, Jason. Beyond the Science Lab. MacLure, Ashley, illus. 2012. 82p. pap. 16.95 *(978-0-9854248-4-8(2))* Pinwheel Bks.

Lockwood, Cate. Science Lab Tools. 2013. (InfoMax Readers Ser.). (ENG.). 24p. (J). (gr. 2-3). pap. 49.50 *(978-1-4777-2304-3(8));* (Illus.). pap. 8.25 *(978-1-4777-2303-6(X),* 9ad4802a-532b-4e26-8554-1c8c8baaa82d) Rosen Publishing Group, Inc., The. (Rosen Classroom).

Madgwick, Wendy. Animals & Plants: 10 Easy-to-Follow Experiments for Learning Fun - Find Out about Nature & How Things Live! 2014. (Illus.). 270p. (J). (gr. -1-12). 8.99 *(978-1-86147-349-3(4),* Armadillo) Anness Publishing GBR. Dist: National Bk. Network.

—First Science Library: Super Materials. 2014. (Illus.). 32p. *(978-1-86147-354-7(0),* Armadillo) Anness Publishing.

Make & Learn, 12 vols. 2014. (Make & Learn Ser.). (ENG.). 32p. (J). (gr. 4-4). 175.62 *(978-1-4777-7095-5(X),* 37862d5d-40ce-4798-9dd6-22dbdc98f9fc, PowerKids Pr.) Rosen Publishing Group, Inc., The.

Make It Work Science, 14 vol. set. 2005. (gr. 4-8). 169.00 *(978-0-7166-4737-9(0))* World Bk., Inc.

Maker Kids. 2014. (Maker Kids Ser.). 32p. (J). (gr. 3-6). pap. 70.50 *(978-1-4777-7232-4(4));* (ENG.). (gr. 4-5). 175.62 *(978-1-4777-6662-0(6),* 07798c52-dd47-4640-bcc9-460aa4466003) Rosen Publishing Group, Inc., The. (PowerKids Pr.).

Maloof, Torrey. What's the Matter with Mr. Fuego? rev. ed. 2015. (Reader's Theater Ser.). (ENG., Illus.). 32p. (gr. 3-4). pap. 11.99 *(978-1-4938-1294-3(7))* Teacher Created Materials, Inc.

Mandell, Muriel. Super Science Experiments. Garbot, Dave, illus. 2005. (No-Sweat Science(r) Ser.). 128p. (J). (gr. 3-7). per. 5.95 *(978-1-4027-2149-6(8))* Sterling Publishing Co., Inc.

Margles, Samantha. Mythbusters - Science Fair Book, 1. 2011. (Mythbusters Science Fair Bks.). (ENG., Illus.). 128p. (J). (gr. 3-6). 26.19 *(978-0-545-23745-1(9))* Scholastic, Inc.

—Star Wars: Science Fair Book. 2013. lib. bdg. 20.85 *(978-0-606-32399-4(6))* Turtleback.

Marks, Jennifer L. How to Make a Bouncing Egg, 1 vol. 2010. (Hands-On Science Fun Ser.). (ENG., Illus.). 24p. (J). (gr. -1-2). pap. 7.29 *(978-1-4296-6214-7(X),* 115374, Capstone Pr.) Capstone.

Martin, Steve. Scientist Academy. Kimpimaki, Essi, illus. 2018. (ENG.). 64p. (J). pap. 12.99 *(978-1-61067-668-7(8))* Kane Miller.

Martineau, Susan. Shadows in the Bedroom, 1 vol. Noyes, Leighton, illus. 2011. (Everyday Science Experiments Ser.). (ENG.). 24p. (J). (gr. 3-4). pap. 11.60 *(978-1-61533-410-0(6),* a3e7efb4-7cd5-4436-9254-007d6ee8b372, Windmill Bks.) Rosen Publishing Group, Inc., The.

Masoff, Joy. Oh, Ick! 117 Science Experiments Guaranteed to Gross Out! 2016. lib. bdg. 26.90 *(978-0-606-38003-4(5))* Turtleback.

McCallum, Ann. Eat Your Science Homework: Recipes for Inquiring Minds. Hernandez, Leeza, illus. 2014. (Eat Your Homework Ser.: 2). 48p. (J). (gr. 2-5). 16.95 *(978-1-57091-298-6(X))* Charlesbridge Publishing, Inc.

McGill, Jordan. Life Science Fair Projects. 2011. (J). *(978-1-61690-330-5(9));* (gr. 3-5). pap. 12.95 *(978-1-61690-658-0(8),* AV2 by Weigl); (Illus.). 24p. (gr. 3-6). 27.13 *(978-1-61690-654-2(5))* Weigl Pubs., Inc.

McGowan, Chris. Abacus. 2010. (Illus.). 312p. (J). (gr. 5-9). *(978-0-9810831-1-7(0));* pap. *(978-0-9810831-0-0(2))* Euphausia Pr.

Meiani, Antonella. Air. 2003. (Experimenting with Science Ser.). (Illus.). 40p. (J). (gr. 4-8). lib. bdg. 23.93 *(978-0-8225-0082-7(5))* Lerner Publishing Group.

—Magnetism. 2003. (Experimenting with Science Ser.). (Illus.). 40p. (J). (gr. 4-8). lib. bdg. 23.93 *(978-0-8225-0085-8(X))* Lerner Publishing Group.

Mercer, Bobby. Junk Drawer Chemistry: 50 Awesome Experiments That Don't Cost a Thing. 2015. (Junk Drawer Science Ser.: 2). (ENG., Illus.). 224p. (J). (gr. 4). pap. 16.99 *(978-1-61373-179-6(5))* Chicago Review Pr., Inc.

—Junk Drawer Engineering: 25 Construction Challenges That Don't Cost a Thing. 2017. (Junk Drawer Science Ser.: 3). (ENG., Illus.). 224p. (J). (gr. 4). pap. 16.99 *(978-1-61373-716-3(5))* Chicago Review Pr., Inc.

Merrill, Amy French. Everyday Physical Science Experiments with Magnetism, 1 vol. 2004. (Science Surprises Ser.). (ENG., Illus.). 24p. (J). (gr. 3-4). lib. bdg. 26.27 *(978-0-8239-5800-9(0),* 339eadb1-8d5c-434c-994b-a6282c2c3e95, PowerKids Pr.) Rosen Publishing Group, Inc., The.

Messner, Kate. Solve This! Forensics: Super Science & Curious Capers for the Daring Detective in You. 2020. (Illus.). 160p. (J). (gr. 3-7). (ENG.). 26.90 *(978-1-4263-3745-1(0));* pap. 16.99 *(978-1-4263-3744-4(2))* Disney Publishing Worldwide. (National Geographic Kids).

Metz, Lorijo. Using Clocks & Stopwatches, 1 vol. 2013. (Science Tools Ser.). (ENG., Illus.). 24p. (J). (gr. 2-3). 26.27 *(978-1-4488-9689-9(4),* 72d3a67c-f101-4f0a-a8c3-a166d868c186); pap. 9.25 *(978-1-4488-9836-7(6),* 59ef4940-8ec8-435a-b67e-e7ae51059ec2) Rosen Publishing Group, Inc., The. (PowerKids Pr.).

—Using Scales & Balances, 1 vol. 2013. (Science Tools Ser.). (ENG., Illus.). 24p. (J). (gr. 2-3). 26.27 *(978-1-4488-9686-8(X),* 54300f7c-04b8-46f2-9f19-293f21528331); pap. 9.25 *(978-1-4488-9830-5(7),* 86d17a2d-4e01-4791-8191-642fa9f111d7) Rosen Publishing Group, Inc., The. (PowerKids Pr.).

Mind-Blowing Science Experiments. 2017. (Mind-Blowing Science Experiments Ser.). 32p. (gr. 4-5). pap. 63.00 *(978-1-5382-0836-6(9));* (ENG.). lib. bdg. 169.62 *(978-1-5382-0827-4(X),* d8bb40f8-c172-4596-9e15-8f084023558f) Stevens, Gareth Publishing LLLP.

Mullins, Matt. Think Like a Scientist in the Kitchen. 2011. (Explorer Junior Library: Science Explorer Junior Ser.). (ENG., Illus.). 32p. (J). (gr. 4-8). lib. bdg. 32.07 *(978-1-61080-165-2(2),* 201100) Cherry Lake Publishing.

Muntz, Kendra & Kenis, Daniel. Dr. Mollie Cule Reboots the Robot: Awesome Science Activities You Can Do at Home. Carrington, Matt, illus. 2014. 160p. (J). *(978-0-7166-0633-8(X))* World Bk., Inc.

Murphy, Brian. Movement. 2004. (Experiment with Ser.). (ENG., Illus.). 32p. (J). (gr. 2-5). 9.95 *(978-1-58728-248-5(8),* Two-Can Publishing) T&N Children's Publishing.

Nagelhout, Ryan. The Unofficial Guide to Science Experiments in Minecraft, 1 vol. 2018. (STEM Projects in Minecraft(r) Ser.). (ENG.). 24p. (gr. 3-3). pap. 9.25 *(978-1-5383-4256-5(1),* edc5bc48-08fd-4ce9-af64-f01213001c96, PowerKids Pr.) Rosen Publishing Group, Inc., The.

Nagy, Frances. Science with Water. 2007. (Usborne Science Activities Ser.). (Illus.). 24p. (J). (gr. 1). lib. bdg. 13.99 *(978-1-58086-976-8(9));* pap. 5.99 *(978-0-7945-1484-6(7))* EDC Publishing. (Usborne).

Naylor, Brenda & Naylor, Stuart. The Snowman's Coat & Other Science Questions, 4 vols. Mitchell, Ged, illus. (ENG.). 32p. (J). pap. *(978-0-340-75755-0(8))* Hodder & Stoughton.

Nelson, M. Rae & Krapp, Kristine. Experiment Central: Understanding Scientific Principles Through Projects, 6 vols. 2nd ed. 2010. (Experiment Central Ser.). (ENG.). 2340p. (J). 634.00 *(978-1-4144-7613-1(2),* UXL) Cengage Gale.

Nelson, M. Rae & Krapp, Kristine M. Experiment Central: Understanding Scientific Principles Through Projects. 2nd ed. 2010. (J). *(978-1-4144-7618-6(3)); (978-1-4144-7617-9(5)); (978-1-4144-7616-2(7)); (978-1-4144-7615-5(9)); (978-1-4144-7619-3(1)); (978-1-4144-7614-8(0))* Cengage Gale. (UXL).

Olinger, Heidi. Leonardo's Science Workshop: Invent, Create, & Make STEAM Projects Like a Genius. 2019. (Leonardo's Workshop Ser.). (ENG., Illus.). 144p. (J). (gr. 5-8). pap. 22.99 *(978-1-63159-524-0(5),* 304041, Rockport Publishers) Quarto Publishing Group USA.

Olson, Elsie. Super Gross Poop, Puke, & Booger Projects. 2018. (Super Simple Super Gross Science Ser.). (ENG., Illus.). 32p. (J). (gr. k-4). lib. bdg. 34.21 *(978-1-5321-1732-9(9),* 30752, Super SandCastle) ABDO Publishing Co.

O'Neal, Claire. A Project Guide to Rocks & Minerals. 2010. (Earth Science Projects for Kids Ser.). (Illus.). 48p. (J). (gr. 4-7). lib. bdg. 29.95 *(978-1-58415-866-0(2))* Mitchell Lane Pubs.

Oxlade, Chris. Excellent Science Experiments, 1 vol. 2015. (Excellent Science Experiments Ser.). (ENG.). 32p. (J). 47.00 *(978-1-4994-0345-9(3),* PowerKids Pr.) Rosen Publishing Group, Inc., The.

—Experiments with Air & Water, 1 vol. 2014. (Excellent Science Experiments Ser.). (ENG., Illus.). 32p. (J). (gr. 4-5). lib. bdg. 29.27 *(978-1-4777-5793-2(7),* aee3547d-3207-48a5-8617-388e6640f6b1, PowerKids Pr.) Rosen Publishing Group, Inc., The.

—Experiments with Electricity & Magnets, 1 vol. 2014. (Excellent Science Experiments Ser.). (ENG., Illus.). 32p. (J). (gr. 4-5). pap. 12.75 *(978-1-4777-5962-2(X),* 62787578-06c9-47df-97ef-aa4f4d0cd21d, PowerKids Pr.) Rosen Publishing Group, Inc., The.

—Experiments with Matter & Materials, 1 vol. 2014. (Excellent Science Experiments Ser.). (ENG.). 32p. (J). (gr. 4-5). lib. bdg. 29.27 *(978-1-4777-5969-1(7),* 4f23ee91-dd3d-42e7-843a-f7f824ef9bc8, PowerKids Pr.) Rosen Publishing Group, Inc., The.

—Experiments with Sound & Light, 1 vol. 2014. (Excellent Science Experiments Ser.). (ENG., Illus.). 32p. (J). (gr. 4-5). lib. bdg. 29.27 *(978-1-4777-5965-3(4),* 8ceee608-5c78-425e-82f9-1b8d9e130ea2, PowerKids Pr.) Rosen Publishing Group, Inc., The.

—Simple Experiments with Inclined Planes, 1 vol. 2013. (Science Experiments with Simple Machines Ser.). (ENG.). 32p. (J). (gr. 2-3). 31.17 *(978-1-61533-752-1(0),* 2c1b48f5-4d72-4d74-885c-1fe571cab294); pap. 12.75 *(978-1-61533-821-4(7),* 81808ed5-9e4b-4eac-b4d7-a06c9973b73f) Rosen Publishing Group, Inc., The. (Windmill Bks.).

—Simple Experiments with Inclined Planes. 2013. (Science Experiments with Simple Machines Ser.). 32p. (J). (gr. k-3). pap. 70.50 *(978-1-61533-822-1(5))* Windmill Bks.

—Simple Experiments with Levers, 1 vol. 2013. (Science Experiments with Simple Machines Ser.). (ENG.). 32p. (J). (gr. 2-3). 31.17 *(978-1-61533-756-9(3),* ee533921-48f4-40a7-b850-2686d2eb5e9b); pap. 12.75 *(978-1-61533-829-0(2),* 3bc4f17b-431c-41b5-9dc9-25cd674a6a2d) Rosen Publishing Group, Inc., The. (Windmill Bks.).

—Simple Experiments with Levers. 2013. (Science Experiments with Simple Machines Ser.). 32p. (J). (gr. k-3). pap. 70.50 *(978-1-61533-830-6(6))* Windmill Bks.

—Simple Experiments with Pulleys, 1 vol. 2013. (Science Experiments with Simple Machines Ser.). (ENG.). 32p. (J). (gr. 2-3). 31.17 *(978-1-61533-751-4(2),* 914a7071-9320-4a2d-9019-f2d9b2a6f206); pap. 12.75 *(978-1-61533-819-1(5),* d0e12c02-fb25-466a-b0e3-c9835b99286e) Rosen Publishing Group, Inc., The. (Windmill Bks.).

—Simple Experiments with Pulleys. 2013. (Science Experiments with Simple Machines Ser.). 32p. (J). (gr. k-3). pap. 70.50 *(978-1-61533-820-7(9))* Windmill Bks.

—Simple Experiments with Screws, 1 vol. 2013. (Science Experiments with Simple Machines Ser.). (ENG.). 32p. (J). (gr. 2-3). 31.17 *(978-1-61533-753-8(9),* 794c1f3d-762a-4660-9613-a117f612ca70); pap. 12.75 *(978-1-61533-823-8(3),* d69dff2a-3da0-419d-9e45-3e55129cd5ba) Rosen Publishing Group, Inc., The. (Windmill Bks.).

—Simple Experiments with Screws. 2013. (Science Experiments with Simple Machines Ser.). 32p. (J). (gr. k-3). pap. 70.50 *(978-1-61533-824-5(1))* Windmill Bks.

—Simple Experiments with Wedges, 1 vol. 2013. (Science Experiments with Simple Machines Ser.). (ENG.). 32p. (J). (gr. 2-3). 31.17 *(978-1-61533-755-2(5),* 5a85d8a3-5a70-41ca-974d-155f945f5a5d); pap. 12.75 *(978-1-61533-827-6(6),* 0cabe58c-94a4-425b-bc57-0b3d2816ffe5) Rosen Publishing Group, Inc., The. (Windmill Bks.).

—Simple Experiments with Wedges. 2013. (Science Experiments with Simple Machines Ser.). 32p. (J). (gr. k-3). pap. 70.50 *(978-1-61533-828-3(4))* Windmill Bks.

—Simple Experiments with Wheels & Axles, 1 vol. 2013. (Science Experiments with Simple Machines Ser.). (ENG.). 32p. (J). (gr. 2-3). 31.17 *(978-1-61533-754-5(7),* f20d8034-caf6-4904-b63c-c3548d2e2bb0); pap. 12.75 *(978-1-61533-825-2(X),* 9561e978-f36e-4a8b-92e4-dbfa4b2bd1d6) Rosen Publishing Group, Inc., The. (Windmill Bks.).

—Simple Experiments with Wheels & Axles. 2013. (Science Experiments with Simple Machines Ser.). 32p. (J). (gr. k-3). pap. 70.50 *(978-1-61533-826-9(8))* Windmill Bks.

—Super Science Air & Water Experiments: 10 Amazing Experiments with Step by Step Photographs - For. 2016. (ENG., Illus.). (J). pap. *(978-1-78209-419-7(9))* Miles Kelly Publishing, Ltd.

—Super Science Experiments. Kelly, Richard, ed. 2017. (Illus.). 96p. (J). pap. 18.95 *(978-1-78209-423-4(7))* Miles Kelly Publishing, Ltd. GBR. Dist: Parkwest Pubns., Inc.

—150 Amazing Science Experiments: Fascinating Projects Using Everyday Materials, Demonstrated. 2014. (Illus.). 256p. (J). (gr. 3-7). pap. 13.99 *(978-1-86147-472-8(5),* Armadillo) Anness Publishing GBR. Dist: National Bk. Network.

Oxlade, Chris & Stockley, Corinne. The World of the Microscope. Chen, Kuo Kang et al, illus. 2008. (Usborne Science & Experiments Ser.). 48p. (J). (gr. 5-11). pap. 8.99 *(978-0-7945-1524-9(X),* Usborne) EDC Publishing.

Oxlade, Chris, et al. The Science & History Project Book: 300 Step-By-Step Fun Science Experiments & History Craft Projects for Home Learning & School Study. 2013. (Illus.). 512p. (J). (gr. 2-7). pap. 17.99 *(978-1-84322-745-8(2),* Armadillo) Anness Publishing GBR. Dist: National Bk. Network.

Parker, Steve & Parker, Jane. My Giant Book of Science Projects: Fun & Easy Learning, with Simple Step-By-Step Experiments. 2019. (Illus.). 24p. (J). (gr. -1-12). pap. 10.00 *(978-1-86147-855-9(0),* Armadillo) Anness Publishing GBR. Dist: National Bk. Network.

—Show Me How: I Can Do Science. 2016. (Illus.). 48p. (J). (gr. -1 — 1). 7.99 *(978-1-86147-404-9(0),* Armadillo) Anness Publishing GBR. Dist: National Bk. Network.

Parker, Steve & Prinja, Raman. Science Club. 2012. (Illus.). 120p. (J). *(978-1-4351-4413-2(9))* Barnes & Noble, Inc.

Pascoe, Elaine. Bugs. Kuhn, Dwight, illus. Kuhn, Dwight, photos by. 2003. 48p. (J). 23.70 *(978-1-56711-458-4(X),* Blackbirch Pr., Inc.) Cengage Gale.

—Flowers. 2003. (Illus.). 48p. (J). 24.95 *(978-1-56711-432-4(6),* Blackbirch Pr., Inc.) Cengage Gale.

Pederson, Bridget & Doudna, Kelly. Don't Be Hasty with Science Safety!, 1 vol. 2007. (Science Made Simple Ser.). (Illus.). 24p. (J). (gr. k-3). lib. bdg. 24.21 *(978-1-59928-580-1(0),* SandCastle) ABDO Publishing Co.

Perelman, Yakov. Amazing Experiments for Young Physicians. Williams, Brian, tr. 2013. 114p. pap. *(978-2-917260-29-6(7))* Prodinnova.

Peterson, Carol. Jump into Science: Themed Science Fairs, 1 vol. 2007. (ENG., Illus.). 152p. (gr. 3-7). per. 40.00 *(978-1-59158-413-1(2),* 900322275, Libraries Unlimited) ABC-CLIO, LLC.

Physical Science with Vernier. 2007. spiral bd. 45.00 *(978-1-929075-47-8(2))* Vernier Software & Technology.

Popular Mechanics Press Editors, ed. The Boy Scientist: 160 Extraordinary Experiments & Adventures. 2012. 242p. pap. 14.99 *(978-1-60796-498-8(8))* Meirovich, Igal.

Presti, Lori;Daronco. Measuring Tools. Schieber, Jennifer, ed. 2011. (Early Connections Ser.). (ENG.). (J). (gr. 1). 8.00 net. *(978-1-61672-641-6(5))* Benchmark Education Co.

Prize-Winning Science Fair Projects, 12 vols. 2015. (Prize-Winning Science Fair Projects Ser.). (ENG.). 128p. (J). (gr. 7-7). lib. bdg. 233.58 *(978-0-7660-6700-4(9),* c1b8141c-654c-40aa-9780-592a60d59236) Enslow Publishing, LLC.

Ragsdale, Tyraine D. Science of Grand Hank Lab Book of Experiments. 2005. pap. 24.95 *(978-0-9767236-0-8(3))* Grand Hank Productions, Inc.

Rau, Dana Meachen. Think Like a Scientist on the Playground. 2011. (Explorer Junior Library: Science Explorer Junior Ser.). (ENG., Illus.). 32p. (gr. 4-8). lib. bdg. 32.07 *(978-1-61080-169-0(5),* 201108) Cherry Lake Publishing.

Reilly, Kathleen M. The Human Body: Get under the Skin with Science Activities for Kids. Cornell, Alexis, illus. 2019. (Build It Yourself Ser.). (ENG.). 128p. (J). (gr. 4-6). 22.95 *(978-1-61930-798-8(7),* 552e8004-ac72-4238-9728-1e85298ccb06); pap. 17.95 *(978-1-61930-801-5(0),* e2eae405-0002-4972-b9db-764b30640e75) Nomad Pr.

Resler, T. J. How Things Work: Discover Secrets & Science Behind Bounce Houses, Hovercraft, Robotics, & Everything in Between. 2016. (Illus.). 208p. (J). (gr. 3-7). 19.99 *(978-1-4263-2555-7(X),* National Geographic Kids) Disney Publishing Worldwide.

Revolutionary Discoveries of Scientific Pioneers, 16 vols. 2013. (Revolutionary Discoveries of Scientific Pioneers Ser.). (ENG.). 80p. (YA). (gr. 6-6). 307.28 *(978-1-4777-1818-6(4),* 44978647-d7c7-4a7d-ac59-5a2c32750025) Rosen Publishing Group, Inc., The.

Rice, Dona Herweck. Science Detectives, 1 vol. rev. ed. 2014. (Science: Informational Text Ser.). (ENG., Illus.). 24p. (gr. 1-2). pap. 9.99 *(978-1-4807-4574-2(X))* Teacher Created Materials, Inc.

Richards, Jon. Air & Flight. 2009. (Science Factory Ser.). 32p. (gr. 4-5). 50.50 *(978-1-60853-018-2(3),* PowerKids Pr.) Rosen Publishing Group, Inc., The.

Robinson, Tim. The Everything Kids' Magical Science Experiments Book: Dazzle Your Friends & Family by Making Magical Things Happen! 2007. (Everything(r) Kids Ser.). (ENG., Illus.). 144p. (gr. 4-7). per. 9.99 *(978-1-59869-426-0(X),* Everything) Adams Media Corp.

Rogers, Kirsteen, et al. The Usborne Science Encyclopedia: Internet-Linked. Bhachu, Verinder, illus. 2009. (Usborne Internet-Linked Encyclopedia Ser.). 448p. (J). (gr. 4-7). 19.99 *(978-0-7945-2629-0(2),* Usborne) EDC Publishing.

Rohrig, Brian. 39 Dazzling Experiments with Dry Ice. 2003. (Illus.). 104p. (YA). per. *(978-0-9718480-3-0(3))* FizzBang Science.

—39 Dazzling Experiments with the Mega-Magnet. 2003. (Illus.). 136p. (YA). per. *(978-0-9718480-4-7(1))* FizzBang Science.

Ross, Michael Elsohn. Kitchen Lab. Seeley, Tim, illus. 2003. (You Are the Scientist Ser.). 48p. (J). (gr. 3-6). lib. bdg. 23.93 *(978-0-87614-625-5(6))* Lerner Publishing Group.

—What's the Matter in Mr. Whiskers' Room? Meisel, Paul, illus. 2007. (ENG.). 48p. (J). (gr. 1-4). pap. 7.99 *(978-0-7636-3566-4(9))* Candlewick Pr.

—What's the Matter in Mr. Whiskers' Room? 2007. 18.40 *(978-1-4177-9071-5(7))* Turtleback.

Roth, Jennifer A. Backyard Laboratory. 2007. (Experiment with Science Ser.). (ENG., Illus.). 32p. (J). (gr. 3-6). 27.00 *(978-0-531-18542-1(7),* Children's Pr.) Scholastic Library Publishing.

Rowe, Brooke. Floating a Paper Clip. Bane, Jeff, illus. 2016. (My Early Library: My Science Fun Ser.). (ENG.). 24p. (J). (gr. k-1). 30.64 *(978-1-63471-032-9(0),* 208208) Cherry Lake Publishing.

—Inflating a Balloon. Bane, Jeff, illus. 2017. (My Early Library: My Science Fun Ser.). (ENG.). 24p. (J). (gr. k-1). lib. bdg. 30.64 *(978-1-63472-822-5(X),* 209714) Cherry Lake Publishing.

—Making Colors Move. Bane, Jeff, illus. 2017. (My Early Library: My Science Fun Ser.). (ENG.). 24p. (J). (gr. k-1). lib. bdg. 30.64 *(978-1-63472-820-1(3),* 209706) Cherry Lake Publishing.

—Melting Ice. Bane, Jeff, illus. 2017. (My Early Library: My Science Fun Ser.). (ENG.). 24p. (J). (gr. k-1). lib. bdg. 30.64 *(978-1-63472-823-2(8),* 209718) Cherry Lake Publishing.

—Separating Colors in Ink. Bane, Jeff, illus. 2017. (My Early Library: My Science Fun Ser.). (ENG.). 24p. (J). (gr. k-1). lib.

S

bdg. 30.64 (978-1-63472-824-9(6), 209722) Cherry Lake Publishing.

—Shining a Penny. Bane, Jeff, illus. 2016. (My Early Library: My Science Fun Ser.). (ENG.). 24p. (J). (gr. k-1). 30.64 (978-1-63471-030-5(4), 208200) Cherry Lake Publishing.

Royston, Angela. Experiments with a Lemon. 2016. (One-Stop Science Ser.). 32p. (gr. 2-5). 31.35 (978-1-62588-140-3(1), Smart Apple Media) Black Rabbit Bks.

—Experiments with a Ruler. 2016. (One-Stop Science Ser.). 32p. (gr. 2-5). 31.35 (978-1-62588-143-4(6), Smart Apple Media) Black Rabbit Bks.

Roza, Greg. Heads or Tails? Exploring Probability Through Games, 1 vol. 2010. (Math for the REAL World Ser.). (ENG., Illus.). 24p. (gr. 3-4). pap. 8.25 (978-0-8239-8894-5(5), 18f44d5a-0b93-4df2-8254-65d16fbfbbd8, PowerKids Pr.) Rosen Publishing Group, Inc., The.

—Heads or Tails: Exploring Probability Through Games. 2004. (Math Big Bookstm Ser.). (ENG.). 24p. (gr. 3-4). 43.95 (978-0-8239-7644-7(0)) Rosen Publishing Group, Inc., The.

—Where We Play Sports: Measuring the Perimeters of Polygons, 1 vol. 2010. (Math for the REAL World Ser.). (ENG., Illus.). 24p. (gr. 3-4). pap. 8.25 (978-0-8239-8895-2(3), 94cbddbf-bd5d-47fc-af1a-91ebc50d354d, PowerKids Pr.) Rosen Publishing Group, Inc., The.

Rybolt, Thomas R. Soda Pop Science Fair Projects, 1 vol. 2015. (Prize-Winning Science Fair Projects Ser.). (ENG., Illus.). 128p. (gr. 7-7). lib. bdg. 38.93 (978-0-7660-7024-0(7), 23d3583c-b8af-4adc-a9ba-9ef5a426ae72) Enslow Publishing, LLC.

Rybolt, Thomas R. & Mebane, Robert C. Science Experiments for Young People, 5 bks., Set. (Illus.). (YA). (gr. 4-9). lib. bdg. 99.75 (978-0-89490-448-6(5)) Enslow Publishing, LLC.

Scholastic Library Publishing. A True Book-Experiments. 2011. (True Book-Experiments Ser.). (J). 174.00 (978-0-531-20912-7(1), Children's Pr.) Scholastic Library Publishing.

Schuette, Sarah L. Science Safety. 2019. (Staying Safe! Ser.). (ENG., Illus.). 24p. (J). (gr. -1-2). 24.65 (978-1-9771-0869-2(5), 140480, Pebble) Capstone.

Schwartz, Heather, et al. Girls Science Club. 2012. (Girls Science Club Ser.). (ENG.). 32p. (J). (gr. 3-9). pap., pap., pap. 31.80 (978-1-4296-8521-4(2), 17801) Capstone.

Science Experiments. 2004. (gr. 4). pap. 14.95 (978-0-7403-0221-3(3), SV0401); (gr. 6). pap. 14.95 (978-1-58095-902-5(4), SV0601); (gr. 7). pap. 14.95 (978-1-58095-903-2(2), SV0701); (gr. 8). pap. 14.95 (978-1-58095-904-9(0), SV0801) Alpha Omega Pubns., Inc. (Lifepac).

Science Experiments (Group 3), 12 vols., Set. 2003. (Science Experiments Ser.). (ENG.). (gr. 4-4). 195.84 (978-0-7614-1465-0(7), 47f2d71e-ab8b-4015-b11b-0d819034109d, Cavendish Square) Cavendish Square Publishing LLC.

Science Experiments Kid Kit. 2004. (Illus.). 64p. (J). 18.95 (978-1-58086-419-0(8)) EDC Publishing.

Science Experiments with Simple Machines. 2013. (Science Experiments with Simple Machines Ser.). 32p. (J). (gr. k-3). pap. 70.50 (978-1-61533-878-8(0)) Windmill Bks.

Science Explorer Junior (Set), 20 vols., Set. Incl. Junior Scientists: Experiment with Bugs. Gray, Susan H. (gr. 3-6). 2010. lib. bdg. 32.07 (978-1-60279-842-7(7), 200550); Junior Scientists: Experiment with Heat. Lockwood, Sophie. (gr. 3-6). 2010. lib. bdg. 32.07 (978-1-60279-843-4(5), 200552); Junior Scientists: Experiment with Liquids. Mullins, Matt. (gr. 3-6). 2010. lib. bdg. 32.07 (978-1-60279-846-5(X), 200558); Junior Scientists: Experiment with Magnets. Taylor-Butler, Christine. (gr. 3-6). 2010. lib. bdg. 32.07 (978-1-60279-844-1(3), 200554); Junior Scientists: Experiment with Plants. Gray, Susan H. (gr. 3-6). 2010. lib. bdg. 32.07 (978-1-60279-839-7(7), 200544); Junior Scientists: Experiment with Rocks. Lockwood, Sophie. (gr. 3-6). 2010. lib. bdg. 32.07 (978-1-60279-836-6(2), 200538); Junior Scientists: Experiment with Seeds. Gray, Susan H. (gr. 3-6). 2010. lib. bdg. 32.07 (978-1-60279-835-9(4), 200536); Junior Scientists: Experiment with Soil. Franchino, Vicky. (gr. 3-6). 2010. lib. bdg. 32.07 (978-1-60279-837-3(0), 200540); Junior Scientists: Experiment with Solar Energy. Taylor-Butler, Christine. (gr. 3-6). 2010. lib. bdg. 32.07 (978-1-60279-840-3(0), 200546); Junior Scientists: Experiment with Solids. Gregory, Josh. (gr. 3-6). 2010. lib. bdg. 32.07 (978-1-60279-845-8(1), 200556); Junior Scientists: Experiment with Water. Simon, Charnan & Kazunas, Ariel. (gr. 3-6). 2010. lib. bdg. 32.07 (978-1-60279-838-0(9), 200542); Junior Scientists: Experiment with Weather. Orr, Tamra B. (gr. 3-6). 2010. lib. bdg. 32.07 (978-1-60279-841-0(9), 200548); Set. Think Like a Scientist (Set) (gr. 4-8). 2011. 256.56 (978-1-61080-249-9(7), 201036); (Explorer Junior Library: Science Explorer Junior Ser.). (ENG., Illus.). 32p. 2011. 641.40 (978-1-61080-247-5(0), 201034) Cherry Lake Publishing.

Science Lab Set, 8 vols. 2008. (Science Lab Ser.). (ENG., Illus.). (J). (gr. 4-4). lib. bdg. 121.08 (978-1-4358-2826-1(7), 2cfcf892-4993-4880-9793-0c67a9140278, PowerKids Pr.) Rosen Publishing Group, Inc., The.

Science Lab (Set), 8 vols., Set. Incl. Science Lab: Gases. Duke, Shirley Smith. lib. bdg. 32.07 (978-1-61080-203-1(9), 201182); Science Lab: Motion & Forces. Hirsch, Rebecca. 32.07 (978-1-61080-205-5(5), 201186); Science Lab: Properties of Matter. Hirsch, Rebecca. lib. bdg. 32.07 (978-1-61080-206-2(3), 201188); Science Lab: Soil. Barker, David M. lib. bdg. 32.07 (978-1-61080-207-9(1), 201190); Science Lab: Technological Design. Sirota, Lyn A. lib. bdg. 32.07 (978-1-61080-208-6(X), 201192); Science Lab: the Life Cycles of Plants. Hirsch, Rebecca. lib. bdg. 32.07 (978-1-61080-204-8(7), 201184); Science Lab: the Transfer of Energy. Zuchora-Walske, Christine. lib. bdg. 32.07 (978-1-61080-209-3(8), 201194); Science Lab: Weather Patterns. Hand, Carol. lib. bdg. 32.07 (978-1-61080-210-9(1), 201196); (gr. 4-8). (Explorer Library: Language Arts Explorer Ser.). (ENG., Illus.). 32p. 2011. 256.56 (978-1-61080-245-1(4), 201032) Cherry Lake Publishing.

The Science Library, 10 vols., Set. Incl. Animal Life. Parker, Steve. lib. bdg. 19.95 (978-1-4222-1547-0(4)); Discovering Science. Farndon, John & Graham, Ian. lib. bdg. 19.95 (978-1-4222-1548-7(2)); Great Scientists. Farndon, John. lib. bdg. 19.95 (978-1-4222-1549-4(0)); How Things Work. Farndon, John. lib. bdg. 19.95 (978-1-4222-1550-0(4)); Human Body. Parker, Steve. lib. bdg. 19.95 (978-1-4222-1551-7(2)); Inventions. Taylor, Barbara. lib. bdg. 19.95 (978-1-4222-1552-4(0)); Planet Earth. Farndon, John. lib. bdg. 19.95 (978-1-4222-1553-1(9)); Plants. Riley, Peter. lib. bdg. 19.95 (978-1-4222-1554-8(7)); Space. Farndon, John. lib. bdg. 19.95 (978-1-4222-1555-5(5)); Wild Animals. Parker, Steve. lib. bdg. 19.95 (978-1-4222-1556-2(3)); 40p. (J). (gr. 3-18). 2010. Set lib. bdg. 199.50 (978-1-4222-1546-3(6)) Mason Crest.

Science Stories Foss Spanish Ideas & Inventions EA CR05. 2005. (J). (978-1-59242-588-4(7)) Delta Education, LLC.

Science Whiz Experiments, 12 vols. 2017. (Science Whiz Experiments Ser.). (ENG.). 128p. (gr. 5-5). lib. bdg. 233.58 (978-0-7660-8597-8(X), 89fe7e69-8367-45cb-b350-cf4fb8c21426) Enslow Publishing, LLC.

Science with Magnets Kid Kit. 2004. (Kid Kits Ser.). (Illus.). 24p. (J). 14.95 (978-1-58086-420-6(1)) EDC Publishing.

The Scientific Method in Action, 12 vols. 2014. (Scientific Method in Action Ser.). 24p. (J). (gr. 3-3). (ENG.). 151.62 (978-1-4777-6386-5(4), 9d85a17f-de98-4afc-b397-ee33d89bba95); pap. 49.50 (978-1-4777-7250-8(2)) Rosen Publishing Group, Inc., The. (PowerKids Pr.).

Sévigny, Eric, illus. The Jungle Explorer. 2010. (Clubhouse Ser.). (ENG.). 24p. (J). (gr. -1-1). pap. 3.99 (978-2-89450-724-7(0)) Caillouet, Gerry.

Shores, Lori. Cómo Hacer un Globo con Olor Misterioso. Translations.com Staff, tr. 2010. (Divertirse con la Ciencia/Hands-On Science Fun Ser.).Tr. of How to Make a Mystery Smell Balloon. (MUL.). 24p. (J). (gr. -1-2). lib. bdg. 27.32 (978-1-4296-6108-9(9), 115132) Capstone.

—How to Build a Fizzy Rocket: A 4D Book. rev. ed. 2018. (Hands-On Science Fun Ser.). (ENG., Illus.). 24p. (J). (gr. -1-2). lib. bdg. 29.32 (978-1-5435-0943-4(6), 137650, Capstone Pr.) Capstone.

—How to Build a Tornado in a Bottle: A 4D Book. rev. ed. 2018. (Hands-On Science Fun Ser.). (ENG., Illus.). 24p. (J). (gr. -1-2). lib. bdg. 29.32 (978-1-5435-0944-1(4), 137651, Capstone Pr.) Capstone.

—How to Make a Liquid Rainbow: A 4D Book. rev. ed. 2018. (Hands-On Science Fun Ser.). (ENG., Illus.). 24p. (J). (gr. -1-2). pap. 6.95 (978-1-5435-0952-6(5), 137659); lib. bdg. 29.32 (978-1-5435-0946-5(0), 137653) Capstone. (Capstone Pr.).

—How to Make a Mystery Smell Balloon: A 4D Book. rev. ed. 2018. (Hands-On Science Fun Ser.). (ENG., Illus.). 24p. (J). (gr. -1-2). pap. 6.95 (978-1-5435-0951-9(7), 137658); lib. bdg. 29.32 (978-1-5435-0945-8(2), 137652) Capstone. (Capstone Pr.).

Shores, Lori & Capstone Press Staff. Hands-On Science Fun, 1 vol. 2010. (Hands-on Science Fun Ser.). (ENG.). 32p. lib. bdg. 95.96 (978-1-4296-5941-3(6), Capstone Pr.) Capstone.

Sian Phys&Chml Changes. 2004. (Science in A Nutshell Ser.). (J). (978-1-59242-055-1(9)) Delta Education, LLC.

Simon, Seymour & Fauteux, Nicole. Let's Try It Out in the Air. Cushman, Doug, illus. 2003. (Let's Try It Out Ser.). 28p. (J). (gr. -1-3). lib. bdg. 14.65 (978-0-7569-1477-6(9)) Perfection Learning Corp.

—Let's Try It Out in the Water: Hands-on Early-Learning Science Activities. Cushman, Doug, illus. 2003. (Let's Try It Out Ser.). (J). (gr. -1-3). 14.65 (978-0-7569-1478-3(7)) Perfection Learning Corp.

SMARTLAB Creative Team. Indoor Outdoor Science Lab. 2010. 12p. mass mkt. 39.99 (978-1-60380-051-8(4)) becker&mayer! books.

Smibert, Angie. Mind-Blowing Physical Science Activities. 2017. (Curious Scientists Ser.). (ENG., Illus.). 24p. (J). (gr. 1-3). lib. bdg. 25.99 (978-1-5157-6887-6(2), 135382, Capstone Pr.) Capstone.

Smith, A. Big Book of Science Experiments. rev. ed. 2011. (Science Experiments Ser.). 96p. (J). pap. 14.99 (978-0-7945-3039-6(7), Usborne) EDC Publishing.

Smith, Chris & Ansell, Dave. Spectacular Science: Exciting Experiments to Try at Home. 2010. (ENG., Illus.). 144p. (gr. 6-18). (978-1-84773-703-8(X)) New Holland Pubs., Ltd.

Smith, Paula. Plan & Investigate It!, 1 vol. 2015. (Science Sleuths Ser.). (ENG., Illus.). 24p. (J). (gr. 2-2). pap. (978-0-7787-1546-7(9)) Crabtree Publishing Co.

—Prove It!, 1 vol. 2015. (Science Sleuths Ser.). (ENG., Illus.). 24p. (J). (gr. 2-2). pap. (978-0-7787-1547-4(7)) Crabtree Publishing Co.

Sohn, Emily. A Crash Course in Forces & Motion with Max Axiom, Super Scientist. Erwin, Steve, illus. rev. ed. 2016. (Graphic Science Ser.). (ENG.). 32p. (J). (gr. 3-9). pap. 8.10 (978-1-5157-4638-6(0), 134305) Capstone.

—Variables & Experiments. 2019. (IScience Ser.). (ENG., Illus.). 48p. (J). (gr. 5-6). 23.94 (978-1-68450-944-7(0)); pap. 13.26 (978-1-68404-408-5(1)) Norwood Hse. Pr.

Somervill, Barbara A. What Did You Find Out? Reporting Conclusions. (Think Like a Scientist Ser.). 24p. (gr. 2-3). 2009. 42.50 (978-1-60854-359-5(5), PowerKids Pr.) 2006. (ENG.). pap. 8.25 (978-1-4358-2684-7(1), 47699ca5-448d-4646-84b9-746cbc2c4ec7, Rosen Classroom) Rosen Publishing Group, Inc., The.

—What Do You Want to Prove? Planning Investigations. (Think Like a Scientist Ser.). 24p. (gr. 2-3). 2009. 42.50 (978-1-60854-360-1(9), PowerKids Pr.) 2006. (ENG.). pap. 8.25 (978-1-4358-2685-4(X), 4da81289-e630-4fa0-8b72-654848549dc3, Rosen Classroom) Rosen Publishing Group, Inc., The.

Stevenson, Victoria & McNeice, Amanda. Gastro Blast: Make Tasty Treats & Learn Great Science: Comics, Quizzes & Questions Answered! Get Ready to Make Science Delicious! 2016. (ENG., Illus.). 128p. (J). (gr. 1-7). pap. 24.95 (978-1-4595-0462-2(3), 0462) Formac Publishing Co., Ltd. CAN. Dist: Formac Lorimer Bks. Ltd.

Stillinger, Doug, ed. Battery Science: Make Widgets That Work & Gadgets That Go. 2003. (ENG., Illus.). 56p. (J). (gr. 3-7). 21.95 (978-1-59174-251-7(X), 53643124) Klutz.

Stone, George K. Science Projects You Can Do. Peck, Stephen R., illus. 12th ed. 2023. Orig. Title: One Hundred One Science Projects. (ENG.). 1288p. (C). (gr. 7-9). pap. 195.17 (978-0-13-795377-6(1), Pearson Higher Ed) Pearson Education.

Strange Science & Explosive Experiments, 12 vols. 2017. (Strange Science & Explosive Experiments Ser.). (ENG.). (J). (gr. 4-5). lib. bdg. 175.62 (978-1-5081-6272-8(7), 7f35f8f8-5472-4283-ac23-b50657b3140b, PowerKids Pr.) Rosen Publishing Group, Inc., The.

Strickling Jacob. Make Science Fun. 2017. (Illus.). 192p. (J). 14.99 (978-1-74257-907-8(8)) New Holland Pubs. Pty, Ltd. AUS. Dist: Independent Pubs. Group.

Strickling, Jacob. Make Science Fun: Experiments. 2018. (Illus.). 192p. (J). pap. 14.99 (978-1-74257-071-6(2)) New Holland Pubs. Pty, Ltd. AUS. Dist: Independent Pubs. Group.

Stuart, Colin. Astonishing Atoms & Matter Mayhem. 2018. (STEM Quest Ser.). lib. bdg. 22.10 (978-0-606-41259-9(X)) Turtleback.

Sturm, Jeanne. Comprension de los Modelos. 2012. (Let's Explore Science Ser.). (SPA.). 48p. (gr. 4-8). pap. 10.95 (978-1-61810-472-4(1), 9781618104724) Rourke Educational Media.

Super Science Tools. 2017. (Super Science Tools Ser.). 24p. (gr. 1-2). pap. 48.90 (978-1-5382-0228-9(X)); (ENG.). lib. bdg. 145.62 (978-1-5382-0227-2(1), 381da9b6-7bce-49e7-b511-3e93debe13bc) Stevens, Gareth Publishing LLLP.

Swanson, Jennifer. Busting Boredom with Experiments. 2017. (Boredom Busters Ser.). (ENG., Illus.). 32p. (J). (gr. 3-9). lib. bdg. 28.65 (978-1-5157-4702-4(6), 134341, Capstone Pr.) Capstone.

Taylor-Butler, Christine. Experiments with Magnets & Metals, 1 vol. 2011. (My Science Investigations Ser.). (ENG.). 32p. (J). (gr. 1-3). pap. 8.29 (978-1-4329-5365-2(6), 116078, Heinemann) Capstone.

Tennant, Carol & Wheeler-Toppen, Jodi. Edible Science: Experiments You Can Eat. 2015. (Illus.). 80p. (J). (gr. 3-7). pap. 12.99 (978-1-4263-2111-5(2), National Geographic Kids) Disney Publishing Worldwide.

The Exploratorium, The. Exploralab. 2013. (ENG.). 128p. (J). 24.95 (978-1-61628-491-6(9)) Weldon Owen, Inc.

Think Like a Scientist (Set), 8 vols., Set. Incl. Think Like a Scientist at the Beach. Rau, Dana Meachen. lib. bdg. 32.07 (978-1-61080-168-3(7), 201106); Think Like a Scientist in the Backyard. Mullins, Matt. lib. bdg. 32.07 (978-1-61080-167-6(9), 201104); Think Like a Scientist in the Car. Mullins, Matt. lib. bdg. 32.07 (978-1-61080-164-5(4), 201098); Think Like a Scientist in the Classroom. Hindman, Susan. lib. bdg. 32.07 (978-1-61080-170-6(9), 201110); Think Like a Scientist in the Garden. Mullins, Matt. lib. bdg. 32.07 (978-1-61080-166-9(0), 201102); Think Like a Scientist in the Gym. Taylor-Butler, Christine. lib. bdg. 32.07 (978-1-61080-163-8(6), 201096); Think Like a Scientist in the Kitchen. Mullins, Matt. lib. bdg. 32.07 (978-1-61080-165-2(2), 201100); Think Like a Scientist on the Playground. Rau, Dana Meachen. lib. bdg. 32.07 (978-1-61080-169-0(5), 201108); (gr. 4-8). (Explorer Junior Library: Science Explorer Junior Ser.). (ENG., Illus.). 32p. 2011. 256.56 (978-1-61080-249-9(7), 201036) Cherry Lake Publishing.

Thompson, Veronica. Earth-Friendly Science Crafts. Thompson, Veronica, photos by. 2018. (Green STEAM Ser.). (ENG., Illus.). 32p. (J). (gr. 3-5). 29.32 (978-1-5415-2416-3(0), b29c50a1-7aec-4605-99f4-6bffce3fc5b0, Lerner Pubns.) Lerner Publishing Group.

Time for Kids Editors. Big Book of Science Experiments: A Step-by-Step Guide. 2011. (ENG., Illus.). 192p. (J). (gr. 3-17). 17.95 (978-1-60320-893-2(3), Time For Kids) Time Inc. Bks.

Tocci, Salvatore. True Books: Experiments with Colors. 2003. (True Bks.). (ENG., Illus.). 48p. (J). 25.00 (978-0-516-22785-6(8), Children's Pr.) Scholastic Library Publishing.

—True Books: Experiments with Sports. 2003. (True Book: Science Experiments Ser.). (ENG., Illus.). 48p. (J). (gr. 3-5). 18.69 (978-0-516-22789-4(0)) Scholastic Library Publishing.

Top That Publishing Staff, ed. Safe & Simple Science Tricks. 2004. (Fun Kits Ser.). (Illus.). 48p. (J). (978-1-904748-75-5(9)) Top That! Publishing PLC.

Unwin, M. Science Activities. 2009. (Science Activities Ser.). 74p. (J). Vol. 2. 13.99 (978-0-7945-2421-0(4)) Vol. 3. 13.99 (978-0-7945-2422-7(2)) EDC Publishing. (Usborne).

VanCleave, Janice. Janice VanCleave's a+ Projects in Physics: Winning Experiments for Science Fairs & Extra Credit. 2003. (VanCleave a+ Science Projects Ser.: 4). (ENG., Illus.). 240p. (gr. 7-12). pap. 16.00 (978-0-471-33098-1(1)) Wiley, John & Sons, Inc.

—Janice VanCleave's a+ Science Fair Projects. 2003. (ENG., Illus.). 168p. (gr. 7-12). pap. 14.95 (978-0-471-33102-5(3), Jossey-Bass) Wiley, John & Sons, Inc.

—Janice VanCleave's Big Book of Play & Find Out Science Projects. 2007. (ENG., Illus.). 224p. (gr. 3-7). per. 19.95 (978-0-7879-8928-6(2), Jossey-Bass) Wiley, John & Sons, Inc.

—Janice VanCleave's Engineering for Every Kid: Easy Activities That Make Learning Science Fun. 2nd ed. 2007. (Science for Every Kid Ser.: 119). (ENG., Illus.). 224p. (gr. 3-7). pap. 14.95 (978-0-471-47182-0(8)) Wiley, John & Sons, Inc.

—Janice VanCleave's Great Science Project Ideas from Real Kids. 2006. (ENG., Illus.). 144p. (gr. 3-7). pap. 16.00 (978-0-471-47204-9(2)) Wiley, John & Sons, Inc.

—Janice VanCleave's Super Science Challenges: Hands-On Inquiry Projects for Schools, Science Fairs, or Just Plain Fun! 2007. (ENG., Illus.). 160p. (gr. 3-7). pap. 14.95 (978-0-471-47183-7(6)) Wiley, John & Sons, Inc.

—More of Janice VanCleave's Wild, Wacky, & Weird Earth Science Experiments, 1 vol. 2016. (Janice VanCleave's Wild, Wacky, & Weird Science Experiments Ser.). (ENG.). 64p. (J). (gr. 5-5). pap. 14.53 (978-1-4994-6549-5(1), 48fe6930-9b18-43d3-b131-63934ac199f9, Rosen Young Adult) Rosen Publishing Group, Inc., The.

Vecchione, Glen. Experimentos Sencillos con la Luz y el Sonido. Elena, Horacio, tr. Elena, Horacio, illus. 2004. (Juego de la Ciencia Ser.). (SPA.). 124p. 10.99 (978-84-9754-043-8(3), 87814) Ediciones Oniro S.A. ESP. Dist: Lectorum Pubns., Inc.

Wakefield, Chris. Dad Did It! 2013. (ENG., Illus.). 32p. pap. 3.25 (978-1-85741-116-4(1)) Southgate Pubs. GBR. Dist: Parkwest Pubns., Inc.

Warner, Penny. Project Book: Ideas, Tips & Techniques for School Projects. Wagner, Amy, ed. Moore, Lishia, illus. Moore, Lishia & Wagner, Amy, photos by. 2007. 80p. pap. 9.98 (978-1-887436-05-2(7)) Woodland Scenics.

Weakland, Mark. Zoom! Wile E. Coyote Experiments with Speed & Velocity. Sordo, Paco, illus. 2017. (Wile E. Coyote, Physical Science Genius Ser.). (ENG.). 32p. (J). (gr. 3-5). lib. bdg. 31.32 (978-1-5157-3734-6(9), 133678, Capstone Pr.) Capstone.

West, Krista. Hands-on Projects about Changes in the Earth. 2009. (Great Earth Science Projects Ser.). 24p. (gr. 3-3). 42.50 (978-1-61513-110-5(8), PowerKids Pr.) Rosen Publishing Group, Inc., The.

—Hands-on Projects about Oceans. 2009. (Great Earth Science Projects Ser.). 24p. (gr. 3-3). 42.50 (978-1-61513-112-9(4), PowerKids Pr.) Rosen Publishing Group, Inc., The.

—Hands-On Projects about Rocks, Minerals & Fossils, 1 vol. 2004. (Great Earth Science Projects Ser.). (ENG., Illus.). 24p. (J). (gr. 3-4). lib. bdg. 26.27 (978-0-8239-5842-9(6), c9db3f00-971e-458d-be3b-09eb1599b156, PowerKids Pr.) Rosen Publishing Group, Inc., The.

Wheeler-Toppen, Jodi. Science Experiments That Explode & Implode: Fun Projects for Curious Kids. 2011. (Kitchen Science Ser.). (ENG.). 32p. (gr. 3-4). pap. 47.70 (978-1-4296-6418-9(5), Capstone Pr.) Capstone.

—Science Experiments That Fizz & Bubble: Fun Projects for Curious Kids. 2011. (Kitchen Science Ser.). (ENG.). 32p. (gr. 3-4). pap. 47.70 (978-1-4296-6419-6(3), Capstone Pr.) Capstone.

Wheeler-Toppen, Jodi, et al. Girls Science Club. 2012. (Girls Science Club Ser.). (ENG.). 32p. (gr. 3-4). pap. 190.80 (978-1-4296-8522-1(0), Capstone Pr.) Capstone.

Whitley, Peggy & Goodwin, Susan Williams. 99 Jumpstarts for Kids' Science Research, 1 vol. 2005. (ENG., Illus.). 264p. per. 42.00 (978-1-59158-261-8(X), 900308586, Libraries Unlimited) ABC-CLIO, LLC.

Williams, Jennifer. Oobleck, Slime & Dancing Spaghetti: Twenty Terrific at Home Science Experiments Inspired by Favorite Children's Books. 2009. (ENG., Illus.). 192p. pap. 14.95 (978-1-933979-34-2(8), 2c6ee899-514f-48ef-9789-08269718bb27) Night Heron Media.

Williams, Zella. Do-It-Yourself Science, 10 vols., Set. Incl. Experiments about Planet Earth. (J). lib. bdg. 28.93 (978-1-4042-3662-2(7), 900d061c-31b4-4610-a017-65017ff668de); Experiments about the Natural World. (J). lib. bdg. 28.93 (978-1-4042-3661-5(9), a5e956c1-e54e-4ed3-8250-9921e544f32d); Experiments on Rocks & the Rock Cycle. (YA). lib. bdg. 28.93 (978-1-4042-3660-8(0), 781c8975-cda2-49cb-beb6-b2ed7849678d); Experiments on the Weather. (J). lib. bdg. 28.93 (978-1-4042-3663-9(5), c9b75c6c-a02f-404c-a62f-8a8dd51b24cd); Experiments with Physical Science. (J). lib. bdg. 28.93 (978-1-4042-3659-2(7), 033aea5c-3b2b-4ab3-80d2-5f52678098b9); (Illus.). 24p. (gr. 2-3). 2007. (Do-It-Yourself Science Ser.). (ENG.). 2006. Set lib. bdg. 144.65 (978-1-4042-3605-9(8), 3d1fefd5-997f-444b-9aa4-eb95f07f6831, PowerKids Pr.) Rosen Publishing Group, Inc., The.

—Experiments with Solids, Liquids, & Gases. 2007. (Do-It-Yourself Science Ser.). (Illus.). 24p. (J). 42.30 (978-1-4042-4013-1(6), PowerKids Pr.) Rosen Publishing Group, Inc., The.

Yomtov, Nel. How to Write a Lab Report. Petelinsek, Kathleen, illus. 2013. (Explorer Junior Library: How to Write Ser.). (ENG.). 24p. (J). (gr. 1-4). 29.21 (978-1-62431-185-7(7), 203064); pap. 12.79 (978-1-62431-317-2(5), 203066) Cherry Lake Publishing.

Young, Karen Romano. Try This Extreme: 50 Fun & Safe Experiments for the Mad Scientist in You. 2017. (Illus.). 160p. (J). (gr. 5-9). pap. 16.99 (978-1-4263-2863-3(X)); (ENG., lib. bdg. 26.90 (978-1-4263-2864-0(8)) Disney Publishing Worldwide. (National Geographic Kids).

Zhang, Selina. The Slime Workshop: 20 DIY Projects to Make Awesome Slimes — All Borax Free! 2017. (Illus.). 80p. (J). (gr. 4-9). pap. 12.95 (978-1-4547-1066-0(7)) Lark Bks.

Zonderkidz. Adventure Bible Book of Daring Deeds & Epic Creations: 60 Ultimate Try-Something-new, Explore-the-world Activities, 1 vol. 2018. (Adventure Bible Ser.). (ENG., Illus.). 160p. (J). 12.99 (978-0-310-76317-8(7)) Zonderkidz.

SCIENCE—EXPERIMENTS—FICTION

Anderson, M. T. The Astonishing Life of Octavian Nothing, Traitor to the Nation, Volume I: The Pox Party, Vol. 1. 2008. (ENG., Illus.). 384p. (YA). (gr. 9-12). pap. 13.99 (978-0-7636-3679-1(7)) Candlewick Pr.

Anderson, Matthew. The Astonishing Life of Octavian Nothing, Traitor to the Nation, Volume I: The Pox Party. 2009. (Astonishing Life of Octavian Nothing, Traitor to the Nation Ser.: Vol. 1). 11.94 (978-0-7848-1900-5(9), Everbind) Marco Bk. Co.

—The Astonishing Life of Octavian Nothing, Traitor to the Nation, Volume I: The Pox Party. 2011. 22.00 (978-1-60686-925-3(6)) Perfection Learning Corp.

—The Astonishing Life of Octavian Nothing, Traitor to the Nation, Volume I: The Pox Party. l.t. ed. 2020. (ENG.). pap. 15.99 (978-1-4328-7401-8(2)) Thorndike Pr.

Andros, Camille. Charlotte the Scientist Finds a Cure. Farley, Brianne, illus. 2019. (Charlotte the Scientist Ser.). (ENG.). 40p. (J). (gr. -1-3). 17.99 (978-0-544-81376-2(6), 1642033, Clarion Bks.) HarperCollins Pubs.

—Charlotte the Scientist Is Squished. Farley, Brianne, illus. 2017. (Charlotte the Scientist Ser.). (ENG.). 40p. (J). (gr. -1-3). 17.99 (978-0-544-78583-0(5), 1638581, Clarion Bks.) HarperCollins Pubs.

Beaty, Andrea. Ada Twist, Scientist. 2016. (Questioneers Ser.). (ENG., Illus.). 32p. (J). (gr. k-2). 19.99 (978-1-4197-2137-3(2), 1119001) Abrams, Inc.

Benton, Jim. Attack of the 50-Ft. Cupid. Benton, Jim, illus. 2004. (Franny K. Stein, Mad Scientist Ser.: 2). (ENG., Illus.). 112p. (J). (gr. 2-5). 17.99 (978-0-689-86292-2(X), Simon &

Schuster Bks. For Young Readers) Simon & Schuster Bks. For Young Readers.

—Attack of the 50-Ft. Cupid. Benton, Jim, illus. 2011. (Franny K. Stein, Mad Scientist Ser.). (ENG., Illus.). 112p. (J). (gr. 2-6). 31.36 *(978-1-59961-818-0(4)*, 7828, Chapter Bks.) Spotlight.

—Bad Hair Day. Benton, Jim, illus. 2019. (Franny K. Stein, Mad Scientist Ser.: 8). (ENG., Illus.). 112p. (J). (gr. 1-5). 15.99 *(978-1-5344-1337-5(5)*, Simon & Schuster Bks. For Young Readers) Simon & Schuster Bks. For Young Readers.

—The Fran with Four Brains. Benton, Jim, illus. 2011. (Franny K. Stein, Mad Scientist Ser.). (ENG., Illus.). 112p. (J). (gr. 2-6). 31.36 *(978-1-59961-822-7(2)*, 7832, Chapter Bks.) Spotlight.

—The Fran with Four Brains. 2007. (Franny K. Stein, Mad Scientist Ser.: 6). lib. bdg. 16.00 *(978-1-4177-9038-8(5))* Turtleback.

—The Frandidate. Benton, Jim, illus. 2009. (Franny K. Stein, Mad Scientist Ser.: 7). (ENG., Illus.). 112p. (J). (gr. 2-5). pap. 6.99 *(978-1-4169-0234-8(1)*, Simon & Schuster Bks. For Young Readers) Simon & Schuster Bks. For Young Readers.

—The Frandidate. Benton, Jim, illus. 2011. (Franny K. Stein, Mad Scientist Ser.). (ENG., Illus.). 128p. (J). (gr. 2-6). 31.36 *(978-1-59961-823-4(0)*, 7833, Chapter Bks.) Spotlight.

—Franny K. Stein, Mad Scientist, 5 vols., Set. Benton, Jim, illus. Incl. Attack of the 50-Ft. Cupid. 112p. 31.36 *(978-1-59961-818-0(4)*, 7828); Fran with Four Brains. 112p. 31.36 *(978-1-59961-822-7(2)*, 7832); Frandidate. 128p. 31.36 *(978-1-59961-823-4(0)*, 7833); Invisible Fran. 112p. 31.36 *(978-1-59961-819-7(2)*, 7829); Lunch Walks among Us. 112p. 31.36 *(978-1-59961-817-3(6)*, 7827); (J). (gr. 2-6). (Franny K. Stein, Mad Scientist Ser.). (ENG., Illus.). 2011. Set lib. bdg. 188.16 *(978-1-59961-816-6(8)*, 7826, Chapter Bks.) Spotlight.

—Lunch Walks among Us. Benton, Jim, illus. (Franny K. Stein, Mad Scientist Ser.: 1). (ENG., Illus.). 112p. (J). (gr. 2-5). 2004. mass mkt. 6.99 *(978-0-689-86295-3(4))* 2003. 17.99 *(978-0-689-86291-5(1))* Simon & Schuster Bks. For Young Readers. (Simon & Schuster Bks. For Young Readers).

—Lunch Walks among Us. Benton, Jim, illus. 2011. (Franny K. Stein, Mad Scientist Ser.). (ENG., Illus.). 112p. (J). (gr. 2-6). 31.36 *(978-1-59961-817-3(6)*, 7827, Chapter Bks.) Spotlight.

Bloch, Robert. The Crowded Earth. 2009. 112p. 22.95 *(978-1-60664-648-9(6))*; pap. 9.95 *(978-1-60664-273-3(1))* Rodgers, Alan Bks.

Bodeen, S. A. The Gardener. 2011. (ENG.). 256p. (YA). (gr. 7-12). pap. 11.99 *(978-0-312-65942-4(3)*, 900070540) Square Fish.

Bower, Eric. The Magnificent Flying Baron Estate. 2017. (Bizarre Baron Inventions Ser.: 1). (ENG., Illus.). 250p. (J). (gr. 4-7). 15.99 *(978-1-944995-13-3(7))* Amberjack Publishing Co.

Brande, Robin. Fat Cat. 2011.Tr. of Fat Cat. (ENG.). 336p. (YA). (gr. 8-12). lib. bdg. 26.19 *(978-0-375-94449-9(4)*, Knopf Bks. for Young Readers) Random Hse. Children's Bks.

Clements, Andrew. Jake Drake, Know-It-All. Frazee, Marla & Pedersen, Janet, illus. 2007. (Jake Drake Ser.: Bk. 2). 88p. (gr. 2-5). 15.00 *(978-0-7569-8212-6(X))* Perfection Learning Corp.

—Jake Drake, Know-It-All. Pedersen, Janet, illus. 2007. (Jake Drake Ser.: Bk. 2). (ENG.). 112p. (J). (gr. 2-5). pap. 6.99 *(978-1-4169-3931-3(8)*, Atheneum Bks. for Young Readers) Simon & Schuster Children's Publishing.

Cooper, Brigitte Henry. Steam & Ice. Heitz, Tim, illus. 2017. (Game Face Ser.). (ENG.). 112p. (J). (gr. 2-5). lib. bdg. 38.50 *(978-1-5321-3046-5(5)*, 27048, Calico Chapter Bks.) ABDO Publishing Co.

Coven, Wanda. Heidi Heckelbeck & the Secret Admirer. 2012. (Heidi Heckelbeck Ser.: 6). lib. bdg. 16.00 *(978-0-606-26905-6(3))* Turtleback.

Dahl, Michael. Maze Monster. Catling, Andy, illus. 2016. (Igor's Lab of Fear Ser.). (ENG.). 40p. (J). (gr. 4-8). lib. bdg. 23.99 *(978-1-4965-3528-3(6)*, 132642, Stone Arch Bks.) Capstone.

DanTDM. DanTDM: Trayaurus & the Enchanted Crystal. 2018. (ENG.). 192p. (J). (gr. 3-7). pap. 9.99 *(978-0-06-257429-9(9)*, HarperAlley) HarperCollins Pubs.

De Marco, Clare. The Mad Scientist Next Door. 2014. (Race Ahead with Reading Ser.). (ENG., Illus.). 32p. (J). (gr. 2-2). *(978-0-7787-1305-0(9))* Crabtree Publishing Co.

Dowell, Frances O'Roark. Phineas L. MacGuire ... Blasts Off! McDaniels, Preston, illus. 2011. (From the Highly Scientific Notebooks of Phineas L. MacGuire Ser.). (ENG.). 224p. (J). (gr. 3-7). pap. 7.99 *(978-1-4424-2204-9(1)*, Atheneum Bks. for Young Readers) Simon & Schuster Children's Publishing.

—Phineas L. MacGuire ... Erupts! The First Experiment. McDaniels, Preston, illus. (From the Highly Scientific Notebooks of Phineas L. MacGuire Ser.). (ENG.). 176p. (J). (gr. 3-7). 2007. pap. 7.99 *(978-1-4169-4734-9(5))* 2006. 18.99 *(978-1-4169-0195-2(7))* Simon & Schuster Children's Publishing. (Atheneum Bks. for Young Readers).

—Phineas L. MacGuire ... Gets Cooking! McDaniels, Preston, illus. (From the Highly Scientific Notebooks of Phineas L. MacGuire Ser.). (ENG.). (J). (gr. 3-7). 2015. 224p. pap. 6.99 *(978-1-4814-0100-5(9))* 2014. 208p. 16.99 *(978-1-4814-0099-2(1)*, Atheneum Bks. for Young Readers) Simon & Schuster Children's Publishing.

—Phineas L. MacGuire ... Gets Slimed! McDaniels, Preston, illus. 2010. (From the Highly Scientific Notebooks of Phineas L. MacGuire Ser.). (ENG.). 224p. (J). (gr. 3-7). pap. 7.99 *(978-1-4169-9775-7(X)*, Atheneum Bks. for Young Readers) Simon & Schuster Children's Publishing.

Fliess, Sue. The Princess & the Petri Dish. Bouloubasis, Petros, illus. 2020. (ENG.). 32p. (J). (gr. -1-3). 16.99 *(978-0-8075-6644-2(6)*, 807566446) Whitman, Albert & Co.

Galardi Mlis, Judith A. Judi Galardi's Thrae Back Atcha! 2011. 128p. (gr. -1). pap. 16.49 *(978-1-4567-2388-0(X))* AuthorHouse.

Glickman, Susan. Bernadette in the Doghouse, 1 vol. 2011. (Lunch Bunch Ser.: 2). (ENG., Illus.). 118p. (J). (gr. 1-4). pap. 8.95 *(978-1-897187-92-0(0))* Second Story Pr. CAN. Dist: Orca Bk. Pubs. USA.

Grunwell, Jeanne Marie. Mind Games. 2006. (ENG., Illus.). 144p. (J). (gr. 5-7). pap. 10.95 *(978-0-618-68947-7(8)*, 410165, Clarion Bks.) HarperCollins Pubs.

Hawking, Stephen & Hawking, Lucy. George & the Big Bang. Parsons, Garry, illus. (George's Secret Key Ser.). (ENG.). (J). (gr. 3-7). 2013. 304p. pap. 13.99 *(978-1-4424-4006-7(6))* 2012. 336p. 22.99 *(978-1-4424-4005-0(8))* Simon & Schuster Bks. For Young Readers. (Simon & Schuster Bks. For Young Readers).

Haynes, Natalie. The Great Escape. 2014. (ENG.). 288p. (J). pap. 8.99 *(978-1-4711-2184-5(4)*, Simon & Schuster Children's) Simon & Schuster, Ltd. GBR. Dist: Simon & Schuster, Inc.

Howe, James. It Came from Beneath the Bed! 2004. (Tales from the House of Bunnicula Ser.). 112p. (J). (gr. 3-6). pap. 17.00 incl. audio *(978-1-4000-8632-0(9)*, Listening Library) Random Hse. Audio Publishing Group.

Hughes, Alison. On a Scale from Idiot to Complete Jerk, 1 vol. 2014. (ENG., Illus.). 144p. (J). (gr. 4-7). pap. 9.95 *(978-1-4598-0484-5(8))* Orca Bk. Pubs. USA.

Hughey, Sue C. Herby's Secret Formula. Hughey, Sue C., illus. 2013. (Illus.). 232p. pap. 11.95 *(978-0-9840358-1-6(8))* Associated Arts Pub.

Khoury, Jessica. Vitro. 2015. 384p. (YA). (gr. 7). pap. 9.99 *(978-1-59514-606-9(7)*, Razorbill) Penguin Young Readers Group.

King, Trey. Wrecking Valentine's Day! Wang, Sean, illus. 2015. 24p. (J). *(978-1-4806-9662-4(5))* Scholastic, Inc.

Knudsen, Michelle. Argus. Wesson, Andrea, illus. 2011. (ENG.). 32p. (J). (gr. -1-3). 17.99 *(978-0-7636-3790-3(4))* Candlewick Pr.

—A Moldy Mystery. Gott, Barry, illus. 2006. (Science Solves It! Ser.). (ENG.). 32p. (J). (gr. 1-3). pap. 5.95 *(978-1-57565-167-5(X)*, c1e381a9-3e25-43db-87fc-1e26ebf5123d, Kane Press) Astra Publishing Hse.

Korman, Gordon. Masterminds: Payback. 2018. (Masterminds Ser.: 3). (ENG.). 320p. (J). (gr. 3-7). pap. 9.99 *(978-0-06-230006-5(7)*, Balzer & Bray) HarperCollins Pubs.

Kravetz, Nathan. A Monkey's Tale. 2012. 64p. (gr. 4-6). pap. 8.95 *(978-1-4759-5825-6(0))* iUniverse, Inc.

LernerClassroom Editors, ed. Science Solves It! en Espanol: Classroom Set. 2008. pap. 22.95 *(978-1-58013-766-9(0))* Astra Publishing Hse.

—Science Solves It! en Espanol: Complete Set. 2008. pap. 138.95 *(978-1-58013-767-6(9))* Astra Publishing Hse.

Lynellen Sullivan & Bryan Castle. Poppers to the Rescue: Book 1 of the Popcorn Series. 2010. 72p. pap. 8.95 *(978-1-4401-9764-2(4))* iUniverse, Inc.

Malia, Jen. Too Sticky! Sensory Issues with Autism. Lew-Vriethoff, Joanne, illus. 2020. (ENG.). 32p. (J). (gr. -1-3). 17.99 *(978-0-8075-8026-4(0)*, 807580260) Whitman, Albert & Co.

Manushkin, Fran. Katie Blows Her Top. Lyon, Tammie, illus. 2018. (Katie Woo Ser.). (ENG.). 32p. (J). (gr. k-2). lib. bdg. 22.65 *(978-1-5158-2265-3(6)*, 136884, Picture Window Bks.) Capstone.

Meister, Cari. Buzz Beaker & the Growing Goo, 1 vol. McGuire, Bill, illus. 2011. (Buzz Beaker Bks.). (ENG.). 32p. (J). (gr. 2-3). pap. 6.25 *(978-1-4342-3056-0(2)*, 114656, Stone Arch Bks.) Capstone.

Mills, Claudia. The Nora Notebooks, Book 1: the Trouble with Ants. Kath, Katie, illus. 2016. (Nora Notebooks Ser.: 1). 176p. (J). (gr. 2-5). 7.99 *(978-0-385-39163-4(3)*, Yearling) Random Hse. Children's Bks.

Mull, David Kenneth. His Date for the Dance was His Science Project. 2012. 80p. pap. 9.99 *(978-0-89824-371-0(8))* Royal Fireworks Publishing Co.

Parish, Herman. Amelia Bedelia, Rocket Scientist? Sweat, Lynn, illus. (I Can Read Level 2 Ser.). 64p. (J). 2007. (ENG.). (gr. k-3). pap. 4.99 *(978-0-06-051889-9(8)*, Greenwillow Bks.) 2005. (gr. 1-18). 15.99 *(978-0-06-051887-5(1))* 2005. (ENG.). (gr. k-4). lib. bdg. 17.89 *(978-0-06-051888-2(X)*, Greenwillow Bks.) HarperCollins Pubs.

Patterson, James. Maximum Ride Boxed Set #1. 2010. (ENG.). 1392p. (YA). (gr. 5-17). pap. 32.99 *(978-0-316-12825-4(2)*, Jimmy Patterson) Little Brown & Co.

Patterson, James & Grabenstein, Chris. Max Einstein: The Genius Experiment. Johnson, Beverly, illus. 2018. 338p. (J). *(978-0-316-45219-9(X)*, Jimmy Patterson) Little Brown & Co.

—Max Einstein: the Genius Experiment. Johnson, Beverly, illus. (Max Einstein Ser.: 1). (ENG.). (J). 2019. 368p. pap. 8.99 *(978-0-316-52397-4(6))* 2018. 352p. (gr. 3-9). 14.99 *(978-0-316-52396-7(8))* Little Brown & Co. (Jimmy Patterson).

Pflugfelder, Bob & Hockensmith, Steve. Nick & Tesla's Secret Agent Gadget Battle: A Mystery with Spy Cameras, Code Wheels, & Other Gadgets You Can Build Yourself. 2014. (Nick & Tesla Ser.: 3). (Illus.). 256p. (J). (gr. 4-7). 12.95 *(978-1-59474-676-5(1))* Quirk Bks.

—Nick & Tesla's Special Effects Spectacular: A Mystery with Animatronics, Alien Makeup, Camera Gear, & Other Movie Magic You Can Make Yourself! 2015. (Nick & Tesla Ser.: 5). (Illus.). 256p. (J). (gr. 4-7). 12.95 *(978-1-59474-760-1(1))* Quirk Bks.

Platt, Cynthia. Parker Bell & the Science of Friendship. Zhai, Rea, illus. 2019. (ENG.). 160p. (J). (gr. 3-7). 16.99 *(978-1-328-97347-4(6)*, 1708149, Clarion Bks.) HarperCollins Pubs.

Roland, Timothy. A Silly Science Experiment. 2007. (Illus.). 91p. (J). *(978-0-545-00400-8(4))* Scholastic, Inc.

Seuling, Barbara. Robert & the Happy Endings. Brewer, Paul, illus. 2007. (Robert Bks.). (ENG.). 160p. (J). (gr. 1-4). 16.95 *(978-0-8126-2748-0(2))* Cricket Bks.

Shelley, Mary. Frankenstein. 2013. (Differentiated Timeless Classics Ser.). (ENG.). 80p. (YA). (gr. 4-12). 14.95 *(978-1-62250-717-7(7))* Saddleback Educational Publishing, Inc.

Tobin, Paul. The Genius Factor: How to Capture an Invisible Cat. Lafontaine, Thierry, illus. 2017. (ENG.). 288p. (J). pap. 8.99 *(978-1-68119-278-9(0)*, 900165496, Bloomsbury USA Childrens) Bloomsbury Publishing USA.

—How to Tame a Human Tornado. 2018. (ENG., Illus.). 368p. (J). 16.99 *(978-1-61963-899-0(1)*, 900151199, Bloomsbury USA Childrens) Bloomsbury Publishing USA.

Wells, H. G. The Invisible Man. Calero, Dennis, illus. 2010. (Classic Fiction Ser.). 72p. pap. 0.60 *(978-1-4342-3208-3(5)*, Stone Arch Bks.) Capstone.

Yasuda, Anita. The Slime Attack, 1 vol. Harpster, Steve, illus. 2013. (Dino Detectives Ser.). (ENG.). 32p. (J). (gr. 1-2). pap. 5.95 *(978-1-4342-4833-6(X)*, 121752, Stone Arch Bks.) Capstone.

SCIENCE—FICTION

see Science Fiction

SCIENCE—HISTORY

Anniss, Matt. James Watson & Francis Crick. 2014. (Dynamic Duos of Science Ser.). 48p. (YA). (gr. 5-8). pap. 84.30 *(978-1-4824-1282-6(9))* Stevens, Gareth Publishing LLLP.

—Science vs. Disease, 1 vol. 2013. (Science Fights Back Ser.). (ENG., Illus.). 48p. (gr. 4-5). 34.60 *(978-1-4339-8687-1(6)*, b466eb66-c0d9-42c2-b751-a62db9415e97); pap. 15.05 *(978-1-4339-8688-8(4)*, 11a8306a-d519-46ef-bcdd-2bd26cad501e) Stevens, Gareth Publishing LLLP. (Gareth Stevens Learning Library).

Atkinson, Mary. Schockwave: the Earth Is Flat! 2007. (Shockwave: Science in Practice Ser.). (ENG., Illus.). 36p. (J). (gr. 3-5). 25.00 *(978-0-531-17580-4(4)*, Children's Pr.) Scholastic Library Publishing.

Balchin, Jon. Science: 100 Scientists Who Changed the World. 2003. (Illus.). 224p. 18.95 *(978-1-59270-017-2(9))* Enchanted Lion Bks., LLC.

Benchmark Education Company, LLC Staff, compiled by. HIST & Nature of Science. 2006. spiral bd. 145.00 *(978-1-4108-6949-4(0))* 2005. spiral bd. 135.00 *(978-1-4108-4515-3(X))* 2005. spiral bd. 165.00 *(978-1-4108-5850-4(2))* 2005. spiral bd. 85.00 *(978-1-4108-5849-8(9))* 2005. spiral bd. 185.00 *(978-1-4108-5437-7(X))* 2005. spiral bd. 185.00 *(978-1-4108-5436-0(1))* 2005. spiral bd. 42.00 *(978-1-4108-3879-7(X))* 2005. spiral bd. 42.00 *(978-1-4108-3878-0(1))* 2005. spiral bd. 145.00 *(978-1-4108-3865-0(X))* 2005. spiral bd. 60.00 *(978-1-4108-3849-0(8))* 2005. spiral bd. 180.00 *(978-1-4108-3848-3(X))* Benchmark Education Co.

—Scientific Achievements: Theme Set. 2006. (J). 131.00 *(978-1-4108-7130-5(4))* Benchmark Education Co.

Biesty, Stephen & Platt, Richard. Stephen Biesty's Incredible Explosions: Exploded Views of Astonishing Things. (Illus.). 32p. (J). pap. 22.99 *(978-0-590-24893-8(6))* Scholastic, Inc.

Brown Bear Books. Chemistry, Earth, & Space Sciences. 2009. (Great Scientists Ser.). (ENG.). 64p. (J). (gr. 8-11). 35.65 *(978-1-933834-47-4(1)*, 16492) Brown Bear Bks.

—Physical Sciences. 2009. (Great Scientists Ser.). (ENG.). 64p. (J). (gr. 8-11). 39.95 *(978-1-933834-46-7(3)*, 16494) Brown Bear Bks.

Bryson, Bill. A Really Short History of Nearly Everything. 2009. (ENG., Illus.). 176p. (J). (gr. 3-7). 21.99 *(978-0-385-73810-1(2)*, Delacorte Bks. for Young Readers) Random Hse. Children's Bks.

Cashin, John. Leonardo Da Vinci, Vol. 11. 2018. (Scientists & Their Discoveries Ser.). (Illus.). 96p. (J). (gr. 7). lib. bdg. 34.60 *(978-1-4222-4032-8(0))* Mason Crest.

Challoner, Jack. Exploring the Mysteries of Genius & Invention, 1 vol. 2016. (STEM Guide to the Universe Ser.). (ENG.). 96p. (J). (gr. 9-9). lib. bdg. 47.80 *(978-1-4994-6410-8(X)*, ef7fec10-188d-4443-a901-65c6c1e00385) Rosen Publishing Group, Inc., The.

Claybourne, Anna. Story of Science Kid Kit. 2010. (Kid Kits Ser.). 96p. (J). pap. 17.99 *(978-1-60130-197-0(9)*, Usborne) EDC Publishing.

Colson, Rob. Scholars of Science. 2018. (STEM-Gineers Ser.). (Illus.). 32p. (J). (gr. 5-5). *(978-0-7787-5738-2(2))* Crabtree Publishing Co.

Craig, Diane. Science History Is No Mystery!, 1 vol. 2007. (Science Made Simple Ser.). (Illus.). 24p. (J). (gr. k-3). lib. bdg. 24.21 *(978-1-59928-616-7(5)*, SandCastle) ABDO Publishing Co.

Duncan, Terri Kaye. Eerie Science Experiments, 1 vol. 2019. (Creepy, Kooky Science Ser.). (ENG.). 48p. (gr. 5-5). pap. 12.70 *(978-1-9785-1374-7(7)*, c9a17a9a-634e-40ae-9589-56ad57c4b4b7) Enslow Publishing, LLC.

Farndon, John. Science & Technology: The Greatest Innovations in Human History. 2016. (Illus.). 64p. (J). (gr. -1-12). 12.99 *(978-1-86147-780-4(5)*, Armadillo) Anness Publishing GBR. Dist: National Bk. Network.

—The Story of Science & Technology, 1 vol. 2010. (Journey Through History Ser.). (ENG.). 64p. (YA). (gr. 5-6). lib. bdg. 37.13 *(978-1-4488-0621-8(6)*, 2918e756-bad8-430b-aae8-83c5e631b0a2, Rosen Reference) Rosen Publishing Group, Inc., The.

Faulkner, Nicholas. A Visual History of Science & Technology, 1 vol. 2016. (Visual History of the World Ser.). (ENG., Illus.). 96p. (J). (gr. 8-8). 38.80 *(978-1-4994-6596-9(3)*, 90bec01a-ee04-4a60-9d4b-d75d5abe2c40) Rosen Publishing Group, Inc., The.

Faulkner, Nicholas, ed. 101 Women of STEM, 1 vol. 2016. (People You Should Know Ser.). (ENG., Illus.). 184p. (J). (gr. 8-8). lib. bdg. 38.84 *(978-1-68048-511-0(3)*, 315dc040-0784-49a3-80dd-a86ebb329319) Rosen Publishing Group, Inc., The.

Fries-Gaither, Jessica. Exemplary Evidence: Scientists & Their Data. 2019. (ENG., Illus.). 32p. (J). (gr. 2-4). pap. 14.95 *(978-1-68140-361-8(7))* National Science Teachers Assn.

Herold, Vickey. Discover Science During the Renaissance. 2006. (J). pap. *(978-1-4108-6467-3(7))* Benchmark Education Co.

—Science During the Renaissance. 2006. (J). pap. *(978-1-4108-6464-2(2))* Benchmark Education Co.

Hibbert, Clare. Beliefs & Ideas That Changed the World. 2017. (Revolutions Ser.). (ENG., Illus.). 64p. (J). (gr. 3-6). 19.99 *(978-0-7123-5680-0(0))* British Library, The GBR. Dist: Independent Pubs. Group.

Hunter, Dru. What Is Out There? (Think Like a Scientist Ser.). (ENG.). 48p. (J). (gr. 4-7). 2016. pap. 12.00 *(978-1-62832-199-9(7)*, 21067, Creative Paperbacks) 2015. (Illus.). *(978-1-60818-594-8(X)*, 21066, Creative Education) Creative Co., The.

Killcoyne, Hope Lourie, ed. Science: Its History & Development, 1 vol. 2014. (Study of Science Ser.). (ENG.). 104p. (YA). (gr. 8-8). 37.82 *(978-1-62275-421-2(2)*, 2e777c2c-3a72-4711-81f8-39a30ec13aa4) Rosen Publishing Group, Inc., The.

Kortemeier, Todd. Unsung Heroes of Science. 2017. (Unsung Heroes Ser.). (ENG., Illus.). 32p. (J). (gr. 3-6). 32.80 *(978-1-63235-309-2(1)*, 11829, 12-Story Library) Bookstaves, LLC.

—Unsung Heroes of Technology. 2017. (Unsung Heroes Ser.). (ENG., Illus.). 32p. (J). (gr. 3-6). 32.80 *(978-1-63235-311-5(3)*, 11831, 12-Story Library) Bookstaves, LLC.

Krull, Kathleen. Lives of the Scientists: Experiments, Explosions (and What the Neighbors Thought) Hewitt, Kathryn, illus. 2016. (Lives Of ... Ser.). (ENG.). 96p. (J). (gr. 5-7). 8.99 *(978-0-544-81087-7(2)*, 1641669, Clarion Bks.) HarperCollins Pubs.

Kuhtz, Russell. Physical Science, 1 vol. 2016. (Study of Science Ser.). (ENG., Illus.). 156p. (YA). (gr. 8-8). lib. bdg. 37.82 *(978-1-5081-0425-4(5)*, 8a0bdce8-b0c3-41f8-8ed8-c2a73ededb28) Rosen Publishing Group, Inc., The.

Kumar Terry, Stuart. The Science That Changed the World: Remarkable Discoveries & Breakthroughs. 2019. (ENG.). 48p. (J). 14.99 *(978-1-921580-48-2(8))* New Holland Pubs. Pty. Ltd. AUS. Dist: Independent Pubs. Group.

Lachner, Elizabeth, ed. Top 101 Scientists, 1 vol. 2016. (People You Should Know Ser.). (ENG., Illus.). 184p. (J). (gr. 8-8). lib. bdg. 38.84 *(978-1-68048-510-3(5)*, e680b7c6-7f82-4698-8db4-de77e580e303) Rosen Publishing Group, Inc., The.

Leavitt, Amie Jane. How STEM Built the Aztec Empire, 1 vol. 2019. (How STEM Built Empires Ser.). (ENG.). 80p. (gr. 7-7). pap. 16.30 *(978-1-7253-4134-0(4)*, 4018fd21-706c-4ecc-975f-0a94efc7e4c3) Rosen Publishing Group, Inc., The.

Loh-Hagan, Virginia. Girl Scientists. 2019. (History's Yearbook Ser.). (ENG., Illus.). 32p. (J). (gr. 4-8). pap. 14.21 *(978-1-5341-5079-9(X)*, 213623); lib. bdg. 32.07 *(978-1-5341-4793-5(4)*, 213622) Cherry Lake Publishing. (45th Parallel Press).

—Weird Science. 2018. (Stranger Than Fiction Ser.). (ENG.). 32p. (J). (gr. 4-8). pap. 14.21 *(978-1-5341-3256-6(2)*, 211789); (Illus.). lib. bdg. 32.07 *(978-1-5341-2936-8(7)*, 211788) Cherry Lake Publishing. (45th Parallel Press).

Machajewski, Sarah. Freaky Science Discoveries, 1 vol. 2015. (Freaky True Science Ser.). (ENG., Illus.). 32p. (J). (gr. 4-5). pap. 11.50 *(978-1-4824-2952-7(7)*, 513dd71f-6a95-4d78-aecc-4cb7fb97e3c2) Stevens, Gareth Publishing LLLP.

McCarthy, Cecilia Pinto. The Science of Warriors, 1 vol. 2016. (Super-Awesome Science Ser.). (ENG., Illus.). 48p. (J). (gr. 4-8). lib. bdg. 35.64 *(978-1-68078-253-0(3)*, 22107) ABDO Publishing Co.

Merlin, Hope, ed. The History of Science, 1 vol., 1. 2013. (Scientific Inquiry Ser.). (ENG.). 112p. (YA). (gr. 10-10). 36.49 *(978-1-62275-116-7(7)*, c3d4436f-61fe-4ad9-9529-863c7641894b) Rosen Publishing Group, Inc., The.

Meyer, Susan. Isaac Newton, 1 vol. 2017. (Leaders of the Scientific Revolution Ser.). (ENG., Illus.). 112p. (J). (gr. 8-8). 38.80 *(978-1-5081-7470-7(9)*, 66a1cb61-49f7-483d-9294-4756e72496bc, Rosen Young Adult) Rosen Publishing Group, Inc., The.

Milestones in Modern Science, 4 vols. 2005. (Milestones in Modern Science Ser.). (ENG.). 48p. (gr. 6-8). lib. bdg. 67.34 *(978-0-8368-5850-1(6)*, e5bed344-c2db-4a10-8722-acf2f0f011cd, Gareth Stevens Secondary Library) Stevens, Gareth Publishing LLLP.

Oachs, Emily Rose. The 12 Most Influential Scientific Discoveries of All Time. 2018. (Most Influential Ser.). (ENG., Illus.). 32p. (J). (gr. 3-6). 32.80 *(978-1-63235-413-6(6)*, 13750, 12-Story Library) Bookstaves, LLC.

Perritano, John. Science & Technology, Vol. 9. van Dijk, Ruud, ed. 2016. (Making of the Modern World: 1945 to the Present Ser.). (Illus.). 64p. (J). (gr. 7). 23.95 *(978-1-4222-3641-3(2))* Mason Crest.

Platt, Richard. Stephen Biesty's Incredible Explosions: Exploded Views of Astonishing Things. Biesty, Stephen, illus. 2004. 32p. (J). (gr. 2-8). reprint ed. 20.00 *(978-0-7567-7680-0(5))* DIANE Publishing Co.

Raum, Elizabeth. The Cold, Hard Facts about Science & Medicine in Colonial America. 2011. (Life in the American Colonies Ser.). (ENG.). 32p. (J). (gr. 3-4). pap. 48.60 *(978-1-4296-7216-0(1)*, 16775, Capstone Pr.); pap. 8.10 *(978-1-4296-7215-3(3)*, 116825) Capstone.

Samuels, Charlie. Ancient Science (Prehistory - A. D. 500), 1 vol. 2010. (Science Highlights: a Gareth Stevens Timeline Ser.). (ENG.). 48p. (J). (gr. 6-8). pap. 15.05 *(978-1-4339-4137-5(6)*, 7472475a-fbf7-4e94-8951-d2ebc3ec2685); lib. bdg. 34.60 *(978-1-4339-4136-8(8)*, d18edd04-27ec-4309-acf2-5befeeb25afe) Stevens, Gareth Publishing LLLP. (Gareth Stevens Secondary Library).

—Medieval Science (500 - 1500), 1 vol. 2010. (Science Highlights: a Gareth Stevens Timeline Ser.). (ENG.). 48p. (J). (gr. 6-8). pap. 15.05 *(978-1-4339-4140-5(6)*, 7f53e548-3ae3-4089-9292-abd78c196f41); lib. bdg. 34.60 *(978-1-4339-4139-9(2)*, ead83189-db33-4574-80b5-01ad0f58cb57) Stevens, Gareth Publishing LLLP. (Gareth Stevens Secondary Library).

—Revolutions in Science (1500 - 1700), 1 vol. 2010. (Science Highlights: a Gareth Stevens Timeline Ser.). (ENG.). 48p. (J). (gr. 6-8). pap. 15.05 *(978-1-4339-4143-6(0)*, a4f92dab-c64d-4cd7-90e6-eed7def9d179); lib. bdg. 34.60 *(978-1-4339-4142-9(2)*, d4d8c93a-b3c9-403a-b20b-5cc5c2d88ecf) Stevens, Gareth Publishing LLLP. (Gareth Stevens Secondary Library).

Scientific Revolution: PowerPoints in World History. 2005. cd-rom 49.95 net. *(978-1-56004-215-0(X))* Social Studies Schl. Service.

Scientific Revolution DBA. 2003. spiral bd. 16.95 *(978-1-56004-168-9(4))* Social Studies Schl. Service.

Winter, Ali. Science & Me: Inspired by the Discoveries of Nobel Prize Laureates in Physics, Chemistry & Medicine, 1 vol. El Fathi, Mickael, illus. 2021. (ENG.). 40p. (J). (gr. 4-6). 18.99 *(978-1-911373-71-1(4)*, 4650fe8e-3175-42a5-82d6-11d2f54c17dd) Lantana Publishing GBR. Dist: Lerner Publishing Group.

SCIENCE—METHODOLOGY

see also Logic

Alkire, Jessie. Super Gross Germ Projects. 2018. (Super Simple Super Gross Science Ser.). (ENG., Illus.). 32p. (J).

S

(gr. k-4). lib. bdg. 34.21 *(978-1-5321-1731-2(0)*, 30750, Super SandCastle) ABDO Publishing Co.

Allegra, Mike. Scampers Thinks Like a Scientist. Zechel, Elizabeth, illus. 2019. 32p. (J). (gr. k-3). 16.95 *(978-1-58469-642-1(7)*, Dawn Pubns.) Sourcebooks, Inc.

Ardizzone, Leonisa. Science — Not Just for Scientists! Easy Explorations for Young Children. 2015. (ENG., Illus.). 96p. pap. 12.95 *(978-0-87659-484-1(4)*, Gryphon House Inc) Gryphon Hse., Inc.

Biskup, Agnieszka. The Amazing Work of Scientists with Max Axiom, Super Scientist. Baez, Marcelo, illus. 2013. (Graphic Science & Engineering in Action Ser.). (ENG.). 32p. (J). (gr. 3-4). pap. 49.60 *(978-1-62065-702-7(3)*, 19300, Capstone Pr.) Capstone.

—The Amazing Work of Scientists with Max Axiom, Super Scientist, 1 vol. Baez, Marcelo & Baez, Marcelo, illus. 2013. (Graphic Science & Engineering in Action Ser.). (ENG.). 32p. (J). (gr. 3-9). pap. 8.10 *(978-1-62065-701-0(5)*, 121698); lib. bdg. 31.32 *(978-1-4296-9936-5(1)*, 120644) Capstone.

Braun, Eric. Mad Margaret Experiments with the Scientific Method, 1 vol. Boyden, Robin Oliver, illus. 2012. (In the Science Lab Ser.). (ENG.). 24p. (J). (gr. k-3). pap. 9.95 *(978-1-4048-7710-8(X)*, 120445, Picture Window Bks.) Capstone.

Carlson Berne, Emma. Answer! Analyze Your Data, 1 vol. 2014. (Scientific Method in Action Ser.). (Illus.). 24p. (J). (gr. 3-3). (ENG.). 25.27 *(978-1-4777-2930-4(5)*, 65980130-6256-493a-9f85-c51e66a8c715); (ENG., pap. 9.25 *(978-1-4777-3017-1(6)*, 8875c218-bafb-4b73-b1e0-ac0d026636fb); pap. 49.50 *(978-1-4777-3088-1(5))* Rosen Publishing Group, Inc., The. (PowerKids Pr.).

—Guess! Research & Form a Hypothesis, 1 vol. 2014. (Scientific Method in Action Ser.). (ENG., Illus.). 24p. (J). (gr. 3-3). 25.27 *(978-1-4777-2926-7(7)*, 7ce4f9b4-eee4-4328-a6cd-84bdd4c82b79, PowerKids Pr.) Rosen Publishing Group, Inc., The.

—Look! Make Observations & Ask Questions, 1 vol. 2014. (Scientific Method in Action Ser.). (ENG., Illus.). 24p. (J). (gr. 3-3). 25.27 *(978-1-4777-2924-3(0)*, 2af49a66-fb93-492c-ae9b-fb139d5cc26e, PowerKids Pr.) Rosen Publishing Group, Inc., The.

—Predict! Plan an Experiment. 2014. (Scientific Method in Action Ser.). (Illus.). 24p. (J). (gr. 3-6). pap. 49.50 *(978-1-4777-3086-7(9)*, PowerKids Pr.) Rosen Publishing Group, Inc., The.

—Share! Present Your Findings. 2014. (Scientific Method in Action Ser.). (Illus.). 24p. (J). (gr. 3-6). pap. 49.50 *(978-1-4777-3089-8(3)*, PowerKids Pr.) Rosen Publishing Group, Inc., The.

—Test! Collect & Document Data, 1 vol. 2014. (Scientific Method in Action Ser.). (ENG., Illus.). 24p. (J). (gr. 3-3). pap. 9.25 *(978-1-4777-3016-4(8)*, 9b68c130-5cf9-414d-b8e0-2246f036ff04, PowerKids Pr.) Rosen Publishing Group, Inc., The.

Chappell, Rachel. Solving Science Questions: A Book about the Scientific Process. 2007. (Big Ideas for Young Scientists Ser.). (Illus.). 24p. (J). (gr. 2-5). lib. bdg. *(978-1-60044-542-2(X))* Rourke Educational Media.

deMarin, Layne. Look & Learn. 2011. (Wonder Readers Fluent Level Ser.). (ENG.). 16p. (gr. -1-2). pap. 35.94 *(978-1-4296-8120-9(9)*, Capstone Pr.) Capstone.

—What Scientists Do, 1 vol. 2011. (Wonder Readers Fluent Level Ser.). (ENG.). 16p. (gr. -1-2). (J). pap. 6.25 *(978-1-4296-7945-9(X)*, 118277); pap. 35.94 *(978-1-4296-8205-3(1))* Capstone. (Capstone Pr.).

Dempski, Seth. Natalie's Nature Walk: Represent & Interpret Data, 1 vol. 2014. (Math Masters: Measurement & Data Ser.). (ENG.). 24p. (J). (gr. 2-2). 25.27 *(978-1-4777-6440-4(2)*, 09a87ac6-290b-41f7-9077-83d9583a8831); pap. 8.25 *(978-1-4777-4828-2(8)*, 412e89a8-6561-4f46-b5a3-dda4db51d115) Rosen Publishing Group, Inc., The. (Rosen Classroom).

Doudna, Kelly. Ill Use Information for My Explanation!, 1 vol. 2007. (Science Made Simple Ser.). (Illus.). 24p. (J). (gr. k-3). lib. bdg. 24.21 *(978-1-59928-588-7(6)*, SandCastle) ABDO Publishing Co.

—It's a Date, Let's Investigate!, 1 vol. 2007. (Science Made Simple Ser.). (Illus.). 24p. (J). (gr. k-3). lib. bdg. 24.21 *(978-1-59928-596-2(7)*, SandCastle) ABDO Publishing Co.

—It's Not Too Late, Let's Communicate!, 1 vol. 2007. (Science Made Simple Ser.). (Illus.). 24p. (J). (gr. k-3). lib. bdg. 24.21 *(978-1-59928-606-8(8)*, SandCastle) ABDO Publishing Co.

—We Are Wise, Let's Hypothesize!, 1 vol. 2007. (Science Made Simple Ser.). (Illus.). 24p. (J). (gr. k-3). lib. bdg. 24.21 *(978-1-59928-622-8(X)*, SandCastle) ABDO Publishing Co.

Editors of YES Mag. Science Detectives: How Scientists Solved Six Real-Life Mysteries. Cowles, Rose, illus. 2006. (ENG.). 48p. (J). (gr. 3-7). pap. 8.95 *(978-1-55337-995-9(0))* Kids Can Pr., Ltd. CAN. Dist: Hachette Bk. Group.

Flatt, Lizann. Collecting Data. 2016. (Get Graphing! Building Data Literacy Skills Ser.). (ENG., Illus.). 24p. (J). (gr. 1-3). *(978-0-7787-2633-3(9))* Crabtree Publishing Co.

Flynn, Riley. Using Facts & Investigating. 2016. (Science & Engineering Practices Ser.). (ENG., Illus.). 24p. (J). (gr. -1-2). pap. 6.95 *(978-1-5157-0981-7(7)*, 132306, Capstone Pr.) Capstone.

Fontichiaro, Kristin. Citizen Science. 2017. (21st Century Skills Library: Data Geek Ser.). (ENG., Illus.). 32p. (J). (gr. 4-7). lib. bdg. 32.07 *(978-1-63472-712-9(6)*, 210106) Cherry Lake Publishing.

Fries-Gaither, Jessica. Exemplary Evidence: Scientists & Their Data. 2019. (ENG., Illus.). 32p. (J). (gr. 2-4). pap. 14.95 *(978-1-68140-361-8(7))* National Science Teachers Assn.

—Notable Notebooks: Scientists & Their Writings. 2017. (ENG., Illus.). 32p. (J). (gr. 2-4). 18.95 *(978-1-68140-379-3(X))*; pap. 38.99 *(978-1-68140-307-6(2)*, P527774) National Science Teachers Assn.

Greek, Joe. Collaborate & Share Results, 1 vol. 2018. (Think Like a Scientist Ser.). (ENG.). 32p. (gr. 3-4). 26.06 *(978-1-5383-0254-5(3)*, 45c280ac-c076-4bc6-a7c9-5f351b7af4cf, Britannica Educational Publishing) Rosen Publishing Group, Inc., The.

Harbo, Christopher L. Frankenstein's Monster & Scientific Methods. Aón, Carlos, illus. 2013. (Monster Science Ser.). (ENG.). 32p. (J). (gr. 3-4). pap. 48.60 *(978-1-62065-817-8(8)*, 19400, Capstone Pr.) Capstone.

Heitkamp, Kristina Lyn. Exploring Field Investigations Through Science Research Projects, 1 vol. 2018. (Project-Based Learning in Science Ser.). (ENG.). 64p. (gr. 5-5). pap. 14.53 *(978-1-5081-8474-4(7)*, 472ea2ee-ca41-4b3b-9a82-59d43e824d5a, Rosen Reference) Rosen Publishing Group, Inc., The.

Hindman, Susan. Think Like a Scientist in the Classroom. 2011. (Explorer Junior Library: Science Explorer Junior Ser.). (ENG., Illus.). 32p. (gr. 4-8). lib. bdg. 32.07 *(978-1-61080-170-6(9)*, 201110) Cherry Lake Publishing.

Horvath, Joan. What Scientists Actually Do. 2008. (Illus.). 208p. (YA). pap. 16.95 *(978-1-933277-08-0(4))* Stargazer Publishing Co.

Hunter, Dru. How Do We Apply Science? 2015. (Think Like a Scientist Ser.). (ENG., Illus.). 48p. (J). (gr. 4-7). *(978-1-60818-592-4(3)*, 21060, Creative Education) Creative Co., The.

—How Does It Work? (Think Like a Scientist Ser.). (ENG.). 48p. (J). (gr. 4-7). 2016. pap. 12.00 *(978-1-62832-198-2(9)*, 21064, Creative Paperbacks) 2015. (Illus.). *(978-1-60818-593-1(1)*, 21063, Creative Education) Creative Co., The.

—What Is Out There? (Think Like a Scientist Ser.). (ENG.). 48p. (J). (gr. 4-7). 2016. pap. 12.00 *(978-1-62832-199-9(7)*, 21067, Creative Paperbacks) 2015. (Illus.). *(978-1-60818-594-8(X)*, 21066, Creative Education) Creative Co., The.

—What Is the Reason? (Think Like a Scientist Ser.). (ENG.). 48p. (J). (gr. 4-7). 2016. pap. 12.00 *(978-1-62832-200-2(4)*, 21070, Creative Paperbacks) 2015. (Illus.). *(978-1-60818-595-5(8)*, 21069, Creative Education) Creative Co., The.

—Where Do We Look for Life? (Think Like a Scientist Ser.). (ENG.). 48p. (J). (gr. 4-7). 2016. pap. 12.00 *(978-1-62832-201-9(2)*, 21073, Creative Paperbacks) 2015. (Illus.). *(978-1-60818-596-2(6)*, 21072, Creative Education) Creative Co., The.

Lemke, Donald B. Investigating the Scientific Method with Max Axiom, Super Scientist, 1 vol. Smith, Tod & Milgram, Al, illus. 2008. (Graphic Science Ser.). (ENG.). 32p. (J). (gr. 3-9). per. 8.10 *(978-1-4296-1760-4(8)*, 94307, Capstone Pr.) Capstone.

Loria, Laura. Develop & Test a Hypothesis, 1 vol. 2018. (Think Like a Scientist Ser.). (ENG.). 32p. (gr. 3-4). lib. bdg. 26.06 *(978-1-5383-0242-2(X)*, c223b0bc-26bb-4fbc-b0ea-0cb523c6469c, Britannica Educational Publishing) Rosen Publishing Group, Inc., The.

Magner, Laura. The Scientific Method in Fairy Tale Forest. 2007. pap. 14.95 *(978-1-931334-94-5(3))* Pieces of Learning.

Maloof, Torrey. Analyze It!, 1 vol. rev. ed. 2014. (Science: Informational Text Ser.). (ENG.). 32p. (gr. 2-3). pap. 10.99 *(978-1-4807-4613-8(4))* Teacher Created Materials, Inc.

McAneney, Caitie. Make a Research Plan, 1 vol. 2018. (Think Like a Scientist Ser.). (ENG.). 32p. (gr. 3-4). lib. bdg. 26.06 *(978-1-5383-0226-2(8)*, 180b42ef-aaa5-439b-9688-40e32a7f3a41, Britannica Educational Publishing) Rosen Publishing Group, Inc., The.

McGill, Jordan. Earth Science Fair Projects. 2011. (gr. 3-5). pap. 12.95 *(978-1-61690-655-9(3)*, AV2 by Weigl); (Illus.). 24p. (J). 27.13 *(978-1-61690-651-1(0))* Weigl Pubs., Inc.

—Life Science Fair Projects. 2011. (J). *(978-1-61690-330-5(9))*; (gr. 3-5). pap. 12.95 *(978-1-61690-658-0(8)*, AV2 by Weigl); (Illus.). 24p. (gr. 3-6). 27.13 *(978-1-61690-654-2(5))* Weigl Pubs., Inc.

—Space Science Fair Projects. 2011. (J). (gr. 3-5). pap. 12.95 *(978-1-61690-657-3(X)*, AV2 by Weigl); (Illus.). 24p. 27.13 *(978-1-61690-653-5(7))* Weigl Pubs., Inc.

—Water Science Fair Projects. 2011. (J). *(978-1-61690-332-9(5))*; (gr. 3-5). pap. 12.95 *(978-1-61690-656-6(1)*, AV2 by Weigl); (Illus.). 24p. (gr. 3-6). 27.13 *(978-1-61690-652-8(9))* Weigl Pubs., Inc.

Montgomery, Anne. I Spy, 1 vol. rev. ed. 2014. (Science: Informational Text Ser.). (ENG., Illus.). 24p. (J). (gr. -1-1). pap. 9.99 *(978-1-4807-4525-4(1))* Teacher Created Materials, Inc.

—Tell Me about It, 1 vol. rev. ed. 2014. (Science: Informational Text Ser.). (ENG., Illus.). 24p. (J). (gr. -1-1). pap. 9.99 *(978-1-4807-4526-1(X))* Teacher Created Materials, Inc.

Morgan, Emily. Never Stop Wondering. 2019. (ENG., Illus.). 32p. (J). (gr. 2-4). pap. 13.99 *(978-1-68140-008-2(1))* National Science Teachers Assn.

Mullins, Matt. Think Like a Scientist in the Car. 2011. (Explorer Junior Library: Science Explorer Junior Ser.). (ENG., Illus.). 32p. (gr. 4-8). lib. bdg. 32.07 *(978-1-61080-164-5(4)*, 201098) Cherry Lake Publishing.

—Think Like a Scientist in the Garden. 2011. (Explorer Junior Library: Science Explorer Junior Ser.). (ENG., Illus.). 32p. (gr. 4-8). lib. bdg. 32.07 *(978-1-61080-166-9(0)*, 201102) Cherry Lake Publishing.

—Think Like a Scientist in the Kitchen. 2011. (Explorer Junior Library: Science Explorer Junior Ser.). (ENG., Illus.). 32p. (gr. 4-8). lib. bdg. 32.07 *(978-1-61080-165-2(2)*, 201100) Cherry Lake Publishing.

National Geographic Learning. Reading Expeditions (Science: Math Behind the Science): Thinking It Through. 2007. (ENG., Illus.). 24p. (J). pap. 15.95 *(978-0-7922-4593-3(8))* CENGAGE Learning.

Niver, Heather Moore. The History of the Scientific Method, 1 vol. 2018. (Think Like a Scientist Ser.). (ENG.). 32p. (gr. 3-4). lib. bdg. 26.06 *(978-1-5383-0230-9(6)*, 5ba8d67f-893c-468b-a7e8-b90a081020b4, Britannica Educational Publishing) Rosen Publishing Group, Inc., The.

Olson, Elsie. Super Gross Poop, Puke, & Booger Projects. 2018. (Super Simple Super Gross Science Ser.). (ENG., Illus.). 32p. (J). (gr. k-4). lib. bdg. 34.21 *(978-1-5321-1732-9(9)*, 30752, Super SandCastle) ABDO Publishing Co.

Pederson, Bridget. Its Not Strange, I Know about Change!, 1 vol. 2007. (Science Made Simple Ser.). (Illus.). 24p. (J). (gr. k-3). lib. bdg. 24.21 *(978-1-59928-604-4(1)*, SandCastle) ABDO Publishing Co.

Porchetta, Renato L. Universal Methodology: UNIVERSAL SCIENTIFIC PROGRAMMING CONTROL-HUMAN INTELLIGENCE AMPLIFICATION MANAGEMENT-SCIENCE of the COMPOSITION of the SIGNIFICANCE,SEMANTICS-SCIENCE of MANAGEMENT-the Mosaic Thinking, 2 vols, Vol.1. 2nd ed. 2007. (ENG., Illus.). 490p. lib. bdg. 100.00 *(978-0-9769931-0-0(4))* Ce Code Efficiency, Inc.

Quinlan, Julia J. Collect & Analyze Data, 1 vol. 2018. (Think Like a Scientist Ser.). (ENG.). 32p. (gr. 3-4). 26.06 *(978-1-5383-0250-7(0)*, bde8ca68-a7a3-480a-b8e8-5bd2e1212a87, Britannica Educational Publishing) Rosen Publishing Group, Inc., The.

Rainis, Kenneth G. Cell & Microbe Science Fair Projects, Using the Scientific Method, 1 vol. rev. exp. ed. 2010. (Biology Science Projects Using the Scientific Method Ser.). (ENG., Illus.). 160p. (gr. 5-6). 38.60 *(978-0-7660-3420-4(8)*, e757c3ee-9023-4b9c-a039-a9b382e225c9) Enslow Publishing, LLC.

Rau, Dana Meachen. Think Like a Scientist on the Playground. 2011. (Explorer Junior Library: Science Explorer Junior Ser.). (ENG., Illus.). 32p. (gr. 4-8). lib. bdg. 32.07 *(978-1-61080-169-0(5)*, 201108) Cherry Lake Publishing.

Rice, Dona Herweck. Predict It!, 1 vol. 2015. (Science: Informational Text Ser.). (ENG., Illus.). 32p. (gr. 3-4). pap. 11.99 *(978-1-4807-4652-7(5))* Teacher Created Materials, Inc.

—Sort It!, 1 vol. rev. ed. 2014. (Science: Informational Text Ser.). (ENG., Illus.). 24p. (J). (gr. k-1). pap. 9.99 *(978-1-4807-4535-3(9))* Teacher Created Materials, Inc.

—What a Scientist Sees. 2015. (Science: Informational Text Ser.). (ENG.). 32p. (J). (gr. 3-5). pap. 11.99 *(978-1-4807-4691-6(6))* Teacher Created Materials, Inc.

—What the Evidence Shows. 2015. (Science: Informational Text Ser.). (ENG., Illus.). 32p. (J). (gr. 4-8). pap. 11.99 *(978-1-4807-4730-2(0))* Teacher Created Materials, Inc.

Riley, Peter D. Light. 2011. (Real Scientist Investigates Ser.). (Illus.). 32p. (J). (gr. 3-5). lib. bdg. 28.50 *(978-1-59771-281-1(7))* Sea-To-Sea Pubns.

—Materials. 2011. (Real Scientist Investigates Ser.). (Illus.). 32p. (J). (gr. 3-5). lib. bdg. 28.50 *(978-1-59771-282-8(5))* Sea-To-Sea Pubns.

—Space. 2011. (Real Scientist Investigates Ser.). (Illus.). 32p. (J). (gr. 3-5). lib. bdg. 28.50 *(978-1-59771-284-2(1))* Sea-To-Sea Pubns.

Rourke, Brigid. Tools of Science, 1 vol. 2013. (Rosen Readers Ser.). (ENG.). 24p. (J). (gr. 2-2). pap. 8.25 *(978-1-4777-2325-8(0)*, d91aa367-b5c0-4f16-8b59-b89cae13723f); pap. 49.50 *(978-1-4777-2326-5(9))* Rosen Publishing Group, Inc., The. (Rosen Classroom).

Rybolt, Thomas R. & Mebane, Robert C. Environmental Science Fair Projects, Using the Scientific Method, 1 vol. 2010. (Earth Science Projects Using the Scientific Method Ser.). (ENG., Illus.). 160p. (gr. 5-6). 38.60 *(978-0-7660-3426-6(7)*, 97149028-67df-48c2-b266-cc3dc48c7454) Enslow Publishing, LLC.

Science Detectives, 12 vols. 2008. (Science Detectives Ser.). (ENG., Illus.). (J). (gr. 2-3). lib. bdg. 157.62 *(978-1-4358-2553-6(5)*, 5bb9e9a9-f84b-449d-9d3a-50e80a1d5a27, PowerKids Pr.) Rosen Publishing Group, Inc., The.

Smith, Paula. Measure It!, 1 vol. 2015. (Science Sleuths Ser.). (ENG., Illus.). 24p. (J). (gr. 2-2). pap. *(978-0-7787-1544-3(2))* Crabtree Publishing Co.

—Model It!, 1 vol. 2015. (Science Sleuths Ser.). (ENG., Illus.). 24p. (J). (gr. 2-2). pap. *(978-0-7787-1545-0(0))* Crabtree Publishing Co.

—Plan & Investigate It!, 1 vol. 2015. (Science Sleuths Ser.). (ENG., Illus.). 24p. (J). (gr. 2-2). pap. *(978-0-7787-1546-7(9))* Crabtree Publishing Co.

—Prove It!, 1 vol. 2015. (Science Sleuths Ser.). (ENG., Illus.). 24p. (J). (gr. 2-2). pap. *(978-0-7787-1547-4(7))* Crabtree Publishing Co.

Somervill, Barbara A. Does This Make Sense? Constructing Explanations. (Think Like a Scientist Ser.). 24p. (gr. 2-3). 2009. 42.50 *(978-1-60854-356-4(0)*, PowerKids Pr.) 2006. (ENG.). pap. 8.25 *(978-1-4358-2681-6(7)*, 3738aae7-9509-4a7b-831d-954013305e1e, Rosen Classroom) Rosen Publishing Group, Inc., The.

—Sorting It Out: Evaluating Data. (Think Like a Scientist Ser.). 24p. (gr. 2-3). 2009. 42.50 *(978-1-60854-357-1(9)*, PowerKids Pr.) 2006. (ENG.). pap. 8.25 *(978-1-4358-2682-3(5)*, fc058202-23bd-47a2-a37a-6be32a7f8bbc, Rosen Classroom) Rosen Publishing Group, Inc., The.

—What Are the Facts? Collecting Information, 1 vol. 2006. (Think Like a Scientist Ser.). (ENG., Illus.). 24p. (YA). (gr. 2-3). lib. bdg. 26.27 *(978-1-4042-3484-0(5)*, 7763489f-16fc-4783-825e-52a18dbb17e0) Rosen Publishing Group, Inc., The.

—What Are the Facts? Collecting Information. (Think Like a Scientist Ser.). 24p. (gr. 2-3). 2009. 42.50 *(978-1-60854-358-8(7)*, PowerKids Pr.) 2006. (ENG.). pap. 8.25 *(978-1-4358-2683-0(3)*, a7eb66ea-5749-41fb-b243-ee0739354128, Rosen Classroom) Rosen Publishing Group, Inc., The.

—What Did You Find Out? Reporting Conclusions. (Think Like a Scientist Ser.). 24p. (gr. 2-3). 2009. 42.50 *(978-1-60854-359-5(5)*, PowerKids Pr.) 2006. (ENG.). pap. 8.25 *(978-1-4358-2684-7(1)*, 47699ca5-448d-4646-84b9-746cbc2c4ec7, Rosen Classroom) Rosen Publishing Group, Inc., The.

—What Do You Want to Prove? Planning Investigations. (Think Like a Scientist Ser.). 24p. (gr. 2-3). 2009. 42.50 *(978-1-60854-360-1(9)*, PowerKids Pr.) 2006. (ENG.). pap. 8.25 *(978-1-4358-2685-4(X)*, 4da81289-e630-4fa0-8b72-654848549dc3, Rosen Classroom) Rosen Publishing Group, Inc., The.

—What's the Big Idea? Forming Hypotheses. (Think Like a Scientist Ser.). 24p. (gr. 2-3). 2009. 42.50 *(978-1-60854-361-8(7)*, PowerKids Pr.) 2006. (ENG.). pap. 8.25 *(978-1-4358-2686-1(8)*, 2368c1ff-7cfd-4776-9d98-7182111a4c31, Rosen Classroom) Rosen Publishing Group, Inc., The.

Stefoff, Rebecca. Astrology & Astronomy, 1 vol. 2014. (Is It Science? Ser.). (ENG.). 48p. (gr. 5-5). lib. bdg. 32.64 *(978-1-62712-506-2(X)*, 1c2619d0-5c63-4905-ba5b-7d7bffa20978) Cavendish Square Publishing LLC.

—Astrology or Astronomy: Is Your Fate in the Stars? 2013. (J). *(978-0-7614-8144-7(3))* Marshall Cavendish.

—Earth or Sun: Which One Is in the Center? 2013. (J). *(978-0-7614-8147-8(8))* Marshall Cavendish.

Swanson, Diane. Nibbling on Einstein's Brain: The Good, the Bad & the Bogus in Science. Blake, Francis, illus. 2nd rev. ed. 2009. (ENG.). 160p. (J). (gr. 1-12). 24.95 *(978-1-55451-187-7(9)*, 9781554511877) Annick Pr., Ltd. CAN. Dist: Publishers Group West (PGW).

Wolny, Philip. Write Like a Scientist, 1 vol. 2018. (Think Like a Scientist Ser.). (ENG.). 32p. (gr. 3-4). 26.06 *(978-1-5383-0234-7(9)*, 35b03750-106d-4e0c-ac31-394a12cea908, Britannica Educational Publishing) Rosen Publishing Group, Inc., The.

Yoder, Eric & Yoder, Natalie. More Short Mysteries You Solve with Science! / ¡Más Misterios Cortos Que Resuelves con Ciencias! Bercovich, Nadia & Bachelet, Esteban, trs. 2016. (One Minute Mysteries Ser.). (ENG & SPA., Illus.). 224p. (J). (gr. 4-8). pap. 12.95 *(978-1-938492-15-0(3))* Science, Naturally!

Zoehfeld, Kathleen. National Geographic Little Kids First Big Book of Science. 2019. (Illus.). 128p. (J). (gr. -1-k). 14.99 *(978-1-4263-3318-7(8))*; (ENG., lib. bdg. 24.90 *(978-1-4263-3319-4(6))* Disney Publishing Worldwide. (National Geographic Kids).

SCIENCE—PHILOSOPHY

Beck, Esther. Ill Help My Chums Learn about Systems!, 1 vol. 2007. (Science Made Simple Ser.). (Illus.). 24p. (J). (gr. k-3). lib. bdg. 24.21 *(978-1-59928-584-9(3)*, SandCastle) ABDO Publishing Co.

Gow, Mary. The Great Thinker: Aristotle & the Foundations of Science, 1 vol. 2010. (Great Minds of Ancient Science & Math Ser.). (ENG.). 128p. (gr. 4-6). 35.93 *(978-0-7660-3121-0(7)*, ec09824d-bd32-4caa-b787-f641068f33b5) Enslow Publishing, LLC.

Harding, Sandra & Figueroa, Robert, eds. Science & Other Cultures: Issues in Philosophies of Science & Technology. 2003. (ENG.). 284p. (C). (gr. 13-18). 51.95 *(978-0-415-93992-8(5)*, RT3570) Routledge.

SCIENCE—POETRY

Rosen, Michael. Centrally Heated Knickers. 2018. (Illus.). 160p. (J). (gr. 4-6). pap. 12.99 *(978-0-14-138896-0(X))* Penguin Bks., Ltd. GBR. Dist: Independent Pubs. Group.

Shields, Carol Diggory. BrainJuice: Science, Fresh Squeezed! Thompson, Richard, illus. 2003. (ENG.). 64p. (J). (gr. -1-7). 14.95 *(978-1-59354-005-0(1))* Chronicle Bks. LLC.

Vergo, Franny. Sciencepalooza: A Collection of Science Poetry for Primary & Intermediate Students. 2012. 118p. pap. 14.95 *(978-1-4772-1598-2(0))* AuthorHouse.

SCIENCE—RESEARCH

Cherfas, Jeremy. El Genoma Humano. Yanez, Cecilia, tr. 2003. (Essential Science Ser.). (SPA.). 72p. (J). pap. 6.95 *(978-970-690-599-4(5))* Planeta Mexicana Editorial S. A. de C. V. MEX. Dist: Lectorum Pubns., Inc.

Garlick, Mark A. El Universo en Expansion. Barois, Valerian Stoopen, tr. 2003. (Ciencia para Todos Ser.). (SPA.). 72p. (J). pap. 6.95 *(978-970-690-600-7(2))* Planeta Mexicana Editorial S. A. de C. V. MEX. Dist: Lectorum Pubns., Inc.

Tudge, Colin. Alimentos para el Futuro. Barois, Lorena Stoopen, tr. 2003. (Essential Science Ser.). (SPA.). 72p. (J). pap. 6.95 *(978-970-690-603-8(7))* Planeta Mexicana Editorial S. A. de C. V. MEX. Dist: Lectorum Pubns., Inc.

SCIENCE—SOCIAL ASPECTS

see Science and Civilization

SCIENCE—STUDY AND TEACHING

see also Nature Study

Ardizzone, Leonisa. Science — Not Just for Scientists! Easy Explorations for Young Children. 2015. (ENG., Illus.). 96p. pap. 12.95 *(978-0-87659-484-1(4)*, Gryphon House Inc) Gryphon Hse., Inc.

Barfield, Mike. Destroy This Book in the Name of Science! Brainiac Edition. 2018. (ENG., Illus.). 56p. (J). (gr. 2-4). pap. 14.99 *(978-1-5247-7194-2(5)*, Crown Books For Young Readers) Random Hse. Children's Bks.

Bendick, Jeanne. Archimedes & the Door of Science: Immortals of Science. 2011. 154p. (gr. 5-8). 41.95 *(978-1-258-01488-9(2))* Literary Licensing, LLC.

Board, Joan. Cambridge Primary Science. Learner's Book. Per la Scuola Media. Con Espansione Online. 2014. (Cambridge Primary Science Ser.). (ENG., Illus.). 110p. pap. 24.40 *(978-1-107-66304-6(0))* Cambridge Univ. Pr.

Brown, Sam Ed. Bubbles, Rainbows & Worms: Science Experiments for Preschool Children. rev. ed. 2004. (ENG., Illus.). 96p. pap. 14.95 *(978-0-87659-241-0(8)*, 10243, Gryphon House Inc) Gryphon Hse., Inc.

Building Blocks of Science: Human Bodyworks Teacher's Guide (Firsthand Learning) 2007. ring bd. *(978-0-89278-337-3(0))* Carolina Biological Supply Co.

Building Blocks of Science: Light Teacher's Guide. 2007. (Illus.). ring bd. *(978-0-89278-339-7(7))* Carolina Biological Supply Co.

Clausen-Grace, Nicki. What Can You Make? 2006. (Science about Me Ser.). (Illus.). 8p. (J). (gr. 3-7). pap. 5.95 *(978-1-59515-932-8(0))* Rourke Educational Media.

Cleland, Jo. I Can Make Colors. 2006. (Science about Me Ser.). (Illus.). 8p. (J). (gr. 3-7). pap. 5.95 *(978-1-59515-925-0(8))* Rourke Educational Media.

Dykstra, Danell. Exploring Design Investigations Through Science Research Projects, 1 vol. 2018. (Project-Based Learning in Science Ser.). (ENG.). 64p. (gr. 5-5). pap. 14.53 *(978-1-5081-8593-2(X)*, 393e39d6-d3a0-465f-92a2-c437b8e988a6, Rosen Reference) Rosen Publishing Group, Inc., The.

Enz, Tammy. Cool Plastic Bottle & Milk Jug Science. 2016. (Recycled Science Ser.). (ENG., Illus.). 32p. (J). (gr. 3-9). lib. bdg. 28.65 *(978-1-5157-0862-9(4)*, 132163, Capstone Pr.) Capstone.

Enz, Tammy & Wheeler-Toppen, Jodi. Recycled Science: Bring Out Your Science Genius with Soda Bottles, Potato Chip Bags, & More Unexpected Stuff. 2016. (Recycled Science Ser.). (ENG., Illus.). 112p. (J). (gr. 3-9). pap., pap., pap. 9.95 *(978-1-62370-697-5(1)*, 132172, Capstone Young Readers) Capstone.

Good, Keith. Hands-on Science Projects: Classroom Library. 2008. pap. 6.95 (978-0-8225-9426-0(9)) Lerner Publishing Group.

Harcourt School Publishers Staff. Harcourt Ciencias: CA & National Big Book. 2003. (Harcourt Ciencias Ser.). (SPA., Illus.). 221.70 (978-0-15-321531-5(3)) Harcourt Schl. Pubs.

—Harcourt Ciencias, Grade 1: Grade Level Set: Texas/National Edition. 2003. (Harcourt Ciencias Ser.). (SPA.). (gr. 1-18). tchr. ed. 145.10 (978-0-15-315172-9(2)) Harcourt Schl. Pubs.

—Harcourt Ciencias, Grade 2: Grade Level Set: Texas/National Edition. 2003. (Harcourt Ciencias Ser.). (SPA.). (gr. 2-18). tchr. ed. 145.10 (978-0-15-315173-6(0)) Harcourt Schl. Pubs.

—Harcourt Ciencias, Grade 3 Unit A&B: Life Science. 2003. (Harcourt Ciencias Ser.). (SPA.). (gr. 3-18). tchr. ed. 67.40 (978-0-15-314808-8(X)) Harcourt Schl. Pubs.

—Harcourt Ciencias, Grade 3 Unit E&F: Physical Science. 2003. (Harcourt Ciencias Ser.). (SPA.). (gr. 3-18). tchr. ed. 67.40 (978-0-15-314810-1(1)) Harcourt Schl. Pubs.

—Harcourt Ciencias, Grade 4 Unit A&B: Life Science. 2003. (Harcourt Ciencias Ser.). (SPA.). (gr. 4-18). tchr. ed. 67.40 (978-0-15-314811-8(X)) Harcourt Schl. Pubs.

—Harcourt Ciencias, Grade 4 Unit E&F: Physical Science. 2003. (Harcourt Ciencias Ser.). (SPA.). (gr. 4-18). tchr. ed. 67.40 (978-0-15-314813-2(6)) Harcourt Schl. Pubs.

—Harcourt Ciencias, Grade 5 Unit A&B: Life Science. 2003. (Harcourt Ciencias Ser.). (SPA.). (gr. 5-18). tchr. ed. 70.00 (978-0-15-314814-9(4)) Harcourt Schl. Pubs.

—Harcourt Ciencias, Grade 5 Unit E&F: Physical Science. 2003. (Harcourt Ciencias Ser.). (SPA.). (gr. 5-18). tchr. ed. 70.00 (978-0-15-315037-1(8)) Harcourt Schl. Pubs.

—Harcourt School Publishers Science California: Lab Manual Student Edition Science 08 Grade 4. 2005. pap. 9.00 (978-0-15-352271-0(2)) Harcourt Schl. Pubs.

—Harcourt Science. 2nd ed. 2003. (Harcourt Science Ser.). (Illus.). (gr. 3-18). wbk. ed. 8.70 (978-0-15-323713-3(9)) Harcourt Schl. Pubs.

Havelka, Jacqueline. STEM in Auto Racing. 2019. (Connecting STEM & Sports Ser.). (Illus.). 80p. (J). (gr. 12). lib. bdg. 34.60 (978-1-4222-4330-5(3)) Mason Crest.

—STEM in Extreme Sports. 2019. (Connecting STEM & Sports Ser.). (Illus.). 80p. (J). (gr. 12). lib. bdg. 34.60 (978-1-4222-4333-6(8)) Mason Crest.

—STEM in Football. 2019. (Connecting STEM & Sports Ser.). (Illus.). 80p. (J). (gr. 12). lib. bdg. 34.60 (978-1-4222-4334-3(6)) Mason Crest.

—STEM in Gymnastics. 2019. (Connecting STEM & Sports Ser.). (Illus.). 80p. (J). (gr. 12). lib. bdg. 34.60 (978-1-4222-4335-0(4)) Mason Crest.

Holt, Rinehart and Winston Staff. Holt Science & Technology: Science Skills Worksheets. 5th ed. 2004. (Illus.). pap., wbk. ed. 11.60 (978-0-03-035197-6(9)) Holt McDougal.

James, Rosemary. What Do Scientists Do? Solve Problems Involving Measurement & Estimation, 1 vol. 2014. (InfoMax Math Readers Ser.). (ENG.). 24p. (J). (gr. 3-3). pap. 8.25 (978-1-4777-4603-5(X), 1b2d1f26-7b3f-40f5-af6d-56833401aee1, Rosen Classroom) Rosen Publishing Group, Inc., The.

Kellett, Sarah, et al, eds. Hands-On Science: 50 Kids' Activities from CSIRO. 2017. (Illus.). 128p. (gr. 7-14). pap. 16.50 (978-1-4863-0614-5(4)) CSIRO Publishing AUS. Dist: Stylus Publishing, LLC.

Kriesberg, Daniel A. Think Green, Take Action: Books & Activities for Kids, 1 vol. 2010. (ENG., Illus.). 148p. pap. 35.00 (978-1-59884-378-1(8), 900316591, Libraries Unlimited) ABC-CLIO, LLC.

Latta, Sara L. Positive Reaction! A Crash Course in Science, 1 vol. 2014. (Crash Course Ser.). (ENG.). 64p. (J). (gr. 4-8). lib. bdg. 35.32 (978-1-4914-0772-1(7), 126001) Capstone.

Leidtke, Amy. Leonardo's Art Workshop: Invent, Create, & Make STEAM Projects Like a Genius. 2018. (Leonardo's Workshop Ser.). (ENG., Illus.). 144p. (J). (gr. 5-8). pap. 22.99 (978-1-63159-522-6(9), 303402, Rockport Publishers) Quarto Publishing Group USA.

Lew, Kristi. Exploring Secondary Research Investigations Through Science Research Projects, 1 vol. 2018. (Project-Based Learning in Science Ser.). (ENG.). 64p. (gr. 5-5). pap. 14.53 (978-1-5081-8480-5(1), b51ce62d-6046-4bcb-9671-b0ab3d9aefae, Rosen Reference) Rosen Publishing Group, Inc., The.

Luke, Andrew. STEM in Ice Hockey. 2019. (Connecting STEM & Sports Ser.). (Illus.). 80p. (J). (gr. 12). lib. bdg. 34.60 (978-1-4222-4336-7(2)) Mason Crest.

Machajewski, Sarah. Discovering STEM at the Restaurant, 1 vol. 2015. (STEM in the Real World Ser.). (ENG., Illus.). 24p. (J). (gr. 2-3). pap. 9.25 (978-1-4994-0924-6(9), a8b2e9a5-a409-4ed5-967c-3ee158a0054e, PowerKids Pr.) Rosen Publishing Group, Inc., The.

Marks, Jennifer L. How to Make a Bouncing Egg. 2010. (Hands-On Science Fun Ser.). (ENG.). 24p. (J). (gr. k-1). pap. 43.74 (978-1-4296-6384-7(7), 16135, Capstone Pr.) Capstone.

Maurer, Daniel D. Do You Really Want to Burn Your Toast? A Book about Heat. Alberini, Teresa, illus. 2016. (Adventures in Science Ser.). (ENG.). 24p. (J). (gr. 1-4). lib. bdg. 20.95 (978-1-60753-961-2(6), 15628) Amicus.

—Do You Really Want to Skate on Thin Ice? A Book about States of Matter. Alberini, Teresa, illus. 2016. (Adventures in Science Ser.). (ENG.). 24p. (J). (gr. 1-4). lib. bdg. 20.95 (978-1-60753-958-2(6), 15631) Amicus.

Miles Kelly Staff. Science. 2003. (Info Bank Ser.). (Illus.). 96p. (J). 7.95 (978-1-84236-152-8(X)) Miles Kelly Publishing, Ltd. GBR. Dist: Independent Pubs. Group.

—Science & Maths. 2003. (Flip Quiz Ser.). (Illus.). 38p. (J). (gr. 10-11). spiral bd. 5.95 (978-1-84236-032-3(9)); (gr. 11-12). spiral bd. 5.95 (978-1-84236-033-0(7)); (gr. 7-9). spiral bd. 5.95 (978-1-84236-030-9(2)); (gr. 9-10). spiral bd. 5.95 (978-1-84236-031-6(0)) Miles Kelly Publishing, Ltd. GBR. Dist: Independent Pubs. Group.

Nagelhout, Ryan. Discovering STEM at the Baseball Game, 1 vol. 2015. (STEM in the Real World Ser.). (ENG., Illus.). 24p. (J). (gr. 2-3). pap. 9.25 (978-1-4994-0916-1(8), e9f895a6-68c3-4437-bf5f-1a0622d027dc, PowerKids Pr.) Rosen Publishing Group, Inc., The.

Pobst, Sandy. Scientific Discovery in the Renaissance: Text Pairs. 2008. (Bridges/Navigators Ser.). (J). (gr. 6). 89.00 (978-1-4108-8448-0(1)) Benchmark Education Co.

Roby, Cynthia. Discovering STEM at the Airport, 1 vol. 2015. (STEM in the Real World Ser.). (ENG., Illus.). 24p. (J). (gr. 2-3). pap. 9.25 (978-1-4994-0907-9(9), 3902fc2a-c1df-4cf3-b3ff-c8a1db451aab, PowerKids Pr.) Rosen Publishing Group, Inc., The.

—Discovering STEM at the Amusement Park, 1 vol. 2015. (STEM in the Real World Ser.). (ENG., Illus.). 24p. (J). (gr. 2-3). pap. 9.25 (978-1-4994-0910-9(9), f6b2f59d-2231-419c-a104-bfee2878d729, PowerKids Pr.) Rosen Publishing Group, Inc., The.

Rourke, Brigid. Tools of Science, 1 vol. 2013. (Rosen Readers Ser.). (ENG.). 24p. (J). (gr. 2-2). pap. 8.25 (978-1-4777-2325-8(0), d91aa367-b5c0-4f16-8b59-b89cae13723f); pap. 49.50 (978-1-4777-2326-5(9)) Rosen Publishing Group, Inc., The. (Rosen Classroom).

Rowe, Brooke. Building a Lava Lamp. Bane, Jeff, illus. 2016. (My Early Library: My Science Fun Ser.). (ENG.). 24p. (J). (gr. k-1). 30.64 (978-1-63471-026-8(6), 208184) Cherry Lake Publishing.

—Building a Volcano. Bane, Jeff, illus. 2016. (My Early Library: My Science Fun Ser.). (ENG.). 24p. (J). (gr. k-1). 30.64 (978-1-63471-025-1(8), 208180) Cherry Lake Publishing.

—Creating Rain. Bane, Jeff, illus. 2016. (My Early Library: My Science Fun Ser.). (ENG.). 24p. (J). (gr. k-1). 30.64 (978-1-63471-027-5(4), 208188) Cherry Lake Publishing.

Shea, Therese. Discovering STEM at the Zoo, 1 vol. 2015. (STEM in the Real World Ser.). (ENG., Illus.). 24p. (J). (gr. 2-3). pap. 9.25 (978-1-4994-0928-4(1), f51373b9-d1eb-41db-be95-b08d6f436aeb, PowerKids Pr.) Rosen Publishing Group, Inc., The.

Skillicorn, Phillipa, et al. International Primary Science Workbook 1. Miller, Jonathan & Pilling, Anne, eds. Robinson, Pete, tr. Hannigan, Pauline et al, illus. 2014. (Collins International Primary Science Ser.). (ENG.). 80p. (J). (gr. -1-k). pap. 6.95 (978-0-00-755148-4(7)) HarperCollins Pubs. Ltd. GBR. Dist: Independent Pubs. Group.

Spilsbury, Richard. I'M Good at Science... What Job Can I Get? 2012. (What's a Good Job for Me? Ser.). (ENG., Illus.). 32p. (J). (gr. 5-6). (978-1-4488-6632-8(4), PowerKids Pr.) Rosen Publishing Group, Inc., The.

Staley, Erin. 10 Great Makerspace Projects Using Science, 1 vol. 2017. (Using Makerspaces for School Projects Ser.). (ENG., Illus.). 64p. (J). (gr. 6-6). 36.13 (978-1-4994-3848-2(6), e7d0ad5d-dc0d-475d-9565-acf73d2dd068, Rosen Central) Rosen Publishing Group, Inc., The.

Sundance/Newbridge LLC Staff. Where Plants Live. 2004. (Reading PowerWorks Ser.). (gr. 1-3). 37.50 (978-0-7608-7799-9(8)); pap. 6.10 (978-0-7608-7800-2(5)) Sundance/Newbridge Educational Publishing.

Suzuki, David T. & Helmer, Barbara. Descubre las Plantas. 2004. (Juego de la Ciencia Ser.). (SPA., Illus.). 96p. 14.99 (978-84-9754-062-9(X), 87817) Ediciones Oniro S.A. ESP. Dist: Lectorum Pubns., Inc.

The Study of Science: Set 1, 28 vols. 2014. (Study of Science Ser.). (ENG.). 88-144p. (YA). (gr. 8-8). 529.48 (978-1-62275-758-9(0), a9daedb4-72ff-49b8-8c76-65b5c636ef7f) Rosen Publishing Group, Inc., The.

The Study of Science: Set 2, 8 vols., Vol. 1. 2016. (Study of Science Ser.). (ENG.). 96p. (YA). (gr. 8-8). 151.28 (978-1-68048-222-5(X), 75af47b3-dcf2-4067-9ea7-59cb97e9ac36, Britannica Educational Publishing) Rosen Publishing Group, Inc., The.

The Study of Science: Set 3, 12 vols. 2016. (Study of Science Ser.). (ENG.). 00104p. (YA). (gr. 8-8). 226.92 (978-1-5081-0294-6(5), f3a86d29-5346-43bb-9880-3ced50cdb0dd, Britannica Educational Publishing) Rosen Publishing Group, Inc., The.

The Study of Science: The Study of Science, 1-7, 14 vols. 2014. (Study of Science Ser.). (ENG.). 160p. (YA). (gr. 8-8). 264.74 (978-1-62275-424-3(7), cb9ea0f1-7818-42a3-81c8-a40916f12675) Rosen Publishing Group, Inc., The.

Timmons, Angie. Exploring Controlled Investigations Through Science Research Projects, 1 vol. 2018. (Project-Based Learning in Science Ser.). (ENG.). 64p. (gr. 5-5). pap. 14.53 (978-1-5081-8471-3(2), 8b92f5d7-e806-4ca8-9fc7-fd902754eec9, Rosen Reference) Rosen Publishing Group, Inc., The.

Twist, Clint. Light & Sound. 2010. (Science Everywhere! Ser.). 24p. 24.25 (978-1-84898-297-0(6)) Black Rabbit Bks.

VanCleave, Janice. Janice VanCleave's Big Book of Play & Find Out Science Projects. 2007. (ENG., Illus.). 224p. (gr. 3-7). per. 19.95 (978-0-7879-8928-6(2), Jossey-Bass) Wiley, John & Sons, Inc.

Ventura, Marne. STEM in Baseball. 2018. (STEM in Sports Ser.). (ENG., Illus.). 48p. (J). (gr. 4-4). pap. 11.95 (978-1-64185-291-3(7), 1641852917, SportsZone) ABDO Publishing Co.

Weikart, Cindy. The Ohio Graduation Test: Science Study Guide. 2004. 288p. pap., stu. ed. 16.95 (978-1-882203-30-7(5)) Orange Frazer Pr.

Wheeler-Toppen, Jodi. Amazing Cardboard Tube Science. 2016. (Recycled Science Ser.). (ENG., Illus.). 32p. (J). (gr. 3-9). lib. bdg. 28.65 (978-1-5157-0860-5(8), 132162, Capstone Pr.) Capstone.

Wiese, Jim. Ancient Science: 40 Time-Traveling, World-Exploring, History-Making Activities for Kids. Shems, Ed, illus. 2003. (ENG.). 128p. (J). (gr. 3-7). pap. 16.00 (978-0-471-21595-0(3)) Wiley, John & Sons, Inc.

Workman Publishing. Everything You Need to Ace Science in One Big Fat Notebook: The Complete Middle School Study Guide. 2016. (Big Fat Notebooks Ser.). (ENG., Illus.). 544p. (J). (gr. 6-9). pap. 16.95 (978-0-7611-6095-3(7), 16095) Workman Publishing Co., Inc.

Yoder, Eric & Yoder, Natalie. More Short Mysteries You Solve with Science! / ¡Más Misterios Cortos Que Resuelves con Ciencias! Bercovich, Nadia & Bachelet, Esteban, trs. 2016. (One Minute Mysteries Ser.). (ENG & SPA., Illus.). 224p. (J). (gr. 4-8). pap. 12.95 (978-1-938492-15-0(3)) Science, Naturally!

SCIENCE—VOCATIONAL GUIDANCE

Brinkerhoff, Shirley. Research Scientist. Riggs, Ernestine G. & Gholar, Cheryl, eds. 2013. (Careers with Character Ser.: 18). 96p. (J). (gr. 7-18). 22.95 (978-1-4222-2765-7(0)) Mason Crest.

Bruno, Nikki. Gross Jobs in Science: 4D an Augmented Reading Experience. 2019. (Gross Jobs 4D Ser.). (ENG., Illus.). 32p. (J). (gr. 3-9). lib. bdg. 31.99 (978-1-5435-5490-8(3), 139361, Capstone Pr.) Capstone.

Burnett, Betty. Cool Careers Without College for Math & Science Wizards. 2009. (Cool Careers Without College Ser.). 144p. (gr. 6-6). 66.50 (978-1-61511-959-2(0)) Rosen Publishing Group, Inc., The.

Byers, Ann. Jobs As Green Builders & Planners. 2010. (Green Careers Ser.). 80p. (YA). (gr. 7-12). E-Book 61.20 (978-1-4488-0131-2(1)) Rosen Publishing Group, Inc., The.

Cool Science Careers (Set), 18 vols. 2011. (21st Century Skills Library: Cool Science Careers Ser.). (ENG., Illus.). 32p. (gr. 4-8). 577.26 (978-1-61080-036-5(2), 200940) Cherry Lake Publishing.

Etingoff, Kim. Women Who Built Our Scientific Foundations. Lee-Karlon, Ann, ed. 2013. (Major Women in Science Ser.: 10). 64p. (J). (gr. 7-18). 22.95 (978-1-4222-2933-0(5)) Mason Crest.

Extreme Science Careers, 12 vols. 2015. (Extreme Science Careers Ser.). (ENG.). 128p. (J). (gr. 7-7). lib. bdg. 233.58 (978-0-7660-6696-0(7), 5dd408d1-79e9-4c6a-a43e-947611b5966a) Enslow Publishing, LLC.

French, Lloyd C. On the Job with an Explorer. 2003. (Adventures in Science Professions Ser.). (J). pap. (978-1-58417-123-2(5)); lib. bdg. (978-1-58417-060-0(3)) Lake Street Pubs.

Harmon, Daniel E. Jobs in Environmental Cleanup & Emergency Hazmat Response. 2010. (Green Careers Ser.). 80p. (YA). (gr. 7-12). E-Book 61.20 (978-1-4488-0132-9(X)) Rosen Publishing Group, Inc., The.

Hoyt, Beth Caldwell & Ritter, Erica. The Ultimate Girls' Guide to Science: From Backyard Experiments to Winning the Nobel Prize. Palen, Debbie, illus. 2004. 128p. (J). (gr. 4-12). pap. (978-1-58270-092-2(3)) Beyond Words Publishing, Inc.

Hynson, Colin. Dream Jobs in Science. 2017. (Cutting-Edge Careers in STEM Ser.). (Illus.). 32p. (J). (gr. 5-5). (978-0-7787-2965-5(6)) Crabtree Publishing Co.

Idzikowski, Lisa. Working in Science. 2018. (Career Files Ser.). (ENG., Illus.). 32p. (J). (gr. 3-6). 32.80 (978-1-63235-448-8(9), 13841, 12-Story Library) Bookstaves, LLC.

Jackson, Donna M. Extreme Scientists: Exploring Nature's Mysteries from Perilous Places. 2014. (Scientists in the Field Ser.). lib. bdg. 20.85 (978-0-606-35330-4(5)) Turtleback.

Klein, Rebecca T. Careers for Tech Girls in Science, 1 vol. 2015. (Tech Girls Ser.). (ENG., Illus.). 80p. (J). (gr. 7-8). 37.47 (978-1-4994-6103-9(8), e68f3614-3665-4ca7-a52b-04b2c080437f, Rosen Young Adult) Rosen Publishing Group, Inc., The.

Liebman, Dan & Liebman, Dan. I Want to Be a Scientist. 2016. (I Want to Be Ser.). (ENG., Illus.). 24p. (J). (gr. -1-2). pap. 3.99 (978-1-77085-789-6(3), 1d95a503-624a-456e-a25a-41cca03ee7fa) Firefly Bks., Ltd.

—Quiero Ser Cientifico. 2016. (Quiero Ser.). (SPA., Illus.). 24p. (J). (gr. -1-2). pap. 6.99 (978-1-77085-865-7(2), 22f7745a-bb3e-4663-b7f7-d6c15d57e546) Firefly Bks., Ltd.

Louv, Barbara. Choose a Career in Science. 2006. (Illus.). 112p. (gr. 3-7). per. 12.95 (978-1-59858-130-0(9)) Dog Ear Publishing, LLC.

Mahaney, Ian F. Energy in Action, 4 vols., Set. Incl. Heat. (YA). lib. bdg. 26.27 (978-1-4042-3477-2(2), c7a457ef-db3c-4391-abdf-b561fd4a3278); Light. (YA). lib. bdg. 26.27 (978-1-4042-3476-5(4), 6f958087-0feb-4b4d-865d-94bbf08a35e0); Solar Energy. (J). lib. bdg. 26.27 (978-1-4042-3479-6(9), caa8fd1d-7f50-4d7e-9267-b4708a556374, PowerKids Pr.); (Illus.). 24p. (gr. 3-3). 2007. (Energy in Action Ser.). (ENG.). 2006. Set lib. bdg. 52.54 (978-1-4042-3504-5(3), 888f1685-a313-4558-9910-008b3766a673) Rosen Publishing Group, Inc., The.

McGuinness, Daniel. Cool Careers Without College for People Who Are Really Good at Science & Math, 1 vol. 2nd ed. 2013. (Cool Careers Without College Ser.). (ENG., Illus.). 144p. (J). (gr. 7-7). 41.12 (978-1-4777-1823-0(0), 34cdd741-e47f-4e0b-9394-f85589747e6d) Rosen Publishing Group, Inc., The.

Objects in the Sky, 12 vols., Set. Incl. Exploring Comets. Way, Jennifer. lib. bdg. 26.27 (978-1-4042-3469-7(1), ffbeff81-f650-4e68-b14a-1fc7e391ef90, PowerKids Pr.); Exploring Earth. Olien, Rebecca. lib. bdg. 26.27 (978-1-4042-3465-9(9), 52a1b5a5-51c2-479a-b460-4096dcb62c56); Exploring Meteors. Olien, Rebecca. lib. bdg. 26.27 (978-1-4042-3468-0(3), 8e585b55-a39f-4814-93fa-3ccf4f62d96d, PowerKids Pr.); Exploring the Moon. Olien, Rebecca. lib. bdg. 26.27 (978-1-4042-3466-6(7), 003b77c6-da98-40f1-897b-ea98f1c4d440, PowerKids Pr.); Exploring the Planets in Our Solar System. Olien, Rebecca. lib. bdg. 26.27 (978-1-4042-3467-3(5), a3e1acfe-1a80-4987-9269-aac56a1fa428, PowerKids Pr.); Exploring the Sun. Olien, Rebecca. lib. bdg. 26.27 (978-1-4042-3464-2(0), b8eed2ba-a2e8-4d34-9503-ec495cb7fd65, PowerKids Pr.); (Illus.). 24p. (J). (gr. 3-3). 2007. (Objects in the Sky Ser.). (ENG.). 2006. Set lib. bdg. 157.62 (978-1-4042-3502-1(7), 12b56598-5968-41e9-855a-4aceb10261a5, PowerKids Pr.) Rosen Publishing Group, Inc., The.

Reeves, Diane Lindsey. Find Your Future in Science. 2016. (Bright Futures Press: Find Your Future in STEAM Ser.). (ENG., Illus.). 32p. (J). (gr. 4-6). 32.07 (978-1-63471-898-1(4), 208913) Cherry Lake Publishing.

—Stem. 2017. (Bright Futures Press: World of Work Ser.). (ENG., Illus.). 32p. (J). (gr. 4-7). lib. bdg. 32.07 (978-1-63472-628-3(6), 209546) Cherry Lake Publishing.

Rhodes, Sam. STEAM Jobs for Workers Willing to Get Dirty. 2018. (STEAM Jobs Ser.). (ENG., Illus.). 32p. (J). (gr. 3-9). lib. bdg. 28.65 (978-1-5435-3095-7(8), 138674, Capstone Pr.) Capstone.

Ring, Susan. Scientists at Work. 2005. (Yellow Umbrella Fluent Level Ser.). (ENG., Illus.). 16p. (gr. k-1). pap. 35.70 (978-0-7368-5303-3(0), Capstone Pr.) Capstone.

Sawyer, Sarah. Careers in DNA Analysis, 1 vol. 2008. (Careers in Forensics Ser.). (ENG., Illus.). 64p. (J). (gr. 5-5). lib. bdg. 37.13 (978-1-4042-1343-2(0), 2fec1b0b-9622-4b71-acf8-34da0c533398) Rosen Publishing Group, Inc., The.

Sheen, Barbara. Careers If You Like Research & Analysis. 2019. (Career Exploration Ser.). (ENG.). 80p. (J). (gr. 6-12). 41.27 (978-1-68282-591-4(4)) ReferencePoint Pr., Inc.

Snyder, Gail. Careers If You Like Science. 2016. (ENG.). 80p. (J). (gr. 5-12). lib. bdg. (978-1-68282-006-3(8)) ReferencePoint Pr., Inc.

Spiro, Ruth. Baby Loves Scientists. Chan, Irene, illus. 2019. (Baby Loves Science Ser.). 24p. (J). (— 1). 12.99 (978-1-62354-149-1(2)) Charlesbridge Publishing, Inc.

Suen, Anastasia. Top STEM Careers in Science, 1 vol. 2014. (Cutting-Edge STEM Careers Ser.). (ENG., Illus.). 128p. (J). (gr. 9-9). 38.80 (978-1-4777-7664-3(8), 37125832-da8b-4594-8b87-788b3b896c8c) Rosen Publishing Group, Inc., The.

Wendinger, Jennifer. Unusual & Awesome Jobs Using Science: Food Taster, Human Lie Detector, & More. 2015. (You Get Paid for THAT? Ser.). (ENG., Illus.). 32p. (J). (gr. 3-9). 28.65 (978-1-4914-2031-7(6), 127509, Capstone Pr.) Capstone.

SCIENCE—YEARBOOKS

Science Year 2006. 2005. (gr. 5-12). 38.50 (978-0-7166-0559-1(7)) World Bk., Inc.

SCIENCE AND CIVILIZATION

Hulick, Kathryn. Citizen Science: How Anyone Can Contribute to Scientific Discovery. 2019. (YA). (978-1-68282-736-9(4)) ReferencePoint Pr., Inc.

Kovacs, Vic. Get into Citizen Science. 2017. (Get-Into-It Guides). (Illus.). 32p. (J). (gr. 4-5). (978-0-7787-3636-3(9)) Crabtree Publishing Co.

Rajczak, Michael. Be a Citizen Scientist!, 1 vol. 2018. (Be the Change! Shaping Your Community Ser.). (ENG.). 32p. (gr. 3-4). 28.27 (978-1-5382-1995-9(6), de0228db-7fe4-428e-a2e1-5b301b7f16f1) Stevens, Gareth Publishing LLLP.

Turney, Jon. Technology - Ethical Debates about the Application of Science. 2008. (Dilemmas in Modern Science Ser.). (ENG., Illus.). 48p. (J). 23.99 (978-0-237-53370-0(7)) Evans Brothers, Ltd. GBR. Dist: Independent Pubs. Group.

SCIENCE AND RELIGION

see Religion and Science

SCIENCE AND SPACE

see Space Sciences

SCIENCE FICTION

see also Time Travel

Aaron, Jason. Vader down: Volume 1. Deodato, Mike & Martin, Laura, illus. 2016. (Star Wars: Vader Down Ser.). (ENG.). 36p. (J). (gr. 6-12). lib. bdg. 31.36 (978-1-61479-561-2(4), 24395, Graphic Novels) Spotlight.

—Vader down: Volume 3. Deodato, Mike & Martin, Laura, illus. 2016. (Star Wars: Vader Down Ser.). (ENG.). 24p. (J). (gr. 6-12). lib. bdg. 31.36 (978-1-61479-563-6(0), 24397, Graphic Novels) Spotlight.

—Vader down: Volume 5. Deodato, Mike & Martin, Laura, illus. 2016. (Star Wars: Vader Down Ser.). (ENG.). 24p. (J). (gr. 6-12). lib. bdg. 31.36 (978-1-61479-565-0(7), 24399, Graphic Novels) Spotlight.

Abbott, Tony. Wizard or Witch? Merrell, David & Jessell, Tim, illus. 2004. (Secrets of Droon Ser.: 2). (ENG.). 161p. (J). (gr. 2-4). 18.69 (978-0-439-56049-8(7)) Scholastic, Inc.

ABDO Publishing Company Staff. Tom Swift, Young Inventor - 4 Titles. 2007. (Tom Swift, Young Inventor Ser.). (ENG.). 165p. 108.28 (978-1-59961-349-9(2)) Spotlight.

ABDO Publishing Company Staff & Parker, Jeff. 4 Titles, 2 vols. 2007. (X-Men: First Class Ser.: 4). (ENG.). 24p. (J). (gr. 2-6). lib. bdg. 62.72 (978-1-59961-397-0(2), 15628, Marvel Age) Spotlight.

Abnett, Dan. The Real Ghostbusters: This Ghost Is Toast! Williams, Anthony, illus. 2007. (Real Ghostbusters Ser.). (ENG.). 96p. per. 8.95 (978-1-84576-143-1(X), Titan Bks.) Titan Bks. Ltd. GBR. Dist: Penguin Random Hse. LLC.

The Abominable Snowman, 6 Vols., Pack. (Bookweb Ser.). 32p. (gr. 3-18). 34.00 (978-0-7635-3935-1(X)) Rigby Education.

Abuhamda, Nasser. A Flower in the Rain. 2009. 40p. pap. 14.95 (978-1-59858-879-8(6)) Dog Ear Publishing, LLC.

Acampora, Michael V. Escape from the Orange Lanterns, 1 vol. Schoening, Dan, illus. 2011. (Green Lantern Ser.). (ENG.). 56p. (J). (gr. 3-6). lib. bdg. 26.65 (978-1-4342-2622-8(0), 113667, Stone Arch Bks.) Capstone.

—Red Lanterns' Revenge, 1 vol. Schoening, Dan, illus. 2011. (Green Lantern Ser.). (ENG.). 56p. (J). (gr. 3-6). pap. 4.95 (978-1-4342-3409-4(6), 116422); lib. bdg. 26.65 (978-1-4342-2623-5(9), 113668) Capstone. (Stone Arch Bks.).

Accardo, Jus. Omega. 2017. (Infinity Division Novel Ser.: 2). (ENG.). 320p. (YA). pap. 9.99 (978-1-63375-825-4(7), 900180795) Entangled Publishing, LLC.

Adams, Jennifer. Frankenstein: A BabyLit(TM) Anatomy Primer, 1 vol. Oliver, Alison, illus. 2014. 22p. (J). (gr. k-1). bds. 9.99 (978-1-4236-3741-7(0)) Gibbs Smith, Publisher.

Adams, John Joseph, ed. Under the Moons of Mars: New Adventures on Barsoom. (ENG., Illus.). 368p. (YA). (gr. 7). 2013. pap. 9.99 (978-1-4424-2030-4(8)) 2012. 16.99 (978-1-4424-2029-8(4)) Simon & Schuster Bks. For Young Readers. (Simon & Schuster Bks. For Young Readers).

Adams, Matthew R. Kord & Harley. O'Reilly, Sean Patrick, ed. 2011. (Illus.). 50p. (YA). pap. 19.95 (978-0-9809204-7-5(7)) Arcana Studio, Inc.

Adams, W. Royce. The Computer's Nerd. 2011. 154p. (gr. 4-7). 22.99 (978-0-9712206-9-0(7)) Rairarubia Bks.

Adina Bates, Shelley. A Lady of Spirit: A Steampunk Adventure Novel. 2014. (ENG.). pap. 13.99 (978-1-939087-15-7(5), Moonshell Bks., Inc.) Shelley Adina.

Adlington, L. J. The Diary of Pelly D. 2008. (ENG.). 304p. (YA). (gr. 9). per. 9.99 (978-0-06-076617-7(4), Greenwillow Bks.) HarperCollins Pubs.

Adventures Beyond the Solar System: Planetron & Me. 2005. (J). audio, cd-rom 24.95 (978-0-9771381-5-9(1)) Williams, Geoffrey T.

Adventures in the Solar System: Planetron & Me. 2005. (J). audio, cd-rom 24.95 (978-0-9771381-4-2(3)) Williams, Geoffrey T.

Aguirre, Ann. Enclave. 2012. (Razorland Trilogy Ser.: 1). (ENG.). 288p. (YA). (gr. 7). pap. 10.99 (978-0-312-55137-7(1), 900074423) Square Fish.

—Horde. 2014. (Razorland Trilogy Ser.: 3). (ENG.). 464p. (YA). (gr. 7). pap. 18.99 (978-1-250-05077-9(4), 900134148) Square Fish.

—Outpost. 2013. (Razorland Trilogy Ser.: 2). (ENG.). 352p. (YA). (gr. 7). pap. 13.99 (978-1-250-03418-2(3), 900120590) Square Fish.

—Vanguard: A Razorland Companion Novel. 2018. (Razorland Trilogy Ser.: 4). (ENG.). 368p. (YA). pap. 15.99 (978-1-250-15867-3(2), 900185525) Square Fish.

Ahmed, Samira. Internment. (ENG.). 400p. (YA). (gr. 7-17). 2020. pap. 11.99 (978-0-316-52270-0(8)) 2019. 17.99 (978-0-316-52269-4(4)) Little, Brown Bks. for Young Readers.

Akinyemi, Rowena. Oxford Bookworms Library: under the Moon: Level 1: 400-Word Vocabulary. 3rd ed. 2008. (ENG., Illus.). 64p. 11.00 (978-0-19-478922-6(5)) Oxford Univ. Pr., Inc.

Alameda, Courtney. Pitch Dark. 2019. (ENG.). 384p. (YA). pap. 10.99 (978-1-250-29457-9(6), 900195082) Square Fish.

Albee, Sarah. Trevor el Ingenioso; Clever Trevor. 2008. pap. 34.95 (978-0-7613-3868-0(3)) Astra Publishing Hse.

Albee, Sarah, et al. To the Center of the Earth! 2008. (Backyardigans Ser.). (ENG.). 24p. (J). pap. 3.99 (978-1-4169-7094-1(0), Simon Spotlight/Nickelodeon) Simon Spotlight/Nickelodeon.

Alexander, Claudia. Windows to Adventure: Windows to the Morning Star. 2012. 68p. pap. 15.99 (978-1-937781-66-8(6)) Blue Pheonix Bks.

Alexander, William. Ambassador. 2015. (ENG.). 256p. (J). (gr. 3-7). pap. 7.99 (978-1-4424-9765-8(3), McElderry, Margaret K. Bks.) McElderry, Margaret K. Bks.

—Ambassador. 2015. lib. bdg. 18.40 (978-0-606-37848-2(0)) Turtleback.

—Nomad. 2015. (ENG., Illus.). 272p. (J). (gr. 3-7). 16.99 (978-1-4424-9767-2(X), McElderry, Margaret K. Bks.) McElderry, Margaret K. Bks.

The Alien Next Door. 2005. (J). audio, cd-rom 24.95 (978-0-9771381-8-0(6)) Williams, Geoffrey T.

Alpert, Mark. The Silence. 2017. (Six Ser.: 3). 384p. (YA). (gr. 6-12). 17.99 (978-1-4926-4896-3(5)) Sourcebooks, Inc.

Alsberg, Sasha & Cummings, Lindsay. Zenith. 2018. (Androma Saga Ser.: 1). (ENG.). 576p. (YA). pap. 9.99 (978-1-335-13973-3(7), Harlequin Teen) Harlequin Enterprises ULC CAN. Dist: HarperCollins Pubs.

Altebrando, Tara. Take Me with You. 2020. (ENG.). 384p. (YA). 17.99 (978-1-68119-748-7(0), 900184215, Bloomsbury Young Adult) Bloomsbury Publishing USA.

Ambassador. 2014. (ENG., Illus.). 240p. (J). (gr. 3-7). 16.99 (978-1-4424-9764-1(5), McElderry, Margaret K. Bks.) McElderry, Margaret K. Bks.

Ames, Mildred. Anna to the Infinite Power. 2003. (J). pap. 2.75 (978-0-590-42707-4(5)) Scholastic, Inc.

Ammann, Michael. Exos. 2003. 108p. (YA). pap. 9.95 (978-0-595-27121-4(9), Writers Club Pr.) iUniverse, Inc.

Anderson, Brian. The Adventures of Commander Zack Proton & the Red Giant. Holgate, Doug, illus. 2006. (Adventures of Commander Zack Proton Ser.: 1). (ENG.). 128p. (J). (gr. 2-5). pap. 5.99 (978-1-4169-1364-1(5), Simon & Schuster/Paula Wiseman Bks.) Simon & Schuster/Paula Wiseman Bks.

—The Adventures of Commander Zack Proton & the Warlords of Nibblecheese. Holgate, Doug, illus. 2006. (Adventures of Commander Zack Proton Ser.: 2). (ENG.). 112p. (J). (gr. 2-5). pap. 6.99 (978-1-4169-1365-8(3), Aladdin) Simon & Schuster Children's Publishing.

Anderson, D. M. Killer Cows. 2010. 274p. (YA). pap. 13.99 (978-1-59080-686-9(7), Quake) Echelon Press Publishing.

Anderson, E. V. The Many Lives of Lilith Lane, 0 vols. unabr. ed. 2012. (ENG.). 162p. (J). (gr. 7-12). pap. 14.95 (978-1-61109-792-4(4), 9781611097924, Skyscape) Amazon Publishing.

Anderson, M. T. Feed. 2012. (ENG., Illus.). 320p. (YA). (gr. 9). pap. 11.99 (978-0-7636-6262-2(3)) Candlewick Pr.

—Landscape with Invisible Hand. (ENG.). 160p. (gr. 9). 2019. (J). pap. 8.99 (978-0-7636-9950-5(0)) 2017. (YA). 16.99 (978-0-7636-8789-2(8)) Candlewick Pr.

—Whales on Stilts! Cyrus, Kurt, illus. 2010. (Pals in Peril Tale Ser.). (ENG.). (J). (gr. 5-9). 224p. pap. 8.99 (978-1-4424-0701-5(8));1. 208p. 17.99 (978-1-4424-0695-7(X)) Beach Lane Bks. (Beach Lane Bks.).

Anderson, Matt & Hutchins, Eric. White Picket Fences: Double Feature One-shot. 2008. (Illus.). 52p. (YA). pap. 6.95 (978-0-9801314-9-9(9)) Ape Entertainment.

Anderson, Matthew. The Astonishing Life of Octavian Nothing, Traitor to the Nation, Volume II: The Kingdom on the Waves. 2009. (ENG., Illus.). 592p. (YA). (gr. 9). pap. 12.99 (978-0-7636-4626-4(1)) Candlewick Pr.

—The Astonishing Life of Octavian Nothing, Traitor to the Nation, Volume II: The Kingdom on the Waves. 2011. 24.00 (978-1-60686-926-0(4)) Perfection Learning Corp.

—Feed. braille ed. 2003. (J). (gr. 2). spiral bd. (978-0-616-15869-2(6)) Canadian National Institute for the Blind/Institut National Canadien pour les Aveugles.

—Feed. 2004. 299p. (YA). (gr. 9-12). 15.65 (978-0-7569-6578-5(0)) Perfection Learning Corp.

—Feed. 2004. 320p. (J). (gr. 7-18). pap. 38.00 incl. audio (978-1-4000-9022-8(9), Listening Library) Random Hse. Audio Publishing Group.

—Feed. 2012. lib. bdg. 19.65 (978-0-606-26941-4(X)) Turtleback.

—Whales on Stilts! Cyrus, Kurt, illus. 2006. (M. T. Anderson's Thrilling Tales Ser.). 188p. (gr. 5-9). 15.95 (978-0-7569-7213-4(2)) Perfection Learning Corp.

Anderson, R. J. Ultraviolet. (ENG.). 312p. (YA). (gr. 7-12). 2013. pap. 9.95 (978-1-4677-0914-9(X), 49905a67-b3d3-4207-afce-401434fab3bd) 2011. 17.95 (978-0-7613-7408-4(6)) Lerner Publishing Group. (Carolrhoda Lab™).

Anderson, Suzette. Cybertreks: Wildest West. 2004. 196p. pap. 13.95 (978-0-595-30840-8(6)) iUniverse, Inc.

Andre Norton. 2010. (ENG., Illus.). 128p. (gr. 6-12). 35.00 (978-1-60413-682-1(0), P178901, Facts On File) Infobase Holdings, Inc.

Andrews, Jefferri & Andrews, Jonathan. The Macos Adventure. 2013. (ENG.). 212p. (YA). pap. 23.99 (978-0-9848980-9-1(3), BTWEYL) Bks. That Will Enhance Your Life.

Andrews, Jerome. The Initiation. 2006. 40p. pap. 8.50 (978-1-4116-9167-4(9)) Lulu Pr., Inc.

Andrews, Jesse. Munmun. 2018. (ENG.). 416p. (YA). (gr. 9-17). 18.99 (978-1-4197-2871-6(7), 1140101, Amulet Bks.) Abrams, Inc.

Ant, Exupery. Journee avec le Petit Prince. pap. 10.95 (978-2-07-054268-0(8)) Gallimard, Editions FRA. Dist: Distribooks, Inc.

Anthony, David & David, Charles. Knightscares #3: (Knightscares): Early Winter's Orb. 2005. (Illus.). 208p. (J). pap. 5.99 (978-0-9728461-2-7(3)) Sigil Publishing.

Antonios, Joseph. Portal:Earth. 2010. (ENG.). 126p. pap. 12.99 (978-0-557-40539-8(4)) Lulu Pr., Inc.

Antram, David. How to Draw Science Fiction. (Illus.). 32p. (J). 2012. 70.50 (978-1-4488-4528-6(9)) 2011. (ENG., (gr. 4-5). pap. 12.75 (978-1-4488-4527-9(0), cfd0c939-e74f-441b-b071-253faadb3c41) Rosen Publishing Group, Inc., The. (PowerKids Pr.).

Applegate, K. A., pseud. Aftermath. 2003. (Remnants Ser.: No. 12). 163p. (J). (gr. 4-8). 12.65 (978-0-7569-5318-8(9)) Perfection Learning Corp.

—The Invasion (Animorphs #1) 2nd ed. 2011. (Animorphs Ser.: 1). (ENG.). 192p. (J). (gr. 3-7). pap. 7.99 (978-0-545-29151-4(8), Scholastic Paperbacks) Scholastic, Inc.

—The Stranger (Animorphs #7) 2012. (Animorphs Ser.: 7). (ENG.). 176p. (J). (gr. 3-7). pap. 8.99 (978-0-545-42414-1(3), Scholastic Paperbacks) Scholastic, Inc.

—Survival. 2003. (Remnants Ser.: No. 13). 165p. (J). (gr. 4-8). 12.65 (978-0-7569-5301-0(4)) Perfection Learning Corp.

—The Visitor (Animorphs #2), 1 vol. 2nd ed. 2011. (Animorphs Ser.: 2). (ENG.). 192p. (J). (gr. 3-7). pap. 8.99 (978-0-545-29152-1(6), Scholastic Paperbacks) Scholastic, Inc.

Applegate, Katherine. The Capture. 2012. (Animorphs Ser.: 6). lib. bdg. 17.20 (978-0-606-26194-4(X)) Turtleback.

—The Stranger. 2012. (Animorphs Ser.: 7). lib. bdg. 17.20 (978-0-606-26195-1(8)) Turtleback.

Appleton, Victor. The Adventures of Tom Swift. 2007. 456p. per. 19.95 (978-1-4344-9982-0(0)) Wildside Pr., LLC.

—The Drone Pursuit. 2019. (Tom Swift Inventors' Academy Ser.: 1). (ENG., Illus.). 144p. (J). (gr. 3-7). pap. 7.99 (978-1-5344-3630-5(8), Simon & Schuster/Paula Wiseman Bks.) Simon & Schuster/Paula Wiseman Bks.

—Into the Abyss. 2007. (Tom Swift, Young Inventor Ser.). (ENG.). 160p. (gr. 3-7). 27.07 (978-1-59961-350-5(6)) Spotlight.

—Restricted Access. 2019. (Tom Swift Inventors' Academy Ser.: 3). (ENG., Illus.). 160p. (J). (gr. 3-7). 17.99 (978-1-5344-3637-4(5), Simon & Schuster/Paula Wiseman Bks.) Simon & Schuster/Paula Wiseman Bks.

—The Sonic Breach. 2019. (Tom Swift Inventors' Academy Ser.: 2). (ENG., Illus.). 144p. (J). (gr. 3-7). pap. 6.99 (978-1-5344-3633-6(2), Simon & Schuster/Paula Wiseman Bks.) Simon & Schuster/Paula Wiseman Bks.

—Tom Swift & His Photo Telephone. 2007. 100p. per. (978-1-4068-1621-1(3)) Echo Library.

—Tom Swift & the Electronic Hydrolung. l.t. ed. 2007. (ENG.). 132p. pap. 19.99 (978-1-4346-3073-5(0)) Creative Media Partners, LLC.

Ariga, Hitoshi. Mega Man Gigamix, 2 vols., Vol. 3. 2011. (ENG., Illus.). 224p. (J). pap. 13.95 (978-1-926778-31-0(6), 0153699d-9923-4f66-bb8d-3b47059957a7) URON Entertainment Corp. CAN. Dist: Diamond Comic Distributors, Inc.

Armentrout, Jennifer L. The Darkest Star. 2019. (Origin Ser.: 1). (ENG.). 384p. (YA). pap. 11.99 (978-1-250-17571-7(2), 900189438, Tor Teen) Doherty, Tom Assocs., LLC.

—Lux: Consequences (Opal & Origin) 2014. (Lux Novel Ser.: Bks. 3-4). (ENG.). 800p. (YA). (gr. 7-12). 19.99 (978-1-62266-481-8(7), 900140857) Entangled Publishing, LLC.

—Lux: Opposition: Special Collector's Edition. collector's ed. 2014. (Lux Novel Ser.: 5). (ENG.). 500p. (YA). 19.99 (978-1-62266-733-8(6), 900146176) Entangled Publishing, LLC.

—Obsidian. 2012. (Lux Novel Ser.: 1). (ENG.). 400p. (YA). pap. 11.99 (978-1-62061-007-7(8), 900148865) Entangled Publishing, LLC.

—Onyx: A Lux Novel. 2012. (Lux Novel Ser.: 2). (ENG.). 416p. (YA). pap. 10.99 (978-1-62061-011-4(6), 900148866) Entangled Publishing, LLC.

—Opal: A Lux Novel. 2012. (Lux Novel Ser.: 3). (ENG.). 452p. (YA). (gr. 9). pap. 11.99 (978-1-62061-009-1(4), 900148867) Entangled Publishing, LLC.

—Opposition. (ENG.). 2016. (Lux Novel Ser.: 5). 300p. (YA). pap. 11.99 (978-1-63375-694-6(7), 900176110) 2013. (Lux Ser.: Bk. 5). (J). pap. 9.99 (978-1-62266-026-1(9), Entangled Teen) Entangled Publishing, LLC.

—Origin. 2013. (ENG.). (Lux Ser.: Bk. 4). (J). pap. 9.99 (978-1-62061-280-4(1)); (Lux Novel Ser.: 4). 400p. (YA). (gr. 7-12). pap. 10.99 (978-1-62266-075-9(7), 900128407) Entangled Publishing, LLC.

Armstrong, Jennifer. The Kiln. 2004. (Fire-Us Ser.: No. 3). (ENG.). 256p. (J). (gr. 7-18). pap. 5.99 (978-0-06-447271-5(X)) HarperCollins Pubs.

Armstrong, Jennifer & Butcher, Nancy. The Kiln. 2003. (Fire-Us Ser.: Bk. 3). (ENG.). 208p. (J). (gr. 7-18). 15.99 (978-0-06-008050-1(7)) HarperCollins Pubs.

Arnett, Mindee. Avalon. 2014. (Avalon Ser.: 1). (ENG.). 432p. (YA). (gr. 8). 17.99 (978-0-06-223559-6(1), Balzer & Bray) HarperCollins Pubs.

—Polaris. 2015. (Avalon Ser.: 2). (ENG.). 432p. (YA). (gr. 8). 17.99 (978-0-06-223562-6(1), Balzer & Bray) HarperCollins Pubs.

Arnold, Michelle Lee. Mathew Sunburst & the Keepers of the Sky. 2003. 141p. (J). pap. 13.95 (978-0-7414-1575-2(5)) Infinity Publishing.

Arnold, Shari. Mystique. 2012. (YA). (978-1-4521-0363-1(1)) Chronicle Bks. LLC.

Artifact Group, The & Shepherd, Jodie. Robot Rampage! 2009. (Backyardigans Ser.). (ENG.). 24p. (J). (gr. -1-1). pap. 3.99 (978-1-4169-9013-0(5), Simon Spotlight/Nickelodeon) Simon Spotlight/Nickelodeon.

Artus, William. The King on the Moon. 2008. 32p. pap. 20.95 (978-1-4092-3044-1(9)) Lulu Pr., Inc.

Ashes, Dustin. Space-Boot Johnny Recharged. 2010. (J). pap. 10.95 (978-0-7414-5900-8(0)) Infinity Publishing.

The Ask & the Answer (with Bonus Short Story) Chaos Walking: Book Two. 2014. (Chaos Walking Ser.: 2). (ENG., Illus.). 560p. (YA). (gr. 9). pap. 12.00 (978-0-7636-7617-9(9)) Candlewick Pr.

Aslan, Austin. The Islands at the End of the World. 2015. (Islands at the End of the World Ser.). (ENG., Illus.). 384p. (YA). (gr. 7). pap. 10.99 (978-0-385-74403-4(X), Ember) Random Hse. Children's Bks.

Astro, Ian. Moon School, 1 vol. 2006. (Neighborhood Readers Ser.). (ENG.). 16p. (gr. 1-2). pap. 6.50 (978-1-4042-7196-8(1), 5462beef-9025-4a84-b0cd-78c50d2a7eb8, Rosen Classroom) Rosen Publishing Group, Inc., The.

Atticus, C. J. Stranded in Space: The Stellar Life of Jpeg the Robot Dog. Domschke, Angelika, illus. 2013. 119p. (J). pap. 6.95 (978-0-9887780-2-3(5)) Atticus, C. J.

Auerbach, Annie. The Grosse Adventures: The Good, the Bad, & the Gassy, Vol. 1. Norton, Mike, illus. 2006. (Grosse Adventures Manga Ser.: 1). (ENG.). 96p. (J). (gr. 4-1). pap. 9.99 (978-1-59816-049-9(4)) TOKYOPOP, Inc.

Avi. Poppy's Return. Floca, Brian, illus. (J). 2020. (Poppy Ser.: 6). (ENG.). 256p. (gr. 3-7). pap. 7.99 (978-0-06-000014-1(7), HarperCollins) 2005. (Poppy Stories Ser.). 240p. lib. bdg. 16.89 (978-0-06-000013-4(9)) HarperCollins Pubs.

AWRP Meet Superkids. (J). pap., stu. ed. (978-0-201-21600-4(0)) Addison-Wesley Longman, Inc.

Bach, Ari. Ragnarok. 2016. (ENG., Illus.). (YA). (gr. 9-12). 32.99 (978-1-63533-067-0(X), Harmony Ink Pr.) Dreamspinner Pr.

—Valhalla. 2nd ed. (ENG., (YA). 2016. Illus.). (gr. 9-12). 29.99 (978-1-63477-990-6(8)) 2014. (Valhalla Ser.: 1). 330p. pap. 17.99 (978-1-62798-718-9(5)) Dreamspinner Pr. (Harmony Ink Pr.).

Bachorz, Pam. Candor. 2011. (ENG.). 256p. (gr. 9-12). lib. bdg. 24.94 (978-1-60684-044-3(4)) Farshore GBR. Dist: Children's Plus, Inc.

—Drought. 2011. (ENG.). 400p. (YA). (gr. 7-12). 17.99 (978-1-60684-016-0(9), 287c1b93-a51d-4c11-892e-c61df04d0ed9, Carolrhoda Lab™) Lerner Publishing Group.

Bacigalupi, Paolo. The Drowned Cities. 2013. (ENG.). 464p. (J). (gr. 10-17). pap. 12.99 (978-0-316-05622-9(7)) 2012. 448p. (YA). 17.99 (978-0-316-20037-0(9)) Little, Brown Bks. for Young Readers.

—The Drowned Cities. 2012. 352p. (978-1-59606-506-2(0)) Subterranean Pr.

—The Drowned Cities. 2013. (J). lib. bdg. 22.10 (978-0-606-31749-8(X)) Turtleback.

—Ship Breaker (National Book Award Finalist) 2011. (ENG.). 352p. (YA). (gr. 10-17). pap. 12.99 (978-0-316-05619-9(7)) Little, Brown Bks. for Young Readers.

—Tool of War. (Ship Breaker Ser.). (ENG.). 384p. (YA). 2018. (gr. 9-17). pap. 19.99 (978-0-316-22081-1(7)) 2017. (gr. 10-17). 17.99 (978-0-316-22083-5(3)) Little, Brown Bks. for Young Readers.

Bacigalupi, Paolo, et al. Diverse Energies, 1 vol. Buckell, Tobias S. & Monti, Joe, eds. 2012. (ENG., Illus.). 368p. (YA). (gr. 8-12). pap. 13.95 (978-1-62014-011-6(X), leelowtu) Lee & Low Bks., Inc.

Bacon, Lee. The Last Human. 2019. (Last Human Ser.). (ENG., Illus.). 288p. (YA). (gr. 3-7). 16.99 (978-1-4197-3691-9(4), 1266301, Amulet Bks.) Abrams, Inc.

Baggott, Julianna. Burn. 2014. (Pure Trilogy Ser.: 3). (ENG.). 432p. 26.00 (978-1-4555-0299-8(5)) Grand Central Publishing.

—Fuse. 2013. (ENG.). 416p. pap. 14.99 (978-1-4555-2169-2(8)) Grand Central Publishing.

Bailey, Kristin. Legacy of the Clockwork Key. (Secret Order Ser.: 1). (ENG., (YA). (gr. 9). 2014. Illus.). 432p. pap. 9.99 (978-1-4424-4027-2(9)) 2013. 416p. 17.99 (978-1-4424-4026-5(0)) Simon Pulse. (Simon Pulse).

—Rise of the Arcane Fire. 2014. (Secret Order Ser.: 2). (ENG., Illus.). 464p. (YA). (gr. 9). 17.99 (978-1-4424-6802-3(5), Simon Pulse) Simon Pulse.

—Shadow of the War Machine. 2015. (Secret Order Ser.: 3). (ENG., Illus.). 448p. (YA). (gr. 9). 17.99 (978-1-4424-6805-4(X), Simon Pulse) Simon Pulse.

Bailey, Mary. Vhan Zeely & the Time Prevaricators. 2009. 192p. 25.50 (978-1-60693-477-7(5), Eloquent Bks.) Strategic Book Publishing & Rights Agency (SBPRA).

Bailey-Peiffer, Stefanie & Bailey-Yarbrough, Caroline. Modie & the Power of the BellKeys. 2004. pap. 8.95 (978-0-9762502-0-3(9)) Hudson Bks.

Baker, Chandler. This Is Not the End. 2018. (ENG.). 384p. (YA). (gr. 9-17). pap. 9.99 (978-1-4847-9009-0(X)) Hyperion Bks. for Children.

Bakowski, Barbara & Brent Sandvold, Lynnette. Superhero Science: Kapow! Comic Book Crime Fighters Put Physics to the Test, 1 vol. 2009. (Current Science Ser.). (ENG.). 48p. (YA). (gr. 4-6). lib. bdg. 33.67 (978-1-4339-2243-5(6), 8d91c020-b1c8-4630-a920-11cc55c995ed) Stevens, Gareth Publishing LLLP.

Balian, Lorna. Humbug Witch: Spanish, 1 vol. 2003.Tr. of Humbug Witch. (SPA., Illus.). 32p. (J). (gr. -1). pap. 4.95 (978-1-59572-011-5(1)) Star Bright Bks., Inc.

Ball, Nate. Alien in My Pocket #3: Radio Active. Pamintuan, Macky, illus. 2014. (Alien in My Pocket Ser.: 3). (ENG.). 144p. (J). (gr. 1-5). pap. 4.99 (978-0-06-221627-4(9), HarperCollins) HarperCollins Pubs.

—Blast Off! 2014. (Alien in My Pocket Ser.: 1). (J). lib. bdg. 14.75 (978-0-606-35181-2(7)) Turtleback.

—Forces of Nature. 2015. (Alien in My Pocket Ser.: 6). (J). lib. bdg. 14.75 (978-0-606-37611-2(9)) Turtleback.

—On Impact! 2014. (Alien in My Pocket Ser.: 4). (J). lib. bdg. 14.75 (978-0-606-35952-8(4)) Turtleback.

—Space Invaders. 2016. (Alien in My Pocket Ser.: 8). (J). lib. bdg. 14.75 (978-0-606-38752-1(8)) Turtleback.

Baltazar, Armand. Timeless: Diego & the Rangers of the Vastlantic. Baltazar, Armand, illus. (Timeless Ser.: 1). (ENG., Illus.). 624p. (J). (gr. 3-7). 2019. pap. 12.99 (978-0-06-240237-0(4)) 2017. 19.99 (978-0-06-240236-3(6)) HarperCollins Pubs. (Tegen, Katherine Bks).

Baltazar, Art. Powers in Action Volume 1. 2020. (ENG., Illus.). 128p. (J). pap. 9.99 (978-1-63229-441-8(9), b832908e-fcc9-4356-bff4-b02c43131429) Action Lab Entertainment.

Banim, Lisa. Case of the Missing She-Geek. 2004. 125p. (J). lib. bdg. 16.92 (978-1-4242-0683-4(9)) Fitzgerald Bks.

Banks, Alex. Jump Boys: Sos. 2013. 200p. pap. (978-0-9918599-6-2(0)) Novel Ninjutsu.

Bankston, John. Ray Bradbury. 2011. (ENG., Illus.). 140p. (gr. 6-12). 35.00 (978-1-60413-778-1(9), P189898, Facts On File) Infobase Holdings, Inc.

Barbara Stathi. Sacrifice. 2009. 312p. pap. 18.95 (978-1-4401-7699-9(X)) iUniverse, Inc.

Barbini, F. T. Tijaran Tales: White Child. 2011. 214p. pap. (978-0-7552-1349-8(1)) Authors OnLine, Ltd.

Bardugo, Leigh. Wonder Woman: Warbringer. (DC Icons Ser.). (ENG.). (YA). (gr. 7). 2019. 464p. pap. 12.99 (978-0-399-54976-2(5), Ember) 2017. 384p. 18.99 (978-0-399-54973-1(0), Random Hse. Bks. for Young Readers) Random Hse. Children's Bks.

—Wonder Woman: Warbringer. Pelea Como una Guerrera (Spanish Edition) 2018. (Dc Icons Ser.: 1). (SPA.). 432p. (YA). (gr. 8-12). pap. 16.95 (978-607-31-5969-2(2), Montena) Penguin Random House Grupo Editorial ESP. Dist: Penguin Random Hse. LLC.

Bardugo, Leigh, et al. The DC Icons Series Boxed Set: Catwoman; Batman; Wonder Woman, 3 vols. 2018. (DC Icons Ser.). 304p. (YA). (gr. 7). 56.97 (978-1-9848-4898-7(4), Random Hse. Bks. for Young Readers) Random Hse. Children's Bks.

Barlow, Dave. The Seekers. 2004. 48p. 3.95 (978-0-9725230-4-2(9)) Wandering Sage Pubns., LLC.

Barlow, Jeremy. Star Wars Adventures: Boba Fett & the Ship of Fear. Daxiong Staff, illus. 2013. (Star Wars Digests Ser.). (ENG.). 80p. (J). (gr. 3-8). lib. bdg. 34.21 (978-1-61479-056-3(6), 13759, Graphic Novels) Spotlight.

Barlow, Steve & Skidmore, Steve. Stone Me! Ross, Tony, illus. 2005. (Mad Myths Ser.). 122p. (J). pap. 5.95 (978-1-903015-43-8(X)) Barn Owl Bks, London GBR. Dist: Independent Pubs. Group.

Barnacott, Anthony Royce. Permanoids of Chilon. 2009. 260p. 27.99 (978-1-4389-3824-0(1)) AuthorHouse.

Barnes, Jennifer Lynn. Nobody. 2014. (ENG.). 400p. (YA). (gr. 7-12). pap. 14.99 (978-1-60684-508-0(X), 929b4dd8-ff43-47e1-b0c4-5807b46bfe3c, Carolrhoda Lab™) Lerner Publishing Group.

Barns, Crosby H. Who Programmed the Species? The Theory of Scientific Coincidence. 2008. 36p. pap. 16.99 (978-1-4389-0727-7(3)) AuthorHouse.

Barr, Lester. Robots Land at Manchester Airport. 2012. (Illus.). 80p. pap. 13.66 (978-1-4772-2248-5(0)) AuthorHouse.

Barrera, J. Mario. Nine Moons. 2005. (ENG & SPA., Illus.). (YA). cd-rom 21.99 (978-0-9752725-2-7(7)) Orion-Cosmos.

Barrowman, John & Barrowman, Carole. Inquisitor. 2018. (Orion Chronicles Ser.: 3). (ENG.). 320p. (YA). (gr. 7). 19.99 (978-1-78185-645-1(1)) Head of Zeus GBR. Dist: Independent Pubs. Group.

Barry, William J. Forever Awakening. 2014. 242p. pap. 18.50 (978-1-61213-113-9(1)) Writer's Coffee Shop, The.

Barth, Kathleen E. The Amazing Adventures of Quigley D Pigley & His Friends: How to Become an Astronaut. 2009. 16p. pap. 8.49 (978-1-4389-8606-7(8)) AuthorHouse.

Bartol, Amy A. Darken the Stars, 0 vols. 2015. (Kricket Ser.: 3). (ENG.). 302p. pap. 14.95 (978-1-5039-4742-9(4), 9781503947429, 47North) Amazon Publishing.

Bartow, Philip. T & the Jello Castle-Book 2: Bio Bots. 2013. 264p. (J). pap. 13.30 (978-0-9835176-3-4(0)) Institute For Outdoor Awareness, Inc.

The Bash Street Kids Annual 2004. annuals 2003. (Illus.). 96p. (978-0-85116-815-9(9)) Thomson, D.C. & Co., Ltd. GBR. Dist: APG Sales & Distribution Services.

Basic, Zdenko, illus. Steampunk: H. G. Wells. 2013. (ENG.). 408p. (YA). (gr. 7-17). 18.95 (978-0-7624-4444-1(4), Running Pr. Kids) Running Pr.

Bassett, Jennifer. Oxford Bookworms Library: the Omega Files DS Short Stories: Level 1: 400-Word Vocabulary. 3rd ed. 2008. (ENG., Illus.). 64p. 11.00 (978-0-19-478913-4(6)) Oxford Univ. Pr., Inc.

Baum, L. Frank, et al. A Children's Treasury. 2007. 792p. per. 24.95 (978-1-60459-011-1(4)) Wilder Pubns., Corp.

Baxendale, Trevor & BBC. Doctor Who: Choose the Future: Terror Moon. 2016. (ENG.). 208p. (J). pap. 9.99 (978-1-4059-2651-5(1), 8d68da6f-aacb-4610-84c3-1e50439fc6c3) Penguin Bks., Ltd. GBR. Dist: Diamond Comic Distributors, Inc.

Baxendale, Trevor & British Broadcasting Corporation Children's Books Staff. Doctor Who: Heart of Stone: Heart of Stone. 2015. (ENG.). 160p. (YA). pap. 9.99 (978-1-4059-2216-6(8), 9b0ad1f0-e6a0-4657-ba31-eb48a4b18968) Penguin Bks., Ltd. GBR. Dist: Diamond Comic Distributors, Inc.

BBC. Doctor Who How to Be a Time Lord: The Official Guide. 2015. (Illus.). 176p. (YA). 16.99 (978-0-7232-9436-8(4), 3388e08b-78bc-47bd-8887-0116bf2d050d) Penguin Bks., Ltd. GBR. Dist: Diamond Comic Distributors, Inc.

—Doctor Who: Tales of Terror. 2018. (ENG., Illus.). 272p. (J). 16.99 (978-1-4059-3003-1(9), 5b2dda25-4965-4f07-80c0-f2db1f01ba94) Penguin Bks., Ltd. GBR. Dist: Diamond Comic Distributors, Inc.

—Doctor Who: the Day She Saved the Doctor: Four Stories from the TARDIS. 2018. (ENG.). 192p. (J). 14.99 (978-1-4059-2997-4(9), abb335a4-a5f1-4d20-9866-f091458cbd87) Penguin Bks., Ltd. GBR. Dist: Diamond Comic Distributors, Inc.

BBC Books Staff. Doctor Who - 12 Doctors 12 Stories. 2014. (ENG.). 528p. (YA). pap. 16.99 (978-0-14-135535-1(2)) Penguin Bks., Ltd. GBR. Dist: Diamond Bk. Distributors.

BBC Children's Books. Doctor Who: Heroes & Monsters Collection. 2015. 336p. (J). pap. 9.99 *(978-1-4059-2268-5(0),* 77b1375f-bd36-433f-b297-691dfcc6084a) Penguin Bks., Ltd. GBR. Dist: Diamond Comic Distributors, Inc.

Beach, John, reader. Moo Cow Kaboom! unabr. ed. 2005. (Picture Book Readalong Ser.). (J). (gr. -1-2). 28.95 incl. audio compact disk *(978-1-59519-502-9(5))* Live Oak Media.

Beacham, Travis. Pacific Rim: Tales from Year Zero. 2013. (ENG., Illus.). 128p. (gr. 8-17). 24.99 *(978-0-7851-5394-8(2))* Legendary Comics.

Beagle, Peter S. & Link, Kelly. Superheroes. Horton, Rich, ed. 2013. (ENG.). 384p. pap. 15.95 *(978-1-60701-380-8(0),* a30345cb-0c89-4eef-82f0-c0b8abc8ded4) Prime.

Beaudoin, Sean. Fade to Blue. 2011. (ENG., Illus.). 208p. (YA). (gr. 6-8). 24.94 *(978-0-316-01417-5(6))* Little Brown & Co.

Beauregard, Lynda. Summer Camp Science Mysteries. Helmer, Der-shing, illus. 2012. (Summer Camp Science Mysteries Ser.). (ENG.). 48p. (J). (gr. 3-6). pap. 52.82 *(978-0-7613-9272-9(6))*;Pack, Set. pap. 316.92 *(978-0-7613-9273-6(4))* Lerner Publishing Group. (Graphic Universe™).

Beck, A. E. Master-E: Travel into Mystical Dragon Dimensions: Collision of Fantasy, Science Fiction & Physics. 2010. 212p. pap. 49.49 *(978-1-4490-3612-6(0))* AuthorHouse.

Becker, Lindsey. The Star Thief. 2018. (ENG., Illus.). 416p. (J). (gr. 3-7). pap. 7.99 *(978-0-316-34853-9(8))* Little, Brown Bks. for Young Readers.

Becker, Savan. Starry Night (2nd Edition) 2008. 60p. pap. 25.95 *(978-0-615-23554-7(9))* Becker, Savan C.

Beecroft, Simon. Beware the Dark Side. 2007. (DK Readers Level 4 Ser.). (ENG., Illus.). 48p. (J). (gr. 2-4). lib. bdg. 16.19 *(978-0-7566-3115-4(7))* Dorling Kindersley Publishing, Inc.

—Chewbacca & the Wookiee Warriors. 2012. (Star Wars: the Clone Wars DK Readers Ser.). lib. bdg. 13.55 *(978-0-606-26456-3(6))* Turtleback.

—DK Readers L4: Star Wars: Beware the Dark Side: Discover the Sith's Evil Schemes ... 2007. (DK Readers Level 4 Ser.). (ENG., Illus.). 48p. (J). (gr. 4-7). pap. 4.99 *(978-0-7566-3114-7(9),* DK Children) Dorling Kindersley Publishing, Inc.

—DK Readers L4: Star Wars: Epic Battles: Find Out about the Galaxy's Scariest Clashes! 2008. (DK Readers Level 4 Ser.). (ENG., Illus.). 48p. (J). (gr. 3-7). pap. 4.99 *(978-0-7566-3603-6(5),* DK Children) Dorling Kindersley Publishing, Inc.

—Jedi Adventures. 2009. (Star Wars: the Clone Wars DK Readers Ser.). lib. bdg. 13.55 *(978-0-606-06254-1(8))* Turtleback.

—R2-D2 & Friends. 2008. (Star Wars DK Readers Level 2 Ser.). (Illus.). 32p. lib. bdg. 13.55 *(978-1-4364-5044-7(6))* Turtleback.

—Star Wars: Death Star Battles. 2016. (Star Wars DK Readers Level 3 Ser.). (ENG., Illus.). 48p. (J). (gr. 2-4). lib. bdg. 13.55 *(978-0-606-39358-4(7))* Turtleback.

Behling, Steve. Iron Man: Invasion of the Space Phantoms. 2016. (Mighty Marvel Chapter Bks.). (J). lib. bdg. 16.00 *(978-0-606-38305-9(0))* Turtleback.

—Iron Man: Invasion of the Space Phantoms. Pham, Khoi & Sotomayor, Chris, illus. 2018. (Mighty Marvel Chapter Bks.). (ENG.). 128p. (J). (gr. 2-7). lib. bdg. 31.36 *(978-1-5321-4217-8(X),* 28554, Chapter Bks.) Spotlight.

Bell, David. Pink Alert! 2007. (Dawn Gray Ser.). (ENG.). 260p. pap. *(978-1-84167-581-7(4))* Ransom Publishing Ltd.

Bell, Janet. Eyes of the Soul. 2003. pap. 24.95 *(978-1-4137-0425-9(5))* America Star Bks.

Belleza, Rhoda. Empress of a Thousand Skies. 2017. (ENG.). 352p. (YA). (gr. 7). pap. 9.99 *(978-1-101-99911-0(X),* Razorbill) Penguin Young Readers Group.

Bellin, Joshua David. Freefall. 2017. (ENG., Illus.). 368p. (YA). (gr. 9). 18.99 *(978-1-4814-9165-5(2),* McElderry, Margaret K. Bks.) McElderry, Margaret K. Bks.

—Scavenger of Souls. 2016. (ENG., Illus.). 368p. (YA). (gr. 9). 18.99 *(978-1-4814-6244-0(X),* McElderry, Margaret K. Bks.) McElderry, Margaret K. Bks.

—Survival Colony 9. 2015. (ENG., Illus.). 336p. (YA). (gr. 9). pap. 12.99 *(978-1-4814-0355-9(9),* McElderry, Margaret K. Bks.) McElderry, Margaret K. Bks.

Bendis, Brian Michael. Spider-Man - Miles Morales, Vol. 3. Brown, Patrick & Kudranski, Szymon, illus. 2017. (Spider-Man Ser.: 3). 160p. (gr. 4-17). pap. 19.99 *(978-1-302-90597-2(X),* Marvel Universe) Marvel Worldwide, Inc.

Benintendi, Steve. Underfire. 2003. (Powermark Comics Ser.). (Illus.). 32p. (J). pap. 2.95 *(978-0-9705669-2-8(1))* PowerMark Productions.

Bennett, Jeffrey. Max Goes to Mars: A Science Adventure with Max the Dog. Okamoto, Alan, illus. 2015. (Science Adventures with Max the Dog Ser.). (ENG.). 32p. (J). (gr. 2-4). 15.00 *(978-1-937548-44-5(9))* Big Kid Science.

—Max Goes to the Moon: A Science Adventure with Max the Dog. Okamoto, Alan, illus. 2nd ed. 2012. (Science Adventures with Max the Dog Ser.). (ENG.). 32p. (J). (gr. 2-4). 15.00 *(978-1-937548-20-9(1))* Big Kid Science.

—Max Goes to the Space Station: A Science Adventure with Max the Dog. Carroll, Michael, illus. 2013. (Science Adventures with Max the Dog Ser.). (ENG.). 32p. (J). (gr. 2-4). 15.00 *(978-1-937548-28-5(7))* Big Kid Science.

Bennett, Jeffrey, et al. Max Goes to Jupiter: A Science Adventure with Max the Dog. Carroll, Michael, illus. 2nd ed. 2018. (Science Adventures with Max the Dog Ser.). (ENG.). 32p. (J). (gr. k-8). 15.00 *(978-1-937548-82-7(1))* Big Kid Science.

Benton, Jim. The Fran That Time Forgot. Benton, Jim, illus. 4th ed. 2005. (Franny K. Stein, Mad Scientist Ser.: 4). (ENG., Illus.). 112p. (J). (gr. 2-5). mass mkt. 6.99 *(978-0-689-86298-4(9))*; 17.99 *(978-0-689-86294-6(6))* Simon & Schuster Bks. For Young Readers. (Simon & Schuster Bks. For Young Readers).

—The Invisible Fran. Benton, Jim, illus. 2005. (Franny K. Stein, Mad Scientist Ser.: 3). (ENG., Illus.). 112p. (J). (gr. 2-5). pap. 7.99 *(978-0-689-86297-7(0),* Simon & Schuster Bks. For Young Readers) Simon & Schuster Bks. For Young Readers.

—The Invisible Fran. Benton, Jim, illus. 2011. (Franny K. Stein, Mad Scientist Ser.). (ENG., Illus.). 112p. (J). (gr. 2-6). 31.36 *(978-1-59961-819-7(2),* 7829, Chapter Bks.) Spotlight.

—Let's Do a Thing! (Victor Shmud, Total Expert #1), 1 vol. Benton, Jim, illus. 2017. (Victor Shmud, Total Expert Ser.: 1). (ENG., Illus.). 128p. (J). (gr. 2-5). pap. 5.99 *(978-0-545-93229-5(7),* Scholastic Paperbacks) Scholastic, Inc.

—Lunch Walks among Us. Benton, Jim, illus. 2004. (Franny K. Stein, Mad Scientist Ser.: 1). (Illus.). 102p. (gr. 2-5). lib. bdg. 16.00 *(978-1-4176-4054-6(5))* Turtleback.

Bergeron, Alain M. Capitaine Static. Sampar, illus. 2021. (Capitaine Static Ser.: 1). (FRE.). 56p. (J). (gr. 1-3). pap. 12.95 *(978-2-7644-0568-0(5))* Quebec Amerique CAN. Dist: Orca Bk. Pubs. USA.

Bergin, Virginia. The XY. 2018. (ENG.). 352p. (YA). (gr. 8-12). 17.99 *(978-1-4926-6217-4(8))* Sourcebooks, Inc.

Bernard, Romily. Never Apart. 2017. (ENG.). 400p. (J). 17.99 *(978-1-63375-822-3(2),* 9781633758223) Entangled Publishing, LLC.

Berne, Emma Carlson. Daring Adventures. 2017. (Illus.). 116p. (J). *(978-1-5444-0002-0(0))* Disney Publishing Worldwide.

Besser, KennethR. Arnie Carver & the Plague of Demeverde. 2007. (Illus.). x, 338p. (J). *(978-1-934316-02-3(4))* RTMC Organization, LLC.

Bethune, Helen. A Bright New Day, 1 vol. rev. ed. 2013. (Literary Text Ser.). (ENG., Illus.). 32p. (J). (gr. 2-4). pap. 11.99 *(978-1-4333-5640-7(6))* Teacher Created Materials, Inc.

Bichoman Vuelve de la Tumba. (Fantasmas de Fear Street Coleccion). (SPA.). (YA). (gr. 5-8). pap. 7.95 *(978-950-04-1718-1(9),* EM9292) Emecé Editores S.A. ARG. Dist: Lectorum Pubns., Inc., Planeta Publishing Corp.

Bick, Ilsa J. Ashes. 2012. (Ashes Trilogy Ser.: Bk. 1). (ENG.). 480p. (YA). (gr. 9-12). pap. 17.99 *(978-1-60684-385-7(0),* 49a7f184-e32c-49cf-ac7d-91c59f25b4dc, Carolrhoda Lab™) Lerner Publishing Group.

—The Dickens Mirror. 2015. (Dark Passages Ser.: 2). (ENG.). 576p. (YA). (gr. 9-12). E-Book 29.32 *(978-1-5124-0177-6(3),* Carolrhoda Lab™) Lerner Publishing Group.

—Monsters. 2014. (Ashes Trilogy Ser.). (ENG.). 688p. (YA). (gr. 9-12). pap. 17.99 *(978-1-60684-544-8(6),* 7d912f36-8c5b-416f-8a24-12a20a671761, Carolrhoda Lab™) Lerner Publishing Group.

—Shadows. 2013. (Ashes Trilogy Ser.: Bk. 2). (ENG.). 528p. (YA). (gr. 9-12). pap. 17.99 *(978-1-60684-445-8(8),* 2bf296e8-9263-4946-aaf1-1b28a02600de, Carolrhoda Lab™) Lerner Publishing Group.

Biggs, Stephen. The Time Barrel. 2009. 152p. pap. *(978-1-84923-434-4(5))* YouWriteOn.

Bily, Ro. My Red Island in the Sky. 2012. 530p. 34.95 *(978-1-4626-6645-4(0))*; pap. 34.95 *(978-1-4626-6971-4(9))* America Star Bks.

Binding, Tim. Sylvie & the Songman. 2011. (ENG.). 352p. (J). (gr. 4-6). lib. bdg. 22.44 *(978-0-385-75159-9(1),* Yearling) Random Hse. Children's Bks.

Birch, Kate Jarvik. Tarnished. (Perfected Ser.: 2). (ENG.). 304p. (YA). 2018. pap. 9.99 *(978-1-63375-904-6(0),* 9781633759046) 2015. (gr. 7-12). 16.99 *(978-1-63375-127-9(9),* 9781633751279) Entangled Publishing, LLC.

Black, Cally. In the Dark Spaces. 2017. (ENG.). 328p. (YA). (gr. 7). pap. 18.99 *(978-1-76012-864-7(3))* Hardie Grant Children?s Publishing AUS. Dist: Independent Pubs. Group.

Black, Holly. Black Heart. (Curse Workers Ser.: 3). (ENG.). (YA). (gr. 9). 2013. 320p. pap. 12.99 *(978-1-4424-0347-5(0))*3. 2012. 304p. 19.99 *(978-1-4424-0346-8(2))* McElderry, Margaret K. Bks. (McElderry, Margaret K. Bks.).

—Red Glove. 2012. (Curse Workers Ser.: 2). (ENG.). 352p. (YA). (gr. 9). pap. 12.99 *(978-1-4424-0340-6(3),* McElderry, Margaret K. Bks.) McElderry, Margaret K. Bks.

—Red Glove, 2. 2011. (Curse Workers Ser.: 2). (ENG.). 336p. (YA). (gr. 9-12). 19.99 *(978-1-4424-0339-0(X))* Simon & Schuster, Inc.

—White Cat. (Curse Workers Ser.: 1). (ENG.). (YA). (gr. 9). 2011. 336p. pap. 11.99 *(978-1-4169-6397-4(9))* 2010. 320p. 17.99 *(978-1-4169-6396-7(0))* McElderry, Margaret K. Bks. (McElderry, Margaret K. Bks.).

Black, Holly & Blackman, Marjorie. Doctor Who 12 Doctors 12 Stories. 2014. (ENG., Illus.). 528p. (YA). pap. 16.99 *(978-0-14-135988-5(9),* 8019dfdc-9e32-4830-bac5-ae0769833a1c) Penguin Bks., Ltd. GBR. Dist: Diamond Comic Distributors, Inc.

Black, Jenna. Replica. 2013. (Replica Ser.: 1). (ENG.). 368p. (YA). (gr. 8-12). pap. 18.99 *(978-0-7653-3371-1(6),* 900086439, Tor Teen) Doherty, Tom Assocs., LLC.

—Resistance. 2014. (Replica Ser.: 2). (ENG.). 368p. (YA). (gr. 8-12). pap. 18.99 *(978-0-7653-3372-8(4),* 900086440, Tor Teen) Doherty, Tom Assocs., LLC.

—Revolution. 2014. (Replica Ser.: 3). (ENG.). 400p. (YA). (gr. 8-12). pap. 19.99 *(978-0-7653-3373-5(2),* 900086441, Tor Teen) Doherty, Tom Assocs., LLC.

Black, Natalie & Black, Melissa. Double Sided: A Teen Novel. 2010. 124p. 23.50 *(978-1-4520-7415-3(1))*; pap. 12.99 *(978-1-4520-7416-0(X))* AuthorHouse.

Blackburn, Sheila M. Stewie Scraps & the Space Racer. 2008. 68p. pap. *(978-1-903853-84-9(2))* Brilliant Pubns.

Blackman, Haden. Darth Vader & the Lost Command. Leonardi, Rick, illus. 2012. (Star Wars: Darth Vader & the Lost Command Ser.). (ENG.). 24p. (J). (gr. 6-12). 31.36 *(978-1-59961-980-4(6),* 13805, Graphic Novels) Spotlight.

—Darth Vader & the Lost Command. Leonardi, Rick et al, illus. 2012. (Star Wars: Darth Vader & the Lost Command Ser.). (ENG.). 24p. (J). (gr. 6-12). 31.36 *(978-1-59961-983-5(0),* 13808, Graphic Novels) Spotlight.

—Darth Vader & the Lost Command, Vol. 2. Leonardi, Rick, illus. 2012. (Star Wars: Darth Vader & the Lost Command Ser.). (ENG.). 24p. (J). (gr. 6-12). 31.36 *(978-1-59961-981-1(4),* 13806, Graphic Novels) Spotlight.

—Darth Vader & the Lost Command, Vol. 3. Leonardi, Rick et al, illus. 2012. (Star Wars: Darth Vader & the Lost Command Ser.). (ENG.). 24p. (J). (gr. 6-12). 31.36 *(978-1-59961-982-8(2),* 13807, Graphic Novels) Spotlight.

—Lost Command. Leonardi, Rick, illus. 2012. (Star Wars: Darth Vader & the Lost Command Ser.). (ENG.). 24p. (J). (gr. 6-12). 31.36 *(978-1-59961-984-2(9),* 13809, Graphic Novels) Spotlight.

Blackout! Individual Title Six-Packs. (Bookweb Ser.). 32p. (gr. 4-18). 34.00 *(978-0-7635-3728-9(4))* Rigby Education.

Blackwell, Paul. Undercurrent. 2014. (ENG.). 320p. (YA). (gr. 9). pap. 9.99 *(978-0-06-212352-7(1),* HarperTeen) HarperCollins Pubs.

Blakemore, Megan Frazer. The Daybreak Bond. 2018. (ENG.). 336p. (J). pap. 9.99 *(978-1-68119-896-5(7),* 900191672, Bloomsbury Children's Bks.) Bloomsbury Publishing USA.

—The Firefly Code. 2017. (ENG.). 368p. (J). pap. 9.99 *(978-1-68119-527-8(5),* 900176380, Bloomsbury USA Childrens) Bloomsbury Publishing USA.

—The Firefly Code. 2017. (J). lib. bdg. 18.40 *(978-0-606-40543-0(7))* Turtleback.

Bland, Ralph. Long Long Time. Barlow, Dave, illus. 2014. 251p. 13.50 *(978-1-933300-00-9(0))* Wandering Sage Pubns., LLC.

Blishen, Edward, compiled by. Out of This World: Science Fiction Stories. 2008. (ENG., Illus.). 272p. (YA). (gr. 5-8). pap. 21.19 *(978-0-7534-6246-1(X),* 9780753462461) Kingfisher Publications, plc GBR. Dist: Children's Plus, Inc.

Bloch, Robert. The Crowded Earth. 2009. 112p. pap. 9.95 *(978-1-60664-273-3(1))* Rodgers, Alan Bks.

Bodeen, S. A. The Gardener. 2011. (ENG.). 256p. (YA). (gr. 7-12). pap. 11.99 *(978-0-312-65942-4(3),* 900070540) Square Fish.

Bon, Kimberly. Mitchie's Amazing Adventures: Good Bye to Pluto. 2012. 48p. pap. 21.99 *(978-1-4685-5133-4(7))* AuthorHouse.

Boné, Thomas H., illus. The Teacher Who Would Not Retire Discovers a New Planet. 2009. (J). 17.95 *(978-0-9792918-3-8(6))* Blue Marlin Pubns.

Bortz, Fred. Envisioning Outer Space: Where Science & Fiction Meet. 2015. (J). lib. bdg. *(978-1-4677-3740-1(2))* Twenty First Century Bks.

Bow, Erin. The Swan Riders. 2017. (Prisoners of Peace Ser.). (ENG.). 384p. (YA). (gr. 9). pap. 11.99 *(978-1-4814-4275-6(9),* McElderry, Margaret K. Bks.) McElderry, Margaret K. Bks.

Bower, Eric. The Magnificent Flying Baron Estate. 2017. (Bizarre Baron Inventions Ser.: 1). (ENG., Illus.). 250p. (J). (gr. 4-7). 15.99 *(978-1-944995-13-3(7))* Amberjack Publishing Co.

Bowkett, Steve. Catch Minitales: Short Science Fiction Stories with a Sting! 2003. (ENG.). 152p. *(978-1-85539-175-8(9),* Network Continuum Education) Bloomsbury Publishing Plc.

Bowman, Erin. Forged. 2016. (Taken Ser.: 3). (ENG.). 384p. (YA). (gr. 8). pap. 10.99 *(978-0-06-211733-5(5),* HarperTeen) HarperCollins Pubs.

—Immunity. 2019. (Contagion Ser.: 2). (ENG., Illus.). 448p. (YA). (gr. 8). 17.99 *(978-0-06-257417-6(5),* HarperTeen) HarperCollins Pubs.

Boyd, Charles O'Halloran. Mountains of the North. 2009. 172p. pap. 13.95 *(978-1-4401-4228-4(9))* iUniverse, Inc.

Bracken, Alexandra. The Darkest Legacy-The Darkest Minds, Book 4. 2018. (Darkest Minds Novel Ser.: 4). (ENG.). 576p. (YA). (gr. 7-12). 18.99 *(978-1-368-02324-5(X),* Disney-Hyperion) Disney Publishing Worldwide.

—The Darkest Minds. 2013. (Darkest Minds Ser.: 1). (YA). lib. bdg. 20.85 *(978-0-606-36533-8(8))* Turtleback.

—The Darkest Minds Series Boxed Set [4-Book Paperback Boxed Set]-The Darkest Minds. 2018. (Darkest Minds Novel Ser.). (ENG.). 2096p. (YA). (gr. 7-12). 39.99 *(978-1-368-02337-5(1),* Disney-Hyperion) Disney Publishing Worldwide.

—Darkest Minds, the-A Darkest Minds Novel, Book 1. 2012. (Darkest Minds Novel Ser.: 1). (ENG.). 496p. (J). (gr. 5-9). 17.99 *(978-1-4231-5737-3(0),* Disney-Hyperion) Disney Publishing Worldwide.

—Darkest Minds, the (Bonus Content) 2018. (Darkest Minds Novel Ser.: 1). (ENG.). 576p. (YA). (gr. 7-12). pap. 11.99 *(978-1-368-02245-3(6),* Disney-Hyperion) Disney Publishing Worldwide.

—In the Afterlight. 2015. (Darkest Minds Ser.: 3). (YA). lib. bdg. 20.85 *(978-0-606-37505-4(8))* Turtleback.

—In the Afterlight (Bonus Content)-A Darkest Minds Novel, Book 3. 2018. (Darkest Minds Novel Ser.: 3). (ENG.). 624p. (YA). (gr. 7-12). pap. 10.99 *(978-1-368-02247-7(2),* Disney-Hyperion) Disney Publishing Worldwide.

—Never Fade. 2014. (Darkest Minds Ser.: 2). (YA). lib. bdg. 20.85 *(978-0-606-36534-5(6))* Turtleback.

—Never Fade (Bonus Content)-The Darkest Minds, Book 2. 2018. (Darkest Minds Novel Ser.: 2). (ENG.). 576p. (YA). (gr. 7-12). pap. 10.99 *(978-1-368-02246-0(4),* Disney-Hyperion) Disney Publishing Worldwide.

—Through the Dark (Bonus Content)-A Darkest Minds Collection. 2018. (Darkest Minds Novel Ser.). (ENG.). 448p. (YA). (gr. 7-12). 10.99 *(978-1-368-02248-4(0),* Disney-Hyperion) Disney Publishing Worldwide.

Brackett, Leigh & Coppel, Jr., Alfred. Planet Stories - Summer 1949. 2008. 128p. (YA). pap. 14.95 *(978-1-59798-181-1(8))* Adventure Hse.

Bradley, Marion Zimmer. The Planet Savers. 2011. 100p. 22.95 *(978-1-4638-9621-8(2))* Rodgers, Alan Bks.

Bradman, Tony. Alien. 2012. (Stoke Books Titles Ser.). 64p. (J). (gr. 5-8). pap. 7.95 *(978-1-78112-026-2(9))*; pap. 45.32 *(978-0-7613-9214-9(9))*; lib. bdg. 22.60 *(978-1-78112-025-5(0))* Stoke Bks.

Brady, Dustin & Brady, Jesse. Trapped in a Video Game: The Final Boss. 2019. (Trapped in a Video Game Ser.: 5). (ENG.). 208p. (J). 13.99 *(978-1-4494-9629-6(6))*;Volume 5. (Illus.). pap. 9.99 *(978-1-4494-9573-2(7))* Andrews McMeel Publishing.

Brallier, Max. Galactic Hot Dogs 1: Cosmoe's Wiener Getaway. Maguire, Rachel & Kelley, Nichole, illus. 2016. (Galactic Hot Dogs Ser.: 1). (ENG.). 304p. (J). (gr. 3-7). 14.99 *(978-1-4814-8098-7(7),* Aladdin) Simon & Schuster Children's Publishing.

—Galactic Hot Dogs 2: The Wiener Strikes Back. Maguire, Rachel & Kelley, Nichole, illus. 2016. (Galactic Hot Dogs Ser.: 2). (ENG.). 288p. (J). (gr. 3-7). 13.99 *(978-1-4814-2496-7(3),* Aladdin) Simon & Schuster Children's Publishing.

—Galactic Hot Dogs 3: Revenge of the Space Pirates. Maguire, Rachel & Kelley, Nichole, illus. 2017. (Galactic Hot Dogs Ser.: 3). (ENG.). 320p. (J). (gr. 3-7). 14.99 *(978-1-4814-2498-1(X),* Aladdin) Simon & Schuster Children's Publishing.

—Galactic Hot Dogs Collection (Boxed Set) Galactic Hot Dogs 1; Galactic Hot Dogs 2; Galactic Hot Dogs 3. Maguire, Rachel & Kelley, Nichole, illus. 2017. (Galactic Hot Dogs Ser.). (ENG.). 912p. (J). (gr. 3-7). 41.99 *(978-1-4814-9802-9(9),* Aladdin) Simon & Schuster Children's Publishing.

Bramlett, Timothy A. Sharkey Explores the Unknown. 2007. pap. 14.95 *(978-0-9796444-0-5(2))* Azuria Bks.

Branley, Franklyn M. The Moon Seems to Change. 2015. (Let's-Read-And-Find-Out Science: Stage 2 Ser.). (J). lib. bdg. 17.20 *(978-0-606-37639-6(9))* Turtleback.

Brashares, Ann. The Here & Now. 2015. lib. bdg. 22.10 *(978-0-606-37649-5(6))* Turtleback.

Braswell, Liz. The Fallen. movie tie-in ed. 2011. (Nine Lives of Chloe King Ser.: 1). (ENG.). 256p. (YA). (gr. 9). pap. 8.99 *(978-1-4424-4134-7(8),* Simon Pulse) Simon Pulse.

Braun, Eric. Rumpelstiltskin: An Interactive Fairy Tale Adventure. Brown, Alan, illus. 2017. (You Choose: Fractured Fairy Tales Ser.). (ENG.). 112p. (J). (gr. 3-7). pap. 6.95 *(978-1-5157-8777-8(X),* 136328); lib. bdg. 32.65 *(978-1-5157-8775-4(3),* 136326) Capstone. (Capstone Pr.).

Bray, Adam. Lego Star Wars: Into Battle! 2015. (DK Adventures Ser.). lib. bdg. 16.00 *(978-0-606-36923-7(6))* Turtleback.

Brege, K. B. Champ... A Wave of Terror! Five Ways to Finish. 2006. (Mick Morris Myth Solver Ser.: No. 3). (J). mass mkt. 6.99 *(978-0-9774119-2-4(3))* Team B Creative LLC.

Brennan, Herbie. The Secret Prophecy. 2012. (ENG.). 368p. (J). (gr. 3-7). 16.99 *(978-0-06-207180-4(7),* Balzer & Bray) HarperCollins Pubs.

Brett, Jan. Hedgie Blasts Off! Brett, Jan, illus. 2006. (Illus.). 32p. (J). (gr. -1-3). 18.99 *(978-0-399-24621-0(5),* G.P. Putnam's Sons Books for Young Readers) Penguin Young Readers Group.

Brezenoff, Steve. The Final Mission. Calle Velez, Juan, illus. 2019. (Michael Dahl Presents: Screams in Space 4D Ser.). (ENG.). 112p. (J). (gr. 3-5). lib. bdg. 27.32 *(978-1-4965-7902-7(X),* 139612, Stone Arch Bks.) Capstone.

—A Hole in the Dome. Calle Velez, Juan, illus. 2019. (Michael Dahl Presents: Screams in Space 4D Ser.). (ENG.). 112p. (J). (gr. 3-5). lib. bdg. 27.32 *(978-1-4965-7903-4(8),* 139613, Stone Arch Bks.) Capstone.

Brickwood, L. M. Children of the Moon. 2007. 216p. pap. 14.95 *(978-1-920153-03-8(9))* Zulu Planet Pubs. ZAF. Dist: APG Sales & Distribution Services.

Briggs, Elizabeth. Future Lost. 2018. (Future Shock Ser.: 3). (ENG.). 256p. (YA). (gr. 8-12). 16.99 *(978-0-8075-2687-3(8),* 807526878); pap. 9.99 *(978-0-8075-2689-7(4),* 807526894) Whitman, Albert & Co.

—Future Shock. 2016. (YA). (Future Shock Ser.: 1). (ENG.). 288p. (gr. 8-12). pap. 9.99 *(978-0-8075-2680-4(0),* 807526800); *(978-0-8075-2683-5(5))*; (Future Shock Ser.: 1). (ENG.). 272p. (gr. 8-12). 16.99 *(978-0-8075-2682-8(7),* 807526827) Whitman, Albert & Co.

—Future Threat. 2017. (Future Shock Ser.: 2). (ENG.). 272p. (YA). (gr. 8-12). 16.99 *(978-0-8075-2684-2(3),* 807526843); pap. 9.99 *(978-0-8075-2686-6(X),* 080752686X) Whitman, Albert & Co.

Bright, J. E. The Man of Steel: Cyborg Superman. Levins, Tim, illus. 2013. (Man of Steel Ser.). (ENG.). 88p. (J). (gr. 3-7). pap. 5.95 *(978-1-4342-4219-8(6),* 120277, Stone Arch Bks.) Capstone.

Brindley, John. The City of Screams. 2009. (Exceptional Reading & Language Arts Titles for Intermediate Grades Ser.). (ENG.). 408p. (YA). (gr. 7-12). 18.95 *(978-0-7613-3908-3(6))* Lerner Publishing Group.

—The Rule of Claw. Benfold Haywood, Ian P., illus. 2009. (Exceptional Reading & Language Arts Titles for Intermediate Grades Ser.). (ENG.). 408p. (YA). (gr. 7-12). 18.95 *(978-1-58013-608-2(7))* Lerner Publishing Group.

Brinley, Bertrand R. The Mad Scientists' Club. Geer, Charles, illus. 50th ed. 2011. (J). 18.95 *(978-1-930900-53-0(8))* Purple Hse. Pr.

Brockington, Drew. CatStronauts: Mission Moon. 2017. (CatStronauts Ser.: 1). (J). lib. bdg. 18.40 *(978-0-606-39900-5(3))* Turtleback.

Brody, Jennifer. Return of the Continuums: The Continuum Trilogy, Book 2. 2016. (Continuum Trilogy Ser.: 2). (ENG.). 432p. (YA). 36.95 *(978-1-68162-259-0(9))*; pap. 14.95 *(978-1-68162-258-3(0))* Turner Publishing Co.

—The United Continuums: The Continuum Trilogy, Book 3. 2017. (Continuum Trilogy Ser.: 3). (ENG.). 464p. (YA). 36.99 *(978-1-68162-263-7(7))*; pap. 15.99 *(978-1-68162-262-0(9))* Turner Publishing Co.

—The 13th Continuum: The Continuum Trilogy, Book 1. 2016. (Continuum Trilogy Ser.: 1). (ENG., Illus.). 416p. (YA). pap. 20.95 *(978-1-68162-254-5(8))* Turner Publishing Co.

Brody, Jessica & Rendell, Joanne. Sky Without Stars. 2019. (System Divine Ser.: 1). (ENG., Illus.). 592p. (YA). (gr. 7). 19.99 *(978-1-5344-1063-3(5),* Simon Pulse) Simon Pulse.

Brooks, Max. Minecraft: the Island: An Official Minecraft Novel. (Minecraft Ser.). (ENG., Illus.). 288p. (gr. 5-7). 2019. pap. 10.99 *(978-0-399-18179-5(2))* 2017. 17.99 *(978-0-399-18177-1(6))* Random Hse. Worlds.

—Minecraft: the Mountain: An Official Minecraft Novel. 2021. 272p. (J). *(978-1-5291-3511-4(7),* Del Rey) Random House Publishing Group.

—Minecraft: the Mountain: An Official Minecraft Novel. 2021. (Minecraft Ser.). (ENG.). 272p. (J). (gr. 5-7). 17.99 *(978-0-593-15915-6(2))* Random Hse. Worlds.

Brooks, Molly. Field Trip. Brooks, Molly, illus. 2019. (Sanity & Tallulah Ser.: 2). (ENG., Illus.). 240p. (J). (gr. 3-7). pap. 12.99 *(978-1-368-02377-1(0))* Little, Brown Bks. for Young Readers.

—Sanity & Tallulah. Brooks, Molly, illus. 2018. (Sanity & Tallulah Ser.: 1). (ENG., Illus.). 240p. (J). (gr. 3-7). 21.99 *(978-1-368-00844-0(5))*; pap. 12.99 *(978-1-368-02280-4(4))* Little, Brown Bks. for Young Readers.

Brown, Bruce, et al. Awol, 3 vols., Vol. 2. Kirkman, Robert, ed. 2008. (ENG., Illus.). 160p. (YA). pap. 14.99 *(978-1-58240-864-4(5),* 0deb1600-a376-4769-8966-2a76a6a23c94) Image Comics.

Brown, Jeff Allan. Floom Shroom the Batting Mushroom. 2009. 100p. pap. 28.99 *(978-1-60693-485-2(6),* Strategic Bk. Publishing) Strategic Book Publishing & Rights Agency (SBPRA).

S

Brown, Jeffrey. Jedi Academy. 2019. (Star Wars: Jedi Academy Ser.). (ENG.). 160p. (J). (gr. 4-5). 16.96 (978-0-87617-580-4(9)) Penworthy Co., LLC, The.

—Jedi Academy. Brown, Jeffrey, illus. 2013. (Star Wars Jedi Academy Ser.: Bk. 1). (Illus.). 160p. (J). pap. (978-0-545-60999-9(2)) Scholastic, Inc.

—Return of the Padawan. 2019. (Star Wars: Jedi Academy Ser.). (ENG.). 176p. (J). (gr. 4-5). 16.96 (978-0-87617-581-1(7)) Penworthy Co., LLC, The.

Brown, Jennifer. How Lunchbox Jones Saved Me from Robots, Traitors, & Missy the Cruel. 2017. (ENG.). 256p. (J). pap. 8.99 (978-1-68119-441-7(4), 900172653, Bloomsbury USA Childrens) Bloomsbury Publishing USA.

Brown, Michele. New Tales from Alice's Wonderland: The Queen of Hearts & the Wibbly Wobbly Jelly. Martyr, Paula, illus. 24p. (J). pap. 7.95 (978-0-233-99536-6(6)) Andre Deutsch GBR. Dist: Trans-Atlantic Pubns., Inc.

Brown, Peter. The Wild Robot Escapes. (Wild Robot Ser.: 2). (ENG.). 288p. (J). (gr. 3-7). 2020. pap. 8.99 (978-0-316-47926-4(8)) 2018. (Illus.). 17.99 (978-0-316-38204-5(3)) Little, Brown Bks. for Young Readers.

—The Wild Robot Escapes, 2. 2020. (Wild Robot Ser.). (ENG.). 288p. (gr. 3-6). 24.94 (978-1-5364-6223-4(3)) Little, Brown Bks. for Young Readers.

Brown, Peter, illus. The Wild Robot Escapes. 2018. 279p. (J). (978-0-316-45375-2(7)) Little Brown & Co.

Brown, Zachary. The Darkside War. 2015. (Icarus Corps Ser.: 1). (ENG., Illus.). 240p. pap. 16.99 (978-1-4814-3035-7(1), SAGA Press) Simon & Schuster Bks. For Young Readers.

Bruce, Karl. Annie Apple & the Teleportation Phantoms from Outer Space. 2006. (YA). pap. 16.00 (978-0-8059-7156-9(4)) Dorrance Publishing Co., Inc.

Bruchac, Joseph. Arrow of Lightning, 1 vol. 2017. (Killer of Enemies Ser.: 3). (ENG.). 400p. (YA). (gr. 7-12). 19.95 (978-1-62014-330-8(5), leelowtu, Tu Bks.) Lee & Low Bks., Inc.

—Killer of Enemies, 1 vol. 2013. (Killer of Enemies Ser.). (ENG.). 400p. (YA). 19.95 (978-1-62014-143-4(4), 1620141434, Tu Bks.) Lee & Low Bks., Inc.

—Trail of the Dead, 1 vol. 2015. (Killer of Enemies Ser.: 2). (ENG.). 400p. (YA). (gr. 7-12). 19.95 (978-1-62014-261-5(9), leelowtu) Lee & Low Bks., Inc.

Brunner, Max. Superfail. Mackay, Dustin, illus. 2017. (ENG.). 208p. (J). (gr. 3-7). 13.99 (978-0-7624-6229-2(9), Running Pr. Kids) Running Pr.

Brunswick, Glen. Non-Humans Volume 1: Runaway American Dream TP: Runaway American Dream TP. 2013. (Illus.). 120p. (YA). pap. 14.99 (978-1-60706-666-8(1)) Image Comics.

Bryers, Paul. Kobal. 2009. 1.00 (978-1-4074-4320-1(8)) Recorded Bks., Inc.

Bryson, Karen Mueller. The Incredibly Awesome Adventures of Puggie Liddel, the Graphic Novel. Tisdel, L. L, illus. 2013. 108p. pap. (978-1-927384-09-1(5)) Zeta Comics.

BubbleGirl, Season. A Doggy Diary. 2006. 93p. (J). per. (978-0-9775120-0-3(2)) Carpe Diem Publishing.

Buckley, Jacob Salpeter. The Great Mistake. 2004. (ENG.). 260p. pap. 13.50 (978-1-4184-9936-5(6)) AuthorHouse.

Buller, Laura. DK Readers L1: Star Wars: What Is a Wookiee? 2015. (DK Readers Level 1 Ser.). (ENG., Illus.). 48p. (J). (gr. k-2). pap. 3.99 (978-1-4654-3386-2(4), DK Children) Dorling Kindersley Publishing, Inc.

—Star Wars: Star Pilot. 2015. (Star Wars DK Readers Level 3 Ser.). lib. bdg. 13.55 (978-0-606-37408-8(6)) Turtleback.

Bunker, Lisa. Felix Yz. (ENG.). 288p. (J). (gr. 5-9). 2018. 8.99 (978-0-425-28851-1(X), Puffin Books) 2017. 16.99 (978-0-425-28850-4(1), Viking Books for Young Readers) Penguin Young Readers Group.

—Felix Yz. 2018. lib. bdg. 19.65 (978-0-606-41316-9(2)) Turtleback.

Bunzl, Peter. Cogheart. 2019. (Cogheart Adventures Ser.). (ENG.). 368p. (J). (gr. 3-7). pap. 12.99 (978-1-63163-287-7(6), 1631632876, Jolly Fish Pr.) North Star Editions.

Burnam, Michael H. The Last Stop. 2016. (ENG., Illus.). 288p. (J). (gr. -1-12). pap. 12.95 (978-1-78535-117-4(6), Lodestone Bks.) Hunt, John Publishing Ltd. GBR. Dist: National Bk. Network.

—The Next Step: Book Two of the Last Stop Series. 2017. (ENG., Illus.). 312p. (YA). (gr. 8-17). pap. 12.95 (978-1-78535-575-2(9), Lodestone Bks.) Hunt, John Publishing Ltd. GBR. Dist: National Bk. Network.

Burns, Dal. The Adventures of Phoo. 2006. 148p. pap. 24.95 (978-1-4241-1773-4(9)) PublishAmerica, Inc.

Burroughs, Edgar Rice. Mars Trilogy: A Princess of Mars; the Gods of Mars; the Warlord of Mars. Fischer, Scott M. et al, illus. 2012. (ENG.). 704p. (gr. 7). pap. 18.99 (978-1-4424-2387-9(0), Simon & Schuster Bks. For Young Readers) Simon & Schuster Bks. For Young Readers.

Burt, Jake. Cleo Porter & the Body Electric. 2020. (ENG., Illus.). 288p. (J). 16.99 (978-1-250-23655-5(X), 900210567) Feiwel & Friends.

—Cleo Porter & the Body Electric. 2022. (ENG., Illus.). 288p. (J). pap. 7.99 (978-1-250-80272-9(5), 900210568) Square Fish.

Butler, Susan. The Hermit Thrush Sings. unabr. ed. 2003. (YA). 76.75 (978-0-7887-3798-5(8), 41042X4) Recorded Bks., Inc.

Byng, Georgia. Molly Moon Detiene el Mundo. 2004. (SPA.). 358p. (gr. 5-8). 18.99 (978-84-348-9610-9(9)) SM Ediciones ESP. Dist: Lectorum Pubns., Inc.

—Molly Moon, Micky Minus, & the Mind Machine. (Molly Moon Ser.). (ENG.). (J). (gr. 3-7). 2007. 384p. 16.99 (978-0-06-075036-7(7))4. 2008. 416p. pap. 7.99 (978-0-06-075038-1(3), HarperCollins) HarperCollins Pubs.

—Molly Moon Stops the World. (Illus.). (J). 2004. 384p. 16.99 (978-0-06-051410-5(8)) 2005. (Molly Moon Ser.: 2). (ENG., 416p. (gr. 3-7). reprint ed. pap. 7.99 (978-0-06-051415-0(9), HarperCollins) HarperCollins Pubs.

—Molly Moon Viaja a Traes del Tiempo. Crispin, Maria Dolores, tr. 2005. (SPA.). 350p. (978-84-675-0570-2(2)) SM Ediciones.

—Molly Moon's Hypnotic Time Travel Adventure. (ENG.). 400p. (J). 2006. (Molly Moon Ser.: 3). (gr. 3-7). pap. 8.99 (978-0-06-075034-3(0), HarperCollins) 2005. (Illus.). 16.99 (978-0-06-075032-9(4)) HarperCollins Pubs.

—Molly Moon's Hypnotic Time-Travel Adventure. 2005. (Illus.). 400p. (J). lib. bdg. 18.89 (978-0-06-075033-6(2)) HarperCollins Pubs.

Byrne, John & Marvel Various. Fantastic Four: Behold... Galactus! Byrne, John & Marvel Various, illus. 2019. (Illus.). 232p. (gr. -1-17). pap. 24.99 (978-1-302-91793-7(5), Marvel Universe) Marvel Worldwide, Inc.

Cabot, Meg. Avalon High: Coronation #3: Hunter's Moon. Coronado, Jinky, illus. 2009. (ENG.). 160p. (J). (gr. 8-18). pap. 9.99 (978-0-06-117710-1(5), HarperCollins) HarperCollins Pubs.

—The Mediator #5: Haunted. 2004. (Mediator Ser.: 5). (ENG.). 288p. (YA). (gr. 8-18). pap. 10.99 (978-0-06-075164-7(9), HarperTeen) HarperCollins Pubs.

Cadenhead, MacKenzie. Buggin' Out! 2018. (Marvel Super Hero Adventures Early Chapter Bks.). (J). lib. bdg. 14.75 (978-0-606-40978-0(5)) Turtleback.

—Marvel Super Hero Adventures: Buggin' Out! An Early Chapter Book. 2018. (Super Hero Adventures Chapter Bks.: 3). (ENG., Illus.). 80p. (J). (gr. 1-3). pap. 4.99 (978-1-368-00857-0(7)) Marvel Worldwide, Inc.

—Sleeper. 2017. (ENG.). 272p. (YA). (gr. 6-12). pap. 10.99 (978-1-4926-3614-4(2)) Sourcebooks, Inc.

Cadenhead, MacKenzie & Ryan, Sean. Buggin' Out! Laufman, Derek, illus. 2019. (Marvel Super Hero Adventures Ser.). (ENG.). 80p. (J). (gr. 1-5). lib. bdg. 31.36 (978-1-5321-4312-0(5), 31842, Chapter Bks.) Spotlight.

Caine, Rachel, pseud. Honor among Thieves. 2018. (Honors Ser.: 1). (ENG., Illus.). 480p. (YA). (gr. 8). 17.99 (978-0-06-257099-4(4), Tegen, Katherine Bks) HarperCollins Pubs.

Caine, Rachel, pseud & Aguirre, Ann. Honor among Thieves. 2019. (Honors Ser.: 1). (ENG.). 496p. (YA). (gr. 8). pap. 9.99 (978-0-06-257100-7(1), Tegen, Katherine Bks) HarperCollins Pubs.

Calabrese, Linda Lee. It Is What It Is: In a Kid's Mind. 2012. 28p. pap. 24.95 (978-1-4626-5643-1(9)) America Star Bks.

Calandrelli, Emily. Ada Lace, on the Case. Kurilla, Renée, illus. 2017. (Ada Lace Adventure Ser.: 1). (ENG.). 128p. (J). (gr. 1-5). pap. 6.99 (978-1-4814-8598-2(9), Simon & Schuster Bks. For Young Readers) Simon & Schuster Bks. For Young Readers.

—Ada Lace Sees Red. Kurilla, Renée, illus. 2017. (Ada Lace Adventure Ser.: 2). (ENG.). 144p. (J). (gr. 1-5). 17.99 (978-1-4814-8602-6(0)); pap. 6.99 (978-1-4814-8601-9(2)) Simon & Schuster Bks. For Young Readers. (Simon & Schuster Bks. For Young Readers).

—Ada Lace, Take Me to Your Leader. Kurilla, Renée, illus. 2018. (Ada Lace Adventure Ser.: 3). (ENG.). 96p. (J). (gr. 1-5). 17.99 (978-1-4814-8605-7(5)); pap. 6.99 (978-1-4814-8604-0(7)) Simon & Schuster Bks. For Young Readers. (Simon & Schuster Bks. For Young Readers).

—Ada Lace, Take Me to Your Leader. 2018. (Ada Lace Adventure Ser.: 3). lib. bdg. 17.20 (978-0-606-41405-0(3)) Turtleback.

Calero, Dennis. You're Not the Captain of Me! 2011. (ENG.). 272p. (J). (gr. 4-7). pap. 9.95 (978-1-59687-375-9(2)) IBks., Inc.

Caletti, Deb. The Last Forever. 2016. (ENG., Illus.). 352p. (YA). (gr. 7-7). pap. 11.99 (978-1-4424-5002-8(9), Simon & Schuster Bks. For Young Readers) Simon & Schuster Bks. For Young Readers.

Calhoun, Bonnie S. Lightning: A Novel. 2015. (Stone Braide Chronicles Ser.: 2). (ENG.). 416p. (YA). pap. 19.00 (978-0-8007-2377-4(5)) Revell.

—Thunder: A Novel. 2014. 425p. (YA). pap. (978-0-8007-2416-0(X)) Revell.

Calleja, Seve. El Planeta del Tesoro. 2003. (Disney Collection). (SPA.). 96p. (J). 6.95 (978-84-670-0305-5(7)) Espasa Calpe, S.A. ESP. Dist: Planeta Publishing Corp.

Cameron, Sharon. The Forgetting. (ENG.). 416p. (YA). (gr. 7-7). 2017. pap. 12.99 (978-1-338-16071-0(0)) 2016. 18.99 (978-0-545-94521-9(6)) Scholastic, Inc. (Scholastic Pr.).

—The Knowing. (ENG.). 448p. (YA). (gr. 7-7). 2018. pap. 10.99 (978-1-338-28196-5(8)) 2017. 18.99 (978-0-545-94524-0(0), Scholastic Pr.) Scholastic, Inc.

Campbell, Hazel D. Ramgoat Dashalong: Magical Tales from Jamaica. 2004. (ENG., Illus.). 74p. pap. 5.99 (978-976-610-269-2(4)) Penguin Publishing Group.

Capetta, Amy Rose. Entangled. 2013. (ENG.). 336p. (YA). (gr. 9). 17.99 (978-0-544-08744-6(5), 1538242, Clarion Bks.) HarperCollins Pubs.

—Unmade. 2016. (ENG.). 384p. (YA). (gr. 9). pap. 9.99 (978-0-544-54258-7(4), 1608916, Clarion Bks.) HarperCollins Pubs.

Capozzi, Suzy. I Am Smart. Unten, Eren, illus. 2018. (Rodale Kids Curious Readers/Level 2 Ser.: 5). 32p. (J). (gr. -1-1). pap. 4.99 (978-1-62336-957-6(6), 9781623369576, Rodale Kids) Random Hse. Children's Bks.

Carbone, Courtney. Butterfly Battle! (DC Super Hero Girls) Orum, Pernille, illus. 2018. (Step into Reading Ser.). (ENG.). 32p. (J). (gr. -1-1). pap. 4.99 (978-1-5247-6917-8(7), Random Hse. Bks. for Young Readers) Random Hse. Children's Bks.

—I Am a Princess. Martinez, Heather, illus. 2016. (J). (978-1-5182-1626-8(9), Golden Bks.) Random Hse. Children's Bks.

—Star Wars: the Phantom Menace (Star Wars) Martinez, Heather, illus. 2015. (Little Golden Book Ser.). (ENG.). 24p. (J). (-k). 4.99 (978-0-7364-3542-0(5), Golden Bks.) Random Hse. Children's Bks.

Carbone, Courtney & Marston, William Moulton. Wonder Woman to the Rescue! Doescher, Erik, illus. 2016. 24p. (J). (978-1-4806-9760-7(5)) Random Hse., Inc.

Card, Orson Scott. Pathfinder. (Pathfinder Trilogy Ser.). (ENG.). 672p. (YA). (gr. 7). 2011. pap. 13.99 (978-1-4169-9179-3(4)) 2010. 21.99 (978-1-4169-9176-2(X)) Simon Pulse. (Simon Pulse).

—Pathfinder. l.t. ed. 2011. (Pathfinder Ser.). (ENG.). 802p. 23.99 (978-1-4104-3681-8(0)) Thorndike Pr.

—Ruins. 2013. (Pathfinder Trilogy Ser.). (ENG.). 544p. (YA). (gr. 7). pap. 14.99 (978-1-4169-9180-9(8), Simon Pulse) Simon Pulse.

—Stonefather. Kidd, Tom, illus. 2008. 112p. 35.00 (978-1-59606-194-1(4)) Subterranean Pr.

—Visitors. 2015. (Pathfinder Trilogy Ser.). (ENG., Illus.). 608p. (YA). (gr. 7). pap. 13.99 (978-1-4169-9181-6(6), Simon Pulse) Simon Pulse.

Carey, Anna. Eve. (Eve Ser.: 1). (ENG.). (YA). (gr. 8). 2012. 352p. pap. 9.99 (978-0-06-204851-6(1)) 2011. 336p. 17.99 (978-0-06-204850-9(3)) HarperCollins Pubs. (HarperCollins).

—Eve. 2012. (SPA.). 224p. (YA). pap. 20.95 (978-84-9918-434-0(0)) Roca Editorial ESP. Dist: Spanish Pubs., LLC.

—Once, 2. 2013. (Eve Ser.: 2). (ENG.). 384p. (YA). (gr. 8-12). pap. 10.99 (978-0-06-204855-4(4), HarperCollins) HarperCollins Pubs.

—Rise. 2013. (Eve Ser.: 3). (ENG.). 336p. (YA). (gr. 8). pap. 10.99 (978-0-06-204858-5(9), HarperCollins) HarperCollins Pubs.

—Rise: An Eve Novel. 2013. (Illus.). 320p. (YA). pap. 9.99 (978-0-06-226273-8(4)) HarperCollins Pubs.

Carlson, Caroline. The Door at the End of the World. 2019. (ENG.). 304p. (J). (gr. 3-7). 16.99 (978-0-06-236830-0(3), HarperCollins) HarperCollins Pubs.

Carlson, Dale. The Human Apes. Carlson, Al & Nicklaus, Carol, illus. 2nd ed. 2005. (ENG.). 155p. (gr. 8-12). reprint ed. pap. 14.95 (978-1-884158-31-5(5)) Bick Publishing Hse.

Carlson, Dale Bick. The Mountain of Truth. Nicklaus, Carol, illus. 2nd ed. 2005. (ENG.). 169p. (gr. 8-12). reprint ed. pap. 14.95 (978-1-884158-30-8(7)) Bick Publishing Hse.

Carman, Patrick. The Dark Planet. 2010. (Atherton Ser.: 3). (ENG., Illus.). 368p. (J). (gr. 3-7). pap. 18.99 (978-0-316-16675-1(8)) Little, Brown Bks. for Young Readers.

—The Dark Planet. 2010. (Atherton Ser.: 3). (J). lib. bdg. 20.85 (978-0-606-14737-8(3)) Turtleback.

—Pulse. 2013. (Pulse Ser.: 1). (ENG.). 384p. (YA). (gr. 8). 17.99 (978-0-06-208576-4(X), Tegen, Katherine Bks) HarperCollins Pubs.

—Quake. (Pulse Ser.: 3). (ENG.). 288p. (YA). (gr. 8). 2016. pap. 10.99 (978-0-06-208597-9(2)) 2015. 17.99 (978-0-06-208590-0(5)) HarperCollins Pubs. (Tegen, Katherine Bks).

—Rivers of Fire, 2. 2008. (Atherton Ser.). (ENG., Illus.). 303p. (J). (gr. 6-8). 18.69 (978-0-316-16672-0(3)) Little Brown & Co.

—Rivers of Fire. 2009. (Atherton Ser.: 2). (ENG., Illus.). 336p. (J). (gr. 3-7). pap. 17.99 (978-0-316-16673-7(1)) Little, Brown Bks. for Young Readers.

—Tremor. (Pulse Ser.: 2). (ENG.). (YA). (gr. 8). 2015. 384p. pap. 9.99 (978-0-06-208581-8(6)) 2014. 368p. 17.99 (978-0-06-208580-1(8)) HarperCollins Pubs. (Tegen, Katherine Bks).

Carmody, Isobelle. The Farseekers. 2003. (Obernewtyn Chronicles: Bk. 2). (Illus.). 316p. (J). 13.65 (978-0-7569-4608-1(5)) Perfection Learning Corp.

Carriger, Gail. Curtsies & Conspiracies. 2014. (Finishing School Ser.: 2). (ENG.). 336p. (YA). (gr. 7-17). pap. 10.99 (978-0-316-19020-6(9)) Little, Brown Bks. for Young Readers.

—Etiquette & Espionage. 2013. (Finishing School Ser.: 1). (ENG.). 336p. (YA). (gr. 7-17). pap. 11.99 (978-0-316-19010-7(1)) Little, Brown Bks. for Young Readers.

—Waistcoats & Weaponry. 2015. (Finishing School Ser.: 3). (ENG.). 320p. (YA). (gr. 7-17). pap. 18.99 (978-0-316-19025-1(X)) Little, Brown Bks. for Young Readers.

Carroll, Michael Owen. Stronger: A Super Human Clash, 3. 3rd ed. 2012. (Super Human Ser.: 3). (ENG.). 384p. (YA). (gr. 6-8). 26.19 (978-0-399-25761-2(6)) Penguin Young Readers Group.

Carter, Liane. The Chronicles of Joy. 2008. 244p. pap. (978-1-84923-001-8(3)) YouWriteOn.

Carter, Mike. Access to the Universe. 2005. (Illus.). 160p. (Orig.). pap. (978-0-7344-0696-5(7), Lothian Children's Bks.) Hachette Australia.

Carter, Rachel. Find Me Where the Water Ends. 2014. (ENG.). 352p. (YA). (gr. 9). 17.99 (978-0-06-208111-7(X), HarperTeen) HarperCollins Pubs.

—This Strange & Familiar Place. 2013. (ENG.). 272p. (YA). (gr. 9). 17.99 (978-0-06-208108-7(X), HarperTeen) HarperCollins Pubs.

Carter-Stephenson, C. J. The Crystal Ship. 2010. (ENG., Illus.). 121p. (J). pap. 12.95 (978-1-4457-1369-4(1)) Lulu Pr., Inc.

Casey, Joe. Godland Finale. 2013. (Illus.). 72p. (YA). pap. 6.99 (978-1-60706-819-8(2)) Image Comics.

Cast, P. C. Sun Warrior: Tales of a New World. 2018. (Tales of a New World Ser.: 2). (ENG., Illus.). 576p. (YA). pap. 11.99 (978-1-250-10076-4(3), 900162489, Wednesday Bks.) St. Martin's Pr.

Castellan, Andrea. Mickey Mouse & the Orbiting Nightmare. 2011. (ENG., Illus.). 128p. (J). pap. (978-1-60886-630-4(0)) BOOM! Studios.

Caterer, Claire M. The Key & the Flame. (ENG.). (J). (gr. 3-7). 2015. 496p. pap. 7.99 (978-1-4424-5742-3(2)) 2013. 480p. 17.99 (978-1-4424-5741-6(4)) McElderry, Margaret K. Bks. (McElderry, Margaret K. Bks.).

Cave, Patrick. The Selected. 2010. (ENG.). 416p. (YA). (gr. 9-18). 17.99 (978-1-4169-1573-7(7), Atheneum Bks. for Young Readers) Simon & Schuster Children's Publishing.

—Sharp North. 2009. (ENG.). 528p. (YA). (gr. 9). pap. 8.99 (978-1-4169-1223-1(1), Atheneum Bks. for Young Readers) Simon & Schuster Children's Publishing.

Center for Learning Network Staff. Slaughterhouse-Five: Curriculum Unit. 2005. (Novel Ser.). 76p. (YA). tchr. ed., spiral bd. 19.95 (978-1-56077-789-2(3)) Center for Learning, The.

Cerasi, Chris. The Hunt for Grievous. 2010. (Star Wars: Clone Wars Readers Ser.). (ENG.). 48p. (J). (gr. 1-3). 16.19 (978-0-448-45394-1(0)) Penguin Young Readers Group.

—Star Wars Adventures: Chewbacca & the Slavers of the Shadowlands. Meyer, Jennifer L., illus. 2013. (Star Wars Digests Ser.). (ENG.). 80p. (J). (gr. 3-8). lib. bdg. 34.21 (978-1-61479-057-0(4), 13760, Graphic Novels) Spotlight.

Chabot, Jason. Above: Broken Sky Chronicles, Book 2. 2017. (Broken Sky Chronicles Ser.: 2). (ENG.). 384p. (YA). pap. 19.95 (978-1-68162-604-8(7)) Turner Publishing Co.

—Below: Broken Sky Chronicles, Book 1. 2016. (Broken Sky Chronicles Ser.: 1). (ENG.). 308p. (YA). 29.95 (978-1-68162-602-4(0)); pap. 16.95 (978-1-68162-601-7(2)) Turner Publishing Co.

—Beyond: Broken Sky Chronicles, Book 3. 2017. (Broken Sky Chronicles Ser.: 3). (ENG.). 432p. (YA). 35.99 (978-1-68162-608-6(X)); pap. 19.99 (978-1-68162-607-9(1)) Turner Publishing Co.

Chan, Marty. Demon Gate, 1 vol. 2013. (Ehrich Weisz Chronicles Ser.). (ENG.). 262p. (YA). (gr. 7-10). pap. 12.95 (978-1-55455-306-8(7), ea320d17-ce0b-4bdd-ad87-d1058c095c34) Trifolium Bks., Inc. CAN. Dist: Firefly Bks., Ltd.

Chang, Ifay, as told by. Outopians. 2007. (Illus.). 27p. (YA). pap. (978-0-9771594-1-3(8)) TLC Information Services.

Charbonneau, Joelle. Independent Study. 2015. (Testing Ser.: 2). lib. bdg. 20.85 (978-0-606-36832-2(9)) Turtleback.

—Independent Study: The Testing, Book 2. (Testing Ser.: 2). (ENG.). (YA). (gr. 7). 2015. 336p. pap. 15.99 (978-0-544-43945-0(7), 1596844) 2014. 320p. 17.99 (978-0-547-95920-7(6), 1520240) HarperCollins Pubs. (Clarion Bks.).

—The Testing. 2015. (Testing Ser.: 1). (ENG.). 352p. (YA). (gr. 7). pap. 15.99 (978-0-544-33623-0(2), 1584169, Clarion Bks.) HarperCollins Pubs.

CHARLES, A. M. A. N. & 1st World Publishing. Dad & Me Go to School. 2006. 24p. per. 9.95 (978-1-4218-9924-4(8)) 1st World Publishing, Inc.

Charretier, Elsa & Jody Houser. Star Wars: Forces of Destiny. 2018. (Illus.). (J). lib. bdg. 24.50 (978-0-606-41292-6(1)) Turtleback.

Chartrand, Kenneth. A Martian's Dream of Christmas. 2006. 48p. pap. 16.95 (978-1-4241-4123-4(0)) PublishAmerica, Inc.

Chase, Jeffrey Scott. Andy the Alien. 2006. (J). pap. 16.00 (978-0-8059-7081-4(9)) Dorrance Publishing Co., Inc.

—Andy the Alien Visits the Outer Planets. 2007. (J). pap. 17.00 (978-0-8059-7488-1(1)) Dorrance Publishing Co., Inc.

Chase, Max. STAR FIGHTERS 2: Deadly Mission. 2012. (ENG., Illus.). 128p. (J). pap. (978-1-4088-1579-3(6)) Bloomsbury Pr.

—STAR FIGHTERS 5: Lethal Combat. 2012. (Star Fighters Ser.: 5). (ENG., Illus.). 128p. (J). (gr. 2-4). pap. (978-1-4088-1582-3(6), 31112, Bloomsbury Children's Bks.) Bloomsbury Publishing Plc.

Cheng, Jack. See You in the Cosmos. 2018. lib. bdg. 19.65 (978-0-606-41314-5(6)) Turtleback.

Cherobin. Zoomy Boomy, the Moon, & the Earth: All in its Season, & Seasons Change. 2010. 24p. pap. 14.99 (978-1-4490-2658-5(3)) AuthorHouse.

Cheverton, Mark. Overworld in Flames: Herobrine?s Revenge Book Two (a Gameknight999 Adventure): an Unofficial Minecrafter?s Adventure. 2016. (Gameknight999 Ser.: Bk. 2). (ENG.). 256p. (J). (gr. 3-3). pap. 9.99 (978-1-5107-0681-1(X), Sky Pony Pr.) Skyhorse Publishing Co., Inc.

Chiaramonti, Gregory. Probie: the Space Probe, Mission One: the Ocean of Europa. 2007. 32p. (J). 16.72 (978-0-615-13848-0(9)) Chiaramonti, Gregory.

Childress, Jamie. Galactic Treasure Hunt: Lost City of Atlantis. Braun, Chris, illus. 2008. (Galactic Treasure Hunt Ser.). (ENG.). 176p. pap. 4.99 (978-1-931882-62-0(2)) Adventures Unlimited Pr.

—Galactic Treasure Hunt #4: Lost in Time. Braun, Chris, illus. 2008. (Galactic Treasure Hunt Ser.). (ENG.). 176p. (J). pap. 5.99 (978-1-931882-89-7(4)) Adventures Unlimited Pr.

—Lost City of the Moon. Braun, Chris, illus. 2005. (ENG.). 115p. (gr. -1-7). per. 4.99 (978-1-931882-45-3(2)) Adventures Unlimited Pr.

—Lost Universe. Braun, Chris, illus. 2007. (ENG.). 162p. (gr. 4-7). per. 4.99 (978-1-931882-74-3(6)) Adventures Unlimited Pr.

Chilton, Claire. Shattered. 2012. 268p. pap. (978-1-908822-10-9(4)) Ragz Bks.

Choyce, Lesley. Deconstructing Dylan. 2006. (ENG.). 180p. (J). (gr. 7). pap. 12.99 (978-1-55002-603-0(8)) Dundurn Pr. CAN. Dist: Publishers Group West (PGW).

Christie, Tory. Curious Mccarthy's Family Chemistry. Price, Mina, illus. 2017. (Curious Mccarthy Ser.). (ENG.). 112p. (J). (gr. 2-4). pap. 6.95 (978-1-5158-1649-2(4), 136304); lib. bdg. 25.32 (978-1-5158-1645-4(1), 136300) Capstone. (Picture Window Bks.).

Christopher, John. Beyond the Burning Lands. 2015. (Sword of the Spirits Ser.: 2). (ENG., Illus.). 272p. (J). (gr. 5-9). pap. 7.99 (978-1-4814-1994-9(3), Aladdin) Simon & Schuster Children's Publishing.

—The City of Gold & Lead. 2003. (Tripods Ser.). 209p. (YA). (gr. 7). 13.65 (978-0-7569-5877-0(6)) Perfection Learning Corp.

—The City of Gold & Lead. 2014. (Tripods Ser.: 2). (ENG., Illus.). 304p. (J). (gr. 4-8). 19.99 (978-1-4814-1476-0(3)); pap. 8.99 (978-1-4814-1475-3(5)) Simon & Schuster Children's Publishing. (Aladdin).

—The Pool of Fire. 2014. (Tripods Ser.: 3). (ENG., Illus.). 272p. (J). (gr. 4-8). pap. 8.99 (978-1-4814-1479-1(8), Aladdin) Simon & Schuster Children's Publishing.

—The Tripods Collection (Boxed Set) The White Mountains; the City of Gold & Lead; the Pool of Fire; When the Tripods Came. 2014. (Tripods Ser.). (ENG., Illus.). 1088p. (J). (gr. 4-8). pap. 31.99 (978-1-4814-1505-7(0), Aladdin) Simon & Schuster Children's Publishing.

—When the Tripods Came. 2014. (Tripods Ser.). (ENG., Illus.). 240p. (J). (gr. 4-8). pap. 8.99 (978-1-4814-1481-4(X), Aladdin) Simon & Schuster Children's Publishing.

—The White Mountains. 2014. (Tripods Ser.: 1). (ENG., Illus.). 272p. (J). (gr. 4-8). pap. 8.99 (978-1-4814-1477-7(1), Aladdin) Simon & Schuster Children's Publishing.

—The White Mountains. 2014. (Tripods Ser.: 1). (ENG., Illus.). 272p. (J). (gr. 4-8). 19.99 (978-1-4814-1478-4(X), Simon & Schuster/Paula Wiseman Bks.) Simon & Schuster/Paula Wiseman Bks.

—Wild Jack. 2015. (ENG., Illus.). 224p. (J). (gr. 5-9). pap. 7.99 (978-1-4814-2006-8(2), Aladdin) Simon & Schuster Children's Publishing.

Chuks-Samuel, Mary. Captain Rainbow & the Agents: Value My Vote. 2012. (Illus.). 24p. pap. 19.82 (978-1-4772-1787-0(8)) AuthorHouse.

Chwast, Seymour. Arno & the MiniMachine. Chwast, Seymour, illus. 2019. (Illus.). 32p. (J). (gr. -1-3). 17.95 *(978-1-60980-879-2(7),* Triangle Square) Seven Stories Pr.

Ciencin, Scott. Attack of the Cling-Ons, 1 vol. Crowther, Jeff, illus. 2011. (Graphic Sparks Ser.). (ENG.). 40p. (J). (gr. 2-4). pap. 5.95 *(978-1-4342-3067-6(8),* 114683); lib. bdg. 23.99 *(978-1-4342-2637-2(9),* 113961) Capstone. (Stone Arch Bks.).

Clark, Henry. The Book That Proves Time Travel Happens. 2016. (ENG., Illus.). 432p. (J). (gr. 3-7). pap. 19.99 *(978-0-316-40616-1(3))* Little, Brown Bks. for Young Readers.

Clark, Kent. Peter Powers & the Swashbuckling Sky Pirates! Bardin, Dave, illus. 2017. (Peter Powers Ser.: 6). (ENG.). 128p. (J). (gr. 1-5). pap. 9.99 *(978-0-316-43793-6(X))* Little, Brown Bks. for Young Readers.

Clark, Kent & Snider, Brandon T. Peter Powers & the League of Lying Lizards! Bardin, Dave, illus. 2017. (Peter Powers Ser.: 4). (ENG.). 128p. (J). (gr. 1-5). pap. 9.99 *(978-0-316-54636-2(4))* Little, Brown Bks. for Young Readers.

—Peter Powers & the Rowdy Robot Raiders! Bardin, Dave, illus. 2017. (Peter Powers Ser.: 2). (ENG.). 128p. (J). (gr. 1-5). pap. 5.99 *(978-0-316-35938-2(6))* Little, Brown Bks. for Young Readers.

Clark, Lisa M. The Messengers: Revealed. 2018. 270p. (YA). *(978-0-7586-5961-3(X))* Concordia Publishing Hse.

Clark, Wook-Jin. Megagogo, Vol. 1. 2014. (ENG., Illus.). 176p. pap. 19.99 *(978-1-62010-117-9(3),* 9781620101179, Lion Forge) Oni Pr., Inc.

Clayton, Emma. The Whisper. 2012. 309p. *(978-0-545-43365-5(7),* Chicken Hse., The) Scholastic, Inc.

CLE, Troy. The Marvelous Effect. 2008. (Marvelous World Ser.: 1). (ENG.). 384p. (J). (gr. 5-9). pap. 16.99 *(978-1-4169-4215-3(7),* Simon & Schuster Bks. For Young Readers) Simon & Schuster Bks. For Young Readers.

Clement, Emily Gillespie. Bea & the Smart Kids. 2012. 188p. pap. *(978-1-105-50303-0(8))* Lulu.com.

Clements, Andrew. Things Not Seen. 2004. 272p. (J). (gr. 5-18). reprint ed. pap. 8.99 *(978-0-14-240076-0(9),* Puffin Books) Penguin Young Readers Group.

—Things Not Seen. 2004. 251p. (gr. 5-9). 17.00 *(978-0-7569-2599-4(1))* Perfection Learning Corp.

—Things Not Seen. 2004. 256p. (J). (gr. 4-7). pap. 38.00 incl. audio *(978-1-4000-9014-3(8),* Listening Library) Random Hse. Audio Publishing Group.

Clenott, Peter. Devolution. 2013. 280p. pap. *(978-1-927792-14-8(2))* Imajin Bks.

Clough, Caroline. Silver Storm, 50 vols. 2016. (Illus.). 256p. (J). 9.95 *(978-1-78250-313-2(7),* Kelpies) Floris Bks. GBR. Dist: Consortium Bk. Sales & Distribution.

Cohen, Rich. Alex & the Amazing Time Machine. Murphy, Kelly, illus. 2013. (ENG.). 176p. (J). (gr. 3-7). pap. 14.99 *(978-1-250-02729-0(2),* 900098301) Square Fish.

Colby, J. Z. Trilogy One. Colby, J. Z. et al, illus. 2010. (Nebador Ser.: Books One, Two, and Three). (ENG.). 641p. (YA). pupil's gde. ed. 49.95 *(978-1-936253-17-3(8))* Nebador Archives.

Colby, J. Z. & Persons, Katelynn. Flight Training, Kibi & the Search for Happiness. Colby, J. Z. & Powers, Mireille Xioulan, illus. 2011. (Nebador Ser.: Book Four). 178p. (YA). pap. 10.95 *(978-1-936253-27-2(5))* Nebador Archives.

Cole, Barry. The Time Bandit. 2016. (ENG., Illus.). v, 115p. (J). *(978-0-9935831-5-5(6))* Elba Publishing.

Cole, Bob. Power Reading: Chapter/Sci-Fi/Dr. Little. Sirrell, Terri, illus. 2004. 25p. (J). (gr. 3-4). vinyl bd. 39.95 *(978-1-883186-63-0(3),* PPSF1) National Reading Styles Institute, Inc.

—Power Reading: Chapter/Sci-Fi/Dr. Little 2. Ford, David, illus. 2005. 25p. (J). (gr. 3-4). vinyl bd. 39.95 *(978-1-883186-76-0(5),* PPSF4) National Reading Styles Institute, Inc.

—Power Reading: Chapter/Sci-Fi/Superhero. Ford, David, illus. 2004. 25p. (J). (gr. 3-4). vinyl bd. 39.95 *(978-1-883186-62-3(5),* PPSF2) National Reading Styles Institute, Inc.

—Power Reading: Chapter/Sci-Fi/Time Warp. Ford, David, illus. 2004. 25p. (J). (gr. 4-18). vinyl bd. 39.95 *(978-1-883186-60-9(9),* PPSF3) National Reading Styles Institute, Inc.

—Power Reading: Chapter/Sci-Fi/Time Warp 2. Ford, David, illus. 2005. 52p. (J). (gr. 4-18). vinyl bd. 39.95 *(978-1-883186-75-3(7),* PPSF5) National Reading Styles Institute, Inc.

Cole, Dylan. The Otherworldly Adventures of Tyler Washburn: the New Kid. 2012. (ENG., Illus.). 48p. (J). (gr. -1). 19.95 *(978-1-933492-77-3(5))* Design Studio Pr.

Cole, Frank L. The World's Greatest Adventure Machine. 2017. 320p. (J). (gr. 4-7). 16.99 *(978-0-399-55282-3(0),* Delacorte Bks. for Young Readers) Random Hse. Children's Bks.

Cole, Gwen. Ride On. 2018. (ENG.). 280p. (YA). (gr. 6-12). 16.99 *(978-1-5107-2993-3(3),* Sky Pony Pr.) Skyhorse Publishing Co., Inc.

Cole, Olivia A. A Conspiracy of Stars. (ENG.). (YA). (gr. 8). 2019. 448p. pap. 9.99 *(978-0-06-264422-0(X))* 2018. 432p. 17.99 *(978-0-06-264421-3(1))* HarperCollins Pubs. (Tegen, Katherine Bks).

Cole, Steve. Z. Rex. (ENG.). (J). 2010. 256p. (gr. 5-18). 8.99 *(978-0-14-241712-6(2),* Puffin Books)1. 2009. 276p. (gr. 6-8). 22.44 *(978-0-399-25253-2(3))* Penguin Young Readers Group.

Cole, T. M. A Slip in Time: The Book of Eventide. Cole, Raymond A., illus. 2006. (YA). per. 10.75 *(978-0-9777677-0-0(1))* Silver Cloak Pubns.

Collingwood, Harry. The Log of the 'Flying Fish' 2011. 236p. 26.95 *(978-1-4638-9645-4(X))* Rodgers, Alan Bks.

—The Strange Adventures of Eric Blackburn. 2017. (ENG., Illus.). (J). 24.95 *(978-1-374-85314-0(3));* pap. 14.95 *(978-1-374-85313-3(5))* Capital Communications, Inc.

—The Strange Adventures of Eric Blackburn. 2008. 164p. 25.95 *(978-1-60664-711-0(3))* Rodgers, Alan Bks.

Collins, A. L. Asylum: Refugees of Mars. Tikulin, Tomislav, illus. 2018. (Redworld Ser.). (ENG.). 128p. (J). (gr. 3-8). lib. bdg. 25.99 *(978-1-4965-5886-2(3),* 137024, Stone Arch Bks.) Capstone.

—Homestead: A New Life on Mars. Tikulin, Tomislav, illus. 2017. (Redworld Ser.). (ENG.). 128p. (J). (gr. 3-8). lib. bdg. 25.99 *(978-1-4965-4819-1(1),* 135341, Stone Arch Bks.) Capstone.

—Legacy: Relics of Mars. Tikulin, Tomislav, illus. 2017. (Redworld Ser.). (ENG.). 128p. (J). (gr. 3-8). lib. bdg. 25.99 *(978-1-4965-4822-1(1),* 135344, Stone Arch Bks.) Capstone.

—Outcry: Defenders of Mars. Tikulin, Tomislav, illus. 2018. (Redworld Ser.). (ENG.). 128p. (J). (gr. 3-8). lib. bdg. 25.99 *(978-1-4965-5887-9(1),* 137025, Stone Arch Bks.) Capstone.

—Raiders: Water Thieves of Mars. Tikulin, Tomislav, illus. 2017. (Redworld Ser.). (ENG.). 128p. (J). (gr. 3-8). lib. bdg. 25.99 *(978-1-4965-4820-7(5),* 135342, Stone Arch Bks.) Capstone.

—Redworld, 6 vols. Tikulin, Tomislav, illus. 2018. (Redworld Ser.). (ENG.). 128p. (J). (gr. 3-8). 163.92 *(978-1-4965-5892-3(8),* 27538, Stone Arch Bks.) Capstone.

—Redworld: Year One. Tikulin, Tomislav, illus. 2018. (Redworld Ser.). (ENG.). 320p. (J). (gr. 3-8). pap., pap., pap. 8.95 *(978-1-62370-986-0(5),* 137317, Capstone Young Readers) Capstone.

—Tharsis City: The Wonder of Mars. Tikulin, Tomislav, illus. 2017. (Redworld Ser.). (ENG.). 128p. (J). (gr. 3-8). lib. bdg. 25.99 *(978-1-4965-4821-4(3),* 135343, Stone Arch Bks.) Capstone.

Collins, Ailynn. Alien Lockdown. Calle Velez, Juan, illus. 2019. (Michael Dahl Presents: Screams in Space 4D Ser.). (ENG.). 112p. (J). (gr. 3-5). lib. bdg. 27.32 *(978-1-4965-7905-8(4),* 139615, Stone Arch Bks.) Capstone.

Collins, Suzanne. The Ballad of Songbirds & Snakes (a Hunger Games Novel) (Unabridged Edition), 2 vols. unabr. ed. 2020. Orig. Title: Untitled Panem Novel (Audio): a Hunger Games Novel. (ENG.). (YA). (gr. 7-7). audio compact disk 44.99 *(978-1-338-63519-5(0))* Scholastic, Inc.

—Catching Fire. 2009. (Hunger Games Trilogy: Bk. 2). (YA). 74.99 *(978-1-61574-572-2(6))* Findaway World, LLC.

—Catching Fire. 2009. 12.04 *(978-0-7848-3842-6(9),* Everbind) Marco Bk. Co.

—Catching Fire. 2011. (ENG.). 448p. pap. *(978-1-4071-3209-9(1))* Scholastic.

—Catching Fire. l.t. ed. (Hunger Games Trilogy: 2). (ENG.). (YA). 2012. 498p. (gr. 7-12). pap. 14.99 *(978-1-59413-585-9(1),* Large Print Pr.) 2009. 499p. 23.95 *(978-1-4104-2044-2(2))* Thorndike Pr.

—Catching Fire. 2013. (Hunger Games Trilogy Ser.: 2). lib. bdg. 24.50 *(978-0-606-32025-2(3))* Turtleback.

—Catching Fire. 2011. (Hunger Games Trilogy: Bk. 2). (CHI.). 344p. (YA). (gr. 7-12). pap. *(978-7-5063-5566-7(3))* Writers' Publishing Hse.

—Catching Fire (Hunger Games, Book Two), 1 vol. (Hunger Games Ser.: 2). (ENG.). 400p. (gr. 7). 2013. (YA). pap. 14.99 *(978-0-545-58617-7(8))* 2009. (J). pap. 22.99 *(978-0-439-02349-8(1))* Scholastic, Inc. (Scholastic Pr.).

—Gregor & the Prophecy of Bane (the Underland Chronicles #2) Gregor the Overlander & the Prophecy of Bane. 2013. (Underland Chronicles Ser.: 2). (ENG.). 320p. (J). (gr. 4-7). pap. 8.99 *(978-0-439-65076-2(3),* Scholastic Paperbacks) Scholastic, Inc.

—The Hunger Games. 2009. (Hunger Games Trilogy: Bk. 1). 10.85 *(978-0-7848-3801-3(1),* Everbind) Marco Bk. Co.

—The Hunger Games. 2010. (Hunger Games Trilogy: Bk. 1). (ENG.). 374p. (gr. 7-12). 21.00 *(978-1-60686-581-1(1))* Perfection Learning Corp.

—The Hunger Games. Fournier, Guillaume, tr. 2011. (Hunger Games Trilogy: Bk. 1). (FRE.). 398p. (YA). (gr. 7-12). pap. *(978-2-266-18269-0(2))* Presses Pocket.

—The Hunger Games. 2011. (Hunger Games Trilogy: 1). (YA). 69.75 *(978-1-4561-3196-8(6))* Recorded Bks., Inc.

—The Hunger Games. 2009. (Hunger Games Trilogy: Bk. 1). (ENG., Illus.). 448p. pap. *(978-1-4071-0908-4(1),* Scholastic) Scholastic, Inc.

—The Hunger Games. l.t. ed. (Hunger Games Trilogy: Bk. 1). (ENG.). (YA). 2012. 484p. (gr. 7-12). pap. 14.99 *(978-1-59413-587-3(8),* Large Print Pr.) 2009. 485p. 23.95 *(978-1-4104-1986-6(X))* Thorndike Pr.

—The Hunger Games. 2010. (Hunger Games Trilogy Ser.: 1). (SWE.). lib. bdg. 22.10 *(978-1-4178-3173-9(1))* Turtleback.

—The Hunger Games. 2010. (Hunger Games Trilogy: Bk. 1). (CHI.). 324p. (YA). (gr. 7-12). pap. *(978-7-5063-5153-9(6))* Writers' Publishing Hse.

—The Hunger Games (Hunger Games, Book One), 1 vol. (Hunger Games Ser.: 1). (ENG.). 384p. (J). (gr. 7-18). 2010. pap. 14.99 *(978-0-439-02352-8(1))* 2008. 22.99 *(978-0-439-02348-1(3))* Scholastic, Inc. (Scholastic Pr.).

—The Hunger Games (Hunger Games, Book One) (Unabridged Edition), 9 vols., Vol. 1. unabr. ed. 2018. (Hunger Games Ser.: 1). (ENG.). 2p. (YA). (gr. 7). audio compact disk 44.99 *(978-1-338-33492-0(1))* Scholastic, Inc.

—Hunger Games Trilogy Boxed Set: Paperback Classic Collection. 2014. (Hunger Games Ser.). (ENG.). (J). (gr. 7-7). 36.97 *(978-0-545-67031-9(4),* Scholastic Pr.) Scholastic, Inc.

—The Hunger Games Trilogy Boxed Set Set. 2010. (Hunger Games Ser.: 1). (ENG.). (J). (gr. 7-7). 53.97 *(978-0-545-26535-5(5),* Scholastic Pr.) Scholastic, Inc.

—Los Juegos del Hambre. 2012. (Hunger Games Trilogy Spanish Ser.: 1).Tr. of Hunger Games. (SPA.). lib. bdg. 33.05 *(978-0-606-26447-1(7))* Turtleback.

—Los Juegos del Hambre (los Juegos del Hambre 1) 2012. (Hunger Games Trilogy: Bk. 1). (SPA.). 400p. (gr. 8-12). pap. 21.99 *(978-84-272-0212-2(1))* Molino, Editorial ESP. Dist: Lectorum Pubns., Inc.

—Mockingjay. 2011. (Hunger Games Trilogy: Bk. 3). (CHI.). 435p. (YA). (gr. 7-12). pap. *(978-986-213-216-6(7))* Locus Publishing Co.

—Mockingjay. (Hunger Games Trilogy: 3). (YA). 2011. 77.75 *(978-1-4561-3203-3(2))* 2010. 1.25 *(978-1-4640-2636-2(X))* 2010. 75.75 *(978-1-4561-3205-7(9))* Recorded Bks., Inc.

—Mockingjay. 2011. (Hunger Games Ser.: Vol. 3). (ENG.). 448p. (YA). (gr. 8-12). pap. *(978-1-4071-3210-5(5))* Scholastic Canada, Ltd.

—Mockingjay. 2010. pap. *(978-0-439-02354-2(8),* Scholastic Pr.) Scholastic, Inc.

—Mockingjay. l.t. ed. (Hunger Games Trilogy: Bk. 3). (ENG.). (YA). 2012. 502p. (gr. 7-12). pap. 14.99 *(978-1-59413-586-6(X),* Large Print Pr.) 2010. 503p. 23.99 *(978-1-4104-2841-7(9))* Thorndike Pr.

—Mockingjay. 2014. (Hunger Games Trilogy Ser.: 3). lib. bdg. 24.50 *(978-0-606-36328-0(9));* lib. bdg. 24.50 *(978-0-606-35133-1(7))* Turtleback.

—Mockingjay (Hunger Games, Book Three), 1 vol. (Hunger Games Ser.: 3). (ENG.). 400p. (J). (gr. 7). 2014. pap. 14.99 *(978-0-545-66326-7(1))* 2010. 19.99 *(978-0-439-02351-1(3))* Scholastic, Inc. (Scholastic Pr.).

—Sinsajo. 2012. (Hunger Games Trilogy Spanish Ser.: 3).Tr. of Mockingjay. (SPA.). lib. bdg. 33.05 *(978-0-606-26449-5(3))* Turtleback.

—Sinsajo (los Juegos del Hambre 3) (Hunger Games Trilogy: Bk. 3). (SPA.). 424p. (gr. 8-12). 2012. pap. 21.99 *(978-84-272-0214-6(8))* 2010. (J). pap. 19.99 *(978-84-272-0038-8(2))* Molino, Editorial ESP. Dist: Lectorum Pubns., Inc.

Collins, Tim. The Long-Lost Secret Diary of the World's Worst Astronaut. 2018. (Long-Lost Secret Diary Ser.). (ENG., Illus.). 216p. (J). (gr. 4-5). pap. 9.99 *(978-1-63163-192-4(6),* 1631631926); lib. bdg. 28.50 *(978-1-63163-191-7(8),* 1631631918) North Star Editions. (Jolly Fish Pr.).

—Sneezy Alien Attack: Cosmic Colin. Bigwood, John, illus. 2014. (Cosmic Colin Ser.: 2). (ENG.). 128p. (J). (gr. 4-6). pap. 9.99 *(978-1-78055-242-2(4))* O'Mara, Michael Bks., Ltd. GBR. Dist: Independent Pubs. Group.

Collins, Tim & Bigwood, John. Cosmic Colin: Ticking Time Bomb. 2017. (Cosmic Colin Ser.: 4). (ENG., Illus.). 128p. (J). (gr. 4-6). pap. 8.99 *(978-1-78055-481-5(8))* O'Mara, Michael Bks., Ltd. GBR. Dist: Independent Pubs. Group.

Condie, Ally. Juntos. 2011.Tr. of Matched. (SPA.). lib. bdg. 22.05 *(978-0-606-26417-4(5))* Turtleback.

Condon, Bill. Planet Puzzle. 1 vol. rev. ed. 2013. (Literary Text Ser.). (ENG., Illus.). 28p. (gr. 2-3). pap. 9.99 *(978-1-4333-5562-2(0))* Teacher Created Materials, Inc.

Connely, Chris L. & Vaughan, Mark. An Alien from Earth. 2003. 175p. per. 9.95 *(978-0-9745544-0-2(5))* Lewis Lynn Bks.

Conner, Jimmie L. The Adventures of Captain Computerman & His Sidekick Mouseman: The Saving of the Toy Websites. 2005. 77p. pap. 19.95 *(978-1-4137-7457-3(1))* America Star Bks.

The Contagious Colors of Mumpley Middle School. 2014. (ENG., Illus.). 288p. (J). (gr. 2-5). pap. 8.99 *(978-1-4424-7830-5(6),* Atheneum Bks. for Young Readers) Simon & Schuster Children's Publishing.

Cook, Donna. The Silly Solar System. 2009. pap. 15.00 *(978-1-61623-557-4(8))* Independent Pub.

Cook, Eileen. Remember. 2015. (ENG., Illus.). 320p. (YA). (gr. 9). 17.99 *(978-1-4814-1696-2(0),* Simon Pulse) Simon Pulse.

Cook, Julia. Hygiene... You Stink!, Volume 5. DuFalla, Anita, illus. 2014. (Building Relationships Ser.). (ENG.). 31p. (J). (gr. k-6). pap. 10.95 *(978-1-934490-62-4(8))* Boys Town Pr.

Cook, Sherry & Johnson, Terri. Gilbert Gas, 26 vols. Kuhn, Jesse, illus. l.t. ed. 2006. (Quirkles — Exploring Phonics through Science Ser.: 7). 32p. (J). 7.99 *(978-1-933815-06-0(X),* Quirkles, The) Creative 3, LLC.

—Inquisitive Inman, 26 vols. Kuhn, Jesse, illus. l.t. ed. 2006. (Quirkles — Exploring Phonics through Science Ser.: 9). 32p. (J). 7.99 *(978-1-933815-08-4(6),* Quirkles, The) Creative 3, LLC.

—Kitchen Chemistry Kal, 26 vols. Kuhn, Jesse, illus. l.t. ed. 2006. (Quirkles — Exploring Phonics through Science Ser.: 11). 32p. (J). 7.99 *(978-1-933815-10-7(8),* Quirkles, The) Creative 3, LLC.

—Mary Motion, 26 vols. Kuhn, Jesse, illus. l.t. ed. 2006. (Quirkles — Exploring Phonics through Science Ser.: 13). 32p. (J). 7.99 *(978-1-933815-12-1(4),* Quirkles, The) Creative 3, LLC.

—Ollie Oxygen, 26 vols. Kuhn, Jesse, illus. l.t. ed. 2006. (Quirkles — Exploring Phonics through Science Ser.: 15). 32p. (J). 7.99 *(978-1-933815-14-5(0),* Quirkles, The) Creative 3, LLC.

—Pressure Pete, 26 vols. Kuhn, Jesse, illus. l.t. ed. 2006. (Quirkles — Exploring Phonics through Science Ser.: 16). 32p. (J). 7.99 *(978-1-933815-15-2(9),* Quirkles, The) Creative 3, LLC.

—Quincy Quake, 26. Kuhn, Jesse, illus. l.t. ed. 2006. (Quirkles — Exploring Phonics through Science Ser.: 17). 32p. (J). 7.99 *(978-1-933815-16-9(7),* Quirkles, The) Creative 3, LLC.

—Zany Science Zeke, 26. Kuhn, Jesse, illus. l.t. ed. 2006. (Quirkles — Exploring Phonics through Science Ser.: 26). 32p. (J). 7.99 *(978-1-933815-25-1(6),* Quirkles, The) Creative 3, LLC.

Cooper, Susan. Green Boy. 2013. (ENG., Illus.). 208p. (J). (gr. 3-7). 17.99 *(978-1-4424-8081-0(5));* pap. 8.99 *(978-1-4424-8082-7(3))* McElderry, Margaret K. Bks. (McElderry, Margaret K. Bks.).

Cooper, T. & Glock-Cooper, Allison. Changers Book One: Drew. 2014. (Changers Ser.). (ENG., Illus.). 288p. (gr. 6). pap. 11.95 *(978-1-61775-195-0(2),* Black Sheep) Akashic Bks.

Coppens, Katie. The Acadia Files: Book Two, Autumn Science, 1 vol. Hatam, Holly, illus. 2018. (Acadia Science Ser.: 2). (ENG.). 80p. (J). (gr. 4-7). 13.95 *(978-0-88448-604-6(4),* 884604) Tilbury Hse. Pubs.

Cory, Adrian A. On the Eighth Tin. 2014. (ENG., Illus.). 194p. (J). (gr. -1-12). pap. 11.95 *(978-1-78279-368-7(2),* Lodestone Bks.) Hunt, John Publishing Ltd. GBR. Dist: National Bk. Network.

Costa, Mike. Venom: The Land Before Crime, Vol. 2. Sandoval, Gerardo & Moore, Tradd, illus. 2017. (Venom Ser.: 2). 120p. (gr. 8-17). pap. 16.99 *(978-1-302-90603-0(8),* Marvel Universe) Marvel Worldwide, Inc.

Cotes, Gilles. OGM et Chant de Mais. Begin, Jean-Guy, illus. 2004. (FRE.). 112p. (J). *(978-2-89599-002-4(6))* Editions de la Paix CAN. Dist: World of Reading, Ltd.

Cotterill, Jo. Electrigirl. Brett, Cathy, illus. 2017. (Electrigirl Ser.). (ENG.). 240p. (J). (gr. 4-8). pap. 8.95 *(978-1-4965-5654-7(2),* 136670); pap., pap., pap. 26.85 *(978-1-4965-5646-2(1),* 27371) Capstone. (Stone Arch Bks.).

—Electrigirl & the Deadly Swarm. Brett, Cathy, illus. 2017. (Electrigirl Ser.). (ENG.). 240p. (J). (gr. 4-8). pap. 8.95 *(978-1-4965-5661-5(5),* 136671, Stone Arch Bks.) Capstone.

—Electrigirl & the Invisible Thieves. Brett, Cathy, illus. 2017. (Electrigirl Ser.). (ENG.). 240p. (J). (gr. 4-8). pap. 8.95 *(978-1-4965-5669-1(0),* 136672, Stone Arch Bks.) Capstone.

Courage, Nick. The Loudness: A Novel. 2015. (ENG.). 336p. (J). (gr. 3-7). 15.99 *(978-1-63220-414-1(2),* Sky Pony Pr.) Skyhorse Publishing Co., Inc.

Cousineau, Craig S. Skippy & Oaf: The Battle Against Oxygen Radicals. 2007. (ENG., Illus.). 48p. (J). (gr. 2-4). per. *(978-1-933255-27-9(7))* DNA Pr.

Coville, Bruce. Aliens Ate My Homework. Coville, Katherine, illus. 2008. (Rod Allbright & the Galactic Patrol Ser.). 179p. (gr. 3-7). 17.00 *(978-0-7569-8466-3(1))* Perfection Learning Corp.

—Aliens Ate My Homework. 179p. (J). (gr. 4-6). pap. 3.99 *(978-0-8072-1503-6(1),* Listening Library) Random Hse. Audio Publishing Group.

—Aliens Ate My Homework. Coville, Katherine, illus. 2007. (Rod Allbright & the Galactic Patrol Ser.). (ENG.). 192p. (J). (gr. 3-7). pap. 7.99 *(978-1-4169-3883-5(4),* Aladdin) Simon & Schuster Children's Publishing.

—Aliens Ate My Homework Collection (Boxed Set) Aliens Ate My Homework; I Left My Sneakers in Dimension X; the Search for Snout; Aliens Stole My Body. Coville, Katherine, illus. 2018. (Rod Allbright & the Galactic Patrol Ser.). (ENG.). 848p. (J). (gr. 3-7). pap. 27.99 *(978-1-5344-1514-0(9),* Aladdin) Simon & Schuster Children's Publishing.

—Aliens Stole My Body. Coville, Katherine, illus. 2008. (Rod Allbright & the Galactic Patrol Ser.). (ENG.). 240p. (J). (gr. 3-7). pap. 7.99 *(978-1-4169-5359-3(0),* Simon & Schuster/Paula Wiseman Bks.) Simon & Schuster/Paula Wiseman Bks.

S

—I Left My Sneakers in Dimension X. Coville, Katherine, illus. 2007. (Rod Allbright & the Galactic Patrol Ser.). (ENG.). 192p. (J). (gr. 3-7). pap. 7.99 *(978-1-4169-3882-8(6),* Simon & Schuster/Paula Wiseman Bks.) Simon & Schuster/Paula Wiseman Bks.

—I Lost My Grandfather's Brain. unabr. ed. 2004. (I Was a Sixth Grade Alien Ser.: Vol. 3). 160p. (J). (gr. 3-6). pap. 29.00 incl. audio *(978-0-8072-8385-1(1),* YA180SP, Listening Library) Random Hse. Audio Publishing Group.

—I Was a Sixth Grade Alien. (I Was a Sixth Grade Alien Ser.: Vol. 1). 170p. (J). (gr. 4-6). pap. 3.99 *(978-0-8072-8202-1(2));* 2004. (gr. 3-6). pap. 29.00 incl. audio *(978-0-8072-8201-4(4),* S YA 138 SP) Random Hse. Audio Publishing Group. (Listening Library).

—The Monsters of Morley Manor. 2003. (Madcap Adventures Ser.). 223p. (gr. 3-7). 17.00 *(978-0-7569-1627-5(5))* Perfection Learning Corp.

—The Monsters of Morley Manor: A Madcap Adventure. 2003. (ENG.). 240p. (J). (gr. 3-7). pap. 7.99 *(978-0-15-204705-4(0),* 1194174, Clarion Bks.) HarperCollins Pubs.

—My Teacher Flunked the Planet. Pierard, John, illus. 2005. (My Teacher Bks.: 4). (ENG.). 176p. (J). (gr. 3-7). pap. 7.99 *(978-1-4169-0331-4(3),* Aladdin) Simon & Schuster Children's Publishing.

—My Teacher Fried My Brains. 2014. (My Teacher Bks.: 2). (ENG., Illus.). 176p. (J). (gr. 3-7). 17.99 *(978-1-4814-0431-0(8),* Aladdin) Simon & Schuster Children's Publishing.

—My Teacher Is an Alien. unabr. ed. 2004. (My Teacher Is an Alien Ser.: Bk. 1). 123p. (J). (gr. 3-6). pap. 29.00 incl. audio *(978-0-8072-8029-4(1),* S YA971 SP, Listening Library) Random Hse. Audio Publishing Group.

—My Teacher Is an Alien. 2005. (My Teacher Bks.: 1). (ENG., Illus.). 160p. (J). (gr. 3-7). pap. 7.99 *(978-1-4169-0334-5(8),* Aladdin) Simon & Schuster Children's Publishing.

—My Teacher Is an Alien. 2014. (My Teacher Bks.: 1). (ENG., Illus.). 160p. (J). (gr. 3-7). 17.99 *(978-1-4814-0430-3(X),* Simon & Schuster/Paula Wiseman Bks.) Simon & Schuster/Paula Wiseman Bks.

—The Search for Snout. Coville, Katherine, illus. 2007. (Rod Allbright & the Galactic Patrol Ser.). (ENG.). 224p. (J). (gr. 3-7). pap. 7.99 *(978-1-4169-4980-0(1),* Simon & Schuster/Paula Wiseman Bks.) Simon & Schuster/Paula Wiseman Bks.

Cowey, James. William Snottengrout - Quapta's Revenge. 2006. 104p. per. *(978-1-84667-023-7(3))* Derwent Pr., The.

Cox, Greg. Riese: Kingdom Falling. 2013. (ENG., Illus.). 288p. (YA). (gr. 7). pap. 9.99 *(978-1-4424-2970-3(4),* Simon & Schuster Bks. For Young Readers) Simon & Schuster Bks. For Young Readers.

Coyle, Katie. Vivian Apple Needs a Miracle. 2017. (ENG.). 304p. (YA). (gr. 7). pap. 9.99 *(978-0-544-81318-2(9),* 1641919, Clarion Bks.) HarperCollins Pubs.

Craig, Joe. Jimmy Coates: Killer. 2007. 261p. (J). (gr. 5-9). 15.99 *(978-0-06-077266-6(2))* HarperCollins Pubs.

Cremer, Andrea. The Inventor's Secret. 2015. (Inventor's Secret Ser.: 1). (ENG.). 416p. (YA). (gr. 7). pap. 10.99 *(978-0-14-751438-7(X),* Speak) Penguin Young Readers Group.

Crew, Gary. The Viewer. Tan, Shaun, illus. 2003. (ENG.). 32p. (J). (gr. 1-6). 16.95 *(978-1-894965-02-6(7))* Simply Read Bks. CAN. Dist: Ingram Publisher Services.

Crewe, Megan. The Clouded Sky, 0 vols. 2015. (Earth & Sky Trilogy Ser.: 2). (ENG.). 354p. (YA). (gr. 7-12). pap. 9.99 *(978-1-4778-2912-7(1),* 9781477829127, Skyscape) Amazon Publishing.

—The Lives We Lost. 2018. (Fallen World Ser.: Vol. 2). (ENG., Illus.). 292p. (YA). (gr. 7-12). pap. 11.99 *(978-0-9952169-8-3(3))* Another World Pr.

—A Sky Unbroken, 0 vols. 2015. (Earth & Sky Trilogy Ser.: 3). (ENG., Illus.). 347p. (YA). (gr. 7-12). pap. 9.99 *(978-1-5039-4657-6(6),* 9781503946576, Skyscape) Amazon Publishing.

—The Way We Fall. 2018. (Fallen World Ser.: Vol. 1). (ENG., Illus.). 336p. (YA). (gr. 7-12). pap. 11.99 *(978-0-9952169-4-5(0))* Another World Pr.

—The Way We Fall, 1. 2013. (Fallen World Trilogy Ser.). (ENG.). 336p. (YA). (gr. 8-12). 24.94 *(978-1-4231-4631-5(X))* Hyperion Bks. for Children.

—The Worlds We Make. 2018. (Fallen World Ser.: Vol. 3). (ENG., Illus.). 298p. (YA). (gr. 7-12). pap. 11.99 *(978-0-9952169-9-0(1))* Another World Pr.

Crews, G. S. Ellen G Goes to the Haunted Planetarium. Designs, Marion, photos by. 2009. (Illus.). 50p. pap. 20.00 *(978-0-9795236-4-9(8))* Crews Pubns., LLC.

Crilley, Mark. Akiko Flights of Fancy. exp. ed. 2007. (Illus.). 264p. pap. 24.95 *(978-1-57989-088-9(1))* Sirius Entertainment, Inc.

—The Battle for Boach's Keep Vol. 7. 2004. (Illus.). 144p. pap. 14.95 *(978-1-57989-064-3(4))* Sirius Entertainment, Inc.

Crilley, Paul. The Osiris Curse: A Tweed & Nightingale Adventure. 2013. (Tweed & Nightingale Adventures Ser.). (ENG.). 287p. (YA). (gr. 7). 17.99 *(978-1-61614-857-7(8))*, Pyr) Start Publishing LLC.

Crockett, S. D. After the Snow. 2013. (After the Snow Ser.: 1). (ENG.). 320p. (YA). (gr. 7-12). pap. 13.99 *(978-1-250-01676-8(2))*, 900087090) Square Fish.

Crofoot, Betty & Arledge, Roo. Battle for the Multiverse - My Genie & Me Series Book 3. 2013. 92p. pap. 8.95 *(978-1-60862-489-8(7))* E-BookTime LLC.

Cross, Julie. Tempest: A Novel. 2012. (Tempest Trilogy Ser.: 1). (ENG.). 368p. (YA). (gr. 9-12). pap. 14.99 *(978-1-250-01120-6(5))*, 900084879, St. Martin's Griffin) St. Martin's Pr.

—Vortex: A Tempest Novel. 2013. (Tempest Trilogy Ser.: 2). (ENG.). 384p. (YA). (gr. 9-12). pap. 14.99 *(978-1-250-04478-5(2))*, 900127471, St. Martin's Griffin) St. Martin's Pr.

Crossan, Sarah. Breathe. 2013. (Breathe Ser.: 1). (ENG.). 400p. (YA). (gr. 9). pap. 11.99 *(978-0-06-211870-7(6))*, Greenwillow Bks.) HarperCollins Pubs.

Crow, E. J. The Eye Pocket. 2006. (Fantastic Society of Peculiar Adventures Ser.). (ENG., Illus.). 48p. (J). (gr. 2-4). per. *(978-1-933255-17-0(X))* DNA Pr.

Crowder, Melanie. A Way Between Worlds. 2020. (Lighthouse Keepers Ser.). (ENG.). 224p. (J). (gr. 3-7). pap. 7.99 *(978-1-5344-0519-6(4))* Simon & Schuster Children's Publishing.

Cunningham, Mary. The Magic Medallion. 2006. (Cynthia's Attic Ser.). 158p. (J). (gr. 4-7). per. 9.99 *(978-1-59080-460-5(0))* Echelon Press Publishing.

A Cup of Tea, A Piece of Pie. 2004. (J). 14.95 *(978-0-9747363-4-1(1))* Kelly, Kimberly.

Curtis, Simon. Boy Robot. 2016. (ENG., Illus.). 432p. (YA). (gr. 9). 17.99 *(978-1-4814-5929-7(5))*, Simon Pulse) Simon Pulse.

Cushman, Doug. Space Cat. Cushman, Doug, illus. 2006. (I Can Read Bks.). (Illus.). 32p. (gr. -1-3). 14.00 *(978-0-7569-6977-6(8))* Perfection Learning Corp.

Cusick, John M. Girl Parts. (ENG., Illus.). 240p. (YA). (gr. 9). 2012. pap. 7.99 *(978-0-7636-5644-7(5))* 2010. 16.99 *(978-0-7636-4930-2(9))* Candlewick Pr.

Czerneda, Julie E., ed. Odyssey, 1 vol. Normand, Jean-Pierre, illus. 2004. (Wonder Zone Ser.). (ENG.). 130p. (J). (gr. 4-7). pap. 9.95 *(978-1-55244-080-3(X))*, 2520cb1b-a57f-44c1-922e-e52d426cf3a2) Fitzhenry & Whiteside, Ltd. CAN. Dist: Firefly Bks., Ltd.

—Polaris: A Celebration of Polar Science, 1 vol. Normand, Jean-Pierre, illus. 2007. (Wonder Zone Ser.). (ENG.). 174p. (YA). (gr. 5-8). per. 6.95 *(978-0-88995-372-7(4))*, 63753e61-0c66-46f2-9525-7e3b0b04cfb2) Red Deer Pr. CAN. Dist: Firefly Bks., Ltd.

Dael, Do Van. Earth Child. 2012. (Illus.). 24p. pap. 19.82 *(978-1-4772-1402-2(X))* AuthorHouse.

Dahl, Michael. Attack of the Drones. Clarey, Patricio, illus. 2019. (Escape from Planet Alcatraz Ser.). (ENG.). 40p. (J). (gr. 3-6). lib. bdg. 24.65 *(978-1-4965-8315-4(9))*, 140490, Stone Arch Bks.) Capstone.

—A Buried Starship. Levins, Tim & Vecchio, Luciano, illus. 2017. (Superman Tales of the Fortress of Solitude Ser.). (ENG.). 40p. (J). (gr. 4-8). lib. bdg. 24.65 *(978-1-4965-4395-0(5))*, 134635, Stone Arch Bks.) Capstone.

—Last Son of Krypton. Delaney, John, illus. 2009. (Superman Ser.). (ENG.). 56p. (J). (gr. 3-6). pap. 4.95 *(978-1-4342-1370-9(6))*, 95667); lib. bdg. 26.65 *(978-1-4342-1155-2(X))*, 95369) Capstone. (Stone Arch Bks.).

—The Museum Monsters. Schoening, Dan, illus. 2009. (Superman Ser.). (ENG.). 56p. (J). (gr. 3-6). pap. 4.95 *(978-1-4342-1372-3(2))*, 95669, Stone Arch Bks.) Capstone.

—The Pit of No Return. Clarey, Patricio, illus. 2019. (Escape from Planet Alcatraz Ser.). (ENG.). 40p. (J). (gr. 3-6). lib. bdg. 24.65 *(978-1-4965-8311-6(6))*, 140486, Stone Arch Bks.) Capstone.

—Voyage to the Metal Moon. Clarey, Patricio, illus. 2019. (Escape from Planet Alcatraz Ser.). (ENG.). 40p. (J). (gr. 3-6). lib. bdg. 24.65 *(978-1-4965-8314-7(0))*, 140489, Stone Arch Bks.) Capstone.

Dahl, Roald. Charlie & the Great Glass Elevator. Blake, Quentin, illus. (ENG.). (J). (gr. 3-7). 2007. 192p. 8.99 *(978-0-14-241032-5(2))* 2005. 176p. pap. 7.99 *(978-0-14-240412-6(8))* Penguin Young Readers Group. (Puffin Books).

—Charlie & the Great Glass Elevator. 2007. 18.40 *(978-1-4177-8610-7(8))* Turtleback.

Dale, Jeremy. Battle at Three Rivers, Vol. 3. 2014. (ENG., Illus.). 96p. (YA). pap. 8.99 *(978-1-939352-55-2(X))*, fe55253b-cd8b-45a6-9727-33403fbc1e11) Action Lab Entertainment.

—Into the Woods. 2014. (ENG., Illus.). 96p. (J). pap. 8.99 *(978-1-939352-50-7(9))*, c037cf7b-7e09-493e-a8a6-fce3c136e6fc) Action Lab Entertainment.

—Strange Creatures, Vol. 2. 2014. (ENG., Illus.). 96p. (J). pap. 8.99 *(978-1-939352-52-1(5))*, 80af0392-9798-499f-a1e5-69705aedd104) Action Lab Entertainment.

Daley, Michael J. Rat Trap. 2008. (ENG.). 272p. (J). (gr. 3-7). 16.95 *(978-0-8234-2093-3(0))* Holiday Hse., Inc.

Dalton, Ryan. The Black Tempest. 2017. (Time Shift Trilogy Ser.). (ENG.). 448p. (YA). (gr. 9-12). pap. 14.99 *(978-1-63163-106-1(3))*, 1631631063, Jolly Fish Pr.) North Star Editions.

—The Genesis Flame. 2018. (Time Shift Trilogy Ser.). (ENG.). 480p. (YA). (gr. 9-12). pap. 14.99 *(978-1-63163-170-2(5))*, 1631631705, Jolly Fish Pr.) North Star Editions.

Daly, Joseph M. Strange Town Volume One: The Woods Behind Trevor Malone's House. 2007. 265p. (YA). pap. 9.99 net. *(978-0-9779921-0-2(1))* Wolfs Corner Publishing.

Dare, Danni. Jake Jett: Adventures in Space. 2010. 32p. pap. 12.99 *(978-1-4520-4981-6(5))* AuthorHouse.

Dashner, James. The Blade of Shattered Hope. 2010. (13th Reality Ser.: Bk. 3). 432p. (J). 18.99 *(978-1-60641-239-8(6))*, Shadow Mountain) Shadow Mountain Publishing.

—The Blade of Shattered Hope. Dorman, Brandon, illus. 2011. (13th Reality Ser.: 3). (ENG.). 528p. (J). (gr. 3-7). pap. 9.99 *(978-1-4424-0871-5(5))*, Aladdin) Simon & Schuster Children's Publishing.

—The Death Cure. 2013. (Maze Runner Ser.: 3). lib. bdg. 20.85 *(978-0-606-27005-2(1))* Turtleback.

—The Death Cure (Maze Runner, Book Three) (Maze Runner Ser.: 3). (ENG.). (YA). (gr. 7). 2013. 368p. pap. 10.99 *(978-0-385-73878-1(1))* 2011. 352p. 19.99 *(978-0-385-73877-4(3))* Random Hse. Children's Bks. (Delacorte Pr.).

—The Eye of Minds. 2013. 310p. (YA). *(978-0-385-38370-7(3))*, Delacorte Pr) Random House Publishing Group.

—The Eye of Minds (the Mortality Doctrine, Book One) 2014. (Mortality Doctrine Ser.: 1). (ENG.). 352p. (YA). (gr. 7). pap. 13.99 *(978-0-385-74140-8(5))*, Ember) Random Hse. Children's Bks.

—The Fever Code (Maze Runner, Book Five; Prequel) 2016. (Maze Runner Ser.: 5). (ENG.). 384p. (YA). (gr. 7). 18.99 *(978-0-553-51309-7(5))*, Delacorte Pr.) Random Hse. Children's Bks.

—The Game of Lives (the Mortality Doctrine, Book Three) 2017. (Mortality Doctrine Ser.: 3). (ENG.). 384p. (YA). (gr. 7). pap. 11.99 *(978-0-385-74144-6(8))*, Ember) Random Hse. Children's Bks.

—A Gift of Ice. 2004. (Jimmy Fincher Saga: Bk. 2). 208p. pap. 14.99 *(978-1-55517-753-9(0))*, 1232041) Cedar Fort, Inc./CFI Distribution.

—The Hunt for Dark Infinity. Beus, Bryan, illus. 2009. (13th Reality Ser.: Bk. 2). 446p. (J). 18.95 *(978-1-60641-034-9(2))*, Shadow Mountain) Shadow Mountain Publishing.

—The Hunt for Dark Infinity. Beus, Bryan, illus. 2010. (13th Reality Ser.: 2). (ENG.). 544p. (J). (gr. 3-7). pap. 9.99 *(978-1-4169-9153-3(0))*, Aladdin) Simon & Schuster Children's Publishing.

—The Journal of Curious Letters. Beus, Bryan, illus. 2008. (13th Reality Ser.: Bk. 1). 434p. (J). (gr. 4-7). 17.95 *(978-1-59038-831-0(3))*, Shadow Mountain) Shadow Mountain Publishing.

—The Journal of Curious Letters. Beus, Bryan, illus. 2009. (13th Reality Ser.: 1). (ENG.). 528p. (J). (gr. 3-7). 240p. pap. 9.99 *(978-1-4169-9152-6(2))*, Aladdin) Simon & Schuster Children's Publishing.

—The Kill Order. 2014. (Maze Runner Ser.: 0). lib. bdg. 20.85 *(978-0-606-35572-8(3))* Turtleback.

—The Maze Runner. 2010. (Maze Runner Ser.: 1). 375p. lib. bdg. 20.85 *(978-0-606-15077-4(3))* Turtleback.

—The Maze Runner: Virus Letal. 2013. 362p. (YA). pap. 15.99 *(978-987-612-565-9(6))* V&R Editoras.

—The Maze Runner (Maze Runner, Book One) Book One. (Maze Runner Ser.: 1). (ENG.). (YA). (gr. 7). 2010. 416p. pap. 10.99 *(978-0-385-73795-1(5))* 2009. 400p. 19.99 *(978-0-385-73794-4(7))* Random Hse. Children's Bks. (Delacorte Pr.).

—The Maze Runner Series Complete Collection Boxed Set (5-Book), 5 vols. 2016. (Maze Runner Ser.). (ENG.). (YA). (gr. 7). 98.95 *(978-1-5247-1434-5(8))*, Delacorte Pr.) Random Hse. Children's Bks.

—The Maze Runner Trilogy, 3 vols. 2013. (Maze Runner Ser.). (ENG.). (YA). pap., pap., pap. 29.97 *(978-0-385-37379-1(1))*, Ember) Random Hse. Children's Bks.

—A Mutiny in Time. 2015. (Infinity Ring Ser.: 1). lib. bdg. 17.20 *(978-0-606-37765-2(4))* Turtleback.

—The Rule of Thoughts (the Mortality Doctrine, Book Two), Bk. 2. 2016. (Mortality Doctrine Ser.: 2). (ENG.). 352p. (YA). (gr. 7). pap. 11.99 *(978-0-385-74142-2(1))*, Ember) Random Hse. Children's Bks.

—The Scorch Trials. 2011. (Maze Runner Ser.: 2). lib. bdg. 20.85 *(978-0-606-23430-6(6))* Turtleback.

—The Scorch Trials (Maze Runner, Book Two) (Maze Runner Ser.: 2). (ENG.). (YA). (gr. 7). 2011. 400p. pap. 10.99 *(978-0-385-73876-7(5))* 2010. 384p. 19.99 *(978-0-385-73875-0(7))* Random Hse. Children's Bks. (Delacorte Pr.).

—The Void of Mist & Thunder. Dorman, Brandon, illus. 2013. (13th Reality Ser.: 4). (ENG.). 496p. (J). (gr. 3-7). pap. 9.99 *(978-1-4424-0873-9(1))*, Aladdin) Simon & Schuster Children's Publishing.

Davenport, Roger. Wanderer. (ENG.). 2016. 268p. (J). (gr. 6-6). pap. 8.99 *(978-1-5107-0389-6(6))* 2013. 288p. (YA). (gr. 8-12). 16.95 *(978-1-62087-541-4(1))*, 620541) Skyhorse Publishing Co., Inc. (Sky Pony Pr.).

David, Charles. Skull in the Birdcage (Knightscares #2, an Epic Fantasy Adventure Series) Knightscares #2. 2003. (Knightscares Ser.: Vol. 2). 208p. (J). per. 5.99 *(978-0-9728461-1-0(5))*, 1222855) Sigil Publishing.

David, Lawrence. El niño escarabajo. 2004. (SPA.). 32p. *(978-84-7720-794-8(1))* Ediciones Obelisco.

Davidson, Ellen. When the Third Moon Wanes. 2004. 123p. pap. 19.95 *(978-1-4137-2233-8(4))* America Star Bks.

Davidson, Lg. Supernova's Unique Family. 2012. 36p. pap. 20.99 *(978-1-4772-6322-8(5))* AuthorHouse.

Davidson, MaryJanice & Alongi, Anthony. The Silver Moon Elm: A Jennifer Scales Novel, 3 vols. 2008. (Jennifer Scales Ser.: 3). (ENG.). 288p. (gr. 12-18). 7.99 *(978-0-441-01601-3(4))*, Ace) Penguin Publishing Group.

Davila, Andrew. Prophecies of the Ancient. 2003. 110p. (YA). pap. 9.95 *(978-0-595-26851-1(X))* iUniverse, Inc.

Davis, Adam. Avengers: Age of Ultron: Hulk to the Rescue. 2015. (Passport to Reading Level 2 Ser.). (J). lib. bdg. 13.55 *(978-0-606-37215-2(6))* Turtleback.

Davis, Pat. Estelle & the Escape from Mars: A Children's Novel By. 2009. 136p. pap. 10.99 *(978-1-4389-5432-5(8))* AuthorHouse.

Davroe, A. L. Nexis. 2015. (Tricksters Novel Ser.: 1). (ENG.). 304p. (YA). pap. 9.99 *(978-1-63375-017-3(5))*, 900147128) Entangled Publishing, LLC.

Dawson, Delilah S. Hit. 2015. (ENG., Illus.). 336p. (YA). (gr. 9). 17.99 *(978-1-4814-2339-7(8))*, Simon Pulse) Simon Pulse.

—Strike. 2016. (ENG., Illus.). 480p. (YA). (gr. 9). 17.99 *(978-1-4814-2342-7(8))*, Simon Pulse) Simon Pulse.

Dayton, Arwen Elys. Stronger, Faster, & More Beautiful. 2018. (ENG.). 384p. (YA). (gr. 9). 18.99 *(978-0-525-58095-9(6))*, Delacorte Pr.) Random Hse. Children's Bks.

DBG. World of Reading Avengers Boxed Set: Level 1. 2015. (World of Reading Ser.: 2). (ENG., Illus.). 192p. (J). (gr. 1-3). 12.99 *(978-1-4847-0438-7(X))* Marvel Worldwide, Inc.

de Campi, Alex. Agent Boo: The Littlest Agent, Vol. 1. Fuijkschot, Edo, illus. 2006. (Agent Boo Manga Ser.: 1). (ENG.). 96p. (J). (gr. 4-1). pap. 4.99 *(978-1-59816-802-0(9))*, a94434fe-1058-4c27-b8c9-1aabbcecc4c2, TOKYOPOP Manga) TOKYOPOP, Inc.

de la Peña, Matt. Superman: Dawnbreaker. 2019. (DC Icons Ser.). (ENG.). 336p. (YA). (gr. 7). lib. bdg. 21.99 *(978-0-399-54966-3(8))*, Random Hse. Bks. for Young Readers) Random Hse. Children's Bks.

De Saint-Exupéry, Antoine. A Day with the Little Prince. 2003. (Illus.). (J). bds. *(978-0-15-204727-6(1))*, Red Wagon Bks.) Harcourt Children's Bks. CAN. Dist: Harcourt Trade Pubs.

DeConnick, Kelly Sue. Bitch Planet, Volume 2: President Bitch, Vol. 2. 2017. lib. bdg. 26.95 *(978-0-606-38898-6(2))* Turtleback.

Dekker, Cees & Oranje, Corien. Science Geek Sam & His Secret Logbook. van Rijssen, Petra & van Rijssen, Petra, trs. 2017. (ENG., Illus.). 208p. (J). (gr. 4-6). pap. 13.99 *(978-0-7459-7724-9(3))*, b9fbce7f-90ad-4c86-ac63-3108b5a87d78, Lion Children's) Lion Hudson PLC GBR. Dist: Baker & Taylor Publisher Services (BTPS).

del Rio, Tania. Warren the 13th & the Whispering Woods: A Novel. Staehle, Will, illus. 2017. (Warren The 13th Ser.: 2). 240p. (J). (gr. 5). 16.95 *(978-1-59474-929-2(9))* Quirk Bks.

DeLonge, Tom & Herbach, Geoff. Strange Times: The Ghost in the Girl. 2016. (ENG.). 288p. (YA). 17.99 *(978-1-943272-21-1(2))* To The Stars...

DeLonge, Tom & Young, Suzanne. Poet Anderson ... in Darkness. 2018. (Poet Anderson Ser.: 2). (ENG.). 280p. (YA). 17.99 *(978-1-943272-32-7(8))* To The Stars...

Denning, Troy. Tempest: Star Wars Legends (Legacy of the Force) 2006. (Star Wars: Legacy of the Force - Legends Ser.: 3). (ENG.). 400p. mass mkt. 9.99 *(978-0-345-47752-1(9))* Random Hse. Worlds.

Denton, Terry. Storymaze 1: the Ultimate Wave. 2003. (Storymaze Ser.: Vol. 1). (ENG., Illus.). 144p. (J). (gr. 3-7). pap. 11.99 *(978-1-86508-378-0(X))* Allen & Unwin AUS. Dist: Independent Pubs. Group.

—Storymaze 2: the Eye of Ulam. 2003. (Storymaze Ser.: Vol. 2). (ENG., Illus.). 132p. (J). (gr. 3-6). pap. 11.99 *(978-1-86508-358-2(5))* Allen & Unwin AUS. Dist: Independent Pubs. Group.

d'Errico, Camilla & Sanders, Scott. Camilla d'Errico's Burn. d'Errico, Camilla, illus. 2009. (ENG., Illus.). 160p. (YA). (gr. 7-18). pap. 9.99 *(978-1-4169-7873-2(9))*, Simon Pulse) Simon Pulse.

DeStefano, Lauren. Fever, 7 vols. 2012. (Chemical Garden Trilogy: Bk. 2). (YA). 102.75 *(978-1-4640-1914-2(2))* Recorded Bks., Inc.

—Fever. (Chemical Garden Trilogy Ser.: 2). (ENG., (YA). (gr. 9). 2013. illus.). 368p. pap. 12.99 *(978-1-4424-0908-8(8))* 2012. 352p. 17.99 *(978-1-4424-0907-1(X))* Simon & Schuster Bks. For Young Readers. (Simon & Schuster Bks. For Young Readers).

—Fiebre. (Chemical Garden Trilogy: Bk. 2).Tr. of Fever. (SPA.). 352p. pap. 18.95 *(978-84-96886-28-5(X))* Ediciones Urano S. A. ESP. Dist: Spanish Pubs., LLC.

—The Girl with the Ghost Machine. 2018. (ENG.). 240p. (J). pap. 8.99 *(978-1-68119-784-5(7))*, 900186906, Bloomsbury Children's Bks.) Bloomsbury Publishing USA.

—The Girl with the Ghost Machine. 2018. (J). lib. bdg. 18.40 *(978-0-606-41072-4(4))* Turtleback.

—Perfect Ruin. 2013. (Internment Chronicles Ser.: 1). (ENG., Illus.). 368p. (YA). (gr. 7). 18.99 *(978-1-4424-8061-2(0))*, Simon & Schuster Bks. For Young Readers) Simon & Schuster Bks. For Young Readers.

—Sever. 2013. (Chemical Garden Trilogy Ser.: 3). (ENG.). 400p. (YA). (gr. 9). pap. 9.99 *(978-1-4424-0910-1(X))* Simon & Schuster.

—Sever. 2013. (Chemical Garden Trilogy Ser.: 3). (ENG.). 384p. (YA). (gr. 9). 17.99 *(978-1-4424-0909-5(6))*, Simon & Schuster Bks. For Young Readers) Simon & Schuster Bks. For Young Readers.

—Wither, 9 vols. (Chemical Garden Ser.: 1). (YA). 90.75 *(978-1-4561-2060-3(3))*; 256.75 *(978-1-4561-2059-7(X))*; 1.25 *(978-1-4561-2064-1(6))*; 2011. 122.75 *(978-1-4561-2061-0(1))*; 2011. 120.75 *(978-1-4561-2063-4(8))* Recorded Bks., Inc.

—Wither. 2011. (Chemical Garden Trilogy Ser.: 1). (ENG.). 384p. (YA). (gr. 9). pap. 13.99 *(978-1-4424-0906-4(1))*, Simon & Schuster Bks. For Young Readers) Simon & Schuster Bks. For Young Readers.

DeYoung, Andrew. The Exo Project. 2017. (ENG.). 455p. (YA). (gr. 7). 18.95 *(978-1-62979-610-9(7))*, Astra Young Readers) Astra Publishing Hse.

Diamond, Laura. Endure. 2013. 268p. pap. 11.99 *(978-1-940223-45-2(8))* Etopia Pr.

Dick, Philip. The Gun. 2011. 26p. pap. 6.95 *(978-1-60664-563-5(3))* Rodgers, Alan Bks.

Diggs, Dylan. Palladium: Second Contact. 2006. (J). mass mkt. 3.80 *(978-1-886366-13-8(6))*, 5,000) Sights Productions.

—Palladium: Trust No One. 2006. (J). mass mkt. 3.80 *(978-1-886366-14-5(4))* Sights Productions.

DiGuardo, Maggie & Leventis, Kelly. Celly. 2012. (J). 14.95 *(978-1-937406-17-2(2))* Amplify Publishing Group.

Dinn, Philip & Jones, Andy. Peg Bearskin. Cohen, Elly, illus. 2003. (ENG.). 32p. (J). pap. *(978-0-9688712-7-0(5))* Running the Goat, Bks. & Broadsides.

Disney Book Group. Trapped in the Death Star! 2016. (Star Wars: World of Reading Ser.). (Illus.). 30p. (J). lib. bdg. 14.75 *(978-0-606-39174-0(6))* Turtleback.

Disney Book Group, et al. Death Star Battle. 2016. (Star Wars: World of Reading Ser.). (Illus.). 30p. (J). lib. bdg. 13.55 *(978-0-606-39171-9(1))* Turtleback.

Disney Book Group Staff & Michaels, Kay. Star Wars Rebels. 2014. (Star Wars: World of Reading Ser.). (J). lib. bdg. 13.55 *(978-0-606-35282-6(1))* Turtleback.

Disney Press. Avengers: Battle with Ultron. 2015. (Marvel World of Reading Level 2 Ser.). (Illus.). 29p. (J). lib. bdg. 13.55 *(978-0-606-36904-6(X))* Turtleback.

Disney Press, et al. Star Wars Rebels: Kanan's Jedi Training. 2015. (Star Wars: World of Reading Ser.). (Illus.). 32p. (J). lib. bdg. 13.55 *(978-0-606-36911-4(2))* Turtleback.

Disney Press Editors. Avengers: The New Team. 2015. (Marvel World of Reading Level 1 Ser.). (J). lib. bdg. 13.55 *(978-0-606-36903-9(1))* Turtleback.

—Star Wars Rebels: Always Bet on Chopper. 2015. (Star Wars: World of Reading Ser.). (Illus.). 32p. (J). lib. bdg. 13.55 *(978-0-606-36910-7(4))* Turtleback.

—Star Wars Rebels: Hera's Phantom Flight. 2015. (Star Wars: World of Reading Ser.). (J). lib. bdg. 13.55 *(978-0-606-36909-1(0))* Turtleback.

—Use the Force! 2015. (Star Wars: World of Reading Ser.). (J). lib. bdg. 13.55 *(978-0-606-35923-8(0))* Turtleback.

Disney Press Staff & Heddle, Jennifer. Sabine's Art Attack. 2015. (Star Wars: World of Reading Ser.). (J). lib. bdg. 13.55 *(978-0-606-35928-3(1))* Turtleback.

Disney Press Staff & Rusu, Meredith. The Inquisitor's Trap. 2014. (Star Wars Rebels 8x8 Ser.). (J). lib. bdg. 14.75 *(978-0-606-35926-9(5))* Turtleback.

DiTerlizzi, Tony. A Hero for WondLa. DiTerlizzi, Tony, illus. 2023. (Search for WondLa Ser.: 2). (ENG., Illus.). (J). (gr. 5). 464p. 22.99 *(978-1-6659-2859-5(X))*; 480p. pap. 13.99 *(978-1-6659-2860-1(3))* Simon & Schuster Bks. For Young Readers. (Simon & Schuster Bks. For Young Readers).

—Jimmy Zangwow's Out-Of-This-World Moon-Pie Adventure. DiTerlizzi, Tony, illus. 2003. (ENG., Illus.). 40p. (J). (gr. k-3). 8.99 *(978-0-689-85563-4(X))*, Simon & Schuster Bks. For Young Readers) Simon & Schuster Bks. For Young Readers.

—The Search for WondLa. DiTerlizzi, Tony, illus. 2023. (Search for WondLa Ser.: 1). (ENG., Illus.). (J). (gr. 5). 496p. 22.99 *(978-1-6659-2857-1(3))*; 512p. pap. 13.99 *(978-1-6659-2858-8(1))* Simon & Schuster Bks. For Young Readers. (Simon & Schuster Bks. For Young Readers).

DiTerlizzi, Tony & Black, Holly. El Arbol Metálico. Abreu, Carlos, tr. 2007. (Escritura desatada Ser.). (SPA., Illus.). 116p. (J). (gr. 4-7). 13.95 *(978-84-666-1658-4(6))* Ediciones B ESP. Dist: Spanish Pubs., LLC.

Dixon, Chuck. Perdition's Gate, Vol. 6. Eaglesham, Dale et al, illus. 2004. (Sigil Ser.: Vol. 6). 160p. (YA). pap. 15.95 *(978-1-59314-048-9(7))* CrossGeneration Comics, Inc.

—Resurrection, Vol. 5. Cariello, Sergio et al, illus. 2004. (Crux Ser.: Vol. 5). 160p. (YA). pap. 15.95 *(978-1-59314-053-3(3))* CrossGeneration Comics, Inc.

Dixon, John. Phoenix Island. 2014. (ENG.). 320p. pap. 17.99 *(978-1-4767-3865-9(3))*, Gallery Bks.) Gallery Bks.

DK. DK Readers L1: Star Wars: the Clone Wars: Don't Wake the Zillo Beast! Beware the Galaxy's Baddest Beasts! 2011. (DK Readers Level 1 Ser.). (ENG.). 32p. (J). (gr. -1-1). 4.99 *(978-0-7566-8279-8(7))*, DK Children) Dorling Kindersley Publishing, Inc.

—Star Wars the Rise of Skywalker Amazing Sticker Adventures. 2019. (Ultimate Sticker Collection). (ENG.). 72p. (J). (gr. k-2). pap. 12.99 *(978-1-4654-7904-4(X))*, DK Children) Dorling Kindersley Publishing, Inc.

Dobson, Carol Anne. Freedom. 2013. 130p. pap. *(978-0-9558324-3-7(8))* Appledrane Bks.

Doctorow, Cory. For the Win. 2012. (ENG.). 480p. (YA). (gr. 9-12). 26.19 *(978-0-7653-2216-6(1))*, 900054863, Tor Bks.) Doherty, Tom Assocs., LLC.

—Pirate Cinema. 2013. (ENG.). 384p. (YA). (gr. 7). pap. 18.99 *(978-0-7653-2909-7(3))*, 900074453, Tor Teen) Doherty, Tom Assocs., LLC.

Doeden, Matt. Can You Survive an Artificial Intelligence Uprising? An Interactive Doomsday Adventure. Fisher-Johnson, Paul, illus. 2016. (You Choose: Doomsday Ser.). (ENG.). 112p. (J). (gr. 3-7). lib. bdg. 32.65 *(978-1-4914-8107-3(2))*, 130598, Capstone Pr.) Capstone.

—Can You Survive an Asteroid Strike? An Interactive Doomsday Adventure. Davidson, Paul, illus. 2016. (You Choose: Doomsday Ser.). (ENG.). 112p. (J). (gr. 3-7). lib. bdg. 32.65 *(978-1-4914-8109-7(9))*, 130600, Capstone Pr.) Capstone.

Donatelli, Jen & Jones, Jen. Stellar Science Fiction Crafts: 4D an Augmented Reading Crafts Experience. 2018. (Next Chapter Crafts 4D Ser.). (ENG., Illus.). 32p. (J). (gr. 1-5). lib. bdg. 33.99 *(978-1-5435-0686-0(0))*, 137432, Capstone Classroom) Capstone.

Donbavand, Tommy. Read on - Cyber Shock. 2014. (Read On Ser.). (ENG., Illus.). 640p. (YA). (gr. 7). 9.99 *(978-0-00-746473-9(8))* HarperCollins Pubs. Ltd. GBR. Dist: Independent Pubs. Group.

Donne, Alexa. Brightly Burning. (ENG.). (YA). (gr. 7). 2020. 416p. pap. 9.99 *(978-1-328-60438-5(1))*, 1732068) 2018. 400p. 17.99 *(978-1-328-94893-9(5))*, 1705605) HarperCollins Pubs. (Clarion Bks.).

—The Stars We Steal. 2020. (ENG.). 400p. (YA). (gr. 7). 17.99 *(978-1-328-94894-6(3))*, 1705521, HarperTeen) HarperCollins Pubs.

Doors, Mason. The I T I P. 2012. 36p. pap. 20.99 *(978-1-4772-2046-7(1))* AuthorHouse.

Doran, Colleen. A Distant Soil: the Gathering TP: The Gathering TP. 2013. (Illus.). 240p. (YA). pap. 16.99 *(978-1-60706-689-7(0))* Image Comics.

Dorling Kindersley Publishing Staff. Attack of the Clones. 2013. (LEGO Star Wars DK Reader Ser.). lib. bdg. 13.55 *(978-0-606-32111-2(X))* Turtleback.

—Even Droids Need Friends! 2013. (Star Wars DK Readers Pre-Level Ser.). lib. bdg. 13.55 *(978-0-606-31478-7(4))* Turtleback.

—The Invincible Iron Man: The Rise of Iron Man. 2010. (DK Readers Level 4 Ser.). (ENG., Illus.). 48p. (J). (gr. 2-4). 16.19 *(978-0-7566-5784-0(9))* Dorling Kindersley Publishing, Inc.

—The Mysterious World of Doctor Strange. 2016. (ENG., Illus.). 176p. *(978-0-241-27857-4(0))* Dorling Kindersley Publishing, Inc.

—Rogue One. 2016. (Star Wars DK Readers Level 4 Ser.). lib. bdg. 13.55 *(978-0-606-39359-1(5))* Turtleback.

Dorling Kindersley Publishing Staff & Newsworthy, Lauren. Rebel Power! 2015. (Star Wars DK Readers Level 2 Ser.). lib. bdg. 13.55 *(978-0-606-36925-1(2))* Turtleback.

Doucette, Gene. The Spaceship Next Door. 2018. (ENG.). 368p. pap. 15.99 *(978-1-328-56746-8(X)*, 1726765, Harper Voyager) HarperCollins Pubs.
Douglas, Helen. Chasing Stars. 2016. (ENG.). 352p. (YA). 17.99 *(978-1-61963-410-7(4)*, 900135715, Bloomsbury USA Childrens) Bloomsbury Publishing USA.
Dowell, Frances O'Roark. Phineas L. MacGuire ... Blasts Off! McDaniels, Preston, illus. 2008. (From the Highly Scientific Notebooks of Phineas L. MacGuire Ser.). (ENG.). 208p. (J). (gr. 3-7). 16.99 *(978-1-4169-2689-4(5))* Simon & Schuster, Inc.
—Phineas L. MacGuire... Gets Slimed! McDaniels, Preston, illus. l.t. ed. 2008. (From the Highly Scientific Notebooks of Phineas L. MacGuire Ser.). 159p. (J). (gr. 3-7). 22.95 *(978-1-4104-0440-4(4))* Thorndike Pr.
Dower, Laura. The Beast with 1000 Eyes #3. Schlafman, Dave, illus. 2009. (Monster Squad Ser.: 3). 144p. (J). (gr. 3-7). pap. 5.99 *(978-0-448-44914-2(5)*, Grosset & Dunlap) Penguin Young Readers Group.
Dowsett, Elizabeth. The Amazing Book of Star Wars: Feel the Force! Learn about Star Wars! 2016. (ENG., Illus.). 48p. (J). (gr. k-2). 14.99 *(978-1-4654-5460-7(8)*, DK Children) Dorling Kindersley Publishing, Inc.
The Dragon Compass: Individual Title Six-Packs. (Bookweb Ser.). 32p. (gr. 6-18). 34.00 *(978-0-7578-0898-2(0))* Rigby Education.
Drake, Raelyn. Realm of Mystics. 2017. (Level Up Ser.). (ENG.). 120p. (YA). (gr. 6-12). pap. 7.99 *(978-1-5124-5359-1(5)*, 2db305fb-5671-42ec-b0de-48cb8df9c814); lib. bdg. 26.65 *(978-1-5124-3989-2(4)*, f51a5363-838f-45b4-b9b7-c89b4fcd2ba4) Lerner Publishing Group. (Darby Creek).
D'Souza, Barbara. If We Were Snowflakes. 2018. (YA). pap. *(978-1-59719-091-6(8))* Pearlsong Pr.
Duane, Diane. High Wizardry, 7 vols. (Young Wizards Ser.: 3). (J). 2006. 90.75 *(978-1-4025-9917-0(X))* 2004. 93.75 *(978-1-4025-8355-1(9))* Recorded Bks., Inc.
Ducie, Joe. Crystal Force. 2016. (ENG.). 288p. (YA). (gr. 7). pap. 9.99 *(978-1-4714-0455-9(2))* Bonnier Publishing GBR. Dist: Independent Pubs. Group.
Duckro, Rebecca S. Adventures of Charlie KeeperTechnobrat. 2006. 156p. per. 12.95 *(978-0-595-40498-8(7))* iUniverse, Inc.
Duey, Kathleen. Time Soldiers, Set. Epstein, Eugene, illus. Gould, Robert, photos by. gif. ed. 2003. (Time Soldiers Ser.). (ENG.). 144p. (J). (gr. k-2). 32.95 *(978-1-929945-23-8(X))* Big Guy Bks., Inc.
Duey, Kathleen & Gould, Robert. Rex. Windler-Cheren, Victoria, tr. Epstein, Eugene, illus. Gould, Robert, photos by. 2003. (Time Soldiers Ser.: Bk. 1). (SPA & ENG.). 48p. (J). (gr. k-4). pap. 8.95 *(978-1-929945-35-1(3))* Big Guy Bks., Inc.
Duffett-Smith, James. Stella & Steve Travel Through Space! Straker, Bethany, illus. 2014. (ENG.). 32p. (J). (gr. -1-k). 14.95 *(978-1-62873-815-5(4)*, Sky Pony Pr.) Skyhorse Publishing Co., Inc.
Dufresne, Michèle. Space Monster Saves the Day. 2007. (Spaceboy Chapter Ser.). (ENG.). (J). per. 7.67 *(978-1-932570-61-8(6))* Pioneer Valley Bks.
—Spaceboy Chapter Books. 2007. (ENG.). (J). per. 29.33 *(978-1-932570-60-1(8))* Pioneer Valley Bks.
Duncan, Alexandra. Blight. 2017. (ENG.). 400p. (YA). (gr. 8). 17.99 *(978-0-06-239699-0(4)*, Greenwillow Bks.) HarperCollins Pubs.
—Salvage. 2014. (Salvage Ser.: 1). (ENG.). 528p. (YA). (gr. 8). 17.99 *(978-0-06-222014-1(4)*, Greenwillow Bks.) HarperCollins Pubs.
Duncan Gurley, Ann. Esbe's Halo. 2009. 108p. (J). pap. 15.95 *(978-1-4327-3453-4(9))* Outskirts Pr., Inc.
Dunkle, Clare B. The Walls Have Eyes. 2009. (ENG.). 240p. (YA). (gr. 7). 16.99 *(978-1-4169-5379-1(5)*, Atheneum Bks. for Young Readers) Simon & Schuster Children's Publishing.
Dunn, Mark. The Age Altertron, Bk. 1. 2009. (ENG.). 175p. (gr. 4). *(978-1-59692-345-4(8))* MacAdam/Cage Publishing, Inc.
Dunn, Pintip. Remember Yesterday. 2017. (Forget Tomorrow Ser.: 2). (ENG.). 420p. (YA). pap. 9.99 *(978-1-63375-832-2(X)*, 900181032) Entangled Publishing, LLC.
Dunnion, Kristyn. Big Big Sky, 1 vol. Hopkinson, Nalo, ed. 2008. (ENG.). 348p. (YA). (gr. 7-12). pap. 9.95 *(978-0-88995-404-5(6)*, 55f940db-88c7-467a-a0d2-091338143b4e) Red Deer Pr. CAN. Dist: Firefly Bks., Ltd.
DuPrau, Jeanne. The City of Ember Deluxe Edition: The First Book of Ember. 2013. (City of Ember Ser.: 1). (ENG., Illus.). 320p. (J). (gr. 3-7). pap. 10.99 *(978-0-385-37135-3(7)*, Random Hse. Bks. for Young Readers) Random Hse. Children's Bks.
A Dusk of Demons. 2014. (ENG., Illus.). 288p. (J). (gr. 4-8). pap. 7.99 *(978-1-4814-2018-1(6)*, Aladdin) Simon & Schuster Children's Publishing.
Dutcher, David. Feebie Brainiac & the Lysis Virus. 2005. (ENG., Illus.). 248p. (YA). (gr. 7). per. *(978-1-933255-14-9(5))* DNA Pr.
Duyvis, Corinne. On the Edge of Gone. 2016. (ENG.). 464p. (J). (gr. 8-17). 17.95 *(978-1-4197-1903-5(3)*, 1104701, Amulet Bks.) Abrams, Inc.
Dyan, Penelope. A Thousand Stars. Dyan, Penelope, illus. 2012. (Illus.). 34p. pap. 11.95 *(978-1-61477-049-7(2))* Bellissima Publishing, LLC.
Earls, J. S. The Realm Unseen. 2010. 266p. (J). pap. 9.00 *(978-1-60039-155-2(9))* Lamp Post Inc.
—The Realm Unseen: Hard Cover. 2010. 266p. 16.00 *(978-1-60039-156-9(7))* Lamp Post Inc.
Earth 8 X 8 #2. 2009. 24p. pap. 3.99 *(978-1-4231-2203-6(8))* Disney Pr.
Eastman, Brock. Hope. 2019. 509p. (J). pap. *(978-1-59638-249-7(X))* P & R Publishing.
Eastman, Brock D. & Eastman, Brock. Taken. 2011. (Illus.). 315p. (J). pap. *(978-1-59638-245-9(7))* P & R Publishing.
Eddleman, Peggy. Sky Jumpers: Book 1. 2014. (Sky Jumpers Ser.: 1). 304p. (J). (gr. 3-7). 7.99 *(978-0-307-98130-1(4)*, Yearling) Random Hse. Children's Bks.
Edmondson, Nathan. The Activity Volume 3. 2015. (ENG., Illus.). 160p. (YA). pap. 16.99 *(978-1-60706-759-7(5)*, 528a26f1-a908-4b59-8aa8-ecfb02740d62) Image Comics.
Edwards, R. Katie King's Journal. 2004. 376p. (YA). 31.95 *(978-0-595-66890-8(9))* iUniverse, Inc.
Egan, Kate. Evil Comes in Pairs. Merkel, Joe F., illus. 2009. (Spider-Man Ser.). 64p. (J). (gr. 2-5). pap. 4.99 *(978-0-06-162625-8(2)*, HarperFestival) HarperCollins Pubs.
Elish, Dan. The Attack of the Frozen Woodchucks. Call, Greg, illus. 2008. (ENG.). 256p. (J). (gr. 3-7). 16.99 *(978-0-06-113870-6(3)*, Geringer, Laura Book) HarperCollins Pubs.
ELLIS, B. J. Mrs. Morgan's Adventures with Aliens. 2008. (ENG.). 249p. 29.50 *(978-0-557-00095-1(5))* Lulu Pr., Inc.
Ellis, Sarah. Odd Man Out, 1 vol. 2006. (ENG.). 160p. (J). (gr. 4-7). pap. 8.95 *(978-0-88899-703-6(5))* Groundwood Bks. CAN. Dist: Publishers Group West (PGW).
Elmer, Robert. Trion Rising, 1 vol. 2008. (Shadowside Trilogy Ser.). (ENG.). 352p. (YA). (gr. 8-11). pap. 9.99 *(978-0-310-71421-7(4))* Zondervan.
Elwood, Tessa. Inherit the Stars. 2015. (ENG.). 304p. (YA). (gr. 7-17). pap. 9.95 *(978-0-7624-5840-0(2)*, Running Pr. Kids) Running Pr.
Elys Dayton, Arwen. Disruptor. 2017. (Seeker Ser.: 3). (ENG.). 384p. (YA). (gr. 9). pap. 14.99 *(978-0-385-74415-7(3)*, Ember) Random Hse. Children's Bks.
—Seeker. 2015. (Seeker Ser.: 1). (ENG.). 480p. (YA). (gr. 9). pap. 9.99 *(978-0-385-74408-9(0)*, Ember) Random Hse. Children's Bks.
—Seeker. 2015. lib. bdg. 20.85 *(978-0-606-38458-2(8))* Turtleback.
Emerson, Kevin. Last Day on Mars. (Chronicle of the Dark Star Ser.: 1). (ENG.). (J). (gr. 3-7). 2018. 352p. pap. 9.99 *(978-0-06-230672-2(3))* 2017. 336p. 16.99 *(978-0-06-230671-5(5))* HarperCollins Pubs. (Walden Pond Pr.).
—The Lost Code. (Atlanteans Ser.: 1). (ENG.). (YA). (gr. 8). 2013. 464p. pap. 9.99 *(978-0-06-206280-2(8))* 2012. 448p. 17.99 *(978-0-06-206279-6(4))* HarperCollins Pubs. (Tegen, Katherine Bks).
—The Oceans Between Stars. (Chronicle of the Dark Star Ser.: 2). (ENG.). (J). (gr. 3-7). 2019. 432p. pap. 7.99 *(978-0-06-230675-3(8))* 2018. (Illus.). 416p. 16.99 *(978-0-06-230674-6(X))* HarperCollins Pubs. (Walden Pond Pr.).
Emmet, Laura. Julie Trent & the Lightning. 2003. 148p. pap. 11.95 *(978-0-595-27380-5(7)*, Writers Club Pr.) iUniverse, Inc.
—Julie Trent & the Tempest. 2003. 136p. pap. 11.95 *(978-0-595-27418-5(8)*, Writers Club Pr.) iUniverse, Inc.
Ende, Michael. La Historia Interminable.Tr. of Unendliche Geschichte. (SPA.). 432p. (YA). (gr. 5-8). 13.95 *(978-84-204-2522-1(2)*, LEC5222) Ediciones Alfaguara ESP. Dist: Lectorum Pubns., Inc.
—La Historia Interminable. Quadflieg, Roswitha & Sáenz, Miguel, trs. Quadflieg, Roswitha, illus.Tr. of Unendliche Geschichte. (SPA.). 424p. (J). 9.95 *(978-84-204-3226-7(1))* Ediciones Alfaguara ESP. Dist: Santillana USA Publishing Co., Inc.
—La Historia Interminable. Quadflieg, Roswitha, tr. 57th ed. 2014.Tr. of Unendliche Geschichte. (SPA., Illus.). 419p. 17.95 *(978-84-204-6439-8(2))* Ediciones Alfaguara ESP. Dist: Santillana USA Publishing Co., Inc.
—La Historia Interminable. 2003.Tr. of Unendliche Geschichte. (SPA., Illus.). 420p. (J). (gr. 5-8). pap. 12.95 *(978-968-19-0254-4(8))* Santillana USA Publishing Co., Inc.
Enderle, Dotti. Book 18: Spaced Out! 2014. (Ghost Detectors Set 3 Ser.). 80p. (J). (gr. 2-5). lib. bdg. 27.07 *(978-1-62402-006-3(2)*, Calico Chapter Bks.) Magic Wagon.
—Ghost Detectors, 6 vols., Set. McWilliam, Howard, illus. Incl. Don't Read This! 35.64 *(978-1-60270-695-8(6)*, 8810); Draw! 35.64 *(978-1-60270-694-1(8)*, 8808); I Dare You! 35.64 *(978-1-60270-693-4(X)*, 8806); I'm Gonna Get You! 35.64 *(978-1-60270-691-0(3)*, 8802); It Creeps! 35.64 *(978-1-60270-690-3(5)*, 8800); Tell No One! 35.64 *(978-1-60270-692-7(1)*, 8804); (J). (gr. 2-5). (Ghost Detectors Ser.: 6). (ENG., Illus.). 80p. 2009. Set lib. bdg. 213.84 *(978-1-60270-689-7(1)*, 8798, Calico Chapter Bks.) ABDO Publishing Co.
—Spaced Out!, 1 vol. McWilliam, Howard, illus. 2015. (Ghost Detectors Ser.: 18). (ENG.). 80p. (J). (gr. 2-5). 35.64 *(978-1-62402-101-5(8)*, 18144, Calico Chapter Bks.) ABDO Publishing Co.
Engdahl, Sylvia. Enchantress from the Stars. 2018. (ENG.). 368p. (J). pap. 10.99 *(978-1-68119-613-8(1)*, 900179035, Bloomsbury USA Childrens) Bloomsbury Publishing USA.
—Enchantress from the Stars. 2003. (ENG.). 304p. (YA). (gr. 7-18). pap. 9.99 *(978-0-14-250037-8(2)*, Firebird) Penguin Young Readers Group.
—The Far Side of Evil. 2005. (ENG.). 336p. (YA). (gr. 7-7). 22.00 *(978-0-14-240293-1(1)*, Firebird) Penguin Young Readers Group.
Engel, Amy. The Book of Ivy. 2014. (YA). lib. bdg. 20.85 *(978-0-606-38239-7(9))* Turtleback.
—The Book of Ivy. 2016. (CHI.). 272p. (YA). (gr. 7-12). pap. *(978-986-133-566-7(8))* Yuan Shen Pr. Co., Ltd.
—The Revolution of Ivy. 2015. (Book of Ivy Ser.: 2). (ENG.). 400p. (YA). pap. 9.99 *(978-1-63375-115-6(5)*, 900150742) Entangled Publishing, LLC.
Engineering is Elementary Team. Michelle's MVP Award: A Chemical Engineering Story. 2005. (J). lib. bdg. 15.99 *(978-0-9774084-7-4(7))* Engineering is Elementary.
England, M. K. The Disasters. (ENG.). (YA). (gr. 9). 2019. 384p. pap. 10.99 *(978-0-06-265768-8(2))* 2018. 368p. 17.99 *(978-0-06-265767-1(4))* HarperCollins Pubs. (HarperTeen).
Epner, Paul. There's a Dachshund in My Bed! Reed, Bill, illus. 2004. 56p. (J). 16.95 *(978-0-9743335-8-8(1))* Imaginative Publishing, Ltd.
Erin, Aileen. Off Planet. 2019. (Off Planet Ser.). 350p. (YA). pap. 16.99 *(978-1-943858-21-7(7))* Ink Monster.
Erin Hicks, Faith. The Adventures of Superhero Girl (Expanded Edition) 2017. (Illus.). 128p. (J). (gr. 5-9). 16.99 *(978-1-5067-0336-7(4)*, Dark Horse Books) Dark Horse Comics.
Evans, Joseph. The Trinity Awakening. 2013. 466p. pap. *(978-0-9572912-1-8(3))* Evans, Joseph.
Evans, Nate. Tyrannosaurus Ralph. Evans, Vince, illus. 2017. (ENG.). 180p. (J). pap. 9.99 *(978-1-4494-7208-5(7))* Andrews McMeel Publishing.
Evans, Richard Paul. Michael Vey: The Prisoner of Cell 25. (Michael Vey Ser.: 1). (ENG., Illus.). (YA). (gr. 7). 2012. 352p. pap. 12.99 *(978-1-4424-6812-2(2))* 2011. 336p. 19.99 *(978-1-4516-5650-3(5))* Simon Pulse/Mercury Ink. (Simon Pulse/Mercury Ink).
—Michael Vey 2: Rise of the Elgen. (Michael Vey Ser.: 2). (ENG., Illus.). 352p. (YA). (gr. 7). 2013. pap. 12.99 *(978-1-4424-7510-6(2))* 2012. 19.99 *(978-1-4424-5414-9(8))* Simon Pulse/Mercury Ink. (Simon Pulse/Mercury Ink).
—Michael Vey 3: Battle of the Ampere. (Michael Vey Ser.: 3). (ENG., Illus.). 320p. (YA). (gr. 7). 2014. pap. 12.99 *(978-1-4424-7512-0(9))* 2013. 19.99 *(978-1-4424-7511-3(0))* Simon Pulse/Mercury Ink. (Simon Pulse/Mercury Ink).
—Michael Vey 4: Hunt for Jade Dragon. 2014. (Michael Vey Ser.: 4). (ENG., Illus.). 336p. (YA). (gr. 7). 19.99 *(978-1-4814-2438-7(6)*, Simon Pulse/Mercury Ink) Simon Pulse/Mercury Ink.
—Michael Vey 5: Storm of Lightning. 2015. (Michael Vey Ser.: 5). (ENG., Illus.). 288p. (YA). (gr. 7). 19.99 *(978-1-4814-4410-1(7)*, Simon Pulse/Mercury Ink) Simon Pulse/Mercury Ink.
Ewing, Al. Royals, Vol. 1. 2017. (YA). lib. bdg. 30.60 *(978-0-606-40703-8(0))* Turtleback.
Faerber, Jay, et al. Universal Heroes. 2006. (Illus.). 136p. (YA). pap. 13.99 *(978-0-7851-1857-2(8))* Marvel Worldwide, Inc.
Fagan, Deva. Circus Galacticus. 2013. (ENG.). 304p. (J). (gr. 4-6). 17.44 *(978-0-547-58136-1(X))* Harcourt Children's Bks.
Falk, Nick & Flowers, Tony. Tyrannosaurus in the Veggie Patch: Saurus Street 1 (Large Print 16pt) 2013. 102p. pap. *(978-1-4596-5771-7(3))* ReadHowYouWant.com, Ltd.
Falkner, Brian. The Assault (Recon Team Angel #1) 2013. (Recon Team Angel Ser.: 1). (ENG.). 304p. (YA). (gr. 7). pap. 9.99 *(978-0-375-87190-0(X)*, Ember) Random Hse. Children's Bks.
—Brain Jack. 2011. (ENG.). 368p. (YA). (gr. 7). pap. 13.99 *(978-0-375-84367-9(1)*, Ember) Random Hse. Children's Bks.
—The Tomorrow Code. 2008. (ENG.). 368p. (J). (gr. 6-8). lib. bdg. 26.19 *(978-0-375-93923-5(7))* Random House Publishing Group.
—The Tomorrow Code. 2009. (ENG.). 372p. (YA). (gr. 7). pap. 9.99 *(978-0-375-84365-5(5)*, Ember) Random Hse. Children's Bks.
Falksen, G. D. The Transatlantic Conspiracy. Iwata, Nat, illus. 2017. 240p. (YA). (gr. 9). pap. 10.99 *(978-1-61695-814-5(6)*, Soho Teen) Soho Pr., Inc.
Falls, Kat. Dark Life, 1. 2011. (ENG.). 304p. (J). (gr. 4-7). pap. 9.99 *(978-0-545-17815-0(0))* Scholastic, Inc.
—Rip Tide. 2011. 314p. (J). pap. *(978-0-545-43175-0(1)*, Scholastic Pr.) Scholastic, Inc.
Falls the Shadow. 2014. (ENG., Illus.). 352p. (YA). (gr. 7). 18.99 *(978-1-4424-9753-5(X)*, Simon & Schuster Bks. For Young Readers) Simon & Schuster Bks. For Young Readers.
Farley, C. J. Game World. 2014. (ENG., Illus.). 288p. (J). (gr. 4). pap. 19.95 *(978-1-61775-197-4(9)*, Black Sheep) Akashic Bks.
Farmer, Nancy. The Ear, the Eye, & the Arm. 2012. (ENG.). 336p. (J). (gr. 4-7). pap. 8.99 *(978-0-545-35661-9(X)*, Scholastic Paperbacks) Scholastic, Inc.
—The Ear, the Eye, & the Arm. 2012. lib. bdg. 18.40 *(978-0-606-23944-8(8))* Turtleback.
—The House of the Scorpion. 2004. 380p. (gr. 6). lib. bdg. 22.10 *(978-1-4176-1900-9(7))* Turtleback.
—The Lord of Opium. 2013. (House of the Scorpion Ser.). (ENG., Illus.). 432p. (YA). (gr. 7). 21.99 *(978-1-4424-8254-8(0))* Simon & Schuster Children's Publishing.
Feasey, Steve. Mutant Rising. 2016. (ENG.). 352p. (YA). (gr. 7). pap. 10.99 *(978-1-4088-5572-0(0)*, 258446, Bloomsbury Children's Bks.) Bloomsbury Publishing Plc.
Feeley, Karen. Project 20/20: The Experiment. 2005. (ENG.). 304p. pap. 19.97 *(978-1-84728-531-7(7))* Lulu Pr., Inc.
Feener, Chani Lynn. Amid Stars & Darkness. 2018. (Xenith Trilogy Ser.: 1). (ENG.). 384p. (YA). pap. 14.99 *(978-1-250-15895-6(8)*, 900185541) Square Fish.
Feldstein, Al. Weird Science, Vol. 2. 2007. (ENG., Illus.). 212p. (YA). 49.95 *(978-1-888472-69-1(3)*, bc3997ef-ed3d-4769-bfeb-b8c5b4305ada, William M. Gaines Agent, INC.) Diamond Bk. Distributors.
Fentiman, David. The Adventures of BB-8. 2016. (Illus.). 47p. (J). *(978-1-5182-1848-4(2))* Dorling Kindersley Publishing, Inc.
—The Adventures of BB-8. 2016. (Star Wars DK Readers Level 2 Ser.). lib. bdg. 13.55 *(978-0-606-38709-5(9))* Turtleback.
—DK Readers L2: Star Wars: the Adventures of BB-8: Discover BB-8's Secret Mission. 2016. (DK Readers Level 2 Ser.). (ENG., Illus.). 48p. (J). (gr. k-2). pap. 4.99 *(978-1-4654-5102-6(1)*, DK Children) Dorling Kindersley Publishing, Inc.
—DK Readers L3: Star Wars: Finn's Mission: Find Out How Finn Can Save the Galaxy! 2016. (DK Readers Level 3 Ser.). (ENG., Illus.). 64p. (J). (gr. 4-7). pap. 3.99 *(978-1-4654-5101-9(3)*, DK Children) Dorling Kindersley Publishing, Inc.
—Finn's Mission. 2016. (Illus.). 63p. (J). *(978-1-5182-1853-8(9))* Dorling Kindersley Publishing, Inc.
—Finn's Mission. 2016. (Star Wars DK Readers Level 3 Ser.). lib. bdg. 13.55 *(978-0-606-38710-1(2))* Turtleback.
—New Adventures. 2015. (Illus.). 47p. (J). *(978-1-4806-9626-6(9))* Dorling Kindersley Publishing, Inc.
Ferguson, Alane. The Angel of Death. 2008. (Forensic Mystery Ser.). 258p. 17.00 *(978-0-7569-8929-3(9))* Perfection Learning Corp.
Fickling, Phillip. Fillmore & Geary Take Off! Shulman, Mark, illus. 2003. 40p. (J). lib. bdg. *(978-1-58717-258-8(5)*, SeaStar Bks.) Chronicle Bks. LLC.
Fields, Bryan W. Lunchbox & the Aliens. Atteberry, Kevan, illus. 2009. (Froonga Ser.: 1). (ENG.). 208p. (J). (gr. 4-6). pap. 14.99 *(978-0-312-56115-4(6)*, 900058845) Square Fish.
Fillbach. Clone Wars Adventures, 7. Fillbach, illus. 2013. (Star Wars Digests Ser.). (ENG., Illus.). 80p. (J). (gr. 3-8). lib. bdg. 34.21 *(978-1-61479-058-7(2)*, 13761, Graphic Novels) Spotlight.
—Star Wars: Clone Wars Adventures. Fillbach, illus. 2013. (Star Wars Digests Ser.). (ENG., Illus.). 80p. (J). (gr. 3-8). lib. bdg. 34.21 *(978-1-61479-059-4(0)*, 13762, Graphic Novels) Spotlight.
Fine, Sarah. Uncanny. 2017. (ENG.). 316p. (YA). (gr. 10-12). pap. 9.99 *(978-1-5420-4646-6(7)*, 9781542046466, Skyscape) Amazon Publishing.
Finlay, Adrianne. Your One & Only. (ENG.). 320p. (YA). (gr. 9). 2019. pap. 9.99 *(978-1-328-59588-1(9)*, 1731274) 2018. 17.99 *(978-0-544-99147-7(8)*, 1666535) HarperCollins Pubs. (Clarion Bks.).
Finley, Leah. The One & Only Mr C. 2009. 82p. pap. 8.95 *(978-1-935118-75-6(7))* Bellissima Publishing, LLC.
Fisch, Sholly. Teen Titans GO! Vol. 1: Party, Party!, Vol. 1. Hernandez, Lea, illus. 2015. 128p. (J). (gr. 1-3). pap. 12.99 *(978-1-4012-5242-7(7))* DC Comics.
Fleury, Mike Stevenson. Natural Disaster 2222. 2003. (ENG.). 112p. 19.95 *(978-0-595-65436-9(3))*; 108p. (YA). pap. 9.95 *(978-0-595-25921-2(9))* iUniverse, Inc. (Writers Club Pr.).
Flintham, Thomas. Super Rabbit Boy Powers Up! 2017. (Press Start! — Branches Ser.: 2). lib. bdg. 14.75 *(978-0-606-40188-3(1))* Turtleback.
Floreen, Tim. Tattoo Atlas. 2016. (ENG., Illus.). 384p. (YA). (gr. 9). 17.99 *(978-1-4814-3280-1(X)*, Simon Pulse) Simon Pulse.
—Willful Machines. 2016. (ENG., Illus.). 384p. (YA). (gr. 9). pap. 12.99 *(978-1-4814-3278-8(8)*, Simon Pulse) Simon Pulse.
Flounders, Anne, ed. Return to Earth. Wolk-Stanley, Jessica; Flounders, illus. 2004. (Reader's Theater Content-Area Concepts Ser.). (ENG.). (J). (gr. 3-5). 5.00 net. *(978-1-4108-2306-9(7)*, A23067) Benchmark Education Co.
Flynn, Ian. Mega Man 2: Time Keeps Slipping. 2012. (Mega Man Ser.: 2). (ENG., Illus.). 112p. (J). (gr. 4-7). pap. 11.99 *(978-1-879794-95-5(0))* Archie Comic Pubns., Inc.
—Mega Man 3: Return of Dr. Wily. Bates, Ben, illus. 2012. (Mega Man Ser.: 3). (ENG.). 112p. (J). (gr. 4-7). pap. 11.99 *(978-1-936975-11-2(4))* Archie Comic Pubns., Inc.
—Mega Man 4: Spiritus Ex Machina. 2012. (Mega Man Ser.: 4). (ENG., Illus.). 112p. (J). (gr. 4-7). pap. 11.99 *(978-1-936975-27-3(0))* Archie Comic Pubns., Inc.
Foley, James. Gastronauts. 2018. (S. Tinker Inc Ser.). (Illus.). 120p. (J). (gr. 3-6). 9.95 *(978-1-925591-68-2(9))* Fremantle Pr. AUS. Dist: Independent Pubs. Group.
Fontana, Shea. DC Super Hero Girls: Past Times at Super Hero High. Garbowska, Agnes & Labat, Yancey, illus. 2017. 132p. (J). (gr. 3-7). pap. 9.99 *(978-1-4012-7383-5(1)*, DC Zoom) DC Comics.
—Summer Olympus. 2017. (DC Super Hero Girls Ser.: 3). lib. bdg. 20.85 *(978-0-606-40123-4(7))* Turtleback.
—Super Hero High Yearbook! (DC Super Hero Girls) Random House, illus. 2016. (ENG.). 96p. (J). (gr. 3-7). pap. 9.99 *(978-1-5247-0106-2(8)*, Random Hse. Bks. for Young Readers) Random Hse. Children's Bks.
Fontes, Justine & Fontes, Ron. Casebook: UFOs and/or Alien Encounter, 1 vol. 2009. (Top Secret Graphica Mysteries Ser.). (ENG., Illus.). 48p. (YA). (gr. 4-4). 33.93 *(978-1-60754-603-0(5)*, 54a778e6-0a9b-4887-9b2d-4d2f9b27c3c6); pap. 12.75 *(978-1-60754-604-7(3)*, aa110e88-94a4-4b4f-a6bc-576eb7411a96) Rosen Publishing Group, Inc., The. (Windmill Bks.).
Ford, Sharon Lea. The Pages of Lost Time. 2010. 212p. 24.95 *(978-1-60911-127-4(3)*, Eloquent Bks.) Strategic Book Publishing & Rights Agency (SBPRA).
Forde, Patricia. The List. (List Ser.). (ENG.). 368p. (J). (gr. 5-8). 2018. pap. 9.99 *(978-1-4926-6085-9(X))* 2017. 16.99 *(978-1-4926-4796-6(9)*, 9781492647966) Sourcebooks, Inc.
Fosgitt, Jay P. Little Green Men. 2010. (ENG., Illus.). 100p. (YA). pap. 9.95 *(978-1-936340-01-9(1)*, 9781936340019) Ape Entertainment.
Fox, Jennifer. Meet Optimus Prime. 2015. (Transformers Passport to Reading Ser.). (J). lib. bdg. 13.55 *(978-0-606-35938-2(9))* Turtleback.
Foxe, Steve. Decepticon Island! 2017. (Transformers Passport to Reading Ser.). (J). lib. bdg. 14.75 *(978-0-606-39908-1(9))* Turtleback.
—Hot Pursuit! (DC Super Friends) Random House, illus. 2023. (Pictureback(R) Ser.). (ENG.). 16p. (J). (gr. -1-2). pap. 5.99 *(978-1-5247-1715-5(0)*, Random Hse. Bks. for Young Readers) Random Hse. Children's Bks.
Frankel, Jordana. The Isle. 2016. (ENG.). 384p. (YA). (gr. 8). 17.99 *(978-0-06-209537-4(4)*, Tegen, Katherine Bks) HarperCollins Pubs.
—The Ward. 2016. (ENG.). 496p. (YA). (gr. 8). pap. 9.99 *(978-0-06-209535-0(8)*, Tegen, Katherine Bks) HarperCollins Pubs.
Franks, Melissa. Warped! An Adventure Through Time Bk. 1: A What-a-saur? 2008. 96p. pap. 19.95 *(978-1-60703-636-4(3))* America Star Bks.
Fraser, Jess, illus. The Legend of the Cosmic Cowboy. 2007. (J). cd-rom 12.99 *(978-0-9795190-7-9(1))* Color & Learn.
Frederick, Milner. Douglas Brain. 2008. 208p. per. *(978-1-84549-290-8(0))* arima publishing.
Fredley, Nichole. The Sirius, 1 vol. 2010. 534p. pap. 34.95 *(978-1-61582-910-1(5))* America Star Bks.
Freestone, Annie. The Little Mars Rovers. 2008. 36p. pap. 13.95 *(978-1-59858-459-2(6))* Dog Ear Publishing, LLC.
Freitas, Donna. The Body Market. 2017. (Unplugged Ser.: 2). (ENG.). 432p. (YA). (gr. 8). pap. 9.99 *(978-0-06-211864-6(1)*, HarperTeen) HarperCollins Pubs.
—The Mind Virus. 2018. (Unplugged Ser.: 3). (ENG.). 432p. (YA). (gr. 8). pap. 9.99 *(978-0-06-211867-7(6)*, HarperTeen) HarperCollins Pubs.
Frewin Jones, Allan. Thunderbolt. (Hunter & Moon Mystery Ser.: Vol. 5). (ENG., Illus.). 171p. (J). pap. 8.99 *(978-0-340-70963-4(4))* Hodder & Stoughton GBR. Dist: Trafalgar Square Publishing.
Frey, James. Endgame: the Complete Fugitive Archives. 2017. (Endgame: the Fugitive Archives Ser.). (ENG.). 352p. (YA). (gr. 9). pap. 9.99 *(978-0-06-233278-3(3)*, HarperCollins) HarperCollins Pubs.
—Endgame: the Complete Training Diaries: Volumes 1, 2, And 3. 2015. (Endgame: the Training Diaries: Nos. 1-3). (ENG.). 416p. (YA). (gr. 9). pap. 9.99 *(978-0-06-233276-9(7)*, HarperCollins) HarperCollins Pubs.

S

Frey, James & Johnson-Shelton, Nils. Endgame: Rules of the Game. (Endgame Ser.: 3). (ENG.). (YA). (gr. 9). 2017. 368p. pap. 10.99 (978-0-06-233265-3(1)) 2016. (Illus.). 352p. 19.99 (978-0-06-233264-6(3)) HarperCollins Pubs. (HarperCollins).

—Endgame: Sky Key. 2015. (Endgame Ser.: 2). (ENG., Illus.). 512p. (YA). (gr. 9). 19.99 (978-0-06-233261-5(9), HarperCollins) HarperCollins Pubs.

—Endgame: the Calling. (Endgame Ser.: 1). (ENG.). (YA). (gr. 9). 2015. 496p. pap. 10.99 (978-0-06-233259-2(7)) 2014. 480p. 19.99 (978-0-06-233258-5(9)) HarperCollins Pubs. (HarperCollins).

—Sky Key. 2015. (Endgame Ser.: Bk. 2). 512p. (YA). (gr. 9). pap. 12.00 (978-0-06-241424-3(0)) HarperCollins Pubs.

Frid, Colt & Frid, Randy. Demons at the Door. 2009. (ENG.). 252p. pap. (978-0-9811847-1-5(5)) Frid Enterprises, Inc.

Fridolfs, Derek. Injustice Gang & the Deadly Nightshade. Levins, Tim, illus. 2017. (Justice League Ser.). (ENG.). 88p. (J). (gr. 2-6). lib. bdg. 26.65 (978-1-4965-5158-0(3), 136171, Stone Arch Bks.) Capstone.

Friedman, Michael Jan, et al. Convergence. Erwin, Steve et al, illus. 2008. (Titan Star Trek Collections). (ENG.). 176p. pap. 14.95 (978-1-84576-320-6(3), Titan Bks.) Titan Bks. Ltd. GBR. Dist: Penguin Random Hse. LLC.

Friedman, Stanley. Quantum Outlaws. 2010. 210p. pap. 11.95 (978-1-935630-09-8(1)) Bellissima Publishing, LLC.

—Quantum Prisoner. 2012. 212p. pap. 11.95 (978-1-61477-029-9(8)) Bellissima Publishing, LLC.

Friedrich, Gary & Lee, Stan. Incredible Hulk Epic Collection - The Hulk Must Die. Everett, Bill & Kane, Gil, illus. 2017. 432p. (gr. -1-17). pap. 39.99 (978-1-302-90445-6(0), Marvel Universe) Marvel Worldwide, Inc.

Fritz, Julie. My Mother Is an Astronaut. 2008. (ENG.). 24p. pap. 10.50 (978-1-4343-7551-3(X)) AuthorHouse.

Frommer, Abbey C. A New Fight: (Sequel to the Nix), 1 vol. 2010. 116p. pap. 19.95 (978-1-4489-7959-2(5)) America Star Bks.

Fry, Jason. Darth Maul: Shadow Conspiracy. 2013. lib. bdg. 16.00 (978-0-606-26775-5(1)) Turtleback.

—DK Readers L4: Star Wars: Rogue One: Secret Mission: Join the Quest to Destroy the Death Star! 2016. (DK Readers Level 4 Ser.). (ENG.). 96p. (J). (gr. 4-7). pap. 3.99 (978-1-4654-5264-1(8), DK Children) Dorling Kindersley Publishing, Inc.

—Edge of the Galaxy. 2014. 172p. (J). lib. bdg. 17.20 (978-0-606-36536-9(2)) Turtleback.

—The Jupiter Pirates: Hunt for the Hydra. 2014. (Jupiter Pirates Ser.: 1). (ENG.). 272p. (J). (gr. 3-7). pap. 6.99 (978-0-06-223021-8(2), HarperCollins) HarperCollins Pubs.

—Rey's Story. 2016. (Star Wars the Force Awakens Chapter Bks.). (Illus.). 138p. (J). lib. bdg. 16.00 (978-0-606-38302-8(6)) Turtleback.

—Star Wars Rebels: Edge of the Galaxy. 2014. 172p. (J). (978-1-4242-6295-3(X), Disney Lucasfilm Press) Disney Publishing Worldwide.

Fry, Jason & Weisman, Greg. Servants of the Empire. 2015. 171p. (J). (978-1-4242-6297-7(6), Disney Lucasfilm Press) Disney Publishing Worldwide.

Fukuda, Andrew. The Prey. 2013. (Hunt Trilogy Ser.: 2). (ENG.). 336p. (YA). (gr. 7-12). pap. 16.99 (978-1-250-00530-4(2), 900080956, St. Martin's Griffin) St. Martin's Pr.

Furman, Simon. Transformers: Spotlight - 6 Titles, 2 vols., Set. Musson, Robby, illus. Incl. Ultra Magnus. (ENG., Illus.). 24p. (gr. 2-7). 2008. 24.21 (978-1-59961-479-3(0)); (Transformers: Spotlight Ser.: 6). (ENG.). Illus.). 24p. 2008. Set lib. bdg. 59.86 o.p. (978-1-59961-473-1(1), 14882, Graphic Novels) Spotlight.

G-Force Gadget Guide. 2009. 48p. pap. 5.99 (978-1-4231-1805-3(7)) Disney Pr.

Gabel, Claudia & Klam, Cheryl. Etherworld. 2016. (Elusion Ser.: 2). (ENG.). 352p. (YA). (gr. 9). pap. 9.99 (978-0-06-212245-2(2), Tegen, Katherine Bks) HarperCollins Pubs.

Gagnon, Michelle. Strangelets. 2014. (Illus.). 296p. (YA). (gr. 9). pap. 11.99 (978-1-61695-420-8(5), Soho Teen) Soho Pr., Inc.

Gaiman, Neil & Reaves, Michael. Interworld. 2008. (Illus.). 181p. (J). (gr. 5-9). 60.00 (978-1-59606-173-6(1)) Subterranean Pr.

—InterWorld. (InterWorld Trilogy Ser.: 1). (ENG.). (YA). (gr. 8). 2013. 304p. pap. 9.99 (978-0-06-212530-9(3), HarperTeen) 2008. 256p. pap. 10.99 (978-0-06-123898-7(8), HarperCollins) HarperCollins Pubs.

Gaiman, Neil, et al. Eternity's Wheel. (InterWorld Trilogy Ser.: 3). (ENG.). 288p. (YA). (gr. 8). 2016. pap. 9.99 (978-0-06-206800-2(8)) 2015. 17.99 (978-0-06-206799-9(0)) HarperCollins Pubs. (HarperTeen).

—The Silver Dream. (InterWorld Trilogy Ser.: 2). (ENG.). (YA). (gr. 8). 2015. 272p. pap. 9.99 (978-0-06-206797-5(4)) 2013. 256p. 18.99 (978-0-06-206796-8(6)) HarperCollins Pubs. (HarperTeen).

Gaither, Stefanie. Into the Abyss. (ENG.). 352p. (YA). (gr. 7). 2017. pap. 11.99 (978-1-4814-4996-0(6)) 2016. (Illus.). 18.99 (978-1-4814-4995-3(8)) Simon & Schuster Bks. For Young Readers. (Simon & Schuster Bks. For Young Readers).

The Galactic Adventures of Team Energy: Episode I: Dr. Slouch & the Candy Factory. 2007. (J). 16.95 (978-0-9778776-1-4(2)) LGE Performance Systems, Inc.

Gallagher, Michael. X-Men, Magneto's Master Plan. Severin, Marie, illus. 24p. (YA). (gr. k-18). 12.95 (978-0-9627001-6-3(9)) Futech Educational Products, Inc.

—X-Men, Scourge of the Savage Land. Severin, Marie, illus. 24p. (YA). (gr. k-18). 12.95 (978-0-9627001-7-0(7)) Futech Educational Products, Inc.

Gamble, Paul. The Knight's Armor: Book 3 of the Ministry of SUITs. 2018. (Ministry of SUITs Ser.: 3). (ENG., Illus.). 368p. (J). 25.99 (978-1-250-07684-7(6), 900152371) Feiwel & Friends.

Gamow, George. Mr Tompkins Learns the Facts of Life. 2011. (ENG., Illus.). 116p. pap. 22.99 (978-1-107-40207-2(7)) Cambridge Univ. Pr.

Gant, Gene. Lessons on Destroying the World. (ENG., 2016. Illus.). (J). 24.99 (978-1-63533-040-3(8)) 2014. 200p. (YA). pap. 14.99 (978-1-62798-792-9(4)) Dreamspinner Pr. (Harmony Ink Pr.).

Gardiner, John Reynolds. ALTO SECRETO. (SPA.). 96p. (YA). (gr. 5-8). (978-84-279-3396-5(7), NG3489) Noguer y Caralt Editores, S. A. ESP. Dist: Lectorum Pubns., Inc.

Garibaldi, Jose. Captain Underpants & the Perilous Plot of Professor Poopypants: The Fourth Epic Novel. Pilkey, Dav, illus. 2016. 149p. (J). (978-1-5182-1145-4(3), 112964869) Scholastic, Inc.

Garing, Ken. Planetoid. 2013. (ENG., Illus.). 164p. (YA). pap. 15.99 (978-1-60706-813-6(3), b64f9724-12a3-45be-8c0c-85ba432b3738) Image Comics.

Garner, Em. Contaminated. 2014. (Contaminated Ser.). (ENG.). 336p. (YA). (gr. 7-12). pap. 9.99 (978-1-60684-542-4(X), 2c54e8bc-3921-4e4c-83a2-24e18c5d6d0c, Carolrhoda Lab™) Lerner Publishing Group.

—Mercy Mode. 2014. (Contaminated Ser.). (ENG.). 341p. (YA). (gr. 7-12). 17.99 (978-1-60684-356-7(7), 2128b0bf-02fc-4d42-8da7-4a7424292054, Carolrhoda Lab™) Lerner Publishing Group.

Garvie, Maureen. Amy by Any Other Name. 2009. (ENG.). 256p. (YA). (gr. 7-18). pap. (978-1-55470-142-1(2)) Me to We.

Gass, Kenneth. Trilobites! 2005. 110p. per. 18.99 net. (978-0-9634906-8-1(0), SQP) Specialized Quality Pubns.

Gathering Place Publishers. Stones' Quest in Search of Its Master. 2010. (ENG., Illus.). 472p. (J). 21.95 (978-0-9754622-5-6(3)) Gathering Place Pubs., Inc.

—Stones' Quest in Search of Its Master: In Search of Its Master 2005. (Stones' Quest Ser.: 1). (ENG., Illus.). 489p. (J). pap. 19.95 (978-0-9754622-0-1(2)) Gathering Place Pubs., Inc.

Gebhart, Ryan. Of Jenny & the Aliens. 2017. 368p. (J). (gr. 11). 17.99 (978-0-7636-8845-5(2)) Candlewick Pr.

Gehrt, Linda. My Trip, My Spaceship. 2004. 26p. pap. 24.95 (978-1-4137-3392-1(1)) PublishAmerica, Inc.

Gellineau, Lloyd. The Alien in the Flashlight. 2012. 24p. (-18). pap. 15.99 (978-1-4797-2339-3(8)) Xlibris Corp.

Geneviève Douyon Flambert. Grace: The Mystical Caribbean Mission. 2009. 152p. pap. 12.95 (978-0-595-51639-1(4)) iUniverse, Inc.

Gerwitz, Felice & Gerwitz, Christina. Dinosaur Quest at Diamond Peak, 3, Vol. 2. 2nd rev. ed. 2007. (Truth Seeker's Mystery Ser.). 208p. (YA). per. 8.99 (978-1-931941-11-2(4)) Media Angels, Inc.

—The Missing Link: Found, 3, Vol. 1. 2nd rev. ed. 2004. (Truth Seeker's Mystery Ser.). 208p. (YA). per. 8.99 (978-1-931941-08-2(4)) Media Angels, Inc.

Giants of Anglesey. 2011. 176p. (gr. 4-6). pap. 13.95 (978-1-4620-3359-1(8)) iUniverse, Inc.

Gibbs, Stuart. Space Case. 2015. (Moon Base Alpha Ser.). (ENG., Illus.). 368p. (J). (gr. 3-7). pap. 8.99 (978-1-4424-9487-9(5), Simon & Schuster Bks. For Young Readers) Simon & Schuster Bks. For Young Readers.

—Space Case. 2015. (Moon Base Alpha Ser.: 1). lib. bdg. 18.40 (978-0-606-37883-3(9)) Turtleback.

—Spaced Out. (Moon Base Alpha Ser.). (ENG.). (J). (gr. 3-7). 2017. 368p. pap. 8.99 (978-1-4814-2337-3(1)) 2016. (Illus.). 352p. 18.99 (978-1-4814-2336-6(3)) Simon & Schuster Bks. For Young Readers. (Simon & Schuster Bks. For Young Readers).

—Spaced Out. 2017. (Moon Base Alpha Ser.: 2). lib. bdg. 18.40 (978-0-606-39762-9(0)) Turtleback.

—Waste of Space. (Moon Base Alpha Ser.). (ENG.). (J). (gr. 3-7). 2019. 368p. pap. 8.99 (978-1-4814-7780-2(3)) 2018. (Illus.). 336p. 18.99 (978-1-4814-7779-6(X)) Simon & Schuster Bks. For Young Readers. (Simon & Schuster Bks. For Young Readers).

Gibson, James E. & Gibson, Sylvia Scott. Treetoe the Space Monster, 1 vol. Gibson, Gregory V., illus. 2010. 28p. 24.95 (978-1-4489-4896-3(7)) PublishAmerica, Inc.

Giles, Lamar. The Last Last-Day-Of-Summer. Adeola, Dapo, illus. 2019. (Legendary Alston Boys Adventure Ser.). (ENG.). 304p. (J). (gr. 3-7). 17.99 (978-1-328-46083-7(5), 1712835, Versify) HarperCollins Pubs.

Gill, David Macinnis. Black Hole Sun. 2012. (Black Hole Sun Ser.: 1). (ENG.). 368p. (YA). (gr. 9). pap. 8.99 (978-0-06-167306-1(4), Greenwillow Bks.) HarperCollins Pubs.

—Invisible Sun. 2013. (Black Hole Sun Ser.: 2). (ENG.). 400p. (YA). (gr. 9). pap. 9.99 (978-0-06-207333-4(8), Greenwillow Bks.) HarperCollins Pubs.

—Shadow on the Sun. 2013. (Black Hole Sun Ser.: 3). (ENG.). 432p. (YA). (gr. 9). 17.99 (978-0-06-207335-8(4), Greenwillow Bks.) HarperCollins Pubs.

Gill, Margaret. The Brain Changers. 2004. 160p. (YA). pap. 12.95 (978-0-595-31161-3(X)) iUniverse, Inc.

Gill, Michael. Mitsuki. 2008. 32p. pap. 19.99 (978-1-4363-0938-7(7)) Xlibris Corp.

Gillen, Kieron. Shadows & Secrets: Volume 1. Larroca, Salvador & Delgado, Edgar, illus. 2016. (Star Wars: Darth Vader Set 2 Ser.). (ENG.). 24p. (J). (gr. 6-12). lib. bdg. 31.36 (978-1-61479-547-6(9), 24381, Graphic Novels) Spotlight.

—Vader. Larroca, Salvador & Delgado, Edgar, illus. 2016. (Star Wars: Darth Vader Ser.). (ENG.). (J). (gr. 6-12). 24p. lib. bdg. 31.36 (978-1-61479-523-0(1), 21423); 24p. lib. bdg. 31.36 (978-1-61479-521-6(5), 21421); Vol. 1. 36p. lib. bdg. 31.36 (978-1-61479-520-9(7), 21420); Vol. 3. 24p. lib. bdg. 31.36 (978-1-61479-522-3(3), 21422); Vol. 5. 24p. lib. bdg. 31.36 (978-1-61479-524-7(X), 21424); Vol. 6. 24p. lib. bdg. 31.36 (978-1-61479-525-4(8), 21425) Spotlight. (Graphic Novels).

—Vader down: Volume 4. Larroca, Salvador & Delgado, Edgar, illus. 2016. (Star Wars: Vader Down Ser.). (ENG.). 24p. (J). (gr. 6-12). lib. bdg. 31.36 (978-1-61479-564-3(9), 24398, Graphic Novels) Spotlight.

—Vader down: Volume 6. Larroca, Salvador & Delgado, Edgar, illus. 2016. (Star Wars: Vader Down Ser.). (ENG.). 24p. (J). (gr. 6-12). lib. bdg. 31.36 (978-1-61479-566-7(5), 24400, Graphic Novels) Spotlight.

Gilliland, Raquel Vasquez. Sia Martinez & the Moonlit Beginning of Everything. 2020. (ENG., Illus.). 432p. (YA). (gr. 7). 19.99 (978-1-5344-4863-6(2), Simon Pulse) Simon Pulse.

Gingeleski, Randolph J. The War of Lord Capani. 2008. 58p. pap. 16.95 (978-1-60563-758-7(0)) America Star Bks.

Gioseffi, Anthony P. Mainframe. 2007. 144p. per. 11.95 (978-0-595-44953-8(0)) iUniverse, Inc.

Girard, Geoffrey. Project Cain. 2013. (ENG., Illus.). 368p. (YA). (gr. 9). 17.99 (978-1-4424-7696-7(6), Simon & Schuster Bks. For Young Readers) Simon & Schuster Bks. For Young Readers.

Glanville, K. L. 2108: Eyes Open. 2012. (ENG.). 280p. (J). pap. 12.99 (978-1-61222-210-3(2)) Luminations Media Group, Inc.

Glass, Calliope. Star Wars: ABC3PO: Alphabet Book. 2016. (ENG., Illus.). 48p. (J). (gr. -1-k). 12.99 (978-1-4847-4142-9(0), Disney Lucasfilm Press) Disney Publishing Worldwide.

—Star Wars at-At Attack! 2015. (Star Wars: World of Reading Ser.). (J). lib. bdg. 13.55 (978-0-606-37538-2(4)) Turtleback.

—Star Wars: OBI123: A Book of Numbers. 2017. (ENG., Illus.). 48p. (J). (gr. 1-3). 12.99 (978-1-4847-6812-9(4), Disney Lucasfilm Press) Disney Publishing Worldwide.

—Star Wars: Search Your Feelings. 2018. (ENG., Illus.). 48p. (J). (gr. 1-3). 12.99 (978-1-368-02736-6(9), Disney Lucasfilm Press) Disney Publishing Worldwide.

Glur, D. L' Empire Contre Attaque.Tr. of Empire Strikes Back. (FRE.). (J). pap. 11.95 (978-2-265-06729-5(6)) Fleuve Noir FRA. Dist: Distribooks, Inc.

Goelman, Ari. The Innocence Treatment. 2018. (ENG.). 272p. (YA). pap. 17.99 (978-1-250-18082-7(1), 900176503) Square Fish.

Golden Books. I Am a Droid (Star Wars) Kennett, Chris, illus. 2016. (Little Golden Book Ser.). (ENG.). 24p. (J). (-k). 5.99 (978-0-7364-3489-8(5), Golden Bks.) Random Hse. Children's Bks.

—I Am a Hero (Star Wars) Golden Books, illus. 2017. (Little Golden Book Ser.). (ENG., Illus.). 24p. (J). (-k). 4.99 (978-0-7364-3587-1(5), Golden Bks.) Random Hse. Children's Bks.

—I Am a Jedi (Star Wars) Cohee, Ron, illus. 2016. (Little Golden Book Ser.). (ENG.). 24p. (J). (-k). 5.99 (978-0-7364-3487-4(9), Golden Bks.) Random Hse. Children's Bks.

—I Am a Pilot (Star Wars) Batson, Alan, illus. 2016. (Little Golden Book Ser.). (ENG.). 24p. (J). (-k). 5.99 (978-0-7364-3621-2(9), Golden Bks.) Random Hse. Children's Bks.

—I Am a Sith (Star Wars) Kennett, Chris, illus. 2016. (Little Golden Book Ser.). (ENG.). 24p. (J). (-k). 5.99 (978-0-7364-3607-6(3), Golden Bks.) Random Hse. Children's Bks.

—The Rise of Skywalker (Star Wars) Golden Books, illus. 2020. (Little Golden Book Ser.). (ENG., Illus.). 24p. (J). (-k). 5.99 (978-0-7364-4076-9(3), Golden Bks.) Random Hse. Children's Bks.

—Star Wars: Attack of the Clones (Star Wars) Beavers, Ethen, illus. 2015. (Little Golden Book Ser.). (ENG.). 24p. (J). (-k). 4.99 (978-0-7364-3546-8(8), Golden Bks.) Random Hse. Children's Bks.

—Star Wars Little Golden Book Collection (Star Wars) Golden Books, illus. 2016. (ENG., Illus.). 176p. (J). (-k). 12.99 (978-0-7364-3609-0(X), Golden Bks.) Random Hse. Children's Bks.

—Star Wars: the Force Awakens (Star Wars) Meurer, Caleb, illus. 2016. (Little Golden Book Ser.). (ENG.). 24p. (J). (-k). 5.99 (978-0-7364-3491-1(7), Golden Bks.) Random Hse. Children's Bks.

—This Is the Way (Star Wars: the Mandalorian) Clester, Shane, illus. 2020. (Little Golden Book Ser.). (ENG.). 24p. (J). (-k). 5.99 (978-0-7364-4171-1(9), Golden Bks.) Random Hse. Children's Bks.

Golden Books, illus. Nine Marvel Super Hero Tales (Marvel) 2017. (ENG.). 224p. (J). (-k). 12.99 (978-1-5247-1783-4(5), Golden Bks.) Random Hse. Children's Bks.

—Star Wars: I Am A... Little Golden Book Library (Star Wars) I Am a Pilot; I Am a Jedi; I Am a Sith; I Am a Droid; I Am a Princess, 5 vols. 2016. (Little Golden Book Ser.). (ENG.). 120p. (J). (-k). 29.95 (978-0-7364-3638-0(3), Golden Bks.) Random Hse. Children's Bks.

—The Star Wars Little Golden Book Library (Star Wars) The Phantom Menace; Attack of the Clones; Revenge of the Sith; a New Hope; the Empire Strikes Back; Return of the Jedi, 6 vols. 2015. (Little Golden Book Ser.). (ENG.). 144p. (J). (-k). 29.94 (978-0-7364-3470-6(4), Golden Bks.) Random Hse. Children's Bks.

Goldman, Stanley M. The Doorway to Forever: September 2nd, 1666, the First Day of Forever. 2008. (ENG.). 186p. (J). (gr. 7). pap. 9.95 (978-1-933255-46-0(3)) DNA Pr.

Gompertz, Haley. Pluto's Planet Problems. 2012. 30p. pap. 10.99 (978-1-60820-712-1(9)) MLR Pr., LLC.

Goodman, Alison. Singing the Dogstar Blues. 2008. (ENG.). 240p. (YA). (978-0-7322-8863-1(0)) HarperCollins Pubs. Australia.

Goodwin, Archie. Episode V Vol. 2: The Empire Strikes Back. Williamson, Al, illus. 2010. (Star Wars Ser.: No. 3). (ENG.). 24p. (J). (gr. 6-12). 31.36 (978-1-59961-702-2(1), 13783, Graphic Novels) Spotlight.

—Episode V Vol. 4: The Empire Strikes Back. Williamson, Al, illus. 2010. (Star Wars Ser.: No. 3). (ENG.). 24p. (J). (gr. 6-12). 31.36 (978-1-59961-704-6(8), 13785, Graphic Novels) Spotlight.

—Episode VI Vol. 2: Return of the Jedi Vol. 2, 1 vol. Williamson, Al, illus. 2010. (Star Wars Ser.: No. 3). (ENG.). 24p. (J). (gr. 6-12). 31.36 (978-1-59961-706-0(4), 13787, Graphic Novels) Spotlight.

—Episode VI Vol. 3: Return of the Jedi Vol. 3, 1 vol. Williamson, Al, illus. 2010. (Star Wars Ser.: No. 3). (ENG.). 24p. (J). (gr. 6-12). 31.36 (978-1-59961-707-7(2), 13788, Graphic Novels) Spotlight.

—Episode VI Vol. 4: Return of the Jedi Vol. 4, 1 vol. Williamson, Al, illus. 2010. (Star Wars Ser.: No. 3). (ENG.). 24p. (J). (gr. 6-12). 31.36 (978-1-59961-708-4(0), 13789, Graphic Novels) Spotlight.

Gordon, Roderick. Closer, 12 vols. (Tunnels Ser.: 4). (J). 296.75 (978-1-4498-2158-6(8)); 121.75 (978-1-4498-2159-3(6)); 1.25 (978-1-4498-2165-4(0)); 2011. 134.75 (978-1-4498-2161-6(8)); 2011. 132.75 (978-1-4498-2163-0(4)) Recorded Bks., Inc.

—Spiral, 9 vols. 2012. (Tunnels Ser.: 5). (J). 132.75 (978-1-4618-4519-5(X)); 121.75 (978-1-4618-4516-4(5)); 134.75 (978-1-4618-4517-1(3)); 296.75 (978-1-4618-4515-7(7)) Recorded Bks., Inc.

Gould, Robert & Duey, Kathleen. Time Soldiers - Rex. Epstein, Eugene, illus. Gould, Robert, photos by. 2005. (Time Soldiers Ser.: Bk. 1). (ENG.). 96p. (J). (gr. k-2). per. 5.95 (978-1-929945-53-5(1)); per. 5.95 (978-1-929945-54-2(X)) Big Guy Bks., Inc.

Graceffa, Joey. Children of Eden: A Novel. 2017. (Children of Eden Ser.: 1). (ENG.). 288p. (gr. 7-12). pap. 12.99 (978-1-5011-4990-0(3), Atria Bks.) Simon & Schuster.

—Elites of Eden: A Novel. 2018. (Children of Eden Ser.: 2). (ENG.). 288p. (gr. 7-12). pap. 15.00 (978-1-5011-7454-4(1), Atria Bks.) Simon & Schuster.

—Rebels of Eden: A Novel. 2019. (Children of Eden Ser.: 3). (ENG.). 384p. (gr. 7-12). pap. 16.99 (978-1-5011-7459-9(2), Atria Bks.) Simon & Schuster.

Graham, Brandon & Roy, Simon. Brothers. 2013. (ENG., Illus.). 172p. (YA). pap. 14.99 (978-1-60706-749-8(8), 2f81e881-88cb-4a34-95dd-f7ba17a5c8fc) Image Comics.

Graham, Brandon, et al. Empire. 2014. (ENG., Illus.). 128p. (YA). pap. 14.99 (978-1-60706-858-7(3), 4f0d4bf1-24b5-4e02-a3e1-016be3530e6b) Image Comics.

Grange, Emma. The Empire Strikes Back. 2014. (LEGO Star Wars DK Reader Ser.). lib. bdg. 13.55 (978-0-606-35734-0(3)) Turtleback.

—A New Hope. 2014. (LEGO Star Wars DK Reader Ser.). lib. bdg. 13.55 (978-0-606-35733-3(5)) Turtleback.

Grant, Michael. Bzrk. (Bzrk Ser.). (ENG.). 400p. (YA). (gr. 9-12). 2013. pap. 9.99 (978-1-60684-418-2(0), be48eae0-186e-42f3-9a8f-7a9a80661ce8) 2012. 17.99 (978-1-60684-312-3(5), ba9d46d5-5aa2-4bc4-bb35-da33ac28de6c) Lerner Publishing Group. (Carolrhoda Lab™).

—BZRK Reloaded. 2013. (Bzrk Ser.). (ENG.). 432p. (YA). (gr. 9-12). 18.99 (978-1-60684-394-9(X), 20fe8bbb-63fa-40af-8c0e-54890e077fe3, Carolrhoda Lab™) Lerner Publishing Group.

—Hero. 2019. (Gone Ser.: 9). (ENG.). 448p. (YA). (gr. 9). 17.99 (978-0-06-246790-4(5), Tegen, Katherine Bks) HarperCollins Pubs.

—Monster. (Gone Ser.: 7). (ENG.). (YA). (gr. 9). 2018. 448p. pap. 11.99 (978-0-06-246785-0(9)) 2017. 432p. 18.99 (978-0-06-246784-3(0)) HarperCollins Pubs. (Tegen, Katherine Bks).

Grant, Sara. Dark Parties. 2013. (ENG.). 352p. (J). (gr. 7-17). pap. 18.99 (978-0-316-08595-3(2)) Little, Brown Bks. for Young Readers.

Gratton, Tessa. Star Wars: the High Republic: Quest for Planet X. 2023. (ENG.). 288p. (J). (gr. 3-7). 14.99 (978-1-368-08287-7(4), Disney Lucasfilm Press) Disney Publishing Worldwide.

Gratz, Alan. The League of Seven. Helquist, Brett, illus. 2015. (League of Seven Ser.: 1). (ENG.). 352p. (J). (gr. 5-9). pap. 10.99 (978-0-7653-3825-9(4), 900126212, Starscape) Doherty, Tom Assocs., LLC.

Graudin, Ryan. Invictus. 2018. (ENG.). 480p. (YA). (gr. 9-17). pap. 10.99 (978-0-316-50308-2(8)) Little, Brown Bks. for Young Readers.

—Invictus. l.t. ed. 2019. (ENG.). 660p. (YA). (gr. 9-17). pap. 12.99 (978-1-4328-6451-4(3), Large Print Pr.) Thorndike Pr.

Gravel, Elise. Odd Creatures. 2019. (Balloon Toons Ser.). (ENG.). 40p. (J). (gr. k-1). 22.96 (978-1-64310-900-8(6)) Penworthy Co., LLC, The.

Gray, Claudia. Defy the Fates. 2019. (Defy the Stars Ser.: 3). (ENG.). 480p. (YA). (gr. 9-17). 18.99 (978-0-316-44075-2(2)) Little, Brown Bks. for Young Readers.

—Defy the Stars. 2018. (Defy the Stars Ser.: 1). (ENG.). 528p. (YA). (gr. 9-17). pap. 23.99 (978-0-316-39404-8(1)) Little, Brown Bks. for Young Readers.

—Defy the Stars. 2018. (YA). lib. bdg. 22.10 (978-0-606-40988-9(2)) Turtleback.

—Defy the Worlds. 2019. (Defy the Stars Ser.: 2). (ENG.). 496p. (YA). (gr. 9-17). pap. 12.99 (978-0-316-39407-9(6)) Little, Brown Bks. for Young Readers.

—Star Wars: Lost Stars. 2017. (ENG.). 576p. (J). (gr. 7-12). pap. 9.99 (978-1-368-01378-9(3), Disney Lucasfilm Press) Disney Publishing Worldwide.

—Ten Thousand Skies above You. (Firebird Ser.: 2). (ENG.). (YA). (gr. 9). 2016. 448p. pap. 11.99 (978-0-06-227900-2(9)) 2015. 432p. 17.99 (978-0-06-227899-9(1)) HarperCollins Pubs. (HarperTeen).

Greenburg, Dan. Weird Planet #1: Dude, Where's My Spaceship. Pamintuan, Macky, illus. 2006. (Weird Planet Ser.: 1). (ENG.). 96p. (J). (gr. 1-4). 6.99 (978-0-375-83344-1(7), Random Hse. Bks. for Young Readers) Random Hse. Children's Bks.

Greene, Janice. Escape from Earth (Science Fiction), 1 vol. 2017. (Pageturners Ser.). (ENG.). 76p. (YA). (gr. 9-12). 10.75 (978-1-68021-394-2(6)) Saddleback Educational Publishing, Inc.

—Under Siege (Science Fiction), 1 vol. 2017. (Pageturners Ser.). (ENG.). 80p. (YA). (gr. 9-12). 10.75 (978-1-68021-397-3(0)) Saddleback Educational Publishing, Inc.

Greenwood, Arin. Your Robot Dog Will Die. 2019. 192p. (YA). (gr. 9). pap. 10.99 (978-1-61695-852-7(9), Soho Teen) Soho Pr., Inc.

Gregory, David. Visions of Reality. 2007. 236p. per. 15.95 (978-0-595-44969-9(7)) iUniverse, Inc.

Grey, Audrey. Shadow Fall. 2016. (Shadow Fall Ser.: 1). (ENG.). 368p. (YA). (gr. 9). pap. 9.95 (978-0-9970104-9-7(5)) Blaze Publishing, LLC.

Griffin, Emily Ziff. Light Years. 2017. (ENG., Illus.). 304p. (YA). (gr. 9-12). 18.99 (978-1-5072-0005-6(6), Simon Pulse) Simon Pulse.

Griffiths, Mark. The Impossible Boy. 2014. (ENG., Illus.). 272p. (J). pap. 8.99 (978-0-85707-539-0(X), Simon & Schuster Children's) Simon & Schuster, Ltd. GBR. Dist: Simon & Schuster, Inc.

—Technoslime Terror! Chatterton, Martin, illus. 2013. (ENG.). 288p. (J). pap. 6.99 (978-0-85707-537-6(3), Simon & Schuster Children's) Simon & Schuster, Ltd. GBR. Dist: Simon & Schuster, Inc.

Grine, Chris. Time Shifters: a Graphic Novel. 2017. (ENG., Illus.). 272p. (J). (gr. 3-7). 24.99 (978-0-545-92659-1(9)); pap. 12.99 (978-0-545-92657-7(2)) Scholastic, Inc. (Graphix).

Grisham, Jonathan. The Death of the Universe. 2005. (YA). per. (978-1-933594-16-3(0)) FBC Pubns. & Printing.

The Guardians. 2014. (ENG., Illus.). 288p. (J). (gr. 4-8). pap. 7.99 (978-1-4814-1834-8(3), Aladdin) Simon & Schuster Children's Publishing.
Guffrey, Lindsey. A Psalm for the Solar System. 2013. 24p. pap. 9.00 (978-0-9896518-0-6(0)) Yorkshire Publishing Group.
Guillet, Jean-Pierre. La Puce Cosmique et le Rayon Bleuge. Guillet, Francois, illus. 2004. (Des 9 Ans. Ser.). (FRE.). 120p. (J). (978-2-922565-98-0(X)) Editions de la Paix CAN. Dist: World of Reading, Ltd.
Gutman, Dan. My Weird School #10: Mr. Docker Is off His Rocker! Paillot, Jim, illus. 2006. (My Weird School Ser.: 10). (ENG.). 112p. (J). (gr. 1-5). pap. 5.99 (978-0-06-082227-9(9), HarperCollins) HarperCollins Pubs.
—My Weird School Daze #3: Mr. Granite Is from Another Planet!, No. 3. Paillot, Jim, illus. 2008. (My Weird School Daze Ser.: 3). (ENG.). 112p. (J). (gr. 1-5). pap. 4.99 (978-0-06-134611-8(X), HarperCollins) HarperCollins Pubs.
Haddix, Margaret Peterson. The Always War. (ENG.). (YA). (gr. 7). 2012. 224p. pap. 8.99 (978-1-4169-9527-2(7)) 2011. 208p. 16.99 (978-1-4169-9526-5(9)) Simon & Schuster Bks. For Young Readers. (Simon & Schuster Bks. For Young Readers).
—Among the Barons. 2004. (Shadow Children Ser.). 182p. (gr. 3-7). 17.00 (978-0-7569-3923-6(2)) Perfection Learning Corp.
—Among the Barons. (Shadow Children Ser.: 4). (ENG.). (J). (gr. 3-7). 2003. 192p. 18.99 (978-0-689-83906-1(5)) 2004. 208p. reprint ed. pap. 7.99 (978-0-689-83910-8(3)) Simon & Schuster Bks. For Young Readers. (Simon & Schuster Bks. For Young Readers).
—Among the Brave. 2004. (Shadow Children Ser.: Bk. 5). 132p. (J). lib. bdg. 20.00 (978-1-4242-0392-5(9)) Fitzgerald Bks.
—Among the Brave. (Shadow Children Ser.: 5). (ENG., Illus.). (J). (gr. 3-7). 2005. 256p. pap. 7.99 (978-0-689-85795-9(0)) 2004. 240p. 18.99 (978-0-689-85794-2(2)) Simon & Schuster Bks. For Young Readers. (Simon & Schuster Bks. For Young Readers).
—Among the Enemy. 2006. (Shadow Children Ser.: Bk. 6). (Illus.). 214p. (gr. 3-7). 17.00 (978-0-7569-6792-5(9)) Perfection Learning Corp.
—Among the Enemy. (Shadow Children Ser.: 6). (ENG., (J). (gr. 3-7). 2006. Illus.). 240p. pap. 7.99 (978-0-689-85797-3(7)) 2005. 224p. 18.99 (978-0-689-85796-6(9)) Simon & Schuster Bks. For Young Readers. (Simon & Schuster Bks. For Young Readers).
—Among the Free. 2007. (Shadow Children Ser.: Bk. 7). 194p. (gr. 3-7). 17.00 (978-0-7569-7953-9(6)) Perfection Learning Corp.
—Among the Free. (Shadow Children Ser.: Bk. 7). (ENG., Illus.). (J). (gr. 3-7). 2007. 224p. pap. 7.99 (978-0-689-85799-7(3)) 2006. 208p. 19.99 (978-0-689-85798-0(5)) Simon & Schuster Bks. For Young Readers. (Simon & Schuster Bks. For Young Readers).
—Among the Free. 2007. (Shadow Children Ser.: 7). lib. bdg. 18.40 (978-1-4178-1424-4(1)) Turtleback.
—Among the Hidden. 2014. (Shadow Children Ser. 1 Ser.). (ENG.). 160p. (J). 11.24 (978-1-63245-178-1(6)) Lectorum Pubns., Inc.
—Caught. (Missing Ser.: 5). (ENG., (J). (gr. 3-7). 2013. Illus.). 368p. pap. 8.99 (978-1-4169-8983-7(8)) 2012. 352p. 16.99 (978-1-4169-8982-0(X)) Simon & Schuster Bks. For Young Readers. (Simon & Schuster Bks. For Young Readers).
—Caught. 2013. (Missing Ser.: 5). lib. bdg. 18.40 (978-0-606-27045-8(0)) Turtleback.
—Children of Exile. 2016. (Children of Exile Ser.: 1). (ENG., Illus.). 304p. (J). (gr. 5). 18.99 (978-1-4424-5003-5(7), Simon & Schuster Bks. For Young Readers) Simon & Schuster Bks. For Young Readers.
—Found. (Missing Ser.: 1). (ENG.). (J). (gr. 3-7). 2009. 336p. pap. 8.99 (978-1-4169-5421-7(X)) 2008. 320p. 19.99 (978-1-4169-5417-0(1)) Simon & Schuster Bks. For Young Readers. (Simon & Schuster Bks. For Young Readers).
—In over Their Heads. 2017. (Under Their Skin Ser.: 2). (ENG., Illus.). 320p. (J). (gr. 3-7). 18.99 (978-1-4814-1761-7(4), Simon & Schuster Bks. For Young Readers) Simon & Schuster Bks. For Young Readers.
—Redeemed. 2015. (Missing Ser.: 8). (ENG.). 416p. (J). (gr. 3-7). 19.99 (978-1-4424-9756-6(4), Simon & Schuster Bks. For Young Readers) Simon & Schuster Bks. For Young Readers.
—Redeemed. 2016. (Missing Ser.: 8). lib. bdg. 18.40 (978-0-606-39234-1(3)) Turtleback.
—Revealed. 2015. (Missing Ser.: 7). lib. bdg. 19.65 (978-0-606-37847-5(2)) Turtleback.
—Risked. 2013. (Missing Ser.: 6). (ENG., Illus.). 320p. (J). (gr. 3-7). 18.99 (978-1-4169-8984-4(6), Simon & Schuster Bks. For Young Readers) Simon & Schuster Bks. For Young Readers.
—Risked. 2014. (Missing Ser.: 6). lib. bdg. 19.65 (978-0-606-36096-8(4)) Turtleback.
—Sabotaged. (Missing Ser.: 3). (ENG.). (J). (gr. 3-7). 2011. 400p. pap. 8.99 (978-1-4169-5425-5(2)) 2010. 384p. 17.99 (978-1-4169-5424-8(4)) Simon & Schuster Bks. For Young Readers. (Simon & Schuster Bks. For Young Readers).
—Sent. (Missing Ser.: 2). (YA). 2011. 82.75 (978-1-4407-2678-1(7)) 2009. 218.75 (978-1-4407-2670-5(1)) 2009. 98.75 (978-1-4407-2675-0(2)) 2009. 1.25 (978-1-4407-2679-8(5)) Recorded Bks., Inc.
—Sent. (Missing Ser.: 2). (ENG.). (J). (gr. 3-7). 2010. 336p. pap. 8.99 (978-1-4169-5423-1(6)) 2009. 320p. 16.99 (978-1-4169-5422-4(8)) Simon & Schuster Bks. For Young Readers. (Simon & Schuster Bks. For Young Readers).
—Sent. abr. ed. 2009. (978-1-4424-0767-1(0)) Simon & Schuster Children's Publishing.
—Sent. l.t. ed. 2010. (Missing Ser.: Bk. 2). (ENG.). 345p. 23.99 (978-1-4104-3245-2(9)) Thorndike Pr.
—Sent. 2010. (Missing Ser.: 2). lib. bdg. 18.40 (978-0-606-14699-9(7)) Turtleback.
—Torn. (Missing Ser.: 4). (ENG.). (J). (gr. 3-7). 2012. 368p. pap. 8.99 (978-1-4169-8981-3(1)) 2011. 352p. 19.99 (978-1-4169-8980-6(3)) Simon & Schuster Bks. For Young Readers. (Simon & Schuster Bks. For Young Readers).
—Torn. l.t. ed. 2011. (Missing Ser.: Bk. 4). (ENG.). 566p. 23.99 (978-1-4104-4078-5(8)) Thorndike Pr.
—Torn. 2012. (Missing Ser.: 4). lib. bdg. 18.40 (978-0-606-26333-7(0)) Turtleback.
—Turnabout. 2012. (ENG.). 224p. (YA). (gr. 7). pap. 8.99 (978-1-4424-4603-8(X), Simon & Schuster Bks. For Young Readers) Simon & Schuster Bks. For Young Readers.
—Under Their Skin. 2016. (Under Their Skin Ser.: 1). (ENG., Illus.). 320p. (J). (gr. 3-7). 18.99 (978-1-4814-1758-7(4), Simon & Schuster Bks. For Young Readers) Simon & Schuster Bks. For Young Readers.
—Under Their Skin. 2017. (Under Their Skins Ser.: 1). lib. bdg. 18.40 (978-0-606-39756-8(6)) Turtleback.
Haddon, Mark. Boom! 2011. (ENG.). 208p. (J). (gr. 3-7). 7.99 (978-0-385-75224-4(5), Yearling) Random Hse. Children's Bks.
Hadland, W. Into the Night. 2010. 312p. (gr. 4-6). pap. 19.13 (978-1-4251-4187-5(0)) Trafford Publishing.
Hager, Mandy. Into the Wilderness. 2014. (Blood of the Lamb Ser.: 2). (ENG.). 335p. (YA). (gr. 9). 17.99 (978-1-61614-863-8(2), Pyr) Start Publishing LLC.
Hager, Robert. Saurcana: Terror from the Sea. 2004. (J). (978-0-9727676-1-3(4)); pap. (978-0-9727676-0-6(6)) Hager, Robert.
Haladay, Max. Max Gets Mad, 1 vol. 2006. (Neighborhood Readers Ser.). (ENG.). 8p. (gr. 1-2). pap. 5.15 (978-1-4042-6811-1(1), 937b21d8-5e4c-4b3c-8801-b2ad27c26bb7, Rosen Classroom) Rosen Publishing Group, Inc., The.
Hale, Bruce. The Adventures of Space Gecko. (Illus.). (J). 8.95 (978-0-9621280-2-8(3)) Words & Pictures Publishing, Inc.
Hale, Nathan. One Trick Pony. (ENG., Illus.). (J). (gr. 3-7). 2018. 144p. pap. 9.99 (978-1-4197-2944-7(6), 1104003) 2017. 128p. 14.95 (978-1-4197-2128-1(3), 1104001) Abrams, Inc. (Amulet Bks.).
Halevy, Hanita H. Dragonlions & the Spacemen. Heler, Shraga, illus. 2012. (ENG.). 140p. (J). pap. 13.00 (978-965-550-085-1(3)) Contento De Semrik ISR. Dist: Baker & Taylor Publisher Services (BTPS).
Hall, Susan, illus. Robot Repairman to the Rescue! 2009. (Backyardigans Ser.). (ENG.). 24p. (J). (gr. -1-2). pap. 3.99 (978-1-4169-9012-3(7), Simon Spotlight/Nickelodeon) Simon Spotlight/Nickelodeon.
Hall, Teri. The Line. 2011. (J). 224p. (gr. 7-12). 21.19 (978-0-8037-3466-1(2)); 240p. (gr. 5-18). 8.99 (978-0-14-241776-8(9), Puffin Books) Penguin Young Readers Group.
Hambrick, Sharon. Tommy's Rocket. Manning, Maurie J., illus. 2003. (Fig Street Kids Ser.). 83p. (J). (gr. 1-2). 7.49 (978-1-59166-186-3(2)) BJU Pr.
Hamilton, Kersten. The Ire of Iron Claw: Gadgets & Gears, Book 2. Hamilton, James, illus. 2016. (Gadgets & Gears Ser.: 2). (ENG.). 192p. (J). (gr. 3-7). pap. 6.99 (978-0-544-66854-6(5), 1625480, Clarion Bks.) HarperCollins Pubs.
Hand, Elizabeth. A New Threat. 2004. (Star Wars Ser.: Vol. 5). 139p. (J). lib. bdg. 20.00 (978-1-4242-0781-7(9)) Fitzgerald Bks.
Hanover, Rebecca. The Similars. 2019. (Similars Ser.). (ENG.). (YA). (gr. 8-12). 416p. pap. 10.99 (978-1-4926-9180-8(1)); 400p. 17.99 (978-1-4926-6510-6(X)) Sourcebooks, Inc.
Hansen, Lynne. Reckless Revolution. 2007. (YA). (978-1-4114-9672-9(8), Spark Publishing Group) Sterling Publishing Co., Inc.
—Shades of Blue & Gray. 2007. (YA). pap. (978-1-4114-9674-3(4), Spark Publishing Group) Sterling Publishing Co., Inc.
—A Time for Witches. 2007. (YA). (978-1-4114-9671-2(X), Spark Publishing Group) Sterling Publishing Co., Inc.
Hantula, Richard & Asimov, Isaac. Science Fiction: Vision of Tomorrow?, 1 vol. 2004. (Isaac Asimov's 21st Century Library of the Universe: Fact & Fantasy Ser.). (ENG., Illus.). 32p. (gr. 3-5). lib. bdg. 28.67 (978-0-8368-3952-4(8), 88ba2be3-3e6c-46e6-9149-e224d6fb5b51) Stevens, Gareth Publishing LLLP.
Hapka, Catherine, pseud. Plants vs. Zombies. 2014. (I Can Read! Level 2 Ser.). (J). lib. bdg. 13.55 (978-0-606-35477-6(8)) Turtleback.
Hardinge, Frances. A Face Like Glass. 2017. (ENG.). 496p. (YA). (gr. 7-17). 19.95 (978-1-4197-2484-8(3), 1172701, Amulet Bks.) Abrams, Inc.
Hardy, Melissa. The Geomancer's Compass. 2012. 256p. (YA). (gr. 7). 17.95 (978-1-77049-292-9(5), Tundra Bks.) Tundra Bks. CAN. Dist: Penguin Random Hse. LLC.
Harper, Benjamin. The Lion & the Mouse & the Invaders from Zurg: A Graphic Novel. Rodriguez, Pedro, illus. 2017. (Far Out Fables Ser.). (ENG.). 40p. (J). (gr. 3-6). pap. 4.95 (978-1-4965-5426-0(4), 136359); lib. bdg. 25.32 (978-1-4965-5422-2(1), 136355) Capstone. (Stone Arch Bks.).
HarperCollins Publishers Ltd. Staff, et al. James Cameron's Avatar. movie tie-in ed. 2009. (James Cameron's Avatar Ser.). (ENG., Illus.). 48p. (J). (gr. -1-2). pap. 7.99 (978-0-06-180124-2(0), HarperFestival) HarperCollins Pubs.
Harrington, Kim. App of the Living Dead (Gamer Squad 3) 2017. (Gamer Squad Ser.). 192p. (J). (gr. 3-7). pap. 6.95 (978-1-4549-2614-6(7)) Sterling Publishing Co., Inc.
Harrison, Harry. Toy Shop. 2011. 18p. pap. 6.95 (978-1-60664-572-7(2)) Rodgers, Alan Bks.
Harrison, S. Infinity Reborn, 0 vols. 2016. (Infinity Trilogy Ser.: 3). (ENG.). 364p. (gr. 7-12). pap. 9.99 (978-1-5039-3346-0(6), 9781503933460, Skyscape) Amazon Publishing.
—Infinity Rises, 0 vols. 2016. (Infinity Trilogy Ser.: 2). (ENG.). 272p. (YA). (gr. 9-13). pap. 9.99 (978-1-5039-5225-6(8), 9781503952256, Skyscape) Amazon Publishing.
Harrison, Zac. Frozen Enemies, 1 vol. 2013. (Hyperspace High Ser.). (ENG.). 288p. (J). (gr. 4-8). 27.32 (978-1-4342-6307-0(X), 123753); pap. 8.95 (978-1-4342-6311-7(8), 123757) Capstone. (Stone Arch Bks.).
Harstad, Johan. 172 Hours on the Moon. 2012. (ENG.). 368p. (YA). (gr. 7-17). 36.99 (978-0-316-18288-1(5)) Little, Brown Bks. for Young Readers.
Hartley Bellows, Carol. Icey. 2009. 32p. pap. 14.99 (978-1-4389-4475-3(6)) AuthorHouse.
Hasany, Syed M. Where Is My Stethoscope? 2012. 24p. pap. 14.93 (978-1-4669-6888-2(5)) Trafford Publishing.
Hatke, Ben. Legends of Zita the Spacegirl. 2012. (Zita the Spacegirl Ser.: 2). (ENG., Illus.). 224p. (J). (gr. 3-7). 22.99 (978-1-59643-806-4(1), 900086236); pap. 14.99 (978-1-59643-447-9(3), 900054804) Roaring Brook Pr. (First Second Bks.).
—Legends of Zita the Spacegirl. 2012. (Zita the Spacegirl Ser.: 2). (J). lib. bdg. 24.50 (978-0-606-26708-3(5)) Turtleback.
—Zita the Spacegirl. 2011. (Zita the Spacegirl Ser.: 1). (ENG., Illus.). 192p. (J). (gr. 3-7). 21.99 (978-1-59643-695-4(6), 900073109); pap. 14.99 (978-1-59643-446-2(5), 900054803) Roaring Brook Pr. (First Second Bks.).
—Zita the Spacegirl. 2011. (Zita the Spacegirl Ser.: 1). (J). lib. bdg. 24.50 (978-0-606-21623-4(5)) Turtleback.
Hautman, Pete. The Cydonian Pyramid. (Klaatu Diskos Ser.: 2). (ENG.). 368p. (YA). (gr. 7). 2014. pap. 8.99 (978-0-7636-6933-1(4)) 2013. 16.99 (978-0-7636-5404-7(3)) Candlewick Pr.
—The Flinkwater Factor. 2015. (Flinkwater Chronicles Ser.: 1). (ENG.). 256p. (J). (gr. 4-8). 19.99 (978-1-4814-3251-1(6), Simon & Schuster Bks. For Young Readers) Simon & Schuster Bks. For Young Readers.
—The Forgetting Machine. 2016. (Flinkwater Chronicles Ser.: 2). (ENG., Illus.). 224p. (J). (gr. 4-8). 16.99 (978-1-4814-6438-3(8), Simon & Schuster Bks. For Young Readers) Simon & Schuster Bks. For Young Readers.
—Hole in the Sky. 2007. (ENG.). 224p. (YA). (gr. 7). pap. 11.95 (978-1-4169-6822-1(9), Simon Pulse) Simon Pulse.
—Rash. 2007. (ENG., Illus.). 272p. (YA). (gr. 7-12). pap. 12.99 (978-0-689-86904-4(5), Simon & Schuster Bks. For Young Readers) Simon & Schuster Bks. For Young Readers.
Hawking, Lucy. George & the Ship of Time. Parsons, Garry, illus. 2019. (George's Secret Key Ser.). (ENG.). 416p. (J). (gr. 3-7). 18.99 (978-1-5344-3730-2(4), Simon & Schuster Bks. For Young Readers) Simon & Schuster Bks. For Young Readers.
Hawking, Lucy & Hawking, Stephen. George's Cosmic Treasure Hunt. Parsons, Garry, illus. 2009. (George's Secret Key Ser.). (ENG.). 320p. (J). (gr. 3-7). 19.99 (978-1-4169-8671-3(5), Simon & Schuster Bks. For Young Readers) Simon & Schuster Bks. For Young Readers.
Hawking, Stephen & Hawking, Lucy. George & the Unbreakable Code. Parsons, Garry, illus. (George's Secret Key Ser.). (ENG.). (J). (gr. 3-7). 2017. 368p. pap. 12.99 (978-1-4814-6628-8(3)) 2016. 352p. 19.99 (978-1-4814-6627-1(5)) Simon & Schuster Bks. For Young Readers. (Simon & Schuster Bks. For Young Readers).
—George's Secret Key to the Universe. Parsons, Garry, illus. (George's Secret Key Ser.). (ENG.). (J). (gr. 3-7). 2009. 336p. pap. 12.99 (978-1-4169-8584-6(0)) 2007. 304p. 22.99 (978-1-4169-5462-0(7)) Simon & Schuster Bks. For Young Readers. (Simon & Schuster Bks. For Young Readers).
Hawkins, Matt. Think Tank, Vol. 1. 2012. (ENG., Illus.). 120p. (YA). pap. 14.99 (978-1-60706-660-6(2), e4632b0e-ae92-4f19-9f67-2dd5bef999e2) Image Comics.
—Think Tank, Vol. 2. 2013. (ENG., Illus.). 160p. (YA). pap. 14.99 (978-1-60706-745-0(5), ce795cc5-a050-44da-8297-acc2c7592dfa) Image Comics.
Hayes, Vicki C. Sky Watchers. 2014. (Red Rhino Ser.). (J). lib. bdg. 18.40 (978-0-606-36197-2(9)) Turtleback.
Healey, Karen. When We Wake. 2014. (ENG.). 320p. (YA). (gr. 7-17). pap. 17.99 (978-0-316-20077-6(8)) Little, Brown Bks. for Young Readers.
Hearn, Julie & Yankus, Marc. Sign of the Raven. 2005. (ENG., Illus.). 336p. (YA). 16.95 (978-0-689-85734-8(9), Atheneum Bks. for Young Readers) Simon & Schuster Children's Publishing.
Heddle, Jennifer & Roux, Stéphane. Star Wars Rebels: Sabine's Art Attack, 1 vol. 2015. (World of Reading Level 1 Ser.). (ENG., Illus.). 32p. (J). (gr. -1-3). lib. bdg. 31.36 (978-1-61479-365-6(4), 18200) Spotlight.
Heidicker, Christian McKay. Attack of the 50 Foot Wallflower. Bosma, Sam, illus. (ENG.). 320p. (YA). (gr. 9). 2019. pap. 11.99 (978-1-4814-9914-9(9)) 2018. 18.99 (978-1-4814-9913-2(0)) Simon & Schuster Bks. For Young Readers. (Simon & Schuster Bks. For Young Readers).
Hein, Connie L. Toliver in Time; for a Journey West: History in a Nutshell. Theobald, Denise, illus. l.t. ed. 2005. 28p. (J). lib. bdg. 17.95 (978-0-9740855-6-2(1)); per. 9.95 (978-0-9740855-7-9(X)) Still Water Publishing.
Hello Mars! 2005. (J). audio, cd-rom 24.95 (978-0-9771381-6-6(X)) Williams, Geoffrey T.
Heltzel, Anne. Circle Nine. 2011. (ENG.). 272p. (YA). (gr. 9). 16.99 (978-0-7636-5333-0(0)) Candlewick Pr.
Hemsworth, Jade. Project Mc2: Smart Is the New Cool. 2016. (ENG., Illus.). 144p. (J). (978-1-250-12632-0(0)) ETT Imprint.
Henighan, Tom. Mercury Man. 2004. (ENG.). 200p. (YA). (gr. 6). pap. 9.99 (978-1-55002-508-8(2)) Dundurn Pr. CAN. Dist: Publishers Group West (PGW).
Henriques, Ben. Max & the Memory Machine. 2010. (J). 12.95 (978-0-615-38727-7(6)) EB Benjamin, LLC.
Hernandez, Carlos. Rick Riordan Presents Sal & Gabi Break the Universe (a Sal & Gabi Novel, Book 1) (Sal & Gabi Novel Ser.: 1). (ENG.). (J). (gr. 3-7). 2020. 416p. pap. 8.99 (978-1-368-02362-7(2)) 2019. 400p. 16.99 (978-1-368-02282-8(0)) Disney Publishing Worldwide. (Riordan, Rick).
Hibbert, Clare. DK Readers L1: Star Wars: Tatooine Adventures. 2011. (DK Readers Level 1 Ser.). (ENG.). 48p. (J). (gr. k-4). 4.99 (978-0-7566-7128-0(0), DK Children) Dorling Kindersley Publishing, Inc.
—DK Readers L2: Star Wars: Clone Troopers in Action: Meet the Elite Soldiers of the Republic. 2010. (DK Readers Level 2 Ser.). (ENG.). 32p. (J). (gr. 1-3). 4.99 (978-0-7566-6691-0(0), DK Children) Dorling Kindersley Publishing, Inc.
Hidalgo, Pablo. The Phantom Menace. 2012. (Star Wars Ser.). (ENG.). 64p. (J). (gr. -1-3). pap. 9.99 (978-0-545-38986-0(0)) Scholastic, Inc.
—Star Wars Rebels: Head to Head. 2014. lib. bdg. 19.65 (978-0-606-36071-5(9)) Turtleback.
Higuera, Donna Barba. The Last Cuentista. 2021. (ENG.). 336p. (J). (gr. 5-9). 18.99 (978-1-64614-089-3(3)) Levine Querido.
—The Last Cuentista. Ahokoivu, Mari, illus. 2022. (J). pap. 8.99 (978-1-7374508-8-7(7)) Literati.
Hill, C. J. Echo in Time. 2014. 387p. (YA). (978-0-06-212395-4(5)) HarperCollins Pubs.
Hill, Nick. Carlton Casey: Alien Incident. 2007. 100p. per. 9.95 (978-1-59800-310-9(0)) Outskirts Pr., Inc.
Hilton, Dave, et al. Star Wars. Rood, Brian, illus. 2015. 8p. (J). (978-1-5037-0033-8(X)) Phoenix International Publications, Inc.
Hilton, Marilyn. Full Cicada Moon. 2017. lib. bdg. 19.65 (978-0-606-39789-6(2)) Turtleback.
Hinkler Books Staff, reader. Barney's Outer Space Adventure. 2004. (J). 9.99 incl. audio compact disk (978-1-86515-996-6(4)) Hinkler Bks. Pty. Ltd. AUS. Dist: Penton Overseas, Inc.
Hirsch, Jeff. Black River Falls. 2017. (ENG.). 336p. (YA). (gr. 7). pap. 9.99 (978-0-544-93885-4(2), 1658463, Clarion Bks.) HarperCollins Pubs.
—Unnatural Disasters. 2019. (ENG.). 352p. (YA). (gr. 7). 17.99 (978-0-544-99916-9(9), 1666807, Clarion Bks.) HarperCollins Pubs.
Hobbs, Constance. Dreamers. 2008. 436p. 50.50 (978-0-9556783-6-3(6)) Hobbs, Constance GBR. Dist: Lulu Pr., Inc.
Hobbs, Will. Go Big or Go Home. 2009. (ENG.). 208p. (J). (gr. 5). pap. 6.99 (978-0-06-074143-3(0), HarperCollins) HarperCollins Pubs.
Hockney, Deborah. Jocasta's Gift. 2012. (ENG.). 248p. pap. (978-1-78088-050-1(2)) Troubador Publishing Ltd.
Hoena, Blake A. Ack's New Pet, 1 vol. Harpster, Steve, illus. 2014. (Eek & Ack Early Chapter Bks.). (ENG.). 32p. (J). (gr. k-2). lib. bdg. 22.65 (978-1-4342-6406-0(8), 123886, Stone Arch Bks.) Capstone.
—Beyond the Black Hole. Harpster, Steve, illus. 2008. (Graphic Sparks Ser.). (ENG.). 40p. (J). (gr. 2-5). pap. 5.95 (978-1-4342-0855-2(9), 95216, Stone Arch Bks.) Capstone.
—The Black Hole Report, 1 vol. Harpster, Steve, illus. 2014. (Eek & Ack Early Chapter Bks.). (ENG.). 32p. (J). (gr. k-2). lib. bdg. 22.65 (978-1-4342-6409-1(2), 123889, Stone Arch Bks.) Capstone.
—Eek & Ack Early Chapter Books, 1 vol. 2014. (Eek & Ack Early Chapter Bks.). (ENG.). 32p. (J). (gr. k-2). 90.60 (978-1-4342-8457-0(3), 20993, Stone Arch Bks.) Capstone.
—Poison Ivy's Deadly Garden. Doescher, Erik, illus. 2009. (Batman Ser.). (ENG.). 56p. (J). (gr. 3-6). lib. bdg. 26.65 (978-1-4342-1152-1(5), 95366, Stone Arch Bks.) Capstone.
—Under the Red Sun, 1 vol. Schoening, Dan, illus. 2009. (Superman Ser.). (ENG.). 56p. (J). (gr. 3-6). pap. 4.95 (978-1-4342-1375-4(7), 95672); lib. bdg. 27.32 (978-1-4342-1159-0(2), 95373) Capstone. (Stone Arch Bks.).
Hoffman, Mary. Trace in Space. (ENG., Illus.). 118p. (J). pap. 8.99 (978-0-340-62669-6(0)) Hodder & Stoughton GBR. Dist: Trafalgar Square Publishing.
Hoffmann, Lou. Key of Behliseth. 2nd ed. 2016. (ENG., Illus.). (J). 27.99 (978-1-63533-037-3(8), Harmony Ink Pr.) Dreamspinner Pr.
Holder, Nancy & Viguie, Debbie. Wicked: Witch & Curse. 2009. (978-1-4351-2000-6(0)) Barnes & Noble, Inc.
Holder, Nancy, et al. Wicked: Witch & Curse. 2008. (Wicked Ser.). (ENG.). 672p. (YA). (gr. 9). pap. 14.99 (978-1-4169-7119-1(X), Simon Pulse) Simon Pulse.
Holliday, Susan. The Time Street Gang & the Rag & Bone Boy. l.t. ed. 2007. 132p. pap. (978-1-905665-64-8(4)) Pollinger In Print.
Holt, Christopher. Dark Waters. 2013. (Last Dogs Ser.: 2). (J). lib. bdg. 18.40 (978-0-606-35308-3(9)) Turtleback.
—Journey's End. 2014. (Last Dogs Ser.: 4). (J). lib. bdg. 18.40 (978-0-606-35944-3(3)) Turtleback.
—The Last Dogs: Dark Waters. Douglas, Allen, illus. 2013. (Last Dogs Ser.: 2). (ENG.). 352p. (J). (gr. 3-7). pap. 8.99 (978-0-316-20009-7(3)) Little, Brown Bks. for Young Readers.
—The Last Dogs: Journey's End. Douglas, Allen, illus. 2014. (Last Dogs Ser.: 4). (ENG.). 320p. (J). (gr. 3-7). 17.00 (978-0-316-20007-3(7)) Little, Brown Bks. for Young Readers.
—The Last Dogs: the Long Road. Douglas, Allen, illus. 2014. (Last Dogs Ser.: 3). (ENG.). 352p. (J). (gr. 3-7). pap. 8.99 (978-0-316-20016-5(6)) Little, Brown Bks. for Young Readers.
—The Long Road. 2014. (Last Dogs Ser.: 3). (J). lib. bdg. 18.40 (978-0-606-35309-0(7)) Turtleback.
Holt, K. A. Mike Stellar: Nerves of Steel. 2009. (ENG.). 272p. (J). (gr. 4-6). lib. bdg. 22.44 (978-0-375-94556-4(3), Yearling) Random Hse. Children's Bks.
—Red Moon Rising. 2016. (ENG., Illus.). 336p. (J). (gr. 5-9). 16.99 (978-1-4814-3626-7(0), McElderry, Margaret K. Bks.) McElderry, Margaret K. Bks.
Holyoke, Polly. The Neptune Challenge. 2016. (ENG.). 352p. (J). (gr. 5-9). pap. 18.99 (978-1-4847-1571-0(3)) Hyperion Bks. for Children.
Hopper, Ada. March of the Mini Beasts. Ricks, Sam, illus. 2016. (DATA Set Ser.: 1). (ENG.). 128p. (J). (gr. k-4). pap. 5.99 (978-1-4814-5728-6(4), Little Simon) Little Simon.
—March of the Mini Beasts. Ricks, Sam, illus. 2018. 125p. (J). (gr. 1-4). 15.96 (978-1-64310-195-8(1)) Penworthy Co., LLC, The.
Horne, Jay. Published Youth Volume Two. 2010. 61p. pap. 10.99 (978-0-557-30674-9(4)) Lulu Pr., Inc.
Hosie, Donna. The 48. 2018. 360p. (YA). (gr. 9). 17.99 (978-0-8234-3856-3(2)) Holiday Hse., Inc.
Houran, Lori Haskins. One Small Step for Spork (Book 12) Warrick, Jessica, illus. 2018. (How to Be an Earthling Ser.). 64p. (J). (gr. 1-4). pap. 6.99 (978-1-63592-027-7(2), ba741b83-e28d-4d53-9417-c7ede2ef66af, Kane Press) Astra Publishing Hse.
House, David James. The Key to Space. 2006. (ENM.). 364p. (YA). 24.95 (978-0-9777086-0-4(8)) House, David.
Houtman, Jacqueline. Reinvention of Edison Thomas. 2012. (ENG.). 192p. (J). (gr. 3-7). pap. 8.95 (978-1-59078-951-3(2), Astra Young Readers) Astra Publishing Hse.
Howard, Roger. Safety First. 2008. 328p. pap. 12.95 (978-1-4327-0449-0(4)) Outskirts Pr., Inc.
Howe, James. Screaming Mummies of the Pharaoh's Tomb II. Helquist, Brett, illus. 2004. (Tales from the House of Bunnicula Ser.: 4). (ENG.). 112p. (J). (gr. 2-5). pap. 6.99 (978-0-689-83954-2(5), Atheneum Bks. for Young Readers) Simon & Schuster Children's Publishing.

S

Howe, Tina Field. Alysa of the Fields: Book One in the Tellings of Xunar-kun. 2006. (Illus.). 320p. (YA). 30.95 *(978-0-9768585-2-2(5))* Howe, Tina Field.

Howson, Imogen. Linked. 2014. (ENG., Illus.). 384p. (YA). (gr. 7). pap. 9.99 *(978-1-4424-4660-1(9)*, Simon & Schuster Bks. For Young Readers) Simon & Schuster Bks. For Young Readers.

—Unravel. 2014. (ENG., Illus.). 480p. (YA). (gr. 7). 17.99 *(978-1-4424-4658-8(7)*, Simon & Schuster Bks. For Young Readers) Simon & Schuster Bks. For Young Readers.

Hoyle, K. B. Criminal. 2016. (ENG., Illus.). (YA). 31.99 *(978-1-61213-395-9(9))*; (Breeder Cycle Ser.: Vol. 2). pap. 21.50 *(978-1-61213-388-1(6))* Writer's Coffee Shop, The.

Hubbell, Mary A. The Miracle of Annie's Ring. 2010. 138p. pap. 11.50 *(978-1-60911-530-2(9)*, Eloquent Bks.) Strategic Book Publishing & Rights Agency (SBPRA).

Huber, Morgan. Nanite. 2013. 140p. pap. 19.95 *(978-1-63004-633-0(7))* America Star Bks.

Hubert, Jerry. They Were Not Gods: A Space-Age Fairytale. 2003. 170p. (YA). 23.95 *(978-0-595-66091-9(6))*; pap. 13.95 *(978-0-595-29970-6(9))* iUniverse, Inc.

Huddleston, Tom. The Rescue. 2018. (Star Wars Adventures in Wild Space Ser.: 6). (J). lib. bdg. 16.00 *(978-0-606-40975-9(0))* Turtleback.

Hueller, Andy. Skipping Stones at the Center of the Earth: A Middle Grade Novel. 2011. 241p. (J). pap. 8.99 *(978-1-59955-488-4(7)*, Bonneville Bks.) Cedar Fort, Inc./CFI Distribution.

Hueller, P. W. The Wish. 2015. (Tartan House Ser.). (ENG.). 96p. (J). (gr. 3-6). *(978-1-63235-059-6(9)*, 11686, 12-Story Library) Bookstaves, LLC.

Hughes, Devon. Unnaturals #2: Escape from Lion's Head. (Unnaturals Ser.: 2). (ENG.). 384p. (J). (gr. 3-7). 2018. pap. 6.99 *(978-0-06-225758-1(7))* 2017. 16.99 *(978-0-06-225757-4(9))* HarperCollins Pubs. (Tegen, Katherine Bks).

Hughes, Mark Peter. A Crack in the Sky. (Greenhouse Chronicles Ser.). (ENG.). 416p. (J). 2011. (gr. 3-7). 9.99 *(978-0-385-73709-8(2))*1. 2012. (gr. 7-12). lib. bdg. 22.44 *(978-0-385-90645-6(5))* Random Hse. Children's Bks. (Yearling).

Hughes, Monica. The Game. 2010. (ENG.). 208p. (YA). (gr. 7). pap. 11.99 *(978-1-4424-0939-2(8)*, Simon Pulse) Simon Pulse.

—The Golden Aquarians. 2009. (ENG.). 192p. (YA). (gr. 7-7). pap. 9.99 *(978-1-4424-0223-2(7)*, Simon & Schuster Bks. For Young Readers) Simon & Schuster Bks. For Young Readers.

—Keeper of the Isis Light. 2008. (ENG.). 240p. (J). (gr. 3-7). pap. 11.99 *(978-1-4169-8963-9(3)*, Atheneum Bks. for Young Readers) Simon & Schuster Children's Publishing.

—Space Trap. (J). pap. 7.95 *(978-0-88899-202-4(5))* Groundwood Bks. CAN. Dist: Publishers Group West (PGW).

Hughes, Ted. The Iron Man. 2013. (ENG., Illus.). 144p. (J). 8.95 *(978-0-571-30224-6(6)*, Faber & Faber Children's Bks.) Faber & Faber, Inc.

—The Iron Man. Davidson, Andrew, illus. 2nd ed. 2005. (ENG.). 80p. (J). pap. 9.95 *(978-0-571-22612-2(4)*, Faber & Faber Children's Bks.) Faber & Faber, Inc.

Hunter, Devin. Betrayal at Salty Springs: An Unofficial Novel for Fortnite Fans. 2018. (Trapped in Battle Royale Ser.). (ENG.). 112p. (J). (gr. 1-5). pap. 7.99 *(978-1-5107-4344-1(8)*, Sky Pony Pr.) Skyhorse Publishing Co., Inc.

—Clash at Fatal Fields: An Unofficial Novel for Fans of Fortnite. 2018. (Trapped in Battle Royale Ser.). (ENG.). 112p. (J). (gr. 1-5). pap. 7.99 *(978-1-5107-4263-5(8)*, Sky Pony Pr.) Skyhorse Publishing Co., Inc.

—The Squad of Lucky Landing: An Unofficial Novel of Fortnite. 2018. (Trapped in Battle Royale Ser.). (ENG.). 112p. (J). (gr. 1-5). pap. 7.99 *(978-1-5107-4346-5(4)*, Sky Pony Pr.) Skyhorse Publishing Co., Inc.

Hunter, Erin. A Dangerous Path. Stevenson, Dave, illus. 2005. (Warriors: the Prophecies Begin Ser.: 5). (ENG.). 336p. (J). (gr. 3-7). pap. 6.99 *(978-0-06-052565-1(7))* HarperCollins Pubs.

Hurst, Melissa E. The Edge of Forever. 2015. (ENG.). 272p. (J). (gr. 6-6). pap. 14.99 *(978-1-63220-424-0(X)*, Sky Pony Pr.) Skyhorse Publishing Co., Inc.

—On Through the Never. 2017. (ENG.). 272p. (J). (gr. 6-6). pap. 14.99 *(978-1-5107-0761-0(1)*, Sky Pony Pr.) Skyhorse Publishing Co., Inc.

Hussey, Don. Chesapeake Station: It Began with Serenity. 2013. 152p. pap. 12.99 *(978-0-9893324-2-2(X))* Westchester Publishing.

Hutchinson, Shaun David. The Apocalypse of Elena Mendoza. 2019. (ENG., Illus.). 464p. (YA). (gr. 9). pap. 12.99 *(978-1-4814-9855-5(X)*, Simon Pulse) Simon Pulse.

Iacobucci, Vincent. The Little Book All about Fluguls. 2006. (Illus.). (J). *(978-0-9779390-0-8(6))* Flugul Pubng.

Ignatow, Amy. The Mighty Odds (the Odds Series #1) 2017. (Odds Ser.). (ENG., Illus.). 248p. (J). (gr. 5-9). pap. 8.99 *(978-1-4197-2371-1(5)*, 1087703, Amulet Bks.) Abrams, Inc.

Indrani, Majumdar. Puffin Classics: the Mystery of Munroe Island & Other Stories. 2015. (ENG.). 392p. (J). pap. 19.99 *(978-0-14-333328-9(3)*, Puffin) Penguin Bks. India PVT, Ltd IND. Dist: Independent Pubs. Group.

Ireland, Justina. Star Wars: the High Republic: Out of the Shadows. 2021. (ENG.). 432p. (YA). (gr. 7-12). 17.99 *(978-1-368-06065-3(X)*, Disney Lucasfilm Press) Disney Publishing Worldwide.

Irvine, Alexander C. Have Robot, Will Travel. 2013. (ENG.). 222p. pap. 19.95 *(978-1-59687-959-1(9))* ibooks, Inc.

Isbell, Tom. The Capture. 2016. (Prey Trilogy Ser.: 2). (ENG.). 448p. (YA). (gr. 8). 17.99 *(978-0-06-221605-2(8)*, HarperTeen) HarperCollins Pubs.

—The Prey. 2015. (Prey Trilogy Ser.: 1). (ENG.). 416p. (YA). (gr. 8). 17.99 *(978-0-06-221601-4(5)*, HarperTeen) HarperCollins Pubs.

Ishwaran, Wobine. A Journey into Space: Kary to the Moon. 2008. 24p. pap. 11.49 *(978-1-4343-6717-4(7))* AuthorHouse.

Ivanoff, George. Gamers' Quest. 2009. (Gamers Ser.: Bk. 1). (ENG.). 172p. (YA). pap. *(978-1-876462-86-4(8))* Ford Street Publishing Pty, Limited.

—How to Make a Fake Death Ray into a Real Laser. 2007. 96p. (J). *(978-1-4207-0735-9(3))* Sundance/Newbridge Educational Publishing.

Izubuchi, Yutaka & Ohnogi, Hiroshi. Rahxephon, Vol. 3. 2006. (RahXephon (Dr Masterbook) Ser.). (ENG., Illus.). 200p. (YA). pap. 7.95 *(978-1-59796-002-1(0))* DrMaster Pubns. Inc.

Jablonski, Carla. Book One of the Travelers, Bk. 1. 2009. (Pendragon: Before the War Ser.: 1). (ENG., Illus.). 256p. (J). (gr. 5-9). pap. 8.99 *(978-1-4169-6522-0(X)*, Aladdin) Simon & Schuster Children's Publishing.

Jackson-Beavers, Rose, et al. A Hole in My Heart. 2004. (ENG.). (YA). per. 10.95 *(978-0-9753634-0-9(9))* Prioritybooks Pubns.

Jackson, Paul B. Luke & Mcnashty's Treasure. 2006. 96p. pap. 16.95 *(978-1-4241-2909-6(5))* PublishAmerica, Inc.

Jacobs, Evan. Emoji of Doom, 1 vol. 2016. (White Lightning Ser.). (ENG.). 91p. (J). (gr. 6-8). pap. 10.95 *(978-1-68021-354-6(7))* Saddleback Educational Publishing, Inc.

Jacques, Brian. Redwall: the Graphic Novel. 2007. (Redwall Ser.). (ENG., illus.). 148p. (J). (gr. 5-18). 12.99 *(978-0-399-24481-0(6)*, Philomel Bks.) Penguin Young Readers Group.

Jae, Ava. Into the Black. 2017. (Beyond the Red Trilogy Ser.: 2). (ENG., Illus.). 372p. (YA). (gr. 7-13). 17.99 *(978-1-5107-2236-1(X)*, Sky Pony Pr.) Skyhorse Publishing Co., Inc.

Jaffe, Charlotte & Doherty, Barbara. The Space Race. 2003. (Illus.). (J). (gr. 2-3). 60.00 *(978-1-57336-395-2(2)*, I5077) Interaction Pubs., Inc.

Jakobs, D. Meet Blades the Copter-Bot. 2014. (Transformers Passport to Reading Ser.). (J). lib. bdg. 14.75 *(978-0-606-35295-6(3))* Turtleback.

James, Dalton. The Heroes of Googley Woogley. 2009. 22p. (J). pap. 10.95 *(978-1-4327-2782-6(6))* Outskirts Pr., Inc.

James, Lauren. The Loneliest Girl in the Universe. (ENG.). 320p. (YA). (gr. 9). 2019. pap. 15.99 *(978-0-06-266026-8(8))* 2018. 17.99 *(978-0-06-266025-1(X))* HarperCollins Pubs. (HarperTeen).

James, Nick. Crimson Rising. 2012. (Skyship Academy Ser.: 2). (ENG.). 360p. (YA). (gr. 9-12). pap. 9.99 *(978-0-7387-2342-6(8)*, 0738723428, Flux) North Star Editions.

—The Pearl Wars. 2011. (Skyship Academy Ser.: 1). (ENG.). 384p. (YA). (gr. 9-12). pap. 11.99 *(978-0-7387-2341-9(X)*, 073872341X, Flux) North Star Editions.

—Strikeforce. 2013. (Skyship Academy Ser.: 3). (ENG., Illus.). 360p. (YA). (gr. 9-12). pap. 9.99 *(978-0-7387-3637-2(6)*, 0738736376, Flux) North Star Editions.

Janicke, Gregory. The Dark Mystery of the Shadow Beasts. 2004. (Illus.). 168p. *(978-983-58-0993-4(3))* Times Edition.

Jansen, Patty. The Far Horizon. 2012. 176p. pap. *(978-0-9872009-4-5(1))* Capricornica Pubns.

Jay, Annabelle. Starsong. 2017. (ENG., Illus.). (YA). (Sun Dragon Ser.: Vol. 3). 25.99 *(978-1-64080-349-7(1))*; (Sun Dragon Ser.: 3). 180p. pap. 14.99 *(978-1-63533-246-9(X))* Dreamspinner Pr. (Harmony Ink Pr.).

Jayasuriya, Michael. The Time MacHine. 2011. 66p. pap. 15.99 *(978-1-4653-3741-2(5))* Xlibris Corp.

Jazwierska, Jennifer & Popiel, Candice Bataille. Discovery of Glow. 2008. (Glowmundo Ser.). (J). (gr. 2-6). pap. 12.95 *(978-0-9814930-0-8(9))* Elora Media, LLC.

Jenkins, Martin. The Squirrels' Busy Year: A First Science Storybook. Jones, Richard, illus. 2018. (Science Storybooks Ser.). (ENG.). 32p. (J). (gr. -1-1). 17.99 *(978-0-7636-9600-9(5))* Candlewick Pr.

Jinks, Catherine. Evil Genius. 2007. 486p. (J). *(978-1-4287-3510-1(0))* Harcourt Trade Pubs.

—Evil Genius. 2011. (ENG., Illus.). 496p. (YA). (gr. 7). pap. 11.99 *(978-0-15-206185-2(1)*, 1198564, Clarion Bks.) HarperCollins Pubs.

—Genius Squad. 2009. (ENG., Illus.). 448p. (YA). (gr. 7). pap. 9.99 *(978-0-15-206650-5(0)*, 1099011, Clarion Bks.) HarperCollins Pubs.

—The Genius Wars. 2010. (ENG., Illus.). 384p. (YA). (gr. 7-12). 24.94 *(978-0-15-206619-2(5))* Houghton Mifflin Harcourt Publishing Co.

—Living Hell. 2011. (ENG.). 264p. (YA). (gr. 7). pap. 14.99 *(978-0-547-54998-9(9)*, 1450165, Clarion Bks.) HarperCollins Pubs.

Johansen, K. V. The Black Box. 2010. (Illus.). 212p. (J). pap. 13.00 *(978-0-9864974-0-7(1))* Sybertooth, Inc. CAN. Dist: Ingram Content Group.

Johnson, Bob. The Lost Mine of the Mechanical Spider. Johnson, Bob, illus. 2006. (Squatland Chronicles Ser.). (Illus.). 53p. (J). (gr. -1-3). per. 11.00 *(978-1-60002-185-5(9)*, 3977) Mountain Valley Publishing, LLC.

Johnson, Cornelius. Escape from Ketan, 1 vol. 2010. 80p. pap. 19.95 *(978-1-4489-5463-6(0))* America Star Bks.

Johnson, Elana. Abandon: A Possession Novel. 2013. (ENG.). 464p. (YA). (gr. 9). 17.99 *(978-1-4424-8482-5(9)*, Simon Pulse) Simon Pulse.

—Possession. 2012. (Possession Novel Ser.). (ENG.). 416p. (YA). (gr. 7-12). 26.19 *(978-1-4424-2125-7(8))* Simon & Schuster, Inc.

—Possession. 2012. (ENG.). 432p. (YA). (gr. 9). pap. 11.99 *(978-1-4424-2126-4(6)*, Simon Pulse) Simon Pulse.

—Surrender: A Possession Novel. (ENG.). (YA). (gr. 9). 2013. 496p. pap. 9.99 *(978-1-4424-4569-7(6))* 2012. 480p. 17.99 *(978-1-4424-4568-0(8))* Simon Pulse. (Simon Pulse).

Johnson, Jennifer & Johnson, Jennifer L. Battle for the Zephyr Badge (Pokémon Classic Chapter Book #13) 2018. (Pokémon Chapter Bks.: 20). (ENG.). 96p. (J). (gr. 2-5). pap. 4.99 *(978-1-338-28406-5(1))* Scholastic, Inc.

Johnson, Mike & Parrott, Ryan. Star Trek: Starfleet Academy. Charm, Derek, illus. 2016. (Star Trek Ser.). 120p. pap. 19.99 *(978-1-63140-663-8(9)*, 9781631406638) Idea & Design Works, LLC.

Johnson, Sandi. Chip Dude from Outer Space. Johnson, Britt, ed. Sturgen, Bobbi, illus. l.t. ed. 2014. (ENG.). 28p. (J). (gr. k-5). pap. 12.99 *(978-1-929063-81-9(4)*, 254) Moons & Stars Publishing For Children.

Johnston, E. K. Star Wars: Ahsoka. 2017. (ENG.). 384p. (J). (gr. 7-12). pap. 10.99 *(978-1-4847-8231-6(3)*, Disney Lucasfilm Press) Disney Publishing Worldwide.

Jolley, Alana L. If You Give a Padre a Peppertree. 2008. 24p. pap. 15.99 *(978-1-4257-9308-1(8))* Xlibris Corp.

Jones, Allan Frewin. Starship. (Hunter & Moon Mystery Ser.: Vol. 5). (ENG.). 169p. (J). pap. 8.99 *(978-0-340-70964-1(2))* Hodder & Stoughton GBR. Dist: Trafalgar Square Publishing.

Jones, Chris. Cameron Jack & the Ghosts of World War 2. 2010. 120p. pap. 12.49 *(978-1-4520-2839-2(7))* AuthorHouse.

Jones, Diana Wynne. A Tale of Time City. 2012. (ENG.). 384p. (YA). (gr. 7-18). 10.99 *(978-0-14-242015-7(8)*, Firebird) Penguin Young Readers Group.

Jordan, Cat. Eight Days on Planet Earth. 2017. (ENG.). 320p. (YA). (gr. 8). 17.99 *(978-0-06-257173-1(7)*, HarperTeen) HarperCollins Pubs.

Jordan, Robert. The Hunt Begins. Keegan, Charles, illus. 2005. (Great Hunt Ser.: Bk. 1). 397p. (gr. 5-9). 16.00 *(978-0-7569-5065-1(1))* Perfection Learning Corp.

Jordan, Sophie. Uninvited. 2015. (Uninvited Ser.: 1). (ENG.). 400p. (YA). (gr. 8). pap. 9.99 *(978-0-06-223364-6(5)*, HarperTeen) HarperCollins Pubs.

Joy, Judith Bourassa. A Doorway Through Space: Winner of Mayhaven Award for Children's Fiction. 2008. (ENG.). 224p. (YA). 14.95 *(978-1-932278-17-0(6))* Mayhaven Publishing, Inc.

Jung, Mike. Geeks, Girls, & Secret Identities. Maihack, Mike, illus. 2012. (J). pap. *(978-0-545-33549-2(3)*, Levine, Arthur A. Bks.) Scholastic, Inc.

Kabaya, Kosuke. Android Angels. 2014. (ENG., Illus.). 158p. (YA). pap. 14.95 *(978-1-939012-10-4(4)*, 37d9e08e-4a3b-4eef-ad96-95d9871aad32) Gen Manga Entertainment, Inc.

Kacvinsky, Katie. Awaken. 2012. (ENG.). 320p. (YA). (gr. 7). pap. 11.99 *(978-0-547-72198-9(6)*, 1482455, Clarion Bks.) HarperCollins Pubs.

—Awaken. 2012. lib. bdg. 20.85 *(978-0-606-24781-8(5))* Turtleback.

—Middle Ground. 2013. (ENG.). 336p. (YA). (gr. 7). pap. 9.99 *(978-0-544-10480-8(3)*, 1540789, Clarion Bks.) HarperCollins Pubs.

Kaczynski, Heather. Dare Mighty Things. 2017. (ENG.). 384p. (YA). (gr. 8). 17.99 *(978-0-06-247986-0(5)*, HarperTeen) HarperCollins Pubs.

Kahaney, Amelia. The Invisible: A Brokenhearted Novel. 2015. (Brokenhearted Ser.: 2). (ENG.). 304p. (YA). (gr. 8). pap. 9.99 *(978-0-06-223193-2(6)*, HarperTeen) HarperCollins Pubs.

Kahn, J. Le Retour du Jedi, Vol. II.Tr. of Return of the Jedi. (FRE.). (J). pap. 11.95 *(978-2-265-06728-8(8))* Fleuve Noir FRA. Dist: Distribooks, Inc.

Kamachi, Kazuma. A Certain Magical Index, Vol. 1 (light Novel), Vol. 1. Haimura, Kiyotaka, illus. 2014. (Certain Magical Index Ser.: 1). (ENG.). 224p. (gr. 8-17). 14.00 *(978-0-316-33912-4(1)*, Yen Pr.) Yen Pr. LLC.

—A Certain Magical Index, Vol. 14 (light Novel) Haimura, Kiyotaka, illus. 2018. (Certain Magical Index Ser.: 14). (ENG.). 192p. (gr. 8-17). pap. 14.00 *(978-0-316-44270-1(4)*, Yen Pr.) Yen Pr. LLC.

Kamat Tarkar, Poorwa Yeshwant. The Cornelius Sign: & the Season Queen Business, 1 vol. 2009. 234p. pap. 24.95 *(978-1-61582-408-3(1))* America Star Bks.

Kammer, Gina. Dream Monsters: A 4D Book. Chalik, Chris, illus. 2018. (Mind Drifter Ser.). (ENG.). 128p. (J). (gr. 3-8). lib. bdg. 27.32 *(978-1-4965-5896-1(0)*, 137057, Stone Arch Bks.) Capstone.

—Enemy Mind: A 4D Book. Chalik, Chris, illus. 2018. (Mind Drifter Ser.). (ENG.). 128p. (J). (gr. 3-8). lib. bdg. 27.32 *(978-1-4965-5898-5(7)*, 137059, Stone Arch Bks.) Capstone.

—Reject Rebound: A 4D Book. Chalik, Chris, illus. 2018. (Mind Drifter Ser.). (ENG.). 128p. (J). (gr. 3-8). lib. bdg. 27.32 *(978-1-4965-5899-2(5)*, 137061, Stone Arch Bks.) Capstone.

Karl, Jean E. The Turning Place: Stories of a Future Past. 2016. (ENG.). 224p. (YA). (gr. 5-8). pap. 7.99 *(978-0-486-80459-0(3)*, 804593) Dover Pubns., Inc.

Karp, Jesse. What We Become. 2013. (ENG.). 432p. (YA). (gr. 7). 16.99 *(978-0-547-55500-3(8)*, 1452456, Clarion Bks.) HarperCollins Pubs.

Katcher, Brian. The Improbable Theory of Ana & Zak. 2016. (ENG.). 352p. (YA). (gr. 8). pap. 9.99 *(978-0-06-227278-2(0)*, Tegen, Katherine Bks) HarperCollins Pubs.

Kaufman, Amie. Illuminae. 2017. lib. bdg. 24.50 *(978-0-606-39847-3(3))* Turtleback.

Kaufman, Amie & Kristoff, Jay. Aurora Rising. (Aurora Cycle Ser.: 1). (ENG., Illus.). (YA). (gr. 7). 2020. 496p. pap. 12.99 *(978-1-5247-2099-5(2)*, Ember) 2019. 480p. 19.99 *(978-1-5247-2096-4(8)*, Knopf Bks. for Young Readers) 2019. 480p. lib. bdg. 21.99 *(978-1-5247-2097-1(6)*, Knopf Bks. for Young Readers) Random Hse. Children's Bks.

—Gemina. (Illuminae Files Ser.: 2). (ENG.). 672p. (YA). (gr. 9). 2018. pap. 12.99 *(978-0-553-49918-6(1)*, Ember) 2016. (Illus.). 21.99 *(978-0-553-49915-5(7)*, Knopf Bks. for Young Readers) Random Hse. Children's Bks.

—Obsidio. (Illuminae Files Ser.: 3). (ENG., Illus.). (YA). (gr. 9). 2019. 640p. pap. 12.99 *(978-0-553-49922-3(X)*, Ember) 2018. 624p. 21.99 *(978-0-553-49919-3(X)*, Knopf Bks. for Young Readers) Random Hse. Children's Bks.

Kaufman, Amie & Spooner, Meagan. Their Fractured Light. 2016. (Starbound Trilogy Ser.: 3). (ENG.). 432p. (YA). (gr. 7-12). pap. 19.99 *(978-1-4847-4783-4(6))* Hyperion Pr.

—These Broken Stars: A Starbound Novel. 2014. (Starbound Trilogy Ser.: 1). (ENG., Illus.). 416p. (YA). (gr. 7-12). pap. 10.99 *(978-1-4231-7121-8(7))* Hyperion Bks. for Children.

—This Shattered World. 2015. (Starbound Trilogy Ser.: 2). (ENG., Illus.). 416p. (YA). (gr. 7-17). pap. 10.99 *(978-1-4231-7122-5(5))* Hyperion Bks. for Children.

Kawahara, Reki. Accel World, Vol. 2 (light Novel) The Red Storm Princess, Vol. 2. 2014. (Accel World Ser.: 2). (ENG., Illus.). 256p. (gr. 8-17). pap. 13.00 *(978-0-316-29636-6(8)*, Yen Pr.) Yen Pr. LLC.

—Sword Art Online 10 (light Novel) Alicization Running. Paul, Stephen, tr. 2017. (Sword Art Online Ser.: 10). (ENG., Illus.). 248p. (gr. 8-17). pap. 14.00 *(978-0-316-39043-9(7)*, Yen Pr.) Yen Pr. LLC.

—Sword Art Online 11 (light Novel) Alicization Turning. 2017. (Sword Art Online Ser.: 11). (ENG., Illus.). 208p. (gr. 8-17). pap. 14.00 *(978-0-316-39044-6(5)*, Yen Pr.) Yen Pr. LLC.

—Sword Art Online 12 (light Novel) Alicization Rising. 2017. (Sword Art Online Ser.: 12). (ENG., Illus.). 216p. (gr. 8-17). 14.00 *(978-0-316-39045-3(3)*, Yen Pr.) Yen Pr. LLC.

—Sword Art Online 15 (light Novel) Alicization Invading. 2018. (Sword Art Online Ser.: 15). (ENG., Illus.). 240p. (gr. 8-17). pap. 14.00 *(978-0-316-39049-1(6)*, Yen Pr.) Yen Pr. LLC.

—Sword Art Online 9 (light Novel) Alicization Beginning. 2016. (Sword Art Online Ser.: 9). (ENG., Illus.). 272p. (gr. 8-17). pap. 14.00 *(978-0-316-39042-2(9)*, Yen Pr.) Yen Pr. LLC.

Keats, Israel. Alien Invasion. 2017. (Level Up Ser.). (ENG.). 120p. (YA). (gr. 6-12). pap. 7.99 *(978-1-5124-5356-0(0)*, b9358e54-28d0-4870-96f3-95ea47d4215e); lib. bdg. 26.65 *(978-1-5124-3984-7(3)*, 4bd61854-84ad-4b3c-a63b-159a2525f4ee) Lerner Publishing Group. (Darby Creek).

—Deserted. 2018. (Attack on Earth Ser.). (ENG.). 112p. (YA). (gr. 6-12). pap. 7.99 *(978-1-5415-2629-7(5)*, a3bd9e3a-6897-4bd1-8082-d17df4bbe7d2); lib. bdg. 26.65 *(978-1-5415-2574-0(4)*, 2cea1cb0-09ce-4573-ba9a-ff8596e35033) Lerner Publishing Group. (Darby Creek).

—Labyrinth. 2017. (Level Up Ser.). (ENG.). 128p. (YA). (gr. 6-12). pap. 7.99 *(978-1-5124-5357-7(9)*, e7f5d859-1e75-4e25-a08a-54652805091b); 26.65 *(978-1-5124-3987-8(8)*, 33c50e5e-c0e4-4b3b-8d1c-e5a349efcbe5) Lerner Publishing Group. (Darby Creek).

—The Zephyr Conspiracy. 2017. (Level Up Ser.). (ENG.). 112p. (YA). (gr. 6-12). pap. 7.99 *(978-1-5124-5361-4(7)*, 7e569a6f-416c-40e8-8dfc-520ae09833c9); lib. bdg. 26.65 *(978-1-5124-3985-4(1)*, 07cc3b67-9541-407e-a23c-ab2e2516b1d9) Lerner Publishing Group. (Darby Creek).

Keene, Carolyn. Green-Eyed Monster: Book One in the Eco Mystery Trilogy. 2009. (Nancy Drew (All New) Girl Detective Ser.: 39). (ENG.). 176p. (J). (gr. 3-7). pap. 6.99 *(978-1-4169-7844-2(5)*, Aladdin) Simon & Schuster Children's Publishing.

Keeper of the Colony. 2006. (Keeper Ser.). 246p. (J). (gr. 3-9). per. 10.95 *(978-1-929976-35-5(6))* Top Pubns., Ltd.

Keller, Julia. Dark Mind Rising: A Dark Intercept Novel. 2019. (Dark Intercept Ser.: 2). (ENG.). 288p. (YA). pap. 16.99 *(978-0-7653-8767-7(0)*, 900161508, Tor Teen) Doherty, Tom Assocs., LLC.

Kellerman, Faye & Kellerman, Aliza. Prism. 2009. 272p. (YA). (gr. 7-18). lib. bdg. 17.89 *(978-0-06-168722-8(7)*, HarperTeen) HarperCollins Pubs.

Kelly, Mark. Project Rescue. 2017. (Astrotwins Ser.: 2). lib. bdg. 18.40 *(978-0-606-39745-2(0))* Turtleback.

Kenah, Katharine. The Best Teacher in Second Grade. Carter, Abby, illus. 2007. (I Can Read Bks.). 48p. (gr. -1-3). 14.00 *(978-0-7569-8105-1(0))* Perfection Learning Corp.

Kennedy, Katie. What Goes Up. 2018. (ENG.). 352p. (YA). pap. 10.99 *(978-1-61963-914-0(9)*, 900151484, Bloomsbury Young Adult) Bloomsbury Publishing USA.

Kent, Lindsay. DK Readers L2: Star Wars: the Adventures of Han Solo. 2011. (DK Readers Level 2 Ser.). (ENG.). 32p. (J). (gr. -1-1). 3.99 *(978-0-7566-8252-1(5)*, DK Children) Dorling Kindersley Publishing, Inc.

Kernaghan, Eileen. The Alchemist's Daughter. 2006. (ENG., Illus.). 144p. pap. 15.95 *(978-1-894345-79-8(7))* Thistledown Pr., Ltd. CAN. Dist: Univ. of Toronto Pr.

Kerner, Charlotte. Blueprint. Crawford, Elizabeth D., tr. from GER. 2003. (Young Adult Fiction Ser.). 192p. (YA). (gr. 9-12). 16.95 *(978-0-8225-0080-3(9)*, Carolrhoda Bks.) Lerner Publishing Group.

Kesel, Barbara. Radiant, Vol. 2. Perez, George et al, illus. 2004. (Solus Ser.: Vol. 2). 160p. (YA). pap. 15.95 *(978-1-59314-057-1(6))* CrossGeneration Comics, Inc.

Khanlu, Nancy Yousefian. A Trip into Space. 2012. 16p. pap. 7.95 *(978-1-4525-0399-8(0))* Get Published.

Khoury, Jessica. Vitro. 2015. 384p. (YA). (gr. 7). pap. 9.99 *(978-1-59514-606-9(7)*, Razorbill) Penguin Young Readers Group.

Kibbie, George Anthon. Bilwok: Dawn of the Trolls. 2015. 183p. (YA). pap. 13.99 *(978-1-4621-1663-8(9))* Cedar Fort, Inc./CFI Distribution.

Kiesling, Ralph W. The Exploration, 1 vol. 2009. 253p. pap. 27.95 *(978-1-61546-668-9(1))* America Star Bks.

Kincaid, S. J. The Diabolic. (Diabolic Ser.: 1). (ENG.). (YA). (gr. 9). 2017. 432p. pap. 12.99 *(978-1-4814-7268-5(2))* 2016. (Illus.). 416p. 19.99 *(978-1-4814-7267-8(4))* Simon & Schuster Bks. For Young Readers. (Simon & Schuster Bks. For Young Readers).

—The Empress. (Diabolic Ser.: 2). (ENG.). 384p. (YA). (gr. 9). 2018. pap. 13.99 *(978-1-5344-0993-4(9))* 2017. (Illus.). 17.99 *(978-1-5344-0992-7(0))* Simon & Schuster Bks. For Young Readers. (Simon & Schuster Bks. For Young Readers).

—Insignia. (Insignia Ser.: 1). (ENG.). (YA). (gr. 8). 2013. 480p. pap. 10.99 *(978-0-06-209300-4(2))* 2012. 464p. 17.99 *(978-0-06-209299-1(5))* HarperCollins Pubs. (Tegen, Katherine Bks).

—Vortex. (Insignia Ser.: 2). (ENG.). (YA). (gr. 8). 2014. 416p. pap. 9.99 *(978-0-06-209303-5(7))* 2013. 400p. 17.99 *(978-0-06-209302-8(9))* HarperCollins Pubs. (Tegen, Katherine Bks).

King, Carrie. The Life in the Wood with Joni-Pip. 2007. (Illus.). 463p. *(978-0-9555246-8-4(7))* Bothy Bks., Corwall, A Div. of Grace & Patrick Pubs., Ltd.

King, J. R. Arianna Kelt & the Renegades of Time: Deluxe Edition, Wizards of Skyhall Book 2. 2008. (ENG.). 252p. (YA). per. 15.95 *(978-1-57545-120-6(4))* RP Media.

—Arianna Kelt & the Wizards of Skyhall. 2008. (ENG.). 200p. (J). 18.95 *(978-1-57545-164-0(6)*, Reagent Pr. Echo) RP Media.

King, Kristin. Project: Noah's Ark. 2005. 201p. pap. 24.95 *(978-1-4137-6521-2(1))* America Star Bks.

King, Sharon. Oops Was Bullied? Hey, Why Did You Hurt Me That Way? LaRoe, Misty Bailey, illus. 2013. (ENG.). 32p. (J). pap. 16.95 *(978-1-4787-1364-7(X))* Outskirts Pr., Inc.

King-Smith, Dick. The Water Horse. Parkins, David, illus. 2007. (ENG.). 128p. (J). (gr. 1-4). 7.99 *(978-0-375-84231-3(4)*, Yearling) Random Hse. Children's Bks.

King, Wesley. The Incredible Space Raiders from Space! 2016. lib. bdg. 18.40 *(978-0-606-38276-2(3))* Turtleback.

—The Vindico. (YA). (gr. 7). 2013. 320p. pap. 8.99 *(978-0-14-242656-2(3)*, Speak)1. 2012. (ENG.). 304p. 24.94 *(978-0-399-25654-7(7))* Penguin Young Readers Group.

The check digit for ISBN-10 appears in parentheses after the full ISBN-13

Kinney, Scott. Kozmik. O'Reilly, Sean Patrick, ed. 2013. (Illus.). 78p. (J). pap. 14.95 *(978-1-927424-51-3(8))* Arcana Studio, Inc.
Kipling, Joe. Blinded by the Light. 2013. 268p. pap. *(978-1-909776-00-5(9))* Cillian Pr. Ltd.
Kirby, Matthew J. The Dark Gravity Sequence (1) The Arctic Code. 2016. (Dark Gravity Sequence Ser.: 1). (ENG.). 352p. (J). (gr. 3-7). pap. 6.99 *(978-0-06-222488-0(3)*, Balzer & Bray) HarperCollins Pubs.
—The Rogue World. 2017. (Dark Gravity Sequence Ser.: 3). (ENG.). 400p. (J). (gr. 3-7). 16.99 *(978-0-06-222493-4(X)*, Balzer & Bray) HarperCollins Pubs.
Kirkman, Robert. Super Dinosaur. (ENG., Illus.). (J). Vol. 1. 2011. 128p. pap. 9.99 *(978-1-60706-420-6(0)*, cc7c7209-2e43-4ed4-99b7-594aca9b395b) Vol. 2. 2012. 112p. pap. 12.99 *(978-1-60706-568-5(1)*, 0931d4ec-4978-4c81-aedb-6c71b824f580) Vol. 3. 2013. 112p. pap. 12.99 *(978-1-60706-667-5(X)*, ef2e1eaa-aa85-4739-9df7-c9387ec7d192) Image Comics.
—Super Dinosaur, Vol. 4. 2015. (ENG., Illus.). 128p. (J). pap. 12.99 *(978-1-60706-843-3(5)*, 25e4d799-0d53-4cab-b558-fb245080a5b2) Image Comics.
Kirsch, R. A. The Big One: (A Bicycle Tale), 1 vol. 2009. 191p. pap. 24.95 *(978-1-60703-341-7(0))* PublishAmerica, Inc.
Kizer, Amber. A Matter of Days. 2016. (ENG.). 288p. (YA). (gr. 7). pap. 9.99 *(978-0-385-73974-0(5)*, Ember) Random Hse. Children's Bks.
Klass, David. Firestorm. rev. l.t. ed. 2007. (Caretaker Trilogy: Bk. 1). 435p. (YA). (gr. 9). 23.95 *(978-0-7862-9364-3(0))* Thorndike Pr.
—Firestorm: The Caretaker Trilogy: Book 1. 1. 2008. (Caretaker Trilogy Ser.: 1). (ENG.). 320p. (YA). (gr. 7-12). pap. 17.99 *(978-0-312-38018-2(6)*, 900050543) Square Fish.
—Timelock: The Caretaker Trilogy: Book 3. 2010. (Caretaker Trilogy Ser.: 3). (ENG.). 272p. (YA). (gr. 9-12). pap. 15.99 *(978-0-312-60863-7(2)*, 900065165) Square Fish.
—Whirlwind: The Caretaker Trilogy: Book 2. 2009. (Caretaker Trilogy Ser.: 2). (ENG.). 320p. (YA). (gr. 9-12). pap. 18.99 *(978-0-312-38429-6(7)*, 900053364) Square Fish.
Klein Bernstein, Sandy. The Door in the Sky. 2012. 268p. pap. 12.95 *(978-1-4575-1111-0(8))* Dog Ear Publishing, LLC.
Klein, Glasko. The Fallout. 2018. (Attack on Earth Ser.). (ENG.). 104p. (YA). (gr. 6-12). 26.65 *(978-1-5415-2577-1(9)*, 83f6c253-cd01-42b2-80d2-20ff18c76b91, Darby Creek) Lerner Publishing Group.
Klein, Joel & Klein, Abby. The Night I Saved the Universe: From the Files of the Galactic Police Department. 2009. 126p. (J). *(978-0-545-12933-6(8))* Scholastic, Inc.
Klement, Jon. Rush & the Grey Fox: Ready to Rumble. 2007. 96p. per. *(978-1-897217-66-5(8))* Coscom Entertainment.
Kloepfer, John. Galaxy's Most Wanted. 2014. (Galaxy's Most Wanted Ser.: 1). (ENG., Illus.). 224p. (J). (gr. 3-7). 12.99 *(978-0-06-223101-7(4)*, HarperCollins) HarperCollins Pubs.
—Galaxy's Most Wanted #2: into the Dorkness. Edwards, Nick, illus. 2016. (Galaxy's Most Wanted Ser.: 2). (ENG.). 272p. (J). (gr. 3-7). pap. 6.99 *(978-0-06-223109-3(X)*, HarperCollins) HarperCollins Pubs.
Knutsson, Catherine. Shadows Cast by Stars. 2013. (ENG., Illus.). 464p. (YA). (gr. 7). pap. 13.99 *(978-1-4424-0192-1(3)*, Atheneum Bks. for Young Readers) Simon & Schuster Children's Publishing.
Kogge, Michael. Rise of the Rebels. 2014. (Star Wars Rebels Chapter Bks.). (J). lib. bdg. 16.00 *(978-0-606-35281-9(3))* Turtleback.
—Star Wars: The Force Awakens. 2016. (Illus.). 186p. (J). *(978-1-338-13324-0(1))* Disney Publishing Worldwide.
—Star Wars: The Force Awakens Junior Novel. 2016. (Illus.). 186p. (J). lib. bdg. 17.20 *(978-0-606-38303-5(4))* Turtleback.
—Star Wars: The Last Jedi. 2018. (Illus.). 203p. (J). *(978-1-5444-1310-5(6)*, Disney Lucasfilm Press) Disney Publishing Worldwide.
Kogge, Michael, adapted by. The Rebellion Begins. 2014. (Illus.). 168p. (J). *(978-1-4242-6294-6(1)*, Disney Lucasfilm Press) Disney Publishing Worldwide.
Kopple, Deborah. A Spear of Golden Grass: Short Stories by Norwalk High School Honors English Students. 2010. 216p. (J). pap. 15.95 *(978-1-4502-1896-2(2))* iUniverse, Inc.
Korman, Gordon. Masterminds. (Masterminds Ser.: 1). (ENG.). (J). (gr. 3-7). 2016. 352p. pap. 9.99 *(978-0-06-229999-4(9))* 2015. 336p. 16.99 *(978-0-06-229996-3(4))* HarperCollins Pubs. (Balzer & Bray).
—Masterminds. 2016. (Masterminds Ser.: 1). (J). lib. bdg. 18.40 *(978-0-606-38138-3(4))* Turtleback.
—Masterminds: Criminal Destiny. 2017. (Masterminds Ser.: 2). (ENG.). 336p. (J). (gr. 3-7). 9.99 *(978-0-06-230003-4(2)*, Balzer & Bray) HarperCollins Pubs.
Korté, Steve. Superman Solar System Adventures. Brizuela, Dario, illus. 2018. (Superman Solar System Adventures Ser.). (ENG.). 32p. (J). (gr. 4-8). 223.92 *(978-1-5435-1607-4(6)*, 28051, Stone Arch Bks.) Capstone.
Kositsky, Lynne. The Plagues of Kondar. 2014. (Trials of Kondar Ser.). (ENG.). 184p. (YA). pap. 12.99 *(978-1-4597-0934-8(9))* Dundurn Pr. CAN. Dist: Publishers Group West (PGW).
Kostick, Conor. Epic. 2004. (Avatar Chronicles Ser.: 1). (ENG.). 320p. (J). pap. 14.00 *(978-0-86278-877-3(3))* O'Brien Pr., Ltd., The IRL. Dist: Casemate Pubs. & Bk. Distributors, LLC.
—Saga. 2006. (Avatar Chronicles Ser.: 2). (ENG.). 320p. (J). pap. 14.00 *(978-0-86278-979-4(6))* O'Brien Pr., Ltd., The IRL. Dist: Casemate Pubs. & Bk. Distributors, LLC.
Kozlowsky, M. P. Frost. 2016. (ENG.). 352p. (J). (gr. 8). 17.99 *(978-0-545-83191-8(1)*, Scholastic Pr.) Scholastic, Inc.
Kraatz, Jeramey. Space Runners #1: the Moon Platoon. (Space Runners Ser.: 1). (ENG.). (J). (gr. 3-7). 2018. 368p. pap. 7.99 *(978-0-06-244598-8(7))* 2017. 352p. 16.99 *(978-0-06-244597-1(9))* HarperCollins Pubs. (HarperCollins).
—Space Runners #2: Dark Side of the Moon. 2018. (Space Runners Ser.: 2). (ENG.). (J). (gr. 3-7). 368p. pap. 6.99 *(978-0-06-244601-5(0))*; 352p. 16.99 *(978-0-06-244600-8(2))* HarperCollins Pubs. (HarperCollins).
—Space Runners #4: the Fate of Earth. 2019. (Space Runners Ser.: 4). (ENG.). 320p. (J). (gr. 3-7). 16.99 *(978-0-06-244606-0(1)*, HarperCollins) HarperCollins Pubs.
Kreie, Chris. Take Shelter. 2018. (Attack on Earth Ser.). (ENG.). 112p. (YA). (gr. 6-12). pap. 7.99 *(978-1-5415-2631-0(7)*, f97b38d8-1c87-40b0-8b19-ebd5c2f36aaf); lib. bdg. 26.65 *(978-1-5415-2578-8(7)*, d2b53f7d-5a7e-42ff-a7fb-3a6c8be8e7ef) Lerner Publishing Group. (Darby Creek).
Kristoff, Jay. Life L1k3. 2018. (Illus.). 402p. (J). *(978-0-525-64459-0(8))* Knopf, Alfred A. Inc.
Kriyananda, Swami. The Time Tunnel: A Tale for All Ages & for the Child in You. 2013. (ENG., Illus.). 180p. (J). (gr. 3-7). 14.95 *(978-1-56589-270-5(4))* Crystal Clarity Pubs.
Krokos, Dan. The Black Stars. 2015. (Planet Thieves Ser.: 2). (ENG., Illus.). 304p. (J). (gr. 3-8). pap. 17.99 *(978-0-7653-7668-8(7)*, 900134306, Starscape) Doherty, Tom Assocs., LLC.
—The Planet Thieves. 2014. (Planet Thieves Ser.: 1). (ENG., Illus.). 256p. (J). (gr. 3-7). pap. 16.99 *(978-0-7653-7538-4(9)*, 900131710, Starscape) Doherty, Tom Assocs., LLC.
Krosoczka, Jarrett J. The Principal Strikes Back. 2018. (Illus.). 176p. (J). *(978-1-76066-157-1(0))* Scholastic, Inc.
Krosoczka, Jarrett J., illus. The Force Oversleeps. 2017. 172p. (J). *(978-1-338-20871-9(3))* Scholastic, Inc.
Kruger, Mark H. Overpowered. 2013. (ENG., Illus.). 432p. (YA). (gr. 7). 17.99 *(978-1-4424-3128-7(8)*, Simon & Schuster Bks. For Young Readers) Simon & Schuster Bks. For Young Readers.
Krumwiede, Lana. Archon. 2013. (Psi Chronicles Ser.: 2). (ENG., Illus.). 320p. (J). (gr. 5). 16.99 *(978-0-7636-6402-2(2))* Candlewick Pr.
—True Son. 2015. (Psi Chronicles Ser.: 3). 288p. (J). (gr. 5). 15.99 *(978-0-7636-7262-1(9))* Candlewick Pr.
Kuhlmann, Torben. Armstrong: The Adventurous Journey of a Mouse to the Moon. Kuhlmann, Torben, illus. 2016. (Mouse Adventures Ser.). (ENG., Illus.). 128p. (J). (gr. 2-6). 19.95 *(978-0-7358-4262-5(0))* North-South Bks., Inc.
—Armstrong Special Edition: The Adventurous Journey of a Mouse to the Moon. 2019. (Mouse Adventures Ser.). (ENG.). 128p. (J). (gr. 2-6). 19.95 *(978-0-7358-4378-3(3))* North-South Bks., Inc.
Kuper, Tonya. Anomaly. 2014. (Schrodinger's Consortium Ser.: 1). (ENG.). 400p. (YA). (gr. 7-12). pap. 9.99 *(978-1-62266-405-4(1)*, 9781622664054) Entangled Publishing, LLC.
Kuykendall, Roger. All Day September. 2011. 28p. 12.95 *(978-1-4638-9782-6(0))*; pap. 6.95 *(978-1-4638-0109-0(2))* Rodgers, Alan Bks.
LaBaff, Stephanie. Draw Aliens & Space Objects in 4 Easy Steps: Then Write a Story, 1 vol. 2012. (Drawing in 4 Easy Steps Ser.). (ENG., Illus.). 48p. (gr. 3-3). pap. 11.53 *(978-1-4644-0014-8(8)*, a0f88a34-fc39-4692-ad7b-703cd730d313, Enslow Elementary) Enslow Publishing, LLC.
LaFleur, James & Massie, Gordon. Order Of 5ive: The Complete First Season. Dalglish, Rich, ed. 2012. (ENG.). 308p. (YA). pap. 8.99 *(978-1-935702-09-2(2))* Unique Coloring.
Lake, Nick. Satellite. (ENG.). 464p. (YA). (gr. 7). 2019. pap. 10.99 *(978-1-5247-1356-0(2)*, Ember) 2017. 17.99 *(978-1-5247-1353-9(8)*, Knopf Bks. for Young Readers) Random Hse. Children's Bks.
Lambert, Eugene. Into the No-Zone (Sign of One Trilogy) 2017. (Sign of One Trilogy Ser.: 2). (ENG.). 368p. (J). (gr. 7). pap. 10.99 *(978-1-4052-7736-5(X)*, Electric Monkey) Farshore GBR. Dist: HarperCollins Pubs.
Lancaster, J. A. Joe Parker's Prophecy of Zargala. 2010. 392p. pap. 21.18 *(978-0-557-26685-2(8))* Lulu Pr., Inc.
Lancaster, Mike A. Dotmeme. 2018. (ENG.). 420p. (YA). (gr. 9-9). 17.99 *(978-1-5107-0807-5(3)*, Sky Pony Pr.) Skyhorse Publishing Co., Inc.
—Dotwav. (ENG.). 2017. 456p. (YA). (gr. 7-7). pap. 9.99 *(978-1-5107-2659-8(4))* 2016. 448p. (J). (gr. 6-6). 17.99 *(978-1-5107-0404-6(3))* Skyhorse Publishing Co., Inc. (Sky Pony Pr.).
Landers, Ace. Anakin to the Rescue. 2012. (LEGO Star Wars 8X8 Ser.). lib. bdg. 13.55 *(978-0-606-26774-8(3))* Turtleback.
—Lego Star Wars: The Yoda Chronicles Trilogy. 2014. (LEGO Star Wars Chapter Bks.). lib. bdg. 18.40 *(978-0-606-35414-1(X))* Turtleback.
—A New Hope: Episode 4. 2015. (LEGO Star Wars 8X8 Ser.). lib. bdg. 13.55 *(978-0-606-38104-8(X))* Turtleback.
—Tales of the Rebellion. 2016. (Illus.). 64p. (J). *(978-1-4806-9634-1(X))* Scholastic, Inc.
—Yoda's Secret Missions. 2014. (LEGO Star Wars Chapter Bks.: 1). (Illus.). 63p. (J). lib. bdg. 14.75 *(978-0-606-36070-8(0))* Turtleback.
Landon, Kristen. The Limit. 2011. (ENG.). 304p. (J). (gr. 3-7). pap. 8.99 *(978-1-4424-0272-0(5)*, Aladdin) Simon & Schuster Children's Publishing.
Lane, Miles. Episode III: Revenge of the Sith. Wheatley, Doug, illus. 2009. (Star Wars Ser.: No. 2). (ENG.). 24p. (J). (gr. 6-12). 31.36 *(978-1-59961-618-6(1)*, 13774); 31.36 *(978-1-59961-620-9(3)*, 13776); 31.36 *(978-1-59961-617-9(3)*, 13773) Spotlight. (Graphic Novels).
Lane, Miles & Wheatley, Doug. Episode III: Revenge of the Sith. 2009. (Star Wars Ser.: No. 2). (ENG., Illus.). 24p. (J). (gr. 6-12). 31.36 *(978-1-59961-619-3(X)*, 13775, Graphic Novels) Spotlight.
Laney, Matt. The Four Guardians. 2019. (Pride Wars Ser.). (ENG., Illus.). 368p. (J). (gr. 5-7). 16.99 *(978-1-328-70738-3(5)*, 1673039); pap. 7.99 *(978-0-358-22942-1(1)*, 1766222) HarperCollins Pubs. (Clarion Bks.).
—The Spinner Prince. 2019. (Pride Wars Ser.). (ENG.). 352p. (J). (gr. 5-7). pap. 7.99 *(978-1-328-61309-7(7)*, 1733493, Clarion Bks.) HarperCollins Pubs.
Lange, Sue. The Perpetual Motion Club. 2013. 208p. pap. 14.95 *(978-0-9887488-6-6(X))* Perpetual Motion Machine Publishing.
Lanning, Andy. God Complex, 3 vols. Abnett, Dan & Eaton, Scot, illus. 2011. (Iron Man & Thor Ser.). (ENG.). 24p. (J). (gr. 4-8). 31.36 *(978-1-59961-944-6(X)*, 10022);Pt. 4. 31.36 *(978-1-59961-945-3(8)*, 10023);Set. 31.36 *(978-1-59961-943-9(1)*, 10021) Spotlight. (Marvel Age).
Larkin, Angela & Haverlock, Catina. Before. 2018. (ENG.). 256p. (YA). pap. 17.99 *(978-1-4621-2205-9(1)*, Sweetwater Bks.) Cedar Fort, Inc./CFI Distribution.
Lasky, Kathryn. The First Collier (Guardians of Ga'Hoole #9) 2006. (Guardians of Ga'hoole Ser.: 9). (ENG.). 208p. (J). (gr. 4-7). 8.99 *(978-0-439-79568-5(0)*, Scholastic Paperbacks) Scholastic, Inc.
—The Rescue. 2004. (Guardians of Ga'Hoole Ser.: 3). (gr. 3-6). lib. bdg. 17.20 *(978-0-613-72136-3(5))* Turtleback.
Lassiter, Rhiannon. Shadows. 2011. (Hex Ser.: 2). (ENG.). 272p. (YA). (gr. 7). pap. 12.99 *(978-1-4424-3103-4(2)*, Simon Pulse) Simon Pulse.
Lathrop, Brandy. Jalen Goes to Mars. 2008. 22p. pap. 24.95 *(978-1-4241-9010-2(X))* America Star Bks.
Lavoie, Rejean. Des Legumes Pour Frank Einstein. Begin, Jean-Guy, illus. 2004. (Des 9 Ans. Ser.: Vol. 44). (FRE.). 120p. (J). 8.95 *(978-2-89599-006-2(9))* Editions de la Paix CAN. Dist: World of Reading, Ltd.
Lawrence, James. Buck Rogers in the 25th Century - The Gray Morrow Years, 1979-1981, Vol. 1. Herman, Daniel, ed. 2013. (ENG., Illus.). 240p. (YA). 49.99 *(978-1-61345-034-5(6)*, 4dad6690-acd3-4fef-bb98-0bb0b4bfb9d7) Hermes Pr.
Lawrence, Kelsey. Rune. 2006. (Illus.). 92p. pap. 13.50 *(978-1-84426-399-8(1))* Upfront Publishing Ltd. GBR. Dist: Printondemand-worldwide.com.
Lawrence, Michael. Small Eternities. (Withern Rise Ser.). 336p. 2006. (Illus.). (J). (gr. 7). pap. 7.99 *(978-0-06-072482-5(X)*, HarperTeen) 2005. (YA). 16.89 *(978-0-06-072481-8(1))* 2005. (ENG.). (J). (gr. 8). 15.99 *(978-0-06-072480-1(3)*, Greenwillow Bks.) HarperCollins Pubs.
—The Underwood See. 2007. (Withern Rise Ser.). 372p. (YA). (gr. 9-18). 16.99 *(978-0-06-072483-2(8))* HarperCollins Pubs.
Lawrence, Mike. Star Scouts: the League of Lasers. 2018. (Star Scouts Ser.: 2). (ENG., Illus.). 208p. (J). pap. 14.99 *(978-1-62672-281-1(1)*, 900148377, First Second Bks.) Roaring Brook Pr.
Layne, Steven L. Mergers, 1 vol. 2006. (ENG., Illus.). 208p. (YA). (gr. 6-10). 15.99 *(978-1-58980-183-7(0)*, Pelican Publishing) Arcadia Publishing.
Le Guin, Ursula. K. A Wizard of Earthsea. 2012. (Earthsea Cycle Ser.: 1). (ENG., Illus.). (YA). (gr. 7). 240p. 19.99 *(978-0-547-85139-6(1)*, 1501135); 320p. mass mkt. 10.99 *(978-0-547-77374-2(9)*, 1490754) HarperCollins Pubs. (Clarion Bks.).
Le Guin, Ursula K. A Wizard of Earthsea. 2012. (Earthsea Cycle Ser.: 1). (ENG., Illus.). 264p. (YA). (gr. 7). pap. 15.99 *(978-0-547-72202-3(8)*, 1482458, Clarion Bks.) HarperCollins Pubs.
Lee, C. B. Not Your Villain. 2017. (Sidekick Squad Ser.: 2). (ENG.). 320p. (YA). pap. 16.99 *(978-1-945053-25-2(9)*, Interlude Pr.) Chicago Review Pr.
Lee, Fonda. Cross Fire: an Exo Novel. (ENG.). 384p. (YA). (gr. 7-7). 2019. pap. 9.99 *(978-1-338-13911-2(8)*, Scholastic Paperbacks) 2018. 17.99 *(978-1-338-13909-9(6)*, Scholastic Pr.) Scholastic, Inc.
—Exo (a Novel) 2017. (ENG.). 384p. (YA). (gr. 7). 17.99 *(978-0-545-93343-8(9)*, Scholastic Pr.) Scholastic, Inc.
—Zeroboxer. 2015. (ENG.). 360p. (YA). (gr. 9-12). pap. 11.99 *(978-0-7387-4338-7(0)*, 0738743380, Flux) North Star Editions.
Lee, Mackenzi. This Monstrous Thing. (ENG.). (YA). (gr. 8). 2017. 400p. pap. 9.99 *(978-0-06-238278-8(0))* 2015. 384p. 17.99 *(978-0-06-238277-1(2))* HarperCollins Pubs. (Tegen, Katherine Bks).
Lee, Pat. DrawbotZ. 2014. (Illus.). 72p. (YA). pap. 12.99 *(978-0-9836131-8-3(4))* Sea Lion Bks.
Lee, Quinlan B. Phonics Pack 2. 2016. (LEGO DC Super Heroes Ser.). (ENG.). 16p. (J). (gr. -1-k). 12.99 *(978-0-545-86802-0(5))* Scholastic, Inc.
—Phonics (Star Wars) 2012. (Star Wars Ser.). (ENG.). 16p. (J). (gr. -1-1). 12.99 *(978-0-545-47952-3(5))* Scholastic, Inc.
Lee, Yoon. Dragon Pearl. 2019. (ENG.). 320p. lib. bdg. 18.80 *(978-1-6636-2730-8(4))* Perfection Learning Corp.
—Rick Riordan Presents Dragon Pearl (a Thousand Worlds Novel, Book 1) 2019. (ENG., Illus.). 320p. (J). (gr. 3-7). 16.99 *(978-1-368-01335-2(X)*, Riordan, Rick) Disney Publishing Worldwide.
—Rick Riordan Presents Dragon Pearl (a Thousand Worlds Novel Book 1) 2020. 320p. (J). (gr. 3-7). pap. 8.99 *(978-1-368-01474-8(7)*, Riordan, Rick) Disney Publishing Worldwide.
Lee, Yoon Ha. Dragon Pearl. 2020. (Thousand Worlds (Trade) Ser.). (ENG.). 320p. (gr. 4-7). 24.94 *(978-1-5364-6113-8(X)*, Riordan, Rick) Disney Pr.
—Dragon Pearl. 2019. 320p. 16.99 *(978-1-368-01519-6(0))* Disney Publishing Worldwide.
Leflore, Henry. The Aftermath: The Curse of the Blue Flamed Meteor. 2009. 112p. pap. 10.99 *(978-1-4389-9588-5(1))* AuthorHouse.
Leiber, Fritz. The Creature from Cleveland Depths. 2009. 76p. pap. 7.95 *(978-1-60664-286-3(3))* Rodgers, Alan Bks.
Leicht, Martin & Neal, Isla. Mothership. 2012. (Ever-Expanding Universe Ser.: 1). (ENG., Illus.). 320p. (YA). (gr. 9). 16.99 *(978-1-4424-2960-4(7)*, Simon & Schuster Bks. For Young Readers) Simon & Schuster Bks. For Young Readers.
—A Stranger Thing. 2013. (Ever-Expanding Universe Ser.: 2). (ENG., Illus.). 288p. (YA). (gr. 9). 17.99 *(978-1-4424-2963-5(1)*, Simon & Schuster Bks. For Young Readers) Simon & Schuster Bks. For Young Readers.
—The World Forgot. 2015. 279p. (YA). pap. *(978-1-4424-2967-3(4)*, Simon & Schuster Bks. For Young Readers) Simon & Schuster Bks. For Young Readers.
Leitich Smith, Greg. Borrowed Time. 2015. (ENG., Illus.). 192p. (J). (gr. 5-7). 16.99 *(978-0-544-23711-7(0)*, 1564706, Clarion Bks.) HarperCollins Pubs.
—Chronal Engine. Henry, Blake, illus. 2013. (ENG.). 192p. (J). (gr. 5-7). pap. 6.99 *(978-0-544-02277-5(7)*, 1528498, Clarion Bks.) HarperCollins Pubs.
Leloup, Roger. The Curious Trio. 2012. (Yoko Tsuno Ser.: 7). (Illus.). 48p. (J). (gr. 3-12). pap. 11.95 *(978-1-84918-127-3(6))* CineBook GBR. Dist: National Bk. Network.
—The Devil's Organ. 2013. (Yoko Tsuno Ser.: 8). (Illus.). 48p. (J). (gr. 3-12). pap. 11.95 *(978-1-84918-164-8(0))* CineBook GBR. Dist: National Bk. Network.
—The Dragon of Hong Kong - Yoko Tsuno, Vol. 5. 2010. (Yoko Tsuno Ser.: 5). (Illus.). 46p. (J). (gr. 3-17). pap. 11.95 *(978-1-84918-041-2(5))* CineBook GBR. Dist: National Bk. Network.
—On the Edge of Life. 2007. (Yoko Tsuno Ser.: 1). (Illus.). 48p. (J). (gr. 4-7). pap. 11.95 *(978-1-905460-32-8(5))* CineBook GBR. Dist: National Bk. Network.
—The Prey & the Ghost. 2009. (Yoko Tsuno Ser.: 3). (Illus.). 48p. pap. 11.95 *(978-1-905460-56-4(2))* CineBook GBR. Dist: National Bk. Network.
—The Time Spiral. 2008. (Yoko Tsuno Ser.: 2). (Illus.). 48p. pap. 11.95 *(978-1-905460-43-4(0))* CineBook GBR. Dist: National Bk. Network.
Lemieux, Jean. Toby Shoots for Infinity. Casson, Sophie, illus. 2005. 61p. (J). lib. bdg. 12.00 *(978-1-4242-1201-9(4))* Fitzgerald Bks.
Lemire, Jeff. Descender: the Deluxe Edition Volume 1. 2017. (ENG., Illus.). 400p. (YA). 49.99 *(978-1-5343-0346-1(4)*, ae035ef5-d60a-4477-8ebf-43bbd2e60aea) Image Comics.
Lemke, Donald. The Amazing Mini-Mutts, 1 vol. Baltazar, Art, illus. 2012. (DC Super-Pets Ser.). (ENG.). 56p. (J). (gr. 1-3). pap. 4.95 *(978-1-4048-7218-9(3)*, 118037); lib. bdg. 25.32 *(978-1-4048-6488-7(1)*, 114169) Capstone. (Stone Arch Bks.).
—Pranking News. 2016. (Justice League Classic: I Can Read! Ser.). (J). lib. bdg. 13.55 *(978-0-606-38772-9(2))* Turtleback.
L'Engle, Madeleine. Una Arruga en el Tiempo. 2003. (SPA., Illus.). 206p. (J). (gr. 5-8). pap. 12.95 *(978-84-204-4074-3(4)*, KZ744) Santillana USA Publishing Co., Inc.
—A Swiftly Tilting Planet. 228p. (YA). (gr. 5-18). pap. 5.50 *(978-0-8072-1495-4(7)*, Listening Library) Random Hse. Audio Publishing Group.
—A Swiftly Tilting Planet. 2007. (Wrinkle in Time Quintet Ser.: 4). (ENG.). 320p. (J). (gr. 5-9). per. 7.99 *(978-0-312-36856-2(9)*, 900042673) Square Fish.
—A Wind in the Door. 211p. (YA). (gr. 5-18). pap. 5.50 *(978-0-8072-1466-4(3)*, Listening Library) Random Hse. Audio Publishing Group.
—A Wind in the Door. 2007. (Wrinkle in Time Quintet Ser.: 2). (ENG.). 256p. (J). (gr. 5-9). per. 8.99 *(978-0-312-36854-8(2)*, 900042671) Square Fish.
—A Wrinkle in Time, 2 vols., Set. 20.00 *(978-0-89064-014-2(9))* National Assn. for Visually Handicapped.
—A Wrinkle in Time. 211p. (YA). (gr. 5-18). pap. 5.99 *(978-0-8072-1460-2(4)*, Listening Library) Random Hse. Audio Publishing Group.
—A Wrinkle in Time. l.t. ed. 2005. 273p. pap. 10.95 *(978-0-7862-7335-5(6)*, Large Print Pr.) Thorndike Pr.
—A Wrinkle in Time. (Madeleine L'Engle's Time Quintet Ser.). (J). 2007. 245p. 17.20 *(978-1-4177-8460-8(1))* 50th anniv. ed. 2012. lib. bdg. 20.85 *(978-0-606-23785-7(2))* Turtleback.
—The Wrinkle in Time Quintet - Digest Size Boxed Set. Set. 2007. (Wrinkle in Time Quintet Ser.). (ENG.). 244p. (J). (gr. 5-9). 44.95 *(978-0-312-37351-1(1)*, 900048381) Square Fish.
—A Wrinkle in Time Trilogy. (Wrinkle in Time Quintet Ser.). (ENG.). (J). 2012. 800p. (gr. 6-9). pap. 21.99 *(978-1-250-00343-0(1)*, 900079905) 2007. 224p. (gr. 5-8). per. 7.99 *(978-0-312-36755-8(4)*, 900042368) 2007. 256p. (gr. 5-9). per. 8.99 *(978-0-312-36754-1(6)*, 900042359) Square Fish.
—The Young Unicorns: Book Three of the Austin Family Chronicles. 2008. (Austin Family Ser.: 3). (ENG.). 304p. (J). (gr. 7-12). pap. 12.99 *(978-0-312-37933-9(1)*, 900050196) Square Fish.
Leo. The Group, 3 vols., Vol. 2. 2009. (Aldebaran Ser.: 2). (Illus.). 96p. pap. 19.95 *(978-1-905460-70-0(8))* CineBook GBR. Dist: National Bk. Network.
Leo & LEO, Inc Staff. Aldebaran Vol. 1, 3 vols., Vol. 1. LEO, Inc Staff, illus. 2008. (Aldebaran Ser.: 1). (Illus.). 104p. pap. 19.95 *(978-1-905460-57-1(0))* CineBook GBR. Dist: National Bk. Network.
Leonard, Krystian. Shining Scars. Kelly, Lucas, illus. 2013. (ENG.). 31p. (J). 16.95 *(978-0-938467-72-4(7))* Headline Bks., Inc.
Lepp, Royden. Rust Vol. 1: Visitor in the Field, Vol. 1. Lepp, Royden, illus. 2016. (Rust Ser.: 1). (ENG., Illus.). 176p. (J). (gr. 8-12). pap. 14.99 *(978-1-60886-894-0(X)*, Archaia Entertainment) BOOM! Studios.
—Rust Vol. 2: Secrets of the Cell, Vol. 2. Lepp, Royden, illus. 2017. (Rust Ser.: 2). (ENG., Illus.). 144p. (J). (gr. 8-12). pap. 14.99 *(978-1-60886-895-7(8)*, Archaia Entertainment) BOOM! Studios.
Lestelle, Wende. Science Mouse. 2004. pap. *(978-1-930493-65-0(7))* Athena Pr.
Lester, Cas. Harvey Drew & the Junk Skunks. 2016. (Harvey Drew Ser.: 3). (ENG., Illus.). 256p. (J). (gr. k-3). pap. 9.99 *(978-1-4714-0334-7(3))* Bonnier Publishing GBR. Dist: Independent Pubs. Group.
Levigne, Michelle. Commonwealth Universe: Modern Era. 2013. 110p. pap. *(978-1-922066-31-2(1))*; 134p. pap. *(978-1-922066-32-9(X))*; 146p. pap. *(978-1-922066-33-6(8))*; 110p. pap. *(978-1-922066-35-0(4))* Writers Exchange E-Publishing.
Levy, Janey. Edwin Visits Earth, 1 vol. 2006. (Neighborhood Readers Ser.). (ENG.). 16p. (J). (gr. 1-2). pap. 6.50 *(978-1-4042-7160-9(0)*, 209947a7-6472-43f9-a407-889f89caad6b, Rosen Classroom) Rosen Publishing Group, Inc., The.
Lewis, Bryan. The Tiny World You Can't See. 2011. 24p. pap. 14.50 *(978-1-4670-2837-0(1))* AuthorHouse.
Liddell Nolen, Laura. The Ark (the Ark Trilogy, Book 1), Book 1. 2015. (Ark Trilogy Ser.: 1). (ENG.). 284p. (YA). 19.99 *(978-0-00-812069-6(2)*, Harper Voyager) HarperCollins Pubs.
Link, Kelly. Pretty Monsters. 2010. (ENG., Illus.). 416p. (YA). (gr. 7-12). pap. 11.99 *(978-0-14-241672-3(X)*, Speak) Penguin Young Readers Group.
Linka, Catherine. A Girl Called Fearless: A Novel. 2014. (Girl Called Fearless Ser.: 1). (ENG.). 368p. (YA). (gr. 7). 34.99 *(978-1-250-03929-3(0)*, 900123214, St. Martin's Griffin) St. Martin's Pr.
Liparulo, Robert. Whirlwind, 1 vol. 2010. (Dreamhouse Kings Ser.: 5). (ENG.). 320p. (YA). pap. 14.99 *(978-1-59554-892-4(0))* Nelson, Thomas Inc.
Lippert-Martin, Kristen. Incognita. 2016. (Tabula Rasa Saga Ser.: 2). (ENG.). 272p. (YA). (gr. 7-12). 17.99 *(978-1-5124-0577-4(9)*, c95eb2b3-fcea-48ff-8ae9-b24c84de25b4, Carolrhoda Lab™) Lerner Publishing Group.

S

Lipsyte, Robert. The Twinning Project. 2014. (ENG.). 288p. (J). (gr. 5-7). pap. 16.99 *(978-0-544-22522-0(8),* 1563389, Clarion Bks.) HarperCollins Pubs.

Liss, David. Randoms. 2016. (Randoms Ser.: 1). (ENG., Illus.). 512p. (J). (gr. 5). pap. 8.99 *(978-1-4814-1780-8(0),* Simon & Schuster Bks. For Young Readers) Simon & Schuster Bks. For Young Readers.

—Rebels. 2016. (Randoms Ser.: 2). (ENG., Illus.). 400p. (J). (gr. 5). 18.99 *(978-1-4814-1782-2(7),* Simon & Schuster Bks. For Young Readers) Simon & Schuster Bks. For Young Readers.

—Renegades. 2017. (Randoms Ser.: 3). (ENG., Illus.). 352p. (J). (gr. 5). 19.99 *(978-1-4814-1785-3(1),* Simon & Schuster Bks. For Young Readers) Simon & Schuster Bks. For Young Readers.

Liu, Liana. The Memory Key. 2015. (ENG.). 368p. (YA). (gr. 8). 17.99 *(978-0-06-230664-7(2),* HarperTeen) HarperCollins Pubs.

Lix, Caryn. Sanctuary. (Sanctuary Novel Ser.). (ENG., Illus.). (YA). (gr. 9). 2019. 496p. pap. 12.99 *(978-1-5344-0534-9(8))* 2018. 480p. 19.99 *(978-1-5344-0533-2(X))* Simon Pulse. (Simon Pulse).

Llongueras, Joan & Masnou, Merce. Kadingir: El Cetro de Zink. 2007. (SPA.). 365p. (J). 18.95 *(978-84-96544-64-2(8))* Roca Editorial ESP. Dist: Spanish Pubs., LLC.

Lloyd, Saci. The Carbon Diaries 2015. 2010. (Carbon Diaries). (ENG.). 384p. (YA). (gr. 7-12). 22.44 *(978-0-8234-2190-9(2))* Holiday Hse., Inc.

Lo, Malinda. Adaptation. 2013. (ENG.). 416p. (YA). (gr. 10-17). pap. 19.99 *(978-0-316-19798-4(X))* Little, Brown Bks. for Young Readers.

—Inheritance. 2014. (ENG.). 480p. (YA). (gr. 10-17). pap. 21.99 *(978-0-316-19799-1(8))* Little, Brown Bks. for Young Readers.

Lochner, Caitlin. A Soldier & a Liar. 2020. (Soldier & a Liar Ser.: 1). (ENG.). 368p. (YA). pap. 17.99 *(978-1-250-16824-5(4),* 900187670) Square Fish.

Locke, Terry. Spencer Hurley & the Aliens: Book One: the Abduction. Hucks, Robin, ed. 2008. (Spencer Hurley & the Aliens Ser.: 1). (ENG., Illus.). 256p. (J). 12.95 *(978-0-9786940-0-5(7),* SHAB1V1E1CB) Dream Workshop Publishing Co., LLC, The.

Locke, Thomas, pseud. Recruits. 2017. (Recruits Ser.: 1). (ENG.). (YA). 378p. pap. 16.00 *(978-0-8007-2789-5(4));* 384p. 25.99 *(978-0-8007-2865-6(3))* Revell.

—Renegades. 2017. (Recruits Ser.). (ENG.). 288p. pap. 16.00 *(978-0-8007-2790-1(8))* Revell.

Loesch, Joe. The Tuskegee Airmen: Raiders of the Skies with Buffalo Biff & Farley's Raiders. Hutchinson, Cheryl, ed. 2004. (Backyard Adventure Ser.). (Illus.). 56p. (J). bds. 16.95 incl. audio compact disk *(978-1-932332-27-8(8))* Toy Box Productions.

Lofficier, Randy & Lofficier, Jean-Marc. Robonocchio. Pijuán Aragón, Miren, tr. Martiniere, Stephan, illus. 2004. (SPA.). 128p. (YA). per. 14.95 *(978-1-932983-25-8(2),* Black Coat Pr.) HollywoodComics.com, LLC.

Lohner, Ryan. The Place Beyond. 2018. (ENG., Illus.). 264p. (YA). (gr. 8-17). pap. 12.95 *(978-1-78279-912-2(5),* Lodestone Bks.) Hunt, John Publishing Ltd. GBR. Dist: National Bk. Network.

Lois, Lowry. Gathering Blue. 2013. (Giver Quartet Ser.: 2). lib. bdg. 20.85 *(978-0-606-31673-6(6))* Turtleback.

—Passeur. pap. 22.95 *(978-2-211-02166-1(2))* Archimede Editions FRA. Dist: Distribooks, Inc.

—Son. l.t. ed. 2013. (Giver Quartet Ser.). (ENG.). 422p. 23.99 *(978-1-4104-5448-5(7))* Thorndike Pr.

—Son. 2014. (Giver Quartet Ser.: 4). lib. bdg. 20.85 *(978-0-606-35979-5(6))* Turtleback.

Long, Christopher E. Hero Worship. 2014. (ENG.). 240p. (YA). (gr. 9-12). pap. 9.99 *(978-0-7387-3909-0(X),* 073873909X, Flux) North Star Editions.

Long, Ethan. Clara & Clem in Outer Space. 2013. (Penguin Young Readers, Level 1 Ser.). (ENG.). 32p. (J). (gr. k-1). pap. 5.99 *(978-0-448-46721-4(6),* Penguin Young Readers) Penguin Young Readers Group.

Long, Melinda & Wyrick, Monica. Art Smart, Science Detective: The Case of the Sliding Spaceship. 2018. (Young Palmetto Bks.). (ENG., Illus.). 64p. pap. 12.99 *(978-1-61117-935-4(1),* P599510) Univ. of South Carolina Pr.

Lord, Pia. The Day the Sun Went Out. 2012. 30p. 24.95 *(978-1-4626-6797-0(X))* America Star Bks.

Lore, Pittacus. The Fate of Ten. 2015. 399p. (YA). *(978-0-06-242452-5(1)); (978-0-06-242751-9(2))* Harper & Row Ltd.

—The Fate of Ten. (Lorien Legacies Ser.: 6). (ENG.). (YA). (gr. 9). 2016. 432p. pap. 15.99 *(978-0-06-219476-3(3))* 2015. 416p. 18.99 *(978-0-06-219475-6(5))* HarperCollins Pubs. (HarperCollins).

—The Fate of Ten. 2016. (Lorien Legacies Ser.: 6). (YA). lib. bdg. 20.85 *(978-0-606-38760-6(9))* Turtleback.

—Fugitive Six. (Lorien Legacies Reborn Ser.: 2). (ENG.). (YA). (gr. 9). 2019. 464p. pap. 11.99 *(978-0-06-249388-0(4))* 2018. 448p. 18.99 *(978-0-06-249376-7(0))* HarperCollins Pubs. (HarperCollins).

—Generation One. (Lorien Legacies Reborn Ser.: 1). (ENG.). 416p. (YA). (gr. 9). 2018. pap. 10.99 *(978-0-06-249370-5(1))* 2017. 18.99 *(978-0-06-249374-3(4))* HarperCollins Pubs. (HarperCollins).

—Generation One. 2018. (YA). lib. bdg. 20.85 *(978-0-606-41372-5(3))* Turtleback.

—I Am Number Four. (Lorien Legacies Ser.: 1). (ENG.). (YA). (gr. 9). 2011. 496p. pap. 15.99 *(978-0-06-196957-7(5))* 2010. 448p. 18.99 *(978-0-06-196955-3(9))* HarperCollins Pubs. (HarperCollins).

—I Am Number Four. 2009. (Lorien Legacies Ser.: Bk. 1). 11.04 *(978-0-7848-3715-3(5),* Everbind) Marco Bk. Co.

—I Am Number Four. 2011. (I Am Number Four Ser.: Vol. 1). (ENG.). 440p. (gr. 9-12). 20.00 *(978-1-61383-207-3(9))* Perfection Learning Corp.

—I Am Number Four. 2011. (Lorien Legacies Ser.: 1). (YA). lib. bdg. 20.85 *(978-0-606-23545-7(0))* Turtleback.

—I Am Number Four Movie Tie-In Edition. movie tie-in ed. 2011. (Lorien Legacies Ser.: 1). (ENG.). (YA). (gr. 9). 496p. pap. 9.99 *(978-0-06-211655-0(X));* 480p. 17.99 *(978-0-06-202624-8(0))* HarperCollins Pubs. (HarperCollins).

—I Am Number Four: the Lost Files: Rebel Allies. 2015. (Lorien Legacies: the Lost Files Ser.). (ENG.). 416p. (YA). (gr. 9). pap. 10.99 *(978-0-06-236404-3(9),* HarperCollins) HarperCollins Pubs.

—I Am Number Four: the Lost Files: Secret Histories. 2013. (Lorien Legacies: the Lost Files Ser.). (ENG.). 416p. (YA). (gr. 9). pap. 10.99 *(978-0-06-222367-8(4),* HarperCollins) HarperCollins Pubs.

—I Am Number Four: the Lost Files: Zero Hour. 2016. (Lorien Legacies: the Lost Files Ser.). (ENG.). 416p. (YA). (gr. 9). pap. 11.99 *(978-0-06-238771-4(5),* HarperCollins) HarperCollins Pubs.

—The Legacies. 2012. (Lorien Legacies: the Lost Files Ser.). (YA). lib. bdg. 20.85 *(978-0-606-26874-5(X))* Turtleback.

—The Power of Six. (Lorien Legacies Ser.: 2). (ENG.). (YA). (gr. 9). 2012. 448p. pap. 11.99 *(978-0-06-197457-1(9))* 2011. 416p. 17.99 *(978-0-06-197455-7(2))* HarperCollins Pubs. (HarperCollins).

—The Power of Six. 2012. (Lorien Legacies Ser.: 2). (YA). lib. bdg. 20.85 *(978-0-606-26289-7(X))* Turtleback.

—Return to Zero. 2019. (Lorien Legacies Reborn Ser.: 3). (ENG.). 464p. (YA). (gr. 9). 18.99 *(978-0-06-249380-4(9),* HarperCollins) HarperCollins Pubs.

—The Revenge of Seven. 2014. 371p. (J). *(978-0-06-236719-8(6))* Harper & Row Ltd.

—The Revenge of Seven. (Lorien Legacies Ser.: 5). (ENG.). 416p. (YA). (gr. 9). 2015. pap. 11.99 *(978-0-06-219473-2(9))* 2014. 17.99 *(978-0-06-219472-5(0))* HarperCollins Pubs. (HarperCollins).

—The Revenge of Seven. 2015. (Lorien Legacies Ser.: 5). 415p. lib. bdg. 20.85 *(978-0-606-36981-7(3))* Turtleback.

—The Rise of Nine. (Lorien Legacies Ser.: 3). (ENG.). 416p. (YA). (gr. 9). 2013. pap. 11.99 *(978-0-06-197460-1(9))* 2012. 17.99 *(978-0-06-197458-8(7))* HarperCollins Pubs. (HarperCollins).

—The Rise of Nine. 2013. (Lorien Legacies Ser.: 3). (YA). lib. bdg. 20.85 *(978-0-606-31830-3(5))* Turtleback.

—Secret Histories. 2013. (Lorien Legacies: the Lost Files Ser.). (YA). lib. bdg. 20.85 *(978-0-606-31823-5(2))* Turtleback.

—United As One. 2017. (Lorien Legacies Ser.: 7). (ENG.). (YA). (gr. 9). lib. bdg. 20.85 *(978-0-606-40055-8(9))* Turtleback.

Lorimer, Janet. Bugged (Science Fiction), 1 vol. 2017. (Pageturners Ser.). (ENG.). 80p. (YA). (gr. 9-12). 10.75 *(978-1-68021-393-5(8))* Saddleback Educational Publishing, Inc.

—Flashback (Science Fiction), 1 vol. 2017. (Pageturners Ser.). (ENG.). 80p. (YA). (gr. 9-12). 10.75 *(978-1-68021-395-9(4))* Saddleback Educational Publishing, Inc.

—Murray's Nightmare (Science Fiction), 1 vol. 2017. (Pageturners Ser.). (ENG.). 76p. (YA). (gr. 9-12). 10.75 *(978-1-68021-396-6(2))* Saddleback Educational Publishing, Inc.

The Lotus Caves. 2014. (ENG., Illus.). 288p. (J). (gr. 4-8). pap. 7.99 *(978-1-4814-1837-9(8),* Aladdin) Simon & Schuster Children's Publishing.

The Lotus Caves. 2014. (ENG., Illus.). 288p. (J). (gr. 4-8). 17.99 *(978-1-4814-1838-6(6),* Simon & Schuster/Paula Wiseman Bks.) Simon & Schuster/Paula Wiseman Bks.

Loux, Matthew. The Time Museum. 2017. (Time Museum Ser.: 1). (ENG., Illus.). 256p. (J). pap. 15.99 *(978-1-59643-849-1(5),* 900097185, First Second Bks.) Roaring Brook Pr.

—The Time Museum. 2017. (J). lib. bdg. 26.95 *(978-0-606-40348-1(5))* Turtleback.

Lovhaug, Lewis J. Angel Armor: The Cassandra Conflict. 2004. 188p. (YA). pap. 13.95 *(978-0-595-30869-9(4))* iUniverse, Inc.

Lowry, Lois. Gathering Blue. (Giver Quartet Ser.: 2). (ENG.). 256p. (YA). (gr. 7). 2013. pap. 11.99 *(978-0-547-90414-6(2),* 1510989) 2012. 19.99 *(978-0-547-99568-7(7),* 1525434) HarperCollins Pubs. (Clarion Bks.).

—The Giver. 2007. (KOR.). 310p. (YA). pap. *(978-89-491-2074-4(7))* Biryongso Publishing Co.

—The Giver. l.t. ed. 2004. (Giver Quartet Ser.). (ENG.). 226p. (YA). (gr. 5-8). pap. 15.99 *(978-0-7862-7153-5(1))* Cengage Gale.

—The Giver. 2014. (ENG.). 192p. (YA). (gr. 3-7). 11.24 *(978-1-63245-036-4(4))* Lectorum Pubns., Inc.

—The Giver. 2009. 9.14 *(978-0-7848-0666-1(7));* 10.52 *(978-0-7848-2389-7(8))* Marco Bk. Co. (Everbind).

—The Giver. 180p. (gr. 5-18). (YA). pap. 5.99 *(978-0-8072-8314-1(2));* 2004. (J). pap. 38.00 incl. audio *(978-0-8072-8313-4(4),* YA159SP) Random Hse. Audio Publishing Group. (Listening Library).

—The Giver, 4 vols. (J). 2009. 55.75 *(978-1-4281-5700-2(X))* 2007. 58.75 *(978-1-4281-5698-2(4))* Recorded Bks., Inc.

—The Giver. l.t. ed. 2004. 226p. 23.95 *(978-0-7862-7154-2(X))* Thorndike Pr.

—The Giver. 2014. (Giver Quartet Ser.: 1). lib. bdg. 19.65 *(978-0-606-35978-8(8))* Turtleback.

—The Giver: A Newbery Award Winner. 25th ed. 2014. (Giver Quartet Ser.: 1). (ENG.). 240p. (YA). (gr. 7). pap. 11.99 *(978-0-544-33626-1(7),* 1584172, Clarion Bks.) HarperCollins Pubs.

—The Giver (for Pob Boxed Set Only) 2014. (Giver Quartet Ser.). (ENG.). 192p. (YA). (gr. 7). 9.99 *(978-0-544-34063-3(9),* Clarion Bks.) HarperCollins Pubs.

—The Giver Movie Tie-In Edition: A Newbery Award Winner. movie tie-in ed. 2014. (Giver Quartet Ser.: 1). (ENG.). 256p. (YA). (gr. 7). pap. 9.99 *(978-0-544-34068-8(X),* 1584762, Clarion Bks.) HarperCollins Pubs.

—The Giver Quartet Box Set. 2014. (Giver Quartet Ser.). (ENG.). 864p. (YA). (gr. 7). 49.99 *(978-0-544-34062-6(0),* 1584756, Clarion Bks.) HarperCollins Pubs.

—The Giver Quartet Omnibus. 2014. (Giver Quartet Ser.). (ENG.). 784p. (YA). (gr. 7). 32.99 *(978-0-544-34097-8(3),* 1584842, Clarion Bks.) HarperCollins Pubs.

—Messenger. (Giver Quartet Ser.: 3). (ENG.). 192p. (YA). (gr. 7). 2018. pap. 10.99 *(978-1-328-46620-4(5),* 1713613) 2012. 17.99 *(978-0-547-99567-0(9),* 1525433) HarperCollins Pubs. (Clarion Bks.).

—Son. (Giver Quartet Ser.: 4). (ENG.). 400p. (YA). (gr. 7). 2014. pap. 9.99 *(978-0-544-33625-4(9),* 1584171) 2012. 17.99 *(978-0-547-88720-3(5),* 1507673) HarperCollins Pubs. (Clarion Bks.).

Lu, Marie. Batman: Nightwalker. 2018. (DC Icons Ser.). (ENG.). 288p. (YA). (gr. 7). pap. *(978-0-525-57856-7(0))* Penguin Random Hse.

—Batman: Nightwalker. 2019. (DC Icons Ser.). (ENG.). 320p. (YA). (gr. 7). pap. 12.99 *(978-0-399-54980-9(3),* Ember) Random Hse. Children's Bks.

—Batman: Nightwalker (Spanish Edition) 2018. (Dc Icons Ser.: 2). (SPA.). 336p. (YA). (gr. 8-12). pap. 16.95 *(978-1-947783-71-3(8),* Montena) Penguin Random House Grupo Editorial ESP. Dist: Penguin Random Hse. LLC.

—Batman: Nightwalker (the Graphic Novel) Wildgoose, Chris, illus. 2019. 208p. (YA). (gr. 7-9). pap. 16.99 *(978-1-4012-8004-8(8),* DC Ink) DC Comics.

—Champion: A Legend Novel. (Legend Ser.: 3). (ENG.). (YA). (gr. 7). 2014. 416p. pap. 12.99 *(978-0-14-751228-4(X),* Speak) 2013. (Illus.). 384p. 19.99 *(978-0-399-25677-6(6),* G.P. Putnam's Sons Books for Young Readers) Penguin Young Readers Group.

—Legend. aut. ltd. collector's ed. 2013. (Legend Trilogy: Bk. 1). (Illus.). 306p. (YA). mass mkt. 100.00 net. *(978-1-934267-38-7(4))* Gauntlet, Inc.

—Legend. 2011. (Legend Trilogy: Bk. 1). (ENG.). (YA). (gr. 8-12). 54.99 *(978-1-61657-044-6(X),* Penguin AudioBooks) Penguin Publishing Group.

—Legend. (Legend Ser.: 1). (ENG.). (YA). (gr. 7). 2013. 352p. pap. 12.99 *(978-0-14-242207-6(X),* Speak) 2011. 320p. 19.99 *(978-0-399-25675-2(X),* G.P. Putnam's Sons Books for Young Readers) Penguin Young Readers Group.

—Legend. l.t. ed. 2012. (Legend Trilogy: Bk. 1). (ENG.). 394p. (J). (gr. 7-12). 23.99 *(978-1-4104-4606-0(9))* Thorndike Pr.

—Legend. (Legend Graphic Novels Ser.: 1). 2015. lib. bdg. 26.95 *(978-0-606-38424-7(3))* 2013. lib. bdg. 20.85 *(978-0-606-31701-6(5))* Turtleback.

—Legend: the Graphic Novel. 2015. (Legend Ser.: 1). (ENG., Illus.). 160p. (YA). (gr. 7). pap. 15.99 *(978-0-399-17189-5(4),* G.P. Putnam's Sons Books for Young Readers) Penguin Young Readers Group.

—Legend Trilogy Boxed Set, 5 vols. 2013. (Legend Ser.: Bk. 1). (ENG.). 1088p. (YA). (gr. 7). 56.97 *(978-0-399-16667-9(X),* G.P. Putnam's Sons Books for Young Readers) Penguin Young Readers Group.

—Prodigy. l.t. ed. 2013. (Legend Trilogy: Bk. 2). (ENG.). 486p. 23.99 *(978-1-4104-5512-3(2))* Thorndike Pr.

—Prodigy. 2014. (Legend Ser.: 2). lib. bdg. 20.85 *(978-0-606-35716-6(5))* Turtleback.

—Prodigy: A Legend Novel. (Legend Ser.: 2). (ENG., (YA). (gr. 7). 2014. Illus.). 416p. pap. 12.99 *(978-0-14-242755-2(1),* Speak) 2013. 384p. 19.99 *(978-0-399-25676-9(8),* G.P. Putnam's Sons Books for Young Readers) Penguin Young Readers Group.

—Prodigy: the Graphic Novel. 2016. (Legend Ser.: 2). (ENG., Illus.). 160p. (YA). (gr. 7). pap. 14.99 *(978-0-399-17190-1(8),* G.P. Putnam's Sons Books for Young Readers) Penguin Young Readers Group.

—Warcross. l.t. ed. 2017. (ENG.). 514p. 24.95 *(978-1-4328-4371-7(0))* Cengage Gale.

—Warcross. (Warcross Ser.: 1). (ENG.). (YA). (gr. 7). 2019. 400p. 9.99 *(978-1-9848-1576-7(8),* Penguin Books) 2018. 416p. pap. 11.99 *(978-0-399-54797-3(5),* Speak) 2017. 368p. 18.99 *(978-0-399-54796-6(7),* G.P. Putnam's Sons Books for Young Readers) Penguin Young Readers Group.

—Warcross. 2018. (SPA.). 520p. (YA). pap. 19.99 *(978-987-747-342-1(9))* V&R Editoras.

Lubar, David. My Rotten Life. 2009. (Nathan Abercrombie, Accidental Zombie Ser.: 1). (ENG., Illus.). 160p. (J). (gr. 3-7). pap. 13.99 *(978-0-7653-1634-9(X),* 900038898, Starscape) Doherty, Tom Assocs., LLC.

Lucas Film Book Group. Luke Skywalker. 2016. (Star Wars: Force Awakens 8X8 Ser.). (J). lib. bdg. 14.75 *(978-0-606-39175-7(4))* Turtleback.

—Trouble on Tatooine. 2017. (Star Wars: World of Reading Ser.). (J). lib. bdg. 14.75 *(978-0-606-39963-0(1))* Turtleback.

Lucas Film Book Group Editors. Poe Dameron. 2017. (Star Wars: Force Awakens 8X8 Ser.). (J). lib. bdg. 14.75 *(978-0-606-39506-9(7))* Turtleback.

Lucas, George. La Guerre des Etoiles, Tome 1.Tr. of Star Wars. (FRE.). (J). pap. 11.95 *(978-2-265-06730-1(X))* Fleuve Noir FRA. Dist: Distribooks, Inc.

Lucasfilm Book Group. The Heist. 2017. (Star Wars Adventures in Wild Space Ser.: 3). (J). lib. bdg. 16.00 *(978-0-606-39961-6(5))* Turtleback.

Lucasfilm Book Group & Huddleston, Tom. The Darkness. 2017. (Star Wars Adventures in Wild Space Ser.: 4). (Illus.). 134p. (J). lib. bdg. 16.00 *(978-0-606-39962-3(3))* Turtleback.

Lucasfilm Press. Han & the Rebel Rescue. 2017. (J). lib. bdg. 14.75 *(978-0-606-39966-1(6))* Turtleback.

Lucasfilm Press, Lucasfilm. Star Wars: 5Minute Star Wars Stories. 2015. (5-Minute Stories Ser.). (ENG.). 176p. (J). (gr. 1-3). 12.99 *(978-1-4847-2820-8(3),* Disney Lucasfilm Press) Disney Publishing Worldwide.

—World of Reading Star Wars Boxed Set: Level 2. 2017. (World of Reading Ser.). (ENG., Illus.). 192p. (J). (gr. 1-3). 12.99 *(978-1-368-00587-6(X),* Disney Lucasfilm Press) Disney Publishing Worldwide.

—5-Minute Star Wars Stories Strike Back. 2017. (Illus.). 20p. (J). (gr. 1-3). 12.99 *(978-1-368-00351-3(6),* Disney Lucasfilm Press) Disney Publishing Worldwide.

LucasFilm Press Staff. Star Wars: Before the Awakening. Noto, Phil, illus. 2015. E-Book *(978-1-4847-3550-3(1))* Disney Publishing Worldwide.

Luper, Eric. Battle of the Bots. 2018. (Key Hunters Ser.: 7). (ENG., Illus.). 128p. (J). (gr. 2-5). pap. 4.99 *(978-1-338-21233-4(8),* Scholastic Paperbacks) Scholastic, Inc.

Lupini, Valerie. The Whistle. 2005. (ENG.). 200p. (J). (gr. 6-9). pap. 4.95 *(978-0-88995-314-7(7),* 4bf69360-1e0e-4592-aaeb-ec1fa95eac81) Trifolium Bks., Inc. CAN. Dist: Firefly Bks., Ltd.

Lyen, Taylor Samuel. Pembroke: The Adventures of Arthur Bacterium & Patty Virus. 2012. 180p. (-18). pap. 13.95 *(978-1-4759-5855-3(2))* iUniverse, Inc.

Lyga, Barry, et al. After the Red Rain. 2015. (ENG.). 400p. (YA). (gr. 10-17). 18.00 *(978-0-316-40603-1(1))* Little, Brown Bks. for Young Readers.

Lynch, Chris. In a Wired Future, Animals Need Our Help. 2010. (Cyberia Ser.: 1). (ENG.). 160p. (J). (gr. 4-6). 18.69 *(978-0-545-02796-0(9))* Scholastic, Inc.

—Monkey See, Monkey Don't. 2011. (Cyberia Ser.: 2). (ENG.). 144p. (J). (gr. 4-7). pap. 5.99 *(978-0-545-02797-7(7))* Scholastic, Inc.

Lyons, Suzanne. Pete Discovers Gravity: Set Of 6. 2011. (Early Connections Ser.). (J). pap. 39.00 net. *(978-1-4108-1559-0(5))* Benchmark Education Co.

Ma, Jyoti & Devi, Chandra. Sparkling Together: Starbright & His Earthling Friends. 2004. (ENG., Illus.). 96p. (J). pap. 19.95 *(978-0-932040-54-1(3),* ddc1ee5d-f71a-4c3b-8b79-8b3ee127a8bb) Integral Yoga Pubns.

Maas, Sarah J. Catwoman: Soulstealer. (DC Icons Ser.). (ENG.). (YA). (gr. 7). 2019. 400p. pap. 11.99 *(978-0-399-54972-4(2),* Ember) 2018. 384p. 18.99 *(978-0-399-54969-4(2),* Random Hse. Bks. for Young Readers) Random Hse. Children's Bks.

Maberry, Jonathan. Mars One. 2017. (ENG., Illus.). 448p. (YA). (gr. 7). 19.99 *(978-1-4814-6161-0(3),* Simon & Schuster Bks. For Young Readers) Simon & Schuster Bks. For Young Readers.

—The Orphan Army. 2015. (Nightsiders Ser.: 1). (ENG., Illus.). 400p. (J). (gr. 3-7). 16.99 *(978-1-4814-1575-0(1),* Simon & Schuster Bks. For Young Readers) Simon & Schuster Bks. For Young Readers.

—The Orphan Army. 2016. (Nightsiders Ser.: 1). lib. bdg. 18.40 *(978-0-606-38959-4(8))* Turtleback.

—Vault of Shadows. (Nightsiders Ser.: 2). (ENG.). 464p. (J). (gr. 3-7). 2017. pap. 8.99 *(978-1-4814-1579-8(4))* 2016. (Illus.). 16.99 *(978-1-4814-1578-1(6))* Simon & Schuster Bks. For Young Readers. (Simon & Schuster Bks. For Young Readers).

Macaw, Grant. Vigil's End. 2005. (ENG.). 310p. (YA). (gr. 7). per. *(978-1-933255-13-2(7))* DNA Pr.

MacDonald, Tom. Secret of the Tree: Marcus Speer's Ecosentinel. Stieber, Joel, illus. 2009. 300p. 28.95 *(978-0-595-51985-9(7))* iUniverse, Inc.

MacHado, Ana Maria. Un Deseo Loco. (Torre de Papel Ser.). (SPA.). (YA). (gr. 6-18). 8.95 *(978-958-04-4529-6(X),* NR30565) Norma S.A. COL. Dist: Lectorum Pubns., Inc., Distribuidora Norma, Inc.

MacHale, D. J. The Reality Bug. 2003. (Pendragon Ser.: 4). (ENG., Illus.). 384p. (J). (gr. 5-9). pap. 10.99 *(978-0-7434-3734-9(9),* Aladdin) Simon & Schuster Children's Publishing.

Mack, Karen. The Magical Adventures of Sun Beams. 2009. 42p. 31.99 *(978-1-4415-3636-5(1))* Xlibris Corp.

Maes, Nicholas. Locksmith: A Felix Taylor Adventure. 2008. (Felix Taylor Adventure Ser.: 1). (ENG.). 240p. (J). (gr. 5-8). pap. 11.99 *(978-1-55002-791-4(3))* Dundurn Pr. CAN. Dist: Publishers Group West (PGW).

Mafi, Tahereh. Defy Me. (Shatter Me Ser.: 5). (ENG.). (YA). (gr. 9). 2020. 384p. pap. 15.99 *(978-0-06-267640-5(7))* 2019. 368p. 19.99 *(978-0-06-267639-9(3))* HarperCollins Pubs. (HarperCollins).

—Ignite Me. 2014. (Shatter Me Ser.: 3). (ENG.). 416p. (YA). (gr. 9). pap. 15.99 *(978-0-06-208558-0(1));* 19.99 *(978-0-06-208557-3(3))* HarperCollins Pubs. (HarperCollins).

—Restore Me. 2018. 435p. (YA). *(978-0-06-284176-6(9))* Harper & Row Ltd.

—Restore Me. (Shatter Me Ser.: 4). (YA). (gr. 9). 2019. (ENG.). 464p. pap. 15.99 *(978-0-06-267637-5(7),* HarperCollins) 2018. (ENG.). 448p. 19.99 *(978-0-06-267636-8(9),* HarperCollins) 2018. 352p. 18.99 *(978-0-06-282045-7(1))* HarperCollins Pubs.

—Shatter Me. 2018. (Shatter Me Ser.: 1). (ENG.). (YA). (gr. 9). 448p. 21.99 *(978-0-06-274173-8(X));* 368p. pap. 15.99 *(978-0-06-208550-4(6))* HarperCollins Pubs. (HarperCollins).

—Shatter Me. 2012. (Shatter Me Ser.: 1). (YA). lib. bdg. 20.85 *(978-0-606-26868-4(5))* Turtleback.

—Unite Me. 2014. (Shatter Me Ser.). (ENG.). 224p. (YA). (gr. 9). pap. 15.99 *(978-0-06-232796-3(8),* HarperCollins) HarperCollins Pubs.

—Unravel Me. 2013. (Shatter Me Ser.: 2). (ENG.). (YA). (gr. 9). 496p. pap. 15.99 *(978-0-06-208554-2(9));* 480p. 19.99 *(978-0-06-208553-5(0))* HarperCollins Pubs. (HarperCollins).

—Unravel Me. 2013. (Shatter Me Ser.: 2). (YA). lib. bdg. 20.85 *(978-0-606-35049-5(7))* Turtleback.

Maguire, K. C. Inside the Palisade. 2015. (ENG., Illus.). 173p. (J). (gr. -1-12). pap. 11.95 *(978-1-78279-715-9(7),* Lodestone Bks.) Hunt, John Publishing Ltd. GBR. Dist: National Bk. Network.

Mahoney, Jerry. Buttheads from Outer Space. 2018. (ENG.). 288p. (J). (gr. 3-7). pap. 7.99 *(978-1-5107-3261-2(6),* Sky Pony Pr.) Skyhorse Publishing Co., Inc.

—Buttheads from Outer Space. 2018. lib. bdg. 18.40 *(978-0-606-41303-9(0))* Turtleback.

Mai, Lily. Bertie Boom's Trip to the Moon. 2010. (Illus.). 20p. 12.49 *(978-1-4520-1379-4(9))* AuthorHouse.

Maihack, Mike. Secret of the Time Tablets, 3. 2019. (Cleopatra in Space Graphic Nvls Ser.). (ENG.). 182p. (J). (gr. 4-5). 23.96 *(978-0-87617-335-0(0))* Penworthy Co., LLC, The.

—Secret of the Time Tablets. 2016. (Cleopatra in Space Ser.: 3). lib. bdg. 24.50 *(978-0-606-38812-2(5))* Turtleback.

Mak, D P. Invisible Pill. 2005. 44p. pap. *(978-1-84401-210-7(7))* Athena Pr.

Maker, Don. Miranda's Magic. 2013. 152p. pap. 6.63 *(978-0-9859707-4-1(X))* Metacognition Pr.

Malley, Gemma. The Declaration. 2008. (Declaration Ser.). (ENG., Illus.). 320p. (YA). (gr. 7). 10.99 *(978-1-59990-295-1(8),* 900053613, Bloomsbury USA Childrens) Bloomsbury Publishing USA.

—The Declaration, 7 vols. (YA). 2008. 119.75 *(978-1-4281-7284-5(X))* 2007. 91.75 *(978-1-4281-7278-4(5))* 2007. 245.75 *(978-1-4281-7279-1(3))* 2007. 1.25 *(978-1-4281-7275-3(0))* 2007. 89.75 *(978-1-4281-7280-7(7))* 2007. 121.75 *(978-1-4281-7282-1(3))* Recorded Bks., Inc.

Mammano, Meredith. The Electronic Adventures of Diga Byte: Wrong Turn, the First of His Adventures. Cesarski, Thomas, photos by. 2008. (ENG.). 50p. pap. 22.49 *(978-1-4343-9636-5(3))* AuthorHouse.

Manchee, William. Tarizon the Liberator: Tarizon Trilogy Vol 1. 2008. 340p. (YA). (gr. 7-18). lib. bdg. 24.00 *(978-1-929976-48-5(8),* TOP) Top Pubns., Ltd.

Manning, Matthew K. Batman Character Encyclopedia. 2016. (ENG., Illus.). 208p. (J). (gr. 4-7). 16.99 *(978-1-4654-4498-1(X),* DK Children) Dorling Kindersley Publishing, Inc.

—Batman/Teenage Mutant Ninja Turtles Adventures. Sommariva, Jon, illus. 2017. 144p. (J). (gr. 4-7). pap. 19.99 *(978-1-63140-909-7(3))* Idea & Design Works, LLC.

—The Face of Two Worlds. Sommariva, Jon, illus. 2018. (Batman / Teenage Mutant Ninja Turtles Adventures Ser.). (ENG.). 32p. (J). (gr. 2-6). lib. bdg. 28.95 *(978-1-4965-7381-0(1)*, 138939, Stone Arch Bks.) Capstone.

—The Terror of the Kraang. Sommariva, Jon, illus. 2018. (Batman / Teenage Mutant Ninja Turtles Adventures Ser.). (ENG.). 32p. (J). (gr. 2-6). lib. bdg. 28.95 *(978-1-4965-7387-2(0)*, 138944, Stone Arch Bks.) Capstone.

Manship, Paul. The Cube. 2006. (ENG.). 128p. (J). pap. 7.50 *(978-1-84323-739-6(3))* Gomer Pr. GBR. Dist: Casemate Pubs. & Bk. Distributors, LLC.

Marazano, Richard. Civilisation, 2 vols. Ponzio, Jean-Michel, illus. 2010. (Chimpanzee Complex Ser.: 3). 55p. pap. 13.95 *(978-1-84918-043-6(1))* CineBook GBR. Dist: National Bk. Network.

—The Sons of Ares, 2 vols. Ponzio, Jean-Michel, illus. 2009. (Chimpanzee Complex Ser.: 1). 56p. pap. 13.95 *(978-1-84918-002-3(4))* CineBook GBR. Dist: National Bk. Network.

March, Julia. Monster Battles. 2016. (Illus.). 63p. (J). *(978-1-5182-1852-1(0))* Dorling Kindersley Publishing, Inc.

Marciano, Johnny & Chenoweth, Emily. Klawde: Evil Alien Warlord Cat #1. Mommaerts, Robb, illus. 2019. (Klawde: Evil Alien Warlord Cat Ser.: 1). 224p. (J). (gr. 3-7). 14.99 *(978-1-5247-8720-2(5)*, Penguin Workshop) Penguin Young Readers Group.

Marie, Anna. Hexon. 2012. (ENG.). 66p. pap. 9.95 *(978-1-4327-9112-4(5))* Outskirts Pr., Inc.

Mario. Arriving to Planet Noah. 2011. 68p. 24.99 *(978-1-4628-5905-4(4))*; pap. 15.99 *(978-1-4628-5904-7(6))* Xlibris Corp.

Mariz, Rae. The Unidentified. 2012. (ENG.). 304p. (YA). (gr. 8). pap. 8.99 *(978-0-06-180209-6(3)*, Balzer & Bray) HarperCollins Pubs.

Marlowe, Paul. Sporeville. 2007. (Wellborn Conspiracy Ser.: Bk. 1). 250p. (YA). (gr. 8-12). pap. 10.95 *(978-0-9739505-4-0(4))* Sybertooth, Inc. CAN. Dist: Ingram Content Group.

Marman, Richard. Mcalister's Spark. Marman, Richard, illus. 2013. (Illus.). 364p. pap. *(978-1-909302-21-1(X))* Abela Publishing.

Marr, Melissa, et al. Shards & Ashes. 2013. (ENG.). 384p. (YA). (gr. 8). pap. 9.99 *(978-0-06-209845-0(4)*, HarperCollins) HarperCollins Pubs.

Marsh, Carole. The Earthshaking Earthquake Mystery. 2007. (Masters of Disasters Ser.). (Illus.). 118p. (J). (gr. 2-9). 14.95 *(978-0-635-06395-3(6))* Gallopade International.

—The Ferocious Forest Fire Mystery. 2008. (Masters of Disasters Ser.). (Illus.). 118p. (J). (gr. 3-5). 14.95 *(978-0-635-06468-4(5))*;6. (ENG., (gr. 2-4). 18.69 *(978-0-635-06465-3(0))* Gallopade International.

—The Treacherous Tornado Mystery. 2007. (Masters of Disasters Ser.). (Illus.). 118p. (J). (gr. 2-9). 14.95 *(978-0-635-06394-6(8))* Gallopade International.

Marshall, G. Skies of Dawn. 2007. 160p. per. 12.95 *(978-0-595-42946-2(7))* iUniverse, Inc.

Martens, J. D. Countdown to Destruction: Book 5. 2017. (Meteor Ser.). (ENG.). 184p. (YA). (gr. 5-12). 31.42 *(978-1-68076-831-2(X)*, 27434, Epic Escape) EPIC Pr.

—Days of Anarchy: Book 2. 2017. (Meteor Ser.). (ENG.). 184p. (YA). (gr. 5-12). 31.42 *(978-1-68076-828-2(X)*, 27431, Epic Escape) EPIC Pr.

Martin, Caroline Jane. The Flow. 2013. (ENG.). 276p. pap. *(978-0-9928101-0-8(8))* Lovell Pr.

Martin-Duttmann, Robin. Zoo on the Moon. 2013. 24p. pap. 12.97 *(978-1-62212-735-1(8)*, Strategic Bk. Publishing) Strategic Book Publishing & Rights Agency (SBPRA).

Martin, Gary & Pennebaker, H. I. Professor Tyme's Timeless Tales: Revenge of the Sargasso Sea Ogre. 2006. (ENG.). 160p. per. 24.95 *(978-1-4241-5701-3(3))* America Star Bks.

Martin, Laura. Edge of Extinction #1: the Ark Plan. Deschamps, Eric, illus. 2017. (Edge of Extinction Ser.: 1). (ENG.). 384p. (J). (gr. 3-7). pap. 6.99 *(978-0-06-241623-0(5)*, HarperCollins) HarperCollins Pubs.

Martin, R. T. The Field Trip. 2018. (Attack on Earth Ser.). (ENG.). 112p. (YA). (gr. 6-12). 26.65 *(978-1-5415-2573-3(6)*, 06e260b9-f5cb-42f2-80c8-692f0c9fe067, Darby Creek) Lerner Publishing Group.

—Safe Zone. 2017. (Level Up Ser.). (ENG.). 112p. (YA). (gr. 6-12). pap. 7.99 *(978-1-5124-5360-7(9)*, 4b340d12-02d0-489e-a9cd-c0f80ec63dde); lib. bdg. 26.65 *(978-1-5124-3986-1(X)*, 239c2cad-d57a-4415-85bc-2ab2fc7ecf43) Lerner Publishing Group. (Darby Creek).

Marvel. Avengers: Age of Ultron: Avengers Save the Day. 2015. (Marvel 8x8s Ser.). (J). lib. bdg. 14.75 *(978-0-606-37214-5(8))* Turtleback.

—Avengers: Age of Ultron: Battle at Avengers Tower. 2015. (Marvel 8x8s Ser.). (J). lib. bdg. 13.55 *(978-0-606-37213-8(X))* Turtleback.

Marvel Editors. Marvel's Guardians of the Galaxy, Vol. 2. 2017. (Passport to Reading Level 2 Ser.). (J). lib. bdg. 14.75 *(978-0-606-39905-0(4))*; lib. bdg. 14.75 *(978-0-606-39906-7(2))* Turtleback.

Marvel Press Book Group, Marvel Press. World of Reading: Marvel 3-In-1 Listen-along Reader-World of Reading Level 1: 3 Tales of Adventure with CD! 2017. (World of Reading Ser.). (ENG.). 96p. (J). (gr. -1-k). pap. 7.99 *(978-1-4847-9948-2(8))* Marvel Worldwide, Inc.

Mashima, Hiro. Rave. 2006. (Rave Ser.). (SPA., Illus.). reprint ed. Vol. 1. 185p. pap. 10.95 *(978-1-59497-175-4(7))* Vol. 3. 184p. pap. 10.95 *(978-1-59497-177-8(3))* Vol. 4. 188p. per. 10.95 *(978-1-59497-178-5(1))* Vol. 5. 192p. pap. 10.95 *(978-1-59497-179-2(X))* Vol. 6. 200p. pap. 10.95 *(978-1-59497-180-8(3))* Public Square Bks.

—Rave: Volume 2, Vol. 2. 2006. (Rave Ser.). (SPA., Illus.). 180p. reprint ed. pap. 10.95 *(978-1-59497-176-1(5))* Public Square Bks.

—Rave: Volume 7, Vol. 7. 2006. (Rave Ser.). (SPA., Illus.). 189p. reprint ed. pap. 10.95 *(978-1-59497-199-0(4))* Public Square Bks.

—Rave: Volume 9, Vol. 9. 2006. (Rave Ser.). (SPA., Illus.). 189p. reprint ed. pap. 10.95 *(978-1-59497-201-0(X))* Public Square Bks.

—Rave, Volume 8, Vol. 8. 2006. (Rave Ser.). (SPA., Illus.). 171p. reprint ed. pap. 10.95 *(978-1-59497-200-3(1))* Public Square Bks.

Mass, Wendy. Pi in the Sky. 2014. (ENG.). 272p. (J). (gr. 3-7). pap. 8.99 *(978-0-316-08917-3(6))* Little, Brown Bks. for Young Readers.

—Voyagers: the Seventh Element (Book 6) 2016. (Voyager Ser.: 6). 208p. (J). (gr. 3-7). 12.99 *(978-0-385-38673-9(7)*, Random Hse. Bks. for Young Readers) Random Hse. Children's Bks.

Mass, Wendy & Brawer, Michael. Archie's Alien Disguise. 2015. (Space Taxi Ser.: 3). (J). lib. bdg. 16.00 *(978-0-606-37517-7(1))* Turtleback.

—B. U. R. P. Strikes Back. 2017. (Space Taxi Ser.: 5). (J). lib. bdg. 16.00 *(978-0-606-40226-2(8))* Turtleback.

—The Galactic B. U. R. P. 2016. (Space Taxi Ser.: 4). (J). lib. bdg. 16.00 *(978-0-606-37518-4(X))* Turtleback.

—Space Taxi: B. U. R. P. Strikes Back. 2017. (Space Taxi Ser.: 5). (ENG., Illus.). 144p. (J). (gr. 1-5). pap. 5.99 *(978-0-316-30840-3(4))* Little, Brown Bks. for Young Readers.

—Space Taxi: the Galactic B. U. R. P. 2016. (Space Taxi Ser.: 4). (ENG., Illus.). 128p. (J). (gr. 1-5). 14.99 *(978-0-316-24331-5(0))*; pap. 5.99 *(978-0-316-24330-8(2))* Little, Brown Bks. for Young Readers.

Mass, Wendy & Michael Brawer. Aliens on Earth. 2017. (Space Taxi Ser.: 6). (J). lib. bdg. 16.00 *(978-0-606-40227-9(6))* Turtleback.

Matheson, Rebecca. Pacific Rim Uprising: the Junior Novel. 2018. (ENG., Illus.). 152p. (J). pap. 6.99 *(978-1-68383-386-4(4))* Insight Editions.

Mathews, Temple. The New Kid. 2010. 288p. (J). (gr. 6-11). pap. 24.95 *(978-1-935618-27-0(X)*, SmartPop) BenBella Bks.

—The Sword of Armageddon. 2010. ix, 291p. *(978-1-935618-17-1(2))* BenBella Bks.

Mattern, Joanne. Batter Up! 2005. (J). pap. *(978-1-4108-4193-3(6))* Benchmark Education Co.

Mayer, Kirsten. Meet Team Prime. 2012. (Transformers Passport to Reading Ser.). (J). lib. bdg. 13.55 *(978-0-606-26148-7(6))* Turtleback.

Maynard, Case. The Surrendered. 2016. (ENG.). 266p. (YA). (gr. 9). pap. 9.95 *(978-0-9970104-7-3(9))* Blaze Publishing, LLC.

Mayne, William. Earthfasts. 2008. (J). (gr. 4-7). 25.25 *(978-0-8446-6430-9(8))* Smith, Peter Pub., Inc.

McBee, Travis. A Little Holiday Thrill. 2008. 66p. pap. 10.99 *(978-0-557-03276-1(8))* Lulu Pr., Inc.

McBride, Earvin, Jr. The Blockheads from Planet Ecto. 2nd unabr. ed. 2003. (Earvin MacBride's Amazing Sci-Fi & Adventure Heroes Ser.). (Illus.). 41p. (YA). (gr. 7-12). pap. 4.95 *(978-1-892511-10-2(X)*, Disposition Sketch Bks.) MacBride, E. J. Pubn., Inc.

McCardle, Meredith. Blackout, 0 vols. 2015. (Annum Guard Ser.: 2). (ENG.). 351p. (YA). (gr. 7-12). pap. 9.99 *(978-1-4778-2711-6(0)*, 9781477827116, Skyscape) Amazon Publishing.

McCarthy, Cory. Breaking Sky. 2015. (ENG.). 416p. (YA). (gr. 7-12). 16.99 *(978-1-4926-0141-8(1)*, 9781492601418) Sourcebooks, Inc.

McCarthy, Cory & Capetta, A. R. Once & Future. (ENG.). (YA). (gr. 9-17). 2020. 384p. pap. 10.99 *(978-0-316-44926-7(1))* 2019. 368p. 18.99 *(978-0-316-44927-4(X))* Little Brown & Co. (Jimmy Patterson).

McClellan, Rachel. Escape to Eden. 2016. (ENG.). 295p. (YA). pap. 17.99 *(978-1-4621-1777-2(5)*, Sweetwater Bks.) Cedar Fort, Inc./CFI Distribution.

McClymer, Kelly. Must Love Black. 2008. (ENG.). 192p. (YA). (gr. 7-18). pap. 8.99 *(978-1-4169-4903-9(8)*, Simon Pulse) Simon Pulse.

McCranie, Stephen. Stephen Mccranie's Space Boy Volume 2. McCranie, Stephen, illus. 2018. (Illus.). 240p. (J). (gr. 5-9). pap. 12.99 *(978-1-5067-0680-1(0)*, Dark Horse Books) Dark Horse Comics.

—Stephen Mccranie's Space Boy Volume 3. McCranie, Stephen, illus. 2019. (ENG., Illus.). 240p. (J). (gr. 5-9). pap. 12.99 *(978-1-5067-0842-3(0)*, Dark Horse Books) Dark Horse Comics.

Mcdonald, Megan. Solar System Superhero. 2013. (Stink Ser.: 5). lib. bdg. 14.75 *(978-0-606-31591-3(8))* Turtleback.

McDougal, Anna. Sam's Solar Panels: If... Then, 1 vol. 2017. (Computer Science for the Real World Ser.). (ENG.). 16p. (gr. 2-3). pap. *(978-1-5383-5224-3(9)*, f3c44c6e-c64d-4306-b3c2-c27ff7616080, Rosen Classroom) Rosen Publishing Group, Inc., The.

McDougall, Sophia. Mars Evacuees. 2015. (ENG.). 416p. (J). (gr. 3-7). 16.99 *(978-0-06-229399-2(0)*, HarperCollins) HarperCollins Pubs.

McElligott, Matthew. Mad Scientist Academy: the Space Disaster. (Mad Scientist Academy Ser.: 3). 40p. (J). (gr. k-3). 2019. 8.99 *(978-0-553-52385-0(6)*, Dragonfly Bks.) 2017. (Illus.). 17.99 *(978-0-553-52382-9(1)*, Crown Books For Young Readers) Random Hse. Children's Bks.

Mcentire, Myra. Hourglass, 1. 2012. (Hourglass Ser.). (ENG.). 400p. (YA). (gr. 9-12). 26.19 *(978-1-60684-144-0(0))* Farshore GBR. Dist: Children's Plus, Inc.

McFarland, Kim. A Refugee in Oz. 2010. 164p. pap. 11.95 *(978-0-557-48706-6(4))* Lulu Pr., Inc.

McGee, Katharine. The Dazzling Heights. 2017. (Thousandth Floor Ser.: 2). (ENG.). 432p. (YA). (gr. 8). 18.99 *(978-0-06-241862-3(9)*, HarperCollins) HarperCollins Pubs.

—The Thousandth Floor. (Thousandth Floor Ser.: 1). (ENG.). (YA). (gr. 8). 2017. 496p. pap. 11.99 *(978-0-06-241860-9(2))* 2016. 448p. 18.99 *(978-0-06-241859-3(9))* HarperCollins Pubs. (HarperCollins).

McGee, Krista. Revolutionary, 1 vol. 2014. (Anomaly Ser.: 3). (ENG.). 320p. (YA). pap. 14.99 *(978-1-4016-8876-9(4))* Nelson, Thomas Inc.

McGoran, Jon. Spliked. 2020. (Spliced Ser.: 3). 352p. (YA). (gr. 9). 18.99 *(978-0-8234-4091-7(5))* Holiday Hse., Inc.

—Spliced. (Spliced Ser.: 1). (YA). 2019. 416p. (gr. 7). pap. 9.99 *(978-0-8234-4234-8(9))* 2017. (ENG.). 400p. (gr. 9). 18.95 *(978-0-8234-3855-6(4))* Holiday Hse., Inc.

—Splintered. 2019. (Spliced Ser.: 2). 352p. (YA). (gr. 9). 18.99 *(978-0-8234-4090-0(7))* Holiday Hse., Inc.

McGowan, Maureen. Compliance, 0 vols. 2014. (Dust Chronicles Ser.: 2). (ENG.). 386p. (J). (gr. 7-12). pap. 9.99 *(978-1-4778-1696-7(8)*, 9781477816967, Skyscape) Amazon Publishing.

—Deviants, 0 vols. 2012. (Dust Chronicles Ser.: 1). (ENG.). 322p. (YA). (gr. 7-12). pap. 9.99 *(978-1-4778-1032-3(3)*, 9781477810323, Skyscape) Amazon Publishing.

—Glory, 0 vols. 2014. (Dust Chronicles Ser.: 3). (ENG.). 326p. (J). (gr. 7-12). pap. 9.99 *(978-1-4778-4797-8(9)*, 9781477847978, Skyscape) Amazon Publishing.

McGrath, Robin. Livyers World. 2007. (ENG.). 150p. (J). (gr. 4-7). per. *(978-1-897174-15-9(2))* Breakwater Bks., Ltd.

McGuiness, Dan. The Next Adventure, 2. 2011. (Pilot & Huxley Ser.: 2). (ENG.). 64p. (J). (gr. 3-6). 24.94 *(978-0-545-26845-5(1))* Scholastic, Inc.

McIntosh, Will. Watchdog. 2019. (ENG.). 192p. (J). (gr. 5). 8.99 *(978-1-5247-1387-4(2)*, Yearling) Random Hse. Children's Bks.

McKeever, Sean & Lee, Stan. Doom with a View! Norton, Mike, illus. 2007. (Spider-Man Ser.: No. 2). (ENG.). 24p. (J). (gr. 2-6). lib. bdg. 31.36 *(978-1-59961-208-9(9)*, 13620, Marvel Age) Spotlight.

McLaughlin, Lauren. Scored. 2012. (ENG.). 240p. (YA). (gr. 9). pap. 10.99 *(978-0-375-86791-0(0)*, Ember) Random Hse. Children's Bks.

McMann, Lisa. Going Wild. (Going Wild Ser.: 1). (ENG.). (J). (gr. 3-7). 2017. 400p. pap. 6.99 *(978-0-06-233715-3(7))* 2016. (Illus.). 384p. 16.99 *(978-0-06-233714-6(9))* HarperCollins Pubs. (HarperCollins).

—Going Wild #2: Predator vs. Prey. 2017. (Going Wild Ser.: 2). (ENG.). 400p. (J). (gr. 3-7). 16.99 *(978-0-06-233717-7(3)*, HarperCollins) HarperCollins Pubs.

—Map of Flames (the Forgotten Five, Book 1) 2022. (Forgotten Five Ser.: 1). (J). (gr. 3-7). (ENG.). 400p. 9.99 *(978-0-593-32542-1(7))*; 384p. 17.99 *(978-0-593-32540-7(0))* Penguin Young Readers Group. (G.P. Putnam's Sons Books for Young Readers).

McMullen, Sean. Before the Storm. 2009. 262p. (Orig.). pap. *(978-1-879462-50-2(8))* Ford Street Publishing Pty, Limited.

McNichol, John. The Tripods Attack! 2008. (Young Chesterton Chronicles Ser.). 367p. (YA). (gr. 8-12). pap. 17.95 *(978-1-933184-26-5(4))* Sophia Institute Pr.

McOmber, Rachel B., ed. McOmber Phonics Storybooks: Tale of the Green Glob. rev. ed. (Illus.). (J). *(978-0-944991-65-7(3))* Swift Learning Resources.

McQuestion, Karen. From a Distant Star, 0 vols. 2015. (ENG.). 280p. (YA). (gr. 7-12). pap. 9.99 *(978-1-4778-3016-1(2)*, 9781477830161, Skyscape) Amazon Publishing.

McTrustry, Chris. Cleopatra's Report, 1 vol. rev. ed. 2013. (Literary Text Ser.). (ENG., Illus.). 32p. (J). (gr. 2-4). pap. 11.99 *(978-1-4333-5639-1(2))* Teacher Created Materials, Inc.

Meachen Rau, Dana. Mi Lugar Preferido: My Special Space. Kim, Julie J., illus. 2005. (Rookie Reader Español Ser.). 32p. (gr. k-2). 19.50 *(978-0-516-25250-6(X)*, Children's Pr.) Scholastic Library Publishing.

Meadows, Daisy. Marissa the Science Fairy. 2018. 64p. (J). (gr. 1-4). 15.36 *(978-1-64310-189-7(7))* Penworthy Co., LLC, The.

—Marissa the Science Fairy. 2016. (Rainbow Magic — the School Day Fairies Ser.: 1). lib. bdg. 14.75 *(978-0-606-38789-7(7))* Turtleback.

Mears, Richard Chase. Saint Nick & the Space Nicks. Westerfield, William Stephen, illus. l.t. ed. 2004. 32p. (J). 16.95 *(978-0-9754056-0-4(8))* Tuxedo Blue, LLC.

Meddaugh, Susan. Space Dogs. 2012. (Martha Speaks Ser.). (ENG., Illus.). 96p. (J). (gr. 1-4). 14.99 *(978-0-547-68119-1(4))*; pap. 5.99 *(978-0-547-68118-4(6))* Houghton Mifflin Harcourt Publishing Co.

Medina, Kathleen. Born into Greyworld. 2008. 220p. 29.99 *(978-1-4363-2619-3(2))*; pap. 19.99 *(978-1-4363-2618-6(4))* Xlibris Corp.

Meehan, William. Amulets of Acacia. 2003. 184p. pap. 13.95 *(978-0-595-27163-4(4))* iUniverse, Inc.

Melbourne, Lois. The STEM Club Goes Exploring. 2016. (ENG., Illus.). 48p. 15.95 *(978-1-62634-303-0(9))* Greenleaf Book Group.

Menge, Dawn & Rhoades, Heath. Queen Vernita Meets Sir HeathyBean the Astronomer. 2010. 33p. (J). pap. 19.95 *(978-1-4327-3120-5(3))* Outskirts Pr., Inc.

Messner, Kate. Wake up Missing. 2014. (ENG.). 288p. (YA). (gr. 5-8). pap. 8.99 *(978-0-8027-3748-9(X)*, 900135674, Bloomsbury USA Childrens) Bloomsbury Publishing USA.

Metzger, Joanna. The Space Program. Elizalde, Marcelo, illus. 2006. 142p. (J). *(978-1-59336-695-7(7))* Mondo Publishing.

Meyer, Marissa. Archenemies. 2018. (Renegades Ser.: 2). (ENG.). 496p. (YA). 19.99 *(978-1-250-07830-8(X)*, 900153576); 474p. (J). *(978-1-250-21418-8(1))* Feiwel & Friends.

—Archenemies. 2021. (Renegades Ser.: 2). (ENG.). 512p. (YA). pap. 12.99 *(978-1-250-07837-7(7)*, 900153626) Square Fish.

—Archenemies. 2018. (Renegades Ser.: Vol. 2). (ENG.). (YA). (gr. 7-12). pap. 11.99 *(978-1-250-31742-1(8))* St. Martin's Pr.

—Cinder. l.t. ed. 2012. (Lunar Chronicles: Bk. 1). (ENG.). 517p. (J). (gr. 7-12). 23.99 *(978-1-4104-4607-7(7))* Thorndike Pr.

—Cinder. 2013. (Lunar Chronicles Ser.: 1). (YA). lib. bdg. 20.85 *(978-0-606-28633-6(0))* Turtleback.

—Cinder. 2015. (Cinder Ser.: 1). (SPA.). 416p. (YA). (gr. 9-12). pap. 20.99 *(978-987-612-927-5(9))* V&R Editoras.

—Cinder: Book One of the Lunar Chronicles. 2012. (Lunar Chronicles Ser.: 1). (ENG.). 400p. (YA). (gr. 7-12). 24.99 *(978-0-312-64189-4(3)*, 900078307) Feiwel & Friends.

—Cinder: Book One of the Lunar Chronicles. 2020. (Lunar Chronicles Ser.: 1). (ENG.). 448p. (YA). pap. 11.99 *(978-1-250-76888-9(8)*, 900233163) Square Fish.

—Cress. 2014. (YA). (Lunar Chronicles Ser.: 3). (ENG.). 560p. (gr. 7-12). 24.99 *(978-0-312-64297-6(0)*, 900078310); 552p. *(978-1-250-05632-0(2))* Feiwel & Friends.

—Fairest: Levana's Story. 2016. (Lunar Chronicles Ser.: 0). (YA). lib. bdg. 20.85 *(978-0-606-38438-4(3))* Turtleback.

—Fairest: The Lunar Chronicles: Levana's Story. 2015. (YA). 222p. *(978-1-250-06959-7(9))*; (ENG.). 272p. (gr. 7-12). 19.99 *(978-1-250-06055-6(9)*, 900141423) Feiwel & Friends.

—Renegades. 2017. (Renegades Ser.: 1). (ENG.). 576p. (YA). 21.99 *(978-1-250-04466-2(9)*, 900128560) Feiwel & Friends.

—Renegades. 2018. (Renegades Ser.: 1). (ENG.). 592p. (YA). pap. 12.99 *(978-1-250-18063-6(5)*, 900190235) Square Fish.

—Scarlet. 2013. (Lunar Chronicles Ser.: 2). (ENG.). 464p. (YA). (gr. 7). 19.99 *(978-0-312-64296-9(2)*, 900078309) Feiwel & Friends.

—Scarlet. l.t. ed. 2013. (Lunar Chronicles: Bk. 2). (ENG.). 572p. 23.99 *(978-1-4104-5623-6(4))* Thorndike Pr.

—Scarlet. 2014. (Lunar Chronicles Ser.: 2). (YA). lib. bdg. 20.85 *(978-0-606-35097-6(7))* Turtleback.

—Scarlet. 2016. (SPA.). 430p. (YA). (gr. 9-12). pap. 20.99 *(978-987-612-990-9(2))* V&R Editoras.

—Stars Above. 2016. (ENG.). 336p. (YA). pap. *(978-1-250-10445-8(9))* Feiwel & Friends.

—Stars above: a Lunar Chronicles Collection. 2016. (Lunar Chronicles Ser.). (ENG.). 400p. (YA). (gr. 7-12). 19.99 *(978-1-250-09184-0(5)*, 900159565) Feiwel & Friends.

—Supernova. 2019. (Renegades Ser.: 3). (ENG.). 560p. (YA). 19.99 *(978-1-250-07838-4(5)*, 900153627) Feiwel & Friends.

—Winter. 2015. (Lunar Chronicles Ser.: 4). (ENG.). 832p. (YA). (gr. 7-12). 28.99 *(978-0-312-64298-3(9)*, 900078311) Feiwel & Friends.

—Winter. 2018. (Lunar Chronicles Ser.: 4). (YA). lib. bdg. 24.50 *(978-0-606-40586-7(0))* Turtleback.

—Wires & Nerve: Volume 1. Holgate, Douglas, illus. 2017. (Wires & Nerve Ser.: 1). (ENG.). 240p. (YA). 21.99 *(978-1-250-07826-1(1)*, 900153572) Feiwel & Friends.

—Wires & Nerve, Volume 2: Gone Rogue. Gilpin, Stephen, illus. 2018. (Wires & Nerve Ser.: 2). (ENG.). 336p. (YA). 21.99 *(978-1-250-07828-5(8)*, 900153574) Feiwel & Friends.

Micheline, David, et al. Freemind - The Origin. 2003. (Freemind Ser.). (Illus.). 112p. 14.95 *(978-0-9744225-0-3(9))* Future Comics.

Mikumo, Gakuto. Strike the Blood, Vol. 6 (light Novel) Return of the Alchemist. 2017. (Strike the Blood (light Novel) Ser.: 6). (ENG., Illus.). 224p. (YA). (gr. 8-17). pap. 14.00 *(978-0-316-34558-3(X)*, Yen Pr.) Yen Pr. LLC.

Milam, Mary Kay. The Zooming Star Babies. Date not set. (J). pap. *(978-1-890622-65-7(6))* Leathers Publishing.

Milan, Maura. Eclipse the Skies. 2019. (Ignite the Stars Ser.: 2). (ENG.). 400p. (YA). (gr. 8-12). 17.99 *(978-0-8075-3638-4(5)*, 807536385) Whitman, Albert & Co.

—Ignite the Stars. (Ignite the Stars Ser.: 1). (ENG.). 400p. (YA). (gr. 8-12). 2019. pap. 9.99 *(978-0-8075-3627-8(X)*, 080753627X) 2018. 17.99 *(978-0-8075-3625-4(3)*, 807536253) Whitman, Albert & Co.

Miles, Brenda S. & Sweet, Susan D. Cinderstella: A Tale of Planets Not Princes. Docampo, Valeria, illus. 2016. 32p. (J). *(978-1-4338-2270-4(9)*, Magination Pr.) American Psychological Assn.

Milky, D. J. Karma Club Novel, 4 vols., Vol. 1. McAdoo, Tyson, illus. 2007. (Karma Club Novel Ser.: 1). (ENG.). 184p. (gr. 7-1). pap. 9.99 *(978-1-59182-263-9(7)*, fe098df8-7874-42d6-ab1e-440f30df2db7) TOKYOPOP, Inc.

Miller, John Jackson, et al. Star Wars - Knights of the Old Republic, 9 vols., Vol. 1. 2007. (Illus.). 152p. *(978-1-84576-371-8(8))* Titan Bks. Ltd.

Miller, Larry W., Jr. Droptroopers: Gauntlet of Fear. 2007. 208p. per. 14.95 *(978-0-595-47591-9(4))* iUniverse, Inc.

Miller, Lauren. Parallel. 2013. (ENG.). 432p. (YA). (gr. 8). 17.99 *(978-0-06-219977-5(3)*, HarperTeen) HarperCollins Pubs.

Miller, Michael & Strickland, AdriAnne. Shadow Run. 2018. (ENG.). 416p. (YA). (gr. 7). pap. 10.99 *(978-0-399-55256-4(1)*, Ember) Random Hse. Children's Bks.

Miller, Sam J. The Art of Starving. (ENG.). (YA). (gr. 8). 2019. 400p. pap. 10.99 *(978-0-06-245672-4(5))* 2017. 384p. 18.99 *(978-0-06-245671-7(7))* HarperCollins Pubs. (HarperTeen).

Miller, Wray. Cerulean Blue. 2003. 506p. (YA). per. 18.95 *(978-0-9723948-1-9(8))* MillerWrite, Inc.

Millet, Lydia. The Shimmers in the Night: A Novel. 2012. (Dissenters Ser.). (ENG.). 256p. (J). (gr. 3-7). 16.95 *(978-1-931520-78-2(X)*, Big Mouth Hse.) Small Beer Pr.

Millett, Peter. Meltdown 4 Voyagers. Campos, Leo, illus. 2017. (Cambridge Reading Adventures Ser.). (ENG.). 32p. pap. 8.30 *(978-1-108-43485-0(1))* Cambridge Univ. Pr.

Millici, Nate. Chaos at the Castle. 2018. (World of Reading Ser.). (ENG.). 29p. (J). (gr. -1-1). 13.89 *(978-1-64310-776-9(3))* Penworthy Co., LLC, The.

—Star Wars: Finn & Poe Team Up! Parisi, Andrea & Krysinski, Grzegorz, illus. 2017. (World of Reading Level 1 Ser.). (ENG.). 32p. (J). (gr. -1-3). 31.36 *(978-1-5321-4054-9(1)*, 25426) Spotlight.

Millici, Nate, et al. Star Wars. Roux, Stéphane, illus. 2017. (J). *(978-1-368-01493-9(3))* Disney Publishing Worldwide.

Mindler, Jason. Giralon. 2003. 122p. (YA). 20.95 *(978-0-595-74854-9(6))*; pap. 10.95 *(978-0-595-28581-5(3))* iUniverse, Inc. (Writers Club Pr.).

Mitchell, J. Barton. Midnight City: A Conquered Earth Novel. 2013. (Conquered Earth Ser.: 1). (ENG.). 400p. (YA). (gr. 7-12). pap. 25.99 *(978-1-250-03628-5(3)*, 900121938, St. Martin's Griffin) St. Martin's Pr.

—Valley of Fires: A Conquered Earth Novel. 2014. (Conquered Earth Ser.: 3). (ENG.). 416p. (YA). (gr. 7-12). 36.99 *(978-1-250-00948-7(0)*, 900084097, Dunne, Thomas Bks.) St. Martin's Pr.

Miyazaki, Yuu. The Asterisk War, Vol. 1 (light Novel) Encounter with a Fiery Princess. 2016. (Asterisk War Ser.: 1). (ENG., Illus.). 192p. (YA). (gr. 8-17). pap. 14.00 *(978-0-316-31527-2(3)*, Yen Pr.) Yen Pr. LLC.

—The Asterisk War, Vol. 2 (light Novel) Awakening of Silver Beauty, Vol. 2. 2016. (Asterisk War Ser.: 2). (ENG., Illus.). 176p. (YA). (gr. 8-17). pap. 14.00 *(978-0-316-39858-9(6)*, Yen Pr.) Yen Pr. LLC.

Mlynowski, Sarah. Bras & Broomsticks. 2006. (Magic in Manhattan Ser.: 1). (ENG.). 320p. (YA). (gr. 7-12). reprint ed. pap. 9.99 *(978-0-385-73184-3(1)*, Delacorte Pr.) Random Hse. Children's Bks.

Moesta, Rebecca & Anderson, Kevin J. Space Station Crisis. 2011. (Star Challengers Ser.). 184p. (J). (gr. 4-7). 11.99 *(978-1-934857-66-3(1)*, Catalyst Game Labs) InMediaRes Productions.

Moesta, Rebecca, et al. Star Challengers Trilogy. 2013. (J). pap. 18.99 *(978-1-61475-124-3(2)*, WordFire Pr.) WordFire Pr.

S

Mohr, L. C. Krumbuckets. Musheno, Erica, illus. 2007. (ENG.). 144p. (J). (gr. 2-7). 13.95 (978-0-9769417-6-7(7)) Blooming Tree Pr.

Monda, Joseph, creator. The Unnaturals. 2007. (Illus.). 32p. (YA). 3.50 (978-0-615-15138-0(8)) Wild Mind Creations.

Monir, Alexandra. The Final Six. 2018. (ENG.). 352p. (YA). (gr. 9). 18.99 (978-0-06-265894-4(8), HarperTeen) HarperCollins Pubs.

Monsters of Men (with Bonus Short Story) Chaos Walking: Book Three. 2014. (Chaos Walking Ser.: 3). (ENG., Illus.). 656p. (YA). (gr. 9). pap. 14.00 (978-0-7636-7619-3(5)) Candlewick Pr.

Montgomery, Anson. Moon Quest. Semionov, Vladimir, illus. 2008. (ENG.). 144p. (J). (gr. 4-8). pap. 7.99 (978-1-933390-26-0(3)) Chooseco LLC.

Montgomery, R. A. Beyond Escape. 2005. (Choose Your Own Adventure Ser.). (Illus.). 118p. (gr. 4-8). pap. 5.50 (978-0-7608-9703-4(4)) Sundance/Newbridge Educational Publishing.

—Beyond Escape! Millet, Jason, illus. 2006. (ENG.). 144p. (J). (gr. 4-8). per. 7.99 (978-1-933390-15-4(8), CHCL15) Chooseco LLC.

—The Brilliant Dr. Wogan. 2005. (Choose Your Own Adventure Ser.). (Illus.). 112p. (J). (gr. 4-8). pap. 5.50 (978-0-7608-9705-8(0)) Sundance/Newbridge Educational Publishing.

—The Brilliant Dr. Wogan. Trod, Mariano et al, illus. 2006. (ENG.). 144p. (J). (gr. 4-8). per. 7.99 (978-1-933390-17-8(4), CHC:17) Chooseco LLC.

—Escape. 2005. (Illus.). 127p. (J). pap. (978-0-7608-9696-9(8)) Sundance/Newbridge Educational Publishing.

—Forecast from Stonehenge. Semionov, Vladimir, illus. 2007. (ENG.). 144p. (J). (gr. 4-8). pap. 7.99 (978-1-933390-19-2(0)) Chooseco LLC.

—Prisoner of the Ant People. 2007. 144p. (J). pap. (978-1-86504-932-8(8)) Chooseco LLC.

—Prisoner of the Ant People. Millet, Jason, illus. 2006. (ENG.). 144p. (J). (gr. 4-8). per. 7.99 (978-1-933390-10-9(7), CHCL10) Chooseco LLC.

—Prisoner of the Ant People. 2005. (Illus.). 115p. (J). pap. (978-0-7608-9698-3(4)) Sundance/Newbridge Educational Publishing.

—Project UFO. Semionov, Vladimir & Cannella, Marco, illus. 2008. (ENG.). 144p. (J). (gr. 4-8). pap. 7.99 (978-1-933390-27-7(1)) Chooseco LLC.

—Space & Beyond. Pornkerd, Vorrarit et al, illus. 2006. (ENG.). 144p. (J). (gr. 4-8). pap. 7.99 (978-1-933390-03-1(4), CHCL03) Chooseco LLC.

—Space Pup. Newton, Keith, illus. 2014. (ENG.). 80p. (J). (gr. 2-2). pap. 8.99 (978-1-937133-43-6(5)) Chooseco LLC.

—War with the Evil Power Master. 2005. (Illus.). 123p. (J). pap. (978-0-7608-9700-3(X)) Sundance/Newbridge Educational Publishing.

—War with the Evil Power Master. Millet, Jason, illus. 2006. (ENG.). 144p. (J). (gr. 4-8). per. 7.99 (978-1-933390-12-3(3), CHCL12) Chooseco LLC.

Montgomery, R. A. & Gilligan, Shannon. Gus vs. the Robot King. Newton, Keith, illus. 2014. (ENG.). 80p. (J). (gr. 3-3). pap. 7.99 (978-1-937133-44-3(3)) Chooseco LLC.

Monti, Joe, ed. Diverse Energies: By 11 Speculative Fiction Authors, 1 vol. 2012. (ENG.). 368p. (YA). 19.95 (978-1-60060-887-2(6), Tu Bks.) Lee & Low Bks., Inc.

Montijo, Rhode. Chews Your Destiny. 2017. (Gum Girl Ser.: 1). (J). lib. bdg. 16.00 (978-0-606-39969-2(0)) Turtleback.

Moore, Stephanie Perry. Getting Home 2018. (Attack on Earth Ser.). (ENG.). 104p. (YA). (gr. 6-12). pap. 7.99 (978-1-5415-2628-0(7), 6c7038c6-4bf9-4551-b3f6-a8e5fdd1c3f5); lib. bdg. 26.65 (978-1-5415-2575-7(2), 300dbd6a-844a-436f-b919-a2b2b67e6f26) Lerner Publishing Group. (Darby Creek).

Mooring, John L. Cricket's Chronicles: The Third Grade Science Fair. 2010. 24p. pap. 12.99 (978-1-4490-3278-4(8)) AuthorHouse.

Mordenga, Michael P. Spirit Box. 2007. 280p. per. 17.95 (978-0-595-43785-6(0)) iUniverse, Inc.

Moreau, Chris. The Professor's Telescope. Marek, Jane, illus. 2006. (YA). 10.95 (978-0-9785399-0-0(7)); cd-rom 7.95 (978-0-9785399-2-4(3)) Windows of Discovery.

Moreira, Carol. Membrane. 2013. 282p. pap. (978-1-927746-04-2(3)) Fierce ink Pr. Co-Op, Ltd.

Morgan, Kass. Day 21. (100 Ser.: 2). (ENG.). 320p. (YA). (gr. 10-17). 2015. pap. 12.99 (978-0-316-23457-3(5)) 2014. 18.00 (978-0-316-23455-9(9)) Little, Brown Bks. for Young Readers.

—Homecoming. 2015. (100 Ser.: 3). (ENG.). 352p. (YA). (gr. 10-17). pap. 12.99 (978-0-316-38196-3(9)) Little, Brown Bks. for Young Readers.

—Light Years. 2018. (ENG.). 384p. (YA). E-Book (978-0-316-51046-2(7)) Little Brown & Co.

—Light Years. (Light Years Ser.: 1). (ENG.). (YA). (gr. 9-17). 2019. 416p. pap. 10.99 (978-0-316-51043-1(2)) 2018. 384p. 17.99 (978-0-316-51044-8(0)) Little, Brown Bks. for Young Readers.

—Supernova. 2019. (ENG.). 368p. (YA). (gr. 9-17). 18.99 (978-0-316-51051-6(3)) Little, Brown Bks. for Young Readers.

Moriarty, Chris. The Inquisitor's Apprentice. Geyer, Mark Edward, illus. 2013. (ENG.). 352p. (J). (gr. 5-7). pap. 7.99 (978-0-547-85084-9(0), 1501042, Clarion Bks.) HarperCollins Pubs.

Morphew, Chris. Life in the Flames, Volume 3. 2017. (Phoenix Files Ser.: 3). (ENG.). 672p. (YA). (gr. 7). pap. 12.99 (978-1-76012-427-4(3)) Hardie Grant Children?s Publishing AUS. Dist: Independent Pubs. Group.

—The Phoenix Files, Contact. 2013. 320p. (YA). pap. 6.99 (978-1-61067-092-0(2)) Kane Miller.

Morrison, Michele. The Comet's Tale. 2007. (ENG.). 136p. pap. 16.95 (978-1-84753-634-1(4)) Lulu Pr., Inc.

Morse, Scott. Magic Pickle: a Graphic Novel. Morse, Scott, illus. 2008. (ENG., Illus.). 112p. (J). (gr. 2-5). pap. 9.99 (978-0-439-87995-8(7), Graphix) Scholastic, Inc.

Moss, Marissa. Max Disaster #3: Alien Eraser Reveals the Secrets of Evolution. Moss, Marissa, illus. 2009. (ENG., Illus.). 56p. (J). (gr. 3-7). 15.99 (978-0-7636-3579-4(0)); pap. 6.99 (978-0-7636-4419-2(6)) Candlewick Pr.

Mould, Paul, ed. The Magnificent Six. 2007. (Illus.). 52p. pap. (978-1-58690-048-9(X)) Mould, Paul Publishing.

Moyer, Jenny. Flashfall. 2016. (Flashfall Ser.: 1). (ENG., Illus.). 352p. (YA). 29.99 (978-1-62779-481-7(6), 900152138, Holt, Henry & Co. Bks. For Young Readers) Holt, Henry & Co.

Mueller, Richard. Zoonauts: The Secret of Animalville. Gosline, Sheldon, ed. Dal Chele, Egido Victor, illus. 2003. 210p. (J). 14.95 (978-0-9719496-6-9(2)) Shangri-La Pubns.

Muller, Jean Powers. Rudolph's Sniffalator. 2011. 20p. pap. 13.77 (978-1-4269-7065-8(X)) Trafford Publishing.

Mullin, Mike. Ashen Winter. 2013. (Ashfall Ser.). (ENG.). 580p. (YA). (gr. 6). pap. 13.99 (978-1-933718-98-9(6)) Tanglewood Pr.

—Ashfall. (Ashfall Ser.). (ENG.). 476p. (gr. 8). 2012. (YA). pap. 13.99 (978-1-933718-74-3(9)) 2011. (J). 17.95 (978-1-933718-55-2(2)) Tanglewood Pr.

Munzel, Alexander. Allí Donde Florece el Cardo Sagrado/Where the Holy Thistle Blooms. 2003. (SPA., Illus.). 196p. (J). per. (978-0-9672566-2-7(3)) Technical Software, Inc.

Murguia, Bethanie Deeney. I Feel Five! Murguia, Bethanie Deeney, illus. 2014. (ENG., Illus.). 32p. (J). (gr. -1-3). 15.99 (978-0-7636-6291-2(7)) Candlewick Pr.

Murray, Helen. Stop the Stone Monsters! 2017. (Illus.). 24p. (J). (978-1-5182-3635-8(9)) Dorling Kindersley Publishing, Inc.

My Teacher Glows in the Dark. 2014. (My Teacher Bks.: 3). (ENG., Illus.). 192p. (J). (gr. 3-7). 17.99 (978-1-4814-0432-7(6), Simon & Schuster/Paula Wiseman Bks.) Simon & Schuster/Paula Wiseman Bks.

Myklusch, Matt. The Accidental Hero. 2011. (Jack Blank Adventure Ser.: 1). (ENG., Illus.). 496p. (J). (gr. 3-7). pap. 9.99 (978-1-4169-9562-3(5), Aladdin) Simon & Schuster Children's Publishing.

—Jack Blank & the Imagine Nation. 2010. (Jack Blank Adventure Ser.: Bk. 1). (ENG., Illus.). 480p. (J). (gr. 3-7). 19.99 (978-1-4169-9561-6(7), Aladdin) Simon & Schuster Children's Publishing.

Naderi, Babak. The Adventures of Captain Zero. 2009. 16p. pap. 9.00 (978-1-4251-8693-7(9)) Trafford Publishing.

—King of the Universe. 2013. (ENG.). 24p. pap. 14.95 (978-1-4669-8136-2(9)) Trafford Publishing.

Nagatsuki, Tappei. Re:ZERO -Starting Life in Another World-Ex, Vol. 1 (light Novel) The Dream of the Lion King. 2017. (Re:ZERO Ex (light Novel) Ser.: 1). (ENG., Illus.). 224p. (YA). (gr. 8-17). pap. 14.00 (978-0-316-41290-2(2), Yen Pr.) Yen Pr. LLC.

—Re:ZERO -Starting Life in Another World-, Vol. 2 (light Novel), Vol. 2. 2016. (Re:ZERO -Starting Life in Another World- Ser.: 2). (ENG., Illus.). 256p. (YA). (gr. 8-17). pap. 14.00 (978-0-316-39837-4(3), Yen Pr.) Yen Pr. LLC.

—Re:ZERO -Starting Life in Another World-, Vol. 4 (light Novel) 2017. (Re:ZERO -Starting Life in Another World- Ser.: 4). (ENG., Illus.). 248p. (gr. 8-17). pap. 14.00 (978-0-316-39842-8(X), Yen Pr.) Yen Pr. LLC.

Nancy, Farmer. The House of the Scorpion. 2014. (ENG.). 400p. (YA). (gr. 3-6). 14.24 (978-1-63245-268-9(5)) Lectorum Pubns., Inc.

Nayeri, Daniel. Straw House, Wood House, Brick House, Blow: Four Novellas by Daniel Nayeri. 2011. (ENG., Illus.). 432p. (YA). (gr. 9). 19.99 (978-0-7636-5526-6(0)) Candlewick Pr.

Neilson, G. E. F. Cosmic Aviators - Book 1 - Flight Edition. 2013. 288p. pap. (978-0-9576132-5-6(3)) Buzzword Pr.

—Cosmic Aviators - Nathaniel's 1st Adventure. 2013. 248p. (978-0-9576132-4-9(5)); 332p. pap. (978-0-9576132-0-1(2)) Buzzword Pr.

Nelson, O. T. The Girl Who Owned a City: Graphic Novel. Delk, Chrissy, illus. 2012. (Single Titles Ser.). (ENG.). 128p. (YA). (gr. 5-12). lib. bdg. 29.27 (978-0-7613-4903-7(0), Graphic Universe™) Lerner Publishing Group.

Nelson, O. T. (Terry). The Girl Who Owned a City. 2012. (ENG.). 208p. (YA). (gr. 5-12). pap. 9.99 (978-0-7613-5086-6(1), 7994c097-e4ac-4e65-a42b-ee32768ba735, Carolrhoda Bks.) Lerner Publishing Group.

Nesbit, E. The Seven Dragons & Other Stories. 2006. 140p. 24.95 (978-1-59818-171-5(8)) Aegypan.

Ness, Patrick. Chaos Walking Movie Tie-In Edition: the Knife of Never Letting Go. 2020. (Chaos Walking Ser.: 1). (ENG.). 496p. (YA). (gr. 9). pap. 12.00 (978-1-5362-0052-2(2)) Candlewick Pr.

—Chaos Walking: the Complete Trilogy: Books 1-3, 3 vols. 2018. (Chaos Walking Ser.). (ENG.). 1744p. (YA). (gr. 9). pap. 36.00 (978-1-5362-0706-4(3)) Candlewick Pr.

—The Knife of Never Letting Go. 2018. (Chaos Walking Ser.: 1). (ENG.). 496p. (YA). (gr. 9). 24.99 (978-1-5362-0053-9(0)) Candlewick Pr.

—The Knife of Never Letting Go. 2010. 20.00 (978-1-60686-704-4(0)) Perfection Learning Corp.

—The Knife of Never Letting Go. 2014. (Chaos Walking Ser.: 1). 479p. lib. bdg. 22.10 (978-0-606-35873-6(0)) Turtleback.

Ness, Patrick & Benedict, A. K. Class: the Stone House. 2017. (Class Ser.: 1). (ENG.). (YA). (gr. 8). 288p. pap. 9.99 (978-0-06-266618-5(5)); 272p. 17.99 (978-0-06-266617-8(7)) HarperCollins Pubs. (Quill Tree Bks.).

Nesworthy, Lauren. Darth Vader, Rebel Hunter! 2016. (Illus.). 48p. (J). (978-1-5182-1849-1(0)) Dorling Kindersley Publishing, Inc.

Nettrour, Nelani. Nunkey's Adventures, Bk. 1. Nettrour, Autumn, illus. 2003. 70p. (J). pap. 11.95 (978-1-929381-17-3(4), Third Millennium Publishing) Sci Fi-Arizona, Inc.

Nevins, Paul. Dante's War. 2003. 168p. (YA). pap. 12.95 (978-0-595-26743-9(2), Writers Club Pr.) iUniverse, Inc.

Newsome, Eric. The Adventures of Eric: Starry Beginnings. 2009. 51p. pap. 14.95 (978-1-4327-4075-7(X)) Outskirts Pr., Inc.

Newton, A. I. The Alien Next Door 2: Aliens for Dinner?! Sarkar, Anjan, illus. 2018. (Alien Next Door Ser.: 2). (ENG.). 112p. (J). (gr. k-3). 16.99 (978-1-4998-0562-8(4)); pap. 5.99 (978-1-4998-0561-1(6)) Little Bee Books Inc.

—The Alien Next Door 3: Alien Scout. Sarkar, Anjan, illus. 2018. (Alien Next Door Ser.: 3). (ENG.). 112p. (J). (gr. k-3). 16.99 (978-1-4998-0581-9(0)); pap. 5.99 (978-1-4998-0580-2(2)) Little Bee Books Inc.

—The Alien Next Door 4: Trick or Cheat? Sarkar, Anjan, illus. 2018. (Alien Next Door Ser.: 4). (ENG.). 112p. (J). (gr. k-3). 16.99 (978-1-4998-0584-0(5)); pap. 5.99 (978-1-4998-0583-3(7)) Little Bee Books Inc.

—The Alien Next Door 5: Baseball Blues. Sarkar, Anjan, illus. 2018. (Alien Next Door Ser.: 5). (ENG.). 112p. (J). (gr. k-3). 16.99 (978-1-4998-0723-3(6)); pap. 5.99 (978-1-4998-0722-6(8)) Little Bee Books Inc.

—The Alien Next Door 6: the Mystery Valentine. Sarkar, Anjan, illus. 2018. (Alien Next Door Ser.: 6). (ENG.). 112p. (J). (gr. k-3). 16.99 (978-1-4998-0726-4(0)); pap. 5.99 (978-1-4998-0725-7(2)) Little Bee Books Inc.

—The Alien Next Door 7: up, up, & Away! Sarkar, Anjan, illus. 2019. (Alien Next Door Ser.: 7). (ENG.). 112p. (J). (gr. k-3). 16.99 (978-1-4998-0806-3(2)); pap. 5.99 (978-1-4998-0805-6(4)) Little Bee Books Inc.

—Alien Scout, 3. 2019. (Alien Next Door Ch Bks). (ENG.). 94p. (J). (gr. 2-3). 15.59 (978-0-87617-269-8(9)) Penworthy Co., LLC, The.

—Aliens for Dinner?!, 2. 2019. (Alien Next Door Ch Bks). (ENG.). 94p. (J). (gr. 2-3). 15.59 (978-0-87617-270-4(2)) Penworthy Co., LLC, The.

—Baseball Blues, 5. 2019. (Alien Next Door Ch Bks). (ENG.). 93p. (J). (gr. 2-3). 15.59 (978-0-87617-271-1(0)) Penworthy Co., LLC, The.

—The Mystery Valentine, 6. 2019. (Alien Next Door Ch Bks). (ENG.). 95p. (J). (gr. 2-3). 15.59 (978-0-87617-272-8(9)) Penworthy Co., LLC, The.

—Trick or Cheat?, 4. 2019. (Alien Next Door Ch Bks). (ENG.). 97p. (J). (gr. 2-3). 15.59 (978-0-87617-274-2(5)) Penworthy Co., LLC, The.

Nguyen, Taohuu. Mighty Mite 3: Good Mites, Bad Mites. Nguyen, Taohuu, illus. 2007. (Illus.). (J). 14.95 (978-0-9790302-3-9(4)) Amazing Factory, The.

Nicholas, Christopher. I Am a Hero. Unten, Eren Blanquet, illus. 2017. (J). (978-1-5379-5736-4(8), Golden Bks.) Random Hse. Children's Bks.

Nicholson, William. Viento en Llamas: Siervos del Maestro. Manero Jiménez, Laura, tr. 2005. (Escritura desatada Ser.). (SPA.). 384p. (J). 17.95 (978-84-666-1178-7(9)) Ediciones B ESP. Dist: Independent Pubs. Group.

Nicieza, Mariano. Phazer: A Man Lost in Alternative Universes. Olivetti, Ariel, illus. 2008. 48p. (YA). per. 14.95 (978-0-9740212-7-0(X)) Cedar Grove Publishing.

Nickel, Scott. The Dozer Strikes! Jennings, Christopher S. & Jennings, Christopher S., illus. 2010. (Incredible Rockhead Ser.). (ENG.). 40p. (J). (gr. 2-5). lib. bdg. 23.99 (978-1-4342-1894-0(5), 102353, Stone Arch Bks.) Capstone.

Nikovics, Anne. The Adventures of Katie Ladybug. 2005. 132p. 21.95 (978-1-4184-4002-2(7)) AuthorHouse.

Nimoy, Leonard. Leonard Nimoy's Primortals Vol. 1, No. 1: Origins. Chambers, James et al, eds. Eaton, Scot & Barreiro, Mike, illus. 36p. (Orig.). (YA). pap. 2.25 (978-0-9645175-1-6(5)) Big Entertainment, Inc.

Nix, Garth. Grim Tuesday, 2. 2004. (Keys to the Kingdom Ser.: 2). (ENG.). 336p. (J). (gr. 4-6). 22.44 (978-0-439-43655-7(9)) Scholastic, Inc.

—Mister Monday, 1. 2003. (Keys to the Kingdom Ser.: 1). (ENG.). 368p. (J). (gr. 4-6). 22.44 (978-0-439-55123-6(4)) Scholastic, Inc.

—Shade's Children. 2012. (ENG.). 368p. (YA). (gr. 8). pap. 10.99 (978-0-06-207598-7(5), HarperCollins) HarperCollins Pubs.

Nojima, Kazushige. Final Fantasy VII: on the Way to a Smile. 2018. (ENG., Illus.). 204p. (YA). (gr. 8-17). pap. 14.00 (978-1-9753-8235-3(8), 9781975382353, Yen Pr.) Yen Pr. LLC.

Nono, Auntie. Solar System Song. Shirasu, Nori, illus. 2004. (J). bds. 1.25 (978-0-9754098-0-0(8)) Accordian Bks.

Norman, Matthew. Domestic Violets: A Novel. 2011. (ENG.). 352p. pap. 14.99 (978-0-06-206511-7(4), Harper Perennial) HarperCollins Pubs.

Norris, Elizabeth. Unbreakable. 2014. (Unraveling Ser.: 2). (ENG.). 496p. (YA). (gr. 9). pap. 9.99 (978-0-06-210377-2(6), Balzer & Bray) HarperCollins Pubs.

—Unraveling. 2013. (Unraveling Ser.: 1). (ENG.). 480p. (YA). (gr. 8). pap. 9.99 (978-0-06-210374-1(1), Balzer & Bray) HarperCollins Pubs.

North, Julian. Fate of Order: Age of Order Saga Book 3. 2017. (ENG.). 278p. (YA). pap. (978-0-9992658-1-9(4)) Plebeian Media.

—State of Order. 2017. (ENG.). 344p. (YA). pap. (978-0-9992658-0-2(6)) Plebeian Media.

North, Phoebe. Starbreak. 2014. (Starglass Sequence Ser.). (ENG., Illus.). 432p. (YA). (gr. 7). 17.99 (978-1-4424-5956-4(5), Simon & Schuster Bks. For Young Readers) Simon & Schuster Bks. For Young Readers.

—Starglass. (Starglass Sequence Ser.). (ENG., Illus.). (YA). (gr. 7). 2014. 464p. pap. 12.99 (978-1-4424-5954-0(9)) 2013. 448p. 17.99 (978-1-4424-5953-3(0)) Simon & Schuster Bks. For Young Readers. (Simon & Schuster Bks. For Young Readers).

Norton, Andre. Key Out of Time. 2007. 140p. per. 11.95 (978-1-60312-081-4(5)) Aegypan.

—The Time Traders. 2007. 236p. per. 12.95 (978-1-4218-2734-6(4)); 27.95 (978-1-4218-2634-9(8)) 1st World Publishing, Inc. (1st World Library - Literary Society).

—The Time Traders. 2006. pap. (978-1-4068-3561-8(7)) Echo Library.

Noth, Paul. How to Properly Dispose of Planet Earth. 2019. (ENG., Illus.). 192p. (J). 13.99 (978-1-68119-659-6(X), 900179851, Bloomsbury Children's Bks.) Bloomsbury Publishing USA.

—How to Win the Science Fair When You're Dead. 2019. (ENG., Illus.). 192p. (J). 13.99 (978-1-68119-661-9(1), 900179847, Bloomsbury Children's Bks.) Bloomsbury Publishing USA.

Novel Units. Among the Hidden Novel Units Student Packet. 2019. (Shadow Children Ser.). (ENG.). (J). (gr. 7-8). pap., stu. ed. 13.99 (978-1-58130-779-5(9), Novel Units, Inc.) Classroom Library Co.

—Z for Zachariah Novel Units Student Packet. 2019. (ENG.). (J). pap. 13.99 (978-1-56137-889-0(5), Novel Units, Inc.) Classroom Library Co.

—Z for Zachariah Novel Units Teacher Guide. 2019. (ENG.). (J). pap. 12.99 (978-1-56137-888-3(7), Novel Units, Inc.) Classroom Library Co.

Nunez, Kent Hamilton. Mish: The Desert. 2007. 152p. per. 11.95 (978-0-595-47808-8(5)) iUniverse, Inc.

Nybo, B. J. Elmo Jackson Great Yellow Ball. 2005. (978-0-9742322-0-1(3)) New Art & Vision, LLC.

Nye, Bill & Mone, Gregory. Jack & the Geniuses: At the Bottom of the World. Iluzada, Nicholas, illus. (ENG.). (J). (gr. 3-7). 2018. 272p. pap. 8.99 (978-1-4197-3288-1(9), 1152603) 2017. 256p. 13.95 (978-1-4197-2303-2(0), 1152601, Amulet Bks.) Abrams, Inc.

—Lost in the Jungle: Jack & the Geniuses Book #3. Iluzada, Nicholas, illus. (Jack & the Geniuses Ser.). (ENG.). 288p. (J). (gr. 3-7). 2019. pap. 7.99 (978-1-4197-3485-4(7), 1158103) 2018. 13.99 (978-1-4197-2867-9(9), 1158101) Abrams, Inc. (Amulet Bks.).

Nye, Jody Lynn & Taylor, Travis S. Moon Tracks. 2019. (ENG.). 256p. (gr. 5). 24.00 (978-1-4814-8383-4(8)) Baen Bks.

Nylund, Eric. The Resisters, 1. 2012. (Resisters Ser.). (ENG.). 224p. (J). (gr. 4-6). lib. bdg. 21.19 (978-0-375-96856-3(3)) Random House Publishing Group.

—The Resisters #1: the Resisters. 2012. (Resisters Ser.: 1). (ENG.). 240p. (J). (gr. 5-9). 7.99 (978-0-375-87224-2(8), Yearling) Random Hse. Children's Bks.

—The Resisters #2: Sterling Squadron. 2012. (Resisters Ser.: 2). (ENG.). 320p. (J). (gr. 5-9). 7.99 (978-0-375-87225-9(6), Yearling) Random Hse. Children's Bks.

—The Resisters #3: Titan Base. 2013. (Resisters Ser.: 3). (ENG.). 288p. (J). (gr. 5-9). 7.99 (978-0-307-97854-7(0), Yearling) Random Hse. Children's Bks.

—The Resisters #4: Operation Inferno. 2013. (Resisters Ser.: 4). (ENG.). 288p. (J). (gr. 5-9). 7.99 (978-0-307-97855-4(9), Yearling) Random Hse. Children's Bks.

Oberne, Sharon. Kelsey. 2006. 88p. (YA). pap. 13.95 (978-1-58909-340-9(2)) Bookstand Publishing.

Obie, Christopher R. Dumisai & the Enchanted Journey. 2003. (J). pap. (978-0-9718530-0-3(2)) Ancestral Light Publishing.

O'Brien, Caragh M. Birthmarked. 2011. (Birthmarked Trilogy Ser.: 1). (ENG.). 384p. (YA). (gr. 7). pap. 15.99 (978-0-312-67472-4(4), 900072883) Square Fish.

O'Brien, Johnny. Day of the Assassins: A Jack Christie Adventure. Hardcastle, Nick, illus. 2010. (Jack Christie Adventure Ser.: 1). (ENG.). 224p. (J). (gr. 4-7). pap. 6.99 (978-0-7636-4995-1(3), Templar) Candlewick Pr.

—Day of the Assassins: A Jack Christie Adventure, 1. Hardcastle, Nick, illus. 2009. (Jack Christie Adventure Ser.: 1). (ENG.). 224p. (J). (gr. 4-7). 15.99 (978-0-7636-4595-3(8), Templar) Candlewick Pr.

O'Callaghan, G. Tektite. 2007. 144p. per. (978-1-84693-025-6(1)) Best Global Publishing Ltd.

O'Connor, Grandma. Rodney the Robot: Why Rodney Rebels. 2008. 52p. pap. 8.95 (978-0-595-51055-9(8)) iUniverse, Inc.

O'Connor, Jane. Fancy Nancy Sees Stars. 2008. (I Can Read Level 1 Ser.). (ENG., Illus.). 32p. (J). (gr. -1-3). pap. 4.99 (978-0-06-123611-2(X), HarperCollins) HarperCollins Pubs.

—Fancy Nancy Sees Stars. Glasser, Robin Preiss, illus. 2008. (I Can Read Level 1 Ser.). (ENG.). 32p. (J). (gr. -1-3). 17.99 (978-0-06-123612-9(8), HarperCollins) HarperCollins Pubs.

Odgers, Sally. Journey to the Center of the Earth, 1 vol. rev. ed. 2013. (Literary Text Ser.). (ENG., Illus.). 24p. (J). (gr. 2-3). pap. 8.99 (978-1-4333-5527-1(2)) Teacher Created Materials, Inc.

Offill, Jenny. 11 Experiments That Failed. Carpenter, Nancy, illus. 2011. (ENG.). 40p. (J). (gr. -1-3). 17.99 (978-0-375-84762-2(6), Schwartz & Wade Bks.) Random Hse. Children's Bks.

Oh, Axie. Rebel Seoul, 1 vol. Hue, Sebastien, illus. 2017. (Rebel Seoul Ser.). (ENG.). 400p. (YA). (gr. 6-12). 21.95 (978-1-62014-299-8(6), leelowtu, Tu Bks.) Lee & Low Bks., Inc.

O'Hely, Eileen. Penny in Space. Phelan, Nicky, illus. 2009. (ENG.). 225p. (J). pap. 14.95 (978-1-85635-571-1(3)) Mercier Pr., Ltd., The IRL. Dist: Dufour Editions, Inc.

Ohnogi, Hiroshi. Rahxephon, Vol. 4. 2006. (RahXephon (Dr Masterbook) Ser.). (ENG., Illus.). 200p. (YA). pap. 7.95 (978-1-59796-003-8(9)) DrMaster Pubns. Inc.

—Rahxephon, Vol. 5. 2006. (RahXephon (Dr Masterbook) Ser.). (ENG., Illus.). 200p. (YA). pap. 7.95 (978-1-59796-004-5(7)) DrMaster Pubns. Inc.

Okorafor, Nnedi. Ikenga. 2020. 240p. (J). (gr. 5). 16.99 (978-0-593-11352-3(7), Viking Books for Young Readers) Penguin Young Readers Group.

Older, Daniel José. Star Wars: the High Republic: Race to Crashpoint Tower. 2021. (ENG., Illus.). 240p. (J). (gr. 3-7). 14.99 (978-1-368-06066-0(8), Disney Lucasfilm Press) Disney Publishing Worldwide.

Oliver, Chad. Far from This Earth & Other Stories. Olson, Priscilla, ed. Dennis, Jane, illus. 2003. (NESFA's Choice Ser.: 25). 480p. 24.00 (978-1-886778-48-1(5), NESFA Pr.) New England Science Fiction Assn., Inc.

—A Star Above It & Other Stories. Olson, Priscilla, ed. Dennis, Jane, illus. 2003. (NESFA's Choice Ser.: 24). 480p. 24.00 (978-1-886778-45-0(0), NESFA Pr.) New England Science Fiction Assn., Inc.

Oliver, Lauren. Delirium, 1. 2016. (Delirium Trilogy Ser.: 1). (ENG.). 480p. (YA). (gr. 9-12). pap. 15.99 (978-0-06-172683-5(4), HarperCollins) HarperCollins Pubs.

—Delirium. 2016. (Delirium Ser.: 1). (YA). lib. bdg. 20.85 (978-0-606-23575-4(2)) Turtleback.

—Delirium Stories: Hana, Annabel, Raven & Alex. (Delirium Ser.). (YA). 2016. lib. bdg. 20.85 (978-0-606-38920-4(2)) 2013. lib. bdg. 20.85 (978-0-606-31834-1(8)) Turtleback.

—Delirium Stories: Hana, Annabel, & Raven. 2013. (Delirium Trilogy Ser.). (ENG.). 224p. (YA). (gr. 9). pap. 9.99 (978-0-06-226778-8(7), HarperCollins) HarperCollins Pubs.

—Delirium Stories: Hana, Annabel, Raven, & Alex. 2016. (Delirium Story Ser.). (ENG.). 224p. (YA). (gr. 9). pap. 9.99 (978-0-06-248432-1(X), HarperCollins) HarperCollins Pubs.

—Delirium: the Special Edition. 2011. (Delirium Trilogy Ser.: 1). (ENG.). 480p. (YA). (gr. 9). 17.99 (978-0-06-211243-9(0), HarperCollins) HarperCollins Pubs.

—Pandemonium. (YA). 2016. (Delirium Trilogy Ser.: 2). (ENG.). 400p. (gr. 9). pap. 11.99 (978-0-06-197807-4(8), HarperCollins) 2012. (Delirium Trilogy Ser.: 2). (ENG.). 384p. (gr. 9-18). 18.99 (978-0-06-197806-7(X), HarperCollins)

2012. (Delirium Trilogy: Bk. 2). 375p. *(978-0-06-213008-2(0))* HarperCollins Pubs.
—Pandemonium. 2016. (Delirium Ser.: 2). (YA). lib. bdg. 20.85 *(978-0-606-27141-7(4))* Turtleback.
—Replica. (Replica Ser.: 1). (ENG.). (YA). (gr. 9). 2017. 560p. pap. 12.99 *(978-0-06-239417-0(7))* 2016. 544p. 19.99 *(978-0-06-239416-3(9))* HarperCollins Pubs. (HarperCollins).
—Réplica. 2017. (ENG.). 480p. (YA). (gr. 9-12). pap. 21.95 *(978-84-666-6144-7(1),* B De Blook) Penguin Random House Grupo Editorial ESP. Dist: Penguin Random Hse. LLC.
—Requiem. 2013. (Delirium Trilogy Ser.: 3). (ENG.). 432p. (YA). (gr. 9). 18.99 *(978-0-06-201453-5(6),* HarperCollins) HarperCollins Pubs.
—Ringer. (Replica Ser.: 2). (ENG.). 528p. (YA). (gr. 9). 2018. pap. 13.99 *(978-0-06-239420-0(7))* 2017. 19.99 *(978-0-06-239419-4(3))* HarperCollins Pubs. (HarperCollins).
Oliver, Lin & Baker, Theo. Sound Bender. 2011. (ENG.). 272p. (J). (gr. 5-9). 16.99 *(978-0-545-19692-5(2),* Scholastic Pr.) Scholastic, Inc.
The Ologies Collection. 2006. (J). 79.96 *(978-0-7636-3509-1(X))* Candlewick Pr.
Olsen, Nora. Swans & Klons. 2013. (ENG.). 192p. (gr. 7). pap. 11.95 *(978-1-60282-874-2(1))* Bold Strokes Bks.
Olson, Kayla. The Sandcastle Empire. 2017. (ENG.). 464p. *(978-0-06-274071-7(7),* HarperTeen) HarperCollins Pubs.
O'Malley, Kevin. Captain Raptor & the Moon Mystery. O'Brien, Patrick, illus. 2005. (Captain Raptor Ser.). (ENG.). 32p. (J). (gr. k-5). 19.99 *(978-0-8027-8935-8(8),* 900034813, Bloomsbury USA Childrens) Bloomsbury Publishing USA.
O'Malley, Kevin & O'Brien, Patrick. Captain Raptor & the Perilous Planet. O'Brien, Patrick, illus. 2018. (Captain Raptor Ser.: 3). (Illus.). 32p. (J). (gr. -1-3). lib. bdg. 17.99 *(978-1-58089-809-6(2))* Charlesbridge Publishing, Inc.
—Captain Raptor & the Space Pirates. O'Brien, Patrick, illus. 2007. (Captain Raptor Ser.). (ENG., Illus.). 32p. (J). (gr. k-3). 17.99 *(978-0-8027-9571-7(4),* 900040057, Bloomsbury USA Childrens) Bloomsbury Publishing USA.
Onyebuchi, Tochi. War Girls. 2019. (ENG.). 464p. (YA). (gr. 7). 18.99 *(978-0-451-48167-2(4),* Razorbill) Penguin Young Readers Group.
Oppel, Kenneth. Bloom. 2020. (Overthrow Ser.: 1). (ENG., Illus.). 320p. (J). (gr. 5-7). 16.99 *(978-1-5247-7300-7(X),* Knopf Bks. for Young Readers) Random Hse. Children's Bks.
Ormand, Kate. Dark Days. (ENG.). (gr. 6-12). 2018. 272p. pap. 8.99 *(978-1-5107-1710-7(2))* 2014. 256p. (J). 16.95 *(978-1-62873-594-9(5))* Skyhorse Publishing Co., Inc. (Sky Pony Pr.).
—The Pack. 2017. (ENG.). 304p. (J). 16.99 *(978-1-5107-1218-8(6),* Sky Pony Pr.) Skyhorse Publishing Co., Inc.
Orme, David. Galactic Shopping Mall, Set. 2008. (Starchasers Ser.). (ENG., Illus.). 48p. pap. *(978-1-84167-764-4(7))* Ransom Publishing Ltd.
—Jungle Planet, Set. 2008. (Starchasers Ser.). (ENG., Illus.). 48p. pap. *(978-1-84167-768-2(X))* Ransom Publishing Ltd.
—Lost Explorers, Set. 2008. (Starchasers Ser.). (ENG., Illus.). 48p. pap. *(978-1-84167-763-7(9))* Ransom Publishing Ltd.
—Planet of the Vampires, Set. 2008. (Starchasers Ser.). (ENG., Illus.). 48p. pap. *(978-1-84167-765-1(5))* Ransom Publishing Ltd.
—Space Explorers. 2004. (Shades Ser.). 64p. (J). pap. *(978-0-237-52646-7(8))* Evans Brothers, Ltd.
—Ultimate Secret, Set. 2008. (Starchasers Ser.). (ENG., Illus.). 48p. pap. *(978-1-84167-766-8(3))* Ransom Publishing Ltd.
Orme, David & Orme, David. Science Fiction. 2008. (Trailblazers Ser.). (ENG., Illus.). 36p. pap. *(978-1-84167-693-7(4))* Ransom Publishing Ltd.
O'Rourke, Erica. Resonance. 2015. (Dissonance Ser.). (ENG., Illus.). 448p. (YA). (gr. 7). 18.99 *(978-1-4424-6027-0(X),* Simon & Schuster Bks. For Young Readers) Simon & Schuster Bks. For Young Readers.
O'Ryan, Ray. The Annoying Crush. Kraft, Jason, illus. 2014. (Galaxy Zack Ser.: 9). (ENG.). 128p. (J). (gr. k-4). 17.99 *(978-1-4424-9364-3(X))*; pap. 5.99 *(978-1-4424-9363-6(1))* Little Simon. (Little Simon).
—The Annoying Crush. 2014. (Galaxy Zack Ser.: 9). lib. bdg. 16.00 *(978-0-606-36093-7(X))* Turtleback.
—Cosmic Blackout! Kraft, Jason, illus. 2017. (Galaxy Zack Ser.: 16). (ENG.). 128p. (J). (gr. k-4). 17.99 *(978-1-4814-9990-3(4))*; pap. 5.99 *(978-1-4814-9989-7(0))* Little Simon. (Little Simon).
—Drake Makes a Splash! Jack, Colin, illus. 2014. (Galaxy Zack Ser.: 8). (ENG.). 128p. (J). (gr. k-4). pap. 6.99 *(978-1-4424-9360-5(7),* Little Simon) Little Simon.
—A Galactic Easter! Jack, Colin, illus. 2014. (Galaxy Zack Ser.: 7). (ENG.). 128p. (J). (gr. k-4). pap. 6.99 *(978-1-4424-9357-5(7),* Little Simon) Little Simon.
—A Galactic Easter! 2014. (Galaxy Zack Ser.: 7). lib. bdg. 16.00 *(978-0-606-35428-8(X))* Turtleback.
—The Galaxy Zack Collection (Boxed Set) A Stellar Four-Book Boxed Set: Hello, Nebulon!; Journey to Juno; the Prehistoric Planet; Monsters in Space! Jack, Colin, illus. 2014. (Galaxy Zack Ser.). (ENG.). 512p. (J). (gr. k-4). pap. 23.99 *(978-1-4814-0665-9(5),* Little Simon) Little Simon.
—A Green Christmas! Jack, Colin, illus. 2013. (Galaxy Zack Ser.: 6). (ENG.). 128p. (J). (gr. k-2). 17.99 *(978-1-4424-8225-8(7))*; pap. 6.99 *(978-1-4424-8224-1(9))*; pap. 6.99 *(978-1-4424-8224-1(9))* Little Simon. (Little Simon).
—A Green Christmas! 2013. (Galaxy Zack Ser.: 6). lib. bdg. 14.75 *(978-0-606-35185-0(X))* Turtleback.
—A Haunted Halloween. Kraft, Jason, illus. 2015. (Galaxy Zack Ser.: 11). (ENG.). 128p. (J). (gr. k-4). 17.99 *(978-1-4814-3491-1(8),* Little Simon) Little Simon.
—Hello, Nebulon! Jack, Colin, illus. 2013. (Galaxy Zack Ser.: 1). (ENG.). 128p. (J). (gr. k-4). 17.99 *(978-1-4424-5387-6(7))*; pap. 6.99 *(978-1-4424-5386-9(9))* Little Simon. (Little Simon).
—Hello, Nebulon! 2013. (Galaxy Zack Ser.: 1). lib. bdg. 16.00 *(978-0-606-32442-7(9))* Turtleback.
—Journey to Juno. Jack, Colin, illus. 2013. (Galaxy Zack Ser.: 2). (ENG.). 128p. (J). (gr. k-4). 17.99 *(978-1-4424-5391-3(5))*; pap. 6.99 *(978-1-4424-5390-6(7))* Little Simon. (Little Simon).
—Journey to Juno. 2013. (Galaxy Zack Ser.: 2). lib. bdg. 16.00 *(978-0-606-32443-4(7))* Turtleback.
—Monsters in Space! Jack, Colin, illus. 2013. (Galaxy Zack Ser.: 4). (ENG.). 128p. (J). (gr. k-2). 16.99 *(978-1-4424-6721-7(5))*; pap. 6.99 *(978-1-4424-6718-7(5))* Little Simon. (Little Simon).
—Monsters in Space! 2013. (Galaxy Zack Ser.: 4). lib. bdg. 16.00 *(978-0-606-32460-1(7))* Turtleback.
—Operation Twin Trouble. Kraft, Jason, illus. 2015. (Galaxy Zack Ser.: 12). (ENG.). 128p. (J). (gr. k-4). pap. 5.99 *(978-1-4814-4399-9(2),* Little Simon) Little Simon.
—The Prehistoric Planet. Jack, Colin, illus. 2013. (Galaxy Zack Ser.: 3). (ENG.). 128p. (J). (gr. k-4). 17.99 *(978-1-4424-6716-3(9))*; pap. 6.99 *(978-1-4424-6715-6(0))* Little Simon. (Little Simon).
—The Prehistoric Planet. 2013. (Galaxy Zack Ser.: 3). lib. bdg. 16.00 *(978-0-606-32461-8(5))* Turtleback.
—Ready, Set, Blast Off! Kraft, Jason, illus. 2017. (Galaxy Zack Ser.: 15). (ENG.). 128p. (J). (gr. k-4). pap. 6.99 *(978-1-4814-8595-1(4),* Little Simon) Little Simon.
—Return to Earth! Kraft, Jason, illus. 2015. (Galaxy Zack Ser.: 10). (ENG.). 128p. (J). (gr. k-4). pap. 6.99 *(978-1-4814-2181-2(6),* Little Simon) Little Simon.
—Science Fair Disaster! Kraft, Jason, illus. 2016. (Galaxy Zack Ser.: 13). (ENG.). 128p. (J). (gr. k-4). pap. 5.99 *(978-1-4814-5876-4(0),* Little Simon) Little Simon.
—Space Camp. Kraft, Jason, illus. 2016. (Galaxy Zack Ser.: 14). (ENG.). 128p. (J). (gr. k-4). pap. 5.99 *(978-1-4814-6300-3(4),* Little Simon) Little Simon.
—Three's a Crowd! Jack, Colin, illus. 2013. (Galaxy Zack Ser.: 5). (ENG.). 128p. (J). (gr. k-4). 17.99 *(978-1-4424-8222-7(2))*; pap. 6.99 *(978-1-4424-8221-0(4))* Little Simon. (Little Simon).
—Three's a Crowd! 2013. (Galaxy Zack Ser.: 5). lib. bdg. 16.00 *(978-0-606-35187-4(6))* Turtleback.
Osborne, Mary Pope. Medianoche en la Luna. 2004. (Casa del Arbol Ser.: 8).Tr. of Midnight on the Moon. (SPA.). (J). pap. 6.99 *(978-1-930332-69-0(6))* Lectorum Pubns., Inc.
—Night of the New Magicians. Murdocca, Sal, illus. 2007. (Magic Tree House (R) Merlin Mission Ser.: 7). 144p. (J). (gr. 2-5). 6.99 *(978-0-375-83036-5(7),* Random Hse. Bks. for Young Readers) Random Hse. Children's Bks.
—Night of the New Magicians. 2007. (Magic Tree House Merlin Missions Ser.: 7). lib. bdg. 16.00 *(978-1-4177-9108-8(X))* Turtleback.
Osterlund, Anne. Academy 7. 2009. 272p. (YA). (gr. 7-18). pap. 8.99 *(978-0-14-241437-8(9),* Speak) Penguin Young Readers Group.
Ottaviani, Jim. T-Minus: The Race to the Moon. Cannon, Kevin & Cannon, Zander, illus. 2009. (ENG.). 128p. (J). (gr. 3-7). 36.19 *(978-1-4169-8682-9(0),* Aladdin) Simon & Schuster Children's Publishing.
Outram, Richard. The Adventures of Exokid: Growing Financial Wings. 2013. 40p. pap. 13.95 *(978-1-4575-2130-0(X))* Dog Ear Publishing, LLC.
Overpowered. 2014. (ENG., Illus.). 432p. (YA). (gr. 7). pap. 11.99 *(978-1-4424-3129-4(6),* Simon & Schuster Bks. For Young Readers) Simon & Schuster Bks. For Young Readers.
Packard, Edward. Through the Black Hole. Willis, Drew, illus. 2012. (U-Ventures Ser.). (ENG.). 160p. (J). (gr. 3-7). pap. 6.99 *(978-1-4424-3426-4(0))* Simon & Schuster, Inc.
Page, Cecelia Frances. Adventures on Ancient Continents. 2007. 172p. per. 13.95 *(978-0-595-46358-9(4))* iUniverse, Inc.
Pallock, Ruth. The Planet Mazol: Book 2 of World Adventures of Jayden. 2011. 82p. pap. 19.95 *(978-1-4560-9004-3(6))* America Star Bks.
Palmer, Kristine. Eigenoids Episode 2: Momentum Sphere Coaster. 2013. 134p. pap. 19.95 *(978-1-63000-928-1(8))* America Star Bks.
Parker, Derek. Children of Zone. 2015. (ENG., Illus.). 142p. pap. *(978-1-925138-91-7(7))* Connor Court Publishing Pty Ltd.
Parker, Jake. Rescue on Tankium3. 2011. (Missile Mouse Ser.: 2). (ENG., Illus.). 160p. (J). (gr. 3-7). 21.99 *(978-0-545-11716-6(X),* Graphix) Scholastic, Inc.
Parker, Jeff. The Leader Has a Big Head. Garcia, Manuel, illus. 2007. (Avengers Ser.: No. 1). (ENG.). 24p. (J). (gr. 2-6). 31.36 *(978-1-59961-384-0(0),* 24, Marvel Age) Spotlight.
—The Masters of Evil. Paniccia, Mark, ed. Garcia, Manuel, illus. 2007. (Avengers Ser.: No. 1). (ENG.). 24p. (J). (gr. 2-6). 31.36 *(978-1-59961-385-7(9),* 25, Marvel Age) Spotlight.
—The Replacements. Paniccia, Mark, ed. Garcia, Manuel, illus. 2007. (Avengers Ser.: No. 1). (ENG.). 24p. (J). (gr. 2-6). 31.36 *(978-1-59961-386-4(7),* 26, Marvel Age) Spotlight.
Parker, Steve. Robots in Fiction & Films. 2010. (Robot World Ser.). (ENG.). 32p. (J). (gr. 4-6). lib. bdg. 28.50 *(978-1-60753-073-2(2),* 17228) Amicus.
Parker, Steve & Pipe, Jim. Robots in Fiction & Films. 2011. (On the Edge Ser.). 32p. (YA). (gr. 3-6). lib. bdg. 28.50 *(978-1-59920-515-1(7))* Black Rabbit Bks.
Parnell, Declan. Brett Meets the Bee Lady, 1 vol., 1. 2015. (Rosen REAL Readers: STEM & STEAM Collection). (ENG.). 12p. (J). (gr. k-1). pap. 6.33 *(978-1-5081-1518-2(4),* 3e5cd911-0fc0-49c4-8099-4362796eccf7, Rosen Classroom) Rosen Publishing Group, Inc., The.
Parry, Jo. Blast Off! 2009. (Wow! Bks.). (Illus.). (J). bds. 12.99 *(978-1-934650-26-4(9))* Just For Kids Pr., LLC.
Parton, Paula. Room 17 - Where History Comes Alive - Missions. Parton, Paula, illus. 2010. (illus.). 126p. pap. 8.95 *(978-1-935630-19-7(9))* Bellissima Publishing, LLC.
Pascoe, Matt. Chaos Island: A Daisy Albright Adventure. 2010. 72p. pap. 9.99 *(978-1-60911-208-0(3),* Eloquent Bks.) Strategic Book Publishing & Rights Agency (SBPRA).
Pat Morrissey/Havlin. The Case of the Crumbling Crystals. 2007. (ENG.). 88p. 24.99 *(978-1-4257-9627-3(3))*; pap. 15.99 *(978-1-4257-9624-2(9))* Xlibris Corp.
Patchett, Mary E. Flight to the Misty Planet. 2011. 236p. 46.95 *(978-1-258-07100-4(2))* Literary Licensing, LLC.
Pati, Geeta. Finny's Voyage Through the Universe: The. 2005. (ENG.). 64p. per. 10.95 *(978-1-59526-019-2(6))* Aeon Publishing Inc.
Patterson, Eric. Carl Nose the Truth. Wright, Christopher, illus. 2007. 104p. (J). pap. 6.95 *(978-0-9797106-6-7(9))* Avid Readers Publishing Group.
Patterson, James. Angel. 2011. (Maximum Ride Ser.). (YA). 54.99 *(978-1-60941-970-7(7))* Findaway World, LLC.
—Angel. 2012. (Maximum Ride Ser.: 7). lib. bdg. 20.85 *(978-0-606-23452-8(7))* Turtleback.
—Angel: A Maximum Ride Novel. (Maximum Ride Ser.: 7). (ENG.). (gr. 5-17). 2012. 352p. pap. 11.99 *(978-0-316-03832-4(6))* 2011. 320p. 33.99 *(978-0-316-03620-7(X))* 2011. 384p. pap. 19.99 *(978-0-316-12201-6(7))* Little Brown & Co. (Jimmy Patterson).
—Crazy House. 2019. (Crazy House Ser.: 1). (ENG.). 352p. mass mkt. 8.99 *(978-1-5387-1406-5(X))* Grand Central Publishing.
—Crazy House. 2018. (Crazy House Ser.: 1). (ENG.). 384p. (YA). (gr. 9-17). pap. 9.99 *(978-0-316-51499-6(3),* Jimmy Patterson) Little Brown & Co.
—The Dangerous Days of Daniel X. 2014. lthr. 79.00 *(978-1-62715-506-9(6))* Leatherbound Bestsellers.
—The Dangerous Days of Daniel X. (Daniel X Ser.: 1). (ENG.). (J). (gr. 3-7). 2010. illus.). 272p. pap. 8.99 *(978-0-316-11970-2(9))* 2009. 288p. mass mkt. 7.99 *(978-0-446-50913-8(2))* 2008. 304p. pap. 19.99 *(978-0-316-03025-0(2))* Little Brown & Co. (Jimmy Patterson).
—The Dangerous Days of Daniel X. 2010. (Daniel X Ser.: 1). (J). lib. bdg. 18.45 *(978-0-606-14720-0(9))* Turtleback.
—Daniel X: Armageddon. (Daniel X Ser.: 5). (ENG.). (J). (gr. 3-7). 2013. 320p. pap. 17.99 *(978-0-316-10177-6(X))* 2012. 304p. 16.99 *(978-0-316-10179-0(6))* 2012. 384p. 28.00 *(978-0-316-22421-5(9))* Little Brown & Co. (Jimmy Patterson).
—Daniel X: Demons & Druids. (Daniel X Ser.: 3). (ENG.). (J). (gr. 3-7). 2011. 304p. pap., pap. 8.99 *(978-0-316-03830-0(X))* 2010. 320p. 33.99 *(978-0-316-08731-5(9))* Little Brown & Co. (Jimmy Patterson).
—Fang: A Maximum Ride Novel. (Maximum Ride Ser.: 6). (ENG.). (gr. 5-17). 2011. 368p. pap. 11.99 *(978-0-316-03831-7(8))* 2010. 336p. 35.99 *(978-0-316-03619-1(6))* 2010. 416p. pap. 21.99 *(978-0-316-07106-2(4))* Little Brown & Co. (Jimmy Patterson).
—The Final Warning. l.t. ed. 2009. (Maximum Ride Ser.: No. 4). 420p. (YA). 23.95 *(978-1-4104-1626-1(7))* Thorndike Pr.
—The Final Warning: A Maximum Ride Novel. 2008. (Maximum Ride Ser.: 4). (ENG.). (gr. 7-17). 304p. pap. 11.99 *(978-0-316-00287-5(9))*; 4th ed. 272p. 32.99 *(978-0-316-00286-8(0))* Little Brown & Co. (Jimmy Patterson).
—Hawk. (Maximum Ride: Hawk Ser.: 1). (ENG.). (YA). (gr. 7-17). 2021. 432p. pap. 10.99 *(978-0-316-28922-1(1))* 2020. 416p. 18.99 *(978-0-316-49440-3(2))* Little Brown & Co. (Jimmy Patterson).
—Max: A Maximum Ride Novel. 2009. (Maximum Ride Ser.: 5). (ENG.). (YA). (gr. 5-17). 352p. pap. 11.99 *(978-0-316-00290-5(9))*; 416p. 38.99 *(978-0-316-03759-4(1))* Little Brown & Co. (Jimmy Patterson).
—Maximum Ride. 2015. (Maximum Ride: the Manga Ser.: 9). lib. bdg. 24.50 *(978-0-606-38045-4(0))* Turtleback.
—Maximum Ride Forever. 2015. (Maximum Ride Ser.: 9). (ENG.). 400p. (YA). (gr. 7-17). 36.99 *(978-0-316-20750-8(0),* Jimmy Patterson) Little Brown & Co.
—Nevermore: The Final Maximum Ride Adventure. 2012. (Maximum Ride Ser.: 8). (ENG.). (YA). (gr. 5-17). 384p. 36.99 *(978-0-316-10184-4(2))*; 448p. 30.99 *(978-0-316-20811-6(6))* Little Brown & Co. (Jimmy Patterson).
—Not So Normal Norbert. Aly, Hatem, illus. 2018. (ENG.). 368p. (J). (gr. 3-9). 13.99 *(978-0-316-46541-0(0),* Jimmy Patterson) Little Brown & Co.
—Saving the World & Other Extreme Sports. 2008. (Maximum Ride Ser.: Bk. 5). 429p. (gr. 4-7). 18.00 *(978-0-7569-8353-6(3))* Perfection Learning Corp.
—Saving the World & Other Extreme Sports. l.t. ed. 2007. (Maximum Ride Ser.: No. 3). 489p. (J). (gr. 3-7). 23.95 *(978-0-7862-9887-7(1))* Thorndike Pr.
—Saving the World & Other Extreme Sports: A Maximum Ride Novel. 3rd ed. (Maximum Ride Ser.: 3). (ENG.). (J). (gr. 5-17). 2007. 416p. 37.99 *(978-0-316-15560-1(8))* 2008. 432p. pap. 10.99 *(978-0-316-15427-7(X))* Little Brown & Co. (Jimmy Patterson).
—School's Out - Forever. 2008. (Maximum Ride Ser.: Bk. 2). 418p. (gr. 4-7). 18.00 *(978-0-7569-8349-9(5))* Perfection Learning Corp.
—School's Out - Forever. 2007. (Maximum Ride Ser.: 2). (YA). lib. bdg. 20.85 *(978-1-4177-7493-7(2))* Turtleback.
—School's Out — Forever: A Maximum Ride Novel. 2nd ed. 2006. (Maximum Ride Ser.: 2). (ENG.). 416p. (J). (gr. 5-17). 38.99 *(978-0-316-15559-5(4),* Jimmy Patterson) Little Brown & Co.
—Watch the Skies. 2014. lthr. 79.00 *(978-1-62715-571-7(6))* Leatherbound Bestsellers.
—Watch the Skies. 2010. (Daniel X Ser.: 2). (J). lib. bdg. 18.45 *(978-0-606-10550-7(6))* Turtleback.
Patterson, James & Grabenstein, Chris. Armageddon. 2013. (Daniel X Ser.: 5). (J). lib. bdg. 18.45 *(978-0-606-31747-4(3))* Turtleback.
—Daniel X: Lights Out. 2015. (Daniel X Ser.: 6). (ENG.). 272p. (J). (gr. 3-7). 32.99 *(978-0-316-20745-4(4),* Jimmy Patterson) Little Brown & Co.
—Katt vs. Dogg. López, Anuki, illus. (ENG.). (J). (gr. 3-7). 2021. (Katt vs. Dogg Ser.: 1). 336p. pap. 8.99 *(978-0-316-39712-4(1))* 2019. 320p. 13.99 *(978-0-316-41156-1(6))* Little Brown & Co. (Jimmy Patterson).
Patterson, James & Rust, Ned. Daniel X: Game Over. 2011. (Daniel X Ser.: 4). (ENG.). 240p. (J). (gr. 3-7). 32.99 *(978-0-316-10178-3(8),* Jimmy Patterson) Little Brown & Co.
—Daniel X: the Manga, Vol. 2. 2011. (Daniel X: the Manga Ser.: 2). (ENG., Illus.). 208p. (gr. 7-17). pap. 12.99 *(978-0-316-07765-1(8),* Yen Pr.) Yen Pr. LLC.
—Daniel X: Watch the Skies. (Daniel X Ser.: 2). (ENG.). (J). (gr. 3-7). 2010. 288p. pap. 8.99 *(978-0-316-11969-6(5))* 2009. 352p. pap. 19.99 *(978-0-316-04363-2(X))* Little Brown & Co. (Jimmy Patterson).
Patterson, James & Sadler, Adam. Daniel X: Demons & Druids. 2010. (Daniel X Ser.: 3). (ENG.). 256p. (J). (gr. 3-7). 31.99 *(978-0-316-03698-6(6),* Jimmy Patterson) Little Brown & Co.
Patterson, Michael. Blam! O'Reilly, Sean Patrick, ed. 2011. (Illus.). 80p. (YA). pap. 14.95 *(978-1-926914-04-6(X))* Arcana Studio, Inc.
Paulsen, Gary. The Time Hackers. 2006. (ENG.). 96p. (J). (gr. 3-7). 5.99 *(978-0-553-48788-6(4),* Yearling) Random Hse. Children's Bks.
Pavlou, Stel. Daniel Coldstar #1: the Relic War. 2019. (Daniel Coldstar Ser.: 1). (ENG.). 320p. (J). (gr. 3-7). pap. 6.99 *(978-0-06-212606-1(7),* HarperCollins) HarperCollins Pubs.
—Daniel Coldstar #2: the Betrayer. 2019. (Daniel Coldstar Ser.: 2). (ENG.). 304p. (J). (gr. 3-7). 16.99 *(978-0-06-212609-2(1),* HarperCollins) HarperCollins Pubs.
Paye, Won-Ldy & Lippert, Margaret H. Head, Body, Legs: A Story from Liberia. Paschkis, Julie, illus. 2006. (gr. -1-3). lib. bdg. 18.00 *(978-0-7569-6925-7(5))* Perfection Learning Corp.
Pearson, Edwin. Will's Galactic Adventure. 2013. (ENG.). 104p. pap. *(978-1-78306-154-9(5))* Troubador Publishing Ltd.
Pearson, Maggie. Alien Draw. (ENG.). 214p. (J). pap. *(978-0-340-68077-3(6))* Hodder & Stoughton.
Pearson, Mary E. The Adoration of Jenna Fox. 2008. (Jenna Fox Chronicles Ser.: 1). (ENG.). 272p. (YA). (gr. 7-12). 26.99 *(978-0-8050-7668-4(9),* 900045743, Holt, Henry & Co. Bks. For Young Readers) Holt, Henry & Co.
—The Adoration of Jenna Fox. 2011. 9.46 *(978-0-7848-3478-7(4),* Everbind) Marco Bk. Co.
—The Adoration of Jenna Fox. 2009. (Jenna Fox Chronicles Ser.: 1). (ENG.). 288p. (YA). (gr. 7-12). pap. 11.99 *(978-0-312-59441-1(0),* 900062867) Square Fish.
—The Fox Inheritance, 2. 2013. (Jenna Fox Chronicles Ser.: 2). (ENG.). 320p. (YA). (gr. 7-12). pap. 12.99 *(978-1-250-01032-2(2),* 900084770) Square Fish.
Pearson, Ridley. Super Sons: the PolarShield Project. Gonzalez, Ile, illus. 2019. 160p. (gr. 3-7). pap. 9.99 *(978-1-4012-8639-2(9),* DC Zoom) DC Comics.
Pease, D. Robert. Noah Zarc: Cataclysm. 2nd l.t. ed. 2013. (ENG.). 234p. (gr. 3-8). pap. 11.95 *(978-1-62253-406-7(9))* Evolved Publishing.
—Noah Zarc: Cataclysm. Diamond, Lane, ed. 3rd ed. 2017. (Noah Zarc Ser.: Vol. 2). (ENG., Illus.). (YA). (gr. 7-12). pap. 16.95 *(978-1-62253-419-7(0))* Evolved Publishing.
—Noah Zarc: Declaration. l.t. ed. 2013. (ENG.). 226p. (gr. 3-8). pap. 11.95 *(978-1-62253-408-1(5))* Evolved Publishing.
—Noah Zarc: Declaration. Diamond, Lane, ed. 3rd ed. 2017. (Noah Zarc Ser.: Vol. 3). (ENG., Illus.). (YA). (gr. 7-12). pap. 15.95 *(978-1-62253-420-3(4))* Evolved Publishing.
—Noah Zarc: Mammoth Trouble. 2nd l.t. ed. 2013. (ENG.). 214p. (gr. 3-8). pap. 11.95 *(978-1-62253-404-3(2))* Evolved Publishing.
—Noah Zarc: Mammoth Trouble. Diamond, Lane, ed. 3rd ed. 2017. (Noah Zarc Ser.: Vol. 1). (ENG., Illus.). (YA). (gr. 7-12). pap. 14.95 *(978-1-62253-418-0(2))* Evolved Publishing.
—Noah Zarc: Omnibus. l.t. ed. 2013. (ENG.). 630p. (gr. 3-8). 36.95 *(978-1-62253-410-4(7))* Evolved Publishing.
—Noah Zarc: Omnibus. Diamond, Lane, ed. 2nd ed. 2017. (Noah Zarc Ser.: Vol. 4). (ENG., Illus.). (YA). (gr. 7-12). 39.95 *(978-1-62253-421-0(2))* Evolved Publishing.
Peers, Bobbie. William Wenton & the Lost City. Chace, Tara F., tr. 2019. (William Wenton Ser.: 3). (ENG., Illus.). 256p. (J). (gr. 3-7). 17.99 *(978-1-4814-7831-1(1),* Aladdin) Simon & Schuster Children's Publishing.
—William Wenton & the Secret Portal. Chace, Tara F., tr. 2019. (William Wenton Ser.: 2). (ENG.). 288p. (J). (gr. 3-7). pap. 7.99 *(978-1-4814-7829-8(X),* Aladdin) Simon & Schuster Children's Publishing.
Peredo, Roberto. Acoyani: El Nino y el Poeta. Sanchez, Andres & Arte Y Diseno, Tane, illus. 2nd rev. ed. 2006. (Castillo de la Lectura Naranja Ser.). (SPA & ENG.). 166p. (J). (gr. 4-7). pap. 7.95 *(978-970-20-0146-1(3))* Castillo, Ediciones, S. A. de C. V. MEX. Dist: Macmillan.
Perritano, John. The Science of Movies, 1 vol. 2016. (Red Rhino Nonfiction Ser.). (ENG., Illus.). 60p. (J). (gr. 4-7). pap. 11.95 *(978-1-68021-050-7(5))* Saddleback Educational Publishing, Inc.
Perritano, Johnrau Dana M. The Science of Movies. 2017. (Red Rhino Nonfiction Ser.). (J). lib. bdg. 19.60 *(978-0-606-39892-3(9))* Turtleback.
Perry, Fred & Dlin, Doug. Gold Digger Tech Manual. 2011. (ENG.). 352p. (YA). pap., pap. 19.99 *(978-0-9844879-7-4(2),* d4b0f957-8fe9-4c47-bc07-786055531e90) Antarctic Pr., Inc.
Perry, Michael. The Scavengers. 2014. (ENG.). 336p. (J). (gr. 3-7). 16.99 *(978-0-06-202616-3(X),* HarperCollins) HarperCollins Pubs.
Peter, David, et al. Star Trek Comics Classics: the Return of the Worthy. 2007. (Titan Star Trek Collections). (ENG., Illus.). 160p. per. 14.95 *(978-1-84576-319-0(X),* Titan Bks.) Titan Bks. Ltd. GBR. Dist: Penguin Random Hse. LLC.
Peterfreund, Diana. For Darkness Shows the Stars. 2013. (Stars Ser.: 1). (ENG.). 448p. (YA). (gr. 8). pap. 10.99 *(978-0-06-200615-8(0),* Balzer & Bray) HarperCollins Pubs.
—Omega City: Infinity Base. 2018. (Omega City Ser.: 3). (ENG.). 304p. (J). (gr. 3-7). 16.99 *(978-0-06-231091-0(7),* Balzer & Bray) HarperCollins Pubs.
Peterson, Megan Cooley. Scooby-Doo! a Science of Electricity Mystery: The Mutant Crocodile. Cornia, Christian, illus. 2017. (Scooby-Doo Solves It with S. T. E. M. Ser.). (ENG.). 32p. (J). (gr. 3-6). lib. bdg. 28.65 *(978-1-5157-3698-1(9),* 133667, Capstone Pr.) Capstone.
—Scooby-Doo! a Science of Light Mystery: The Angry Alien. Brizuela, Dario, illus. 2017. (Scooby-Doo Solves It with S. T. E. M. Ser.). (ENG.). 32p. (J). (gr. 3-6). lib. bdg. 28.65 *(978-1-5157-3700-1(4),* 133669, Capstone Pr.) Capstone.
—Scooby-Doo! a Science of Magnetism Mystery: The Magnetic Monster. Cornia, Christian, illus. 2017. (Scooby-Doo Solves It with S. T. E. M. Ser.). (ENG.). 32p. (J). (gr. 3-6). lib. bdg. 28.65 *(978-1-5157-3699-8(7),* 133668, Capstone Pr.) Capstone.
Peterson, Scott. The Joker Virus. Cavallaro, Mike, illus. 2012. (Dark Knight Ser.). (ENG.). 88p. (J). (gr. 3-7). lib. bdg. 26.65 *(978-1-4342-4096-5(7),* 119815, Stone Arch Bks.) Capstone.

S

—The Ultimate Returns. 4th ed. 2009. (Spectrobes Ser.: No. 3). (ENG.). 144p. (J). (gr. 3-7). pap. 4.99 *(978-1-4231-0811-5(6))* Disney Pr.

Petri, Michelle. The Fvantom: Omegapocalypse. 2007. 212p. per. 14.95 *(978-0-595-45723-6(1))* iUniverse, Inc.

Pfeffer, Susan Beth. The Dead & the Gone. 2010. (Last Survivors Ser.: 2). 321p. lib. bdg. 19.65 *(978-0-606-14464-3(1))* Turtleback.

—Life As We Knew It. (Life As We Knew It Ser.: 1). (ENG., Illus.). 352p. (YA). (gr. 7-18). 2008. pap. 15.99 *(978-0-15-206154-8(1)*, 1060872) 2006. 13.99 *(978-0-15-205826-5(5)*, 1197505) HarperCollins Pubs. (Clarion Bks.).

—Life As We Knew It. 2008. (Last Survivors Ser.: 1). 347p. (gr. 7-12). lib. bdg. 19.65 *(978-1-4178-1541-8(8))* Turtleback.

—The Life As We Knew It 4-Book Collection. 2015. (Life As We Knew It Ser.). (ENG.). 1252p. (YA). (gr. 7). pap. 29.99 *(978-0-544-54263-1(0)*, 1608921, Clarion Bks.) HarperCollins Pubs.

—The Shade of the Moon. 2014. (Life As We Knew It Ser.: 4). (ENG.). 304p. (YA). (gr. 7). pap. 9.99 *(978-0-544-33615-5(1)*, 1584161, Clarion Bks.) HarperCollins Pubs.

—This World We Live In, Bk. 3. 2011. (Life As We Knew It Ser.: 3). (ENG.). 256p. (YA). (gr. 7). pap. 9.99 *(978-0-547-55028-2(6)*, 1450237, Clarion Bks.) HarperCollins Pubs.

Pflugfelder, Bob & Hockensmith, Steve. Nick & Tesla & the High-Voltage Danger Lab: A Mystery with Gadgets You Can Build Yourself Ourself. 2013. (Nick & Tesla Ser.: 1). (ENG., Illus.). 240p. (J). (gr. 4-7). 12.99 *(978-1-59474-648-2(6))* Quirk Bks.

Phelan, James. The Last Thirteen Book Six: 8. 2014. (ENG., Illus.). 192p. (J). pap. *(978-1-4431-3352-4(3))* Kane Miller.

Philbrick, Rodman. The Last Book in the Universe. unabr. ed. 2004. 224p. (J). (gr. 5-9). pap. 36.00 incl. audio *(978-0-8072-8844-3(6)*, LYA 272 SP, Listening Library) Random Hse. Audio Publishing Group.

Phillips, Terrie. The Ski Trip. 2006. (Illus.). 38p. (J). lib. bdg. 12.95 *(978-0-9789449-0-2(9))* Tbooks Publishing Co.

Phineas and Ferb. Phineas & Ferb Batter Up! 2010. pap. 5.99 *(978-1-4231-2408-5(1))* Disney Pr.

PI Kids. Marvel Avengers: Assembled We Stand Sound Book. 2018. (ENG., Illus.). 12p. (J). bds. 14.99 *(978-1-5037-3406-7(4)*, 2828, PI Kids) Phoenix International Publications, Inc.

Pierce, Meredith Ann. Waters Luminous & Deep. 2005. 320p. (YA). (gr. 7-7). 9.99 *(978-0-14-240356-3(3)*, Firebird) Penguin Young Readers Group.

Pierce, Tamora. Alanna: The First Adventure. unabr. ed. 2004. (Song of the Lioness Ser.: Bk. 1). 216p. (J). (gr. 6-18). pap. 36.00 incl. audio *(978-0-8072-8772-9(5)*, YA263SP, Listening Library) Random Hse. Audio Publishing Group.

Pillsbury, Samuel H. The Invasion of Planet Wampetter. Angom, Matthew, illus. 2003. (Planet Wampetter Adventure Ser.). 133p. (J). (gr. 3-8). 15.00 *(978-0-9622036-6-4(1))*; pap. 8.95 *(978-1-930085-05-3(2))* Perspective Publishing, Inc.

Pinkwater, Daniel M. Adventures of a Cat-Whiskered Girl. 2011. (ENG., Illus.). 288p. (J). (gr. 5-7). pap. 16.95 *(978-0-547-55002-2(2)*, 1450215, Clarion Bks.) HarperCollins Pubs.

—Lizard Music. Pinkwater, Daniel M., illus. 2017. (Illus.). 160p. (J). (gr. 4-7). pap. 11.99 *(978-1-68137-184-9(7)*, NYRB Kids) New York Review of Bks., Inc., The.

Piper, Henry Beam. Little Fuzzy. Lt. ed. 2007. (ENG.). 188p. per. 21.99 *(978-1-4346-2952-4(X))* Creative Media Partners, LLC.

Pittman, Eddie. Red's Planet. 2016. (Red's Planet Ser.: 1). (J). lib. bdg. 20.80 *(978-0-606-38203-8(8))* Turtleback.

—Red's Planet: Book 2: Friends & Foes. 2017. (ENG., Illus.). 192p. (J). (gr. 3-7). pap. 9.99 *(978-1-4197-2315-5(4)*, Amulet Bks.) Abrams, Inc.

Plum, Amy. Neverwake. (Dreamfall Ser.: 2). (ENG.). (YA). (gr. 9). 2019. 320p. pap. 9.99 *(978-0-06-242991-9(4))* 2018. 304p. 17.99 *(978-0-06-242990-2(6))* HarperCollins Pubs. (HarperTeen).

Plummer, Todd. Superhero Science: Kapow! Comic Book Crime Fighters Put Physics to the Test. 2009. (Current Science Ser.). (ENG.). 48p. (J). (gr. 4-6). pap. 8.95 *(978-1-4339-2247-3(9)*, Gareth Stevens Learning Library) Stevens, Gareth Publishing LLLP.

Pohl, Laura. The Last 8. (Last 8 Ser.: 1). (YA). (gr. 8-12). 2020. 384p. pap. 10.99 *(978-1-4926-9156-3(9))* 2019. (ENG.). 368p. 17.99 *(978-1-4926-6989-0(X))* Sourcebooks, Inc.

Pon, Cindy. Ruse. 2019. (ENG., Illus.). 304p. (YA). (gr. 9). 18.99 *(978-1-5344-1992-6(6)*, Simon Pulse) Simon Pulse.

—Want. (ENG.). (YA). (gr. 9). 2019. 352p. pap. 12.99 *(978-1-4814-8923-2(2))* 2017. (Illus.). 336p. 19.99 *(978-1-4814-8922-5(4))* Simon Pulse. (Simon Pulse).

Pope, P. R. Queens of Antares: Volume 1 of the Bloodline Trilogy: Bloodline Returned: Bloodline Returned. 2012. (ENG., Illus.). 224p. pap. *(978-1-908168-01-6(3)*, Elsewhen Pr.) Alnpete Ltd.

Popescu, Petru. Footprints in Time. 2008. 256p. (J). (gr. 5). lib. bdg. 17.89 *(978-0-06-088400-0(2)*, Geringer, Laura Book) HarperCollins Pubs.

Porter, Sarah. Tentacle & Wing. 2017. (ENG.). 272p. (J). (gr. 5-7). 16.99 *(978-1-328-70733-8(4)*, 1672696, Clarion Bks.) HarperCollins Pubs.

Poston, Ashley. Heart of Iron. 2019. (ENG.). 496p. (YA). (gr. 8). pap. 9.99 *(978-0-06-265286-7(9))* 2018. 467p. (J). *(978-0-06-284485-9(7))* HarperCollins Pubs. (Balzer & Bray).

Pratchett, Terry. The Bromeliad Trilogy: Truckers, Diggers, & Wings. 2003. 512p. (J). (gr. 5-18). 18.89 *(978-0-06-054855-1(X))*; (ENG.). 19.99 *(978-0-06-009493-5(1)*, Clarion Bks.) HarperCollins Pubs.

Pratt, Jeffrey. Team Player. 2019. (AI High Ser.). (ENG.). 112p. (YA). (gr. 6-12). pap. 7.99 *(978-1-5415-7294-2(7)*, 179e9c99-a9e7-43fc-90d3-3828427be6be, Darby Creek) Lerner Publishing Group.

Prendergast, G. S. Cold Falling White. (Nahx Invasions Ser.: 2). (ENG.). 576p. (YA). (gr. 9). 2020. pap. 13.99 *(978-1-4814-8188-5(6))* 2019. 19.99 *(978-1-4814-8187-8(8))* Simon & Schuster Bks. For Young Readers. (Simon & Schuster Bks. For Young Readers).

—Cold Falling White. 2019. (ENG.). 368p. (YA). *(978-1-5011-4714-2(5))* Simon & Schuster Children's Publishing.

—Zero Repeat Forever. (Nahx Invasions Ser.: 1). (ENG.). (YA). (gr. 9). 2019. 512p. pap. 13.99 *(978-1-4814-8185-4(1))* 2017. (Illus.). 496p. 17.99 *(978-1-4814-8184-7(3))* Simon & Schuster Bks. For Young Readers. (Simon & Schuster Bks. For Young Readers).

Preston, L. M. Explorer X: Beta. 2012. (ENG.). 264p. (YA). pap. 11.99 *(978-0-9841989-5-5(4))* Phenomenal One Pr.

—The Pack. 2010. (ENG.). 316p. (J). pap. 14.99 *(978-0-9841989-7-9(0))* Phenomenal One Pr.

—The Pack - Retribution: Retribution. 2012. (ENG.). 250p. (YA). (gr. 8-12). pap. 11.99 *(978-0-9850251-0-6(7))* Phenomenal One Pr.

Price, Kevin, ed. The Mystery of Love: A Born Storyteller Collection of Mystery Adventure & Science Fiction Stories. 2013. (Illus.). 308p. pap. *(978-0-9872559-6-9(7)*, Crotchet Quaver) Logorythm.

Price, Lissa. Starters. (Starters Ser.: 1). (ENG.). (YA). (gr. 7). 2013. 384p. pap. 10.99 *(978-0-385-74248-1(7)*, Ember)1. 2012. 352p. lib. bdg. 26.19 *(978-0-375-99060-1(7)*, Delacorte Pr.) Random Hse. Children's Bks.

Price, Susan. A Sterkarm Kiss. 2004. (ENG.). 288p. (J). (gr. 7-18). 16.99 *(978-0-06-072197-8(9))* HarperCollins Pubs.

Project Cain. 2014. (ENG., Illus.). 384p. (YA). (gr. 9). pap. 11.99 *(978-1-4424-7698-1(2)*, Simon & Schuster Bks. For Young Readers) Simon & Schuster Bks. For Young Readers.

Psycho Backho: Arc of Fury - the Cataclysm. 2005. (YA). per. *(978-1-59620-003-6(0))* Science of Knowledge Pr.

Publications International Ltd. Staff. Wall E Large Sound BK. 2008. 24p. (J). 17.98 *(978-1-4127-8991-2(5)*, PIL Kids) Publications International, Ltd.

Publications International Ltd. Staff, ed. Star Wars: Revenge of the Sith: Play-a-Sound. 2005. (Illus.). 24p. (J). 16.98 *(978-1-4127-3487-5(8)*, 7262800) Publications International, Ltd.

Pullman, Philip. The Adventures of John Blake: Mystery of the Ghost Ship. Fordham, Fred, illus. 2017. lib. bdg. 33.05 *(978-0-606-40195-1(4))* Turtleback.

—La Daga. Gallart, Dolors, tr. 7th ed. 2005. (Escritura desatada Ser.).Tr. of Subtle Knife. (SPA., Illus.). 283p. (YA). (gr. 7-11). 13.95 *(978-84-406-8409-7(6))* Ediciones B ESP. Dist: Independent Pubs. Group.

Quintana, Adrienne. Eruption. 2015. 282p. (YA). pap. 16.99 *(978-1-4621-1536-5(5))* Cedar Fort, Inc./CFI Distribution.

Ralles, H. J. Darok 10. 2005. 230p. (J). pap. 9.95 *(978-1-929976-31-7(3))* Top Pubns., Ltd.

—Keeper of the Realm, Vol. 2. 2003. (Illus.). 248p. (J). pap. 9.95 *(978-1-929976-21-8(6))* Top Pubns., Ltd.

Rauch, Earl Mac. Buckaroo Banzai TP Vol 02 No Matter Where You Go. 2014. (ENG., Illus.). 158p. (YA). pap. 16.95 *(978-1-936814-72-5(2)*, 6593acc1-d7d2-4f81-ad60-ecbc4ffc1276) Moonstone.

Rauch, Mac & Richter, W. D. BUCKAROO BANZAI: TPB Vol. 1: Return of the Screw: TPB Vol. 1: Return of the Screw. 2014. (ENG., Illus.). 120p. (YA). pap. 15.95 *(978-1-936814-71-8(4)*, 4c0d5e6f-61ab-41a2-a04c-6031951094d7) Moonstone.

Raughley, Sarah. Legacy of Light. (Effigies Ser.: 3). (ENG.). 512p. (YA). (gr. 9). 2019. pap. 14.99 *(978-1-4814-6684-4(4))* 2018. (Illus.). 21.99 *(978-1-4814-6683-7(6))* Simon Pulse. (Simon Pulse).

—Siege of Shadows. (Effigies Ser.: 2). (ENG.). (YA). (gr. 9). 2018. 464p. pap. 12.99 *(978-1-4814-6681-3(X))* 2017. (Illus.). 448p. 18.99 *(978-1-4814-6680-6(1))* Simon Pulse. (Simon Pulse).

Rawson, Christopher. Gnomes & Goblins. Cartwright, Stephen, illus. 2004. (Young Reading Series One Ser.). 48p. (J). (gr. 2-18). pap. 5.95 *(978-0-7945-0407-6(8)*, Usborne) EDC Publishing.

Reese, Jenn. Above World. 2013. (Above World Ser.: 1). (ENG.). 368p. (J). (gr. 5). pap. 8.99 *(978-0-7636-6259-2(3))* Candlewick Pr.

—Mirage. 2013. (Above World Ser.: 2). (ENG.). 368p. (J). (gr. 5). 16.99 *(978-0-7636-5418-4(3))* Candlewick Pr.

Reeve, Philip. Black Light Express. 2017. (Railhead Ser.). (ENG.). 352p. (YA). (gr. 7-12). 17.95 *(978-1-63079-096-7(6)*, 136360, Switch Pr.) Capstone.

—A Darkling Plain, 4. 2012. (Predator Cities Ser.: 4). (ENG.). 544p. (J). (gr. 7-12). 24.94 *(978-0-545-22214-3(1))* Scholastic, Inc.

—A Darkling Plain (Mortal Engines, Book 4) 2017. (Mortal Engines Ser.: 4). (ENG.). 544p. (YA). (gr. 7-7). pap. 12.99 *(978-1-338-20115-4(8)*, Scholastic Pr.) Scholastic, Inc.

—Fever Crumb (the Fever Crumb Trilogy, Book 1), Bk. 1. 2011. (Fever Crumb Ser.: 1). (ENG.). 336p. (YA). (gr. 7-7). pap. 12.99 *(978-0-545-22215-0(X))* Scholastic, Inc.

—Infernal Devices. 2012. (Predator Cities Ser.: 3). lib. bdg. 19.65 *(978-0-606-23951-6(0))* Turtleback.

—Infernal Devices (Mortal Engines, Book 3) 2017. (Mortal Engines Ser.: 3). (ENG.). 352p. (YA). (gr. 7-7). pap. 9.99 *(978-1-338-20114-7(X)*, Scholastic Pr.) Scholastic, Inc.

—Mortal Engines (Mortal Engines, Book 1) 2017. (Mortal Engines Ser.: 1). (ENG.). 320p. (YA). (gr. 7-7). pap. 12.99 *(978-1-338-20112-3(3)*, Scholastic Pr.) Scholastic, Inc.

—Predator's Gold (Mortal Engines, Book 2) 2017. (Mortal Engines Ser.: 2). (ENG.) 336p. (YA). (gr. 7-7). pap. 12.99 *(978-1-338-20113-0(1)*, Scholastic Pr.) Scholastic, Inc.

—Station Zero. 2019. (Railhead Ser.). (ENG.). 320p. (YA). (gr. 7-12). lib. bdg. 17.95 *(978-1-68446-053-3(0)*, 140333, Capstone Editions) Capstone.

—A Web of Air (the Fever Crumb Trilogy, Book 2), 2. Seife, Emily, ed. 2013. (Fever Crumb Ser.: 2). (ENG.). 304p. (YA). (gr. 7-12). pap. 9.99 *(978-0-545-22217-4(6))* Scholastic, Inc.

Reichs, Brendan. Chrysalis. 2019. (Project Nemesis Ser.: 3). (ENG.). 416p. (YA). (gr. 7). 18.99 *(978-0-525-51705-4(7)*, G.P. Putnam's Sons Books for Young Readers) Penguin Young Readers Group.

—Genesis. 2019. (Project Nemesis Ser.: 2). (ENG.). 528p. (YA). (gr. 7). pap. 10.99 *(978-0-399-54497-2(6)*, Penguin Books) Penguin Young Readers Group.

—Nemesis. 2018. (Project Nemesis Ser.: 1). (ENG.). 480p. (YA). (gr. 7). pap. 12.99 *(978-0-399-54494-1(1)*, Penguin Books) Penguin Young Readers Group.

Reichs, Kathy. Code: A Virals Novel. 2013. (Virals Ser.: 3). (ENG.). 432p. (J). (gr. 5). pap. 11.99 *(978-1-59514-572-7(9)*, Puffin Books) Penguin Young Readers Group.

—Virals. 2014. lthr. 79.00 *(978-1-62715-582-3(1))* Leatherbound Bestsellers.

—Virals. 2011. (Virals Ser.: 1). (ENG.). 480p. (J). (gr. 5-18). 11.99 *(978-1-59514-426-3(9)*, Puffin Books) Penguin Young Readers Group.

—Virals. 2011. 20.00 *(978-1-61383-226-4(5))* Perfection Learning Corp.

Reichs, Kathy & Reichs, Brendan. Code. 2013. (Virals Ser.: 3). lib. bdg. 19.65 *(978-0-606-32140-2(3))* Turtleback.

—Trace Evidence. 2016. (Virals Ser.). lib. bdg. 20.85 *(978-0-606-38400-1(6))* Turtleback.

—Virals. 2011. (Virals Ser.: 1). lib. bdg. 20.85 *(978-0-606-23069-8(6))* Turtleback.

Reid, Kate. Operation Timewarp. 2003. (ENG.). 195p. pap. *(978-1-84255-203-2(1)*, Orion Children's Bks.) Hachette Children's Group.

Reilly, Carmel & Young, Karen. Buzz Takes Over. 2008. (Rigby Focus Forward: Level I Ser.). (Illus.). 24p. (J). (gr. 4-7). pap. *(978-1-4190-3743-6(9)*, Rigby) Pearson Education Australia.

Reintgen, Scott. Nyxia Unleashed. (Nyxia Triad Ser.: 2). (ENG.). (YA). (gr. 7). 2019. 416p. pap. 10.99 *(978-0-399-55686-9(9)*, Ember) 2018. 400p. 17.99 *(978-0-399-55683-8(4)*, Crown Books For Young Readers) Random Hse. Children's Bks.

—Nyxia Uprising. 2019. (Nyxia Triad Ser.: 3). (ENG.). 368p. (YA). (gr. 7). 17.99 *(978-0-399-55687-6(7)*, Crown Books For Young Readers) Random Hse. Children's Bks.

Reiss, Kathryn. Paint by Magic. 2003. (ENG.). 288p. (J). (gr. 5-7). pap. 17.95 *(978-0-15-204925-6(8)*, 1194872, Clarion Bks.) HarperCollins Pubs.

Renick, Sam X. The Adventures of Sammy the Saver In: Will Sammy Ride the World's First Space Coaster?, Vol. 2. Alvarado, Juan, illus. 2003. 32p. (J). pap. 8.95 *(978-0-9713664-1-1(1))* It's A Habit! Co., The.

Revealed. 2014. (Missing Ser.: 7). (ENG., Illus.). 448p. (J). (gr. 3-7). 19.99 *(978-1-4169-8986-8(2)*, Simon & Schuster Bks. For Young Readers) Simon & Schuster Bks. For Young Readers.

Revis, Beth. Across the Universe. 2012. (Across the Universe Trilogy: Bk. 1). (ENG.). (YA). (gr. 7-12). 54.99 *(978-1-61587-857-4(2)*, Penguin AudioBooks) Penguin Publishing Group.

—Across the Universe, 1. 2011. (Across the Universe Ser.: 1). (ENG.). 448p. (YA). (gr. 9-12). pap. 11.99 *(978-1-59514-467-6(6)*, Razorbill) Penguin Young Readers Group.

—Across the Universe. 2011. (Across the Universe Trilogy Ser.: 1). lib. bdg. 20.85 *(978-0-606-23139-8(0))* Turtleback.

—A Million Suns. 2012. (Across the Universe Trilogy: 2). lib. bdg. 20.85 *(978-0-606-26632-1(1))* Turtleback.

—Shades of Earth. 2013. (Across the Universe Trilogy: 3). lib. bdg. 20.85 *(978-0-606-32117-4(9))* Turtleback.

—Shades of Earth: An Across the Universe Novel. 2013. (Across the Universe Ser.: 3). (ENG.). 448p. (YA). (gr. 9). pap. 10.99 *(978-1-59514-615-1(6)*, Razorbill) Penguin Young Readers Group.

Rex, Adam. The True Meaning of Smekday, 1. Rex, Adam, illus. 2009. (Smek Smeries Ser.: 1). (ENG., Illus.). 432p. (J). (gr. 3-7). pap. 8.99 *(978-0-7868-4901-7(0))* Little, Brown Bks. for Young Readers.

—The True Meaning of Smekday. 2009. (Illus.). 423p. 18.00 *(978-1-60686-525-5(0))* Perfection Learning Corp.

Rex, Michael. The Egg of Misery: Fangbone, Third Grade Barbarian. Rex, Michael, illus. 2012. (Fangbone! Third Grade Barbarian Ser.: 2). (Illus.). 128p. (J). (gr. 2-4). 9.99 *(978-0-399-25522-9(2)*, G.P. Putnam's Sons Books for Young Readers) Penguin Young Readers Group.

—Fangbone! Third-Grade Barbarian. 2012. (Illus.). 120p. (J). *(978-0-545-44042-4(4)*, Putnam Juvenile) Penguin Publishing Group.

Reynolds, Jason. Miles Morales. 2018. (YA). lib. bdg. 20.85 *(978-0-606-40966-7(1))* Turtleback.

—Miles Morales: Spider-Man. 2018. (Marvel YA Novel Ser.). (ENG., Illus.). 272p. (YA). (gr. 7-12). pap. 10.99 *(978-1-4847-8850-9(8))* Marvel Worldwide, Inc.

—Miles Morales: SpiderMan. 2017. (Marvel YA Novel Ser.). (ENG., Illus.). 272p. (YA). (gr. 7-12). 17.99 *(978-1-4847-8748-9(X))* Marvel Worldwide, Inc.

RH Disney. WALL-E (Disney/Pixar WALL-e) RH Disney, illus. 2008. (Little Golden Book Ser.). (ENG., Illus.). 24p. (J). (gr. -1-2). 5.99 *(978-0-7364-2422-6(9)*, RH/Disney) Random Hse. Children's Bks.

Richard Richtmyer. A Bit of Magic: A Novel. 2009. 116p. pap. 10.95 *(978-1-4401-5565-9(8))* iUniverse, Inc.

Richards, C. J. Battle of the Bots. 2017. (Robots Rule Ser.: 3). (ENG.). (J). (gr. 2-5). lib. bdg. 17.20 *(978-0-606-39811-4(2))* Turtleback.

Richards, Justin. Rewind Assassin. 2007. (Time Runners Ser.: 2). (ENG.). 208p. (J). (gr. 4-7). pap. 8.99 *(978-1-4169-2643-6(7))* Simon & Schuster, Ltd. GBR. Dist: Simon & Schuster, Inc.

Richardson, D. L. Feedback. 2013. 254p. pap. 11.99 *(978-1-939194-83-1(0))* Etopia Pr.

Richardson, Fay Lapka. Dark is a Color. 2004. 264p. (J). pap. 12.95 *(978-0-9744989-6-6(3))* Fox Song Bks.

Riggs, Carol. The Body Institute. 2015. (ENG.). 368p. (J). pap. 9.99 *(978-1-63375-125-5(2)*, 9781633751255) Entangled Publishing, LLC.

—The Lying Planet. 2016. (ENG., Illus.). (YA). (gr. 7). pap. 17.99 *(978-1-68281-304-1(5))* Entangled Publishing, LLC.

Riggs, Ransom. Miss Peregrine's Journal for Peculiar Children. 2016. (Miss Peregrine's Peculiar Children Ser.). 192p. (YA). (gr. 9). 14.99 *(978-1-59474-940-7(X))* Quirk Bks.

Riis, Jon. Something for Nothing: A Diploma for Your Life Experience. 2010. 192p. (YA). pap. 17.00 *(978-1-934376-21-8(3))* Balona Bks.

Ripley, T. P. Lily Lovebug & the Unconquered Planet. 2013. 170p. pap. *(978-1-908910-43-1(7))* Crooked Cat Publishing.

Ritchie, Brendan. Beyond Carousel. 2017. (Carousel Ser.). 368p. (YA). (gr. 7). 19.99 *(978-1-925164-03-9(9))* Fremantle Pr. AUS. Dist: Independent Pubs. Group.

Rivera, Lilliam. Dealing in Dreams. 2019. (ENG., Illus.). 336p. (YA). (gr. 9). 18.99 *(978-1-4814-7214-2(3)*, Simon & Schuster Bks. For Young Readers) Simon & Schuster Bks. For Young Readers.

Robbins, Trina. The Bark in Space: Book 5, No. 5. Page, Tyler, illus. 2013. (Chicagoland Detective Agency Ser.: 5). (ENG.). 64p. (J). (gr. 4-8). pap. 6.95 *(978-1-4677-0725-1(2)*, 659d0711-80dc-41a4-866d-7c460cfaabf5, Graphic Universe™) Lerner Publishing Group.

—The Drained Brains Caper: Book 1, No. 1. Page, Tyler, illus. 2010. (Chicagoland Detective Agency Ser.: 1). (ENG.). 64p. (J). (gr. 4-8). pap. 8.99 *(978-0-7613-5635-6(5)*, 3b3c032d-e980-466a-9075-55d5ee724833, Graphic Universe™) Lerner Publishing Group.

—Night of the Living Dogs. Page, Tyler, illus. 2012. (Chicagoland Detective Agency Ser.). 64p. (J). (gr. 4-8). pap. 39.62 *(978-0-7613-9313-9(7)*, Graphic Universe™) Lerner Publishing Group.

Roberts, Jeyn. Dark Inside. (ENG.). (YA). (gr. 9). 2012. 352p. pap. 12.99 *(978-1-4424-2352-7(8))* 2011. 336p. 17.99 *(978-1-4424-2351-0(X))* Simon & Schuster Bks. For Young Readers. (Simon & Schuster Bks. For Young Readers).

—Rage Within. (ENG., 368p. (YA). (gr. 9). 2013. Illus.). pap. 11.99 *(978-1-4424-2355-8(2))* 2012. 17.99 *(978-1-4424-2354-1(4))* Simon & Schuster Bks. For Young Readers. (Simon & Schuster Bks. For Young Readers).

Roberts, Willo Davis. The Girl with the Silver Eyes. 2011. (ENG.). 192p. (J). (gr. 3-7). pap. 8.99 *(978-1-4424-2170-7(3)*, Aladdin) Simon & Schuster Children's Publishing.

Robinson, Anitha. Broken Worlds. 2014. (Broken Worlds Ser.). (ENG.). 200p. (YA). (gr. 7-11). pap. 8.95 *(978-1-933767-37-6(5))* CBAY Bks.

Robinson, Kelley. Naming: Book One of the Magic of Io Series. Curtiss, Melody, illus. 2013. 138p. pap. 8.95 *(978-0-9745865-1-9(X)*, SarahRose Children's Bks.) SarahRose Publishing.

Robinson, Michelle. Goodnight Spaceman: The Perfect Bedtime Book! East, Nick, illus. 2017. (Goodnight Ser.). (ENG.). 32p. (J). (gr. -1 — 1). pap. 7.99 *(978-1-4380-1086-1(9))* Sourcebooks, Inc.

Robinson, R. M. Death by Paradox. 2014. (Illus.). 320p. 29.95 *(978-1-939434-14-2(9))* Firefall Editions.

Robson, Jenny. Savannah 2116 Ad. 2005. 144p. pap. *(978-0-624-04230-3(8))* Tafelberg Pubs., Ltd.

Rockwell, Carey. On the Trail of Space Pirates. Ley, Willy, ed. 2007. 140p. per. 11.95 *(978-1-60312-283-2(4))* Aegypan.

—On the Trail of Space Pirates. 2007. 140p. 24.95 *(978-1-60312-781-3(X))* Aegypan.

—The Revolt on Venus: The TOM CORBETT Space Cadet Adventure. 2007. (ENG.). 180p. pap. 19.99 *(978-1-4264-9548-9(X))* Creative Media Partners, LLC.

—Sabotage in Space. 2007. 108p. per. *(978-1-4068-3959-3(0))* Echo Library.

—Treachery in Outer Space. 2017. (ENG., Illus.). (J). 23.95 *(978-1-374-97145-5(6))*; pap. 13.95 *(978-1-374-97144-8(8))* Capital Communications, Inc.

Rockwell, Carey & Ley, Willy. The Space Pioneers: A Tom Corbett Space Cadet Adventure. Glanzman, Louis, illus. 2011. 220p. 44.95 *(978-1-258-10097-1(5))* Literary Licensing, LLC.

Rockwood, Roy. Lost on the Moon. 2008. 132p. pap. 10.95 *(978-1-60664-236-8(7))* Rodgers, Alan Bks.

—Through Space to Mars. 2008. 128p. (gr. 4-7). 23.95 *(978-1-60664-801-8(2))*; pap. 11.95 *(978-1-60664-173-6(5))* Aegypan.

Rodda, Emily. Isle of the Dead. 2004. (Dragons of Deltora Ser.: No. 3). 195p. (J). lib. bdg. 16.92 *(978-1-4242-0273-7(6))* Fitzgerald Bks.

—Shadowgate. 2004. (Dragons of Deltora Ser.: No. 2). 195p. (J). lib. bdg. 16.92 *(978-1-4242-0274-4(4))* Fitzgerald Bks.

Roe, David & Reader's Digest Editors. Mix & Match. Milne, Alex & Ruffolo, Rob, illus. 2007. (ENG.). 12p. (J). (gr. -1-1). bds. 14.99 *(978-0-7944-1286-9(6))* Reader's Digest Assn., Inc., The.

Rogers, Anne. The magic rainbow large Print. 2008. 332p. pap. 30.95 *(978-1-4092-3059-5(7))* Lulu Pr., Inc.

—The magic rainbow very large Print. 2008. 502p. pap. 39.50 *(978-1-4092-3065-6(1))* Lulu Pr., Inc.

Roland, Timothy. Monkey Me & the School Ghost. Roland, Timothy, illus. 2014. (Monkey Me Ser.: 4). (ENG., Illus.). 96p. (J). (gr. 1-3). pap. 4.99 *(978-0-545-55989-8(8))* Scholastic, Inc.

Rollins, Danielle. Stolen Time. (Dark Stars Ser.: 1). (ENG.). (YA). (gr. 9). 2020. 432p. pap. 10.99 *(978-0-06-267995-6(3))* 2019. 416p. 17.99 *(978-0-06-267994-9(5))* HarperCollins Pubs. (HarperTeen).

Rollins, James. Jake Ransom & the Howling Sphinx. 2012. (Jake Ransom Ser.: 2). (ENG.). 160p. (J). (gr. 5). pap. 7.99 *(978-0-06-147384-5(7)*, HarperCollins) HarperCollins Pubs.

Rooper, Leah. Jane Unwrapped. 2015. (ENG., Illus.). 290p. (J). pap. 16.99 *(978-1-943892-66-2(0))* Entangled Publishing, LLC.

Rose, Imogen. Initiation: Japanese Language Edition. Galeano, Tomomi, tr. 2013. 482p. pap. 16.99 *(978-1-940015-04-0(9))* Imogen Rose.

Rose, Sue. Jinxed! 2006. (Unfabulous! Ser.). (Illus.). 118p. (J). *(978-1-4156-5170-4(1))* Scholastic, Inc.

Rosenberg, Michael. The Story of Bendalot Part: The Return Home. 2009. (Illus.). 36p. pap. 15.49 *(978-1-4389-8294-6(1))* AuthorHouse.

Rosenblum, Gregg. Revolution 19. (Revolution 19 Ser.: 1). (ENG.). (YA). (gr. 8). 2014. 288p. pap. 9.99 *(978-0-06-212596-5(6))* 2013. 272p. 17.99 *(978-0-06-212595-8(8))* HarperCollins Pubs. (HarperTeen).

Rosenow, Ty. The Historical Adventures of Thomas Balfour. 2012. (ENG.). 184p. pap. 17.95 *(978-1-105-94011-8(X))* Lulu Pr., Inc.

Ross, Joel. The Fog Diver. 2015. (Fog Diver Ser.: 1). (ENG.). 336p. (J). (gr. 3-7). 16.99 *(978-0-06-235293-4(8)*, HarperCollins) HarperCollins Pubs.

—The Lost Compass. 2016. (Fog Diver Ser.: 2). (ENG.). 352p. (J). (gr. 3-7). 16.99 *(978-0-06-235297-2(0)*, HarperCollins) HarperCollins Pubs.

Rossi, Veronica. Into the Still Blue. 2014. 392p. (YA). *(978-0-06-229518-7(7))* Harper & Row Ltd.

—Under the Never Sky. 2012. (Under the Never Sky Trilogy Ser.: 1). (ENG.). 400p. (YA). (gr. 9). pap. 10.99 *(978-0-06-207204-7(8)*, HarperCollins) HarperCollins Pubs.

Rossing, Nina. Supermassive. 2016. (ENG., Illus.). (J). 27.99 *(978-1-63533-076-2(9)*, Harmony Ink Pr.) Dreamspinner Pr.

Roth, Jonathan. Party Crashers, 2. 2019. (Beep & Bob Ser.). (ENG.). 128p. (J). (gr. 2-4). 15.59 *(978-1-64310-827-8(1))* Penworthy Co., LLC, The.

—Party Crashers. Roth, Jonathan, illus. 2018. (Beep & Bob Ser.: 2). (ENG., Illus.). 128p. (J). (gr. 1-4). 16.99 *(978-1-4814-8856-3(2))*; pap. 6.99 *(978-1-4814-8855-6(4))* Simon & Schuster Children's Publishing. (Aladdin).

—Too Much Space!, 1. 2019. (Beep & Bob Ser.). (ENG.). 128p. (J). (gr. 2-4). 15.59 *(978-1-64310-829-2(8))* Penworthy Co., LLC, The.

—Too Much Space! Roth, Jonathan, illus. 2018. (Beep & Bob Ser.: 1). (ENG., Illus.). 128p. (J). (gr. 1-4). 17.99 *(978-1-4814-8853-2(8))*; pap. 5.99 *(978-1-4814-8852-5(X))* Simon & Schuster Children's Publishing. (Aladdin).

Roth, Veronica. Allegiant. (Divergent Ser.: 3). (ENG.). (YA). (gr. 9). 2016. 592p. pap. 15.99 *(978-0-06-202407-7(8))* 2013. 544p. 19.99 *(978-0-06-202406-0(X))* HarperCollins Pubs. (Tegen, Katherine Bks).

—Allegiant. l.t. ed. 2016. (Divergent Ser.: 3). (ENG.). 580p. pap. 15.99 *(978-1-59413-960-4(1)*, Large Print Pr.) Thorndike Pr.

—Allegiant. 2016. (Divergent Ser.: 3). lib. bdg. 24.50 *(978-0-606-38141-3(4))*; lib. bdg. 24.50 *(978-0-606-38182-6(1))* Turtleback.

—Allegiant Movie Tie-In Edition. 2016. (Divergent Ser.: 3). (ENG.). 592p. (YA). (gr. 9). pap. 12.99 *(978-0-06-242009-1(7))*; 19.99 *(978-0-06-242008-4(9))* HarperCollins Pubs. (Tegen, Katherine Bks).

—Carve the Mark. 2017. (Carve the Mark Ser.: 1). (ENG.). (YA). (gr. 9). 512p. pap. 12.99 *(978-0-06-234864-7(7))*; (Illus.). 480p. 22.99 *(978-0-06-234863-0(9))* HarperCollins Pubs. (Tegen, Katherine Bks).

—Carve the Mark. 2018. (YA). lib. bdg. 24.50 *(978-0-606-41030-4(9))* Turtleback.

—Divergent. 2013. (KOR.). *(978-89-5660-710-8(9))* Eunhaeng Namu Publishing Co.

—Divergent. (ENG.). 576p. (gr. 9-12). 10.91 *(978-1-63245-531-4(5))* HF Group, LLC., The.

—Divergent. Delort, Nicolas, photos by. 2014. (Divergent Ser.: 1). (ENG., Illus.). 576p. (YA). (gr. 9). pap. 16.99 *(978-0-06-238724-0(3)*, Tegen, Katherine Bks) HarperCollins Pubs.

—Divergent. 2012. (ENG.). 512p. pap. *(978-0-06-219406-0(2))* HarperCollins Pubs.

—Divergent, 3 vols. Delort, Nicolas, photos by. 2011. (Divergent Ser.: 1). (ENG., Illus.). 496p. (YA). (gr. 9-18). 21.99 *(978-0-06-202402-2(7)*, Tegen, Katherine Bks) HarperCollins Pubs.

—Divergent, Book 1. 2012. (ENG.). 496p. *(978-0-00-742042-1(0))* HarperCollins Pubs. Ltd.

—Divergent. 2009. (Divergent Ser.: Bk. 1). 11.04 *(978-0-7848-3786-3(4)*, Everbind) Marco Bk. Co.

—Divergent. 2014. (Divergent Trilogy Ser.). (ENG.). (YA). (gr. 9). lib. bdg. 23.60 *(978-1-62765-593-4(X))* Perfection Learning Corp.

—Divergent. l.t. ed. 2014. (Divergent Ser.: Bk. 1). (ENG.). 530p. pap. 12.99 *(978-1-59413-745-7(5)*, Large Print Pr.) Thorndike Pr.

—Divergent. 2014. (Divergent Ser.: 1). (YA). lib. bdg. 24.50 *(978-0-606-36515-4(X))* Turtleback.

—Divergent Collector's Edition. Delort, Nicolas, photos by. collector's ed. 2014. (Divergent Ser.: 1). (ENG., Illus.). 576p. (YA). (gr. 9). 19.99 *(978-0-06-235217-0(2)*, Tegen, Katherine Bks) HarperCollins Pubs.

—Divergent Movie Tie-In Edition. Delort, Nicolas, photos by. movie tie-in ed. 2014. (Divergent Ser.: 1). (ENG.). 496p. (YA). (gr. 9). 17.99 *(978-0-06-228984-1(5)*, Tegen, Katherine Bks) HarperCollins Pubs.

—Divergent Series 3-Book Box Set: Divergent, Insurgent, Allegiant, 3 vols., Set. 2013. (Divergent Ser.: Bks. 1-3). (ENG.). (YA). (gr. 9). 55.97 *(978-0-06-227878-4(9)*, Tegen, Katherine Bks) HarperCollins Pubs.

—The Fates Divide. l.t. ed. 2018. (ENG.). 602p. (YA). lib. bdg. 24.99 *(978-1-4328-5197-2(7))* Cengage Gale.

—The Fates Divide. 2019. (Carve the Mark Ser.: 2). (ENG.). 480p. (YA). (gr. 9). pap. 14.99 *(978-0-06-242696-3(6))* 2018. (ENG.). 464p. (J). *(978-0-00-819220-4(0))* 2018. (Illus.). 443p. (J). *(978-0-06-284238-1(2))*Bk. 2. 2018. (Carve the Mark Ser.: 2). (ENG., Illus.). 464p. (YA). (gr. 9). 21.99 *(978-0-06-242695-6(8))* HarperCollins Pubs. (Tegen, Katherine Bks).

—Four: a Divergent Collection. 2014. (Divergent Series Story Ser.). (ENG.). 304p. (YA). (gr. 9). 19.99 *(978-0-06-234521-9(4)*, Tegen, Katherine Bks) HarperCollins Pubs.

—Insurgent. 2014. (KOR.). *(978-89-5660-758-0(3))* Eunhaeng Namu Publishing Co.

—Insurgent. 2015. pap. *(978-0-06-238845-2(2))* 2015. (Divergent Ser.: 2). (ENG.). 592p. (YA). (gr. 9). pap. 14.99 *(978-0-06-202405-3(1))* 2012. (Divergent Ser.: 2). (ENG.). 544p. (YA). (gr. 9). 18.99 *(978-0-06-202404-6(3))* 2012. (Divergent Ser.: 2). 544p. (YA). (gr. 9). pap. 12.00 *(978-0-06-212784-6(5))* HarperCollins Pubs. (Tegen, Katherine Bks).

—Insurgent. 2015. (Divergent Trilogy Ser.). (ENG.). (YA). (gr. 9). lib. bdg. 23.60 *(978-1-62765-988-8(9))* Perfection Learning Corp.

—Insurgent. 2015. (Divergent Ser.: 2). (YA). lib. bdg. 24.50 *(978-0-606-36475-1(7))* Turtleback.

—Insurgent Collector's Edition. collector's ed. 2012. (Divergent Ser.: 2). (ENG.). 592p. (YA). (gr. 9). 19.99 *(978-0-06-223493-3(5)*, Tegen, Katherine Bks) HarperCollins Pubs.

—Insurgent Movie Tie-In Edition. movie tie-in ed. 2015. (Divergent Ser.: 2). (ENG.). 592p. (YA). (gr. 9). pap. 12.99 *(978-0-06-237285-7(8)*, Tegen, Katherine Bks) HarperCollins Pubs.

Rothenberg, Jess. The Kingdom. 2019. (Illus.). 340p. (YA). *(978-1-250-25935-6(5))* Holt, Henry & Co.

Routley, Becky. Moon Golf. 2009. (Illus.). 28p. pap. 12.49 *(978-1-4490-4713-9(0))* AuthorHouse.

Roza, Greg. The Messy Robot, 1 vol. 2006. (Neighborhood Readers Ser.). (ENG., Illus.). 16p. (gr. 1-2). pap. 6.50 *(978-1-4042-7184-5(8)*, ab104137-9707-4ea4-b9ca-64861955aa1d, Rosen Classroom) Rosen Publishing Group, Inc., The.

Rubin, Lance. Denton Little's Deathdate. 2015. (Denton Little Ser.: 1). (ENG.). 352p. (YA). (gr. 9). 17.99 *(978-0-553-49696-3(4)*, Knopf Bks. for Young Readers) Random Hse. Children's Bks.

Rubinstein, Gillian. Space Demons. 2018. (Space Demons Ser.: Vol. 1). (ENG.). 204p. (YA). (gr. 7). pap. *(978-1-925883-04-6(3))* Ligature.

Ruby, Laura. York: the Shadow Cipher. Stevenson, Dave, illus. 2017. (York Ser.: 1). (ENG.). 496p. (J). (gr. 3-7). E-Book *(978-0-06-230695-1(2)*, 9780062306951); 17.99 *(978-0-06-230693-7(6))* HarperCollins Pubs. (Walden Pond Pr.).

Rucka, Greg. Journey to Star Wars: The Force Awakens — Shattered Empire. 2015. (Star Wars Graphic Novels Ser.). (YA). lib. bdg. 29.40 *(978-0-606-37933-5(9))* Turtleback.

—Star Wars the Force Awakens: Before the Awakening. 2016. (JPN.). 191p. (J). pap. *(978-4-06-219884-4(3))* Kodansha, Ltd.

Runberg, Sylvain. Orbital Vol. 1: Scars. Saincatin, Jerome, tr. Pellé, Serge, illus. 2009. (Orbital Ser.: 1). 47p. pap. 11.95 *(978-1-905460-89-2(9))* CineBook GBR. Dist: National Bk. Network.

—Orbital Vol. 5: Justice. Pelle, Serge, illus. 2014. (Orbital Ser.: 5). 56p. pap. 13.95 *(978-1-84918-172-3(1))* CineBook GBR. Dist: National Bk. Network.

Rush, Jennifer. Altered. 2013. (Altered Ser.: 1). (ENG.). 352p. (YA). (gr. 7-17). pap. 10.00 *(978-0-316-19709-0(2))* Little, Brown Bks. for Young Readers.

Russell, P. M. The Wormhole Adventures: Travel Is Relative. 2007. 57p. pap. 16.95 *(978-1-60441-426-4(X))* America Star Bks.

Russell, Romina. Black Moon. 2017. (Zodiac Ser.: 3). 416p. (YA). (gr. 7). pap. 11.99 *(978-1-59514-746-2(2)*, Razorbill) Penguin Young Readers Group.

—Thirteen Rising. (Zodiac Ser.: 4). (YA). (gr. 7). 2018. 368p. pap. 10.99 *(978-0-448-49356-5(X))* 2017. 352p. 18.99 *(978-0-448-49355-8(1))* Penguin Young Readers Group. (Razorbill).

—Zodiac. 2015. (Zodiac Ser.: 1). 480p. (YA). (gr. 7). 13.99 *(978-1-59514-741-7(1)*, Razorbill) Penguin Young Readers Group.

Rust, Ned. Patrick Griffin's First Birthday on Ith. 2018. (Patrick Griffin & the Three Worlds Ser.: 2). (ENG., Illus.). 304p. (J). pap. 15.99 *(978-1-250-15892-5(3)*, 900185538) Square Fish.

Rutkoski, Marie. The Shadow Society. 2013. (ENG.). 448p. (YA). (gr. 7-12). pap. 17.99 *(978-1-250-03424-3(8)*, 900120597) Square Fish.

Rymer, Alta M. Stars of Obron: Chambo Returns. Rymer, Alta M., illus. (Tales of Planet Artembo Ser.: Bk. 3). (Illus.). 56p. (Orig.). (J). (gr. 5-7). pap. 20.00 *(978-0-9600792-3-0(8))* Rymer Bks.

Sadler, Karen. Rebellion, 1 vol. 2014. (Tankborn Ser.: 3). (ENG.). 400p. (YA). (gr. 7-12). 19.95 *(978-1-60060-984-8(8)*, leelowtu) Lee & Low Bks., Inc.

Sage, Angie. Maximillian Fly. 2019. (ENG.). 384p. (J). (gr. 3-7). 16.99 *(978-0-06-257116-8(8)*, Tegen, Katherine Bks) HarperCollins Pubs.

Said, S. F. Phoenix. McKean, Dave, illus. 2016. (ENG.). 496p. (J). (gr. 5). 19.99 *(978-0-7636-8850-9(9))* Candlewick Pr.

Saito, Chiho. Revolutionary Girl Utena, Vol. 3. Be-Papas, illus. 2003. (Revolutionary Girl Utena Ser.: 3). (ENG.). 200p. pap. 9.95 *(978-1-56931-812-6(3))* Viz Media.

Salvatierra, Dante. The Latchkey Kids & the Trip Through T. 2005. (ENG.). 234p. pap. 12.99 *(978-1-4116-3814-3(X))* Lulu Pr., Inc.

Samphire, Patrick. The Emperor of Mars. Holmes, Jeremy, illus. 2017. (Secrets of the Dragon Tomb Ser.: 2). (ENG.). 368p. (J). 34.99 *(978-0-8050-9908-9(5)*, 900125300, Holt, Henry & Co. Bks. For Young Readers) Holt, Henry & Co.

Sanderson, Brandon. Calamity. 2016. (Reckoners Ser.: 3). (ENG.). 432p. (YA). (gr. 7-10). 19.99 *(978-0-385-74360-0(2)*, Delacorte Pr.) Random House Publishing Group.

—Firefight. (Reckoners Ser.: 2). (ENG.). (YA). (gr. 7). 2020. 496p. 10.99 *(978-0-593-30713-7(5)*, Delacorte Pr.) 2016. 464p. pap. 11.99 *(978-0-385-74359-4(9)*, Ember) 2015. 432p. 19.99 *(978-0-385-74358-7(0)*, Delacorte Pr.) Random Hse. Children's Bks.

—Firefight. 2016. (Reckoners Ser.: 2). lib. bdg. 22.10 *(978-0-606-38447-6(2))* Turtleback.

—The Reckoners Series Hardcover Boxed Set: Steelheart; Firefight; Calamity, 3 vols. 2016. (Reckoners Ser.). (ENG.). (YA). (gr. 7). 59.97 *(978-0-399-55168-0(9)*, Delacorte Pr.) Random Hse. Children's Bks.

—Steelheart. 2013. 386p. (YA). *(978-0-385-38371-4(1)*, Delacorte Pr) Random House Publishing Group.

—Steelheart. (Reckoners Ser.: 1). (ENG.). (YA). (gr. 7). 2020. 496p. 9.99 *(978-0-593-30712-0(7)*, Delacorte Pr.) 2014. 432p. pap. 11.99 *(978-0-385-74357-0(2)*, Ember) 2013. 400p. 19.99 *(978-0-385-74356-3(4)*, Delacorte Pr.) Random Hse. Children's Bks.

—Steelheart. 2014. (Reckoners Ser.: 1). lib. bdg. 20.85 *(978-0-606-36027-2(1))* Turtleback.

—STEELHEART (TRILOGÍA DE LOS RECKONERS 1) (SPA.). 416p. pap. 27.95 *(978-84-666-5296-4(5))* Ediciones B ESP. Dist: Spanish Pubs., LLC.

—Steelheart(Spanish Edition), Vol. 2. 2021. (Trilogía de Los Reckoners / the Reckoners Ser.: 1). (SPA.). 416p. pap. 14.95 *(978-84-9070-095-2(8))* Ediciones B Mexico MEX. Dist: Penguin Random Hse. LLC.

Sandford, John, pseud & Cook, Michele. Outrage (the Singular Menace, 2) 2016. (Singular Menace Ser.: 2). (ENG.). 336p. (YA). (gr. 9). pap. 10.99 *(978-0-385-75311-1(X)*, Ember) Random Hse. Children's Bks.

—Rampage (the Singular Menace, 3) 2017. (Singular Menace Ser.: 3). (ENG.). 336p. (YA). (gr. 9). pap. 11.99 *(978-0-385-75315-9(2)*, Ember) Random Hse. Children's Bks.

—Uncaged (the Singular Menace, 1) 2015. (Singular Menace Ser.: 1). (ENG.). 416p. (YA). (gr. 9). pap. 14.99 *(978-0-385-75305-0(5)*, Ember) Random Hse. Children's Bks.

Sandler, Karen. Awakening. 2013. (ENG.). 400p. (YA). 18.95 *(978-1-60060-982-4(1)*, Tu Bks.) Lee & Low Bks., Inc.

—Awakening: A Tankborn Novel #2, 1 vol. 2019. (Tankborn Ser.: 2). (ENG.). 400p. (YA). (gr. 7-12). pap. 16.95 *(978-1-64379-092-3(7)*, leelowtu, Tu Bks.) Lee & Low Bks., Inc.

Sanna, Alessandro, illus. Pinocchio: The Origin Story. 2016. 48p. (J). (gr. k-9). 19.95 *(978-1-59270-191-9(4))* Enchanted Lion Bks., LLC.

Sant, Sharon. Runners. 2013. 286p. pap. *(978-1-907737-52-7(9))* Immanion Pr.

Santos, Ray. I Am Green Lantern. 2013. (Justice League Classic: I Can Read! Ser.). (J). lib. bdg. 13.55 *(978-0-606-32152-5(7))* Turtleback.

Sargent, Pamela. Homesmind (Watchstar Trilogy: Book 3) 2010. 200p. pap. 16.95 *(978-0-7592-1542-9(1))* Open Road Integrated Media, Inc.

Sasaki, Chris & Wells, H. G. The War of the Worlds. Akib, Jamel, illus. 2007. (Classic Starts Ser.). 151p. (J). *(978-1-4287-4208-6(5))* Sterling Publishing Co., Inc.

Saunders, Catherine. The Jedi & the Force. 2014. (Illus.). 144p. (J). *(978-1-4351-5416-2(9))* Dorling Kindersley Publishing, Inc.

—The Story of Darth Vader. 2015. (Star Wars DK Readers Level 3 Ser.). lib. bdg. 13.55 *(978-0-606-37409-5(4))* Turtleback.

Saunders, Jami Lynn. Feral: Book I of the Werecat Saga. 2011. 86p. (YA). pap. 4.99 *(978-1-936307-15-9(4)*, 711Press) Vendera Publishing.

—Rabid: Book II of the Werecat Saga. 2012. 94p. (YA). pap. 4.99 *(978-1-936307-16-6(2)*, 711Press) Vendera Publishing.

Sava, Scott Christian. Hyperactive. 2008. (Illus.). 112p. 12.95 *(978-0-9789168-4-8(0))* Blue Dream Studios.

—My Grandparents Are Secret Agents. 2008. (Illus.). 112p. (J). 12.95 *(978-0-9789168-6-2(7))* Blue Dream Studios.

Savage, J. Scott. Embers of Destruction. (Mysteries of Cove Ser.: 3). (ENG., Illus.). (J). (gr. 3-6). 2018. 352p. pap. 7.99 *(978-1-62972-420-1(3)*, 5194505) 2017. 336p. 17.99 *(978-1-62972-339-6(8)*, 5177716) Shadow Mountain Publishing. (Shadow Mountain).

—Fires of Invention. 2016. (Mysteries of Cove Ser.: 1). (ENG., Illus.). 320p. (J). (gr. 5). pap. 7.99 *(978-1-62972-156-9(5)*, 5145180, Shadow Mountain) Shadow Mountain Publishing.

—Gears of Revolution. (Mysteries of Cove Ser.: 2). (ENG., Illus.). 352p. (J). (gr. 3-6). 2017. pap. 7.99 *(978-1-62972-295-5(2)*, 5166096) 2016. 17.99 *(978-1-62972-223-8(5)*, 5155663) Shadow Mountain Publishing. (Shadow Mountain).

Scarborough, R. A. Starblade: The Beginning, 1 vol. 2010. 128p. pap. 19.95 *(978-1-4489-3906-0(2))* America Star Bks.

Scarrow, Alex. Plague Land. 2017. (Plague Land Ser.: 1). (ENG.). 384p. (YA). (gr. 8-12). pap. 10.99 *(978-1-4926-5210-6(5))* Sourcebooks, Inc.

—Plague Land: Reborn. 2018. (Plague Land Ser.: 2). (ENG.). 416p. (YA). (gr. 8-12). pap. 10.99 *(978-1-4926-6023-1(X))* Sourcebooks, Inc.

Scarrow, Alex & Bale, Tim. TimeRiders, 1. 2011. (TimeRiders Ser.). (ENG.). 416p. (YA). (gr. 7-12). 26.19 *(978-0-8027-2172-3(9)*, 9780802721723) Walker & Co.

Schade, Susan. Simon's Dream. Buller, Jon, illus. 2009. (Fog Mound Ser.: 3). (ENG.). 208p. (J). (gr. 3-7). pap. 12.99 *(978-0-689-87689-9(0)*, Aladdin) Simon & Schuster Children's Publishing.

—Travels of Thelonious. Buller, Jon, illus. 2007. (Fog Mound Ser.: 1). (ENG.). 224p. (J). (gr. 3-7). pap. 12.99 *(978-0-689-87685-1(8)*, Aladdin) Simon & Schuster Children's Publishing.

Schaefer, Elizabeth. The Force Awakens: Episode VII. White, Dave, illus. 2016. (LEGO Star Wars 8X8 Ser.). (ENG.). 24p. (J). (gr. -1-3). 13.55 *(978-0-606-39117-7(7))* Turtleback.

—Star Wars: the Last Jedi (Star Wars) Batson, Alan, illus. 2018. (Little Golden Book Ser.). (ENG.). 24p. (J). (-k). 5.99 *(978-0-7364-3586-4(7)*, Golden Bks.) Random Hse. Children's Bks.

Schembra, John. A Vince Torelli Novel Book 2: Retribution. Cummins, Sandy, ed. 2007. (Shadows Trilogy). (ENG.). pap. *(978-1-876962-68-5(2)*, Writers Exchange) Writers Exchange E-Publishing.

Schindler, Roslyn. Zeon. Schindler, Roslyn, illus. 2013. (Illus.). 28p. pap. 13.95 *(978-1-61493-192-8(5))* Peppertree Pr., The.

Schleich, James J. The Sound Man. (Illus.). 64p. (J). pap. 7.00 *(978-0-615-12142-0(X))* Schleich, James.

Schmitz, James H. Trigger & Friends. 2004. (ENG.). 480p. mass mkt. 6.99 *(978-0-671-31966-3(3))* Baen Bks.

Schneider, John Lee. Extinction: Dragons of Earth: A Novel. 2005. 173p. (YA). pap. *(978-1-890109-79-0(7)*, Cross Time) Crossquarter Publishing Group.

Schoening, Dan, illus. Green Lantern, 12 vols., Set. Incl. Battle of the Blue Lanterns. Acampora, Michael V. & Acampora, Michael V. lib. bdg. 26.65 *(978-1-4342-2608-2(5)*, 113653); Beware Our Power! Sonneborn, Scott. 26.65 *(978-1-4342-2607-5(7)*, 113652); Escape from the Orange Lanterns. Acampora, Michael V. lib. bdg. 26.65 *(978-1-4342-2622-8(0)*, 113667); Fear the Shark. Sutton, Laurie S. lib. bdg. 26.65 *(978-1-4342-2620-4(4)*, 113665); Guardian of Earth. Dahl, Michael. lib. bdg. 27.32 *(978-1-4342-2611-2(5)*, 113656); High-Tech Terror. Steele, Michael Anthony. lib. bdg. 26.65 *(978-1-4342-2609-9(3)*, 113654); Light King Strikes! Sutton, Laurie S. lib. bdg. 26.65 *(978-1-4342-2610-5(7)*, 113655); Prisoner of the Ring. Sonneborn, Scott. lib. bdg. 26.65 *(978-1-4342-2624-2(7)*, 113669); Red Lanterns' Revenge. Acampora, Michael V. lib. bdg. 26.65 *(978-1-4342-2623-5(9)*, 113668); Savage Sands. Bright, J. E. lib. bdg. 26.65 *(978-1-4342-2619-8(0)*, 113664); Web of Doom. Steele, Michael Anthony. lib. bdg. 26.65 *(978-1-4342-2621-1(2)*, 113666); (Illus.). (J). (gr. 3-6). (Green Lantern Ser.). (ENG.). 56p. 2011. 300.52 *(978-1-4342-3240-3(9)*, 171278, Stone Arch Bks.) Capstone.

Scholastic Editors. Space Justice! 2015. (LEGO DC Super Heroes Ser.). lib. bdg. 13.55 *(978-0-606-37077-6(3))* Turtleback.

Scholastic, Inc. Staff, ed. Chicken Soup for Little Souls: The Never Forgotten Doll. Date not set. (Star Wars Ser.). (J). pap. 4.95 *(978-0-590-39635-6(8))* Scholastic, Inc.

Scholastic, Inc. Staff & Windham, Ryder. Fire Ring Race, 1. 2010. (Star Wars Adventures in Hyperspace Ser.). (ENG.). 96p. (J). (gr. 2-4). 17.44 *(978-0-545-21358-5(4))* Scholastic, Inc.

Scholte, Astrid. Four Dead Queens. (ENG.). (YA). (gr. 7). 2020. 464p. pap. 12.99 *(978-0-525-51394-0(9)*, Penguin Books) 2019. 432p. 17.99 *(978-0-525-51392-6(2)*, G.P. Putnam's Sons Books for Young Readers) Penguin Young Readers Group.

Schoon, Christian. Under Nameless Stars. 2014. (ENG.). 368p. (J). (gr. 9). pap. 9.99 *(978-1-908844-87-3(6)*, Strange Chemistry) Watkins Media Limited GBR. Dist: Penguin Random Hse. LLC.

Schraff, Anne. Roses Red As Blood (Suspense), 1 vol. 2017. (Pageturners Ser.). (ENG.). 76p. (YA). (gr. 9-12). 10.75 *(978-1-68021-405-5(5))* Saddleback Educational Publishing, Inc.

Schreiber, Joe. Solo: A Star Wars Story. 2018. (Illus.). 201p. (J). *(978-1-5444-2608-2(9))* Disney Publishing Worldwide.

Schrieve, Hal. Out of Salem. 2019. 448p. (YA). (gr. 7). 19.95 *(978-1-60980-901-0(7)*, Triangle Square) Seven Stories Pr.

Schwartz, Tom. Spaceship Earth: A Beginning Without End. 2010. 172p. pap. 10.99 *(978-1-57545-151-0(4))*; 19.99 *(978-1-57545-143-5(3))* RP Media. (Reagent Pr. Bks. for Young Readers).

Scieszka, Jon. Baloney (Henry P.) Smith, Lane, illus. 2005. 40p. (J). (gr. k-k). pap. 8.99 *(978-0-14-240430-0(6)*, Puffin Books) Penguin Young Readers Group.

—Frank Einstein & the Antimatter Motor. Biggs, Brian, illus. 2014. (Frank Einstein Ser.). 192p. (J). (gr. 3-7). pap. 7.95 *(978-1-4197-1506-8(2))* Abrams, Inc.

—Frank Einstein & the Antimatter Motor. 2017. (Frank Einstein Ser.: 1). (J). lib. bdg. 18.40 *(978-0-606-39683-7(7))* Turtleback.

—Frank Einstein & the Antimatter Motor (Frank Einstein Series #1) Book One. Biggs, Brian, illus. 2014. (Frank Einstein Ser.). (ENG.). 192p. (J). (gr. 3-7). 13.95 *(978-1-4197-1601-0(8)*, Amulet Bks.) Abrams, Inc.

—Frank Einstein & the BrainTurbo (Frank Einstein Series #3), 3. Biggs, Brian, illus. 2015. (ENG.). 192p. (J). (gr. 3-7). 13.95 *(978-1-4197-1643-0(3)*, 1070201, Amulet Bks.) Abrams, Inc.

—Frank Einstein & the EvoBlaster B, Bk. 4. 2016. (Frank Einstein Ser.). (ENG., Illus.). 208p. (J). (gr. 3-7). pap. 7.95 *(978-1-4197-2379-7(0))* Abrams, Inc.

—Frank Einstein & the EvoBlaster Belt (Frank Einstein Series #4) Book Four. Biggs, Brian, illus. (Frank Einstein Ser.). (ENG.). (J). (gr. 3-7). 2017. 224p. pap. 7.99 *(978-1-4197-2736-8(2)*, 1070303) 2016. 208p. 13.95 *(978-1-4197-1887-8(8)*, 1070301, Amulet Bks.) Abrams, Inc.

—Frank Einstein & the Space-Time Zipper (Frank Einstein Series #6) Book Six. Biggs, Brian, illus. 2019. (ENG.). 176p. (J). (gr. 3-7). pap. 7.99 *(978-1-4197-3384-0(2)*, 1070603, Amulet Bks.) Abrams, Inc.

—Frank Einstein Book 2. 2015. (Frank Einstein Ser.). (ENG., Illus.). 176p. (YA). (gr. 3-7). pap. 7.95 *(978-1-4197-1666-9(2))* Abrams, Inc.

—It's All Greek to Me #8, No. 8. Smith, Lane, illus. 2004. (Time Warp Trio Ser.: 8). 80p. (J). (gr. 2-4). pap. 5.99 *(978-0-14-240116-3(1)*, Puffin Books) Penguin Young Readers Group.

Scieszka, Jon & Brian Biggs. Frank Einstein & the Electro-Finger. 2017. (Frank Einstein Ser.: 2). (J). lib. bdg. 18.40 *(978-0-606-39684-4(5))* Turtleback.

Scollon, Bill & Rabb, Michael. Doc Mcstuffins: Starry, Starry Night. Character Building Studio & Disney Storybook Art Team, illus. 2018. (World of Reading Level 1 Ser.). (ENG.). 32p. (J). (gr. -1-3). lib. bdg. 31.36 *(978-1-5321-4187-4(4)*, 31064) Spotlight.

Scollon, William. Doc Mcstuffins: Starry, Starry Night. 2014. (World of Reading Ser.). (Illus.). 32p. (J). lib. bdg. 13.55 *(978-0-606-35257-4(0))* Turtleback.

Scott, Cavan. A Han & Chewie Adventure, 1. 2019. (Star Wars Choose Your Destiny Ser.). (ENG.). 144p. (J). (gr. 2-4). 15.59 *(978-1-64310-797-4(6))* Penworthy Co., LLC, The.

—Star Wars: a Luke & Leia Adventure: A Choose Your Destiny Chapter Book. 2018. (Choose Your Destiny Chapter Book Ser.). (ENG., Illus.). 144p. (J). (gr. 1-3). pap. 5.99 *(978-1-368-02424-2(6)*, Disney Lucasfilm Press) Disney Publishing Worldwide.

Sedgwick, Marcus. The Ghosts of Heaven. 2016. (ENG.). 384p. (YA). pap. 10.99 *(978-1-250-07367-9(7)*, 900150798) Square Fish.

Seegert, Scott & Martin, John. Sci-Fi Junior High. 2018. (Sci-Fi Junior High Ser.: 1). (ENG., Illus.). 336p. (J). (gr. 3-7). pap. 7.99 *(978-0-316-31517-3(6)*, Jimmy Patterson) Little Brown & Co.

—Sci-Fi Junior High: Crash Landing. 2018. (Sci-Fi Junior High Ser.: 2). (ENG., Illus.). 336p. (J). (gr. 3-7). 13.99 *(978-0-316-31521-0(4)*, Jimmy Patterson) Little Brown & Co.

Seeley, Tim. Guardians of the Galaxy, 3 vols. 2015. (Guardians of the Galaxy Ser.: Vol. 3). (ENG.). 24p. (J). (gr. 3-6). 94.08 *(978-1-61479-389-2(1)*, 18220, Marvel Age) Spotlight.

—Tim Seeley's Action Figure Collection Volume 1. 2017. (ENG., Illus.). 160p. (YA). pap. 12.99 *(978-1-5343-0370-6(7)*, 0e2f77e3-68ff-4258-9b4a-691e681febbf) Image Comics.

Segel, Jason & Miller, Kirsten. OtherEarth. 2018. (Last Reality Ser.: 2). (ENG.). 320p. (YA). (gr. 7). 18.99 *(978-1-101-93936-9(2)*, Delacorte Pr.) Random Hse. Children's Bks.

—Otherearth. 2018. 310p. (YA). *(978-0-525-70794-3(8)*, Delacorte Pr) Random House Publishing Group.

—Otherworld. 2018. (Last Reality Ser.: 1). (ENG.). 384p. (YA). (gr. 7). pap. 10.99 *(978-1-101-93935-2(4)*, Ember) Random Hse. Children's Bks.

Senior, Patricia. Mischief on Mumpit Mountain. 2009. 36p. pap. 14.75 *(978-1-60693-661-0(1)*, Eloquent Bks.) Strategic Book Publishing & Rights Agency (SBPRA).

Service, Pamela F. Alien Encounter. Gorman, Mike, illus. 2010. (Alien Agent Ser.: 4). (ENG.). 152p. (J). (gr. 4-6). 16.95 *(978-0-8225-8873-3(0)*, 07e31f3f-08b4-4f75-89d0-8685b56dd365, Darby Creek) Lerner Publishing Group.

—Alien Envoy. Gorman, Mike, illus. (Alien Agent Ser.). 176p. (J). (gr. 4-6). 2012. pap. 33.92 *(978-0-7613-9208-8(4))*No. 6. 2012. (ENG.). pap. 8.99 *(978-0-7613-7298-1(9)*, 587338f8-a9b5-4dd7-b81d-3c34842e3f13)No. 6. 2011. (ENG.). 16.95 *(978-0-7613-5364-5(X)*, dbf8a334-7399-415b-b37c-3f8980a16eb0) Lerner Publishing Group. (Darby Creek).

—Alien Expedition. 2010. pap. 33.92 *(978-0-7613-6958-5(9))* Lerner Publishing Group.

—Camp Alien. 2010. pap. 33.92 *(978-0-7613-6955-4(4))* Lerner Publishing Group.

—Escape from Planet Yastol, No. 1. Gorman, Mike, illus. 2011. (Way-Too-Real Aliens Ser.: 1). (ENG.). 112p. (J). (gr. 4-6). pap. 5.95 *(978-0-7613-7921-8(5),* Darby Creek) Lerner Publishing Group.

—My Cousin, the Alien. Gorman, Mike, illus. 2008. (Alien Agent Ser.: 1). (ENG.). 160p. (J). (gr. 4-6). 16.95 *(978-0-8225-7627-3(9),* Carolrhoda Bks.) Lerner Publishing Group.

—The Not-So-Perfect Planet. Gorman, Mike, illus. (Way-Too-Real Aliens Ser.: 2). (ENG.). 120p. (J). (gr. 4-6). 2012. pap. 6.95 *(978-0-7613-7923-2(1),* Darby Creek) 2015. E-Book 53.32 *(978-1-4677-5961-8(9),* 9781467759618, Lerner Digital) Lerner Publishing Group.

—Stinker's Return. 2018. (ENG.). 96p. (gr. 2-5). pap. 6.99 *(978-0-486-81887-0(X))* Dover Pubns., Inc.

—The Wizards of Wyrd World. Gorman, Mike, illus. 2015. (Way-Too-Real Aliens Ser.: 3). (ENG.). 112p. (J). (gr. 4-6). E-Book 53.32 *(978-1-4677-5962-5(7),* 9781467759625, Lerner Digital) Lerner Publishing Group.

—#4 Alien Encounter. Gorman, Mike, illus. 2011. (Alien Agent Ser.). 152p. (J). pap. 33.92 *(978-0-7613-7608-8(9),* Darby Creek) Lerner Publishing Group.

—#5 Alien Contact. Gorman, Mike, illus. 2011. (Alien Agent Ser.). pap. 33.92 *(978-0-7613-8347-5(6),* Darby Creek) Lerner Publishing Group.

Seven, John. The Alchemist War, 1 vol. Phillips, Craig, illus. 2013. (Time-Tripping Faradays Ser.). (ENG.). 160p. (J). (gr. 4-8). 9.95 *(978-1-62370-011-9(6),* 123720, Capstone Young Readers); pap. 5.95 *(978-1-4342-6438-1(6),* 124129, Stone Arch Bks.) Capstone.

—The Dragon of Rome, 1 vol. Phillips, Craig, illus. 2013. (Time-Tripping Faradays Ser.). (ENG.). 160p. (J). (gr. 4-8). pap. 5.95 *(978-1-4342-6439-8(4),* 124130, Stone Arch Bks.) Capstone.

—The Outlaw of Sherwood Forest, 1 vol. Hans, Stephanie, illus. 2014. (Time-Tripping Faradays Ser.). (ENG.). 192p. (J). (gr. 4-8). lib. bdg. 26.65 *(978-1-4342-9174-5(X),* 125644, Stone Arch Bks.) Capstone.

—The Terror of the Tengu, 1 vol. Hans, Stephanie, illus. 2014. (Time-Tripping Faradays Ser.). (ENG.). 192p. (J). (gr. 4-8). 26.65 *(978-1-4342-9173-8(1),* 125643, Stone Arch Bks.) Capstone.

SFX Fantasy. Tween Tales - Robots, Dragons & the Interworld Machine. 2007. (ENG.). 131p. pap. 12.99 *(978-1-4303-2546-8(1))* Lulu Pr., Inc.

S.H., Addan. Guardabosque Del Ano 3000: Canis Familiaris Evolucion. 2004. (SPA., Illus.). 340p. pap. *(978-1-84401-133-9(X))* Athena Pr.

Shadow, Jak. The F. E. A. R. Agency. 2006. (F. E. A. R. Adventures S. Ser.). (ENG., Illus.). 80p. (J). 4.00 *(978-1-84046-726-0(6),* Wizard Books) Icon Bks., Ltd. GBR. Dist: Publishers Group Canada.

Shand, Patrick. Marvel Guardians of the Galaxy: Space Riot. 2017. lib. bdg. 24.50 *(978-0-606-40199-9(7))* Turtleback.

Shea, Therese. One More Floor!, 1 vol. 2006. (Neighborhood Readers Ser.). (ENG.). 16p. (gr. 1-2). pap. 6.50 *(978-1-4042-7244-6(5),* 2dcda1d1-5e34-4ca9-b623-6c75f0c4b4b8, Rosen Classroom) Rosen Publishing Group, Inc., The.

Shearer, Alex. The Cloud Hunters. 2013. (ENG.). 288p. (J). (gr. 6-8). 14.95 *(978-1-62636-216-1(5),* 263216, Sky Pony Pr.) Skyhorse Publishing Co., Inc.

—Sky Run. 2014. (Cloud Hunters Ser.). (ENG.). 288p. (J). (gr. 2-7). 14.95 *(978-1-62873-593-2(7),* Sky Pony Pr.) Skyhorse Publishing Co., Inc.

Sheehan, Anna. A Long, Long Sleep. 2011. (ENG., Illus.). 352p. (YA). (gr. 9). 16.99 *(978-0-7636-5260-9(1))* Candlewick Pr.

Sheehy, Shawn. Beyond the Sixth Extinction: A Post-Apocalyptic Pop-Up. Solano, Jordi, illus. 2018. (ENG.). 40p. (J). (gr. 9). 65.00 *(978-0-7636-8738-5(X))* Candlewick Pr.

Shein, Erik. The Pillow Princess: Mystoryland Friends Brand. 2014. (ENG., Illus.). 32p. (J). 8.95 *(978-0-9765358-0-5(7))* Ark Watch Holdings LLC.

Sheley, Kristen. Partners in Time #4: Family Matters. 2008. 216p. pap. 15.95 *(978-0-595-51850-0(8))* iUniverse, Inc.

—Partners in Time #5: A Change of Course. 2010. 236p. 25.95 *(978-1-4502-6658-1(4));* pap. 15.95 *(978-1-4502-6657-4(6))* iUniverse, Inc.

Shelton, C. M. Cosmic Chaos. 2015. (ENG., Illus.). 226p. (J). pap. 8.99 *(978-1-941720-25-7(0))* Ashberry Lane.

Shepherd, Megan. The Cage. 2016. (Cage Ser.: 1). (ENG.). 416p. (YA). (gr. 8). pap. 9.99 *(978-0-06-224306-5(3),* Balzer & Bray) HarperCollins Pubs.

—The Gauntlet. 2018. (Cage Ser.: 3). (ENG.). 400p. (YA). (gr. 8). pap. 9.99 *(978-0-06-224313-3(6),* Balzer & Bray) HarperCollins Pubs.

—Her Dark Curiosity. 2014. (Madman's Daughter Ser.: 2). (ENG.). 432p. (YA). (gr. 8). 17.99 *(978-0-06-212805-8(1),* Balzer & Bray) HarperCollins Pubs.

—The Madman's Daughter. 2013. (Madman's Daughter Ser.: 1). (ENG.). (YA). (gr. 8). 464p. pap. 10.99 *(978-0-06-212803-4(5));* 432p. 17.99 *(978-0-06-212802-7(7))* HarperCollins Pubs. (Balzer & Bray).

Shiga, Jason. Meanwhile: Pick Any Path. 3,856 Story Possibilities. 2010. (ENG., Illus.). 80p. (J). (gr. 3-9). 17.99 *(978-0-8109-8423-3(7),* 665501, Amulet Bks.) Abrams, Inc.

Shine, Joe. I Become Shadow. 2015. (ENG.). 336p. (YA). (gr. 9). pap. 10.99 *(978-1-61695-537-3(6),* Soho Teen) Soho Pr., Inc.

Shipton, Paul. The Games Player of Zob: Band 15/Emerald (Collins Big Cat) McCafferty, Jan, illus. 2007. (Collins Big Cat Ser.). (ENG.). 48p. (J). (gr. 3-4). pap. 10.99 *(978-0-00-723094-5(X))* HarperCollins Pubs. Ltd. GBR. Dist: Independent Pubs. Group.

Shirvington, Jessica. Disruption. 2016. (Disruption Ser.: 01). 410p. (YA). (gr. 9). 9.99 *(978-0-7322-9810-4(5),* HarperCollins) HarperCollins Pubs.

Shmakov, Efim. The Return of Hezzord. 2010. 280p. pap. *(978-1-921731-15-0(X))* Zeus Pubns.

Shore, Diane Z. This Is the Earth. Minor, Wendell, illus. 2016. (ENG.). 40p. (J). (gr. -1-3). 17.99 *(978-0-06-055526-9(2),* HarperCollins) HarperCollins Pubs.

Shusterman, Neal. The Dark Side of Nowhere. unabr. ed. 2004. 192p. (J). (gr. 4-7). pap. 36.00 incl. audio *(978-0-8072-8757-6(1),* YA258SP, Listening Library) Random Hse. Audio Publishing Group.

—The Dark Side of Nowhere. 2012. (ENG.). 256p. (YA). (gr. 7). pap. 11.99 *(978-1-4424-2281-0(5),* Simon & Schuster Bks. For Young Readers) Simon & Schuster Bks. For Young Readers.

—Scythe. (Arc of a Scythe Ser.: 1). (ENG., Illus.). (YA). (gr. 7). 2017. 464p. pap. 13.99 *(978-1-4424-7243-3(X))* 2016. 448p. 19.99 *(978-1-4424-7242-6(1))* Simon & Schuster Bks. For Young Readers. (Simon & Schuster Bks. For Young Readers).

—Thunderhead. (Arc of a Scythe Ser.: 2). (ENG., Illus.). 512p. (YA). (gr. 7). 2019. pap. 13.99 *(978-1-4424-7246-4(4))* 2018. 19.99 *(978-1-4424-7245-7(6))* Simon & Schuster Bks. For Young Readers. (Simon & Schuster Bks. For Young Readers).

—Thunderhead. 2018. (Arc of a Scythe Ser.: 2). (ENG., Illus.). 512p. (YA). (gr. 7). pap. 12.99 *(978-1-5344-1786-1(9))* Simon & Schuster Children's Publishing.

—Thunderhead. l.t. ed. 2020. (Arc of a Scythe Ser.: 2). (ENG.). lib. bdg. 22.99 *(978-1-4328-7667-8(8))* Thorndike Pr.

—The Toll. (Arc of a Scythe Ser.: 3). (ENG.). 640p. (YA). (gr. 7). 2020. pap. 13.99 *(978-1-4814-9707-7(3))* 2019. (Illus.). 19.99 *(978-1-4814-9706-0(5))* Simon & Schuster Bks. For Young Readers. (Simon & Schuster Bks. For Young Readers).

—UnBound: Stories from the Unwind World. (Unwind Dystology Ser.). (ENG.). (YA). (gr. 7). 2016. 336p. pap. 12.99 *(978-1-4814-5724-8(1))* 2015. (Illus.). 320p. 18.99 *(978-1-4814-5723-1(3))* Simon & Schuster Bks. For Young Readers. (Simon & Schuster Bks. For Young Readers).

—Undivided. 2015. (Unwind Dystology Ser.: 4). lib. bdg. 23.30 *(978-0-606-37863-5(4))* Turtleback.

—UnDivided. 2014. (Unwind Dystology Ser.: 4). (ENG., Illus.). 384p. (YA). (gr. 7). 19.99 *(978-1-4814-0975-9(1),* Simon & Schuster Bks. For Young Readers) Simon & Schuster Bks. For Young Readers.

—UnSouled. (Unwind Dystology Ser.: 3). (ENG., Illus.). (YA). (gr. 7). 2014. 432p. pap. 12.99 *(978-1-4424-2370-1(6))* 2013. 416p. 19.99 *(978-1-4424-2369-5(2))* Simon & Schuster Bks. For Young Readers. (Simon & Schuster Bks. For Young Readers).

—Unsouled. 2014. (Unwind Dystology Ser.: 3). lib. bdg. 23.30 *(978-0-606-36107-1(3))* Turtleback.

—UnWholly. (Unwind Dystology Ser.: 2). (ENG.). 416p. (YA). (gr. 7). 2013. pap. 12.99 *(978-1-4424-2367-1(6),* Simon & Schuster Bks. For Young Readers) 2012. 19.99 *(978-1-4424-2366-4(8))* Simon & Schuster Bks. For Young Readers.

—UnWholly. 2013. (Unwind Dystology Ser.: 2). lib. bdg. 23.30 *(978-0-606-32336-9(8))* Turtleback.

—Unwind. 2011. 10.36 *(978-0-7848-3496-1(2),* Everbind) Marco Bk. Co.

—Unwind. (Unwind Dystology Ser.: 1). (ENG., Illus.). (YA). 2009. 384p. (gr. 8). pap. 12.99 *(978-1-4169-1205-7(3))* 2007. 352p. (gr. 7-12). 19.99 *(978-1-4169-1204-0(5))* Simon & Schuster Bks. For Young Readers. (Simon & Schuster Bks. For Young Readers).

—Unwind. 2009. (Unwind Dystology Ser.: 1). lib. bdg. 23.30 *(978-0-606-10700-6(2))* Turtleback.

Shusterman, Neal & Elfman, Eric. Edison's Alley. 2016. (Accelerati Trilogy Ser.: 2). (ENG.). 256p. (J). (gr. 5-9). pap. 7.99 *(978-1-4231-5517-1(3))* Little, Brown Bks. for Young Readers.

—Hawking's Hallway. (Accelerati Trilogy Ser.: 3). (ENG.). 368p. (J). (gr. 5-9). 2017. pap. 8.99 *(978-1-4231-5521-8(1))* 2016. 16.99 *(978-1-4231-4805-0(3))* Little, Brown Bks. for Young Readers.

—I Am the Walrus. 2023. (N. O. A. H Files Ser.: 1). (ENG.). 400p. (J). (gr. 5-9). 17.99 *(978-0-7595-5524-2(9))* Little, Brown Bks. for Young Readers.

Siegel, Mark & Siegel, Alexis. The Sand Warrior. Bouma, Xanthe et al, illus. 2017. (5 Worlds Ser.: 1). lib. bdg. 24.50 *(978-0-606-40243-9(8))* Turtleback.

—5 Worlds Book 1: the Sand Warrior: (a Graphic Novel) Bouma, Xanthe et al, illus. 2017. (5 Worlds Ser.: 1). 256p. (J). (gr. 3-7). 21.99 *(978-1-101-93586-6(3));* pap. 12.99 *(978-1-101-93588-0(X))* Penguin Random Hse. LLC.

—5 Worlds Book 3: the Red Maze: (a Graphic Novel) Bouma, Xanthe et al, illus. 2019. (5 Worlds Ser.: 3). 256p. (J). (gr. 3-7). 21.99 *(978-1-101-93592-7(8));* pap. 13.99 *(978-1-101-93594-1(4))* Penguin Random Hse. LLC.

Sierra, Donn. Candin Book 2: The Visitors. 2012. 214p. pap. 14.50 *(978-1-62212-619-4(X),* Strategic Bk. Publishing) Strategic Book Publishing & Rights Agency (SBPRA).

Siglain, Michael. Finn & Rey Escape! 2015. (Star Wars: Force Awakens 8X8 Ser.). (J). lib. bdg. 14.75 *(978-0-606-38311-0(5))* Turtleback.

—Han & Chewie Return! 2015. (Star Wars: Force Awakens 8X8 Ser.). (J). lib. bdg. 13.55 *(978-0-606-38310-3(7))* Turtleback.

—Rescue from Jabba's Palace. 2017. (World of Reading Level 2 (Leveled Readers) Ser.). (ENG., Illus.). 32p. (J). (gr. k-3). lib. bdg. 31.36 *(978-1-5321-4064-8(9),* 25435) Spotlight.

—Use the Force! Roux, Stéphane, illus. 2017. (World of Reading Level 2 (Leveled Readers) Ser.). (ENG.). 32p. (J). (gr. k-3). 31.36 *(978-1-5321-4065-5(7),* 25436) Spotlight.

Sigler, Scott. Alive. 2016. (Generations Trilogy Ser.: 1). 384p. (gr. 9). pap. 14.00 *(978-0-553-39312-5(X),* Del Rey) Random House Publishing Group.

—The Starter, 2. 2012. (Galactic Football League Ser.: 2). (ENG.). 463p. (J). (gr. 7-12). 26.19 *(978-1-938120-10-7(8),* Diversion Bks.) Diversion Publishing Corp.

Silver, Eve. Rush. 2014. (Game Ser.: 1). (ENG.). 384p. (YA). (gr. 9). pap. 10.99 *(978-0-06-219214-1(0),* Tegen, Katherine Bks) HarperCollins Pubs.

Silvestri, Marc & Hawkins, Matt. Cyber Force Rebirth, Vol. 1. 2013. (ENG., Illus.). 160p. (YA). pap. 9.99 *(978-1-60706-671-2(8),* d95a6fa2-4c6c-4536-b905-17379991e64f) Image Comics.

Sim, Tara. Chainbreaker. 2018. (Timekeeper Ser.: 2). (Illus.). 488p. (YA). (gr. 9-9). 18.99 *(978-1-5107-0619-4(4),* Sky Pony Pr.) Skyhorse Publishing Co., Inc.

—Firestarter. 2019. (Timekeeper Ser.: 3). (ENG., Illus.). 528p. (YA). (gr. 9-9). 26.99 *(978-1-5107-0620-0(8),* Sky Pony Pr.) Skyhorse Publishing Co., Inc.

Simmons, Kristen. The Glass Arrow. 2016. (ENG.). 352p. (YA). pap. 18.99 *(978-0-7653-3664-4(2),* 900121071, Tor Teen) Doherty, Tom Assocs., LLC.

—Pacifica. 2019. (ENG.). 384p. (YA). pap. 19.99 *(978-0-7653-3666-8(9),* 900121077, Tor Teen) Doherty, Tom Assocs., LLC.

Singer, Maurene, et al. A Place in the Sky. Marino, Natalie & Marino, Illustrator, Natalie, Natalie, illus. 2005. 52p. (J). 16.00 *(978-0-9759382-0-1(7))* Carousel Pubns., Inc.

Skillchecks for Science Fiction. rev. ed. 2005. (Fastback Ser.). 32p. (J). (gr. 6-12). pap. 5.95 *(978-0-13-024450-5(3))* Globe Fearon Educational Publishing.

Skrimager, R. J. The Making: Volume One of the Golden Isle. 2003. 380p. (YA). pap. 20.95 *(978-0-595-26705-7(X),* Writers Club Pr.) iUniverse, Inc.

Skrutskie, Emily. The Edge of the Abyss. 2017. (Abyss Ser.). (ENG., Illus.). 296p. (YA). (gr. 9-12). pap. 11.99 *(978-1-63583-000-2(1),* 1635830001, Flux) North Star Editions.

—The Edge of the Abyss. 2017. lib. bdg. 23.30 *(978-0-606-40232-3(2))* Turtleback.

—Hullmetal Girls. 2018. 320p. (YA). (gr. 9). 17.99 *(978-1-5247-7019-8(1),* Delacorte Pr.) Random Hse. Children's Bks.

Skurzynski, Gloria. Afterwar. 2011. (ENG., Illus.). 528p. (YA). (gr. 7). pap. 9.99 *(978-1-4424-1681-9(5),* Atheneum Bks. for Young Readers) Simon & Schuster Children's Publishing.

—The Clones Bk. 2: The Virtual War Chronologs — Book 2. 2007. (ENG.). 192p. (YA). (gr. 7). pap. 10.95 *(978-1-4169-5560-3(7),* Simon Pulse) Simon Pulse.

—Virtual War: The Virtual War Chronologs — Book 1. 2008. (ENG.). 188p. (YA). (gr. 7). pap. 10.99 *(978-1-4169-7577-9(2),* Simon Pulse) Simon Pulse.

Skvarch, Angela & Skvarch, Jeffrey. Dinosaurs in Space. 2004. 48p. (J). per. 9.95 *(978-1-932560-35-0(1))* Aeon Publishing Inc.

Slade, Arthur G. The Hunchback Assignments, 1. 2010. (Hunchback Assignments Ser.). (ENG.). 288p. (YA). (gr. 7-12). lib. bdg. 24.94 *(978-0-385-90694-4(3))* Random House Publishing Group.

Slivensky, Katie. The Seismic Seven. 2018. (ENG., Illus.). 352p. (J). (gr. 3-7). 16.99 *(978-0-06-246318-0(7),* HarperCollins) HarperCollins Pubs.

Sloane, William, ed. Space, Space, Space: Stories about the Time When Men Will Be Adventuring to the Stars. 2011. 288p. 48.95 *(978-1-258-10156-5(4))* Literary Licensing, LLC.

SMARTLAB Creative Team. Space Exploration. 2010. 10p. mass mkt. 39.99 *(978-1-60380-050-1(6))* becker&mayer! books.

Smibert, Angie. The Meme Plague, 0 vols. 2016. (Memento Nora Ser.: 3). (ENG.). 240p. (YA). (gr. 7-12). pap. 9.99 *(978-1-4778-1689-9(5),* 9781477816899, Skyscape) Amazon Publishing.

—Memento Nora, 0 vols. 2013. (Memento Nora Ser.: 1). (ENG.). 192p. (YA). (gr. 7-12). pap. 9.99 *(978-1-4778-1624-0(0),* 9781477816240, Skyscape) Amazon Publishing.

Smith, Alexander Gordon. Death Sentence: Escape from Furnace 3. 2012. (Escape from Furnace Ser.: 3). (ENG.). 288p. (YA). (gr. 7-11). pap. 12.99 *(978-0-312-67441-0(4),* 900072856) Square Fish.

—The Devil's Engine: Hellfighters: (Book 2) 2016. (Devil's Engine Ser.: 2). (ENG.). 320p. (YA). 29.99 *(978-0-374-30172-9(7),* 900140532, Farrar, Straus & Giroux (BYR)) Farrar, Straus & Giroux.

—The Devil's Engine: Hellfighters: (Book 2) 2017. (Devil's Engine Ser.: 2). (ENG.). 336p. (YA). pap. 10.99 *(978-1-250-12965-9(6),* 900176103) Square Fish.

—The Devil's Engine: Hellraisers: (Book 1) 2015. (Devil's Engine Ser.: 1). (ENG.). 352p. (YA). (gr. 7). 29.99 *(978-0-374-30169-9(7),* 900140530, Farrar, Straus & Giroux (BYR)) Farrar, Straus & Giroux.

—The Devil's Engine: Hellwalkers: (Book 3) 2017. (Devil's Engine Ser.: 3). (ENG.). 320p. (YA). 29.99 *(978-0-374-30174-3(3),* 900140534, Farrar, Straus & Giroux (BYR)) Farrar, Straus & Giroux.

—Execution: Escape from Furnace 5. 2013. (Escape from Furnace Ser.: 5). (ENG.). 336p. (YA). (gr. 7-11). pap. 13.99 *(978-1-250-02942-3(2),* 900118576) Square Fish.

—Fugitives: Escape from Furnace 4. 2012. (Escape from Furnace Ser.: 4). (ENG.). 304p. (YA). (gr. 7-11). pap. 15.99 *(978-1-250-00339-3(3),* 900079878) Square Fish.

—Hellfighters. 2017. (Devil's Engine Ser.: 2). (YA). lib. bdg. 22.10 *(978-0-606-40588-1(7))* Turtleback.

—Lockdown: Escape from Furnace 1. 2010. (Escape from Furnace Ser.: 1). (ENG.). 304p. (YA). (gr. 7-11). pap. 10.99 *(978-0-312-61193-4(5),* 900065537) Square Fish.

—Solitary: Escape from Furnace 2. 2011. (Escape from Furnace Ser.: 2). (ENG.). 256p. (YA). (gr. 7-11). pap. 11.99 *(978-0-312-67476-2(7),* 900072887) Square Fish.

Smith, Andrew. Exile from Eden: Or, after the Hole. Smith, Andrew, illus. 2019. (ENG., Illus.). 368p. (YA). (gr. 9). 18.99 *(978-1-5344-2223-0(4),* Simon & Schuster Bks. For Young Readers) Simon & Schuster Bks. For Young Readers.

—Grasshopper Jungle. 2015. (ENG.). 416p. (YA). (gr. 9). pap. 11.99 *(978-0-14-242500-8(1),* Speak) Penguin Young Readers Group.

—Rabbit & Robot. 2018. (ENG., Illus.). 448p. (YA). (gr. 9). 18.99 *(978-1-5344-2220-9(X),* Simon & Schuster Bks. For Young Readers) Simon & Schuster Bks. For Young Readers.

Smith, Geof. Everything I Need to Know I Learned from a Star Wars Little Golden Book (Star Wars) Kennett, Chris & Batson, Alan, illus. 2016. (Little Golden Book Ser.). (ENG.). 96p. (J). (gr. 7-12). 10.99 *(978-0-7364-3656-4(1),* Golden Bks.) Random Hse. Children's Bks.

—Star Wars: Return of the Jedi (Star Wars) Cohee, Ron, illus. 2015. (Little Golden Book Ser.). (ENG.). 24p. (J). (-k). 5.99 *(978-0-7364-3548-2(4),* Golden Bks.) Random Hse. Children's Bks.

—Star Wars: Revenge of the Sith (Star Wars) Spaziante, Patrick, illus. 2015. (Little Golden Book Ser.). (ENG.). 24p. (J). (-k). 4.99 *(978-0-7364-3540-6(9),* Golden Bks.) Random Hse. Children's Bks.

—Star Wars: the Empire Strikes Back (Star Wars) Kennett, Chris, illus. 2015. (Little Golden Book Ser.). (ENG.). 24p. (J). (-k). 4.99 *(978-0-7364-3544-4(1),* Golden Bks.) Random Hse. Children's Bks.

Smith, Greg Leitich. Ninjas, Piranhas, & Galileo. 2013. 178p. (J). pap. 14.95 *(978-1-62352-029-8(0))* IntoPrint Publishing LLC.

Smith, J. E. Complex City: All in a Day's Work. 2003. 120p. per. 12.95 *(978-0-9728070-0-5(4))* Better Comics.

Smith, Kim, illus. The X-Files: Earth Children Are Weird: A Picture Book. 2017. (Pop Classics Ser.: 2). 40p. (J). (gr. -1-3). 18.99 *(978-1-59474-979-7(5))* Quirk Bks.

Smith, Larry. Cloud Realm. 2003. (Chronicles of Ingarde: Bk. 1). 218p. (YA). pap. 15.95 *(978-0-595-30149-2(5))* iUniverse, Inc.

Smith, Ronald L. Black Panther: The Young Prince. 2018. *(978-1-368-01222-5(1))* Disney Publishing Worldwide.

—Black Panther: the Young Prince. 2019. (Young Prince Ser.: 1). (ENG.). 272p. (J). (gr. 3-7). pap. 7.99 *(978-1-368-00849-5(6))* Marvel Worldwide, Inc.

Smith, Shane W. The Lesser Evil, Book 3 Comic Book. Smith, Shane W., illus. 2012. (Illus.). 114p. pap. *(978-1-927384-04-6(4))* Zeta Comics.

Snider, Brandon T. Black Panther:: the Battle for Wakanda. 2018. (Mighty Marvel Chapter Book Ser.). (ENG., Illus.). 128p. (J). (gr. 3-7). pap. 5.99 *(978-1-368-02014-5(3))* Marvel Worldwide, Inc.

—Guardians of the Galaxy: Gamora's Galactic Showdown! 2017. (Mighty Marvel Chapter Bks.). (J). lib. bdg. 16.00 *(978-0-606-39965-4(8))* Turtleback.

—Guardians of the Galaxy: Gamora's Galactic Showdown. Qualano, Pascale & Sotomayor, Chris, illus. 2018. (Mighty Marvel Chapter Bks.). (ENG.). 128p. (J). (gr. 2-7). lib. bdg. 31.36 *(978-1-5321-4216-1(1),* 28553, Chapter Bks.) Spotlight.

Sniegoski, Thomas E. Monstrous. (Savage Ser.). (ENG.). 448p. (YA). (gr. 9). 2018. pap. 12.99 *(978-1-4814-7719-2(6))* 2017. (Illus.). 18.99 *(978-1-4814-7718-5(8))* Simon Pulse. (Simon Pulse).

—Savage. (Savage Ser.). (ENG.). (YA). (gr. 9). 2017. 432p. pap. 9.99 *(978-1-4814-4374-6(7))* 2016. (Illus.). 416p. 17.99 *(978-1-4814-4373-9(9))* Simon Pulse. (Simon Pulse).

Sniegoski, Thomas E. & Golden, Christopher. Dragon Secrets. 2013. (Magic Zero Ser.: 2). (ENG.). 320p. (J). (gr. 3-7). pap. 6.99 *(978-1-4424-7309-6(6));* 2. 17.99 *(978-1-4424-7310-2(X))* Simon & Schuster Children's Publishing. (Aladdin).

Sonneborn, Scott. Prisoner of the Ring, 1 vol. Schoening, Dan, illus. 2011. (Green Lantern Ser.). (ENG.). 56p. (J). (gr. 3-6). pap. 4.95 *(978-1-4342-3410-0(X),* 116423); lib. bdg. 26.65 *(978-1-4342-2624-2(7),* 113669) Capstone. (Stone Arch Bks.).

Sorrells, Walter. Book Two of the Travelers, Bk. 2. 2009. (Pendragon: Before the War Ser.: 2). (ENG.). 240p. (J). (gr. 5-9). pap. 8.99 *(978-1-4169-6523-7(8),* Aladdin) Simon & Schuster Children's Publishing.

Souders, J. A. Revelations: A Novel. 2016. (Elysium Chronicles Ser.: 2). (ENG.). 368p. (YA). (gr. 8-12). pap. 18.99 *(978-0-7653-3249-3(3),* 900082997, Tor Teen) Doherty, Tom Assocs., LLC.

Space Case. 2014. (Moon Base Alpha Ser.). (ENG., Illus.). 352p. (J). (gr. 3-7). 18.99 *(978-1-4424-9486-2(7),* Simon & Schuster Bks. For Young Readers) Simon & Schuster Bks. For Young Readers.

Sparkes, Ali. Alligator Action, No. 14. Collins, Ross, illus. 2014. (S. W. I. T. C. H. Ser.: 14). (ENG.). 112p. (J). (gr. 2-5). lib. bdg. 27.99 *(978-1-4677-2117-2(4),* a29ee350-23b8-409b-9c6f-f08687ada878, Darby Creek) Lerner Publishing Group.

—Chameleon Chaos, No. 10. Collins, Ross, illus. 2014. (S. W. I. T. C. H. Ser.: 10). (ENG.). 112p. (J). (gr. 2-5). lib. bdg. 27.99 *(978-1-4677-2113-4(1),* 8c574e9c-1868-42a1-83d2-b86d8afe583a, Darby Creek) Lerner Publishing Group.

—Frozen in Time. 2011. (ENG.). 320p. (J). (gr. 4-6). 22.44 *(978-1-60684-077-1(0))* Farshore GBR. Dist: Children's Plus, Inc.

—Gecko Gladiator, No. 12. Collins, Ross, illus. 2014. (S. W. I. T. C. H. Ser.: 12). (ENG.). 104p. (J). (gr. 2-5). lib. bdg. 27.99 *(978-1-4677-2115-8(8),* cc532572-06e9-4568-a918-8e1b276481a3, Darby Creek) Lerner Publishing Group.

—Lizard Loopy, Bk. 9. Collins, Ross, illus. 2014. (S. W. I. T. C. H. Ser.: 9). (ENG.). 104p. (J). (gr. 2-5). lib. bdg. 27.99 *(978-1-4677-2112-7(3),* b130a932-7a79-4525-84ae-ef15db1971ce, Darby Creek) Lerner Publishing Group.

—Newt Nemesis, No. 8. Collins, Ross, illus. 2014. (S. W. I. T. C. H. Ser.: 8). (ENG.). 88p. (J). (gr. 2-5). lib. bdg. 27.99 *(978-1-4677-3233-8(8),* 929674af-dfcb-4fe0-abb2-b77ab1d219ad, Darby Creek) Lerner Publishing Group.

Spiegelman, Art. Jack & the Box: Toon Books Level 1. 2008. (ENG., Illus.). 32p. (J). (gr. -1-3). 12.95 *(978-0-9799238-3-8(2),* Toon Books) Astra Publishing Hse.

Spiegelman, Nadja. Zig & Wikki in Something Ate My Homework: Toon Books Level 3. Loeffler, Trade, illus. (Toon Ser.). (ENG.). 40p. (J). (gr. -1-3). 2013. pap. 7.99 *(978-1-935179-38-2(1))* 2010. 12.95 *(978-1-935179-02-3(0))* Astra Publishing Hse. (Toon Books).

Spiegelman, Nadja & Loeffler, Trade. Zig & Wikki in Something Ate My Homework. 2013. (Toon Books Level 3 Ser.). lib. bdg. 14.75 *(978-0-606-32252-2(3))* Turtleback.

Spoor, Mike, illus. The Emperor's Guards: Concepts of Time, 1 vol. 2010. (Mandril! Mountain Math Mysteries Ser.). (ENG.). 32p. (J). (gr. 2-3). lib. bdg. 27.27 *(978-1-60754-922-2(0),* 85dd0127-799d-49a7-b02c-a55c0fa8b8a4, Windmill Bks.) Rosen Publishing Group, Inc., The.

Spradlin, Michael P. Menace from the Deep. 2013. (Killer Species Ser.: 1). lib. bdg. 16.00 *(978-0-606-32447-2(X))* Turtleback.

Spring, Manda. Emerald & the Magic of Raynon. 2004. 118p. pap. 19.95 *(978-1-4137-3708-0(0))* America Star Bks.

Springham, James. Earth-n-Bones: Blue Things. 2006. 54p. pap. 16.95 *(978-1-4137-9738-1(5))* America Star Bks.

—Earth-n-Bones: Toxic. 2005. 56p. pap. 16.95 *(978-1-4137-9755-8(5))* America Star Bks.

St. Mark Kindergarten. Kindergarten Goes to Outer Space for the Day. 2009. 28p. pap. 12.49 *(978-1-4490-0587-0(X))* AuthorHouse.

Stahler, David, Jr. The Seer. 2008. 320p. (J). pap. 6.99 *(978-0-06-052290-2(9)*, Eos) HarperCollins Pubs.

Stamps, Sarah. Our Gang & the Shrinking Machine. Workman, Paula J., illus. 2008. 33p. pap. 24.95 *(978-1-60610-953-3(7))* PublishAmerica, Inc.

Stanek, Robert, pseud. Explore the Solar System. 2010. 42p. pap. 11.99 *(978-1-57545-179-4(4)*, Reagent Pr. Bks. for Young Readers) RP Media.

—The Kingdoms & the Elves of the Reaches Iii (Reader's Choice Edition, Keeper Martin's Tales Book 3) 2008. (Illus.). 244p. pap. 15.95 *(978-1-57545-198-5(0))* RP Media.

Stanford, Cody L. Sinews of the Heart. 2013. 186p. pap. 10.99 *(978-1-62757-059-6(4))* Storm Moon Pr., LLC.

Stanley, Diane. Joplin, Wishing. 2017. (ENG.). 272p. (J). (gr. 3-7). 16.99 *(978-0-06-242370-2(3)*, HarperCollins) HarperCollins Pubs.

Star Wars Digests, 4 vols. 2013. (Star Wars Digests Ser.: 4). (ENG.). 80p. (J). (gr. 3-8). lib. bdg. 125.44 *(978-1-61479-055-6(8)*, 13758, Graphic Novels) Spotlight.

Star Wars Staff & Valois, Rob. Sticker Storyteller. 2008. (Star Wars). (ENG.). 48p. (J). (gr. 1-3). pap. 12.99 *(978-0-448-45058-2(5))* Penguin Publishing Group.

Stasse, Lisa M. The Defiant: The Forsaken Trilogy. 2014. (ENG., Illus.). 352p. (YA). (gr. 7). 17.99 *(978-1-4424-3271-0(3)*, Simon & Schuster Bks. For Young Readers) Simon & Schuster Bks. For Young Readers.

—The Defiant: The Forsaken Trilogy. 2015. (ENG., Illus.). 352p. (YA). (gr. 7). pap. 10.99 *(978-1-4424-3272-7(1))* Simon & Schuster Children's Publishing.

—The Forsaken: The Forsaken Trilogy. (ENG., (YA). (gr. 7). 2013. illus.). 400p. pap. 11.99 *(978-1-4424-3266-6(7))* 2012. 384p. 16.99 *(978-1-4424-3265-9(9))* Simon & Schuster Bks. For Young Readers. (Simon & Schuster Bks. For Young Readers).

—The Uprising: The Forsaken Trilogy. 2013. (ENG.). 384p. (YA). (gr. 7). 16.99 *(978-1-4424-3268-0(3)*, Simon & Schuster Bks. For Young Readers) Simon & Schuster Bks. For Young Readers.

Steele, Andrew. The Galaxy Boys & the Sphere. 2008. (ENG.). 285p. (J). (gr. 4-7). pap. *(978-1-85756-687-1(4))* Janus Publishing Co.

Steele, Michael Anthony. Web of Doom, 1 vol. Schoening, Dan, illus. 2011. (Green Lantern Ser.). (ENG.). 56p. (J). (gr. 3-6). lib. bdg. 26.65 *(978-1-4342-2621-1(2)*, 113666, Stone Arch Bks.) Capstone.

Steiger, A. J. Mindstormer. 2017. (ENG.). 432p. (J). (gr. 6). pap. 12.99 *(978-1-78074-926-6(0)*, 1780749260, Rock the Boat) Oneworld Pubns. GBR. Dist: Grantham Bk. Services.

Stephanie. The Beginning of Gerald. 2012. 28p. pap. 24.95 *(978-1-62709-212-8(9))* America Star Bks.

Stephens, Berin L. Time Gangsters. 2012. pap. 14.99 *(978-1-59955-966-7(8))* Cedar Fort, Inc./CFI Distribution.

Steps To Literacy Staff, compiled by. The Mysterious Benedict Society Collection: Class Pack (3 titles, 6 Each) 2010. (ENG.). (J). pap. 125.82 *(978-1-61267-335-6(X))* Steps To Literacy, LLC.

—The Mysterious Benedict Society Collection: Variety Pack (3 titles, 1 Each) 2010. (ENG.). (J). pap. 20.97 *(978-1-61267-334-9(1))* Steps To Literacy, LLC.

Sterling, L. E. True North. 2018. (True Born Ser.: 2). (ENG.). 304p. (YA). pap. 9.99 *(978-1-63375-915-2(6)*, 900185555) Entangled Publishing, LLC.

Stevens, Cara J. The Alien Conspiracy: An Unofficial Fortnite Novel. 2018. (Battle Royale: Secrets of the Island Ser.). 112p. (J). (gr. 1-5). pap. 7.99 *(978-1-5107-4434-9(7)*, Sky Pony Pr.) Skyhorse Publishing Co., Inc.

—Battle Storm: An Unofficial Novel of Fortnite. 2018. (Battle Royale: Secrets of the Island Ser.). (ENG.). 112p. (J). (gr. 1-5). pap. 7.99 *(978-1-5107-4433-2(9)*, Sky Pony Pr.) Skyhorse Publishing Co., Inc.

Stevens, Eric. The Menace of Metallo, 1 vol. McManus, Shawn, illus. 2009. (Superman Ser.). (ENG.). 56p. (J). (gr. 3-6). pap. 4.95 *(978-1-4342-1371-6(4)*, 95668, Stone Arch Bks.) Capstone.

—The Revenge of Clayface. Schigiel, Gregg, illus. 2009. (Batman Ser.). (ENG.). 56p. (J). (gr. 3-6). lib. bdg. 26.65 *(978-1-4342-1149-1(5)*, 95364, Stone Arch Bks.) Capstone.

Stevens, Noel. From the Farthest Hills of Elsewhere. 2008. 172p. pap. 13.95 *(978-0-595-52835-6(X))* iUniverse, Inc.

Stevenson, Robin. Desolación, 1 vol. 2012. (Spanish Soundings Ser.). (SPA.). 160p. (YA). (gr. 8-12). pap. 9.95 *(978-1-4598-0305-3(1))* Orca Bk. Pubs. USA.

Stevermer, Caroline & Collin, Francesca. River Rats. 2005. (ENG., Illus.). 320p. (YA). (gr. 7-12). pap. 19.95 *(978-0-15-205554-7(1)*, 1196703) Houghton Mifflin Harcourt Publishing Co.

Stewart, Trenton Lee. The Mysterious Benedict Society. Ellis, Carson, illus. (Mysterious Benedict Society Ser.: 1). (ENG.). (J). (gr. 3-7). 2008. 512p. pap. 9.99 *(978-0-316-00395-7(6))* 2007. 496p. 19.99 *(978-0-316-05777-6(0))* Little, Brown Bks. for Young Readers.

—The Mysterious Benedict Society. 2021. (Mysterious Benedict Society Ser.). (ENG., Illus.). 496p. (J). (gr. 3-7). pap. 9.99 *(978-0-316-29760-8(7))* Little, Brown Bks. for Young Readers.

—The Mysterious Benedict Society. 2009. 17.45 *(978-1-60686-527-9(7))* Perfection Learning Corp.

—The Mysterious Benedict Society. 2010. (Mysterious Benedict Society Ser.: 3). (J). lib. bdg. 19.65 *(978-0-606-15117-7(6))* Turtleback.

—The Mysterious Benedict Society. Ellis, Carson, illus. 2008. (Mysterious Benedict Society Ser.: 1). 485p. (J). (gr. 3-7). lib. bdg. 19.65 *(978-1-4178-1817-4(4))* Turtleback.

—The Mysterious Benedict Society & the Perilous Journey. Sudyka, Diana, illus. (Mysterious Benedict Society Ser.: 2). (ENG.). (J). (gr. 3-7). 2009. 464p. pap. 9.99 *(978-0-316-03673-3(0))* 2008. 448p. 19.99 *(978-0-316-05780-6(0))* Little, Brown Bks. for Young Readers.

—The Mysterious Benedict Society & the Perilous Journey. 2009. (Mysterious Benedict Society Ser.: 2). (J). lib. bdg. 19.65 *(978-0-606-07462-9(7))* Turtleback.

—The Mysterious Benedict Society & the Prisoner's Dilemma. Sudyka, Diana, illus. (Mysterious Benedict Society Ser.: 3). (ENG.). 400p. (J). (gr. 3-7). 2010. pap. 9.99 *(978-0-316-04550-6(0))* 2009. 36.99 *(978-0-316-04552-0(7))* Little, Brown Bks. for Young Readers.

Stiefvater, Maggie. Ballad: A Gathering of Faerie. 2009. (Lament Novel Ser.: 2). (ENG.). 360p. (YA). (gr. 9-12). pap. 11.99 *(978-0-7387-1484-4(4)*, 0738714844, Flux) North Star Editions.

Stilton, Gerónimo. The Galactic Goal. 2015. (Geronimo Stilton Spacemice Ser.: 4). lib. bdg. 18.40 *(978-0-606-37059-2(5))* Turtleback.

Stilton, Gerónimo & Pizzelli, Anna. The Underwater Planet. Facciotto, Giuseppe & Verzini, Daniele, illus. 2016. 113p. (J). *(978-1-5182-0303-9(5))* Scholastic, Inc.

Stine, Fay. Star Ship Fantasy: The New Frontier of Space. 2008. 52p. pap. 10.95 *(978-1-4327-2703-1(6))* Outskirts Pr., Inc.

Stock, Lisa. Battle for Naboo. 2012. (Star Wars DK Readers Level 3 Ser.). lib. bdg. 13.55 *(978-0-606-26564-5(3))* Turtleback.

—DK Readers L2: Star Wars: Rey to the Rescue! 2017. (Star Wars DK Readers Level 2 Ser.). lib. bdg. 13.55 *(978-0-606-39899-2(6))* Turtleback.

—DK Readers L2: Star Wars: Rey to the Rescue! Discover Rey's Force Powers! 2017. (DK Readers Level 2 Ser.). (ENG., Illus.). 48p. (J). (gr. k-2). pap. 3.99 *(978-1-4654-5580-2(9)*, DK Children) Dorling Kindersley Publishing, Inc.

—Rey to the Rescue! 2017. (Illus.). 48p. (J). *(978-1-5182-2634-2(5))* Dorling Kindersley Publishing, Inc.

Stohl, Kevin. Time Chronicles Ozone, Vol. 3. 2004. 170p. (YA). 22.95 *(978-0-595-66639-3(6))* iUniverse, Inc.

Stohl, Margaret. Icons. 2014. (Icons Ser.: 1). (ENG.). 464p. (YA). (gr. 7-17). pap. 21.99 *(978-0-316-20519-1(2))* Little, Brown Bks. for Young Readers.

Stone, Emma. Loholt Scrimminge & the Moor-Land Quest. 2007. 140p. per. *(978-1-906210-19-9(5))* Grosvenor Hse. Publishing Ltd.

Stories Beyond Time & Space. (J). pap. 15.50 *(978-0-8359-0158-1(0))* Globe Fearon Educational Publishing.

Storm, Michael. Pulp7: A Sweet Deal, a Killer Calling, & a Man Inside. 2nd enl. ed. 2005. (YA). 23.95 *(978-0-9744929-6-4(5))* Leeway Pubs.

Stracher, Cameron. The Water Wars. 2011. (ENG.). 256p. (YA). (gr. 7-12). pap. 18.99 *(978-1-4022-6759-8(2)*, 9781402267598) Sourcebooks, Inc.

Strange, Jason. Realm of Ghosts, 1 vol. Parks, Phil, illus. 2011. (Jason Strange Ser.). (ENG.). 72p. (J). (gr. 3-6). 25.32 *(978-1-4342-2962-5(9)*, 114195); pap. 6.25 *(978-1-4342-3096-6(1)*, 114736) Capstone. (Stone Arch Bks.).

Strickland, Brad & Fuller, Thomas E. Missing! 2004. (Mars Year One Ser.: 2). (ENG., Illus.). 176p. (J). (gr. 3-7). pap. 9.99 *(978-0-689-86401-8(9)*, Aladdin) Simon & Schuster Children's Publishing.

Stroud, David Wayne. Wiggies the White Blood Cell. Stroud, David Wayne, illus. 2005. (Illus.). (J). 14.95 *(978-0-9762835-1-5(4))* Shooting Star Publishing.

Strungis, Elaine. Sammi & Danny Learn about Jupiter. 2012. 32p. pap. 14.50 *(978-1-4669-5411-3(6))* Trafford Publishing.

—Sammi & Danny Learn about Mercury. 2012. 28p. pap. 13.55 *(978-1-4669-5413-7(2))* Trafford Publishing.

—Sammi & Danny Learn about the Earth. 2012. 32p. pap. 14.50 *(978-1-4669-3731-4(9))* Trafford Publishing.

—Sammi & Danny Learn about Uranus. 2012. 32p. pap. 14.50 *(978-1-4669-6297-2(6))* Trafford Publishing.

—Sammi & Danny Learn about Venus. 2012. 32p. pap. 14.50 *(978-1-4669-3733-8(5))* Trafford Publishing.

Struyk-Bonn, Chris. Whisper, 1 vol. 2014. (ENG.). 352p. (YA). (gr. 8-12). pap. 12.95 *(978-1-4598-0475-3(9))* Orca Bk. Pubs. USA.

Stupniker, Yehudit. The Remarkable Invention That Saves Zion: A Tale of Triz. 2007. 292p. 18.95 *(978-1-932687-74-3(2)*, Devora Publishing) Simcha Media Group.

Suen, Anastasia. A Prize Inside: A Robot & Rico Story, 1 vol. Laughead, Michael, illus. 2009. (Robot & Rico Ser.). (ENG.). 32p. (J). (gr. 1-2). pap. 6.25 *(978-1-4342-1749-3(3)*, 102221, Stone Arch Bks.) Capstone.

Sumerak, Marc. Big Trouble at the Big Top! Gurihiru Staff, illus. 2006. (X-Men Power Pack - 4 Titles Ser.). 24p. lib. bdg. 22.78 *(978-1-59961-219-5(4))* Spotlight.

—Costumes On! Gurihiru Staff, illus. 2006. (X-Men Power Pack - 4 Titles Ser.). 24p. lib. bdg. 22.78 *(978-1-59961-220-1(8))* Spotlight.

Sumner, M. C. Lost Soul. 2013. (Extreme Zone Ser.: 7). (ENG., Illus.). 192p. (YA). (gr. 11). pap. 13.99 *(978-1-4814-2117-1(4)*, Simon Pulse) Simon Pulse.

—Unseen Powers. 2013. (Extreme Zone Ser.: 3). (ENG., Illus.). 192p. (YA). (gr. 11). pap. 13.99 *(978-1-4814-2114-0(X)*, Simon Pulse) Simon Pulse.

Suparna. The Science Playground: Fun with Science Concepts & Nature. 2009. (ENG.). 46p. pap. 24.99 *(978-1-4389-3466-2(1))* AuthorHouse.

Sutherland, Tui T. Shadow Falling. 2007. (Avatars Ser.: Bk.2). 356p. (YA). (gr. 7-12). lib. bdg. 17.89 *(978-0-06-085147-7(3)*, Eos) HarperCollins Pubs.

Sutton, Laurie S. Bug Team Alpha, 6 vols. Clarey, Patricio, illus. 2018. (Bug Team Alpha Ser.). (ENG.). 112p. (J). (gr. 3-6). 159.90 *(978-1-4965-5972-2(X)*, 27621, Stone Arch Bks.) Capstone.

—The Dig. Nathan, James, illus. 2017. (Bug Team Alpha Ser.). (ENG.). 112p. (J). (gr. 3-6). lib. bdg. 26.65 *(978-1-4965-5183-2(4)*, 136186, Stone Arch Bks.) Capstone.

—The Draco. Nathan, James, illus. 2017. (Bug Team Alpha Ser.). (ENG.). 112p. (J). (gr. 3-6). lib. bdg. 26.65 *(978-1-4965-5186-3(9)*, 136189, Stone Arch Bks.) Capstone.

—Invisible Enemy. Nathan, James, illus. 2017. (Bug Team Alpha Ser.). (ENG.). 112p. (J). (gr. 3-6). lib. bdg. 26.65 *(978-1-4965-5184-9(2)*, 136187, Stone Arch Bks.) Capstone.

—Juggernaut. Clarey, Patricio, illus. 2018. (Bug Team Alpha Ser.). (ENG.). 112p. (J). (gr. 3-6). lib. bdg. 26.65 *(978-1-4965-5958-6(4)*, 137178, Stone Arch Bks.) Capstone.

—The Man of Steel: Superman vs. the Doomsday Army, 1 vol. Levins, Tim & Vecchio, Luciano, illus. 2013. (Man of Steel Ser.). (ENG.). 88p. (J). (gr. 3-7). 26.65 *(978-1-4342-4487-1(3)*, 120486); pap. 5.95 *(978-1-4342-4827-5(5)*, 121744) Capstone. (Stone Arch Bks.).

—Stranded. Nathan, James, illus. 2017. (Bug Team Alpha Ser.). (ENG.). 112p. (J). (gr. 3-6). lib. bdg. 26.65 *(978-1-4965-5185-6(0)*, 136188, Stone Arch Bks.) Capstone.

—The Time Vortex. Clarey, Patricio, illus. 2018. (Bug Team Alpha Ser.). (ENG.). 112p. (J). (gr. 3-6). lib. bdg. 26.65 *(978-1-4965-5957-9(6)*, 137177, Stone Arch Bks.) Capstone.

Suvada, Emily. This Cruel Design. 2018. (Mortal Coil Ser.). (ENG., Illus.). 400p. (YA). (gr. 9). 19.99 *(978-1-4814-9636-0(0)*, Simon Pulse) Simon Pulse.

Suzanne, Collins. Los juegos del hambre. 2009. (Hunger Games Trilogy: Bk. 1). (SPA.). pap. 19.99 *(978-84-9867-539-9(1))* RBA Libros, S.A. ESP. Dist: Lectorum Pubns., Inc.

Suzukaze, Ryo. Attack on Titan: Kuklo Unbound. Shibamoto, Thores, illus. 2015. (Attack on Titan Ser.: 2). 298p. (J). (gr. 7). pap. 14.95 *(978-1-939130-87-7(5)*, Vertical) Kodansha America, Inc.

Swain, H. A. Gifted. 2016. (ENG.). 320p. (YA). 27.99 *(978-1-250-02830-3(2)*, 900118076) Feiwel & Friends.

Swanson, David. Tube World. Burke, Shane, illus. 2012. 158p. pap. 10.00 *(978-0-9830830-4-7(5))* Swanson, David.

Swindells, Robert. Timesnatch. Riley, Jon, illus. 2008. 176p. (YA). (gr. 7). pap. 12.99 *(978-0-552-55592-0(4)*, Corgi) Transworld Publishers Ltd. GBR. Dist: Independent Pubs. Group.

Sykes, Harold S. The Beacon of Airport Seven. 2004. reprint ed. pap. 1.99 *(978-1-4192-5375-1(1))* Kessinger Publishing, LLC.

Sylvester, Kevin. MiNRS. (MiNRS Ser.: 1). (ENG., Illus.). (J). (gr. 3-7). 2016. 352p. pap. 8.99 *(978-1-4814-4040-0(3))* 2015. 336p. 18.99 *(978-1-4814-4039-4(X))* McElderry, Margaret K. Bks. (McElderry, Margaret K. Bks.).

—MiNRS 2. 2016. (MiNRS Ser.: 2). (ENG., Illus.). 352p. (J). (gr. 3-7). 17.99 *(978-1-4814-4042-4(X)*, McElderry, Margaret K. Bks.) McElderry, Margaret K. Bks.

Szpirglas, Jeff. Evil Eye. 2013. 192p. pap. *(978-0-9867914-7-5(4))* Star Crossed Pr.

Tamura, Yumi. Book of Justice. Tamura, Yumi, illus. 2003. (Chicago Ser.: Vol. 2). (ENG., Illus.). 200p. pap. 15.95 *(978-1-56931-829-4(8))* Viz Media.

Tan, Shaun. The Lost Thing. (Illus.). 32p. pap. *(978-0-7344-0388-9(7)*, Lothian Children's Bks.) Hachette Australia.

Tanner, Lian. Battlesong: Book Three in the Icebreaker Trilogy. 2018. (Icebreaker Trilogy Ser.: 3). (ENG.). 304p. (J). pap. 15.99 *(978-1-250-15871-0(0)*, 900185527) Square Fish.

Tarkoff, Sarah. Sinless. 2018. (Eye of the Beholder Ser.: 1). (ENG.). 304p. pap. 15.99 *(978-0-06-245638-0(5)*, Harper Voyager) HarperCollins Pubs.

Tarore, Martha. The Runaway Bubble. 2011. (ENG.). 35p. (J). pap. 16.95 *(978-1-4327-5898-1(5))* Outskirts Pr., Inc.

Taylor, Cora. On Wings of Evil, 1 vol. 2005. (ENG.). 250p. (J). (gr. 7-9). 8.95 *(978-1-55041-929-0(3)*, aff69785-dd94-4f6e-a639-e5b4cd202da4) éditeur, Annika Parance CAN. Dist: Firefly Bks., Ltd.

Taylor, G. P. El Hechicero de las Sombras. Attrache, Ismael, tr. 2005. (SPA.). 328p. pap. 9.95 *(978-950-511-910-3(0))* Santillana USA Publishing Co., Inc.

—Wormwood. 2004. (Illus.). 272p. (J). (gr. 3-6). 17.99 *(978-1-59185-626-9(4))* Charisma Media.

Taylor, Travis S. & Nye, Jody Lynn. Moon Beam. 2017. (ENG.). 384p. (J). (gr. 5). 18.99 *(978-1-4814-8252-3(1))* Baen Bks.

Teacher Talk: Individual Title Six-Packs. (gr. -1-2). 27.00 *(978-0-7635-9477-0(6))* Rigby Education.

Teagan, Erin. Luciana. Truman, Lucy, illus. 2018. 164p. (J). *(978-1-5490-0282-3(1))* Scholastic, Inc.

Teague, David. How Oscar Indigo Broke the Universe (and Put It Back Together Again) 2017. (ENG.). 256p. (J). (gr. 3-7). 16.99 *(978-0-06-237749-4(3)*, HarperCollins) HarperCollins Pubs.

Tebbetts, Chris. Me Myself & Him. 2019. (ENG.). 304p. (YA). (gr. 9). 17.99 *(978-1-5247-1522-9(0)*, Delacorte Pr.) Random Hse. Children's Bks.

Teitelbaum, Michael. I Am Superman. 2009. (Justice League Classic: I Can Read! Ser.). (J). lib. bdg. 13.55 *(978-0-606-06951-9(8))* Turtleback.

—The Secret Life of Black Cat. Sazaklis, John, illus. 2009. (Spider-Man Ser.). 64p. (J). (gr. 2-5). pap. 4.99 *(978-0-06-162626-5(0)*, HarperFestival) HarperCollins Pubs.

Terrell, Brandon. Limbo's Diner. 2016. (Tartan House Ser.). (ENG., Illus.). 96p. (J). (gr. 3-6). *(978-1-63235-164-7(1)*, 11895, 12-Story Library) Bookstaves, LLC.

Terry, Teri. Deception. 2019. (Dark Matter Trilogy Ser.). (ENG., Illus.). 368p. (YA). (gr. 7). lib. bdg. 18.99 *(978-1-62354-106-4(9)*, Charlesbridge Teen) Charlesbridge Publishing, Inc.

—Fractured: Book Two in the Slated Trilogy. 2014. (Slated Ser.: 2). (ENG.). 352p. (YA). (gr. 7). pap. 10.99 *(978-0-14-242504-6(4)*, Speak) Penguin Young Readers Group.

—Shattered: Book Three in the Slated Trilogy. 2015. (Slated Ser.: 3). (ENG.). 336p. (YA). (gr. 7). pap. 9.99 *(978-0-14-242507-7(9)*, Speak) Penguin Young Readers Group.

Tesler, Monica. Bounders. 2016. (Bounders Ser.: 1). (ENG., Illus.). 384p. (J). (gr. 5-9). 16.99 *(978-1-4814-4593-1(6)*, Aladdin) Simon & Schuster Children's Publishing.

—The Forgotten Shrine. (Bounders Ser.: 3). (ENG.). (J). (gr. 5-9). 2018. 400p. pap. 8.99 *(978-1-4814-4600-6(2))* 2017. (Illus.). 384p. 17.99 *(978-1-4814-4599-3(5))* Simon & Schuster Children's Publishing. (Aladdin).

—The Heroes Return. 2018. (Bounders Ser.: 4). (ENG., Illus.). 400p. (J). (gr. 5-9). 17.99 *(978-1-5344-0247-8(0)*, Aladdin) Simon & Schuster Children's Publishing.

—The Tundra Trials. 2017. (Bounders Ser.: 2). (ENG.). 384p. (J). (gr. 5-9). pap. 8.99 *(978-1-4814-4597-9(9)*, Aladdin) Simon & Schuster Children's Publishing.

—The Tundra Trials. 2016. (Bounders Ser.: 2). (ENG., Illus.). 384p. (J). (gr. 5-9). 16.99 *(978-1-4814-4596-2(0)*, Simon & Schuster/Paula Wiseman Bks.) Simon & Schuster/Paula Wiseman Bks.

Testa, Dom. Galahad 1: The Comet's Curse. 2005. 224p. (YA). per. 8.95 *(978-0-9760564-0-9(2))* Profound Impact Group, Inc.

—Galahad 2: The Web of Titan. 2006. (YA). per. 8.95 *(978-0-9760564-1-6(0))* Profound Impact Group, Inc.

—Galahad 3: The Cassini Code. 2008. 272p. (YA). pap. 9.95 *(978-0-9760564-4-7(5))* Profound Impact Group, Inc.

Tezuka, Osamu. Phoenix, Vol. 1. Tezuka, Osamu, illus. 2003. (ENG., Illus.). 344p. pap. 15.95 *(978-1-56931-868-3(9))* Viz Media.

—Yamato/Space, Vol. 3. Tezuka, Osamu, illus. 2003. (Phoenix Ser.). (ENG., Illus.). 336p. pap. 15.95 *(978-1-59116-100-4(2))* Viz Media.

Thame, Val. Witches in Trouble. I.t. ed. 2006. 104p. per. *(978-1-905665-27-3(X))* Pollinger In Print.

The Guide Dog, Thelma. For the Love of My Pet. Hartley, Joshua, illus. 2012. (ENG.). 26p. (gr. k-5). pap. 14.95 *(978-1-61448-338-0(8))* Morgan James Publishing.

Thomas, Brandon. Horizon Volume 1. 2017. (ENG., Illus.). 136p. (YA). pap. 9.99 *(978-1-5343-0047-7(3)*, ed1e26a4-3148-4580-bc57-fb64c7be6eb0) Image Comics.

—Remnant. 2017. (ENG., Illus.). 128p. (YA). pap. 16.99 *(978-1-5343-0227-3(1)*, 4cb62148-11bd-46ed-9b26-e7181ed5dcb7) Image Comics.

Thomas, Jane. Zioc Saves His Planet. 2009. (Illus.). 208p. pap. 14.49 *(978-1-4389-4930-7(8))* AuthorHouse.

S

Thomas, Lex. The Burnouts. 2016. (Quarantine Ser.: 3). (ENG.). 296p. (YA). (gr. 9-12). pap. 9.99 *(978-1-5124-0419-7(5)*, e71b4da5-69dd-42c0-af43-1a1b573637a4, Carolrhoda Lab™) Lerner Publishing Group.

—The Giant. (Quarantine Ser.). (ENG.). 352p. (YA). (gr. 9-12). 2018. pap. 9.99 *(978-1-5415-3846-7(3)*, ba896617-e02e-4086-8dbc-3a543f00f30a) 2016. E-Book 27.99 *(978-1-5124-0159-2(5))* Lerner Publishing Group. (Carolrhoda Lab™).

—The Loners. (Quarantine Ser.: No. 1). (ENG.). 416p. (gr. 9). 2012. 17.99 *(978-1-60684-329-1(X)*Bk. 1. 2013. (YA). pap. 9.99 *(978-1-60684-438-0(5)*, a4290b32-f23c-40fb-9b34-385c9b02c589) Lerner Publishing Group. (Carolrhoda Lab™).

—The Saints, Bk. 2. 2014. (Quarantine Ser.: No. 2). (ENG.). 416p. (YA). (gr. 9-12). pap. 9.99 *(978-1-60684-540-0(3)*, 9b2df3a0-3933-41db-aeb0-259ae3dfdc73, Carolrhoda Lab™) Lerner Publishing Group.

Thomas, Nigel. Tom Travis: The Lost People of Orion. 2006. 193p. pap. 24.95 *(978-1-4241-0382-9(7))* PublishAmerica, Inc.

Thomas, Rich. The Amazing Spider-Man. Clark, Jeff, illus. 2012. (Marvel Origins Ser.). (ENG.). 48p. (J). (gr. k-5). lib. bdg. 31.36 *(978-1-61479-007-5(8)*, 11335, Marvel Age) Spotlight.

—The Incredible Hulk. Semeiks, Val, illus. 2012. (Marvel Origins Ser.). (ENG.). 48p. (J). (gr. k-5). lib. bdg. 31.36 *(978-1-61479-009-9(4)*, 11337, Marvel Age) Spotlight.

Thompson, Colin. In the Pink. 2017. (Watch This Space Ser.: 2). 224p. (J). (gr. 4-7). pap. 9.99 *(978-1-74275-618-9(2))* Random Hse. Australia AUS. Dist: Independent Pubs. Group.

Thompson, Craig. Space Dumplins. 2015. lib. bdg. 26.95 *(978-0-606-37760-7(3))* Turtleback.

—Space Dumplins: a Graphic Novel. Thompson, Craig, illus. 2015. (ENG., Illus.). 320p. (J). (gr. 3-7). pap. 18.99 *(978-0-545-56543-1(X)*, Graphix) Scholastic, Inc.

Thompson, Hannah. Living with the Fall. 2016. (ENG., Illus.). (J). 27.99 *(978-1-63533-043-4(2)*, Harmony Ink Pr.) Dreamspinner Pr.

Thompson, Kirk Robert. Paradise Lost: Earth First. 2004. 384p. (YA). per. 18.95 *(978-0-9716681-3-3(2))* Magic Valley Pubs.

Thompson, Paul B. Lost Republic, 1 vol. 2015. (Scarlet Voyage Ser.). (ENG.). 256p. (gr. 6-7). 23.61 *(978-1-62324-000-4(X)*, 7d18d20e-88c8-4879-b024-02bdf91c8627) Enslow Publishing, LLC.

Thorne, Frank. Prodigal: Egg of First Light: Egg of First Light. 2012. (ENG., Illus.). 96p. (YA). pap. 12.95 *(978-1-934944-14-1(9)*, 9781934944141) Ape Entertainment.

A Thousand Pieces of You. 2014. (Firebird Ser.: 1). (ENG.). 368p. (YA). (gr. 9). 18.99 *(978-0-06-227896-8(7)*, HarperTeen) HarperCollins Pubs.

Tintera, Amy. Rebel. (Reboot Ser.: 2). 352p. (YA). (gr. 8). 2015. (ENG.). pap. 10.99 *(978-0-06-221711-0(9))* 2014. pap. 12.00 *(978-0-06-233790-0(4))* HarperCollins Pubs. (HarperTeen).

—Reboot. (Reboot Ser.: 1). (ENG.). (YA). (gr. 8). 2014. 400p. pap. 10.99 *(978-0-06-221708-0(9))* 2013. 384p. 17.99 *(978-0-06-221707-3(0))* HarperCollins Pubs. (HarperTeen).

Tobey, Danny. The God Game: A Novel. 2020. (ENG., Illus.). 464p. (YA). pap. *(978-1-250-27079-5(0))* St. Martin's Pr.

Tobin, Paul. The Genius Factor: How to Capture an Invisible Cat. Lafontaine, Thierry, illus. 2016. (ENG.). 272p. (J). 16.99 *(978-1-61963-840-2(1)*, 900150260, Bloomsbury USA Childrens) Bloomsbury Publishing USA.

—Plants vs. Zombies: Garden Warfare Volume 2. Lattie, Tim, illus. 2018. 88p. (J). (gr. 3-7). 10.99 *(978-1-5067-0548-4(0)*, Dark Horse Books) Dark Horse Comics.

—Plants vs. Zombies Volume 6: Boom Boom Mushroom. Chabot, Jacob, illus. 2017. (Plants vs. Zombies Ser.: 6). 80p. (J). (gr. 3-7). 10.99 *(978-1-5067-0037-3(3)*, Dark Horse Books) Dark Horse Comics.

Tocco, John V. Meet the Gizmos: The First Kids on the International Space Station. Tocco, Douglas, illus. 2003. 32p. 16.95 *(978-0-9711665-2-3(8))*; per. 9.95 *(978-0-9711665-3-0(6))* Favorite Uncle Bks., LLC.

Todd, Ilima. Remake. 2014. (Remake Ser.: 1). (ENG.). 304p. (YA). (gr. 7). 17.99 *(978-1-60907-924-6(8)*, 5123870, Shadow Mountain) Shadow Mountain Publishing.

Todd, Ruthven. Space Cat. 2008. (J). (gr. k-4). 27.50 *(978-0-8446-6561-0(4))* Smith, Peter Pub., Inc.

Tolar, Kathy. I Must Be from Another Planet. 2009. 20p. pap. 12.99 *(978-1-4389-9378-2(1))* AuthorHouse.

Tomizawa, Hitoshi. Alien Nine: Emulators. Pannone, Frank, ed. Jackson, Laura & Kobayashi, Yoko, trs. from JPN. Tomizawa, Hitoshi, illus. 2004. (Illus.). 248p. pap. 9.99

(978-1-58664-924-1(8), CMX 65004G, CPM Manga) Central Park Media Corp.

Toole, Anne. Crystal Cadets Vol. 1. O'Neill, K., illus. 2016. (ENG.). 128p. (J). pap. 12.99 *(978-1-941302-16-3(5)*, 7e636ac5-2ec6-4bab-be53-c19c34c9ab48, Lion Forge) Oni Pr., Inc.

Torday, Piers. The Last Wild. 2015. (Last Wild Ser.: 1). (ENG.). 352p. (J). (gr. 3-7). 9.99 *(978-0-14-750965-9(3)*, Puffin Books) Penguin Young Readers Group.

Torres, J. Power Lunch Vol. 2 Bk. 2: Seconds. Trippe, Dean, illus. 2014. (Power Lunch Ser.: 2). (ENG.). 40p. (J). 12.99 *(978-1-62010-011-0(8)*, 9781620100110, Lion Forge) Oni Pr., Inc.

Torres, Jennifer. The Battle: The Briny Deep Mysteries Book 3, 1 vol. 2014. (Briny Deep Mysteries Ser.: Bk. 3). (ENG., Illus.). 96p. (J). (gr. 4-6). pap. 13.88 *(978-1-62285-187-4(0)*, 51cf6dd5-1a8a-4473-9858-9caf72f84df1) Enslow Publishing, LLC.

—The Disappearing: The Briny Deep Mysteries Book 1, 1 vol. 2014. (Briny Deep Mysteries Ser.: Bk. 1). (ENG., Illus.). 96p. (J). (gr. 4-6). pap. 13.88 *(978-1-62285-173-7(0)*, 585ba180-2450-4cac-a487-b9bd7d4e81a9) Enslow Publishing, LLC.

—The Return: The Briny Deep Mysteries Book 2, 1 vol. 2014. (Briny Deep Mysteries Ser.: Bk. 2). (ENG., Illus.). 96p. (J). (gr. 4-6). pap. 13.88 *(978-1-62285-182-9(X)*, 469249a8-6de1-4339-a610-4d64bcb9e170) Enslow Publishing, LLC.

Torres, Mario J. The Incredible Adventures of Kaplan & Dylan: Book One: Present, 1 vol. 2009. 159p. pap. 24.95 *(978-1-4489-9513-4(2))* PublishAmerica, Inc.

Torrey, Michele. The Case of the Gasping Garbage. Torrey, Michele & Newman, Barbara Johansen, illus. 2009. (Doyle & Fossey, Science Detectives Ser.: 1). (ENG.). 96p. (J). (gr. 4-7). pap. 6.99 *(978-1-4027-4960-5(0))* Sterling Publishing Co., Inc.

—The Case of the Graveyard Ghost. Newman, Barbara Johansen, illus. 2009. (Doyle & Fossey, Science Detectives Ser.: 3). (ENG.). 96p. (J). pap. 6.95 *(978-1-4027-4963-6(5))* Sterling Publishing Co., Inc.

—The Case of the Mossy Lake Monster. Torrey, Michele & Newman, Barbara Johansen, illus. 2009. (Doyle & Fossey, Science Detectives Ser.: 2). (ENG.). 96p. (J). (gr. 4-7). pap. 6.99 *(978-1-4027-4962-9(7))* Sterling Publishing Co., Inc.

The TrailFolk of Xunar-kun: Book Two in the Tellings of Xunar-kun. 2008. (YA). 30.95 *(978-0-9768585-5-3(X))*; pap. 16.95 *(978-0-9768585-4-6(1))* Howe, Tina Field.

Treggiari, Jo. Ashes, Ashes. (ENG.). 352p. (YA). (gr. 7). 2013. pap. 9.99 *(978-0-545-25564-6(3)*, Scholastic Paperbacks) 2011. 17.99 *(978-0-545-25563-9(5)*, Scholastic Pr.) Scholastic, Inc.

Trevayne, Emma. Gamescape: Overworld. 2016. (Gamescape Ser.: 1). (ENG.). 416p. (YA). (gr. 9). 17.99 *(978-0-06-240876-1(3)*, Greenwillow Bks.) HarperCollins Pubs.

Troupe, Thomas Kingsley. Carma Comes Home. Tayal, Amit, illus. 2017. (Star Belchers Ser.). (ENG.). 128p. (J). (gr. 3-6). pap. 7.95 *(978-1-4965-4877-1(9)*, 135642); lib. bdg. 25.99 *(978-1-4965-4873-3(6)*, 135638) Capstone. (Stone Arch Bks.).

—Robot Ruckus. Tayal, Amit, illus. 2017. (Star Belchers Ser.). (ENG.). 128p. (J). (gr. 3-6). lib. bdg. 25.99 *(978-1-4965-4872-6(8)*, 135637, Stone Arch Bks.) Capstone.

—A Spaceship Named Judy. Tayal, Amit, illus. 2017. (Star Belchers Ser.). (ENG.). 128p. (J). (gr. 3-6). pap. 7.95 *(978-1-4965-4875-7(2)*, 135640); lib. bdg. 25.99 *(978-1-4965-4871-9(X)*, 135636) Capstone. (Stone Arch Bks.).

—Star Belchers, 4 vols. 2017. (Star Belchers Ser.). (ENG., Illus.). 128p. (J). (gr. 3-6). 101.28 *(978-1-4965-4891-7(4)*, 26716, Stone Arch Bks.) Capstone.

Tullien, Sean. Meltdown Town. 2016. (Tartan House Ser.). (ENG.). 96p. (J). (gr. 3-6). *(978-1-63235-165-4(X)*, 11896, 12-Story Library) Bookstaves, LLC.

Tzvi, G. J. The Great Adventure of la Gang du Sept. 2006. (ENG.). 177p. pap. 14.95 *(978-1-4116-8291-7(2))* Lulu Pr., Inc.

Ueno, Haruki. Big Hero 6, Vol. 2. 2015. (Big Hero 6 Graphic Novel Ser.: 2). lib. bdg. 23.30 *(978-0-606-37926-7(6))* Turtleback.

Ueyama, Michiro. Chaotic Century. Ueyama, Michiro, illus. (Zoids Ser.). (ENG., Illus.). Vol. 11. 2004. 82p. pap. 5.95 *(978-1-56931-858-4(1))* Vol. 12. 2003. 72p. pap. 5.95 *(978-1-56931-867-6(0))* Viz Media.

Uncle Henry. Biode. Uncle Henry, illus. 100th ed. 2004. (Illus.). 216p. pap. 7.99 *(978-1-932568-02-8(6)*, UHB003) Uncle Henry Bks.

Urey, Gary. Escaped. 2018. (Secrets of the X-Point Ser.: 2). (ENG.). 272p. (J). (gr. 3-7). pap. 9.99 *(978-0-8075-6689-3(6)*, 807566896) Whitman, Albert & Co.

Valentine, James. The Past Is Gone. 2007. (TimeJumpers Ser.: 1). (ENG.). 288p. (J). (gr. 3-7). pap. 13.99 *(978-1-4169-3955-9(5)*, Simon & Schuster/Paula Wiseman Bks.) Simon & Schuster/Paula Wiseman Bks.

—The Present Never Happens. 2007. (TimeJumpers Ser.: 2). (ENG.). 304p. (J). (gr. 3-7). pap. 13.99 *(978-1-4169-3956-6(3)*, Simon & Schuster/Paula Wiseman Bks.) Simon & Schuster/Paula Wiseman Bks.

Valentine, Nicole. A Time Traveler's Theory of Relativity. 2019. (ENG., Illus.). 352p. (J). (gr. 4-8). 17.99 *(978-1-5415-5538-9(4)*, 2b60b16e-6e91-4b27-b7dd-76c86cce49dc, Carolrhoda Bks.) Lerner Publishing Group.

Van Der Watt, Tony. Balthazar, the Wolf Who Reformed. 2010. 48p. pap. 12.50 *(978-1-60911-125-0(7)*, Eloquent Bks.) Strategic Book Publishing & Rights Agency (SBPRA).

Van Dolzer, Krista. Earth to Dad. 2018. (ENG.). 320p. (J). (gr. 4-8). 15.95 *(978-1-68446-012-0(3)*, 138859, Capstone Editions) Capstone.

van Eekhout, Greg. Voyage of the Dogs. (ENG.). (J). (gr. 3-7). 2019. 240p. pap. 7.99 *(978-0-06-268601-5(1))* 2018. 224p. 16.99 *(978-0-06-268600-8(3))* HarperCollins Pubs. (HarperCollins).

Van Hamme, Jean. Beyond the Shadows. Rosinski, Grzegorz, illus. 2008. (Thorgal Ser.: 3). 96p. pap. 19.95 *(978-1-905460-45-8(7))* CineBook GBR. Dist: National Bk. Network.

—Child of the Stars. Rosinski, Adolf, illus. 2007. (Thorgal Ser.: 1). 96p. per. 19.95 *(978-1-905460-23-6(6))* CineBook GBR. Dist: National Bk. Network.

van Hamme, Jean. Thorgal - City of the Lost God, Vol. 6. Rosinski, Grzegorz, illus. 2009. (Thorgal Ser.: 6). 96p. pap. 19.95 *(978-1-84918-001-6(6))* CineBook GBR. Dist: National Bk. Network.

Van Hamme, Jean. The Three Elders of Aran. Rosinski, illus. 2007. (Thorgal Ser.: 2). 96p. (J). (gr. 4-7). pap. 19.95 *(978-1-905460-31-1(7))* CineBook GBR. Dist: National Bk. Network.

Vande Velde, Vivian. Heir Apparent. 2004. (ENG., Illus.). 352p. (J). (gr. 5-7). reprint ed. pap. 8.99 *(978-0-15-205125-9(2)*, 1060977, Clarion Bks.) HarperCollins Pubs.

Vargas, George. The Prophecy of the Ages: Of War & Choices. 2004. 458p. (YA). pap. 24.95 *(978-0-595-29607-1(6))* iUniverse, Inc.

Varma, Eric. The Orphaned Knight. 2004. (Caviant Ser.: Bk. 1). 200p. (YA). 24.95 *(978-0-595-66668-3(X))* iUniverse, Inc.

Varsell, Linda. Ends of Rainbow. Curtis, E., illus. 2003. 260p. (J). per. 8.00 *(978-0-9725479-5-6(9))* Rainbow Communications.

—The Humane Touch. Curtis, E., illus. 2003. 316p. per. 10.00 *(978-0-9728737-0-3(8))* Rainbow Communications.

—The Rainbow Breakers. Curtis, E., illus. 2003. 232p. per. 7.00 *(978-0-9725479-3-2(2))* Rainbow Communications.

—The Rainbow Circle. Curtis, E., illus. 2003. 428p. (J). per. 10.00 *(978-0-9725479-9-4(1))* Rainbow Communications.

—The Rainbow Dreamers. Curtis, E., illus. 2003. 262p. per. 8.00 *(978-0-9725479-4-9(0))* Rainbow Communications.

—The Rainbow Makers. Curtis, E., illus. 2003. 148p. per. 6.00 *(978-0-9725479-2-5(4))* Rainbow Communications.

—The Rainbow Planet. Curtis, E., illus. 2003. 162p. (J). per. 6.00 *(978-0-9725479-7-0(5))* Rainbow Communications.

—The Rainbow Remnants. Curtis, E., illus. 2003. 204p. (J). per. 7.00 *(978-0-9725479-8-7(3))* Rainbow Communications.

—The Rainbow Rescue. Curtis, E., illus. 2003. 200p. (J). per. 7.00 *(978-0-9725479-6-3(7))* Rainbow Communications.

—With a Human Touch. Curtis, E., illus. 2003. 178p. per. 6.00 *(978-0-9725479-0-1(8))* Rainbow Communications.

Vaughan, M. M. The Ability. Bruno, Iacopo, illus. (Ability Ser.). (ENG.). (YA). (gr. 3-7). 2014. 352p. pap. 8.99 *(978-1-4424-5201-5(3))* 2013. 336p. 15.99 *(978-1-4424-5200-8(5))* McElderry, Margaret K. Bks. (McElderry, Margaret K. Bks.).

—Mindscape. Bruno, Iacopo, illus. 2015. (Ability Ser.). (ENG.). 336p. (YA). (gr. 3-7). pap. 7.99 *(978-1-4424-5205-3(6)*, McElderry, Margaret K. Bks.) McElderry, Margaret K. Bks.

—Six. 2015. (ENG., Illus.). 368p. (J). (gr. 3-7). 16.99 *(978-1-4814-2069-3(0)*, McElderry, Margaret K. Bks.) McElderry, Margaret K. Bks.

Vaughn, C. L. I See Aliens. 2007. 15p. 10.95 *(978-1-4357-0117-5(8))* Lulu Pr., Inc.

Velvet, Black. The Adventures of Sam in Space: Planet of the Sweets. 2007. 32p. (J). pap. 8.00 *(978-0-8059-7367-9(2))* Dorrance Publishing Co., Inc.

Verba, Joan Marie. Action Alert. 2008. 176p. (YA). pap. 15.95 *(978-0-9653575-8-6(9))* FTL Pubns.

Vern, Jules. From the Earth to the Moon. 2008. (Bring the Classics to Life Ser.). (ENG., Illus.). 72p. (gr. 4-12). pap., act. bk. ed. 10.95 *(978-1-55576-181-3(X)*, EDCTR-407B) EDCON Publishing Group.

—A Journey to the Center of the Earth, 1 vol. Fisher, Eric Scott, illus. 2011. (Calico Illustrated Classics Ser.: No. 3). (ENG.). 112p. (J). (gr. 2-5). 38.50 *(978-1-61641-104-6(X)*, 4015, Calico Chapter Bks.) ABDO Publishing Co.

—A Journey to the Interior of the Earth. 2006. 196p. per. 13.95 *(978-1-59818-461-7(X))* Aegypan.

—Topsy-Turvy. 2020. (ENG.). 118p. (J). pap. 9.95 *(978-1-63637-172-6(8))* Bibliotech Pr.

—Topsy-Turvy. Ogilvie, J. G., tr. 2009. 108p. 22.95 *(978-1-60664-685-4(0))*; pap. 9.95 *(978-1-60664-314-3(2))* Rodgers, Alan Bks.

—Voyage au Centre de la Terre.Tr. of Voyage to the Center of the Earth. (FRE.). (J). pap. 14.95 *(978-2-07-051437-3(4))* Gallimard, Editions FRA. Dist: Distribooks, Inc.

—20,000 Leagues under the Sea. 2004. (Fast Track Classics Ser.). (Illus.). 48p. (J). pap. *(978-0-237-52688-7(3))* Evans Brothers, Ltd.

—20,000 Leagues under the Sea, 1 vol. Fisher, Eric Scott, illus. 2011. (Calico Illustrated Classics Ser.: No. 3). (ENG.). 112p. (J). (gr. 2-5). 38.50 *(978-1-61641-110-7(4)*, 4027, Calico Chapter Bks.) ABDO Publishing Co.

Verne, Jules. Classic Starts(r): Journey to the Center of the Earth. Freeberg, Eric, illus. 2011. (Classic Starts(r) Ser.). (ENG.). 160p. (J). (gr. 2-4). 7.99 *(978-1-4027-7313-6(7))* Sterling Publishing Co., Inc.

Villeneuve, Kevin J. The Adventures of Nick the Ecologist & His Robot O-Zone: The Mystery of the Missing Trees. 2007. 96p. per. 9.95 *(978-0-595-42362-0(0))* iUniverse, Inc.

Vincent, Rachel. Brave New Girl. 2017. 272p. (YA). (gr. 7). 17.99 *(978-0-399-55245-8(6)*, Delacorte Pr.) Random Hse. Children's Bks.

—Strange New World. 2018. 368p. (YA). (gr. 7). 17.99 *(978-0-399-55249-6(9)*, Delacorte Pr.) Random Hse. Children's Bks.

Vlock, Rob. Sven Carter & the Android Army. 2018. (Max Ser.). (ENG.). 368p. (J). (gr. 4-8). 18.99 *(978-1-4814-9017-7(6))*; (Illus.). pap. 7.99 *(978-1-4814-9016-0(8))* Simon & Schuster Children's Publishing. (Aladdin).

Vyff, Shannon. 21st Century Kids. 2007. 280p. pap. 14.95 *(978-1-886057-00-5(1))* Warren Publishing, Inc.

Wadsworth, Kay. Daisy Moon & the Worm Armies. 2011. (Illus.). 100p. pap. 12.52 *(978-1-4567-7043-3(8))* AuthorHouse.

Walden, Mark. Aftershock. 2014. (H. I. V. E. Ser.: 7). (ENG., Illus.). 304p. (J). (gr. 3-7). 19.99 *(978-1-4424-9467-1(0)*, Simon & Schuster Bks. For Young Readers) Simon & Schuster Bks. For Young Readers.

—Deadlock. 2015. (H. I. V. E. Ser.: 8). (ENG., Illus.). 304p. (J). (gr. 3-7). 18.99 *(978-1-4424-9470-1(0)*, Simon & Schuster Bks. For Young Readers) Simon & Schuster Bks. For Young Readers.

—Dreadnought. (H. I. V. E. Ser.: 4). (ENG.). (J). (gr. 3-7). 2012. 320p. pap. 8.99 *(978-1-4424-1368-9(9))* 2011. 304p. 18.99 *(978-1-4424-2186-8(X))* Simon & Schuster Bks. For Young Readers. (Simon & Schuster Bks. For Young Readers).

—Escape Velocity. (H. I. V. E. Ser.: 3). (ENG.). (J). (gr. 3-7). 2012. 368p. pap. 8.99 *(978-1-4424-1367-2(0))* 2011. 352p. 18.99 *(978-1-4424-2185-1(1))* Simon & Schuster Bks. For Young Readers. (Simon & Schuster Bks. For Young Readers).

—H. I. V. E. Higher Institute of Villainous Education. (H. I. V. E. Ser.: 1). (ENG.). 320p. (J). (gr. 3-7). 2008. pap. 8.99 *(978-1-4169-3572-8(X))* 2007. (Illus.). 19.99 *(978-1-4169-3571-1(1))* Simon & Schuster Bks. For Young Readers. (Simon & Schuster Bks. For Young Readers).

—The Overlord Protocol. (H. I. V. E. Ser.: 2). (ENG.). 384p. (J). (gr. 3-7). 2009. pap. 8.99 *(978-1-4169-3574-2(6))* 2008. 18.99 *(978-1-4169-3573-5(8))* Simon & Schuster Bks. For Young Readers. (Simon & Schuster Bks. For Young Readers).

—Redemption. 2018. (Earthfall Trilogy Ser.: 3). (ENG., Illus.). 304p. (J). (gr. 3-7). 17.99 *(978-1-4424-9421-3(2)*, Simon & Schuster Bks. For Young Readers) Simon & Schuster Bks. For Young Readers.

—Retribution. 2015. (Earthfall Trilogy Ser.: 2). (ENG., Illus.). 272p. (J). (gr. 3-7). 17.99 *(978-1-4424-9418-3(2)*, Simon & Schuster Bks. For Young Readers) Simon & Schuster Bks. For Young Readers.

—Rogue. (H. I. V. E. Ser.: 5). (ENG.). (J). (gr. 3-7). 2012. 320p. pap. 8.99 *(978-1-4424-1369-6(7))* 2011. 304p. 18.99 *(978-1-4424-2187-5(8))* Simon & Schuster Bks. For Young Readers. (Simon & Schuster Bks. For Young Readers).

—Zero Hour. 2012. (H. I. V. E. Ser.: 6). (ENG.). 304p. (J). (gr. 3-7). 18.99 *(978-1-4424-2188-2(6)*, Simon & Schuster Bks. For Young Readers) Simon & Schuster Bks. For Young Readers.

Wallach, Tommy. Slow Burn. 2018. (Anchor & Sophia Ser.: 2). (ENG., Illus.). 416p. (YA). (gr. 9). 18.99 *(978-1-4814-6841-1(3)*, Simon & Schuster Bks. For Young Readers) Simon & Schuster Bks. For Young Readers.

—Strange Fire. 2017. (Anchor & Sophia Ser.: 1). (ENG., Illus.). 400p. (YA). (gr. 9). 17.99 *(978-1-4814-6838-1(3)*, Simon & Schuster Bks. For Young Readers) Simon & Schuster Bks. For Young Readers.

—We All Looked Up. 2015. (ENG., Illus.). 384p. (YA). (gr. 9). 17.99 *(978-1-4814-1877-5(7)*, Simon & Schuster Bks. For Young Readers) Simon & Schuster Bks. For Young Readers.

Wallenfels, Stephen. Pod. 2012. (ENG.). 304p. (gr. 12). 7.99 *(978-1-937007-43-0(X)*, Ace) Penguin Publishing Group.

Walsh, Jill Paton. The Green Book. Bloom, Lloyd, illus. 2012. (ENG.). 80p. (J). (gr. 4-6). pap. 7.99 *(978-0-312-64122-1(2)*, 900077672) Square Fish.

Walters, Eric. Fourth Dimension. 2018. (Neighborhood Ser.: 4). (ENG.). 384p. (YA). (gr. 7). 17.99 *(978-0-14-319844-4(0)*, Penguin Teen) PRH Canada Young Readers CAN. Dist: Penguin Random Hse. LLC.

—The Rule of Three: Fight for Power. 2015. (Rule of Three Ser.: 2). (ENG.). 352p. (YA). (gr. 7). 27.99 *(978-0-374-30179-8(4)*, 900140944, Farrar, Straus & Giroux (BYR)) Farrar, Straus & Giroux.

Wang, Jack & Wang, Holman. Star Wars Epic Yarns: Return of the Jedi. 2015. (ENG., Illus.). 24p. (J). (gr. -1 — 1). 9.95 *(978-1-4521-3500-7(2))* Chronicle Bks. LLC.

Ward, David. Beneath the Mask: The Grassland Trilogy: Book Two, Bk. 2. 2008. (ENG.). 272p. (YA). (gr. 5-17). 16.95 *(978-0-8109-7074-8(0)*, 6255, Amulet Bks.) Abrams, Inc.

Warner Brothers. Supergirl: the Secret Files of Kara Danvers: The Ultimate Guide to the Hit TV Show. 2019. (Supergirl Ser.). (ENG., Illus.). 192p. (J). (gr. 3-7). 16.99 *(978-1-4197-3170-9(X)*, 1205601, Amulet Bks.) Abrams, Inc.

Warrington, Dean Grey. Perfiction. 2007. 188p. per. 13.95 *(978-0-595-43758-0(3))* iUniverse, Inc.

Wasserman, Robin. Crashed. 2009. (ENG.). 448p. (YA). (gr. 9-18). 16.99 *(978-1-4169-7453-6(9)*, Simon Pulse) Simon Pulse.

—Torn. 2011. (Cold Awakening Ser.: 3). (ENG.). 384p. (YA). (gr. 9). pap. 9.99 *(978-1-4169-3636-7(X)*, Simon Pulse) Simon Pulse.

—Truth, 3. 2007. (Chasing Yesterday Ser.: No. 3). (ENG.). 235p. (J). (gr. 6-8). 18.69 *(978-0-439-93342-1(0))* Scholastic, Inc.

—Wired. 2010. (ENG.). 400p. (YA). (gr. 9-18). 15.99 *(978-1-4169-7454-3(7)*, Simon Pulse) Simon Pulse.

Waters, Galadriel, ed. The Plot Thickens... Harry Potter Investigated by Fans for Fans. Rogers, Melissa & Heran, Michelle, illus. 2004. (ENG.). 100p. pap. 18.95 *(978-0-9723936-3-8(3))* Wizarding World Pr.

Watson, Jacqueline. Mattie-Jo-Calico. 2003. 109p. pap. 19.95 *(978-1-59286-920-6(3))* America Star Bks.

Watson, Jude. Death on Naboo. 2006. (Star Wars Ser.: No. 4). 135p. (J). lib. bdg. 13.00 *(978-1-4242-0777-0(0))* Fitzgerald Bks.

—The Desperate Mission. 2005. (Star Wars Ser.: No. 1). 168p. (J). lib. bdg. 20.00 *(978-1-4242-0774-9(6))* Fitzgerald Bks.

—Underworld. 2005. (Star Wars Ser.: No. 3). 137p. (J). lib. bdg. 20.00 *(978-1-4242-0776-3(2))* Fitzgerald Bks.

Watson, Vicki. Bob & the Alien Escapade. 2013. 226p. pap. *(978-0-9574062-2-3(3))* Green, Callisto.

Waugh, Sylvia. Carrera Espacial. (SPA.). (YA). 8.95 *(978-958-04-6028-2(0))* Norma S.A. COL. Dist: Distribuidora Norma, Inc.

Weber, David & Lindskold, Jane. Fire Season. 2013. (Star Kingdom (Weber) Ser.: 2). (ENG., Illus.). 304p. (YA). (gr. 7). pap. 9.99 *(978-1-4516-3921-6(X))* Baen Bks.

Webster, Christy. Teenage Mutant Ninga Turtles: Double-Team! 2014. (Step into Reading Level 4 Ser.). lib. bdg. 13.55 *(978-0-606-36283-2(5))* Turtleback.

Webster, David Scott. Book One of the Naxos Island Mages: The Grand Adventure. 2003. 200p. 24.95 *(978-0-595-75137-2(7))*; pap. 14.95 *(978-0-595-29933-1(4))* iUniverse, Inc.

Weekes, Patrick. Feeder. 2018. (ENG., Illus.). 304p. (YA). (gr. 9). 17.99 *(978-1-5344-0016-0(8)*, McElderry, Margaret K. Bks.) McElderry, Margaret K. Bks.

Weinman, Logan & Bennett, Jeffrey. Max's Ice Age Adventure. 2007. (Science Adventures with Max the Dog Ser.). (ENG., Illus.). 32p. (J). (gr. k-2). 12.00 *(978-0-9721819-2-1(X))* Big Kid Science.

Weitz, Chris. The Young World. 2015. (Young World Ser.: 1). (ENG.). 400p. (YA). (gr. 10-17). pap. 19.99 *(978-0-316-22628-8(9))* Little, Brown Bks. for Young Readers.

Wells, Dan. Bluescreen. 2017. 456p. (YA). (gr. 9-12). pap. 17.99 *(978-987-747-261-5(9))* V&R Editoras.

—Ones & Zeroes. 2018. (Mirador Ser.: 2). (ENG.). 432p. (YA). (gr. 8). pap. 9.99 *(978-0-06-234791-6(8)*, Balzer & Bray) HarperCollins Pubs.

—Partials. (ENG.). (YA). 2013. (Partials Sequence Ser.: 1). 528p. (gr. 9). pap. 11.99 *(978-0-06-207105-7(X)*, Balzer & Bray) 2012. (Partials Sequence Ser.: 1). 480p. (gr. 9). 17.99 *(978-0-06-207104-0(1)*, Balzer & Bray) 2012. 496p. pap. 9.99 *(978-0-06-213569-8(4))* HarperCollins Pubs.

—Ruins. 2014. (Partials Sequence Ser.: 3). (ENG.). 464p. (YA). (gr. 9). 17.99 *(978-0-06-207110-1(6)*, Balzer & Bray) HarperCollins Pubs.

Wells, H. G. The Invisible Man. Fisher, Eric Scott, illus. 2011. (Calico Illustrated Classics Ser.: No. 3). (ENG.). 112p. (J). (gr. 2-5). 38.50 *(978-1-61641-103-9(1)*, 4013, Calico Chapter Bks.) ABDO Publishing Co.

—The Lost World. 2004. (Fast Track Classics Ser.). (Illus.). 48p. (J). pap. *(978-0-237-52404-3(X))* Evans Brothers, Ltd.

—The Time Machine. 2008. (Bring the Classics to Life Ser.). (Illus.). 72p. (gr. 4-12). pap., act. bk. ed. 10.95 *(978-0-931334-43-6(8)*, EDCTR-403B) EDCON Publishing Group.

—The Time Machine. 2004. (Fast Track Classics Ser.). (Illus.). 48p. (J). pap. *(978-0-237-52406-7(6))* Evans Brothers, Ltd.

—The War of the Worlds. 2008. (Bring the Classics to Life Ser.). (ENG., Illus.). 72p. (gr. 3-12). pap., act. bk. ed. 10.95 *(978-1-55576-097-7(X)*, EDCTR-306B) EDCON Publishing Group.

—The War of the Worlds. 2008. 256p. (J). (gr. 3-7). 29.95 *(978-1-4344-6610-5(8))*; pap. 14.95 *(978-1-4344-6609-9(4))* Wildside Pr., LLC.

—The War of the Worlds. 2004. (Fast Track Classics Ser.). (Illus.). 48p. (J). pap. *(978-0-237-52405-0(8))* Evans Brothers, Ltd.

—War of the Worlds. Bennet, Felix, illus. 2013. (Classics of Science Fiction Ser.). (ENG.). 64p. pap. 7.95 *(978-1-906230-12-8(9))* Real Reads Ltd. GBR. Dist: Casemate Pubs. & Bk. Distributors, LLC.

—The War of the Worlds, 1 vol. Fisher, Eric Scott, illus. 2011. (Calico Illustrated Classics Ser.: No. 3). (ENG.). 112p. (J). (gr. 2-5). 38.50 *(978-1-61641-111-4(2)*, 4029, Calico Chapter Bks.) ABDO Publishing Co.

Wells, H. G. & Geary, Rick. The Invisible Man. (Classics Illustrated Ser.). (Illus.). 52p. (YA). pap. 4.95 *(978-1-57209-020-0(0))* Classics International Entertainment, Inc.

Wells, H. G., et al. The Island of Doctor Moreau. (Illus.). 52p. (YA). pap. 4.95 *(978-1-57209-012-5(X))* Classics International Entertainment, Inc.

Wells, Robison. Blackout. 2014. (Blackout Ser.: 1). (ENG.). 448p. (YA). (gr. 8). pap. 9.99 *(978-0-06-202613-2(5)*, HarperTeen) HarperCollins Pubs.

—Dead Zone. 2014. (Blackout Ser.: 2). (ENG.). 384p. (YA). (gr. 8). 17.99 *(978-0-06-227502-8(X)*, HarperTeen) HarperCollins Pubs.

—Feedback. (ENG.). (YA). 2013. (Variant Ser.: 2). 336p. (gr. 8). pap. 10.99 *(978-0-06-202611-8(9))* 2012. 320p. pap. 9.99 *(978-0-06-222830-7(7))* HarperCollins Pubs. (HarperTeen).

—Variant. (Variant Ser.: 1). (ENG.). (YA). (gr. 8-18). 2011. 384p. 17.99 *(978-0-06-202608-8(9))*1. 2012. 400p. pap. 10.99 *(978-0-06-202609-5(7))* HarperCollins Pubs. (HarperTeen).

Werner, Jane. Mickey Mouse & His Spaceship (Disney: Mickey Mouse) RH Disney, illus. 2016. (Little Golden Book Ser.). (ENG.). 24p. (J). (-k). 5.99 *(978-0-7364-3633-5(2)*, Golden/Disney) Random Hse. Children's Bks.

West, Alexandra C. These Are the Avengers. 2018. (Marvel World of Reading Level 1 Ser.). (J). lib. bdg. 14.75 *(978-0-606-40977-3(7))* Turtleback.

—World of Reading: Black Panther:: This Is Black Panther-Level 1: Level 1. 2018. (World of Reading Ser.). (ENG., Illus.). 32p. (J). (gr. 1-3). pap. 4.99 *(978-1-368-00853-2(4))* Marvel Worldwide, Inc.

—World of Reading: Marvel Super Hero Adventures: These Are the Avengers-Level 1. 2018. (World of Reading Ser.). (ENG., Illus.). 32p. (J). (gr. 1-3). pap. 4.99 *(978-1-368-02353-5(3))* Marvel Worldwide, Inc.

West, Melissa. Hover. 2013. (Taking Ser.: 2). (ENG.). 352p. (YA). (gr. 7-12). pap. 9.99 *(978-1-62266-008-7(0)*, 9781622660087) Entangled Publishing, LLC.

West, Robert. Attack of the Spider Bots, 1 vol. 2008. (Star-Fighters of Murphy Street Ser.: 2). (ENG., Illus.). 160p. (J). (gr. 4-7). pap. 6.99 *(978-0-310-71426-2(5))* Zonderkidz.

—Escape from the Drooling Octopod!, 1 vol., 3. 2008. (Star-Fighters of Murphy Street Ser.: 3). (ENG., Illus.). 144p. (J). (gr. 4-6). pap. 6.99 *(978-0-310-71427-9(3))* Zonderkidz.

West, Tracey. Talent Showdown (Pokémon: Chapter Book) 2017. (Pokémon Chapter Bks.). (ENG.). 96p. (J). (gr. 2-5). pap. 4.99 *(978-1-338-17591-2(2))* Scholastic, Inc.

West, Tracey, adapted by. Independence Day Resurgence Movie Novelization: Young Readers Edition. 2016. (ENG., Illus.). 144p. (J). (gr. 3-7). pap. 6.99 *(978-1-4814-7858-8(3)*, Simon Spotlight) Simon Spotlight.

Westerfeld, Scott. Behemoth. Thompson, Keith, illus. (Leviathan Trilogy Ser.). (ENG.). (YA). (gr. 7). 2011. 512p. pap. 14.99 *(978-1-4169-7176-4(9))* 2010. 496p. 18.99 *(978-1-4169-7175-7(0))* Simon Pulse. (Simon Pulse).

—Behemoth. l.t. ed. 2010. (Leviathan Trilogy: Bk. 2). (ENG., Illus.). 540p. 23.99 *(978-1-4104-3066-3(9))* Thorndike Pr.

—Behemoth. 2011. (Leviathan Ser.: 2). lib. bdg. 24.50 *(978-0-606-22407-9(6))* Turtleback.

—Bogus to Bubbly: An Insider's Guide to the World of Uglies. Phillips, Craig, illus. 2008. (Uglies Ser.). (ENG.). 224p. (YA). (gr. 7). pap. 11.99 *(978-1-4169-7436-9(9)*, Simon Pulse) Simon Pulse.

—Extras. (Uglies Ser.: 4). (YA). 2008. 83.49 *(978-1-4281-8889-1(4))* 2007. 130.75 *(978-1-4281-7244-9(0))* 2007. 132.75 *(978-1-4281-7242-5(4))* 2007. 267.75 *(978-1-4281-7239-5(4))* 2007. 110.75 *(978-1-4281-7240-1(8))* 2007. 112.75

(978-1-4281-7238-8(6)) 2007. 1.25 *(978-1-4281-7235-7(1))* Recorded Bks., Inc.
—Extras. 2011. (Uglies Ser.). (ENG.). 416p. (YA). (gr. 7). pap. 12.99 *(978-1-4424-1978-0(4))*; lib. bdg. 21.99 *(978-1-4424-3007-5(9))* Simon Pulse. (Simon Pulse).
—Goliath. 2011. (YA). 1.25 *(978-1-4640-3062-8(6))*; 122.75 *(978-1-4618-0617-2(8))*; 122.75 *(978-1-4618-0614-1(3))*; 124.75 *(978-1-4618-0613-4(5))*; 305.75 *(978-1-4618-0618-9(6))* Recorded Bks., Inc.
—Goliath. Thompson, Keith, illus. (Leviathan Trilogy Ser.). (ENG.). (YA). (gr. 7). 2012. 576p. pap. 14.99 *(978-1-4169-7178-8(5))* 2011. 560p. 24.99 *(978-1-4169-7177-1(7))* Simon Pulse. (Simon Pulse).
—Goliath. 2012. (Leviathan Ser.: 3). lib. bdg. 24.50 *(978-0-606-26355-9(1))* Turtleback.
—Impostors, 1 vol. (Impostors Ser.). (ENG.). 416p. (YA). (gr. 7-7). 2021. 12.99 *(978-1-338-75790-3(3))* 2018. 18.99 *(978-1-338-15151-0(7)*, Scholastic Pr.) Scholastic, Inc.
—Leviathan. Thompson, Keith, illus. (Leviathan Trilogy Ser.). (ENG.). (YA). (gr. 7-18). 2010. 464p. pap. 14.99 *(978-1-4169-7174-0(2))* 2009. 448p. 24.99 *(978-1-4169-7173-3(4))* Simon Pulse. (Simon Pulse).
—Leviathan. l.t. ed. 2010. (Leviathan Trilogy: Bk. 1). (ENG.). 525p. 23.95 *(978-1-4104-2572-0(X))* Thorndike Pr.
—The Manual of Aeronautics: An Illustrated Guide to the Leviathan Series. Thompson, Keith, illus. 2012. (ENG.). 64p. (YA). (gr. 7). 19.99 *(978-1-4169-7179-5(3)*, Simon Pulse) Simon Pulse.
—Midnighters #2: Touching Darkness. 2008. (Midnighters Ser.: 2). (ENG.). 336p. (YA). (gr. 8-12). reprint ed. pap. 9.99 *(978-0-06-051956-8(8)*, HarperTeen) HarperCollins Pubs.
—Midnighters #3: Blue Noon. 2008. (Midnighters Ser.: 3). (ENG., Illus.). 384p. (YA). (gr. 8-12). pap. 9.99 *(978-0-06-051959-9(2)*, HarperTeen) HarperCollins Pubs.
—Pretties, 10 vols. (Uglies Ser.: 2). (YA). 2008. 124.75 *(978-1-4281-1126-4(3))* 2008. 75.75 *(978-1-4281-8039-0(7))* 2007. 1.25 *(978-1-4281-1117-2(4))* 2007. 97.75 *(978-1-4281-1120-2(4))* 2006. 94.75 *(978-1-4281-1122-6(0))* 2006. 127.75 *(978-1-4281-1124-0(7))* 2006. 199.75 *(978-1-4281-1121-9(2))* Recorded Bks., Inc.
—Pretties. 2011. (Uglies Ser.). (ENG.). 368p. (YA). (gr. 7). 21.99 *(978-1-4169-3639-8(4))*; pap. 12.99 *(978-1-4424-1980-3(6))* Simon Pulse. (Simon Pulse).
—The Secret Hour. 2006. 304p. *(978-1-904233-82-4(1)*, Atom Books) Little, Brown Book Group Ltd.
—Shatter City (Impostors, Book 2) 2019. (Impostors Ser.: 2). (ENG.). 416p. (YA). (gr. 7-7). 18.99 *(978-1-338-15041-4(3)*, Scholastic Pr.) Scholastic, Inc.
—Specials. (Uglies Ser.: 3). (YA). 2010. 1.25 *(978-1-4281-3456-0(5))* 2010. 247.75 *(978-1-4281-3460-7(3))* 2008. 87.49 *(978-1-4281-8042-0(7))* 2007. 101.75 *(978-1-4281-3459-1(X))* 2007. 131.75 *(978-1-4281-3463-8(8))* 2007. 129.75 *(978-1-4281-3465-2(4))* 2007. 99.75 *(978-1-4281-3461-4(1))* Recorded Bks., Inc.
—Specials. 2011. (Uglies Ser.). (ENG.). 384p. (YA). (gr. 7). pap. 12.99 *(978-1-4424-1979-7(2))*; lib. bdg. 21.99 *(978-1-4424-3008-2(7))* Simon Pulse. (Simon Pulse).
—Spill Zone Book 2: The Broken Vow. Puvilland, Alex, illus. 2019. (Spill Zone Ser.: 2). (ENG.). 240p. (YA). pap. 17.99 *(978-1-250-30942-6(5)*, 900198487, First Second Bks.) Roaring Brook Pr.
—Uglies. 2009. (Uglies Ser.: Bk. 1). 10.36 *(978-0-7848-3338-4(9)*, Everbind) Marco Bk. Co.
—Uglies. Fournier, Guillaume, tr. 2007. (Uglies Trilogy). (FRE.). 432p. (YA). (gr. 7-12). pap. *(978-2-266-15924-1(0))* Presses Pocket.
—Uglies. (Uglies Ser.: 1). (J). 2008. 80.49 *(978-1-4281-8028-4(1))* 2007. 199.75 *(978-1-4281-1334-3(7))* 2007. 1.25 *(978-1-4281-1330-5(4))* 2006. 127.75 *(978-1-4281-1337-4(1))* 2006. 124.75 *(978-1-4281-1339-8(8))* 2006. 97.75 *(978-1-4281-1333-6(9))* 2006. 94.75 *(978-1-4281-1335-0(5))* Recorded Bks., Inc.
—Uglies. 2011. (Uglies Ser.). (ENG.). 432p. (YA). (gr. 7). pap. 12.99 *(978-1-4424-1981-0(4))*; (Illus.). 21.99 *(978-1-4169-3638-1(6))* Simon Pulse. (Simon Pulse).
—Uglies (Boxed Set) Uglies; Pretties; Specials; Extras. 2012. (Uglies Ser.). (ENG.). 1600p. (YA). (gr. 7). pap. 51.99 *(978-1-4424-7939-5(6)*, Simon Pulse) Simon Pulse.
Westerfeld, Scott & Grayson, Devin. Cutters. 2012. (Uglies Graphic Novel Ser.: 2). lib. bdg. 22.10 *(978-0-606-26828-8(6))* Turtleback.
—Shay's Story. 2012. (Uglies Graphic Novel Ser.: 1). lib. bdg. 24.50 *(978-0-606-26475-4(2))* Turtleback.
Westerfeld, Scott & Lanagan, Margo. Swarm. 2018. (Zeroes Ser.: 2). lib. bdg. 24.50 *(978-0-606-40832-5(0))* Turtleback.
Westerfeld, Scott, et al. Swarm. (Zeroes Ser.: 2). (ENG.). (YA). (gr. 9). 2018. 480p. pap. 12.99 *(978-1-4814-4340-1(2))* 2016. (Illus.). 464p. 19.99 *(978-1-4814-4339-5(9))* Simon Pulse. (Simon Pulse).
—Zeroes. (Zeroes Ser.: 1). (ENG.). (YA). (gr. 9). 2016. 576p. pap. 12.99 *(978-1-4814-4337-1(2))* 2015. (Illus.). 560p. 19.99 *(978-1-4814-4336-4(4))* Simon Pulse. (Simon Pulse).
Westlake, Donald. The Risk Profession. 2009. 60p. pap. 7.95 *(978-1-60664-380-8(0))* Rodgers, Alan Bks.
Weston, Robert Paul. Zorgamazoo. 2010. (ENG.). 288p. (J). (gr. 3-7). 8.99 *(978-1-59514-295-5(9)*, Razorbill) Penguin Young Readers Group.
Westover, Alli. My Daddy Works at NASA. 2005. (J). 15.95 *(978-1-888237-59-7(7))* Baxter Pr.
Weyn, Suzanne. The Bar Code Tattoo (the Bar Code Trilogy, Book 1) 2012. (Bar Code Ser.: 1). (ENG.). 256p. (YA). (gr. 7). pap. 12.99 *(978-0-545-47054-4(4)*, Scholastic Paperbacks) Scholastic, Inc.
Whaley, John Corey. Noggin. (ENG., Illus.). (YA). (gr. 9). 2015. 368p. pap. 12.99 *(978-1-4424-5873-4(9))* 2014. 352p. 19.99 *(978-1-4424-5872-7(0))* Simon & Schuster Children's Publishing. (Atheneum Bks. for Young Readers).
Wheeler, Alex. Firefight, 4. 2009. (Star Wars: Rebel Force Ser.: 4). (ENG.). 160p. (J). (gr. 4-6). 21.19 *(978-0-545-14084-3(6))* Scholastic, Inc.
Wheeler, Kim. Even More Adventures of Jonny Plumb. 2013. 186p. pap. *(978-0-7552-1570-6(2)*, Bright Pen) Authors OnLine, Ltd.
—Jonny Plumb's New Adventures... 2013. 172p. pap. *(978-0-7552-1569-0(9)*, Bright Pen) Authors OnLine, Ltd.
White, Andrea. Windows on the World. 2011. 238p. (J). 18.95 *(978-1-60898-105-2(3))*; pap. 9.95 *(978-1-60898-106-9(1))* namelos llc.
White, Ruth. You'll Like It Here (Everybody Does) 2012. 272p. (J). (gr. 4-6). (ENG.). lib. bdg. 21.19 *(978-0-385-90813-9(X)*, Delacorte Pr.); 7.99 *(978-0-375-86596-1(9)*, Yearling) Random Hse. Children's Bks.
Whittemore, Jo. Supergirl: Age of Atlantis: (Supergirl Book 1) 2019. (ENG.). 256p. (J). (gr. 4-7). pap. 8.99 *(978-1-4197-3609-4(4)*, 1205303, Amulet Bks.) Abrams, Inc.
—Supergirl: Master of Illusion. 2019. (ENG.). 256p. (J). (gr. 5-9). 13.99 *(978-1-4197-3142-6(4)*, 1205501, Amulet Bks.) Abrams, Inc.
Wiggins, Bethany. Stung. 2014. (ENG.). 320p. (YA). (gr. 9). pap. 10.99 *(978-0-8027-3589-8(4)*, 900123276, Bloomsbury USA Childrens) Bloomsbury Publishing USA.
Wiley. The Extraordinary Adventures of Ordinary Basil: Island of the Volcano Monkeys. 2007. (Ordinary Basil Ser.). (J). pap. *(978-0-439-86133-5(0))* Blue Sky Pr.
William H. Sadlier Staff. At Space Camp, Vol. 2. 2005. (Early Library). (gr. k-2). 24.00 net. *(978-0-8215-8945-8(8))* Sadlier, William H. Inc.
Williams, Heather L. & Muench-Williams, Heather. Caillou Learns about Space. Storch, Ellen N., illus. l.t. ed. 2005. (HRL Board Book Ser.). (J). (gr. -1-k). bds. 10.95 *(978-1-57332-308-6(X)*, HighReach Learning, Incorporated) Carson-Dellosa Publishing, LLC.
Williams, Rozanne. Jump! 2017. (Learn-To-Read Ser.). (ENG., Illus.). (J). pap. 3.49 *(978-1-68310-342-4(4))* Pacific Learning, Inc.
Williams, Sean. Twinmaker. 2013. (Twinmaker Ser.: 1). (ENG.). 496p. (YA). (gr. 8). 17.99 *(978-0-06-220321-2(5)*, Balzer & Bray) HarperCollins Pubs.
Williams, Suzanna. Ninety-Five Percent Human. 2013. 270p. pap. *(978-0-9574662-2-7(6))* Beresford Publishing Hse.
Wills, Joseph. The World. 2013. 200p. pap. *(978-1-906954-76-5(3))* Live It Publishing.
Windham, Ryder. Ezra's Gamble. 2014. (Star Wars Rebels Chapter Bks.). 154p. (J). lib. bdg. 17.20 *(978-0-606-35283-3(X))* Turtleback.
—Ezra's Gamble: An Original Novel. 2014. 154p. (J). *(978-1-4242-6296-0(8))* Disney Publishing Worldwide.
—Island of Lost Masks. 2015. lib. bdg. 16.00 *(978-0-606-37793-5(X))* Turtleback.
—A New Hope: The Life of Luke Skywalker. 2009. 208p. (J). *(978-0-545-16177-0(0))* Scholastic, Inc.
—The Shape-Shifter Strikes. 2003. 85p. (J). *(978-0-439-45884-9(6))* Scholastic, Inc.
—The Wrath of Darth Maul. 2012. 216p. (J). *(978-0-545-43367-9(3))* Scholastic, Inc.
Windham, Ryder & Beecroft, Simon. DK Readers L3: Star Wars: I Want to Be a Jedi: What Does It Take to Join the Jedi Order? 2007. (DK Readers Level 3 Ser.). (ENG., Illus.). 48p. (J). (gr. 2-4). pap. 4.99 *(978-0-7566-3112-3(2)*, DK Children) Dorling Kindersley Publishing, Inc.
Windham, Ryder & Scholastic, Inc. Staff. Shinebone Showdown, 2. 2010. (Star Wars Adventures in Hyperspace Ser.). (ENG.). 96p. (J). (gr. 2-4). 17.44 *(978-0-545-21359-2(2))* Scholastic, Inc.
Winick, Judd. Hilo Book 1: the Boy Who Crashed to Earth: (a Graphic Novel) 2015. (Hilo Ser.: 1). (ENG., Illus.). 208p. (J). (gr. 3-7). 16.99 *(978-0-385-38618-0(4))* Penguin Random Hse. LLC.
—Hilo Book 2: Saving the Whole Wide World: (a Graphic Novel) 2016. (Hilo Ser.: 2). (ENG., Illus.). 208p. (J). (gr. 3-7). 16.99 *(978-0-385-38624-1(9))*;Bk. 2. 13.99 *(978-0-385-38623-4(0))* Penguin Random Hse. LLC.
—Hilo Book 4: Waking the Monsters: (a Graphic Novel) 2018. (Hilo Ser.: 4). (Illus.). 208p. (J). (gr. 3-7). 13.99 *(978-1-5247-1493-2(3))* Penguin Random Hse. LLC.
—Hilo Book 6: All the Pieces Fit: (a Graphic Novel) 2020. (Hilo Ser.: 6). (Illus.). 224p. (J). (gr. 3-7). 13.99 *(978-0-525-64406-4(7))*; (ENG.). 16.99 *(978-0-525-64407-1(5))* Penguin Random Hse. LLC.
Winterfeld, Henry. Star Girl. Schabert, Kyrill, tr. Wegner, Fritz, illus. 2015. (ENG.). 192p. (J). (gr. 3-8). pap. 9.99 *(978-0-486-79468-6(7)*, 794687) Dover Pubns., Inc.
Wolf, Fred Alan. Dr. Quantum in the Grandfather Paradox. 2007. (Dr. Quantum Ser.). (Illus.). 176p. (J). (gr. 4-7). per. 12.95 *(978-0-9786813-3-3(9))* Elora Media, LLC.
Wolf, Mari. An Empty Bottle. 2011. 30p. 13.95 *(978-1-4638-9995-0(5))* Rodgers, Alan Bks.
Wolfe, D. K. Flap Doodle & the Incredible Kibbil Caper 2005. (Illus.). 247p. (J). (gr. 4-6). 16.95 *(978-1-59810-031-0(9))* Jeriger Pr.
Wolff, Tracy. Book 1: Crisis. Kinsella, Pat, illus. 2016. (Mars Bound Ser.). (ENG.). 48p. (J). (gr. 3-7). lib. bdg. 34.21 *(978-1-62402-197-8(2)*, 24573, Spellbound) Magic Wagon.
—Book 2: Sabotage. Kinsella, Pat, illus. 2016. (Mars Bound Ser.). (ENG.). 48p. (J). (gr. 3-7). lib. bdg. 34.21 *(978-1-62402-198-5(0)*, 24575, Spellbound) Magic Wagon.
—Book 3: Restoration. Kinsella, Pat, illus. 2016. (Mars Bound Ser.). (ENG.). 48p. (J). (gr. 3-7). lib. bdg. 34.21 *(978-1-62402-199-2(9)*, 24577, Spellbound) Magic Wagon.
Wong, Clarissa. Guardians of the Galaxy: These Are the Guardians, 1 vol. Lim, Ron & Pinto, Marcelo, illus. 2015. (World of Reading Level 1 Ser.). (ENG.). 32p. (J). (gr. -1-3). 31.36 *(978-1-61479-360-1(3)*, 18195) Spotlight.
Wood, Dorreya. Planet Cannibal. 2009. (Illus.). 90p. (YA). pap. *(978-0-615-26795-1(5))* World Awake Bks.
Wood, Greg V. & Benchmark Education Co. Opinions about Themes in Science Fiction: Two Stories about Valerie Logan, Interstellar Troubleshooter. Retwick, Roy, illus. 2014. (Text Connections Ser.). (J). (gr. 3). *(978-1-4509-9665-5(5))* Benchmark Education Co.
Wooding, Chris. Pale. 2012. (Stoke Books Titles Ser.). (ENG.). 72p. (YA). (gr. 8-12). pap. 6.95 *(978-1-78112-091-0(9))*; lib. bdg. 22.60 *(978-1-78112-092-7(7))* Lerner Publishing Group.
Woolley, Justin. A City Called Smoke: the Territory 2. 2015. (Territory Ser.: Bk. 2). (ENG., Illus.). 286p. (YA). pap. *(978-1-76030-089-0(6))* Momentum.
—A Town Called Dust: the Territory 1. 2015. (Territory Ser.: Bk. 1). (ENG., Illus.). 302p. (YA). pap. *(978-1-76030-037-1(3))* Momentum.
—A World of Ash: the Territory 3. 2016. (Territory Ser.: Bk. 3). (ENG., Illus.). 324p. (YA). pap. *(978-1-76030-245-0(7))* Momentum.
Wright Johnson, Shelli. Falcon in the Nest: A Story of Bes Adventure. 2004. 273p. pap. 27.95 *(978-1-4137-5263-2(2))* America Star Bks.
Wright, Julie. Hazzardous Universe. Wasden, Kevin, illus. 2011. 242p. (J). pap. *(978-1-60861-206-2(6))* Covenant Communications.
Wright, Marcus. Raincloud. 2006. (ENG.). 172p. pap. 9.88 *(978-0-615-15579-1(0))* Digitex-U Pubns.
Wronski, Gareth. Holly Farb & the Princess of the Galaxy. (ENG.). 320p. (J). (gr. 3-7). 2018. pap. 7.99 *(978-1-4814-7178-7(3))* 2017. (Illus.). 16.99 *(978-1-4814-7177-0(5))* Simon & Schuster Children's Publishing. (Aladdin).
Wyatt, Chris. Falcon: Fight or Flight. 2015. (Mighty Marvel Chapter Bks.). (J). lib. bdg. 16.00 *(978-0-606-36905-3(8))* Turtleback.
—Star-Lord: Knowhere to Run. 2014. (Mighty Marvel Chapter Bks.). (J). lib. bdg. 16.00 *(978-0-606-35920-7(6))* Turtleback.
X-Men. 2003. (J). *(978-1-57657-859-9(3))* Paradise Pr., Inc.
Yager, Fred. Sound from a Star: A Novel. 2011. 150p. (YA). 31.95 *(978-1-889262-90-1(0))* Hannacroix Creek Bks., Inc.
Yamamoto, Lun Lun. Swan in Space, Vol. 1. 2009. (ENG., Illus.). 160p. (J). pap. 8.99 *(978-1-897376-93-5(6)*, a605f8c0-be59-4181-a4bb-565df99efcb2) URON Entertainment Corp. CAN. Dist: Diamond Comic Distributors, Inc.
—Swans in Space, Vol. 3. 2011. (ENG., Illus.). 128p. (J). pap. 8.99 *(978-1-897376-95-9(2)*, c3e02c59-9b09-431b-b309-d84af4538c18) URON Entertainment Corp. CAN. Dist: Diamond Comic Distributors, Inc.
Yancey, Rick. The Infinite Sea. 2015. (5th Wave Ser.: 2). lib. bdg. 22.10 *(978-0-606-38204-5(6))* Turtleback.
—The Infinite Sea: The Second Book of the 5th Wave. 2015. (5th Wave Ser.: 2). (ENG.). 352p. (YA). (gr. 9-12). pap. 12.99 *(978-1-101-99698-0(6)*, Penguin Books) Penguin Young Readers Group.
—The Last Star: The Final Book of the 5th Wave. 2016. (5th Wave Ser.: 3). (ENG.). 352p. (YA). (gr. 9). 18.99 *(978-0-399-16243-5(7)*, G.P. Putnam's Sons Books for Young Readers) Penguin Young Readers Group.
—The 5th Wave. 2015. (5th Wave Ser.: Vol. 1). (ENG.). (YA). (gr. 9). lib. bdg. 21.60 *(978-1-62765-623-8(5))* Perfection Learning Corp.
—The 5th Wave. l.t. ed. 2016. (5th Wave Ser.: 1). 630p. pap. 12.99 *(978-1-59413-981-9(4)*, Large Print Pr.) Thorndike Pr.
—The 5th Wave. 2015. (5th Wave Ser.: 1). lib. bdg. 22.10 *(978-0-606-36640-3(7))*; lib. bdg. 22.10 *(978-0-606-37680-8(1))* Turtleback.
—The 5th Wave: The First Book of the 5th Wave Series. 2015. (5th Wave Ser.: 1). (ENG.). 512p. (YA). (gr. 9). pap. 12.99 *(978-0-14-242583-1(4)*, Penguin Books) Penguin Young Readers Group.
—The 5th Wave Collection, 3 vols. 2017. (5th Wave Ser.). (ENG.). (YA). (gr. 9). pap., pap., pap. 35.97 *(978-0-425-29032-3(8)*, Speak) Penguin Young Readers Group.
Yang, Gene Luen. The Shadow Hero. Liew, Sonny, illus. 2014. (Shadow Hero Ser.). (ENG.). 176p. (YA). (gr. 7-12). pap. 19.99 *(978-1-59643-697-8(2)*, 900073186, First Second Bks.) Roaring Brook Pr.
—The Shadow Hero. Liew, Sonny, illus. 2014. (YA). lib. bdg. 30.60 *(978-0-606-35521-6(9))* Turtleback.
Yates, Alexander. How We Became Wicked. 2019. (ENG., Illus.). 368p. (YA). (gr. 9). 19.99 *(978-1-4814-1984-0(6)*, Atheneum Bks. for Young Readers) Simon & Schuster Children's Publishing.
Yeager, Jackie. Flip the Silver Switch. 2018. (Crimson Five Ser.: 2). (ENG., Illus.). 296p. (J). (gr. 4-7). 15.99 *(978-1-944995-69-0(2))* Amberjack Publishing Co.
Yee, Lisa. Bumblebee at Super Hero High (DC Super Hero Girls) Random House, illus. 2018. (ENG.). 208p. (J). (gr. 4-7). 13.99 *(978-1-5247-6926-0(6)*, Random Hse. Bks. for Young Readers) Random Hse. Children's Bks.
Young, Helen Ann. Hello to Hellie's World. Young, Tim Blair, illus. 2013. 46p. pap. *(978-1-908353-00-9(7))* Young Editions.
Young, Moira. Blood Red Road. (Dust Lands Ser.: 1). (ENG.). (YA). (gr. 9). 2012. 480p. pap. 12.99 *(978-1-4424-2999-4(2))* 2011. (Illus.). 464p. 17.99 *(978-1-4424-2998-7(4))* McElderry, Margaret K. Bks. (McElderry, Margaret K. Bks.).
—Blood Red Road, 9 vols. 2011. (YA). 122.75 *(978-1-4618-0629-5(1))*; 286.75 *(978-1-4618-0634-9(8))*; 1.25 *(978-1-4640-2632-4(7))*; 120.75 *(978-1-4618-0633-2(X))*; 120.75 *(978-1-4618-0630-1(5))* Recorded Bks., Inc.
—Raging Star. (Dust Lands Ser.: 3). (ENG., Illus.). 448p. (YA). (gr. 9). 2015. pap. 13.99 *(978-1-4424-3003-7(6))* 2014. 17.99 *(978-1-4424-3002-0(8))* McElderry, Margaret K. Bks. (McElderry, Margaret K. Bks.).
—Rebel Heart. 2013. (Dust Lands Ser.: 2). (ENG., Illus.). 448p. (YA). (gr. 9). pap. 13.99 *(978-1-4424-3001-3(X)*, McElderry, Margaret K. Bks.) McElderry, Margaret K. Bks.
Young, Shaun. Castor. 2016. (ENG., Illus.). 230p. (YA). pap. 14.99 *(978-1-63476-886-3(8)*, Harmony Ink Pr.) Dreamspinner Pr.
Young, Suzanne. The Adjustment. 2017. (Program Ser.: 5). (ENG., Illus.). 416p. (YA). (gr. 9). 19.99 *(978-1-4814-7132-9(5)*, Simon Pulse) Simon Pulse.
—The Adjustment. 2018. (Program Ser.: 5). (ENG., Illus.). 480p. (YA). (gr. 9). pap. 12.99 *(978-1-4814-7133-6(3)*, Simon Pulse) Simon Pulse.
—The Complication. (Program Ser.: 6). (ENG.). (YA). (gr. 9). 2019. 496p. pap. 12.99 *(978-1-4814-7136-7(8))* 2018. (Illus.). 464p. 17.99 *(978-1-4814-7135-0(X))* Simon Pulse. (Simon Pulse).
—The Epidemic. 2016. (Program Ser.: 4). (ENG., Illus.). 384p. (YA). (gr. 9). 19.99 *(978-1-4814-4470-5(0)*, Simon Pulse) Simon Pulse.
—Girls with Sharp Sticks. 2019. (Girls with Sharp Sticks Ser.: 1). (ENG., Illus.). 400p. (YA). (gr. 9). 19.99 *(978-1-5344-2613-9(2)*, Simon Pulse) Simon Pulse.
—The Program. (Program Ser.: 1). (ENG., Illus.). (YA). (gr. 9). 2014. 432p. pap. 12.99 *(978-1-4424-4581-9(5))* 2013. 416p. 19.99 *(978-1-4424-4580-2(7))* Simon Pulse. (Simon Pulse).
—The Remedy. 2015. (Program Ser.: 3). (ENG., Illus.). 416p. (YA). (gr. 9). 19.99 *(978-1-4814-3765-3(8)*, Simon Pulse) Simon Pulse.
—The Treatment. (Program Ser.: 2). (ENG., Illus.). (YA). (gr. 9). 2015. 368p. pap. 12.99 *(978-1-4424-4584-0(X))* 2014. 352p. 19.99 *(978-1-4424-4583-3(1))* Simon Pulse. (Simon Pulse).
Young, Timothy. I'm Going to Outer Space!, 1 vol. 2017. (ENG., Illus.). 32p. (J). (gr. -1-3). 16.99 *(978-0-7643-5385-7(3)*, 8936) Schiffer Publishing, Ltd.
Zachary, Alyson A. Earth Helpers: Count the Ways to Save Our Planet. 2009. (ENG.). 12p. 8.95 *(978-1-58117-906-4(5)*, Intervisual/Piggy Toes) Bendon, Inc.
Zakour, John. Baxter Moon Galactic Scout. 2008. 198p. (J). (gr. 5-10). per. 8.95 *(978-0-9768126-9-2(X))* Brown Barn Bks.
Zappa, Shana Muldoon, et al. Leona's Unlucky Mission, 3. 2016. (Star Darlings Ser.). (ENG., Illus.). 176p. (J). (gr. 3-6). 21.19 *(978-1-4844-7387-0(6))* Disney Pr.
—Scarlet Discovers True Strength, 5. 2016. (Star Darlings Ser.). (ENG., Illus.). 176p. (J). (gr. 3-6). 21.19 *(978-1-4844-7390-0(6))* Disney Pr.
Zenescope Entertainment Staff, et al. Never Underestimate a Hermit Crab. 2014. (ENG., Illus.). 48p. (J). pap. 9.99 *(978-1-939683-25-0(4)*, 3a14a419-1b5e-4587-8656-0524d045c377) Zenescope Entertainment.
Zevin, Gabrielle. Because It Is My Blood: A Novel. 2013. (Birthright Ser.: 2). (ENG.). 384p. (YA). (gr. 7). pap. 19.99 *(978-1-250-03422-9(1)*, 900120595) Square Fish.
Zhang, Kat. Echoes of Us. 2015. (Hybrid Chronicles Ser.: 3). (ENG.). 368p. (YA). (gr. 8). pap. 10.99 *(978-0-06-211494-5(8)*, HarperCollins) HarperCollins Pubs.
—What's Left of Me. 2012. (Hybrid Chronicles Ser.: 1). (ENG.). 352p. (YA). (gr. 8). 17.99 *(978-0-06-211487-7(5)*, HarperCollins) HarperCollins Pubs.
Zub, Jim. Avengers vs. Ultron #4. Choi, Woo Bin et al, illus. 2016. (Avengers K Ser.). (ENG.). 28p. (J). (gr. 2-8). lib. bdg. 31.36 *(978-1-61479-571-1(1)*, 24352, Marvel Age) Spotlight.
—Avengers vs. Ultron #5. Choi, Woo Bin et al, illus. 2016. (Avengers K Ser.). (ENG.). 28p. (J). (gr. 2-8). lib. bdg. 31.36 *(978-1-61479-572-8(X)*, 24353, Marvel Age) Spotlight.
—Avengers vs. Ultron #6. Choi, Woo Bin et al, illus. 2016. (Avengers K Ser.). (ENG.). 28p. (J). (gr. 2-8). lib. bdg. 31.36 *(978-1-61479-573-5(8)*, 24354, Marvel Age) Spotlight.

SCIENCE FICTION—HISTORY AND CRITICISM

Benjamin, Kathy, Lisa and Kafer & Benchmark Education Co. Staff. Opinions about Science Fiction Technology - from Fiction to Fact. 2014. (Text Connections Ser.). (J). (gr. 5). *(978-1-4900-1372-5(5))* Benchmark Education Co.
Bodden, Valerie. Science Fiction. 2013. (Stories Well Told Ser.). (ENG., Illus.). 48p. (J). (gr. 4-7). 35.65 *(978-1-60818-181-0(2)*, 21700, Creative Education) Creative Co., The.
Bortz, Fred. Envisioning Outer Space: Where Science & Fiction Meet. 2015. (J). *(978-1-4677-6305-9(5))* Twenty First Century Bks.
Friedland, Joyce, ed. Ender's Game: Novel-Ties Study Guide. 2011. 38p. pap. 16.95 *(978-0-7675-4510-5(9))* Learning Links Inc.
Gagne, Tammy. The Giver. 2016. *(978-1-5105-2015-8(5))* SmartBook Media, Inc.
Hamen, Susan E. Science Fiction. 2016. (Essential Literary Genres Ser.). (ENG.). 112p. (J). (gr. 6-12). lib. bdg. 41.36 *(978-1-68078-383-4(1)*, 23531, Essential Library) ABDO Publishing Co.
Hoppa, Jocelyn. Isaac Asimov: Science Fiction Trailblazer, 1 vol. 2007. (Authors Teens Love Ser.). (ENG., Illus.). 104p. (gr. 6-7). lib. bdg. 35.93 *(978-0-7660-2961-3(1)*, 6b5ddc4b-6da2-42a2-a0ab-49fd81ab8d63) Enslow Publishing, LLC.
Nagle, Jeanne, ed. Great Authors of Science Fiction & Fantasy, 1 vol. 2013. (Essential Authors for Children & Teens Ser.). (ENG., Illus.). 176p. (YA). (gr. 8-8). 48.59 *(978-1-62275-090-0(X)*, 3af134dc-ba89-4d8d-9663-676c5f95db2d) Rosen Publishing Group, Inc., The.

SCIENCE PROJECTS

Adamick, Mike. Dad's Book of Awesome Science Experiments: From Boiling Ice & Exploding Soap to Erupting Volcanoes & Launching Rockets, 30 Inventive Experiments to Excite the Whole Family! 2014. (ENG., Illus.). 192p. pap. 18.99 *(978-1-4405-7077-3(9))* Adams Media Corp.
Adolph, Jonathan. Mason Jar Science: 40 Slimy, Squishy, Super-Cool Experiments; Capture Big Discoveries in a Jar, from the Magic of Chemistry & Physics to the Amazing Worlds of Earth Science & Biology. 2018. (ENG., Illus.). 136p. (J). (gr. 3-7). 14.95 *(978-1-61212-986-0(2)*, 622986) Storey Publishing, LLC.
Ahrens, Niki. Aladdin Idea Lab. Ahrens, Niki, photos by. 2019. (Disney STEAM Projects Ser.). (ENG., Illus.). 32p. (J). (gr. 2-5). pap. 8.99 *(978-1-5415-7400-7(1)*, 9781541574007, Lerner Pubns.) Lerner Publishing Group.
Alkire, Jessie. Construct It! Architecture You Can Build, Break, & Build Again. 2017. (Cool Makerspace Gadgets & Gizmos Ser.). (ENG.). 32p. (J). (gr. 3-6). lib. bdg. 34.21 *(978-1-5321-1252-2(1)*, 27583, Checkerboard Library) ABDO Publishing Co.
—Super Gross Slime & Snot Projects. 2018. (Super Simple Super Gross Science Ser.). (ENG., Illus.). 32p. (J). (gr. k-4). lib. bdg. 34.21 *(978-1-5321-1733-6(7)*, 30754, Super SandCastle) ABDO Publishing Co.
—Super Simple Earthquake Projects: Science Activities for Future Seismologists. 2017. (Super Simple Earth Investigations Ser.). (ENG., Illus.). 32p. (J). (gr. k-4). lib. bdg. 34.21 *(978-1-5321-1236-2(X)*, 27623, Super SandCastle) ABDO Publishing Co.
—Super Simple Mineral Projects: Science Activities for Future Mineralogists. 2017. (Super Simple Earth Investigations Ser.). (ENG.). 32p. (J). (gr. k-4). lib. bdg. 34.21 *(978-1-5321-1238-6(6)*, 27625, Super SandCastle) ABDO Publishing Co.
—Super Simple Rock Cycle Projects: Science Activities for Future Petrologists. 2017. (Super Simple Earth Investigations Ser.). (ENG.). 32p. (J). (gr. k-4). lib. bdg. 34.21 *(978-1-5321-1239-3(4)*, 27626, Super SandCastle) ABDO Publishing Co.

S

—Super Simple Weather Projects: Science Activities for Future Meteorologists. 2017. (Super Simple Earth Investigations Ser.). (ENG., Illus.). 32p. (J). (gr. k-4). lib. bdg. 34.21 *(978-1-5321-1241-6(6)*, 27628, Super SandCastle) ABDO Publishing Co.

Alpert, Barbara. How to Make a Box Guitar: A 4D Book. 2019. (Hands-On Science Fun Ser.). (ENG., Illus.). 24p. (J). (gr. -1-2). lib. bdg. 29.32 *(978-1-9771-0225-6(5)*, 139238, Capstone Pr.) Capstone.

—How to Make a Pom-Pom Flyer: A 4D Book. 2019. (Hands-On Science Fun Ser.). (ENG., Illus.). 24p. (J). (gr. -1-2). lib. bdg. 29.32 *(978-1-9771-0224-9(7)*, 139237, Capstone Pr.) Capstone.

—How to Make a Wind Speed Meter: A 4D Book. 2019. (Hands-On Science Fun Ser.). (ENG., Illus.). 24p. (J). (gr. -1-2). lib. bdg. 29.32 *(978-1-9771-0227-0(1)*, 139240, Capstone Pr.) Capstone.

—How to Make Ice Cream in a Bag: A 4D Book. 2019. (Hands-On Science Fun Ser.). (ENG., Illus.). 24p. (J). (gr. -1-2). lib. bdg. 29.32 *(978-1-9771-0226-3(3)*, 139239, Capstone Pr.) Capstone.

Anderson, Maxine. Amazing Leonardo Da Vinci Inventions: You Can Build Yourself. 2006. (Build It Yourself Ser.). (Illus.). 128p. (J). (gr. 3-7). pap. 15.95 *(978-0-9749344-2-6(9)*, 18fa9126-fd2c-4938-afe1-1738ffa9ce49) Nomad Pr.

Bailey, Loren. 30-Minute Rainy Day Science Projects. 2019. (30-Minute Makers Ser.). (ENG., Illus.). 32p. (J). (gr. 2-5). 27.99 *(978-1-5415-3892-4(7)*, 05968502-973a-40d7-81fe-471ce3c5dda4); pap. 8.99 *(978-1-5415-5714-7(X)*, 20baf092-33bc-4f7a-b6b6-2ac9315d9a11) Lerner Publishing Group. (Lerner Pubns.).

Barfield, Mike. Destroy This Book in the Name of Science: Galileo Edition. 2020. (Wreck This Activity Book Ser.). (ENG.). 56p. (J). (gr. 4-6). pap. 12.99 *(978-1-78055-482-2(6)*, Buster Bks.) O'Mara, Michael Bks., Ltd. GBR. Dist: Independent Pubs. Group.

Benbow, Ann & Mably, Colin. Master the Scientific Method with Fun Life Science Projects, 1 vol. 2010. (Real Life Science Experiments Ser.). (ENG., Illus.). 48p. (gr. 3-3). lib. bdg. 27.93 *(978-0-7660-3151-7(9)*, 7dd1b3f1-6c27-4162-9674-44956affe4f4) Enslow Publishing, LLC.

Blobaum, Cindy. Explore Night Science! With 25 Great Projects. Stone, Bryan, illus. 2012. (Explore Your World Ser.). (ENG.). 96p. (J). (gr. k-4). pap. 12.95 *(978-1-61930-156-6(3)*, bb6e0d07-c57a-4d90-9a6e-8f86955def8c) Nomad Pr.

—Skulls & Skeletons! With 25 Science Activities for Kids. Casteel, Tom, illus. 2019. (Explore Your World Ser.). (ENG.). 96p. (J). (gr. 3-4). pap. 14.95 *(978-1-61930-809-1(6)*, 520e6fdb-2d5a-4ad2-ae61-06a14a2e2478) Nomad Pr.

—Skulls & Skeletons! With 25 Science Projects for Kids. Casteel, Tom, illus. 2019. (Explore Your World Ser.). 96p. (J). (gr. 3-4). 19.95 *(978-1-61930-806-0(1)*, 14d6a3f4-639d-4789-bad2-d39e1e249c33) Nomad Pr.

Bochinski, Julianne Blair. More Award-Winning Science Fair Projects. DiBiase, Judy, illus. 2003. (ENG.). 242p. (J). (gr. 6-12). pap. 22.00 *(978-0-471-27337-0(6))* Wiley, John & Sons, Inc.

Bolte, Mari. Super Science Projects You Can Make & Share. 2015. (Sleepover Girls Crafts Ser.). (ENG., Illus.). 32p. (J). (gr. 2-5). lib. bdg. 28.65 *(978-1-62065-177-3(7)*, 120875, Capstone Young Readers) Capstone.

Bonnet, Robert L. & Keen, Dan. Home Run! Science Projects with Baseball & Softball, 1 vol. 2009. (Score! Sports Science Projects Ser.). (ENG., Illus.). 104p. (gr. 5-6). lib. bdg. 35.93 *(978-0-7660-3365-8(1)*, dba14f41-8d17-48fa-a413-92e4bc29a7a0) Enslow Publishing, LLC.

Brown, Patrica A. & Krelle, Ginger R. Classroom Hydroponic Plant Factory, Vol. 2. 2nd rev. ed. 2004. (Illus.). 102p. (YA). (gr. 7-12). pap. 19.95 *(978-0-9669557-1-2(4))* Foothill-Hydroponics.

Buczynski, Sandra. Designing a Winning Science Fair Project. 2014. (Explorer Junior Library: Information Explorer Junior Ser.). (ENG., Illus.). 24p. (J). (gr. 1-4). lib. bdg. 32.07 *(978-1-63137-790-7(6)*, 205403) Cherry Lake Publishing.

—Get Ready for a Winning Science Project. 2011. (Explorer Library: Information Explorer Ser.). (ENG., Illus.). 32p. (gr. 4-8). lib. bdg. 32.07 *(978-1-61080-124-9(5)*, 201134) Cherry Lake Publishing.

—Super Smart Information Strategies: Get Ready for a Winning Science Project. 2011. (Explorer Library: Information Explorer Ser.). (ENG.). 32p. (gr. 4-8). pap. 14.21 *(978-1-61080-270-3(5)*, 201231) Cherry Lake Publishing.

Burillo-Kirch, Christine. Bioengineering: Discover How Nature Inspires Human Designs. Cornell, Alexis, illus. 2016. (Build It Yourself Ser.). (ENG.). 128p. (J). (gr. 3-7). 22.95 *(978-1-61930-366-9(3)*, 3f9ccb79-c97a-40a7-9db7-a1de407192f0) Nomad Pr.

Burling, Alexis. Exploring Journal Writing Through Science Research Projects, 1 vol. 2018. (Project-Based Learning in Science Ser.). (ENG.). 64p. (gr. 5-5). pap. 14.53 *(978-1-5081-8477-5(1)*, 6f589ea9-557a-4461-9193-2dfe2f96ae20, Rosen Reference) Rosen Publishing Group, Inc., The.

Calhoun, Yael. Earth Science Fair Projects, Using the Scientific Method, 1 vol. 2010. (Earth Science Projects Using the Scientific Method Ser.). (ENG., Illus.). 160p. (gr. 5-6). 38.60 *(978-0-7660-3425-9(9)*, c86f9e82-18a8-47a9-8419-c8f56b6d2a7d) Enslow Publishing, LLC.

—Plant & Animal Science Fair Projects, Using the Scientific Method, 1 vol. rev. exp. ed. 2010. (Biology Science Projects Using the Scientific Method Ser.). (ENG., Illus.). 160p. (gr. 5-6). 38.60 *(978-0-7660-3421-1(6)*, 8ae7af5a-08b1-45a9-a40b-1297a418d155) Enslow Publishing, LLC.

Candlewick Press. FETCH! with Ruff Ruffman: Ruff Ruffman's 44 Favorite Science Activities. WGBH, illus. 2015. (Fetch! with Ruff Ruffman Ser.). (ENG.). 132p. (J). (gr. 3-7). pap. 12.99 *(978-0-7636-7432-8(X)*, Candlewick Entertainment) Candlewick Pr.

Carlson, Laurie. Thomas Edison for Kids: His Life & Ideas, 21 Activities. 2006. (For Kids Ser.: 19). (ENG., Illus.). 160p. (J). (gr. 4-7). pap. 19.99 *(978-1-55652-584-1(2)*, 1248637) Chicago Review Pr., Inc.

Carson, Mary Kay. Weather Projects for Young Scientists: Experiments & Science Fair Ideas. 2007. (ENG., Illus.). 144p. (J). (gr. 4-7). pap. 16.95 *(978-1-55652-629-9(6))* Chicago Review Pr., Inc.

Challoner, Jack. Maker Lab: 28 Super Cool Projects. 2016. (DK Activity Lab Ser.). (ENG., Illus.). 160p. (J). (gr. 3-7). 19.99 *(978-1-4654-5135-4(8)*, DK Children) Dorling Kindersley Publishing, Inc.

—Maker Lab: Outdoors: 25 Super Cool Projects. 2018. (DK Activity Lab Ser.). (ENG., Illus.). 160p. (J). (gr. 3-7). 19.99 *(978-1-4654-6887-1(0)*, DK Children) Dorling Kindersley Publishing, Inc.

—Maker Lab Outdoors: 25 Super Cool Projects: Build, Invent, Create, Discover. 2018. (Illus.). 160p. (J). *(978-1-4654-7392-9(0))* Dorling Kindersley Publishing, Inc.

—STEM Lab. 2019. (DK Activity Lab Ser.). (ENG., Illus.). 160p. (J). (gr. 4-7). 19.99 *(978-1-4654-7561-9(3)*, DK Children) Dorling Kindersley Publishing, Inc.

Chudler, Eric H. Brain Lab for Kids: 52 Mind-Blowing Experiments, Models, & Activities to Explore Neuroscience, Volume 15. 2018. (Lab for Kids Ser.: 15). (ENG., Illus.). 144p. (J). (gr. 2-5). pap. 24.99 *(978-1-63159-396-3(X)*, 225966, Quarry Bks.) Quarto Publishing Group USA.

Cobb, Allan B. Psyched for Science, 6 bks. Incl. Super Science Projects about Animals in Their Habitats. lib. bdg. 34.47 *(978-0-8239-3175-0(7)*, 57b80348-5db2-4687-a859-9b5287a21ebe); Super Science Projects about Light & Optics. lib. bdg. 34.47 *(978-0-8239-3177-4(3)*, 83f10959-208b-4f04-9d49-871621b847c4); Super Science Projects about Oceans. lib. bdg. 34.47 *(978-0-8239-3174-3(9)*, d72dc43a-11ab-45f1-a795-148b5d2c7caa); Super Science Projects about Sound. lib. bdg. 34.47 *(978-0-8239-3176-7(5)*, 2f867990-7400-47f6-88b5-67b2f1ebfcad); 48p. (YA). (gr. 5-8). 1999. (Illus.). Set lib. bdg. 143.70 Rosen Publishing Group, Inc., The.

Cobb, Vicki. Science Experiments You Can Eat. Carpenter, Tad, illus. 2016. (ENG.). 256p. (J). (gr. 3-7). pap. 9.99 *(978-0-06-237729-6(9)*, HarperCollins) HarperCollins Pubs.

—See for Yourself! More Than 100 Amazing Experiments for Science Fairs & School Projects. 2nd ed. 2010. (ENG., Illus.). 192p. (J). (gr. 1-3). pap. 14.95 *(978-1-61608-083-9(3)*, 608083) Skyhorse Publishing Co., Inc.

Do It Yourself Projects! Set, 8 vols. 2008. (Do It Yourself Projects! Ser.). (ENG., Illus.). (J). (gr. 4-4). lib. bdg. 115.72 *(978-1-4358-3004-2(0)*, 179239c0-9210-4730-a89a-2fb17c492f5c, PowerKids Pr.) Rosen Publishing Group, Inc., The.

Doudna, Kelly. The Kid's Book of Simple Everyday Science. 2013. (ENG., Illus.). 112p. (J). (gr. k-4). pap. 13.95 *(978-1-938063-34-3(1)*, Mighty Media Kids) Mighty Media Pr.

Dragotta, Nick, et al. Howtoons: Tools of Mass Construction. 2014. (ENG., Illus.). 360p. (J). pap. 17.99 *(978-1-63215-101-8(4)*, 4de65120-4aec-4e27-863d-b7cb0baecc8b) Image Comics.

Dykstra, Danell. Exploring Design Investigations Through Science Research Projects, 1 vol. 2018. (Project-Based Learning in Science Ser.). (ENG.). 64p. (gr. 5-5). pap. 14.53 *(978-1-5081-8593-2(X)*, 393e39d6-d3a0-465f-92a2-c437b8e988a6, Rosen Reference) Rosen Publishing Group, Inc., The.

Dziengel, Ana. STEAM Projects 101: Fun Step-By-step Projects to Teach Kids about STEAM. 2019. (Little Engineers Ser.). (ENG., Illus.). 32p. (J). (gr. -1-2). 26.65 *(978-1-942875-80-2(0)*, 907d93e9-c566-4283-8e00-2ec337e53e59, Walter Foster Jr) Quarto Publishing Group USA.

Earth Instructional Guide. 2009. (Grade 8: Science Exit Project Kits Ser.). spiral bd. *(978-1-4042-4022-3(5)*, Rosen Classroom) Rosen Publishing Group, Inc., The.

Ebner, Aviva. Environmental Science Experiments. 2011. (ENG., Illus.). 160p. (gr. 5-8). 35.00 *(978-1-60413-851-1(3)*, P189921, Facts On File) Infobase Holdings, Inc.

Edom, H. Science Activities, Vol. 1. 2010. (Science Activities Ser.). 72p. (J). 13.99 *(978-0-7945-2752-5(3)*, Usborne) EDC Publishing.

Enz, Tammy. Dynamic Planet: Exploring Changes on Earth with Science Projects. 2015. (Discover Earth Science Ser.). (ENG., Illus.). 32p. (J). (gr. 3-6). lib. bdg. 27.99 *(978-1-4914-4815-1(6)*, 128713, Capstone Pr.) Capstone.

Enz, Tammy Laura Lynn. Liquid Planet: Exploring Water on Earth with Science Projects. 2016. (ENG., Illus.). 32p. (J). lib. bdg. *(978-1-4747-0325-3(9))* Capstone.

Felix, Rebecca. Crayola (r) Super Easy Crafts. 2019. (Colorful Crayola (r) Crafts Ser.). (ENG., Illus.). 32p. (J). (gr. 1-4). pap. 7.99 *(978-1-5415-4598-4(2)*, 1c719bff-3d26-4d79-80eb-61969cebedf1); 29.32 *(978-1-5415-1099-9(2)*, ec2001e5-12b4-41dd-b196-8b3068e17e29) Lerner Publishing Group. (Lerner Pubns.).

Friedhoffer, Bob. More Winning Science Fair Projects. 2006. (Scientific American Winning Science Fair Projects Ser.). (ENG., Illus.). 48p. (gr. 4-6). 27.00 *(978-0-7910-9057-2(4)*, P114524, Facts On File) Infobase Holdings, Inc.

—Simple Science Fair Projects. 2006. (Scientific American Winning Science Fair Projects Ser.). (ENG., Illus.). 48p. (gr. 3-5). lib. bdg. 27.00 *(978-0-7910-9054-1(X)*, P114521, Facts On File) Infobase Holdings, Inc.

Friedhoffer, Bob & Tocci, Salvatore. Scientific American Science Fair Projects, 4 Vols., Set. 2006. (Scientific American Winning Science Fair Projects Ser.). 48p. (gr. 3-7). 108.00 *(978-0-7910-9097-8(3)*, Chelsea Clubhse.) Infobase Holdings, Inc.

Fulcher, Roz. Science Around the House: Simple Projects Using Household Recyclables. 2010. (Dover Science for Kids Ser.). (ENG., Illus.). 80p. (J). (gr. 3-5). pap. 6.99 *(978-0-486-47645-2(6)*, 476456) Dover Pubns., Inc.

Gabrielson, Curt. Stomp Rockets, Catapults, & Kaleidoscopes: 30+ Amazing Science Projects You Can Build for Less Than $1. 2008. (ENG., Illus.). 176p. (J). (gr. 4-18). pap. 16.95 *(978-1-55652-737-1(3))* Chicago Review Pr., Inc.

Gagliardi, Sue. Making a Raft for the Three Billy Goats Gruff. 2020. (Fairy Tale Science Ser.). (ENG., Illus.). 32p. (J). (gr. 2-3). pap. 9.95 *(978-1-64493-109-7(5)*, 1644931095); lib. bdg. 31.35 *(978-1-64493-030-4(7)*, 1644930307) North Star Editions. (Focus Readers).

Gardner, Robert. Ace Your Math & Measuring Science Project: Great Science Fair Ideas, 1 vol. 2009. (Ace Your Physics Science Project Ser.). (ENG., Illus.). 128p. (gr. 5-6). lib. bdg. 35.93 *(978-0-7660-3224-8(8)*, 3e2f0053-4afa-4ce7-ae09-8351cd47fc5e) Enslow Publishing, LLC.

—Ace Your Science Project Using Chemistry Magic & Toys: Great Science Fair Ideas, 1 vol. 2009. (Ace Your Science Project Ser.). (ENG., Illus.). 128p. (gr. 5-6). lib. bdg. 35.93 *(978-0-7660-3226-2(4)*, 2ddcb01b-d092-4687-bdb1-7d70fd78d371) Enslow Publishing, LLC.

—Chemistry Science Fair Projects Using Inorganic Stuff, Using the Scientific Method, 1 vol. rev. exp. ed. 2010. (Chemistry Science Projects Using the Scientific Method Ser.). (ENG., Illus.). 160p. (gr. 5-6). 38.60 *(978-0-7660-3413-6(5)*, 58bc50b8-1c8a-4f7a-b167-858a0343c0c4) Enslow Publishing, LLC.

—Desert Experiments: 11 Science Experiments in One Hour or Less, 1 vol. 2014. (Last Minute Science Projects with Biomes Ser.). (ENG., Illus.). 48p. (gr. 5-6). 26.93 *(978-0-7660-5917-7(0)*, df526d53-e8a1-45a7-93b8-84df33183cf5); pap. 11.53 *(978-0-7660-5918-4(9)*, dc2e64ad-4f06-432b-a212-90635e69f8fc, Enslow Elementary) Enslow Publishing, LLC.

—Easy Genius Science Projects with Electricity & Magnetism: Great Experiments & Ideas, 1 vol. 2008. (Easy Genius Science Projects Ser.). (ENG., Illus.). 128p. (gr. 5-6). lib. bdg. 35.93 *(978-0-7660-2923-1(9)*, 9961177c-44c3-4566-93d4-de7b73146222) Enslow Publishing, LLC.

—Easy Genius Science Projects with Light: Great Experiments & Ideas, 1 vol. 2008. (Easy Genius Science Projects Ser.). (ENG., Illus.). 128p. (gr. 5-6). lib. bdg. 35.93 *(978-0-7660-2926-2(3)*, 536e0326-ced6-4dbb-9ac3-95cf79547ba6) Enslow Publishing, LLC.

—Easy Genius Science Projects with the Human Body: Great Experiments & Ideas, 1 vol. 2008. (Easy Genius Science Projects Ser.). (ENG., Illus.). 112p. (gr. 5-6). lib. bdg. 35.93 *(978-0-7660-2927-9(1)*, 81fcf0aa-fffc-417e-a31b-35562fadb975) Enslow Publishing, LLC.

—Easy Genius Science Projects with Weather: Great Experiments & Ideas, 1 vol. 2008. (Easy Genius Science Projects Ser.). (ENG., Illus.). 128p. (J). (gr. 5-6). lib. bdg. 35.93 *(978-0-7660-2924-8(7)*, fe626b97-ebcc-4bb8-9384-cd0e1f203d33) Enslow Publishing, LLC.

—Electricity & Magnetism Science Fair Projects, Using the Scientific Method, 1 vol. 2010. (Physics Science Projects Using the Scientific Method Ser.). (ENG., Illus.). 160p. (gr. 5-6). 38.60 *(978-0-7660-3418-1(6)*, b57da7f6-a4df-44a7-9e44-7597feee5c2c) Enslow Publishing, LLC.

—Energy: Green Science Projects about Solar, Wind, & Water Power, 1 vol. 2011. (Team Green Science Projects Ser.). (ENG., Illus.). 128p. (gr. 5-6). lib. bdg. 35.93 *(978-0-7660-3643-7(X)*, 7bbbfa62-fcc7-4ac6-af68-c2aa75b8ac5e) Enslow Publishing, LLC.

—Experiments with Chemistry, 1 vol. 2017. (Science Whiz Experiments Ser.). (ENG.). 128p. (gr. 5-5). lib. bdg. 38.93 *(978-0-7660-8676-0(3)*, c6f8ecd5-08d1-46b6-8b1c-9ae66adbbaf8) Enslow Publishing, LLC.

—Genetics & Evolution Science Fair Projects, Using the Scientific Method, 1 vol. 2010. (Biology Science Projects Using the Scientific Method Ser.). (ENG., Illus.). 160p. (gr. 5-6). 38.60 *(978-0-7660-3422-8(4)*, 17bab87a-64b4-489d-b330-59084e6496e2) Enslow Publishing, LLC.

—Grasslands Experiments: 11 Science Experiments in One Hour or Less, 1 vol. 2014. (Last Minute Science Projects with Biomes Ser.). (ENG., Illus.). 48p. (gr. 5-6). 26.93 *(978-0-7660-5927-6(8)*, dd98eb73-a108-40ed-a43b-b1e77fcc8ed7); pap. 11.53 *(978-0-7660-5928-3(6)*, b6fc64bc-5d9f-4809-82a4-e603d601dfea, Enslow Elementary) Enslow Publishing, LLC.

—How Big Is Big? Science Projects with Volume, 1 vol. 2014. (Hot Science Experiments Ser.). (ENG.). 48p. (gr. 3-4). 26.93 *(978-0-7660-6620-5(7)*, 59e2ffbd-3dfa-44d1-a217-89a1d798828c) Enslow Publishing, LLC.

—How Fast Is Fast? Science Projects with Speed, 1 vol. 2014. (Hot Science Experiments Ser.). (ENG.). 48p. (gr. 3-4). 26.93 *(978-0-7660-6615-1(0)*, 29456ae8-f1b0-4655-be51-d3e2a910adb8); pap. 11.53 *(978-0-7660-6616-8(9)*, 07c9a8fc-9197-4b00-bcf4-8b7e6f45bbef, Enslow Elementary) Enslow Publishing, LLC.

—How Heavy Is Heavy? Science Projects with Weight, 1 vol. 2014. (Hot Science Experiments Ser.). (ENG.). 48p. (gr. 3-4). 26.93 *(978-0-7660-6600-7(2)*, 6a136b12-c3ea-40af-8e30-a924c9a4b6ba) Enslow Publishing, LLC.

—How High Is High? Science Projects with Height & Depth, 1 vol. 2014. (Hot Science Experiments Ser.). (ENG.). 48p. (gr. 3-4). 26.93 *(978-0-7660-6595-6(2)*, 3cad5a94-5695-4045-846d-a3bd3ab5b215); pap. 11.53 *(978-0-7660-6596-3(0)*, 838c9331-738e-46a8-a4eb-3ea4d563b092, Enslow Elementary) Enslow Publishing, LLC.

—How Hot Is Hot? Science Projects with Temperature, 1 vol. 2014. (Hot Science Experiments Ser.). (ENG.). 48p. (gr. 3-4). 26.93 *(978-0-7660-6605-2(3)*, 2e3c465c-b479-444d-8478-b27294a9e448); pap. 11.53 *(978-0-7660-6606-9(1)*, 0b01b06e-aeb3-48ac-b846-ec3cc2fa07dc, Enslow Elementary) Enslow Publishing, LLC.

—How Quick Is Quick? Science Projects with Time, 1 vol. 2014. (Hot Science Experiments Ser.). (ENG.). 48p. (gr. 3-4). 26.93 *(978-0-7660-6610-6(X)*, 993bab8a-20f7-4396-8a4a-baa95afa850d); pap. 11.53 *(978-0-7660-6611-3(8)*, 11faf6c4-6e12-4cc7-9354-506c48ea6676, Enslow Elementary) Enslow Publishing, LLC.

—Light, Sound, & Waves Science Fair Projects, Using the Scientific Method, 1 vol. 2010. (Physics Science Projects Using the Scientific Method Ser.). (ENG., Illus.). 160p. (gr. 5-6). 38.60 *(978-0-7660-3416-7(X)*, a9e26572-5a3f-47d1-bd08-f3116b6e00ac) Enslow Publishing, LLC.

—Meteorology Projects with a Weather Station You Can Build, 1 vol. 2008. (Build-A-Lab! Science Experiments Ser.). (ENG., Illus.). 128p. (gr. 5-6). lib. bdg. 35.93 *(978-0-7660-2807-4(0)*, 618a523a-009c-4ed9-af2b-7fbdb4c1e576) Enslow Publishing, LLC.

—The Physics of Sports Science Projects, 1 vol. 2013. (Exploring Hands-On Science Projects Ser.). (ENG.). 128p. (gr. 5-6). pap. 13.88 *(978-1-4644-0222-7(1)*, 0257ffe0-eddf-4a37-8257-690a9f6c4745); lib. bdg. 30.60 *(978-0-7660-4146-2(8)*, 1cfcb805-a91a-4b9a-91f7-951871acdc1a) Enslow Publishing, LLC.

—The Physics of Toys & Games Science Projects, 1 vol. 2013. (Exploring Hands-On Science Projects Ser.). (ENG.). 128p. (gr. 5-6). pap. 13.88 *(978-1-4644-0219-7(1)*, 51857e6a-ef0b-453d-91ad-9147775c17ea); lib. bdg. 30.60 *(978-0-7660-4143-1(3)*, 06eb0f09-d618-462e-b5ba-bdb9acad4c7b) Enslow Publishing, LLC.

—Planet Earth Science Fair Projects, Using the Scientific Method, 1 vol. 2010. (Earth Science Projects Using the Scientific Method Ser.). (ENG., Illus.). 160p. (gr. 5-6). 38.60 *(978-0-7660-3423-5(2)*, 3412cb22-51d3-4203-a20f-ff27c69f732) Enslow Publishing, LLC.

—Rain Forest Experiments: 10 Science Experiments in One Hour or Less, 1 vol. 2014. (Last Minute Science Projects with Biomes Ser.). (ENG., Illus.). 48p. (gr. 5-6). lib. bdg. 26.93 *(978-0-7660-5937-5(5)*, 913a7198-86a3-488a-8eb9-9f47d4513223) Enslow Publishing, LLC.

—The Science Behind Magic Science Projects, 1 vol. 2013. (Exploring Hands-On Science Projects Ser.). (ENG.). 128p. (gr. 5-6). 30.60 *(978-0-7660-4147-9(6)*, 61d4e8fc-867f-4e58-8fba-ee01fad5a7f2); pap. 13.88 *(978-1-4644-0223-4(X)*, d309281d-6071-4681-ad53-44a2b82d6486) Enslow Publishing, LLC.

—Science Fair Projects about Planet Earth, 1 vol. 2016. (Hands-On Science Ser.). (ENG.). 48p. (gr. 4-4). 29.60 *(978-0-7660-8219-9(9)*, e0e28ba7-0905-46b1-8d05-32b1f811c32b) Enslow Publishing, LLC.

—Science Fair Projects about the Atmosphere, 1 vol. 2016. (Hands-On Science Ser.). (ENG.). 48p. (gr. 4-4). pap. 12.70 *(978-0-7660-8220-5(2)*, 41b5c0ed-1fda-4ae8-8c11-52bb0e4b9cea) Enslow Publishing, LLC.

—Science Fair Projects about the Properties of Matter, Using the Scientific Method, 1 vol. 2010. (Physics Science Projects Using the Scientific Method Ser.). (ENG., Illus.). 160p. (gr. 5-6). 38.60 *(978-0-7660-3417-4(8)*, af76a3b3-d47f-4afb-8acc-dd7aa224aad6) Enslow Publishing, LLC.

—Science Fair Projects about Water & Soil, 1 vol. 2016. (Hands-On Science Ser.). (ENG.). 48p. (gr. 4-4). pap. 12.70 *(978-0-7660-8211-3(3)*, a401950b-3da0-424a-a345-84a667eafd0f) Enslow Publishing, LLC.

—Science Fair Projects about Weather, 1 vol. 2016. (Hands-On Science Ser.). (ENG.). 48p. (gr. 4-4). pap. 12.70 *(978-0-7660-8204-5(0)*, a8eb04cd-1b8e-43f0-9782-9b369eaa9cab) Enslow Publishing, LLC.

—Soil: Green Science Projects for a Sustainable Planet, 1 vol. 2011. (Team Green Science Projects Ser.). (ENG., Illus.). 128p. (gr. 5-6). lib. bdg. 35.93 *(978-0-7660-3647-5(2)*, 4e4025f5-d910-4e34-aeef-00c93859fee4) Enslow Publishing, LLC.

—Solids, Liquids, & Gases Science Projects, 1 vol. 2013. (Exploring Hands-On Science Projects Ser.). (ENG.). 128p. (gr. 5-6). pap. 13.88 *(978-1-4644-0221-0(3)*, 7f9c7a33-bc58-4744-a37a-98b85e39527d); lib. bdg. 30.60 *(978-0-7660-4145-5(X)*, 8b552e68-1f05-4dcc-87a5-747e774f7443) Enslow Publishing, LLC.

—Temperate Forest Experiments: 8 Science Experiments in One Hour or Less, 1 vol. 2014. (Last Minute Science Projects with Biomes Ser.). (ENG.). 48p. (gr. 5-6). 26.93 *(978-0-7660-5922-1(7)*, f6dd3daf-1662-4970-9e07-34fd8e1e6c9d); (Illus.). pap. 11.53 *(978-0-7660-5923-8(5)*, fddb4e6b-2498-48d6-8d42-b5cd0a0f260b, Enslow Elementary) Enslow Publishing, LLC.

—Tundra Experiments: 14 Science Experiments in One Hour or Less, 1 vol. 2014. (Last Minute Science Projects with Biomes Ser.). (ENG., Illus.). 48p. (gr. 5-6). lib. bdg. 26.93 *(978-0-7660-5942-9(1)*, 7874380a-2829-4c35-a83f-ee3736a9c97e) Enslow Publishing, LLC.

—Water: Green Science Projects for a Sustainable Planet, 1 vol. 2011. (Team Green Science Projects Ser.). (ENG., Illus.). 128p. (gr. 5-6). lib. bdg. 35.93 *(978-0-7660-3645-1(6)*, 649f9824-3db9-48ab-a0c9-fbe53efa7f04) Enslow Publishing, LLC.

—Who Can Solve the Crime? Science Projects Using Detective Skills, 1 vol. 2010. (Who Dunnit? Forensic Science Experiments Ser.). (ENG., Illus.). 48p. (gr. 3-3). 27.93 *(978-0-7660-3247-7(7)*, 2a8ff8d5-4a72-408b-919f-e1654850f858) Enslow Publishing, LLC.

—Who Forged This Document? Crime-Solving Science Projects, 1 vol. 2010. (Who Dunnit? Forensic Science Experiments Ser.). (ENG., Illus.). 48p. (gr. 3-3). 27.93 *(978-0-7660-3246-0(9)*,

640c9120-dae0-434c-869e-4a34248dacb1) Enslow Publishing, LLC.

—Whose Bones Are These? Crime-Solving Science Projects, 1 vol. 2010. (Who Dunnit? Forensic Science Experiments Ser.). (ENG., Illus.). 48p. (gr. 3-3). 27.93 *(978-0-7660-3248-4(5)*, 344fbdde-efa4-4e59-aa93-041cacf77d15) Enslow Publishing, LLC.

—Whose Fingerprints Are These? Crime-Solving Science Projects, 1 vol. 2010. (Who Dunnit? Forensic Science Experiments Ser.). (ENG., Illus.). 48p. (gr. 3-3). 27.93 *(978-0-7660-3245-3(0)*, 1f4f4c75-b1f7-4146-82a2-1adcb14621d7) Enslow Publishing, LLC.

Gardner, Robert & Conklin, Joshua. Experiments for Future Chemists, 1 vol. 2016. (Experiments for Future STEM Professionals Ser.). (ENG.). 128p. (gr. 6-6). lib. bdg. 38.93 *(978-0-7660-7856-7(6)*, ea68f0f5-6b5a-465c-a7b7-a7431ea3b20c) Enslow Publishing, LLC.

—Experiments for Future Engineers, 1 vol. 2016. (Experiments for Future STEM Professionals Ser.). (ENG.). 128p. (gr. 6-6). 38.93 *(978-0-7660-7853-6(1)*, c2dd6370-5739-446b-9a3d-0cf16e8f454f) Enslow Publishing, LLC.

—A Kid's Book of Experiments with Light, 1 vol. 2015. (Surprising Science Experiments Ser.). (ENG., Illus.). 48p. (gr. 4-4). 29.60 *(978-0-7660-7205-3(3)*, 415607dd-2f50-4b02-999e-94bc995993f7) Enslow Publishing, LLC.

—A Kid's Book of Experiments with Sound, 1 vol. 2015. (Surprising Science Experiments Ser.). (ENG., Illus.). 48p. (gr. 4-4). 29.60 *(978-0-7660-7209-1(6)*, 7844d024-d3f5-421c-a5f1-7b20dd35cc1d) Enslow Publishing, LLC.

Gardner, Robert & Gardner Conklin, Barbara. Ace Your Human Biology Science Project: Great Science Fair Ideas, 1 vol. 2009. (Ace Your Biology Science Project Ser.). (ENG., Illus.). 128p. (gr. 5-6). lib. bdg. 35.93 *(978-0-7660-3219-4(1)*, 7a323de3-2d12-4b18-8ccb-dd5cefa2db71) Enslow Publishing, LLC.

—Organic Chemistry Science Fair Projects, Using the Scientific Method, 1 vol. 2010. (Chemistry Science Projects Using the Scientific Method Ser.). (ENG., Illus.). 160p. (gr. 5-6). 38.60 *(978-0-7660-3414-3(3)*, aab1d46b-f42c-49d4-905c-75d03efc773b) Enslow Publishing, LLC.

Gardner, Robert & Goodstein, Madeline. Ace Your Forces & Motion Science Project: Great Science Fair Ideas, 1 vol. 2009. (Ace Your Physics Science Project Ser.). (ENG., Illus.). 128p. (gr. 5-6). lib. bdg. 35.93 *(978-0-7660-3222-4(1)*, 2f7dfd04-9bf2-4ab5-9294-0acb62f03bc1) Enslow Publishing, LLC.

—Ace Your Space Science Project: Great Science Fair Ideas, 1 vol. 2009. (Ace Your Science Project Ser.). (ENG., Illus.). 128p. (gr. 5-6). lib. bdg. 35.93 *(978-0-7660-3230-9(2)*, 4b435834-8e1d-493e-94dc-af7e8e16e91a) Enslow Publishing, LLC.

Gardner, Robert & Kemer, Eric. Easy Genius Science Projects with Temperature & Heat: Great Experiments & Ideas, 1 vol. 2008. (Easy Genius Science Projects Ser.). (ENG., Illus.). 128p. (gr. 5-6). lib. bdg. 35.93 *(978-0-7660-2939-2(5)*, d70be169-fe0d-4539-b5b2-7db03444ca01) Enslow Publishing, LLC.

Gardner, Robert & Rybolt, Thomas R. Ace Your Science Project about the Senses: Great Science Fair Ideas, 1 vol. 2009. (Ace Your Biology Science Project Ser.). (ENG., Illus.). 112p. (gr. 5-6). lib. bdg. 35.93 *(978-0-7660-3217-0(5)*, 1b53ee8f-8906-435b-895f-6452810b6f56) Enslow Publishing, LLC.

Gardner, Robert & Shortelle, Dennis. Slam Dunk! Science Projects with Basketball, 1 vol. 2009. (Score! Sports Science Projects Ser.). (ENG., Illus.). 104p. (gr. 5-6). lib. bdg. 35.93 *(978-0-7660-3366-5(X)*, 3a1ecb7c-3db4-4917-9411-3322e74f5780) Enslow Publishing, LLC.

Gardner, Robert & Tocci, Salvatore. Ace Your Weather Science Project: Great Science Fair Ideas, 1 vol. 2009. (Ace Your Physics Science Project Ser.). (ENG., Illus.). 104p. (gr. 5-6). lib. bdg. 35.93 *(978-0-7660-3223-1(X)*, abb9e9fa-ea2b-4d59-8dc1-544cfff132b9) Enslow Publishing, LLC.

Gardner, Robert, et al. Ace Your Animal Science Project: Great Science Fair Ideas, 1 vol. 2009. (Ace Your Biology Science Project Ser.). (ENG., Illus.). 104p. (gr. 5-6). lib. bdg. 35.93 *(978-0-7660-3220-0(5)*, 125f46d0-ce8d-44b5-b737-6f29d441bc23) Enslow Publishing, LLC.

—Ace Your Chemistry Science Project: Great Science Fair Ideas, 1 vol. 2009. (Ace Your Science Project Ser.). (ENG., Illus.). 112p. (gr. 5-6). lib. bdg. 35.93 *(978-0-7660-3227-9(2)*, 118113ed-b5f9-43e7-9126-f350774d1e57) Enslow Publishing, LLC.

—Ace Your Ecology & Environmental Science Project: Great Science Fair Ideas, 1 vol. 2009. (Ace Your Science Project Ser.). (ENG., Illus.). 112p. (gr. 5-6). lib. bdg. 35.93 *(978-0-7660-3216-3(7)*, cd06592b-05ff-496f-a0e7-80ae4f0493a8) Enslow Publishing, LLC.

—Ace Your Exercise & Nutrition Science Project: Great Science Fair Ideas, 1 vol. 2009. (Ace Your Biology Science Project Ser.). (ENG., Illus.). 128p. (gr. 5-6). lib. bdg. 35.93 *(978-0-7660-3218-7(3)*, 89019949-f036-4c97-8705-b72bdc5a442d) Enslow Publishing, LLC.

—Ace Your Food Science Project: Great Science Fair Ideas, 1 vol. 2009. (Ace Your Science Project Ser.). (ENG., Illus.). 128p. (gr. 5-6). lib. bdg. 35.93 *(978-0-7660-3228-6(0)*, 37c58d8b-ebcb-44dc-9057-f1e80d83c023) Enslow Publishing, LLC.

—Ace Your Physical Science Project: Great Science Fair Ideas, 1 vol. 2009. (Ace Your Physics Science Project Ser.). (ENG., Illus.). 128p. (J). (gr. 5-6). lib. bdg. 35.93 *(978-0-7660-3225-5(6)*, 9b932f2c-8b79-482c-a7a7-89f386b3f7ab) Enslow Publishing, LLC.

Goodstein, Madeline. Goal! Science Projects with Soccer, 1 vol. 2009. (Score! Sports Science Projects Ser.). (ENG., Illus.). 104p. (gr. 5-6). lib. bdg. 35.93 *(978-0-7660-3106-7(3)*, 4e2da253-e69d-416f-a848-a59dec36c85f) Enslow Publishing, LLC.

—Plastics & Polymers Science Fair Projects, Using the Scientific Method, 1 vol. rev. exp. ed. 2010. (Chemistry Science Projects Using the Scientific Method Ser.). (ENG., Illus.). 160p. (gr. 5-6). 38.60 *(978-0-7660-3412-9(7)*, f3dfba6c-ef48-41a9-ab5d-d360bd356248) Enslow Publishing, LLC.

Gregory, Josh. Junior Scientists: Experiment with Solids. 2010. (Explorer Junior Library: Science Explorer Junior Ser.). (ENG., Illus.). 32p. (gr. 3-6). lib. bdg. 32.07 *(978-1-60279-845-8(1)*, 200556) Cherry Lake Publishing.

Hagler, Gina. Electricity. 2016. (J). *(978-1-4896-5274-4(4))* Weigl Pubs., Inc.

—Magnets. 2016. (J). *(978-1-4896-5286-7(8))* Weigl Pubs., Inc.

—Sound. 2016. (J). *(978-1-4896-5292-8(2))* Weigl Pubs., Inc.

Hall, Kevin. 10 Great Makerspace Projects Using Math, 1 vol. 2017. (Using Makerspaces for School Projects Ser.). (ENG., Illus.). 64p. (J). (gr. 6-6). 36.13 *(978-1-4994-3846-8(X)*, 6f6d6b7b-7efc-4cf3-af77-0b27c21fd0a7, Rosen Central) Rosen Publishing Group, Inc., The.

Halls, Kelly. Goo Makers. 2018. (Project: STEAM Ser.). (ENG., Illus.). 48p. (gr. 4-8). pap. 10.95 *(978-1-64156-591-2(8)*, 9781641565912) Rourke Educational Media.

Harris, Elizabeth Snoke. Weird & Wonderful Science Experiments Volume 2: Cool Creations: Make Slime, Crystals, Invisible Ink, & More! 2018. (Weird & Wonderful Science Ser.). (ENG., Illus.). 64p. (J). (gr. 5-8). 33.32 *(978-1-942875-58-1(4)*, 9e2901ee-5a08-4fb8-b2e6-354e47cc7b19, Moondance) Quarto Publishing Group USA.

—Weird & Wonderful Science Experiments Volume 3: Build It: Build Rockets & Racers & Test Energy & Forces! 2018. (Weird & Wonderful Science Ser.). (ENG., Illus.). 64p. (J). (gr. 5-8). 33.32 *(978-1-942875-59-8(2)*, 98e32b7d-afef-4f38-b331-65715ff981e4, Moondance) Quarto Publishing Group USA.

—Weird & Wonderful Science Experiments Volume 4: the World Around Us: Get Dirty Outdoors, Test Your Brain, & More! 2018. (Weird & Wonderful Science Ser.). (ENG., Illus.). 64p. (J). (gr. 5-8). 33.32 *(978-1-942875-60-4(6)*, fa626b50-5e58-4d98-b3f9-2d39a98fb0db, Moondance) Quarto Publishing Group USA.

Haysom, John. Science Fair Warm-Up: Learning the Practice of Scientists. (ENG., Illus.). 2013. 55p. (J). pap. *(978-1-936959-20-4(8))* 2012. 65p. pap. 19.99 *(978-1-936959-21-1(6)*, P218227) 2012. 75p. pap. 19.99 *(978-1-936959-22-8(4)*, P218651) National Science Teachers Assn.

Heitkamp, Kristina Lyn. Exploring Field Investigations Through Science Research Projects, 1 vol. 2018. (Project-Based Learning in Science Ser.). (ENG.). 64p. (gr. 5-5). pap. 14.53 *(978-1-5081-8474-4(7)*, 472ea2ee-ca41-4b3b-9a82-59d43e824d5a, Rosen Reference) Rosen Publishing Group, Inc., The.

Henneberg, Susan. Creating Science Fair Projects with Cool New Digital Tools. 2013. (Way Beyond PowerPoint: Making 21st Century Presentations Ser.). (Illus.). 48p. (J). (gr. 5-8). pap. 70.50 *(978-1-4777-1848-3(6))*; (ENG., (gr. 6-6). 34.41 *(978-1-4777-1836-0(2)*, e288a670-f185-4f38-9096-f589c89dcae9); (ENG., (gr. 6-6). pap. 12.75 *(978-1-4777-1847-6(8)*, 6428893d-7e06-40a1-85f4-25bd8a88b19f) Rosen Publishing Group, Inc., The. (Rosen Reference).

Holt, Rinehart and Winston Staff. Holt Science & Technology: Long-Term Projects & Research Ideas. 5th ed. 2004. (Illus.). pap. 11.13 *(978-0-03-035191-4(X))* Holt McDougal.

—Holt Science & Technology: Science Fair Guide. 5th ed. 2004. (Illus.). pap. 11.60 *(978-0-03-035199-0(5))* Holt McDougal.

Howell, Izzi, et al. Adventures in STEAM. 2018. (Adventures in STEAM Ser.). (ENG.). 48p. (J). (gr. 3-6). 179.94 *(978-1-5435-3556-3(9)*, 28609, Capstone Pr.) Capstone.

Ives, Rob. Fun Experiments with Matter: Invisible Ink, Giant Bubbles, & More. Sassin, Eva, illus. 2017. (Amazing Science Experiments Ser.). (ENG.). 32p. (J). (gr. 3-6). lib. bdg. 27.99 *(978-1-5124-3216-9(4)*, a8503d73-4445-434c-bf6d-2da4ebd9590f, Hungry Tomato (r)) Lerner Publishing Group.

Jacobson, Ryan. Light & Vision. 2016. (J). *(978-1-4896-5283-6(3))* Weigl Pubs., Inc.

Juliano, Larissa. How to Build a Leprechaun Trap. 2018. 96p. (J). (gr. k-5). pap. 10.99 *(978-1-4926-6388-1(3))* Sourcebooks, Inc.

Kessler, Colleen. A Project Guide to Electricity & Magnetism. 2011. (Physical Science Projects for Kids Ser.). (Illus.). 48p. (J). (gr. 3-6). lib. bdg. 29.95 *(978-1-58415-966-7(9)*, 1327821) Mitchell Lane Pubs.

—A Project Guide to Reptiles & Birds. 2010. (Life Science Projects for Kids Ser.). (Illus.). 48p. (J). (gr. 4-8). lib. bdg. 29.95 *(978-1-58415-874-5(3))* Mitchell Lane Pubs.

Kjelle, Marylou Morano. A Project Guide to Wind, Weather, & the Atmosphere. 2010. (Earth Science Projects for Kids Ser.). (Illus.). 48p. (J). (gr. 4-7). lib. bdg. 29.95 *(978-1-58415-869-1(7))* Mitchell Lane Pubs.

Latham, Donna. Biomes: Discover the Earth's Ecosystems with Environmental Science Activities for Kids. Casteel, Tom, illus. 2019. (Build It Yourself Ser.). 128p. (J). (gr. 4-6). 22.95 *(978-1-61930-736-0(7)*, 45a7c594-0297-4186-b678-56063cdf5af7); (ENG.). pap. 17.95 *(978-1-61930-739-1(1)*, d6830206-86d4-455c-87cf-edf928c5fd2c) Nomad Pr.

—Garbage: Follow the Path of Your Trash with Environmental Science Activities for Kids. Casteel, Tom, illus. 2019. (Build It Yourself Ser.). (ENG.). 128p. (J). (gr. 4-6). 22.95 *(978-1-61930-744-5(8)*, 568bd6cc-1b8c-4739-9a54-a54711d56cac); pap. 17.95 *(978-1-61930-747-6(2)*, f4e812b2-c8a8-4871-9a6e-19a0dd649ddc) Nomad Pr.

Latta, Sara L. All about Earth: Exploring the Planet with Science Projects. 2016. (ENG., Illus.). 32p. (J). lib. bdg. *(978-1-4747-0323-9(2))* Capstone.

Lee, Ji Sun & Dec, Jaymes. Make: Tech DIY: Easy Electronics Projects for Parents & Kids. 2016. (ENG., Illus.). 192p. pap. 19.99 *(978-1-68045-177-1(4))* O'Reilly Media, Inc.

Leigh, Anna. 30-Minute Chemistry Projects. 2019. (30-Minute Makers Ser.). (ENG., Illus.). 32p. (J). (gr. 2-5). 27.99 *(978-1-5415-3893-1(5)*, 24a06a26-f910-4263-b735-0ca47d897810, Lerner Pubns.) Lerner Publishing Group.

—30-Minute Edible Science Projects. 2019. (30-Minute Makers Ser.). (ENG., Illus.). 32p. (J). (gr. 2-5). 27.99 *(978-1-5415-3891-7(9)*, 28bb05a8-975b-4ada-8346-f7710d8d846d, Lerner Pubns.) Lerner Publishing Group.

—30-Minute Outdoor Science Projects. 2019. (30-Minute Makers Ser.). (ENG., Illus.). 32p. (J). (gr. 2-5). 27.99 *(978-1-5415-3889-4(7)*, dd4c77ec-de4f-4ded-af5b-0026f9e9f813); pap. 8.99 *(978-1-5415-5713-0(1)*, 7eaba67d-e59c-416b-b5bb-abd70681eb55) Lerner Publishing Group. (Lerner Pubns.).

Lew, Kristi. Exploring Secondary Research Investigations Through Science Research Projects, 1 vol. 2018. (Project-Based Learning in Science Ser.). (ENG.). 64p. (gr. 5-5). pap. 14.53 *(978-1-5081-8480-5(1)*, b51ce62d-6046-4bcb-9671-b0ab3d9aefae, Rosen Reference) Rosen Publishing Group, Inc., The.

Lockwood, Sophie. Junior Scientists: Experiment with Heat. 2010. (Explorer Junior Library: Science Explorer Junior Ser.). (ENG., Illus.). 32p. (gr. 3-6). lib. bdg. 32.07 *(978-1-60279-843-4(5)*, 200552) Cherry Lake Publishing.

—Junior Scientists: Experiment with Rocks. 2010. (Explorer Junior Library: Science Explorer Junior Ser.). (ENG., Illus.). 32p. (gr. 3-6). lib. bdg. 32.07 *(978-1-60279-836-6(2)*, 200538) Cherry Lake Publishing.

Lopez, Delano. The Solar System: Out of This World with Science Activities for Kids. Slater, Jason, illus. 2019. (Build It Yourself Ser.). (ENG.). 128p. (J). (gr. 4-6). 22.95 *(978-1-61930-794-0(4)*, 329dacbf-73b3-4968-82a1-3ee65b64455a); pap. 17.95 *(978-1-61930-797-1(9)*, dda7d1f8-af61-46a6-a5fa-223afd67b1a8) Nomad Pr.

Margles, Samantha. Mythbusters - Science Fair Book, 1. 2011. (Mythbusters Science Fair Bks.). (ENG., Illus.). 128p. (J). (gr. 3-6). 26.19 *(978-0-545-23745-1(9))* Scholastic, Inc.

Marsico, Katie. Insects. 2016. (J). *(978-1-4896-5277-5(9))* Weigl Pubs., Inc.

McFarren, Kathleen & Graf, Mike. Science Fair Projects & Activities: Creative Ideas Using Easy-to-Find Materials. Valko, Diane & Corbin, Hillam, illus. 2005. 144p. (J). pap. 18.99 *(978-0-88160-376-7(7)*, LW407, Learning Works, The) Creative Teaching Pr., Inc.

McGill, Jordan. Earth Science Fair Projects. 2011. (gr. 3-5). pap. 12.95 *(978-1-61690-655-9(3)*, AV2 by Weigl); (Illus.). 24p. (J). 27.13 *(978-1-61690-651-1(0))* Weigl Pubs., Inc.

—Space Science Fair Projects. 2011. (J). (gr. 3-5). pap. 12.95 *(978-1-61690-657-3(X)*, AV2 by Weigl); (Illus.). 24p. 27.13 *(978-1-61690-653-5(7))* Weigl Pubs., Inc.

—Water Science Fair Projects. 2011. (J). *(978-1-61690-332-9(5))*; (gr. 3-5). pap. 12.95 *(978-1-61690-656-6(1)*, AV2 by Weigl); (Illus.). 24p. (gr. 3-6). 27.13 *(978-1-61690-652-8(9))* Weigl Pubs., Inc.

Mullins, Matt. Junior Scientists: Experiment with Liquids. 2010. (Explorer Junior Library: Science Explorer Junior Ser.). (ENG., Illus.). 32p. (gr. 3-6). lib. bdg. 32.07 *(978-1-60279-846-5(X)*, 200558) Cherry Lake Publishing.

Nash, Kimberley. Lab Reports: 10 Experiments. 2007. (ENG., Illus.). 140p. spiral bd., wbk. ed. 20.00 *(978-0-9710950-8-3(6))* Resurrection Resources LLC.

Neuhaus, Richard A. Science Projects: Book 1. Project Ideas in the Life Sciences, Vol. 1. Gormley, Julia Ann, illus. 2008. (ENG.). 184p. (gr. 7-12). pap. 24.95 *(978-0-9794500-1-3(2))* Gormley Publishing.

—Science Projects: Book 2. Project Ideas in Chemistry & Biochemistry, Vol. 2. Gormley, Julia Ann, illus. 2008. (ENG.). 196p. (gr. 7-12). pap. 24.95 *(978-0-9794500-4-4(7))* Gormley Publishing.

—Science Projects: How to Collect, Analyze, & Present Your Data. Gormley, Julia Ann, illus. 2007. (ENG.). 184p. (gr. 7-12). pap. 24.95 *(978-0-9794500-0-6(4))* Gormley Publishing.

Olson, Elsie. Super Gross Creepy-Crawly Projects. 2018. (Super Simple Super Gross Science Ser.). (ENG., Illus.). 32p. (J). (gr. k-4). lib. bdg. 34.21 *(978-1-5321-1730-5(2)*, 30748, Super SandCastle) ABDO Publishing Co.

—Super Gross Stinky, Smelly Projects. 2018. (Super Simple Super Gross Science Ser.). (ENG., Illus.). 32p. (J). (gr. k-4). lib. bdg. 34.21 *(978-1-5321-1734-3(5)*, 30756, Super SandCastle) ABDO Publishing Co.

O'Neal, Claire. A Project Guide to Earthquakes. 2010. (Earth Science Projects for Kids Ser.). (Illus.). 48p. (J). (gr. 4-7). lib. bdg. 29.95 *(978-1-58415-870-7(0))* Mitchell Lane Pubs.

—A Project Guide to Volcanoes. 2010. (Earth Science Projects for Kids Ser.). (Illus.). 48p. (J). (gr. 4-7). lib. bdg. 29.95 *(978-1-58415-868-4(9))* Mitchell Lane Pubs.

—Projects in Genetics. 2010. (Life Science Projects for Kids Ser.). (Illus.). 48p. (J). (gr. 4-8). lib. bdg. 29.95 *(978-1-58415-877-6(8))* Mitchell Lane Pubs.

Orr, Tamra B. Junior Scientists: Experiment with Weather. 2010. (Explorer Junior Library: Science Explorer Junior Ser.). (ENG., Illus.). 32p. (gr. 3-6). lib. bdg. 32.07 *(978-1-60279-841-0(9)*, 200548) Cherry Lake Publishing.

O'Sullivan, J. K. Marshes & Swamps! With 25 Science Projects for Kids. Casteel, Tom, illus. 2018. (Explore Your World Ser.). (ENG.). 96p. (J). (gr. 3-4). 19.95 *(978-1-61930-705-6(7)*, 284372aa-bcd9-4f5f-8fd0-714ad199f44e) Nomad Pr.

Perdew, Laura. Biodiversity: Explore the Diversity of Life on Earth with Environmental Science Activities for Kids. Casteel, Tom, illus. 2019. (Build It Yourself Ser.). (ENG.). 128p. (J). (gr. 4-6). pap. 17.95 *(978-1-61930-751-3(0)*, 78250de4-7cad-4841-96a6-f9d85843390d) Nomad Pr.

Petersen, Christine. A Project Guide to Mammals. 2010. (Life Science Projects for Kids Ser.). (Illus.). 48p. (J). (gr. 4-8). lib. bdg. 29.95 *(978-1-58415-875-2(1))* Mitchell Lane Pubs.

Peterson, Carol. Jump into Science: Themed Science Fairs, 1 vol. 2007. (ENG., Illus.). 152p. (gr. 3-7). per. 40.00 *(978-1-59158-413-1(2)*, 900322275, Libraries Unlimited) ABC-CLIO, LLC.

Prize-Winning Science Fair Projects, 12 vols. 2015. (Prize-Winning Science Fair Projects Ser.). (ENG.). 128p. (J). (gr. 7-7). lib. bdg. 233.58 *(978-0-7660-6700-4(9)*, c1b8141c-654c-40aa-9780-592a60d59236) Enslow Publishing, LLC.

Reilly, Kathleen M. Energy: 25 Projects Investigate Why We Need Power & How We Get It. Takacs-Moore, Mary, illus. 2009. (Build It Yourself Ser.). (ENG.). 128p. (J). (gr. 3-7). pap. 15.95 *(978-1-934670-34-7(0)*, c81158d2-1583-4f24-8352-3603fa6cd8fa) Nomad Pr.

—Planet Earth: Finding Balance on the Blue Marble with Environmental Science Activities for Kids. Casteel, Tom, illus. 2019. (Build It Yourself Ser.). (ENG.). 128p. (J). (gr. 4-6). 22.95 *(978-1-61930-740-7(5)*, 33ec5fae-afee-4647-816d-addb4ac676f1); pap. 17.95 *(978-1-61930-743-8(X)*, 45ddd69d-b67c-4b41-90ff-5575fd96d227) Nomad Pr.

Riley, Karen. Agarranderas Plasticas y Otras Cosas: Plastic Rings & Other Things. 2003. (ENG & SPA., Illus.). 16p. (J). (gr. 2-5). pap. 4.50 *(978-0-9708135-2-7(X))* S.C.R.A.P. Gallery.

Robertson, Charmaine. Stephanie's Science Project, 1 vol. 2016. (Rosen REAL Readers: STEM & STEAM Collection). (ENG.). 8p. (gr. k-1). pap. 5.46 *(978-1-5081-2619-5(4)*, 9eebd6cc-ed60-4cb1-a35c-859e6dca48ce, Rosen Classroom) Rosen Publishing Group, Inc., The.

Romaine, Garret. Cool Crystal Creations: Exploring the Wonders of the Earth with Single Strand & Crystal Clusters. 2018. (Geology Lab for Kids Ser.). (ENG., Illus.). 32p. (J). (gr. 3-6). lib. bdg. 27.99 *(978-1-63159-455-7(9)*, 9ef68724-6a0a-49a8-8dc2-57b0e68a7fee, Quarry Bks.) Quarto Publishing Group USA.

—Geology Lab for Kids: 52 Projects to Explore Rocks, Gems, Geodes, Crystals, Fossils, & Other Wonders of the Earth's Surface, Volume 13. 2017. (Lab for Kids Ser.: 13). (ENG., Illus.). 144p. (J). (gr. 1-7). pap. 24.99 *(978-1-63159-285-0(8)*, 224245, Quarry Bks.) Quarto Publishing Group USA.

—Understanding the Earth: Exploring the Wonders of the Earth's Surface & Its Amazing Geological Events. 2018. (Geology Lab for Kids Ser.). (ENG., Illus.). 32p. (J). (gr. 3-6). lib. bdg. 27.99 *(978-1-63159-458-8(3)*, df617031-918f-4d88-8eab-747b01b0da99, Quarry Bks.) Quarto Publishing Group USA.

Rowe, Brooke. Building a Volcano. Bane, Jeff, illus. 2016. (My Early Library: My Science Fun Ser.). (ENG.). 24p. (J). (gr. k-1). 30.64 *(978-1-63471-025-1(8)*, 208180) Cherry Lake Publishing.

Rybolt, Leah M. & Rybolt, Thomas R. Smelly Science Fair Projects, 1 vol. 2015. (Prize-Winning Science Fair Projects Ser.). (ENG.). 128p. (gr. 7-7). lib. bdg. 38.93 *(978-0-7660-7022-6(0)*, a75e5cd0-58a2-4208-8c96-c743084731c3) Enslow Publishing, LLC.

Rybolt, Thomas R. & Mebane, Robert C. Environmental Science Fair Projects, Using the Scientific Method, 1 vol. 2010. (Earth Science Projects Using the Scientific Method Ser.). (ENG., Illus.). 160p. (gr. 5-6). 38.60 *(978-0-7660-3426-6(7)*, 97149028-67df-48c2-b266-cc3dc48c7454) Enslow Publishing, LLC.

Schneider, Christa. Light It! Creations That Glow, Shine, & Blink. 2017. (Cool Makerspace Gadgets & Gizmos Ser.). (ENG.). 32p. (J). (gr. 3-6). lib. bdg. 34.21 *(978-1-5321-1253-9(X)*, 27584, Checkerboard Library) ABDO Publishing Co.

Schuh, Mari. Yes I Can! A Story of Grit. Byrne, Mike, illus. 2018. (Cloverleaf Books (tm) — Stories with Character Ser.). (ENG.). 24p. (J). (gr. k-2). pap. 8.99 *(978-1-5415-1071-5(2)*, a571e9a6-945e-4e83-a096-ef82e3ecf5f8); lib. bdg. 25.32 *(978-1-5124-8646-9(9)*, 144339d8-c88a-40fd-aa02-ef7d3d967dd3) Lerner Publishing Group. (Millbrook Pr.).

Schwartz, Heather E. Cool Engineering Activities for Girls. 2012. (Girls Science Club Ser.). (ENG.). 32p. (gr. 3-4). pap. 47.70 *(978-1-4296-8519-1(0)*, Capstone Pr.); (Illus.). (J). pap. 8.19 *(978-1-4296-8021-9(0)*, 118353) Capstone.

Science Lab Set, 8 vols. 2008. (Science Lab Ser.). (ENG., Illus.). (J). (gr. 4-4). lib. bdg. 121.08 *(978-1-4358-2826-1(7)*, 2cfcf892-4993-4880-9793-0c67a9140278, PowerKids Pr.) Rosen Publishing Group, Inc., The.

Slade, Suzanne. Splat! Wile E. Coyote Experiments with States of Matter, 1 vol. Cornia, Christian, illus. 2014. (Wile E. Coyote, Physical Science Genius Ser.). (ENG.). 32p. (J). (gr. 3-6). 31.32 *(978-1-4765-4224-9(4)*, 124336, Capstone Pr.) Capstone.

—Zap! Wile E. Coyote Experiments with Energy, 1 vol. Ricci, Andrés, illus. 2014. (Wile E. Coyote, Physical Science Genius Ser.). (ENG.). 32p. (J). (gr. 3-6). 31.32 *(978-1-4765-4223-2(6)*, 124335); pap. 8.95 *(978-1-4765-5214-9(2)*, 124521) Capstone. (Capstone Pr.).

Smibert, Angie. Game Logic: Level up & Create Your Own Games with Science Activities for Kids. Chandhok, Lena, illus. 2019. (Build It Yourself Ser.). 128p. (J). (gr. 4-6). (ENG.). 22.95 *(978-1-61930-802-2(9)*, 8046bcce-4e0f-4979-8651-10aa7d9e3c9a); pap. 17.95 *(978-1-61930-805-3(3)*, 1d27a7ba-2821-40b3-a208-08d802b0304e) Nomad Pr.

Sobey, Ed. Electric Motor Experiments, 1 vol. 2011. (Cool Science Projects with Technology Ser.). (ENG., Illus.). 128p. (gr. 5-6). lib. bdg. 35.93 *(978-0-7660-3306-1(6)*, a44732ac-6ec1-4fd4-bd05-bd6eda25e11c) Enslow Publishing, LLC.

—Radio-Controlled Car Experiments, 1 vol. 2011. (Cool Science Projects with Technology Ser.). (ENG., Illus.). 128p. (gr. 5-6). lib. bdg. 35.93 *(978-0-7660-3304-7(X)*, f5235405-7b74-4362-a3c5-56362d8d0cd2) Enslow Publishing, LLC.

Taylor-Butler, Christine. Experiments with Magnets & Metals, 1 vol. 2011. (My Science Investigations Ser.). (ENG.). 32p. (J). (gr. 1-3). pap. 8.29 *(978-1-4329-5365-2(6)*, 116078, Heinemann) Capstone.

—Experiments with Plants. 2011. (True Bk Ser.). (Illus.). 48p. (J). (ENG.). pap. 6.95 *(978-0-531-26647-2(8))*; lib. bdg.

29.00 *(978-0-531-26347-1(9))* Scholastic Library Publishing. (Children's Pr.).

—Junior Scientists: Experiment with Magnets. 2010. (Explorer Junior Library: Science Explorer Junior Ser.). (ENG., Illus.). 32p. (gr. 3-6). lib. bdg. 32.07 *(978-1-60279-844-1(3),* 200554) Cherry Lake Publishing.

—Junior Scientists: Experiment with Solar Energy. 2010. (Explorer Junior Library: Science Explorer Junior Ser.). (ENG., Illus.). 32p. (gr. 3-6). lib. bdg. 32.07 *(978-1-60279-840-3(0),* 200546) Cherry Lake Publishing.

Tennant, Carol & Wheeler-Toppen, Jodi. Edible Science: Experiments You Can Eat. 2015. (Illus.). 80p. (J). (gr. 3-7). pap. 12.99 *(978-1-4263-2111-5(2),* National Geographic Kids) Disney Publishing Worldwide.

Tocci, Salvatore. Science Fair Projects with Everyday Stuff, 1 vol. 2015. (Prize-Winning Science Fair Projects Ser.). (ENG.). 128p. (gr. 7-7). lib. bdg. 38.93 *(978-0-7660-7020-2(4),* b422dee1-a367-4adf-b864-3b2aeadd7bc3) Enslow Publishing, LLC.

Van Vleet, Carmella. Amazing Ben Franklin Inventions. 2007. (Build It Yourself Ser.). (ENG., Illus.). 128p. (J). (gr. 3-7). 19.95 *(978-0-9792268-8-5(0),* 9976ad60-c354-42ab-b89e-7266f5ebfe8c) Nomad Pr.

—Amazing Ben Franklin Inventions: You Can Build Yourself. 2007. (Build It Yourself Ser.). (ENG., Illus.). 128p. (J). (gr. 3-7). per. 15.95 *(978-0-9771294-7-8(0),* a830d2b8-e5a4-4ed5-93e1-dcb07622ded9) Nomad Pr.

—Robotics! With 25 Science Projects for Kids. Casteel, Tom, illus. 2019. (Explore Your World Ser.). 96p. (J). (gr. 3-4). 19.95 *(978-1-61930-810-7(X),* 0506c5df-f10b-48b8-9b0b-4eae2d6cca02); pap. 14.95 *(978-1-61930-813-8(4),* bc5b5cb3-e4f0-4726-8df8-3def753af60a) Nomad Pr.

VanCleave, Janice. Even More of Janice VanCleave's Wild, Wacky, & Weird Earth Science Experiments, 1 vol. 2017. (Janice VanCleave's Wild, Wacky, & Weird Science Experiments Ser.). (ENG.). 64p. (J). (gr. 5-5). 38.47 *(978-1-4994-6689-8(7),* c22dafba-6f5d-4a46-9fb6-faffa62484a4, Rosen Central) Rosen Publishing Group, Inc., The.

—Janice VanCleave's a+ Science Fair Projects. 2003. (ENG., Illus.). 168p. (gr. 7-12). pap. 14.95 *(978-0-471-33102-5(3),* Jossey-Bass) Wiley, John & Sons, Inc.

—Janice VanCleave's a+ Science Fair Workbook & Project Journal, Grades 7-12. 2003. (ENG., Illus.). 354p. (gr. 7-12). pap. 24.95 *(978-0-471-46719-9(7))* Wiley, John & Sons, Inc.

—Janice VanCleave's Big Book of Play & Find Out Science Projects. 2007. (ENG., Illus.). 224p. (gr. 3-7). per. 19.95 *(978-0-7879-8928-6(2),* Jossey-Bass) Wiley, John & Sons, Inc.

—Janice VanCleave's Great Science Project Ideas from Real Kids. 2006. (ENG., Illus.). 144p. (gr. 3-7). pap. 16.00 *(978-0-471-47204-9(2))* Wiley, John & Sons, Inc.

—Janice VanCleave's Super Science Challenges: Hands-On Inquiry Projects for Schools, Science Fairs, or Just Plain Fun! 2007. (ENG., Illus.). 160p. (gr. 3-7). pap. 14.95 *(978-0-471-47183-7(6))* Wiley, John & Sons, Inc.

—Step-by-Step Science Experiments in Astronomy, 1 vol. 2012. (Janice VanCleave's First-Place Science Fair Projects Ser.). (ENG., Illus.). 80p. (J). (gr. 5-5). 38.47 *(978-1-4488-6978-7(1),* 86fff42e-48ab-40c2-87bc-91e74bd372e4); pap. 15.15 *(978-1-4488-8461-2(6),* 5cd51228-b6cd-4d12-b3a2-1d06b47810dd) Rosen Publishing Group, Inc., The. (Rosen Reference).

—Step-by-Step Science Experiments in Energy, 1 vol. 2012. (Janice VanCleave's First-Place Science Fair Projects Ser.). (ENG., Illus.). 80p. (J). (gr. 5-5). 38.47 *(978-1-4488-6979-4(X),* 1c72a9fe-c4de-4eb1-b8ab-9b42c6b0ddcc); pap. 15.15 *(978-1-4488-8471-1(3),* 3adf76f6-75f1-45cb-808b-86b08c7f7ed6) Rosen Publishing Group, Inc., The. (Rosen Reference).

VanCleave, Janice Pratt. Janice VanCleave's Crazy, Kooky, & Quirky Chemistry Experiments, 1 vol. 2018. (Janice VanCleave's Crazy, Kooky, & Quirky Science Experiments Ser.). (ENG.). 64p. (gr. 5-5). 38.47 *(978-1-5081-8097-5(0),* c62203c0-f548-4999-87a4-ade206a3f216, Rosen Reference) Rosen Publishing Group, Inc., The.

—Janice VanCleave's Crazy, Kooky, & Quirky Earth Science Experiments, 1 vol. 2018. (Janice VanCleave's Crazy, Kooky, & Quirky Science Experiments Ser.). (ENG.). 64p. (gr. 5-5). 38.47 *(978-1-5081-8098-2(9),* 73472e8f-c09c-436b-a742-d85794979ad3, Rosen Reference) Rosen Publishing Group, Inc., The.

—Janice VanCleave's Wild, Wacky, & Weird Earth Science Experiments, 1 vol. 2016. (Janice VanCleave's Wild, Wacky, & Weird Science Experiments Ser.). (ENG., Illus.). 64p. (J). (gr. 5-5). pap. 14.53 *(978-1-4777-8973-5(1),* eeaef485-9961-48ec-b4f6-7c2c6727ecbb, Rosen Reference) Rosen Publishing Group, Inc., The.

—Many More of Janice Vancleave's Wild, Wacky, & Weird: Earth Science Experiments, 1 vol. 2017. (Janice VanCleave's Wild, Wacky, & Weird Science Experiments Ser.). (ENG.). 64p. (J). (gr. 5-5). 38.47 *(978-1-4994-3951-9(2),* 41c317bc-37f3-4297-afc8-9024ed6f85ac, Rosen Reference) Rosen Publishing Group, Inc., The.

Warner, Penny. Project Book: Ideas, Tips & Techniques for School Projects. Wagner, Amy, ed. Moore, Lishia, illus. Moore, Lishia & Wagner, Amy, photos by. 2007. 80p. pap. 9.98 *(978-1-887436-05-2(7))* Woodland Scenics.

Weakland, Mark. Smash! Wile E. Coyote Experiments with Simple Machines, 1 vol. Cornia, Christian, illus. 2014. (Wile E. Coyote, Physical Science Genius Ser.). (ENG.). 32p. (J). (gr. 3-6). 31.32 *(978-1-4765-4222-5(8),* 124334, Capstone Pr.) Capstone.

—Thud! Wile E. Coyote Experiments with Forces & Motion, 1 vol. Cornia, Christian, illus. 2014. (Wile E. Coyote, Physical Science Genius Ser.). (ENG.). 32p. (J). (gr. 3-6). 31.32 *(978-1-4765-4221-8(X),* 124333, Capstone Pr.) Capstone.

—Whoosh! Wile E. Coyote Experiments with Flight & Gravity. Brown, Alan, illus. 2017. (Wile E. Coyote, Physical Science Genius Ser.). (ENG.). 32p. (J). (gr. 3-5). lib. bdg. 31.32 *(978-1-5157-3732-2(2),* 133676, Capstone Pr.) Capstone.

Wheeler-Toppen, Jodi Lyn. Gross Science Projects, 1 vol. 2013. (Gross Guides). (ENG.). 32p. (J). (gr. 3-9). lib. bdg. 28.65 *(978-1-4296-9924-2(8),* 120635, Capstone Pr.) Capstone.

Young, Karen Romano. Try This! 50 Fun Experiments for the Mad Scientist in You. 2014. (Illus.). 160p. (J). (gr. 5-9). pap. 16.99 *(978-1-4263-1711-8(5),* National Geographic Kids) Disney Publishing Worldwide.

—Try This Extreme: 50 Fun & Safe Experiments for the Mad Scientist in You. 2017. (Illus.). 160p. (J). (gr. 5-9). pap. 16.99 *(978-1-4263-2863-3(X));* (ENG., lib. bdg. 26.90 *(978-1-4263-2864-0(8))* Disney Publishing Worldwide. (National Geographic Kids).

Zonderkidz. Adventure Bible Book of Daring Deeds & Epic Creations: 60 Ultimate Try-Something-new, Explore-the-world Activities, 1 vol. 2018. (Adventure Bible Ser.). (ENG., Illus.). 160p. (J). 12.99 *(978-0-310-76317-8(7))* Zonderkidz.

SCIENCE PROJECTS—FICTION

Abrams, Kelsey. Llama Drama: A Grace Story. Tejido, Jomike, illus. 2019. (Second Chance Ranch Set 2 Ser.). (ENG.). 120p. (J). (gr. 3-4). pap. 7.99 *(978-1-63163-264-8(7),* 1631632647); lib. bdg. 27.13 *(978-1-63163-263-1(9),* 1631632639) North Star Editions. (Jolly Fish Pr.).

Allbright, Lauren. Exit Strategy. (Max Ser.). (ENG.). 176p. (J). (gr. 4-8). 2018. pap. 7.99 *(978-1-4814-7913-4(X))* 2017. (Illus.). 16.99 *(978-1-4814-7912-7(1))* Simon & Schuster Children's Publishing. (Aladdin).

Andersen, Jill. Tanya's Craft Project, 1 vol. 2016. (Rosen REAL Readers: STEM & STEAM Collection). (ENG.). 8p. (gr. k-1). pap. 5.46 *(978-1-5081-2586-0(4),* 04f659e3-eecc-4959-8e51-5d003bde5d88, Rosen Classroom) Rosen Publishing Group, Inc., The.

Barnes, John L. C. Clara's Clever Custard. 2010. (ENG.). 212p. (J). mass mkt. 8.99 *(978-0-9566042-0-0(X))* Five Valleys Publishing GBR. Dist: Ingram Content Group.

Barnett, Mac. Oh No! Or How My Science Project Destroyed the World. Santat, Dan, illus. 2010. (ENG.). 40p. (J). (gr. -1-2). 18.99 *(978-1-4231-2312-5(3))* Little, Brown Bks. for Young Readers.

Barrows, Annie & Blackall, Sophie. Ivy & Bean What's the Big Idea?, 7. 2011. (Ivy & Bean Ser.). (ENG., Illus.). 132p. (J). (gr. 2-5). 31.36 *(978-1-59961-934-7(2),* 10114, Chapter Bks.) Spotlight.

Barrows, Annie, et al. Ivy & Bean What's the Big Idea? (Book 7) Blackall, Sophie, illus. 2010. (ENG.). 128p. (J). (gr. 1-5). 14.99 *(978-0-8118-6692-7(0))* Chronicle Bks. LLC.

Bean, Raymond. Sweet Farts #2: Rippin' It Old School, 0 vols. unabr. ed. 2010. (Sweet Farts Ser.: 2). (ENG.). 184p. (J). (gr. 2-6). pap. 9.95 *(978-1-935597-08-7(6),* 9781935597087, Two Lions) Amazon Publishing.

—Sweet Farts #3: Blown Away, 0 vols. unabr. ed. 2012. (Sweet Farts Ser.: 3). (ENG.). 172p. (J). (gr. 2-6). pap. 9.95 *(978-1-61218-251-3(8),* 9781612182513, Two Lions) Amazon Publishing.

Birney, Betty G. Humphrey's Playful Puppy Problem. Burris, Priscilla, illus. 2014. (Humphrey's Tiny Tales Ser.: 2). (ENG.). 96p. (J). (gr. k-3). pap. 6.99 *(978-0-14-751484-4(3),* Puffin Books) Penguin Young Readers Group.

Boniface, William. The Extraordinary Adventures of Ordinary Boy: Book 2: the Return of Mete or Boy. 2008. (Extraordinary Adventures of Ordinary Boy Ser.: 2). (ENG., Illus.). 368p. (J). (gr. 3-7). pap. 9.99 *(978-0-06-077469-1(X),* HarperCollins) HarperCollins Pubs.

Bryant, Megan E. Fly to the Rescue (Tiny Geniuses #1) 2018. (Tiny Geniuses Ser.: 1). (ENG.). 128p. (J). (gr. 2-5). pap. 5.99 *(978-0-545-90951-8(1),* Scholastic Paperbacks) Scholastic, Inc.

Chabert, Jack. The Science Fair Is Freaky! 2016. (Eerie Elementary — Branches Ser.: bk.4). (ENG.). (J). lib. bdg. 14.75 *(978-0-606-38806-1(0))* Turtleback.

—The Science Fair Is Freaky! a Branches Book (Eerie Elementary #4) Ricks, Sam, illus. 2016. (Eerie Elementary Ser.: 4). (ENG.). 96p. (J). (gr. 1-3). pap. 5.99 *(978-0-545-87368-0(1))* Scholastic, Inc.

Cheng, Andrea. The Year of the Baby. Barton, Patrice, illus. 2014. (Anna Wang Novel Ser.: 2). (ENG.). 176p. (J). (gr. 1-4). pap. 6.99 *(978-0-544-22525-1(2),* 1563367, Clarion Bks.) HarperCollins Pubs.

Clements, Andrew. Jake Drake, Know-It-All. Frazee, Marla & Pedersen, Janet, illus. 2007. (Jake Drake Ser.: Bk. 2). 88p. (gr. 2-5). 15.00 *(978-0-7569-8212-6(X))* Perfection Learning Corp.

—Jake Drake, Know-It-All. Pedersen, Janet, illus. 2007. (Jake Drake Ser.: Bk. 2). (ENG.). 112p. (J). (gr. 2-5). pap. 6.99 *(978-1-4169-3931-3(8),* Atheneum Bks. for Young Readers) Simon & Schuster Children's Publishing.

Cook, Eileen. Gnome Invasion, 3. 2011. (Fourth Grade Fairy Ser.: 3). (ENG.). 160p. (J). (gr. 3-7). pap. 6.99 *(978-1-4169-9813-6(6))* Simon & Schuster, Inc.

Coven, Wanda. Heidi Heckelbeck & the Secret Admirer. Burris, Priscilla, illus. 2012. (Heidi Heckelbeck Ser.: 6). (ENG.). 128p. (J). (gr. k-4). 17.99 *(978-1-4424-4175-0(5));* pap. 6.99 *(978-1-4424-4174-3(7))* Little Simon. (Little Simon).

Dahl, Michael. A Jar of Eyeballs. Sinkovec, Igor, illus. 2015. (Igor's Lab of Fear Ser.). (ENG.). 40p. (J). (gr. 4-8). lib. bdg. 23.99 *(978-1-4965-0455-5(0),* 128480, Stone Arch Bks.) Capstone.

Derting, Kimberly & Johannes, Shelli R. Cece Loves Science. Harrison, Vashti, illus. 2018. (Loves Science Ser.: 1). (ENG.). 40p. (J). (gr. -1-3). 17.99 *(978-0-06-249960-8(2),* Greenwillow Bks.) HarperCollins Pubs.

Ecton, Emily. Project Jackalope. 2012. (ENG., Illus.). 256p. (J). (gr. 3-7). 15.99 *(978-1-4521-0155-2(8))* Chronicle Bks. LLC.

English, Karen. Trouble Next Door: The Carver Chronicles, Book Four. Freeman, Laura, illus. 2018. (Carver Chronicles Ser.). (ENG.). 144p. (J). (gr. 1-4). pap. 6.99 *(978-1-328-90011-1(8),* 1700039, Clarion Bks.) HarperCollins Pubs.

Frazier, Sundee T. Brendan Buckley's Sixth-Grade Experiment. 2013. (ENG.). 288p. (J). (gr. 4-7). 7.99 *(978-0-385-74051-7(4),* Yearling) Random Hse. Children's Bks.

Gagnon, Mary. Are Those Your Shoes? 2008. 120p. pap. 11.95 *(978-1-4357-2942-1(0))* Lulu Pr., Inc.

Gallagher, Diana G. Mice Capades, 1 vol. Puglisi, Adriana & Puglisi, Adriana, illus. 2013. (Pet Friends Forever Ser.). (ENG.). 88p. (J). (gr. 1-3). pap. 5.95 *(978-1-4795-1863-0(8),* 123501, Picture Window Bks.) Capstone.

Green, D. L. Zeke Meeks vs the Stinkin' Science Fair, 1 vol. Alves, Josh, illus. 2012. (Zeke Meeks Ser.). (ENG.). 128p. (J). (gr. 2-4). pap. 5.95 *(978-1-4048-7222-6(1),* 118074); lib. bdg. 22.65 *(978-1-4048-6802-1(X),* 116247) Capstone. (Picture Window Bks.).

Greene, Stephanie. Owen Foote, Mighty Scientist. Smith, Catharine Bowman, illus. 2004. (ENG.). 96p. (J). (gr. 1-4). tchr. ed. 15.00 *(978-0-618-43016-1(4),* 100349, Clarion Bks.) HarperCollins Pubs.

Grunwell, Jeanne Marie. Mind Games. 2006. (ENG., Illus.). 144p. (J). (gr. 5-7). pap. 10.95 *(978-0-618-68947-7(8),* 410165, Clarion Bks.) HarperCollins Pubs.

Haynes, Marilee. A. K. A. Genius. 2013. (ENG.). 208p. (J). 9.95 *(978-0-8198-0830-1(X))* Pauline Bks. & Media.

Helget, Nicole. The End of the Wild. 2018. (ENG., Illus.). 288p. (J). (gr. 3-7). pap. 7.99 *(978-0-316-24513-5(5))* Little, Brown Bks. for Young Readers.

Holm, Jennifer L. & Holm, Matthew. Babymouse #14: Mad Scientist. Holm, Jennifer L. & Holm, Matthew, illus. 2011. (Babymouse Ser.: 14). (ENG., Illus.). 96p. (J). (gr. 2-5). pap. 7.99 *(978-0-375-86574-9(8));* lib. bdg. 12.99 *(978-0-375-96574-6(2))* Penguin Random Hse. LLC.

Hughes, Alison. On a Scale from Idiot to Complete Jerk, 1 vol. 2014. (ENG., Illus.). 144p. (J). (gr. 4-7). pap. 9.95 *(978-1-4598-0484-5(8))* Orca Bk. Pubs. USA.

Humphrey, Anna. Ruby Goldberg's Bright Idea. Brantley-Newton, Vanessa, illus. 2013. (ENG.). 144p. (J). (gr. 3-7). 17.99 *(978-1-4424-8027-8(0),* Simon & Schuster Bks. For Young Readers) Simon & Schuster Bks. For Young Readers.

Jette, Sarah Marie. What the Wind Can Tell You, 1 vol. 2018. (ENG.). 200p. (J). pap. 14.95 *(978-1-944762-41-4(8),* fc663e39-efc7-4487-a1c0-96325ef48495) Islandport Pr., Inc.

Johnson, Sonia M. Tyler's Third Grade Science Project. 2009. (Illus.). 20p. pap. 12.49 *(978-1-4343-5553-9(5))* AuthorHouse.

Kelly, Erin Entrada. We Dream of Space: A Newbery Honor Award Winner. 2020. (ENG., Illus.). 400p. (J). (gr. 3-7). 16.99 *(978-0-06-274730-3(4),* Greenwillow Bks.) HarperCollins Pubs.

Kerley, Barbara. Greetings from Planet Earth. 2010. (ENG.). 256p. (J). (gr. 4-6). 21.19 *(978-0-439-80204-8(0))* Scholastic, Inc.

Kinard, Kami. The Boy Project: a Wish Novel: Notes & Observations of Kara Mcallister. 2016. (Wish Ser.). (ENG.). 272p. (J). (gr. 4-7). pap. 6.99 *(978-0-545-34516-3(2),* Scholastic Paperbacks) Scholastic, Inc.

Komechak, Marilyn Gilbert. Paisano Pete: Snake-Killer Bird. Eckhardt, Jason C., illus. 2003. 100p. (J). (gr. 3-7). per. 11.95 *(978-1-57168-770-8(X),* Eakin Pr.) Eakin Pr.

Krulik, Nancy & Burwasser, Amanda. Science No Fair! Project Droid #1. Moran, Mike, illus. 2016. (Project Droid Ser.). (ENG.). 112p. (J). (gr. 1-4). 13.99 *(978-1-5107-1018-4(3),* Sky Pony Pr.) Skyhorse Publishing Co., Inc.

—Soccer Shocker! Project Droid #2. Moran, Mike, illus. 2016. (Project Droid Ser.). (ENG.). 104p. (J). (gr. 1-4). pap. 5.99 *(978-1-5107-1029-0(9),* Sky Pony Pr.) Skyhorse Publishing Co., Inc.

Manushkin, Fran. Pedro Goes Buggy. Lyon, Tammie, illus. 2016. (Pedro Ser.). (ENG.). 32p. (J). (gr. k-2). lib. bdg. 21.32 *(978-1-5158-0085-9(7),* 132124, Picture Window Bks.) Capstone.

—Pedro's Tricky Tower. Lyon, Tammie, illus. 2017. (Pedro Ser.). (ENG.). 32p. (J). (gr. k-2). lib. bdg. 21.32 *(978-1-5158-1903-5(5),* 136537, Picture Window Bks.) Capstone.

—Ready, Set, Oops! 2008. pap. 34.95 *(978-1-58013-762-1(8))* Astra Publishing Hse.

—La Torre Embromada de Pedro. Trusted Translations, Trusted, tr. Lyon, Tammie, illus. 2018. (Pedro en Español Ser.). (SPA.). 32p. (J). (gr. k-2). lib. bdg. 21.32 *(978-1-5158-2513-5(2),* 137572, Picture Window Bks.) Capstone.

McCann, Jesse Leon. The Science Project. Fruchter, Jason, illus. 2003. 61p. (J). *(978-0-439-56271-3(6))* Scholastic, Inc.

McElligott, Matthew & Tuxbury, Larry David. Benjamin Franklinstein Lives!, 1. McElligott, Matthew, illus. 2011. (Benjamin Franklinstein Ser.: 1). (ENG., Illus.). 128p. (J). (gr. 4-6). 22.44 *(978-0-399-25229-7(0))* Penguin Young Readers Group.

McMullan, Kate. Pearl & Wagner: Two Good Friends. Alley, R. W., illus. 2011. (Pearl & Wagner Ser.: 2). 48p. (J). (gr. 1-3). pap. 4.99 *(978-0-448-45690-4(7),* Penguin Young Readers) Penguin Young Readers Group.

Miller, Amanda. The Library's Secret: A Hidden Adventure. 2010. 88p. pap. 10.49 *(978-1-4520-7012-4(1))* AuthorHouse.

Mills, Claudia. How Oliver Olson Changed the World. Maione, Heather, illus. 2011. (ENG.). 128p. (J). (gr. 2-5). pap. 8.99 *(978-0-312-67282-9(9),* 900072371) Square Fish.

O'Ryan, Ray. Science Fair Disaster! Kraft, Jason, illus. 2016. (Galaxy Zack Ser.: 13). (ENG.). 128p. (J). (gr. k-4). pap. 5.99 *(978-1-4814-5876-4(0),* Little Simon) Little Simon.

Parish, Herman. Amelia Bedelia, Rocket Scientist? Sweat, Lynn, illus. (I Can Read Level 2 Ser.). 64p. (J). 2007. (ENG.). (gr. k-3). pap. 4.99 *(978-0-06-051889-9(8),* Greenwillow Bks.) 2005. (gr. 1-18). 15.99 *(978-0-06-051887-5(1))* 2005. (ENG.). (gr. k-4). lib. bdg. 17.89 *(978-0-06-051888-2(X),* Greenwillow Bks.) HarperCollins Pubs.

—Amelia Bedelia, Rocket Scientist? Sweat, Lynn, illus. 2007. (I Can Read Ser.). 64p. 14.00 *(978-0-7569-8058-0(5))* Perfection Learning Corp.

—Amelia Bedelia, Rocket Scientist? Sweat, Lynn, illus. 2007. (Amelia Bedelia: I Can Read! Ser.: 19). (J). lib. bdg. 13.55 *(978-1-4177-8068-6(1))* Turtleback.

Perry, Phyllis Jean. The Alien, the Giant, & Rocketman. Francis, Guy, illus. 2006. (J). pap. *(978-1-59336-723-7(6))* Mondo Publishing.

Reynolds, Paul A. Sydney & Simon: to the Moon! Reynolds, Peter H., illus. 2017. (Sydney & Simon Ser.: 3). 48p. (J). (gr. 1-4). lib. bdg. 12.99 *(978-1-58089-679-5(0))* Charlesbridge Publishing, Inc.

Sateren, Shelley Swanson. Max & Zoe: the Science Fair, 1 vol. Sullivan, Mary, illus. 2013. (Max & Zoe Ser.). (ENG.). 32p. (J). (gr. k-2). pap. 5.19 *(978-1-4795-2330-6(5),* 124368, Picture Window Bks.) Capstone.

Sierra, Judy. The Secret Science Project That Almost Ate the School. Gammell, Stephen, illus. 2006. (ENG.). 32p. (J). (gr. 1-4). 19.99 *(978-1-4169-1175-3(8),* Simon & Schuster/Paula Wiseman Bks.) Simon & Schuster/Paula Wiseman Bks.

Stadelmann, Amy Marie. Olive & Beatrix: The Super-Smelly Moldy Blob, Vol. 2. Stadelmann, Amy Marie, illus. 2016. (Olive & Beatrix Ser.: 2). (ENG., Illus.). 80p. (J). (gr. k-2). 15.99 *(978-0-545-81485-0(5))* Scholastic, Inc.

Suen, Anastasia. Girls Can, Too! A Tolerence Story, 1 vol. Ebbeler, Jeff, illus. 2008. (Main Street School~ Kids with Character Ser.). (ENG.). 32p. (J). (gr. k-4). 32.79 *(978-1-60270-271-4(3),* 11277, Looking Glass Library) Magic Wagon.

Terrell, Brandon. Science Fair Sabotage. Epelbaum, Mariano, illus. 2017. (Snoops, Inc Ser.). (ENG.). 112p. (J). (gr. 4-8). lib. bdg. 27.32 *(978-1-4965-4347-9(5),* 134264, Stone Arch Bks.) Capstone.

Thaler, Mike. The Science Fair from the Black Lagoon. Lee, Jared, illus. 2011. (Black Lagoon Adventures Ser.: No. 1). (ENG.). 64p. (J). (gr. 2-6). 31.36 *(978-1-59961-814-2(1),* 3600, Chapter Bks.) Spotlight.

Watson, J. A. Crab Campaign: An Invasive Species Tracker's Journal. Olbey, Arpad, illus. 2019. (Science Squad Set 2 Ser.). (ENG.). 192p. (J). (gr. 3-4). 28.50 *(978-1-63163-295-2(7),* 1631632957, Jolly Fish Pr.) North Star Editions.

—Monarch Mystery: A Butterfly Researcher's Journal. 2018. (Science Squad Ser.). (ENG., Illus.). 192p. (J). (gr. 3-4). lib. bdg. 28.50 *(978-1-63163-183-2(7),* 1631631837, Jolly Fish Pr.) North Star Editions.

—Monarch Mystery: A Butterfly Researcher's Journal. Olbey, Arpad, illus. 2018. (Science Squad Ser.). (ENG.). 192p. (J). (gr. 3-4). pap. 9.99 *(978-1-63163-184-9(5),* 1631631845, Jolly Fish Pr.) North Star Editions.

—Nocturnal Symphony: A Bat Detector's Journal. Olbey, Arpad, illus. 2019. (Science Squad Set 2 Ser.). (ENG.). 192p. (J). (gr. 3-4). 28.50 *(978-1-63163-299-0(X),* 163163299X, Jolly Fish Pr.) North Star Editions.

—Pigeon Problems: An Urban Bird Researcher's Journal. 2018. (Science Squad Ser.). (ENG., Illus.). 192p. (J). (gr. 3-4). lib. bdg. 28.50 *(978-1-63163-187-0(X),* 163163187X, Jolly Fish Pr.) North Star Editions.

—Pigeon Problems: An Urban Bird Researcher's Journal. Olbey, Arpad, illus. 2018. (Science Squad Ser.). (ENG.). 192p. (J). (gr. 3-4). pap. 9.99 *(978-1-63163-188-7(8),* 1631631888, Jolly Fish Pr.) North Star Editions.

Weaver, Verity. Sandwich Shenanigans. Huddleston, Courtney, illus. 2019. (What Happened? Ser.). (ENG.). 120p. (J). (gr. 3-4). pap. 7.99 *(978-1-63163-316-4(3),* 1631633163); lib. bdg. 27.13 *(978-1-63163-315-7(5),* 1631633155) North Star Editions. (Jolly Fish Pr.).

SCIENTIFIC APPARATUS AND INSTRUMENTS

see also names of groups of instruments, e.g. Aeronautical Instruments; Astronomical Instruments; Chemical Apparatus; Electric Apparatus and Appliances; Meteorological Instruments

Besel, Jennifer M. Compass Roses & Directions, 1 vol. 2013. (Maps Ser.). (ENG.). 24p. (J). (gr. -1-2). pap. 6.95 *(978-1-4765-3524-1(8),* 123574) Capstone.

Bortz, Alfred B. Seven Wonders of Exploration Technology. 2010. (Seven Wonders Ser.). (YA). (gr. 5-9). lib. bdg. 33.26 *(978-0-7613-4241-0(9))* Twenty First Century Bks.

Cardenas, Ernesto & Saavedra, Patricia. El laboratorio de Ciencias. l.t. ed. 2006. (SPA., Illus.). 16p. pap. 4.95 *(978-1-933668-24-6(5))* Milo Educational Bks. & Resources.

Cardenas, Ernesto A. What Does A Scientist Use? 2009. 19.95 *(978-1-60698-020-0(3));* pap. 3.95 *(978-1-60698-018-7(1))* Milo Educational Bks. & Resources.

Deane-Pratt, Ade. Sensors, 1 vol. 2011. (How Things Work Ser.). (ENG., Illus.). 32p. (YA). (gr. 4-4). lib. bdg. 30.27 *(978-1-4488-5281-9(1),* 1d93a544-838d-49b9-88ba-89dcec8e85bc) Rosen Publishing Group, Inc., The.

deMarin, Layne. Look & Learn, 1 vol. 2011. (Wonder Readers Fluent Level Ser.). (ENG.). 16p. (gr. -1-2). (J). pap. 6.25 *(978-1-4296-7939-8(5),* 118271); pap. 35.94 *(978-1-4296-8120-9(9))* Capstone. (Capstone Pr.).

Duhig, Holly. Invisibility Cloaks, 1 vol. 2017. (Science Fiction to Science Fact Ser.). (ENG.). 32p. (J). (gr. 4-5). pap. 11.50 *(978-1-5382-1495-4(4),* c8780f9b-1f16-4b92-845b-576c887d67e9); lib. bdg. 28.27 *(978-1-5382-1384-1(2),* 5cd4c626-8077-41fc-9033-5275891500ac) Stevens, Gareth Publishing LLLP.

—Replicators, 1 vol. 2017. (Science Fiction to Science Fact Ser.). (ENG.). 32p. (J). (gr. 4-5). pap. 11.50 *(978-1-5382-1493-0(8),* 54ac1bb2-c4d9-4c39-a9a7-74d2d3d5a4c7); lib. bdg. 28.27 *(978-1-5382-1386-5(9),* 111d7be7-cd56-42d7-b9f1-d9312be8eb6a) Stevens, Gareth Publishing LLLP.

—Tractor Beams, 1 vol. 2017. (Science Fiction to Science Fact Ser.). (ENG.). 32p. (J). (gr. 4-5). pap. 11.50 *(978-1-5382-1489-3(X),* 496c8e06-4bb5-4140-bcf7-7314b9823d7d); lib. bdg. 28.27 *(978-1-5382-1390-2(7),* 23b6365a-729d-4eb1-96d6-33d825076439) Stevens, Gareth Publishing LLLP.

Enz, Tammy. Build Your Own Periscope, Flashlight, & Other Useful Stuff. 2011. (Build It Yourself Ser.). (ENG.). 32p. (gr. 3-4). pap. 47.70 *(978-1-4296-6431-8(2),* Capstone Pr.) Capstone.

Furgang, Kathy. Science Measuring Tools & Instrumentos para medir en Ciencias: 6 English, 6 Spanish Adaptations. 2011. (ENG & SPA.). (J). 101.00 net. *(978-1-4108-5727-9(1))* Benchmark Education Co.

Gulati, Annette. Scientists Use Tools. 2018. (Starting with STEAM Ser.). (ENG., Illus.). 24p. (J). (gr. 1-3). lib. bdg. 28.50 *(978-1-64156-426-7(1),* 9781641564267) Rourke Educational Media.

Harris, Michael C. Spare Parts for People, 1 vol. 2011. (Cool Science Ser.). (ENG.). 48p. (J). (gr. 4-4). 31.21 *(978-1-60870-080-6(1),* 889f7953-eb8c-4238-96ee-0d497a50a76d) Cavendish Square Publishing LLC.

Helbrough, Emma. A Day in the Life of a Pirate, 1 vol. Firenze, Inklink, illus. 2007. (Day in the Life Ser.: Vol. 4). (ENG.). 32p. (J). (gr. 4-5). lib. bdg. 28.93 *(978-1-4042-3853-4(0),* 6d457101-4920-4c92-b2b4-34ad753b04d6) Rosen Publishing Group, Inc., The.

Hicks, Kelli. Using Tools to Understand Our World. 2012. (My Science Library). (ENG.). 24p. (gr. 3-4). pap. 8.95 *(978-1-61810-230-0(3),* 9781618102300) Rourke Educational Media.

Holt, Rinehart and Winston Staff. Holt Science & Technology: Calculator for Biological Science Labs. 5th ed. 2004. (Illus.). pap. 14.60 *(978-0-03-035177-8(4))* Holt McDougal.

Koontz, Robin Michal. Binoculars. 2014. (How It Works). (ENG.). (J). (gr. k-3). lib. bdg. 19.55 *(978-1-62765-597-2(2))* Perfection Learning Corp.

Larson, Kirsten. Tools of the Trade: Using Scientific Equipment. 2016. (Let's Explore Science Ser.). (ENG.). 48p. (gr. 5-8). 35.64 *(978-1-68191-400-8(X),* 9781681914008) Rourke Educational Media.

Marsico, Katie. Scientific Instruments. Bane, Jeff, illus. 2018. (My Early Library: My World of Science Ser.). (ENG.). 24p. (gr. k-1). lib. bdg. 30.64 *(978-1-5341-2891-0(3),* 211608) Cherry Lake Publishing.

Martin, Elena. Seeing Is Believing. 2005. (Yellow Umbrella Fluent Level Ser.). (ENG., Illus.). 16p. (gr. k-1). pap. 35.70 *(978-0-7368-5299-9(9),* Capstone Pr.) Capstone.

Meredith, Susan. Using Scientific Tools. 2009. (Let's Explore Science Ser.). (ENG., Illus.). 48p. (gr. 4-8). pap. 10.95 *(978-1-60694-531-5(9),* 9781606945315) Rourke Educational Media.

—Uso de Instrumentos Cientificos. 2012. (Let's Explore Science Ser.). (SPA.). 48p. (gr. 4-8). pap. 10.95 *(978-1-61810-471-7(3),* 9781618104717) Rourke Educational Media.

Metz, Lorijo. Using Beakers & Graduated Cylinders, 1 vol. 2013. (Science Tools Ser.). (ENG., Illus.). 24p. (J). (gr. 2-3). 26.27 *(978-1-4488-9685-1(1),* 79699b11-ce93-4d40-9d7f-84030d356b6e); pap. 9.25 *(978-1-4488-9828-2(5),* 753fd99d-638a-406c-a59b-719e9379e089) Rosen Publishing Group, Inc., The. (PowerKids Pr.).

Rau, Dana Meachen. Become an Explorer: Make & Use a Compass. 2010. (Creative Adventure Guides). 48p. (J). (gr. 3-6). lib. bdg. 26.60 *(978-1-59953-383-4(9))* Norwood Hse. Pr.

Rourke, Brigid. Tools of Science, 1 vol. 2013. (Rosen Readers Ser.). (ENG.). 24p. (J). (gr. 2-2). pap. 8.25 *(978-1-4777-2325-8(0),* d91aa367-b5c0-4f16-8b59-b89cae13723f); pap. 49.50 *(978-1-4777-2326-5(9))* Rosen Publishing Group, Inc., The. (Rosen Classroom).

Science Lab Set, 8 vols. 2008. (Science Lab Ser.). (ENG., Illus.). (J). (gr. 4-4). lib. bdg. 121.08 *(978-1-4358-2826-1(7),* 2cfcf892-4993-4880-9793-0c67a9140278, PowerKids Pr.) Rosen Publishing Group, Inc., The.

Sharkawy, Azza. Observe It! 2014. (Science Sleuths Ser.). (ENG., Illus.). 24p. (J). (gr. 2-2). *(978-0-7787-0765-3(2))* Crabtree Publishing Co.

Smith, Paula. Measure It!, 1 vol. 2015. (Science Sleuths Ser.). (ENG., Illus.). 24p. (J). (gr. 2-2). pap. *(978-0-7787-1544-3(2))* Crabtree Publishing Co.

—Model It!, 1 vol. 2015. (Science Sleuths Ser.). (ENG., Illus.). 24p. (J). (gr. 2-2). pap. *(978-0-7787-1545-0(0))* Crabtree Publishing Co.

Ward, Lesley. The Science of Glass. rev. ed. 2018. (Smithsonian: Informational Text Ser.). (ENG., Illus.). 32p. (J). (gr. 4-8). pap. 11.99 *(978-1-4938-6716-5(4))* Teacher Created Materials, Inc.

SCIENTIFIC DISCOVERIES

see Discoveries in Science

SCIENTIFIC EDUCATION

see Science—Study and Teaching

SCIENTIFIC EXPEDITIONS

see also names of regions explored, e.g. Antarctic Regions; Arctic Regions; and names of expeditions

Johnson, Rebecca L. Journey into the Deep: Discovering New Ocean Creatures. (ENG., Illus.). 64p. (J). (gr. 4-8). 2010. lib. bdg. 31.99 *(978-0-7613-4148-2(X),* f2f61c84-d06a-4e20-80f6-33973b2f5e36, Millbrook Pr.) 2015. E-Book 53.32 *(978-1-4677-5923-6(6),* 9781467759236, Lerner Digital) Lerner Publishing Group.

SCIENTIFIC EXPEDITIONS—FICTION

Alzial, Sylvain. Panthera Tigris. Rajcak, Hélène, illus. 2019. (ENG.). 32p. (J). *(978-0-8028-5529-9(6),* Eerdmans Bks For Young Readers) Eerdmans, William B. Publishing Co.

Doyle, Arthur Conan. The Lost World, 1 vol. 2009. (Real Reads Ser.). (ENG., Illus.). 64p. (J). (gr. 5-5). pap. 14.55 *(978-1-60754-395-4(8),* 49a60ade-2b66-439a-88f7-600b078eef55); lib. bdg. 33.93 *(978-1-60754-394-7(X),* 222eeae2-6661-460a-8103-8cfc7225ef8f) Rosen Publishing Group, Inc., The. (Windmill Bks.).

Lane, Jean E. Lill & Mewe Journey to the Ocean of Runa. 2013. 122p. pap. 11.95 *(978-1-62212-538-8(X),* Strategic Bk. Publishing) Strategic Book Publishing & Rights Agency (SBPRA).

Sniegoski, Tom. Quest for the Spark: Book Three: a BONE Companion, Bk. 3. Smith, Jeff, illus. 2013. (BONE: Quest for the Spark Ser.). (ENG.). 288p. (J). (gr. 3-7). 26.99 *(978-0-545-14105-5(2),* Graphix) Scholastic, Inc.

Whitmore, Andrew. Beast of the Jungle. 2007. 96p. (YA). pap. *(978-1-4207-0728-1(0))* Sundance/Newbridge Educational Publishing.

SCIENTIFIC EXPERIMENTS

see Science—Experiments

also particular branches of science with the subdivision Experiments, e.g. Chemistry—Experiments

SCIENTIFIC INSTRUMENTS

see Scientific Apparatus and Instruments

SCIENTIFIC MANAGEMENT

see Management

SCIENTIFIC METHOD

see Science—Methodology

SCIENTIFIC RECREATIONS

see also Mathematical Recreations

Blum, Raymond, et al. Giant Book of Science Fun/Giant Book of Math Fun: Flip Book. Sterling Publishing Company Staff, ed. (Illus.). 512p. pap. 9.98 *(978-1-4027-0469-7(0))* Sterling Publishing Co., Inc.

Brown, Cynthia Light & Brown, Grace. Explore Fossils! With 25 Great Projects. Stone, Bryan, illus. 2016. (Explore Your World Ser.). (ENG.). 96p. (J). (gr. 1-5). 19.95 *(978-1-61930-331-7(0),* 6c592174-b1d9-4454-b9fa-1f96e3e8c7f4) Nomad Pr.

Cleary, Brian P. Mrs. Riley Bought Five Itchy Aardvarks & Other Painless Tricks for Memorizing Science Facts. Sandy, J. P., illus. 2008. (Adventures in Memory Ser.). (ENG.). 48p. (gr. 4-6). 26.60 *(978-0-8225-7819-2(0))* Lerner Publishing Group.

Cobb, Vicki. We Dare You: Hundreds of Fun Science Bets, Challenges, & Experiments You Can Do at Home. 2009. (ENG., Illus.). 336p. (J). (gr. 2-7). pap. 14.95 *(978-1-60239-775-0(9),* 239775) Skyhorse Publishing Co., Inc.

—We Dare You! Hundreds of Fun Science Bets, Challenges, & Experiments You Can Do at Home. rev. ed. 2015. (ENG., Illus.). 336p. (J). (gr. 2-7). pap. 12.95 *(978-1-62914-631-7(5),* Sky Pony Pr.) Skyhorse Publishing Co., Inc.

Dragotta, Nick, et al. Howtoons: Tools of Mass Construction. 2014. (ENG., Illus.). 360p. (J). pap. 17.99 *(978-1-63215-101-8(4),* 4de65120-4aec-4e27-863d-b7cb0baecc8b) Image Comics.

Dyer, Janice. Get into Wow-Factor Science. 2017. (Get-Into-It Guides). (Illus.). 32p. (J). (gr. 4-5). *(978-0-7787-3643-1(1))* Crabtree Publishing Co.

Falk, John H., et al. Bubbie Monster: And Other Science Fun. 2003. (Illus.). 176p. (J). (gr. -1-3). pap. 17.95 *(978-1-55652-301-4(7))* Chicago Review Pr., Inc.

Gardner, Martin. Martin Gardner's Science Magic: Tricks & Puzzles. 2011. (Dover Magic Bks.). (ENG., Illus.). 96p. (gr. 4). pap. 4.99 *(978-0-486-47657-5(X),* 47657X) Dover Pubns., Inc.

Hanson, Anders Mann & Mann, Elissa. Cool String Art: Creative Activities That Make Math & Science Fun for Kids! 2013. (Cool Art with Math & Science Ser.). (ENG.). 32p. (J). (gr. 3-6). lib. bdg. 34.21 *(978-1-61783-824-8(1),* 4594, Checkerboard Library) ABDO Publishing Co.

—Cool Structures: Creative Activities That Make Math & Science Fun for Kids! 2013. (Cool Art with Math & Science Ser.). (ENG.). 32p. (J). (gr. 3-6). lib. bdg. 34.21 *(978-1-61783-825-5(X),* 4596, Checkerboard Library) ABDO Publishing Co.

Hickman, Pamela & Federation of Ontario Naturalists. Naturaleza Divertida. Shore, Judie, illus. (SPA.). 92p. *(978-84-9754-095-7(6),* 87821) Ediciones Oniro S.A.

—La Naturaleza y Tú. Shore, Judie, illus. (SPA.). 63p. *(978-84-9754-106-0(5),* 87822) Ediciones Oniro S.A.

El Libro de los Acertijos Cientificos. (Coleccion Acertijos). (SPA.). (YA). (gr. 5-8). *(978-950-724-614-2(2),* LM8237) Lumen ARG. Dist: Lectorum Pubns., Inc.

Low, A. M. Popular Scientific Recreations - Science. 2006. 292p. per. *(978-1-4067-9717-6(0),* Hesperides Pr.) Read Bks.

Martineau, Susan. Crazy Contraptions, 1 vol. Ursell, Martin, illus. 2011. (Awesome Activities Ser.). (ENG.). 24p. (J). (gr. 4-4). lib. bdg. 29.93 *(978-1-61533-367-7(3),* aa683d12-a380-4d04-930f-85450f7a335e, Windmill Bks.) Rosen Publishing Group, Inc., The.

Press, Judy. Little Hands Sea Life Art & Activities: Creative Learning Experiences for 3-7-Year Olds. 2004. (Williamson's Little Hands Book Ser.). (Illus.). 128p. (J). pap. 12.95 *(978-1-885593-94-8(5),* Ideals Pubns.) Worthy Publishing.

Roth, Jennifer A. Backyard Laboratory. 2007. (Experiment with Science Ser.). (ENG., Illus.). 32p. (J). (gr. 3-6). 27.00 *(978-0-531-18542-1(7),* Children's Pr.) Scholastic Library Publishing.

VanCleave, Janice. Janice VanCleave's Super Science Challenges: Hands-On Inquiry Projects for Schools, Science Fairs, or Just Plain Fun! 2007. (ENG., Illus.). 160p. (gr. 3-7). pap. 14.95 *(978-0-471-47183-7(6))* Wiley, John & Sons, Inc.

SCIENTISTS

see also Science—Vocational Guidance

also classes of scientists, e.g. Astronomers; Chemists; Geologists; Mathematicians; Naturalists; Physicists, etc.; and names of scientists

Ackerman, Jane. Louis Pasteur & the Founding of Microbiology. 2004. (Profiles in Science Ser.). (Illus.). 144p. (YA). (gr. 6-12). 26.95 *(978-1-931798-13-6(3))* Reynolds, Morgan Inc.

Adams, Colleen. Benjamin Franklin: American Inventor. 2009. (Reading Room Collection 2 Ser.). 24p. (gr. 3-4). 42.50 *(978-1-60851-959-0(7),* PowerKids Pr.) Rosen Publishing Group, Inc., The.

Adler, David A. A Picture Book of Benjamin Franklin. Wallner, John & Wallner, Alexandra, illus. 2008. (Picture Book Biography Ser.). (J). (gr. k-3). 28.95 incl. audio compact disk *(978-1-4301-0340-0(X));* Set. pap. 37.95 incl. audio *(978-1-4301-0338-7(8))* Live Oak Media.

—A Picture Book of George Washington Carver. Brown, Dan, illus. 2008. (Picture Book Biography Ser.). (J). (gr. -1-2). 28.95 incl. audio compact disk *(978-1-4301-0348-6(5))* Live Oak Media.

Allen, John. Robert Boyle: Father of Chemistry. 2005. (Giants of Science Ser.). (ENG., Illus.). 64p. (J). (gr. 3-7). lib. bdg. 28.35 *(978-1-56711-887-2(9),* Blackbirch Pr., Inc.) Cengage Gale.

Alphin, Elaine Marie. Germ Hunter: A Story about Louis Pasteur. Verstraete, Elaine, illus. 2003. (Creative Minds Biography Ser.). 64p. (J). lib. bdg. 22.60 *(978-1-57505-179-6(6),* Carolrhoda Bks.); (ENG.). (gr. 4-8). per. 9.99 *(978-0-87614-929-4(8),* 136cda8a-5a1e-4dc9-9e0b-6b7431df4759) Lerner Publishing Group.

Anastasio, Dina & Who HQ. Who Was Steve Irwin? Eldridge, Jim, illus. 2015. (Who Was? Ser.). (ENG.). 112p. (J). (gr. 3-7). 6.99 *(978-0-448-48838-7(8),* Penguin Workshop) Penguin Young Readers Group.

Anderson, Margaret J. & Stephenson, Karen F. Aristotle: Genius Philosopher & Scientist, 1 vol. 2014. (Genius Scientists & Their Genius Ideas Ser.). (ENG.). 96p. (gr. 5-5). (J). 29.60 *(978-0-7660-6535-2(9),* 459c9f5a-2af5-44aa-bf25-accba6b3ee96); pap. 13.88 *(978-0-7660-6536-9(7),* ac311030-e0fa-4387-98d2-2507ddcf9eaf) Enslow Publishing, LLC.

Anderson, Michael, ed. Pioneers of the Green Movement: Environmental Solutions, 1 vol. 2012. (Inventors & Innovators Ser.). (ENG., Illus.). 152p. (gr. 8-8). (J). 38.82 *(978-1-61530-698-5(6),* b90a75f7-38d4-4718-b884-26aab1cc3a6a); (YA). 77.64 *(978-1-61530-788-3(5),* 659d664a-c938-4bb0-98d5-1baeb712b0f3) Rosen Publishing Group, Inc., The.

Anniss, Matt. James Watson & Francis Crick. 2014. (Dynamic Duos of Science Ser.). 48p. (YA). (gr. 5-8). pap. 84.30 *(978-1-4824-1282-6(9))* Stevens, Gareth Publishing LLLP.

Apel, Melanie Ann. Virginia Apgar: Innovative Female Physician & Inventor of the Apgar Score. (Women Hall of Famers in Mathematics & Science Ser.). 112p. (gr. 5-8). 2009. 63.90 *(978-1-60854-815-6(5))* 2003. (ENG., Illus.). lib. bdg. 39.80 *(978-0-8239-3880-3(8),* ce7edbfa-c582-4033-985e-5cccc3ea2c50) Rosen Publishing Group, Inc., The. (Rosen Reference).

Ashby, Ruth. The Amazing Mr. Franklin: Or the Boy Who Read Everything, 1 vol. 2019. (Illus.). 112p. (J). (gr. 2-5). pap. 7.95 *(978-1-68263-102-7(8))* Peachtree Publishing Co. Inc.

Bailey, Gerry & Foster, Karen. Galileo's Telescope. Noyes, Leighton & Radford, Karen, illus. 2008. (Stories of Great People Ser.). (ENG.). 40p. (J). (gr. 3-6). lib. bdg. *(978-0-7787-3694-3(6));* pap. *(978-0-7787-3716-2(0))* Crabtree Publishing Co.

Balchin, Jon. Science: 100 Scientists Who Changed the World. 2003. (Illus.). 224p. 18.95 *(978-1-59270-017-2(9))* Enchanted Lion Bks., LLC.

Bankston, John. Gregor Mendel & the Discovery of the Gene. 2004. (Uncharted, Unexplored, & Unexplained Ser.). (Illus.). 48p. (J). (gr. 4-8). lib. bdg. 29.95 *(978-1-58415-266-8(4))* Mitchell Lane Pubs.

Bardoe, Cheryl. Gregor Mendel: The Friar Who Grew Peas. 2015. (ENG., Illus.). 32p. (J). (gr. k-4). pap. 10.99 *(978-1-4197-1840-3(1),* 591503, Abrams Bks. for Young Readers) Abrams, Inc.

Baxter, Roberta. Skeptical Chemist: The Story of Robert Boyle. 2006. (Profiles in Science Ser.). (Illus.). 128p. (gr. 6-12). lib. bdg. 27.95 *(978-1-59935-025-7(4))* Reynolds, Morgan Inc.

Be a Scientist!, 12 vols. 2014. (Be a Scientist! Ser.). 32p. (J). (gr. 3-4). (ENG.). 169.62 *(978-1-4824-1177-5(6),* 6b492b5a-fe77-437d-8c9c-7a7efd37ea42); pap. 63.00 *(978-1-4824-1553-7(4))* Stevens, Gareth Publishing LLLP.

Be a Space Scientist!, 12 vols. 2017. (Be a Space Scientist! Ser.). (ENG.). (J). (gr. 5-5). lib. bdg. 191.58 *(978-1-5081-6263-6(8),* 57e8e602-518d-4f5c-8189-a0948105350a, PowerKids Pr.) Rosen Publishing Group, Inc., The.

Belton, Blair. Be a Zoologist, 1 vol. 2014. (Be a Scientist! Ser.). 32p. (J). (gr. 3-4). (ENG.). pap. 11.50 *(978-1-4824-1286-4(1),* 089f14d6-6a23-4624-beeb-b63a31d359b3); pap. 63.00 *(978-1-4824-1188-1(1))* Stevens, Gareth Publishing LLLP.

Bendick, Jeanne. Archimedes & the Door of Science: Immortals of Science. 2011. 154p. (gr. 5-8). 41.95 *(978-1-258-01488-9(2))* Literary Licensing, LLC.

Benge, Janet & Benge, Geoff. Heroes of History - Benjamin Franklin: Live Wire. 2005. (Heroes of History Ser.). (ENG., Illus.). 208p. (YA). (gr. 5). pap. 11.99 *(978-1-932096-14-9(0))* Emerald Bks.

Bennett, Doraine & Scott, Clark C. Benjamin Franklin. 2012. (Illus.). 24p. (J). *(978-1-935884-38-5(7));* pap. *(978-1-935884-47-7(6))* State Standards Publishing, LLC.

Biskup, Agnieszka. The Amazing Work of Scientists with Max Axiom, Super Scientist. Baez, Marcelo, illus. 2013. (Graphic Science & Engineering in Action Ser.). (ENG.). 32p. (J). (gr. 3-4). pap. 49.60 *(978-1-62065-702-7(3),* 19300, Capstone Pr.) Capstone.

—The Amazing Work of Scientists with Max Axiom, Super Scientist, 1 vol. Baez, Marcelo & Baez, Marcelo, illus. 2013. (Graphic Science & Engineering in Action Ser.). (ENG.). 32p. (J). (gr. 3-9). pap. 8.10 *(978-1-62065-701-0(5),* 121698); lib. bdg. 31.32 *(978-1-4296-9936-5(1),* 120644) Capstone.

Boekhoff, P. M. Galileo. 2003. (Inventors & Creators Ser.). (Illus.). 48p. (J). 23.70 *(978-0-7377-1891-1(9),* Greenhaven Pr., Inc.) Cengage Gale.

Boekhoff, P. M. & Kallen, Stuart A. Benjamin Franklin. 2006. (Illus.). 48p. (J). (gr. 4-8). 17.00 *(978-1-4223-5322-6(2))* DIANE Publishing Co.

Bolton, Sarah K. Famous Men of Science. 2017. (ENG., Illus.). (YA). (gr. 7-12). pap. *(978-93-86423-11-5(1))* Alpha Editions.

Boone, Mary. George Washington Carver: Botanist & Inventor. 2018. (STEM Scientists & Inventors Ser.). (ENG., Illus.). 24p. (J). (gr. 1-3). lib. bdg. 27.99 *(978-1-5435-0646-4(1),* 137409, Capstone Pr.) Capstone.

—Thomas Edison: Physicist & Inventor. 2018. (STEM Scientists & Inventors Ser.). (ENG.). 24p. (J). (gr. 1-3). pap. 7.95 *(978-1-5435-0653-2(4),* 137417, Capstone Pr.) Capstone.

Bortz, Fred. The Laws of Genetics & Gregor Mendel, 1 vol. 2013. (Revolutionary Discoveries of Scientific Pioneers Ser.). (ENG., Illus.). 80p. (J). (gr. 6-6). 38.41 *(978-1-4777-1806-3(0),* 0f692ffb-d9d7-4d54-bcee-2cbec240cc9d) Rosen Publishing Group, Inc., The.

Borus, Audrey. James Watson, Francis Crick, Rosalind Franklin, & Maurice Wilkins: The Scientists Who Revealed the Structure of DNA. 2019. (J). pap. *(978-1-9785-1455-3(7))* Enslow Publishing, LLC.

BourkeKenna. Jeff Corwin: Wild Man Beginning Book with Online Access, 1 vol. 2014. (ENG., Illus.). 24p. pap., E-Book, E-Book 9.50 *(978-1-107-68039-5(5))* Cambridge Univ. Pr.

Bozzone, Donna M. Famous Immigrant Computer Scientists, 1 vol. 2017. (Making America Great: Immigrant Success Stories Ser.). (ENG.). 112p. (gr. 7-7). 38.93 *(978-0-7660-9246-4(1),* 315a068f-f9b1-4f9e-99f5-633da72b0498); pap. 20.95 *(978-0-7660-9592-2(4),* 4ee40efc-1810-42e7-a65a-9fdf65710de4) Enslow Publishing, LLC.

Brasch, Nicholas. Leonardo Da Vinci, 1 vol. 2013. (Discovery Education: Discoveries & Inventions Ser.). (ENG.). 32p. (J). (gr. 4-5). 28.93 *(978-1-4777-1330-3(1),* ea95200d-a82b-4e89-b3c2-9514b425abf7, PowerKids Pr.) Rosen Publishing Group, Inc., The.

—Leonardo Da Vinci: The Greatest Inventor. 2013. (Discovery Education: Discoveries & Inventions Ser.). 32p. (J). (gr. 3-6). pap. 60.00 *(978-1-4777-1503-1(7),* PowerKids Pr.) Rosen Publishing Group, Inc., The.

Brasch, Nicolas. Leonardo Da Vinci: The Greatest Inventor, 1 vol. 2013. (Discovery Education: Discoveries & Inventions Ser.). (ENG., Illus.). 32p. (J). (gr. 4-5). pap. 11.00 *(978-1-4777-1502-4(9),* 3020c0f3-c19e-4c49-91d5-84e39db0f080, PowerKids Pr.) Rosen Publishing Group, Inc., The.

Brezina, Corona. Careers as a Medical Examiner. (Careers in Forensics Ser.). 64p. (gr. 5-5). 2009. 58.50 *(978-1-61511-799-4(7),* Rosen Reference) 2008. (ENG., Illus.). (J). lib. bdg. 37.13 *(978-1-4042-1347-0(3),* 5559df5e-914e-48e2-b6d6-18de6e33a566) Rosen Publishing Group, Inc., The.

Brinkerhoff, Shirley. Research Scientist. Riggs, Ernestine G. & Gholar, Cheryl, eds. 2013. (Careers with Character Ser.: 18). 96p. (J). (gr. 7-18). 22.95 *(978-1-4222-2765-7(0))* Mason Crest.

Brown Bear Books. Chemistry, Earth, & Space Sciences. 2009. (Great Scientists Ser.). (ENG.). 64p. (J). (gr. 8-11). 35.65 *(978-1-933834-47-4(1),* 16492) Brown Bear Bks.

—Life Sciences. 2009. (Great Scientists Ser.). (ENG.). 64p. (J). (gr. 8-11). 39.95 *(978-1-933834-45-0(5),* 16493) Brown Bear Bks.

—Physical Sciences. 2009. (Great Scientists Ser.). (ENG.). 64p. (J). (gr. 8-11). 39.95 *(978-1-933834-46-7(3),* 16494) Brown Bear Bks.

Burling, Alexis. Robert Boyle, 1 vol. 2017. (Leaders of the Scientific Revolution Ser.). (ENG., Illus.). 112p. (YA). (gr. 8-8). 38.80 *(978-1-5081-7476-9(8),* d25c293b-ed44-426c-8ec8-8c45789db0ba, Rosen Young Adult) Rosen Publishing Group, Inc., The.

Byman, Jeremy. Carl Sagan: In Contact with the Cosmos. 2004. (Great Scientists Ser.). (Illus.). 112p. (YA). (gr. 6-12). 21.95 *(978-1-883846-55-8(2),* First Biographies) Reynolds, Morgan Inc.

Byrd, Robert. Electric Ben: The Amazing Life & Times of Benjamin Franklin. 2012. 40p. (J). (gr. k-3). 17.99 *(978-0-8037-3749-5(1),* Dial Bks) Penguin Young Readers Group.

Calkhoven, Laurie. Women Who Launched the Computer Age: Ready-To-Read Level 3. Petersen, Alyssa, illus. 2016. (You Should Meet Ser.). (ENG.). 48p. (J). (gr. 1-3). pap. 4.99 *(978-1-4814-7046-9(9),* Simon Spotlight) Simon Spotlight.

Cardona, Ruby. Temple Grandin (Women in Science) (Library Edition) Lundie, Isobel, illus. 2019. (Women in Science Ser.). (ENG.). 32p. (J). (gr. 2-3). lib. bdg. 29.00 *(978-0-531-23536-2(X),* Watts, Franklin) Scholastic Library Publishing.

Carson, Mary Kay. The Bat Scientists. (Scientists in the Field Ser.). (ENG., Illus.). 80p. (J). (gr. 5-7). 2013. pap. 10.99 *(978-0-544-10493-8(5),* 1540800) 2010. 18.99 *(978-0-547-19956-6(2),* 1058461) HarperCollins Pubs. (Clarion Bks.).

Castro, Rachel. Temple Grandin. 2019. (STEM Superstars Ser.). (ENG., Illus.). 24p. (J). (gr. k-2). 22.60 *(978-1-68450-922-5(X))* Norwood Hse. Pr.

Challoner, Jack. Exploring the Mysteries of Genius & Invention, 1 vol. 2016. (STEM Guide to the Universe Ser.). (ENG.). 96p. (J). (gr. 9-9). lib. bdg. 47.80 *(978-1-4994-6410-8(X),* ef7fec10-188d-4443-a901-65c6c1e00385) Rosen Publishing Group, Inc., The.

Clovacco, Justine. Leonardo Da Vinci, 1 vol. 2014. (Britannica Beginner Bios Ser.). (ENG., Illus.). 32p. (J). (gr. 2-3). 26.06 *(978-1-62275-677-3(0),* 0c6a37f7-5c23-4479-9483-d8fa300ed764, Britannica Educational Publishing) Rosen Publishing Group, Inc., The.

Citro, Asia. Pigeon Math. Watson, Richard, illus. 2019. (ENG.). 40p. (J). (gr. k-5). 16.99 *(978-1-943147-62-5(0),* b0b01c77-c2cc-438d-bb9a-f16d4f6aa9eb) Innovation Pr., The.

Cohen, Sheila & Terman Cohen, Sheila. Gaylord Nelson: Champion for Our Earth. 2010. (Badger Biographies Ser.). (ENG., Illus.). 120p. (J). pap. 12.95 *(978-0-87020-443-2(2))* Wisconsin Historical Society.

Cohn, Jessica. Parasite Collector, 1 vol. 2011. (Dirty & Dangerous Jobs Ser.). (ENG.). 32p. (gr. 3-3). 31.21 *(978-1-60870-175-9(1),* 7dc95fac-bfb6-4cfc-93b1-088f460bb909) Cavendish Square Publishing LLC.

Colbert, David. Benjamin Franklin. 2008. (10 Days Ser.). (ENG.). 160p. (J). (gr. 3-8). pap. 8.99 *(978-1-4169-6446-9(0),* Simon & Schuster/Paula Wiseman Bks.) Simon & Schuster/Paula Wiseman Bks.

Coleman, Miriam. Mujeres en Las Ciencias (Women in Science), 1 vol. 2015. (Ellas Abrieron Camino (Women Groundbreakers) Ser.). (SPA.). 32p. (J). (gr. 4-5). 27.93 *(978-1-4994-0539-2(1),* bf53c40c-2012-41a7-8935-dba1ef4097e7, PowerKids Pr.) Rosen Publishing Group, Inc., The.

Collard, Sneed B., III. Benjamin Franklin: The Man Who Could Do Just about Anything, 1 vol. 2007. (American Heroes Ser.). (ENG., Illus.). 48p. (gr. 3-3). lib. bdg. 32.64 *(978-0-7614-2161-0(0),* 92ba54e7-6855-43a1-b3f4-276d6a5eef30) Cavendish Square Publishing LLC.

—Science Adventures, 8 vols., Set. Incl. In the Deep Sea. lib. bdg. 32.64 *(978-0-7614-1952-5(7),* 51a1271b-3391-4430-aee9-cd04cde8adbb); In the Rain Forest Canopy. lib. bdg. 32.64 *(978-0-7614-1954-9(3),* bc7e6cf1-bc45-4030-b1ad-9735ea8337cc); In the Wild. lib. bdg. 32.64 *(978-0-7614-1955-6(1),* f6a29e18-2839-462e-97d0-11e8759beac6); On the Coral Reefs. lib. bdg. 32.64 *(978-0-7614-1953-2(5),* 1835758b-57a9-4fe7-93d6-a5287c1d13aa); (Illus.). 48p. (gr. 4-4). (Science Adventures Ser.). (ENG.). 2007. 130.56 *(978-0-7614-1951-8(9),* 135734b4-2f5a-45d5-b44b-727df55abccb, Cavendish Square) Cavendish Square Publishing LLC.

Colson, Rob. Scholars of Science. 2018. (STEM-Gineers Ser.). (Illus.). 32p. (J). (gr. 5-5). *(978-0-7787-5738-2(2))* Crabtree Publishing Co.

S

Conklin, Wendy. 16th Century Superstar: Da Vinci. 2nd rev. ed. 2017. (TIME(r): Informational Text Ser.). (ENG., Illus.). 32p. (gr. 6-8). pap. 13.99 *(978-1-4938-3630-7(7))* Teacher Created Materials, Inc.

Conlan, Kathy & Canadian Museum of Nature Staff. Under the Ice: A Marine Biologist at Work. 2004. (Illus.). 56p. (J). (gr. 4-6). 11.95 *(978-1-55337-060-4(0))* Kids Can Pr., Ltd. CAN. Dist: Hachette Bk. Group.

Cornell, Kari. Urban Biologist Danielle Lee. 2016. (STEM Trailblazer Bios Ser.). (ENG., Illus.). 32p. (J). (gr. 2-5). 26.65 *(978-1-4677-9529-6(1),* 3e654c34-7ad3-459f-8484-dc1009ffc2dc, Lerner Pubns.) Lerner Publishing Group.

Cregan, Elizabeth R. C. Pioneers in Cell Biology, 1 vol. rev. ed. 2007. (Science: Informational Text Ser.). (ENG.). 32p. (gr. 3-6). pap. 12.99 *(978-0-7439-0586-2(5))* Teacher Created Materials, Inc.

Crompton, Samuel Willard. Thomas Paine: Fighting for American Independence, 1 vol. 2017. (Rebels with a Cause Ser.). (ENG.). 128p. (gr. 8-8). lib. bdg. 38.93 *(978-0-7660-8515-2(5),* 9bbb932c-af6f-4b5e-9b36-0aa7fa6f6bff) Enslow Publishing, LLC.

Csiszar, John. Facebook. 2018. (J). *(978-1-4222-4060-1(6))* Mason Crest.

Curtis, Suzanne. John Wesley Powell: American Hero. 2013. (ENG & SPA., Illus.). 78p. (J). pap. 8.95 *(978-0-86541-178-4(6))* Filter Pr., LLC.

Dakers, Diane. Dian Fossey: Animal Rights Activist & Protector of Mountain Gorillas. 2016. (ENG., Illus.). 112p. (J). lib. bdg. *(978-0-7787-2563-3(4))* Crabtree Publishing Co.

Davis, Lynn. Thomas Edison, 1 vol. 2015. (Amazing Inventors & Innovators Ser.). (ENG., Illus.). 24p. (J). (gr. k-3). 32.79 *(978-1-62403-723-8(2),* 17952, Super SandCastle) ABDO Publishing Co.

De Angelis, Gina & Bianco, David J. Computers: Processing the Data. 2005. (Innovators Ser.: Vol. 13). (Illus.). 144p. (J). (gr. 5-18). lib. bdg. 24.95 *(978-1-881508-87-8(0))* Oliver Pr., Inc.

deMarin, Layne. What Scientists Do, 1 vol. 2011. (Wonder Readers Fluent Level Ser.). (ENG.). 16p. (gr. -1-2). (J). pap. 6.25 *(978-1-4296-7945-9(X),* 118277); pap. 35.94 *(978-1-4296-8205-3(1))* Capstone. (Capstone Pr.).

Di Piazza, Domenica. Space Engineer & Scientist Margaret Hamilton. 2017. (STEM Trailblazer Bios Ser.). (ENG., Illus.). 32p. (J). (gr. 2-5). 26.65 *(978-1-5124-3450-7(7),* 00361086-11f1-4e7d-80a7-8140621d335a, Lerner Pubns.) Lerner Publishing Group.

DK. Look I'm a Scientist. 2017. (Look! I'm Learning Ser.). (ENG., Illus.). 48p. (J). (gr. -1-2). 12.99 *(978-1-4654-5963-3(4),* DK Children) Dorling Kindersley Publishing, Inc.

Dolan, Ellen M. Thomas Alva Edison: American Inventor & Businessman, 1 vol. 2014. (Legendary American Biographies Ser.). (ENG.). 96p. (gr. 6-6). 29.60 *(978-0-7660-6510-9(3),* 6e9706d2-6897-496b-9aeb-918625305770); pap. 13.88 *(978-0-7660-6511-6(1),* ed8adaea-d7c0-4744-8fda-3cfb3a7edba0) Enslow Publishing, LLC.

Don Nardo. The Trial of Galileo. 2003. (Famous Trials Ser.). (ENG., Illus.). 112p. (J). 29.95 *(978-1-59018-423-3(8))* Cengage Gale.

Driscoll, Laura. George Washington Carver: The Peanut Wizard. Weber, Jill, illus. 2003. (Smart about History Ser.). 32p. (J). (gr. k-4). mass mkt. 7.99 *(978-0-448-43243-4(9),* Grosset & Dunlap) Penguin Young Readers Group.

Duignan, Brian, ed. The Britannica Guide to the World's Most Influential People (Print/Ebook Combo Set) Print/Ebook Combo Set, 64 vols. Incl. 100 Most Influential Philosophers of All Time. (ENG.). 368p. (YA). (gr. 10-10). 2010. 113.18 *(978-1-61530-072-3(4),* 247aac42-c737-4e0d-8e4a-b7306f082367); (Britannica Guide to the World's Most Influential People Ser.). (ENG.). 336-384p. 2010. 905.44 *(978-1-61530-165-2(8),* ea8db089-fd00-4db0-8986-b9239413f7c8) Rosen Publishing Group, Inc., The.

Duling, Kaitlyn. Benjamin Franklin: Inventor & Founding Father, 1 vol. 2019. (Great American Entrepreneurs Ser.). (ENG.). 128p. (gr. 9-9). pap. 22.16 *(978-1-5026-4536-4(X),* 466b4ac5-f5a1-400d-bd8d-c6e4a33af683) Cavendish Square Publishing LLC.

—Benjamin Franklin: Inventor & Founding Father. 2018. (J). pap. *(978-1-5026-4023-9(6))* Musa Publishing.

Dynamic Duos of Science, 12 vols. 2014. (Dynamic Duos of Science Ser.). (ENG.). 48p. (YA). (gr. 5-6). 201.60 *(978-1-4824-1183-6(0),* 295721c3-86b5-401a-85f6-4d7a7f1febeb) Stevens, Gareth Publishing LLLP.

Edwards, Linda McMurry. George Washington Carver: The Life of the Great American Agriculturist. 2009. (Library of American Lives & Times Ser.). 112p. (gr. 5-5). 69.20 *(978-1-60853-485-2(5))* Rosen Publishing Group, Inc., The.

Elliot, Henry. John Muir: Protecting & Preserving the Environment. 2009. (Voices for Green Choices Ser.). (ENG., Illus.). 48p. (J). (gr. 5-9). lib. bdg. *(978-0-7787-4668-3(2))* Crabtree Publishing Co.

Endres, Hollie J. Shockwave: Scientists Try, Try Again. 2007. (Shockwave: Life Stories Ser.). (ENG., Illus.). 36p. (J). (gr. 3-5). 25.00 *(978-0-531-17744-0(0),* Children's Pr.) Scholastic Library Publishing.

Fandel, Jennifer. Louis Pasteur. 2003. (World Was Never the Same Ser.). (J). *(978-1-58417-266-6(5))* Lake Street Pubs.

Farndon, John. Great Scientists. 2010. (Science Library). 40p. (J). (gr. 3-18). lib. bdg. 19.95 *(978-1-4222-1549-4(0))* Mason Crest.

Flath, Camden. Tomorrow's Enterprising Scientists: Computer Software Designers & Specialists. 2010. (New Careers for the 21st Century Ser.). 64p. (YA). (gr. 7-18). pap. 9.95 *(978-1-4222-2043-6(5));* lib. bdg. 22.95 *(978-1-4222-1822-8(8))* Mason Crest.

Fleming, Candace. Ben Franklin's Almanac: Being a True Account of the Good Gentleman's Life. 2003. (ENG., Illus.). 128p. (J). (gr. 5-9). 22.99 *(978-0-689-83549-0(3),* Atheneum Bks. for Young Readers) Simon & Schuster Children's Publishing.

Fleming, Thomas. Ben Franklin: Inventing America. 2017. (Great Leaders & Events Ser.). (ENG., Illus.). 208p. (J). (gr. 4-8). lib. bdg. 35.99 *(978-1-942875-23-9(1),* ddb56499-e1ab-4552-9b39-62486bda3151, Voyageur Pr.) Quarto Publishing Group USA.

Forbes, Charlotte & Forbes, Charlotte. Those Amazing Scientists. Pillion, Dean, illus. 2007. 26p. (J). *(978-0-9772799-1-3(X))* Trilogy Pubns. LLC.

Fradin, Dennis Brindell. Nicolaus Copernicus: The Earth Is a Planet. von Buhler, Cynthia, tr. von Buhler, Cynthia, illus. 2003. 32p. (J). (gr. 2-6). 15.95 *(978-1-59336-006-1(1));* pap. *(978-1-59336-007-8(X))* Mondo Publishing.

—Who Was Ben Franklin? O'brien, John, illus. 2003. (Who Was... ? Ser.). 105p. (gr. 4-7). 15.00 *(978-0-7569-1589-6(9))* Perfection Learning Corp.

Franco, Michou. I Can Be a Scientist, 1 vol. 2017. (I Can Be Anything! Ser.). (ENG.). 24p. (gr. k-k). pap. 9.15 *(978-1-4824-6329-3(6),* d7e30da4-aca8-427f-af6c-2ff3bb697cde) Stevens, Gareth Publishing LLLP.

Franklin, Benjamin. Benjamin Franklin's Wise Words: How to Work Smart, Play Well, & Make Real Friends. 2017. (Illus.). 128p. (J). (gr. 3-7). 16.99 *(978-1-4263-2699-8(8),* National Geographic Kids) Disney Publishing Worldwide.

Freedman, Claire. Monstersaurus. Cort, Ben, illus. 2013. (J). *(978-1-4351-4952-6(1))* Barnes & Noble, Inc.

Fries-Gaither, Jessica. Exemplary Evidence: Scientists & Their Data. 2019. (ENG., Illus.). 32p. (J). (gr. 2-4). pap. 14.95 *(978-1-68140-361-8(7))* National Science Teachers Assn.

—Notable Notebooks: Scientists & Their Writings. 2017. (ENG., Illus.). 32p. (J). (gr. 2-4). 18.95 *(978-1-68140-379-3(X));* pap. 38.99 *(978-1-68140-307-6(2),* P527774) National Science Teachers Assn.

Frisch, Aaron. Albert Einstein. 2005. (Genius Ser.). (Illus.). 48p. (J). (gr. 5-9). lib. bdg. 21.95 *(978-1-58341-328-9(6),* Creative Education) Creative Co., The.

Frydenborg, Kay. Wild Horse Scientists. 2012. (Scientists in the Field Ser.). (ENG., Illus.). 80p. (J). (gr. 5-7). 18.99 *(978-0-547-51831-2(5),* 1445015, Clarion Bks.) HarperCollins Pubs.

Gaustad, Edwin S. Benjamin Franklin: Inventing America. 2006. 143p. (J). (gr. 4-8). reprint ed. 22.00 *(978-1-4223-5227-4(7))* DIANE Publishing Co.

Gazlay, Suzy. David Suzuki: Doing Battle with Climate Change. 2009. (Voices for Green Choices Ser.). (ENG., Illus.). 48p. (J). (gr. 5-9). lib. bdg. *(978-0-7787-4665-2(8))* Crabtree Publishing Co.

Gholz, Sophia. The Boy Who Grew a Forest: The True Story of Jadav Payeng. Harren, Kayla, illus. 2019. (ENG.). 32p. (J). (gr. k-3). 16.99 *(978-1-5341-1024-3(0),* 204656) Sleeping Bear Pr.

Giblin, James Cross. The Amazing Life of Benjamin Franklin. Dooling, Michael, illus. 2006. 48p. (gr. -1-3). 18.00 *(978-0-7569-6551-8(9))* Perfection Learning Corp.

Gibson, Brylee. Extreme Scientists. 2007. (Connectors Ser.). (gr. 2-5). pap. *(978-1-877453-08-3(0))* Global Education Systems Ltd.

Gilman, Sarah. Ben Franklin, 1 vol. 2016. (Explore Colonial America Ser.). (ENG., Illus.). 48p. (gr. 4-5). 29.60 *(978-0-7660-7873-4(6),* 42aeadd0-ba2b-4e55-9437-cc525a643fff) Enslow Publishing, LLC.

Glass, Maya. Benjamin Franklin: Early American Genius. (Primary Sources of Famous People in American History Ser.). 32p. 2009. (gr. 2-3). 47.90 *(978-1-60851-654-4(7))* 2003. (ENG., Illus.). (gr. 3-4). pap. 10.00 *(978-0-8239-4175-9(2),* b45187dc-6b5e-4b22-9e71-9d53ecc04d6a) 2003. (ENG., Illus.). (J). (gr. 3-4). lib. bdg. 29.13 *(978-0-8239-4103-2(5),* 8b464c67-53c0-43ed-99f2-2206fe1f6d9d) Rosen Publishing Group, Inc., The.

—Benjamin Franklin: Early American Genius / Político e inventor Estadounidense. 2009. (Famous People in American History/Grandes personajes en la historia de los Estados Unidos Ser.). (ENG & SPA.). 32p. (gr. 2-3). 47.90 *(978-1-61512-538-8(8),* Editorial Buenas Letras) Rosen Publishing Group, Inc., The.

—Benjamin Franklin: Político e inventor Estadounidense, 1 vol. 2003. (Grandes Personajes en la Historia de Los Estados Unidos (Famous People in American History) Ser.). (SPA.). 32p. (gr. 3-4). pap. 10.00 *(978-0-8239-4221-3(X),* c2496fbf-eecd-4e55-90ef-221234038279, Rosen Classroom) Rosen Publishing Group, Inc., The.

—Benjamin Franklin: Político e inventor estadounidense (Benjamin Franklin: Early American Genius) 2009. (Grandes personajes en la historia de los Estados Unidos (Famous People in American History) Ser.). (SPA.). 32p. (gr. 2-3). 47.90 *(978-1-61512-790-0(9),* Editorial Buenas Letras) Rosen Publishing Group, Inc., The.

Goldsmith, Mike. Eureka! The Most Amazing Scientific Discoveries of All Time. 2016. (ENG., Illus.). 96p. (J). (gr. 4-6). pap. 13.95 *(978-0-500-29227-3(2),* 529227) Thames & Hudson.

Goodridge, Catherine. Jane Goodall (Spanish) 2011. (SPA.). (J). pap. 40.00 net. *(978-1-4108-2426-4(8),* A24268) Benchmark Education Co.

Gosman, Gillian. Benjamin Franklin, 1 vol. 2011. (Life Stories Ser.). (ENG., Illus.). 24p. (J). (gr. 3-3). pap. 9.25 *(978-1-4488-2759-6(0),* d96f395d-ae34-43c9-9680-8de06d8c53e6); lib. bdg. 26.27 *(978-1-4488-2585-1(7),* 0ce2f8ab-182f-4f36-8495-052334f7703d) Rosen Publishing Group, Inc., The. (PowerKids Pr.).

—Benjamin Franklin, 1 vol. 2011. (Life Stories / Biografías Ser.). (ENG & SPA., Illus.). 24p. (J). (gr. 3-3). lib. bdg. 26.27 *(978-1-4488-3219-4(5),* bcceb801-fe7d-4a54-bb4d-51e934d4ffff) Rosen Publishing Group, Inc., The.

Gould, Jane H. Benjamin Franklin, 1 vol. 2012. (Jr. Graphic Founding Fathers Ser.). (ENG., Illus.). 24p. (J). (gr. 2-3). pap. 11.60 *(978-1-4488-7990-8(6),* c2607bf3-41ea-46f1-90c5-06cc7b530046); lib. bdg. 28.93 *(978-1-4488-7896-3(9),* 4e9506b1-7138-494a-9292-34a30a1d094c) Rosen Publishing Group, Inc., The. (PowerKids Pr.).

—George Washington Carver, 1 vol. 2013. (Jr. Graphic American Inventors Ser.). (ENG., Illus.). 24p. (J). (gr. 2-3). pap. 11.60 *(978-1-4777-0141-6(9),* e782a57e-6e23-4b3f-a6f4-28864818392e); lib. bdg. 28.93 *(978-1-4777-0078-5(1),* a7abf2c5-2474-43e8-8544-988b45a6fe20) Rosen Publishing Group, Inc., The. (PowerKids Pr.).

Gow, Mary. The Great Thinker: Aristotle & the Foundations of Science, 1 vol. 2010. (Great Minds of Ancient Science & Math Ser.). (ENG.). 128p. (gr. 4-6). 35.93 *(978-0-7660-3121-0(7),* ec09824d-bd32-4caa-b787-f641068f33b5) Enslow Publishing, LLC.

Graham, Amy. Astonishing Ancient World Scientists: Eight Great Brains, 1 vol. 2009. (Great Scientists & Famous Inventors Ser.). (ENG., Illus.). 128p. (gr. 6-7). lib. bdg. 37.27 *(978-1-59845-079-8(4),* 4e5b556f-9694-404a-a25e-3fa0eafcb78a) Enslow Publishing, LLC.

Gray, Leon. Animal Scientists. 2015. (Animal Scientists Ser.). (ENG.). 32p. (gr. 3-4). 139.95 *(978-1-4914-7010-7(0),* Capstone Pr.) Capstone.

Grayson, Robert. Ed Begley, Jr. Living Green. 2009. (Voices for Green Choices Ser.). (ENG., Illus.). 48p. (J). (gr. 5-9). lib. bdg. *(978-0-7787-4667-6(4))* Crabtree Publishing Co.

Great Scientific Questions & the Scientists Who Answered Them: Sets 1 - 2, 18 vols. 2004. (Great Scientific Questions & the Scientists Who Answered Them Ser.). (ENG., Illus.). 112p. (gr. 7-12). lib. bdg. 358.20 *(978-1-4042-0356-3(7),* 692abd0f-e42c-4b52-9e1c-ac7dbd00e263) Rosen Publishing Group, Inc., The.

Greenstein, Elaine. The Goose Man: The Story of Konrad Lorenz. Greenstein, Elaine, illus. 2010. (ENG., Illus.). 32p. (J). (gr. -1-3). 16.00 *(978-0-547-08459-6(5),* 1043412, Clarion Bks.) HarperCollins Pubs.

Gregory, Josh. Hydrologist. 2013. (21st Century Skills Library: Cool STEM Careers Ser.). (ENG., Illus.). 32p. (gr. 4-8). (J). pap. 14.21 *(978-1-62431-025-6(7),* 202457); 32.07 *(978-1-62431-001-0(X),* 202455) Cherry Lake Publishing.

Gregory, Joy. Biologist. 2020. (J). *(978-1-7911-1696-5(5),* AV2 by Weigl) Weigl Pubs., Inc.

Guglielmo, Amy & Tourville, Jacqueline. How to Build a Hug: Temple Grandin & Her Amazing Squeeze Machine. Potter, Giselle, illus. 2018. (ENG.). 48p. (J). (gr. -1-3). 18.99 *(978-1-5344-1097-8(X))* Simon & Schuster Children's Publishing.

Haldy, Emma E. Benjamin Franklin. Bane, Jeff, illus. 2016. (My Early Library: My Itty-Bitty Bio Ser.). (ENG.). 24p. (J). (gr. k-1). 30.64 *(978-1-63470-478-6(9),* 207643) Cherry Lake Publishing.

—Benjamin Franklin SP. Bane, Jeff, illus. 2018. (My Early Library: Mi Mini Biografía (My Itty-Bitty Bio) Ser.). (SPA.). 24p. (J). (gr. k-1). lib. bdg. 30.64 *(978-1-5341-2994-8(4),* 212024) Cherry Lake Publishing.

Hall, Derek, ed. Philosophy, Invention, & Engineering. 2009. (FAYFT: Great Scientists Ser.). 64p. (gr. 4-10). 39.95 *(978-1-933834-48-1(X))* Brown Bear Bks.

Hand, Carol. Jane Goodall, 1 vol. 2014. (Great Science Writers Ser.). (ENG., Illus.). 112p. (J). (gr. 7-7). 38.80 *(978-1-4777-7685-8(0),* 1e07e3f0-5d47-4a5c-a94d-856fb2601132) Rosen Publishing Group, Inc., The.

Hansen, Grace. Jane Goodall: Chimpanzee Expert & Activist, 1 vol. 2015. (History Maker Biographies (Abdo Kids Jumbo) Ser.). (ENG., Illus.). 24p. (J). (gr. -1-2). lib. bdg. 32.79 *(978-1-62970-702-0(3),* 17011, Abdo Kids) ABDO Publishing Co.

—Jane Goodall: Chimpanzee Expert & Activist. 2017. (History Maker Biographies Ser.). (ENG.). 24p. (J). (gr. -1-2). pap. 7.95 *(978-1-4966-1225-0(6),* 134989, Capstone Classroom) Capstone.

Hantula, Richard. Jonas Salk, 1 vol. 2004. (Trailblazers of the Modern World Ser.). (ENG., Illus.). 48p. (J). (gr. 5-8). lib. bdg. 33.67 *(978-0-8368-5100-7(5),* 91b76e1b-e792-41ca-b702-2c41f73c8f78, Gareth Stevens Secondary Library) Stevens, Gareth Publishing LLLP.

Harris, Godfrey & Brockwell, Maurice Walter. The Life & Contributions of Leonardo Da Vinci. 2006. (ENG., Illus.). 58p. (J). pap. *(978-0-935047-60-8(3))* Americas Group, The.

Harris, Laurie Lanzen. Biography for Beginners: Inventors. 2006. (J). lib. bdg. 55.00 *(978-1-931360-27-2(8))* Favorable Impressions.

Haynie, Rachel & Cook, Trahern. First, You Explore: The Story of Young Charles Townes 2014. (Young Palmetto Bks.). (ENG., Illus.). 40p. 29.95 *(978-1-61117-343-7(4),* P231851) Univ. of South Carolina Pr.

Heinrichs, Ann. Nanotechnologist. 2009. (21st Century Skills Library: Cool Science Careers Ser.). (ENG., Illus.). 32p. (gr. 4-8). lib. bdg. 32.07 *(978-1-60279-307-1(7),* 200203) Cherry Lake Publishing.

Heitkamp, Kristina Lyn. Rachel Carson: Pioneering Environmental Activist. 2017. (Spotlight on Civic Courage: Heroes of Conscience Ser.). (Illus.). 48p. (J). (gr. 10-15). 70.50 *(978-1-5383-8075-8(7));* (ENG., (gr. 6-6). pap. 12.75 *(978-1-5383-8074-1(9),* 119b7370-d960-44cd-9967-4d11a6da74e4) Rosen Publishing Group, Inc., The.

Heller, Esther Susan. Menorah under the Sea. Ginsburg, David, photos by. 2009. (Hanukkah Ser.). (Illus.). 32p. (J). (gr. k-2). 17.95 *(978-0-8225-7386-9(5),* Kar-Ben Publishing) Lerner Publishing Group.

Heos, Bridget. Stronger Than Steel: Spider Silk DNA & the Quest for Better Bulletproof Vests, Sutures, & Parachute Rope. Comins, Andy, illus. 2013. (Scientists in the Field Ser.). (ENG.). 80p. (J). (gr. 5-7). 18.99 *(978-0-547-68126-9(7),* 1475667, Clarion Bks.) HarperCollins Pubs.

Hesieden, Michael. Benjamin Franklin: American Diplomat, 1 vol. 2015. (Spotlight on American History Ser.). (ENG., Illus.). 24p. (J). (gr. 4-6). pap. 11.00 *(978-1-4994-1782-1(9),* 9e07a93f-8acc-4758-91cb-ca59c6005d7f, PowerKids Pr.) Rosen Publishing Group, Inc., The.

Hilliam, Rachel. Galileo Galilei: Father of Modern Science. 2009. (Rulers, Scholars, & Artists of the Renaissance Ser.). 112p. (gr. 5-8). 66.50 *(978-1-60852-941-4(X),* Rosen Reference) Rosen Publishing Group, Inc., The.

Hirsch, Rebecca E. Climate Scientists at Work. 2018. (Taking Earth's Temperature Ser.). (ENG., Illus.). 48p. (gr. 4-8). pap. 10.95 *(978-1-64156-578-3(0),* 9781641565783) Rourke Educational Media.

Holmes, Parker. Oceanographers, 1 vol., 1. 2015. (Out of the Lab: Extreme Jobs in Science Ser.). (ENG., Illus.). 32p. (J). (gr. 4-5). pap. 11.00 *(978-1-5081-4517-2(2),* ecf50f7a-d5ae-42c1-81ad-c02d34f36257, PowerKids Pr.) Rosen Publishing Group, Inc., The.

Holub, Joan. This Little Scientist: A Discovery Primer. Roode, Daniel, illus. 2018. (This Little Ser.). (ENG.). 26p. (J). (gr. -1-k). bds. 7.99 *(978-1-5344-0108-2(3),* Little Simon) Little Simon.

Hoppa, Jocelyn. Isaac Asimov: Science Fiction Trailblazer, 1 vol. 2007. (Authors Teens Love Ser.). (ENG., Illus.). 104p. (gr. 6-7). lib. bdg. 35.93 *(978-0-7660-2961-3(1),* 6b5ddc4b-6da2-42a2-a0ab-49fd81ab8d63) Enslow Publishing, LLC.

Horvath, Joan. What Scientists Actually Do. 2008. (Illus.). 208p. (YA). pap. 16.95 *(978-1-933277-08-0(4))* Stargazer Publishing Co.

Houran, Lori Haskins. How to Spy on a Shark. Marquez, Francisca, illus. 2019. (ENG.). 24p. (J). (-3). pap. 7.99 *(978-0-8075-3406-9(4),* 807534064) Whitman, Albert & Co.

Housel, Debra J. Pioneering Ecologists, 1 vol. rev. ed. 2007. (Science: Informational Text Ser.). (ENG.). 32p. (J). (gr. 3-6). pap. 12.99 *(978-0-7439-0592-3(X))* Teacher Created Materials, Inc.

Hudak, Heather C. Sam J. Porcello: Oreo Innovator. 2017. (Food Dudes Set 3 Ser.). (ENG., Illus.). 32p. (J). (gr. 3-6). lib. bdg. 32.79 *(978-1-5321-1084-9(7),* 25744, Checkerboard Library) ABDO Publishing Co.

Hunter, Dru. How Do We Apply Science? 2015. (Think Like a Scientist Ser.). (ENG., Illus.). 48p. (J). (gr. 4-7). *(978-1-60818-592-4(3),* 21060, Creative Education) Creative Co., The.

—How Does It Work? (Think Like a Scientist Ser.). (ENG.). 48p. (J). (gr. 4-7). 2016. pap. 12.00 *(978-1-62832-198-2(9),* 21064, Creative Paperbacks) 2015. (Illus.). *(978-1-60818-593-1(1),* 21063, Creative Education) Creative Co., The.

—What Is Out There? 2015. (Think Like a Scientist Ser.). (ENG., Illus.). 48p. (J). (gr. 4-7). *(978-1-60818-594-8(X),* 21066, Creative Education) Creative Co., The.

—What Is the Reason? 2015. (Think Like a Scientist Ser.). (ENG., Illus.). 48p. (J). (gr. 4-7). *(978-1-60818-595-5(8),* 21069, Creative Education) Creative Co., The.

—Where Do We Look for Life? (Think Like a Scientist Ser.). (ENG.). 48p. (J). (gr. 4-7). 2016. pap. 12.00 *(978-1-62832-201-9(2),* 21073, Creative Paperbacks) 2015. (Illus.). *(978-1-60818-596-2(6),* 21072, Creative Education) Creative Co., The.

Ignotofsky, Rachel. Women in Science: 50 Fearless Pioneers Who Changed the World. 2016. (Women in Science Ser.). (Illus.). 128p. (YA). (gr. 5-12). 16.99 *(978-1-60774-976-9(9),* Ten Speed Pr.) Potter/Ten Speed/Harmony/Rodale.

—Women in Science: 100 Postcards. 2017. (Women in Science Ser.). (Illus.). 100p. 20.00 *(978-1-60774-981-3(5),* Clarkson Potter) Potter/Ten Speed/Harmony/Rodale.

Indovino, Shaina. Women in Anthropology. Lee-Karlon, Ann, ed. 2013. (Major Women in Science Ser.: 10). 64p. (J). (gr. 7-18). 22.95 *(978-1-4222-2924-8(6))* Mason Crest.

—Women in Information Technology. Lee-Karlon, Ann, ed. 2013. (Major Women in Science Ser.: 10). 64p. (J). (gr. 7-18). 22.95 *(978-1-4222-2928-6(9))* Mason Crest.

Ingram, Scott. Nicolaus Copernicus: Father of Modern Astronomy. 2004. (Illus.). 64p. (J). 26.20 *(978-1-56711-489-8(X),* Blackbirch Pr., Inc.) Cengage Gale.

Isaac Newton: Organizing the Universe. 2004. (Great Scientists Ser.). (Illus.). 144p. (YA). (gr. 6-12). 26.95 *(978-1-931798-01-3(X))* Reynolds, Morgan Inc.

Isle, Mick. Aristotle: Pioneering Philosopher & Founder of the Lyceum. 2009. (Library of Greek Philosophers Ser.). 112p. (gr. 6-6). 66.50 *(978-1-60853-658-0(0),* Rosen Reference) Rosen Publishing Group, Inc., The.

Iyer, Rani & Smibert, Angie. Curious Scientists. 2017. (Curious Scientists Ser.). (ENG., Illus.). 24p. (J). (gr. 1-3). 111.96 *(978-1-5157-6910-1(0),* 26599, Capstone Pr.) Capstone.

Jackson, Donna M. The Bug Scientists. 2004. (Illus.). 48p. (J). lib. bdg. 13.60 *(978-0-7569-5192-4(5))* Perfection Learning Corp.

Jackson, Donna M. & O'Connell, Caitlin. The Elephant Scientist. 2016. (Scientists in the Field Ser.). lib. bdg. 20.85 *(978-0-606-37983-0(5))* Turtleback.

James, Emily. Great Scientists & Inventors. 2017. (Great Scientists & Inventors Ser.). (ENG.). 24p. (J). (gr. -1-2). 163.92 *(978-1-5157-3910-4(4),* 25530, Capstone Pr.) Capstone.

—Rachel Carson. 2017. (Great Scientists & Inventors Ser.). (ENG., Illus.). 24p. (J). (gr. -1-2). lib. bdg. 27.32 *(978-1-5157-3881-7(7),* 133785, Capstone Pr.) Capstone.

James, Wayan. Scientists Look for Patterns & Rules, 1 vol. 2016. (Rosen REAL Readers: STEM & STEAM Collection). (ENG.). 12p. (gr. k-1). pap. 6.33 *(978-1-5081-2431-3(0),* b1f2a018-2ca2-4b2c-b484-4a9d9223fa2a, Rosen Classroom) Rosen Publishing Group, Inc., The.

Jankowski, Connie. Jane Goodall: Animal Scientist & Friend, 1 vol. rev. ed. 2007. (Science: Informational Text Ser.). (ENG.). 32p. (gr. 3-6). pap. 12.99 *(978-0-7439-0594-7(6))* Teacher Created Materials, Inc.

—Pioneers of Light & Sound, 1 vol. rev. ed. 2007. (Science: Informational Text Ser.). (ENG.). 32p. (gr. 3-6). pap. 12.99 *(978-0-7439-0580-0(6))* Teacher Created Materials, Inc.

Jeffrey, Gary. Hurricane Hunters & Tornado Chasers, 1 vol. Garofalo, Gianluca, illus. 2008. (Graphic Careers Ser.). (ENG.). 48p. (gr. 5-5). per. 14.05 *(978-1-4042-1459-0(3),* d963ad23-fe8f-4c78-8a53-dcb6c4522b93); (YA). lib. bdg. 37.13 *(978-1-4042-1458-3(5),* 3486897e-4cf0-4e1a-83f8-3b59a796e2cf) Rosen Publishing Group, Inc., The.

Jenner, Caryn. DK Readers L4: Thomas Edison: the Great Inventor. 2007. (DK Readers Level 4 Ser.). (ENG.). 48p. (J). (gr. 3-7). pap. 4.99 *(978-0-7566-2946-5(2),* DK Children) Dorling Kindersley Publishing, Inc.

Jones, Grace. People Who Changed the World: Science & Arts. 2018. (Ideas, Inventions, & Innovators Ser.). (Illus.). 32p. (J). (gr. 4-4). *(978-0-7787-5828-0(1))* Crabtree Publishing Co.

Kamberg, Mary-Lane. Stephen Hawking, 1 vol. 2014. (Great Science Writers Ser.). (ENG., Illus.). 112p. (J). (gr. 7-7). 38.80 (978-1-4777-7683-4(4), e79ad039-6fbb-4d47-acac-1d756ff4ae2f) Rosen Publishing Group, Inc., The.

Katz, Alan. Awesome Achievers in Science: Super & Strange Facts about 12 Almost Famous History Makers. Judge, Chris, illus. 2019. (Awesome Achievers Ser.: 2). (ENG.). 112p. (J). (gr. 3-7). pap. 11.99 (978-0-7624-6338-1(4), Running Pr. Kids) Running Pr.

Kawa, Katie. Forensic Detectives, 1 vol., 1. 2015. (Out of the Lab: Extreme Jobs in Science Ser.). (ENG., Illus.). 32p. (J). (gr. 4-5). pap. 11.00 (978-1-5081-4521-9(0), 1fe05cc6-ed3c-477d-b3b8-fdb11bb9a2b9, PowerKids Pr.) Rosen Publishing Group, Inc., The.

Kelly, Jack. Benjamin Franklin. Tafalla, Ortiz, illus. 2005. (Heroes of America Ser.). 239p. (gr. 3-8). 27.07 (978-1-59679-257-9(4), Abdo & Daughters) ABDO Publishing Co.

Kennon, Caroline. Leonardo Da Vinci in His Own Words, 1 vol. 2015. (Eyewitness to History Ser.). (ENG.). 32p. (J). (gr. 4-5). pap. 11.50 (978-1-4824-4074-4(1), d1c607ef-02d8-4160-a02b-5560c7538834) Stevens, Gareth Publishing LLLP.

Kepnes, Caroline. Stephen Crane. 2004. (Classic Storytellers Ser.). (Illus.). 48p. (J). (gr. 4-8). lib. bdg. 29.95 (978-1-58415-272-9(9)) Mitchell Lane Pubs.

Keppeler, Jill. Be an Anthropologist, 1 vol. 2018. (Be a Scientist! Ser.). (ENG.). 32p. (gr. 3-4). 28.27 (978-1-5382-3000-8(3), 45f3bc96-d835-46a4-b031-37365d35e21f) Stevens, Gareth Publishing LLLP.

Koontz, Robin Michal. Marine Biologists. 2015. (Scientists in the Field Ser.). (ENG.). 48p. (gr. 3-6). 35.64 (978-1-63430-408-5(X), 9781634304085) Rourke Educational Media.

Kortemeier, Todd. Unsung Heroes of Science. 2017. (Unsung Heroes Ser.). (ENG., Illus.). 32p. (J). (gr. 3-6). 32.80 (978-1-63235-309-2(1), 11829, 12-Story Library) Bookstaves, LLC.

Kraft Rector, Rebecca. Alan Turing, 1 vol., 1. 2015. (Tech Pioneers Ser.). (ENG.). 112p. (J). (gr. 7-7). 38.80 (978-1-4994-6280-7(8), 3eec5ae5-0253-486e-bf62-5554f45c9c4c, Rosen Young Adult) Rosen Publishing Group, Inc., The.

Krensky, Stephen & Dorling Kindersley Publishing Staff. Benjamin Franklin. 2008. (DK Biography Ser.). (ENG., Illus.). 128p. (J). (gr. 5-8). 17.44 (978-0-7566-3529-9(2)) Dorling Kindersley Publishing, Inc.

Krull, Kathleen. Benjamin Franklin. Kulikov, Boris, illus. 2014. (Giants of Science Ser.). 128p. (J). (gr. 3-7). pap. 7.99 (978-0-14-751178-2(X), Puffin Books) Penguin Young Readers Group.

—Leonardo Da Vinci. Kulikov, Boris, illus. 2008. (Giants of Science Ser.). 128p. (J). (gr. 3-7). 7.99 (978-0-14-240821-6(2), Puffin Books) Penguin Young Readers Group.

—Lives of the Scientists: Experiments, Explosions (and What the Neighbors Thought) Hewitt, Kathryn, illus. (Lives Of ... Ser.). (ENG.). 96p. (J). (gr. 5-7). 2016. 8.99 (978-0-544-81087-7(2), 1641669) 2013. 20.99 (978-0-15-205909-5(1), 1197743) HarperCollins Pubs. (Clarion Bks.).

Kumar Terry, Stuart. The Science That Changed the World: Remarkable Discoveries & Breakthroughs. 2019. (ENG.). 48p. (J). 14.99 (978-1-921580-48-2(8)) New Holland Pubs. Pty, Ltd. AUS. Dist: Independent Pubs. Group.

Kurtz, Jane. Mister Bones: Dinosaur Hunter (Ready-To-Read Level 1) Haverfield, Mary, illus. 2004. (Ready-To-Read Ser.). (ENG.). 32p. (J). (gr. -1-1). pap. 4.99 (978-0-689-85960-1(0), Simon Spotlight) Simon Spotlight.

Lace, William W. Benjamin Franklin. 2010. (ENG., Illus.). 120p. (gr. 5-8). 35.00 (978-1-60413-737-8(1), P210466, Facts On File) Infobase Holdings, Inc.

Lachner, Elizabeth, ed. Top 101 Scientists, 1 vol. 2016. (People You Should Know Ser.). (ENG., Illus.). 184p. (J). (gr. 8-8). lib. bdg. 38.84 (978-1-68048-510-3(5), e680b7c6-7f82-4698-8db4-de77e580e303) Rosen Publishing Group, Inc., The.

Lantier, Patricia. Rachel Carson: Fighting Pesticides & Other Chemical Pollutants. 2009. (Voices for Green Choices Ser.). (ENG., Illus.). 48p. (J). (gr. 5-9). lib. bdg. (978-0-7787-4663-8(1)) Crabtree Publishing Co.

Larson, Kirsten. Tools of the Trade: Using Scientific Equipment. 2016. (Let's Explore Science Ser.). (ENG.). 48p. (gr. 5-8). 35.64 (978-1-68191-400-8(X), 9781681914008) Rourke Educational Media.

Latta, Sara L. Ice Scientist: Careers in the Frozen Antarctic, 1 vol. 2009. (Wild Science Careers Ser.). (ENG., Illus.). 128p. (gr. 5-6). lib. bdg. 35.93 (978-0-7660-3048-0(2), bfc92540-f7a2-456a-9694-7c881999ee5b) Enslow Publishing, LLC.

—Polar Scientists: Studying the Antarctic, 1 vol. 2015. (Extreme Science Careers Ser.). (ENG., Illus.). 128p. (gr. 7-7). 38.93 (978-0-7660-6966-4(4), 6d3e77f8-911a-4630-9914-94b78d91c8d7) Enslow Publishing, LLC.

—Who Fixed Babies' Hearts? Vivien Thomas, 1 vol. 2012. (I Like Inventors! Ser.). (ENG., Illus.). 24p. (gr. k-2). pap. 10.35 (978-1-4644-0130-5(6), c0cf9514-8617-4cbf-8a20-7013f980f543, Enslow Elementary) Enslow Publishing, LLC.

Lawlor, Laurie. Rachel Carson & Her Book That Changed the World. Beingessner, Laura, illus. 2014. (ENG.). 32p. (J). (gr. 1-4). 7.99 (978-0-8234-3193-9(2)) Holiday Hse., Inc.

Leaders of the Scientific Revolution, 16 vols. 2017. (Leaders of the Scientific Revolution Ser.). (ENG.). 112p. (gr. 8-8). 310.40 (978-1-4994-6634-8(X), 7e7b7fc5-3cb2-4533-be92-3bab2a5625b9, Rosen Young Adult) Rosen Publishing Group, Inc., The.

Leavitt, Amie Jane. Becoming a Software Engineer, 1 vol. 2017. (Tech Track: Building Your Career in IT Ser.). (ENG., Illus.). 80p. (J). (gr. 7-7). 37.47 (978-1-5081-7554-4(3), a5147794-2621-4c05-9921-85cc03e42871, Rosen Young Adult) Rosen Publishing Group, Inc., The.

Lee, Fekany Kimberly. Cell Scientists: Discovering How Cells Work, 1 vol. rev. ed. 2007. (Science: Informational Text Ser.). (ENG.). 32p. (gr. 3-6). pap. 12.99 (978-0-7439-0584-8(9)) Teacher Created Materials, Inc.

Lee, Sally. Mad Scientists: The Not-So-Crazy Work of Amazing Scientists, 1 vol. 2014. (Scary Science Ser.). (ENG., Illus.). 32p. (J). (gr. 3-6). lib. bdg. 27.99 (978-1-4765-3928-7(6), 123926) Capstone.

Levine, Ellen S. Up Close: Rachel Carson. 2008. (Up Close Ser.). (ENG., Illus.). 224p. (YA). (gr. 7-18). 7.99 (978-0-14-241046-2(2), Puffin Books) Penguin Young Readers Group.

Levit, Joe. Let's Explore Science. 2018. (Bumba Books (r) — a First Look at STEM Ser.). (ENG., Illus.). 24p. (J). (gr. -1-1). pap. 8.99 (978-1-5415-2701-0(1), 129407c9-853a-4bc9-bb0c-095d0018ed81) Lerner Publishing Group.

Liebman, Dan & Liebman, Dan. I Want to Be a Scientist. 2016. (I Want to Be Ser.). (ENG., Illus.). 24p. (J). (gr. -1-2). pap. 3.99 (978-1-77085-789-6(3), 1d95a503-624a-456e-a25a-41cca03ee7fa) Firefly Bks., Ltd.

—Quiero Ser Cientifico. 2016. (Quiero Ser.). (SPA., Illus.). 24p. (J). (gr. -1-2). pap. 6.99 (978-1-77085-865-7(2), 22f7745a-bb3e-4663-b7f7-d6c15d57e546) Firefly Bks., Ltd.

Llanas, Sheila. Jonas Salk: Medical Innovator & Polio Vaccine Developer, 1 vol. 2013. (Essential Lives Set 8 Ser.). (ENG., Illus.). 112p. (YA). (gr. 6-12). lib. bdg. 41.36 (978-1-61783-896-5(9), 6769, Essential Library) ABDO Publishing Co.

Lo Bosco, Maryellen. Famous Immigrant Scientists, 1 vol. 2017. (Making America Great: Immigrant Success Stories Ser.). (ENG.). 112p. (gr. 7-7). 38.93 (978-0-7660-9244-0(5), ae4ecab6-755a-4647-b5f3-8a4a24233a23); pap. 20.95 (978-0-7660-9590-8(8), 55315889-46db-4469-8d5c-01ac41cf5b35) Enslow Publishing, LLC.

Loh-Hagan, Virginia. Rosalyn Sussman Yalow. Bane, Jeff, illus. 2018. (Mi Mini Biografía (My Itty-Bitty Bio): My Early Library). (ENG.). 24p. (J). (gr. k-1). pap. 12.79 (978-1-5341-0813-4(0), 210616); lib. bdg. 30.64 (978-1-5341-0714-4(2), 210615) Cherry Lake Publishing.

Lourie, Peter. The Manatee Scientists: Saving Vulnerable Species. 2016. (Scientists in the Field Ser.). (ENG., Illus.). 80p. (J). (gr. 5-7). pap. 10.99 (978-0-544-22529-9(5), 1563372, Clarion Bks.) HarperCollins Pubs.

—The Manatee Scientists: The Science of Saving the Vulnerable. 2016. (Scientists in the Field Ser.). lib. bdg. 20.85 (978-0-606-37985-4(1)) Turtleback.

MacBain, Jennifer. Gertrude Elion: Nobel Prize Winner in Physiology & Medicine. (Women Hall of Famers in Mathematics & Science Ser.). 112p. (gr. 5-8). 2009. 63.90 (978-1-60854-811-8(2)) 2003. (ENG., Illus.). (YA). lib. bdg. 39.80 (978-0-8239-3876-6(X), d9dba5e4-16b2-44bb-b119-f6cd5270e474) Rosen Publishing Group, Inc., The. (Rosen Reference).

Mahoney, Emily. Antarctic Researchers, 1 vol., 1. 2015. (Out of the Lab: Extreme Jobs in Science Ser.). (ENG., Illus.). 32p. (J). (gr. 4-5). pap. 11.00 (978-1-5081-4505-9(9), 9d55e9b1-7808-480a-b4ec-1a95833457df, PowerKids Pr.) Rosen Publishing Group, Inc., The.

Malnor, Bruce & Malnor, Carol L. Earth Heroes: Champions of the Wilderness, 1 vol. Hovemann, Anisa Claire, illus. 2011. (ENG.). 143p. (J). (gr. 5-8). pap. 12.95 (978-1-58469-116-7(6), Dawn Pubns.) Sourcebooks, Inc.

Maloof, Torrey. Analyze It!, 1 vol. rev. ed. 2014. (Science: Informational Text Ser.). (ENG.). 32p. (gr. 2-3). pap. 10.99 (978-1-4807-4613-8(4)) Teacher Created Materials, Inc.

Mara, Wil. Benjamin Franklin. (Rookie Biographies(tm) Ser.). (Illus.). (J). 2014. (ENG.). 32p. lib. bdg. 25.00 (978-0-531-20558-7(4)) 2007. 31p. (gr. 1-2). pap. 4.95 (978-0-531-12591-5(2), Children's Pr.) Scholastic Library Publishing.

—Benjamin Franklin (Rookie Biographies) 2014. (Rookie Biographies Ser.). (ENG., Illus.). 32p. (J). (gr. 1-2). pap. 5.95 (978-0-531-21201-1(7), Children's Pr.) Scholastic Library Publishing.

Marsh, Carole. Marie Curie, Nobel Prize Winning Scientist. 2004. 12p. (gr. k-4). 2.95 (978-0-635-02374-2(1)) Gallopade International.

Martin, Jacqueline Briggs. Snowflake Bentley. 2004. (Illus.). (J). (gr. -1-3). spiral bd. (978-0-616-01714-2(6)) Canadian National Institute for the Blind/Institut National Canadien pour les Aveugles.

—Snowflake Bentley: A Caldecott Award Winner. Azarian, Mary, illus. 2009. (ENG.). 32p. (J). (gr. -1-3). pap. 8.99 (978-0-547-24829-5(6), 1100744, Clarion Bks.) HarperCollins Pubs.

Mason, Paul. Barmy Biogs: Bonkers Boffins, Inventors & Other Eccentric Eggheads. 2017. (Barmy Biogs Ser.). (ENG., Illus.). 96p. (J). (gr. 4-6). pap. 7.99 (978-0-7502-8391-5(2), Wayland) Hachette Children's Group GBR. Dist: Hachette Bk. Group.

Maxwell, Cassandre. Fur, Fins, & Feathers: Abraham Dee Bartlett & the Invention of the Modern Zoo. 2015. (ENG., Illus.). 34p. (J). 17.00 (978-0-8028-5432-2(X), Eerdmans Bks For Young Readers) Eerdmans, William B. Publishing Co.

Maynard, Charles W. John Wesley Powell: Soldier, Scientist, & Explorer. 2009. (Famous Explorers of the American West Ser.). 24p. (gr. 3-4). 42.50 (978-1-61512-505-0(1), PowerKids Pr.) Rosen Publishing Group, Inc., The.

McCully, Emily Arnold. Caroline's Comets: A True Story. 2017. (ENG.). 40p. (J). (gr. 1-4). 16.95 (978-0-8234-3664-4(0)) Holiday Hse., Inc.

McCurdy, Michael, illus. So Said Ben. 2007. (ENG.). 32p. (J). (gr. 1-3). 17.95 (978-1-56846-147-2(X), 22702, Creative Editions) Creative Co., The.

McDaniel, Jequita Potts. Mardy Murie Did! Grandmother of Conservation. Van Zyle, Jon, illus. 2011. (J). (978-1-58979-525-9(3)) Taylor Trade Publishing.

McDaniel, Jequite Po & Van Zyle, Jon. Mardi Murie Did! Grandmother of Conservation. 2011. (ENG., Illus.). 32p. (J). (gr. -1-2). 15.95 (978-1-58979-565-5(2)) Taylor Trade Publishing.

McDowell, Pamela. Benjamin Franklin. 2013. (978-1-62127-307-3(5)); pap. (978-1-62127-313-4(X)) Weigl Pubs., Inc.

McGowan, Joseph. Al Gore, 1 vol. 2009. (People We Should Know (Second Series) Ser.). (ENG.). 48p. (J). (gr. 3-5). pap. 11.50 (978-1-4339-2146-9(4), d085d240-5610-4f6c-a156-448650d8b212); lib. bdg. 33.67 (978-1-4339-1947-3(8), 30467b93-158a-4097-996b-f59ce266e739) Stevens, Gareth Publishing LLLP. (Gareth Stevens Learning Library).

McLeese, Don. Benjamin Franklin. 2005. (Heroes of the American Revolution Ser.). (Illus.). 32p. (gr. 2-5). 19.95 (978-1-59515-216-9(4)) Rourke Educational Media.

McNeil, Niki, et al. HOCPP 1107 Steve Irwin. 2006. spiral bd. 21.00 (978-1-60308-107-8(0)) In the Hands of a Child.

Medina, Nico & Putra, Dede. Who Was Jacques Cousteau? 2015. (Who Was... ? Ser.). lib. bdg. 16.00 (978-0-606-36599-4(0)) Turtleback.

Meltzer, Brad. I Am Jane Goodall. Eliopoulos, Christopher, illus. 2016. (Ordinary People Change the World Ser.). 32p. (J). (gr. k-4). 16.99 (978-0-525-42849-7(6), Dial Bks) Penguin Young Readers Group.

Merrell Foster, Leila. Benjamin Franklin: Statesman & Inventor, 1 vol. 2014. (Legendary American Biographies Ser.). (ENG.). 96p. (gr. 6-6). 29.60 (978-0-7660-6445-4(X), 6f71ffbe-8abd-4301-95fb-7c002da289d3) Enslow Publishing, LLC.

Miller, Brandon Marie. Benjamin Franklin, American Genius: His Life & Ideas with 21 Activities. 2009. (For Kids Ser.: 28). (ENG., Illus.). 144p. (J). (gr. 4-7). pap. 18.99 (978-1-55652-757-9(8)) Chicago Review Pr., Inc.

Mills, Andrea. 100 Scientists Who Made History. 2018. (DK 100 Things That Made History Ser.). (ENG., Illus.). 128p. (J). (gr. 3-7). 17.99 (978-1-4654-6889-5(7), DK Children) Dorling Kindersley Publishing, Inc.

Montgomery, Sy. The Great White Shark Scientist. 2016. (Scientists in the Field Ser.). (ENG., Illus.). 80p. (J). (gr. 5-7). 18.99 (978-0-544-35298-8(X), 1586364, Clarion Bks.) HarperCollins Pubs.

—The Quest for the Tree Kangaroo: An Expedition to the Cloud Forest of New Guinea. Bishop, Nic, photos by. 2009. (Scientists in the Field Ser.). (ENG., Illus.). 80p. (J). (gr. 5-7). pap. 10.99 (978-0-547-24892-9(X), 1100904, Clarion Bks.) HarperCollins Pubs.

Morrison, Heather S. Inventors of Computer Technology, 1 vol. 2015. (Designing Engineering Solutions Ser.). (ENG.). 144p. (YA). (gr. 8-8). lib. bdg. 44.50 (978-1-5026-0654-9(2), 5e8869e4-5338-4d85-8915-3a401916ae1a) Cavendish Square Publishing LLC.

Mosca, Julia Finley. The Girl Who Thought in Pictures: The Story of Dr. Temple Grandin. Rieley, Daniel, illus. 2017. (Amazing Scientists Ser.: 1). 40p. (J). (gr. k-5). 17.99 (978-1-943147-30-4(2), 5ae02658-cb15-4cd2-a907-670448522514) Innovation Pr., The.

Mould, Steve. How to Be a Scientist. 2017. (Careers for Kids Ser.). (ENG., Illus.). 144p. (J). (gr. 2-4). 19.99 (978-1-4654-6121-6(3), DK Children) Dorling Kindersley Publishing, Inc.

Mullins, Matt. Geoscientist. 2013. (21st Century Skills Library: Cool STEM Careers Ser.). (ENG.). 32p. (gr. 4-8). (J). pap. 14.21 (978-1-62431-028-7(1), 202469); (Illus.). 32.07 (978-1-62431-004-1(4), 202467) Cherry Lake Publishing.

Nelson, Maria. The Life of Ben Franklin, 1 vol. 2012. (Famous Lives Ser.). (ENG.). 24p. (J). (gr. 1-2). pap. 9.15 (978-1-4339-6347-6(7), 26557dd4-7694-49cb-9a64-92978e1c931d); lib. bdg. 25.27 (978-1-4339-6345-2(0), 46c95f44-0445-407d-a54d-e09def9de09c) Stevens, Gareth Publishing LLLP.

—The Life of Ben Franklin / la Vida de Benjamín Franklin, 1 vol. 2012. (Famous Lives / Vidas Extraordinarias Ser.). (ENG & SPA., Illus.). 24p. (J). (gr. 1-2). 25.27 (978-1-4339-6653-8(0), 9e202cf7-e254-4a33-8484-e8019e733ad8) Stevens, Gareth Publishing LLLP.

Newman, Patricia. Zoo Scientists to the Rescue. Crawley, Annie, photos by. 2017. (ENG., Illus.). 64p. (J). (gr. 4-8). lib. bdg. 33.32 (978-1-5124-1571-1(5), 85e5e5e1-e4d4-40b1-a39a-cfa8a6664d14, Millbrook Pr.) Lerner Publishing Group.

Nichols, Catherine. Leonardo Da Vinci, 1 vol. 2005. (Primary Source Library of Famous Artists Ser.). (ENG., Illus.). 32p. (J). (gr. 3-4). lib. bdg. 27.60 (978-1-4042-2762-0(8), 75695994-479b-4ca3-a08b-bef4d09cabba, PowerKids Pr.) Rosen Publishing Group, Inc., The.

—Leonardo da Vinci. 2009. (Primary Source Library of Famous Artists Ser.). 32p. (gr. 3-4). 42.50 (978-1-60854-101-0(0), PowerKids Pr.) Rosen Publishing Group, Inc., The.

Norlander, Britt. I've Discovered Electricity!, 1 vol. 2009. (Eureka! Ser.). (ENG.). 32p. (gr. 4-4). lib. bdg. 31.21 (978-0-7614-3195-4(0), 4213b5c7-4b77-48e2-83c0-17b425e8a501) Cavendish Square Publishing LLC.

Northrup, Mary. Pioneering American Computer Geniuses, 1 vol. 2013. (Inspiring Collective Biographies Ser.). (ENG.). 112p. (gr. 5-6). lib. bdg. 35.93 (978-0-7660-4167-7(0), 911670fd-c29a-469a-9388-fba3031b760c) Enslow Publishing, LLC.

Novelli, Luca. Leonardo Da Vinci & the Pen That Drew the Future. 2017. (Flashes of Genius Ser.). (ENG., Illus.). 112p. (J). (gr. 3). pap. 9.99 (978-1-61373-869-6(2)) Chicago Review Pr., Inc.

O'Connell, Caitlin & Jackson, Donna M. The Elephant Scientist. Rodwell, Timothy, illus. 2016. (Scientists in the Field Ser.). (ENG.). 80p. (J). (gr. 5-7). 11.99 (978-0-544-66830-0(8), 1625422, Clarion Bks.) HarperCollins Pubs.

O'Donnell, Kerri. Galileo: Man of Science. 2009. (Reading Room Collection 2 Ser.). 24p. (gr. 3-4). 42.50 (978-1-60851-964-4(3), PowerKids Pr.) Rosen Publishing Group, Inc., The.

Olsen, Alana. A Day at Work with a Molecular Biologist, 1 vol., 1. 2015. (Super STEM Careers Ser.). (ENG., Illus.). 24p. (J). (gr. 3-4). pap. 9.25 (978-1-5081-4410-6(9), 667bb165-e2be-4ffd-b517-0562e7c691fa, PowerKids Pr.) Rosen Publishing Group, Inc., The.

Orozco, Julia & Mulfinger, George. Christian Men of Science. 2004. (Illus.). 304p. (YA). pap. 14.99 (978-1-932307-22-1(2), Ambassador-Emerald, International) Emerald Hse. Group, Inc.

Osborne, Mary Pope & Boyce, Natalie Pope. Benjamin Franklin: A Nonfiction Companion to Magic Tree House #32: to the Future, Ben Franklin! 2019. (Magic Tree House (R) Fact Tracker Ser.: 41). (Illus.). 128p. (J). (gr. 2-5). pap. 6.99 (978-1-9848-9317-8(3), Random Hse. Bks. for Young Readers) Random Hse. Children's Bks.

Owen, Ruth. Marine Biologists. 2013. (Out of the Lab: Extreme Jobs in Science Ser.). 32p. (J). (gr. 3-6). pap. 60.00 (978-1-4777-1386-0(7)); (ENG.). (gr. 4-5). pap. 11.00 (978-1-4777-1381-5(6), 5a9acbb8-9c54-4208-8a68-65ab5d187441); (ENG.). (gr. 4-5). lib. bdg. 28.93 (978-1-4777-1291-7(7), 99da8f07-6bd6-4951-b3c1-1ad4c78d0211) Rosen Publishing Group, Inc., The. (PowerKids Pr.).

Owens, L. L. Benjamin Franklin, 1 vol. 2007. (Essential Lives Set 1 Ser.). (ENG., Illus.). 112p. (YA). (gr. 6-12). lib. bdg. 41.36 (978-1-59928-840-6(0), 6633, Essential Library) ABDO Publishing Co.

Patent, Dorothy Hinshaw. Call of the Osprey. Muñoz, William, illus. 2015. (Scientists in the Field Ser.). (ENG.). 80p. (J). (gr. 5-7). 18.99 (978-0-544-23268-6(2), 1564093, Clarion Bks.) HarperCollins Pubs.

Payment, Simone. Biologists at Work, 1 vol. 2017. (Scientists at Work Ser.). (ENG., Illus.). 32p. (J). (gr. 2-3). pap. 13.90 (978-1-68048-749-7(3), 052b5448-cbd6-40d8-97b1-40e81480a9d3, Britannica Educational Publishing) Rosen Publishing Group, Inc., The.

Peters, Marilee. The Man Who Knew Everything: The Strange Life of Athanasius Kircher. Bikadoroff, Roxanna, illus. 2017. (ENG.). 60p. (J). (gr. 5-8). 19.95 (978-1-55451-974-3(8)); pap. 12.95 (978-1-55451-973-6(X)) Annick Pr., Ltd. CAN. Dist: Publishers Group West (PGW).

Peterson, Judy Monroe. Underwater Explorers: Marine Biologists. (Extreme Scientists Ser.). 24p. (gr. 2-3). 2009. 42.50 (978-1-61512-453-4(5), PowerKids Pr.) 2008. (ENG., Illus.). (YA). lib. bdg. 26.27 (978-1-4042-4526-6(X), e5708052-f6ba-4088-a012-c2f3a5d06e0d) Rosen Publishing Group, Inc., The.

Pezzi, Bryan. David Suzuki. 2010. (Illus.). 24p. (978-1-77071-595-0(9)); pap. (978-1-77071-601-8(7)) Weigl Educational Pubs. Ltd.

Phillips, Cynthia & Priwer, Shana. 101 Things You Didn't Know about Da Vinci: Inventions, Intrigue, & Unfinished Works. 2018. (101 Things Ser.). (ENG., Illus.). 256p. pap. 14.99 (978-1-5072-0659-1(3)) Adams Media Corp.

Phillips, Dee. Rachel Carson: Environmental Pioneer, 1 vol. 2013. (Rosen Readers Ser.). (ENG.). 24p. (J). (gr. 3-3). pap. 8.25 (978-1-4777-2465-1(6), bad5ad21-acb4-443f-ba02-4520cf175b2d, Rosen Classroom) Rosen Publishing Group, Inc., The.

Phillips, Dorian. Rachel Carson: Environmental Pioneer. 2013. (Rosen Readers Ser.). (ENG.). 24p. (J). (gr. 3-4). pap. 49.50 (978-1-4777-2466-8(4), Rosen Classroom) Rosen Publishing Group, Inc., The.

Phillips, John. World History Biographies: Leonardo Da Vinci: The Genius Who Defined the Renaissance. 2008. (National Geographic World History Biographies Ser.). (Illus.). 64p. (J). (gr. 3-7). pap. 7.99 (978-1-4263-0248-0(7), National Geographic Kids) Disney Publishing Worldwide.

Physicians, Scientists, & Mathematicians of the Islamic World, 14 vols. 2016. (Physicians, Scientists, & Mathematicians of the Islamic World Ser.). (ENG.). 112p. (gr. 6-6). 271.60 (978-1-4777-8547-8(7), 23f8ead9-d594-41aa-b370-3a45f56f2952, Rosen Young Adult) Rosen Publishing Group, Inc., The.

Piddock, Charles. Rachel Carson: a Voice for the Natural World, 1 vol. 2009. (Life Portraits Ser.). (ENG., Illus.). 112p. (YA). (gr. 6-8). lib. bdg. 38.67 (978-1-4339-0058-7(0), 3353b49b-e652-433f-83d8-e82720b990f5) Stevens, Gareth Publishing LLLP.

Polcovar, Jane. Rosalind Franklin & the Structure of Life. 2006. (Profiles in Science Ser.). (Illus.). 144p. (J). (gr. 3-7). lib. bdg. 27.95 (978-1-59935-022-6(X)) Reynolds, Morgan Inc.

Polinsky, Paige. Sara Seager: Planetary Scientist. 2019. (Women Leading the Way Ser.). (ENG., Illus.). 24p. (J). (gr. k-3). pap. 7.99 (978-1-61891-505-4(3), 12155, Blastoff! Readers) Bellwether Media.

Polinsky, Paige V. Sara Seager: Planetary Scientist. 2019. (Women Leading the Way Ser.). (ENG., Illus.). 24p. (J). (gr. k-3). lib. bdg. 26.95 (978-1-62617-944-8(1), Blastoff! Readers) Bellwether Media.

Porterfield, Jason. Tim Berners-Lee, 1 vol., 1. 2015. (Tech Pioneers Ser.). (ENG.). 112p. (J). (gr. 7-7). 38.80 (978-1-4994-6290-6(5), 634d8e95-2000-46a6-a1a2-aec3f6879496, Rosen Young Adult) Rosen Publishing Group, Inc., The.

Puerta, Germán. Galileo Galilei - Y Sin Embargo se Mueve. 2005. (SPA.). 108p. (YA). (978-958-30-1700-1(0)) Panamericana Editorial.

Rabinowitz, Alan. A Boy & a Jaguar. Chien, Cátia, illus. 2014. (ENG.). 32p. (J). (gr. -1-3). 17.99 (978-0-547-87507-1(X), 1505753, Clarion Bks.) HarperCollins Pubs.

Rae, Rowena. Rachel Carson & Ecology for Kids: Her Life & Ideas, with 21 Activities & Experiments. 2020. (For Kids Ser.: 74). (ENG., Illus.). 144p. (J). (gr. 4-7). pap. 18.99 (978-0-89733-933-9(9)) Chicago Review Pr., Inc.

Randolph, Ryan P. Benjamin Franklin: Inventor, Writer, & Patriot. 2009. (Library of American Lives & Times Ser.). 112p. (gr. 5-5). 69.20 (978-1-60853-472-2(3)) Rosen Publishing Group, Inc., The.

Rauf, Don. Thomas Paine: Author of Common Sense, 1 vol. 2017. (Spotlight on Civic Courage: Heroes of Conscience Ser.). (ENG., Illus.). 48p. (J). (gr. 6-6). 33.47 (978-1-5383-8100-7(1), 82c374e6-6b8f-4c4a-a82d-9d449ee2c3ad) Rosen Publishing Group, Inc., The.

Raum, Elizabeth. The Life of Marie Curie. 2019. (Sequence Change Maker Biographies Ser.). (ENG.). 32p. (J). (gr. 2-5). lib. bdg. (978-1-68151-678-3(0), 10810) Amicus.

Rausch, Monica. Benjamin Franklin, 1 vol. 2007. (Great Americans Ser.). (ENG., Illus.). 24p. (gr. 2-4). pap. 9.15 (978-0-8368-7689-5(X), f9d7d902-1989-4c9f-a6ea-a5c5f1ef3960); lib. bdg. 24.67 (978-0-8368-7682-6(2), e5fe2671-81d7-496f-bd45-9a1d7ab28aad) Stevens, Gareth Publishing LLLP. (Weekly Reader Leveled Readers).

—Benjamín Franklin, 1 vol. 2007. (Grandes Personajes (Great Americans) Ser.). (SPA., Illus.). 24p. (gr. 2-4). lib. bdg. 24.67 *(978-0-8368-7981-0(3)*, 1de6ba44-ef15-450a-bd7c-2aa5e00e911c) Stevens, Gareth Publishing LLLP.

Raynham, Alex. Leonardo Da Vinci. 3rd ed. 2013. (Illus.). 64p. pap. 11.00 *(978-0-19-423670-6(6))* Oxford Univ. Pr., Inc.

Reid, Struan & Fara, Patricia. El Libro de los Cientificos: Desde Arquimedes a Einstein. (SPA.). (YA). (gr. 5-8). pap. *(978-950-724-272-4(4)*, LMA8234) Lumen ARG. Dist: Lectorum Pubns., Inc.

Revolutionary Discoveries of Scientific Pioneers, 16 vols. 2013. (Revolutionary Discoveries of Scientific Pioneers Ser.). (ENG.). 80p. (YA). (gr. 6-6). 307.28 *(978-1-4777-1818-6(4)*, 44978647-d7c7-4a7d-ac59-5a2c32750025) Rosen Publishing Group, Inc., The.

Rice, Dona Herweck. What a Scientist Sees. 2015. (Science: Informational Text Ser.). (ENG.). 32p. (J). (gr. 3-5). pap. 11.99 *(978-1-4807-4691-6(6))* Teacher Created Materials, Inc.

—What the Evidence Shows. 2015. (Science: Informational Text Ser.). (ENG., Illus.). 32p. (J). (gr. 4-8). pap. 11.99 *(978-1-4807-4730-2(0))* Teacher Created Materials, Inc.

Rice, William B. The First Geologists, 1 vol. rev. ed. 2007. (Science: Informational Text Ser.). (ENG.). 32p. (gr. 4-6). pap. 12.99 *(978-0-7439-0554-1(7))* Teacher Created Materials, Inc.

—Jane Goodall, 1 vol. 2nd rev. ed. 2012. (TIME for KIDS(r): Informational Text Ser.). (ENG.). 32p. (gr. 3-5). pap. 12.99 *(978-1-4333-3684-3(7))* Teacher Created Materials, Inc.

Rich, Mari. Computer Science, Vol. 10. Gilmore, Malinda & Pouson, Mel, eds. 2016. (Black Achievement in Science Ser.). (Illus.). 64p. (J). (gr. 7). 23.95 *(978-1-4222-3557-7(2))* Mason Crest.

—Technology, Vol. 10. Gilmore, Malinda & Pouson, Mel, eds. 2016. (Black Achievement in Science Ser.). (Illus.). 64p. (J). (gr. 7). 23.95 *(978-1-4222-3564-5(5))* Mason Crest.

Richard, Orlin. 12 Scientists Who Changed the World. 2016. (Change Makers Ser.). (ENG., Illus.). 32p. (J). (gr. 3-6). 32.80 *(978-1-63235-149-4(8)*, 11939, 12-Story Library) Bookstaves, LLC.

Riley, Gail Blasser. Cornerstones of Freedom: Benjamin Franklin & Electricity. 2004. (Cornerstones of Freedom Ser.). (ENG., Illus.). 48p. (J). (gr. 4-7). 26.00 *(978-0-516-24240-8(7))* Scholastic Library Publishing.

Riley, John B. Benjamin Franklin: A Photo Biography. l.t. ed. 2004. (First Biographies Ser.). (Illus.). 24p. (YA). (gr. 5-18). 16.95 *(978-1-883846-64-0(1)*, First Biographies) Reynolds, Morgan Inc.

Rinaldo, Denise. Jane Goodall: With a Discussion of Responsibility. 2003. (Values in Action Ser.). (J). *(978-1-59203-062-0(9))* Learning Challenge, Inc.

—Leonardo Da Vinci: With a Discussion of Imagination. 2003. (Values in Action Ser.). (J). *(978-1-59203-066-8(1))* Learning Challenge, Inc.

Ring, Susan. Scientists at Work. 2005. (Yellow Umbrella Fluent Level Ser.). (ENG., Illus.). 16p. (gr. k-1). pap. 35.70 *(978-0-7368-5303-3(0)*, Capstone Pr.) Capstone.

Rock, Meghan. Rachel Carson: Marine Biologist & Winner of the National Book Award, 1 vol. 2016. (Women in Science Ser.). (ENG., Illus.). 128p. (J). (gr. 9-9). 47.36 *(978-1-5026-2319-5(6)*, 590270de-ea00-487a-b74f-e776c37c06f7) Cavendish Square Publishing LLC.

Romero, Libby. National Geographic Readers: Ibn AlHaytham: The Man Who Discovered How We See. 2016. (Readers Bios Ser.). (Illus.). 48p. (J). (gr. 1-3). pap. 4.99 *(978-1-4263-2500-7(2)*, National Geographic Kids) Disney Publishing Worldwide.

Rooney, Anne. Biologists in Action. 2018. (Scientists in Action Ser.). (Illus.). 32p. (J). (gr. 5-5). pap. *(978-0-7787-5208-0(9))* Crabtree Publishing Co.

Roscoe, Kelly & Isle, Mick. Aristotle: The Father of Logic, 1 vol. 2015. (Greatest Greek Philosophers Ser.). (ENG.). 112p. (J). (gr. 7-8). 38.80 *(978-1-4994-6126-8(7)*, 2bbe47fc-070e-4c62-b4c9-ea47550e0b0e, Rosen Young Adult) Rosen Publishing Group, Inc., The.

Roselli, Stephanie, ed. The Budding Scientist. 2012. (Budding Ser.). (ENG., Illus.). 72p. pap. 9.95 *(978-0-87659-385-1(6)*, Gryphon House Inc) Gryphon Hse., Inc.

Rubin, Elizabeth. The Curies & Radium. Moyler, Alan, illus. 2011. 122p. 40.95 *(978-1-258-09479-9(7))* Literary Licensing, LLC.

Saddleback Educational Publishing Staff, ed. Albert Einstein, 1 vol. unabr. ed. 2007. (Graphic Biographies Ser.). (ENG., Illus.). 25p. (YA). (gr. 4-12). pap. 9.75 *(978-1-59905-212-0(1))* Saddleback Educational Publishing, Inc.

Salt, Zelda. Be a Geneticist, 1 vol. 2018. (Be a Scientist! Ser.). (ENG.). 32p. (gr. 3-4). 28.27 *(978-1-5382-2996-5(X)*, 4ccd5d4a-0f4f-48f2-94dd-6d4e49e67b65) Stevens, Gareth Publishing LLLP.

—Be a Marine Biologist, 1 vol. 2018. (Be a Scientist! Ser.). (ENG.). 32p. (gr. 3-4). 28.27 *(978-1-5382-2997-2(8)*, 5454289c-cc80-402e-a458-7b0b33492e7d) Stevens, Gareth Publishing LLLP.

—Be a Microbiologist, 1 vol. 2018. (Be a Scientist! Ser.). (ENG.). 32p. (gr. 3-4). 28.27 *(978-1-5382-2998-9(6)*, ea9c305a-b697-49e4-9819-dace66b7239f) Stevens, Gareth Publishing LLLP.

Sammons, Sandra. Marjory Stoneman Douglas & the Florida Everglades. 2010. (Pineapple Press Biography Ser.). (ENG.). 70p. (J). (gr. -1-12). pap. 14.95 *(978-1-56164-471-1(4))* Pineapple Pr., Inc.

Satterfield, Kathryn Hoffman. Benjamin Franklin A Man of Many Talents. 2005. 44p. (J). lib. bdg. 15.00 *(978-1-4242-0846-3(7))* Fitzgerald Bks.

Scheppler, Bill. Al-Biruni: Master Astronomer & Muslim Scholar of the Eleventh Century. 2009. (Great Muslim Philosophers & Scientists of the Middle Ages Ser.). 112p. (gr. 6-6). 66.50 *(978-1-61513-177-8(9)*, Rosen Reference) Rosen Publishing Group, Inc., The.

Scherer, Glenn & Fletcher, Marty. Who on Earth Is Rachel Carson? Mother of the Environmental Movement, 1 vol. 2009. (Scientists Saving the Earth Ser.). (ENG., Illus.). 112p. (gr. 5-6). lib. bdg. 35.93 *(978-1-59845-116-0(2)*, 343dce81-2eda-49de-b291-3e1571389d7d) Enslow Publishing, LLC.

Scientists at Work, 12 vols. 2017. (Scientists at Work Ser.). 32p. (ENG.). (gr. 2-3). 156.36 *(978-1-5081-0544-2(8)*, 2b9c4dfb-1084-4ffb-aab9-8440432b7456); (gr. 6-8). pap. 77.40 *(978-1-5081-0546-6(4))* Rosen Publishing Group, Inc., The. (Britannica Educational Publishing).

Scott, Celicia. YouTube: How Steve Chen Changed the Way We Watch Videos. 2014. (Wizards of Technology Ser.: 10). (Illus.). 64p. (J). (gr. 7-18). 23.95 *(978-1-4222-3188-3(7))* Mason Crest.

Shetty, B. Vithal. World as Seen under the Lens of a Scientist: Negro Zero to American Hero Who Changed United States from American Hypocrisy to Greatest Democracy. 2009. 552p. 34.99 *(978-1-4415-0472-2(9))*; pap. 23.99 *(978-1-4415-0471-5(0))* Xlibris Corp.

Sidman, Joyce. The Girl Who Drew Butterflies: How Maria Merian's Art Changed Science. 2018. (ENG., Illus.). 160p. (J). (gr. 5-7). 17.99 *(978-0-544-71713-8(9)*, 1630630, Clarion Bks.) HarperCollins Pubs.

Simon, Samantha. Clinical & Medical Laboratory Scientists. 2017. (Careers in Healthcare Ser.: Vol. 13). (ENG., Illus.). 64p. (J). (gr. 7-12). 23.95 *(978-1-4222-3796-0(6))* Mason Crest.

Simons, Lisa M. Bolt. Benjamin Banneker: Self-Educated Scientist. 2018. (STEM Scientists & Inventors Ser.). (ENG., Illus.). 24p. (J). (gr. 1-3). pap. 7.95 *(978-1-5435-0651-8(8)*, 137415, Capstone Pr.) Capstone.

Slade, Suzanne. The Inventor's Secret: What Thomas Edison Told Henry Ford. Reinhardt, Jennifer Black, illus. 2015. (ENG.). 48p. (J). (gr. 1-4). lib. bdg. 17.99 *(978-1-58089-667-2(7))* Charlesbridge Publishing, Inc.

Small, Cathleen. Barbara Mcclintock: Cytogeneticist & Discoverer of Mobile Genetic Elements, 1 vol. 2016. (Women in Science Ser.). (ENG., Illus.). 128p. (J). (gr. 9-9). lib. bdg. 47.36 *(978-1-5026-2311-9(0)*, 9a9e424b-2bc1-4eff-83ce-6de7ab66b444) Cavendish Square Publishing LLC.

Smith, Paula. Measure It!, 1 vol. 2015. (Science Sleuths Ser.). (ENG., Illus.). 24p. (J). (gr. 2-2). pap. *(978-0-7787-1544-3(2))* Crabtree Publishing Co.

—Model It!, 1 vol. 2015. (Science Sleuths Ser.). (ENG., Illus.). 24p. (J). (gr. 2-2). pap. *(978-0-7787-1545-0(0))* Crabtree Publishing Co.

—Plan & Investigate It!, 1 vol. 2015. (Science Sleuths Ser.). (ENG., Illus.). 24p. (J). (gr. 2-2). pap. *(978-0-7787-1546-7(9))* Crabtree Publishing Co.

—Prove It!, 1 vol. 2015. (Science Sleuths Ser.). (ENG., Illus.). 24p. (J). (gr. 2-2). pap. *(978-0-7787-1547-4(7))* Crabtree Publishing Co.

Somervill, Barbara A. Marine Biologist. 2009. (21st Century Skills Library: Cool Science Careers Ser.). (ENG., Illus.). 32p. (gr. 4-8). lib. bdg. 32.07 *(978-1-60279-504-4(5)*, 200306) Cherry Lake Publishing.

Souza, D. M. John Wesley Powell. 2004. (Watts Library). (ENG., Illus.). 64p. (J). (gr. 5-7). pap. 8.95 *(978-0-531-16653-6(8)*, Watts, Franklin) Scholastic Library Publishing.

Spiller, Sara. Tu Youyou. Bane, Jeff, illus. 2018. (My Early Library: My Itty-Bitty Bio Ser.). (ENG.). 24p. (J). (gr. k-1). lib. bdg. 30.64 *(978-1-5341-2882-8(4)*, 211572) Cherry Lake Publishing.

Spilsbury, Louise. Zoologists in the Field. 2010. (Big Picture: People & Culture Ser.). (ENG.). 24p. (gr. 1-2). pap. 41.70 *(978-1-4296-5822-5(3)*, Capstone Pr.) Capstone.

Spiro, Ruth. Baby Loves Scientists. Chan, Irene, illus. 2019. (Baby Loves Science Ser.). 24p. (J). (— 1). 12.99 *(978-1-62354-149-1(2))* Charlesbridge Publishing, Inc.

Spotlight on Kids Can Code: Set 3, 24 vols. 2017. (Spotlight on Kids Can Code Ser.). 24p. (ENG.). (gr. 4-5). 335.16 *(978-1-5081-5590-4(9)*, 6e6cbf63-d5be-41ce-806a-d286da79dc86); (gr. 8-10). pap. 141.00 *(978-1-5081-5591-1(7))* Rosen Publishing Group, Inc., The. (PowerKids Pr.).

Stabler, David. Kid Scientists: True Tales of Childhood from Science Superstars. Syed, Anoosha, illus. 2018. (Kid Legends Ser.: 5). 208p. (J). (gr. 3-7). 13.99 *(978-1-68369-074-0(5))* Quirk Bks.

Strand, Jennifer. Jacques Cousteau. 2016. (Pioneering Explorers Ser.). (ENG.). 24p. (J). (gr. -1-2). 49.94 *(978-1-68079-410-6(8)*, 23031, Abdo Zoom-Launch) ABDO Publishing Co.

—Jane Goodall. 2016. (Great Women Ser.). (ENG.). 24p. (J). (gr. -1-2). 49.94 *(978-1-68079-389-5(6)*, 23010, Abdo Zoom-Launch) ABDO Publishing Co.

Strauss, Holden. Jobs in Science: Solve Problems Involving Measurement & Estimation, 1 vol. 2014. (Rosen Math Readers Ser.). (ENG.). 24p. (J). (gr. 3-3). pap. 8.25 *(978-1-4777-4912-8(8)*, 2b2acbf9-aab4-4bf1-8097-eff8c54572c7, PowerKids Pr.) Rosen Publishing Group, Inc., The.

Streissguth, Tom. Benjamin Franklin. 2005. (Bios for Challenged Readers Ser.). (Illus.). 112p. (J). (gr. 6-12). lib. bdg. 27.93 *(978-0-8225-2210-2(1))* Lerner Publishing Group.

—Biotech Careers. 2018. (STEM Careers Ser.). (ENG.). 80p. (YA). (gr. 6-12). 39.93 *(978-1-68282-427-6(6))* ReferencePoint Pr., Inc.

Strom, Laura Layton. Shockwave: Leonardo Da Vinci. 2007. (Shockwave: Life Stories Ser.). (ENG., Illus.). 36p. (J). (gr. 3-5). 25.00 *(978-0-531-17771-6(8)*, Children's Pr.) Scholastic Library Publishing.

Sullivan, Anne Marie. Sir Isaac Newton: Famous English Scientist. 2004. (Great Names Ser.). (Illus.). 32p. (J). (gr. 3-18). lib. bdg. 19.95 *(978-1-59084-139-6(5))* Mason Crest.

Superheroes of Science. 2015. (Superheroes of Science Ser.). (ENG.). 48p. (J). (gr. 6-6). pap., pap., pap. 505.80 *(978-1-4824-3507-8(1))* Stevens, Gareth Publishing LLLP.

Taylor, Diane C. The Renaissance Thinkers: With History Projects for Kids. 2018. (the Renaissance for Kids Ser.). (ENG., Illus.). 112p. (J). (gr. 5-10). 22.95 *(978-1-61930-692-9(1)*, 3c9390fe-bce0-49a7-bc51-b4d53654767b) Nomad Pr.

Teacher Created Materials Staff, ed. Biographies III Science Pioneers: Themed Classroom Readers- 2007. (Themed Reader Sets Ser.). pap. 439.99 *(978-1-4333-0157-5(1))* Teacher Created Materials, Inc.

Thayer, William Makepeace. From Boyhood to Manhood: Life of Benjamin Franklin. 2006. pap. *(978-1-4068-0906-0(3))* Echo Library.

Thomas, William David. Marine Biologist, 1 vol. 2009. (Cool Careers: Cutting Edge Ser.). (ENG., Illus.). 32p. (J). (gr. 3-3). pap. 11.50 *(978-1-4339-2156-8(1)*, 80994c2a-1031-49c8-936a-3bfbe27203b8); lib. bdg. 28.67 *(978-1-4339-1957-2(5)*, 1655f66a-f139-4886-a668-8148d44cef98) Stevens, Gareth Publishing LLLP.

Thompson, Clifford. Climatologists!, Vol. 10. 2015. (Scientists in Action Ser.). (Illus.). 48p. (J). (gr. 5). 20.95 *(978-1-4222-3422-8(3))* Mason Crest.

Time for Kids Editors. Benjamin Franklin - A Man of Many Talents. 2005. (Time for Kids Ser.). (ENG., Illus.). 48p. (J). (gr. 2-4). pap. 3.99 *(978-0-06-057609-7(X))* HarperCollins Pubs.

Todd, Kim D. Jean Jennings Bartik: Computer Pioneer. 2015. (Notable Missourians Ser.). (ENG., Illus.). 48p. (J). pap. 24.00 *(978-1-61248-145-6(0))* Truman State Univ. Pr.

Tracy, Kathleen. Leonardo Da Vinci. 2008. (Art Profiles for Kids Ser.). (Illus.). 48p. (YA). (gr. 4-7). lib. bdg. 29.95 *(978-1-58415-711-3(9))* Mitchell Lane Pubs.

—Robert Koch & the Study of Anthrax. 2004. (Uncharted, Unexplored, & Unexplained Ser.). (Illus.). 48p. (J). (gr. 4-8). lib. bdg. 29.95 *(978-1-58415-261-3(3))* Mitchell Lane Pubs.

Tuffen, Hugh & Waldron, Melanie. Volcanologist: The Coolest Jobs on the Planet, 1 vol. HL Studios, illus. 2014. (Coolest Jobs on the Planet Ser.). (ENG.). 48p. (J). (gr. 5-8). 35.32 *(978-1-4109-6643-8(7)*, 126143); pap. 8.99 *(978-1-4109-6649-0(6)*, 126148) Capstone. (Raintree).

Tupper, Susan. Fran & Frederick Hamerstrom: Wildlife Conservation Pioneers. 2016. (Badger Biographies Ser.). (ENG., Illus.). 136p. (J). (gr. 4-6). pap. 12.95 *(978-0-87020-732-7(6))* Wisconsin Historical Society.

Unlocking the Secrets of Science: Set of 15 Scientists. (Illus.). (gr. 4-10). lib. bdg. *(978-1-58415-233-0(8))* Mitchell Lane Pubs.

Valice, Kim Perez. The Orca Scientists. 2018. (Scientists in the Field Ser.). (ENG., Illus.). 80p. (J). (gr. 5-7). 18.99 *(978-0-544-89826-4(5)*, 1653794, Clarion Bks.) HarperCollins Pubs.

Van Gorp, Lynn. Gregor Mendel: Genetics Pioneer, 1 vol. rev. ed. 2007. (Science: Informational Text Ser.). (ENG.). 32p. (J). (gr. 3-6). pap. 12.99 *(978-0-7439-0598-5(9))* Teacher Created Materials, Inc.

Vander Hook, Sue. Louis Pasteur: Groundbreaking Chemist & Biologist, 1 vol. 2011. (Essential Lives Set 6 Ser.). (ENG., Illus.). 112p. (J). (gr. 6-12). lib. bdg. 41.36 *(978-1-61714-783-8(4)*, 6731, Essential Library) ABDO Publishing Co.

Venezia, Mike. Getting to Know the World's Greatest Inventors & Scientists, 4 vols., Set. Venezia, Mike, illus. Incl. Charles Drew: Doctor Who Got the World Pumped up to Donate Blood. 28.00 *(978-0-531-23725-0(7))*; Mary Leakey - Archaeologist Who Really Dug Her Work. 28.00 *(978-0-531-23727-4(3))*; Stephen Hawking: Cosmologist Who Gets a Big Bang Out of the Universe. 28.00 *(978-0-531-23728-1(1))*; 32p. (J). (gr. 2-5). 2009. (Illus.). 2009. Set lib. bdg. 112.00 *(978-0-531-26130-9(1)*, Watts, Franklin) Scholastic Library Publishing.

—Leonardo Da Vinci (Revised Edition) (Getting to Know the World's Greatest Artists) Venezia, Mike, illus. rev. ed. 2015. (Getting to Know the World's Greatest Artists Ser.). (ENG., Illus.). 40p. (J). (gr. 3-4). pap. 7.95 *(978-0-531-21289-9(0)*, Children's Pr.) Scholastic Library Publishing.

—Rachel Carson (Getting to Know the World's Greatest Inventors & Scientists) Venezia, Mike, illus. 2010. (Getting to Know the World's Greatest Inventors & Scientists Ser.). (ENG., Illus.). 32p. (J). (gr. 3-4). pap. 6.95 *(978-0-531-20778-9(1)*, Children's Pr.) Scholastic Library Publishing.

Verstraete, Larry. S Is for Scientists: A Discovery Alphabet. Geister, David, illus. 2010. (Science Alphabet Ser.). (ENG.). 40p. (J). (gr. 1-4). 16.95 *(978-1-58536-470-1(3)*, 202189) Sleeping Bear Pr.

Vittachi, Nury. Young Scientists Series, the (in 12 Volumes) 2017. (ENG., Illus.). 12p. pap. *(978-981-322-130-7(5))* World Scientific Publishing Co. Pte Ltd.

Wallace, Ian. The Slippers' Keeper, 1 vol. 2015. (ENG., Illus.). 36p. (J). (gr. k-3). 18.95 *(978-1-55498-414-5(9))* Groundwood Bks. CAN. Dist: Publishers Group West (PGW).

Wasmer Smith, Linda. Louis Pasteur: Genius Disease Fighter, 1 vol. 2014. (Genius Scientists & Their Genius Ideas Ser.). (ENG.). 96p. (gr. 5-5). 29.60 *(978-0-7660-6575-8(8)*, 1caafcef-6933-4d89-a0a7-dfa51ab0bfd5); pap. 13.88 *(978-0-7660-6576-5(6)*, 1d5493be-8ec4-4f56-9eed-c81e0d260546) Enslow Publishing, LLC.

Waxman, Laura Hamilton. Genetics Expert Joanna L. Kelley. 2015. (STEM Trailblazer Bios Ser.). (ENG., Illus.). 32p. (J). (gr. 2-5). pap. 8.99 *(978-1-4677-6120-8(6)*, 1ae4f21a-d87b-46a5-ba6d-c4d4df4593df); lib. bdg. 26.65 *(978-1-4677-5795-9(0)*, 118a4846-3980-4448-998d-79f5954ddf0e, Lerner Pubns.) Lerner Publishing Group.

Webster, Christine. Who on Earth Is Archie Carr? Protector of Sea Turtles, 1 vol. 2009. (Scientists Saving the Earth Ser.). (ENG., Illus.). 112p. (J). (gr. 5-6). lib. bdg. 35.93 *(978-1-59845-120-7(0)*, c0c9a912-9d14-44cd-895e-e4892875f9a3) Enslow Publishing, LLC.

Wendinger, Jennifer. Unusual & Awesome Jobs Using Science: Food Taster, Human Lie Detector, & More. 2015. (You Get Paid for THAT? Ser.). (ENG., Illus.). 32p. (J). (gr. 3-9). 28.65 *(978-1-4914-2031-7(6)*, 127509, Capstone Pr.) Capstone.

Weston Woods Staff, creator. Snowflake Bentley. 2004. 29.95 *(978-1-55592-624-3(X))* Weston Woods Studios, Inc.

What Do Scientists Do? Big Book: Level E. 8p. 20.95 *(978-0-322-00346-0(6))* Wright Group/McGraw-Hill.

Wheeler, Jill C. Grace Hopper: Computer Scientist. 2017. (Women in Science Ser.). (ENG., Illus.). 112p. (J). (gr. 6-12). lib. bdg. 41.36 *(978-1-5321-1044-3(8)*, 25664, Essential Library) ABDO Publishing Co.

Whiting, Jim. Benjamin Franklin. 2006. (Profiles in American History Ser.). (Illus.). 48p. (J). (gr. 3-7). lib. bdg. 29.95 *(978-1-58415-435-8(7))* Mitchell Lane Pubs.

Williams, Judith. Forensic Scientist: Careers Solving Crimes & Scientific Mysteries, 1 vol. 2009. (Wild Science Careers Ser.). (ENG., Illus.). 128p. (J). (gr. 5-6). lib. bdg. 35.93 *(978-0-7660-3051-0(2)*, a9aa346f-9417-4465-bd17-77be1fc9769c) Enslow Publishing, LLC.

Wilson, Janet. Our Earth: How Kids Are Saving the Planet, 1 vol. 2010. (Kids Making a Difference Ser.: 1). (ENG., Illus.). 32p. (J). (gr. 3-6). lib. bdg. 18.95 *(978-1-897187-84-5(X))* Second Story Pr. CAN. Dist: Orca Bk. Pubs. USA.

—Severn & the Day She Silenced the World, 1 vol. 2014. (Kids' Power Book Ser.: 5). (ENG., Illus.). 184p. (J). (gr. 4-7). pap. 14.95 *(978-1-927583-23-4(3))* Second Story Pr. CAN. Dist: Orca Bk. Pubs. USA.

Winter, Ali. Science & Me: Inspired by the Discoveries of Nobel Prize Laureates in Physics, Chemistry & Medicine, 1 vol. El Fathi, Mickael, illus. 2021. (ENG.). 40p. (J). (gr. 4-6). 18.99 *(978-1-911373-71-1(4)*, 4650fe8e-3175-42a5-82d6-11d2f54c17dd) Lantana Publishing GBR. Dist: Lerner Publishing Group.

Winter, Jeanette. The Watcher: Jane Goodall's Life with the Chimps. Winter, Jeanette, illus. 2011. (ENG., Illus.). 48p. (J). (gr. -1-3). 18.99 *(978-0-375-86774-3(0)*, Schwartz & Wade Bks.) Random Hse. Children's Bks.

Wiseman, Blaine. Ecologist. 2020. (J). *(978-1-7911-1676-7(0)*, AV2 by Weigl) Weigl Pubs., Inc.

Wolny, Philip. Geologists at Work, 1 vol. 2017. (Scientists at Work Ser.). (ENG., Illus.). 32p. (J). (gr. 2-3). pap. 13.90 *(978-1-68048-760-2(4)*, 3a5785c6-6124-4900-b9d1-a4d92d9c474b, Britannica Educational Publishing) Rosen Publishing Group, Inc., The.

World Book's Biographical Encyclopedia of Scientists, 8 vols. 2005. 1,536p. (YA). (gr. 6-18). 329.00 *(978-0-7166-7601-0(X)*, 20170) World Bk., Inc.

Wright, A. Gilbert. In the Steps of the Great American Herpetologist. Kalmenoff, Matthew, illus. 2014. (ENG.). 128p. (J). (gr. 2-6). pap. 11.95 *(978-1-59077-360-4(8))* Evans, M. & Co., Inc.

Wyborny, Sheila. Nikola Tesla. 2012. (Innovators Ser.). (ENG., Illus.). 64p. (gr. 4-8). lib. bdg. 29.60 *(978-0-7377-5528-2(8)*, Kidhaven) Cengage Gale.

Yasuda, Anita. Forensics: Cool Women Who Investigate. Bruce, Allison, illus. 2016. (Girls in Science Ser.). (ENG.). 112p. (J). (gr. 3-7). 19.95 *(978-1-61930-346-1(9)*, f123d08a-2e0b-41e8-9cfd-70a23d72cd8b) Nomad Pr.

Yount, Lisa. Antoni Van Leeuwenhoek: First to See Microscopic Life, 1 vol. rev. ed. 2009. (Great Minds of Science Ser.). (ENG., Illus.). 128p. (gr. 5-6). lib. bdg. 35.93 *(978-0-7660-3012-1(1)*, dac680c1-ca1a-41f8-af72-aaeff98dce53) Enslow Publishing, LLC.

Zannos, Susan. Dmitri Mendeleyev & the Periodic Table. 2004. (Uncharted, Unexplored, & Unexplained Ser.). (Illus.). 48p. (J). (gr. 4-8). lib. bdg. 29.95 *(978-1-58415-267-5(2))* Mitchell Lane Pubs.

—The Life & Times of Archimedes. 2004. (Biography from Ancient Civilizations Ser.). (Illus.). 48p. (J). (gr. 4-8). lib. bdg. 29.95 *(978-1-58415-242-2(7))* Mitchell Lane Pubs.

SCIENTISTS—FICTION

Abela, Deborah. In Search of the Time & Space Machine: Max Remy Superspy 1. Murphy, Jobi, illus. 2005. (Spy Force Ser.). 256p. (Orig.). (J). 14.95 *(978-1-74051-765-2(2)*, Simon & Schuster Bks. For Young Readers) Simon & Schuster Bks. For Young Readers.

Amo, Montserrat del. Montes, Pájaros y Amigos. 2007. (SPA.). 104p. (gr. 5-8). pap. 13.99 *(978-84-207-2788-2(1)*, GS6293) Grupo Anaya, S.A. ESP. Dist: Lectorum Pubns., Inc.

Anderson, M. T. Whales on Stilts! Cyrus, Kurt, illus. 2010. (Pals in Peril Tale Ser.). (ENG.). (J). (gr. 5-9). 224p. pap. 8.99 *(978-1-4424-0701-5(8))*;1. 208p. 17.99 *(978-1-4424-0695-7(X))* Beach Lane Bks. (Beach Lane Bks.).

Anderson, Matthew. Whales on Stilts! Cyrus, Kurt, illus. 2006. (M. T. Anderson's Thrilling Tales Ser.). 188p. (gr. 5-9). 15.95 *(978-0-7569-7213-4(2))* Perfection Learning Corp.

Atkins, Jeannine. Finding Wonders: Three Girls Who Changed Science. (ENG., Illus.). 208p. (J). (gr. 5). 2017. pap. 7.99 *(978-1-4814-6566-3(X))* 2016. 18.99 *(978-1-4814-6565-6(1)*, Atheneum Bks. for Young Readers) Simon & Schuster Children's Publishing.

Baker, Chandler. Teen Frankenstein: High School Horror. 2017. (High School Horror Ser.: 1). (ENG.). 336p. (YA). pap. 14.99 *(978-1-250-06887-3(8)*, 900147303) Square Fish.

Bass, Guy. The Pirate's Eye, 1 vol. Williamson, Pete, illus. 2013. (Stitch Head Ser.). (ENG.). 208p. (J). (gr. 3-6). 10.95 *(978-1-62370-008-9(6)*, 123265, Capstone Young Readers) Capstone.

Beaty, Andrea. Ada Twist & the Perilous Pants: The Questioneers Book #2. 2019. (Questioneers Ser.). (ENG., Illus.). 144p. (J). (gr. 1-4). 12.99 *(978-1-4197-3422-9(9)*, 1203901) Abrams, Inc.

—Ada Twist, Scientist. 2016. (Questioneers Ser.). (ENG., Illus.). 32p. (J). (gr. k-2). 19.99 *(978-1-4197-2137-3(2)*, 1119001) Abrams, Inc.

Bennett, Sandra. Gingerbread Aliens. Welsh, Hayley, illus. 2012. (ENG.). 56p. (J). pap. *(978-0-9872356-4-0(8))* Australian Self Publishing Group/ Inspiring Pubs.

Benton, Jim. Attack of the 50-Ft. Cupid. Benton, Jim, illus. 2005. (Franny K. Stein, Mad Scientist Ser.: 2). (ENG., Illus.). 112p. (J). (gr. 2-5). pap. 6.99 *(978-0-689-86296-0(2)*, Simon & Schuster Bks. For Young Readers) Simon & Schuster Bks. For Young Readers.

—Franny K. Stein, Mad Scientist (Boxed Set) Lunch Walks among Us; Attack of the 50-Ft. Cupid; the Invisible Fran; the Fran That Time Forgot; Frantastic Voyage; the Fran with Four Brains; the Frandidate. Benton, Jim, illus. 2012. (Franny K. Stein, Mad Scientist Ser.). (ENG., Illus.). 784p. (J). (gr. 2-5). pap. 44.99 *(978-1-4424-7424-6(6)*, Simon & Schuster Bks. For Young Readers) Simon & Schuster Bks. For Young Readers.

Biskup, Agnieszka. The Dynamic World of Chemical Reactions with Max Axiom, Super Scientist. Martin, Cynthia, illus. 2010. (Graphic Science Ser.). (ENG.). 32p. (J). (gr. 3-4). pap. 49.60 *(978-1-4296-5719-8(7)*, 15498, Capstone Pr.) Capstone.

Blaine, John. The Caves of Fear: A Rick Brant Science Adventure Story. 2011. 220p. 44.95 *(978-1-258-09271-9(9))* Literary Licensing, LLC.
—Smuggler's Reef: A Rick Brant Science Adventure Story. 2011. 220p. 44.95 *(978-1-258-04085-7(9))* Literary Licensing, LLC.
Blaine, John & Goodwin, Harold Leland. The Caves of Fear. 2011. 150p. 24.95 *(978-1-4638-9614-0(X))*; pap. 13.95 *(978-1-4638-0073-4(8))* Rodgers, Alan Bks.
Brinley, Bertrand R. The Big Chunk of Ice: The Last Known Adventure of the Mad Scientists' Club. Geer, Charles, illus. 2005. (Mad Scientist Club Ser.). 275p. (J). (gr. 3-7). 18.95 *(978-1-930900-29-5(5))* Purple Hse. Pr.
—The Mad Scientists' Club Complete Collection. Geer, Charles, illus. 2010. 619p. (YA). pap. 29.99 *(978-1-930900-51-6(1))* Purple Hse. Pr.
Broad, Michael. Ghost Diamond!, No. 1. Broad, Michael, illus. 2011. (Agent Amelia Ser.: 1). (ENG., Illus.). 144p. (J). (gr. 2-5). lib. bdg. 22.60 *(978-0-7613-8056-6(6))* Lerner Publishing Group.
—#1 Ghost Diamond! 2011. (Agent Amelia Ser.). pap. 33.92 *(978-0-7613-8341-3(7)*, Darby Creek) Lerner Publishing Group.
—#3 Hypno Hounds! 2011. (Agent Amelia Ser.). pap. 33.92 *(978-0-7613-8343-7(3)*, Darby Creek) Lerner Publishing Group.
Bryers, Paul. Kobal. 2009. 1.00 *(978-1-4074-4320-1(8))* Recorded Bks., Inc.
Campbell, Howard. A Dog Named Pavlov: Un Perro Llamado Pavlov. McCloskey, Kevin, illus. 2010. 44p. (J). pap. 12.95 *(978-0-9790350-4-3(X))* Stanley Publishing Co.
Castle, M. E. Game of Clones, No. 3. 2014. (Clone Chronicles Ser.: No. 3). (ENG., Illus.). 256p. (J). (gr. 3-6). pap. 6.99 *(978-1-60684-538-7(1)*, ba3c56fd-6d94-42af-be8a-35582221b366, Darby Creek) Lerner Publishing Group.
Chabert, Jack. Classes Are Canceled! 2017. (Eerie Elementary — Branches Ser.: 7). (J). lib. bdg. 14.75 *(978-0-606-40669-7(7))* Turtleback.
—Classes Are Canceled!: a Branches Book (Eerie Elementary #7) Loveridge, Matt, illus. 2017. (Eerie Elementary Ser.: 7). (ENG.). 96p. (J). (gr. 1-3). pap. 5.99 *(978-1-338-18180-7(7))* Scholastic, Inc.
—The End of Orson Eerie? a Branches Book (Eerie Elementary #10) Loveridge, Matt, illus. 2019. (Eerie Elementary Ser.: 10). (ENG.). 96p. (J). (gr. 1-3). pap. 5.99 *(978-1-338-31856-2(X))* Scholastic, Inc.
—Sam Battles the Machine! 2017. (Eerie Elementary — Branches Ser.: bk.6). (ENG.). (J). lib. bdg. 14.75 *(978-0-606-40191-3(1))* Turtleback.
—Sam Battles the Machine!: a Branches Book (Eerie Elementary #6) Ricks, Sam, illus. 2017. (Eerie Elementary Ser.: 6). (ENG.). 96p. (J). (gr. 1-3). pap. 5.99 *(978-0-545-87378-9(9))* Scholastic, Inc.
—The Science Fair Is Freaky! 2016. (Eerie Elementary — Branches Ser.: bk.4). (ENG.). (J). lib. bdg. 14.75 *(978-0-606-38806-1(0))* Turtleback.
—The Science Fair Is Freaky! a Branches Book (Eerie Elementary #4) Ricks, Sam, illus. 2016. (Eerie Elementary Ser.: 4). (ENG.). 96p. (J). (gr. 1-3). pap. 5.99 *(978-0-545-87368-0(1))* Scholastic, Inc.
Christie, Tory. Curious Mccarthy, 4 vols. Price, Mina, illus. 2017. (Curious Mccarthy Ser.). (ENG.). 112p. (J). (gr. 2-4). pap., pap., pap. 27.80 *(978-1-5158-1665-2(6)*, 27121, Picture Window Bks.) Capstone.
—Curious Mccarthy's Power of Observation. Price, Mina, illus. 2017. (Curious Mccarthy Ser.). (ENG.). 112p. (J). (gr. 2-4). pap. 6.95 *(978-1-5158-1650-8(8)*, 136305); lib. bdg. 25.32 *(978-1-5158-1646-1(X)*, 136301) Capstone. (Picture Window Bks.).
Clenott, Peter. Devolution. 2013. 280p. pap. *(978-1-927792-14-8(2))* Imajin Bks.
Cole, Olivia A. An Anatomy of Beasts. 2019. (ENG.). 432p. (YA). (gr. 8). 17.99 *(978-0-06-264424-4(6)*, Tegen, Katherine Bks) HarperCollins Pubs.
—A Conspiracy of Stars. (ENG.). (YA). (gr. 8). 2019. 448p. pap. 9.99 *(978-0-06-264422-0(X))* 2018. 432p. 17.99 *(978-0-06-264421-3(1))* HarperCollins Pubs. (Tegen, Katherine Bks).
Collins ELT Readers: Amazing Mathematicians (Level 2), 1 vol. 2014. (Collins English Readers Ser.). (ENG.). 80p. audio compact disk 13.95 *(978-0-00-754503-2(7))* HarperCollins Pubs. Ltd. GBR. Dist: Independent Pubs. Group.
Collins, Janet Ann. The Peril of the Sinister Scientist. 2009. 98p. pap. 7.95 *(978-1-935137-79-5(4))* Guardian Angel Publishing, Inc.
Colvin, S. R. R. The Krybosian Stairpath: Magnetic Reversal. 2009. 200p. pap. 14.95 *(978-1-4401-5927-5(0))* iUniverse, Inc.
CortAs, Ricardo. Sea Creatures from the Sky. 2018. (ENG., Illus.). 48p. (J). 16.95 *(978-1-61775-616-0(4)*, Black Sheep) Akashic Bks.
Cousteau, Fabien & Fraioli, James O. Great White Shark Adventure. St.Pierre, Joe, illus. 2019. (Fabien Cousteau Expeditions Ser.). (ENG.). 112p. (J). (gr. 3-7). 12.99 *(978-1-5344-2087-8(8)*, McElderry, Margaret K. Bks.) McElderry, Margaret K. Bks.
Cowan, Jennifer. Earthgirl. 2013. 272p. pap. *(978-1-4596-6502-6(3))* ReadHowYouWant.com, Ltd.
Crichton, Michael & Koepp, David. Jurassic Park. Holtsclaw, Josh, illus. 2018. (J). *(978-1-5444-0887-3(0)*, Golden Bks.) Random Hse. Children's Bks.
Cummings, Troy. Sneeze of the Octo-Schnozz. 2016. (Notebook of Doom Ser.: 11). lib. bdg. 14.75 *(978-0-606-39714-8(0))* Turtleback.
DanTDM. DanTDM: Trayaurus & the Enchanted Crystal. 2018. (ENG.). 192p. (J). (gr. 3-7). pap. 9.99 *(978-0-06-257429-9(9)*, HarperAlley) HarperCollins Pubs.
Davis, Kent. A Riddle in Ruby #3: the Great Unravel. (Riddle in Ruby Ser.: 3). (ENG.). 448p. (J). (gr. 3-7). 2018. pap. 7.99 *(978-0-06-236841-6(9))* 2017. 17.99 *(978-0-06-236840-9(0))* HarperCollins Pubs. (Greenwillow Bks.).
Dean, Ramsey. Riding on a Beam of Light: Albert Einstein. Hamdan, Noah, illus. 2013. 48p. pap. 10.48 *(978-0-9893372-1-2(9))* Ramsey Dean, Inc.
Del Toro, Gladys. The Mutation of Black Cat, 1 vol. 2009. 76p. pap. 16.95 *(978-1-61546-487-6(5))* PublishAmerica, Inc.
Derting, Kimberly & Johannes, Shelli R. Cece Loves Science. Harrison, Vashti, illus. 2018. (Loves Science Ser.: 1). (ENG.). 40p. (J). (gr. -1-3). 17.99 *(978-0-06-249960-8(2)*, Greenwillow Bks.) HarperCollins Pubs.
—Cece Loves Science & Adventure. Harrison, Vashti, illus. 2019. (Loves Science Ser.: 2). (ENG.). 40p. (J). (gr. -1-3). 17.99 *(978-0-06-249962-2(9)*, Greenwillow Bks.) HarperCollins Pubs.
Dexter & Missy the Kitten. 2004. (J). per. 15.99 *(978-0-9753533-1-8(4))* Golden Eagle Publishing Hse., Inc.
Dexter Rescues Matt the Duckling. 2004. (J). per. 15.99 *(978-0-9753533-3-2(0))* Golden Eagle Publishing Hse., Inc.
Dexter the Hamster Gets Lost. 2004. (J). per. 15.99 *(978-0-9753533-2-5(2))* Golden Eagle Publishing Hse., Inc.
Durst, Sarah Beth. Ice. 2010. (ENG.). 336p. (YA). (gr. 7). pap. 8.99 *(978-1-4169-8644-7(8)*, McElderry, Margaret K. Bks.) McElderry, Margaret K. Bks.
Eagar, Lindsay. Race to the Bottom of the Sea. (ENG.). 432p. (J). (gr. 3-7). 2019. pap. 9.99 *(978-0-7636-9877-5(6))* 2017. 17.99 *(978-0-7636-7923-1(2))* Candlewick Pr.
Ferrie, Chris. Goodnight Lab: A Scientific Parody. 2017. (Illus.). 32p. (J). (gr. -1-3). 17.99 *(978-1-4926-5617-3(8))* Sourcebooks, Inc.
Fisher, Justin. The Gold Thief (Ned's Circus of Marvels, Book 2) 2018. (Ned's Circus of Marvels Ser.: 2). (ENG.). 432p. (J). 6.99 *(978-0-00-826221-1(7)*, HarperCollins Children's Bks.) HarperCollins Pubs. Ltd. GBR. Dist: HarperCollins Pubs.
Furlong, C. T. Killer Genes. 2012. (Arctic6 Adventure Ser.). 192p. (YA). (gr. 4-6). pap. 45.54 *(978-0-7613-9209-5(2))* Lerner Publishing Group.
—Killer Strangelets. 2011. (Arctic6 Ser.). 208p. (J). pap. *(978-0-9562315-6-7(X))* Inside Pocket Publishing, Ltd.
Furlong, Carol T. Killer Genes. 2012. (Arctic6 Adventure Ser.). 192p. (YA). (gr. 4-6). pap. 7.99 *(978-0-9562315-7-4(8))* Lerner Publishing Group.
Gamble, Paul. The Knight's Armor: Book 3 of the Ministry of SUITs. 2018. (Ministry of SUITs Ser.: 3). (ENG., Illus.). 368p. (J). 25.99 *(978-1-250-07684-7(6)*, 900152371) Feiwel & Friends.
Graves, Annie. Frankenkids, No. 5. McElhinney, Glenn, illus. 2015. (Nightmare Club Ser.: 5). (ENG.). 64p. (J). (gr. 2-5). lib. bdg. 25.32 *(978-1-4677-4352-5(6)*, 3873901b-8a1c-4968-a1e0-0b6d38b34a01, Darby Creek) Lerner Publishing Group.
Hawking, Stephen & Hawking, Lucy. George's Secret Key to the Universe. Parsons, Garry, illus. 2009. (George's Secret Key Ser.). (ENG.). 336p. (J). (gr. 3-7). pap. 12.99 *(978-1-4169-8584-6(0)*, Simon & Schuster Bks. For Young Readers) Simon & Schuster Bks. For Young Readers.
Hawkins, Matt. Think Tank, Vol. 1. 2012. (ENG., Illus.). 120p. (YA). pap. 14.99 *(978-1-60706-660-6(2)*, e4632b0e-ae92-4f19-9f67-2dd5bef999e2) Image Comics.
Himmelman, John. Albert Hopper, Science Hero. Himmelman, John, illus. 2020. (Albert Hopper, Science Hero Ser.: 1). (ENG., Illus.). 144p. (J). 13.99 *(978-1-250-23016-4(0)*, 900209343, Holt, Henry & Co. Bks. For Young Readers) Holt, Henry & Co.
Holm, Jennifer L. The Fourteenth Goldfish. 2015. (CHI.). 264p. (J). pap. *(978-986-320-783-2(7))* Commonwealth Publishing Co., Ltd.
—The Fourteenth Goldfish. (ENG.). (J). (gr. 3-7). 2016. 240p. 8.99 *(978-0-375-87114-6(4)*, Yearling) 2014. 208p. 16.99 *(978-0-375-87064-4(4)*, Random Hse. Bks. for Young Readers) Random Hse. Children's Bks.
—The Fourteenth Goldfish. 2016. lib. bdg. 18.40 *(978-0-606-38465-0(0))* Turtleback.
—The Third Mushroom. 2018. (ENG., Illus.). 240p. (J). (gr. 3-7). 16.99 *(978-1-5247-1980-7(3)*, Random Hse. Bks. for Young Readers) Random Hse. Children's Bks.
Jayasuriya, Michael. The Time MacHine. 2011. 66p. pap. 15.99 *(978-1-4653-3741-2(5))* Xlibris Corp.
Jones, C. B. The Cats' Meow. Green, Chris, illus. 2017. (Bog Hollow Boys Ser.). (ENG.). 72p. (J). (gr. 4-8). lib. bdg. 25.32 *(978-1-4965-4057-7(3)*, 133365, Stone Arch Bks.) Capstone.
Kelly, Jacqueline. La Evolución de Calpurnia Tate. 2010.Tr. of Evolution of Calpurnia Tate. (SPA.). 272p. (YA). pap. 20.95 *(978-84-9918-103-5(1))* Roca Editorial ESP. Dist: Spanish Pubs., LLC.
—La evolución de Calpurnia Tate, Vol. 2. 2011. (SPA.). 272p. pap. 12.95 *(978-84-92833-15-3(7))* Roca Editorial ESP. Dist: Spanish Pubs., LLC.
—La Evolución de Calpurnia Tate, Vol. 3. 2015.Tr. of Evolution of Calpurnia Tate. (SPA.). 320p. (YA). (gr. 5-8). 19.95 *(978-84-15729-78-5(2))* Roca Editorial ESP. Dist: Spanish Pubs., LLC.
—The Evolution of Calpurnia Tate. 2010. (CHI.). 344p. (J). (gr. 5-9). pap. *(978-986-216-538-6(3))* Commonwealth Publishing Co., Ltd.
—The Evolution of Calpurnia Tate. 2018. (CHI.). (J). (gr. 5-9). pap. *(978-7-221-14182-8(7))* Guizhou People's Publishing Hse.
—The Evolution of Calpurnia Tate. 2011. (JPN.). 412p. (J). (gr. 5-9). *(978-4-593-53474-6(7))* Holp Shuppan, Publishing.
—The Evolution of Calpurnia Tate. 2009. (Calpurnia Tate Ser.: 1). (ENG.). 352p. (J). (gr. 4-7). 19.99 *(978-0-8050-8841-0(5)*, 900051792, Holt, Henry & Co. Bks. For Young Readers) Holt, Henry & Co.
—The Evolution of Calpurnia Tate. 2010. 340p. 18.00 *(978-1-60686-849-2(7))* Perfection Learning Corp.
—The Evolution of Calpurnia Tate. 2011. (Calpurnia Tate Ser.: 1). (ENG.). 368p. (J). (gr. 4-7). pap. 8.99 *(978-0-312-65930-1(X)*, 900070517) Square Fish.
—The Evolution of Calpurnia Tate. 2011. (Calpurnia Tate Ser.: 1). (J). lib. bdg. 18.40 *(978-0-606-20974-8(3))* Turtleback.
King, J. Eric & Graham, Greg. Byron Carmichael Book One: The Human Corpse Trade. Mizer, Lindsay, ed. Warner, Michael, illus. 2008. (ENG.). 408p. (gr. 8-12). 18.95 *(978-0-615-15770-2(X))* G & K Publishing.
Kirby, Matthew J. The Arctic Code. 2015. (Dark Gravity Sequence Ser.: 1). (ENG.). 336p. (J). (gr. 3-7). 16.99 *(978-0-06-222487-3(5)*, Balzer & Bray) HarperCollins Pubs.
Klages, Ellen. The Green Glass Sea. 2008. (Gordon Family Saga Ser.: 1). 368p. (J). (gr. 3-7). 9.99 *(978-0-14-241149-0(3)*, Puffin Books) Penguin Young Readers Group.
—The Green Glass Sea. 2008. 321p. (gr. 4-7). 19.00 *(978-0-7569-8931-6(0))* Perfection Learning Corp.
Langdale, Mark Roland. Professor Doppelganger & the Fantastical Cloud Factory. 2012. 106p. pap. *(978-1-78003-267-2(6))* Pen Pr. Pubs., Ltd.
Larry, H. I. Zac Power #1: Poison Island: 24 Hours to Save the World ... & Walk the Dog. Oswald, Ash, illus. 2008. (Zac Power Ser.: 1). (ENG.). 96p. (J). (gr. 3-6). pap. 6.99 *(978-0-312-34659-1(X)*, 900042759) Square Fish.
Lassiter, Rhiannon. Shadows. 2011. (Hex Ser.: 2). (ENG.). 272p. (YA). (gr. 7). pap. 12.99 *(978-1-4424-3103-4(2)*, Simon Pulse) Simon Pulse.
Latham, Jean Lee & Walsh, Mary R. Carry on, Mr. Bowditch: A Newbery Award Winner. 2003. (ENG., Illus.). 256p. (YA). (gr. 7). pap. 9.99 *(978-0-618-25074-5(3)*, 489709, Clarion Bks.) HarperCollins Pubs.
Linke, Glenn Colin. The Gargantuan Boy. 2011. 102p. pap. 30.50 *(978-1-60976-079-3(4)*, Eloquent Bks.) Strategic Book Publishing & Rights Agency (SBPRA).
Lopuszynski, Barbara. Angel & Brie. 2013. (ENG.). 246p. (YA). pap. 14.95 *(978-1-4787-0886-5(7))* Outskirts Pr., Inc.
Lumry, Amanda & Hurwitz, Laura. Operation Orangutan. 2007. (Adventures of Riley (Unnumbered) Ser.). (Illus.). 36p. (J). (gr. -1-3). 15.95 *(978-0-9748411-4-4(5))* Eaglemont Pr.
Lyons, Kelly Starling. Sleepover Scientist #3. Myers, Nneka & Brantley-Newton, Vanessa, illus. 2019. (Jada Jones Ser.: 3). 96p. (J). (gr. 1-3). 6.99 *(978-1-5247-9055-4(9))*; lib. bdg. 15.99 *(978-1-5247-9056-1(7))* Penguin Young Readers Group. (Penguin Workshop).
MacDonald, Tom. Secret of the Tree: Marcus Speer's Ecosentinel. Stieber, Joel, illus. 2009. 300p. pap. 18.95 *(978-0-595-52402-0(8))* iUniverse, Inc.
The Mad Scientist, 6 vols. (Woodland Mysteriestm Ser.). 133p. (gr. 3-7). 42.50 *(978-0-7802-7928-5(X))* Wright Group/McGraw-Hill.
Manga University Staff. My First PC: The Comic Book That Teaches You about the Internet. 2012. 128p. (J). pap. 9.99 *(978-4-921205-28-7(0))* Japanime Co., Ltd. JPN. Dist: Diamond Bk. Distributors.
Marsh, Carole. The Behemoth Blizzard Mystery. (Masters of Disasters Ser.). (Illus.). 118p. (J). (gr. 3-5). 2008. per. 5.99 *(978-0-635-06464-6(2))* 2007. 14.95 *(978-0-635-06467-7(7))* Gallopade International.
—The Earthshaking Earthquake Mystery!, 1. 2009. (Carole Marsh's Masters of Disasters Ser.). (ENG., Illus.). 118p. (J). (gr. 3-6). 18.69 *(978-0-635-06339-7(5))* Gallopade International.
—The Ferocious Forest Fire Mystery. 2008. (Masters of Disasters Ser.). (Illus.). 118p. (J). (gr. 3-5). 14.95 *(978-0-635-06468-4(5))*;6. (ENG., (gr. 2-4). 18.69 *(978-0-635-06465-3(0))* Gallopade International.
—The Horrendous Hurricane Mystery. 2007. (Masters of Disasters Ser.). (Illus.). 118p. (J). (gr. 2-9). 14.95 *(978-0-635-06396-0(4))*; per. 7.99 *(978-0-635-06340-3(9))* Gallopade International.
—The Treacherous Tornado Mystery. 2007. (Masters of Disasters Ser.). (Illus.). 118p. (J). (gr. 2-9). 14.95 *(978-0-635-06394-6(8))*; per. 5.99 *(978-0-635-06338-0(7))* Gallopade International.
—The Voracious Volcano Mystery. 2008. (Masters of Disasters Ser.). (Illus.). 118p. (J). (gr. 3-5). 14.95 *(978-0-635-06466-0(9))*; per. 5.99 *(978-0-635-06463-9(4))* Gallopade International.
Mazzola, Lori E. The Forbidden Forest: Tales of the Tree People, 1 vol. 2009. 151p. pap. 24.95 *(978-1-4489-2656-5(4))* America Star Bks.
McElligott, Matthew & Tuxbury, Larry David. Benjamin Franklinstein Lives!, 1. McElligott, Matthew, illus. 2011. (Benjamin Franklinstein Ser.: 1). (ENG., Illus.). 128p. (J). (gr. 4-6). 22.44 *(978-0-399-25229-7(0))* Penguin Young Readers Group.
—Benjamin Franklinstein Meets the Fright Brothers, 2. McElligott, Matthew, illus. 2012. (Benjamin Franklinstein Ser.: 2). (ENG., Illus.). 160p. (J). (gr. 4-6). 22.44 *(978-0-399-25480-2(3))* Penguin Young Readers Group.
Mead, Richelle. Silver Shadows: A Bloodlines Novel. 2015. (Bloodlines Ser.: 5). (ENG.). 416p. (YA). (gr. 7). pap. 12.99 *(978-1-59514-632-8(6)*, Razorbill) Penguin Young Readers Group.
Melville, V. H. Livia the Scientist. 2007. 20p. per. 24.95 *(978-1-4241-8547-4(5))* America Star Bks.
Mills, Rachel. Wraiths. 2010. 269p. pap. 18.95 *(978-1-4461-4326-1(0))* Lulu Pr., Inc.
Miss Gomez's Third Grade Class Staff. Wacky Stories from Wisdom Academy for Young Scientists. 2013. (ENG.). 63p. (YA). pap. 16.95 *(978-1-4787-1103-2(5))* Outskirts Pr., Inc.
Montgomery, R. A. The Brilliant Dr. Wogan. 2005. (Choose Your Own Adventure Ser.). (Illus.). 112p. (J). (gr. 4-8). pap. 5.50 *(978-0-7608-9705-8(0))* Sundance/Newbridge Educational Publishing.
—The Brilliant Dr. Wogan. Trod, Mariano et al, illus. 2006. (ENG.). 144p. (J). (gr. 4-8). per. 7.99 *(978-1-933390-17-8(4)*, CHC:17) Chooseco LLC.
Morgen, A. M. The Inventors & the Lost Island. 2019. (ENG., Illus.). 384p. (J). (gr. 3-7). 16.99 *(978-0-316-47153-4(4))* Little, Brown Bks. for Young Readers.
—The Inventors at No. 8. (ENG., Illus.). (J). (gr. 3-7). 2019. 368p. pap. 7.99 *(978-0-316-47151-0(8))* 2018. 352p. 16.99 *(978-0-316-47149-7(6))* Little, Brown Bks. for Young Readers.
Munday, Dj. The Secret Dummy of Joshua Bean. 2008. 84p. pap. *(978-1-84923-029-2(3))* YouWriteOn.
Nye, Bill & Mone, Gregory. Jack & the Geniuses: At the Bottom of the World. Iluzada, Nicholas, illus. (ENG.). (J). (gr. 3-7). 2018. 272p. pap. 8.99 *(978-1-4197-3288-1(9)*, 1152603) 2017. 256p. 13.95 *(978-1-4197-2303-2(0)*, 1152601, Amulet Bks.) Abrams, Inc.
—Lost in the Jungle: Jack & the Geniuses Book #3. Iluzada, Nicholas, illus. (Jack & the Geniuses Ser.). (ENG.). 288p. (J). (gr. 3-7). 2019. pap. 7.99 *(978-1-4197-3485-4(7)*, 1158103) 2018. 13.99 *(978-1-4197-2867-9(9)*, 1158101) Abrams, Inc. (Amulet Bks.).
Onion Head Monster Attacks. 2007. (YA). per. 12.95 *(978-0-9793676-0-1(3))* Friedrich, Paul.
Onion Head Monster Attacks (XL) 2006. per. 19.99 *(978-0-9793676-3-2(8))* Friedrich, Paul.
Osorio, Rick. The Great Adventure of Sally Rock & el Lobo. 2007. (ENG.). 96p. per. 19.95 *(978-1-4241-5869-0(9))* America Star Bks.
The Perfect Person, 6 Packs. (Bookweb Ser.). 32p. (gr. 4-18). 34.00 *(978-0-7635-3734-0(9))* Rigby Education.
The Perfect Pet, 6 Packs. (Bookweb Ser.). 32p. (gr. 5-18). 34.00 *(978-0-7635-3781-4(0))* Rigby Education.
Rand, Johnathan. American Chillers #23 Wicked Velociraptors of West Virginia. 2008. 208p. (J). pap. 5.99 *(978-1-893699-94-6(3))* AudioCraft Publishing, Inc.
Random House. Monkey Business (Teenage Mutant Ninja Turtles) Spaziante, Patrick, illus. 2013. (Pictureback(R) Ser.). (ENG.). 16p. (J). (gr. -1-2). 3.99 *(978-0-449-81852-7(7)*, Random Hse. Bks. for Young Readers) Random Hse. Children's Bks.
Reiche, Dietlof & Brownjohn, John. Freddy in Peril: Book Two in the Golden Hamster Saga. Cepeda, Joe, illus. 2004. 202p. (J). pap. *(978-0-439-64984-1(6))* Scholastic, Inc.
Reid, Roger. Space. 2008. (ENG.). 160p. (J). 19.95 *(978-1-58838-230-6(3)*, 9002, NewSouth Bks.) NewSouth, Inc.
Richards, C. J. Battle of the Bots. 2017. (Robots Rule Ser.: 3). (ENG.). (J). (gr. 2-5). lib. bdg. 17.20 *(978-0-606-39811-4(2))* Turtleback.
Richmond, Susan Edwards. Bird Count, 1 vol. Coleman, Stephanie Fizer, illus. 2019. 32p. (J). (gr. -1-3). 18.99 *(978-1-56145-954-4(2))* Peachtree Publishing Co. Inc.
Rose, John. Wikker. 2007. 248p. pap. 17.95 *(978-1-4303-1523-0(7))* Lulu Pr., Inc.
Rossiter, Nan Parson. The Fo'c'sle: Henry Beston's Outermost House. 2012. (ENG., Illus.). 32p. (J). (gr. 5-18). 17.95 *(978-1-56792-433-6(6))* Godine, David R. Pub.
Roy, Philip. Me & Mr. Bell: A Novel, 1 vol. 2013. (ENG.). 140p. pap. *(978-1-927492-55-0(6))* Cape Breton Univ. Pr.
Schwartz, Tom. Spaceship Earth: A Beginning Without End. 2010. 172p. pap. 10.99 *(978-1-57545-151-0(4))*; 19.99 *(978-1-57545-143-5(3))* RP Media. (Reagent Pr. Bks. for Young Readers).
Scieszka, Jon. Frank Einstein & the BrainTurbo (Frank Einstein Series #3) Book Three. Biggs, Brian, illus. 2017. (Frank Einstein Ser.). (ENG.). 208p. (J). (gr. 3-7). pap. 7.99 *(978-1-4197-2735-1(4)*, 1070203) Abrams, Inc.
Shelley, Mary. Frankenstein. Irving, Frazer, illus. 2005. 176p. (gr. 3-7). 21.00 *(978-0-7569-5809-1(1))* Perfection Learning Corp.
—Frankenstein: The Graphic Novel, 1 vol. 2010. (Classic Graphic Novel Collection). (ENG., Illus.). 144p. (gr. 7-10). 41.03 *(978-1-4205-0374-6(X)*, d221a00b-4501-4809-ba3c-c9c335f54c95, Lucent Pr.) Greenhaven Publishing LLC.
Shreve, Steve. Stan & the Toilet Monster. Shreve, Steve, illus. 2019. (ENG., Illus.). 160p. (J). (gr. 2-6). pap. 9.99 *(978-1-4778-4744-2(8)*, 9781477847442, Two Lions) Amazon Publishing.
Simonson, Louise. Snow White & the Seven Robots: A Graphic Novel. Sanchez, Jimena S., illus. 2015. (Far Out Fairy Tales Ser.). (ENG.). 40p. (J). (gr. 3-6). lib. bdg. 25.32 *(978-1-4342-9648-1(2)*, 126939, Stone Arch Bks.) Capstone.
Sonneborn, Scott. The Frankenstein Journals, 1 vol. Banks, Timothy, illus. 2014. (Frankenstein Journals). (ENG.). 160p. (J). (gr. 2-4). 9.95 *(978-1-4342-9130-1(8)*, 125575, Stone Arch Bks.) Capstone.
—A Pain in the Butt. Banks, Timothy, illus. 2015. (Frankenstein Journals). (ENG.). 80p. (J). (gr. 2-4). 22.65 *(978-1-4965-0222-3(1)*, 128036, Stone Arch Bks.) Capstone.
Spradlin, Michael P. Menace from the Deep. 2013. (Killer Species Ser.: 1). lib. bdg. 16.00 *(978-0-606-32447-2(X))* Turtleback.
Springham, James. Earth-n-Bones: Toxic. 2005. 56p. pap. 16.95 *(978-1-4137-9755-8(5))* America Star Bks.
Stine, R. L. Frankenstein's Dog. 2013. (Goosebumps Most Wanted Ser.: 4). 136p. (J). lib. bdg. 17.20 *(978-0-606-32006-1(7))* Turtleback.
Tatulli, Mark. Lio: Making Friends. 2013. (Lio Ser.: 8). (ENG., Illus.). 224p. (J). pap. 9.99 *(978-1-4494-2558-6(5))* Andrews McMeel Publishing.
Teagan, Erin. The Friendship Experiment. (ENG.). 256p. (J). (gr. 5-7). 2019. pap. 7.99 *(978-1-328-91125-4(X)*, 1701810) 2016. 16.99 *(978-0-544-63622-4(8)*, 1619956) HarperCollins Pubs. (Clarion Bks.).
Thomas, Carroll, creator. Under the Open Sky: A Matty Trescott Novel. 2005. (Illus.). 184p. (J). per. 12.95 *(978-0-9762091-2-6(8))* Antrim Hse.
Thomas, Rich. The Incredible Hulk. Semeiks, Val, illus. 2012. (Marvel Origins Ser.). (ENG.). 48p. (J). (gr. k-5). lib. bdg. 31.36 *(978-1-61479-009-9(4)*, 11337, Marvel Age) Spotlight.
Thrasher, Amanda M. A Fairy Match in the Mushroom Patch. 2013. (Mischief Ser.: 2). (ENG., Illus.). 162p. (J). (gr. 2-4). pap. 8.99 *(978-0-9888568-1-3(6))* Progressive Rising Phoenix Pr., LLC.
Torres, Mario J. The Incredible Adventures of Kaplan & Dylan: Book One: Present, 1 vol. 2009. 159p. pap. 24.95 *(978-1-4489-9513-4(2))* PublishAmerica, Inc.
Toufexis, George. MONSTER MASH-Up — Rise of the Predators. 2014. (ENG., Illus.). 48p. (J). (gr. 4). pap. 4.99 *(978-0-486-49224-7(9))* Dover Pubns., Inc.
—MONSTER MASH-Up — Robots' Revenge. 2014. (ENG., Illus.). 48p. (J). (gr. 4). pap. 4.99 *(978-0-486-49225-4(7))* Dover Pubns., Inc.
Trent, Tiffany. The Unnaturalists. 2013. (ENG., Illus.). 336p. (YA). (gr. 7). pap. 9.99 *(978-1-4424-2207-0(6)*, Simon & Schuster Bks. For Young Readers) Simon & Schuster Bks. For Young Readers.
Trine, Greg. Attack of the Valley Girls, 6. Montijo, Rhode, illus. 6th ed. 2008. (Melvin Beederman, Superhero Ser.: 6). (ENG.). 137p. (J). (gr. 2-4). 22.44 *(978-0-8050-8160-2(7)*, Holt, Henry & Co.) Holt, Henry & Co.
—Attack of the Valley Girls (6) Montijo, Rhode, illus. 6th ed. 2008. (Melvin Beederman, Superhero Ser.: 6). (ENG.). 144p. (J). (gr. 2-5). pap. 9.99 *(978-0-8050-8161-9(5)*, 900040235) Square Fish.
Villeneuve, Kevin J. The Adventures of Nick the Ecologist & His Robot O-Zone: The Mystery of the Missing Trees. 2007. 96p. per. 9.95 *(978-0-595-42362-0(0))* iUniverse, Inc.

S

Walsh, Ann. Flower Power. 2006. (Orca Currents Ser.). 107p. (gr. 5-9). 19.95 *(978-0-7569-6874-8(7))* Perfection Learning Corp.
Walters, Eric. Visions. 2011. (ENG.). 208p. (J). pap. *(978-1-55455-122-4(6))* Fitzhenry & Whiteside, Ltd.
Wells, H. G. The Invisible Man. Calero, Dennis, illus. 2010. (Classic Fiction Ser.). 72p. pap. 0.60 *(978-1-4342-3208-3(5)*, Stone Arch Bks.) Capstone.
White, Kiersten. The Dark Descent of Elizabeth Frankenstein. 2019. 320p. (YA). (gr. 7). pap. 11.99 *(978-0-525-57796-6(3)*, Ember) Random Hse. Children's Bks.

SCIENTISTS, AFRICAN AMERICAN
see African American Scientists

SCOOBY-DOO (FICTITIOUS CHARACTER)—FICTION
Abdo Publishing & Gelsey, James. Scooby-Doo Mysteries, 4 vols., Set. Sur, Duendes Del, illus. 2013. (Scooby-Doo Mysteries Ser.: 6). (ENG.). 64p. (J). (gr. 3-6). lib. bdg. 125.44 *(978-1-61479-041-9(8)*, 13221, Chapter Bks.) Spotlight.
ABDO Publishing Company Staff. Scooby-Doo Early Reading Adventures, 14 vols. Sur, Duendes del, illus. 2016. (Scooby-Doo Early Reading Adventures Ser.). (ENG.). 24p. (J). (gr. -1-2). lib. bdg. 439.04 *(978-1-61479-463-9(4)*, 21376) Spotlight.
ABDO Publishing Company Staff & Howard, Lee. Scooby-Doo Comic Storybook, 3 vols. Alcadia SNC Staff, illus. 2014. (Scooby-Doo Comic Storybook Ser.: 4). (ENG.). 32p. (J). (gr. -1-3). lib. bdg. 94.08 *(978-1-61479-280-2(1)*, 1634, Graphic Novels) Spotlight.
Adamson, Heather & Adamson, Thomas K. Scooby-Doo! a Time Mystery: The Case of the Spinning Spook. Neely, Scott, illus. 2017. (Solve It with Scooby-Doo!: Math Ser.). (ENG.). 24p. (J). (gr. k-2). lib. bdg. 28.65 *(978-1-5157-7910-0(6)*, 136025, Capstone Pr.) Capstone.
—Scooby-Doo! an Estimation Mystery: The Case of the Greedy Ghost. Neely, Scott, illus. 2017. (Solve It with Scooby-Doo!: Math Ser.). (ENG.). 24p. (J). (gr. k-2). lib. bdg. 28.65 *(978-1-5157-7905-6(X)*, 136020, Capstone Pr.) Capstone.
—Solve It with Scooby-Doo!: Math. Neely, Scott, illus. 2017. (Solve It with Scooby-Doo!: Math Ser.). (ENG.). 24p. (J). (gr. k-2). 183.90 *(978-1-5157-7924-7(6)*, 26952, Capstone Pr.) Capstone.
Auerbach, Annie. Scooby-Doo in the Coolsville Contraption Contest, 1 vol. 2015. (Scooby-Doo! Ser.). (ENG., Illus.). 32p. (J). (gr. k-4). lib. bdg. 31.36 *(978-1-61479-409-7(X)*, 19448, Picture Bk.) Spotlight.
—Scooby-Doo in the Mystery Mansion, 1 vol. 2015. (Scooby-Doo! Ser.). (ENG., Illus.). 32p. (J). (gr. k-4). lib. bdg. 31.36 *(978-1-61479-411-0(1)*, 19450, Picture Bk.) Spotlight.
Balaban, Mariah. Scooby-Doo! & the Haunted Diner. 2010. (Illus.). 31p. (J). *(978-0-545-20882-6(3))* Scholastic, Inc.
—Scooby-Doo & the Rotten Robot, 1 vol. Sur, Duendes Del, illus. 2011. (Scooby-Doo! Ser.: No. 2). (ENG.). 24p. (J). (gr. k-4). lib. bdg. 31.36 *(978-1-59961-868-5(0)*, 13246, Picture Bk.) Spotlight.
—Scooby-Doo & the Scary Snowman, 1 vol. Sur, Duendes Del, illus. 2011. (Scooby-Doo! Ser.: No. 2). (ENG.). 24p. (J). (gr. k-4). lib. bdg. 31.36 *(978-1-59961-869-2(9)*, 13247, Picture Bk.) Spotlight.
—Scooby-Doo & the Thanksgiving Terror, 1 vol. Duendes Del Sur Staff, illus. 2011. (Scooby-Doo! Ser.: No. 2). (ENG.). 24p. (J). (gr. k-4). lib. bdg. 31.36 *(978-1-59961-870-8(2)*, 13248, Picture Bk.) Spotlight.
Barbo, Maria S. Scooby-Doo & the Kitty Cat Caper, 1 vol. Sur, Duendes del, illus. 2016. (Scooby-Doo Early Reading Adventures Ser.). (ENG.). 24p. (J). (gr. -1-2). lib. bdg. 31.36 *(978-1-61479-465-3(0)*, 21378) Spotlight.
—Treasure Hunt, 1 vol. Sur, Duendes Del, illus. 2013. (Scooby-Doo! Picture Clue Bks.). (ENG.). 24p. (J). (gr. k-2). lib. bdg. 31.36 *(978-1-61479-040-2(X)*, 13234) Spotlight.
Busch, Robbie. Scooby-Doo in Don't Play Dummy with Me, 1 vol. Deporter, Vincent, illus. 2010. (Scooby-Doo Graphic Novels Ser.: No. 1). (ENG.). 24p. (J). (gr. 2-6). 31.36 *(978-1-59961-693-3(9)*, 561, Graphic Novels) Spotlight.
—Scooby-Doo in Ready-to-Werewolf, 1 vol. Matchette, Karen, illus. 2010. (Scooby-Doo Graphic Novels Ser.: No. 1). (ENG.). 24p. (J). (gr. 2-6). 31.36 *(978-1-59961-696-4(3)*, 564, Graphic Novels) Spotlight.
—Scooby-Doo in the Agony of de Feet! Pope, Robert, illus. 2010. (Scooby-Doo Graphic Novels Ser.: No. 1). (ENG.). 24p. (J). (gr. 2-6). 31.36 *(978-1-59961-690-2(4)*, 558, Graphic Novels) Spotlight.
Class 1-208. Pizza Place Ghost, 1 vol. Sur, Duendes Del, illus. 2013. (Scooby-Doo! Picture Clue Bks.). (ENG.). 24p. (J). (gr. k-2). lib. bdg. 31.36 *(978-1-61479-038-9(8)*, 13232) Spotlight.
Cunningham, Scott. Scooby-Doo & the Hungry Ghost. Duendes Del Sur Staff, illus. 2005. (Scooby Doo Ser.). (ENG.). 12p. (J). (gr. -1-3). 8.99 *(978-0-439-74882-7(8))* Scholastic, Inc.
—Scooby-Doo in Terror Is Afoot! Neely, Scott & Pope, Robert, illus. 2010. (Scooby-Doo Graphic Novels Ser.: No. 1). (ENG.). 24p. (J). (gr. 2-6). 31.36 *(978-1-59961-698-8(X)*, 566, Graphic Novels) Spotlight.
Cunningham, Scott & Barrios, Roberto. Scooby-Doo & the Shadow Goblin, 1 vol. 2011. (Scooby-Doo Graphic Novels Ser.: No. 2). (ENG., Illus.). 24p. (J). (gr. 2-6). 31.36 *(978-1-59961-917-0(2)*, 571, Graphic Novels) Spotlight.
Fertig, Michael P. Musical Mystery Scooby Doo! McKee, Darren, illus. 2007. (Scooby Doo Ser.). (J). (gr. -1-3). 12.98 *(978-1-4127-7429-1(2))* Publications International, Ltd.
Fisch, Sholly. Scooby-Doo in Fangs, but No Fangs!, 1 vol. Deporter, Vincent, illus. 2013. (Scooby-Doo Graphic Novels Ser.). (ENG.). 24p. (J). (gr. 2-6). lib. bdg. 31.36 *(978-1-61479-051-8(5)*, 584, Graphic Novels) Spotlight.
Gelsey, James. The Baseball Boogeyman. 2004. (Illus.). 44p. (J). *(978-0-439-55713-9(5))* Scholastic, Inc.
—Scooby-Doo! & the Carnival Creeper, 1 vol. Sur, Duendes Del, illus. 2013. (Scooby-Doo Mysteries Ser.). (ENG.). 64p. (J). (gr. 3-6). lib. bdg. 31.36 *(978-1-61479-042-6(6)*, 13222, Chapter Bks.) Spotlight.
—Scooby-Doo! & the Groovy Ghost, 1 vol. Sur, Duendes Del, illus. 2013. (Scooby-Doo Mysteries Ser.). (ENG.). 64p. (J). (gr. 3-6). lib. bdg. 31.36 *(978-1-61479-044-0(2)*, 13224, Chapter Bks.) Spotlight.
—Scooby-Doo! & the Gruesome Goblin, 1 vol. Sur, Duendes Del, illus. 2013. (Scooby-Doo Mysteries Ser.). (ENG.). 64p. (J). (gr. 3-6). lib. bdg. 31.36 *(978-1-61479-045-7(0)*, 13225, Chapter Bks.) Spotlight.
—Scooby-Doo! & the Spooky Strikeout, 1 vol. Sur, Duendes Del, illus. 2013. (Scooby-Doo Mysteries Ser.). (ENG.). 64p. (J). (gr. 3-6). lib. bdg. 31.36 *(978-1-61479-047-1(7)*, 13227, Chapter Bks.) Spotlight.
Giffen, Keith. Scooby Apocalypse Vol. 1. 2017. lib. bdg. 29.40 *(978-0-606-39806-0(6))* Turtleback.
Griep, Heinrich & Laguna, Fabio. Scooby-Doo in Sumo A-Go-Go, 1 vol. 2011. (Scooby-Doo Graphic Novels Ser.: No. 2). (ENG., Illus.). 24p. (J). (gr. 2-6). 31.36 *(978-1-59961-923-1(7)*, 577, Graphic Novels) Spotlight.
Griep, Terrance & Batic, Leo. Scooby-Doo in Chills & Spills!, 1 vol. 2011. (Scooby-Doo Graphic Novels Ser.: No. 2). (ENG., Illus.). 24p. (J). (gr. 2-6). 31.36 *(978-1-59961-919-4(9)*, 573, Graphic Novels) Spotlight.
Griep, Terrence, Jr. Scooby-Doo in Screechy Keen, 1 vol. Matchette, Karen, illus. 2010. (Scooby-Doo Graphic Novels Ser.: No. 1). (ENG.). 24p. (J). (gr. 2-6). 31.36 *(978-1-59961-697-1(1)*, 565, Graphic Novels) Spotlight.
Guidone, Ellen. Scooby-Doo in Lights Out at the Ball Game, 1 vol. Sur, Duendes del, illus. 2016. (Scooby-Doo Early Reading Adventures Ser.). (ENG.). 24p. (J). (gr. -1-2). lib. bdg. 31.36 *(978-1-61479-475-2(8)*, 21388) Spotlight.
Herman, Gail. Fall Fright. Duendes Del Sur Staff, illus. 2005. (Hello Reader! Ser.). 32p. (J). pap. *(978-0-439-78358-3(5))* Scholastic, Inc.
—Scooby-Doo: A Scooby-Rific Reader. 2012. (Illus.). (J). *(978-1-4351-3986-2(0))* Scholastic, Inc.
—Scooby-Doo in the Lighthouse Mystery, 1 vol. 2015. (Scooby-Doo! Ser.). (ENG., Illus.). 32p. (J). (gr. k-4). lib. bdg. 31.36 *(978-1-61479-410-3(3)*, 19449, Picture Bk.) Spotlight.
—Scooby-Doo in up, up, & Away!, 1 vol. 2015. (Scooby-Doo! Ser.). (ENG., Illus.). 32p. (J). (gr. k-4). lib. bdg. 31.36 *(978-1-61479-412-7(X)*, 19451, Picture Bk.) Spotlight.
—A Scooby-Rific Reader. Duendes Del Sur Staff, illus. 2005. (Scooby Doo Ser.). 290p. (J). *(978-0-681-15349-3(0))* Scholastic, Inc.
Hinkler Books, ed. Scooby Doo! & the Gang's Spooky Snacks. 2012. 48p. (J). 19.99 *(978-1-74308-544-8(3))* Hinkler Bks. Pty, Ltd. AUS. Dist: Ideals Pubns.
Howard, Kate. Hotel of Horrors. 2012. (Scooby Doo 8X8 Ser.). lib. bdg. 14.75 *(978-0-606-31559-3(4))* Turtleback.
Howard, Lee. Giddy-Up, Scooby-Doo, 1 vol. Alcadia, S. N. C., illus. 2015. (Scooby-Doo Leveled Readers Ser.). (ENG.). 32p. (J). (gr. k-4). lib. bdg. 31.36 *(978-1-61479-414-1(6)*, 19437) Spotlight.
—Scooby-Doo & the Snow Monster Mystery, 1 vol. Alcadia, S. N. C., illus. 2015. (Scooby-Doo Leveled Readers Ser.). (ENG.). 32p. (J). (gr. k-4). lib. bdg. 31.36 *(978-1-61479-417-2(0)*, 19440) Spotlight.
—Scooby-Doo & the Unnatural, 1 vol. 2015. (Scooby-Doo Comic Readers Ser.). (ENG., Illus.). 32p. (J). (gr. -1-3). lib. bdg. 31.36 *(978-1-61479-453-0(7)*, 19432, Graphic Novels) Spotlight.
—Scooby-Doo in Bake-Off Mayhem, 1 vol. Alcadia, S. N. C., illus. 2015. (Scooby-Doo Leveled Readers Ser.). (ENG.). 32p. (J). (gr. k-4). lib. bdg. 31.36 *(978-1-61479-418-9(9)*, 19441) Spotlight.
—Scooby-Doo in Monkey See, Monkey Doo, 1 vol. Alcadia, S. N. C., illus. 2015. (Scooby-Doo Leveled Readers Ser.). (ENG.). 32p. (J). (gr. k-4). lib. bdg. 31.36 *(978-1-61479-419-6(7)*, 19442) Spotlight.
—Scooby-Doo in There's No Creature Like Snow Creature, 1 vol. 2015. (Scooby-Doo Comic Readers Ser.). (ENG., Illus.). 32p. (J). (gr. k-3). lib. bdg. 31.36 *(978-1-61479-456-1(1)*, 19435, Graphic Novels) Spotlight.
Hurley, Jo. Scooby-Doo! & the Phantom Prankster. 2005. (Illus.). 44p. *(978-0-439-73708-1(7))* Scholastic, Inc.
Ip, Ivy S. Clues at the Carnival, 1 vol. Sur, Duendes Del, illus. 2013. (Scooby-Doo! Picture Clue Bks.). (ENG.). 24p. (J). (gr. k-2). lib. bdg. 31.36 *(978-1-61479-036-5(1)*, 13230) Spotlight.
Korté, Steve. Curse of the Stage Fright. Neely, Scott, illus. 2016. (Scooby-Doo Comic Chapter Bks.). (ENG.). 88p. (J). (gr. 3-7). pap. 5.95 *(978-1-4965-3587-0(1)*, 132733); lib. bdg. 27.32 *(978-1-4965-3583-2(9)*, 132729) Capstone. (Stone Arch Bks.).
Korté, Steve & Manning, Matthew K. Scooby-Doo Comic Chapter Books. Neely, Scott, illus. 2016. (Scooby-Doo Comic Chapter Bks.). (ENG.). 88p. (J). (gr. 3-7). 111.96 *(978-1-4965-3603-7(7)*, 25085) Capstone.
Kravitz, Darryl Taylor & Pope, Robert. Scooby-Doo in Nothing S'More Terrifying!, 1 vol. 2011. (Scooby-Doo Graphic Novels Ser.: No. 2). (ENG., Illus.). 24p. (J). (gr. 2-6). 31.36 *(978-1-59961-921-7(0)*, 575, Graphic Novels) Spotlight.
Kress, Earl. Scooby-Doo in Hear No Evil, 1 vol. Delaney, John, illus. 2010. (Scooby-Doo Graphic Novels Ser.: No. 1). (ENG.). 24p. (J). (gr. 2-6). 31.36 *(978-1-59961-694-0(7)*, 562, Graphic Novels) Spotlight.
Kupperberg, Paul. Scooby-Doo in over the Boardwalk, 1 vol. Laguna, Fabio, illus. 2013. (Scooby-Doo Graphic Novels Ser.). (ENG.). 24p. (J). (gr. 2-6). lib. bdg. 31.36 *(978-1-61479-052-5(3)*, 585, Graphic Novels) Spotlight.
—Scooby-Doo in Read All about It!, 1 vol. Laguna, Fabio, illus. 2013. (Scooby-Doo Graphic Novels Ser.). (ENG.). 24p. (J). (gr. 2-6). lib. bdg. 31.36 *(978-1-61479-053-2(1)*, 586, Graphic Novels) Spotlight.
Kupperberg, Paul & Barrios, Roberto. Scooby-Doo & the Black Katz, 1 vol. 2011. (Scooby-Doo Graphic Novels Ser.: No. 2). (ENG., Illus.). 24p. (J). (gr. 2-6). 31.36 *(978-1-59961-915-6(6)*, 569, Graphic Novels) Spotlight.
—Scooby-Doo in the Phantom of the Opal!, 1 vol. 2011. (Scooby-Doo Graphic Novels Ser.: No. 2). (ENG., Illus.). 24p. (J). (gr. 2-6). 31.36 *(978-1-59961-924-8(5)*, 578, Graphic Novels) Spotlight.
Kupperberg, Paul & Laguna, Fabio. Scooby-Doo in Scooba Doo!, 1 vol. 2011. (Scooby-Doo Graphic Novels Ser.: No. 2). (ENG., Illus.). 24p. (J). (gr. 2-6). 31.36 *(978-1-59961-922-4(9)*, 576, Graphic Novels) Spotlight.
—Scooby-Doo Versus Them!, 1 vol. 2011. (Scooby-Doo Graphic Novels Ser.: No. 2). (ENG., Illus.). 24p. (J). (gr. 2-6). 31.36 *(978-1-59961-926-2(1)*, 580, Graphic Novels) Spotlight.
Manning, Matthew K. The Mystery of the Mayhem Mansion. Neely, Scott, illus. 2016. (You Choose Stories: Scooby-Doo Ser.). (ENG.). 112p. (J). (gr. 2-6). lib. bdg. 32.65 *(978-1-4965-2661-8(9)*, 131220, Stone Arch Bks.) Capstone.
—Mystery of the Mist Monster. Neely, Scott, illus. 2016. (Scooby-Doo Comic Chapter Bks.). (ENG.). 88p. (J). (gr. 3-7). lib. bdg. 27.32 *(978-1-4965-3586-3(3)*, 132732, Stone Arch Bks.) Capstone.
—The Salem Witch Showdown. Neely, Scott, illus. 2017. (You Choose Stories: Scooby-Doo Ser.). (ENG.). 112p. (J). (gr. 2-6). lib. bdg. 32.65 *(978-1-4965-4334-9(3)*, 134223, Stone Arch Bks.) Capstone.
—Secret of the Haunted Cave. Neely, Scott, illus. 2016. (Scooby-Doo Comic Chapter Bks.). (ENG.). 88p. (J). (gr. 3-7). lib. bdg. 27.32 *(978-1-4965-3585-6(5)*, 132731, Stone Arch Bks.) Capstone.
McCann, Jesse Leon. Scooby-Doo & Museum Madness, 1 vol. Sur, Duendes Del, illus. 2011. (Scooby-Doo! Ser.: No. 2). (ENG.). 24p. (J). (gr. k-4). lib. bdg. 31.36 *(978-1-59961-867-8(2)*, 13245, Picture Bk.) Spotlight.
—Scooby-Doo & the Fishy Phantom, 1 vol. Sur, Duendes Del, illus. 2011. (Scooby-Doo! Ser.: No. 2). (ENG.). 24p. (J). (gr. k-4). lib. bdg. 31.36 *(978-1-59961-866-1(4)*, 13244, Picture Bk.) Spotlight.
Musacchia, Vince, illus. Scooby-Doo! The Case of the Disappearing Scooby Snacks. 2005. (Media Favorites!! Ser.). 22p. (J). 9.95 *(978-1-58117-214-0(1)*, Intervisual/Piggy Toes) Bendon, Inc.
Nagler, Michelle H. Scooby-Doo & the Monster in the Woods, 1 vol. Sur, Duendes del, illus. 2016. (Scooby-Doo Early Reading Adventures Ser.). (ENG.). 24p. (J). (gr. -1-2). lib. bdg. 31.36 *(978-1-61479-468-4(5)*, 21381) Spotlight.
—Scooby-Doo in Lost at Sea, 1 vol. Sur, Duendes del, illus. 2016. (Scooby-Doo Early Reading Adventures Ser.). (ENG.). 24p. (J). (gr. -1-2). lib. bdg. 31.36 *(978-1-61479-476-9(6)*, 21389) Spotlight.
Panini Publishing, creator. Scooby Doo! Summer Annual. 2011. (Illus.). 63p. (J). (gr. 4-7). pap. *(978-1-84653-145-3(4))* Panini Publishing.
Penney, Shannon. Decodes a Mystery. 2005. 22p. *(978-0-439-67841-4(2))* Scholastic, Inc.
Peterson, Megan Cooley. Scooby-Doo! a Science of Chemical Reactions Mystery: The Overreacting Ghost. Brizuela, Dario, illus. 2017. (Scooby-Doo Solves It with S. T. E. M. Ser.). (ENG.). 32p. (J). (gr. 3-6). lib. bdg. 28.65 *(978-1-5157-3697-4(0)*, 133666, Capstone Pr.) Capstone.
—Scooby-Doo! a Science of Electricity Mystery: The Mutant Crocodile. Cornia, Christian, illus. 2017. (Scooby-Doo Solves It with S. T. E. M. Ser.). (ENG.). 32p. (J). (gr. 3-6). lib. bdg. 28.65 *(978-1-5157-3698-1(9)*, 133667, Capstone Pr.) Capstone.
—Scooby-Doo! a Science of Light Mystery: The Angry Alien. Brizuela, Dario, illus. 2017. (Scooby-Doo Solves It with S. T. E. M. Ser.). (ENG.). 32p. (J). (gr. 3-6). lib. bdg. 28.65 *(978-1-5157-3700-1(4)*, 133669, Capstone Pr.) Capstone.
—Scooby-Doo! a Science of Magnetism Mystery: The Magnetic Monster. Cornia, Christian, illus. 2017. (Scooby-Doo Solves It with S. T. E. M. Ser.). (ENG.). 32p. (J). (gr. 3-6). lib. bdg. 28.65 *(978-1-5157-3699-8(7)*, 133668, Capstone Pr.) Capstone.
—Scooby-Doo Solves It with S. T. E. M. Brizuela, Dario, illus. 2017. (Scooby-Doo Solves It with S. T. E. M. Ser.). (ENG.). 32p. (J). (gr. 3-6). 245.20 *(978-1-5157-3717-9(9)*, 25460, Capstone Pr.) Capstone.
Publications International Ltd. Staff, ed. Scooby Doo Message in a Bottle Sound Book. 2004. (Illus.). 24p. 15.98 *(978-1-4127-0600-1(9)*, 7222600) Publications International, Ltd.
—Scooby Doo: Spooky Shadows: Flashlight Adventure Sound Book. 2013. 14p. (J). (gr. 1-3). 17.98 *(978-1-4508-6598-2(4)*, f7a3c6e7-aa63-4615-8fc2-d9e099fdce9c) Publications International, Ltd.
Rozum, Fred & Gross, Scott. Scooby-Doo & Those Meddling Kids, 1 vol. 2011. (Scooby-Doo Graphic Novels Ser.: No. 2). (ENG., Illus.). 24p. (J). (gr. 2-6). 31.36 *(978-1-59961-918-7(0)*, 572, Graphic Novels) Spotlight.
Rozum, John. Scooby-Doo in Yankee Doodle Danger, 1 vol. Laguna, Fabio, illus. 2013. (Scooby-Doo Graphic Novels Ser.). (ENG.). 24p. (J). (gr. 2-6). lib. bdg. 31.36 *(978-1-61479-054-9(X)*, 587, Graphic Novels) Spotlight.
Rozum, John & Laguna, Fabio. Scooby-Doo in Fright Ride, 1 vol. 2011. (Scooby-Doo Graphic Novels Ser.: No. 2). (ENG., Illus.). 24p. (J). (gr. 2-6). 31.36 *(978-1-59961-920-0(2)*, 574, Graphic Novels) Spotlight.
Rozum, John & Pope, Robert. Scooby-Doo & the Monster of a Thousand Faces!, 1 vol. 2011. (Scooby-Doo Graphic Novels Ser.: No. 2). (ENG., Illus.). 24p. (J). (gr. 2-6). 31.36 *(978-1-59961-916-3(4)*, 570, Graphic Novels) Spotlight.
Sander, Sonia. Big-Top Scooby-Doo! Movie Reader. 2012. (Scooby Doo Reader Ser.). lib. bdg. 13.55 *(978-0-606-26542-3(2))* Turtleback.
—Scooby-Doo & the Battle of the Snowboarders, 1 vol. Alcadia, S. N. C., illus. 2015. (Scooby-Doo Leveled Readers Ser.). (ENG.). 32p. (J). (gr. k-4). lib. bdg. 31.36 *(978-1-61479-415-8(4)*, 19438) Spotlight.
—Scooby-Doo & the Big Catch, 1 vol. Alcadia, S. N. C., illus. 2015. (Scooby-Doo Leveled Readers Ser.). (ENG.). 32p. (J). (gr. k-4). lib. bdg. 31.36 *(978-1-61479-416-5(2)*, 19439) Spotlight.
—Scooby-Doo & the Chocolate Phantom, 1 vol. 2015. (Scooby-Doo Comic Readers Ser.). (ENG., Illus.). 32p. (J). (gr. -1-3). lib. bdg. 31.36 *(978-1-61479-451-6(0)*, 19430, Graphic Novels) Spotlight.
—Scooby-Doo & the International Express. 2009. (Illus.). 32p. (J). pap. *(978-0-545-16283-8(1))* Scholastic, Inc.
—Scooby-Doo in Food Fight!, 1 vol. 2015. (Scooby-Doo Comic Readers Ser.). (ENG., Illus.). 32p. (J). (gr. -1-3). lib. bdg. 31.36 *(978-1-61479-454-7(5)*, 19433, Graphic Novels) Spotlight.
—Scooby-Doo in Keepaway Camp, 1 vol. Gross, Scott, illus. 2015. (Scooby-Doo! Ser.). (ENG.). 32p. (J). (gr. k-3). lib. bdg. 31.36 *(978-1-61479-407-3(3)*, 19446, Picture Bk.) Spotlight.
—Scooby-Doo in Raging River Adventure, 1 vol. Alcadia, S. N. C., illus. 2015. (Scooby-Doo Leveled Readers Ser.). (ENG.). 32p. (J). (gr. k-4). lib. bdg. 31.36 *(978-1-61479-420-2(0)*, 19443) Spotlight.
—Scooby-Doo in Shiver Me Timbers, 1 vol. 2015. (Scooby-Doo! Ser.). (ENG., Illus.). 32p. (J). (gr. k-4). lib. bdg. 31.36 *(978-1-61479-408-0(1)*, 19447, Picture Bk.) Spotlight.
—Scooby-Doo Steals the Dog Show, 1 vol. Alcadia, S. N. C., illus. 2015. (Scooby-Doo Leveled Readers Ser.). (ENG.). 32p. (J). (gr. k-4). lib. bdg. 31.36 *(978-1-61479-421-9(9)*, 19444) Spotlight.
—Werewolf Watch. 2012. (Scooby Doo Reader Ser.). lib. bdg. 13.55 *(978-0-606-23961-5(8))* Turtleback.
—Witching Hour. 2009. (Scooby Reader 25 Ser.). (ENG., Illus.). 32p. (J). (gr. -1-3). pap. 3.99 *(978-0-545-16106-0(1))* Scholastic, Inc.
Sazaklis, John. The Mystery of the Maze Monster, 1 vol. Neely, Scott, illus. 2014. (You Choose Stories: Scooby-Doo Ser.). (ENG.). 112p. (J). (gr. 2-6). pap. 6.95 *(978-1-4342-7928-6(6)*, 124639, Stone Arch Bks.) Capstone.
Scholastic. Peppa's Storybook Collection (Peppa Pig) 2017. (ENG., Illus.). 192p. (J). (gr. -1-k). 12.99 *(978-1-338-21199-3(4))* Scholastic, Inc.
Scholastic, Inc. Staff. Scooby-Doo: Frankencreepy Movie Reader. 2014. (Scooby Doo Reader Ser.). lib. bdg. 13.55 *(978-0-606-36270-2(3))* Turtleback.
Scholastic, Inc. Staff & Duendes Del Sur Staff, contrib. by. Scooby-Doo! & the Mummy's Curse. 2005. (Illus.). 24p. (J). *(978-1-4156-3913-9(2))* Scholastic, Inc.
Scooby-Do! Scooby. . . Don't! 2005. (Media Favorites!! Ser.). 14p. (J). 10.95 *(978-1-58117-215-7(X)*, Intervisual/Piggy Toes) Bendon, Inc.
Scooby-Doo & the Case of the Disappearing Scooby Snacks. 2004. (Media Favorites!! Ser.). 12p. (J). 4.95 *(978-1-58117-329-1(6)*, Intervisual/Piggy Toes) Bendon, Inc.
Scooby-Doo Comic Readers: Set. 4 vols. 2015. (Scooby-Doo Comic Readers Ser.: 6). (ENG.). 32p. (J). (gr. -1-3). lib. bdg. 125.44 *(978-1-61479-450-9(2)*, 19429, Graphic Novels) Spotlight.
Scooby-Doo! el caso de las Scooby-galletas Misteriosas. 2005.Tr. of Scooby Doo! The Case of the Disappearing Scooby Snacks. (SPA.). 12p. (J). 4.95 *(978-1-58117-330-7(X)*, Intervisual/Piggy Toes) Bendon, Inc.
Scooby-Doo Graphic Novels, 4 vols. 2013. (Scooby-Doo Graphic Novels Ser.: 6). (ENG.). 24p. (J). (gr. 2-6). lib. bdg. 125.44 *(978-1-61479-048-8(5)*, 581, Graphic Novels) Spotlight.
Simmons, Alex. Scooby-Doo in Dead & Let Spy, 1 vol. Pope, Robert, illus. 2010. (Scooby-Doo Graphic Novels Ser.: No. 1). (ENG.). 24p. (J). (gr. 2-6). 31.36 *(978-1-59961-692-6(0)*, 560, Graphic Novels) Spotlight.
Soderberg, Erin. Scooby-Doo & the Dinosaur Ghost, 1 vol. Sur, Duendes del, illus. 2016. (Scooby-Doo Early Reading Adventures Ser.). (ENG.). 24p. (J). (gr. -1-2). lib. bdg. 31.36 *(978-1-61479-464-6(2)*, 21377) Spotlight.
—Scooby-Doo & the Mystery at the Park, 1 vol. Sur, Duendes del, illus. 2016. (Scooby-Doo Early Reading Adventures Ser.). (ENG.). 24p. (J). (gr. -1-2). lib. bdg. 31.36 *(978-1-61479-469-1(3)*, 21382) Spotlight.
Steele, Michael Anthony. The Case of the Fright Flight. Neely, Scott, illus. 2016. (You Choose Stories: Scooby-Doo Ser.). (ENG.). 112p. (J). (gr. 2-6). lib. bdg. 32.65 *(978-1-4965-2662-5(7)*, 131221, Stone Arch Bks.) Capstone.
—Creepy Cowboy Caper. Jeralds, Scott, illus. 2017. (Scooby-Doo! Beginner Mysteries Ser.). (ENG.). 112p. (J). (gr. 1-3). lib. bdg. 23.99 *(978-1-4965-4768-2(3)*, 135305, Stone Arch Bks.) Capstone.
—Monster Mutt Madness. Jeralds, Scott, illus. 2017. (Scooby-Doo! Beginner Mysteries Ser.). (ENG.). 112p. (J). (gr. 1-3). lib. bdg. 22.65 *(978-1-4965-4767-5(5)*, 135304, Stone Arch Bks.) Capstone.
—Scooby-Doo! Beginner Mysteries. 2017. (Scooby-Doo! Beginner Mysteries Ser.). (ENG.). 112p. (J). (gr. 1-3). 95.96 *(978-1-4965-4796-5(9)*, 26568, Stone Arch Bks.) Capstone.
—Skeleton Crew Showdown. Jeralds, Scott, illus. 2017. (Scooby-Doo! Beginner Mysteries Ser.). (ENG.). 112p. (J). (gr. 1-3). lib. bdg. 22.65 *(978-1-4965-4769-9(1)*, 135306, Stone Arch Bks.) Capstone.
—Vampire Zoo Hullabaloo. Jeralds, Scott, illus. 2017. (Scooby-Doo! Beginner Mysteries Ser.). (ENG.). 112p. (J). (gr. 1-3). lib. bdg. 22.65 *(978-1-4965-4770-5(5)*, 135307, Stone Arch Bks.) Capstone.
Strom, Frank & Barrios, Roberto. Scooby-Doo in Welcome to the Jungle, 1 vol. 2011. (Scooby-Doo Graphic Novels Ser.: No. 2). (ENG., Illus.). 24p. (J). (gr. 2-6). 31.36 *(978-1-59961-925-5(3)*, 579, Graphic Novels) Spotlight.
Sturk, Karl. Movie Star Mystery. 2010. (Scooby Doo Reader Ser.: 24). lib. bdg. 13.55 *(978-0-606-07085-0(0))* Turtleback.
Sur, Duendes Del, illus. Scooby-Doo! Picture Clue Books, 3 vols. 2013. (Scooby-Doo! Picture Clue Bks.: 6). (ENG.). 24p. (J). (gr. -1-2). lib. bdg. 94.08 *(978-1-61479-034-1(5)*, 13228) Spotlight.
Sutton, Laurie S. The Case of the Clown Carnival. Neely, Scott, illus. 2017. (You Choose Stories: Scooby-Doo Ser.). (ENG.). 112p. (J). (gr. 2-6). lib. bdg. 32.65 *(978-1-4965-4333-2(5)*, 134222, Stone Arch Bks.) Capstone.
—The Curse of Atlantis. Neely, Scott, illus. 2015. (You Choose Stories: Scooby-Doo Ser.). (ENG.). 112p. (J). (gr. 2-6). lib. bdg. 32.65 *(978-1-4965-0477-7(1)*, 128503, Stone Arch Bks.) Capstone.
—The Fright at Zombie Farm. Neely, Scott, illus. 2015. (You Choose Stories: Scooby-Doo Ser.). (ENG.). 112p. (J). (gr. 2-6). lib. bdg. 32.65 *(978-1-4342-9713-6(6)*, 127039, Stone Arch Bks.) Capstone.
—The Ghost of the Bermuda Triangle, 1 vol. Neely, Scott, illus. 2014. (You Choose Stories: Scooby-Doo Ser.). (ENG.). 112p. (J). (gr. 2-6). 32.65 *(978-1-4342-9126-4(X)*, 125571, Stone Arch Bks.) Capstone.
—The House on Spooky Street. Neely, Scott, illus. 2015. (You Choose Stories: Scooby-Doo Ser.). (ENG.). 112p. (J). (gr. 2-6). lib. bdg. 32.65 *(978-1-4342-9714-3(4)*, 127040, Stone Arch Bks.) Capstone.
—Legend of the Gator Man. Neely, Scott, illus. 2016. (Scooby-Doo Comic Chapter Bks.). (ENG.). 88p. (J). (gr. 3-7). lib. bdg. 27.32 *(978-1-4965-3584-9(7)*, 132730, Stone Arch Bks.) Capstone.
—The Mystery of the Aztec Tomb, 1 vol. Neely, Scott, illus. 2014. (You Choose Stories: Scooby-Doo Ser.). (ENG.). 112p. (J). (gr. 2-6). 32.65 *(978-1-4342-9127-1(8)*, 125572, Stone Arch Bks.) Capstone.
—The Secret of the Flying Saucer. Neely, Scott, illus. 2015. (You Choose Stories: Scooby-Doo Ser.). (ENG.). 112p. (J).

(gr. 2-6). lib. bdg. 32.65 (978-1-4965-0478-4(X), 128504, Stone Arch Bks.) Capstone.
—The Secret of the Sea Creature, 1 vol. Neely, Scott, illus. 2014. (You Choose Stories: Scooby-Doo Ser.). (ENG.). 112p. (J). (gr. 2-6). pap. 6.95 (978-1-4342-7925-5(1), 124637, Stone Arch Bks.) Capstone.
—The Terror of the Bigfoot Beast, 1 vol. Neely, Scott, illus. 2014. (You Choose Stories: Scooby-Doo Ser.). (ENG.). 112p. (J). (gr. 2-6). pap. 6.95 (978-1-4342-7926-2(X), 124636, Stone Arch Bks.) Capstone.
Sutton, Laurie S. & Manning, Matthew K. You Choose Stories: Scooby-Doo. Neely, Scott, illus. 2017. (You Choose Stories: Scooby-Doo Ser.). (ENG.). 112p. (J). (gr. 2-6). 457.10 (978-1-4965-4341-7(6), 25802, Stone Arch Bks.) Capstone.
Wasserman, Robin. Scooby-Doo & the Missing Scooby-Snacks, 1 vol. Sur, Duendes del, illus. 2016. (Scooby-Doo Early Reading Adventures Ser.). (ENG.). 24p. (J). (gr. -1-2). lib. bdg. 31.36 (978-1-61479-467-7(7), 21380) Spotlight.
—Scooby-Doo & the Snow Monster Scare, 1 vol. Sur, Duendes del, illus. 2016. (Scooby-Doo Early Reading Adventures Ser.). (ENG.). 24p. (J). (gr. -1-2). lib. bdg. 31.36 (978-1-61479-473-8(1), 21386) Spotlight.
Weakland, Mark. Unearthing Ancient Civilizations with Scooby-Doo! Comia, Christian & Brizuela, Dario, illus. 2018. (Unearthing Ancient Civilizations with Scooby-Doo! Ser.). (ENG.). 32p. (J). (gr. 3-6). 119.96 (978-1-5157-7532-4(1), 26799, Capstone Pr.) Capstone.

SCOPES, JOHN THOMAS, 1900-1970

Crewe, Sabrina & Uschan, Michael V. The Scopes Monkey Trial, 1 vol. 2004. (Events That Shaped America Ser.). (ENG., Illus.). 32p. (gr. 3-5). lib. bdg. 28.67 (978-0-8368-3415-4(1), b329797a-64db-4fba-8ac0-4e4ac4579fee, Gareth Stevens Learning Library) Stevens, Gareth Publishing LLLP.
Kowalski, Kathiann M. Evolution on Trial: From the Scopes Monkey Case to Inherit the Wind, 1 vol. 2009. (Famous Court Cases That Became Movies Ser.). (ENG., Illus.). 112p. (gr. 6-7). lib. bdg. 35.93 (978-0-7660-3056-5(3), 76add179-e7a4-46bc-977e-9e0245876ce4) Enslow Publishing, LLC.
The Scopes Monkey Trial: Debate over Evolution. 2010. (ENG., Illus.). 128p. (gr. 6-12). 35.00 (978-1-60413-679-1(0), P174395, Facts On File) Infobase Holdings, Inc.
Uschan, Michael V. The Scopes Monkey Trial, 1 vol. 2004. (Landmark Events in American History Ser.). (ENG., Illus.). 48p. (gr. 5-8). pap. 15.05 (978-0-8368-5424-4(1), dc45e062-7940-404a-87bf-311422683e68); lib. bdg. 33.67 (978-0-8368-5396-4(2), e62fff93-f673-4984-ae44-76ee6988972f) Stevens, Gareth Publishing LLLP. (Gareth Stevens Secondary Library).

SCORPIONS

Black, Nessa. Scorpions. 2019. (Spot Creepy Crawlies Ser.). (ENG.). 16p. (J). (gr. -1-2). lib. bdg. (978-1-68151-539-7(3), 14500) Amicus.
Blake, Kevin. Deadly Scorpion Sting! 2018. (Envenomators Ser.). (ENG., Illus.). 24p. (J). (gr. 2-7). 19.45 (978-1-68402-659-3(8)) Bearport Publishing Co., Inc.
Bodden, Valerie. Creepy Creatures: Scorpions. 2011. (Creepy Creatures Ser.). (ENG.). 24p. (J). (gr. 1-3). pap. 8.99 (978-0-89812-568-9(5), 22140, Creative Paperbacks) Creative Co., The.
—Scorpions. 2011. (Creepy Creatures Ser.). (ENG.). 24p. (J). (gr. 1-4). 24.25 (978-1-58341-995-3(0), 22135, Creative Education) Creative Co., The.
—Scorpions. 2010. (ENG., Illus.). 24p. (J). pap. 8.95 (978-1-926853-75-8(X)) Saunders Bk. Co. CAN. Dist: Creative Co., The.
Davin, Rose. Scorpions. 2017. (Meet Desert Animals Ser.). (ENG., Illus.). 24p. (J). (gr. -1-2). lib. bdg. 27.32 (978-1-5157-4601-0(1), 134285, Capstone Pr.) Capstone.
Feltes Taylor, Kimberly. Scorpion vs. Centipede: Duel to the Death. 2016. (Bug Wars Ser.). (ENG., Illus.). 32p. (J). (gr. 3-9). lib. bdg. 28.65 (978-1-4914-8066-3(1), 130570, Capstone Pr.) Capstone.
Franchino, Vicky. Nature's Children: Scorpions. 2015. (ENG.). 48p. (J). pap. 6.95 (978-0-531-21188-5(6), Orchard Bks.) Scholastic Library Publishing.
Goldish, Meish. Bark Scorpion. 2015. (Desert Animals Searchin' for Shade Ser.). (ENG.). 24p. (J). (gr. -1-3). lib. bdg. 26.99 (978-1-62724-535-7(9)) Bearport Publishing Co., Inc.
Gonzales, Doreen. Scorpions in the Dark, 1 vol. 2009. (Creatures of the Night Ser.). (ENG.). 24p. (gr. 2-3). (YA). pap. 9.25 (978-1-4358-3257-2(4), 8c962ee3-f6c1-4d97-a1f7-c7c1499fa95d); (Illus.). (J). 26.27 (978-1-4042-8100-4(2), e123172f-5292-45cb-987c-62c52b26ad5b) Rosen Publishing Group, Inc., The.
Lunis, Natalie. Stinging Scorpions. 2009. (No Backbone! Ser.). (Illus.). 24p. (J). (gr. k-3). lib. bdg. 26.99 (978-1-59716-756-7(8)) Bearport Publishing Co., Inc.
Lynette, Rachel. Scorpions, 1 vol. 2013. (Monsters of the Animal Kingdom Ser.). (ENG., Illus.). 24p. (J). (gr. 2-3). pap. 9.25 (978-1-4488-9722-3(X), 7939f2ae-f61d-494f-8042-4ec30843acae); lib. bdg. 26.27 (978-1-4488-9633-2(9), 8cb91de2-9d7f-4a4a-a5ab-5829f1bc5772) Rosen Publishing Group, Inc., The. (PowerKids Pr.).
Markovics, Joyce. MIS Pinzas Son Negras y Enormes (Scorpion) 2016. (Pistas de Animales 2/Zoo Clues 2 Ser.). (SPA.). 24p. (J). (gr. -1-3). 26.99 (978-1-944102-78-4(7)) Bearport Publishing Co., Inc.
Markovics, Joyce L. My Claws Are Huge & Black. 2016. (Zoo Clues 2 Ser.). (ENG & SPA.). 24p. (J). (gr. -1-3). 26.99 (978-1-944102-60-9(4)) Bearport Publishing Co., Inc.
McAneney, Caitie. Scorpion vs. Black Widow, 1 vol. 2015. (Bizarre Beast Battles Ser.). (ENG., Illus.). 24p. (J). (gr. 2-3). pap. 9.15 (978-1-4824-2792-9(3), 8c506fca-aaf9-4e8e-8d82-63f4c477db2) Stevens, Gareth Publishing LLLP.
McFee, Shane. Scorpions. (Poison! Ser.). 24p. (gr. 2-3). 2009. 42.50 (978-1-60851-325-3(4), PowerKids Pr.) 2007. (ENG., Illus.). (J). lib. bdg. 26.27 (978-1-4042-3794-0(1), 0ed7b70e-9349-4825-954f-d710db12a61e) Rosen Publishing Group, Inc., The.
Otfinoski, Steven. Scorpions, 1 vol. 2012. (Animals, Animals Ser.). (ENG., Illus.). 48p. (gr. 5-5). 32.64 (978-0-7614-4878-5(0), 6834db48-dc51-4961-92dd-c4343d3a4a90) Cavendish Square Publishing LLC.
Owings, Lisa. The Deathstalker Scorpion. 2013. (Nature's Deadliest Ser.). (ENG., Illus.). 24p. (J). (gr. 3-8). lib. bdg. 27.95 (978-1-60014-879-8(4), Pilot Bks.) Bellwether Media.
Pallotta, Jerry. Tarantula vs. Scorpion (Who Would Win?) Bolster, Rob, illus. 2016. (Who Would Win? Ser.). (ENG.). 32p. (J). (gr. 1-3). pap. 3.99 (978-0-545-30172-5(6)) Scholastic, Inc.
Pringle, Laurence. Scorpions! Strange & Wonderful. Henderson, Meryl Learnihan, illus. 2013. (Strange & Wonderful Ser.). (ENG.). 32p. (J). (gr. 2-5). 16.95 (978-1-59078-473-0(1), Astra Young Readers) Astra Publishing Hse.
Raum, Elizabeth. Scorpions. 2015. (Poisonous Animals Ser.). (ENG., Illus.). 32p. (J). (gr. 2-5). lib. bdg. 19.95 (978-1-60753-788-5(5), 15304) Amicus.
Roza, Greg. Sting! The Scorpion & Other Animals That Sting, 1 vol. 2011. (Armed & Dangerous Ser.). (ENG., Illus.). 24p. (J). (gr. 2-3). 26.27 (978-1-4488-2548-6(2), 9e9b4535-819e-480c-a0ed-dd6cb5799b2c); pap. 9.25 (978-1-4488-2680-3(2), 286ac118-1094-450e-a17c-2cc64979c994, PowerKids Pr.) Rosen Publishing Group, Inc., The.
Schuetz, Kari. Scorpions. 2015. (Creepy Crawlies Ser.). (ENG., Illus.). 24p. (J). (gr. k-3). lib. bdg. 26.95 (978-1-62617-226-5(9), Blastoff! Readers) Bellwether Media.
Shea, Therese M. Scorpions, 1 vol. 2015. (Things That Sting Ser.). (ENG., Illus.). 24p. (J). (gr. 2-3). lib. bdg. 24.27 (978-1-4824-1714-2(6), 53a1decd-3764-4be8-b486-2fc65843e19a) Stevens, Gareth Publishing LLLP.
Siemens, Jared. Scorpions. 2017. (Illus.). 24p. (J). (978-1-5105-0644-2(6)) SmartBook Media, Inc.
Sirota, Lyn. Los Escorpiones. 2019. (Criaturas Rastreras Ser.). (SPA., Illus.). 32p. (J). (gr. 4-6). lib. bdg. (978-1-62310-201-2(4), 12849, Bolt) Black Rabbit Bks.
—Scorpions. 2019. (Crawly Creatures Ser.). (ENG.). 32p. (J). (gr. 4-6). pap. 9.99 (978-1-64466-023-2(7), 12681); (Illus.). lib. bdg. (978-1-68072-812-5(1), 12680) Black Rabbit Bks. (Bolt).
Stark, Kristy. Terrarium Pets: Volume (Grade 6) 2019. (Mathematics in the Real World Ser.). (ENG., Illus.). 32p. (gr. 5-8). pap. 11.99 (978-1-4258-5891-9(0)) Teacher Created Materials, Inc.
Sullivan, Laura L. The Deathstalker Scorpion. 2017. (Toxic Creatures Ser.). 32p. (gr. 3-3). pap. 63.48 (978-1-5026-2577-9(6), Cavendish Square) Cavendish Square Publishing LLC.
Thomas, Isabel. Scorpion vs. Tarantula. 2017. (Animal Rivals Ser.). (ENG., Illus.). 24p. (J). (gr. k-2). lib. bdg. 25.99 (978-1-4846-4070-8(5), 135681, Heinemann) Capstone.

SCOTLAND

Ainsley, Dominic J. United Kingdom, Vol. 16. 2018. (European Countries Today Ser.). (Illus.). 96p. (J). (gr. 7). 34.60 (978-1-4222-3993-3(4)) Mason Crest.
Bodden, Valerie. To the Heart of Africa. 2011. (Great Expeditions Ser.). (ENG., Illus.). 48p. (J). (gr. 5-8). 35.65 (978-1-60818-066-0(2), 22152, Creative Education) Creative Co., The.
Carr, Simonetta. John Knox. Abraxas, Matt, illus. 2014. (ENG.). 64p. (J). 18.00 (978-1-60178-289-2(6)) Reformation Heritage Bks.
Day, Anna. Scotland 123: A Counting Book for Cool Kids. Gentry, Lauren, illus. 2015. (ENG.). 20p. (J). pap. 10.95 (978-0-9575456-2-5(2)) Playroom Pr.
Kirkby, Mandy. Pick Your Brains about Scotland. Williams, Caspar, illus. 2005. (Pick Your Brains Ser.). 128p. pap. 9.95 (978-1-86011-223-2(4)) Cadogan Guides GBR. Dist: Globe Pequot Pr., The.
MacDonald, Fiona. Meet a Body Snatcher! Criminals & Murderers You'D Rather Avoid. 2009. (You Wouldn't Want To... Ser.). (ENG., Illus.). 32p. (J). (gr. 4-6). 26.19 (978-0-531-20822-9(2), Watts, Franklin) Scholastic Library Publishing.
MacKenzie, Catherine. Scottish Highland Adventures. 2007. (Adventure Ser.). (ENG., Illus.). 96p. (J). per. 8.99 (978-1-84550-281-2(7), 790df1fd-063a-4fc3-8fa4-17d4063ada97) Christian Focus Pubns. GBR. Dist: Baker & Taylor Publisher Services (BTPS).
Zocchi, Judy. In Scotland. Brodie, Neale, illus. 2005. (Global Adventures II Ser.). 32p. (J). per. 10.95 (978-1-59646-149-9(7)) Dingles & Co.
—In Scotland/en Escocia. Brodie, Neale, illus. 2005. (Global Adventures II Ser.).Tr. of En Escocia. (ENG & SPA.). 32p. (J). per. 10.95 (978-1-59646-151-2(9)) Dingles & Co.

SCOTLAND—FICTION

Alexander, Sarah. The Art of Not Breathing. 2017. (ENG.). 288p. (YA). (gr. 9). pap. 9.99 (978-0-544-93687-4(6), 1658695, Clarion Bks.) HarperCollins Pubs.
Anderson, Sandra. Rockcliffe. 2007. 156p. per. 8.95 (978-1-59800-893-7(5)) Outskirts Pr., Inc.
Arbuthnott, Gill. Beneath, 30 vols. 2014. 288p. (YA). 9.95 (978-1-78250-052-0(9), Kelpies) Floris Bks. GBR. Dist: Consortium Bk. Sales & Distribution.
Atkin, Jean. The Crow House. 2013. 270p. pap. (978-1-78299-650-7(8)) FeedARead.com.
Baccalario, P. D. Suitcase of Stars, 1 vol. Pernigotti, Chiara, tr. Bruno, Iacopo, illus. 2014. (Enchanted Emporium Ser.). (ENG.). 240p. (J). (gr. 4-8). 26.65 (978-1-4342-6516-6(1), 124272, Stone Arch Bks.) Capstone.
Baccalario, Pierdomenico. Compass of Dreams, 1 vol. Pernigotti, Chiara, tr. Bruno, Iacopo, illus. 2014. (Enchanted Emporium Ser.). (ENG.). 240p. (J). (gr. 4-8). 26.65 (978-1-4342-6517-3(X), 124273, Stone Arch Bks.) Capstone.
—Map of the Passages. McGuinness, Nanette, tr. Bruno, Iacopo, illus. 2015. (Enchanted Emporium Ser.). (ENG.). 240p. (J). (gr. 4-8). 12.95 (978-1-62370-204-5(6), 127181, Capstone Young Readers) Capstone.
Bach, Ari. Valhalla. 2nd ed. (ENG., (YA). 2016. Illus.). (gr. 9-12). 29.99 (978-1-63477-990-6(8)) 2014. (Valhalla Ser.: 1). 330p. pap. 17.99 (978-1-62798-718-9(5)) Dreamspinner Pr. (Harmony Ink Pr.).
Barrowman, John & Barrowman, Carole E. Bone Quill. 2014. (Hollow Earth Ser.). (ENG., Illus.). 304p. (J). (gr. 3-7). pap. 8.99 (978-1-4424-8929-5(4), Aladdin) Simon & Schuster Children's Publishing.
—Hollow Earth. 2012. (Hollow Earth Ser.). (ENG.). 400p. (J). (gr. 3-7). 16.99 (978-1-4424-5852-9(6), Aladdin) Simon & Schuster Children's Publishing.
Bayham, Dalan J. The Loch Ness Monster Incident - Junior Explorers Society Episode 2. 2007. 160p. pap. 12.95 (978-1-4303-2291-7(8)) Lulu Pr., Inc.
Bennett, Paul. Freddie, Bill & Irving. Shannon, Kate, illus. 2009. 112p. (gr. 2-2). pap. 25.16 (978-1-4251-7692-1(5)) Trafford Publishing.
Black, Sean. Extolziby Gruff & the 39th College. 2013. 236p. pap. (978-1-909062-25-2(1)) Sean Black Digital.
Blackford. The Eskdale Herd Boy A Scottish Tale for the Instruction & Amusement of Young Persons. 2004. reprint ed. pap. 15.95 (978-1-4191-6125-4(3)) Kessinger Publishing, LLC.
Bold, Emily. Breath of Yesterday, 0 vols. Bell, Katja, tr. 2014. (Curse Ser.: 2). (ENG.). 376p. (YA). (gr. 9-12). pap. 9.99 (978-1-4778-4714-5(6), 9781477847145, Skyscape) Amazon Publishing.
—The Curse: Touch of Eternity, 0 vols. Heron, Jeanette, tr. 2013. (Curse Ser.: 1). (ENG.). 318p. (YA). (gr. 9-12). pap. 9.99 (978-1-4778-0735-4(7), 9781477807354, Skyscape) Amazon Publishing.
Bond, Doug. Crown & Covenant, 3 bks. Bird, Matthew, illus. 2004. (Crown & Covenant Ser.). (J). per. 26.99 (978-0-87552-671-3(3)) P & R Publishing.
Brown, Hazel. Prince Henry St. Clair Earl of Orkney. Bramadat, Dawn, ed. Brown, Hazel, illus. 2013. (Illus.). 106p. pap. 25.95 (978-1-935786-57-3(1)) St. Clair Pubns.
Brown, Kathryn. Adventures at Aaron Loch Farm. 2009. (ENG.). 50p. pap. 23.50 (978-1-4092-6961-8(2)) Lulu Pr., Inc.
Bruce Clarke, Margaret. Hunter's Marjory. 2007. 244p. 27.95 (978-1-4218-4203-5(3)); per. 12.95 (978-1-4218-4301-8(3)) 1st World Publishing, Inc. (1st World Library - Literary Society).
Bunting, Eve. Forbidden. 2017. (ENG.). 224p. (YA). (gr. 7). pap. 9.99 (978-0-544-93881-6(X), 1658455, Clarion Bks.) HarperCollins Pubs.
Butler, Berwyn. Dinky the Doorknob: The Adventures of Sir Dinkum Wilhelm, the Third Earl of Surridge. 2005. (J). per. 11.95 (978-1-933732-02-2(4)) Big Ransom Studio.
Butler, Berwyn & McClean, Shorty. Dinky the Doorknob. 2006. (J). lib. bdg. 21.95 (978-1-933732-04-6(0)) Big Ransom Studio.
Claire, Bethany. Morna's Magic: A Sweet Scottish Time Travel Romance. 2017. 258p. pap. 12.99 (978-1-947731-08-0(4)) Bethany Claire Bks.
Clarke, Margaret Bruce. Hunter's Marjory. 2007. 148p. per. (978-1-4068-4613-3(9)) Echo Library.
Clayton, Coo. Maggie's Monsters. Soye, Alison, illus. 2018. (Maggie Ser.). (ENG.). 36p. (J). (gr. -1-k). pap. 12.99 (978-1-78530-177-3(2)) Black and White Publishing Ltd. GBR. Dist: Independent Pubs. Group.
Cohen, Rosalind. Scotland Yard, Us. 2008. 28p. pap. 13.99 (978-1-4389-4328-2(8)) AuthorHouse.
Cole, Steve. Z. Rex. 2010. (ENG.). 256p. (J). (gr. 5-18). 8.99 (978-0-14-241712-6(2), Puffin Books) Penguin Young Readers Group.
Collins, Tim. Fangs a Lot: Final Notes from a Totally Lame Vampire. Pinder, Andrew, illus. 2014. (ENG.). 320p. (J). (gr. 5-9). 13.99 (978-1-4814-2134-8(4), Aladdin) Simon & Schuster Children's Publishing.
Conan Doyle, Arthur. Sherlock Holmes & the Adventure of the Speckled Band: Case 5, No. 5. Rohrbach, Sophie, illus. 2010. (On the Case with Holmes & Watson Ser.: 5). (ENG.). 48p. (J). (gr. 4-6). pap. 9.99 (978-0-7613-6198-5(7), da1d6bdc-4673-4aa3-94e6-93dad2ea71a5, Graphic Universe™) Lerner Publishing Group.
Cooper, Susan. The Boggart. 2018. (Boggart Ser.). (ENG.). 240p. (J). (gr. 3-7). pap. 7.99 (978-1-5344-2011-3(8), McElderry, Margaret K. Bks.) McElderry, Margaret K. Bks.
—The Boggart. 2004. 196p. (gr. 3-7). 17.00 (978-0-7569-3932-8(1)) Perfection Learning Corp.
—The Boggart & the Monster. 2018. (Boggart Ser.). (ENG.). 224p. (J). (gr. 3-7). pap. 7.99 (978-1-5344-2012-0(6), McElderry, Margaret K. Bks.) McElderry, Margaret K. Bks.
—The Boggart Fights Back. 2018. (Boggart Ser.). (ENG., Illus.). 224p. (J). (gr. 3-7). 16.99 (978-1-5344-0629-2(8), McElderry, Margaret K. Bks.) McElderry, Margaret K. Bks.
Cummings, Mag. Fishplates & Frogs. 2007. 272p. per. (978-1-905529-99-5(6)) Grosvenor Hse. Publishing Ltd.
Dawley, Linda. Wee Mac. 2014. (ENG.). 146p. (J). pap. (978-0-9941011-8-1(X), The Little Red Hen Community Pr.) CCB Publishing.
De Saulles, Tony. Early Reader: the Loch Ness Monster Spotters. 2017. (Early Reader Ser.). (ENG., Illus.). 64p. (J). (gr. 1-3). 4.99 (978-1-5101-0185-2(3), Orion Children's Bks.) Hachette Children's Group GBR. Dist: Hachette Bk. Group.
Derwent, Lavinia. Sula, 56 vols. (ENG., Illus.). 144p. 10.00 (978-0-86315-487-4(5)) Floris Bks. GBR. Dist: SteinerBooks, Inc.
Destiny, A. & Helms, Rhonda. Sparks in Scotland. 2015. (Flirt Ser.). (ENG.). 224p. (YA). (gr. 7). pap. 9.99 (978-1-4814-2121-8(2), Simon Pulse) Simon Pulse.
Dickinson, Peter. Emma Tupper's Diary. 2014. (ENG.). 212p. (J). (gr. 4). pap. 12.00 (978-1-61873-063-3(0), Big Mouth Hse.) Small Beer Pr.
Dodd, Emily. Ollie & the Otter: A Scottish Osprey Story, 30 vols. Harris-Jones, Kirsteen, illus. 2023. (Picture Kelpies Ser.). 24p. 11.95 (978-1-78250-369-9(2), Kelpies) Floris Bks. GBR. Dist: Consortium Bk. Sales & Distribution.
Don, Lari. First Aid for Fairies & Other Fabled Beasts, 20 vols. 2008. (ENG.). 224p. (J). pap. (978-0-86315-636-6(3)) Floris Bks.
—First Aid for Fairies & Other Fabled Beasts, 28 vols. 2nd rev. ed. 2014. (Fabled Beasts Chronicles Ser.: 1). 224p. (J). 9.95 (978-1-78250-137-4(1), Kelpies) Floris Bks. GBR. Dist: Consortium Bk. Sales & Distribution.
—Wolf Notes & Other Musical Mishaps, 24 vols. 2nd rev. ed. 2014. (Fabled Beasts Chronicles Ser.: 2). (Illus.). 272p. (J). 9.95 (978-1-78250-138-1(X), Kelpies) Floris Bks. GBR. Dist: Consortium Bk. Sales & Distribution.
Douglas, Margaret. Spirit of Meradoon. 2012. 192p. (gr. 2-2). 30.95 (978-1-4497-6471-5(1)); pap. 13.95 (978-1-4497-6470-8(3)) Author Solutions, LLC. (WestBow Pr.).
Downer, Ann. The Dragon of Never-Was. Rayyan, Omar, illus. 2008. (ENG.). 320p. (J). (gr. 3-6). pap. 14.99 (978-1-4169-5453-8(8), Atheneum Bks. for Young Readers) Simon & Schuster Children's Publishing.
Duckers, John. The Amazing Adventures of the Silly Six. 2013. (Illus.). 188p. pap. (978-1-78148-626-9(3)) Grosvenor Hse. Publishing Ltd.
Ehrenhaft, Daniel. Drawing a Blank: Or How I Tried to Solve a Mystery, End a Feud, & Land the Girl of My Dreams. Ristow, Trevor, illus. 2009. (ENG.). 352p. (J). pap. 8.99 (978-0-06-075254-5(8), HarperTeen) HarperCollins Pubs.
Farmer, Nancy. The Islands of the Blessed. (ENG., Illus.). 496p. (YA). (gr. 7). 2012. pap. 13.99 (978-1-4169-0738-1(6), Atheneum Bks. for Young Readers) 2009. 18.99 (978-1-4169-0737-4(8), Atheneum/Richard Jackson Bks.) Simon & Schuster Children's Publishing.
—The Islands of the Blessed. l.t. ed. 2010. (Sequel to the Land of the Silver Apples Ser.). (ENG.). 607p. (J). 23.95 (978-1-4104-2253-8(4)) Thorndike Pr.
Ferchaud, Steve, illus. Glen Robbie: A Scottish Fairy Tale. 2006. (J). 22.95 (978-1-58478-013-7(4), Highland Children's Pr.) Heather & Highlands Publishing.
—The Man Who Spoke with Cats. 2006. (ENG.). 48p. (J). 18.95 (978-1-58478-019-9(3), Highland Children's Pr.) Heather & Highlands Publishing.
Fidler, Kathleen. The Desperate Journey, 30 vols. 2012. (Classic Kelpies Ser.). (Illus.). 192p. (J). 9.95 (978-0-86315-881-0(1), Kelpies) Floris Bks. GBR. Dist: Consortium Bk. Sales & Distribution.
—Flash the Sheep Dog, 30 vols. 4th rev. ed. 2018. (Illus.). 176p. (J). 9.95 (978-1-78250-492-4(3), Kelpies) Floris Bks. GBR. Dist: Consortium Bk. Sales & Distribution.
—Haki the Shetland Pony, 28 vols. 3rd rev. ed. 2018. (Illus.). 144p. (J). pap. 9.95 (978-1-78250-493-1(1), Kelpies) Floris Bks. GBR. Dist: Consortium Bk. Sales & Distribution.
Flaherty, Alice Weaver. Luck of the Loch Ness Monster: A Tale of Picky Eating. Magoon, Scott, illus. 2007. (ENG.). 40p. (J). (gr. 3-7). 16.00 (978-0-618-55644-1(3), 585613, Clarion Bks.) HarperCollins Pubs.
Flitcroft, Jean. The Loch Ness Monster. 2010. (Cryptid Files Ser.: No. 1). xii, 176p. (J). pap. (978-1-84840-940-8(0)) Little Island.
Foreman, Colin. A Moment Comes. Colin Foreman. 2007. (Keepers & Seekers Ser.). (ENG., Illus.). 320p. pap. (978-0-9548949-2-4(8)) Myroy Bks. Ltd.
Forest, Heather. The Woman Who Flummoxed the Fairies. Gaber, Susan, illus. 2013. (ENG.). 32p. (J). (gr. -1-3). 8.95 (978-1-939160-71-3(5)) August Hse. Pubs., Inc.
Forster, David. Dreamer in the Snows. 2017. (ENG.). 312p. pap. 15.95 (978-1-78629-823-2(6), 88116579-8ebb-4025-83b0-81635dd9e28f) Austin Macauley Pubs. Ltd. GBR. Dist: Baker & Taylor Publisher Services (BTPS).
Galer, Chris. Ross Gang. 2006. 136p. per. (978-1-905529-84-1(8)) Grosvenor Hse. Publishing Ltd.
Glaser, Mechthild. The Book Jumper. 2018. (ENG.). 400p. (YA). pap. 12.99 (978-1-250-14423-2(X), 900180625) Square Fish.
Gliori, Debi. The Tobermory Cat Postal Book. 2015. (Illus.). 32p. (J). pap. 7.95 (978-1-78027-329-7(0), BC Bks.) Birlinn, Ltd. GBR. Dist: Casemate Pubs. & Bk. Distributors, LLC.
Gosling, Cherie & Disney Storybook Artists Staff. Mulan Is Loyal: Merida Is Brave. 2017. (Illus.). 24p. (J). (978-1-5379-5745-6(7)) Random Hse., Inc.
Graham, H. P. & De Bats, M. On the Heels of the Hunted. 2013. 346p. pap. (978-1-78148-067-0(2)) Grosvenor Hse. Publishing Ltd.
Grant, Michael. The Magnificent 12: the Key. 2013. (Magnificent 12 Ser.: 3). (ENG.). 304p. (J). (gr. 3-7). pap. 5.99 (978-0-06-183371-7(1), Tegen, Katherine Bks) HarperCollins Pubs.
Greig, Louise. The Island & the Bear, 50 vols. Nastanlieva, Vanya, illus. 2017. 24p. (J). 11.95 (978-1-78250-368-2(4), Kelpies) Floris Bks. GBR. Dist: Consortium Bk. Sales & Distribution.
Gurrea, Susana, illus. A Super Scotland Sticker Book, 30 vols. 2018. (Super Scotland Ser.). 24p. (J). 11.95 (978-1-78250-422-1(2), Kelpies) Floris Bks. GBR. Dist: Consortium Bk. Sales & Distribution.
Harris, Robert J. Thor Is Locked in My Garage!!, 28 vols. 2014. (World's Gone Loki Ser.). 192p. (J). 9.95 (978-1-78250-122-0(3), Kelpies) Floris Bks. GBR. Dist: Consortium Bk. Sales & Distribution.
Hartley, James. The Invisible Hand: Shakespeare's Moon, Act I. 2017. (ENG., Illus.). 168p. (J). (gr. 6-12). pap. 11.95 (978-1-78535-498-4(1), Lodestone Bks.) Hunt, John Publishing Ltd. GBR. Dist: National Bk. Network.
Henderson, Lauren. Kisses & Lies. 2. 2009. (Scarlett Wakefield Novels Ser.). (ENG.). 320p. (J). (gr. 9-12). lib. bdg. 26.19 (978-0-385-90486-5(X), Delacorte Pr.) Random Hse. Children's Bks.
Hendry, Frances. Quest for a Kelpie. l.t. ed. 2007. 248p. per. (978-1-905665-17-4(2)) Pollinger In Print.
Hergé. The Black Island. (Illus.). 62p. (J). 19.95 (978-0-8288-5012-4(7)) French & European Pubns., Inc.
—L' Ile Noire.Tr. of Black Island. (FRE., Illus.). (J). (gr. 7-9). ring bd. 19.95 (978-0-8288-5039-1(9)) French & European Pubns., Inc.
Hinds, Gareth. Macbeth. Hinds, Gareth, illus. 2015. (ENG., Illus.). 152p. (YA). (gr. 7). 21.99 (978-0-7636-6943-0(1)) Candlewick Pr.
Howell, Gill. Selkie Child. Keen, Sophie, illus. 2005. (ENG.). 24p. (J). lib. bdg. 23.65 (978-1-59646-750-7(9)) Dingles & Co.
Hunter, Donna K. Hunterston Happenings: Kilts, Casts & Castles. 2013. (Illus.). 60p. pap. 24.99 (978-1-4772-2400-7(9)) AuthorHouse.
Hunter, Mollie. A Stranger Came Ashore, 30 vols. 2012. (Classic Kelpies Ser.). 192p. (J). 9.95 (978-0-86315-883-4(8), Kelpies) Floris Bks. GBR. Dist: Consortium Bk. Sales & Distribution.
Jakobsen, Lars. The Mysterious Manuscript. Jakobsen, Lars, illus. 2012. (Mortensen's Escapades Ser.: 1). (Illus.). 48p. (gr.

S

6-12). pap. 6.95 (978-0-8225-9409-3(9), Graphic Universe™) Lerner Publishing Group.

Johnson, C. Homecoming. 2007. (Illus.). 64p. per. 10.00 (978-1-4251-1358-2(3)) Trafford Publishing.

Kane, James. Tom & Katie's Greatest Adventure. 2005. 73p. pap. 14.95 (978-1-4241-0776-6(8)) PublishAmerica, Inc.

Kay, Susan. Abby & Gabby Tales. 2009. 16p. pap. 9.99 (978-1-4389-6467-6(6)) AuthorHouse.

Kellerhals-Stewart, Heather. Brave Highland Heart. 2004. (Illus.). (J). (gr. k-3). spiral bd. (978-0-616-01688-6(3)) Canadian National Institute for the Blind/Institut National Canadien pour les Aveugles.

King-Smith, Dick. The Water Horse. Parkins, David, illus. 2007. (ENG.). 128p. (J). (gr. 1-4). 7.99 (978-0-375-84231-3(4), Yearling) Random Hse. Children's Bks.

Klaassen, Sandra. Peg & Uan: Making Friends, 52 vols. 2017. (Illus.). 14p. (J). 9.95 (978-1-78250-441-2(9), Kelpies) Floris Bks. GBR. Dist: Consortium Bk. Sales & Distribution.

—Peg the Little Sheepdog, 44 vols. 2015. (Illus.). 32p. (J). 11.95 (978-1-78250-181-7(9), Kelpies) Floris Bks. GBR. Dist: Consortium Bk. Sales & Distribution.

Klise, Kate. The Loch Ness Punster. Klise, M. Sarah, illus. 2016. (43 Old Cemetery Road Ser.: 7). (ENG.). 144p. (J). (gr. 3-7). pap. 7.99 (978-0-544-81085-3(6), 1641667, Clarion Bks.) HarperCollins Pubs.

Knight, Eric. Lassie Come-Home. Kirmse, Marguerite, illus. rev. ed. 2003. (ENG.). 256p. (J). (gr. 3-7). 26.99 (978-0-8050-7206-8(3), 900018916, Holt, Henry & Co. Bks. For Young Readers) Holt, Henry & Co.

Krech, Bob. Love Puppies & Corner Kicks. 2010. (ENG.). 192p. (J). (gr. 6-8). 22.44 (978-0-525-42197-9(1)) Penguin Young Readers Group.

Kudina Steinberg, Ganna V. The Princess Conspiracy: an Inspector Poopchyk Mystery. 2009. 143p. 30.00 (978-0-557-08936-9(0)) Lulu Pr., Inc.

Lang, Andrew. Prince Ricardo of Pantouflia. 2006. (Illus.). pap. 24.95 (978-1-4286-0645-6(9)) Kessinger Publishing, LLC.

Leaf, Munro. Wee Gillis. Lawson, Robert, illus. 2006. 80p. (J). (gr. -1-2). 16.95 (978-1-59017-206-3(X), NYR Children's Collection) New York Review of Bks., Inc., The.

Lemley, Ronald W. The Wee Bannock: A Scottish Fairy Tale. 2008. 43p. pap. 24.95 (978-1-60610-122-3(6)) America Star Bks.

Lewis, Gill. Wild Wings. Onoda, Yuta, illus. (ENG.). 304p. (J). (gr. 3-7). 2012. pap. 8.99 (978-1-4424-1446-4(4)) 2011. 21.99 (978-1-4424-1445-7(6)) Simon & Schuster Children's Publishing. (Atheneum Bks. for Young Readers).

Lindenbaum, Pija. Mini Mia & Her Darling Uncle. Dyssegaard, Elisabeth Kallick, tr. from SWE. 2007. (Illus.). 40p. (J). (gr. -1-3). 16.00 (978-91-29-66734-9(8)) R & S Bks. SWE. Dist: Macmillan.

Linklater, Eric. The Pirates in the Deep Green Sea. 2013. (ENG.). 314p. (YA). pap. (978-1-4482-0582-0(4), 150371, Bloomsbury Reader) Bloomsbury Publishing Plc.

Lund, Celia. Square Sails & Dragons. 2006. 284p. per. 19.95 (978-1-4120-5758-5(2)) Trafford Publishing.

Lunetta, Demitria. Bad Blood. 2017. 272p. (YA). (gr. 7). 17.99 (978-1-101-93805-8(6), Delacorte Pr.) Random Hse. Children's Bks.

MacDonald, George. A Double Story. 2008. 108p. 22.95 (978-1-60664-983-1(3)) Aegypan.

—The Elect Lady. 2008. 148p. 24.95 (978-1-60664-792-9(X)) Aegypan.

—The History of Gutta-Percha Willie. 2006. 116p. per. 9.95 (978-1-59818-578-2(0)) Aegypan.

—The History of Gutta-Percha Willie. 2007. 136p. per. (978-1-4065-2998-2(2)) Dodo Pr.

—Ranald Bannermans Boyhood. 2006. 168p. per. 13.95 (978-1-59818-238-5(2)) Aegypan.

MacKenzie, C. A. The Search for a Golden Eagle. 2013. (Illus.). 48p. pap. 10.95 (978-0-7552-0712-1(2)) Authors OnLine, Ltd. GBR. Dist: Printondemand-worldwide.com.

MacKenzie, Ross. The Nowhere Emporium, 30 vols. 2015. 280p. (J). 12.95 (978-1-78250-125-1(8), Kelpies) Floris Bks. GBR. Dist: Consortium Bk. Sales & Distribution.

MacKie, Ian. The Adventures of Hamish the Sea Eagle. Mackie, Marie-Anne, illus. 2013. 24p. (978-1-78148-614-6(X)) Grosvenor Hse. Publishing Ltd.

Maclean, Heather. Toward a Secret Sky, 1 vol. 2018. (ENG.). 384p. (YA). pap. 10.99 (978-0-310-75487-9(9)) Blink.

MacPhail, Cathy. Devil You Know, 22 vols. 2015. 240p. (YA). pap. 9.95 (978-1-78250-179-4(7), Kelpies) Floris Bks. GBR. Dist: Consortium Bk. Sales & Distribution.

MacPhail, David. Thorfinn & the Awful Invasion, 32 vols., Bk. 1. Morgan, Richard, illus. 2015. (Thorfinn the Nicest Viking Ser.). 136p. (J). pap. 8.95 (978-1-78250-158-9(4), Kelpies) Floris Bks. GBR. Dist: Consortium Bk. Sales & Distribution.

—Thorfinn & the Terrible Treasure, 30 vols. Morgan, Richard, illus. 2016. (Thorfinn the Nicest Viking Ser.). 136p. (J). pap. 6.95 (978-1-78250-235-7(1), Kelpies) Floris Bks. GBR. Dist: Consortium Bk. Sales & Distribution.

Matthews, Rodney, illus. Tales of King Arthur. rev. ed. 2007. (Usborne Classics Retold Ser.). 139p. (J). (gr. 4-7). per. 4.99 (978-0-7945-1483-9(9), Usborne) EDC Publishing.

May, Elizabeth. The Vanishing Throne: Book Two of the Falconer Trilogy. 2016. (Falconer Ser.: 2). (ENG., Illus.). 458p. (YA). (gr. 7-12). 17.99 (978-1-4521-2882-5(0)) Chronicle Bks. LLC.

—The Vanishing Throne: Book Two of the Falconer Trilogy (Young Adult Books, Fantasy Novels, Trilogies for Young Adults) 2017. (Falconer Ser.: 2). (ENG.). 480p. (YA). pap. 10.99 (978-1-4521-6140-2(2)) Chronicle Bks. LLC.

McCall, Alex. Attack of the Giant Robot Chickens, 30 vols. 2014. 208p. (J). 9.95 (978-1-78250-008-7(1), Kelpies) Floris Bks. GBR. Dist: Consortium Bk. Sales & Distribution.

McCartney, Tania. A Scottish Year: Twelve Months in the Life of Scotland's Kids. Snerling, Tina, illus. 2015. (Kids' Year Ser.). (ENG.). 32p. (J). (gr. -1-3). 17.99 (978-1-921966-87-3(4), EK Bks.) Exisle Publishing Pty Ltd. AUS. Dist: Two Rivers Distribution.

McCaughrean, Geraldine. Where the World Ends. 2019. (ENG., Illus.). 336p. (YA). 18.99 (978-1-250-22549-8(3), 900208586) Flatiron Bks.

McKay, Kirsty. Unfed. 2015. (Undead Ser.: 2). (YA). 1.25 (978-1-4906-3511-8(4)) Recorded Bks., Inc.

—Unfed. 2013. (YA). (978-0-545-53674-5(X), Chicken Hse., The) Scholastic, Inc.

McLean, Allan Campbell. The Hill of the Red Fox, 40 vols. (Kelpies Ser.). 272p. (J). 2nd ed. 2006. (ENG.). 11.95 (978-0-86315-556-7(1)) 3rd rev. ed. 2015. 9.95 (978-1-78250-206-7(8), Kelpies) Floris Bks. GBR. Dist: SteinerBooks, Inc., Consortium Bk. Sales & Distribution.

McLelland, Kate. Isla & Pickle: Best Friends, 30 vols. 2017. (Isla & Pickle Ser.). (Illus.). 24p. (J). 11.95 (978-1-78250-421-4(4), Kelpies) Floris Bks. GBR. Dist: Consortium Bk. Sales & Distribution.

—Isla & Pickle: the Highland Show, 25 vols. 2018. (Isla & Pickle Ser.). (Illus.). 24p. (J). pap. 11.95 (978-1-78250-509-9(1), Kelpies) Floris Bks. GBR. Dist: Consortium Bk. Sales & Distribution.

Mehrabi, Jacqueline. Discovering the Sun. Reed, Susan, illus. 2015. (Discovering Ser.). (ENG.). 177p. (J). (gr. 6-11). pap. 12.00 (978-1-61851-079-2(7)) Baha'i Publishing.

Miles, Cindy. Forevermore. 2013. (ENG.). 288p. (YA). (gr. 7). pap. 9.99 (978-0-545-42622-0(7)) Scholastic, Inc.

Millar, Martin. Lonely Werewolf Girl. 2008. (ENG.). 560p. per. 16.95 (978-0-9796636-6-6(0), Soft Skull Pr.) Counterpoint Pr.

Nicholson, Mike. Catscape, 24 vols. 2005. 192p. (J). 9.95 (978-0-86315-531-4(6)) Floris Bks. GBR. Dist: Consortium Bk. Sales & Distribution.

Nye, Alex. Chill, 30 vols. 2nd rev. ed. 2014. (Illus.). 208p. (J). 9.95 (978-1-78250-149-7(5), Kelpies) Floris Bks. GBR. Dist: Consortium Bk. Sales & Distribution.

—Shiver, 28 vols. 2nd rev. ed. 2014. 248p. (J). 9.95 (978-1-78250-150-3(9), Kelpies) Floris Bks. GBR. Dist: Consortium Bk. Sales & Distribution.

Ollivant, Alfred. Bob, Son of Battle. 2016. (ENG., Illus.). (J). 28.95 (978-1-358-94410-9(5)) Creative Media Partners, LLC.

Paterson, Judy. Scottish Folk Tales for Children. 2017. (Folk Tales for Children Ser.). (ENG., Illus.). 192p. (J). (gr. 2-4). pap. 16.99 (978-0-7509-6844-7(3)) History Pr. Ltd.,The GBR. Dist: Independent Pubs. Group.

Paul, Colette. Whoever You Chose to Love. 2004. 256p. pap. (978-0-297-84717-5(1), Weidenfeld & Nicolson) Orion Publishing Group, Ltd.

Pelley, Kathleen T. & Manning, Maurie J. The Giant King. 2003. (ENG., Illus.). 32p. (gr. -1-4). 14.95 (978-0-87868-880-7(3), P544300, Child & Family Pr.) Child Welfare League of America, Inc.

Perkins, Lucy Fitch. The Scotch Twins. 2004. reprint ed. pap. 15.95 (978-1-4191-8160-3(2)); pap. 1.99 (978-1-4192-8160-0(7)) Kessinger Publishing, LLC.

Peyton, K. M. Stealaway. Wyatt, David, illus. 2004. (ENG.). 96p. (J). 12.95 (978-0-8126-2722-0(9)) Cricket Bks.

Phelps, Piki Nestares. The Art of Falconry. 2009. (ENG.). 34p. pap. 14.99 (978-1-4415-5421-5(1)) Xlibris Corp.

Poulsen, David A. Shivers & Shakes. 2009. (Salt & Pepper Chronicles Ser.). (ENG.). 176p. (J). (gr. 3-7). pap. (978-1-55470-144-5(9)) Me to We.

Rae, Milne. Geordie's Tryst. 2007. 72p. per. (978-1-4068-3682-0(6)) Echo Library.

Redbank, Tennant. Brave Little Golden Book (Disney/Pixar Brave) RH Disney, illus. 2012. (Little Golden Book Ser.). (ENG.). 24p. (J). (gr. k-k). 5.99 (978-0-7364-2901-6(8), Golden/Disney) Random Hse. Children's Bks.

Richardson, Alex. Gladigator & the Legend of Auchinle. 2009. (Illus.). 96p. pap. 31.99 (978-1-4490-1968-6(4)) AuthorHouse.

—Gladigator & the legend of Auchinlea. 2010. (Illus.). 96p. pap. 11.99 (978-1-4520-3324-2(2)) AuthorHouse.

Roberts, Scott A. The Rollicking Adventures of Tam O'Hare. 2007. (Illus.). 228p. (J). (gr. 4-7). per. 16.95 (978-1-60037-289-6(9)) Morgan James Publishing.

Rooney-Freedman, Isabelle. Angus MacDream & the Roktopus Rogue. 2011. 206p. pap. 11.95 (978-0-9843064-3-5(9)) Word with You Pr., A.

Russel, Mary. Flickertail & Paint, Barnyard Sleuths, 1 vol. 2010. 96p. pap. 19.95 (978-1-4489-7248-7(5)) America Star Bks.

Scribner, Meagen & Jensen, Angelina. Princess & the Peasant. 2013. 40p. pap. (978-1-4602-3308-5(5)) FriesenPress.

Shakespeare, William. Macbeth, 1 vol. Ferran, Daniel, illus. 2011. (Shakespeare Graphics Ser.). (ENG.). 88p. (J). (gr. 5-9). pap. 7.15 (978-1-4342-3447-6(9), 116468); lib. bdg. 28.65 (978-1-4342-2506-1(2), 113327) Capstone. (Stone Arch Bks.).

Simons, D. M. Keep Her Safe. 2011. (ENG.). 232p. pap. (978-1-84876-697-6(1)) Troubador Publishing Ltd.

Spirn, Michele Sobel. The Bridges in Edinburgh. 2004. (Going to Ser.). 144p. (J). pap. 6.95 (978-1-893577-11-4(2)) Four Corners Publishing Co., Inc.

Stemple, Adam & Yolen, Jane. Sanctuary: Book 2. Zangara, Orion, illus. 2018. (Stone Man Mysteries Ser.). (ENG.). 88p. (YA). (gr. 7-12). pap. 8.99 (978-1-5415-1043-2(7), 56cb1424-a16d-418a-a0c5-52e2dda42a46);No. 2. 29.32 (978-1-4677-4197-2(3), 96ca54a0-3352-4fc3-8226-178cee1ddbb1) Lerner Publishing Group. (Graphic Universe™).

—Stone Cold: Book 1. Zangara, Orion, illus. 2016. (Stone Man Mysteries Ser.: 1). (ENG.). 80p. (gr. 7-12). (J). E-Book 43.99 (978-1-5124-0903-1(0), 9781512409031);No. 1. (YA). pap. 8.99 (978-1-5124-1155-3(8), f2275e16-f0aa-4e03-9423-302d12617e07);No. 1. (YA). lib. bdg. 29.32 (978-1-4677-4196-5(5), 1ced9530-2931-4585-8c9c-adff2d2724ca) Lerner Publishing Group. (Graphic Universe™).

Stevenson, Robert Louis. Kidnapped. 2020. (ENG.). (J). (gr. 5). 180p. 19.95 (978-1-64799-263-7(X)); 178p. pap. 9.95 (978-1-64799-262-0(1)) Bibliotech Pr.

—Kidnapped. (ENG.). (J). (gr. 5). 2020. 240p. pap. 11.95 (978-1-714-68474-8(1)) 2019. 224p. 20.99 (978-0-368-65626-2(8)) 2019. 224p. 23.99 (978-0-368-65625-5(X)) 2019. 224p. pap. 7.99 (978-0-368-65627-9(6)) Blurb, Inc.

—Kidnapped. 2018. (ENG., Illus.). 324p. (J). pap. 16.95 (978-1-377-49570-5(1)) Creative Media Partners, LLC.

—Kidnapped. (ENG.). (J). (gr. 5). 2019. 218p. pap. 24.99 (978-1-7077-8899-6(5)) 2019. 310p. pap. 13.99 (978-1-7018-8473-1(9)) 2019. 754p. pap. 43.99 (978-1-6965-8428-9(0)) 2019. 216p. pap. 15.99 (978-1-0891-4601-8(9)) 2019. 474p. pap. 26.99 (978-1-6913-9137-0(9)) 2019. 236p. pap. 14.45 (978-1-6927-5856-1(X)) 2019. 754p. pap. 43.99 (978-1-6958-4227-4(8)) 2019. 326p. pap. 12.99 (978-1-6896-0376-8(3)) 2019. 472p. pap. 26.99 (978-1-0898-6789-0(1)) 2019. 516p. pap. 32.99 (978-1-0827-4762-5(9)) 2019. 472p. pap. 31.99 (978-1-0809-0466-2(2)) 2019. 472p. pap. 32.99 (978-1-0774-0928-6(1)) 2019. 474p. pap. 31.00 (978-1-0754-0548-8(3)) 2019. 754p. pap. 43.99 (978-1-0726-7197-8(2)) 2019. 354p. pap. 19.99 (978-1-0726-3706-6(5)) 2019. 472p. pap. 26.99 (978-1-0707-1013-6(X)) 2019. 228p. pap. 13.99 (978-1-0995-5205-2(2)) 2019. 494p. pap. 26.99 (978-1-0952-4192-9(3)) 2019. 756p. pap. 43.99 (978-1-0987-6220-9(7)) 2019. 474p. pap. 26.99 (978-1-0971-5449-4(1)) 2019. 472p. pap. 30.99 (978-1-0913-7211-5(X)) 2019. 332p. pap. 18.00 (978-1-7988-4185-3(1)) 2019. 490p. pap. 29.99 (978-1-7962-8303-7(7)) 2018. 522p. pap. 31.99 (978-1-7916-6452-7(0)) 2018. (Illus.). 222p. pap. 13.99 (978-1-7919-1519-3(1)) Independently Published.

—Kidnapped. 2020. (ENG.). (J). (gr. 5). 190p. 19.95 (978-1-64439-331-4(X)); 188p. pap. 10.95 (978-1-64439-330-7(1)) IndoEuropeanPublishing.com.

—Kidnapped. 2006. per. 8.95 (978-1-57646-970-5(0)) Quiet Vision Publishing.

—Kidnapped. 2018. (ENG., Illus.). 190p. (J). 19.99 (978-1-5154-2229-7(1)) Wilder Pubns., Corp.

—Kidnapped: Adapted for Young Readers. Kliros, Thea, illus. abr. ed. 2011. (Dover Children's Thrift Classics Ser.). (ENG.). 96p. (J). (gr. 3-8). reprint ed. pap. 4.00 (978-0-486-29354-7(8), 293548) Dover Pubns., Inc.

—Kidnapped: Bring the Classics to Life. 2008. (Bring the Classics to Life Ser.). (ENG., Illus.). 72p. (gr. 3-12). pap., act. bk. ed. 10.95 (978-0-931334-65-8(9), EDCTR-303B) EDCON Publishing Group.

Stevenson, Robert Louis & Hole, W. B. Kidnapped. 2017. (ENG.). 334p. (J). (gr. 5). pap. (978-3-7447-6112-3(6)) Creation Pubs.

Stevenson, Robert Louis & Rhead, Louis. Kidnapped. 2020. (ENG., Illus.). 224p. (J). (gr. 5). (978-1-78943-112-4(3)); pap. (978-1-78943-111-7(5)) Benediction Classics.

Stevenson, Steve. The King of Scotland's Sword. 2013. (Agatha Girl of Mystery Ser.: 3). lib. bdg. 16.00 (978-0-606-31688-0(4)) Turtleback.

Stilton, Thea. Thea Stilton & the Secret of the Old Castle. 2012. (Thea Stilton Ser.: 10). lib. bdg. 19.65 (978-0-606-23930-1(8)) Turtleback.

Stoddart, Lady. The Eskdale Herd Boy: A Scottish Tale for the Instruction & Amusement of Young Persons. 2005. reprint ed. pap. 20.95 (978-1-4179-6691-2(2)) Kessinger Publishing, LLC.

Strachan, Linda. Hamish Mchaggis & the Ghost of Glamis. Collins, Sally J., illus. 2005. (Hamish Mchaggis Ser.). 26p. (J). per. 9.00 (978-0-9546701-9-1(1)) GW Publishing GBR. Dist: Gatewood Pr.

—Hamish Mchaggis & the Search for the Loch Ness Monster. Collins, Sally J., illus. 2005. 32p. (J). pap. 9.00 (978-0-9546701-5-3(9)) GW Publishing GBR. Dist: Gatewood Pr.

—Hamish Mchaggis & the Skye Surprise. Collins, Sally J., illus. 2005. (Hamish Mchaggis Ser.). 26p. (J). pap. 9.00 (978-0-9546701-8-4(3)) GW Publishing GBR. Dist: Gatewood Pr.

Sutcliff, Rosemary. The Mark of the Horse Lord. 2015. (Rediscovered Classics Ser.: 21). (ENG.). 296p. (YA). (gr. 7). pap. 12.95 (978-1-61373-154-3(X)) Chicago Review Pr., Inc.

—Sword Song. 2005. (ENG., Illus.). 288p. (YA). (gr. 7-12). per. 13.99 (978-0-374-46984-9(9), 900028277, Farrar, Straus & Giroux (BYR)) Farrar, Straus & Giroux.

Taylor, Janet B. Into the Dim. 2017. lib. bdg. 20.85 (978-0-606-39929-6(1)) Turtleback.

Tracey, Rhian. When Isla Meets Luke Meets Isla. 2003. 224p. (YA). (gr. 7). pap. 12.95 (978-0-7475-6344-0(6)) Bloomsbury Publishing Plc GBR. Dist: Independent Pubs. Group.

Turnbull, Betty. Abigail & the Royal Thread. Adasikov, Igor, illus. 2014. 44p. (J). pap. 8.95 (978-1-61153-008-7(3)) Light Messages Publishing.

—The Man Who Saved the King. Adasikov, Igor, illus. 2014. 44p. (J). pap. 8.95 (978-1-61153-004-9(0)) Light Messages Publishing.

Tuxford, Jenny & Brazier, Jenny. Fredd Boggitt & the Loch Ness Monster. 2009. 152p. pap. 11.99 (978-1-4389-9593-9(8)) AuthorHouse.

Vanderwal, Andrew H. The Battle for Duncragglin. 2009. 320p. (J). (gr. 5-18). 19.95 (978-0-88776-886-6(5), Tundra Bks.) Tundra Bks. CAN. Dist: Penguin Random Hse. LLC.

Wallace, Karen. Flash Harriet & the Loch Ness Monster: Band 13/Topaz (Collins Big Cat) Nayler, Sarah, illus. 2007. (Collins Big Cat Ser.). (ENG.). 32p. (J). (gr. 2-4). pap. 9.99 (978-0-00-723082-2(6)) HarperCollins Pubs. Ltd. GBR. Dist: Independent Pubs. Group.

Watson, Sally. Witch of the Glens. 2004. (YA). pap. 12.95 (978-1-59511-001-5(1), 800-691-7779) Image Cascade Publishing.

Weatherstone, Hollie. When the Pandas Came to Scotland. Cochrane, Claire, illus. 2012. (ENG.). 24p. pap. 19.82 (978-1-4772-3528-7(0)) AuthorHouse.

Wein, Elizabeth. The Pearl Thief. (ENG.). (YA). (gr. 7-12). 2018. 352p. pap. 10.99 (978-1-4847-2370-8(8)) 2017. 336p. 18.99 (978-1-4847-1716-5(3)) Hyperion Bks. for Children.

—The Pearl Thief. 2018. (YA). lib. bdg. 20.85 (978-0-606-40964-3(5)) Turtleback.

Weston, Danny. Scarecrow. 2017. (ENG.). 288p. (J). (gr. 6-9). pap. 15.99 (978-1-78344-531-8(9)) Andersen Pr. GBR. Dist: Independent Pubs. Group.

Whitney, Barbara I. Barbara's Quest to Find a Messenger Journeys III & IV: Journeys III & IV. 2009. (ENG.). 48p. pap. 31.99 (978-1-4415-1551-3(8)) Xlibris Corp.

Wiggin, Kate Douglas. Penelope's Experiences in Scotland. 2008. 156p. (gr. 4-7). pap. 13.95 (978-1-60664-127-9(1)) Aegypan.

—Penelope's Experiences in Scotland. 2004. reprint ed. pap. 1.99 (978-1-4192-4071-3(4)); pap. 21.95 (978-1-4191-4071-6(X)) Kessinger Publishing, LLC.

Wightman, Jillian C. The Adventures of Erin Mctavitt. 2008. 68p. pap. 19.95 (978-1-4327-3164-9(5)) Outskirts Pr., Inc.

Wiley, Melissa. Little House in the Highlands. 2007. (Little House Prequel Ser.). (ENG.). 160p. (J). (gr. 3-7). pap. 7.99 (978-0-06-114817-0(2), HarperCollins) HarperCollins Pubs.

Williamson, Victoria. The Fox Girl & the White Gazelle, 26 vols. 2018. 272p. (J). 9.95 (978-1-78250-490-0(7), Kelpies) Floris Bks. GBR. Dist: Consortium Bk. Sales & Distribution.

Wilson, Barbara-Ann. The Faerie Hill. 2008. (ENG.). 124p. pap. 20.95 (978-1-4092-1845-6(7)) Lulu Pr., Inc.

Wilson, Db. Teale Tales: Wyv Land of Magik. 2012. 266p. pap. (978-1-78176-345-2(3)) FeedARead.com.

Young, Francis Kerr. The Paperweight. Steele, Andrew & Clement, Devyn, illus. 2008. 39p. pap. 24.95 (978-1-60610-034-9(3)) America Star Bks.

Young, Jessica. Howl at the Moon: a Branches Book (Haggis & Tank Unleashed #3) Burks, James, illus. 2017. (Haggis & Tank Unleashed Ser.: 3). (ENG.). 80p. (J). (gr. k-2). pap. 5.99 (978-1-338-04525-3(3)) Scholastic, Inc.

Young, John. Farewell Tour of a Terminal Optimist, 30 vols. 2017. 288p. (YA). 9.95 (978-1-78250-424-5(9), Kelpies) Floris Bks. GBR. Dist: Consortium Bk. Sales & Distribution.

SCOTLAND—HISTORY

Blathwayt, Benedict. The Sticker Atlas of Scotland. 2019. (Illus.). 32p. (J). pap. 14.95 (978-1-78027-412-6(2), BC Bks.) Birlinn, Ltd. GBR. Dist: Casemate Pubs. & Bk. Distributors, LLC.

Burnett, Alan & Burnett, Allan. Mary Queen of Scots & All That. Anderson, Scoular, illus. 2016. (and All That Ser.). 112p. (gr. 4-8). pap. 7.95 (978-1-78027-388-4(6)) Birlinn, Ltd. GBR. Dist: Casemate Pubs. & Bk. Distributors, LLC.

Capt, E. Raymond. Isle of Iona. 2003. 160p. per. 11.95 (978-0-934666-58-9(X)) Artisan Pubs.

Carruth, J. A., text. Mary Queen of Scots. (Scotland in Words & Pictures Ser.). (Illus.). 32p. pap. 3.95 (978-0-7117-0147-2(4)) Jarrold Publishing GBR. Dist: 7 Hills Bk. Distributors.

Gagne, Tammy. My Home Is My Castle Glamis Castle: Glamis. 2015. (ENG., Illus.). 48p. (J). 29.95 (978-1-62469-134-8(X)) Purple Toad Publishing, Inc.

Gliori, Debi. A Hebridean Alphabet. 2018. (ENG., Illus.). 32p. (J). pap. 10.95 (978-1-78027-510-9(2), BC Bks.) Birlinn, Ltd. GBR. Dist: Casemate Pubs. & Bk. Distributors, LLC.

Kelly, Terri B. Mary Slessor: Missionary Mother. 2014. (Illus.). 164p. (J). (978-1-60682-630-0(1)) BJU Pr.

Kiehm, Eve Begley. B Is for Bagpipes: A Scotland Alphabet. Rutherford, Alexa, illus. 2010. (Discover the World Ser.). (ENG.). 40p. (J). (gr. 1-3). 19.99 (978-1-58536-453-4(3), 202177) Sleeping Bear Pr.

Klepeis, Alicia Z. Scotland. 2019. (Country Profiles Ser.). (ENG., Illus.). 32p. (J). (gr. 3-8). lib. bdg. 27.95 (978-1-64487-053-2(3), Blastoff! Discovery) Bellwether Media.

Knox, Barbara. Edinburgh Castle: Scotland's Haunted Fortress. 2006. (Castles, Palaces, & Tombs Ser.). (Illus.). 32p. (YA). (gr. 2-5). lib. bdg. 28.50 (978-1-59716-248-7(5)) Bearport Publishing Co., Inc.

Leavitt, Amie Jane. My Home Is My Castle Balmoral Castle: Balmoral Castle. 2015. (ENG., Illus.). 48p. (J). 29.95 (978-1-62469-136-2(6)) Purple Toad Publishing, Inc.

Levy, Patricia & Ong, Jacqueline. Scotland, 1 vol. 2nd rev. ed. 2011. (Cultures of the World (Second Edition)(r) Ser.). (ENG.). 144p. (gr. 5-5). lib. bdg. 49.79 (978-1-60870-218-3(9), 8b08e5f1-aeca-4bcb-80dc-478ca6fa83d4) Cavendish Square Publishing LLC.

Levy, Patricia, et al. Scotland, 1 vol. 3rd ed. 2019. (Cultures of the World (Third Edition)(r) Ser.). (ENG.). 144p. (gr. 5-5). lib. bdg. 48.79 (978-1-5026-5078-8(9), ce1d4218-eaa3-40bc-aa94-b2971926d2a0) Cavendish Square Publishing LLC.

MacAndrewRichard. Scotland Level 3 Lower-Intermediate. 2009. (Cambridge Experience Readers Ser.). (ENG., Illus.). 80p. pap. 14.75 (978-84-8323-579-9(X)) Cambridge Univ. Pr.

Marshall, H. E. Scotland's Story (Yesterday's Classics) Skelton, J. R. et al, illus. 2005. 552p. (J). per. 17.95 (978-1-59915-056-7(5)) Yesterday's Classics.

Muldoon, Eilidh. The Colouring Book of Scotland. 2016. (Illus.). 48p. pap. 13.95 (978-1-78027-405-8(X), 178027405X) Birlinn, Ltd. GBR. Dist: Casemate Pubs. & Bk. Distributors, LLC.

Porteus, Tim. East Lothian Folk Tales for Children. Graham, Morvern, illus. 2019. (ENG.). 192p. pap. 18.95 (978-0-7509-8899-5(1)) History Pr. Ltd.,The GBR. Dist: Independent Pubs. Group.

Rodgers, Alan & Streluk, Angella. Scotland, 1 vol. 2013. (Step up Geography Ser.). (ENG., Illus.). 32p. (J). pap. 12.99 (978-0-237-54377-8(X)) Evans Brothers, Ltd. GBR. Dist: Independent Pubs. Group.

Rudolph, Jessica. Scotland. 2017. (Countries We Come From Ser.). (ENG., Illus.). 32p. (J). (gr. k-3). 19.95 (978-1-68402-255-7(X)) Bearport Publishing Co., Inc.

Turnbull, Betty. Isobel's New World. Adasikov, Igor, illus. 2014. 48p. (J). pap. 8.95 (978-1-61153-006-3(7)) Light Messages Publishing.

Zobel, Derek. Scotland. 2012. (Exploring Countries Ser.). (ENG., Illus.). 32p. (J). (gr. 3-7). lib. bdg. 27.95 (978-1-60014-734-0(8), Blastoff! Readers) Bellwether Media.

Zocchi, Judy. In Scotland. Brodie, Neale, illus. 2005. (Global Adventures I Ser.). 32p. (J). pap. 10.95 (978-1-59646-147-5(0)); lib. bdg. 21.65 (978-1-59646-012-6(1)) Dingles & Co.

—In Scotland/en Escocia. Brodie, Neale, illus. 2005. (Global Adventures I Ser.).Tr. of En Escocia. (ENG & SPA.). 32p. (J). pap. 10.95 (978-1-59646-150-5(0)); lib. bdg. (978-1-59646-013-3(X)) Dingles & Co.

SCOTLAND—HISTORY—FICTION

Belli, Alfredo, illus. Speed Bonnie Boat: A Tale from Scottish History Inspired by the Skye Boat Song, 30 vols. 2017. (Traditional Scottish Tales Ser.). 24p. (J). 11.95 (978-1-78250-367-5(6), Kelpies) Floris Bks. GBR. Dist: Consortium Bk. Sales & Distribution.

Bond, Douglas. King's Arrow. Bird, Matthew, illus. 2003. (Crown & Covenant Ser.). 208p. (J). per. 10.99 (978-0-87552-743-7(4)) P & R Publishing.

—Rebel's Keep. Bird, Matthew, illus. 2004. (Crown & Covenant Ser.). 285p. (J). per. 9.99 (978-0-87552-744-4(2)) P & R Publishing.

Breslin, Theresa. Mary, Queen of Scots: Escape from Lochleven Castle, 48 vols. Martinez, Teresa, illus. 2018. (Traditional Scottish Tales Ser.). 32p. (J). 14.95 (978-1-78250-512-9(1), Kelpies) Floris Bks. GBR. Dist: Consortium Bk. Sales & Distribution.
Cameron, Ian. Stirling Bridge. (Illus.). 32p. pap. 6.95 (978-1-899827-07-7(2)) Scottish Children's Pr. GBR. Dist: Gatewood Pr.
Cooney, Caroline B. Enter Three Witches: A Story of Macbeth. l.t. ed. 2007. (Thorndike Literacy Bridge Young Adult Ser.). 343p. (YA). (gr. 8-12). 22.95 (978-0-7862-9889-1(8)) Thorndike Pr.
Cooney, Caroline B. & Shakespeare, William. Enter Three Witches: A Story of Macbeth. 2007. 281p. (YA). pap. (978-0-545-01972-9(9)) Scholastic, Inc.
Cremer, Andrea. Rift. 2013. (Nightshade Novels Ser.). (ENG.). 464p. (YA). (gr. 8-12). 26.19 (978-0-399-25613-4(X)) Penguin Young Readers Group.
Davidson, Jenny. The Explosionist. 2008. 464p. (YA). (gr. 7-18). lib. bdg. 18.89 (978-0-06-123976-2(3), HarperTeen) HarperCollins Pubs.
Hendry, Frances. Quest for a Queen: The Falcon. 2006. pap. (978-1-905665-06-8(7)) Pollinger In Print.
Henty, George. Bonnie Prince Charlie: A Tale of Fontenoy & Culloden. 2007. (ENG.). 280p. pap. 21.99 (978-1-4264-2121-1(4)); 268p. pap. 23.99 (978-1-4264-2189-1(3)) Creative Media Partners, LLC.
—In Freedom's Cause: A Story of Wallace & Bruce. 2004. reprint ed. pap. 1.99 (978-1-4192-2572-7(3)) Kessinger Publishing, LLC.
—In Freedom's Cause: A Story of Wallace & Bruce. 2004. 176p. (YA). pap. 8.95 (978-1-57646-886-9(0)) Quiet Vision Publishing.
—In Freedom's Cause: A Tale of Wallace & Bruce. 2011. 372p. pap. 19.95 (978-1-61179-152-5(9)) Fireship Pr.
Jenkins, Sara D. The Prose Marmion a Tale of the Scottish. 2004. reprint ed. pap. 15.95 (978-1-4191-7925-9(X)) Kessinger Publishing, LLC.
—The Prose Marmion A Tale of the Scottish Border. 2004. reprint ed. pap. 1.99 (978-1-4192-7925-6(4)) Kessinger Publishing, LLC.
Lennon, Joan. Silver Skin. 2015. (ENG.). 208p. pap. 12.95 (978-1-78027-284-9(7)) Birlinn, Ltd. GBR. Dist: Casemate Pubs. & Bk. Distributors, LLC.
Lightwood, Donald. The Long Revenge. 128p. pap. 7.95 (978-1-899827-94-7(3)) Scottish Children's Pr. GBR. Dist: Gatewood Pr.
Mackay, Janis. The Reluctant Time Traveller, 30 vols. 2014. (Time Traveller Ser.). 240p. (J). 9.95 (978-1-78250-111-4(8), Kelpies) Floris Bks. GBR. Dist: Consortium Bk. Sales & Distribution.
Maclean, Fiona. Death or Victory: Tales of the Clan Maclean. Turnbull, Brian, illus. 2011. 128p. (YA). pap. (978-2-930583-06-8(1)) White & MacLean Publishing BEL. Dist: Gardners Bks. Ltd.
MacPhail, David. Thorfinn & the Raging Raiders, 30 vols. Morgan, Richard, illus. 2016. (Thorfinn the Nicest Viking Ser.). 136p. (J). pap. 6.95 (978-1-78250-233-3(5), Kelpies) Floris Bks. GBR. Dist: Consortium Bk. Sales & Distribution.
—Thorfinn the Nicest Viking & the Gruesome Games, 30 vols. Morgan, Richard, illus. 2015. (Thorfinn the Nicest Viking Ser.). 136p. (J). 8.95 (978-1-78250-159-6(2), Kelpies) Floris Bks. GBR. Dist: Consortium Bk. Sales & Distribution.
Marston, Hope Irvin. Against the Tide: The Valor of Margaret Wilson. 2007. (Chosen Daughters Ser.). 219p. (J). (gr. 3-7). per. 11.99 (978-1-59638-061-5(6)) P & R Publishing.
Meyer, Carolyn. The Wild Queen: The Days & Nights of Mary, Queen of Scots. 2013. (Young Royals Ser.). (ENG.). 432p. (YA). (gr. 7). pap. 8.99 (978-0-544-02219-5(X), 1528477, Clarion Bks.) HarperCollins Pubs.
Morgan, Nicola. Fleshmarket. 2003. (ENG.). 272p. (J). (gr. 7-17). pap. 9.99 (978-0-340-85557-7(6)) Hachette Children's Group GBR. Dist: Hachette Bk. Group.
—The Highwayman's Curse. 2009. (J). (978-0-7636-4066-8(2)) Candlewick Pr.
Shakespeare, William. Macbeth: The Graphic Novel, 1 vol. 2010. (Classic Graphic Novel Collection). (ENG., Illus.). 144p. (J). (gr. 7-10). 41.03 (978-1-4205-0373-9(1), 8beacdff-6ff3-4c8d-8b26-7888a357344f, Lucent Pr.) Greenhaven Publishing LLC.
Stevenson, Robert Louis. Kidnapped. 2009. (Puffin Classics Ser.). (ENG.). 352p. (J). (gr. 5-7). 8.99 (978-0-14-132602-3(6), Puffin Books) Penguin Young Readers Group.
—Kidnapped. Wyeth, N. C., illus. 2004. (Scribner Storybook Classics Ser.). (ENG.). 64p. (J). (gr. 3-7). 19.99 (978-0-689-86542-8(2), Atheneum Bks. for Young Readers) Simon & Schuster Children's Publishing.
—Kidnapped, 1 vol. Fisher, Eric Scott, illus. 2011. (Calico Illustrated Classics Ser.: No. 3). (ENG.). 112p. (J). (gr. 2-5). 38.50 (978-1-61641-105-3(8), 4017, Calico Chapter Bks.) ABDO Publishing Co.
—Kidnapped & Catriona. 2007. 480p. per. 15.00 (978-1-84697-033-7(4)) Birlinn, Ltd. GBR. Dist: Casemate Pubs. & Bk. Distributors, LLC.
Strachan, Linda. Hamish Mchaggis & the Edinburgh Adventure. Collins, Sally J., illus. 2005. (Hamish Mchaggis Ser.). 26p. (J). per. 9.00 (978-0-9546701-7-7(5)) GW Publishing GBR. Dist: Gatewood Pr.
Vanderwal, Andrew H. Death of a King. 2013. (Illus.). 304p. (J). (gr. 5). 19.95 (978-1-77049-398-6(0), Tundra Bks.) Tundra Bks. CAN. Dist: Penguin Random Hse. LLC.
Weigand, Edith S. If Mandy Ruled the World. 2003. (Illus.). 16p. 7.95 (978-0-9618904-9-0(5)) Zhera Pubns.
Wiley, Melissa. Beyond the Heather Hills. Graef, Renee, illus. 2003. (Little House Ser.). 189p. (J). (gr. 3-7). 14.65 (978-0-7569-3467-5(2)) Perfection Learning Corp.
Wright, Peter M. The Stone Prince, 1 vol. 2009. 48p. pap. 16.95 (978-1-4489-2591-9(6)) America Star Bks.
Yolen, Jane & Harris, Robert J. Girl in a Cage. 2004. 234p. (gr. 5-9). 17.00 (978-0-7569-2946-6(6)) Perfection Learning Corp.

SCOTLAND—HISTORY—WAR OF INDEPENDENCE, 1285-1371

Clare, John. Braveheart. 2009. (Hodder History: Concepts & Processes Ser.). (ENG., Illus.). 48p. pap. 23.50 (978-0-340-95771-4(9)) Hodder Education Group GBR. Dist: Trans-Atlantic Pubns., Inc.

SCOTS—UNITED STATES—FICTION

Gratz, Alan M. Something Wicked. 2009. 288p. (YA). (gr. 7-18). 10.99 (978-0-14-241496-5(4), Speak) Penguin Young Readers Group.
Namioka, Lensey. Half & Half. 2005. 136p. (gr. 3-7). 16.00 (978-0-7569-5680-6(3)) Perfection Learning Corp.
Wibberley, Leonard. Peter Treegate's War. 2009. (ENG.). 134p. (J). (gr. 10-12). pap. 12.95 (978-1-932350-21-0(7)) Ignatius Pr.

SCOTT, DRED, 1809-1858

Herda, D. J. The Dred Scott Case: Slavery & Citizenship, 1 vol. rev. ed. 2010. (Landmark Supreme Court Cases, Gold Edition Ser.). (ENG., Illus.). 104p. (gr. 6-7). 35.93 (978-0-7660-3427-3(5), 93b18d2b-b363-4fc5-b99b-7b1b87095065) Enslow Publishing, LLC.
—Slavery & Citizenship: The Dred Scott Case, 1 vol. 2016. (U. S. Supreme Court Landmark Cases Ser.). (ENG., Illus.). 128p. (J). (gr. 7-7). 38.93 (978-0-7660-8426-1(4), ffcb8d36-7c36-4d76-8da3-8ca5072dc032) Enslow Publishing, LLC.
McNeese, Tim. Dred Scott V. Sandford. 2006. (Great Supreme Court Decisions Ser.). (ENG., Illus.). 120p. (J). (gr. 5-9). lib. bdg. 32.95 (978-0-7910-9236-1(4), P114570, Facts On File) Infobase Holdings, Inc.
Naden, Corinne & Flum Galvin, Irene. Dred Scott: Person or Property?, 1 vol. 2006. (Supreme Court Milestones Ser.). (ENG., Illus.). 128p. (J). (gr. 8-8). 45.50 (978-0-7614-1841-2(5), c0c31031-3114-488f-83a3-2d4a01460e85) Cavendish Square Publishing LLC.
Rosen, Daniel. Dred Scott & the Supreme Court: Set Of 6. 2011. (Navigators Ser.). (J). pap. 48.00 net. (978-1-4108-6258-7(5)) Benchmark Education Co.
—Dred Scott & the Supreme Court: Text Pairs. 2008. (Bridges/Navigators Ser.). (J). (gr. 5). 94.00 (978-1-4108-8413-8(9)) Benchmark Education Co.
Skog, Jason. The Dred Scott Decision. 2006. (We the People: Civil War Era Ser.). (ENG., Illus.). 48p. (gr. 5-6). 7.95 (978-0-7565-2038-0(X), Compass Point Bks.) Capstone.

SCOTT, ROBERT FALCON, 1868-1912

Dowdeswell, Evelyn, et al. Scott of the Antarctic, 1 vol. 2012. (ENG., Illus.). 32p. (gr. 1-3). pap. 8.29 (978-1-4329-6891-5(2), 119837, Heinemann) Capstone.
Grochowicz, Joanna. Into the White: Scott's Antarctic Odyssey. 2017. (ENG.). 288p. (J). (gr. 5-9). pap. 14.99 (978-1-76029-365-9(2)) Allen & Unwin AUS. Dist: Independent Pubs. Group.
Llanas, Sheila Griffin. Who Reached the South Pole First? (Race for History Ser.). (ENG.). 32p. (gr. 3-4). 2011. pap. 47.70 (978-1-4296-6413-4(4)) 2010. (J). lib. bdg. 27.99 (978-1-4296-3344-4(1), 95851) Capstone. (Capstone Pr.).
McNeil, Niki, et al. HOCPP 1132 Robert Falcon Scott. 2006. spiral bd. 18.50 (978-1-60308-132-0(1)) In the Hands of a Child.
Pipe, Jim. The Race to the South Pole. 2006. (Stories from History Ser.). (ENG., Illus.). 48p. (J). (gr. 3-6). 21.19 (978-0-7696-4722-7(7)) School Specialty, Incorporated.
Riddle, John. Robert F. Scott: British Explorer of the South. 2004. (Great Names Ser.). (Illus.). 32p. (J). (gr. 3-18). lib. bdg. 19.95 (978-1-59084-146-4(8)) Mason Crest.

SCOTTISH POETRY

Aigner-Clark, Julie. Baby Einstein Poemas Preciosos: Pretty Poems & Wonderful Words. Zaidi, Nadeem, illus. 2004. (SPA.). 10p. (J). 9.95 (978-970-718-210-3(5), Silver Dolphin Bks.) Readerlink Distribution Services, LLC.
Stevenson, Robert Louis. A Child's Garden of Verses. McClintock, Barbara, illus. 2011. (ENG.). 80p. (J). (gr. -1-3). 18.99 (978-0-06-028228-8(2), HarperCollins) HarperCollins Pubs.
—A Child's Garden of Verses, 1 vol. Wildsmith, Brian, illus. 2008. (ENG.). 32p. (J). 21.99 (978-1-59572-057-3(X)) Star Bright Bks., Inc.
—My Shadow. Lang, Glenna, illus. 2019. (ENG.). 32p. (gr. 1-18). 17.95 (978-0-87923-788-2(0)) Godine, David R. Pub.
—Poetry For Young People: Robert Louis Stevenson. 2003. cd-rom 19.00 (978-0-931968-62-4(3)) Seltzer Bks.

SCOUTS AND SCOUTING

see also Boy Scouts; Girl Scouts

Buckley, James. Coaching & Scouting, Vol. 10. Ferrer, Al, ed. 2015. (Careers off the Field Ser.). (Illus.). 64p. (J). (gr. 7). lib. bdg. 23.95 (978-1-4222-3267-5(0)) Mason Crest.
Calvert, Patricia. Kit Carson: He Led the Way, 1 vol. 2007. (Great Explorations Ser.). (ENG., Illus.). 80p. (gr. 6-6). lib. bdg. 36.93 (978-0-7614-2223-5(4), 963e1330-9bef-4967-b147-72bb2846fbe9) Cavendish Square Publishing LLC.
Girl Scouts of the USA, creator. The Senior Girl's Guide to Girl Scouting. 2011. spiral bd. 22.50 (978-0-88441-779-8(4)) Girl Scouts of the USA.
Kalar, Bonnie. The Scouts. Spreen, Kathe, illus. Date not set. 8p. (J). (gr. -1-2). pap. (978-1-891619-26-7(8)) Corona Pr.
Rice, Dona Herweck. Juliette Gordon Low: The First Girl Scout. rev. ed. 2018. (Social Studies: Informational Text Ser.). (ENG., Illus.). 32p. (J). (gr. 2-4). pap. 11.99 (978-1-4938-8781-1(5)) Teacher Created Materials, Inc.
Russell, Wendy Thomas & Goodman, Sarah. MEdia. 2010. (Illus.). 96p. (J). (978-0-88441-752-1(2)) Girl Scouts of the USA.
Sanford, William R. & Green, Carl R. Kit Carson: Courageous Mountain Man, 1 vol. 2013. (Courageous Heroes of the American West Ser.). (ENG., Illus.). 48p. (J). (gr. 5-7). 25.27 (978-0-7660-4011-3(9), 757f65d3-b04f-4e69-b4da-2cf66fb6c127); pap. 11.53 (978-1-4644-0094-0(6), c76bd838-258d-431a-a120-4cfb04bb164f) Enslow Publishing, LLC.
Savage, Jeff. Fearless Scouts: True Tales of the Wild West, 1 vol. 2012. (True Tales of the Wild West Ser.). (ENG., Illus.). 48p. (gr. 5-7). pap. 11.53 (978-1-4644-0032-2(6), 1e23d9c1-b183-4644-b14d-d34ef5487bc1); lib. bdg. 25.27 (978-0-7660-4024-3(0), 2b158bfd-477d-4d23-ae67-76b93dbaa2c3) Enslow Publishing, LLC.
Studio 2b: Focus - Express It. 2004. (YA). pap. (978-0-88441-671-5(2)) Girl Scouts of the USA.
Studio 2b Focus - Don't Sweat It. 2004. (YA). pap. (978-0-88441-669-2(0)) Girl Scouts of the USA.
Studio 2b Focus - Mind Your Own Business. 2004. (YA). pap. (978-0-88441-668-5(2)) Girl Scouts of the USA.
STUDIO 2B Guide for Councils Phase II: Strategies & Models. 2004. (YA). (978-0-88441-686-9(0)) Girl Scouts of the USA.
Tuchman, Laura. Welcome to the Daisy Flower Garden. Kalis, Jennifer, illus. 2008. 88p. (J). (978-0-88441-709-5(3)) Girl Scouts of the USA.
Vander Pluym, Andrea. Mission: Sisterhood. Waters, Susy Pilgrim, illus. 2010. 80p. (YA). (978-0-88441-753-8(0)) Girl Scouts of the USA.
Warren, Andrea. The Boy Who Became Buffalo Bill: Growing up Billy Cody in Bleeding Kansas, 0 vols. 2015. (ENG., Illus.). 256p. (J). (gr. 4-9). 19.99 (978-1-4778-2718-5(8), 9781477827185, Two Lions) Amazon Publishing.
Wiese, Jim & Melton, H. Keith. The Spy's Guide to Scouting & Reconnaissance. 2003. (Illus.). 48p. (J). (978-0-439-33647-5(3)) Scholastic, Inc.

SCOUTS AND SCOUTING—FICTION

Appelt, Kathi. The True Blue Scouts of Sugar Man Swamp. (ENG., Illus.). (J). (gr. 3-7). 2014. 352p. pap. 8.99 (978-1-4424-2108-0(8), Atheneum Bks. for Young Readers) 2013. 336p. 19.99 (978-1-4424-2105-9(3)) Simon & Schuster Children's Publishing.
August, John. Arlo Finch in the Valley of Fire. 2019. (Arlo Finch Ser.: 1). (ENG.). 352p. (J). pap. 8.99 (978-1-250-29425-8(8), 900174830) Square Fish.
Berenstain, Jan & Berenstain, Mike. Help the Homeless, 1 vol. 2012. (I Can Read! / Berenstain Bears / Good Deed Scouts / Living Lights: a Faith Story Ser.). (ENG., Illus.). 32p. (J). pap. 4.99 (978-0-310-72102-4(4)) Zonderkidz.
—Honey Hunt Helpers, 1 vol. 2012. (I Can Read! / Berenstain Bears / Good Deed Scouts / Living Lights: a Faith Story Ser.). (ENG., Illus.). 32p. (J). pap. 4.99 (978-0-310-72101-7(6)) Zonderkidz.
—Let the Bible Be Your Guide. 2011. (Berenstain Bears/Living Lights Ser.). (ENG., Illus.). 40p. (J). 6.99 (978-0-310-72714-9(6)) Zonderkidz.
Bowen, Robert Sidney. Dave Dawson, Flight Lieutenant. 2011. 248p. 46.95 (978-1-258-01820-7(9)) Literary Licensing, LLC.
D'Ath, Justin. Grizzly Trap. 2015. (ENG.). 144p. (J). pap. 4.99 (978-1-61067-359-4(X)) Kane Miller.
Dillard, Sarah. Mouse Scouts: Make Friends. 2018. (Mouse Scouts Ser.: 4). (Illus.). 160p. (J). (gr. 2-5). pap. 7.99 (978-0-385-75612-9(7), Yearling) Random Hse. Children's Bks.
Garis, Lilian C. The Girl Scout Pioneers; or, Winning the First B C. 2007. 148p. per. (978-1-4065-2775-9(0)) Dodo Pr.
Gatewood, June S. Mandy Miller & the Brownie Troop. Connors, Mary, illus. 2009. 48p. pap. 17.49 (978-1-4389-1727-6(9)) AuthorHouse.
Hapka, Catherine, pseud. Pony Scouts: Pony Crazy. Kennedy, Anne, illus. 2009. (I Can Read Level 2 Ser.). (ENG.). 32p. (J). (gr. -1-3). 16.99 (978-0-06-125533-5(5), HarperCollins) HarperCollins Pubs.
Hawke, Jay Jordan. A Scout Is Brave. 2nd ed. 2016. (ENG., Illus.). (J). 24.99 (978-1-63477-929-6(0), Harmony Ink Pr.) Dreamspinner Pr.
Kipling, Rudyard. Land & Sea Tales for Scouts & Scout. 2005. pap. 30.95 (978-1-885529-84-8(8)) Stevens Publishing.
McCormick, Wilfred. Eagle Scout: A Bronc Burnett Story. 2011. 192p. 42.95 (978-1-258-07309-1(9)) Literary Licensing, LLC.
Newton, A. I. The Alien Next Door 3: Alien Scout. Sarkar, Anjan, illus. 2018. (Alien Next Door Ser.: 3). (ENG.). 112p. (J). (gr. k-3). 16.99 (978-1-4998-0581-9(0)); pap. 5.99 (978-1-4998-0580-2(2)) Little Bee Books Inc.
—Alien Scout, 3. 2019. (Alien Next Door Ch Bks). (ENG.). 94p. (J). (gr. 2-3). 15.59 (978-0-87617-269-8(9)) Penworthy Co., LLC, The.
Osmond, Joanne H. A Fishy Adventure. Osmond, Jack, illus. 2013. 152p. pap. 12.99 (978-1-933334-26-4(6)) Vision Tree, Ltd., The.
Ralphson, G. Harvey. Boy Scouts on the Open Plain. 2005. pap. 27.95 (978-1-885529-55-8(4)) Stevens Publishing.
Rubino, Tony. Who Ate the Brownies. 2013. 28p. pap. 24.95 (978-1-63004-481-7(4)) America Star Bks.
Shotz, Jennifer Li. Scout: National Hero. 2018. (Scout Ser.: 1). (ENG.). 224p. (J). (gr. 3-7). pap. 9.99 (978-0-06-280247-7(X), HarperCollins) HarperCollins Pubs.
—Scout: Firefighter. 2018. (Scout Ser.: 2). (ENG.). 208p. (J). (gr. 3-7). 17.99 (978-0-06-280250-7(X)); 12.99 (978-0-06-288989-8(3)); pap. 7.99 (978-0-06-280261-3(5)) HarperCollins Pubs. (HarperCollins).
Swanson, Matthew. The Real Mccoys: Wonder Undercover. Behr, Robbi, illus. 2019. (Real Mccoys Ser.: 3). (ENG.). 352p. (J). 16.99 (978-1-250-30782-8(1), 900198140) Imprint IND. Dist: Macmillan.
Uss, Christina. The Colossus of Roads. 2020. 208p. (J). (gr. 4-7). 17.99 (978-0-8234-4450-2(3), Margaret Ferguson Books) Holiday Hse., Inc.
Welcome to the Nature Scouts. 2003. (J). per. (978-1-57657-874-2(7)) Paradise Pr., Inc.

SCRIPTURES, HOLY

see Bible

SCREEN PROCESS PRINTING

Luidens, Lyz & Griffin, Camille. Silk Screening. 2015. (21st Century Skills Innovation Library: Makers As Innovators Ser.). (ENG., Illus.). 32p. (J). (gr. 4-8). 32.07 (978-1-63362-379-8(3), 206936) Cherry Lake Publishing.

SCROOGE, EBENEZER (FICTITIOUS CHARACTER)—FICTION

Block, Shelly, et al. Uncle Scrooge, No. 351. Clark, John, ed. 2006. (ENG., Illus.). 64p. pap. 6.95 (978-1-888472-15-8(4), 9781888472158) Gemstone Publishing, Inc.
A Christmas Carol. 2004. (J). cd-rom 7.99 (978-0-9740847-9-4(4)) GiGi Bks.
A Christmas Carol. 2003. (Illus.). 32p. (J). 9.98 (978-1-4054-0997-1(5)) Parragon, Inc.
Dickens, Charles. A Christmas Carol. 2008. (Illus.). 116p. (Orig.). pap. 7.99 (978-1-60450-545-0(1), Serenity Pubs.) Arc Manor.
—A Christmas Carol. Collins, Mike, illus. 2012. (ENG.). 160p. (Orig.). (gr. 6). lib. bdg. 24.95 (978-1-907127-40-3(2)) Classical Comics GBR. Dist: Publishers Group West (PGW).
—A Christmas Carol. 2008. (ENG., Illus.). 160p. (Orig.). (gr. 4-18). pap. 16.95 (978-1-906332-52-5(5), Classical Comics, Ltd.) Classical Comics GBR. Dist: Publishers Group West (PGW).
—A Christmas Carol. 2006. (Illus.). 61p. (Orig.). (J). lib. bdg. 30.77 (978-1-4242-1016-9(X)) Fitzgerald Bks.
—A Christmas Carol. 2009. 84p. (Orig.). (gr. -1-18). pap. 19.99 (978-1-4432-6003-9(7)) General Bks. LLC.
—A Christmas Carol. Helquist, Brett, illus. 2009. (ENG.). 40p. (Orig.). (J). (gr. k). 17.99 (978-0-06-165099-4(4), Balzer & Bray) HarperCollins Pubs.
—A Christmas Carol. 2008. (Puffin Classics Ser.). (Illus.). 160p. (Orig.). (J). (gr. 5-7). 7.99 (978-0-14-132452-4(X), Puffin Books) Penguin Young Readers Group.
—A Christmas Carol. 2004. 224p. (Orig.). (YA). pap. 29.00 incl. audio (978-1-4000-9005-1(9), Listening Library) Random Hse. Audio Publishing Group.
—A Christmas Carol. Donnelly, Karen, illus. 2013. (Charles Dickens Ser.). (ENG.). 64p. (Orig.). pap. 7.95 (978-1-906230-02-9(1)) Real Reads Ltd. GBR. Dist: Casemate Pubs. & Bk. Distributors, LLC.
—A Christmas Carol. Andrews, Gary, illus. 2008. (Fast Track Classics Ser.). 46p. (Orig.). (J). (gr. 4-7). pap. 10.00 (978-1-4190-5087-9(7)) Steck-Vaughn.
—A Christmas Carol. 2008. 160p. (Orig.). (gr. 5-6). pap. 11.95 (978-1-4341-0214-0(9)) The Editorium, LLC.
—Christmas Carol. Innocenti, Roberto, illus. 2005. 152p. (J). (gr. 4-6). 35.00 (978-1-56846-182-3(8)) Creative Co., The.
—A Christmas Carol, 1 vol. 2009. (Foundation Classics Ser.). (ENG.). 56p. (J). (gr. 5-5). lib. bdg. 32.60 (978-1-60754-850-8(X), 7827880d-6e02-4a5c-b454-0e2162825350, Windmill Bks.) Rosen Publishing Group, Inc., The.
—A Christmas Carol. Blake, Quentin, illus. unabr. ed. 2004. (Chrysalis Childrens Classics Ser.). (ENG.). 190p. (Orig.). (YA). pap. (978-1-84365-063-8(0), Pavilion Children's Books) Pavilion Bks.
—A Christmas Carol Graphic Novel. 2010. (Illustrated Classics Ser.). (ENG., Illus.). 64p. (YA). (gr. 4-12). pap. 11.95 (978-1-56254-890-2(5)) Saddleback Educational Publishing, Inc.
—A Christmas Carol the Graphic Novel: Original Text. 2008. (ENG., Illus.). 160p. (Orig.). (gr. 4-18). pap. 16.95 (978-1-906332-51-8(7), Classical Comics, Ltd.) Classical Comics GBR. Dist: Publishers Group West (PGW).
Dickens, Charles & Wilson, Sean Michael. A Christmas Carol - Original Text. 2008. (Illus.). 160p. (Orig.). (J). pap. (978-1-906332-17-4(7)) Classical Comics.
Marks, Alan, illus. A Christmas Carol. 2013. (ENG.). 24p. (J). 18.99 (978-0-7945-2910-9(0), Usborne) EDC Publishing.
Wilson, Matthew. Scrooge & Santa GN. 2011. (Illus.). 100p. pap. 14.95 (978-1-897548-98-1(2)) Arcana Studio, Inc.

SCUBA DIVING

Here are entered works on free diving with the use of a self-contained underwater breathing apparatus. Works on free diving with the use of mask, fins and snorkel are entered under Skin Diving.

Arroyo, Sheri L. & Stewart, Rhea A. How Deep Sea Divers Use Math. 2009. (Math in the Real World Ser.). (ENG.). 32p. (gr. 4-6). 28.00 (978-1-60413-611-1(1), P466913, Chelsea Clubhse.) Infobase Holdings, Inc.
Bodden, Valerie. Scuba Diving. 2009. (Active Sports Ser.). (J). (gr. 1-5). 24.25 (978-1-58341-701-0(X), Creative Education) Creative Co., The.
Broadbent, Paul. Scuba Diving. 2007. (Trackers-Math Ser.). (gr. 2-5). pap. 5.00 (978-1-59055-938-3(X)) Pacific Learning, Inc.
Gilkerson, Patricia. My Adventure Scuba Diving. 2006. (My Adventure Ser.). 44p. (J). (gr. -1-3). pap. 8.99 (978-1-59092-286-6(7)) Blue Forge Pr.
Huntrods, David. For the Love of Scuba. 2006. (For the Love of Sports Ser.). (Illus.). 24p. lib. bdg. 24.45 (978-1-59036-382-9(5)); per. 8.95 (978-1-59036-383-6(3)) Weigl Pubs., Inc.
—Scuba. 2013. (J). (978-1-62127-320-2(2)); pap. (978-1-62127-325-7(3)) Weigl Pubs., Inc.
Lopatka, Michael. Scuba Divers Sign Language: A Guide to Underwater Communications of Tropical Reef Inhabitants. 2003. (Illus.). 75p. 12.95 (978-0-9723218-9-1(6), 0-9723218-9-6) Awesome Guides, Inc.
McFee, Shane. Scuba Diving. (Living on the Edge Ser.). 24p. (gr. 2-3). 2009. 42.50 (978-1-61514-298-9(3), PowerKids Pr.) 2008. (ENG., Illus.). (J). lib. bdg. 26.27 (978-1-4042-4217-3(1), cfa8d091-27e7-4543-8cf8-320b672f8857) Rosen Publishing Group, Inc., The.
Murray, Laura K. Scuba Diver. 2018. (Wild Jobs Ser.). (ENG., Illus.). 24p. (J). (gr. 1-4). (978-1-60818-925-0(2), 19647, Creative Education); pap. 9.99 (978-1-62832-541-6(0), 19645, Creative Paperbacks) Creative Co., The.
Nagelhout, Ryan. Diving with Sharks. 2014. (Illus.). 32p. (J). (978-1-4824-3287-9(0)) Stevens, Gareth Publishing LLLP.
Ryback, Carol. Scuba Diving, 1 vol. 2004. (Extreme Sports Ser.). (ENG., Illus.). 24p. (gr. 2-4). pap. 9.15 (978-0-8368-4549-5(8), 6701c145-01ef-4305-b75a-c3776d46a161); lib. bdg. 25.67 (978-0-8368-4542-6(0), 82e28786-5db1-41ba-b1e1-63aed3acef75) Stevens, Gareth Publishing LLLP. (Gareth Stevens Learning Library).
Woolf, Alex. Sailing the Great Barrier Reef. 2014. (Traveling Wild Ser.). 32p. (J). (gr. 3-6). pap. 63.00 (978-1-4824-1252-9(7)) Stevens, Gareth Publishing LLLP.

SCULLING

see Rowing

SCULLY, DANA (FICTITIOUS CHARACTER)—FICTION

Smith, Kim, illus. The X-Files: Earth Children Are Weird: A Picture Book. 2017. (Pop Classics Ser.: 2). 40p. (J). (gr. -1-3). 18.99 (978-1-59474-979-7(5)) Quirk Bks.

SCULPTORS

D'Aquino, Andrea. A Life Made by Hand: The Story of Ruth Asawa. 2019. (ENG., Illus.). 40p. (J). (gr. k-3). 18.95 (978-1-61689-836-6(4)) Princeton Architectural Pr.

S

Di Cagno, Gabriella. Michelangelo. 2008. (Art Masters Ser.). 64p. (YA). (gr. 6-18). lib. bdg. 24.95 net. *(978-1-934545-01-0(5))* Oliver Pr., Inc.

Dunn, L. Kerr, et al. Dreaming with Animals: Anna Hyatt Huntington & Brookgreen Gardens. 2017. (Young Palmetto Bks.). (ENG., Illus.). 40p. 18.99 *(978-1-61117-820-3(7),* P544770) Univ. of South Carolina Pr.

Etinde-Crompton, Charlotte & Crompton, Samuel Willard. Augusta Savage: Sculptor of the Harlem Renaissance, 1 vol. 2019. (Celebrating Black Artists Ser.). (ENG.). 104p. (gr. 7-7). 38.93 *(978-1-9785-0361-8(X),* aec30130-812d-454f-944c-ee1713e42444) Enslow Publishing, LLC.

—Edmonia Lewis: Internationally Renowned Sculptor, 1 vol. 2019. (Celebrating Black Artists Ser.). (ENG.). 104p. (gr. 7-7). 38.93 *(978-1-9785-1471-3(9),* 6921823c-3c41-4da5-ab0e-436b232739e0) Enslow Publishing, LLC.

Kuiper, Kathleen, ed. The 100 Most Influential Painters & Sculptors of the Renaissance, 1 vol. 2010. (Britannica Guide to the World's Most Influential People Ser.). (ENG., Illus.). 376p. (YA). (gr. 10-10). lib. bdg. 56.59 *(978-1-61530-004-4(X),* deb5d486-8e60-40ab-9222-0c87fd73c880) Rosen Publishing Group, Inc., The.

Morrison, Taylor. The Buffalo Nickel. Morrison, Taylor, illus. 2006. (Illus.). 32p. (J). (gr. 4-8). reprint ed. 16.00 *(978-1-4223-5858-0(5))* DIANE Publishing Co.

O'Reilly, Sally. Henry Moore. 2003. (Artists in Their Time Ser.). (ENG., Illus.). 48p. (J). 24.00 *(978-0-531-12241-9(7),* Watts, Franklin) Scholastic Library Publishing.

Rosenstock, Barb. The Secret Kingdom: Nek Chand, a Changing India, & a Hidden World of Art. Nivola, Claire A., illus. 2018. (ENG.). 48p. (J). (gr. 2-5). 17.99 *(978-0-7636-7475-5(3))* Candlewick Pr.

Schoettler, Joan. Ruth Asawa: A Sculpting Life, 1 vol. Van Van Wagoner, Traci, illus. 2018. (ENG.). 32p. (gr. 1-4). 16.99 *(978-1-4556-2397-6(0),* Pelican Publishing) Arcadia Publishing.

Schroeder, Alan & National Geographic Learning Staff. In Her Hands: The Story of Sculptor Augusta Savage, 1 vol. Bereal, JaeMe, illus. 2009. (ENG.). 48p. (J). (gr. 1-5). pap. 13.95 *(978-1-60060-989-3(9),* leelowbooks) Lee & Low Bks., Inc.

Stock, Catherine. Vinnie & Abraham. unabr. ed. 2008. (J). (gr. 2-5). 27.95 incl. audio *(978-0-8045-6967-5(3));* 29.95 incl. audio compact disk *(978-0-8045-4190-9(6))* Spoken Arts, Inc.

Stone, Tanya Lee. Sandy's Circus: A Story about Alexander Calder. Kulikov, Boris, illus. 2008. 40p. (J). (gr. 1-3). 18.99 *(978-0-670-06268-3(5),* Viking Books for Young Readers) Penguin Young Readers Group.

Wenzel, Angela. 13 Sculptures Children Should Know. 2010. (13 Children Should Know Ser.). (ENG., Illus.). 48p. (J). (gr. 3-7). 14.95 *(978-3-7913-7010-1(3))* Prestel Verlag GmbH & Co KG. DEU. Dist: Penguin Random Hse. LLC.

SCULPTORS—FICTION

Arnold, Elana K. Infandous. 2015. (ENG.). 200p. (YA). (gr. 8-12). 18.99 *(978-1-4677-3849-1(2),* 5f116506-df41-46d9-aaec-833557c7c676, Carolrhoda Lab™) Lerner Publishing Group.

Atkins, Jeannine. Stone Mirrors: The Sculpture & Silence of Edmonia Lewis. 2018. (ENG.). 192p. (YA). (gr. 7). pap. 12.99 *(978-1-4814-5906-8(6))* Simon & Schuster Children's Publishing.

Bedard, Michael. The Clay Ladies. braille ed. 2004. (J). (gr. k-3). spiral bd. *(978-0-616-01544-5(5))* Canadian National Institute for the Blind/Institut National Canadien pour les Aveugles.

Bradbury, Jennifer. Outside In. 2017. (ENG., Illus.). 288p. (J). (gr. 3-7). 17.99 *(978-1-4424-6827-6(0),* Atheneum/Caitlyn Dlouhy Books) Simon & Schuster Children's Publishing.

Carmichael, Clay. Wild Things. 2012. (ENG.). 184p. (J). (gr. 4-7). pap. 9.99 *(978-1-59078-914-8(6),* Astra Young Readers) Astra Publishing Hse.

—Wild Things, 6 vols. 2010. (J). 77.75 *(978-1-4498-0632-3(5))* Recorded Bks., Inc.

Daly, Jude. Sivu's Six Wishes: A Taoist Tale. 2010. (ENG., Illus.). 36p. (J). (gr. 1-5). 17.00 *(978-0-8028-5369-1(2),* Eerdmans Bks For Young Readers) Eerdmans, William B. Publishing Co.

Henkes, Kevin. Sweeping up the Heart. 2019. (ENG.). 192p. (J). (gr. 3-7). 16.99 *(978-0-06-285254-0(X));* E-Book *(978-0-06-285257-1(4),* 9780062852571) HarperCollins Pubs. (Greenwillow Bks.).

Stanley, Diane. The Trouble with Wishes. Stanley, Diane, illus. 2007. (Illus.). 32p. (J). (gr. k-3). lib. bdg. 17.89 *(978-0-06-055452-1(5))* HarperCollins Pubs.

SCULPTURE

see also Mobiles (Sculpture); Modeling; Monuments; Soap Sculpture

Alexander, Heather. A Child's Introduction to Art: The World's Greatest Paintings & Sculptures. Hamilton, Meredith, illus. 2014. (Child's Introduction Ser.). (ENG.). 96p. (J). (gr. -1-17). 19.99 *(978-1-57912-956-9(0),* 81956, Black Dog & Leventhal Pubs. Inc.) Running Pr.

Beak, Nick Huckleberry. How to Bend Balloons. 2013. (Illus.). 64p. (J). (gr. 3-7). 9.99 *(978-1-84322-864-6(5),* Armadillo) Anness Publishing GBR. Dist: National Bk. Network.

Briggs, Paula. Make Build Create: Sculpture Projects for Children. 2016. (ENG., Illus.). 144p. pap. 24.95 *(978-1-910433-70-6(5))* Black Dog Publishing Ltd. GBR. Dist: Consortium Bk. Sales & Distribution.

deMarin, Layne. Built from Stone, 1 vol. 2011. (Wonder Readers Fluent Level Ser.). (ENG.). 16p. (J). (gr. -1-2). pap. 6.25 *(978-1-4296-7911-4(5),* 118243, Capstone Pr.) Capstone.

Hill, Isabel. Urban Animals, 1 vol. 2009. (ENG., Illus.). 32p. (J). (gr. 2-7). 17.95 *(978-1-59572-209-6(2))* Star Bright Bks., Inc.

Hove, Carol. Make It Yourself! Collages & Sculptures. 2017. (Cool Makerspace Ser.). (ENG., Illus.). 32p. (J). (gr. 3-6). lib. bdg. 34.21 *(978-1-5321-1067-2(7),* 25710, Checkerboard Library) ABDO Publishing Co.

Howse, Jennifer. Totem Poles: Canadian Icons. 2010. (Illus.). 24p. *(978-1-77071-574-5(6));* pap. *(978-1-77071-581-3(9))* Weigl Educational Pubs. Ltd.

James, Sara. Sculpting. 2014. (Art Today! Ser.: 10). (Illus.). 64p. (J). (gr. 7-18). 23.95 *(978-1-4222-3176-0(3))* Mason Crest.

Jiang, Helga. Clay Charm Magic! 25 Amazing, Teeny-Tiny Projects to Make with Polymer Clay. 2014. (ENG.). 128p. (J). (gr. k). 12.95 *(978-1-63220-398-4(7),* Sky Pony Pr.) Skyhorse Publishing Co., Inc.

Jones, Mark. Do You Want to Build a Snowman? Your Guide to Creating Exciting Snow-Sculptures. 2017. (ENG., Illus.). 80p. (J). (gr. k-8). pap. 12.99 *(978-1-63158-121-2(X),* Racehorse Publishing) Skyhorse Publishing Co., Inc.

Kallen, Stuart. Sculpture. 2014. (Discovering Art). (ENG., Illus.). 80p. (J). lib. bdg. *(978-1-60152-678-6(4))* ReferencePoint Pr., Inc.

Krempel, Ulrich. Niki's World: Niki de Saint Phalle. 2004. (Adventures in Art Ser.). (Illus.). 30p. (J). 14.95 *(978-3-7913-3068-6(3))* Prestel Publishing.

Kuiper, Kathleen, ed. The 100 Most Influential Painters & Sculptors of the Renaissance, 1 vol. 2010. (Britannica Guide to the World's Most Influential People Ser.). (ENG., Illus.). 376p. (YA). (gr. 10-10). lib. bdg. 56.59 *(978-1-61530-004-4(X),* deb5d486-8e60-40ab-9222-0c87fd73c880) Rosen Publishing Group, Inc., The.

Loh-Hagan, Virginia. Green Man. 2017. (Urban Legends: Don't Read Alone! Ser.). (ENG., Illus.). 32p. (J). (gr. 4-8). lib. bdg. 32.07 *(978-1-63472-902-4(1),* 210034, 45th Parallel Press) Cherry Lake Publishing.

May, Susie & Whitely, Heather. Shape. 2006. (Children's Art Ser. from the National Gallery of Victoria Ser.). (Illus.). 28p. pap. 9.95 *(978-0-7241-0239-6(6))* National Gallery of Victoria AUS. Dist: Antique Collectors' Club.

Nardo, Don. Sculpture, 1 vol. 2006. (Eye on Art Ser.). (ENG., Illus.). 104p. (gr. 7-7). lib. bdg. 41.03 *(978-1-59018-966-5(3),* 779c3ac0-17d4-4e85-bbb2-4bf1cd3afbc6, Lucent Pr.) Greenhaven Publishing LLC.

Nelson, Robin. From Wax to Crayon. 2013. (Start to Finish, Second Ser.). (ENG., Illus.). 24p. (J). (gr. k-3). pap. 7.99 *(978-1-4677-0798-5(8),* a99fd755-5d3c-47c5-80d4-8d3cd49aaf10) Lerner Publishing Group.

Oachs, Emily Rose. The Terra-Cotta Army. 2019. (Digging up the Past Ser.). (ENG., Illus.). 24p. (J). (gr. 3-7). lib. bdg. 26.95 *(978-1-64487-070-9(3),* 12262, Torque Bks.) Bellwether Media.

Pitamic, Maja & Laidlaw, Jill. Three-Dimensional Art Adventures: 36 Creative, Artist-Inspired Projects in Sculpture, Ceramics, Textiles, & More. 2016. (Art Adventures Ser.). (ENG., Illus.). 144p. (J). (gr. 1). pap. 19.99 *(978-1-61373-659-3(2))* Chicago Review Pr., Inc.

Pym, Tasha. Super Sculptures: Band 05/Green (Collins Big Cat) 2006. (Collins Big Cat Ser.). (ENG., Illus.). 24p. (J). (gr. 1-1). pap. 8.99 *(978-0-00-718686-0(X))* HarperCollins Pubs. Ltd. GBR. Dist: Independent Pubs. Group.

QEB Let's Start! Art National Book Stores Edition: Sculpture. 2006. (J). per. *(978-1-59566-302-3(9))* QEB Publishing Inc.

Raczka, Bob. 3-D ABC: A Sculptural Alphabet. 2006. (Bob Raczka's Art Adventures Ser.). (ENG., Illus.). 32p. (J). (gr. k-12). lib. bdg. 25.26 *(978-0-7613-9456-3(7),* Millbrook Pr.) Lerner Publishing Group.

Schoettler, Joan. Ruth Asawa: A Sculpting Life, 1 vol. Van Van Wagoner, Traci, illus. 2018. (ENG.). 32p. (gr. 1-4). 16.99 *(978-1-4556-2397-6(0),* Pelican Publishing) Arcadia Publishing.

Schwake, Susan. Art Lab for Kids: Express Yourself: 52 Creative Adventures to Find Your Voice Through Drawing, Painting, Mixed Media, & Sculpture, Volume 19. 2018. (Lab for Kids Ser.: 19). (ENG., Illus.). 144p. (J). (gr. -1-5). pap. 24.99 *(978-1-63159-592-9(X),* 305221, Quarry Bks.) Quarto Publishing Group USA.

Taylor, Terry. Sand Play! 20+ SANDsational Ideas. 2014. (ENG., Illus.). 48p. (J). (gr. 2-6). pap. 7.99 *(978-0-486-79479-2(2),* 794792) Dover Pubns., Inc.

Tullet, Hervé & Tullet, Hervé. The Giant Game of Sculpture. 2014. (ENG., Illus.). 16p. (gr. k-3). 29.95 *(978-0-7148-6800-4(0))* Phaidon Pr., Inc.

VanVoorst, Jenny Fretland. La Escultura. 2016. (El Estudio del Artista (Artist's Studio)).Tr. of Sculpture. (SPA., Illus.). 24p. (J). (gr. k-2). lib. bdg. 25.65 *(978-1-62031-323-7(5),* Bullfrog Bks.) Jump! Inc.

—Sculpture. 2016. (Artist's Studio Ser.). (Illus.). 24p. (J). (gr. k-2). lib. bdg. 25.65 *(978-1-62031-284-1(0),* Bullfrog Bks.) Jump! Inc.

Weill, Cynthia. Mi Familia Calaca / My Skeleton Family, 1 vol. Zárate, Jesús Canseco, illus. 2017. (First Concepts in Mexican Folk Art Ser.). (ENG.). 32p. (J). (gr. -1-2). pap. 11.95 *(978-1-941026-34-2(6),* 23353382, Cinco Puntos Press) Lee & Low Bks., Inc.

Wenzel, Angela. 13 Sculptures Children Should Know. 2010. (13 Children Should Know Ser.). (ENG., Illus.). 48p. (J). (gr. 3-7). 14.95 *(978-3-7913-7010-1(3))* Prestel Verlag GmbH & Co KG. DEU. Dist: Penguin Random Hse. LLC.

SCULPTURE—FICTION

Balliett, Blue. The Calder Game. Helquist, Brett, illus. 2010. (ENG.). 416p. (J). (gr. 4-7). 7.99 *(978-0-439-85208-1(0),* Scholastic Paperbacks) Scholastic, Inc.

Campos, Tito. Muffler Man el Hombre Mofle. Alvarez, Lamberto, illus. 2009. 32p. (J). pap. 7.95 *(978-1-55885-557-1(2),* Piñata Books) Arte Publico Pr.

Howse, Jennifer. Les Totems: Les Emblèmes Canadiens. McMann, Julie, tr. from ENG. 2011. (FRE.). 24p. (YA). (gr. 2-4). *(978-1-77071-412-0(X))* Weigl Educational Pubs. Ltd.

Kusmierski, Janet & Colin, Paul. Snowman's Big Job. 2004. (Illus.). (J). *(978-0-439-58392-3(6))* Scholastic, Inc.

Marsoli, Lisa Ann & Bridwell, Norman. The Snow Dog. Haefele, Steve, illus. 2004. (Big Red Reader Ser.). (J). pap. *(978-0-439-58559-0(7))* Scholastic, Inc.

Parker, Emma. The Snowman Olympics. 2010. (Illus.). 20p. pap. *(978-1-877561-36-8(3))* First Edition Ltd.

Reynolds, Aaron. Metal Man. Hoppe, Paul, illus. 2010. (ENG.). 32p. (J). (gr. k-3). pap. 7.95 *(978-1-58089-151-6(9))* Charlesbridge Publishing, Inc.

Styles, Walker. The Case of the Missing Tiger's Eye. Whitehouse, Ben, illus. 2016. (Rider Woofson Ser.: 1). (ENG.). 128p. (J). (gr. k-4). 16.99 *(978-1-4814-5738-5(1),* Little Simon) Little Simon.

Sullivan, Kate. On Linden Square. Sullivan, Kate, illus. 2013. (ENG., Illus.). 40p. (J). (gr. 1-3). 15.99 *(978-1-58536-832-7(6),* 202894) Sleeping Bear Pr.

Tegen, Katherine. Snowman Magic: A Winter & Holiday Book for Kids. Dorman, Brandon, illus. 2012. (ENG.). 32p. (J). (gr. -1-3). 12.99 *(978-0-06-201445-0(5),* HarperCollins) HarperCollins Pubs.

Thielbar, Melinda. The Book Bandit: A Mystery with Geometry. Chow, Candice & Lee, Jennifer A., illus. 2011. (Manga Math Mysteries Ser.: 7). (ENG.). 48p. (J). (gr. 3-5). pap. 7.99 *(978-0-7613-8136-5(8),* e0e0aea2-a276-4124-9f9e-f3e70f31022c, Graphic Universe™) Lerner Publishing Group.

—#7 the Book Bandit: A Mystery with Geometry. Lee, Jenn Manley & Chow, Candice, illus. 2011. (Manga Math Mysteries Set II Ser.). pap. 39.62 *(978-0-7613-8364-2(6),* Graphic Universe™) Lerner Publishing Group.

Trice, Linda. Kenya's Art. Mitchell, Hazel, illus. 2016. (ENG.). 32p. (J). (gr. -1-3). 16.95 *(978-1-57091-848-3(1))* Charlesbridge Publishing, Inc.

SCULPTURE—HISTORY

Osier, Peter. The History of Western Sculpture, 1 vol. 2015. (Britannica Guide to the Visual & Performing Arts Ser.). (ENG., Illus.). 224p. (J). (gr. 9-10). 47.59 *(978-1-68048-085-6(5),* 1b6482c1-286b-4970-8259-16d0b11b06a0, Britannica Educational Publishing) Rosen Publishing Group, Inc., The.

Osier, Peter, ed. The History of Western Sculpture, 4 vols. 2015. (Britannica Guide to the Visual & Performing Arts Ser.). (ENG.). 224p. (YA). (gr. 9-10). 95.18 *(978-1-68048-086-3(3),* f7ac37bd-e7f0-4bb9-87f3-2ee3e4b3aa3a, Britannica Educational Publishing) Rosen Publishing Group, Inc., The.

SCULPTURE, RELIGIOUS

see Christian Art and Symbolism

SCULPTURE—TECHNIQUE

see also Modeling

Kuhtz, Cleo, ed. Sculpture: Materials, Technique, Styles, & Practice, 1 vol. 2016. (Britannica's Practical Guide to the Arts Ser.). (ENG., Illus.). 128p. (J). (gr. 10-10). lib. bdg. 37.82 *(978-1-68048-375-8(7),* ae5390fe-19a7-4d4d-970d-0f9ac4430832) Rosen Publishing Group, Inc., The.

Reid, Emily. Space Claymation, 1 vol. 2016. (Claymation Sensation Ser.). (ENG.). 32p. (gr. 3-3). pap. 12.75 *(978-1-4994-8100-6(4),* 2acb6b4e-e396-40f0-a8ad-eef704259d0e, Windmill Bks.) Rosen Publishing Group, Inc., The.

—Sports Claymation, 1 vol. 2016. (Claymation Sensation Ser.). (ENG.). 32p. (gr. 3-3). pap. 12.75 *(978-1-4994-8104-4(7),* 39ca1238-4448-4e52-987f-c6f370df48e3, Windmill Bks.) Rosen Publishing Group, Inc., The.

Spilsbury, Richard. Sculpture, 1 vol. 2008. (Stories in Art Ser.). (ENG., Illus.). 32p. (J). (gr. 4-4). lib. bdg. 30.27 *(978-1-4042-4435-1(2),* 92a7cb8d-0204-4acb-85f5-6f99f91f8c5f, PowerKids Pr.) Rosen Publishing Group, Inc., The.

Watt, Fiona. Complete Book of Art Ideas. 2005. (Art Ideas Ser.). 288p. (J). 39.95 *(978-0-7945-0900-2(2),* Usborne) EDC Publishing.

Yates, Jane. 3-D Art Skills Lab. 2018. (Art Skills Lab Ser.). (Illus.). 32p. (J). (gr. 4-4). pap. *(978-0-7787-5225-7(9))* Crabtree Publishing Co.

SEA

see Ocean

SEA ANIMALS

see Marine Animals

SEA FISHERIES

see Fisheries

SEA HORSES

Bell, Samantha. Sea Horses. 2014. (21st Century Skills Library: Exploring Our Oceans Ser.). (ENG., Illus.). 32p. (J). (gr. 3-6). 32.07 *(978-1-62431-604-3(2),* 203200) Cherry Lake Publishing.

Berger, Melvin & Berger, Gilda. Caballitos de Mar: Sea Horses. 2006. (SPA & ENG., Illus.). (J). *(978-0-439-87988-0(4))* Scholastic, Inc.

Bozzo, Linda. How Seahorses Grow Up. 2019. (Animals Growing Up Ser.). (ENG.). 24p. (gr. 1-2). 56.10 *(978-1-9785-1238-2(4))* Enslow Publishing, LLC.

Butterworth, Chris. Sea Horse: Read & Wonder: the Shyest Fish in the Sea. Lawrence, John, illus. 2009. (Read & Wonder Ser.). (ENG.). 32p. (J). (gr. -1-3). pap. 7.99 *(978-0-7636-4140-5(5))* Candlewick Pr.

Butterworth, Christine. Sea Horse: The Shyest Fish in the Sea. Lawrence, John, illus. 2006. (Read & Wonder Ser.). (ENG.). 32p. (J). (gr. k-2). 22.44 *(978-0-7636-2989-2(8))* Candlewick Pr.

Clinging Sea Horses 6-Pack. 2004. (Illus.). (J). lib. bdg. 39.99 *(978-0-8225-5192-8(6))* Lerner Publishing Group.

Duhaime, Darla. Sea Horses. 2017. (Ocean Animals Ser.). (ENG.). 24p. (gr. k-2). pap. 9.95 *(978-1-68342-424-6(7),* 9781683424246) Rourke Educational Media.

George, Twig C. Seahorses. (gr. k-3). 2005. (Illus.). 31p. (J). per. 8.95 *(978-0-8225-3390-0(1))* 2003. 32p. lib. bdg. 24.90 *(978-0-7613-2869-8(6),* Millbrook Pr.) Lerner Publishing Group.

Gibbs, Maddie. Sea Horses, 1 vol. 2013. (PowerKids Readers: Fun Fish Ser.). 24p. (J). (gr. k-k). (ENG.). 26.27 *(978-1-4777-0761-6(1),* cee18873-8a7c-4c57-b95e-9e7445cad95b); pap. 49.50 *(978-1-4777-0856-9(1));* (ENG., Illus.). pap. 9.25 *(978-1-4777-0855-2(3),* 62063407-60e7-436a-8d74-82859cba93ff) Rosen Publishing Group, Inc., The. (PowerKids Pr.).

—Sea Horses / Los Caballos de Mar, 1 vol. De La Vega, Eida, ed. 2013. (PowerKids Readers: Peces Divertidos / Fun Fish Ser.). (ENG & SPA.). 24p. (J). (gr. k-k). 26.27 *(978-1-4777-1219-1(4),* 824930f3-c030-46f3-baa8-9e5e115899e7, PowerKids Pr.) Rosen Publishing Group, Inc., The.

Gilkerson, Patricia. My Adventure with Sea Horses. 2009. (ENG.). 44p. (J). 8.99 *(978-1-59092-465-5(7))* Blue Forge Pr.

Gish, Melissa. Living Wild: Seahorses. 2017. (Living Wild Ser.). (ENG., Illus.). 48p. (J). (gr. 5-7). pap. 12.00 *(978-1-62832-437-2(6),* 20208, Creative Paperbacks) Creative Co., The.

—Seahorses. 2017. (Living Wild Ser.). (ENG., Illus.). 48p. (J). (gr. 4-7). *(978-1-60818-834-5(5),* 20207, Creative Education) Creative Co., The.

Hansen, Grace. Caballitos de Mar (Seahorses), 1 vol. 2016. (Vida en el Océano (Ocean Life) Ser.). (SPA., Illus.). 24p. (J). (gr. -1-2). lib. bdg. 32.79 *(978-1-68080-748-6(X),* 22658, Abdo Kids) ABDO Publishing Co.

—Seahorses, 1 vol. 2015. (Ocean Life Ser.). (ENG.). 24p. (J). (gr. -1-2). lib. bdg. 32.79 *(978-1-62970-711-2(2),* 17221, Abdo Kids) ABDO Publishing Co.

Herriges, Ann & National Geographic Learning Staff. Sea Horses. 2006. (Oceans Alive Ser.). (ENG., Illus.). 24p. (J). (gr. k-3). lib. bdg. 26.95 *(978-1-60014-020-4(3),* Blastoff! Readers) Bellwether Media.

Is it a Fish? 6 Each of 1, 6 vols. (Sunshinetm Science Ser.). 24p. (gr. 1-2). 41.95 *(978-0-7802-1428-6(5))* Wright Group/McGraw-Hill.

Is it a Fish? Big Book. (Sunshinetm Science Ser.). 24p. (gr. 1-2). 37.50 *(978-0-7802-1429-3(3))* Wright Group/McGraw-Hill.

James, Helen Foster. Discover Sea Horses. 2015. (21st Century Basic Skills Library: Splash! Ser.). (ENG., Illus.). 24p. (J). (gr. 2-4). 26.35 *(978-1-63362-605-8(9),* 206604) Cherry Lake Publishing.

Jango-Cohen, Judith. Clinging Sea Horses. 2005. (Pull Ahead Bks.). (Illus.). 32p. (gr. k-3). lib. bdg. 22.60 *(978-0-8225-3764-9(8))* Lerner Publishing Group.

Kalman, Bobbie. Les Hippocampes. 2010. (FRE., Illus.). 32p. (J). pap. 9.95 *(978-2-89579-286-4(0))* Bayard Canada Livres CAN. Dist: Crabtree Publishing Co.

—The Life Cycle of a Sea Horse, 1 vol. 2003. (Life Cycle Ser.). (ENG., Illus.). 32p. (J). pap. *(978-0-7787-0693-9(1));* lib. bdg. *(978-0-7787-0663-2(X))* Crabtree Publishing Co.

Laughlin, Kara L. Sea Horses. 2017. (In the Deep Blue Sea Ser.). (ENG.). 24p. (J). (gr. k-3). lib. bdg. 32.79 *(978-1-5038-1688-6(5),* 211524) Child's World, Inc, The.

Leaf, Christina. Sea Horses. 2016. (Ocean Life up Close Ser.). (ENG., Illus.). 24p. (J). (gr. k-3). 26.95 *(978-1-62617-420-7(2));* pap. 7.99 *(978-1-61891-267-1(4),* 12057) Bellwether Media. (Blastoff! Readers).

Meister, Cari. Sea Horses. 2013. (ENG., Illus.). 24p. (J). lib. bdg. 25.65 *(978-1-62031-033-5(3))* Jump! Inc.

Otfinoski, Steven. Seahorses, 1 vol. 2008. (Animals, Animals Ser.). (ENG., Illus.). 48p. (gr. 5-5). lib. bdg. 32.64 *(978-0-7614-2529-8(2),* f28b09ed-f2f9-4573-9521-33cb7a8aa731) Cavendish Square Publishing LLC.

Owen, Ruth. Seahorse Fry. 2012. (Water Babies Ser.). 24p. (J). (gr. -1-3). lib. bdg. 25.65 *(978-1-61772-604-0(4))* Bearport Publishing Co., Inc.

Proudfit, Benjamin. Seahorses, 1 vol. 2019. (Ocean Animals Ser.). (ENG.). 24p. (gr. k-k). pap. 9.15 *(978-1-5382-4465-4(9),* 2e923d08-34c3-46ba-9cbd-c97b37a9e409) Stevens, Gareth Publishing LLLP.

Rhodes, Mary Jo & Hall, David. Seahorses & Sea Dragons. Hall, David, photos by. 2005. (Undersea Encounters Ser.). (ENG., Illus.). 48p. (J). (gr. 3-7). lib. bdg. 27.00 *(978-0-516-24393-1(4),* Children's Pr.) Scholastic Library Publishing.

Schuh, Mari. Sea Horses. 2019. (Spot Ocean Animals Ser.). (ENG.). 16p. (J). (gr. -1-2). lib. bdg. *(978-1-68151-631-8(4),* 10763) Amicus.

Sexton, Colleen. The Life Cycle of a Sea Horse. 2010. (Life Cycles Ser.). (ENG., Illus.). 24p. (J). (gr. k-3). lib. bdg. 26.95 *(978-1-60014-312-0(1),* Blastoff! Readers) Bellwether Media.

Shofner, Melissa Raé. Sea Horses. 2017. (Freaky Fish Ser.). 24p. (J). (gr. 2-3). pap. 48.90 *(978-1-5382-0250-0(6))* Stevens, Gareth Publishing LLLP.

Statts, Leo. Seahorses. 2016. (Ocean Animals Ser.). (ENG., Illus.). 24p. (J). (gr. -1-2). lib. bdg. 31.36 *(978-1-68079-914-9(2),* 24132, Abdo Zoom-Launch) ABDO Publishing Co.

Terp, Gail. Seahorses. 2022. (Super Sea Creatures Ser.). (ENG.). 32p. (J). (gr. 4-6). *(978-1-62310-285-2(5),* 13468, Bolt) Black Rabbit Bks.

Turner, Pamela S. Project Seahorse. Tuason, Scott, illus. 12th ed. 2010. (Scientists in the Field Ser.). (ENG.). 64p. (J). (gr. 5-7). 18.99 *(978-0-547-20713-1(1),* 1059611, Clarion Bks.) HarperCollins Pubs.

Walker, Sally M. Sea Horses. 2004. (Early Bird Nature Bks.). (Illus.). 47p. (J). 25.26 *(978-0-8225-3051-0(1),* Lerner Pubns.) Lerner Publishing Group.

Wearing, Judy. Seahorses. 2009. (World of Wonder Ser.). (Illus.). 24p. (J). (gr. 2-4). lib. bdg. 24.45 *(978-1-60596-102-6(7))* Weigl Pubs., Inc.

—Seahorses: World of Wonder: Underwater Life. 2009. (Illus.). 24p. (J). pap. 8.95 *(978-1-60596-103-3(5))* Weigl Pubs., Inc.

Weber, Valerie J. Sea Horses, 1 vol. 2008. (Animals That Live in the Ocean Ser.). (ENG., Illus.). 24p. (gr. 1-1). pap. 9.15 *(978-0-8368-9342-7(5),* c12f5ef7-6ace-49de-83aa-36580aff3775, Weekly Reader Leveled Readers) Stevens, Gareth Publishing LLLP.

—Sea Horses / Caballitos de Mar, 1 vol. 2008. (Animals That Live in the Ocean / Animales Que Viven en el Océano Ser.). (SPA & ENG.). 24p. (J). (gr. 1-1). lib. bdg. 25.27 *(978-0-8368-9249-9(6),* 559f6309-9aa6-4121-950f-9d7d1e9b3015, Weekly Reader Leveled Readers) Stevens, Gareth Publishing LLLP.

Weber, Valerie J. & Weber, Valerie J. Sea Horses, 1 vol. 2008. (Animals That Live in the Ocean Ser.). (ENG., Illus.). 24p. (J). (gr. 1-1). lib. bdg. 25.27 *(978-0-8368-9243-7(7),* 2508d9e5-03c2-4b25-ae74-62b349e87293, Weekly Reader Leveled Readers) Stevens, Gareth Publishing LLLP.

—Sea Horses / Caballitos de Mar, 1 vol. 2008. (Animals That Live in the Ocean / Animales Que Viven en el Océano Ser.). (SPA & ENG.). 24p. (gr. 1-1). pap. 9.15 *(978-0-8368-9348-9(4),* 5132442a-5725-422b-801a-fd569c33537e, Weekly Reader Leveled Readers) Stevens, Gareth Publishing LLLP.

SEA HORSES—FICTION

Bardhan-Quallen, Sudipta. Purrmaids #3: Seasick Sea Horse. Wu, Vivien, illus. 2018. (Purrmaids Ser.: 3). (ENG.). 96p. (J).

(gr. 1-4). 5.99 *(978-1-5247-0167-3(X)*, Random Hse. Bks. for Young Readers) Random Hse. Children's Bks.

Bellón, Teresa, illus. Splish Splash, Seahorse! 2018. (J). bds. 7.99 *(978-1-61067-780-6(3))* Kane Miller.

Bise, Jr. J. David & Bise, Jr. In Search of a Name a Seahorse Story. 2011. 44p. pap. 15.50 *(978-1-60976-288-9(6)*, Strategic Bk. Publishing) Strategic Book Publishing & Rights Agency (SBPRA).

Carle, Eric. Mister Seahorse. Carle, Eric, illus. 2004. (ENG., Illus.). 32p. (J). (gr. -1-k). 18.99 *(978-0-399-24269-4(4))* Penguin Young Readers Group.

—Mister Seahorse: Board Book. Carle, Eric, illus. 2011. (ENG., Illus.). 64p. (J). (gr. -1 — 1). bds. 9.99 *(978-0-399-25490-1(0))* Penguin Young Readers Group.

Dadey, Debbie. The Secret Sea Horse. Avakyan, Tatevik, illus. 2013. (Mermaid Tales Ser.: 6). (ENG.). 112p. (J). (gr. 1-4). 17.99 *(978-1-4424-8261-6(3))*; pap. 6.99 *(978-1-4424-8260-9(5))* Simon & Schuster Children's Publishing. (Aladdin).

Dadey, Debby & Dadey, Debbie. Secret Sea Horse, Bk. 6. Avakyan, Tatevik, illus. 2015. (Mermaid Tales Ser.). (ENG.). 96p. (J). (gr. 1-4). 31.36 *(978-1-61479-327-4(1)*, 17149, Chapter Bks.) Spotlight.

Davis, Caroline. Seahorse. 2017. (ENG., Illus.). 8p. (J). (gr. -1 — 1). 5.99 *(978-1-4380-7842-7(0))* Sourcebooks, Inc.

Dean, James, illus. Pete the Cat: Scuba-Cat. 2016. (I Can Read Book: My First Ser.). (ENG.). 32p. (J). (gr. -1-1). 17.44 *(978-1-4844-7052-7(4))* HarperCollins Pubs.

Dean, James & Dean, Kimberly. Pete the Cat: Scuba-Cat. Dean, James, illus. 2016. (My First I Can Read Ser.). (ENG., Illus.). 32p. (J). (gr. -1-3). pap. 4.99 *(978-0-06-230388-2(0)*, HarperCollins) HarperCollins Pubs.

Giulieri, Anne. Little Sea Horse & the Big Crab. Aranda, Omar, illus. 2012. (Engage Literacy Yellow Ser.). (ENG.). 16p. (J). (gr. k-2). pap. 36.94 *(978-1-4296-8969-4(2)*, 18381); pap. 6.99 *(978-1-4296-8968-7(4)*, 119989) Capstone. (Capstone Pr.).

—Little Sea Horse & the Big Storm. Aranda, Omar, illus. 2012. (Engage Literacy Blue Ser.). (ENG.). 16p. (J). (gr. k-2). pap. 36.94 *(978-1-4296-8993-9(5)*, 18393); pap. 6.99 *(978-1-4296-8992-2(7)*, 120002) Capstone. (Capstone Pr.).

Hendra, Sue. Barry the Fish with Fingers & the Hairy Scary Monster. 2011. 32p. *(978-1-74276-025-4(2)*, Koala Books) Scholastic Australia.

King, Karen. Sparkle the Seahorse. Hicks, Angie, illus. 2012. (ENG.). 24p. (J). 9.95 *(978-1-84135-879-6(7))* Award Pubns. Ltd. GBR. Dist: Parkwest Pubns., Inc.

Krosoczka, Jarrett J. Peanut Butter & Jellyfish. 2014. (ENG., Illus.). 40p. (J). (gr. -1-2). 18.99 *(978-0-375-87036-1(9)*, Knopf Bks. for Young Readers) Random Hse. Children's Bks.

Lee, Julia Elizabeth. Seahorses Down Under. Weiser, Robert, ed. (Defenders of Wildlife Ser.). (Illus.). 50+p. (J). (gr. k-3). lib. bdg. 9.95 *(978-0-9666857-0-1(9))* Dawn of Day Childrens Publishing Co., Inc.

Meadows, Daisy. Rihanna the Seahorse Fairy. 2012. (Illus.). 65p. (J). *(978-0-545-42599-5(9))* Scholastic, Inc.

Spickett, D. M. The Adventures of Sarah the Seahorse, 1 vol. 2009. 21p. pap. 24.95 *(978-1-61546-205-6(8))* America Star Bks.

Steele, Margaret. Wuz Da Nite Befo: A Pidgin Christmas Story in Hawaii. Chang, Roy, illus. 2005. 24p. 10.95 *(978-1-56647-750-5(6))* Mutual Publishing LLC.

Voyage to Shelter Cove. 2006. (Illus.). (J). pap., act. bk. ed. 2.00 *(978-0-9724425-5-8(3)*, White Tiger Pr.) Homes for the Homeless Institute, Inc.

Walker, Sally M. Seahorse Reef: A Story of the South Pacific. Petruccio, Steven James, illus. 2005. (ENG.). 32p. (J). (gr. -1-2). pap. 6.95 *(978-1-56899-938-8(0)*, S4020) Soundprints.

Wyllie, Jim & Wyllie, Miggie. Cedric's Day at the Castle. 2003. (Illus.). 24p. (J). (gr. -1-1). pap. 7.95 *(978-1-85149-712-6(9))* Antique Collectors' Club.

SEA IN ART

Baumbusch, Brigitte. Oceans in Art, 1 vol. 2004. (What Makes a Masterpiece? Ser.). (ENG., Illus.). 32p. (gr. 2-4). lib. bdg. 25.67 *(978-0-8368-4782-6(2)*, 7e409b0d-36a5-4401-b1c8-26db556befa0, Gareth Stevens Learning Library) Stevens, Gareth Publishing LLLP.

Harbo, Christopher L. Easy Ocean Origami, 1 vol. 2010. (Easy Origami Ser.). (ENG.). 24p. (J). (gr. 1-3). lib. bdg. 25.99 *(978-1-4296-5385-5(X)*, 113811, Capstone Pr.) Capstone.

Montgomery, Kelly & Creative Haven Staff. Sea Life Designs Coloring Book. 2012. (Adult Coloring Books: Sea Life Ser.). (ENG., Illus.). 64p. (gr. 3). pap. 6.99 *(978-0-486-49088-5(2)*, 490882) Dover Pubns., Inc.

SEA LIFE

see Seafaring Life

also names of countries with the subhead Navy, e.g., United States—Navy

SEA LIONS

see Seals (Animals)

SEA MOSSES

see Algae

SEA POETRY

Downey, Shirley. Fishes in the Seas, 1 vol. Manchester, Peter, illus. 2008. (ENG.). 24p. (J). pap. 12.95 *(978-0-9686586-3-5(6)*, 10e3992e-000b-489a-9e9e-4347573b7591) Muddle Puddle Bks. CAN. Dist: Baker & Taylor Publisher Services (BTPS).

Hughes, Langston. Sail Away. Bryan, Ashley, illus. 2015. (ENG.). 40p. (J). (gr. -1-3). 19.99 *(978-1-4814-3085-2(8))* Simon & Schuster Children's Publishing.

SEA POWER

see also Disarmament; Naval History; Warships

also names of countries with the subhead Navy or the subdivision History, Naval, e.g. United States—Navy; United States—History, Naval, etc.

Dougherty, Martin J. Sea Warfare, 1 vol. 2010. (Modern Warfare Ser.). (ENG., Illus.). 32p. (J). (gr. 3-5). lib. bdg. 28.67 *(978-1-4339-2734-8(9)*, 45af19c0-ebb4-47bd-acbf-dcc391772edf) Stevens, Gareth Publishing LLLP.

Mueller, Richard. Naval Warfare of the Future. (Library of Future Weaponry Ser.). 64p. (gr. 6-6). 2009. 58.50 *(978-1-60853-640-5(8))* 2006. (ENG., Illus.). (J). lib. bdg. 37.13 *(978-1-4042-0526-0(8)*, 79362953-5812-48a5-999a-e68a85d71840) Rosen Publishing Group, Inc., The.

SEA ROUTES

see Trade Routes

SEA SHELLS

see Shells

SEA SHORE

see Seashore

SEA STORIES

Adams, Jennifer. Moby Dick Playset: A BabyLit(TM) Ocean Primer Board Book & Playset, 1 vol. Oliver, Alison, illus. 2015. (ENG.). 22p. (J). 19.99 *(978-1-4236-3871-1(9))* Gibbs Smith, Publisher.

Anton, Amy Way. Ina the Octopus & Her Shipwreck Adventure. Way, MaryFaye, illus. 2008. 28p. pap. 13.99 *(978-1-4389-2177-8(2))* AuthorHouse.

Avi. The True Confessions of Charlotte Doyle. l.t. ed. 2005. 337p. pap. 10.95 *(978-0-7862-7252-5(X)*, Large Print Pr.) Thorndike Pr.

—The True Confessions of Charlotte Doyle. 2012. lib. bdg. 17.20 *(978-0-606-26779-3(4))* Turtleback.

—The True Confessions of Charlotte Doyle (Scholastic Gold), 1 vol. 2012. (ENG.). 240p. (J). (gr. 4-7). pap. 9.99 *(978-0-545-47711-6(5)*, Scholastic Paperbacks) Scholastic, Inc.

Babbitt, Natalie. The Eyes of the Amaryllis. 2007. (ENG.). 144p. (J). (gr. 5-8). per. 9.99 *(978-0-312-37008-4(3)*, 900044345) Square Fish.

Beck, Patricia. Prince Hasmir's High Seas Adventure. 2011. 24p. pap. 15.99 *(978-1-4628-6151-4(2))* Xlibris Corp.

Bently, Peter. Captain Jack & the Pirates. Oxenbury, Helen, illus. 2016. (ENG.). 32p. (J). (-k). 18.99 *(978-0-525-42950-0(6)*, Dial Bks) Penguin Young Readers Group.

Bleu, Kennedy. Cotter Otter in Treasure Water. Goembel, Ponder, illus. 2014. (ENG.). 24p. (J). pap. 24.95 *(978-1-63004-814-3(3))* America Star Bks.

Bodeen, S. A. The Raft. 2013. (ENG.). 256p. (YA). (gr. 7-12). pap. 11.99 *(978-1-250-02739-9(X)*, 900098311) Square Fish.

Bringsvaerd, Tor Age. Ruffen: The Escape to Loch Ness. Hansen, Thore, illus. 2009. (Ruffen Ser.). 72p. (J). (gr. 1-4). 16.95 *(978-0-9815761-2-1(5))* Mackenzie Smiles, LLC.

Collingwood, Harry. The Castaways. 2017. (ENG., Illus.). (J). 24.95 *(978-1-374-98145-4(1))*; pap. 14.95 *(978-1-374-98144-7(3))* Capital Communications, Inc.

—The Castaways. 2008. 172p. 25.95 *(978-1-60664-710-3(5))*; pap. 13.95 *(978-1-60664-209-2(X))* Rodgers, Alan Bks.

—The Rover's Secret. 2011. 274p. 29.95 *(978-1-4638-9505-1(4))* Rodgers, Alan Bks.

—Under the Chilean Flag. 2009. 184p. 26.95 *(978-1-60664-598-7(6))*; pap. 13.95 *(978-1-60664-330-3(4))* Rodgers, Alan Bks.

Cooper, Susan. Victory. 2013. (ENG., Illus.). 224p. (J). (gr. 5-9). 17.99 *(978-1-4424-8079-7(3))*; pap. 7.99 *(978-1-4424-8080-3(7))* McElderry, Margaret K. Bks. (McElderry, Margaret K. Bks.).

Croce, Pat & Slutsky, Adam. Plunder. 2015. (Plunder Ser.: 1). (ENG.). 336p. 31.95 *(978-1-68162-373-3(0))*; 338p. (J). pap. 16.95 *(978-1-63026-893-0(3))* Turner Publishing Co.

Cummings, Mary. And the Baker's Boy Went to Sea. 2006. (Illus.). 195p. (YA). 16.95 *(978-0-9774855-0-5(1))* Sparkling Pr.

Dalmatian Press Staff, adapted by. Moby Dick. (J). 9.95 *(978-1-56156-308-1(0))* Kidsbooks, LLC.

De Valor, Diana. The Great Adventures of Sea Worthy with the I Can Crew: The Treasure of Captain Blue Beard. 2011. 32p. pap. 19.95 *(978-1-4269-6627-9(X))* Trafford Publishing.

Duncan, Daniel. South. 2017. (ENG., Illus.). 40p. (J). (gr. k-2). 17.95 *(978-1-4197-2299-8(9)*, 1159001, Abrams Bks. for Young Readers) Abrams, Inc.

Eagar, Lindsay. Race to the Bottom of the Sea. (ENG.). 432p. (J). (gr. 3-7). 2019. pap. 9.99 *(978-0-7636-9877-5(6))* 2017. 17.99 *(978-0-7636-7923-1(2))* Candlewick Pr.

Eames, Brian. The Dagger Quick. (Dagger Chronicles Ser.). (ENG., (J). (gr. 3-7). 2013. Illus.). 352p. pap. 6.99 *(978-1-4424-8368-2(7))* 2011. 336p. 15.99 *(978-1-4424-2311-4(0))* Simon & Schuster/Paula Wiseman Bks. (Simon & Schuster/Paula Wiseman Bks.).

Eisner, Will & Melville, Herman. Moby Dick. 2003. (ENG., Illus.). 32p. (J). pap. 7.95 *(978-1-56163-294-7(5))* NBM Publishing Co.

Faiella, Graham. Moby Dick & the Whaling Industry of the 19th Century. 2009. (Looking at Literature Through Primary Sources Ser.). 64p. (gr. 5-8). 58.50 *(978-1-61514-305-4(X))* Rosen Publishing Group, Inc., The.

Farjeon, Eleanor. Jim at the Corner. Ardizzone, Edward, illus. 2017. (ENG.). 96p. (J). (gr. 2-4). 15.95 *(978-1-68137-164-1(2)*, NYR Children's Collection) New York Review of Bks., Inc., The.

Fenton, Geleta. Joel's Adventure at Sea. Siniard, Ricky, illus. 2013. 50p. (J). mass mkt. 9.95 *(978-0-9824433-2-3(3))* Octopus Publishing Co.

Flanagan, John. The Ghostfaces. 2016. (Brotherband Chronicles Ser.: 6). (ENG.). 400p. (J). (gr. 5). 18.99 *(978-0-399-16357-9(3)*, Philomel Bks.) Penguin Young Readers Group.

Fultz, Steven D. The Adventures of the Barnyard Detectives: Where's Mr. Peacock, 1 vol. 2009. 79p. pap. 19.95 *(978-1-60749-965-7(7))* America Star Bks.

George, Jessica Day. Saturdays at Sea. 2018. (Tuesdays at the Castle Ser.). (ENG.). 288p. (J). pap. 8.99 *(978-1-68119-606-0(9)*, 900179030, Bloomsbury USA Childrens) Bloomsbury Publishing USA.

Gilkerson, William. Pirate's Passage. 2014. (ENG., Illus.). 376p. (J). (gr. 4-7). pap. 16.95 *(978-1-61180-247-4(4)*, Trumpeter) Shambhala Pubns., Inc.

Golden, Christopher & Lebbon, Tim. The Sea Wolves Bk. 2, Bk. 2. Ruth, Greg, illus. 2012. (Secret Journeys of Jack London Ser.: 2). (ENG.). 400p. (YA). (gr. 8). 16.99 *(978-0-06-186320-2(3)*, HarperTeen) HarperCollins Pubs.

González, Jorge. Captain Barbosa & the Pirate Hat Chase. González, Jorge, illus. 2019. (ENG., Illus.). 32p. (J). (gr. k-3). pap. 7.99 *(978-1-5415-4527-4(3)*, c373e22a-df24-482f-80bd-fbc9df5288e1); 26.65 *(978-1-5415-4154-2(5)*, 2f468433-a2c4-4821-a24c-13da048a68d8) Lerner Publishing Group. (Graphic Universe™).

Hart, Alison. Leo, Dog of the Sea, 1 vol. Montgomery, Michael G., illus. 2019. (Dog Chronicles Ser.). 176p. (J). (gr. 2-5). pap. 7.95 *(978-1-68263-089-1(7))* Peachtree Publishing Co. Inc.

Hawes, Charles Boardman. The Dark Frigate. Chappell, Warren, illus. 2018. (ENG.). 240p. (gr. 3-7). pap. 7.99 *(978-0-486-82392-8(X)*, 82392X) Dover Pubns., Inc.

—The Dark Frigate. 2005. pap. 27.95 *(978-1-4179-3209-2(0))* Kessinger Publishing, LLC.

Hesse, Karen. Stowaway. unabr. ed. 2004. 328p. (J). (gr. 5-9). pap. 48.00 incl. audio *(978-0-8072-8760-6(1)*, LYA 259 SP, Listening Library) Random Hse. Audio Publishing Group.

Hodgson, William Hope. The Sea Horses. 2004. reprint ed. pap. 1.99 *(978-1-4192-8166-2(6))* Kessinger Publishing, LLC.

Hopkins, William J. The Sandman: His Sea Stories (Yesterday's Classics) Home, Diantha W., illus. 2009. 188p. pap. 9.95 *(978-1-59915-303-2(3))* Yesterday's Classics.

Horrigan, David J. The Spark in the Sea: Adventures in Marine Science, 1. 2003. 152p. pap. 24.00 *(978-0-9743712-0-7(3)*, 001) Home Planet Bks.

Jacobson, Bonny B. Whale Fables. 2011. 68p. pap. 31.99 *(978-1-4535-9956-3(8))* Xlibris Corp.

Jolivet, Joëlle, illus. Moby-Dick: A Pop-Up Book from the Novel by Herman Melville (Pop up Books for Adults & Kids, Classic Books for Kids, Interactive Books for Adults & Children) 2019. (ENG.). 16p. 40.00 *(978-1-4521-7384-9(2))* Chronicle Bks. LLC.

Katar, Al. Captain Scratch: The Island of Sirmarj. 2008. 48p. pap. 21.99 *(978-1-4363-4188-2(4))* Xlibris Corp.

Kipling, Rudyard. Land & Sea Tales for Scouts & Scout. 2005. pap. 30.95 *(978-1-885529-84-8(8))* Stevens Publishing.

Kirker, Solveig. The Florida Pod. 2009. 32p. pap. 12.99 *(978-1-4389-3137-1(9))* AuthorHouse.

Kositsky, Lynne. Minerva's Voyage. 2009. (ENG., Illus.). 240p. (YA). (gr. 6-18). pap. 10.99 *(978-1-55488-439-1(X))* Dundurn Pr. CAN. Dist: Publishers Group West (PGW).

LaBaff, Stephanie. Draw Pirates in 4 Easy Steps: Then Write a Story, 1 vol. 2012. (Drawing in 4 Easy Steps Ser.). (ENG., Illus.). 48p. (gr. 3-3). pap. 11.53 *(978-1-4644-0012-4(1)*, 3836b10f-8c0c-4974-9bd5-5cd19df96f16, Enslow Elementary) Enslow Publishing, LLC.

Lasky, Kathryn. Pirate Bob. Clark, David, illus. alt. ed. 2008. (ENG.). 32p. (J). (gr. k-3). per. 8.95 *(978-1-57091-647-2(0))* Charlesbridge Publishing, Inc.

Lawrence, Iain. The Buccaneers. 2003. (High Seas Trilogy). (Illus.). 244p. (gr. 5-9). 16.50 *(978-0-7569-1454-7(X))* Perfection Learning Corp.

LeBrun, Barbie. Porter Horse Finds Blackbeard's Treasure. 2013. (ENG.). 24p. (J). pap. 21.95 *(978-1-4787-1604-4(5))* Outskirts Pr., Inc.

Lees, Caroline. Silly Sea Stories. 2010. (Illus.). 48p. pap. 19.49 *(978-1-4389-0701-7(X))* AuthorHouse.

Lindgren, Astrid. Pippi in the South Seas. (Pippi Longstocking Ser.). 125p. (J). (gr. 3-5). pap. 3.99 *(978-0-8072-1392-6(6)*, Listening Library) Random Hse. Audio Publishing Group.

Liora, Iimma. Flick Goes under the Sea! 2012. 32p. (-18). pap. 16.95 *(978-1-4525-0663-0(9))* Balboa Pr.

LoDolce, Jodi. Johnny's Adventure at Sea. 2013. 18p. pap. 8.99 *(978-1-62839-102-2(2))* Salem Author Services.

London, Jack. The Mutiny of the 'ElsinoreApos. 2006. 264p. per. 15.95 *(978-1-59818-834-9(8))* Aegypan.

—Sea Wolf, Vol. 3. 2008. (Bring the Classics to Life Ser.). (ENG., Illus.). 72p. (gr. 3-12). pap., act. bk. ed. 10.95 *(978-1-55576-180-6(1)*, EDN307B) EDCON Publishing Group.

McCall Smith, Alexander. School Ship Tobermory. 2016. (School Ship Tobermory Ser.: 1). (ENG., Illus.). 224p. (J). (gr. 3-7). 15.99 *(978-0-399-55261-8(8)*, Delacorte Bks. for Young Readers) Random Hse. Children's Bks.

McDonnell, Vincent. The Catalpa Adventure: Escape to Freedom. 2010. (ENG.). 128p. (J). pap. 12.95 *(978-1-84889-038-1(9)*, Collins Pr., The) M.H. Gill & Co. U. C. IRL. Dist: Dufour Editions, Inc.

Meadows, Daisy. Ally the Dolphin Fairy. 2011. (Illus.). 63p. (J). *(978-0-545-28871-2(1))* Scholastic, Inc.

—Courtney the Clownfish Fairy. 2011. (Illus.). 62p. (J). *(978-0-545-28877-4(0))* Scholastic, Inc.

—Stephanie the Starfish Fairy. 2011. (Illus.). 65p. (J). *(978-0-545-28875-0(4))* Scholastic, Inc.

—Tess the Sea Turtle Fairy. 2011. (Illus.). 65p. (J). *(978-0-545-28874-3(6))* Scholastic, Inc.

—Whitney the Whale Fairy. 2011. (Illus.). 64p. (J). *(978-0-545-28876-7(2))* Scholastic, Inc.

Melville, Herman. Cities of the Fantastic: Brusel. Eisner, Will, illus. 2003. (Cities of the Fantastic Ser.). (ENG.). 120p. 19.95 *(978-1-56163-291-6(0))* NBM Publishing Co.

—Classic Starts(r): Moby-Dick. Freeberg, Eric, illus. 2010. (Classic Starts(r) Ser.). 160p. (J). (gr. 2-4). 7.99 *(978-1-4027-6644-2(0))* Sterling Publishing Co., Inc.

—Moby Dick. Eisner, Will, illus. 2003. (ENG.). 32p. (J). (gr. 4-7). 15.95 *(978-1-56163-293-0(7))* NBM Publishing Co.

—Moby Dick. 2008. (Bring the Classics to Life Ser.). (Illus.). 72p. (gr. 5-12). pap., act. bk. ed. 10.95 *(978-1-55576-326-8(X)*, EDCTR-508B) EDCON Publishing Group.

—Moby Dick. 2019. (ENG.). 320p. (J). (gr. 3-7). *(978-1-989631-64-5(9))* OMNI Publishing.

—Moby Dick. Elphinstone, Katy, illus. 2014. (Travel & Adventure Ser.). (ENG.). 64p. pap. 7.95 *(978-1-906230-72-2(2))* Real Reads Ltd. GBR. Dist: Casemate Pubs. & Bk. Distributors, LLC.

—Moby Dick. 2003. (Historias de Siempre Ser.). (SPA., Illus.). 92p. (J). (gr. 5-8). pap. 9.95 *(978-84-204-5732-1(9))* Santillana USA Publishing Co., Inc.

—Moby Dick: Or, the Whale. 2019. (ENG.). 316p. (YA). (gr. 7-12). pap. 12.18 *(978-1-6995-4001-5(2))* Independently Published.

—Moby Dick, Grades 5-12. adapted ed. pap., tchr. ed. 4.95 *(978-0-8359-0123-9(8))* Globe Fearon Educational Publishing.

Melville, Herman., creator. Moby Dick. 2020. (ENG.). 582p. (J). (gr. 3-7). pap. *(978-0-371-37815-1(X))* HardPr.

Melville, Herman., et al. Moby Dick. (Classics Illustrated Ser.). (Illus.). 52p. (YA). pap. 4.95 *(978-1-57209-003-3(0))* Classics International Entertainment, Inc.

Meyer, L. A. The Mark of the Golden Dragon: Being an Account of the Further Adventures of Jacky Faber, Jewel of the East, Vexation of the West. 2013. (Bloody Jack Adventures Ser.: 9). (ENG.). 400p. (YA). (gr. 9). pap. 9.99 *(978-0-544-00328-6(4)*, 1526370, Clarion Bks.) HarperCollins Pubs.

—The Mark of the Golden Dragon: Being an Account of the Further Adventures of Jacky Faber, Jewel of the East, Vexation of the West, & Pearl of the South China Sea. 2011. (Bloody Jack Adventures Ser.: 9). (ENG.). 384p. (YA). (gr. 9). 16.99 *(978-0-547-51764-3(5)*, 1444890, Clarion Bks.) HarperCollins Pubs.

—The Wake of the Lorelei Lee: Being an Account of the Further Adventures of Jacky Faber, on Her Way to Botany Bay. 2010. (Bloody Jack Adventures Ser.: Bk. 8). audio compact disk 29.95 *(978-1-59316-484-3(X))* Listen & Live Audio, Inc.

Milbourne, Anna. How Deep Is the Sea? Riglietti, Serena, illus. 2010. (Picture Bks). 24p. (J). 10.99 *(978-0-7945-2311-4(0))* EDC Publishing.

Milford, Kate. The Left-Handed Fate. Wheeler, Eliza, illus. 2017. (ENG.). 384p. (J). pap. 13.99 *(978-1-250-12183-7(3)*, 900157594) Square Fish.

Moniz, Michael. The Whalemaster. 2016. (ENG., Illus.). 235p. (J). (gr. 4-7). pap. 9.95 *(978-1-927018-79-8(X))* Simply Read Bks. CAN. Dist: Ingram Publisher Services.

Mowat, Farley. The Black Joke. 2009. (ENG.). 192p. pap. 9.95 *(978-0-7710-6469-2(1)*, Emblem Editions) McClelland & Stewart CAN. Dist: Random Hse., Inc.

Niedworok, Claudio O. Seafarers: Chronicles of the Suspense & Romance of the Sea. Knight, Tori, ed. Cooper, Paul, illus. Date not set. 80p. (Orig.). (YA). pap. 11.95 *(978-1-882133-05-5(6))* Barefoot Pr.

Ocean, Davy. Fishin' Impossible, 8. Blecha, Aaron, illus. 2017. (Shark School Ser.). (ENG.). 144p. (J). (gr. 1-3). 21.19 *(978-1-5364-1675-6(4)*, Aladdin) Simon & Schuster Children's Publishing.

—Fishin': Impossible. Blecha, Aaron, illus. 2017. (Shark School Ser.: 8). (ENG.). 144p. (J). (gr. 1-4). pap. 6.99 *(978-1-4814-6549-6(X)*, Aladdin) Simon & Schuster Children's Publishing.

Penrose, Margaret. The Motor Girls on the Coast or the Waif from the Se. 2011. 140p. pap. 9.99 *(978-1-61203-219-1(2))* Bottom of the Hill Publishing.

Pierse, Maurice, illus. South - Ernest Shackleton. 2016. (ENG.). 64p. pap. 7.95 *(978-1-911091-03-5(4))* Real Reads Ltd. GBR. Dist: Casemate Pubs. & Bk. Distributors, LLC.

Pryor, Bonnie. Captain Hannah Pritchard: The Hunt for Pirate Gold, 1 vol. 2012. (Historical Fiction Adventures Ser.). (ENG., Illus.). 160p. (J). (gr. 3-5). pap. 13.88 *(978-1-59845-283-9(5)*, 249245aa-07ef-41ea-a6ac-68d5be3db404); lib. bdg. 31.93 *(978-0-7660-3817-2(3)*, d1bf7ad2-c916-402c-ba83-61c0f084aac6) Enslow Publishing, LLC.

—Hannah Pritchard: Pirate of the Revolution, 1 vol. 2008. (Historical Fiction Adventures Ser.). (ENG., Illus.). 160p. (J). (gr. 3-5). lib. bdg. 31.93 *(978-0-7660-2851-7(8)*, 26121413-8628-47dc-9a2d-81661c6d5db1) Enslow Publishing, LLC.

Pyle, Howard, illus. The Book of Pirates. 2020. (ENG.). 336p. (J). (gr. 3). pap. 39.95 *(978-0-486-84096-3(4)*, 840964) Dover Pubns., Inc.

Ransome, Arthur. We Didn't Mean to Go to Sea: Stage Play. 2010. (ENG., Illus.). 100p. (gr. 2). pap. 17.99 *(978-1-906582-05-0(X))* Aurora Metro Pubns. Ltd. GBR. Dist: Publishers Group West (PGW).

Rees, Celia. Pirates! The True & Remarkable Adventures of Minerva Sharpe & Nancy Kington, Female Pirates. 2005. (Illus.). 379p. (YA). (gr. 9-12). 16.60 *(978-0-7569-6304-0(4))* Perfection Learning Corp.

RH Disney. Beware the Kakamora! (Disney Moana) RH Disney, illus. 2016. (Pictureback(R) Ser.). (ENG., Illus.). 24p. (J). (gr. -1-2). 4.99 *(978-0-7364-3601-4(4)*, RH/Disney) Random Hse. Children's Bks.

—Moana Big Golden Book (Disney Moana) RH Disney, illus. 2016. (Big Golden Book Ser.). (ENG., Illus.). 48p. (J). (gr. -1-2). 10.99 *(978-0-7364-3602-1(2)*, Golden/Disney) Random Hse. Children's Bks.

—Moana: the Junior Novelization (Disney Moana) RH Disney, illus. 2016. (ENG., Illus.). 144p. (J). (gr. 2-5). 6.99 *(978-0-7364-3600-7(6)*, RH/Disney) Random Hse. Children's Bks.

Rockwood, Roy. The Wizard of the Sea. 2007. 84p. per. *(978-1-4068-3969-2(8))* Echo Library.

Rosen, Michael J. Sailing the Unknown: Around the World with Captain Cook. Pritelli, Maria Cristina, illus. 2012. (ENG.). 40p. (J). (gr. 5-9). 19.99 *(978-1-56846-216-5(6)*, 22025, Creative Editions) Creative Co., The.

Ruby, Anne. Children of the Sea. Meier, Ty, illus. 2007. (YA). per. *(978-0-9787881-0-0(9))* Seachild.

Sante, Andrew R. The Silver Heart Chronicles: The Voyage. 2012. 50p. 24.99 *(978-1-4771-4700-9(4))*; pap. 15.99 *(978-1-4771-4699-6(7))* Xlibris Corp.

Scollon, Bill. Beware the Kakamora! 2016. (Illus.). (J). *(978-1-5182-2416-4(4))* Random Hse., Inc.

Shelton, Dave. A Boy & a Bear in a Boat. 2013. (ENG.). 304p. (J). (gr. 2-5). 7.99 *(978-0-449-81060-6(7)*, Yearling) Random Hse. Children's Bks.

Slater, Dashka. The Antlered Ship. Fan, Terry & Fan, Eric, illus. 2017. (ENG.). 48p. (J). (gr. -1-3). 17.99 *(978-1-4814-5160-4(X)*, Beach Lane Bks.) Beach Lane Bks.

Smith, Barbara. Ghost Stories of the Sea, 1 vol., Vol. 1. rev. ed. 2003. (Ghost Stories Ser.: 36). (ENG., Illus.). 224p. (gr. 4). pap. 12.95 *(978-1-894877-23-7(3)*, dbf8fc73-43e1-4a32-a672-4626fe2f1d8e, Ghost Hse. Bks.) Lone Pine Publishing USA.

Soundprints Staff. Ocean Adventures: Story-Time Treasury. 2005. (Smithsonian Institution Story-Time Treasures Ser.). (Illus.). 256p. (J). (gr. -1-2). 14.95 *(978-1-59069-226-4(8)*, HT1001) Studio Mouse LLC.

Squid-Napped! 2014. (Shark School Ser.: 3). (ENG., Illus.). 144p. (J). (gr. 1-4). pap. 6.99 *(978-1-4814-0684-0(1)*, Aladdin) Simon & Schuster Children's Publishing.

Stevenson, Robert Louis. Secuestrado. 3rd ed. (Coleccion Clasicos en Accion).Tr. of Kidnapped. (SPA., Illus.). 80p. (YA). (gr. 5-8). 15.95 *(978-84-241-5781-4(8)*, EV1487) Everest Editora ESP. Dist: Lectorum Pubns., Inc.

Taylor, Theodore. The Odyssey of Ben O'neal. 2004. (ENG., Illus.). 264p. (J). (gr. 3-7). pap. 15.95 *(978-0-15-205295-9(X)*, 1195954, Clarion Bks.) HarperCollins Pubs.

Terry, Alana. What Hurricane? My Solar-Powered History on a Supply Ship to the Jamestown Colony. Steffen, Jeremy, illus. 2013. 136p. pap. 12.99 *(978-1-937848-05-7(1))* Do Life Right, Inc.

Thomas, David, ed. Teenage Sea Stories. 2011. 252p. 46.95 *(978-1-258-10166-4(1))* Literary Licensing, LLC.

Troncale, Steven L. Yankee Boys of War. 2003. 171p. pap. 24.95 *(978-1-59286-879-7(7))* America Star Bks.

Tweed, Susan Larned. A Sailor's Adventure: Sailing Stormy Seas. 2012. 24p. pap. 11.50 *(978-1-61897-522-5(6)*, Strategic Bk. Publishing) Strategic Book Publishing & Rights Agency (SBPRA).

Valor, De. Pirate Adventures of Sea Worthy: Featuring: the Treasure of Captain Blue Beard & the Return of Captain Blue Beard. 2013. 150p. (gr. 2-2). 20.35 *(978-1-4669-7483-8(4))*; pap. 10.35 *(978-1-4269-9551-4(2))* Trafford Publishing.

Vern, Jules. Dick Sand. Munro, George, tr. 2008. 296p. 29.95 *(978-1-60664-752-3(0))* Rodgers, Alan Bks.

—Twenty Thousand Leagues under the Sea. abr. ed. 2019. (ENG.). (J). 232p. 19.95 *(978-1-61895-531-9(4))*; 230p. pap. 12.95 *(978-1-61895-530-2(6))* Bibliotech Pr.

—Twenty Thousand Leagues under the Sea. 2018. (ENG., Illus.). 170p. (J). (gr. 5). pap. 7.99 *(978-1-9779-9837-8(2))* CreateSpace Independent Publishing Platform.

—Twenty Thousand Leagues under the Sea. (ENG., Illus.). (J). 2017. (gr. 5). pap. 17.95 *(978-1-376-13408-7(X))* 2015. (gr. 3-7). 27.95 *(978-1-296-82308-5(3))* Creative Media Partners, LLC.

—Twenty Thousand Leagues under the Sea. 2019. (ENG.). 238p. (J). (gr. 5). pap. *(978-1-989201-88-6(1))* East India Publishing Co.

—Twenty Thousand Leagues under the Sea. l.t. ed. 2006. 592p. pap. *(978-1-84702-222-6(7))* Echo Library.

—Twenty Thousand Leagues under the Sea. 2019. (ENG.). 662p. (J). (gr. 3-7). pap. 25.99 *(978-1-7033-4221-5(6))* Independently Published.

—Twenty Thousand Leagues under the Sea. 2020. (ENG.). 230p. (J). (gr. 3-7). 19.95 *(978-1-64439-407-6(3))* IndoEuropeanPublishing.com.

—Twenty Thousand Leagues under the Sea. 2018. (ENG., Illus.). 254p. (J). (gr. 5). *(978-3-7326-2412-6(9))* Klassik Literatur. ein Imprint der Salzwasser Verlag GmbH.

—Twenty Thousand Leagues under the Sea. 2018. (ENG., Illus.). 388p. (J). (gr. 5). pap. 16.95 *(978-0-940075-35-1(0))* Quillquest Books.

—Twenty Thousand Leagues under the Sea. 2016. (ENG.). 376p. (J). (gr. 3-7). pap. *(978-93-5304-941-6(5))* Rupa & Co.

—20,000 Leagues under the Sea, 1 vol. Fisher, Eric Scott, illus. 2011. (Calico Illustrated Classics Ser.: No. 3). (ENG.). 112p. (J). (gr. 2-5). 38.50 *(978-1-61641-110-7(4)*, 4027, Calico Chapter Bks.) ABDO Publishing Co.

Verne, Julio & Vern, Jules. Veinte Mil Leguas de Viaje Submarino. 2019. (Brújula y la Veleta Ser.).Tr. of Twenty Thousand Leagues under the Sea. (SPA.). 64p. (J). (gr. 2-4). pap. 9.95 *(978-987-718-566-9(0))* Ediciones Lea S.A. ARG. Dist: Independent Pubs. Group.

West, Tracey & Bader, Bonnie. Stowaway! Adventures at Sea. 2008. (Club Penguin Ser.: 1). (ENG.). 80p. (J). (gr. k-3). 16.19 *(978-0-448-45055-1(0))* Penguin Young Readers Group.

Weston Woods Staff, creator. Burt Dow: Deep Water Man. 2004. (J). 18.95 *(978-1-55592-374-7(7))*; 38.75 *(978-1-55592-376-1(3))* Weston Woods Studios, Inc.

Wheeler, Lisa. Seadogs: An Epic Ocean Operetta. Siegel, Mark, illus. 2006. (ENG.). 40p. (J). (gr. 2-5). reprint ed. 8.99 *(978-1-4169-4103-3(7)*, Atheneum Bks. for Young Readers) Simon & Schuster Children's Publishing.

Whistler, Charles W. A Sea Queen's Sailing. 2017. (ENG., Illus.). (J). 24.95 *(978-1-374-93134-3(9))*; pap. 14.95 *(978-1-374-93133-6(0))* Capital Communications, Inc.

—A Sea-Queen's Sailing. Groome, W. H. C., illus. 2011. 346p. 24.95 *(978-1-934671-42-9(8))* Salem Ridge Press LLC.

Whybrow, Ian. A Tale of Two Sinbads 3 Explorers. Shamshirsaz, Shabab, illus. 2017. (Cambridge Reading Adventures Ser.). (ENG.). 32p. pap. 8.60 *(978-1-108-43097-5(X))* Cambridge Univ. Pr.

Williams, Geoffrey T. The Great White Red Alert. Artful Doodlers, illus. Campbell, Tom, photos by. 2008. (Save Our Seas Adventure Bks.). (ENG.). 64p. (J). (gr. 4-7). 8.95 *(978-0-9800444-0-9(5))* Save Our Seas, Ltd.

Zuhdi, Daria. A South Sea Adventure, Vol. 4. 2005. (Cat Detectives Present Ser.: 4). (Illus.). 104p. (J). per. 6.99 *(978-0-9706062-6-6(5))* catBOX Entertainment, Inc.

2nd and 7 Foundation. The Hog Mollies & the Amazing Aquatic Adventure (Soft Cover) rev. ed. 2011. (ENG.). 32p. pap. 6.95 *(978-0-7575-9147-1(7))* Kendall Hunt Publishing Co.

2nd and 7 Foundation Staff. The Hog Mollies & the Amazing Aquatic Adventure. rev. ed. 2011. 32p. pap. 12.95 *(978-0-7575-9148-8(5))* Kendall Hunt Publishing Co.

SEA WAVES

see Ocean Waves

SEAFARING LIFE

Baum, L. Frank. Navy Alphabet Book. 2004. (Applewood Bks.). (ENG., Illus.). 60p. (gr. -1-3). per. 14.95 *(978-1-55709-570-1(1))* Applewood Bks.

Branse, J. L. A Day in the Life of a Colonial Sea Captain. 2009. (Library of Living & Working in Colonial Times Ser.). 24p. (gr. 3-3). 42.50 *(978-1-60853-737-2(4)*, PowerKids Pr.) Rosen Publishing Group, Inc., The.

Brewster, Joy. El mundo bajo las Olas. Hanner, Albert, illus. 2011. (SPA.). 32p. (J). pap. 49.00 net. *(978-1-4108-2339-7(3)*, A23393) Benchmark Education Co.

Brook, Henry. Sea Adventures. 2008. (True Adventure Stories Ser.). 153p. (J). pap. 4.99 *(978-0-7945-2195-0(9)*, Usborne) EDC Publishing.

Bruce, Julia. Sail! Can You Command a Sea Voyage?, 1 vol. 2009. (Step into History Ser.). (ENG., Illus.). 32p. (gr. 3-3). lib. bdg. 26.60 *(978-0-7660-3477-8(1)*, 2179b596-e7be-4db3-ad0d-ec836e43f26d) Enslow Publishing, LLC.

Dover & Printworks KMG Staff. Sea Life Field Guide. 2013. (Dover Science for Kids Ser.). (ENG.). 48p. (J). (gr. 3-8). pap. 5.99 *(978-0-486-49157-8(9)*, 491579) Dover Pubns., Inc.

Duder, Tessa, ed. Down to the Sea Again: True Sea Stories for Young Newzealanders. 2005. 256p. (J). *(978-1-86950-476-2(3))* HarperCollins Pubs. New Zealand NZL. Dist: HarperCollins Pubs. Australia.

Hirschi, Ron. Swimming with Humuhumu: A Young Snorkeler's First Guide to Hawaiian Sea Life. Yee, Tammy, illus. 32p. (J). 14.99 *(978-0-931548-67-3(5)*, 25098-000) Island Heritage Publishing.

Meredith, Susan Markowitz. Hiding in the Sea: Set Of 6. 2011. (Early Connections Ser.). (J). pap. 37.00 net. *(978-1-4108-1080-9(1))* Benchmark Education Co.

Meyer, L. A. The Wake of the Lorelei Lee: Being an Account of the Further Adventures of Jacky Faber, on Her Way to Botany Bay. 2012. (Bloody Jack Adventures Ser.: 8). (ENG.). 576p. (YA). (gr. 9). pap. 12.99 *(978-0-547-72194-1(3)*, 1482451, Clarion Bks.) HarperCollins Pubs.

O'Donnell, Liam. Hop on the Pirate History Boat. 2017. (Pirates! Ser.). (ENG., Illus.). 32p. (J). (gr. 3-5). lib. bdg. 32.65 *(978-1-4109-8703-7(5)*, 135774, Raintree) Capstone.

Petrillo, Valerie. Sailors, Whalers, Fantastic Sea Voyages: An Activity Guide to North American Sailing Life. 2003. (ENG., Illus.). 224p. (J). (gr. 4-7). pap. 14.95 *(978-1-55652-475-2(7))* Chicago Review Pr., Inc.

Platt, Richard. Stephen Biesty's Cross-Sections Man-Of-War. Biesty, Stephen, illus. 2019. (DK Stephen Biesty Cross-Sections Ser.). (ENG.). 32p. (J). (gr. 4-7). 19.99 *(978-1-4654-8471-0(X)*, DK Children) Dorling Kindersley Publishing, Inc.

Rice, Dona Herweck. Navigating at Sea (Grade 3) rev. ed. 2018. (Smithsonian: Informational Text Ser.). (ENG., Illus.). 32p. (J). (gr. 3-4). pap. 11.99 *(978-1-4938-6680-9(X))* Teacher Created Materials, Inc.

—Sea Life, 1 vol. 2nd rev. ed. 2011. (TIME for KIDS(r): Informational Text Ser.). (ENG.). 20p. (gr. 1-2). 8.99 *(978-1-4333-3590-7(5))* Teacher Created Materials, Inc.

Soffer, Ruth, et al. Big Book of Sea Life to Color. 2008. (Dover Sea Life Coloring Bks.). (ENG., Illus.). 144p. (J). (gr. 3-5). 9.95 *(978-0-486-46681-1(7)*, 466817) Dover Pubns., Inc.

Sohl, Marcia & Dackerman, Gerald. Two Years Before the Mast: Student Activity Book. Cruz, Ernesto R, illus. (Now Age Illustrated Ser.). (J). (gr. 4-12). stu. ed. 1.25 *(978-0-88301-294-9(4))* Pendulum Pr., Inc.

Steele, Philip. The Amazing History of Pirates: See What a Buccaneer's Life Was Really Like, with over 350 Exciting Pictures. 2016. (Illus.). 64p. (J). (gr. 3-7). 12.99 *(978-1-86147-711-8(2)*, Armadillo) Anness Publishing GBR. Dist: National Bk. Network.

West, David. Ten of the Best Adventures on the Seas. 2015. (Ten of the Best: Stories of Exploration & Adventure Ser.). (ENG., Illus.). 24p. (J). (gr. 3-4). *(978-0-7787-1839-0(5))* Crabtree Publishing Co.

SEALS (ANIMALS)

Adamson, Heather. Sea Lions. 2017. (Ocean Life up Close Ser.). (ENG., Illus.). 24p. (J). (gr. k-3). lib. bdg. 26.95 *(978-1-62617-645-4(0)*, Blastoff! Readers) Bellwether Media.

Alderman, Christine Thomas. Baby Harp Seals. 2018. (Adorable Animals Ser.). (ENG.). 32p. (J). (gr. 4-6). pap. 9.99 *(978-1-64466-241-0(8)*, 12219); (Illus.). lib. bdg. *(978-1-68072-394-6(4)*, 12218) Black Rabbit Bks. (Bolt).

Alkire, Jessie. Harp Seals. 2018. (Arctic Animals at Risk Ser.). (ENG., Illus.). 32p. (J). (gr. 3-6). lib. bdg. 32.79 *(978-1-5321-1696-4(9)*, 30680, Checkerboard Library) ABDO Publishing Co.

Arnold, Quinn M. Seals. 2017. (Seedlings Ser.). (ENG., Illus.). 24p. (J). (gr. -1-k). pap. 9.99 *(978-1-62832-401-3(5)*, 20153, Creative Paperbacks); *(978-1-60818-781-2(0)*, 20155, Creative Education) Creative Co., The.

Beltran, Roxanne & Robinson, Patrick. A Seal Named Patches. 2017. (ENG., Illus.). 40p. (J). (gr. k-2). 17.95 *(978-1-60223-331-7(4))* Univ. of Alaska Pr.

Blake, Jason. Focas Fabulosas. 2008. (SPA., Illus.). 24p. (J). pap. *(978-0-545-02283-5(5))* Scholastic, Inc.

Bozzo, Linda. How Seals Grow Up, 1 vol. 2019. (Animals Growing Up Ser.). (ENG.). 24p. (gr. 1-2). 24.27 *(978-1-9785-0722-7(4)*, 0056bcb0-24b4-43b6-a43e-d84ac1e75d8f) Enslow Publishing, LLC.

Brannon, Cecelia H. Baby Seals at the Zoo. 2016. (All about Baby Zoo Animals Ser.). 24p. (J). (gr. k-1). pap. 56.10 *(978-0-7660-7520-7(6)*, Enslow Publishing) Enslow Publishing, LLC.

Butterworth, Christine. See What a Seal Can Do. Nelms, Kate, illus. 2015. (Read & Wonder Ser.). (ENG.). 32p. (J). (gr. -1-3). 8.99 *(978-0-7636-7649-0(7))* Candlewick Pr.

Clay, Kathryn. Seals: A 4D Book. 2018. (Mammals in the Wild Ser.). (ENG., Illus.). 24p. (J). (gr. -1-2). lib. bdg. 24.65 *(978-1-9771-0078-8(3)*, 138284, Pebble) Capstone.

Cleave, Andrew. Seals & Sea Lions. 2019. (Creatures of the Ocean Ser.). (Illus.). 80p. (J). (gr. 12). lib. bdg. 34.60 *(978-1-4222-4309-1(5))* Mason Crest.

Coleman, Miriam. Swimming with Sea Lions, 1 vol. 2009. (Flippers & Fins Ser.). (ENG., Illus.). 24p. (J). (gr. 2-3). pap. 9.25 *(978-1-4358-3247-3(7)*, 3993b3f3-f93b-45bf-9812-71d2e431d4a2, PowerKids Pr.); lib. bdg. 26.27 *(978-1-4042-8095-3(2)*, ffa72a2a-b6c9-45d9-9432-1784c8c2220d) Rosen Publishing Group, Inc., The.

Crossingham, John & Kalman, Bobbie. Seals & Sea Lions. 2005. (Living Ocean Ser.). (ENG., Illus.). 32p. (J). (gr. -1-3). lib. bdg. *(978-0-7787-1301-2(6))*; (gr. 3-4). pap. *(978-0-7787-1323-4(7))* Crabtree Publishing Co.

Dessen, Maci. Elephant Seals, 1 vol., 1. 2015. (Ocean Friends Ser.). (ENG., Illus.). 24p. (J). (gr. 1-1). pap. 9.25 *(978-1-5081-4168-6(1)*, 7af5a787-fcc6-404f-8849-1ec24181d0cf, PowerKids Pr.) Rosen Publishing Group, Inc., The.

Drumlin, Sam. Harp Seals, 1 vol. 2013. (PowerKids Readers: Sea Friends Ser.). (ENG., Illus.). 24p. (J). (gr. k-k). pap. 9.25 *(978-1-4488-9750-6(5)*, bd8c6b80-88f0-4d5e-b74e-4ffe7bbf496c); lib. bdg. 26.27 *(978-1-4488-9646-2(0)*, e8df3a52-7428-48e7-b967-74d1f60e224b) Rosen Publishing Group, Inc., The. (PowerKids Pr.).

—Harp Seals: Las Focas de Groenlandia, 1 vol. Alamán, Eduardo, tr. 2013. (PowerKids Readers: Los Amigos Del Mar / Sea Friends Ser.). (SPA & ENG., Illus.). 24p. (J). (gr. k-k). lib. bdg. 26.27 *(978-1-4488-9973-9(7)*, 0cadf811-e5fe-4576-9ec9-1bca5e6b3b19, PowerKids Pr.) Rosen Publishing Group, Inc., The.

Emily Rose Townsend. Seals [Scholastic]. 2009. (Polar Animals Ser.). 24p. (gr. k-1). pap. 0.34 *(978-1-4296-4226-2(2)*, Pebble) Capstone.

Fetty, Margaret. Sea Lions. 2006. (Smart Animals! Ser.). (Illus.). 32p. (J). (gr. 2-5). lib. bdg. 25.27 *(978-1-59716-274-6(4))* Bearport Publishing Co., Inc.

Franks, Katie. Sea Lions, 1 vol. 2014. (Zoo's Who's Who Ser.). (ENG., Illus.). 24p. (J). (gr. 1-2). pap. 9.25 *(978-1-4777-6585-2(9)*, 11037f1f-ded6-40a8-be18-4ff734d26aa1, PowerKids Pr.) Rosen Publishing Group, Inc., The.

Gallagher, Debbie. Seals & Sea Lions, 1 vol. 2010. (Zoo Animals Ser.). (ENG.). 32p. (gr. 2-2). lib. bdg. 21.27 *(978-0-7614-4748-1(2)*, 9f05e3ae-e51a-4bdb-b382-e17cad3799e8) Cavendish Square Publishing LLC.

Gish, Ashley. Elephant Seals. 2019. (X-Books: Marine Mammals Ser.). (ENG.). 32p. (J). (gr. 3-5). pap. 9.99 *(978-1-62832-752-6(9)*, 19209, Creative Paperbacks); *(978-1-64026-189-1(3)*, 19212, Creative Education) Creative Co., The.

Gish, Melissa. Living Wild: Sea Lions. 2013. (Living Wild Ser.). (ENG., Illus.). 48p. (J). (gr. 4-7). pap. 12.00 *(978-0-89812-776-8(9)*, 21903, Creative Paperbacks) Creative Co., The.

—Sea Lions. 2012. (Living Wild Ser.). (ENG.). 48p. (J). (gr. 4-7). 23.95 *(978-1-60818-169-8(3)*, 21895, Creative Education) Creative Co., The.

Goldish, Meish. Sea Lions in the Navy. 2012. (America's Animal Soldiers Ser.). 24p. (J). (gr. 1-6). lib. bdg. 26.99 *(978-1-61772-450-3(5))* Bearport Publishing Co., Inc.

—Southern Elephant Seal: The Biggest Seal in the World. 2010. (More SuperSized! Ser.). (Illus.). 24p. (J). (gr. k-3). lib. bdg. 26.99 *(978-1-936087-26-6(X))* Bearport Publishing Co., Inc.

Goyette, AnneReneé. Journey of the Elephant Seals, 1 vol. 2018. (Massive Animal Migrations Ser.). (ENG.). 24p. (gr. 2-3). 24.27 *(978-1-5382-1645-3(0)*, c6d64198-8ade-4c0f-978d-22b89577881e) Stevens, Gareth Publishing LLLP.

Gray, Susan H. Elephant Seal. 2007. (21st Century Skills Library: Road to Recovery Ser.). (ENG., Illus.). 32p. (gr. 4-8). lib. bdg. 32.07 *(978-1-60279-038-4(8)*, 200078) Cherry Lake Publishing.

Green, Jen. California Sea Lion. 2013. (Science Slam: the Deep End-Animal Life Underwater Ser.). 24p. (J). (gr. -1-3). lib. bdg. 26.99 *(978-1-61772-919-5(1))* Bearport Publishing Co., Inc.

—Sea Lions. 2008. (Illus.). 52p. (J). *(978-0-7172-6285-4(5))* Grolier, Ltd.

Haller, Christine A. Chippy: The sea lion that lost its Way. Lund, Nancy M., illus. 2006. 20p. (J). 11.95 *(978-0-9771129-0-6(X))* Oxbow Bks.

Haney, Johannah. Seals, 1 vol. 2010. (Endangered! Ser.). (ENG.). 48p. (gr. 3-3). lib. bdg. 32.64 *(978-0-7614-4053-6(4)*, a09d879a-9a85-4e8a-952f-82f7bfd746b1) Cavendish Square Publishing LLC.

Harvey, Jeanne Walker. Honey Girl: the Hawaiian Monk Seal. Bersani, Shennen, illus. 2017. (ENG.). 32p. (J). (gr. k-3). 17.95 *(978-1-62855-921-7(7))*; pap. 9.95 *(978-1-62855-922-4(5))* Arbordale Publishing.

Hendrix, Emilia. Seals & Pups, 1 vol. 2015. (Animal Family Ser.). (ENG., Illus.). 24p. (J). (gr. k-k). pap. 9.15 *(978-1-4824-3787-4(2)*, a009510f-6e7d-452d-a817-b813f5a047a4) Stevens, Gareth Publishing LLLP.

Hirschi, Ron. Seals, 1 vol. 2003. (Animals, Animals Ser.). (ENG., Illus.). 48p. (gr. 5-5). 32.64 *(978-0-7614-1445-2(2)*, 43f1e2e7-7a5c-42d5-bb92-5a324d4e74b8) Cavendish Square Publishing LLC.

Hodgkins, Fran. Do Seals Ever ... ? Leggitt, Marjorie, illus. 2017. 32p. (J). (gr. -1-3). 16.95 *(978-1-60893-467-6(5))* Down East Bks.

Jackson, Tom. Seals. 2008. (Nature's Children Ser.). (Illus.). 52p. (J). *(978-0-7172-6243-4(X))* Grolier, Ltd.

Jaycox, Jaclyn. Seals Are Awesome. 2019. (Polar Animals Ser.). (ENG., Illus.). 32p. (J). (gr. -1-2). pap. 7.95 *(978-1-9771-1000-8(2)*, 140943, Pebble) Capstone.

Kalman, Bobbie. Endangered Monk Seals. 2004. (Earth's Endangered Animals Ser.). (ENG., Illus.). 32p. (J). pap. *(978-0-7787-1897-0(2))* Crabtree Publishing Co.

Kalman, Bobbie & Crossingham, John. Les Phoques et les Otaries. Briere, Marie-Josee, tr. from ENG. 2007. (Petit Monde Vivant Ser.). (FRE., Illus.). 32p. (J). pap. 9.95 *(978-2-89579-165-2(1))* Bayard Canada Livres CAN. Dist: Crabtree Publishing Co.

Kawa, Katie. Baby Seals, 1 vol. 2011. (Cute & Cuddly: Baby Animals Ser.). (Illus.). 24p. (gr. k-k). (ENG.). (J). pap. 9.15 *(978-1-4339-5536-5(9)*, 146c21df-40f8-40f8-ae4f-34630e611214); (ENG., (J). lib. bdg. 25.27 *(978-1-4339-5534-1(2)*, 2e712dbe-93e4-4bd0-b38c-ef3420dcb53f); 69.20 *(978-1-4339-6894-5(0))* Stevens, Gareth Publishing LLLP.

Keller, Susanna. Meet the Sea Lion, 1 vol. 2010. (At the Zoo Ser.). (ENG.). 24p. (J). (gr. 1-1). pap. 9.25 *(978-1-4358-9728-1(5)*, ba142775-e87c-4f40-8eff-d4e46c81d911); (Illus.). lib. bdg. 26.27 *(978-1-4358-9308-5(5)*, f8553a4b-f814-4fe8-b008-cba6eff658dd) Rosen Publishing Group, Inc., The. (PowerKids Pr.).

King, Aven. Harp Seals, 1 vol., 1. 2015. (Ocean Friends Ser.). (ENG., Illus.). 24p. (J). (gr. 1-1). pap. 9.25 *(978-1-5081-4172-3(X)*, e6b38a1e-0770-4c85-9e21-fa9d8af6f51d, PowerKids Pr.) Rosen Publishing Group, Inc., The.

King, Zelda. Seals. (Illus.). 24p. (J). 2012. 49.50 *(978-1-4488-5144-7(0)*, PowerKids Pr.) 2011. (ENG., (gr. 2-3). pap. 9.25 *(978-1-4488-5143-0(2)*, bcc3db2c-3774-4222-82fe-3070b1553562, PowerKids Pr.) 2011. (ENG., (gr. 2-3). lib. bdg. 26.27 *(978-1-4488-5006-8(1)*, 28b360c9-b346-4d80-b754-76f446435858) Rosen Publishing Group, Inc., The.

Lamm, Drew. Sea Lion Swims. Cohen, Jessie, photos by. 2005. (Let's Go to the Zoo! Ser.). (ENG., Illus.). 16p. (J). (gr. -1-k). 5.95 *(978-1-56899-976-0(3)*, B9010) Soundprints.

Landau, Elaine. Harp Seals: Animals of the Snow & Ice, 1 vol. 2010. (Animals of the Snow & Ice Ser.). (ENG., Illus.). 32p. (J). (gr. 3-3). 26.60 *(978-0-7660-3460-0(7)*, 899a1da2-7964-4169-9384-b027946cac16) Enslow Publishing, LLC.

Lang, Aubrey. Baby Seal, 1 vol. Lynch, Wayne, photos by. 2004. (Nature Babies Ser.). (ENG., Illus.). 36p. (J). (gr. k-3). pap. 7.95 *(978-1-55041-726-5(6)*, a224862a-f658-4ffc-b144-b77d1286af7a) Trifolium Bks., Inc. CAN. Dist: Firefly Bks., Ltd.

Laughlin, Kara L. Seals. 2017. (In the Deep Blue Sea Ser.). (ENG.). 24p. (J). (gr. k-3). lib. bdg. 32.79 *(978-1-5038-1691-6(5)*, 211525) Child's World, Inc, The.

Lawrence, Ellen. Harbor Seals. 2018. (Day at the Beach: Animal Life on the Shore Ser.). (ENG.). 24p. (J). (gr. -1-3). lib. bdg. 26.99 *(978-1-68402-448-3(X))*; E-Book 41.36 *(978-1-68402-506-0(0))* Bearport Publishing Co., Inc.

Leaf, Christina. Baby Seals. 2014. (Super Cute! Ser.). (ENG., Illus.). 24p. (J). (gr. -1-3). lib. bdg. 26.95 *(978-1-60014-977-1(4)*, Blastoff! Readers) Bellwether Media.

Leon, Vicki. A Colony of Seals: The Captivating Life of a Deep Sea Diver. 2nd ed. 2005. (Jean-Michel Cousteau Presents Ser.). (ENG., Illus.). 48p. (J). (gr. 4). per. 9.95 *(978-0-9766134-0-4(9))* London Town Pr.

Lunis, Natalie. California Sea Lion: Fast & Smart! 2010. (Blink of an Eye: Superfast Animals Ser.). 24p. (J). (gr. k-3). lib. bdg. 26.99 *(978-1-936088-08-9(8))* Bearport Publishing Co., Inc.

Macheske, Felicia. Sunny Swimmers: Monk Seal. 2017. (Guess What Ser.). (ENG., Illus.). 24p. (J). (gr. k-2). lib. bdg. 30.64 *(978-1-63472-175-2(6)*, 209272) Cherry Lake Publishing.

Markle, Sandra. Leopard Seals. 2009. (Animal Predators Ser.). (ENG.). 40p. (gr. 3-6). 26.60 *(978-1-58013-540-5(4))* Lerner Publishing Group.

Markovics, Joyce L. Weddell Seal: Fat & Happy. 2008. (Uncommon Animals Ser.). (Illus.). 32p. (YA). (gr. 2-5). lib. bdg. 28.50 *(978-1-59716-734-5(7)*, 1284362) Bearport Publishing Co., Inc.

Martin-James, Kathleen. Harp Seals. 2008. (Early Bird Nature Bks.). (ENG.). 48p. (gr. 2-5). 26.60 *(978-0-8225-7889-5(1))* Lerner Publishing Group.

Meister, Cari. Seals. 2012. (ENG., Illus.). 24p. (J). lib. bdg. 25.65 *(978-1-62031-011-3(2))* Jump! Inc.

Metz, Lorijo. Discovering Sea Lions, 1 vol. 2011. (Along the Shore Ser.). (ENG., Illus.). 24p. (J). (gr. 2-3). lib. bdg. 26.27 *(978-1-4488-4992-5(6)*, 2cc91396-d670-4a79-b32f-69f2a41b736f) Rosen Publishing Group, Inc., The.

Miller, Sara Swan. Seals of the Antarctic. 2009. (Brrr! Polar Animals Ser.). 24p. (gr. 2-3). 42.50 *(978-1-61511-754-3(7)*, PowerKids Pr.); (ENG.). (J). lib. bdg. 26.27 *(978-1-4358-2745-5(7)*, a5293e07-7167-4826-96a4-03c451f05ead); (ENG., Illus.). (J). pap. 9.25 *(978-1-4358-3149-0(7)*, b54d4ca2-65bf-457b-bcdc-4b7534f9f012, PowerKids Pr.) Rosen Publishing Group, Inc., The.

Orr, Tamra. Seal or Sea Lion. 2019. (21st Century Junior Library: Which Is Which? Ser.). (ENG., Illus.). 24p. (J). (gr. 2-5). pap. 12.79 *(978-1-5341-5021-8(8)*, 213391); lib. bdg. 30.64 *(978-1-5341-4735-5(7)*, 213390) Cherry Lake Publishing.

Owen, Ruth. Seal Pups. 2012. (Water Babies Ser.). 24p. (J). (gr. -1-3). lib. bdg. 25.65 *(978-1-61772-605-7(2))* Bearport Publishing Co., Inc.

Owings, Lisa. Elephant Seal. 2014. (Extremely Weird Animals Ser.). (ENG., Illus.). 24p. (J). (gr. 3-8). lib. bdg. 27.95 *(978-1-62617-074-2(6)*, Pilot Bks.) Bellwether Media.

Peterson, Megan C. California Sea Lions, 1 vol. 2012. (Marine Mammals Ser.). (ENG., Illus.). 24p. (J). (gr. -1-2). lib. bdg. 27.32 *(978-1-4296-8573-3(5)*, 118545, Capstone Pr.) Capstone.

Pettiford, Rebecca. Harp Seals. 2019. (Animals of the Arctic Ser.). (ENG., Illus.). 24p. (J). (gr. k-3). lib. bdg. 26.95 *(978-1-62617-937-0(9)*, Blastoff! Readers) Bellwether Media.

—Seals. 2017. (Ocean Life up Close Ser.). (ENG., Illus.). 24p. (J). (gr. k-3). lib. bdg. 26.95 *(978-1-62617-574-7(8)*, Blastoff! Readers) Bellwether Media.

Phillips, Dee. Harp Seal. 2015. (Arctic Animals: Life Outside the Igloo Ser.). (ENG.). 24p. (J). (gr. -1-3). lib. bdg. 26.99 *(978-1-62724-531-9(6))* Bearport Publishing Co., Inc.

Proudfit, Benjamin. Seals, 1 vol. 2019. (Ocean Animals Ser.). (ENG.). 24p. (gr. k-k). pap. 9.15 *(978-1-5382-4469-2(1)*, 024d8c92-cf7d-421d-b61a-ead25f018269) Stevens, Gareth Publishing LLLP.

Read, Tracy C. Exploring the World of Seals & Walruses. 2011. (Exploring the World Of Ser.). (ENG., Illus.). 24p. (J). (gr. 3-7). 16.95 *(978-1-55407-784-7(2)*, 869a160e-bf4a-4da2-8356-79ceabdca1d0); pap. 6.95 *(978-1-55407-797-7(4)*, 7cd2e8c5-ab0a-45f4-b309-a26ab05b26a6) Firefly Bks., Ltd.

Riggs, Kate. Amazing Animals: Sea Lions. 2014. (Amazing Animals Ser.). (ENG.). 24p. (J). (gr. 1-3). pap. 9.99 *(978-0-89812-928-1(1)*, 21475, Creative Paperbacks) Creative Co., The.

—Sea Lions. (Seedlings Ser.). (J). 2015. (ENG.). 24p. (gr. -1-k). *(978-1-60818-516-0(8)*, 21249) 2014. 25.65 *(978-1-60818-349-4(1))* Creative Co., The. (Creative Education).

—Seedlings: Sea Lions. 2015. (Seedlings Ser.). (ENG.). 24p. (J). (gr. -1-1). pap. 10.99 *(978-1-62832-116-6(4)*, 21250, Creative Paperbacks) Creative Co., The.

Rockwood, Leigh. Tell Me the Difference Between a Seal & a Sea Lion, 1 vol. 2013. (How Are They Different? Ser.). (ENG., Illus.). 24p. (J). (gr. 2-3). pap. 9.25 *(978-1-4488-9738-4(6)*, 92edcc09-9f23-49fc-a986-6b08f37ce829); lib. bdg. 26.27 *(978-1-4488-9640-0(1)*, bbc413bb-7d8b-49e7-a6f2-e5c0a861e363) Rosen Publishing Group, Inc., The. (PowerKids Pr.).

Ryndak, Rob. Seal or Sea Lion?, 1 vol. 2015. (Animal Look-Alikes Ser.). (ENG., Illus.). 24p. (J). (gr. 1-2). lib. bdg. 24.27 *(978-1-4824-2726-4(5),* 561a74c2-d59d-420f-807c-f0ea4f49173e) Stevens, Gareth Publishing LLLP.

Sellers, Charles. Subtracting with Seals, 1 vol. 2011. (Animal Math Ser.). (ENG.). 24p. (J). (gr. 1-2). pap. 9.15 *(978-1-4339-5672-0(1),* 868b3bee-4d0d-4562-8094-c9a2f904b63b); lib. bdg. 25.27 *(978-1-4339-5670-6(5),* 750f06a6-ee7d-4721-bcaa-55d5f87be6d8) Stevens, Gareth Publishing LLLP.

Sexton, Colleen. Sea Lions. 2008. (Oceans Alive Ser.). (ENG., Illus.). 24p. (J). (gr. k-3). lib. bdg. 26.95 *(978-1-60014-174-4(9))* Bellwether Media.

—Seal Pups. 2008. (Watch Animals Grow Ser.). (ENG., Illus.). 24p. (J). (gr. k-3). lib. bdg. 26.95 *(978-1-60014-171-3(4))* Bellwether Media.

—Seals. 2007. (Oceans Alive Ser.). (ENG., Illus.). 24p. (J). (gr. k-3). lib. bdg. 26.95 *(978-1-60014-056-3(4))* Bellwether Media.

Shofner, Melissa Raé. Sea Lions on the Shore, 1 vol. 2017. (Critters by the Sea Ser.). (ENG.). 24p. (J). (gr. 3-3). 25.27 *(978-1-5383-2519-3(5),* a03f1512-1cb2-40e3-8905-49e0a1e04ded, PowerKids Pr.) Rosen Publishing Group, Inc., The.

Silverman, Buffy. Can You Tell a Seal from a Sea Lion? 2012. (Animal Look-Alikes Ser.). 32p. (gr. k-2). pap. 45.32 *(978-0-7613-9257-6(2))* Lerner Publishing Group.

Soundprints Staff, ed. Oceanic Collection III: Beluga Whale, Harp Seal, Walrus & Lobster Books, 4 micro bks. (Smithsonian Oceanic Collection). (Illus.). 128p. (J). (gr. -1-2). 18.95 *(978-1-56899-633-2(0))* Soundprints.

Statts, Leo. Seals. 2016. (Polar Animals Ser.). (ENG.). 24p. (J). (gr. -1-2). 49.94 *(978-1-68079-358-1(6),* 22979, Abdo Zoom-Launch) ABDO Publishing Co.

Stearns, Precious. Steller Sea Lions. 2009. (Eye to Eye with Endangered Species Ser.). (Illus.). 24p. (J). (gr. 3-6). lib. bdg. 27.07 *(978-1-60694-402-8(9))* Rourke Educational Media.

The Story of Small Fry: Individual Title Six-Packs. (Action Packs Ser.). 104p. (gr. 3-5). 44.00 *(978-0-7635-8405-4(3))* Rigby Education.

Taylor, Trace. Seals. 2012. (Marine Life Ser.). (ENG.). 12p. (J). (gr. k-2). pap. 8.00 *(978-1-59301-760-6(X))* American Reading Co.

Taylor, Trace & Sanchez, Lucia M. Focas (Seals) 2011. (poder de 100 - Animales marinos Ser.). (SPA.). 12p. pap. 39.62 *(978-1-61541-277-8(8))* American Reading Co.

Townsend, Emily Rose. Seals, 1 vol. 2004. (Polar Animals Ser.). (ENG., Illus.). 24p. (gr. k-1). 21.32 *(978-0-7368-2359-3(X),* Pebble) Capstone.

Twine, Alice. Seals. (Baby Animals Ser.). 24p. (gr. 1-1). 2009. 42.50 *(978-1-61511-496-2(3),* PowerKids Pr.) 2007. (ENG., Illus.). (J). lib. bdg. 26.27 *(978-1-4042-3773-5(9),* 704224c2-05ea-4e50-ae39-b71dc04eb604) Rosen Publishing Group, Inc., The.

—Seals/Focas. 2009. (Baby Animals/Animales bebé Ser.). (ENG & SPA.). 24p. (gr. 1-1). 42.50 *(978-1-61511-508-2(0),* Editorial Buenas Letras) Rosen Publishing Group, Inc., The.

—Seals/Focas, 1 vol. Obregon, Jose Maria, tr. 2007. (Baby Animals / Animales Bebé Ser.). (ENG & SPA., Illus.). 24p. (J). (gr. 1-1). lib. bdg. 26.27 *(978-1-4042-7632-1(7),* 0c47d21f-f1ae-4679-a7c7-ef1b34dccc28) Rosen Publishing Group, Inc., The.

Walker Harvey, Jeanne. Astro: the Steller Sea Lion, 1 vol. Bersani, Shennen, illus. 2010. (ENG.). 32p. (J). (gr. 2-3). pap. 10.95 *(978-1-60718-874-2(0),* bfba7161-c404-4b8d-bbeb-72553eefc548) Arbordale Publishing.

Wexo, John Bonnett. Seals & Sea Lions. rev. ed. 2003. (Illus.). 24p. (J). (gr. 1-7). 10.95 *(978-1-932396-00-3(4),* Zoo Bks.) National Wildlife Federation.

Wildlife Education, compiled by. Seals. 2007. (Illus.). 12p. (J). 5.99 *(978-1-932396-41-6(1),* Critters Up Close) National Wildlife Federation.

Wilsdon, Christina. Seals, 1 vol. 2010. (Amazing Animals Ser.). (ENG.). 48p. (J). (gr. 3-5). pap. 11.50 *(978-1-4339-4026-2(4),* 00d70462-4b0d-4bd6-b5d1-bcf56d94cb40); lib. bdg. 30.67 *(978-1-4339-4025-5(6),* 3a3d1ef1-dd22-4202-9a4c-c26fe5c9ef4f) Stevens, Gareth Publishing LLLP. (Gareth Stevens Learning Library).

—Seals. 2007. (J). *(978-1-59939-127-4(9),* Reader's Digest Young Families, Inc.) Studio Fun International.

SEALS (ANIMALS)—FICTION

Aronson, Rosy. A Tale of Serendipity: the Adventure Begins! 2010. 370p. pap. 24.84 *(978-0-557-12641-5(X))* Lulu Pr., Inc.

Brezenoff, Steve. Field Trip Mysteries: the Seals That Wouldn't Swim. Calo, Marcos, illus. 2011. (Field Trip Mysteries Ser.). (ENG.). 88p. (J). (gr. 3-6). pap. 5.95 *(978-1-4342-3428-5(2),* 116449, Stone Arch Bks.) Capstone.

Brown, Dolores. A Wave of Stars. Wimmer, Sonja, illus. 2020. 44p. (J). 16.95 *(978-84-17673-41-3(5))* NubeOcho Ediciones ESP. Dist: Consortium Bk. Sales & Distribution.

Butterworth, Chris. See What a Seal Can Do. Nelms, Kate, illus. 2013. (ENG.). 32p. (J). (gr. k-4). 14.99 *(978-0-7636-6574-6(6))* Candlewick Pr.

Call of the Selkie: Individual Title Six-Packs. (Action Packs Ser.). 104p. (gr. 3-5). 44.00 *(978-0-7635-2991-8(5))* Rigby Education.

Chronicle Books & ImageBooks. Little Seal: Finger Puppet Book: (Finger Puppet Book for Toddlers & Babies, Baby Books for First Year, Animal Finger Puppets) 2012. (Little Finger Puppet Board Bks.: FING). (ENG., Illus.). 12p. (J). (gr. -1 — 1). 7.99 *(978-1-4521-0812-4(9))* Chronicle Bks. LLC.

Cobb, Amelia. The Silky Seal Pup (Zoe's Rescue Zoo #3) 2016. (Zoe's Rescue Zoo Ser.: 3). (ENG., Illus.). 128p. (J). (gr. 2-5). pap. 4.99 *(978-0-545-84224-2(7),* Scholastic Paperbacks) Scholastic, Inc.

Collins, Lynette. Codi & Tamaka: The Lost Seal. 2016. (ENG., Illus.). 70p. (J). pap. 36.28 *(978-1-5245-2034-2(9))* Xlibris Corp.

Cook, Sherry & Johnson, Terri. Susie Sound, 26. Kuhn, Jesse, illus. l.t. ed. 2006. 32p. (J). 7.99 *(978-1-933815-18-3(3),* Quirkles, The) Creative 3, LLC.

Crowley, Peter. J T Seavey. 2012. (ENG.). 35p. (J). pap. 18.95 *(978-1-4327-8712-7(8))* Outskirts Pr., Inc.

Don, Lari. Never Trust a Tiger: A Story from Korea. Williamson, Melanie, illus. 2012. (Animal Stories Ser.). 48p. (J). (gr. 1-4). pap. 8.99 *(978-1-84686-776-7(2))* Barefoot Bks., Inc.

Dynamo. Googly Eyes: Flipper the Seal Makes a Discovery! 2014. (ENG., Illus.). 12p. (J). (gr. -1-2). bds. 6.99 *(978-1-84322-905-6(6),* Armadillo) Anness Publishing GBR. Dist: National Bk. Network.

Ferry, Beth. Sealed with a Kiss. Tallec, Olivier, illus. 2019. (ENG.). 32p. (J). (gr. -1-3). 19.99 *(978-0-06-247577-0(0),* HarperCollins) HarperCollins Pubs.

Foreman, Michael. Seal Surfer. Foreman, Michael, illus. 2007. (ENG., Illus.). 32p. (J). (gr. k-4). pap. 12.99 *(978-1-84270-578-0(4))* Andersen Pr. GBR. Dist: Independent Pubs. Group.

French, Sarah. Summer Friends. 2011. (ENG., Illus.). 32p. (J). 17.95 *(978-0-9827146-5-2(3))* Vineyard Stories.

Fry, Rosalie K. Secret of the Ron Mor Skerry. Fry, Rosalie K., illus. 2017. (Illus.). 104p. (J). (gr. 3-7). 16.95 *(978-1-68137-166-5(9),* NYR Children's Collection) New York Review of Bks., Inc., The.

Harris, Sue. Little Seal Finds a Friend. Boey, Stephanie, illus. 2007. (ENG.). 24p. (J). *(978-1-55168-295-2(8))* Fenn, H. B. & Co., Ltd.

He Who Listens: Individual Title Six-Packs. (Literatura 2000 Ser.). (gr. 2-3). 33.00 *(978-0-7635-0171-6(9))* Rigby Education.

Hoff, Syd. Sammy the Seal. Hoff, Syd, illus. 2017. (I Can Read Level 1 Ser.). (ENG., Illus.). 72p. (J). (gr. -1-3). 9.99 *(978-0-06-257274-5(1),* HarperCollins) HarperCollins Pubs.

Holden, Pam. Seal on the Loose, 1 vol. Hatam, Samer, illus. 2015. (ENG.). 16p. (-1). pap. *(978-1-77654-134-8(0),* Red Rocket Readers) Flying Start Bks.

Hollenbeck, Kathleen M. Islands of Ice: The Story of a Harp Seal. Genzo, John Paul, illus. (Smithsonian Oceanic Collection Ser.). (ENG.). 32p. (J). (gr. -1-3). 2011. 19.95 *(978-1-60727-652-4(6))* 2005. 9.95 *(978-1-56899-970-8(4),* PB4071) 2005. 19.95 *(978-1-56899-967-8(4),* BC4021) 2005. 4.95 *(978-1-56899-966-1(6),* B4071) 2005. 15.95 *(978-1-56899-965-4(8),* B4021) Soundprints.

Holloway, Christina. Irish Selkie. 2008. 12p. pap. 24.95 *(978-1-60610-693-8(7))* America Star Bks.

Horn, Sandra. Silkie. (ENG., Illus.). 89p. pap. 7.95 *(978-0-340-67265-5(X))* Hodder & Stoughton GBR. Dist: Trafalgar Square Publishing.

—The Silkie. Perks, Anne-Marie, illus. 2017. (ENG.). 46p. (J). pap. *(978-1-909568-11-2(2))* Clucket Pr., The.

Howell, Gill. Selkie Child. Keen, Sophie, illus. 2005. (ENG.). 24p. (J). lib. bdg. 23.65 *(978-1-59646-750-7(9))* Dingles & Co.

Kaczka, Fallon. What about Oysters. 2010. 24p. 13.00 *(978-1-4520-2066-2(3))* AuthorHouse.

Kipling, Rudyard. The White Seal. Jones, Chuck, illus. 2006. (ENG.). 32p. (J). (gr. -1-3). 8.95 *(978-0-8249-6598-3(1),* Ideals Pubns.) Worthy Publishing.

LaFaye, A. Water Steps. 2009. (ENG., Illus.). 208p. (J). (gr. 2-7). 16.95 *(978-1-57131-687-5(6));* pap. 6.95 *(978-1-57131-686-8(8))* Milkweed Editions.

Lawton, Diana. Paulie the Penguin Meets Sammy the Seal. 2012. 30p. 24.95 *(978-1-4626-6782-6(1))* America Star Bks.

Leach, Cheryl. Sally to the Rescue. 2012. 36p. pap. 20.99 *(978-1-4772-9974-6(2))* AuthorHouse.

MacGregor, Jill. Swim Safe Little Seals. 2006. (Illus.). 31p. (J). 14.95 *(978-0-9774062-0-3(2))* Seal Publishing, LLC.

Mackay, Janis. Magnus Fin & the Moonlight Mission, 72 vols. 2011. (Magnus Fin Ser.). 192p. (J). 9.95 *(978-0-86315-796-7(3),* Kelpies) Floris Bks. GBR. Dist: Consortium Bk. Sales & Distribution.

Marsaw, Roy. Swim, Swam, Swum. Harris, Phyllis, illus. 2007. 32p. (J). pap. 14.95 *(978-0-9744446-8-0(5))* All About Kids Publishing.

McGrath, Barbara Barbieri. Five Flying Penguins. Coleman, Stephanie Fizer, illus. 2018. (ENG.). 32p. (J). (gr. -1-2). lib. bdg. 12.99 *(978-1-58089-805-8(X))* Charlesbridge Publishing, Inc.

McRaven, William H. Make Your Bed with Skipper the Seal. McWilliam, Howard, illus. 2021. (ENG.). 48p. (J). (gr. -1-3). 18.99 *(978-0-316-59235-2(8))* Little, Brown Bks. for Young Readers.

Meadows, Daisy. Amelie the Seal Fairy. 2011. (Illus.). 65p. (J). *(978-0-545-28872-9(X))* Scholastic, Inc.

Medina, Larry. The Adventures of Peek a Boo the Sea Lion. 2010. 40p. 21.00 *(978-1-4520-1499-9(X))* AuthorHouse.

Muldrow, Diane. How Do Penguins Play? Walker, David M., illus. 2011. (Little Golden Book Ser.). 24p. (J). (gr. -1-k). 5.99 *(978-0-375-86501-5(2),* Golden Bks.) Random Hse. Children's Bks.

Murphy, T. M. Saving Santa's Seals. Taylor, Adam, illus. 2009. (LeapKids Ser.). (ENG.). 170p. (J). (gr. 1-5). pap. 10.95 *(978-0-9815148-8-8(X))* Leapfrog Pr.

Papish, Ram. The Little Seal: An Alaska Adventure. 2009. (ENG., Illus.). 24p. (J). 17.95 *(978-1-60223-068-2(4))* Univ. of Alaska Pr.

Patterson, Ellie. Baby Bear & the Big, Wide World. Kolanovic, Dubravka, illus. 2013. (J). *(978-1-4351-4929-8(7))* Barnes & Noble, Inc.

Patterson, Sherri, et al. No-No & the Secret Touch: The Gentle Story of a Little Seal Who Learns to Stay Safe, Say "No" & Tell! Krupp, Marian N., illus. unabr. ed. 70p. (J). (gr. 1-6). pap. 14.95 incl. audio *(978-0-9632276-2-1(9))* National Self-Esteem Resources & Development Ctr.

Resnicoff, Stan. Stanley, the Seal of Approval. 2012. (ENG.). (J). pap. *(978-1-4675-1535-1(3))* Independent Pub.

Rylant, Cynthia. The Sea Lion. McDaniels, Preston, illus. (Lighthouse Family Ser.: 7). (ENG.). 48p. (J). (gr. 1-5). 2018. pap. 5.99 *(978-1-4814-6026-2(9))* 2017. 17.99 *(978-1-4814-6025-5(0))* Beach Lane Bks. (Beach Lane Bks.).

Seeger, Laura Vaccaro. What If? Seeger, Laura Vaccaro, illus. 2010. (ENG., Illus.). 32p. (J). (gr. -1-2). 18.99 *(978-1-59643-398-4(1),* 900051552) Roaring Brook Pr.

Shaw-MacKinnon, Margaret. Tiktala, 1 vol. Gal, Laszlo, illus. 2005. (ENG.). 32p. (J). (gr. 1-4). per. 9.95 *(978-1-55005-143-8(1),* e1d19284-7c03-4f56-a262-c414345d9bdb) Fitzhenry & Whiteside, Ltd. CAN. Dist: Firefly Bks., Ltd.

Sherrow, Victoria. Galapagos Fur Seal. 2012. (ENG., Illus.). 24p. (J). pap. 3.95 *(978-1-60727-725-5(5))* Soundprints.

—Galapagos Fur Seal: At Home in the Tropics. Wertheim, Anne, illus. 2011. (ENG.). 32p. (J). pap. 8.95 *(978-1-60727-613-5(5))* Soundprints.

Sobel, Deane. Philip the Sea Lion. 2012. (ENG.). (J). pap. *(978-1-4675-2347-9(X))* Independent Pub.

Spalding, Andrea. Seal Song, 1 vol. Milelli, Pascal, illus. 2011. (ENG.). 32p. (J). (gr. -1-k). 19.95 *(978-1-55469-242-2(3))* Orca Bk. Pubs. USA.

Sue-A-Quan, Goomatie. A Seal Fascination at Sea: A Fascinating Seal. 2008. (Illus.). 38p. (J). pap. 19.00 *(978-0-8059-7517-8(9))* Dorrance Publishing Co., Inc.

Sundaram, Renuka. Sammy, the Galapagos Sea Lion. 2011. 32p. pap. 15.00 *(978-1-61286-015-2(X))* Avid Readers Publishing Group.

Temple, Kate. Room on Our Rock. Baynton, Terri Rose, illus. 2019. (J). 12.99 *(978-1-61067-902-2(4))* Kane Miller.

Virgo, Seán. Shadow Mother, 1 vol. Serrano Pérez, Javier, illus. 2014. (ENG.). 64p. (J). (gr. 6). 21.95 *(978-0-88899-971-9(2))* Groundwood Bks. CAN. Dist: Publishers Group West (PGW).

Waters, Summer. Stormy Skies (Silver Dolphins, Book 8), Book 8. 2010. (Silver Dolphins Ser.: 8). (ENG.). 176p. (J). (gr. 2-4). pap. 7.99 *(978-0-00-734813-8(4),* HarperCollins Children's Bks.) HarperCollins Pubs. Ltd. GBR. Dist: HarperCollins Pubs.

Zoehfeld, Kathleen Weidner. Seal Pup Grows Up: The Story of a Harbor Seal. Bonforte, Lisa, illus. 2011. (Smithsonian Oceanic Collection Ser.). (ENG.). 32p. (J). (gr. -1-3). 19.95 *(978-1-60727-663-0(1))* Soundprints.

SEAMANSHIP

see also Navigation

Pelling. Getting Afloat. 2003. (Illus.). 80p. pap. *(978-0-7136-5278-9(0),* Adlard Coles) Bloomsbury Publishing Plc.

SEAMEN

see Sailors

SEARCH AND RESCUE OPERATIONS

see Rescue Work

SEASHORE

Amery, Heather. The Seaside. Cartwright, Stephen, illus. 2008. (Usborne Talkabout Bks.). 12p. (J). bds. 8.99 *(978-0-7945-1794-6(3),* Usborne) EDC Publishing.

—What's Happening at the Seaside? Cartwright, Stephen, illus. rev. ed. 2006. (What's Happening Ser.). 16p. (J). (gr. -1-3). 5.99 *(978-0-7945-1290-3(9),* Usborne) EDC Publishing.

Anderson, Sheila. Coasts. 2008. (First Step Nonfiction - Landforms Ser.). (Illus.). 23p. (J). (gr. -1). lib. bdg. 18.60 *(978-0-8225-8595-4(2),* Lerner Pubns.); pap. 34.95 *(978-0-8225-9935-7(X))* Lerner Publishing Group.

Andrews, Alexa. At the Beach. Keimig, Candice, illus. 2013. (Penguin Young Readers, Level 1 Ser.). 32p. (J). (gr. k-1). pap. 4.99 *(978-0-448-46471-8(3),* Penguin Young Readers) Penguin Young Readers Group.

Arnosky, Jim. Beachcombing: Exploring the Seashore. 2014. (ENG.). 32p. (J). (gr. 2-5). 8.99 *(978-0-14-751163-8(1),* Puffin Books) Penguin Young Readers Group.

Beckett-Bowman, Lucy. Seashore. Donaera, Patrizia & Haggerty, Tim, illus. 2008. (Beginners Nature Ser.). 32p. (J). (gr. -1-3). 4.99 *(978-0-7945-2061-8(8),* Usborne) EDC Publishing.

Benjamin, Tina. Let's Visit the Beach, 1 vol. 2015. (Let's Go Outdoors! Ser.). (ENG., Illus.). 24p. (J). (gr. k-k). lib. bdg. 24.27 *(978-1-4824-2631-1(5),* 5812dc37-e78d-40a8-bd40-db5c19bc93ea) Stevens, Gareth Publishing LLLP.

Berne, Emma Carlson. Bays, 1 vol. 2008. (Geography Zone: Landforms Ser.). (ENG., Illus.). 24p. (J). (gr. 2-3). lib. bdg. 26.27 *(978-1-4042-4206-7(6),* 9c9b6d06-a8b5-485f-9a3f-d74725afedd7) Rosen Publishing Group, Inc., The.

Beylon, Cathy. At the Beach. 2004. (Dover Kids Coloring Bks.). (ENG., Illus.). 32p. (J). (gr. -1-2). pap. 3.99 *(978-0-486-43643-2(8),* 436438) Dover Pubns., Inc.

Bluemel Oldfield, Dawn. Patterns at the Seashore. 2014. (Math Blast!: Seeing Patterns All Around Ser.). (ENG.). 32p. (J). (gr. -1-3). lib. bdg. 28.50 *(978-1-62724-335-3(6))* Bearport Publishing Co., Inc.

Bone, Emily. Seashore. 2018. (Young Beginners Ser.). (ENG.). 32p. (J). 4.99 *(978-0-7945-4031-9(7),* Usborne) EDC Publishing.

Brinker, Spencer. At the Beach. 2019. (I Spy Ser.). (ENG., Illus.). 16p. (J). (gr. -1-1). 6.99 *(978-1-64280-397-6(9))* Bearport Publishing Co., Inc.

Brown, Carron. Secretos de la Costa: Shine-A-light. Nassner, Alyssa, illus. 2019.Tr. of Secrets of the Seashore. (SPA.). (J). 12.99 *(978-1-61067-912-1(1))* Kane Miller.

—Secrets of the Seashore. 2014. (ENG., Illus.). 36p. (J). 12.99 *(978-1-61067-309-9(3))* Kane Miller.

Burgess, Thornton W. Burgess Sea Shore Book for Children. (J). 26.95 *(978-0-8488-0403-9(1))* Amereon Ltd.

Burton, Margie, et al. Clean Beaches. 2011. (Early Connections Ser.). (J). *(978-1-61672-518-1(4))* Benchmark Education Co.

—Clean Beaches & Playas Limpias: 6 English, 6 Spanish Adaptations. 2011. (J). spiral bd. 75.00 net. *(978-1-4108-5625-8(9))* Benchmark Education Co.

Carlson Berne, Emma. Bays. 2009. (Geography Zone: Landforms Ser.). 24p. (gr. 2-3). 42.50 *(978-1-61512-690-3(2),* PowerKids Pr.) Rosen Publishing Group, Inc., The.

Carlson-Berne, Emma. Beaches, 1 vol. 2008. (Geography Zone: Landforms Ser.). (ENG., Illus.). 24p. (J). (gr. 2-3). lib. bdg. 26.27 *(978-1-4042-4205-0(8),* e0fff50d-31f8-4f8b-86fa-5f228813ef2a) Rosen Publishing Group, Inc., The.

Carlson Berne, Emma. Beaches. 2009. (Geography Zone: Landforms Ser.). 24p. (gr. 2-3). 42.50 *(978-1-61512-691-0(0),* PowerKids Pr.) Rosen Publishing Group, Inc., The.

Carolan. B Is for Beach: An Alphabet Book. 2007. 64p. 18.95 incl. audio compact disk *(978-0-9715333-8-7(5))* Banana Patch Pr.

Crossingham, John & Kalman, Bobbie. Cadenas Alimentarias de la Costa Marina. 2006. (Cadenas Alimentarias Ser.). (SPA., Illus.). 32p. (J). (gr. 3-7). pap. *(978-0-7787-8547-7(5))* Crabtree Publishing Co.

Crow, Marilee. Down by the Shore. Roberts, Mary Sue, photos by. 2011. (Illus.). 30p. 19.95 *(978-1-61633-087-3(2))* Guardian Angel Publishing, Inc.

Davidson, Avelyn. Beach Biology. 2007. (Shockwave: Life Science & Medicine Ser.). (Illus.). 36p. (J). (gr. 4-6). pap. 6.95 *(978-0-531-15495-3(5),* Children's Pr.) Scholastic Library Publishing.

Day, Amelia. Olivia's Ocean Adventure, 1 vol. 2013. (Core Math Skills: Numbers & Operations in Base 10 Ser.). (ENG.). 24p. (J). (gr. 1-1). 26.27 *(978-1-4777-2222-0(X),* 9cd40fa0-788a-48a7-a127-f99db4a6fc4b, Rosen Classroom) Rosen Publishing Group, Inc., The.

—Olivia's Ocean Adventure: Understand Place Value, 1 vol. 2013. (Rosen Math Readers Ser.). (ENG.). 24p. (J). (gr. 1-1). pap. 8.25 *(978-1-4777-2037-0(5),* f8c1f145-b20c-4523-87fa-f66a833f86c0); pap. 49.50 *(978-1-4777-2038-7(3))* Rosen Publishing Group, Inc., The. (Rosen Classroom).

De la Bédoyère, Camilla & Philip, Claire. Seashore. Kelly, Richard, ed. 2017. (ENG., Illus.). 96p. (J). pap. 9.95 *(978-1-78209-168-4(8))* Miles Kelly Publishing, Ltd. GBR. Dist: Parkwest Pubns., Inc.

Dunn, Mary. My Adventure Building the Eiffel Tower. 2007. 44p. (J). 8.99 *(978-1-59092-413-6(4))* Blue Forge Pr.

Early Macken, JoAnn. Beaches, 1 vol. 2006. (Water Habitats Ser.). (ENG., Illus.). 24p. (gr. k-2). lib. bdg. 24.67 *(978-0-8368-4882-3(9),* 328820a1-484c-41da-8e67-e726827f7a03, Weekly Reader Leveled Readers) Stevens, Gareth Publishing LLLP.

—Beaches / Playas, 1 vol. 2005. (Water Habitats / Hábitats Acuáticos Ser.). (SPA & ENG., Illus.). 24p. (gr. k-2). pap. 9.15 *(978-0-8368-6034-4(9),* 20f8d626-b152-4db0-81f9-335a6d7cb500, Weekly Reader Leveled Readers) Stevens, Gareth Publishing LLLP.

Editors of Storey Publishing. Backpack Explorer: Beach Walk. Befort, Oana, illus. 2019. (Backpack Explorer Ser.). (ENG.). 48p. (J). (gr. -1-3). 12.95 *(978-1-61212-902-0(1),* 622902) Storey Publishing, LLC.

Evans, Shira. National Geographic Readers: at the Beach. 2017. (Readers Ser.). (Illus.). 24p. (J). (gr. -1-k). pap. 4.99 *(978-1-4263-2807-7(9));* (ENG., lib. bdg. 13.90 *(978-1-4263-2808-4(7))* Disney Publishing Worldwide. (National Geographic Kids).

Felix, Rebecca. Visiting the Beach in Summer. 2014. (21st Century Basic Skills Library: Let's Look at Summer Ser.). (ENG., Illus.). 24p. (J). (gr. k-3). 26.35 *(978-1-63137-598-9(9),* 205175) Cherry Lake Publishing.

Foxxe, Ellen. The Rising Seas: Shorelines under Threat. 2009. (Extreme Environmental Threats Ser.). 64p. (gr. 6-6). 58.50 *(978-1-61512-436-7(5))* Rosen Publishing Group, Inc., The.

Fretland VanVoorst, Jenny. Las Formas en la Playa. 2015.Tr. of Shapes by the Sea. (SPA., Illus.). 24p. (J). lib. bdg. *(978-1-62031-249-0(2),* Bullfrog Bks.) Jump! Inc.

—Shapes by the Sea. 2015. (Illus.). 24p. (J). lib. bdg. *(978-1-62031-202-5(6),* Bullfrog Bks.) Jump! Inc.

From Rocks to Sand: Level L, 6 vols. (Wonder Worldtm Ser.). 16p. 34.95 *(978-0-7802-4575-4(X))* Wright Group/McGraw-Hill.

Gates, Margo. Maya Likes the Beach. Hartley, Brian, illus. 2019. (Seasons All Around Me (Pull Ahead Readers — Fiction) Ser.). (ENG.). 16p. (J). (gr. -1-1). 27.99 *(978-1-5415-5873-1(1),* 9d43d5af-33bc-4bb7-b018-0443403a2874, Lerner Pubns.) Lerner Publishing Group.

Geatches, Hazel, ed. At the Beach. 2012. (ENG., Illus.). 32p. 11.00 *(978-0-19-464628-4(9))* Oxford Univ. Pr., Inc.

Goldman, Laurie. A Walk on the Beach: Into the Field Guide. 2013. (ENG.). 112p. (J). (gr. k). 19.99 *(978-1-935703-24-2(2))* Downtown Bookworks.

Grandma Fudgie. A Day at the Beach. 2011. 24p. pap. 14.99 *(978-1-4567-5548-5(X))* AuthorHouse.

Grassby, Donna. A Seaside Alphabet. Tooke, Susan, illus. 2009. (ABC Our Country Ser.). 32p. (J). (gr. 1-4). pap. 7.95 *(978-0-88776-938-2(1),* Tundra Bks.) Tundra Bks. CAN. Dist: Penguin Random Hse. LLC.

Green, Jen. Coastlines Around the World, 1 vol. 2008. (Geography Now! Ser.). (ENG.). 32p. (gr. 5-5). (YA). lib. bdg. 30.27 *(978-1-4358-2871-1(2),* d1338d59-41a2-4b52-b964-78497c91288b); (Illus.). (J). pap. 11.00 *(978-1-4358-2957-2(3),* 11e4f3c7-e8da-44eb-b8d2-e1da749437af, PowerKids Pr.) Rosen Publishing Group, Inc., The.

—Coasts, 1 vol. 2011. (Geography Wise Ser.). (ENG., Illus.). 32p. (YA). (gr. 2-3). lib. bdg. 30.27 *(978-1-4488-3279-8(9),* aea3e351-47d2-486c-840e-b34bbbf12ff8) Rosen Publishing Group, Inc., The.

—Projects with the Seaside, 1 vol. 2014. (Make & Learn Ser.). (ENG., Illus.). 32p. (J). (gr. 4-4). lib. bdg. 29.27 *(978-1-4777-7173-0(5),* 581753bf-7736-4cd6-8e0d-3143aebee92e, PowerKids Pr.) Rosen Publishing Group, Inc., The.

Greenaway, Theresa, ed. Ocean: A Foldout Book & Wall Chart. 2005. (Illus.). 12p. (J). (gr. k-4). reprint ed. 10.00 *(978-0-7567-8533-8(2))* DIANE Publishing Co.

Gregoire, Maryellen. At the Beach. 2012. (Wonder Readers Emergent Level Ser.). (ENG.). 16p. (J). (gr. -1-k). pap. 38.50 *(978-1-4296-9205-2(7),* 18494); pap. 6.25 *(978-1-4296-9195-6(6),* 120180) Capstone. (Capstone Pr.).

—En la Playa. 2012. (Wonder Readers Spanish Emergent Ser.). (SPA.). 16p. (J). (gr. -1-1). pap. 38.00 *(978-1-62065-566-5(7),* 19231) Capstone.

Hale, Wendy A. & Lantz, Peggy. The Coastlines of Florida. 2014. (Florida Water Story Ser.). (Illus.). 36p. (J). (gr. -1-12). pap. 6.95 *(978-1-56164-702-6(0))* Pineapple Pr., Inc.

Harbo, Rick. Guide to the Western Seashore: Introductory Marinelife Guide to the Pacific Coast. 2005. (Act Ser.). (ENG., Illus.). 48p. (Orig.). pap. 7.95 *(978-0-88839-201-5(X))* Hancock Hse. Pubs.

Harvey, Stephanie. Ladders Social Studies 3: Living on the Coast, (below-Level) 2014. 24p. pap. 9.95 *(978-1-285-34803-2(6))* National Geographic School Publishing, Inc.

Hewitt, Sally. By the Sea. 2010. (Starting Geography Ser.). 32p. (J). (gr. 2-5). 28.50 *(978-1-60753-123-4(2))* Amicus Learning.

—By the Sea. 2012. (Deadly & Incredible Animals Ser.). 32p. (gr. 2-6). 27.10 (978-1-59920-409-3(6)) Black Rabbit Bks.

Holland, Gini. I Live near the Ocean, 1 vol. 2004. (Where I Live Ser.). (ENG., Illus.). 24p. (gr. k-2). pap. 9.15 (978-0-8368-4089-6(5), d3ef8710-e9a9-45c7-8479-de3b7fddc8b4, Weekly Reader Leveled Readers) Stevens, Gareth Publishing LLLP.

—I Live near the Ocean / Vivo Cerca Del Mar, 1 vol. 2004. (Where I Live / Donde Vivo Ser.). (SPA & ENG., Illus.). 24p. (gr. k-2). lib. bdg. 24.67 (978-0-8368-4130-5(1), 06abee9a-6c92-4cdf-95ed-03ab6c52a049) Stevens, Gareth Publishing LLLP.

I Feel Hot, 6 Packs. (gr. -1-2). 23.00 (978-0-7635-9014-7(2)) Rigby Education.

Kalman, Bobbie. Earth's Coasts. 2008. (Looking at Earth Ser.). (ENG., Illus.). 32p. (J). (gr. 1-4). lib. bdg. (978-0-7787-3206-8(1)) Crabtree Publishing Co.

—Las Costas de la Tierra. 2009. (SPA.). 32p. (J). (978-0-7787-8237-7(9)); pap. (978-0-7787-8254-4(9)) Crabtree Publishing Co.

Kawa, Katie. My First Trip to the Beach, 1 vol. 2012. (My First Adventures Ser.). (Illus.). 24p. (gr. k-k). (ENG.). (J). pap. 9.15 (978-1-4339-7309-3(X), 200bde70-bbc4-4e19-9ae9-f7acefe0923d); (ENG., (J). lib. bdg. 25.27 (978-1-4339-7308-6(1), 97db5ed4-d6b4-4f9d-8c62-66872c81af0b); 69.20 (978-1-4339-8049-7(5)) Stevens, Gareth Publishing LLLP.

—My First Trip to the Beach /Mi Primer Viaje a la Playa, 1 vol. 2012. (My First Adventures / Mis Primeras Aventuras Ser.). (SPA & ENG., Illus.). 24p. (J). (gr. k-k). lib. bdg. 25.27 (978-1-4339-7376-5(6), 8e1488b1-5120-422c-bd86-7d236c38020c) Stevens, Gareth Publishing LLLP.

Kent, Lorna, illus. At the Beach. 2004. 8p. (J). bds. 3.99 (978-1-85854-087-0(9)) Brimax Books Ltd. GBR. Dist: Byeway Bks.

Kerrigan, Michael. Coastlines. 2004. (Geography Fact Files Ser.). (J). lib. bdg. 28.50 (978-1-58340-424-9(4)) Black Rabbit Bks.

King, Zelda. Examining Tide Pool Habitats. 2009. (Graphic Organizers: Habitats Ser.). 24p. (gr. 2-3). 42.50 (978-1-61513-103-7(5)); (ENG.). (J). lib. bdg. 26.27 (978-1-4358-2719-6(8), fa5cb5a2-7f22-4b2c-8c61-13d944b5b322) Rosen Publishing Group, Inc., The. (PowerKids Pr.).

Kingsley, Charles. Glaucus or the Wonders of the Shore. 2004. reprint ed. pap. 15.95 (978-1-4191-2183-8(9)); pap. 1.99 (978-1-4192-2183-5(3)) Kessinger Publishing, LLC.

Kittinger, Jo S. Going to the Beach. Warren, Shari, illus. 2011. (Rookie Ready to Learn Ser.). 32p. (J). (ENG.). pap. 5.95 (978-0-531-26801-8(2)); (gr. -1-k). lib. bdg. 23.00 (978-0-531-25641-1(3)) Scholastic Library Publishing. (Children's Pr.).

Kochanoff, Peggy. Be a Beach Detective: Solving the Mysteries of Lakes, Swamps, & Pools, 1 vol. 2015. (Be a Nature Detective Ser.). (ENG., Illus.). 48p. (J). (gr. 1-3). pap. 14.95 (978-1-77108-267-9(4), f6d2e803-7d10-4a4a-811d-0538fedff4dd) Nimbus Publishing, Ltd. CAN. Dist: Baker & Taylor Publisher Services (BTPS).

Koeppel, Ruth. At the Seashore. McBee, Scott, illus. 2009. (ENG.). 10p. (J). (gr. -1-1). 12.99 (978-1-58476-817-3(7)) Innovative Kids.

Kopp, Megan. What Do You Find in a Tide Pool? 2016. (ENG., Illus.). 24p. (J). (978-0-7787-2263-2(5)) Crabtree Publishing Co.

Ladders Social Studies 3: Living on the Coast, (above-Level) 2014. 24p. pap. 9.95 (978-1-285-34802-5(8)) National Geographic School Publishing, Inc.

Laughing Elephant Staff, ed. By the Sea: Shape Book. 2013. (Children's Die-Cut Shape Book Ser.). (ENG., Illus.). 16p. (J). 10.95 (978-1-59583-702-8(7)) Laughing Elephant.

Lawrence, Ellen. Beach Fleas & Other Tiny Sand Animals. 2018. (Day at the Beach: Animal Life on the Shore Ser.). (ENG.). 24p. (J). (gr. -1-3). 17.95 (978-1-68402-449-0(8)) Bearport Publishing Co., Inc.

—Bloodworms & Other Wriggly Beach Dwellers. 2018. (Day at the Beach: Animal Life on the Shore Ser.). (ENG.). 24p. (J). (gr. -1-3). lib. bdg. 26.99 (978-1-68402-444-5(7)); E-Book 41.36 (978-1-68402-502-2(8)) Bearport Publishing Co., Inc.

Lindeen, Mary. At the Beach. 2015. (Beginning-To-Read Ser.). (ENG.). 32p. (J). (gr. k-2). pap. 13.26 (978-1-60357-758-8(0)); lib. bdg. 22.60 (978-1-59953-698-9(6)) Norwood Hse. Pr.

Litchfield, Jo. Beach. 2004. (Look & Say Board Books Ser.). (ENG., Illus.). 12p. (J). bds. 7.95 (978-0-7945-0703-9(4), Usborne) EDC Publishing.

Lynch, Annabelle. The Seaside, 1 vol., 1. 2015. (Nature Explorers Ser.). (ENG., Illus.). 24p. (J). (gr. k-1). pap. 9.25 (978-1-5081-9073-8(9), a82b11f1-4fae-4e2d-8ba7-01b6f92cddb6, Windmill Bks.) Rosen Publishing Group, Inc., The.

Marsh, Laura. National Geographic Readers: Tide Pools (L1) 2019. (Readers Ser.). (Illus.). 32p. (J). (gr. -1-k). pap. 4.99 (978-1-4263-3343-9(9), National Geographic Kids) Disney Publishing Worldwide.

McCormick, Anita Louise. Creating Sand Beaches with Poop, 1 vol. 2017. (Power of Poop Ser.). (ENG.). 32p. (gr. 3-4). pap. 11.52 (978-0-7660-9104-7(X), a33e0a15-10b2-46f7-9fa0-9bb7d27b81df) Enslow Publishing, LLC.

McFarlane, Sheryl. A Pod of Orcas, 1 vol. Wakelin, Kirsti Anne, illus. 2006. (ENG.). 28p. (J). (gr. -1-k). per. 9.95 (978-1-55041-722-7(3), f375b4e2-3abe-43cd-a538-3e956e1ab82f) Trifolium Bks., Inc. CAN. Dist: Firefly Bks., Ltd.

Meachen Rau, Dana. At the Beach, 1 vol. 2008. (Fun Time Ser.). (ENG., Illus.). 24p. (gr. k-1). lib. bdg. 25.50 (978-0-7614-2609-7(4), 81df4d12-166c-4e8d-857e-526ee8d52a8f) Cavendish Square Publishing LLC.

—En la Playa (at the Beach), 1 vol. 2009. (Tiempo de la Diversión (Fun Time) Ser.). (SPA., Illus.). 24p. (gr. k-1). lib. bdg. 25.50 (978-0-7614-2748-3(1), d4c12fb7-eb50-4738-a48d-55aac6da10e1) Cavendish Square Publishing LLC.

Meredith, Susan Markowitz. Patterns at the Beach. 2011. (Early Connections Ser.). (J). (978-1-61672-371-2(8)) Benchmark Education Co.

Michaels, Chris. Finding Stripes. 2010. (Sight Word Readers Ser.). (J). 3.49 (978-1-60719-626-6(3)) Newmark Learning LLC.

Milbourne, Anna. On the Seashore. Waters, Erica-Jane, illus. 2006. 24p. (J). (gr. -1-3). 9.99 (978-0-7945-1069-5(8), Usborne) EDC Publishing.

Mis, Melody S. Exploring Peninsulas, 1 vol. 2009. (Geography Zone: Landforms Ser.). (ENG.). 24p. (J). (gr. 2-3). pap. 9.25 (978-1-4358-3109-4(8), f80c1eb2-204f-42d1-b077-04308026a7e6, PowerKids Pr.) Rosen Publishing Group, Inc., The.

Moses, Jessie. My Day at the Beach. Boyer, Lyn, illus. 2017. (Text Connections Guided Close Reading Ser.). (J). (gr. k). (978-1-4900-1769-3(0)) Benchmark Education Co.

Munson, Victoria. The Seashore, 1 vol. 2018. (My First Book of Nature Ser.). (ENG., Illus.). 24p. (J). (gr. 2-2). 26.27 (978-1-5081-9619-8(2), 1a57059a-c72a-454a-8f2e-836ebf9e3d1a, Windmill Bks.) Rosen Publishing Group, Inc., The.

Murray, W. On the Beach. (Sunstart Ser.: No. 747-2). (Illus.). 50p. (J). (gr. -1-5). 3.50 (978-0-7214-8001-5(2), Dutton Juvenile) Penguin Publishing Group.

On the Beach: Individual Title-Six Packs. (Chiquilibros Ser.). (gr. k-1). 23.00 (978-0-7635-0448-9(3)) Rigby Education.

Owen, Ruth. Welcome to the Seashore. 2016. (Nature's Neighborhoods: All about Ecosystems Ser.). (ENG., Illus.). 32p. (J). (gr. -1-3). lib. bdg. 30.65 (978-1-910549-68-1(1), 91add997-a08b-4ed0-b305-5972ce03573f) Ruby Tuesday Books Limited GBR. Dist: Lerner Publishing Group.

Parker, Steve. The Seashore. 2010. (Unpredictable Nature Ser.). (Illus.). 48p. (J). (gr. 3-18). lib. bdg. 19.95 (978-1-4222-2006-1(0)) Mason Crest.

Patrizzi, Barbara. O Is for Oystercatcher: A Book of Seaside ABCs. Patrizzi, Barbara, illus. 2003. (Illus.). 55p. 15.95 (978-1-59322-008-2(1)) Down The Shore Publishing.

Phillips, Clifton. Waterworld Wonderways. 2007. 36p. 9.99 (978-0-9797106-2-9(6)) Avid Readers Publishing Group.

Picthall, Chez & Award, Anna. Beach. 2017. (Illus.). 10p. (J). bds. 9.00 (978-1-907604-75-1(8)) Award Pubns. Ltd. GBR. Dist: Parkwest Pubns., Inc.

La Playa: Individual Title Six-Packs. (Literatura 2000 Ser.). (SPA.). (gr. -1-1). 28.00 (978-0-7635-1001-5(7)) Rigby Education.

Randall, Jory. My Day at the Beach, 1 vol. 2009. (Kid's Life! Ser.). (ENG.). 24p. (J). (gr. 1-1). pap. 9.25 (978-1-4358-2467-6(9), 13d1db64-bf0d-43d6-9561-d7786c688691); (Illus.). lib. bdg. 26.27 (978-1-4042-8074-8(X), 12bac136-dec7-4f22-a064-00796edb002b) Rosen Publishing Group, Inc., The. (PowerKids Pr.).

Rau, Dana Meachen. Think Like a Scientist at the Beach. 2011. (Explorer Junior Library: Science Explorer Junior Ser.). (ENG., Illus.). 32p. (gr. 4-8). lib. bdg. 32.07 (978-1-61080-168-3(7), 201106) Cherry Lake Publishing.

Richter, A. By the Ocean: Learning the Long O Sound. 2009. (PowerPhonics Ser.). 24p. (gr. 1-1). 39.90 (978-1-60851-436-6(6), PowerKids Pr.) Rosen Publishing Group, Inc., The.

Rigby Education Staff. Look up, Look down, Look All Around. (Illus.). 8p. (J). bds. 3.95 (978-0-7635-6504-6(0), 765040C99) Rigby Education.

Roza, Greg. My First Trip to the Beach, 1 vol. 2019. (My First Trip Ser.). (ENG.). 24p. (gr. 1-1). 25.27 (978-1-5383-4434-7(3), 222dfe14-816d-459d-b3ef-726670042ab3, PowerKids Pr.) Rosen Publishing Group, Inc., The.

A Seaside Ecosystem. 2012. (Nature Trail Ser.). (ENG., Illus.). 32p. (J). (gr. k-5). 23.95 (978-1-4488-6628-1(6), PowerKids Pr.) Rosen Publishing Group, Inc., The.

Sexton, Colleen. Tide Pools. 2008. (Learning about the Earth Ser.). (ENG., Illus.). 24p. (J). (gr. k-3). lib. bdg. 26.95 (978-1-60014-231-4(1)) Bellwether Media.

—Tide Pools. 2011. (Blastoff! Readers Ser.). 24p. (J). pap. 5.95 (978-0-531-26037-1(2), Children's Pr.) Scholastic Library Publishing.

Shah, Keiran. Math by the Ocean, 1 vol. 2016. (Math Is Everywhere! Ser.). (ENG., Illus.). 24p. (J). (gr. k-k). pap. 9.15 (978-1-4824-5508-3(0), bf09ed32-c144-42b3-8af2-7eadf22ca419) Stevens, Gareth Publishing LLLP.

Smith, Alastair & Howell, Laura. On the Beach. 2004. (Luxury Lift-the-Flap Ser.). 16p. (J). (gr. 1-18). 11.95 (978-0-7945-0740-4(9), Usborne) EDC Publishing.

Smith, Carrie & Swain, Cameron. Fun at the Beach. 2006. (Early Explorers Ser.). (J). pap. (978-1-4108-6021-7(3)) Benchmark Education Co.

Spalding, Maddie. A Trip to the Beach. 2018. (Welcoming the Seasons Ser.). (ENG.). 24p. (J). (gr. -1-2). lib. bdg. 32.79 (978-1-5038-2376-1(8), 212219) Child's World, Inc, The.

Steele, Phillip W. Changing Coastlines. 2004. (Earth's Changing Landscape Ser.). (Illus.). 46p. (J). lib. bdg. 28.50 (978-1-58340-476-8(7)) Black Rabbit Bks.

Taylor, Barbara. Coastal Habitats, 1 vol. 2006. (Exploring Habitats Ser.). (ENG., Illus.). 36p. (gr. 4-6). lib. bdg. 28.67 (978-0-8368-7252-1(5), 0bccb321-ab39-4ebb-9548-f26d32a3f30e, Gareth Stevens Learning Library) Stevens, Gareth Publishing LLLP.

Taylor, Trace & Zorzi, Gina. At the Beach. 2017. (1-3Y in My World Ser.). (ENG., Illus.). 20p. (J). (gr. k-1). pap. 9.60 (978-1-59301-261-8(6)) American Reading Co.

Thomas, M. Summer at the Beach: Learning the EA Sound. 2009. (PowerPhonics Ser.). 24p. (gr. 1-1). 39.90 (978-1-60851-472-4(2), PowerKids Pr.) Rosen Publishing Group, Inc., The.

Thomson, Ruth. Coasts. 2012. (Geography Corner Ser.). (ENG., Illus.). 24p. (J). (gr. k-3). 21.25 (978-1-4488-6616-8(2), PowerKids Pr.) Rosen Publishing Group, Inc., The.

Unstead, Sue. Seashore. 2006. (Illus.). 32p. (J). (978-0-439-91178-8(8), Scholastic) Scholastic, Inc.

Vogel, Carole Garbuny. Shifting Shores. 2003. (Restless Sea Ser.). (ENG.). 80p. (gr. 5-8). pap. 12.95 (978-0-531-16683-3(X)); (Illus.). (J). 30.50 (978-0-531-12322-5(7)) Scholastic Library Publishing. (Watts, Franklin).

Watt, Fiona. Seaside Stroller Book. Baggott, Stella, illus. 2010. 8p. (J). 7.99 (978-0-7945-2810-2(4), Usborne) EDC Publishing.

When the Tide Goes Out: Individual Title, 6 packs. (Story Steps Ser.). (gr. k-2). 20.00 (978-0-7635-9590-6(X)) Rigby Education.

Wood, Susan. Sandy Feet! Whose Feet? Footprints at the Shore. Doneva, Steliyana, illus. 2019. (ENG.). 32p. (J). (gr. k-3). 16.99 (978-1-58536-409-1(6), 204652) Sleeping Bear Pr.

Woodward, John. Along the Shore. 2010. (Oceans Alive! Ser.). 32p. lib. bdg. 28.50 (978-1-933834-61-0(7)) Brown Bear Bks.

Wynne, Patricia J. Seashore Activity Book. 2005. (Dover Kids Activity Books: Nature Ser.). (ENG., illus.). 48p. (J). (gr. 3-8). per., act. bk. ed. 4.99 (978-0-486-44434-5(1), 444341) Dover Pubns., Inc.

SEASHORE—FICTION

Adler, David A. Young Cam Jansen & the Double Beach Mystery. Natti, Susanna, illus. 2003. (Young Cam Jansen Ser.: 8). (ENG.). 32p. (J). (gr. 1-3). mass mkt. 4.99 (978-0-14-250079-8(8), Penguin Young Readers) Penguin Young Readers Group.

Adrian, Mikel. Iza & Her Magic Seashell. Cotton, Sue, illus. 2018. (ENG.). 28p. (J). (gr. k-2). pap. 15.95 (978-1-61493-631-2(5)) Peppertree Pr., The.

—Iza & Her Magic Seashell. Cotton, Sue Lynn, illus. 2012. 28p. 24.95 (978-1-61493-077-8(5)) Peppertree Pr., The.

Alley, R. W. Gretchen over the Beach. 2016. (ENG., Illus.). 32p. (J). (gr. -1-3). 14.99 (978-0-547-90708-6(7), 1512358, Clarion Bks.) HarperCollins Pubs.

Anderson, Sorrel. The Clumsies Make a Mess of the Seaside (the Clumsies, Book 2), Book 2. 2010. (Clumsies Ser.: 2). (ENG., Illus.). 112p. (J). pap. 5.99 (978-0-00-733935-8(6), HarperCollins Children's Bks.) HarperCollins Pubs. Ltd. GBR. Dist: HarperCollins Pubs.

Arena, Felice & Kettle, Phil. Hit the Beach. Vane, Mitch, illus. 2004. (J). pap. (978-1-59336-361-1(3)) Mondo Publishing.

At the Beach. 2004. (Out & about Ser.). 12p. (J). bds. 4.99 (978-1-85997-807-8(X)) Byeway Bks.

Bancks, Tristan. Mac Slater Hunts the Cool. (Mac Slater Hunts the Cool Ser.). (ENG.). 224p. (J). (gr. 3-7). 2011. pap. 6.99 (978-1-4169-8575-4(1)) 2010. 15.99 (978-1-4169-8574-7(3)) Simon & Schuster Bks. For Young Readers. (Simon & Schuster Bks. For Young Readers).

Barefoot Books. Out of the Blue. Jay, Alison, illus. 2014. (ENG.). 32p. (J). (gr. -1-k). 16.99 (978-1-78285-042-7(2)) Barefoot Bks., Inc.

Barkley, Callie. Liz & the Sand Castle Contest. Riti, Marsha, illus. 2015. (Critter Club Ser.: 11). (ENG.). 128p. (J). (gr. k-4). pap. 5.99 (978-1-4814-2405-9(X), Little Simon) Little Simon.

Barron, T. A. The Lost Years of Merlin. unabr. ed. 2004. (Lost Years of Merlin Ser.: Bk. 1). 284p. (J). (gr. 5-9). pap. 46.00 incl. audio (978-0-8072-8766-8(0), YA261SP, Listening Library) Random Hse. Audio Publishing Group.

Beam, Emily. Tumtum & Nutmeg: Adventures Beyond Nutmouse Hall. 2011. (Tumtum & Nutmeg Ser.: 1). (ENG., Illus.). 512p. (J). (gr. 3-7). pap. 14.99 (978-0-316-07574-9(4)) Little, Brown Bks. for Young Readers.

—The Tumtum & Nutmeg: the Rose Cottage Adventures. Price, Nick, illus. 2013. (Tumtum & Nutmeg Ser.: 2). (ENG.). 416p. (J). (gr. 3-7). pap. 14.99 (978-0-316-08598-4(7)) Little, Brown Bks. for Young Readers.

Beil, Michael D. Summer at Forsaken Lake. Kneen, Maggie, illus. 2013. (ENG.). 336p. (J). (gr. 5). pap. 10.99 (978-0-375-86496-4(2), Yearling) Random Hse. Children's Bks.

Bentley, Sue. Seaside Mystery. 2013. (Magic Kitten Ser.: 9). lib. bdg. 16.00 (978-0-606-32121-1(7)) Turtleback.

—A Splash of Magic #3. Swan, Angela, illus. 2013. (Magic Bunny Ser.: 3). (ENG.). 128p. (J). (gr. 1-3). pap. 6.99 (978-0-448-46729-0(1), Grosset & Dunlap) Penguin Young Readers Group.

Berenstain, Jan. Berenstain Bears Go on Vacation. 2010. (Berenstain Bears Ser.). (ENG., Illus.). 32p. (J). (gr. -1-3). pap. 7.99 (978-0-06-057433-8(X), HarperCollins) HarperCollins Pubs.

Berenstain, Jan & Berenstain, Stan. The Berenstain Bears' Seashore Treasure. Berenstain, Jan, illus. 2005. (I Can Read Level 1 Ser.). (ENG., Illus.). 32p. (J). (gr. k-3). pap. 4.99 (978-0-06-058341-5(X), HarperCollins) HarperCollins Pubs.

Bixley, Donovan. My First Board Book: a Day at the Beach. 2022. (My First Board Book Ser.). (ENG., Illus.). 24p. (J). (gr. -1-k). bds. 13.99 (978-1-86971-365-2(6)) Hachette New Zealand NZL. Dist: Hachette Bk. Group.

Blackaby, Susan. El Lugar de Luis, 1 vol. Ruíz, Carlos & Ruíz, Carlos, trs. Gallagher-Cole, Mernie, illus. 2006. (Read-It! Readers en Español: Story Collection).Tr. of Place for Mike. (SPA.). 24p. (J). (gr. -1-3). 22.65 (978-1-4048-1688-6(7), 90854, Picture Window Bks.) Capstone.

Blackstone, Stella. Secret Seahorse. Beaton, Clare, illus. 2005. (ENG.). (J). (gr. -1-2). 24p. bds. 8.99 (978-1-905236-15-2(8)); 24p. 15.99 (978-1-84148-704-5(X)); 32p. pap. 9.99 (978-1-84148-937-7(9)) Barefoot Bks., Inc.

Bles, Riemke. Beene & What He Learned about the Atlantic Ocean. 2011. 32p. pap. 28.99 (978-1-4634-1633-1(4)) AuthorHouse.

Blumberg, Margie. Sunny Bunnies. Goulding, June, illus. 2008. (ENG.). 32p. (gr. -1-k). 15.95 (978-0-9624166-4-4(9)) MB Publishing, LLC.

Blumenthal, Deborah. The Lifeguard. (ENG.). 288p. (YA). (gr. 8-12). 2013. 9.99 (978-0-8075-4536-2(8), 807545368) 2012. 16.99 (978-0-8075-4535-5(X), 080754535X) Whitman, Albert & Co.

Bonacci, Ross. Rossi & Lucy Go to the Beach. Karla, Nicolee, illus. 2013. 38p. pap. (978-0-9873831-2-9(4)) Bonacci Publishing.

Bond, Michael. Paddington at the Beach. Alley, R. W., illus. 2015. (Paddington Ser.). (ENG.). 32p. (J). (gr. -1-3). 17.99 (978-0-06-231720-9(2), HarperCollins) HarperCollins Pubs.

—Paddington Sets Sail. Alley, R. W., illus. 2016. (I Can Read Level 1 Ser.). (ENG.). 32p. (J). (gr. -1-3). pap. 4.99 (978-0-06-243064-9(5), HarperCollins) HarperCollins Pubs.

Booth, Tom. Day at the Beach. Booth, Tom, illus. 2018. (Jeter Publishing Ser.). (ENG., Illus.). 40p. (J). (gr. -1-3). 19.99 (978-1-5344-1105-0(4), Aladdin) Simon & Schuster Children's Publishing.

Bourke, Debra. First Day at Bouddi School. Cowley, Ray B., illus. 2012. 32p. pap. 18.00 (978-1-4349-8469-2(9), RoseDog Bks.) Dorrance Publishing Co., Inc.

Branford, Henrietta & Beardshaw, Rosalind. Splash! (ENG., Illus.). 32p. (J). 19.99 (978-0-340-85550-8(9)) Macmillan Pubs., Ltd. GBR. Dist: Trafalgar Square Publishing.

Brooks, Brian. Oopsy Daisy's Bad Day. Brooks, Brian, illus. 2007. (Illus.). 62p. (J). reprint ed. 13.00 (978-1-4223-9004-7(7)) DIANE Publishing Co.

Brouillette, Kathy. What Makes me Smile. 2010. 16p. 8.99 (978-1-4520-1112-7(5)) AuthorHouse.

Buggs, Matthews. Beach Party. 2006. (J). 10.00 (978-0-9790515-3-1(3)) Pinkston, Anastasia.

Bulion, Leslie. Uncharted Waters, 1 vol. 2009. 192p. (J). (gr. 3-7). pap. 7.95 (978-1-56145-485-3(0)) Peachtree Publishing Co. Inc.

The Busy Beach. 2003. (J). 12.75 (978-0-89610-768-7(X)) Island Heritage Publishing.

Byars, Betsy. The Animal, the Vegetable, & John D. Jones. 150p. (J). (gr. 4-6). pap. 3.50 (978-0-8072-1414-5(0), Listening Library) Random Hse. Audio Publishing Group.

Caine, Paul. Jake's Journey. 2010. 68p. pap. 10.49 (978-1-4520-0508-9(7)) AuthorHouse.

Canale, Suzie Hearl. The Candy Roses of Cape Care. Coffey, Kevin, illus. 2012. 38p. (J). 14.95 (978-1-937406-67-7(9)) Amplify Publishing Group.

Candlewick Press. Peppa Pig & the Great Vacation. 2014. (Peppa Pig Ser.). (ENG.). 32p. (J). (-k). 14.99 (978-0-7636-6986-7(5), Candlewick Entertainment) Candlewick Pr.

Carestio, Michael A. Black Jack Jetty: A Boy's Journey Through Grief. 2010. (Illus.). 64p. (J). (gr. 3-8). (ENG.). 14.95 (978-1-4338-0784-8(X)); pap. 9.95 (978-1-4338-0786-2(6)) American Psychological Assn. (Magination Pr.).

Catrow, David. Fun in the Sun. 2017. (I Like to Read Ser.). (ENG.). 32p. (J). (gr. -1-3). 7.99 (978-0-8234-3845-7(7)) Holiday Hse., Inc.

Cepeda, Joe. I Dig. 2019. (I Like to Read Ser.). (Illus.). 32p. (J). (gr. -1-3). 15.99 (978-0-8234-3975-1(5)) Holiday Hse., Inc.

Chapman, Carlene. Jackson Goes to the Beach. 2010. 24p. pap. 11.95 (978-1-4490-9768-4(5)) AuthorHouse.

Chichester Clark, Emma. Beside the Sea (Melrose & Croc) Chichester Clark, Emma, illus. 2007. (Melrose & Croc Ser.). (ENG., Illus.). 32p. (gr. -1-2). pap. 8.95 (978-0-00-718244-2(9), HarperCollins Children's Bks.) HarperCollins Pubs. Ltd. GBR. Dist: HarperCollins Pubs.

Child's Play. Off to the Beach! Cocoretto, illus. 2017. (Tactile Bks.). 12p. (J). spiral bd. (978-1-84643-923-0(X)) Child's Play International Ltd.

Clark, Joyce. Katie. 2006. 196p. 27.43 (978-1-4122-0067-7(9)) Trafford Publishing.

Clements, Andrew. Because Your Daddy Loves You. Alley, R. W., illus. (ENG.). 32p. (J). (gr. -1-3). 2009. pap. 8.99 (978-0-547-23764-0(2), 1083875) 2005. 16.99 (978-0-618-00361-7(4), 112735) HarperCollins Pubs. (Clarion Bks.).

Collins, Izola. Pip, Squeak, & Zoom. 2009. 68p. pap. 23.49 (978-1-4490-0717-1(1)) AuthorHouse.

Condra, Estelle. See the Ocean. 7.95 (978-1-57102-178-6(7), Ideals Pubns.) Worthy Publishing.

Cooper, Elisha. Beach. Cooper, Elisha, illus. 2006. (ENG., Illus.). 40p. (J). (gr. -1-k). 18.99 (978-0-439-68785-0(3), Orchard Bks.) Scholastic, Inc.

Coste, Marion. Wild Beach. Gray, Cissy, illus. 2005. (ENG.). 32p. (J). pap. 8.25 (978-0-89317-062-2(3), WW-623); lib. bdg. 17.95 (978-0-89317-061-5(5), WW-0615) Finney Co., Inc. (Windward Publishing).

Couloumbis, Audrey. Lexie. Denos, Julia, illus. 2012. (ENG.). 208p. (J). (gr. 3-7). pap. 6.99 (978-0-375-85633-4(1), Yearling) Random Hse. Children's Bks.

Cousins, Lucy. Maisy Goes on Vacation: A Maisy First Experiences Book. Cousins, Lucy, illus. 2012. (Maisy Ser.). (ENG., Illus.). 32p. (J). (gr. -1-2). pap. 7.99 (978-0-7636-6039-0(6)) Candlewick Pr.

Cowley, Joy. Mrs. WishyWashy & the Big Tub. 2009. pap. 8.25 (978-1-60559-233-6(1)) Hameray Publishing Group, Inc.

Crimi, Carolyn. There Might Be Lobsters. Molk, Laurel, illus. 2017. (ENG.). 32p. (J). (gr. -1-2). 18.99 (978-0-7636-7542-4(3)) Candlewick Pr.

Crockett-Blassingame, Linda, illus. See the Ocean. 2006. 32p. (J). 14.95 (978-0-9778143-0-5(0)) Inclusive Books LLC.

Crupi, Jaclyn. Theo at the Beach. Verdoux, Aurélia, illus. 2013. (J). (978-1-4351-4722-5(7)) Barnes & Noble, Inc.

Cummings, Priscilla. Meet Chadwick & His Chesapeake Bay Friends, 1 vol. 2019. (ENG., Illus.). 32p. (J). pap. 9.99 (978-0-7643-5700-8(X), 16396) Schiffer Publishing, Ltd.

Curry, Jane Louise. Over the Sea's Edge. 2017. (ENG., Illus.). (J). pap. 19.99 (978-1-62524-319-5(7), Candlewood Pr.) Harding Hse. Publishing Sebice Inc.

Daffney. The Birthday Fairy. 2009. 16p. pap. 8.49 (978-1-4490-0095-0(9)) AuthorHouse.

Davis, Jacky. Ladybug Girl at the Beach. Soman, David, illus. 2010. (Ladybug Girl Ser.). 40p. (J). (gr. -1-k). 18.99 (978-0-8037-3416-6(6), Dial Bks) Penguin Young Readers Group.

Dean, James & Dean, Kimberly. Pete the Cat: Pete at the Beach. Dean, James, illus. 2013. (My First I Can Read Ser.). (ENG., Illus.). 32p. (J). (gr. -1-3). pap. 5.99 (978-0-06-211072-5(1), HarperCollins) HarperCollins Pubs.

deGroat, Diane. Gilbert, the Surfer Dude. 2009. (Illus.). 31p. (J). lib. bdg. 18.89 (978-0-06-125212-9(3)) HarperCollins Pubs.

Dubose, Sarah. Uncharted Waters. 2013. 440p. pap. (978-1-4596-6282-7(2)) ReadHowYouWant.com, Ltd.

Dudar, Judy. I Spy a Bunny, 1 vol. Rudnicki, Richard, illus. 2009. (ENG.). 32p. (J). (gr. -1-k). 17.95 (978-1-55109-700-8(1), c7f6750d-91ca-4dd9-86b7-0cbc864d538f) Nimbus Publishing, Ltd. CAN. Dist: Baker & Taylor Publisher Services (BTPS).

Dyan, Penelope. Courtney's Beach. Dyan, Penelope, illus. 2008. (Illus.). 44p. pap. 11.95 (978-1-935118-35-0(8)) Bellissima Publishing, LLC.

Eastman, Peter Anthony. Fred & Ted Like to Fly. Eastman, Peter Anthony, illus. 2007. (Beginner Books(R) Ser.). (Illus.). 48p. (J). (gr. -1-2). 9.99 *(978-0-375-84064-7(8),* Random Hse. Bks. for Young Readers) Random Hse. Children's Bks.

Edelson, Madelyn. The Proud Beech: A Long Island Folk Tale. Tucker, Diane, illus. 2004. 48p. (J). pap. 14.95 *(978-0-9658920-7-0(7))* Edelson, Madelyn.

Elliot, Margaret. Cat & Tiger Go to the Seaside. 2012. 24p. pap. 28.03 *(978-1-4691-7674-1(2))* Xlibris Corp.

Elliott, Rebecca. Eva at the Beach: a Branches Book (Owl Diaries #14) Elliott, Rebecca, illus. 2021. (Owl Diaries: 14). (ENG., Illus.). 80p. (J). (gr. k-2). pap. 5.99 *(978-1-338-29879-6(8))* Scholastic, Inc.

—Eva at the Beach: a Branches Book (Owl Diaries #14) (Library Edition) Elliott, Rebecca, illus. 2021. (Owl Diaries: 14). (ENG., Illus.). 80p. (J). (gr. k-2). lib. bdg. 24.99 *(978-1-338-29881-9(X))* Scholastic, Inc.

Ellis, Dianne. Rusty Rumble's Day at the Beach. 2012. 40p. pap. 32.70 *(978-1-4797-0360-9(5))* Xlibris Corp.

Elmquist, Laurie. Beach Baby, 1 vol. MacKay, Elly, illus. 2016. (ENG.). 24p. (J). (gr. -1 — 1). bds. 10.95 *(978-1-4598-0954-3(8))* Orca Bk. Pubs. USA.

Ernshaw, Shea. The Wicked Deep. (ENG.). (YA). (gr. 9). 2019. 336p. pap. 12.99 *(978-1-4814-9735-0(9))* 2018. (Illus.). 320p. 19.99 *(978-1-4814-9734-3(0))* Simon Pulse. (Simon Pulse).

Fernandez, Joy C. Rockman. 2010. 36p. pap. 16.45 *(978-1-4520-6751-3(1))* AuthorHouse.

Ferrante, Elena. The Beach at Night. Goldstein, Ann, tr. Cerri, Mara, illus. 2016. (ENG.). 48p. 13.00 *(978-1-60945-370-1(0))* Europa Editions, Inc.

Fineman, Kelly Ramsdell. At the Boardwalk. Armiño, Mónica, illus. 2012. (ENG.). 32p. (J). *(978-1-58925-104-5(0));* pap. *(978-1-58925-431-2(7))* Tiger Tales.

Fleming, Candace. Tippy-Tippy-Tippy, Splash! Karas, G. Brian, illus. 2014. (ENG.). 40p. (J). (gr. -1-3). 16.99 *(978-1-4169-5403-3(1),* Atheneum Bks. for Young Readers) Simon & Schuster Children's Publishing.

Flowers, Luke. Surf's up!: an Acorn Book (Moby Shinobi & Toby, Too! #1) (Library Edition) Flowers, Luke, illus. 2019. (Moby Shinobi & Toby Too! Ser.: 1). (ENG., Illus.). 64p. (J). (gr. k-2). 23.99 *(978-1-338-54753-5(4))* Scholastic, Inc.

Forton-Barnes, Therese. Zaki & Venus. 2007. 13.95 *(978-1-59526-388-9(8))* Aeon Publishing Inc.

Frazee, Marla. A Couple of Boys Have the Best Week Ever. Frazee, Marla, illus. 2008. (ENG., Illus.). 40p. (J). (gr. 1-4). 17.99 *(978-0-15-206020-6(0),* 1198080, Clarion Bks.) HarperCollins Pubs.

French, Sarah. Summer Friends. 2011. (ENG., Illus.). 32p. (J). 17.95 *(978-0-9827146-5-2(3))* Vineyard Stories.

Fry, Sonali. Eloise Goes to the Beach. Lyon, Tammie, illus. 2007. (Eloise Ser.). (ENG.). 12p. (J). (gr. -1-2). 9.99 *(978-1-4169-3344-1(1),* Little Simon) Little Simon.

Gallup, Zd. Nap Time at the Beach. 2013. 34p. pap. 14.95 *(978-1-4575-2129-4(6))* Dog Ear Publishing, LLC.

Gamble, Adam. Good Night Beach. Stevenson, Harvey, illus. 2007. (Good Night Our World Ser.). (ENG.). 28p. (J). (gr. k — 1). bds. 9.95 *(978-1-60219-002-3(X))* Good Night Bks.

Garcia, Jesus E. Tim & Ann's First Day at the Beach. 2013. 24p. pap. 24.95 *(978-1-62709-341-5(9))* America Star Bks.

Gateley, Edwina. God Goes on Vacation. Gateley, Edwina, illus. 2009. (ENG., Illus.). 32p. (Orig.). (J). pap. 9.95 *(978-0-8091-6747-0(6))* Paulist Pr.

Gay, Marie-Louise. Stella, Star of the Sea, 1 vol. (Illus.). 32p. (J). 2010. (Stella & Sam Ser.: 5). (gr. -1-k). pap. 9.99 *(978-0-88899-992-4(5))* 2004. (ENG., 7.95 *(978-0-88899-572-8(5))* Groundwood Bks. CAN. Dist: Publishers Group West (PGW).

Geraldi, Michele J. A Shell Story. 2009. 28p. pap. 13.99 *(978-1-4389-2827-2(0))* AuthorHouse.

Gibbs, Stuart. Whale Done. 2023. (FunJungle Ser.). (ENG., Illus.). 320p. (J). (gr. 3-7). 17.99 *(978-1-5344-9931-7(8),* Simon & Schuster Bks. For Young Readers) Simon & Schuster Bks. For Young Readers.

Gibson, Mary, illus. Buried Treasure. 2007. 12p. (J). 5.95 *(978-0-9801269-0-7(8))* Scribe's Closet Pubns., The.

Gillespie, Elizabeth. Robbie's Beach Adventure. 2011. 28p. pap. 15.99 *(978-1-4628-7992-2(6))* Xlibris Corp.

Gompper, Gail. Every Day by the Bay. Gompper, Gail, illus. 2011. (ENG., Illus.). 24p. (J). bds. 9.95 *(978-0-9726487-7-6(1))* Puddle Jump Pr., Ltd.

Gorbachev, Valeri. Not Me! 2016. (I Like to Read Ser.). (ENG., Illus.). 24p. (J). (gr. -1-3). pap. 7.99 *(978-0-8234-3547-0(4))* Holiday Hse., Inc.

Gordon, Marie Elaina. My Grand-Mom Told Me-down by the Sea. 2008. 108p. pap. 19.95 *(978-1-4241-9095-9(9))* America Star Bks.

Gow, Kailin. Loving Summer. 2012. 250p. (-18). pap. 9.99 *(978-1-59748-044-4(4),* The Edge) Sparklesoup LLC.

Green, Judy. The Little Blue Octopus. 2009. 28p. pap. 21.99 *(978-1-4415-3393-7(1))* Xlibris Corp.

Green, Ruth. Hedgehog Holidays. 2017. (ENG., Illus.). 32p. (J). (gr. k-3). 14.95 *(978-1-84976-484-1(0),* 1306901) Tate Publishing, Ltd. GBR. Dist: Abrams, Inc.

Greenwald, Lisa. Dog Beach Unleashed: The Seagate Summers Book Two. 2015. (Seagate Summers Ser.). (ENG., Illus.). 36p. (J). (gr. 5-9). 15.95 *(978-1-4197-1481-8(3),* 1072001, Amulet Bks.) Abrams, Inc.

Guerras Safia. Lou Lou. Kemble, Mai S., illus. 2013. (ENG.). 24p. (J). pap. 16.95 *(978-1-4787-2359-2(9))* Outskirts Pr., Inc.

H & T Imaginations Unlimited, Inc. Sand Castles with Professor Woodpecker. 2009. 12p. pap. 8.49 *(978-1-4389-7262-6(8))* AuthorHouse.

Han, Jenny. The Complete Summer I Turned Pretty Trilogy (Boxed Set) The Summer I Turned Pretty; It's Not Summer Without You; We'll Always Have Summer. 2013. (Summer I Turned Pretty Ser.). (ENG., Illus.). 928p. (YA). (gr. 7). pap. 35.99 *(978-1-4424-9832-7(3),* Simon & Schuster Bks. For Young Readers) Simon & Schuster Bks. For Young Readers.

—It's Not Summer Without You. (Summer I Turned Pretty Ser.). (ENG.). (YA). (gr. 7). 2011. 320p. pap. 11.99 *(978-1-4169-9556-2(0))* 2010. 288p. 19.99 *(978-1-4169-9555-5(2))* 2022. (Illus.). 320p. pap. 11.99 *(978-1-6659-3799-3(8))* Simon & Schuster Bks. For Young Readers. (Simon & Schuster Bks. For Young Readers).

—The Summer I Turned Pretty. (Summer I Turned Pretty Ser.). (ENG.). (YA). (gr. 7). 2010. 304p. pap. 11.99 *(978-1-4169-6829-0(6))* 2009. 288p. 19.99 *(978-1-4169-6823-8(7))* Simon & Schuster Bks. For Young Readers. (Simon & Schuster Bks. For Young Readers).

—The Summer I Turned Pretty. 2010. lib. bdg. 22.10 *(978-0-606-14529-9(X))* Turtleback.

—We'll Always Have Summer. 2011. (YA). 1.25 *(978-1-4640-1977-7(0))* Recorded Bks., Inc.

—We'll Always Have Summer. (Summer I Turned Pretty Ser.). (ENG., Illus.). (YA). (gr. 7). 2012. 320p. pap. 11.99 *(978-1-4169-9559-3(5))* 2011. 304p. 19.99 *(978-1-4169-9558-6(7))* Simon & Schuster Bks. For Young Readers. (Simon & Schuster Bks. For Young Readers).

Heady, Heather. What's at the Beach? Storch, Ellen N., illus. I.t. ed. 2005. 10p. (J). (gr. -1-k). pap. 10.95 *(978-1-57332-355-0(1),* HighReach Learning, Incorporated) Carson-Dellosa Publishing, LLC.

Henkes, Kevin. Junonia. Henkes, Kevin, illus. (ENG., Illus.). 192p. (J). (gr. 3-7). 2012. pap. 6.99 *(978-0-06-196419-0(0))* 2011. 15.99 *(978-0-06-196417-6(4))* HarperCollins Pubs. (Greenwillow Bks.).

Hennessy, B. G. Corduroy Goes to the Beach. McCue, Lisa, illus. 2006. (Corduroy Ser.). 20p. (J). (gr. 1-k). 12.99 *(978-0-670-06052-8(6),* Viking Books for Young Readers) Penguin Young Readers Group.

Hill, Eric. Spot Goes to the Beach. Hill, Eric, illus. 2019. (Spot Ser.). (ENG., Illus.). 12p. (J). (-k). bds. 6.99 *(978-0-241-35182-6(0),* Warne) Penguin Young Readers Group.

Hillert, Margaret. Dear Dragon Goes to the Beach. Pullan, Jack, illus. 2015. (BeginningtoRead Ser.). (ENG.). 32p. (J). (gr. k-2). lib. bdg. 22.60 *(978-1-59953-704-7(4))* Norwood Hse. Pr.

—Let's Go, Dear Dragon. Pullan, Jack, illus. 2016. (BeginningtoRead Ser.). (ENG.). 32p. (J). (-2). lib. bdg. 22.60 *(978-1-59953-774-0(5))* Norwood Hse. Pr.

Hills, Tad. Duck & Goose Go to the Beach. Hills, Tad, illus. 2014. (Duck & Goose Ser.). (ENG., Illus.). 40p. (J). (gr. -1-2). 18.99 *(978-0-385-37235-0(3))* Random Hse. Children's Bks.

Hines, Anna Grossnickle. Gramma's Walk. Hines, Anna Grossnickle, illus. 2016. (ENG., Illus.). (J). (gr. -1-3). 18.95 *(978-1-930900-66-0(X))* Purple Hse. Pr.

Hochman, Marisa. A Walk in Pirate's Cove, 1 vol. 2012. (ENG., Illus.). 32p. (J). *(978-0-9865679-0-2(6))* Fitzhenry & Whiteside, Ltd.

Hoff, Syd. Danny & the Dinosaur & the Sand Castle Contest. No. 5. 2018. (I Can Read Level 1 Ser.). (ENG., Illus.). 32p. (J). (gr. -1-3). 16.99 *(978-0-06-241049-8(0));* pap. 5.99 *(978-0-06-241048-1(2))* HarperCollins Pubs. (HarperCollins).

Hofmeister, Alan, et al. The Shell. (Reading for All Learners Ser.). (Illus.). (J). pap. *(978-1-56861-103-7(X))* Swift Learning Resources.

Holland, Amy L. The Adventures of Bubba & Sis: Book One. 2009. 16p. pap. 8.49 *(978-1-4389-5941-2(9))* AuthorHouse.

Holm, Jennifer L. & Holm, Matthew. Babymouse #3: Beach Babe. 2006. (Babymouse Ser.: 3). (ENG., Illus.). 96p. (J). (gr. 2-5). pap. 6.99 *(978-0-375-83231-4(9))* Penguin Random Hse. LLC.

—Beach Babe. 2008. (Babymouse Ser.: No. 3). (Illus.). 91p. (gr. 2-5). 17.00 *(978-0-7569-8345-1(2))* Perfection Learning Corp.

Hope, Laura Lee. The Bobbsey Twins at the Seashore. 2005. 26.95 *(978-1-4218-1070-6(0));* 176p. pap. 11.95 *(978-1-4218-1170-3(7))* 1st World Publishing, Inc. (1st World Library - Literary Society).

Hoppner, Gabi. Beach Fun. 2004. (What A Series of Fun! Ser.). (Illus.). 10p. (J). bds. 3.99 *(978-1-59384-053-2(5))* Parklane Publishing.

Horvath, Polly. My One Hundred Adventures. 2010. (My One Hundred Adventures Ser.: 1). (Illus.). 272p. (J). (gr. 3-7). 8.99 *(978-0-375-85526-9(2),* Yearling) Random Hse. Children's Bks.

Howell, Gail L. Sarah's World: Sarah Meets her Cousins by the Sea. 2009. 24p. pap. 11.49 *(978-1-4389-4864-5(6))* AuthorHouse.

Hughes, Shirley. Lucy & Tom at the Seaside. 2016. (Illus.). 32p. (J). (-k). pap. 12.99 *(978-1-78295-516-0(X),* Red Fox) Random House Children's Books GBR. Dist: Independent Pubs. Group.

Hurley, Jorey. Fetch. Hurley, Jorey, illus. 2015. (ENG., Illus.). 40p. (J). (gr. -1-2). 17.99 *(978-1-4424-8969-1(3),* Simon & Schuster Bks. For Young Readers) Simon & Schuster Bks. For Young Readers.

Hutchings, Tony, illus. A Week at the Seaside. 2014. (J). *(978-1-4351-5464-3(9))* Barnes & Noble, Inc.

Hutton, John. Beach: Baby Unplugged. Kang, Andrea, illus. 2012. (Baby Unplugged Ser.). (ENG.). 14p. (J). (— 1). bds. 7.99 *(978-1-936669-07-3(2))* Blue Manatee Press.

Idle, Molly. Sea Rex. Idle, Molly, illus. 2015. (Rex Book Ser.). (Illus.). 40p. (J). (-k). 17.99 *(978-0-670-78574-2(1),* Viking Books for Young Readers) Penguin Young Readers Group.

Jackson, Kathryn, et al. A Day at the Seashore. 2010. (Little Golden Book Ser.). (Illus.). 24p. (J). (gr. -1-2). 5.99 *(978-0-375-85425-5(8),* Golden Bks.) Random Hse. Children's Bks.

Jardine Stoddart, Heidi. Back to the Beach, 1 vol. 2009. (ENG., Illus.). 32p. (J). (gr. 1-3). 12.95 *(978-1-55109-702-2(8),* d7c26c62-ea19-4d5f-bd53-296e3752f163) Nimbus Publishing, Ltd. CAN. Dist: Baker & Taylor Publisher Services (BTPS).

—East to the Sea, 1 vol. 2006. (ENG., Illus.). 32p. (J). (gr. -1-3). pap. 11.95 *(978-1-55109-577-6(7),* 3cfbcb0f-f867-4d00-a28a-91cd0f76dc07) Nimbus Publishing, Ltd. CAN. Dist: Baker & Taylor Publisher Services (BTPS).

Jeanba, Malahkee. Makeda Goes to the Beach. 2012. 24p. pap. 15.99 *(978-1-4691-9129-4(6))* Xlibris Corp.

Jessell, Tim, illus. The Boardwalk Mystery. 2013. (Boxcar Children Mysteries Ser.: 131). (ENG.). 144p. (J). (gr. 2-5). pap. 6.99 *(978-0-8075-0803-9(9),* 807508039);131. 15.99 *(978-0-8075-0802-2(0),* 807508020) Random Hse. Children's Bks. (Random Hse. Bks. for Young Readers).

Johnson, C. Homecoming. 2007. (Illus.). 64p. per. 10.00 *(978-1-4251-1358-2(3))* Trafford Publishing.

Jules, Jacqueline. The Beach Trip. Smith, Kim, illus. 2016. (Sofia Martinez Ser.). (ENG.). 32p. (J). (gr. k-2). lib. bdg. 21.32 *(978-1-4795-8719-3(2),* 131113, Picture Window Bks.) Capstone.

Kalar, Bonnie. A Trip to the Beach. Spreen, Kathe, illus. Date not set. 12p. (J). (gr. -1-2). pap. *(978-1-891619-42-7(X))* Corona Pr.

Kann, Victoria. Aqualicious. Kann, Victoria, illus. 2015. (ENG., Illus.). 40p. (J). (gr. -1-3). 18.99 *(978-0-06-233016-1(0),* HarperCollins) HarperCollins Pubs.

Katz, Karen. Where Is Baby's Beach Ball? A Lift-The-Flap Book. Katz, Karen, illus. 2009. (ENG., Illus.). 14p. (J). (gr. -1 — 1). bds. 7.99 *(978-1-4169-4962-6(3),* Little Simon) Little Simon.

Keller, Holly. Miranda's Beach Day. Keller, Holly, illus. 2009. (Illus.). 32p. (J). (gr. -1). lib. bdg. 18.89 *(978-0-06-158300-1(6),* Greenwillow Bks.) HarperCollins Pubs.

Kettle, Shey. Surf Girls. Thomas, Meredith, illus. 2005. (Girlz Rock! Ser.). (J). pap. *(978-1-59336-708-4(2))* Mondo Publishing.

Kirby, Jessi. Moonglass. 2012. (ENG.). 256p. (YA). (gr. 7). pap. 11.99 *(978-1-4424-1695-6(5),* Simon & Schuster Bks. For Young Readers) Simon & Schuster Bks. For Young Readers.

Kondrchek, Jamie & Rasemas, Joe. What Day Is It? (Que Dia Es Hoy?) Vega, Eida de la, tr. Rasemas, Joe, illus. 2009. (Day in the Life Ser.). (SPA & ENG., Illus.). 32p. (J). (gr. -1-1). 25.70 *(978-1-58415-838-7(7))* Mitchell Lane Pubs.

Koss, Amy Goldman. Kailey. Howe, Philip, illus. 2003. (American Girl of Today Ser.). (ENG.). 160p. (J). pap. 6.95 *(978-1-58485-591-0(6))* American Girl Publishing, Inc.

Krulik, Nancy. Catch That Wave. 2013. (Magic Bone Ser.: 2). lib. bdg. 14.75 *(978-0-606-31681-1(7))* Turtleback.

—Catch That Wave #2. Braun, Sebastien, illus. 2013. (Magic Bone Ser.: 2). 128p. (J). (gr. 1-3). pap. 6.99 *(978-0-448-46444-2(6),* Grosset & Dunlap) Penguin Young Readers Group.

Kurtz, Carmen. Veva y el Mar.Tr. of Veva & the Sea. (SPA.). 144p. (J). (gr. 3-5). *(978-84-279-3129-9(8))* Noguer y Caralt Editores, S. A. ESP. Dist: Lectorum Pubns., Inc.

Laberje, Reji. Max Explores the Beach. Fenech, Liza, illus. 2015. (Max Explores Ser.). (ENG.). 20p. (J). (— 1). bds. 9.95 *(978-1-62937-101-6(7))* Triumph Bks.

Lakin, Patricia. Dad & Me in the Morning. Steele, Robert G., illus. 2019. (ENG.). 32p. (J). (gr. -1-3). pap. 7.99 *(978-0-8075-1420-7(9),* 807514209) Whitman, Albert & Co.

Lantz, Francess L. Sea for Yourself. 2004. (Luna Bay Ser.: No. 8). 176p. mass mkt. 4.99 *(978-0-06-059520-3(5),* Harper Entertainment) HarperCollins Pubs.

Lasaracina, Barbara. Mermaid Tears: A Magical Sea Tale. Peer, Nancy, illus. 2010. 28p. pap. 11.99 *(978-1-60844-451-9(1))* Dog Ear Publishing, LLC.

Latimer, Alex. Lula & the Sea Monster, 1 vol. 2019. (ENG., Illus.). 32p. (J). (gr. -1-3). 16.95 *(978-1-68263-122-5(2))* Peachtree Publishing Co. Inc.

Le Clézio, J. M. G. Lullaby. Lemoine, Georges, illus. 2007. (FRE.). 72p. (J). (gr. 5-10). pap. *(978-2-07-061258-1(9))* Gallimard, Editions.

LeapFrog Staff. Imagination Desk Counting Day at the Beach. 2003. (Illus.). 9.99 *(978-1-59319-025-5(5))* LeapFrog Enterprises, Inc.

Leblanc, A. J. Donnie the Little Knee Boarder. 2012. 28p. pap. 24.95 *(978-1-4626-8313-0(4))* PublishAmerica, Inc.

Lee, Quinlan B. Beach Day. Haefele, Steve, illus. 2006. (J). *(978-0-439-81618-2(1))* Scholastic, Inc.

Lee, Suzy. Wave: (Books about Ocean Waves, Beach Story Children's Books) 2008. (ENG., Illus.). 40p. (J). (gr. -1-17). 15.99 *(978-0-8118-5924-0(X))* Chronicle Bks. LLC.

Lehrhaupt, Adam. Chicken on Vacation. Kober, Shahar, illus. 2018. (I Can Read Level 1 Ser.). (ENG.). 32p. (J). (gr. -1-3). 16.99 *(978-0-06-236419-7(7));* pap. 4.99 *(978-0-06-236418-0(9))* HarperCollins Pubs. (HarperCollins).

Lester, Alison. Magic Beach. 2006. (ENG., Illus.). 32p. (J). (gr. -1-k). pap. 11.99 *(978-1-74114-488-8(4))* Allen & Unwin AUS. Dist: Independent Pubs. Group.

—Noni the Pony Goes to the Beach. Lester, Alison, illus. 2015. (Noni the Pony Ser.). (ENG., Illus.). 32p. (J). (gr. -1-3). 17.99 *(978-1-4814-4625-9(8),* Beach Lane Bks.) Beach Lane Bks.

Lewis, Gill. One White Dolphin. Aparicio, Raquel, illus. 2013. (ENG.). 368p. (J). (gr. 3-7). pap. 8.99 *(978-1-4424-1448-8(0),* Atheneum Bks. for Young Readers) Simon & Schuster Children's Publishing.

Lies, Brian. Bats at the Beach. 2006. (Bat Book Ser.). (ENG., Illus.). 32p. (J). (gr. -1-3). 18.99 *(978-0-618-55744-8(X),* 529911, Clarion Bks.) HarperCollins Pubs.

Lilienstein, Jennel. Day at the Beach. 2003. (Illus.). 36p. (J). 8.99 *(978-0-9741215-1-2(7))* Stories of My Life, The.

Linder, Karen A. Jack the Curly Black Dog: Goes to the Beach. 2010. 20p. 13.80 *(978-1-4520-3434-8(6))* AuthorHouse.

Logan, Dottie Colegrove. Picnic on the Beach: Nana & Me Series, Book Three. 2010. 16p. 12.99 *(978-1-4490-3689-8(9))* AuthorHouse.

Lorimer, Janet. Ring of Fear, 1 vol. unabr. ed. 2010. (Q Reads Ser.). (ENG.). 32p. (YA). (gr. 9-12). pap. 8.50 *(978-1-61651-194-4(X))* Saddleback Educational Publishing, Inc.

Lubar, David. Dunk. 2004. (ENG.). 272p. (YA). (gr. 7-18). reprint ed. pap. 9.99 *(978-0-618-43909-6(9),* 490005, Clarion Bks.) HarperCollins Pubs.

Lucas, Sally. Dancing Dinos at the Beach. Lucas, Margeaux, illus. 2010. (Step into Reading Ser.). 32p. (J). (gr. -1-1). pap. 5.99 *(978-0-375-85640-2(4),* Random Hse. Bks. for Young Readers) Random Hse. Children's Bks.

Lynch, Chris. The Gravedigger's Cottage. 2004. (ENG.). 208p. (J). (gr. 7-18). 15.99 *(978-0-06-623940-8(0))* HarperCollins Pubs.

MacVeety, Sue Maney. Singing Sea/el Mar Que Canta. Zantay, Valerie, tr. 2005. (ENG., Illus.). 36p. per. 15.99 *(978-1-4134-7275-2(3))* Xlibris Corp.

Maddox, Tony & Wen, Dref. Ffred Ar y Môr. Cyfres Ffred Ci'r Fferm. 2005. (WEL., Illus.). 32p. pap. *(978-1-85596-666-6(2))* Dref Wen.

Magill, Sharon L. Chloe Madison & the Beach Heists. 2009. 60p. pap. 10.49 *(978-1-4389-4191-2(9))* AuthorHouse.

Mann, Jennifer K. Sam & Jump. Mann, Jennifer K., illus. 2016. (ENG., Illus.). 32p. (J). (gr. -1-2). 15.99 *(978-0-7636-7947-7(X))* Candlewick Pr.

Manushkin, Fran. La Jefa Del Mundo, 1 vol. Lyon, Tammie & Lyon, Tammie, illus. 2012. (Katie Woo en Español Ser.). (SPA.). 32p. (J). (gr. k-2). pap. 6.95 *(978-1-4048-7679-8(0),* 120353); lib. bdg. 21.32 *(978-1-4048-7523-4(9),* 119825) Capstone. (Picture Window Bks.).

Marquess, Dana. Night of the Lighted Freedom - A Firefly Fantasy. 2006. (ENG., Illus.). 32p. (J). 19.95 *(978-1-932278-06-4(0))* Mayhaven Publishing, Inc.

May, Eleanor. A Beach for Albert. Melmon, Deborah, illus. 2013. (Mouse Math Ser.). 32p. (J). (gr. -1-1). lib. bdg. 22.60 *(978-1-57565-530-7(6));* (J). pap. 7.99 *(978-1-57565-531-4(4),* b38f0cb2-7040-4d3e-87c6-7c42db43b2cb, Kane Press) Astra Publishing Hse.

—A Beach for Albert. 2018. (Mouse Math Ser.). (ENG.). 32p. (J). (gr. -1-1). lib. bdg. 34.28 *(978-1-4896-8285-7(6),* AV2 by Weigl) Weigl Pubs., Inc.

Mayer, Mercer. Just Grandma, Grandpa, & Me. 2016. (Little Critter Ser.). lib. bdg. 16.00 *(978-0-606-38482-7(0))* Turtleback.

—Just Grandma, Grandpa, & Me (Little Critter) 2016. (Pictureback(R) Ser.). (Illus.). 48p. (J). (gr. -1-2). 5.99 *(978-0-553-53986-8(8),* Random Hse. Bks. for Young Readers) Random Hse. Children's Bks.

McCarty, Peter. Hondo & Fabian. unabr. ed. 2006. (Illus.). (J). (gr. -1-3). 29.95 *(978-0-439-84906-7(3),* WHCD688) Weston Woods Studios, Inc.

McClure, Nikki. Waiting for High Tide. 2016. (ENG., Illus.). 48p. (J). (gr. k-2). 19.95 *(978-1-4197-1656-0(5),* 1090101, Abrams Bks. for Young Readers) Abrams, Inc.

McDonald, Kirsten. The Sandy Weekend, 1 vol. Meza, Erika, illus. 2016. (Carlos & Carmen Ser.). (ENG.). 32p. (J). (gr. -1-3). 32.79 *(978-1-62402-142-8(5),* 21551, Calico Chapter Bks) Magic Wagon.

McHeffey, Adam. Asiago, 0 vols. McHeffey, Adam, illus. 2012. (ENG., Illus.). 32p. (J). (gr. 1-3). 16.99 *(978-0-7614-6138-8(8),* 9780761461388, Two Lions) Amazon Publishing.

McNamara, Margaret. Summer Treasure: Ready-To-Read Level 1. Gordon, Mike, illus. 2012. (Robin Hill School Ser.). (ENG.). 32p. (J). (gr. -1-1). 17.99 *(978-1-4424-3646-6(8));* pap. 4.99 *(978-1-4424-3645-9(X))* Simon Spotlight. (Simon Spotlight).

Meadows, Daisy. Nicole the Beach Fairy. 2014. (Rainbow Magic — the Earth Fairies Ser.). lib. bdg. 14.75 *(978-0-606-35830-9(7))* Turtleback.

Meckel, Jamie & BeachHouse Publishing. Down at the Beach. 2011. (ENG.). 16p. (J). (gr. -1-1). bds. 7.95 *(978-1-933067-41-4(1))* Beachhouse Publishing, LLC.

Meister, Cari. Seaside Escape: A 4D Book. Burns, Heather, illus. 2018. (Three Horses Ser.). (ENG.). 56p. (J). (gr. k-2). pap. 4.95 *(978-1-5158-2953-9(7),* 138500); lib. bdg. 23.99 *(978-1-5158-2949-2(9),* 138496) Capstone. (Picture Window Bks.).

Merveille, David. Mr. Hulot at the Beach. 2016. (ENG., Illus.). 32p. (J). 18.95 *(978-0-7358-4254-0(X))* North-South Bks., Inc.

Miedoso, Andres. Surf's up, Creepy Stuff! Rivas, Victor, illus. 2018. (Desmond Cole Ghost Patrol Ser.: 3). (ENG.). 128p. (J). (gr. k-4). 17.99 *(978-1-5344-1802-8(4));* pap. 6.99 *(978-1-5344-1801-1(6))* Little Simon. (Little Simon).

Militello, Vincent. Nicholas the Naked Sicilian, & Other Stories. 2007. 140p. pap. 3.95 *(978-1-4259-6966-0(6))* AuthorHouse.

Miller, Suzanne. Pirates! That Is Who We Be! 2010. 28p. pap. 13.50 *(978-1-4490-6362-7(4))* AuthorHouse.

Mills-Darlow, Beryl C. My Beach Granny. 2012. 36p. pap. 14.50 *(978-1-61897-681-9(8),* Strategic Bk. Publishing) Strategic Book Publishing & Rights Agency (SBPRA).

Milord, Susan. Pebble: A Story about Belonging. Milord, Susan, illus. 2007. (ENG., Illus.). 32p. (J). (gr. -1-2). 15.99 *(978-0-06-085807-0(9),* HarperCollins) HarperCollins Pubs.

Montgomery, L. M. Along the Shore: Tales by the Sea. (YA). 22.95 *(978-0-8488-2655-0(8))* Amereon Ltd.

Moon, Jonny. The Beach Buoy, Book 5. 2011. (GUNK Aliens Ser.). (ENG., Illus.). 112p. (J). (gr. 2-4). 7.99 *(978-0-00-732616-7(5))* HarperCollins Pubs. Ltd. GBR. Dist: Independent Pubs. Group.

Moskowitz, Hannah. Invincible Summer. 2011. (ENG.). 288p. (YA). (gr. 9-18). pap. 9.99 *(978-1-4424-0751-0(4),* Simon Pulse) Simon Pulse.

Munsch, Robert. The Sandcastle Contest. 2007. 15.00 *(978-0-7569-7690-3(1))* Perfection Learning Corp.

Murphy, Stuart J. Camila y Su Equipo. 2012. (I See I Learn Ser.: 21). (Illus.). 32p. (J). (-k). 14.95 *(978-1-58089-490-6(9))* Charlesbridge Publishing, Inc.

—Camille's Team. 2011. (I See I Learn Ser.: 5). (Illus.). 32p. (J). (gr. -1-k). 14.95 *(978-1-58089-458-6(5));* pap. 6.95 *(978-1-58089-459-3(3))* Charlesbridge Publishing, Inc.

Myers, Matt. Hum & Swish. 2019. (Illus.). 40p. (J). (gr. -1-3). 18.99 *(978-0-8234-4286-7(1),* Neal Porter Bks) Holiday Hse., Inc.

Nesbit, E. Wet Magic. 2006. 188p. (gr. -1-7). 26.95 *(978-1-59818-174-6(2))* Aegypan.

Nicoll, David. Bean at the Beach. 2012. 24p. pap. 15.99 *(978-1-4691-7042-8(6))* Xlibris Corp.

Nugent, Cynthia. Fred & Pete at the Beach, 1 vol. 2009. (ENG., Illus.). 32p. (J). (gr. -1-k). 19.95 *(978-1-55469-126-5(5))* Orca Bk. Pubs. USA.

O'Connor, Jane. Fancy Nancy: Sand Castles & Sand Palaces. Glasser, Robin Preiss, illus. 2014. (Fancy Nancy Ser.). (ENG.). 24p. (J). (gr. -1-3). pap. 5.99 *(978-0-06-226954-6(2),* HarperFestival) HarperCollins Pubs.

—Sand Castles & Sand Palaces. 2014. (Fancy Nancy Picture Bks.). (J). lib. bdg. 14.75 *(978-0-606-36477-5(3))* Turtleback.

Olker, Constance. The Punctuation Pals Go to the Beach. Guzman, Minerva, illus. 2005. (Punctuation Pals Ser.). 36p. (J). per. 18.95 *(978-1-933449-12-8(8))* Nightengale Pr.

O'Reilly, Sean. Monster Beach, 1 vol. Arcana Studio Staff, illus. 2012. (Mighty Mighty Monsters Ser.). (ENG.). 48p. (J). (gr. 2-4). pap. 6.10 *(978-1-4342-4608-0(6),* 120596, Stone Arch Bks.) Capstone.

Pace, Anne Marie. Vampirina at the Beach-Vampirina Ballerina. 2017. (Vampirina Ser.: 3). (ENG., Illus.). 40p. (J). (gr. -1-k). 17.99 *(978-1-4847-7342-0(X),* Disney-Hyperion) Disney Publishing Worldwide.

S

Palka, Yvonne. Dragon Fire Ocean Mist. 2009. pap. 12.95 *(978-0-9817668-0-5(3))* Heartrock Pr.
Paquette, Ammi-Joan. The Tiptoe Guide to Tracking Mermaids. LeTourneau, Marie, illus. 2012. (ENG.). 32p. (J). (gr. k-5). 16.95 *(978-1-933718-59-0(5))* Tanglewood Pr.
Parish, Herman. Amelia Bedelia Chapter Book #7: Amelia Bedelia Sets Sail. Avril, Lynne, illus. 2015. (Amelia Bedelia Ser.). (ENG.). 160p. (J). (gr. 1-5). 15.99 *(978-0-06-233405-3(0))*; pap. 5.99 *(978-0-06-233404-6(2))* HarperCollins Pubs. (Greenwillow Bks.).
—Amelia Bedelia Digs in. 2018. (Amelia Bedelia Chapter Book Ser.: 12). (J). lib. bdg. 14.75 *(978-0-606-40061-9(3))* Turtleback.
Parr, todd. Otto Goes to the Beach. 2014. (Passport to Reading Level 1 Ser.). (ENG., Illus.). 32p. (J). (gr. -1-1). 4.99 *(978-0-316-24602-6(6))* Little, Brown Bks. for Young Readers.
Parvensky Barwell, Catherine A. Tommi Goes to the Beach, 4 vols. Barwell, Matthew W. & Parvensky, Mary T., eds. 2006. (Illus.). 40p. (J). *(978-0-9774409-2-4(3)*, TL003) ILT Publishing.
Patterson, Sandra Jean. Crabby Crab. 2006. bds. 12.95 *(978-1-59700-246-2(1))* Island Heritage Publishing.
Perkins, Lynne Rae. Secret Sisters of the Salty Sea. Perkins, Lynne Rae, illus. 2019. (ENG., Illus.). 256p. (J). (gr. 3-7). pap. 6.99 *(978-0-06-249967-7(X)*, Greenwillow Bks.) HarperCollins Pubs.
—Secret Sisters of the Salty Sea. 2018. (ENG., Illus.). 240p. (J). (gr. 3-7). 16.99 *(978-0-06-249966-0(1)*, Greenwillow Bks.) HarperCollins Pubs.
Perry, Robert. Down at the Seaweed Cafe. Guzek, Greta, illus. unabr. ed. 2010. (ENG.). 32p. (J). pap. 9.95 *(978-0-88971-246-1(8)*, d81e6a73-3fa8-4ade-abf2-e74b316542bc) Nightwood Editions CAN. Dist: Harbour Publishing Co., Ltd.
Pfister, Marcus. The Rainbow Fish Colors. 2013. (Rainbow Fish Ser.). (ENG., Illus.). 12p. (J). (gr. -1-k). bds. 7.95 *(978-0-7358-4147-5(0))* North-South Bks., Inc.
Pliscou, Lisa. Dude: Fun with Dude & Betty. Dunne, Tom, illus. 2011. (ENG.). 40p. (J). (gr. 1-3). 14.99 *(978-0-06-175690-0(3)*, HarperCollins) HarperCollins Pubs.
Pritelli, Maria Cristina, creator. Seaside Lullaby. 2018. 32p. (J). (gr. -1-1). 17.99 *(978-1-56846-328-5(6)*, 19705, Creative Editions) Creative Co., The.
Raven, Margot Theis. Circle Unbroken. Lewis, E. B., illus. 2007. (ENG.). 48p. (J). (gr. -1-3). per. 9.99 *(978-0-312-37603-1(0)*, 900048323) Square Fish.
Reasoner, Charles. Shapes at the Beach. Pitt, Sarah, illus. 2009. (3D Board Bks.). 12p. (J). (gr. -1-k). bds. 9.99 *(978-1-934650-36-3(6))* Just For Kids Pr., LLC.
Rebello, Kevin. Julia & Mckinley's Day at the Beach. 2009. 32p. pap. 12.99 *(978-1-4389-7330-2(6))* AuthorHouse.
Reid, Hunter. Beach Day! Hinton, Stephanie, illus. 2016. (Fluorescent Pop! Ser.). (ENG.). 14p. (J). (gr. -1-k). bds. 5.99 *(978-1-4998-0219-1(6))* Little Bee Books Inc.
Renaud, Anne. How the Sea Came to Marissa. Durland, Maud, illus. 2006. 32p. (J). *(978-1-58270-129-5(6))* Beyond Words Publishing, Inc.
Resnicoff, Stan. Stanley, the Seal of Approval. 2012. (ENG.). (J). pap. *(978-1-4675-1535-1(3))* Independent Pub.
Rey, Margret & Rey, H. A. Curious George Goes to the Beach. 2014. (Curious George 8x8 Ser.). (gr. k-3). lib. bdg. 13.55 *(978-0-613-21392-9(0))* Turtleback.
Reynolds Naylor, Phyllis. Roxie & the Hooligans at Buzzard's Roost. Boiger, Alexandra, illus. (ENG.). 208p. (J). (gr. 2-5). 2019. pap. 7.99 *(978-1-4814-3783-7(6))* 2018. 16.99 *(978-1-4814-3782-0(8))* Simon & Schuster Children's Publishing. (Atheneum Bks. for Young Readers).
Ricchiazzi, Lisa Gail. The Little Lost Seashell: (Never Lose Hope) 2011. (ENG.). 24p. (gr. -1). pap. 11.59 *(978-1-4269-6505-0(2))* Trafford Publishing.
Richburg, Sheila. The Story of Panhandle Pete Part One. 2010. 19p. 16.95 *(978-0-557-15382-4(4))* Lulu Pr., Inc.
Roberts, Roxanne. Angel Wings, Faery Dust & Other Magical Things: A Story about Merpeople. 2011. 24p. pap. 11.50 *(978-1-61204-588-7(X)*, Strategic Bk. Publishing) Strategic Book Publishing & Rights Agency (SBPRA).
Rockwell, Anne. At the Beach. Rockwell, Harlow & Rockwell, Lizzy, illus. 2014. (ENG.). 24p. (J). (gr. -1-3). 14.99 *(978-1-4814-1133-2(0)*, Aladdin) Simon & Schuster Children's Publishing.
—At the Beach. Rockwell, Harlow, illus. 2016. (ENG.). 24p. (J). (gr. -1-3). lib. bdg. 17.20 *(978-0-606-39423-9(0))* Turtleback.
Rogers, Lauren. Skyler & the Se. Sexton, Jessa, ed. Keaggy, Sarah, illus. 2012. 36p. pap. 8.00 *(978-0-9860150-1-4(6))* O'More Publishing.
Romolino, Kimberly. A Day at Sea. 2009. 15p. pap. 24.95 *(978-1-60813-803-6(8))* America Star Bks.
Rookie Reader Boxed Set: the Beach Box. 2008. (Rookie Reader Ser.). (ENG., Illus.). 88p. (J). (gr. k-3). 9.95 *(978-0-516-29687-6(6)*, Children's Pr.) Scholastic Library Publishing.
Rotner, Shelley. Senses at the Seashore. Rotner, Shelley, photos by. (Shelley Rotner's Early Childhood Library). (ENG., Illus.). 32p. (gr. -1-2). 2010. (J). pap. 8.99 *(978-0-7613-6530-3(3)*, 5739b8eb-3fd2-4581-9738-40913bdb4d7a, Millbrook Pr.) 2006. lib. bdg. 22.60 *(978-0-7613-2897-1(1))* Lerner Publishing Group.
Rouncville, Bibi. Sea Bugs & Moose Eggs. 2009. 52p. pap. 9.50 *(978-1-4357-4004-4(1))* Lulu Pr., Inc.
Rylant, Cynthia. The Bear. McDaniels, Preston, illus. (Lighthouse Family Ser.: 8). (ENG.). 48p. (J). (gr. 1-5). 2019. pap. 5.99 *(978-1-4814-6029-3(3))* 2018. 17.99 *(978-1-4814-6028-6(5))* Beach Lane Bks. (Beach Lane Bks.).
—The Octopus. McDaniels, Preston, illus. 2005. (Lighthouse Family Ser.: 5). (ENG.). 64p. (J). (gr. 1-5). 17.99 *(978-0-689-86246-5(6)*, Simon & Schuster Bks. For Young Readers) Simon & Schuster Bks. For Young Readers.
—The Otter. McDaniels, Preston, illus. 2016. (Lighthouse Family Ser.: 6). (ENG.). 48p. (J). (gr. 1-5). 17.99 *(978-1-4814-6045-3(5)*, Beach Lane Bks.) Beach Lane Bks.
—The Sea Lion. McDaniels, Preston, illus. (Lighthouse Family Ser.: 7). (ENG.). 48p. (J). (gr. 1-5). 2018. pap. 5.99 *(978-1-4814-6026-2(9))* 2017. 17.99 *(978-1-4814-6025-5(0))* Beach Lane Bks. (Beach Lane Bks.).
Santillo, LuAnn. The Snack Shack. Santillo, LuAnn, ed. 2003. (Half-Pint Kids Readers Ser.). (Illus.). 7p. (J). (gr. -1-1). pap. 1.00 *(978-1-59256-086-8(5))* Half-Pint Kids, Inc.
Sattler, Jennifer. Pig Kahuna Pirates! 2014. (Pig Kahuna Ser.). (ENG., Illus.). 32p. (J). E-Book 6.39 *(978-1-61963-203-5(9)*, Bloomsbury USA Childrens) Bloomsbury Publishing USA.
Schroder, Jack. A Fun Day at the Beach. 2005. 170p. (YA). per. 6.95 net. *(978-0-9763810-0-6(1))* Catalpa Pr.
Schroeder, Lisa. The Day Before. 2012. (ENG.). 336p. (YA). (gr. 9). pap. 12.99 *(978-1-4424-1744-1(7)*, Simon Pulse) Simon Pulse.
Schueler, M. A. Penny the Beach Westie Big Trouble for a Little Dog. 2009. 24p. pap. 16.50 *(978-1-60860-424-1(1)*, Eloquent Bks.) Strategic Book Publishing & Rights Agency (SBPRA).
Schwartz, Joanne. Pinny in Summer, 1 vol. Malenfant, Isabelle, illus. 2016. (ENG.). 32p. (J). (gr. -1-2). 16.95 *(978-1-55498-782-5(2))* Groundwood Bks. CAN. Dist: Publishers Group West (PGW).
—Town Is by the Sea, 1 vol. Smith, Sydney, illus. 2017. (ENG.). 52p. (J). (gr. k-4). 19.95 *(978-1-55498-871-6(3))* Groundwood Bks. CAN. Dist: Publishers Group West (PGW).
Scotton, Rob. A Whale of a Tale. 2013. (Splat the Cat: I Can Read Ser.). (J). lib. bdg. 13.55 *(978-0-606-31814-3(3))* Turtleback.
Seashore Touch & See Hi? 2004. (J). 11.95 *(978-0-89610-999-5(2))* Island Heritage Publishing.
Shernock, Judith. Sammi the Seahorse. 2012. 28p. pap. 15.99 *(978-1-4691-3293-8(1))* Xlibris Corp.
Shortcake 99. The Beach Day. 2011. 24p. pap. 13.00 *(978-1-4634-1337-8(8))* AuthorHouse.
Slate, Kelly. The Adventures of Santa Claws: At Amelia Island. 2012. 28p. pap. 16.99 *(978-1-4772-2093-1(3))* AuthorHouse.
Smith, Carrie. Going to the Beach: Small Book. 2004. (Shared Connections Ser.). (J). pap. *(978-1-4108-1639-9(7))* Benchmark Education Co.
Smith, John D. H. The Whale Whisperers, 1 vol. Smith, Anne, illus. 2009. 17p. pap. 24.95 *(978-1-60749-211-5(3))* America Star Bks.
Smith Matheson, Shirlee. Fastback Beach, 1 vol. 2003. (Orca Soundings Ser.). (ENG.). 128p. (YA). (gr. 8-12). pap. 9.95 *(978-1-55143-267-0(6))* Orca Bk. Pubs. USA.
Spinelli, Eileen. Summerhouse Time. Lew-Vriethoff, Joanne, illus. 2009. (ENG.). 224p. (J). (gr. 3-7). 8.99 *(978-0-440-42224-2(8)*, Yearling) Random Hse. Children's Bks.
Spinelli, Patti. Mackenzie & Emme Visit York Beach. Spinelli, Patti, illus. 2003. (Illus.). (J). *(978-0-9742328-0-5(7))* Spinelli, Patti.
Spohn, Kate. Turtle & Snake's Day at the Beach. Spohn, Kate, illus. 2004. (Puffin Easy-to-Read Ser.). (Illus.). 32p. (gr. k-3). 14.00 *(978-0-7569-2826-1(5))* Perfection Learning Corp.
Sprenger, Luke. Sommer in Canvas Bay. 2008. (GER.). 92p. pap. 13.95 *(978-1-4092-3213-1(1))* Lulu Pr., Inc.
Spurr, Elizabeth. At the Beach, 1 vol. Oliphant, Manelle, illus. 2013. 22p. (J). (gr. -1 — 1). bds. 6.99 *(978-1-56145-583-6(0))* Peachtree Publishing Co. Inc.
Stein, David Ezra. Ice Boy. 2017. (Illus.). 32p. (J). *(978-1-4063-7691-3(4))* Candlewick Pr.
Stella, Lennon & Stella, Maisy. In the Waves. Bjorkman, Steve, illus. 2015. (ENG.). 40p. (J). (gr. -1-3). 17.99 *(978-0-06-235939-1(8)*, HarperCollins) HarperCollins Pubs.
Stewart, Nancy. Bella Saves the Beach. Bell, Samantha, illus. 2013. 24p. 19.95 *(978-1-61633-370-6(7))*; pap. 11.95 *(978-1-61633-371-3(5))* Guardian Angel Publishing, Inc.
—One Pelican at a Time: A Story of the Gulf Oil Spill. Bell, Samantha, illus. 2011. 26p. (J). 19.95 *(978-1-61633-138-2(0))*; pap. 11.95 *(978-1-61633-139-9(9))* Guardian Angel Publishing, Inc.
Stine, R. L. Attack of the Jack. 2017. (Goosebumps SlappyWorld Ser.: 2). lib. bdg. 17.20 *(978-0-606-40169-2(5))* Turtleback.
—Attack of the Jack (Goosebumps SlappyWorld #2) 2017. (Goosebumps SlappyWorld Ser.: 2). (ENG.). 160p. (J). (gr. 3-7). pap. 7.99 *(978-1-338-06836-8(9)*, Scholastic Paperbacks) Scholastic, Inc.
Strasser, Todd & Thacker, Nola. The Shore: Shirt & Shoes Not Required; LB (Laguna Beach) 2011. (ENG.). 480p. (YA). (gr. 9). pap. 9.99 *(978-1-4424-1970-4(9)*, Simon Pulse) Simon Pulse.
Takhar, Jodi. Four Seasons of Fun. Takhar, Jodi & Jones, Paul, illus. 14p. (J). (gr. -1-3). 19.95 *(978-1-886000-02-5(6))* Takhar's, Jodi Spilt Milk Collection.
Tarshis, Lauren. I Survived the Shark Attacks of 1916. 2010. (I Survived Ser.: No. 2). lib. bdg. 14.75 *(978-0-606-23742-0(9))* Turtleback.
—I Survived the Shark Attacks of 1916 (I Survived #2) Dawson, Scott, illus. 2010. (I Survived Ser.: 2). (ENG.). 112p. (J). (gr. 2-5). pap. 5.99 *(978-0-545-20695-2(2)*, Scholastic Paperbacks) Scholastic, Inc.
Telma, Tante. Telma's Day at Magens Bay. 2012. 16p. pap. 15.99 *(978-1-4772-7776-8(5))* AuthorHouse.
Thrasher, Grady. Tim & Sally's Beach Adventure. Rabon, Elaine Hearn, illus. 2008. (ENG.). 48p. (J). (gr. -1-3). 18.95 *(978-1-58818-161-9(8))* Hill Street Pr., LLC.
Torres, J. Checkers & Dot at the Beach. Lum, J., illus. 2013. (Checkers & Dot Ser.: 4). 16p. (J). (— 1). bds. 7.95 *(978-1-77049-444-2(8)*, Tundra Bks.) Tundra Bks. CAN. Dist: Penguin Random Hse. LLC.
Tripp, Valerie. Camille's Mermaid Tale. Thai, Thu, illus. 2017. 100p. (J). *(978-1-5182-4321-9(5)*, American Girl) American Girl Publishing, Inc.
Tucker, Valerie Neil. The Hermit's Box. 2009. 36p. pap. 15.49 *(978-1-4490-2285-3(5))* AuthorHouse.
Tunks, Karyn. Jubilee!, 1 vol. Buckner, Julie, illus. 2012. (ENG.). 32p. (J). (gr. k-3). 16.99 *(978-1-58980-880-5(0)*, Pelican Publishing) Arcadia Publishing.
Twitty, Mary F. Ashley Visits Urchin Village. 2008. 92p. pap. 51.99 *(978-1-4363-5578-0(6))* Xlibris Corp.
Tyler, Jenny & Cartwright, S. Duck by the Sea. 2004. (SPA.). 6p. (J). vinyl bd. 7.95 *(978-0-7945-0569-1(4))* EDC Publishing.
Valentin, Karen. When Are We Going to the Beach? 2009. 32p. 6.95 *(978-1-60349-020-7(5)*, Marimba Bks.) Just Us Bks., Inc.
Van Dusen, Chris. Down to the Sea with Mr. Magee: (Kids Book Series, Early Reader Books, Best Selling Kids Books) 2006. (Mr. Magee Ser.). (ENG., Illus.). 36p. (J). (gr. -1-7). pap. 8.99 *(978-0-8118-5225-8(3))* Chronicle Bks. LLC.
Vasiliu, Mircea. A Day at the Beach. 2007. (Illus.). 36p. (J). 7.95 *(978-1-59091-068-9(0))* Eastern National.
Veranda, Molly. Molly & Tucker get Shanghaied. 2009. (ENG.). 41p. pap. 9.96 *(978-0-557-04210-4(0))* Lulu Pr., Inc.
Voake, Steve. Daisy Dawson at the Beach. Meserve, Jessica, illus. 2012. (Daisy Dawson Ser.: 4). (ENG.). 96p. (J). (gr. 1-4). pap. 5.99 *(978-0-7636-5946-2(0))* Candlewick Pr.
Wade, Judith. Faelen, the Horse from the Sea. 2007. 107p. (J). mass mkt. 5.99 *(978-0-9728958-5-9(X))* Riley Pr.
Wagner, Jenny. High Hopes on Sea. Rogers, Gregory, illus. 2005. (UQP Children's Fiction Ser.). 80p. (Orig.). (J). pap. *(978-0-7022-3525-2(3))* Univ. of Queensland Pr.
Waite, Lance. A Day with Dad at the Beach. 2008. (J). 17.99 *(978-1-60131-016-3(1)*, Parents Publishing Group) Big Tent Bks.
Walker, Anna. I Love Vacations. Walker, Anna, illus. 2011. (ENG., Illus.). 32p. (J). (gr. -1-1). 9.99 *(978-1-4169-8321-7(X)*, Simon & Schuster Bks. For Young Readers) Simon & Schuster Bks. For Young Readers.
Walker, Jorge L. Little Winston's Desire. 2011. (ENG.). 24p. pap. 9.49 *(978-1-4567-2396-5(0))* AuthorHouse.
Wallace, Nancy Elizabeth. Shells! Shells! Shells!, 0 vols. Wallace, Nancy Elizabeth, illus. 2013. (ENG.). 40p. (J). (gr. 1-3). pap. 9.99 *(978-1-4778-1679-0(8)*, 9781477816790, Two Lions) Amazon Publishing.
Webb, Holly. The Rescued Puppy. Williams, Sophy, illus. 2017. 124p. (J). *(978-1-5182-4904-4(3))* Tiger Tales.
Webb, Jane K. My Super Stupendous Day at the Beach. Cupolo, Eileen, illus. 2012. 24p. pap. 12.95 *(978-1-61493-044-0(9))* Peppertree Pr., The.
Wells, Carolyn. Marjorie at Seacote. 2011. 296p. 48.95 *(978-1-258-08998-6(X))* Literary Licensing, LLC.
—Marjorie at Seacote. 2006. 29.95 *(978-1-55742-656-7(2))*; pap. 14.95 *(978-1-55742-653-6(8))* Wildside Pr., LLC.
—Patty's Butterfly Days. 2005. 28.95 *(978-1-4218-0309-8(7)*, 1st World Library - Literary Society) 1st World Publishing, Inc.
Wen, Dref. Traeth Prysur. 2005.Tr. of Busy Beach. (WEL., Illus.). 12p. *(978-1-85596-661-1(1))* Dref Wen.
White, Amanda. Sand Sister. 2016. (ENG.). 32p. (J). (gr. -1-2). pap. 8.99 *(978-1-78285-279-7(4))* Barefoot Bks., Inc.
—Sand Sister. Morales, Yuyi, illus. 2004. (ENG.). 32p. (J). 16.99 *(978-1-84148-617-8(5))* Barefoot Bks., Inc.
White, Pam. Buddy Goes to the Beach. 2010. 20p. 12.50 *(978-1-4520-3065-4(0))* AuthorHouse.
Williams, Karen Lynn. A Beach Tail. Cooper, Floyd, illus. 2010. (ENG.). 32p. (J). (gr. -1-2). 17.99 *(978-1-59078-712-0(9)*, Astra Young Readers) Astra Publishing Hse.
Woodcock, Fiona. Hello. Woodcock, Fiona, illus. 2019. (ENG., Illus.). 40p. (J). (gr. -1-3). 17.99 *(978-0-06-264456-5(4)*, Greenwillow Bks.) HarperCollins Pubs.
Wright, Kiyah. Vacation Fun. 2011. 24p. pap. 14.95 *(978-1-4634-4055-8(3))* AuthorHouse.
Yasuda, Anita. The Beach Bandit, 1 vol. Harpster, Steve, illus. 2013. (Dino Detectives Ser.). (ENG.). 32p. (J). (gr. 1-2). pap. 5.95 *(978-1-4342-4830-5(5)*, 121749); lib. bdg. 22.65 *(978-1-4342-4154-2(8)*, 119898) Capstone. (Stone Arch Bks.).
Yoon, Salina. Penguin on Vacation. (Penguin Ser.). (ENG., Illus.). (J). (gr. -1-1). 2015. 34p. bds. 7.99 *(978-0-8027-3837-0(0)*, 900142737) 2013. 40p. 14.99 *(978-0-8027-3397-9(2)*, 900084821) Bloomsbury Publishing USA. (Bloomsbury USA Childrens).
Young, Ruth. Aunty Marmalade. 2009. 218p. pap. 13.78 *(978-1-60693-893-5(2)*, Eloquent Bks.) Strategic Book Publishing & Rights Agency (SBPRA).
Zadunajsky, Donna M. Tayla's Day at the Beach. Bicking, Judith, illus. 2013. (ENG.). 26p. pap. 6.99 *(978-1-938037-34-4(0))* Zadunajsky, Donna M.
Zeigler, Robbie. Down by the Se. 2011. 16p. pap. 13.99 *(978-1-4634-2056-7(0))* AuthorHouse.
Zolotow, Charlotte. The Seashore Book. Minor, Wendell, illus. 2017. 32p. (J). (-k). lib. bdg. 18.99 *(978-1-58089-787-7(8))* Charlesbridge Publishing, Inc.
—The Seashore Book. Minor, Wendell, illus. 2004. (Reading Rainbow Bks.). (gr. -1-3). 17.00 *(978-0-7569-4234-2(9))* Perfection Learning Corp.

SEASONS

see also names of the seasons, e.g. Autumn, etc.

Alary, Laura. Look! A Child's Guide to Advent & Christmas. Boyajian, Ann, illus. 2017. (ENG.). 32p. (J). (gr. -1-5). pap. 16.99 *(978-1-61261-866-1(9))* Paraclete Pr., Inc.
Aloian, Molly. How Do We Know It Is Fall? 2013. (Seasons Close-Up Ser.). (ENG., Illus.). 24p. (J). (gr. 2-2). pap. *(978-0-7787-0965-7(5))* Crabtree Publishing Co.
—How Do We Know It Is Spring? 2013. (ENG., Illus.). 24p. (J). *(978-0-7787-0959-6(0))*; (gr. 2-2). pap. *(978-0-7787-0963-3(9))* Crabtree Publishing Co.
—How Do We Know It Is Summer? 2013. (ENG., Illus.). 24p. (J). *(978-0-7787-0960-2(4))*; (gr. 2-2). pap. *(978-0-7787-0964-0(7))* Crabtree Publishing Co.
—How Do We Know It Is Winter? 2013. (ENG., Illus.). 24p. (J). *(978-0-7787-0962-6(0))*; (gr. 2-2). pap. *(978-0-7787-0966-4(3))* Crabtree Publishing Co.
—How Do We Know It's Fall? 2013. (ENG., Illus.). 24p. (J). *(978-0-7787-0961-9(2))* Crabtree Publishing Co.
Appleby, Alex. ¿Qué Sucede en Invierno? / What Happens in Winter?, 1 vol., Vol. 1. 2013. (Cuatro Estaciones Estupendas / Four Super Seasons Ser.). (SPA & ENG.). 24p. (J). (gr. k-k). 25.27 *(978-1-4824-0132-5(0)*, d8b53b9b-a8b9-4f7b-b6c0-b503bb196a6e) Stevens, Gareth Publishing LLLP.
—¿Qué Sucede en Otoño? / What Happens in Fall?, 1 vol., Vol. 1. 2013. (Cuatro Estaciones Estupendas / Four Super Seasons Ser.). (SPA & ENG.). 24p. (J). (gr. k-k). 25.27 *(978-1-4824-0101-1(0)*, 9853e31f-b81b-4f7c-a21b-890526796f76) Stevens, Gareth Publishing LLLP.
—¿Qué Sucede en Primavera? / What Happens in Spring?, 1 vol., Vol. 1. 2013. (Cuatro Estaciones Estupendas / Four Super Seasons Ser.). (SPA & ENG.). 24p. (J). (gr. k-k). 25.27 *(978-1-4824-0119-6(3)*, 3ce3c190-4f18-4c1f-b30b-50c350bb6fe4) Stevens, Gareth Publishing LLLP.
—¿Qué Sucede en Verano? / What Happens in Summer?, 1 vol., Vol. 1. 2013. (Cuatro Estaciones Estupendas / Four Super Seasons Ser.). (SPA & ENG.). 24p. (J). (gr. k-k). 25.27 *(978-1-4824-0128-8(2)*, e493c895-3347-4056-8e4d-deacb496bd98) Stevens, Gareth Publishing LLLP.
Aspen-Baxter, Linda & Kissock, Heather. Las Estaciones. 2012. (Mirando Al Cielo Ser.). (SPA., Illus.). 24p. (J). (gr. k-2). lib. bdg. 27.13 *(978-1-61913-217-7(6)*, AV2 by Weigl) Weigl Pubs., Inc.
Baker, Chris. A Year in Barrowswold Forest: Band 15/Emerald. 2017. (Collins Big Cat Ser.). (ENG.). 48p. (J). pap. 10.99 *(978-0-00-820886-8(7))* HarperCollins Pubs. Ltd. GBR. Dist: Independent Pubs. Group.
Barnham, Kay & Frost, Maddie. A Stroll Through the Seasons. 2018. (ENG., Illus.). 32p. (J). (gr. k-3). 10.99 *(978-1-4380-5041-6(0))* Sourcebooks, Inc.
Barraclough, Sue. Seasons, 1 vol. 2009. (Me & My World Ser.). (ENG., Illus.). 24p. (J). (gr. -1-2). pap. 9.15 *(978-1-60754-066-3(5)*, d41f6773-eea4-443d-8f45-a2945b6546ef); lib. bdg. 27.27 *(978-1-60754-059-5(2)*, 6ea20a10-bfed-486a-8100-96207a2d2f5e) Rosen Publishing Group, Inc., The. (Windmill Bks.).
Beckett, Sydney. My Favorite Season, 1 vol. 2012. (InfoMax Readers Ser.). (ENG., Illus.). 16p. (J). (gr. k-k). pap. 7.00 *(978-1-4488-8914-3(6)*, b56957f0-0829-4f26-9600-1ab2d449d39d, Rosen Classroom) Rosen Publishing Group, Inc., The.
Benchmark Education Company. Weather & Climate (Teacher Guide) 2005. *(978-1-4108-4635-8(0))* Benchmark Education Co.
Benchmark Education Company, LLC Staff, compiled by. Weather & Seasons. 2006. (J). 265.00 *(978-1-4108-7031-5(6))* Benchmark Education Co.
Bernay, Emma & Berne, Emma Carlson. The Seasons of the Year. Palin, Tim, illus. 2019. (Patterns of Time Ser.). (ENG.). 24p. (J). (gr. -1-2). 33.99 *(978-1-68410-410-9(6)*, 141220) Cantata Learning.
Branley, Franklyn M. Sunshine Makes the Seasons. Rex, Michael, illus. 2005. (Let's-Read-And-Find-Out Science 2 Ser.). (ENG.). 40p. (J). (gr. k-4). pap. 5.99 *(978-0-06-059205-9(2)*, Collins) HarperCollins Pubs.
—Sunshine Makes the Seasons. Rex, Michael, illus. 2016. (Let's-Read-And-Find-Out Science 2 Ser.). (ENG.). 40p. (J). (gr. -1-3). pap. 8.99 *(978-0-06-238209-2(8)*, HarperCollins) HarperCollins Pubs.
Branley, Franklyn Mansfield. Sunshine Makes the Seasons. Rex, Michael, illus. 2005. (Let's-Read-and-Find-Out-Science Ser.). (ENG.). 40p. (J). (gr. -1 — 1). 15.99 *(978-0-06-059203-5(6))* HarperCollins Pubs.
Braun, Eric. Curious Pearl Identifies the Reason for Seasons: 4D an Augmented Reality Science Experience. Dehennin, Stephanie, illus. 2017. (Curious Pearl, Science Girl 4D Ser.). (ENG.). 24p. (J). (gr. k-2). lib. bdg. 25.99 *(978-1-5158-1343-9(6)*, 135145, Picture Window Bks.) Capstone.
Brennan, Linda Crotta. Leaves Change Color. 2014. (Tell Me Why Library). (ENG., Illus.). 24p. (J). (gr. 2-5). 29.21 *(978-1-63188-008-7(X)*, 205439) Cherry Lake Publishing.
Bridge, Chris Helene. Spring Is Coming! 2018. (ENG., Illus.). 32p. (J). 19.95 *(978-1-942945-48-2(5)*, f8784901-b803-4cb9-94e3-3a165a836043) Night Heron Media.
Brown, Janet Allison & Brown, Janet Allison. Seasons, Vol. 4. 2005. (Our Seasons & Weather Ser.). (YA). (gr. k-3). 118.80 *(978-0-7368-4201-3(2)*, Pebble) Capstone.
Brown, Jeremy. God Makes the Seasons. 2011. 28p. pap. 14.93 *(978-1-4269-4946-3(4))* Trafford Publishing.
Burningham, John. Las Estaciones. (SPA., Illus.). (J). (gr. k-3). *(978-84-88342-14-0(4)*, KK7662) S.A. Kokinos ESP. Dist: Lectorum Pubns., Inc.
Capstone Press. First Graphics: Seasons, 1 vol. 2010. (First Graphics: Seasons Ser.). (ENG.). 32p. lib. bdg. 106.60 *(978-1-4296-5936-9(X))* Capstone.
Cardenas, Ernesto A. The Four Seasons of the Year. 2009. pap. 4.95 *(978-1-60698-092-7(0))* Milo Educational Bks. & Resources.
—Spring, Summer, Fall, & Winter. 2009. 19.95 *(978-1-60698-011-8(4))*; pap. 3.95 *(978-1-60698-009-5(2))* Milo Educational Bks. & Resources.
Carr, Aaron. Spring. 2013. 25.00 *(978-1-62127-493-3(4))* Weigl Pubs., Inc.
—Summer. 2013. 25.00 *(978-1-62127-494-0(2))* Weigl Pubs., Inc.
—Winter. 2013. pap. 17.95 *(978-1-62127-495-7(0))* Weigl Pubs., Inc.
Carroll. Lbd Gka Nf Fun for All Seasons. 2009. (C). pap. 8.53 *(978-1-4189-3337-1(6))* Rigby Education.
Ceanadach, Siusaidh. Let's Talk about Elements & the Pagan Wheel. 2013. (ENG., Illus.). 73p. (J). (gr. -1-12). pap. 9.95 *(978-1-78099-561-8(X)*, Moon Bks.) Hunt, John Publishing Ltd. GBR. Dist: National Bk. Network.
Chapman, Simon. In the African Bush: Band 08/Purple, Bd. 8. 2018. (Collins Big Cat Ser.). (ENG.). 24p. (J). pap. 7.99 *(978-0-00-823035-7(8))* HarperCollins Pubs. Ltd. GBR. Dist: Independent Pubs. Group.
Curious George Discovers the Seasons. 2016. (Curious George Ser.). (ENG., Illus.). 32p. (J). (gr. -1-3). pap. 6.99 *(978-0-544-78509-0(6)*, 1638633, Clarion Bks.) HarperCollins Pubs.
DeGezelle, Terri. Exploring the Seasons. 2012. (Exploring the Seasons Ser.). (ENG.). 24p. (gr. k-1). pap. 166.80 *(978-1-4296-8355-5(4)*, Capstone Pr.) Capstone.
deMarin, Layne. Desert Seasons. 2011. (Wonder Readers Fluent Level Ser.). (ENG.). 16p. (gr. -1-2). pap. 35.94 *(978-1-4296-8082-0(2)*, Capstone Pr.) Capstone.
Dinmont, Kerry. Nora's Busy Year: A Book about the Four Seasons. 2017. (My Day Readers Ser.). (ENG.). 24p. (J). (gr. -1-2). lib. bdg. 32.79 *(978-1-5038-2018-0(1)*, 211865) Child's World, Inc, The.
DK. Is It Warm Enough for Ice Cream? 2018. (ENG., Illus.). 18p. (J). (-k). bds. 9.99 *(978-1-4654-6786-7(6)*, DK Children) Dorling Kindersley Publishing, Inc.

—Weather & the Seasons. 2019. (Projects to Make & Do Ser.). (ENG., Illus.). 32p. (J). (-k). 8.99 *(978-1-4654-6649-5(5),* DK Children) Dorling Kindersley Publishing, Inc.

Dompierre, Judith E. No More Than Four of a Kind. 2012. 36p. pap. 24.95 *(978-1-4626-9329-0(6))* America Star Bks.

Dorling Kindersley Publishing Staff. Is It Warm Enough for Ice Cream? 2018. (ENG., Illus.). 18p. (J). bds. *(978-0-241-31305-3(8))* Dorling Kindersley Publishing, Inc.

Droop, Constanza. Que? Como? Por Que?: Las Estaciones del Ano. Caballero, D., tr. Droop, Constanza, illus. 2007. (Junior (Silver Dolphin) Ser.). (Illus.). 16p. (J). (gr. -1). *(978-970-718-492-3(2),* Silver Dolphin en Español) Advanced Marketing, S. de R. L. de C. V.

Duling, Kaitlyn. The Sun & Plant. 2019. (Power of the Sun Ser.). (ENG.). 32p. (gr. 3-3). 63.48 *(978-1-5026-4675-0(7))* Cavendish Square Publishing LLC.

—The Sun & Plants, 1 vol. 2019. (Power of the Sun Ser.). (ENG.). 32p. (gr. 3-3). pap. 11.58 *(978-1-5026-4674-3(9),* e40f5afa-98f9-4418-8fd5-4c3b2ef89b15) Cavendish Square Publishing LLC.

Eckart, Edana. Watching the Seasons. 2004. (Wel-Watching Nature Ser.). (J). 19.00 *(978-0-516-27600-7(X),* Children's Pr.) Scholastic Library Publishing.

—Welcome Books: Watching the Seasons. 2004. (Welcome Bks.). (ENG.). 24p. (J). (gr. -1-2). pap. 4.95 *(978-0-516-25937-6(7),* Children's Pr.) Scholastic Library Publishing.

Education.com. Celebrate the Seasons: A Workbook of Seasons, Holidays, Weather, & Time. 2015. (Dover Kids Activity Books: Nature Ser.). (ENG.). 128p. (J). (gr. -1-k). pap. 7.99 *(978-0-486-80257-2(4),* 802574) Dover Pubns., Inc.

Las Estaciones del Ano, 4 vols. 2006. (SPA.). (J). (gr. k-2). 69.08 *(978-0-8225-3322-1(7),* Ediciones Lerner) Lerner Publishing Group.

Evans, David & Williams, Claudette. Seasons & Weather. (Let's Explore Science Ser.). (Illus.). (J). 12.95 *(978-0-590-74592-5(1))* Scholastic, Inc.

Feeney, Stephanie. Sun & Rain: Exploring Seasons in Hawaii. 2007. (ENG., Illus.). 48p. (gr. -1-3). 15.99 *(978-0-8248-3088-5(1),* 2037) Univ. of Hawaii Pr.

Feldman, Thea. Kingfisher Readers L1: Seasons. 2013. (Kingfisher Readers Ser.). (ENG., Illus.). 32p. (J). (gr. k-3). pap. 3.99 *(978-0-7534-6898-2(0),* 900085129, Kingfisher) Roaring Brook Pr.

Ferguson, Gloria. What Season Is It? Weir, Carrie & Weir, Nolet, illus. Frigon, Kerry, photos by. 2011. 28p. pap. 24.95 *(978-1-4626-4136-9(9))* America Star Bks.

Ferris, Diane J. Weather Watcher. 2009. (Illus.). 20p. pap. 13.00 *(978-1-4490-1218-2(3))* AuthorHouse.

Fisher, Valorie. Everything I Need to Know Before I'm Five. Fisher, Valorie, illus. 2011. (Illus.). 40p. (J). (gr. k-k). 17.99 *(978-0-375-86865-8(8),* Schwartz & Wade Bks.) Random Hse. Children's Bks.

Fort, Holli, et al. Teachers' Favorites Fun Activities for Fall! Hamblin, George, illus. 2010. 96p. (J). *(978-1-4508-2765-2(9))* Publications International, Ltd.

The Four Seasons. 16.95 incl. audio compact disk *(978-0-9700489-5-0(5))* Little Fiddle Co., Inc., The.

The Four Seasons, 1 vol. 2015. (Our Wonderful World Ser.). 8p. (J). (gr. -1-1). pap. 9.35 *(978-1-5081-1226-6(6),* 2f97c8e1-ffa5-4afa-9c0a-b6beddd6399f); pap. 9.35 *(978-1-5081-1238-9(X),* 7eeda04c-05b7-4195-a4e8-dcc745b8db6a); pap. 9.35 *(978-1-5081-1244-0(4),* bc7e61ae-bee9-47ed-a730-580615548ecb); pap. 9.35 *(978-1-5081-1250-1(9),* e40d203d-7b21-4852-a012-b7549c5d078f); pap. 9.35 *(978-1-5081-1262-4(2),* 87d5c37b-aaf3-457a-9e04-45ab34bdb8eb) Rosen Publishing Group, Inc., The. (Rosen Classroom).

The Four Seasons: Las Cuatro Estaciones, 1 vol. 2015. (Our Wonderful World Ser.). (ENG & SPA.). 8p. (J). (gr. -1-1). pap. 9.35 *(978-1-5081-1256-3(8),* 88850be6-e035-4350-a23b-046c9e587e74, Rosen Classroom) Rosen Publishing Group, Inc., The.

Fun in Fall, 12 vols. 2014. (Fun in Fall Ser.). (ENG.). 24p. (J). (gr. k-k). lib. bdg. 145.62 *(978-1-4824-1631-2(X),* 77b6a4af-7066-4d62-8412-acf48f853690) Stevens, Gareth Publishing LLLP.

George, Jean Craighead. Spring Moon. 2003. (J). (gr. 3-7). 20.75 *(978-0-8446-7242-7(4))* Smith, Peter Pub., Inc.

Gibbons, Gail. The Reasons for Seasons (New & Updated Edition) 2019. (Illus.). 32p. (J). (gr. -1-3). 18.99 *(978-0-8234-4273-7(X));* pap. 8.99 *(978-0-8234-4272-0(1))* Holiday Hse., Inc.

Gladstone, James. Turtle Pond. Reczuch, Karen, illus. 2018. (ENG.). 32p. E-Book *(978-1-55498-911-9(6))* Groundwood Bks.

Glaser, Linda. It's Fall! Swan, Susan, illus. 2003. (Celebrate the Seasons Ser.). (ENG.). 32p. (J). (gr. k-3). pap. 7.99 *(978-0-7613-1342-7(7),* 4690b963-35b0-429f-ad88-437697692864, First Avenue Editions) Lerner Publishing Group.

Gold, Kimberley. Four Seasons. (Flip Flap Fun Book Ser.). (Illus.). 10p. (J). bds. *(978-2-89393-934-6(1))* Phidal Publishing, Inc./Editions Phidal, Inc.

Green, Jen. Weather & Seasons, 1 vol. 2007. (Our Earth Ser.). (ENG., Illus.). 24p. (J). (gr. 2-3). lib. bdg. 26.27 *(978-1-4042-4272-2(4),* 292c8d5e-5eb9-4a04-ad80-3f6d4410b662) Rosen Publishing Group, Inc., The.

Guy, Ginger Foglesong. Dias y Dias/Days & Days: Bilingual English-Spanish. Moreno, Rene King, illus. 2019. (ENG.). 40p. (J). (gr. -1-3). 17.99 *(978-0-06-173182-2(X),* Greenwillow Bks.) HarperCollins Pubs.

Hansen, Amy S. Where Does the Sun Go at Night? An Earth Science Mystery, 1 vol. Scott, Korey, illus. 2011. (First Graphics: Science Mysteries Ser.). (ENG.). 24p. (J). (gr. k-3). pap. 6.29 *(978-1-4296-7176-7(9),* 116796) Capstone.

—Where Does the Sun Go at Night? An Earth Science Mystery. Scott, Korey, illus. 2011. (First Graphics: Science Mysteries Ser.). (ENG.). 24p. (J). (gr. 1-2). pap. 38.74 *(978-1-4296-7180-4(7),* 16734) Capstone.

Helenek, Sophie. My First Book FRUITS: GOLD Mom's Choice Awards. 2014. (My First Book Ser.). (ENG., Illus.). 16p. (J). (gr. -1-k). bds. 5.99 *(978-0-9894505-0-8(3))* Nursery Bks.

Heuninck, Ronald. Rain or Shine, 1 vol. Heuninck, Ronald, illus. Orig. Title: Buiten Spelen. (ENG., Illus.). 12p. (J). 5.50 *(978-0-86315-089-0(6),* 20269) Floris Bks. GBR. Dist: Gryphon Hse., Inc.

—Rain or Shine, 40 vols. 2nd rev. ed. 2014. Orig. Title: Buiten Spelen. (Illus.). 14p. (J). 9.95 *(978-1-78250-044-5(8))* Floris Bks. GBR. Dist: Consortium Bk. Sales & Distribution.

Hibbert, Clare. My Busy Year. Raga, Silvia, illus. 2011. (Busy Times Ser.). 24p. (J). (gr. -1-k). lib. bdg. 25.65 *(978-1-60753-103-6(8))* Amicus Learning.

Hirschi, Ron. Winter Is for Whales: A Book of Hawaiian Seasons. Green, Yuko, illus. 2007. (ENG.). 36p. (J). (gr. -1-3). *(978-1-59700-504-3(5))* Island Heritage Publishing.

Hudson, Cheryl Willis. Book of Seasons. Simpson, Howard, illus. (Afro-Bets Ser.). (J). pap. 4.95 *(978-0-940975-15-6(7))* Just Us Bks., Inc.

Hunt, Jeanne. Celebrating Saints & Seasons: Hundreds of Activities for Catholic Children. 2010. (ENG.). 192p. pap. 15.99 *(978-0-86716-959-1(1))* Franciscan Media.

Jackson, Ellen B. The Spring Equinox: The Greening of the Earth. 2003. (Illus.). 32p. (J). (gr. 3-6). pap. 7.95 *(978-0-7613-1963-2(2),* Millbrook Pr.) Lerner Publishing Group.

James, Wayan. Daylight in Winter, Summer, Fall, & Spring, 1 vol. 2016. (Rosen REAL Readers: STEM & STEAM Collection). (ENG.). 12p. (gr. 1-2). pap. 6.33 *(978-1-5081-2446-7(9),* 9c0bbfb3-395b-40a5-aa65-a581288bffd4, Rosen Classroom) Rosen Publishing Group, Inc., The.

Johnson, T. Seasons of the Year. 2010. 16p. (J). pap. 13.95 *(978-1-4327-5070-1(4))* Outskirts Pr., Inc.

Jones, Tammy. Look at the Weather. 2009. (Sight Word Readers Set A Ser.). (J). *(978-1-60719-140-7(7))* Newmark Learning LLC.

Kalman, Bobbie. ¿Qué Es el Tiempo? 2009. (SPA.). 24p. (J). *(978-0-7787-8703-7(6));* pap. *(978-0-7787-8742-6(7))* Crabtree Publishing Co.

—What Time Is It? 2008. (Looking at Nature Ser.). (ENG., Illus.). 24p. (J). (gr. -1-2). pap. *(978-0-7787-3345-4(9));* lib. bdg. *(978-0-7787-3325-6(4))* Crabtree Publishing Co.

—Which Season Is It? 2011. (ENG.). 16p. (J). *(978-0-7787-9553-7(5));* pap. *(978-0-7787-9578-0(0))* Crabtree Publishing Co.

Kalman, Bobbie & MacAulay, Kelley. Changing Seasons, 1 vol. 2005. (ENG., Illus.). 32p. (J). pap. *(978-0-7787-2309-7(7))* Crabtree Publishing Co.

Kelley, K. C. Seasons. 2018. (Spot Awesome Nature Ser.). (ENG.). 16p. (J). (gr. -1-2). pap. 7.99 *(978-1-68152-245-6(4),* 14824) Amicus.

Kissock, Heather. Seasons. 2011. (J). 27.13 *(978-1-61690-956-7(0)); (978-1-61690-602-3(2))* Weigl Pubs., Inc.

Kniffke, Sophie, et al. El Tiempo. (Coleccion Mundo Maravilloso).Tr. of Seasons & Weather. (SPA., Illus.). 40p. (J). (gr. 2-4). *(978-84-348-3470-5(7),* SM5473) SM Ediciones.

Lane, Bonnie. Bob the Inchworm & the Four Seasons. 2009. 20p. pap. 11.00 *(978-1-4389-9833-6(3))* AuthorHouse.

Latta, Sara L. Why Is It Fall?, 1 vol. 2012. (Why Do We Have Seasons? Ser.). (ENG., Illus.). 24p. (gr. k-2). pap. 10.35 *(978-1-59845-388-1(2),* 9053c121-33da-4fe3-9f7e-e3f42bdee3ab, Enslow Elementary) Enslow Publishing, LLC.

—Why Is It Spring?, 1 vol. 2012. (Why Do We Have Seasons? Ser.). (ENG., Illus.). 24p. (gr. k-2). 25.27 *(978-0-7660-3986-5(2),* ee79cb96-5d69-4305-8286-91f597a2d7e0); pap. 10.35 *(978-1-59845-389-8(0),* 482a48cf-0736-49d7-81d6-82605ae602da, Enslow Elementary) Enslow Publishing, LLC.

—Why Is It Summer?, 1 vol. 2012. (Why Do We Have Seasons? Ser.). (ENG., Illus.). 24p. (gr. k-2). pap. 10.35 *(978-1-59845-390-4(4),* aab9d43d-370e-4c92-99c6-11018ca4bca1, Enslow Elementary) Enslow Publishing, LLC.

—Why Is It Winter?, 1 vol. 2012. (Why Do We Have Seasons? Ser.). (ENG., Illus.). 24p. (gr. k-2). 25.27 *(978-0-7660-3988-9(9),* db8e83fd-6c54-419a-a375-58ee8ee4bc33); pap. 10.35 *(978-1-59845-391-1(2),* 6815eee9-38c1-4c79-8926-22e29bbefa47, Enslow Elementary) Enslow Publishing, LLC.

LernerClassroom Editors. First Step Nonfiction-Seasons Teaching Guide. 2009. pap. 7.95 *(978-0-8225-5628-2(6))* Lerner Publishing Group.

Lin, Grace & McKneally, Ranida T. Our Seasons. Lin, Grace, illus. 2007. (ENG., Illus.). 32p. (J). (gr. k-3). pap. 7.95 *(978-1-57091-361-7(7))* Charlesbridge Publishing, Inc.

Linde, Barbara M. Weather & Climate. 2005. (J). pap. *(978-1-4108-4587-0(7))* Benchmark Education Co.

Linus, Benjamin. Spring, Summer, Fall, Winter, 1 vol. 2012. (InfoMax Readers Ser.). (ENG., Illus.). 16p. (J). (gr. k-k). pap. 7.00 *(978-1-4488-8959-4(6),* f16a02c6-6a37-47ac-84a9-af37bb8409e4, Rosen Classroom) Rosen Publishing Group, Inc., The.

Lucas, Diane & Searle, Ken. Walking with the Seasons in Kakadu. 2005. (ENG., Illus.). 32p. (J). (gr. 2-4). pap. 12.95 *(978-1-74114-471-0(X))* Allen & Unwin AUS. Dist: Independent Pubs. Group.

MacDonald, Margaret. What Season Is It? 2011. (Learn-Abouts Ser.). (Illus.). 16p. (J). pap. 7.95 *(978-1-59920-617-2(X))* Black Rabbit Bks.

Manushkin, Fran. Katie Woo Spring 2010, 6 vols., Set. Lyon, Tammie, illus. Incl. Best Season Ever. lib. bdg. 21.32 *(978-1-4048-5730-8(3),* 102308); Katie Goes Camping. lib. bdg. 21.32 *(978-1-4048-5731-5(1),* 102309); Katie in the Kitchen. lib. bdg. 21.32 *(978-1-4048-5724-7(9),* 102301); Make-Believe Class. lib. bdg. 21.32 *(978-1-4048-5732-2(X),* 102311); Nervous Night. lib. bdg. 21.32 *(978-1-4048-5725-4(7),* 102302); (J). (gr. k-2). (Katie Woo Ser.). (ENG., Illus.). 32p. 2010. 127.92 o.p. *(978-1-4048-5973-9(X),* 13889, Picture Window Bks.) Capstone.

Markovics, Joyce L. Los Colores de Las Estaciones: Cómo Cambian. 2014. (Los Colores Cuentan una Historia Ser.). (SPA.). 24p. (J). (gr. -1-3). lib. bdg. 23.93 *(978-1-62724-469-5(7))* Bearport Publishing Co., Inc.

—The Seasons' Colors: How They Change. 2015. (Illus.). 24p. (J). lib. bdg. 26.99 *(978-1-62724-327-8(5))* Bearport Publishing Co., Inc.

Maskell, Hazel. A Year in Nature: A Carousel Book of the Seasons. Taylor, Eleanor, illus. 2018. (ENG.). 8p. (J). (gr. 1-4). 21.99 *(978-1-78627-306-2(3),* King, Laurence Publishing) Orion Publishing Group, Ltd. GBR. Dist: Hachette Bk. Group.

Meachen Rau, Dana. Las Estaciones / Seasons, 1 vol. 2010. (Los Ciclos de la Naturaleza / Nature's Cycles Ser.). (ENG & SPA.). 32p. (gr. 1-2). lib. bdg. 25.50 *(978-0-7614-4791-7(1),* 865814af-bc63-4bda-9cba-f3553e601c26) Cavendish Square Publishing LLC.

—Seasons, 1 vol. 2010. (Nature's Cycles Ser.). (ENG.). 32p. (gr. 1-2). 25.50 *(978-0-7614-4098-7(4),* 38183a44-2664-46df-8a69-0808a7042d24) Cavendish Square Publishing LLC.

—Space & Time, 1 vol. 2009. (Earth Matters Ser.). (ENG.). 32p. (gr. 1-2). pap. 9.23 *(978-0-7614-3573-0(5),* e4668759-d4ab-49ff-a79f-c0f71b32a844); lib. bdg. 25.50 *(978-0-7614-3049-0(0),* 91797fe1-a50e-4ea7-b87b-7e4d7caab1a8) Cavendish Square Publishing LLC.

—El Tiempo y el Espacio / Space & Time, 1 vol. 2010. (Nuestro Planeta Es Importante / Earth Matters Ser.). (ENG & SPA.). 32p. (gr. 1-2). lib. bdg. 25.50 *(978-0-7614-3496-2(8),* 363b2c2d-4381-40c1-8cc1-c313d066b158) Cavendish Square Publishing LLC.

—El Tiempo y el Espacio (Space & Time), 1 vol. 2010. (Nuestro Planeta Es Importante (Earth Matters) Ser.). (SPA.). 32p. (gr. 1-2). lib. bdg. 25.50 *(978-0-7614-3470-2(4),* 2f501a84-2a44-4e71-b2bd-84314a5f4c7d) Cavendish Square Publishing LLC.

Meister, Cari. First Graphics - Seasons, Set. Lingenfelter, Jim, illus. Incl. Summer Is Super. lib. bdg. 24.65 *(978-1-4296-4730-4(2),* 103274); Winter Is Wonderful. lib. bdg. 24.65 *(978-1-4296-4732-8(9),* 103276); (Illus.). (J). (gr. 1-3). (First Graphics: Seasons Ser.). (ENG.). 24p. 2010. 98.60 o.p. *(978-1-4296-4733-5(7),* 169325) Capstone.

Miller, Derek L. Earth, Sun, & Moon: Cyclic Patterns of Lunar Phases, Eclipses, & the Seasons, 1 vol. 2016. (Space Systems Ser.). (ENG., Illus.). 112p. (J). (gr. 8-8). 44.50 *(978-1-5026-2291-4(2),* 57747697-6be6-413c-89a6-556ec9ddfb6e) Cavendish Square Publishing LLC.

Mills, Nathan & Rodgers, Katherine. What Season Is It?, 1 vol. 2012. (Rosen Readers Ser.). (ENG., Illus.). 16p. (J). (gr. k-k). pap. 7.00 *(978-1-4488-8695-1(3),* cd056a02-9366-4711-a5e6-3d5e754caf76, Rosen Classroom) Rosen Publishing Group, Inc., The.

Moon, Walt K. ¡el Otoño Es Divertido! (Fall Is Fun!) 2017. (Bumba Books (r) en Español — Diviértete con Las Estaciones (Season Fun) Ser.). (SPA., Illus.). 24p. (J). (gr. -1-1). 26.65 *(978-1-5124-2860-5(4),* 47ac3250-e64d-4611-803f-b21a06bc995e, Ediciones Lerner) Lerner Publishing Group.

—¡el Verano Es Divertido! (Summer Is Fun!) 2017. (Bumba Books (r) en Español — Diviértete con Las Estaciones (Season Fun) Ser.). (SPA., Illus.). 24p. (J). (gr. -1-1). 26.65 *(978-1-5124-2862-9(0),* 1353f998-bcca-449a-968a-524c8282993d, Ediciones Lerner) Lerner Publishing Group.

—Fall Is Fun! 2016. (Bumba Books (r) — Season Fun Ser.). (ENG., Illus.). 24p. (J). (gr. -1-1). 26.65 *(978-1-5124-1409-7(3),* 3a04ed47-5fb1-4919-a76e-49e343e5221d, Lerner Pubns.) Lerner Publishing Group.

—¡la Primavera Es Divertida! (Spring Is Fun!) 2017. (Bumba Books (r) en Español — Diviértete con Las Estaciones (Season Fun) Ser.). (SPA., Illus.). 24p. (J). (gr. -1-1). 26.65 *(978-1-5124-2861-2(2),* 4b55454e-9e54-4ab8-a9d8-fc24b45cf0dd, Ediciones Lerner) Lerner Publishing Group.

—Spring Is Fun! 2016. (Bumba Books (r) — Season Fun Ser.). (ENG., Illus.). 24p. (J). (gr. -1-1). 26.65 *(978-1-5124-1411-0(5),* fbacb6ce-d925-4510-94e7-50bb06305071, Lerner Pubns.) Lerner Publishing Group.

Morgan, Sally. Seasons. 2011. (Earth Cycles Ser.). 32p. (YA). (gr. 3-6). lib. bdg. 28.50 *(978-1-59920-526-7(2))* Black Rabbit Bks.

Muller, Gerda. The Gerda Muller Seasons Gift Collection: Spring, Summer, Autumn & Winter, 4 vols. 2018. (Seasons Board Bks.). (Illus.). 48p. 30.00 *(978-1-78250-473-3(7))* Floris Bks. GBR. Dist: Consortium Bk. Sales & Distribution.

Murray, Julie. Fall, 1 vol. 2015. (Seasons Ser.). (ENG., Illus.). 24p. (J). (gr. -1-2). 31.36 *(978-1-62970-919-2(0),* 18296, Abdo Kids) ABDO Publishing Co.

—Spring, 1 vol. 2015. (Seasons Ser.). (ENG., Illus.). 24p. (J). (gr. -1-2). 31.36 *(978-1-62970-920-8(4),* 18298, Abdo Kids) ABDO Publishing Co.

—Summer, 1 vol. 2015. (Seasons Ser.). (ENG., Illus.). 24p. (J). (gr. -1-2). 31.36 *(978-1-62970-921-5(2),* 18300, Abdo Kids) ABDO Publishing Co.

—Winter, 1 vol. 2015. (Seasons Ser.). (ENG., Illus.). 24p. (J). (gr. -1-2). 31.36 *(978-1-62970-922-2(0),* 18302, Abdo Kids) ABDO Publishing Co.

My First Book of Seasons. (Butterfly Bks.). (ARA., Illus.). (J). 14.95 *(978-0-86685-711-6(7))* International Bk. Ctr., Inc.

Nelson, Robin. Estaciones (Seasons) 2012. (Mi Primer Paso Al Mundo Real — Descubriendo Los Ciclos de la Naturaleza (First Step Nonfiction — Discovering Nature's Cycles) Ser.). (SPA., Illus.). 24p. (J). (gr. k-2). pap. 6.99 *(978-0-7613-9357-3(9),* 64ec8efa-0487-42e3-bb5f-1c4d0cfb2c16, Ediciones Lerner) Lerner Publishing Group.

—Seasons. 2010. (First Step Nonfiction — Discovering Nature's Cycles Ser.). (gr. k-2). (ENG., Illus.). 24p. (J). pap. 6.99 *(978-0-7613-5684-4(3),* bb8b1803-cde2-4be6-941d-90a8c3a8e452); pap. 33.92 *(978-0-7613-6916-5(3))* Lerner Publishing Group.

Nichols, Catherine. An Arctic Year, 1 vol. 2003. (We Can Read about Nature! Ser.). (ENG., Illus.). 32p. (gr. 1-2). 25.50 *(978-0-7614-1430-8(4),* a925ab7a-2859-4ad6-99f8-5a230ceb9cda) Cavendish Square Publishing LLC.

O'Mara, Mary. Monsoon! An Extreme Weather Season, 1 vol. 2009. (Science Kaleidoscope Ser.). (ENG.). 32p. (J). (gr. 4-4). lib. bdg. 28.93 *(978-1-4358-2988-6(3),* a111e878-8a86-49c5-ba2b-b2d3c425b414, PowerKids Pr.) Rosen Publishing Group, Inc., The.

Owen, Ruth. What's the Season? 2017. (Get Started with STEM Ser.). (ENG., Illus.). 32p. (J). (gr. k-3). 9.99 *(978-1-78856-122-8(8),* 7f585476-e554-4265-b054-ff4621235280) Ruby Tuesday Books Limited GBR. Dist: Lerner Publishing Group.

Pebble Books: Our Seasons & Weather. 2005. (YA). (gr. k-3). 712.80 *(978-0-7368-4219-8(5),* Pebble) Capstone.

Pendergast, George. A Year of Seasons, 1 vol. 2015. (Cycles in Nature Ser.). (ENG., Illus.). 24p. (J). (gr. 1-2). lib. bdg. 24.27 *(978-1-4824-1654-1(9),* bb89c215-9098-495f-8027-3358f8510d0f) Stevens, Gareth Publishing LLLP.

Perez, Marlene. Colors of the Seasons. 2004. (Shared Connections Ser.). (J). pap. *(978-1-4108-1628-3(1))* Benchmark Education Co.

—Colors of the Seasons (Big Book) 2004. (Shared Connections Ser.). (J). pap., instr.'s gde. ed. 27.00 *(978-1-4108-1604-7(4))* Benchmark Education Co.

Peters, Katie. We Like the Summer. 2019. (Seasons All Around Me (Pull Ahead Readers — Nonfiction) Ser.). (ENG., Illus.). 16p. (J). (gr. -1-1). pap. 8.99 *(978-1-5415-7346-8(3),* 58d5867c-6574-4f91-bb56-574cd3e7e71a, Lerner Pubns.) Lerner Publishing Group.

—Winter Fun. 2019. (Seasons All Around Me (Pull Ahead Readers — Nonfiction) Ser.). (ENG., Illus.). 16p. (J). (gr. -1-1). pap. 8.99 *(978-1-5415-7347-5(1),* eeaed2e3-0b79-4877-9525-e3ae86394391); lib. bdg. 27.99 *(978-1-5415-5869-4(3),* 177f8cda-46f2-4478-9683-55e02492ae7c) Lerner Publishing Group. (Lerner Pubns.).

Powell, Jillian. Projects with Weather & Seasons, 1 vol. 2014. (Make & Learn Ser.). (ENG., Illus.). 32p. (J). (gr. 4-4). lib. bdg. 29.27 *(978-1-4777-7181-5(6),* 2f54b9ed-114d-48e3-a826-76e46cead893, PowerKids Pr.) Rosen Publishing Group, Inc., The.

Priddy, Roger. Bright Baby Touch & Feel Fall. 2010. (Bright Baby Touch & Feel Ser.). (ENG., Illus.). 10p. (J). (gr. -1 — 1). bds. 5.99 *(978-0-312-50922-4(7),* 900070097) St. Martin's Pr.

Provensen, Alice & Provensen, Martin. A Book of Seasons. 32p. (J). Random Hse. Children's Bks.

Radtke, Becky J. Four Seasons of Fun Activity Book. 2013. (ENG.). 48p. (J). (gr. 1-4). pap. 4.99 *(978-0-486-49894-2(8))* Dover Pubns., Inc.

Randolph, Joanne. All about the Seasons. (It's about Time Ser.). 24p. (gr. 1-1). 2009. 42.50 *(978-1-61513-633-9(9),* PowerKids Pr.) 2007. (ENG., Illus.). (J). lib. bdg. 26.27 *(978-1-4042-3768-1(2),* 5bc8ded1-a0e9-4987-9aa1-e925237a1750) Rosen Publishing Group, Inc., The.

—All about the Seasons/Las Estaciones. 2009. (It's about Time/Los libros del tiempo Ser.). (ENG & SPA.). 24p. (gr. 1-1). 42.50 *(978-1-61513-629-2(0),* Editorial Buenas Letras) Rosen Publishing Group, Inc., The.

—All about the Seasons/Las Estaciones, 1 vol. Brusca, Maria Cristina, tr. 2007. (It's about Time / Los Libros Del Tiempo Ser.). (ENG & SPA., Illus.). 24p. (J). (gr. 1-1). lib. bdg. 26.27 *(978-1-4042-7629-1(7),* d7934608-b9b2-4f32-a868-a819127930a0) Rosen Publishing Group, Inc., The.

Rice, Dona Herweck. Living in Sunlight Extremes. rev. ed. 2019. (Smithsonian: Informational Text Ser.). (ENG.). 32p. (J). (gr. 2-3). pap. 10.99 *(978-1-4938-6666-3(4))* Teacher Created Materials, Inc.

Rice, William. The Seasons, 1 vol. rev. ed. (Science: Informational Text Ser.). (ENG., Illus.). 24p. (gr. 1-2). 2015. lib. bdg. 22.96 *(978-1-4938-1156-4(8))* 2014. (J). pap. 9.99 *(978-1-4807-4569-8(3))* Teacher Created Materials, Inc.

Richard, Orlin. Investigating Seasons. 2015. (Searchlight Books (tm) — What Are Earth's Cycles? Ser.). (ENG., Illus.). 40p. (J). (gr. 3-5). 30.65 *(978-1-4677-8059-9(6),* d26b7ac3-4da1-4e83-ab2f-793026ffa3ac, Lerner Pubns.) Lerner Publishing Group.

Rideout, Flora. Mona Nantow, 1 vol. 2016. (ENG., Illus.). 32p. (J). 10.95 *(978-1-926506-02-9(2),* 21095d79-3920-4671-8141-b46e436b9310) Pemmican Pubns., Inc. CAN. Dist: Firefly Bks., Ltd.

Rigby Education Staff. Discovery World Yel Seasons. (Discovery World Ser.). (Illus.). 12p. (gr. k-1). 23.00 *(978-0-7635-2694-8(0))* Rigby Education.

Rissman, Rebecca. Seasons, 1 vol. 2013. (Picture This! Ser.). (ENG.). 24p. (J). (gr. -1-k). pap. 9.95 *(978-1-4109-5257-8(6),* Raintree) Capstone.

Robinson, Julie. Seasons in Our Garden. Lindsay, Pattie, illus. 2017. 28p. (J). spiral bd. *(978-0-692-71414-0(6))* Robinson, Julia.

Rockwell, Anne. Four Seasons Make a Year. Halsey, Megan, illus. 2004. (ENG.). 32p. (J). (gr. k-3). 17.99 *(978-0-8027-8883-2(1),* 900032718, Bloomsbury USA Childrens) Bloomsbury Publishing USA.

Rookie Ready to Learn - Seasons & Weather, 5 vols., Set. Incl. Animal Babies. Hamsa, Bobbie. Dunnington, Tom, illus. 40p. lib. bdg. 23.00 *(978-0-531-25640-4(5));* Going to the Beach. Kittinger, Jo S. Warren, Shari, illus. 32p. lib. bdg. 23.00 *(978-0-531-25641-1(3));* Pumpkin Fever. Simon, Charnan. Bryan-Hunt, Jan, illus. 40p. lib. bdg. 23.00 *(978-0-531-25643-5(X));* Snow Joe. Greene, Carol. Sharp, Paul, illus. 40p. lib. bdg. 23.00 *(978-0-531-25644-2(8));* (J). (gr. -1-k). (Rookie Ready to Learn Ser.). 2011. Set lib. bdg. 115.00 *(978-0-531-26724-0(5),* Children's Pr.) Scholastic Library Publishing.

Rustad, Martha E. H. Diversión con Calabazas en Otoño (Fall Pumpkin Fun) Enright, Amanda, illus. 2019. (Diversión en Otoño (Fall Fun) (Early Bird Stories (tm) en Español) Ser.). (SPA.). 24p. (J). (gr. k-2). pap. 8.99 *(978-1-5415-4539-7(7),* c59b7691-7b94-48bd-829a-46981b248a67); lib. bdg. 29.32 *(978-1-5415-4083-5(2),* 2673506f-7186-4461-962e-aee818da3026) Lerner Publishing Group. (Ediciones Lerner).

S

—Diversión con Las Hojas de Otoño (Fall Leaves Fun) Enright, Amanda, illus. 2019. (Diversión en Otoño (Fall Fun) (Early Bird Stories (tm) en Español) Ser.). (SPA.). 24p. (J). (gr. k-2). 29.32 (978-1-5415-4082-8(4), 403d05ba-cb5c-4885-9716-4e8d2a344d9f, Ediciones Lerner) Lerner Publishing Group.

—Fall Leaves Fun. Enright, Amanda, illus. 2018. (Fall Fun (Early Bird Stories (tm)) Ser.). (ENG.). 24p. (J). (gr. k-2). pap. 9.99 (978-1-5415-2720-1(8), c659dbe0-7852-496f-a2ed-4f5682f0485e) Lerner Publishing Group.

—Fall Pumpkin Fun. Enright, Amanda, illus. 2018. (Fall Fun (Early Bird Stories (tm)) Ser.). (ENG.). 24p. (J). (gr. k-2). lib. bdg. 29.32 (978-1-5415-2004-2(1), 49859806-2f42-467d-978d-61ac70dffbbc, Lerner Pubns.) Lerner Publishing Group.

Salas, Laura Purdie. Snowman - Cold = Puddle: Spring Equations. Archer, Micha, illus. 2019. 32p. (J). (gr. -1-3). lib. bdg. 16.99 (978-1-58089-798-3(3)) Charlesbridge Publishing, Inc.

Sayre, April Pulley. Full of Fall. 2017. (Weather Walks Ser.). (ENG., Illus.). 40p. (J). (gr. -1-3). 19.99 (978-1-4814-7984-4(9), Beach Lane Bks.) Beach Lane Bks.

Schuette, Sarah L. Investigate the Seasons. rev. ed. 2018. (Investigate the Seasons Ser.). (ENG.). 24p. (J). (gr. -1-2). 117.28 (978-1-5435-0885-7(5), 27759, Capstone Pr.) Capstone.

—Let's Look at Fall: A 4D Book. rev. ed. 2018. (Investigate the Seasons Ser.). (ENG., Illus.). 24p. (J). (gr. -1-2). lib. bdg. 29.32 (978-1-5435-0860-4(X), 137611, Capstone Pr.) Capstone.

—Let's Look at Spring: A 4D Book. rev. ed. 2018. (Investigate the Seasons Ser.). (ENG., Illus.). 24p. (J). (gr. -1-2). lib. bdg. 29.32 (978-1-5435-0858-1(8), 137609, Capstone Pr.) Capstone.

—Let's Look at Winter: A 4D Book. rev. ed. 2018. (Investigate the Seasons Ser.). (ENG., Illus.). 24p. (J). (gr. -1-2). lib. bdg. 29.32 (978-1-5435-0845-1(6), 137608, Capstone Pr.) Capstone.

Schuh, Mari. L' automne. 2019. (Spot les Saisons Ser.). (FRE.). 16p. (J). (gr. -1-2). (978-1-77092-441-3(8), 14536) Amicus.

—Colores Del Otoño Crayola (r) (Crayola (r) Fall Colors) 2018. (Estaciones Crayola (r) (Crayola (r) Seasons) Ser.). (SPA., Illus.). 24p. (J). (gr. -1-3). 29.32 (978-1-5415-0953-5(6), 5552e67e-d144-41b3-a58c-b12e971cf301, Ediciones Lerner) Lerner Publishing Group.

—Fall. 2019. (Spot Seasons Ser.). (ENG.). 16p. (J). (gr. -1-2). lib. bdg. (978-1-68151-552-6(0), 14513) Amicus.

—L' hiver. 2019. (Spot les Saisons Ser.). (FRE.). 16p. (J). (gr. -1-2). (978-1-77092-442-0(6), 14537) Amicus.

—I Feel Fall Weather. 2016. (First Step Nonfiction — Observing Fall Ser.). (ENG., Illus.). 24p. (J). (gr. k-2). 23.99 (978-1-5124-0797-6(6), 8fb0eb1f-79e9-4770-a953-bd2d0a2c359d, Lerner Pubns.) Lerner Publishing Group.

—El Invierno. 2019. (Estaciones Ser.). (SPA.). 16p. (J). (gr. -1-2). lib. bdg. (978-1-68151-629-5(2), 14530) Amicus.

—L'été. 2019. (Spot les Saisons Ser.). (FRE.). 16p. (J). (gr. -1-2). (978-1-77092-440-6(X), 14535) Amicus.

—El Otoño. 2019. (Estaciones Ser.). (SPA.). 16p. (J). (gr. -1-2). (978-1-68151-628-8(4), 14529) Amicus.

—La Primavera. 2019. (Estaciones Ser.). (SPA.). 16p. (J). (gr. -1-2). (978-1-68151-626-4(8), 14527) Amicus.

—Le Printemps. 2019. (Spot les Saisons Ser.). (FRE.). 16p. (J). (gr. -1-2). (978-1-77092-439-0(6), 14528) Amicus.

—Spring. 2019. (Spot Seasons Ser.). (ENG.). 16p. (J). (gr. -1-2). lib. bdg. (978-1-68151-550-2(4), 14511) Amicus.

—Summer. 2019. (Spot Seasons Ser.). (ENG.). 16p. (J). (gr. -1-2). lib. bdg. (978-1-68151-551-9(2), 14512) Amicus.

—El Verano. 2019. (Estaciones Ser.). (SPA.). 16p. (J). (gr. -1-2). lib. bdg. (978-1-68151-627-1(6), 18667) Amicus.

—Winter. 2019. (Spot Seasons Ser.). (ENG.). 16p. (J). (gr. -1-2). lib. bdg. (978-1-68151-553-3(9), 14514) Amicus.

Schwartz, Heather E. Conteo: Las Estaciones. rev. ed. 2018. (TIME for KIDS(r): Informational Text Ser.). (SPA., Illus.). 16p. (J). (gr. 1-2). 8.99 (978-1-4258-2692-5(X)) Teacher Created Materials, Inc.

—Counting: The Seasons. 2018. (TIME for KIDS(r): Informational Text Ser.). (ENG., Illus.). 16p. (J). (gr. 1-2). 8.99 (978-1-4258-4955-9(5)) Teacher Created Materials, Inc.

Seasons: Individual Title, 6 packs. (Discovery World Ser.). 12p. (gr. k-1). 28.00 (978-0-7635-8445-0(2)) Rigby Education.

The Seasons: Individual Title Two-Packs. (Chiquilibros Ser.). (gr. -1-1). 12.00 (978-0-7635-8543-3(2)) Rigby Education.

Seasons of the Year, 8 vols. 2017. (Seasons of the Year Ser.). 24p. (ENG.). (gr. 1-1). 105.08 (978-1-4994-8274-4(4), 497a7a72-c9f9-4edd-888b-69ccf6ac0bcb); (gr. 5-6). pap. 33.00 (978-1-4994-8411-3(9)) Rosen Publishing Group, Inc., The. (Windmill Bks.).

Seelig, Renate, illus. Mein Kleiner Brockhaus: Jahreszeiten. (GER.). 28p. (J). (gr. -1-18). (978-3-7653-2571-7(6)) Brockhaus, F. A., GmbH DEU. Dist: International Bk. Import Service, Inc.

Serio, Marie L. Hello Autumn Goodbye Autumn. 2011. (Illus.). 16p. (gr. 1-2). pap. 9.75 (978-1-4634-0215-0(5)) AuthorHouse.

Sesame Workshop Staff. Toddler Time Explore Seasons with Cookie Monster. 2011. (J). (gr. k-1). pap. 3.99 (978-1-59922-883-9(1)) Twin Sisters IP, LLC.

Shapiro, Sara. What Do You See? A Book about the Seasons. 2009. (Illus.). 16p. (J). pap. (978-0-545-16154-1(1)) Scholastic, Inc.

Shepherd, Jodie. Colores de la Primavera Crayola (r) (Crayola (r) Spring Colors) 2018. (Estaciones Crayola (r) (Crayola (r) Seasons) Ser.). (SPA., Illus.). 24p. (J). (gr. -1-3). 29.32 (978-1-5415-0954-2(4), 1bd4009c-60cb-49df-87ed-f8af08142635, Ediciones Lerner) Lerner Publishing Group.

—Colores Del Invierno Crayola (r) (Crayola (r) Winter Colors) 2018. (Estaciones Crayola (r) (Crayola (r) Seasons) Ser.). (SPA., Illus.). 24p. (J). (gr. -1-3). 29.32 (978-1-5415-0956-6(0), a6e43e28-0ae8-44dc-a978-7d4cdbc89819, Ediciones Lerner) Lerner Publishing Group.

Sikkens, Crystal. The Four Seasons. 2019. (Full STEAM Ahead! - Science Starters Ser.). (Illus.). 24p. (J). (gr. 1-1). (978-0-7787-6188-4(6)); pap. (978-0-7787-6235-5(1)) Crabtree Publishing Co.

Slade, Suzanne. The Four Seasons. (Cycles in Nature Ser.). (gr. 3-3). 2009. 24p. 42.50 (978-1-61512-111-3(0)) 2007. 28p. pap. 21.25 (978-1-4358-3827-7(0)) Rosen Publishing Group, Inc., The. (PowerKids Pr.).

Smith, Ian. Scholastic Clubs Animal Kingdom Pack (5 x PB QAL Titles) 2004. (QEB Start Talking Ser.). (Illus.). 24p. (J). per. 15.95 (978-1-59566-162-3(X)) QEB Publishing Inc.

Smith, Lori Joy. I Love You Like ... 2018. (ENG., Illus.). 32p. (J). (gr. -1-3). 16.95 (978-1-77147-157-2(3)) Owlkids Bks. Inc. CAN. Dist: Publishers Group West (PGW).

Spilsbury, Richard & Spilsbury, Louise. Weather & Seasons, 1 vol. 2018. (Flowchart Smart Ser.). (ENG.). 48p. (gr. 4-5). pap. 15.05 (978-1-5382-3482-2(3), 47e5a693-74a0-4796-a037-bcdc2e31bef0) Stevens, Gareth Publishing LLLP.

Stark, Ryan. Why Do Seasons Change?, 1 vol. 2013. (Nature's Super Secrets Ser.). (ENG., Illus.). 24p. (J). (gr. 1-2). 25.27 (978-1-4339-8185-2(8), e5d57bcf-3790-448b-908b-81b9ca87dbbd); pap. 9.15 (978-1-4339-8186-9(6), f3b212dd-4d39-4e21-9b97-7f4ffd326ec8) Stevens, Gareth Publishing LLLP.

Steffora, Tracey. Seasons of the Year, 1 vol. 2011. (Measuring Time Ser.). (ENG.). 24p. (J). (gr. -1-1). pap. 6.29 (978-1-4329-4909-9(8), 114810, Heinemann) Capstone.

Stewart, Melissa. Why Do the Seasons Change?, 1 vol. (Tell Me Why, Tell Me How Ser.). (ENG., Illus.). 32p. (gr. 3-3). 2008. pap. 9.23 (978-0-7614-3367-5(8), 067bb11d-0ce8-45aa-854d-db452d7ced50) 2007. lib. bdg. 32.64 (978-0-7614-2112-2(2), 8d5f452d-8651-44fd-9be0-52fd79e07367) Cavendish Square Publishing LLC.

Storad, Conrad J. Earth Is Tilting! Lew, Kristi, ed. 2011. (My Science Library). (ENG.). (J). (gr. 2-3). lib. bdg. 19.55 (978-1-68065-000-6(9)) Perfection Learning Corp.

—Earth Is Tilting! 2011. (My Science Library). (ENG., Illus.). 24p. (gr. 2-3). pap. 9.95 (978-1-61741-952-2(4), 9781617419522) Rourke Educational Media.

Storey, Rita. Art for Fall, 1 vol. 2017. (Outdoor Art Room Ser.). (ENG.). 32p. (J). (gr. 3-3). 30.27 (978-1-5081-9417-0(3), 651088bd-8009-49eb-8bc5-66c46b756a19); pap. 12.75 (978-1-5081-9466-8(1), d60a4488-2c59-4a09-b034-5a8e87a275b7) Rosen Publishing Group, Inc., The. (Windmill Bks.).

Strudwick, Leslie. The Science of Seasons. 2003. (Living Science Ser.). (Illus.). 32p. (J). (gr. 1-3). pap. 9.95 (978-1-930954-16-8(6)) Weigl Pubs., Inc.

Sundance/Newbridge LLC Staff. The Four Seasons. 2007. (Early Science Ser.). (gr. k-3). 18.95 (978-1-4007-6143-2(3)); pap. 6.10 (978-1-4007-6139-5(5)) Sundance/Newbridge Educational Publishing.

Trumbauer, Lisa. A Year in the Desert, 6 vols., Set. 2005. (Yellow Umbrella Fluent Level Ser.). (ENG., Illus.). 16p. (gr. k-1). pap. 35.70 (978-0-7368-5302-6(2), Capstone Pr.) Capstone.

Vickers, Roy Henry & Budd, Robert. Sockeye Silver, Saltchuck Blue. Vickers, Roy Henry, illus. 2019. (First West Coast Bks.: 3). (ENG., Illus.). 20p. (J). bds. (978-1-55017-870-8(9), 520ce3c0-4f6a-4af7-9ce5-9d7f6dd08fa5) Harbour Publishing Co., Ltd.

Walpole, Brenda. I Wonder Why the Sun Rises: And Other Questions about Time & Seasons. Tremblay, Marie-Ave, illus. 2011. (I Wonder Why Ser.). (ENG.). 32p. (J). (gr. k-3). pap. 6.99 (978-0-7534-6529-5(9), 900070356, Kingfisher) Roaring Brook Pr.

—I Wonder Why the Sun Rises & Other Questions about Time & Seasons. 2008. (I Wonder Why Ser.). (Illus.). 32p. (gr. k-3). 17.00 (978-0-7569-9054-1(8)) Perfection Learning Corp.

Watt, Fiona. Rainy Day Stroller Book. Baggott, Stella, illus. 2010. 8p. (J). 7.99 (978-0-7945-2850-8(3), Usborne) EDC Publishing.

Weather & Seasons Classroom Library. (gr. k-2). lib. bdg. 128.95 (978-0-7368-1828-5(6), Red Brick Learning) Capstone.

Weather & Seasons Complete Program. (gr. k-2). 642.95 (978-0-7368-1829-2(4), Red Brick Learning) Capstone.

Weiner, Miriam. Shakespeare's Seasons. Whitt, Shannon, illus. 2012. (ENG.). 32p. (J). (gr. -1). 16.99 (978-1-935703-57-0(9)) Downtown Bookworks.

Welzen, Jon. I Know the Seasons, 1 vol. 2016. (What I Know Ser.). (ENG., Illus.). 24p. (J). (gr. k-k). pap. 9.15 (978-1-4824-5473-4(4), 361118bb-6997-461d-b15a-48ed02821f4b) Stevens, Gareth Publishing LLLP.

White, Teagan. Adventures with Barefoot Critters. (Illus.). (J). 2017. 30p. (— 1). bds. 9.99 (978-1-101-91913-2(2)) 2014. 32p. (gr. -1-3). 16.99 (978-1-77049-624-8(6)) Tundra Bks. CAN. (Tundra Bks.). Dist: Penguin Random Hse. LLC.

Willis, John & Gillespie, Katie. Seasons. 2018. (Illus.). 24p. (J). (978-1-4896-5689-6(8), AV2 by Weigl) Weigl Pubs., Inc.

World Book, Inc. Staff, contrib. by. Seasonal Forests. 2012. (J). (978-0-7166-0444-0(2)) World Bk., Inc.

Ziefert, Harriet. One Red Apple. Gudeon, Karla, illus. 2009. 36p. (J). 15.99 (978-1-934706-46-6(9)) Blue Apple Bks.

SEASONS—FICTION

Agell, Charlotte. Mud, Sand, & Snow, 1 vol. 2019. (ENG., Illus.). 24p. (J). bds. 10.95 (978-1-944762-63-6(9), d78dec78-9cf2-4564-827f-b22713342f84) Islandport Pr., Inc.

Allen, Elise & Stanford, Halle. Autumn's Secret Gift. Pooler, Paige, illus. 2014. (Enchanted Sisters Ser.: 1). (J). lib. bdg. 16.00 (978-0-606-35519-3(7)) Turtleback.

—Jim Henson's Enchanted Sisters: Autumn's Secret Gift. 2014. (Enchanted Sisters Ser.). (ENG., Illus.). 128p. (J). (gr. 2-4). pap. 5.99 (978-1-61963-254-7(3), 900131787, Bloomsbury USA Childrens) Bloomsbury Publishing USA.

—Winter's Flurry Adventure. Pooler, Paige, illus. 2014. (Enchanted Sisters Ser.: 2). (YA). lib. bdg. 16.00 (978-0-606-36217-7(7)) Turtleback.

Arrhenius, Ingela P., illus. Bookscape Board Books: a Forest's Seasons: (Colorful Children?s Shaped Board Book, Forest Landscape Toddler Book) 2019. (Bookscape Board Bks.). (ENG.). 10p. (J). (gr. -1 — 1). bds. 8.99 (978-1-4521-7494-5(6)) Chronicle Bks. LLC.

AZ Books Staff. Our Cozy Forest. Zayceva, Irina, ed. 2012. (Hook-And-Loop-Pictures Ser.). (ENG.). 8p. (J). (-k). bds. 11.95 (978-1-61889-157-0(X)) AZ Bks. LLC.

Baker, Keith. Hap-Pea All Year. Baker, Keith, illus. 2016. (Peas Ser.). (ENG., Illus.). 40p. (J). (gr. -1-3). 18.99 (978-1-4814-5854-2(X), Beach Lane Bks.) Beach Lane Bks.

Barklem, Jill. Spring Story. Barklem, Jill, illus. 2011. (Brambly Hedge Ser.). (ENG., Illus.). 32p. (J). 9.99 (978-0-00-183922-9(5), HarperCollins Children's Bks.) HarperCollins Pubs. Ltd. GBR. Dist: HarperCollins Pubs.

—Summer Story. Barklem, Jill, illus. 2011. (Brambly Hedge Ser.). (ENG., Illus.). 32p. (J). 9.99 (978-0-00-183923-6(3), HarperCollins Children's Bks.) HarperCollins Pubs. Ltd. GBR. Dist: HarperCollins Pubs.

Berger, Carin. Finding Spring: A Springtime Book for Kids. Berger, Carin, illus. 2015. (ENG., Illus.). 40p. (J). (gr. -1-3). 17.99 (978-0-06-225019-3(1), Greenwillow Bks.) HarperCollins Pubs.

—Forever Friends. Berger, Carin, illus. 2010. (ENG., Illus.). 40p. (J). (gr. -1-1). 17.99 (978-0-06-191528-4(9), Greenwillow Bks.) HarperCollins Pubs.

Berger, Samantha & Chanko, Pamela. It's Spring! Sweet, Melissa, illus. 2003. (ENG.). 30p. (J). (gr. -1-3). bds. 6.99 (978-0-439-44238-1(9), Cartwheel Bks.) Scholastic, Inc.

Bergren, Lisa Tawn. God Gave Us Thankful Hearts. Hohn, David, illus. 2016. (ENG.). 40p. (J). (gr. -1-2). 10.99 (978-1-60142-874-5(X), WaterBrook Pr.) Crown Publishing Group, The.

Beskow, Elsa. Children of the Forest, 30 vols. gif. ed. 2005. (Illus.). 32p. (J). (gr. -1-3). 9.95 (978-0-86315-497-3(2)) Floris Bks. GBR. Dist: Consortium Bk. Sales & Distribution.

Bishop, Celeste. It's Fall, 1 vol. 2016. (Four Seasons Ser.). (ENG., Illus.). 24p. (gr. 1-1). pap. 9.25 (978-1-5081-5179-1(2), 321f863f-a0f5-4b35-8bac-5406d551092c, PowerKids Pr.) Rosen Publishing Group, Inc., The.

—It's Raining, 1 vol. 2016. (What's the Weather Like? Ser.). (ENG.). 24p. (gr. 1-1). pap. 9.25 (978-1-4994-2351-8(9), 7700f540-cbaa-4c5c-bbb3-e63b80bd55f8, PowerKids Pr.) Rosen Publishing Group, Inc., The.

Bissonette, Aimee. North Woods Girl. McGehee, Claudia, illus. 2015. (ENG.). 32p. (J). 17.95 (978-0-87351-966-3(3)) Minnesota Historical Society Pr.

Blackford, Cheryl. Hungry Coyote. Caple, Laurie, illus. 2015. (ENG.). 32p. (J). (gr. -1-2). 16.95 (978-0-87351-964-9(7)) Minnesota Historical Society Pr.

Blackstone, Stella. On y Danse les Saisons. Carluccio, Maria, illus. 2016. (FRE.). (J). pap. (978-1-78285-298-8(0)) Barefoot Bks., Inc.

—Skip Through the Seasons. Carluccio, Maria, illus. 2009. 32p. (J). 16.99 (978-1-84686-293-9(0)) Barefoot Bks., Inc.

Blexbolex. Seasons. 2010.Tr. of Saisons. (ENG., Illus.). 180p. (J). (gr. -1-2). 22.95 (978-1-59270-095-0(0)) Enchanted Lion Bks., LLC.

Boom Boom. 2014. (ENG., Illus.). 40p. (J). (gr. -1-3). 17.99 (978-1-4424-3412-7(0), Beach Lane Bks.) Beach Lane Bks.

Brennan, Martin. I Saw It in the Garden. Monroe, Michael Glenn, illus. 2006. 32p. (J). (gr. -1-3). 17.95 (978-1-58726-296-8(7), Mitten Pr.) Ann Arbor Editions LLC.

Broach, Elise. Barnyard Baby. Doerrfeld, Cori, illus. 2013. (Baby Seasons Ser.). (ENG.). 14p. (J). (gr. -1 — 1). bds. 7.99 (978-0-316-21203-8(2)) Little, Brown Bks. for Young Readers.

Brown, Kimberly. Autumn Castles. 2012. 28p. pap. 12.50 (978-1-61897-032-9(1), Strategic Bk. Publishing) Strategic Book Publishing & Rights Agency (SBPRA).

Bush, Leanne. Sarah's Happy Harvest Time, 1 vol. Briggs, Charlotte, illus. 2009. 32p. pap. 24.95 (978-1-60813-818-0(6)) America Star Bks.

Camden, Marian Louise. An Earth Child's Book of the Year. Wright, Diane Beem, illus. 2011. 32p. pap. (978-1-77067-742-5(9)) FriesenPress.

Candlewick Press. Peppa Pig & the Year of Family Fun. 2016. (Peppa Pig Ser.). (ENG., Illus.). 10p. (J). (gr. -1-2). 17.99 (978-0-7636-8739-7(1), Candlewick Entertainment) Candlewick Pr.

Capucilli, Alyssa Satin. My Mom & Me. Mitchell, Susan, illus. 2009. (ENG.). 16p. (J). (gr. -1-1). 7.99 (978-1-4169-5829-1(0), Little Simon) Little Simon.

Carter, David A. Snow Bugs: A Wintery Pop-Up Book. Carter, David A., illus. 2009. (David Carter's Bugs Ser.). (ENG., Illus.). 20p. (J). (gr. -1-3). 14.99 (978-1-4169-5054-7(0), Little Simon) Little Simon.

Cherobin. Zoomy Boomy, the Moon, & the Earth: All in its Season, & Seasons Change. 2010. 24p. pap. 14.99 (978-1-4490-2658-5(3)) AuthorHouse.

Child's Play. Fall. Busby, Ailie, illus. 2015. (Seasons Ser.: 4). (ENG.). 12p. (J). (gr. 1-1). bds. (978-1-84643-744-1(X)) Child's Play International Ltd.

—Spring. Busby, Ailie, illus. 2015. (Seasons Ser.: 4). 12p. (J). (gr. 1-1). spiral bd. (978-1-84643-741-0(5)) Child's Play International Ltd.

Christenson, Lisa & Christenson, Emme Jo. Seasons on the Sofa. Christenson, Lisa & Christenson, Emme Jo, illus. 2006. (Illus.). per. (978-0-9725311-3-9(0), Pickled Eggs Press (TM)) Loucks Studios Inc.

Churchman, Jennifer & Churchman, John. Alpaca Lunch. 2018. (Sweet Pea & Friends Ser.: 4). (ENG., Illus.). 40p. (J). (gr. -1-3). 17.99 (978-0-316-41160-8(4)) Little, Brown Bks. for Young Readers.

Cochran, Jean M. Off I Go! Gullens, Lee M., illus. 2008. (ENG.). 32p. (J). (gr. -1-k). 16.95 (978-0-9792035-1-0(1)) Pleasant St. Pr.

Cook, Maureen McNamee. Is There Magic in the Mountains, Mamma? Connell, Jacqueline, illus. 2008. 23p. pap. 24.95 (978-1-60672-673-0(0)) America Star Bks.

Courtney-Tickle, Jessica, illus. The Story Orchestra: Four Seasons in One Day: Press the Note to Hear Vivaldi's Music, Volume 1. 2016. (Story Orchestra Ser.: 1). (ENG.). 24p. (J). (gr. 1-4). 24.99 (978-1-84780-877-6(8), 314669, Frances Lincoln Children's Bks.) Quarto Publishing Group UK GBR. Dist: Hachette UK Distribution.

Crayton, Tina Anderson. Sniffles: Each Season Brings New Sniffles. 2012. 12p. pap. 15.99 (978-1-4772-8454-4(0)) AuthorHouse.

Crilley, Mark. Miki Falls: Autumn. Crilley, Mark, illus. 2007. (Miki Falls Ser.: 3). (ENG., Illus.). 176p. (J). (gr. 8-12). pap. 9.99 (978-0-06-084618-3(6), HarperCollins) HarperCollins Pubs.

Curato, Mike. Little Elliot, Fall Friends. Curato, Mike, illus. 2017. (Little Elliot Ser.: 4). (ENG., Illus.). 40p. (J). 18.99 (978-1-62779-640-8(1), 900157312, Holt, Henry & Co. Bks. For Young Readers) Holt, Henry & Co.

Davis, Rachayl Eckstein & Schram, Peninnah. The Apple Tree's Discovery. Lee, Wendy W., illus. 2012. (ENG.). 24p. (J). (gr. -1-2). pap. 7.99 (978-0-7613-5132-0(9), 6adca0a0-d419-4ca4-82b0-6ee930438a2e, Kar-Ben Publishing) Lerner Publishing Group.

de Brunhoff, Laurent. Babar & His Family. 2012. (ENG., Illus.). 24p. (J). (gr. -1 — 1). bds. 8.99 (978-1-4197-0263-1(7), 1019801, Abrams Appleseed) Abrams, Inc.

Deady, Kathleen W. All Year Long. Bronson, Linda, illus. 2004. (Carolrhoda Picture Books Ser.). 32p. (J). (gr. -1-3). 15.95 (978-1-57505-537-4(6)) Lerner Publishing Group.

dePaola, Tomie. Four Friends in Autumn. dePaola, Tomie, illus. 2004. (ENG., Illus.). 32p. (J). (gr. -1-3). 18.99 (978-0-689-85980-9(5), Simon & Schuster Bks. For Young Readers) Simon & Schuster Bks. For Young Readers.

Derby, Sally. Mi Escalera (Spanish Edition), 1 vol. 2005. (SPA., Illus.). 32p. (J). (gr. k-2). pap. 12.95 (978-1-880000-75-5(X), leelowbooks) Lee & Low Bks., Inc.

—My Steps, 1 vol. Burrowes, Adjoa J., illus. 2005. (ENG.). 32p. (J). (gr. k-2). pap. 11.95 (978-1-880000-84-7(9), leelowbooks) Lee & Low Bks., Inc.

Desrochers, Diane O. The Little Tree That Would Be Great. Boucher, Julie, illus. 2009. 36p. pap. 14.95 (978-0-9819727-7-0(2)) Fiction Publishing, Inc.

Dierenfeldt, Jane. A Time for Everything. Hanawalt, Josh, illus. 2012. 36p. 24.95 (978-1-4626-6146-6(7)) America Star Bks.

Diesen, Deborah. Hello, Fall! Fleming, Lucy, illus. 2018. (ENG.). 32p. (J). 17.99 (978-0-374-30754-7(7), 900180736, Farrar, Straus & Giroux (BYR)) Farrar, Straus & Giroux.

Disney Publishing Staff. My Favorite Season, 15 vols. 2003. (It's Fun to Learn Ser.). (Illus.). 32p. (J). (gr. -1-3). 3.99 (978-1-57973-129-8(5)) Advance Pubs. LLC.

Doty, Linda. In Search of the Robin. 2003. 35p. pap. 24.95 (978-1-4137-0231-6(7)) PublishAmerica, Inc.

Dougherty, Brandi. Poppy's Harvest Hullabaloo. Kurilla, Renée, illus. 2019. (J). (978-1-63565-139-3(5)) Random Hse., Inc.

Drescher, Daniela. In the Land of Elves, 25 vols. Orig. Title: Im Zwergenland. (Illus.). 24p. (ENG.). 14.95 (978-0-86315-484-3(0)); 2nd rev. ed. 2016. (J). 15.95 (978-1-78250-242-5(4)) Floris Bks. GBR. Dist: SteinerBooks, Inc., Consortium Bk. Sales & Distribution.

—Pippa & Pelle in the Autumn Wind, 30 vols. 2017. (Pippa & Pelle Ser.). Orig. Title: Pippa und Pelle Im Brausewind. (Illus.). 12p. (J). 9.95 (978-1-78250-442-9(7)) Floris Bks. GBR. Dist: Consortium Bk. Sales & Distribution.

Dubuc, Marianne, creator. The Lion & the Bird. 2014. (ENG., Illus.). 64p. (J). (gr. -1). 17.95 (978-1-59270-151-3(5)) Enchanted Lion Bks., LLC.

Edwards, Pamela Duncan. Four Seasons of Fun: Egg Hunts! Fireworks! Pumpkins! Reindeer! Daigneault, Sylvie, illus. 2018. (ENG.). 32p. (J). (gr. k-2). 16.99 (978-1-58536-403-9(7), 204584) Sleeping Bear Pr.

Ehlert, Lois. Leaf Man Big Book. Ehlert, Lois, illus. 2014. (ENG., Illus.). 40p. (J). (gr. -1-3). pap. 26.99 (978-0-544-33916-3(9), 1584487, Clarion Bks.) HarperCollins Pubs.

Elya, Susan Middleton. Maya Papaya & Amigos Play Dress-Up. Mola, Maria, illus. 2018. 32p. (J). (gr. -1-2). lib. bdg. 16.99 (978-1-58089-803-4(3)) Charlesbridge Publishing, Inc.

Emanuel, Effie Ann. Charles Chameleon. 2007. 32p. per. 24.95 (978-1-4241-8621-1(8)) America Star Bks.

Espluga, Maria. I, Farmer: Yo, Campesino. 2009. (SPA & ENG.). 28p. (J). 13.95 (978-1-931398-54-1(2)) Me+Mi Publishing.

Estes, Don. Willy & Friends traveling through the Seasons: The continuing story of Willy the little fire Jeep. Glass, Eric, illus. 2006. (J). (978-1-883551-75-9(7), Maple Corners Press) Attic Studio Publishing Hse.

Ferrier, Florian & Ferrier, Katherine. Wake up, Spring: Book 1, Bk. 1. Ferrier, Katherine, illus. 2015. (Hotel Strange Ser.). (ENG., Illus.). 40p. (J). (gr. 2-5). 26.65 (978-1-4677-8584-6(9), bd9f62cf-32a6-470f-88b2-c8f499a248ab, Graphic Universe™) Lerner Publishing Group.

Fischer, Jean. Little Book of Thanks, 1 vol. 2018. (Precious Moments Ser.). (ENG., Illus.). 32p. (J). bds. 9.99 (978-0-7180-9864-3(1), Tommy Nelson) Nelson, Thomas Inc.

Fleming, Meg. Sometimes Rain. Sudyka, Diana, illus. 2018. (ENG.). 40p. (J). (gr. -1-3). 17.99 (978-1-4814-5918-1(X), Beach Lane Bks.) Beach Lane Bks.

Fliess, Sue. The Earth Gives More. Engel, Christiane, illus. 2019. (ENG.). 32p. (J). (gr. -1-3). 16.99 (978-0-8075-7710-3(3), 807577103) Whitman, Albert & Co.

Florian, Douglas. The Curious Cares of Bears. Sánchez, Sonia, illus. 2017. (ENG.). 32p. (J). (gr. -1-3). 16.99 (978-1-4998-0462-1(8)) Little Bee Books Inc.

The Four Seasons, 8 vols. 2016. (Four Seasons Ser.). 24p. (gr. 1-1). (ENG.). 101.08 (978-1-4994-2436-2(1), d3e15852-49ae-44da-b231-2482e9a66808); pap. 33.00 (978-1-4994-2490-4(6)) Rosen Publishing Group, Inc., The. (PowerKids Pr.).

Fraggalosch, Audrey. Let's Explore, Moose! Forest, Crista, illus. 2005. (ENG.). 32p. (J). (gr. -1-1). pap. 3.95 (978-1-59249-151-3(0), S2017) Soundprints.

Frost, Helen. Applesauce Weather. Bates, Amy June, illus. 2016. 112p. (J). (gr. 3-7). 14.99 (978-0-7636-7576-9(8)) Candlewick Pr.

—Applesauce Weather. Bates, Amy June, illus. 2018. 112p. (J). (gr. 3-7). pap. 6.99 (978-1-5362-0361-5(0)) Candlewick Pr.

Frost, Maddie, illus. Candy Apple Blessings, 1 vol. 2018. (Sweet Blessings Ser.). (ENG.). 20p. (J). bds. 8.99 (978-1-4003-1779-0(7), Tommy Nelson) Nelson, Thomas Inc.

Galloway, Fhiona, illus. Fall Is Here! 2015. (ENG.). 16p. (J). (gr. -1 — 1). bds. 5.99 (978-1-4998-0110-1(6)) Little Bee Books Inc.

—Where's the Pumpkin? 2015. (ENG.). 16p. (J). (gr. -1 — 1). bds. 5.99 *(978-1-4998-0097-5(5))* Little Bee Books Inc.

George, Lynn. The Leaf Pile, 1 vol. 2006. (Neighborhood Readers Ser.). (ENG.). 16p. (gr. 1-2). pap. 6.50 *(978-1-4042-7120-3(1),* eb28fcd8-46b5-4310-bbff-9d8e2396137c, Rosen Classroom) Rosen Publishing Group, Inc., The.

Gershator, Phillis. Listen, Listen. Jay, Alison, illus. (ENG.). 32p. (J). (gr. -1-2). 2008. bds. 14.99 *(978-1-84686-201-4(9))* 2007. 16.99 *(978-1-84686-084-3(9))* Barefoot Bks., Inc.

Giuliano, Kevin. When I Was Young. 2010. 36p. pap. 18.99 *(978-1-4520-6314-0(1))* AuthorHouse.

Gravett, Emily. The Rabbit Problem. Gravett, Emily, illus. 2010. (ENG., Illus.). 32p. (J). (gr. -1-3). 24.99 *(978-1-4424-1255-2(0),* Simon & Schuster Bks. For Young Readers) Simon & Schuster Bks. For Young Readers.

Griffin, Adele & Sheinmel, Courtney. Agnes & Clarabelle. 2018. (Read & Bloom Ser.). (J). lib. bdg. 17.20 *(978-0-606-41069-4(4))* Turtleback.

Hall, Kirsten. Good Times: All about the Seasons. Luedecke, Bev, illus. 2004. (Beastieville Ser.). (J). 19.50 *(978-0-516-23648-3(2),* Children's Pr.) Scholastic Library Publishing.

Hall, Michael. Wonderfall. 2016. (ENG., Illus.). 40p. (J). (gr. -1-3). 17.99 *(978-0-06-238298-6(5),* Greenwillow Bks.) HarperCollins Pubs.

Halperin, Wendy Anderson, illus. Peace. 2013. (ENG.). 40p. (J). (gr. -1-3). 18.99 *(978-0-689-82552-1(8),* Atheneum Bks. for Young Readers) Simon & Schuster Children's Publishing.

Harris, Harris. Union Cross: New Seasons. 2013. 234p. (J). pap. 9.00 *(978-1-60039-202-3(4))* Lamp Post Inc.

Harris, Nicholas. A Year at a Farm. 2008. (Time Goes By Ser.). (ENG., Illus.). 24p. (gr. k-3). lib. bdg. 22.60 *(978-1-58013-553-5(6))* Lerner Publishing Group.

Harrison, Nicholas. A Year at a Farm. 2008. (Time Goes By Ser.). (ENG.). (gr. k-3). pap. 39.62 *(978-0-7613-4713-2(5))* Lerner Publishing Group.

Harshman, Marc & Ryan, Cheryl. Red Are the Apples. Zahares, Wade, illus. 2007. (ENG.). 32p. (J). (gr. -1-3). pap. 7.99 *(978-0-15-206065-7(0),* 1198217, Clarion Bks.) HarperCollins Pubs.

Hemming, Alice. The Leaf Thief. Slater, Nicola, illus. 2021. (Squirrel & Bird Book Ser.). (ENG.). 32p. (J). (gr. -1-3). 17.99 *(978-1-7282-3520-2(0),* Sourcebooks Jabberwocky) Sourcebooks, Inc.

Henkes, Kevin. In the Middle of Fall. Dronzek, Laura, illus. (ENG.). 40p. (J). (gr. -1-3). 2019. pap. 8.99 *(978-0-06-274724-2(X))* 2017. 18.99 *(978-0-06-257311-7(X))* HarperCollins Pubs. (Greenwillow Bks.).

—Old Bear. Henkes, Kevin, illus. 2008. (ENG., Illus.). 32p. (J). (gr. -1-5). 17.99 *(978-0-06-155205-2(4));* lib. bdg. 18.89 *(978-0-06-155206-9(2))* HarperCollins Pubs. (Greenwillow Bks.).

—Old Bear Board Book. Henkes, Kevin, illus. 2011. (ENG., Illus.). 28p. (J). (gr. -1 — 1). bds. 7.99 *(978-0-06-208963-2(3),* Greenwillow Bks.) HarperCollins Pubs.

—Summer Song. Dronzek, Laura, illus. 2020. (ENG.). 40p. (J). (gr. -1-3). 18.99 *(978-0-06-286613-4(3));* lib. bdg. 19.89 *(978-0-06-286614-1(1))* HarperCollins Pubs. (Greenwillow Bks.).

—Summer Song Board Book. Dronzek, Laura, illus. 2021. (ENG.). 36p. (J). (gr. -1 — 1). bds. 8.99 *(978-0-06-286616-5(8),* Greenwillow Bks.) HarperCollins Pubs.

—When Spring Comes. Dronzek, Laura, illus. 2016. (ENG.). 40p. (J). (gr. -1-3). 18.89 *(978-0-06-233140-3(X),* Greenwillow Bks.) HarperCollins Pubs.

—When Spring Comes: An Easter & Springtime Book for Kids. Dronzek, Laura, illus. 2019. (ENG.). 40p. (J). (gr. -1-3). pap. 8.99 *(978-0-06-274167-7(5),* Greenwillow Bks.) HarperCollins Pubs.

—Winter Is Here. Dronzek, Laura, illus. 2018. (ENG.). 40p. (J). (gr. -1-3). 17.99 *(978-0-06-274718-1(5));* lib. bdg. 18.89 *(978-0-06-274719-8(3))* HarperCollins Pubs. (Greenwillow Bks.).

Hensel, Rita. Humble Stew in Going Country. 2008. 41p. pap. 24.95 *(978-1-60563-219-3(8))* America Star Bks.

Hillert, Margaret. It's Fall, Dear Dragon. Schimmell, David, illus. 2009. (BeginningtoRead Ser.). 32p. (J). (gr. k-2). lib. bdg. 22.60 *(978-1-59953-311-7(1))* Norwood Hse. Pr.

Holland, Loretta. Fall Leaves. MacKay, Elly, illus. 2014. (ENG.). 32p. (J). (gr. -1-3). 17.99 *(978-0-544-10664-2(4),* 1540825, Clarion Bks.) HarperCollins Pubs.

Holloway, Jamie. Let's Go Pumpkin Picking, 1 vol. 2015. (Rosen REAL Readers: STEM & STEAM Collection). (ENG.). 8p. (gr. k-1). pap. 5.46 *(978-1-4994-9542-3(0),* 2b2bd034-9a89-4107-98ce-4d0b3374dc64, Rosen Classroom) Rosen Publishing Group, Inc., The.

Holmes, Ardy. 4 Seasons of Color. 2007. 48p. per. 16.95 *(978-1-4241-7249-8(7))* America Star Bks.

Horácek, Petr. A Surprise for Tiny Mouse. Horácek, Petr, illus. 2015. (ENG., Illus.). 16p. (J). (— 1). bds. 8.99 *(978-0-7636-7967-5(4))* Candlewick Pr.

Huisingh, Rosemary. Vocabulary Stories for Toddlers: Seasons. 2012. (Illus.). *(978-0-7606-1348-1(6))* LinguiSystems, Inc.

Igl, Janeane. Winter, Spring, Summer, Fall: (A Sing-Song Book) 2008. 20p. pap. 24.95 *(978-1-60563-279-7(1))* America Star Bks.

Jackson, Richard. A Kiss for Akaraka. Goodale, E. B., illus. 2018. (ENG.). 40p. (J). (gr. -1-3). 17.99 *(978-0-06-265196-9(X),* Greenwillow Bks.) HarperCollins Pubs.

James, Lauren & Kisloski, Carolyn. Building a Snowman. de Polonia, Nina, illus. 2017. (Play Time Ser.). (ENG.). 24p. (gr. -1-2). pap. 9.95 *(978-1-68342-784-1(X),* 9781683427841) Rourke Educational Media.

—Kindergarten Seasons. Bassani, Srimalie, illus. 2017. (School Days Ser.). (ENG.). 24p. (gr. -1-2). pap. 9.95 *(978-1-68342-786-5(6),* 9781683427865) Rourke Educational Media.

—Planting Seeds. Grott, Isabella, illus. 2017. (Seasons Around Me Ser.). (ENG.). 24p. (gr. -1-2). pap. 9.95 *(978-1-68342-789-6(0),* 9781683427896) Rourke Educational Media.

Jones, Lara, illus. Poppy Cat's Garden. 2008. (ENG.). 8p. (J). (gr. 3-6). bds. 16.95 *(978-0-230-01715-3(0),* Macmillan) Pan Macmillan GBR. Dist: Trans-Atlantic Pubns., Inc.

Jordan, Apple. A Fairy-Tale Fall. 2010. (Disney Princess Step into Reading Ser.). lib. bdg. 13.55 *(978-0-606-14879-5(5))* Turtleback.

—A Fairy-Tale Fall (Disney Princess) Legramandi, Francesco, illus. 2010. (Step into Reading Ser.). (ENG.). 32p. (J). (gr. k-3). pap. 5.99 *(978-0-7364-2674-9(4),* RH/Disney) Random Hse. Children's Bks.

Katz, Karen. Baby Loves Fall! A Karen Katz Lift-The-Flap Book. Katz, Karen, illus. 2013. (ENG., Illus.). 14p. (J). (gr. -1 — 1). bds. 7.99 *(978-1-4424-5209-1(9),* Little Simon) Little Simon.

Keeler, Renee, illus. Seasons. 2006. (Learn to Write Ser.). 8p. (J). (gr. k-2). pap. 3.49 *(978-1-59198-291-3(X),* 6185) Creative Teaching Pr., Inc.

Kondrchek, Jamie & Rasemas, Joe. What Should I Wear Today? (Que Ropa Me Pondre Hoy?) Vega, Elda de la, tr. Rasemas, Joe, illus. 2009. (Day in the Life Ser.). (ENG & SPA., Illus.). 32p. (J). (gr. -1-1). 25.70 *(978-1-58415-839-4(5))* Mitchell Lane Pubs.

Koopmans, Loek. Frog, Bee & Snail Look for Snow, 44 vols. 2006. Orig. Title: Samen Op Zoek. (ENG., Illus.). 28p. (J). (gr. -1-3). 15.95 *(978-0-86315-559-8(6))* Floris Bks. GBR. Dist: SteinerBooks, Inc.

Kosinski, Colleen Rowan, illus. Lilla's Sunflowers. 2016. (ENG.). 32p. (J). (gr. -1-k). 16.99 *(978-1-5107-0464-0(7),* Sky Pony Pr.) Skyhorse Publishing Co., Inc.

Kreloff, Elliot. The Luckiest Snowball. 2019. (Illus.). 40p. (J). (gr. -1-2). 17.99 *(978-0-8234-4105-1(9))* Holiday Hse., Inc.

Kroner, David & Du Houx, Ramona. Seasons. Du Houx, E. M. Cornell, illus. 2007. 70p. (J). per. 6.95 *(978-1-882190-54-6(8))* Solon Ctr. for Research & Publishing.

Kruusval, Catarina. Ellen's Apple Tree. Sandin, Joan, tr. from SWE. 2008. (Illus.). 32p. (J). (gr. -1-3). 16.00 *(978-91-29-66905-3(7))* R & S Bks. SWE. Dist: Macmillan.

LaMarche, Jim. Pond. LaMarche, Jim, illus. 2016. (ENG., Illus.). 40p. (J). (gr. -1-3). 18.99 *(978-1-4814-4735-5(1),* Simon & Schuster/Paula Wiseman Bks.) Simon & Schuster/Paula Wiseman Bks.

Las Cuatro Estaciones / the Four Seasons, 8 vols. 2016. (Las Cuatro Estaciones / the Four Seasons Ser.). (ENG & SPA.). 24p. (gr. 1-1). 101.08 *(978-1-4994-2467-6(1),* 1488e487-d836-4328-99e7-e2c66b6c91fc, PowerKids Pr.) Rosen Publishing Group, Inc., The.

Leahy, Sandy & Tarentino, Kathy. The Hibernating House. 2013. 26p. 19.95 *(978-1-4575-1753-2(1));* pap. 12.95 *(978-1-4575-1670-2(5))* Dog Ear Publishing, LLC.

Lee, Nancy. Hoover's Funny Little Kids. 2005. (J). spiral bd. 8.95 *(978-0-9748087-8-9(4))* Journey Pubns., LLC.

Lee, Uk-Bae. When Spring Comes to the DMZ. Lee, Uk-Bae, illus. 2019. (Illus.). 40p. (J). (gr. -1-3). 17.95 *(978-0-87486-972-9(2))* Plough Publishing Hse.

Lenart, Claudia, illus. Seasons of Joy: Every Day Is for Outdoor Play. 2017. 27p. (J). pap. *(978-1-61599-317-8(7))* Loving Healing Pr., Inc.

Lester, James D. Corn Flower on the Great Plains. 2019. 110p. (J). pap. *(978-1-63293-250-1(4))* Sunstone Pr.

Levine, Rhoda. Arthur. Aison, Everett, illus. 2015. 48p. (J). (gr. -1-2). 15.95 *(978-1-59017-935-2(8),* NYR Children's Collection) New York Review of Bks., Inc., The.

Lin, Grace. Ling & Ting: Together in All Weather. 2016. (Passport to Reading Level 3 Ser.). (J). lib. bdg. 14.75 *(978-0-606-39187-0(8))* Turtleback.

—Ling & Ting: Together in All Weather. 2016. (ENG.). 48p. (J). (gr. 1-4). pap. 4.99 *(978-0-316-33548-5(7))* Little, Brown Bks. for Young Readers.

Lister, Mary. Winter King, Summer Queen. Mayo, Diana, illus. 2007. 32p. (J). (gr. -1-3). (ENG.). pap. 7.99 *(978-1-84686-080-5(6));* pap. 9.99 *(978-1-84686-009-6(1))* Barefoot Bks., Inc.

Lloyd-Jones, Sally. Bunnys First Spring, 1 vol. McPhail, David, illus. 2015. (ENG.). 32p. (J). 16.99 *(978-0-310-73386-7(3))* Zonderkidz.

Long, Loren. Little Tree. Long, Loren, illus. 2015. (Illus.). 40p. (J). (gr. k-3). 18.99 *(978-0-399-16397-5(2),* Philomel Bks.) Penguin Young Readers Group.

Mahoney, Liana. Forest Green: A Walk Through the Adirondack Seasons. Henry, Maggie, illus. 2014. (ENG.). (J). *(978-1-59531-047-7(9))* North Country Bks., Inc.

Manushkin, Fran. Best Season Ever, 1 vol. Lyon, Tammie, illus. 2010. (Katie Woo Ser.). (ENG.). 32p. (J). (gr. k-2). lib. bdg. 21.32 *(978-1-4048-5730-8(3),* 102308, Picture Window Bks.) Capstone.

Matheson, Christie. Tap the Magic Tree. Matheson, Christie, illus. 2013. (ENG., Illus.). 40p. (J). (gr. -1-3). 18.99 *(978-0-06-227445-8(7),* Greenwillow Bks.) HarperCollins Pubs.

Mayer, Mercer. The Fall Festival. 2012. (Illus.). 32p. (J). *(978-1-4351-4384-5(1)); (978-0-06-222992-2(3))* HarperCollins Pubs.

—Little Critter Fall Storybook Favorites: Includes 7 Stories Plus Stickers! Mayer, Mercer, illus. 2019. (Little Critter Ser.). (ENG., Illus.). 192p. (J). (gr. -1-3). 14.99 *(978-0-06-289460-1(9),* HarperCollins) HarperCollins Pubs.

McAllister, Angela. Winter's Child. Baker-Smith, Grahame, illus. 2015. (ENG.). 40p. (J). (gr. -1-2). 16.99 *(978-0-7636-7964-4(X),* Templar) Candlewick Pr.

McBratney, Sam. Guess How Much I Love You Coloring Book. Jeram, Anita, illus. 2017. (Guess How Much I Love You Ser.). (ENG.). 96p. (J). (gr. k-k). pap. 7.99 *(978-0-7636-9467-8(3))* Candlewick Pr.

—A Surprise for the Nutbrown Hares. Jeram, Anita, illus. 2009. (J). *(978-0-7636-4903-6(1))* Candlewick Pr.

McClure, Nikki. Mama, Is It Summer Yet? 2018. (ENG., Illus.). 30p. (J). (gr. -1 — 1). bds. 9.99 *(978-1-4197-2828-0(8),* 1202510, Abrams Appleseed) Abrams, Inc.

McGhee, Alison. Making a Friend. Rosenthal, Marc, illus. 2011. (ENG.). 40p. (J). (gr. -1-3). 16.99 *(978-1-4169-8998-1(6),* Atheneum Bks. for Young Readers) Simon & Schuster Children's Publishing.

McNamara, Margaret. Fall Leaf Project: Ready-To-Read Level 1. Gordon, Mike, illus. 2006. (Robin Hill School Ser.). (ENG.). 32p. (J). (gr. -1-1). pap. 4.99 *(978-1-4169-1537-9(0),* Simon Spotlight) Simon Spotlight.

Menge, Dawn & Rhoades, Heath. Queen Vernita Meets Sir HeathyBean the Astronomer. 2010. 33p. (J). pap. 19.95 *(978-1-4327-3120-5(3))* Outskirts Pr., Inc.

Messersmith, Heather. Seasons. 2005. pap. 23.50 *(978-1-4208-6698-8(2))* AuthorHouse.

Metzger, Steve. I Love You All Year Long. Keay, Claire, illus. 2009. 20p. (J). (gr. -1-k). 8.95 *(978-1-58925-847-1(9))* Tiger Tales.

—We're Going on a Leaf Hunt. Sakamoto, Miki, illus. 2005. (J). pap. *(978-0-439-77361-4(X))* Scholastic, Inc.

Micklos, John, Jr. & Micklos, John. One Leaf, Two Leaves, Count with Me! McFarland, Clive, illus. 2017. 32p. (J). (— 1). 16.99 *(978-0-399-54471-2(2),* Nancy Paulsen Books) Penguin Young Readers Group.

Miller, Sara. Vampirina in the Fall. 2018. (Illus.). 32p. (J). *(978-1-5444-0806-4(4))* Disney Publishing Worldwide.

Mills, Nathan & Francis, Bill. Hannah's Four Seasons, 1 vol. 2012. (Rosen Readers Ser.). (ENG., Illus.). 16p. (J). (gr. k-k). pap. 7.00 *(978-1-4488-8740-8(2),* c1b66f27-406d-4deb-8448-5e2f4413896f, Rosen Classroom) Rosen Publishing Group, Inc., The.

Miniver, William. Driftwood Days. Vess, Charles, illus. 2019. (ENG.). 48p. (J). *(978-0-8028-5370-7(6),* Eerdmans Bks For Young Readers) Eerdmans, William B. Publishing Co.

Mioduchowska, Anna. In Between Season. 67p. (J). 12.95 *(978-1-895836-56-1(5))* River Bks. CAN. Dist: Coteau Bks.

Moonah, Karen. Spring into Summer! 2012. (Cat in the Hat Knows a Lot about That Ser.). lib. bdg. 14.75 *(978-0-606-23849-6(2))* Turtleback.

Moreel, Yvette. Whirly's Autumn Surprise. 2011. 44p. pap. 21.99 *(978-1-4628-9686-8(3))* Xlibris Corp.

Moroney, Tracey, illus. Little Fox's Surprise. 2015. (J). *(978-0-545-84956-2(X))* Scholastic, Inc.

Moss, Marissa. Amelia's 5th-Grade Notebook. Moss, Marissa, illus. 2006. (Amelia Ser.). (ENG., Illus.). 40p. (J). (gr. 2-5). 14.99 *(978-1-4169-0912-5(5),* Simon & Schuster/Paula Wiseman Bks.) Simon & Schuster/Paula Wiseman Bks.

Muller, Gerda. A Year Around the Great Oak, 24 vols. 2nd rev. ed. 2019. Orig. Title: Unser Baum. (ENG., Illus.). 40p. (J). 18.95 *(978-1-78250-602-7(0))* Floris Bks. GBR. Dist: Consortium Bk. Sales & Distribution.

Nettrour, Nelani. Jodi & the Seasons. Nettrour, Heather, illus. l.t. ed. 2004. 88p. pap. 11.95 *(978-1-932657-16-6(9))* Third Millennium Pubns.

Nicholas, Nicki. Peter & Lil's Amazing Autumn Day. 2011. 24p. (gr. 1-2). pap. 15.50 *(978-1-4269-6047-5(6))* Trafford Publishing.

Norman, Kim. Come Next Season. Miyares, Daniel, illus. 2019. (ENG.). 40p. (J). 17.99 *(978-0-374-30598-7(6),* 900173047, Farrar, Straus & Giroux (BYR)) Farrar, Straus & Giroux.

O'Brien, Anne Sibley & Gal, Susan. Abracadabra, It's Spring! 2016. (Seasonal Magic Ser.). (ENG., Illus.). 24p. (J). (gr. -1-k). 15.99 *(978-1-4197-1891-5(6),* 1121301, Abrams Appleseed) Abrams, Inc.

O'Connor, Jane. Fancy Nancy & the Fall Foliage. 2014. (Fancy Nancy Ser.). (ENG., Illus.). 24p. (J). (gr. -1-3). pap. 4.99 *(978-0-06-208630-3(8),* HarperFestival) HarperCollins Pubs.

Owens, Katherine. Tree Seasons Ball, 1 bk. l.t. ed. 2004. (Illus.). 40p. (J). per. 19.99 *(978-0-9760419-0-0(1),* TREESEASONSBALL) ThatsMyLife Co.

Pak, Kenard. Goodbye Autumn, Hello Winter. Pak, Kenard, illus. 2017. (ENG., Illus.). 32p. (J). 18.99 *(978-1-62779-416-9(6),* 900149958, Holt, Henry & Co. Bks. For Young Readers) Holt, Henry & Co.

—Goodbye Summer, Hello Autumn. Pak, Kenard, illus. 2016. (ENG., Illus.). 32p. (J). 18.99 *(978-1-62779-415-2(8),* 900149957, Holt, Henry & Co. Bks. For Young Readers) Holt, Henry & Co.

Parker, Amy. Tiny Blessings: for All Seasons. Walsh, Sarah, illus. 2017. (ENG.). 10p. (J). (gr. -1 — 1). bds. 7.99 *(978-0-7624-6180-6(2),* Running Pr. Kids) Running Pr.

Plourde, Lynn. Wild Child. Couch, Greg, illus. 2003. (ENG.). 32p. (J). (gr. -1-3). 8.99 *(978-0-689-86349-3(7),* Aladdin) Simon & Schuster Children's Publishing.

—Wild Child. 2003. 18.40 *(978-0-613-69321-9(3))* Turtleback.

Polacco, Patricia. For the Love of Autumn. Polacco, Patricia, illus. 2008. (Illus.). 40p. (J). (gr. 1-4). 18.99 *(978-0-399-24541-1(3),* Philomel Bks.) Penguin Young Readers Group.

Posner, Renee & Quinton, Sasha. Suzy Season Loves Spring. D'Argo, Laura, illus. (Be Mine Bears Ser.). (J). bds. 4.99 *(978-1-58209-350-5(4))* Bks. Are Fun, Ltd.

Precious Moments: Happy Harvest, 1 vol. 2016. (Precious Moments Ser.). (ENG., Illus.). 32p. (J). bds. 9.99 *(978-0-7180-3241-8(1),* Tommy Nelson) Nelson, Thomas Inc.

Pritelli, Maria Cristina, creator. Seaside Lullaby. 2018. 32p. (J). (gr. -1-1). 17.99 *(978-1-56846-328-5(6),* 19705, Creative Editions) Creative Co., The.

Pugliano-Martin, Carol. Glooscap Makes the Seasons: A Canadian Legend. 2006. (J). pap. *(978-1-4108-7159-6(2))* Benchmark Education Co.

—Ready for Fall! 2006. (Early Explorers Ser.). (J). pap. *(978-1-4108-6103-0(1))* Benchmark Education Co.

Raczka, Robert. Fall Mixed Up. Cameron, Chad, illus. 2011. (ENG.). 32p. (J). (gr. -1-3). lib. bdg. 19.99 *(978-0-7613-4606-7(6),* a231a1d6-f87a-4711-bd25-c1d4eb362f4a, Carolrhoda Bks.) Lerner Publishing Group.

Rawlinson, Julia. Fletcher & the Falling Leaves. 2011. (J). (gr. -1-2). 18.95 *(978-0-545-19705-2(8));* 29.95 *(978-0-545-19699-4(X))* Weston Woods Studios, Inc.

Remenar, Kristen. Groundhog's Dilemma. Faulkner, Matt, illus. 2015. (ENG.). 32p. (J). (gr. -1-2). lib. bdg. 18.99 *(978-1-58089-600-9(6))* Charlesbridge Publishing, Inc.

Reynolds, Michael, tr. The River. 2014. (Illus.). 110p. (J). (gr. k). 22.95 *(978-1-59270-149-0(3))* Enchanted Lion Bks., LLC.

Rhode, Paul. Presents for Phoebe: Growing Independent. Margolis, Al, illus. 2011. 24p. (YA). pap. 9.95 *(978-1-935706-05-2(5))* Wiggles Pr.

Riggs, Kate. Colors of Nature. Paolo, Domeniconi, illus. 2017. (ENG.). 14p. (J). (gr. -1 — 1). bds. 8.99 *(978-1-56846-299-8(9),* 20160, Creative Education) Creative Co., The.

Rim, Sujean. Birdie's Happiest Halloween. 2016. (ENG., Illus.). 40p. (J). (gr. -1-3). 16.99 *(978-0-316-40746-5(1))* Little, Brown Bks. for Young Readers.

Ringler, Matt. It's Fall! Shearing, Leonie, illus. 2006. 28p. (J). pap. *(978-0-439-87146-4(8))* Scholastic, Inc.

—One Little, Two Little, Three Little Apples. Kennedy, Anne, illus. 2005. (J). pap. *(978-0-439-77500-7(0))* Scholastic, Inc.

Rinker, Sherri Duskey. Construction Site: Farming Strong, All Year Long. Ford, A. G., illus. 2022. (Goodnight, Goodnight, Construc Ser.). (ENG.). 40p. (J). (gr. -1 — 1). 17.99 *(978-1-7972-1387-3(3))* Chronicle Bks. LLC.

Rockwell, Anne. Apples & Pumpkins. Rockwell, Lizzy, illus. 2014. (Classic Board Bks.). (ENG.). 28p. (J). (gr. -1-k). bds. 7.99 *(978-1-4424-9977-5(X),* Little Simon) Little Simon.

—Apples & Pumpkins. Rockwell, Lizzy, illus. 2012. (ENG.). 24p. (J). (gr. -1-3). 7.99 *(978-1-4424-7656-1(7),* Aladdin) Simon & Schuster Children's Publishing.

Rodhe, Paul & Wallas Reidy, Sarah. The Little Plum Tree. Margolis, Al & Young, Bill, illus. 2010. 24p. (J). pap. 9.95 *(978-1-935706-06-9(3))* Wiggles Pr.

Rohmann, Eric. A Kitten Tale. 2012. 32p. (J). (gr. -1-2). pap. 8.99 *(978-0-307-97774-8(9),* Dragonfly Bks.) Random Hse. Children's Bks.

Rosas, Heather. Red Riding Hood's Rainbow. 2009. (ENG.). 16p. (J). bds. 8.95 *(978-1-58117-863-0(8),* Intervisual/Piggy Toes) Bendon, Inc.

Rosen, Michael J. The Forever Flowers. Danowski, Sonja, illus. 2014. (ENG.). 32p. (J). (gr. 1-3). 18.99 *(978-1-56846-273-8(5),* 21316, Creative Editions) Creative Co., The.

Rosenstiehl, Agnès. Silly Lilly & the Four Seasons, 1 vol. Rosenstiehl, Agnès, illus. 2013. (Toon Bks.). (ENG., Illus.). 36p. (J). (gr. -1-1). lib. bdg. 32.79 *(978-1-61479-155-3(4),* 14847) Spotlight.

Rosenstiehl, Agnes. Silly Lilly & the Four Seasons: Toon Books Level 1. (Toon Ser.). (ENG., Illus.). (J). (gr. -1-3). 2013. 32p. pap. 7.99 *(978-1-935179-23-8(3))* 2008. 36p. 12.99 *(978-0-9799238-1-4(6))* Astra Publishing Hse. (TOON Books).

Rossiter, Nan Parson. The Fo'c'sle: Henry Beston's Outermost House. 2012. (ENG., Illus.). 32p. (J). (gr. 5-18). 17.95 *(978-1-56792-433-6(6))* Godine, David R. Pub.

Ruffenach, Jessie, ed. Baby Learns about Seasons. Thomas, Peter, tr. from ENG. Blacksheep, Beverly, illus. 2005. (NAV & ENG.). 16p. (J). (gr. 4-7). 7.95 *(978-1-893354-61-6(X))* Salina Bookshelf Inc.

Rylant, Cynthia. In November. Kastner, Jill, illus. 2014. 32p. pap. 7.00 *(978-1-61003-180-6(6))* Center for the Collaborative Classroom.

—In November. Kastner, Jill, illus. 2008. (ENG.). 32p. (J). (gr. -1-3). pap. 7.99 *(978-0-15-206342-9(0),* 1198996, Clarion Bks.) HarperCollins Pubs.

—Long Night Moon. Siegel, Mark, illus. 2004. (ENG.). 32p. (J). (gr. -1-3). 18.99 *(978-0-689-85426-2(9),* Simon & Schuster Bks. For Young Readers) Simon & Schuster Bks. For Young Readers.

—Mr. Putter & Tabby Ring the Bell. Howard, Arthur, illus. 2012. (Mr. Putter & Tabby Ser.). (ENG.). 44p. (J). (gr. 1-4). pap. 5.99 *(978-0-547-85075-7(1),* 1501053, Clarion Bks.) HarperCollins Pubs.

—Poppleton in Fall: an Acorn Book (Poppleton #4), 5. Teague, Mark, illus. 2020. (Poppleton Ser.: 4). (ENG.). 64p. (J). (gr. k-2). pap. 4.99 *(978-1-338-56673-4(3))* Scholastic, Inc.

Ryski, Dawid. My Four Seasons. 2017. (ENG., Illus.). 32p. (J). (gr. -1-3). 19.95 *(978-3-89955-784-8(0))* Die Gestalten Verlag DEU. Dist: Ingram Publisher Services.

Sargent, David M., Jr. Autumn's Emergency. Huff, Jeane Lirley, illus. 2003. (Doggie Tails Ser.). 32p. (J). lib. bdg. 19.95 *(978-1-56763-845-5(7))* Ozark Publishing.

Savard, Remi, et al. First Spring: An Innu Tale of North America. 2006. (Illus.). 44p. (J). (gr. -1-k). 16.95 *(978-1-894965-34-7(5))* Simply Read Bks. CAN. Dist: Ingram Publisher Services.

Schertle, Alice. Such a Little Mouse. Yue, Stephanie, illus. 2015. (ENG.). 32p. (J). (gr. -1-k). 16.99 *(978-0-545-64929-2(3))* Scholastic, Inc.

—Very Hairy Bear. Phelan, Matt, illus. 2012. lib. bdg. 17.20 *(978-0-606-26605-5(4))* Turtleback.

Scholastic, Inc. Staff. Peppa's Windy Fall Day. 2015. (Peppa Pig 8X8 Ser.). (Illus.). (J). lib. bdg. 13.55 *(978-0-606-37088-2(9))* Turtleback.

Scholastic, Inc. Staff, contrib. by. The Seasons. 2014. (Rookie Toddler(r) Ser.). (ENG.). 12p. (J). bds. 6.95 *(978-0-531-20914-1(8))* Scholastic Library Publishing.

Schram, Peninnah & Davis, Rachayl Eckstein. The Apple Tree's Discovery. Lee, Wendy W., illus. 2012. (Kar-Ben Favorites Ser.). (ENG.). 24p. (J). (gr. -1-2). lib. bdg. 16.95 *(978-0-7613-5130-6(2),* Kar-Ben Publishing) Lerner Publishing Group.

Spinelli, Eileen. I Know It's Autumn. Hayashi, Nancy, tr. Hayashi, Nancy, illus. 2004. 32p. (J). (gr. -1-2). lib. bdg. 17.89 *(978-0-06-029423-6(X))* HarperCollins Pubs.

—I Know It's Autumn. Hayashi, Nancy, illus. 2004. (ENG.). 32p. (J). (gr. -1-2). 16.99 *(978-0-06-029422-9(1),* HarperCollins) HarperCollins Pubs.

—Now It Is Summer. DePalma, Mary, illus. 2011. (ENG.). 36p. (YA). (gr. -1-3). 16.00 *(978-0-8028-5340-0(4),* Eerdmans Bks For Young Readers) Eerdmans, William B. Publishing Co.

Steers, Billy. Tractor Mac: Autumn Is Here. Steers, Billy, illus. 2019. (Tractor Mac Ser.: 1). (ENG., Illus.). 40p. (J). 19.99 *(978-0-374-30920-6(5),* 900189990, Farrar, Straus & Giroux (BYR)) Farrar, Straus & Giroux.

—Tractor Mac Harvest Time. 2015. (Tractor Mac Ser.: 1). (ENG., Illus.). 32p. (J). (gr. -1-2). 8.99 *(978-0-374-30111-8(5),* 900138389, Farrar, Straus & Giroux (BYR)) Farrar, Straus & Giroux.

Stein, David Ezra. Leaves. Stein, David Ezra, illus. (Illus.). (J). (gr. -1 — 1). 2010. 30p. bds. 7.99 *(978-0-399-25497-0(8))* 2007. (ENG., 32p. 16.99 *(978-0-399-24636-4(3))* Penguin Young Readers Group. (G.P. Putnam's Sons Books for Young Readers).

Stringer, Lauren. Winter Is the Warmest Season: A Winter & Holiday Book for Kids. Stringer, Lauren, illus. 2006. (ENG., Illus.). 40p. (J). (gr. -1-3). 18.99 *(978-0-15-204967-6(3),* 1194999, Clarion Bks.) HarperCollins Pubs.

—Yellow Time. Stringer, Lauren, illus. 2016. (ENG., Illus.). 40p. (J). (gr. -1-3). 19.99 *(978-1-4814-3156-9(0),* Beach Lane Bks.) Beach Lane Bks.

S

SungJa, Cho. Bubbly & Grumpy. SukWon, Sa, illus. rev. ed. 2014. (MySELF Bookshelf Ser.). (ENG.). 32p. (J). (gr. k-2). pap. 11.94 *(978-1-60357-660-4(6))* Norwood Hse. Pr.

Symons, Brandy. Lemonade Kisses. 2009. 24p. pap. 12.95 *(978-1-4389-7251-0(2))* AuthorHouse.

Teckentrup, Britta. Tree: a Peek-Through Picture Book. 2016. (ENG.). 32p. (J). (gr. -1-2). 16.99 *(978-1-101-93242-1(2),* Doubleday Bks. for Young Readers) Random Hse. Children's Bks.

Thompson, Lauren. Mouse's First Fall. Erdogan, Buket, illus. 2010. (Classic Board Bks.). (ENG.). 34p. (J). (gr. -1 — 1). bds. 8.99 *(978-1-4169-9477-0(7),* Little Simon) Little Simon.

Trinco, Trish. The Leaf That Wouldn't Leave. Langdo, Bryan, illus. 2008. (ENG.). 32p. (J). 16.95 *(978-0-931674-90-7(5),* Waldman House Pr.) TRISTAN Publishing, Inc.

Tsiang, Sarah. A Flock of Shoes. Leng, Qin, illus. 3rd ed. 2010. (ENG.). 32p. (J). (gr. -1-k). pap. 8.95 *(978-1-55451-248-5(4),* 9781554512485) Annick Pr., Ltd. CAN. Dist: Publishers Group West (PGW).

Van Laan, Nancy. Busy, Busy Moose. Rusch, Amy, illus. 2003. (ENG.). 48p. (J). (gr. k-2). tchr. ed. 21.19 *(978-0-395-96091-2(6))* Houghton Mifflin Harcourt Publishing Co.

Wagner Lloyd, Megan. Fort-Building Time. Halpin, Abigail, illus. 2017. 32p. (J). (gr. -1-2). 17.99 *(978-0-399-55655-5(9),* Knopf Bks. for Young Readers) Random Hse. Children's Bks.

Wallace, Nancy Elizabeth. Leaves! Leaves! Leaves!, 1 vol. 2003. (ENG., Illus.). 32p. (J). 16.95 *(978-0-7614-5140-2(4))* Marshall Cavendish Corp.

Walsh, Susanne. My Very Favorite Time of Year: Featuring the Whimsy Kids. 2007. 34p. pap. 24.95 *(978-1-4241-9090-4(8))* America Star Bks.

Waters, Tony. Cinnamon's Busy Year. Waters, Tony, illus. 2003. (Illus.). 32p. (J). (gr. -1-3). pap. 5.95 *(978-0-9710278-2-4(X))* All About Kids Publishing.

Watt, Fiona. Hide-and-Seek Bunnies. Danson, Lesley, illus. 2007. (Touchy-Feely Flap Bks). 10p. (J). (gr. -1-k). bds. 16.99 *(978-0-7945-1566-9(5),* Usborne) EDC Publishing.

Wayne, Viv. Bloom Where You Are Planted: A garden story about overcoming your Challenges. 2012. 28p. pap. 19.99 *(978-1-4685-4791-7(7))* AuthorHouse.

Weiss, Ellen. Winter Spring Summer Fall: A Touch-and-Feel Seasons Book. Bennett, Andy, illus. 2006. (PBS Kids Ser.). 8p. (J). (gr. -1-k). bds. 6.95 *(978-1-57791-312-2(4))* Brighter Minds Children's Publishing.

Weston Woods Staff, creator. Fletcher & the Falling Leaves. 2011. 38.75 *(978-0-545-19710-6(4))* Weston Woods Studios, Inc.

—In the Small, Small Pond. 2011. 38.75 *(978-0-439-84578-6(5))* Weston Woods Studios, Inc.

—Inch by Inch. 2011. 38.75 *(978-0-439-90543-5(5))* Weston Woods Studios, Inc.

Williams, Rozanne Lanczak. Seasons. Maio, Barbara & Faulkner, Stacey, eds. 2006. (J). per. 6.99 *(978-1-59198-342-2(8))* Creative Teaching Pr., Inc.

Wilson, Pamela J. Tales from Tubblewood Too. 2009. (Illus.). 164p. 23.50 *(978-1-4389-4064-9(5))* AuthorHouse.

—Tales from Tubblewood Too: Miss Duck to the Rescue. 2009. (Illus.). 164p. pap. 13.50 *(978-1-4389-4063-2(7))* AuthorHouse.

Wilson, Steve. Hedgehugs: Autumn Hide-And-Squeak. Tapper, Lucy, illus. 2017. (Hedgehugs Ser.: 3). (ENG.). 32p. (J). 16.99 *(978-1-250-11248-4(6),* 900170464, Holt, Henry & Co. Bks. For Young Readers) Holt, Henry & Co.

Witek, Jo. My Tree & Me: A Book of Seasons. 2019. (Growing Hearts Ser.). (ENG., Illus.). 32p. (J). (gr. -1 — 1). 16.99 *(978-1-4197-3503-5(9),* 1268201) Abrams, Inc.

Wright, Maureen. Sneeze, Big Bear, Sneeze!, 0 vols. Hillenbrand, Will, illus. 2012. (ENG.). 32p. (J). (gr. -1-2). 16.99 *(978-0-7614-5959-0(6),* 9780761459590, Two Lions) Amazon Publishing.

Yeoman, John. All the Year Round. Blake, Quentin, illus. 2019. (ENG.). 32p. (J). (gr. k-2). pap. 16.99 *(978-1-78344-613-1(7))* Andersen Pr. GBR. Dist: Independent Pubs. Group.

Yolen, Jane. Sing a Season Song. Ashlock, Lisel, illus. 2015. (ENG.). 48p. (J). (gr. 1-3). 22.95 *(978-1-56846-255-4(7),* 20829, Creative Editions) Creative Co., The.

Yoon, Salina. Penguin & Pumpkin. 2014. (Penguin Ser.). (ENG., Illus.). 40p. (J). (gr. -1-1). 15.99 *(978-0-8027-3732-8(3),* 900134209); E-Book 6.39 *(978-0-8027-3770-0(6))* Bloomsbury Publishing USA. (Bloomsbury USA Childrens).

SEASONS—POETRY

Diaz, David, illus. Sharing the Seasons: A Book of Poems. 2010. (ENG.). 96p. (J). (gr. 3-7). 24.99 *(978-1-4169-0210-2(4),* McElderry, Margaret K. Bks.) McElderry, Margaret K. Bks.

Franco, Betsy & Salerno, Steven. Mathematickles! 2006. (Illus.). (gr. k-5). 18.00 *(978-0-7569-6709-3(0))* Perfection Learning Corp.

Giovanni, Nikki. The Sun Is So Quiet. Bryan, Ashley, illus. 2014. (ENG.). 32p. (J). (gr. -1-3). 8.99 *(978-1-250-04669-7(6),* 900131698) Square Fish.

Jenkins, Ellie, illus. Poems for the Seasons, 1 vol. 2017. (Poems Just for Me Ser.). (ENG.). 32p. (J). (gr. 3-3). 28.93 *(978-1-4994-8387-1(2),* 8bff6233-686e-42b0-bc40-1bf02ce1cd16, Windmill Bks.) Rosen Publishing Group, Inc., The.

Low, Elizabeth Cothen. Big Book of Seasons, Holidays, & Weather: Rhymes, Fingerplays, & Songs for Children. 2011. (ENG., Illus.). 168p. E-Book 45.00 *(978-1-59884-624-9(8),* A3162E, Libraries Unlimited) ABC-CLIO, LLC.

O'Rourke, Ryan, illus. One Big Rain: Poems for Every Season. 2014. (ENG.). 32p. (J). (gr. 2-5). pap. 7.95 *(978-1-57091-717-2(5))* Charlesbridge Publishing, Inc.

Raczka, Bob. Guyku: A Year of Haiku for Boys. Reynolds, Peter H., illus. (ENG.). 48p. (J). (gr. -1-3). 2018. pap. 6.99 *(978-1-328-86930-2(X),* 1696693) 2010. 16.99 *(978-0-547-24003-9(1),* 1098616) HarperCollins Pubs. (Clarion Bks.).

Randolph, Joanne, ed. Poems about Spring, 1 vol. 2018. (Poet's Journal: Exploring Nature & the Seasons Ser.). (ENG.). 24p. (gr. 2-4). 26.27 *(978-1-5081-9705-8(9),* 98ee7818-679d-47c4-a2e1-804744dc8eee); pap. 9.25 *(978-1-5081-9706-5(7),* 30875b2e-84f4-456e-b5d3-c2ad63f4a4a1) Rosen Publishing Group, Inc., The. (Windmill Bks.).

—Poems about Summer, 1 vol. 2018. (Poet's Journal: Exploring Nature & the Seasons Ser.). (ENG.). 24p. (gr. 2-4). 26.27 *(978-1-5081-9709-6(1),* a6201814-0051-4b62-9f88-0b85924fac3d); pap. 9.25 *(978-1-5081-9710-2(5),* 7aab9cab-2e92-4268-80c8-ab5b0e676d83) Rosen Publishing Group, Inc., The. (Windmill Bks.).

—Poems about Weather, 1 vol. 2018. (Poet's Journal: Exploring Nature & the Seasons Ser.). (ENG.). 24p. (gr. 2-4). 26.27 *(978-1-5081-9713-3(X),* cbf3ec7f-0ee5-4fe3-bb6c-60d4e22f36d2); pap. 9.25 *(978-1-5081-9714-0(8),* 281c94f1-34c9-4a87-978d-dd8c4c6b7400) Rosen Publishing Group, Inc., The. (Windmill Bks.).

—Poems about Winter, 1 vol. 2018. (Poet's Journal: Exploring Nature & the Seasons Ser.). (ENG.). 24p. (gr. 2-4). 26.27 *(978-1-5081-9717-1(2),* eab8f2ba-cbf7-4b41-8310-0a57fca846ad); pap. 9.25 *(978-1-5081-9718-8(0),* f1e0b8db-98dc-4f6e-af14-0e7ebdb88264) Rosen Publishing Group, Inc., The. (Windmill Bks.).

Seasons Come Seasons Go. 2nd ed. 2005. per. *(978-0-9763958-0-5(0))* Aceybee Publishing.

Sidman, Joyce. Red Sings from Treetops: A Caldecott Honor Award Winner. Zagarenski, Pamela, illus. 2009. (ENG.). 32p. (J). (gr. -1-3). 18.99 *(978-0-547-01494-4(5),* 1031109, Clarion Bks.) HarperCollins Pubs.

—Red Sings from Treetops: A Year in Colors. 2010. (J). 36.75 *(978-1-4498-2606-2(7));* 38.75 *(978-1-4498-2608-6(3));* 184.75 *(978-1-4498-2605-5(9));* 36.75 *(978-1-4498-2610-9(5))* Recorded Bks., Inc.

Siebert, Diane. Spring, Summer, Autumn, Winter. Burckhardt, Marc, illus. 2005. (J). *(978-1-59336-299-7(4));* pap. *(978-1-59336-300-0(1))* Mondo Publishing.

Thomas, Patricia. Nature's Paintbox: A Seasonal Gallery of Art & Verse. Orback, Craig, illus. 2007. (Millbrook Picture Books Ser.). (ENG.). 32p. (J). (gr. 2-4). lib. bdg. 16.95 *(978-0-8225-6807-0(1),* Millbrook Pr.) Lerner Publishing Group.

Waters, Fiona, ed. Sing a Song of Seasons: A Nature Poem for Each Day of the Year. Preston-Gannon, Frann, illus. 2018. (ENG.). 336p. (J). (gr. k-4). 40.00 *(978-1-5362-0247-2(9))* Candlewick Pr.

Williams, Rozanne. The Four Seasons. 2017. (Learn-To-Read Ser.). (ENG., Illus.). (J). pap. 3.49 *(978-1-68310-169-7(3))* Pacific Learning, Inc.

SEATTLE, CHIEF, 1790-1866

Carew-Miller, Anna. Chief Seattle: Great Chief. 2004. (Great Names Ser.). (Illus.). 32p. (J). (gr. 3-18). lib. bdg. 19.95 *(978-1-59084-154-9(9))* Mason Crest.

SEATTLE (WASH.)

Cotton, Jacqueline S. Seattle. 2018. (Illus.). 24p. (J). pap. *(978-1-4896-9473-7(0),* AV2 by Weigl) Weigl Pubs., Inc.

Dyan, Penelope. Smile Seattle! a Kid's Guide to Seattle, Washington. Weigand, John D., photos by. 2013. (Illus.). 34p. pap. 11.95 *(978-1-61477-109-8(X))* Bellissima Publishing, LLC.

Filer, Patricia & Fulton, Cathy. Welcome to the Greenland: A Children's Activity Guide to the Birthplace of Seattle. 2003. (Illus.). 40p. (J). spiral bd. 24.95 *(978-0-9727759-5-3(1))* Capturing Memories.

Laberje, Reji. Max Explores Seattle. Fenech, Liza, illus. 2015. (Max Explores Ser.). (ENG.). 20p. (J). (— 1). bds. 9.95 *(978-1-62937-103-0(3))* Triumph Bks.

Mad Libs. I Love Seattle Mad Libs: World's Greatest Word Game. 2015. (Mad Libs Ser.). 48p. (J). (gr. 3-7). bds. 5.99 *(978-0-8431-8268-2(7),* Mad Libs) Penguin Young Readers Group.

Murray, Julie. Space Needle. 2018. (Super Structures Ser.). (ENG., Illus.). 24p. (J). (gr. k-4). lib. bdg. 31.36 *(978-1-5321-2314-6(0),* 28395, Abdo Zoom-Dash) ABDO Publishing Co.

Skewes, John. New York City ABC: a Larry Gets Lost Book. 2018. (Larry Gets Lost Ser.). (Illus.). 32p. (J). (-k). 14.99 *(978-1-63217-167-2(8),* Little Bigfoot) Sasquatch Bks.

—Seattle ABC: a Larry Gets Lost Book. 2017. (Larry Gets Lost Ser.). (Illus.). 32p. (J). (-k). 14.99 *(978-1-63217-093-4(0),* Little Bigfoot) Sasquatch Bks.

Tracy, Kathleen. Seattle. 2010. (Class Trip Ser.). (Illus.). 48p. (J). (gr. 2-5). lib. bdg. 29.95 *(978-1-58415-880-6(8))* Mitchell Lane Pubs.

SEATTLE (WASH.)—FICTION

Anonymous. Calling Maggie May. 2015. (Anonymous Diaries). (ENG., Illus.). 272p. (YA). (gr. 9). pap. 11.99 *(978-1-4814-3901-5(4),* Simon Pulse) Simon Pulse.

Barden, Stephanie. Cinderella Smith. Goode, Diane, illus. 2011. (Cinderella Smith Ser.: 1). (ENG.). 160p. (J). (gr. 3-7). 16.99 *(978-0-06-196423-7(9),* HarperCollins) HarperCollins Pubs.

—Cinderella Smith: the Super Secret Mystery, Vol. 3. Goode, Diane, illus. 2013. (Cinderella Smith Ser.: 3). (ENG.). 144p. (J). (gr. 1-5). 16.99 *(978-0-06-200443-7(3),* HarperCollins) HarperCollins Pubs.

Bennett, Jenn. Serious Moonlight. 2019. (ENG., Illus.). 432p. (YA). (gr. 9). 19.99 *(978-1-5344-2514-9(4),* Simon Pulse) Simon Pulse.

Butler, Dori Hillestad. The Underground Ghosts #10: A Super Special. Damant, Aurore, illus. 2017. (Haunted Library: 10). 192p. (J). (gr. 1-3). 7.99 *(978-0-515-15711-6(2),* Grosset & Dunlap) Penguin Young Readers Group.

Caletti, Deb. The Nature of Jade. 2007. (ENG.). 320p. (YA). (gr. 7-12). 24.94 *(978-1-4169-1005-3(0))* Simon & Schuster, Inc.

—The Nature of Jade. 2008. (ENG.). 320p. (YA). (gr. 7-12). pap. 10.99 *(978-1-4169-1006-0(9),* Simon Pulse) Simon Pulse.

Colbert, Cory. Sammy the Sea Otter Makes New Friends: Adventures of Sammy the Sea Otter. 2011. 18p. pap. 11.95 *(978-1-4327-7648-0(7))* Outskirts Pr., Inc.

Cosgrove, Stephen. Good Night, Wheedle. James, Robin, illus. 2016. 20p. (J). (— 1). bds. 9.99 *(978-1-63217-075-0(2),* Little Bigfoot) Sasquatch Bks.

—Wheedle on the Needle. James, Robin, illus. 2009. (ENG.). 32p. (J). (gr. -1-2). 18.99 *(978-1-57061-628-0(0),* Little Bigfoot) Sasquatch Bks.

Dokey, Cameron. How Not to Spend Your Senior Year. 2012. (Romantic Comedies Ser.). (ENG.). 304p. (YA). (gr. 9). pap. 14.99 *(978-1-4424-6056-0(3),* Simon Pulse) Simon Pulse.

Hobbs, Will. Jackie's Wild Seattle. (ENG.). 208p. (J). (gr. 5-18). 2004. pap. 6.99 *(978-0-380-73311-8(0))* 2003. 19.99 *(978-0-688-17474-3(4))* HarperCollins Pubs. (HarperCollins).

Holtzen, Mark. A Ticket to the Pennant: A Tale of Baseball in Seattle. Skewes, John, illus. 2016. 32p. (J). (gr. -1-3). 17.99 *(978-1-63217-003-3(5),* Little Bigfoot) Sasquatch Bks.

Hudspeth, Jodi. Unconditional Love. 2009. 80p. pap. 28.99 *(978-1-4343-6383-1(X))* AuthorHouse.

Ingold, Jeanette. Paper Daughter. 2013. (ENG.). 224p. (YA). (gr. 7). pap. 15.99 *(978-0-544-10484-6(6),* 1540793, Clarion Bks.) HarperCollins Pubs.

James, Wilson. SONS & BROTHERS in SEATTLE. 2009. 158p. pap. 14.95 *(978-0-557-07436-5(3))* Lulu Pr., Inc.

Kehret, Peg. Abduction! 2006. (ENG.). 224p. (J). (gr. 5-18). 8.99 *(978-0-14-240617-5(1),* Puffin Books) Penguin Young Readers Group.

—Abduction! 2007. 215p. (gr. 3-7). 17.00 *(978-0-7569-8282-9(0))* Perfection Learning Corp.

Lockhart, E. The Boyfriend List: 15 Guys, 11 Shrink Appointments, 4 Ceramic Frogs & Me, Ruby Oliver, 1. 2006. (Ruby Oliver Quartet Ser.: 1). (ENG.). 256p. (YA). (gr. 7-12). reprint ed. pap. 9.99 *(978-0-385-73207-9(4),* Delacorte Pr.) Random Hse. Children's Bks.

—Real Live Boyfriends: Yes. Boyfriends, Plural. If My Life Weren't Complicated, I Wouldn't Be Ruby Oliver. 2011. (Ruby Oliver Quartet Ser.: 4). (ENG.). 240p. (YA). (gr. 7). pap. 9.99 *(978-0-385-73429-5(8),* Ember) Random Hse. Children's Bks.

—The Treasure Map of Boys: Noel, Jackson, Finn, Hutch, Gideon — And Me, Ruby Oliver. 2010. (Ruby Oliver Quartet Ser.: 3). (ENG.). 256p. (YA). (gr. 7). pap. 8.99 *(978-0-385-73427-1(1),* Delacorte Pr.) Random Hse. Children's Bks.

Loyd, Mark. Big Ben: A Little Known Story. Loyd, Mark, illus. 2005. (Illus.). (J). *(978-0-9773317-1-0(7))* Too Fun Publishing.

Marsh, Carole. Mystery at the Space Needle. 2016. (Real Kids, Real Places Ser.). (ENG.). (J). (gr. 3-7). pap. 7.99 *(978-0-635-12432-6(7),* Marsh, Carole Mysteries) Gallopade International.

Mathieson, Karen. Liza, Elizabeth: Book Three of the Rosemary Ridge Trilogy. 2013. 164p. (J). pap. 7.99 *(978-1-940350-08-0(5))* Mathieson Creative Media.

McKernan, Victoria. The Devil's Paintbox. 1. 2010. (Devil's Paintbox Ser.). (ENG.). 368p. (J). (gr. 9-12). lib. bdg. 22.44 *(978-0-375-93750-7(1))* Random House Publishing Group.

—The Devil's Paintbox. (ENG.). (YA). (gr. 9). 2013. 384p. pap. 9.99 *(978-0-449-81655-4(9),* Ember) 2010. 368p. mass mkt. 8.99 *(978-0-440-23962-8(1),* Laurel Leaf) Random Hse. Children's Bks.

Mochizuki, Ken. Beacon Hill Boys. 2004. 200p. 16.00 *(978-0-7569-4281-6(0))* Perfection Learning Corp.

Powell, Randy. Tribute to Another Dead Rock Star. 2003. (ENG.). 224p. (YA). (gr. 7-12). pap. 15.99 *(978-0-374-47968-8(2),* 900021239, Farrar, Straus & Giroux (BYR)) Farrar, Straus & Giroux.

Reed, Amy. Beautiful. 2009. (ENG.). 240p. (YA). (gr. 9-12). 16.99 *(978-1-4169-7830-5(5))* Simon & Schuster, Inc.

—Beautiful. 2010. (ENG.). 256p. (YA). (gr. 9). pap. 10.99 *(978-1-4169-7831-2(3),* Simon Pulse) Simon Pulse.

—Clean. (ENG.). (YA). (gr. 9). 2012. 304p. pap. 12.99 *(978-1-4424-1345-0(X))* 2011. 288p. 16.99 *(978-1-4424-1344-3(1))* Simon Pulse. (Simon Pulse).

Renn, Diana. Tokyo Heist. 2013. (ENG.). 384p. (YA). (gr. 7). pap. 8.99 *(978-0-14-242654-8(7),* Speak) Penguin Young Readers Group.

Rollins, Danielle. Stolen Time. (Dark Stars Ser.: 1). (ENG.). (YA). (gr. 9). 2020. 432p. pap. 10.99 *(978-0-06-267995-6(3))* 2019. 416p. 17.99 *(978-0-06-267994-9(5))* HarperCollins Pubs. (HarperTeen).

Savage, J. Scott. Gears of Revolution. 2016. (Mysteries of Cove Ser.: 2). (ENG., Illus.). 352p. (J). (gr. 3-6). 17.99 *(978-1-62972-223-8(5),* 5155663, Shadow Mountain) Shadow Mountain Publishing.

Skewes, John & Ode, Eric. Larry Gets Lost in Seattle: 10th Anniversary Edition. 10th ed. 2017. (Larry Gets Lost Ser.). (Illus.). 32p. (J). (gr. -1-2). 17.99 *(978-1-63217-092-7(2),* Little Bigfoot) Sasquatch Bks.

Solomon, Rachel Lynn. Our Year of Maybe. 2019. (ENG., Illus.). 384p. (YA). (gr. 9). 18.99 *(978-1-4814-9776-3(6),* Simon Pulse) Simon Pulse.

—You'll Miss Me When I'm Gone. 2018. (ENG., Illus.). 384p. (YA). (gr. 9). 19.99 *(978-1-4814-9773-2(1),* Simon Pulse) Simon Pulse.

Steere, Jay. Good Night Seattle. Veno, Joe, illus. 2007. (Good Night Our World Ser.). (ENG.). 20p. (J). (gr. k — 1). bds. 9.95 *(978-1-60219-014-6(3))* Good Night Bks.

Thomas, Teri. The Barge Ghost, 1 vol. unabr. ed. 2010. (Q Reads Ser.). (ENG.). 32p. (YA). (gr. 9-12). pap. 8.50 *(978-1-61651-211-8(3))* Saddleback Educational Publishing, Inc.

Trueman, Terry. Life Happens Next. 2012. (Stuck in Neutral Ser.: 3). (ENG.). 144p. (YA). (gr. 9). 17.99 *(978-0-06-202803-7(0),* HarperTeen) HarperCollins Pubs.

Warner, Gertrude Chandler, creator. The Seattle Puzzle. 2007. (Boxcar Children Mysteries Ser.: 111). (ENG., Illus.). (J). (gr. 2-5). 128p. lib. bdg. 14.99 *(978-0-8075-5560-6(6),* 807555606); 112p. per. 5.99 *(978-0-8075-5561-3(4),* 807555614) Random Hse. Children's Bks. (Random Hse. Bks. for Young Readers).

SEATTLE MARINERS (BASEBALL TEAM)

Freedman, Lew. Seattle Mariners, 1 vol. 2015. (Inside MLB Ser.). (ENG., Illus.). 48p. (J). (gr. 3-6). lib. bdg. 34.21 *(978-1-62403-485-5(3),* 17133, SportsZone) ABDO Publishing Co.

LeBoutillier, Nate. The Story of the Seattle Mariners. 2011. (Baseball: the Great American Game Ser.). (Illus.). 48p. (J). (gr. 5-8). lib. bdg. 34.25 *(978-1-60818-056-1(5),* Creative Education) Creative Co., The.

Peterson, Sheryl. The Story of the Seattle Mariners. 2007. (Baseball, the Great American Game Ser.). (Illus.). 48p. (YA). (gr. 4-7). lib. bdg. 32.80 *(978-1-58341-500-9(9))* Creative Co., The.

Stewart, Mark. The Seattle Mariners. 2012. (Team Spirit Ser.). 48p. (J). (gr. 3-6). lib. bdg. 29.27 *(978-1-59953-497-8(5))* Norwood Hse. Pr.

SEATTLE SEAHAWKS (FOOTBALL TEAM)

Adamson, Thomas K. The Seattle Seahawks Story. 2016. (NFL Teams Ser.). (ENG., Illus.). 32p. (J). (gr. 3-7). lib. bdg. 26.95 *(978-1-62617-382-8(6),* Torque Bks.) Bellwether Media.

Burgess, Zack. Meet the Seattle Seahawks. 2016. (Big Picture Sports Ser.). (ENG., Illus.). 24p. (J). (gr. k-3). lib. bdg. 22.60 *(978-1-59953-748-1(6))* Norwood Hse. Pr.

Gilbert, Sara. The History of the Seattle Seahawks. 2004. (NFL Today Ser.). (Illus.). 32p. (YA). (gr. 5-9). 18.95 *(978-1-58341-314-2(6))* Creative Co., The.

—The Story of the Seattle Seahawks. 2009. (NFL Today Ser.). 48p. (YA). (gr. 5-9). 22.95 *(978-1-58341-771-3(0))* Creative Co., The.

McGee, Earl & Mason, Tyler. Seattle Seahawks, 1 vol. 2016. (NFL up Close Ser.). (ENG., Illus.). 32p. (J). (gr. 3-9). lib. bdg. 32.79 *(978-1-68078-233-2(9),* 22069, SportsZone) ABDO Publishing Co.

Morey, Allan. Superstars of the Seattle Seahawks. 2018. (Pro Sports Superstars - NFL Ser.). (ENG.). 24p. (J). (gr. 1-4). lib. bdg. *(978-1-68151-411-6(7),* 15078) Amicus.

Sandler, Michael. Malcolm Smith & the Seattle Seahawks: Super Bowl XLVIII. 2015. (Illus.). 24p. (J). lib. bdg. 26.99 *(978-1-62724-295-0(3))* Bearport Publishing Co., Inc.

Stewart, Mark. The Seattle Seahawks. rev. ed. 2012. (Team Spirit Ser.). (ENG.). 48p. (J). (gr. 3-6). lib. bdg. 29.27 *(978-1-59953-539-5(4))* Norwood Hse. Pr.

Storm, Marysa. Highlights of the Seattle Seahawks. 2019. (Team Stats — Football Edition Ser.). (ENG., Illus.). 32p. (J). (gr. 4-6). lib. bdg. *(978-1-68072-889-7(X),* 12832, Bolt) Black Rabbit Bks.

Whiting, Jim. Seattle Seahawks. rev. ed. 2019. (NFL Today Ser.). (ENG.). 48p. (J). (gr. 4-7). pap. 12.00 *(978-1-62832-721-2(9),* 19081, Creative Paperbacks) Creative Co., The.

—The Story of the Seattle Seahawks. (NFL Today Ser.). 48p. (J). 2019. (ENG.). (gr. 3-6). *(978-1-64026-158-7(3),* 19084) 2013. (Illus.). 35.65 *(978-1-60818-320-3(3))* Creative Co., The. (Creative Education).

Wyner, Zach. Seattle Seahawks. 2015. (Illus.). 32p. (J). pap. *(978-1-4896-0891-8(5))* Weigl Pubs., Inc.

Zappa, Marcia. Seattle Seahawks, 1 vol. 2015. (NFL's Greatest Teams Ser.). (ENG.). 32p. (J). (gr. 2-5). 34.21 *(978-1-62403-591-3(4),* 17209, Big Buddy Bks.) ABDO Publishing Co.

SEAWEED

see Algae

SECONDARY EDUCATION

see Education, Secondary

SECONDARY SCHOOLS

see Education, Secondary; High Schools; Public Schools

SECRET SERVICE

see also Detectives; Spies

also subdivision Secret Service under individual wars, e.g. World War, 1939-1945—Secret Service.

Bascomb, Neal. The Nazi Hunters: How a Team of Spies & Survivors Captured the World's Most Notorious Nazi, 1 vol. (ENG., Illus.). (YA). (gr. 7-7). 2018. 272p. pap. 9.99 *(978-0-545-43100-2(X))* 2013. 256p. 17.99 *(978-0-545-43099-9(2))* Scholastic, Inc. (Levine, Arthur A. Bks.).

Caravantes, Peggy. Petticoat Spies: Six Women Spies of the US Civil War. 2004. (Notable Americans Ser.). (Illus.). 112p. (YA). (gr. 6-12). 23.95 *(978-1-883846-88-6(9),* First Biographies) Reynolds, Morgan Inc.

Costain, Meredith. Spies Revealed, 1 vol. 2013. (Discovery Education: Sensational True Stories Ser.). (ENG., Illus.). 32p. (J). (gr. 4-5). pap. 11.00 *(978-1-4777-0103-4(6),* 11898d18-742b-418f-a4b6-6bfb0c8a0c6b); lib. bdg. 28.93 *(978-1-4777-0059-4(5),* 3bf85882-32bd-485b-be1e-1a7ad9c1868a) Rosen Publishing Group, Inc., The. (PowerKids Pr.).

Croce, Nicholas. Detectives: Life Investigating Crime. 2009. (Extreme Careers Ser.). 64p. (gr. 5-5). 58.50 *(978-1-61512-390-2(3),* Rosen Reference) Rosen Publishing Group, Inc., The.

Larson, Kirsten W. U. S. Secret Service. 2016. (Protecting Our People Ser.). (ENG., Illus.). 32p. (J). (gr. 2-5). lib. bdg. 20.95 *(978-1-60753-987-2(X),* 15778) Amicus.

Newcomb, Tim. Secret Service Agent, Vol. 12. 2015. (On a Mission Ser.). (Illus.). 48p. (J). (gr. 5). 20.95 *(978-1-4222-3400-6(2))* Mason Crest.

Polisar, Patti. Inside France's DGSE: The General Directorate for External Security. 2005. (Illus.). 63p. (gr. 4-8). reprint ed. 20.00 *(978-0-7567-8670-0(3))* DIANE Publishing Co.

Ryan, Bernard. The Secret Service. 2010. (Law Enforcement Agencies Ser.). (Illus.). 128p. (gr. 6-12). 35.00 *(978-1-60413-623-4(5),* Facts On File) Infobase Holdings, Inc.

Shea, Therese. A Career As a Secret Service Agent, 1 vol. 2015. (Federal Forces: Careers As Federal Agents Ser.). (ENG., Illus.). 32p. (J). (gr. 4-5). 27.93 *(978-1-4994-1117-1(0),* 1b2177a2-21b1-41f2-b2b8-cc7f0e061aa2, PowerKids Pr.) Rosen Publishing Group, Inc., The.

Woog, Adam. Careers in the Secret Service, 1 vol. 2014. (Law & Order Jobs Ser.). (ENG.). 112p. (gr. 6-6). 42.63 *(978-1-62712-434-8(9),* b731810a-5b8e-4283-89fc-94e8a69ff4de) Cavendish Square Publishing LLC.

—Careers in the Secret Service. 2013. (J). 34.21 *(978-1-60870-960-1(4))* Marshall Cavendish Corp.

SECRET SERVICE—FICTION

Blum, Paul. Dawn of the Zombies, 1 vol. 2007. (Extraordinary Files Ser.). (ENG., Illus.). 48p. (J). (gr. 4-7). pap. 10.99 *(978-1-84680-250-8(4))* Evans Brothers, Ltd. GBR. Dist: Independent Pubs. Group.

—Day of Judgement, 1 vol. 2007. (Extraordinary Files Ser.). (ENG., Illus.). 48p. (J). (gr. 4-7). pap. 11.99 *(978-1-84680-251-5(2))* Evans Brothers, Ltd. GBR. Dist: Independent Pubs. Group.

—Gene Machine, 1 vol. 2007. (Extraordinary Files Ser.). (ENG., Illus.). 48p. (J). (gr. 4-7). pap. 10.99 *(978-1-84680-252-2(0))* Evans Brothers, Ltd. GBR. Dist: Independent Pubs. Group.

—Killer Robot, 1 vol. 2007. (Extraordinary Files Ser.). (ENG., Illus.). 48p. (J). (gr. 4-7). pap. 10.99 *(978-1-84680-178-5(8))* Evans Brothers, Ltd. GBR. Dist: Independent Pubs. Group.

—Puppet Master, 1 vol. 2007. (Extraordinary Files Ser.). (ENG., Illus.). 48p. (J). (gr. 4-7). pap. 10.99 *(978-1-84680-182-2(6))* Evans Brothers, Ltd. GBR. Dist: Independent Pubs. Group.

—Secrets & Lies, 1 vol. 2007. (Extraordinary Files Ser.). (ENG., Illus.). 48p. (J). (gr. 4-7). pap. 10.99 *(978-1-84680-249-2(0))* Evans Brothers, Ltd. GBR. Dist: Independent Pubs. Group.

—Sleep Walker, 1 vol. 2007. (Extraordinary Files Ser.). (ENG., Illus.). 48p. (J). (gr. 4-7). pap. 10.99 *(978-1-84680-174-7(5))* Evans Brothers, Ltd. GBR. Dist: Independent Pubs. Group.

—Spider Invasion, 1 vol. 2007. (Extraordinary Files Ser.). (ENG., Illus.). 48p. (J). (gr. 4-7). pap. 10.99 *(978-1-84680-183-9(4))* Evans Brothers, Ltd. GBR. Dist: Independent Pubs. Group.

—Werewolf Eclipse, 1 vol. 2007. (Extraordinary Files Ser.). (ENG., Illus.). 48p. (J). (gr. 4-7). pap. 10.99 *(978-1-84680-180-8(X))* Evans Brothers, Ltd. GBR. Dist: Independent Pubs. Group.

Cox, Joseph J. Grobar & the Mind Control Potion. Becker, Rebecca J., illus. 2005. 168p. (J). per. 9.95 *(978-0-9764659-3-5(0))* Suckerfish Bks.

Dautel, Daniel. Mission to Mount Everest. 2009. 90p. pap. 9.96 *(978-0-557-09695-4(2))* Lulu Pr., Inc.

de Groot, Bob. Clifton Vol. 6: Kidnapping. 2009. (Clifton Ser.: 6). (Illus.). 48p. (J). (gr. 3-17). pap. 11.95 *(978-1-905460-87-8(2))* CineBook GBR. Dist: National Bk. Network.

Goldsmann, Henri. Secret Agent Spanky Sheep in the mystery of: the Pooperous Pizza Plunderer. 2006. 140p. pap. 11.99 *(978-1-4116-8094-4(4))* Lulu Pr., Inc.

Groot, Bob de. Jade Vol. 5. Rodrigue, illus. 2008. (Clifton Ser.: 5). 48p. pap. 11.95 *(978-1-905460-52-6(X))* CineBook GBR. Dist: National Bk. Network.

Groot, De. Black Moon. Spear, Luke, tr. Rodrigue, illus. 2007. (Clifton Ser.: 4). 48p. (J). (gr. 4-7). pap. 9.99 *(978-1-905460-30-4(9))* CineBook GBR. Dist: National Bk. Network.

Harvey, Paul E., Jr. The Adventures of Shamus the Leprechaun. 2009. 48p. pap. 15.50 *(978-1-60693-924-6(6)*, Strategic Bk. Publishing) Strategic Book Publishing & Rights Agency (SBPRA).

Hunt, Elizabeth Singer. Secret Agent Jack Stalwart: Book 5: the Secret of the Sacred Temple: Cambodia. 2008. (Secret Agent Jack Stalwart Ser.: 5). (ENG., Illus.). 128p. (J). (gr. 1-4). per. 5.99 *(978-1-60286-003-2(3)*, Da Capo Lifelong) Hachette Bks.

—Secret Agent Jack Stalwart: Book 7: the Puzzle of the Missing Panda: China, Bk. 7. 2008. (Secret Agent Jack Stalwart Ser.: 7). (ENG., Illus.). 128p. (J). (gr. 1-4). pap. 5.99 *(978-1-60286-020-9(3))* Hachette Bk. Group.

Payson, Howard. The Boy Scouts under Sealed Orders. 2005. (Illus.). pap. 30.95 *(978-1-885529-57-2(0))* Stevens Publishing.

Smith, Roland. Independence Hall. (I, Q Ser.: Bk. 1). (ENG., 312p. (YA). (gr. 6-8). 2009. Illus.). 15.95 *(978-1-58536-468-8(1)*, 202188) 2008. pap. 12.99 *(978-1-58536-325-4(1)*, 202289) Sleeping Bear Pr.

Turk, Judy Vanslyke, et al. Laughing Thief. 2007. (Clifton Ser.: 2). (Illus.). 48p. (J). (gr. 4-7). per. 11.95 *(978-1-905460-07-6(4))* CineBook GBR. Dist: National Bk. Network.

Van Draanen, Wendelin. Sammy Keyes & the Dead Giveaway. 2008. (Sammy Keyes Ser.: Bk. 10). (J). 64.99 *(978-1-60640-639-7(6))* Findaway World, LLC.

—Sammy Keyes & the Dead Giveaway. unabr. ed. 2006. (Sammy Keyes Ser.: Bk. 10). (J). (gr. 5-7). pap. 54.95 incl. audio compact disk *(978-1-59519-771-9(0))*; pap. 36.95 incl. audio *(978-1-59519-770-2(2))* Live Oak Media.

—Sammy Keyes & the Dead Giveaway. 2007. (Sammy Keyes Ser.: 10). (ENG., Illus.). 304p. (J). (gr. 5-7). per. 7.99 *(978-0-440-41911-2(5)*, Yearling) Random Hse. Children's Bks.

SECRET WRITING

see Cryptography

SECRETARIES

Kidde, Rita. What Do School Secretaries Do?, 1 vol. 2014. (Jobs in My School Ser.). (ENG., Illus.). 24p. (J). (gr. 1-2). pap. 9.25 *(978-1-4777-6538-8(7)*, a3c1def1-4ee9-4142-92ba-4dc1e02a8fd8, PowerKids Pr.) Rosen Publishing Group, Inc., The.

—What Do School Secretaries Do? (¿Qué Hacen los Secretarios de la Escuela?), 1 vol. de la Vega, Eida, ed. 2014. (Oficios en Mi Escuela / Jobs in My School Ser.). (SPA & ENG.). 24p. (J). (gr. 1-2). lib. bdg. 25.27 *(978-1-4777-6795-5(9)*, 69838fc8-d412-4d34-a42b-8a7b88555389, PowerKids Pr.) Rosen Publishing Group, Inc., The.

Syrewicz, Connor. Personal Assistant. 2013. (Earning $50,000 - $100,000 with a High School Diploma or Less Ser.: 14). 64p. (J). (gr. 7-18). 22.95 *(978-1-4222-2897-5(5))* Mason Crest.

SECRETARIES—FICTION

Stockton, Frank Richard. What Might Have Been Expected. 2009. 128p. 23.95 *(978-1-60664-676-2(1))*; pap. 10.95 *(978-1-60664-305-1(3))* Rodgers, Alan Bks.

Thaler, Mike. The School Secretary from the Black Lagoon. Lee, Jared, illus. 2006. (J). *(978-0-439-80077-8(3))* Scholastic, Inc.

SECTS

see also names of churches and sects, e.g. Methodist Church, etc.

Calvert, John. Divisions in Islam. 2010. (World of Islam Ser.). (Illus.). 64p. (YA). (gr. 4-7). lib. bdg. 22.95 *(978-1-4222-0533-4(9))* Mason Crest.

Espejo, Roman, ed. Cults, 1 vol. 2012. (Opposing Viewpoints Ser.). (ENG., Illus.). 224p. (gr. 10-12). 50.43 *(978-0-7377-3994-7(0)*, 5d28239c-fecc-47a2-b11d-858fce7d3104); pap. 34.80 *(978-0-7377-3995-4(9)*, 3954a273-c346-4957-a922-59ed3afdee30) Greenhaven Publishing LLC. (Greenhaven Publishing).

Kiesbye, Stefan, ed. Drunk Driving, 1 vol. 2008. (Social Issues Firsthand Ser.). (ENG., Illus.). 112p. (gr. 10-12). lib. bdg. 39.93 *(978-0-7377-4031-8(0)*, 1fc505d0-5336-4094-8033-4e45a4a70fa2, Greenhaven Publishing) Greenhaven Publishing LLC.

Owen, Ruth. Voodoo Zombies. 2018. (Zombie Zone Ser.). (ENG.). 24p. (J). (gr. 2-7). 18.95 *(978-1-68402-439-1(0))* Bearport Publishing Co., Inc.

Person, Stephen. Voodoo in New Orleans. 2010. (HorrorScapes Ser.). 32p. (YA). (gr. 4-7). lib. bdg. 28.50 *(978-1-936087-99-0(5))* Bearport Publishing Co., Inc.

Piehl, Norah, ed. Cults, 1 vol. 2013. (Issues That Concern You Ser.). (ENG., Illus.). 128p. (gr. 7-10). lib. bdg. 43.63 *(978-0-7377-6286-0(1)*, 4ece0d8f-2eb3-4442-9496-dd91c10edd7d, Greenhaven Publishing) Greenhaven Publishing LLC.

Schauer, Pete. The People Behind Cult Murders, 1 vol. 2016. (Psychology of Mass Murderers Ser.). (ENG., Illus.). 144p. (gr. 8-8). 38.93 *(978-0-7660-7610-5(5)*, f26f5969-ad8d-4808-bae8-6092ae96b6af) Enslow Publishing, LLC.

SECURITIES

see also Bonds; Investments; Stocks

Mahoney, Emily. Learn Capitalization with Wizards, 1 vol. 2020. (Grammar Magic! Ser.). (ENG.). 24p. (gr. 2-3). pap. 9.15 *(978-1-5382-4727-3(5)*, 747219ca-b071-411f-855b-eaf3afdd2ca1) Stevens, Gareth Publishing LLLP.

SECURITIES EXCHANGE

see Stock Exchanges

SECURITY (PSYCHOLOGY)

Schulz, Charles. Seguridad es un Pulgar y una Manta. (SPA.). (J). 7.00 *(978-84-7655-664-1(0)*, PI3929) Plaza Joven, S.A. ESP. Dist: Lectorum Pubns., Inc.

SECURITY (PSYCHOLOGY)—FICTION

Littman, Sarah Darer. Want to Go Private? (ENG.). 336p. (YA). (gr. 9-9). 2019. pap. 10.99 *(978-0-545-15147-4(3))* 2011. 17.99 *(978-0-545-15146-7(5)*, Scholastic Pr.) Scholastic, Inc.

Rylant, Cynthia. The Stars Will Still Shine. Beeke, Tiphanie, illus. 2005. 40p. (J). lib. bdg. 17.89 *(978-0-06-054640-3(9))*; (ENG.). (gr. -1-3). 17.99 *(978-0-06-054639-7(5)*, HarperCollins) HarperCollins Pubs.

Simon, Coco. Katie Starting from Scratch. 2014. (Cupcake Diaries: 21). (ENG., Illus.). 160p. (J). (gr. 3-7). pap. 7.99 *(978-1-4814-0471-6(7)*, Simon Spotlight) Simon Spotlight.

Spinelli, Jerry. Eggs. 2008. (ENG., Illus.). 240p. (J). (gr. 3-7). pap. 8.99 *(978-0-316-16647-8(2))* Little, Brown Bks. for Young Readers.

SECURITY, INTERNATIONAL

see also Disarmament; International Organization

Hudak, Heather C. McCarthyism & the Red Scare. 2017. (Uncovering the Past: Analyzing Primary Sources Ser.). 48p. (J). (gr. 5-6). *(978-0-7787-3939-5(2))* Crabtree Publishing Co.

Van Dijk, Ruud. The Making of the Modern World: 1945 to the Present: Governance & the Quest for Security, Vol. 9. 2016. (Making of the Modern World: 1945 to the Present Ser.: Vol. 9). (ENG., Illus.). 64p. (J). (gr. 7-12). 23.95 *(978-1-4222-3638-3(2))* Mason Crest.

SEDITION

see Political Crimes and Offenses; Revolutions

SEEDS

Allyn, Daisy. Seeds & Plants, 1 vol. 2012. (InfoMax Readers Ser.). (ENG., Illus.). 16p. (J). (gr. k-k). pap. 7.00 *(978-1-4488-8932-7(4)*, 2876ca2a-4ec7-453a-91e9-5b812c8eda1a, Rosen Classroom) Rosen Publishing Group, Inc., The.

Aloian, Molly. What Are Seeds? 2012. (ENG., Illus.). 24p. (J). *(978-0-7787-4221-0(0))*; pap. *(978-0-7787-4226-5(1))* Crabtree Publishing Co.

Amstutz, Lisa J. Which Seed Is This?, 1 vol. 2012. (Nature Starts Ser.). (ENG.). 32p. (J). (gr. -1-2). pap. 8.10 *(978-1-4296-7851-3(8)*, 118164); (J). (gr. -1-2). lib. bdg. 27.99 *(978-1-4296-7552-9(7)*, 117129); (gr. 1-2). pap. 47.70 *(978-1-4296-8297-8(3)*, Capstone Pr.) Capstone.

Anderson, Judith. Once There Was a Seed. Gordon, Mike, illus. 2010. (Nature's Miracles Ser.). (ENG.). 32p. (J). (gr. k-3). 18.69 *(978-0-7641-4493-6(6)*, B.E.S. Publishing) Peterson's.

Aston, Dianna Hutts. A Seed Is Sleepy. 2014. (J). lib. bdg. 18.40 *(978-0-606-35291-8(0))* Turtleback.

Austen, Elizabeth. Seeds, 1 vol. rev. ed. 2014. (Science: Informational Text Ser.). (ENG., Illus.). 24p. (gr. k-1). pap. 9.99 *(978-1-4807-4522-3(7))* Teacher Created Materials, Inc.

Balsavar, Deepa & Kaushal, Tara. The Seed. 2005. (HIN & ENG., Illus.). (J). *(978-81-8146-110-0(X))* Tulika Pubs.

Benbow, Ann & Mably, Colin. Sprouting Seed Science Projects, 1 vol. 2009. (Real Life Science Experiments Ser.). (ENG., Illus.). 48p. (gr. 3-3). lib. bdg. 27.93 *(978-0-7660-3147-0(0)*, ed8b4b8a-3453-4a17-9e11-e2f5bebfb593) Enslow Publishing, LLC.

Benchmark Education Co., LLC. We Need a Seed Big Book. 2014. (Shared Reading Foundations Ser.). (J). (gr. -1). *(978-1-4509-9449-1(0))* Benchmark Education Co.

Bishop, Celeste. ¿Por Qué Las Plantas Tienen Flores? / Why Do Plants Have Flowers?, 1 vol., 1. 2015. (Partes de la Planta / Plant Parts Ser.). (ENG & SPA., Illus.). 24p. (J). (gr. 1-1). 25.27 *(978-1-5081-4739-8(6)*, 0c55f5cf-54f3-451e-bd50-8fa6bb1505bc, PowerKids Pr.) Rosen Publishing Group, Inc., The.

—¿Por Qué Las Plantas Tienen Frutas? / Why Do Plants Have Fruits?, 1 vol., 1. 2015. (Partes de la Planta / Plant Parts Ser.). (ENG & SPA., Illus.). 24p. (J). (gr. 1-1). 25.27 *(978-1-5081-4740-4(X)*, 73d89ba0-3b5a-4759-8bd2-abdb0214dcf2, PowerKids Pr.) Rosen Publishing Group, Inc., The.

—¿Por Qué Las Plantas Tienen Semillas? / Why Do Plants Have Seeds?, 1 vol., 1. 2015. (Partes de la Planta / Plant Parts Ser.). (ENG & SPA., Illus.). 24p. (J). (gr. 1-1). 25.27 *(978-1-5081-4732-9(9)*, d861f168-84d1-4b2b-8132-424f3c292c9f, PowerKids Pr.) Rosen Publishing Group, Inc., The.

—Why Do Plants Have Flowers?, 1 vol., 1. 2015. (Plant Parts Ser.). (ENG., Illus.). 24p. (J). (gr. 1-1). pap. 9.25 *(978-1-5081-4213-3(0)*, 41352a7c-4026-4b29-a441-0ac97319edd3, PowerKids Pr.) Rosen Publishing Group, Inc., The.

—Why Do Plants Have Fruits?, 1 vol., 1. 2015. (Plant Parts Ser.). (ENG., Illus.). 24p. (J). (gr. 1-1). pap. 9.25 *(978-1-5081-4217-1(3)*, 477aa2b2-ca34-48b7-910a-460bf4a63fdd, PowerKids Pr.) Rosen Publishing Group, Inc., The.

—Why Do Plants Have Seeds?, 1 vol., 1. 2015. (Plant Parts Ser.). (ENG., Illus.). 24p. (J). (gr. 1-1). pap. 9.25 *(978-1-5081-4229-4(7)*, c1e04ee5-1e8c-429c-99c6-96a5ec588e84, PowerKids Pr.) Rosen Publishing Group, Inc., The.

Blackaby, Susan. Plant Packages: A Book about Seeds, 1 vol. Delage, Charlene, illus. 2003. (Growing Things Ser.). (ENG.). 24p. (J). (gr. -1-2). per. 8.95 *(978-1-4048-0384-8(X)*, 92535, Picture Window Bks.) Capstone.

Blanchard, Emma. Seeds I See: Work with 11-19 to Gain Foundations for Place Value. 2013. (Rosen Math Readers Ser.). (ENG.). 16p. (J). (gr. k-1). pap. 42.00 *(978-1-4777-1606-9(8))*; (Illus.). pap. 7.00 *(978-1-4777-1605-2(X)*, 1d65d968-7ed5-4152-aedc-77b62fd3c96e) Rosen Publishing Group, Inc., The. (Rosen Classroom).

Bodach, Vijaya K. Seeds [Scholastic]. 2010. (Plant Parts Ser.). 24p. pap. 0.52 *(978-1-4296-5060-1(5)*, Capstone Pr.) Capstone.

Bodach, Vijaya Khisty. Seeds. rev. ed. 2016. (Plant Parts Ser.). (ENG.). 24p. (J). (gr. -1-2). pap. 7.29 *(978-1-5157-4246-3(6)*, 134004, Capstone Pr.) Capstone.

Bone, Emily. How Food Grows. 2017. (Big Picture Books* Ser.). (ENG.). 32p. 14.99 *(978-0-7945-4032-6(5)*, Usborne) EDC Publishing.

Buchanan, Shelly. Plant Reproduction. 2015. (Science: Informational Text Ser.). (ENG., Illus.). 32p. (J). (gr. 3-5). pap. 11.99 *(978-1-4807-4676-3(2))* Teacher Created Materials, Inc.

Carle, Eric. La Semillita (the Tiny Seed) Romay, Alexis, tr. Carle, Eric, illus. 2016. (World of Eric Carle Ser.). (SPA., Illus.). 40p. (J). (gr. -1-3). 8.99 *(978-1-4814-7834-2(6)*, Libros Para Ninos) Libros Para Ninos.

—The Tiny Seed/Ready-To-Read Level 2. Carle, Eric, illus. 2015. (World of Eric Carle Ser.). (ENG., Illus.). 32p. (J). (gr. k-2). pap. 4.99 *(978-1-4814-3575-8(2)*, Simon Spotlight) Simon Spotlight.

Cartw, Paul. Where Are the Seeds/Ww/E. (Wonder Worldtm Ser.). 16p. 29.95 *(978-0-7802-2042-3(0))* Wright Group/McGraw-Hill.

Clay, Kathryn. Planting Seeds. 2016. (Celebrate Spring Ser.). (ENG., Illus.). 24p. (J). (gr. -1-2). lib. bdg. 22.65 *(978-1-4914-8305-3(9)*, 130781) Capstone.

Colby, Jennifer. Burrs to Velcro. 2019. (21st Century Junior Library: Tech from Nature Ser.). (ENG., Illus.). 24p. (J). (gr. 2-5). lib. bdg. 30.64 *(978-1-5341-4290-9(8)*, 212612) Cherry Lake Publishing.

—Thistle Burrs to Velcro. 2019. (21st Century Junior Library: Tech from Nature Ser.). (ENG.). 24p. (J). (gr. 2-5). pap. 12.79 *(978-1-5341-3946-6(X)*, 212613) Cherry Lake Publishing.

Dodson Wade, Mary. Seeds Sprout!, 1 vol. 2009. (I Like Plants! Ser.). (ENG., Illus.). 24p. (gr. k-2). pap. 10.35 *(978-0-7660-3614-7(6)*, c671c95c-4b63-406e-85f0-5fc891a28b1c, Enslow Elementary); lib. bdg. 25.27 *(978-0-7660-3154-8(3)*, 7487ebb3-16e6-4ebf-a649-cf8c6b226bfe) Enslow Publishing, LLC.

Dunn, Mary R. A Bean's Life Cycle. 2017. (Explore Life Cycles Ser.). (ENG., Illus.). 24p. (J). (gr. -1-2). lib. bdg. 27.32 *(978-1-5157-7051-0(6)*, 135481, Capstone Pr.) Capstone.

Galbraith, Kathryn O. Planting the Wild Garden, 1 vol. Halperin, Wendy Anderson, illus. 32p. (J). (gr. -1-3). 2015. pap. 7.99 *(978-1-56145-791-5(4))* 2011. 16.99 *(978-1-56145-563-8(6))* Peachtree Publishing Co. Inc.

Gibbons, Gail. From Seed to Plant. Gibbons, Gail, illus. 2012. (Illus.). audio compact disk 18.95 *(978-1-4301-1079-8(1))* Live Oak Media.

Glaser, Rebecca. Seeds. 2012. (ENG., Illus.). 24p. (J). lib. bdg. 25.65 *(978-1-62031-029-8(5))* Jump! Inc.

Gray, Susan H. Junior Scientists: Experiment with Seeds. 2010. (Explorer Junior Library: Science Explorer Junior Ser.). (ENG., Illus.). 32p. (gr. 3-6). lib. bdg. 32.07 *(978-1-60279-835-9(4)*, 200536) Cherry Lake Publishing.

—Seeds. 2009. (Explorer Library: Science Explorer Ser.). (ENG., Illus.). 32p. (gr. 4-8). lib. bdg. 32.07 *(978-1-60279-514-3(2)*, 200293) Cherry Lake Publishing.

Gregory, Josh. From Thistle Burrs to... Velcro. 2012. (21st Century Skills Innovation Library: Innovations from Nature Ser.). (ENG.). 32p. (gr. 4-8). pap. 14.21 *(978-1-61080-668-8(9)*, 202278); (Illus.). 32.07 *(978-1-61080-494-3(5)*, 202104) Cherry Lake Publishing.

Haakonsen, Jens. What Are Seeds?, 1 vol. 2017. (Plants in My World Ser.). (ENG.). 24p. (gr. 1-1). pap. 9.25 *(978-1-5081-6155-4(0)*, 555a27b8-c866-45df-9149-0d904aa47e98, PowerKids Pr.) Rosen Publishing Group, Inc., The.

Hayes, Amy. A Seed Becomes a Dandelion, 1 vol. 2015. (Transformations in Nature Ser.). (ENG., Illus.). 24p. (gr. 1-1). pap. 9.23 *(978-1-5026-0826-0(X)*, afde8727-87da-4a52-9dd1-b0af5c468156) Cavendish Square Publishing LLC.

Heller, Ruth. The Reason for a Flower. (FRE.). (J). 6.99 *(978-0-590-71999-5(8))* Scholastic, Inc.

Hutts Aston, Dianna. A Seed Is Sleepy. Long, Sylvia, illus. 2007. (Family Treasure Nature Encylopedias Ser.). (ENG.). 40p. (J). (gr. k-5). 16.99 *(978-0-8118-5520-4(1))* Chronicle Bks. LLC.

Jordan, Helene J. Como Crece una Semilla: How a Seed Grows (Spanish Edition), 1 vol. Krupinski, Loretta, illus. 2006. (Let's-Read-And-Find-Out Science 1 Ser.).Tr. of How a Seed Grows. (SPA.). 32p. (J). (gr. -1-3). pap. 6.99 *(978-0-06-088716-2(8)*, HarperCollins) HarperCollins Pubs.

Juettner, Bonnie. The Seed Vault. 2009. (Great Idea Ser.). (Illus.). 48p. (J). (gr. 4-6). lib. bdg. 26.60 *(978-1-59953-343-8(X))* Norwood Hse. Pr.

Kababik, Dana. From Seed to Flower. 2003. (Grow up! Ser.). (J). *(978-1-58417-170-6(7))*; pap. *(978-1-58417-176-8(6))* Lake Street Pubs.

Kim, Sue. How Does a Seed Grow? A Book with Foldout Pages. 2010. (ENG., Illus.). 14p. (J). (gr. -1-1). bds. 9.99 *(978-1-4169-9435-0(1)*, Little Simon) Little Simon.

Kirkman, Marissa. Seeds. 2019. (Plant Parts Ser.). (ENG., Illus.). 24p. (J). (gr. -1-2). pap. 6.95 *(978-1-9771-1024-4(X)*, 141100, Pebble) Capstone.

Lawrence, Ellen. From Bird Poop to Wind: How Seeds Get Around. 2012. (Science Slam: Plant-Ology Ser.). (Illus.). 24p. (J). (gr. -1-3). lib. bdg. 26.99 *(978-1-61772-585-2(4))* Bearport Publishing Co., Inc.

Levine, Amy-Jill & Eisenberg Sasso, Sandy. The Marvelous Mustard Seed. Meganck, Margaux, illus. 2018. (ENG.). 48p. (J). (gr. -1-3). 16.00 *(978-0-664-26275-4(9)*, 664262759, Flyaway Bks.) Westminster John Knox Pr.

Levy, Janey. How Plants Spread Seeds, 1 vol. 2019. (Top Secret Life of Plants Ser.). (ENG.). 24p. (gr. 2-3). pap. 9.15 *(978-1-5382-3383-2(5)*, b2073707-89ef-4982-9429-a61c5a98311c) Stevens, Gareth Publishing LLLP.

Macken, JoAnn Early. Flip, Float, Fly: Seeds on the Move. Paparone, Pam, illus. 2016. (ENG.). 32p. (J). (gr. 1-4). 8.99 *(978-0-8234-3758-0(2))* Holiday Hse., Inc.

Mann, Rachel. Plants Grow from Seeds, 6 vols., Set. 2003. (Phonics Readers 1-36 Ser.). (ENG.). 8p. (gr. k-1). pap. 29.70 *(978-0-7368-3207-6(6))* Capstone.

Mitchell, Melanie. Seeds. (First Step Nonfiction — Parts of Plants Ser.). (ENG., Illus.). 8p. (J). (gr. k-2). 2004. pap. 5.99 *(978-0-8225-3920-9(9)*, 63341e0a-5172-4e75-9af5-d150bb93e709) 2015. E-Book 23.99 *(978-1-5124-1052-5(7))* Lerner Publishing Group.

Moore, David. National Geographic Science 1-2 (Life Science: Plants & Animals): Explore on Your Own: Trees, Seeds, & Leaves. 2009. (C). pap. 8.95 *(978-0-7362-5563-9(X))* National Geographic School Publishing, Inc.

Morgan, Emily. Next Time You See a Maple Seed. 2014. (Next Time You See Ser.). (ENG.). 32p. (J). (gr. -1-k). 13.99 *(978-1-938946-35-6(9))* National Science Teachers Assn.

Morgan, Sally. Flowers, Fruits & Seeds. (Looking at Plants Ser.). (Illus.). 32p. (J). lib. bdg. 24.25 *(978-1-931983-10-5(0))* Chrysalis Education.

Morley, Margaret W. Little Wanderers. 2009. (Illus.). 116p. pap. 8.95 *(978-1-59915-317-9(3))* Yesterday's Classics.

—Seed-Babies. 2009. (Illus.). 88p. pap. 7.95 *(978-1-59915-316-2(5))* Yesterday's Classics.

O'Donnell, K. So Many Seeds: Learning the S Sound. 2009. (PowerPhonics Ser.). 24p. (gr. 1-1). 39.90 *(978-1-60851-471-7(4)*, PowerKids Pr.) Rosen Publishing Group, Inc., The.

Ohanesian, Diane C. Seeds & Plants: Grades 2 & 3. (Illus.). (J). pap., wbk. ed. 4.99 *(978-0-88743-961-2(6))* School Zone Publishing Co.

Owen, Ruth. How Do Plants Make & Spread Their Seeds?, 1 vol. 2014. (World of Plants Ser.). (ENG.). 32p. (J). (gr. 2-3). lib. bdg. 27.93 *(978-1-4777-7145-7(X)*, c8f9d4dd-9ae5-4afe-956e-97471f999c90, PowerKids Pr.) Rosen Publishing Group, Inc., The.

—Science & Craft Projects with Plants & Seeds, 1 vol. 2013. (Get Crafty Outdoors Ser.). (ENG., Illus.). 32p. (J). (gr. 2-3). 30.27 *(978-1-4777-0247-5(4)*, 7d5a3b0c-ada1-4af8-a0f7-023eb105439d); pap. 12.75 *(978-1-4777-0257-4(1)*, 145185e6-8bb6-44f9-9b9f-db3c07dde47a) Rosen Publishing Group, Inc., The. (PowerKids Pr.).

Page, Robin. Seeds Move! Page, Robin, illus. 2019. (ENG., Illus.). 32p. (J). (gr. -1-3). 18.99 *(978-1-5344-0915-6(7)*, Beach Lane Bks.) Beach Lane Bks.

Pallotta, Jerry. Who Will Plant a Tree? Leonard, Tom, illus. 2010. (ENG.). 32p. (J). (gr. 1-4). 16.99 *(978-1-58536-502-9(5)*, 202196) Sleeping Bear Pr.

Peterson, Cris. Seed, Soil, Sun: Earth's Recipe for Food. Lundquist, David R., photos by. 2012. (ENG., Illus.). 32p. (J). (gr. k-3). pap. 8.99 *(978-1-59078-947-6(4)*, Astra Young Readers) Astra Publishing Hse.

Plants & Seeds, 6 vols. (Sunshinetm Science Ser.). 24p. (gr. 1-2). 31.50 *(978-0-7802-0291-7(0))* Wright Group/McGraw-Hill.

Prokos, Anna. Seed Power: Discovering How Plants Grow. Clegg, Dave, illus. 2017. (Imagine That! Ser.). (ENG.). 32p. (J). (gr. 2-4). lib. bdg. 26.65 *(978-1-63440-151-7(4)*, 13b73175-3636-42d7-94ca-565c8bc54281); E-Book 39.99 *(978-1-63440-163-0(8))* Red Chair Pr.

Puri, Devi. Seeds, Bulbs, & Sprouts, 1 vol. 2015. (Garden Squad! Ser.). (ENG., Illus.). 24p. (J). (gr. 3-4). pap. 9.25 *(978-1-4994-0977-2(X)*, 911b40a8-7696-4945-94b5-7db88d9964fc, PowerKids Pr.) Rosen Publishing Group, Inc., The.

Reid, Barbara. Seed to Sunflower: A First Look Board Book. Crysler, Ian, photos by. 2004. (Illus.). 12p. (J). (gr. k-2). reprint ed. 10.00 *(978-0-7567-7853-8(0))* DIANE Publishing Co.

Relf, Patricia. Magic School Plants Seeds. 2014. 14.00 *(978-1-63419-672-7(4))* Perfection Learning Corp.

Rhodes, Evan. How Do Seeds Sprout?, 1 vol. 2013. (Nature's Super Secrets Ser.). (ENG., Illus.). 24p. (J). (gr. 1-2). pap. 9.15 *(978-1-4339-8166-1(1)*, 219a8c82-eb27-475d-8577-4b1827b0ebee); lib. bdg. 25.27 *(978-1-4339-8165-4(3)*, 0abcf1e5-2c76-4e72-a851-e1ce43f74d8f) Stevens, Gareth Publishing LLLP.

Richards, Jean. A Fruit Is a Suitcase for Seeds. Hariton, Anca, illus. 2006. (ENG.). 32p. (J). (gr. -1-3). pap. 9.99 *(978-0-8225-5991-7(9)*, e41a0fd6-4f03-4277-bced-b9980242b94f, First Avenue Editions) Lerner Publishing Group.

Rigby Education Staff. From Here to There. (Sails Literacy Ser.). (Illus.). 16p. (gr. 2-3). 27.00 *(978-0-7635-9958-4(1)*, 699581C99) Rigby Education.

Riggs, Kate. A Seed Needs Sun. Dogi, Fiammetta, illus. 2014. 14p. (J). (gr. -1-k). bds. 9.99 *(978-1-56846-254-7(9)*, 21594, Creative Editions) Creative Co., The.

—Sunflower. 2012. (Grow with Me Ser.). (ENG., Illus.). 32p. (J). (gr. 3-6). 19.95 *(978-1-60818-218-3(5)*, 21976, Creative Education) Creative Co., The.

Robbins, Ken. Seeds. Robbins, Ken, illus. 2005. (ENG., Illus.). 32p. (J). (gr. 1-4). 17.99 *(978-0-689-85041-7(7)*, Atheneum

Bks. for Young Readers) Simon & Schuster Children's Publishing.

Rockwell, Anne. One Bean. 2014. 17.00 *(978-1-63419-723-6(2))* Perfection Learning Corp.

Roemer, Heidi. What Kind of Seeds Are These? Kassian, Olena, illus. 2006. (ENG.). 32p. (J). (gr. k-1). 16.95 *(978-1-55971-955-1(9))* Cooper Square Publishing Llc.

Sayre, April Pulley. Let's Go Nuts! Seeds We Eat. Sayre, April Pulley, illus. 2013. (ENG., Illus.). 32p. (J). (gr. -1-3). 17.99 *(978-1-4424-6728-6(2)*, Beach Lane Bks.) Beach Lane Bks.

Schaefer, Lola M. Pick, Pull, Snap! Where Once a Flower Bloomed. 2003. (ENG., Illus.). 32p. (J). (gr. k-5). 17.99 *(978-0-688-17834-5(0)*, Greenwillow Bks.) HarperCollins Pubs.

School Zone Publishing Company Staff. Seeds & Plants. (Illus.). (J). 19.99 incl. audio compact disk *(978-0-88743-922-3(5))* School Zone Publishing Co.

Scraper, Katherine. A Seed Needs Help. 2006. (Early Explorers Ser.). (J). pap. *(978-1-4108-6026-2(4))* Benchmark Education Co.

Seeds... (Early Intervention Levels Ser.). 23.10 *(978-0-7362-0011-0(8))* CENGAGE Learning.

Seeds Grow, 6 vols. (Sunshinetm Science Ser.). 24p. (gr. 1-2). 31.50 *(978-0-7802-0290-0(2))*; 36.95 *(978-0-7802-0541-3(3))* Wright Group/McGraw-Hill.

Seeds, Seeds, Seeds, 6 vols. (Sunshinetm Science Ser.). 24p. (gr. 1-2). 31.50 *(978-0-7802-0289-4(9))* Wright Group/McGraw-Hill.

Sian revision seed Mysteries. 2004. (J). *(978-1-59242-065-0(6))* Delta Education, LLC.

Sterling, Kristin. Exploring Seeds. 2011. (First Step Nonfiction — Let's Look at Plants Ser.). (gr. k-2). (ENG., Illus.). 24p. (J). pap. 6.99 *(978-0-7613-7835-8(9)*, 47f5a4eb-c679-44f6-b0fe-186f47e0b906); pap. 33.92 *(978-0-7613-8617-9(3))*; lib. bdg. 21.27 *(978-0-7613-5782-7(3))* Lerner Publishing Group.

Stewart, Melissa. How Does a Seed Sprout? And Other Questions about Plants. Schwartz, Carol, illus. 2014. (Good Question! Ser.). (ENG.). 32p. (J). (gr. 1). pap. 6.95 *(978-1-4549-0671-1(5))* Sterling Publishing Co., Inc.

—A Seed Is the Start. 2018. (Illus.). 32p. (J). (gr. 1-3). 17.99 *(978-1-4263-2977-7(6))*; (ENG., lib. bdg. 27.90 *(978-1-4263-2978-4(4))* Disney Publishing Worldwide. (National Geographic Kids).

Stone, Lynn. Seeds. 2007. (Plant Parts Ser.). (ENG., Illus.). 24p. (gr. 2-3). per. 8.95 *(978-1-60044-695-5(7)*, 9781600446955) Rourke Educational Media.

Sundance/Newbridge LLC Staff. Seeds Get Around. 2007. (Early Science Ser.). (gr. k-3). 18.95 *(978-1-4007-6341-2(X))*; pap. 6.10 *(978-1-4007-6337-5(1))* Sundance/Newbridge Educational Publishing.

Thomson, Ruth. The Life Cycle of a Bean, 1 vol. 2007. (Learning about Life Cycles Ser.). (ENG., Illus.). 24p. (J). (gr. 2-2). lib. bdg. 26.27 *(978-1-4042-3714-8(3)*, d6883220-1731-47bb-af4a-520a84aadc0d, PowerKids Pr.) Rosen Publishing Group, Inc., The.

Throp, Claire. All about Seeds. rev. ed. 2016. (All about Plants Ser.). (ENG.). 24p. (J). (gr. -1-1). pap. 5.99 *(978-1-4846-3849-1(2)*, 134790, Heinemann) Capstone.

Ward, Jennifer. What Will Grow? Ghahremani, Susie, illus. 2017. (ENG.). 40p. (J). 17.99 *(978-1-68119-030-3(3)*, 900156309, Bloomsbury USA Childrens) Bloomsbury Publishing USA.

Weakland, Mark. Seeds Go, Seeds Grow. 2010. (Science Starts Ser.). (ENG.). 32p. (J). (gr. 1-2). pap. 49.60 *(978-1-4296-6146-1(1)*, 16038); (Illus.). (gr. -1-2). pap. 8.10 *(978-1-4296-6145-4(3)*, 115296) Capstone. (Capstone Pr.).

SEEING EYE DOGS

see Guide Dogs

SEGHERS, CHARLES JOHN, 1839-1886

Bosco, Antoinette. Charles John Seghers: Pioneer in Alaska. Kalmenoff, Matthew, illus. 2011. 194p. 42.95 *(978-1-258-01868-9(3))* Literary Licensing, LLC.

SEGREGATION IN EDUCATION

see also Discrimination in Education

Aretha, David. Brown V. Board of Education. 2013. (The Civil Rights Movement Ser.). (Illus.). 128p. (YA). 28.95 *(978-1-59935-370-8(9))* Reynolds, Morgan Inc.

—With All Deliberate Speed: Court-Ordered Busing & American Schools. 2012. (Civil Rights Movement Ser.). (YA). (gr. 7-12). 28.95 *(978-1-59935-181-0(1))* Reynolds, Morgan Inc.

Bailey, Budd. School Desegregation: Brown V. Board of Education of Topeka, 1 vol. 2018. (Courting History Ser.). (ENG.). 64p. (J). (gr. 6-6). pap. 16.87 *(978-1-5026-3952-3(1)*, 8019b94c-0e9d-4c56-8df5-3bff1cbd30c8) Cavendish Square Publishing LLC.

Bridges, Ruby. Ruby Bridges Goes to School: My True Story. 2009. (Scholastic Reader Level 2 Ser.). lib. bdg. 13.55 *(978-0-606-06808-6(2))* Turtleback.

—Ruby Bridges Goes to School: My True Story. 2009. (Scholastic Reader, Level 2 Ser.). (ENG., Illus.). 32p. (J). (gr. -1-3). pap. 3.99 *(978-0-545-10855-3(1))* Scholastic, Inc.

—This Is Your Time. 2020. (ENG., Illus.). 64p. (J). (gr. 5). lib. bdg. 18.99 *(978-0-593-37853-3(9))*; 15.99 *(978-0-593-37852-6(0))* Random Hse. Children's Bks. (Delacorte Bks. for Young Readers).

—Through My Eyes: Ruby Bridges. Lundell, Margo, ed. Lundell, Margo, illus. 2018. (Follow Me Around... Ser.). (ENG.). 64p. (J). (gr. 3-4). E-Book 27.00 *(978-0-545-70803-6(6))* Scholastic, Inc.

Bridges, Ruby & Maccarone, Grace. Let's Read About — Ruby Bridges. Van Wright, Cornelius & Hu, Ying-Hwa, illus. 2003. (Scholastic First Biographies Ser.). (J). *(978-0-439-51362-3(6))* Scholastic, Inc.

Coles, Robert. The Story of Ruby Bridges. 2009. 8.44 *(978-0-7848-3016-1(9)*, Everbind) Marco Bk. Co.

—The Story of Ruby Bridges. 2011. 17.00 *(978-1-61383-173-1(0))* Perfection Learning Corp.

—The Story of Ruby Bridges. Ford, George, illus. 50th anniv. ed. 2010. (ENG.). 32p. (J). (gr. -1-3). pap. 7.99 *(978-0-439-47226-5(1)*, Scholastic Paperbacks) Scholastic, Inc.

—The Story of Ruby Bridges. 2010. lib. bdg. 17.20 *(978-0-606-23189-3(7))* Turtleback.

Derosier, M. Michelle. Ruby Bridges: Get to Know the Girl Who Took a Stand for Education. 2019. (People You Should Know Ser.). (ENG., Illus.). 32p. (J). (gr. 3-6). lib. bdg. 27.99 *(978-1-5435-5527-1(6)*, 139387, Capstone Pr.) Capstone.

Donaldson, Madeline. Ruby Bridges. 2009. (History Maker Biographies Ser.). (ENG., Illus.). 48p. (J). (gr. 3-6). 27.93 *(978-0-7613-4220-5(6)*, 1299456, Lerner Pubns.) Lerner Publishing Group.

Dudley Gold, Susan. Brown V. Board of Education: Separate but Equal?, 1 vol. 2006. (Supreme Court Milestones Ser.). (ENG., Illus.). 128p. (YA). (gr. 8-8). 45.50 *(978-0-7614-1842-9(3)*, cd8e87c5-57bb-44e5-8e90-9eada1f95aa2) Cavendish Square Publishing LLC.

Furgang, Kathy. Brown V. Board of Education, 1 vol. 2017. (Spotlight on the Civil Rights Movement Ser.). (ENG., Illus.). 48p. (J). (gr. 6-6). pap. 12.75 *(978-1-5383-8021-5(8)*, d98e4a06-825e-4f48-b9d4-86d94722e4f3) Rosen Publishing Group, Inc., The.

Garbus, Julia, ed. The Brown V. Board of Education Trial, 1 vol. 2014. (Perspectives on Modern World History Ser.). (ENG., Illus.). 208p. (gr. 10-12). lib. bdg. 49.43 *(978-0-7377-7307-1(3)*, 052caf0e-5658-49d6-be35-fcda53ed4ae7, Greenhaven Publishing) Greenhaven Publishing LLC.

Goodman, Susan E. The First Step: How One Girl Put Segregation on Trial. Lewis, E. B., illus. 2016. (ENG.). 40p. (J). 17.99 *(978-0-8027-3739-7(0)*, 900135323); (gr. 1-3). E-Book 12.59 *(978-0-8027-3741-0(2))* Bloomsbury Publishing USA. (Bloomsbury USA Childrens).

Hale, Christy. Todos Iguales/All Equal: Un Corrido de Lemon Grove/a Ballad of Lemon Grove, 1 vol. 2019. (SPA., Illus.). 40p. (J). (gr. 3-7). 20.95 *(978-0-89239-427-2(7)*, leelowcbp, Children's Book Press) Lee & Low Bks., Inc.

Hamby, Rachel. Barbara Rose Johns Jump-Starts the Civil Rights Movement. 2018. (J). *(978-1-64185-354-5(9)*, Focus Readers) North Star Editions.

Harris, Duchess & Lawrence, Blythe. Daisy Bates & the Little Rock Nine. 2018. (Freedom's Promise Ser.). (ENG., Illus.). 48p. (J). (gr. 4-8). lib. bdg. 35.64 *(978-1-5321-1768-8(X)*, 30824) ABDO Publishing Co.

Hinton, KaaVonia. Brown V. Board of Education, Topeka, KS, 1954. 2009. (Monumental Milestones Ser.). 48p. (YA). (gr. 4-7). lib. bdg. 29.95 *(978-1-58415-738-0(0))* Mitchell Lane Pubs.

—Desegregating America's Schools. 2009. (Monumental Milestones Ser.). 48p. (YA). (gr. 4-7). lib. bdg. 29.95 *(978-1-58415-737-3(2))* Mitchell Lane Pubs.

Kanefield, Teri. The Girl from the Tar Paper School: Barbara Rose Johns & the Advent of the Civil Rights Movement. 2014. (ENG., Illus.). 56p. (J). (gr. 5-9). 19.95 *(978-1-4197-0796-4(5)*, 1005601, Abrams Bks. for Young Readers) Abrams, Inc.

Klein, J. M. Sylvia Mendez: Education Equality Activist, 1 vol. 2019. (Barrier-Breaker Bios Ser.). (ENG.). 32p. (gr. 2-2). pap. 11.58 *(978-1-5026-4972-0(1)*, e3b45b76-9434-49ca-90d1-ff0fa4ec73ba) Cavendish Square Publishing LLC.

Klein, Rebecca T. School Integration: Brown V. Board of Education of Topeka, 1 vol. 2014. (Celebration of the Civil Rights Movement Ser.). (ENG., Illus.). 80p. (J). (gr. 6-6). 37.47 *(978-1-4777-7743-5(1)*, dd01ddfb-2d0d-4011-a138-4444fa6c37de) Rosen Publishing Group, Inc., The.

—Your Legal Rights in School, 1 vol. 2014. (Know Your Rights Ser.). (ENG., Illus.). 64p. (J). (gr. 6-7). 36.47 *(978-1-4777-8048-0(3)*, 61b2da81-d4cf-43c5-b71b-2e8a412fb7ce, Rosen Reference) Rosen Publishing Group, Inc., The.

Looye, Juliette. Ruby Bridges. (Voices Reading Ser.). (Illus.). 16p. (J). pap. *(978-0-7367-2913-0(5))* Zaner-Bloser, Inc.

Lucas, Eileen. Cracking the Wall: The Struggles of the Little Rock Nine. Anthony, Mark, illus. 2007. pap. 37.95 incl. audio *(978-1-59519-939-3(X))*; pap. 39.95 incl. audio compact disk *(978-1-59519-943-0(8))* Live Oak Media.

—The Little Rock Nine Stand up for Their Rights. Gustavson, Adam, illus. 2011. (History Speaks: Picture Books Plus Reader's Theater Ser.). 48p. pap. 56.72 *(978-0-7613-7634-7(8))*; pap. 9.95 *(978-0-7613-7118-2(4))* Lerner Publishing Group.

Miller, Jake. Brown vs. Board of Education of Topeka: Challenging School Segregation in the Supreme Court, 1 vol. 2003. (Library of the Civil Rights Movement Ser.). (ENG., Illus.). 24p. (J). (gr. 3-3). lib. bdg. 26.27 *(978-0-8239-6250-1(4)*, 184de3f3-dc5b-4394-bb50-bc67c24250b5) Rosen Publishing Group, Inc., The.

Mooney, Carla. Little Rock Nine, 1 vol. 2015. (Stories of the Civil Rights Movement Ser.). (ENG.). 48p. (J). (gr. 4-8). 35.64 *(978-1-62403-880-8(8)*, 18130) ABDO Publishing Co.

Morretta, Alison. Rosa Parks & Civil Disobedience, 1 vol. 2016. (Primary Sources of the Civil Rights Movement Ser.). (ENG., Illus.). 64p. (gr. 6-6). 35.93 *(978-1-5026-1870-2(2)*, aab07914-02e2-4aa5-9164-fec426698f87) Cavendish Square Publishing LLC.

Perritano, John. Little Rock Nine. 2018. (Red Rhino Nonfiction Ser.). lib. bdg. 20.80 *(978-0-606-41252-0(2))* Turtleback.

Ribke, Simone T. Ruby Bridges (Rookie Biographies) 2015. (Rookie Biographies Ser.). (ENG., Illus.). 32p. (J). (gr. 1-2). pap. 5.95 *(978-0-531-20993-6(8)*, Children's Pr.) Scholastic Library Publishing.

Rotberg, Iris C. Choosing Charters: Better Schools or More Segregation? Glazer, Joshua L., ed. 2018. (ENG., Illus.). 264p. pap. 36.95 *(978-0-8077-5899-1(X)*, P570868) Teachers College Pr., Teachers College, Columbia Univ.

Rubin, Susan Goldman. Brown V. Board of Education: A Fight for Simple Justice. (ENG.). 144p. (J). (gr. 5). 2018. pap. 15.99 *(978-0-8234-4035-1(4))* 2016. (Illus.). 18.95 *(978-0-8234-3646-0(2))* Holiday Hse., Inc.

Taylor, Charlotte & Miller, Mara. The Little Rock Nine & School Desegregation, 1 vol. 2015. (Our Shared History Ser.). (ENG., Illus.). 128p. (gr. 7-7). lib. bdg. 38.93 *(978-0-7660-7010-3(7)*, 3a650216-cbd1-4bc3-b8e7-77de47b11b20) Enslow Publishing, LLC.

Tisdale, Rachel. Brown V. Board of Education, 1 vol., 1. 2014. (We Shall Overcome Ser.). (ENG.). 32p. (J). (gr. 4-5). 28.93 *(978-1-4777-6073-4(3)*, 436458e0-8bc8-4b5d-b295-263ec6b52c1e, PowerKids Pr.) Rosen Publishing Group, Inc., The.

—The Little Rock Nine, 1 vol., 1. 2014. (We Shall Overcome Ser.). (ENG.). 32p. (J). (gr. 4-5). 28.93 *(978-1-4777-6057-4(1)*, 4a01ffb3-b725-4d3c-8134-23788bf3affe, PowerKids Pr.) Rosen Publishing Group, Inc., The.

Tonatiuh, Duncan. Separate Is Never Equal: Sylvia Mendez & Her Family's Fight for Desegregation. 2014. (ENG., Illus.). 40p. (J). (gr. 1-4). 19.99 *(978-1-4197-1054-4(0)*, 1073301) Abrams, Inc.

Tougas, Shelley. Little Rock Girl 1957: How a Photograph Changed the Fight for Integration, 1 vol. 2011. (Captured History Ser.). (ENG.). 64p. (J). (gr. 5-8). lib. bdg. 35.32 *(978-0-7565-4440-9(8)*, 114961); pap. 8.95 *(978-0-7565-4512-3(9)*, 116901) Capstone. (Compass Point Bks.).

SEGREGATION IN EDUCATION—FICTION

Conkling, Winifred. Sylvia & Aki. 2013. 160p. (J). (gr. 4-7). 7.99 *(978-1-58246-345-2(X)*, Yearling) Random Hse. Children's Bks.

Michelson, Richard. Busing Brewster. Roth, R. G., illus. 2018. (ENG.). 32p. (J). pap. 10.95 *(978-1-56792-644-6(4))* Godine, David R. Pub.

Sharenow, Robert. My Mother the Cheerleader. 2007. 304p. (J). (gr. 7-18). 16.99 *(978-0-06-114896-5(2))*; lib. bdg. 17.89 *(978-0-06-114897-2(0))* HarperCollins Pubs. (Geringer, Laura Book).

Walvoord, Linda. Rosetta, Rosetta, Sit by Me!, 0 vols. Velasquez, Eric, illus. 2012. (ENG.). 98p. (J). (gr. 1-3). 14.95 *(978-0-7614-5171-6(4)*, 9780761451716, Two Lions) Amazon Publishing.

SEISMOGRAPHY

see Earthquakes

SEISMOLOGY

see Earthquakes

SELECTION, NATURAL

see Natural Selection

SELECTIVE SERVICE

see Draft

SELF-ACCEPTANCE

Beaupré, Nathalie. Why Am I Perfect? An Empowering Book Written for Children First. 2012. 72p. 24.99 *(978-1-4797-1114-7(4))*; pap. 15.99 *(978-1-4797-1113-0(6))* Xlibris Corp.

Conway, Celeste. Body Image & the Media. 2013. (Hot Topics in Media Ser.). (ENG.). 48p. (J). (gr. 4-8). lib. bdg. 18.50 *(978-1-61783-782-1(2)*, 10756) ABDO Publishing Co.

Cooper, T. & Glock-Cooper, Allison. Changers Book Four: Forever. 2018. (Changers Ser.). (ENG.). (J). 284p. 35.95 *(978-1-61775-733-4(0))*; 280p. pap. 12.95 *(978-1-61775-528-6(1))* Akashic Bks. (Black Sheep).

Esherick, Joan. Physical Challenges. Albers, Lisa et al, eds. 2014. (Living with a Special Need Ser.: 16). 128p. (J). (gr. 7-18). 25.95 *(978-1-4222-3041-1(4))* Mason Crest.

Freeland, Claire A.B. & Toner, Jacqueline B. What to Do When Mistakes Make You Quake: A Kid's Guide to Accepting Imperfection. McDonnell, Janet, illus. 2015. 96p. (J). pap. *(978-1-4338-1930-8(9)*, Magination Pr.) American Psychological Assn.

Gaines, Joanna. The World Needs Who You Were Made to Be, 1 vol. Swaney, Julianna, illus. 2020. (ENG.). 32p. (J). 19.99 *(978-1-4003-1423-2(2)*, Tommy Nelson) Nelson, Thomas Inc.

Grossman, Laurie & Musumeci's 5th Grade Class, Musumeci's. Master of Mindfulness: How to Be Your Own Superhero in Times of Stress. 2016. (ENG., Illus.). 72p. (J). (gr. k-5). pap. 14.95 *(978-1-62625-464-0(8)*, 34640) New Harbinger Pubns.

Jones, Viola & Willett, Edward. Conquering Negative Body Image, 1 vol., 1. 2015. (Conquering Eating Disorders Ser.). (ENG.). 64p. (J). (gr. 6-6). 36.13 *(978-1-4994-6205-0(0)*, d14e3a9e-9895-4de9-8be4-63dfc74410d9, Rosen Young Adult) Rosen Publishing Group, Inc., The.

Kelly, Dorothy A. Developing a Sense of Self: A Workbook of Tenets & Tactics for Adolescent Girls. 2006. (Illus.). 146p. (J). pap. 29.99 *(978-0-87101-366-8(5)*, NASW Pr.) National Assn. of Social Workers/NASW Pr.

Lite, Lori. Affirmation Weaver: A Believe in Yourself Story Designed to Help Children Increase Self-Esteem While Decreasing Stress & Anxiety. 2nd ed. 2011. 24p. pap. 14.95 *(978-0-9836256-9-8(7))* Stress Free Kids.

—Angry Octopus: An Anger Management Story Introducing Active Progressive Muscular Relaxation & Deep Breathing. 2011. (Illus.). 30p. (gr. -1-3). pap. 14.95 *(978-0-9836256-8-1(9))* Stress Free Kids.

—A Boy & a Turtle: A Relaxation Story Teaching Young Children Visualization Techniques to Increase Creativity While Lowering Stress & Anxiety. Lev. 3rd ed. 2012. Tr. of niño y una Tortuga. (ENG.). 16p. (J). pap. 12.95 *(978-1-937985-13-4(X))* Stress Free Kids.

—Bubble Riding: A Relaxation Story Designed to Teach Children Visualization Techniques to Increase Creativity While Lowering Stress & Anxiety. 2012. Tr. of Montando Burbujas. (ENG.). (J). pap. 14.95 *(978-1-937985-03-5(2))* Stress Free Kids.

—Buenas Noches Oruga: Una Historia para la Relajación Que Ayuda a Los Niños a Controlar la Ira y el Estrés para Que Se Queden Dormidos Sosegadamente. 2012. Tr. of Goodnight Caterpillar. (SPA., Illus.). 16p. (J). pap. 12.95 *(978-1-937985-16-5(4))* Stress Free Kids.

—Caleta de la Nutria Marina: Un Cuento para la Ansiedad Infantil, Enseña la Relajación, la Respiración Profunda para Reducir la Ansiedad, el Estrés y la Ira, a la Vez Que Fomenta el Sueño Sosegado. 2011. Tr. of Sea Otter Cove. (SPA., Illus.). 28p. (J). pap. 14.95 *(978-1-937985-11-0(3))* Stress Free Kids.

—The Goodnight Caterpillar: A Children's Relaxation Story to Improve Sleep, Manage Stress, Anxiety, Anger. 3rd abr. ed. 2011. Tr. of Buenas Noches, Oruga. (ENG.). 18p. (J). pap. 12.95 *(978-1-937985-00-4(8))* Stress Free Kids.

—Montando Burbujas: Un Cuento con Ejercicios de Relajación para Niños, Diseñada para Enseñar a Los Niños Técnicas de Visualización para Aumentar la Creatividad Mientras Disminuyen Sus Niveles de Ansiedad y de Estrés. 2012. Tr. of Bubble Riding. (SPA., Illus.). 32p. (J). pap. 14.95 *(978-1-937985-12-7(1))* Stress Free Kids.

—El Niño y la Tortuga: Un Cuento para Promover la Relajación. 2012. Tr. of Boy & a Turtle. (SPA., Illus.). 16p. (J). pap. 12.95 *(978-1-937985-17-2(2))* Stress Free Kids.

—El Pulpo Enojado: Un Cuento Sobre Cómo Controlar la Ira Que Enseña la Relajación Muscular Activa y Progresiva, y la Respiración: un Cuento Sobre Cómo Controlar la Ira Que Enseña la Relajación Muscular Activa y Progresiva, y la Respiración. 2012. Tr. of Angry Octopus. (SPA., Illus.). 30p. (J). pap. 14.95 *(978-1-937985-01-1(6))* Stress Free Kids.

—Sea Otter Cove: A Relaxation Story, Introducing Deep Breathing to Decrease Anxiety, Stress & Anger While Promoting Peaceful Sleep. 2nd ed. 2012. Tr. of Caleta de la Nutria Marina. (SPA & ENG., Illus.). 24p. (J). 14.95 *(978-1-937985-08-0(3))* Stress Free Kids.

—Tejedor de Afirmaciones: Un Cuento Que Aumenta la Autoestima en Los Niños, Creer en Ellos Mismos, Mientras Que Reducen Su Estrés y Su Ansiedad. 2012. Tr. of Affirmation Weaver. (SPA., Illus.). 24p. (J). pap. 14.95 *(978-1-937985-02-8(4))* Stress Free Kids.

Lukasiak, Chloe. Girl on Pointe: Chloe's Guide to Taking on the World. 2018. (ENG., Illus.). 208p. (J). 18.99 *(978-1-68119-737-1(5)*, 900183717, Bloomsbury USA Childrens) Bloomsbury Publishing USA.

Lyn, Jenipher. Find Your Rainbow: Color & Create Your Way to a Calm & Happy Life. 2018. (Illus.). 128p. (J). (gr. 3-7). pap. 12.99 *(978-1-5247-1850-3(5)*, Crown Books For Young Readers) Random Hse. Children's Bks.

Miller, Ruth L. The Power of Self Ralph Waldo Emerson's Wonder Filled Life. Shonkwiler, Martha, illus. 2013. 66p. pap. 12.00 *(978-0-945385-85-1(4))* WiseWoman Pr.

Murphy Payne, Lauren. Just Because I Am: A Child's Book of Affirmation. Iwai, Melissa, illus. 2nd rev. ed. 2015. (ENG.). 36p. (J). (gr. -1-2). 16.99 *(978-1-63198-051-0(3))* Free Spirit Publishing Inc.

—Just Because I Am / Solo Porque Soy Yo: A Child's Book of Affirmation / un Libro de Afirmaciones para Ninos. Iwai, Melissa, illus. 2018. (ENG.). 44p. (J). (gr. -1-3). pap. 12.99 *(978-1-63198-335-1(0)*, 83351) Free Spirit Publishing Inc.

Ottaviano, Patricia. Girl World: How to Ditch the Drama & Find Your Inner Amazing. 2015. (ENG.). 160p. (YA). (gr. 6-12). pap. 12.99 *(978-1-4926-0912-4(9)*, 9781492609124) Sourcebooks, Inc.

Palmer, Pat. Liking Myself. Shondeck, Betty, illus. 2010. 102p. (J). pap. 12.99 *(978-0-9622834-2-0(8))* Uplift Pr.

Parr, todd. The Okay Book. 2004. (ENG., Illus.). 24p. (J). (gr. -1 — 1). bds. 7.99 *(978-0-316-90809-2(6))* Little, Brown Bks. for Young Readers.

Skeen, Michelle & Skeen, Kelly. Just As You Are: A Teen's Guide to Self-Acceptance & Lasting Self-Esteem. 2018. (Instant Help Solutions Ser.). (ENG.). 176p. (YA). pap. 17.95 *(978-1-62625-590-6(3)*, 35906) New Harbinger Pubns.

Tool Kits for Kids LLC Staff, creator. Outsmart Your Worry - Tool Kit for Kids: Elementary School Edition. 2008. (Illus.). 23p. (J). 39.95 *(978-0-9819483-0-0(8))* Tool Kits For Kids LLC.

—Outsmart Your Worry - Tool Kit for Kids: High School / Middle School Edition. 2008. (Illus.). (J). 39.95 *(978-0-9819483-1-7(6))* Tool Kits For Kids LLC.

Van Hollander, Tammi. Casey's Greatness Wings: Teaching Mindfulness, Connection & Courage to Children. 2018. (Illus.). 62p. pap. 24.99 *(978-1-64316-778-7(2))* Primedia eLaunch LLC.

SELF-ACCEPTANCE—FICTION

Al-Ghani, K. I. Baby Blue Has the Blues, 1 vol. 2011. (ENG., Illus.). 32p. (J). (gr. -1-3). 16.99 *(978-0-7643-3732-1(7)*, 4089, Schiffer Publishing Ltd) Schiffer Publishing, Ltd.

Archambault, Marc. Teevert the Little Green Leaf. 2010. 31p. 18.98 *(978-0-557-17967-1(X))* Lulu Pr., Inc.

Arkangel, Brian. Cow Story. Moffat, Ross, illus. 2009. 24p. pap. 24.95 *(978-1-60703-272-4(4))* America Star Bks.

Atamer, Billie. The Little Purple Pumpkin. 2013. 28p. (gr. -1-3). pap. 11.95 *(978-1-61244-235-8(8))* Halo Publishing International.

Ayton, Shalanna. The Adventures of Missy the Moose. 2009. 68p. pap. 26.99 *(978-1-4389-7827-7(8))* AuthorHouse.

Baird, Noah. Southpaw. McMaugh, Kimberly, illus. 2013. 40p. pap. 13.95 *(978-1-938101-35-9(9))* Indigo Sea Pr., LLC.

Baker, Keith. Sometimes. Baker, Keith, illus. 2003. (Green Light Readers Level 1 Ser.). (ENG., Illus.). 24p. (J). (gr. -1-3). pap. 5.99 *(978-0-15-204847-1(2)*, 1194636, Clarion Bks.) HarperCollins Pubs.

—Sometimes. 2003. (Green Light Readers Level 1 Ser.). (gr. -1-2). lib. bdg. 13.50 *(978-0-613-64597-3(9))* Turtleback.

—Sometimes/Algunas Veces: Bilingual English-Spanish. Baker, Keith, illus. 2007. (Green Light Readers Level 1 Ser.). (ENG., Illus.). 28p. (J). (gr. -1-3). pap. 4.99 *(978-0-15-205961-3(X)*, 1197901, Clarion Bks.) HarperCollins Pubs.

Bar-el, Dan. Not Your Typical Dragon. Bowers, Tim, illus. 2013. (ENG.). 40p. (J). (gr. -1-k). 18.99 *(978-0-670-01402-6(8)*, Viking Books for Young Readers) Penguin Young Readers Group.

Beaumont, Karen. Wild about Us! Stevens, Janet, illus. 2015. (ENG.). 40p. (J). (gr. -1-3). 17.99 *(978-0-15-206294-1(7)*, 1198860, Clarion Bks.) HarperCollins Pubs.

Beck, Rachel. Bella & the Little Gray Kitten. 2011. 40p. (gr. -1). pap. 18.50 *(978-1-4567-3365-0(6))* AuthorHouse.

Bedrick, Claudia, tr. Jerome by Heart. 2018. (ENG., Illus.). 32p. (J). 16.95 *(978-1-59270-250-3(3))* Enchanted Lion Bks., LLC.

Bell, Davina. All the Ways to Be Smart. Colpoys, Allison, illus. 2019. (ENG.). 32p. (J). (gr. -1-1). 17.99 *(978-1-947534-96-4(3))* Scribe Pubns. AUS. Dist: Consortium Bk. Sales & Distribution.

Benedetto, K. & Barlow, J. I See the World. 2009. pap. *(978-1-61584-125-7(3))* Independent Pub.

Berenstain, Stan, et al. God Loves You!, 1 vol. 2008. (Berenstain Bears/Living Lights: a Faith Story Ser.). (ENG., Illus.). 32p. (J). pap. 4.99 *(978-0-310-71250-3(5))* Zonderkidz.

Bergen, Lara. Sophie the Awesome. Tallardy, Laura, illus. 2010. 99p. (J). *(978-0-545-24231-8(2))* Scholastic, Inc.

Berger, Samantha. Rock What Ya Got. 2018. (ENG., Illus.). 40p. (J). (gr. -1-3). 17.99 *(978-0-316-56150-1(9))* Little, Brown Bks. for Young Readers.

Bingham, Kelly. Shark Girl. (ENG., Illus.). 288p. (YA). (gr. 7). 2010. pap. 9.99 *(978-0-7636-4627-1(X))*1. 2007. 16.99 *(978-0-7636-3207-6(4))* Candlewick Pr.
Bloom, Denise. More Than a Spoonful. 2007. 28p. (J). (gr. -1-2). pap. 5.95 *(978-0-9778113-2-8(8))* HeartFelt Stories LLC.
Bloom, Denise, et al. More Than a Spoonful. 2007. (Heartfelt Stories Ser.). (Illus.). 28p. (J). 12.95 *(978-0-9778113-0-4(1))* HeartFelt Stories LLC.
Blume, Judy. Otherwise Known As Sheila the Great. 2007. (ENG.). 176p. (J). (gr. 3-7). 8.99 *(978-0-14-240879-7(4),* Puffin Books) Penguin Young Readers Group.
—Otherwise Known as Sheila the Great. 2007. 154p. (gr. 4-7). 16.00 *(978-0-7569-7915-7(3))* Perfection Learning Corp.
—Otherwise Known as Sheila the Great. 2007. (Fudge Bks.: 2). 138p. (gr. 4-7). lib. bdg. 18.40 *(978-1-4177-8370-0(2))* Turtleback.
Boulden, James. Buddy Learns from His Mistakes: Student Involvement Pack. 2003. (Illus.). 21p. (J). 24.95 *(978-1-892421-78-4(X))* Boulden Publishing.
Bramsen, Carin. Just a Duck? 2018. (Illus.). 34p. (J). (— 1). bds. 7.99 *(978-1-5247-6600-9(3),* Random Hse. Bks. for Young Readers) Random Hse. Children's Bks.
Briceno, Carole. Turtle's Journey, 1 vol. White, Tina Jorgenson, illus. 2009. 28p. pap. 24.95 *(978-1-60813-934-7(4))* America Star Bks.
Bridge, Chris Helene. The Same Heart. 2015. (ENG., Illus.). 32p. (J). 19.95 *(978-1-942945-06-2(X),* ab5ff38e-fd54-4dec-9465-debe103cfacc) Night Heron Media.
Brown, Peter. Mr. Tiger Goes Wild. 2014. (CHI & ENG.). 52p. (J). (gr. -1-2). *(978-986-320-369-8(6))* Commonwealth Publishing Co., Ltd.
—Mr. Tiger Goes Wild. 2013. (ENG., Illus.). 48p. (J). (gr. -1-3). 18.99 *(978-0-316-20063-9(8))* Little, Brown Bks. for Young Readers.
Burkhart, Kiersi & Keyser, Amber J. The Long Trail Home. 2017. (Quartz Creek Ranch Ser.). (ENG.). 240p. (J). (gr. 4-8). E-Book 42.65 *(978-1-5124-2698-4(9),* Darby Creek) Lerner Publishing Group.
Burn, Doris. Andrew Henry's Meadow. Burn, Doris, illus. 2012. (Illus.). 48p. (J). (gr. 1-4). 18.99 *(978-0-399-25608-0(3),* Philomel Bks.) Penguin Young Readers Group.
Burns, Marilyn. The Greedy Triangle. Silveria, Gordon, illus. 2008. (Scholastic Bookshelf Ser.). (ENG.). 32p. (J). (gr. -1-3). pap. 7.99 *(978-0-545-04220-8(8),* Scholastic Paperbacks) Scholastic, Inc.
Cabral, Noel. Rachel's Four-Legged Friend. 2012. 24p. 24.95 *(978-1-4626-6089-6(4))* America Star Bks.
Caminada, Janet Barnett. Yoga, the Kid & the Cricket: A fun & easy illustrated guide to beginner's yoga. A complete yoga workout that follows along with the story. Written. 2011. 36p. pap. 22.88 *(978-1-4634-4478-5(8))* AuthorHouse.
Campbell, Jennifer. Elise the Elephant. Cox, Nancy, illus. 2012. 32p. pap. 16.99 *(978-1-4567-9920-5(7))* AuthorHouse.
Cardin, Jodi. Bernice's Bad Hair Days. Chin, Todd, illus. 2009. 56p. (J). pap. *(978-1-60800-004-3(4))* LifeReloaded Specialty Publishing LLC.
Carter, Catherine. Anna's Choice. Pittman, Gail, illus. 2005. 24p. (J). (gr. 3-7). 12.95 *(978-1-893062-79-5(1))* Quail Ridge Pr., Inc.
Cavanaugh, Nancy J. This Journal Belongs to Ratchet. 2014. (ENG.). 320p. (J). (gr. 3-6). pap. 12.99 *(978-1-4926-0109-8(8),* 9781492601098) Sourcebooks, Inc.
Cento, Nucci. Maverick & Miss Murphy at Rascal's Rescue Ranch. 2009. 48p. pap. 12.50 *(978-1-60860-388-6(1),* Eloquent Bks.) Strategic Book Publishing & Rights Agency (SBPRA).
Claverie, Jean & Chapouton, Anne Marie. Julian. 2003. (SPA., Illus.). 28p. *(978-84-85334-71-1(X))* Lóguez Ediciones ESP. Dist: Lectorum Pubns., Inc.
Cole, Hana. Hooray! I'm Catholic. Steege, Joanna, illus. 2010. 32p. (J). 14.95 *(978-0-8091-6746-3(8),* Ambassador Bks.) Paulist Pr.
Colfer, Chris. The Curvy Tree: A Tale from the Land of Stories. Dorman, Brandon, illus. 2015. (Land of Stories Ser.). (ENG.). 32p. (J). (gr. -1-3). 18.99 *(978-0-316-40685-7(6))* Little, Brown Bks. for Young Readers.
Collins, Ross. Medusa Jones. 2008. (Illus.). 134p. (J). *(978-0-439-90101-7(4),* Levine, Arthur A. Bks.) Scholastic, Inc.
Cooper, Abby. Sticks & Stones. 2017. (J). lib. bdg. 18.40 *(978-0-606-39950-0(X))* Turtleback.
Cotterill, Colin. Average Alan. 2013. 150p. pap. *(978-616-7503-18-9(4))* Asia Document Bureau, Ltd.
Coven, Wanda. Heidi Heckelbeck Gets Glasses. Burris, Priscilla, illus. 2012. (Heidi Heckelbeck Ser.: 5). (ENG.). 128p. (J). (gr. k-4). 17.99 *(978-1-4424-4172-9(0));* pap. 6.99 *(978-1-4424-4171-2(2))* Little Simon. (Little Simon).
—Heidi Heckelbeck Gets Glasses. 2012. (Heidi Heckelbeck Ser.: 5). lib. bdg. 16.00 *(978-0-606-26888-2(X))* Turtleback.
Cuthand, Beth. Sikiihpsis. Cuthand, Stan, tr. Longman, Mary, illus. ed. 2007. (Little Duck Ser.). (ENG.). 28p. 17.00 *(978-1-894778-44-2(8))* Theytus Bks., Ltd. CAN. Dist: Univ. of Toronto Pr.
Dakos, Kalli. Why Am I Blue? A Story about Being Yourself. Garofoli, Viviana, illus. 2017. 32p. (J). 15.95 *(978-1-4338-2734-1(4),* Magination Pr.) American Psychological Assn.
Davis, Rachayl Eckstein & Schram, Peninnah. The Apple Tree's Discovery. Lee, Wendy W., illus. 2012. (ENG.). 24p. (J). (gr. -1-2). pap. 7.99 *(978-0-7613-5132-0(9),* 6adca0a0-d419-4ca4-82b0-6ee930438a2e, Kar-Ben Publishing) Lerner Publishing Group.
de la Peña, Matt. Mexican WhiteBoy. 2010. (ENG.). 272p. (YA). (gr. 9). pap. 12.99 *(978-0-440-23938-3(9),* Ember) Random Hse. Children's Bks.
De La Peña, Matt. Mexican WhiteBoy. 2010. lib. bdg. 20.85 *(978-0-606-12316-7(4))* Turtleback.
Dean, James & Dean, Kimberly. Pete the Cat & the Cool Cat Boogie. Dean, James, illus. (Pete the Cat Ser.). (ENG., Illus.). 40p. (J). (gr. -1-3). 2023. pap. 9.99 *(978-0-06-240435-0(0))* 2017. 17.99 *(978-0-06-240434-3(2))* 2017. lib. bdg. 18.89 *(978-0-06-240909-6(3))* HarperCollins Pubs. (HarperCollins).
Dean, Kimberly. Pete the Cat & the Cool Cat Boogie. 2023. (Pete the Cat Ser.). 40p. (gr. -1-1). 26.19 ***(978-1-5364-7890-7(3))*** HarperCollins Pubs.
Demonia, Lori. Leah's Voice. 2013. 28p. 16.95 *(978-1-61244-240-2(4))* Halo Publishing International.
Denton, Kiwi. Freddie's Magical Glasses, 1 vol. 2010. 18p. 24.95 *(978-1-4489-3309-9(9))* PublishAmerica, Inc.
Deuker, Carl. On the Devil's Court. 2008. (ENG.). 208p. (YA). (gr. 7-17). pap. 10.99 *(978-0-316-06727-0(X))* Little, Brown Bks. for Young Readers.
Diggs, Taye. Chocolate Me! Evans, Shane W., illus. (ENG.). (J). 2019. 32p. bds. 7.99 *(978-1-250-20785-2(1),* 900201772) 2011. 40p. (gr. -1-3). 18.99 *(978-0-312-60326-7(6),* 900064334) Feiwel & Friends.
Dole, Mayra Lazara. Down to the Bone. 2008. 384p. (gr. 9). lib. bdg. 17.89 *(978-0-06-084311-3(X),* HarperTeen) HarperCollins Pubs.
Doren, Greg Van. Obieo. 2010. 24p. pap. 11.49 *(978-1-4490-8811-8(2))* AuthorHouse.
Doyle, Marissa. Courtship & Curses. 2013. (ENG.). 368p. (YA). (gr. 9-13). pap. 19.99 *(978-1-250-02744-3(6),* 900098317) Square Fish.
Drachman, Eric. A Frog Thing. Muscarello, James, illus. 2006. (ENG.). 32p. (J). (gr. -1-2). 18.95 incl. audio compact disk *(978-0-9703809-3-7(3))* Kidwick Bks.
Driskell, Cheryl. Child & Youth Reiki Program: Mount Kurama & the Emerald Lake. 2005. 84p. (J). pap. 15.95 *(978-1-4116-3900-3(6))* Lulu Pr., Inc.
Dufayet, Danielle. Fantastic You. Zivoin, Jennifer, illus. 2019. 32p. (J). *(978-1-4338-3028-0(0),* Magination Pr.) American Psychological Assn.
Duvoisin, Roger. Donkey-Donkey. 2016. (Illus.). 56p. (J). (-k). 17.95 *(978-1-59017-964-2(1),* NYR Children's Collection) New York Review of Bks., Inc., The.
Ebeling, Vicki. The Winners Group. 2007. (J). per. 7.95 *(978-0-9779768-0-5(7))* Ebeling, Vicki.
Eland, Lindsay. A Summer of Sundays. (ENG.). 336p. (J). (gr. 3-6). 2014. pap. 9.99 *(978-1-60684-541-7(1),* 67648b2b-690e-453b-a2e4-e48665b96786) 2013. 16.99 *(978-1-60684-030-6(4))* Lerner Publishing Group. (Carolrhoda Bks.).
Elliott, Sherria L. My Shaking Eyes. Moore, Sasha & Tilak, Brian, illus. 2013. 30p. pap. 12.99 *(978-0-9846963-2-1(6))* 4Elliott Publishing, Inc.
Erskine, Kathryn. The Absolute Value of Mike. 2012. 272p. (J). (gr. 5-18). pap. 7.99 *(978-0-14-242101-7(4),* Puffin Books) Penguin Young Readers Group.
Escott, Maria. Green Anole Meets Brown Anole, a Love Story. Wigal, Mike, illus. 2010. 28p. pap. 12.95 *(978-1-936051-82-3(6))* Peppertree Pr., The.
Ewert, Marcus. She Wanted to Be Haunted. Ghahremani, Susie, illus. 2020. (ENG.). 40p. (J). 17.99 *(978-1-68119-791-3(X),* 900187075, Bloomsbury Children's Bks.) Bloomsbury Publishing USA.
Ferguson, Terrence. Stuttering Sammie: I'm Just Like You, I Just Repeat Some Letters or Words When I Talk. 2012. 24p. 24.95 *(978-1-4626-6267-8(6));* pap. 24.95 *(978-1-4626-8326-0(6))* America Star Bks.
Flesher, Vivienne. Alfred's Nose. Flesher, Vivienne, illus. 2008. (Illus.). 32p. (J). (gr. -1-2). lib. bdg. 17.89 *(978-0-06-084314-4(4))* HarperCollins Pubs.
Folz, Alexandra. Indigo's Bracelet. 2010. 84p. pap. 9.95 *(978-1-4525-0058-4(4))* Get Published.
Forester, Victoria. The Girl Who Could Fly. 2015. (Piper Mccloud Ser.: 1). (ENG.). 352p. (J). (gr. 4-7). pap. 8.99 *(978-1-250-07246-7(8),* 900150204) Square Fish.
Fortmeyer, Kendra. Hole in the Middle. 2019. (ENG.). 360p. (YA). (gr. 9). pap. 10.99 *(978-1-64129-033-3(1),* Soho Teen) Soho Pr., Inc.
Frank, E. R. Wrecked. (ENG., (YA). 2015. Illus.). 336p. (gr. 9). pap. 10.99 *(978-1-4814-5137-6(5))* 2007. 256p. (gr. 7-12). pap. 9.99 *(978-0-689-87384-3(0))* Simon & Schuster Children's Publishing. (Atheneum Bks. for Young Readers).
Frye, Karen. Flake, 1 vol. 2010. 16p. 24.95 *(978-1-4489-4935-9(1))* PublishAmerica, Inc.
Furukawa, Masumi, illus. The Ugly Duckling. 2007. (Flip-Up Fairy Tales Ser.). 24p. (J). (gr. -1-2). *(978-1-84643-095-4(X))* Child's Play International Ltd.
Garland, Michael. Fish Had a Wish. 2013. (I Like to Read Ser.). (ENG., Illus.). 24p. (J). (gr. -1-3). pap. 7.99 *(978-0-8234-2757-4(9))* Holiday Hse., Inc.
Gawade, Akansha A. This Is Who I Am. 2006. (J). pap. 8.00 *(978-0-8059-6886-6(5))* Dorrance Publishing Co., Inc.
Genhart, Michael. Love Is Love. Min, Ken, illus. 2018. (ENG.). 32p. (J). (gr. -1-3). 18.99 *(978-1-939775-13-9(2),* Little Pickle Pr.) Sourcebooks, Inc.
—Mac & Geeeez! ... being Real Is What It's All About. Mack, Steve, illus. 2017. 32p. (J). *(978-1-4338-2723-5(9),* Magination Pr.) American Psychological Assn.
Gibney, Shannon. See No Color. 2015. (ENG.). 192p. (YA). (gr. 7-12). 18.99 *(978-1-4677-7682-0(3),* 0d801875-6153-4314-be00-0db6e51b029f); E-Book 29.32 *(978-1-4677-8814-4(7))* Lerner Publishing Group. (Carolrhoda Lab™).
Giff, Patricia Reilly. All the Way Home. 2003. (ENG., Illus.). 176p. (J). (gr. 3-7). pap. 7.99 *(978-0-440-41182-6(3),* Yearling) Random Hse. Children's Bks.
Gil, Carmen. Story of a Cockroach. Brokenbrow, Jon, tr. Wimmer, Sonja, illus. 2012. (Mini-Animalist Ser.). (ENG.). 32p. (J). (gr. -1-2). 14.95 *(978-84-15241-22-5(4))* Cuento de Luz SL ESP. Dist: Publishers Group West (PGW).
Glickman, Susan. Bernadette & the Lunch Bunch, 1 vol. 2008. (Lunch Bunch Ser.: 1). (ENG., Illus.). 124p. (J). (gr. 1-4). pap. 6.95 *(978-1-897187-51-7(3))* Second Story Pr. CAN. Dist: Orca Bk. Pubs. USA.
Golden, Laura. Every Day After. 2014. 224p. (J). (gr. 4-7). 7.99 *(978-0-307-98314-5(5),* Yearling) Random Hse. Children's Bks.
Goobie, Beth. Ni un Dia Más, 1 vol. 2009. (Spanish Soundings Ser.). Orig. Title: Kicked Out. (SPA.). 112p. (YA). (gr. 8-12). pap. 9.95 *(978-1-55469-137-1(0))* Orca Bk. Pubs. USA.
Goss, Leon. I'm Good, I'm Beautiful, I'm Smart. Mailey, Maria C. & Neuburger, Jenny, illus. 2005. (J). per. *(978-1-933156-02-6(3),* VisionQuest Kids) GSVQ Publishing.
Grammy Sunshine. The Adventures of Mouse: The Mouse Who Wanted to Be A Pig. 2009. 20p. pap. 12.49 *(978-1-4389-9268-6(8))* AuthorHouse.
Grateful Steps Publishing & Tipton, Angela. Butterflies Don't Crawl. Irvine, Wil, illus. 2009. 32p. (J). 16.95 *(978-1-935130-14-7(5))* Grateful Steps.
Gray, Diane. The Bears with Unruly Hairs. 2011. 28p. pap. 15.99 *(978-1-4568-8129-0(9))* Xlibris Corp.
Green, George & Brooke, Amy/ J. George Green's, the Lion Who Couldn't Roar. 2008. (Illus.). (J). per. 16.99 *(978-1-933156-14-9(7),* Visikid Bks.) GSVQ Publishing.
Greenley, Wendy. Lola Shapes the Sky. Domeniconi, Paolo, illus. 2019. (ENG.). 32p. (J). (gr. 1-3). 19.99 *(978-1-56846-319-3(7),* 18668, Creative Editions) Creative Co., The.
Guerrero, Tanya. How to Make Friends with the Sea. 2020. (ENG.). 368p. (J). 16.99 *(978-0-374-31199-5(4),* 900197455, Farrar, Straus & Giroux (BYR)) Farrar, Straus & Giroux.
Guidroz, Rukhsanna. Leila in Saffron. Mirtalipova, Dinara, illus. 2019. (ENG.). 32p. (J). (gr. -1-3). 18.99 *(978-1-5344-2564-4(0),* Salaam Reads) Simon & Schuster Bks. For Young Readers.
Gunderson, Jessica. Desastre en el Musical. Aparicio Publishing LLC, Aparicio Publishing, tr. Cho, Sumin, illus. 2020. (Drama en la Secundaria Ser.). (SPA.). 64p. (J). (gr. 3-6). pap. 6.95 *(978-1-4965-9318-4(9),* 142348); lib. bdg. 25.99 *(978-1-4965-9163-0(1),* 142080) Capstone. (Stone Arch Bks.).
—The School Musical Meltdown. Cho, Sumin, illus. 2018. (Junior High Drama Ser.). (ENG.). 64p. (J). (gr. 3-6). 25.99 *(978-1-4965-4711-8(X),* 135225, Stone Arch Bks.) Capstone.
Harrison, Hannah E. Extraordinary Jane. 2014. 40p. (J). (gr. -1-k). 17.99 *(978-0-8037-3914-7(1),* Dial Bks) Penguin Young Readers Group.
Harrison, Vashti. Big. 2023. (ENG.). 60p. (J). (gr. -1-3). 19.99 *(978-0-316-35322-9(1))* Little Brown & Co.
Headley, Justina Chen. The Patch. Vane, Mitch, illus. 2007. (ENG.). 32p. (J). (gr. k-3). pap. 7.95 *(978-1-58089-170-7(5))* Charlesbridge Publishing, Inc.
Henshon, Suzanna E. Spiders on the Ceiling. 2006. (J). *(978-0-88092-614-0(7))* Royal Fireworks Publishing Co.
Hilb, Jessie. The Calculus of Change. 2018. (ENG.). 336p. (YA). (gr. 9). 17.99 *(978-0-544-95333-8(9),* 1660557, Clarion Bks.) HarperCollins Pubs.
Hill, Julia. Cyril the Serious Cirrus Cloud. (ENG., Illus.). (J). 2018. 26p. 19.95 *(978-1-949231-43-4(7))* 2017. pap. 9.95 *(978-1-947825-18-5(6))* Yorkshire Publishing Group.
Hofmann-Maniyar, Ariane. That's NOT How You Do It! Hofmann-Maniyar, Ariane, illus. 2017. (Child's Play Library). (ENG., Illus.). 32p. (J). *(978-1-84643-929-2(9))* Child's Play International Ltd.
Hogan, Mary. Pretty Face. (ENG.). 224p. 2009. (J). pap. 8.99 *(978-0-06-084113-3(3))* 2008. (YA). (gr. 9-18). 16.99 *(978-0-06-084111-9(7))* HarperCollins Pubs. (HarperTeen).
Hudson, Katy. Bear & Duck. Hudson, Katy, illus. 2015. (ENG., Illus.). 32p. (J). (gr. -1-3). 17.99 *(978-0-06-232051-3(3),* HarperCollins) HarperCollins Pubs.
Jackson, Richard. Puddle. Raschka, Chris, illus. 2019. (ENG.). 40p. (J). (gr. -1-3). 17.99 *(978-0-06-265195-2(1),* Greenwillow Bks.) HarperCollins Pubs.
James, LeBron. I Promise. Mata, Niña, illus. 2020. (ENG.). 40p. (J). (gr. -1-3). 19.99 *(978-0-06-297106-7(9),* HarperCollins) HarperCollins Pubs.
Jerry, Spinelli. Loser. 2014. (ENG.). 224p. (J). (gr. 7-7). 11.24 *(978-1-63245-207-8(3))* Lectorum Pubns., Inc.
John, Jory. Giraffe Problems. Smith, Lane, illus. 2018. (Animal Problems Ser.). (ENG.). 42p. (J). (gr. -1-2). 17.99 *(978-1-5247-7203-1(8),* Random Hse. Bks. for Young Readers) Random Hse. Children's Bks.
Jovanovic, Katarina. The King Has Goat Ears, 1 vol. Béha, Phillippe, illus. 2008. (ENG.). 32p. (J). (gr. -1-k). 16.95 *(978-1-896580-22-7(X))* Tradewind Bks. CAN. Dist: Orca Bk. Pubs. USA.
Kaiser, Lori. Megan the Moody Moose. Kaiser, Lori, illus. 2013. (Illus.). 26p. pap. *(978-0-9883770-5-9(5))* Roxby Media Ltd.
Katrana, Carol. Charlie, the Christmas Camel: A Christmas Story to Remember. 2012. 120p. (gr. 4-6). pap. 16.95 *(978-1-4772-7710-2(2))* AuthorHouse.
Keith, Brooke. Chrissie's Shell. Bausman, Mary, illus. 2010. 32p. (J). 14.99 *(978-1-59317-398-2(9))* Warner Pr., Inc.
Kent, Renee Holmes. Robyn Flies Home, Vol. 4. 2004. (Adventures in Misty Falls Ser.: Vol. 4). (Illus.). 100p. (gr. 4-7). pap. 4.99 *(978-1-56309-764-5(8),* N007106, New Hope Pubs.) Iron Stream Media.
Keyser, Amber J. & Burkhart, Kiersi. The Long Trail Home. 2017. (Quartz Creek Ranch Ser.). (ENG.). 240p. (J). (gr. 4-8). 6.99 *(978-1-5124-3090-5(0),* 237da2bf-d64a-47f5-9377-07661a1f1425, Darby Creek) Lerner Publishing Group.
Kimmel, Elizabeth Cody. Lily B. on the Brink of Love. 2005. (ENG.). 192p. (J). 15.99 *(978-0-06-075541-6(5))* HarperCollins Pubs.
—Suddenly Supernatural: Scaredy Kat. 2010. (Suddenly Supernatural Ser.: 2). (ENG.). 272p. (J). (gr. 3-7). pap. 15.99 *(978-0-316-08745-2(9))* Little, Brown Bks. for Young Readers.
Kittle, Katrina. Reasons to Be Happy. 2011. 288p. (J). (gr. 6-8). pap. 10.99 *(978-1-4022-6020-9(2))* Sourcebooks, Inc.
Knapp, J. Richard. Bobby's Story: An Amazing Story of Teen Courage. 2006. (ENG.). 224p. (YA). per. 14.95 *(978-0-9774761-7-6(0),* Books To Believe In) Thornton Publishing, Inc.
Knight, Chris. Karen Bighead: The Story of a Little Girl with a Big Head. 2011. (Illus.). 24p. 12.12 *(978-1-4520-7730-7(4))* AuthorHouse.
Koffman, Donna Carol. Different Kinds of Special. Biggar, Breanne, illus. 2011. 36p. pap. *(978-1-55483-897-4(5))* Insomniac Pr.
Kogler, Jennifer. The Otherworldlies. 2008. 400p. (J). lib. bdg. 17.89 *(978-0-06-073960-7(6));* (ENG.). (gr. 5-18). 16.99 *(978-0-06-073959-1(2))* HarperCollins Pubs. (Eos).
Kowalski, Bernard. Alexis & Ralph the Dragon, 1 vol. 2010. 32p. 24.95 *(978-1-4512-1008-8(6))* PublishAmerica, Inc.
Kranz, Linda. You Be You. (Illus.). 32p. (J). 2013. (gr. -1 — 1). 7.95 *(978-1-58979-747-5(7))* 2011. (ENG., E-Book *(978-1-58979-667-6(5))* 2011. (gr. -1-1). 12.95 *(978-1-58979-666-9(7))* Taylor Trade Publishing.
—You Be You/Sé Siempre Tú. Mlawer, Teresa, tr. 2014. (Illus.). 32p. (J). (gr. -1-1). 12.95 *(978-1-63076-021-2(8))* Taylor Trade Publishing.
Kredensor, Diane. Buck's Tooth. Kredensor, Diane, illus. 2015. (Pix Ser.). (ENG., Illus.). 64p. (J). (gr. 1-4). 12.99 *(978-1-4814-2382-3(7),* Aladdin) Simon & Schuster Children's Publishing.
Krupic, Janice. Felicia's Family Divorces. 2004. 72p. *(978-0-9745219-0-9(6))* Children Concept Publishing.
Kwaymullina, Ezekiel. Colour Me. Court, Moira, illus. 2018. (ENG.). 32p. (J). (gr. -1-k). pap. 12.95 *(978-1-925164-66-4(7))* Fremantle Pr. AUS. Dist: Independent Pubs. Group.
Kyrja. Rupert's Tales: The Nature of Elements, 1 vol. Pringle-Burke, Lesli, illus. 2017. (ENG.). 72p. (J). (gr. -1-3). 16.99 *(978-0-7643-5387-1(X),* 7672, Red Feather) Schiffer Publishing, Ltd.
Laubenstein, Sharon. Something about Sally. 2013. 24p. pap. 10.95 *(978-1-4908-0723-2(3),* WestBow Pr.) Author Solutions, LLC.
Le Guin, Ursula. K. Very Far Away from Anywhere Else. 2004. (ENG.). 144p. (YA). (gr. 7-12). pap. 7.99 *(978-0-15-205208-9(9),* 1195706, Clarion Bks.) HarperCollins Pubs.
Leppard, Laura Jennifer. The Duchess of Sao Paulo. 2006. 49p. (J). pap. 17.89 *(978-1-4116-6635-1(6))* Lulu Pr., Inc.
Levine, Gail Carson. Fairest. (J). (gr. 3-7). 2012. (ENG.). 352p. pap. 7.99 *(978-0-06-073410-7(8),* HarperCollins) 2006. 326p. lib. bdg. 18.89 *(978-0-06-073409-1(4))* HarperCollins Pubs.
—Fairest. l.t. rev. ed. 2007. (Literacy Bridge Young Adult Ser.). 349p. (J). (gr. 3-7). 23.95 *(978-0-7862-9270-7(9))* Thorndike Pr.
Licker, Laura. Frogs & Dragons, 1 vol. 2009. 28p. pap. 24.95 *(978-1-60836-475-6(5))* America Star Bks.
Little Gestalten, Little, ed. Goliath: The Boy Who Was Different. Abadía, Ximo, illus. 2019. (ENG.). 48p. 19.95 *(978-3-89955-826-5(X))* Die Gestalten Verlag DEU. Dist: Ingram Publisher Services.
Lopez, Diana. Choke. 2012. (ENG.). 240p. (YA). (gr. 7-7). 17.99 *(978-0-545-41822-5(4))* Scholastic, Inc.
Louise, Kate. Tough Cookie. Sandford, Grace, illus. 2015. (ENG.). 32p. (J). (gr. -1-k). 16.99 *(978-1-63450-197-2(7),* Sky Pony Pr.) Skyhorse Publishing Co., Inc.
—The Upside-Down Fish. Matine, Laura, illus. 2015. 32p. (J). (gr. -1-k). 16.95 *(978-1-62914-628-7(5),* Sky Pony Pr.) Skyhorse Publishing Co., Inc.
Love, Katie. Fruit to Live By..., 1 vol. 2009. 62p. pap. 16.95 *(978-1-60836-122-9(5))* PublishAmerica, Inc.
Lucado, Max. Punchinello & the Most Marvelous Gift: And, Your Special Gift. Martinez, Sergio, illus. 2007. (J). *(978-1-58134-877-4(0))* Crossway.
—Your Special Gift. Wenzel, David, illus. 2006. (Max Lucado's Wemmicks Ser.: 6). (ENG.). 32p. (J). (gr. -1-3). 16.99 *(978-1-58134-698-5(0))* Crossway.
Luciani, Brigitte. The Wild Cat: Book 6. Tharlet, Eve, illus. 2018. (Mr. Badger & Mrs. Fox Ser.). (ENG.). 32p. (J). (gr. k-3). 26.65 *(978-1-5415-0086-0(5),* db60c918-cf2b-4049-8c66-c81a69da77ae, Graphic Universe™) Lerner Publishing Group.
Lytton, Deborah. Silence. 2015. (ENG.). 320p. (YA). (gr. 7). 17.99 *(978-1-60907-945-1(0),* 5125977, Shadow Mountain) Shadow Mountain Publishing.
MacDonald, Alan. The Pig in a Wig. Hess, Paul, illus. 2003. 32p. (J). (gr. k-3). pap. 6.95 *(978-1-56145-299-6(8),* Q32523) Peachtree Publishing Co. Inc.
MacHale, D. J. The Monster Princess. Bolger, Alexandra, illus. 2010. (ENG.). 40p. (J). (gr. -1-1). 17.99 *(978-1-4169-4809-4(0),* Aladdin) Simon & Schuster Children's Publishing.
Malik, Katherine. Giselle's Magical World, 1 vol. 2009. 150p. pap. 24.95 *(978-1-4489-1902-4(9))* America Star Bks.
Manning, Jane. Millie Fierce. Manning, Jane, illus. 2012. (Millie Fierce Ser.). (Illus.). 32p. (J). (gr. -1-2). 17.99 *(978-0-399-25642-4(3),* Philomel Bks.) Penguin Young Readers Group.
Marie, Lynne. The Star in the Christmas Play. Hussey, Lorna, illus. 2018. 32p. (J). 16.99 *(978-1-5064-3813-9(X),* Beaming Books) 1517 Media.
Markes, Julie. Good Thing You're Not an Octopus. Smith, Maggie, illus. 2006. (ENG.). 40p. (J). (gr. -1-3). pap. 8.99 *(978-0-06-443586-4(5),* HarperCollins) HarperCollins Pubs.
Marlowe, Sara. My New Best Friend. Salom, Ivette, illus. 2016. (ENG.). 32p. (J). 15.95 *(978-1-61429-353-8(8))* Wisdom Pubns.
McClintock, Norah. Dooley Takes the Fall, 1 vol. 2007. (Dooley Ser.). (ENG.). 256p. (YA). (gr. 7-12). per. 12.95 *(978-0-88995-403-8(8),* 4f86ceaa-f9c8-4d68-a820-8fb4039fda28) Trifolium Bks., Inc. CAN. Dist: Firefly Bks., Ltd.
McClure, Brian D. The Up down Day. Plumlee, Buddy, illus. 2009. (Brian D. Mcclure Childrens Book Collection). 47p. (J). (gr. -1-3). 14.95 *(978-1-933426-07-5(1))* Universal Flag Publishing.
McDonald, Fiona. Ghost Doll & Jasper. 2012. (ENG., Illus.). 112p. (J). (gr. 2-7). 12.95 *(978-1-62087-174-4(2),* 620174, Sky Pony Pr.) Skyhorse Publishing Co., Inc.
McGann, Amber Ann. Windrush the Crooked Llama. 2008. 34p. pap. 24.95 *(978-1-60563-728-0(9))* PublishAmerica, Inc.
McGregor, Janet C. Happy for a Honk & a Wave. Craft, Donna, illus. 2010. 20p. pap. 12.95 *(978-1-936343-04-1(5))* Peppertree Pr., The.
Midden, Maribeth Grubb. Rosie: The Patchwork Bunny. Techau, Ashlyn, illus. 2011. 24p. (gr. 1-2). pap. 12.99 *(978-1-4269-5671-3(1))* Trafford Publishing.
Millard, Glenda. The Naming of Tishkin Silk. Magerl, Caroline, illus. 2019. (Kingdom of Silk Ser.: 01). 96p. mass mkt. 4.99 *(978-0-7333-1314-1(0))* ABC Bks. AUS. Dist: HarperCollins Pubs.
Mith with an Itch. 2008. (Illus.). 34p. (J). 10.95 *(978-0-9800259-0-3(7))* Dream Weaver Ministries, Inc.
Moore, Julianne. Best Friends Forever. 2015. (CHI.). 40p. (J). (gr. -1-8). pap. *(978-7-5133-1778-8(X))* New Star Publishing Hse.

S

—Freckleface Strawberry. Pham, LeUyen, illus. 2007. (Freckleface Strawberry Ser.). (ENG.). 40p. (J). (gr. -1-3). 18.99 *(978-1-59990-107-7(2)*, 900044746, Bloomsbury USA Childrens) Bloomsbury Publishing USA.
Moore, Leslie. Right Left: A Boy Named Grey. 2013. 48p. pap. 20.45 *(978-1-4497-8649-6(9)*, WestBow Pr.) Author Solutions, LLC.
Morgan, Sally & Kwaymullina, Ambelin. I Love Me. 2019. (ENG., Illus.). 24p. (J). bds. 8.99 *(978-1-5248-5116-3(7))* Andrews McMeel Publishing.
Moulton, Erin E. Tracing Stars. 2013. (ENG.). 256p. (J). (gr. 3-7). pap. 6.99 *(978-0-14-242653-1(9)*, Puffin Books) Penguin Young Readers Group.
Murray, Lisa A. Portend Learns That We Need Each Other. 2011. 32p. pap. 15.99 *(978-1-4634-0132-0(9))* AuthorHouse.
Murrell, Diane. Oliver Onion: The Onion Who Learns to Accept & Be Himself. Murrell, Diane, illus. 2004. (Illus.). 40p. (J). (gr. -1-4). 16.95 *(978-1-931282-64-2(1))* Autism Asperger Publishing Co.
Nanette. Little Red. 2004. (Life on Granny's Farm Ser.). (J). 12.95 *(978-0-9741269-1-3(8))* St. Bernard Publishing, LLC.
—Oinky the Yellow Pig. 2004. (Life on Granny's Farm Ser.). (J). 12.95 *(978-0-9741269-4-4(2))* St. Bernard Publishing, LLC.
Nasser, Amal. Falfoul's Trunk, 1 vol. Abul-Maati, Rania, illus. 2016. (Stories & Fables from Around the World Ser.). (ENG.). 24p. (J). (gr. 1-2). lib. bdg. 26.27 *(978-1-4777-5693-5(0)*, 9e3fe07f-261e-4b5a-a376-60d3e9bcc3bd, Windmill Bks.) Rosen Publishing Group, Inc., The.
Nevers, Merri B. Lonely Lucille. 2012. 28p. pap. 16.95 *(978-1-4497-4246-1(7)*, WestBow Pr.) Author Solutions, LLC.
Nyong'o, Lupita. Sulwe. Harrison, Vashti, illus. 2019. Orig. Title: Sulwe. (ENG.). 48p. (J). (gr. -1-3). 17.99 *(978-1-5344-2536-1(5)*, Simon & Schuster Bks. For Young Readers) Simon & Schuster Bks. For Young Readers.
Oliver, Amanda Eaddy. Cheyenne the Cat. 2010. 28p. 13.99 *(978-1-4520-6218-1(8))* AuthorHouse.
Palacio, R. J. Wonder. 2015. (JPN.). 420p. (J). *(978-4-593-53495-1(X))* Holp Shuppan, Publishing.
—Wonder. 2017. (Illus.). 341p. (J). *(978-1-5247-6446-3(9))* Knopf, Alfred A. Inc.
—Wonder. 2012. (Wonder Ser.). (ENG.). 320p. (J). (gr. 3-7). 17.99 *(978-0-375-86902-0(6))*; lib. bdg. 19.99 *(978-0-375-96902-7(0))* Random Hse. Children's Bks. (Knopf Bks. for Young Readers).
—Wonder. Lt. ed. 2013. (ENG.). 482p. 23.99 *(978-1-4104-5741-7(9))* Thorndike Pr.
—Wonder. 2012. lib. bdg. 29.40 *(978-0-606-36646-5(6))* Turtleback.
—The Wonder Journal. 2015. (Wonder Ser.). (ENG.). 176p. (J). (gr. 3-7). 12.99 *(978-0-553-49907-0(6)*, Knopf Bks. for Young Readers) Random Hse. Children's Bks.
—Wonder: la Historia de Julián / the Julian Chapter: a Wonder Story. 2015. (SPA.). 160p. (J). (gr. 3-7). pap. 9.95 *(978-607-31-3242-8(5)*, Nube De Tinta) Penguin Random House Grupo Editorial ESP. Dist: Penguin Random Hse. LLC.
Paley, Sasha. Huge. 2008. (ENG.). 272p. (YA). (gr. 7-12). pap. 8.99 *(978-1-4169-5795-9(2)*, Simon & Schuster Bks. For Young Readers) Simon & Schuster Bks. For Young Readers.
Petty, Dini. The Queen, the Bear & the Bumblebee. Cowles, Rose, illus. 32p. (J). 19.95 *(978-1-55285-151-7(6))* Whitecap Bks., Ltd. CAN. Dist: Graphic Arts Ctr. Publishing Co.
Phyllarry (Rittmueller), Kathryn. Beauregart the Bear. 2009. (ENG., Illus.). 64p. (J). 12.95 *(978-0-943972-80-0(9))* Homestead Publishing.
Pitino, Donna Marie. Too-Tall Tina. Woodruff, Liza, illus. 2005. (Math Matters Ser.). 32p. (J). (gr. k-2). pap. 5.95 *(978-1-57565-150-7(5)*, ab8f34ba-7005-4f87-9d67-ed858dd707cd, Kane Press) Astra Publishing Hse.
Pride, Wallace. The Mighty Christmas Oak. 2008. 19p. pap. 24.95 *(978-1-60672-752-2(4))* PublishAmerica, Inc.
Purkapile, Susan & Peck, Amy. Mumbles the Bumble Bee: The Bee Who Couldn't Buzz. Ducommun, Barbara, illus. 2008. (J). *(978-1-930596-87-0(1))* Amherst Pr.
Raschka, Chris, illus. Crabby Crab. 2014. (Thingy Things Ser.). (ENG.). 24p. (J). (gr. -1-k). 6.95 *(978-1-4197-1056-8(7)*, 1072801, Abrams Appleseed) Abrams, Inc.
Raymundo, Peter. I Am Not a Fish! Raymundo, Peter, illus. 2019. (Illus.). 32p. (J). (-k). 18.99 *(978-0-525-55459-2(9)*, Dial Bks) Penguin Young Readers Group.
Reade, O. K. The Little Girl & Her Shadow. 2015. (Illus.). (J). 12.99 *(978-1-4621-1618-8(3))* Cedar Fort, Inc./CFI Distribution.
Redbank, Tennant. The Saggy Baggy Elephant. Hathi, Garva, illus. 2016. (Step into Reading Ser.). 32p. (J). (gr. -1-1). pap. 4.99 *(978-0-553-53588-4(9)*, Random Hse. Bks. for Young Readers) Random Hse. Children's Bks.
Regan, Anne, ed. First Time for Everything. 2016. (ENG., Illus.). (J). 32.99 *(978-1-63533-015-1(7)*, Harmony Ink Pr.) Dreamspinner Pr.
Richmond, Marianne. Hooray for You! 2019. (Illus.). 40p. (J). (gr. -1-2). 9.99 *(978-1-4926-7516-7(4)*, Sourcebooks Jabberwocky) Sourcebooks, Inc.
Ritter, John H. Choosing up Sides. 2004. 166p. (gr. 5-9). 16.00 *(978-0-7569-4094-2(X))* Perfection Learning Corp.
Robinson, Christian. You Matter. Robinson, Christian, illus. 2020. (ENG., Illus.). 40p. (J). (gr. -1-3). 17.99 *(978-1-5344-2169-1(6)*, Atheneum Bks. for Young Readers) Simon & Schuster Children's Publishing.
Romig, Hilary. Meet Ruby & Louise. 2009. 16p. pap. 8.49 *(978-1-4389-4609-2(0))* AuthorHouse.
Roos, Stephen. The Gypsies Never Came. 2010. (ENG., Illus.). 128p. (J). (gr. 3-7). pap. 7.99 *(978-1-4424-2940-6(2)*, Simon & Schuster Bks. For Young Readers) Simon & Schuster Bks. For Young Readers.
Rosenthal, Amy Krouse. The OK Book. 2007. (ENG., Illus.). 40p. (J). (gr. -1-2). 13.99 *(978-0-06-115255-9(2)*, HarperCollins) HarperCollins Pubs.
Rosenthal, Amy Krouse & Lichtenheld, Tom. The OK Book. Rosenthal, Amy Krouse & Lichtenheld, Tom, illus. 2007. (Illus.). 40p. (J). (gr. -1-3). lib. bdg. 14.89 *(978-0-06-115256-6(0))* HarperCollins Pubs.
Rosenthal, Amy Krouse & Rosenthal, Paris. Dear Girl, A Celebration of Wonderful, Smart, Beautiful You! Hatam, Holly, illus. 2017. (ENG.). 40p. (J). (gr. -1-3). 17.99 *(978-0-06-242250-7(2)*, HarperCollins) HarperCollins Pubs.
Rudolph, Shaina & Royer, Danielle. All My Stripes: A Story for Children with Autism. Zivoin, Jennifer, illus. 2014. (J). pap. *(978-1-4338-1917-9(1)*, Magination Pr.) American Psychological Assn.
Ryan, P. E. Saints of Augustine. 2007. 308p. (YA). (gr. 7-18). 16.99 *(978-0-06-085810-0(9))*; lib. bdg. 17.89 *(978-0-06-085811-7(7))* HarperCollins Pubs. (HarperTeen).
Salter, Sydney. My Big Nose & Other Natural Disasters. 2009. (ENG., Illus.). 352p. (YA). (gr. 7-18). pap. 19.95 *(978-0-15-206643-7(8)*, 1099023, Clarion Bks.) HarperCollins Pubs.
Savageau, Cheryl. Muskrat Will Be Swimming, 1 vol. Hynes, Robert, illus. 2006. (ENG.). 32p. (J). (gr. 3-7). 9.95 *(978-0-88448-280-2(4)*, 884280) Tilbury Hse. Pubs.
Scanlon, Liz Garton. Noodle & Lou. Howard, Arthur, illus. 2011. (ENG.). 32p. (J). (gr. -1-1). 15.99 *(978-1-4424-0288-1(1)*, Beach Lane Bks.) Beach Lane Bks.
Scheier, Leah. Your Voice Is All I Hear. 2015. 336p. (YA). (gr. 8-12). pap. 9.99 *(978-1-4926-1441-8(6))* Sourcebooks, Inc.
Schoonmaker, Elizabeth. Square Cat. Schoonmaker, Elizabeth, illus. 2011. (ENG., Illus.). 32p. (J). (gr. -1-3). 19.99 *(978-1-4424-0619-3(4)*, Aladdin) Simon & Schuster Children's Publishing.
Schram, Peninnah & Davis, Rachayl Eckstein. The Apple Tree's Discovery. Lee, Wendy W., illus. 2012. (Kar-Ben Favorites Ser.). (ENG.). 24p. (J). (gr. -1-2). lib. bdg. 16.95 *(978-0-7613-5130-6(2)*, Kar-Ben Publishing) Lerner Publishing Group.
Shelton, Crystal G. Theodore's Rings. 2013. 24p. pap. 24.95 *(978-1-62709-378-1(8))* America Star Bks.
Shimberg, Elaine Fantle. Helga, the Hippopotamouse. Walling, Sandy Seeley, illus. 2008. (ENG.). 36p. (J). 7.95 *(978-0-9741940-4-2(2))* Abernathy Hse. Publishing.
Silverstein, Shel. The Missing Piece Meets the Big O. Silverstein, Shel, illus. 2006. (ENG., Illus.). 104p. (J). (gr. -1-3). 19.99 *(978-0-06-025657-9(5)*, HarperCollins) HarperCollins Pubs.
—The Missing Piece Meets the Big O. 2005. (CHI., Illus.). 60p. (J). *(978-7-5442-2517-5(8))* Nanhai Publishing Co.
Simon, Coco. Alexis: The Icing on the Cupcake. 2014. (Cupcake Diaries: 20). lib. bdg. 17.20 *(978-0-606-35786-9(6))* Turtleback.
—Alexis the Icing on the Cupcake. 2014. (Cupcake Diaries: 20). (ENG., Illus.). 160p. (J). (gr. 3-7). pap. 7.99 *(978-1-4814-0468-6(7)*, Simon Spotlight) Simon Spotlight.
—Mia: A Matter of Taste. 2013. (Cupcake Diaries: 14). lib. bdg. 16.00 *(978-0-606-32042-9(3))* Turtleback.
—Mia a Matter of Taste. 2013. (Cupcake Diaries: 14). (ENG., Illus.). 160p. (J). (gr. 3-7). 17.99 *(978-1-4424-7480-2(7))*; pap. 6.99 *(978-1-4424-7435-2(1))* Simon Spotlight. (Simon Spotlight).
Sloan, Holly Goldberg. Short. (ENG.). (J). (gr. 3-7). 2018. 320p. 9.99 *(978-0-399-18622-6(0)*, Puffin Books) 2017. 304p. 17.99 *(978-0-399-18621-9(2)*, Dial Bks) Penguin Young Readers Group.
—Short. 2018. lib. bdg. 19.65 *(978-0-606-40875-2(4))* Turtleback.
Small, David. Imogene's Antlers. 2020. (ENG., Illus.). 32p. (J). (gr. -1-2). 17.99 *(978-0-375-81048-0(X)*, Knopf Bks. for Young Readers) Random Hse. Children's Bks.
Smith, Bryan. Is There an App for That? Wish, Katia, illus. 2015. (ENG.). 31p. (J). (gr. k-6). pap. 10.95 *(978-1-934490-74-7(1))* Boys Town Pr.
Smithem, Beth. Cocoa Bean & Squirt. 2010. 68p. pap. 10.49 *(978-1-4520-1929-1(0))* AuthorHouse.
Sommer, Carl. If Only I Were- James, Kennon, illus. 2014. (J). pap. *(978-1-57537-954-8(6))* Advance Publishing, Inc.
—If Only I Were...(Si Yo Fuese...) James, Kennon, illus. 2009. (Another Sommer-Time Story Bilingual Ser.). (SPA & ENG.). 48p. (J). lib. bdg. 16.95 *(978-1-57537-154-2(5))* Advance Publishing, Inc.
Spinelli, Eileen. Another Day As Emily. Lew-Vriethoff, Joanne, illus. 2015. 240p. (J). (gr. 3-7). 8.99 *(978-0-449-80989-1(7)*, Yearling) Random Hse. Children's Bks.
Spinelli, Jerry. Loser. 2018. (ENG.). 240p. (J). (gr. 3-7). pap. 9.99 *(978-0-06-054074-6(5)*, HarperCollins) HarperCollins Pubs.
—Loser. 2003. (J). (gr. 3-6). lib. bdg. 17.20 *(978-0-613-66899-6(5))* Turtleback.
Stanton, Elizabeth Rose. Henny. Stanton, Elizabeth Rose, illus. 2014. (ENG., Illus.). 40p. (J). (gr. -1-3). 18.99 *(978-1-4424-8436-8(5)*, Simon & Schuster/Paula Wiseman Bks.) Simon & Schuster/Paula Wiseman Bks.
Steers, Billy. Tractor Mac Learns to Fly. (Tractor Mac Ser.). (ENG., Illus.). (J). 2016. 24p. pap. 5.99 *(978-0-374-30537-6(4)*, 900163423) 2015. 32p. (gr. -1-2). 9.99 *(978-0-374-30103-3(4)*, 900138381) Farrar, Straus & Giroux. (Farrar, Straus & Giroux (BYR)).
—Tractor Mac Learns to Fly. 2016. (Tractor Mac Ser.). (J). lib. bdg. 14.75 *(978-0-606-39558-8(X))* Turtleback.
Steers, Billy, illus. Tractor Mac Learns to Fly. 2007. (J). 7.95 *(978-0-9788496-2-7(0))* Tractor Mac Inc.
Stokes, Maura Ellen. Fadeaway. 2018. (ENG.). 304p. (J). (gr. 4-9). 16.99 *(978-1-4998-0674-8(4)*, Yellow Jacket) Bonnier Publishing USA.
Stone, Tamara Ireland. Every Last Word. 2017. (ENG.). (YA). (gr. 7-12). lib. bdg. 20.85 *(978-0-606-39885-5(6))* Turtleback.
Streitz Haber, Tiffany. The Monster Who Lost His Mean. Edmunds, Kirstie, illus. 2012. (ENG.). 40p. (J). (gr. -1-3). 18.99 *(978-0-8050-9375-9(3)*, 900073740, Holt, Henry & Co. Bks. For Young Readers) Holt, Henry & Co.
Stuart, Tara. Tara's Tales: Trees. 2013. 60p. pap. 17.99 *(978-1-4575-2186-7(5))* Dog Ear Publishing, LLC.
Sullivan, Candida. Zippy & the Stripes of Courage. 2011. (J). pap. 13.99 *(978-1-937331-08-5(3))* ShadeTree Publishing, LLC.
Taddonio, Lea. Pain in the Neck. 2019. (Shiverwood Academy Ser.). (ENG., Illus.). 48p. (J). (gr. 3-7). lib. bdg. 34.21 *(978-1-5321-3504-0(1)*, 31927, Spellbound) Magic Wagon.
Taylor-Chiarello, Robin. The Blue Lobster. Bohart, Lisa, illus. 2011. 36p. pap. 15.95 *(978-1-936343-84-3(3))* Peppertree Pr., The.
Taylor, Helen. Emu Can't Fly. Gilles-Gray, Carolyn, illus. 2013. 24p. pap. *(978-1-921883-39-2(1)*, MBS Pr.) Pick-a-Woo Woo Pubs.
Terry, Michael. Rhinos Horns. 2003. (Illus.). (J). *(978-1-58234-796-7(4)*, Bloomsbury USA Childrens) Bloomsbury Publishing USA.
Thurston, Alecia Frances. Shumalady's Butterfly Tree. 2010. 40p. pap. 18.49 *(978-1-4490-5609-4(1))* AuthorHouse.
Todd, Ilima. Remake. 2014. (Remake Ser.: 1). (ENG.). 304p. (YA). (gr. 7). 17.99 *(978-1-60907-924-6(8)*, 5123870, Shadow Mountain) Shadow Mountain Publishing.
Tokio, Marnelle. More Than You Can Chew. 2003. (Illus.). 240p. (YA). (gr. 9-18). pap. 12.95 *(978-0-88776-639-8(0)*, Tundra Bks.) Tundra Bks. CAN. Dist: Penguin Random Hse. LLC.
Townsend, Wendy. Lizard Love. 2013. 198p. 18.95 *(978-1-60898-151-9(7))* namelos llc.
Ure, Daylene Mary. Today I'm Going to be a Hedgehog. 2008. 36p. 16.50 *(978-0-615-25326-8(1))* Ure, Daylene.
Vezeau, Sheila. Sky, the Blue Bunny. Ostrowski, Justin, illus. 2012. 16p. pap. 24.95 *(978-1-4626-7533-3(6))* America Star Bks.
Walter, Debbie. Introducing Russell. Walter, Debbie, illus. 2007. (Illus.). 68p. (J). per. 6.95 *(978-0-9766315-2-1(0))* Moose Run Productions.
Westheimer, Ruth K. & Neusner, Dena. Crocodile, You're Beautiful. Decker, C. B., illus. 2019. (ENG.). 38p. (J). 17.95 *(978-1-68115-551-7(6)*, 0dfd1964-4a86-4f76-ae32-c0318aeee416, Apples & Honey Pr.) Behrman Hse., Inc.
White, Pamela. Poppa Full of Pictures. 2012. 16p. pap. 15.99 *(978-1-4772-9223-5(3))* AuthorHouse.
Williams, Bonnie. Pete Can Fly! Ready-To-Read Level 1. Gordon, John, illus. 2014. (Dino School Ser.). (ENG.). 24p. (J). (gr. -1-1). pap. 4.99 *(978-1-4814-0465-5(2)*, Simon Spotlight) Simon Spotlight.
Williams, Laura E. Slant. 2008. (ENG.). 160p. (J). (gr. 2-8). pap. 6.95 *(978-1-57131-682-0(5))* Milkweed Editions.
Wilson, Diane Lee. Black Storm Comin' 2006. (ENG.). 240p. (J). (gr. 5-9). pap. 8.99 *(978-0-689-87138-2(4)*, McElderry, Margaret K. Bks.) McElderry, Margaret K. Bks.
—Black Storm Comin' 2006. (Illus.). 291p. (gr. 5-9). 17.00 *(978-0-7569-6908-0(5))* Perfection Learning Corp.
Winter, Laurel. Growing Wings. 2010. (ENG.). 208p. (J). (gr. 3-7). pap. 13.95 *(978-0-547-24904-9(7)*, 1100910, Clarion Bks.) HarperCollins Pubs.
Wojtowicz, Jen. The Boy Who Grew Flowers. Adams, Steve, illus. 2012. (ENG.). 32p. (J). (gr. k-5). pap. 9.99 *(978-1-84686-749-1(5))* Barefoot Bks., Inc.
Wojtowicz, Jen & Wojtowitz, Jen. The Boy Who Grew Flowers. Adams, Steve, illus. 2005. (ENG.). 32p. (J). (gr. -1-3). 16.99 *(978-1-84148-686-4(8))* Barefoot Bks., Inc.
Wonder/365 Days of Wonder Boxed Set, 2 vols., Set. 2014. (Wonder Ser.). (ENG.). 432p. (J). (gr. 3-7). 31.98 *(978-0-553-49906-3(8)*, Knopf Bks. for Young Readers) Random Hse. Children's Bks.
Yaccarino, Dan. Giant Tess. Yaccarino, Dan, illus. 2019. (ENG., Illus.). 40p. (J). (gr. -1-3). 17.99 *(978-0-06-267027-4(1)*, HarperCollins) HarperCollins Pubs.
Yee, Paul. Money Boy. 2013. 192p. pap. *(978-1-4596-6450-0(7))* ReadHowYouWant.com, Ltd.
Zia, Farhana. The Garden of My Imaan, 1 vol. 2016. 192p. (J). (gr. 3-7). pap. 8.99 *(978-1-56145-921-6(6))* Peachtree Publishing Co. Inc.

SELF-CONFIDENCE

see also Self-reliance

Adams, Jennifer. I Am a Warrior Goddess. 2018. (I Am a Warrior Goddess Ser.: 1). (ENG., Illus.). 32p. (J). 17.95 *(978-1-68364-005-9(5)*, 900220842) Sounds True, Inc.
Calland, Chris & Hutchinson, Nicky. Minnie & Max are Ok! Smid, Emmi, illus. 2017. 40p. (J). 17.95 *(978-1-78592-233-6(5)*, 696284) Kingsley, Jessica Pubs. GBR. Dist: Hachette UK Distribution.
Chinn, Jacqueline. How Can I Be Special? Mondragon, Manny, illus. 2003. (J). pap. 15.95 *(978-0-929526-55-3(4))* Double B Pubns.
Domoney, Cathy. Madeleine, Maddy & Midge: Positive Thinking for Children. 2012. 36p. pap. 15.95 *(978-1-4525-0761-3(9))* Balboa Pr.
Dreaming Bigger Dreams. 2005. (YA). per. *(978-1-59872-127-0(5))* Instant Pub.
Etingoff, Kim. Confidence. 2013. (Junior Martial Arts Ser.: 9). 32p. (J). (gr. 4-18). 19.95 *(978-1-4222-2734-3(0))* Mason Crest.
Everly, Nita. Early Social Behavior Books Can You Keep Trying? 2007. (J). spiral bd. 11.95 *(978-0-7606-0738-1(9))* LinguiSystems, Inc.
Fox, Annie. Be Confident in Who You Are, Vol. 1. Kindt, Matt, illus. 2008. (Middle School Confidential Ser.: Bk. 1). (ENG.). 96p. (YA). (gr. 6-18). pap. 14.99 *(978-1-57542-302-9(2)*, 23029) Free Spirit Publishing Inc.
Frankel, Erin. Weird! A Story about Dealing with Bullying in Schools. Heaphy, Paula, illus. 2013. (Weird! Ser.). (ENG.). 48p. (J). (gr. k-4). pap. 11.99 *(978-1-57542-437-8(1))* Free Spirit Publishing Inc.
Green, Edna. My Special Thoughts. 2003. (J). (gr. -1-5). bds. 11.95 *(978-0-9743019-0-7(6))* My Special Thoughts.
Harris, Destiny. Beauty Secrets for Girls. 2004. (J). per. *(978-0-9754380-2-2(6)*, 100) Harris, Pleshette Communications Inc. Publishing.
Hodgson, David. The Buzz: A Practical Confidence Builder for Teenagers, 1 vol. 2nd ed. 2015. (ENG., Illus.). 176p. (C). pap. 14.95 *(978-1-84590-998-7(4))* Crown Hse. Publishing LLC.
Jeffers, Susan & Gradstein, Donna. I Can Handle It! 50 Confidence-Building Stories to Empower Your Child. 2006. (ENG., Illus.). 160p. per. 9.95 *(978-0-9777618-0-7(0))* Jeffers Pr.
Kay, Katty. Living the Confidence Code: Real Girls, Real Stories, Real Confidence. 2021. (ENG., Illus.). 400p. (J). (gr. 3-7). 14.99 *(978-0-06-295411-4(3)*, HarperCollins) HarperCollins Pubs.
Kenney, Karen Latchana. Quiet Confidence: The Shy Guide to Using Your Strengths. 2019. (Shy Guides). (ENG., Illus.). 48p. (J). (gr. 4-8). pap. 8.95 *(978-0-7565-6025-6(X)*, 139144); lib. bdg. 31.99 *(978-0-7565-6021-8(7)*, 139140) Capstone. (Compass Point Bks.).
Meiners, Cheri J. Feel Confident! A Book about Self-Esteem. Allen, Elizabeth, illus. 2013. (Being the Best Me(r) Ser.). (ENG.). 40p. (J). (gr. -1-3). pap. 11.99 *(978-1-57542-442-2(8))* Free Spirit Publishing Inc.
Miller, Ruth L. The Power of Self Ralph Waldo Emerson's Wonder Filled Life. Shonkwiler, Martha, illus. 2013. 66p. pap. 12.00 *(978-0-945385-85-1(4))* WiseWoman Pr.
Moss, Wendy L. Being Me: A Kid's Guide to Boosting Confidence & Self-Esteem. 2010. (Illus.). 112p. (J). (gr. 3-8). 14.95 *(978-1-4338-0883-8(8))*; pap. 9.95 *(978-1-4338-0884-5(6))* American Psychological Assn. (Magination Pr.).
Payne, Lauren Murphy. Just Because I Am. 2015. lib. bdg. 20.85 *(978-0-606-37402-6(7))* Turtleback.
Piper, Watty & Hart, Charlie. You Can! Words of Wisdom from the Little Engine That Could. Howarth, Jill, illus. 2018. (Little Engine That Could Ser.). 80p. (J). (gr. 5-12). 12.99 *(978-1-5247-8468-3(0)*, Grosset & Dunlap) Penguin Young Readers Group.
Rice, Ashley. Girls Rule: A very special book created especially for girls — UPDATED EDITION —, 1 vol. 2011. 64p. pap. 12.95 *(978-1-59842-598-7(6))* Blue Mountain Arts Inc.
Rodriguez, Joshua. Embracing the Awkward: A Guide for Teens to Succeed at School, Life & Relationships. 2018. (ENG.). 236p. (YA). (gr. 7-9). pap. 18.99 *(978-1-63353-736-1(6))* Mango Media.
Rooks, Jo. Hector's Favorite Place. Rooks, Jo, illus. 2018. (Illus.). 32p. (J). *(978-1-4338-2868-3(5)*, Magination Pr.) American Psychological Assn.
Rotner, Shelley. We All Do Something Well. 2013. (Shelley Rotner's World Ser.). (ENG.). 24p. (J). (gr. 1-2). pap. 47.70 *(978-1-62065-755-3(4)*, Capstone Pr.) Capstone.
Schab, Lisa M. Cool, Calm, Confident: A Workbook to Help Kids Learn Assertiveness Skills. 2009. (ENG.). 184p. (J). (gr. k-5). pap. 18.95 *(978-1-57224-630-0(8)*, 6300, Instant Help Books) New Harbinger Pubns.
Shipp, Josh. The Teen's Guide to World Domination: Advice on Life, Liberty, & the Pursuit of Awesomeness. 2010. (ENG., Illus.). 304p. (YA). (gr. 8-18). pap., instr.'s gde. ed. 16.99 *(978-0-312-64154-2(0)*, 900067551, St. Martin's Griffin) St. Martin's Pr.
Siwa, JoJo. JoJo's Guide to the Sweet Life: #PeaceOutHaterz. 2020. (ENG.). 256p. (J). (gr. 5-17). pap. 12.99 *(978-1-4197-4865-3(3)*, 1206303, Amulet Bks.) Abrams, Inc.
Smith, Sarah. Self-Confidence, Vol. 7. 2018. (Leadership Skills & Character Building Ser.). 64p. (J). (gr. 7). lib. bdg. 31.93 *(978-1-4222-3999-5(3))* Mason Crest.
Straight Talk about Self-Confidence. (YA). (gr. 6-8). 69.95 *(978-1-55942-197-3(5)*, 9239V9) Witcher Productions.
Summers, Barbara. Open the Unusual Door: True Life Stories of Challenge, Adventure, & Success by Black Americans. 2005. (ENG., Illus.). 224p. (YA). (gr. 7-18). pap. 12.99 *(978-0-618-58531-1(1)*, 430075, Clarion Bks.) HarperCollins Pubs.
Syed, Matthew. The You Are Awesome Journal. 2020. (ENG.). 144p. (J). (gr. 4-8). pap. 10.99 *(978-1-7282-0950-0(1))* Sourcebooks, Inc.
Tool Kits for Kids LLC Staff, creator. Charge up Your Confidence - Tool Kit for Kids: Elementary School Edition. 2008. (Illus.). (J). 39.95 *(978-0-9819483-2-4(4))* Tool Kits For Kids LLC.
—Charge up Your Confidence - Tool Kit for Kids: High School / Middle School Edition. 2009. (Illus.). (J). 39.95 *(978-0-9819483-3-1(2))* Tool Kits For Kids LLC.
Van Hollander, Tammi. Casey's Greatness Wings: Teaching Mindfulness, Connection & Courage to Children. 2018. (Illus.). 62p. pap. 24.99 *(978-1-64316-778-7(2))* Primedia eLaunch LLC.
Van Wagenen, Maya. Popular: A Memoir. 2015. lib. bdg. 22.10 *(978-0-606-36796-7(9))* Turtleback.
—Popular: How a Geek in Pearls Discovered the Secret to Confidence. 2015. (ENG.). 272p. (YA). (gr. 7). pap. 10.99 *(978-0-14-751254-3(9)*, Speak) Penguin Young Readers Group.
Yankee, Kris & Nelson, Marian. Are You Confident Today? 2014. (ENG., Illus.). 32p. (J). pap. 9.95 *(978-1-938326-24-0(5)*, Ferne Pr.) Nelson Publishing & Marketing.

SELF-CONFIDENCE—FICTION

Abela, Deborah. The Stupendously Spectacular Spelling Bee. (Spectacular Spelling Bee Ser.: 1). (ENG.). (J). (gr. 3-7). 2019. 240p. pap. 7.99 *(978-1-4926-6822-0(2))* 2018. 224p. 16.99 *(978-1-4926-6211-2(9))* Sourcebooks, Inc.
Aisha. Parsley, Sage, Rosemary & Thyme. 2012. 24p. 24.95 *(978-1-4626-5122-1(4))* America Star Bks.
Alexander, Jill S. The Sweetheart of Prosper County. 2010. (ENG.). 240p. (YA). (gr. 7-12). pap. 18.99 *(978-0-312-54857-5(5)*, 900055795) Square Fish.
Allen, Debbie. Dancing in the Wings. Nelson, Kadir, illus. 2003. (ENG.). 32p. (J). (gr. -1-3). 8.99 *(978-0-14-250141-2(7)*, Puffin Books) Penguin Young Readers Group.
—Dancing in the Wings. Nelson, Kadir, illus. 2003. (J). (gr. -1-3). 14.65 *(978-0-7569-7022-2(9))* Perfection Learning Corp.
Anderson, Jodi Lynn. Among the Stars. 2014. (May Bird Ser.: 2). (ENG., Illus.). 304p. (J). (gr. 3-7). pap. 7.99 *(978-1-4424-9578-4(2)*, Aladdin) Simon & Schuster Children's Publishing.
—Among the Stars. 2014. (May Bird Ser.: 2). (ENG., Illus.). 304p. (J). (gr. 3-7). 18.99 *(978-1-4424-9579-1(0)*, Simon & Schuster/Paula Wiseman Bks.) Simon & Schuster/Paula Wiseman Bks.
Anderson, John David. Sidekicked. 2013. (ENG.). 384p. (J). (gr. 3-7). 16.99 *(978-0-06-213314-4(4)*, Waldon Pond Pr.) HarperCollins Pubs.
Andros, Camille. Charlotte the Scientist Finds a Cure. Farley, Brianne, illus. 2019. (Charlotte the Scientist Ser.). (ENG.). 40p. (J). (gr. -1-3). 17.99 *(978-0-544-81376-2(6)*, 1642033, Clarion Bks.) HarperCollins Pubs.
Applegate, Katherine. Don't Tap-Dance on Your Teacher. Biggs, Brian, illus. 2009. (Roscoe Riley Rules Ser.: 5). (ENG.). 96p. (J). (gr. 1-5). pap. 4.99 *(978-0-06-114889-7(X))* HarperCollins Pubs.
—Don't Tap-Dance on Your Teacher. Biggs, Brian, illus. 2016. (Roscoe Riley Rules Ser.: 5). (ENG.). 112p. (J). (gr. 1-5). 14.75 *(978-0-606-39252-5(1))* Turtleback.

—Don't Tap-Dance on Your Teacher. 2009. (Roscoe Riley Rules Ser.: 5). (J). lib. bdg. 14.75 *(978-0-606-05007-4(8))* Turtleback.
Arreola, Perla. Weenz the Cat: What about Me? Arreola, Manuel, illus. 2013. 30p. 14.99 *(978-0-9859298-7-9(1))* Dream&Achieve Bks.
Baguchinsky, Jill. Mammoth. 2018. (Illus.). 304p. (YA). (ENG.). 26.99 *(978-1-68442-195-4(0))*; pap. 17.99 *(978-1-68442-194-7(2))* Turner Publishing Co.
Baker, E. D. More Than a Princess. (More Than a Princess Ser.). (ENG.). (J). 2019. 304p. pap. 8.99 *(978-1-5476-0211-7(2)*, 900203281) 2018. 288p. 16.99 *(978-1-68119-768-5(5)*, 900185875) Bloomsbury Publishing USA. (Bloomsbury Children's Bks.).
Bandsuh, Jim. Helmet Hank. 2007. (Illus.). (J). per. 15.99 *(978-1-933156-19-4(8)*, Visikid Bks.) GSVQ Publishing.
Bang, Molly. When Sophie Thinks She Can't... Bang, Molly, illus. 2018. (ENG., Illus.). 40p. (J). (gr. -1-3). 18.99 *(978-1-338-15298-2(X)*, Blue Sky Pr., The) Scholastic, Inc.
Barnes, Derrick. Crown: An Ode to the Fresh Cut. James, Gordon C., illus. 2017. 32p. (J). (gr. -1-3). 18.95 *(978-1-57284-224-3(5))* Agate Publishing, Inc.
—I Am Every Good Thing. James, Gordon C., illus. 2020. (ENG.). 32p. (J). (gr. -1-2). 18.99 *(978-0-525-51877-8(0)*, Nancy Paulsen Books) Penguin Young Readers Group.
—The King of Kindergarten. Brantley-Newton, Vanessa, illus. 2019. 32p. (J). (-k). 17.99 *(978-1-5247-4074-0(8)*, Nancy Paulsen Books) Penguin Young Readers Group.
—The Queen of Kindergarten. Brantley-Newton, Vanessa, illus. 2022. (ENG.). 32p. (J). (-k). 17.99 *(978-0-593-11142-0(7)*, Nancy Paulsen Books) Penguin Young Readers Group.
Barrett, Kendra J., et al. Yes I Can! A Girl & Her Wheelchair. Lemay, Violet, illus. 2018. 32p. (J). *(978-1-4338-2869-0(3)*, Magination Pr.) American Psychological Assn.
Bartha, Alysa. Petal's Wish. 2010. 32p. 14.99 *(978-1-4490-7417-3(0))* AuthorHouse.
Bashford, Taryn. The Harper Effect. 2018. (ENG.). 408p. (YA). (gr. 8-8). 17.99 *(978-1-5107-2665-9(9)*, Sky Pony Pr.) Skyhorse Publishing Co., Inc.
Bee, Sarah. The Yes. Kitamura, Satoshi, illus. 2015. (ENG.). 32p. (J). 16.00 *(978-0-8028-5449-0(4)*, Eerdmans Bks For Young Readers) Eerdmans, William B. Publishing Co.
Belavilas, Charlotte. Walter, the Carpenter Bee. 2007. pap. 9.00 *(978-0-8059-8504-7(2))* Dorrance Publishing Co., Inc.
Bell, Krista & Smith, Craig. If the Shoe Fits. 2008. (Illus.). 60p. (Orig.). (J). (gr. -1-3). 14.95 *(978-1-58089-338-1(4))* Charlesbridge Publishing, Inc.
Bell, Lucy. Hal & the Very Long Race: A Book about Self-Acceptance. Garton, Michael, illus. 2017. (Frolic First Faith Ser.). 32p. (J). (gr. -1-k). 12.99 *(978-1-5064-1789-9(2)*, Sparkhouse Family) 1517 Media.
Benedetto, K. & Barlow, J. I See the World. 2009. pap. *(978-1-61584-125-7(3))* Independent Pub.
Benton, Jim. Howard Hubbins Half Hour Hero. 2008. (J). pap. 4.99 *(978-0-06-059774-0(7))* HarperCollins Pubs.
Berkowitz, Barbara. The Talent Show. 2009. 108p. 21.49 *(978-1-4389-9826-8(0))*; pap. 10.99 *(978-1-4389-9825-1(2))* AuthorHouse.
Bertrand, Diane Gonzales. The F Factor. 2010. 256p. (J). (gr. 6-18). pap. 12.95 *(978-1-55885-598-4(X)*, Piñata Books) Arte Publico Pr.
Bloom, Stephanie. The Drummer Who Lost His Beat. Keylon, Joe, illus. 2005. 40p. (J). lib. bdg. 16.95 *(978-1-931969-47-5(7))* Bloom & Grow Bks.
Blume, Lesley M. M. Cornelia & the Audacious Escapades of the Somerset Sisters. 2008. 272p. (J). (gr. 3-7). 8.99 *(978-0-440-42110-8(1)*, Yearling) Random Hse. Children's Bks.
Bowe, Julie. Pompom Problems. 2015. (Victoria Torres, Unfortunately Average Ser.). (ENG., Illus.). 160p. (J). (gr. 4-8). lib. bdg. 27.99 *(978-1-4965-0532-3(8)*, 128604, Stone Arch Bks.) Capstone.
Bowen, Carl. BMX Breakthrough, 1 vol. Sandoval, Gerardo, illus. 2011. (Sports Illustrated Kids Graphic Novels Ser.). (ENG.). 56p. (J). (gr. 3-8). pap. 7.19 *(978-1-4342-3401-8(0)*, 116414); lib. bdg. 26.65 *(978-1-4342-2240-4(3)*, 103103) Capstone. (Stone Arch Bks.).
—Quarterback Rush, 1 vol. Garcia, Eduardo, illus. 2014. (Sports Illustrated Kids Graphic Novels Ser.). (ENG.). 72p. (J). (gr. 3-8). 26.65 *(978-1-4342-6489-3(0)*, 124177, Stone Arch Bks.) Capstone.
Bowen, Fred. Full Court Fever, 1 vol. rev. ed. 2009. (Fred Bowen Sports Story Ser.: 6). (Illus.). 103p. (J). (gr. 2-6). pap. 6.95 *(978-1-56145-508-9(3))* Peachtree Publishing Co. Inc.
—The Golden Glove, 1 vol. rev. ed. 2009. (Fred Bowen Sports Story Ser.: 1). (Illus.). 120p. (J). (gr. 2-6). pap. 6.99 *(978-1-56145-505-8(9))* Peachtree Publishing Co. Inc.
—Hardcourt Comeback, 1 vol. 2010. (Fred Bowen Sports Story Ser.: 14). (Illus.). 152p. (J). (gr. 2-6). pap. 6.99 *(978-1-56145-516-4(4))* Peachtree Publishing Co. Inc.
—Lucky Enough, 1 vol. 2018. (Fred Bowen Sports Story Ser.: 22). 144p. (J). (gr. 2-6). pap. 6.99 *(978-1-56145-958-2(5))* Peachtree Publishing Co. Inc.
—On the Line, 1 vol. 2nd rev. ed. 2009. (Fred Bowen Sports Story Ser.: 7). (Illus.). 103p. (J). (gr. 2-6). pap. 6.95 *(978-1-56145-511-9(3))* Peachtree Publishing Co. Inc.
Brantz, Loryn, illus. Not Just a Dot. 2014. (ENG.). 32p. (J). (-k). 16.95 *(978-1-62914-622-5(6)*, Sky Pony Pr.) Skyhorse Publishing Co., Inc.
Braunstein, M. & Braunstein, J. Don't I Look Smart. 2009. *(978-1-61584-845-4(2))* Independent Pub.
—Don't Look Smart?! 2009. (J). pap. *(978-1-61623-138-5(6))* Independent Pub.
Brennan-Nelson, Denise. Buzzy the Bumblebee. Monroe, Michael Glenn, illus. 2003. (ENG.). 32p. (J). (gr. 1-4). pap. 6.95 *(978-1-58536-166-3(6)*, 202260) Sleeping Bear Pr.
Brian, Kate, pseud. Megan Meade's Guide to the Mcgowan Boys. 2006. (ENG.). 288p. (YA). (gr. 7-12). pap. 11.99 *(978-1-4169-0031-3(4)*, Simon & Schuster Bks. For Young Readers) Simon & Schuster Bks. For Young Readers.
Bright, Rachel. The Koala Who Could. Field, Jim, illus. 2017. (ENG.). 32p. (J). (gr. -1-k). 18.99 *(978-1-338-13908-2(8)*, Scholastic Pr.) Scholastic, Inc.
Brightwood, Laura, illus. The Woodsman & His Ax. Brightwood, Laura, . 2007. (J). DVD *(978-1-934409-07-7(3))* 3-C Institute for Social Development.
Britton, Faith. If You'D Only Believe. 2009. 24p. pap. 12.99 *(978-1-4490-1741-5(X))* AuthorHouse.
Brown, Tricia. Charlie & the Blanket Toss. Martinsen, Sarah, illus. 2015. (ENG.). 32p. (J). (gr. 1-2). pap. 12.99 *(978-1-941821-66-4(9)*, Alaska Northwest Bks.) West Margin Pr.
Brown-Wood, Janay. Imani's Moon. Mitchell, Hazel, illus. 2014. (ENG.). 32p. (J). (gr. 1-4). pap. 7.95 *(978-1-934133-58-3(2))* Charlesbridge Publishing, Inc.
Bruchac, Joseph. The Way. 2013. (ENG.). 160p. (YA). (gr. 6-12). pap. 9.95 *(978-1-4677-0862-3(3)*, dd3043d8-11f7-4c45-a484-7bef255f2f84) 2007. 156p. (J). (gr. 4-7). 16.95 *(978-1-58196-062-4(X))* Lerner Publishing Group. (Darby Creek).
Brun, Laura. Frosty the Craft Maker. 2012. 24p. pap. 24.95 *(978-1-62709-700-0(7))* America Star Bks.
Bunting, Eve. One Green Apple. Lewin, Ted, illus. 2006. (ENG.). 32p. (J). (gr. -1-3). 17.99 *(978-0-618-43477-0(1)*, 100359, Clarion Bks.) HarperCollins Pubs.
Burch, Christian. The Manny Files. 2008. (Mix Ser.). (ENG.). 304p. (J). (gr. 4-8). pap. 14.99 *(978-1-4169-5534-4(8)*, Aladdin) Simon & Schuster Children's Publishing.
Burk, Josh. The Summer of Saint Nick. 2007. (ENG.). 152p. (YA). per. 12.95 *(978-0-9768042-2-2(0))* Maven Of Memory Publishing.
Cabot, Meg. The Princess Diaries, Volume IX: Princess Mia, Vol. 9. 2009. (Princess Diaries: 9). (ENG.). 304p. (YA). (gr. 8). pap. 10.99 *(978-0-06-072463-4(3)*, HarperTeen) HarperCollins Pubs.
—Princess Mia. 2008. (Princess Diaries: Vol. 9). (ENG.). 256p. (J). (gr. 7-18). 16.99 *(978-0-06-072461-0(7))* HarperCollins Pubs.
—Princess Mia. 2009. (Princess Diaries: 9). (YA). lib. bdg. 20.85 *(978-0-606-02178-4(7))* Turtleback.
Calabrese, Dianne. The Inspirational Guide, 1 vol. 2010. 24p. 24.95 *(978-1-4489-4844-4(4))* PublishAmerica, Inc.
Calonita, Jen. The Real Z. 2017. 147p. (J). *(978-1-338-14809-1(5))* Scholastic, Inc.
Canby, Kelly. Rodney. 2019. (Illus.). 32p. (J). (gr. -1-k). 17.95 *(978-1-925815-32-0(3))* Fremantle Pr. AUS. Dist: Independent Pubs. Group.
Caruso, Rosalie. How I taught my mom... the Law of Attraction. 2010. 48p. 17.45 *(978-1-4525-0135-2(1))* Get Published.
Cellucci, Lucy Lemay. True Colours. 2010. (ENG., Illus.). 240p. (YA). (gr. 7-10). pap. 9.95 *(978-1-926607-13-9(9)*, Napoleon & Co.) Dundurn Pr. CAN. Dist: Publishers Group West (PGW).
Cervantes, Angela. Allie, First at Last: a Wish Novel. 2016. (ENG.). 208p. (J). (gr. 3-7). 16.99 *(978-0-545-81223-8(2)*, Scholastic Pr.) Scholastic, Inc.
Chandler, Bill & Chandler, Marie. The Reindeer That Couldn't Fly. Kling, Leslie, illus. 2009. 48p. pap. 19.99 *(978-1-933817-40-8(2))* Profits Publishing.
Chidebelu-Eze / Dove Publishing, Chibueze Obi. The Lion That Finally Roared: Inspirational Story of Purpose & Destiny. Newborne, David / F., illus. 2008. 80p. (J). 17.99 *(978-0-9766578-5-9(6))*; pap. 11.99 *(978-0-9766578-6-6(4))* Dove Publishing, Inc.
Chin, Oliver. The Year of the Rooster: Tales from the Chinese Zodiac. Calle, Juan, illus. 2016. (Tales from the Chinese Zodiac Ser.: 12). (ENG.). 40p. (J). (gr. -1). 15.95 *(978-1-59702-125-8(3))* Immedium.
Choyce, Lesley. Book of Michael, 1 vol. 2008. (ENG.). 224p. (YA). (gr. 9-12). pap. 9.95 *(978-0-88995-417-5(8)*, 46f6c2d9-d965-4aff-bb00-a2db42ea87fb) Trifolium Bks., Inc. CAN. Dist: Firefly Bks., Ltd.
—Carrie Loses Her Nerve, 1 vol. Thurman, Mark, illus. 2003. (Formac First Novels Ser.: 26). (ENG.). 64p. (J). (gr. 1-5). 4.95 *(978-0-88780-591-2(4)*, 591); 14.95 *(978-0-88780-592-9(2)*, 592) Formac Publishing Co., Ltd. CAN. Dist: Formac Lorimer Bks. Ltd.
Christopher, Matt. The Dog That Pitched a No-Hitter. Bjorkman, Steve, illus. 2013. (Passport to Reading Level 3 Ser.). (ENG.). 48p. (J). (gr. 1-4). 4.99 *(978-0-316-21848-1(0))* Little, Brown Bks. for Young Readers.
—The Dog That Pitched a No-Hitter. Bjorkman, Steve, illus. 2018. (Matt Christopher Sports Readers Ser.). (ENG.). 48p. (J). (gr. 1-4). lib. bdg. 31.36 *(978-1-5321-4255-0(2)*, 31055) Spotlight.
—Fairway Phenom. 2003. (Matt Christopher Sports Bio Bookshelf Ser.). 132p. (J). (gr. 4-7). 12.65 *(978-0-7569-1565-1(X))* Perfection Learning Corp.
—Hook Shot Hero: A Nothin' but Net Sequel. 2011. (ENG.). 144p. (J). (gr. 3-7). pap. 5.99 *(978-0-316-10296-4(2))* Little, Brown Bks. for Young Readers.
—The Lucky Baseball Bat. Henneberger, Robert, illus. 2019. (ENG.). 128p. (J). pap. 6.99 *(978-0-316-53132-0(4))* Little, Brown Bks. for Young Readers.
—The Lucky Baseball Bat. Henneberger, Robert, illus. 2005. 123p. (gr. -1-3). 16.00 *(978-0-7569-4890-0(8))* Perfection Learning Corp.
—Man Out at First. Beier, Ellen, illus. 2009. (New Peach Street Mudders Sports Library). 64p. (J). (gr. 2-4). lib. bdg. 23.93 *(978-1-59953-319-3(7))* Norwood Hse. Pr.
Ciara & Wilson, Russell. Why Not You? Gibson, Jessica, illus. 2022. 32p. (J). (gr. -1-3). 18.99 *(978-0-593-37440-5(1))*; (ENG.). lib. bdg. 21.99 *(978-0-593-37441-2(X))* Random Hse. Children's Bks. (Random Hse. Bks. for Young Readers).
Ciencin, Scott. Snowboard Standoff, 1 vol. Aburto, Jesus & Cobos, Fabian, illus. 2011. (Sports Illustrated Kids Graphic Novels Ser.). (ENG.). 56p. (J). (gr. 3-8). pap. 7.19 *(978-1-4342-3403-2(7)*, 116416); lib. bdg. 26.65 *(978-1-4342-2242-8(X)*, 103104) Capstone. (Stone Arch Bks.).
Clark, Ruth. Airport Mouse Works the Nightshift. 2008. (ENG.). 32p. (J). 15.95 *(978-0-9792963-3-8(1))* Hibiscus Publishing.
Clough, Paige. The Jumping Orie Story. Yates, Bridget & Ward, Karen, illus. 2015. (J). *(978-1-942945-24-6(8))* Night Heron Media.
—The Jumping Orie Story. Yates, Bridget & Ward, Karen, illus. 2015. (J). *(978-0-9915511-2-5(5))* Rule 2 Bks.
Cohen, Miriam. Layla's Head Scarf, 1 vol. Himler, Ronald, illus. 2009. (ENG.). 32p. (J). (gr. -1-3). 15.95 *(978-1-59572-177-8(0))*; pap. 5.95 *(978-1-59572-178-5(9))* Star Bright Bks., Inc.
Condie, Ally. The Last Voyage of Poe Blythe. 2019. (ENG.). 336p. (YA). (gr. 7). 18.99 *(978-0-525-42645-5(0)*, Dutton Books for Young Readers) Penguin Young Readers Group.
Cooner, Donna. Worthy. 2017. (ENG.). 288p. (YA). (gr. 7). 17.99 *(978-0-545-90393-6(9))* Scholastic, Inc.
Copeland, Misty. Firebird. Myers, Christopher, illus. 2014. 40p. (J). (gr. k-3). 17.99 *(978-0-399-16615-0(7)*, G.P. Putnam's Sons Books for Young Readers) Penguin Young Readers Group.
Cornish, D. M. Foundling. Cornish, D. M., illus. 2007. (Monster Blood Tattoo Ser.). (Illus.). 434p. (gr. 7-12). 20.00 *(978-0-7569-7957-7(9))* Perfection Learning Corp.
Cosgrove, Stephen. Mizz Buggly: Doing Your Best. Arroyo, Fian, illus. 2004. (J). *(978-1-58804-380-1(0))* P C I Education.
Cowing, Sue. Call Me Drog. 2014. (ENG.). 320p. (J). 13.99 *(978-0-00-757804-7(0))* HarperCollins Pubs. Ltd. GBR. Dist: Independent Pubs. Group.
Curtis, Kelli. Amber & the Fallen Bridge. 2009. 32p. pap. 13.00 *(978-1-60860-631-3(7)*, Strategic Bk. Publishing) Strategic Book Publishing & Rights Agency (SBPRA).
Cushman, Karen. Grayling's Song. 2020. (ENG.). 240p. (J). (gr. 3-7). pap. 7.99 *(978-0-358-09748-8(7)*, 1747604, Clarion Bks.) HarperCollins Pubs.
Cuyler, Margery. Bonaparte Falls Apart. Terry, Will, illus. 2020. 40p. (J). (gr. -1-2). 8.99 *(978-1-101-93772-3(6)*, Dragonfly Bks.) Random Hse. Children's Bks.
Cuyler, Margery & Terry, Will. Bonaparte Falls Apart. 2017. (Illus.). 40p. (J). (gr. -1-2). 17.99 *(978-1-101-93768-6(8)*, Crown Books For Young Readers) Random Hse. Children's Bks.
Davis, Jacky. Black Belt Bunny. Fleck, Jay, illus. 2017. 40p. (J). (-k). 16.99 *(978-0-525-42902-9(6)*, Dial Bks) Penguin Young Readers Group.
Defillippo, Steve. Growing up Nicely! Grammy Helps Adam Grow up & Develop Social Skills & Moral Values. 2012. 24p. (-18). pap. 15.99 *(978-1-4797-0957-1(3))* Xlibris Corp.
Delle Donne, Elena. Out of Bounds. 2018. (Hoops Ser.: 3). (ENG., Illus.). 176p. (J). (gr. 3-7). 16.99 *(978-1-5344-1237-8(9)*, Simon & Schuster Bks. For Young Readers) Simon & Schuster Bks. For Young Readers.
Desir, C. & Perry, Jolene. Love Blind. (ENG.). (YA). (gr. 9). 2017. 336p. pap. 10.99 *(978-1-4814-1694-8(4))* 2016. (Illus.). 320p. 17.99 *(978-1-4814-1693-1(6))* Simon Pulse. (Simon Pulse).
DeVillers, Julia. Lynn Visible. 2011. (ENG.). 160p. (gr. 6-8). 18.69 *(978-0-525-47691-7(1))* Penguin Young Readers Group.
Diesen, Deborah. The Pout-Pout Fish Goes to School. Hanna, Dan, illus. (Pout-Pout Fish Adventure Ser.). (ENG.). 32p. (J). 2018. bds. 7.99 *(978-0-374-30852-0(7)*, 900187130) 2014. (gr. -1-k). 18.99 *(978-0-374-36095-5(2)*, 900085614) Farrar, Straus & Giroux. (Farrar, Straus & Giroux (BYR)).
Diggle, David Mark. Barbara: A Sssslithering Adventure of Self Discovery. Diggle, Daniel James, illus. 2011. 24p. (J). pap. *(978-0-9871657-9-4(8))* Diggle de Doo Productions Pty. Ltd.
Dillon, Diane. I Can Be Anything! Don't Tell Me I Can't. Dillon, Diane, illus. 2018. (ENG., Illus.). 32p. (J). (gr. -1-3). 18.99 *(978-1-338-16690-3(5)*, Blue Sky Pr., The) Scholastic, Inc.
Dinolfo, Louann S. The Calico Kite. 2011. 28p. pap. 15.99 *(978-1-4628-6356-3(6))* Xlibris Corp.
Double Reverse, 1 vol. 2014. (Fred Bowen Sports Story Ser.: 19). 144p. (J). (gr. 2-6). pap. 6.99 *(978-1-56145-807-3(4))* Peachtree Publishing Co. Inc.
Dowell, Frances O'Roark. The Second Life of Abigail Walker. (ENG., Illus.). (J). (gr. 3-7). 2013. 272p. pap. 8.99 *(978-1-4424-0594-3(5))* 2012. 240p. 16.99 *(978-1-4424-0593-6(7))* Simon & Schuster Children's Publishing. (Atheneum Bks. for Young Readers).
Dower, Laura. Gabi & the Great Big Bakeover. Lazuli, Lilly, illus. 2016. (Dessert Diaries). (ENG.). 160p. (J). (gr. 4-8). lib. bdg. 26.65 *(978-1-4965-3119-3(1)*, 132190, Stone Arch Bks.) Capstone.
—Gabi & the Great Big Bakeover. Lazuli, Lilly, illus. 2017. (ENG.). 160p. (J). pap. *(978-1-4747-2213-1(X)*, Stone Arch Bks.) Capstone.
Drachman, Eric. Leo the Lightning Bug. Muscarello, James, illus. l.t. ed. 2005. (ENG.). 32p. (J). (gr. -1-2). 18.95 incl. audio compact disk *(978-0-9703809-0-6(9))* Kidwick Bks.
Draper, Sharon M. Out of My Heart. 2021. (Out of My Mind Ser.). (ENG., Illus.). 352p. (J). (gr. 5). 18.99 *(978-1-6659-0216-8(7)*, Atheneum/Caitlyn Dlouhy Books) Simon & Schuster Children's Publishing.
Drouhard, Brianne. Billie the Unicorn. 2011. (ENG., Illus.). 36p. (J). (gr. -1-3). 15.95 *(978-1-59702-024-4(9))* Immedium.
Duff, Hilary. My Little Brave Girl. Garrity-Riley, Kelsey, illus. 2021. (ENG.). 32p. (J). (gr. -1-2). 18.99 *(978-0-593-30072-5(6))*; lib. bdg. 21.99 *(978-0-593-30073-2(4))* Random Hse. Children's Bks. (Random Hse. Bks. for Young Readers).
Dunlap, Sonya K. Responza the Bull Learns the Ropes. 2008. 24p. pap. 17.95 *(978-0-9815245-5-9(9))* Accelerator Bks.
Durso, Diana T. Did You Know That's Not My Name? Bentz, Jill M., illus. 2009. (ENG.). 50p. pap. 19.95 *(978-1-4389-3182-1(4))* AuthorHouse.
Dyan, Penelope. Mikey & Me & the Se. 2011. 36p. pap. 11.95 *(978-1-935630-63-0(6))* Bellissima Publishing, LLC.
Easton, Kelly. To Be Mona. (ENG.). 224p. (YA). (gr. 7). 2009. pap. 7.99 *(978-1-4169-0055-9(1))* 2008. 16.99 *(978-1-4169-0054-2(3))* McElderry, Margaret K. Bks. (McElderry, Margaret K. Bks.).
Efaw, Amy. Battle Dress. 2003. 400p. (J). (gr. 7-18). pap. 6.99 *(978-0-06-053520-9(2))* HarperCollins Pubs.
—Battle Dress. 2010. (ENG.). 304p. (YA). (gr. 7-18). 8.99 *(978-0-14-241397-5(6)*, Speak) Penguin Young Readers Group.
Fagan, Cary. I Wish I Could Draw, 1 vol. 2014. (ENG., Illus.). 32p. (J). (gr. k-3). 12.95 *(978-1-55498-318-6(5))* Groundwood Bks. CAN. Dist: Publishers Group West (PGW).
Faruqi, Saadia. Meet Yasmin! Aly, Hatem, illus. 2018. (Yasmin Ser.). (ENG.). 96p. (J). (gr. k-2). pap., pap., pap. 5.95 *(978-1-68436-022-2(6)*, 137937, Picture Window Bks.) Capstone.
—Yasmin the Painter. Aly, Hatem, illus. 2018. (Yasmin Ser.). (ENG.). 32p. (J). (gr. k-2). 22.65 *(978-1-5158-2728-3(3)*, 137932, Picture Window Bks.) Capstone.
Feldman, Eve B. Seymour, the Formerly Fearful. Singh, Parwinder, illus. 2019. (ENG.). (J). (gr. 3-6). pap. 8.99 *(978-1-5415-3951-8(6)*, def5e665-e8c7-4bc2-a8fe-04cb2a223083, Kar-Ben Publishing) Lerner Publishing Group.
Ferguson, Sarah. Ballerina Rosie. Goode, Diane, illus. 2012. (ENG.). 32p. (J). (gr. -1-3). 16.99 *(978-1-4424-3066-2(4)*, Simon & Schuster/Paula Wiseman Bks.) Simon & Schuster/Paula Wiseman Bks.
Flinn, Alex. Diva. 2013. (ENG.). 304p. (YA). (gr. 9). pap. 9.99 *(978-0-06-212434-0(X))* 2007. (ENG.). 304p. (J). (gr. 9-12). pap. 8.99 *(978-0-06-056846-7(1))* 2006. 263p. (YA). (gr. 7-12). 16.99 *(978-0-06-056843-6(7))* 2006. 263p. (YA). (gr. 7-12). lib. bdg. 18.89 *(978-0-06-056845-0(3))* HarperCollins Pubs. (HarperTeen).
Foard, Sheila Wood. Harvey Girl. 2006. (ENG., Illus.). 176p. (J). (gr. 7-12). per. 18.95 *(978-0-89672-570-6(7)*, P171685) Texas Tech Univ. Pr.
The Fold. 2017. (ENG., Illus.). (YA). (gr. 7). 256p. 19.99 *(978-1-4814-4239-8(2))*; 272p. pap. 12.99 *(978-1-4814-4240-4(6))* Simon & Schuster Children's Publishing. (Atheneum/Caitlyn Dlouhy Books).
Ford, Adam B. Jam-Bo, Litta-Girl, & the Bullies. Huddleston, Courtney, illus. 2013. 44p. pap. 12.95 *(978-0-9794104-9-9(5))* H Bar Pr.
Forman, Gayle. Sisters in Sanity. (YA). 2016. (ENG.). 304p. (gr. 8). pap. 9.99 *(978-0-06-088749-0(4))* 2007. 290p. (gr. 7-12). lib. bdg. 17.89 *(978-0-06-088748-3(6))* 2007. (ENG.). 304p. (gr. 7-18). 16.99 *(978-0-06-088747-6(8))* HarperCollins Pubs. (HarperTeen).
Franklin, Ashley. Not Quite Snow White. Glenn, Ebony, illus. 2019. (ENG.). 32p. (J). (gr. -1-3). 17.99 *(978-0-06-279860-2(X)*, HarperCollins) HarperCollins Pubs.
Friedman, Aimee. Two Summers. 2016. (ENG.). 368p. (YA). (gr. 7). 17.99 *(978-0-545-51807-9(5))* Scholastic, Inc.
Friedman, Laurie. Game Time, Mallory! Kalis, Jennifer, illus. 2015. (Mallory Ser.). (ENG.). 160p. (J). (gr. 2-5). E-Book 23.99 *(978-1-4677-6188-8(5)*, Darby Creek) Lerner Publishing Group.
Gelin, Antoinette. Captain Underfish: Superhero for the Underworld. 2011. 40p. pap. 25.95 *(978-1-4634-2662-0(3))* AuthorHouse.
Gerbay, Susanne. I Am Jack. 2013. (ENG., Illus.). 144p. (J). pap. 5.99 *(978-1-61067-128-6(7))* Kane Miller.
Gervay, Susanne. Being Jack. Wilcox, Cathy, illus. (J). 2016. (ENG.). 192p. pap. 5.99 *(978-1-61067-379-2(4))* 2015. 167p. *(978-1-61067-455-3(3))* Kane Miller.
Gibbs, Lynne. Molly Mouse Is Shy: A Story of Shyness, 1 vol. Mitchell, Missy, illus. 2009. (Let's Grow Together Ser.). (ENG.). 32p. (J). (gr. k-1). pap. 11.55 *(978-1-60754-761-7(9)*, 6aac5f9c-dab3-409a-95c2-a45eaeb14dcd); lib. bdg. 27.27 *(978-1-60754-756-3(2)*, 2e202d76-3c52-42a4-b9bb-002ce24a3c6d) Rosen Publishing Group, Inc., The. (Windmill Bks.).
Giff, Patricia Reilly. Number One Kid. Bright, Alasdair, illus. 2010. (Zigzag Kids Ser.: 1). (ENG.). 80p. (J). (gr. 1-4). pap. 4.99 *(978-0-553-49468-6(6)*, Yearling) Random Hse. Children's Bks.
Going, K. L. The Liberation of Gabriel King. (ENG.). (J). 2007. 160p. (gr. 3-7). 7.99 *(978-0-14-240766-0(6)*, Puffin Books) 2005. 151p. (gr. 6-8). 21.19 *(978-0-399-23991-5(X))* Penguin Young Readers Group.
—The Liberation of Gabriel King. 2007. 151p. (gr. 3-7). 17.00 *(978-0-7569-7762-7(2))* Perfection Learning Corp.
Goobie, Beth. Kicked Out. 2004. (Orca Soundings Ser.). 92p. 19.95 *(978-0-7569-4309-7(4))* Perfection Learning Corp.
—El Qué Dirán, 1 vol. 2019. (Spanish Soundings Ser.). Tr. of Sticks & Stones. (SPA.). 112p. (YA). (gr. 8-12). pap. 10.95 *(978-1-4598-2241-2(2))* Orca Bk. Pubs. USA.
Goss, Michael Anthony. The Bat Who Wore Glasses. Longabough, Kristen, illus. 2005. (J). pap. *(978-1-933156-13-2(9))*; per. 16.99 *(978-1-933156-06-4(6))* GSVQ Publishing. (VisionQuest Kids).
Grannis, Greg. Lottie Bright & the Starmaker's Universe. Vargas, Robert, illus. 2006. (ENG.). 280p. (J). per. *(978-0-9778205-9-7(9))* Helm Publishing.
Grant, Crystal. Warrior Boy. 2007. (ENG.). 92p. per. 16.95 *(978-1-4241-3978-1(3))* PublishAmerica, Inc.
Grennan, Conor. The Hadley Academy for the Improbably Gifted, 1 vol. Valdrighi, Alessandro, illus. 2019. (ENG.). 368p. (J). 16.99 *(978-1-4002-1534-8(X)*, Tommy Nelson) Nelson, Thomas Inc.
Griffie, Sandra. The Snow Dancer. 2012. 28p. 24.95 *(978-1-4626-6777-2(5))* America Star Bks.
Griffin, Lisa M. Hey Goose! What's Your Excuse? 2017. (ENG., Illus.). 31p. (J). (gr. -1-4). pap. 10.95 *(978-1-944882-18-1(9))* Boys Town Pr.
Groeneweg, Nicole. One Word Pearl. Mitchell, Hazel, illus. 2013. 32p. (J). (gr. k-3). 17.95 *(978-1-934133-53-8(1))* Charlesbridge Publishing, Inc.
Gurevich, Margaret. Ballet Breakdown. Almon, Claire, illus. 2018. (Academy of Dance Ser.). (ENG.). 72p. (J). (gr. 3-6). lib. bdg. 25.32 *(978-1-4965-6206-7(2)*, 137815, Stone Arch Bks.) Capstone.
—Design Disaster. Hagel, Brooke, illus. 2015. (Chloe by Design Ser.). (ENG.). 96p. (J). (gr. 5-8). 25.32 *(978-1-4965-0505-7(0)*, 128577, Stone Arch Bks.) Capstone.
—Gina's Balance. 2016. (What's Your Dream? Ser.). (ENG., Illus.). 96p. (J). (gr. 4-6). lib. bdg. 25.99 *(978-1-4965-3443-9(3)*, 132565) Capstone.
—Unraveling, 1 vol. Hagel, Brooke, illus. 2014. (Chloe by Design Ser.). (ENG.). 96p. (J). (gr. 5-8). 25.32 *(978-1-4342-9179-0(0)*, 125653, Stone Arch Bks.) Capstone.
Hale, Shannon. Palace of Stone. 2015. (Princess Academy Ser.: 2). (YA). lib. bdg. 18.40 *(978-0-606-36439-3(0))* Turtleback.
—Princess Academy. (Princess Academy Ser.: 1). (ENG.). (gr. 5-8). 2005. 320p. (YA). 17.99 *(978-1-58234-993-0(2)*, 900031142) 2nd ed. 2015. 336p. (J). pap. 9.99 *(978-1-61963-613-2(1)*, 900142415) Bloomsbury Publishing USA. (Bloomsbury USA Childrens).
—Princess Academy. 2009. (Princess Academy Ser.: No. 1). 8.86 *(978-0-7848-2867-0(9)*, Everbind) Marco Bk. Co.

—Princess Academy. 2007. (Princess Academy Ser.: No. 1). 314p. (gr. 5-9). 18.00 *(978-0-7569-8180-8(3))* Perfection Learning Corp.

—Princess Academy. (Princess Academy Ser.: No. 1). *(978-0-439-88811-0(5)*, Scholastic) Scholastic, Inc.

—Princess Academy. l.t. ed. 2006. (Princess Academy Ser.: No. 1). 339p. (J). (gr. 5-9). 23.95 *(978-0-7862-8733-8(0))* Thorndike Pr.

—Princess Academy. 2015. (Princess Academy Ser.: 1). (YA). lib. bdg. 18.40 *(978-0-606-36438-6(2))* Turtleback.

—Princess Academy: Palace of Stone. (Princess Academy Ser.: 2). (ENG.). (gr. 5-8). 2015. 352p. (J). pap. 8.99 *(978-1-61963-257-8(8)*, 900131475) 2012. 336p. (YA). 17.99 *(978-1-59990-873-1(5)*, 900082614) Bloomsbury Publishing USA. (Bloomsbury USA Childrens).

—Princess Academy: the Forgotten Sisters. (Princess Academy Ser.: 3). (ENG.). 2016. 352p. (J). pap. 9.99 *(978-1-61963-933-1(5)*, 900152540) 2015. 336p. (YA). (gr. 5-8). 18.99 *(978-1-61963-485-5(6)*, 900138574) Bloomsbury Publishing USA. (Bloomsbury USA Childrens).

Hamilton, Arlene. Only a Cow, 1 vol. Griffiths, Dean, illus. 2008. (ENG.). 32p. (J). (gr. k-3). pap. 7.95 *(978-1-55455-088-3(2)*, 0ec3dad9-f456-42e5-8448-d7ff8f1fba9a) éditeur, Annika Parance CAN. Dist: Firefly Bks., Ltd.

Harkness, Karen. Coralee's Best Run Yet. 2007. (Illus.). 40p. (J). per. 7.99 net. *(978-0-9800934-0-7(6))* H&W Publishing Inc.

Hart, Lauri J. A Day in the Life of Nicholas B. 2009. 28p. pap. 14.99 *(978-1-4490-1935-8(8))* AuthorHouse.

Haynes, Marilee. Pictures of Me. 2016. 149p. (J). pap. *(978-0-8198-6019-4(0))* Pauline Bks. & Media.

Heard, B. R. If. 2007. (ENG.). 176p. pap. 15.95 *(978-0-615-16192-1(8))* Lulu Pr., Inc.

Hector, Julian. The Gentleman Bug. Hector, Julian, illus. 2010. (ENG., Illus.). 40p. (J). (gr. -1-k). 16.99 *(978-1-4169-9467-1(X)*, Atheneum Bks. for Young Readers) Simon & Schuster Children's Publishing.

Heller, Alyson. After-School Sports Club Adventures. Björkman, Steve, illus. 2016. (J). *(978-1-4814-7741-3(2))* Simon & Schuster Children's Publishing.

Hernandez, Laurie. She's Got This. Mata, Niña, illus. 2018. (ENG.). 32p. (J). (gr. -1-3). 18.99 *(978-0-06-284058-5(4)*, HarperCollins) HarperCollins Pubs.

Ho, Joanna. Eyes That Kiss in the Corners. Ho, Dung, illus. 2021. (ENG.). 40p. (J). (gr. -1-3). 17.99 *(978-0-06-291562-7(2)*, HarperCollins) HarperCollins Pubs.

Hobbs, Valerie. Minnie Mcclary Speaks Her Mind. 2013. (ENG.). 240p. (J). (gr. 4-8). pap. 17.99 *(978-1-250-03408-3(6)*, 900120578) Square Fish.

Hoblin, Paul. The Clutch. 2017. (Gridiron Ser.). (ENG.). 120p. (YA). (gr. 6-12). 26.65 *(978-1-5124-3980-9(0)*, 47ffa938-3ceb-4a46-920e-6e8b99db3406, Darby Creek) Lerner Publishing Group.

Hoffmann, Kerry Cohen. It's Not You, It's Me. 2011. (ENG.). 192p. (YA). (gr. 8-12). lib. bdg. 22.44 *(978-0-385-90638-8(2))* Random House Publishing Group.

Hopkins, Cathy. Mates, Dates, & Chocolate Cheats. 2011. (Mates, Dates Ser.). (ENG.). 224p. (YA). (gr. 7). pap. 10.99 *(978-1-4424-3081-5(8)*, Simon Pulse) Simon Pulse.

Hopkinson, Deborah. Butterflies Belong Here: A Story of One Idea, Thirty Kids, & a World of Butterflies. So, Meilo, illus. 2020. (ENG.). 68p. (J). (gr. k-3). 18.99 *(978-1-4521-7680-2(9))* Chronicle Bks. LLC.

Howling, Eric. Drive, 1 vol. 2008. (Lorimer Sports Stories Ser.). (ENG.). 120p. (J). (gr. 4-8). 9.95 *(978-1-55277-009-2(5)*, 05eecbd4-6f9e-45a0-a7b9-4452969f9bb0); 16.95 *(978-1-55277-010-8(9)*, 010) James Lorimer & Co. Ltd., Pubs. CAN. Dist: Lerner Publishing Group, Formac Lorimer Bks. Ltd.

Hueller, Andy. Dizzy Fantastic & Her Flying Bicycle. 2010. (Illus.). 155p. (J). pap. 8.99 *(978-1-59955-395-5(3))* Cedar Fort, Inc./CFI Distribution.

Hurwitz, Michele Weber. Calli Be Gold. 2012. 208p. (J). (gr. 3-7). 7.99 *(978-0-375-86528-2(4)*, Yearling) Random Hse. Children's Bks.

Jakubowski, Michele. The Big Bike. Waters, Erica-Jane, illus. 2015. (Perfectly Poppy Ser.). (ENG.). 32p. (J). (gr. k-2). 22.65 *(978-1-4795-5801-8(X)*, 126831, Picture Window Bks.) Capstone.

John, Jory. The Cool Bean. Oswald, Pete, illus. 2019. (Food Group Ser.). (ENG.). 40p. (J). (gr. -1-3). 18.99 *(978-0-06-295452-7(0)*, HarperCollins) HarperCollins Pubs.

—The Smart Cookie. Oswald, Pete, illus. 2021. (Food Group Ser.). (ENG.). 40p. (J). (gr. -1-3). 19.99 *(978-0-06-304540-8(0)*, HarperCollins) HarperCollins Pubs.

Johnson, Kathleen A. A Voice Came to Me. 2006. lib. bdg. 17.95 *(978-0-9785623-0-4(5))* Voice of Light Pubns.

Johnson, Lauren. Beastly Basketball, 1 vol. Garcia, Eduardo, illus. 2014. (Sports Illustrated Kids Graphic Novels Ser.). (ENG.). 72p. (J). (gr. 3-8). lib. bdg. 26.65 *(978-1-4342-6490-9(4)*, 124178, Stone Arch Bks.) Capstone.

Jones, Christianne C. Fuchsia Fierce. Canby, Kelly, illus. 2016. (ENG.). 32p. (J). (gr. -1-2). 15.95 *(978-1-62370-786-6(2)*, 133092, Capstone Young Readers); lib. bdg. 22.65 *(978-1-5158-0553-3(0)*, 133091, Picture Window Bks.) Capstone.

Jones, Debra M. What in the World Should I Be. Collier, Kevin, illus. 2010. 16p. pap. 9.95 *(978-1-61633-037-8(6))* Guardian Angel Publishing, Inc.

Jones, Diana Wynne & Jones, Ursula. The Islands of Chaldea. 2015. (ENG.). 368p. (J). (gr. 3-7). pap. 10.99 *(978-0-06-229508-8(X)*, Greenwillow Bks.) HarperCollins Pubs.

Jones, Jen. Brooke's Quest for Captain: #2, No. 2. 2011. (Team Cheer Ser.). (ENG., Illus.). 112p. (J). (gr. 4-6). lib. bdg. 25.32 *(978-1-4342-2995-3(5)*, 114388, Stone Arch Bks.) Capstone.

Jones, Traci L. Standing Against the Wind. 2010. (ENG.). 208p. (YA). (gr. 7-12). pap. 11.99 *(978-0-312-62293-0(7)*, 900066262) Square Fish.

Jonsberg, Barry. A Song Only I Can Hear. 2020. (ENG.). 304p. (J). (gr. 3-7). 17.99 *(978-1-5344-4252-8(9)*, Simon & Schuster Bks. For Young Readers) Simon & Schuster Bks. For Young Readers.

Jordan, Apple. A Princess Can! (Disney Princess) Legramandi, Francesco & Matta, Gabriella, illus. 2015. (Step into Reading Ser.). (ENG.). 24p. (J). (gr. -1-1). 5.99 *(978-0-7364-3341-9(4)*, RH/Disney) Random Hse. Children's Bks.

Jordan, Deloris. Michael's Golden Rules. Nelson, Kadir, illus. 2007. (ENG.). 32p. (J). (gr. 1-5). 18.99 *(978-0-689-87016-3(7)*, Simon & Schuster/Paula Wiseman Bks.) Simon & Schuster/Paula Wiseman Bks.

Jordan, Dream. Bad Boy: A Novel. 2012. (ENG.). 208p. (YA). (gr. 6-11). pap. 17.99 *(978-0-312-54997-8(0)*, 900055718, St. Martin's Griffin) St. Martin's Pr.

Judge, Lita. When You Need Wings. Judge, Lita, illus. 2020. (ENG., Illus.). 40p. (J). (gr. -1-3). 17.99 *(978-1-5344-3755-5(X)*, Atheneum Bks. for Young Readers) Simon & Schuster Children's Publishing.

Jungle Crossing. 2011. (ENG.). 228p. (J). (gr. 5-7). pap. 13.99 *(978-0-547-55009-1(X)*, 1450218, Clarion Bks.) HarperCollins Pubs.

Kakakios, Melissa. I Love Taekwondo: My First Taekwondo Books. 2013. 28p. pap. 16.95 *(978-1-4525-7668-8(8)*, Balboa Pr.) Author Solutions, LLC.

Kane, Kim. The New Friend. 2018. (Ginger Green, Playdate Queen Ser.). (ENG., Illus.). 64p. (J). (gr. 1-3). pap. 5.95 *(978-1-5158-1952-3(3)*, 136635, Picture Window Bks.) Capstone.

—The New Friend. Davis, Jon, illus. 2017. (Ginger Green, Playdate Queen Ser.). (ENG.). 64p. (J). (gr. 1-3). lib. bdg. 23.32 *(978-1-5158-1946-2(9)*, 136629, Picture Window Bks.) Capstone.

—The Only Friend. Davis, Jon, illus. 2018. (Ginger Green, Playdate Queen Ser.). (ENG.). 64p. (J). (gr. 1-3). pap. 5.95 *(978-1-5158-2012-3(2)*, 136659, Picture Window Bks.) Capstone.

Kang, A. N. My Big Bad Monster. Kang, A. N., illus. 2019. (ENG., Illus.). 40p. (J). (gr. -1-3). 16.99 *(978-1-4847-2882-6(3))* Disney Pr.

Kay, Karin. Floppy Cat. 2009. (J). 16.95 *(978-0-9823818-0-9(8))* Floppy Cat Co.

Kelley, Jane. Nature Girl. 2011. (ENG., Illus.). 256p. (J). (gr. 3-7). pap. 7.99 *(978-0-375-85635-8(8)*, Yearling) Random Hse. Children's Bks.

Kim, YeShil. We Are Proud of You. The Pope Twins, illus. rev. ed. 2014. (MySELF Bookshelf Ser.). (ENG.). 32p. (J). (gr. k-2). pap. 11.94 *(978-1-60357-651-2(7))*; lib. bdg. 25.27 *(978-1-59953-642-2(0))* Norwood Hse. Pr.

King, A. S. Everybody Sees the Ants. 2012. (ENG.). 320p. (YA). (gr. 10-17). pap. 11.99 *(978-0-316-12927-5(5))* Little, Brown Bks. for Young Readers.

Kinra, Richa, illus. The Princess Panda Tea Party: A Cerebral Palsy Fairy Tale. 2014. 45p. (J). pap. 14.95 *(978-1-61599-219-5(7))* Loving Healing Pr., Inc.

Kirby, Matthew J. Icefall. 2013. (ENG.). 336p. (J). (gr. 3-7). pap. 10.99 *(978-0-545-27425-8(7)*, Scholastic Paperbacks) Scholastic, Inc.

Kirouac, Bn, Nicole. I Am Unique. 2013. 32p. pap. 13.99 *(978-1-4525-7594-0(0)*, Balboa Pr.) Author Solutions, LLC.

Knight, Richard, et al. Finn at Clee Point. Hurst, Oliver, illus. 2012. 128p. (J). pap. 12.99 *(978-1-84686-401-8(1))* Barefoot Bks., Inc.

Konigsburg, E. L. The View from Saturday. 280p. (YA). (gr. 5-18). pap. 4.95 *(978-0-8072-1511-1(2)*, Listening Library) Random Hse. Audio Publishing Group.

Kravitz, Danny. Tommy Mcknight & the Great Election. 2016. (Presidential Politics Ser.). (ENG.). (J). 48p. pap. 48.70 *(978-1-4965-2752-3(6)*, 174780); (Illus.). 96p. (gr. 3-6). lib. bdg. 26.65 *(978-1-4965-2585-7(X)*, 130712) Capstone. (Stone Arch Bks.).

Kreloff, Elliot. Please Don't Make Me Fly! A Growing-Up Story of Self-Confidence. Kreloff, Elliot, illus. 2017. (Growing Up Ser.). (ENG., Illus.). 32p. (J). (gr. -1 — 1). lib. bdg. 19.99 *(978-1-63440-179-1(4)*, 91dc9305-ef53-4b8a-8e2c-83ce13291ce8); E-Book 30.65 *(978-1-63440-183-8(2))* Red Chair Pr. (Rocking Chair Kids).

Krishnaswami, Uma. El árbol más feliz: un cuento sobre Yoga, 1 vol. Jeyaveeran, Ruth, illus. 2008. (SPA.). 32p. (J). (gr. k-5). pap. 12.95 *(978-1-62014-149-6(3)*, leelowbooks) Lee & Low Bks., Inc.

Kroll, Steven. When I Dream of Heaven: Angelina's Story. 2004. 156p. (J). lib. bdg. 16.92 *(978-1-4242-0770-1(3))* Fitzgerald Bks.

Kylie's Song: Evaluation Guide. 2006. (J). *(978-1-55942-414-1(1))* Witcher Productions.

Lamb. Bianca the Dancing Crocodile. Skon, Sandy, illus. 2008. 30p. pap. 24.95 *(978-1-60563-447-0(6))* America Star Bks.

Landry, Cristy. Snowboarding with Courage. 2016. 116p. (YA). (gr. 8-12). pap. 10.95 *(978-0-9963756-0-3(0))* All About Kids Publishing.

Langston, Laura. Exit Point, 1 vol. 2006. (Orca Soundings Ser.). (ENG.). 136p. (YA). (gr. 8-12). per. 9.95 *(978-1-55143-505-3(5))* Orca Bk. Pubs. USA.

Larsen, Ramonita. Yes, I Can Do It/Si, lo Puedo Hacer. Larsen, Ramonita, illus. l.t. ed. 2006. (Illus.). 18p. (J). per. 10.99 *(978-1-59879-292-8(X))* Lifevest Publishing, Inc.

Law, Felicia. Alice the Armadillo: A Tale of Self Discovery, 1 vol. Messina, Lilli, illus. 2009. (Animal Fair Values Ser.). (ENG.). 32p. (J). (gr. 2-2). pap. 11.55 *(978-1-60754-809-6(7)*, 8a68dd81-a5ab-4cf1-ba70-8da519c28b56); lib. bdg. 27.27 *(978-1-60754-805-8(4)*, be84d1fe-62bf-4c6f-adfd-871f539a98bd) Rosen Publishing Group, Inc., The. (Windmill Bks.).

Levine, Gail Carson. The Two Princesses of Bamarre. (J). 2012. (ENG.). 272p. (gr. 3-7). pap. 9.99 *(978-0-06-440966-7(X)*, HarperCollins) 2004. (Illus.). 304p. (gr. 7-18). reprint ed. pap. 6.99 *(978-0-06-057580-9(8))* HarperCollins Pubs.

Levy, Debbie. Underwater. 2007. (Darby Creek Exceptional Titles Ser.). 155p. (J). (gr. 4-7). 16.95 *(978-1-58196-053-2(0)*, Darby Creek) Lerner Publishing Group.

Lewin, Betsy. You Can Do It! 2014. (I Like to Read Ser.). (ENG., Illus.). 24p. (J). (gr. -1-3). 7.99 *(978-0-8234-3055-0(3))* Holiday Hse., Inc.

L'Heureux, Christine. Caillou: I Can Do It Myself! Kary, illus. 2019. (Caillou's Essentials Ser.). (ENG.). 24p. (J). (gr. -1-k). bds. 7.99 *(978-2-89718-438-9(4))* Caillouet, Gerry.

Lippmann, Wilfried. The Gift of Eye. 2008. 140p. (gr. 7-12). pap. 11.95 *(978-0-595-52251-4(3))* iUniverse, Inc.

Lombardo, Constance. Mr. Puffball: Stunt Cat to the Stars. Lombardo, Constance, illus. 2015. (Mr. Puffball Ser.: 1). (ENG., Illus.). 240p. (J). (gr. 3-7). 12.99 *(978-0-06-232065-0(3)*, HarperCollins) HarperCollins Pubs.

Lonczak, Heather. Mookey the Monkey Gets over Being Teased. Ramsey, Marcy, illus. 2006. 32p. (J). (gr. -1-3). 14.95 *(978-1-59147-479-1(5)*, Magination Pr.) American Psychological Assn.

Lonczak, Heather Suzanne. Mookey the Monkey Gets over Being Teased. Ramsey, Marcy Dunn, illus. 2006. 32p. (J). (gr. -1-3). 9.95 *(978-1-59147-480-7(9)*, Magination Pr.) American Psychological Assn.

Look, Lenore. Alvin Ho: Allergic to Birthday Parties, Science Projects, & Other Man-Made Catastrophes. Pham, LeUyen, illus. 2011. (Alvin Ho Ser.: 3). 192p. (J). (gr. 1-4). 7.99 *(978-0-375-87369-0(4)*, Yearling) Random Hse. Children's Bks.

—Alvin Ho: Allergic to Camping, Hiking, & Other Natural Disasters. Pham, LeUyen, illus. 2010. (Alvin Ho Ser.: 2). 192p. (J). (gr. 1-4). 7.99 *(978-0-375-85750-8(8)*, Yearling) Random Hse. Children's Bks.

—Alvin Ho: Allergic to Dead Bodies, Funerals, & Other Fatal Circumstances. Pham, LeUyen, illus. 2012. (Alvin Ho Ser.: 4). 208p. (J). (gr. 1-4). 6.99 *(978-0-307-97695-6(5)*, Yearling) Random Hse. Children's Bks.

Lord, Michelle. The Quick Quarterback, 1 vol. Harpster, Steve, illus. 2012. (My First Graphic Novel Ser.). (ENG.). 32p. (J). (gr. k-2). pap. 6.25 *(978-1-4342-3861-0(X)*, 118043, Stone Arch Bks.) Capstone.

Lubar, David. My Rotten Life. 2009. (Nathan Abercrombie, Accidental Zombie Ser.: 1). (ENG., Illus.). 160p. (J). (gr. 3-7). pap. 13.99 *(978-0-7653-1634-9(X)*, 900038898, Starscape) Doherty, Tom Assocs., LLC.

—Sleeping Freshmen Never Lie. 2007. (ENG.). 288p. (YA). (gr. 7-18). 11.99 *(978-0-14-240780-6(1)*, Speak) Penguin Young Readers Group.

Ludwig, Trudy. Just Kidding. Gustavson, Adam, illus. 2006. 32p. (J). (gr. 1-4). 18.99 *(978-1-58246-163-2(5)*, Tricycle Pr.) Random Hse. Children's Bks.

Lukachko, Mary Louise. Peter the Blue Penguin. 2012. 28p. pap. 24.95 *(978-1-4626-8186-0(7))* America Star Bks.

Lupica, Mike. Batting Order. (ENG.). (J). (gr. 3-7). 2020. 320p. pap. 8.99 *(978-1-5344-2156-1(4))* 2019. (Illus.). 304p. 19.99 *(978-1-5344-2155-4(6))* Simon & Schuster Bks. For Young Readers. (Simon & Schuster Bks. For Young Readers).

—Qb 1. 2014. (ENG.). 288p. (J). (gr. 5). pap. 8.99 *(978-0-14-751152-2(6)*, Puffin Books) Penguin Young Readers Group.

Lyssenko, Taras. Wendy's Fear of Heights. 2003. 14p. (J). *(978-0-9740542-0-9(8))* Prairie Shore Creative, Inc.

Mabille, Christine. Potato-Kid & the Adventure: Treasures Within, 1 vol. 2009. 76p. pap. 19.95 *(978-1-61582-981-1(4))* America Star Bks.

Mack, Winnie. After All, You're Callie Boone. 2013. (ENG.). 192p. (J). (gr. 4-7). pap. 14.99 *(978-1-250-02735-1(7)*, 900098307) Square Fish.

Mackler, Carolyn. Tangled. 2011. (ENG.). 336p. (YA). (gr. 9-12). pap. 10.99 *(978-0-06-173106-8(4)*, HarperTeen) HarperCollins Pubs.

Maddox, Jake. Aerials & Envy. 2018. (Jake Maddox JV Girls Ser.). (ENG., Illus.). 96p. (J). (gr. 4-8). lib. bdg. 26.65 *(978-1-4965-5914-2(2)*, 137121, Stone Arch Bks.) Capstone.

—Bad-Luck Basketball, 1 vol. Ray, Michael, illus. 2014. (Jake Maddox JV Ser.). (ENG.). 96p. (J). (gr. 4-6). 26.65 *(978-1-4342-9156-1(1)*, 125606, Stone Arch Bks.) Capstone.

—Basketball Breakdown. 2016. (Jake Maddox JV Girls Ser.). (ENG., Illus.). 96p. (J). (gr. 4-8). pap. 5.95 *(978-1-4965-3676-1(2)*, 132927); lib. bdg. 26.65 *(978-1-4965-3166-7(3)*, 133202) Capstone. (Stone Arch Bks.).

—Beyond Basketball. 2018. (Jake Maddox JV Girls Ser.). (ENG., Illus.). 96p. (J). (gr. 4-8). pap. 5.95 *(978-1-4965-6345-3(X)*, 138069); lib. bdg. 25.99 *(978-1-4965-6343-9(3)*, 138067) Capstone. (Stone Arch Bks.).

—BMX Bravery. 2016. (Jake Maddox JV Ser.). (ENG., Illus.). 96p. (J). (gr. 4-6). lib. bdg. 26.65 *(978-1-4965-2630-4(9)*, 131192, Stone Arch Bks.) Capstone.

—BMX Challenge, 1 vol. Tiffany, Sean, illus. 2011. (Jake Maddox Sports Stories Ser.). (ENG.). 72p. (J). (gr. 3-6). pap. 5.95 *(978-1-4342-3423-0(1)*, 116444, Stone Arch Bks.) Capstone.

—Catching Confidence. 2018. (Jake Maddox JV Girls Ser.). (ENG., Illus.). 96p. (J). (gr. 4-8). lib. bdg. 26.65 *(978-1-4965-5915-9(0)*, 137122, Stone Arch Bks.) Capstone.

—Cowboy Up, 1 vol. Tiffany, Sean, illus. 2011. (Jake Maddox Sports Stories Ser.). (ENG.). 72p. (J). (gr. 3-6). pap. 5.95 *(978-1-4342-3425-4(8)*, 116446); lib. bdg. 25.99 *(978-1-4342-2989-2(0)*, 114319) Capstone. (Stone Arch Bks.).

—Cowgirl Grit. Wood, Katie, illus. 2018. (Jake Maddox Girl Sports Stories Ser.). (ENG.). 72p. (J). (gr. 3-6). lib. bdg. 25.32 *(978-1-4965-5847-3(2)*, 136932, Stone Arch Bks.) Capstone.

—Dancing Solo, 1 vol. Wood, Katie, illus. 2014. (Jake Maddox Girl Sports Stories Ser.). (ENG.). 72p. (J). (gr. 3-6). 25.32 *(978-1-4342-4142-9(4)*, 119877, Stone Arch Bks.) Capstone.

—Diamond Double Play. Tiffany, Sean, illus. 2019. (Jake Maddox Sports Stories Ser.). (ENG.). 72p. (J). (gr. 3-6). 25.99 *(978-1-4965-8329-1(9)*, 140498); pap. 5.95 *(978-1-4965-8452-6(X)*, 140977) Capstone. (Stone Arch Bks.).

—Double-Axel Doubt, 1 vol. Pulsar Studio (Beehive), Pulsar Studio, illus. 2011. (Jake Maddox Girl Sports Stories Ser.). (ENG.). 72p. (J). (gr. 3-6). lib. bdg. 25.32 *(978-1-4342-2499-6(6)*, 112978, Stone Arch Bks.) Capstone.

—Double Scribble. Aburto, Jesus, illus. 2017. (Jake Maddox Graphic Novels Ser.). (ENG.). 72p. (J). (gr. 3-8). lib. bdg. 26.65 *(978-1-4965-3701-0(7)*, 132940, Stone Arch Bks.) Capstone.

—Free Throw Fail. 2017. (Jake Maddox JV Ser.). (ENG., Illus.). 96p. (J). (gr. 4-6). lib. bdg. 26.65 *(978-1-4965-4941-9(4)*, 135846, Stone Arch Bks.) Capstone.

—Half-Pipe Panic. Muñiz, Berenice, illus. 2018. (Jake Maddox Graphic Novels Ser.). (ENG.). 72p. (J). (gr. 3-8). lib. bdg. 27.99 *(978-1-4965-6044-5(2)*, 137425, Stone Arch Bks.) Capstone.

—Heavyweight Takedown. 2015. (Jake Maddox JV Ser.). (ENG., Illus.). 96p. (J). (gr. 4-6). lib. bdg. 26.65 *(978-1-4342-9638-2(5)*, 126917, Stone Arch Bks.) Capstone.

—Home Safe Home. 2018. (Jake Maddox JV Ser.). (ENG., Illus.). 96p. (J). (gr. 4-6). lib. bdg. 26.65 *(978-1-4965-5931-9(2)*, 137133, Stone Arch Bks.) Capstone.

—Hoop Hustle. Aburto, Jesus, illus. 2015. (Jake Maddox Sports Stories Ser.). (ENG.). 72p. (J). (gr. 3-6). lib. bdg. 25.99 *(978-1-4965-0494-4(1)*, 128566, Stone Arch Bks.) Capstone.

—Horseback Hurdles, 1 vol. Wood, Katie, illus. 2012. (Jake Maddox Girl Sports Stories Ser.). (ENG.). 72p. (J). (gr. 3-6). pap. 5.95 *(978-1-4342-3905-1(5)*, 118090); lib. bdg. 25.32 *(978-1-4342-3294-6(8)*, 116258) Capstone. (Stone Arch Bks.).

—Longboard Letdown. Wood, Katie, illus. 2017. (Jake Maddox Girl Sports Stories Ser.). (ENG.). 72p. (J). (gr. 3-6). lib. bdg. 25.32 *(978-1-4965-4972-3(4)*, 135864, Stone Arch Bks.) Capstone.

—On the Line, 1 vol. Tiffany, Sean, illus. 2006. (Jake Maddox Sports Stories Ser.). (ENG.). 72p. (J). (gr. 3-6). 25.99 *(978-1-59889-062-4(X)*, 86533); pap. 5.95 *(978-1-59889-240-6(1)*, 91592) Capstone. (Stone Arch Bks.).

—Pick & Roll. Tiffany, Sean, illus. 2018. (Jake Maddox Sports Stories Ser.). (ENG.). 72p. (J). (gr. 3-6). pap. 5.95 *(978-1-4965-6320-0(4)*, 138059); lib. bdg. 25.99 *(978-1-4965-6318-7(2)*, 138050) Capstone. (Stone Arch Bks.).

—Pool Panic. Wood, Katie, illus. 2016. (Jake Maddox Girl Sports Stories Ser.). (ENG.). 72p. (J). (gr. 3-6). lib. bdg. 25.32 *(978-1-4965-2618-2(X)*, 131174, Stone Arch Bks.) Capstone.

—Rodeo Challenge. Aburto, Jesus, illus. 2018. (Jake Maddox Sports Stories Ser.). (ENG.). 72p. (J). (gr. 3-6). lib. bdg. 25.99 *(978-1-4965-5865-7(0)*, 136944, Stone Arch Bks.) Capstone.

—Rookie Runner. 2018. (Jake Maddox JV Ser.). (ENG., Illus.). 96p. (J). (gr. 4-6). pap. 5.95 *(978-1-4965-6334-7(4)*, 138064); lib. bdg. 25.99 *(978-1-4965-6332-3(8)*, 138063) Capstone. (Stone Arch Bks.).

—Secondhand Slice. Aburto, Jesus, illus. 2018. (Jake Maddox Sports Stories Ser.). (ENG.). 72p. (J). (gr. 3-6). lib. bdg. 25.99 *(978-1-4965-5864-0(2)*, 136940, Stone Arch Bks.) Capstone.

—Slam Dunk Shoes, 1 vol. Tiffany, Sean, illus. 2007. (Jake Maddox Sports Stories Ser.). (ENG.). 72p. (J). (gr. 3-6). 25.99 *(978-1-59889-842-2(6)*, 94239); per. 5.95 *(978-1-59889-894-1(9)*, 94318) Capstone. (Stone Arch Bks.).

—Slap-Shot Slump. 2015. (Jake Maddox JV Ser.). (ENG., Illus.). 96p. (J). (gr. 4-6). lib. bdg. 26.65 *(978-1-4342-9635-1(0)*, 126914, Stone Arch Bks.) Capstone.

—Soccer Step-Up. 2016. (Jake Maddox JV Girls Ser.). (ENG., Illus.). 96p. (J). (gr. 4-8). lib. bdg. 26.65 *(978-1-4965-3675-4(4)*, 132926, Stone Arch Bks.) Capstone.

—Softball Switch-Up. Wood, Katie, illus. 2019. (Jake Maddox Girl Sports Stories Ser.). (ENG.). 72p. (J). (gr. 3-6). pap. 5.95 *(978-1-4965-8450-2(3)*, 140975, Stone Arch Bks.) Capstone.

—Squad Struggles. Wood, Katie, illus. 2017. (Jake Maddox Girl Sports Stories Ser.). (ENG.). 72p. (J). (gr. 3-6). lib. bdg. 25.32 *(978-1-4965-4971-6(6)*, 135859, Stone Arch Bks.) Capstone.

—Storm Surfer, 1 vol. Mourning, Tuesday, illus. 2008. (Jake Maddox Girl Sports Stories Ser.). (ENG.). 72p. (J). (gr. 3-6). lib. bdg. 25.32 *(978-1-4342-0471-4(5)*, 94419); per. 5.95 *(978-1-4342-0521-6(5)*, 94461) Capstone. (Stone Arch Bks.).

—Striker's Sister. Wood, Katie, illus. 2018. (Jake Maddox Girl Sports Stories Ser.). (ENG.). 72p. (J). (gr. 3-6). lib. bdg. 25.32 *(978-1-4965-6355-2(7)*, 138071, Stone Arch Bks.) Capstone.

—Touchdown Turmoil. 2018. (Jake Maddox JV Ser.). (ENG., Illus.). 96p. (J). (gr. 4-6). pap. 5.95 *(978-1-4965-6333-0(6)*, 138065); lib. bdg. 25.99 *(978-1-4965-6331-6(X)*, 138062) Capstone. (Stone Arch Bks.).

Madkins, Dorenda W. Smiley Face: A Smile a Day Takes the Frown Away. 2012. 28p. pap. 24.95 *(978-1-4626-6553-2(5))* America Star Bks.

Magnus, Kellie. Little Lion Goes to School. Robinson, Michael, illus. l.t. ed. 2003. 16p. (J). 9.99 *(978-0-9744211-0-0(3))* Media Magic New York.

Mahony, Mary. Harry Scores A Hat Trick, Pawns, Pucks, & Scoliosis: The Sequel to Stand Tall, Harry. Pasternack, Susan, ed. Larkin, Catherine, illus. 2003. 130p. (YA). (gr. 5-8). per. 14.95 *(978-0-9658879-3-9(6))* Redding Pr.

Maier, Inger. When Lizzy Was Afraid of Trying New Things. Candon, Jennifer, illus. 2004. (ENG.). 32p. (J). 14.95 *(978-1-59147-170-7(2)*, Magination Pr.) American Psychological Assn.

Maier, Inger M. When Lizzie Was Afraid: Of Trying New Things. Candon, Jennifer, illus. 2004. 32p. (J). pap. 9.95 *(978-1-59147-171-4(0)*, Magination Pr.) American Psychological Assn.

Margolis, Leslie. We Are Party People. 2018. (ENG.). 304p. (J). pap. 7.99 *(978-1-250-17725-4(1)*, 900158350) Square Fish.

Markey, Kevin. Rainmaker. 2012. (Illus.). 230p. (J). lib. bdg. 16.89 *(978-0-06-115229-0(3))* HarperCollins Pubs.

—The Super Sluggers: Slumpbuster. 2010. (ENG., Illus.). 208p. (J). (gr. 3-7). pap. 7.99 *(978-0-06-115220-7(X)*, HarperCollins) HarperCollins Pubs.

Marshall, Joseph. In the Footsteps of Crazy Horse. Yellowhawk, James Mark, illus. 2015. (ENG.). 176p. (J). (gr. 5-9). 18.99 *(978-1-4197-0785-8(X)*, 1059701) Abrams, Inc.

Martin, Sheila. Muddy Water. 2005. pap. 16.95 *(978-1-4137-8551-7(4))* PublishAmerica, Inc.

Masino, Brian. Cabbage Patch Kids: We Are All Best Friends. Karl, Linda, illus. 2006. (J). pap. *(978-0-439-76820-7(9))* Scholastic, Inc.

McAnulty, Stacy. Beautiful. Lew-Vriethoff, Joanne, illus. 2016. (ENG.). 32p. (J). (gr. -1-1). 17.99 *(978-0-7624-5781-6(3),* Running Pr. Kids) Running Pr.
McClure, Kim. Edgar the Seagull who was Afraid to Fly. 2009. (ENG.). 34p. pap. 16.70 *(978-0-557-05920-1(8))* Lulu Pr., Inc.
McCrimmon, Linda. Can You Please tie My Shoes? 2007. (J). 10.95 *(978-0-9796978-2-1(4))* G Publishing LLC.
McDonald, Avril. The Wolf Is Not Invited, 1 vol. Minina, Tatiana, illus. 2016. (Feel Brave Ser.). (ENG.). 32p. (J). pap. 12.95 *(978-1-78583-017-4(1))* Crown Hse. Publishing LLC.
McGowan, Keith. The Witch's Guide to Cooking with Children: A Modern-Day Retelling of Hansel & Gretel, 1. Tanaka, Yoko, illus. 2011. (ENG.). 192p. (J). (gr. 4-6). pap. 12.99 *(978-0-312-67486-1(4),* 900072904) Square Fish.
McKay, Hilary. Permanent Rose. 2006. (ENG.). 256p. (J). (gr. 3-7). reprint ed. per. 8.99 *(978-1-4169-2804-1(9),* McElderry, Margaret K. Bks.) McElderry, Margaret K. Bks.
McKissack, Robert. Try Your Best. Cepeda, Joe, illus. 2004. (ENG.). 24p. (J). (gr. -1-3). pap. 4.99 *(978-0-15-205090-0(6),* 1195368, Clarion Bks.) HarperCollins Pubs.
McKissack, Robert L. Try Your Best. Cepeda, Joe, illus. 2005. (Green Light Readers Level 2 Ser.). (gr. k-2). 13.95 *(978-0-7569-5630-1(7))* Perfection Learning Corp.
McKnight, Marty. Jim Nasium Is a Basket Case. Jones, Chris B., illus. 2015. (Jim Nasium Ser.). (ENG.). 88p. (J). (gr. 2-3). pap. 5.95 *(978-1-4965-0526-2(3),* 128598, Stone Arch Bks.) Capstone.
—Jim Nasium Is a Football Fumbler. Jones, Chris B., illus. 2015. (Jim Nasium Ser.). (ENG.). 88p. (J). (gr. 2-3). lib. bdg. 25.32 *(978-1-4965-0522-4(0),* 128595, Stone Arch Bks.) Capstone.
—Jim Nasium Is a Hockey Hazard. Jones, Chris B., illus. 2015. (Jim Nasium Ser.). (ENG.). 88p. (J). (gr. 2-3). pap. 5.95 *(978-1-4965-0524-8(7),* 128596, Stone Arch Bks.) Capstone.
—Jim Nasium Is a Soccer Goofball. Jones, Chris B., illus. 2015. (Jim Nasium Ser.). (ENG.). 88p. (J). (gr. 2-3). pap. 5.95 *(978-1-4965-0525-5(5),* 128597, Stone Arch Bks.) Capstone.
McMann, Lisa. Island of Silence. (Unwanteds Ser.: 2). (ENG., (J). (gr. 3-7). 2013. illus.). 432p. pap. 8.99 *(978-1-4424-0772-5(7))* 2012. 416p. 19.99 *(978-1-4424-0771-8(9))* Simon & Schuster Children's Publishing. (Aladdin).
—Island of Silence. 2013. (Unwanteds Ser.: 2). lib. bdg. 18.40 *(978-0-606-32044-3(X))* Turtleback.
McMullan, Akilah. The Best Me I Can Be. 2010. 28p. pap. 13.99 *(978-1-4490-1840-5(8))* AuthorHouse.
McNamara, Margaret. A Poem in Your Pocket (Mr. Tiffin's Classroom Series) Karas, G. Brian, illus. 2015. (Mr. Tiffin's Classroom Ser.). 40p. (J). (gr. -1-3). 17.99 *(978-0-307-97947-6(4),* Schwartz & Wade Bks.) Random Hse. Children's Bks.
McStay, Moriah. Everything That Makes You. 2015. (ENG.). 352p. (YA). (gr. 8). 17.99 *(978-0-06-229548-4(9),* Tegen, Katherine Bks) HarperCollins Pubs.
McVoy, Terra Elan. Being Friends with Boys. (ENG., (YA). (gr. 9). 2013. illus.). 384p. pap. 10.99 *(978-1-4424-2160-8(6))* 2012. 368p. 16.99 *(978-1-4424-2159-2(2))* Simon Pulse. (Simon Pulse).
Meister, Cari. The Fancy Octopus, 1 vol. Harpster, Steve, illus. 2011. (Ocean Tales Ser.). (ENG.). 32p. (J). (gr. 2-3). lib. bdg. 22.65 *(978-1-4342-3201-4(8),* 114965, Stone Arch Bks.) Capstone.
Mendoza, Jessica & Mendoza, Alana. There's No Base Like Home, 1 vol. McNally Barshaw, Ruth, illus. 2018. (ENG.). 240p. (J). (gr. 3-7). 18.95 *(978-1-62014-588-3(X),* leelowtu, Tu Bks.) Lee & Low Bks., Inc.
Meng, Cece. Tough Chicks Lap Board Book: An Easter & Springtime Book for Kids. Suber, Melissa, illus. 2018. (ENG.). 28p. (J). (— 1). bds. 12.99 *(978-1-328-95985-0(6),* 1706952, Clarion Bks.) HarperCollins Pubs.
Merschel, Michael. Revenge of the Star Survivors. 2018. (ENG.). 320p. (J). (gr. 5). pap. 8.99 *(978-0-8234-4041-2(9))* Holiday Hse., Inc.
Messner, Kate. All the Answers. 2016. (ENG.). 272p. (J). pap. 8.99 *(978-1-68119-020-4(6),* 900156128, Bloomsbury USA Childrens) Bloomsbury Publishing USA.
Milanes, Janelle. Analee, in Real Life. (ENG.). (YA). (gr. 7). 2019. 432p. pap. 12.99 *(978-1-5344-1030-5(9))* 2018. (Illus.). 416p. 18.99 *(978-1-5344-1029-9(5))* Simon Pulse. (Simon Pulse).
Miles, Brenda S. & Sweet, Susan D. Cinderstella: A Tale of Planets Not Princes. Docampo, Valeria, illus. 2016. 32p. (J). *(978-1-4338-2270-4(9),* Magination Pr.) American Psychological Assn.
Mills, Joyce C. & Crowley, Richard J. Sammy the Elephant & Mr. Camel: A Story to Help Children Overcome Bedwetting. Ramsey, Marcy, illus. 2nd ed. 2005. (ENG.). 32p. (J). 14.95 *(978-1-59147-247-6(4),* Magination Pr.) American Psychological Assn.
—Sammy the Elephant & Mr. Camel: A Story to Help Children Overcome Bedwetting. Pillo, Cary, illus. 2nd ed. 2005. 32p. (J). pap. 9.95 *(978-1-59147-248-3(2),* Magination Pr.) American Psychological Assn.
Minou: Evaluation Guide. 2006. (J). *(978-1-55942-416-5(8))* Witcher Productions.
Montalbano, Andrea. One on One. 2018. (Soccer Sisters Ser.: 3). (Illus.). 192p. (J). (gr. 3-7). pap. 7.99 *(978-1-4926-4487-3(0))* Sourcebooks, Inc.
Monteiro, Francelina. The Star That Couldn't Shine. 2009. 24p. pap. 12.99 *(978-1-4490-3775-8(5))* AuthorHouse.
Moore-Malinos, Jennifer. Winning Isn't Everything! Fabrega, Marta, illus. 2007. (Live & Learn Ser.). (ENG.). 36p. (J). (gr. k-3). 21.19 *(978-0-7641-3791-4(3),* B.E.S. Publishing) Peterson's.
Morgan, Alex. In the Zone. 2018. (Kicks Ser.). (ENG., Illus.). 128p. (J). (gr. 3-7). 17.99 *(978-1-4814-8153-3(3),* Simon & Schuster Bks. For Young Readers) Simon & Schuster Bks. For Young Readers.
—Shaken Up. 2015. (Kicks Ser.). (ENG., Illus.). 128p. (J). (gr. 3-7). 16.99 *(978-1-4814-5100-0(6),* Simon & Schuster Bks. For Young Readers) Simon & Schuster Bks. For Young Readers.
Ms. Sue. Where Is Your Name? Ducy, George, illus. 2009. 24p. pap. 24.95 *(978-1-60672-711-9(7))* America Star Bks.
Mullarkey, Lisa. Daniela, 1 vol. Franco, Paula, illus. 2015. (Pony Girls Ser.). Tr. of Daniela. (ENG.). 112p. (J). (gr. 2-5). 38.50 *(978-1-62402-128-2(X),* 19377, Calico Chapter Bks.) ABDO Publishing Co.
Murray, Stuart A. P. Matty in the Goal. 1 vol. 2012. (Champion Sports Story Ser.). (ENG.). 104p. (J). (gr. 3-5). 30.60 *(978-0-7660-3877-6(7),* 7cd5aacf-9446-4eco-a170-384455d3c3f5); pap. 13.88 *(978-1-4644-0003-2(2),* cf8888ef-6c05-46e8-828c-b0584784f0c5) Enslow Publishing, LLC.
Nanette. Blue the Frog. 2004. (Life on Granny's Farm Ser.). (J). 12.95 *(978-0-9741269-2-0(6))* St. Bernard Publishing, LLC.
Neilly, Lori Ann. The Oracle & the Mirror. 2013. 56p. pap. 24.20 *(978-1-4669-8403-5(1))* Trafford Publishing.
Newman, Lesléa. Miss Tutu's Star. Armstrong-Ellis, Carey, illus. 2010. (ENG.). 32p. (J). (gr. -1-3). 17.95 *(978-0-8109-8396-0(6),* 647801, Abrams Bks. for Young Readers) Abrams, Inc.
Newman, Patrice Tomasetti. Where Oh Where? It's in My Hair! 2012. 26p. 24.95 *(978-1-4626-6284-5(6))* America Star Bks.
Novel Units. The View from Saturday Novel Units Student Packet. 2019. (ENG.). (J). pap. 13.99 *(978-1-56137-936-1(0),* Novel Units, Inc.) Classroom Library Co.
Oates, Joyce Carol. Sexy. 2005. 272p. (J). (gr. 7-18). 16.99 *(978-0-06-054149-1(0),* HarperTeen) HarperCollins Pubs.
Oliver, Sarah. Be the Best. 2008. (Illus.). 104p. pap. 25.50 *(978-0-9559820-0-2(6))* Oliver, Sarah GBR. Dist: Lulu Pr., Inc.
Olsen, Elizabeth & Arnett, Robbie. Hattie Harmony: Worry Detective. Valdez, Marissa, illus. 2022. 40p. (J). (gr. -1-3). 17.99 *(978-0-593-35144-4(4),* Viking Books for Young Readers) Penguin Young Readers Group.
Osburn, Jacquelyn. Willy, the Worried Worm. 2008. 24p. pap. 12.99 *(978-1-4343-8183-5(8))* AuthorHouse.
Paratore, Coleen Murtagh. Sunny Holiday. 2008. (Sunny Holiday Ser.: 1). (ENG.). 176p. (J). (gr. 2-4). 18.69 *(978-0-545-07588-6(2))* Scholastic, Inc.
Parr, todd. Be Who You Are. 2016. (ENG., Illus.). 32p. (J). (gr. -1-1). 18.99 *(978-0-316-26523-2(3))* Little, Brown Bks. for Young Readers.
Paulsen, Gary. Molly Mcginty Has a Really Good Day. 2006. (Illus.). 105p. (J). (gr. 3-7). 13.15 *(978-0-7569-6621-8(3))* Perfection Learning Corp.
—Notes from the Dog. 2011. (ENG.). 144p. (YA). (gr. 7). pap. 8.99 *(978-0-375-85542-9(4),* Ember) Random Hse. Children's Bks.
Pearsall, Shelley. All of the Above. 2008. (ENG., Illus.). 256p. (J). (gr. 3-7). per. 8.00 *(978-0-316-11526-1(6))* Little, Brown Bks. for Young Readers.
Pennington, Beverly A. Jonathan's Discovery. Pennington, Beverly A., illus. 2006. (Illus.). 29p. (J). (gr. -1-3). pap. 12.95 *(978-1-56167-920-1(8))* American Literary Pr.
Peoples-Riley, Daria. I Got Next. Peoples-Riley, Daria, illus. 2019. (ENG., Illus.). 40p. (J). (gr. -1-3). 17.99 *(978-0-06-265777-0(1),* Greenwillow Bks.) HarperCollins Pubs.
—This Is It. Peoples-Riley, Daria, illus. 2018. (ENG., Illus.). 40p. (J). (gr. -1-3). 17.99 *(978-0-06-265776-3(3),* Greenwillow Bks.) HarperCollins Pubs.
Pequeña the Burro: Evaluation Guide. 2006. (J). *(978-1-55942-420-2(6))* Witcher Productions.
Perl, Erica S. When Life Gives You O. J. 2013. (When Life Gives You O. J. Ser.). (ENG.). (J). 208p. (gr. 4-6). 21.19 *(978-0-375-95924-0(6),* Knopf Bks. for Young Readers); 224p. (gr. 3-7). 8.99 *(978-0-375-85902-1(0),* Yearling) Random Hse. Children's Bks.
Perry, Gina. Small. 2017. (ENG., Illus.). 40p. (J). (gr. -1-3). 17.99 *(978-1-4998-0401-0(6))* Little Bee Books Inc.
Perry, Laurie. Brown Bear, 1 vol. Mackay, Hugh, illus. 2010. 22p. pap. 24.95 *(978-1-4489-5702-6(8))* PublishAmerica, Inc.
Phipps, Ben. I'm a Winner You're a Winner: Remembering How Great You Are. 2006. (J). per. 9.95 *(978-0-9779374-0-0(2))* One Source Publishing, LLC.
Piper, Deb. From A — to Zulinski. 2008. (J). pap. *(978-0-88092-713-0(5));* lib. bdg. *(978-0-88092-712-3(7))* Royal Fireworks Publishing Co.
Pitchford, Dean. Captain Nobody. 208p. (J). 2010. (gr. 3-7). 8.99 *(978-0-14-241667-9(3),* Puffin Books) 2009. (ENG.). (gr. 4-6). 21.19 *(978-0-399-25034-7(4))* Penguin Young Readers Group.
Poulsen, David A. Numbers. 2nd ed. 2015. (ENG.). 200p. (YA). pap. 12.99 *(978-1-4597-3248-3(0))* Dundurn Pr. CAN. Dist: Publishers Group West (PGW).
—Numbers. 2008. (ENG.). 232p. (YA). (gr. 6-18). *(978-1-55470-095-0(7))* Me to We.
Powers, David M. F. Ein Schmetterling Ohne Flügel. Vail, Sue, tr. Nesterova, Natalia, illus. 2013. 42p. pap. 9.99 *(978-0-9860373-3-7(8))* Pants On Fire Pr.
Qualey, Marsha. Gracie Laroo at Pig Jubilee. Litten, Kristyna, illus. 2017. (Gracie Laroo Ser.). (ENG.). 40p. (J). (gr. k-2). lib. bdg. 21.32 *(978-1-5158-1442-9(4),* 135712, Picture Window Bks.) Capstone.
—Gracie Laroo Goes to School. Litten, Kristyna, illus. 2017. (Gracie Laroo Ser.). (ENG.). 40p. (J). (gr. k-2). lib. bdg. 21.32 *(978-1-5158-1440-5(8),* 135710, Picture Window Bks.) Capstone.
—The Marvelous, Amazing, Pig-Tastic Gracie Laroo! Litten, Kristyna & Litten, Kristyna, illus. 2018. (Gracie Laroo Ser.). (ENG.). 128p. (J). (gr. k-2). pap., pap., pap. 5.95 *(978-1-5158-1458-0(0),* 135717, Picture Window Bks.) Capstone.
Queen Latifah. Queen of the Scene. Morrison, Frank, illus. 2006. 32p. (J). (gr. -1-3). 17.89 incl. audio compact disk *(978-0-06-077857-6(1),* Geringer, Laura Book) HarperCollins Pubs.
Raskin, Joyce. My Misadventures As a Teenage Rock Star. Chu, Carol, illus. 2011. (ENG.). 112p. (YA). (gr. 7-18). pap. 8.99 *(978-0-547-39311-7(3),* 1426898, Clarion Bks.) HarperCollins Pubs.
Reichman, Justin. The Green. 2003. (Touchdown Editions Ser.: Vol. 9). (ENG.). 150p. (gr. 7-12). 26.19 *(978-0-9708992-9-3(7))* Scobre Pr. Corp.
Rennison, Louise. Withering Tights. 2012. (Misadventures of Tallulah Casey Ser.: 1). (ENG.). 304p. (YA). (gr. 8). pap. 8.99 *(978-0-06-179933-4(5),* HarperTeen) HarperCollins Pubs.
Resau, Laura. Red Glass. 2009. (ENG.). 304p. (YA). (gr. 7). pap. 9.99 *(978-0-440-24025-9(5),* Delacorte Bks. for Young Readers) Random Hse. Children's Bks.
Reynolds Naylor, Phyllis. Including Alice. 2005. (Alice McKinley Ser.: No. 16). 277p. (J). (gr. 4-7). 13.65 *(978-0-7569-5460-4(6))* Perfection Learning Corp.
Reynolds, Peter H. The Dot. Reynolds, Peter H., illus. 2003. (Creatrilogy Ser.). (ENG., Illus.). 32p. (J). (gr. k-4). 15.00 *(978-0-7636-1961-9(2),* 53509533) Candlewick Pr.
—Ish. Reynolds, Peter H., illus. 2004. (Creatrilogy Ser.). (ENG., Illus.). 32p. (J). (gr. k-4). 15.00 *(978-0-7636-2344-9(X))* Candlewick Pr.
Rigby, Jill. I Put It Right There! I Swear! The story of one boy's master plan to overcome executive functioning Difficulties! 2011. 28p. pap. 12.77 *(978-1-4634-3710-7(2))* AuthorHouse.
Riley, Zach. Surprise Kick. Ricci, Andrés, illus. 2012. (Zach Riley Ser.). (ENG.). 80p. (J). (gr. 2-5). lib. bdg. 35.64 *(978-1-61783-536-0(6),* 15863, Calico Chapter Bks.) ABDO Publishing Co.
Ripken Jr., Cal. The Closer. 2017. (Cal Ripken Jr. 's All Stars Ser.: 6). (ENG.). 208p. (J). (gr. 3-7). pap. 6.99 *(978-1-4847-2788-1(6))* Hyperion Bks. for Children.
Robinson, Gary. Tribal Journey. 2013. (PathFinders Ser.). (ENG.). 96p. (YA). (gr. 8-12). pap. 9.95 *(978-1-939053-01-5(3),* 7th Generation) BPC.
Rodda, Emily. The Flower Fairies. Vitale, Raoul, illus. 2003. (Fairy Realm Ser.). 128p. (J). 8.99 *(978-0-06-009586-4(5))* HarperCollins Pubs.
Rosciti, Donna. The Birthday Train: Book 1. 2013. (ENG.). 48p. (J). 24.95 *(978-1-4787-2236-6(3))* Outskirts Pr., Inc.
Rosenlund, Ranee. Benny the Frog's Leap of Faith. 2010. 16p. 8.49 *(978-1-4490-5408-3(0))* AuthorHouse.
Roth, Sarra J. Not the Quitting Kind. Bishop, Tracy, illus. 2014. (ENG.). 32p. (J). 16.99 *(978-1-4413-1415-4(6),* 1449d677-112d-4408-b198-ea19b3cef1c3) Peter Pauper Pr. Inc.
Rush, Jennifer. Devils & Thieves. 2017. (Devils & Thieves Ser.: 1). (ENG.). 336p. (YA). (gr. 9-17). 17.99 *(978-0-316-39089-7(5))* Little, Brown Bks. for Young Readers.
Ryder, Chloe. Princess Ponies 8: a Singing Star. 2015. (Princess Ponies Ser.). (ENG., Illus.). 128p. (J). (gr. 2-4). pap. 5.99 *(978-1-61963-567-8(4),* 900140704, Bloomsbury USA Childrens) Bloomsbury Publishing USA.
Saltzberg, Barney. Star of the Week. Saltzberg, Barney, illus. 2010. (ENG., Illus.). 32p. (J). (gr. k-3). pap. 7.99 *(978-0-7636-3076-8(4))* Candlewick Pr.
Sauer, Tammi. Wordy Birdy. Mottram, Dave, illus. 32p. (J). (gr. -1-2). 2019. pap. 8.99 *(978-0-593-11898-6(7),* Dragonfly Bks.) 2018. 16.99 *(978-1-5247-1929-6(3),* Doubleday Bks. for Young Readers) Random Hse. Children's Bks.
Schafer, Milton. I'm Big! Lew-Vriethoff, Joanne, illus. 2006. (J). *(978-1-4156-8150-3(3),* Dial) Penguin Publishing Group.
Schraff, Anne. I Am Underdog. 2014. (Red Rhino Ser.). (J). lib. bdg. 18.40 *(978-0-606-36198-9(7))* Turtleback.
Schroeder, Lisa. Keys to the City. 2017. (ENG.). 240p. (J). (gr. 3-7). 16.99 *(978-0-545-90738-5(1),* Scholastic Pr.) Scholastic, Inc.
Scieszka, Jon. The Great Truck Rescue. Shannon, David et al, illus. 2010. (Jon Scieszka's Trucktown Ser.). (ENG.). 40p. (J). (gr. -1-3). pap. 4.99 *(978-1-4424-0932-3(0),* Simon & Schuster Bks. For Young Readers) Simon & Schuster Bks. For Young Readers.
Sebra, Diane. Making Mountains Out of Moles. 2003. 120p. pap. 9.95 *(978-1-55517-712-6(3),* 77123) Cedar Fort, Inc./CFI Distribution.
Sellers, Bakari. Who Are Your People? 2022. (ENG., Illus.). 32p. (J). (gr. -1-3). 18.99 *(978-0-06-308285-4(3),* Quill Tree Bks.) HarperCollins Pubs.
Serluca-Foster, Rosemary. Genevieve's Gift: A Child's Joyful Tale of Connecting with Her Intuitive Heart. 2007. (ENG.). 32p. pap. 11.99 *(978-1-4196-7321-4(1))* CreateSpace Independent Publishing Platform.
Sheldon, Dyan. Sophie Pitt-Turnbull Discovers America. 2007. (ENG.). 192p. (YA). (gr. 7-12). per. 7.99 *(978-0-7636-3295-3(3))* Candlewick Pr.
Sileo, Frank J. Don't Put Yourself down in Circus Town: A Story about Self-Confidence. Cornelison, Sue, illus. 2014. (ENG.). 32p. (J). pap. *(978-1-4338-1914-8(7),* Magination Pr.) American Psychological Assn.
Skovron, Jon. Struts & Frets. 2011. (ENG.). 288p. (YA). (gr. 8-17). pap. 7.95 *(978-1-4197-0028-6(6),* 657403, Amulet Bks.) Abrams, Inc.
Small Acts of Amazing Courage. 2013. (ENG., Illus.). 240p. (J). (gr. 4-7). pap. 8.99 *(978-1-4424-9495-4(6),* Simon & Schuster/Paula Wiseman Bks.) Simon & Schuster/Paula Wiseman Bks.
Small, Lily. Bella the Bunny: Fairy Animals of Misty Wood. 2015. (Fairy Animals of Misty Wood Ser.: 2). (ENG., Illus.). 144p. (J). (gr. k-3). pap. 6.99 *(978-1-62779-142-7(6),* 900137175, Holt, Henry & Co. Bks. For Young Readers) Holt, Henry & Co.
Small, Tanya. What You Say Is What You Are. 2007. pap. 7.50 *(978-0-9705090-1-7(4))* MorningGlory Publishing.
Sorenson, Margo. Ambrose & the Cathedral Dream. Szegedi, Katalin, illus. 2006. (ENG.). 32p. (J). (gr. -1-3). pap. 4.24 *(978-0-8146-3004-4(9))* Liturgical Pr.
Spieller, Lauren. Your Destination Is on the Left. 2018. (ENG., Illus.). 304p. (YA). (gr. 9). 18.99 *(978-1-4814-9212-6(8))* Simon & Schuster, Inc.
Standish, Burt L. Frank Merriwell's Confidence. Rudman, Jack, ed. 2003. (Frank Merriwell Ser.). 29.95 *(978-0-8373-9349-0(3));* pap. 9.95 *(978-0-8373-9049-9(4))* Merriwell, Frank Inc.
Steers, Billy. Tractor Mac: New Friend. 2019. (Tractor Mac Ser.). (J). lib. bdg. 16.00 *(978-0-606-41573-6(4))* Turtleback.
—Tractor Mac New Friend. 2015. (Tractor Mac Ser.). (ENG., Illus.). 32p. (J). (gr. -1-k). 9.99 *(978-0-374-30110-1(7),* 900138388, Farrar, Straus & Giroux (BYR)) Farrar, Straus & Giroux.
Stein, David Ezra. Pouch! Stein, David Ezra, illus. 2012. (ENG., Illus.). 32p. (J). (gr. -1 — 1). bds. 8.99 *(978-0-399-25738-4(1),* Nancy Paulsen Books) Penguin Young Readers Group.
Stevens, Elizabeth. Mister D. Frongia, Daniela, illus. 2012. 24p. (J). 16.95 *(978-1-60131-114-6(1))* Big Tent Bks.
Stier, Catherine. The Terrible Secrets of the Tell-All Club. 2011. (ENG.). 128p. (J). (gr. 4-6). lib. bdg. 18.69 *(978-0-8075-7798-1(7))* Whitman, Albert & Co.
Stone, Phoebe. Paris for Two. 2016. (J). (ENG.). 272p. (gr. 3-7). 16.99 *(978-0-545-44362-3(8));* 257p. *(978-1-338-04510-9(5))* Scholastic, Inc. (Levine, Arthur A. Bks.).
Struyk-Bonn, Chris. Nice Girls Endure. 2016. (ENG.). 256p. (YA). (gr. 9-12). 16.95 *(978-1-63079-047-9(8),* 131502, Switch Pr.) Capstone.
Supplee, Suzanne. Somebody Everybody Listens To. 2011. 288p. (YA). (gr. 7-12). 8.99 *(978-0-14-241886-4(2),* Speak) Penguin Young Readers Group.
Swift, Amanda. Big Bones. 2005. (ENG.). 144p. (J). (gr. 4-7). per. 9.95 *(978-0-689-87547-2(9))* Simon & Schuster, Ltd. GBR. Dist: Simon & Schuster, Inc.
Tatum, Channing. The One & Only Sparkella. Barnes, Kim, illus. 2021. (Sparkella Ser.: 1). (ENG.). 48p. (J). 18.99 *(978-1-250-75075-4(X),* 900224690) Feiwel & Friends.
Taylor-Butler, Christine. I Am Smart. Borlasca, Hector, illus. (My First Reader Ser.). (ENG.). 32p. (J). (gr. k-1). 2006. per. 3.95 *(978-0-516-24971-1(1))* 2005. lib. bdg. 18.50 *(978-0-516-25176-9(7))* Scholastic Library Publishing. (Children's Pr.).
Taylor, Helen. Emu Can't Fly. Gilles-Gray, Carolyn, illus. 2013. 24p. pap. *(978-1-921883-39-2(1),* MBS Pr.) Pick-a-Woo Woo Pubs.
Terrell, Brandon. Quarterback Scramble, 1 vol. Sandoval, Gerardo, illus. 2011. (Sports Illustrated Kids Graphic Novels Ser.). (ENG.). 56p. (J). (gr. 3-8). pap. 7.19 *(978-1-4342-3070-6(8),* 1321221); lib. bdg. 26.65 *(978-1-4342-2220-6(9),* 1321221) Capstone. (Stone Arch Bks.).
—8-Bit Baseball, 1 vol. Ferrara, Eduardo, illus. 2014. (Sports Illustrated Kids Graphic Novels Ser.). (ENG.). 72p. (J). (gr. 3-8). 26.65 *(978-1-4342-4164-1(5),* Stone Arch Bks.) Capstone.
Thomas, Jane Resh. Blind Mountain. 2006. (ENG.). 128p. (J). (gr. 5-7). 15.00 *(978-0-618-64872-6(0),* 100463, Clarion Bks.) HarperCollins Pubs.
Thompson, Carol. Run! Thompson, Carol, illus. 2013. (Little Movers Ser.). (Illus.). 12p. (J). spiral bd. *(978-1-84643-616-1(8))* Child's Play International Ltd.
Thompson, Colin & Lissiat, Amy. Norman & Brenda. 2009. (ENG., Illus.). 32p. (J). 6.99 *(978-1-933605-86-9(3))* Kane Miller.
Thompson, Lauren. Wee Little Chick. Butler, John, illus. 2008. (Wee Little Ser.). (ENG.). 32p. (J). (gr. -1-3). 19.99 *(978-1-4169-3468-4(5),* Simon & Schuster Bks. For Young Readers) Simon & Schuster Bks. For Young Readers.
Tracy, Roseann. Do You Love Me When I Am Upside Down? 2008. 28p. pap. 12.99 *(978-1-4389-0503-7(3))* AuthorHouse.
van Genechten, Guido. Kangaroo Christine. van Genechten, Guido, illus. 2005. (Illus.). 24p. (J). (gr. 3-7). pap. 6.95 *(978-1-58925-396-4(5))* Tiger Tales.
VanDenberg, Saidat. Tadias & the Pitbully Tree. 2012. 36p. pap. 21.99 *(978-1-4797-0172-8(6))* Xlibris Corp.
Vega, Denise. Rock On: A Story of Guitars, Gigs, Girls, & a Brother (not Necessarily in That Order) 2013. (ENG., Illus.). 304p. (YA). (gr. 7-17). pap. 8.99 *(978-0-316-13309-8(4))* Little, Brown Bks. for Young Readers.
Ventura, Marne. Edgy Estella Aces the Sleepover Party. Trinidad, Leo, illus. 2016. (Worry Warriors Ser.). (ENG.). 96p. (J). (gr. 2-4). lib. bdg. 25.99 *(978-1-4965-3610-5(X),* 132816, Stone Arch Bks.) Capstone.
Vision, David & Vision, Mutiya Sahar. If Only I Could! Alcantara, Ignacio, illus. 2009. 32p. 17.00 *(978-0-9659538-8-7(2))* Von Curtis Publishing.
Vivian, Siobhan. Same Difference. 2014. (ENG.). 304p. (YA). (gr. 7-7). pap. 10.99 *(978-0-545-75802-4(5))* Scholastic, Inc.
Vizzini, Med. Be More Chill. 2011. 9.68 *(978-0-7848-3414-5(8),* Everbind) Marco Bk. Co.
Vizzini, Ned. Be More Chill. 2005. (ENG.). 320p. (YA). (gr. 7-12). per. 8.99 *(978-0-7868-0996-7(5),* Disney-Hyperion) Disney Publishing Worldwide.
Wade, Rebecca. The Theft & the Miracle. 2007. 351p. (J). (gr. 4-7). lib. bdg. 17.89 *(978-0-06-077495-0(9))* HarperCollins Pubs.
Wallace, Rich. Between the Sticks, 1 vol. Heitz, Tim, illus. 2015. (Game Face Ser.). (ENG.). 112p. (J). (gr. 2-5). 38.50 *(978-1-62402-132-9(8),* 19192, Calico Chapter Bks.) ABDO Publishing Co.
—Dunk under Pressure #7: Winning Season, Vol. 7. 7th ed. 2007. (Winning Season Ser.: 7). 128p. (J). (gr. 3-7). 5.99 *(978-0-14-240858-2(1),* Puffin Books) Penguin Young Readers Group.
—Pressure Point, 1 vol. Heitz, Tim, illus. 2015. (Game Face Ser.). (ENG.). 112p. (J). (gr. 2-5). 38.50 *(978-1-62402-135-0(2),* 19198, Calico Chapter Bks.) ABDO Publishing Co.
—Roar of the Crowd. 2004. 101p. (J). lib. bdg. 15.38 *(978-1-4242-2165-3(X))* Fitzgerald Bks.
Warren, Dotti M. Dreama Lynn & the Magic Tu Tu. 2008. 16p. pap. 9.49 *(978-1-4389-2983-5(8))* AuthorHouse.
Weinberger, Justin. Reformed. 2017. (ENG.). 208p. (J). (gr. 3-7). 16.99 *(978-0-545-90252-6(5),* Scholastic Pr.) Scholastic, Inc.
Westcott, Anne & Hu, C. C. Alicia. How Little Coyote Found His Secret Strength: A Story about How to Get Through Hard Times. Kuo, Ching-Pang, illus. 2017. (Hidden Strengths Therapeutic Children's Bks.). 32p. (C). pap. 17.95 *(978-1-78592-771-3(X),* 696597) Kingsley, Jessica Pubs. GBR. Dist: Hachette UK Distribution.
Weston Woods Staff, creator. Casi. 2011. (SPA.). 29.95 *(978-0-439-90592-3(3))* Weston Woods Studios, Inc.
Whelan, Gloria. Small Acts of Amazing Courage. 2011. (ENG.). 224p. (J). (gr. 4-7). 15.99 *(978-1-4424-0931-6(2),* Simon & Schuster/Paula Wiseman Bks.) Simon & Schuster/Paula Wiseman Bks.
Whelen-Banks, Jane. Liam Goes Poo in the Toilet: A Story about Trouble with Toilet Training. 2008. (Illus.). 32p. 13.95 *(978-1-84310-900-6(X),* 695773) Kingsley, Jessica Pubs. GBR. Dist: Hachette UK Distribution.

Wigington, Patti. Summer's Ashes. 2007. (ENG.). 208p. (gr. 8-12). per. 15.00 *(978-0-9766805-9-8(9))* Keene Publishing.
Wilkerson, L. Kobie, 3rd, reader. Fred & Mary. 2008. (Illus.). 32p. (J). 24.95 incl. DVD, audio compact disk *(978-0-9796679-0-9(9))* Love I! Learn Bks.
Williams, Laura E. Slant. 2008. (ENG.). 160p. (J). (gr. 2-8). pap. 6.95 *(978-1-57131-682-0(5))* Milkweed Editions.
Willow, Bim. I-Can't & I-Can! Morales, Jose, illus. 2012. 28p. pap. 8.99 *(978-0-9853574-3-6(6))* Mountain Creek Pubns.
Wood, David & Wood, Aimee. The Beautiful Swan. 2008. 24p. pap. 14.95 *(978-1-59858-624-4(6))* Dog Ear Publishing, LLC.
Woods, Brenda. Zoe in Wonderland. 2017. 224p. (J). (gr. 3-7). 8.99 *(978-0-425-28891-7(9),* Puffin Books) Penguin Young Readers Group.
Wright-McAdoo, Joyce & Wright-Mcadoo, Joyce. Zimb: Believe. 2009. (Illus.). 28p. pap. 15.99 *(978-1-4415-8051-1(4))* Xlibris Corp.
Yaccarino, Dan. Morris Mole. Yaccarino, Dan, illus. 2017. (ENG., Illus.). 40p. (J). (gr. -1-3). 17.99 *(978-0-06-241107-5(1),* HarperCollins) HarperCollins Pubs.
Yang, Kelly. Front Desk (Front Desk #1) (Scholastic Gold) (Front Desk Ser.). (ENG., (J). (gr. 3-7). 2019. Illus.). 320p. pap. 8.99 *(978-1-338-15782-6(5))* 2018. 304p. E-Book *(978-1-338-15780-2(9))*Vol .1. 2018. (Illus.). 304p. 18.99 *(978-1-338-15779-6(5))* Scholastic, Inc. (Levine, Arthur A. Bks.).
—Room to Dream (Front Desk #3) 2021. (Front Desk Ser.). (ENG.). 320p. (J). (gr. 3-7). 17.99 *(978-1-338-62112-9(2),* Scholastic Pr.) Scholastic, Inc.
You Can Be Anything! 2006. (Illus.). 32p. (J). 14.95 *(978-0-9786813-1-9(2))* Elora Pr.
Youyou, Ruth. The Bird That Could Not Fly. 2007. (ENG.). 24p. pap. 12.99 *(978-1-4257-6183-7(6))* Xlibris Corp.
Zobel Nolan, Allia. What I Like about Me! A Book Celebrating Differences. Yamamoto, Miki, illus. 2009. (What I Like About Ser.). (ENG.). 14p. (J). (gr. -1-k). 6.99 *(978-0-7944-1945-5(3),* Studio Fun International) Printers Row Publishing Group.
Zuill, Andrea. Sweety. 2019. (Illus.). 32p. (J). (gr. -1-2). 18.99 *(978-0-525-58000-3(X),* Schwartz & Wade Bks.) Random Hse. Children's Bks.

SELF-CONTROL

Antill, Sara. Self-Control, 1 vol. 2013. (Character Strength Ser.). 24p. (J). (ENG.). (gr. 2-3). pap. 9.25 *(978-1-4488-9816-9(1),* abdf7a51-c7ec-4635-8ff2-8ce55e8ce2f2); (ENG.). (gr. 2-3). lib. bdg. 26.27 *(978-1-4488-9679-0(7),* b46a96f3-bd60-4975-bb11-a6f58748e7a9); (gr. 3-6). pap. 49.50 *(978-1-4488-9817-6(X))* Rosen Publishing Group, Inc., The. (PowerKids Pr.).
Baruch-Feldman, Caren. The Grit Guide for Teens: A Workbook to Help You Build Perseverance, Self-Control, & a Growth Mindset. 2017. (ENG.). 152p. (YA). (gr. 6-12). pap. 18.95 *(978-1-62625-856-3(2),* 38563) New Harbinger Pubns.
Brukner, Lauren. How to Be a Superhero Called Self-Control! Super Powers to Help Younger Children to Regulate Their Emotions & Senses. Apsley, illus. 2015. 112p. 21.95 *(978-1-84905-717-2(6),* 693908) Kingsley, Jessica Pubs. GBR. Dist: Hachette UK Distribution.
Doron. Look in the Mirror... 2005. 228p. pap. 15.00 *(978-1-4116-0109-3(2))* Lulu Pr., Inc.
—Look in the Mirror. 2nd ed. 2005. 335p. pap. 16.56 *(978-1-4116-0197-0(1))* Lulu Pr., Inc.
Doudna, Kelly. Keep Your Cool!, 1 vol. 2007. (Character Concepts Ser.). (Illus.). 24p. (J). (gr. k-3). lib. bdg. 24.21 *(978-1-59928-736-2(6),* SandCastle) ABDO Publishing Co.
Esherick, Joan. Physical Challenges. Albers, Lisa et al, eds. 2014. (Living with a Special Need Ser.: 16). 128p. (J). (gr. 7-18). 25.95 *(978-1-4222-3041-1(4))* Mason Crest.
Hansen, Sharon A. The Executive Functioning Workbook for Teens: Help for Unprepared, Late, & Scattered Teens. 2013. (ENG.). 144p. (YA). (gr. 6-12). pap. 18.95 *(978-1-60882-656-8(2),* 26568) New Harbinger Pubns.
James, Sara. Self-Discipline. 2013. (Junior Martial Arts Ser.: 9). 32p. (J). (gr. 4-18). 19.95 *(978-1-4222-2739-8(1))* Mason Crest.
Lawler, Jean C. Experience Media: How Your Media Choices Make You Feel. 2018. (Experience Personal Power Ser.). (ENG., Illus.). 24p. (J). (gr. 2-4). pap. 6.99 *(978-1-63440-380-1(0),* 60935072-586b-4cc3-864c-766a38ee2fe4); lib. bdg. 23.99 *(978-1-63440-376-4(2),* 4a6ce30d-ef1a-4b30-8f50-7b5cf0ad3dd5) Red Chair Pr.
—Experience Mindfulness: How Quiet-Time Makes You Feel. 2018. (Experience Personal Power Ser.). (ENG., Illus.). 24p. (J). (gr. 2-4). pap. 6.99 *(978-1-63440-379-5(7),* 99c76723-9470-4819-855a-92318e19dcfd); lib. bdg. 23.99 *(978-1-63440-375-7(4),* ea5724e9-66a4-470d-97a8-bcc8b31f76df) Red Chair Pr.
Lisbona, Margie Taylor. Rock & Rhino Learn Responsibility. Roberts, J. P., illus. 2011. 48p. pap. *(978-1-77067-530-8(2))* FriesenPress.
Manolis, Kay & Todd, Anne. George Washington: A Life of Self-Discipline. 2007. (People of Character Ser.). (ENG., Illus.). 24p. (J). (gr. 2-5). lib. bdg. 26.95 *(978-1-60014-094-5(7))* Bellwether Media.
Phelan, Thomas & Lee, Tracy. 1-2-3 Magic for Kids: Helping Your Kids Understand the New Rules. 2nd. ed. 2017. (Illus.). 128p. pap. 11.99 *(978-1-4926-4786-7(1),* 9781492647867) Sourcebooks, Inc.
Pryor, Kimberley Jane. Self Discipline, 1 vol. 2011. (Values Ser.). (ENG., Illus.). 32p. (gr. 1-1). 31.21 *(978-1-60870-147-6(6),* ace36c3c-ee64-4479-8d46-7b19013ec9ae) Cavendish Square Publishing LLC.
Purcell, Sherry L. Using Assistive Technology. 2004. 325p. (gr. 4-6). spiral bd. 29.00 incl. audio compact disk *(978-1-57861-493-6(7),* IEP Resources) Attainment Co., Inc.
Regan, Lisa. Don't Get Angry, Annie: Stay Calm, 1 vol. 2017. (You Choose Ser.). (ENG.). 32p. (gr. 2-2). lib. bdg. 26.93 *(978-0-7660-8700-2(X),* 479b2854-51a2-4b83-aee6-d61a5b013484) Enslow Publishing, LLC.
Siddoway, Ramona. Self-Control. 2013. (7 Character Strengths of Highly Successful Students Ser.). 64p. (J). (gr. 5-8). pap. 77.70 *(978-1-4488-9564-9(2));* (ENG., Illus.). (gr. 6-6). pap. 13.95 *(978-1-4488-9563-2(4),* 3d763f9f-d267-468a-be81-d3269f04b46d, Rosen Classroom); (ENG., Illus.). (gr. 6-6). lib. bdg. 37.12 *(978-1-4488-9543-4(X),* 910d5e68-b1ff-475b-9d3f-45d221c07452, Rosen Classroom) Rosen Publishing Group, Inc., The.
Smith, Sarah. Self-Discipline & Responsibility, Vol. 7. 2018. (Leadership Skills & Character Building Ser.). 64p. (J). (gr. 7). lib. bdg. 31.93 *(978-1-4222-4000-7(2))* Mason Crest.
Verdick, Elizabeth. Waiting Is Not Forever. Heinlen, Marieka, illus. 2019. (Best Behavior(r) Board Book Ser.). (ENG.). 26p. (J). (— 1). bds. 9.99 *(978-1-63198-466-2(7),* 84662) Free Spirit Publishing Inc.

SELF-CULTURE

see also Books and Reading

Asugha, Ruby. Little Sisters, Listen Up! A Message of Hope for Girls Growing up in Poverty Racism, & Despair. 2004. 138p. 9.95 *(978-1-889322-61-2(X),* 25-017) Boys Town Pr.
Bishop, John. Goal Setting for Students: Winner of three national parenting book Awards. 2003. (Illus.). (YA). pap. 11.95 *(978-0-9743700-0-2(2))* Accent On Success.
Bright Ideas: Level O, 6 vols. (Explorers Ser.). 32p. (gr. 3-6). 44.95 *(978-0-7699-0598-3(6))* Shortland Pubns. (U. S. A.) Inc.
Cox, Scott, Sr. Love Your Ego As Your SELF. 2004. (J). per. 12.95 *(978-0-9753817-1-7(7))* Unlimited Horizons.
Douglas, Marianne. How to Deal When Your Middle Name Is Stress: Real Teens - Real Advice. 2004. (J). per. 4.95 *(978-1-59196-643-2(4))* Instant Pub.
Renaud, Andrea. The Goal Keeper Journal. 2003. (Illus.). 160p. (YA). per. *(978-0-9717041-1-4(2))* A Happy Friend, Inc.
Stone, Penny. Complicated Mourning & Grief Blocks: How to Move Forward Past Our Pain. 2004. (New Line of Grief Guides). 64p. pap. 15.00 *(978-1-891400-10-0(X))* Sourcebooks, Inc.
—My World Is Upside Down: Making Sense of Life after Confronting Death. 2004. (New Line of Grief Guides). 9.95 *(978-1-891400-24-7(X))* Sourcebooks, Inc.
—Surviving the Loss of a Parent. 2005. (New Line of Grief Guides). 9.95 *(978-1-891400-57-5(6))* Sourcebooks, Inc.
—Taste of Cultures: Italy. 2004. (New Line of Grief Guides). 9.95 *(978-1-891400-76-6(2))* Sourcebooks, Inc.
Wambach, Abby. Wolfpack (Young Readers Edition) 2020. (ENG., Illus.). 112p. (J). 16.99 *(978-1-250-76686-1(9),* 900232554) Roaring Brook Pr.
Wolff, Ariana. Khan Academy & Salman Khan, 1 vol. 2014. (Internet Biographies Ser.). (ENG.). 128p. (YA). (gr. 7-7). 39.80 *(978-1-4777-7927-9(2),* c017de9d-2737-4c81-b2b1-213a40a1fdf7, Rosen Young Adult) Rosen Publishing Group, Inc., The.

SELF-DEFENSE

see also Boxing; Judo; Karate

Berry, Joy. Help Me Be Good Fighting. Bartholomew, illus. 2010. (Help Me Be Good Ser.). (ENG.). 32p. (J). (gr. -1-2). pap. 4.99 *(978-1-60577-135-9(X))* Berry, Joy Enterprises.
Chaline, Eric. Martial Arts for Women: Winning Ways. James, Adam, ed. 2015. (Mastering Martial Arts Ser.). (Illus.). 96p. (J). (gr. 5). lib. bdg. 24.95 *(978-1-4222-3243-9(3))* Mason Crest.
Feigh, Alison. I Can Play It Safe. Logan, Laura, illus. 2008. (ENG.). 32p. (J). (gr. -1-3). 16.99 *(978-1-57542-285-5(9),* 1275) Free Spirit Publishing Inc.
Holt, Rinehart and Winston Staff. Holt Science & Technology Chapter 27: Life Science: Body Defenses. 5th ed. 2004. (Illus.). pap. 12.86 *(978-0-03-030256-5(0))* Holt McDougal.
James, Sara. Self-Defense. 2013. (Junior Martial Arts Ser.: 9). 32p. (J). (gr. 4-18). 19.95 *(978-1-4222-2738-1(3))* Mason Crest.
Klimchuk, David. Aikido, 1 vol. 2019. (Enter the Dojo! Martial Arts for Kids Ser.). (ENG.). 24p. (gr. 3-4). pap. 9.25 *(978-1-7253-0998-2(X),* 51d28fd8-889a-4016-a7e8-ffa95ea2aabb, PowerKids Pr.) Rosen Publishing Group, Inc., The.
McNab, Chris. Martial Arts for People with Disabilities. 2004. (Martial & Fighting Arts Ser.). (Illus.). 96p. (YA). (gr. 7). lib. bdg. 22.95 *(978-1-59084-399-4(1))* Mason Crest.
Mitchell, Susan K. Animal Chemical Combat: Poisons, Smells, & Slime, 1 vol. 2008. (Amazing Animal Defenses Ser.). (ENG., Illus.). 48p. (gr. 5-7). lib. bdg. 27.93 *(978-0-7660-3294-1(9),* cda2101d-2349-4010-ab44-17eee5d5b9c3) Enslow Publishing, LLC.
Safe Kids USA Staff. Self-Defense for Kids: Learn Practical & Effective Techniques to Help You Defend Yourself. 2004. (Illus.). 48p. (J). (gr. -1-12). pap. 6.95 *(978-0-9718609-5-7(5))* Escher, Ursula.
Thompson, Tamara, ed. Self-Defense Laws, 1 vol. 2014. (At Issue Ser.). (ENG.). 104p. (gr. 10-12). pap. 28.80 *(978-0-7377-6855-8(X),* 1aabb90d-2ad1-4b97-91a1-07503cc1bf31); lib. bdg. 41.03 *(978-0-7377-6854-1(1),* 172487c1-b72d-42b0-b5c6-c532e7a8ef12) Greenhaven Publishing LLC. (Greenhaven Publishing).
Williamson, Wendy. Christian Martial Arts 101. 2004. (ENG.). 256p. per. 29.95 *(978-0-9721328-1-7(3))* Agapy Publishing.
—Christian Martial Arts 101 (Instructor's Edition) 2004. (ENG.). 288p. per. 18.95 *(978-0-9721328-2-4(1))* Agapy Publishing.
Wood, Alix. Aikido, 1 vol. 2013. (Kid's Guide to Martial Arts Ser.). (ENG., Illus.). 32p. (J). (gr. 2-3). pap. 12.75 *(978-1-4777-0352-6(7),* 648cf281-21f9-4f19-bb7f-097c2405106a); lib. bdg. 30.27 *(978-1-4777-0315-1(2),* 3a74afd4-54e6-46ae-a69f-d15d90e64d8a) Rosen Publishing Group, Inc., The. (PowerKids Pr.).

SELF-ESTEEM

Abolaffio, Ariella. You Are a Star. Abolaffio, Ariella, illus. 2019. (Illus.). (J). 8.99 *(978-1-61067-813-1(3))* Kane Miller.
Ajayi Jones, Luvvie. Rising Troublemaker: A Fear-Fighter Manual for Teens. 2022. (ENG., Illus.). 272p. (YA). (gr. 7). 17.99 *(978-0-593-52603-3(1),* Philomel Bks.) Penguin Young Readers Group.
Allman, Toney. Understanding Self-Image & Confidence. 2017. (Understanding Psychology Ser.). (ENG.). 80p. (YA). (gr. 5-12). *(978-1-68282-279-1(6))* ReferencePoint Pr., Inc.
Anana, Christy Lynn. I Can Feel Better: a Tapping Story: Emotional Freedom Technique (EFT): Effective Step by Step Mind & Body Relaxation for Kids, Teens & Adults. 2021. pap. 15.00 *(978-1-957400-00-6(5))* Anana Pr.
Andrus, Aubre. Lonely Planet Kids 101 Small Ways to Change the World 1. 2018. (Lonely Planet Kids Ser.). (ENG., Illus.). 112p. (J). (gr. 4-7). 14.99 *(978-1-78701-487-9(8),* 5863) Lonely Planet Global Ltd. IRL. Dist: Hachette Bk. Group.
Apel, Melanie Ann. Let's Talk About When You Think Nobody Likes You. 2009. (Let's Talk Library). 24p. (gr. 2-3). 42.50 *(978-1-60853-449-4(9),* PowerKids Pr.) Rosen Publishing Group, Inc., The.
Asgedom, Mawi. The Code: The 5 Secrets of Teen Success. 2003. (ENG., Illus.). 160p. (YA). (gr. 7-17). pap. 10.99 *(978-0-316-73689-3(9))* Little, Brown Bks. for Young Readers.
Avant-garde, Zaila. It's Not Bragging If It's True: How to Be Awesome at Life, from a Winner of the Scripps National Spelling Bee. 2023. (ENG., Illus.). 144p. (J). (gr. 3-7). 17.99 ***(978-0-593-56899-6(0))***; lib. bdg. 20.99 ***(978-0-593-56900-9(8))*** Random Hse. Children's Bks. (Random Hse. Bks. for Young Readers).
Baldoni, Justin. Boys Will Be Human: A Get-Real Gut-Check Guide to Becoming the Strongest, Kindest, Bravest Person You Can Be. 2022. (ENG.). 304p. (J). (gr. 6). 14.99 *(978-0-06-306718-9(8),* HarperCollins) HarperCollins Pubs.
Becnel, Barbara, ed. Gangs & Self-Esteem: Stanley Tookie Williams Street Peace Series, 8 bks., Vol. 1, Bk. 4. 2008. 24p. (J). 6.95 *(978-0-9753584-1-2(3))* Damamli Publishing Co.
Bell, Latarcia. The Looking Glass. 2011. 28p. pap. 24.95 *(978-1-4626-3234-3(3))* America Star Bks.
Bender, Alexandra Sabina. Alana's Advice... When There's a Clique, You've Got to Think Quick. 2007. (ENG., Illus.). 152p. (C). (gr. 4-10). per. 14.95 *(978-1-84590-075-5(8))* Crown Hse. Publishing LLC.
Bolden, Tanisha N. This Is Why I Rock: A Self-Empowerment Journal for Youth. 2011. 112p. pap. 11.95 *(978-0-9831743-2-5(6))* Second Time Media & Communications.
Bowen, Shane. Out of the Darkness. 2010. 220p. pap. 21.95 *(978-0-557-26249-6(6))* Lulu Pr., Inc.
Boyd, Beverly L. I Am a Blessing in Disguise Journal for Children. 2012. (Illus.). 65p. (J). per. 14.95 *(978-0-9742367-8-0(0))* ABR Pubns.
Cain, Susan, et al. Quiet Power: The Secret Strengths of Introverted Kids. Snider, Grant, illus. 2017. (ENG.). 288p. (J). (gr. 5). 9.99 *(978-0-14-750992-5(0),* Puffin Books) Penguin Young Readers Group.
—Quiet Power: The Secret Strengths of Introverts. Snider, Grant, illus. 2016. (ENG.). 288p. (J). (gr. 5). 17.99 *(978-0-8037-4060-0(3),* Dial Bks) Penguin Young Readers Group.
Calhoun, Dorothy Sweet. Six Bees for Children: A Collection of Educational Wisdoms for Children. 2012. (ENG.). 30p. (J). pap. 14.95 *(978-1-4327-8870-4(1))* Outskirts Pr., Inc.
Cassius, Sonya. My Beautiful World. 2009. (Illus.). 32p. pap. 12.99 *(978-1-4343-0061-4(7))* AuthorHouse.
Cavell-Clarke, Steffi. Respecting Others. 2017. (Our Values - Level 2 Ser.). (Illus.). 24p. (J). (gr. 2-3). *(978-0-7787-3263-1(0))* Crabtree Publishing Co.
Chargualaf, Cathy. Animal Storybook No. 1: Building Self-Esteem Through Animal Stories. 2013. (ENG.). 32p. (J). pap. 13.99 *(978-1-4525-7575-9(4),* Balboa Pr.) Author Solutions, LLC.
—Animal Storybook No. 2: Building Self-Esteem Through Animal Stories. 2013. (ENG.). 30p. (J). pap. 13.99 *(978-1-4525-7583-4(5),* Balboa Pr.) Author Solutions, LLC.
Child, Maria. Girls Own Book 1834. 2006. 292p. per. *(978-1-4067-9133-4(4),* Pomona Pr.) Read Bks.
Chinn, Jacqueline. How Can I Be Special? Mondragon, Manny, illus. 2003. (J). pap. 15.95 *(978-0-929526-55-3(4))* Double B Pubns.
Claybourne, Anna. Healthy for Life: Self-Esteem & Mental Health. 2018. (Healthy for Life Ser.). (ENG., Illus.). 32p. (J). (gr. 4-6). pap. 11.99 *(978-1-4451-4980-6(X),* Franklin Watts) Hachette Children's Group GBR. Dist: Hachette Bk. Group.
Collins-Donnelly, Kate. Banish Your Self-Esteem Thief: A Cognitive Behavioural Therapy Workbook on Building Positive Self-Esteem for Young People. 2014. (Gremlin & Thief CBT Workbooks Ser.). (Illus.). 240p. pap. 26.95 *(978-1-84905-462-1(2),* 694272) Kingsley, Jessica Pubs. GBR. Dist: Hachette UK Distribution.
Costanzo, Charlene. The Twelve Gifts of Birth. 2011. (Twelve Gifts Ser.: 1). (ENG., Illus.). 64p. 23.99 *(978-0-06-621104-6(2),* Morrow, William & Co.) HarperCollins Pubs.
Coster, Patience. How to Handle Low SelfEsteem. 2014. (Under Pressure Ser.). 48p. (gr. 4-7). 37.10 *(978-1-59920-828-2(8))* Black Rabbit Bks.
Crayton, Lisa A. Beating Bullying as a Teen with a Disability, 1 vol. 2019. (Equal Access: Fighting for Disability Protections Ser.). (ENG.). 64p. (gr. 5-5). pap. 13.95 *(978-1-5081-8333-4(3),* 611488ec-a67c-494d-bcb1-c023eb829ee6) Rosen Publishing Group, Inc., The.
Criswell, Patti Kelley. Stand up for Yourself & Your Friends: Dealing with Bullies & Bossiness & Finding a Better Way. Martini, Angela, illus. 2016. (American Girl(r) Wellbeing Ser.). (ENG.). 64p. (J). pap. 9.99 *(978-1-60958-738-3(3))* American Girl Publishing, Inc.
Domoney, Cathy. Madeleine, Maddy & Midge: Positive Thinking for Children. 2012. 36p. pap. 15.95 *(978-1-4525-0761-3(9))* Balboa Pr.
Doron. Look in the Mirror... 2005. 228p. pap. 15.00 *(978-1-4116-0109-3(2))* Lulu Pr., Inc.
—Look in the Mirror. 2nd ed. 2005. 335p. pap. 16.56 *(978-1-4116-0197-0(1))* Lulu Pr., Inc.
Dunn, Michael P. What's the Big Secret? 2003. (Illus.). 192p. per. 13.95 *(978-0-9724924-3-0(7))* Big Secret, The.
Elisha, . & Elyssa. I Love Me: Self-Esteem in Seven Easy Steps. 2014. (ENG., Illus.). 72p. pap. 9.95 *(978-1-63047-140-8(2))* Morgan James Publishing.
Engelbreit, Mary. Mary Engelbreit's the World Is Yours. Engelbreit, Mary, illus. 2019. (ENG., Illus.). 48p. (J). (gr. -1-3). 12.99 *(978-0-06-288994-2(X),* HarperCollins) HarperCollins Pubs.
Ferguson, Addy. Group Bullying: Exclusion & Ganging Up, 1 vol. 2013. (Stand up: Bullying Prevention Ser.). (ENG., Illus.). 24p. (J). (gr. 2-3). pap. 9.25 *(978-1-4488-9796-4(3),* dbe1c144-fd59-4e25-8757-0af7e0324160); lib. bdg. 26.27 *(978-1-4488-9669-1(X),* 5532e85d-47d1-4270-a2fe-b538b83ee48c) Rosen Publishing Group, Inc., The. (PowerKids Pr.).
—What to Do When You Are Bullied for Being Different, 1 vol. 2014. (Stand up: Bullying Prevention Ser.). (ENG.). 24p. (J). (gr. 2-3). lib. bdg. 26.27 *(978-1-4777-6892-1(0),* 238bcb20-9270-4514-8e47-5eb59f2ce7d5, PowerKids Pr.) Rosen Publishing Group, Inc., The.
Fixman, Jennifer. Make a Difference with Miss Jenny. 2009. 64p. 19.99 *(978-1-930979-14-7(2))* Edutunes.
Forche, Carolyn A. Colors Come from God ... Just Like Me! 2015. (ENG.). 32p. pap. 11.99 *(978-1-5018-0838-8(9),* 14429) Abingdon Pr.
Girard, Vanessa, DM. Diversity Is U & Me (high school survival Guide) 2010. 92p. pap. 10.99 *(978-0-557-54094-5(1))* Lulu Pr., Inc.
Harper, Hill. Letters to a Young Sister: DeFINE Your Destiny. 2009. 320p. (gr. 12-18). 18.00 *(978-1-59240-459-6(6),* Avery) Penguin Publishing Group.
How to Be a S. T. A. R. The Young Person's Guide to Finding Success & Living Your Dreams. 2nd ed. 2003. (J). *(978-0-9728626-0-8(9))* Gems International, LLC.
Hudson, Wade & Hudson, Cheryl Willis, eds. The Talk: Conversations about Race, Love & Truth. (Illus.). 160p. (J). (gr. 5). 2021. 7.99 *(978-0-593-12164-1(3),* Yearling) 2020. 16.99 *(978-0-593-12161-0(9),* Crown Books For Young Readers) 2020. (ENG., lib. bdg. 19.99 *(978-0-593-12162-7(7),* Crown Books For Young Readers) Random Hse. Children's Bks.
Jain, Renee & Tsabary, Shefali. Superpowered: Transform Anxiety into Courage, Confidence, & Resilience. (Illus.). (J). (gr. 3-7). 2022. (ENG.). 352p. 9.99 *(978-0-593-12642-4(4),* Yearling) 2020. 336p. 17.99 *(978-0-593-12639-4(4),* Random Hse. Bks. for Young Readers) 2020. (ENG., 336p. lib. bdg. 20.99 *(978-0-593-12641-7(6),* Random Hse. Bks. for Young Readers) Random Hse. Children's Bks.
James, Sara. Self-Esteem. 2013. (Junior Martial Arts Ser.: 9). 32p. (J). (gr. 4-18). 19.95 *(978-1-4222-2740-4(5))* Mason Crest.
Jones, Luvvie Ajayi, contrib. by. Rising Troublemaker: A Fear-Fighter Manual for Teens. 2023. (ENG.). 272p. (YA). (gr. 7). pap. 10.99 ***(978-0-593-52604-0(X),*** Philomel Bks.) Penguin Young Readers Group.
Kalman, Izzy C. Bullies to Buddies - How to Turn Your Enemies into Friends! How to Turn Your Enemies into Friends! Kalman, Lola, illus. 2005. (ENG.). 128p. (YA). per. 15.00 *(978-0-9706482-1-1(9))* The Wisdom Pages, Inc.
Kaufman, Gershen & Raphael, Lev. Stick up for Yourself! Every Kid's Guide to Personal Power & Positive Self-Esteem. 3rd rev. ed. 2019. (ENG., Illus.). 152p. (J). (gr. 4-7). pap. 15.99 *(978-1-63198-322-1(9),* 83221) Free Spirit Publishing Inc.
Keep Empowering Yourself Successfully: Raising Your Self Esteem. 2004. (YA). *(978-0-9762009-1-8(0))* Keep Empowering Yourself Successfully.
Kent, Susan. Learning How to Feel Good about Yourself. 2009. (Violence Prevention Library). 24p. (gr. 2-3). 42.50 *(978-1-60854-265-9(3),* PowerKids Pr.) Rosen Publishing Group, Inc., The.
Koya, Lena & Kamberg, Mary-Lane. Female Body Image & Self-Perception, 1 vol. 2017. (Women in the World Ser.). (ENG., Illus.). 112p. (J). (gr. 6-6). 38.80 *(978-1-5081-7726-5(0),* f3982b64-a3de-4ae1-bf79-0fc07d713210) Rosen Publishing Group, Inc., The.
Kunjufu, Jawanza & Prescott, Folami. SETCLAE, Eighth Grade: Self-Esteem Through Culture Leads to Academic Excellence. 2003. (ENG.). 60p. (J). (gr. 8). pap. 9.95 *(978-0-913543-93-1(4))* African American Images.
—SETCLAE, Fifth Grade: Self-Esteem Through Culture Leads to Academic Excellence. 2003. (ENG.). 60p. (J). (gr. 5). pap. 14.95 *(978-0-913543-90-0(X))* African American Images.
—SETCLAE, First Grade: Self-Esteem Through Culture Leads to Academic Excellence. 2003. (ENG.). 60p. (J). (gr. 1). pap. 9.95 *(978-0-913543-86-3(1))* African American Images.
—SETCLAE, Fourth Grade: Self-Esteem Through Culture Leads to Academic Excellence. 2003. (ENG.). 60p. (J). (gr. 4). pap. 9.95 *(978-0-913543-89-4(6))* African American Images.
—SETCLAE, High School: Self-Esteem Through Culture Leads to Academic Excellence. 2003. (ENG.). 60p. (J). (gr. 9-12). pap. 14.95 *(978-0-913543-94-8(2))* African American Images.
—SETCLAE, Kindergarten: Self-Esteem Through Culture Leads to Academic Excellence. 2003. (ENG.). 60p. (J). (gr. k). pap. 9.95 *(978-0-913543-85-6(3))* African American Images.
—SETCLAE, Second Grade: Self-Esteem Through Culture Leads to Academic Excellence. 2003. (ENG.). 60p. (J). (gr. 2). pap. 9.95 *(978-0-913543-87-0(X))* African American Images.
—SETCLAE, Seventh Grade: Self-Esteem Through Culture Leads to Academic Excellence. 2003. (ENG.). 60p. (J). (gr. 7). pap. 9.95 *(978-0-913543-92-4(6))* African American Images.
—SETCLAE, Sixth Grade: Self-Esteem Through Culture Leads to Academic Excellence. 2003. (ENG.). 60p. (J). (gr. 6). pap. 9.95 *(978-0-913543-91-7(8))* African American Images.
—SETCLAE, Third Grade: Self-Esteem Through Culture Leads to Academic Excellence. 2003. (ENG., Illus.). 60p. (J). (gr. 3). pap. 9.95 *(978-0-913543-88-7(8))* African American Images.
Landau, Jennifer, ed. Teens Talk about Self-Esteem & Self-Confidence. 2017. (Teen Voices: Real Teens Discuss Real Problems Ser.). (Illus.). 64p. (J). (gr. 12-17). 77.70 *(978-1-5081-7637-4(X))* Rosen Publishing Group, Inc., The.
Lazurek, Michelle S. Uniquely you. Wright, Alison H., illus. 2018. pap. 9.99 *(978-1-946638-70-0(6))* Elk Lake Publishing, Inc.
—Uniquely You. Wright, Alison H., illus. 2018. pap. 9.99 *(978-1-946638-69-4(2))* Elk Lake Publishing, Inc.

Levine, Amy-Jill & Eisenberg Sasso, Sandy. ¿Quién Cuenta? 100 Ovejas, 10 Monedas y 2 Hijos. Meganck, Margaux, illus. 2018. (ENG & SPA.). 40p. (J). (gr. -1-3). pap. 10.00 *(978-0-664-26406-2(9))* Westminster John Knox Pr.

Lewis, Jacqueline J. You Are So Wonderful. Tugeau, Jeremy, illus. 2020. 32p. (J). (gr. -1-2). 16.99 *(978-1-5064-6376-6(2),* Beaming Books) 1517 Media.

Lishinski, Ann King. Let Your Light Shine. Morello, Charles, ed. Lishinski, Jamie, illus. 2003. (J). pap. 9.95 *(978-0-9709575-0-4(5))* Singing River Pubns.

Lite, Lori. Affirmation Weaver: A Believe in Yourself Story, Designed to Help Children Boost Self-Esteem While Decreasing Stress & Anxiety (Indigo Dreams) 2008. (Illus.). 35p. (J). 14.95 *(978-0-9787781-5-6(4))* Stress Free Kids.

—Affirmation Weaver: A Believe in Yourself Story Designed to Help Children Increase Self-Esteem While Decreasing Stress & Anxiety. 2nd ed. 2011. 24p. pap. 14.95 *(978-0-9836256-9-8(7))* Stress Free Kids.

—Angry Octopus: An Anger Management Story Introducing Active Progressive Muscular Relaxation & Deep Breathing. 2011. (Illus.). 30p. (gr. -1-3). pap. 14.95 *(978-0-9836256-8-1(9))* Stress Free Kids.

—A Boy & a Turtle: A Relaxation Story Teaching Young Children Visualization Techniques to Increase Creativity While Lowering Stress & Anxiety Lev. 3rd ed. 2012.Tr. of niño y una Tortuga. (ENG.). 16p. (J). pap. 12.95 *(978-1-937985-13-4(X))* Stress Free Kids.

—Bubble Riding: A Relaxation Story Designed to Teach Children Visualization Techniques to Increase Creativity While Lowering Stress & Anxiety. 2012.Tr. of Montando Burbujas. (ENG.). (J). pap. 14.95 *(978-1-937985-03-5(2))* Stress Free Kids.

—Buenas Noches Oruga: Una Historia para la Relajación Que Ayuda a Los Niños a Controlar la Ira y el Estrés para Que Se Queden Dormidos Sosegadamente. 2012.Tr. of Goodnight Caterpillar. (SPA., Illus.). 16p. (J). pap. 12.95 *(978-1-937985-16-5(4))* Stress Free Kids.

—Caleta de la Nutria Marina: Un Cuento para la Ansiedad Infantil, Enseña la Relajación, la Respiración Profunda para Reducir la Ansiedad, el Estrés y la Ira, a la Vez Que Fomenta el Sueño Sosegado. 2011.Tr. of Sea Otter Cove. (SPA., Illus.). 28p. (J). pap. 14.95 *(978-1-937985-11-0(3))* Stress Free Kids.

—Children's Wellness Curriculum: Lessons, Stories & Techniques Designed to Decrease Bullying, Anxiety, Anger & Obesity While Promoting Self-Esteem & Healthy Food Choices. 2007. (J). (gr. k-5). 89.95 incl. audio compact disk *(978-0-9787781-2-5(X),* 5) Stress Free Kids.

—The Goodnight Caterpillar: A Children's Relaxation Story to Improve Sleep, Manage Stress, Anxiety, Anger. 3rd abr. ed. 2011.Tr. of Buenas Noches, Oruga. (ENG.). 18p. (J). pap. 12.95 *(978-1-937985-00-4(8))* Stress Free Kids.

—Montando Burbujas: Un Cuento con Ejercicios de Relajación para Niños, Diseñada para Enseñar a Los Niños Técnicas de Visualización para Aumentar la Creatividad Mientras Disminuyen Sus Niveles de Ansiedad y de Estrés. 2012.Tr. of Bubble Riding. (SPA., Illus.). 32p. (J). pap. 14.95 *(978-1-937985-12-7(1))* Stress Free Kids.

—El Niño y la Tortuga: Un Cuento para Promover la Relajación. 2012.Tr. of Boy & a Turtle. (SPA., Illus.). 16p. (J). pap. 12.95 *(978-1-937985-17-2(2))* Stress Free Kids.

—El Pulpo Enojado: Un Cuento Sobre Cómo Controlar la Ira Que Enseña la Relajación Muscular Activa y Progresiva, y la Respiración: un Cuento Sobre Cómo Controlar la Ira Que Enseña la Relajación Muscular Activa y Progresiva, y la Respiración. 2012.Tr. of Angry Octopus. (SPA., Illus.). 30p. (J). pap. 14.95 *(978-1-937985-01-1(6))* Stress Free Kids.

—Sea Otter Cove: A Relaxation Story, Introducing Deep Breathing to Decrease Anxiety, Stress & Anger While Promoting Peaceful Sleep. 2nd ed. 2012.Tr. of Caleta de la Nutria Marina. (SPA & ENG., Illus.). 24p. (J). 14.95 *(978-1-937985-08-0(3))* Stress Free Kids.

—Tejedor de Afirmaciones: Un Cuento Que Aumenta la Autoestima en Los Niños, Creer en Ellos Mismos, Mientras Que Reducen Su Estrés y Su Ansiedad. 2012.Tr. of Affirmation Weaver. (SPA., Illus.). 24p. (J). pap. 14.95 *(978-1-937985-02-8(4))* Stress Free Kids.

Markowitz, Siri. HELP with RAISING YOUR NURSERY or PRESCHOOL CHILDREN - 26 great ideas for parents & preschool Teachers. 2009. 44p. pap. 19.99 *(978-0-557-09610-7(3))* Lulu Pr., Inc.

McCloud, Carol. Have You Filled a Bucket Today? A Guide to Daily Happiness for Kids. Messing, David, illus. 2006. (ENG.). 32p. (J). (gr. -1-3). pap. 9.95 *(978-0-9785075-1-0(7),* Ferne Pr.) Nelson Publishing & Marketing.

Mccloud, Carol. Have You Filled a Bucket Today: A Guide to Daily Happiness for Kids. 2015. lib. bdg. 20.80 *(978-0-606-38236-6(4))* Turtleback.

McNulty John. I Am Your Self-Esteem. Gilmour, Karen, illus. 2006. 32p. (J). *(978-0-9769580-5-5(8))* I Am Your Playground LLC.

Mitchell-Tulloss, Delores. ABCs of Character for People Around the World. Hardison, Brian, illus. 2007. 32p. (J). pap. *(978-0-9670712-6-8(7))* zReyomi Publishing.

Moe, Barbara. Understanding Negative Body Image. 2009. (Teen Eating Disorder Prevention Book Ser.). 192p. (gr. 7-12). 63.90 *(978-1-61511-242-5(1))* Rosen Publishing Group, Inc., The.

Morse, Philip C. Kick Out Stress - Teen Stress Reduction Program: Improving Self-Esteem, Optimizing Performance in School & Sports & Improving Physical & Emotional Health. 2004. (YA). (gr. 8-12). pap. *(978-0-9748548-0-9(8))* Mind/Body Workshops.

Moss, Wendy L. Being Me: A Kid's Guide to Boosting Confidence & Self-Esteem. 2010. (Illus.). 112p. (J). (gr. 3-8). 14.95 *(978-1-4338-0883-8(8));* pap. 9.95 *(978-1-4338-0884-5(6))* American Psychological Assn. (Magination Pr.).

Mulcahy, William. Zach Hangs in There. McKee, Darren, illus. 2017. (Zach Rules Ser.). (ENG.). 32p. (J). (gr. k-3). 15.99 *(978-1-63198-162-3(5),* 81623) Free Spirit Publishing Inc.

Naik, Anita. Think Yourself Gorgeous: How to Feel Good - Inside & Out. 2012. (ENG., Illus.). 176p. (YA). (gr. 7). pap. 11.99 *(978-0-7499-5244-0(X),* Piatkus Bks.) Little, Brown Book Group Ltd. GBR. Dist: Independent Pubs. Group.

Noah, Michal Y. A-Z the Universe in Me. 2012. 18.95 *(978-0-7414-7841-2(2));* pap. 13.95 *(978-0-7414-7840-5(4))* Infinity Publishing.

O'Keefe, Susan Heyboer. Be the Star That You Are: A Book for Kids Who Feel Different. Alley, R. W., illus. 2005. (Elf-Help Books for Kids). (J). per. 7.95 *(978-0-87029-391-7(5))* Abbey Pr.

Onuoha-Ezemma, Glory. Don't Make Fun of My Name: My Name Is Special to My Parents & Me. unabr. ed. 2003. (Illus.). 47p. (J). (gr. k-6). pap. 9.95 *(978-0-9661598-6-8(1))* Orange County Publishing.

Onyett, Nicola & Williams, Tennessee. Study & Revise for AS/A Level: A Streetcar Named Desire by Tennessee Williams. 2011. (Philip Allan Literature Guide for A-Level Ser.). (ENG., Illus.). 96p. (gr. 10-12). pap. 24.95 *(978-1-4441-2156-8(1))* Trans-Atlantic Pubns., Inc.

Ornelas, Lourdes. So Can I. 2013. 32p. 25.99 *(978-1-4808-0189-9(5));* pap. 16.99 *(978-1-4808-0187-5(9))* Archway Publishing.

Ottaviano, Patricia. Girl World: How to Ditch the Drama & Find Your Inner Amazing. 2015. (ENG.). 160p. (YA). (gr. 6-12). pap. 12.99 *(978-1-4926-0912-4(9),* 9781492609124) Sourcebooks, Inc.

Rice, Ashley. Make Your Dreams Come True: A Girl's Guide to Always Believing in Yourself. 2015. 96p. pap. *(978-1-59842-865-0(9),* Blue Mountain Pr.) Blue Mountain Arts Inc.

Rodi, Robert & Ross, Laura. Staying Mentally Healthy, Vol. 10. Jennings, Kevin, ed. 2016. (Living Proud! Growing up LGBTQ Ser.). (Illus.). 64p. (J). (gr. 7). 23.95 *(978-1-4222-3510-2(6))* Mason Crest.

Rogers, Jennifer. While the Stars Are at Play. 2013. 30p. pap. 13.99 *(978-1-4525-6681-8(X))* Balboa Pr.

Rothenberg, B. Annye. Mommy & Daddy Are Always Supposed to Say Yes— Aren't They? Eldridge, Marion, illus. 2007. 40p. (J). pap. 9.95 *(978-0-9790420-0-3(3))* Perfecting Parenting Pr.

Rue, Nancy N. Everybody Tells Me to Be Myself but I Don't Know Who I Am. 2007. (Faithgirlz! Ser.). (ENG., Illus.). 144p. (J). (gr. 3-7). pap. 7.99 *(978-0-310-71295-4(5))* Zonderkidz.

Schab, Lisa M. Cool, Calm, Confident: A Workbook to Help Kids Learn Assertiveness Skills. 2009. (ENG.). 184p. (J). (gr. k-5). pap. 18.95 *(978-1-57224-630-0(8),* 6300, Instant Help Books) New Harbinger Pubns.

—Self-Esteem for Teens: Six Principles for Creating the Life You Want. 2016. (Instant Help Solutions Ser.). (ENG.). 184p. (YA). (gr. 6-12). pap. 23.95 *(978-1-62625-419-0(2),* 34190) New Harbinger Pubns.

—The Self-Esteem Habit for Teens: 50 Simple Ways to Build Your Confidence Every Day. 2018. (Instant Help Solutions Ser.). (ENG.). 200p. (YA). pap. 19.95 *(978-1-62625-919-5(4),* 39195) New Harbinger Pubns.

Schoenberg, Jill. Journal Buddies: A Girl's Journal for Sharing & Celebrating Magnificence. 2nd ed. 2007. (J). per. 16.95 *(978-0-9768623-0-7(1))* Blue Sky at Night Publishing.

Self-Esteem Garden. 2003. *(978-1-57543-116-1(5))* MAR*CO Products, Inc.

The Self-Esteem Handbook for Kids. 2004. (J). 24.95 *(978-0-9725836-0-2(2))* Long Life Publishing Co.

Serwaa, Maame. Perfect As I Am. Forkuo, Fleance, illus. 2018. (ENG.). 30p. (J). pap. 9.99 *(978-1-62676-800-0(5),* Melanin Origins, LLC) Grivante Pr.

Snow, Todd. You Are Important. Strong, Melodee, illus. 2007. (You Are Important Ser.). (ENG.). 24p. (J). (gr. -1-k). bds. 7.99 *(978-1-934277-06-5(1))* Maren Green Publishing, Inc.

Sommer, Carl. If Only I Were. . . 2003. (Another Sommer-Time Story Ser.). (Illus.). 48p. (J). (gr. 1-4). 16.95 incl. audio *(978-1-57537-551-9(6))* Advance Publishing, Inc.

—If Only I Were. . . James, Kennon, illus. 2003. (Another Sommer-Time Story Ser.). (ENG.). 48p. (J). 16.95 incl. audio compact disk *(978-1-57537-502-1(8))* Advance Publishing, Inc.

Standard Publishing Staff. Self Esteem. 2006. cd-rom 24.99 *(978-0-7847-1886-5(5))* Standard Publishing.

Stewart, Sheila. I Like Me. (Kids Have Troubles Too Ser.). 48p. (YA). (gr. 5-18). 2010. lib. bdg. 19.95 *(978-1-4222-1699-6(3))* 2009. pap. 7.95 *(978-1-4222-1912-6(7))* Mason Crest.

Stokes, Trinitee. Bold & Blessed: How to Stay True to Yourself & Stand Out from the Crowd. 1 vol. 2018. (ENG., Illus.). 224p. (J). pap. 14.99 *(978-0-310-76642-1(7))* Zondervan.

Storck, Kelly. The Gender Identity Workbook for Kids: A Guide to Exploring Who You Are. Grigni, Noah, illus. 2018. (ENG.). 176p. (J). (gr. k-5). pap. 18.95 *(978-1-68403-030-9(7),* 40309) New Harbinger Pubns.

Sunderland, Margot. Helping Children with Low Self-Esteem: A Guidebook. 2017. (Helping Children with Feelings Ser.). (ENG., Illus.). 96p. (C). pap. 37.95 *(978-0-86388-466-5(0),* Y329814) Routledge.

Swan, Richard. The Pardoner's Prologue & Tale. 2011. (Philip Allan Literature Guide for A-Level Ser.). (ENG., Illus.). 96p. (gr. 10-12). pap. 24.95 *(978-1-4441-2159-9(6))* Trans-Atlantic Pubns., Inc.

Tammen, Christina. C h u m P. 2010. 42p. pap. 13.95 *(978-1-935268-21-5(X))* Halo Publishing International.

Telgemeier, Raina. Smile. 2010. 21.00 *(978-1-60686-896-6(9))* Perfection Learning Corp.

—Smile. Telgemeier, Raina, illus. 2010. (ENG., Illus.). 224p. (J). (gr. 3-7). pap. 10.99 *(978-0-545-13206-0(1),* Graphix) Scholastic, Inc.

—Smile. 2010. lib. bdg. 22.10 *(978-0-606-14082-9(4))* Turtleback.

—Smile: a Graphic Novel. Telgemeier, Raina, illus. 2010. (ENG.). 224p. (J). (gr. 3-7). 24.99 *(978-0-545-13205-3(3),* Graphix) Scholastic, Inc.

Thomas, Natasha. Mommy & Daddy Is There Really Greatness in Me? 2013. (ENG.). 24p. (J). pap. 34.95 *(978-1-4327-8767-7(5))* Outskirts Pr., Inc.

Tiger Woods Foundation & Woods, Earl. Start Something: You Can Make a Difference. 2006. (ENG., Illus.). 144p. (gr. 4-7). pap. 14.00 *(978-1-4165-3704-5(X))* Simon & Schuster.

Tool Kits for Kids LLC Staff, creator. Charge up Your Confidence - Tool Kit for Kids: Elementary School Edition. 2008. (Illus.). (J). 39.95 *(978-0-9819483-2-4(4))* Tool Kits For Kids LLC.

—Charge up Your Confidence - Tool Kit for Kids: High School / Middle School Edition. 2009. (Illus.). (J). 39.95 *(978-0-9819483-3-1(2))* Tool Kits For Kids LLC.

Van Leeuwen, Michele D., creator. Summer Bridge Activities: Grades PK to K. 2012. (Summer Bridge Activities Ser.). (ENG., Illus.). 150p. pap. 14.95 *(978-1-60996-440-5(3))* Carson-Dellosa Publishing, LLC.

Vaughn, Wendy. For Children of the World with Love. 2003. 63p. pap. 19.95 *(978-1-4137-0124-1(8))* America Star Bks.

Viglione, Steve. The I AM! Affirmation Book (English-Spanish Edition) Discovering the Value of Who You Are. 2007. (Love - Wisdom Ser.). (Illus.). (J). 6.95 *(978-0-9645224-7-3(0))* I AM Foundation, The.

Vinci, Daniela V. Hi, My Name Is Daniela & I Want to Be a Great Woman: How I Found Me. 2008. 72p. pap. 10.95 *(978-0-595-52116-6(9))* iUniverse, Inc.

Weeber, Jochen. What in the World Is Wrong with Gisbert? Gholizadeh, Fariba, illus. 2018. (ENG.). 32p. (J). (gr. -1-3). 16.00 *(978-1-947888-02-9(1),* Flyaway Bks.) Westminster John Knox Pr.

Weiss, S. I. Coping with the Beauty Myth: A Guide for Real Girls. 2009. (Coping Ser.). 192p. (gr. 7-12). 63.90 *(978-1-61512-014-7(9))* Rosen Publishing Group, Inc., The.

West, Lorraine, illus. The Mirror & Me. 2005. 40p. (J). per. 12.95 *(978-0-9768674-0-1(0))* Hip Hop Schl. Hse.

Wilde, Jerry. Hot Stuff to Help Kids Cheer Up: The Depression & Self-Esteem Workbook. 2007. 80p. (J). (gr. 4-7). pap. 14.99 *(978-1-4022-0926-0(6))* Sourcebooks, Inc.

Wiley, Judith Gupton. Something More Special. 2011. 16p. 8.32 *(978-1-4567-4283-6(3))* AuthorHouse.

Yankee, Kris & Nelson, Marian. Are You Confident Today? 2014. (ENG., Illus.). 32p. (J). pap. 9.95 *(978-1-938326-24-0(5),* Ferne Pr.) Nelson Publishing & Marketing.

SELF-ESTEEM—FICTION

Abromovitz, Jaime. Baby Dreamer Ding-A-Ling: Ding-A-Lings. 2004. (Illus.). (J). per. 9.95 *(978-0-9762587-1-4(4))* StoryGirl Productions, LLC.

—Dreamer Ding-A-Ling: Ding-A-Lings: the Banana Phone. 2004. (Illus.). (J). per. 9.95 *(978-0-9762587-0-4(6))* StoryGirl Productions, LLC.

—Zazzy-Q Ding-A-Ling: Ding-A-Lings: the Magic Wand. 2004. (Illus.). (J). per. 9.95 *(978-0-9762587-2-8(2))* StoryGirl Productions, LLC.

Akerson, Julie Chicos. The Life of Riley the Cat. Taylor, Jennifer, illus. 2005. 28p. (J). 15.50 *(978-1-4120-5858-2(9))* Trafford Publishing.

Aldrich, Jodi. Bee Mumble & Wug. 2011. 36p. (J). pap. 20.95 *(978-1-4327-6808-9(5))* Outskirts Pr., Inc.

Alexander, Kwame. Booked. (Crossover Ser.). (ENG.). (J). (gr. 5-7). 2019. 336p. pap. 9.99 *(978-1-328-59630-7(3),* 1731272) 2016. 320p. 16.99 *(978-0-544-57098-6(7),* 1612557) HarperCollins Pubs. (Clarion Bks.).

—Booked. 2016. lib. bdg. 29.40 *(978-0-606-37992-2(4))* Turtleback.

Almada, Ariel Andrés. Walking Through a World of Aromas. Brokenbrow, Jon, tr. Wimmer, Sonja, illus. 2013. (ENG.). 24p. (J). (gr. k-3). 16.95 *(978-84-15619-48-2(0))* Cuento de Luz SL ESP. Dist: Publishers Group West (PGW).

Amenii, Nehprii. Memories of the Little Elephant. 2008. (Illus.). 60p. (J). 24.95 *(978-0-9797010-0-9(7))* Khunum Productions, Inc.

Ana, Reverend & Binkow, Howard. Howard B. Wigglebottom Listens to His Heart. Cornelison, Susan F., illus. 2nd ed. 2008. (Howard B. Wigglebottom Ser.). (ENG.). 32p. (J). (gr. -1-3). 15.00 *(978-0-9715390-2-0(2),* ac6db1e7-fc6b-47b5-b36f-019875126f32, We Do Listen) We Do Listen Foundation.

Appelt, Kathi. Incredible Me! Karas, G. Brian, illus. 2003. (ENG.). 32p. (J). (gr. -1-3). 17.99 *(978-0-06-028622-4(9),* HarperCollins) HarperCollins Pubs.

Applehead, Zippy. You Are Who You Be. 2012. 28p. pap. 24.95 *(978-1-4626-6505-1(5))* America Star Bks.

Attaway-Young, Andrea & Lane Durbin, Deborah. The Secret Treasure - A Fairy Tale. 2010. (ENG.). 40p. 9.95 *(978-1-934363-70-6(7))* Zoe Life Christian Communications.

Bakker, Merel. Maks & Mila on a Special Journey. Mini Pois Etc. illus. 2013. 54p. *(978-2-9700865-0-5(6))* Mila Publishing, Merel Bakker.

Balash, Sue Beth. Mimi the Inchworm. 2009. (ENG.). 32p. pap. 10.95 *(978-1-933916-44-6(3),* Ferne Pr.) Nelson Publishing & Marketing.

Banks, Piper. Geek Abroad, 2 vols. 2008. (Geek High Ser.: 2). (ENG.). 256p. (YA). (gr. 9-18). 9.99 *(978-0-451-22393-7(4),* Berkley) Penguin Publishing Group.

—Revenge of the Geek. 2010. (Geek High Ser.: 4). (ENG.). 256p. (gr. 12-18). 9.99 *(978-0-451-23134-5(1),* Berkley) Penguin Publishing Group.

—Summer of the Geek. 2010. (Geek High Ser.: 3). (ENG.). 256p. (YA). (gr. 5-18). 9.99 *(978-0-451-22984-7(3),* Berkley) Penguin Publishing Group.

Banting, Celia. I Only Said Yes So That They'd Like Me. 2006. (Illus.). 224p. (YA). per. 14.99 *(978-0-9786648-1-7(7))* Wighita Pr.

Baratz-Logsted, Lauren. Me, in Between. 2008. (ENG.). 208p. (J). (gr. 4-8). pap. 5.99 *(978-1-4169-5068-4(0),* Simon & Schuster/Paula Wiseman Bks.) Simon & Schuster/Paula Wiseman Bks.

Beaudoin, Sean. Going Nowhere Faster. 2008. (ENG.). 256p. (J). (gr. 7-17). pap. 13.99 *(978-0-316-01416-8(8))* Little, Brown Bks. for Young Readers.

Beaumont, Karen. I Like Myself! Catrow, David, illus. 2004. (ENG.). 32p. (J). (gr. -1-3). 18.99 *(978-0-15-202013-2(6),* 1191551, Clarion Bks.) HarperCollins Pubs.

—I Like Myself! Board Book. Catrow, David, illus. 2016. (ENG.). 32p. (J). (gr. -1 — 1). bds. 9.99 *(978-0-544-64101-3(9),* 1620821, Clarion Bks.) HarperCollins Pubs.

—I Like Myself! Lap Board Book. Catrow, David, illus. 2010. (ENG.). 32p. (J). (gr. -1 — 1). bds. 14.99 *(978-0-547-40163-8(9),* 1427978, Clarion Bks.) HarperCollins Pubs.

Bellingham, Brenda. Lilly Takes the Lead. MacDonald, Clarke, illus. 2006. (Formac First Novels Ser.: 34). (ENG.). 64p. (gr. 2-5). 14.95 *(978-0-88780-703-9(8),* 703); (J). 4.95 *(978-0-88780-701-5(1),* 701) Formac Publishing Co., Ltd. CAN. Dist: Formac Lorimer Bks. Ltd.

Benoff-Nadel, Phyllis. The Magical Garden. 2013. 32p. pap. 16.99 *(978-1-4525-7445-5(6),* Balboa Pr.) Author Solutions, LLC.

Biancakrystal. Clap to Beauty: A toddler self-esteem Book. 2011. 16p. pap. 10.00 *(978-1-4634-1693-5(8))* AuthorHouse.

Birkholz, Gay Lyn. Veneti: Lake Michigan's Treasure. Williamson, Linda K., illus. 2010. 52p. pap. 17.00 *(978-1-60860-129-5(3),* Strategic Bk. Publishing) Strategic Book Publishing & Rights Agency (SBPRA).

Black, Cassandra. Twinkle: The Only Firefly Who Couldn't Light Up. Kirk, Tim, illus. 3rd ed. 2012. (ENG.). 111p. (J). (gr. 4-7). pap. 12.99 *(978-0-9742739-3-8(7))* Lavender Bks.

Bowe, Julie. Pompom Problems. 2015. (Victoria Torres, Unfortunately Average Ser.). (ENG., Illus.). 160p. (J). (gr. 4-8). lib. bdg. 27.99 *(978-1-4965-0532-3(8),* 128604, Stone Arch Bks.) Capstone.

Bowser, Ken. Bobbi's Big Brake: Self-Confidence. Bowser, Ken, illus. 2016. (Funny Bone Readers (tm) — Truck Pals on the Job Ser.). (ENG., Illus.). 24p. (J). (gr. k-2). E-Book 30.65 *(978-1-63440-064-0(X))* Red Chair Pr.

—Lawni Takes the Field: Teamwork. Bowser, Ken, illus. 2016. (Funny Bone Readers (tm) — Truck Pals on the Job Ser.). (ENG., Illus.). 24p. (J). (gr. k-2). E-Book 30.65 *(978-1-63440-076-3(3))* Red Chair Pr.

Boynton, Sandra. Woo Hoo! You're Doing Great! 2023. (ENG., Illus.). 40p. (J). (gr. k-3). 17.99 *(978-0-316-48679-8(5))* Little, Brown Bks. for Young Readers.

Briggs, Mayke Beckmann. Here You Are. Briggs, Mayke Beckmann, illus. 2007. (Illus.). 44p. (J). 16.95 *(978-0-9776469-1-3(2))* BoathouseBooks.

Brosgol, Vera. Anya's Ghost. Brosgol, Vera, illus. 2011. (ENG., Illus.). 224p. (YA). (gr. 7-12). 24.99 *(978-1-59643-713-5(8),* 900075181, First Second Bks.) Roaring Brook Pr.

Broski, Julie. Being Me. Vigia, Vincent, illus. 2011. (Rookie Ready to Learn Ser.). 40p. (J). (ENG.). pap. 5.95 *(978-0-531-26653-3(2));* (gr. -1-k). lib. bdg. 23.00 *(978-0-531-26428-7(9))* Scholastic Library Publishing. (Children's Pr.).

Brown, Ayanna. I Am Beautiful, for All the Children of the World, 1 vol. Elliot, Lee, photos by. 2010. (Illus.). 20p. pap. 24.95 *(978-1-4489-8112-0(3))* PublishAmerica, Inc.

Brudos, Susan E. & Rubino, Alisa A., illus. Wayne's Trail. 2004. (J). pap. *(978-0-932991-62-1(9))* Place In The Woods, The.

Burk, Josh. The Summer of Saint Nick. 2007. (ENG.). 152p. (YA). per. 12.95 *(978-0-9768042-2-2(0))* Maven Of Memory Publishing.

Byers, Grace. I Am Enough. Bobo, Keturah A., illus. 2018. (ENG.). 32p. (J). (gr. -1-3). 18.99 *(978-0-06-266712-0(2),* Balzer & Bray) HarperCollins Pubs.

Byrd, Jeff, illus. A Tale of Two Tails, el Perro con Dos Colas: A children's story in English & Spanish. 2004.Tr. of Perro con Dos Colas. (SPA.). (J). (gr. -1-3). per. 14.95 *(978-0-9746024-0-0(X))* One Arm Publishing.

Campisi, Stephanie. The Ugly Dumpling. Kober, Shahar, illus. 2016. (ENG.). 32p. (J). (-3). 15.95 *(978-1-938063-67-1(8),* Mighty Media Kids) Mighty Media Pr.

Cannistra, Meg. The Trouble with Shooting Stars. 2019. (ENG., Illus.). 336p. (J). (gr. 3-7). 17.99 *(978-1-5344-2896-6(8),* Simon & Schuster Bks. For Young Readers) Simon & Schuster Bks. For Young Readers.

Carlson, Nancy. ¡Piensa en Grande! 2005. (Libros Ilustrados (Picture Bks.)). (SPA., Illus.). 32p. (J). (gr. k-2). lib. bdg. 15.95 *(978-0-8225-3192-0(5),* Ediciones Lerner) Lerner Publishing Group.

—Think Big! 2005. (Illus.). 28p. (J). (gr. -1-3). 15.95 *(978-1-57505-622-7(4),* Carolrhoda Bks.) Lerner Publishing Group.

Carman, Debby. I'm Maximum Cat. That's a Fact! 2007. (Illus.). 28p. (J). 14.99 *(978-0-9777340-2-3(1))* Faux Paw Media Group.

—Kittywimpuss Got Game. Carman, Debby, illus. 2007. (Illus.). 28p. (J). (gr. -1-1). 14.99 *(978-0-9777340-4-7(8))* Faux Paw Media Group.

Caruso, Rosalie. How I taught my mom... the Law of Attraction. 2010. 48p. 17.45 *(978-1-4525-0135-2(1))* Get Published.

Cattanach, Ann. Malpas the Dragon. Renouf, Michael, illus. 2007. 28p. (C). (gr. 3-7). per. 17.95 *(978-1-84310-572-5(1),* 691969) Kingsley, Jessica Pubs. GBR. Dist: Hachette UK Distribution.

Chandler Goldstein. Georgette: A Little Frog Discovers the Value in Revealing Her True Self! 2012. 20p. pap. 15.99 *(978-1-4772-0835-9(6))* AuthorHouse.

Charaipotra, Sona & Clayton, Dhonielle. Shiny Broken Pieces: a Tiny Pretty Things Novel. 2017. (ENG.). 384p. (YA). (gr. 9). pap. 10.99 *(978-0-06-234243-0(6),* HarperTeen) HarperCollins Pubs.

Chartier, Brent & Jones, Patrick. The Franchise. 2013. (Opportunity Ser.). (ENG.). 104p. (YA). (gr. 6-12). pap. 7.95 *(978-1-4677-1496-9(8),* 4c2e72dc-bf80-48ba-b1f0-f567f0997a91, Darby Creek) Lerner Publishing Group.

Chen, Eva. Juno Valentine & the Magical Shoes. Desierto, Derek, illus. 2018. (Juno Valentine Ser.). (ENG.). 32p. (J). 18.99 *(978-1-250-29726-6(5),* 900195905) Feiwel & Friends.

Chen, Justina. Nothing but the Truth (and a Few White Lies). 2007. (Justina Chen Novel Ser.). (ENG.). 256p. (J). (gr. 7-17). per. 15.99 *(978-0-316-01131-0(2))* Little, Brown Bks. for Young Readers.

Choyce, Lesley. Book of Michael, 1 vol. 2008. (ENG.). 224p. (YA). (gr. 9-12). pap. 9.95 *(978-0-88995-417-5(8),* 46f6c2d9-d965-4aff-bb00-a2db42ea87fb) Trifolium Bks., Inc. CAN. Dist: Firefly Bks., Ltd.

Clanton, Ben. Rot, the Cutest in the World! Clanton, Ben, illus. 2017. (ENG., Illus.). 40p. (J). (gr. -1-3). 17.99 *(978-1-4814-6762-9(X),* Atheneum Bks. for Young Readers) Simon & Schuster Children's Publishing.

Clarion Books, Clarion. Girl Power 5-Minute Stories. 2015. (5-Minute Stories Ser.). (ENG., Illus.). 224p. (J). (gr. -1-3). 12.99 *(978-0-544-33925-5(8),* 1584496, Clarion Bks.) HarperCollins Pubs.

Clarissa - Evaluation Guide: Evaluation Guide. 2006. (J). *(978-1-55942-402-8(8))* Witcher Productions.

Clarke, Jane. Plodney Creeper, Supersloth. 2006. (Blue Bananas Ser.). (ENG., Illus.). 48p. (J). (gr. -1-3). *(978-0-7787-0896-4(9))* Crabtree Publishing Co.

Clevenger, Lee. IncrediBoy: Be Careful What You Wish. 2004. 267p. (J). pap. 12.95 *(978-0-9764052-0-7(2))* Thomas Max Publishing.

S

Codell, Esmé Raji & Codell, Esmé Raji. Sahara Special. 2004. (ENG.). 192p. (J). (gr. 3-7). pap. 7.99 (978-0-7868-1611-8(2)) Little, Brown Bks. for Young Readers.

Cohn, Rachel. You Know Where to Find Me. 2009. (ENG.). 224p. (YA). (gr. 7). pap. 8.99 (978-0-689-87860-2(5), Simon & Schuster Bks. For Young Readers) Simon & Schuster Bks. For Young Readers.

—You Know Where to Find Me. 2008. (ENG.). 204p. (YA). (gr. 7-12). 22.44 (978-0-689-87859-6(1)) Simon & Schuster, Inc.

Colagiovanni, Marc. When Things Aren't Going Right, Go Left. Reynolds, Peter H., illus. 2023. (ENG.). 32p. (J). (gr. -1-3). 18.99 (978-1-338-83118-4(6), Orchard Bks.) Scholastic, Inc.

Cole, Kathryn. Never Give Up: A Story about Self-Esteem, 1 vol. Leng, Qin, illus. 2015. (I'm a Great Little Kid Ser.: 7). (ENG.). 24p. (J). (gr. 1-3). 15.95 (978-1-927583-60-9(8)) Second Story Pr. CAN. Dist: Orca Bk. Pubs. USA.

Conner, Wendy Simpson. Princess of the Moon. (Illus.). (J). 16.95 (978-1-889599-20-5(4)) Interstellar Publishing Co.

Cook, Julia. Cliques Just Don't Make Cents, Volume 1. DuFalla, Anita, illus. 2012. (Building Relationships Ser.). (ENG.). 31p. (J). (gr. k-6). pap. 11.95 (978-1-934490-39-6(3)) Boys Town Pr.

Cottswold, Wooley. Rose & the Bald-Headed Elephant. 2009. (Illus.). 28p. (J). 16.95 (978-0-9779064-0-6(X)) Archie Publishing.

Covey, Sean. Just the Way I Am: Habit 1. Curtis, Stacy, illus. 2018. (7 Habits of Happy Kids Ser.: 1). (ENG.). 32p. (J). (gr. -1-1). 6.99 (978-1-5344-1577-5(7), Simon & Schuster Bks. For Young Readers) Simon & Schuster Bks. For Young Readers.

—Just the Way I Am: Habit 1 (Ready-To-Read Level 2) Curtis, Stacy, illus. 2019. (7 Habits of Happy Kids Ser.: 1). (ENG.). 32p. (J). (gr. k-2). 17.99 (978-1-5344-4445-4(9)); pap. 4.99 (978-1-5344-4444-7(0)) Simon Spotlight. (Simon Spotlight).

Crane, Stephen. The Red Badge of Courage: With a Discussion of Self-Esteem. Clift, Eva, illus. 2003. (Values in Action Illustrated Classics Ser.). 190p. (J). (978-1-59203-034-7(3)) Learning Challenge, Inc.

CUNNINGHAM, WHO AM I SAUNDA. Who am I? 2008. 75p. pap. 14.95 (978-1-4357-0475-6(4)) Lulu Pr., Inc.

Curtis, Jamie Lee. I'm Gonna Like Me: Letting off a Little Self-Esteem. Cornell, Laura, illus. 2007. (ENG.). 32p. (J). (gr. -1-3). 19.99 (978-0-06-028761-0(6), HarperCollins) HarperCollins Pubs.

Dahl, Michael. A Jar of Eyeballs. Sinkovec, Igor, illus. 2015. (Igor's Lab of Fear Ser.). (ENG.). 40p. (J). (gr. 4-8). lib. bdg. 23.99 (978-1-4965-0455-5(0), 128480, Stone Arch Bks.) Capstone.

Dahnke, Julie. I'm Not Perfect So What? 2012. 20p. pap. 15.99 (978-1-4772-5662-6(8)) AuthorHouse.

Danziger, Paula. I, Amber Brown. Ross, Tony, illus. 2011. (Amber Brown Ser.: 8). (ENG.). 160p. (J). (gr. 2-5). 6.99 (978-0-14-241965-6(6), Puffin Books) Penguin Young Readers Group.

—I, Amber Brown. 2004. (Amber Brown Ser.: No. 8). 144p. (J). (gr. 2-4). pap. 17.00 incl. audio (978-0-8072-2064-1(7), Listening Library) Random Hse. Audio Publishing Group.

Darden, Hunter. Pete's Angel. Vaca, Sally, illus. 2008. 44p. pap. 12.00 (978-1-60693-264-3(0), Strategic Bk. Publishing) Strategic Book Publishing & Rights Agency (SBPRA).

Debeer, Kristen. I Believe in You: A Mother's Message to Her Son with Learning Differences. Santy, Elizabeth & Fisher, Jessie, illus. 2012. 32p. pap. 12.97 (978-1-61897-802-8(0), Strategic Bk. Publishing) Strategic Book Publishing & Rights Agency (SBPRA).

Defillippo, Steve. Growing up Nicely! Grammy Helps Adam Grow up & Develop Social Skills & Moral Values. 2012. 24p. (-18). pap. 15.99 (978-1-4797-0957-1(3)) Xlibris Corp.

DelleCava, Karen. A Closer Look. 2011. 304p. (YA). (gr. 9-18). 16.95 (978-1-934813-49-2(4)) Westside Bks.

deVos, Kelly. Fat Girl on a Plane. 2018. (ENG.). 384p. (YA). 18.99 (978-0-373-21253-8(4), Harlequin Teen) Harlequin Enterprises ULC CAN. Dist: HarperCollins Pubs.

Dewdney, Anna. Little Excavator. 2017. (Illus.). 40p. (J). (-k). 18.99 (978-1-101-99920-2(9), Viking Books for Young Readers) Penguin Young Readers Group.

Diggle, David Mark. Barbara: A Sssslithering Adventure of Self Discovery. Diggle, Daniel James, illus. 2011. 24p. (J). pap. (978-0-9871657-9-4(8)) Diggle de Doo Productions Pty, Ltd.

Dipucchio, Kelly. Clink. Myers, Matthew, illus. 2011. (ENG.). 32p. (J). (gr. -1-2). 17.99 (978-0-06-192928-1(X), Balzer & Bray) HarperCollins Pubs.

Dixon, Tiffany. Everyone Is Special. 2008. 16p. per. 24.95 (978-1-60441-231-4(3)) America Star Bks.

Docherty, Helen. Do You Remember? Beech, Mark, illus. 2018. (ENG.). 32p. pap. 8.95 (978-0-571-32114-8(3), Faber & Faber Children's Bks.) Faber & Faber, Inc.

Donovan, Rebecca. Out of Breath, 0 vols. unabr. ed. 2013. (Breathing Ser.: 3). (ENG.). 432p. (YA). (gr. 7-12). pap. 9.99 (978-1-4778-1718-6(2), 9781477817186, Skyscape) Amazon Publishing.

Douglas, Babette. Curly Hare Gets It Straight. Williams, Ted, illus. 2006. (Kiss a Me Teacher Creature Stories Ser.). (J). (gr. -1-3). (978-1-890343-35-4(8)) Kiss A Me Productions, Inc.

Dowell, Frances O'Roark. Chicken Boy. 2007. (ENG., Illus.). 224p. (J). (gr. 5-9). pap. 7.99 (978-1-4169-3482-0(0), Atheneum Bks. for Young Readers) Simon & Schuster Children's Publishing.

Doyle, Malachy. Long Gray Norris. 2006. (Yellow Bananas Ser.). (ENG., Illus.). 48p. (J). (gr. -1-3). (978-0-7787-1002-8(5)) Crabtree Publishing Co.

Dreiling, Christy. Holes in My Socks. 2005. pap. 16.95 (978-0-9771891-0-6(4)) Holes In My Socks Publishing.

Dubovoy, Silvia. Turquesita. (SPA.). (J). pap. (978-968-6465-18-1(9)) Casa de Estudios de Literatura y Talleres Artisticos Amaquemecan A.C. MEX. Dist: Lectorum Pubns., Inc.

Dufayet, Danielle. Fantastic You. Zivoin, Jennifer, illus. 2019. 32p. (J). (978-1-4338-3028-0(0), Magination Pr.) American Psychological Assn.

Dyan, Penelope. You Are Okay! Dyan, Penelope, illus. 2013. (Illus.). 34p. pap. 11.95 (978-1-61477-070-1(0)) Bellissima Publishing, LLC.

Echols, Jennifer. The One That I Want. 2012. (ENG., Illus.). 288p. (YA). (gr. 7). pap. 9.99 (978-1-4424-5236-7(6), Simon Pulse) Simon Pulse.

Ewart, Franzeska G. Speak up, Spike. Oliver, Mark, illus. 2005. (Yellow Go Bananas Ser.). (ENG.). 48p. (J). (gr. 3-4). (978-0-7787-2744-6(0)); lib. bdg. (978-0-7787-2722-4(X)) Crabtree Publishing Co.

Flake, Sharon G. The Skin I'm In. 2007. (J). lib. bdg. 19.65 (978-1-4178-0860-1(8)) Turtleback.

Fleischman, Paul. Breakout. 2003. (ENG.). 160p. (J). 15.95 (978-0-8126-2696-4(6)) Cricket Bks.

—Breakout. 2005. (ENG.). 144p. (YA). (gr. 7). reprint ed. pap. 6.99 (978-0-689-87189-4(9), Simon Pulse) Simon Pulse.

Foltz, Joanna "Gwen". The Owl Tree. 2011. 28p. pap. 13.59 (978-1-4634-1199-2(5)) AuthorHouse.

Folz, Alexandra. Indigo's Bracelet. 2010. 84p. pap. 9.95 (978-1-4525-0058-4(4)) Get Published.

Franklin, Ashley. Not Quite Snow White. Glenn, Ebony, illus. 2019. (ENG.). 32p. (J). (gr. -1-3). 17.99 (978-0-06-279860-2(X), HarperCollins) HarperCollins Pubs.

Franklin, Shirley A. Lupita's Quinciner: A Celebration to Remember. 2008. 48p. pap. 8.95 (978-1-4401-0234-9(1)) iUniverse, Inc.

Fredericks, Mariah. Life. Watkins, Liselotte, illus. 2009. (In the Cards Ser.: No. 3). (ENG.). 272p. (J). pap. 5.99 (978-0-689-87659-2(9), Simon & Schuster/Paula Wiseman Bks.) Simon & Schuster/Paula Wiseman Bks.

Furtado, Sierra. Life Uploaded. 2016. 242p. (YA). pap. (978-1-5011-4396-0(4), Gallery Bks.) Gallery Bks.

Gadot, Eran. Supernatural Hero. 2019. (ENG., Illus.). 176p. (J). (gr. 3-6). pap. 7.99 (978-1-58270-688-7(3), Beyond Words) Simon & Schuster.

Gallucci, Susie. Believe I-Can. Sellers, Amy, illus. 2006. (J). (978-0-9776074-1-9(0)) Pounce To Success International, Inc.

—Dream I-Can. Sellers, Amy, illus. 2006. (J). (978-0-9776074-2-6(9)) Pounce To Success International, Inc.

Gano, Debra. Beauty's Secret. Pitre, Dawn, illus. 2008. (Heartlight Girls Ser.). 54p. (J). 17.95 (978-0-9787689-0-4(6)) Heartlight Girls.

Garcia, Mary. Play with Me: Togetherness Time for Your Preschooler & You. (J). 2007. 16.95 (978-0-9790931-2-8(0)) 2006. 16.95 (978-0-9790931-0-4(4)) SMARTseeds Co., LLC, The.

—Play with Me: Togetherness Time for Your Preschooler & You: St. Valentine's Day. 2007. (J). (978-0-9790931-1-1(2)) SMARTseeds Co., LLC, The.

Gayle, Sherri. Bubbles of Faith. 2013. 48p. pap. 11.95 (978-1-61244-076-7(2)) Halo Publishing International.

Genhart, Michael. Rainbow: A First Book of Pride. Passchier, Anne, illus. 2019. 24p. (J). (978-1-4338-3087-7(6), Magination Pr.) American Psychological Assn.

Gerbay, Susanne. Butterflies. 2012. (Fiction Ser.). (ENG.). 256p. (J). pap. 4.99 (978-1-61067-043-2(4)) Kane Miller.

Gifaldi, David. Toby Scudder, King of the School. 2005. (ENG.). 208p. (J). (gr. 5-7). pap. 12.95 (978-0-618-55158-3(1), 100824, Clarion Bks.) HarperCollins Pubs.

Going, K. L. King of the Screwups. 2009. (ENG., Illus.). 320p. (YA). (gr. 7-12). 22.44 (978-0-15-206258-3(0)) Harcourt Children's Bks.

Goobie, Beth. Something Girl, 1 vol. 2005. (Orca Soundings Ser.). (ENG.). 128p. (YA). (gr. 8-12). pap. 9.95 (978-1-55143-347-9(8), 1551433478) Orca Bk. Pubs. USA.

Goodman, Shawn. Kindness for Weakness. 2015. (ENG.). 272p. (YA). (gr. 9). pap. 9.99 (978-0-385-74325-9(4), Ember) Random Hse. Children's Bks.

Gordon, David. The Ugly Truckling. Gordon, David, illus. 2004. (Illus.). 32p. (J). (gr. -1-2). lib. bdg. 16.89 (978-0-06-054601-4(8), Geringer, Laura Book) HarperCollins Pubs.

Goss, Leon. Selfus Esteemus Personalitus Low. Tunell, Ken, illus. 2005. (J). pap. (978-1-933156-08-8(2), VisionQuest Kids) GSVQ Publishing.

Goss, Leon, 3rd. Selfus Esteemus Personalitus Low. Tunell, Ken, illus. 2005. 32p. (J). per. 16.99 (978-1-933156-00-2(7), VisionQuest Kids) GSVQ Publishing.

Greene, Bette. Summer of My German Soldier (Puffin Modern Classics) 2006. (Puffin Modern Classics Ser.). (ENG.). 240p. (J). (gr. 5-18). 8.99 (978-0-14-240651-9(1), Puffin Books) Penguin Young Readers Group.

Griffin, Saundra J. Which Should I Be? 2004. 21p. pap. 24.95 (978-1-4137-3167-5(8)) PublishAmerica, Inc.

Hairston, Lisa Lee. Victoria Has A Secret. 2011. 36p. 23.00 (978-1-4269-4994-4(4)) Trafford Publishing.

Hale, Bruce. Danny & the Dinosaur: Too Tall. Cutting, David, illus. 2015. 29p. (J). (978-1-4806-8575-8(5)) Harper & Row Ltd.

Hale, Shannon. Forest Born. 2017. (Books of Bayern Ser.). (ENG.). 400p. (YA). pap. 10.99 (978-1-68119-319-9(1), 900165750, Bloomsbury USA Childrens) Bloomsbury Publishing USA.

Hall, Deirdre Riordan. Sugar, 0 vols. 2015. (ENG.). 276p. (YA). (gr. 7-12). pap. 9.99 (978-1-4778-2938-7(5), 9781477829387, Skyscape) Amazon Publishing.

Halley, Marilyn. Apple-Green Eyes. 2005. pap. 8.00 (978-0-8059-6681-7(1)) Dorrance Publishing Co., Inc.

Hallmark, Danna G. How Do I Feel Happy? How Do I Feel Sad? 2008. 36p. pap. 24.95 (978-1-4241-9178-9(5)) PublishAmerica, Inc.

Han, Jenny. Shug. 2007. (ENG.). 256p. (J). (gr. 4-8). pap. 8.99 (978-1-4169-0943-9(5), Simon & Schuster/Paula Wiseman Bks.) Simon & Schuster Bks. For Young Readers.

—Shug. 2006. (ENG., Illus.). 256p. (YA). (gr. 7-8). 19.99 (978-1-4169-0942-2(7)) Simon & Schuster, Inc.

Hansen, MaryAnn Shelley. Sam the Second. 2010. 32p. 14.49 (978-1-4520-2408-0(1)) AuthorHouse.

Harper, Charise Mericle. Cupcake. Harper, Charise Mericle, illus. 2010. (ENG., Illus.). 32p. (J). (gr. -1-3). 14.99 (978-1-4231-1897-8(9)) Hyperion Pr.

Harris, Devon D. Yes I Can. 2006. (Illus.). 48p. (J). (978-0-9764082-4-6(4)) Waterhouse Publishing.

Hartnett, Sonya. Butterfly. 2013. (ENG.). 240p. (YA). (gr. 9). pap. 7.99 (978-0-7636-6334-6(4)) Candlewick Pr.

Hawley, Bobby. By Golly, Molly, You're Right. 2006. 48p. pap. 16.95 (978-1-4241-2085-7(3)) PublishAmerica, Inc.

Hayes, Sonia. Ms. Thang. 2009. (ENG.). 200p. (YA). per. 9.95 (978-0-9777573-0-5(7)) NUA Multimedia.

—Urban Goddess. 2007. 224p. (YA). per. 9.95 (978-0-9777573-1-2(5)) NUA Multimedia.

Haynes, Marilee. A. K. A. Genius. 2013. (ENG.). 208p. (J). 9.95 (978-0-8198-0830-1(X)) Pauline Bks. & Media.

Hearth, Liese. My Dog Burps. 2008. 14p. pap. 24.95 (978-1-4241-9608-1(6)) America Star Bks.

Heinz, Renata Perpetua. Nali's Life. 2008. 17p. pap. 24.95 (978-1-4241-9245-8(5)) America Star Bks.

Helen, Grace. Vicky Sticky Lips: Putting Others to the Test. 2012. 24p. 24.95 (978-1-4626-5975-3(6)) America Star Bks.

Hernandez, Jo Ann Yolanda. The Throwaway Piece. 2006. 246p. (J). (gr. 6). per. 9.95 (978-1-55885-353-9(7), Piñata Books) Arte Publico Pr.

Herrndorf, Wolfgang. You, Me, & a Russian Jeep. 2013. 245p. (YA). pap. (978-0-545-48181-6(3), Levine, Arthur A. Bks.) Scholastic, Inc.

Hill, Janet Muirhead. Kendall's Storm. Leonhard, Herb, illus. 2011. (J). pap. 12.00 (978-0-9820893-0-9(9)) Raven Publishing Inc. of Montana.

—Kyleah's Tree. Leonhard, Herb, illus. 2011. (J). pap. 12.00 (978-0-9827377-9-8(3)) Raven Publishing Inc. of Montana.

Holder, Amy. The Lipstick Laws. 2011. (ENG.). 240p. (YA). (gr. 7-18). pap. 13.99 (978-0-547-36306-6(0), 1421941, Clarion Bks.) HarperCollins Pubs.

Homzie, Hillary. Things Are Gonna Get Ugly. 2009. (Mix Ser.). (ENG.). 272p. (J). (gr. 4-8). pap. 5.99 (978-1-4169-7563-2(2), Aladdin) Simon & Schuster Children's Publishing.

Honsinger, Linda. Leonard Lou: Beautiful, Brave, Strong, & True. Honsinger, Alise, illus. 2012. 38p. 24.95 (978-1-4626-6872-4(0)) America Star Bks.

Hoog, Mark. Your Song: A Growing Field Adventure. Aukerman, Robert J., illus. 2007. (ENG.). 43p. (J). (gr. -1-3). 16.95 (978-0-9770391-2-8(9)) Growing Field Bks.

Hoog, Mark E. Dream Machine: A Growing Field Adventure. Aukerman, Robert J., illus. 2007. (Growing Field Adventure Ser.). (ENG.). 35p. (J). (gr. -1-3). 16.95 (978-0-9770391-1-1(0), 5000) Growing Field Bks.

Hopkins, Ellen. Perfect. (ENG., (YA). (gr. 9). 2013. Illus.). 656p. pap. 14.99 (978-1-4169-8325-5(2)) 2011. 640p. 18.99 (978-1-4169-8324-8(4)) McElderry, Margaret K. Bks. (McElderry, Margaret K. Bks.).

Howard, Chloe. Stand Beautiful, 1 vol. Melmon, Deborah, illus. 2018. (ENG.). 32p. (J). 16.99 (978-0-310-76495-3(5)) Zonderkidz.

—Stand Beautiful: A Story of Brokenness, Beauty & Embracing It All, 1 vol. 2018. (ENG., Illus.). 208p. (YA). pap. 16.99 (978-0-310-76513-4(7)) Zondervan.

Howland, Leila. Hello, Sunshine. 2018. (ENG.). 368p. (YA). (gr. 9-17). pap. 9.99 (978-1-4847-2850-5(5)) Hyperion Bks. for Children.

Jacono, Mary Kaye. Lenny's Gift. 2005. 27p. pap. 10.95 (978-0-7414-2602-4(1)) Infinity Publishing.

Jenkins, Toye L. The Way God Made Me: A Self Image Book for Girls. 2009. 28p. pap. 12.49 (978-1-4389-9363-8(3)) AuthorHouse.

Jiries, Nariman. Grace-A-Lena Learns the Meaning of Self-Esteem. 2012. 36p. pap. 21.99 (978-1-4771-0476-7(3)) Xlibris Corp.

Johnson, Felicia P. Shuck Shuck Shuck. 2011. 28p. pap. 21.99 (978-1-4568-6343-2(6)) Xlibris Corp.

Johnson, Harvell. What about Johnson? Howard, Vanetta, ed. Clark, Donna Osborn, illus. 2013. 132p. pap. 11.95 (978-0-9885056-0-5(6)) Word on Da Street Publishing.

Johnson, Kathleen A. A Voice Came to Me. 2006. lib. bdg. 17.95 (978-0-9785623-0-4(5)) Voice of Light Pubns.

Johnson, Maerryane. I Am Still the Same Aubrey! 2013. 24p. pap. 24.95 (978-1-4626-9878-3(6)) America Star Bks.

Jones, Greg. Timmy the Toaster. 2016. (ENG., Illus.). 34p. (J). pap. (978-1-7751919-0-2(7)) Goldie, Gregory.

Jones, Patrick & Chartier, Brent. The Franchise. 2015. (Opportunity Ser.). (ENG.). 104p. (YA). (gr. 6-12). E-Book 53.32 (978-1-4677-6015-7(3), 9781467760157, Lerner Digital) Lerner Publishing Group.

K. Elizabeth, Sterling. Austin's First Puppy. 2007. 48p. (J). pap. 10.95 (978-0-7414-3263-6(3)) Infinity Publishing.

Kade, Stacey. Finding Felicity. 2018. (ENG., Illus.). 304p. (YA). (gr. 9). 17.99 (978-1-4814-6425-3(6), Simon & Schuster Bks. For Young Readers) Simon & Schuster Bks. For Young Readers.

Kamins, Julie Firstenberg. Why Am I at the Red Table? Long, Carlos, illus. 2008. 32p. (J). 13.95 (978-0-9771566-9-6(9)) Librujas.

Kang, Anna. You Are (Not) Small. 2018. (My Arabic Library). (ARA.). 32p. (J). (gr. -1-1). pap. 7.99 (978-1-338-26784-6(1)) Scholastic, Inc.

Kares, P. S. The Prairie Orphans' Journey. 2008. 32p. per. 24.95 (978-1-4241-8396-8(0)) America Star Bks.

Kelly, Erin Entrada. Blackbird Fly. Peterschmidt, Betsy, illus. 2016. (ENG.). 320p. (J). (gr. 3-7). pap. 7.99 (978-0-06-223862-7(0), Greenwillow Bks.) HarperCollins Pubs.

Kessler, Jackie Morse. Loss. 2012. (Riders of the Apocalypse Ser.: 3). (ENG.). 272p. (YA). (gr. 7-12). pap. 8.99 (978-0-547-71215-4(4), 1480762, Clarion Bks.) HarperCollins Pubs.

—Loss. 2012. (Riders of the Apocalypse Ser.: 3). lib. bdg. 19.65 (978-0-606-24742-9(4)) Turtleback.

Kirouac Bn, Nicole. I Am Unique. 2013. 32p. pap. 13.99 (978-1-4525-7594-0(0), Balboa Pr.) Author Solutions, LLC.

Knowles, Alison. Ollie & the Silver Stripe. Wiltshire, Sophie, illus. 2017. 64p. (J). 17.95 (978-1-78592-241-1(6), 696459) Kingsley, Jessica Pubs. GBR. Dist: Hachette UK Distribution.

Kobert, Michael Gilead & Donato, Dona. Who Goes with That Nose? The Wild Adventures of Juicy Coppertoes. Fuller, Laurie, illus. 2005. 40p. (J). per. 9.95 (978-0-9770700-0-8(X)) Giggling Gorilla Productions, LLC.

Koehler, Lora. The Little Snowplow. Parker, Jake, illus. (ENG.). (J). 2022. 32p. (gr. -1-2). 7.99 (978-1-5362-2777-2(3)) 2018. 30p. (— 1). bds. 8.99 (978-1-5362-0340-0(8)) 2015. 32p. (gr. -1-2). 17.99 (978-0-7636-7074-0(X)) Candlewick Pr.

Koller, Jackie French. A Wizard Named Nell. 2003. (ENG., Illus.). 208p. (J). (gr. 3-7). pap. 11.95 (978-0-689-85591-7(5), Aladdin) Simon & Schuster Children's Publishing.

Kreloff, Elliot. Worth the Wait: A Growing-Up Story of Self-Esteem. Kreloff, Elliot, illus. 2017. (Growing Up Ser.). (ENG., Illus.). 32p. (J). (gr. -1 — 1). lib. bdg. 19.99 (978-1-63440-180-7(8), da348a2c-efee-4749-b0dd-42052c6cfd7f); E-Book 30.65 (978-1-63440-184-5(0)) Red Chair Pr. (Rocking Chair Kids).

Krohberger, Dawn. Jack Out of the Box: Self-Esteem Elevation for Children. 2013. 24p. pap. 12.99 (978-1-4525-8253-5(X), Balboa Pr.) Author Solutions, LLC.

Lakes, Lofton & Metu, illus. The Dream Team. 2007. 48p. (YA). pap. (978-0-9799320-0-7(9)) Pinkney, Gail.

Lane, Deborah Jean. I Am an Individual. 2004. pap. 8.00 (978-0-8059-6527-8(0)) Dorrance Publishing Co., Inc.

Lane, Melaina. Chubs. . Another Day at School. 2011. 20p. 9.14 (978-1-4251-7330-2(6)) Trafford Publishing.

Larsen, Jen. Future Perfect. 2015. (ENG.). 320p. (YA). (gr. 8-12). 17.99 (978-0-06-232123-7(4), HarperTeen) HarperCollins Pubs.

Larsen, Ramonita. Yes, I Can Do It/Si, lo Puedo Hacer. Larsen, Ramonita, illus. l.t. ed. 2006. (Illus.). 18p. (J). per. 10.99 (978-1-59879-292-8(X)) Lifevest Publishing, Inc.

Lea, Audry. Scott the Dot. 2005. (Illus.). 32p. (J). 16.00 (978-1-4120-4927-6(X)) Trafford Publishing.

Lechelt, Karen. What Do You Love about You? 2016. (ENG., Illus.). 32p. (J). 16.99 (978-1-68119-093-8(1), 900158424, Bloomsbury USA Childrens) Bloomsbury Publishing USA.

Lee, Jeffrey Lyndon. Locked in the Box. 2013. 40p. pap. 24.95 (978-1-4626-6218-0(8)) America Star Bks.

Leshem-Pelly, Miri. Scribble & Author. 2017. (ENG., Illus.). 32p. (J). 12.99 (978-1-61067-575-8(4)) Kane Miller.

Levy, Joanne. Crushing It. 2017. (Mix Ser.). (ENG., Illus.). 240p. (J). (gr. 4-8). pap. 8.99 (978-1-4814-6473-4(6), Aladdin) Simon & Schuster Children's Publishing.

Lewis-Cook, Ashley. Beautiful Me! 2012. (Illus.). 16p. pap. 15.99 (978-1-4772-1291-2(4)) AuthorHouse.

Lockhart, Kendra. Marvelous Misadventures of Magnificent Madelaine. 2010. (Illus.). 24p. (J). pap. 14.95 (978-0-9843883-4-9(6), Green Lady Pr., The) RealityIsBooks.com, Inc.

London, Adam. Lucky the Rubber Ducky. Atherton, Jim, illus. 2009. 14p. (J). pap. 14.95 (978-0-578-00865-3(3)) AthertonCustoms.

Lotorto-Soroka, Mary. Who Needs Spots Anyways? 2009. 24p. pap. 12.99 (978-1-4490-3947-9(2)) AuthorHouse.

Love, D. Anne. Defying the Diva. 2008. (ENG., Illus.). 272p. (YA). (gr. 7-12). 17.99 (978-1-4169-3481-3(2), McElderry, Margaret K. Bks.) McElderry, Margaret K. Bks.

Ludwig, Trudy. Better Than You. Gustavson, Adam, illus. 2011. 32p. (J). (gr. 1-4). 18.99 (978-1-58246-380-3(8), Knopf Bks. for Young Readers) Random Hse. Children's Bks.

Luftner, Kai. Lily Loves. Drews, Judith, illus. 2012. (ENG.). 32p. (J). (gr. -1-3). 16.95 (978-1-897476-94-9(9)) Simply Read Bks. CAN. Dist: Ingram Publisher Services.

Luyken, Corinna. The Tree in Me. 2021. (Illus.). 56p. (J). (gr. -1-3). 18.99 (978-0-593-11259-5(8), Dial Bks) Penguin Young Readers Group.

Lyga, Barry. Hero-Type. 2009. (ENG.). 312p. (YA). (gr. 7). pap. 17.99 (978-0-547-24877-6(6), 1100781, Clarion Bks.) HarperCollins Pubs.

MacMillan, Ian C. Khala Maninge - the Little Elephant That Cried a Lot: An African Fable. MacMillan, Eric G., illus. 2nd ed. 2003. lib. bdg. 5.00 (978-0-9729698-0-2(2)) Maninge Mali.

Madonna, Lenae. Lost & Found. Conde, Manuel, illus. 2012. 38p. (J). 16.95 (978-1-60131-115-3(X), Castlebridge Bks.) Big Tent Bks.

Maier, Inger. When Lizzy Was Afraid of Trying New Things. Candon, Jennifer, illus. 2004. (ENG.). 32p. (J). 14.95 (978-1-59147-170-7(2), Magination Pr.) American Psychological Assn.

Maier, Inger M. When Lizzie Was Afraid: Of Trying New Things. Candon, Jennifer, illus. 2004. 32p. (J). pap. 9.95 (978-1-59147-171-4(0), Magination Pr.) American Psychological Assn.

Mangum, Kay Lynn. When the Bough Breaks. 2007. 352p. (YA). pap. 15.95 (978-1-59038-748-1(1)) Deseret Bk. Co.

Mann, Gerre. Cora the Caterpillar. Brody, Joyce, illus. 2012. 20p. pap. 14.99 (978-1-61170-088-6(4)) Robertson Publishing.

Marchese, Stephen, illus. The Flights of Marceau: Week Two. 2007. (ENG.). 60p. (J). 16.95 (978-0-9797495-1-3(4)) Majestic Eagle Publishing.

Marino, Peter. Dough Boy. 2007. (ENG.). 176p. (YA). (gr. 7-12). pap. 6.95 (978-0-8234-2096-4(5)) Holiday Hse., Inc.

Mauzy, Barbara E. Don't Be a Schwoe: Fitness: Fitness, 1 vol. 2013. (ENG., Illus.). 64p. (J). (gr. -1-3). 16.99 (978-0-7643-4295-0(9), 4777) Schiffer Publishing, Ltd.

Mayeaux, Stacy. Not Just Any Donkey. Schultz, Rebecca, illus. 2008. (ENG.). 24p. pap. 12.49 (978-1-4343-6598-9(0)) AuthorHouse.

McBratney, Sam. You're All My Favorites. Jeram, Anita, illus. 2008. (ENG.). 32p. (J). (gr. k-k). bds. 7.99 (978-0-7636-4297-6(5)) Candlewick Pr.

McVay, Kinsy. Just Line Around. 2009. 52p. pap. 18.50 (978-1-60860-423-4(3), Eloquent Bks.) Strategic Book Publishing & Rights Agency (SBPRA).

Michelle, Nelson-Schmidt. Jonathan James & the Whatif Monster. 2013. (ENG., Illus.). 32p. (J). pap. 6.99 (978-1-61067-118-7(X)) Kane Miller.

—Jonathan James & Whatif Monster. 2012. (ENG., Illus.). (J). 12.99 (978-1-61067-131-6(7)) Kane Miller.

Michie, Brandon J. Andie the Ant: Animal Lessons. 2012. 16p. pap. 14.97 (978-1-4670-2585-0(2)) AuthorHouse.

Mills, Joyce C. Little Tree: A Story for Children with Serious Medical Illness. Sebern, Brian, illus. 2nd ed. 2003. 32p. (J). pap. 9.95 (978-1-59147-042-7(0)); 14.95 (978-1-59147-041-0(2)) American Psychological Assn. (Magination Pr.).

Mitchell, P. S. I Don't Wanna Be Me. 2013. 48p. 15.95 (978-0-615-80354-8(7)) Mitchell, P. S.

Moger, Susan. Of Better Blood. 2016. (ENG.). 304p. (YA). (gr. 8-12). 16.99 (978-0-8075-4774-8(3), 807547743) Whitman, Albert & Co.

Montgomery, L. M. Mistress Pat: From the Author of Anne of Green Gables. 2014. (ENG.). 384p. (YA). (gr. 5-12). pap. 13.99 (978-1-4022-8927-9(8)) Sourcebooks, Inc.

Moore, Stephanie Perry. Icing on the Cake, No. 5. 2014. (Sharp Sisters Ser.: 5). (ENG.). 160p. (YA). (gr. 6-12). pap. 7.95 (978-1-4677-4487-4(5), 29998c09-e540-4b5a-8fc4-8602f7f158b6); lib. bdg. 27.99

(978-1-4677-3728-9(3), f405893c-9260-48ce-94ea-f4ca879855dc) Lerner Publishing Group. (Darby Creek).

Morgan, Dennis W. Stubby the Giraffe Who Wouldn't Take Chances. 2013. 40p. pap. 14.99 (978-0-9892295-0-0(5)) Dreamstreet Studios, Inc. (A Div. of DSMV Industries, Inc.).

Mosier, Paul. Train I Ride. 2018. (ENG.). 208p. (J). (gr. 3-7). pap. 6.99 (978-0-06-245574-1(5), HarperCollins) HarperCollins Pubs.

—Train I Ride. 2019. (Penworthy Picks Middle School Ser.). (ENG.). 181p. (J). (gr. 4-5). 18.96 (978-1-64310-914-5(6)) Penworthy Co., LLC, The.

Ms. Sue. Where Is Your Name? Ducy, George, illus. 2009. 24p. pap. 24.95 (978-1-60672-711-9(7)) America Star Bks.

Mucklow, Hope. Rojo the Baby Red Panda at the Zoo: An Allegory about Self-Worth Through a Red Panda & Giant Panda Comparison. 2014. (ENG., Illus.). 32p. (J). (gr. -1-3). 14.95 (978-1-62086-593-4(9)) Amplify Publishing Group.

Murcray, Rod. Tuttle Stories. McDaniel, Rick, illus. 2012. 40p. pap. 14.95 (978-1-61897-654-3(0), Strategic Bk. Publishing) Strategic Book Publishing & Rights Agency (SBPRA).

Murdoch, Patricia. Exposure, 1 vol. 2006. (Orca Soundings Ser.). (ENG.). 128p. (YA). (gr. 8-12). pap. 9.95 (978-1-55143-493-3(8)) Orca Bk. Pubs. USA.

Murphy, Julie. Dear Sweet Pea. 2019. (ENG.). 288p. (J). (gr. 3-7). 16.99 (978-0-06-247307-3(7)); E-Book (978-0-06-247309-7(3), 9780062473097) HarperCollins Pubs. (Balzer & Bray).

—Dumplin' (Dumplin' Ser.: 1). (ENG.). (YA). (gr. 8). 2017. 400p. pap. 10.99 (978-0-06-232719-2(4)) 2015. 384p. 17.99 (978-0-06-232718-5(6)) HarperCollins Pubs. (Balzer & Bray).

—Dumplin' 2017. (YA). lib. bdg. 20.85 (978-0-606-39647-9(0)) Turtleback.

—Dumplin' Movie Tie-In Edition. movie tie-in ed. 2018. (Dumplin' Ser.: 1). (ENG.). 400p. (YA). (gr. 8). pap. 9.99 (978-0-06-293467-3(8), Balzer & Bray) HarperCollins Pubs.

—Puddin' (Dumplin' Ser.: 2). (ENG.). (YA). (gr. 8). 2019. 464p. pap. 9.99 (978-0-06-241839-5(4)) 2018. 448p. 17.99 (978-0-06-241838-8(6)) HarperCollins Pubs. (Balzer & Bray).

Murray, Fisher C & Murray, Colleen O. One & Only Bernadette P. McMull. 2009. (ENG.). 32p. pap. 10.95 (978-1-933916-52-1(4), Ferne Pr.) Nelson Publishing & Marketing.

Myers, Lily. This Impossible Light. 2017. 352p. (YA). (gr. 7). 17.99 (978-0-399-17372-1(2), Philomel Bks.) Penguin Young Readers Group.

Mystic. Talon Hawke: A Journey Through Darkness. 2007. 228p. per. 15.95 (978-0-595-46386-2(X)) iUniverse, Inc.

Nanette. The Black Alligator. 2004. (Life on Granny's Farm Ser.). (J). 12.95 (978-0-9741269-3-7(4)) St. Bernard Publishing, LLC.

Nelson, Jacob. And Then There Was Jake. 2012. (ENG.). (YA). pap. (978-1-4675-4158-9(3)) Independent Pub.

Nelson-Schmidt, Michelle. Jonathan James & the Whatif Monster. 2013. (ENG., Illus.). (J). 26.99 (978-1-61067-194-1(5)) Kane Miller.

—José Juan y el Monstruo Ysi. Nelson-Schmidt, Michelle, illus. 2019.Tr. of Jonathan James & the Whatif Monster. (SPA., Illus.). (J). pap. 6.99 (978-1-61067-924-4(5)) Kane Miller.

Newman, Patrice Tomasetti. Where Oh Where? It's in My Hair! 2012. 26p. 24.95 (978-1-4626-6284-5(6)) America Star Bks.

Nolan, Lucy. Jack Quack, 1 vol. Wesson, Andrea, illus. 2003. (ENG.). 32p. (J). (gr. k-3). pap. 5.95 (978-0-7614-5153-2(6)) Marshall Cavendish Corp.

Oates, Joyce Carol. Two or Three Things I Forgot to Tell You. (ENG.). (YA). (gr. 9). 2013. 304p. pap. 9.99 (978-0-06-211048-0(9)) 2012. 288p. 17.99 (978-0-06-211047-3(0)) HarperCollins Pubs. (HarperTeen).

Oceanak, Karla. Mooch. Spanjer, Kendra, illus. 2018. (Aldo Zelnick Comic Novel Ser.: 13). (ENG.). 160p. (J). 12.95 (978-1-934649-76-3(7)) Bailiwick Pr.

Olien, Jessica. Right Now. Olien, Jessica, illus. 2018. (ENG., Illus.). 40p. (J). (gr. -1-3). 17.99 (978-0-06-256828-1(0), Balzer & Bray) HarperCollins Pubs.

Olizon-Chikiamco, Norma. Pan de Sal Saves the Day: An Award-Winning Children's Story from the Philippines [New Bilingual English & Tagalog Edition]. Salvatus, Mark, illus. 2017. 28p. (J). (gr. -1-6). pap. 8.95 (978-0-8048-4754-4(1)) Tuttle Publishing.

Ostrovski, Emil. Away We Go. 2016. (ENG.). 272p. (YA). (gr. 9). 17.99 (978-0-06-223855-9(8), Greenwillow Bks.) HarperCollins Pubs.

Owens, Connie S. I know I am Special! 2003. pap. 5.99 (978-1-59317-010-3(6)) Warner Pr., Inc.

Paige, D. M. Going to Press. (Opportunity Ser.). (ENG.). 104p. (YA). (gr. 6-12). 2013. pap. 7.95 (978-1-4677-1495-2(X), 9781467714952, Darby Creek) 2013. lib. bdg. 27.99 (978-1-4677-1373-3(2), 1c70bf7b-24bf-4cd8-ae36-e34ad0c2c525, Darby Creek) 2015. E-Book 53.32 (978-1-4677-6016-4(1), 9781467760164, Lerner Digital) Lerner Publishing Group.

Paley, Sasha. Huge. 2007. (ENG.). 272p. (YA). (gr. 9-12). 15.99 (978-1-4169-3517-9(7), Simon & Schuster Bks. For Young Readers) Simon & Schuster Bks. For Young Readers.

Parr, todd. Be Who You Are. 2016. (ENG., Illus.). 32p. (J). (gr. -1-1). 18.99 (978-0-316-26523-2(3)) Little, Brown Bks. for Young Readers.

—It's Okay to Be Different. 2009. (ENG., Illus.). 32p. (J). (gr. -1-1). pap. 8.99 (978-0-316-04347-2(8)) Little, Brown Bks. for Young Readers.

—It's Okay to Be Different. Parr, todd, illus. 2019. (Todd Parr Picture Bks.). (ENG., Illus.). 32p. (J). (gr. -1-2). 31.36 (978-1-5321-4374-8(5), 31824, Picture Bk.) Spotlight.

—It's Okay to Make Mistakes. 2014. (ENG., Illus.). 32p. (J). (gr. -1-1). 18.99 (978-0-316-23053-7(7)) Little, Brown Bks. for Young Readers.

—It's Okay to Make Mistakes. Parr, todd, illus. 2019. (Todd Parr Picture Bks.). (ENG., Illus.). 32p. (J). (gr. -1-2). 31.36 (978-1-5321-4375-5(3), 31825, Picture Bk.) Spotlight.

Parsley, Elise. Neck & Neck. 2018. (ENG., Illus.). 40p. (J). (gr. -1-3). 17.99 (978-0-316-46674-5(3)) Little, Brown Bks. for Young Readers.

Patel, Sonia. Rani Patel in Full Effect, 1 vol. 2016. (ENG.). 224p. (J). (gr. 9-12). 16.95 (978-1-941026-49-6(4), 23353362, Cinco Puntos Press) Lee & Low Bks., Inc.

Pearlman, Robb. Pink Is for Boys. Kaban, Eda, illus. 2018. (ENG.). 40p. (J). (gr. -1-3). 18.99 (978-0-7624-6247-6(7), Running Pr. Kids) Running Pr.

Penn, Audrey. A Kiss Goodbye. Gibson, Barbara, illus. 2007. (Kissing Hand Ser.). (ENG.). 32p. (J). (gr. -1-3). 16.99 (978-1-933718-04-0(8)) Tanglewood Pr.

—Sassafras. Harper, Ruth, illus. 2006. (ENG.). 32p. (J). (gr. -1-3). 16.95 (978-1-933718-03-3(X)) Tanglewood Pr.

Phillips, Dee. Mirror, 1 vol. 2014. (Right Now! Ser.). (ENG.). 48p. (YA). (gr. 9-12). pap. 10.75 (978-1-62250-879-2(3)) Saddleback Educational Publishing, Inc.

Pielichaty, Helena. Starring Alex ... 2006. (Girls of Avenue Z Ser.). (ENG.). 128p. (J). (gr. 3-6). 17.44 (978-1-4169-0063-4(2)) Simon & Schuster, Inc.

Pilling, Ann. The Year of the Worm. 172p. (J). (gr. 4-7). pap. 7.50 (978-0-7459-4294-0(6), Lion Books) Lion Hudson PLC GBR. Dist: Trafalgar Square Publishing.

Plummer, Deborah. The Adventures of the Little Tin Tortoise: A Self-Esteem Story with Activities for Teachers, Parents & Carers. 2005. (Illus.). 144p. (J). per. 35.00 (978-1-84310-406-3(7), 695331) Kingsley, Jessica Pubs. GBR. Dist: Hachette UK Distribution.

Pokeberry, P. J. The Huckenpuck Papers: The Tales of a Family's Secret & a Young Girls Search for Self-Esteem. 2003. (Illus.). 87p. (J). pap. 8.95 (978-0-943962-03-0(X)) Viewpoint Pr.

Polacco, Patricia. The Junkyard Wonders. Polacco, Patricia, illus. 2010. (ENG., Illus.). 48p. (J). (gr. 1-4). 18.99 (978-0-399-25078-1(6), Philomel Bks.) Penguin Young Readers Group.

Poland, Pitch & Poland, Inglan. Lost & Found. Rose, Drew, illus. 2013. 30p. (J). (978-0-9853430-0-2(1)) Little P Pr. Co.

Provenzano, Stella Marie. How Rusty Rooster Found His Do. 2008. 16p. per. 24.95 (978-1-4241-9362-2(1)) America Star Bks.

Pukac, Michael & Stephen, Marchesi, illus. The Flights of Marceau: Week Three. 2008. (ENG.). 64p. (J). 16.95 (978-0-9797495-2-0(2)) Majestic Eagle Publishing.

Pulley, Kelly. Ten Unusual Features of Lulu McDunn. Pulley, Kelly, illus. 2010. (Illus.). 32p. (J). (gr. -1). 16.95 (978-0-9820812-7-3(8), Frog Legs Ink) Gauthier Pubns. Inc.

Rainey. School Is Cool. Huggens, Karin, illus. 2004. (J). (978-0-9666199-9-7(4)) DreamDog Pr.

Rallison, Janette. My Fair Godmother. 2009. (ENG.). 384p. (J). (gr. 6-8). 21.19 (978-0-8027-9780-3(6), 900051897) Walker & Co.

Rankin, Heather & Rankin, Heather. All It Takes Is One Friend. 2012. 46p. pap. (978-0-9878945-0-2(1)) Our Farm Bks.

Rayburn, Tricia. Maggie Bean Stays Afloat. 2008. (ENG.). 320p. (J). (gr. 4-8). pap. 6.99 (978-1-4169-3347-2(6), Aladdin) Simon & Schuster Children's Publishing.

—The Melting of Maggie Bean. 2007. (ENG.). 256p. (J). (gr. 4-8). pap. 6.99 (978-1-4169-3348-9(4), Aladdin) Simon & Schuster Children's Publishing.

Redmond, Valerie. Emma & the African Wishing Bead. Victoria, Kirton, illus. 2013. 28p. pap. 13.95 (978-1-61244-115-3(7)) Halo Publishing International.

Reed, Amy. Beautiful. 2009. (ENG.). 240p. (YA). (gr. 9-12). 16.99 (978-1-4169-7830-5(5)) Simon & Schuster, Inc.

—Beautiful. 2010. (ENG.). 256p. (YA). (gr. 9). pap. 10.99 (978-1-4169-7831-2(3), Simon Pulse) Simon Pulse.

Reynolds, Cynthia Furlong. Grammie's Secret Cupboard. Dodson, Bert, illus. 2007. 32p. (J). (gr. -1-3). 17.95 (978-1-58726-310-1(6), Mitten Pr.) Ann Arbor Editions LLC.

Reynolds Naylor, Phyllis. I Like Him, He Likes Her: Alice Alone; Simply Alice; Patiently Alice. 2010. (Alice Ser.). (ENG.). 640p. (J). (gr. 7). pap. 12.99 (978-1-4424-0978-1(9), Atheneum Bks. for Young Readers) Simon & Schuster Children's Publishing.

Reynolds, Peter H. Be You! Reynolds, Peter H., illus. 2020. (ENG., Illus.). 32p. (J). (gr. -1-3). 17.99 (978-1-338-57231-5(8), Orchard Bks.) Scholastic, Inc.

—¡Di Algo! (Say Something!), 1 vol. Reynolds, Peter H., illus. 2019. (SPA., Illus.). 40p. (J). (gr. -1-k). pap. 7.99 (978-1-338-56596-6(6), Scholastic en Espanol) Scholastic, Inc.

—Say Something! Reynolds, Peter H., illus. 2019. (ENG., Illus.). 40p. (J). (gr. -1-3). 17.99 (978-0-545-86503-6(4), Orchard Bks.) Scholastic, Inc.

Richards, Arlene. That's Bingzy! Busy Building Self-Esteem. Zimmerman, Louis, illus. 2007. 32p. (J). (gr. -1-3). 19.95 incl. audio compact disk (978-0-9794323-4-7(0)) Bing Note, Inc.

Richmond, Marianne. Hooray for You! A Celebration of You-Ness. 2015. (Marianne Richmond Ser.: 0). 24p. (J). (gr. -1-2). bds. 7.99 (978-1-4926-1555-2(2), Sourcebooks Jabberwocky) Sourcebooks, Inc.

Rivadeneira, Caryn. The Wrong Shoes: A Book about Money & Self-Esteem. Ross, Graham, illus. 2018. 62p. (J). 14.99 (978-1-5064-4681-3(7), Beaming Books) 1517 Media.

Robinson, Christian. You Matter. Robinson, Christian, illus. 2020. (ENG., Illus.). 40p. (J). (gr. -1-3). 17.99 (978-1-5344-2169-1(6), Atheneum Bks. for Young Readers) Simon & Schuster Children's Publishing.

Robinson, Gary. Tribal Journey. 2013. (PathFinders Ser.). (ENG.). 96p. (YA). (gr. 8-12). pap. 9.95 (978-1-939053-01-5(3), 7th Generation) BPC.

Rodriguez, Grisell. Chaka the Cow. 2010. 32p. pap. 13.99 (978-1-60844-153-2(9)) Dog Ear Publishing, LLC.

Roe, Mechal Renee. Happy Hair. 2019. (Happy Hair Ser.). (ENG., Illus.). 32p. (J). (gr. -1-2). 16.99 (978-1-9848-9554-7(0), Doubleday Bks. for Young Readers) Random Hse. Children's Bks.

Roy, Wendy. Kelly Confident Shows You Why... It's POWERFUL to be a GIRL! It's POWERFUL to be a GIRL! 2012. (ENG.). 34p. (J). pap. 10.95 (978-0-615-59502-3(2)) Roy, Wendy.

Salter, Sydney. My Big Nose & Other Natural Disasters. 2009. (ENG., Illus.). 352p. (YA). (gr. 7-18). pap. 19.95 (978-0-15-206643-7(8), 1099023, Clarion Bks.) HarperCollins Pubs.

Samuels, Arthur. Old Flames: Teen Bullies & Prep School Cruelty. 2013. 238p. pap. 14.00 (978-0-9882394-4-9(2)) STARR Publishing.

Santomero, Angela C., adapted by. You Are Special, Daniel Tiger! 2014. (Daniel Tiger's Neighborhood Ser.). (ENG., Illus.). 26p. (J). (gr. -1-2). 12.99 (978-1-4814-1915-4(3), Simon Spotlight) Simon Spotlight.

Schraff, Anne. Outrunning the Darkness, 1 vol. unabr. ed. 2010. (Urban Underground Ser.). (ENG.). 191p. (YA). (gr. 9-12). pap. 11.95 (978-1-61651-000-8(5)) Saddleback Educational Publishing, Inc.

—To Be Somebody. 2008. (Passages Ser.). 120p. (J). (gr. 4-6). lib. bdg. 13.95 (978-0-7569-8390-1(8)) Perfection Learning Corp.

—To Catch a Dream, 1 vol. unabr. ed. 2010. (Urban Underground Ser.). (ENG.). 198p. (YA). (gr. 9-12). pap. 11.95 (978-1-61651-269-9(5)) Saddleback Educational Publishing, Inc.

Schraff, Anne E. Hurting Time. 2012. (Urban Underground — Cesar Chavez High School Ser.: 27). (YA). lib. bdg. 20.80 (978-0-606-26597-3(X)) Turtleback.

Serluca-Foster, Rosemary. Genevieve's Gift: A Child's Joyful Tale of Connecting with Her Intuitive Heart. 2007. (ENG.). 32p. pap. 11.99 (978-1-4196-7321-4(1)) CreateSpace Independent Publishing Platform.

Sesame Workshop. Just One You! 2015. (Sesame Street Scribbles Ser.: 0). (ENG.). 32p. (J). (gr. -1-3). 10.99 (978-1-4022-9735-9(1)) Sourcebooks, Inc.

—Love: From Sesame Street. 2018. (Sesame Street Scribbles Ser.: 0). (ENG., Illus.). 32p. (J). (gr. k-3). 12.99 (978-1-4926-7749-9(3)) Sourcebooks, Inc.

Siegert, Mia. Somebody Told Me. 2020. (ENG.). 272p. (YA). (gr. 8-12). 18.99 (978-1-5415-7819-7(8), 222e1ba4-28dd-488e-8818-a2000e061510, Carolrhoda Lab™) Lerner Publishing Group.

Simon, Jazmyn & Hill, Dulé. Repeat after Me: Big Things to Say Every Day. Knight-Justice, Shamar, illus. 2023. 32p. (J). (gr. -1-3). 18.99 (978-0-593-42697-5(5)); (ENG.). lib. bdg. 21.99 (978-0-593-42698-2(3)) Random Hse. Children's Bks. (Random Hse. Bks. for Young Readers).

Simonson, Louise. Las Malvadas de la Escuela Secundaria. Aparicio Publishing LLC, Aparicio Publishing, tr. from ENG. Cho, Sumin, illus. 2020. (Drama en la Secundaria Ser.).Tr. of Middle School Mean Queens. (SPA.). 64p. (J). (gr. 3-6). pap. 6.95 (978-1-4965-9317-7(0), 142347); lib. bdg. 25.99 (978-1-4965-9162-3(3), 142079) Capstone. (Stone Arch Bks.).

Small, Tanya. What You Say Is What You Are. 2007. pap. 7.50 (978-0-9705090-1-7(4)) MorningGlory Publishing.

Smillie, Bryan. A Time for Evron. Rooth, Mike, illus. 2004. 190p. 11.95 (978-0-9689516-0-6(0)) Shabrya Publishing CAN. Dist: Hushion Hse. Publishing, Ltd.

Smith, Bryan. Is There an App for That? Wish, Katia, illus. 2015. (ENG.). 31p. (J). (gr. k-6). pap. 10.95 (978-1-934490-74-7(1)) Boys Town Pr.

—Mindset Matters, Volume 2. Griffin, Lisa M., illus. 2017. (Without Limits Ser.: 2). (ENG.). 31p. (J). (gr. k-6). pap. 10.95 (978-1-944882-12-9(X)) Boys Town Pr.

Smith, M. Jane. The First Fry Bread: A Gitxsan Story. Wheeler, Jordan, ed. Mowatt, Ken N., illus. 2012. 32p. pap. (978-1-4602-0226-5(0)) FriesenPress.

Smith, Suzanne C. Peter Cottontail & the Easter Bunny Imposter. Brittingham, Geoffrey, illus. 24p. (J). pap. 3.25 (978-0-8249-5372-0(X), Ideals Pubns.) Worthy Publishing.

Sohaili, Monira. Stories from Earth & Beyond: Enchanting & Inspirational Stories. 2006. (Illus.). 94p. per. 9.95 (978-1-60002-044-5(5), 2833) Mountain Valley Publishing, LLC.

Sommer, Carl. The Eagle & the Chickens. Noé, illus. 2016. (J). (978-1-57537-945-6(7)) Advance Publishing, Inc.

—The Ugly Princess. Martinez, Jorge, illus. 2016. 32p. (J). (978-1-57537-948-7(1)) Advance Publishing, Inc.

Sones, Sonya. What My Girlfriend Doesn't Know. 2011. 9.68 (978-0-7848-3389-6(3), Everbind) Marco Bk. Co.

—What My Girlfriend Doesn't Know. 2013. (ENG., Illus.). 320p. (YA). (gr. 7). pap. 12.99 (978-1-4424-9384-1(4), Simon & Schuster Bks. For Young Readers) Simon & Schuster Bks. For Young Readers.

Spencer, Mignon. I'm Living My Dream: An Inspirationsl Rhyme for all Ages in English & Spanish. Mack, Travis, illus. 2008.Tr. of Hago mi sueno Realidad. (ENG & SPA.). 32p. (J). 12.99 (978-0-9763871-2-1(3)) Solomon's Bks.

Spero, Mitch & Spero, Maria. Florida the Turtle: Who Thinks He's a Dog Finds His Feelings. 2012. 28p. pap. 21.99 (978-1-4771-0184-1(5)) Xlibris Corp.

Starcher, Michele. The Ornery Angel. 2005. 68p. per. 13.95 (978-1-59858-039-6(6)) Dog Ear Publishing, LLC.

Stenger, D. L. Pumpkn's Secret. 2006. (ENG.). 44p. per. 18.49 (978-1-4259-5055-2(8)) AuthorHouse.

Stoehr, Shelley. Crosses. 2003. 161p. (YA). pap. 13.95 (978-0-595-26952-5(4), Writers Club Pr.) iUniverse, Inc.

Storti, Jill. Keiko the Koala. 2011. 24p. (gr. -1 — 1). pap. 12.95 (978-1-4567-3110-6(6)) AuthorHouse.

Strasnick, Lauren. Nothing Like You. 2010. (ENG.). 240p. (YA). (gr. 9). pap. 8.99 (978-1-4169-8265-4(5), Simon Pulse) Simon Pulse.

StVil, Yves Lola. Girls Like Me. (ENG.). 320p. (YA). (gr. 7). 2018. pap. 8.99 (978-1-328-90102-6(5), 1700156) 2016. 17.99 (978-0-544-70674-3(9), 1628646) HarperCollins Pubs. (Clarion Bks.).

Sue. The Whinermans. 2010. 72p. (gr. 1-2). pap. 8.95 (978-1-4502-4998-0(1)) iUniverse, Inc.

Sunderland, Margot, et al. Ruby & the Rubbish Bin: A Story for Children with Low Self-Esteem. 2003. (Helping Children with Feelings Ser.). (ENG., Illus.). 32p. pap. 18.95 (978-0-86388-462-7(8), Y329066) Routledge.

Supplee, Suzanne. Artichoke's Heart. 2009. 288p. (YA). (gr. 7-18). 8.99 (978-0-14-241427-9(1), Speak) Penguin Young Readers Group.

Tanaka, Usa. Give Me That! Tanaka, Usa, illus. 2007. (ENG., Illus.). 32p. (J). 15.95 (978-0-9741319-0-0(3)) 4N Publishing LLC.

Tatum, Channing. The One & Only Sparkella. Barnes, Kim, illus. 2021. (Sparkella Ser.: 1). (ENG.). 48p. (J). 18.99 (978-1-250-75075-4(X), 900224690) Feiwel & Friends.

Taylor, Carol K. Behind the Fence. 2009. 24p. pap. 12.99 (978-1-4389-4352-7(0)) AuthorHouse.

Taylor, Helen. Emu Can't Fly. Gilles-Gray, Carolyn, illus. 2013. 24p. pap. (978-1-921883-39-2(1), MBS Pr.) Pick-a-Woo Woo Pubs.

Tennant, Kim. Thin Club. 2007. 52p. per. 10.00 (978-1-4257-2619-5(4)) Xlibris Corp.

Terrill Holdman, Shirley. The Adventures of Giggles & Owen: Adventure Three - Unlimited Pawsibilities. Leeds, Marjorie M., illus. 2013. 50p. pap. 17.95 (978-1-4575-2175-1(X)) Dog Ear Publishing, LLC.

Thomas, E. J. Brooster Rooster: King of the Farmyard, 1 vol. 2009. 22p. pap. 24.95 (978-1-60813-936-1(0)) America Star Bks.

Thompson, Kay. Eloise's What I Absolutely Love Love Love. 2005. (Eloise Ser.). (ENG., Illus.). 32p. (J). 13.99 (978-0-689-84965-7(6), Simon & Schuster Bks. For Young Readers) Simon & Schuster Bks. For Young Readers.

Thurman, Carol. Molly's Field of Dreams. 2011. 24p. pap. 11.99 (978-1-4567-3101-4(7)) AuthorHouse.

Tillman, Nancy. The Crown on Your Head. Tillman, Nancy, illus. (ENG., Illus.). (J). (gr. -1-3). 2014. 34p. bds. 8.99 (978-1-250-04045-9(0), 900123921) 2011. 32p. 17.99 (978-0-312-64521-2(X), 900068684) Feiwel & Friends.

—On the Night You Were Born. Tillman, Nancy, illus. 2006. (ENG., Illus.). 32p. (J). (gr. -1 — 1). 18.99 (978-0-312-34606-5(9), 900041898) Feiwel & Friends.

—You're Here for a Reason. (ENG., Illus.). (J). 2017. 16p. bds. 8.99 (978-1-250-10650-6(8), 900164479) 2015. 32p. (gr. -1-3). 18.99 (978-1-250-05626-9(8), 900138737) Feiwel & Friends.

Treasure Island: A Growing Field Adventure. 2011. (Illus.). 64p. (J). 16.95 (978-0-9770391-4-2(5)) Growing Field Bks.

Treisman, Karen. Gilly the Giraffe Self-Esteem Activity Book: A Therapeutic Story with Creative Activities for Children Aged 5-10. 2019. (Therapeutic Treasures Collection). (Illus.). 144p. (C). 29.95 (978-1-78592-552-8(0), 696895) Kingsley, Jessica Pubs. GBR. Dist: Hachette UK Distribution.

Tsiang, Sarah. Sugar & Snails. Wimmer, Sonja, illus. 2018. (J). pap. (978-1-77321-004-9(1)) Annick Pr., Ltd.

Vail, Rachel. Gorgeous. 2009. (Avery Sisters Trilogy Ser.: 2). (ENG.). 288p. (YA). (gr. 8-18). 16.99 (978-0-06-089046-9(0), HarperTeen) HarperCollins Pubs.

Viknesh, R. My Fantasy Your Treat. 2012. 32p. pap. 28.55 (978-1-4669-2733-9(X)) Trafford Publishing.

Vivian, Siobhan. The List. 2014. (ENG.). 336p. (YA). (gr. 9). pap. 10.99 (978-0-545-16918-9(6), Scholastic Paperbacks) Scholastic, Inc.

Walton, K. M. Cracked. 2012. (ENG.). (YA). (gr. 9). 336p. pap. 13.99 (978-1-4424-2917-8(8)); 320p. 16.99 (978-1-4424-2916-1(X)) Simon Pulse. (Simon Pulse).

—Empty. 2013. (ENG., Illus.). 272p. (YA). (gr. 9). pap. 12.99 (978-1-4424-5358-6(3), Simon Pulse) Simon Pulse.

Wan, Joyce. You Are My Magical Unicorn. Wan, Joyce, illus. 2018. (ENG., Illus.). 14p. (J). (gr. -1-k). bds. 6.99 (978-1-338-33410-4(7), Cartwheel Bks.) Scholastic, Inc.

Webster, Wendy. Magicus Perfecticum. 2009. (Illus.). 60p. pap. 11.49 (978-1-4490-0765-2(1)) AuthorHouse.

Weeks, Sarah. I'm a Pig. Berry, Holly, illus. 2005. 32p. (J). (gr. -1-2). lib. bdg. 16.89 (978-0-06-074344-4(1), Geringer, Laura Book) HarperCollins Pubs.

Weinberger, Kimberly. Dolphin's Big Leap. Ziss, Debra, illus. 2003. (Hello Reader! Ser.). 30p. (J). (978-0-439-44159-9(5)) Scholastic, Inc.

Weiner, Marcella Bakur & Neimark, Jill. I Want Your Moo: A Story for Children about Self-Esteem. Adinolfi, JoAnn, illus. 2nd ed. 2009. 32p. (J). (gr. -1-3). 14.95 (978-1-4338-0542-4(1)); pap. 9.95 (978-1-4338-0552-3(9)) American Psychological Assn. (Magination Pr.).

What Do You See When You Look at Me? 2003. (J). 12.00 (978-0-9724442-7-9(0)) LightHouse Pr.

Wild, Margaret. Fox. 2006. (ENG., Illus.). 32p. (J). (gr. 1). pap. 7.99 (978-1-933605-15-9(4)) Kane Miller.

Wilkerson, L. Kobie, 3rd, reader. Fred & Mary. 2008. (Illus.). 32p. (J). 24.95 incl. DVD, audio compact disk (978-0-9796679-0-9(9)) Love II Learn Bks.

Williams, Alicia D. Genesis Begins Again. 2019. (ENG., Illus.). 384p. (J). (gr. 4-8). 17.99 (978-1-4814-6580-9(5), Atheneum/Caitlyn Dlouhy Books) Simon & Schuster Children's Publishing.

Williams, Maggy. "I'm Mixed!" Agresta, Elizabeth, illus. 2018. 38p. (J). pap. (978-1-61599-359-8(2)) Loving Healing Pr., Inc.

Wilson, Jacqueline. Cookie. Sharratt, Nick, illus. 2010. (ENG.). 352p. (J). (gr. 4-7). pap. 17.99 (978-0-312-64290-7(3), 900068061) Square Fish.

Wilson, Troy. Perfect Man, 1 vol. Griffiths, Dean, illus. 2005. (ENG.). 32p. (J). (gr. 1-3). per. 9.95 (978-1-55143-435-3(0)) Orca Bk. Pubs. USA.

Witherow, Wendy. Miranda's Makeover. Pulley, Kelly, illus. 2007. 93p. (J). (978-1-934306-11-6(8)) Mission City Pr., Inc.

Withers, Pam. Breathless, 1 vol. 2005. (Orca Soundings Ser.). (ENG.). 128p. (YA). (gr. 8-12). per. 9.95 (978-1-55143-480-3(6)) Orca Bk. Pubs. USA.

Wright-McAdoo, Joyce & Wright-Mcadoo, Joyce. Zimb: Believe. 2009. (Illus.). 28p. pap. 15.99 (978-1-4415-8051-1(4)) Xlibris Corp.

Yamada, Kobi. What Do You Do with an Idea? Besom, Mae, illus. 2014. (ENG.). 36p. (J). (gr. -1-3). 16.95 (978-1-938298-07-3(1)) Compendium, Inc., Publishing & Communications.

—What You Do Matters: Boxed Set: What Do You Do with an Idea?, What Do You Do with a Problem?, What Do You Do with a Chance?, 3 vols. 2018. (ENG., Illus.). (J). (gr. k-3). 49.95 (978-1-946873-14-9(4)) Compendium, Inc., Publishing & Communications.

Yep, Laurence. When the Circus Came to Town. Wang, Suling, illus. 2004. 112p. (J). (gr. 3-5). 13.65 (978-0-7569-2969-5(5)) Perfection Learning Corp.

Young, Karen Romano. Cobwebs. 400p. 2005. (ENG.). (YA). pap. 7.99 (978-0-06-441028-1(5), HarperTeen) 2004. (J). (gr. 7-18). lib. bdg. 16.89 (978-0-06-029762-6(X)) HarperCollins Pubs.

Zarr, Sara. Story of a Girl. 2007. (ENG.). 208p. (YA). (gr. 7-17). 29.99 (978-0-316-01453-3(2)) Little, Brown Bks. for Young Readers.

Zevgolis, Irene. The Dreamer & the Moon: An Inspirational Story with a Ballet Theme. Zevgolis, Irene, illus. 2008. (ENG., Illus.). 32p. (J). (gr. -1-6). 9.95 (978-0-615-17590-4(2)) E-City Publishing.

Zobel Nolan, Allia. What I Like about Me! Yamamoto, Miki, illus. 2005. (What I Like About Ser.). (ENG.). 14p. (J). (gr. -1-k). 14.99 (978-0-7944-0763-6(3), Studio Fun International) Printers Row Publishing Group.

Zusak, Markus. I Am the Messenger. 2009. 10.52 (978-0-7848-2491-7(6), Everbind) Marco Bk. Co.

S

—I Am the Messenger. 2006. 21.00 *(978-0-7569-7034-5(2))* Perfection Learning Corp.

—I Am the Messenger. 368p. (YA). (gr. 7). 2005. (ENG.). 16.95 *(978-0-375-83099-0(5))* 2006. (Illus.). reprint ed. pap. 12.99 *(978-0-375-83667-1(5))* Random Hse. Children's Bks. (Knopf Bks. for Young Readers).

—I Am the Messenger. (J). 2007. 1.25 *(978-1-4281-2308-3(3))* 2007. 77.75 *(978-1-4281-2309-0(1))* 2006. 74.75 *(978-1-4281-2311-3(3))* Recorded Bks., Inc.

SELF-GOVERNMENT

see Democracy

SELF-INSTRUCTION

see Self-Culture

SELF-MUTILATION

Allman, Toney. Self-Harm, 1 vol. 2016. (Hot Topics Ser.). (ENG.). 112p. (YA). (gr. 7-7). lib. bdg. 41.03 *(978-1-5345-6017-8(3),* 2ff2d5a5-e5bc-4894-971f-9f92846e7237, Lucent Pr.) Greenhaven Publishing LLC.

—Self-Injury, 1 vol. 2011. (Hot Topics Ser.). (ENG.). 112p. (gr. 7-7). lib. bdg. 41.03 *(978-1-4205-0552-8(1),* d9859398-ff26-403a-8548-79e8ad5bfa95, Lucent Pr.) Greenhaven Publishing LLC.

Eagen, Rachel. Cutting & Self-Injury, 1 vol. 2010. (ENG.). 48p. (J). pap. *(978-0-7787-2137-6(X))*; lib. bdg. *(978-0-7787-2130-7(2))* Crabtree Publishing Co.

Parks, Peggy J. Self-Injury Disorder. 2010. (Compact Research Ser.). (YA). (gr. 7-12). 41.27 *(978-1-60152-112-5(X))* ReferencePoint Pr., Inc.

—Teens: Cutting & Self-Injury. 2015. (ENG., Illus.). 96p. (J). lib. bdg. *(978-1-60152-770-7(5))* ReferencePoint Pr., Inc.

Pomere, Jonas. Frequently Asked Questions about Self Mutilation & Cutting. 2009. (FAQ: Teen Life Ser.). 64p. (gr. 5-6). 58.50 *(978-1-61512-587-6(6))* Rosen Publishing Group, Inc., The.

Shapiro, Lawrence E. Stopping the Pain: A Workbook for Teens Who Cut & Self Injure. 2008. (ENG., Illus.). 168p. (YA). (gr. 6-12). pap. 18.95 *(978-1-57224-602-7(2),* 6027, Instant Help Books) New Harbinger Pubns.

Shea, John M. Self-Injury & Cutting: Stopping the Pain, 1 vol. 2013. (Helpline: Teen Issues & Answers Ser.). (ENG., Illus.). 80p. (YA). (gr. 5-6). lib. bdg. 38.41 *(978-1-4488-9448-2(4),* 6ad61855-2f3d-4de8-93cc-633919557690, Rosen Classroom) Rosen Publishing Group, Inc., The.

Williams, Mary E., ed. Self-Injury, 1 vol. 2013. (Introducing Issues with Opposing Viewpoints Ser.). (ENG., Illus.). 128p. (gr. 7-10). lib. bdg. 43.63 *(978-0-7377-6280-8(2),* 2b70df2e-b389-48d8-9c69-105f79c8d56b, Greenhaven Publishing) Greenhaven Publishing LLC.

—Self-Mutilation, 1 vol. 2008. (Introducing Issues with Opposing Viewpoints Ser.). (ENG., Illus.). 112p. (gr. 7-10). 43.63 *(978-0-7377-4173-5(2),* 3f7022ce-2e3a-40f3-8a31-b6766c783052, Greenhaven Publishing) Greenhaven Publishing LLC.

SELF-MUTILATION—FICTION

Dzidrums, Christine. Cutters Don't Cry. Allison, Elizabeth, ed. Dzidrums, Joseph, photos by. 2010. (Illus.). 132p. (YA). 24.99 *(978-0-9826435-2-5(7))*; pap. 14.99 *(978-0-9826435-1-8(9))* Creative Media Publishing.

Glasgow, Kathleen. Girl in Pieces. 2018. (ENG.). 448p. (YA). (gr. 9). pap. 10.99 *(978-1-101-93474-6(3),* Ember) Random Hse. Children's Bks.

Hoban, Julia. Willow. (ENG.). (YA). (gr. 9-18). 2010. 336p. 9.99 *(978-0-14-241666-2(5),* Speak) 2009. 224p. 26.19 *(978-0-8037-3356-5(9))* Penguin Young Readers Group.

McCormick, Patricia. Cut. unabr. ed. 2004. 168p. (J). (gr. 7-18). pap. 36.00 incl. audio *(978-0-8072-0868-7(X),* LYA 320 SP, Listening Library) Random Hse. Audio Publishing Group.

—Cut. 2011. (gr. 7-12). lib. bdg. 19.65 *(978-0-613-49394-9(X))* Turtleback.

Rainfield, Cheryl. Scars. 2011. 8.67 *(978-0-7848-3439-8(3),* Everbind) Marco Bk. Co.

Stoehr, Shelley. Crosses. 2003. 161p. (YA). pap. 13.95 *(978-0-595-26952-5(4),* Writers Club Pr.) iUniverse, Inc.

SELF-PERCEPTION

Adson, Patricia R. A Princess & Her Garden: A Fable of Awakening & Arrival. 2nd ed. 2011. (J). *(978-0-935652-93-2(0))* Myers & Briggs Foundation, Inc.

Allman, Toney. Understanding Self-Image & Confidence. 2017. (Understanding Psychology Ser.). (ENG.). 80p. (YA). (gr. 5-12). *(978-1-68282-279-1(6))* ReferencePoint Pr., Inc.

Apel, Melanie Ann. Let's Talk about When You Think Nobody Likes You. 2009. (Let's Talk Library). 24p. (gr. 2-3). 42.50 *(978-1-60853-449-4(9),* PowerKids Pr.) Rosen Publishing Group, Inc., The.

Carlson, Dale. Understand Your Self: Teen Manual for the Understanding of Oneself. 2013. (Illus.). 192p. (gr. 9-13). pap. 14.95 *(978-1-884158-36-0(6),* 21540f59-9618-4de6-80e4-f5fe89e31805) Bick Publishing Hse.

Conway, Celeste. Body Image & the Media. 2013. (Hot Topics in Media Ser.). (ENG.). 48p. (J). (gr. 4-8). pap. 18.50 *(978-1-61783-782-1(2),* 10756) ABDO Publishing Co.

Espeland, Pamela. Knowing Me, Knowing You: The I-Sight Way to Understand Yourself & Others. 2004. (Illus.). 128p. (YA). (gr. 8-12). pap. 13.95 *(978-1-57542-090-5(2))* Free Spirit Publishing Inc.

Gitlin, Martin. I'm Being Targeted by a Gang. Now What?, 1 vol. 2016. (Teen Life 411 Ser.). (ENG., Illus.). 112p. (J). (gr. 7-7). 38.80 *(978-1-5081-7191-1(2),* eb7f4a0e-6835-4a65-8123-e5b3f79c83ab, Rosen Young Adult) Rosen Publishing Group, Inc., The.

Hawkins, Frank C. & Laube, Greta L. B. The Book of Bad Habits for Young (and Not So Young!) Men & Women: How to Chuck the Worst & Turn the Rest to Your Advantage. Hong, Richard, illus. 2010. (ENG.). 148p. (J). (gr. 7). pap. 12.95 *(978-0-9793219-3-1(X))* Big Book Pr., LLC.

Kelly, Dorothy A. Developing a Sense of Self: A Workbook of Tenets & Tactics for Adolescent Girls. 2006. (Illus.). 146p. (J). pap. 29.99 *(978-0-87101-366-8(5),* NASW Pr.) National Assn. of Social Workers/NASW Pr.

Lazear, Jonathon. Come On, Get Happy. 2004. (ENG., Illus.). 384p. *(978-0-00-717532-1(9),* HarperElement) HarperCollins Pubs. Ltd.

Lindsey, Brooklyn. Confessions of a Not-So-Supermodel: Faith, Friends, & Festival Queens, 1 vol. 2008. (Invert Ser.). (ENG., Illus.). 176p. (YA). (gr. 7-14). pap. 9.99 *(978-0-310-27753-8(1))* Zondervan.

Mills, J. Elizabeth. Expectations for Women: Confronting Stereotypes. 2010. (Young Woman's Guide to Contemporary Issues Ser.). 112p. (YA). (gr. 9-12). lib. bdg., E-Book 63.90 *(978-1-61532-907-6(2))* Rosen Publishing Group, Inc., The.

Mirriam-Goldberg, Caryn. Write Where You Are: How to Use Writing to Make Sense of Your Life: A Guide for Teens. 2004. (Illus.). 168p. (YA). (gr. 7-12). pap. 14.95 *(978-1-57542-060-8(0))* Free Spirit Publishing Inc.

Moe, Barbara. Understanding Negative Body Image. 2009. (Teen Eating Disorder Prevention Book Ser.). 192p. (gr. 7-12). 63.90 *(978-1-61511-242-5(1))* Rosen Publishing Group, Inc., The.

Monchamp, Genny. God Made Wonderful Me! Kaminski, Karol, illus. 2008. 14p. (J). (gr. -1). 8.95 *(978-0-8198-3108-8(5))* Pauline Bks. & Media.

Murphy Payne, Lauren. Just Because I Am: A Child's Book of Affirmation. Iwai, Melissa, illus. 2nd rev. ed. 2015. (ENG.). 36p. (J). (gr. -1-2). 16.99 *(978-1-63198-051-0(3))* Free Spirit Publishing Inc.

—Just Because I Am / Solo Porque Soy Yo: A Child's Book of Affirmation / un Libro de Afirmaciones para Ninos. Iwai, Melissa, illus. 2018. (ENG.). 44p. (J). (gr. -1-3). pap. 12.99 *(978-1-63198-335-1(0),* 83351) Free Spirit Publishing Inc.

Strickland, Jennifer. Pretty from the Inside Out: Discover All the Ways God Made You Special. 2015. (ENG.). 128p. (J). (gr. 2-6). pap. 11.99 *(978-0-7369-5634-5(4),* 6956345) Harvest Hse. Pubs.

Ward, Lesley. Showdown: Underdogs (Level 7) 2018. (TIME(r): Informational Text Ser.). (ENG., Illus.). 48p. (J). (gr. 6-8). pap. 11.99 *(978-1-4258-5007-4(3))* Teacher Created Materials, Inc.

Weiss, S. I. Coping with the Beauty Myth: A Guide for Real Girls. 2009. (Coping Ser.). 192p. (gr. 7-12). 63.90 *(978-1-61512-014-7(9))* Rosen Publishing Group, Inc., The.

Willett, Edward. Negative Body Image. (Danger Zone: Dieting & Eating Disorders Ser.). 64p. (gr. 5-6). 2009. 55.90 *(978-1-61512-125-0(0))* 2007. (ENG., Illus.). (YA). lib. bdg. 37.13 *(978-1-4042-1995-3(1),* f6b5288b-4dd7-49d8-9ab5-76419a56a291) Rosen Publishing Group, Inc., The.

Wooster, Patricia. Ignite Your Spark: Discovering Who You Are from the Inside Out. 2017. (ENG., Illus.). 224p. (YA). (gr. 7). pap. 12.99 *(978-1-58270-564-4(X))* Simon Pulse/Beyond Words.

SELF-PERCEPTION—FICTION

Alfonsi, Alice, adapted by. Face-off. 2006. (Hannah Montana Ser.). (Illus.). 126p. (J). (gr. 3-7). 12.65 *(978-0-7569-8315-4(0))* Perfection Learning Corp.

Allen, Crystal. The Laura Line. 2016. (ENG.). 352p. (J). (gr. 3-7). pap. 6.99 *(978-0-06-249021-6(4),* Balzer & Bray) HarperCollins Pubs.

Andrews, Julie & Hamilton, Emma Walton. The Very Fairy Princess. Davenier, Christine, illus. 2010. (Very Fairy Princess Ser.). (ENG.). 32p. (J). (gr. -1-3). 18.99 *(978-0-316-04050-1(9))* Little, Brown Bks. for Young Readers.

Angelou, Maya. Cedric of Jamaica. Rockwell, Lizzy, illus. 2005. (Random House Pictureback Book Ser.). (J). *(978-0-375-83269-7(6))* Random Hse., Inc.

Anonymous. Letting Ana Go. 2013. (Anonymous Diaries). (ENG.). 304p. (YA). (gr. 9). 17.99 *(978-1-4424-7223-5(5))*; (Illus.). pap. 11.99 *(978-1-4424-7213-6(8))* Simon Pulse. (Simon Pulse).

Auerbach, Annie. Spongebob Superstar, Vol. 5. 2004. 64p. (J). (gr. 2-5). pap. 17.00 incl. audio *(978-1-4000-8628-3(0),* Listening Library) Random Hse. Audio Publishing Group.

Avi. The True Confessions of Charlotte Doyle. 2012. lib. bdg. 17.20 *(978-0-606-26779-3(4))* Turtleback.

—The True Confessions of Charlotte Doyle (Scholastic Gold), 1 vol. 2012. (ENG.). 240p. (J). (gr. 4-7). pap. 9.99 *(978-0-545-47711-6(5),* Scholastic Paperbacks) Scholastic, Inc.

Ballard, Alexandra. What I Lost. 2018. (ENG.). 400p. (YA). pap. 19.99 *(978-1-250-15842-0(7),* 900160480) Square Fish.

Barnwell, Ysaye M. No Mirrors in My Nana's House: Musical CD & Book. Saint James, Synthia, illus. 2005. (ENG.). 32p. (J). (gr. -1-3). reprint ed. audio compact disk 10.99 *(978-0-15-205243-0(7),* 1195796, Clarion Bks.) HarperCollins Pubs.

Barreto, Sandra Maciel. No Fundo Do Fundo Do Mar. Rodrigues, Felipe Lima, illus. 2014. (POR.). 59p. (J). *(978-85-420-0460-1(4))* Expressao Grafica e Editora Ltda.

Bencastro, Mario. A Promise to Keep. Giersbach-Rascon, Susan, tr. from SPA. 2005. 134p. (J). (gr. 3-7). pap. 9.95 *(978-1-55885-457-4(6),* Piñata Books) Arte Publico Pr.

Billingsley, Franny. Chime. 2011. (Playaway Young Adult Ser.). (YA). 59.99 *(978-1-61707-143-0(9))* Findaway World, LLC.

—Chime. 2012. (ENG.). 320p. (YA). (gr. 7-12). 26.19 *(978-0-8037-3552-1(9),* Dial) Penguin Publishing Group.

—Chime. 2012. (ENG.). 384p. (YA). (gr. 7-18). 8.99 *(978-0-14-242092-8(1),* Speak) Penguin Young Readers Group.

Bloom, Denise. More Than a Spoonful. 2007. 28p. (J). (gr. -1-2). pap. 5.95 *(978-0-9778113-2-8(8))* HeartFelt Stories LLC.

Bloom, Denise, et al. More Than a Spoonful. 2007. (Heartfelt Stories Ser.). (Illus.). 28p. (J). 12.95 *(978-0-9778113-0-4(1))* HeartFelt Stories LLC.

Bowman, Akemi Dawn. Starfish. (ENG.). (YA). (gr. 7). 2018. 368p. pap. 12.99 *(978-1-4814-8773-3(6))* 2017. (Illus.). 352p. 19.99 *(978-1-4814-8772-6(8))* Simon Pulse. (Simon Pulse).

Brande, Robin. Fat Cat. 2011.Tr. of Fat Cat. (ENG.). 336p. (YA). (gr. 8-12). lib. bdg. 26.19 *(978-0-375-94449-9(4),* Knopf Bks. for Young Readers) Random Hse. Children's Bks.

Brian, Kate, pseud. Sweet 16. 2007. (ENG.). 288p. (YA). (gr. 7-12). pap. 9.99 *(978-1-4169-0033-7(0),* Simon & Schuster Bks. For Young Readers) Simon & Schuster Bks. For Young Readers.

Brightwood, Laura, illus. Look What You've Done. Brightwood, Laura, . 2007. (J). DVD *(978-1-934409-03-9(0))* 3-C Institute for Social Development.

Broski, Julie. Being Me. Vigla, Vincent, illus. 2011. (Rookie Ready to Learn Ser.). 40p. (J). (ENG.). pap. 5.95 *(978-0-531-26653-3(2))*; (gr. -1-k). lib. bdg. 23.00 *(978-0-531-26428-7(9))* Scholastic Library Publishing. (Children's Pr.).

Brown, Devin. Not Exactly Normal. 2006. (ENG.). 238p. (J). (gr. 4). per. 8.00 *(978-0-8028-5287-8(4),* Eerdmans Bks For Young Readers) Eerdmans, William B. Publishing Co.

Brown, Lisa. How to Be. Brown, Lisa, illus. 2006. (ENG., Illus.). 32p. (J). (gr. -1 — 1). 17.99 *(978-0-06-054635-9(2),* HarperCollins) HarperCollins Pubs.

Burns, Suzanne. The Moon Painters. 2003. 192p. 14.00 *(978-1-894942-36-2(1))* Zumaya Pubns. LLC.

Caletti, Deb. Honey, Baby, Sweetheart. 2008. (ENG.). 336p. (YA). (gr. 7-12). pap. 9.99 *(978-1-4169-5783-6(9),* Simon Pulse) Simon Pulse.

Cameron, Ann. The Secret Life of Amanda K. Woods. 2014. (ENG.). 208p. (J). (gr. 5-9). pap. 14.99 *(978-1-250-04419-8(7),* 900128307) Square Fish.

Cameron, Peter. Someday This Pain Will Be Useful to You: A Novel. 2009. (ENG.). 240p. (YA). (gr. 9-13). pap. 18.00 *(978-0-312-42816-7(2),* 900054659) Picador.

Canfield, Dorothy. Understood Betsy. 2004. reprint ed. pap. 1.99 *(978-1-4192-9201-9(3))*; pap. 24.95 *(978-1-4179-0955-1(2))* Kessinger Publishing, LLC.

Cash, M. A. Edward of Canterbury & the King of Red. Adams, Craig, illus. 2003. (J). *(978-0-9772711-0-8(2))* Jama Kids.

Castellucci, Cecil. Beige. (ENG., 320p. (YA). 2009. Illus.). (gr. 9). pap. 8.99 *(978-0-7636-4232-7(0))* 2007. (Illus.). (gr. 9-18). 16.99 *(978-0-7636-3066-9(7))* 2007. 25.66 *(978-1-4287-4767-8(2))* Candlewick Pr.

Christopher, Matt. Center Court Sting. 2005. (Sports Classics II Ser.). 140p. (J). lib. bdg. 15.00 *(978-1-59054-749-6(7))* Fitzgerald Bks.

—Center Court Sting. l.t. ed. 2007. (New Matt Christopher Sports Library). 160p. (J). (gr. 4-6). lib. bdg. 26.60 *(978-1-59953-106-9(2))* Norwood Hse. Pr.

—Slam Dunk. 2004. (ENG., Illus.). 128p. (J). (gr. 3-7). pap. 6.99 *(978-0-316-60762-9(2))* Little, Brown Bks. for Young Readers.

Coburn, Jake. Prep. 2005. 192p. (YA). (gr. 7-7). 6.99 *(978-0-14-240307-5(5),* Speak) Penguin Young Readers Group.

Connelly, Wendy. Fiona the Firefly! 2003. (Illus.). (J). 12.95 *(978-1-929039-16-6(6))* Ambassador Bks., Inc.

Conrad, Lauren. L. A. Candy. (L. A. Candy Ser.: 1). (ENG.). (YA). (gr. 9-18). 2010. 352p. pap. 9.99 *(978-0-06-176759-3(X))* 2009. 336p. 17.99 *(978-0-06-176758-6(1))* HarperCollins Pubs. (HarperCollins).

Conway, Celeste. When You Open Your Eyes. 2012. (ENG.). 320p. (YA). (gr. 9). pap. 9.99 *(978-1-4424-3031-0(1),* Simon Pulse) Simon Pulse.

Cook, Eileen. The Education of Hailey Kendrick. 2011. (ENG.). 288p. (YA). (gr. 9). pap. 9.99 *(978-1-4424-1326-9(3),* Simon Pulse) Simon Pulse.

Copeland, Cynthia L. The 15 Best Things about Being the New Kid. Vargo, Sharon, illus. 2006. (Silly Millies Ser.). 32p. (J). (gr. -1-3). lib. bdg. 21.27 *(978-0-7613-2889-6(0),* Millbrook Pr.); (gr. 2). per. 5.95 *(978-0-8225-6473-7(4),* First Avenue Editions) Lerner Publishing Group.

Coyle, Carmela Lavigna. Do Princesses Wear Hiking Boots? Gordon, Mike & Gordon, Carl, illus. 2003. (Do Princesses Ser.). (ENG.). 32p. (J). (gr. -1-2). 15.95 *(978-0-87358-828-7(2))* Cooper Square Publishing Llc.

Crutcher, Chris. Deadline. (ENG.). (YA). (gr. 9). 2009. 336p. pap. 10.99 *(978-0-06-085091-3(4))* 2007. 320p. 17.99 *(978-0-06-085089-0(2))* HarperCollins Pubs. (Greenwillow Bks.).

—Deadline. 2011. 10.36 *(978-0-7848-3487-9(3),* Everbind) Marco Bk. Co.

Cumyn, Alan. Hot Pterodactyl Boyfriend. 2016. (ENG., Illus.). 416p. (YA). (gr. 9). 17.99 *(978-1-4814-3980-0(4),* Atheneum/Caitlyn Dlouhy Books) Simon & Schuster Children's Publishing.

Cuyler, Margery. Bullies Never Win. Howard, Arthur, illus. 2009. (ENG.). 32p. (J). (gr. k-3). 18.99 *(978-0-689-86187-1(7),* Simon & Schuster Bks. For Young Readers) Simon & Schuster Bks. For Young Readers.

Dean, Myers Walter. Monster. 2014. (ENG.). 304p. (J). (gr. 12-12). 14.24 *(978-1-63245-060-9(7))* Lectorum Pubns., Inc.

Dessen, Sarah. Saint Anything. 2016. (ENG.). 448p. (YA). (gr. 7). pap. 12.99 *(978-0-14-751603-9(X),* Speak) Penguin Young Readers Group.

—Saint Anything. 2016. lib. bdg. 22.10 *(978-0-606-38833-7(8))* Turtleback.

Durrant, George D. Shakespeare's Best Work: A Novel of Unexpected Family Ties & Uncommon Faith. 2003. 130p. pap. 10.95 *(978-1-55517-709-6(3),* 77093) Cedar Fort, Inc./CFI Distribution.

Echols, Jennifer. Biggest Flirts. 2014. (Superlatives Ser.). (ENG., Illus.). 336p. (YA). (gr. 9). pap. 9.99 *(978-1-4424-7445-1(9),* Simon Pulse) Simon Pulse.

Fisher, Dorothy Canfield. Understood Betsy. 2018. (ENG., Illus.). 108p. (J). 12.99 *(978-1-5154-3494-8(X))* Wilder Pubns., Corp.

Fox, Mem. The Goblin & the Empty Chair. Dillon, Leo & Dillon, Diane, illus. 2009. (ENG.). 32p. (J). (gr. k-3). 17.99 *(978-1-4169-8585-3(9),* Beach Lane Bks.) Beach Lane Bks.

Gantos, Jack. Best in Show for Rotten Ralph. Rubel, Nicole, illus. 2008. (Rotten Ralph Rotten Readers Ser.). (J). 28.95 incl. audio compact disk *(978-1-4301-0451-3(1))*; 25.95 incl. audio *(978-1-4301-0448-3(1))* Live Oak Media.

Gerber, Linda. Now & Zen. 2006. (S. A. S. S. Ser.). (Illus.). 224p. (YA). (gr. 7-18). 7.99 *(978-0-14-240657-1(0),* Speak) Penguin Young Readers Group.

Gologan, Trena. Esther's Younique Crown. 2008. 32p. pap. 16.25 *(978-1-4357-3544-6(7))* Lulu Pr., Inc.

Goss, Leon. Selfus Esteemus Personalitus Low. Tunell, Ken, illus. 2005. (J). pap. 26.19 *(978-1-933156-08-8(2),* VisionQuest Kids) GSVQ Publishing.

Goss, Leon, 3rd. Selfus Esteemus Personalitus Low. Tunell, Ken, illus. 2005. 32p. (J). per. 16.99 *(978-1-933156-00-2(7),* VisionQuest Kids) GSVQ Publishing.

Green, John. An Abundance of Katherines. 2008. (J). 69.99 *(978-1-60514-809-0(1))* Findaway World, LLC.

—An Abundance of Katherines. 2009. 9.68 *(978-0-7848-1947-0(5),* Everbind) Marco Bk. Co.

—An Abundance of Katherines. (ENG., Illus.). (YA). 2008. 264p. (gr. 7-18). 12.99 *(978-0-14-241070-7(5),* Penguin Books) 2006. 240p. (gr. 9-18). 19.99 *(978-0-525-47688-7(1),* Dutton Books for Young Readers) Penguin Young Readers Group.

—An Abundance of Katherines. 2008. 227p. 20.00 *(978-1-60686-090-8(9))* Perfection Learning Corp.

—Penguin Minis: an Abundance of Katherines. 2018. (ENG.). 576p. (YA). (gr. 9). pap. 12.00 *(978-0-525-55572-8(2),* Dutton Books for Young Readers) Penguin Young Readers Group.

Greene, Stephanie. Moose's Big Idea, 0 vols. Mathieu, Joe, illus. 2012. (Moose & Hildy Ser.: 1). (ENG.). 64p. (J). (gr. 1-3). pap. 6.99 *(978-0-7614-5698-8(8),* 9780761456988, Two Lions) Amazon Publishing.

Griffin, Bethany. Handcuffs. 2008. (ENG.). 320p. (YA). (gr. 9-12). lib. bdg. 22.44 *(978-0-385-90529-9(7))* Random House Publishing Group.

Grover, Lorie Ann. On Pointe. 2008. (ENG.). 320p. (J). (gr. 3-7). pap. 14.99 *(978-1-4169-7826-8(7),* McElderry, Margaret K. Bks.) McElderry, Margaret K. Bks.

Hall, Angela Marie. Priscilla Pennybrook: Hello World, I Have Arrived!, 1 vol. 2009. 55p. pap. 16.95 *(978-1-61582-899-9(0))* America Star Bks.

Halpern, Julie. Get Well Soon. 2009. (ENG.). 224p. (YA). (gr. 7-12). pap. 18.99 *(978-0-312-58148-0(3),* 900062005) Square Fish.

Harris-Wyrick, Wayne. Why Am I Me? Macquignon, Stephen, illus. 2011. 32p. pap. 17.99 *(978-0-9828346-2-6(4))* 4RV Pub.

Hayes, Sonia. Ms. Thang. 2009. (ENG.). 200p. (YA). per. 9.95 *(978-0-9777573-0-5(7))* NUA Multimedia.

—Urban Goddess. 2007. 224p. (YA). per. 9.95 *(978-0-9777573-1-2(5))* NUA Multimedia.

Henkes, Kevin. Olive's Ocean: A Newbery Honor Award Winner. (ENG.). 224p. (J). (gr. 3-7). 2003. 16.99 *(978-0-06-053543-8(1,* 53396925) 2005. reprint ed. pap. 8.99 *(978-0-06-053545-2(8))* HarperCollins Pubs. (Greenwillow Bks.).

Hijuelos, Oscar. Dark Dude. 2009. (ENG., Illus.). 464p. (YA). (gr. 8-18). pap. 14.99 *(978-1-4169-4945-9(3),* Atheneum Bks. for Young Readers) Simon & Schuster Children's Publishing.

Hoffman, Alice. Indigo. 2003. (ENG.). 96p. (gr. 4-7). pap. 6.99 *(978-0-439-25636-0(4),* Scholastic Paperbacks) Scholastic, Inc.

Holm, Jennifer L. Boston Jane: an Adventure. 2010. (Boston Jane Ser.: 1). (ENG.). 272p. (J). (gr. 3-7). 8.99 *(978-0-375-86204-5(8),* Yearling) Random Hse. Children's Bks.

—Wilderness Days. unabr. ed. 2004. (Boston Jane Ser.: No. 2). 288p. (J). (gr. 5-9). pap. 38.00 incl. audio *(978-0-8072-0787-1(X),* S YA 307 SP, Listening Library) Random Hse. Audio Publishing Group.

Holstein, Barbara Becker. Secrets: Diary of a Gutsy Teen. 2015. (ENG.). 144p. (J). (gr. 2-7). 12.95 *(978-1-62914-626-3(9),* Sky Pony Pr.) Skyhorse Publishing Co., Inc.

Hundal, Nancy. Kaleidoscopes & Butterfly Dreams. 2009. (ENG.). 112p. (YA). (gr. 5-9). pap. 12.95 *(978-0-88982-256-6(5))* Oolichan Bks. CAN. Dist: Univ. of Toronto Pr.

Jaffe, Gail Lois. The Enchanted Mirror. Holmes, Jon, ed. 32p. (YA). (gr. 6-18). 24.95 *(978-0-9667476-0-7(7))* Papillon Pr., Inc.

Jenkins, A. M. Out of Order. 2003. 256p. (J). lib. bdg. 16.89 *(978-0-06-623969-9(9))* HarperCollins Pubs.

Johnson, LouAnne. Muchacho: a Novel. 2011. (ENG.). 208p. (YA). (gr. 7). pap. 9.99 *(978-0-375-85903-8(9),* Ember) Random Hse. Children's Bks.

Johnson, Vincent L. Of Corn Silk & Black Braids. Crockett, Linda, illus. 2005. 32p. (J). (gr. k-3). 17.95 *(978-0-9657033-2-1(0))* Marzetta Bks.

Jones, Diana Wynne. The Merlin Conspiracy. 480p. (J). 2004. (Magids Ser.: 2). (ENG.). (gr. 3-7). pap. 9.99 *(978-0-06-052320-6(4),* Greenwillow Bks.) 2003. (gr. 5-18). 17.89 *(978-0-06-052319-0(0))* HarperCollins Pubs.

Kazmierczak, Jean. National Chrome 2: The Good, the Bad & the Indifferent. 2008. 76p. pap. 16.95 *(978-1-60703-641-8(X))* PublishAmerica, Inc.

Keplinger, Kody. The DUFF: (Designated Ugly Fat Friend) (ENG.). (YA). (gr. 10-17). 2011. 304p. pap., pap. 10.99 *(978-0-316-08424-6(7))* 2015. 320p. pap. 10.00 *(978-0-316-38180-2(2))* Little, Brown Bks. for Young Readers. (Poppy).

Kimmel, Elizabeth Cody. The Reinvention of Moxie Roosevelt. (ENG.). (J). 2011. 256p. (gr. 5-18). 6.99 *(978-0-14-241870-3(6),* Puffin Books) 2010. 208p. (gr. 6-8). 21.19 *(978-0-8037-3303-9(8))* Penguin Young Readers Group.

Kishimoto, Masashi. Naruto: Chapter Book, Vol. 1: The Boy Ninja. 2008. (Naruto: Chapter Bks.: 1). (ENG., Illus.). 80p. (J). (gr. 1-5). pap. 4.99 *(978-1-4215-2056-8(7))* Viz Media.

Klass, David. You Don't Know Me. 2010. (ENG.). 288p. (YA). (gr. 9-12). pap. 12.99 *(978-0-312-65302-6(6),* 900069443) Square Fish.

Klimo, Kate. Twinky the Dinky Dog. Fleming, Michael, illus. 2013. (Step into Reading Ser.). 48p. (J). (gr. k-3). pap. 5.99 *(978-0-307-97667-3(X),* Random Hse. Bks. for Young Readers) Random Hse. Children's Bks.

Koertge, Ron. Boy Girl Boy. 2007. (ENG., Illus.). 180p. (YA). (gr. 9-18). pap. 12.95 *(978-0-15-205865-4(6),* 1197613, Clarion Bks.) HarperCollins Pubs.

Kogler, Jennifer Anne. Ruby Tuesday. 2005. (ENG.). 320p. (J). (gr. 7-18). 15.99 *(978-0-06-073956-0(8))* HarperCollins Pubs.

Koja, Kathe. Talk. 2008. (ENG.). 144p. (YA). (gr. 7-12). per. 16.99 *(978-0-312-37605-5(7),* 900048334) Square Fish.

LaFaye, A. Nissa's Place. 2010. (ENG.). 256p. (J). (gr. 2-8). pap. 8.00 *(978-1-57131-697-4(3))* Milkweed Editions.

Leavy, Patricia. Blue. 2016. (Social Fictions Ser.: 18). (ENG., Illus.). 168p. pap. *(978-94-6300-353-7(3))* BRILL.

Littman, Sarah Darer. Purge. 2010. (ENG.). 240p. (J). (gr. 7). 8.99 *(978-0-545-05237-5(8),* Scholastic Paperbacks) Scholastic, Inc.

Lockhart, E. Real Live Boyfriends: Yes. Boyfriends, Plural. If My Life Weren't Complicated, I Wouldn't Be Ruby Oliver.

2011. (Ruby Oliver Quartet Ser.: 4). (ENG.). 240p. (YA). (gr. 7). pap. 9.99 *(978-0-385-73429-5(8)*, Ember) Random Hse. Children's Bks.
Lowry, Brigid. Follow the Blue: A Novel. 2006. (ENG.). 208p. (YA). (gr. 8-12). pap. 18.99 *(978-0-312-34297-5(7)*, 900030648, St. Martin's Griffin) St. Martin's Pr.
Lyga, Barry. The Astonishing Adventures of Fanboy & Goth Girl. 2007. (ENG.). 320p. (YA). (gr. 7-12). pap. 9.99 *(978-0-618-91652-8(0)*, 1015005, Clarion Bks.) HarperCollins Pubs.
Lynch, Chris. Me, Dead Dad, & Alcatraz. 3rd ed. 2005. (ENG.). 240p. (J). 15.99 *(978-0-06-059709-2(7))* HarperCollins Pubs.
Mackler, Carolyn. The Earth, My Butt, & Other Big Round Things. 2018. (ENG.). 288p. (YA). pap. 11.99 *(978-1-68119-798-2(7)*, 900187324, Bloomsbury USA Childrens) Bloomsbury Publishing USA.
—The Earth, My Butt, & Other Big Round Things, 1. 2012. (Earth, My Butt, & Other Big Round Things Ser.). (ENG., Illus.). 246p. (YA). (gr. 9). 24.94 *(978-0-7636-1958-9(2))* Candlewick Pr.
—Guyaholic. 2009. (ENG., Illus.). 192p. (YA). (gr. 9). pap. 7.99 *(978-0-7636-2801-7(8))* Candlewick Pr.
—The Universe Is Expanding & So Am I. 2019. (ENG.). 304p. (YA). pap. 10.99 *(978-1-68119-982-5(3)*, 900194721, Bloomsbury Young Adult) Bloomsbury Publishing USA.
Marchetta, Melina. Jellicoe Road. 2008. (ENG.). 432p. (YA). (gr. 8-18). 17.99 *(978-0-06-143183-8(4)*, HarperTeen) HarperCollins Pubs.
McCranie, Stephen. Stephen Mccranie's Space Boy Volume 2. McCranie, Stephen, illus. 2018. (Illus.). 240p. (J). (gr. 5-9). pap. 12.99 *(978-1-5067-0680-1(0)*, Dark Horse Books) Dark Horse Comics.
—Stephen Mccranie's Space Boy Volume 3. McCranie, Stephen, illus. 2019. (ENG., Illus.). 240p. (J). (gr. 5-9). pap. 12.99 *(978-1-5067-0842-3(0)*, Dark Horse Books) Dark Horse Comics.
McDonald, Abby. Boys, Bears, & a Serious Pair of Hiking Boots. (ENG., Illus.). 304p. (YA). (gr. 9). 2011. pap. 7.99 *(978-0-7636-4994-4(5))* 2010. 16.99 *(978-0-7636-4382-9(3))* Candlewick Pr.
McHay, Micki. The Ugly Snowflake (children's hard cover book with musical C. D.) 2006. (Illus.). (J). 15.95 *(978-0-9786826-0-6(2))* McHay, Micki.
McNamara, Margaret. How Many Seeds in a Pumpkin? (Mr. Tiffin's Classroom Series) Karas, G. Brian, illus. 2007. (Mr. Tiffin's Classroom Ser.). (ENG.). 40p. (J). (gr. -1-2). 17.99 *(978-0-375-84014-2(1)*, Schwartz & Wade Bks.) Random Hse. Children's Bks.
Messer, Celeste M. Andi's Choice. Hoeffner, Deb, illus. 2004. 82-92p. 4.95 *(978-0-9702171-6-5(1))* AshleyAlan Enterprises.
Mohler, Marie. Leonard's Song. 2008. 32p. 18.95 *(978-1-4357-1372-7(9))* Lulu Pr., Inc.
Montgomery, L. M. Anne of the Island. 2006. (ENG.). pap. *(978-1-4068-2171-0(3))*; pap. *(978-1-4068-3175-7(1))* Echo Library.
—Anne of the Island. 2004. reprint ed. pap. 1.99 *(978-1-4192-0718-1(0))*; pap. 30.95 *(978-1-4179-0885-1(8))* Kessinger Publishing, LLC.
—Anne of the Island. l.t. ed. 2004. 396p. 26.00 *(978-1-58287-640-5(1))* North Bks.
—Anne of the Island. 2010. (Puffin Classics Ser.). (ENG.). 368p. (J). (gr. 5-7). pap. 7.99 *(978-0-14-132736-5(7)*, Puffin Books) Penguin Young Readers Group.
Moranville, Sharelle Byars. 27 Magic Words. (ENG.). 208p. (J). (gr. 3-7). 2018. pap. 7.99 *(978-0-8234-4034-4(6))* 2016. 16.95 *(978-0-8234-3657-6(8))* Holiday Hse., Inc.
Moss, Marissa. The All-New Amelia. Moss, Marissa, illus. (ENG., Illus.). (J). 2013. 5.99 *(978-1-4169-1289-7(4))* 2007. 40p. (gr. 2-5). 14.99 *(978-1-4169-0908-8(7))* Simon & Schuster/Paula Wiseman Bks. (Simon & Schuster/Paula Wiseman Bks.).
Munsch, Robert. Makeup Mess. 2004. (Illus.). (J). (gr. k-3). spiral bd. *(978-0-616-11125-3(8))* Canadian National Institute for the Blind/Institut National Canadien pour les Aveugles.
—Makeup Mess. Martchenko, Michael, illus. 2004. (J). (gr. k-3). spiral bd. *(978-0-616-11124-6(X))* Canadian National Institute for the Blind/Institut National Canadien pour les Aveugles.
—Makeup Mess. Martchenko, Michael, illus. 2019. (ENG.). 32p. (J). pap. 7.99 *(978-0-439-98896-4(9))* Scholastic Canada, Ltd. CAN. Dist: Publishers Group West (PGW).
Myers, Walter Dean. Lockdown. (ENG.). (YA). (gr. 8). 2011. 272p. pap. 10.99 *(978-0-06-121482-0(5))* 2010. 256p. 16.99 *(978-0-06-121480-6(9))* HarperCollins Pubs. (Amistad).
—Monster. 2019. (ENG., Illus.). 336p. (YA). (gr. 8). reprint ed. pap. 12.99 *(978-0-06-440731-1(4)*, Amistad) HarperCollins Pubs.
—Monster: A Graphic Novel. Anyabwile, Dawud, illus. 2015. (Monster Ser.). (ENG.). 160p. (J). (gr. 8). pap. 15.99 *(978-0-06-227499-1(6)*, Quill Tree Bks.) HarperCollins Pubs.
Myracle, Lauren. Ten. 2012. (Winnie Years Ser.: 1). (ENG.). 240p. (J). (gr. 3-7). pap. 9.99 *(978-0-14-242134-5(0)*, Puffin Books) Penguin Young Readers Group.
—Twelve, 2. 2008. (Winnie Years Ser.: 3). (ENG.). 224p. (J). (gr. 5-8). 8.99 *(978-0-14-241091-2(8)*, Puffin) Penguin Young Readers Group.
Nash, Andy. Tatum & Her Tiger: For Kids Blessed with Passion. 2007. (Illus.). (J). 9.99 *(978-0-8127-0451-8(7))* Autumn Hse. Publishing Co.
Neasi, Barbara J. So Many Me's. 2004. (Rookie Reader Español Ser.). (ENG.). 32p. (J). (gr. k-2). pap. 4.95 *(978-0-516-27786-8(3)*, Children's Pr.) Scholastic Library Publishing.
Nolan, Han. Send Me down a Miracle. 2003. (ENG.). 276p. (YA). (gr. 7-12). pap. 15.95 *(978-0-15-204680-4(1)*, 252782, Clarion Bks.) HarperCollins Pubs.
Novel Units. Dogsong Novel Units Teacher Guide. 2019. (ENG.). (YA). pap. 12.99 *(978-1-56137-342-0(7)*, Novel Units, Inc.) Classroom Library Co.
Oliver, Lauren. Before I Fall. (ENG.). (YA). (gr. 9). 2021. 544p. pap. 11.99 *(978-0-06-172681-1(8))* 2010. 480p. 17.99 *(978-0-06-172680-4(X))* HarperCollins Pubs. (HarperCollins).
—Before I Fall. 2010. 368p. pap. *(978-0-340-98090-3(7)*, Hodder Paperbacks) Hodder & Stoughton.
—Before I Fall. 2016. (YA). lib. bdg. 22.10 *(978-0-606-23576-1(0))* Turtleback.
Óscar, Hijuelos. Dark Dude. 2010. (SPA.). 430p. (YA). (gr. 9-18). 19.99 *(978-84-441-4316-3(2))* Everest Editora ESP. Dist: Lectorum Pubns., Inc.
Palatini, Margie. Geek Chic: the Zoey Zone. Palatini, Margie, illus. 2010. (ENG., Illus.). 192p. (J). (gr. 3-6). pap. 6.99 *(978-0-06-113900-0(9)*, Tegen, Katherine Bks) HarperCollins Pubs.
Paulsen, Gary. Dogsong. 2007. (ENG.). 192p. (J). (gr. 5-9). pap. 8.99 *(978-1-4169-3962-7(8)*, Simon & Schuster Bks. For Young Readers) Simon & Schuster Bks. For Young Readers.
—Dogsong. 2007. (ENG.). 192p. (YA). (gr. 7). mass mkt. 7.99 *(978-1-4169-3919-1(9)*, Simon Pulse) Simon Pulse.
Pearce, Jackson. Ellie, Engineer: in the Spotlight. 2019. (Ellie, Engineer Ser.). (ENG., Illus.). 208p. (J). 16.99 *(978-1-5476-0185-1(X)*, 900203119, Bloomsbury Children's Bks.) Bloomsbury Publishing USA.
Pearson, Mary E. The Adoration of Jenna Fox. 2008. (Jenna Fox Chronicles Ser.: 1). (ENG.). 272p. (YA). (gr. 7-12). 26.99 *(978-0-8050-7668-4(9)*, 900045743, Holt, Henry & Co. Bks. For Young Readers) Holt, Henry & Co.
—The Adoration of Jenna Fox. 2011. 9.46 *(978-0-7848-3478-7(4)*, Everbind) Marco Bk. Co.
—The Adoration of Jenna Fox. 2009. (Jenna Fox Chronicles Ser.: 1). (ENG.). 288p. (YA). (gr. 7-12). pap. 11.99 *(978-0-312-59441-1(0)*, 900062867) Square Fish.
Pelley, Kathleen T. Raj the Bookstore Tiger. Keiser, Paige, illus. 2011. 32p. (J). (gr. -1-3). 15.95 *(978-1-58089-230-8(2))* Charlesbridge Publishing, Inc.
Pennington, Jessica. When Summer Ends: A Novel. 2020. (ENG.). 288p. (YA). pap. 16.99 *(978-1-250-18731-4(1)*, 900191792, Tor Teen) Doherty, Tom Assocs., LLC.
Pennypacker, Sara. The Talented Clementine. Frazee, Marla, illus. (Clementine Ser.: 2). (ENG.). (J). (gr. 1-5). 2008. 160p. pap. 5.99 *(978-0-7868-3871-4(X))* 2007. 144p. 28.99 *(978-0-7868-3870-7(1))* Little, Brown Bks. for Young Readers.
Peters, Julie Anne. Pretend You Love Me. 2011. (ENG.). 304p. (YA). (gr. 10-17). pap. 16.99 *(978-0-316-12741-7(8))* Little, Brown Bks. for Young Readers.
Polacco, Patricia. Gracias, Senor Falker. 2006. (SPA., Illus.). 34p. (J). (gr. 2-3). per. 9.99 *(978-1-933032-02-3(2)*, LC34004) Lectorum Pubns., Inc.
—Thank You, Mr. Falker. Polacco, Patricia, illus. 2012. (Illus.). 40p. (J). (gr. k-3). 15.99 *(978-0-399-25762-9(4)*, Philomel Bks.) Penguin Young Readers Group.
Proimos III, James, Jr. 12 Things to Do Before You Crash & Burn. 2011. (ENG.). 128p. (YA). (gr. 9-13). 18.99 *(978-1-59643-595-7(X)*, 900065550) Roaring Brook Pr.
Queen Latifah. Queen of the Scene. Morrison, Frank, illus. 2006. 32p. (J). (gr. -1-3). 17.89 incl. audio compact disk *(978-0-06-077857-6(1)*, Geringer, Laura Book) HarperCollins Pubs.
Quick, Matthew. Every Exquisite Thing. 2016. (ENG.). 272p. (YA). (gr. 10-17). 17.99 *(978-0-316-37959-5(X))* Little, Brown Bks. for Young Readers.
Rahlens, Holly-Jane. Prince William, Maximilian Minsky, & Me. 2007. (ENG.). 320p. (YA). (gr. 7-11). per. 7.99 *(978-0-7636-3299-1(6))* Candlewick Pr.
Randle, Kristen D. Slumming. 2003. (Illus.). 240p. (J). lib. bdg. 16.89 *(978-0-06-001023-2(1)*, HarperTeen) HarperCollins Pubs.
Raschke, Erik. The Book of Samuel: A Novel. 2009. (ENG.). 256p. (YA). (gr. 4-7). pap. 19.99 *(978-0-312-37969-8(2)*, 900050340, St. Martin's Griffin) St. Martin's Pr.
Ratzlaff, Aaron J. Quills. 2011. (ENG.). 40p. (J). pap. 13.99 *(978-0-8361-9509-5(4))* Herald Pr.
Resau, Laura. What the Moon Saw. 2008. (ENG.). 272p. (J). (gr. 3-7). pap. 8.99 *(978-0-440-23957-4(5)*, Yearling) Random Hse. Children's Bks.
Rex, Adam. Why? Keane, Claire, illus. 2019. (ENG.). 60p. (J). (gr. k-3). 17.99 *(978-1-4521-6863-0(6))* Chronicle Bks. LLC.
Reynolds Naylor, Phyllis. Dangerously Alice. 2007. (Alice Ser.: 19). (ENG.). 304p. (YA). (gr. 9-12). 15.99 *(978-0-689-87094-1(9)*, Atheneum Bks. for Young Readers) Simon & Schuster Children's Publishing.
—Dangerously Alice. 2008. (Alice Ser.: No. 19). (ENG.). 320p. (YA). mass mkt. 6.99 *(978-0-689-87095-8(7)*, Simon Pulse) Simon Pulse.
—The Grooming of Alice. 2012. (Alice Ser.: 12). (ENG., Illus.). 240p. (J). (gr. 5-9). pap. 7.99 *(978-1-4424-3496-7(1)*, Atheneum Bks. for Young Readers) Simon & Schuster Children's Publishing.
—Please Don't Be True: Dangerously Alice; Almost Alice; Intensely Alice. 2011. (Alice Ser.). (ENG., Illus.). 768p. (YA). (gr. 9). pap. 12.99 *(978-1-4424-1721-2(8)*, Atheneum Bks. for Young Readers) Simon & Schuster Children's Publishing.
Reynolds, Peter H. Peter Reynolds Creatrilogy Box Set (Dot, Ish, Sky Color). 3 vols. 2012. (Creatrilogy Ser.). (ENG.). 96p. (J). (gr. k-4). 45.00 *(978-0-7636-6327-8(1))* Candlewick Pr.
—So Few of Me. Reynolds, Peter H., illus. 2006. (ENG., Illus.). 32p. (J). (gr. k-4). 15.00 *(978-0-7636-2623-5(6))* Candlewick Pr.
Rivers, Karen. The Girl in the Well Is Me. 2017. (ENG.). 224p. (J). (gr. 5-8). pap. 6.95 *(978-1-61620-696-3(9)*, 73696) Algonquin Young Readers.
Rue, Ginger. Rock 'n' Roll Rebel. 2016. (Tig Ripley Ser.). (ENG.). 349p. (J). (gr. 4-7). 16.99 *(978-1-58536-945-4(4)*, 204106) Sleeping Bear Pr.
Ryan, Amy Kathleen. Vibes. 2010. (ENG.). 264p. (YA). (gr. 9). pap. 14.95 *(978-0-547-24889-9(X)*, 1100901, Clarion Bks.) HarperCollins Pubs.
Salm, Arthur. Anyway* *a Story about Me with 138 Footnotes, 27 Exaggerations, & 1 Plate of Spaghetti. (ENG., Illus.). 192p. (J). (gr. 3-7). 2013. pap. 7.99 *(978-1-4424-2931-4(3))* 2012. 15.99 *(978-1-4424-2930-7(5))* Simon & Schuster Bks. For Young Readers. (Simon & Schuster Bks. For Young Readers).
Schraff, Anne. To Be Somebody. 2008. (Passages Ser.). 120p. (J). (gr. 4-6). lib. bdg. 13.95 *(978-0-7569-8390-1(8))* Perfection Learning Corp.
Schulte, Mary. Who Do I Look Like? Roos, Maryn, illus. 2006. (Rookie Reader Skill Set Ser.). (ENG.). 32p. (J). (gr. k-2). pap. 4.95 *(978-0-516-24758-8(1)*, Children's Pr.) Scholastic Library Publishing.
Scott, Elizabeth. Between Here & Forever. 2012. (ENG.). 272p. (YA). (gr. 9). pap. 9.99 *(978-1-4169-9485-5(8)*, Simon Pulse) Simon Pulse.
—Love You Hate You Miss You. 2010. (ENG.). 304p. (YA). (gr. 8). pap. 9.99 *(978-0-06-112285-9(8)*, HarperTeen) HarperCollins Pubs.
Scott, Lisa Ann. School of Charm. 2014. (ENG.). 304p. (J). (gr. 3-7). 16.99 *(978-0-06-220758-6(X)*, Tegen, Katherine Bks) HarperCollins Pubs.
Sedoti, Chelsea. Hundred Lies of Lizzie Lovett. 2017. (ENG.). 400p. (YA). (gr. 8-12). 17.99 *(978-1-4926-3608-3(8)*, 9781492636083) Sourcebooks, Inc.
Sellers, Bakari. Who Are Your People? 2022. (ENG., Illus.). 32p. (J). (gr. -1-3). 18.99 *(978-0-06-308285-4(3)*, Quill Tree Bks.) HarperCollins Pubs.
Sharif, Medeia. Bestest. Ramadan. Ever. 2011. (ENG.). 312p. (YA). (gr. 9-12). pap. 9.95 *(978-0-7387-2323-5(1)*, 0738723231, Flux) North Star Editions.
Sharp, Michael. Vayda Jane Bean - Chocolate. Van Tine, Laura, illus. 2007. 20p. pap. *(978-1-897455-70-8(4))* Avatar Pubns., Inc.
Shusterman, Neal. Full Tilt. 2009. (ENG.). 224p. (YA). (gr. 7). pap. 12.99 *(978-1-4169-9748-1(2)*, Simon & Schuster Bks. For Young Readers) Simon & Schuster Bks. For Young Readers.
—Full Tilt. 2003. (Neal Shusterman Collection). (ENG., Illus.). 201p. (YA). (gr. 7-12). 29.94 *(978-0-689-80374-1(5))* Simon & Schuster, Inc.
—Full Tilt. 2004. (ENG.). 208p. (YA). (gr. 7). mass mkt. 8.99 *(978-0-689-87325-6(5)*, Simon Pulse) Simon Pulse.
—The Schwa Was Here. 2006. 240p. (YA). (gr. 7-18). reprint ed. 10.99 *(978-0-14-240577-2(9)*, Puffin Books) Penguin Young Readers Group.
Smallman, Steve. Bumbletum. Warnes, Tim, illus. 2006. 24p. (J). (gr. -1-3). 15.95 *(978-1-58925-060-4(5))* Tiger Tales.
Snider, Cindy Gay. Finding Anna Bee. Chambers, Mary, illus. 2007. 163p. (J). (gr. 3-7). per. 9.99 *(978-0-8361-9392-3(X))* Herald Pr.
Sonnenblick, Jordan. Notes from the Midnight Driver. 2009. 265p. 18.00 *(978-1-60686-516-3(1))* Perfection Learning Corp.
—Notes from the Midnight Driver. 2007. (ENG.). 288p. (J). (gr. 7-12). pap. 11.99 *(978-0-439-75781-2(9)*, Scholastic Paperbacks) Scholastic, Inc.
Steig, William. Toby, Who Are You? Euvremer, Teryl, illus. 2004. 32p. (J). (gr. -1-3). lib. bdg. 15.89 *(978-0-06-000706-5(0)*, Cotler, Joanna Books) HarperCollins Pubs.
Stein, Gertrude, et al. The World Is Round. 75th ed. 2013. (ENG., Illus.). 128p. 19.99 *(978-0-06-220307-6(X)*, Harper) HarperCollins Pubs.
Talley, Gigi T. Fairest Florabell. 2012. 34p. 24.95 *(978-1-4560-0628-0(2))* America Star Bks.
Tamaki, Mariko. Saving Montgomery Sole. 2017. (YA). lib. bdg. 20.85 *(978-0-606-39584-7(9))* Turtleback.
Tamaki, Mariko & Mariko, Tamaki. Saving Montgomery Sole. 2017. (ENG.). 240p. (YA). pap. 11.99 *(978-1-250-10440-3(8)*, 900163717) Square Fish.
Thomas, Rob. Satellite Down. 2018. (ENG.). 272p. (YA). (gr. 7). pap. 11.99 *(978-1-5344-3010-5(5)*, Simon & Schuster Bks. For Young Readers) Simon & Schuster Bks. For Young Readers.
Thompson, Alicia. Psych Major Syndrome. 2010. (ENG.). 336p. pap. 8.99 *(978-1-4231-1549-6(X))* Disney Pr.
Tracy, Kristen. The Reinvention of Bessica Lefter. 2012. (Bessica Lefter Ser.). (ENG.). 320p. (J). (gr. 5). 7.99 *(978-0-375-84547-5(X)*, Yearling) Random Hse. Children's Bks.
Van Draanen, Wendelin. Flipped. 2003. 224p. (YA). (gr. 7-9). pap. 10.99 *(978-0-375-82544-6(4)*, Ember) Random Hse. Children's Bks.
Van Dusen, Chris. King Hugo's Huge Ego. 2011. (ENG., Illus.). 40p. (J). (gr. -1-2). 18.99 *(978-0-7636-5004-9(8))* Candlewick Pr.
Velmans, Hester. Isabel of the Whales. 2006. (ENG.). 192p. (J). (gr. 3-7). per. 6.99 *(978-0-440-42025-5(3)*, Yearling) Random Hse. Children's Bks.
Vipont, Elfrida. The Lark in the Morn. Freeman, T. R., illus. 2007. (Young Adult Historical Bookshelf Ser.). (ENG.). 196p. (J). (gr. 7-9). pap. 12.95 *(978-1-932350-22-7(5))* Ignatius Pr.
Vision, Mutiya Sahar. Disabilities. Alcantara, Ignacio, illus. 2009. 32p. 17.00 *(978-0-9659538-9-4(0))* Von Curtis Publishing.
Vivian, Siobhan. The List. 2014. (ENG.). 336p. (YA). (gr. 9). pap. 10.99 *(978-0-545-16918-9(6)*, Scholastic Paperbacks) Scholastic, Inc.
Vizzini, Med. Be More Chill. 2011. 9.68 *(978-0-7848-3414-5(8)*, Everbind) Marco Bk. Co.
Vizzini, Ned. Be More Chill. 2005. (ENG.). 320p. (YA). (gr. 7-12). per. 8.99 *(978-0-7868-0996-7(5)*, Disney-Hyperion) Disney Publishing Worldwide.
Vrettos, Adrienne Maria. Skin. (ENG.). (YA). (gr. 7-12). 2007. 272p. pap. 12.99 *(978-1-4169-0656-8(8))* 2006. (Illus.). 240p. 16.95 *(978-1-4169-0655-1(X))* McElderry, Margaret K. Bks. (McElderry, Margaret K. Bks.).
Wild, Margaret. Jinx. 2004. (ENG., Illus.). 224p. (YA). (gr. 9). reprint ed. pap. 11.95 *(978-0-689-86541-1(4)*, Simon Pulse) Simon Pulse.
Willner-Pardo, Gina. Prettiest Doll. 2012. (ENG.). 240p. (J). (gr. 5-7). 16.99 *(978-0-547-68170-2(4)*, 1476079, Clarion Bks.) HarperCollins Pubs.
Witherow, Wendy. Miranda's Makeover. Pulley, Kelly, illus. 2007. 93p. (J). *(978-1-934306-11-6(8))* Mission City Pr., Inc.
Wolcott, P. A. The Fox, the Badger, & the Bunny: A Dales Tale. Wolcott, K. Hannah, ed. Schweitzer, Patty, illus. 2009. 20p. pap. 24.95 *(978-1-60749-525-3(2))* America Star Bks.
Wolfson, Jill. What I Call Life. 2008. (ENG.). 288p. (J). (gr. 5-9). pap. 19.99 *(978-0-312-37752-6(5)*, 900049142) Square Fish.
Yaccarino, Dan. Unlovable. Yaccarino, Dan, illus. rev. ed. 2004. (ENG., Illus.). 32p. (J). (gr. -1-1). reprint ed. pap. 8.99 *(978-0-8050-7532-8(1)*, 900021844) Square Fish.
Zadoff, Allen. Food, Girls, & Other Things I Can't Have. 2011. (ENG., Illus.). 320p. (gr. 9). pap. 9.99 *(978-1-60584-151-8(3)*, Carolrhoda Lab™) Lerner Publishing Group.

SELF-RELIANCE

see also Self-confidence

Adams, Jennifer. I Am a Warrior Goddess. 2018. (I Am a Warrior Goddess Ser.: 1). (ENG., Illus.). 32p. (J). 17.95 *(978-1-68364-005-9(5)*, 900220842) Sounds True, Inc.
Berry, Joy. Getting Dressed. 2009. (ENG.). 40p. (J). (gr. k — 1). bds. 7.95 *(978-1-60577-009-3(4))* Berry, Joy Enterprises.
Child, Maria. Girls Own Book 1834. 2006. 292p. per. *(978-1-4067-9133-4(4)*, Pomona Pr.) Read Bks.
Dyer, Wayne & Dyer, Summer. 10 Secrets for Success & Inner Peace for Teens. 2004. 12.95 *(978-1-4019-0270-4(7)*, 2707, Hay Hse. Lifestyles) Hay Hse., Inc.
Farrin, Patty. The Teacup Café. Davis, Hilary, illus. 2018. (J). 19.95 *(978-1-63381-142-3(5))*; pap. 15.95 *(978-1-63381-143-0(3))* Maine Authors Publishing.
Noah, Michal Y. A-Z the Universe in Me. 2012. 18.95 *(978-0-7414-7841-2(2))*; pap. 13.95 *(978-0-7414-7840-5(4))* Infinity Publishing.
Tapper, Alice Paul. Raise Your Hand. Kissi, Marta, illus. 2019. 32p. (J). (gr. -1-3). 17.99 *(978-1-5247-9120-9(2)*, Penguin Workshop) Penguin Young Readers Group.

SELF-RELIANCE—FICTION

Adams, Diane. I Can Do It Myself!, 1 vol. Hayashi, Nancy, illus. 2013. 32p. (J). (gr. -1-k). 7.99 *(978-1-56145-725-0(6))* Peachtree Publishing Co. Inc.
Alger, Horatio. Frank & Fearless or the Fortunes of Jasper Kent. 2007. 228p. 20.99 *(978-1-4280-7465-1(1))*; per. 14.99 *(978-1-4280-7470-5(8))* IndyPublish.com.
Aliki. All by Myself! Aliki, illus. 2003. (ENG., Illus.). 32p. (J). (gr. -1-1). pap. 7.99 *(978-0-06-446253-2(6)*, HarperCollins) HarperCollins Pubs.
—All by Myself! 2003. (J). (gr. k-3). lib. bdg. 17.20 *(978-0-613-65685-6(7))* Turtleback.
Auch, M. J. One-Handed Catch. 2009. (ENG.). 272p. (J). (gr. 5-9). pap. 12.99 *(978-0-312-53575-9(9)*, 900054755) Square Fish.
Auch, Mary Jane. One-Handed Catch. 2009. 272p. (J). (gr. 5-9). pap. 6.99 *(978-0-312-58002-5(9))* Square Fish.
Baratz-Logsted, Lauren. Me, in Between. 2008. (ENG.). 208p. (J). (gr. 4-8). pap. 5.99 *(978-1-4169-5068-4(0)*, Simon & Schuster/Paula Wiseman Bks.) Simon & Schuster/Paula Wiseman Bks.
Boochever, Annie. Bristol Bay Summer. 2014. (ENG., Illus.). 258p. (gr. 3-7). (YA). 28.99 *(978-0-88240-994-8(8))* West Margin Pr. (Alaska Northwest Bks.).
Bruchac, Joseph. The Long Run. 2016. (PathFinders Ser.). (ENG.). 116p. (YA). (gr. 8-12). pap. 9.95 *(978-1-939053-09-1(9)*, 7th Generation) BPC.
Cameron, Ann. Gloria Rising. Toft, Lis, illus. 2004. (Julian's World Ser.). (ENG.). 112p. (J). (gr. 1-4). 6.99 *(978-0-440-41998-3(0)*, Random Hse. Bks. for Young Readers) Random Hse. Children's Bks.
Carmichael, Clay. Wild Things. 2012. (ENG.). 184p. (J). (gr. 4-7). pap. 9.99 *(978-1-59078-914-8(8)*, Astra Young Readers) Astra Publishing House.
—Wild Things, 6 vols. 2010. (J). 77.75 *(978-1-4498-0632-3(5))* Recorded Bks., Inc.
Clark, Shawnie. Wonder Wheels Dyslexic Font. 2017. (ENG., Illus.). (J). (gr. k-6). 17.99 *(978-1-365-86143-7(0))* Lulu Pr., Inc.
Climo, Liz. Rory the Dinosaur: Me & My Dad. 2015. (ENG., Illus.). 40p. (J). (gr. -1-3). 17.99 *(978-0-316-27728-0(2))* Little, Brown Bks. for Young Readers.
Coles, Michael Joseph, et al. The Land of Caring Bou. Banks, Timothy, illus. 2006. (J). *(978-0-87483-814-5(2))* August Hse. Pubs., Inc.
Connor, Leslie. Crunch. 2012. (ENG.). 336p. (J). (gr. 5). pap. 9.99 *(978-0-06-169234-5(4)*, Tegen, Katherine Bks) HarperCollins Pubs.
—Waiting for Normal. (ENG.). (J). (gr. 5). 2010. 320p. pap. 7.99 *(978-0-06-089090-2(8))* 2008. 304p. 16.99 *(978-0-06-089088-9(6))* HarperCollins Pubs. (Tegen, Katherine Bks).
Coon, Kelly. Gravemaidens. 416p. (YA). (gr. 9). 2020. pap. 11.99 *(978-0-525-64784-3(8)*, Ember) 2019. (ENG.). lib. bdg. 21.99 *(978-0-525-64785-0(6)*, Delacorte Pr.) Random Hse. Children's Bks.
Cooper, Brigitte Henry. Balancing Act. Heitz, Tim, illus. 2017. (Game Face Ser.). (ENG.). 112p. (J). (gr. 2-5). lib. bdg. 38.50 *(978-1-5321-3043-4(0)*, 27045, Calico Chapter Bks.) ABDO Publishing Co.
Decker, Tim. The Punk Ethic. Decker, Tim, illus. 2012. (ENG., Illus.). 188p. (YA). 18.95 *(978-1-60898-120-5(7))*; pap. 9.95 *(978-1-60898-121-2(5))* namelos llc.
Denise, Carolyn. I Can Do It Myself! Chatterji, Somnath, illus. 2012. (ENG.). 16p. (J). (gr. -1-3). pap. 19.95 *(978-0-9835651-4-7(7))* Levi Bass Publishing.
Deshone, Jerry Michael. Bear in Mind. 2011. 24p. pap. 24.95 *(978-1-4626-2973-2(3))* America Star Bks.
Diesen, Deborah. The Pout-Pout Fish, Far, Far from Home. Hanna, Dan, illus. (Pout-Pout Fish Adventure Ser.). (ENG.). 32p. (J). 2019. bds. 8.99 *(978-0-374-31078-3(5)*, 900194752) 2017. 16.99 *(978-0-374-30194-1(8)*, 900141733) Farrar, Straus & Giroux. (Farrar, Straus & Giroux (BYR)).
Dorfman, Craig. I Knew You Could! A Book for All the Stops in Your Life. Ong, Cristina, illus. 2003. (Little Engine That Could Ser.). 32p. (J). (gr. -1-2). 12.99 *(978-0-448-43148-2(3)*, Grosset & Dunlap) Penguin Young Readers Group.
Duey, Kathleen. Korow: A Baby Chimpanzee's Story. Gurin, Lara, illus. 2008. (My Animal Family Ser.). (ENG.). 32p. (J). (gr. -1-3). 12.99 *(978-0-8249-1816-3(9)*, Ideals Pubns.) Worthy Publishing.
—Leo: A Baby Lion's Story. Gurin, Lara, illus. 2008. (My Animal Family Ser.). 32p. (J). (gr. -1-3). 12.99 *(978-0-8249-1817-0(7)*, Ideals Pubns.) Worthy Publishing.
—Nanuq: A Baby Polar Bear's Story. Gurin, Lara, illus. 2008. (ENG.). 32p. (J). (gr. -1-3). 12.99 *(978-0-8249-1818-7(5)*, Ideals Pubns.) Worthy Publishing.
Duncan, Alexandra. Salvage. 2014. (Salvage Ser.: 1). (ENG.). 528p. (YA). (gr. 8). 17.99 *(978-0-06-222014-1(4)*, Greenwillow Bks.) HarperCollins Pubs.
Ellis, Edward Sylvester. Through Forest & Fire. 2005. pap. 14.95 *(978-1-59224-221-4(9))* Wildside Pr., LLC.
Fleming, Candace. Imogene's Last Stand. Carpenter, Nancy, illus. 2014. 40p. (J). (gr. -1-3). 7.99 *(978-0-385-38654-8(0)*, Dragonfly Bks.) Random Hse. Children's Bks.

Ghigna, Charles. First Times, 1 vol. Smith, Lori Joy, illus. 2017. (ENG.). 32p. (J). (gr. -1-k). 19.95 *(978-1-4598-1198-0(4))* Orca Bk. Pubs. USA.
Giff, Patricia Reilly. Genevieve's War. 2019. (ENG.). 240p. (J). (gr. 3-7). pap. 7.99 *(978-0-8234-4178-5(4))* Holiday Hse., Inc.
—R My Name Is Rachel. 2012. (ENG.). 176p. (J). (gr. 4-7). pap. 6.99 *(978-0-440-42176-4(4)*, Yearling) Random Hse. Children's Bks.
Harazin, S. A. Painless. 2015. (ENG.). 304p. (YA). (gr. 8-12). 16.99 *(978-0-8075-6288-8(2)*, 807562882) Whitman, Albert & Co.
Henderson, Leah. One Shadow on the Wall. (ENG.). 448p. (J). (gr. 3-7). 2018. pap. 8.99 *(978-1-4814-6296-9(2))* 2017. (Illus.). 18.99 *(978-1-4814-6295-2(4))* Simon & Schuster Children's Publishing. (Atheneum Bks. for Young Readers).
Hengel, Katherine. Taking Control, 1 vol. unabr. ed. 2010. (District 13 Ser.). (ENG.). 48p. (YA). (gr. 9-12). 9.75 *(978-1-61651-276-7(8))* Saddleback Educational Publishing, Inc.
Holstein, Barbara Becker. The Truth: Diary of a Gutsy Tween. 2014. (ENG.). 176p. (J). (gr. 2-7). 12.95 *(978-1-62873-611-3(9)*, Sky Pony Pr.) Skyhorse Publishing Co., Inc.
Horvath, Polly. Everything on a Waffle, 1 vol. (ENG., Illus.). 160p. (J). pap. 8.95 *(978-0-88899-442-4(7))* Groundwood Bks. CAN. Dist: Publishers Group West (PGW).
—Everything on a Waffle. 2008. (Illus.). 154p. (gr. 5-9). 18.00 *(978-0-7569-8776-3(8))* Perfection Learning Corp.
—Everything on a Waffle. 2008. (ENG., Illus.). 176p. (J). (gr. 5-9). pap. 8.99 *(978-0-312-38004-5(6)*, 900050527) Square Fish.
—One Year in Coal Harbor. 2014. 224p. (J). (gr. 4-7). 7.99 *(978-0-385-38653-1(2)*, Yearling) Random Hse. Children's Bks.
Katherine, Paterson. Lyddie. 2014. (Puffin Modern Classics Ser.). (ENG.). 192p. (J). (gr. 1-4). 11.24 *(978-1-63245-222-1(7))* Lectorum Pubns., Inc.
Killion, Bette. Little Lek Longtail Learns to Sleep. Vidal, Beatriz, illus. 2016. 28p. (J). (gr. k-3). 17.95 *(978-1-937786-63-2(3)*, Wisdom Tales) World Wisdom, Inc.
Lanagan, Margo. Tintinnabula. Cai, Rovina, illus. 2018. (ENG.). 24p. (J). (gr. k-2). 19.99 *(978-1-74297-525-2(9))* Little Hare Bks. AUS. Dist: Independent Pubs. Group.
Larson, Kirby. Hattie Big Sky. (Hattie Ser.: 1). (YA). (gr. 7-7). 2008. (ENG.). 304p. 8.99 *(978-0-385-73595-7(2)*, Yearling) 2007. 336p. pap. 9.99 *(978-0-440-23941-3(9)*, Ember) Random Hse. Children's Bks.
—Hattie Big Sky. Lt. ed. 2007. (Literacy Bridge Young Adult Ser.). 381p. (YA). (gr. 7-12). 23.95 *(978-0-7862-9697-2(6))* Thorndike Pr.
—Hattie Ever After. 2014. (Hattie Ser.: 2). (ENG.). 256p. (YA). (gr. 7). pap. 8.99 *(978-0-375-85090-5(2)*, Ember) Random Hse. Children's Bks.
Law, Felicia. Kimberly the Koala: A Tale of Independence, 1 vol. Danson, Lesley, illus. 2010. (Animal Fair Values Ser.). (ENG.). 32p. (J). (gr. 2-2). pap. 11.55 *(978-1-60754-909-3(3)*, cfc08d6e-6671-4d78-b1c8-6b6c65e4a58d); lib. bdg. 27.27 *(978-1-60754-902-4(6)*, 97439e9a-18c3-41f8-b3c4-63f83053636a) Rosen Publishing Group, Inc., The. (Windmill Bks.).
—Limpopo the Lion: A Tale of Laziness & Lethargy, 1 vol. Messina, Lilli, illus. 2009. (Animal Fair Values Ser.). (ENG.). 32p. (J). (gr. 2-2). pap. 11.55 *(978-1-60754-808-9(9)*, d1903f80-3c78-4770-9a62-d63b8bbb7a33); lib. bdg. 27.27 *(978-1-60754-804-1(6)*, 5bbbc020-d15b-4a7e-8b61-201f65278e1c) Rosen Publishing Group, Inc., The. (Windmill Bks.).
Leguin, Ursula K. Jane on Her Own. Schindler, S. D., illus. 2003. (Catwings Ser.: No. 4). (ENG.). 48p. (J). (gr. 2-5). 5.99 *(978-0-439-55192-2(7))* Scholastic, Inc.
Leshem-Pelly, Miri. Scribble & Author. 2017. (ENG., Illus.). 32p. (J). 12.99 *(978-1-61067-575-8(4))* Kane Miller.
Maddox, Jake. Skateboard Struggle, 1 vol. Tiffany, Sean, illus. 2011. (Jake Maddox Sports Stories Ser.). (ENG.). 72p. (J). (gr. 3-6). pap. 5.95 *(978-1-4342-3424-7(X)*, 116445, Stone Arch Bks.) Capstone.
Maggiore, Lisa. Ava the Monster Slayer. Felten, Ross, illus. 2015. (Ava the Monster Slayer Ser.: 1). (ENG.). 36p. (J). (gr. -1-k). 16.99 *(978-1-63450-151-4(9)*, Sky Pony Pr.) Skyhorse Publishing Co., Inc.
Matson, Morgan. Since You've Been Gone. 2015. (ENG., Illus.). 480p. (YA). (gr. 7). pap. 12.99 *(978-1-4424-3501-8(1)*, Simon & Schuster Bks. For Young Readers) Simon & Schuster Bks. For Young Readers.
Mayer, Mercer. All by Myself. 2014. 24p. pap. 4.00 *(978-1-61003-371-8(X))* Center for the Collaborative Classroom.
McGinnis, Mindy. Not a Drop to Drink. 2013. (ENG.). 320p. (YA). (gr. 9). 17.99 *(978-0-06-219850-1(5)*, Tegen, Katherine Bks) HarperCollins Pubs.
Mikaelsen, Ben. Stranded. rev. ed. 2010. (ENG.). 288p. (J). (gr. 3-7). pap. 7.99 *(978-1-4231-3362-9(5))* Hyperion Bks. for Children.
Mlynowski, Sarah. Ten Things We Did (and Probably Shouldn't Have) (ENG.). (YA). (gr. 9). 2017. 384p. pap. 10.99 *(978-0-06-268303-8(9))* 2012. 368p. pap. 9.99 *(978-0-06-170126-9(2))* HarperCollins Pubs. (HarperTeen).
Mothershead, Martha Fulford. Petoskey Stone Soup. Clarkson, Janet M., illus. 2006. 32p. (J). 18.95 *(978-0-9785465-0-2(4))* Leelanau Pr.
Parrott, Darcie. Ladybug's Walk. 2007. (ENG.). 32p. (J). (gr. -1-k). 10.95 *(978-0-9772692-8-0(0))* Birch Island.
Paterson, Katherine. The Same Stuff As Stars. 2015. (ENG.). 256p. (J). (gr. 5-7). pap. 7.99 *(978-0-544-54030-9(1)*, 1608841, Clarion Bks.) HarperCollins Pubs.
—The Same Stuff as Stars. 2004. 270p. (gr. 3-7). 17.00 *(978-0-7569-2801-8(X))* Perfection Learning Corp.
Patterson, James & Tebbetts, Chris. Middle School: Save Rafe! Park, Laura, illus. 2014. (Middle School Ser.: 6). (ENG.). 288p. (J). (gr. 3-7). 13.99 *(978-0-316-32212-6(1)*, Jimmy Patterson) Little Brown & Co.
Patterson, James & Tebbetts, Christopher. Save Rafe! Park, Laura, illus. 2014. 269p. (J). *(978-0-316-28629-9(X))* Little Brown & Co.
Paulsen, Gary. Brian's Return. unabr. ed. 2004. (Middle Grade Cassette Librariestm Ser.). 115p. (J). (gr. 5-9). pap. 29.00 incl. audio *(978-0-8072-0658-4(X)*, S YA 292 SP, Listening Library) Random Hse. Audio Publishing Group.
—Brian's Return. 2012. (Hatchet Adventure Ser.: 4). (ENG.). 160p. (YA). (gr. 5). pap. 10.99 *(978-0-307-92960-0(4)*, Ember) Random Hse. Children's Bks.
—Fishbone's Song. 2016. (ENG., Illus.). 160p. (J). (gr. 5). 18.99 *(978-1-4814-5226-7(6)*, Simon & Schuster Bks. For Young Readers) Simon & Schuster Bks. For Young Readers.
—The River. unabr. ed. 2004. (Middle Grade Cassette Librariestm Ser.). 132p. (J). (gr. 5-9). pap. 29.00 incl. audio *(978-0-8072-8704-0(0)*, S YA 241 SP, Listening Library) Random Hse. Audio Publishing Group.
—The River. 2012. (Hatchet Adventure Ser.: 2). (ENG.). 176p. (YA). (gr. 5). pap. 9.99 *(978-0-307-92961-7(2)*, Ember) Random Hse. Children's Bks.
—The River. 2012. lib. bdg. 20.85 *(978-0-606-23880-9(8))* Turtleback.
Peralta, Joaquin. Emma Snow: At the Edge of the World. 2009. 206p. (J). pap. 17.00 *(978-1-934376-19-5(1))* Balona Bks.
Pérez, Ashley Hope. What Can't Wait. 2011. (Carolrhoda YA Ser.). (ENG.). 240p. (YA). (gr. 9-12). 17.95 *(978-0-7613-6155-8(3)*, Carolrhoda Bks.) Lerner Publishing Group.
Petrillo, Genevieve. Keep Your Ear on the Ball, 1 vol. Lyon, Lea, illus. 2007. (ENG.). 32p. (J). (gr. -1-3). 16.95 *(978-0-88448-296-3(0))* Tilbury Hse. Pubs.
Pratt, Drusilla. What Do I Love. 2012. (ENG.). 26p. 13.00 *(978-1-105-73983-5(X))* Lulu Pr., Inc.
Reynolds, Peter H. ¡Di Algo! (Say Something!), 1 vol. Reynolds, Peter H., illus. 2019. (SPA., Illus.). 40p. (J). (gr. -1-k). pap. 7.99 *(978-1-338-56596-6(6)*, Scholastic en Espanol) Scholastic, Inc.
—Say Something! Reynolds, Peter H., illus. 2019. (ENG., Illus.). 40p. (J). (gr. -1-3). 17.99 *(978-0-545-86503-6(4)*, Orchard Bks.) Scholastic, Inc.
Rinaldi, Ann. Juliet's Moon. 2010. (ENG., Illus.). 256p. (YA). (gr. 7). pap. 14.99 *(978-0-547-25874-4(7)*, 1402328, Clarion Bks.) HarperCollins Pubs.
Ross, Tony. I Want to Do It Myself! Ross, Tony, illus. 2011. (Andersen Press Picture Bks). (ENG., Illus.). 32p. (J). (gr. -1-3). 16.95 *(978-0-7613-7412-1(4))* Lerner Publishing Group.
Sarno-Doyle, Christine. Your Inside Shape. 2012. (ENG., Illus.). 32p. (J). 17.95 *(978-0-9824461-0-2(1))* SDP Publishing.
Schulz, Kathy. I Need a Little Help. Iosa, Ann, illus. 2011. (Rookie Ready to Learn — All about Me! Ser.). 32p. (J). (gr. -1-k). lib. bdg. 25.00 *(978-0-531-26526-0(9)*, Children's Pr.) Scholastic Library Publishing.
—Rookie Ready to Learn en Español: Necesito una Ayudita. Iosa, Ann, illus. 2011. (Rookie Ready to Learn Español Ser.). Orig. Title: Rookie Ready to Learn: I Need a Little Help. (SPA.). 32p. (J). pap. 5.95 *(978-0-531-26782-0(2)*, Children's Pr.) Scholastic Library Publishing.
Shank, Marilyn Sue. Child of the Mountains. 2013. 272p. (J). (gr. 4-7). 7.99 *(978-0-375-87331-7(7)*, Yearling) Random Hse. Children's Bks.
Sharafeddine, Fatima. The Servant, 1 vol. 2017. (ENG.). 160p. (J). (gr. 6). pap. 9.95 *(978-1-55498-308-7(8))* Groundwood Bks. CAN. Dist: Publishers Group West (PGW).
Smith, Bryan. Mindset Matters, Volume 2. Griffin, Lisa M., illus. 2017. (Without Limits Ser.: 2). (ENG.). 31p. (J). (gr. k-6). pap. 10.95 *(978-1-944882-12-9(X))* Boys Town Pr.
Sternberg, Julie. Like Pickle Juice on a Cookie. Cordell, Matthew, illus. 2011. (ENG.). 128p. (J). (gr. 3-5). 15.95 *(978-0-8109-8424-0(5)*, 658801, Amulet Bks.) Abrams, Inc.
Stott, Ann. I'll Be There. Phelan, Matt, illus. 2011. (ENG.). 32p. (J). (gr. -1-2). 14.99 *(978-0-7636-4711-7(X))* Candlewick Pr.
Stratton-Porter, Gene. A Girl of the Limberlost. (J). reprint ed. lib. bdg. 33.95 *(978-0-89190-948-4(6)*, Rivercity Pr.) Amereon Ltd.
—A Girl of the Limberlost. Benda, Wladyslaw T., illus. 2005. reprint ed. pap. 38.95 *(978-0-7661-9424-3(8))* Kessinger Publishing, LLC.
—A Girl of the Limberlost. 2006. 336p. (YA). 21.95 *(978-1-934169-30-8(7))*; pap. 10.95 *(978-1-934169-31-5(5))* Norilana Bks.
—A Girl of the Limberlost. (Twelve-Point Ser.). 2003. (J). lib. bdg. 25.00 *(978-1-58287-232-2(5))* 2004. 463p. 26.00 *(978-1-58287-716-7(5))* North Bks.
—A Girl of the Limberlost. 2011. 266p. pap. 17.99 *(978-1-61279-071-8(2))* Publishing in Motion.
Tarsky, Sue. Brown Bear Starts School. Aizen, Marina, illus. 2019. (ENG.). 32p. (J). (gr. -1-3). 16.99 *(978-0-8075-0773-5(3)*, 807507733) Whitman, Albert & Co.
Tennant, Kim. Thin Club. 2007. 52p. per. 10.00 *(978-1-4257-2619-5(4))* Xlibris Corp.
Trigiani, Adriana. Viola in Reel Life. 2011. (Viola Ser.: 1). (ENG.). 304p. (YA). (gr. 8). pap. 8.99 *(978-0-06-145104-1(5)*, HarperTeen) HarperCollins Pubs.
van Genechten, Guido. Alex & the Tart. 2005. (Von Hamm Family Ser.). (Illus.). 32p. (J). (gr. -1-2). 6.95 *(978-1-58925-393-3(0))* Tiger Tales.
Van Leeuwen, Jean. Cabin on Trouble Creek. 2008. (ENG.). 224p. (J). (gr. 3-7). 7.99 *(978-0-14-241164-3(7)*, Puffin Books) Penguin Young Readers Group.
Voigt, Cynthia. Mister Max: the Book of Kings: Mister Max 3. Bruno, Iacopo, illus. 2016. (Mister Max Ser.: 3). (ENG.). 352p. (J). (gr. 3-7). 8.99 *(978-0-307-97688-8(2)*, Yearling) Random Hse. Children's Bks.
—Mister Max: the Book of Lost Things: Mister Max 1. Bruno, Iacopo, illus. 2014. (Mister Max Ser.: 1). (ENG.). 400p. (J). (gr. 3-7). 10.99 *(978-0-307-97682-6(3)*, Yearling) Random Hse. Children's Bks.
Vrabel, Beth. A Blind Guide to Stinkville. 2015. (ENG.). 264p. (J). (gr. 2-7). 16.99 *(978-1-63450-157-6(8)*, Sky Pony Pr.) Skyhorse Publishing Co., Inc.
Waber, Bernard. Betty's Day Off. Date not set. (J). *(978-0-618-46875-1(7))* Houghton Mifflin Harcourt Publishing Co.
Weston Woods Staff, creator. I Like Me! 2011. 18.95 *(978-0-545-23376-7(3))*; 29.95 *(978-0-545-23373-6(9))*; 38.75 *(978-0-545-23378-1(X))* Weston Woods Studios, Inc.
White, Dianne & Wiseman, Daniel. Goodbye Brings Hello: A Book of Firsts. 2018. (ENG., Illus.). 40p. (J). (gr. -1-3). 17.99 *(978-0-544-79875-5(9)*, 1640192, Clarion Bks.) HarperCollins Pubs.
Wiles, Deborah. Love, Ruby Lavender. 2005. (ENG., Illus.). 240p. (J). (gr. 3-7). reprint ed. pap. 9.99 *(978-0-15-205478-6(2)*, 1196483, Clarion Bks.) HarperCollins Pubs.
—Love, Ruby Lavender. 2004. 216p. (J). (gr. 3-7). pap. 36.00 incl. audio *(978-0-8072-2096-2(5)*, Listening Library) Random Hse. Audio Publishing Group.
Young, Rebecca. Teacup. Ottley, Matt, illus. 2016. (ENG.). 40p. (J). (gr. -1-3). 17.99 *(978-0-7352-2777-4(2)*, Dial Bks) Penguin Young Readers Group.

SELF-RESPECT

Asher, Sandy, ed. With All My Heart, with All My Mind: Thirteen Stories about Growing up Jewish. 2004. Orig. Title: Today I Am. 164p. (J). (gr. 4-8). reprint ed. pap. 18.00 *(978-0-7567-7692-3(9))* DIANE Publishing Co.
Greene, Ida. Looking for Love in All the Wrong Places. 2013. 90p. (Orig.). (gr. 10-18). pap. 19.95 *(978-1-881165-05-7(1))* People Skills International.
Hood, Christine. Just Like Me. 2017. (Learn-To-Read Ser.). (ENG., Illus.). (J). pap. 3.49 *(978-1-68310-252-6(5))* Pacific Learning, Inc.
Jordano, Kimberly. I Am Special. 2017. (Learn-To-Read Ser.). (ENG., Illus.). (J). (gr. -1-2). pap. 3.49 *(978-1-68310-247-2(9))* Pacific Learning, Inc.
The Need to Know Library: Guidance for Today's Problems, 8 bks. Incl. Everything You Need to Know about Bipolar Disorder & Manic Depressive Illness. Sommers, Michael A. (J). (gr. 4-6). 2000. lib. bdg. 25.25 *(978-0-8239-3106-4(4)*, NTBIDI); Everything You Need to Know about Diabetes. Apel, Melanie Ann. (YA). (gr. 5-5). 1999. lib. bdg. 37.13 *(978-0-8239-3090-6(4)*, 1eb24220-8fee-4e52-a7cd-fd7616bee7d1); Everything You Need to Know about Family Court. Bianchi, Anne. (YA). (gr. 5-5). 1999. lib. bdg. 37.13 *(978-0-8239-3163-7(3)*, 3c810f7b-10f0-44b3-9532-bf3b3ee168c6); Everything You Need to Know about Hepatitis. Aronson, Virginia. (YA). (gr. 5-5). 1999. lib. bdg. 37.13 *(978-0-8239-3100-2(5)*, cbcc0226-a2d1-4f26-afc0-035aecb6c0f4); 64p. (Illus.). Set lib. bdg. 202.00 *(978-0-8239-9282-9(9))* Rosen Publishing Group, Inc., The.
Romain, Trevor. Cliques, Phonies, & Other Baloney. 2012. (Laugh & Learn Ser.). (ENG., Illus.). 136p. (J). (gr. 3-6). pap. 24.94 *(978-1-57542-045-5(7))* Free Spirit Publishing Inc.
Story Rhyme Staff. Self-Esteem: Stories, Poetry & Activity Pages. Story Rhyme Staff, illus. Date not set. (Illus.). 28p. (YA). (gr. 4-9). ring bd. 19.95 *(978-1-56820-107-8(9))* Story Time Stories That Rhyme.

SELLING

see Sales Personnel

SEMANTICS

Carr, Aaron. Opposites, with Code. 2012. (Science Kids Ser.). (ENG., Illus.). 24p. (J). (gr. -1-1). pap. 12.95 *(978-1-61913-308-2(3))*; lib. bdg. 27.13 *(978-1-61913-085-2(8))* Weigl Pubs., Inc. (AV2 by Weigl).

SEMMES, RAPHAEL, 1809-1877

Bailey, Tom. Raphael Semmes: Commander of the Alabama. 2011. (Illus.). 120p. (J). *(978-1-59421-062-4(4))* Seacoast Publishing, Inc.

SENATORS—UNITED STATES

see Legislators—United States; United States—Congress—Senate—Biography

SENEGAL

Berg, Elizabeth & Wan, Ruth. Senegal, 1 vol. 2nd rev. ed. 2010. (Cultures of the World (Second Edition)(r) Ser.). (ENG.). 144p. (gr. 5-5). 49.79 *(978-0-7614-4481-7(5)*, 079d697f-2e3d-4a7c-8e70-819f934aeb49) Cavendish Square Publishing LLC.
Bjorklund, Ruth. Senegal (Enchantment of the World) (Library Edition) 2019. (Enchantment of the World. Second Ser.). (ENG., Illus.). 144p. (J). (gr. 5-9). lib. bdg. 40.00 *(978-0-531-12695-0(1)*, Children's Pr.) Scholastic Library Publishing.
Mulroy, Tanya. Senegal. 2012. (J). pap. *(978-1-4222-2229-4(2))* Mason Crest.
—Senegal. Rotberg, Robert I., ed. 2012. (Evolution of Africa's Major Nations Ser.). (Illus.). 80p. (J). (gr. 7). 22.95 *(978-1-4222-2201-0(2))* Mason Crest.
Nevins, Debbie, et al. Senegal, 1 vol. 2018. (Cultures of the World (Third Edition)(r) Ser.). (ENG.). 144p. (J). (gr. 5-5). lib. bdg. 48.79 *(978-1-5026-3642-3(5)*, 2d1446a9-6f61-46b2-bb7c-74aa3fb7caf0) Cavendish Square Publishing LLC.
Obiols, Anna. Senegal, 1 vol. 2018. (On the Way to School Ser.). (ENG.). 32p. (gr. 3-3). 28.93 *(978-1-5081-9587-0(0)*, 5ef827c4-279f-4582-9146-e08a610b9b20); pap. 11.00 *(978-1-5081-9588-7(9)*, 1a60c19d-7eb6-4723-86b6-0cfc2744a2a6) Rosen Publishing Group, Inc., The. (Windmill Bks.).
Streissguth, Thomas & Streissguth, Tom. Senegal in Pictures. 2009. (Visual Geography Series, Second Ser.). (ENG., Illus.). 80p. (J). (gr. 5-12). 31.93 *(978-1-57505-951-8(7))* Lerner Publishing Group.

SENSES AND SENSATION

see also Hearing; Smell; Touch; Vision

Aliki. My Five Senses. Aliki, illus. 2015. (Let's-Read-And-Find-Out Science 1 Ser.). (ENG., Illus.). 32p. (J). (gr. -1-3). 17.99 *(978-0-06-238191-0(1)*, HarperCollins) HarperCollins Pubs.
—My Five Senses. 2014. (Let's-Read-And-Find-Out Science 1 Ser.). (ENG.). 32p. (J). (gr. k-3). 10.24 *(978-1-63245-272-6(3))* Lectorum Pubns., Inc.
All about My Senses. 2017. (All about My Senses Ser.). 24p. (gr. k-1). pap. 56.10 *(978-0-7660-8813-9(8))*; (ENG.). lib. bdg. 145.62 *(978-0-7660-8601-2(1)*, e4547c5b-c3ce-4ca6-ace7-3789e61e581f) Enslow Publishing, LLC.
Aloian, Molly. What Is Taste? 2013. (ENG., Illus.). 24p. (J). *(978-0-7787-0967-1(1))*; (gr. 1-2). pap. *(978-0-7787-0972-5(8))* Crabtree Publishing Co.
Animals & Their Senses, 4 vols. 2005. (Animals & Their Senses Ser.). (ENG.). 24p. (gr. k-2). lib. bdg. 49.34 *(978-0-8368-4801-4(2)*, e3a44f71-21b6-4067-9e17-5fa704f3a659, Weekly Reader Leveled Readers) Stevens, Gareth Publishing LLLP.
Animals & Their Senses/Los Sentidos de los Animales, 6 vols., Set. 2005. (Animals & Their Senses / Los Sentidos de Los Animales Ser.). (SPA & ENG.). 24p. (gr. k-2). lib. bdg. 74.01 *(978-0-8368-4813-7(6)*, d6f3be77-7ac1-4cc5-bc78-9cdb62ca2158, Weekly Reader Leveled Readers) Stevens, Gareth Publishing LLLP.
Appleby, Alex. Dinosaur's Five Senses, 1 vol. 2013. (Dinosaur School Ser.). 24p. (J). (gr. k-k). (ENG.). pap. 9.15 *(978-1-4339-9050-2(4)*, cbca5f8e-95cf-438b-a085-70bf63bcd585); pap. 48.90 *(978-1-4339-9051-9(2))*; (ENG., Illus.). lib. bdg. 25.27 *(978-1-4339-9049-6(0)*, 80fb95df-3648-4451-9dec-6c25c6ba7172) Stevens, Gareth Publishing LLLP.
—Lo Que Oigo / What I Hear, 1 vol. 2014. (Mis Cinco Sentidos / My Five Senses Ser.). (SPA & ENG.). 24p. (J). (gr. k-k). 24.27 *(978-1-4824-0869-0(4)*, 5af715a4-fe82-4a1d-9bb7-f08d22b7bbf8) Stevens, Gareth Publishing LLLP.
—Lo Que Toco / What I Touch, 1 vol. 2014. (Mis Cinco Sentidos / My Five Senses Ser.). (SPA & ENG.). 24p. (J). (gr. k-k). 24.27 *(978-1-4824-0877-5(5)*, eaa24db5-9dd7-476d-9819-f4ffbe35e3c5) Stevens, Gareth Publishing LLLP.
—What I Hear, 1 vol. 2014. (My Five Senses Ser.). (ENG., Illus.). 24p. (J). (gr. k-k). pap. 9.15 *(978-1-4824-0776-1(0)*, 0727c5d0-487f-458b-88ad-7deecc1b8a4f) Stevens, Gareth Publishing LLLP.
—What I See, 1 vol. 2014. (My Five Senses Ser.). (ENG.). 24p. (J). (gr. k-k). 24.27 *(978-1-4824-0808-9(2)*, 956e203e-c476-4591-a994-19b891c34901) Stevens, Gareth Publishing LLLP.
—What I Smell, 1 vol. 2014. (My Five Senses Ser.). (ENG.). 24p. (J). (gr. k-k). 24.27 *(978-1-4824-0813-3(9)*, 482ee750-d1df-44bc-b53b-c8ab9e786947); pap. 9.15 *(978-1-4824-0814-0(7)*, 5c2fb743-023e-42b3-ac04-ecaecd2885f1) Stevens, Gareth Publishing LLLP.
—What I Taste, 1 vol. 2014. (My Five Senses Ser.). (ENG., Illus.). 24p. (J). (gr. k-k). 24.27 *(978-1-4824-0818-8(X)*, 5ee37574-93d5-4980-82e9-f81d66a3e0f0) Stevens, Gareth Publishing LLLP.
—What I Touch, 1 vol. 2014. (My Five Senses Ser.). 24p. (J). (gr. k-k). (ENG.). pap. 9.15 *(978-1-4824-0823-2(6)*, 9ea243d7-cfb0-4a26-9b01-8849cfa8176d); pap. 48.90 *(978-1-4824-0824-9(4))* Stevens, Gareth Publishing LLLP.
Aragó, Mª Rosa. El pastel de chocolate. (SPA.). 32p. (J). 10.00 *(978-84-342-2515-2(8))* Parramon Ediciones S.A. ESP. Dist: Distribuidora Norma, Inc.
Baby Shakespeare. (Baby Einstein Ser.). (Illus.). 28p. (J). (gr. -1). pap. 19.98 incl. audio, VHS *(978-1-892309-15-0(7))* Baby Einstein Co., LLC, The.
Bailey, Jacqui. What Happens When You Use Your Senses?, 1 vol. 2008. (How Your Body Works (2008) Ser.). (ENG.). 32p. (gr. 3-3). pap. 10.60 *(978-1-4358-2616-8(7)*, 213b9c42-a9fe-4369-b095-f0cea982fb97, Rosen Classroom); (Illus.). (J). lib. bdg. 30.27 *(978-1-4042-4427-6(1)*, f58e93b6-4a41-47bd-82c8-427d722715bc) Rosen Publishing Group, Inc., The.
Ballard, Carol. Understanding the Senses, 1 vol. (Understanding the Human Body Ser.). (ENG., Illus.). 48p. (gr. 7-7). 2010. (YA). lib. bdg. 34.47 *(978-1-4358-9683-3(1)*, 25b20a02-45fe-431e-a791-d70e4100513e) 2009. (J). pap. 12.75 *(978-1-4358-9689-5(0)*, 5db284e5-27cb-47b5-a01f-0484de854b6d) Rosen Publishing Group, Inc., The. (Rosen Reference).
—Your Sense of Touch, 1 vol. 2010. (Your Body at Work Ser.). (ENG.). 32p. (YA). (gr. 2-4). lib. bdg. 29.27 *(978-1-4339-4115-3(5)*, 3585c295-56ff-43c0-a6ca-8170da28a2fc) Stevens, Gareth Publishing LLLP.
Barraclough, Sue. What Can I Taste? 2005. (J). *(978-1-4034-7081-2(2))*; (ENG.). 32p. pap. *(978-1-4034-7087-4(1))* Steck-Vaughn.
Beattie, Steven M., II. These Are My Sensors. Beattie, Steven M., II, illus. 2007. (Illus.). 32p. (gr. -1-k). 19.99 *(978-1-59879-310-9(1))* Lifevest Publishing, Inc.
Beaumont, Susanna. Baby Senses Taste. 2005. (Baby Senses Ser.). (Illus.). 12p. (gr. -1-k). per., bds. *(978-1-905051-50-2(6))* Make Believe Ideas.
Bellamy, Adam. What's Intuition?, 1 vol. 2017. (All about My Senses Ser.). (ENG.). 24p. (gr. k-1). lib. bdg. 24.27 *(978-0-7660-8722-4(0)*, 969ec410-c1ac-4191-96d7-4f63a2392173) Enslow Publishing, LLC.
—What's That I Feel?, 1 vol. 2017. (All about My Senses Ser.). (ENG.). 24p. (gr. k-1). lib. bdg. 24.27 *(978-0-7660-8720-0(4)*, 59c87403-bf41-483f-9854-3f01352a5e30) Enslow Publishing, LLC.
—What's That I Hear?, 1 vol. 2017. (All about My Senses Ser.). (ENG.). 24p. (gr. k-1). lib. bdg. 24.27 *(978-0-7660-8603-6(8)*, 1b61493e-7788-4e75-bcfd-813279a6ab34) Enslow Publishing, LLC.
—What's That Smell?, 1 vol. 2017. (All about My Senses Ser.). (ENG.). 24p. (gr. k-1). lib. bdg. 24.27 *(978-0-7660-8607-4(0)*, a6b1ff3a-84cd-4d1d-b401-31739f184159) Enslow Publishing, LLC.
—What's That Taste?, 1 vol. 2017. (All about My Senses Ser.). (ENG.). 24p. (gr. k-1). lib. bdg. 24.27 *(978-0-7660-8609-8(7)*, 160a54b5-dc4b-4ed4-8663-ad3e7c6fab06) Enslow Publishing, LLC.
Benbow, Ann & Mably, Colin. Sensational Human Body Science Projects, 1 vol. 2010. (Real Life Science Experiments Ser.). (ENG., Illus.). 48p. (gr. 3-3). lib. bdg. 27.93 *(978-0-7660-3149-4(7)*, f43b4cf3-f2e3-4245-87d5-828cf077ff6d) Enslow Publishing, LLC.
Benchmark Education Company, LLC Staff, compiled by. Senses. 2006. (J). 91.00 *(978-1-4108-7033-9(2))* Benchmark Education Co.
Bentley, Joyce. Soft. 2006. (Things Around Us Ser.). (J). *(978-1-59389-278-4(0))* Chrysalis Education.

—Wet. 2006. (Things Around Us Ser.). (J). *(978-1-59389-279-1(9))* Chrysalis Education.

Bjorklund, Ruth. The Senses, 1 vol. 2010. (Amazing Human Body Ser.). (ENG.). 80p. (gr. 6-6). lib. bdg. 36.93 *(978-0-7614-4043-7(7),* 899eb052-895b-4ed8-bd05-de7932f18b51) Cavendish Square Publishing LLC.

Bodach, Vijaya Khisty. Making Observations. 2008. (Discovering & Exploring Science Ser.). (Illus.). 16p. (J). (gr. -1-3). lib. bdg. 12.95 *(978-0-7569-8431-1(9))* Perfection Learning Corp.

Boothroyd, Jennifer. Lightning Bolt Books: Your Amazing Senses, 5 vols., Set. Incl. What Is Taste? (Illus.). 32p. (J). (gr. 1-3). 2009. 29.32 *(978-0-7613-4251-9(6),* a8c9808e-0164-43d7-8cf5-951821e4084d, Lerner Pubns.); 2009. Set lib. bdg. 126.30 *(978-0-7613-4246-5(X),* Lerner Pubns.) Lerner Publishing Group.

—What Is Taste? 2009. (Lightning Bolt Books (r) — Your Amazing Senses Ser.). (ENG., Illus.). 32p. (J). (gr. 1-3). 29.32 *(978-0-7613-4251-9(6),* a8c9808e-0164-43d7-8cf5-951821e4084d, Lerner Pubns.); pap. 9.99 *(978-0-7613-5017-0(9),* 9e85326b-8c89-487d-94da-947238e7a1a7) Lerner Publishing Group.

Boynton, Jeannette. God Loves Variety. Boynton, Jeannette & Holdeen, Bonnie, illus. 2007. (J). per. 10.99 *(978-1-59879-264-5(4))* Lifevest Publishing, Inc.

Brocket, Jane. Cold, Crunchy, Colorful: Using Our Senses. Brocket, Jane, photos by. 2014. (Jane Brocket's Clever Concepts Ser.). (ENG., Illus.). 32p. (J). (gr. -1-2). lib. bdg. 26.65 *(978-1-4677-0233-1(1),* e6434536-167e-4e83-86d1-0a1bc96cc0a9, Millbrook Pr.) Lerner Publishing Group.

Buchanan, Shelly. Animal Senses. 2015. (Science: Informational Text Ser.). (ENG.). 32p. (J). (gr. 3-5). pap. 11.99 *(978-1-4807-4678-7(9))* Teacher Created Materials, Inc.

Burton, Margie, et al. My Five Senses. 2011. (Early Connections Ser.). (J). *(978-1-61672-263-0(0))* Benchmark Education Co.

Canavan, Thomas. Do You Really Taste with Your Nose? Questions about the Senses, 1 vol. 2016. (Human Body FAQ Ser.). (ENG.). 32p. (J). (gr. 3-3). pap. 11.00 *(978-1-4994-3163-6(5),* c2ec545a-6dac-453d-9906-ec564b59dc1f, PowerKids Pr.) Rosen Publishing Group, Inc., The.

Cardenas, Ernesto A. The Five Senses. 2009. pap. 4.95 *(978-1-60698-074-3(2))* Milo Educational Bks. & Resources.

—With My Senses. 2009. 19.95 *(978-1-60698-029-3(7));* pap. 3.95 *(978-1-60698-027-9(0))* Milo Educational Bks. & Resources.

Carlson-Berne, Emma. Let's Explore the Sense of Taste. 2020. (Bumba Books (r) — Discover Your Senses Ser.). (ENG., Illus.). 24p. (J). (gr. -1-1). 26.65 *(978-1-5415-7688-9(8),* e07731df-6c3d-4c15-98b4-6acc59869b14, Lerner Pubns.) Lerner Publishing Group.

Carr, Aaron. El Gusto. 2013. (Mis Sentidos Ser.). (SPA., Illus.). 24p. (J). (gr. 3-7). lib. bdg. 27.13 *(978-1-62127-581-7(7),* AV2 by Weigl) Weigl Pubs., Inc.

—El Oido. 2013. (Mis Sentidos Ser.). (SPA., Illus.). 24p. (J). (gr. -1-3). lib. bdg. 27.13 *(978-1-62127-575-6(2),* AV2 by Weigl) Weigl Pubs., Inc.

—El Olfato. 2013. (Mis Sentidos Ser.). (SPA., Illus.). 24p. (J). (gr. 3-7). lib. bdg. 27.13 *(978-1-62127-579-4(5),* AV2 by Weigl) Weigl Pubs., Inc.

—Tacto. 2014. (SPA., Illus.). 24p. (J). *(978-1-62127-583-1(3))* Weigl Pubs., Inc.

—Vista. 2014. (SPA., Illus.). 24p. (J). *(978-1-62127-577-0(9))* Weigl Pubs., Inc.

Casado, Dami & Casado, Alicia. El Gusto. 2005. (Sentidos y Algo Más). (SPA.). 10p. *(978-84-272-6414-4(3))* Molino, Editorial.

—El Oido. 2005. (Sentidos y Algo Más). (SPA & ESP.). 16p. 8.99 *(978-84-272-6412-0(7))* Molino, Editorial ESP. Dist: Santillana USA Publishing Co., Inc.

—La Palabra. 2005. (Sentidos y Algo Más). (SPA & ESP.). 16p. 8.99 *(978-84-272-6416-8(X))* Molino, Editorial ESP. Dist: Santillana USA Publishing Co., Inc.

—El Tacto. 2005. (Sentidos y Algo Más). (SPA & ESP.). 16p. 8.99 *(978-84-272-6415-1(1))* Molino, Editorial ESP. Dist: Santillana USA Publishing Co., Inc.

—La Vista. 2005. (Sentidos y Algo Más). (SPA & ESP.). 16p. 8.99 *(978-84-272-6411-3(9))* Molino, Editorial ESP. Dist: Santillana USA Publishing Co., Inc.

Chancellor, Deborah. Lemons Taste Sour: And Other Questions about the Senses. 2008. (I Wonder Why Ser.). (ENG., Illus.). 32p. (J). (gr. k-3). pap. 21.19 *(978-0-7534-6232-4(X),* 9780753462324) Kingfisher Publications, plc GBR. Dist: Children's Plus, Inc.

Chara, Kathleen A. & Chara, Paul J. Sensory Smarts: A Book for Kids with ADHD or Autism Spectrum Disorders Struggling with Sensory Integration Problems. 2004. (Illus.). 80p. pap. 22.95 *(978-1-84310-783-5(X),* 692212) Kingsley, Jessica Pubs. GBR. Dist: Hachette UK Distribution.

Chudler, Eric H. Brain Lab for Kids: 52 Mind-Blowing Experiments, Models, & Activities to Explore Neuroscience, Volume 15. 2018. (Lab for Kids Ser.: 15). (ENG., Illus.). 144p. (J). (gr. 2-5). pap. 24.99 *(978-1-63159-396-3(X),* 225966, Quarry Bks.) Quarto Publishing Group USA.

Claymation Sensation, 12 vols. 2016. (Claymation Sensation Ser.). 32p. (gr. 3-3). (ENG.). 181.62 *(978-1-4994-8096-2(2),* c7f86336-4ddd-47bc-ba1a-a8a76055c935); pap. 70.50 *(978-1-5081-9271-8(5))* Rosen Publishing Group, Inc., The. (Windmill Bks.).

Coan, Sharon. Message Received!, 1 vol. rev. ed. 2014. (Science: Informational Text Ser.). (ENG., Illus.). 24p. (gr. 1-2). pap. 9.99 *(978-1-4807-4565-0(0))* Teacher Created Materials, Inc.

Cobb, Vicki. Perk up Your Ears: Discover Your Sense of Hearing. Lewis, Cynthia, illus. 2003. (Five Senses Ser.). (ENG.). 32p. (gr. 3-5). pap. 7.95 *(978-0-7613-1981-8(6),* Millbrook Pr.) Lerner Publishing Group.

Colligan, L. H. Pain Treatments, 1 vol. 2013. (Advances in Medicine Ser.). (ENG.). 64p. (gr. 6-6). pap. 16.28 *(978-1-62712-011-1(4),* f3419940-d6d2-4da8-a9e9-f91655d1dd4d); (Illus.). 36.93 *(978-1-60870-468-2(8),* 992b1060-69ab-4438-b690-055a3350afe2) Cavendish Square Publishing LLC.

Como Funcionan Nuestros Sentidos. (SPA.). 92p. (J). 10.00 *(978-84-342-1809-3(7))* Parramon Ediciones S.A. ESP. Dist: Distribuidora Norma, Inc.

Cornell, Kari. Our Senses. 2016. (Illus.). 16p. (J). *(978-0-87659-701-9(0))* Gryphon Hse., Inc.

Dalmatian Press Staff. Pop & Sniff Fruit. 2008. (ENG.). 12p. (J). 10.95 *(978-1-58117-676-6(7),* Intervisual/Piggy Toes) Bendon, Inc.

Dayton, Connor. El Gusto / Taste, 1 vol., 1. De La Vega, Eida, ed. 2014. (Tus Cinco Sentidos y Tu Sexto Sentido / Your Five Senses & Your Sixth Sense Ser.). (SPA & ENG.). 24p. (J). (gr. 1-2). 26.27 *(978-1-4777-3274-8(8),* 3f0ea143-4fb7-4f56-8fc6-cb8a9741cbb6, PowerKids Pr.) Rosen Publishing Group, Inc., The.

—El Oido / Hearing, 1 vol. De La Vega, Eida, ed. 2014. (Tus Cinco Sentidos y Tu Sexto Sentido / Your Five Senses & Your Sixth Sense Ser.). (SPA & ENG.). 24p. (J). (gr. 1-2). 26.27 *(978-1-4777-3268-7(3),* 52b631dc-b902-4c03-af3a-7c3855b53533, PowerKids Pr.) Rosen Publishing Group, Inc., The.

—Taste, 1 vol., 1. 2014. (Your Five Senses & Your Sixth Sense Ser.). (ENG.). 24p. (J). (gr. 1-2). 26.27 *(978-1-4777-2856-7(2),* 14beaf71-9fb3-4e02-ba8f-81a946f50575, PowerKids Pr.) Rosen Publishing Group, Inc., The.

—Touch, 1 vol., 1. 2014. (Your Five Senses & Your Sixth Sense Ser.). (ENG.). 24p. (J). (gr. 1-2). pap. 9.25 *(978-1-4777-2948-9(8),* 7616ca68-b312-4063-8615-221e4db89f7f, PowerKids Pr.) Rosen Publishing Group, Inc., The.

Del Moral, Susana. Que Flota? Un Libro para Banarse y Disfrutar. Zaidi, Nadeem, illus. 2006. (Baby Einstein Ser.). (SPA.). 8p. (J). (gr. -1). *(978-970-718-453-4(1),* Silver Dolphin en Español) Advanced Marketing, S. de R. L. de C. V.

Delafosse, Claude. El tacto. (Coleccion Mundo Maravilloso). (SPA., Illus.). 42p. (J). (gr. 2-4). *(978-84-348-5207-5(1),* SM8406) SM Ediciones.

Dell, J. A. The Gateways of Knowledge: An Introduction to the Study of the Senses. 2013. (ENG.). 186p. pap. 39.99 *(978-1-107-65583-6(8))* Cambridge Univ. Pr.

DK. Baby Touch & Feel I Love You. 2016. (Baby Touch & Feel Ser.). (ENG., Illus.). 14p. (J). (— 1). bds. 7.99 *(978-1-4654-5763-9(1),* DK Children) Dorling Kindersley Publishing, Inc.

—Look I'm a Cook. 2017. (Look! I'm Learning Ser.). (ENG., Illus.). 48p. (J). (gr. -1-2). 12.99 *(978-1-4654-5964-0(2),* DK Children) Dorling Kindersley Publishing, Inc.

Douglas, Lloyd G. My Ears. 2004. (Wel-My Body Ser.). (J). 19.00 *(978-0-516-24062-6(5),* Children's Pr.) Scholastic Library Publishing.

—My Eyes. 2004. (Wel-My Body Ser.). (J). 19.00 *(978-0-516-24060-2(9),* Children's Pr.) Scholastic Library Publishing.

—My Nose. 2004. (Welcome Books: My Body Ser.). (ENG.). 24p. (J). (gr. k-3). 17.44 *(978-0-516-24063-3(3),* Children's Pr.) Scholastic Library Publishing.

Durrie, Karen. Taste. 2012. (J). *(978-1-61913-312-9(1));* pap. 12.95 *(978-1-61913-317-4(2))* Weigl Pubs., Inc.

Editions Phidal Staff, ed. Senses. (Jump Ser.). (Illus.). 32p. (J). (gr. 2-7). pap. 4.95 *(978-1-882210-30-5(1))* Action Publishing, Inc.

—Senses. 2004. (Illus.). lib. bdg. 7.95 *(978-0-8225-5162-1(4))* Lerner Publishing Group.

Farndon, John. Stickmen's Guide to Your Brilliant Brain. Dean, Venitia, illus. 2017. (Stickmen's Guides to Your Awesome Body Ser.). (ENG.). 32p. (J). (gr. 3-6). 27.99 *(978-1-5124-3213-8(X),* 64319f2f-57f9-4d90-a986-883c311327e5, Hungry Tomato (r)) Lerner Publishing Group.

Ferguson, Beth. The Ears, 1 vol. 2005. (Kaleidoscope: Human Body Ser.). (ENG., Illus.). 48p. (gr. 4-4). lib. bdg. 32.64 *(978-0-7614-1592-3(0),* 45864ed0-4ac7-4381-a7b4-4568a495e458) Cavendish Square Publishing LLC.

—The Eyes, 1 vol. 2005. (Kaleidoscope: Human Body Ser.). (ENG., Illus.). 48p. (gr. 4-4). lib. bdg. 32.64 *(978-0-7614-1590-9(4),* f6f2592c-9c38-427e-898c-7eb04f1caf7d) Cavendish Square Publishing LLC.

Furgang, Kathy. My Eyes. 2009. (My Body Ser.). 24p. (gr. 3-3). 42.50 *(978-1-61514-688-8(1),* PowerKids Pr.) Rosen Publishing Group, Inc., The.

—My Nose. 2009. (My Body Ser.). 24p. (gr. 3-3). 42.50 *(978-1-61514-691-8(1),* PowerKids Pr.) Rosen Publishing Group, Inc., The.

Gagne, Tammy. Extra Senses. 2019. (Engineering the Human Body Ser.). (ENG., Illus.). 32p. (J). (gr. 3-5). pap. 9.95 *(978-1-64185-833-5(8),* 1641858338); lib. bdg. 31.35 *(978-1-64185-764-2(1),* 1641857641) North Star Editions. (Focus Readers).

Ganeri, Anita. Taste. 2013. (Senses Ser.). (Illus.). 24p. (gr. k-3). 28.50 *(978-1-59920-854-1(7))* Black Rabbit Bks.

Gardner, Robert & Rybolt, Thomas R. Ace Your Science Project about the Senses: Great Science Fair Ideas, 1 vol. 2009. (Ace Your Biology Science Project Ser.). (ENG., Illus.). 112p. (gr. 5-6). lib. bdg. 35.93 *(978-0-7660-3217-0(5),* 1b53ee8f-8906-435b-895f-6452810b6f56) Enslow Publishing, LLC.

Gibson, Brylee. Keeping in Touch. 2007. (Connectors Ser.). (gr. 2-5). pap. *(978-1-877453-05-2(6))* Global Education Systems Ltd.

Gillespie, Katie. My Senses: Touch. 2017. (Eyediscover Ser.). (ENG., Illus.). 24p. (J). (gr. k-2). 28.55 *(978-1-4896-5707-7(X),* AV2 by Weigl) Weigl Pubs., Inc.

Glover, David & Glover, Penny. Senses. 2005. (Humans & Animals Ser.). (Illus.). 30p. (J). (gr. 2-4). lib. bdg. 27.10 *(978-1-58340-692-2(1))* Black Rabbit Bks.

Gregoire, Maryellen. Your Five Senses, 1 vol. 2011. (Wonder Readers Early Level Ser.). (ENG.). 16p. (gr. -1-1). (J). pap. 6.25 *(978-1-4296-7880-3(1),* 118212); pap. 35.94 *(978-1-4296-8211-4(6))* Capstone. (Capstone Pr.).

Group/McGraw-Hill, Wright. Nuestros Cinco Sentidos, 6 vols. (First Explorers. Primeros Exploradores Nonfiction Sets Ser.). (SPA.). (gr. 1-2). 29.95 *(978-0-7699-1476-3(4))* Shortland Pubns. (U. S. A.) Inc.

Haddon, Jean. Make Sense! DiRocco, Carl, illus. 2006. (Silly Millies Ser.). 32p. (J). (gr. 3-7). per. 5.95 *(978-0-8225-6472-0(6),* First Avenue Editions); (ENG.). (gr. k-2). lib. bdg. 21.27 *(978-0-7613-3403-3(3),* Millbrook Pr.) Lerner Publishing Group.

Hall, Kirsten. Animal Taste, 1 vol. 2005. (Animals & Their Senses Ser.). (ENG., Illus.). 24p. (gr. k-2). lib. bdg. 24.67 *(978-0-8368-4805-2(5),* 1c4122a8-5a3b-42ce-861e-1434d313c80f, Weekly Reader Leveled Readers) Stevens, Gareth Publishing LLLP.

—Animal Taste / el Gusto en Los Animales, 1 vol. 2005. (Animals & Their Senses / Los Sentidos de Los Animales Ser.). (ENG & SPA., Illus.). 24p. (gr. k-2). pap. 9.15 *(978-0-8368-4823-6(3),* dca12a8a-aba8-432b-97e2-b44604f60e75, Weekly Reader Leveled Readers) Stevens, Gareth Publishing LLLP.

—Animal Touch / el Tacto en Los Animales, 1 vol. 2005. (Animals & Their Senses / Los Sentidos de Los Animales Ser.). (ENG & SPA., Illus.). 24p. (gr. k-2). pap. 9.15 *(978-0-8368-4824-3(1),* d9f3564f-2522-41ac-935f-144b3c11e3bf); lib. bdg. 24.67 *(978-0-8368-4818-2(7),* 01529c73-9d4f-4068-9a32-3d700ac7962d) Stevens, Gareth Publishing LLLP. (Weekly Reader Leveled Readers).

Hanel, Rachael. Smell. 2003. 24p. (J). lib. bdg. 21.35 *(978-1-58340-306-8(X))* Black Rabbit Bks.

Hardyman, Robyn. The Senses & Your Brain, 1 vol. 2018. (What Goes on Inside Your Brain? Ser.). (ENG.). 48p. (gr. 4-5). pap. 15.05 *(978-1-5382-3557-7(9),* 5f8723b0-285c-43ac-a542-7ac2f96bc4a5) Stevens, Gareth Publishing LLLP.

Hartley Steiner. This Is Gabriel Making Sense of School: A Book about Sensory Processing Disorder. 2010. 28p. pap. 13.95 *(978-1-4269-2777-5(0))* Trafford Publishing.

Helenek, Sophie. My First Book MUSICAL INSTRUMENTS: GOLD Mom's Choice Awards Recipient. 2014. (My First Book Ser.). (ENG., Illus.). 16p. (J). (gr. -1 — 1). bds. 5.99 *(978-0-9894505-2-2(X))* Nursery Bks.

Hellebuyck, Adam & Medvinsky, Mike. Sight & Sound in Minecraft. 2019. (21st Century Skills Innovation Library: Minecraft & STEAM Ser.). (ENG., Illus.). 32p. (J). (gr. 4-8). pap. 14.21 *(978-1-5341-3971-8(0),* 212713) Cherry Lake Publishing.

—Sight & Sound in Minecraft: Art. 2019. (21st Century Skills Innovation Library: Minecraft & STEAM Ser.). (ENG., Illus.). 32p. (J). (gr. 4-8). lib. bdg. 32.07 *(978-1-5341-4315-9(7),* 212712) Cherry Lake Publishing.

Hewitt, Sally. Tastes Good! 2008. (Let's Start Science Ser.). (ENG., Illus.). 24p. (J). (gr. 3-7). pap. *(978-0-7787-4061-2(7))* Crabtree Publishing Co.

Hickman, Pamela. How Animals Use Their Senses. Stephens, Pat, illus. 2006. (Kids Can Read Ser.). 32p. (J). (gr. 1-3). 14.95 *(978-1-55337-902-7(0))* Kids Can Pr., Ltd. CAN. Dist: Hachette Bk. Group.

Hidalgo, Maria. Taste. 2003. 24p. (J). lib. bdg. 21.35 *(978-1-58340-305-1(1))* Black Rabbit Bks.

—Touch. 2003. 24p. (J). lib. bdg. 21.35 *(978-1-58340-307-5(8))* Black Rabbit Bks.

Hilton, Jennifer & McCurry, Kristen. God's Wonderful World: A Book about the Five Senses. 2016. (Frolic First Faith Ser.). (Illus.). 22p. (J). (gr. -1 — 1). bds. 6.99 *(978-1-5064-1047-0(2),* Sparkhouse Family) 1517 Media.

Hilton, Jennifer Sue & McCurry, Kristen. El Mundo Maravilloso de Dios. Rimmington, Natasha, illus. 2016. (SPA.). (J). *(978-1-5064-2094-3(X))* 1517 Media.

Holland, Mary. Animal Noses. 2019. (ENG., Illus.). 32p. (J). (gr. 1-4). 17.95 *(978-1-60718-805-6(8),* 9781607188056); 9.95 *(978-1-60718-806-3(6),* 9781607188063) Arbordale Publishing.

—Animal Noses. 2019. (Animal Adaptations Pic Bks). (ENG.). 32p. (J). (gr. k-2). 19.96 *(978-1-64310-836-0(0))* Penworthy Co., LLC, The.

Honders, Christine. How Sharks & Other Animals Sense Electricity, 1 vol. 2015. (Superior Animal Senses Ser.). (ENG., Illus.). 24p. (J). (gr. 3-4). pap. 9.25 *(978-1-4994-0994-9(X),* 9816b148-89c1-4151-a0bc-ea398fb91c1f, PowerKids Pr.) Rosen Publishing Group, Inc., The.

Howells, Shelley. Making Sense of Your Senses: Set Of 6. 2011. (Navigators Ser.). (J). pap. 44.00 net. *(978-1-4108-0407-5(0))* Benchmark Education Co.

—Making Sense of Your Senses & Tus sentidos tienen Sentido: 6 English, 6 Spanish Adaptations. 2011. (ENG & SPA.). (J). 89.00 net. *(978-1-4108-5677-7(1))* Benchmark Education Co.

Ikids Staff. The Five Senses. 2009. (ENG., Illus.). 20p. (J). (gr. -1-1). 6.99 *(978-1-58476-812-8(6))* Innovative Kids.

Issa, Joanna. These Are My Senses, 1 vol. 2014. (These Are My Senses Ser.). (ENG.). 24p. (J). (gr. -1-1). pap., pap., pap. 29.95 *(978-1-4846-0435-9(0),* 21800, Heinemann) Capstone.

—What Can I Taste?, 1 vol. 2014. (These Are My Senses Ser.). (ENG., Illus.). 24p. (J). (gr. -1-1). pap. 5.99 *(978-1-4846-0430-4(X),* 126586, Heinemann) Capstone.

Jenkins, Steve & Page, Robin. What Do You Do with a Tail Like This? A Caldecott Honor Award Winner. Calvo, Carlos, tr. Jenkins, Steve, illus. 2008. (ENG., Illus.). 32p. (J). (gr. -1-3). pap. 7.95 *(978-0-618-99713-8(X),* 1028080, Clarion Bks.) HarperCollins Pubs.

Jones, Ayesha. Allah Gave Me a Tongue to Taste. Stratford, Stevan, illus. 2016. (ENG.). 32p. (J). 8.95 *(978-0-86037-338-4(X))* Kube Publishing Ltd. GBR. Dist: Consortium Bk. Sales & Distribution.

Kalman, Bobbie. How Does It Feel? 2007. (Looking at Nature Ser.). (ENG., Illus.). 24p. (J). (gr. -1-2). pap. *(978-0-7787-3334-8(3));* lib. bdg. *(978-0-7787-3314-0(9))* Crabtree Publishing Co.

—MIS Sentidos Me Ayudan. 2010. (SPA & ENG.). 16p. (J). pap. *(978-0-7787-8584-2(X))* Crabtree Publishing Co.

—My Senses Help Me. 2010. (My World Ser.). (ENG., Illus.). 16p. (J). (gr. k-2). *(978-0-7787-9428-8(8));* pap. *(978-0-7787-9472-1(5))* Crabtree Publishing Co.

—What Senses Do Animals Have?, 1 vol. 2009. (Big Science Ideas Ser.). (ENG., Illus.). 32p. (J). (gr. 1-4). pap. *(978-0-7787-3305-8(X));* (gr. 2-4). *(978-0-7787-3285-3(1))* Crabtree Publishing Co.

Karim, Joseph & Karim, Silvana. What Does Happy Look Like? Karim, Joseph & Karim, Silvana, illus. 2009. (Illus.). 47p. (J). pap. 18.95 *(978-1-934575-54-3(2))* Autism Asperger Publishing Co.

Kashman, Nancy & Mora, Janet. The Sensory Connection: Sensory & Communication Strategies That Work, 1. 2nd ed. 2005. Orig. Title: An OT & SLP Team Approach. (Illus.). 192p. per. 19.95 *(978-1-931615-21-1(7))* Sensory Resources.

Katz, Karen. A Potty for Me! Katz, Karen, illus. 2005. (ENG., Illus.). 26p. (J). (gr. -1-k). tchr. ed. 7.99 *(978-0-689-87423-9(5),* Little Simon) Little Simon.

—Wiggle Your Toes. Katz, Karen, illus. 2006. (ENG., Illus.). 14p. (J). (gr. -1-k). bds. 11.99 *(978-1-4169-0365-9(8),* Little Simon) Little Simon.

Kirk, Bill. Great Gobs of Gustation- the Sum of Our Parts. Ruble, Eugene, illus. 2013. 24p. pap. 10.95 *(978-1-61633-358-4(8))* Guardian Angel Publishing, Inc.

Klepeis, Alicia Z. How Animals Smell, 1 vol. 2018. (Science of Senses Ser.). (ENG.). 32p. (gr. 3-3). pap. 11.58 *(978-1-5026-4208-0(5),* 9b13e895-4f4e-4687-b708-6791b75408df) Cavendish Square Publishing LLC.

Klingel, Cynthia & Noyed, Robert B. Nose, 1 vol. 2010. (Let's Read about Our Bodies (Second Edition) Ser.). (ENG., Illus.). 24p. (gr. k-2). pap. 9.15 *(978-1-4339-3372-1(1),* 0fba4b99-b136-4f40-afde-bd52b6e6ec8e); (J). lib. bdg. 24.67 *(978-1-4339-3371-4(3),* ba20bc52-5f23-4e5c-9ec3-f0515eb949ed) Stevens, Gareth Publishing LLLP.

—Nose / la Nariz, 1 vol. 2010. (Let's Read about Our Bodies / Hablemos Del Cuerpo Humano Ser.). (SPA & ENG., Illus.). 24p. (gr. k-2). pap. 9.15 *(978-1-4339-3748-4(4),* 78273cbd-e597-47e1-b311-29989cac650c); (J). lib. bdg. 24.67 *(978-1-4339-3747-7(6),* 86aed606-2438-4275-9026-266bcfe8a324) Stevens, Gareth Publishing LLLP.

Kopp, Megan. Senses. 2016. (Illus.). 24p. (J). *(978-1-5105-0939-9(9))* SmartBook Media, Inc.

Kroneberger, Abigail Grace. The Sensory Room Kids Get in Sync. Kroneberger, Abigail Grace, illus. 2008. (Illus.). 24p. per. 12.95 *(978-1-934246-98-6(0))* Peppertree Pr., The.

Kurtz, John. The World Around Us! Tasting. 2011. (Dover Science for Kids Coloring Bks.). (ENG.). 32p. (J). (gr. k-3). pap. 4.99 *(978-0-486-48037-4(2),* 480372) Dover Pubns., Inc.

Larson, Kirsten W. Super Powers in Nature. 2015. (Freaky Nature Ser.). (ENG., Illus.). 32p. (J). (gr. 2-5). lib. bdg. 19.95 *(978-1-60753-781-6(8),* 15297) Amicus.

Lay, Kathryn. Extreme Senses: Animals with Unusual Senses for Hunting Prey: Animals with Unusual Senses for Hunting Prey. Wald, Christina, illus. 2012. (Sensing Their Prey Ser.). (ENG.). 32p. (J). (gr. -1-4). E-Book 29.93 *(978-1-61478-860-7(X),* 13278, Looking Glass Library) Magic Wagon.

Layton, Neil. Go Wild with Noises. 2004. (Illus.). 12p. (J). bds. *(978-1-84458-043-9(1),* Pavilion Children's Books) Pavilion Bks.

LernerClassroom Editors. First Step Nonfiction-Senses Teaching Guide. 2009. pap. 7.95 *(978-0-8225-5973-3(0))* Lerner Publishing Group.

L'Heureux, Christine. Caillou Tries New Foods. Kary, illus. 2018. (Caillou's Essentials Ser.). (ENG.). 24p. (J). (gr. -1-k). bds. 7.99 *(978-2-89718-439-1(6))* Caillouet, Gerry.

Libra, Anna. Why Does Loud Music Hurt My Ears? An Inside Look at the Ear. 2003. (J). pap. *(978-1-58417-072-3(7));* lib. bdg. *(978-1-58417-009-9(3))* Lake Street Pubs.

—Why Does That Taste Bad? An Inside Look at the Tongue. 2003. (J). pap. *(978-1-58417-069-3(7));* lib. bdg. *(978-1-58417-006-8(9))* Lake Street Pubs.

Llewellyn, Claire. Our Senses Red Band. 2016. (Cambridge Reading Adventures Ser.). (ENG., Illus.). 16p. pap. 7.95 *(978-1-316-60568-4(X))* Cambridge Univ. Pr.

Loh-Hagan, Virginia. Top 10: Super Senses. 2017. (Wild Wicked Wonderful Ser.). (ENG., Illus.). 32p. (J). (gr. 4-8). lib. bdg. 32.07 *(978-1-63472-141-7(1),* 209136, 45th Parallel Press) Cherry Lake Publishing.

Lowery, Lawrence F. Fragrant As a Flower. 2017. (I Wonder Why Ser.). (ENG., Illus.). 36p. (J). (gr. k-2). pap. 13.99 *(978-1-68140-353-3(6),* P531926) National Science Teachers Assn.

—Look & See. 2017. (I Wonder Why Ser.). (ENG., Illus.). 36p. (J). (gr. k-2). pap. 13.99 *(978-1-68140-355-7(2),* P531927) National Science Teachers Assn.

—Quiet As a Butterfly. 2017. (I Wonder Why Ser.). (ENG., Illus.). 36p. (J). (gr. k-2). pap. 13.99 *(978-1-68140-354-0(4),* P531929) National Science Teachers Assn.

MacKenzie, Catherine. God Gave Me Smell. rev. ed. 2010. (Board Books Sense Ser.). (ENG.). 16p. (J). (gr. -1-3). bds. 3.99 *(978-1-85792-564-7(5),* fc237af7-ea30-4b8e-bf85-b4467785d7fd) Christian Focus Pubns. GBR. Dist: Baker & Taylor Publisher Services (BTPS).

—God Gave Me Taste. rev. ed. 2010. (Board Books Sense Ser.). (ENG.). 16p. (J). (gr. -1-3). bds. 3.99 *(978-1-85792-561-6(0),* 8dcae5e9-7e54-4b21-97cb-4ee4c0f9b10e) Christian Focus Pubns. GBR. Dist: Baker & Taylor Publisher Services (BTPS).

Martineau, Susan. Understanding Feelings. 2011. (Positive Steps Ser.). 32p. (gr. 2-5). lib. bdg. 31.35 *(978-1-59920-494-9(0))* Black Rabbit Bks.

Mattern, Joanne. How Animals Feel, 1 vol. 2018. (Science of Senses Ser.). (ENG.). 32p. (gr. 3-3). pap. 11.58 *(978-1-5026-4196-0(8),* 45b756da-a825-4674-a75a-644ad1c52f1e) Cavendish Square Publishing LLC.

—How Animals Hear, 1 vol. 2018. (Science of Senses Ser.). (ENG.). 32p. (gr. 3-3). pap. 11.58 *(978-1-5026-4200-4(X),* d04acf24-f999-418b-9adb-4ab11824cce2) Cavendish Square Publishing LLC.

—How Animals See, 1 vol. 2018. (Science of Senses Ser.). (ENG.). 32p. (gr. 3-3). pap. 11.58 *(978-1-5026-4204-2(2),* 6afbf8aa-971c-4d17-9cba-fc6cb6e42c4f) Cavendish Square Publishing LLC.

S

—Super Senses. 2019. (Core Content Science — Animal Superpowers Ser.). (ENG., Illus.). 32p. (J). (gr. 2-4). lib. bdg. 23.99 *(978-1-63440-423-5(8),* c9a9b259-e282-47bc-bb79-aed7498b5583) Red Chair Pr.

McAneney, Caitlin. How Elephants & Other Animals Hear the Earth, 1 vol. 2015. (Superior Animal Senses Ser.). (ENG., Illus.). 24p. (J). (gr. 3-4). pap. 9.25 *(978-1-4994-0991-8(5),* 70e65fe8-e3fc-4a08-9917-ae6e2a5a6cfb, PowerKids Pr.) Rosen Publishing Group, Inc., The.

McKendry, Sam. Are You Ticklish?/Tienes Cosquillas? Mitchell, Melanie, illus. 2005. (ENG.). 12p. (gr. -1-k). 10.95 *(978-1-58117-472-4(1),* Intervisual/Piggy Toes) Bendon, Inc.

McNeil, Niki, et al. HOCPP 1067 the Five Senses. 2006. spiral bd. 15.50 *(978-1-60308-067-5(8))* In the Hands of a Child.

Michael, Joan. The Five Senses/Opposites & Position Words, 4 bks., Set. Incl. Let's Play a Five Senses Guessing Game. Miller, Amanda. 18.00 *(978-0-531-14871-6(8));* Let's Talk about Opposites, Morning to Night. Falk, Laine. 18.00 *(978-0-531-14872-3(6));* (Illus.). 24p. (J). (gr. -1-3). 2007. (Let's Find Out Early Learning Bks.). 2007. 72.00 o.p. *(978-0-531-17574-3(X),* Children's Pr.) Scholastic Library Publishing.

Miller, Amanda & Michael, Joan. Let's Play a Five Senses Guessing Game. 2007. (Let's Find Out Early Learning Bks.). (ENG., Illus.). 24p. (J). (gr. -1-3). 18.00 *(978-0-531-14871-6(8),* Children's Pr.) Scholastic Library Publishing.

Miller, Derek. Eyes, Ears, & Noses, 1 vol. 2018. (Animal Structures Ser.). (ENG.). 24p. (J). (gr. 1-1). pap. 9.22 *(978-1-5026-4180-9(1),* 0126d668-9e73-4ab6-9472-4cc62dadd307) Cavendish Square Publishing LLC.

Miller-Schroeder, Patricia. Senses. 2007. (Life Science (Weigl Hardcover) Ser.). (Illus.). 32p. (J). (gr. 4-7). lib. bdg. 26.00 *(978-1-59036-715-5(4));* per. 9.95 *(978-1-59036-716-2(2))* Weigl Pubs., Inc.

Mills, Nathan & Diggory, Nikki. Our Five Senses, 1 vol. 2012. (Rosen Readers Ser.). (ENG., Illus.). 16p. (J). (gr. k-k). pap. 7.00 *(978-1-4488-8686-9(4),* 3050459c-e612-44b8-983e-051284a568d2, Rosen Classroom) Rosen Publishing Group, Inc., The.

Mis Cinco Sentidos / My Five Senses, 10 vols. 2014. (Mis Cinco Sentidos / My Five Senses Ser.). (SPA & ENG.). 24p. (J). (gr. k-k). 121.35 *(978-1-4824-1040-2(0),* da893625-4eac-4702-9014-c3aed08e1855) Stevens, Gareth Publishing LLLP.

Mitchell, Melanie. Ears. 2004. (First Step Nonfiction — Animal Traits Ser.). (ENG., Illus.). 8p. (J). (gr. k-2). pap. 5.99 *(978-0-8225-3910-0(1),* 260b7fd7-1eb0-4574-a4d1-fefbd08106ba) Lerner Publishing Group.

Mlawer, Teresa, tr. What Do I Feel? / ¿Qué Siento? Kubler, Annie, illus. 2015. (Small Senses Bilingual Ser.: 5). (ENG.). 12p. (J). bds. *(978-1-84643-721-2(0))* Child's Play International Ltd.

—What Do I Hear? / ¿Qué Oigo? Kubler, Annie, illus. 2015. (Small Senses Bilingual Ser.: 5). (ENG.). 12p. (J). bds. *(978-1-84643-724-3(5))* Child's Play International Ltd.

—What Do I See? / ¿Qué Veo? Kubler, Annie, illus. 2015. (Small Senses Bilingual Ser.: 5). (ENG.). 12p. (J). bds. *(978-1-84643-725-0(3))* Child's Play International Ltd.

—What Do I Smell? / ¿Qué Huelo? Kubler, Annie, illus. 2015. (Small Senses Bilingual Ser.: 5). (ENG.). 12p. (J). bds. *(978-1-84643-723-6(7))* Child's Play International Ltd.

—What Do I Taste? / ¿Qué Saboreo? Kubler, Annie, illus. 2015. (Small Senses Bilingual Ser.: 5). (ENG.). 12p. (J). bds. *(978-1-84643-722-9(9))* Child's Play International Ltd.

Morgan, Philip. Sending Messages. 2010. (How Your Body Works). 32p. (YA). (gr. 4-7). 28.50 *(978-1-60753-056-5(2))* Amicus Learning.

—Sensing the World. 2012. (ENG., Illus.). 32p. (J). (gr. 4-7). pap. 8.95 *(978-1-926722-66-5(3))* Saunders Bk. Co. CAN. Dist: RiverStream Publishing.

Morgan, Sally. How Taste Works. 2010. (Our Senses Ser.). 24p. (J). (gr. k-2). pap. 8.25 *(978-1-61532-563-4(8),* PowerKids Pr.); (ENG., Illus.). (gr. 1-1). lib. bdg. 25.27 *(978-1-61532-555-9(7),* b620edf3-6546-4c78-8a0f-4b7028eab09b) Rosen Publishing Group, Inc., The.

—Our Senses, 5 vols., Set. Incl. How Smell Works. lib. bdg. 26.27 *(978-1-61532-554-2(9),* 78b672e1-e74a-47ec-93d3-42663ce91ff6); How Taste Works. lib. bdg. 25.27 *(978-1-61532-555-9(7),* b620edf3-6546-4c78-8a0f-4b7028eab09b); (J). (gr. 1-1). (Illus.). 24p. 2010. Set lib. bdg. 106.25 *(978-1-61532-845-1(9),* PowerKids Pr.) Rosen Publishing Group, Inc., The.

Mucklow, Nancy. The Sensory Team Handbook: A Hands-on Tool to Help Young People Make Sense of Their Senses & Take Charge of Their Sensory Processing. 2nd ed. 2009. (Illus.). 180p. (YA). pap. *(978-0-9811439-2-7(X))* Grass, Michael Hse.

Murphy, Patricia J. Smell. 2003. (True Book: Health Ser.). (ENG., Illus.). 48p. (J). (gr. 3-5). 18.69 *(978-0-516-22598-2(7))* Scholastic Library Publishing.

—True Books: Taste. 2003. (True Bks.). (ENG.). 48p. (gr. 3-5). pap. 6.95 *(978-0-516-26971-9(2),* Children's Pr.) Scholastic Library Publishing.

Murray, Julie. The Five Senses, 1 vol. 2015. (Senses Ser.). (ENG., Illus.). 24p. (J). (gr. -1-2). 31.36 *(978-1-62970-924-6(7),* 18306, Abdo Kids) ABDO Publishing Co.

—I Can See, 1 vol. 2015. (Senses Ser.). (ENG., Illus.). 24p. (J). (gr. -1-2). 31.36 *(978-1-62970-926-0(3),* 18310, Abdo Kids) ABDO Publishing Co.

—I Can Taste, 1 vol. 2015. (Senses Ser.). (ENG., Illus.). 24p. (J). (gr. -1-2). 31.36 *(978-1-62970-928-4(X),* 18314, Abdo Kids) ABDO Publishing Co.

My Five Senses, 10 vols. 2014. (My Five Senses Ser.). (ENG.). 24p. (J). (gr. k-k). 121.35 *(978-1-4824-1036-5(2),* c3de77f3-705f-4f3c-8abe-06fffe9f83c3) Stevens, Gareth Publishing LLLP.

Nagelhout, Ryan. How Pigeons & Other Animals Sense Magnetic Fields, 1 vol. 2015. (Superior Animal Senses Ser.). (ENG., Illus.). 24p. (J). (gr. 3-4). pap. 9.25 *(978-1-4994-0992-5(3),* 635d5109-0afb-41ee-9280-02a9f566a421, PowerKids Pr.) Rosen Publishing Group, Inc., The.

Nelson, Robin. El Gusto. Translations.com Staff, tr. from ENG. 2006. (Mi Primer Paso Al Mundo Real - Los Sentidos (First Step Nonfiction - Senses) Ser.). (SPA., Illus.). 24p. (gr. k-2). lib. bdg. 23.93 *(978-0-8225-6224-5(3),* Ediciones Lerner) Lerner Publishing Group.

—Hearing. 2005. (First Step Nonfiction Ser.). (Illus.). 24p. (gr. k-2). lib. bdg. 17.27 *(978-0-8225-1264-6(5))* Lerner Publishing Group.

—Tasting. 2005. (Senses Ser.). (Illus.). 24p. (gr. k-2). lib. bdg. 17.27 *(978-0-8225-1265-3(3))* Lerner Publishing Group.

—Touching. 2005. (First Step Nonfiction Ser.). (Illus.). 24p. (gr. k-2). lib. bdg. 17.27 *(978-0-8225-1266-0(1))* Lerner Publishing Group.

The Nervous System/The Senses/The Skin. 2006. (World Book's Human Body Works). (Illus.). 48p. (J). *(978-0-7166-4430-9(4))* World Bk., Inc.

Nettleton, Pamela Hill. Look, Listen, Taste, Touch, & Smell: Learning about Your Five Senses. Shipe, Becky, illus. 2004. (Amazing Body Ser.). (ENG.). 24p. (J). (gr. k-3). per. 8.95 *(978-1-4048-0508-8(7),* 92524, Picture Window Bks.) Capstone.

O'Hara, Nicholas. Textura / Sort It by Texture, 1 vol. de la Vega, Eida, tr. 2015. (Vamos a Agrupar Por... / Sort It Out! Ser.). (ENG & SPA., Illus.). 24p. (J). (gr. k-1). lib. bdg. 24.27 *(978-1-4824-3223-7(4),* 32406b75-0bcb-4198-89ec-623e31fa474f) Stevens, Gareth Publishing LLLP.

Oliendo. (Coleccion Mil Preguntas). (SPA., Illus.). 24p. (J). pap. 4.50 *(978-950-11-0659-6(4),* SGM628) Sigmar ARG. Dist: Continental Bk. Co., Inc.

Olson, Karen W. Eyes, Ears, Nose & Mouth. George, Leonard, Jr., illus. 2005. (ENG.). 20p. (J). pap. 10.95 *(978-1-894778-34-3(0))* Theytus Bks., Ltd. CAN. Dist: Univ. of Toronto Pr.

Our Senses. (Early Intervention Levels Ser.). 23.10 *(978-0-7362-0030-1(4));* Vol. 4. 3.85 *(978-1-56334-978-2(7))* CENGAGE Learning.

Our Senses, 10 vols., 5 Vols. 2004. (Our Senses Ser.). (ENG.). 24p. (gr. 1-3). lib. bdg. 128.35 *(978-0-8368-4405-4(X),* d029dddc-42b5-423a-9ed0-d099304e9327, Gareth Stevens Learning Library) Stevens, Gareth Publishing LLLP.

Owen, Ruth. My Senses. 2017. (Get Started with STEM Ser.). (ENG., Illus.). 32p. (J). (gr. k-3). 9.99 *(978-1-78856-120-4(1),* 4ac20e4e-d0bb-4754-a580-d4e22b1b7e67) Ruby Tuesday Books Limited GBR. Dist: Lerner Publishing Group.

Owings, Lisa. Hearing. 2018. (Five Senses Ser.). (ENG., Illus.). 24p. (J). (gr. k-3). pap. 7.99 *(978-1-61891-296-1(8),* 12101, Blastoff! Readers) Bellwether Media.

—Seeing. 2018. (Five Senses Ser.). (ENG., Illus.). 24p. (J). (gr. k-3). pap. 7.99 *(978-1-61891-297-8(6),* 12102, Blastoff! Readers) Bellwether Media.

—Smelling. 2018. (Five Senses Ser.). (ENG., Illus.). 24p. (J). (gr. k-3). lib. bdg. 26.95 *(978-1-62617-770-3(8),* Blastoff! Readers) Bellwether Media.

—Tasting. 2018. (Five Senses Ser.). (ENG., Illus.). 24p. (J). (gr. k-3). pap. 7.99 *(978-1-61891-299-2(2),* 12104, Blastoff! Readers) Bellwether Media.

—Touching. 2018. (Five Senses Ser.). (ENG., Illus.). 24p. (J). (gr. k-3). pap. 7.99 *(978-1-61891-300-5(X),* 12105, Blastoff! Readers) Bellwether Media.

Oyendo. (Coleccion Mil Preguntas). (SPA., Illus.). 24p. (J). pap. 5.50 *(978-950-11-0662-6(4),* SGM624) Sigmar ARG. Dist: Continental Bk. Co., Inc.

Paine, Penelope C. Gift of Taste. Maeno, Itoko, illus. 2006. 24p. 5.95 *(978-0-9707944-6-8(0))* Paper Posie Publishing Co., The.

Pat Them Gently w/ Plush. 2007. 14.95 *(978-1-58117-626-1(0),* Intervisual/Piggy Toes) Bendon, Inc.

Petersen, Christine. Does Everyone Have ADHD? A Teen's Guide to Diagnosis & Treatment. (ENG., Illus.). 144p. (YA). (gr. 9-13). 2007. pap. 17.95 *(978-0-531-17975-8(3))* 2006. 30.50 *(978-0-531-16794-6(1),* Watts, Franklin) Scholastic Library Publishing.

Phidal Publishing Staff, ed. Senses. (Turn & Learn Ser.). 12p. (J). *(978-2-7643-0140-1(5))* Phidal Publishing, Inc./Editions Phidal, Inc.

Piggy Toes Press Staff. Dog Walk. 2006. (ENG.). 14p. 9.95 *(978-1-58117-481-6(0),* Intervisual/Piggy Toes) Bendon, Inc.

Pizza, Andy J. & Miller, Sophie. Invisible Things. 2023. (ENG., Illus.). 52p. (J). (gr. k-3). 17.99 *(978-1-7972-1520-4(5))* Chronicle Bks. LLC.

Priddy, Roger. Baby Touch & Feel: Quack! Quack! These Baby Animals Can't Wait to Meet You. rev. ed. 2004. (Baby Touch & Feel Ser.). (ENG., Illus.). 12p. (J). (gr. -1 — 1). bds. 8.95 *(978-0-312-49250-2(2),* 900024403) St. Martin's Pr.

—Bright Baby Touch & Feel Slipcase: Includes Words, Colors, Numbers, & Shapes. 2008. (Bright Baby Touch & Feel Ser.). (ENG.). 12p. (J). (gr. -1 — 1). bds., bds., bds. 19.99 *(978-0-312-50428-1(4),* 900055418) St. Martin's Pr.

Prior, Jennifer. The Five Senses, 1 vol. 2nd rev. ed. 2012. (TIME for KIDS(r): Informational Text Ser.). (ENG.). 32p. (gr. 3-5). pap. 12.99 *(978-1-4333-3676-8(6))* Teacher Created Materials, Inc.

Pryor, Kimberley Jane. Seeing. 2003. (Senses Ser.). (Illus.). 32p. (gr. 2-4). 23.00 *(978-0-7910-7555-5(9),* Facts On File) Infobase Holdings, Inc.

Rajczak, Kristen. How Snakes & Other Animals Taste the Air, 1 vol. 2015. (Superior Animal Senses Ser.). (ENG., Illus.). 24p. (J). (gr. 3-4). pap. 9.25 *(978-1-4994-0995-6(8),* 02837a1d-a1c3-46f9-b600-653fe26203b3, PowerKids Pr.) Rosen Publishing Group, Inc., The.

Randolph, Joanne, ed. Taste & Digestion, 1 vol. 2017. (Amazing Human Body Ser.). (ENG.). 48p. (gr. 6-6). pap. 12.70 *(978-0-7660-8989-1(4),* 51340689-265a-4848-9da4-68faf1919865) Enslow Publishing, LLC.

Ransom, Candice. Let's Explore the Five Senses. 2020. (Bumba Books (r) — Discover Your Senses Ser.). (ENG., Illus.). 24p. (J). (gr. -1-1). 26.65 *(978-1-5415-7690-2(X),* fef7b1a2-829f-4dd6-834a-e498e1b8cdff, Lerner Pubns.) Lerner Publishing Group.

Rappaport, Carrie, et al. The Best Sense for Safety. 2017. (Text Connections Guided Close Reading Ser.). (J). (gr. 1). *(978-1-4900-1828-7(X))* Benchmark Education Co.

Rauf, Don. The Senses. 2017. (Freaky Phenomena Ser.: Vol. 8). (ENG., Illus.). 48p. (YA). (gr. 5-8). 20.95 *(978-1-4222-3780-9(X))* Mason Crest.

Rescek, Sanja, illus. Bounce & Jiggle. 2007. (Baby Gym Ser.). 12p. (J). (gr. -1). spiral bd. *(978-1-84643-131-9(X))* Child's Play International Ltd.

—Calm & Soothe. 2007. (Baby Gym Ser.). 12p. (J). (gr. -1). spiral bd. *(978-1-84643-133-3(6))* Child's Play International Ltd.

—Touch & Tickle. 2007. (Baby Gym Ser.). 12p. (J). (gr. -1). bds. *(978-1-84643-130-2(1))* Child's Play International Ltd.

—Wiggle & Move. 2007. (Baby Gym Ser.). 12p. (J). (gr. -1). spiral bd. *(978-1-84643-132-6(8))* Child's Play International Ltd.

Rissman, Rebecca. Using Your Senses, 1 vol. 2011. (ENG.). 24p. (J). (gr. -1-1). pap. 9.95 *(978-1-4329-5495-6(4),* 116338, Heinemann) Capstone.

Robert, Na'ima Bint & Petrova-Browning, Nina. Welcome to the World Baby. Brazell, Derek, illus. 2005. (ENG & BUL.). 32p. (J). pap. *(978-1-84444-721-3(9))* Mantra Lingua.

Rofé, April, illus. The SENSEsational Alphabet: See-Read, Touch-Feel, Scratch & Smell, Hear-Learn, Have Fun! 2006. (J). *(978-0-9779189-1-1(2))* Waldenhouse Pubs., Inc.

Rosa-Mendoza, Gladys. My Five Senses, 1 vol. Merer, Laura, illus. 2010. (My World Ser.). (ENG.). 24p. (J). (gr. k-1). pap. 9.15 *(978-1-61533-029-4(1),* 0be13867-e3da-48ce-83e9-93ba5b004d81); lib. bdg. 27.27 *(978-1-60754-948-2(4),* 87768b01-61a6-4cdc-b6cf-d6c5dc827046) Rosen Publishing Group, Inc., The. (Windmill Bks.).

—My Senses/Mis Sentidos. Merer, Laura, illus. 2007. (English Spanish Foundations Ser.). (ENG & SPA.). 20p. (J). (gr. -1-k). bds. 6.95 *(978-1-931398-21-3(6))* Me+Mi Publishing.

Rotner, Shelley. Senses on the Farm. 2008. (Illus.). 32p. (J). (gr. -1-2). 23.93 *(978-0-8225-8623-4(1),* Millbrook Pr.) Lerner Publishing Group.

Royston, Angela. Senses. 2011. (Your Body Inside & Out Ser.). (Illus.). 32p. (J). (gr. 3-6). lib. bdg. 28.50 *(978-1-59771-267-5(1))* Sea-To-Sea Pubns.

Rustad, Martha E. H. Touching. 2014. (Illus.). 24p. (J). lib. bdg. 25.65 *(978-1-62031-119-6(4),* Bullfrog Bks.) Jump! Inc.

Saab, Carl Y. Seeing, Hearing, & Smelling the World. Chudler, Eric H., ed. 2007. (ENG., Illus.). 101p. (gr. 5-9). lib. bdg. 32.95 *(978-0-7910-8945-3(2),* P114487, Facts On File) Infobase Holdings, Inc.

SAMI Staff. Look, Baby! 2009. (ENG., Illus.). 20p. (J). (— 1). 9.95 *(978-1-934706-26-8(4))* Blue Apple Bks.

Scholastic Clubs US Five Senses Pack: Let's Start Science. 2006. (J). 34.75 *(978-1-59566-323-8(1))* QEB Publishing Inc.

Schuh, Mari. The Sense of Hearing. 2007. (Senses Ser.). (ENG., Illus.). 24p. (J). (gr. 2-5). lib. bdg. 26.95 *(978-1-60014-070-9(X))* Bellwether Media.

—The Sense of Sight. 2007. (Senses Ser.). (ENG., Illus.). 24p. (J). (gr. 2-5). lib. bdg. 26.95 *(978-1-60014-071-6(8))* Bellwether Media.

—The Sense of Smell. 2007. (Senses Ser.). (ENG., Illus.). 24p. (J). (gr. 2-5). lib. bdg. 26.95 *(978-1-60014-072-3(6))* Bellwether Media.

—The Sense of Taste. 2007. (Senses Ser.). (ENG., Illus.). 24p. (J). (gr. 2-5). lib. bdg. 26.95 *(978-1-60014-073-0(4))* Bellwether Media.

—The Sense of Touch. 2007. (Senses Ser.). (ENG., Illus.). 24p. (J). (gr. 2-5). lib. bdg. 26.95 *(978-1-60014-074-7(2),* 11283) Bellwether Media.

Sensational , 6 Pack. (Bookweb Ser.). 32p. (gr. 3-18). 34.00 *(978-0-7635-3949-8(X))* Rigby Education.

Shea, Therese. How Dolphins & Other Animals Use Sonar, 1 vol. 2015. (Superior Animal Senses Ser.). (ENG., Illus.). 24p. (J). (gr. 3-4). pap. 9.25 *(978-1-4994-0988-8(5),* f7c31867-bb07-43f1-9cba-3e4689c22f2e, PowerKids Pr.) Rosen Publishing Group, Inc., The.

Sheldon, Kaylene Kauwila. I Know Ka'a'awa. 2008.Tr. of Ike Au la Ka'a'awa. (ENG & HAW., Illus.). 17p. (J). lib. bdg. *(978-0-9773495-6-2(X))* Na Kamalei Koolauloa Early Education Program.

Sian revision smell taste Touch. 2004. (J). *(978-1-59242-069-8(9))* Delta Education, LLC.

Sights And Sounds. (YA). (gr. 8). 48.95 *(978-0-673-72661-2(4),* Scott Foresman) Addison Wesley Schl.

Silver Dolphin en Español Editors, creator. El Gusto. 2007. (Baby Senses (Silver Dolphin en Espanol) Ser.). (Illus.). 10p. (J). (gr. -1). bds. *(978-970-718-473-2(6),* Silver Dolphin en Español) Advanced Marketing, S. de R. L. de C. V.

—El Olfato. 2007. (Baby Senses (Silver Dolphin en Espanol) Ser.). (Illus.). 10p. (J). (gr. 5). bds. *(978-970-718-471-8(X),* Silver Dolphin en Español) Advanced Marketing, S. de R. L. de C. V.

—La Vista. 2007. (Baby Senses (Silver Dolphin en Espanol) Ser.). (Illus.). 8p. (J). (gr. -1). bds. *(978-970-718-472-5(8),* Silver Dolphin en Español) Advanced Marketing, S. de R. L. de C. V.

Simon, Seymour. Eyes & Ears. (ENG., Illus.). 32p. (J). (gr. k-5). 2005. pap. 7.99 *(978-0-06-073302-5(0),* HarperCollins) 2003. 15.99 *(978-0-688-15303-8(8))* HarperCollins Pubs.

—Eyes & Ears. 2005. (Illus.). (gr. k-3). 17.00 *(978-0-7569-5398-0(7))* Perfection Learning Corp.

Slegers, Liesbet. Que Veo?/ What Do I See? 2008. 24p. bds. 11.95 *(978-84-263-6705-1(4))* Vives, Luis Editorial (Edelvives) ESP. Dist: Baker & Taylor Bks.

Smart Kids Publishing Staff. What's That Sound. Sharp, Chris, illus. 2005. 10p. (J). (gr. -1-k). 12.95 *(978-0-8249-6624-9(4),* Ideals Pubns.) Worthy Publishing.

Sounds & Hearing. 2005. (J). *(978-0-9767850-0-2(5))* Success for All Foundation.

Spilsbury, Louise & Spilsbury, Richard. The Science of the Senses. 2017. (Flowchart Smart Ser.). 48p. (gr. 4-5). pap. 84.30 *(978-1-5382-0685-0(4))* Stevens, Gareth Publishing LLLP.

Spiro, Ruth. Baby Loves the Five Senses: Hearing! Chan, Irene, illus. 2019. (Baby Loves Science Ser.). 20p. (J). (— 1). bds. 8.99 *(978-1-62354-102-6(6))* Charlesbridge Publishing, Inc.

—Baby Loves the Five Senses: Smell! Chan, Irene, illus. 2020. (Baby Loves Science Ser.). 20p. (J). (— 1). bds. 8.99 *(978-1-62354-153-8(0))* Charlesbridge Publishing, Inc.

Steffora, Tracey. My Five Senses, 1 vol. 2014. (These Are My Senses Ser.). (ENG., Illus.). 24p. (J). (gr. -1-1). 26.00 *(978-1-4846-0442-7(3),* 195271, Heinemann) Capstone.

Steps To Literacy Staff, compiled by. Read about the Five Sense Collection: Lib052. 2005. (ENG., Illus.). (J). pap. *(978-1-60015-011-1(X))* Steps To Literacy, LLC.

Stihler, Cherie B. Squishy, Squishy: A Book about My Five Senses. Rose, Heidi, illus. 2005. 23p. (J). pap. 5.95 *(978-0-8198-7078-0(1),* 332-374) Pauline Bks. & Media.

Strading, Jan. Sense This: Level I, 6 vols. (First Explorers Ser.). 24p. (gr. 1-2). 29.95 *(978-0-7699-1452-7(7))* Shortland Pubns. (U. S. A.) Inc.

Studio Mouse Staff. Learn about Five Senses with JoJo! - My Five Senses. 2006. (ENG., Illus.). 60p. (J). (gr. -1-3). 12.99 *(978-1-59069-478-7(3))* Studio Mouse LLC.

Sullivan, Laura L. How Animals Taste, 1 vol. 2018. (Science of Senses Ser.). (ENG.). 32p. (gr. 3-3). pap. 11.58 *(978-1-5026-4212-7(3),* 3201cdc9-3fed-4ccf-bcf1-864b2606fb00) Cavendish Square Publishing LLC.

Sundance/Newbridge LLC Staff. See, Hear, Touch, Taste, Smell. 2007. (Early Science Ser.). (gr. k-3). 18.95 *(978-1-4007-6197-5(2));* pap. 6.10 *(978-1-4007-6193-7(X))* Sundance/Newbridge Educational Publishing.

Superior Animal Senses. 2015. (Superior Animal Senses Ser.). (ENG.). 24p. (J). (gr. 3-4). pap., pap., pap. 297.00 *(978-1-4994-1317-5(3),* PowerKids Pr.) Rosen Publishing Group, Inc., The.

Tatchell, Judy. How Do Your Senses Work? Wheatley, Maria, illus. rev. ed. 2004. (Flip Flaps Ser.). 16p. (J). (gr. 2-18). pap. 7.95 *(978-0-7945-0642-1(9),* Usborne) EDC Publishing.

Taylor, Kristen Fitz & McDonald, Cheryl. Danceland: Fun Songs & Activities to Improve Sensory Skills. 2nd ed. 2008. 32p. (gr. -1-k). audio 19.95 *(978-1-931615-04-4(7))* Sensory Resources.

Thames, Susan. Our Senses. 2007. (ENG., Illus.). 24p. (gr. k-1). 28.50 *(978-1-60472-112-6(X));* pap. 9.95 *(978-1-60044-674-0(4),* 9781600446740) Rourke Educational Media.

Treays, Rebecca. Understanding Your Senses. 2005. (Illus.). 31p. (J). pap. *(978-0-439-79805-1(1))* Scholastic, Inc.

Tsiang, Sarah Yi-Mei. Toesy Toes, 1 vol. 2018. (ENG., Illus.). 26p. (J). (gr. -1 — 1). bds. 9.95 *(978-1-4598-1342-7(1))* Orca Bk. Pubs. USA.

Tullet, Hervé & Tullet, Hervé. The Five Senses. 2005. (ENG., Illus.). 144p. (J). (gr. -1-3). pap. 19.95 *(978-1-85437-581-0(4))* Tate Publishing, Ltd. GBR. Dist: Abrams, Inc.

Tyler, Jenny. Jugamos Al Escondite? 2004. (Titles in Spanish Ser.). (SPA., Illus.). 10p. (J). 15.95 *(978-0-7460-6114-5(5),* Usborne) EDC Publishing.

Walt & Wells. Este No Es Mi Dinosaurio. 2004. (Touchy-Feely Board Bks.).Tr. of This Is Not My Dinosaur. (SPA., Illus.). 12p. (J). (gr. -1-18). 7.99 *(978-0-7460-5079-8(8))* EDC Publishing.

Wang, Margaret. Baby Mine Touch & Feel Flashcards. 2006. (ENG.). 10p. 12.95 *(978-1-58117-502-8(7),* Intervisual/Piggy Toes) Bendon, Inc.

Waters, John F. Sharks Have Six Senses. Barner, Bob, illus. 2015. (Let's-Read-And-Find-Out Science 2 Ser.). (ENG.). 40p. (J). (gr. -1-3). 17.99 *(978-0-06-028140-3(5),* HarperCollins) HarperCollins Pubs.

Watt, Fiona. Baby Monster Cloth Book. Wells, Rachel, illus. 2007. (Usborne Cloth Bks.). 10p. (J). (gr. -1-k). 10.99 *(978-0-7945-1428-0(6),* Usborne) EDC Publishing.

—Cuddly Baby: Snuggletime. MacKinnon, Catherine-Anne, illus. 2006. 10p. (J). (gr. -1-k). bds. 8.99 *(978-0-7945-1070-1(1),* Usborne) EDC Publishing.

—Esta No Es Mi Muneca. Wells, Rachel, illus. 2005. (Titles in Spanish Ser.). (SPA.). 10p. (J). 7.95 *(978-0-7460-6102-2(1),* Usborne) EDC Publishing.

—Este No es Mi Sirenita. 2006. 10p. (J). bds. 9.99 *(978-0-7460-7386-5(0),* Usborne) EDC Publishing.

—Hide-and-seek baby board Book. 2005. 10p. (J). 8.99 *(978-0-7945-1055-8(8),* Usborne) EDC Publishing.

—Snuggletime Busy Baby. MacKinnon, Catherine-Anne, illus. 2005. 10p. (J). (gr. -1-k). per., bds. 8.99 *(978-0-7945-1054-1(X),* Usborne) EDC Publishing.

—That's Not My Mermaid: Her Hair Is Too Fluffy. Wells, Rachel, illus. 2006. (Usborne Touchy-Feely Board Bks.). 10p. (J). (gr. -1-k). bds. 9.99 *(978-0-7945-1083-1(3),* Usborne) EDC Publishing.

—That's Not My Robot... Wells, Rachel, illus. 2005. (Usborne Touchy-Feely Board Bks.). 10p. (J). (gr. -1-k). bds. 7.95 *(978-0-7945-1169-2(4),* Usborne) EDC Publishing.

Wearing, Judy. Taste. 2009. (World of Wonder Ser.). (Illus.). 24p. (J). (gr. 2-4). pap. 8.95 *(978-1-60596-057-9(8));* lib. bdg. 24.45 *(978-1-60596-056-2(X))* Weigl Pubs., Inc.

Wheeler-Toppen, Jodi Lyn. Our Mouths Can Taste. 2017. (Our Amazing Senses Ser.). (ENG., Illus.). 24p. (J). (gr. -1-2). lib. bdg. 22.65 *(978-1-5157-6707-7(8),* 135268, Pebble) Capstone.

Willis, John & Gillespie, Katie. Taste. 2018. (Illus.). 24p. (J). *(978-1-4896-5704-6(5),* AV2 by Weigl) Weigl Pubs., Inc.

Woodward, Kay. Taste, 1 vol. 2004. (Our Senses Ser.). (ENG., Illus.). 24p. (gr. 1-3). lib. bdg. 25.67 *(978-0-8368-4409-2(2),* 29b01ac6-536e-4e46-9b4e-50f12c955b87, Gareth Stevens Learning Library) Stevens, Gareth Publishing LLLP.

World of Wonder: Senses, 6 vols., Set. Incl. Common Sense. De Medeiros, Michael. lib. bdg. 24.45 *(978-1-60596-062-3(4));* Hearing. Winnick, Nick. lib. bdg. 24.45 *(978-1-60596-054-8(3));* Sight. Bekkering, Annalise. lib. bdg. 24.45 *(978-1-60596-052-4(7));* Smell. Wearing, Judy. lib. bdg. 24.45 *(978-1-60596-060-9(8));* Taste. Wearing, Judy. lib. bdg. 24.45 *(978-1-60596-056-2(X));* Touch. DeMedeiros, James. lib. bdg. 24.45 *(978-1-60596-058-6(6));* (Illus.). 24p. (J). (gr. 2-4). 2009. 2010. Set lib. bdg. 146.70 *(978-1-60596-668-7(1))* Weigl Pubs., Inc.

Wright, Frankie. Taste. 2016. (Illus.). 16p. (J). pap. *(978-1-338-03051-8(5))* Scholastic, Inc.

Wynne, Patricia J. My First Book about the Five Senses. 2017. (Dover Science for Kids Coloring Bks.). (ENG., Illus.). 48p. (J). (gr. 3-6). pap. 5.99 *(978-0-486-81748-4(2),* 817482) Dover Pubns., Inc.

Young, Laurie. I See a Monster! Mahoney, Daniel J. & Mahoney, Daniel, illus. 2006. (ENG.). 12p. (J). (gr. -1-k). bds.

10.95 *(978-1-58117-483-0(7)*, Intervisual/Piggy Toes) Bendon, Inc.

SENSES AND SENSATION—FICTION

Almada, Ariel Andrés. Walking Through a World of Aromas. Brokenbrow, Jon, tr. Wimmer, Sonja, illus. 2013. (ENG.). 24p. (J). (gr. k-3). 16.95 *(978-84-15619-48-2(0))* Cuento de Luz SL ESP. Dist: Publishers Group West (PGW).

Baker, Keith. Sometimes. Baker, Keith, illus. 2003. (Green Light Readers Level 1 Ser.). (ENG., Illus.). 24p. (J). (gr. -1-3). pap. 5.99 *(978-0-15-204847-1(2)*, 1194636, Clarion Bks.) HarperCollins Pubs.

—Sometimes. 2003. (Green Light Readers Level 1 Ser.). (gr. -1-2). lib. bdg. 13.50 *(978-0-613-64597-3(9))* Turtleback.

—Sometimes/Algunas Veces: Bilingual English-Spanish. Baker, Keith, illus. 2007. (Green Light Readers Level 1 Ser.). (ENG., Illus.). 28p. (J). (gr. -1-3). pap. 4.99 *(978-0-15-205961-3(X)*, 1197901, Clarion Bks.) HarperCollins Pubs.

Beavin, John. The Parable of the Stars. 2009. 24p. pap. 11.50 *(978-1-60693-368-8(X)*, Strategic Bk. Publishing) Strategic Book Publishing & Rights Agency (SBPRA).

Blackstone, Stella. Bear's Busy Family / la Familia Ocupada de Oso. Harter, Debbie, illus. 2014. (Bear Ser.). (ENG.). 32p. (J). (gr. -1-1). pap. 8.99 *(978-1-84686-771-2(1))* Barefoot Bks., Inc.

—La Famille Active de l'Ours. 2012.Tr. of Bear's Busy Family. (FRE & ENG., Illus.). (J). pap. 6.99 *(978-1-84686-772-9(X))* Barefoot Bks., Inc.

Book Company Staff. Are You a Dinosaur? 2003. (Novelty Bks.). (J). 12.95 *(978-1-74047-319-4(1))* Book Co. Publishing Pty, Ltd., The AUS. Dist: Penton Overseas, Inc.

—Are You a Frog? 2003. (Novelty Bks.). (Illus.). (J). 12.95 *(978-1-74047-318-7(3))* Book Co. Publishing Pty, Ltd., The AUS. Dist: Penton Overseas, Inc.

Brown, Gina Bates. Zen & Bodhi's Snowy Day. Hinder, Sarah Jane, illus. 2014. (ENG.). 24p. (J). 15.95 *(978-1-61429-165-7(9))* Wisdom Pubns.

Bryant, Gerry. Metamorphosed: Sun's Gift. 2006. (ENG.). 116p. (YA). 20.95 *(978-0-595-67412-1(7))*; pap. 10.95 *(978-0-595-36729-0(1))* iUniverse, Inc.

Coll, Ivar Da. Cinco Amigos. (SPA.). (J). bds. *(978-958-04-4909-6(0))* Norma S.A. COL. Dist: Lectorum Pubns., Inc.

Cotterill, Samantha. This Beach Is Loud! Cotterill, Samantha, illus. 2019. (Little Senses Ser.). (ENG., Illus.). 32p. (J). (gr. -1-2). 17.99 *(978-0-525-55345-8(2)*, Dial Bks) Penguin Young Readers Group.

Crupi, Jaclyn. Theo at the Beach. Verdoux, Aurélia, illus. 2013. (J). *(978-1-4351-4722-5(7))* Barnes & Noble, Inc.

Curious George Discovers the Senses. 2015. (Curious George Ser.). (ENG., Illus.). 32p. (J). (gr. -1-3). 6.99 *(978-0-544-50023-5(7)*, 1604222, Clarion Bks.) HarperCollins Pubs.

Del Moral, Susana. La Casa de Violet. Zaidi, Nadeem, illus. 2005. (Baby Einstein: Libros de Carton Ser.). (SPA.). 10p. (J). (gr. -1). bds. *(978-970-718-305-6(5)*, Silver Dolphin en Español) Advanced Marketing, S. de R. L. de C. V.

Derubertis, Barbara. Sammy Skunk's Super Sniffer. Alley, R. W., illus. 2011. (Animal Antics A to Z Set III Ser.). pap. 45.32 *(978-0-7613-8428-1(6))* Astra Publishing Hse.

deRubertis, Barbara. Sammy Skunk's Super Sniffer. Alley, R. W., illus. 2011. (Animal Antics a to Z Ser.). 32p. (J). (gr. -1-3). pap. 7.95 *(978-1-57565-344-0(3)*, 16bcbd5e-f8d1-4d8e-aeb0-6d16e78957fc, Kane Press) Astra Publishing Hse.

Disney Books. Winnie the Pooh: Pooh's Honey Trouble. 2012. (ENG.). 16p. (J). (gr. -1-k). bds. 6.99 *(978-1-4231-3579-1(2)*, Disney Press Books) Disney Publishing Worldwide.

Doudna, Kelly. Rabbit Ears. Nobens, C. A., illus. 2006. (Fact & Fiction Ser.). 24p. (J). pap. 48.42 *(978-1-59679-962-2(5))* ABDO Publishing Co.

Emma Treehouse Ltd. My Pets. Davis, Caroline, illus. 2007. (Easy Flaps Ser.). 10p. (J). (gr. -1). bds. 6.95 *(978-1-58925-824-2(X))* Tiger Tales.

Farrington Wilson, Lynda. Squirmy Wormy: How I Learned to Help Myself. 2009. (ENG., Illus.). 32p. (gr. 1). pap. 14.95 *(978-1-935567-18-9(7)*, 9781935567189) Sensory Resources.

Flesher, Vivienne. Alfred's Nose. Flesher, Vivienne, illus. 2008. (Illus.). 32p. (J). (gr. -1-2). lib. bdg. 17.89 *(978-0-06-084314-4(4))* HarperCollins Pubs.

Hale, Ohara. Be Still;Life. 2018. (ENG., Illus.). 48p. (J). (gr. -1). 17.95 *(978-1-59270-257-2(0))* Enchanted Lion Bks., LLC.

Hall, Kirsten. A Perfect Day: All about the Five Senses. Luedecke, Bev, illus. (Beastieville Ser.). (J). (gr. k-1). 2005. (ENG.). 32p. pap. 3.95 *(978-0-516-25521-7(5))* 2004. 19.50 *(978-0-516-24437-2(X))* Scholastic Library Publishing. (Children's Pr.).

Hamilton, Robert M. Mia's Five Senses, 1 vol. 2012. (InfoMax Readers Ser.). (ENG., Illus.). 16p. (J). (gr. k-k). pap. 7.00 *(978-1-4488-8905-1(7)*, 9a22228c-a649-4f18-b935-328bd983b908, Rosen Classroom) Rosen Publishing Group, Inc., The.

Harris, Shawn, illus. Have You Ever Seen a Flower? 2021. (ENG.). 48p. (J). (gr. -1-k). 17.99 *(978-1-4521-8270-4(1))* Chronicle Bks. LLC.

Hayward, Mark Brauner. I See Without My Eyes. Hartman, Nancy Lee, illus. 2009. 32p. pap. 12.99 *(978-1-4343-3823-5(1))* AuthorHouse.

Hughes, Jack. Rex's Specs, 1 vol. 2014. (Dinosaur Friends Ser.). (ENG., Illus.). 32p. (J). (gr. 2-3). lib. bdg. 28.93 *(978-1-4777-9226-1(0)*, d22e2e23-7684-4a5f-81ce-dadac3f7f784, Windmill Bks.) Rosen Publishing Group, Inc., The.

Isadora, Rachel. I Hear a Pickle: And Smell, See, Touch, & Taste It, Too! Isadora, Rachel, illus. (Illus.). (J). (— 1). 2017. 30p. bds. 8.99 *(978-1-5247-3958-4(8))* 2016. 32p. 17.99 *(978-0-399-16049-3(3))* Penguin Young Readers Group. (Nancy Paulsen Books).

Jeffers, Oliver. The Incredible Book Eating Boy. Jeffers, Oliver, illus. (ENG., Illus.). 32p. pap. *(978-0-00-718231-2(7)*, HarperCollins Children's Bks.) HarperCollins Pubs. Ltd.

Kranowitz, Carol Stock. The Goodenoughs Get in Sync: A Story for Kids about the Tough Day When Filibuster Grabbed Darwin's Rabbit's Foot... Wylie, T. J., illus. 2004. 86p. (J). 14.95 *(978-1-931615-17-4(9)*, 978-1-931615-17-4) Sensory Resources.

Ladd, Debbie. Don't Pick Your Nose, one. 2003. (Illus.). 24p. (J). 12.95 *(978-0-9727615-1-2(9))* Deb on Air Bks.

Malia, Jen. Too Sticky! Sensory Issues with Autism. Lew-Vriethoff, Joanne, illus. 2020. (ENG.). 32p. (J). (gr. -1-3). 17.99 *(978-0-8075-8026-4(0)*, 807580260) Whitman, Albert & Co.

Mandy and Ness Staff, et al. Hattie's House: A First Book about Sound. 2005. (Senses Ser.). (URD, ENG, VIE, CHI & BEN., Illus.). 16p. (J). pap. 9.95 *(978-1-84059-156-9(0))* Milet Publishing.

Marshall, Rita. Taste the Clouds. 2016. (ENG., Illus.). 14p. (J). (gr. -1-k). bds. 8.99 *(978-1-56846-285-1(9)*, 20558, Creative Editions) Creative Co., The.

Mass, Wendy. A Mango-Shaped Space. 2005. (ENG.). 240p. (YA). (gr. 5-8). per. 8.99 *(978-0-316-05825-4(4))* Little, Brown Bks. for Young Readers.

McKendry, Sam. Are You Ticklish? A Touch & Tickle Book. Mitchell, Melanie, illus. 2007. 15.95 *(978-1-58117-571-4(X)*, Intervisual/Piggy Toes) Bendon, Inc.

Moore, Ann C. Looking for a Place to Take a Long Winter Nap. 2009. 32p. pap. 14.49 *(978-1-4490-0852-9(6))* AuthorHouse.

Muntean, Michaela. Elmo Can... Taste! Touch! Smell! See! Hear! (Sesame Street) Swanson, Maggie, illus. 2013. (Big Bird's Favorites Board Bks.). (ENG.). 24p. (J). (— 1). bds. 4.99 *(978-0-307-98078-6(2)*, Random Hse. Bks. for Young Readers) Random Hse. Children's Bks.

Nex, Anthony, photos by. Little Feet Love. 2009. (Illus.). 12p. 7.95 *(978-1-58117-881-4(6)*, Intervisual/Piggy Toes) Bendon, Inc.

Nichols, Kathleen. My Five Senses. 2008. (ENG., Illus.). 12p. (J). (gr. k-k). bds. *(978-1-59700-581-4(9))* Island Heritage Publishing.

O'Brien, Gerry. Bubba Begonia, You'll Be Sorry. Jones, Brenda, illus. 2006. (ENG.). 80p. (J). per. 6.95 *(978-1-894838-23-8(8))* Acorn Pr., The CAN. Dist: Univ. of Toronto Pr.

Patricelli, Leslie. Binky. Patricelli, Leslie, illus. 2005. (Leslie Patricelli Board Bks.). (ENG., Illus.). 24p. (J). (— 1). bds. 7.99 *(978-0-7636-2364-7(4))* Candlewick Pr.

—Blankie. Patricelli, Leslie, illus. 2005. (Leslie Patricelli Board Bks.). (ENG., Illus.). 24p. (J). (— 1). bds. 7.99 *(978-0-7636-2363-0(6))* Candlewick Pr.

—Yummy Yucky/¡Ñam! ¡Puaj! Patricelli, Leslie, illus. 2016. (Leslie Patricelli Board Bks.). (Illus.). 24p. (J). (— 1). bds. 8.99 *(978-0-7636-8776-2(6))* Candlewick Pr.

Payne, Laurie. Mush & the Big Blue Flower. 2007. (ENG., Illus.). 104p. (J). (gr. -1). pap. 12.95 *(978-0-88982-242-9(5))* Oolichan Bks. CAN. Dist: Univ. of Toronto Pr.

Piggy Toes Press Staff, creator. Little Feet Like: A Tiny Tootsie Touch & Feel Book. 2008. (ENG., Illus.). 12p. (gr. -1-k). 9.95 *(978-1-58117-692-6(9)*, Intervisual/Piggy Toes) Bendon, Inc.

Quinton, Sasha, text. Ears. 2010. (Illus.). 10p. (J). *(978-1-936199-15-0(7))* Book Shop, Ltd., The.

—Noses. 2010. (Illus.). 10p. (J). *(978-1-936199-17-4(3))* Book Shop, Ltd., The.

—Paws. 2010. (Illus.). 10p. (J). *(978-1-936199-16-7(5))* Book Shop, Ltd., The.

Raschka, Chris. Five for a Little One. Raschka, Chris, illus. 2006. (ENG., Illus.). 48p. (J). (gr. -1-2). 19.99 *(978-0-689-84599-4(5)*, Atheneum/Richard Jackson Bks.) Simon & Schuster Children's Publishing.

Romano, Annie Cronin. Before You Sleep: A Bedtime Book of Gratitude. Hobai, Ioana, illus. 2018. (ENG.). 40p. (J). 17.99 *(978-1-62414-578-0(7)*, 900192299) Page Street Publishing Co.

Roth, Judith L. & Rothshank, Brooke, illus. Julia's Words. 2008. (J). (gr. -1-3). pap. 12.99 *(978-0-8361-9417-3(9))* Herald Pr.

Rotner, Shelley. Senses at the Seashore. Rotner, Shelley, photos by. (Shelley Rotner's Early Childhood Library). (ENG., Illus.). 32p. (gr. -1-2). 2010. (J). pap. 8.99 *(978-0-7613-6530-3(3)*, 5739b8eb-3fd2-4581-9738-40913bdb4d7a, Millbrook Pr.) 2006. lib. bdg. 22.60 *(978-0-7613-2897-1(1))* Lerner Publishing Group.

Ruffenach, Jessie, ed. Baby Learns about Senses. Thomas, Peter, tr. from ENG. Blacksheep, Beverly, illus. 2005. (NAV & ENG.). 16p. (J). (gr. 4-7). 7.95 *(978-1-893354-63-0(6))* Salina Bookshelf Inc.

Rummel, Verna. I Can Too, 1 vol. 2009. 12p. pap. 24.95 *(978-1-60836-089-5(X))* America Star Bks.

Ryan, Pam Muñoz. Hello Ocean. Astrella, Mark, illus. 2014. 32p. pap. 8.00 *(978-1-61003-319-0(1))* Center for the Collaborative Classroom.

—Hola Mar / Hello Ocean. Astrella, Mark, illus. 2003. (Charlesbridge Bilingual Bks.).Tr. of Hello Ocean (Bilingual). 32p. (J). (gr. -1-2). pap. 7.95 *(978-1-57091-372-3(2))* Charlesbridge Publishing, Inc.

Salati, Doug. Hot Dog: (Winner of the 2023 Caldecott Medal) 2022. (ENG.). 40p. (J). (gr. -1-3). 20.99 *(978-0-593-30844-8(1))*; 18.99 *(978-0-593-30843-1(3))* Random Hse. Children's Bks. (Knopf Bks. for Young Readers).

Shannon, David. David Smells! a Diaper David Book. Shannon, David, illus. 2005. (ENG., Illus.). 12p. (J). (gr. -1-k). bds. 6.99 *(978-0-439-69138-3(9)*, Cartwheel Bks.) Scholastic, Inc.

Steiner, Hartley. This Is Gabriel: Making Sense of School - 2nd Edition: A Book about Sensory Processing Disorder. 2nd rev. ed. 2012. (ENG., Illus.). 32p. pap. 12.95 *(978-1-935567-34-9(9)*, P217127) Future Horizons, Inc.

Stojic, Manya. Rain. Stojic, Manya, illus. 2009. (ENG., Illus.). 32p. (J). (gr. -1-2). pap. 8.99 *(978-0-385-73729-6(7)*, Dragonfly Bks.) Random Hse. Children's Bks.

Taylor, Alastair. Mr. Blewitt's Nose. 2005. (J). (gr. k-3). 16.00 *(978-0-618-58111-5(1))* Houghton Mifflin Harcourt Trade & Reference Pubs.

Van Fleet, Matthew. Lick! Mini Board Book. Van Fleet, Matthew, illus. 2013. (ENG., Illus.). 14p. (J). (gr. -1-1). 12.99 *(978-1-4424-6049-2(0)*, Simon & Schuster/Paula Wiseman Bks.) Simon & Schuster/Paula Wiseman Bks.

—Sniff! Mini Board Book. Van Fleet, Matthew, illus. 2012. (ENG., Illus.). 14p. (J). (gr. -1-1). 9.99 *(978-1-4424-6050-8(4)*, Simon & Schuster/Paula Wiseman Bks.) Simon & Schuster/Paula Wiseman Bks.

Veenendall, Jennifer. Why Does Izzy Cover Her Ears? Dealing with Sensory Overload. 2009. (Illus.). 39p. (J). 18.95 *(978-1-934575-46-8(1))* Autism Asperger Publishing Co.

Vonthron, Satanta C. Marsy's Perfect Eyesight. Teeple, Jackie, illus. l.t. ed. 2005. (J). (gr. -1-k). pap. 10.95 *(978-1-57332-344-4(6))*; pap. 10.95 *(978-1-57332-345-1(4))* Carson-Dellosa Publishing, LLC. (HighReach Learning, Incorporated).

Wagner, Brian. 10 Things Not to Do with Your Eyeball. 2005. 20p. 9.99 *(978-1-4116-5977-3(5))* Lulu Pr., Inc.

Wagner Lloyd, Megan. Finding Wild. Halpin, Abigail, illus. 2016. 32p. (J). (gr. -1-2). 18.99 *(978-1-101-93281-0(3)*, Knopf Bks. for Young Readers) Random Hse. Children's Bks.

Watt, Fiona. That's Not My Hamster. 2012. (Touchy-Feely Board Bks). 10p. (J). bds. 8.99 *(978-0-7945-3277-2(2)*, Usborne) EDC Publishing.

—That's Not My Train. rev. ed. 2008. (Touchy-Feely Board Bks). 10p. (J). bds. 8.99 *(978-0-7945-2168-4(1)*, Usborne) EDC Publishing.

Watt, Fiona & Wells, Rachel. That's Not My Train: Its Wheels Are Too Slippery. 2004. (Touchy-Feely Board Bks.). (SPA & ENG., Illus.). 1p. (J). (gr. -1-18). bds. 7.95 *(978-0-7460-3779-9(1))* EDC Publishing.

Wax, Wendy. Look Who's Buzzing. 2009. 12p. 9.95 *(978-1-58117-911-8(1)*, Intervisual/Piggy Toes) Bendon, Inc.

Werber, Yael. Spring for Sophie. Hill, Jen, illus. 2017. (ENG.). 32p. (J). (gr. -1-3). 19.99 *(978-1-4814-5134-5(0)*, Simon & Schuster Bks. For Young Readers) Simon & Schuster Bks. For Young Readers.

Whose Ears. 2005. (J). bds. 5.99 *(978-1-933200-06-4(5))* Family Bks. at Home.

Whose Feet. 2005. (J). bds. 5.99 *(978-1-933200-02-6(2))* Family Bks. at Home.

Whose Nose. 2005. (J). bds. 5.99 *(978-1-933200-03-3(0))* Family Bks. at Home.

Zaidi, Nadeem, illus. Baby Mozart: Musica Por Todas Partes. 2005. (Baby Einstein: Libros de Carton Ser.). (SPA.). 16p. (J). (gr. -1). bds. *(978-970-718-309-4(8)*, Silver Dolphin en Español) Advanced Marketing, S. de R. L. de C. V.

SEPARATION (LAW)

see Divorce

SEPARATION ANXIETY

Berry, Joy. Let's Talk about Being Away from Your Parents. Smith, Maggie, illus. 2010. (Let's Talk About Ser.). (ENG.). 32p. (J). (gr. -1-k). pap. 4.99 *(978-1-60577-202-8(X))* Berry, Joy Enterprises.

Lavallee, Kristen & Schneider, Silvia. What to Do When You Don't Want to Be Apart: A Kid's Guide to Overcoming Separation Anxiety. McDonnell, Janet, illus. 2017. 88p. (J). pap. *(978-1-4338-2713-6(1)*, Magination Pr.) American Psychological Assn.

Zeavin, Carol & Silverbush, Rhona. Bye-Bye! Davis, Jon, illus. 2018. 16p. (J). *(978-1-4338-2876-8(6)*, Magination Pr.) American Psychological Assn.

SEPARATION ANXIETY—FICTION

Dewdney, Anna. Llama Llama Misses Mama. (Llama Llama Ser.). (Illus.). (J). 2019. (ENG.). 36p. (— 1). bds. 9.99 *(978-0-593-11671-5(2))* 2009. 40p. (gr. -1-k). 18.99 *(978-0-670-06198-3(0))* Penguin Young Readers Group. (Viking Books for Young Readers).

Edwards, Becky. My First Day at Nursery School. Flintoft, Anthony, illus. 2004. (ENG.). 32p. (J). (gr. -1-1). pap. 7.99 *(978-1-58234-909-1(6)*, 900024733, Bloomsbury USA Childrens) Bloomsbury Publishing USA.

Freeman, Suzanne. The Cuckoo's Child. 249p. (YA). (gr. 5-8). pap. 5.95 *(978-0-8072-1510-4(4)*, Listening Library) Random Hse. Audio Publishing Group.

Greene, Marjorie. Cassie's Big Day. 2003. (Illus.). (J). 16.95 *(978-0-9741764-0-6(0))* Greene, Marjorie A.

Haughton, Chris. Little Owl Lost. Haughton, Chris, illus. 2010. (ENG., Illus.). 32p. (J). (gr. -1-k). 17.99 *(978-0-7636-5022-3(6))* Candlewick Pr.

Hughes, Shirley. Don't Want to Go! Hughes, Shirley, illus. 2010. (ENG., Illus.). 32p. (J). (gr. -1-2). 16.99 *(978-0-7636-5091-9(9))* Candlewick Pr.

Kaufmann, Nancy. Bye, Bye! Spetter, Jung-Hee, illus. 2004. (ENG.). 32p. (J). (gr. -1-1). 14.95 *(978-1-886910-95-9(2)*, Lemniscaat) Highlights Pr., c/o Highlights for Children, Inc.

Maier, Inger. When Fuzzy Was Afraid of Losing His Mother. Candon, Jennifer, illus. 2004. 32p. (J). 14.95 *(978-1-59147-168-4(0)*, Magination Pr.) American Psychological Assn.

Maier, Inger M. When Fuzzy Was Afraid: Of Losing His Mother. Candon, Jennifer, illus. 2004. 32p. (J). pap. 9.95 *(978-1-59147-169-1(9)*, Magination Pr.) American Psychological Assn.

Peck, Judith. The Bright Blue Button & the Button-Hole. Stasolla, Mario, illus. 2004. 28p. (J). 18.95 *(978-0-9746119-5-2(6))* Imagination Arts Pubns.

Penn, Audrey. Un Beso en Mi Mano (the Kissing Hand) Harper, Ruth, illus. 2006. (ENG.). 32p. (J). (gr. -1-3). 18.99 *(978-1-933718-01-9(3))* Tanglewood Pr.

—The Kissing Hand. Harper, Ruth, illus. 2007. (ENG.). 32p. (J). (gr. -1-3). 28.95 *(978-1-933718-07-1(2))* Tanglewood Pr.

—A Kissing Hand for Chester Raccoon. Gibson, Barbara, illus. 2014. (Kissing Hand Ser.). (ENG.). 14p. (J). (gr. -1-2). bds. 8.99 *(978-1-933718-77-4(3))* Tanglewood Pr.

Penn, Audrey, et al, illus. The Kissing Hand. 2010. 23.05 *(978-0-7569-9299-6(0))* Natl Bk. Network.

Potvin, Amy K. I Miss Daddy. 2009. 28p. pap. 13.99 *(978-1-4259-1705-0(4))* AuthorHouse.

Sederman, Marty & Epstein, Seymour. The Magic Box: When Parents Can't Be There to Tuck You In. Brooks, Karen Stormer, illus. 2003. 32p. (J). (gr. -1-3). 14.95 *(978-1-55798-807-2(2)*, Magination Pr.) American Psychological Assn.

Stratford, Anne Margaret. My Daddy Is A Soldier. 2008. (Illus.). 40p. (J). 17.99 *(978-0-9817938-0-1(0))* Diamond Fly Publishing, Inc.

Thomas, Christie. Quinn's Promise Rock: No Matter Where, God Is Always There. 2019. (ENG., Illus.). 32p. (J). (gr. -1-2). 17.99 *(978-0-7369-7432-5(6)*, 6974325) Harvest Hse. Pubs.

Wells, Rosemary. Love Waves: Midi Edition. Wells, Rosemary, illus. 2012. (ENG., Illus.). 32p. (J). (gr. k — 1). 8.99 *(978-0-7636-6224-0(0))* Candlewick Pr.

Woodson, Jacqueline. Coming on Home Soon. Lewis, E. B., illus. 2004. (ENG.). 32p. (J). (gr. k-3). 18.99 *(978-0-399-23748-5(8)*, G.P. Putnam's Sons Books for Young Readers) Penguin Young Readers Group.

Wright, Michael. Jake Starts School. Wright, Michael, illus. 2010. (ENG., Illus.). 48p. (J). (gr. -1-1). 21.19 *(978-0-312-60884-2(5)*, 900065180) Square Fish.

SEPTEMBER 11 TERRORIST ATTACKS, 2001

Anderson, Dale. The Terrorist Attacks of September 11 2001, 1 vol. 2003. (Landmark Events in American History Ser.). (ENG., Illus.). 48p. (gr. 5-8). pap. 15.05 *(978-0-8368-5408-4(X)*, 09da09bc-b75b-4b60-97eb-c06300161720); lib. bdg. 33.67 *(978-0-8368-5380-3(6)*, 731c0e2e-4f9b-4b9e-be7c-4c7faabe1171) Stevens, Gareth Publishing LLLP. (Gareth Stevens Secondary Library).

Andryszewski, Tricia. Terrorism in America. 2003. (Headliners Ser.). (Illus.). 64p. (J). (gr. 5-8). lib. bdg. 25.90 *(978-0-7613-2803-2(3)*, Millbrook Pr.) Lerner Publishing Group.

Baurys, Tamra. The World Will Never Forget. Bouchal, Renee', illus. 2011. 34p. pap. 12.95 *(978-0-9833354-2-9(7))* Amira Rock Publishing.

Benoit, Peter. September 11, 2001: The 10th Anniversary. 2011. (Cornerstones of Freedom, Third Ser.). (Illus.). 64p. (J). (gr. 4-6). lib. bdg. 30.00 *(978-0-531-25040-2(7)*, Children's Pr.) Scholastic Library Publishing.

—September 11 Then & Now. 2011. (True Book-Disasters Ser.). (ENG., Illus.). 48p. (J). (gr. 3-5). lib. bdg. 29.00 *(978-0-531-25424-0(0)*, Children's Pr.) Scholastic Library Publishing.

Blohm, Craig E. The 9/11 Investigation, 1 vol. 2009. (Crime Scene Investigations Ser.). (ENG., Illus.). 104p. (gr. 7-7). 37.08 *(978-1-4205-0136-0(4)*, 1bc469f1-91f6-4283-937f-8665435465ea, Lucent Pr.) Greenhaven Publishing LLC.

Bodden, Valerie. The 9/11 Terror Attacks. (Odysseys in History Ser.). (J). 2016. (ENG.). 80p. (gr. 7-10). pap. 15.99 *(978-1-62832-130-2(X)*, 20960, Creative Paperbacks) 2007. (Illus.). 48p. (gr. 4-7). lib. bdg. 31.35 *(978-1-58341-549-8(1)*, Creative Education) Creative Co., The.

—The 9/11 Terror Attacks: Days of Change. 2015. (Illus.). 80p. (J). *(978-1-60818-529-0(X)*, Creative Education) Creative Co., The.

Brewer, Paul. September 11 & Radical Islamic Terrorism, 1 vol. 2005. (Terrorism in Today's World Ser.). (ENG., Illus.). 48p. (gr. 5-8). pap. 15.05 *(978-0-8368-6567-7(7)*, 31845189-b9d0-47d8-9837-bc9c8a5dfdd0); lib. bdg. 33.67 *(978-0-8368-6560-8(X)*, 492237bb-a90b-44d3-a93c-2c1facf10515) Stevens, Gareth Publishing LLLP. (Gareth Stevens Secondary Library).

Brindell Fradin, Dennis. 9/11/01, 1 vol. 2010. (Turning Points in U. S. History Ser.). (ENG.). 48p. (gr. 4-4). 34.07 *(978-0-7614-4259-2(6)*, 75002057-d3bf-4e16-9278-148fda1efa7d) Cavendish Square Publishing LLC.

Brown, Don. America Is under Attack: September 11, 2001: the Day the Towers Fell. 2014. (Actual Times Ser.: 4). (ENG., Illus.). 64p. (J). (gr. 1-5). pap. 10.99 *(978-1-250-04415-0(4)*, 900128302) Square Fish.

Burgan, Michael. Captured! Bringing in 9/11 Planner Khalid Sheik Mohammed, Vol. 8. 2018. (Special Forces Stories Ser.). 64p. (J). (gr. 7). 31.93 *(978-1-4222-4078-6(9))* Mason Crest.

Casil, Amy Sterling. Coping with Terrorism, 1 vol. 2003. (Coping (1982-2004) Ser.). (ENG.). 112p. (YA). (gr. 7-12). lib. bdg. 39.80 *(978-0-8239-4484-2(0)*, fef21c5c-5f8e-4158-bc5b-9dacc5367610) Rosen Publishing Group, Inc., The.

Challen, Paul C. Surviving 9/11, 1 vol. 2015. (Surviving Disaster Ser.). (ENG., Illus.). 48p. (J). (gr. 5-6). 33.47 *(978-1-4994-3657-0(2)*, a6e838c6-ff2e-44cc-8721-69dc469493ed, Rosen Central) Rosen Publishing Group, Inc., The.

Corrigan, Jim. Causes of the War on Terrorism. 2009. (J). lib. bdg. *(978-1-59556-035-3(1))* OTTN Publishing.

Deedy, Carmen Agra. 14 Cows for America, 1 vol. Gonzalez, Thomas, illus. 36p. (J). (gr. 2-5). 2016. pap. 8.99 *(978-1-56145-961-2(5))* 2009. 17.99 *(978-1-56145-490-7(7))* Peachtree Publishing Co. Inc.

—14 Cows for America. Gonzalez, Thomas, illus. 2016. (ENG.). 36p. (J). (gr. -1-3). lib. bdg. 19.60 *(978-0-606-39065-1(0))* Turtleback.

—14 Vacas para América, 1 vol. Gonzalez, Thomas, illus. 2008.Tr. of 14 Cows for America. 36p. (J). (gr. 2-5). 17.95 *(978-1-56145-550-8(4))*; pap. 8.95 *(978-1-56145-555-3(5))* Peachtree Publishing Co. Inc.

Doeden, Matt. Impact: The Story of the September 11 Terrorist Attacks. 2015. (Tangled History Ser.). (ENG., Illus.). 112p. (J). (gr. 3-9). lib. bdg. 32.65 *(978-1-4914-7079-4(8)*, 129461, Capstone Pr.) Capstone.

Gard, Carolyn. The Attack on the Pentagon on September 11 2001. 2009. (Terrorist Attacks Ser.). 64p. (gr. 5-5). 58.50 *(978-1-60853-310-7(7))* Rosen Publishing Group, Inc., The.

Gassman, Julie. Saved by the Boats: The Heroic Sea Evacuation of September 11. Moors, Steve, illus. 2016. (Encounter: Narrative Nonfiction Picture Bks.). (ENG.). 32p. (J). (gr. 3-6). lib. bdg. 27.99 *(978-1-5157-0269-6(3)*, 131908, Capstone Pr.) Capstone.

Goldish, Meish. Ground Zero Dogs. 2012. (Dog Heroes Ser.). 32p. (J). (gr. 2-7). lib. bdg. 28.50 *(978-1-61772-576-0(5))* Bearport Publishing Co., Inc.

Green, Robert. Cause & Effect the September 11 Attacks: The September 11 Attacks. 2015. (ENG., Illus.). 80p. (J). lib. bdg. *(978-1-60152-788-2(8))* ReferencePoint Pr., Inc.

—Debates on the 9/11 Attacks. 2018. (Debating History Ser.). (ENG.). 80p. (YA). (gr. 6-12). 39.93 *(978-1-68282-377-4(6))* ReferencePoint Pr., Inc.

Greene, Jacqueline Dembar. The 2001 World Trade Center Attack. 2007. (Code Red Ser.). (Illus.). 32p. (YA). (gr. 2-5). lib. bdg. 28.50 *(978-1-59716-365-1(1))* Bearport Publishing Co., Inc.

Halberstam, David. Firehouse. 2003. (ENG., Illus.). 208p. (gr. 8-17). pap. 19.99 *(978-0-7868-8851-1(2)*, Hachette Bks.) Hachette Bks.

Hampton, Wilborn. September 11 2001: Attack on New York City. 2011. (ENG., Illus.). 160p. (J). (gr. 5). pap. 14.99 *(978-0-7636-5767-3(0))* Candlewick Pr.
Haulley, Fletcher. Critical Perspectives on 9/11, 1 vol. 2004. (Critical Anthologies of Nonfiction Writing Ser.). (ENG.). 176p. (J). (gr. 8-8). lib. bdg. 42.47 *(978-1-4042-0060-9(6),* 3b3fe485-b729-4454-b7a5-4c5a477535d8) Rosen Publishing Group, Inc., The.
Haulley, Fletcher, ed. Critical Perspectives On 9/11. 2009. (Critical Anthologies of Nonfiction Writing Ser.). 176p. (gr. 8-8). 63.90 *(978-1-61512-072-7(6))* Rosen Publishing Group, Inc., The.
Hirsch, Judd, reader. Fireboat: The Heroic Adventures of the John J. Harvey. (Illus.). (J). 2006. pap. incl. audio *(978-1-59112-985-1(0))* 2004. pap. 39.95 incl. audio compact disk *(978-1-59112-989-9(3))* Live Oak Media.
Johnson, Linda Carlson & Johnson, Keri. 9.11 Helping the Heroes: A Salvation Army Story. 2011. (Illus.). (J). *(978-0-89216-130-0(2))* Salvation Army.
Kalman, Maira. Fireboat: The Heroic Adventures of the John J. Harvey. Kalman, Maira, illus. 2005. (Illus.). 48p. (J). (gr. -1-3). reprint ed. pap. 7.99 *(978-0-14-240362-4(8),* Puffin Books) Penguin Young Readers Group.
Koya, Lena & Buell, Tonya. Investigating the Crash of Flight 93, 1 vol. 2017. (Terrorism in the 21st Century: Causes & Effects Ser.). (ENG., Illus.). 64p. (gr. 6-6). 36.13 *(978-1-5081-7459-2(8),* 6c0a7b54-6ade-4ce1-81cb-ae527e8a843a, Rosen Young Adult) Rosen Publishing Group, Inc., The.
Koya, Lena & Gard, Carolyn. Investigating the Attack on the Pentagon, 1 vol. 2017. (Terrorism in the 21st Century: Causes & Effects Ser.). (ENG., Illus.). 64p. (J). (gr. 6-6). 36.13 *(978-1-5081-7453-0(9),* bc1e9ec9-7801-4ace-bd71-16cffa37ffa8, Rosen Young Adult) Rosen Publishing Group, Inc., The.
—Investigating the Attacks on the World Trade Center, 1 vol. 2017. (Terrorism in the 21st Century: Causes & Effects Ser.). (ENG.). 64p. (J). (gr. 6-6). 36.13 *(978-1-5081-7455-4(5),* d0bd35c2-5fcc-4264-bbc2-d1fdae8e1bd0, Rosen Young Adult) Rosen Publishing Group, Inc., The.
Lynch, Kelly Ann. He Said Yes: The Story of Father Mychal Judge. Oatman, M. Scott, illus. 2007. (ENG.). 32p. (J). (gr. -1-3). 12.95 *(978-0-8091-6740-1(9),* 6740-1) Paulist Pr.
Margulies, Phillip. Al Qaeda: Osama bin Laden's Army of Terrorists. 2009. (Inside the World's Most Infamous Terrorist Organizations Ser.). 64p. (gr. 5-5). 58.50 *(978-1-61513-573-8(1))* Rosen Publishing Group, Inc., The.
Marin, Dale Diane. Rachel Beth & the Day the Towers Came Down, 1 vol. Marin, Liz, illus. 2009. 27p. pap. 24.95 *(978-1-60813-328-4(1))* America Star Bks.
McNeil, Niki, et al. HOCPP 1105 September 11th 2001. 2006. spiral bd. 21.00 *(978-1-60308-105-4(4))* In the Hands of a Child.
McNeilly, Linden. Living Through the Post 9-11 Era. 2018. (American Culture & Conflict Ser.). (ENG., Illus.). 48p. (gr. 4-8). lib. bdg. 35.64 *(978-1-64156-420-5(2),* 9781641564205) Rourke Educational Media.
Miller, Mara. Remembering September 11 2001: What We Know Now, 1 vol. 2011. (Issues in Focus Today Ser.). (ENG.). 112p. (gr. 6-7). 35.93 *(978-0-7660-2931-6(X),* ef1bb047-74cb-4c5f-a4f2-b80a04b76535) Enslow Publishing, LLC.
Murdico, Suzanne J. Osama Bin Laden, 1 vol. 2006. (Middle East Leaders Ser.). (ENG., Illus.). 112p. (J). (gr. 5-8). lib. bdg. 39.80 *(978-1-4042-0875-9(5),* 9faeacea-bc57-4b4f-b1eb-e8ac34879793, Rosen Reference) Rosen Publishing Group, Inc., The.
—Osama bin Laden. 2009. (Middle East Leaders Ser.). 112p. (gr. 5-8). 66.50 *(978-1-61514-647-5(4),* Rosen Reference) Rosen Publishing Group, Inc., The.
Murray, Laura K. The 9/11 Terror Attacks. 2016. (Turning Points Ser.). (ENG.). 48p. (J). (gr. 4-7). *(978-1-60818-750-8(0),* 20798, Creative Education) Creative Co., The.
Nolan, Janet. Seven & a Half Tons of Steel, 1 vol. Gonzalez, Thomas, illus. 2016. 36p. (J). (gr. 1-4). 17.95 *(978-1-56145-912-4(7))* Peachtree Publishing Co. Inc.
Orr, Tamra B. September 11 & Terrorism in America. 2017. (Perspectives Library: Modern Perspectives Ser.). (ENG., Illus.). 32p. (J). (gr. 4-7). lib. bdg. 32.07 *(978-1-63472-858-4(0),* 209858) Cherry Lake Publishing.
Ringgold, Faith, intro. What Will You Do for Your Peace? Impact of 9/11 on New York City Youth. 2004. (Illus.). 32p. (YA). 16.95 net. *(978-0-9761753-0-8(4))* InterRelations Collaborative, Inc.
Roleff, Tamara L., ed. The World Trade Center Attack. 2003. (History Firsthand Ser.). (Illus.). 202p. (YA). (gr. 7-10). pap. 21.20 *(978-0-7377-1469-2(7),* Greenhaven Pr., Inc.) Cengage Gale.
Sanderson, Whitney. The September 11 Attacks Transform America. 2018. (Events That Changed America Ser.). (ENG.). 32p. (J). (gr. 3-6). lib. bdg. 35.64 *(978-1-5038-2522-2(1),* 212326, MOMENTUM) Child's World, Inc, The.
Santora, Maureen Crethan. The Day the Towers Fell: The Story of September 11 2001. Cardona, Patricia Santora, illus. 2008. (ENG.). 34p. pap. 21.99 *(978-1-4257-7869-9(0));* 31.99 *(978-1-4257-7872-9(0))* Xlibris Corp.
—My Son Christopher: A 9/11 Mother's Tale of Remembrance. 2008. 36p. 31.99 *(978-1-4363-3044-2(0))* Xlibris Corp.
Scheppler, Bill. Guantánamo Bay & Military Tribunals: The Detention & Trial of Suspected Terrorists. 2009. (Frontline Coverage of Current Events Ser.). 48p. (gr. 5-5). 53.00 *(978-1-61512-655-2(4))* Rosen Publishing Group, Inc., The.
Smith, Katrina M. This Is My Flag. 2011. 44p. pap. 18.46 *(978-1-4634-4785-4(X))* AuthorHouse.
The\September 11 Generation. Freedom's Answer: When the Twin Towers Fell, the Next Generation Rose! 2004. 160p. pap. *(978-0-9720227-7-4(5))* Little Moose Pr.
Williams, Brian. America under Attack. 2003. (Dates with History Ser.). 45p. (J). lib. bdg. 28.50 *(978-1-58340-406-5(6))* Black Rabbit Bks.
Yeager, Allison Blair. If I Could Change the World. Mesch, Kate, ed. (Illus.). 32p. (YA). (gr. 1-18). pap. 8.95 *(978-0-9715322-0-5(6),* LUBOITCCW) Luv U Bks.
Zullo, Allan. Heroes of 9/11. 2011. (Illus.). 181p. (J). pap. *(978-0-545-25506-6(6))* Scholastic, Inc.
13 Unknown Souls. 2003. (YA). 13.00 *(978-0-9745360-0-2(8))* Burney Enterprises Unlimited.

SEQUOIA NATIONAL FOREST (CALIF.)

Nicholas, Jeff D. Sequoia & Kings Canyon. 2004. (Illus.). per. 4.95 *(978-1-58071-054-1(9),* Wish You Were Here) Sierra Pr.

SEQUOYAH, 1770?-1843

Bennett, Doraine. Sequoyah. 2008. *(978-1-935077-05-3(8));* pap. *(978-1-935077-12-1(0))* State Standards Publishing, LLC.
Levine, Michelle. Sequoyah. 2004. (History Maker Bios Ser.). (J). pap. 8.95 *(978-0-8225-2071-9(0))* Lerner Publishing Group.
Marsh, Carole. Sequoyah. 2003. 12p. (gr. k-4). 2.95 *(978-0-635-02363-6(6))* Gallopade International.
Micklos, John & Micklos, John, Jr. Sequoyah, 1 vol. 2020. (Inside Guide: Famous Native Americans Ser.). (ENG.). 32p. (J). (gr. 4-5). pap. 11.58 *(978-1-5026-5128-0(9),* fa7bb66a-495b-460f-b594-43b58487b383) Cavendish Square Publishing LLC.
Rodgers, Kelly. Sequoyah & the Written Word. rev. ed. 2016. (Social Studies: Informational Text Ser.). (ENG., Illus.). 32p. (gr. 2-4). pap. 10.99 *(978-1-4938-2554-7(2))* Teacher Created Materials, Inc.
Rumford, James. Sequoyah: The Cherokee Man Who Gave His People Writing. 2004. (ENG., Illus.). 32p. (J). (gr. -1-3). tchr. ed. 18.99 *(978-0-618-36947-8(3),* 595398, Clarion Bks.) HarperCollins Pubs.
Strand, Jennifer. Sequoyah. 2017. (Native American Leaders Ser.). (ENG., Illus.). 24p. (J). (gr. -1-2). lib. bdg. 31.36 *(978-1-5321-2026-8(5),* 25316, Abdo Zoom-Launch) ABDO Publishing Co.
Summitt, April R. Sequoyah & the Invention of the Cherokee Alphabet, 1 vol. 2012. (Landmarks of the American Mosaic Ser.). (ENG., Illus.). 184p. 45.00 *(978-0-313-39177-4(7),* 790551, Greenwood) Bloomsbury Publishing USA.
Townsend, Dana E. Sequoyah & the Cherokee Alphabet. Gabriel, Andrea, illus. 2005. (Voices Reading Ser.). 32p. (J). *(978-0-7367-2953-6(4))* Zaner-Bloser, Inc.
Waxman, Laura Hamilton. Sequoyah. 2004. (History Maker Biographies Ser.). (ENG., Illus.). 48p. (gr. 3-6). 27.93 *(978-0-8225-0697-3(1),* Carolrhoda Bks.) Lerner Publishing Group.
Waya, Joe. We Should Honor Sequoyah. 2017. (Text Connections Guided Close Reading Ser.). (J). (gr. 2). *(978-1-4900-1856-0(5))* Benchmark Education Co.

SEQUOYAH, 1770?-1843—FICTION

Browin, Frances Williams. Captured Words: The Story of A Great Indian. Bjorklund, L. F., illus. 2011. 192p. 42.95 *(978-1-258-09914-5(4))* Literary Licensing, LLC.
Bruchac, Joseph. Talking Leaves. 2017. 288p. (J). (gr. 5). pap. 8.99 *(978-0-14-242298-4(3),* Puffin Books) Penguin Young Readers Group.

SERIALS (PUBLICATIONS)

see Periodicals

SERIGRAPHY

see Screen Process Printing

SERMON ON THE MOUNT

Gortler, Rosemarie & Piscitelli, Donna. The Beatitudes for Children. Sternhagen, Mimi, illus. 2009. 64p. (J). (gr. -1-3). pap. 6.95 *(978-1-59276-545-4(9))* Our Sunday Visitor, Publishing Div.
Halpin, D. Thomas. The Beatitudes Coloring & Activity Book. Richards, Virginia Helen, illus. 2006. (J). 1.95 *(978-0-8198-2359-5(7))* Pauline Bks. & Media.
Larsen, Carolyn. Teachings of Jesus. 2012. (Standard Bible Storybook Ser.). (ENG., Illus.). 32p. (J). 7.99 *(978-0-7847-3565-7(4))* Standard Publishing.
Rylant, Cynthia. Nativity. Rylant, Cynthia, illus. 2017. (ENG., Illus.). 40p. (J). (gr. -1-3). 18.99 *(978-1-4814-7041-4(8),* Beach Lane Bks.) Beach Lane Bks.

SERMONS

Beeching, Henry Charles. Seven Sermons to Schoolboys. 2006. pap. 20.95 *(978-1-4286-3591-3(2))* Kessinger Publishing, LLC.
Brennan, Gerald T. Angel Food for Boys & Girls - Vol. I, vol. 1. 2013. (Angel Food Ser.: 1). (ENG.). 114p. (J). (gr. k-3). 16.95 *(978-0-911845-66-2(6),* NP9020, Neumann Pr.) TAN Bks.
—Angel Food for Boys & Girls - Vol. II, vol. 2. 2013. (Angel Food Ser.: 2). (ENG.). 126p. (J). (gr. k-4). reprint ed. 16.95 *(978-0-911845-67-9(4),* NP9021, Neumann Pr.) TAN Bks.
—Angel Food for Boys & Girls - Vol. III, Vol. III. 2013. (Angel Food Ser.: 3). (ENG., Illus.). 114p. (J). (gr. k-4). 16.95 *(978-0-911845-94-5(1),* NP9022, Neumann Pr.) TAN Bks.
—Angel Food for Boys & Girls - Vol. IV, 4 vols. , Vol. IV. 2013. (Angel Food Ser.: 4). (ENG.). 126p. (J). (gr. k-4). 16.95 *(978-0-911845-95-2(X),* NP9023, Neumann Pr.) TAN Bks.
Dyan, Penelope. Beatitudes Are Attitudes. 2011. 34p. pap. 11.95 *(978-1-935630-90-6(3))* Bellissima Publishing, LLC.
Group Publishing Staff, ed. Quick Children's Sermons: Did Adam & Eve Have Bellybuttons? 2004. (Illus.). 96p. (gr. -1-6). pap. 17.99 *(978-0-7644-2296-6(0),* Flagship Church Resources) Group Publishing, Inc.
Hewitt, Beth Edington. Sermones Que Cautivan A los Ninos: Como Preparar y Presentar Sermones Infantiles Poderosos. Ballesta, Alfredo, tr. 2006. (SPA.). 208p. pap. 9.50 *(978-0-311-43030-7(9),* Editorial Mundo Hispano) Casa Bautista de Publicaciones.
Newton, Richard. Bible Promises: Sermons for Children on. 2006. pap. 15.99 *(978-1-59925-057-1(8))* Solid Ground Christian Bks.
—Bible Warnings: Sermons to Children. 2006. pap. 25.00 *(978-1-59925-083-0(7))* Solid Ground Christian Bks.
—Leaves from the Tree of Life: Sermons for Children. 2011. 164p. pap. 17.00 *(978-1-59925-150-9(7))* Solid Ground Christian Bks.
—Pebbles from the Brook: Sermons for Children Fighting the Good Fight of Faith. 2011. 316p. pap. 23.00 *(978-1-59925-151-6(5))* Solid Ground Christian Bks.
Phillips, Mary. Children'S Sermons with Humor. 2009. 56p. pap. 15.99 *(978-1-4415-1156-0(3))* Xlibris Corp.
Smith, Rodney Gipsy. The Lost Christ. 2003. (Illus.). 32p. 2.99 *(978-1-931393-05-8(2))* Christian Life Bks.
Staf, Edie. Christmas Novena: For Home or Classroom. 22p. (J). (gr. 2-8). pap. 1.50 *(978-0-8198-1456-2(3),* 332-032) Pauline Bks. & Media.
Vanissery, Matthew. Awesome Homilies: The Power of His Word. 2004. 236p. pap. 29.95 *(978-0-9759906-0-5(8))* Vanissery, Matthew.
Wehrheim, Carol A. Feasting on the Word Childrens's Sermons for Year A. 2016. (ENG.). 178p. pap. 24.00 *(978-0-664-26107-8(8))* Westminster John Knox Pr.
Wezeman, Phyllis Vos & Liechty, Anna L. Tell Me a Story: 30 Children's Sermons Based on Best-Loved Books. 2005. (New Brown Bag Ser.). (Illus.). 96p. pap. 12.00 *(978-0-8298-1635-8(6))* Pilgrim Pr., The/United Church Pr.
Wezeman, Phyllis Vos, et al. Wipe the Tears: 30 Children's Sermons on Death. 2005. (New Brown Bag Ser.). (Illus.). 96p. 10.00 *(978-0-8298-1520-7(1))* Pilgrim Pr., The/United Church Pr.

SERPENTS

see Snakes

SERRA, JUNIPERO, 1713-1784

Améz, Lynda & Améz, Lynda. Father Junipero Serra: Founder of the California Missions, 1 vol. 2015. (Exceptional Latinos Ser.). (ENG.). 24p. (gr. 3-4). pap. 10.35 *(978-0-7660-6710-3(6),* 0f4490d7-4307-473c-90b9-d935e8b061b1) Enslow Publishing, LLC.
Marsh, Carole. Father Junipero Serra: California Missions Founder: California Missions Founder. 2003. 12p. (gr. k-4). 2.95 *(978-0-635-02136-6(6))* Gallopade International.
Nussbaum, Ben. Junipero Serra: A Spanish Missionary. rev. ed. 2017. (Social Studies: Informational Text Ser.). (ENG., Illus.). 32p. (J). (gr. 3-5). pap. 11.99 *(978-1-4258-3235-3(0))* Teacher Created Materials, Inc.

SERVICE, COMPULSORY MILITARY

see Draft

SET THEORY

see also Arithmetic; Number Theory

Aboff, Marcie. If You Were a Set [LTD Commodities]. Dillard, Sarah, illus. 2010. (Math Fun Ser.). 24p. pap. 3.50 *(978-1-4048-6258-6(7),* Picture Window Bks.) Capstone.
—Sorting Fur, Feathers, Tails, & Scales. 2011. (Data Mania Ser.). (ENG & ABK.). 24p. (gr. 1-2). pap. 41.70 *(978-1-4296-6467-7(3),* Capstone Pr.) Capstone.
Alexander, Emmett. Sort It by Size, 1 vol. 2015. (Sort It Out! Ser.). (ENG., Illus.). 24p. (J). (gr. k-1). pap. 9.15 *(978-1-4824-2573-4(4),* a84356cb-8115-4a18-9a57-6d0bdb071a8d) Stevens, Gareth Publishing LLLP.
Becker, Ann & Peppas, Lynn. Sorting. 2009. (ENG.). 24p. (J). lib. bdg. *(978-0-7787-4349-1(7));* pap. *(978-0-7787-4367-5(5))* Crabtree Publishing Co.
Brunner- Jass, Renata. Hidden Ducks: Describing & Interpreting Data. 2013. (iMath Ser.). (ENG., Illus.). 48p. (J). (gr. 5-6). pap. 13.26 *(978-1-60357-511-9(1))* Norwood Hse. Pr.
Corcorane, Ann. Sorting, 1 vol. 2011. (Wonder Readers Early Level Ser.). (ENG.). 16p. (gr. -1-1). (J). pap. 6.25 *(978-1-4296-7870-4(4),* 118202); pap. 35.94 *(978-1-4296-8151-3(9),* Capstone Pr.) Capstone.
Coss, Lauren. Let's Sort by Color. 2014. (21st Century Basic Skills Library: Sorting Ser.). (ENG., Illus.). 24p. (J). (gr. k-3). 26.35 *(978-1-63137-634-4(9),* 205319) Cherry Lake Publishing.
—Let's Sort by Size. 2014. (21st Century Basic Skills Library: Sorting Ser.). (ENG., Illus.). 24p. (J). (gr. k-3). 26.35 *(978-1-63137-635-1(7),* 205323) Cherry Lake Publishing.
—Let's Sort Money. 2014. (21st Century Basic Skills Library: Sorting Ser.). (ENG., Illus.). 24p. (J). (gr. k-3). 26.35 *(978-1-63137-633-7(0),* 205315) Cherry Lake Publishing.
—Let's Sort Shapes. 2014. (21st Century Basic Skills Library: Sorting Ser.). (ENG., Illus.). 24p. (J). (gr. k-3). 26.35 *(978-1-63137-632-0(2),* 205311) Cherry Lake Publishing.
Day, Nancy Raines. What in the World? Numbers in Nature. Cyrus, Kurt, illus. 2015. (ENG.). 32p. (J). (gr. -1-3). 17.99 *(978-1-4814-0060-2(6),* Beach Lane Bks.) Beach Lane Bks.
Doudna, Kelly. Use Your Eye, Let's Classify!, 1 vol. 2007. (Science Made Simple Ser.). (Illus.). 24p. (J). (gr. k-3). lib. bdg. 24.21 *(978-1-59928-620-4(3),* SandCastle) ABDO Publishing Co.
Editorial Staff, Gareth. I Know Same & Different, 1 vol. 2005. (I'm Ready for Math Ser.). (ENG., Illus.). 16p. (gr. k-1). pap. 6.30 *(978-0-8368-6481-6(6),* c3600deb-894f-446a-943c-e971486edaab, Weekly Reader Leveled Readers) Stevens, Gareth Publishing LLLP.
GER Set Square. 2006. (J). 2.90 *(978-1-934046-11-1(6))* Global Education Resources, LLC.
Hawley, Ella. The Number 1. 2010. (Numbers in My World Ser.). (ENG.). 16p. (J). bds. 11.95 *(978-1-4358-9319-1(0),* PowerKids Pr.) Rosen Publishing Group, Inc., The.
—The Number 2. 2010. (Numbers in My World Ser.). (ENG.). 16p. (J). bds. 11.95 *(978-1-4358-9320-7(4),* PowerKids Pr.) Rosen Publishing Group, Inc., The.
—The Number 3. 2010. (Numbers in My World Ser.). (ENG.). 16p. (J). bds. 11.95 *(978-1-4358-9321-4(2),* PowerKids Pr.) Rosen Publishing Group, Inc., The.
—The Number 4. 2010. (Numbers in My World Ser.). (ENG.). 16p. (J). bds. 11.95 *(978-1-4358-9322-1(0),* PowerKids Pr.) Rosen Publishing Group, Inc., The.
—The Number 5. 2010. (Numbers in My World Ser.). (ENG.). 16p. (J). bds. 11.95 *(978-1-4358-9323-8(9),* PowerKids Pr.) Rosen Publishing Group, Inc., The.
—Numbers 1, 2, 3, 4, 5. 2010. (Numbers in My World Ser.). (ENG.). 16p. (J). bds. 11.95 *(978-1-4358-9324-5(7),* PowerKids Pr.) Rosen Publishing Group, Inc., The.
Jocelyn, Marthe. Same Same. Slaughter, Tom, illus. (J). (gr. k-k). 2010. 16p. 7.95 *(978-0-88776-987-0(X))* 2009. 24p. 15.95 *(978-0-88776-885-9(7))* Tundra Bks. CAN. (Tundra Bks.). Dist: Penguin Random Hse. LLC.
Kompelien, Tracy. There Is Order on the Border!, 1 vol. 2007. (Math Made Fun Ser.). (Illus.). 24p. (J). (gr. k-3). lib. bdg. 24.21 *(978-1-59928-547-4(9),* SandCastle) ABDO Publishing Co.
Loughran, Donna & Brunner-Jass, Renata. Hidden Ducks: Describing & Interpreting Data. 2013. (iMath Ser.). (Illus.). 48p. (J). (gr. 5-6). lib. bdg. 23.94 *(978-1-59953-572-2(6))* Norwood Hse. Pr.
McDonnell, Mary Rose. Sorting with Snakes, 1 vol. 2013. (Animal Math Ser.). (ENG.). 24p. (J). (gr. 1-2). 25.27 *(978-1-4339-9328-2(7),* 67bc28f8-0d19-4fbb-8d9c-e1064f7d6a5d) Stevens, Gareth Publishing LLLP.
Miller, Reagan & Berry, Minta. What Comes in Sets? Crabtree Publishing Staff, ed. 2011. (My Path to Math Ser.: No. 38). (ENG., Illus.). 24p. (J). (gr. k-3). pap. *(978-0-7787-5268-4(2))* Crabtree Publishing Co.
—What Comes in Sets? 2011. (ENG., Illus.). 24p. (J). lib. bdg. *(978-0-7787-5279-0(8))* Crabtree Publishing Co.
Mineo, Kate. Compare with Bears, 1 vol. 2011. (Animal Math Ser.). (ENG., Illus.). 24p. (J). (gr. 1-2). pap. 9.15 *(978-1-4339-5660-7(8),* b95cafc9-5301-4171-b168-dce070d9c152); lib. bdg. 25.27 *(978-1-4339-5658-4(6),* 846b0876-4e3a-449b-8271-f0ac949558a6) Stevens, Gareth Publishing LLLP.
Murphy, Stuart J. 3 Little Firefighters. 2003. (Mathstart Level 1 Ser.). (J). (gr. k-3). 16.00 *(978-0-613-68469-9(9))* Turtleback.
Pluckrose, Henry. Sorting (Math Counts: Updated Editions) 2018. (Math Counts, New & Updated Ser.). (ENG., Illus.). 32p. (J). (gr. k-3). pap. 5.95 *(978-0-531-13522-8(5),* Children's Pr.) Scholastic Library Publishing.
Ribke, Simone T. Grouping at the Dog Show. 2006. (Rookie Read-About Math Ser.). (ENG., Illus.). 32p. (J). (gr. 1-2). lib. bdg. 20.50 *(978-0-516-24959-9(2),* Children's Pr.) Scholastic Library Publishing.
Rice, Dona. Sombreros. rev. ed. 2019. (Mathematics in the Real World Ser.). (SPA.). 20p. (J). (gr. k-1). 8.99 *(978-1-4258-2824-0(8))* Teacher Created Materials, Inc.
Rozines Roy, Jennifer & Roy, Gregory. Sorting at the Ocean, 1 vol. (Math All Around Ser.). (ENG.). 32p. (gr. 2-2). 2008. pap. 9.23 *(978-0-7614-3408-5(9),* 97bf28ce-a3a4-4891-b240-ed8fb1ad238f) 2007. (Illus.). lib. bdg. 32.64 *(978-0-7614-1998-3(5),* 54de353d-d644-4c59-92d1-520f7cfeadba) Cavendish Square Publishing LLC.
Shepherd, Jodie. The Crayola (r) Sorting Book. 2017. (Crayola (r) Concepts Ser.). (ENG., Illus.). 24p. (J). (gr. -1-3). 29.32 *(978-1-5124-3286-2(5),* 2977e247-5da5-4613-90a0-8f546cb2e7b6, Lerner Pubns.) Lerner Publishing Group.
Snyder, Jane. Days of the Week: Learning Ordinal Numbers, 1 vol. 2010. (Math for the REAL World Ser.). (ENG.). 12p. (gr. 1-2). pap. 5.90 *(978-0-8239-8913-3(5),* 0becf867-7afa-4107-bbc5-f44c333665a4, Rosen Classroom) Rosen Publishing Group, Inc., The.
Staff, Gareth Editorial Staff. I Know Same & Different, 1 vol. 2005. (I'm Ready for Math Ser.). (ENG., Illus.). 16p. (gr. k-1). lib. bdg. 21.67 *(978-0-8368-6476-2(X),* 9a9009fe-9247-4e76-8c09-fb73aca7b1be, Weekly Reader Leveled Readers) Stevens, Gareth Publishing LLLP.
Steffora, Tracey. Sorting at the Market, 1 vol. 2011. (Math Around Us Ser.). (ENG.). 24p. (J). (gr. -1-1). 25.32 *(978-1-4329-4927-3(6),* 114828); pap. 6.29 *(978-1-4329-4935-8(7),* 114834) Capstone. (Heinemann).
Tang, Greg. Math-Terpieces: the Art of Problem-Solving. Paprocki, Greg, illus. 2003. (ENG.). 32p. (gr. 2-5). 18.99 *(978-0-439-44388-3(1))* Scholastic, Inc.

SETON, ERNEST THOMPSON, 1860-1946

Moss, Leila & Knox, Linda L. The Storyteller. 2015. (Illus.). xiv, 107p. 24.95 *(978-1-935204-53-4(X))* Salem Author Services.

SETS (MATHEMATICS)

see Set Theory

SETTLEMENTS, SOCIAL

see Social Settlements

SEUSS, DR., 1904-1991

Carlson, Cheryl. Dr. Seuss [Scholastic]. 2011. (First Biographies - Writers, Artists, & Athletes Ser.). 24p. pap. 0.50 *(978-1-4296-6317-5(0),* Pebble) Capstone.
Foran, Jill. Dr. Seuss. 2012. (J). 13.95 *(978-1-61913-059-3(9));* pap. 28.55 *(978-1-61913-595-6(7))* Weigl Pubs., Inc.
Grahame-Smith, Deborah. Dr. Seuss, 1 vol. 2014. (Spotlight on Children's Authors Ser.). (ENG.). 48p. (gr. 4-4). lib. bdg. 31.64 *(978-1-62712-846-9(8),* 50312738-8906-40c8-87f4-43e55132ba9c) Cavendish Square Publishing LLC.
Krull, Kathleen. The Boy on Fairfield Street: How Ted Geisel Grew up to Become Dr. Seuss. Johnson, Steve & Fancher, Lou, illus. 2010. (ENG.). 48p. (J). (gr. k-4). pap. 7.99 *(978-0-375-85550-4(5),* Dragonfly Bks.) Random Hse. Children's Bks.
—The Boy on Fairfield Street: How Ted Geisel Grew up to Become Dr. Seuss. 2010. lib. bdg. 18.40 *(978-0-606-12416-4(0))* Turtleback.
Kudlinski, Kathleen. Dr. Seuss: Young Author & Artist. Henderson, Meryl, illus. 2005. 184p. (J). lib. bdg. 18.46 *(978-1-4242-2201-8(X))* Fitzgerald Bks.
Landau, Jennifer. Dr. Seuss, 1 vol., 1. 2015. (Britannica Beginner Bios Ser.). (ENG., Illus.). 32p. (J). (gr. 2-3). pap. 13.90 *(978-1-5081-0063-8(2),* 85406712-b206-485b-bd15-89f958410abc, Britannica Educational Publishing) Rosen Publishing Group, Inc., The.
Pascal, Janet B. & Who HQ. Who Was Dr. Seuss? Harrison, Nancy, illus. 2011. (Who Was? Ser.). 112p. (J). (gr. 3-7). pap. 5.99 *(978-0-448-45585-3(4),* Penguin Workshop) Penguin Young Readers Group.
Schuetz, Kari. Dr. Seuss. 2015. (Children's Storytellers Ser.). (ENG., Illus.). 24p. (J). (gr. 2-5). lib. bdg. 26.95 *(978-1-62617-265-4(X),* Blastoff! Readers) Bellwether Media.
Waxman, Laura Hamilton. Dr. Seuss. 2010. (History Maker Biographies Ser.). (ENG.). 48p. (gr. 3-6). lib. bdg. 27.93 *(978-0-7613-5206-8(6),* Lerner Pubns.) Lerner Publishing Group.

SEVEN WONDERS OF THE WORLD

Benchmark Education Company. The Seven Wonders of the Ancient World (Teacher Guide) 2004. *(978-1-4108-2582-7(5))* Benchmark Education Co.
Gonzales, Doreen. What Are the 7 Wonders of the Modern World?, 1 vol. 2013. (What Are the Seven Wonders of the World? Ser.). (ENG.). 48p. (gr. 4-6). 27.93 *(978-0-7660-4152-3(2),* fddaafab-b0bb-4798-a3ca-70a45b3a5222); pap. 11.53 *(978-1-4644-0231-9(0),*

b5947b0e-db4e-4642-a8b8-8d35c0157a2b) Enslow Publishing, LLC.
Graham, Amy. What Are the 7 Wonders of the Natural World?, 1 vol. 2013. (What Are the Seven Wonders of the World? Ser.). (ENG.). 48p. (gr. 4-6). 27.93 *(978-0-7660-4153-0(0),* af6a964e-2dd9-4996-b6ec-350ba4d998dd); pap. 11.53 *(978-1-4644-0232-6(9),* 33939e7a-ef2d-4ea9-a044-7ce3d21da59b) Enslow Publishing, LLC.
HarrisNic. Wonders of the World High Beginning Book with Online Access, 1 vol. 2014. (ENG., Illus.). 24p. (J). pap., E-Book, E-Book 9.50 *(978-1-107-64298-0(1))* Cambridge Univ. Pr.
Hibbert, Adam. World Wonders. 2010. (Unpredictable Nature Ser.). 48p. (J). (gr. 3-18). lib. bdg. 19.95 *(978-1-4222-2008-5(7))* Mason Crest.
Kenah, Katharine. Amazing Creations. 2006. (Extreme Readers: Level 2 Ser.). (Illus.). 32p. (gr. 4-7). 13.95 *(978-0-7569-6844-1(5))* Perfection Learning Corp.
Koll, Hilary & Mills, Steve. A Math Journey Around the Wonders of the World. 2016. (ENG., Illus.). 32p. (J). *(978-0-7787-2321-9(6))* Crabtree Publishing Co.
Laliberte, Michelle. What Are the 7 Wonders of the Ancient World?, 1 vol. 2013. (What Are the Seven Wonders of the World? Ser.). (ENG.). 48p. (gr. 4-6). 27.93 *(978-0-7660-4151-6(4),* 63b83078-f9f1-42f5-87e7-40a7de690883); pap. 11.53 *(978-1-4644-0230-2(2),* 23514bb1-e725-4518-935c-f9dcc9d7dd7f) Enslow Publishing, LLC.
McDonough, Yona Z. & Who HQ. Where Were the Seven Wonders of the Ancient World? Putra, Dede, illus. 2020. (Where Is? Ser.). 112p. (J). (gr. 3-7). 5.99 *(978-0-593-09330-6(5),* Penguin Workshop) Penguin Young Readers Group.
Mchugh, Arianne. Seven Wonders of the Ancient World. 2015. (Red Rhino Nonfiction Ser.). (J). lib. bdg. 20.80 *(978-0-606-37197-1(4))* Turtleback.
Miller, Ron. Seven Wonders, 7 vols., Set. Incl. Seven Wonders of the Gas Giants & Their Moons. lib. bdg. 33.26 *(978-0-7613-5449-9(2));* Seven Wonders of the Rocky Planets & Their Moons. lib. bdg. 33.26 *(978-0-7613-5448-2(4));* 80p. (gr. 5-8). 2011. 2011. Set lib. bdg. 232.82 *(978-0-7613-7469-5(8),* Twenty-First Century Bks.) Lerner Publishing Group.
Piano, Maureen. My Adventure to the Wonders of the World. 2006. 44p. (J). 8.99 *(978-1-59092-445-7(2))* Blue Forge Pr.
Sullivan, Erin Ash. The Seven Wonders of the Ancient World. 2011. (Navigators Ser.). (J). pap. 50.00 net. *(978-1-4108-2567-4(1))* Benchmark Education Co.
—The Seven Wonders of the Ancient World & Las siete maravillas del mundo Antiguo: 6 English, 6 Spanish Adaptations. 2011. (ENG & SPA.). (J). 101.00 net. *(978-1-4108-5728-6(X))* Benchmark Education Co.
Top That Publishing Staff, ed. 7 Wonders of World. 2004. (Know How Know Why Ser.). (Illus.). 48p. (J). pap. *(978-1-84510-073-5(5))* Top That! Publishing PLC.
Van Vleet, Carmella. Seven Wonders of the World: Discover Amazing Monuments to Civilization with 20 Projects. Rizvi, Farah, illus. 2011. (Build It Yourself Ser.). (ENG.). 128p. (J). (gr. 3-7). 21.95 *(978-1-934670-82-8(0),* 152e57d1-692d-4b5c-8276-348801a25dda); pap. 15.95 *(978-1-936313-73-0(1),* b4919469-a2d5-4fef-b58d-5bdbb836f9e6) Nomad Pr.
Woods, Michael & Woods, Mary B. Seven Wonders of the Ancient World. 2008. (Seven Wonders Ser.). (ENG., Illus.). 80p. (gr. 5-8). lib. bdg. 33.26 *(978-0-8225-7568-9(X))* Lerner Publishing Group.
World Book, Inc. Staff, contrib. by. Wonders of the World. 2011. (J). *(978-0-7166-1794-5(3))* World Bk., Inc.

SEWAGE DISPOSAL

see also Refuse and Refuse Disposal; Water—Pollution
Bowles, Stella. My River: Cleaning up the Lahave River. 2018. (ENG.). 96p. (J). (gr. 3-6). pap. 8.99 *(978-1-4595-0551-3(4),* a5c560da-b2bc-49df-80f9-c4b26c017a7e) Formac Publishing Co., Ltd. CAN. Dist: Lerner Publishing Group.
Flynn, Riley. Sewers Stink! How Does Waste Go Down? 2018. (Story of Sanitation Ser.). (ENG., Illus.). 32p. (J). (gr. 3-6). lib. bdg. 27.99 *(978-1-5435-3113-8(X),* 138711, Capstone Pr.) Capstone.
—Toilets Tank! Their Inner Workings. 2018. (Story of Sanitation Ser.). (ENG., Illus.). 32p. (J). (gr. 3-6). lib. bdg. 27.99 *(978-1-5435-3114-5(8),* 138714, Capstone Pr.) Capstone.
Furgang, Kathy. Zoom in on Water & Sewage Systems, 1 vol. 2017. (Zoom in on Engineering Ser.). (ENG.). 24p. (gr. 2-2). pap. 10.95 *(978-0-7660-8840-5(5),* f596da04-3edd-4812-8c38-ea3864bfb9c6); lib. bdg. 25.60 *(978-0-7660-8714-9(X),* 691d8a52-7224-45eb-bc11-18dde139506a) Enslow Publishing, LLC.
LaPlante, Walter. What Happens When I Flush the Toilet?, 1 vol. 2015. (Everyday Mysteries Ser.). (ENG.). 24p. (J). (gr. 1-2). pap. 9.15 *(978-1-4824-3825-3(9),* 2cdd320c-8262-4ce0-9b09-50f7c80b235e) Stevens, Gareth Publishing LLLP.
Mahoney, Emily. Wasted Waters, 1 vol. 2017. (Unnatural Disasters Ser.). (ENG.). 32p. (J). (gr. 4-5). pap. 11.50 *(978-1-5382-0527-3(0),* abd4f13d-4974-49f9-bcde-7b09e3680cf3) Stevens, Gareth Publishing LLLP.
Newman, Patricia. Plastic, Ahoy! Investigating the Great Pacific Garbage Patch. Crawley, Annie, illus. 2014. (ENG.). 48p. (J). (gr. 3-6). lib. bdg. 30.65 *(978-1-4677-1283-5(3),* 79120d0d-5b42-47f6-80e4-e7af8c1d8d00, Millbrook Pr.) Lerner Publishing Group.
Porter, Esther. What's Sprouting in My Trash? A Book about Composting. 2013. (Earth Matters Ser.). (ENG.). 32p. (J). (gr. 1-2). pap. 48.60 *(978-1-62065-746-1(5),* 19326, Capstone Pr.) Capstone.
Rhatigan, Joe. Get a Job at the Landfill. 2016. (Bright Futures Press: Get a Job Ser.). (ENG., Illus.). 32p. (J). (gr. 4-6). 32.07 *(978-1-63471-905-6(0),* 208941) Cherry Lake Publishing.
Roza, Greg. How Do Sewers Work?, 1 vol. 2016. (STEM Waterworks Ser.). (ENG.). 32p. (J). (gr. 5-5). pap. 12.75 *(978-1-4994-2003-6(X),* f2054283-5648-4f69-9e25-8ac5ba720812, PowerKids Pr.) Rosen Publishing Group, Inc., The.

SEWING

see also Dressmaking; Embroidery; Needlework
Blake, Susannah. Crafts for Styling Your Wardrobe, 1 vol. 2013. (Eco Chic Ser.). (ENG.). 32p. (gr. 4-6). lib. bdg. 26.61 *(978-0-7660-4316-9(9),* 77d822aa-6253-4cca-aed2-2a5119f0fa53) Enslow Publishing, LLC.
Butcher, Alice & Farquhar, Ginny. Sewing for Kids: Easy Projects to Sew at Home. 2013. (ENG., Illus.). 80p. pap. 14.99 *(978-1-4463-0261-3(X))* David & Charles Pubs. GBR. Dist: Two Rivers Distribution.
Carlson, Laurie M. Queen of Inventions: How the Sewing Machine Changed the World. 2003. (Illus.). 32p. lib. bdg. 22.90 *(978-0-7613-2706-6(1),* Millbrook Pr.) Lerner Publishing Group.
Cherry, Winky. My First Doll Book KIT: Hand Sewing. 2nd ed. 2011. (My First Sewing Book Kit Ser.). (ENG.). 40p. (J). (gr. 3-7). pap. 16.95 *(978-0-935278-87-3(7))* Palmer-Pletsch Assocs.
—My First Machine Sewing Book KIT: Straight Stitching. 2nd ed. 2011. (My First Sewing Book Kit Ser.). (ENG.). 40p. (J). (gr. 3-7). pap. 16.95 *(978-0-935278-88-0(5))* Palmer-Pletsch Assocs.
—My First Quilt Book: Machine Sewing. 2nd ed. 2011. (My First Sewing Book Kit Ser.). (ENG., Illus.). 40p. (J). (gr. 2). pap. 16.95 *(978-0-935278-90-3(7))* Palmer-Pletsch Assocs.
—My First Sewing Book KIT: Hand Sewing. 2nd ed. 2011. (My First Sewing Book Kit Ser.). (ENG.). 40p. (J). (gr. 3-7). pap. 16.95 *(978-0-935278-85-9(0))* Palmer-Pletsch Assocs.
Editors of Klutz. Sew Mini Animals: More Than 12 Animal Plushies to Stitch & Stuff. 2017. (ENG.). 48p. (J). (gr. 3-7). 21.99 *(978-1-338-10644-2(9))* Klutz.
Fryer, Jane Eayre. The Mary Frances Sewing Book 100th Anniversary Edition: A Childrens Story-Instruction Sewing Book with Doll Clothes Patterns for American Girl & Other 18-Inch Dolls. 2011. (ENG., Illus.). 284p. (J). pap. 19.95 *(978-1-937564-01-8(0),* Classic Bookwrights) Lindaloo Enterprises.
Hardy, Emma. My First Sewing Machine Book: 35 Fun & Easy Projects for Children Aged 7 Years + 2014. (ENG., Illus.). 128p. (J). (gr. 7-11). pap. 16.99 *(978-1-78249-101-9(5),* 1782491015, CICO Books) Ryland Peters & Small GBR. Dist: WIPRO.
Hines Stephens, Sarah. Show Off: How to Do Absolutely Everything. One Step at a Time. Mann, Bethany, illus. 2009. (ENG.). 224p. (J). (gr. 5-9). pap. 18.99 *(978-0-7636-4599-1(0))* Candlewick Pr.
Kachidurian, Debbie, et al. Accessorize Yourself! 66 Projects to Personalize Your Look. 2016. (Craft It Yourself Ser.). (ENG., Illus.). 144p. (J). (gr. 3-9). pap., pap. 14.95 *(978-1-62370-645-6(9),* 131410, Capstone Young Readers) Capstone.
Kenney, Karen Latchana & Chagollan, Samantha. No Sew, No Problem. 2018. (No Sew, No Problem Ser.). (ENG.). 32p. (J). (gr. 3-9). 122.60 *(978-1-5435-2566-3(0),* 28128, Capstone Pr.) Capstone.
Kerr, Sophie. A Kid's Guide to Sewing: 16 Projects You'll Love to Make & Use. 2013. (ENG., Illus.). 144p. (J). (gr. 6-9). pap. 21.95 *(978-1-60705-751-2(4),* FunStitch Studio) C & T Publishing.
Kuskowski, Alex. Cool Sewing for Kids: A Fun & Creative Introduction to Fiber Art. 2014. (Cool Fiber Art Ser.). (ENG.). 32p. (J). (gr. 3-6). lib. bdg. 34.21 *(978-1-62403-311-7(3),* 1284, Checkerboard Library) ABDO Publishing Co.
Lan, Angela. #OOTD Sew & Style: Make Your Dream Wardrobe with Angela. 2016. (ENG., Illus.). 128p. (J). (gr. 6-12). pap. 24.95 *(978-1-61745-136-2(3),* Stash Bks.) C & T Publishing.
Lisle, Andria & Plumley, Amie Petronis. Sewing School (r) 2: Lessons in Machine Sewing; 20 Projects Kids Will Love to Make. 2013. (Sewing School Ser.). (ENG., Illus.). 160p. (J). (gr. 3-7). pap. 19.95 *(978-1-61212-049-2(0),* 622049) Storey Publishing, LLC.
Low, Rachel. Girl's Guide to DIY Fashion: Design & Sew 5 Complete Outfits * Mood Boards * Fashion Sketching * Choosing Fabric * Adding Style. 2015. (ENG., Illus.). 192p. (J). (gr. 2-8). pap. 19.95 *(978-1-60705-995-0(9),* FunStitch Studio) C & T Publishing.
Maloney, Brenna. This Is Mouse - An Adventure in Sewing: Make Mouse & Friends * Travel with Them from Africa to Outer Space. 2015. (ENG., Illus.). 112p. (J). (gr. -1-12). pap. 16.95 *(978-1-60705-977-6(0),* FunStitch Studio) C & T Publishing.
McNicol, Alison. My First Learn to Sew Book. 2012. (Illus.). 42p. pap. *(978-1-908707-04-8(6))* Kyle Craig Publishing.
—My First Sewing Machine Book: Learn to Sew Kids. 2011. (ENG., Illus.). 40p. pap. *(978-1-908707-00-0(3))* Kyle Craig Publishing.
Milligan, Lynda & Smith, Nancy. The Best of Sewing Machine Fun for Kids: Ready, Set, Sew - 37 Projects & Activities. 2nd ed. 2016. (ENG., Illus.). 128p. (J). (gr. 4-9). pap. 16.95 *(978-1-61745-263-5(7),* FunStitch Studio) C & T Publishing.
Nelson, Brandy. Sew with Me: 60 Fun & Easy Projects to Make Your Own Fabulous décor & Accessories. 2018. (ENG., Illus.). 192p. pap. 21.99 *(978-1-62414-631-2(7),* 900195273) Page Street Publishing Co.
Nicoll, Allison. Sew It! Make 17 Projects with Yummy Precut Fabric - Jelly Rolls, Layer Cakes, Charm Packs & Fat Quarters. 2014. (ENG., Illus.). 128p. (J). (gr. 1). pap. 29.95 *(978-1-60705-874-8(X),* FunStitch Studio) C & T Publishing.
O'Donoghue, Sean. Create a Quilt: Understand Concepts of Area, 1 vol. 2014. (Rosen Math Readers Ser.). (ENG., Illus.). 24p. (J). (gr. 3-3). pap. 8.25 *(978-1-4777-4894-7(6),* 885ae316-bbd3-490b-84b5-31eee6afc89b, Rosen Classroom) Rosen Publishing Group, Inc., The.
Paredes, L. Magical Forest Fairy Crafts Through Seas. 2018. (ENG., Illus.). 144p. (J). (gr. 2-6). pap. 21.95 *(978-1-61745-661-9(6),* FunStitch Studio) C & T Publishing.
Petelinsek, Kathleen. Learning to Sew. Petelinsek, Kathleen, illus. 2014. (How-To Library). (ENG., Illus.). 32p. (J). (gr. 3-6). 32.07 *(978-1-63137-780-8(9),* 205363) Cherry Lake Publishing.
Phillips, Jennifer. Picture Perfect! Glam Scarves, Belts, Hats, & Other Fashion Accessories for All Occassions. 2016. (Accessorize Yourself! Ser.). (ENG., Illus.). 48p. (J). (gr. 4-8). lib. bdg. 35.32 *(978-1-4914-8229-2(X),* 130691, Capstone Pr.) Capstone.
Pittman, Janet. Colorful Quilts for Playful Kids: 14 Colorful Projects with Dozens of Designs to Mix & Match. 2012. (ENG., Illus.). 128p. pap. 24.95 *(978-1-935726-25-8(0),* 258) Landauer Publishing, LLC.
Plumley, Amie Petronis & Lisle, Andria. Sewing School (r) Box Set, Set. 2018. (Sewing School Ser.). (ENG., Illus.). 304p. (J). (gr. 1-7). spiral bd. 40.00 *(978-1-63586-117-4(9),* 626117) Storey Publishing, LLC.
—Sewing School (r) Fashion Design: Make Your Own Wardrobe with Mix-And-Match Projects Including Tops, Skirts & Shorts. 2019. (Sewing School Ser.). (ENG., Illus.). 160p. (J). (gr. 3-7). spiral bd. 22.95 *(978-1-61212-860-3(2),* 622860) Storey Publishing, LLC.
Ross, Kathy. Things to Make for Your Doll. Garvin, Elaine, illus. (Girl Crafts Ser.). 48p. 2005. (ENG.). (gr. 2-5). lib. bdg. 26.60 *(978-0-7613-2861-2(0),* Millbrook Pr.) 2003. (J). (gr. k-2). pap. 7.95 *(978-0-7613-1781-4(3),* First Avenue Editions) Lerner Publishing Group.
Sadler, Ann. Sewing.Tr. of Couture. (FRE., Illus.). (J). (gr. k-5). pap. 7.99 *(978-0-590-24055-0(2))* Scholastic, Inc.
Trail, Sara. Sew with Sara: Fun Stuff to Keep, Give, Sell! 2009. (ENG., Illus.). 112p. pap. 19.95 *(978-1-57120-603-9(5))* C & T Publishing.
Turnbull, Stephanie. Cool Stuff to Sew. 2014. (Cool Stuff Ser.). (ENG.). 32p. (J). (gr. 2-5). 31.35 *(978-1-62588-191-5(6),* 19265, Smart Apple Media) Black Rabbit Bks.
—Sewing. 2015. (Try This! Ser.). (ENG., Illus.). 24p. (J). (gr. 3-6). 27.10 *(978-1-62588-375-9(7),* 17449) Black Rabbit Bks.
Warwick, Ellen. Stuff to Hold Your Stuff. Lum, Bernice, illus. 2006. (Planet Girl Ser.). 80p. (J). (gr. 5-9). 12.95 *(978-1-55337-745-0(1))* Kids Can Pr., Ltd. CAN. Dist: Hachette Bk. Group.
Wrigley, Annabel. We Love to Sew: 28 Pretty Things to Make. 2013. (ENG., Illus.). 176p. (J). (gr. -1-12). pap. 22.95 *(978-1-60705-632-4(1))* C & T Publishing.
—We Love to Sew — Bedrooms: 23 Projects, Cool Stuff for Your Space. 2014. (ENG., Illus.). 176p. (J). (gr. 2-8). pap. 21.95 *(978-1-60705-824-3(3),* FunStitch Studio) C & T Publishing.
Yang, Veronica. Seamless Sewing Projects. 2018. (Crafty Creations Ser.). (ENG., Illus.). 48p. (J). (gr. 4-8). lib. bdg. 31.99 *(978-1-5157-7445-7(7),* 135793, Capstone Pr.) Capstone.

SEX

see also Reproduction
also headings beginning with the word Sexual
Adams, Gloria G. Coping with Sexism & Misogyny, 1 vol. 2017. (Coping (2017-2020) Ser.). (ENG., Illus.). 112p. (J). (gr. 7-7). 40.13 *(978-1-5081-7693-0(0),* a318945e-5e16-465d-9954-0145f37bc20c) Rosen Publishing Group, Inc., The.
Ascension Press, creator. Theology of the Body for Teens Student Workbook: Discovering God's Plan for Love & Life. 2006. (Illus.). 210p. per. 14.95 *(978-1-932927-86-3(7))* Ascension Pr.
Attwood, Sarah. Making Sense of Sex: A Forthright Guide to Puberty, Sex & Relationships for People with Asperger's Syndrome. 2008. (Illus.). 320p. (J). (gr. 4-12). pap. 23.95 *(978-1-84310-374-5(5),* 691701) Kingsley, Jessica Pubs. GBR. Dist: Hachette UK Distribution.
Baldino, Greg. Everything You Need to Know about Bisexuality, 1 vol. 2019. (Need to Know Library). (ENG.). 64p. (gr. 6-6). 36.13 *(978-1-5081-8752-3(5),* 9c0c906b-ee49-40cf-8261-d43d6c559e88) Rosen Publishing Group, Inc., The.
Buckey, A. W. LGBT Intolerance: Intolerance & Violence in Society. 2019. (Intolerance & Violence in Society Ser.). (ENG.). 80p. (J). (gr. 6-12). 41.27 *(978-1-68282-685-0(6))* ReferencePoint Pr., Inc.
Cart, Michael. Necessary Noise: Stories about Our Families as They Really Are. Noruzi, Charlotte, illus. 2003. 256p. (J). (gr. 12-18). lib. bdg. 16.89 *(978-0-06-027500-6(6))* HarperCollins Pubs.
Choosing The Best Publishing. Choosing the Best Path 6th Edition Leader Kit. Choosing The Best Publishing, ed. 3rd ed. 2004. *(978-0-9724890-2-7(9))* Choosing The Best Publishing.
Crabtree Publishing Company Staff & Bow, James. Sex. 2012. (ENG., Illus.). 48p. (J). *(978-0-7787-2186-4(8));* pap. *(978-0-7787-2193-2(0))* Crabtree Publishing Co.
Craig, Joe. A Guy's Guide to Sexuality & Sexual Identity in the 21st Century, 1 vol. 2011. (Young Man's Guide to Contemporary Issues Ser.). (ENG.). 104p. (YA). (gr. 8-9). lib. bdg. 39.80 *(978-1-4488-5524-7(1),* b76a2d41-ed20-48da-a669-9379c574fbbb) Rosen Publishing Group, Inc., The.
Cross, Craig, et al. Questions You Can't Ask Your Mama about Sex, 1 vol. 2005. (Invert Ser.). (ENG.). 128p. (YA). pap. 9.99 *(978-0-310-25812-4(X))* Zondervan.
Culp, Jennifer. Dating Etiquette & Sexual Respect, 1 vol. 2016. (Etiquette Rules! Ser.). (ENG., Illus.). 48p. (J). (gr. 6-6). pap. 12.75 *(978-1-4994-6492-4(4),* 5188d290-cd9f-45dc-a950-028b94db54dc) Rosen Publishing Group, Inc., The.
Custom Curricul Staff. What about Sex, Drugs, And... ? 2004. (Custom Curriculum Ser.). 256p. pap., pap. 19.99 *(978-0-7814-4093-6(9),* 0781440939) Cook, David C.
DeCarlo, Carolyn. Everything You Need to Know about the Risks of Unprotected Sex, 1 vol. 2018. (Need to Know Library). (ENG., Illus.). 64p. (J). (gr. 6-6). pap. 13.95 *(978-1-5081-8360-0(0),* fc6e3251-2207-4be9-a69e-953c68ef3315) Rosen Publishing Group, Inc., The.
Ferguson, Olivia & Mitchell Haugen, Hayley, eds. Is Childhood Becoming Too Sexualized?, 1 vol. 2010. (At Issue Ser.). (ENG.). 120p. (gr. 10-12). 41.03 *(978-0-7377-4884-0(2),* ecfc422d-62d7-4ab8-8849-57dce615cd3b); pap. 28.80 *(978-0-7377-4885-7(0),* 9b276424-8f09-4c55-bac1-82439a704d26) Greenhaven Publishing LLC. (Greenhaven Publishing).
Friedman, Lauri S., ed. Sexual Orientation, 1 vol. 2012. (Introducing Issues with Opposing Viewpoints Ser.). (ENG., Illus.). 128p. (gr. 7-10). lib. bdg. 43.63 *(978-0-7377-6281-5(0),* 8d84096a-8db1-4d26-bb0e-578d9857c135, Greenhaven Publishing) Greenhaven Publishing LLC.
Gay & Lesbian Writers. 2005. (Gay & Lesbian Writers Ser.). (Illus.). 144p. (gr. 6-12). 175.00 *(978-0-7910-8477-9(9),* Facts On File) Infobase Holdings, Inc.
Gerdes, Louise I., ed. What Are the Causes of Prostitution?, 1 vol. 2007. (At Issue Ser.). (ENG.). 104p. (gr. 10-12). pap. 28.80 *(978-0-7377-2738-8(1),* c45d4119-7a1b-4c9f-b5c6-590fd70fd033, Greenhaven Publishing) Greenhaven Publishing LLC.
Gilbert, Laura. Everything You Need to Know about Compulsive Sexual Behavior. 2009. (Need to Know Library). 64p. (gr. 5-5). 58.50 *(978-1-60854-059-4(6))* Rosen Publishing Group, Inc., The.
Gross, Craig & Foster, Mike. Questions You Can't Ask Your Mama: 68 1/2 Questions for Craig & Mike. 2003. (C). per. 11.99 *(978-0-9741849-0-6(X))* Fireproof Ministries.
Harris, Robie H. It's So Amazing! A Book about Eggs, Sperm, Birth, Babies, & Families. Emberley, Michael, illus. 2014. (Family Library). (ENG.). 88p. (J). (gr. 2-5). 22.99 *(978-0-7636-6873-0(7))* Candlewick Pr.
—Sexo... Que Es? 2003. (SPA., Illus.). (YA). (gr. 7-8). pap. *(978-84-95040-35-0(2),* RR7144) Serres, Ediciones, S. L. ESP. Dist: Lectorum Pubns., Inc.
Hickman, Pamela. Animals & Their Mates: How Animals Attract, Fight for & Protect Each Other. Stephens, Pat, illus. 2004. (Animal Behavior Ser.). (ENG.). 40p. (J). (gr. 2-6). 5.95 *(978-1-55337-546-3(7))* Kids Can Pr., Ltd. CAN. Dist: Hachette Bk. Group.
Hill, Z. B. Romantic Attraction. Croft, Cindy, ed. 2014. (Causes & Effects of Emotions Ser.: 13). 64p. (J). (gr. 7-18). 23.95 *(978-1-4222-3077-0(5))* Mason Crest.
Human Sexuality: Human Sexuality (Windows/Macintosh) 36p. (gr. 7-12). cd-rom 126.00 *(978-1-59070-357-1(X))* Goodheart-Willcox Pub.
Johnson, Kathryn T. & Balczon, Mary-Lynne J. The Sexual Dictionary: Terms & Expressions for Teens & Parents. St. John, Charlotte, ed. Date not set. (Life Management Ser.). (Illus.). 176p. (YA). pap. 12.95 *(978-0-89896-400-4(8))* Larksdale.
La Bella, Laura. Confronting Sexism, 1 vol. 2017. (Speak up! Confronting Discrimination in Your Daily Life Ser.). (ENG.). 64p. (YA). (gr. 7-7). pap. 13.95 *(978-1-5383-8180-9(X),* 12267065-283c-47b3-b030-38597bf97998) Rosen Publishing Group, Inc., The.
Lickona, Tom & Lickona, Judy. Sex, Love & You: Making the Right Decision. rev. ed. 2003. (Illus.). 192p. (YA). pap. 15.95 *(978-0-87793-987-0(X))* Ave Maria Pr.
Lucy, Cousins. El show de maisy. 2005. (SPA., Illus.). 96p. (gr. 6-8). pap. 12.99 *(978-84-8488-181-0(4))* Serres, Ediciones, S. L. ESP. Dist: Lectorum Pubns., Inc.
Machowski, Marty. God Made Boys & Girls: Helping Children Understand the Gift of Gender. 2019. (ENG., Illus.). 32p. (J). 15.99 *(978-1-64507-031-3(X))* New Growth Pr.
Marcovitz, Hal. Teens & Sex. Developed in Association with the Gallup Organization Staff, ed. 2013. (Gallup Youth Survey: Major Issues & Trends Ser.: 14). 112p. (J). (gr. 7-18). 24.95 *(978-1-4222-2957-6(2))* Mason Crest.
Mirk, Sarah. You Do You: Figuring Out Your Body, Dating, & Sexuality. 2019. (ENG., Illus.). 120p. (YA). (gr. 6-12). 37.32 *(978-1-5415-4022-4(0),* aef64119-3944-4b93-8221-7ad043de9e05, Twenty-First Century Bks.) Lerner Publishing Group.
Nardo, Don. LGBT Issues (Thinking Critically) LGBT Issues. 2019. (Thinking Critically Ser.). (ENG.). 80p. (YA). (gr. 6-12). 41.27 *(978-1-68282-661-4(9))* ReferencePoint Pr., Inc.
Navarre, Sam. Masculinity, Bullying, & Aggression: A Guy's Guide, 1 vol. 2011. (Young Man's Guide to Contemporary Issues Ser.). (ENG.). 104p. (J). (gr. 8-9). lib. bdg. 39.80 *(978-1-4488-5525-4(X),* fa266102-feec-48ec-a62d-b7e48e4d834f) Rosen Publishing Group, Inc., The.
Orr, Tamra. Home & Family Relationships, 1 vol. 2010. (Teens: Being Gay, Lesbian, Bisexual, or Transgender Ser.). (ENG., Illus.). 80p. (YA). (gr. 6-6). lib. bdg. 38.47 *(978-1-4358-3579-5(4),* 201cec76-f0db-4e89-94af-cbb94ee32ee4) Rosen Publishing Group, Inc., The.
Penne, Barbra & Renehan, Patrick. Your Rights As an LGBTQ+ Teen, 1 vol. 2017. (LGBTQ+ Guide to Beating Bullying Ser.). (ENG., Illus.). 64p. (J). (gr. 6-6). 36.13 *(978-1-5081-7439-4(3),* 7f5511ac-a4e9-4874-9f82-82d288f98fbf, Rosen Young Adult) Rosen Publishing Group, Inc., The.
Planned Parenthood Federation of America, Inc. Staff. Teensex? It's Okay to Say: No Way! 2003. (YA). pap. 3.00 net. *(978-0-934586-79-5(9))* Planned Parenthood Federation of America, Inc.
Rodi, Robert & Ross, Laura. Living with Religion & Faith, Vol. 10. Jennings, Kevin, ed. 2016. (Living Proud! Growing up LGBTQ Ser.). (Illus.). 64p. (J). (gr. 7). 23.95 *(978-1-4222-3507-2(6))* Mason Crest.
Rose, Lyman Hinckley. Pure & Chased. 2004. ix, 86p. pap. 7.95 *(978-1-55517-774-4(3))* Cedar Fort, Inc./CFI Distribution.
Santos, Rita. Beyond Gender Binaries: The History of Trans, Intersex, & Third-Gender Individuals, 1 vol. 2018. (History of the LGBTQ+ Rights Movement Ser.). (ENG., Illus.). 112p. (J). (gr. 7-7). pap. 18.65 *(978-1-5081-8307-5(4),* 881415a4-d31d-4ecf-80af-bfdddffa3252) Rosen Publishing Group, Inc., The.
Scherrer, David L. & Klepacki, Linda M. Fearless Love: Making Sexual Choices That Honor God. 2004. (Worth Waiting for Ser.). (Illus.). 176p. (YA). (gr. 13-18). 19.99 *(978-0-7814-4076-9(9),* 0781440769) Cook, David C.
Schiffer, Howard B. First Love: Remembrances. 2004. (YA). 29.95 *(978-0-9723639-2-1(0))* Heartful Loving Pr.
Smiler, Andrew P. Dating & Sex: A Guide for the 21st Century Teen Boy. 2015. 226p. (J). pap. *(978-1-4338-2045-8(5),* Magination Pr.) American Psychological Assn.
Smith, Louis. Sexual Sins of the Bible: Everything You Want to Know, but Wouldn't Ask! 2004. 200p. pap. 14.99 *(978-0-9744519-1-6(6))* Smith, Kasper.
Stenzel, Pam. Sex Has a Price Tag: Discussions about Sexuality, Spirituality, & Self-Respect, 1 vol. 2015. (ENG.). 144p. (YA). pap. 9.99 *(978-0-310-74885-4(2))* Zondervan.
Stenzel, Pam & Kirgiss, Crystal. Sex Has a Price Tag: Discussions about Sexuality, Spirituality, & Self Respect.

S

2003. (Invert Ser.). (ENG., illus.). 144p. (YA). pap. 9.99 *(978-0-310-24971-9(6))* Zondervan.

Vitale, Ann. Drug Therapy & Sexual Disorders. 2003. (Psychiatric Disorders: Drugs & Psychology for the Mind & Bod Ser.). (Illus.). 123p. (YA). pap. 14.95 *(978-1-4222-0399-6(9))* Mason Crest.

—Sexual Disorders. McDonnell, Mary Ann & Esherick, Donald, eds. 2013. (State of Mental Illness & Its Therapy Ser.: 19). (Illus.). 128p. (J). (gr. 7-18). 24.95 *(978-1-4222-2836-4(3))* Mason Crest.

Vitale, Ann E. Drug Therapy & Sexual Disorders. 2004. (Encyclopedia of Psychiatric Drugs & Their Disorders Ser.). (Illus.). 128p. (YA). lib. bdg. 24.95 *(978-1-59084-575-2(7))* Mason Crest.

Witton, Hannah. Doing It. 2018. (ENG., Illus.). 352p. (YA). (gr. 8-12). pap. 10.99 *(978-1-4926-6502-1(9))* Sourcebooks, Inc.

World Book, Inc. Staff, contrib. by. Animals Finding Mates. 2018. (Illus.). 48p. (J). *(978-0-7166-2731-9(0))* World Bk., Inc.

SEX—FICTION

Angelchild, P. Erotic Memoirs Volume 1. 2007. pap. *(978-1-84747-127-7(7))* Chipmunkapublishing.

Arnold, Elana K. Infandous. 2015. (ENG.). 200p. (YA). (gr. 8-12). 18.99 *(978-1-4677-3849-1(2),* 5f116506-df41-46d9-aaec-833557c7c676, Carolrhoda Lab™) Lerner Publishing Group.

—What Girls Are Made Of. 2017. (ENG.). 208p. (YA). (gr. 8-12). 18.99 *(978-1-5124-1024-2(1),* 848dcd61-90fb-4012-8f86-538e2bd27fd2); E-Book 29.32 *(978-1-5124-2694-6(6))*; E-Book 9.99 *(978-1-5124-3437-8(X),* 9781512434378); E-Book 29.32 *(978-1-5124-3438-5(8),* 9781512434385) Lerner Publishing Group. (Carolrhoda Lab™).

Banting, Celia. I Only Said Yes So That They'd Like Me. 2006. (Illus.). 224p. (YA). per. 14.99 *(978-0-9786648-1-7(7))* Wighita Pr.

Beth, Robinson. God Made Me: The Safe Touch Coloring Book. Noel, Green, illus. 2007. 20p. (J). pap. 3.99 *(978-0-9799092-0-7(1))* Robinson, Beth.

Blake, Ashley Herring. The Mighty Heart of Sunny St. James. 2019. (ENG.). 384p. (J). (gr. 3-7). 16.99 *(978-0-316-51553-5(1))* Little, Brown Bks. for Young Readers.

The Boy I Love. 2014. (ENG., Illus.). 288p. (YA). (gr. 7). 17.99 *(978-1-4424-8056-8(4),* Atheneum Bks. for Young Readers) Simon & Schuster Children's Publishing.

Cabot, Meg. The Princess Diaries, Volume VIII: Princess on the Brink. 2007. (Princess Diaries: 8). (ENG.). 272p. (YA). (gr. 8). pap. 10.99 *(978-0-06-072460-3(9),* HarperTeen) HarperCollins Pubs.

—Ready or Not. 2008. (All-American Girl Ser.: 2). (ENG.). 336p. (YA). (gr. 8). pap. 10.99 *(978-0-06-147996-0(9),* HarperTeen) HarperCollins Pubs.

Cart, Michael, et al. How Beautiful the Ordinary: Twelve Stories of Identity. 2009. (ENG.). 368p. (YA). (gr. 9-18). 17.99 *(978-0-06-115498-0(9),* HarperTeen) HarperCollins Pubs.

Downing, Erin. Kiss It. 2010. (ENG.). 288p. (YA). (gr. 9-18). pap. 9.99 *(978-1-4169-9700-9(8),* Simon Pulse) Simon Pulse.

French, Gillian. Grit: A Novel. (ENG.). (YA). (gr. 9). 2018. 320p. pap. 9.99 *(978-0-06-264256-1(1))* 2017. 304p. 17.99 *(978-0-06-264255-4(3))* HarperCollins Pubs. (HarperTeen).

Gingras, Charlotte. Pieces of Me. Ouriou, Susan, tr. 2009. 144p. (J). (gr. 7-9). 17.95 *(978-1-55453-242-1(6))* Kids Can Pr., Ltd. CAN. Dist: Hachette Bk. Group.

Gonsalves, Florence. Love & Other Carnivorous Plants. 2018. (ENG.). 352p. (YA). (gr. 9-17). 17.99 *(978-0-316-43672-4(0))* Little, Brown Bks. for Young Readers.

Honowitz, Stacey. Genius with a Penis, Don't Touch! 2012. 24p. 19.95 *(978-1-4575-1326-8(9))* Dog Ear Publishing, LLC.

Hopkins, Ellen. Burned. 2013. (ENG., Illus.). 560p. (YA). (gr. 9). pap. 14.99 *(978-1-4424-9461-9(1),* McElderry, Margaret K. Bks.) McElderry, Margaret K. Bks.

—Tricks. (ENG.). (YA). (gr. 9). 2017. 656p. pap. 14.99 *(978-1-4814-9824-1(X))* 2009. 640p. 24.99 *(978-1-4169-5007-3(9))* McElderry, Margaret K. Bks. (McElderry, Margaret K. Bks.).

—Tricks. 2011. lib. bdg. 24.50 *(978-0-606-23290-6(7))* Turtleback.

Hopper, Laura. I Never. 2019. (ENG.). 304p. (YA). (gr. 9). pap. 9.99 *(978-1-328-59587-4(0),* 1730762, Clarion Bks.) HarperCollins Pubs.

Karre, Elizabeth. The Fight. 2013. (Surviving Southside Ser.). (ENG.). 128p. (YA). (gr. 6-12). pap. 7.95 *(978-1-4677-0709-1(0),* 554aa69c-e617-40b7-bf91-a64fd0acb6c7, Darby Creek) Lerner Publishing Group.

Kenley, Holli. Another Way: A Novel. 2015. 155p. (YA). pap. *(978-1-61599-259-1(6))* Loving Healing Pr., Inc.

Keplinger, Kody. The DUFF: (Designated Ugly Fat Friend) (ENG.). (YA). (gr. 10-17). 2011. 304p. pap., pap. 10.99 *(978-0-316-08424-6(7))* 2015. 320p. pap. 10.00 *(978-0-316-38180-2(2))* Little, Brown Bks. for Young Readers. (Poppy).

Kiely, Brendan. Tradition. 2018. (ENG., Illus.). 352p. (YA). (gr. 9). 18.99 *(978-1-4814-8034-5(0),* McElderry, Margaret K. Bks.) McElderry, Margaret K. Bks.

Logsted, Greg. Something Happened. 2008. (ENG.). 208p. (J). (gr. 7-9). pap. 8.99 *(978-1-4169-5078-3(8),* Simon Pulse) Simon Pulse.

Mackler, Carolyn. Guyaholic. 2009. (ENG., Illus.). 192p. (YA). (gr. 9). pap. 7.99 *(978-0-7636-2801-7(8))* Candlewick Pr.

Martin, C. K. Kelly. The Lighter Side of Life & Death. 2010. (YA). pap. *(978-0-375-84590-1(9))* Random Hse. Children's Bks.

Mayfield, Jamie. Destiny. 2016. (ENG., Illus.). (J). 29.99 *(978-1-63533-000-7(9),* Harmony Ink Pr.) Dreamspinner Pr.

Mesrobian, Carrie. Cut Both Ways. 2015. (ENG.). 352p. (YA). (gr. 9). 17.99 *(978-0-06-234988-0(0),* HarperCollins) HarperCollins Pubs.

—Perfectly Good White Boy. 2014. (ENG.). 304p. (YA). (gr. 8-12). 17.95 *(978-1-4677-3480-6(2),* e7f9b1e7-dbd7-4f67-97d9-e3c14d2f823a, Carolrhoda Lab™) Lerner Publishing Group.

Miller, Sarah. The Other Girl: A Midvale Academy Novel. 2010. (Midvale Academy Ser.: 2). (ENG.). 304p. (YA). (gr. 8). pap. 20.99 *(978-0-312-33416-1(8),* 900026448, St. Martin's Griffin) St. Martin's Pr.

Moore, Stephanie Perry. Give It Up, No. 1. 2015. (Swoop List Ser.: 1). (ENG., Illus.). 128p. (YA). (gr. 6-12). lib. bdg. 27.99 *(978-1-4677-5804-8(3),* 03890806-974c-4ceb-8661-7ba91c6d43ae, Darby Creek) Lerner Publishing Group.

Murphy, Julie. Ramona Blue. (ENG.). (YA). (gr. 8). 2018. 448p. pap. 11.99 *(978-0-06-241836-4(X))* 2017. 432p. 17.99 *(978-0-06-241835-7(1))* HarperCollins Pubs. (Balzer & Bray).

Ramsey, Jo. High Heels & Lipstick. 2016. (ENG., Illus.). (J). 24.99 *(978-1-63533-029-8(7),* Harmony Ink Pr.) Dreamspinner Pr.

Reed, Amy. Beautiful. 2009. (ENG.). 240p. (YA). (gr. 9-12). 16.99 *(978-1-4169-7830-5(5))* Simon & Schuster, Inc.

—Beautiful. 2010. (ENG.). 256p. (YA). (gr. 9). pap. 10.99 *(978-1-4169-7831-2(3),* Simon Pulse) Simon Pulse.

—Nowhere Girls. 2017. (ENG.). (YA). (gr. 9). pap. 12.99 *(978-1-5344-1555-3(6))* Simon & Schuster.

—The Nowhere Girls. (ENG., Illus.). (YA). (gr. 9). 2019. 432p. pap. 12.99 *(978-1-4814-8174-8(6))* 2017. 416p. 19.99 *(978-1-4814-8173-1(8))* Simon Pulse. (Simon Pulse).

Reynolds Naylor, Phyllis. Alice on the Outside. 2012. (Alice Ser.: 11). (ENG., Illus.). 208p. (J). (gr. 5-9). pap. 7.99 *(978-1-4424-3495-0(3),* Atheneum Bks. for Young Readers) Simon & Schuster Children's Publishing.

—Lovingly Alice. 2004. (Alice Bks.). 166p. (J). (gr. 4-6). 13.65 *(978-0-7569-6604-1(3))* Perfection Learning Corp.

Robar, Serena. Giving up the V. 2009. (ENG.). 272p. (YA). (gr. 9-18). pap. 9.99 *(978-1-4169-7558-8(6),* Simon Pulse) Simon Pulse.

Rosin, Lindsey. Cherry. 2016. (ENG., Illus.). 400p. (YA). (gr. 9). 17.99 *(978-1-4814-5908-2(2),* Simon Pulse) Simon Pulse.

Ruby, Laura. Good Girls. 2008. (ENG.). 304p. (YA). (gr. 9-12). pap. 8.99 *(978-0-06-088225-9(5))* 2006. 288p. (J). lib. bdg. 17.89 *(978-0-06-088224-2(7))* 2006. (ENG.). 288p. (YA). (gr. 9-12). 16.99 *(978-0-06-088223-5(9))* HarperCollins Pubs. (HarperTeen).

Shaddix, M. K. Aisling's Summer Diary. 2012. 200p. pap. 6.99 *(978-0-9567500-8-2(7))* BeActive Publishing Co.

Smith, Amber. The Last to Let Go. 2018. (ENG.). 384p. (YA). (gr. 9). pap. 12.99 *(978-1-5344-2601-6(9))*; (Illus.). 17.99 *(978-1-4814-8073-4(1),* McElderry, Margaret K. Bks.) McElderry, Margaret K. Bks.

Snadowsky, Daria. Anatomy of a Boyfriend. 2008. (Anatomy of A... Ser.). (ENG.). 272p. (YA). (gr. 9). pap. 10.99 *(978-0-440-23944-4(3),* Ember) Random Hse. Children's Bks.

Strasnick, Lauren. Her & Me & You. (ENG.). 208p. (YA). (gr. 9). 2011. pap. 9.99 *(978-1-4169-8267-8(1))* 2010. 16.99 *(978-1-4169-8266-1(3))* Simon Pulse. (Simon Pulse).

Zarr, Sara. Story of a Girl. 2007. (ENG.). 208p. (YA). (gr. 7-17). 29.99 *(978-0-316-01453-3(2))* Little, Brown Bks. for Young Readers.

SEX CRIMES

see also Child Sexual Abuse; Incest; Rape

Buckey, A. W. Sexual Violence. 2019. (Intolerance & Violence in Society Ser.). (ENG.). 80p. (J). (gr. 6-12). 41.27 *(978-1-68282-693-5(7))* ReferencePoint Pr., Inc.

Byers, Ann. Sexual Assault & Abuse, 1 vol. 2015. (Confronting Violence Against Women Ser.). (ENG., Illus.). 64p. (J). (gr. 6-7). 36.13 *(978-1-4994-6042-1(2),* d12763ff-cadc-420e-b093-c166cc0a251b, Rosen Young Adult) Rosen Publishing Group, Inc., The.

Denton, Michelle. Rape Culture: How Can We End It?, 1 vol. 2017. (Hot Topics Ser.). (ENG.). 104p. (YA). (gr. 7-7). pap. 20.99 *(978-1-5345-6292-9(3),* b808f388-fa77-4bd2-89bb-e17a27d47ca7); lib. bdg. 41.03 *(978-1-5345-6207-3(9),* 51b2a8d2-3058-4886-9240-3787614e5f98) Greenhaven Publishing LLC. (Lucent Pr.).

Eboch, M. M., ed. The #MeToo Movement, 1 vol. 2019. (Opposing Viewpoints Ser.). (ENG.). 200p. (gr. 10-12). pap. 34.80 *(978-1-5345-0596-4(2),* b65c6140-6a2b-4e58-afbc-b5cb05eeb12f) Greenhaven Publishing LLC.

Erickson, Marty. The #MeToo Movement. 2019. (In Focus Ser.). (ENG.). 80p. (J). (gr. 6-12). 41.27 *(978-1-68282-717-8(8),* BrightPoint Pr.) ReferencePoint Pr., Inc.

Ghafoerkhan, Olivia. Sexual Assault: The Ultimate Teen Guide. 2016. (It Happened to Me Ser.: 51). (Illus.). 216p. 59.00 *(978-1-4422-5247-9(2))* Rowman & Littlefield Publishers, Inc.

Gitlin, Marty. Combatting Discrimination Against Women in the Gamer Community, 1 vol. 2016. (Combatting Shaming & Toxic Communities Ser.). (ENG., Illus.). 64p. (J). (gr. 7-7). 36.13 *(978-1-5081-7118-8(1),* 91d7845c-e891-48c3-8a74-49f8b27438dd) Rosen Publishing Group, Inc., The.

Haerens, Margaret, ed. Human Trafficking, 1 vol. 2011. (Global Viewpoints Ser.). (ENG., Illus.). 216p. (gr. 10-12). 47.83 *(978-0-7377-5658-6(6),* 5b533785-38bd-48a8-8ebf-19afe817c566); pap. 32.70 *(978-0-7377-5659-3(4),* c97d637a-aeb6-44f6-a034-6aed74683e8c) Greenhaven Publishing LLC. (Greenhaven Publishing).

Haugen, David M. & Musser, Susan, eds. Sex, 1 vol. 2013. (Teen Rights & Freedoms Ser.). (ENG., Illus.). 160p. (gr. 10-12). lib. bdg. 43.63 *(978-0-7377-6404-8(X),* bc95c851-279b-4758-b7df-e0e4f736cd1d, Greenhaven Publishing) Greenhaven Publishing LLC.

Hudak, Heather C. #MeToo Movement. 2018. (Get Informed — Stay Informed Ser.). (Illus.). 48p. (J). (gr. 5-6). *(978-0-7787-4960-8(6))* Crabtree Publishing Co.

Keyser, Amber J. No More Excuses: Dismantling Rape Culture. 2019. (ENG., Illus.). 144p. (YA). (gr. 8-12). 37.32 *(978-1-5415-4020-0(4),* 0f66f534-2e67-4337-b1be-8f33c7f62b6a, Twenty-First Century Bks.) Lerner Publishing Group.

Leese, Vickie. When God Created Little Girls... 2011. 22p. pap. 17.99 *(978-1-61379-521-7(1))* Salem Author Services.

Lohmann, Raychelle Cassada & Raja, Sheela. The Sexual Trauma Workbook for Teen Girls: A Guide to Recovery from Sexual Assault & Abuse. 2016. (ENG.). 200p. (YA). (gr. 6-12). pap. 18.95 *(978-1-62625-399-5(4),* 33995) New Harbinger Pubns.

Mayer, Melissa. Coping with Date Rape & Acquaintance Rape, 1 vol. 2018. (Coping Ser.). (ENG.). 112p. (gr. 7-7). pap. 19.24 *(978-1-5081-8315-0(5),* 6f829b59-c72c-4633-9631-1a99b88b5b59) Rosen Publishing Group, Inc., The.

McGee, Kathleen M. & Buddenberg, Laura J. Unmasking Sexual Con Games: Helping Teens Avoid Emotional Grooming & Dating Violence. 3rd ed. 2004. (Leader's Guide with Session Plans Ser.). (ENG., Illus.). 199p. pap. 29.95 *(978-1-889322-54-4(7),* 25-015) Boys Town Pr.

Parks, Peggy J. The #MeToo Movement. 2020. (ENG.). 80p. (YA). (gr. 6-12). 41.27 *(978-1-68282-761-1(5))* ReferencePoint Pr., Inc.

Penney, Betty. Tell Your Mother. 2004. (Illus.). 32p. (J). pap. 8.95 *(978-0-9631975-4-2(1))* Morgan, E. A.

Poole, H. W. Coping with Sexual Violence & Harassment. 2019. (Sexual Violence & Harassment Ser.). (Illus.). 80p. (J). (gr. 12). lib. bdg. 34.60 *(978-1-4222-4201-8(3))* Mason Crest.

—Dealing with Dating & Romance. 2019. (Sexual Violence & Harassment Ser.). (Illus.). 80p. (J). (gr. 12). lib. bdg. 34.60 *(978-1-4222-4202-5(1))* Mason Crest.

—Preventing Sexual Assault & Harassment. 2019. (Sexual Violence & Harassment Ser.). (Illus.). 80p. (J). (gr. 12). lib. bdg. 34.60 *(978-1-4222-4203-2(X))* Mason Crest.

Roach, Nicole. Private Parts. 2012. 24p. (-18). pap. 14.93 *(978-1-4669-5233-1(4))* Trafford Publishing.

Sorensen McGee, Kathleen & Holmes Buddenberg, Laura. Unmasking Sexual Con Games Teen's Guide: A Teen's Guide to Avoiding Emotional Grooming & Dating Violence. 3rd ed. 2004. (Leader's Guide with Session Plans Ser.). (ENG.). 79p. pap. 5.95 *(978-1-889322-55-1(5),* 25-016) Boys Town Pr.

Staley, Erin. Coping with Sexual Consent, 1 vol. 2019. (Coping (2017-2020) Ser.). (ENG., Illus.). 112p. (J). (gr. 7-7). 40.13 *(978-1-5081-8743-1(6),* f47ca517-b32f-4d5e-b26d-bfc8d221bd1c) Rosen Publishing Group, Inc., The.

Timmons, Angie. Everything You Need to Know about Reporting Sexual Assault, 1 vol. 2019. (Need to Know Library). (ENG., Illus.). 64p. (J). (gr. 6-6). pap. 13.95 *(978-1-5081-8764-6(9),* fa441f69-77f6-49da-b3ee-d7b0f7867a69) Rosen Publishing Group, Inc., The.

SEX CRIMES—FICTION

Akers, Ellery. Sarah's Waterfall: A Healing Story about Sexual Abuse. Benicio, Angelique, illus. 2009. (J). *(978-1-884444-79-1(2))* Safer Society Pr.

Barth, Amy. Annabelle's Secret. Kinra, Richa, illus. 2009. (J). pap. 12.95 *(978-1-932690-95-8(6))* Loving Healing Pr., Inc.

—Will Was All Boy: A Story about Sexual Abuse. Kinra, Richa, illus. 2009. (J). pap. *(978-1-61599-000-9(3))* Loving Healing Pr., Inc.

Blake, Ashley Herring. Girl Made of Stars. (ENG.). 304p. (YA). (gr. 9). 2019. pap. 9.99 *(978-0-358-10822-1(5),* 1748885) 2018. 17.99 *(978-1-328-77823-9(1),* 1681853) HarperCollins Pubs. (Clarion Bks.).

Bradley, Kimberly Brubaker. Fighting Words. 2020. (ENG.). 272p. (J). (gr. 5-7). 17.99 *(978-1-9848-1568-2(7),* Dial Bks) Penguin Young Readers Group.

Gray, Laurie. Maybe I Will. 2013. 212p. pap. 14.95 *(978-1-935462-72-9(5))* Luminis Bks., Inc.

Hebert, Marie-Francine. This Side of the Sky, 1 vol. Ouriou, Susan, tr. 2006. (ENG.). 112p. (YA). (gr. 9-18). per. 6.95 *(978-0-88995-369-7(4),* 6769f377-a38f-45b0-b953-5cf946544e52) Trifolium Bks., Inc. CAN. Dist: Firefly Bks., Ltd.

Hopkins, Ellen. Traffick. (ENG., Illus.). 528p. (YA). (gr. 9). 2017. pap. 14.99 *(978-1-4424-8288-3(5))* 2015. 19.99 *(978-1-4424-8287-6(7))* McElderry, Margaret K. Bks. (McElderry, Margaret K. Bks.).

Jiron, Betsy. Sing for Me. 2013. 170p. 29.99 *(978-0-9897380-4-0(3))* Zaloli, LLC.

Kiely, Brendan. The Gospel of Winter. 2014. (ENG., Illus.). 304p. (YA). (gr. 9). 19.99 *(978-1-4424-8489-4(6),* McElderry, Margaret K. Bks.) McElderry, Margaret K. Bks.

Phillips, Suzanne. Chloe Doe. 2008. (ENG.). 208p. (J). (gr. 10-17). pap. 12.99 *(978-0-316-01414-4(1))* Little, Brown Bks. for Young Readers.

Polak, Monique. On the Game, 1 vol. 2005. (SideStreets Ser.). (ENG.). 184p. (YA). (gr. 9-12). 17.44 *(978-1-55028-877-3(6),* 877); 8.99 *(978-1-55028-876-6(8),* 26f8f32a-30a0-4413-a9c9-7d44eb7afa76) James Lorimer & Co. Ltd., Pubs. CAN. Dist: Children's Plus, Inc., Lerner Publishing Group.

Riggs, Shannon. Not in Room 204: Breaking the Silence of Abuse. Zollars, Jaime, illus. 2017. (ENG.). 32p. (J). (gr. -1-3). pap. 7.99 *(978-0-8075-5766-2(8),* 807557668) Whitman, Albert & Co.

Sanchez, Alex. Bait. 2010. (ENG.). 256p. (YA). (gr. 7). pap. 12.99 *(978-1-4169-3774-6(9),* Simon & Schuster Bks. For Young Readers) Simon & Schuster Bks. For Young Readers.

—Bait. 2009. (ENG.). 256p. (YA). (gr. 7-12). 17.99 *(978-1-4169-3772-2(2))* Simon & Schuster, Inc.

Sinel, Natasha. The Fix. 2018. (ENG.). 344p. (gr. 6-12). pap. 9.99 *(978-1-5107-3119-6(9),* Sky Pony Pr.) Skyhorse Publishing Co., Inc.

Stang, Debra L. Visiting Grandma. 2003. 136p. (YA). pap. 12.95 *(978-1-59113-322-3(X))* Booklocker.com, Inc.

Weeks, Sarah. Jumping the Scratch. 2007. (J). 1.25 *(978-1-4193-8222-2(5))* Recorded Bks., Inc.

Woodson, Jacqueline. I Hadn't Meant to Tell You This. 2010. (ENG.). 160p. (YA). (gr. 7-18). 8.99 *(978-0-14-241704-1(1),* Puffin Books) Penguin Young Readers Group.

—I Hadn't Meant to Tell You This. 2006. 114p. (YA). (gr. 7-12). 13.65 *(978-0-7569-6730-7(9))* Perfection Learning Corp.

SEX INSTRUCTION

Amos, Janine. Is Helen Pregnant. 2003. (Body Matters Ser.: 1). (ENG., Illus.). 32p. (YA). 19.99 *(978-1-84234-107-0(3))* Evans Brothers, Ltd. GBR. Dist: Independent Pubs. Group.

Attwood, Sarah. Making Sense of Sex: A Forthright Guide to Puberty, Sex & Relationships for People with Asperger's Syndrome. 2008. (Illus.). 320p. (J). (gr. 4-12). pap. 23.95 *(978-1-84310-374-5(5),* 691701) Kingsley, Jessica Pubs. GBR. Dist: Hachette UK Distribution.

Bailey, Jacqui. Sex, Puberty, & All That Stuff: A Guide to Growing Up. 2nd rev. ed. 2016. (ENG., Illus.). 124p. (J). (gr. 5-10). pap. 14.99 *(978-1-4380-0857-8(0))* Sourcebooks, Inc.

Ballman, Swanee. Where Do Babies Come From? 2003. (Illus.). 32p. (J). per. 6.95 *(978-1-59094-023-5(7),* 1590940237) Jawbone Publishing Corp.

Barlow, C. E. Scary Man. Tharp, Lauren R., illus. 2009. 44p. pap. 18.99 *(978-1-4269-1060-9(6))* Trafford Publishing.

Basso, Michael J. The Underground Guide to Teenage Sexuality. 2nd ed. 2003. (Illus.). 320p. pap. 16.95 *(978-1-57749-131-6(9))* Taylor Trade Publishing.

Bourgeois, Paulette & Martyn, Kim. Changes in You & Me: A Book about Puberty Mostly for Boys. Phillips, Louise, illus. rev. ed. 2005. (ENG.). 63p. (J). pap. 16.95 *(978-1-55263-668-8(2))* Leaf Storm Pr.

—Changes in You & Me: A Book about Puberty Mostly for Girls. Phillips, Louise, illus. rev. ed. 2005. (ENG.). 64p. (J). pap. 16.95 *(978-1-55263-670-1(4))* Kollath-Stensaas Pubs.

Brynie, Faith Hickman. 101 Questions about Sex & Sexuality: With Answers for the Curious, Cautious, & Confused. Holm, Sharon, illus. 2003. (101 Questions... Ser.). (ENG.). 176p. (gr. 7-12). lib. bdg. 30.60 *(978-0-7613-2310-5(4),* Twenty-First Century Bks.) Lerner Publishing Group.

Burns, Jim. How God Makes Babies. 2009. (Pure Foundations Ser.). (ENG., Illus.). 48p. (gr. 1-4). 16.99 *(978-0-7642-0210-0(3))* Bethany Hse. Pubs.

—The Purity Code: God's Plan for Sex & Your Body. 2008. (Pure Foundations Ser.). (ENG., Illus.). 176p. pap. 15.99 *(978-0-7642-0209-4(X))* Bethany Hse. Pubs.

Daldry, Jeremy. The Teenage Guy's Survival Guide: The Real Deal on Going Out, Growing up, & Other Guy Stuff. 2nd rev. ed. 2018. (ENG., Illus.). 192p. (J). (gr. 7-17). 17.99 *(978-0-316-56142-6(8))* Little, Brown Bks. for Young Readers.

Feinstein, Stephen. Do You Wonder about Sex & Sexuality?, 1 vol. 2015. (Got Issues? Ser.). (ENG., Illus.). 128p. (gr. 7-7). 38.93 *(978-0-7660-6989-3(3),* 888c3211-3824-4bfb-80cb-c3c5e3e015cb) Enslow Publishing, LLC.

Ferguson, Olivia, ed. Teen Sex, 1 vol. 2010. (At Issue Ser.). (ENG.). 112p. (gr. 10-12). 41.03 *(978-0-7377-5095-9(2),* 68d489f6-2f30-47bc-ba17-e4a1eefc6e8c); pap. 28.80 *(978-0-7377-5096-6(0),* 5afc66e6-636a-4022-abd6-fa1b1ff74fb1) Greenhaven Publishing LLC. (Greenhaven Publishing).

Fonda, Jane. Being a Teen: Everything Teen Girls & Boys Should Know about Relationships, Sex, Love, Health, Identity & More. 2014. (Illus.). 288p. (YA). (gr. 7). pap. 18.00 *(978-0-8129-7861-2(7),* Random Hse. Trade Paperbacks) Random House Publishing Group.

—Being a Teen: Everything Teen Girls & Boys Should Know about Relationships, Sex, Love, Health, Identity & More. 2014. lib. bdg. 29.40 *(978-0-606-35596-4(0))* Turtleback.

Gitchel, Sam & Foster, Lorri. Let's Talk about S-E-X: A Guide for Kids 9 to 12 & Their Parents. 2nd ed. 2005. (ENG., Illus.). 100p. pap. 9.99 *(978-1-931863-18-6(0))* Book Peddlers.

Greene, Carol. Why Boys & Girls Are Different. 2008. (Illus.). 32p. pap. 12.99 *(978-0-7586-1415-5(2))* Concordia Publishing Hse.

—Why Boys & Girls Are Different. Dorankamp, Michelle, illus. 2008. (J). pap. 12.99 *(978-0-7586-1409-4(8))* Concordia Publishing Hse.

Harris, Robie H. It's Not the Stork! A Book about Girls, Boys, Babies, Bodies, Families & Friends. Emberley, Michael, illus. (Family Library). (ENG.). 64p. (J). (gr. -1-3). 2008. pap. 12.99 *(978-0-7636-3331-8(3))* 2006. 18.99 *(978-0-7636-0047-1(4))* Candlewick Pr.

—It's Perfectly Normal. 2014. lib. bdg. 24.50 *(978-0-606-35863-7(3))* Turtleback.

—What's in There? All about Before You Were Born. Bernard Westcott, Nadine, illus. 2013. (Let's Talk about You & Me Ser.). (ENG.). 40p. (J). (-k). 17.99 *(978-0-7636-3630-2(4))* Candlewick Pr.

—Who Has What? All about Girls' Bodies & Boys' Bodies. Westcott, Nadine B., illus. 2011. (Let's Talk about You & Me Ser.). (ENG.). 32p. (J). (gr. -1-2). 17.99 *(978-0-7636-2931-1(6))* Candlewick Pr.

Hirschmann, Kris. Your Sexuality. 2007. (Ripped from the Headlines Ser.). 64p. (YA). (gr. 7-12). 23.95 *(978-1-60217-009-4(6))* Erickson Pr.

Jamiolkowski, Raymond M. A Baby Doesn't Make the Man: Alternative Sources of Power & Manhood for Young Men. 2009. (Teen Pregnancy Prevention Library). 64p. (gr. 5-5). 58.50 *(978-1-60854-244-4(0))* Rosen Publishing Group, Inc., The.

Kahaner, Ellen. Everything You Need to Know about Growing up Female. 2009. (Need to Know Library). 64p. (gr. 5-5). 58.50 *(978-1-60854-070-9(7))* Rosen Publishing Group, Inc., The.

Kemp, Kristen. Healthy Sexuality. 2005. (Life Balance Ser.). (ENG., Illus.). 80p. (J). (gr. 5-8). pap. 6.95 *(978-0-531-16689-5(9),* Watts, Franklin) Scholastic Library Publishing.

Lickona, Tom & Lickona, Judy. Sex, Love & You: Making the Right Decision. rev. ed. 2003. (Illus.). 192p. (YA). pap. 15.95 *(978-0-87793-987-0(X))* Ave Maria Pr.

Loper, Ami M. The Miracle of Life. Loper, Carol J., illus. 2007. (J). *(978-0-9678798-1-9(7))* Biblical Standards Pubns.

Luadzers, Darcy. Virgin S.e.x: A Girl's No-Regrets Guide to Happy, Healthy Sex... the First Time & Every Time. 2004. 261p. (YA). per. 18.95 *(978-0-9742532-7-5(8))* Palmetto Tree Pr.

Madaras, Lynda. My Body, My Self for Boys. 2nd rev. ed. 2007. (What's Happening to My Body? Ser.). (ENG., Illus.). 128p. (gr. 4-6). pap. 16.99 *(978-1-55704-767-0(7),* William Morrow Paperbacks) HarperCollins Pubs.

—My Body, My Self for Girls. 3rd rev. ed. 2007. (What's Happening to My Body? Ser.). (ENG., Illus.). 160p. (gr. 4-6). pap. 13.99 *(978-1-55704-766-3(9),* William Morrow Paperbacks) HarperCollins Pubs.

—What's Happening to My Body? Book for Boys. 3rd rev. ed. 2007. (What's Happening to My Body? Ser.). (ENG., Illus.). 256p. (gr. 7-9). 24.99 *(978-1-55704-769-4(3),* Morrow, William & Co.) HarperCollins Pubs.

Madaras, Lynda & Madaras, Area. Que Pasa en Mi Cuerpo? el Libro para Muchachos: La Guía de Mayor Venta Sobre el Desarrollo, Escrita para Adolescentes y Preadolescentes.

2012. (What's Happening to My Body? Ser.). (ENG., Illus.). 256p. (gr. 4-18). pap. 14.99 (978-1-55704-940-7(8), William Morrow Paperbacks) HarperCollins Pubs.
—Que Pasa en Mi Cuerpo? Libro para Muchachas: La Guía de Mayor Venta Sobre el Desarrollo Escrita para Adolescentes y Preadolescentes. 2011. (What's Happening to My Body? Ser.). (ENG., Illus.). 288p. (gr. 4-18). pap. 14.99 (978-1-55704-939-1(4), William Morrow Paperbacks) HarperCollins Pubs.
Madaras, Lynda, et al. What's Happening to My Body? Book for Boys: Revised Edition. 3rd rev. ed. 2007. (What's Happening to My Body? Ser.). (ENG., Illus.). 256p. (gr. 5-7). pap. 16.99 (978-1-55704-765-6(0), William Morrow Paperbacks) HarperCollins Pubs.
—What's Happening to My Body? Book for Girls: Revised Edition. 3rd rev. ed. 2007. (What's Happening to My Body? Ser.). (ENG., Illus.). 288p. (gr. 7-9). pap. 16.99 (978-1-55704-764-9(2), William Morrow Paperbacks) HarperCollins Pubs.
Martyn, Kim. All the Way: Sex for the First Time, 1 vol. 2004. (ENG., Illus.). 216p. (YA). (gr. 8-12). pap. (978-1-894549-26-4(0), Sumach Pr.) Canadian Scholars.
Paonessa, Mary. Growth & Development with Friends, 8 vols. 3rd rev. ed. 2003. (Human Growth & Development Ser.). (Illus.). 41p. (J). (gr. 5-18). pap. 9.00 (978-0-9711721-0-4(2), 388) Paon Pubns.
—Growth & Development with Friends & School, 8 vols. 3rd ed. 2003. (Human Growth & Development Ser.). (Illus.). (J). (gr. 7-18). 112p. pap., tchr. ed. 15.00 (978-0-9711721-5-9(3), 393); 91p. pap. (978-0-9711721-4-2(5), 392) Paon Pubns.
Pardes, Bronwen. Doing It Right: Making Smart, Safe, & Satisfying Choices about Sex. (ENG., Illus.). (YA). (gr. 9). 2013. 160p. 18.99 (978-1-4424-8370-5(9)) 2013. 146p. pap. 12.99 (978-1-4424-8371-2(7)) 2007. 160p. pap. 14.99 (978-1-4169-1823-3(X)) Simon Pulse. (Simon Pulse).
parks, peggy j. Teenage Sex & Pregnancy. 2011. (Compact Research Ser.). 96p. (YA). (gr. 7-12). lib. bdg. 43.93 (978-1-60152-168-2(5)) ReferencePoint Pr., Inc.
Planned Parenthood Federation of America, Inc. Staff. A Young Woman's Guide to Sexuality. 2003. (Illus.). (YA). pap. 3.00 net. (978-1-930996-17-5(9)) Planned Parenthood Federation of America, Inc.
Ratcliff, Ace. Disabilities, Sexual Health, & Consent, 1 vol. 2019. (Equal Access: Fighting for Disability Protections Ser.). (ENG.). 64p. (gr. 5-5). 36.13 (978-1-5081-8337-2(6), 8f3d719d-2aff-44c7-93db-2821fe4ad8c7, Rosen Young Adult) Rosen Publishing Group, Inc., The.
Roberts, Jillian. Where Do Babies Come From? Our First Talk about Birth, 1 vol. Revell, Cindy, illus. 2015. (Just Enough Ser.: 1). (ENG.). 32p. (J). (gr. -1-k). 19.95 (978-1-4598-0942-0(4)) Orca Bk. Pubs. USA.
Schiffer, Howard B. How to Be the Best Lover - a Guide for Teenage Boys. 2004. (YA). 19.95 (978-0-9723639-0-7(4)) Heartful Loving Pr.
Silverberg, Cory. Sex Is a Funny Word: A Book about Bodies, Feelings, & YOU. Smyth, Fiona, illus. 2015. 160p. (J). (gr. 2-5). 25.95 (978-1-60980-606-4(9), Triangle Square) Seven Stories Pr.
Stephens, Aarti D., ed. Teenage Sexuality, 1 vol. 2012. (Opposing Viewpoints Ser.). (ENG., Illus.). 248p. (gr. 10-12). 50.43 (978-0-7377-5763-7(9), 307560b7-00df-48ef-941e-79a5e41e31a8); pap. 34.80 (978-0-7377-5764-4(7), ceda39ee-52a0-4f6c-a423-82dfe2fbd20e) Greenhaven Publishing LLC. (Greenhaven Publishing).
Thiel, Kristin. Dealing with Teen Pregnancy, 1 vol. 2019. (Helping Yourself, Helping Others Ser.). (ENG.). 112p. (gr. 7-7). pap. 20.99 (978-1-5026-4635-4(8), 40935b11-ee92-4455-99ff-286df23110db) Cavendish Square Publishing LLC.
Vermond, Kira. Growing Up, Inside & Out. 2013. 104p. (978-1-77147-036-0(4)) Owlkids Bks. Inc.
Williams, Heidi, ed. Teen Pregnancy, 1 vol. 2009. (Issues That Concern You Ser.). (ENG., Illus.). 144p. (gr. 7-10). 43.63 (978-0-7377-4498-9(7), ee468f84-382b-4745-a8f1-ea677dee1107, Greenhaven Publishing) Greenhaven Publishing LLC.
Witton, Hannah. Doing It. 2018. (ENG., Illus.). 352p. (YA). (gr. 8-12). pap. 10.99 (978-1-4926-6502-1(9)) Sourcebooks, Inc.
Wright, Sally Ann. Where Do Babies Come From? Ayres, Honor, illus. 2007. 29p. (J). 9.95 (978-0-8198-8311-7(5)) Pauline Bks. & Media.
X. Before You Were Born - Our Wish for A Baby - Donor Insemination: Version 2: Donor Insemination. 2004. (ENG., Illus.). 16p. (J). pap. 17.95 (978-0-9755028-1-5(6)) X, Y, & Me LLC.
—Before You Were Born - Our Wish for A Baby - Donor Sperm/IVF: Version 8: Donor Sperm (IVF) 2004. (ENG., Illus.). 16p. (J). pap. 17.95 (978-0-9755028-7-7(5)) X, Y, & Me LLC.
—Before You Were Born - Our Wish for A Baby - Embryo Donation: Version 7: Embryo Donation. 2004. (ENG., Illus.). 16p. (J). pap. 17.95 (978-0-9755028-6-0(7)) X, Y, & Me LLC.
—Before You Were Born - Our Wish for A Baby - Female Partners: Version 9: Female Partners. 2004. (ENG., Illus.). 16p. (J). pap. 17.95 (978-0-9755028-8-4(3)) X, Y, & Me LLC.
—Before You Were Born - Our Wish for A Baby - Frozen Embryo: Version 6: Frozen Embryo. 2004. (ENG., Illus.). 16p. (J). pap. 17.95 (978-0-9755028-5-3(9)) X, Y, & Me LLC.
—Before You Were Born - Our Wish for A Baby - Gestational Carrier: Version 5: Gestational Carrier. 2004. (ENG., Illus.). 16p. (J). pap. 17.95 (978-0-9755028-4-6(0)) X, Y, & Me LLC.
—Before You Were Born - Our Wish for A Baby - IVF: Version 1: in Vitro Fertilization. 2004. (ENG., Illus.). 16p. (J). pap. 17.95 (978-0-9755028-0-8(8)) X, Y, & Me LLC.
—Before You Were Born - Our Wish for A Baby - Male Partners: Version 10: Male Partners. 2004. (ENG., Illus.). 16p. (J). pap. 17.95 (978-0-9755028-9-1(1)) X, Y, & Me LLC.
—Before You Were Born - Our Wish for A Baby - Traditional Surrogate: Version 4: Traditional Surrogate. 2004. (ENG., Illus.). 16p. (J). pap. 17.95 (978-0-9755028-3-9(2)) X, Y, & Me LLC.
Zep. What's Going on down There? All the Stuff Your Body Won't Tell You about Sex. Zimmerman, Dwight Jon, ed. 2005. (Illus.). 96p. pap. 14.95 (978-1-4165-0458-0(3)) ibooks, Inc.

SEX INSTRUCTION—FICTION

Blackall, Sophie. The Baby Tree. Blackall, Sophie, illus. 2014. (Illus.). 40p. (J). (gr. k-3). 18.99 (978-0-399-25718-6(7), Nancy Paulsen Books) Penguin Young Readers Group.
Ryan, Patrick. In Mike We Trust. 2009. 321p. (J). lib. bdg. 17.89 (978-0-06-085814-8(1), HarperTeen) HarperCollins Pubs.

SEX ROLE

Ashour, Monica & Harrald-Pilz, Marilee. God Has a Plan for Boys & for Girls. 2015. (Illus.). 25p. (J). pap. 12.95 (978-0-8198-3131-6(X)) Pauline Bks. & Media.
Cook, Maria. Gender Identity: Beyond Pronouns & Bathrooms. Cornell, Alexis, illus. 2019. (Inquire & Investigate Ser.). (ENG.). 128p. (YA). (gr. 7-9). 22.95 (978-1-61930-756-8(1), 553a9d71-ec5f-41fc-b354-d7412b2ca075); pap. 17.95 (978-1-61930-759-9(6), f650d554-4380-470d-a61f-3d194d5cd572) Nomad Pr.
Eboch, M. M., ed. Gender in the 21st Century, 1 vol. 2019. (Opposing Viewpoints Ser.). (ENG.). 176p. (gr. 10-12). pap. 34.80 (978-1-5345-0592-6(X), 504748ff-e075-4313-81ae-a929072c3706, Greenhaven Publishing) Greenhaven Publishing LLC.
Gagne, Tammy. Women in the Workplace. 2019. (Women & Society Ser.). (ENG.). 80p. (YA). (gr. 6-12). (978-1-68282-553-2(1)) ReferencePoint Pr., Inc.
Gitlin, Martin, ed. Transgender Rights, 1 vol. 2017. (Issues That Concern You Ser.). (ENG.). 112p. (YA). (gr. 7-10). pap. 29.30 (978-1-5345-0283-3(1), 070381e3-7129-4974-a3f3-e5de23e20491) Greenhaven Publishing LLC.
Gonzales, Kathryn & Rayne, Karen. Trans+ Love, Sex, Romance, & Being You. Passchier, Anne, illus. 2019. 304p. (J). (978-1-4338-2983-3(5), Magination Pr.) American Psychological Assn.
Hand, Carol. Everything You Need to Know about Sexism, 1 vol. 2017. (Need to Know Library). (ENG., Illus.). 64p. (J). (gr. 6-6). pap. 13.95 (978-1-5081-7679-4(5), dcecfacb-d556-49ed-845a-93325a6ea67b) Rosen Publishing Group, Inc., The.
Harris, Robie H. It's Not the Stork! A Book about Girls, Boys, Babies, Bodies, Families & Friends. Emberley, Michael, illus. 2006. (Family Library). (ENG.). 64p. (J). (gr. -1-3). 18.99 (978-0-7636-0047-1(4)) Candlewick Pr.
Haughton, Emma. Equality of the Sexes? 2005. (Viewpoints (Sea to Sea) Ser.). (Illus.). 32p. (YA). (gr. 5-9). lib. bdg. 27.10 (978-1-932889-58-1(2)) Sea-To-Sea Pubns.
Henneberg, Susan, ed. Gender Politics, 1 vol. 2016. (At Issue Ser.). (ENG.). 120p. (YA). (gr. 10-12). pap. 28.80 (978-1-5345-0041-9(3), 52f77ffb-b619-480e-bc4e-71b562834b7b); lib. bdg. 41.03 (978-1-5345-0014-3(6), fcc4c713-c3f2-4b16-a860-e5fcf5126551) Greenhaven Publishing LLC. (Greenhaven Publishing).
Kawa, Katie. What's Gender Identity?, 1 vol. 2019. (What's the Issue? Ser.). (ENG.). 24p. (gr. 3-3). lib. bdg. 26.23 (978-1-5345-3218-2(8), e42a6b50-0e07-4d96-bdc5-9ceed23b5a63, KidHaven Publishing) Greenhaven Publishing LLC.
Kilodavis, Cheryl. My Princess Boy. DeSimone, Suzanne, illus. 2010. (ENG.). 36p. (J). (gr. -1-3). 17.99 (978-1-4424-2988-8(7), Aladdin) Simon & Schuster Children's Publishing.
Kim Ko, Yon-Ju. Na Ui Ch'ot Chendo Suop. 2017. (KOR., Illus.). 201p. (YA). (978-89-364-5227-8(4)) Chang-jag and Bipyeong Co.
Light, Kate. Gender Identity: The Search for Self, 1 vol. 2016. (Hot Topics Ser.). (ENG.). 104p. (YA). (gr. 7-7). lib. bdg. 41.03 (978-1-5345-6023-9(8), f2e6c575-fa38-44b9-8230-ba8800ffddcc, Lucent Pr.) Greenhaven Publishing LLC.
Lowery, Zoe & Mills, J. Elizabeth. Social Roles & Stereotypes, 1 vol. 2017. (Women in the World Ser.). (ENG., Illus.). 112p. (J). (gr. 6-6). 38.80 (978-1-5081-7441-7(5), 461dd125-e5a7-4467-9223-6b78b507b25a, Rosen Young Adult) Rosen Publishing Group, Inc., The.
Lundquist-Arora, Stephanie. Coping with Gender Fluidity, 1 vol. 2019. (Coping Ser.). (ENG., Illus.). 112p. (J). (gr. 7-7). pap. 19.24 (978-1-7253-4125-8(5), 6c6f1951-e323-449a-9b28-7026280977fd) Rosen Publishing Group, Inc., The.
Marsh, Sarah Glenn. Alice Across America: The Story of the First Women's Cross-Country Road Trip. Ford, Gilbert, illus. 2020. (ENG.). 48p. (J). 18.99 (978-1-250-29702-0(8), 900195861, Holt, Henry & Co. Bks. For Young Readers) Holt, Henry & Co.
Merino, Noël, ed. Gender, 1 vol. 2010. (Issues on Trial Ser.). (ENG.). 216p. (gr. 10-12). 45.58 (978-0-7377-4948-9(2), 9ebb67a6-f474-4cbf-b00f-97e5880cf505, Greenhaven Publishing) Greenhaven Publishing LLC.
—Sex Discrimination, 1 vol. 2010. (Issues on Trial Ser.). (ENG., Illus.). 192p. (gr. 10-12). 49.93 (978-0-7377-4740-9(4), f6def051-4b6c-43c1-a0da-ab92c22e6b6a, Greenhaven Publishing) Greenhaven Publishing LLC.
Negley, Keith. Mary Wears What She Wants. Negley, Keith, illus. 2019. (ENG., Illus.). 48p. (J). (gr. -1-3). 18.99 (978-0-06-284679-2(5), Balzer & Bray) HarperCollins Pubs.
Rajczak Nelson, Kristen. 20 Fun Facts about Women in Ancient Greece & Rome, 1 vol. 2015. (Fun Fact File: Women in History Ser.). (ENG., Illus.). 32p. (J). (gr. 2-3). 27.93 (978-1-4824-2818-6(0), 4d434707-8ead-41ea-a037-4a8b7544ab7a) Stevens, Gareth Publishing LLLP.
Sands, Crystal. Women & Feminism Today. 2019. (Women & Society Ser.). (ENG.). 80p. (J). (gr. 6-12). (978-1-68282-547-1(7)) ReferencePoint Pr., Inc.
Seba, Jaime A. Feeling Wrong in Your Own Body: Understanding What It Means to Be Transgender. 2009. (Gallup's Guide to Modern Gay, Lesbian, & Transgender Lifestyle Ser.). (Illus.). 64p. (YA). (gr. 7-18). lib. bdg. 22.95 (978-1-4222-1746-7(9)) Mason Crest.
Swisher, Clarice. Women of Victorian England. 2004. (Women in History Ser.). (ENG., Illus.). 112p. (YA). (gr. 7-12). lib. bdg. 33.45 (978-1-59018-571-1(4), Lucent Bks.) Cengage Gale.
Wenzel, Anna, ed. Male Privilege, 1 vol. 2019. (At Issue Ser.). (ENG.). 128p. (gr. 10-12). 41.03 (978-1-5345-0521-6(0), c9b2d82d-1b5c-46df-879a-8b8bccec859b) Greenhaven Publishing LLC.

SEX ROLE—FICTION

Ahdieh, Renée. Flame in the Mist. (Flame in the Mist Ser.: 1). (ENG.). (YA). (gr. 7). 2018. 448p. pap. 11.99 (978-0-14-751387-8(1), Penguin Books) 2017. 416p. 17.99 (978-0-399-17163-5(0), G.P. Putnam's Sons Books for Young Readers) Penguin Young Readers Group.
—Flame in the Mist. 2018. lib. bdg. 22.10 (978-0-606-40878-3(9)) Turtleback.
—Smoke in the Sun. 2018. (Flame in the Mist Ser.: 2). (ENG.). 432p. (YA). (gr. 7). 18.99 (978-1-5247-3814-3(X), G.P. Putnam's Sons Books for Young Readers) Penguin Young Readers Group.
Anton, Maggie. Rashi's Daughter, Secret Scholar. 2008. (ENG.). 160p. (gr. 4-7). pap. 14.00 (978-0-8276-0869-6(1)) Jewish Pubn. Society.
Ashley, Jonathan. Lily & Kosmo in Outer Outer Space. Ashley, Jonathan, illus. 2018. (ENG., Illus.). 208p. (J). (gr. 2-5). 16.99 (978-1-5344-1364-1(2), Simon & Schuster Bks. For Young Readers) Simon & Schuster Bks. For Young Readers.
Atkins, Jeannine. Finding Wonders: Three Girls Who Changed Science. (ENG., Illus.). 208p. (J). (gr. 5). 2017. pap. 7.99 (978-1-4814-6566-3(X)) 2016. 18.99 (978-1-4814-6565-6(1), Atheneum Bks. for Young Readers) Simon & Schuster Children's Publishing.
Avi. The Secret School. 2003. 157p. (J). (gr. 3-7). 13.60 (978-0-7569-1625-1(9)) Perfection Learning Corp.
—The True Confessions of Charlotte Doyle. 2012. lib. bdg. 17.20 (978-0-606-26779-3(4)) Turtleback.
—The True Confessions of Charlotte Doyle (Scholastic Gold), 1 vol. 2012. (ENG.). 240p. (J). (gr. 4-7). pap. 9.99 (978-0-545-47711-6(5), Scholastic Paperbacks) Scholastic, Inc.
Axel, Brett. Goblinheart: A Fairy Tale. Biddlespacher, Tara, illus. 2012. (J). 15.00 (978-0-9769771-2-4(5)) Eastwaterfront Pr.
Baer, Jill. Just One of the Princes. 2014. (Sofia the First World of Reading Ser.). (Illus.). 32p. (J). lib. bdg. 13.55 (978-0-606-35263-5(5)) Turtleback.
Banghart, Tracy. Grace & Fury. 2019. (Grace & Fury Ser.: 1). (ENG.). 336p. (YA). (gr. 9-17). pap. 10.99 (978-0-316-47142-8(9)) Little, Brown Bks. for Young Readers.
Baratz-Logsted, Lauren. The Education of Bet. 2011. (ENG.). 192p. (YA). (gr. 7). pap. 11.99 (978-0-547-55024-4(3), 1450234, Clarion Bks.) HarperCollins Pubs.
Barbieri, Kara. White Stag: A Permafrost Novel. 2019. (ENG.). 368p. (YA). pap. (978-1-250-22619-8(8), Wednesday Bks.) St. Martin's Pr.
Bare, Bart. Girl. 2010. 188p. (YA). pap. 11.95 (978-0-9825396-4-4(9)) Canterbury Hse. Publishing, Ltd.
Beck-Jacobson, Darlene. Wheels of Change. 2014. (ENG., Illus.). 197p. (J). (gr. 2-5). 12.95 (978-1-939547-13-2(X), fea434e9-1ddd-40eb-b4bd-f71744c8d3e9) Creston Bks.
Bell, Alex. The Polar Bear Explorers' Club. Tomic, Tomislav, illus. 2018. (Polar Bear Explorers' Club Ser.: 1). (ENG.). 320p. (J). (gr. 3-7). 17.99 (978-1-5344-0646-9(8), Simon & Schuster Bks. For Young Readers) Simon & Schuster Bks. For Young Readers.
Bergin, Virginia. The XY. 2018. (ENG.). 352p. (YA). (gr. 8-12). 17.99 (978-1-4926-6217-4(8)) Sourcebooks, Inc.
Blake, Stephanie J. The Marble Queen, 0 vols. 2012. (ENG.). 190p. (J). (gr. 4-6). 16.99 (978-0-7614-6227-9(9), 9780761462279, Two Lions) Amazon Publishing.
Bradman, Tony. Rapunzel Lets Her Hair Down, 1 vol. Warburton, Sarah, illus. (After Happily Ever After Ser.). (ENG.). 56p. (J). (gr. 3-6). 2014. pap. 4.95 (978-1-4342-7965-1(0), 124715) 2009. lib. bdg. 25.99 (978-1-4342-1307-5(2), 95632) Capstone. (Stone Arch Bks.).
Bunting, Eve. Girls a to Z. Bloom, Suzanne, illus. 2013. (ENG.). 32p. (J). (gr. k-2). pap. 7.95 (978-1-62091-028-3(4), Astra Young Readers) Astra Publishing Hse.
—The Pirate Captain's Daughter. 2011. (Eve Bunting's Pirate Ser.). (ENG.). 208p. (J). (gr. 7-11). pap. 8.95 (978-1-58536-525-8(4), 202318);1. lib. bdg. 15.95 (978-1-58536-526-5(2), 202212) Sleeping Bear Pr.
Burch, Christian. The Manny Files. 2008. (Mix Ser.). (ENG.). 304p. (J). (gr. 4-8). pap. 14.99 (978-1-4169-5534-4(8), Aladdin) Simon & Schuster Children's Publishing.
Carlson, Caroline. The Buccaneers' Code. (Very Nearly Honorable League of Pirates Ser.: 3). (ENG.). 320p. (J). (gr. 3-7). 2016. pap. 7.99 (978-0-06-219440-4(2)) 2015. 16.99 (978-0-06-219439-8(9)) HarperCollins Pubs. (HarperCollins).
—The Terror of the Southlands. Phillips, Dave, illus. 2014. (ENG.). 336p. (J). pap. (978-0-06-236178-3(3)) Harper & Row Ltd.
Carlson, Nancy. Louanne Pig in Making the Team. 2005. (Louanne Pig Ser.). (Illus.). 32p. (J). (gr. k-2). lib. bdg. 15.95 (978-1-57505-914-3(2)) Lerner Publishing Group.
Chibbaro, Julie. Deadly. Sovak, Jean-Marc Superville, illus. 2012. (ENG.). 304p. (YA). (gr. 7). pap. 11.99 (978-0-689-85739-3(X), Atheneum Bks. for Young Readers) Simon & Schuster Children's Publishing.
Cochrane, Mick. The Girl Who Threw Butterflies. 2010. (ENG.). 192p. (J). (gr. 3-7). 7.99 (978-0-375-84610-6(7), Yearling) Random Hse. Children's Bks.
Colfer, Chris. A Tale of Magic... (Tale of Magic... Ser.: 1). (ENG.). (J). (gr. 3-7). 2020. 512p. pap. 9.99 (978-0-316-52351-6(8)) 2019. (Illus.). 496p. 18.99 (978-0-316-52347-9(X)) 2019. 720p. pap. 30.99 (978-0-316-42633-6(4)) Little, Brown Bks. for Young Readers.
Collins, Pat Lowery. The Fattening Hut. 2005. (ENG.). 192p. (YA). (gr. 7). pap. 12.95 (978-0-618-55209-2(X), 491911, Clarion Bks.) HarperCollins Pubs.
Corey, Shana. Players in Pigtails. Gibbon, Rebecca, illus. 2006. 28p. (YA). (gr. 8-11). reprint ed. 17.00 (978-1-4223-5848-1(8)) DIANE Publishing Co.
Cornwell, Betsy. The Forest Queen. (ENG.). (YA). (gr. 7). 2020. 320p. pap. 9.99 (978-0-358-13361-2(0), 1749855) 2018. 304p. 17.99 (978-0-544-88819-7(7), 1653253) HarperCollins Pubs. (Clarion Bks.).
Courgeon, Remi. Feather. Bedrick, Claudia Zoe, tr. 2017. (ENG., Illus.). 36p. (J). (gr. k-4). 17.95 (978-1-59270-210-7(4)) Enchanted Lion Bks., LLC.
Coy, John. Top of the Order: The 4 for 4 Series. 2010. (4 For 4 Ser.: 1). (ENG.). 208p. (J). (gr. 3-6). pap. 14.99 (978-0-312-61111-8(0), 900065447) Square Fish.
Cremer, Andrea. Rift. 2013. (Nightshade Novels Ser.). (ENG.). 464p. (YA). (gr. 8-12). 26.19 (978-0-399-25613-4(X)) Penguin Young Readers Group.
Dale, Elizabeth. Cara the Cowgirl. Lombardo, Serena, illus. 2021. (Early Bird Readers — Gold (Early Bird Stories (tm)) Ser.). (ENG.). 32p. (J). (gr. k-3). 30.65 (978-1-5415-9007-6(4), 2c85c67a-e715-4717-9395-1ee97d95bee3, Lerner Pubns.) Lerner Publishing Group.
Day, Karen. No Cream Puffs. 224p. (J). 2010. (gr. 3-7). 8.99 (978-0-375-83776-0(0), Yearling) 2008. (ENG.). (gr. 6-8). lib. bdg. 21.19 (978-0-375-93775-0(7), Lamb, Wendy Bks.) Random Hse. Children's Bks.
Deborah, Ellis. The Breadwinner. 2014. (ENG.). 176p. (J). 13.20 (978-1-63245-145-3(X)) Lectorum Pubns., Inc.
Delaney, Rachelle. Guardians of Island X, 2. Guerlais, Gérald, illus. 2012. (Ship of Lost Souls Ser.). (ENG.). 224p. (J). (gr. 4-6). 22.44 (978-0-448-45778-9(4), Grosset & Dunlap) Penguin Publishing Group.
—The Ship of Lost Souls #1, 1. Guerlais, Gérald, illus. 2012. (Ship of Lost Souls Ser.). (ENG.). 256p. (J). (gr. 4-6). 22.44 (978-0-448-45776-5(8), Grosset & Dunlap) Penguin Publishing Group.
Demont, Belle. I Love My Purse. Wimmer, Sonja, illus. 2017. (ENG.). 34p. (J). (gr. k-2). 18.95 (978-1-55451-954-5(3)) Annick Pr., Ltd. CAN. Dist: Publishers Group West (PGW).
dePaola, Tomie. Oliver Button Is a Sissy. dePaola, Tomie, illus. 2017. (ENG., Illus.). 48p. (J). (gr. -1-3). 17.99 (978-1-4814-7757-4(9), Simon & Schuster Bks. For Young Readers) Simon & Schuster Bks. For Young Readers.
Dines, Carol. The Queen's Soprano. 2007. (ENG., Illus.). 336p. (YA). (gr. 9). pap. 18.95 (978-0-15-206102-9(9)) Houghton Mifflin Harcourt Publishing Co.
Dole, Mayra L. Drum, Chavi, Drum!, 1 vol. Tonel, illus. 2014. (Chavi Ser.).Tr. of ¡Toca, Chavi, Toca! (ENG.). 32p. (J). (gr. k-3). pap. 11.95 (978-0-89239-302-2(5), leelowcbp, Children's Book Press) Lee & Low Bks., Inc.
—Toca, Chavi, Toca! Tonel, illus. 2003.Tr. of Drum, Chavi, Drum! (ENG & SPA.). 32p. (J). 16.95 (978-0-89239-186-8(3)) Lee & Low Bks., Inc.
Donaldson, Julia. Zog & the Flying Doctors. Scheffler, Axel, illus. 2017. (ENG.). 32p. (J). (gr. -1-3). 17.99 (978-1-338-13417-9(5), Levine, Arthur A. Bks.) Scholastic, Inc.
Donnelly, Jennifer. These Shallow Graves. 2016. (ENG.). 512p. (YA). (gr. 7). pap. 11.99 (978-0-385-73766-1(1), Ember) Random Hse. Children's Bks.
—These Shallow Graves. 2016. (ENG.). 496p. (YA). (gr. 7). 22.10 (978-0-606-39341-6(2)) Turtleback.
Double Reverse, 1 vol. 2014. (Fred Bowen Sports Story Ser.: 19). 144p. (J). (gr. 2-6). pap. 6.99 (978-1-56145-807-3(4)) Peachtree Publishing Co. Inc.
Echols, Jennifer. The Ex Games. 2011. (Romantic Comedies Ser.). (ENG.). 240p. (YA). (gr. 7). pap. 11.99 (978-1-4424-3083-9(4), Simon Pulse) Simon Pulse.
Echols, Jennifer & Hapka, Catherine. Winter's Kiss: The Ex Games; the Twelve Dates of Christmas. 2012. (ENG.). 496p. (YA). (gr. 7). pap. 9.99 (978-1-4424-5040-0(1), Simon Pulse) Simon Pulse.
Ellis, Deborah. The Breadwinner. 2013. 164p. pap. (978-1-4596-6483-8(3)) ReadHowYouWant.com, Ltd.
—The Breadwinner (movie Tie-In Edition), 1 vol. 2017. (Breadwinner Ser.: 1). (ENG., Illus.). 160p. (J). (gr. 5-9). pap. 10.99 (978-1-77306-071-2(6)) Groundwood Bks. CAN. Dist: Publishers Group West (PGW).
—Mud City. 2013. 156p. pap. (978-1-4596-6445-6(0)) ReadHowYouWant.com, Ltd.
Ellison, Laura. Hard Rock, Hard Times: Coming of Age in Butte Montana, 1911-1917. 2005. 195p. (YA). per. (978-0-9722217-7-1(8)) Horse Creek Pubns.
Engle, Margarita. Drum Dream Girl: How One Girl's Courage Changed Music. López, Rafael & López, Rafael, illus. 2015. (ENG.). 48p. (J). (gr. -1-3). 19.99 (978-0-544-10229-3(0), 1540161, Clarion Bks.) HarperCollins Pubs.
Evans, Loralee. The King's Heir. 2006. 287p. (YA). (gr. 8-12). per. 18.99 (978-1-55517-865-9(0), Bonneville Bks.) Cedar Fort, Inc./CFI Distribution.
Feinstein, John. Benchwarmers. 2019. (Benchwarmers Ser.: 1). (ENG.). 320p. (J). 16.99 (978-0-374-31203-9(6), 900198272, Farrar, Straus & Giroux (BYR)) Farrar, Straus & Giroux.
Ferrari, Michael. Born to Fly. 2011. 224p. (J). (ENG.). (gr. 4-6). lib. bdg. 21.19 (978-0-385-90649-4(8), Delacorte Pr.); (gr. 3-7). 7.99 (978-0-375-84607-6(7), Yearling) Random Hse. Children's Bks.
Fierstein, Harvey. The Sissy Duckling: Book & CD. Cole, Henry, illus. 2014. (ENG.). 40p. (J). (gr. -1-3). pap. 10.99 (978-1-4424-9817-4(X), Little Simon) Little Simon.
Filak, Stacey. The Queen Underneath. 2018. (ENG.). 288p. (YA). 16.99 (978-1-62414-560-5(4), 900191141) Page Street Publishing Co.
Fisher, Linda C. A Will of Her Own. 2006. (YA). pap. (978-0-88092-641-6(4)); lib. bdg. (978-0-88092-640-9(6)) Royal Fireworks Publishing Co.
FitzGerald, Dawn. Getting in the Game. 2007. (ENG.). 144p. (J). (gr. 4-8). pap. 16.99 (978-0-312-37753-3(3), 900049148) Square Fish.
Florence, Debbi Michiko. Jasmine Toguchi, Mochi Queen. 2017. (J). pap. (978-0-374-30411-9(4)) Farrar, Straus & Giroux.
Friesner, Esther. Nobody's Princess. 2008. (Princesses of Myth Ser.). (ENG., Illus.). 336p. (YA). (gr. 7-11). pap. 8.99 (978-0-375-87529-8(8), Ember) Random Hse. Children's Bks.
—Spirit's Chosen. 2014. (Princesses of Myth Ser.). (ENG., Illus.). 512p. (YA). (gr. 7). pap. 10.99 (978-0-375-87316-4(3), Ember) Random Hse. Children's Bks.
Friesner, Esther M. Spirit's Princess. 2012. 449p. (YA). (978-0-375-87315-7(5)) Random Hse., Inc.
Gag, Wanda. Gone Is Gone: Or the Story of a Man Who Wanted to Do Housework. 2003. (Fesler-Lampert Minnesota Heritage Ser.). (ENG., Illus.). 64p. 14.95 (978-0-8166-4243-4(5)) Univ. of Minnesota Pr.

Garvin, Jeff. Symptoms of Being Human. (ENG.). (YA). (gr. 9). 2017. 368p. pap. 11.99 *(978-0-06-238287-0(X))* 2016. 352p. 17.99 *(978-0-06-238286-3(1))* HarperCollins Pubs. (Balzer & Bray).

Geeslin, Campbell. Elena's Serenade. Juan, Ana, illus. 2004. (ENG.). 40p. (J). (gr. -1-2). 19.99 *(978-0-689-84908-4(7),* Atheneum Bks. for Young Readers) Simon & Schuster Children's Publishing.

Gehl, Laura. Except When They Don't. Heinsz, Joshua, illus. 2019. (ENG.). 32p. (J). (gr. -1-3). 16.99 *(978-1-4998-0804-9(6))* Little Bee Books Inc.

Gilbert, Frances. Go, Girls, Go! Black, Allison, illus. 2019. (ENG.). 40p. (J). (gr. -1-3). 17.99 *(978-1-5344-2482-1(2),* Beach Lane Bks.) Beach Lane Bks.

Girard, M-E. Girl Mans Up. (ENG.). (YA). (gr. 9). 2018. 400p. pap. 11.99 *(978-0-06-240418-3(0))* 2016. 384p. 17.99 *(978-0-06-240417-6(2))* HarperCollins Pubs. (HarperCollins).

Goldstein, Lori. Screen Queens. 2019. (ENG., Illus.). 368p. (YA). (gr. 7). 17.99 *(978-0-451-48159-7(3),* Razorbill) Penguin Young Readers Group.

Goodman, Alison. Eon. 2010. Orig. Title: The Two Pearls of Wisdom. (ENG.). 576p. (YA). (gr. 7-18). 13.99 *(978-0-14-241711-9(4),* Firebird) Penguin Young Readers Group.

—Eon: Dragoneye Reborn. 2010. (Eon Ser.: 1). lib. bdg. 22.10 *(978-0-606-23647-8(3))* Turtleback.

Gould, Sasha. Cross My Heart. 2013. (ENG.). 272p. (YA). (gr. 8-12). lib. bdg. 24.94 *(978-0-375-99007-6(0),* Delacorte Pr.) Random Hse. Children's Bks.

Grambling, Lois G. Nicky Jones & the Roaring Rhinos. Geer, William J., illus. 2004. 32p. (J). 6.95 *(978-1-877810-14-5(2))* Rayve Productions, Inc.

Green, Connie Jordan. The War at Home. 2nd ed. 2003. 144p. (J). pap. 15.00 *(978-0-916078-75-1(2))* Iris Publishing Group, Inc., The.

Green, D. L. Zeke Meeks vs the Gruesome Girls, 1 vol. Alves, Josh, illus. 2012. (Zeke Meeks Ser.). (ENG.). 128p. (J). (gr. 2-4). pap. 5.95 *(978-1-4048-7221-9(3),* 118073, Picture Window Bks.) Capstone.

Gregory, Kristiana. My Darlin' Clementine. 2009. (ENG.). 192p. (J). (gr. 5-18). 16.95 *(978-0-8234-2198-5(8))* Holiday Hse., Inc.

Grosso, Mike. I Am Drums. (ENG.). 256p. (J). (gr. 5-7). 2019. pap. 7.99 *(978-1-328-90013-5(4),* 1700043) 2016. 17.99 *(978-0-544-70710-8(9),* 1628642) HarperCollins Pubs. (Clarion Bks.).

Guthrie, Savannah & Oppenheim, Allison. Princesses Wear Pants. Byrne, Eva, illus. 2017. (ENG.). 32p. (J). (gr. -1-2). 18.99 *(978-1-4197-2603-3(X),* 1186101) Abrams, Inc.

Gutierrez, Amy. Smarty Marty Steps up Her Game. Killora, Ariana, illus. 2017. (ENG.). 132p. (J). (gr. 2-5). 13.95 *(978-1-944903-08-4(9),* 1330301, Cameron Kids) Cameron + Co.

Gutman, Dan. Mickey & Me. 2004. (Baseball Card Adventures Ser.). (ENG., Illus.). 160p. (J). (gr. 5-9). pap. 7.99 *(978-0-06-447258-6(2),* HarperCollins) HarperCollins Pubs.

—Mickey & Me. 2004. (Baseball Card Adventures Ser.). (J). lib. bdg. 16.00 *(978-0-613-99233-6(4))* Turtleback.

Haddix, Margaret Peterson. Just Ella. 2015. (Palace Chronicles Ser.: 1). (ENG., Illus.). 208p. (YA). (gr. 7). pap. 10.99 *(978-1-4814-2021-1(6),* Simon & Schuster Bks. For Young Readers) Simon & Schuster Bks. For Young Readers.

Hahn, Mary Downing. The Gentleman Outlaw & Me — Eli. 2007. (ENG.). 224p. (YA). (gr. 7-7). pap. 6.99 *(978-0-618-83000-8(6),* 100560, Clarion Bks.) HarperCollins Pubs.

Hale, Shannon. Palace of Stone. 2015. (Princess Academy Ser.: 2). (YA). lib. bdg. 18.40 *(978-0-606-36439-3(0))* Turtleback.

—Princess Academy: Palace of Stone. (Princess Academy Ser.: 2). (ENG.). (gr. 5-8). 2015. 352p. (J). pap. 8.99 *(978-1-61963-257-8(8),* 900131475) 2012. 336p. (YA). 17.99 *(978-1-59990-873-1(5),* 900082614) Bloomsbury Publishing USA. (Bloomsbury USA Childrens).

Harlow, Joan Hiatt. Midnight Rider. 2006. (ENG.). 384p. (J). (gr. 4-9). pap. 8.99 *(978-0-689-87010-1(8),* McElderry, Margaret K. Bks.) McElderry, Margaret K. Bks.

Hawes, Louise. The Vanishing Point. 2007. (ENG.). 240p. (J). (gr. 5-7). pap. 15.95 *(978-0-618-74788-7(5),* 487465, Clarion Bks.) HarperCollins Pubs.

Healy, Christopher. A Perilous Journey of Danger & Mayhem #1: a Dastardly Plot. 2018. (Perilous Journey of Danger & Mayhem Ser.: 1). (ENG.). (J). (gr. 3-7). 384p. 16.99 *(978-0-06-234197-6(9));* 400p. E-Book *(978-0-06-234199-0(5),* 9780062341990) HarperCollins Pubs. (Walden Pond Pr.).

Heller, Alyson. Touchdown! Ready-To-Read Level 1. Björkman, Steve & Björkman, Steve, illus. 2010. (After-School Sports Club Ser.). (ENG.). 32p. (J). (gr. -1-1). pap. 4.99 *(978-1-4169-9413-8(0),* Simon Spotlight) Simon Spotlight.

Hidden. 2014. (ENG., Illus.). 384p. (YA). (gr. 7). 17.99 *(978-1-4424-8300-2(8),* Simon & Schuster/Paula Wiseman Bks.) Simon & Schuster/Paula Wiseman Bks.

Holm, Jennifer L. Our Only May Amelia. 2019. (ENG., Illus.). 272p. (J). (gr. 3-7). pap. 9.99 *(978-0-06-288177-9(9),* HarperCollins) HarperCollins Pubs.

—Our Only May Amelia. unabr. ed. 2004. 253p. (J). (gr. 5-9). pap. 36.00 incl. audio *(978-0-8072-8366-0(5),* YA191SP, Listening Library) Random Hse. Audio Publishing Group.

—The Trouble with May Amelia. Gustavson, Adam, illus. (ENG.). 224p. (J). (gr. 3-7). 2012. pap. 5.99 *(978-1-4169-1374-0(2))*2. 2011. 17.99 *(978-1-4169-1373-3(4))* Simon & Schuster Children's Publishing. (Atheneum Bks. for Young Readers).

Howard, Elizabeth Fitzgerald. Virgie Goes to School with Us Boys. Lewis, E. B., illus. 2005. (gr. k-3). 18.00 *(978-0-7569-5088-0(0))* Perfection Learning Corp.

Jefferson, Joanne. Lightning & Blackberries, 1 vol. 2008. (ENG.). 186p. (J). (gr. 8-12). pap. 10.95 *(978-1-55109-654-4(4),* 5d828963-4abb-416d-b5fb-d9c30a459078) Nimbus Publishing, Ltd. CAN. Dist: Baker & Taylor Publisher Services (BTPS).

Johnson, Angela. Just Like Josh Gibson. Peck, Beth, illus. 2007. (J). 14.65 *(978-0-7569-8088-7(7))* Perfection Learning Corp.

—Just Like Josh Gibson. Peck, Beth, illus. (ENG.). 32p. (J). 2004. (gr. -1-2). 19.99 *(978-0-689-82628-3(1))* 2007. (gr. k-2). reprint ed. 8.99 *(978-1-4169-2728-0(X))* Simon & Schuster Bks. For Young Readers. (Simon & Schuster Bks. For Young Readers).

Jones Yang, Dori. Daughter of Xanadu. 2012. (ENG.). 352p. (YA). (gr. 7). pap. 9.99 *(978-0-385-73924-5(9),* Ember) Random Hse. Children's Bks.

Kahler, Alex R. Playing Wicked. Whitehouse, Ben, illus. 2020. (ENG.). 32p. (J). (gr. -1-3). 16.99 *(978-0-8075-8739-3(7),* 807587397) Whitman, Albert & Co.

Kay, Alan N. No Girls Allowed. 2003. (Young Heroes of History Ser.: Vol. 5). (Illus.). 140p. (J). pap. 6.95 *(978-1-57249-324-7(0),* White Mane Kids) White Mane Publishing Co., Inc.

Kellerhals-Stewart, Heather. Skookum Sal, Birling Gal. Blaine, Janice, illus. unabr. ed. 2003. (ENG.). 32p. (J). *(978-1-55017-285-0(9),* 1e2eff2c-7cc2-442f-ab71-ac66903cba23) Harbour Publishing Co., Ltd.

Kelly, Erin Entrada. Lalani of the Distant Sea. 2019. (ENG., Illus.). 400p. (J). (gr. 3-7). 16.99 *(978-0-06-274727-3(4),* Greenwillow Bks.) HarperCollins Pubs.

Kelly, Jacqueline. Counting Sheep: Calpurnia Tate, Girl Vet. White, Teagan & Meyer, Jennifer L., illus. 2017. (Calpurnia Tate, Girl Vet Ser.: 2). (ENG.). 128p. (J). pap. 6.99 *(978-1-250-12945-1(1),* 900161283) Square Fish.

—The Curious World of Calpurnia Tate. 2017. (Calpurnia Tate Ser.: 2). (J). lib. bdg. 18.40 *(978-0-606-39939-5(9))* Turtleback.

Kenneally, Miranda. Catching Jordan. (Hundred Oaks Ser.: 1). (YA). 2011. (ENG.). 288p. (gr. 7-12). pap. 14.99 *(978-1-4022-6227-2(2))* 2nd ed. 2020. 384p. (gr. 8-12). pap. 10.99 *(978-1-7282-1061-2(5))* Sourcebooks, Inc.

Kirsch, Vincent. From Archie to Zack. 2020. (ENG., Illus.). 40p. (J). (gr. -1-3). 17.99 *(978-1-4197-4367-2(8),* 1685701, Abrams Bks. for Young Readers) Abrams, Inc.

Kittinger, Jo S. Cuando Sea Grande. Lucas, Margeaux, illus. 2005. (Rookie Reader Español Ser.). (SPA.). 23p. (J). (gr. k-2). per. 4.95 *(978-0-516-24692-5(5),* Children's Pr.) Scholastic Library Publishing.

Kreie, Chris. The Extra Point. 2017. (Gridiron Ser.). (ENG.). 112p. (YA). (gr. 6-12). pap. 7.99 *(978-1-5124-5353-9(6),* a69990e5-5999-4950-8756-d26bf9597ba0); lib. bdg. 26.65 *(978-1-5124-3981-6(9),* c05bca7d-a773-4c86-bcdf-ad09f17f6750) Lerner Publishing Group. (Darby Creek).

Kupchella, Rick. Girls Can! Make it Happen. Brown, Marilyn, illus. 2004. (ENG.). 40p. (J). 16.95 *(978-0-9726504-3-4(1))* TRISTAN Publishing, Inc.

Lavender, William. Aftershocks. 2006. (ENG., Illus.). 352p. (YA). (gr. 7-12). 17.00 *(978-0-15-205882-1(6),* 1197660, Clarion Bks.) HarperCollins Pubs.

Lecesne, James. Trevor: A Novella. (Illus.). (J). (gr. 5-9). 2013. 112p. pap. 9.95 *(978-1-60980-487-9(2))* 2012. (ENG., 114p. 14.95 *(978-1-60980-420-6(1))* Seven Stories Pr. (Triangle Square).

Lee, Y. S. The Agency 2: the Body at the Tower. 2010. (Agency Ser.: 2). (ENG., Illus.). 352p. (YA). (gr. 7-18). 16.99 *(978-0-7636-4968-5(6))* Candlewick Pr.

—The Agency 3: the Traitor in the Tunnel. 2012. (Agency Ser.: 3). (ENG., Illus.). 384p. (YA). (gr. 7). 16.99 *(978-0-7636-5316-3(0))* Candlewick Pr.

—The Agency: a Spy in the House. 2016. (Agency Ser.: 1). (ENG.). 352p. (YA). (gr. 7). pap. 9.99 *(978-0-7636-8748-9(0))* Candlewick Pr.

—A Spy in the House, 1. 2010. (Agency Ser.: Bk. 1). (ENG., Illus.). 352p. (YA). (gr. 7-12). 22.44 *(978-0-7636-4067-5(0))* Candlewick Pr.

Liggett, Kim. The Grace Year: A Novel. (ENG., Illus.). 416p. (YA). 2020. pap. 11.99 *(978-1-250-14545-1(7),* 900181039) 2019. 16.99 *(978-1-250-14544-4(9),* 900181038) St. Martin's Pr. (Wednesday Bks.).

Lough, Amber. Open Fire. 2020. (ENG.). 264p. (YA). (gr. 6-12). 18.99 *(978-1-5415-7289-8(0),* 26390117-2d45-4720-a977-2ce45d9ddfb3, Carolrhoda Lab™) Lerner Publishing Group.

Lukoff, Kyle. Too Bright to See. (J). (gr. 5). 2022. 224p. 8.99 *(978-0-593-11117-8(6))* 2021. 192p. 17.99 *(978-0-593-11115-4(X))* Penguin Young Readers Group. (Dial Bks).

Luper, Eric. Jeremy Bender vs. the Cupcake Cadets. 2011. (ENG.). 240p. (J). (gr. 3-7). 16.99 *(978-0-06-201512-9(5),* Balzer & Bray) HarperCollins Pubs.

Mackall, Dandi Daley. A Girl Named Dan. Graef, Renée, illus. 2008. (ENG.). 32p. (J). (gr. 1-4). 16.95 *(978-1-58536-351-3(0),* 202138) Sleeping Bear Pr.

MacLeod, Jennifer Tzivia. Joan & the Secrets of the Universe. Brereton, Alice, illus. 2018. (J). *(978-1-5124-4437-7(5),* Kar-Ben Publishing) Lerner Publishing Group.

Maid of Deception. 2014. (Maids of Honor Ser.). (ENG., Illus.). 416p. (YA). (gr. 7). 17.99 *(978-1-4424-4141-5(0),* Simon & Schuster Bks. For Young Readers) Simon & Schuster Bks. For Young Readers.

Mann, J. Albert. What Every Girl Should Know: Margaret Sanger's Journey. (ENG.). (YA). (gr. 9). 2020. 256p. pap. 11.99 *(978-1-5344-1933-9(0))* 2019. (Illus.). 240p. 18.99 *(978-1-5344-1932-2(2))* Simon & Schuster Children's Publishing. (Atheneum Bks. for Young Readers).

Matas, Carol. Rosie in New York City: Gotcha! 2003. (ENG., Illus.). 128p. (J). (gr. 4-7). pap. 9.95 *(978-0-689-85714-0(4),* Simon & Schuster/Paula Wiseman Bks.) Simon & Schuster/Paula Wiseman Bks.

McCullough, Joy. Blood Water Paint. 2019. 320p. (YA). (gr. 9). pap. 11.99 *(978-0-7352-3213-6(X),* Penguin Books) Penguin Young Readers Group.

McElroy, Lisa Tucker. Love, Lizzie: Letters to a Military Mom. Paterson, Diane, illus. 2009. (ENG.). 32p. (J). (gr. -1-3). pap. 7.99 *(978-0-8075-4778-6(6),* 807547786) Whitman, Albert & Co.

McGowan, Jennifer. Maid of Secrets. (Maids of Honor Ser.). (ENG.). (YA). (gr. 7). 2014. 432p. pap. 9.99 *(978-1-4424-4139-2(9))* 2013. 416p. 17.99 *(978-1-4424-4138-5(0))* Simon & Schuster Bks. For Young Readers. (Simon & Schuster Bks. For Young Readers).

—Maid of Wonder. 2015. (Maids of Honor Ser.). (ENG., Illus.). 336p. (YA). (gr. 7). 17.99 *(978-1-4814-1826-3(2))* Simon & Schuster Children's Publishing.

McNamara, Margaret. The Dinosaur Expert. Karas, G. Brian, illus. 2018. (Mr. Tiffin's Classroom Ser.). 40p. (J). (gr. -1-3). 17.99 *(978-0-553-51143-7(2),* Schwartz & Wade Bks.) Random Hse. Children's Bks.

—Playground Problem: Ready-To-Read Level 1. Gordon, Mike, illus. 2004. (Robin Hill School Ser.). (ENG.). 32p. (J). (gr. -1-1). pap. 4.99 *(978-0-689-85876-5(0),* Simon Spotlight) Simon Spotlight.

Messner, Kate. Spitfire. 2007. (ENG.). (J). pap. *(978-1-59531-018-7(5))* North Country Bks., Inc.

Meyer, L. A. Boston Jacky: Being an Account of the Further Adventures of Jacky Faber, Taking Care of Business. 2015. (Bloody Jack Adventures Ser.: 11). (ENG.). 384p. (YA). (gr. 9). pap. 9.99 *(978-0-544-43914-6(7),* 1596825, Clarion Bks.) HarperCollins Pubs.

—The Mark of the Golden Dragon: Being an Account of the Further Adventures of Jacky Faber, Jewel of the East, Vexation of the West. 2013. (Bloody Jack Adventures Ser.: 9). (ENG.). 400p. (YA). (gr. 9). pap. 9.99 *(978-0-544-00328-6(4),* 1526370, Clarion Bks.) HarperCollins Pubs.

—The Mark of the Golden Dragon: Being an Account of the Further Adventures of Jacky Faber, Jewel of the East, Vexation of the West, & Pearl of the South China Sea. 2011. (Bloody Jack Adventures Ser.: 9). (ENG.). 384p. (YA). (gr. 9). 16.99 *(978-0-547-51764-3(5),* 1444890, Clarion Bks.) HarperCollins Pubs.

—The Wake of the Lorelei Lee: Being an Account of the Further Adventures of Jacky Faber, on Her Way to Botany Bay. 2012. (Bloody Jack Adventures Ser.: 8). (ENG.). 576p. (YA). (gr. 9). pap. 12.99 *(978-0-547-72194-1(3),* 1482451, Clarion Bks.) HarperCollins Pubs.

—The Wake of the Lorelei Lee: Being an Account of the Further Adventures of Jacky Faber, on Her Way to Botany Bay. 2010. (Bloody Jack Adventures Ser.: Bk. 8). audio compact disk 29.95 *(978-1-59316-484-3(X))* Listen & Live Audio, Inc.

Michiko Florence, Debbi. Jasmine Toguchi, Mochi Queen. Vukovic, Elizabet, illus. 2017. (Jasmine Toguchi Ser.: 1). (ENG.). 128p. (J). 15.99 *(978-0-374-30410-2(6),* 900158910, Farrar, Straus & Giroux (BYR)) Farrar, Straus & Giroux.

Miller, Bobbi. The Girls of Gettysburg. 2014. (ENG.). 160p. (J). (gr. 3-7). 16.95 *(978-0-8234-3163-2(0))* Holiday Hse., Inc.

Mortensen, Lori. The End Zone, 1 vol. Sullivan, Mary, illus. 2009. (My First Graphic Novel Ser.). (ENG.). 32p. (J). (gr. k-2). pap. 6.25 *(978-1-4342-1408-9(7),* 95686, Stone Arch Bks.) Capstone.

Murphy, Claire Rudolf. Marching with Aunt Susan: Susan B. Anthony & the Fight for Women's Suffrage, 1 vol. Schuett, Stacey, illus. 2011. 36p. (J). (gr. 1-4). 17.99 *(978-1-56145-593-5(8))* Peachtree Publishing Co. Inc.

Napoli, Donna Jo. Bound. 2006. (ENG., Illus.). 192p. (YA). (gr. 7-12). reprint ed. mass mkt. 7.99 *(978-0-689-86178-9(8),* Simon Pulse) Simon Pulse.

—Daughter of Venice. 2003. (ENG.). 288p. (YA). (gr. 7). mass mkt. 9.99 *(978-0-440-22928-5(6),* Laurel Leaf) Random Hse. Children's Bks.

Nix, Garth. Newt's Emerald. 2015. (ENG.). 304p. (YA). (gr. 8-12). 18.99 *(978-0-06-236004-5(3),* Tegen, Katherine Bks) HarperCollins Pubs.

Nixon, Joan Lowery. Ann's Story, 1747. 2004. (J). *(978-0-87935-198-4(5))* Colonial Williamsburg Foundation.

—Maria's Story, 1773. 2004. (J). *(978-0-87935-227-1(2))* Colonial Williamsburg Foundation.

Not Every Princess. 2014. (ENG., Illus.). 32p. (J). *(978-1-4338-1647-5(4),* Magination Pr.) American Psychological Assn.

Osborne, Mary Pope. La Hora de Los Juegos Olimpicos. Brovelli, Marcela, tr. Murdocca, Sal, illus. 2007. (Casa del Arbol Ser.: 16).Tr. of Hour of the Olympics Games. (ENG & SPA.). 68p. (J). per. 6.99 *(978-1-933032-22-1(7))* Lectorum Pubns., Inc.

—Hour of the Olympics. unabr. ed. 2004. (Magic Tree House Ser.: No. 16). 70p. (J). (gr. k-3). pap. 17.00 incl. audio *(978-0-8072-0785-7(3),* LFTR 244 SP, Listening Library) Random Hse. Audio Publishing Group.

Ostertag, Molly Knox. The Witch Boy: a Graphic Novel (the Witch Boy Trilogy #1) 2017. (Witch Boy Ser.). (ENG., Illus.). 224p. (J). (gr. 3-7). 27.99 *(978-1-338-08952-3(8));* pap. 12.99 *(978-1-338-08951-6(X))* Scholastic, Inc. (Graphix).

Ostrom, Melissa. The Beloved Wild. 2018. (ENG.). 320p. (YA). 29.99 *(978-1-250-13279-6(7),* 900177171) Feiwel & Friends.

Park, Linda Sue. Seesaw Girl. Tseng, Mou-Sien & Tseng, Jean, illus. 2009. (ENG.). 96p. (J). (gr. 3-7). pap. 8.99 *(978-0-547-24888-2(1),* 1100900, Clarion Bks.) HarperCollins Pubs.

Parker, Natalie C. Seafire. (Seafire Ser.: 1). (ENG.). (YA). (gr. 7). 2019. 400p. pap. 11.99 *(978-0-451-47882-5(7))* 2018. 384p. 18.99 *(978-0-451-47880-1(0))* Penguin Young Readers Group. (Razorbill).

Pau Preto, Nicki. Crown of Feathers. 2019. (Crown of Feathers Ser.). (ENG., Illus.). 496p. (YA). (gr. 7). 21.99 *(978-1-5344-2462-3(8),* Simon Pulse) Simon Pulse.

Pearce, Jackson. Ellie, Engineer: in the Spotlight. 2019. (Ellie, Engineer Ser.). (ENG., Illus.). 208p. (J). 16.99 *(978-1-5476-0185-1(X),* 900203119, Bloomsbury Children's Bks.) Bloomsbury Publishing USA.

—Ellie, Engineer: the Next Level. (Ellie, Engineer Ser.). (ENG., Illus.). (J). 2019. 208p. pap. 7.99 *(978-1-5476-0206-3(6),* 900203290) 2018. 192p. 15.99 *(978-1-68119-521-6(6),* 900175873) Bloomsbury Publishing USA. (Bloomsbury Children's Bks.).

Pearlman, Robb. Pink Is for Boys. Kaban, Eda, illus. 2018. (ENG.). 40p. (J). (gr. -1-3). 18.99 *(978-0-7624-6247-6(7),* Running Pr. Kids) Running Pr.

Perkins, Mitali. Rickshaw Girl. Hogan, Jamie, illus. 96p. (J). (gr. 2-5). 2008. (ENG.). pap. 7.99 *(978-1-58089-309-1(0))* 2007. 14.95 *(978-1-58089-308-4(2))* Charlesbridge Publishing, Inc.

Pierce, Tamora. Alanna: The First Adventure. 1. Heyer, illus. 2011. (Song of the Lioness Ser.: Bk. 1). (ENG.). 240p. (J). (gr. 7-12). 26.19 *(978-0-689-85323-4(8))* Simon & Schuster, Inc.

—Lioness Rampant. 2011. (Song of the Lioness Ser.: 4). (ENG., Illus.). 368p. (YA). (gr. 7). pap. 12.99 *(978-1-4424-2766-2(3),* Atheneum Bks. for Young Readers) Simon & Schuster Children's Publishing.

—Mastiff, 3. 2012. (Beka Cooper Ser.: Bk. 3). (ENG.). 608p. (J). (gr. 7-12). lib. bdg. 26.19 *(978-0-375-91470-6(6))* Random Hse. Bks. for Young Readers.

—The Woman Who Rides Like a Man. (Song of the Lioness Ser.: 3). (ENG., Illus.). (YA). (gr. 7). 2014. 288p. 22.99 *(978-1-4814-3962-6(6))* 2011. 272p. pap. 12.99 *(978-1-4424-2765-5(5))* Simon & Schuster Children's Publishing. (Atheneum Bks. for Young Readers).

Pryor, Bonnie. Captain Hannah Pritchard: The Hunt for Pirate Gold, 1 vol. 2012. (Historical Fiction Adventures Ser.). (ENG., Illus.). 160p. (J). (gr. 3-5). pap. 13.88 *(978-1-59845-283-9(5),* 249245aa-07ef-41ea-a6ac-68d5be3db404); lib. bdg. 31.93 *(978-0-7660-3817-2(3),* d1bf7ad2-c916-402c-ba83-61c0f084aac6) Enslow Publishing, LLC.

—Hannah Pritchard: Pirate of the Revolution, 1 vol. 2008. (Historical Fiction Adventures Ser.). (ENG., Illus.). 160p. (J). (gr. 3-5). lib. bdg. 31.93 *(978-0-7660-2851-7(8),* 26121413-8628-47dc-9a2d-81661c6d5db1) Enslow Publishing, LLC.

—Pirate Hannah Pritchard: Captured!, 1 vol. 2010. (Historical Fiction Adventures Ser.). (ENG., Illus.). 160p. (J). (gr. 3-5). lib. bdg. 31.93 *(978-0-7660-3310-8(4),* 03ee45a8-be09-4257-aaca-0cd2071fb5cf) Enslow Publishing, LLC.

Qamar, Amjed. Beneath My Mother's Feet. (ENG.). 208p. (YA). (gr. 7). 2011. pap. 12.99 *(978-1-4424-1451-8(0))* 2008. 16.99 *(978-1-4169-4728-8(0))* Simon & Schuster Children's Publishing. (Atheneum Bks. for Young Readers).

Quinn, Jordan. Let the Games Begin! McPhillips, Robert, illus. 2015. (Kingdom of Wrenly Ser.: 7). (ENG.). 128p. (J). (gr. k-4). pap. 6.99 *(978-1-4814-2379-3(7),* Little Simon) Little Simon.

Railey, Shawna. The Messy Life of Blue. 2020. (ENG.). 240p. (J). (gr. 3-7). 16.99 *(978-1-4998-1025-7(3),* Yellow Jacket) Bonnier Publishing USA.

Redgate, Riley. Noteworthy. 2017. (ENG.). 400p. (YA). (gr. 8-17). 17.95 *(978-1-4197-2373-5(1),* 1164601, Amulet Bks.) Abrams, Inc.

Reedy, Trent. Words in the Dust. 2013. (ENG.). 272p. (J). (gr. 5-9). pap. 8.99 *(978-0-545-26126-5(0),* Levine, Arthur A. Bks.) Scholastic, Inc.

Rees, Celia. Sovay. 2010. (ENG.). 432p. (YA). (gr. 7). pap. 9.99 *(978-1-59990-483-2(7),* 900066312, Bloomsbury USA Childrens) Bloomsbury Publishing USA.

—Sovay. 2009. 1.00 *(978-1-4074-4516-8(2))* Recorded Bks., Inc.

Reeve, Philip. Fever Crumb (the Fever Crumb Trilogy, Book 1), Bk. 1. 2011. (Fever Crumb Ser.: 1). (ENG.). 336p. (YA). (gr. 7-7). pap. 12.99 *(978-0-545-22215-0(X))* Scholastic, Inc.

Reich, Susanna. Penelope Bailey Takes the Stage, 1 vol. 2006. (ENG.). 32p. (J). (gr. 3-7). 16.95 *(978-0-7614-5287-4(7))* Marshall Cavendish Corp.

Rennert, Laura Joy. Royal Princess Academy: Dragon Dreams. Florian, Melanie, illus. 2012. (Royal Princess Academy Ser.). (ENG.). 112p. (J). (gr. 1-4). 18.69 *(978-0-8037-3750-1(5))* Penguin Young Readers Group.

Rinaldi, Ann. The Family Greene. 2011. (ENG.). 256p. (YA). (gr. 7). pap. 14.95 *(978-0-547-57723-4(0),* 1458519, Clarion Bks.) HarperCollins Pubs.

Russo, Meredith. If I Was Your Girl. 2018. (YA). lib. bdg. 22.10 *(978-0-606-41084-7(8))* Turtleback.

Salisbury, Linda G. The Wild Women of Lake Anna: A Bailey Fish Adventure. 2005. (Illus.). 159p. (J). *(978-1-881539-37-7(7))* Tabby Hse. Bks.

Sass, A. J. Ana on the Edge. 2020. (ENG.). 384p. (J). (gr. 3-7). 16.99 *(978-0-316-45861-0(9))* Little, Brown Bks. for Young Readers.

Scott, Kate. Spies in Disguise: Boy in Tights. 2016. (ENG., Illus.). 192p. (J). (gr. 1-5). pap. 7.99 *(978-1-63450-689-2(8),* Sky Pony Pr.) Skyhorse Publishing Co., Inc.

Searching for Silverheels. 2014. (ENG., Illus.). 304p. (J). (gr. 5-9). 16.99 *(978-1-4814-0029-9(0),* McElderry, Margaret K. Bks.) McElderry, Margaret K. Bks.

Selfors, Suzanne. A Semi-Charming Kind of Life. 2015. (Ever after High Ser.: Bk. 3). (ENG., Illus.). 224p. (J). E-Book *(978-0-316-40135-7(8))* Little Brown & Co.

Shickman, Allan Richard. Zan-Gah: A Prehistoric Adventure. 2007. 160p. (J). (gr. 4-7). per. 9.95 *(978-0-9790357-0-8(8))* Earthshaker Bks.

Simmons, Kristen. The Glass Arrow. 2016. (ENG.). 352p. (YA). pap. 18.99 *(978-0-7653-3664-4(2),* 900121071, Tor Teen) Doherty, Tom Assocs., LLC.

Skinner, Constance Lindsay. Becky Landers: Frontier Warrior. 2006. (Living History Library). (ENG.). 198p. (J). (gr. 4-6). per. 12.95 *(978-1-932350-06-7(3))* Ignatius Pr.

Sleiman, Dina L. Chivalrous. 2015. (Valiant Hearts Ser.: 2). (ENG.). 360p. (YA). pap. 16.00 *(978-0-7642-1313-7(X))* Bethany Hse. Pubs.

Smith, Lane. Madam President. Smith, Lane, illus. 2008. (ENG., Illus.). 40p. (J). (gr. -1-3). 16.99 *(978-1-4231-0846-7(9))* Hyperion Pr.

—Madam President. 2011. (J). (gr. 1-4). 29.95 *(978-0-545-10688-7(5))* Weston Woods Studios, Inc.

Smith, Matthew Ross. Lizzy Legend. 2019. (ENG., Illus.). 240p. (J). (gr. 3-7). 17.99 *(978-1-5344-2024-3(X),* Aladdin) Simon & Schuster Children's Publishing.

Snow, Maya. Blade's Edge. 2009. 245p. (J). lib. bdg. 17.89 *(978-0-06-124391-2(4))* HarperCollins Pubs.

—Sisters of the Sword. 2008. (Sisters of the Sword Ser.). (J). (gr. 5-18). 288p. 16.99 *(978-0-06-124387-5(6));* 275p. lib. bdg. 17.89 *(978-0-06-124388-2(4))* HarperCollins Pubs.

Spinelli, Jerry. There's a Girl in My Hammerlock. 2008. 199p. (gr. 4-8). 16.00 *(978-0-7569-8465-6(3))* Perfection Learning Corp.

Spinner, Stephanie. Quiver. 2005. 192p. (YA). (gr. 7). reprint ed. per. 5.99 *(978-0-440-23819-5(6),* Laurel Leaf) Random Hse. Children's Bks.

Stanley, Diane. Bella at Midnight. Ibatoulline, Bagram, illus. 2007. (ENG.). 304p. (J). (gr. 3-7). pap. 7.99 *(978-0-06-077575-9(0)*, HarperCollins) HarperCollins Pubs.
Staples, Suzanne Fisher. Haveli. 2012. (Shabanu Ser.). 336p. (YA). (gr. 7). pap. 9.99 *(978-0-307-97789-2(7)*, Ember) Random Hse. Children's Bks.
—Haveli. 2006. 21.50 *(978-0-8446-7291-5(2))* Smith, Peter Pub., Inc.
—The House of Djinn. 2012. (Shabanu Ser.). (ENG.). 224p. (YA). (gr. 7). pap. 8.99 *(978-0-307-97642-0(4)*, Ember) Random Hse. Children's Bks.
—Shabanu: Daughter of the Wind. 3rd ed. (J). pap. 3.99 *(978-0-13-800053-0(0))* Prentice Hall (Schl. Div.).
—Shabanu: Daughter of the Wind. 2012. (Shabanu Ser.). (Illus.). 288p. (YA). (gr. 7). pap. 10.99 *(978-0-307-97788-5(9)*, Ember) Random Hse. Children's Bks.
Stewart, Jennifer J. Close Encounters of a Third World Kind. 2004. (ENG.). 128p. (J). (gr. 4-6). tchr. ed. 16.95 *(978-0-8234-1850-3(2))* Holiday Hse., Inc.
—Close Encounters of a Third-World Kind. 2008. (ENG., Illus.). 181p. (J). (gr. 3-7). 6.95 *(978-0-8234-2161-9(9))* Holiday Hse., Inc.
Stolz, Joelle. The Shadows of Ghadames. 2006. (ENG.). 128p. (J). (gr. 3-7). 5.99 *(978-0-440-41949-5(2)*, Yearling) Random Hse. Children's Bks.
Stratton-Porter, Gene. A Daughter of the Land. 2017. (ENG., Illus.). (J). 27.95 *(978-1-374-91652-4(8))*; pap. 17.95 *(978-1-374-91651-7(X))* Capital Communications, Inc.
—A Daughter of the Land. 2017. (ENG., Illus.). (J). pap. 19.95 *(978-1-376-05950-2(9))* Creative Media Partners, LLC.
—A Daughter of the Land. 2008. pap. *(978-1-84830-034-7(4)*, Wildhern Pr.) Echo Library.
—A Daughter of the Land. 2007. 340p. 22.95 *(978-1-934169-46-9(3))*; pap. 11.95 *(978-1-934169-47-6(1))* Norilana Bks.
Sykes, Shelley & Szymanski, Lois. A Whisper of War. 2003. (J). 5.95 *(978-1-57249-327-8(5)*, White Mane Kids) White Mane Publishing Co., Inc.
Theule, Larissa. Born to Ride: A Story about Bicycle Face. Garrity-Riley, Kelsey, illus. 2019. (ENG.). 32p. (J). (gr. -1-3). 18.99 *(978-1-4197-3412-0(1)*, 1207001, Abrams Bks. for Young Readers) Abrams, Inc.
Thomas, Carroll. The Town on Rambling Creek: A Matty Trescott Novel. 2004. (Illus.). ix, 185p. (J). *(978-1-57525-376-3(3))* Smith & Kraus Pubs., Inc.
Thomas, Carroll, creator. Under the Open Sky: A Matty Trescott Novel. 2005. (Illus.). 184p. (J). per. 12.95 *(978-0-9762091-2-6(8))* Antrim Hse.
Trent, Tiffany. The Unnaturalists. 2013. (ENG., Illus.). 336p. (YA). (gr. 7). pap. 9.99 *(978-1-4424-2207-0(6)*, Simon & Schuster Bks. For Young Readers) Simon & Schuster Bks. For Young Readers.
Underwood, Deborah. Interstellar Cinderella: (Princess Books for Kids, Books about Science) Hunt, Meg, illus. 2015. (Future Fairy Tales Ser.). (ENG.). 40p. (J). (gr. -1-k). 17.99 *(978-1-4521-2532-9(5))* Chronicle Bks. LLC.
—Ogilvy. McBeth, T. L., illus. 2019. (ENG.). 40p. (J). 18.99 *(978-1-250-15176-6(7)*, 900183400, Holt, Henry & Co. Bks. For Young Readers) Holt, Henry & Co.
Walter, Mildred Pitts. Justin & the Best Biscuits in the World. Stock, Catherine, illus. 2010. (ENG.). 144p. (J). (gr. 3-7). pap. 9.99 *(978-0-06-195891-5(3)*, Amistad) HarperCollins Pubs.
—Justin & the Best Biscuits in the World. 2011. 8.32 *(978-0-7848-3586-9(1)*, Everbind) Marco Bk. Co.
Weil, Sylvie. Elvina's Mirror. 2009. (ENG.). 150p. (gr. 5-18). pap. 14.00 *(978-0-8276-0885-6(3))* Jewish Pubn. Society.
—My Guardian Angel. Rosner, Gillian, tr. 2014. (ENG., Illus.). 208p. (J). pap. 14.95 *(978-0-8276-1211-2(7))* Jewish Pubn. Society.
West, Kasie. On the Fence. 2014. (ENG.). 304p. (YA). (gr. 8). pap. 11.99 *(978-0-06-223567-1(2)*, HarperTeen) HarperCollins Pubs.
Weston Woods Staff, creator. Players in Pigtails. 2004. 29.95 *(978-0-7882-0518-7(8))* Weston Woods Studios, Inc.
Whelan, Gloria. Chu Ju's House. 2004. 240p. (J). (gr. 5-18). lib. bdg. 17.89 *(978-0-06-050725-1(X))* HarperCollins Pubs.
Whitney, Kim Ablon. See You down the Road. 14.85 *(978-0-7569-5710-0(9))* Perfection Learning Corp.
Wiles, Deborah. The Aurora County All-Stars. 2009. (ENG., Illus.). 256p. (J). (gr. 2-5). pap. 7.99 *(978-0-15-206626-0(8)*, 1063363, Clarion Bks.) HarperCollins Pubs.
Williams, Susan. Wind Rider. 2006. 309p. (J). (gr. 5-9). 16.99 *(978-0-06-087236-6(5))* HarperCollins Pubs.
Wilson, Diane Lee. Firehorse. (ENG.). 336p. (YA). (gr. 7). 2010. pap. 8.99 *(978-1-4424-0331-4(4))* 2006. (Illus.). 17.99 *(978-1-4169-1551-5(6))* McElderry, Margaret K. Bks. (McElderry, Margaret K. Bks.).
Yeung Russell, Ching. The Tofu Quilt. 2009. (ENG.). 144p. (J). (gr. 3-8). 16.95 *(978-1-60060-423-2(4))* Lee & Low Bks., Inc.
—Tofu Quilt, 1 vol. 2017. (ENG.). 136p. (J). (gr. 3-7). pap. 13.95 *(978-1-62014-354-4(2)*, leelowbooks) Lee & Low Bks., Inc.
Yolen, Jane & Stemple, Heidi E. Y. Not All Princesses Dress in Pink. Lanquetin, Anne-Sophie, illus. 2010. (ENG.). 32p. (J). (gr. -1-3). 17.99 *(978-1-4169-8018-6(0)*, Simon & Schuster Bks. For Young Readers) Simon & Schuster Bks. For Young Readers.
Zielin, Lara. Donut Days. 2010. (ENG.). 256p. (YA). (gr. 6-8). 22.44 *(978-0-399-25066-8(2))* Penguin Young Readers Group.

SEXUAL ABSTINENCE

Ascension Press, creator. Theology of the Body for Teens Student Workbook: Discovering God's Plan for Love & Life. 2006. (Illus.). 210p. per. 14.95 *(978-1-932927-86-3(7))* Ascension Pr.
Gitchel, Sam & Foster, Lorri. Let's Talk about S-E-X: A Guide for Kids 9 to 12 & Their Parents. 2nd ed. 2005. (ENG., Illus.). 100p. pap. 9.99 *(978-1-931863-18-6(0))* Book Peddlers.
Rose, Lyman Hinckley. Pure & Chased. 2004. ix, 86p. pap. 7.95 *(978-1-55517-774-4(3))* Cedar Fort, Inc./CFI Distribution.
Stenzel, Pam. Sex Has a Price Tag: Discussions about Sexuality, Spirituality, & Self-Respect, 1 vol. 2015. (ENG.). 144p. (YA). pap. 9.99 *(978-0-310-74885-4(2))* Zondervan.
The True Love Waits Youth Bible. 2004. (Illus.). 1294p. pap. 19.99 *(978-1-55819-621-6(8))* B&H Publishing Group.

SEXUAL ABSTINENCE—FICTION

Hebert, Marie-Francine. This Side of the Sky, 1 vol. Ourlou, Susan, tr. 2006. (ENG.). 112p. (YA). (gr. 9-18). per. 6.95 *(978-0-88995-369-7(4)*, 6769f377-a38f-45b0-b953-5cf946544e52) Trifolium Bks., Inc. CAN. Dist: Firefly Bks., Ltd.

SEXUAL EDUCATION

see Sex Instruction

SEXUAL ETHICS

see also Birth Control

Dennis, Rainey. Passport 2 Purity. 2004. 29.99 *(978-1-57229-656-5(9))* FamilyLife.
Denton, Michelle. Rape Culture: How Can We End It?, 1 vol. 2017. (Hot Topics Ser.). (ENG.). 104p. (YA). (gr. 7-7). pap. 20.99 *(978-1-5345-6292-9(3)*, b808f388-fa77-4bd2-89bb-e17a27d47ca7); lib. bdg. 41.03 *(978-1-5345-6207-3(9)*, 51b2a8d2-3058-4886-9240-3787614e5f98) Greenhaven Publishing LLC. (Lucent Pr.).
Feinstein, Stephen. Sexuality & Teens: What You Should Know about Sex, Abstinence, Birth Control, Pregnancy, & STDs, 1 vol. 2010. (Issues in Focus Today Ser.). (ENG., Illus.). 104p. (gr. 6-7). lib. bdg. 35.93 *(978-0-7660-3312-2(0)*, 63a283a4-5717-4f01-8da3-5a3e9c2d21da) Enslow Publishing, LLC.
Gilbert, Laura. Everything You Need to Know about Compulsive Sexual Behavior. 2009. (Need to Know Library). 64p. (gr. 5-5). 58.50 *(978-1-60854-059-4(6))* Rosen Publishing Group, Inc., The.
Jamiolkowski, Raymond M. A Baby Doesn't Make the Man: Alternative Sources of Power & Manhood for Young Men. 2009. (Teen Pregnancy Prevention Library). 64p. (gr. 5-5). 58.50 *(978-1-60854-244-4(0))* Rosen Publishing Group, Inc., The.
Lickona, Tom & Lickona, Judy. Sex, Love & You: Making the Right Decision. rev. ed. 2003. (Illus.). 192p. (YA). pap. 15.95 *(978-0-87793-987-0(X))* Ave Maria Pr.
Marcovitz, Hal. Teens & Sex. 2008. (Gallup Youth Survey, Major Issues & Trends Ser.). (Illus.). 112,128p. (YA). (gr. 7-9). lib. bdg. 22.95 *(978-1-59084-722-0(9))* Mason Crest.
Mooney, Carla. Everything You Need to Know about Sexual Consent, 1 vol. 2017. (Need to Know Library). (ENG., Illus.). 64p. (J). (gr. 5-6). 36.13 *(978-1-5081-7412-7(1)*, 5a1239c5-59f4-48d8-bad2-aa25d6b19c20); pap. 13.95 *(978-1-5081-7410-3(5)*, c6007614-5526-4901-8454-9f172a11b561) Rosen Publishing Group, Inc., The. (Rosen Young Adult).
Nakaya, Andrea C. Teens & Sex. 2015. (J). *(978-1-60152-912-1(0))* ReferencePoint Pr., Inc.
Rose, Lyman Hinckley. Pure & Chased. 2004. ix, 86p. pap. 7.95 *(978-1-55517-774-4(3))* Cedar Fort, Inc./CFI Distribution.
The True Love Waits Youth Bible. 2004. (Illus.). 1294p. pap. 19.99 *(978-1-55819-621-6(8))* B&H Publishing Group.

SEXUAL ETHICS—FICTION

Hamilton, Elizabeth L. Date with Responsibility. 2004. (Character-in-Action Ser.: No. 2). (Illus.). 384p. (YA). per. 19.95 *(978-0-9713749-0-4(2)*, Character-in-Action) Quiet Impact, Inc.
Ruditis, Paul. Rainbow Party. 2005. (ENG.). 256p. (YA). (gr. 9-18). pap. 12.95 *(978-1-4169-0235-5(X)*, Simon Pulse) Simon Pulse.

SEXUAL HARASSMENT

Bouchard, Elizabeth. Everything You Need to Know about Sexual Harassment. 2009. (Need to Know Library). 64p. (gr. 5-5). 58.50 *(978-1-60854-085-3(5))* Rosen Publishing Group, Inc., The.
Currie, Stephen. Thinking Critically: Sexual Harassment. 2018. (Thinking Critically Ser.). (ENG.). 80p. (YA). (gr. 6-12). 39.93 *(978-1-68282-443-6(8))* ReferencePoint Pr., Inc.
Gillard, Arthur, ed. Sexual Harassment, 1 vol. 2014. (Issues That Concern You Ser.). (ENG., Illus.). 120p. (gr. 7-10). lib. bdg. 43.63 *(978-0-7377-6933-3(5)*, ec03f732-fbcc-4d3b-bad4-a6b6953ce6b5, Greenhaven Publishing) Greenhaven Publishing LLC.
Harris, Duchess. Sexism in the Media. 2017. (Being Female in America Ser.). (ENG.). 112p. (J). (gr. 6-12). lib. bdg. 41.36 *(978-1-5321-1311-6(0)*, 27519, Essential Library) ABDO Publishing Co.
Harris, Duchess & Morris, Rebecca. The Silence Breakers & the #MeToo Movement. 2018. (Special Reports). (ENG., Illus.). 112p. (J). (gr. 6-12). lib. bdg. 41.36 *(978-1-5321-1683-4(7)*, 30618, Essential Library) ABDO Publishing Co.
Harris, Duchess & Zuchora-Walske, Christine. Sexism in Politics. 2017. (Being Female in America Ser.). (ENG., Illus.). 112p. (J). (gr. 6-12). lib. bdg. 41.36 *(978-1-5321-1310-9(2)*, 27518, Essential Library) ABDO Publishing Co.
Keyser, Amber J. No More Excuses: Dismantling Rape Culture. 2019. (ENG., Illus.). 144p. (YA). (gr. 8-12). 37.32 *(978-1-5415-4020-0(4)*, 0f66f534-2e67-4337-b1be-8f33c7f62b6a, Twenty-First Century Bks.) Lerner Publishing Group.
Lindin, Emily. UnSlut: A Diary & a Memoir. 2015. (ENG., Illus.). 272p. (YA). (gr. 9-12). 14.99 *(978-1-942186-00-7(2)*, 5d5e5227-8b5d-4bd2-b66e-fbbc818a2dbe, Zest Bks.) Lerner Publishing Group.
Miller, Caitlyn. Dealing with Sexual Harassment, 1 vol. 2019. (Helping Yourself, Helping Others Ser.). (ENG.). 112p. (gr. 7-7). pap. 20.99 *(978-1-5026-4632-3(3)*, f34d9b8a-309b-420b-8562-a6632eeae988) Cavendish Square Publishing LLC.
Parks, Peggy. Sex Discrimination. 2018. (Discrimination in Society Ser.). (ENG.). 80p. (YA). (gr. 6-12). 39.93 *(978-1-68282-389-7(X))* ReferencePoint Pr., Inc.
Parks, Peggy J. The #MeToo Movement. 2020. (ENG.). 80p. (YA). (gr. 6-12). 41.27 *(978-1-68282-761-1(5))* ReferencePoint Pr., Inc.
Poole, H. W. Preventing Sexual Assault & Harassment. 2019. (Sexual Violence & Harassment Ser.). (Illus.). 80p. (J). (gr. 12). lib. bdg. 34.60 *(978-1-4222-4203-2(X))* Mason Crest.
Radley, Gail & Harris, Duchess. Sexism at Work. 2017. (Being Female in America Ser.). (ENG., Illus.). 112p. (J). (gr. 6-12). lib. bdg. 41.36 *(978-1-5321-1309-3(9)*, 27517, Essential Library) ABDO Publishing Co.
Tamar's Dilemma: An Overview of Sexual Exploitation. 2003. 32p. (YA). per. *(978-0-9746327-0-4(8)*, 1196490) Trammel, Crystal.

SEXUAL HARASSMENT—FICTION

Banting, Celia. I only said I was telling the Truth. 2006. 240p. (YA). per. 14.99 *(978-0-9786648-4-8(1))* Wighita Pr.
Conford, Ellen. To All My Fans, with Love, From Sylvie. 2013. (ENG.). 200p. (gr. 4). pap. 12.95 *(978-1-939601-01-8(0))* Ig Publishing, Inc.
Dee, Barbara. Maybe He Just Likes You. 2019. (ENG., Illus.). 304p. (J). (gr. 4-8). 19.99 *(978-1-5344-3237-6(X)*, Simon & Schuster/Paula Wiseman Bks.) Simon & Schuster/Paula Wiseman Bks.
Torres, J. Degrassi The Next Generation Extra Credit Turning Japanese. 2006. (Degrassi the Next Generation Ser.). (ENG., Illus.). 120p. (J). pap. *(978-1-55168-318-8(0))* Fenn, H. B. & Co., Ltd.
West-Smith, Sandy. Who Will Teach Johnny: The Difference Between Good Touches & Bad Touches? 2006. (Illus.). 19p. (J). (gr. -1-2). pap. *(978-1-56167-914-0(3))* American Literary Pr.
Woodson, Marion. Charlotte's Vow. 2006. (ENG.). 144p. (J). (gr. 4). pap., tchr. ed. 8.95 *(978-0-88878-413-1(9))* Dundurn Pr. CAN. Dist: Publishers Group West (PGW).

SEXUALLY TRANSMITTED DISEASES

Ambrose, Marylou & Deisler, Veronica. Investigating STDs (Sexually Transmitted Diseases) Real Facts for Real Lives, 1 vol. 2010. (Investigating Diseases Ser.). (ENG., Illus.). 160p. (gr. 9-10). 38.60 *(978-0-7660-3342-9(2)*, c9d16c19-003d-476e-bd6a-abcf6f9d2721) Enslow Publishing, LLC.
—Sexually Transmitted Diseases: Examining STDs, 1 vol. 2014. (Diseases, Disorders, Symptoms Ser.). (ENG., Illus.). 96p. (gr. 9-10). 31.61 *(978-1-62293-080-7(0)*, 7f09b70c-1c64-4c0c-8eef-a37c2b925948); pap. 13.88 *(978-1-62293-081-4(9)*, f0ee17cf-17a4-4858-83de-3507902f34c1) Enslow Publishing, LLC.
Cefrey, Holly. Syphilis & Other Sexually Transmitted Diseases. 2009. (Epidemics Ser.). 64p. (gr. 5-5). 58.50 *(978-1-61512-303-2(2))* Rosen Publishing Group, Inc., The.
Collins, Nicholas & Woods, Samuel G. Frequently Asked Questions about STDs, 1 vol. 2011. (FAQ: Teen Life Ser.). (ENG.). 64p. (J). (gr. 5-6). lib. bdg. 37.13 *(978-1-4488-4630-6(7)*, 73dda564-f6d3-4904-ba7d-e6b56b529573) Rosen Publishing Group, Inc., The.
Egendorf, Laura K., ed. Sexually Transmitted Diseases, 1 vol. 2007. (At Issue Ser.). (ENG.). 104p. (gr. 10-12). pap. 28.80 *(978-0-7377-1976-5(1)*, a9fe2d92-579a-4491-bc1f-05bf1318829a); (Illus.). lib. bdg. 41.03 *(978-0-7377-1975-8(3)*, d08fd578-cb6c-4682-9d10-735adbbca4d3) Greenhaven Publishing LLC. (Greenhaven Publishing).
Farris Naff, Clay, ed. Sexually Transmitted Diseases, 1 vol. 2008. (Perspectives on Diseases & Disorders Ser.). (ENG., Illus.). 168p. (gr. 10-12). lib. bdg. 45.93 *(978-0-7377-4248-0(8)*, 45becea4-1939-4cb4-bd8f-4bed52bf33b0, Greenhaven Publishing) Greenhaven Publishing LLC.
Haugen, David M., et al, eds. Sexually Transmitted Diseases, 1 vol. 2014. (Introducing Issues with Opposing Viewpoints Ser.). (ENG., Illus.). 136p. (gr. 7-10). lib. bdg. 43.63 *(978-0-7377-6928-9(9)*, 9272e166-feb5-457e-a647-16fe49eef7fa, Greenhaven Publishing) Greenhaven Publishing LLC.
Hunter, Miranda & Hunter, William. Sexually Transmitted Infections. McDonnell, Mary Ann & Forman, Sara, eds. 2013. (Young Adult's Guide to the Science of Health Ser.: 15). 128p. (J). (gr. 7-18). 24.95 *(978-1-4222-2814-2(2))* Mason Crest.
—Sexually Transmitted Infections. Forman, Sara & McDonnell, Mary Ann, eds. 2013. (Young Adult's Guide to the Science of Health Ser.). (Illus.). 128p. (J). (gr. 7-18). pap. 14.95 *(978-1-4222-3007-7(4))* Mason Crest.
Kolesnikow, Tassia. Sexually Transmitted Diseases. 2003. (Diseases & Disorders Ser.). (Illus.). 112p. (J). (gr. 6-9). 32.45 *(978-1-56006-910-2(4)*, Lucent Bks.) Cengage Gale.
Michaud, Christopher. Gonorrhea. (Library of Sexual Health Ser.). 64p. (gr. 6-6). 2009. 58.50 *(978-1-60853-845-4(1))* 2006. (ENG., Illus.). (YA). lib. bdg. 37.13 *(978-1-4042-0908-4(5)*, d8c23d12-c5d9-4e58-bc55-6822c6167162) Rosen Publishing Group, Inc., The.
Planned Parenthood Federation of America, Inc. Staff. The Condom. 2003. (YA). pap. 3.00 net. *(978-0-934586-80-1(2))* Planned Parenthood Federation of America, Inc.
—Sexually Transmitted Infections: The Facts. 2003. (YA). pap. 3.00 net. *(978-0-934586-82-5(9))* Planned Parenthood Federation of America, Inc.
Saulmon, Greg. Genital Herpes. 2009. (Library of Sexual Health Ser.). 64p. (gr. 6-6). 58.50 *(978-1-60853-844-7(3))* Rosen Publishing Group, Inc., The.
Slade, Suzanne. The Phases of the Moon, 1 vol. 2007. (Cycles in Nature Ser.). (ENG., Illus.). 24p. (YA). (gr. 3-3). lib. bdg. 26.27 *(978-1-4042-3488-8(8)*, 1cce415b-79c9-45ad-8a2f-b70c02dbe5dc) Rosen Publishing Group, Inc., The.
Strehle Hartman, Ashley. Teens & STDs. 2018. (Teen Health & Safety Ser.). (ENG.). 80p. (YA). (gr. 6-12). 39.93 *(978-1-68282-513-6(2))* ReferencePoint Pr., Inc.
WHO Regional Office for the Western Pacific. Responding to Questions about the 100% Condom Use Programme: A Job Aid for Programme Staff. 2nd rev. ed. 2009. (Public Health Ser.). (ENG.). 49p. pap. 12.00 *(978-92-9061-425-8(0))* World Health Organization.
Winters, Adam. Syphilis. (Library of Sexual Health Ser.). 64p. (gr. 6-6). 2009. 58.50 *(978-1-60853-849-2(4))* 2006. (ENG., Illus.). (YA). lib. bdg. 37.13 *(978-1-4042-0906-0(9)*, 4d2f493e-873b-4db9-9314-ae0057d7776e) Rosen Publishing Group, Inc., The.
Wolny, Philip. I Have an STD. Now What?, 1 vol. 2014. (Teen Life 411 Ser.). (ENG.). 112p. (YA). (gr. 7-7). 38.80 *(978-1-4777-7980-4(9)*, f0e7b747-38a3-4ae1-ad2c-cfa6177f104a, Rosen Young Adult) Rosen Publishing Group, Inc., The.
WSTDTV: Being Informed Is the First Step to HIV/STD Prevention. 2004. (YA). cd-rom *(978-0-9754754-8-5(7))* Academic Edge, Inc.

SHACKLETON, ERNEST HENRY, SIR, 1874-1922

Benge, Janet & Benge, Geoff. Heroes of History - Ernest Shackleton: Going South. 2017. (Heroes of History Ser.). (ENG.). 227p. (J). pap. 11.99 *(978-1-62486-093-5(1))* Emerald Bks.
Bertozzi, Nick. Shackleton: Antarctic Odyssey. Bertozzi, Nick, illus. 2014. (ENG., Illus.). 128p. (YA). (gr. 7-12). pap. 19.99 *(978-1-59643-451-6(1)*, 900054960, First Second Bks.) Roaring Brook Pr.
Bodden, Valerie. To the South Pole. 2011. (Great Expeditions Ser.). (ENG.). 48p. (J). (gr. 5-8). pap. 12.00 *(978-0-89812-667-9(3)*, 22161, Creative Paperbacks) Creative Co., The.
Brasch, Nicolas. Ernest Shackleton's Antarctic Expedition, 1 vol. 2013. (Discovery Education: Sensational True Stories Ser.). (ENG., Illus.). 32p. (J). (gr. 4-5). pap. 11.00 *(978-1-4777-0111-9(7)*, 1db24a9b-1280-4a67-964f-a1e3f67c8b29); lib. bdg. 28.93 *(978-1-4777-0063-1(3)*, 5ad601a2-cf86-4fa5-947a-e09efc57ab59) Rosen Publishing Group, Inc., The. (PowerKids Pr.).
Buckley, James, Jr. & Who HQ. Who Was Ernest Shackleton? Hergenrother, Max, illus. 2013. (Who Was? Ser.). 112p. (J). (gr. 3-7). 5.99 *(978-0-448-47931-6(1)*, Penguin Workshop) Penguin Young Readers Group.
Buckley, James. Who Was Ernest Shackleton? 2013. (Who Was... ? Ser.). lib. bdg. 16.00 *(978-0-606-34162-2(5))* Turtleback.
Calvert, Patricia. Sir Ernest Shackleton: By Endurance We Conquer, 1 vol. 2003. (Great Explorations Ser.). (ENG., Illus.). 80p. (gr. 6-6). 36.93 *(978-0-7614-1485-8(1)*, c420ba55-b637-4fc9-9090-db60567f8753) Cavendish Square Publishing LLC.
Doeden, Matt. Surviving Antarctica: Ernest Shackleton. 2019. (They Survived (Alternator Books (r)) Ser.). (ENG., Illus.). 32p. (J). (gr. 3-6). lib. bdg. 29.32 *(978-1-5415-2349-4(0)*, 4e55d2da-8917-48f5-8f52-9e871c46393a, Lerner Pubns.) Lerner Publishing Group.
Grill, William. Shackleton's Journey. 2014. (ENG., Illus.). 80p. (J). (gr. 2-2). 19.99 *(978-1-909263-10-9(9))* Flying Eye Bks. GBR. Dist: Penguin Random Hse. LLC.
Johnson, Rebecca L. Ernest Shackleton: Gripped by the Antarctic. 2003. (Trailblazer Biographies Ser.). (ENG., Illus.). 112p. (gr. 5-9). 31.93 *(978-0-87614-920-1(4))* Lerner Publishing Group.
Kostyal, K. M. Trial by Ice: A Photobiography of Sir Ernest Shackleton. 2006. (Illus.). 64p. pap. 7.99 *(978-0-15-356619-6(1))* Houghton Mifflin Harcourt School Pubs.
Loh-Hagan, Virginia. Ernest Shackleton: Survival in the Antarctic. 2018. (True Survival Ser.). (ENG.). 32p. (J). (gr. 4-8). pap. 14.21 *(978-1-5341-0868-4(8)*, 210836); (Illus.). lib. bdg. 32.07 *(978-1-5341-0769-4(X)*, 210835) Cherry Lake Publishing. (45th Parallel Press).
McCumiskey, Gavin. Shackleton the Voyage of the James Caird: A Graphic Account. 2016. (ENG., Illus.). 96p. (J). pap. 12.99 *(978-1-84889-281-1(0)*, Collins Pr., The) M.H. Gill & Co. U. C. IRL. Dist: Casemate Pubs. & Bk. Distributors, LLC.
Olson, Tod. Lost in the Antarctic: the Doomed Voyage of the Endurance (Lost #4), Vol. 4. 2019. (Lost Ser.: 4). (ENG., Illus.). 224p. (J). (gr. 3-7). pap. 7.99 *(978-1-338-20734-7(2))* Scholastic, Inc.
Smith, Michael. Shackleton: The Boss. 2nd rev. ed. 2016. (ENG., Illus.). 128p. (J). pap. 7.50 *(978-1-905172-27-6(3)*, Collins Pr., The) M.H. Gill & Co. U. C. IRL. Dist: Casemate Pubs. & Bk. Distributors, LLC.

SHADES AND SHADOWS

see Shadows

SHADOW PANTOMIMES AND PLAYS

see Shadow Shows

SHADOW SHOWS

Fontichiaro, Kristin. Using Light to Make Shadow Puppets. 2018. (21st Century Skills Innovation Library: Makers As Innovators Junior Ser.). (ENG., Illus.). 24p. (J). (gr. 2-5). pap. 12.79 *(978-1-5341-0880-6(7)*, 210884); lib. bdg. 30.64 *(978-1-5341-0781-6(9)*, 210883) Cherry Lake Publishing.
Rice, Dona Herweck. The Art of Shadow Puppets. rev. ed. 2019. (Smithsonian: Informational Text Ser.). (ENG., Illus.). 24p. (J). (gr. 1-2). pap. 8.99 *(978-1-4938-6652-6(4))* Teacher Created Materials, Inc.

SHADOWS

Boothroyd, Jennifer. Playing with Light & Shadows. 2014. (First Step Nonfiction — Light & Sound Ser.). (ENG., Illus.). 24p. (J). (gr. k-2). pap. 6.99 *(978-1-4677-4503-1(0)*, 071b5ea1-3d71-4aea-999d-b65c550ed5c3) Lerner Publishing Group.
Brasch, Nicolas. Why Do Shadows Change? Level 5 Factbook. 2010. (Cambridge Young Readers Ser.). (ENG., Illus.). 24p. pap. 7.16 *(978-0-521-13731-7(4))* Cambridge Univ. Pr.
Canetti, Yanitzia. De quien es esta Sombra? Adivina Adivinador. 2010. (J). pap. 8.99 *(978-1-59835-129-3(X)*, BrickHouse Education) Cambridge BrickHouse, Inc.
Claybourne, Anna. Light & Dark. 2012. (ENG., Illus.). 24p. (gr. k-4). pap. 7.95 *(978-1-926853-57-4(1))* Saunders Bk. Co. CAN. Dist: RiverStream Publishing.
Coan, Sharon. Shadows, 1 vol. rev. ed. 2014. (Science: Informational Text Ser.). (ENG., Illus.). 24p. (gr. 1-2). pap. 9.99 *(978-1-4807-4567-4(7))* Teacher Created Materials, Inc.
Gregoire, Maryellen. We All Have Shadows, 1 vol. 2011. (Wonder Readers Early Level Ser.). (ENG.). 16p. (gr. -1-1). (J). pap. 6.25 *(978-1-4296-7877-3(1)*, 118209); pap. 35.94 *(978-1-4296-8199-5(3))* Capstone. (Capstone Pr.).
Higgins, Nadia. Super Shadows Site CD+Book. Martinez Ricci, Andres, illus. 2010. (Science Rocks! Set 2 Site CD+Book Ser.). 32p. lib. bdg. 84.14 incl. cd-rom *(978-1-61641-013-1(2))* ABDO Publishing Co.
Jennings, Terry. Light & Dark. 2009. (Science Alive Ser.). (ENG., Illus.). 32p. (J). (gr. 4-7). pap. *(978-1-897563-56-4(6))* Saunders Bk. Co.
Jennings, Terry J. Light & Dark. 2009. (J). 28.50 *(978-1-59920-270-9(0))* Black Rabbit Bks.

S

Johnson, Robin. What Are Shadows & Reflections? 2014. (Light & Sound Waves Close-Up Ser.). (ENG., Illus.). 24p. (J). (gr. 1-2). *(978-0-7787-0521-5(8))* Crabtree Publishing Co.

Lowery, Lawrence F. Dark As a Shadow. 2014. (I Wonder Why Ser.). (ENG., Illus.). 36p. (gr. k-3). pap. 11.95 *(978-1-941316-06-1(9),* P241370) National Science Teachers Assn.

Rice, Dona Herweck. The Art of Shadow Puppets. rev. ed. 2019. (Smithsonian: Informational Text Ser.). (ENG., Illus.). 24p. (J). (gr. 1-2). pap. 8.99 *(978-1-4938-6652-6(4))* Teacher Created Materials, Inc.

Robertson, Charmaine. Umbrellas & Tents Make Shade, 1 vol. 2016. (Rosen REAL Readers: STEM & STEAM Collection). (ENG.). 12p. (gr. 1-2). pap. 6.33 *(978-1-5081-2443-6(4),* ee4efe35-b1ca-4059-b97c-2fad017a9c78, Rosen Classroom) Rosen Publishing Group, Inc., The.

Royston, Angela. Light & Dark, 1 vol. 2011. (Science Corner Ser.). (ENG., Illus.). 24p. (J). (gr. 2-2). lib. bdg. 26.27 *(978-1-4488-5258-1(7),* 6770ef8e-d5ef-4169-8405-7c3a87b7831e) Rosen Publishing Group, Inc., The.

Schuh, Mari. How Are Shadows & Reflections Made? 2019. (Let's Look at Light Ser.). (ENG., Illus.). 24p. (J). (gr. -1-2). pap. 6.95 *(978-1-9771-1041-1(X),* 141117, Pebble) Capstone.

Stott-Thornton, Janet. Shadows. Barrett, Virginia, illus. 2007. (Literacy 2000 Satellites: Stage 2 Ser.). 8p. (J). (gr. -1-3). pap. *(978-0-7327-1173-3(8),* Rigby) Pearson Education Australia.

SHADOWS—FICTION

Alexander, William. Ghoulish Song. (ENG., Illus.). (J). (gr. 3-7). 2014. 192p. pap. 6.99 *(978-1-4424-2730-3(2))* 2013. 176p. 16.99 *(978-1-4424-2729-7(9))* McElderry, Margaret K. Bks. (McElderry, Margaret K. Bks.).

Allen, Lisa & Sharp, Julis. Time for Bed - The Secret of Shadows: Shadow Theater Inside. Johnson, Vickie, illus. 26p. (J). (gr. -1-2). pap. *(978-1-56021-355-0(8),* 206) W.J. Fantasy, Inc.

Alvarez, Leticia Herrera. El Pais de las Sombras. Martinez, Enrique & Graullera, Fabiola, illus. 2003. (SPA.). 48p. (J). (gr. 3-5). pap. 7.95 *(978-968-19-0535-4(0))* Santillana USA Publishing Co., Inc.

Asch, Frank. Moonbear's Shadow. Asch, Frank, illus. 2014. (Moonbear Ser.). (ENG., Illus.). 32p. (J). (gr. -1-3). 8.99 *(978-1-4424-9426-8(3),* Aladdin) Simon & Schuster Children's Publishing.

Auerbach, Joshua. Baby Shadows. 1. Auerbach, Joshua, illus. 2003. (Illus.). 8p. (J). bds. 10.00 *(978-0-9744928-0-3(9))* Baby Shadows.

Barry, Dave & Pearson, Ridley. Peter & the Shadow Thieves. Call, Greg, illus. 2007. (Starcatchers Ser.: Bk. 2). 556p. (gr. 5-9). 19.00 *(978-0-7569-8060-3(7))* Perfection Learning Corp.

Bartalos, Michael. Shadowville. 2013. (ENG., Illus.). 32p. (J). (gr. -1-2). 16.95 *(978-1-57687-645-9(4),* powerHouse Bks.) powerHse. Bks.

Cali, Davide. George & His Shadow. Bloch, Serge, illus. 2017. (ENG.). 40p. (J). (gr. -1-3). 17.99 *(978-0-06-256830-4(2),* HarperCollins) HarperCollins Pubs.

Calvert, Deanna. Rookie Reader Español: Las Sombras. Lester, Mike, illus. 2005. (Rookie Reader Español Ser.). (SPA.). 32p. (J). (gr. k-2). per. 4.95 *(978-0-516-24697-0(6),* Children's Pr.) Scholastic Library Publishing.

—Shadows. Lester, Mike, illus. 2004. (Rookie Readers Ser.). 23p. (J). 12.60 *(978-0-7569-4333-2(7))* Perfection Learning Corp.

Connolly, MarcyKate. Comet Rising. 2019. (Shadow Weaver Ser.: 2). (ENG.). (J). (gr. 3-9). 320p. pap. 12.99 *(978-1-4926-9152-5(6));* 304p. 16.99 *(978-1-4926-4998-4(8))* Sourcebooks, Inc.

—Shadow Weaver. 2018. (Shadow Weaver Ser.: 1). (ENG.). 336p. (J). (gr. 3-9). pap. 7.99 *(978-1-4926-6798-8(6))* Sourcebooks, Inc.

Cosgrove, Stephen. Snugg N. Flitter: Facing Your Fears. Arroyo, Fian, illus. 2004. (J). *(978-1-58804-377-1(0))* P C I Education.

Cuevas, Michelle. Smoot: A Rebellious Shadow. Smith, Sydney , illus. 2017. 48p. (J). (gr. -1-3). 17.99 *(978-0-525-42969-2(7),* Dial Bks) Penguin Young Readers Group.

Cummings, Troy. Attack of the Shadow Smashers. 2013. (Notebook of Doom Ser.: 3). lib. bdg. 14.75 *(978-0-606-32369-7(4))* Turtleback.

—Attack of the Shadow Smashers: a Branches Book (the Notebook of Doom #3) Cummings, Troy, illus. 2013. (Notebook of Doom Ser.: 3). (ENG.). 96p. (J). (gr. 1-3). pap. 5.99 *(978-0-545-55297-4(4))* Scholastic, Inc.

Cyr, Joe. Shadi, the Shadow Who Wanted to Be Free. Owen, Ramon, illus. 2010. 40p. pap. 14.95 *(978-1-936343-08-9(8))* Peppertree Pr., The.

Diamond, Donna. The Shadow. Diamond, Donna, illus. 2010. (ENG., Illus.). 32p. (J). (gr. k-3). 15.99 *(978-0-7636-4878-7(7))* Candlewick Pr.

Flynn, S. E. That Night. 2009. 24p. pap. 11.95 *(978-1-4389-6699-1(7))* AuthorHouse.

Freeman, Don. Gregory's Shadow. Freeman, Don, illus. 2003. (Illus.). pap. 39.95 incl. audio compact disk *(978-1-59112-536-5(7))* Live Oak Media.

Grant, Holly. The League of Beastly Dreadfuls Book 1. 2015. (League of Beastly Dreadfuls Ser.: 1). (Illus.). 320p. (J). (gr. 3-7). 16.99 *(978-0-385-37007-3(5),* Random Hse. Bks. for Young Readers) Random Hse. Children's Bks.

Graves, Jennifer. Ava's Awful Fright! 2009. 28p. pap. 15.99 *(978-1-4415-0482-1(6))* Xlibris Corp.

Gundel, Jean. The Mystery Key at Camp Green Meadow. Robertson, R. H., illus. 2011. (J). pap. 14.95 *(978-1-59571-730-6(7))* Word Association Pubs.

Hayward, Linda. Monster Bug. Palmisciano, Diane, illus. 2004. 32p. (J). lib. bdg. 20.00 *(978-1-4242-1097-8(6))* Fitzgerald Bks.

—Monster Bug. Palmisciano, Diane, illus. 2004. (Science Solves It Ser.). 32p. (gr. -1-3). 15.00 *(978-0-7569-4313-4(2))* Perfection Learning Corp.

Hodgkinson, Leigh. Boris & the Wrong Shadow. 2012. (ENG.). 32p. (J). pap. *(978-1-58925-434-3(1))* Tiger Tales.

Hopkins, Douglas. Princess June & the Shadow Pirates, 1 vol. 2007. (ENG., Illus.). 32p. (J). (gr. -1-2). per. *(978-1-894294-88-1(2))* Breakwater Bks., Ltd.

Leathers, Philippa. The Black Rabbit. Leathers, Philippa, illus. 2016. (ENG., Illus.). 40p. (J). (gr. -1-2). 7.99 *(978-0-7636-8879-0(7))* Candlewick Pr.

McKinley, Robin. Shadows. 2013. 356p. (YA). *(978-0-399-25625-7(3))* Penguin Publishing Group.

Meomi. The Octonauts & the Sea of Shade. 2007. (Octonauts Ser.). (Illus.). 36p. (J). (gr. k-2). 15.95 *(978-1-59702-010-7(9))* Immedium.

Mitchell, Saundra. Defy the Dark. 2013. (ENG.). 496p. (YA). (gr. 8). pap. 9.99 *(978-0-06-212353-4(X),* HarperTeen) HarperCollins Pubs.

O'Hara, Natalia. Hortense & the Shadow. 2017. (ENG., Illus.). 32p. (J). (gr. -1-3). 17.99 *(978-0-316-44079-0(5))* Little, Brown Bks. for Young Readers.

Pace, Anne Marie. Groundhug Day. Denise, Christopher, illus. 2017. (ENG.). 48p. (J). (gr. -1-k). 18.99 *(978-1-4847-5356-9(9))* Little, Brown Bks. for Young Readers.

Peoples-Riley, Daria. I Got Next. Peoples-Riley, Daria, illus. 2019. (ENG., Illus.). 40p. (J). (gr. -1-3). 17.99 *(978-0-06-265777-0(1),* Greenwillow Bks.) HarperCollins Pubs.

Powell, Jillian. Henry & the Hand-Me-Downs. Worsley, Belinda, illus. 2005. 32p. (J). lib. bdg. 9.00 *(978-1-4242-0886-9(6))* Fitzgerald Bks.

Reade, O. K. The Little Girl & Her Shadow. 2015. (Illus.). (J). 12.99 *(978-1-4621-1618-8(3))* Cedar Fort, Inc./CFI Distribution.

Rice, Clay. The Lonely Shadow. 2013. (ENG., Illus.). 64p. (gr. k-3). 19.95 *(978-1-938301-08-7(0),* 559108) Familius LLC.

Rogers-Busboom, Kimberly. My Secret Best Friend. Dee, Kati, illus. 2009. 24p. lib. bdg. 16.99 *(978-0-9823145-2-4(3))* Dirks Publishing, LLC.

Stack, David Martin. Good Morning Captain. 2009. 58p. pap. 10.99 *(978-0-557-06575-2(5))* Lulu Pr., Inc.

Valente, Catherynne M. The Girl Who Fell Beneath Fairyland & Led the Revels There. Juan, Ana, illus. 2013. (Fairyland Ser.: 2). (ENG.). 304p. (YA). (gr. 5-9). pap. 9.99 *(978-1-250-03412-0(4),* 900120582) Square Fish.

Young, Timothy. Shadows on My Wall, 1 vol. 2012. (ENG., Illus.). 40p. (J). 16.99 *(978-0-7643-4224-0(X),* 4586) Schiffer Publishing, Ltd.

Zafon, Carlos Ruiz. The Watcher in the Shadows. (ENG.). (YA). (gr. 7-17). 2014. 288p. pap. 15.99 *(978-0-316-04475-2(X))* 2013. 272p. 18.00 *(978-0-316-04476-9(8))* Little, Brown Bks. for Young Readers.

Zarraonandia, Thomas. Johnny Jingle. Zarraonandia, Thomas, illus. 2nd ed. 2003. (Illus.). 30p. (J). (gr. -1-7). per. 20.00 *(978-0-9741070-0-4(X))* Zarraonandia, Anne.

SHAKERS

Pérez-Reverte, Arturo. The Queen of the South. 2004. (Illus.). 384p. (J). (gr. 2-5). pap. *(978-0-9655018-2-8(5))* Knot Garden Pr.

Raschka, Chris. Simple Gifts. Raschka, Chris, illus. 2003. (Illus.). pap. 41.95 incl. audio *(978-0-87499-642-5(2));* pap. 43.95 incl. audio compact disk *(978-1-59112-604-1(5))* Live Oak Media.

Thorne-Thomsen, Kathleen. A Shaker's Dozen: Counting Book. Thorne-Thomsen, Kathleen, illus. Rocheleau, Paul, photos by. 2003. (Illus.). 27p. (J). (gr. k-13). reprint ed. 16.00 *(978-0-7567-9041-7(7))* DIANE Publishing Co.

Turner, Ann Warren. Shaker Hearts. Minor, Wendell, illus. 2006. 35p. (J). (gr. 4-8). pap. 11.00 *(978-1-4223-5856-6(9))* DIANE Publishing Co.

SHAKESPEARE, WILLIAM, 1564-1616

Adams, Jennifer. Romeo & Juliet: A BabyLit(TM) Counting Primer, 1 vol. Oliver, Alison, illus. 2011. (ENG.). 22p. (J). (gr. k-1). bds. 9.99 *(978-1-4236-2205-5(7))* Gibbs Smith, Publisher.

All's Well That Ends Well - William Shakespeare. 2010. (ENG.). 240p. (gr. 9-18). 50.00 *(978-1-60413-708-8(8),* P174402, Facts On File) Infobase Holdings, Inc.

Bailey, Gerry & Foster, Karen. Shakespeare's Quill. Radford, Karen & Noyes, Leighton, illus. 2008. (Stories of Great People Ser.). (ENG.). 40p. (J). (gr. 3-7). lib. bdg. *(978-0-7787-3691-2(1));* pap. *(978-0-7787-3713-1(6))* Crabtree Publishing Co.

Berne, Emma Carlson. William Shakespeare: Playwright & Poet, 1 vol. 2008. (Essential Lives Set 2 Ser.). (ENG., Illus.). 112p. (YA). (gr. 6-12). lib. bdg. 41.36 *(978-1-60453-042-1(1),* 6665, Essential Library) ABDO Publishing Co.

Bosco, Maryellen Lo. Fall from Grace, 1 vol. 2015. (Essential Literary Themes Ser.). (ENG., Illus.). 112p. (YA). (gr. 6-12). 41.36 *(978-1-62403-804-4(2),* 17806, Essential Library) ABDO Publishing Co.

Carew-Miller, Anna. William Shakespeare: Great English Playwright & Poet. (Illus.). 32p. (J). 2013. (People of Importance Ser.: 21). (gr. 4-18). 19.95 *(978-1-4222-2859-3(2))* 2004. (Great Names Ser.). (gr. 3-18). lib. bdg. 19.95 *(978-1-59084-157-0(3))* Mason Crest.

Claybourne, A. & Treays, R. World of Shakespeare. 2004. (Internet-Linked Library of Science). (Illus.). (J). (ENG.). 1p. pap. 9.95 *(978-0-7945-0014-6(5),* Usborne); 64p. lib. bdg. 17.95 *(978-1-58086-391-9(4))* EDC Publishing.

Claybourne, Anna. Where's Will? Find Shakespeare Hidden in His Plays. Tilly, illus. 2015. (J). *(978-1-61067-407-2(3))* Kane Miller.

Cooke, Tim. William Shakespeare, 1 vol. 2016. (Meet the Greats Ser.). (ENG.). 48p. (J). (gr. 5-5). pap. 15.65 *(978-1-4824-5964-7(7),* f811a31c-17b4-4a7d-8ad6-c4d548a5fbec) Stevens, Gareth Publishing LLLP.

Crystal, David & Crystal, Ben. Oxford Illustrated Shakespeare Dictionary. 2015. (ENG., Illus.). 352p. pap. 17.95 *(978-0-19-273750-2(3))* Oxford Univ. Pr., Inc.

Davidson, Rebecca Piatt. All the World's a Stage. Lobel, Anita, illus. 2003. 32p. (J). 16.89 *(978-0-06-029627-8(5))* HarperCollins Pubs.

Dickins, Rosie. William Shakespeare - Internet Referenced. 2008. (Young Reading Series 3 Gift Books - Famous Lives Ser.). 64p. (J). 8.99 *(978-0-7945-2096-0(0),* Usborne) EDC Publishing.

Doder, Joshua. Time Traveler's Guide to Shakespeare's London. 2004. (Timetraveller's Guides). (ENG., Illus.). 96p. (J). pap. 8.99 *(978-1-904153-10-8(0))* Watling St., Ltd. GBR. Dist: Independent Pubs. Group.

Fandel, Jennifer. William Shakespeare. (Voices in Poetry Ser.). 48p. 2014. (ENG.). (J). (gr. 5-8). *(978-1-60818-328-9(9),* 21462, Creative Education) 2014. (ENG.). (J). (gr. 5-8). pap. 12.00 *(978-1-62832-056-5(7),* 21463, Creative Paperbacks) 2003. (Illus.). 19.95 *(978-1-58341-283-1(2),* Creative Education) Creative Co., The.

Fischel, Emma. William Shakespeare. Remphry, Martin, illus. 2010. (Famous People, Famous Lives Ser.). (KOR.). 46p. (J). *(978-89-491-8826-3(0))* Biryongso Publishing Co.

Fowler, Will. Level 4: Shakespeare-His Life & Plays. 2nd ed. 2008. (Pearson English Graded Readers Ser.). (ENG., Illus.). 72p. pap. 12.71 *(978-1-4058-8231-6(X),* Pearson ELT) Pearson Education.

Harmon, Daniel E. William Shakespeare: Playwright & Poet, 1 vol. 2017. (Britannica Beginner Bios Ser.). (ENG.). 32p. (J). (gr. 2-3). 26.06 *(978-1-68048-815-9(5),* 7434e4b0-bfd5-4e25-a6f9-8f8c1910b73c); pap. 13.90 *(978-1-68048-814-2(7),* b4fd04b7-725f-4d31-a2a9-849c310c0de6) Rosen Publishing Group, Inc., The. (Britannica Educational Publishing).

Hill Nettleton, Pamela. William Shakespeare: The Inspiring Life Story of the Playwright Extraordinaire. 2016. (Inspiring Stories Ser.). (ENG., Illus.). 112p. (J). (gr. 5-7). lib. bdg. 38.65 *(978-0-7565-5163-6(3),* 128791, Compass Point Bks.) Capstone.

Hilliam, David. William Shakespeare: England's Greatest Playwright & Poet. 2009. (Rulers, Scholars, & Artists of the Renaissance Ser.). 112p. (gr. 5-8). 66.50 *(978-1-60852-945-2(2),* Rosen Reference) Rosen Publishing Group, Inc., The.

Johnson, Robin. William Shakespeare, 1 vol. 2016. (Crabtree Chrome Ser.). (ENG., Illus.). 48p. (J). (gr. 2-2). pap. *(978-0-7787-2229-8(5))* Crabtree Publishing Co.

Lamb, Charles & Lamb, Mary. Shakespeare Cuenta. 6th ed. (SPA., Illus.). 136p. (YA). (gr. 5-8). 7.96 *(978-84-239-8860-0(0))* Espasa Calpe, S.A. ESP. Dist: Lectorum Pubns., Inc.

Lamb, Mary. Shakespeare Cuenta. 2003. (Advanced Reading Ser.). (SPA.). 136p. (J). (gr. 5-8). 11.95 *(978-84-239-7082-7(5),* EC3412) Espasa Calpe, S.A. ESP. Dist: Lectorum Pubns., Inc., Planeta Publishing Corp.

Lebscky, Ibi. William. Cardoni, Paolo, illus. (Coleccion Seran Famosos).Tr. of Little Wm. Shakespeare. (SPA.). 28p. (J). (gr. 2-4). 10.36 *(978-84-233-1663-2(7))* Ediciones Destino ESP. Dist: Lectorum Pubns., Inc.

Maloof, Torrey. Stepping into William Shakespeare's World. 2nd rev. ed. 2017. (TIME(r): Informational Text Ser.). (ENG., Illus.). 48p. (J). (gr. 6-8). pap. 13.99 *(978-1-4938-3618-5(8))* Teacher Created Materials, Inc.

—Stepping into William Shakespeare's World. 2017. (Time for Kids Nonfiction Readers Ser.). lib. bdg. 20.85 *(978-0-606-40286-6(1))* Turtleback.

Mannis, Celeste & Who HQ. Who Was William Shakespeare? O'Brien, John, illus. 2006. (Who Was? Ser.). 112p. (J). (gr. 3-7). pap. 5.99 *(978-0-448-43904-4(2),* Penguin Workshop) Penguin Young Readers Group.

Mannis, Celeste Davidson & Kramer, Sydelle. Who Was William Shakespeare? O'brien, John, illus. 2006. (Who Was... ? Ser.). 105p. (gr. 2-6). 15.00 *(978-0-7569-6952-3(2))* Perfection Learning Corp.

Mayhew, James & Ryan, Patrick. Shakespeare's Storybook. 2011. (Illus.). 120p. (J). (gr. 4-6). pap. 12.99 *(978-1-84686-541-1(7))* Barefoot Bks., Inc.

Mulherin, Jennifer & Frost, Abigail. Richard III, 1 vol. 2003. (Shakespeare for Everyone Ser.). (ENG., Illus.). 32p. (J). (gr. 4-7). pap. 11.99 *(978-1-84234-049-3(2))* Cherrytree Bks. GBR. Dist: Independent Pubs. Group.

Mussari, Mark. The Sonnets, 1 vol. 2011. (Shakespeare Explained Ser.). (ENG., Illus.). 112p. (YA). (gr. 7-7). 45.50 *(978-1-60870-018-9(6),* 94b0e1ba-18a4-4941-bb9f-c8d48f4f29c0) Cavendish Square Publishing LLC.

Nesbit, E. Shakespeare Retold. Caparo, Antonio Javier, illus. 2016. (ENG.). 128p. (J). (gr. 1-5). 19.99 *(978-0-06-240453-4(9),* HarperCollins) HarperCollins Pubs.

Page, Philip & Pettit, Marilyn. Richard III. 2005. (ENG., Illus.). 64p. pap. *(978-0-340-88811-7(3))* Cambridge Univ. Pr.

Purkiss, Sue. The Life & Times of William Shakespeare: Band 18/Pearl. 2017. (Collins Big Cat Ser.). (ENG., Illus.). 80p. (J). pap. 12.99 *(978-0-00-820898-1(0))* HarperCollins Pubs. Ltd. GBR. Dist: Independent Pubs. Group.

Ray, Caitlin. Revenge, 1 vol. 2015. (Essential Literary Themes Ser.). (ENG., Illus.). 112p. (YA). (gr. 6-12). 41.36 *(978-1-62403-808-2(5),* 17814, Essential Library) ABDO Publishing Co.

Rosen, Michael. What's So Special about Shakespeare? Nayler, Sarah, illus. 2018. (ENG.). 160p. (J). (gr. 3-7). pap. 6.99 *(978-0-7636-9995-6(0));* 14.99 *(978-0-7636-9994-9(2))* Candlewick Pr.

Ryan, Patrick. Shakespeare's Storybook: Folk Tales That Inspired the Bard. Mayhew, James, illus. (ENG.). (J). 2009. 21.99 *(978-1-84686-271-7(X))* 2006. 80p. (gr. 4-7). pap. 16.99 *(978-1-905236-86-2(7))* Barefoot Bks., Inc.

Shakespeare Explained, 5 bks., Set. Incl. Hamlet. Sobran, Joseph. lib. bdg. 45.50 *(978-0-7614-3027-8(X),* 7c368e82-3ea9-42cb-9a2c-6262a9621cdf); Julius Caesar. Sobran, Joseph. lib. bdg. 45.50 *(978-0-7614-3028-5(8),* 772531cb-a96e-4696-b883-5c62c6a56c6d); Macbeth. Andersen, Richard. lib. bdg. 45.50 *(978-0-7614-3029-2(6),* d43a4573-bbe0-4de7-8fae-6e1d4d35b830); Midsummer Night's Dream. Sobran, Joseph. lib. bdg. 45.50 *(978-0-7614-3030-8(X),* d6290319-8efe-4ed8-8f89-eea21e45fe25); Romeo & Juliet. Naden, Corinne. (Illus.). lib. bdg. 45.50 *(978-0-7614-3031-5(8),* 68fe9643-55e5-462e-bdda-b40f1fb228e2); 112p. (YA). (gr. 7-7). 2008. 2008. Set lib. bdg. 149.75 net. *(978-0-7614-3026-1(1),* Cavendish Square) Cavendish Square Publishing LLC.

Shakespeare, William. Romeo & Juliet: The Inessential Shakespeare. 2003. 52p. (J). (gr. 8-12). pap. 7.00 *(978-0-948662-02-7(6))* Kabet Pr. GBR. Dist: Empire Publishing Service.

—The Tempest. 2008. (Shakespeare Ser.: Level 2). (Illus.). 72p. pap., act. bk. ed. 10.95 *(978-1-55576-327-5(8),* EDSC-201B) EDCON Publishing Group.

—Twelfth Night: The Inessential Shakespeare. Hort, John & Hort, Leela, eds. 2003. 52p. (YA). (gr. 8-12). pap. 7.00 *(978-0-948662-00-3(X))* Kabet Pr. GBR. Dist: Empire Publishing Service.

Shakespeare, William & Gill, Roma. Measure for Measure: Oxford School Shakespeare. 2nd ed. 2013. (Oxford School Shakespeare Ser.). (ENG., Illus.). 176p. pap. 9.95 *(978-0-19-839335-1(0))* Oxford Univ. Pr., Inc.

Shakespeare, William, et al. Hamlet. (Classics Illustrated Ser.). (Illus.). 52p. (YA). pap. 4.95 *(978-1-57209-004-0(9))* Classics International Entertainment, Inc.

Stanley, Diane & Vennema, Peter. Bard of Avon: the Story of William Shakespeare. Stanley, Diane, illus. 2015. (ENG., Illus.). 48p. (J). (gr. 1-5). pap. 7.99 *(978-0-06-241925-5(0),* HarperCollins) HarperCollins Pubs.

Sutcliffe, Jane. Will's Words: How William Shakespeare Changed the Way You Talk. Shelley, John, illus. 2018. 40p. (J). (gr. 2-5). pap. 8.99 *(978-1-58089-639-9(1))* Charlesbridge Publishing, Inc.

Wallace, Elise. The Prehistoric Masters of Literature Volume 1: Discover Literary History with a Prehistoric Twist! Isik, Semur, illus. 2018. (Jurassic Classics Ser.). (ENG.). 32p. (J). (gr. 4-7). lib. bdg. 26.65 *(978-1-942875-55-0(X),* 5dd27ad0-30fb-4ce7-a68e-d1ced05396be, Walter Foster Jr) Quarto Publishing Group USA.

—The Prehistoric Masters of Literature Volume 2: Discover Literary History with a Prehistoric Twist! Isik, Semur, illus. 2018. (Jurassic Classics Ser.). (ENG.). 32p. (J). (gr. 4-7). lib. bdg. 26.65 *(978-1-942875-56-7(8),* 83333adc-1433-4bd6-b1f8-7de331dd16e6, Walter Foster Jr) Quarto Publishing Group USA.

Whiting, Jim. William Shakespeare. 2007. (Poets & Playwrights Ser.). (Illus.). 112p. (J). (gr. 3-7). lib. bdg. 37.10 *(978-1-58415-426-6(8))* Mitchell Lane Pubs.

Williams, Colleen Madonna Flood. My Adventure with Shakespeare. 2009. (ENG.). 44p. (J). 8.99 *(978-1-59092-467-9(3))* Blue Forge Pr.

SHAKESPEARE, WILLIAM, 1564-1616—ADAPTATIONS

Barlow, Steve & Skidmore, Steve. The Lost Diary of Shakespeare's Ghostwriter. 2011. (ENG., Illus.). 128p. pap. 7.99 *(978-0-00-694588-8(0),* HarperCollins Children's Bks.) HarperCollins Pubs. Ltd. GBR. Dist: HarperCollins Pubs.

Blackman, Malorie. Naughts & Crosses. 2005. (ENG., Illus.). 400p. (YA). (gr. 9-18). 21.99 *(978-1-4169-0016-0(0),* Simon & Schuster Bks. For Young Readers) Simon & Schuster Bks. For Young Readers.

Fearn, Laura. Usborne Stories from Shakespeare. Temporin, Elena, illus. 2006. 191p. pap. *(978-0-439-88984-1(7))* Scholastic, Inc.

Garfield, Leon. Leon Garfield's Shakespeare Stories. Foreman, Michael, illus. 2015. (ENG.). 576p. (J). (gr. 5). 27.95 *(978-1-59017-931-4(5),* NYR Children's Collection) New York Review of Bks., Inc., The.

Hinds, Gareth. Romeo & Juliet. Hinds, Gareth, illus. 2013. (ENG., Illus.). 144p. (YA). (gr. 7). pap. 15.99 *(978-0-7636-6807-5(9))* Candlewick Pr.

—Romeo & Juliet (Graphic Adaptation) 2013. lib. bdg. 24.50 *(978-0-606-32098-6(9))* Turtleback.

Lamb, Charles. Tales from Shakespeare. 2017. (ENG., Illus.). (J). 25.95 *(978-1-374-82872-8(6))* Capital Communications, Inc.

—Tales from Shakespeare, 2 vols. 2013. 425p. reprint ed. lthr. 69.00 *(978-0-7426-2085-8(9))* Classic Bks.

Lamb, Charles & Lamb, Mary. Tales from Shakespeare. 2007. (Illus.). 352p. (gr. 12-18). 7.95 *(978-0-451-53064-6(0),* Signet) Penguin Publishing Group.

Lamb, Mary & Lamb, Charles. Tales from Shakespeare. 2018. (Alma Junior Classics Ser.). (ENG., Illus.). 288p. (J). pap. 14.00 *(978-1-84749-677-5(6),* 900193597, Alma Classics) Bloomsbury Publishing USA.

Nesbit, E. Beautiful Stories from Shakespeare for Children. Rackham, Arthur, illus. 2018. 192p. (J). (gr. 3-8). 14.99 *(978-1-63158-274-5(7),* Racehorse Publishing) Skyhorse Publishing Co., Inc.

—Shakespeare's Stories for Young Readers. 2006. (Dover Children's Classics Ser.). (ENG., Illus.). 80p. (YA). (gr. 3-8). per. 4.99 *(978-0-486-44762-9(6),* 447626) Dover Pubns., Inc.

Novel Units. King Lear Novel Units Teacher Guide. 2019. (ENG.). (YA). pap. 12.99 *(978-1-56137-923-1(9),* Novel Units, Inc.) Classroom Library Co.

—Much Ado about Nothing Novel Units Student Packet. 2019. (ENG.). (YA). pap. 13.99 *(978-1-56137-926-2(3),* Novel Units, Inc.) Classroom Library Co.

—The Tempest Novel Units Student Packet. 2019. (ENG.). (YA). pap. 13.99 *(978-1-56137-628-5(0),* Novel Units, Inc.) Classroom Library Co.

Page, Philip & Pettit, Marilyn, eds. Romeo & Juliet. Page, Philip, illus. 2005. (Picture This! Shakespeare Ser.). (ENG., Illus.). 58p. (gr. 5-8). 22.44 *(978-0-7641-3144-8(3),* B.E.S. Publishing) Peterson's.

Robert, Thando Bint, adapted by. Macbeth: Dual Language Set. 2004. (J). cd-rom *(978-1-84444-474-8(0));* cd-rom *(978-1-84444-475-5(9));* cd-rom *(978-1-84444-476-2(7));* cd-rom *(978-1-84444-472-4(4));* cd-rom *(978-1-84444-471-7(6));* cd-rom *(978-1-84444-470-0(8));* cd-rom *(978-1-84444-469-4(4));* cd-rom *(978-1-84444-473-1(2))* Mantra Lingua.

Rokison-Woodall, Abigail. Shakespeare for Young People: Productions, Versions & Adaptations. 2013. (ENG.). 256p. pap. 40.95 *(978-1-4411-2556-9(6),* 900100430, The Arden Shakespeare) Bloomsbury Publishing USA.

Ross, Lesley & Shakespeare, William. The 40 Minute Tempest/King Ram. 2003. (Oberon Modern Plays Ser.). (ENG.). 96p. pap. 16.95 *(978-1-84002-313-8(9),* 900242709) Oberon Bks., Ltd. GBR. Dist: Macmillan.

Shakespeare, William. As You Like It: Classicscript. Landes, William-Alan, ed. abr. ed. 2003. (Shakespeare Ser.: Vol. 2). 60p. (YA). (gr. 4-12). pap. 7.00 *(978-0-88734-532-6(8))* Players Pr., Inc.

—King Lear. abr. ed. 2011. (Go Shakespeare - Set 1 Ser.). (ENG.). (YA). (gr. 9-12). 49.93 *(978-1-61641-424-5(3),* Abdo & Daughters) ABDO Publishing Co.

—Twelfth Night: Classicscript. Landes, William-Alan, ed. abr. ed. 2003. (Shakespeare Ser.: Vol. 3). 68p. (J). (gr. 4-12). pap. 7.00 *(978-0-88734-530-2(1))* Players Pr., Inc.

Young, Eleanor Patmore, ed. Shakespeare for Young Actors. 2011. 284p. 48.95 *(978-1-258-08532-2(1))* Literary Licensing, LLC.

SHAKESPEARE, WILLIAM, 1564-1616—ANTONY AND CLEOPATRA

Bloom, Harold, ed. Antony & Cleopatra. 2008. (ENG.). 290p. (gr. 9-12). 50.00 *(978-0-7910-9630-7(0)*, P145733, Facts On File) Infobase Holdings, Inc.

SHAKESPEARE, WILLIAM, 1564-1616—AS YOU LIKE IT

Naden, Corinne. As You Like It, 1 vol. 2011. (Shakespeare Explained Ser.). (ENG., Illus.). 112p. (YA). (gr. 7-7). 45.50 *(978-1-60870-015-8(1)*, fb99fe65-f769-4579-865e-9303d2565683) Cavendish Square Publishing LLC.

Shakespeare, William. As You Like It: Classicscript. Landes, William-Alan, ed. abr. ed. 2003. (Shakespeare Ser.: Vol. 2). 60p. (YA). (gr. 4-12). pap. 7.00 *(978-0-88734-532-6(8))* Players Pr., Inc.

Shakespeare, William. Oxford School Shakespeare: As You Like It. 2009. (Oxford School Shakespeare Ser.). (ENG., Illus.). 160p. pap. 9.95 *(978-0-19-832869-8(9))* Oxford Univ. Pr., Inc.

SHAKESPEARE, WILLIAM, 1564-1616—CRITICISM AND INTERPRETATION

Andersen, Richard. Richard III, 1 vol. 2011. (Shakespeare Explained Ser.). (ENG., Illus.). 112p. (YA). (gr. 7-7). 45.50 *(978-1-60870-017-2(8)*, 5112502d-e8b8-4558-9c74-2ff45948bd9a) Cavendish Square Publishing LLC.

Gleed, Paul. Bloom's How to Write about William Shakespeare. 2008. (Bloom's How to Write About Ser.). (ENG.). 244p. (gr. 9-18). 45.00 *(978-0-7910-9484-6(7)*, P129244, Facts On File) Infobase Holdings, Inc.

Mittelstaedt, Walt. Reading & Interpreting the Works of William Shakespeare, 1 vol. 2016. (Lit Crit Guides). (ENG., Illus.). 176p. (gr. 6-6). 41.60 *(978-0-7660-7912-0(0)*, 8fff7d0e-0e67-4690-a135-aa524545dff1) Enslow Publishing, LLC.

Novel Units. The Merchant of Venice Novel Units Student Packet. 2019. (ENG.). (YA). pap. 13.99 *(978-1-58130-567-8(2)*, NU5672SP, Novel Units, Inc.) Classroom Library Co.

Rokison-Woodall, Abigail. Shakespeare for Young People: Productions, Versions & Adaptations. 2013. (ENG.). 256p. pap. 40.95 *(978-1-4411-2556-9(6)*, 900100430, The Arden Shakespeare) Bloomsbury Publishing USA.

Shakespeare, William. Othello Everything You Need to Catch up, Study & Prepare for & 2023 & 2024 Exams & Assessments. 2nd ed. 2003. (ENG., Illus.). 152p. pap. 20.00 *(978-0-582-78431-4(X))* Pearson Education, Ltd. GBR. Dist: Trans-Atlantic Pubns., Inc.

The Reduced Shakespeare Co., The Reduced, et al. Pop-Up Shakespeare: Every Play & Poem in Pop-Up 3-d. Maizels, Jennie, illus. 2017. (ENG.). 10p. (J). (gr. 2-5). 19.99 *(978-0-7636-9874-4(1))* Candlewick Pr.

Thompson, Stephen P., ed. Sexuality in the Comedies of William Shakespeare, 1 vol. 2014. (Social Issues in Literature Ser.). (ENG., Illus.). 160p. (gr. 10-12). lib. bdg. 48.03 *(978-0-7377-6982-1(3)*, fdb12a57-f00f-4992-88a4-46c54da329c0, Greenhaven Publishing) Greenhaven Publishing LLC.

SHAKESPEARE, WILLIAM, 1564-1616—FICTION

Abrams, Dennis. I Was Cleopatra, 1 vol. 2018. (ENG.). 192p. (YA). (gr. 7). 16.95 *(978-1-77306-022-4(8))* Groundwood Bks. CAN. Dist: Publishers Group West (PGW).

Blackwood, Gary. Shakespeare's Spy. 2005. 288p. (J). (gr. 3-7). 6.99 *(978-0-14-240311-2(3)*, Puffin Books) Penguin Young Readers Group.

—Shakespeare's Spy. 2005. 281p. (gr. 5-9). 17.00 *(978-0-7569-5216-7(6))* Perfection Learning Corp.

Boecker, Virginia. An Assassin's Guide to Love & Treason. 2018. (ENG.). 320p. (YA). E-Book *(978-0-316-32731-2(X))* Little Brown & Co.

—An Assassin's Guide to Love & Treason. 2019. (ENG.). 384p. (YA). (gr. 7-17). pap. 10.99 *(978-0-316-32729-9(8))* Little, Brown Bks. for Young Readers.

Bowe, Julie. So Much Drama. 2016. (Victoria Torres, Unfortunately Average Ser.). (ENG., Illus.). 160p. (J). (gr. 4-8). pap. 5.95 *(978-1-4965-3807-9(2)*, 133115); lib. bdg. 27.99 *(978-1-4965-3799-7(8)*, 133112) Capstone. (Stone Arch Bks.).

Broach, Elise. Shakespeare's Secret. 2007. (Illus.). 258p. (gr. 4-9). 17.00 *(978-0-7569-8204-1(9))* Perfection Learning Corp.

—Shakespeare's Secret. 2007. (ENG.). 272p. (YA). (gr. 6-8). pap. 8.99 *(978-0-312-37132-6(2)*, 900044660) Square Fish.

—Shakespeare's Secret. l.t. ed. 2006. (Thorndike Literacy Bridge Ser.). (Illus.). 263p. (J). (gr. 5-10). 22.95 *(978-0-7862-8735-2(7))* Thorndike Pr.

Castle, M. E. Fakespeare: Something Stinks in Hamlet. Jennewein, Daniel, illus. 2017. 261p. (J). pap. *(978-1-250-10157-0(3))* St. Martin's Pr.

—Fakespeare: Starcrossed in Romeo & Juliet. Jennewein, Daniel, illus. 2017. 295p. (J). pap. *(978-1-250-10160-0(3))* St. Martin's Pr.

Cohen, Paula Marantz. Beatrice Bunson's Guide to Romeo & Juliet. 2016. (ENG.). 223p. (YA). (gr. 4-9). pap. 11.95 *(978-1-58988-105-1(2))* Dry, Paul Bks., Inc.

Dakos, Kalli. Our Principal Promised to Kiss a Pig. 2018. (2019 Av2 Fiction Ser.). (ENG.). 32p. (J). lib. bdg. 34.28 *(978-1-4896-8275-8(9)*, AV2 by Weigl) Weigl Pubs., Inc.

Dakos, Kalli & DesMarteau, Alicia. Our Principal Promised to Kiss a Pig. DiRocco, Carl, illus. (ENG.). 32p. (J). 2017. (gr. -1-3). pap. 7.99 *(978-0-8075-6635-0(7)*, 807566357) 2004. (gr. 2-5). 16.99 *(978-0-8075-6629-9(2))* Whitman, Albert & Co.

Durrant, George D. Shakespeare's Best Work: A Novel of Unexpected Family Ties & Uncommon Faith. 2003. 130p. pap. 10.95 *(978-1-55517-709-6(3)*, 77093) Cedar Fort, Inc./CFI Distribution.

Fisher, Linda C. Runaway Will. 2010. (J). pap. *(978-0-88092-720-8(8))* Royal Fireworks Publishing Co.

—A Will of Her Own. 2006. (YA). pap. *(978-0-88092-641-6(4))*; lib. bdg. *(978-0-88092-640-9(6))* Royal Fireworks Publishing Co.

French, Jackie. The Diary of William Shakespeare, Gentleman. 2020. 288p. 9.99 *(978-1-4607-5057-5(8)*, HarperCollins) HarperCollins Pubs.

Harper, Suzanne. The Juliet Club. (YA). 2010. (ENG.). 416p. (gr. 8). pap. 9.99 *(978-0-06-136693-2(5)*, Greenwillow Bks.) 2008. 402p. (gr. 7-18). lib. bdg. 18.89 *(978-0-06-136692-5(7)*, HarperTeen) HarperCollins Pubs.

Hartley, James. Cold Fire: Shakespeare's Moon, Act II. 2018. (ENG., Illus.). 208p. (YA). (gr. 8-17). pap. 11.95 *(978-1-78535-762-6(X)*, Lodestone Bks.) Hunt, John Publishing Ltd. GBR. Dist: National Bk. Network.

—The Invisible Hand: Shakespeare's Moon, Act I. 2017. (ENG., Illus.). 168p. (J). (gr. 6-12). pap. 11.95 *(978-1-78535-498-4(1)*, Lodestone Bks.) Hunt, John Publishing Ltd. GBR. Dist: National Bk. Network.

Hassinger, Peter W. Shakespeare's Daughter. 2004. (ENG., Illus.). 320p. (J). (gr. 5-18). 15.99 *(978-0-06-028467-1(6)*, Geringer, Laura Book) HarperCollins Pubs.

Hicks, Deron R. Tower of the Five Orders: The Shakespeare Mysteries, Book 2. Geyer, Mark Edward, illus. 2014. (Shakespeare Mysteries Ser.). (ENG.). 320p. (J). (gr. 5-7). pap. 7.99 *(978-0-544-33630-8(5)*, 1584176, Clarion Bks.) HarperCollins Pubs.

Korman, Gordon. Whatshisface. 2019. (ENG.). 240p. (J). (gr. 3-7). pap. 8.99 *(978-1-338-20018-8(6))* Scholastic, Inc.

MacDonald, Bailey. Wicked Will: A Mystery of Young William Shakespeare. 2010. (ENG.). 224p. (J). (gr. 4-7). pap. 5.99 *(978-1-4169-8661-4(8)*, Aladdin) Simon & Schuster Children's Publishing.

Magnuson, Gregory. Crab & Will, a Tale of Shakespeare's Dog. 2012. (ENG.). 36p. pap. 19.95 *(978-1-105-95102-2(2))* Lulu Pr., Inc.

Mayhew, James. Ella Bella Ballerina & a Midsummer Night's Dream. 2015. (Ella Bella Ballerina Ser.). (ENG., Illus.). 32p. (J). (gr. -1-3). 14.99 *(978-0-7641-6797-3(9)*, Sourcebooks Jabberwocky) Sourcebooks, Inc.

Ortiz, Michael J. Swan Town: The Secret Journal of Susanna Shakespeare. 2006. (Illus.). 197p. (J). (gr. 5-9). 15.99 *(978-0-06-058126-8(3))* HarperCollins Pubs.

Shakespeare, William. Romeo & Juliet, 1 vol. Cabrera, Eva, illus. 2011. (Shakespeare Graphics Ser.). (ENG.). 88p. (J). (gr. 5-9). pap. 7.15 *(978-1-4342-3448-3(7)*, 116469, Stone Arch Bks.) Capstone.

Sutherland, Tui T. This Must Be Love. 256p. (J). 2005. pap. 7.99 *(978-0-06-056477-3(6)*, Harper Trophy) 2004. (gr. 7-18). lib. bdg. 16.89 *(978-0-06-056476-6(8))* HarperCollins Pubs.

Sylvester, Kevin. Neil Flambé & the Bard's Banquet. Sylvester, Kevin, illus. 2015. (Neil Flambe Capers Ser.: 5). (ENG., Illus.). 320p. (J). (gr. 3-7). 12.99 *(978-1-4814-1038-0(5)*, Simon & Schuster Bks. For Young Readers) Simon & Schuster Bks. For Young Readers.

SHAKESPEARE, WILLIAM, 1564-1616—HAMLET

Christensen, Caitlyn. Hamlet, 1 vol. 2015. (Reading Shakespeare Today Ser.). (ENG.). 112p. (YA). (gr. 9-9). 44.50 *(978-1-5026-1034-8(5)*, 3bd2e4fb-e0e1-47e1-8358-190e0db97967) Cavendish Square Publishing LLC.

Johnson, Vernon Elso, ed. Corruption in William Shakespeare's Hamlet, 1 vol. 2010. (Social Issues in Literature Ser.). (ENG., Illus.). 176p. (gr. 10-12). 48.03 *(978-0-7377-4809-3(5)*, b2085b79-0a5a-4742-a7d9-aa7db0c8d7d2); pap. 33.00 *(978-0-7377-4810-9(9)*, 430845a8-13d0-408b-94b7-e9e4a2e3c0bc) Greenhaven Publishing LLC. (Greenhaven Publishing).

Shakespeare, William. Hamlet: York Notes Advanced Everything You Need to Catch up, Study & Prepare for & 2023 & 2024 Exams & Assessments. 2003. (ENG., Illus.). 160p. pap. 20.00 *(978-0-582-78428-4(X))* Pearson Education, Ltd. GBR. Dist: Trans-Atlantic Pubns., Inc.

Shakespeare, William. Oxford School Shakespeare: Hamlet. 2009. (Oxford School Shakespeare Ser.). (Illus.). 208p. pap. 9.95 *(978-0-19-832870-4(2))* Oxford Univ. Pr., Inc.

Sobran, Joseph. Hamlet, 1 vol. 2008. (Shakespeare Explained Ser.). (ENG.). 112p. (YA). (gr. 7-7). lib. bdg. 45.50 *(978-0-7614-3027-8(X)*, 7c368e82-3ea9-42cb-9a2c-6262a9621cdf) Cavendish Square Publishing LLC.

SHAKESPEARE, WILLIAM, 1564-1616—JULIUS CAESAR

Griffiths, Katie. Julius Caesar, 1 vol. 2015. (Reading Shakespeare Today Ser.). (ENG., Illus.). 112p. (YA). (gr. 9-9). 44.50 *(978-1-5026-1043-0(4)*, 48c9df58-a007-400c-90d7-ca21a707486b) Cavendish Square Publishing LLC.

Literature Connections English: Julius Caesar. 2004. (gr. 6-12). *(978-0-395-77542-4(6)*, 2-80111) Holt McDougal.

Novel Units. Julius Caesar Novel Units Student Packet. 2019. (ENG.). (YA). pap. 13.99 *(978-1-56137-304-8(4)*, NU3044SP, Novel Units, Inc.) Classroom Library Co.

Shakespeare, William. Oxford School Shakespeare: Julius Caesar. 2010. (Oxford School Shakespeare Ser.). (Illus.). 160p. (YA). pap. 9.95 *(978-0-19-832868-1(0))* Oxford Univ. Pr., Inc.

Sobran, Joseph. Julius Caesar, 1 vol. 2008. (Shakespeare Explained Ser.). (ENG.). 112p. (YA). (gr. 7-7). lib. bdg. 45.50 *(978-0-7614-3028-5(8)*, 772531cb-a96e-4696-b883-5c62c6a56c6d) Cavendish Square Publishing LLC.

SHAKESPEARE, WILLIAM, 1564-1616—KING HENRY IV

Sobran, Joseph. Henry IV, Part 1, 1 vol. 2010. (Shakespeare Explained Ser.). (ENG.). 112p. (YA). (gr. 7-7). 45.50 *(978-0-7614-3419-1(4)*, fc3bb2f2-de7a-445b-8c43-8177a864d651) Cavendish Square Publishing LLC.

SHAKESPEARE, WILLIAM, 1564-1616—KING HENRY V

Langston, David & Shakespeare, William. Henry V: York Notes for GCSE. 2003. (ENG., Illus.). 80p. pap. 15.00 *(978-0-582-77268-7(0))* Pearson Education, Ltd. GBR. Dist: Trans-Atlantic Pubns., Inc.

SHAKESPEARE, WILLIAM, 1564-1616—KING LEAR

Paley, Caitlyn. King Lear, 1 vol. 2015. (Reading Shakespeare Today Ser.). (ENG., Illus.). 112p. (YA). (gr. 9-9). 44.50 *(978-1-5026-1047-8(7)*, 071eb421-1033-4c31-bb6d-57a3785404d3) Cavendish Square Publishing LLC.

Richert, Scott P. King Lear, 1 vol. 2011. (Shakespeare Explained Ser.). (ENG., Illus.). 112p. (YA). (gr. 7-7). 45.50 *(978-1-60870-016-5(X)*, e380ac47-69fa-4173-8b66-bff7cfa54b1e) Cavendish Square Publishing LLC.

Shakespeare, William. King Lear: Classicscript. Landes, William-Alan, ed. 2003. (Shakespeare Ser.: Vol. 8). 71p. (YA). (gr. 6-12). pap. 7.00 *(978-0-88734-537-1(9))* Players Pr., Inc.

—King Lear: York Notes Advanced Everything You Need to Catch up, Study & Prepare for & 2023 & 2024 Exams & Assessments. 2003. (ENG., Illus.). 144p. pap. 20.00 *(978-0-582-78429-1(8))* Pearson Education, Ltd. GBR. Dist: Trans-Atlantic Pubns., Inc.

SparkNotes. King Lear (No Fear Shakespeare) 2003. (No Fear Shakespeare Ser.: 6). (Illus.). 320p. pap. 7.99 *(978-1-58663-853-5(X)*, Spark Notes) Sterling Publishing Co., Inc.

SHAKESPEARE, WILLIAM, 1564-1616—MACBETH

Andersen, Richard. Macbeth, 1 vol. 2008. (Shakespeare Explained Ser.). (ENG.). 112p. (YA). (gr. 7-7). lib. bdg. 45.50 *(978-0-7614-3029-2(6)*, d43a4573-bbe0-4de7-8fae-6e1d4d35b830) Cavendish Square Publishing LLC.

Cunningham, Patrick. How to Dazzle at Macbeth. 2004. (Illus.). 48p. pap. 30.00 *(978-1-897675-93-9(3))* Brilliant Pubns. GBR. Dist: Parkwest Pubns., Inc.

Griffiths, Katie. Macbeth, 1 vol. 2015. (Reading Shakespeare Today Ser.). (ENG., Illus.). 112p. (YA). (gr. 9-9). 44.50 *(978-1-5026-1041-6(8)*, 205c4f69-3995-4dfd-b0a4-11d726d74b16) Cavendish Square Publishing LLC.

Kohl, Brian. Macbeth Worldview Guide. 2016. (Illus.). 43p. (J). pap. *(978-1-944503-42-0(0))* Canon Pr.

Novel Units. Macbeth Novel Units Student Packet. 2019. (ENG.). (YA). pap. 13.99 *(978-1-56137-437-3(7)*, NU4377SP, Novel Units, Inc.) Classroom Library Co.

Shakespeare, William. Macbeth: The Graphic Novel, 1 vol. 2010. (Classic Graphic Novel Collection). (ENG., Illus.). 144p. (J). (gr. 7-10). 41.03 *(978-1-4205-0373-9(1)*, 8beacdff-6ff3-4c8d-8b26-7888a357344f, Lucent Pr.) Greenhaven Publishing LLC.

Shakespeare, William. Oxford School Shakespeare: Macbeth. 2009. (Oxford School Shakespeare Ser.). (ENG., Illus.). 160p. pap. 9.95 *(978-0-19-832400-3(6))* Oxford Univ. Pr., Inc.

Shakespeare, William. The Tragedy of Macbeth. 2008. (Easy Reading Shakespeare Ser.). (ENG., Illus.). 72p. pap., act. bk. ed. 10.95 *(978-1-55576-331-2(6)*, EDSC401B) EDCON Publishing Group.

—The Tragedy of Macbeth. 2004. (Classic Retelling Ser.). (Illus.). 176p. (gr. 6-12). 13.32 *(978-0-618-03147-4(2)*, 2-00141) Holt McDougal.

SparkNotes. Macbeth (No Fear Shakespeare) 2003. (No Fear Shakespeare Ser.: 1). (Illus.). 240p. pap. 7.99 *(978-1-58663-846-7(7)*, Spark Notes) Sterling Publishing Co., Inc.

SHAKESPEARE, WILLIAM, 1564-1616—MERCHANT OF VENICE

Collins GCSE. The Merchant of Venice: AQA GCSE 9-1 English Literature Text Guide: Ideal for the 2024 & 2025 Exams. 2017. (ENG.). 80p. (YA). (gr. 9-11). pap. 5.99 *(978-0-00-824709-6(9))* HarperCollins Pubs. Ltd. GBR. Dist: Independent Pubs. Group.

Novel Units. The Merchant of Venice Novel Units Student Packet. 2019. (ENG.). (YA). pap. 13.99 *(978-1-58130-567-8(2)*, NU5672SP, Novel Units, Inc.) Classroom Library Co.

Paley, Caitlyn. The Merchant of Venice, 1 vol. 2015. (Reading Shakespeare Today Ser.). (ENG., Illus.). 112p. (YA). (gr. 9-9). 44.50 *(978-1-5026-1045-4(0)*, 0e97cf91-be5a-456c-8e1a-ff79f9c7d0ba) Cavendish Square Publishing LLC.

Schupack, Sara. The Merchant of Venice, 1 vol. 2010. (Shakespeare Explained Ser.). (ENG.). 112p. (YA). (gr. 7-7). 45.50 *(978-0-7614-3421-4(6)*, 5cb81545-c094-42ac-b653-33d7c6d83b77) Cavendish Square Publishing LLC.

Shakespeare, William. Oxford School Shakespeare: Merchant of Venice. 2010. (Oxford School Shakespeare Ser.). (ENG., Illus.). 160p. (YA). pap. 9.95 *(978-0-19-832867-4(2))* Oxford Univ. Pr., Inc.

SparkNotes. The Merchant of Venice (No Fear Shakespeare) 2003. (No Fear Shakespeare Ser.: 10). (Illus.). 256p. pap. 6.95 *(978-1-58663-850-4(5)*, Spark Notes) Sterling Publishing Co., Inc.

SHAKESPEARE, WILLIAM, 1564-1616—MIDSUMMER NIGHT'S DREAM

A Midsummer Night's Dream - William Shakespeare. 2nd rev. ed. 2010. (ENG.). 198p. (gr. 9-18). 45.00 *(978-1-60413-817-7(3)*, P174399, Facts On File) Infobase Holdings, Inc.

Shakespeare, William. A Midsummer Night's Dream the Graphic Novel: Original Text. Nicholson, Kat, illus. 2012. (ENG.). 144p. (gr. 6). lib. bdg. 24.95 *(978-1-907127-44-1(5))* Classical Comics GBR. Dist: Publishers Group West (PGW).

Shakespeare, William. & Gill, Roma. Midsummer Night's Dream: Oxford School Shakespeare. 2009. (Oxford School Shakespeare Ser.). (ENG., Illus.). 128p. pap. 9.95 *(978-0-19-832866-7(4))* Oxford Univ. Pr., Inc.

Sobran, Joseph. A Midsummer Night's Dream, 1 vol. 2008. (Shakespeare Explained Ser.). (ENG.). 112p. (YA). (gr. 7-7). lib. bdg. 45.50 *(978-0-7614-3030-8(X)*, d6290319-8efe-4ed8-8f89-eea21e45fe25) Cavendish Square Publishing LLC.

Walker, Geof. William Shakespeare's 'A Midsummer Night's Dream' - a playscript for younger Students. 2006. 49p. pap. 19.45 *(978-1-4116-4407-6(7))* Lulu Pr., Inc.

SHAKESPEARE, WILLIAM, 1564-1616—MUCH ADO ABOUT NOTHING

Page, Philip & Pettit, Marilyn. Much Ado about Nothing. 2005. (ENG., Illus.). 64p. pap. *(978-0-340-88808-7(3))* Cambridge Univ. Pr.

Shakespeare, William. Much Ado about Nothing (2010 Edition) Oxford School Shakespeare. 2010. (Oxford School Shakespeare Ser.). (ENG., Illus.). 160p. (YA). pap. 9.95 *(978-0-19-832872-8(9))* Oxford Univ. Pr., Inc.

SHAKESPEARE, WILLIAM, 1564-1616—OTHELLO

Mussari, Mark. Othello, 1 vol. 2010. (Shakespeare Explained Ser.). (ENG., Illus.). 112p. (YA). (gr. 7-7). 45.50 *(978-0-7614-3422-1(4)*, 34d81c7f-69e2-4fb4-90ed-31fdd387cb98) Cavendish Square Publishing LLC.

Ryckman, Tatiana & Jones, Edith. Othello, 1 vol. 2016. (Reading Shakespeare Today Ser.). (ENG., Illus.). 112p. (YA). (gr. 9-9). lib. bdg. 44.50 *(978-1-5026-2333-1(1)*, a07cce3e-6d68-4be4-bb9d-cb2f23804585) Cavendish Square Publishing LLC.

Shakespeare, William. Othello. abr. ed. 2011. (Go Shakespeare - Set 2 Ser.). (ENG.). (YA). (gr. 9-12). 49.93 *(978-1-61641-428-3(6)*, Abdo & Daughters) ABDO Publishing Co.

—Othello: Classicscript. Landes, William-Alan, ed. abr. ed. 2003. (Shakespeare Ser.: Vol. 9). 64p. (YA). (gr. 4-12). pap. 7.00 *(978-0-88734-538-8(7))* Players Pr., Inc.

—Othello Everything You Need to Catch up, Study & Prepare for & 2023 & 2024 Exams & Assessments. 2nd ed. 2003. (ENG., Illus.). 152p. pap. 20.00 *(978-0-582-78431-4(X))* Pearson Education, Ltd. GBR. Dist: Trans-Atlantic Pubns., Inc.

Shakespeare, William. Oxford School Shakespeare: Othello. 2009. (Oxford School Shakespeare Ser.). (Illus.). 208p. pap. 9.95 *(978-0-19-832873-5(7))* Oxford Univ. Pr., Inc.

Smith, Emma. Othello. 2005. (Writers & Their Work Ser.). (ENG., Illus.). 144p. (C). 99.00 *(978-0-7463-1082-3(X)*, 9780746310823); pap. 32.95 *(978-0-7463-0999-5(6)*, 9780746309995) Liverpool Univ. Pr. GBR. Dist: Oxford Univ. Pr., Inc.

SHAKESPEARE, WILLIAM, 1564-1616—QUOTATIONS

Shakespeare, William. A Treasury of Shakespeare's Verse. Pollinger, Gina, ed. Chichester Clark, Emma, illus. 2006. 96p. (J). (gr. 4-8). reprint ed. pap. 12.00 *(978-1-4223-5444-5(X))* DIANE Publishing Co.

Weiner, Miriam. Shakespeare's Seasons. Whitt, Shannon, illus. 2012. (ENG.). 32p. (J). (gr. -1). 16.99 *(978-1-935703-57-0(9))* Downtown Bookworks.

SHAKESPEARE, WILLIAM, 1564-1616—ROMEO AND JULIET

Griffiths, Katie. Romeo & Juliet, 1 vol. 2015. (Reading Shakespeare Today Ser.). (ENG.). 112p. (YA). (gr. 9-9). 44.50 *(978-1-5026-1036-2(1)*, 828a507f-2412-4e71-ab15-15307e99b28a) Cavendish Square Publishing LLC.

Naden, Corinne. Romeo & Juliet, 1 vol. 2008. (Shakespeare Explained Ser.). (ENG., Illus.). 112p. (YA). (gr. 7-7). lib. bdg. 45.50 *(978-0-7614-3031-5(8)*, 68fe9643-55e5-462e-bdda-b40f1fb228e2) Cavendish Square Publishing LLC.

Shakespeare, William. Romeo & Juliet: The Graphic Novel, 1 vol. 2011. (Classic Graphic Novel Collection). (ENG., Illus.). 168p. (gr. 7-10). lib. bdg. 41.03 *(978-1-4205-0631-0(5)*, cce53f3d-222c-4b3a-aa77-2b1188cff1bc, Lucent Pr.) Greenhaven Publishing LLC.

SparkNotes. Romeo & Juliet (No Fear Shakespeare) 2003. (No Fear Shakespeare Ser.: 2). (Illus.). 304p. pap. 7.99 *(978-1-58663-845-0(9)*, Spark Notes) Sterling Publishing Co., Inc.

SHAKESPEARE, WILLIAM, 1564-1616—STAGE HISTORY

Morley, Jacqueline. You Wouldn't Want to Be a Shakespearean Actor! Antram, David, illus. 2010. (You Wouldn't Want to Ser.). (ENG.). 32p. (J). 29.00 *(978-0-531-20471-9(5))* Scholastic Library Publishing.

—You Wouldn't Want to Be a Shakespearean Actor! Some Roles You Might Not Want to Play. Antram, David, illus. 2010. (You Wouldn't Want to Ser.). (ENG.). 32p. (J). (gr. 3-18). pap. 9.95 *(978-0-531-22826-5(6))* Scholastic Library Publishing.

SHAKESPEARE, WILLIAM, 1564-1616—TAMING OF THE SHREW

Naden, Corinne. The Taming of the Shrew, 1 vol. 2011. (Shakespeare Explained Ser.). (ENG., Illus.). 112p. (YA). (gr. 7-7). 45.50 *(978-1-60870-019-6(4)*, 5ae940cb-6bf0-4ae2-bc2f-e979b6278cb6) Cavendish Square Publishing LLC.

Shakespeare, William. The Taming of the Shrew. 2008. (Easy Reading Shakespeare Ser.). (ENG., Illus.). 72p. pap., act. bk. ed. 10.95 *(978-1-55576-348-0(0)*, EDSC-504B) EDCON Publishing Group.

West, Summar & Warner, Hailey. The Taming of the Shrew, 1 vol. 2016. (Reading Shakespeare Today Ser.). (ENG., Illus.). 112p. (YA). (gr. 9-9). lib. bdg. 44.50 *(978-1-5026-2343-0(9)*, 4e810208-6b01-49fd-b669-3caef7fcbfb5) Cavendish Square Publishing LLC.

SHAKESPEARE, WILLIAM, 1564-1616—TEMPEST

Krueger, Susan Heidi. The Tempest, 1 vol. 2010. (Shakespeare Explained Ser.). (ENG., Illus.). 112p. (YA). (gr. 7-7). lib. bdg. 45.50 *(978-0-7614-3423-8(2)*, 46a0baca-a4cd-452b-88e3-e7bf017a2ffb) Cavendish Square Publishing LLC.

Shakespeare, William. Oxford School Shakespeare: the Tempest. 2010. (Oxford School Shakespeare Ser.). (Illus.). 160p. (YA). pap. 9.95 *(978-0-19-832500-0(2))* Oxford Univ. Pr., Inc.

Shakespeare, William. The Tempest. 2010. 140p. pap. 20.75 *(978-1-141-55192-7(6))* Creative Media Partners, LLC.

Shakespeare, William & Todd, Loreto. The Tempest: York Notes Advanced Everything You Need to Catch up, Study & Prepare for & 2023 & 2024 Exams & Assessments. 3rd ed. 2003. (ENG., Illus.). 120p. pap. 20.00 *(978-0-582-78437-6(9))* Pearson Education, Ltd. GBR. Dist: Trans-Atlantic Pubns., Inc.

S

Walker, Geof. William Shakespeare's 'the Tempest' - a playscript for younger Students. 2005. (ENG.). 28p. 19.46 (978-1-4116-7138-6(4)) Lulu Pr., Inc.

West, Summar & Penny, Katherine. The Tempest, 1 vol. 2016. (Reading Shakespeare Today Ser.). (ENG., Illus.). 112p. (YA). (gr. 9-9). lib. bdg. 44.50 (978-1-5026-2339-3(0), f6c507c1-f8b7-490e-b2cf-c109411f1754) Cavendish Square Publishing LLC.

SHAKESPEARE, WILLIAM, 1564-1616—TWELFTH NIGHT

Schmermund, Elizabeth & Robeson, Dale. Twelfth Night, 1 vol. 2016. (Reading Shakespeare Today Ser.). (ENG., Illus.). 112p. (YA). (gr. 9-9). lib. bdg. 44.50 (978-1-5026-2337-9(4), c2da7342-31d5-4e82-b107-5545538ed634) Cavendish Square Publishing LLC.

Shakespeare, William. Oxford School Shakespeare: Twelfth Night. 2010. (Oxford School Shakespeare Ser.). (Illus.). 144p. (YA). (gr. 8-12). pap. 9.95 (978-0-19-832871-1(0)) Oxford Univ. Pr., Inc.

Sobran, Joseph. Twelfth Night, 1 vol. 2010. (Shakespeare Explained Ser.). (ENG.). 112p. (YA). (gr. 7-7). 45.50 (978-0-7614-3425-2(9), 488cd734-7470-4abf-b85f-6e4cfabea213) Cavendish Square Publishing LLC.

Walker, Geof. William Shakespeare's 'Twelfth Night' - a playscript for younger Students. 2006. 52p. pap. 19.51 (978-1-4116-7137-9(6)) Lulu Pr., Inc.

SHAPE

see Size and Shape

SHARES OF STOCK

see Stocks

SHARING

Adams, Kenneth. Sharing with Others, 1 vol. 2021. (Being Polite Ser.). (ENG.). 24p. (gr. 1-1). 25.27 (978-1-5383-4447-7(5), 22515b45-0969-4877-99b8-42326afbdd51, PowerKids Pr.) Rosen Publishing Group, Inc., The.

Amos, Janine & Spenceley, Annabel. Let's Share, 1 vol. 2009. (Best Behavior Ser.). (ENG., Illus.). 32p. (J). (gr. -1-2). 27.27 (978-1-60754-508-8(X), 2415d6d4-8d01-4f24-856a-2f9228f8d381); pap. 11.55 (978-1-60754-509-5(8), 679df1ae-7f0d-4584-895e-ca6db862eed4) Rosen Publishing Group, Inc., The. (Windmill Bks.).

Bozek, Rachel, ed. Uber, Lyft, Airbnb, & the Sharing Economy, 1 vol. 2017. (Opposing Viewpoints Ser.). (ENG.). 208p. (J). (gr. 10-12). pap. 34.80 (978-1-5345-0046-4(4), 82238a1f-73cc-4fac-82b2-c9410de426c3); lib. bdg. 50.43 (978-1-5345-0048-8(0), 0ead2237-f78c-4966-b827-32e2b703700e) Greenhaven Publishing LLC.

Burton, Margie, et al. One for You & One for Me. 2011. (Early Connections Ser.). (J). (978-1-61672-501-3(X)) Benchmark Education Co.

Carlson, Amie. My Princesses Learn to Share. Heyworth, Heather, illus. 2014. (ENG.). 24p. (J). 6.99 (978-1-4143-9662-0(7), 4608652) Tyndale Hse. Pubs.

Cauchy, Véronique. Line & Dot. Simon, Laurent, illus. 2018. 32p. (J). (978-1-4338-2873-7(1), Magination Pr.) American Psychological Assn.

Colby, Jennifer. Stories of Sharing. 2018. (21st Century Skills Library: Social Emotional Library). (ENG.). 32p. (J). (gr. 4-7). pap. 14.21 (978-1-5341-0846-2(7), 210748); (Illus.). lib. bdg. 32.07 (978-1-5341-0747-2(9), 210747) Cherry Lake Publishing.

Deen, Marilyn. Share & Be Fair, 1 vol. 2011. (Wonder Readers Fluent Level Ser.). (ENG.). 16p. (gr. -1-2). (J). pap. 6.25 (978-1-4296-7935-0(2), 118267); pap. 35.94 (978-1-4296-8149-0(7)) Capstone. (Capstone Pr.).

English, Alex. Mine, Mine, Mine Said the Porcupine. Levey, Emma, illus. 2019. (Early Bird Readers — Blue (Early Bird Stories (tm)) Ser.). (ENG.). 32p. (J). (gr. -1-2). 30.65 (978-1-5415-4173-3(1), b037c99e-c022-438e-9914-09036213cf0c, Lerner Pubns.) Lerner Publishing Group.

Marie, Tina. Isabella Learns to Share. 2010. 20p. 12.49 (978-1-4520-3913-8(5)) AuthorHouse.

Marsico, Katie. Taking Turns! 2012. (21st Century Basic Skills Library: Kids Can Make Manners Count Ser.). (ENG.). 24p. (gr. k-3). pap. 12.79 (978-1-61080-606-0(9), 202216); (Illus.). 26.35 (978-1-61080-432-5(5), 202042) Cherry Lake Publishing.

McClure, Leigh. My School Supplies: Sharing & Reusing, 1 vol. 2017. (Computer Science for the Real World Ser.). (ENG.). 8p. (gr. k-1). pap. (978-1-5383-5093-5(9), 3da1d9c4-7f13-4516-b2db-3b8cc0e4f0b9, Rosen Classroom) Rosen Publishing Group, Inc., The.

Meiners, Cheri J. I Play: A Board Book about Discovery & Cooperation. Weber, Penny, illus. 2018. (Learning about Me & You Ser.). (ENG.). 26p. (J). (-k). bds. 9.99 (978-1-63198-220-0(6), 82200) Free Spirit Publishing Inc.

—I Share: A Board Book about Being Kind & Generous. Weber, Penny, illus. 2018. (Learning about Me & You Ser.). (ENG.). 26p. (J). (-k). bds. 9.99 (978-1-63198-223-1(0), 82231) Free Spirit Publishing Inc.

—Share & Take Turns. Johnson, Meredith, illus. 2003. (Learning to Get Along(r) Ser.). (ENG.). 40p. (J). (gr. -1-3). pap. 11.99 (978-1-57542-124-7(0), 786) Free Spirit Publishing Inc.

—Share & Take Turns / Comparte y Turna. Johnson, Meredith, illus. 2014. (Learning to Get Along(r) Ser.). (ENG.). 48p. (J). (gr. -1-3). pap. 12.99 (978-1-57542-474-3(6)) Free Spirit Publishing Inc.

Nelson, Maria. I Can Share. 2013. (Kids of Character Ser.). 24p. (J). (gr. 1-3). pap. 48.90 (978-1-4339-9035-9(0)); (ENG., Illus.). 25.27 (978-1-4339-9033-5(4), 11e16541-255e-43c2-bc5f-9e05859c8971); (ENG., Illus.). pap. 9.15 (978-1-4339-9034-2(2), 89e5e0a7-e305-4e0d-8b23-dbd30443d37b) Stevens, Gareth Publishing LLLP.

Nunn, Daniel. I Can Take Turns, 1 vol. 2014. (Me & My Friends Ser.). (ENG.). 24p. (J). (gr. -1-1). pap. 5.99 (978-1-4846-0248-5(X), 126301, Heinemann) Capstone.

Orr, Tamra. Sharing Economy. 2019. (21st Century Skills Library: Global Citizens: Social Media Ser.). (ENG., Illus.). 32p. (J). (gr. 4-7). pap. 14.21 (978-1-5341-3967-1(2), 212697); lib. bdg. 32.07 (978-1-5341-4311-1(4), 212696) Cherry Lake Publishing.

Redford, Marjorie & Rice, Courtney. God's Special Rule. Burroughs, Scott, illus. 2013. (Happy Day Ser.). (ENG.). 16p. (J). pap. 2.99 (978-1-4143-9300-1(8), 4608290, Happy Day) Tyndale Hse. Pubs.

Reynolds, Mattie. Sharing with Others: An Introduction to Financial Literacy. 2013. (Start Smart (tm) — Money Ser.). (ENG., Illus.). 24p. (J). (gr. k-2). lib. bdg. 23.99 (978-1-937529-44-4(4), dbaf55ba-4638-4e7e-95ad-036ad1eeed33) Red Chair Pr.

Ricciuti, Edward R. We Share, 1 vol. 2008. (Ready for School Ser.). (ENG.). 24p. (gr. k-1). pap. 9.23 (978-0-7614-3276-0(0), e6d5aeb0-d113-42d9-b070-7e59a7bf1a80) Cavendish Square Publishing LLC.

Williams, Sam. Sharing. 2012. (Little World Social Skills Ser.). (ENG.). 24p. (gr. k-2). pap. 9.95 (978-1-61810-264-5(8), 9781618102645) Rourke Educational Media.

SHARING—FICTION

Ahmed, Said Salah. The Lion's Share/Qayb Libaax: A Somali Folktale. Dupre, Kelly, illus. 2006. 32p. (J). (gr. -1-3). pap. 7.95 (978-1-931016-13-1(5)) Minnesota Humanities Ctr.

Albee, Sarah. One for Me, One for You: A Book about Sharing. Craig, Karen, illus. 2006. (Blue's Clues Ser.: 20). (ENG.). 24p. (J). (gr. -1-3). pap. 3.99 (978-1-4169-1300-9(9), Simon Spotlight/Nickelodeon) Simon Spotlight/Nickelodeon.

Alberts, Katharine O. Boo on the Loose. 2006. (J). 14.00 (978-0-8059-7071-5(1)) Dorrance Publishing Co., Inc.

Allepuz, Anuska. That Fruit Is Mine! 2018. (Illus.). 32p. (J). (978-1-4063-7548-0(9)) Whitman, Albert & Co.

Ardwin, Juanita. Remember When, 1 vol. 2009. 40p. pap. 19.95 (978-1-4489-2008-2(6)) PublishAmerica, Inc.

Arnone, T. I. The Magic Kazoo. 2009. (ENG., Illus.). 48p. pap. 25.00 (978-0-557-12017-8(9)) Lulu Pr., Inc.

Ashby, Gaylene. STORY TIME A Collection of Three Children's Stories. 2008. 28p. 14.95 (978-1-4357-1929-3(8)) Lulu Pr., Inc.

Audho, Gaitree. Moral Stories for Kids. 2011. (ENG.). 32p. pap. 12.77 (978-1-4634-4709-0(4)) AuthorHouse.

Azúa Kramer, Jackie. The Green Umbrella. Sassouni, Maral, illus. 2017. (ENG.). 32p. (J). (gr. -1-3). 17.95 (978-0-7358-4218-2(3)) North-South Bks., Inc.

Barner, Bob. Tengo un Jardín. 2020. (¡Me Gusta Leer! Ser.). (Illus.). 32p. (J). (gr. -1-3). pap. 8.99 (978-0-8234-4693-3(X)) Holiday Hse., Inc.

Berenstain, Jan & Berenstain, Mike. The Berenstain Bears' Caring & Sharing Treasury, 1 vol. 2016. (Berenstain Bears/Living Lights: a Faith Story Ser.). (ENG.). 160p. (J). 12.99 (978-0-310-75358-2(9)) Zonderkidz.

Berenstain, Stan, et al. The Berenstain Bears Learn to Share, 1 vol. 2010. (Berenstain Bears/Living Lights: a Faith Story Ser.). (ENG., Illus.). 40p. (J). (gr. -1-2). 6.99 (978-0-310-71939-7(9)) Zonderkidz.

Bernstein, Ariel. I Have a Balloon. Magoon, Scott, illus. 2017. (ENG.). 40p. (J). (gr. -1-3). 19.99 (978-1-4814-7250-0(X), Simon & Schuster/Paula Wiseman Bks.) Simon & Schuster/Paula Wiseman Bks.

Bethers, Linda, retold by. Christmas Oranges. 2004. 13p. pap. 3.95 (978-1-57734-546-6(0), 01114387) Covenant Communications, Inc.

Blabey, Aaron. Pig the Monster. Blabey, Aaron, illus. 2021. (Pig the Pug Ser.). (ENG.). 32p. (J). (gr. -1-k). 14.99 (978-1-338-76401-7(2), Scholastic Pr.) Scholastic, Inc.

—Pig the Pug. 2016. (Pig the Pug Ser.). (ENG., Illus.). 32p. (J). (gr. -1-k). 14.99 (978-1-338-11245-0(7), Scholastic Pr.) Scholastic, Inc.

Bland, Nick. The Very Brave Bear. 2013. (Illus.). (J). pap. (978-0-545-65137-0(9)) Scholastic, Inc.

—The Very Hungry Bear. 2013. (Illus.). (J). pap. (978-0-545-52290-8(0)) Scholastic, Inc.

Bodden, Michelle, adapted by. Obara the Gatekeeper. 2007. (J). 14.95 (978-0-9753089-1-2(2)) Water Daughter Publishing.

Brandy. WILL & WON't Learn to Share: Big Life Lessons for Little Kids. 2017. (Illus.). 272p. (J). 14.99 (978-981-4771-33-7(3)) Marshall Cavendish International (Asia) Private Ltd. SGP. Dist: Independent Pubs. Group.

Bright, Rachel. Love Monster & the Last Chocolate. 2015. (Love Monster Ser.). (ENG., Illus.). 32p. (J). (gr. -1-k). 21.99 (978-0-374-34690-4(9), 900149206, Farrar, Straus & Giroux (BYR)) Farrar, Straus & Giroux.

Brooks, Felicity. Take Turns, Max & Millie. 2011. (Toddler Bks). 24p. (J). ring bd. 7.99 (978-0-7945-3000-6(1), Usborne) EDC Publishing.

Bryan-Brown, Kim. The Leaf That Was Left. Curren, Cindy, illus. l.t. ed. 2006. 32p. (J). 16.95 (978-0-9772564-0-2(5)) Them Potatoes.

Burnell, Heather Ayris. Friends Rock: an Acorn Book (Unicorn & Yeti #3) Quintanilla, Hazel, illus. 2019. (Unicorn & Yeti Ser.: 3). (ENG.). 64p. (J). (gr. k-2). pap., act. bk. ed. 4.99 (978-1-338-32907-0(3)) Scholastic, Inc.

—Friends Rock: an Acorn Book (Unicorn & Yeti #3) (Library Edition) Quintanilla, Hazel, illus. 2019. (Unicorn & Yeti Ser.: 3). (ENG.). 64p. (J). (gr. k-2). 23.99 (978-1-338-32908-7(1)) Scholastic, Inc.

Cali, Davide & Dek, Maria. Good Morning, Neighbor: (Picture Book on Sharing, Kindness, & Working As a Team, Ages 4-8) 2018. (ENG., Illus.). 48p. (J). (gr. -1-2). 18.95 (978-1-61689-699-7(X)) Princeton Architectural Pr.

Cannon, Sherrill S. Gimme-Jimmy. 2012. 32p. pap. 13.00 (978-1-61897-267-5(7), Strategic Bk. Publishing) Strategic Book Publishing & Rights Agency (SBPRA).

Carmi, Giora. A Circle of Friends, 1 vol. (ENG., Illus.). 32p. (J). (gr. k-9). 2006. pap. 5.95 (978-1-59572-060-3(X)) 2003. 15.95 (978-1-932065-00-8(8)) Star Bright Bks., Inc.

Childs, Barbara. Sammy & the Cow Bird. 2009. 48p. pap. 21.99 (978-1-4389-8025-6(6)) AuthorHouse.

Cohen, Miriam. Mine! (Spanish/English) A Backpack Baby Story, 1 vol. Fiol, Maria A., tr. 2005. (ENG., Illus.). 32p. (J). (gr. -1 — 1). bds. 5.95 (978-1-59572-019-1(7)) Star Bright Bks., Inc.

Cohen, Penny L. Tapuchim & Dvash. Polsky, Beanie, illus. 2012. 36p. 24.95 (978-1-4626-7769-6(X)); pap. 24.95 (978-1-4626-6667-6(1)) PublishAmerica, Inc.

Collingridge, Richard. Tiny Little Rocket. Collingridge, Richard, illus. 2018. (ENG., Illus.). 32p. (J). (gr. -1-k). 17.99 (978-1-338-18949-0(2)) Scholastic, Inc.

Collins, Carleen. Everyone Loves Chocolate. 2009. 60p. pap. 23.99 (978-1-4490-3049-0(1)) AuthorHouse.

Collins, Jordan. Let's Get along!: It's Great to Share. Lynch, Stuart, illus. 2017. (ENG.). 32p. (J). (gr. -1-3). pap. 3.99 (978-1-78598-858-5(1)) Make Believe Ideas GBR. Dist: Scholastic, Inc.

Cook, Julia. I Want to Be the Only Dog!, Volume 6. DuFalla, Anita, illus. 2015. (Building Relationships Ser.). (ENG.). 31p. (J). (gr. k-6). pap. 11.95 (978-1-934490-86-0(5)) Boys Town Pr.

—Teamwork Isn't My Thing, & I Don't Like to Share!, Volume 4. De Weerd, Kelsey, illus. 2012. (Best Me I Can Be Ser.). (ENG.). 31p. (J). (gr. k-6). pap. 10.95 (978-1-934490-35-8(0)) Boys Town Pr.

Cook, Teri Ann. The Adventures of Mrs. Patsy's Farm: A Gift! Is a Gift! Is a Gift!, 1 vol. 2009. 24p. pap. 24.95 (978-1-60749-549-9(X)) America Star Bks.

Cooper, Helen. Pumpkin Soup: A Picture Book. Cooper, Helen, illus. 2005. (ENG., Illus.). 32p. (J). (gr. -1-3). per. 8.99 (978-0-374-46031-0(0), 900030431) Square Fish.

Corchin, D. J. I Feel... Awesome. 2020. (I Feel... Ser.). (Illus.). 56p. (J). (gr. -1-3). 14.99 (978-1-7282-1973-8(6)) Sourcebooks, Inc.

Cosgrove, Stephen. Big Bubba Bigg, Jr. Dealing with Bullies. Arroyo, Fian, illus. 2004. (J). (978-1-58804-352-8(5)) P C I Education.

Cotter, Bill. Don't Touch This Book! 2016. (Illus.). (J). (gr. -1-k). 28p. bds. 6.99 (978-1-4926-4804-8(3), 9781492648048); 32p. 16.99 (978-1-4926-3224-5(4), 9781492632245) Sourcebooks, Inc. (Sourcebooks Jabberwocky).

Crimi, Carolyn. I Am the Boss of This Chair. Morea, Marisa, illus. 2018. 32p. (J). (gr. -1-2). 16.95 (978-1-4549-2322-0(9)) Sterling Publishing Co., Inc.

Dahl, Michael. Playdate for Panda. Vidal, Oriol, illus. 2016. (Hello Genius Ser.). (ENG.). 20p. (J). (gr. -1 — 1). bds. 7.99 (978-1-4795-8741-4(9), 131130, Picture Window Bks.) Capstone.

Daly, Catherine. Double or Nothing: A Makers Story about 3D Printing. Lyon, Tammie, illus. 2018. (Makers Make It Work Ser.). 32p. (J). (gr. k-3). pap. 6.99 (978-1-57565-989-3(1), 1b82b37e-f971-49a5-bd2a-c3b5e07aa673, Kane Press) Astra Publishing Hse.

Daywalt, Drew. This Is MY Fort! (Monkey & Cake) Tallec, Olivier, illus. 2019. (Monkey & Cake Ser.: 2). (ENG.). 56p. (J). (gr. -1-3). 9.99 (978-1-338-14390-4(5), Orchard Bks.) Scholastic, Inc.

Dean, James. Pete's Big Lunch. 2013. (Pete the Cat I Can Read Ser.). (J). lib. bdg. 13.55 (978-0-606-27146-2(5)) Turtleback.

Degroat, Diane. Last One in Is a Rotten Egg! 2011. (Gilbert Ser.). (ENG., Illus.). 32p. (J). (gr. -1-3). pap. 7.99 (978-0-06-089296-8(X), HarperCollins) HarperCollins Pubs.

DelaHaye, Rachel. The Mean Monkey Blue Band. Mosedale, Julian, illus. 2017. (Cambridge Reading Adventures Ser.). (ENG.). 16p. pap. 6.15 (978-1-108-43971-8(3)) Cambridge Univ. Pr.

Dewdney, Anna. Llama Llama Time to Share. 2012. (Llama Llama Ser.). (ENG., Illus.). 40p. (J). (gr. -1-k). 18.99 (978-0-670-01233-6(5), Viking Books for Young Readers) Penguin Young Readers Group.

Divine, Miss Jill. Miles Smiles. 2008. 88p. pap. 15.95 (978-1-4092-5052-4(0)) Lulu Pr., Inc.

Dixon, Dallas L. Shelby's Collection Day. Williams, Nancy E., ed. Forrest, Grace Metzger, illus. 2013. 24p. (J). pap. 12.98 (978-1-938526-54-1(6)) Laurus Co., Inc., The.

Domney, Alexis. Splish, Splat!, 1 vol. Crawford, Alice, illus. 2011. (ENG.). 24p. (J). (gr. 1-3). 15.95 (978-1-897187-88-3(2)) Second Story Pr. CAN. Dist: Orca Bk. Pubs. USA.

Dungy, Tony & Dungy, Lauren. Ruby's New Home: Ready-To-Read Level 2. Brantley-Newton, Vanessa, illus. 2011. (Tony & Lauren Dungy Ready-To-Reads Ser.). (ENG.). 32p. (J). (gr. k-2). lib. bdg. 17.99 (978-1-4424-2948-2(8), Simon Spotlight) Simon & Schuster Children's Publishing.

Dunrea, Olivier. Ollie's Halloween Board Book. Dunrea, Olivier, illus. 2013. (Gossie & Friends Ser.). (ENG., Illus.). 30p. (J). (gr. -1 — 1). bds. 9.99 (978-0-544-05720-3(1), 1533611, Clarion Bks.) HarperCollins Pubs.

Durnil, Lari. A Tale of Two Sisters. 2009. (J). pap. 11.89 (978-0-88144-455-1(3), Total Publishing & Media) Yorkshire Publishing Group.

Easton, Tom. Pirates Can Share, 1 vol., 1. 2015. (Pirate Pals Ser.). (ENG.). 32p. (J). (gr. 1-2). pap. 11.00 (978-1-5081-9155-1(7), 2d0334a5-b737-493e-b5fc-bfe6902603bf, Windmill Bks.) Rosen Publishing Group, Inc., The.

Edwards, W M, illus. Booger Boogie. 2007. (Playdate Kids Musical Ser.). 27p. (J). (gr. -1-3). 14.95 incl. audio compact disk (978-1-933721-13-2(8)) Playdate Kids Publishing.

Elkins, Christy. The Seedling Heart. 2011. (ENG.). 33p. pap. 12.00 (978-0-557-23498-1(0)) Lulu Pr., Inc.

Elliott, Rebecca. Trip to the Pumpkin Farm, 11. 2020. (Branches Early Ch Bks). (ENG.). 72p. (J). (gr. 2-3). 15.36 (978-1-64697-304-0(6)) Penworthy Co., LLC, The.

—Trip to the Pumpkin Farm: a Branches Book (Owl Diaries #11) Elliott, Rebecca, illus. 2019. (Owl Diaries: 11). (ENG., Illus.). 80p. (J). (gr. k-2). pap. 6.99 (978-1-338-29864-2(X)) Scholastic, Inc.

—Trip to the Pumpkin Farm: a Branches Book (Owl Diaries #11) (Library Edition) Elliott, Rebecca, illus. 2019. (Owl Diaries: 11). (ENG., Illus.). 80p. (J). (gr. k-2). lib. bdg. 24.99 (978-1-338-29865-9(8)) Scholastic, Inc.

Evans, Christine. Emily's Idea. 2020. (ENG., Illus.). 32p. (J). 17.99 (978-1-68364-416-3(6), 900220964) Sounds True, Inc.

Fagan, Cary. Ella May & the Wishing Stone. Côté, Geneviève, illus. 2011. 32p. (J). (gr. -1-1). 17.95 (978-1-77049-225-7(9), Tundra Bks.) Tundra Bks. CAN. Dist: Penguin Random Hse. LLC.

farahay, m. l. The BUTTERFLY, the BEE & the SPIDER. 2009. (ENG.). 32p. pap. 6.94 (978-0-557-14043-5(9)) Lulu Pr., Inc.

—The BUTTERFLY, the BEE & the SPIDER, Sc3. 2009. (ENG.). 32p. pap. 14.94 (978-0-557-15287-2(9)) Lulu Pr., Inc.

Fielder, Barbara L. & Broady, Brianna. Missy, the Kitty, Learns about Sharing. (Illus.). 13p. (J). 6.95 (978-0-9639986-2-0(5)) Fielder Group.

Fotso, Serge. The Little Girl & the Lost Bag. Woods, Michele, illus. 2011. 20p. pap. 24.95 (978-1-4626-1741-8(7)) America Star Bks.

Fraser, Mary Ann. Milton & Odie & the Bigger-Than-Bigmouth Bass. Fraser, Mary Ann, illus. 2019. (Illus.). 32p. (J). (gr. -1-3). lib. bdg. 16.99 (978-1-62354-098-2(4)) Charlesbridge Publishing, Inc.

Frayre, A. R. Shannon Cabbage-Head. 2008. 33p. pap. 14.28 (978-0-557-00442-3(X)) Lulu Pr., Inc.

Friedman, Becky. Daniel Learns to Share. 2016. (Simon & Schuster Ready-To-Read Level 1 Ser.). lib. bdg. 13.55 (978-0-606-39754-4(X)) Turtleback.

Fruchter, Jason, illus. Daniel Learns to Share: Ready-To-Read Pre-Level 1. 2016. (Daniel Tiger's Neighborhood Ser.). (ENG.). 32p. (J). (gr. -1-k). pap. 4.99 (978-1-4814-6751-3(4), Simon Spotlight) Simon Spotlight.

Gehl, Laura. One Big Pair of Underwear. Lichtenheld, Tom, illus. 2018. (Classic Board Bks.). (ENG.). 36p. (J). (gr. -1-k). bds. 8.99 (978-1-5344-2036-6(3), Little Simon) Little Simon.

Gibbs, Lynne. Time to Share: A Story of Sharing, 1 vol. Mitchell, Missy, illus. 2009. (Let's Grow Together Ser.). (ENG.). 32p. (J). (gr. k-1). lib. bdg. 27.27 (978-1-60754-757-0(0), a262b884-7f2d-4103-aad4-a1ff78ae63e4, Windmill Bks.) Rosen Publishing Group, Inc., The.

Gilbert, Hary. Oxford Bookworms Library: the Year of Sharing: Level 2: 700-Word Vocabulary. 3rd ed. 2008. (ENG., Illus.). 64p. 11.00 (978-0-19-479077-2(0)) Oxford Univ. Pr., Inc.

Goodspeed, Judy. Perky Turkey Finds a Friend. (Illus.). 24p. (J). 2007. per. 11.99 (978-0-9797574-2-6(8)) 2006. lib. bdg. 24.95 (978-0-9778651-2-3(6)) Dragonfly Publishing, Inc.

Graham, Judith A. The Didley-Doo's, 1 vol. 2009. 36p. pap. 24.95 (978-1-60836-035-2(0)) America Star Bks.

Graham, Oakley. The Bear Who Would Not Share. Walkley, Lizzie, illus. 2015. (J). (978-1-4351-6485-7(7)) Barnes & Noble, Inc.

Gravett, Emily. Bear & Hare Share! Gravett, Emily, illus. 2016. (Bear & Hare Ser.). (ENG., Illus.). 32p. (J). (gr. -1-3). 16.99 (978-1-4814-6217-4(2), Simon & Schuster Bks. For Young Readers) Simon & Schuster Bks. For Young Readers.

Gray, Laurel. The Selfish Shellfish. 2012. 16p. pap. (978-1-909039-83-4(7)) Legend Pr.

Greve, Meg. Let's Get Pizza. Poole, Helen, illus. 2012. (Little Birdie Bks.). (ENG.). 24p. (gr. k-1). pap. 9.95 (978-1-61810-306-2(7), 9781618103062) Rourke Educational Media.

Hale, Bruce. Clark the Shark Dares to Share. Francis, Guy, illus. 2013. (Clark the Shark Ser.). (ENG.). 32p. (J). (gr. -1-3). 17.99 (978-0-06-227905-7(X), HarperCollins) HarperCollins Pubs.

Hallinan, P. K. Let's Play As a Team. 2003. (ENG., Illus.). 28p. (J). 8.75 (978-0-8249-5452-9(1), Ideals Pubns.) Worthy Publishing.

Hamilton, Katharine E. Susie at Your Service. 2012. 24p. pap. 17.99 (978-1-4772-2426-7(2)) AuthorHouse.

Harper, Charise Mericle. The Cookie. 2013. (Bean Dog & Nugget Ser.). lib. bdg. 14.75 (978-0-606-31945-4(X)) Turtleback.

Harris, Tumeka. The Goody Bag. Sea Breeze Productions, ed. Miller, Linzi, illus. 2006. 36p. (J). 14.95 (978-0-9769366-2-6(3)) Dividion Group, LLC, The.

Hendricks, Brenda K. What's Better Than That, Seren Dippity? Hendricks, Brenda K., illus. 2013. (Illus.). 32p. pap. 9.99 (978-0-9826582-4-6(9)) Two Small Fish Pubns.

Henry, Kristina. The Rat Tank, 1 vol. 2011. (ENG., Illus.). 40p. (J). (gr. -1-3). 16.99 (978-0-7643-3842-7(0), 4271, Schiffer Publishing Ltd) Schiffer Publishing, Ltd.

Hensdill, Norma Mae. Friends Are Forever. 2009. 36p. pap. 17.99 (978-1-4389-5053-2(5)) AuthorHouse.

Hibbert, Dee. Share Day, 1 vol. Hibbert, Rhonda, illus. 2009. 31p. pap. 24.95 (978-1-60813-294-2(3)) America Star Bks.

Horowitz, Alena Netia. The Tlytiettlym Tree. Horowitz, Alena Netia & De La Fuente, Mary, illus. l.t. ed. 2003. 64p. (J). per. 12.95 (978-0-923550-42-4(9)) Tetrahedron Publishing LLC.

Hudson, Katy. Too Many Carrots. Hudson, Katy, illus. 2016. (ENG., Illus.). 32p. (J). (gr. -1-1). 14.95 (978-1-62370-638-8(6), 131389, Capstone Young Readers) Capstone.

Hudson, Wade. Feelings I Love to Share. 2009. 24p. 5.95 (978-1-60349-011-5(6), Marimba Bks.) Just Us Bks., Inc.

—Puddin', Jeffrey & Leah. 2008. (Illus.). 16p. (gr. -1). 6.95 (978-1-60349-006-1(X), Marimba Bks.) Just Us Bks., Inc.

Hulme, Joy N. Mary Clare Likes to Share: A Math Reader. Rockwell, Lizzy, illus. 2006. (Step into Reading: Step 2 Ser.). (ENG.). 32p. (J). (gr. -1-1). lib. bdg. 16.19 (978-0-375-93421-6(9)) Random House Publishing Group.

—Mary Clare Likes to Share: A Math Reader. Rockwell, Lizzy, illus. 2006. (Step into Reading Ser.: Vol. 2). 32p. (J). (gr. -1-1). pap. 4.99 (978-0-375-83421-9(4), Random Hse. Bks. for Young Readers) Random Hse. Children's Bks.

Humphrey, Eleanor Cairns. Building Santa's Work Shop from Tales of the Crystal Cave. 2012. 268p. pap. 27.95 (978-1-4626-7820-4(3)) America Star Bks.

I Can Share. 2004. (J). per. (978-1-57657-392-1(3)) Paradise Pr., Inc.

Irwin, Gayle. Sage Learns to Share, 1 vol. Araujo, Katie, illus. 2009. 45p. pap. 24.95 (978-1-60836-409-1(7)) America Star Bks.

Jacobs, Sheila. Jake Earns A Treat: A Life & Money Book. 2011. 24p. 11.99 (978-1-4567-3001-7(0)) AuthorHouse.

—Jake Saves the Day: A Life & Money Book. 2011. 24p. 11.99 (978-1-4520-9929-3(4)) AuthorHouse.

Jaekel, Susan M., illus. Stone Soup: A Tale about Sharing. 2006. (J). (978-1-59939-080-2(9), Reader's Digest Young Families, Inc.) Studio Fun International.

Kane, Kim. The Fancy Friend. 2018. (Ginger Green, Playdate Queen Ser.). (ENG., Illus.). 64p. (J). (gr. 1-3). pap. 5.95 (978-1-5158-1954-7(X), 136637, Picture Window Bks.) Capstone.

—The Fancy Friend. Davis, Jon, illus. 2017. (Ginger Green, Playdate Queen Ser.). (ENG.). 64p. (J). (gr. 1-3). lib. bdg. 23.32 (978-1-5158-1948-6(5), 136631, Picture Window Bks.) Capstone.

Karapetkova, Holly & Picou, Lin. Ouch! Stitches. Reese, Bob, illus. 2011. (Little Birdie Readers Ser.). (ENG.). 24p. (gr. 1-2). pap. 9.95 *(978-1-61236-023-2(8)*, 9781612360232) Rourke Educational Media.

Katz, Alan. Me! Me! Mine! Lemaitre, Pascal, illus. 2011. (ENG.). 16p. (J). (gr. -1-1). bds. 7.99 *(978-1-4169-8993-6(5)*, Little Simon) Little Simon.

Katz, Karen. I Can Share! 2011. 24p. (J). (gr. -1-k). mass mkt. 5.99 *(978-0-448-45592-1(7)*, Grosset & Dunlap) Penguin Young Readers Group.

Kaufman Orloff, Karen. I Wanna New Room. Catrow, David, illus. 2010. 32p. (J). (gr. k-3). 18.99 *(978-0-399-25405-5(6)*, G.P. Putnam's Sons Books for Young Readers) Penguin Young Readers Group.

Kaufman, Suzanne. Confiscated! Kaufman, Suzanne, illus. 2017. (ENG., Illus.). 32p. (J). (gr. -1-3). 17.99 *(978-0-06-241086-3(5)*, Balzer & Bray) HarperCollins Pubs.

Kemnitz, Dianna. A New Hat for Jack. 2012. 38p. 24.95 *(978-1-4626-6816-8(X))* America Star Bks.

Khan, Farheen. Ibrahim Khan & the Mystery of the Roaring Lion. 2010. (Ibrahim Khan Ser.). (ENG., Illus.). 56p. (J). (gr. 2-6). pap. 7.50 *(978-0-86037-467-1(X))* Kube Publishing Ltd. GBR. Dist: Consortium Bk. Sales & Distribution.

Kiernan, Tim. Liams Luck & Finnegans Fortune. 2009. (ENG.). 144p. pap. 10.95 *(978-1-933916-48-4(6)*, Ferne Pr.) Nelson Publishing & Marketing.

Kirk, David. Happy Heartwood Day. 2005. (Illus.). (J). *(978-1-4156-3888-0(8)*, Grosset & Dunlap) Penguin Publishing Group.

Kittinger, Jo S. A Lunch with Punch. 2004. (Rookie Reader Español Ser.). (ENG., Illus.). 32p. (J). (gr. k-2). pap. 4.95 *(978-0-516-27785-1(5)*, Children's Pr.) Scholastic Library Publishing.

Klein, Abby. Thanks for Giving. McKinley, John, illus. 2009. (Ready, Freddy! Reader List: No. 4). 32p. (J). pap. *(978-0-545-14176-5(1))* Scholastic, Inc.

Krans, Kim. Whose Moon Is That? 2017. (Illus.). 48p. (J). (gr. -1-2). 17.99 *(978-1-101-93227-8(9)*, Random Hse. Bks. for Young Readers) Random Hse. Children's Bks.

Kroll, Steven. Jungle Bullies, 0 vols. Nguyen, Vincent, illus. 2013. (ENG.). 34p. (J). (gr. -1-2). pap. 7.99 *(978-0-7614-5620-9(1)*, 9780761456209, Two Lions) Amazon Publishing.

Kumiega, Michelle. The Greedy Bunny. 2008. 28p. pap. 24.95 *(978-1-60672-966-3(7))* America Star Bks.

Lakritz, Deborah. Joey & the Giant Box. Byrne, Mike, illus. 2015. (ENG.). 32p. (J). (gr. -1-2). lib. bdg. 9.99 *(978-1-4677-1953-7(6)*, edd32a84-7290-406d-8c23-7cba166d7843); E-Book 27.99 *(978-1-4677-6205-2(9))* Lerner Publishing Group. (Kar-Ben Publishing).

Lallemand, Orianne & Strickland, Tessa. The Blue Bird's Palace. Hénaff, Carole, illus. 2016. (J). *(978-1-78285-308-4(1))* Barefoot Bks., Inc.

LaReau, Kara. Ugly Fish. Magoon, Scott, illus. 2006. (ENG.). 40p. (J). (gr. -1-3). 17.99 *(978-0-15-205082-5(5)*, 1195349, Clarion Bks.) HarperCollins Pubs.

Larsen, Kirsten. It's Sharing Day! Zalme, Ron, illus. 2007. (SPA & ENG.). (J). pap. *(978-0-439-92237-1(2)*, Scholastic) Scholastic, Inc.

—It's Sharing Day! Zalme, Ron, illus. 2007. (Dora the Explorer Ser.: 22). (ENG & SPA.). 24p. (J). pap. 3.99 *(978-1-4169-1575-1(3)*, Simon Spotlight/Nickelodeon) Simon Spotlight/Nickelodeon.

Lawson, Jessica. Sharing & Making Friends. 2010. 20p. pap. 10.00 *(978-1-60911-707-8(7)*, Eloquent Bks.) Strategic Book Publishing & Rights Agency (SBPRA).

Layne, Steven L. Share with Brother, 1 vol. Hoyt, Ard, illus. 2010. (ENG.). 32p. (J). (gr. k-3). 16.99 *(978-1-58980-860-7(6)*, Pelican Publishing) Arcadia Publishing.

Ledyard, Stephanie Parsley. Pie Is for Sharing. 2018. (ENG., Illus.). 32p. (J). 18.99 *(978-1-62672-562-1(4)*, 900161300) Roaring Brook Pr.

Lee, HaeDa. Ida's Present. Kim, IhHyeon, illus. 2014. (MySELF Bookshelf Ser.). (ENG.). 32p. (J). (gr. k-2). pap. 11.94 *(978-1-60357-694-9(0))*; lib. bdg. 25.27 *(978-1-59953-659-0(5))* Norwood Hse. Pr.

Leung, Hilary. Will Bear Share? 2018. (ENG., Illus.). 38p. (J). (gr. -1 — 1). bds. 7.99 *(978-1-338-21559-5(0)*, Cartwheel Bks.) Scholastic, Inc.

Lionni, Leo. It's Mine! 2015. 32p. pap. 7.00 *(978-1-61003-547-7(X))* Center for the Collaborative Classroom.

Lister, Mary. Winter King, Summer Queen. Mayo, Diana, illus. 2007. 32p. (J). (gr. -1-3). pap. 9.99 *(978-1-84686-009-6(1))*; (ENG.). pap. 7.99 *(978-1-84686-060-5(6))* Barefoot Bks., Inc.

Litwin, Eric. Ice Cream & Dinosaurs (Groovy Joe #1) Lichtenheld, Tom, illus. 2016. (Groovy Joe Ser.: 1). (ENG.). 40p. (J). (gr. -1-k). 17.99 *(978-0-545-88378-8(4)*, Orchard Bks.) Scholastic, Inc.

Lordon, Claire. Lorenzo, the Pizza-Loving Lobster. 2016. (ENG., Illus.). 32p. (J). (gr. -1-3). 16.99 *(978-1-4998-0228-3(5))* Little Bee Books Inc.

Ludmila's Way - Teaching Guide. 2003. (J). 17.95 *(978-1-55942-192-8(4))* Witcher Productions.

Ludmila's Way: Evaluation Guide. 2006. (J). *(978-1-55942-415-8(X))* Witcher Productions.

Luedtke, Courtney. Baby Boo: The Happy Beginning. 2009. (Illus.). 72p. pap. 27.49 *(978-1-4389-2696-4(0))* AuthorHouse.

Mack, Jeff. Mine! (Read Aloud Books for Kids, Funny Children's Books) 2017. (ENG., Illus.). 40p. (J). 16.99 *(978-1-4521-5234-9(9))* Chronicle Bks. LLC.

Mackall, Dandi Daley. Natalie & the Downside-Up Birthday, 1 vol. Blakeslee, Lys, illus. 2009. (That's Nat! Ser.: 4). (ENG.). 96p. (J). (gr. 1-4). pap. 4.99 *(978-0-310-71569-6(5))* Zonderkidz.

Mackall, Dandi Daley & Bowman, Crystal. Jake Learns to Share, 1 vol. 2008. (I Can Read! / the Jake Ser.). (ENG., Illus.). 32p. (J). pap. 4.99 *(978-0-310-71679-2(9))* Zonderkidz.

Maisner, Heather & Stephenson, Kristina. It's My Turn! 2005. (First-Time Stories Ser.). (ENG., Illus.). 24p. (J). (gr. -1-1). pap. 16.19 *(978-0-7534-5740-5(7)*, 9780753457405) Kingfisher Publications, plc GBR. Dist: Children's Plus, Inc.

Mardinly, Berdan. Fresh Tarhana Soup: Story in English & in Turkish. 2008. (ENG & TUR., Illus.). 24p. (J). 8.75 *(978-0-9801675-4-2(X))* Robertson Publishing.

Mattern, Joanne. The Tricky Garden. 2005. (J). pap. *(978-1-4108-4191-9(X))* Benchmark Education Co.

Mcevoy, Ariane. Little Monkey Learns to Share. 2012. 28p. pap. 15.99 *(978-1-4691-5830-3(2))* Xlibris Corp.

McKee, David. Elmer & the Hippos. McKee, David, illus. 2010. (Elmer Ser.). (ENG., Illus.). 32p. (J). (gr. -1-3). 17.99 *(978-0-7613-6442-9(0)*, c2f08435-936a-4921-99d8-7352eceff1a8) Lerner Publishing Group.

McKissack, Patricia C. The All-I'll-Ever-Want Christmas Doll. Pinkney, Jerry, illus. 2007. (ENG.). 40p. (J). (gr. -1-3). 17.99 *(978-0-375-83759-3(0)*, Schwartz & Wade Bks.) Random Hse. Children's Bks.

—What Is Given from the Heart. Harrison, April, illus. 2019. 40p. (J). (gr. -1-3). 17.99 *(978-0-375-83615-2(2)*, Schwartz & Wade Bks.) Random Hse. Children's Bks.

McNease, Mitzy. Chester's Presents. Cox, Kim, illus. 2006. 28p. (J). 10.95 *(978-0-9779488-0-2(3))* Blancmange Publishing LLC.

Meachen Rau, Dana. Let's Share. 2004. (Compass Point Early Reader Ser.). (J). 18.60 *(978-0-7565-0573-8(9)*, Compass Point Bks.) Capstone.

Meddaugh, Susan. Toy Trouble. 2010. (Martha Speaks Ser.). (ENG., Illus.). 24p. (J). (gr. -1-3). pap. 3.99 *(978-0-547-21078-0(7))* Houghton Mifflin Harcourt Publishing Co.

Metzger, Steve. Ice Cream King. Downing, Julie, illus. 2011. (ENG.). 32p. (J). (gr. -1-2). 15.95 *(978-1-58925-096-3(6))*; pap. 7.95 *(978-1-58925-427-5(9))* Tiger Tales.

Mims-Word, Marsha. The Great Vacation. 2011. 36p. pap. 21.99 *(978-1-4568-9675-1(X))* Xlibris Corp.

Moore, Marcia. Wind & Oyster Jack, 1 vol. Crow, Heather, illus. 2017. (ENG.). 32p. (J). 14.99 *(978-0-7643-5422-9(1)*, 7745) Schiffer Publishing, Ltd.

Moores, Susanna. It's Not Yours, It's Mine! 2013. (Child's Play Library). (Illus.). 32p. (J). (gr. -1-2). *(978-1-84643-600-0(1))* Child's Play International Ltd.

Moroney, Tracey, illus. A Snowman for Little Bear. 2016. (J). *(978-0-545-84958-6(6))* Scholastic, Inc.

Muller, Lisa M. Master smokey & mr. Duck. 2006. 15p. (J). 9.99 *(978-1-4276-0027-1(9))* Aardvark Global Publishing.

Muth, Jon J. Stone Soup. 2011. (J). (gr. -1-3). 29.95 *(978-0-545-32741-1(5))* Weston Woods Studios, Inc.

Naish, Sarah & Jefferies, Rosie. Callum Kindly & the Very Weird Child: A Story about Sharing Your Home with a New Child. Evans, Megan, illus. 2017. (Therapeutic Parenting Bks.). (ENG.). 32p. (C). pap. 17.95 *(978-1-78592-300-5(5)*, 696531) Kingsley, Jessica Pubs. GBR. Dist: Hachette UK Distribution.

Nash, Damien K. H. & Nash, Kathy. Big Box, Little Box: The Forecast Calls for Potential Rain! Miller, Steve, illus. 2012. 80p. pap. 13.99 *(978-0-9846507-1-2(7))* Faith Bks. & MORE.

Nesselrode, Sandra. Princess Kelsie & Her Special Gifts. 2008. 28p. pap. 19.95 *(978-1-4327-1708-7(1))* Outskirts Pr., Inc.

Newman, Jeff. The Greedy Worm. Newman, Jeff, illus. 2023. (ENG., Illus.). 32p. (J). (gr. -1-3). 18.99 *(978-1-4424-7195-5(6)*, Simon & Schuster Bks. For Young Readers) Simon & Schuster Bks. For Young Readers.

Nicholson, Doris. A Day with Grandma. 2006. 9.00 *(978-0-8059-9914-3(0))* Dorrance Publishing Co., Inc.

Nolan, Gwen. Steadfast Love. 2016. 182p. spiral bd. 19.95 *(978-1-60789-218-2(9))* Glorybound Publishing.

O'Connor, Jane. Too Many Tutus. 2012. (Fancy Nancy - I Can Read! Ser.). (J). lib. bdg. 13.55 *(978-0-606-27124-0(4))* Turtleback.

Ode, Eric. Too Many Tomatoes. Culotta, Kent, illus. 2016. (ENG.). 32p. (J). 11.99 *(978-1-61067-400-3(6))* Kane Miller.

Olson, D. A. The Treasure Map. 2011. 36p. pap. 24.95 *(978-1-4626-3655-6(1))* America Star Bks.

One Big Pair of Underwear. 2014. (ENG., Illus.). 40p. (J). (gr. -1-3). 19.99 *(978-1-4424-5336-4(2)*, Beach Lane Bks.) Beach Lane Bks.

Opal, Paola, illus. Saffy & Ollie. 2012. (ENG.). 24p. (J). (gr. -1 — 1). bds. 7.95 *(978-1-897476-69-7(8))* Simply Read Bks. CAN. Dist: Ingram Publisher Services.

Oram, Hiawyn. My Friend Fred. Reeve, Rosie, illus. 2012. (ENG.). 32p. (J). *(978-1-58925-105-2(9))* Tiger Tales.

Oxley, Jennifer & Aronson, Billy. Peg + Cat: the Pirate Problem: a Level 2 Reader. 2017. (Peg + Cat Ser.). (ENG.). 48p. (J). (gr. k-3). 14.99 *(978-0-7636-9786-0(9)*, Candlewick Entertainment) Candlewick Pr.

Parenteau, Shirley. Bears on Chairs. Walker, David M., illus. 2011. (Bears on Chairs Ser.). (ENG.). 32p. (J). (gr. -1 — 1). bds. 6.99 *(978-0-7636-5092-6(7))* Candlewick Pr.

Parker, David. I Can Share! Dubin, Jill, illus. 2005. (J). *(978-0-439-73587-2(4))* Scholastic, Inc.

—Sharing My Room. Lucas, Margeaux, illus. 2007. (J). *(978-0-545-00386-5(5))* Scholastic, Inc.

Pearson, Mary E. Generous Me. Krejca, Gary, illus. 2011. (Rookie Ready to Learn — All about Me! Ser.). 40p. (J). (gr. -1-k). lib. bdg. 25.00 *(978-0-531-26427-0(0))*; (ENG.). pap. 5.95 *(978-0-531-26652-6(4))* Scholastic Library Publishing. (Children's Pr.).

Pepper, Louise. Got your Back... A Story of Friendship & Caring. 2011. 24p. (gr. -1). pap. 11.50 *(978-1-4567-5527-0(7))* AuthorHouse.

Pilkey, Dav. Dragon's Merry Christmas: an Acorn Book (Dragon #5) Pilkey, Dav, illus. 2020. (Dragon Ser.: 5). (ENG., Illus.). 64p. (J). (gr. k-2). pap. 4.99 *(978-1-338-34752-4(7))* Scholastic, Inc.

Price, Marilyn. Grandma's Cookies. 2011. 32p. pap. 12.95 *(978-1-934527-28-3(9))* Torah Aura Productions.

Priddy, Roger. Shiny Shapes: Hooray for Thanksgiving! 2018. (Shiny Shapes Ser.). (ENG., Illus.). 10p. (J). bds. 7.99 *(978-0-312-52724-2(1)*, 900189781) St. Martin's Pr.

Principe, Tami. The Green Rabbit: Rabbits Aren't Supposed to Be Green! 2012. 32p. pap. 10.95 *(978-1-4626-7509-8(3))* America Star Bks.

Publications International Ltd. Staff, ed. Finding Nemo - Let's Go to School. 2011. 12p. (J). bds. *(978-1-4508-0510-0(8))* Publications International, Ltd.

—Sesame Street: Potty Time with Elmo (Look & Find) 2010. 20p. (J). pap. 5.98 *(978-1-4508-1471-3(9))* Publications International, Ltd.

Rabei, Carolina. Crunch! Rabei, Carolina, illus. 2016. (Child's Play Library). (ENG., Illus.). 36p. (J). *(978-1-84643-733-5(4))* Child's Play International Ltd.

Raczka, Bob. Beware! Day, Larry, illus. 2019. 32p. (J). (gr. -1-2). lib. bdg. 15.99 *(978-1-58089-683-2(9))* Charlesbridge Publishing, Inc.

Ramsey, Dave. The Big Birthday Surprise: Junior Discovers Giving. Ramsey, Marshall, illus. 2003. 26p. (J). 7.95 *(978-0-9726323-2-4(8))* Ramsey Pr.

Randall, Marilyn. A Hard Nut to Crack. 2009. 36p. pap. 18.95 *(978-0-557-15891-1(5))* Lulu Pr., Inc.

Ranganathan, Babu G. The Selfish Apple Tree. 2010. 12p. 7.95 *(978-1-4497-0312-7(7)*, WestBow Pr.) Author Solutions, LLC.

Ransome, James E. New Red Bike! 2017. (I Like to Read Ser.). (ENG.). 32p. (J). (gr. -1-3). 7.99 *(978-0-8234-3852-5(X))* Holiday Hse., Inc.

—New Red Bike! 2019. (I Like to Read Ser.). (ENG.). 26p. (J). (gr. k-1). 17.96 *(978-0-87617-957-4(X))* Penworthy Co., LLC, The.

Reiss, Mike & Reiss, Mike. The Boy Who Wouldn't Share. Catrow, David, illus. 2008. (ENG.). 32p. (J). (gr. 1-3). 17.99 *(978-0-06-059132-8(3)*, HarperCollins) HarperCollins Pubs.

Rickerty, Simon. The Crayon: A Colorful Tale about Friendship. Rickerty, Simon, illus. 2014. (ENG., Illus.). 32p. (J). (gr. -1-2). 15.99 *(978-1-4814-0475-4(X)*, Aladdin) Simon & Schuster Children's Publishing.

—The Peanut: A Nutty Tale about Sharing. Rickerty, Simon, illus. 2013. (ENG., Illus.). 40p. (J). (gr. -1-2). 15.99 *(978-1-4424-8364-4(4)*, Simon & Schuster/Paula Wiseman Bks.) Simon & Schuster/Paula Wiseman Bks.

Rivadeneira, Caryn. Mine! A Counting Book about Sharing. Gulliver, Amanda, illus. 2018. 28p. (J). bds. 7.99 *(978-1-5064-4679-0(5)*, Beaming Books) 1517 Media.

Rosenthal, Amy Krouse. Plant a Kiss. Reynolds, Peter H., illus. 2011. (ENG.). 40p. (J). (gr. -1-3). 15.99 *(978-0-06-198675-8(5)*, HarperCollins) HarperCollins Pubs.

—Plant a Kiss Board Book. Reynolds, Peter H., illus. 2015. (ENG.). 36p. (J). (gr. -1 — 1). bds. 7.99 *(978-0-06-241652-0(9)*, HarperFestival) HarperCollins Pubs.

Rusu, Meredith. Learning to Share. 2018. (Peppa Pig 8x8 Bks). (ENG.). 24p. (J). (gr. -1-k). 13.89 *(978-1-64310-231-3(1))* Penworthy Co., LLC, The.

—Learning to Share. 2018. (Peppa Pig 8X8 Ser.). lib. bdg. 14.75 *(978-0-606-41179-0(8))* Turtleback.

Santillo, LuAnn. Gum. Santillo, LuAnn, ed. 2003. (Half-Pint Kids Readers Ser.). (Illus.). 7p. (J). (gr. -1-1). pap. 1.00 *(978-1-59256-087-5(3))* Half-Pint Kids, Inc.

Sattler, Jennifer. Bully. Sattler, Jennifer, illus. 2018. (ENG., Illus.). 32p. (J). (gr. k-2). 16.99 *(978-1-58536-416-9(9)*, 204579) Sleeping Bear Pr.

Schmauss, Judy Kentor. Luke's Mule. 2006. (Reader's Clubhouse Level 2 Reader Ser.). (Illus.). 24p. (J). (gr. k-1). pap. 3.99 *(978-0-7641-3297-1(0))* Sourcebooks, Inc.

Schwarz, Evelyn. The Hummingbird Garden. Quinn, Kitty, illus. 2012. (ENG.). 34p. (J). pap. 16.95 *(978-1-4327-9815-4(4))* Outskirts Pr., Inc.

Segarini, Brian. A Belly Buff Duff Shared His Stuff. 2009. (ENG.). 28p. pap. 21.99 *(978-1-4415-5817-6(9))* Xlibris Corp.

Shea, Therese. Bear Likes to Share, 1 vol. 2006. (Neighborhood Readers Ser.). (ENG.). 8p. (gr. k-1). pap. 5.15 *(978-1-4042-5696-5(2)*, 3c922660-348b-4775-a9a8-3ca5c1e27aa4, Rosen Classroom) Rosen Publishing Group, Inc., The.

Smith, D. K. Sock 'n Boots - Share. 2010. 32p. pap. 13.60 *(978-0-557-52614-7(0))* Lulu Pr., Inc.

Sohn, Emily. Astro the Alien Learns about Sharing, 28 vols. Carlos Aón, illus. 2019. (Beginning-To-Read Ser.). (ENG.). 32p. (J). (gr. 1-2). pap. 13.26 *(978-1-68404-442-9(1))* Norwood Hse. Pr.

Soleim, Heather. God's Incredible Creatures: The Gift of Sharing. Greisen, Steve, ed. Hedgecock, Sean, illus. 2005. 24p. (J). bds. 14.95 *(978-0-9707422-9-2(0))* Reel Productions, LLC.

Sommer, Carl. Stone Soup. Denman, Michael, illus. 2014. (Sommer-Time Story Classics Ser.). (ENG.). 32p. (J). (gr. k-4). 16.95 *(978-1-57537-078-1(6))* Advance Publishing, Inc.

—Tied up in Knots(Enredados) Budwine, Greg, illus. 2009. (Another Sommer-Time Story Bilingual Ser.). (SPA & ENG.). 48p. (J). lib. bdg. 16.95 *(978-1-57537-169-6(3))* Advance Publishing, Inc.

Sowards, Ben, illus. Christmas Oranges. 2004. 32p. 17.95 *(978-1-59156-098-2(5))* Covenant Communications, Inc.

Sterer, Gideon. Not Your Nest! Tsurumi, Andrea, illus. 2019. 40p. (J). (gr. -1-2). 17.99 *(978-0-7352-2827-6(2)*, Dial Bks) Penguin Young Readers Group.

Stoop, Naoko. Red Knit Cap Girl & the Reading Tree. 2014. (ENG., Illus.). 40p. (J). (gr. -1-3). 17.99 *(978-0-316-22886-2(9))* Little, Brown Bks. for Young Readers.

Studio Mouse Staff. Sesame Street Share & Care, It's Only Fair. 2009. (ENG.). 60p. (J). (gr. -1). 12.99 *(978-1-59069-739-9(1))* Studio Mouse LLC.

SungJa, Cho. Bubbly & Grumpy. SukWon, Sa, illus. rev. ed. 2014. (MySELF Bookshelf Ser.). (ENG.). 32p. (J). (gr. k-2). pap. 11.94 *(978-1-60357-660-4(6))* Norwood Hse. Pr.

Szymona, Marlene L. My Sister Beth's Pink Birthday. Battuz, Christine, illus. 2014. 32p. (J). pap. *(978-1-4338-1655-0(5)*, Magination Pr.) American Psychological Assn.

—My Sister Beth's Pink Birthday: A Story about Sibling Relationships. Battuz, Christine, illus. 2014. 32p. (J). *(978-1-4338-1654-3(7)*, Magination Pr.) American Psychological Assn.

Talley, Linda. Ludmila's Way. Chase, Andra, illus. 2003. (J). 17.95 *(978-1-55942-190-4(8))* Witcher Productions.

Tan, Richard. George's Banana, 1 vol. 2015. (Rosen REAL Readers: STEM & STEAM Collection). (ENG.). 8p. (gr. k-1). pap. 5.46 *(978-1-4994-9530-0(7)*, 66bc11ab-663e-4bc6-8e61-5e4180048906, Rosen Classroom) Rosen Publishing Group, Inc., The.

Taylor, Myonna. Show & Tell. Phillips, Hope Ann, illus. 2012. 32p. 24.95 *(978-1-4626-7798-6(3))* America Star Bks.

Tineo, Suzanne Nicoll. Danny the Damsel: Sharing. 2012. 44p. pap. 22.65 *(978-1-4771-1510-7(2))* Xlibris Corp.

Tomlinson, Mark K. Share the Grain. 2010. 12p. pap. 8.49 *(978-1-4490-6059-6(5))* AuthorHouse.

Trilling, Richard J. Stories of Stephanie & Friends. 2010. 42p. pap. 15.50 *(978-1-60860-410-4(1)*, Eloquent Bks.) Strategic Book Publishing & Rights Agency (SBPRA).

Trimmer, Christian. Simon's New Bed. van der Paardt, Melissa, illus. 2015. (ENG.). 32p. (J). (gr. -1-3). 17.99 *(978-1-4814-3019-7(X))* Simon & Schuster Children's Publishing.

Tym, Kate. Time to Share. 2008. (Manners Ser.). (Illus.). 24p. (J). (gr. -1-1). lib. bdg. 16.95 *(978-1-59566-591-1(9))* QEB Publishing Inc.

Van Slyke, Rebecca. Monster's Trucks. Sutphin, Joe, illus. 2020. (ENG.). 40p. (J). 17.99 *(978-1-68119-301-4(9)*, 900165544, Bloomsbury Children's Bks.) Bloomsbury Publishing USA.

Waldman, Debby & Feutl, Rita. Room Enough for Daisy, 1 vol. Revell, Cindy, illus. 2011. (ENG.). 32p. (J). (gr. -1-k). 19.95 *(978-1-55469-255-2(5))* Orca Bk. Pubs. USA.

Weaver, Susan. My Goofy Girls. 2007. 24p. per. 24.95 *(978-1-4241-8933-5(0))* America Star Bks.

Wezeman, Phyllis Vos. Petra's Pier Picnic. Joyo, Oscar, illus. 2019. (ENG.). 32p. 19.95 *(978-0-87946-670-1(7))* ACTA Pubns.

Wheeler, Lisa. People Share with People. Idle, Molly, illus. 2019. (People Bks.). (ENG.). 40p. (J). (gr. -1-3). 17.99 *(978-1-5344-2559-0(4)*, Atheneum Bks. for Young Readers) Simon & Schuster Children's Publishing.

Wilhelm, Hans. I Won't Share! Wilhelm, Hans, illus. 2010. (Scholastic Reader Level 1 Ser.). (ENG.). 32p. (J). (gr. -1-2). pap. 3.99 *(978-0-439-77353-9(9))* Scholastic, Inc.

Willems, Mo. ¿Debo Compartir Mi Helado?-An Elephant & Piggie Book, Spanish Edition. 2015. (Elephant & Piggie Book Ser.). (SPA., Illus.). 64p. (J). (gr. -1-k). 10.99 *(978-1-4847-2291-6(4)*, Hyperion Books for Children) Disney Publishing Worldwide.

—¡la Paloma Encuentra un Perro Caliente! 2011. (ENG., Illus.). 40p. (J). (gr. -1-k). pap. 9.99 *(978-1-4231-4051-1(6)*, Hyperion Books for Children) Disney Publishing Worldwide.

—The Pigeon Finds a Hot Dog! 2004. (Pigeon Ser.). (ENG., Illus.). 40p. (J). (gr. -1-k). 17.99 *(978-0-7868-1869-3(7)*, Hyperion Books for Children) Disney Publishing Worldwide.

—Should I Share My Ice Cream?-An Elephant & Piggie Book. 2011. (Elephant & Piggie Book Ser.). (ENG., Illus.). 64p. (J). (gr. -1-k). 9.99 *(978-1-4231-4343-7(4)*, Hyperion Books for Children) Disney Publishing Worldwide.

Williams, Karen Lynn & Mohammed, Khadra. Four Feet, Two Sandals. Chayka, Doug, illus. rev. ed. 2016. 32p. (gr. 2-5). 18.70 *(978-0-8028-5296-0(3))* Kendall Hunt Publishing Co.

Wilson, Geraline. Billy & Willy Learn to Share. 2012. 24p. pap. 24.95 *(978-1-4626-8135-8(2))* America Star Bks.

Wilson, Karma. Bear Says Thanks. Chapman, Jane, illus. 2020. (Classic Board Bks.). (ENG.). 34p. (J). (gr. -1-k). bds. 7.99 *(978-1-5344-7418-5(8)*, Little Simon) Little Simon.

—Bear Says Thanks. Chapman, Jane, illus. (Bear Bks.). (ENG.). 40p. (J). (gr. -1-3). 2023. 9.99 ***(978-1-6659-4244-7(4))*** 2012. 18.99 *(978-1-4169-5856-7(8))* McElderry, Margaret K. Bks. (McElderry, Margaret K. Bks.).

Winkler, Henry & Oliver, Lin. Dump Trucks & Dogsleds #16: I'm on My Way, Mom! 2009. (Hank Zipzer Ser.: 16). (ENG., Illus.). 160p. (J). (gr. 3-7). pap. 6.99 *(978-0-448-44380-5(5)*, Grosset & Dunlap) Penguin Young Readers Group.

Witek, Jo. My Little Gifts: A Book of Sharing. Roussey, Christine, illus. 2018. (Growing Hearts Ser.). (ENG.). 30p. (J). (gr. -1 — 1). 16.99 *(978-1-4197-3320-8(6)*, 1257701, Abrams Appleseed) Abrams, Inc.

Witte, Anna. El Loro Tico Tango. Witte, Anna, illus. 2011. (SPA., Illus.). 24p. (J). (gr. -1-1). 9.99 *(978-1-84686-670-8(7))* Barefoot Bks., Inc.

Woodson, Jacqueline. Pecan Pie Baby. Blackall, Sophie, illus. 2010. (ENG.). 32p. (J). (gr. k-3). 17.99 *(978-0-399-23987-8(1)*, G.P. Putnam's Sons Books for Young Readers) Penguin Young Readers Group.

Yates-Velez, C. My Baby Brother & Me. 2011. (Illus.). 24p. pap. *(978-1-4269-6130-4(8))* Trafford Publishing (UK) Ltd.

Yerrid, Gable. Marley's Treasure. Fitzgerald, Jennifer, illus. 2007. 28p. (J). (gr. -1-3). 15.95 *(978-0-9767442-6-9(0))* Yorkville Pr.

Yim, Natasha. Goldy Luck & the Three Pandas. Zong, Grace, illus. 32p. (J). (gr. -1-3). 2015. (ENG.). pap. 7.95 *(978-1-58089-653-5(7))* 2014. lib. bdg. 17.99 *(978-1-58089-652-8(9))* Charlesbridge Publishing, Inc.

Zake, Daiga. Oranges for Everyone. Stojanova, Elena, illus. 2007. 32p. (J). (POL & ENG.). pap. 12.95 *(978-1-60195-104-5(3))*; (ARA.). pap. 12.95 *(978-1-60195-306-3(2))* International Step by Step Assn.

SHARKS

Abramovitz, Melissa. Deadliest Sharks. 2016. (ENG.). 80p. (J). (gr. 5-12). lib. bdg. *(978-1-68282-054-4(8))* ReferencePoint Pr., Inc.

Alderman, Christine Thomas. Bull Sharks. 2020. (J). pap. *(978-1-62310-108-4(5))* Black Rabbit Bks.

—Goblin Sharks. 2020. (J). pap. *(978-1-62310-109-1(3))* Black Rabbit Bks.

—Great White Sharks. 2020. (J). pap. *(978-1-62310-110-7(7))* Black Rabbit Bks.

—Hammerhead Sharks. 2019. (Swimming with Sharks Ser.). (ENG., Illus.). 32p. (J). (gr. 4-6). pap. 9.99 *(978-1-64466-049-2(0)*, 12805, Bolt) Black Rabbit Bks.

—Sand Tiger Sharks. 2020. (J). pap. *(978-1-62310-112-1(3))* Black Rabbit Bks.

—Tiger Sharks. (J). 2020. (Illus.). 31p. pap. *(978-1-62310-113-8(1))* 2019. (ENG.). 32p. (gr. 4-6). pap. 9.99 *(978-1-64466-051-5(2)*, 12813, Bolt) Black Rabbit Bks.

Alderton, David. Sharks & Sea Creatures Around the World. 2014. (Animals Around the World Ser.). (ENG., Illus.). 32p. (J). (gr. 2-5). 31.35 *(978-1-62588-196-0(7)*, 19262, Smart Apple Media) Black Rabbit Bks.

Antill, Sara. A Shark's Life. (Illus.). 24p. (J). 2012. 49.50 *(978-1-4488-5111-9(4)*, PowerKids Pr.) 2011. (ENG., (gr. 2-3). pap. 9.25 *(978-1-4488-5110-2(6)*, e2822b69-bc41-4bb0-a9bd-4b2a5c778f9a, PowerKids Pr.) 2011. (ENG., (gr. 2-3). lib. bdg. 26.27 *(978-1-4488-4981-9(0)*,

28167eba-e7f9-4dc4-bc3d-24d6d1e95d04) Rosen Publishing Group, Inc., The.

Aparicio, Eduardo. Sharks in the Dark. 2014. (Illus.). 32p. (J). pap. *(978-0-545-72502-6(X))* Scholastic, Inc.

—Sharks vs. Humans. 2014. (Illus.). 32p. (J). *(978-0-545-72499-9(6))* Scholastic, Inc.

Arlon, Penelope. Super Sharks. 2018. (LEGO Nonfiction Ser.: 7). (ENG., Illus.). 32p. (J). (gr. -1-3). pap. 4.99 *(978-1-338-26193-6(2))* Scholastic, Inc.

Arlon, Penelope & Lee, Paul. Super Sharks: A LEGO Adventure in the Real World. Arlon, Penelope & Lee, Paul, illus. 2018. (Illus.). 32p. (J). *(978-1-5490-3571-2(8))* Scholastic, Inc.

Arnold, Tedd. Fly Guy Presents: Sharks (Scholastic Reader, Level 2) Arnold, Tedd, illus. 2013. (Scholastic Reader, Level 2 Ser.). (ENG., Illus.). 32p. (J). (gr. -1-3). pap. 4.99 *(978-0-545-50771-4(5),* Scholastic Nonfiction) Scholastic, Inc.

—Sharks. 2013. (Fly Guy Presents Ser.). lib. bdg. 13.55 *(978-0-606-31968-3(9))* Turtleback.

Bader, Bonnie. My Little Golden Book about Sharks. Laberis, Steph, illus. 2016. (Little Golden Book Ser.). 24p. (J). (-k). 5.99 *(978-1-101-93092-2(6),* Golden Bks.) Random Hse. Children's Bks.

Balfour, Barbara. Great White Sharks. 2006. (Amazing Animals Ser.). (Illus.). 24p. (J). (gr. 3-7). pap. 8.95 *(978-1-59036-397-3(3));* lib. bdg. 24.45 *(978-1-59036-391-1(4))* Weigl Pubs., Inc.

Bantin, John. Shark Bytes: Tales of Diving with the Bizarre & the Beautiful. 2015. (ENG., Illus.). 224p. pap. 30.60 *(978-1-909911-45-1(3))* Fernhurst Bks. GBR. Dist: Casemate Pubs. & Bk. Distributors, LLC.

Barnes, J. Lou. 101 Facts about Sharks, 1 vol. 2004. (101 Facts about Predators Ser.). (ENG., Illus.). 32p. (gr. 2-4). lib. bdg. 28.67 *(978-0-8368-4039-1(9),* 48863134-5218-4b5e-9450-d9076f0176f4, Gareth Stevens Learning Library) Stevens, Gareth Publishing LLLP.

Barnes, Nico. Basking Sharks, 1 vol. 2014. (Sharks (Abdo Kids) Ser.). (ENG.). 24p. (J). (gr. -1-2). lib. bdg. 32.79 *(978-1-62970-064-9(9),* 1643, Abdo Kids) ABDO Publishing Co.

—Great White Sharks, 1 vol. 2014. (Sharks (Abdo Kids) Ser.). (ENG.). 24p. (J). (gr. -1-2). lib. bdg. 32.79 *(978-1-62970-065-6(7),* 1644, Abdo Kids) ABDO Publishing Co.

—Hammerhead Sharks, 1 vol. 2014. (Sharks (Abdo Kids) Ser.). (ENG.). 24p. (J). (gr. -1-2). lib. bdg. 32.79 *(978-1-62970-066-3(5),* 1645, Abdo Kids) ABDO Publishing Co.

—Mako Sharks, 1 vol. 2014. (Sharks (Abdo Kids) Ser.). (ENG.). 24p. (J). (gr. -1-2). lib. bdg. 32.79 *(978-1-62970-067-0(3),* 1646, Abdo Kids) ABDO Publishing Co.

—Whale Sharks, 1 vol. 2014. (Sharks (Abdo Kids) Ser.). (ENG.). 24p. (J). (gr. -1-2). lib. bdg. 32.79 *(978-1-62970-068-7(1),* 1647, Abdo Kids) ABDO Publishing Co.

—Zebra Sharks, 1 vol. 2014. (Sharks (Abdo Kids) Ser.). (ENG.). 24p. (J). (gr. -1-2). lib. bdg. 32.79 *(978-1-62970-069-4(X),* 1648, Abdo Kids) ABDO Publishing Co.

Barnes, Nico, et al. Tiburones Martillo. 2015. (Tiburones Ser.). (SPA., Illus.). 24p. (J). (gr. -1-2). pap. 7.95 *(978-1-4966-0521-4(7),* 130338, Capstone Classroom) Capstone.

Beer, Julie. Sharks vs. Sloths. 2019. (Illus.). 64p. (J). (gr. 1-3). 17.99 *(978-1-4263-3523-5(7),* National Geographic Kids) Disney Publishing Worldwide.

Believe It Or Not!, Ripleys, compiled by. Ripley Twists PB: Sharks & Other Scary Sea Creatures. 2018. (Twist Ser.: 9). (ENG.). 48p. (J). pap. 7.99 *(978-1-60991-231-4(4))* Ripley Entertainment, Inc.

Bell, Samantha. Hammerhead Sharks. 2013. (21st Century Skills Library: Exploring Our Oceans Ser.). (ENG., Illus.). 32p. (J). (gr. 3-6). 32.07 *(978-1-62431-408-7(2),* 202752); pap. 14.21 *(978-1-62431-484-1(8),* 202754) Cherry Lake Publishing.

—Tiger Sharks. 2013. (21st Century Skills Library: Exploring Our Oceans Ser.). (ENG., Illus.). 32p. (J). (gr. 3-6). 32.07 *(978-1-62431-410-0(4),* 202760); pap. 14.21 *(978-1-62431-486-5(4),* 202762) Cherry Lake Publishing.

Benchley, Peter. Shark Life: True Stories about Sharks & the Sea. 2007. (ENG.). 208p. (J). (gr. 3-7). 7.99 *(978-0-440-41954-9(9),* Yearling) Random Hse. Children's Bks.

Berger, Melvin & Berger, Gilda. Sharks. 2003. (Scholastic Reader Ser.). (Illus.). (J). pap. *(978-0-439-47388-0(8))* Scholastic, Inc.

Bergeron, Alain M., et al. Les Requins. 2008. (FRE., Illus.). 64p. (J). pap. 8.95 *(978-2-89435-369-1(3))* Quintin Pubs./Editions Michel Quintin CAN. Dist: Crabtree Publishing Co.

Berman, Ruth. Sharks. rev. ed. 2009. (Nature Watch Ser.). (ENG.). 48p. (gr. 4-8). 27.93 *(978-0-7613-4243-4(5))* Lerner Publishing Group.

Best, Arthur. Sharks, 1 vol. 2018. (Migrating Animals Ser.). (ENG.). 24p. (J). (gr. 1-1). 27.36 *(978-1-5026-3717-8(0),* b48bb4e1-a4e2-405e-b5a6-defe0509bf1c) Cavendish Square Publishing LLC.

Betz, Adrienne & Time for Kids Editors. Sharks! 2005. (Time for Kids Science Scoops Ser.). (ENG., Illus.). 32p. (J). (gr. 1-3). pap. 3.99 *(978-0-06-057632-5(4))* HarperCollins Pubs.

Bodden, Valerie. Sharks. 2010. (Amazing Animals Ser.). (Illus.). 24p. (J). (gr. -1-3). 16.95 *(978-1-58341-812-3(1),* Creative Education) Creative Co., The.

Borgert-Spaniol, Megan. The Sand Tiger Shark. 2012. (Shark Fact Files Ser.). (ENG., Illus.). 24p. (J). (gr. 3-8). lib. bdg. 27.95 *(978-1-60014-806-4(9),* Pilot Bks.) Bellwether Media.

—The Whale Shark. 2012. (Shark Fact Files Ser.). (ENG., Illus.). 24p. (J). (gr. 3-8). lib. bdg. 27.95 *(978-1-60014-807-1(7),* Pilot Bks.) Bellwether Media.

Boyd, Ian, et al. Animal Bites: Sharks. 2005. (Illus.). 24p. (J). pap. *(978-0-439-81500-0(2),* Scholastic) Scholastic, Inc.

Boyer, Crispin. So Cool! Sharks. 2019. (Cool/Cute Ser.). (Illus.). 32p. (J). (gr. -1-k). 6.99 *(978-1-4263-3361-3(7),* National Geographic Kids) Disney Publishing Worldwide.

Braun, Eric. Great White Shark vs. Mosquito. 2018. (Versus! Ser.). (ENG.). 24p. (J). (gr. 4-6). pap. 9.99 *(978-1-64466-332-5(5),* 12163); (Illus.). lib. bdg. *(978-1-68072-349-6(9),* 12162) Black Rabbit Bks. (Hi Jinx).

Bredeson, Carmen. Great White Sharks up Close, 1 vol. 2006. (Zoom in on Animals! Ser.). (ENG., Illus.). 24p. (gr. k-2). lib. bdg. 25.60 *(978-0-7660-2495-3(4),* 322356c4-f708-41ef-b1b5-35a43eb619d7, Enslow Elementary) Enslow Publishing, LLC.

Bright, Michael. Spectacular Sharks: An Exciting Investigation into the Most Powerful Predator in the Ocean, Shown in More Than 200 Images. 2016. (Illus.). 64p. (J). (gr. -1-12). 12.99 *(978-1-86147-496-4(2),* Armadillo) Anness Publishing GBR. Dist: National Bk. Network.

Brown, Laaren. Icky Sticky: Super Sharks (Scholastic Reader, Level 2) 2015. (Scholastic Reader, Level 2 Ser.). (ENG., Illus.). 32p. (J). (gr. 1-3). pap. 4.99 *(978-0-545-87231-7(6),* Scholastic Nonfiction) Scholastic, Inc.

—Super Sharks. 2016. (Illus.). 32p. (J). *(978-1-5182-0105-9(9))* Scholastic, Inc.

Bullard, Lisa. We Need Sharks. 2019. (Animal Files Ser.). (ENG., Illus.). 32p. (J). (gr. 3-5). 31.35 *(978-1-64185-314-9(X),* 164185314X, Focus Readers) North Star Editions.

Bulletpoints Sharks. 2005. (Illus.). (J). per. 4.99 *(978-1-933581-07-1(7))* Byeway Bks.

Calver, Paul & Reynolds, Toby. How to Draw Incredible Sharks & Other Ocean Giants: Packed with over 80 Creatures of the Sea. Gowen, Fiona, illus. 2016. (How to Draw Ser.). (ENG.). 32p. (J). (gr. 2-6). pap. 6.99 *(978-1-4380-0853-0(8))* Sourcebooks, Inc.

Camilla, De La Bedoyere. Sharks. Kelly, Richard, ed. 2017. (Illus.). 96p. (J). pap. 9.95 *(978-1-78209-565-1(9))* Miles Kelly Publishing, Ltd. GBR. Dist: Parkwest Pubns., Inc.

Candelaria, Michael. Sharks! 2003. (World Discovery Science Readers Ser.). (Illus.). 32p. (J). *(978-0-439-56629-2(0))* Scholastic, Inc.

Capstone Press. Shark Zone. 2010. (Shark Zone Ser.). (ENG.). 32p. lib. bdg. 101.28 *(978-1-4296-5913-0(0),* Capstone Pr.) Capstone.

Carrington, Stephanie. Gigantic Whale Sharks, 1 vol. 2017. (Great Big Animals Ser.). (ENG.). 24p. (J). (gr. k-k). pap. 9.15 *(978-1-5382-0899-1(7),* 9fd8b8c1-738a-4db2-b2e5-a066ddd7d0e2); lib. bdg. 25.27 *(978-1-5382-0901-1(2),* 452777b2-25e5-4536-b923-be6ae9b39fbe) Stevens, Gareth Publishing LLLP.

Cerullo, Mary M. Journey to Shark Island: A Shark Photographer's Close Encounters, 1 vol. Rotman, Jeffrey L., illus. Rotman, Jeffrey L., photos by. 2014. (Shark Expedition Ser.). (ENG.). 40p. (J). (gr. 5-9). lib. bdg. 32.65 *(978-0-7565-4887-2(X),* 124954, Compass Point Bks.) Capstone.

Chanko, Pamela. The Shark Book (Side by Side) (Library Edition) 2019. (Side by Side Ser.). (ENG., Illus.). 24p. (J). (gr. k-k). lib. bdg. 26.00 *(978-0-531-23841-7(5),* Children's Pr.) Scholastic Library Publishing.

Chilson, Martin. In Search of Great White Sharks, 1 vol., 1. 2015. (Shark Search Ser.). (ENG., Illus.). 24p. (J). (gr. 3-4). pap. 9.25 *(978-1-5081-4339-0(0),* 821a0a81-ba87-4be8-a3cd-e0aaecc7245e, PowerKids Pr.) Rosen Publishing Group, Inc., The.

Clark, Willow. Shark!, 1 vol. 2010. (Animal Danger Zone Ser.). (ENG.). 24p. (J). (gr. 2-3). lib. bdg. 27.27 *(978-1-60754-957-4(3),* 22ff0d98-69a0-4d77-9295-88dcd6ea9e9b); (Illus.). pap. 9.15 *(978-1-60754-964-2(6),* 675fdecf-4761-434e-bb4e-59c8385122c4) Rosen Publishing Group, Inc., The. (Windmill Bks.).

Clarke, Catriona. Sharks: Information for Young Readers - Level 1. Relf, Adam, illus. 2007. (Usborne Beginners Ser.). 32p. (J). (gr. -1-3). 4.99 *(978-0-7945-1581-2(9),* Usborne) EDC Publishing.

Clarke, Phil. Sharks. 2005. (Usborne Lift the Flap Bks.). (Illus.). 16p. (J). (gr. -1-3). 11.99 *(978-0-7945-1109-8(0),* Usborne) EDC Publishing.

Clarke, Phillip & Furnival, Keith. Sharks. Scott, Peter David, illus. 2005. (J). *(978-0-439-86358-2(9))* Scholastic, Inc.

Clausen-Grace, Nicki. Great White Sharks. 2018. (Wild Animal Kingdom (Continuation) Ser.). (ENG.). 32p. (gr. 2-7). 9.95 *(978-1-68072-734-0(6));* (J). (gr. 4-6). pap. 9.99 *(978-1-64466-287-8(6),* 12401); (J). (gr. 4-6). lib. bdg. *(978-1-68072-440-0(1),* 12400) Black Rabbit Bks. (Bolt).

Claybourne, Anna. Sharks — Predators of the Sea. 2016. (ENG., Illus.). 80p. (J). (gr. 4-7). pap. 9.95 *(978-1-77085-739-1(7),* df31491d-c74b-4fec-845f-6d1910b0bae9) Firefly Bks., Ltd.

Cleave, Andrew. Sharks. 2019. (Creatures of the Ocean Ser.). (Illus.). 80p. (J). (gr. 12). lib. bdg. 34.60 *(978-1-4222-4310-7(9))* Mason Crest.

Cline, Gina. Great White Sharks. Dibble, Traci, illus. 2009. (1B Animal Behaviors Ser.). (ENG.). 36p. (J). pap. 9.60 *(978-1-61406-045-1(2))* American Reading Co.

Coleman, Miriam. Swimming with Sharks, 1 vol. 2009. (Flippers & Fins Ser.). (ENG., Illus.). 24p. (J). (gr. 2-3). pap. 9.25 *(978-1-4358-3239-8(6),* 67a27201-0443-4750-b77a-fc66d748a5c6, PowerKids Pr.); lib. bdg. 26.27 *(978-1-4042-8091-5(X),* e4ce4143-7afe-4884-b8a5-f0eb191fced9) Rosen Publishing Group, Inc., The.

Corwin, Jeff. The World of Sharks. 2014. (Wildlife & Nature Identification Ser.). (ENG., Illus.). 12p. (J). (gr. -1-12). 7.95 *(978-1-58355-816-4(0))* Waterford Pr., Inc.

Crossingham, John & Kalman, Bobbie. El Ciclo de Vida del Tiburon. 2007. (Ciclos de Vida Ser.). (SPA., Illus.). 32p. (J). (gr. 1-4). pap. *(978-0-7787-8719-8(2));* (gr. 3-7). lib. bdg. *(978-0-7787-8673-3(0))* Crabtree Publishing Co.

—The Life Cycle of a Shark. 2005. (Life Cycle Ser.). (ENG., Illus.). 32p. (J). (gr. 2-3). pap. *(978-0-7787-0699-1(0))* Crabtree Publishing Co.

Csotonyi, Julius T. Discovering Sharks: The Ultimate Guide to the Fiercest Predators in the Ocean Deep. 2016. (Discovering Ser.). (ENG., Illus.). 96p. (J). 24.95 *(978-1-60433-604-7(8),* Applesauce Pr.) Cider Mill Pr. Bk. Pubs., LLC.

Dakota, Heather. Shark Bites. Jankowski, Daniel, illus. 2016. 48p. (J). pap. *(978-1-338-13718-7(2))* Scholastic, Inc.

—Sharks: Menacing or Misunderstood? 2007. (Illus.). 48p. (J). *(978-0-439-92829-8(X))* Scholastic, Inc.

Davies, Nicola. Surprising Sharks: Read & Wonder. Croft, James, illus. 2005. (Read & Wonder Ser.). (ENG.). 32p. (J). (gr. -1-3). reprint ed. pap. 8.99 *(978-0-7636-2742-3(9))* Candlewick Pr.

De la Bédoyère, Camilla. Action Files: Sharks. 2008. 24p. (J). *(978-1-84810-022-0(1))* Miles Kelly Publishing, Ltd.

—The Complete Guide to Sharks. 2015. (Illus.). 144p. (J). *(978-1-4351-6164-1(5))* Barnes & Noble, Inc.

—My Little Book of Sharks. 2014. (Illus.). 64p. (J). *(978-1-4351-5529-9(7))* Barnes & Noble, Inc.

—The Wild Life of Sharks, 1 vol. 2014. (Wild Side Ser.). (ENG., Illus.). 24p. (J). (gr. 2-2). lib. bdg. 26.27 *(978-1-4777-5498-6(9),* c2ce57b6-050f-44e2-9c53-a3fcdc24e3d4, Windmill Bks.) Rosen Publishing Group, Inc., The.

Dempski, Seth. In Search of Blue Sharks, 1 vol., 1. 2015. (Shark Search Ser.). (ENG., Illus.). 24p. (J). (gr. 3-4). pap. 9.25 *(978-1-5081-4331-4(5),* 6ef6ef33-7a94-4ce9-bd4c-1beb137e4d5c, PowerKids Pr.) Rosen Publishing Group, Inc., The.

Dibble, Traci. Hammerhead Sharks. Dibble, Traci, illus. 2009. (1-3Y Marine Life Ser.). (ENG., Illus.). 16p. (J). pap. 8.00 *(978-1-61406-037-6(1))* American Reading Co.

DK. DKfindout! Sharks. 2017. (DK Findout! Ser.). (ENG., Illus.). 64p. (J). (gr. 1-4). pap. 10.99 *(978-1-4654-5751-6(8),* DK Children) Dorling Kindersley Publishing, Inc.

—Pocket Genius: Sharks: Facts at Your Fingertips. 2016. (Pocket Genius Ser.: 15). (ENG., Illus.). 160p. (J). (gr. 3-7). pap. 6.99 *(978-1-4654-4592-6(7),* DK Children) Dorling Kindersley Publishing, Inc.

—Sharks & Other Deadly Ocean Creatures Visual Encyclopedia. 2016. (DK Children's Visual Encyclopedias Ser.). (ENG., Illus.). 208p. (J). (gr. 4-7). 17.99 *(978-1-4654-5084-5(X),* DK Children) Dorling Kindersley Publishing, Inc.

—Super Shark Encyclopedia: And Other Creatures of the Deep. 2015. (DK Super Nature Encyclopedias Ser.). (ENG., Illus.). 208p. (J). (gr. 3-7). 24.99 *(978-1-4654-3584-2(0),* DK Children) Dorling Kindersley Publishing, Inc.

—Super Tiburones (Super Shark Encyclopedia) Y Otras Criaturas de Las Profundidades. 2018. (DK Super Nature Encyclopedias Ser.). Orig. Title: Super Shark Encyclopedia. (SPA., Illus.). 208p. (J). (gr. 3-7). 24.99 *(978-1-4654-7924-2(4),* DK Children) Dorling Kindersley Publishing, Inc.

Donaldson, Chelsea. Great White Shark: An Up-Close Look at Senses. 2014. (Illus.). 16p. (J). pap. *(978-0-545-75172-8(1))* Scholastic, Inc.

—Hammerhead Shark: An Up-Close Look at the Body. 2014. (Illus.). 16p. (J). *(978-0-545-75173-5(X))* Scholastic, Inc.

Durrie, Karen. Gran Tiburón Blanco. 2013. (SPA.). (J). *(978-1-62127-567-1(1))* Weigl Pubs., Inc.

—I Am a Great White Shark. 2012. (J). *(978-1-61913-223-8(0));* pap. *(978-1-61913-224-5(9))* Weigl Pubs., Inc.

Einstein, Erin. Sharks, 1 vol. 2016. (KidsWorld Ser.). (ENG., Illus.). 64p. (J). pap. 6.99 *(978-0-9940069-5-0(0),* 48dbc1f6-d81e-4345-8c64-af5c5aa85906) KidsWorld Bks. CAN. Dist: Lone Pine Publishing USA.

Equipo Staff. Tiburones. 2004.Tr. of Sharks. (SPA., Illus.). 64p. (J). pap. 8.95 *(978-0-7460-4515-2(8))* EDC Publishing.

Fact Atlas: Sharks. 2009. (FACT ATLAS Ser.). 72p. (J). 15.95 *(978-0-8416-1095-8(9))* Hammond World Atlas Corp.

Field, Nancy H. Discovering Sharks & Rays. Maydak, Michael S., illus. 2003. (Discovering Nature Library). 40p. (J). (gr. 2-6). pap. 7.95 *(978-0-941042-33-8(2))* Dog-Eared Pubns.

Flood, Joe. Science Comics: Sharks: Nature's Perfect Hunter. 2018. (Science Comics Ser.). (ENG., Illus.). 128p. (J). 21.99 *(978-1-62672-787-8(2),* 900173583); pap. 12.99 *(978-1-62672-788-5(0),* 900173584) Roaring Brook Pr. (First Second Bks.).

Foreman, Niki. DK Readers L3: Shark Reef. 2014. (DK Readers Level 3 Ser.). (ENG.). 48p. (J). (gr. 2-4). pap. 4.99 *(978-1-4654-2007-7(X),* DK Children) Dorling Kindersley Publishing, Inc.

Furstinger, Nancy. Great White Shark Paperback. 2013. (Great Predators Ser.). (ENG.). (J). (gr. 4-8). pap. 18.50 *(978-1-62403-012-3(2),* 10788) ABDO Publishing Co.

Gagne, Tammy. Sharks: Built for the Hunt. 2015. (Predator Profiles Ser.). (ENG., Illus.). 24p. (J). (gr. 1-3). lib. bdg. 27.99 *(978-1-4914-5037-6(1),* 128761, Capstone Pr.) Capstone.

Gibbons, Gail. Sharks (New & Updated Edition) 2020. (Illus.). 32p. (J). (gr. -1-3). 18.99 *(978-0-8234-4571-4(2))* Holiday Hse., Inc.

Gibbons, Lynn. Sharks. 2009. (Up Close Ser.). 24p. (gr. 3-3). 47.90 *(978-1-60854-702-9(7),* PowerKids Pr.) Rosen Publishing Group, Inc., The.

Gibbons, Lynn & Coode, Chris. Sharks, 1 vol. 2006. (Up Close Ser.). (ENG., Illus.). 24p. (J). (gr. 3-3). lib. bdg. 28.93 *(978-1-4042-3762-9(3),* 4b925ea0-5f34-43c0-9b50-e34f393f0d81, PowerKids Pr.) Rosen Publishing Group, Inc., The.

Gilkerson, Patricia. My Adventure with Sharks. 2009. (ENG.). 44p. (J). 8.99 *(978-1-59092-468-6(1))* Blue Forge Pr.

Gish, Melissa. Sharks. (X-Books: Predators Ser.). (Illus.). (J). 2017. (ENG.). 32p. (gr. 3-6). *(978-1-60818-821-5(3),* 20396) 2009. 48p. 22.95 *(978-1-58341-742-3(7))* Creative Co., The. (Creative Education).

—X-Books: Sharks. 2017. (X-Bks.). (ENG., Illus.). 32p. (J). (gr. 3-7). pap. 9.99 *(978-1-62832-424-2(4),* 20397, Creative Paperbacks) Creative Co., The.

Goldish, Meish. Shark. 2018. (Afraid of the Water Ser.). (ENG.). 24p. (J). (gr. 1-6). 7.99 *(978-1-64280-063-0(5))* Bearport Publishing Co., Inc.

—Shark: The Shredder. 2009. (Afraid of the Water Ser.). (Illus.). 24p. (YA). (gr. 2-5). lib. bdg. 26.99 *(978-1-59716-942-4(0))* Bearport Publishing Co., Inc.

—Tiger Sharks: Blue Blenders. (Disappearing Acts Ser.). (Illus.). 24p. (J). (gr. k-3). 2016. (ENG.). pap. 7.99 *(978-1-944998-37-0(3))* 2010. lib. bdg. 26.99 *(978-1-936087-43-3(X))* Bearport Publishing Co., Inc.

—Whale Shark: The World's Biggest Fish. 2007. (SuperSized! Ser.). (Illus.). 24p. (J). (gr. k-3). lib. bdg. 26.99 *(978-1-59716-397-2(X))* Bearport Publishing Co., Inc.

—Whale Shark: The World's Longest Fish. 2019. (J). pap. *(978-1-64280-758-5(3))* Bearport Publishing Co., Inc.

Gray, Susan H. Mako Sharks. 2013. (21st Century Skills Library: Exploring Our Oceans Ser.). (ENG., Illus.). 32p. (J). (gr. 3-6). 32.07 *(978-1-62431-409-4(0),* 202756) Cherry Lake Publishing.

Gray, Susan Heinrichs. Mako Sharks. 2013. (21st Century Skills Library: Exploring Our Oceans Ser.). (ENG., Illus.). 32p. (J). (gr. 3-6). pap. 14.21 *(978-1-62431-485-8(6),* 202758) Cherry Lake Publishing.

Great White Sharks, 6 bks. 2005. (Animal Predators Ser.). (Illus.). 40p. (J). (gr. 3-6). pap. 46.95 *(978-0-8225-5488-2(7))* Lerner Publishing Group.

Green, Jen. Great White Shark. 2013. (Science Slam: the Deep End-Animal Life Underwater Ser.). 24p. (J). (gr. -1-3). lib. bdg. 26.99 *(978-1-61772-918-8(3))* Bearport Publishing Co., Inc.

—Sharks. 2010. (Amazing Animal Hunters Ser.). (ENG., Illus.). 32p. (J). (gr. 3-5). lib. bdg. 28.50 *(978-1-60753-046-6(5),* 17200) Amicus.

—Sharks. 2008. (Nature's Children Ser.). (Illus.). 52p. (J). *(978-0-7172-6262-5(6))* Grolier, Ltd.

—Sharks. 2012. (ENG., Illus.). 32p. (gr. 3-5). pap. 8.95 *(978-1-926722-50-4(7))* Saunders Bk. Co. CAN. Dist: RiverStream Publishing.

Green, Sara. The Blue Shark. 2012. (Shark Fact Files Ser.). (ENG., Illus.). 24p. (J). (gr. 3-8). lib. bdg. 27.95 *(978-1-60014-802-6(6),* Pilot Bks.) Bellwether Media.

—The Goblin Shark. 2013. (Shark Fact Files Ser.). (ENG., Illus.). 24p. (J). (gr. 3-8). lib. bdg. 27.95 *(978-1-60014-870-5(0),* Pilot Bks.) Bellwether Media.

—The Great White Shark. 2012. (Shark Fact Files Ser.). (ENG., Illus.). 24p. (J). (gr. 3-8). lib. bdg. 27.95 *(978-1-60014-803-3(4),* Pilot Bks.) Bellwether Media.

—The Mako Shark. 2012. (Shark Fact Files Ser.). (ENG., Illus.). 24p. (J). (gr. 3-8). lib. bdg. 27.95 *(978-1-60014-804-0(2),* Pilot Bks.) Bellwether Media.

—The Oceanic Whitetip Shark. 2012. (Shark Fact Files Ser.). (ENG., Illus.). 24p. (J). (gr. 3-8). lib. bdg. 27.95 *(978-1-60014-805-7(0),* Pilot Bks.) Bellwether Media.

Gregory, Josh. Great White Sharks. 2013. (ENG.). 48p. (J). 28.00 *(978-0-531-23359-7(6));* pap. 6.95 *(978-0-531-25157-7(8))* Scholastic Library Publishing.

Griffith, Christine. Perfect Hunter. 2014. (Illus.). 32p. (J). *(978-0-545-72494-4(5))* Scholastic, Inc.

—Shark Attack! 2014. (Illus.). 32p. (J). *(978-0-545-72493-7(7))* Scholastic, Inc.

Gurevich, Margaret. National Geographic Kids Chapters: Diving with Sharks! And More True Stories of Extreme Adventures! 2016. (NGK Chapters Ser.). (Illus.). 112p. (J). (gr. 3-7). pap. 5.99 *(978-1-4263-2461-1(8));* (ENG., lib. bdg. 15.90 *(978-1-4263-2462-8(6))* Disney Publishing Worldwide. (National Geographic Kids).

Hall, Howard. A Frenzy of Sharks: The Surprising Life of a Perfect Predator. Leon, Vicki, ed. 2nd ed. 2006. (Jean-Michel Cousteau Presents Ser.). (ENG., Illus.). 48p. (J). (gr. 3-7). pap. 9.95 *(978-0-9766134-4-2(1))* London Town Pr.

Hamilton, S. L. Sharks. 2010. (Xtreme Predators Ser.). (ENG.). 32p. (J). (gr. 3-9). lib. bdg. 32.79 *(978-1-60453-993-6(3),* 15730, Abdo & Daughters) ABDO Publishing Co.

Hammerhead Sharks. 2014. (ENG.). 48p. (J). lib. bdg. 28.00 *(978-0-531-20668-3(8))* Scholastic Library Publishing.

Hardyman, Robyn. Sharks. 2008. (World of Animals Ser.). (ENG.). 32p. (J). (gr. 2-4). 31.35 *(978-1-933834-33-7(1),* 16825) Brown Bear Bks.

Hayes, Jennifer. Face to Face with Sharks. 2018. (Face to Face with Animals Ser.). (Illus.). 32p. (J). (gr. 3-7). pap. 6.99 *(978-1-4263-3259-3(9),* National Geographic Kids) Disney Publishing Worldwide.

Hibbert, Clare. If You Were a Shark. 2013. (If You Were A... Ser.). 32p. (gr. 2-5). 31.35 *(978-1-59920-962-3(4))* Black Rabbit Bks.

Hirsch, James. The Great White Shark. 2009. (Underwater World of Sharks Ser.). 24p. (gr. 3-3). 42.50 *(978-1-60854-245-1(9),* PowerKids Pr.) Rosen Publishing Group, Inc., The.

Honders, Christine. How Sharks & Other Animals Sense Electricity, 1 vol. 2015. (Superior Animal Senses Ser.). (ENG., Illus.). 24p. (J). (gr. 3-4). pap. 9.25 *(978-1-4994-0994-9(X),* 9816b148-89c1-4151-a0bc-ea398fb91c1f, PowerKids Pr.) Rosen Publishing Group, Inc., The.

Hopper, Whitney. In Search of Bull Sharks, 1 vol., 1. 2015. (Shark Search Ser.). (ENG., Illus.). 24p. (J). (gr. 3-4). pap. 9.25 *(978-1-5081-4335-2(8),* fb7800f0-3a7d-4d51-a763-fa036f9bd932, PowerKids Pr.) Rosen Publishing Group, Inc., The.

Houran, Lori Haskins. How to Spy on a Shark. Marquez, Francisca, illus. 2019. (ENG.). 24p. (J). (-3). pap. 7.99 *(978-0-8075-3406-9(4),* 807534064) Whitman, Albert & Co.

Huggins-Cooper, Lynn. Savage Sharks. 2006. (Killer Nature! Ser.). (Illus.). 32p. (J). lib. bdg. 28.50 *(978-1-58340-933-6(5))* Black Rabbit Bks.

Hull, Joyce A. Deepwater Sharks, Vol. 10. 2018. (Amazing World of Sharks Ser.). (Illus.). 64p. (J). (gr. 7). lib. bdg. 31.93 *(978-1-4222-4124-0(6))* Mason Crest.

—Hammerhead Sharks, Vol. 10. 2018. (Amazing World of Sharks Ser.). (Illus.). 64p. (J). (gr. 7). lib. bdg. 31.93 *(978-1-4222-4127-1(0))* Mason Crest.

Humphrey, Natalie K. Sharks & Pups, 1 vol. 2020. (Animal Family Ser.). (ENG.). 24p. (J). (gr. k-k). pap. 9.15 *(978-1-5382-5590-2(1),* 4b1523d5-3b2c-4204-b941-384b8eb898e3) Stevens, Gareth Publishing LLLP.

Hutchison, Patricia. Sharks Are Awesome. 2018. (Animals Are Awesome Ser.). (ENG., Illus.). 32p. (J). (gr. 3-6). 32.80 *(978-1-63235-438-9(1),* 13816, 12-Story Library) Bookstaves, LLC.

Jackson, Tom. Ferocious Sharks, 1 vol. 2010. (Dangerous Animals Ser.). (ENG., Illus.). 32p. (gr. 2-4). (J). pap. 11.50 *(978-1-4339-4044-6(2),* 870d0a03-2b0b-449d-a625-b3dc78cf77af, Gareth Stevens Learning Library); (YA). lib. bdg. 29.27 *(978-1-4339-4043-9(4),* 360dbbe5-3472-46b5-b64e-f05db33dd951) Stevens, Gareth Publishing LLLP.

—Inside the Mind of a Killer Shark, 1 vol. 2012. (Animal Instincts Ser.). (ENG., Illus.). 32p. (J). (gr. 3-3). pap. 11.00 *(978-1-4488-7072-1(0),* 806cf3eb-dc7f-4802-8771-aa9a6f37f370); lib. bdg. 28.93 *(978-1-4488-7031-8(3),* 0b42acfe-1a58-4959-aed8-0380e8a0c10) Rosen Publishing Group, Inc., The. (PowerKids Pr.).
—Shark Attack. 2008. (Crabtree Contact Ser.). (ENG., Illus.). 32p. (J). (gr. 3-7). lib. bdg. *(978-0-7787-3765-0(9))* Crabtree Publishing Co.
—Sharks. 2010. (Illus.). (J). *(978-1-74089-957-4(1))* Fog City Pr.
Jeffrey, Gary. Mega Shark. 2017. (Graphic Prehistoric Animals Ser.). (ENG., Illus.). 32p. (J). (gr. 5-8). lib. bdg. 31.35 *(978-1-62588-410-7(9),* 19279, Smart Apple Media) Black Rabbit Bks.
John, Gee. Tiger Sharks. 2011. (Power 100 - Marine Life Ser.). 24p. pap. 39.62 *(978-1-61541-234-1(4))* American Reading Co.
Johnson, Gee & Zorzi, Gina. Tiger Sharks. 2015. (2G Marine Life Ser.). (ENG.). 24p. (J). (gr. k-2). pap. 8.00 *(978-1-61541-167-2(4))* American Reading Co.
Kalman, Bobbie. Tiburones Espectaculares. 2006. (Libro de Bobbie Kalman Ser.). (SPA., Illus.). 32p. (J). pap. *(978-0-7787-8415-9(0))* Crabtree Publishing Co.
Kalman, Bobbie & Aloian, Molly. Spectacular Sharks. 2003. (Living Ocean Ser.). (ENG., Illus.). 32p. (J). (gr. 3-4). pap. *(978-0-7787-1320-3(2))* Crabtree Publishing Co.
—Tiburones Espectaculares. 2006. (Libro de Bobbie Kalman Ser.). (SPA., Illus.). 32p. (J). (gr. 3-7). lib. bdg. *(978-0-7787-8401-2(0))* Crabtree Publishing Co.
Kasso, Martin. Sharks. Jeffris, Matt, illus. 2008. (ENG.). 24p. (J). (gr. 3-18). 19.95 *(978-1-58117-797-8(6),* Intervisual/Piggy Toes) Bendon, Inc.
Katschke, Judy. Sink or Swim: Exploring Schools of Fish: a Branches Book (the Magic School Bus Rides Again) Artful Doodlers Ltd., illus. 2017. (Magic School Bus Rides Again Ser.: 1). (ENG.). 96p. (J). (gr. 1-3). pap. 5.99 *(978-1-338-19445-6(3))* Scholastic, Inc.
—Unidos o Nada: Explora Bancos de Peces (el Autobus Mágico Vuelve a Despegar) Artful Doodlers Ltd., illus. 2018. (Autobús Mágico Vuelve a Despegar Ser.: 1).Tr. of (el Autobus Mágico Vuelve a Despegar). (SPA.). 96p. (J). (gr. 1-3). pap. 5.99 *(978-1-338-29956-4(5),* Scholastic en Espanol) Scholastic, Inc.
Keating, Jess & Miguéns, Marta Álvarez. Shark Lady: The True Story of How Eugenie Clark Became the Ocean's Most Fearless Scientist. 2017. (Illus.). 40p. (J). (gr. k-4). 18.99 *(978-1-4926-4204-6(5))* Sourcebooks, Inc.
Kelly, Joni. 400-Year-Old Sharks!, 1 vol. 2018. (World's Longest-Living Animals Ser.). (ENG.). 24p. (gr. 1-2). 24.27 *(978-1-5382-1686-6(8),* de6978d2-c880-402c-9744-6f90ff1fa426) Stevens, Gareth Publishing LLLP.
Kenan, Tessa. Look, a Shark! 2016. (Bumba Books (r) — I See Ocean Animals Ser.). (ENG., Illus.). 24p. (J). (gr. -1-1). lib. bdg. 26.65 *(978-1-5124-1419-6(0),* 711d9e07-72a4-40e9-9fb5-0726f32d5773, Lerner Pubns.) Lerner Publishing Group.
—¡Mira, un Tiburón! (Look, a Shark!) 2017. (Bumba Books (r) en Español — Veo Animales Marinos (I See Ocean Animals) Ser.). (SPA., Illus.). 24p. (J). (gr. -1-1). 26.65 *(978-1-5124-2868-1(X),* 73d81de2-1f52-4805-a27c-8d8f558e7c9c, Ediciones Lerner) Lerner Publishing Group.
Kennington, Tammy. Blue Sharks. 2013. (21st Century Skills Library: Exploring Our Oceans Ser.). (ENG., Illus.). 32p. (J). (gr. 3-6). 32.07 *(978-1-62431-404-9(X),* 202736); pap. 14.21 *(978-1-62431-480-3(5),* 202738) Cherry Lake Publishing.
—Bull Sharks. 2013. (21st Century Skills Library: Exploring Our Oceans Ser.). (ENG., Illus.). 32p. (J). (gr. 3-6). 32.07 *(978-1-62431-405-6(8),* 202740); pap. 14.21 *(978-1-62431-481-0(3),* 202742) Cherry Lake Publishing.
Keppeler, Jill. Sharks Lived with the Dinosaurs!, 1 vol. 2016. (Living with the Dinosaurs Ser.). (ENG.). 24p. (J). (gr. 2-3). pap. 9.15 *(978-1-4824-5675-2(3),* a906787a-dd6f-49e6-938b-a10becda960f) Stevens, Gareth Publishing LLLP.
King, H. Elizabeth. Kemo Shark. Date not set. 14p. (J). pap. 2.95 *(978-0-9647798-0-8(3))* Kidscope, Inc.
King, Trey. Training Academy: Sharks & Other Sea Life! (Illus.). 32p. (J). *(978-1-5182-4448-3(3),* Reagan Arthur Bks.) Little Brown & Co.
Kirkman, Marissa. Goblin Sharks: A 4D Book. 2018. (All about Sharks Ser.). (ENG., Illus.). 24p. (J). (gr. -1-2). lib. bdg. 29.32 *(978-1-9771-0157-0(7),* 138322, Capstone Pr.) Capstone.
Kosara, Tori. Big Sharks. 2010. (Illus.). (J). *(978-0-545-30044-5(4))* Scholastic, Inc.
Kratt, Chris & Kratt, Martin. Wild Sea Creatures: Sharks, Whales & Dolphins! (Wild Kratts) 2014. (Step into Reading Ser.). (Illus.). 32p. (J). (gr. -1-1). 5.99 *(978-0-553-49901-8(7),* Random Hse. Bks. for Young Readers) Random Hse. Children's Bks.
Kris Hirschmann. The Whale Shark. 2004. (CREATURES of the SEA Ser.). (ENG., Illus.). 48p. (J). 27.50 *(978-0-7377-2059-4(X),* Kidhaven) Cengage Gale.
Kurtz, Kevin. Sharks & Dolphins: a Compare & Contrast Book, 1 vol. 2016. (Compare & Contrast Ser.). (ENG., Illus.). 39p. (J). (gr. k-3). 17.95 *(978-1-62855-732-9(X))* Arbordale Publishing.
—Sharks & Dolphins: a Compare & Contrast Book: Spanish, 1 vol. 2016. (SPA., Illus.). 39p. (J). (gr. k-1). pap. 11.95 *(978-1-62855-746-6(X),* 676a6ffd-b416-4bb7-862f-9797937f72e6) Arbordale Publishing.
Lacey, Saskia. Amazing Animals: Sharks: Skip Counting (Grade 2) 2018. (Mathematics in the Real World Ser.). (ENG., Illus.). 32p. (J). (gr. 2-3). pap. 10.99 *(978-1-4258-5743-1(4))* Teacher Created Materials, Inc.
—Animales Asombrosos: Tiburones: Conteo Salteado (Amazing Animals: Sharks: Skip Counting) rev. ed. 2018. (Mathematics in the Real World Ser.). (SPA., Illus.). 32p. (J). (gr. 2-3). pap. 10.99 *(978-1-4258-2860-8(4))* Teacher Created Materials, Inc.
Ladybird. Sharks: Ladybird Readers Level 3, Vol. 3. 2016. (Ladybird Readers Ser.). (Illus.). 64p. (J). (gr. 2-4). pap. 9.99 *(978-0-241-25382-3(9))* Penguin Bks., Ltd. GBR. Dist: Independent Pubs. Group.
Lang, Heather. Swimming with Sharks: The Daring Discoveries of Eugenie Clark. Solano, Jordi, illus. 2016. (ENG.). 32p. (J). (gr. -1-3). 17.99 *(978-0-8075-2187-8(6),* 807521876) Whitman, Albert & Co.
Laughlin, Kara L. Sharks. 2017. (In the Deep Blue Sea Ser.). (ENG.). 24p. (J). (gr. k-3). lib. bdg. 32.79 *(978-1-5038-1692-3(3),* 211526) Child's World, Inc, The.
Lawrence, Ellen. Bull Shark. 2016. (Apex Predators of the Amazon Rain Forest Ser.). (ENG., Illus.). 24p. (J). (gr. -1-3). 26.99 *(978-1-68402-035-5(2))* Bearport Publishing Co., Inc.
Le Bloas-Julienne, Renee. The Shark: Silent Hunter. Bios Agency, photos by. 2007. (Animal Close-Ups Ser.). (Illus.). 26p. (J). (gr. 1-4). pap. 6.95 *(978-1-57091-631-1(4))* Charlesbridge Publishing, Inc.
Leavitt, Amie Jane. A Daredevil's Guide to Swimming with Sharks, 1 vol. 2013. (Daredevils' Guides). (ENG., Illus.). 48p. (J). (gr. 5-9). lib. bdg. 32.65 *(978-1-4296-9985-3(X),* 120686) Capstone.
LeBreton, Sue. Whale Shark. 2014. (J). pap. *(978-1-4896-1083-6(9))* Weigl Pubs., Inc.
Lee, Justin. How to Draw Sharks. 2009. (Kid's Guide to Drawing Ser.). 24p. (gr. 3-4). 47.90 *(978-1-61511-040-7(2),* PowerKids Pr.) Rosen Publishing Group, Inc., The.
Lindeen, Carol K. Sharks [Scholastic]. 2010. (Under the Sea Ser.). 24p. pap. 0.50 *(978-1-4296-5064-9(8),* Capstone Pr.) Capstone.
Little & Large Sticker Activity Sharks. 2008. 24p. pap. *(978-1-84810-062-6(0))* Miles Kelly Publishing, Ltd.
Loh-Hagan, Virginia. Discover Great White Shark. 2015. (21st Century Basic Skills Library: Splash! Ser.). (ENG., Illus.). 24p. (J). (gr. 2-4). 26.35 *(978-1-63362-598-3(2),* 206576) Cherry Lake Publishing.
—Discover Hammerhead Shark. 2015. (21st Century Basic Skills Library: Splash! Ser.). (ENG., Illus.). 24p. (J). (gr. 2-4). 26.35 *(978-1-63362-599-0(0),* 206580) Cherry Lake Publishing.
Lynette, Rachel. Bluntnose Sixgill Sharks & Other Strange Sharks, 1 vol. 2011. (Creatures of the Deep Ser.). (ENG., Illus.). 32p. (J). (gr. 3-5). pap. 8.95 *(978-1-4109-4203-6(1),* 115565, Raintree) Capstone.
Magby, Meryl. Hammerhead Sharks, 1 vol. 2012. (Under the Sea Ser.). (ENG., Illus.). 24p. (J). (gr. 2-3). pap. 9.25 *(978-1-4488-7477-4(7),* 01beb9bc-6238-4fd8-9be3-2066d887aec2); lib. bdg. 26.27 *(978-1-4488-7398-2(3),* 8cb5f4f9-7092-4341-9cab-bf52b2d25664) Rosen Publishing Group, Inc., The. (PowerKids Pr.).
Markle, Sandra. The Great Shark Rescue: Saving the Whale Sharks. 2019. (Sandra Markle's Science Discoveries Ser.). (ENG., Illus.). 48p. (J). (gr. 4-6). 33.32 *(978-1-5415-1041-8(0),* 8547381d-d1ef-441b-8cfc-60d92fa97508, Millbrook Pr.) Lerner Publishing Group.
—Great White Sharks. 2005. (Animal Predators Ser.). (ENG., Illus.). 40p. (J). (gr. 3-6). pap. 8.99 *(978-1-57505-747-6(6),* 026fa7d9-f749-4390-bc4e-86177297f177, First Avenue Editions) Lerner Publishing Group.
—Los Tiburones Blancos: Great White Sharks. 2008. pap. 46.95 *(978-0-8225-7091-2(2))* Lerner Publishing Group.
—Sharks: Biggest! Littlest! Perrine, Doug, photos by. 2011. (Biggest! Littlest! Ser.). (ENG., Illus.). 32p. (J). (gr. k-2). pap. 10.95 *(978-1-59078-873-8(7),* Astra Young Readers) Astra Publishing Hse.
—Los Tiburones Blancos. 2006. (Animales Depredadores (Animal Predators) Ser.). (SPA., Illus.). 39p. (J). (gr. 3-7). lib. bdg. 25.26 *(978-0-8225-6490-4(4),* Ediciones Lerner) Lerner Publishing Group.
Markovics, Joyce L. Great White Shark. 2016. (J). lib. bdg. *(978-1-62724-819-8(6))* Bearport Publishing Co., Inc.
Marsico, Katie. Sharks. 2012. (Nature's Children Ser.). (ENG., Illus.). 48p. (J). (gr. 3-5). pap. 6.95 *(978-0-531-21082-6(0));* lib. bdg. 28.00 *(978-0-531-20907-3(5))* Scholastic Library Publishing. (Children's Pr.).
Mason, Paul. The Shark Attack Files. 2018. (Wild World of Sharks Ser.). (ENG., Illus.). 32p. (J). (gr. 3-6). 27.99 *(978-1-5124-5978-4(X),* 5f0b4d47-9da7-4c58-b55c-dea43b2928dc, Hungry Tomato (r)) Lerner Publishing Group.
—Sharks in Danger. 2018. (Wild World of Sharks Ser.). (ENG., Illus.). 32p. (J). (gr. 3-6). lib. bdg. 27.99 *(978-1-5124-5977-7(1),* f2888ea5-a1c0-4758-8db8-0130cd00b770, Hungry Tomato (r)) Lerner Publishing Group.
—Sharks on the Hunt. 2018. (Wild World of Sharks Ser.). (ENG., Illus.). 32p. (J). (gr. 3-6). 27.99 *(978-1-5124-5975-3(5),* aca041c7-3071-4065-8764-c8add15a1190, Hungry Tomato (r)) Lerner Publishing Group.
—World's Weirdest Sharks. 2018. (Wild World of Sharks Ser.). (ENG., Illus.). 32p. (J). (gr. 3-6). 27.99 *(978-1-5124-5976-0(3),* be0a8de1-0190-4597-8c02-5cc90ca8f1e2, Hungry Tomato (r)) Lerner Publishing Group.
Maydak, Michael S., illus. Wild Stickers - Sharks & Rays. 2003. 4p. (J). 2.50 *(978-0-941042-34-5(0))* Dog-Eared Pubns.
McAneney, Caitie. Great White Sharks, 1 vol. 2019. (Killers of the Animal Kingdom Ser.). (ENG.). 24p. (J). (gr. 3-3). pap. 9.25 *(978-1-7253-0601-1(8),* 5ab8edbc-8141-451c-8a80-c1f6234f3e09, PowerKids Pr.) Rosen Publishing Group, Inc., The.
—In Search of Whale Sharks, 1 vol., 1. 2015. (Shark Search Ser.). (ENG., Illus.). 24p. (J). (gr. 3-4). pap. 9.25 *(978-1-5081-4351-2(X),* 42307a1f-823a-4ffd-9df7-230a4bd219b1, PowerKids Pr.) Rosen Publishing Group, Inc., The.
McKay, Sindy. We Both Read Bilingual Edition-Sharks!/Tiburones. Hunt, Judith & Smith, Wendy, illus. 2015.Tr. of Tiburones. (ENG & SPA.). 44p. (J). (gr. 1-2). pap. 5.99 *(978-1-60115-068-4(7))* Treasure Bay, Inc.
—We Both Read-Sharks! Hunt, Judith & Smith, Wendy, illus. 2012. 44p. (J). 9.95 *(978-1-60115-261-9(2));* pap. 5.99 *(978-1-60115-262-6(0))* Treasure Bay, Inc.
McMillan, Beverly & Musick, John A. Sharks. 2008. (Insiders Ser.). (ENG.). 64p. (J). (gr. 3-7). 19.99 *(978-1-4169-3867-5(2),* Simon & Schuster Bks. For Young Readers) Simon & Schuster Bks. For Young Readers.
McNeil, Niki, et al. HOCPP 1085 Sharks. 2006. spiral bd. 19.50 *(978-1-60308-085-9(6))* In the Hands of a Child.
Meister, Cari. Do You Really Want to Meet a Shark? Fabbri, Daniele, illus. 2015. (Do You Really Want to Meet ... ? Ser.). (ENG.). 24p. (J). (gr. 1-4). lib. bdg. 19.95 *(978-1-60753-737-3(0),* 15268) Amicus.
—Sharks. 2013. (ENG.). 24p. (J). lib. bdg. 25.65 *(978-1-62031-035-9(X))* Jump! Inc.
Michael Paul, Michael. Chomp: a Shark Romp. 2019. (Illus.). 40p. (J). (-k). 16.99 *(978-1-5247-6702-0(6),* Crown Books For Young Readers) Random Hse. Children's Bks.
Miller, Jonathan. Sharks. 2004. (Discovery Program Ser.). (SPA., Illus.). 64p. (J). (gr. 2-18). lib. bdg. 16.95 *(978-1-58086-335-3(3))* EDC Publishing.
Mitchell, Susan K. Biggest vs. Smallest Sea Creatures, 1 vol. 2010. (Biggest vs. Smallest Animals Ser.). (ENG., Illus.). 24p. (gr. k-2). 25.27 *(978-0-7660-3580-5(8),* b870c237-3a34-4d45-82c2-5f3439953602, Enslow Elementary) Enslow Publishing, LLC.
Montgomery, Sy. The Great White Shark Scientist. 2016. (Scientists in the Field Ser.). (ENG., Illus.). 80p. (J). (gr. 5-7). 18.99 *(978-0-544-35298-8(X),* 1586364, Clarion Bks.) HarperCollins Pubs.
Moore Niver, Heather. Bull Sharks after Dark, 1 vol. 2016. (Animals of the Night Ser.). (ENG., Illus.). 32p. (gr. 3-3). 26.93 *(978-0-7660-7712-6(8),* 37b70ea2-7eaf-4763-91d7-ec6eb1fa44e1) Enslow Publishing, LLC.
—20 Fun Facts about Sharks, 1 vol. 2012. (Fun Fact File: Animals! Ser.). (ENG., Illus.). 32p. (J). (gr. 2-3). pap. 11.50 *(978-1-4339-6527-2(5),* 4fe7a2a9-6aca-41af-a14f-0398861e67fc); lib. bdg. 27.93 *(978-1-4339-6525-8(9),* d88cbf96-b481-4d90-9ffd-a27e342458f9) Stevens, Gareth Publishing LLLP. (Gareth Stevens Learning Library).
Morey, Allan. Blacktip Reef Sharks. 2016. (Sharks Ser.). (ENG., Illus.). 32p. (J). (gr. 2-5). pap. 9.99 *(978-1-68152-088-9(5),* 15733); lib. bdg. 20.95 *(978-1-60753-975-9(6),* 15725) Amicus.
—Hammerhead Sharks. 2016. (Sharks Ser.). (ENG., Illus.). 32p. (J). (gr. 2-5). pap. 9.99 *(978-1-68152-091-9(5),* 15736); lib. bdg. 20.95 *(978-1-60753-978-0(0),* 15728) Amicus.
—Mako Sharks. 2016. (Sharks Ser.). (ENG., Illus.). 32p. (J). (gr. 2-5). pap. 9.99 *(978-1-68152-092-6(3),* 15737); lib. bdg. 20.95 *(978-1-60753-979-7(9),* 15729) Amicus.
—Whale Sharks. 2016. (Sharks Ser.). (ENG., Illus.). 32p. (J). (gr. 2-5). pap. 9.99 *(978-1-68152-094-0(X),* 15739); lib. bdg. 20.95 *(978-1-60753-981-0(0),* 15731) Amicus.
Morgan, Sally. Sharks. 2004. (QEB Animal Lives Ser.). (Illus.). 32p. (J). lib. bdg. 18.95 *(978-1-59566-034-3(8))* QEB Publishing Inc.
Morgan, Sally & Teacher Created Resources Staff. Sharks. 2006. (Animal Lives Ser.). (ENG., Illus.). 32p. (gr. 2-9). pap. 7.99 *(978-1-4206-8160-4(5))* Teacher Created Resources, Inc.
Mortensen, Lori. Killer Sharks, 1 vol. 2008. (Monsters Ser.). (ENG., Illus.). 48p. (gr. 4-8). lib. bdg. 36.83 *(978-0-7377-4044-8(2),* 4e7d87cf-6008-433f-9859-07fb225679ef, KidHaven Publishing) Greenhaven Publishing LLC.
Mugford, Simon. Shark. 2004. (Twenty4Sevens Ser.). (Illus.). 48p. (J). pap. *(978-0-439-68102-5(2))* Scholastic, Inc.
Murphy, Julie. Whale Sharks. 2013. (21st Century Skills Library: Exploring Our Oceans Ser.). (ENG., Illus.). 32p. (J). (gr. 3-6). 32.07 *(978-1-62431-411-7(2),* 202764); pap. 14.21 *(978-1-62431-487-2(2),* 202766) Cherry Lake Publishing.
Murray, Julie. Great White Sharks. 2019. (Animal Kingdom Ser.). (ENG.). 32p. (J). (gr. 2-5). lib. bdg. 34.21 *(978-1-5321-1634-6(9),* 32379, Big Buddy Bks.) ABDO Publishing Co.
—Hammerhead Sharks. 2019. (Animal Kingdom Ser.). (ENG.). 32p. (J). (gr. 2-5). lib. bdg. 34.21 *(978-1-5321-1636-0(5),* 32383, Big Buddy Bks.) ABDO Publishing Co.
—Sharks. 2016. (I Like Animals! Set 2 Ser.). (ENG., Illus.). 24p. (J). (gr. -1-2). lib. bdg. 31.36 *(978-1-68080-908-4(3),* 23291, Abdo Kids) ABDO Publishing Co.
Musgrave, Ruth A. National Geographic Kids Everything Sharks: All the Shark Facts, Photos, & Fun That You Can Sink Your Teeth Into. 2011. (National Geographic Kids Everything Ser.). (Illus.). 64p. (J). (gr. 3-7). pap. 12.95 *(978-1-4263-0769-0(1),* National Geographic Kids) Disney Publishing Worldwide.
—National Geographic Kids Mission: Shark Rescue: All about Sharks & How to Save Them. 2016. (NG Kids Mission: Animal Rescue Ser.). (Illus.). 112p. (J). (gr. 5-9). pap. 12.99 *(978-1-4263-2090-3(6),* National Geographic Kids) Disney Publishing Worldwide.
Nagelhout, Ryan. Diving with Sharks. 2014. (Illus.). 32p. (J). *(978-1-4824-3287-9(0))* Stevens, Gareth Publishing LLLP.
—Sharks, 1 vol. 2013. (Underwater World Ser.). (ENG., Illus.). 24p. (J). (gr. k-k). pap. 9.15 *(978-1-4339-8576-8(4),* 5ec66474-e020-458a-8b1a-c431429fddb9); lib. bdg. 25.27 *(978-1-4339-8575-1(6),* 944ed05a-004b-468f-bd16-844ba7f91822) Stevens, Gareth Publishing LLLP.
—Sharks / Tiburones, 1 vol. 2013. (Underwater World / el Mundo Submarino Ser.). (SPA & ENG., Illus.). 24p. (J). (gr. k-k). lib. bdg. 25.27 *(978-1-4339-8784-7(8),* 0f665ced-7c41-4954-82ad-d4aa2713f691) Stevens, Gareth Publishing LLLP.
National Geographic Kids. National Geographic Kids Sharks Sticker Activity Book: Over 1,000 Stickers! 2014. (NG Sticker Activity Bks.). 56p. (J). (gr. -1-k). pap., act. bk. ed. 6.99 *(978-1-4263-1774-3(3),* National Geographic Kids) Disney Publishing Worldwide.
Nelson, Kristin L. Hunting Sharks. 2003. (Pull Ahead Bks.). (Illus.). 32p. (J). (gr. 2-6). 22.60 *(978-0-8225-4671-9(X),* Lerner Pubns.) Lerner Publishing Group.
—Let's Look at Sharks. 2010. (Lightning Bolt Books (r) — Animal Close-Ups Ser.). (ENG., Illus.). 32p. (J). (gr. 1-3). pap. 9.99 *(978-0-7613-6041-4(7),* 945788b0-bbf9-4973-95d0-a4ed3911d436); pap. 45.32 *(978-0-7613-6982-0(1))* Lerner Publishing Group.
Nobleman, Marc Tyler. Sharks, 1 vol. 2009. (Endangered! Ser.). (ENG.). 48p. (gr. 3-3). lib. bdg. 32.64 *(978-0-7614-2988-3(3),* efe848f2-c7ea-4614-b0e3-0dbe5a061653) Cavendish Square Publishing LLC.
Northcutt, Ellen. Extreme Sharks. 2014. (Illus.). 32p. (J). *(978-0-545-72501-9(1))* Scholastic, Inc.
Nuzzolo, Deborah. Bull Shark [Scholastic]. 2010. (Sharks Ser.). (ENG.). 24p. pap. 0.52 *(978-1-4296-5043-4(5),* Capstone Pr.) Capstone.
—Bull Sharks. 2017. (All about Sharks Ser.). (ENG., Illus.). 24p. (J). (gr. -1-2). pap. 6.95 *(978-1-5157-7010-7(9),* 135457, Capstone Pr.) Capstone.
—Great White Shark [Scholastic]. 2010. (Sharks Ser.). (ENG.). 24p. pap. 0.52 *(978-1-4296-5041-0(9),* Capstone Pr.) Capstone.
—Hammerhead Shark [Scholastic]. 2010. (Sharks Ser.). (ENG.). 24p. pap. 0.52 *(978-1-4296-5042-7(7),* Capstone Pr.) Capstone.
—Hammerhead Sharks. 2017. (All about Sharks Ser.). (ENG., Illus.). 24p. (J). (gr. -1-2). pap. 6.95 *(978-1-5157-7009-1(5),* 135456, Capstone Pr.) Capstone.
—Mako Sharks. 2017. (All about Sharks Ser.). (ENG., Illus.). 24p. (J). (gr. -1-2). pap. 6.95 *(978-1-5157-7007-7(9),* 135454, Capstone Pr.) Capstone.
—Tiger Shark [Scholastic]. 2010. (Sharks Ser.). (ENG.). 24p. pap. 0.52 *(978-1-4296-5044-1(3),* Capstone Pr.) Capstone.
—Whale Sharks. 2017. (All about Sharks Ser.). (ENG., Illus.). 24p. (J). (gr. -1-2). lib. bdg. 27.32 *(978-1-5157-6999-6(2),* 135446, Capstone Pr.) Capstone.
O'DellKathryn. SHARK ATTACK LOW INTERMEDIATE BOOK WITH ONLINE ACCESS, 1 vol. 2014. (ENG., Illus.). 28p. (J). pap., E-Book, E-Book 9.50 *(978-1-107-66183-7(8))* Cambridge Univ. Pr.
O'Neill, Michael Patrick, photos by. Shark Encounters. O'Neill, Michael Patrick, . 2008. (Illus.). 48p. (J). (gr. 1-4). 19.95 *(978-0-9728653-4-0(9))* Batfish Bks.
Orme, David. Sea Killers. 2007. (Trailblazers Ser.). (ENG., Illus.). 36p. pap. *(978-1-84167-592-3(X))* Ransom Publishing Ltd.
Orme, Helen. Sharks. 2011. (Fact to Fiction Grafx Ser.). (ENG., Illus.). 36p. (J). (gr. 4-7). lib. bdg. 17.45 *(978-1-61384-021-4(7))* Perfection Learning Corp.
Osborne, Mary Pope & Boyce, Natalie Pope. Dolphins & Sharks: A Nonfiction Companion to Magic Tree House #9: Dolphins at Daybreak. Murdocca, Sal, illus. 2003. (Magic Tree House (R) Fact Tracker Ser.: 9). 128p. (J). (gr. 2-5). 6.99 *(978-0-375-82377-0(8),* Random Hse. Bks. for Young Readers) Random Hse. Children's Bks.
—Sharks & Other Predators: A Nonfiction Companion to Magic Tree House #53: Shadow of the Shark. Molinari, Carlo, illus. 2015. (Magic Tree House (R) Fact Tracker Ser.: 32). (ENG.). 128p. (J). (gr. 2-5). 12.99 *(978-0-385-38642-5(7),* Random Hse. Bks. for Young Readers) Random Hse. Children's Bks.
Otfinoski, Steven. Hammerheads & More! 2012. (Illus.). 64p. (J). pap. 10.99 *(978-1-62267-002-4(7))* Bright Connections Media.
Owen, Ruth. Great White Shark, 1 vol., 1. 2014. (Real Life Sea Monsters Ser.). (ENG.). 32p. (J). (gr. 3-3). 28.93 *(978-1-4777-6249-3(3),* e410746a-a8d5-4c06-b875-c9dd254d933a, PowerKids Pr.) Rosen Publishing Group, Inc., The.
—Stealthy Sharks, 1 vol. 2012. (Eye to Eye with Animals Ser.). (ENG., Illus.). 32p. (J). (gr. 2-2). pap. 11.00 *(978-1-4488-8108-6(0),* ebf7e7e4-ce93-4b5e-a8b6-b627b2be38fe, Windmill Bks.) Rosen Publishing Group, Inc., The.
Owings, Lisa. Bull Shark Attack. 2012. (Animal Attacks Ser.). (ENG., Illus.). 24p. (J). (gr. 3-7). lib. bdg. 26.95 *(978-1-60014-787-6(9),* Torque Bks.) Bellwether Media.
—The Great White Shark. 2011. (Nature's Deadliest Ser.). (ENG., Illus.). 24p. (J). (gr. 3-8). lib. bdg. 27.95 *(978-1-60014-665-7(1),* Pilot Bks.) Bellwether Media.
Pallotta, Jerry. Hammerhead vs. Bull Shark (Who Would Win?) Bolster, Rob, illus. 2016. (Who Would Win? Ser.). (ENG.). 32p. (J). (gr. 1-3). pap. 4.95 *(978-0-545-30170-1(X))* Scholastic, Inc.
Parker, Steve. Amazing Sharks, 1 vol. 2016. (Animals Are Wild! Ser.). (ENG.). 40p. (gr. 3-4). pap. 15.05 *(978-1-4824-5018-7(6),* 29b94b87-483f-40ca-bf48-a72dee4d6ac9) Stevens, Gareth Publishing LLLP.
—Sharks. 2010. (Remarkable Man & Beast Ser.). (Illus.). 48p. (J). (gr. 3-18). lib. bdg. 19.95 *(978-1-4222-1974-4(7))* Mason Crest.
—Sharks, 1 vol. Butler, John, illus. 2010. (I Love Animals Ser.). (ENG.). 24p. (J). (gr. 2-2). 27.27 *(978-1-61533-249-6(9),* 76904c5b-9eff-4c21-a6ba-55c200f73ae7); pap. 9.15 *(978-1-61533-254-0(5),* 0cdca43d-e846-41b1-86f9-7fdb00bdc174) Rosen Publishing Group, Inc., The. (Windmill Bks.).
—10 Things You Should Know about Sharks. Gallagher, Belinda & Borton, Paula, eds. Butler, John, illus. 2004. (10 Things You Should Know Ser.). 24p. (J). 6.99 *(978-1-84236-118-4(X))* Miles Kelly Publishing, Ltd. GBR. Dist: Independent Pubs. Group.
Pearl, Norman. Sharks: Ocean Hunters. (Powerful Predators Ser.). 24p. (gr. 2-3). 2009. 42.50 *(978-1-60851-349-9(1))* 2008. (ENG., Illus.). (J). lib. bdg. 26.27 *(978-1-4042-4509-9(X),* 7ebf672c-15b8-4a3c-836b-4b527056e2b7) Rosen Publishing Group, Inc., The. (PowerKids Pr.).
Peterson, Megan Cooley & Rustad, Martha E. H. Sharks, 1 vol. 2013. (Little Scientist Ser.). (ENG., Illus.). 32p. (J). (gr. -1-2). 28.65 *(978-1-4765-0246-5(3),* 122301); pap. 6.95 *(978-1-4765-3546-3(9),* 123592) Capstone. (Capstone Pr.).
Pettiford, Rebecca. Great White Sharks. 2016. (Ocean Life up Close Ser.). (ENG., Illus.). 24p. (J). (gr. k-3). 26.95 *(978-1-62617-416-0(4));* pap. 7.99 *(978-1-61891-264-0(X),* 12054) Bellwether Media. (Blastoff! Readers).
Pfeffer, Wendy & American Museum of Natural History Staff. The World of Sharks. 2011. (Amer Museum of Nat History Easy Readers Ser.: 2). (ENG., Illus.). 32p. (J). (gr. -1-k). pap. 4.95 *(978-1-4027-7783-7(3))* Sterling Publishing Co., Inc.
Phelps, Bonnie. In Search of Mako Sharks, 1 vol., 1. 2015. (Shark Search Ser.). (ENG., Illus.). 24p. (J). (gr. 3-4). pap. 9.25 *(978-1-5081-4343-7(9),*

S

92d0bf85-dbe4-4be0-b9a5-1efdde9da1c3, PowerKids Pr.) Rosen Publishing Group, Inc., The.

Priddy, Roger. Smart Kids: Sharks: And Other Dangers of the Deep. l.t. rev. ed. 2005. (Smart Kids Ser.). (ENG., Illus.). 32p. (J). (gr. -1-2). 10.99 *(978-0-312-49533-6(1)*, 900034543) St. Martin's Pr.

—Smart Kids Sharks: With More Than 30 Stickers. 2018. (Smart Kids Ser.). (ENG., Illus.). 24p. (J). pap. 5.99 *(978-0-312-50602-5(3)*, 900175820) St. Martin's Pr.

Pringle, Laurence. Sharks! Strange & Wonderful. Henderson, Meryl Learnihan, illus. 2008. (Strange & Wonderful Ser.). (ENG.). 32p. (J). (gr. 2-5). pap. 9.95 *(978-1-59078-571-3(1)*, Astra Young Readers) Astra Publishing Hse.

Rafferty, John P. Meat Eaters: Raptors, Sharks, & Crocodiles, 1 vol. 2011. (Britannica Guide to Predators & Prey Ser.). (ENG., Illus.). 208p. (YA). (gr. 10-10). lib. bdg. 55.29 *(978-1-61530-342-7(1)*, 79dfbe61-4f48-44f6-9e67-6e8c0588e97b) Rosen Publishing Group, Inc., The.

Rake, Jody S. Oceanic Whitetip Sharks: A 4D Book. 2018. (All about Sharks Ser.). (ENG., Illus.). 24p. (J). (gr. -1-2). lib. bdg. 29.32 *(978-1-9771-0155-6(0)*, 138320, Capstone Pr.) Capstone.

—Sand Tiger Sharks: A 4D Book. 2018. (All about Sharks Ser.). (ENG., Illus.). 24p. (J). (gr. -1-2). lib. bdg. 29.32 *(978-1-9771-0158-7(5)*, 138323, Capstone Pr.) Capstone.

—Thresher Sharks: A 4D Book. 2018. (All about Sharks Ser.). (ENG., Illus.). 24p. (J). (gr. -1-2). lib. bdg. 29.32 *(978-1-9771-0156-3(9)*, 138321, Capstone Pr.) Capstone.

Randolph, Joanne. The Great White Shark: King of the Ocean. (Sharks: Hunters of the Deep Ser.). 24p. (gr. 2-3). 2009. 42.50 *(978-1-60853-108-0(2))* 2007. (ENG., Illus.). (J). lib. bdg. 26.27 *(978-1-4042-3624-0(4)*, b50e04de-0421-4f2b-8d23-869e43872ac4) Rosen Publishing Group, Inc., The. (PowerKids Pr.).

—The Hammerhead Shark: Coastal Killer. (Sharks: Hunters of the Deep Ser.). 24p. (gr. 2-3). 2009. 42.50 *(978-1-60853-109-7(0))* 2007. (ENG., Illus.). (J). lib. bdg. 26.27 *(978-1-4042-3625-7(2)*, 25fb9774-67ec-47f3-b8e1-7ebe789474e9) Rosen Publishing Group, Inc., The. (PowerKids Pr.).

—The Mako Shark: Built for Speed. (Sharks: Hunters of the Deep Ser.). 24p. (gr. 2-3). 2009. 42.50 *(978-1-60853-110-3(4)*, PowerKids Pr.) 2007. (ENG., Illus.). (J). lib. bdg. 26.27 *(978-1-4042-3627-1(9)*, ea404c11-50d1-4798-ab5c-3ec8e8df1d7c) Rosen Publishing Group, Inc., The.

—Sharks: Hunters of the Deep Set, 8 vols. Incl. Great White Shark: King of the Ocean. lib. bdg. 26.27 *(978-1-4042-3624-0(4)*, b50e04de-0421-4f2b-8d23-869e43872ac4, PowerKids Pr.); Hammerhead Shark: Coastal Killer. lib. bdg. 26.27 *(978-1-4042-3625-7(2)*, 25fb9774-67ec-47f3-b8e1-7ebe789474e9, PowerKids Pr.); Mako Shark: Built for Speed. lib. bdg. 26.27 *(978-1-4042-3627-1(9)*, ea404c11-50d1-4798-ab5c-3ec8e8df1d7c); Whale Shark: Gentle Giant. lib. bdg. 26.27 *(978-1-4042-3626-4(0)*, 44b7fc7c-212c-47ee-ab3d-41fa4c647d5e, PowerKids Pr.); (Illus.). 24p. (J). (gr. 2-3). 2007. (Sharks: Hunters of the Deep Ser.). (ENG.). 2006. Set lib. bdg. 105.08 *(978-1-4042-3599-1(X)*, aca939e6-1b08-4998-bd57-9a7599996555, PowerKids Pr.) Rosen Publishing Group, Inc., The.

—The Whale Shark: Gentle Giant. (Sharks: Hunters of the Deep Ser.). 24p. (gr. 2-3). 2009. 42.50 *(978-1-60853-111-0(2))* 2007. (ENG., Illus.). (J). lib. bdg. 26.27 *(978-1-4042-3626-4(0)*, 44b7fc7c-212c-47ee-ab3d-41fa4c647d5e) Rosen Publishing Group, Inc., The. (PowerKids Pr.).

Rebman, Nick. Sharks. 2018. (Animals Ser.). (ENG., Illus.). 16p. (J). (gr. k-1). pap. 7.95 *(978-1-63517-955-2(6)*, 1635179556); lib. bdg. 25.64 *(978-1-63517-854-8(1)*, 1635178541) North Star Editions. (Focus Readers).

Reher, Matt. The Book of Sharks. 2017. (1G Marine Life Ser.). (ENG., Illus.). 32p. (J). pap. 9.60 *(978-1-63437-671-6(4))* American Reading Co.

Reynolds, Hunter. Hunting with Great White Sharks, 1 vol. 2012. (Animal Attack! Ser.). (ENG., Illus.). 24p. (J). (gr. 2-3). 25.27 *(978-1-4339-7075-7(9)*, c427341a-f382-44fe-8e6a-33d344fdcfa9); pap. 9.15 *(978-1-4339-7076-4(7)*, 6f45edd6-3524-44ff-8353-4e45224e416a) Stevens, Gareth Publishing LLLP. (Gareth Stevens Learning Library).

Reynolds, Shaye. In Search of Tiger Sharks, 1 vol., 1. 2015. (Shark Search Ser.). (ENG., Illus.). 24p. (J). (gr. 3-4). pap. 9.25 *(978-1-5081-4347-5(1)*, a1f01ced-1be2-40c3-ae5b-b3ad9c89e1c0, PowerKids Pr.) Rosen Publishing Group, Inc., The.

Ricciuti, Edward R. Adivina Quién Muerde / Guess Who Bites, 1 vol. 2009. (Adivina Quién / Guess Who? Ser.). (ENG & SPA.). 32p. (gr. k-2). 25.50 *(978-0-7614-2882-4(8)*, ca1e5844-f9d5-4c73-be59-55bc9f47c49e) Cavendish Square Publishing LLC.

—Adivina Quién Muerde (Guess Who Bites), 1 vol. 2009. (Adivina Quién (Guess Who?) Ser.). (SPA.). 32p. (gr. k-2). 25.50 *(978-0-7614-2865-7(8)*, 8942245c-0e32-4181-ba66-f5d823cdc7a1) Cavendish Square Publishing LLC.

—Guess Who Bites, 1 vol. 2006. (Guess Who? Ser.). (ENG.). 32p. (gr. k-1). 25.50 *(978-0-7614-1766-8(4)*, 13ddbac0-9d08-422f-a000-36b414f81498); pap. 9.23 *(978-0-7614-3552-5(2)*, ac47fc84-dbf7-4802-a5d0-734532e18119) Cavendish Square Publishing LLC.

Riehecky, Janet. Megalodon, 1 vol. Hughes, Jon, illus. 2006. (Dinosaurs & Prehistoric Animals Ser.). (ENG.). 24p. (J). (gr. -1-2). 27.32 *(978-0-7368-5354-5(5)*, 86869, Capstone Pr.) Capstone.

Riggs, Kate. Seedlings: Sharks. 2014. (Seedlings Ser.). (ENG.). 24p. (J). (gr. -1-k). pap. 10.99 *(978-0-89812-887-1(0)*, 21679, Creative Paperbacks) Creative Co., The.

—Sharks. 2013. (Seedlings Ser.). (ENG.). 24p. (J). (gr. -1-k). 25.65 *(978-1-60818-342-5(4)*, 21678, Creative Education) Creative Co., The.

Ripley's Believe It Or Not, Ripley's Believe. Ripley Twists: Sharks: And Other Scary Sea Creatures. 2013. (Twist Ser.: 9). (ENG.). 48p. (J). (gr. 1-4). 12.95 *(978-1-60991-083-9(4))* Ripley Entertainment, Inc.

Roseborough, Elizabeth. Blue Sharks, Vol. 10. 2018. (Amazing World of Sharks Ser.). (Illus.). 64p. (J). (gr. 7). lib. bdg. 31.93 *(978-1-4222-4122-6(X))* Mason Crest.

—Bull Sharks, Vol. 10. 2018. (Amazing World of Sharks Ser.). (Illus.). 64p. (J). (gr. 7). lib. bdg. 31.93 *(978-1-4222-4123-3(8))* Mason Crest.

—Freshwater Sharks, Vol. 10. 2018. (Amazing World of Sharks Ser.). (Illus.). 64p. (J). (gr. 7). lib. bdg. 31.93 *(978-1-4222-4125-7(4))* Mason Crest.

—Great White Sharks. 2018. (J). *(978-1-4222-4121-9(1))* Mason Crest.

—Mako Sharks, Vol. 10. 2018. (Amazing World of Sharks Ser.). (Illus.). 64p. (J). (gr. 7). 31.93 *(978-1-4222-4128-8(9))* Mason Crest.

—Thresher Sharks, Vol. 10. 2018. (Amazing World of Sharks Ser.). (Illus.). 64p. (J). (gr. 7). lib. bdg. 31.93 *(978-1-4222-4130-1(0))* Mason Crest.

—Tiger Sharks, Vol. 10. 2018. (Amazing World of Sharks Ser.). (Illus.). 64p. (J). (gr. 7). lib. bdg. 31.93 *(978-1-4222-4131-8(9))* Mason Crest.

Ross, Jeff. Shark. 2018. (Orca Soundings Ser.). lib. bdg. 20.80 *(978-0-606-41423-4(1))* Turtleback.

Roy, Katherine. Neighborhood Sharks: Hunting with the Great Whites of California's Farallon Islands. 2014. (ENG., Illus.). 48p. (J). (gr. 2-6). 18.99 *(978-1-59643-874-3(6)*, 900118022, Macaulay, David Studio) Roaring Brook Pr.

Royston, Angela. Shark, 1 vol. 2013. (Top of the Food Chain Ser.). (ENG.). 32p. (J). (gr. 2-3). 29.92 *(978-1-61533-737-8(7)*, 24926f0b-1309-4bb7-90dd-9a225bee3c45); pap. 11.00 *(978-1-61533-791-0(1)*, 5166e2a8-255a-4494-a611-612b2b10d086) Rosen Publishing Group, Inc., The. (Windmill Bks.).

—Shark: Killer King of the Ocean. 2013. (Top of the Food Chain Ser.). 32p. (J). (gr. k-5). pap. 60.00 *(978-1-61533-792-7(X))* Windmill Bks.

Rustad, Martha E. H. Sharks [Scholastic]. 2009. (Ocean Life Ser.). 24p. (gr. k-1). pap. 2.99 *(978-1-4296-3675-9(0)*, Pebble) Capstone.

Sandler, Michael. Bethany Hamilton: Follow Your Dreams! 2006. (Defining Moments Ser.). (Illus.). 32p. (J). (gr. 2-5). lib. bdg. 28.50 *(978-1-59716-270-8(1))* Bearport Publishing Co., Inc.

Sandy Creek (Firm) Staff, contrib. by. My First Book of Sharks: Learn about Great Whites, Hammerheads, Goblin Sharks, & More with Fun Facts! 2016. (Illus.). 51p. (J). *(978-1-4351-6321-8(4))* Barnes & Noble, Inc.

Scholastic. Great White Sharks (Wild Life LOL!) (Library Edition) 2019. (Wild Life LOL! Ser.). (ENG., Illus.). 32p. (J). (gr. 1-3). lib. bdg. 25.00 *(978-0-531-24037-3(1)*, Children's Pr.) Scholastic Library Publishing.

Schreiber, Anne. National Geographic Readers: Sharks! 2008. (Readers Ser.). (Illus.). 32p. (J). (gr. 1-3). pap. 4.99 *(978-1-4263-0286-2(X)*, National Geographic Kids) Disney Publishing Worldwide.

—National Geographic Readers: Sharks. 2008. (Readers Ser.). (ENG., Illus.). 32p. (J). (gr. 1-3). 14.90 *(978-1-4263-0288-6(6)*, National Geographic Children's Bks.) Disney Publishing Worldwide.

Schroeter, Chloe. Sharks, 1 vol. 2014. (Animal Q & A Ser.). (ENG., Illus.). 24p. (J). (gr. 2-2). lib. bdg. 26.27 *(978-1-4777-9198-1(1)*, 22861eb6-0c56-4b73-a160-9c53386e60aa, Windmill Bks.) Rosen Publishing Group, Inc., The.

—Why Why Why... Are Sharks so Scary? 2010. (Why Why Why Ser.). 32p. (J). (gr. 1-3). lib. bdg. 18.95 *(978-1-4222-1571-5(7))* Mason Crest.

Schuetz, Kari. Oceanic Whitetip Sharks & Pilot Fish. 2019. (Animal Tag Teams Ser.). (ENG., Illus.). 24p. (J). (gr. k-3). lib. bdg. 26.95 *(978-1-62617-957-8(3)*, Blastoff! Readers) Bellwether Media.

Schuh, Mari. Sharks. 2018. (Spot Ocean Animals Ser.). (ENG.). 16p. (J). (gr. -1-2). pap. 9.99 *(978-1-68152-303-3(5)*, 15005); lib. bdg. *(978-1-68151-383-6(8)*, 14999) Amicus.

Sexton, Colleen. Sharks. 2007. (Oceans Alive Ser.). (ENG., Illus.). 24p. (J). (gr. k-3). lib. bdg. 26.95 *(978-1-60014-057-0(2))* Bellwether Media.

Shaffer, Lindsay. Whitetip Reef Sharks. 2020. (Animals of the Coral Reef Ser.). (ENG., Illus.). 24p. (J). (gr. k-3). lib. bdg. 26.95 *(978-1-64487-136-2(X)*, Blastoff! Readers) Bellwether Media.

Shark: Level 2, 6 vols. (Fluency Strand Ser.). (gr. 4-8). 45.00 *(978-1-4045-1210-8(1))* Wright Group/McGraw-Hill.

Shark Discovery [Scholastic]. 2010. (Sharks Ser.). 24p. pap. 2.08 *(978-1-4296-5045-8(1)*, Capstone Pr.) Capstone.

Sharks! (Creatures Corner Ser.). 16p. (J). *(978-2-7643-0121-0(9))* Phidal Publishing, Inc./Editions Phidal, Inc.

Sharks. (Eyes on Nature Ser.). 32p. (J). (gr. 1). pap. *(978-1-882210-55-8(7))* Action Publishing, Inc.

Sharks: An Amazing Discovery Book. 2009. (Amazing Animal Discovery Bks.). (ENG., Illus.). 12p. (J). (gr. -1). 5.95 *(978-1-58117-864-7(6)*, Intervisual/Piggy Toes) Bendon, Inc.

Sharks: Hunters of the Deep, 6 vols. (Book2WebTM Ser.). (gr. 4-8). 36.50 *(978-0-322-02973-6(2))* Wright Group/McGraw-Hill.

Sharks: Level M, 6 vols. (Wonder Worldtm Ser.). 16p. 34.95 *(978-0-7802-2906-8(1))* Wright Group/McGraw-Hill.

Sharks: Monsters of the Deep. 2008. (Illus.). 32p. (J). (gr. -1-3). 9.99 *(978-1-57755-724-1(7))* Flying Frog Publishing, Inc.

Sharks & Rays: Level O, 6 vols. (Explorers Ser.). 32p. (gr. 3-6). 44.95 *(978-0-7699-0590-7(0))* Shortland Pubns. (U. S. A.) Inc.

Sharon the Shark 6 Packs. Set D. (Supersonic Phonics Ser.). (gr. k-3). 29.00 *(978-0-7635-0553-0(6))* Rigby Education.

Shea, Therese. Hammerhead Sharks. 2009. (Ugly Animals Ser.). 24p. (gr. 2-3). 42.50 *(978-1-60854-599-5(7)*, PowerKids Pr.) Rosen Publishing Group, Inc., The.

—Sharks. 2009. (Big Bad Biters Ser.). 24p. (gr. 2-3). 42.50 *(978-1-61511-563-1(3)*, PowerKids Pr.) Rosen Publishing Group, Inc., The.

Shea, Therese M. Hammerhead Sharks, 1 vol. 2006. (Ugly Animals Ser.). (ENG., Illus.). 24p. (J). (gr. 2-3). lib. bdg. 26.27 *(978-1-4042-3529-8(9)*, 0992adb7-b19d-4632-b878-79f2431e8cb6, PowerKids Pr.) Rosen Publishing Group, Inc., The.

Sheikh-Miller, Jonathan. Sharks. 2009. (Discovery Nature Ser.). 64p. (YA). (gr. 3-18). 8.99 *(978-0-7945-2241-4(6)*, Usborne) EDC Publishing.

Shingu, Susumu. Wandering Whale Sharks. 2015. Orig. Title: Whale Shark. (ENG., Illus.). 48p. (J). (gr. k-5). 18.95 *(978-1-77147-130-5(1)*, Owlkids) Owlkids Bks. Inc. CAN. Dist: Publishers Group West (PGW).

Shulman, Mark. Shark Attack: Top 10 Attack Sharks. 2007. (Discovery Channel Bks.). (ENG., Illus.). 48p. (J). (gr. 3-6). 21.19 *(978-0-696-23692-1(3))* Meredith Bks.

Silverman, Buffy. Angel Sharks in Action. 2017. (Lightning Bolt Books (r) — Shark World Ser.). (ENG., Illus.). 24p. (J). (gr. 1-3). 29.32 *(978-1-5124-3381-4(0)*, 1e518dbe-3407-4c1a-851f-ec272a8d5043, Lerner Pubns.) Lerner Publishing Group.

—Great White Sharks in Action. 2017. (Lightning Bolt Books (r) — Shark World Ser.). (ENG., Illus.). 24p. (J). (gr. 1-3). pap. 9.99 *(978-1-5124-5594-6(6)*, fd9e9db7-8299-4e60-94c3-7fed3f304129) Lerner Publishing Group.

—Mako Sharks in Action. 2017. (Lightning Bolt Books (r) — Shark World Ser.). (ENG., Illus.). 24p. (J). (gr. 1-3). 29.32 *(978-1-5124-3378-4(0)*, ee9494a6-1c3a-4590-a75b-d61049453c41, Lerner Pubns.) Lerner Publishing Group.

Simon, Seymour. SeeMore Readers: Incredible Sharks - Level 1. 2003. (SeeMore Readers Ser.: SEMR). (ENG., Illus.). 32p. (J). (gr. -1-7). pap. 5.99 *(978-1-58717-239-7(9))* Chronicle Bks. LLC.

—Sharks. 2006. (ENG., Illus.). 32p. (J). (gr. k-4). pap. 7.99 *(978-0-06-087713-2(8)*, HarperCollins) HarperCollins Pubs.

—Sharks. 2006. (Illus.). 32p. (gr. k-4). 17.00 *(978-0-7569-6751-2(1))* Perfection Learning Corp.

—Sharks. 2005. (Illus.). 24p. (J). *(978-0-439-77699-8(6))* Scholastic, Inc.

—Sharks. 2006. (J). 17.20 *(978-1-4177-7522-4(X))* Turtleback.

Skerry, Brian. The Ultimate Book of Sharks. 2018. (Illus.). 192p. (J). (gr. 3-7). 19.99 *(978-1-4263-3071-1(5))*; (ENG., lib. bdg. 28.90 *(978-1-4263-3072-8(3))* Disney Publishing Worldwide. (National Geographic Kids).

SMARTLAB Creative Team. Mega 3D Puzzle Play Sharks. 2010. 3p. mass mkt. 19.99 *(978-1-60380-094-5(8))* becker&mayer! books.

Smith, Elizabeth. The Magic School Bus & the Shark Adventure. Bracken, Carolyn, illus. 2007. (Scholastic Reader Ser.). (J). *(978-0-545-03464-7(7))* Scholastic, Inc.

Smith, Miranda. Sharks. 2008. (Kingfisher Knowledge Ser.). (ENG., Illus.). 64p. (J). (gr. 3-8). 22.44 *(978-0-7534-6194-5(3)*, 9780753461945) Kingfisher Publications, plc GBR. Dist: Children's Plus, Inc.

Sovak, Jan. Shiny Sharks Stickers. 2007. (Dover Little Activity Books Stickers Ser.). (ENG., Illus.). 2p. (J). (gr. 1-4). 1.50 *(978-0-486-46228-8(5))* Dover Pubns., Inc.

Staff, Gareth Editorial Staff. Sharks, 1 vol. 2004. (All about Wild Animals Ser.). (ENG., Illus.). 32p. (gr. 2-4). lib. bdg. 28.67 *(978-0-8368-4188-6(3)*, 0d64ba2d-7fa3-4547-ba87-20da017b0fbb, Gareth Stevens Learning Library) Stevens, Gareth Publishing LLLP.

Statts, Leo. Great White Sharks. 2017. (Sharks (Launch!) Ser.). (ENG., Illus.). 24p. (J). (gr. -1-2). lib. bdg. 31.36 *(978-1-5321-2008-4(7)*, 25364, Abdo Zoom-Launch) ABDO Publishing Co.

—Hammerhead Sharks. 2017. (Sharks (Launch!) Ser.). (ENG., Illus.). 24p. (J). (gr. -1-2). lib. bdg. 31.36 *(978-1-5321-2009-1(5)*, 25366, Abdo Zoom-Launch); E-Book 57.08 *(978-1-61479-776-0(5)*, 26181) ABDO Publishing Co.

—Mako Sharks. 2017. (Sharks (Launch!) Ser.). (ENG., Illus.). 24p. (J). (gr. -1-2). lib. bdg. 31.36 *(978-1-5321-2010-7(9)*, 25368, Abdo Zoom-Launch) ABDO Publishing Co.

—Sand Sharks. 2017. (Sharks (Launch!) Ser.). (ENG., Illus.). 24p. (J). (gr. -1-2). lib. bdg. 31.36 *(978-1-5321-2011-4(7)*, 25370, Abdo Zoom-Launch) ABDO Publishing Co.

—Tiger Sharks. 2017. (Sharks (Launch!) Ser.). (ENG., Illus.). 24p. (J). (gr. -1-2). lib. bdg. 31.36 *(978-1-5321-2012-1(5)*, 25372, Abdo Zoom-Launch) ABDO Publishing Co.

—Whale Sharks. 2017. (Sharks (Launch!) Ser.). (ENG., Illus.). 24p. (J). (gr. -1-2). lib. bdg. 31.36 *(978-1-5321-2013-8(3)*, 25374, Abdo Zoom-Launch) ABDO Publishing Co.

Stefoff, Rebecca. Whale Sharks, 1 vol. 2014. (Giant Animals Ser.). (ENG.). 48p. (gr. 4-4). lib. bdg. 33.07 *(978-1-62712-954-1(5)*, d655e1d3-bff0-4134-ac6b-47403b901973) Cavendish Square Publishing LLC.

Stein, Lori. Shark-Tastic! 2011. (Science with Stuff Ser.: 1). (ENG.). 64p. (J). (gr. 1). lib. bdg. 12.99 *(978-1-935703-29-7(3))* Downtown Bookworks.

Stephens, David. Sharks: Predators of the Ocean, 1 vol. 2014. (Discovery Education: Animals Ser.). (ENG.). 32p. (J). (gr. 4-5). 27.93 *(978-1-4777-6926-3(9)*, 0d86c558-c779-4c86-b99b-ab90339035ca); pap. 11.00 *(978-1-4777-6927-0(7)*, 87808b17-afb4-4d15-b210-d2a0ac993670) Rosen Publishing Group, Inc., The. (PowerKids Pr.).

Stewart, Melissa. Shark or Dolphin? How Do You Know?, 1 vol. 2011. (Which Animal Is Which? Ser.). (ENG., Illus.). 24p. (gr. k-2). pap. 10.35 *(978-1-59845-239-6(8)*, b469386c-28e0-45c8-9777-4487b639a22e, Enslow Elementary); lib. bdg. 25.27 *(978-0-7660-3680-2(4)*, 230990ca-1669-4eec-9dac-423f8d7f1a3d) Enslow Publishing, LLC.

Stone, Tanya Lee. Sharks. 2003. (Wild Wild World Ser.). 24p. (YA). 24.94 *(978-1-56711-822-3(4)*, Blackbirch Pr., Inc.) Cengage Gale.

Strain Trueit, Trudi. Sharks, 1 vol. 2011. (Ocean Life Ser.). (ENG.). 24p. (gr. k-1). 25.50 *(978-0-7614-4896-9(9)*, 59259463-eb10-4bc4-b060-c9d3c5831cc0) Cavendish Square Publishing LLC.

Taylor, Barbara. Encyclopedia of Sharks. Kelly, Richard, ed. 2017. (ENG., Illus.). 512p. (J). 39.95 *(978-1-78617-021-7(3))* Miles Kelly Publishing, Ltd. GBR. Dist: Parkwest Pubns., Inc.

—Sharks. 2015. (Illus.). 384p. (J). pap. *(978-1-78617-175-7(9))* Barnes & Noble, Inc.

Taylor, Leighton. Great White Sharks. 2005. (Early Bird Nature Bks.). (ENG., Illus.). 48p. (gr. 2-5). lib. bdg. 26.60 *(978-0-8225-2868-5(1)*, Lerner Pubns.) Lerner Publishing Group.

Taylor, Trace. Sharks. 2012. (Marine Life Ser.). (ENG.). 12p. (J). (gr. k-2). pap. 8.00 *(978-1-59301-759-0(6))* American Reading Co.

Taylor, Trace & Sanchez, Lucia M. Tiburones (Sharks) 2011. (poder de 100 - Animales marinos Ser.). (SPA.). 12p. pap. 39.62 *(978-1-61541-279-2(4))* American Reading Co.

Thomas, Elizabeth. Goblin Sharks. 2013. (21st Century Skills Library: Exploring Our Oceans Ser.). (ENG., Illus.). 32p. (J). (gr. 3-6). 32.07 *(978-1-62431-406-3(6)*, 202744); pap. 14.21 *(978-1-62431-482-7(1)*, 202746) Cherry Lake Publishing.

—Great White Sharks. 2013. (21st Century Skills Library: Exploring Our Oceans Ser.). (ENG., Illus.). 32p. (J). (gr. 3-6). 32.07 *(978-1-62431-407-0(4)*, 202748); pap. 14.21 *(978-1-62431-483-4(X)*, 202750) Cherry Lake Publishing.

Thomas, Isabel. Shark vs. Killer Whale. 2017. (Animal Rivals Ser.). (ENG., Illus.). 24p. (J). (gr. k-2). lib. bdg. 25.99 *(978-1-4846-4071-5(3)*, 135682, Heinemann) Capstone.

Thomson, Sarah L. Amazing Sharks! (I Can Read Level 2 Ser.). (ENG., Illus.). 32p. (J). (gr. k-3). 2006. pap. 4.99 *(978-0-06-054456-0(2)*, HarperCollins) 2005. 15.99 *(978-0-06-054458-4(9))* HarperCollins Pubs.

—Amazing Sharks! Wildlife Conservation Society, photos by. 2006. (I Can Read Bks.). (Illus.). 31p. (gr. -1-3). 14.00 *(978-0-7569-6957-8(3))* Perfection Learning Corp.

Los tiburones blancos (Great White Sharks) 2006. (J). pap. 7.95 *(978-0-8225-6627-4(3)*, Ediciones Lerner) Lerner Publishing Group.

Los Tiburones y Las Rayas, 6 vols. (Explorers. Exploradores Nonfiction Sets Ser.). (SPA.). 32p. (gr. 3-6). 44.95 *(978-0-7699-0626-3(5))* Shortland Pubns. (U. S. A.) Inc.

Top That Publishing Staff, ed. Sharks. 2006. (Illus.). 48p. *(978-1-84510-011-7(5))* Top That! Publishing PLC.

Toufexis, George. Ultimate Shark-Athon Facts & Activity Book. 2013. (Dover Kids Activity Books: Animals Ser.). (ENG.). 48p. (J). (gr. 3-8). pap. 4.99 *(978-0-486-49185-1(4)*, 491854) Dover Pubns., Inc.

Toufexis, George & Coloring Books Staff. Sharks! Coloring Book. 2013. (Dover Sea Life Coloring Bks.). (ENG.). 32p. (J). (gr. 2-5). pap. 3.99 *(978-0-486-49028-1(9)*, 490289) Dover Pubns., Inc.

Toufexis, George, et al. Sharks. 2011. (Dover Sea Life Coloring Bks.). (ENG., Illus.). 32p. (J). (gr. 2-6). 5.99 *(978-0-486-48426-6(2)*, 484262) Dover Pubns., Inc.

Troller, Leah. The Great White Shark. 2017. (1-3Y Marine Life Ser.). (ENG., Illus.). 20p. (J). pap. 9.60 *(978-1-63437-678-5(1))* American Reading Co.

Tuchman, Gail. Shark Attack! 2013. (Illus.). 32p. (J). *(978-0-545-62401-5(0))* Scholastic, Inc.

Tunby, Benjamin. Whale Sharks in Action. 2017. (Lightning Bolt Books (r) — Shark World Ser.). (ENG., Illus.). 24p. (J). (gr. 1-3). 29.32 *(978-1-5124-3382-1(9)*, 7a55fd0e-1e0b-45ce-b7ef-ce4cbdc91318, Lerner Pubns.) Lerner Publishing Group.

Turnbull, Stephanie. Shark. 2015. (Big Beasts Ser.). (ENG., Illus.). 24p. (J). (gr. 1-4). 28.50 *(978-1-62588-170-0(3)*, 17284) Black Rabbit Bks.

—Shark. 2015. (ENG., Illus.). 24p. (J). pap. 8.95 *(978-1-77092-218-1(0))* RiverStream Publishing.

Vadon, Catherine. Meet the Shark. 2007. (ENG., Illus.). 45p. (J). (gr. 4-7). 15.95 *(978-1-58728-598-1(3))* Cooper Square Publishing Llc.

Wagner, Kathi. The Everything Kids' Sharks Book: Dive into Fun-Infested Waters! 2005. (Everything(r) Kids Ser.). (ENG., Illus.). 144p. pap. 9.99 *(978-1-59337-304-7(X))* Adams Media Corp.

Waters, John F. Sharks Have Six Senses. Barner, Bob, illus. 2015. (Let's-Read-And-Find-Out Science 2 Ser.). (ENG.). 40p. (J). (gr. -1-3). 17.99 *(978-0-06-028140-3(5)*, HarperCollins) HarperCollins Pubs.

Waxman, Laura Hamilton. Basking Sharks. 2016. (Sharks Ser.). (ENG., Illus.). 32p. (J). (gr. 2-5). pap. 9.99 *(978-1-68152-087-2(7)*, 15732); lib. bdg. 20.95 *(978-1-60753-974-2(8)*, 15724) Amicus.

—Bull Sharks. 2016. (Sharks Ser.). (ENG., Illus.). 32p. (J). (gr. 2-5). pap. 9.99 *(978-1-68152-089-6(3)*, 15734); lib. bdg. 20.95 *(978-1-60753-976-6(4)*, 15726) Amicus.

—Great White Sharks. 2016. (Sharks Ser.). (ENG., Illus.). 32p. (J). (gr. 2-5). pap. 9.99 *(978-1-68152-090-2(7)*, 15735); lib. bdg. 20.95 *(978-1-60753-977-3(2)*, 15727) Amicus.

—Tiger Sharks. 2016. (Sharks Ser.). (ENG., Illus.). 32p. (J). (gr. 2-5). pap. 9.99 *(978-1-68152-093-3(1)*, 15738); lib. bdg. 20.95 *(978-1-60753-980-3(2)*, 15730) Amicus.

Weber, Valerie J. Sharks, 1 vol. 2008. (Animals That Live in the Ocean Ser.). (ENG., Illus.). 24p. (gr. 1-1). (J). lib. bdg. 25.27 *(978-0-8368-9245-1(3)*, 0fcac860-e40d-4c1d-b378-ac7b6807ab64); pap. 9.15 *(978-0-8368-9344-1(1)*, 4e9c55e6-6b78-4e05-a511-99fe5ca82a29) Stevens, Gareth Publishing LLLP. (Weekly Reader Leveled Readers).

—Sharks / Tiburones, 1 vol. 2008. (Animals That Live in the Ocean / Animales Que Viven en el Océano Ser.). (SPA & ENG.). 24p. (gr. 1-1). (J). lib. bdg. 25.27 *(978-0-8368-9251-2(8)*, dca0805d-5f9e-4b75-8034-4b6c5df4a5ef); pap. 9.15 *(978-0-8368-9350-2(6)*, 6fe356ec-37c2-42d1-bb7d-df55cc7e3f09) Stevens, Gareth Publishing LLLP. (Weekly Reader Leveled Readers).

West, David. Sharks & Other Fish, 1 vol. 2017. (Inside Animals Ser.). (ENG.). 24p. (J). (gr. 3-3). 26.27 *(978-1-5081-9391-3(6)*, e2bfa22c-9c45-499c-99ce-7b710c0c52ad, Windmill Bks.) Rosen Publishing Group, Inc., The.

West, David, contrib. by. Sharks & Other Fish, 1 vol. 2017. (Inside Animals Ser.). (ENG.). 24p. (J). (gr. 3-3). pap. 9.25 *(978-1-5081-9429-3(7)*, c4974616-6512-4144-8cb3-2ec6c14320cc, Windmill Bks.) Rosen Publishing Group, Inc., The.

Wexo, John Bonnett. Sharks. rev. ed. 2003. (Illus.). 24p. (J). (gr. 1-7). 10.95 *(978-1-932396-05-8(5)*, Zoo Bks.) National Wildlife Federation.

Wildlife Education. Sharks. 2007. (Illus.). 10p. (J). 5.99 *(978-1-932396-30-0(6)*, Critters Up Close) National Wildlife Federation.

William H. Sadlier Staff. Getting to Know Sharks. 2005. (Fluent Library). (gr. 1-3). 29.34 *(978-0-8215-8963-2(6))* Sadlier, William H. Inc.

Williams, Lily. If Sharks Disappeared. Williams, Lily, illus. 2017. (If Animals Disappeared Ser.). (ENG., Illus.). 40p. (J). 18.99 *(978-1-62672-413-6(X),* 900156281) Roaring Brook Pr.

Wilsdon, Christina. Sharks, 1 vol. 2009. (Amazing Animals Ser.). (ENG.). 48p. (YA). (gr. 3-5). lib. bdg. 30.67 *(978-0-8368-9111-9(2),* dc212612-931f-46ac-8e39-b19de65bf9fc) Stevens, Gareth Publishing LLLP.

—Sharks. 2007. (J). *(978-1-59939-130-4(9),* Reader's Digest Young Families, Inc.) Studio Fun International.

Wood, I. Sharks: Learning the SH Sound. 2009. (PowerPhonics Ser.). 24p. (gr. 1-1). 39.90 *(978-1-60851-470-0(6),* PowerKids Pr.) Rosen Publishing Group, Inc., The.

Worth, Bonnie. Hark! a Shark! All about Sharks. Ruiz, Aristides & Mathieu, Joe, illus. 2013. (Cat in the Hat's Learning Library). 48p. (J). (gr. k-3). 9.99 *(978-0-375-87073-6(3),* Random Hse. Bks. for Young Readers) Random Hse. Children's Bks.

Yin, Robert, illus. & photos by. Sharks & Rays. Yin, Robert, photos by. 2004. (ENG.). 24p. (J). (gr. 1-2). pap. 7.47 net. *(978-0-7685-0357-9(4),* Dominie Elementary) Savvas Learning Co.

Yomtov, Nelson. Terrors from the Deep: True Tales of Surviving Shark Attacks. 2015. (True Stories of Survival Ser.). (ENG., Illus.). 32p. (J). (gr. 3-9). lib. bdg. 31.32 *(978-1-4914-6573-8(5),* 129053, Capstone Pr.) Capstone.

Young, Karen Romano. Shark Quest: Protecting the Ocean's Top Predators. 2018. (ENG., Illus.). 128p. (YA). (gr. 6-12). 37.32 *(978-1-5124-9805-9(X),* 0e31553f-a364-4b28-abd9-4ed33c70da87, Twenty-First Century Bks.) Lerner Publishing Group.

Zoehfeld, Kathleen Weidner. Great White Shark: Ruler of the Sea. Petruccio, Steven James, illus. (Smithsonian Oceanic Collection). (J). 2009. 24.95 incl. audio compact disk *(978-1-59249-664-8(4))* 2005. (ENG.). 32p. (gr. -1-2). per. 6.95 *(978-1-59249-196-4(0),* S4006) Soundprints.

—Great White Shark: Ruler of the Sea. 2005. (ENG., Illus.). 32p. (J). (gr. -1-2). 8.95 *(978-1-59249-224-4(X),* SC4006) Soundprints.

Zoldak, Joyce. Danger in the Deep: Surviving Shark Attacks. 2010. (Survivors Ser.). 128p. (YA). (gr. 7-12). 24.95 *(978-1-4222-0511-2(8))* Mason Crest.

—Danger in the Deep: Survivors of Shark Attacks. 2009. (J). pap. 25.95 *(978-1-4222-1475-6(3))* Mason Crest.

SHARKS—FICTION

Adamson, Ged. Shark Dog & the School Trip Rescue! 2018. (ENG., Illus.). 40p. (J). (gr. -1-3). 17.99 *(978-0-06-245718-9(7),* HarperCollins) HarperCollins Pubs.

Aldrich, Sandra D. Trouble in the Park. 2012. 28p. 19.95 *(978-1-4626-8818-0(7))* America Star Bks.

Allen, Kate. The Line Tender. 2019. (Illus.). 384p. (J). (gr. 5). 17.99 *(978-0-7352-3160-3(5),* Dutton Books for Young Readers) Penguin Young Readers Group.

Alten, Steve. Sharkman. 2014. (Illus.). 272p. (J). (gr. 7-12). 22.95 *(978-1-63076-019-9(6))* Taylor Trade Publishing.

Arroyo, Yvonne. How the Octopus Got Eight Arms: Two Arms Are Never Enough. 2013. (ENG., Illus.). 45p. (J). pap. 23.95 *(978-1-4327-9369-2(1));* pap. 31.95 *(978-1-4327-9644-0(5))* Outskirts Pr., Inc.

Awdry, W. Thomas & the Shark (Thomas & Friends) Courtney, Richard, illus. 2013. (Step into Reading Ser.). (ENG.). 32p. (J). (gr. -1-1). pap. 5.99 *(978-0-307-98200-1(9),* Random Hse. Bks. for Young Readers) Random Hse. Children's Bks.

Awdry, Wilbert V. Thomas & the Shark. 2013. (Thomas & Friends Step into Reading Ser.). lib. bdg. 13.55 *(978-0-606-26996-4(7))* Turtleback.

Bailey, Lin. Stanley - the Shark Who Lost His Fin. 2012. 38p. pap. *(978-1-909395-87-9(0))* Legend Pr.

Ballantyne, R. The Coral Island. 2006. pap. 14.95 *(978-1-55742-666-6(X))* Wildside Pr., LLC.

Barton, Chris. Shark vs. Train. Lichtenheld, Tom, illus. 2010. (ENG.). 40p. (J). (gr. -1-3). 18.99 *(978-0-316-00762-7(5))* Little, Brown Bks. for Young Readers.

Believe It Or Not!, Ripleys, compiled by. Sharkee & the Teddy Bear. 2018. (Story Book Ser.: 1). (ENG., Illus.). 40p. (J). 16.99 *(978-1-60991-208-6(X))* Ripley Entertainment, Inc.

Beserra, Donna. Twirly Shirley in Hurricane Shirley. 2005. 22p. (J). 8.00 *(978-0-9729484-4-9(9))* Seventh Street Pr.

Bise, Jr. J. David & Bise, Jr. In Search of a Name a Seahorse Story. 2011. 44p. pap. 15.50 *(978-1-60976-288-9(6),* Strategic Bk. Publishing) Strategic Book Publishing & Rights Agency (SBPRA).

Cafaro, Phyllis. The Legend of Captain McFinn & Friends. 2012. (ENG.). 24p. (J). 17.99 *(978-0-9799283-3-8(8),* 9780979928338) Captain McFinn and Friends LLC, McFinn Pr.

Chronicle Books & ImageBooks. Little Shark: Finger Puppet Book: (Puppet Book for Baby, Little Toy Board Book, Baby Shark) 2013. (Little Finger Puppet Board Bks.). (ENG., Illus.). 12p. (J). (gr. -1 — 1). 7.99 *(978-1-4521-1251-0(7))* Chronicle Bks. LLC.

Coombs, Bob. Ted P Bear - A Bitter Tale. 2005. (ENG.). 83p. (YA). pap. 8.69 *(978-1-4116-4260-7(0))* Lulu Pr., Inc.

CortAs, Ricardo. Sea Creatures from the Sky. 2018. (ENG., Illus.). 48p. (J). 16.95 *(978-1-61775-616-0(4),* Black Sheep) Akashic Bks.

Cottringer, Anne. Mary Is Scary. Gale, Cathy, illus. 2007. (Bloomsbury Paperbacks Ser.). 32p. (J). (gr. k-2). pap. 9.99 *(978-0-7475-7927-4(X))* Bloomsbury Publishing Plc GBR. Dist: Independent Pubs. Group.

Cousteau, Fabien & Fraioli, James O. Great White Shark Adventure. St.Pierre, Joe, illus. 2019. (Fabien Cousteau Expeditions Ser.). (ENG.). 112p. (J). (gr. 3-7). 12.99 *(978-1-5344-2087-8(8),* McElderry, Margaret K. Bks.) McElderry, Margaret K. Bks.

Cox, Phil Roxbee. Shark in the Park. Tyler, Jenny, ed. Cartwright, Stephen, illus. rev. ed. 2006. (Phonics Readers Ser.). 16p. (J). (gr. -1-k). pap. 6.99 *(978-0-7945-1509-6(6),* Usborne) EDC Publishing.

Cruz, Stefanie. Delta & Dawn: Mother & Baby Whales' Journey. Toppenberg, Lily, illus. 2007. 32p. (J). lib. bdg. 15.95 *(978-0-9791233-2-0(1))* Big Tomato Pr.

Curtis, Manley. Shawn Loves Sharks. 2017. (ENG., Illus.). 32p. (J). 17.99 *(978-1-62672-134-0(3),* 900139956) Roaring Brook Pr.

Dahl, Michael. Blood Shark! Sinkovec, Igor, illus. 2015. (Igor's Lab of Fear Ser.). (ENG.). 40p. (J). (gr. 4-8). lib. bdg. 23.99 *(978-1-4965-0456-2(9),* 128481, Stone Arch Bks.) Capstone.

Diesen, Deborah. The Pout-Pout Fish & the Bully-Bully Shark. Hanna, Dan, illus. (Pout-Pout Fish Adventure Ser.). (ENG.). 32p. (J). 2019. bds. 8.99 *(978-0-374-31222-0(2),* 900200299) 2017. 18.99 *(978-0-374-30402-7(5),* 900158632) Farrar, Straus & Giroux. (Farrar, Straus & Giroux (BYR)).

Downer, Ann. Shark Baby, 1 vol. Bersani, Shennen, illus. 2013. 32p. (J). (ENG.). (gr. -1-3). 17.95 *(978-1-60718-622-9(5));* (ENG.). (gr. -1-3). pap. 9.95 *(978-1-60718-634-2(9));* (SPA.). (gr. 2-3). pap. 11.95 *(978-1-62855-351-2(0),* 30d907ee-6c53-4f54-ab9f-06d37fefc8ad) Arbordale Publishing.

Dyckman, Ame. Misunderstood Shark. Magoon, Scott, illus. 2018. (ENG.). 48p. (J). (gr. -1-k). 18.99 *(978-1-338-11247-4(3),* Orchard Bks.) Scholastic, Inc.

—Misunderstood Shark: Friends Don't Eat Friends. Magoon, Scott, illus. 2019. (ENG.). 48p. (J). (gr. -1-k). 17.99 *(978-1-338-11388-4(7),* Orchard Bks.) Scholastic, Inc.

Ellis, Julie. Shark & Crab Big Book Edition, 1 vol. Hawley, Kelvin, illus. 2014. (ENG.). 16p. (gr. 1-1). pap. *(978-1-77654-094-5(8),* Red Rocket Readers) Flying Start Bks.

Ferry, Beth. Land Shark. Mantle, Ben, illus. 2015. (ENG.). 36p. (J). (gr. -1-k). 16.99 *(978-1-4521-2458-2(2))* Chronicle Bks. LLC.

Gaines, Pat. O. O. Octopus: Sheriff of Blue Ribbon Sound. 2008. (Illus.). 24p. (J). lib. bdg. *(978-0-9801376-4-4(0));* per. *(978-0-9801376-5-1(9))* Dragonfly Publishing, Inc.

Galloway, Ruth. Smiley Shark. Galloway, Ruth, illus. (Illus.). 32p. (J). 2005. 6.95 *(978-1-58925-391-9(4))* 2003. tchr. ed. 15.95 *(978-1-58925-028-4(1))* Tiger Tales.

Geist, Ken. The Three Little Fish & the Big Bad Shark. Gorton, Julia, illus. 2007. (ENG.). 32p. (J). (gr. -1-1). 7.99 *(978-0-439-71962-9(3))* Scholastic, Inc.

George, Jean Craighead. Shark Beneath the Reef. (J). pap. 3.50 *(978-0-13-800038-7(7))* Prentice Hall (Schl. Div.).

Gill, Timothy. Flip & Fin: Super Sharks to the Rescue! 2016. (ENG., Illus.). 32p. (J). (gr. -1-3). 15.99 *(978-0-06-224301-0(2),* Greenwillow Bks.) HarperCollins Pubs.

—Flip & Fin: We Rule the School! 2014. (ENG., Illus.). 32p. (J). (gr. -1-3). 14.99 *(978-0-06-224300-3(4),* Greenwillow Bks.) HarperCollins Pubs.

Glover, Matt. But It's True. 2012. (Illus.). 32p. pap. 13.50 *(978-1-78035-330-2(8),* Fastprint Publishing) Upfront Publishing Ltd. GBR. Dist: Printondemand-worldwide.com.

Griffin, Wiley Chase. Chase the Shark: Flies Like a Bird. 2010. 28p. pap. 12.50 *(978-1-4520-5173-4(9))* AuthorHouse.

Gruber, Penelope. Paul Bunyan & Babe the Blue Whale: A Graphic Novel. Frampton, Otis, illus. 2019. (Far Out Folktales Ser.). (ENG.). 40p. (J). (gr. 3-6). lib. bdg. 26.65 *(978-1-4965-7842-6(2),* 139308, Stone Arch Bks.) Capstone.

Hale, Bruce. Clark the Shark. Francis, Guy, illus. 2013. (Clark the Shark Ser.). (ENG.). 32p. (J). (gr. -1-3). 18.99 *(978-0-06-219226-4(4),* HarperCollins) HarperCollins Pubs.

—Clark the Shark. 2016. (Clark the Shark: I Can Read Level 1 Ser.). (J). lib. bdg. 13.55 *(978-0-606-38774-3(9))* Turtleback.

—Clark the Shark: Lost & Found. Francis, Guy, illus. 2016. (I Can Read Level 1 Ser.). (ENG.). 32p. (J). (gr. -1-3). pap. 4.99 *(978-0-06-227910-1(6),* HarperCollins) HarperCollins Pubs.

—Clark the Shark: Tooth Trouble. Francis, Guy, illus. 2014. (I Can Read Level 1 Ser.). (ENG.). 32p. (J). (gr. -1-3). 16.99 *(978-0-06-227908-8(4),* HarperCollins) HarperCollins Pubs.

—Clark the Shark: Afraid of the Dark. Francis, Guy, illus. 2015. (Clark the Shark Ser.). (ENG.). 32p. (J). (gr. -1-3). 18.99 *(978-0-06-237450-9(8),* HarperCollins) HarperCollins Pubs.

—Clark the Shark & the Big Book Report. Francis, Guy, illus. 2017. (I Can Read Level 1 Ser.). 32p. (J). (ENG.). (gr. -1-3). pap. 4.99 *(978-0-06-227912-5(2),* HarperCollins); *(978-1-5182-4609-8(5))* HarperCollins Pubs.

—Clark the Shark Dares to Share. Francis, Guy, illus. 2013. (Clark the Shark Ser.). (ENG.). 32p. (J). (gr. -1-3). 17.99 *(978-0-06-227905-7(X),* HarperCollins) HarperCollins Pubs.

—Clark the Shark Loves Christmas: A Christmas Holiday Book for Kids. Francis, Guy, illus. 2016. (Clark the Shark Ser.). (ENG.). 32p. (J). (gr. -1-3). 18.99 *(978-0-06-237452-3(4),* HarperCollins) HarperCollins Pubs.

—Clark the Shark Takes Heart. Francis, Guy, illus. 2014. (Clark the Shark Ser.). (ENG.). 32p. (J). (gr. -1-3). 17.99 *(978-0-06-219227-1(2),* HarperCollins) HarperCollins Pubs.

—Clark the Shark: Tooth Trouble. Francis, Guy, illus. 2014. (I Can Read Level 1 Ser.). (ENG.). 32p. (J). (gr. -1-3). pap. 4.99 *(978-0-06-227906-4(8),* HarperCollins) HarperCollins Pubs.

Harvey, M. A. The Shark Island Mystery: Dare to Take the Test. 2004. (Illus.). 128p. (J). pap. *(978-1-84458-147-4(0),* Pavilion Children's Books) Pavilion Bks.

High, Linda Oatman. The Shark [1]. 2016. (Boosters Ser.). (ENG.). 48p. (YA). (gr. 9-12). pap. 9.75 *(978-1-68021-155-9(2))* Saddleback Educational Publishing, Inc.

Ice Water Press Staff. Secrets of the Deep. 2010. (J). pap. *(978-1-921639-95-1(4))* Ripley Entertainment, Inc.

Janacone, Matt. Finny the Friendly Shark. Druschel, Bob, illus. 2005. 40p. (J). per. 20.99 *(978-1-58939-655-5(3))* Virtualbookworm.com Publishing, Inc.

Kapai, Tommy. Cuzzies Meet the Motuhoa Shark. Henry, Mike, illus. 2006. (Cuzzies Adventures Ser.). (MAO & ENG.). 32p. (J). (gr. -1-3). pap. 9.00 *(978-1-86969-100-4(8))* Huia Pubs. NZL. Dist: Univ. of Hawaii Pr.

Laird, Donivee M. Ula Li'i & the Magic Shark. Jossem, Carol, illus. 2003. 49p. (J). (gr. k-3). 9.95 *(978-0-940350-23-6(8))* Barnaby Bks., Inc.

Laird, Donivee Martin. The Magic Shark Learns to Cook. Johnson, Carol Ann, illus. 2004. 48p. (J). 9.95 *(978-1-57306-233-6(2))* Bess Pr., Inc.

Landers, Ace. Shark Attack. 2013. (Scholastic Reader Level 1 Ser.). (Illus.). 32p. (J). lib. bdg. 13.55 *(978-0-606-32391-8(0))* Turtleback.

Lloyd, Sam R. Yummy Yummy! Food for My Tummy. Tickle, Jack, illus. 2004. 32p. (J). tchr. ed. 15.95 *(978-1-58925-035-2(4))* Tiger Tales.

Lucas, Nancy T. Peppy's Coral Kingdom. 2008. (ENG.). 24p. pap. 12.99 *(978-1-4196-9046-4(9))* CreateSpace Independent Publishing Platform.

Luebbe, Tara & Cattie, Becky. Shark Nate-O. Duncan, Daniel, illus. 2018. (ENG.). 40p. (J). (gr. -1-3). 17.99 *(978-1-4998-0496-6(2))* Little Bee Books Inc.

Maddox, Jake. Shark Attack! A Survive! Story. Tiffany, Sean, illus. 2009. (Jake Maddox Sports Stories Ser.). (ENG.). 72p. (J). (gr. 3-6). 25.99 *(978-1-4342-1210-8(6),* 95406, Stone Arch Bks.) Capstone.

Maestro, Betsy & Maestro, Giulio. A Sea Full of Sharks.Tr. of Mer Pleine de Requins. (FRE., Illus.). (J). pap. 7.99 *(978-0-590-74409-6(7))* Scholastic, Inc.

Manushkin, Fran. Pedro & the Shark. Lyon, Tammie, illus. 2017. (Pedro Ser.). (ENG.). 32p. (J). (gr. k-2). lib. bdg. 21.32 *(978-1-5158-0873-2(4),* 134404, Picture Window Bks.) Capstone.

—Pedro y el Tiburón. Trusted Translations, Trusted, tr. Lyon, Tammie, illus. 2018. (Pedro en Español Ser.). (SPA.). 32p. (J). (gr. k-2). lib. bdg. 21.32 *(978-1-5158-2507-4(8),* 137566, Picture Window Bks.) Capstone.

Marin, Cheech. Captain Cheech. Ramirez, Orlando L., illus. 2008. 32p. (J). (gr. -1-3). lib. bdg. 17.89 *(978-0-06-113208-7(X))* HarperCollins Pubs.

Markel, Michelle. The Shark That Taught Me English/El Tiburon Que Me Enseno Ingles. Kim, Bo-Young, illus. 2008. (SPA & ENG.). 28p. (J). pap. 8.95 *(978-1-60448-003-0(3))* Lectura Bks.

—The Shark That Taught Me English/El Tiburon Que Me Enseno Ingles. Guerrero, Ernesto, tr. Kim, Bo-Young, illus. 2008. (ENG & SPA.). 28p. (J). (gr. 1-2). 15.95 *(978-1-60448-002-3(5))* Lectura Bks.

Martin, R. T. Riptide. 2019. (To the Limit Ser.). (ENG.). 104p. (YA). (gr. 6-12). 26.65 *(978-1-5415-4036-1(0),* 13d54020-f345-4b90-8213-09d1d5ea8f63, Darby Creek) Lerner Publishing Group.

Martin, Rafe. The Shark God. Shannon, David, illus. 2007. (Scholastic Bookshelf Ser.). (ENG.). 32p. (J). (gr. k-2). 18.69 *(978-0-590-39570-0(X))* Scholastic, Inc.

Mcdonald, Megan. Stink & the Shark Sleepover. Reynolds, Peter H., illus. 2019. (Stink Ser.). (ENG.). 168p. (J). (gr. 1-5). lib. bdg. 31.36 *(978-1-5321-4333-5(8),* 31863, Chapter Bks.) Spotlight.

—Stink & the Shark Sleepover. 2015. (Stink Ser.: 9). lib. bdg. 14.75 *(978-0-606-36859-9(0))* Turtleback.

McKenzie, J. Lee. Vampires Don't Believe in Mermaids. 2011. 54p. pap. 16.95 *(978-1-4560-1157-4(X))* America Star Bks.

Meister, Cari. The Brave Puffer Fish, 1 vol. Harpster, Steve, illus. 2011. (Ocean Tales Ser.). (ENG.). 32p. (J). (gr. 2-3). pap. 6.25 *(978-1-4342-3389-9(8),* 116396, Stone Arch Bks.) Capstone.

—The Shivery Shark, 1 vol. Harpster, Steve, illus. 2011. (Ocean Tales Ser.). (ENG.). 32p. (J). (gr. 2-3). lib. bdg. 22.65 *(978-1-4342-3200-7(X),* 114964, Stone Arch Bks.) Capstone.

Membrino, Anna. Big Shark, Little Shark. Budgen, Tim, illus. 2017. (Step into Reading Ser.). 32p. (J). (gr. -1-1). pap. 5.99 *(978-0-399-55728-6(8),* Random Hse. Bks. for Young Readers) Random Hse. Children's Bks.

—Big Shark, Little Shark Go to School. Budgen, Tim, illus. 2019. (Step into Reading Ser.). 32p. (J). (gr. -1-1). pap. 5.99 *(978-1-9848-9349-9(1),* Random Hse. Bks. for Young Readers) Random Hse. Children's Bks.

Metzger, Steve. Big Shark's Valentine Surprise. Hohnstadt, Cedric, illus. 2007. (J). pap. *(978-0-439-92251-7(8))* Scholastic, Inc.

—Five Little Sharks Swimming in the Sea. Bryant, Laura, illus. 2004. (J). *(978-0-439-66139-3(0));* pap. *(978-0-439-59228-4(3))* Scholastic, Inc.

Metzger, Steve & Hohnstadt, Cedric. Big Shark's Halloween Mystery. 2007. (Illus.). (J). pap. *(978-0-545-00237-0(0))* Scholastic, Inc.

Morgan, Michaela. Shy Shark. Gomez, Elena, illus. 2005. (ENG.). 24p. (J). lib. bdg. 23.65 *(978-1-59646-722-4(3))* Dingles & Co.

Northrop, Michael. Surrounded by Sharks. 2014. (ENG.). 224p. (YA). (gr. 4-7). 18.99 *(978-0-545-61545-7(3),* Scholastic Pr.) Scholastic, Inc.

Ocean, Davy. Deep-Sea Disaster. Blecha, Aaron, illus. 2014. (Shark School Ser.: 1). (ENG.). 128p. (J). (gr. 1-4). 17.99 *(978-1-4814-0679-6(5),* Aladdin) Simon & Schuster Children's Publishing.

—Deep-Sea Treasury: Deep-Sea Disaster; Lights! Camera! Hammerhead!; Squid-Napped; the Boy Who Cried Shark. Blecha, Aaron, illus. 2015. (Shark School Ser.). (ENG.). 528p. (J). (gr. 1-4). 14.99 *(978-1-4814-5115-4(4),* Aladdin) Simon & Schuster Children's Publishing.

—Fishin' Impossible, 8. Blecha, Aaron, illus. 2017. (Shark School Ser.). (ENG.). 144p. (J). (gr. 1-3). 21.19 *(978-1-5364-1675-6(4),* Aladdin) Simon & Schuster Children's Publishing.

—Fishin': Impossible. Blecha, Aaron, illus. 2017. (Shark School Ser.: 8). (ENG.). 144p. (J). (gr. 1-4). pap. 6.99 *(978-1-4814-6549-6(X),* Aladdin) Simon & Schuster Children's Publishing.

—Long Fin Silver. Blecha, Aaron, illus. 2018. (Shark School Ser.: 9). (ENG.). 144p. (J). (gr. 1-4). 16.99 *(978-1-4814-6553-3(8));* pap. 6.99 *(978-1-4814-6552-6(X))* Simon & Schuster Children's Publishing. (Aladdin).

—Shark Party. Blecha, Aaron, illus. 2014. (ENG.). 128p. (J). pap. *(978-1-84877-926-6(7))* Templar Publishing.

—Splash Dance. Blecha, Aaron, illus. 2015. (Shark School Ser.: 6). (ENG.). 128p. (J). (gr. 1-4). pap. 5.99 *(978-1-4814-0694-9(9),* Aladdin) Simon & Schuster Children's Publishing.

—Tooth or Dare. Blecha, Aaron, illus. 2016. (Shark School Ser.: 7). (ENG.). 128p. (J). (gr. 1-4). pap. 6.99 *(978-1-4814-6546-5(5),* Aladdin) Simon & Schuster Children's Publishing.

Olien, Jessica. Shark Detective! 2015. (ENG., Illus.). 32p. (J). (gr. -1-3). 17.99 *(978-0-06-235714-4(X),* Balzer & Bray) HarperCollins Pubs.

Page, Nick & Page, Claire. Read with Me Jonah the Moaner: Sticker Activity Book. Loy, Nikki, illus. 2006. (Read with Me (Make Believe Ideas) Ser.). 12p. (J). (gr. k-2). pap. *(978-1-84610-183-0(2))* Make Believe Ideas.

Paterakis, Paul. Henry the Friendly Shark. 2013. 24p. pap. 24.95 *(978-1-62709-447-4(4))* America Star Bks.

Pennington, Stacey & Pennington, J. C. D. Let's Go Aquarium: A Magnetic Storybook. Allen, Marie, illus. 2008. 6p. (J). (gr. -1-1). bds. 10.99 *(978-2-7641-2184-9(9))* Gardner Pubns.

Pfister, Marcus. Rainbow Fish to the Rescue! 2018. (Rainbow Fish Ser.: 1).Tr. of Regenbogenfisch, Komm Hilf Mir! (ENG., Illus.). 14p. (J). (gr. -1 — 1). bds. 9.95 *(978-1-55858-880-6(9))* North-South Bks., Inc.

Pinkfong. Baby Shark: Baby Shark & the Balloons. 2019. (My First I Can Read Ser.). (ENG.). 32p. (J). (gr. -1-3). pap. 4.99 *(978-0-06-296584-4(0),* HarperCollins) HarperCollins Pubs.

Quinn, Spencer, pseud. Bow Wow: a Bowser & Birdie Novel. 2018. (ENG.). 304p. (J). (gr. 3-7). pap. 8.99 *(978-1-338-09136-6(0),* Scholastic Pr.) Scholastic, Inc.

Rash, Ron, et al. The Shark's Tooth. 2015. (Young Palmetto Bks.). (ENG., Illus.). 40p. pap. 12.99 *(978-1-61117-527-1(5),* P450702) Univ. of South Carolina Pr.

R.D.Haire & Francis, Richard E. When Good Got Better: The Adventures of Fred the Friendly Shark. 2012. 24p. pap. 15.99 *(978-1-4797-3797-0(6))* Xlibris Corp.

Reed, Lynn Rowe. Benny Shark Goes to Friend School. Montijo, Rhode, illus. 2017. (ENG.). 32p. (J). (gr. -1-2). 17.99 *(978-1-4778-2803-8(6),* 9781477828038, Two Lions) Amazon Publishing.

—Shark Kiss, Octopus Hug. Cornell, Kevin, illus. 2014. (ENG.). 32p. (J). (gr. -1-3). 14.99 *(978-0-06-220320-5(7),* Balzer & Bray) HarperCollins Pubs.

Rentala, Sita Kanaka Valli. Ocean Flows: In Prose: Zcumby's Judo (on Global Warming) 2010. 44p. (J). pap. 19.99 *(978-1-4490-8780-7(9))* AuthorHouse.

Ripley's Believe It Or Not! Ripley's Bureau of Investigation 4: Secrets of the Deep. 2010. (Rbi Ser.: 4). (ENG.). 128p. (J). pap. 4.99 *(978-1-893951-54-9(5))* Ripley Entertainment, Inc.

Rogers, Jewels. The Princess & the Dolphin. 2011. 28p. 12.50 *(978-1-4567-3278-3(1))* AuthorHouse.

—The Princess & the Dolphin. 2010. 28p. pap. 16.99 *(978-1-4269-3966-2(3))* Trafford Publishing.

Rouss, Sylvia & Avalone, C. The Littlest Fish. 2008. 32p. 12.95 *(978-1-934440-53-7(1),* Pitspopany Pr.) Simcha Media Group.

Saddleback Educational Publishing Staff, ed. Sail, 1 vol. unabr. ed. 2011. (Heights Ser.). (ENG.). 50p. (gr. 4-8). 9.75 *(978-1-61651-622-2(4))* Saddleback Educational Publishing, Inc.

—Treasure, 1 vol. 2013. (Heights Ser.). (ENG.). 50p. (gr. 4-8). 9.75 *(978-1-62250-048-2(2))* Saddleback Educational Publishing, Inc.

Sauer, Tammi. Nugget & Fang. 2015. (Nugget & Fang Ser.). lib. bdg. 17.20 *(978-0-606-36825-4(6))* Turtleback.

—Nugget & Fang: Friends Forever — Or Snack Time? Slack, Michael, illus. (Nugget & Fang Ser.). (ENG.). 40p. (J). (gr. -1-3). 2015. 7.99 *(978-0-544-48171-8(2),* 1602585) 2013. 18.99 *(978-0-547-85285-0(1),* 1501493) HarperCollins Pubs. (Clarion Bks.).

—Nugget & Fang Go to School. Slack, Michael, illus. 2019. (Nugget & Fang Ser.). (ENG.). 32p. (J). (gr. -1-3). 17.99 *(978-1-328-54826-9(0),* 1724057, Clarion Bks.) HarperCollins Pubs.

—Nugget & Fang Lap Board Book: Friends Forever — Or Snack Time? Slack, Michael, illus. 2018. (Nugget & Fang Ser.). (ENG.). 38p. (J). (— 1). bds. 12.99 *(978-1-328-76839-1(2),* 1681072, Clarion Bks.) HarperCollins Pubs.

Schwarz, Viviane. Shark & Lobster's Amazing Undersea Adventure. Stewart, Joel, illus. 2006. 34p. (J). *(978-1-4156-8140-4(6))* Candlewick Pr.

Shea, Bob. I'm a Shark. Shea, Bob, illus. 2011. (ENG., Illus.). 40p. (J). (gr. -1-1). 17.99 *(978-0-06-199846-1(X),* Balzer & Bray) HarperCollins Pubs.

Simpkins, Debra Burke. The Luna Tuna. 2010. 32p. 12.99 *(978-1-4520-0213-2(4))* AuthorHouse.

Soileau, Hodges, illus. The Great Shark Mystery. 2003. (Boxcar Children Special Ser.). 130p. (gr. 4-7). 15.50 *(978-0-7569-1616-9(X))* Perfection Learning Corp.

Squid-Napped! 2014. (Shark School Ser.: 3). (ENG., Illus.). 144p. (J). (gr. 1-4). pap. 6.99 *(978-1-4814-0684-0(1),* Aladdin) Simon & Schuster Children's Publishing.

Steele, Michael Anthony. Hunt for the Octo-Shark: A 4D Book. Reeves, Pauline, illus. 2018. (Nearly Fearless Monkey Pirates Ser.). (ENG.). 48p. (J). (gr. k-2). lib. bdg. 23.99 *(978-1-5158-2680-4(5),* 137835, Picture Window Bks.) Capstone.

Stephens, Ann Marie. Christmas for Bly & Ray. Bolan, Michael P., illus. 2003. 45p. (J). per. 11.95 *(978-0-9729285-0-2(2),* 0-9729285-0-2) Kinkachoo Pr., The.

—A Surprise for Ray. Bolan, Michael P., illus. 2003. 47p. (J). per. 11.95 *(978-0-9729285-1-9(0),* 0-9729285-1-0) Kinkachoo Pr., The.

Tarshis, Lauren. I Survived the Shark Attacks of 1916. 2010. (I Survived Ser.: No. 2). lib. bdg. 14.75 *(978-0-606-23742-0(9))* Turtleback.

—I Survived the Shark Attacks of 1916 (I Survived #2) Dawson, Scott, illus. 2010. (I Survived Ser.: 2). (ENG.). 112p. (J). (gr. 2-5). pap. 5.99 *(978-0-545-20695-2(5),* Scholastic Paperbacks) Scholastic, Inc.

Tate, Suzanne. Great Sharky Shark: A Tale of a Big Hunter. Melvin, James, illus. 2004. (Suzanne Tate's Nature Ser.: No. 20). 32p. (J). per. 10.95 *(978-1-878405-46-3(2))* Nags Head Art, Inc.

Verrone, Patric C. W. Sharktooth. 2009. 229p. pap. 14.76 *(978-0-557-09535-3(2))* Lulu Pr., Inc.

Vcake, Steve. Hooey Higgins & the Shark. Dodson, Emma, illus. 2012. (Hooey Higgins Ser.). (ENG.). 112p. (J). (gr. 2-5). 14.99 *(978-0-7636-5782-6(4))* Candlewick Pr.

Walker, Anna. Lottie & Walter. Walker, Anna, illus. 2019. (ENG., Illus.). 40p. (J). (gr. -1-3). 17.99 *(978-1-328-47038-6(5),* 1714020, Clarion Bks.) HarperCollins Pubs.

S

Wheeler, J. D. Gummery & Lubber. 2008. 56p. pap. 16.95 *(978-1-60563-432-6(8))* America Star Bks.
Williams, Geoffrey T. The Great White Red Alert. Artful Doodlers, illus. Campbell, Tom, photos by. 2008. (Save Our Seas Adventure Bks.). (ENG.). 64p. (J). (gr. 4-7). 8.95 *(978-0-9800444-0-9(5))* Save Our Seas, Ltd.
Wrecks, Billy. Shark Attack! Doescher, Erik, illus. 2017. 24p. (J). *(978-1-5182-2649-6(3))* Random Hse., Inc.
—Shark Attack! 2017. (Step into Reading Level 2 Ser.). lib. bdg. 14.75 *(978-0-606-39852-7(X))* Turtleback.
—Shark Attack! (DC Super Friends) Doescher, Erik, illus. 2017. (Step into Reading Ser.). (ENG.). 24p. (J). (gr. -1-1). pap. 4.99 *(978-0-399-55846-7(2),* Random Hse. Bks. for Young Readers) Random Hse. Children's Bks.

SHAVUOT

Marks, Allison & Marks, Wayne. The Art Lesson: A Shavuot Story. Wilkinson, Annie, illus. 2017. (ENG.). 32p. (J). (gr. -1-2). E-Book 27.99 *(978-1-5124-2720-2(9),* 9781512427202, Kar-Ben Publishing) Lerner Publishing Group.
Stern, Ariella. Shavous Guess Who? Argoff, Patti, illus. 2017. (ENG.). 28p. (J). 11.95 *(978-1-945560-00-2(2))* Hachai Publishing.

SHAVUOT—FICTION

Goldin, Barbara Diamond. A Mountain of Blintzes, 0 vols. McGrory, Anik, illus. 2012. (ENG.). 32p. (J). (gr. k-3). pap. 6.99 *(978-0-7614-5790-9(9),* 9780761457909, Two Lions) Amazon Publishing.
MacLeod, Jennifer Tzivia. Yossi & the Monkeys: A Shavuot Story. Waisman, Shirley, illus. 2017. (ENG.). 32p. (J). (gr. -1-3). 17.99 *(978-1-4677-8932-5(1),* 56456978-1d54-4322-b8a3-6987dd47787f, Kar-Ben Publishing) Lerner Publishing Group.
Rouss, Sylvia A. Sammy Spider's First Shavuot. Kahn, Katherine Janus, illus. 2008. (ENG.). 32p. (J). (gr. -1-3). lib. bdg. 9.99 *(978-0-8225-7224-4(9),* c79a4b2f-eed5-4ab2-97f9-40e1c8e3bbca); per. 8.99 *(978-0-8225-7225-1(7),* 4ac00b78-7450-41c1-8879-8889127582ea) Lerner Publishing Group. (Kar-Ben Publishing).

SHAYS' REBELLION, 1786-1787

Roxburgh, Ellis. Shays' Rebellion. 2017. (Rebellions, Revolts, & Uprisings Ser.). 48p. (gr. 5-5). pap. 84.30 *(978-1-5382-0756-7(7))* Stevens, Gareth Publishing LLLP.

SHEEP

Arnold, Quinn M. Sheep. 2017. (Seedlings Ser.). (ENG., Illus.). 24p. (J). (gr. -1-k). pap. 7.99 *(978-1-62832-396-2(5),* 20138, Creative Paperbacks); *(978-1-60818-788-1(8),* 20140, Creative Education) Creative Co., The.
Barlow, Helen. Easy Read with Grandma Read: Book 1, Stage 3. 2009. (Illus.). 48p. pap. *(978-1-84743-507-6(3))* Athena Pr.
Beck, Isabel L., et al. Trophies Kindergarten: The Big Ram. 2003. (Trophies Ser.). (gr. k-6). 13.80 *(978-0-15-329540-9(6))* Harcourt Schl. Pubs.
Boothroyd, Jennifer. Meet a Baby Sheep. 2016. (Lightning Bolt Books (r) — Baby Farm Animals Ser.). (ENG., Illus.). 32p. (J). (gr. 1-3). 29.32 *(978-1-5124-0800-3(X),* fadcb48c-0e67-4f0d-b8cf-788f238e29ce, Lerner Pubns.) Lerner Publishing Group.
Borgert-Spaniol, Megan. Bighorn Sheep. 2015. (North American Animals Ser.). (ENG., Illus.). 24p. (J). (gr. k-3). lib. bdg. 26.95 *(978-1-62617-257-9(9),* Blastoff! Readers) Bellwether Media.
Canetti, Yanitzia. Canta y Cuenta Las Ovejas. 2010. (J). *(978-1-59835-224-5(5))* Cambridge BrickHouse, Inc.
—1-2-3 Do, Re, Mi Sheep. 2010. (J). *(978-1-59835-223-8(7))* Cambridge BrickHouse, Inc.
Carraway, Rose. Sheep on the Farm, 1 vol. 2012. (Farm Animals Ser.). (Illus.). 24p. (gr. k-k). (ENG.). (J). 25.27 *(978-1-4339-7364-2(2),* cc3e5775-aa3b-42e6-8747-71ee4e0a039a); (ENG., (J). pap. 9.15 *(978-1-4339-7365-9(0),* 5a33f56f-8c51-4bf9-9447-6b39fd6f8ffd); 69.20 *(978-1-4339-8057-2(6))* Stevens, Gareth Publishing LLLP.
—Sheep on the Farm / Ovejas de Granja, 1 vol. 2012. (Farm Animals / Animales de Granja Ser.). (SPA & ENG., Illus.). 24p. (gr. k-k). lib. bdg. 25.27 *(978-1-4339-7404-5(5),* d89cdcbf-f2ef-4de8-9022-8e6cd750ad0a) Stevens, Gareth Publishing LLLP.
Carter, Denzel T. Lambs, Lambs, Lambs, 1 vol. 2015. (Rosen REAL Readers: STEM & STEAM Collection). (ENG.). 8p. (gr. k-1). pap. 5.46 *(978-1-4994-9669-7(9),* 2794ae59-1903-487b-a342-5a5b379bbe94, Rosen Classroom) Rosen Publishing Group, Inc., The.
Dicker, Katie. Sheep. 2014. (Farm Animals Ser.). (Illus.). 24p. (gr. 2-5). 28.50 *(978-1-62588-024-6(3))* Black Rabbit Bks.
Dieker, Wendy Strobel. Sheep. 2012. (Illus.). 24p. (J). lib. bdg. 25.65 *(978-1-62031-006-9(6))* Jump! Inc.
Doubleday Entertainment USA - Sheep: Down on the Farm. 2006. (J). per. 6.95 *(978-1-59566-227-9(8))* QEB Publishing Inc.
Dunn, Joeming & Denham, Brian. Dolly: The 1st Cloned Sheep, 1 vol. 2011. (Famous Firsts: Animals Making History Ser.). (ENG., Illus.). 32p. (J). (gr. 3-8). 32.79 *(978-1-61641-640-9(8),* 7210, Graphic Planet - Fiction) Magic Wagon.
Early Macken, JoAnn. Bighorn Sheep, 1 vol. (Animals That Live in the Mountains (First Edition) Ser.). (ENG., 24p. (gr. 1-1). 2005. Illus.). pap. 9.15 *(978-0-8368-6322-2(4),* 8fcc8711-92dd-4fb9-9fca-7af85112d431) 2nd rev. ed. 2009. (J). pap. 9.15 *(978-1-4339-2492-7(7),* 0a9510e3-2ef6-4d82-9046-a838322d30f8) 2nd rev. ed. 2009. (J). lib. bdg. 25.27 *(978-1-4339-2409-5(9),* dcce2fd7-4507-461a-89c5-56fd268f3682) Stevens, Gareth Publishing LLLP. (Weekly Reader Leveled Readers).
—Bighorn Sheep / Carnero de Canadá, 1 vol. 2nd rev. ed. 2009. (Animals That Live in the Mountains / Animales de Las Montañas (Second Edition) Ser.). (ENG & SPA.). 24p. (J). (gr. 1-1). pap. 9.15 *(978-1-4339-2499-6(4),* ed1251a9-f16b-4c35-a92c-0f974d79d02e, Weekly Reader Leveled Readers); lib. bdg. 25.27 *(978-1-4339-2441-5(2),* 1190e02b-1287-4147-929d-ea16d0cbd1bc) Stevens, Gareth Publishing LLLP.
—Mountain Goats / Cabra Montés, 1 vol. 2nd rev. ed. 2009. (Animals That Live in the Mountains / Animales de Las Montañas (Second Edition) Ser.). 24p. (J). (gr. 1-1). (ENG & SPA.). pap. 9.15 *(978-1-4339-2504-7(4),* 5f8ace75-51e7-4e4b-9413-ea029279fddb, Weekly Reader Leveled Readers); (SPA & ENG.). lib. bdg. 25.27 *(978-1-4339-2446-0(3),* ce280275-9c66-4400-b8c8-2edd537a7c6e) Stevens, Gareth Publishing LLLP.
—Sheep, 1 vol. (Animals That Live on the Farm (First Edition) Ser.). (ENG., 24p. (gr. 1-1). 2004. Illus.). pap. 9.15 *(978-0-8368-4283-8(9),* 381dead7-8c42-475d-b2d7-b7c79e80c2a4) 2nd rev. ed. 2009. (J). pap. 9.15 *(978-1-4339-2469-9(2),* cdda8bb8-f973-476d-adf5-260c7f1c4b54) 2nd rev. ed. 2009. (J). lib. bdg. 25.27 *(978-1-4339-2400-2(5),* fbf51095-2f74-46a9-b94f-2190a7691c0d) Stevens, Gareth Publishing LLLP. (Weekly Reader Leveled Readers).
—Sheep / Las Ovejas, 1 vol. (Animals That Live on the Farm / Animales Que Viven en la Granja (First Edition) Ser.). 24p. (gr. 1-1). 2004. (SPA & ENG., Illus.). lib. bdg. 23.67 *(978-0-8368-4290-6(1),* 135f5a10-2fdc-4398-8400-0f7bdc7b9599) 2nd rev. ed. 2009. (ENG & SPA.). (J). pap. 9.15 *(978-1-4339-2476-7(5),* 8dc7ad47-c753-48e1-a1f3-001d5f240c7a, Weekly Reader Leveled Readers) 2nd rev. ed. 2009. (ENG & SPA.). (J). lib. bdg. 25.27 *(978-1-4339-2432-3(3),* daa2732d-9a36-4525-b0d0-a4f46aad3442) Stevens, Gareth Publishing LLLP.
Esquivel, Rosaura. Merino Sheep, 1 vol. 2017. (Wild & Woolly Ser.). (ENG.). 24p. (J). (gr. 3-3). 25.27 *(978-1-5383-2533-9(0),* 37d12e3b-298c-4a89-b4ad-45450b30c606); pap. 9.25 *(978-1-5383-2603-9(5),* 822b659a-8041-4c42-9b11-757964c4d7ce) Rosen Publishing Group, Inc., The. (PowerKids Pr.).
Esseltine, Bruce. At the Sheep Farm, 1 vol. 2016. (Fun on the Farm Ser.). (ENG.). 24p. (J). (gr. k-k). pap. 9.15 *(978-1-4824-5532-8(3),* 5eaf2958-03c6-4afa-a8a7-914832214036) Stevens, Gareth Publishing LLLP.
Frankenhuyzen, Robbyn Smith van. Itsy Bitsy & Teeny Weeny. Frankenhuyzen, Gijsbert van, illus. 2009. (Hazel Ridge Farm Stories Ser.). (ENG.). 48p. (J). (gr. 1-4). 16.95 *(978-1-58536-417-6(7),* 202152) Sleeping Bear Pr.
Gagne, Tammy. Bighorn Sheep. 2017. (Animals of North America Ser.). (ENG., Illus.). 32p. (J). (gr. 2-3). pap. 9.95 *(978-1-63517-088-7(5),* 1635170885, Focus Readers) North Star Editions.
Gandolfo, Glora. Sheep. 2009. (Illus.). 52p. (J). *(978-0-7172-8054-4(3))* Grolier, Ltd.
Gish, Melissa. Bighorn Sheep. (Living Wild Ser.). (ENG.). 48p. (J). 2016. (gr. 5-9). pap. 12.00 *(978-1-62832-165-4(2),* 20878, Creative Paperbacks) 2015. (Illus.). (gr. 4-7). *(978-1-60818-564-1(8),* 20877, Creative Education) Creative Co., The.
Green, Emily K. Sheep. 2007. (Farm Animals Ser.). (ENG., Illus.). 24p. (J). (gr. k-3). lib. bdg. 26.95 *(978-1-60014-069-3(6))* Bellwether Media.
Hasselius, Michelle. Sheep. 2016. (Farm Animals Ser.). (ENG., Illus.). 24p. (J). (gr. -1-2). lib. bdg. 27.32 *(978-1-5157-0927-5(2),* 132229, Capstone Pr.) Capstone.
Hudak, Heather C. Sheep. 2006. (Farm Animals Ser.). (Illus.). 24p. (J). (gr. 3-7). lib. bdg. 24.45 *(978-1-59036-428-4(7));* per. 8.95 *(978-1-59036-435-2(X))* Weigl Pubs., Inc.
Jackson, Tom. Bighorn Sheep. 2008. (Nature's Children Ser.). (Illus.). 52p. (J). *(978-0-7172-6218-2(9))* Grolier, Ltd.
Kawa, Katie. Lambs, 1 vol. 2011. (Cute & Cuddly: Baby Animals Ser.). (Illus.). 24p. (gr. k-k). (ENG.). (J). pap. 9.15 *(978-1-4339-5547-1(4),* f8c5b353-706b-4f94-973a-e27327f823e3); (ENG., (J). lib. bdg. 25.27 *(978-1-4339-5546-4(6),* 96b4f2d3-2473-42a8-930b-6b51c0bc6c0a); 69.20 *(978-1-4339-6897-6(5))* Stevens, Gareth Publishing LLLP.
Kopp, Megan. Ovejas. 2013. (Animales en la Granja Ser.). (SPA., Illus.). 24p. (J). (gr. -1-3). lib. bdg. 27.13 *(978-1-62127-591-6(4),* AV2 by Weigl) Weigl Pubs., Inc.
—Sheep. 2012. (J). *(978-1-61913-278-8(8));* *(978-1-61913-282-5(6))* Weigl Pubs., Inc.
Lang, Aubrey. Baby Mountain Sheep, 1 vol. Lynch, Wayne, photos by. 2007. (Nature Babies Ser.). (ENG., Illus.). 36p. (J). (gr. k-3). 7.95 *(978-1-55455-043-2(2),* 6deec32a-d37c-4852-9d9c-0a9a1e1c3d92); 16.95 *(978-1-55455-042-5(4),* 55c7f00d-f315-44e2-a359-134dc5864e49) Trifolium Bks., Inc. CAN. Dist: Firefly Bks., Ltd.
Leaf, Christina. Baby Sheep. 2014. (Super Cute! Ser.). (ENG., Illus.). 24p. (J). (gr. k-3). lib. bdg. 26.95 *(978-1-60014-978-8(2),* Blastoff! Readers) Bellwether Media.
Leighton, Christina. Sheep. 2018. (Animals on the Farm Ser.). (ENG., Illus.). 24p. (J). (gr. k-3). lib. bdg. 26.95 *(978-1-62617-726-0(0),* Blastoff! Readers) Bellwether Media.
Loh-Hagan, Virginia. Bighorn Sheep. Bane, Jeff, illus. 2017. (My Early Library: My Favorite Animal Ser.). (ENG.). 24p. (J). (gr. k-1). lib. bdg. 30.64 *(978-1-63472-837-9(8),* 209774) Cherry Lake Publishing.
Magby, Meryl. Bighorn Sheep, 1 vol. 2012. (American Animals Ser.). (ENG., Illus.). 24p. (J). (gr. 2-3). pap. 9.25 *(978-1-4488-6321-1(X),* 60aad123-7da9-4e77-8f62-e74fe53782a8, PowerKids Pr.); lib. bdg. 26.27 *(978-1-4488-6181-1(0),* dfe14487-4ed0-4525-afb2-829ddfceb2cc) Rosen Publishing Group, Inc., The.
Mercer, Abbie. Sheep on a Farm. 2009. (Barnyard Animals Ser.). (J). 49.50 *(978-1-4042-8062-5(6));* (ENG.). 24p. (gr. 1-1). pap. 9.25 *(978-1-4042-8061-8(8),* aa6825ee-3e61-492f-bb5a-e06a95237d39); (ENG., Illus.). 24p. (gr. 1-1). lib. bdg. 26.27 *(978-1-4042-8050-2(2),* db37af4b-9392-4717-a7f5-4de8a7eb95cb) Rosen Publishing Group, Inc., The. (PowerKids Pr.).
Metz, Lorijo. Sheep: Ewes, Rams, & Lambs, 1 vol. 2010. (On the Farm Ser.). (ENG.). 24p. (J). (gr. 2-3). pap. 9.25 *(978-1-4488-1341-4(7),* aba89e64-ec9f-499c-b3e3-d4ba9dec97d4); lib. bdg. 26.27 *(978-1-4488-0690-4(9),* 8b8d77af-f12d-4381-9887-ae6c15b262e4) Rosen Publishing Group, Inc., The. (PowerKids Pr.).
Minden, Cecilia. Farm Animals: Sheep. 2009. (21st Century Junior Library: Farm Animals Ser.). (ENG., Illus.). 24p. (gr. 2-4). lib. bdg. 29.21 *(978-1-60279-544-0(4),* 200276) Cherry Lake Publishing.
Mower, Christine Stevens. Little Lamb from Bethlehem. 2017. (Illus.). (J). 26.99 *(978-1-62972-369-3(X))* Deseret Bk. Co.
Murray, Julie. Sheep, 1 vol. 2015. (Farm Animals (Abdo Kids Junior) Ser.). (ENG., Illus.). 24p. (J). (gr. -1-2). 31.36 *(978-1-62970-943-7(3),* 18264, Abdo Kids) ABDO Publishing Co.
Nelid, Piper. At the Sheep Farm, 1 vol., 1. 2015. (Rosen REAL Readers: STEM & STEAM Collection). (ENG.). 8p. (J). (gr. k-1). pap. 5.46 *(978-1-5081-1432-1(3),* e4e77c96-a4c9-486f-bbe6-d1d33cd819d4, Rosen Classroom) Rosen Publishing Group, Inc., The.
Nelson, Robin. From Sheep to Sweater. 2003. (Start to Finish Ser.). (Illus.). 24p. (J). 18.60 *(978-0-8225-0716-1(1),* Lerner Pubns.) Lerner Publishing Group.
—Sheep. 2009. pap. 34.95 *(978-0-7613-4095-9(5));* (ENG.). 24p. 23.93 *(978-0-7613-4062-1(9),* Lerner Pubns.) Lerner Publishing Group.
Osburn, Mary Grace. Shapes with Sheep, 1 vol. 2017. (Animal Math Ser.). (ENG.). 24p. (J). (gr. 1-2). pap. 9.15 *(978-1-5382-0855-7(5),* 825ee072-6dcd-4e4d-afbd-f95756a19f2b) Stevens, Gareth Publishing LLLP.
Owen, Ruth. Meat! Life on a Sheep Farm, 1 vol. 2012. (Food from Farmers Ser.). (ENG., Illus.). 32p. (J). (gr. 1-2). pap. 12.75 *(978-1-61533-542-8(0),* aa7eb670-f961-42e4-a5b2-128f7b61ed72); lib. bdg. 29.93 *(978-1-61533-533-6(1),* f7b9318c-5b3f-40d6-8306-f025d12e244d) Rosen Publishing Group, Inc., The. (Windmill Bks.).
Perish, Patrick. Bighorn Sheep. 2019. (Animals of the Desert Ser.). (ENG., Illus.). 24p. (J). (gr. k-3). lib. bdg. 26.95 *(978-1-62617-920-2(4),* Blastoff! Readers) Bellwether Media.
Ray, Hannah. Sheep. 2008. (Down on the Farm (N.Y.) Ser.). (ENG., Illus.). 24p. (J). (gr. 3-7). pap. *(978-0-7787-4056-8(0))* Crabtree Publishing Co.
—Sheep. 2006. (Down on the Farm Ser.). (Illus.). 24p. (J). (gr. 4-7). lib. bdg. 15.95 *(978-1-59566-182-1(4))* QEB Publishing Inc.
Shanks, Cindy. Alfonso Grows up on the Sheep Trail. 2010. 40p. pap. 18.99 *(978-1-4520-7980-6(3))* AuthorHouse.
Sherman, Jill. Bighorn Sheep. 2018. (North American Animals Ser.). (ENG.). 24p. (J). (gr. 1-4). pap. 8.99 *(978-1-68152-335-4(3),* 15120); lib. bdg. *(978-1-68151-415-4(X),* 15112) Amicus.
—El Borrego Cimarrón. 2018. (Animales Norteamericanos Ser.). (SPA.). 24p. (J). (gr. 1-4). lib. bdg. *(978-1-68151-621-9(7),* 15229) Amicus.
Siemens, Jared. Sheep. 2018. *(978-1-4896-9528-4(1),* AV2 by Weigl) Weigl Pubs., Inc.
Snelbaker, Carmela. Thank You for Your Service, Sheep! 2013. pap. 17.49 *(978-1-4797-4659-0(2))* Xlibris.
Statts, Leo. Sheep. 2016. (Farm Animals Ser.). (ENG., Illus.). 24p. (J). (gr. -1-2). lib. bdg. 31.36 *(978-1-68079-907-1(X),* 24118, Abdo Zoom-Launch) ABDO Publishing Co.
Stiefel, Chana. Sheep on the Family Farm, 1 vol. 2013. (Animals on the Family Farm Ser.). (ENG.). 24p. (gr. k-2). pap. 10.35 *(978-1-4644-0361-3(9),* d07e345c-43f0-4f19-8463-65ac8fc38fa0, Enslow Elementary); lib. bdg. 25.27 *(978-0-7660-4209-4(X),* 4ecd23cf-cb16-4c09-b926-6f1e9a781c75) Enslow Publishing, LLC.
Suen, Anastasia. Lambs. 2019. (Spot Baby Farm Animals Ser.). (ENG.). 16p. (J). (gr. -1-2). lib. bdg. *(978-1-68151-534-2(2),* 14495) Amicus.
Ticktock Media, Ltd. Staff. What Do Sheep Do? 2008. (What Do Animals Do? Ser.). (ENG.). 10p. (J). (gr. k — 1). bds. 4.95 *(978-1-84696-793-1(7),* TickTock Books) Octopus Publishing Group GBR. Dist: Independent Pubs. Group.
Top That Publishing Staff, ed. Wacky Sheep. 2004. (Wacky Animals Ser.). (Illus.). 10p. (J). pap. *(978-1-84510-089-6(1))* Top That! Publishing PLC.
Wendorff, Anne. Lambs. 2009. (Watch Animals Grow Ser.). (ENG., Illus.). 24p. (J). (gr. k-3). lib. bdg. 26.95 *(978-1-60014-241-3(9))* Bellwether Media.
—Lambs. 2009. (Blastoff! Readers Ser.). (ENG., Illus.). 24p. (J). (gr. k-3). 20.00 *(978-0-531-21629-3(2),* Children's Pr.) Scholastic Library Publishing.
Wendt, Jennifer. Showing Sheep at the Fair, 1 vol. 2018. (Blue Ribbon Animals Ser.). (ENG.). 24p. (gr. 2-3). lib. bdg. 24.27 *(978-1-5382-2932-3(3),* 75ccd62e-3ba2-4f68-98d6-03c032e3e852) Stevens, Gareth Publishing LLLP.
Wilsdon, Christina. Sheep, 1 vol. 2010. (Amazing Animals Ser.). (ENG.). 48p. (J). (gr. 3-5). pap. 11.50 *(978-1-4339-4029-3(9),* 831b6d3f-0170-4490-8249-8270251f8b49); lib. bdg. 30.67 *(978-1-4339-4028-6(0),* e2c4b1aa-c9a2-410c-bd65-cda331d14f3e) Stevens, Gareth Publishing LLLP. (Gareth Stevens Learning Library).
—Sheep. 2006. (J). *(978-1-59939-079-6(5),* Reader's Digest Young Families, Inc.) Studio Fun International.
Wolfman, Judy. Life on a Sheep Farm. Winston, David Lorenz, illus. Winston, David Lorenz, photos by. 2004. (Life on a Farm Ser.). (ENG.). 48p. (gr. 2-5). lib. bdg. 23.93 *(978-1-57505-192-5(3))* Lerner Publishing Group.
Wood, Alix. Babydoll Sheep, 1 vol. 2016. (Mini Animals Ser.). (ENG., Illus.). 32p. (J). (gr. 2-3). pap. 11.00 *(978-1-4994-8149-5(7),* 6ae1c96f-e028-40db-a067-041360be22f5, Windmill Bks.) Rosen Publishing Group, Inc., The.

SHEEP—FICTION

Aesop, Aesop. The Wolf in Sheep's Clothing: A Tale about Appearances. 2006. (J). *(978-1-59939-086-4(8),* Reader's Digest Young Families, Inc.) Studio Fun International.
Allard, Harry & Marshall, James. Sheep Out to Eat. 2015. 32p. pap. 7.00 *(978-1-61003-508-8(9))* Center for the Collaborative Classroom.
Alphabetical Sleepy Sheep. 2005. (J). bds. 7.95 *(978-0-9749305-7-2(1));* (ENG.). bds. 7.95 *(978-0-9749305-4-1(7))* Castle Pacific Publishing.
Amery, Heather. Where's Woolly? Tyler, Jenny, ed. Cartwright, Stephen, illus. 2006. (Treasury of Farmyard Tales Ser.). 16p. (J). (gr. -1-18). 15.95 *(978-1-58086-531-9(3))* EDC Publishing.
—Woolly the Sheep. Cartwright, Stephen, illus. 2004. (Young Farmyard Tales Board Books Ser.). 10p. (J). bds. 3.95 *(978-0-7945-0467-0(1),* Usborne) EDC Publishing.
Amundson, Susan D. Three Little Lambs — Somewhere. Geiken, Brenda Joy, illus. 2006. 40p. (J). *(978-1-59984-002-4(2))* Bluedoor, llc.
Anderson, Susan C. Why the Rooster Crowed. 2009. (ENG.). 26p. pap. 15.99 *(978-1-4500-0702-3(3))* Xlibris Corp.
Animal I can hear s/s - Sheep. 2005. (J). bds. *(978-1-4194-0060-5(6))* Paradise Pr., Inc.
Arant, Bruce. Simpson's Sheep Just Want to Sleep! 2017. (ENG., Illus.). 32p. (J). 16.99 *(978-1-4413-2429-0(1),* d1d43977-002e-4650-9006-9d38e13ced02) Peter Pauper Pr. Inc.
Archer, Dosh. Baaad Sheep. Archer, Dosh, illus. 2016. (Urgency Emergency! Ser.). (ENG., Illus.). 48p. (J). (gr. k-2). 12.99 *(978-0-8075-8349-4(9),* 807583499) Whitman, Albert & Co.
Auerbach, Annie. Furry Lamb. Rigo, Laura, illus. 2018. (ENG.). 10p. (J). (gr. -1-k). bds. 5.99 *(978-1-4380-5013-3(5))* Sourcebooks, Inc.
AZ Books, creator. Lamb Searches for Her Mom. 2012. (Plush Baby Ser.). (ENG., Illus.). 10p. (J). (gr. -1 — 1). 11.95 *(978-1-61889-218-8(5))* AZ Bks. LLC.
Baa, Baa Black Sheep. 2003. (J). per. *(978-1-57657-799-8(6))* Paradise Pr., Inc.
Bad Boys. 2007. (J). (gr. k-3). 27.95 incl. audio *(978-0-8045-6956-9(8));* 29.95 incl. audio compact disk *(978-0-8045-4179-4(5))* Spoken Arts, Inc.
Barclay, Eric. Sheep Dog & Sheep Sheep. Barclay, Eric, illus. 2019. (ENG., Illus.). 40p. (J). (gr. -1-3). 17.99 *(978-0-06-267738-9(1),* HarperCollins) HarperCollins Pubs.
Bauer, Michael. The Adventures of Steel Wooly: And my Place on the Farm. 2012. (ENG.). 25p. (J). pap. 12.95 *(978-1-4327-8568-0(0))* Outskirts Pr., Inc.
Beaty, Andrea. Hide & Sheep. Mayer, Bill, illus. 2011. (ENG.). 32p. (J). (gr. -1-3). 15.99 *(978-1-4169-2544-6(9),* McElderry, Margaret K. Bks.) McElderry, Margaret K. Bks.
Bee, Granny. Laffy the Lamb. Werthiemer, Beverly, ed. Sohn, Jeana, illus. 2006. 32p. (J). 16.95 *(978-1-932367-00-3(4))* BookBound Publishing.
Bell, Cece. You Loves Ewe! Bell, Cece, illus. 2019. (Yam & Donkey Book Ser.). (ENG., Illus.). 32p. (J). (gr. -1-3). 17.99 *(978-1-328-52611-3(9),* 1721549, Clarion Bks.) HarperCollins Pubs.
Bell, Lucy. Ava & the Big Ouch: A Book about Feeling Better. Garton, Michael, illus. 2018. (Frolic First Faith Ser.). 32p. (J). (gr. -1-3). 12.99 *(978-1-5064-2504-7(6),* Sparkhouse Family) 1517 Media.
Bell-Martin, Janelle. Mary Had a Little Lamb. 2011. (Early Literacy Ser.). (ENG.). 16p. (gr. k-1). 19.99 *(978-1-4333-2358-4(3));* 6.99 *(978-1-4333-2357-7(5))* Teacher Created Materials, Inc.
Belloni, Giulia. Anything Is Possible. Trevisan, Marco, illus. 2013. (ENG.). 32p. (J). (gr. -1-3). 16.95 *(978-1-926973-91-3(7),* Owlkids) Owlkids Bks. Inc. CAN. Dist: Publishers Group West (PGW).
Bender, Chris. The Lion & the Lamb. 2011. 24p. 14.93 *(978-1-4269-5732-1(7))* Trafford Publishing.
Bently, Peter. The Great Sheep Shenanigans. Matsuoka, Mei, illus. 2012. (Andersen Press Picture Bks). (ENG.). 32p. (J). (gr. -1-3). 16.95 *(978-0-7613-8990-3(3))* Lerner Publishing Group.
Beskow, Elsa. Pelle's New Suit: Mini Edition, 30 vols. 2007. Orig. Title: Pelles Nya Kläder. (Illus.). 32p. (J). (gr. -1-4). 9.95 *(978-0-86315-584-0(7))* Floris Bks. GBR. Dist: Consortium Bk. Sales & Distribution.
Bingham, Mark Jay. Woolie & the Bully. 2013. 52p. 30.95 *(978-1-4582-0843-9(5));* pap. 23.95 *(978-1-4582-0844-6(3))* Author Solutions, LLC. (Abbott Pr.).
Blair, Eric. El Pastorcito Mentiroso: Versión de la Fábula de Esopo. Abello, Patricia, tr. Silverman, Dianne, illus. 2006. (Read-It! Readers en Español: Fábulas Ser.). Tr. of Boy Who Cried Wolf - A Retelling of Aesop's Fable. (SPA.). 24p. (J). (gr. k-3). 22.65 *(978-1-4048-1616-9(X),* 91876, Picture Window Bks.) Capstone.
Bland, Nick, illus. King Pig. 2013. (J). pap. *(978-0-545-67013-5(6))* Scholastic, Inc.
Blyton, Enid. Don't Be Silly Mr Twiddle! (Illus.). 111p. (J). pap. 7.95 *(978-0-7475-3858-5(1))* Bloomsbury Publishing Plc GBR. Dist: Trafalgar Square Publishing.
Bowater, Alan. A Pig Called Pete Meets a Sheep Called Sean, 1 vol. Pascoe, Pete, illus. 2009. (Pig Called Pete Ser.). (ENG.). 32p. (J). (gr. 1-2). 27.27 *(978-1-60754-570-5(5),* 8b646817-e167-43ce-8f24-7259135fe187); pap. 11.55 *(978-1-60754-571-2(3),* 41e4b4d7-04af-4691-87e0-bd9043543e3f) Rosen Publishing Group, Inc., The. (Windmill Bks.).
Brennan, Sarah. The Tale of Rodney Ram. Harrison, Harry, illus. 2014. (J). *(978-1-937160-60-9(2))* Eliassen Creative.
Brents, Alan. Sheldon the Sheep. 2011. 24p. pap. 12.79 *(978-1-4634-8728-7(2))* AuthorHouse.
Brown, Margaret Wise. The Little Lost Lamb. Date not set. 40p. (J). (gr. -1-3). 15.89 *(978-0-06-027291-3(0));* 14.99 *(978-0-06-027290-6(2))* HarperCollins Pubs.
Butler, Dori. A Sheep in Wolf's Clothing. 2006. (J). pap. *(978-1-4108-6185-6(6))* Benchmark Education Co.
Cabrera, Jane. Baa, Baa, Black Sheep. 2016. (Jane Cabrera's Story Time Ser.). (ENG., Illus.). 24p. (J). (gr. -1-k). bds. 7.99 *(978-0-8234-3631-6(4))* Holiday Hse., Inc.
Carr, Elias. Ava & the Skimpy Picnic: A Book about Sharing. Garton, Michael, illus. 2016. (Frolic First Faith Ser.). 32p. (J). (gr. -1-k). 12.99 *(978-1-5064-1051-7(0),* Sparkhouse Family) 1517 Media.
—Ava y el Picnic Raquítico. Garton, Michael, illus. 2016. (SPA.). (J). *(978-1-5064-2095-0(8))* 1517 Media.
—Hal & the New Kid: A Book about Making Friends. Garton, Michael, illus. 2016. (Frolic First Faith Ser.). 32p. (J). (gr. -1-k). 12.99 *(978-1-5064-1050-0(2),* Sparkhouse Family) 1517 Media.
—Hal y el Nuevo Compañero. Garton, Michael, illus. 2016. (SPA.). (J). *(978-1-5064-2098-1(2))* 1517 Media.
—Jo & the Slow Soup: A Book about Patience. Rimmington, Natasha, illus. 2016. (Frolic First Faith Ser.). 32p. (J). (gr. -1-k). 12.99 *(978-1-5064-1048-7(0),* Sparkhouse Family) 1517 Media.

—Rufus & His Angry Tail: A Book about Anger. Garton, Michael, illus. 2016. (Frolic First Faith Ser.). 32p. (J). (gr. -1-k). 12.99 *(978-1-5064-1049-4(9),* Sparkhouse Family) 1517 Media.

—Rufus y Su Cola Enojada. Garton, Michael, illus. 2016. (SPA.). (J). *(978-1-5064-2096-7(6))* 1517 Media.

Cartwright, Stephen. Little Book of Train Stories. rev. ed. 2011. (Farmyard Tales Readers Ser.). 64p. (J). ring bd. 8.99 *(978-0-7945-3070-9(2),* Usborne) EDC Publishing.

Cerato, Mattia. Sheep in the Closet. Cerato, Mattia, illus. 2014. (Family Snaps Ser.). (ENG., Illus.). 32p. (J). (gr. k-2). pap. 6.99 *(978-1-939656-62-9(1),* f68e09c9-632d-4352-b030-9244c1166965) Red Chair Pr.

Chalekian, Bobbie. The Legend of the Lamb & the Lion. 2011. 32p. (gr. 2-4). pap. 14.99 *(978-1-4567-2713-0(3))* AuthorHouse.

Chance, Robyn. Ewela's Unbaalievable Journey. 2012. 46p. (-18). 23.95 *(978-1-936850-87-7(7))* Rhemalda Publishing.

Charles, Kaye Ellen. Macarthur & Martha. 2013. 56p. pap. 20.95 *(978-1-4525-8512-3(1),* Balboa Pr.) Author Solutions, LLC.

Chin, Oliver. The Year of the Sheep. Chau, Alina, illus. 2014. (Tales from the Chinese Zodiac Ser.: 10). (ENG.). 36p. (J). (gr. -1-3). 15.95 *(978-1-59702-104-3(0))* Immedium.

Chronicle Books, Chronicle & ImageBooks. Little Lamb: Finger Puppet Book: (Finger Puppet Book for Toddlers & Babies, Baby Books for First Year, Animal Finger Puppets) 2006. (Little Finger Puppet Board Bks.: FING). (ENG., Illus.). 12p. (J). (gr. -1-7). bds. 7.99 *(978-0-8118-5235-7(0))* Chronicle Bks. LLC.

Churchman, Jennifer & Churchman, John. Brave Little Finn. 2016. (Sweet Pea & Friends Ser.: 2). (ENG., Illus.). 40p. (J). (gr. -1-3). 17.99 *(978-0-316-27359-6(7))* Little, Brown Bks. for Young Readers.

—A Farm for Maisie. 2017. (Sweet Pea & Friends Ser.: 3). (ENG., Illus.). 40p. (J). (gr. -1-3). 17.99 *(978-0-316-27360-2(0))* Little, Brown Bks. for Young Readers.

—The SheepOver. (Sweet Pea & Friends Ser.: 1). (ENG., Illus.). (J). (gr. -1 — 1). 2017. 24p. bds. 7.99 *(978-0-316-27355-8(4))* 2015. 44p. 17.99 *(978-0-316-27356-5(2))* Little, Brown Bks. for Young Readers.

Colorful Sleepy Sheep. 2005. (J). bds. 7.95 *(978-0-9749305-5-8(5))* Castle Pacific Publishing.

Conrad, Liz, illus. Little Lamb. 2009. (My Sparkling Springtime Friends Ser.). (ENG.). 10p. (J). bds. 3.95 *(978-1-58117-868-5(9),* Intervisual/Piggy Toes) Bendon, Inc.

Cordell, Matthew. Another Brother. Cordell, Matthew, illus. 2018. (ENG., Illus.). 40p. (J). pap. 8.99 *(978-1-250-20762-3(2),* 900201653) Square Fish.

Cotter, Natasha. The Christmas Blessing. 2012. 24p. 24.95 *(978-1-4626-6925-7(5))* America Star Bks.

Cox, Phil Roxbee. Sam Sheep Can't Sleep. Tyler, Jenny, ed. Cartwright, Stephen, illus. rev. ed. 2006. (Usborne Phonics Bks.). 16p. (J). (gr. -1-k). 6.99 *(978-0-7945-1508-9(8),* Usborne) EDC Publishing.

Cox, Phil Roxbee & Cartwright, S. Sam Sheep Can't Sleep. 2004. (Phonics Board Bks.). (ENG.). 1p. (J). bds. 4.99 *(978-0-7945-0060-3(9),* Usborne) EDC Publishing.

—Ted's Shed, Toad Makes a Road, Fat Cat on a Mat & Sam Sheep Can't Sleep. 2004. (Easy Words to Read Ser.). (Illus.). 16p. (J). (gr. 1-18). pap. 9.95 *(978-0-7945-0245-4(8),* Usborne) EDC Publishing.

Crangle, Claudine. Woolfred Cannot Eat Dandelions: A Tale of Being True to Your Tummy. 2014. (ENG., Illus.). 32p. (J). *(978-1-4338-1672-7(5),* Magination Pr.) American Psychological Assn.

Crangle, Claudine, illus. Woolfred Does Not Eat Dandelions. 2014. 32p. (J). pap. *(978-1-4338-1673-4(3),* Magination Pr.) American Psychological Assn.

Crayton, Tina Lorice. The Lost Sheep. 2010. (ENG.). 24p. pap. 10.50 *(978-1-4490-7707-5(2))* AuthorHouse.

Crayton, Tina Lorice (Anderson). The Wolf in Sheep's Clothing: The Impostor. 2011. 20p. 10.50 *(978-1-4567-3011-6(8))* AuthorHouse.

Cvetkovic, Judith. Mandy & Star's Sheep Ranch Getaway, 1 vol. 2010. 108p. pap. 19.95 *(978-1-4489-5673-9(0))* America Star Bks.

Dahl, Michael. Story Time for Lamb, 1 vol. Vidal, Oriol, illus. 2011. (Hello Genius Ser.). (ENG.). 20p. (J). (gr. -1 — 1). bds. 7.99 *(978-1-4048-6495-5(4),* 114177, Picture Window Bks.) Capstone.

Dalmatian Press Staff. One Little Sheep. 2008. (ENG.). 6p. bds. 4.95 *(978-1-58117-719-0(4),* Intervisual/Piggy Toes) Bendon, Inc.

Dalton, Sherry A. A New Day - a New Beginning: All about a Day on the Farm. Whitlatch, Jessica A., illus. 2011. 40p. pap. 24.95 *(978-1-4560-7462-3(8))* America Star Bks.

Davies, Gill & Freeman, Tina. Lucy Lamb. 2004. (Tales from Yellow Barn Farm Ser.). (Illus.). 24p. (J). 3.99 *(978-1-85854-322-2(3))* Brimax Books Ltd. GBR. Dist: Byeway Bks.

Debesay, Samson. Cubby, the Lionsheep: Son, you are a lion, live like One! 2011. (Illus.). 24p. pap. 14.89 *(978-1-4567-7899-6(4))* AuthorHouse.

DePrisco, Dorothea. One Little Sheep. 2006. (ENG.). 12p. (J). 12.95 *(978-1-58117-488-5(8),* Intervisual/Piggy Toes) Bendon, Inc.

deRubertis, Barbara. Lana Llama's Little Lamb. Alley, R. W., illus. 2011. (Animal Antics A to Z Ser.). 32p. (J). pap. 45.32 *(978-0-7613-7658-3(5));* (ENG.). lib. bdg. 22.60 *(978-1-57565-333-4(8))* Astra Publishing Hse.

deRubertis, Barbara & DeRubertis, Barbara. Lana Llama's Little Lamb. Alley, R. W., illus. 2012. (Animal Antics A to Z Ser.). 32p. (J). (gr. 2 — 1). cd-rom 7.95 *(978-1-57565-405-8(9))* Astra Publishing Hse.

Devine, Ginger. Hooray for the Circus: A Story of Sam the Lamb. 2008. 36p. pap. 16.99 *(978-1-4389-1826-6(7))* AuthorHouse.

Don, Lari. The Hungry Wolf: A Story from North America. Williamson, Melanie, illus. 2013. (Animal Stories Ser.). 48p. (J). (gr. 1-4). pap. 8.99 *(978-1-84686-872-6(6))* Barefoot Bks., Inc.

Dorner, V. K. The Little Lambs & the Rainbow Zebra. 2011. 36p. 13.95 *(978-1-4497-0889-4(7),* WestBow Pr.) Author Solutions, LLC.

Doudna, Kelly. Lamb Chops. Chawla, Neena, illus. 2006. (Fact & Fiction Ser.). 24p. (J). pap. 48.42 *(978-1-59679-948-6(X))* ABDO Publishing Co.

Dumont, Jean-Francois. The Sheep Go on Strike. 2014. (ENG., Illus.). 34p. (J). 16.00 *(978-0-8028-5470-4(2),* Eerdmans Bks For Young Readers) Eerdmans, William B. Publishing Co.

Durant, Alan. Little Bo-Peep's Missing Sheep. Heming, Leah-Ellen, illus. 2012. (ENG.). 32p. (J). *(978-0-7787-8029-8(5))* Crabtree Publishing Co.

Durkee, Noura. The King, the Prince & the Naughty Sheep. Durkee, Noura, illus. 2007. (ENG., Illus.). 24p. (J). (gr. k-5). 16.00 *(978-1-879402-58-4(0))* Tahrike Tarsile Quran, Inc.

Dykes, Tami J. Being Too Small Is Big Enough. 2013. 42p. pap. 20.45 *(978-1-4497-8483-6(6),* WestBow Pr.) Author Solutions, LLC.

Eglin, Lorna. A Boy of Two Worlds. 2014. (Flamingo Fiction 9-13s Ser.). (ENG., Illus.). 208p. (J). (gr. 4-7). per. 8.99 *(978-1-84550-126-6(8),* 7bd05c30-c5cc-437e-98b4-54dcc88bc3ca) Christian Focus Pubns. GBR. Dist: Baker & Taylor Publisher Services (BTPS).

Eulate, Ana. Little Cloud Lamb. Brokenbrow, Jon, tr. Carretero, Mónica, illus. 2011. (Light (Cuento de Luz) Ser.). 28p. (J). (gr. 1-3). 14.95 *(978-84-938240-2-0(X))* Cuento de Luz SL ESP. Dist: Publishers Group West (PGW).

Falconer, Mary. The Spotted Sheep with the Worthless Wool. 2011. 24p. pap. 10.49 *(978-1-4520-9636-0(8))* AuthorHouse.

Fenwick, Margaret. Lonnie the Lost Lamb. 2010. 32p. pap. 13.00 *(978-1-60911-038-3(2),* Eloquent Bks.) Strategic Book Publishing & Rights Agency (SBPRA).

Fliess, Sue. Mary Had a Little Lab. Bouloubasis, Petros, illus. 2018. (ENG.). 32p. (J). (gr. -1-3). 16.99 *(978-0-8075-4982-7(7),* 807549827) Whitman, Albert & Co.

Following Isabella - Evaluation Guide: Evaluation Guide. 2006. (J). *(978-1-55942-406-6(0))* Witcher Productions.

Fox, Mem & Horacek, Judy. Where Is the Green Sheep? Board Book. Horacek, Judy, illus. alt. ed. 2009. (ENG., Illus.). 32p. (J). (gr. -1 — 1). bds. 6.99 *(978-0-15-206704-5(3),* 1098965, Clarion Bks.) HarperCollins Pubs.

—Where Is the Green Sheep?/Donde Esta la Oveja Verde? Board Book: Bilingual English-Spanish. Horacek, Judy, illus. 2010. (ENG., Illus.). 32p. (J). (gr. -1-k). bds. 5.99 *(978-0-547-39694-1(5),* 1427473, Clarion Bks.) HarperCollins Pubs.

Fraggalosch, Audrey. Trails above the Tree Line: A Story of a Rocky Mountain Meadow. Bond, Higgins, illus. 2005. (Soundprints' Wild Habitats Ser.). (ENG.). (J). (gr. 1-4). 36p. 15.95 *(978-1-56899-941-8(0),* B7021); 32p. pap. 6.95 *(978-1-56899-942-5(9),* S7021) Soundprints.

Françoise. Jeanne-Marie Counts Her Sheep. 2003. (Illus.). 32p. (J). mass mkt. 9.99 *(978-0-9740599-0-7(0),* 1) Omnibus Publishing.

Freitag, Fred. On Hills & Meadows by the River. 2013. 28p. pap. 24.95 *(978-1-63000-584-9(3))* America Star Bks.

French, Jackie. Pete the Sheep. Whatley, Bruce, illus. 2008. 30p. (J). bds. *(978-0-7322-8794-8(4))* HarperCollins Pubs. Australia.

—Pete the Sheep-Sheep. Whatley, Bruce, illus. 2005. (ENG.). 32p. (J). (gr. -1-3). 14.00 *(978-0-618-56862-8(X),* 100414, Clarion Bks.) HarperCollins Pubs.

French, Jackie & Whatley, Bruce. Pete the Sheep. 2006. (ENG., Illus.). 32p. pap. *(978-0-207-19974-5(4))* HarperCollins Pubs. Australia.

Galvin, Laura Gates. Baby Lamb Finds a Friend. (Smithsonian Baby Animals Ser.). (ENG., Illus.). 16p. (gr. -1-k). 2008. 13.95 *(978-1-59249-790-4(X))* 2007. 6.95 *(978-1-59249-746-1(2))* Soundprints.

Gehl, Laura. And Then Another Sheep Turned Up. Adele, Amy, illus. 2015. (ENG.). 32p. (J). (gr. -1-3). E-Book 23.99 *(978-1-4677-1190-6(X),* Kar-Ben Publishing) Lerner Publishing Group.

Gentry, Beatrice. Piep. Gentry, Beatrice, illus. 2016. (ENG., Illus.). 36p. (J). *(978-1-78222-453-2(X))* Paragon Publishing, Rothersthorpe.

Giles, Lisa. The Adventures of Sunny the Bunny: The Easter Egg Hunt. 2010. 20p. 10.49 *(978-1-4520-1842-3(1))* AuthorHouse.

Gonzalez Jensen, Margarita. Botas Negras. Sanchez, Enrique O., illus. (SPA.). (J). (gr. 2-4). 3.96 net. *(978-0-590-26842-4(2))* Scholastic, Inc.

Graham, Oakley. I'm Just a Little Sheep. Green, Barry, illus. 2014. (ENG.). 12p. (gr. -1). *(978-1-78244-591-3(9))* Top That! Publishing PLC.

Griver, Jeanette A. Curio, a Shetland Sheepdog Meets the Crow: A Story of Friendship For Children of All Ages 2004. (Illus.). 44p. (J). pap. 6.95 *(978-0-929948-04-1(1))* Compsych Systems, Inc., Pubns. Div.

Gummelt, Donna & Melchiorre, Dondino. Cow Puppies. Wall, Randy Hugh, ed. Varela, Juan D., tr. Varela, Juan D., illus. 2006.Tr. of Cachorros Vaqueros. (SPA.). 32p. (J). 14.95 *(978-0-9764798-7-1(7))* Story Store Collection Publishing.

Hanlin, Beverly Austin. Little Lamb: A Christmas Story. 2006. (J). pap. 8.00 *(978-0-8059-7128-6(9))* Dorrance Publishing Co., Inc.

Harper, Stephan J. The Black Sheep Beach, Mary FitzGerald, illus. Lt. ed. 2005. 32p. (J). lib. bdg. 16.95 *(978-0-9741800-1-4(7))* Inspire Press, Inc.

Harrington, Claudia. Book 4: Elmer the Very Sneaky Sheep. Syed, Anoosha, illus. 2016. (Hank the Pet Sitter Ser.). (ENG.). 32p. (J). (gr. -1-3). lib. bdg. 32.79 *(978-1-62402-190-9(5),* 24559, Calico Chapter Bks) Magic Wagon.

Hathorn, Libby & Magerl, Caroline. Over the Moon. 2005. (Illus.). 32p. *(978-0-7344-0480-0(8),* Lothian Children's Bks.) Hachette Australia.

Helakoski, Leslie. Ready or Not, Woolbur Goes to School! Harper, Lee & Harper, Lee, illus. 2018. (ENG.). 32p. (J). (gr. -1-3). 17.99 *(978-0-06-136657-4(9),* HarperCollins) HarperCollins Pubs.

—Woolbur. Harper, Lee & Harper, Lee, illus. 2008. (ENG.). 32p. (J). (gr. -1-3). 17.89 *(978-0-06-084727-2(1),* HarperCollins) HarperCollins Pubs.

—Woolbur. Harper, Lee, illus. 2008. (ENG.). 32p. (J). (gr. -1-3). 17.99 *(978-0-06-084726-5(3),* HarperCollins) HarperCollins Pubs.

—Woolbur. 2008. (J). (gr. -1-2). 29.95 incl. audio *(978-0-8045-6971-2(1))* Spoken Arts, Inc.

Heos, Bridget. Twinkle, Twinkle, Little Lamb. Jennings, Sarah, illus. 2018. 32p. (J). (gr. k-3). 17.99 *(978-1-68152-405-4(8),* 15236) Amicus.

Herget, Gundi & Garlid, Ann. Arnold the Brave. Renger, Nikolai, illus. 2018. (ENG.). 32p. (J). 16.99 *(978-1-4413-2650-8(2),* 9de439e7-7f69-4835-bb80-46c50697dede) Peter Pauper Pr. Inc.

Hobbs, Valerie. Sheep. 2009. (ENG.). 144p. (J). (gr. 3-7). pap. 11.99 *(978-0-312-56116-1(4),* 900058846) Square Fish.

Howard, Martin. Blast to the Past, 6. Janes, Andy, illus. 2017. (Shaun the Sheep: Tales from Mossy Bottom Farm Ser.). (ENG.). 112p. (J). (gr. 1-3). 17.44 *(978-1-5364-1044-0(6))* Candlewick Pr.

Hub, Ulrich & Ragg-Kirkby, Helena. Becoming the Wolf. Mühle, Jörg, illus. 2012. (ENG.). 64p. (J). 12.00 *(978-0-8028-5409-4(5),* Eerdmans Bks For Young Readers) Eerdmans, William B. Publishing Co.

Hughes, Mair Wynn & Jones, Steven. Dwyn Afalau. 2005. (WEL., Illus.). 15p. pap. *(978-0-86243-457-1(2))* Y Lolfa.

Hunt, Susan. Sammy & His Shepherd. Godbey, Corey, illus. 2008. (ENG.). 56p. (J). (gr. 3-7). 18.00 *(978-1-56769-109-2(9))* Ligonier Ministries.

Imai, Ayano. The 108th Sheep. Imai, Ayano, illus. 2007. (ENG., Illus.). 32p. (J). (gr. -1-1). 22.44 *(978-1-58925-063-5(X))* Tiger Tales.

Jåho. What if Sheep Could Fly? JudyBee, tr. from FRE. 2nd ed. 2011. (Illus.). 28p. pap. *(978-1-78092-006-1(7))* MX Publishing, Ltd.

Jamieson, Victoria. Bea Rocks the Flock. 2009. (J). (gr. -1-3). 17.89 *(978-1-59990-357-6(1))* Bloomsbury Publishing USA.

Jeffs, Dixie. A Baby to Love. 2012. 20p. pap. 24.95 *(978-1-4626-6780-2(5))* America Star Bks.

Jones, V. M. & Tulloch, Scott. Echo & Hush. 2008. (Illus.). 32p. pap. *(978-1-86950-690-2(1))* HarperCollins Pubs. Australia.

Kitamura, Satoshi. Cuando los Borregos No Pueden Dormir. Kitamura, Satoshi, illus. 2nd ed. 2003. (Picture Books Collection). (SPA., Illus.). 26p. (J). (gr. k-3). pap. 12.95 *(978-84-372-2182-3(X))* Santillana USA Publishing Co., Inc.

—When Sheep Can't Sleep (Cuando los Borregos no Pueden Dormir) (SPA.). (J). (gr. 1-6). 19.95 *(978-84-372-6605-3(X))* Santillana USA Publishing Co., Inc.

Kleyn, Diana & Beeke, Joel R. How God Used a Drought & an Umbrella. rev. ed. 2006. (Building on the Rock Ser.). (ENG., Illus.). 176p. (J). pap. 8.99 *(978-1-85792-818-1(0),* 08d4fa0a-8d5c-4674-9c86-05c01cfb7936, CF4Kids) Christian Focus Pubns. GBR. Dist: Baker & Taylor Publisher Services (BTPS).

Koch, Miriam. Digby Differs. Garlid, Ann, tr. from GER. Koch, Miriam, illus. 2013. (ENG., Illus.). 40p. (J). 17.99 *(978-1-4413-1306-5(0),* 6b7bbe2b-520e-48e6-af5e-7e92c1e47acb) Peter Pauper Pr. Inc.

Krone, Thelma Smith. Nosey. 2007. (J). 7.95 *(978-1-56167-974-4(7))* American Literary Pr.

Lamont, Priscilla. Nursery Rhyme Crimes: Little Bo Peep. 2012. (Illus.). 24p. (J). pap. *(978-1-84780-354-2(7),* White Lion Publishing) Quarto Publishing Group UK.

The Legend of Teton Tony: King of the Mountain Rams. 2005. (Illus.). 32p. (J). 14.95 *(978-0-9767265-0-0(5))* Fisher Enterprises.

Lenski, Lois. Strawberry Girl 60th Anniversary Edition: A Newbery Award Winner. Lenski, Lois, illus. 60th anniv. ed. 2005. (ENG., Illus.). 208p. (J). (gr. 5-18). pap. 7.99 *(978-0-06-440585-0(0),* HarperCollins) HarperCollins Pubs.

Leslie, Emma. For Merrie England: A Tale of the Weavers of Norfolk. Taylor, R., illus. 2010. 168p. 20.95 *(978-1-934671-38-2(X));* pap. 10.95 *(978-1-934671-39-9(8))* Salem Ridge Press LLC.

Lester, Helen. The Sheep in Wolf's Clothing. Munsinger, Lynn, illus. 2014. (Laugh-Along Lessons Ser.). (ENG.). 32p. (J). (gr. -1-3). 8.99 *(978-0-544-23300-3(X),* 1563484, Clarion Bks.) HarperCollins Pubs.

Leung, Hilary. Will Sheep Sleep? 2018. (ENG., Illus.). 38p. (J). (gr. -1 — 1). bds. 7.99 *(978-1-338-21562-5(0),* Cartwheel Bks.) Scholastic, Inc.

Lewis, Kim. Emma's Lamb. 2004. (J). (gr. k-3). spiral bd. *(978-0-616-07563-0(4))* Canadian National Institute for the Blind/Institut National Canadien pour les Aveugles.

The Littlest Lamb: Lap Book. (Pebble Soup Explorations Ser.). 16p. (gr. -1-18). 21.00 *(978-0-7578-1658-1(4))* Rigby Education.

Litton, Jonathan. Planet Pop-Up: Sheep Rules the Roost! Anderson, Nicola, illus. 2015. (Planet Pop-Up Ser.). (ENG.). 12p. (J). (gr. -1). 12.95 *(978-1-62686-354-5(7),* Silver Dolphin Bks.) Readerlink Distribution Services, LLC.

Lodding, Linda Ravin. Little Red Riding Sheep. Atkinson, Cale, illus. 2017. (ENG.). 40p. (J). (gr. -1-3). 17.99 *(978-1-4814-5748-4(9))* Simon & Schuster Children's Publishing.

Loewen, Nancy. The Boy Who Cried Wolf, Narrated by the Sheepish but Truthful Wolf. Moreno, Juan M., illus. 2018. (Other Side of the Fable Ser.). (ENG.). 24p. (J). (gr. -1-3). lib. bdg. 27.99 *(978-1-5158-2869-3(7),* 138407, Picture Window Bks.) Capstone.

Lucy Lamb. 2006. (J). per. 3.99 *(978-1-934004-16-6(2))* Byeway Bks.

Lunn, Janet. Amos's Sweater, 1 vol. Lafave, Kim, illus. 2nd ed. 2007. (ENG.). 32p. (J). (gr. -1-2). pap. 9.99 *(978-0-88899-845-3(7))* Groundwood Bks. CAN. Dist: Publishers Group West (PGW).

Lyon, George Ella. Weaving the Rainbow. Anderson, Stephanie, illus. 2004. (ENG.). 40p. (J). (gr. -1-2). 19.99 *(978-0-689-85169-8(3),* Atheneum/Richard Jackson Bks.) Simon & Schuster Children's Publishing.

Lyon, Tammie Speer, illus. Mary Had a Little Lamb. 2006. 8p. (J). bds. 10.95 *(978-1-57791-210-1(1))* Brighter Minds Children's Publishing.

Mackall, Dandi Daley. Little Shepherd. 2004. 32p. (J). 6.99 *(978-0-7586-0324-1(X))* Concordia Publishing Hse.

—The Lost Lamb & the Good Shepherd. Manuzak, Lisa, illus. 2016. (Flipside Stories Ser.). (ENG.). 48p. (J). 14.99 *(978-1-4964-1121-1(8),* 4612796) Tyndale Hse. Pubs.

Maguire, Thomas Aquinas. Three Little Dreams, 3 vols. 2010. (ENG., Illus.). 36p. (J). (gr. -1). 16.95 *(978-1-894965-79-8(5))* Simply Read Bks. CAN. Dist: Ingram Publisher Services.

Maier, Inger. When Fuzzy Was Afraid of Big & Loud Things. Candon, Jennifer, illus. 2005. (Fuzzy the Little Sheep Ser.). 32p. (J). (gr. -1-3). 14.95 *(978-1-59147-322-0(5),* Magination Pr.) American Psychological Assn.

—When Fuzzy Was Afraid of Losing His Mother. Candon, Jennifer, illus. 2004. 32p. (J). 14.95 *(978-1-59147-168-4(0),* Magination Pr.) American Psychological Assn.

—When Lizzy Was Afraid of Trying New Things. Candon, Jennifer, illus. 2004. (ENG.). 32p. (J). 14.95 *(978-1-59147-170-7(2),* Magination Pr.) American Psychological Assn.

Maier, Inger M. When Fuzzy Was Afraid: Of Losing His Mother. Candon, Jennifer, illus. 2004. 32p. (J). pap. 9.95 *(978-1-59147-169-1(9),* Magination Pr.) American Psychological Assn.

—When Fuzzy Was Afraid of Big & Loud Things. Candon, Jennifer, illus. 2005. 32p. (J). (gr. -1-3). per. 9.95 *(978-1-59147-323-7(3),* Magination Pr.) American Psychological Assn.

—When Lizzie Was Afraid: Of Trying New Things. Candon, Jennifer, illus. 2004. 32p. (J). pap. 9.95 *(978-1-59147-171-4(0),* Magination Pr.) American Psychological Assn.

Malandrinos, Cheryl C. Little Shepherd. Ruble, Eugene, illus. 2010. 16p. pap. 9.95 *(978-1-61633-085-9(6))* Guardian Angel Publishing, Inc.

Marcoux, Tom. Crystal Pegasus. 2012. 92p. pap. 18.24 *(978-0-9800511-9-3(3))* Marcoux, Tom Media, LLC.

Mary, Ms. Little Lambie No-No's Great Escape. 2008. 48p. per. 9.95 *(978-1-4327-1917-3(3))* Outskirts Pr., Inc.

Matthews-Dodd, Melissa. Chase Coming Home. 2003. (J). pap. 9.95 *(978-0-7414-1522-6(4))* Infinity Publishing.

McAllister, Margaret. Emily & the Lamb. Vince, Dawn, illus. 2005. (ENG.). 24p. (J). lib. bdg. 23.65 *(978-1-59646-756-9(8))* Dingles & Co.

Melling, David. Hugless Douglas & the Big Sleepover. 2013. (ENG., Illus.). 32p. (J). *(978-1-58925-116-8(4))* Tiger Tales.

Merino, Gemma. The Sheep Who Hatched an Egg. Merino, Gemma, illus. 2017. (ENG., Illus.). 32p. (J). (gr. -1-3). 16.99 *(978-0-8075-7338-9(8),* 807573388) Whitman, Albert & Co.

Metlen, Ryan W. & Metlen, Ryan. Ewe. 2009. (J). *(978-1-58768-054-0(8),* HiddenSpring) Paulist Pr.

Meyer, Lisa O. The Sheep & the Chicken. Winward, Makenzie, illus. 2011. 16p. pap. 24.95 *(978-1-4626-0478-4(1))* America Star Bks.

Miura, Taro. Crazy Days. 2009. (ENG., Illus.). 24p. (J). (gr. -1-3). 14.50 *(978-1-85437-850-7(3))* Tate Publishing, Ltd. GBR. Dist: Abrams, Inc.

More Than a Meal. (Early Intervention Levels Ser.). 28.56 *(978-0-7362-1049-2(0))* CENGAGE Learning.

Moriarty, Kathleen M. Wil Waal: A Somali Folktale. Adam, Jamal, tr. Amir, Amin Abd al-Fattah Mahmud, illus. 2007. (SOM & ENG.). 32p. (J). (gr. -1-3). 15.95 *(978-1-931016-16-2(X));* pap. 7.95 *(978-1-931016-17-9(8))* Minnesota Humanities Ctr.

Morris, Richard T. Sheep 101. Pham, LeUyen, illus. 2018. (ENG.). 48p. (J). (gr. -1-3). 17.99 *(978-0-316-21359-2(4))* Little, Brown Bks. for Young Readers.

Mullarkey, Lisa. Sweet Pea the Sheep. Franco, Paula, illus. 2019. (Farmyard Friends Ser.). (ENG.). 32p. (J). (gr. -1-3). lib. bdg. 32.79 *(978-1-5321-3489-0(4),* 31897, Calico Chapter Bks) Magic Wagon.

Mustaine Hettinger, Cynthia. Travis, the Shetland Sheep. Ramsey, Jayne, illus. 2004. (Electra's Acres Ser.: Bk. 5). 32p. (J). per. 14.95 *(978-0-9746330-6-0(2))* Anton Berkshire Publishing.

Nation, Kay. Jamie Learns to Love. 2006. pap. 10.00 *(978-1-4257-0534-3(0))* Xlibris Corp.

Noble, Val. Elsie the Sheep & the Kings of the Castle. 2009. (Illus.). 52p. pap. 20.49 *(978-1-4389-5083-9(7))* AuthorHouse.

North, Laura. The Boy Who Cried Sheep! 2016. (ENG., Illus.). 32p. (J). *(978-0-7787-2471-1(9))* Crabtree Publishing Co.

Northfield, Gary. Derek the Sheep. Northfield, Gary, illus. 2009. (Illus.). 64p. (J). (gr. k-2). 16.95 *(978-0-7475-9424-6(4))* Bloomsbury Publishing Plc GBR. Dist: Independent Pubs. Group.

Ogorek, Keith. Eli the Stable Boy. 2009. (ENG.). 28p. pap. 13.99 *(978-1-4490-4116-8(7))* AuthorHouse.

Paglia, Rhonda. The Little Lambs & the Very Special Mission. Paglia, Rhonda & Galaska, Taylor, illus. 2013. 44p. pap. 12.95 *(978-0-9899141-1-6(9))* Angels Landing.

Palatini, Margie. Bad Boys. Cole, Henry, illus. 40p. (J). (gr. -1-2). 2003. lib. bdg. 16.89 *(978-0-06-000103-2(8))* 2003. (ENG.). 15.99 *(978-0-06-000102-5(X),* Tegen, Katherine Bks) 2006. (ENG.). reprint ed. 8.99 *(978-0-06-000104-9(6),* Tegen, Katherine Bks) HarperCollins Pubs.

Patchett, Ann. Lambslide. Glasser, Robin Preiss, illus. 2019. (ENG.). 32p. (J). (gr. -1-3). 18.99 *(978-0-06-288338-4(0),* HarperCollins) HarperCollins Pubs.

Paul, Dwain. The Fox the Hare the Wolf & the Sheep. 2011. 28p. 16.10 *(978-1-4269-5573-0(1))* Trafford Publishing.

Phelps, Karen. The Grass Is Always Greener & Let Sleeping Dogs Lie: Two Original Fables. 2006. (J). pap. *(978-1-4108-7155-8(X))* Benchmark Education Co.

Pileggi, Joe. No Greater Love. McDonald, Susan, illus. 2009. (ENG.). 24p. pap. 10.49 *(978-1-4389-9377-5(3))* AuthorHouse.

Pinson, Joseph. Joey & Big Wooley's Adventures. 2010. 88p. pap. 30.49 *(978-1-4520-4718-8(9))* AuthorHouse.

Piper, Sophie. The Angel & the Lamb: A Story for Christmas, 1 vol. Stephenson, Kristina, illus. 2009. 32p. (J). 12.99 *(978-0-8254-7887-1(1),* Lion Children's) Lion Hudson PLC GBR. Dist: Kregel Pubns.

popular, Cancionero. Juguemos en el bosque. 2004. (SPA., Illus.). 28p. (J). (gr. k-18). pap. 6.50 *(978-980-257-282-3(9))* Ekare, Ediciones VEN. Dist: Iaconi, Mariuccia Bk. Imports.

Rae, Philippa. Count the Sheep to Sleep. Röhr, Stéphanie, illus. 2012. (ENG.). 28p. (J). (gr. -1-k). 12.95 *(978-1-61608-660-2(2),* 608660, Sky Pony Pr.) Skyhorse Publishing Co., Inc.

Raum, Elizabeth. The Christmas Star. Johnson, Meredith, illus. 2005. (ENG.). 28p. (J). (gr. -1-k). bds. 7.95 *(978-0-8249-6620-1(1),* Ideals Pubns.) Worthy Publishing.

S

Redmon, Jaylyle. Gracie the Lop-Eared Burro. 2008. 17p. pap. 24.95 *(978-1-60672-626-6(9))* America Star Bks.

Repicci, Albert. The Littlest Angel: A Christmas Story. 2012. 36p. pap. 21.99 *(978-1-4691-9547-6(X))* Xlibris Corp.

Risco, Elle D. Dora Had a Little Lamb. Savitsky, Steve, illus. 2007. (Dora the Explorer Ser.). (J). (gr. -1-2). 11.65 *(978-0-7569-8294-2(4))* Perfection Learning Corp.

Roche, Jackie, illus. The Derby Ram. 2010. (First Steps in Music Ser.). (ENG.). 32p. (J). (gr. -1-k). 17.95 *(978-1-57999-783-0(X))* G I A Pubns., Inc.

Rock, Michelle L. Nighttime Adventures Counting Sheep. Longmore, Nickolai, illus. 2006. 32p. (J). 3.99 net. *(978-0-9771700-1-2(2))* Mystic Arts, LLC.

Rothstein, Gloria L. Sheep Asleep. Date not set. 224p. (J). (gr. -1-1). pap. 4.99 *(978-0-06-443717-2(5))* HarperCollins Pubs.

Rundstrom, Teressa. Cherry the Sheep Finds Her Sheep Sound. Miller, Bryan & Marshall, H. Keene, illus. 2004. 25p. (J). per. *(978-1-932062-40-3(8))* Idea Magic Bks.

Russell, Christopher & Russell, Christine. The Quest of the Warrior Sheep. 2011. (Warrior Sheep Ser.). (ENG.). 224p. (gr. 4-6). 18.69 *(978-1-4022-5511-3(X))* Sourcebooks, Inc.

Rwakasisi, Rose. How Goats Lost Their Beautiful Tails. 2004. (Illus.). 19p. pap. *(978-9970-02-436-0(1))* Fountain Pubs. Ltd. UGA. Dist: Michigan State Univ. Pr.

Saillard, Remi, illus. Funny Machines for George the Sheep: A Children's Book Inspired by Leonardo Da Vinci. 2014. (Children's Books Inspired by Famous Artworks Ser.). (ENG.). 32p. (J). (gr. -1-3). 14.95 *(978-3-7913-7166-5(5))* Prestel Verlag GmbH & Co KG. DEU. Dist: Penguin Random Hse. LLC.

Samuel, Janet, illus. One Sneaky Sheep: A Touch-and-Feel Fluffy Tale. 2007. (ENG.). 20p. (gr. -1). 14.95 *(978-1-58117-560-8(4),* Intervisual/Piggy Toes) Bendon, Inc.

—One Sneaky Sheep: The Sheep Who Didn't Want to Get Sheared. 2009. (ENG.). 20p. (J). 9.95 *(978-1-58117-841-8(7),* Intervisual/Piggy Toes) Bendon, Inc.

Sanders, Scott Russell. Warm as Wool. Cogancherry, Helen, illus. 2007. (J). lib. bdg. 18.00 *(978-1-59098-421-5(8))* Wooster Bk. Co., The.

Santillo, LuAnn. Shag. Santillo, LuAnn, ed. 2003. (Half-Pint Readers Ser.). (Illus.). 7p. (J). (gr. -1-1). pap. 1.00 *(978-1-59256-068-4(7))* Half-Pint Kids, Inc.

Sargent, Dave & Sargent, David M., Jr. Petie Pelican: Be Proud of Yourself, 19 vols., Vol. 14. Lenoir, Jane, illus. 2003. (Feather Tales Ser.: 14). 42p. (J). pap. 10.95 *(978-1-56763-746-5(9))* Ozark Publishing.

Savitsky, Steven, illus. Dora Had a Little Lamb. 2007. (Dora the Explorer Ser.: 23). (ENG.). 24p. (J). (gr. -1-2). pap. 3.99 *(978-1-4169-3368-7(9),* Simon Spotlight/Nickelodeon) Simon Spotlight/Nickelodeon.

Schwinn, Ruth E. Henry & Dale. Flores, Justin, illus. 2010. (ENG.). 24p. (J). 14.95 *(978-0-578-04719-5(5),* 9780578047195) PRF Pubs.

Scotton, Rob. Russell & the Lost Treasure. Scotton, Rob, illus. 2006. (ENG., Illus.). 32p. (J). (gr. -1-2). 19.99 *(978-0-06-059851-8(4),* HarperCollins) HarperCollins Pubs.

—Russell the Sheep. Scotton, Rob, illus. (ENG., Illus.). 32p. (J). (gr. -1-3). 2015. pap. 6.99 *(978-0-06-239243-5(3),* HarperFestival) 2011. pap. 6.99 *(978-0-06-059850-1(6))* 2005. 17.99 *(978-0-06-059848-8(4),* HarperCollins) HarperCollins Pubs.

—Russell the Sheep Board Book. Scotton, Rob, illus. 2009. (ENG., Illus.). 32p. (J). (gr. -1-3). bds. 7.99 *(978-0-06-170996-8(4),* HarperFestival) HarperCollins Pubs.

—Russell's Christmas Magic. Scotton, Rob, illus. 2007. (Illus.). 32p. (J). (gr. -1-2). lib. bdg. 17.89 *(978-0-06-059855-6(7))* HarperCollins Pubs.

Scraper, Katherine. The Boy Who Cried Wolf: An Aesop's Fable. 2006. (J). pap. *(978-1-4108-6166-5(X))* Benchmark Education Co.

Shanks, Cindy. Emilia Camina la Vereda de Borregos. 2009. 48p. pap. 19.95 *(978-1-4490-2388-1(6))* AuthorHouse.

—Emily Walks the Sheep Trail. 2009. (ENG.). 48p. pap. 19.95 *(978-1-4490-2208-2(1))* AuthorHouse.

Shapely Sleepy Sheep. 2005. (J). bds. 7.95 *(978-0-9749305-6-5(3))* Castle Pacific Publishing.

Shaw, Elizabeth. The Little Black Sheep. Shaw, Elizabeth, illus. 2007. (Pandas Ser.: 06). (ENG., Illus.). 64p. (J). pap. 9.95 *(978-0-86278-463-8(8))* O'Brien Pr., Ltd., The IRL. Dist: Dufour Editions, Inc.

—An T-Uan Beag Dubh. MacPhaidan, Daire, tr. 2004. (Sraith Sos Ser.: 10). (GLE., Illus.). 64p. (J). pap. 11.00 *(978-0-86278-867-4(6))* O'Brien Pr., Ltd., The IRL. Dist: Casemate Pubs. & Bk. Distributors, LLC.

Shaw, Nancy. Me First. Apple, Margot, illus. 2015. 32p. pap. 7.00 *(978-1-61003-505-7(4))* Center for the Collaborative Classroom.

Shaw, Nancy E. Sheep Blast Off! Apple, Margot, illus. 2011. (Sheep in a Jeep Ser.). (ENG.). 32p. (J). (gr. -1-3). pap. 6.99 *(978-0-547-52025-4(5),* 1445464, Clarion Bks.) HarperCollins Pubs.

—Sheep Go to Sleep. Apple, Margot, illus. (Sheep in a Jeep Ser.). (ENG.). 32p. (J). (gr. -1-3). 2019. pap. 7.99 *(978-1-328-60368-5(7),* 1732077) 2015. 16.99 *(978-0-544-30989-0(8),* 1581244) HarperCollins Pubs. (Clarion Bks.).

—Sheep Go to Sleep Board Book. Apple, Margot, illus. 2016. (Sheep in a Jeep Ser.). (ENG.). 30p. (J). (gr. -1-3). bds. 7.99 *(978-0-544-64053-5(5),* 1620828, Clarion Bks.) HarperCollins Pubs.

—Sheep Go to Sleep Lap Board Book. Apple, Margot, illus. 2018. (Sheep in a Jeep Ser.). (ENG.). 30p. (J). (— 1). bds. 12.99 *(978-1-328-91049-3(0),* 1701058, Clarion Bks.) HarperCollins Pubs.

—Sheep in a Jeep. Apple, Margot, illus. 2013. (Sheep in a Jeep Ser.). (ENG.). 32p. (J). (gr. -1-3). pap. 26.99 *(978-0-547-99383-6(8),* 1525236, Clarion Bks.) HarperCollins Pubs.

—Sheep in a Jeep Book & Cd, 1 vol. Apple, Margot, illus. 2006. (Sheep in a Jeep Ser.). (ENG.). 32p. (J). (gr. -1-3). audio compact disk 10.99 *(978-0-618-69522-5(2),* 441919, Clarion Bks.) HarperCollins Pubs.

—Sheep Out to Eat Board Book. Apple, Margot, illus. 2005. (Sheep in a Jeep Ser.). (ENG.). 28p. (J). (gr. k — 1). bds. 6.99 *(978-0-618-58339-3(4),* 587642, Clarion Bks.) HarperCollins Pubs.

Simon, Mary Manz. Lamb Is Joyful. Harris, Phyllis & Clearwater, Linda, illus. 2006. (First Virtuestm for Toddlers Ser.). 20p. (J). 5.99 *(978-0-7847-1575-8(0),* 04069) Standard Publishing.

Smallman, Steve. The Lamb Who Came for Dinner. Dreidemy, Joëlle, illus. 2007. 32p. (J). (gr. -1-2). 15.95 *(978-1-58925-067-3(2))* Tiger Tales.

Smith, Brooke. Mimi & Maty to the Rescue! Book 2: Sadie the Sheep Disappears Without a Peep! Arnold, Alli, illus. 2014. (ENG.). 96p. (J). (gr. 1-5). 14.95 *(978-1-62636-344-1(7),* Sky Pony Pr.) Skyhorse Publishing Co., Inc.

Smith, Carrie. Little Bo Peep. Abbott, Jason, illus. 2010. (Rising Readers Ser.). (J). 3.49 *(978-1-60719-700-3(6))* Newmark Learning LLC.

Smith, Jodene Lynn & Thompson, Chad. Baa, Baa, Black Sheep. 2010. (Early Literacy Ser.). (ENG., Illus.). 16p. (gr. k-1). 19.99 *(978-1-4333-1484-1(3));* 6.99 *(978-1-4333-1483-4(5))* Teacher Created Materials, Inc.

—Beh, Beh, Borreguito Negro. rev. ed. 2010. (Early Literacy Ser.). (SPA., Illus.). 16p. (gr. k-1). 19.99 *(978-1-4333-2095-8(9));* 6.99 *(978-1-4333-2094-1(0))* Teacher Created Materials, Inc.

Snow, Ravay L. Hildegarde & the Great Green Shirt Factory. Snow, Ravay L., illus. 2005. (Hildegarde Ser.). (Illus.). 32p. (J). 16.95 *(978-1-932362-10-7(X))* Snowbound Pr., Inc.

Sommerset, Mark. Baa Baa Smart Sheep. Sommerset, Rowan, illus. 2016. (ENG.). 32p. (J). (gr. k-3). 14.00 *(978-0-7636-8066-4(4))* Candlewick Pr.

—I Love Lemonade. Sommerset, Rowan, illus. 2016. (ENG.). 32p. (J). (gr. k-3). 14.00 *(978-0-7636-8067-1(2))* Candlewick Pr.

Starfall Education. Pete's Sheep. Starfall Education, ed. 2004. (ENG., Illus.). 8p. (J). pap. *(978-1-59577-007-3(0))* Starfall Education.

Stewart, Paul. Brian the Brave. Porter, Jane, illus. 2019. (ENG.). 32p. (J). (gr. -1-1). 17.00 *(978-1-947888-18-0(8),* Flyaway Bks.) Westminster John Knox Pr.

Stiver, Megan, illus. The Great Bellybutton Cover-Up. 2011. 32p. *(978-0-9810634-7-8(0))* Susan Ross (self publishing).

—Say Please to the Honeybees. 2010. 33p. *(978-0-9810634-3-0(8))* Susan Ross (self publishing).

Stohner, Anu. Brave Charlotte. Wilson, Henrike, illus. 2014. 32p. pap. 8.00 *(978-1-61003-341-1(8))* Center for the Collaborative Classroom.

Suzie Sheep & her Friends. 2004. (Play Pals Ser.). (Illus.). 12p. (J). bds. *(978-1-84229-649-3(3))* Top That! Publishing PLC.

Taplin, Sam. Who's Fallen Asleep? 2018. (Who's That... Baby Board Bks.). (ENG.). 10p. (J). 6.99 *(978-0-7945-4271-9(9),* Usborne) EDC Publishing.

Teddy Bear-Sheep. 2003. (J). per. *(978-1-57657-163-7(7))* Paradise Pr., Inc.

Terborg-Hershman, Donna M. Why Sheep Don't Shrink. 2008. 28p. pap. 12.49 *(978-1-4389-3720-5(2))* AuthorHouse.

Theobald, Joseph. Marvin Gets Mad! 2013. pap. *(978-0-545-55294-3(X))* Scholastic, Inc.

—Marvin Wanted More! 2007. (Bloomsbury Paperbacks Ser.). (Illus.). 32p. (J). (gr. -1-k). 13.99 *(978-0-7475-8873-3(2))* Bloomsbury Publishing Plc GBR. Dist: Independent Pubs. Group.

—Marvin Wanted More! Theobald, Joseph, illus. (Illus.). 32p. (J). (gr. -1-k). 2005. pap. 12.99 *(978-0-7475-6481-2(7))* 2004. 16.99 *(978-0-7475-5631-2(8))* Bloomsbury Publishing Plc GBR. Dist: Independent Pubs. Group.

Thomas, Jan. My Friends Make Me Happy! 2018. (Giggle Gang Ser.). (ENG., Illus.). 48p. (J). (gr. -1-3). 9.99 *(978-0-544-96655-0(4),* 1662287, Clarion Bks.) HarperCollins Pubs.

Thompson, Kate. I'm Just a Little Sheep. Green, Barry, illus. 2017. (Googley-Eye Bks.). (ENG.). 12p. (J). (gr. -1-k). bds. 8.99 *(978-1-78445-869-0(4))* Top That! Publishing PLC GBR. Dist: Independent Pubs. Group.

Thompson, Lauren. Little Lamb. Butler, John, illus. 2014. (J). *(978-1-4351-5352-3(9),* Simon & Schuster Bks. For Young Readers) Simon & Schuster Bks. For Young Readers.

—Wee Little Lamb. Butler, John, illus. 2009. (Wee Little Ser.). (ENG.). 32p. (J). (gr. -1-3). 19.99 *(978-1-4169-3469-1(3),* Simon & Schuster Bks. For Young Readers) Simon & Schuster Bks. For Young Readers.

Tnt. God's Zoo. 2005. (On the Way Ser.). (ENG., Illus.). 96p. (J). per. 17.99 *(978-1-84550-069-6(5),* 9f2c21ba-f254-4919-a2e2-f25087a3997b) Christian Focus Pubns. GBR. Dist: Baker & Taylor Publisher Services (BTPS).

Twohy, Mike. Wake up, Rupert! Twohy, Mike, illus. 2014. (ENG., Illus.). 32p. (J). (gr. -1-3). 16.99 *(978-1-4424-5998-4(0),* Simon & Schuster/Paula Wiseman Bks.) Simon & Schuster/Paula Wiseman Bks.

van Haeringen, Annemarie. How to Knit a Monster. van Haeringen, Annemarie, illus. 2018. (ENG., Illus.). 32p. (J). (gr. -1-3). 17.99 *(978-1-328-94210-7(X),* 1691968, Clarion Bks.) HarperCollins Pubs.

Van Slyke, Rebecca. Lana Lynn Howls at the Moon, 1 vol. Sandu, Anca, illus. 2019. 32p. (J). (gr. -1-3). 16.95 *(978-1-68263-050-1(1))* Peachtree Publishing Co. Inc.

Vasquez, Paula. Lily Wool, 1 vol. 2017. (ENG., Illus.). 40p. (J). (gr. k-3). 14.99 *(978-1-4236-4728-7(9))* Gibbs Smith, Publisher.

Voake, Steve. Daisy Dawson & the Big Freeze. Meserve, Jessica, illus. 2011. (Daisy Dawson Ser.). (ENG.). 96p. (J). (gr. 1-4). pap. 5.99 *(978-0-7636-5627-0(5))* Candlewick Pr.

Warden, Evelyn. Oh, Please, Cricket. 2006. 144p. pap. 24.95 *(978-1-4241-1860-1(3))* America Star Bks.

Watts, Frances. Extraordinary Ernie & Marvelous Maud. Watson, Judy, illus. 2010. (ENG.). 80p. (J). (gr. 2-5). pap. 6.00 *(978-0-8028-5363-9(3),* Eerdmans Bks For Young Readers) Eerdmans, William B. Publishing Co.

—Heroes of the Year. Watson, Judy, illus. 2012. (ENG.). 80p. (J). pap. 6.00 *(978-0-8028-5412-4(5),* Eerdmans Bks For Young Readers) Eerdmans, William B. Publishing Co.

—The Middle Sheep. Watson, Judy, illus. 2010. (ENG.). 80p. (J). (gr. 2-5). pap. 6.00 *(978-0-8028-5368-4(4))* Eerdmans, William B. Publishing Co.

Weeks, Sarah. Baa-Choo! Manning, Jane, illus. 2006. (I Can Read Level 1 Ser.). (ENG.). 32p. (J). (gr. k-3). pap. 4.99 *(978-0-06-443740-0(X),* HarperCollins) HarperCollins Pubs.

—Counting Ovejas. Diaz, David, illus. 2006. (ENG.). 40p. (J). (gr. -1-2). 19.99 *(978-0-689-86750-7(6),* Atheneum Bks. for Young Readers) Simon & Schuster Children's Publishing.

Wegwerth, A. L. Little Bo Peep & Her Bad, Bad Sheep: A Mother Goose Hullabaloo. Flowers, Luke, illus. 2016. (Fiction Picture Bks.). (ENG.). 40p. (J). (gr. -1-2). lib. bdg. 22.65 *(978-1-4795-6483-5(4),* 128336, Picture Window Bks.) Capstone.

Will Mcallister. Sam Rivers & the Night Rustlers. 2009. 88p. pap. 9.95 *(978-0-595-46287-2(1))* iUniverse, Inc.

Williams, Kristen. Sheepy Sue & the Bedtime Blues. 2012. 28p. pap. 12.95 *(978-1-105-48819-1(5))* Lulu.com GBR. Dist: Lulu Pr., Inc.

Wolfe, Jane. Sleepy Sheep. Benham, Tors, illus. 2013. 8p. (J). (gr. -1-k). bds. 6.99 *(978-1-84322-778-6(9),* Armadillo) Anness Publishing GBR. Dist: National Bk. Network.

Wonderley, Stanley. My Lamb. 2011. 22.95 *(978-0-7414-6357-9(1))* Infinity Publishing.

SHELLFISH

see Mollusks

SHELLS

see also Mollusks

Berkes, Marianne Collins. Seashells by the Seashore. Noreika, Robert, illus. 2004. (Sharing Nature with Children Book Ser.). 32p. (J). (gr. -1-5). 16.95 *(978-1-58469-035-1(6))* Take Heart Pubns.

Boothroyd, Jennifer. Shells. 2011. (First Step Nonfiction — Body Coverings Ser.). (gr. k-2). (ENG., Illus.). 24p. (J). pap. 6.99 *(978-0-7613-7830-3(8),* cd062e6f-906d-457c-8a42-d66b6571ce41); pap. 33.92 *(978-0-7613-8610-0(6));* (ENG., Illus.). 24p. lib. bdg. 23.93 *(978-0-7613-5788-9(2))* Lerner Publishing Group.

Bredeson, Carmen & Cousins, Lindsey. Can You Find These Seashells?, 1 vol. 2012. (All about Nature Ser.). (ENG.). 24p. (gr. -1-1). 25.27 *(978-0-7660-3978-0(1),* 414cbb75-3776-4b6d-b842-b5a2cc02e2ba); (Illus.). pap. 10.35 *(978-1-4644-0068-1(7),* f5ed2e6f-ea53-48af-9308-db185c58be8e) Enslow Publishing, LLC. (Enslow Publishing).

Cleave, Andrew. Seashells. 2019. (Creatures of the Ocean Ser.). (Illus.). 80p. (J). (gr. 12). lib. bdg. 34.60 *(978-1-4222-4308-4(7))* Mason Crest.

Fiedler, Heidi. Coral: A Close-Up Photographic Look Inside Your World. 2017. (Up Close Ser.). (ENG., Illus.). 32p. (J). (gr. k-6). lib. bdg. 27.99 *(978-1-942875-35-2(5),* 72176bbf-f721-4c01-b574-ce234718829c, Walter Foster Jr) Quarto Publishing Group USA.

Green, Jen. Projects with the Seaside, 1 vol. 2014. (Make & Learn Ser.). (ENG., Illus.). 32p. (J). (gr. 4-4). lib. bdg. 29.27 *(978-1-4777-7173-0(5),* 581753bf-7736-4cd6-8e0d-3143aebee92e, PowerKids Pr.) Rosen Publishing Group, Inc., The.

Hansen, Judith. Seashells in My Pocket: AMC's Family Guide to Exploring the Coast from Maine to Florida. Sabaka, Donna, illus. 3rd ed. 2008. (ENG.). 160p. (gr. 3-7). per. 14.95 *(978-1-929173-61-7(X))* Appalachian Mountain Club Bks.

Hopkins, Therese. Shells. 2009. (Home Sweet Home Ser.). 24p. (gr. 1-1). 42.50 *(978-1-61513-405-2(0),* PowerKids Pr.); (ENG.). (J). pap. 9.25 *(978-1-4358-3070-7(9),* d48a888e-e899-4e59-a000-ae6dfeb58a45, PowerKids Pr.); (ENG.). (J). lib. bdg. 26.27 *(978-1-4358-2696-0(5),* 0959ecd2-3b2f-4bd3-9c65-662b936778fc) Rosen Publishing Group, Inc., The.

Mazurkiewicz, Jessica. Seashell Patterns Coloring Book. 2011. (Dover Sea Life Coloring Bks.). (ENG.). 32p. (J). (gr. 3-5). pap. 3.99 *(978-0-486-47559-2(X),* 47559X) Dover Pubns., Inc.

Miller, Derek. Shells, Scales, & Skin, 1 vol. 2018. (Animal Structures Ser.). (ENG.). 24p. (gr. 1-1). 25.93 *(978-1-5026-4251-6(4),* fe62fd7d-93f9-4029-bd0e-aa8b56ea43b0) Cavendish Square Publishing LLC.

Moore, David. National Geographic Science 1-2 (Physical Science: Solids, Liquids, & Gases): Explore on Your Own: Shell Shapes. 2009. (Illus.). 12p. (C). pap. 8.95 *(978-0-7362-5603-2(2))* National Geographic School Publishing, Inc.

Morgan, Emily. Next Time You See a Seashell. 2012. (Next Time You See Ser.). (ENG., Illus.). 32p. (J). (gr. -1-k). pap. 13.99 *(978-1-936959-15-0(1),* P218554) National Science Teachers Assn.

Pether, Lesley. Shells. 2008. (Discovering & Exploring Science Ser.). (Illus.). 16p. (J). (gr. -1-3). lib. bdg. 12.95 *(978-0-7569-8409-0(2))* Perfection Learning Corp.

Richardson, Adele D. Seashells. (Illus.). 32p. pap. 8.95 *(978-0-89812-320-3(8))* Creative Co., The.

Sea Shells of the United States & Canada. 2004. (World Book's Science & Nature Guides Ser.). (Illus.). 80p. (J). *(978-0-7166-4218-3(2))* World Bk., Inc.

Skeie, Shari. Sea Shells. 2008. (Oceans Alive Ser.). (ENG., Illus.). 24p. (J). (gr. k-3). lib. bdg. 26.95 *(978-1-60014-208-6(7))* Bellwether Media.

Stewart, Melissa. Seashells: More Than a Home. Brannen, Sarah S., illus. 2019. 32p. (J). (gr. 1-4). lib. bdg. 16.99 *(978-1-58089-810-2(6))* Charlesbridge Publishing, Inc.

Weber, Valerie J. Por Qué Algunos Animales Tienen Caparazón (Why Animals Live in Shells), 1 vol. 2008. (Donde Viven Los Animales (Where Animals Live) Ser.). (SPA., Illus.). 24p. (gr. 2-4). lib. bdg. 24.67 *(978-0-8368-8811-9(1),* f2707d25-aeb8-4748-8b4b-511074c7a202, Weekly Reader Leveled Readers) Stevens, Gareth Publishing LLLP.

—Why Animals Live in Shells, 1 vol. 2008. (Where Animals Live Ser.). (ENG., Illus.). 24p. (gr. 2-4). lib. bdg. 24.67 *(978-0-8368-8797-6(2),* 413d799c-3df9-463e-8590-3e1f68bf0b83, Weekly Reader Leveled Readers) Stevens, Gareth Publishing LLLP.

Weber, Valerie J. & Weber, Valerie J. Why Animals Live in Shells, 1 vol. 2008. (Where Animals Live Ser.). (ENG.). 24p. (gr. 2-4). pap. 9.15 *(978-0-8368-8804-1(9),* c1ce335f-ce71-4f54-9414-369d2b7a5f86, Weekly Reader Leveled Readers) Stevens, Gareth Publishing LLLP.

Yin, Robert, illus. & photos by. Seashells. Yin, Robert, photos by. 2004. (ENG.). 24p. (J). (gr. 1-2). pap. 6.50 *(978-0-7685-0355-5(8),* Dominie Elementary) Savvas Learning Co.

Zoehfeld, Kathleen Weidner. What Lives in a Shell? 2015. (Let's Read & Find Out Science Stage 1 Ser.). (J). lib. bdg. 17.20 *(978-0-606-37740-9(9))* Turtleback.

SHEPARD, ALAN B. (ALAN BARTLETT), 1923-1998

Benge, Janet & Benge, Geoff. Christian Heroes Then & Now - Alan Shepard: Higher & Faster. 2007. (Heroes of History Ser.). 229p. (YA). (gr. 3-7). per. 11.99 *(978-1-932096-41-5(8))* Emerald Bks.

Orr, Tamra. Alan Shepard: The First American in Space. 2009. (Library of Astronaut Biographies Ser.). 112p. (gr. 5-8). 63.90 *(978-1-60853-518-7(5),* Rosen Reference) Rosen Publishing Group, Inc., The.

SHEPHERDS

Pastores en el Campo (Shepherd's Fields) (SPA.). (J). *(978-0-7899-0877-3(8),* 496236) Editorial Unilit.

Peregrinos & Extranjeros. El Buen Pastor (The Good Shepherd) (SPA.). (J). 1.59 *(978-1-56063-854-4(0),* 494016) Editorial Unilit.

Urbigkit, Cat. A Young Shepherd. 2006. (Illus.). (J). *(978-1-4156-6559-6(1))* Highlights Pr., c/o Highlights for Children, Inc.

SHEPHERDS—FICTION

Adams, Elizabeth. The Boy Who Cried Wolf, 1 vol. 2012. (ENG., Illus.). 24p. (J). pap. *(978-0-7787-7902-5(5))* Crabtree Publishing Co.

Banks, Celia. Jacob's Promise: A Story about Faith. Unalp, Janet & Perry, Matt, illus. 2006. 32p. 14.99 *(978-0-9764460-6-4(5))* HonorNet.

Blackford. The Eskdale Herd Boy A Scottish Tale for the Instruction & Amusement of Young Persons. 2004. reprint ed. pap. 15.95 *(978-1-4191-6125-4(3))* Kessinger Publishing, LLC.

Blanco, César. Hoky the Caring Wolf. Brokenbrow, Jon, tr. Bk, Blanca, illus. 2013. (ENG.). 32p. (J). (gr. k-3). 15.95 *(978-84-15241-92-8(5))* Cuento de Luz SL ESP. Dist: Publishers Group West (PGW).

Cerpok, M. L. The Mobile Monk: A Zen Tale. Wagner, Gavin, illus. 2008. 73p. pap. 19.95 *(978-1-60610-138-4(2))* America Star Bks.

Cottrell, Stephen. The Sleepy Shepherd: A Timeless Retelling of the Christmas Story. Hagan, Chris, illus. 2018. (ENG.). 48p. (J). pap. 14.99 *(978-0-281-07802-8(5),* d3c4ce1e-9bfe-4b68-810f-58e524ae21e4) SPCK Publishing GBR. Dist: Baker & Taylor Publisher Services (BTPS).

Dateno, Maria Grace. Shepherds to the Rescue, 6 vols., Vol. 1. Cunningham, Paul, illus. 2013. 71p. (J). pap. 5.95 *(978-0-8198-7251-7(2))* Pauline Bks. & Media.

Fine, Maureen. My Two Shepherds in the Garden: A Lesson in Listening. 2012. (ENG.). 24p. pap. 14.93 *(978-1-4669-1991-4(4))* Trafford Publishing.

Flinn, Lisa & Younger, Barbara. The Christmas Garland. Corvino, Lucy, tr. Corvino, Lucy, illus. 2003. 32p. (J). 14.95 *(978-0-8249-5460-4(2),* Ideals Pubns.) Worthy Publishing.

Fogle, Robin. The Shepherd Boy's Christmas. 2005. (J). pap. 1.79 *(978-1-59317-105-6(6))* Warner Pr., Inc.

Hallinan, P. K. That's What a Friend Is! 2003. (ENG.). 24p. (J). bds. 6.95 *(978-0-8249-5468-0(8),* Ideals Pubns.) Worthy Publishing.

Hecket, Jessica. The Lamb, That Got Away. 2018. (ENG., Illus.). 42p. (J). 16.99 *(978-0-9994364-5-5(7))* Jeriel Works.

Hennessy, B. G. The Boy Who Cried Wolf. Kulikov, Boris, illus. 2011. (J). (gr. -1-2). 29.95 *(978-0-545-09452-8(6))* Weston Woods Studios, Inc.

Henry, Juliann. The Little Shepherd Girl: A Christmas Story. Madsen, Jim, illus. 2007. 32p. (J). (gr. -1-3). 14.99 *(978-0-7814-4513-9(2))* Cook, David C.

Herzing, Nancy. The Night the Angels Came. 2012. 46p. pap. 19.99 *(978-1-62419-373-6(0))* Salem Author Services.

Hill, Judith J. Champion for Grace. 2012. 128p. pap. 15.00 *(978-1-936688-22-7(0))* AKA:yoLa.

Howell, Trisha Adelena. The Stinky Shepherd. Marshall, Jamie, illus. 2005. 32p. (J). 15.95 *(978-1-931210-25-6(X))* Howell Canyon Pr.

Jaeger, Elizabeth. The Little Shepherd. Montano, Irene, illus. 2019. 32p. (J). (gr. -1-k). 16.99 *(978-1-5064-4873-2(9),* Beaming Books) 1517 Media.

Laurel Carter, Anne. The Shepherd's Granddaughter. 2013. 236p. pap. *(978-1-4596-6490-6(6))* ReadHowYouWant.com, Ltd.

Mackall, Dandi Daley, adapted by. El Pastorcito: Para ninos de 4-7 Anos.Tr. of Little Shepherd. (SPA.). 32p. 3.99 *(978-0-7586-0362-3(2))* Concordia Publishing Hse.

Metlen, Ryan W. & Metlen, Ryan. Ewe. 2009. (J). *(978-1-58768-054-0(8),* HiddenSpring) Paulist Pr.

North, Laura. The Boy Who Cried Sheep! 2016. (ENG., Illus.). 32p. (J). *(978-0-7787-2471-1(9))* Crabtree Publishing Co.

Ogorek, Keith. Eli the Stable Boy. 2009. (ENG.). 28p. pap. 13.99 *(978-1-4490-4116-8(7))* AuthorHouse.

Rousay II, Richard A. Choose the Right & Walk with Noah. 2008. (ENG.). 82p. pap. 17.50 *(978-0-615-19773-9(6))* P.F.P. Pubs.

Schaefer, Jack. Old Ramon. West, Harold E., illus. 2016. (ENG.). 112p. (J). pap. 19.95 *(978-0-8263-5764-9(4),* P509800) Univ. of New Mexico Pr.

Stockham, Jess, illus. The Boy Who Cried Wolf. 2011. (Flip-Up Fairy Tales Ser.). 24p. (J). (gr. 2-2). *(978-1-84643-368-9(1))* Child's Play International Ltd.

Van Dyke, Henry. The Sad Shepherd: A Christmas Story, & the Unruly Sprite. 2007. 48p. per. *(978-1-4065-4725-2(5))* Dodo Pr.

Weiss, Ellen & Friedman, Mel. The Stinky Giant. 2012. (Step into Reading Ser.). (Illus.). 48p. (J). (gr. k-3). pap. 5.99 *(978-0-375-86743-9(0),* Random Hse. Bks. for Young Readers) Random Hse. Children's Bks.

—The Stinky Giant. Girasole, Alessia, illus. 2012. (Step into Reading Level 3 Ser.). lib. bdg. 13.55 *(978-0-606-23858-8(1))* Turtleback.

Wright, Harold Bell. The Shepherd of the Hills. 2017. (ENG., Illus.). (J). 24.95 *(978-1-374-93262-3(0))* Capital Communications, Inc.

—The Shepherd of the Hills. 2018. (ENG., Illus.). (J). 190p. 19.95 *(978-1-64439-017-7(5));* 188p. pap. 10.95 *(978-1-64439-016-0(7))* IndoEuropeanPublishing.com.

—The Shepherd of the Hills. 2018. (ENG., Illus.). 188p. (J). 19.99 *(978-1-5154-2506-9(1))* Wilder Pubns., Corp.

The check digit for ISBN-10 appears in parentheses after the full ISBN-13

SHERMAN, WILLIAM T. (WILLIAM TECUMSEH), 1820-1891

Hoogenboom, Lynn. William Tecumseh Sherman: The Fight to Preserve the Union. (Library of American Lives & Times Ser.). 112p. (gr. 5-5). 2009. 69.20 *(978-1-60853-511-8(8))* 2003. (ENG., Illus.). (J). lib. bdg. 38.27 *(978-0-8239-6625-7(9),* 6abaef9e-c62b-4dbe-ad9c-82208b1d0928) Rosen Publishing Group, Inc., The.

Koestler-Grack, Rachel A. William Tecumseh Sherman. 2009. (ENG., Illus.). 149p. (gr. 6-12). 35.00 *(978-1-60413-300-4(7),* P162096, Facts On File) Infobase Holdings, Inc.

Streissguth, Tom. Sherman's March to the Sea. 2020. (Civil War Ser.). (ENG., Illus.). 48p. (J). (gr. 5-6). lib. bdg. 34.21 *(978-1-64493-084-7(6),* 1644930846, Focus Readers) North Star Editions.

—Sherman's March to the Sea. 2020. (Civil War Ser.). (ENG., Illus.). 48p. (J). (gr. 5-6). pap. 11.95 *(978-1-64493-163-9(X),* 164493163X, Focus Readers) North Star Editions.

Whitelaw, Nancy. William Tecumseh Sherman: Defender & Destroyer. rev. exp. ed. 2004. (Illus.). 176p. (J). (gr. 6-12). 26.95 *(978-1-931798-31-0(1))* Reynolds, Morgan Inc.

SHERMAN'S MARCH TO THE SEA

Hoogenboom, Lynn. William Tecumseh Sherman: The Fight to Preserve the Union, 1 vol. 2003. (Library of American Lives & Times Ser.). (ENG., Illus.). 112p. (J). (gr. 5-5). lib. bdg. 38.27 *(978-0-8239-6625-7(9),* 6abaef9e-c62b-4dbe-ad9c-82208b1d0928) Rosen Publishing Group, Inc., The.

SHERMAN'S MARCH TO THE SEA—FICTION

Bolden, Tonya. Crossing Ebenezer Creek. (ENG.). 240p. (YA). 2018. pap. 10.99 *(978-1-68119-699-2(9),* 900182277, Bloomsbury Young Adult) 2017. 17.99 *(978-1-59990-319-4(9),* 900054246, Bloomsbury USA Childrens) Bloomsbury Publishing USA.

—Crossing Ebenezer Creek. 2018. (YA). lib. bdg. 22.10 *(978-0-606-41078-6(3))* Turtleback.

Streissguth, Tom. Sherman's March to the Sea. 2020. (Civil War Ser.). (ENG., Illus.). 48p. (J). (gr. 5-6). lib. bdg. 34.21 *(978-1-64493-084-7(6),* 1644930846, Focus Readers) North Star Editions.

—Sherman's March to the Sea. 2020. (Civil War Ser.). (ENG., Illus.). 48p. (J). (gr. 5-6). pap. 11.95 *(978-1-64493-163-9(X),* 164493163X, Focus Readers) North Star Editions.

SHIP BUILDING

see Shipbuilding

SHIP MODELS

Green, Cathy, et al. Great Ships on the Great Lakes Teacher's Guide: A Maritime History. 2013. (ENG., Illus.). cd-rom 49.95 *(978-0-87020-583-5(8))* Wisconsin Historical Society.

Holloway, Jamie. My Toy Boat, 1 vol. 2015. (Rosen REAL Readers: STEM & STEAM Collection). (ENG.). 8p. (gr. k-1). pap. 5.46 *(978-1-4994-9711-3(3),* 6913726b-fa43-40e4-9280-ef3cd98825b5, Rosen Classroom) Rosen Publishing Group, Inc., The.

Sobey, Ed. The Motorboat Book: Build & Launch 20 Jet Boats, Paddle-Wheelers, Electric Submarines & More. 2013. (Science in Motion Ser.). (ENG., Illus.). 224p. (J). (gr. 4). pap. 14.95 *(978-1-61374-447-5(1))* Chicago Review Pr., Inc.

SHIPBUILDING

see also Boatbuilding; Ships; Steamboats

Aloian, Sam. How a Ship Is Built, 1 vol. 2015. (Engineering Our World Ser.). (ENG., Illus.). 24p. (J). (gr. 2-3). pap. 9.15 *(978-1-4824-3915-1(8),* 331a45b7-e343-444c-afca-6186f7c7023a) Stevens, Gareth Publishing LLLP.

Blake, Kevin. Creating Titanic: The Ship of Dreams. 2018. (Titanica Ser.). (ENG.). 32p. (J). (gr. 2-7). 19.95 *(978-1-68402-430-8(7))* Bearport Publishing Co., Inc.

Bow, James. Your Guide to Trade in the Middle Ages. 2017. (Destination: Middle Ages Ser.). (ENG., Illus.). 32p. (J). (gr. 5-5). *(978-0-7787-2996-9(6))*; pap. *(978-0-7787-3052-1(2))* Crabtree Publishing Co.

Curley, Robert, ed. The Complete History of Ships & Boats: From Sails & Oars to Nuclear-Powered Vessels, 4 vols. 2011. (Transportation & Society Ser.). (ENG.). 192p. (gr. 10-10). (YA). 84.70 *(978-1-61530-770-8(2),* 14d746ca-ecbd-4370-843e-a416ccf0ebd7); (Illus.). (J). lib. bdg. 42.35 *(978-1-61530-670-1(6),* ab6de80a-e2b6-48a1-8127-90fcd7acc8e8) Rosen Publishing Group, Inc., The.

Dougherty, Terri, et al. Eyewitness to Titanic: From Building the Great Ship to the Search for Its Watery Grave. 2015. (ENG., Illus.). 160p. (J). (gr. 5-9). pap., pap., pap. 9.95 *(978-1-62370-131-4(7),* 125876, Capstone Young Readers) Capstone.

Heinrichs, Ann. The Shipbuilder, 1 vol. 2013. (Colonial People Ser.). (ENG.). 48p. (gr. 4-4). 34.07 *(978-0-7614-0005-9(2),* b7bd16c4-cc1f-4847-850b-5417894fcd33); pap. 13.93 *(978-1-62712-048-7(3),* d51ce8f1-e09a-4a09-b755-73bb6e5b92f0) Cavendish Square Publishing LLC.

Krebs, Laurie. A Day in the Life of a Colonial Shipwright. 2009. (Library of Living & Working in Colonial Times Ser.). 24p. (gr. 3-3). 42.50 *(978-1-60853-738-9(2),* PowerKids Pr.) Rosen Publishing Group, Inc., The.

Macaulay, David. Crossing on Time: Steam Engines, Fast Ships, & a Journey to the New World. 2019. (ENG., Illus.). 128p. (J). 24.99 *(978-1-59643-477-6(5),* 900055833) Roaring Brook Pr.

Spray, Sally. Awesome Engineering Trains, Planes, & Ships. 2018. (Awesome Engineering Ser.). (ENG., Illus.). 32p. (J). (gr. 3-6). pap. 8.10 *(978-1-5435-1342-4(5),* 137773); lib. bdg. 27.99 *(978-1-5435-1336-3(0),* 137767) Capstone. (Capstone Pr.).

SHIPPING

Bailey, Gerry. Sea Transportation, 1 vol. 2008. (Simply Science Ser.). (ENG., Illus.). 32p. (YA). (gr. 3-5). lib. bdg. 28.67 *(978-0-8368-9230-7(5),* efd3f887-3ce4-4750-ada8-9feaef58a5b7) Stevens, Gareth Publishing LLLP.

Evans, Lesli. Transport Math, 1 vol. 2009. (Math Alive! Ser.). (ENG.). 32p. (gr. 4-4). lib. bdg. 31.21 *(978-0-7614-3211-1(6),* f815c05c-ff16-4bb7-8c4a-9970b7b8027a) Cavendish Square Publishing LLC.

Friend, Robyn C. & Cohen, Judith Love. A Cleaner Port; A Brighter Future: The Greening of the Port of Los Angeles. Katz, David Arthur, illus. 2011. 46p. (J). 13.95 *(978-1-935999-01-0(X))*; pap. 7.00 *(978-1-935999-00-3(1))* Cascade Pass, Inc.

Green, Cathy, et al. Great Ships on the Great Lakes: A Maritime History. 2013. (ENG., Illus.). 144p. (J). pap. 18.95 *(978-0-87020-582-8(X))* Wisconsin Historical Society.

—Great Ships on the Great Lakes Teacher's Guide: A Maritime History. 2013. (ENG., Illus.). cd-rom 49.95 *(978-0-87020-583-5(8))* Wisconsin Historical Society.

Heiligman, Deborah. Torpedoed: The True Story of the World War II Sinking of the Children's Ship. 2019. (ENG., Illus.). 288p. (J). 19.99 *(978-1-62779-554-8(5),* 900155418, Holt, Henry & Co. Bks. For Young Readers) Holt, Henry & Co.

Hinton, Kerry. All about Ships, 1 vol. 2016. (Let's Find Out! Transportation Ser.). (ENG., Illus.). 32p. (J). (gr. 2-3). lib. bdg. 26.06 *(978-1-68048-443-4(5),* 0c96a812-3dc8-487e-bcba-8fc0b229c3ec) Rosen Publishing Group, Inc., The.

Meister, Cari. Ships. 2013. (ENG., Illus.). 24p. (J). lib. bdg. 25.65 *(978-1-62031-047-2(3))* Jump! Inc.

Miller, Marlene. I Know Where the Freighters Go. Miller, Marlene, illus. 2008. (ENG., Illus.). 32p. pap. 9.95 *(978-1-933916-29-3(X))* Nelson Publishing & Marketing.

SHIPPING—FICTION

Kellogg, Elijah. The Ark of Elm Island by Rev Elijah Kellogg. 2006. 300p. per. 23.99 *(978-1-4255-2817-1(1))* Michigan Publishing.

Maurer, Tracy Nelson. Storm Codes. Rodriguez, Christina, illus. 2007. (ENG.). 40p. (J). pap. 8.95 *(978-0-89317-064-6(X),* WW-064X); (gr. 1-7). lib. bdg. 17.95 *(978-0-89317-063-9(1),* WW-0631) Finney Co., Inc. (Windward Publishing).

SHIPS

see also Boats and Boating; Navigation; Sailing; Steamboats; Submarines (Ships); Warships; Yachts and Yachting

Adamson, Thomas K. Ships. 2017. (Mighty Machines in Action Ser.). (ENG., Illus.). 24p. (J). (gr. k-3). lib. bdg. 26.95 *(978-1-62617-608-9(6),* Blastoff! Readers) Bellwether Media.

Alter, Judy. Passenger Ships. 2008. (21st Century Skills Innovation Library: Innovation in Transportation Ser.). (ENG., Illus.). 32p. (gr. 4-8). lib. bdg. 32.07 *(978-1-60279-236-4(4),* 200166) Cherry Lake Publishing.

Amato, William. Cruceros, 1 vol. 2003. (Vehículos de Alta Tecnología (High-Tech Vehicles) Ser.). (SPA., Illus.). 24p. (J). (gr. 2-2). lib. bdg. 26.27 *(978-0-8239-6884-8(7),* bf7e0ddf-2b6f-46cd-8b7b-3464eb219baf) Rosen Publishing Group, Inc., The.

—Cruceros (Cruise Ships) 2009. (Vehículos de alta tecnología (High-Tech Vehicles) Ser.). (SPA.). 24p. (gr. 2-3). 42.50 *(978-1-60854-718-0(3),* Editorial Buenas Letras) Rosen Publishing Group, Inc., The.

—Cruise Ships. 2009. (High-Tech Vehicles Ser.). 24p. (gr. 2-3). 42.50 *(978-1-61513-305-5(4),* PowerKids Pr.) Rosen Publishing Group, Inc., The.

Anderson, Scoular. Ships, Boats & Things That Float. Cambridge Reading Adventures. Purple Band. 2016. (Cambridge Reading Adventures Ser.). (ENG., Illus.). 24p. pap. 8.80 *(978-1-107-56041-3(1))* Cambridge Univ. Pr.

Arnold, Quinn M. Oasis of the Seas. 2016. (Now That's Big! Ser.). (ENG., Illus.). 24p. (J). (gr. 1-3). *(978-1-60818-715-7(2),* 20647, Creative Education) Creative Co., The.

AZ Books Staff. Sailing Ships. Tulup, Natasha, ed. 2012. (Workshop Ser.). (ENG.). 10p. (J). (gr. -1-k). bds. 10.95 *(978-1-61889-162-4(6))* AZ Bks. LLC.

Bailey, Gerry. Sea Transportation, 1 vol. 2008. (Simply Science Ser.). (ENG., Illus.). 32p. (YA). (gr. 3-5). lib. bdg. 28.67 *(978-0-8368-9230-7(5),* efd3f887-3ce4-4750-ada8-9feaef58a5b7) Stevens, Gareth Publishing LLLP.

Beech, Linda Ward. The Exxon Valdez's Deadly Oil Spill. 2007. (Code Red Ser.). (Illus.). 32p. (YA). (gr. 2-5). lib. bdg. 28.50 *(978-1-59716-366-8(X))* Bearport Publishing Co., Inc.

Bender, Lionel. Ships & Boats. 2006. (J). *(978-1-59389-268-5(3))* Chrysalis Education.

Benoit, Peter. The Exxon Valdez Oil Spill. 2011. (J). pap. *(978-0-531-29028-6(X))* Children's Pr., Ltd.

—The Exxon Valdez Oil Spill. 2011. (True Bks.). 48p. (J). (gr. 3-5). 29.00 *(978-0-531-20629-4(7),* Children's Pr.) Scholastic Library Publishing.

Best, B. J. Coast Guard Boats. 2017. (Riding to the Rescue! Ser.). (Illus.). 24p. (J). (gr. 1-1). pap. 49.32 *(978-1-5026-2556-4(3))* Cavendish Square Publishing LLC.

Biesty, Stephen & Butterfield, Moira. Look Inside Cross-Sections: Ships. (ENG., Illus.). 32p. (J). mass mkt. 8.99 *(978-0-590-24342-1(X))* Scholastic, Inc.

Bingham, Jane. The Story of Ships. King, Colin, illus. 2004. (Young Reading Ser.: Vol. 2). 62p. (J). (gr. 2-18). lib. bdg. 13.95 *(978-1-58086-700-9(6),* Usborne) EDC Publishing.

Bone, Emily. Ships. King, Colin, illus. 2009. (Beginner's Science Ser.). 32p. (J). 4.99 *(978-0-7945-2507-1(5),* Usborne) EDC Publishing.

Bow, James. Water Vehicles. 2018. (Vehicles on the Job Ser.). (ENG.). 24p. (J). (gr. 1-3). 25.27 *(978-1-59953-946-1(2))* Norwood Hse. Pr.

Bowler, Peter J. An Interview with Charles Darwin, 1 vol. 2014. (Meet the Masters Ser.). (ENG.). 112p. (YA). (gr. 9-9). lib. bdg. 44.50 *(978-1-62712-909-1(X),* 0ea5fed2-1157-4273-82fd-9e8d089c1f23) Cavendish Square Publishing LLC.

Bowman, Chris. Monster Ships. 2014. (Monster Machines Ser.). (ENG., Illus.). 24p. (J). (gr. k-3). lib. bdg. 26.95 *(978-1-62617-054-4(1),* Blastoff! Readers) Bellwether Media.

Build Your Own Pirate Ship. Date not set. (Build Your Own Ser.). (Illus.). 16p. (J). 3.98 *(978-0-7525-7658-9(5))* Parragon, Inc.

Burgan, Michael. Exxon Valdez: How a Massive Oil Spill Triggered an Environmental Catastrophe. 2018. (Captured Science History Ser.). (ENG., Illus.). 64p. (J). (gr. 5-9). lib. bdg. 35.32 *(978-0-7565-5743-0(7),* 137539, Compass Point Bks.) Capstone.

Calvert, Patricia. Sir Ernest Shackleton: By Endurance We Conquer, 1 vol. 2003. (Great Explorations Ser.). (ENG., Illus.). 80p. (gr. 6-6). 36.93 *(978-0-7614-1485-8(1),* c420ba55-b637-4fc9-9090-db60567f8753) Cavendish Square Publishing LLC.

Carr, Aaron. Cruise Ships. 2014. (J). *(978-1-4896-3216-6(6))* Weigl Pubs., Inc.

Carriere, Nicholle. Ships & Boats, 1 vol. 2017. (Mega Machines Ser.). (ENG., Illus.). 64p. (J). pap. 6.99 *(978-1-926700-76-2(7),* 6ddf74d1-a685-4c91-814c-1a9507b2b4ff) Blue Bike Bks. CAN. Dist: Lone Pine Publishing USA.

Close, Edward. Wheels, Wings, & Motors, 1 vol., 1. 2014. (Discovery Education: How It Works). (ENG.). 32p. (gr. 4-5). 28.93 *(978-1-4777-6313-1(9),* 803af42f-58c3-43fd-81fa-5099de611187, PowerKids Pr.) Rosen Publishing Group, Inc., The.

Coffin, Rebecca J., et al, eds. Boats: The Work They Do & the Way They Do It. 2011. 28p. 35.95 *(978-1-258-06539-3(8))* Literary Licensing, LLC.

Cottman, Michael H. Shackles from the Deep: Tracing the Path of a Sunken Slave Ship, a Bitter Past, & a Rich Legacy. 2017. 128p. (J). (gr. 5-9). 17.99 *(978-1-4263-2663-9(7),* National Geographic Kids) Disney Publishing Worldwide.

Disney Editions, creator. Birnbaum's Disney Cruise Line. 2006. (Birnbaum's Disney Cruise Line Ser.). (ENG., Illus.). 224p. (gr. -1-17). per. 13.95 *(978-1-4231-0052-2(2),* Disney Editions) Disney Pr.

Domiano, Gloria. Ship Shapes: Identify & Describe Shapes. 2013. (Rosen Math Readers Ser.). (ENG.). 16p. (J). (gr. k-1). pap. 42.00 *(978-1-4777-1666-3(1))*; (Illus.). pap. 7.00 *(978-1-4777-1665-6(3),* 009e772f-1da8-472c-9149-9c657f2b92ae) Rosen Publishing Group, Inc., The. (Rosen Classroom).

Eggers, Dave. The Lights & Types of Ships at Night. Dills, Annie, illus. 2020. 32p. (J). 18.99 *(978-1-952119-07-1(3),* d4bd153f-5743-440f-87b9-47476f71591b) McSweeney's Publishing.

Ellis, Catherine. Ships. (Mega Military Machines Ser.). 24p. (gr. 1-1). 2009. 42.50 *(978-1-61514-637-6(7),* PowerKids Pr.) 2007. (ENG., Illus.). (J). lib. bdg. 26.27 *(978-1-4042-3668-4(6),* 3dfa74f4-cc52-4ffd-a6df-b85d5b75d593) Rosen Publishing Group, Inc., The.

—Ships/Barcos. 2009. (Mega Military Machines/Megamaquinas militares Ser.). (SPA.). 24p. (gr. 1-1). 42.50 *(978-1-61514-642-0(3),* Editorial Buenas Letras) Rosen Publishing Group, Inc., The.

—Ships/Barcos, 1 vol. Brusca, Maria Cristina, tr. 2007. (Mega Military Machines / Megamaquinas Militares Ser.). (ENG & SPA., Illus.). 24p. (J). (gr. 1-1). lib. bdg. 26.27 *(978-1-4042-7623-9(8),* ee86b61d-8efc-438e-bb0e-06fbe9ea62ed) Rosen Publishing Group, Inc., The.

Farndon, John. Stickmen's Guide to Watercraft. Paul de Quay, John, illus. 2016. (Stickmen's Guides to How Everything Works). (ENG.). 32p. (J). (gr. 3-6). E-Book 42.65 *(978-1-5124-0699-3(6),* 9781512406993); E-Book 42.65 *(978-1-4677-9594-4(1))* Lerner Publishing Group. (Hungry Tomato (r)).

Fein, Eric. The USS Greeneville Submarine Disaster. 2009. (When Disaster Strikes! Ser.). 48p. (gr. 5-8). 53.00 *(978-1-60854-783-8(3),* Rosen Reference) Rosen Publishing Group, Inc., The.

Flammang, James M. Cargo Ships. 2008. (21st Century Skills Innovation Library: Innovation in Transportation Ser.). (ENG., Illus.). 32p. (gr. 4-8). lib. bdg. 32.07 *(978-1-60279-233-3(X),* 200163) Cherry Lake Publishing.

Gagne, Tammy. Haunted Ships. 2018. (Ghosts & Hauntings Ser.). (ENG., Illus.). 32p. (J). (gr. 4-6). lib. bdg. 28.65 *(978-1-5435-4149-6(6),* 139103, Capstone Pr.) Capstone.

Gamble, Adam & Jasper, Mark. Good Night Boats. Veno, Joe, illus. 2016. (Good Night Our World Ser.). (ENG.). 20p. (J). (— 1). bds. 9.95 *(978-1-60219-500-4(5))* Good Night Bks.

Gibbons, Gail. Boat Book. 2018. (ENG., Illus.). 20p. (J). (— 1). bds. 7.99 *(978-0-8234-3978-2(X))* Holiday Hse., Inc.

Glaser, Rebecca. Boats Float. 2018. (Amicus Ink Board Bks.). 14p. (J). (gr. -1 — 1). bds. 7.99 *(978-1-68152-243-2(8),* 14941) Amicus.

Goldish, Meish. Marine Firefighters. 2014. (Fire Fight! the Bravest Ser.). 32p. (J). (gr. 2-7). lib. bdg. 28.50 *(978-1-62724-098-7(5))* Bearport Publishing Co., Inc.

Gould, Jane H. The Flying Dutchman, 1 vol. 2014. (Jr. Graphic Ghost Stories Ser.). (ENG.). 24p. (J). (gr. 2-3). lib. bdg. 28.93 *(978-1-4777-7088-7(7),* e31f6beb-0403-42bb-8ca8-0c573e342a41, PowerKids Pr.) Rosen Publishing Group, Inc., The.

Graham, Ian. On the Water. 2006. (QEB Machines at Work Ser.). (Illus.). 36p. (J). lib. bdg. 16.95 *(978-1-59566-190-6(5))* QEB Publishing Inc.

—Ships. (Mighty Machines Ser.). (Illus.). 2009. 31p. (J). (gr. 4-7). pap. 7.95 *(978-1-59920-257-0(3))* 2006. 32p. (YA). (gr. 3-6). lib. bdg. 28.50 *(978-1-58340-921-3(1))* Black Rabbit Bks.

Green, Cathy, et al. Great Ships on the Great Lakes: A Maritime History. 2013. (ENG., Illus.). 144p. (J). pap. 18.95 *(978-0-87020-582-8(X))* Wisconsin Historical Society.

Gunston, Bill Tudor & Parker, Steve. Fasten Your Seatbelt! Mind-Boggling Machines. 2010. (ENG.). 96p. (J). (gr. 2-4). pap. 9.95 *(978-1-84696-205-9(6),* TickTock Books) Octopus Publishing Group GBR. Dist: Independent Pubs. Group.

Harris, Nicholas. Let's Explore a Pirate Ship. Lee, Brian, illus. 2010. 36p. (J). 13.99 *(978-0-8437-1378-7(X))* Hammond World Atlas Corp.

Harrison, Paul. Superboats. 2015. 32p. (gr. 1-5). lib. bdg. 31.35 *(978-1-78404-076-5(2))* Arcturus Publishing GBR. Dist: Black Rabbit Bks.

Hickman, Pamela. Righting Canada's Wrongs: the Komagata Maru & Canada's Anti-Indian Immigration Policies in the Twentieth Century. 2014. (Righting Canada's Wrongs Ser.). (ENG., Illus.). 104p. (YA). (gr. 8-12). 34.95 *(978-1-4594-0437-3(8),* 0437) James Lorimer & Co. Ltd., Pubs. CAN. Dist: Formac Lorimer Bks. Ltd.

Hinton, Kerry. All about Ships, 1 vol. 2016. (Let's Find Out! Transportation Ser.). (ENG., Illus.). 32p. (J). (gr. 2-3). lib. bdg. 26.06 *(978-1-68048-443-4(5),* 0c96a812-3dc8-487e-bcba-8fc0b229c3ec) Rosen Publishing Group, Inc., The.

Hopkins, Andrea. Viking Longships. 2009. (Viking Library). 24p. (gr. 3-3). 42.50 *(978-1-60854-259-8(9),* PowerKids Pr.) Rosen Publishing Group, Inc., The.

Ipcizade, Catherine. BIG Boats. 2010. (Big Ser.). (ENG.). 24p. (J). (gr. -1-2). lib. bdg. 27.32 *(978-1-4296-3993-4(8),* 102603, Capstone Pr.) Capstone.

Kacer, Kathy. To Hope & Back: The Journey of the St. Louis, 1 vol. 2011. (Holocaust Remembrance Series for Young Readers Ser.: 11). (ENG., Illus.). 204p. (J). (gr. 6-8). pap. 14.95 *(978-1-897187-96-8(3))* Second Story Pr. CAN. Dist: Orca Bk. Pubs. USA.

Kerr, Daisy. Ships. 2015. (Wonderwise Ser.). (Illus.). 32p. (gr. 2-6). 31.35 *(978-1-62588-362-9(5))* Black Rabbit Bks.

Key Porter Books Staff. Gymboree on a Pirate Ship. rev. ed. 2007. (ENG., Illus.). 1p. (J). *(978-1-55263-921-4(5))* Magma.

Lacey, Minna. Big Book of Big Ships. Chisholm, Jane, ed. 2012. (Big Bks). 16p. (J). ring bd. 14.99 *(978-0-7945-3077-8(X),* Usborne) EDC Publishing.

Let's Look at Boats. 2009. (Let's Go! Ser.). (Illus.). 18p. (J). (gr. -1-k). bds. 12.75 *(978-1-60754-417-3(2))* Windmill Bks.

Levy, Janey. At Sea on a Viking Ship: Solving Problems of Length & Weight Using the Four Math Operations, 1 vol. 2010. (Math for the REAL World Ser.). (ENG., Illus.). 24p. (gr. 3-4). pap. 8.25 *(978-0-8239-8922-5(4),* eea2e498-a9d8-46c5-badc-b0088a52f6bd, PowerKids Pr.) Rosen Publishing Group, Inc., The.

Libretto, Ellen V. The General Slocum Steamboat Fire of 1904, 1 vol. 2003. (Tragic Fires Throughout History Ser.). (ENG., Illus.). 48p. (J). (gr. 5-8). lib. bdg. 34.47 *(978-0-8239-4486-6(7),* eec2e48c-b32f-493d-8d4f-cc9e5ebce7cf, Rosen Reference) Rosen Publishing Group, Inc., The.

—The General Slocum Steamboat Fire Of 1904. 2009. (Tragic Fires Throughout History Ser.). 48p. (gr. 5-8). 53.00 *(978-1-60854-581-0(4),* Rosen Reference) Rosen Publishing Group, Inc., The.

Lindeen, Mary. All about Boats, 1 vol. 2011. (Wonder Readers Fluent Level Ser.). (ENG.). 16p. (gr. -1-2). (J). pap. 6.25 *(978-1-4296-7906-0(9),* 118238); pap. 35.94 *(978-1-4296-8065-3(2))* Capstone. (Capstone Pr.).

—Ships. 2007. (Mighty Machines Ser.). (ENG., Illus.). 24p. (J). (gr. k-3). lib. bdg. 26.95 *(978-1-60014-060-0(2))* Bellwether Media.

MacDumont, Sean. Boats Go!, 1 vol. 2017. (Ways to Go Ser.). (ENG.). 24p. (J). (gr. k-k). pap. 9.15 *(978-1-5382-1013-0(4),* eb96d96e-2e2f-494e-a047-4309af775815) Stevens, Gareth Publishing LLLP.

Margulies, Phillip. The Exxon Valdez Oil Spill. 2009. (When Disaster Strikes! Ser.). 48p. (gr. 5-8). 53.00 *(978-1-60854-780-7(9),* Rosen Reference) Rosen Publishing Group, Inc., The.

Martin, Jacqueline Briggs. The Lamp, the Ice, & the Boat Called Fish: Based on a True Story. 2005. (ENG., Illus.). 48p. (J). (gr. -1-3). 9.99 *(978-0-618-54895-8(5),* 410272, Clarion Bks.) HarperCollins Pubs.

Mason, Conrad. See Inside Ships. King, Colin, illus. 2011. (See Inside Board Books Ser.). 16p. (J). ring bd. 12.99 *(978-0-7945-3005-1(2),* Usborne) EDC Publishing.

Maynard, Chris. I Wonder Why Planes Have Wings: And Other Questions about Transportation. 2012. (I Wonder Why Ser.). (ENG., Illus.). 32p. (J). (gr. k-3). pap. 6.99 *(978-0-7534-6703-9(8),* 900076420, Kingfisher) Roaring Brook Pr.

McNab, Chris. Defending the Seas: The Navy. 2017. (Illus.). 80p. (J). *(978-1-4222-3763-2(X))* Mason Crest.

Meister, Cari. Boats & Ships. 2019. (Transportation in My Community Ser.). (ENG.). 32p. (J). (gr. -1-2). pap. 7.95 *(978-1-9771-0502-8(5),* 139891, Pebble) Capstone.

—Ships. 2013. (ENG., Illus.). 24p. (J). lib. bdg. 25.65 *(978-1-62031-047-2(3))* Jump! Inc.

Meredith, Susan Markowitz & Voege, Debra. Why Do Ships Float? 2009. (Science in the Real World Ser.). (ENG., Illus.). 32p. (gr. 4-6). 28.00 *(978-1-60413-466-7(6),* P173436, Chelsea Clubhse.) Infobase Holdings, Inc.

Mighty Machines: A Lego Adventure in the Real World. 2017. (Illus.). 32p. (J). *(978-1-5182-4494-0(7))* Scholastic, Inc.

Mitton, Tony & Parker, Ant. Busy Boats. 2005. (Amazing Machines Ser.). (ENG., Illus.). 24p. (J). (gr. -1-k). 5.99 *(978-0-7534-5916-4(7),* 900052725, Kingfisher) Roaring Brook Pr.

Olson, Tod. Lost in the Antarctic: the Doomed Voyage of the Endurance (Lost #4), Vol. 4. 2019. (Lost Ser.: 4). (ENG., Illus.). 224p. (J). (gr. 3-7). pap. 7.99 *(978-1-338-20734-7(2))* Scholastic, Inc.

Oxlade, Chris. Ships & Boats: Sail; Navigation; Radar; Anchor; Keel. 2015. (Illus.). 64p. (J). (gr. 3-7). 12.99 *(978-1-86147-412-4(1),* Armadillo) Anness Publishing GBR. Dist: National Bk. Network.

Parker, Steve. On the Sea. 2010. (J). 28.50 *(978-1-59920-286-0(7))* Black Rabbit Bks.

—On Water, 1 vol. West, David, illus. 2012. (Future Transport Ser.). (ENG.). 32p. (gr. 5-5). 31.21 *(978-1-60870-780-5(6),* b9062f54-e70d-448a-ad76-b3f9c7785aef) Cavendish Square Publishing LLC.

Peppas, Lynn. Boats on the Water. 2011. (ENG.). 32p. (J). lib. bdg. *(978-0-7787-2727-9(0))*; (Vehicles on the Move Ser.: No. 13). pap. *(978-0-7787-2734-7(3))* Crabtree Publishing Co.

—Piracy. 2013. (ENG., Illus.). 48p. (J). *(978-0-7787-1103-2(X))*; pap. *(978-0-7787-1123-0(4))* Crabtree Publishing Co.

Platt, Richard & Biesty, Stephen. Man-of-War. (Illus.). (J). pap. 21.95 *(978-0-590-74610-6(3))* Scholastic, Inc.

Renaud, Anne. Into the Mist: The Story of the Empress of Ireland. 2010. (ENG., Illus.). 112p. (YA). (gr. 6). pap. 14.99 *(978-1-55488-759-0(3))* Dundurn Pr. CAN. Dist: Publishers Group West (PGW).

Richter, A. Boats that Float: Learning the OA Sound. 2009. (PowerPhonics Ser.). 24p. (gr. 1-1). 39.90 *(978-1-60851-435-9(8),* PowerKids Pr.) Rosen Publishing Group, Inc., The.

Ring, Susan. Boats, Boats, Boats. 2005. (Yellow Umbrella Fluent Level Ser.). (ENG., Illus.). 16p. (gr. k-1). pap. 35.70 *(978-0-7368-5309-5(X),* Capstone Pr.) Capstone.

Rooney, Anne. The Science of Seafaring: the Float-Tastic Facts about Ships (the Science of Engineering) (Library Edition) Affonso, Alexandre & Beach, Bryan, illus. 2019. (Science Of... Ser.). (ENG.). 32p. (J). (gr. 3-3). lib. bdg. 29.00

(978-0-531-13196-1(3), Watts, Franklin) Scholastic Library Publishing.

Sandler, Martin W. The Impossible Rescue: The True Story of an Amazing Arctic Adventure. 2014. (ENG.). 176p. (J). (gr. 5). pap. 16.99 *(978-0-7636-7093-1(6))* Candlewick Pr.

Sandy Creek (Firm) Staff, contrib. by. Liners & Merchant Ships. 2014. (Illus.). 48p. (J). *(978-1-4351-5369-1(3))* Barnes & Noble, Inc.

Scarry, Richard. Richard Scarry's Boats. Scarry, Richard, illus. 2015. (Illus.). 24p. (J). (— 1). bds. 4.99 *(978-0-385-39269-3(9)*, Golden Bks.) Random Hse. Children's Bks.

Scher, Linda. The Texas City Disaster. 2007. (Code Red Ser.). (Illus.). 32p. (YA). (gr. 2-5). lib. bdg. 28.50 *(978-1-59716-363-7(5))* Bearport Publishing Co., Inc.

Schuh, Mari. Ships. 2017. (Transportation Ser.). (ENG., Illus.). 24p. (J). (gr. -1-2). pap. 6.95 *(978-1-5157-7307-8(8)*, 135656, Pebble) Capstone.

Ships. (Make it Work Ser.). 42p. (J). (gr. 4-8). pap. *(978-1-882210-50-3(6))* Action Publishing, Inc.

Ships: Level N, 6 vols. (Wonder Worldtm Ser.). 48p. 34.95 *(978-0-7802-2030-0(7))* Wright Group/McGraw-Hill.

Sirota, Lyn A. Ships & Subs. 2017. (Rank It! Ser.). (ENG.). 32p. (J). (gr. 4-6). pap. 9.99 *(978-1-64466-213-7(2)*, 11480); (Illus.). lib. bdg. *(978-1-68072-179-9(8)*, 10542) Black Rabbit Bks. (Bolt).

Smith, Steven Michael. New Carissa: The Ship That Refused to Die. 2010. 52p. pap. 22.99 *(978-1-4520-6612-7(4))* AuthorHouse.

Stille, Darlene R. Ships, 1 vol. 2004. (Transportation Ser.). (ENG., Illus.). 32p. (gr. 2-3). 21.32 *(978-0-7565-0608-7(5)*, Compass Point Bks.) Capstone.

Stone, Lynn M. Amphibious Assault Ships. 2005. (Fighting Forces Ser.). (Illus.). 32p. (J). (gr. 4-8). lib. bdg. 28.50 *(978-1-59515-460-6(4))* Rourke Educational Media.

Sutherland, Johnathan & Canwell, Diane. Container Ships & Oil Tankers, 1 vol. 2007. (Amazing Ships Ser.). (ENG., Illus.). 32p. (gr. 3-5). lib. bdg. 28.67 *(978-0-8368-8377-0(2)*, 94ffc712-2f28-4888-a16f-9c5c9ab8303c, Gareth Stevens Learning Library) Stevens, Gareth Publishing LLLP.

Tatge, Cathy. Boats. 2007. (My First Look at: Vehicles Ser.). (Illus.). 24p. (J). (gr. -1-3). lib. bdg. 24.25 *(978-1-58341-526-9(2)*, Creative Education) Creative Co., The.

Thomas, Mark. Discoverer Enterprise: La plataforma de perforación más grande del mundo (the Discoverer Enterprise: World's Largest Offshore Drilling Rig) 2009. (Estructuras extraordinarias (Record-Breaking Structures) Ser.). (SPA.). 24p. (gr. 1-2). 42.50 *(978-1-61512-310-0(5)*, Editorial Buenas Letras) Rosen Publishing Group, Inc., The.

—The Discoverer Enterprise: World's Largest Offshore Drilling Rig. 2009. (Record-Breaking Structures Ser.). 24p. (gr. 1-2). 42.50 *(978-1-60852-454-9(X)*, PowerKids Pr.) Rosen Publishing Group, Inc., The.

Tiner, John Hudson. Ships & Boats. (Illus.). 32p. 2004. pap. 8.95 *(978-0-89812-390-6(9)*, Creative Paperbacks) 2003. (J). lib. bdg. 18.95 *(978-1-58341-257-2(3)*, Creative Education) Creative Co., The.

Tomljanovic, Tatiana. Bluenose: Canadian Icons. 2010. (Illus.). 24p. *(978-1-77071-576-9(2))*; pap. *(978-1-77071-583-7(5))* Weigl Educational Pubs. Ltd.

Tripp, Will. Water Adventures. 2005. (Real Deal Ser.). (Illus.). 32p. (J). pap. *(978-0-7608-9636-5(4))* Sundance/Newbridge Educational Publishing.

Veitch, Catherine. Big Machines Float!, 1 vol. 2014. (Big Machines Ser.). (ENG., Illus.). 24p. (J). (gr. -1-1). 25.99 *(978-1-4846-0587-5(X)*, 126689, Heinemann) Capstone.

Vescia, Monique. Choose a Career Adventure on a Cruise Ship. 2016. (Bright Futures Press: Choose a Career Adventure Ser.). (ENG., Illus.). 32p. (J). (gr. 4-6). 32.07 *(978-1-63471-910-0(7)*, 208961) Cherry Lake Publishing.

West, David. Ships. 2015. (Mechanic Mike's Machines Ser.). (ENG., Illus.). 24p. (J). (gr. k-3). 27.10 *(978-1-62588-066-6(9)*, 19317, Smart Apple Media) Black Rabbit Bks.

Wright, Nicola. Ships. 2006. (Illus.). 24p. (YA). (gr. 1-18). lib. bdg. 22.80 *(978-1-931983-56-3(9))* Chrysalis Education.

SHIPS—FICTION

Altebrando, Tara. The Opposite of Here. 2018. (ENG.). 256p. (YA). 17.99 *(978-1-68119-706-7(5)*, 900182256, Bloomsbury Young Adult) Bloomsbury Publishing USA.

Arato, Rona. The Ship to Nowhere: On Board the Exodus, 1 vol. 2016. (Holocaust Remembrance Series for Young Readers Ser.: 16). (ENG.). 176p. (J). (gr. 4-7). pap. 14.95 *(978-1-77260-018-6(0))* Second Story Pr. CAN. Dist: Orca Bk. Pubs. USA.

Averill, Esther. Jenny Goes to Sea. Averill, Esther, illus. 2005. (Jenny's Cat Club Ser.). (Illus.). 140p. (J). (gr. k-4). reprint ed. 18.95 *(978-1-59017-155-4(1)*, NYR Children's Collection) New York Review of Bks., Inc., The.

Avi. The True Confessions of Charlotte Doyle. 2012. lib. bdg. 17.20 *(978-0-606-26779-3(4))* Turtleback.

—The True Confessions of Charlotte Doyle (Scholastic Gold), 1 vol. 2012. (ENG.). 240p. (J). (gr. 4-7). pap. 9.99 *(978-0-545-47711-6(5)*, Scholastic Paperbacks) Scholastic, Inc.

Awdry, W. The Lost Ship (Thomas & Friends) Courtney, Richard, illus. 2015. (Step into Reading Ser.). (ENG.). 32p. (J). (gr. -1-1). 5.99 *(978-0-553-52171-9(3)*, Random Hse. Bks. for Young Readers) Random Hse. Children's Bks.

Barton, Bob. Trouble on the Voyage. 2010. (ENG., Illus.). 240p. (J). (gr. 4-7). pap. 10.95 *(978-1-926607-10-8(4)*, Napoleon & Co.) Dundurn Pr. CAN. Dist: Publishers Group West (PGW).

Bell, Loman. Old Glory Faces the Hurricane. Bell, Loman, illus. 2013. (Illus.). 46p. pap. *(978-0-9918033-2-3(9))* Wood Islands Prints.

Bentley, Sue. Snowy Wishes. 2013. (Magic Puppy Ser.). lib. bdg. 16.00 *(978-0-606-32124-2(1))* Turtleback.

Boné, Thomas H., illus. The Teacher Who Would Not Retire Retires. 2017. (J). *(978-0-9885295-7-1(2))* Blue Marlin Pubns.

Brown, Corinne. The Stowaway on the Titanic. 2004. 110p. 20.95 *(978-0-595-66754-3(6))* iUniverse, Inc.

Bruton, Georgia. Escape. 2012. 210p. pap. 11.95 *(978-1-938083-10-5(5))* Black Forge.

Burke, Maria. The Ark of Dun Ruah. 2013. (Ark of Dun Ruah Ser.: 01). (ENG., Illus.). 256p. (J). pap. 26.00 *(978-1-85607-794-1(2))* Currach Pr. IRL. Dist: Dufour Editions, Inc.

Butterman, Stephen. Rootbeer Beard. 2012. 74p. pap. 8.95 *(978-1-61477-055-8(7))* Bellissima Publishing, LLC.

Carroll, Claudia. Missy Mouse & the Rocket Ship. 2008. (ENG.). 39p. pap. 9.95 *(978-0-557-01769-0(6))* Lulu Pr., Inc.

Clark, Joyce. Katie. 2006. 196p. 27.43 *(978-1-4122-0067-7(9))* Trafford Publishing.

Coatsworth, Elizabeth Jane & Sewell, Helen. The Fair American. 2005. (ENG., Illus.). 137p. (J). (gr. 3-4). pap. 11.95 *(978-1-883937-85-0(X))* Ignatius Pr.

Collingwood, Harry. The Strange Adventures of Eric Blackburn. 2008. 164p. pap. 13.95 *(978-1-60664-210-8(3))* Rodgers, Alan Bks.

Collins, David Paul. Shanghaied. 2011. (ENG.). 320p. 29.95 *(978-1-4620-3184-9(6))*; pap. 19.95 *(978-1-4620-3183-2(8))* iUniverse, Inc.

Costello, David Hyde. Little Pig Saves the Ship. Costello, David Hyde, illus. 2017. (Illus.). 32p. (J). (gr. -1-2). 14.99 *(978-1-58089-715-0(0))* Charlesbridge Publishing, Inc.

Courtauld, Sarah. On a Pirate Ship. Davies, Benji, illus. 2007. (Picture Bks). 24p. (J). (gr. -1-3). 9.99 *(978-0-7945-1712-0(9)*, Usborne) EDC Publishing.

Cummings, Quasheba Giri. The World's First Submarine. 2008. 20p. pap. 15.49 *(978-1-4389-1273-8(0))* AuthorHouse.

Dafoe, Daniel. Robinson Crusoe. 2008. (Bring the Classics to Life Ser.). (ENG., Illus.). 72p. (gr. 3-12). pap., act. bk. ed. 10.95 *(978-0-931334-30-6(6)*, EDCTR-301B) EDCON Publishing Group.

Danielski, A. The Nick & Austin Chronicles: The Pirate Ship's Magic & a New Home. 2013. 28p. pap. 24.95 *(978-1-4626-7709-2(6))* America Star Bks.

David, Christopher. Denholme & the Skeleton Mystery. 2006. 274p. pap. 22.52 *(978-1-4120-8014-9(2))* Trafford Publishing.

de la Peña, Matt. The Living. 2015. (Living Ser.). (ENG.). 336p. (YA). (gr. 9). pap. 10.99 *(978-0-385-74121-7(9)*, Ember) Random Hse. Children's Bks.

Demarest, Chris. Ship Board Book. 2017. (ENG., Illus.). 16p. (J). (— 1). bds. 6.99 *(978-0-544-97702-0(5)*, 1663470, Clarion Bks.) HarperCollins Pubs.

Dixon, Franklin. Ship of Secrets. 2014. (Hardy Boys: Secret Files Ser.: 15). lib. bdg. 14.75 *(978-0-606-35781-4(5))* Turtleback.

Doucette, Gene. The Spaceship Next Door. 2018. (ENG.). 368p. pap. 15.99 *(978-1-328-56746-8(X)*, 1726765, Harper Voyager) HarperCollins Pubs.

Fitzgerald, D. M. The True Story of the Big Red Onion. Cudd, Savannah, illus. 2013. 36p. 18.99 *(978-0-9890288-7-5(9))*; pap. 10.99 *(978-0-9890288-5-1(2))* Mindstir Media.

Flanagan, John. Scorpion Mountain. 2015. (Brotherband Chronicles Ser.: 5). (ENG.). 480p. (J). (gr. 5). 8.99 *(978-0-14-242727-9(6)*, Puffin Books) Penguin Young Readers Group.

—Scorpion Mountain. 2015. (Brotherband Chronicles Ser.: 5). lib. bdg. 19.65 *(978-0-606-37563-4(5))* Turtleback.

—Slaves of Socorro. 2015. (Brotherband Chronicles Ser.: 4). (ENG.). 496p. (J). (gr. 5). pap. 9.99 *(978-0-14-242726-2(8)*, Puffin Books) Penguin Young Readers Group.

—Slaves of Socorro. 2015. (Brotherband Chronicles Ser.: 4). lib. bdg. 19.65 *(978-0-606-36771-4(3))* Turtleback.

Forward, Toby. The Quayside Cat. Brown, Ruth, illus. 2014. (ENG.). 32p. (J). (gr. -1-3). 16.95 *(978-1-4677-3452-3(7)*, 5794c544-507e-4083-9287-754dd130dea3) Lerner Publishing Group.

Fox, Nita. Captain Benjamin Dale. Wallace, Andrea, illus. 2008. 32p. (J). (gr. -1-3). pap. 5.99 *(978-0-9816107-0-2(6))* Fox's Den Publishing.

Fredley, Nichole. The Sirius, 1 vol. 2010. 534p. pap. 34.95 *(978-1-61582-910-1(5))* America Star Bks.

Friedman, Laurie. Mallory on Board. 2008. pap. 34.95 *(978-0-8225-9440-6(4))* Lerner Publishing Group.

Green, Poppy. It's Raining, It's Pouring. Bell, Jennifer A., illus. 2017. (Adventures of Sophie Mouse Ser.: 10). (ENG.). 128p. (J). (gr. k-4). 17.99 *(978-1-4814-8590-6(3)*, Little Simon) Little Simon.

Gutman, Dan. Flashback Four #2: the Titanic Mission. (Flashback Four Ser.: 2). (ENG.). (J). (gr. 3-7). 2018. 256p. pap. 7.99 *(978-0-06-223636-4(9))* 2017. (Illus.). 240p. 16.99 *(978-0-06-223635-7(0))* HarperCollins Pubs. (HarperCollins).

Hansen, Andra. The Quest: A Story of a Stow Away, Who Eventually Ends up Owning the Ship. For the Barton Reading & Spelling System. 2003. (J). pap. 7.95 *(978-0-9744343-2-2(9)*, SA-305) Bright Solutions for Dyslexia, LLC.

Havercroft, Elizabeth. A Year on a Pirate Ship. 2009. (Time Goes By Ser.). (ENG., Illus.). 24p. (J). (gr. k-3). pap. 8.99 *(978-1-58013-799-7(7)*, 0e71397e-7b0b-489e-80d4-2c57ef622365, First Avenue Editions) Lerner Publishing Group.

Herlong, M. H. The Great Wide Sea. 2010. 304p. (YA). (gr. 7-18). 9.99 *(978-0-14-241670-9(3)*, Puffin Books) Penguin Young Readers Group.

Hofmeister, Alan, et al. The Ship. (Reading for All Learners Ser.). (Illus.). (J). pap. *(978-1-56861-133-4(1))* Swift Learning Resources.

Hopkins, William J. The Sandman: His Sea Stories (Yesterday's Classics) Horne, Diantha W., illus. 2009. 188p. pap. 9.95 *(978-1-59915-303-2(3))* Yesterday's Classics.

—The Sandman: His Ship Stories (Yesterday's Classics) Horne, Diantha W., illus. 2009. 174p. pap. 9.95 *(978-1-59915-302-5(5))* Yesterday's Classics.

Hulme-Cross, Benjamin. Ship of Death. Evergreen, Nelson, illus. 2015. (Dark Hunter Ser.). (ENG.). 64p. (J). (gr. 4-8). pap. 4.99 *(978-1-4677-8090-2(1)*, 82a3aab9-b7a0-4867-a530-ce2eba732b58, Darby Creek) Lerner Publishing Group.

Icanberry, Mark. A Pirate's Feast. 2011. (Illus.). 48p. 14.95 *(978-1-893327-08-5(6))*; pap. 7.95 *(978-1-893327-09-2(4))* Ten Speed Pr. (Tricycle Pr.).

Innocenti, Roberto. My Clementine. 2018. (ENG.). 40p. (J). (gr. 3-6). 18.99 *(978-1-56846-323-0(5)*, 19708, Creative Editions) Creative Co., The.

Jarman, Julia. Stowaway!: Band 14/Ruby (Collins Big Cat) Oldroyd, Mark, illus. 2007. (Collins Big Cat Ser.). (ENG.). 48p. (J). (gr. 3-4). pap. 11.99 *(978-0-00-723088-4(5))* HarperCollins Pubs. Ltd. GBR. Dist: Independent Pubs. Group.

Johnston, James D. The Adventures of Lucas & Celi: Lucas Stows Away. 2009. 32p. pap. 12.99 *(978-1-4343-6372-5(4))* AuthorHouse.

Jones, Rob Lloyd. See Inside Pirate Ships. Muhle, Jorg, illus. 2007. (See Inside Board Bks). 15p. (J). (gr. -1-3). bds. 12.99 *(978-0-7945-1601-7(7)*, Usborne) EDC Publishing.

Keene, Carolyn. Curse of the Arctic Star. 2013. (Nancy Drew Diaries: 1). (ENG.). 208p. (J). (gr. 3-7). pap. 7.99 *(978-1-4169-9072-7(0)*, Aladdin) Simon & Schuster Children's Publishing.

Kellogg, Elijah. The Young Shipbuilders of Elm Island by Rev Elijah Kellogg. 2006. 316p. per. 23.99 *(978-1-4255-3063-1(X))* Michigan Publishing.

Kerkow, Larry. Angel Goes to Sea. 2010. 24p. 12.56 *(978-1-4269-3490-2(4))* Trafford Publishing.

Kimberly Vogel. Everyone's Price: Book 4 of Rae's Story. 2006. 91p. 20.00 *(978-1-4257-1610-3(5))*; pap. 10.00 *(978-1-4257-1611-0(3))* Xlibris Corp.

Kloepfer, John. The Zombie Chasers #6: Zombies of the Caribbean. DeGrand, David, illus. 2014. (Zombie Chasers Ser.: 6). (ENG.). 224p. (J). (gr. 3-7). 16.99 *(978-0-06-229024-3(X)*, HarperCollins) HarperCollins Pubs.

Krulik, Nancy. Super Special: Going Overboard! John and Wendy, illus. 2012. (Katie Kazoo, Switcheroo Ser.: No. 9). 144p. (J). (gr. 2-4). pap. 6.99 *(978-0-448-45681-2(8)*, Grosset & Dunlap) Penguin Young Readers Group.

Lawrence, Iain. The Buccaneers. 2003. (High Seas Trilogy). (Illus.). 244p. (gr. 5-9). 16.50 *(978-0-7569-1454-7(X))* Perfection Learning Corp.

—The Buccaneers. 2003. (High Seas Trilogy Ser.). (ENG., Illus.). 256p. (J). (gr. 3-7). 8.99 *(978-0-440-41671-5(X)*, Yearling) Random Hse. Children's Bks.

Lee, Brian, illus. A Pirate Ship. 2005. (What's Inside? Ser.). *(978-0-7607-6809-9(9))* backpackbook.

Lefroy, Joy, et al. The Catalpa Escape. 2007. 36p. pap. 13.50 *(978-1-921064-60-9(9))* Fremantle Pr. AUS. Dist: Independent Pubs. Group.

Lewis, Amanda West. September 17: A Novel, 1 vol. 2013. (ENG., Illus.). 244p. (J). (gr. 5-8). pap. 14.95 *(978-0-88995-507-3(7)*, 4ca5045b-dd5f-4bbe-a6aa-ef53aee55a8f) Trifolium Bks., Inc. CAN. Dist: Firefly Bks., Ltd.

Light, Steve. Swap! Light, Steve, illus. 2016. (ENG., Illus.). 40p. (J). (gr. -1-2). 16.99 *(978-0-7636-7990-3(9))* Candlewick Pr.

Mateboer, Hans. Peter the Cruise Ship. 2007. (Illus.). 32p. (J). 16.95 *(978-0-9759487-1-2(7))* Mateboer, Johannes Aart.

—Peter the Cruise Ship - to Alaska. 2007. (Illus.). 32p. (J). 16.95 *(978-0-9759487-2-9(5))* Mateboer, Johannes Aart.

Mather, Adriana. Haunting the Deep. (ENG.). (YA). (gr. 7). 2018. 368p. pap. 9.99 *(978-0-553-53954-7(X)*, Ember) 2017. 352p. lib. bdg. 20.99 *(978-0-553-53952-3(3)*, Knopf Bks. for Young Readers) Random Hse. Children's Bks.

McAlister, Hugh. The Flight of the Silver Ship: Around the World Aboard a Giant Dirigible. 2004. reprint ed. pap. 26.95 *(978-1-4179-2616-9(3))* Kessinger Publishing, LLC.

McCanna, Tim. Bitty Bot's Big Beach Getaway. Carpenter, Tad, illus. 2018. (Bitty Bot Ser.). (ENG.). 32p. (J). (gr. -1-3). 17.99 *(978-1-4814-4931-1(1)*, Simon & Schuster/Paula Wiseman Bks.) Simon & Schuster/Paula Wiseman Bks.

McMullan, Kate. I'm Mighty! McMullan, Jim, illus. 2003. (ENG.). 40p. (J). (gr. -1-3). 17.99 *(978-0-06-009290-0(4)*, HarperCollins) HarperCollins Pubs.

Meigs, Cornelia. Clearing Weather. 2018. (ENG., Illus.). 320p. (YA). (gr. 2-6). pap. 8.99 *(978-0-486-81742-2(3)*, 817423) Dover Pubns., Inc.

Miller, Peggy Reiff. The Seagoing Cowboy. Ewart, Claire, illus. 2016. 39p. (J). *(978-0-87178-212-0(X))* Brethren Pr.

Mireles, Debbie. The Map & the Pirate Ship. 2009. 74p. pap. 19.95 *(978-1-61582-417-5(0))* America Star Bks.

Mitchen, Scott. Will of the Pirates. 2008. 180p. 22.95 *(978-0-595-70652-5(5))* iUniverse, Inc.

Morris, Dudley. Mike the Monk. 2011. 58p. 36.95 *(978-1-258-02967-8(7))* Literary Licensing, LLC.

Mowat, Farley. The Black Joke. 2009. (ENG.). 192p. pap. 9.95 *(978-0-7710-6469-2(1)*, Emblem Editions) McClelland & Stewart CAN. Dist: Random Hse., Inc.

Mulazzi, Paola, et al. Disney Fairies Graphic Novel #4: Tinker Bell to the Rescue. 2010. (Disney Fairies Ser.: 4). (ENG., Illus.). 80p. (J). (gr. 1-6). 12.99 *(978-1-59707-230-4(3))* Papercutz.

Newberry, Geoffrey C. The Cape Don Adventure. 2011. 48p. pap. 6.99 *(978-1-61667-262-1(5))* Raider Publishing International.

Nickel, Scott. Blastoff to the Secret Side of the Moon!, 1 vol. Bradley, Jess, illus. 2013. (Comics Land Ser.). (ENG.). 32p. (J). (gr. k-2). 7.95 *(978-1-4342-4273-0(0)*, 120359, Stone Arch Bks.) Capstone.

Northrop, Michael. Polaris. 2017. (ENG., Illus.). 288p. (J). (gr. 4-7). 16.99 *(978-0-545-29716-5(8)*, Scholastic Pr.) Scholastic, Inc.

O'Brien, Duncan. Matson the Mouse. Drage, Robyn, illus. 2011. (J). *(978-0-9686734-2-3(2))* Pier 10 Media.

Osborne, Mary Pope. Dark Day in the Deep Sea. 2009. (Magic Tree House Merlin Missions Ser.: 11). lib. bdg. 16.00 *(978-0-606-01778-7(X))* Turtleback.

Pearson, Ridley. Shell Game. 2013. (Kingdom Keepers Ser.: 5). (J). lib. bdg. 19.65 *(978-0-606-27067-0(1))* Turtleback.

Pighin, Marcel. Tickles the Bear Goes on a Cruise, 1 bk. Mitchell, Hazel, illus. 2006. 48p. (J). per. 10.49 *(978-0-9776679-7-0(9))* MP2ME Enterprise LLC.

Qualey, Marsha. Gracie Laroo Sets Sail. Litten, Kristyna, illus. 2017. (Gracie Laroo Ser.). (ENG.). 40p. (J). (gr. k-2). lib. bdg. 21.32 *(978-1-5158-1439-9(4)*, 135709, Picture Window Bks.) Capstone.

Ransom, Candice. The Life-Saving Adventure of Sam Deal, Shipwreck Rescuer. 2010. pap. 51.02 *(978-0-7613-6918-9(X))* Lerner Publishing Group.

Reasoner, Charles. Inside Jolly Roger's Pirate Ship. Reasoner, Charles, illus. 2007. (Story Book Ser.). (Illus.). 12p. (J). (gr. k). bds. *(978-1-84666-149-5(8)*, Tide Mill Pr.) Top That! Publishing PLC.

Reynolds Naylor, Phyllis. Alice on Board. 2012. (Alice Ser.: 24). (ENG., Illus.). 288p. (YA). (gr. 9). 17.99 *(978-1-4424-4588-8(2)*, Atheneum Bks. for Young Readers) Simon & Schuster Children's Publishing.

Rodda, Emily. The Hungry Isle. 2017. 170p. (J). lib. bdg. *(978-1-61067-638-0(6))* Kane Miller.

—The Hungry Isle: Star of Deltora. 2017. 176p. (J). pap. 5.99 *(978-1-61067-528-4(2))* Kane Miller.

—Shadows of the Master. 2017. 176p. (J). pap. 5.99 *(978-1-61067-525-3(8))* Kane Miller.

—Shadows of the Master: Star of Deltora. 2016. (ENG.). 165p. (J). *(978-1-61067-569-7(X))* Kane Miller.

—The Towers of Illica. 2017. 170p. (J). *(978-1-61067-637-3(8))* Kane Miller.

—The Towers of Illica: Star of Deltora. 2017. 176p. (J). pap. 5.99 *(978-1-61067-527-7(4))* Kane Miller.

—Two Moons. 2016. 165p. (J). *(978-1-61067-570-3(3))* Kane Miller.

—Two Moons: Star of Deltora. 2017. 176p. (J). pap. 5.99 *(978-1-61067-526-0(6))* Kane Miller.

Roddy, Lee. Case of the Dangerous Cruise. 2007. (Ladd Family Adventure Ser.: Vol. 11). (Illus.). 145p. (J). (gr. 3-7). per. 7.99 *(978-0-88062-260-8(1))* Mott Media.

Roots, Arleen. Except Ye Abide in the Ship. Reed, Andreana, illus. 2013. (ENG.). 32p. pap. 12.79 *(978-1-4251-6752-3(7))* Trafford Publishing.

Rothwell, Barbara Yates. The Boy from the Hulks. 2011. 264p. (gr. 4-6). 27.08 *(978-1-4269-9414-2(1))*; pap. 17.08 *(978-1-4269-9415-9(X))* Trafford Publishing.

Roy, Philip. Eco Warrior. 2015. (ENG., Illus.). 232p. pap. 11.95 *(978-1-55380-347-8(7))* Ronsdale Pr. CAN. Dist: SPD-Small Pr. Distribution.

Sanabria, José & Sanabria, José. As Time Went By. 2016. (ENG., Illus.). 48p. (J). (gr. -1-2). 18.95 *(978-0-7358-4248-9(5))* North-South Bks., Inc.

Schrowang, Irene. Sam & Joey's Pirate Ship Adventure. 2013. 16p. pap. 15.99 *(978-1-4817-0333-8(1))* AuthorHouse.

Shearer, Alex. Sea Legs. 2006. (ENG.). 320p. (J). (gr. 5-9). per. 17.99 *(978-0-689-87144-3(9)*, Simon & Schuster/Paula Wiseman Bks.) Simon & Schuster/Paula Wiseman Bks.

The Ship in a Bottle, 6 vols. (Ragged Island Mysteriestm Ser.). 161p. (gr. 5-7). 42.50 *(978-0-322-01648-4(7))* Wright Group/McGraw-Hill.

Sidney, Margaret. Five Little Peppers Abroad. 2008. 212p. per. 14.95 *(978-1-60312-546-8(9))* Aegypan.

Soto, Gary. Chato Goes Cruisin' Guevara, Susan, illus. 2008. (Chato Ser.). (J). 25.95 incl. audio *(978-1-59519-906-5(3))* Live Oak Media.

—Chato Goes Cruisin' Guevara, Susan, illus. 2007. (Chato Ser.). (J). (gr. -1-3). 14.65 *(978-0-7569-8147-1(6))* Perfection Learning Corp.

Southard, Patricia. Captain Andre's Adventure in the Sky. 2008. 27p. pap. 24.95 *(978-1-4241-8613-6(7))* America Star Bks.

Spradlin, Michael P. Into the Killing Seas. 2015. (ENG.). 224p. (J). (gr. 3-7). 16.99 *(978-0-545-72602-3(6)*, Scholastic Pr.) Scholastic, Inc.

Standish, Burt L. Frank Merriwell's Cruise. Rudman, Jack, ed. 2003. (Frank Merriwell Ser.). (YA). (gr. 9-18). 29.95 *(978-0-8373-9326-1(4))*; pap. 9.95 *(978-0-8373-9026-0(5)*, FM-026) Merriwell, Frank Inc.

Stanley, Robert. Nelly Goes Out to Sea, 1 vol. 2010. 46p. pap. 24.95 *(978-1-4489-8828-0(4))* PublishAmerica, Inc.

Stanmore, Tony. Tide of Chance: A Holiday Adventure. 2010. (Illus.). 60p. pap. 10.49 *(978-1-4520-0650-5(4))* AuthorHouse.

Stewart, Paul & Riddell, Chris. Far-Flung Adventures: Corby Flood. 2012. (Far-Flung Adventures Ser.). (ENG.). 256p. (J). (gr. 3-7). 7.99 *(978-0-385-75097-4(8)*, Yearling) Random Hse. Children's Bks.

—Far-Flung Adventures: Fergus Crane. 2011. (Far-Flung Adventures Ser.). (ENG.). 240p. (J). (gr. 3-7). 7.99 *(978-0-385-75112-4(5)*, Yearling) Random Hse. Children's Bks.

Stuchner, Joan Betty. Bagels on Board!, 1 vol. Whamond, Dave, illus. 2015. (Orca Echoes Ser.). (ENG.). 80p. (J). (gr. 1-3). pap. 7.95 *(978-1-4598-0695-5(6))* Orca Bk. Pubs. USA.

Sutton, Laurie S. The Ghost of the Bermuda Triangle, 1 vol. Neely, Scott, illus. 2014. (You Choose Stories: Scooby-Doo Ser.). (ENG.). 112p. (J). (gr. 2-6). 32.65 *(978-1-4342-9126-4(X)*, 125571, Stone Arch Bks.) Capstone.

—The Planet Collector, 1 vol. Vecchio, Luciano, illus. 2014. (Superman: Comic Chapter Bks.). (ENG.). 88p. (J). (gr. 3-7). 21.32 *(978-1-4342-9133-2(2)*, 125579, Stone Arch Bks.) Capstone.

Titelman, Becky. The Wonky Witch & the Witching Well. 2009. 364p. pap. 19.99 *(978-1-4490-2673-8(7))* AuthorHouse.

Troupe, Thomas Kingsley. Robot Ruckus. Tayal, Amit, illus. 2017. (Star Belchers Ser.). (ENG.). 128p. (J). (gr. 3-6). lib. bdg. 25.99 *(978-1-4965-4872-6(8)*, 135637, Stone Arch Bks.) Capstone.

Tzvieli, Neta. The Private Eyes & the Mysterious Submarine. 2009. 149p. 17.99 *(978-1-59826-286-5(6))* Feldheim Pubs.

Umansky, Kaye. Solomon Snow & the Stolen Jewel. Nash, Scott, illus. 2007. (ENG.). 256p. (J). (gr. 2-5). 12.99 *(978-0-7636-2793-5(3))* Candlewick Pr.

Van Dusen, Chris. The Circus Ship. Van Dusen, Chris, illus. (ENG., Illus.). 40p. (J). (gr. -1-3). 2015. 8.99 *(978-0-7636-5592-1(9))* 2009. 18.99 *(978-0-7636-3090-4(X))* Candlewick Pr.

Venable Jr, Al B. Captain Tom, the Sea Adventurer. 2013. 40p. pap. 16.95 *(978-1-63004-037-6(1))* America Star Bks.

Weiland, Peter. So Big yet So Small. Coffey, Kevin, illus. 2012. (J). 14.95 *(978-1-937406-16-5(4))* Amplify Publishing Group.

Wells, Helen. Cherry Ames, Cruise Nurse. 2007. (Cherry Ames Nurse Stories Ser.). 224p. (YA). (gr. 7-12). 14.95 *(978-0-8261-0411-3(8))* Springer Publishing Co., Inc.

Wexler, Django. Ship of Smoke & Steel. 2020. (Wells of Sorcery Trilogy Ser.: 1). (ENG., Illus.). 368p. (YA). pap. 18.99 *(978-0-7653-9725-6(0)*, 900181138, Tor Teen) Doherty, Tom Assocs., LLC.

Whitney, Kim Ablon. The Other Half of Life. 2010. 256p. (YA). (gr. 7). mass mkt. 7.99 *(978-0-375-84422-5(8)*, Laurel Leaf) Random Hse. Children's Bks.

Wolff, Tracy. Book 4: Arrival. Kinsella, Pat, illus. 2016. (Mars Bound Ser.). (ENG.). 48p. (J). (gr. 3-7). lib. bdg. 34.21 *(978-1-62402-200-5(6)*, 24579, Spellbound) Magic Wagon.

Woods, Matilda. The Girl Who Sailed the Stars. Allepuz, Anuska, illus. 2019. (ENG.). 272p. (J). (gr. 3-7). 16.99 *(978-0-525-51524-1(0)*, Philomel Bks.) Penguin Young Readers Group.

SHIPS—HISTORY

Beyer, Mark. Barcos del pasado (Boats of the Past) 2009. (transporte ayer y hoy (Transportation Through the Ages) Ser.). (SPA.). 24p. (gr. 1-2). 42.50 *(978-1-61512-253-0(2)*, Editorial Buenas Letras) Rosen Publishing Group, Inc., The.

—Boats of the Past. 2009. (Transportation Through the Ages Ser.). 24p. (gr. 1-1). 42.50 *(978-1-60854-587-2(3)*, PowerKids Pr.) Rosen Publishing Group, Inc., The.

Burns, Phyllis B. Iron Lady at Sea: From Shipyard to Voyage, A Story of the Great Iron-Hulled Sailing Ship, Star of India. 2nd ed. 2003. (Illus.). 112p. (J). pap. 21.95 *(978-0-9620065-0-0(5))* Burns, Phillys.

Curley, Robert, ed. The Complete History of Ships & Boats: From Sails & Oars to Nuclear-Powered Vessels, 4 vols. 2011. (Transportation & Society Ser.). (ENG.). 192p. (gr. 10-10). (YA). 84.70 *(978-1-61530-770-8(2)*, 14d746ca-ecbd-4370-843e-a416ccf0ebd7); (Illus.). (J). lib. bdg. 42.35 *(978-1-61530-670-1(6)*, ab6de80a-e2b6-48a1-8127-90fcd7acc8e8) Rosen Publishing Group, Inc., The.

Faulkner, Nicholas. A Visual History of Ships & Navigation, 1 vol. 2016. (Visual History of the World Ser.). (ENG., Illus.). 96p. (J). (gr. 8-8). 38.80 *(978-1-4994-6594-5(7)*, 6100f876-8ced-48ff-b09a-6b0a423d36a9) Rosen Publishing Group, Inc., The.

Ireland, Charles E. Toolbox. Diienno, Trish, illus. 2006. (J). *(978-1-892142-30-6(9))* Cedar Tree Bks.

Macaulay, David. Crossing on Time: Steam Engines, Fast Ships, & a Journey to the New World. 2019. (ENG., Illus.). 128p. (J). 24.99 *(978-1-59643-477-6(5)*, 900055833) Roaring Brook Pr.

Macdonald, Fiona. You Wouldn't Want to Sail with Christopher Columbus! 2014. (You Wouldn't Want to... Ser.). (ENG.). 32p. (J). lib. bdg. 29.00 *(978-0-531-21177-9(0)*, Watts, Franklin) Scholastic Library Publishing.

Morris, Neil. Ships. (Past & Present Ser.). (Illus.). 32p. lib. bdg. 24.25 *(978-1-931983-38-9(0))* Chrysalis Education.

Richardson, Gillian. 10 Ships That Rocked the World. Rosen, Kim, illus. 2015. (World of Tens Ser.). (ENG.). 176p. (J). (gr. 4-7). pap. 14.95 *(978-1-55451-781-7(8)*, 9781554517817) Annick Pr., Ltd. CAN. Dist: Publishers Group West (PGW).

Ships to Forts. Date not set. (Illus.). 32p. (YA). (gr. 6-18). pap. 4.00 *(978-1-890541-16-3(8))* Americana Souvenirs & Gifts.

Wolny, Philip. 21st-Century Ships, 1 vol. 2018. (Feats of 21st-Century Engineering Ser.). (ENG.). 48p. (gr. 4-4). 29.60 *(978-0-7660-9700-1(5)*, 91123e9e-9beb-4cfe-a71d-2fe0e732e594) Enslow Publishing, LLC.

SHIPS—MODELS

see Ship Models

SHIPS IN ART

Brecke, Nicole & Stockland, Patricia M. Airplanes & Ships You Can Draw. Brecke, Nicole, illus. 2010. (Ready, Set, Draw! Ser.). (ENG., Illus.). 32p. (gr. 2-4). lib. bdg. 25.26 *(978-0-7613-4166-6(8)*, Millbrook Pr.) Lerner Publishing Group.

Calver, Paul & Reynolds, Toby. How to Draw Cool Ships & Boats: From Sailboats to Ocean Liners. Gowen, Fiona, illus. 2018. (How to Draw Ser.). (ENG.). 32p. (J). (gr. 2-6). pap. 4.99 *(978-1-4380-1056-4(7))* Sourcebooks, Inc.

Curto, Rosa M. Fun & Easy Drawing at Sea, 1 vol. 2013. (Fun & Easy Drawing Ser.). (ENG.). 36p. (gr. k-2). pap. 10.35 *(978-0-7660-6040-1(3)*, a58d07f7-8977-4414-9f7b-dd09764a155d, Enslow Elementary) Enslow Publishing, LLC.

SHIPWRECKS

see also Salvage; Survival

also names of wrecked ships

Addario, Yvonne. Treasure Diving with Captain Dom - Special Archival Section: Special Archival Section. 2007. (ENG., Illus.). 56p. (YA). per. 15.99 *(978-0-9743414-1-5(X))* Adventure in Discovery.

Amstutz, Lisa. The Science of a Shipwreck. 2014. (21st Century Skills Library: Disaster Science Ser.). (ENG., Illus.). 32p. (J). (gr. 4-8). 32.07 *(978-1-63137-627-6(6)*, 205291) Cherry Lake Publishing.

Axelrod-Contrada, Joan. The 12 Worst Shipwrecks of All Time. 2019. (All-Time Worst Disasters Ser.). (ENG., Illus.). 32p. (J). (gr. 3-6). 14.25 *(978-1-63235-605-5(8)*, 13922, 12-Story Library) Bookstaves, LLC.

Benoit, Peter. The Titanic. 2013. (Cornerstones of Freedom™, Third Ser.). (ENG., Illus.). 64p. (J). pap. 8.95 *(978-0-531-21965-2(8))* Scholastic Library Publishing.

—The Titanic Disaster. 2011. (J). pap. *(978-0-531-29026-2(3))* Children's Pr., Ltd.

—The Titanic Disaster. 2011. (True Bks.). 48p. (J). (gr. 3-5). 29.00 *(978-0-531-20627-0(0)*, Children's Pr.) Scholastic Library Publishing.

Bingham, Jane. The Bermuda Triangle, 1 vol. 2013. (Solving Mysteries with Science Ser.). (ENG., Illus.). 48p. (gr. 3-6). pap. 9.95 *(978-1-4109-4991-2(5)*, 121049, Raintree) Capstone.

Blake, Kevin. Titanic's Fatal Voyage. 2018. (Titanica Ser.). (ENG.). 32p. (J). (gr. 2-7). 19.95 *(978-1-68402-432-2(3))* Bearport Publishing Co., Inc.

Blohm, Craig E. The Sinking of the Titanic. 2019. (Historic Disasters & Mysteries Ser.). (ENG.). 64p. (J). (gr. 6-12). 41.27 *(978-1-68282-635-5(X))* ReferencePoint Pr., Inc.

Bodden, Valerie. The Sinking of Titanic. 2018. (Disasters for All Time Ser.). (ENG.). 48p. (J). (gr. 4-7). *(978-1-64026-004-7(8)*, 19722, Creative Education) Creative Co., The.

Brook, Henry. True Sea Stories. 2005. (True Adventure Stories Ser.). (Illus.). 154p. (J). (gr. 5). lib. bdg. 12.95 *(978-1-58086-693-4(X))* EDC Publishing.

Brown, Don. All Stations! Distress! April 15, 1912: the Day the Titanic Sank. Brown, Don, illus. 2010. (Actual Times Ser.: 2). (ENG., Illus.). 64p. (J). (gr. 1-5). pap. 10.99 *(978-1-59643-644-2(1)*, 900068840) Square Fish.

Burlingame, Jeff. The Titanic Tragedy: The Price of Prosperity in a Gilded Age, 1 vol. 2012. (Perspectives On Ser.). (ENG.). 112p. (YA). (gr. 8-8). 42.64 *(978-1-60870-450-7(5)*, a919bc2c-906f-4261-970b-44a50982ee01) Cavendish Square Publishing LLC.

Capek, Michael. The Wilhelm Gustloff Story. 2017. (Famous Ships Ser.). (ENG., Illus.). 112p. (J). (gr. 6-12). lib. bdg. 41.36 *(978-1-5321-1323-9(4)*, 27531, Essential Library) ABDO Publishing Co.

Caper, William. Nightmare on the Titanic. (Code Red Ser.). 32p. (gr. 2-7). 2018. (ENG.). (J). 7.99 *(978-1-64280-066-1(X))* 2007. (Illus.). (YA). lib. bdg. 28.50 *(978-1-59716-362-0(7))* Bearport Publishing Co., Inc.

Claybourne, Anna & Daynes, Katie. Titanic. McNee, Ian, illus. 2006. (Usborne Young Reading Ser.). 64p. (J). (gr. 3-7). 8.99 *(978-0-7945-1269-9(0)*, Usborne) EDC Publishing.

Cook, Peter & Salariya, David. Sail on a 19th-Century Whaling Ship! Grisly Tasks You'd Rather Not Do. Antram, David, illus. 2004. (You Wouldn't Want to Ser.). (ENG.). (J). 29.00 *(978-0-531-12356-0(1))* Scholastic Library Publishing.

Cottman, Michael H. Shackles from the Deep: Tracing the Path of a Sunken Slave Ship, a Bitter Past, & a Rich Legacy. 2017. 128p. (J). (gr. 5-9). 17.99 *(978-1-4263-2663-9(7)*, National Geographic Kids) Disney Publishing Worldwide.

DK. Story of the Titanic. Noon, Steve, illus. 2012. (DK a History Of Ser.). (ENG.). 48p. (J). (gr. 3-7). 18.99 *(978-0-7566-9171-4(0)*, DK Children) Dorling Kindersley Publishing, Inc.

Driscoll, Laura. Titanic: The Story Lives On! Kayganich, Bob, illus. 2012. (Penguin Young Readers: Level 4 Ser.). 48p. (J). (ENG.). (gr. 2-4). 17.44 *(978-0-448-45902-8(7))*; (gr. 3-4). mass mkt. 4.99 *(978-0-448-45757-4(1)*, Penguin Young Readers) Penguin Young Readers Group.

Dubowski, Mark. DK Readers L3: Titanic: The Disaster That Shocked the World! 2015. (DK Readers Level 3 Ser.). (ENG., Illus.). 64p. (J). (gr. 2-4). pap. 4.99 *(978-1-4654-2840-0(2)*, DK Children) Dorling Kindersley Publishing, Inc.

Dunn, Joe & Dunn, Ben. The Titanic, 1 vol. 2007. (Graphic History Ser.). (ENG., Illus.). 32p. (J). (gr. 3-8). 32.79 *(978-1-60270-079-6(6)*, 9044, Graphic Planet - Fiction) Magic Wagon.

Fein, Eric. The USS Greeneville Submarine Disaster. 2009. (When Disaster Strikes! Ser.). 48p. (gr. 5-8). 53.00 *(978-1-60854-783-8(3)*, Rosen Reference) Rosen Publishing Group, Inc., The.

FIONA, Macdonald. Shipwrecks. Kelly, Richard, ed. 2017. 48p. (J). pap. 9.95 *(978-1-78209-395-4(8))* Miles Kelly Publishing, Ltd. GBR. Dist: Parkwest Pubns., Inc.

Fredeen, Charles. Eyewitness to the Sinking of the Lusitania. 2018. (Eyewitness to World War I Ser.). (ENG.). 32p. (J). (gr. 4-7). lib. bdg. 35.64 *(978-1-5038-1607-7(9)*, 211165) Child's World, Inc, The.

Fullman, Joe. The Story of Titanic for Children: Astonishing Little-Known Facts & Details about the Most Famous Ship in the World. 2018. (Y Ser.). (ENG., Illus.). 48p. (J). (gr. 3-7). pap. 12.95 *(978-1-78312-335-3(4))* Carlton Kids GBR. Dist: Two Rivers Distribution.

Gaetán-Beltrán, Daniel, ed. The Titanic, 1 vol. 2015. (Perspectives on Modern World History Ser.). (ENG., Illus.). 200p. (J). (gr. 10-12). 49.43 *(978-0-7377-7310-1(3)*, 9f14e413-e3c9-44a0-9212-6fe18e5ed2bc, Greenhaven Publishing) Greenhaven Publishing LLC.

Ganeri, Anita & West, David. The Sinking of the Titanic & Other Shipwrecks, 1 vol. 2011. (Incredible True Adventures Ser.). (ENG.). 48p. (YA). (gr. 5-5). pap. 12.75 *(978-1-4488-6663-2(4)*, c075d297-3b57-4a61-8423-9a4230f8e669); lib. bdg. 34.47 *(978-1-4488-6659-5(6)*, ca753712-ff23-45c0-846d-1d9707f33019) Rosen Publishing Group, Inc., The. (Rosen Reference).

Glasman, Gabriel., et al. The Secrets of the World's Seas: Atlantis, the Legend of the Lost Continent, & the Bermuda Triangle, 1 vol. 2017. (Secrets of History Ser.). (ENG.). 96p. (YA). (gr. 8-8). pap. 20.99 *(978-1-5026-3442-9(2)*, d8b0ee00-4922-41e9-95c8-720138aae3cc); lib. bdg. 44.50 *(978-1-5026-3275-3(6)*, ee8e6d46-29ed-4cb8-9383-938eeef7e4ea) Cavendish Square Publishing LLC.

Goldish, Meish. Discovering Titanic's Remains. 2018. (Titanica Ser.). (ENG.). 32p. (J). (gr. 2-7). lib. bdg. 28.50 *(978-1-68402-434-6(X))* Bearport Publishing Co., Inc.

—Titanic's Last Hours: The Facts. 2018. (Titanica Ser.). (ENG.). 32p. (J). (gr. 2-7). 19.95 *(978-1-68402-429-2(3))* Bearport Publishing Co., Inc.

Hanel, Rachael, et al. You Choose: Can You Survive Collection. 2017. (You Choose: Survival Ser.). (ENG., Illus.). 328p. (J). (gr. 3-7). pap., pap., pap. 9.99 *(978-1-5157-9081-5(9)*, 136490, Capstone Pr.) Capstone.

Hook. Shipwrecks - Mysteries of the Past. 2004. pap. 48.30 *(978-1-4109-0284-9(6))* Harcourt Schl. Pubs.

Hopkinson, Deborah. Titanic: Voices from the Disaster (Scholastic Focus) 2014. (ENG.). 304p. (J). (gr. 3-7). pap. 8.99 *(978-0-545-11675-6(9))* Scholastic, Inc.

Hunter, Nick. Shipwrecks, 1 vol. 2013. (Treasure Hunters Ser.). (ENG.). 48p. (J). (gr. 5-8). lib. bdg. 32.65 *(978-1-4109-4954-7(0)*, 120946); (Illus.). pap. 9.25 *(978-1-4109-4961-5(3)*, 120952) Capstone. (Raintree).

Jankowski, Susan. True Ocean Rescue Stories, 1 vol. 2011. (True Rescue Stories Ser.). (ENG.). 48p. (gr. 5-7). lib. bdg. 25.27 *(978-0-7660-3665-9(0)*, 0d13b1d8-1968-4595-8f21-5e0acb1bb4bd) Enslow Publishing, LLC.

Jeffrey, Gary. Spectacular Shipwrecks. 2009. (Graphic Discoveries Ser.). (ENG.). 48p. (YA). (gr. 5-5). 58.50 *(978-1-61512-935-5(9)*, Rosen Reference) Rosen Publishing Group, Inc., The.

—Spectacular Shipwrecks, 1 vol. Saraceni, Claudia, illus. 2007. (Graphic Discoveries Ser.). (ENG.). 48p. (gr. 5-5). (J). lib. bdg. 37.13 *(978-1-4042-1091-2(1)*, 8c85c30a-3a0b-49e4-9404-8fd8af57d7bf); pap. 14.05 *(978-1-4042-9597-1(6)*, 17ddbe15-c674-4c53-bb8b-1021e6af496e) Rosen Publishing Group, Inc., The.

Jenkins, Martin. Titanic. Sanders, Brian, illus. 2012. (ENG.). 32p. (J). (gr. 3-7). pap. 6.99 *(978-0-7636-6034-5(5))* Candlewick Pr.

—Titanic: Disaster at Sea. 2012. (Illus.). 31p. lib. bdg. 17.20 *(978-0-606-23811-3(5))* Turtleback.

Karwoski, Gail Langer. Miracle: The True Story of the Wreck of the Sea Venture. MacDonald, John, illus. 2004. (Junior Library Guild Selection Ser.). 64p. (J). (gr. 4-18). 17.95 *(978-1-58196-015-0(8)*, Darby Creek) Lerner Publishing Group.

Kupperberg, Paul. The Tragedy of the Titanic. 2009. (When Disaster Strikes! Ser.). 48p. (gr. 5-8). 53.00 *(978-1-60854-782-1(5)*, Rosen Reference) Rosen Publishing Group, Inc., The.

Lassieur, Allison. Can You Survive the Titanic? An Interactive Survival Adventure, 1 vol. 2011. (You Choose: Survival Ser.). (ENG., 112p. (J). (gr. 3-7). Illus.). lib. bdg. 32.65 *(978-1-4296-6586-5(6)*, 115708); pap. 6.95 *(978-1-4296-7351-8(6)*, 116887) Capstone. (Capstone Pr.).

Loh-Hagan, Virginia. Harrison Okene: Sixty Hours Underwater. 2019. (True Survival Ser.). (ENG., Illus.). 32p. (J). (gr. 4-8). pap. 14.21 *(978-1-5341-3986-2(9)*, 212773); lib. bdg. 32.07 *(978-1-5341-4330-2(0)*, 212772) Cherry Lake Publishing. (45th Parallel Press).

—Mary Celeste. 2017. (Urban Legends: Don't Read Alone! Ser.). (ENG., Illus.). 32p. (J). (gr. 4-8). lib. bdg. 32.07 *(978-1-63472-899-7(8)*, 210022, 45th Parallel Press) Cherry Lake Publishing.

—The Real Violet Jessop. 2019. (History Uncut Ser.). (ENG., Illus.). 32p. (J). (gr. 4-8). pap. 14.21 *(978-1-5341-3992-3(3)*, 212797); lib. bdg. 32.07 *(978-1-5341-4336-4(X)*, 212796) Cherry Lake Publishing. (45th Parallel Press).

—Steven Callahan: Adrift in the Atlantic. 2018. (True Survival Ser.). (ENG., Illus.). 32p. (J). (gr. 4-8). pap. 14.21 *(978-1-5341-0874-5(2)*, 210860); lib. bdg. 32.07 *(978-1-5341-0775-5(4)*, 210859) Cherry Lake Publishing. (45th Parallel Press).

—Women & Children First: Sinking of the Titanic. 2019. (Behind the Curtain Ser.). (ENG., Illus.). 32p. (J). (gr. 4-8). pap. 14.21 *(978-1-5341-3996-1(6)*, 212813); lib. bdg. 32.07 *(978-1-5341-4340-1(8)*, 212812) Cherry Lake Publishing. (45th Parallel Press).

Lusted, Marcia Amidon. The Sinking of the Titanic: A History Perspectives Book. 2013. (Perspectives Library). (ENG., Illus.). 32p. (J). (gr. 4-8). 32.07 *(978-1-62431-421-6(X)*, 202804); pap. 14.21 *(978-1-62431-497-1(X)*, 202806) Cherry Lake Publishing.

MacDonald, Fiona. Shipwrecks. 2010. (Discovery of Life Ser.). 48p. (YA). lib. bdg. 19.95 *(978-1-4222-1527-2(X))* Mason Crest.

Macdonald, Fiona. Shipwrecks, 1 vol. 2014. (100 Facts You Should Know Ser.). (ENG.). 48p. (J). (gr. 4-5). lib. bdg. 33.60 *(978-1-4824-2189-7(5)*, 685b3b9b-f9ff-402a-b28e-3f1d73676352) Stevens, Gareth Publishing LLLP.

Marsh Nigel. Exploring Shipwrecks: Young Reed. 2016. (ENG., Illus.). 48p. (J). (gr. 3-9). 14.99 *(978-1-921580-17-8(8))* New Holland Pubs. Pty, Ltd. AUS. Dist: Independent Pubs. Group.

McCarthy, Tom. Pirates & Shipwrecks: True Stories. 2016. (Mystery & Mayhem Ser.). (ENG., Illus.). 128p. (J). (gr. 3-6). 19.95 *(978-1-61930-471-0(6)*, 106a9167-bf27-46d2-891a-440cbdec514f) Nomad Pr.

McClellan, Ray. The Bermuda Triangle. 2014. (Unexplained Mysteries Ser.). (ENG., Illus.). 24p. (J). (gr. 3-7). lib. bdg. 26.95 *(978-1-62617-102-2(5)*, Epic Bks.) Bellwether Media.

McDonnell, Vincent. Titanic Tragedy. 2007. (ENG.). 160p. (J). (gr. -1-3). per. 12.95 *(978-1-905172-41-2(9)*, Collins Pr., The) M.H. Gill & Co. U. C. IRL. Dist: Dufour Editions, Inc.

McPherson, Stephanie Sammartino. Iceberg, Right Ahead! The Tragedy of the Titanic. (Single Titles Ser.). (ENG., Illus.). 112p. (gr. 6-12). 2011. lib. bdg. 33.26 *(978-0-7613-6756-7(X))* 2015. (YA). E-Book 53.32 *(978-1-4677-5932-8(5)*, 9781467759328, Lerner Digital) Lerner Publishing Group.

Merwin, E. A Haunted Titanic. 2018. (Titanica Ser.). (ENG.). 32p. (J). (gr. 2-7). 19.95 *(978-1-68402-433-9(1))* Bearport Publishing Co., Inc.

Miller, Connie Colwell. The Biggest Shipwrecks. 2018. (History's Biggest Disasters Ser.). (ENG., Illus.). 32p. (J). (gr. 3-9). lib. bdg. 27.32 *(978-1-5157-9988-7(3)*, 136977, Capstone Pr.) Capstone.

Mitchell, Mark. Raising la Belle. Mitchell, Mark, illus. (Professor Wigglestix & the Weather Ser.). (Illus.). 112p. 10.95 *(978-1-57168-703-6(3))* Eakin Pr.

Montgomerie, Adrienne. Ghost Ships. 2012. (ENG.). 32p. (J). *(978-0-7787-8008-3(2))*; pap. *(978-0-7787-8013-7(9))* Crabtree Publishing Co.

Mullenbach, Cheryl. Torpedoed! A World War II Story of a Sinking Passenger Ship & Two Children's Survival at Sea. 2017. (ENG., Illus.). 176p. (J). (gr. 5). 17.99 *(978-1-61373-824-5(2))* Chicago Review Pr., Inc.

Navratil, Elisabeth. Survivors: A True-Life Titanic Story. de Sola Pinto, Joan, tr. 2018. (ENG.). 224p. 15.00 *(978-1-78849-057-3(6))* O'Brien Pr., Ltd., The IRL. Dist: Casemate Pubs. & Bk. Distributors, LLC.

Oachs, Emily Rose. The Titanic. 2019. (Digging up the Past Ser.). (ENG., Illus.). 24p. (J). (gr. 3-7). lib. bdg. 26.95 *(978-1-64487-071-6(1)*, Torque Bks.) Bellwether Media.

Ohlin, Nancy. The Titanic. Larkum, Adam, illus. 2016. (Blast Back! Ser.). (ENG.). 112p. (J). (gr. 2-5). pap. 5.99 *(978-1-4998-0273-3(0))* Little Bee Books Inc.

Otfinoski, Steven. Smooth Sea & a Fighting Chance: The Story of the Sinking of Titanic. 2016. (Tangled History Ser.). (ENG., Illus.). 112p. (J). (gr. 3-9). lib. bdg. 32.65 *(978-1-4914-8453-1(5)*, 130900, Capstone Pr.) Capstone.

Owings, Lisa. Ghost Ships. 2015. (Unexplained Mysteries Ser.). (ENG., Illus.). 24p. (J). (gr. 3-7). lib. bdg. 26.95 *(978-1-62617-202-9(1)*, Epic Bks.) Bellwether Media.

Park, Louise. The Sinking of the Titanic, 1 vol. 2013. (Discovery Education: Sensational True Stories Ser.). (ENG., Illus.). 32p. (J). (gr. 4-5). pap. 11.00 *(978-1-4777-0099-0(4)*, 395291a0-7c6d-4e04-a217-88b3819fbdc3); lib. bdg. 28.93 *(978-1-4777-0057-0(9)*, 595f2e90-803e-4f97-9b07-5777c37e2880) Rosen Publishing Group, Inc., The. (PowerKids Pr.).

Peterson, Megan Cooley. Ghost Ships: Are Ships Really Haunted? 2018. (History's Mysteries Ser.). (ENG.). 32p. (J). (gr. 4-6). pap. 9.99 *(978-1-64466-257-1(4)*, 12281); (Illus.). lib. bdg. *(978-1-68072-410-3(X)*, 12280) Black Rabbit Bks. (Bolt).

Philbrick, Nathaniel. In the Heart of the Sea (Young Readers Edition) The True Story of the Whaleship Essex. 2015. (Illus.). 208p. (J). (gr. 3-7). 8.99 *(978-1-101-99776-5(1)*, Puffin Books) Penguin Young Readers Group.

Pipe, Jim. Sail on an Irish Famine Ship! A Trip Across Teh Atlantic You'd Rather Not Make. Antram, David, illus. 2008. (You Wouldn't Want To... Ser.). (ENG.). 32p. (J). (gr. 4-6). 26.19 *(978-0-531-13913-4(1)*, Watts, Franklin) Scholastic Library Publishing.

—You Wouldn't Want to Sail on an Irish Famine Ship! A Trip Across the Atlanic You'd Rather Not Make. Antram, David, illus. 2008. (You Wouldn't Want to...: History of the World Ser.). (ENG.). 32p. (J). (gr. 4-7). pap. 9.95 *(978-0-531-14854-9(8)*, Watts, Franklin) Scholastic Library Publishing.

Poehlmann, Tristan. The Titanic Story. 2017. (Famous Ships Ser.). (ENG., Illus.). 112p. (J). (gr. 6-12). lib. bdg. 41.36 *(978-1-5321-1321-5(8)*, 27529, Essential Library) ABDO Publishing Co.

Polinsky, Paige V. Ghost Ships. 2019. (Investigating the Unexplained Ser.). (ENG., Illus.). 32p. (J). (gr. 3-8). lib. bdg. 27.95 *(978-1-64487-041-9(X)*, Blastoff! Discovery) Bellwether Media.

Porterfield, Jason. Shipwreck: True Stories of Survival. (Survivor Stories Ser.). 48p. (gr. 5-5). 2009. 53.00 *(978-1-60853-256-8(9)*, Rosen Reference) 2007. (ENG., Illus.). (YA). lib. bdg. 34.47 *(978-1-4042-1000-4(8)*, 9ba7d99f-743b-45f4-b41a-c009cdda42cd) Rosen Publishing Group, Inc., The.

Renaud, Anne. Into the Mist: The Story of the Empress of Ireland. 2010. (ENG., Illus.). 112p. (YA). (gr. 6). pap. 14.99 *(978-1-55488-759-0(3))* Dundurn Pr. CAN. Dist: Publishers Group West (PGW).

Ridley, Frances. Lost at Sea. 2008. (Crabtree Contact Ser.). (ENG., Illus.). 32p. (J). (gr. 3-7). lib. bdg. *(978-0-7787-3809-1(4))* Crabtree Publishing Co.

Roland, James. Frightful Ghost Ships. 2017. (Searchlight Books (tm) — Fear Fest Ser.). (ENG., Illus.). 32p. (J). (gr. 3-5). 30.65 *(978-1-5124-3402-6(7)*, 35f84eeb-eda5-4dd3-b885-1ac409f61014, Lerner Pubns.) Lerner Publishing Group.

Sandler, Martin W. The Whydah: a Pirate Ship Feared, Wrecked, & Found. 2017. (ENG., Illus.). 176p. (J). (gr. 5). 19.99 *(978-0-7636-8033-6(8))* Candlewick Pr.

Schaefer, Lola M. Tow Trucks in Action. 2012. (Transportation Zone Ser.). (ENG.). 24p. (gr. 1-2). pap. 41.70 *(978-1-4296-8396-8(1)*, Capstone Pr.) Capstone.

Shea, Therese M. The Sinking of the Titanic, 1 vol. 2015. (Doomed! Ser.). (ENG.). 32p. (J). (gr. 4-5). pap. 11.50 *(978-1-4824-2944-2(6)*, 8973557f-77b2-4330-973a-b5ffe77c3dfd) Stevens, Gareth Publishing LLLP.

Shoulders, Michael & Shoulders, Debbie. T Is for Titanic: A Titanic Alphabet. Frankenhuyzen, Gijsbert van, illus. 2011. (ENG.). 32p. (J). (gr. 1-4). 17.95 *(978-1-58536-176-2(3)*, 202264) Sleeping Bear Pr.

Silverman, Buffy. Surviving a Shipwreck: The Titanic. 2019. (They Survived (Alternator Books (r)) Ser.). (ENG., Illus.). 32p. (J). (gr. 3-6). 29.32 *(978-1-5415-2352-4(0)*, 29d250a4-cadd-4a1c-a9b6-6d16cb32a121, Lerner Pubns.) Lerner Publishing Group.

Smith, Steven Michael. New Carissa: The Ship That Refused to Die. 2010. 52p. pap. 22.99 *(978-1-4520-6612-7(4))* AuthorHouse.

Stewart, David. You Wouldn't Want to Sail on the Titanic! (Revised Edition) (You Wouldn't Want to...: History of the World) Antram, David, illus. rev. ed. 2013. (You Wouldn't Want To — Ser.). (ENG.). 32p. (J). (gr. 3). pap. 9.95 *(978-0-531-24505-7(5)*, Watts, Franklin) Scholastic Library Publishing.

Stewart, James. Shipwrecks. 2008. (Illus.). 32p. (J). 14.25 *(978-1-59920-206-8(9))*; (gr. 2-6). lib. bdg. 28.50 *(978-1-59920-105-4(4))* Black Rabbit Bks.

Stewart, Melissa. National Geographic Readers: Titanic. 2012. (Readers Ser.). 48p. (J). (gr. 1-3). (ENG.). lib. bdg. 14.90 *(978-1-4263-1060-7(9)*, National Geographic Children's Bks.); (Illus.). pap. 4.99 *(978-1-4263-1059-1(5)*, National Geographic Kids) Disney Publishing Worldwide.

Stine, Megan & Who HQ. Where Is the Bermuda Triangle? Foley, Tim, illus. 2018. (Where Is? Ser.). 112p. (J). (gr. 3-7). 5.99 *(978-1-5247-8626-7(8)*, Penguin Workshop) Penguin Young Readers Group.

Stone, Adam. The Bermuda Triangle. (Illus.). 24p. (J). 2011. *(978-0-531-26400-3(9))* 2010. (ENG., (gr. 3-7). lib. bdg. 26.95 *(978-1-60014-497-4(7)*, Torque Bks.) Bellwether Media.

—The Titanic Disaster. 2014. (Disaster Stories Ser.). (ENG., Illus.). 24p. (J). (gr. 3-8). 29.95 *(978-1-62617-154-1(8)*, Black Sheep) Bellwether Media.

Storm, Marysa. The Bermuda Triangle. 2020. (Little Bit Spooky Ser.). (ENG.). 24p. (J). (gr. k-3). *(978-1-62310-178-7(6)*, 14458, Bolt Jr.) Black Rabbit Bks.

Temple, Bob. The Titanic [Scholastic]: An Interactive History Adventure. 2010. (You Choose: History Ser.). 112p. pap. 0.86 *(978-1-4296-5119-6(9)*, Capstone Pr.) Capstone.

Thompson, Gare. The Monitor: The Iron Warship That Changed the World. Day, Larry, illus. 2003. (All Aboard Reading: Station Stop 3 Ser.). (ENG.). 48p. (J). (gr. 2-4). 16.19 *(978-0-448-43283-0(8))* Penguin Young Readers Group.

Tougias, Michael J. & Sherman, Casey. The Finest Hours. 2015. (True Rescue Ser.). (ENG., Illus.). 208p. (J). (gr. 4-8). pap. 7.99 *(978-1-250-04423-5(5)*, 900128311) Square Fish.

—The Finest Hours (Young Readers Edition) The True Story of a Heroic Sea Rescue. 2014. (True Rescue Ser.). (ENG., Illus.). 176p. (J). (gr. 4-8). 19.99 *(978-0-8050-9764-1(3)*, 900118783, Holt, Henry & Co. Bks. For Young Readers) Holt, Henry & Co.

Troupe, Thomas Kingsley. Surviving a Shipwreck at Sea. 2018. (Survival Guides You Didn't Know You Needed Ser.). (ENG., Illus.). 24p. (J). (gr. 4-6). 28.50 *(978-1-68072-343-4(X)*, 12140, Hi Jinx) Black Rabbit Bks.

—Titanic's Tragic Journey: A Fly on the Wall History. Tejido, Jomike, illus. 2018. (Fly on the Wall History Ser.). (ENG.).

32p. (J). (gr. 1-3). lib. bdg. 27.99 (978-1-5158-1599-0(4), 136252, Picture Window Bks.) Capstone.
Vale, Jenna & Rosenberg, Aaron. Tracking the Bermuda Triangle, 1 vol. 2018. (Paranormal Seekers Ser.). (ENG., Illus.). 64p. (J). (gr. 5-8). pap. 13.95 (978-1-5081-8570-3(0), 43b71e94-3f39-412b-b973-b2aad9cfc457) Rosen Publishing Group, Inc., The.
Walsh, Alice. A Change of Heart, 1 vol. Bennett Banks, Erin, illus. 2018. (ENG.). 32p. (J). pap. 12.95 (978-1-77108-564-9(9), 99931dea-92fc-432b-960d-a95aea5b649a) Nimbus Publishing, Ltd. CAN. Dist: Baker & Taylor Publisher Services (BTPS).
Wargin, Kathy-jo. The Edmund Fitzgerald: The Song of the Bell. Frankenhuyzen, Gijsbert van, illus. 2003. (ENG.). 48p. (J). (gr. 1-4). 17.95 (978-1-58536-126-7(7), 201989) Sleeping Bear Pr.
Wedge, Hayden. Examining Shipwrecks. 2015. (ENG., Illus.). 48p. (J). lib. bdg. 24.95 net. (978-1-934545-67-6(8)) Oliver Pr., Inc.
Welldon, Christine. Children of the Titanic, 1 vol. 2012. (Compass: True Stories for Kids Ser.). (ENG., Illus.). 96p. (J). (gr. 4-7). pap. 14.95 (978-1-55109-892-0(X), 79691984-0924-40d3-8b21-486265a7823d) Nimbus Publishing, Ltd. CAN. Dist: Baker & Taylor Publisher Services (BTPS).
Wick, Walter. Can You See What I See? Treasure Ship: Picture Puzzles to Search & Solve. Wick, Walter, photos by. 2010. (Can You See What I See? Ser.). (ENG., Illus.). 40p. (J). (gr. -1-3). 14.99 (978-0-439-02643-7(1), Cartwheel Bks.) Scholastic, Inc.
Wilkinson, Carole. How to Wreck a Ship. 2007. 96p. (J). pap. (978-1-4207-0737-3(X)) Sundance/Newbridge Educational Publishing.
Wishinsky, Frieda. Remembering the Titanic. 2012. (Scholastic Reader Level 3 Ser.). (ENG.). 32p. (J). (gr. 1-3). pap. 3.99 (978-0-545-35844-6(2), Scholastic Paperbacks) Scholastic, Inc.
Woods, Michael & Woods, Mary B. Disasters at Sea. 2008. (Disasters up Close Ser.). (ENG., Illus.). 64p. (gr. 4-8). lib. bdg. 27.93 (978-0-8225-6773-8(3), Lerner Pubns.) Lerner Publishing Group.
World Book, Inc. Staff, contrib. by. The Bermuda Triangle & Other Mysteries of the Deep. 2015. (Illus.). 48p. (J). (978-0-7166-2672-5(1)) World Bk., Inc.
Yasuda, Anita. Sinking of the Titanic, 1 vol. 2013. (History's Greatest Disasters Ser.). (ENG., Illus.). 48p. (J). (gr. 4-8). lib. bdg. 35.64 (978-1-61783-960-3(4), 9491) ABDO Publishing Co.
—Sinking of the Titanic Paperback. 2013. (History's Greatest Disasters Ser.). (ENG.). (J). (gr. 4-8). pap. 18.50 (978-1-62403-025-3(4), 10774) ABDO Publishing Co.
Yomtov, Nelson. Adrift & Alone: True Tales of Survival at Sea. 2015. (True Stories of Survival Ser.). (ENG.). 32p. (J). (gr. 3-9). lib. bdg. 31.32 (978-1-4914-6572-1(7), 129052, Capstone Pr.) Capstone.
Zullo, Allan. Titanic: Young Survivors (10 True Tales) 2015. (10 True Tales Ser.). (ENG.). 192p. (J). (gr. 3-7). pap. 5.99 (978-0-545-81839-1(7), Scholastic Nonfiction) Scholastic, Inc.

SHIPWRECKS—FICTION

Alger, Horatio. Facing the World. 2006. pap. (978-1-4065-0704-1(0)) Dodo Pr.
Allison, T. A. Noah's Harbour. 2013. 116p. pap. (978-1-78299-579-1(X)) FeedARead.com.
Anton, Amy Way. Ina the Octopus & Her Shipwreck Adventure. Way, MaryFaye, illus. 2008. 28p. pap. 13.99 (978-1-4389-2177-8(2)) AuthorHouse.
Ashley, Bernard. Solitaire. 2012. (Fiction Ser.). 338p. (J). pap. 6.99 (978-0-7945-3031-0(1), Usborne) EDC Publishing.
Autio, Karen. Second Watch, 1 vol. 2005. (ENG., Illus.). 208p. (J). (gr. 4-7). per. 8.95 (978-1-55039-151-0(8)) Sono Nis Pr. CAN. Dist: Orca Bk. Pubs. USA.
Ballantyne, R. The Coral Island. 2006. pap. 14.95 (978-1-55742-666-6(X)) Wildside Pr., LLC.
Ballantyne, R. M. The Young Trawler. 2011. 250p. 27.95 (978-1-4638-9496-2(1)) Rodgers, Alan Bks.
Barnum, P. T. Dick Broadhead: A Story of Perilous Adve. 2006. pap. 30.95 (978-1-4286-1959-3(3)) Kessinger Publishing, LLC.
Bayle, B. J. Perilous Passage. 2007. (ENG.). 184p. (YA). (gr. k-7). pap. 11.99 (978-1-55002-689-4(5)) Dundurn Pr. CAN. Dist: Publishers Group West (PGW).
Bingley, Thomas. Tales of Shipwrecks & Other Disasters. 2006. pap. 26.95 (978-1-4286-5637-6(5)) Kessinger Publishing, LLC.
Black. El MAPA PERDIDO: SPIDERWICK. LAS CRONICAS (VOLUMEN III) 2007. (Escritura desatada Ser.). (SPA., Illus.). 114p. (J). (gr. 4-7). 13.95 (978-84-666-1513-6(X)) Ediciones B ESP. Dist: Spanish Pubs., LLC.
Bodeen, S. A. Found: Book 4 of the Shipwreck Island Series. 2018. (Shipwreck Island Ser.: 4). (ENG.). 160p. (J). pap. 9.99 (978-1-250-02784-9(5), 900104992) Square Fish.
Brezenoff, Steve. Time Voyage, 1 vol. Murphy, Scott, illus. 2012. (Return to Titanic Ser.). (ENG.). 112p. (J). (gr. 3-6). pap. 6.95 (978-1-4342-3909-9(8), 118094, Stone Arch Bks.) Capstone.
Bunting, Eve. S. O. S. Titanic. 2012. (ENG.). 256p. (YA). (gr. 7-12). pap. 7.99 (978-0-15-201305-9(9), 1189458, Clarion Bks.) HarperCollins Pubs.
Charman, Katrina. The Survival Tails: the Titanic. 2018. (Survival Tails Ser.: 1). (ENG., Illus.). 224p. (J). (gr. 3-7). pap. 7.99 (978-0-316-47783-3(4)) Little, Brown Bks. for Young Readers.
—Titanic. 2018. (Survival Tails Ser.: 1). (J). lib. bdg. 18.40 (978-0-606-40981-0(5)) Turtleback.
Collingwood, Harry. The Castaways. 2017. (ENG., Illus.). (J). 24.95 (978-1-374-98145-4(1)); pap. 14.95 (978-1-374-98144-7(3)) Capital Communications, Inc.
—The Castaways. 2008. 172p. 25.95 (978-1-60664-710-3(5)); pap. 13.95 (978-1-60664-209-2(X)) Rodgers, Alan Bks.
Crew, Gary. Pig on the Titanic: A True Story. Whatley, Bruce, illus. 2005. 32p. (J). 15.99 (978-0-06-052305-3(0)) HarperCollins Pubs.
Dafoe, Daniel. Robinson Crusoe. 2012. 338p. pap. 10.99 (978-1-61382-256-2(1)) Simon & Brown.
—Robinson Crusoe: With a Discussion of Resourcefulness. Landgraf, Kenneth, illus. 2003. (Values in Action Illustrated Classics Ser.). 190p. (J). (978-1-59203-035-4(1)) Learning Challenge, Inc.
Dafoe, Daniel, et al. Robinson Crusoe. (Classics Illustrated Ser.). (Illus.). 52p. (YA). pap. 4.95 (978-1-57209-021-7(9)) Classics International Entertainment, Inc.
Defoe, Daniel. Classic Starts(r): Robinson Crusoe: Retold from the Daniel Defoe Original. Akib, Jamel, illus. 2006. (Classic Starts(r) Ser.). 160p. (J). (gr. 2-4). 6.95 (978-1-4027-2664-4(3)) Sterling Publishing Co., Inc.
—Robinson Crusoe: A Graphic Novel. Cabrera, Eva, illus. 2015. (Graphic Revolve: Common Core Editions Ser.). (ENG.). 72p. (J). (gr. 5-9). lib. bdg. 27.99 (978-1-4965-0371-8(6), 128350, Stone Arch Bks.) Capstone.
Dillsworth-Swift, Tammy. The Bermuda Triangle & the Lost Island. 2009. (ENG.). 182p. pap. 16.53 (978-0-557-14503-4(1)) Lulu Pr., Inc.
DiTerlizzi, Tony & Black, Holly. El Arbol Metálico. Abreu, Carlos, tr. 2007. (Escritura desatada Ser.). (SPA., Illus.). 116p. (J). (gr. 4-7). 13.95 (978-84-666-1658-4(6)) Ediciones B ESP. Dist: Spanish Pubs., LLC.
Duey, Kathleen & Bale, Karen A. Titanic: April 1912. 2014. (Survivors Ser.). (ENG., Illus.). 192p. (J). (gr. 3-7). pap. 7.99 (978-1-4424-9051-2(9), Aladdin) Simon & Schuster Children's Publishing.
—Titanic: April 1912. 2014. (Survivors Ser.). (ENG., Illus.). 192p. (J). (gr. 3-7). 15.99 (978-1-4424-9052-9(7), Simon & Schuster/Paula Wiseman Bks.) Simon & Schuster/Paula Wiseman Bks.
Edwards, Garth. #01 Shipwrecked! Stasyuk, Max, illus. 2011. (Adventures of Titch & Mitch, the Ser.). (J). pap. (978-0-7613-8421-2(9)) Inside Pocket Publishing, Ltd.
Fletcher, Corina. Playbook Pirates. Teckentrup, Britta, illus. 2013. (ENG.). 12p. (J). (gr. -1-2). 24.00 (978-0-7636-6606-4(8)) Candlewick Pr.
Garis, Howard Roger. Lulu, Alice & Jammie Wibble Wobble. 2005. 152p. pap. 11.95 (978-1-4218-1564-0(8), 1st World Library - Literary Society) 1st World Publishing, Inc.
—Lulu, Alice & Jimmie Wibblewobble. 2005. 26.95 (978-1-4218-1464-3(1), 1st World Library - Literary Society) 1st World Publishing, Inc.
Grylls, Bear. The Sea Challenge. McCann, Emma, illus. 2017. 118p. (J). pap. (978-1-61067-759-1(2)) Kane Miller.
Hope, Laura Lee. Moving Picture Girls at Sea. 2006. 26.95 (978-1-4218-2979-1(7)); pap. 11.95 (978-1-4218-3079-7(5)) 1st World Publishing, Inc.
—Moving Picture Girls under the Palms. 2006. 26.95 (978-1-4218-2980-7(0)); pap. 11.95 (978-1-4218-3080-3(9)) 1st World Publishing, Inc.
Hunt, Elizabeth Singer. The Search for the Sunken Treasure Bk. 2: Australia. 2007. (Illus.). 110p. (J). (978-1-4242-4190-3(1)) Hachette Bk. Group.
Jane, Sarah. Maiden Voyage: a Titanic Story. 2018. (ENG.). 256p. (J). (gr. 7-7). pap. 9.99 (978-1-338-22665-2(7), Scholastic Pr.) Scholastic, Inc.
Johnson, Sandi. Lost Island. Johnson, Britt & Durant, Sybrina, eds. Sturgeon, Bobbi, illus. l.t. ed. 2014. 28p. (J). (gr. k-5). pap. 12.99 (978-1-929063-69-7(5), 168) Moons & Stars Publishing For Children.
Kingston, William Henry Giles, tr. The Swiss Family Robinson. Wyss, Johann David, illus. 2005. 188p. per. 6.95 (978-1-4209-2269-1(6)) Digireads.com Publishing.
Klimo, Kate. Dog Diaries #14: Sunny. Jessell, Tim, illus. 2019. (Dog Diaries: 14). 160p. (J). (gr. 2-5). pap. 7.99 (978-0-525-64823-9(2), Random Hse. Bks. for Young Readers) Random Hse. Children's Bks.
Korman, Gordon. Escape. 2008. (Island (Playaway Audio) Ser.). (J). 34.99 (978-1-60514-854-0(7)) Findaway World, LLC.
—Island Trilogy. 2005. 404p. (YA). pap. (978-0-681-15634-0(1)) Scholastic, Inc.
—Unsinkable (Titanic, Book 1), Bk. 1. 2011. (Titanic Ser.: 1). (ENG.). 176p. (J). (gr. 4-7). pap. 6.99 (978-0-545-12331-0(3), Scholastic Paperbacks) Scholastic, Inc.
Kositsky, Lynne. Minerva's Voyage. 2009. (ENG., Illus.). 240p. (YA). (gr. 6-18). pap. 10.99 (978-1-55488-439-1(X)) Dundurn Pr. CAN. Dist: Publishers Group West (PGW).
Law, Felicia & Way, Steve. A Storm at Sea: Sorting, Mapping, & Grids in Action, 1 vol. Spoor, Mike, illus. 2009. (Mandrill Mountain Math Mysteries Ser.). (ENG.). 32p. (J). (gr. 2-3). 27.27 (978-1-60754-815-7(1), 8ef36f64-756f-4e9e-ba11-50de241ce395); pap. 11.55 (978-1-60754-820-1(8), 97b78dc7-e6a6-4efd-9acc-1d62e87eeaf2) Rosen Publishing Group, Inc., The. (Windmill Bks.).
Marsh, Carole. The Mystery of the Graveyard of the Atlantic. 2009. (Real Kids, Real Places Ser.). (Illus.). 144p. (J). lib. bdg. 18.99 (978-0-635-07046-3(4), Marsh, Carole Mysteries) Gallopade International.
—The Mystery on the Great Lakes. 2010. (Real Kids, Real Places Ser.). (Illus.). 158p. (J). 18.99 (978-0-635-07449-2(4), Marsh, Carole Mysteries) Gallopade International.
Marsh, Mike. The Efelant Hunters Part One: Shipwreck! Jain, Priti, illus. 2013. 28p. pap. (978-1-927506-21-9(2)) Yellow Toadstool Pr.
Matthews, Andrew. Shakespeare Stories: The Tempest. Ross, Tony, illus. 2003. (ENG.). 64p. (J). (gr. 4-6). pap. 6.99 (978-1-84121-346-0(2), Orchard Bks.) Hachette Children's Group GBR. Dist: Hachette Bk. Group.
McKain, Kelly. The Haunted Shipwreck. Johansson, Cecilia, illus. 2004. (Mermaid Rock Ser.). 48p. (J). (978-0-439-62647-7(1)) Scholastic, Inc.
McKenzie, Lyn. Lavinia's Shoes. 2007. (J). pap. 12.95 (978-0-9788628-5-5(6)) Just Write Bks.
McMann, Lisa. Island of Shipwrecks. 2015. (Unwanteds Ser.: 5). (ENG., Illus.). 480p. (J). (gr. 3-7). pap. 9.99 (978-1-4424-9332-2(1), Aladdin) Simon & Schuster Children's Publishing.
Mead, Richelle. The Emerald Sea. 2018. (Glittering Court Ser.: 3). (ENG.). 496p. (YA). (gr. 7). 19.99 (978-1-59514-845-2(0), Razorbill) Penguin Young Readers Group.
Millet, Lydia. The Fires Beneath the Sea. 2012. (Dissenters Ser.). (ENG.). 256p. (J). (gr. 3-7). pap. 12.00 (978-1-931520-47-8(X), Big Mouth Hse.) Small Beer Pr.
Nielsen, Jennifer A. Iceberg. 2023. (ENG.). 352p. (J). (gr. 3-7). 17.99 (978-1-338-79502-8(3), Scholastic Pr.) Scholastic, Inc.
Osborne, Mary Pope. Tonight on the Titanic. unabr. ed. 2004. (Magic Tree House Ser.: No. 17). 71p. (J). (gr. k-3). pap. 17.00 incl. audio (978-0-8072-0926-4(0), S FTR 249 SP, Listening Library) Random Hse. Audio Publishing Group.
Osborne, Mary Pope & Murdocca, Sal. Esta Noche en el Titanic. Murdocca, Sal, illus. 2008. (Casa del Arbol Ser.: 17).Tr. of Tonight on the Titanic. (SPA., Illus.). (J). (gr. 2-4). pap. 6.99 (978-1-933032-47-4(2)) Lectorum Pubns., Inc.
Phillips, Dee. Titanic. 2014. (Yesterday's Voices Ser.). (YA). lib. bdg. 19.60 (978-0-606-35583-4(9)) Turtleback.
Polacco, Patricia. The Bravest Man in the World. Polacco, Patricia, illus. 2019. (ENG., Illus.). 56p. (J). (gr. -1-3). 17.99 (978-1-4814-9461-8(9), Simon & Schuster Bks. For Young Readers) Simon & Schuster Bks. For Young Readers.
Prager, Ellen. The Shark Whisperer. Caparo, Antonio Javier, illus. 2014. (Tristan Hunt & the Sea Guardians Ser.). (ENG.). 288p. (J). (gr. 3-7). pap. 9.95 (978-1-938063-44-2(9), Mighty Media Junior Readers) Mighty Media Pr.
Prins, Piet. Stefan Derksen's Polar Adventure. 2004. (Illus.). 237p. (J). pap. (978-1-894666-67-1(4)) Inheritance Pubns.
Probst, Jeff & Tebbetts, Chris. Stranded. 2013. (Stranded Ser.: 1). lib. bdg. 17.20 (978-0-606-36788-2(8)) Turtleback.
Probst, Jeff & Tebbetts, Christopher. Desperate Measures. 2016. (Stranded, Shadow Island Ser.: 3). 172p. (J). lib. bdg. 17.20 (978-0-606-37562-7(7)) Turtleback.
—Shadow Island: Desperate Measures. 2016. (Stranded Ser.: 6). (ENG.). 192p. (J). (gr. 3-7). 6.99 (978-0-14-751390-8(1), Puffin Books) Penguin Young Readers Group.
—Shadow Island: the Sabotage. 2015. (Stranded Ser.: 5). (ENG.). 224p. (J). (gr. 3-7). 6.99 (978-0-14-751389-2(8), Puffin Books) Penguin Young Readers Group.
—Stranded. 2013. (Stranded Ser.: 1). (ENG.). 208p. (J). (gr. 3-7). pap. 8.99 (978-0-14-242424-7(2), Puffin Books) Penguin Young Readers Group.
—Trial by Fire. 2013. 174p. (J). (978-0-14-751195-9(X)) Penguin Publishing Group.
—Trial by Fire. 2013. (Stranded Ser.: 2). (ENG.). 208p. (J). (gr. 3-7). pap. 8.99 (978-0-14-242425-4(0), Puffin Books) Penguin Young Readers Group.
R. M. Ballantyne. The Coral Island. 2007. 316p. per. 14.95 (978-1-4218-4004-8(9), 1st World Library - Literary Society) 1st World Publishing, Inc.
Ransome, Arthur. Swallowdale. 2010. (Swallows & Amazons Ser.). (ENG., Illus.). 431p. (J). pap. 15.95 (978-1-56792-421-3(2)) Godine, David R. Pub.
Raver-Lampman, Greg. Adrift: Lost in Life, Marooned at Sea. 2006. 132p. 14.95 (978-1-888842-32-6(6)) Absey & Co.
Reilly, Carmel, et al. Shipwreck. 2008. (Rigby Focus Forward: Level O Ser.). (Illus.). 24p. (J). (gr. 4-7). pap. (978-1-4190-3850-1(8), Rigby) Pearson Education Australia.
Romeu, Emma. Naufragio en las Filipinas. 2003.Tr. of Shipwrecked in the Philippines. (SPA., Illus.). 162p. (J). (gr. 5-8). pap. 9.95 (978-968-19-0555-2(5)) Santillana USA Publishing Co., Inc.
Saddleback Educational Publishing Staff, ed. River, 1 vol. unabr. ed. 2010. (Heights Ser.). (ENG.). 50p. (gr. 4-8). pap. 9.75 (978-1-61651-281-1(4)) Saddleback Educational Publishing, Inc.
Shakespeare, William. The Tempest: The Graphic Novel, 1 vol. 2011. (Classic Graphic Novel Collection). (ENG.). 144p. (gr. 7-10). lib. bdg. 41.03 (978-1-4205-0632-7(3), 33031fef-3bcc-4f2b-b6b1-9b876d12a7ce, Lucent Pr.) Greenhaven Publishing LLC.
Shipwrecked!, 6 vols., Pack. (Bookweb Ser.). 32p. (gr. 4-18). 34.00 (978-0-7635-3736-4(5)) Rigby Education.
Smith, Nikki Shannon. Noelle at Sea: A Titanic Survival Story. Forsyth, Matt, illus. 2019. (Girls Survive Ser.). (ENG.). 112p. (J). (gr. 3-7). lib. bdg. 25.99 (978-1-4965-7850-1(3), 139368, Stone Arch Bks.) Capstone.
Spickett, D. M. The Adventures of Sarah the Seahorse, 1 vol. 2009. 21p. pap. 24.95 (978-1-61546-205-6(8)) America Star Bks.
Stewart, Whitney. Marshall: A Nantucket Sea Rescue. Lyall, Dennis, illus. 2008. (ENG.). 32p. (J). (gr. -1-2). 2.95 (978-1-59249-856-7(6)); 6.95 (978-1-59249-855-0(8)); 10.95 (978-1-59249-857-4(4)) Soundprints.
—Marshall, the Sea Dog. 2010. (ENG.). 56p. (J). (gr. 4-7). 17.95 (978-1-60727-183-3(4)) Soundprints.
Stilton, Gerónimo & Stilton, Thea. Thea Stilton & the Ghost of the Shipwreck. 2010. (Thea Stilton Ser.: 3). lib. bdg. 19.65 (978-0-606-06843-7(0)) Turtleback.
Stilton, Thea. Thea Stilton & the Ghost of the Shipwreck (Thea Stilton #3) A Geronimo Stilton Adventure. 2010. (Thea Stilton Ser.: 3). Orig. Title: Il Vascello Fantasma. (ENG., Illus.). 176p. (J). (gr. 2-5). pap. 8.99 (978-0-545-15059-0(0), Scholastic Paperbacks) Scholastic, Inc.
Swift, Jonathan. Los Viajes de Gulliver. (SPA., Illus.). 144p. (YA). 14.95 (978-84-7281-080-8(1), AF1080) Auriga, Ediciones S.A. ESP. Dist: Continental Bk. Co., Inc.
—Los Viajes de Gulliver. (Coleccion Clasicos de la Juventud). (SPA., Illus.). 204p. (J). 12.95 (978-84-7189-062-7(3), ORT322) Ortells, Alfredo Editorial S.L. ESP. Dist: Continental Bk. Co., Inc.
Tarshis, Lauren. I Survived the Sinking of the Titanic 1912. 2010. (I Survived Ser.: No. 1). lib. bdg. 14.75 (978-0-606-23741-3(0)) Turtleback.
—I Survived the Sinking of the Titanic, 1912 (I Survived #1) Dawson, Scott, illus. 2010. (I Survived Ser.: 1). (ENG.). 112p. (J). (gr. 2-5). 4.99 (978-0-545-20694-5(4), Scholastic Paperbacks) Scholastic, Inc.
Taylor, Theodore. The Cay. 2003. (ENG.). 160p. (J). (gr. 5-7). mass mkt. 7.99 (978-0-440-22912-4(X), Laurel Leaf) Random Hse. Children's Bks.
—Teetoncey. 2004. (ENG., Illus.). 228p. (J). (gr. 3-7). pap. 13.95 (978-0-15-205294-2(1), 1195951, Clarion Bks.) HarperCollins Pubs.
—Teetoncey & Ben O'neal. 2004. (ENG., Illus.). 240p. (J). (gr. 3-7). pap. 15.95 (978-0-15-205297-3(6), 1195960, Clarion Bks.) HarperCollins Pubs.
—Timothy of the Cay. 2007. (ENG., Illus.). 176p. (J). (gr. 5-7). pap. 7.99 (978-0-15-206320-7(X), 1198928, Clarion Bks.) HarperCollins Pubs.
Taylor, Theodore & Taylor, Theodore. The Cay. 2003. (gr. 5-8). lib. bdg. 17.20 (978-0-613-72282-7(5)) Turtleback.
Taylor, Will. Maggie & Abby & the Shipwreck Treehouse. 2019. (ENG.). 400p. (J). (gr. 3-7). 16.99 (978-0-06-264434-3(3), HarperCollins) HarperCollins Pubs.
Thompson, Paul B. Lost Republic, 1 vol. 2015. (Scarlet Voyage Ser.). (ENG.). 256p. (gr. 6-7). 23.61 (978-1-62324-000-4(X), 7d18d20e-88c8-4879-b024-02bdf91c8627) Enslow Publishing, LLC.
Trimper, Marty. Hermione: Shipwrecked! in Ocean City, Maryland. Amy, Holloway, illus. 2004. (J). (978-1-886068-28-5(3)) Fruitbearer Publishing, LLC.
Van Dusen, Chris. The Circus Ship. Van Dusen, Chris, illus. 2015. (ENG., Illus.). 40p. (J). (gr. -1-3). 8.99 (978-0-7636-5592-1(9)) Candlewick Pr.
Vern, Jules. Dick Sand. Munro, George, tr. 2008. 296p. pap. 15.95 (978-1-60664-253-5(7)) Rodgers, Alan Bks.
Vicary, Tim. Oxford Bookworms Library: Grace Darling: Level 2: 700-Word Vocabulary. 3rd ed. 2008. (ENG., Illus.). 64p. pap. 11.00 (978-0-19-479061-1(4)) Oxford Univ. Pr., Inc.
Wade, Judith. The Mermaid's Gift. 2004. 140p. (J). per. 5.99 (978-0-9728958-1-1(7), 750) Riley Pr.
Walsh, Alice. Heroes of Isle aux Morts. 2004. (J). (gr. k-3). spiral bd. (978-0-616-11139-0(8)); spiral bd. (978-0-616-11138-3(X)) Canadian National Institute for the Blind/Institut National Canadien pour les Aveugles.
Watson, Jude. Mission Titanic (the 39 Clues: Doublecross, Book 1) 2014. (Geronimo Stilton Ser.: 1). (ENG.). 240p. (J). (gr. 2-5). E-Book 7.99 (978-0-545-76918-1(3)) Scholastic, Inc.
White, Ellen Emerson. Voyage on the Great Titanic. 2010. (Dear America Ser.). (ENG., Illus.). 208p. (J). (gr. 3-9). 12.99 (978-0-545-23834-2(X), Scholastic Pr.) Scholastic, Inc.
Wilkes, Angela & Rawson, Christopher. Robinson Crusoe. 2004. (Young Reading Ser.). (Illus.). 64p. (J). (gr. 2-18). pap. 5.95 (978-0-7945-0410-6(8), Usborne) EDC Publishing.
Wilkinson, Carole. Buried at Sea. 2007. 96p. (YA). pap. (978-1-4207-0738-0(8)) Sundance/Newbridge Educational Publishing.
Wyss, Johann David. The Swiss Family Robinson. Monahan, Liz, illus. 2014. 46p. (J). (978-1-4351-5826-9(1)) Barnes & Noble, Inc.
—The Swiss Family Robinson. 2007. (Aladdin Classics Ser.). (ENG.). 576p. (J). (gr. 3-7). pap. 7.99 (978-1-4169-3490-5(1), Aladdin) Simon & Schuster Children's Publishing.
Yomtov, Nel. Titanic Disaster! Nickolas Flux & the Sinking of the Great Ship. Simmons, Mark, illus. 2015. (Nickolas Flux History Chronicles Ser.). (ENG.). 40p. (J). (gr. 3-9). lib. bdg. 33.32 (978-1-4914-2070-6(7), 127548, Capstone Pr.) Capstone.
Zafon, Carlos Ruiz. The Prince of Mist. 2011. (ENG.). 256p. (YA). (gr. 7-17). pap., pap. 14.99 (978-0-316-04480-6(6)) Little, Brown Bks. for Young Readers.
Zajonc, Taylor. The Iron Island. Rodriguez, Geraldine, illus. 2018. (Adventures of Samuel Oliver Ser.). (ENG.). 48p. (J). (gr. 3-7). lib. bdg. 34.21 (978-1-5321-3373-2(1), 31169, Spellbound) Magic Wagon.
Zullo, Allan. Titanic Young Survivors. 2012. 181p. (J). (978-0-545-33315-3(6)) Scholastic, Inc.

SHIRLEY, ANNE (FICTITIOUS CHARACTER)—FICTION

George, Kallie. Anne Arrives: Inspired by Anne of Green Gables. Halpin, Abigail, illus. 2018. (Anne Chapter Book Ser.: 1). 72p. (J). (gr. 1-4). 12.99 (978-1-77049-930-0(X), Tundra Bks.) Tundra Bks. CAN. Dist: Penguin Random Hse. LLC.
—Goodnight, Anne: Inspired by Anne of Green Gables. Godbout, Geneviève, illus. 2018. 40p. (J). (gr. -1-2). 17.99 (978-1-77049-926-3(1), Tundra Bks.) Tundra Bks. CAN. Dist: Penguin Random Hse. LLC.
—If I Couldn't Be Anne. Godbout, Geneviève, illus. 2020. (ENG.). 40p. (J). (gr. -1-2). 17.99 (978-1-77049-928-7(8), Tundra Bks.) Tundra Bks. CAN. Dist: Penguin Random Hse. LLC.
Helldorfer, M. C. Anne of Green Gables. Beier, Ellen, illus. 2003. 40p. (J). (gr. -1-2). pap. 7.99 (978-0-440-41614-2(0), Dragonfly Bks.) Random Hse. Children's Bks.
Hill, Kelly, illus. Anne's Numbers: Inspired by Anne of Green Gables. 2018. (Anne of Green Gables Ser.). 22p. (J). (— 1). bds. 8.99 (978-0-7352-6285-0(3), Tundra Bks.) Tundra Bks. CAN. Dist: Penguin Random Hse. LLC.
Montgomery, L. M. Anne of Avonlea. 2018. (ENG., Illus.). 250p. (J). (gr. 3-7). pap. (978-93-5297-101-5(9)) Alpha Editions.
—Anne of Avonlea. (ENG., Illus.). (J). 2018. 400p. pap. 17.95 (978-1-376-49928-5(2)) 2015. 27.95 (978-1-297-91573-4(9)) Creative Media Partners, LLC.
—Anne of Avonlea. 2018. (Anne of Green Gables: the Complete Collection: 2). (ENG.). 336p. (J). (gr. 6-12). 8.99 (978-1-78226-444-6(2), 5ab6e735-475a-4e0f-a18b-99628df1f473) Sweet Cherry Publishing GBR. Dist: Baker & Taylor Publisher Services (BTPS).
—Anne of Avonlea. 2018. (ENG., Illus.). 276p. (YA). 24.99 (978-1-5287-0644-5(7), Classic Bks. Library) The Editorium, LLC.
—Anne of Avonlea. 2019. (ENG.). 262p. (J). pap. 11.89 (978-1-7278-8486-9(8)) CreateSpace Independent Publishing Platform.
—Anne of Avonlea. (ENG.). 2019. 268p. (J). pap. 12.99 (978-1-7018-6034-6(1)) 2019. 386p. (J). pap. 22.99 (978-1-0899-1022-0(3)) 2019. 818p. (J). pap. 46.99 (978-1-0781-0625-2(8)) 2019. 544p. (J). pap. 35.99 (978-1-0780-6471-2(7)) 2019. 546p. (J). pap. 35.99 (978-1-0800-7977-3(7)) 2019. 386p. (J). pap. 22.99 (978-1-0807-5704-6(X)) 2019. 546p. (J). pap. 36.99 (978-1-0825-6163-4(0)) 2019. 386p. (J). pap. 22.99 (978-1-0830-1790-1(X)) 2019. 546p. (J). pap. 31.99 (978-1-0753-6837-0(5)) 2019. 386p. (YA). pap. 22.99 (978-1-0726-8331-5(8)) 2019. 364p. (YA). pap. 19.99 (978-1-0968-7536-9(5)) 2019. 568p. (YA). pap. 33.99 (978-1-0987-6527-9(3)) 2019. 268p. (YA). pap. 18.99 (978-1-0705-9376-0(1)) 2019. 546p. (YA). pap. 30.99 (978-1-0707-5140-5(5)) 2019. 268p. (YA). pap. 16.99 (978-1-0954-6547-9(3)) 2019. 546p. (YA). pap. 34.99 (978-1-0916-4683-4(X)) 2019. 506p. (YA). pap. 29.99 (978-1-7965-5870-8(2)) 2019. (Illus.). 546p. (YA). pap. 34.99

(978-1-7929-7537-0(6)) 2018. (Illus.). 240p. (YA). pap. 15.99 *(978-1-7919-1487-5(X))* Independently Published.
—Anne of Avonlea. 2019. (ENG.). 252p. (J). pap. 27.99 *(978-1-7077-7448-7(X))* Independently Published.
—Anne of Avonlea. 2012. (World Classics Ser.). (ENG.). 228p. pap. 19.99 *(978-1-909438-94-1(4),* Sovereign) Bollinger, Max GBR. Dist: Gardners Bks. Ltd., Lightning Source UK, Ltd.
—Anne of Green Gables. 400p. 2005. 33.95 *(978-1-4218-0660-0(6),* 1st World Library - Literary Society) 2004. per. 16.95 *(978-1-59540-110-6(5))* 1st World Publishing, Inc.
—Anne of Green Gables. 2009. 292p. 27.99 *(978-1-60512-375-2(7));* pap. 14.99 *(978-1-60512-475-9(3))* Akasha Publishing, LLC. (Akasha Classics).
—Anne of Green Gables. 2012. (World Classics Ser.). (ENG.). 260p. pap. 19.99 *(978-1-909438-96-5(0),* Sovereign) Bollinger, Max GBR. Dist: Lightning Source UK, Ltd.
—Anne of Green Gables. 2008. 316p. 28.99 *(978-0-554-32848-5(8))* 2008. 316p. 29.99 *(978-0-554-23545-5(5))* 2007. (ENG.). 312p. pap. 24.99 *(978-1-4264-4662-7(4))* Creative Media Partners, LLC.
—Anne of Green Gables. 2008. (Anne of Green Gables Ser.). (ENG.). 366p. (J). (gr. 4-7). pap. 9.95 *(978-0-9782552-6-8(7))* Davenport Pr. CAN. Dist: Independent Pubs. Group.
—Anne of Green Gables. 2007. per. 6.99 *(978-1-4209-2922-5(4))* Digireads.com Publishing.
—Anne of Green Gables. 2007. 284p. per. *(978-1-4065-6399-3(4))* Dodo Pr.
—Anne of Green Gables. 2007. 572p. *(978-1-84702-773-3(3))* 2006. pap. *(978-1-4068-2170-3(5))* 2006. pap. *(978-1-4068-3174-0(3))* Echo Library.
—Anne of Green Gables. 2009. 242p. pap. 8.58 *(978-0-217-43952-7(7))* General Bks. LLC.
—Anne of Green Gables. 2005. (My First Classics Ser.). 112p. (J). (gr. k-3). pap., pap. 4.99 *(978-0-06-079147-6(0),* HarperFestival) HarperCollins Pubs.
—Anne of Green Gables. 2005. 21.99 *(978-1-4142-5125-7(4))* IndyPublish.com.
—Anne of Green Gables. 2004. reprint ed. pap. 1.99 *(978-1-4192-0717-4(2));* pap. 27.95 *(978-1-4191-0717-7(8))* Kessinger Publishing, LLC.
—Anne of Green Gables. l.t. ed. 2009. (World Classics Ser.). (ENG.). 384p. pap. 21.95 *(978-1-59688-123-5(2))* Large Print Bk. Co., The.
—Anne of Green Gables. 2003. (ENG.). 320p. (gr. 5-7). 5.95 *(978-0-451-52882-7(4),* Signet) Penguin Publishing Group.
—Anne of Green Gables. 2008. (Puffin Classics Ser.). (Illus.). 464p. (J). (gr. 3-7). 8.99 *(978-0-14-132159-2(8),* Puffin Books) Penguin Young Readers Group.
—Anne of Green Gables. 2003. 320p. (J). (gr. 4-7). 12.60 *(978-0-7569-1848-4(0))* Perfection Learning Corp.
—Anne of Green Gables. 2008. (Modern Library Classics Ser.). (ENG.). 320p. pap. 11.00 *(978-0-8129-7903-9(6),* Modern Library) Random House Publishing Group.
—Anne of Green Gables. 2014. (Official Anne of Green Gables Ser.: 1). 352p. (YA). (gr. 5-12). pap. 13.99 *(978-1-4022-8894-4(8))* Sourcebooks, Inc.
—Anne of Green Gables. 2009. 224p. pap. 15.45 *(978-1-4385-1847-3(1),* Bk. Jungle) Standard Publications, Inc.
—Anne of Green Gables. 2008. 316p. pap. 16.95 *(978-1-60096-565-4(2));* pap. 16.95 *(978-1-60096-101-4(0))* The Editorium, LLC.
—Anne of Green Gables: Norton Critical Edition. Rubio, Mary Henley & Waterston, Elizabeth, eds. 2007. (Norton Critical Editions Ser.: 0). (ENG., Illus.). 464p. (C). (gr. 9-12). per. 16.00 net. *(978-0-393-92695-8(8),* 92695) Norton, W. W. & Co., Inc.
—The Anne of Green Gables Collection: Six Complete & Unabridged Novels in One Volume. 2013. 1140p. *(978-1-78139-344-4(3))* Benediction Classics.
—Anne of Green Gables Cookbook. 22.95 *(978-0-8488-2657-4(4))* Amereon Ltd.
—Anne of Green Gables Diary. 22.95 *(978-0-8488-2654-3(X))* Amereon Ltd.
—Anne of the Island. 2018. (ENG., Illus.). 240p. (J). (gr. 2-5). pap. *(978-93-5297-102-2(7))* Alpha Editions.
—Anne of the Island. 2017. (ENG., Illus.). (J). 28.99 *(978-1-366-55836-7(7))* Blurb, Inc.
—Anne of the Island. 2017. (ENG., Illus.). (J). 25.95 *(978-1-374-89884-4(8));* pap. 15.95 *(978-1-374-89883-7(X))* Capital Communications, Inc.
—Anne of the Island. (ENG., Illus.). (J). 2017. pap. 15.90 *(978-1-375-53109-2(3))* 2015. 26.95 *(978-1-297-59159-4(3))* Creative Media Partners, LLC.
—Anne of the Island. 2008. (Anne of Green Gables Ser.). (ENG.). 272p. (J). (gr. 4-7). pap. 9.95 *(978-0-9782552-8-2(3))* Davenport Pr. CAN. Dist: Independent Pubs. Group.
—Anne of the Island. 2006. (ENG.). pap. *(978-1-4068-2171-0(3))* Echo Library.
—Anne of the Island. 2010. (Puffin Classics Ser.). (ENG.). 368p. (J). (gr. 5-7). pap. 7.99 *(978-0-14-132736-5(7),* Puffin Books) Penguin Young Readers Group.
—Anne of the Island. 2018. (Anne of Green Gables: the Complete Collection: 3). (ENG.). 312p. (J). (gr. 6-12). 8.99 *(978-1-78226-445-3(0),* 6a902ad3-6883-4c7e-8532-21673815d7a9) Sweet Cherry Publishing GBR. Dist: Baker & Taylor Publisher Services (BTPS).
—Anne of the Island. 2018. (ENG., Illus.). 258p. (YA). 24.99 *(978-1-5287-0650-6(1),* Classic Bks. Library) The Editorium, LLC.
—Anne of the Island. 2019. (ENG.). 250p. (J). pap. 11.89 *(978-1-7278-8584-2(8))* CreateSpace Independent Publishing Platform.
—Anne of the Island. (ENG.). (J). 2019. 252p. pap. 11.99 *(978-1-7018-6205-0(0))* 2019. 352p. pap. 19.99 *(978-1-0899-1090-9(8))* 2019. 498p. pap. 33.99 *(978-1-0825-6062-0(6))* 2019. 788p. pap. 45.99 *(978-1-0804-7520-9(6))* 2019. 466p. pap. 32.99 *(978-1-0799-0876-3(5))* 2019. 740p. pap. 43.99 *(978-1-0776-6557-6(1))* 2019. 788p. pap. 45.99 *(978-1-0828-3158-4(1))* 2019. 498p. pap. 31.99 *(978-1-0753-6839-4(1))* 2019. 352p. pap. 19.99 *(978-1-0726-8332-2(6))* 2019. 342p. pap. 19.99 *(978-1-0968-7543-7(8))* 2019. 252p. pap. 17.99 *(978-1-0705-9734-8(1))* 2019. 500p. pap. 29.99 *(978-1-0707-5185-6(5))* 2019. 526p. pap. 29.99 *(978-1-0985-3618-3(5))* 2019. 498p. pap. 32.99 *(978-1-0916-4685-8(6))* 2019. 462p. pap. 25.99 *(978-1-7965-5869-2(9))* 2019. 136p. pap. 8.60 *(978-1-7953-3769-4(9))* 2018. (Illus.). 224p. pap. 14.99 *(978-1-7919-1456-1(X))* Independently Published.
—Anne of the Island. 2019. (ENG.). 232p. (J). pap. 27.99 *(978-1-7077-7514-9(1))* Independently Published.
—Anne of the Island. 2012. (World Classics Ser.). (ENG.). 212p. pap. 19.99 *(978-1-909438-92-7(8),* Sovereign) Bollinger, Max GBR. Dist: Lightning Source UK, Ltd.
—Anne of the Island. l.t. ed. 2006. (ENG.). pap. *(978-1-4068-3175-7(1))* Echo Library.
—Anne of the Island. 2004. reprint ed. pap. 1.99 *(978-1-4192-0718-1(0));* pap. 30.95 *(978-1-4179-0885-1(8))* Kessinger Publishing, LLC.
—Anne of the Island. l.t. ed. 2004. 396p. 26.00 *(978-1-58287-640-5(1))* North Bks.
—Rilla of Ingleside. 2004. 224p. (YA). pap. 10.95 *(978-1-57646-891-3(7))* Quiet Vision Publishing.
Montgomery, Lucy Maud. Anne of Avonlea. 2019. (ENG.). (J). (gr. 3-7). 276p. pap. 12.95 *(978-0-368-78940-3(3));* 96p. pap. 12.71 *(978-0-368-28129-7(9))* Blurb, Inc.
—Anne of Avonlea. (ENG.). (J). (gr. 3-7). 2020. 170p. (YA). pap. 9.99 *(978-1-6594-8477-9(4))* 2018. (Illus.). 594p. (J). pap. 34.99 *(978-1-7916-6454-1(7))* Independently Published.
—Anne of Avonlea. Blake, Sheba, ed. 2020. (ENG.). 254p. (YA). (gr. 3-7). pap. 14.99 *(978-1-222-29341-8(2))* Indy Pub.
—Anne of Avonlea. 2008. (ENG., Illus.). 268p. (J). (gr. 3-7). 18.99 *(978-1-4341-1489-1(9),* Waking Lion Press) The Editorium, LLC.
—Anne of Green Gables: Stories for Young Readers, 1 vol. Smith, David Preston, illus. 2008. (ENG.). 46p. (J). (gr. 1-3). pap. 12.95 *(978-1-55109-662-9(5),* 3b164d3e-d44c-49e5-9188-05373178fc3d) Nimbus Publishing, Ltd. CAN. Dist: Baker & Taylor Publisher Services (BTPS).
—Anne of the Island. 2019. (ENG.). (J). (gr. 2-5). 276p. pap. 12.95 *(978-0-368-79656-2(6));* 94p. pap. 12.55 *(978-0-368-28130-3(2))* Blurb, Inc.
—Anne of the Island. 2018. (ENG.). 328p. (J). (gr. 2-5). 44.95 *(978-0-343-91137-9(X));* pap. 27.95 *(978-0-343-91136-2(1))* Creative Media Partners, LLC.
—Anne of the Island. 2019. (ENG.). (J). (gr. 2-5). 734p. pap. 46.99 *(978-1-6681-5126-0(5));* 736p. pap. 43.99 *(978-1-0968-8163-6(2));* 448p. pap. 25.99 *(978-1-0932-8992-3(9))* Independently Published.
Montgomery, Lucy Maud & Grandma's Treasures. Anne of Avonlea. 2019. (ENG.). 252p. (YA). (gr. 3-7). *(978-1-7948-2437-9(5))* Lulu Pr., Inc.
Montgomery, Lucy Maud & Treasures, Grandma's. Anne of Avonlea. 2019. (ENG.). 252p. (YA). (gr. 3-7). pap. *(978-1-7948-2462-1(6))* Lulu Pr., Inc.
Stellings, Caroline. The Contest, 1 vol. 2009. (ENG.). 160p. (J). (gr. 4-7). pap. 9.95 *(978-0-9779183-5-5(1),* 7th Generation) BPC.
Sullivan, Kevin. A New Beginning. 2009. (Anne of Green Gables Ser.). (ENG.). 290p. (J). (gr. 7). pap. 19.95 *(978-0-9811418-1-7(1))* Davenport Pr. CAN. Dist: Independent Pubs. Group.
Sullivan, Kevin & Goldman, Leslie. Anne & the Bully. 2010. (Anne of Green Gables for Young Readers Ser.). (ENG.). 64p. (J). (gr. 2-4). pap. 4.95 *(978-0-9736803-8-6(5))* Davenport Pr. CAN. Dist: Independent Pubs. Group.
—Anne's Babysitting Blues. 2010. (Anne of Green Gables for Young Readers Ser.). (ENG.). 64p. (J). (gr. 2-4). pap. 4.95 *(978-0-9736803-1-7(8))* Davenport Pr. CAN. Dist: Independent Pubs. Group.
—Anne's Red Hair. 2010. (Anne of Green Gables Picture Bks.). (ENG.). 32p. (J). (gr. k-2). pap. 4.95 *(978-0-9736803-3-1(4))* Davenport Pr. CAN. Dist: Independent Pubs. Group.
Sullivan, Kevin & Morgan, Elizabeth. Anne's New Home. 2010. (Anne of Green Gables Picture Bks.). (ENG.). 32p. (J). (gr. k-2). pap. 4.95 *(978-0-9736803-7-9(7))* Davenport Pr. CAN. Dist: Independent Pubs. Group.

SHOES

Blaxland, Wendy. Sneakers, 1 vol. 2009. (How Are They Made? Ser.). (ENG.). 32p. (gr. 4-4). lib. bdg. 21.27 *(978-0-7614-3810-6(6),* 4865c803-4127-4111-82e3-e488b914e616) Cavendish Square Publishing LLC.
Cobb, Vicki. Sneakers. 2008. pap. 52.95 *(978-0-8225-9451-2(X))* Lerner Publishing Group.
D'Cruz, Anna-Marie. Make Your Own Shoes & Slippers, 1 vol. (Do It Yourself Projects! Ser.). (ENG.). 24p. (J). (gr. 4-4). 2009. pap. 10.40 *(978-1-4358-2921-3(2),* 49a5439d-98e2-400c-94d0-9938763f9a8a) 2008. lib. bdg. 28.93 *(978-1-4358-2852-0(6),* 59480fee-3224-4ddc-8650-f5e37c3c25b2) Rosen Publishing Group, Inc., The. (PowerKids Pr.).
Englehart, Victoria. Whose Shoes? 2012. (Illus.). 34p. (-18). pap. 16.99 *(978-1-4525-6056-4(0))* Balboa Pr.
Frisch, Aaron. The Story of Nike. 2003. (Built for Success Ser.). (Illus.). 48p. (J). lib. bdg. 19.95 *(978-1-58340-295-5(0))* Black Rabbit Bks.
Jacobson, Ryan. Shoes. 2016. (J). *(978-1-4896-4541-8(1))* Weigl Pubs., Inc.
Kahalewai, Marilyn. Whose Slippers Are Those? Kobayashi, Gavin, illus. 2005. 24p. (J). (gr. -1-3). 10.95 *(978-1-57306-238-1(3))* Bess Pr., Inc.
Keyser, Amber J. Sneaker Century: A History of Athletic Shoes. 2015. (ENG., Illus.). 64p. (YA). (gr. 6-12). lib. bdg. 34.65 *(978-1-4677-2640-5(0),* bd0cfe6d-b33a-4fc9-95e5-585a554dba27, Twenty-First Century Bks.) Lerner Publishing Group.
Kulot, Daniela. Un Lio de Cordones. 2006. (Illus.). 32p. (J). (gr. 5-7). 15.99 *(978-84-934641-7-2(1))* Lectorum Pubns., Inc.
Lindeen, Mary. If the Shoe Fits, 1 vol. 2011. (Wonder Readers Fluent Level Ser.). (ENG.). 16p. (gr. -1-2). (J). pap. 6.25 *(978-1-4296-7928-2(X),* 118260); pap. 35.94 *(978-1-4296-8097-4(0))* Capstone. (Capstone Pr.).
MacDonald, Margaret. Boots & Shoes. 2011. (Learn-Abouts: Level 10 Ser.). (Illus.). 16p. (J). pap. 7.95 *(978-1-59920-604-2(8))* Black Rabbit Bks.
McNeil, Niki, et al. HOCPP 1094 Red Clogs. 2006. spiral bd. 15.50 *(978-1-60308-094-1(5))* In the Hands of a Child.
Meinking, Mary. Stylish Shoes for the Crafty Fashionista, 1 vol. 2011. (Fashion Craft Studio Ser.). (ENG.). 32p. (J). (gr. 3-9). lib. bdg. 28.65 *(978-1-4296-6554-4(8),* 115668) Capstone.
Merberg, Julie. My Favorite Shoes: A Touch-And-feel Shoe-stravaganza. Rucker, Georgia, illus. 2013. (ENG.). 16p. (J). (gr. -1 — 1). bds. 12.99 *(978-1-935703-64-8(1))* Downtown Bookworks.
Miller, Derek L. Sneakers. 2019. (Making of Everyday Things Ser.). (ENG.). 24p. (gr. 1-1). 49.32 *(978-1-5026-4687-3(0))* Cavendish Square Publishing LLC.
Nelson, Robin. From Leather to Basketball Shoes. 2014. (Start to Finish, Second Ser.). (ENG., Illus.). 24p. (J). (gr. k-3). lib. bdg. 23.99 *(978-1-4677-3893-4(X),* fbdba409-a7a6-492f-ae27-5e107351fedb, Lerner Pubns.) Lerner Publishing Group.
Rice, Dona. Zapatos. rev. ed. 2019. (Mathematics in the Real World Ser.). (SPA.). 20p. (J). (gr. k-1). 8.99 *(978-1-4258-2823-3(X))* Teacher Created Materials, Inc.
Rice, Dona Herweck. Your World:: Shoes. rev. ed. 2018. (Mathematics in the Real World Ser.). (ENG., Illus.). 20p. (J). (gr. k-1). 8.99 *(978-1-4258-5616-8(0))* Teacher Created Materials, Inc.
Ross, Samantha B. "Momby" Wears Combat Boots: Where did she Go? 2011. 28p. pap. 15.99 *(978-1-4568-7129-1(3))* Xlibris Corp.
Sneaker Factory. (J). pap. 13.15 *(978-0-8136-4301-4(5))* Modern Curriculum Pr.
Sneakers. 2006. (Where's the Science Here? Ser.). (J). pap. 8.95 *(978-0-8225-9044-6(1))* Lerner Publishing Group.
Steinberg, D. J. King Louie's Shoes. Neubecker, Robert, illus. 2017. (ENG.). 48p. (J). (gr. -1-3). 17.99 *(978-1-4814-2657-2(5),* Beach Lane Bks.) Beach Lane Bks.
Swinburne, Stephen R. Whose Shoes? A Shoe for Every Job. 2018. (ENG., Illus.). 32p. (J). (— 1). bds. 7.99 *(978-1-62979-691-8(3),* Astra Young Readers) Astra Publishing Hse.

SHOES—FICTION

Anderson, Charoletta. Mizz Goodie 2 Shoez. 2013. 24p. pap. 17.99 *(978-1-4772-9475-8(9))* AuthorHouse.
Andrews, John. Beck's Missing Shoes. 2013. 28p. pap. 9.95 *(978-1-4787-2524-4(9))* Outskirts Pr., Inc.
Applegate, Katherine. Never Walk in Shoes That Talk. Biggs, Brian, illus. 2009. (Roscoe Riley Rules Ser.: 6). (ENG.). 96p. (J). (gr. 1-5). pap. 4.99 *(978-0-06-114891-0(1))* HarperCollins Pubs.
—Never Walk in Shoes That Talk. 2009. (Roscoe Riley Rules Ser.: 06). lib. bdg. 14.75 *(978-0-606-05019-7(1))* Turtleback.
—Roscoe Riley Rules #6: Never Walk in Shoes That Talk. Biggs, Brian, illus. 2009. (Roscoe Riley Rules Ser.: 6). (ENG.). 96p. (J). (gr. 1-5). 14.99 *(978-0-06-114892-7(X),* HarperCollins) HarperCollins Pubs.
Baldwin, Sherry. Santa's Tatty Old Boots. 2016. (ENG., Illus.). (J). 17.95 *(978-1-937721-37-4(X))* Randall, Peter E. Pub.
Barrett, Mary Brigid. Shoebox Sam, 1 vol. Morrison, Frank, illus. 2011. (ENG.). 32p. (J). 15.99 *(978-0-310-71549-8(0))* Zonderkidz.
Beck, Crystall. The Adventures of Carter & Vincent. 2012. 28p. pap. 9.95 *(978-1-4787-1662-4(2))* Outskirts Pr., Inc.
Berting, Judy. There's Poo on My Shoe. 2010. 36p. 17.25 *(978-1-4269-4300-3(8))* Trafford Publishing.
Boelts, Maribeth. Esos Zapatos. Jones, Noah Z., illus. 2018. (SPA.). 40p. (J). (gr. k-3). 8.99 *(978-0-7636-9979-6(9))* Candlewick Pr.
—Those Shoes. 2014. 17.00 *(978-1-63419-735-9(6))* Perfection Learning Corp.
Boileau, Kim. My New Blue Shoes, 1 vol. 2010. 28p. pap. 24.95 *(978-1-4489-8847-1(0))* PublishAmerica, Inc.
Bonar, Troy A. Safety = Caring. 2013. 28p. pap. 9.95 *(978-1-4787-0745-5(3))* Outside the Box Publishing, LLC.
Boyd, Sonya. I Have What It Takes. 2011. 28p. pap. 9.95 *(978-1-4327-7975-7(3))* Outskirts Pr., Inc.
Brannen, Sarah S. Bear Needs Help. Brannen, Sarah S., illus. 2019. (Illus.). 32p. (J). (gr. -1-2). 16.99 *(978-0-525-51650-7(6),* Philomel Bks.) Penguin Young Readers Group.
Brott, Wayne. Shoes! Delosh. Diana Ting, illus. 2013. (ENG.). (J). (gr. -1-3). 14.95 *(978-1-62086-239-1(5))* Amplify Publishing Group.
Bunting, Eve. Whose Shoe? Ruzzier, Sergio, illus. 2015. (ENG.). 32p. (J). (gr. -1-3). 16.99 *(978-0-544-30210-5(9),* 1575895, Clarion Bks.) HarperCollins Pubs.
Burket, Shelia. Detective Morris Norris & the Case of the Missing Socks. 2011. 20p. pap. 24.95 *(978-1-4626-2822-3(2))* America Star Bks.
Carillo, Christina Martin. Mr Plaid. 2011. 24p. pap. 24.95 *(978-1-4560-6930-8(6))* America Star Bks.
Cathy Smentkowski. If the Shoe Fits. 2010. 24p. pap. 15.99 *(978-1-4535-6417-2(9))* Xlibris Corp.
Chen, Eva. Juno Valentine & the Magical Shoes. Desierto, Derek, illus. 2018. (Juno Valentine Ser.). (ENG.). 32p. (J). 18.99 *(978-1-250-29726-6(5),* 900195905) Feiwel & Friends.
Chu, Carol. Shoes, Shoes, Shoes: A Delightful Book of Imaginary Footwear for Coloring, Decorating, & Dreaming. Chwast, Seymour, illus. 2014. (ENG.). 128p. (J). (gr. 7). pap. 12.99 *(978-0-544-30137-5(4),* 1574510, Clarion Bks.) HarperCollins Pubs.
Church, Peggy Pond. Shoes for the Santo Niño. Carrillo, Charles M., illus. 2013. 64p. 25.95 *(978-1-936744-23-7(6),* Rio Grande Bks.) LPD Pr.
—Shoes for the Santo Niño: Zapititos para el Santo Niño: A Bilingual Tale. Carrillo, Charles M., illus. 2009. (SPA & ENG.). 61p. (J). pap. *(978-1-890689-64-3(5),* Rio Grande Bks.) LPD Pr.
Ciesa, Mary E. Dina Prima the Ballerina. 2013. 36p. pap. 16.99 *(978-1-4525-8313-6(7),* Balboa Pr.) Author Solutions, LLC.
Cobb, Daryl K. Do Pirates Go to School. 2010. pap. 11.99 *(978-0-578-05535-0(X))* 10 To 2 Children's Bks.
Coleman, Tamala J. Donovan's Shoes. 2010. 28p. pap. 9.95 *(978-1-4327-5801-1(2))* Outskirts Pr., Inc.
Conti, Alexis. One Blue Shoe. Beth, Shannon, illus. 2013. (ENG.). (J). (gr. -1-3). 14.95 *(978-1-937406-11-0(3))* Amplify Publishing Group.
Conway, Portia. Where My Shoes Have Been, 1 vol. 2010. 22p. 24.95 *(978-1-4512-9671-6(1))* PublishAmerica, Inc.
Cooper, William Y. Nakai & the Red Shoes. 2011. 52p. (gr. 4-6). pap. 19.39 *(978-1-4269-6048-2(4))* Trafford Publishing.
Cowley, Joy. The Hungry Giant's Shoe. 2009. pap. 8.25 *(978-1-60559-223-7(4))* Hameray Publishing Group, Inc.
—The Hungry Giant's Shoe Big Book. 2010. 48.25 *(978-1-60559-250-3(1))* Hameray Publishing Group, Inc.
Crawford, Jaleesa. Teeny Tot. 2013. 28p. pap. 24.95 *(978-1-62709-372-9(9))* America Star Bks.
Creghan, Brian C. Pauly: The alligator who wore tennis Shoes. 2010. 48p. pap. 24.00 *(978-1-4269-3614-2(1))* Trafford Publishing.
Crouch, Cheryl Lynne. Tennis Shoes Trouble. 2006. 48p. 6.50 *(978-0-8341-2227-7(8))* Beacon Hill Pr. of Kansas City.
Dara Cicciarelli. Sam Loses His Sneaker. Hoke, Jason, illus. 2011. 20p. pap. 24.95 *(978-1-4560-9178-1(6))* America Star Bks.
Davis, Jacky. Do You Like These Boots? Soman, David, illus. 2014. (Ladybug Girl Ser.). 32p. (J). (gr. k-1). pap. 4.99 *(978-0-448-46503-6(5),* Penguin Young Readers) Penguin Young Readers Group.
Dean, James, illus. I Love My White Shoes. 2010. (Pete the Cat Ser.). (J). lib. bdg. *(978-0-06-107623-7(6))* HarperCollins Pubs.
Dixon, Dallas L. Shelby's Shoes. Williams, Nancy E., ed. Cappoen, Jennifer Tipton, illus. 2013. 24p. (J). pap. 12.98 *(978-1-938526-33-6(3))* Laurus Co., Inc., The.
Dlugos, Josephine. Josie's Red Shoes. 2012. 24p. pap. 15.99 *(978-1-4771-4097-0(2))* Xlibris Corp.
Dtpolk. The Shoes & the Laces. Barge Ill, John, illus. 2011. 32p. pap. 24.95 *(978-1-4560-3141-1(4))* America Star Bks.
Dubel, Dorothy. The Magical Shoes of Santa's Elves(c). 2011. 24p. pap. 15.99 *(978-1-4568-7883-2(2))* Xlibris Corp.
Dunrea, Olivier. Gossie. Dunrea, Olivier, illus. 2014. (Gossie & Friends Ser.). (ENG., Illus.). 32p. (J). (gr. -1-3). pap. 5.99 *(978-0-544-10573-7(7),* 1540523, Clarion Bks.) HarperCollins Pubs.
—Gossie/Gansi: Bilingual English-Spanish. Dunrea, Olivier, illus. 2011. (Gossie & Friends Ser.). (ENG., Illus.). 32p. (J). (gr. -1-3). bds. 6.99 *(978-0-547-51072-9(1),* 1443769, Clarion Bks.) HarperCollins Pubs.
—Ollie the Stomper. Dunrea, Olivier, illus. 2014. (Gossie & Friends Ser.). (ENG., Illus.). 32p. (J). (gr. -1-3). pap. 4.99 *(978-0-544-14676-1(X),* 1547359, Clarion Bks.) HarperCollins Pubs.
Dyan, Penelope. New Shoes for Hand Me down Rose. Dyan, Penelope, illus. 2012. (Illus.). 34p. pap. 11.95 *(978-1-61477-041-1(7))* Bellissima Publishing, LLC.
Eddy, Catherine J. Sandbox Sandshoes. Krupnek, Joann J., illus. 2009. 38p. pap. 10.95 *(978-0-9818488-5-3(0))* Ajoyin Publishing, Inc.
Edwards, Garth. The Magic Boots. Stasyuk, Max, illus. 2011. (Adventures of Titch & Mitch Ser.). (J). pap. *(978-0-9567449-8-2(2))* Inside Pocket Publishing, Ltd.
—The #04 Magic Boots. Stasyuk, Max, illus. 2011. (Adventures of Titch & Mitch, the Ser.). (J). pap. *(978-0-7613-8424-3(3))* Inside Pocket Publishing, Ltd.
Erickson, Patricia. The Shiny New Shoes. 2011. 24p. pap. 11.50 *(978-1-4670-2544-7(5))* AuthorHouse.
Farley, Robin. Mia & the Tiny Toe Shoes. Ivanov, Aleksey & Ivanov, Olga, illus. 2012. (My First I Can Read Ser.). (ENG.). 32p. (J). (gr. -1-3). 16.99 *(978-0-06-208683-9(9));* pap. 4.99 *(978-0-06-208682-2(0))* HarperCollins Pubs. (HarperCollins).
—Mia Jazzes It Up! 2013. (Mia I Can Read Bks.). (J). lib. bdg. 13.55 *(978-0-606-32164-8(0))* Turtleback.
Finnan, Kristie. Mommy's High Heel Shoes. Achilles, Pat, illus. 2008. 32p. (J). 16.99 *(978-0-9817565-2-3(2))* Mommy Workshop Bks.
Fisher, James C. Oh No! My Shoe! 2013. 24p. pap. 15.99 *(978-1-4797-8210-9(6))* Xlibris Corp.
Flinn, Alex. Cloaked. 2011. 341p. (YA). lib. bdg. 17.89 *(978-0-06-087423-0(6),* HarperTeen) HarperCollins Pubs.
Foster, Evelyn. The Elves & the Trendy Shoes. Venturini, Claudia, illus. 2015. (Tadpoles: Fairytale Twists Ser.). (ENG.). 32p. (J). (gr. 1-2). *(978-0-7787-1932-8(4))* Crabtree Publishing Co.
Franks, Alison. On My Feet! 2013. 24p. pap. 28.03 *(978-1-4797-6958-2(4))* Xlibris Corp.
Gamble, Rev. Vivian T. I Think All the Time... . Ummm. 2012. 28p. pap. 9.95 *(978-1-4787-1359-3(3))* Outskirts Pr., Inc.
—Just to Be Myself. 2012. 28p. pap. 9.95 *(978-1-4787-1358-6(5))* Outskirts Pr., Inc.
Gibson, Beatrice. The Legend of the Sandals. 2008. (ENG.). 26p. pap. 15.99 *(978-1-4363-9169-6(5))* Xlibris Corp.
Graham, Cheryl. Stephanie's Shoes. 2010. 28p. pap. 9.95 *(978-1-4327-5944-5(2))* Outskirts Pr., Inc.
Grande, Gabrielle. Fluffy's Book. 2013. 24p. (J). pap. 12.99 *(978-1-4808-0067-0(8));* (Illus.). 22.99 *(978-1-4808-0068-7(6))* Archway Publishing.
Gregory, Lorraine NAR NEEDED. One, Two, Tie Your Shoes! Carlson, Nancy Gayle, illus. 2010. (J). *(978-0-545-26482-2(0))* Scholastic, Inc.
Guarino, Deborah. If the Shoe Fits. (J). 14.95 *(978-0-8118-3774-3(2))* Chronicle Bks. LLC.
—If the Shoe Fits, 1 vol. Hippen, Seth, illus. 2019. (ENG.). 32p. pap. 9.99 *(978-0-7643-5882-1(0),* 20593); (J). (gr. -1-3). 16.99 *(978-0-7643-5843-2(X),* 9962) Schiffer Publishing, Ltd.
Hannigan, Jana. What Good Will Come. Warren, Henry, illus. 2016. (ENG.). 25p. (J). (gr. 3-7). 14.00 *(978-1-61851-103-4(3))* Baha'i Publishing.
Harlan. My Best Friend. 2011. 28p. pap. 9.95 *(978-1-4327-7164-5(7))* Outskirts Pr., Inc.
Harlow, Honey. Honey's Shoes. 2013. 28p. pap. 9.95 *(978-1-4327-9921-2(5))* Outskirts Pr., Inc.
Harris, Wendell. Elton's Shoes. 2012. 100p. (gr. -1). pap. 13.95 *(978-1-4520-8143-4(3))* AuthorHouse.
Hart, Caryl. One Shoe Two Shoes. Underwood, Edward, illus. 2019. (ENG.). 32p. (J). 17.99 *(978-1-5476-0094-6(2),* 900198463, Bloomsbury Children's Bks.) Bloomsbury Publishing USA.
Hartt-Sussman, Heather. Seamus's Short Story, 1 vol. Pavlović, Milan, illus. 2017. (ENG.). 32p. (J). (gr. k-2). 16.95 *(978-1-55498-793-1(8))* Groundwood Bks. CAN. Dist: Publishers Group West (PGW).
Hayes, Joe. The Lovesick Skunk, 1 vol. Castro L., Antonio, illus. 2010. (ENG.). 32p. (J). (gr. k-7). 16.95

S

(978-1-933693-81-1(9), 41f5c7d6-6dd6-4b56-af34-fe1790e53e54, Cinco Puntos Press) Lee & Low Bks., Inc.

Hinbest, Wendy. Frizzy Tizzy Gets New Shoes. 2011. 24p. pap. 11.95 *(978-1-4583-5827-1(5))* Lulu Pr., Inc.

Hoffman, Mary. The Twelve Dancing Princesses. Clara, Miss, illus. 2013. 40p. (J). (gr. 1-5). 17.99 *(978-1-84686-966-2(8))* Barefoot Bks., Inc.

Holmes, Julienne R. The Girl Who Wore Her Shoes on the Wrong Feet. 2012. 24p. pap. 24.95 *(978-1-4626-8726-8(1))* America Star Bks.

Holub, Joan. Mini Myths: Good Job, Athena! Patricelli, Leslie, illus. 2016. (Mini Myths Ser.). (ENG.). 24p. (J). (gr. -1 — 1). bds. 6.95 *(978-1-4197-1898-4(3)*, 1110410, Abrams Appleseed) Abrams, Inc.

Howell, Heather. Emily's Ballet Recital. 2010. 32p. pap. 12.99 *(978-1-4490-8457-8(5))* AuthorHouse.

I Can Tie My Own Shoes. 2016. (Illus.). 13p. (J). *(978-1-4351-6291-4(9))* Barnes & Noble, Inc.

Ireland, Cameron Robert. The Missing Left Shoe. 2012. 24p. 24.95 *(978-1-4626-6138-1(6))* America Star Bks.

Jannazo, Michelle A. Isabella's Shoes. 2012. 28p. pap. 11.95 *(978-1-4327-9019-6(6))* Outskirts Pr., Inc.

Jones, A. I Can Make a Shoe for You. 2011. 36p. pap. 24.95 *(978-1-4560-9118-7(2))* PublishAmerica, Inc.

Jones, Cheryl. Where Are My Shoes? 2011. 28p. pap. 9.95 *(978-1-4327-7157-7(4))* Outskirts Pr., Inc.

Jones, Lonetha. Big Brother's Missing Shoes. 2010. 28p. pap. 9.95 *(978-1-4327-5926-1(4))* Outskirts Pr., Inc.

Jules, Jacqueline. Freddie Ramos Makes a Splash. Benítez, Miguel, illus. 2013. (Zapato Power Ser.: 4). (ENG.). 96p. (J). (gr. 1-5). pap. 6.99 *(978-0-8075-9486-5(5)*, 807594865) Whitman, Albert & Co.

—Sofia's Party Shoes. Smith, Kim, illus. 2018. (Sofia Martinez Ser.). (ENG.). 32p. (J). (gr. k-2). lib. bdg. 21.32 *(978-1-5158-2336-0(9)*, 137017, Picture Window Bks.) Capstone.

Keast, Jennifer H. Dora the Explorer (Giant First Play-a-Sound) 2010. 10p. (J). bds. 17.98 *(978-1-60553-544-9(3))* Publications International, Ltd.

Kitchen, David. The Adventures of Chesed & Cadence. 2012. 28p. pap. 9.95 *(978-1-4787-1712-6(2))* Outskirts Pr., Inc.

Kliman, Susie. Jonathon's Thongs. Erlich, Esther, illus. 2013. 35p. pap. *(978-0-9875296-1-9(7))* Aly's Bks.

Knapp, Kate. Ruby Red Shoes. 2012. *(978-0-7304-9640-3(6))* HarperCollins Pubs. Australia.

Kosara, Tori. Big Kid Shoes. Borlasca, Hector, illus. 2011. (J). *(978-0-545-36967-1(3))* Scholastic, Inc.

Kucharski, Linda. Sneak the Sneaker. 2010. 44p. pap. 15.50 *(978-1-60911-487-9(6)*, Eloquent Bks.) Strategic Book Publishing & Rights Agency (SBPRA).

Litwin, Eric, ed. Rocking in My School Shoes. 2011. *(978-0-545-50106-4(7))* Scholastic, Inc.

Litwin, Eric & Dean, James. I Love My White Shoes. 2010. (Pete the Cat Ser.). pap. *(978-0-545-41966-6(2))* Scholastic, Inc.

Litwin, Eric & Dean, Kimberly. Pete the Cat: I Love My White Shoes. Dean, James, illus. 2010. (Pete the Cat Ser.). (ENG.). 40p. (J). (gr. -1-3). 19.99 *(978-0-06-190622-0(0))*; lib. bdg. 21.89 *(978-0-06-190623-7(9))* HarperCollins Pubs. (HarperCollins).

—Pete the Cat: Rocking in My School Shoes: A Back to School Book for Kids. Dean, James, illus. 2011. (Pete the Cat Ser.). (ENG.). 40p. (J). (gr. -1-3). 19.99 *(978-0-06-191024-1(4))*; lib. bdg. 17.89 *(978-0-06-191025-8(2))* HarperCollins Pubs. (HarperCollins).

Lopez, Joe. Solemates. 2013. 28p. pap. 9.95 *(978-1-4787-2494-0(3))* Outskirts Pr., Inc.

Lorang, C. J. Where Are My Shoes. 2011. 28p. pap. 9.95 *(978-1-4327-8290-0(8))* Outskirts Pr., Inc.

Lucas & His Long Loopy Laces. 2013. (Illus.). 48p. 16.99 *(978-0-9823519-4-9(1))* Tall Tails Publishing Hse.

Macy, Tana. Tap Shoes & Horse Shoes. Gardiner, Nancy, illus. 2011. 50p. pap. 18.00 *(978-1-60976-086-1(7)*, Eloquent Bks.) Strategic Book Publishing & Rights Agency (SBPRA).

Mantlo, Mickey A. & Cook, Darren A. Tennis Shoes & Toe Clips, 1 vol. 2010. 204p. pap. 24.95 *(978-1-4512-9683-9(5))* America Star Bks.

Manushkin, Fran. Katie's New Shoes, 1 vol. Lyon, Tammie, illus. 2011. (Katie Woo Ser.). (ENG.). 32p. (J). (gr. k-2). pap. 5.95 *(978-1-4048-6855-7(0)*, 116436); lib. bdg. 21.32 *(978-1-4048-6519-8(5)*, 114215) Capstone. (Picture Window Bks.).

Marrero, Rosa M. Nickolas Loves Toby. 2011. 28p. pap. 9.95 *(978-1-4327-7452-3(2))* Outskirts Pr., Inc.

Marrone, Amanda. Master of Mirrors. 2011. (Magic Repair Shop Ser.: 3). (ENG.). 192p. (J). (gr. 3-7). pap. 5.99 *(978-1-4169-9035-2(6)*, Aladdin) Simon & Schuster Children's Publishing.

Melanson, Caroline. Two Old Shoes. 2011. 24p. pap. 15.99 *(978-1-4628-9238-9(8))* Xlibris Corp.

Meyer, Susan Lynn. New Shoes. Velasquez, Eric, illus. (ENG.). 32p. (J). (gr. 1-4). 2016. 7.99 *(978-0-8234-3573-9(3))* 2015. 17.99 *(978-0-8234-2528-0(2))* Holiday Hse., Inc.

Mihai, Adriana. The Inner of the Diamond Shoes. 2011. 28p. pap. 24.95 *(978-1-4560-0979-3(6))* America Star Bks.

Miller, Denise. Annie's Shoes. 2012. 28p. pap. 9.95 *(978-1-4787-2020-1(4))* Outskirts Pr., Inc.

Miracle, Joan. Tia's Shoes. 2013. 28p. pap. 9.95 *(978-1-4787-2603-6(2))* Outskirts Pr., Inc.

Nance, Andrew Jordan. The Barefoot King: A Story about Feeling Frustrated. Holden, Olivia, illus. 2020. 32p. (J). (gr. -1-3). 16.95 *(978-1-61180-748-6(4)*, Bala Kids) Shambhala Pubns., Inc.

Nichols, Cherrie L. Curtiz Says: I Hate My Shoestrings. 2012. 24p. pap. 17.99 *(978-1-4772-7341-8(7))* AuthorHouse.

Orloff, Karen Kaufman. Nightlight Detective: Big Top Circus Mystery. Smith, Jamie, illus. 2013. 42p. spiral bd. 12.99 *(978-1-4413-1227-3(7))* Peter Pauper Pr. Inc.

Oroge, Sabinah. Oluwatofarati & Friends. 2013. 28p. pap. 9.95 *(978-1-4787-0520-8(5))* Outskirts Pr., Inc.

Osborne, Jill. Riley Mae & the Sole Fire Safari, 1 vol. 2014. (Faithgirlz / the Good News Shoes Ser.: 3). (ENG.). 256p. (J). pap. 7.99 *(978-0-310-74283-8(8))* Zonderkidz.

Owens, C. Denise. Help! I Can't Find My Shoes. 2013. 28p. pap. 9.95 *(978-1-4787-2550-3(8))* Outskirts Pr., Inc.

P., Angie. Sneakers. 2012. 32p. pap. 19.99 *(978-1-4772-4548-4(0))* AuthorHouse.

Parker, Emma. Snafu & the Shoes. 2010. (Illus.). pap. *(978-1-877561-00-9(2))* First Edition Ltd.

Patterson, Eric. The Legend of Skylar Swift, the Fastest Boy on Earth. Chris, Wright, illus. 2010. 122p. pap. 6.95 *(978-1-935105-49-7(3))* Avid Readers Publishing Group.

Pemberton, Bernadette. Marshall's Marvelous Shoes. 2012. 24p. pap. 15.99 *(978-1-4771-4309-4(2))* Xlibris Corp.

Pemberton, Teresa. Trissy's New Shoes. 2013. 32p. pap. 13.95 *(978-1-4497-9337-1(1)*, WestBow Pr.) Author Solutions, LLC.

Perry, Daniel. The Case of the Missing Shoes. 2013. 28p. pap. 9.95 *(978-1-4787-2649-4(0))* Outskirts Pr., Inc.

Peters, L. T. Slippery Willie's Stupid, Ugly Shoes, 1 vol. 2010. 20p. 24.95 *(978-1-4512-1511-3(8))* PublishAmerica, Inc.

Primavera, Elise. Louise the Big Cheese & the la-Di-da Shoes. Goode, Diane, illus. 2010. (ENG.). 40p. (J). (gr. k-3). 19.99 *(978-1-4169-7181-8(5)*, Simon & Schuster/Paula Wiseman Bks.) Simon & Schuster/Paula Wiseman Bks.

Pruitt, Lisa A. Savanna & the Magic Boots. 2011. 24p. (gr. 1-2). pap. 11.32 *(978-1-4634-0090-3(X))* AuthorHouse.

Raschka, Chris. New Shoes. 2018. (ENG., Illus.). 32p. (J). (gr. -1-3). 17.99 *(978-0-06-265752-7(6)*, Greenwillow Bks.) HarperCollins Pubs.

Roadhouse, Patricia. Gah Reen Galoshes. 2009. 28p. pap. 16.99 *(978-1-4389-7318-0(7))* AuthorHouse.

Robinson, Jennifer. Isabella's Shoes. 2009. 20p. pap. 10.95 *(978-1-60860-553-8(1)*, Strategic Bk. Publishing) Strategic Book Publishing & Rights Agency (SBPRA).

Rodriguez, Marisela. Violet's Shoes. 2012. 28p. pap. 9.95 *(978-1-4327-9616-7(X))* Outskirts Pr., Inc.

Schmid, Susan Maupin. The Starlight Slippers. 2018. (100 Dresses Ser.: 3). (Illus.). 336p. (J). (gr. 3-7). 16.99 *(978-0-553-53377-4(0)*, Random Hse. Bks. for Young Readers) Random Hse. Children's Bks.

Schuette, Leslie Elaine. Kristina's Shoes. 2013. 24p. pap. 24.95 *(978-1-62709-670-6(1))* America Star Bks.

Searor, Jullie. Can You Help Me? 2010. (ENG.). 26p. pap. 15.99 *(978-1-4535-0856-5(2))* Xlibris Corp.

Seibers, Elexis. Jasmine & the Mystery of the Disappearing Shoes. 2011. 28p. pap. 9.95 *(978-1-4327-7626-8(6))* Outskirts Pr., Inc.

Sparrow, Leilani. My New Shoes. Taylor, Dan, illus. (Mini Bee Board Bks.). (ENG.). (J). (gr. -1-1). 2018. 24p. bds. 7.99 *(978-1-4998-0729-5(5))* 2016. 32p. 16.99 *(978-1-4998-0363-1(X))* Little Bee Books Inc.

Stiles, Dan. Put on Your Shoes! 2013. (ENG., Illus.). 16p. (J). (-k). bds. 9.95 *(978-1-57687-646-6(2)*, powerHouse Bks.) powerHse. Bks.

Stone, Laura. Miss Clarissa & Her Musical Shoes. 2010. 32p. pap. 16.95 *(978-0-557-33226-7(5))* Lulu Pr., Inc.

The Wiggles, The. The Wiggles Emma!: Emma & the Mystery Shoes Storybook. 2017. (Wiggles Ser.). (ENG.). 24p. (J). (gr. -1-k). 10.99 *(978-1-76040-405-5(5))* Bonnier Publishing GBR. Dist: Independent Pubs. Group.

Toussaint, Simone. Sharing My Shoes. 2010. 28p. pap. 9.95 *(978-1-4327-5701-4(6))* Outskirts Pr., Inc.

Ungerer, Tomi. One, Two, Where's My Shoe? 2014. (ENG., Illus.). 32p. (gr. -1-k). 14.95 *(978-0-7148-6798-4(5))* Phaidon Pr., Inc.

Varon, Sara. New Shoes. 2018. (ENG., Illus.). 208p. (J). 19.99 *(978-1-59643-920-7(3)*, 900121340, First Second Bks.) Roaring Brook Pr.

Verde, Susan. My Kicks: A Sneaker Story! Kath, Katie, illus. 2017. (ENG.). 40p. (J). (gr. k-2). 16.95 *(978-1-4197-2309-4(X)*, 1142201) Abrams, Inc.

Wallace, Clinton. H. The Adventures of Roger Eldemire. 2013. 28p. pap. 9.95 *(978-1-4787-2493-3(5))* Outskirts Pr., Inc.

Wardlow, Lynn. Friends with My Brother. 2012. 28p. pap. 9.95 *(978-1-4787-1384-5(4))* Outskirts Pr., Inc.

Wheeler, Lisa. The Christmas Boot. Pinkney, Jerry, illus. 2016. 32p. (J). (gr. -1-3). 18.99 *(978-0-8037-4134-8(0)*, Dial Bks) Penguin Young Readers Group.

Wheeler, Ron. Stinky Stevens: The Missing Soggy Soccer Shoe (Book 3) 2012. 114p. pap. 6.95 *(978-0-9829377-6-1(8))* Written World Communications.

Wilder, Beth. Bugs in Shoes, 1 vol. 2012. (ENG., Illus.). 64p. (J). 14.99 *(978-0-7643-3967-7(2)*, 4351) Schiffer Publishing, Ltd.

Williams, Dawn. Cyril T. Centipede Looks for New Shoes, 1. Chou, Joey, illus. 2006. 48p. (J). (gr. -1-3). 15.00 *(978-0-9770783-0-1(2))* SunriseHouse Pubs.

Williams, Vanessa A. The Missing Penny. 2013. 28p. pap. 9.95 *(978-1-4787-2429-2(3))* Outskirts Pr., Inc.

Wojtowicz, Jen. The Boy Who Grew Flowers. Adams, Steve, illus. 2012. (ENG.). 32p. (J). (gr. k-5). pap. 9.99 *(978-1-84686-749-1(5))* Barefoot Bks., Inc.

SHOOTING

see also Hunting

Barton, Jen. School Shootings. 2019. (In Focus Ser.). (ENG.). 80p. (J). (gr. 6-12). 41.27 *(978-1-68282-721-5(6)*, BrightPoint Pr.) ReferencePoint Pr., Inc.

Braun, Eric. Never Again: The Parkland Shooting & the Teen Activists Leading a Movement. 2019. (Gateway Biographies Ser.). (ENG., Illus.). 48p. (J). (gr. 4-8). lib. bdg. 31.99 *(978-1-5415-5270-8(9)*, 1d67ab4e-63d9-4275-93c9-da0dd22e15c6, Lerner Pubns.) Lerner Publishing Group.

Browne, Bellmore H. Hunting & Shooting: A Vintage Classic. Beard, Daniel, ed. 2017. (ENG., Illus.). 112p. (J). pap. 8.95 *(978-0-486-81327-1(4)*, 813274) Dover Pubns., Inc.

Cashin, John. Firearms Safety. 2014. (J). 33.95 *(978-1-61900-048-3(2))* Eldorado Ink.

Drayton, Tiffanie. Coping with Gun Violence, 1 vol. 2018. (Coping Ser.). (ENG.). 112p. (gr. 7-7). pap. 19.24 *(978-1-4994-6716-1(8)*, b1de98ff-d81f-4344-818b-b0ee882ba172) Rosen Publishing Group, Inc., The.

Gerdes, Louise I., ed. The Columbine School Shooting, 1 vol. 2012. (Perspectives on Modern World History Ser.). (ENG., Illus.). 208p. (gr. 10-12). lib. bdg. 49.43 *(978-0-7377-5788-0(4)*, 1779cc54-8355-4902-9b84-49ce331817c1, Greenhaven Publishing) Greenhaven Publishing LLC.

Hemstock, Annie Wendt. Hunting with Rifles, 1 vol. 2014. (Open Season Ser.). (ENG.). 32p. (J). (gr. 4-5). lib. bdg. 28.93 *(978-1-4777-6710-8(X)*, 0b337683-ad7d-4822-a378-79fae7af74e6, PowerKids Pr.) Rosen Publishing Group, Inc., The.

—Hunting with Shotguns, 1 vol. 2014. (Open Season Ser.). (ENG., Illus.). 32p. (J). (gr. 4-5). lib. bdg. 28.93 *(978-1-4777-6705-4(3)*, b9bb1d64-3300-4990-958b-bd0b493e2e09, PowerKids Pr.) Rosen Publishing Group, Inc., The.

Lambert, Hines. Hunting Ducks, 1 vol. 2013. (Let's Go Hunting Ser.). (ENG., Illus.). 32p. (J). (gr. 4-5). 28.93 *(978-1-4488-9661-5(4)*, 0393e9be-d169-48c8-bc06-9efb284f6722); pap. 11.00 *(978-1-4488-9780-3(7)*, 52a81e87-6aed-4afa-966e-b8cc139e7b9e) Rosen Publishing Group, Inc., The. (PowerKids Pr.).

Lusted, Marcia Amidon. Florida School Shooting. 2018. (Special Reports). (ENG., Illus.). 112p. (J). (gr. 6-12). lib. bdg. 41.36 *(978-1-5321-1610-0(1)*, 29792, Essential Library) ABDO Publishing Co.

Mebane, Jeanie. Pheasant Hunting, 1 vol. 2011. (Wild Outdoors Ser.). (ENG.). 32p. (J). (gr. 3-9). lib. bdg. 27.32 *(978-1-4296-6005-1(8)*, 114942, Capstone Pr.) Capstone.

Omoth, Tyler. Duck Hunting for Kids, 1 vol. 2012. (Into the Great Outdoors Ser.). (ENG.). 32p. (J). (gr. 3-9). pap. 7.95 *(978-1-4296-9268-7(5)*, 120319); lib. bdg. 28.65 *(978-1-4296-8616-7(2)*, 118637) Capstone. (Capstone Pr.).

Pound, Blake. Duck Hunting. 2012. (Outdoor Adventures Ser.). (ENG., Illus.). 24p. (J). (gr. 3-8). lib. bdg. 27.95 *(978-1-60014-797-5(6)*, 11529, Pilot Bks.) Bellwether Media.

—Pheasant Hunting. 2012. (Outdoor Adventures Ser.). (ENG., Illus.). 24p. (J). (gr. 3-8). lib. bdg. 27.95 *(978-1-60014-801-9(8)*, Pilot Bks.) Bellwether Media.

Shooter's Dictionary. 2003. cd-rom 0.00 *(978-0-9747407-1-3(3))* Southwest guns & stuff.

Shoup, Kate. Dealing with School Shootings, 1 vol. 2019. (Helping Yourself, Helping Others Ser.). (ENG.). 112p. (gr. 7-7). lib. bdg. 44.50 *(978-1-5026-4630-9(7)*, bbbc2f24-7c45-4ea2-90d6-d33c0e4668c6) Cavendish Square Publishing LLC.

Steffens, Bradley. Gun Violence & Mass Shootings. 2018. (ENG.). 80p. (YA). (gr. 6-12). 39.93 *(978-1-68282-515-0(9))* ReferencePoint Pr., Inc.

Wolny, Philip. Water Fowl, 1 vol. 2011. (Hunting: Pursuing Wild Game! Ser.). (ENG.). 64p. (YA). (gr. 5-5). pap. 13.95 *(978-1-4488-2273-7(4)*, 0e55910f-5741-48bf-889d-3391512089a2, Rosen Reference); (Illus.). lib. bdg. 37.13 *(978-1-4488-1243-1(7)*, d64a9f6f-5ae9-4e2c-a3e5-c5f1249f0d57) Rosen Publishing Group, Inc., The.

SHOOTING STARS

see Meteors

SHOP COMMITTEES

see Management—Employee Participation

SHOPLIFTING

Sonneborn, Liz. Frequently Asked Questions about Shoplifting & Theft, 1 vol. 2011. (FAQ: Teen Life Ser.). (ENG.). 64p. (YA). (gr. 5-6). lib. bdg. 37.13 *(978-1-4488-5558-2(6)*, f4597a3d-d8da-4f0b-a235-e9bfd62d8811) Rosen Publishing Group, Inc., The.

SHOPLIFTING—FICTION

Cosgrove, Stephen. The Bugglar Brothers: Consequences of Stealing. Arroyo, Fian, illus. 2007. (J). *(978-1-58804-381-8(9))* P C I Education.

Phillips, Rebecca. The Girl You Thought I Was. 2018. (ENG.). 368p. (J). (gr. 9). 17.99 *(978-0-06-257094-9(3)*, HarperTeen) HarperCollins Pubs.

Pollack, Jenny. Klepto. 2008. (ENG.). 288p. (YA). (gr. 7-18). 8.99 *(978-0-14-241072-1(1)*, Speak) Penguin Young Readers Group.

Smith, Kirsten. Trinkets. 2019. (ENG.). 288p. (YA). (gr. 9-17). pap. 10.99 *(978-0-316-45762-0(0))* Little, Brown Bks. for Young Readers.

Tracy, Kristen. Crimes of the Sarahs. 2014. (ENG., Illus.). 384p. (YA). (gr. 9). pap. 9.99 *(978-1-4424-8100-8(5)*, Simon Pulse) Simon Pulse.

Weber, Lori. Klepto, 1 vol. 2004. (Lorimer SideStreets Ser.). (ENG.). 160p. (YA). (gr. 9-12). 8.99 *(978-1-55028-836-0(9)*, b20dc03d-4ed9-46db-9f5b-ee3d8c7b0a79); 16.95 *(978-1-55028-837-7(7)*, 837) James Lorimer & Co. Ltd., Pubs. CAN. Dist: Lerner Publishing Group, Formac Lorimer Bks. Ltd.

SHOPPERS' GUIDES

see Consumer Education; Shopping

SHOPPING

see also Consumer Education

Anderson, Karin. Compradores Inteligentes. rev. ed. 2018. (TIME for KIDS(r): Informational Text Ser.). (SPA., Illus.). 16p. (J). (gr. 1-2). 8.99 *(978-1-4258-2693-2(8))* Teacher Created Materials, Inc.

—Life in Numbers: Smart Shoppers (Level 1) 2018. (TIME for KIDS(r): Informational Text Ser.). (ENG., Illus.). 16p. (J). (gr. 1-2). 8.99 *(978-1-4258-4956-6(3))* Teacher Created Materials, Inc.

At the Toyshop: Individual Title Six-Packs. (gr. -1-2). 23.00 *(978-0-7635-9005-5(3))* Rigby Education.

Big Picture Press. Sticker Style: Shop. Bowers, Jenny, illus. 2015. (ENG.). 12p. (J). (gr. k-3). pap. 12.99 *(978-0-7636-7770-1(1)*, Big Picture Press) Candlewick Pr.

Christmas Shopping: Individual Title Six-Packs. (Literatura 2000 Ser.). (gr. 1-2). 28.00 *(978-0-7635-0088-7(7))* Rigby Education.

Dakers, Diane. Getting Your Money's Worth: Making Smart Financial Choices. 2017. (Financial Literacy for Life Ser.). (ENG.). 48p. (J). (gr. 5-5). *(978-0-7787-3097-2(2))*; pap. *(978-0-7787-3106-1(5))* Crabtree Publishing Co.

Deen, Marilyn. Dollars & Cents, 1 vol. 2011. (Wonder Readers Fluent Level Ser.). (ENG.). 16p. (gr. -1-2). (J). pap. 6.25 *(978-1-4296-7915-2(8)*, 118247); pap. 35.94 *(978-1-4296-8084-4(9))* Capstone. (Capstone Pr.).

Donovan, Sandy. Thrift Shopping: Discovering Bargains & Hidden Treasures. 2015. (ENG., Illus.). 64p. (YA). (gr. 6-12). lib. bdg. 33.32 *(978-1-4677-5783-6(7)*, 2027bef6-4405-44cc-8696-6bf45dc5dd75); E-Book 50.65 *(978-1-4677-6310-3(1))* Lerner Publishing Group. (Twenty-First Century Bks.).

Encyclopaedia Britannica, Inc. Staff, compiled by. Discover English with Ben & Bella: Series 6: Shopping. 2010. 180.00 *(978-1-61535-353-8(4))* Encyclopaedia Britannica, Inc.

Enz, Tammy. Behind the Racks: Exploring the Secrets of a Shopping Mall, 1 vol. 2010. (Hidden Worlds Ser.). (ENG.). 32p. (J). (gr. 3-9). lib. bdg. 27.32 *(978-1-4296-3386-4(7)*, 95892, Capstone Pr.) Capstone.

Ganeri, Anita. Super Malls Orange Band. 2016. (Cambridge Reading Adventures Ser.). (ENG., Illus.). 16p. pap. 7.95 *(978-1-316-50335-5(6))* Cambridge Univ. Pr.

Gillis, Jennifer B. Neighborhood Shopping. 2006. (My Neighborhood Ser.). (Illus.). 24p. (gr. 3-7). 18.50 *(978-0-7569-6930-1(1))* Perfection Learning Corp.

Gillis, Jennifer Blizin. Neighborhood Shopping. 2006. (Readers for Writers Emergent Ser.). (Illus.). 24p. (J). pap. 7.95 *(978-1-59515-559-7(7))* Rourke Educational Media.

Giulieri, Anne. My Food, 1 vol. 2012. (Engage Literacy Magenta Ser.). (ENG.). 16p. (J). (gr. k-2). pap. 6.99 *(978-1-4296-8884-0(X)*, 119945); pap. 36.94 *(978-1-4296-8885-7(8)*, 18338) Capstone. (Capstone Pr.).

Gosman, Gillian. Earth-Friendly Shopping, 1 vol. 2011. (How to Be Earth Friendly Ser.). (ENG., Illus.). 32p. (gr. 3-4). (J). pap. 11.00 *(978-1-4488-2771-8(X)*, 50fb79be-53c4-4ac2-89f0-1fd3145886bc, PowerKids Pr.); (YA). lib. bdg. 28.93 *(978-1-4488-2591-2(1)*, d858ba7b-b337-4783-a67c-50c31138b877) Rosen Publishing Group, Inc., The.

Hamen, Susan E. Before Online Shopping. 2020. (What Did We Do? Ser.). (ENG.). 32p. (J). (gr. 2-3). pap. 9.95 *(978-1-64493-122-6(2)*, 1644931222); lib. bdg. 31.35 *(978-1-64493-043-4(9)*, 1644930439) North Star Editions. (Focus Readers).

Hill, Mary. Signs at the Store. 2003. (Welcome Bks.). (ENG., Illus.). 24p. (J). (gr. -1-2). pap. 4.95 *(978-0-516-24363-4(2)*, Children's Pr.) Scholastic Library Publishing.

Hollander, Barbara. What Are Saving & Spending?, 1 vol. 2016. (Let's Find Out! Community Economics Ser.). (ENG.). 32p. (J). (gr. 2-3). lib. bdg. 26.06 *(978-1-68048-405-2(2)*, 64a5e472-908b-49f3-bfae-f56891a47fd6) Rosen Publishing Group, Inc., The.

Hollander, Barbara Gottfried. Buyers & Sellers, 1 vol. 2018. (Understanding Economics Ser.). (ENG.). 48p. (gr. 6-7). lib. bdg. 28.41 *(978-1-5383-0258-3(6)*, 74995da6-3d86-43de-9e38-337af86a6d90, Britannica Educational Publishing) Rosen Publishing Group, Inc., The.

Houghton, Gillian. Goods & Services. 2009. (Invest Kids Ser.). 24p. (gr. 2-3). 42.50 *(978-1-61513-617-9(7))*; (ENG., Illus.). (J). pap. 9.25 *(978-1-4358-3210-7(8)*, f8895fab-da59-4c48-8d13-f1613b5804f7); (ENG., Illus.). (J). lib. bdg. 26.27 *(978-1-4358-2775-2(9)*, b7b07655-5df7-4a23-afdf-0d3cadb35cf5) Rosen Publishing Group, Inc., The. (PowerKids Pr.).

Hubbard, Ben. Spending Money. Castro, Beatriz, illus. 2020. 32p. (J). *(978-0-7787-7373-3(6))* Crabtree Publishing Co.

James, Dawn L. Store Math, 1 vol. 2014. (Math Around Us Ser.). (ENG.). 24p. (gr. 1-1). pap. 9.23 *(978-1-5026-0165-0(6)*, 4eb2a109-15bb-4616-97a9-2569d398e362) Cavendish Square Publishing LLC.

Keogh, Josie. A Trip to the Grocery Store, 1 vol. 2012. (PowerKids Readers: My Community Ser.). (ENG., Illus.). 24p. (J). (gr. k-k). 26.27 *(978-1-4488-7403-3(3)*, 7cc8fa8d-fd5f-4bac-8aa1-a41f790bab09); pap. 9.25 *(978-1-4488-7482-8(3)*, 62d0588e-f7d1-431a-b519-4be2c26d25ff) Rosen Publishing Group, Inc., The. (PowerKids Pr.).

LaCamera, Breanne. E-Commerce. 2019. (21st Century Skills Innovation Library: Disruptors in Tech Ser.). (ENG., Illus.). 32p. (J). (gr. 4-8). pap. 14.21 *(978-1-5341-5041-6(2)*, 213471); lib. bdg. 32.07 *(978-1-5341-4755-3(1)*, 213470) Cherry Lake Publishing.

Laks Gorman, Jacqueline. The Shopping Mall, 1 vol. 2004. (I Like to Visit Ser.). (ENG., Illus.). 24p. (gr. k-2). pap. 9.15 *(978-0-8368-4462-7(9)*, 1260e7e0-5713-4f4c-ae8c-d3863b579909, Weekly Reader Leveled Readers) Stevens, Gareth Publishing LLLP.

—The Shopping Mall / el Centro Comercial, 1 vol. 2004. (I Like to Visit / Me Gusta Visitar Ser.). (ENG & SPA., Illus.). 24p. (gr. k-2). pap. 9.15 *(978-0-8368-4606-5(0)*, ec033e9a-a6c6-452f-9d23-363c0915c3d4); lib. bdg. 24.67 *(978-0-8368-4599-0(4)*, ba7ad4e3-e187-46fd-a4bf-bb537b371fdd) Stevens, Gareth Publishing LLLP. (Weekly Reader Leveled Readers).

Lanz, Helen. Shopping Choices. 2012. (Go Green Ser.). (ENG., Illus.). 32p. (gr. 3-6). lib. bdg. 28.50 *(978-1-59771-304-7(X))* Sea-To-Sea Pubns.

Larson, Jennifer S. What Can You Do with Money? Earning, Spending, & Saving. 2010. (Lightning Bolt Books (r) — Exploring Economics Ser.). (ENG., Illus.). 32p. (J). (gr. 1-3). pap. 9.99 *(978-0-7613-5666-0(5)*, fd82f1d7-457f-4ab7-a73f-70e41b39f3e1) Lerner Publishing Group.

McLaren, Jimmy. A Better Grocery Cart. 2019. (21st Century Skills Innovation Library: Design a Better World Ser.). (ENG., Illus.). 32p. (J). (gr. 4-7). pap. 14.21 *(978-1-5341-3975-6(3)*, 212729); lib. bdg. 32.07 *(978-1-5341-4319-7(X)*, 212728) Cherry Lake Publishing.

Minden, Cecilia. Smart Shopping. (21st Century Skills Library: Real World Math Ser.). (ENG., 32p. (gr. 4-7). 2015. Illus.). (J). 32.07 *(978-1-63362-575-4(3)*, 206484) 2007. lib. bdg. 32.07 *(978-1-60279-005-6(1)*, 200073) Cherry Lake Publishing.

—What Can I Get at the Shop? 2018. (What to Put On? Ser.). (ENG.). 16p. (J). (gr. -1-2). pap. 11.36 *(978-1-5341-2870-5(0)*, 211531, Cherry Blossom Press) Cherry Lake Publishing.

Morgan, Elizabeth. My Shopping Trip, 1 vol. 2012. (InfoMax Readers Ser.). (ENG., Illus.). 16p. (J). (gr. k-k). pap. 7.00 *(978-1-4488-8893-1(X)*, 0d808b66-2116-440e-a016-e6f9c5c69a9a, Rosen Classroom) Rosen Publishing Group, Inc., The.

Murphy, Stuart J. & Andriani, Renee. Mall Mania. 2006. (Mathstart Ser.). (Illus.). 33p. (gr. 1-4). 16.00 *(978-0-7569-6666-9(3))* Perfection Learning Corp.

Reynolds, Mattie. Super-Smart Shopping: An Introduction to Financial Literacy. 2013. (Start Smart (tm) — Money Ser.). (ENG., Illus.). 24p. (J). (gr. k-2). lib. bdg. 23.99

(978-1-937529-43-7(6), 59e7a73a-8323-44a8-af52-61b14dbc445b) Red Chair Pr.

Rice, Dona Herweck. Store Map (Grade 1) 2018. (See Me Read! Everyday Words Ser.). (ENG., Illus.). 12p. (J). (gr. k-1). 6.99 (978-1-4938-9878-7(7)) Teacher Created Materials, Inc.

Rozines Roy, Jennifer & Roy, Gregory. Money at the Store, 1 vol. (Math All Around Ser.). (ENG.). 32p. (gr. 2-2). 2008. pap. 9.23 (978-0-7614-3385-9(6), 55d54d22-45e0-4ddc-b7ca-87c1c6c663e4) 2007. (Illus.). lib. bdg. 32.64 (978-0-7614-2264-8(1), 862dc996-0f48-4325-82f9-b2b9d2809718) Cavendish Square Publishing LLC.

Santos, Edson. Cool Careers Without College for People Who Love Buying Things, 1 vol. 2017. (Cool Careers Without College Ser.). (ENG., Illus.). 112p. (J). (gr. 7-7). 41.12 (978-1-5081-7544-5(6), 209408d1-146b-4950-8fa2-05393154f5e9, Rosen Young Adult) Rosen Publishing Group, Inc., The.

—Cool Careers Without College for People who Love to Buy Things. 2009. (Cool Careers Without College Ser.). 144p. (gr. 6-6). 66.50 (978-1-61511-971-4(X)) Rosen Publishing Group, Inc., The.

—People Who Love to Buy Things, 1 vol. 2006. (Cool Careers Without College (2002-2006) Ser.). (ENG., Illus.). 144p. (YA). (gr. 7-7). lib. bdg. 41.13 (978-1-4042-0751-6(1), a6c84d0e-a368-479c-8c59-bc9bc5b54bcc) Rosen Publishing Group, Inc., The.

Schwartz, Heather E. Spend Wisely. 2015. (Money Smarts Ser.). (ENG.). 32p. (J). (gr. 2-5). lib. bdg. 19.95 (978-1-60753-795-3(8), 15311) Amicus.

Shopping. (Butterfly Bks.). (ARA., Illus.). 15p. (J). 11.95 (978-0-86685-619-5(6), LDL360) International Bk. Ctr., Inc.

Thompson, Helen. Shopping Math. 2013. (Math 24/7 Ser.: 10). 48p. (J). (gr. 5-18). 19.95 (978-1-4222-2908-8(4)) Mason Crest.

Ticktock Media, Ltd. Staff. Shopping Day. 2009. (Busy Tots Ser.). (ENG.). 10p. (J). (gr. -1-k). bds. 6.95 (978-1-84696-799-3(6), TickTock Books) Octopus Publishing Group GBR. Dist: Independent Pubs. Group.

Tracey, Michele. What Can You Buy at the Mall? 2012. (Level F Ser.). (ENG., Illus.). 16p. (J). (gr. k-2). pap. 7.95 (978-1-927136-52-2(0), 19418) RiverStream Publishing.

Waxman, Laura Hamilton. Let's Explore Saving Money. 2019. (Bumba Books (r) — a First Look at Money Ser.). (ENG., Illus.). 24p. (J). (gr. -1-1). 26.65 (978-1-5415-3854-2(4), 51de5b53-a288-4962-9eee-332f175ab39a, Lerner Pubns.); pap. 8.99 (978-1-5415-4573-1(7), bae5dcab-0f0f-41e8-a00a-7e285e88d0cc) Lerner Publishing Group.

SHOPPING—FICTION

Ashley, Bernard. A Present for Paul. Mitchell, David, illus. 2004. 28p. (J). (978-1-85269-360-2(6)); (978-1-85269-359-6(2)) Mantra Lingua.

Barry, Debra R. Let's Go to the Market. 2012. 28p. pap. 24.95 (978-1-4626-8533-2(1)) America Star Bks.

Bauer, Joan. Best Foot Forward. 2006. 183p. (gr. 7-12). 18.00 (978-0-7569-6767-3(8)) Perfection Learning Corp.

Benenfeld, Rikki. Let's Go Shopping. Benenfeld, Rikki, illus. 2005. (Toddler Experience Ser.). (ENG., Illus.). 24p. (J). 11.95 (978-1-929628-20-9(X)) Hachai Publishing.

Bloor, Edward. Crusader. 2007. (ENG., Illus.). 496p. (YA). (gr. 7). pap. 6.95 (978-0-15-206314-6(5), 1198914, Clarion Bks.) HarperCollins Pubs.

Bohmer, Kara Dale. Walking Sarah: First Day Out. 2013. 32p. (978-1-4602-0076-6(4)); pap. (978-1-4602-0077-3(2)) FriesenPress.

Bond, Michael. Paddington Bear Goes to Market Board Book. Alley, R. W., illus. 2014. (Paddington Ser.). (ENG.). 14p. (J). (gr. -1-3). bds. 7.99 (978-0-06-231722-3(9), HarperFestival) HarperCollins Pubs.

Brokamp, Elizabeth. Back to School, Picky Little Witch!, 1 vol. Welling, Peter, illus. 2014. (Picky Little Witch Ser.). (ENG.). 32p. (J). (gr. k-3). 16.99 (978-1-4556-1887-3(X), Pelican Publishing) Arcadia Publishing.

Christelow, Eileen. Five Little Monkeys Go Shopping. 2012. (Five Little Monkeys Story Ser.). lib. bdg. 17.20 (978-0-606-23990-5(1)) Turtleback.

Coulton, Mia. Danny & Dad Go Shopping. Coulton, Mia, photos by. 2003. (ENG., Illus.). pap. 5.35 (978-0-9720295-4-4(0)) Maryruth Bks., Inc.

Curry, Peter. Millie Goes Shopping. 2004. (First Words with Millie Ser.). (Illus.). 12p. (J). bds. 3.99 (978-1-85854-505-9(6)) Brimax Books Ltd. GBR. Dist: Byeway Bks.

Dames-Johnson, Angela. What's Gerald Done Now? Supermarket Fun. 2009. 24p. pap. 24.95 (978-1-60749-474-4(4)) America Star Bks.

Derby Miller, Sally. Sunday Shopping, 1 vol. Strickland, Shadra, illus. 2019. (ENG.). 32p. (J). (gr. k-3). pap. 10.95 (978-1-62014-833-4(1), leelowbooks) Lee & Low Bks., Inc.

Derby, Sally. Sunday Shopping, 1 vol. Strickland, Shadra, illus. 2015. (ENG.). 32p. (J). 17.95 (978-1-60060-438-6(2), 9781600000000) Lee & Low Bks., Inc.

Dewdney, Anna. Llama Llama Mad at Mama. Dewdney, Anna, illus. 2007. (Llama Llama Ser.). (ENG., Illus.). 40p. (J). (gr. -1-k). 18.99 (978-0-670-06240-9(5), Viking Books for Young Readers) Penguin Young Readers Group.

—Llama Llama Mad at Mama. 2009. (Illus.). (J). (978-0-545-15933-3(4)) Scholastic, Inc.

Donaldson, Julia. Hippo Has a Hat. Sharratt, Nick, illus. 2007. (ENG.). 24p. (J). (gr. k-k). pap. 12.99 (978-1-4050-2192-0(6), 900326073, Macmillan Children's Bks.) Pan Macmillan GBR. Dist: Macmillan.

Dufresne, Michèle. Mom Goes Shopping. 2003. (Mom & Dad Ser.). (ENG.). (J). pap. 7.33 (978-1-58453-251-4(3)) Pioneer Valley Bks.

Dyan, Penelope. A New Bag! Dyan, Penelope, illus. 2012. (Illus.). 34p. pap. 11.95 (978-1-61477-054-1(9)) Bellissima Publishing, LLC.

Elya, Susan Middleton. Bebé Goes Shopping. Salerno, Steven, illus. 2008. (ENG.). 36p. (J). (gr. -1-3). pap. 7.99 (978-0-15-206142-5(8), 1198442, Clarion Bks.) HarperCollins Pubs.

Enderle, Dotti & Sansum, Vicki. Grandpa for Sale. Gentry, T. Kyle, illus. 2007. (ENG.). 32p. (J). (gr. k-3). 17.95 (978-0-9729225-8-6(X)) Flashlight Pr.

Esckilsen, Erik E. The Last Mall Rat. 2005. (ENG.). 192p. (YA). (gr. 7). pap. 11.95 (978-0-618-60896-6(6), 443210, Clarion Bks.) HarperCollins Pubs.

Evans, K. D. Corey, the Little Purple Shopping Cart. 2008. 28p. per. 24.95 (978-1-4241-8457-6(6)) America Star Bks.

Florence, Tyler. Tyler Makes Pancakes! 2012. (ENG., Illus.). 40p. (J). (gr. -1-2). 16.99 (978-0-06-204752-6(3), HarperCollins) HarperCollins Pubs.

Fuerst, Jeffrey B. At the Comma Store. Knuvers, Onno, illus. 2013. (Reader's Theater Word Plays Ser.). (J). (gr. 1-2). (978-1-4509-8921-3(7)) Benchmark Education Co.

Goodier, Eleanor, et al. The Vermin Family Adventures (Book 1) 2010. 68p. pap. 9.50 (978-1-4457-5617-2(X)) Lulu Pr., Inc.

Gooding-Alber, Karry. Red Shoelace, 1 vol. 2010. 16p. pap. 24.95 (978-1-4489-6255-6(2)) America Star Bks.

Goodrich, C. C. Barnabee: Goes Shopping. 2009. (Illus.). 32p. pap. 13.99 (978-1-4389-9728-5(0)) AuthorHouse.

Hammelef, Danielle S. Shopping with the Nicholas Family. 2006. (Early Explorers Ser.). (J). pap. (978-1-4108-6117-7(1)) Benchmark Education Co.

Harvey, Matt. Shopping with Dad. Latimer, Miriam, illus. 2008. 32p. (J). (gr. -1-3). 16.99 (978-1-84686-172-7(1)) Barefoot Bks., Inc.

Hay, Sam. Jam Jar Genie (Reading Ladder Level 2) Watson, Richard, illus. 2017. (Reading Ladder Level 2 Ser.). (ENG.). 48p. (gr. k-2). pap. 4.99 (978-1-4052-8310-6(6), Reading Ladder) Farshore GBR. Dist: HarperCollins Pubs.

Henderson, Sara. Howie Goes Shopping, 1 vol. Zenz, Aaron, illus. 2008. (I Can Read! / Howie Ser.). (ENG.). 32p. (J). (gr. -1-3). pap. 4.99 (978-0-310-71606-8(3)) Zonderkidz.

Henderson, Sara & Zenz, Aaron. Howie Goes Shopping(Fido Va de Compras), 1 vol. Henderson, Sara & Zenz, Aaron, illus. 2009. (I Can Read! / Howie Series / ¡Yo Sé Leer! / Serie: Fido Ser.). (ENG., Illus.). 32p. (J). pap. 3.99 (978-0-310-71874-1(0)) Zonderkidz.

Hill, Eric. Spot Goes Shopping. Hill, Eric, illus. 2014. (Spot Ser.). (ENG., Illus.). 14p. (J). (gr. -1-k). bds. 6.99 (978-0-7232-8997-5(2), Warne) Penguin Young Readers Group.

Hillert, Margaret. Dear Dragon Goes to the Market. Schimmell, David, illus. 2010. (BeginningtoRead Ser.). 32p. (J). (gr. k-2). lib. bdg. 22.60 (978-1-59953-347-6(2)) Norwood Hse. Pr.

—Querido Dragón Va Al Mercado/Dear Dragon Goes to the Market. Schimmell, David, illus. 2011. (BeginningtoRead Ser.). 32p. (J). (-2). pap. 11.94 (978-1-60357-553-9(7)) Norwood Hse. Pr.

Husar, Stephane. Cat & Mouse Let's Go Shopping! Mehee, Loic, illus. 2015. (Av2 Fiction Readalong 2016 Ser.). (ENG.). (J). lib. bdg. 34.28 (978-1-4896-3816-8(4), AV2 by Weigl) Weigl Pubs., Inc.

Johnstone, Jan. Tom the Grocery Trolley. 2009. (Illus.). 28p. pap. 12.49 (978-1-4389-3616-1(8)) AuthorHouse.

Jules, Jacqueline. Un Paseo de Compras Problemático. Smith, Kim, illus. 2018. (Sofia Martinez en Español Ser.). (SPA.). 32p. (J). (gr. k-2). lib. bdg. 21.32 (978-1-5158-2451-0(9), 137554, Picture Window Bks.) Capstone.

—Shopping Trip Trouble Smith, Kim, illus. 2018. (Sofia Martinez Ser.). (ENG.). 32p. (J). (gr. k-2). pap. 5.95 (978-1-5158-0731-5(2), 133613, Picture Window Bks.) Capstone.

Kaplan, Michael. Betty Bunny Wants Everything. Jorisch, Stéphane, illus. 2012. (Betty Bunny Ser.). 32p. (J). (gr. -1-k). 17.99 (978-0-8037-3408-1(5), Dial Bks) Penguin Young Readers Group.

LeapFrog Staff, compiled by. Tad Goes Shopping - U. K. 2003. spiral bd. 18.00 (978-1-58605-950-7(5)) LeapFrog Enterprises, Inc.

Leonard, Marcia. Pantalones Nuevos, No! Handelman, Dorothy, photos by. 2005.Tr. of No New Pants! (Illus.). 32p. (J). (ENG & SPA.). (gr. -1-1). pap. 4.99 (978-0-8225-3297-2(2)); (SPA., (gr. 1-1). per. 5.95 (978-0-8225-3296-5(4), Ediciones Lerner) Lerner Publishing Group.

Lobel, Arnold. On Market Street: 25th Anniversary Edition. 25th anniv. ed. 2006. (ENG., Illus.). 40p. (J). (gr. -1-3). pap. 7.99 (978-0-688-08745-6(0), Greenwillow Bks.) HarperCollins Pubs.

Maisner, Heather. Little Bears Go Shopping. Zlatic, Tomislav, illus. 2015. (J). (978-1-4351-6516-8(0)) Barnes & Noble, Inc.

Manushkin, Fran. Katie Woo, Where Are You?, 1 vol. Lyon, Tammie, illus. 2011. (Katie Woo Ser.). (ENG.). 32p. (J). (gr. k-2). pap. 5.95 (978-1-4048-6853-3(4), 116434, Picture Window Bks.) Capstone.

—Katie's New Shoes, 1 vol. Lyon, Tammie, illus. 2011. (Katie Woo Ser.). (ENG.). 32p. (J). (gr. k-2). pap. 5.95 (978-1-4048-6855-7(0), 116436); lib. bdg. 21.32 (978-1-4048-6519-8(5), 114215) Capstone. (Picture Window Bks.).

Mass, Wendy. Heaven Looks a Lot Like the Mall. 2008. (ENG.). 256p. (J). (gr. 7-17). pap. 14.99 (978-0-316-05850-6(5)) Little, Brown Bks. for Young Readers.

McKune, Lauren. Olivia & Marmalade Go to Town: A Tale of Two Kitties. 2008. (ENG.). 44p. pap. 19.95 (978-1-4343-6999-4(4)) AuthorHouse.

Mealue, Monique. Johnny Goes Shopping. 2010. 24p. 12.95 (978-1-4520-0227-9(4)) AuthorHouse.

Meister, Cari. Buzz Beaker & the Growing Goo, 1 vol. McGuire, Bill, illus. 2011. (Buzz Beaker Bks.). (ENG.). 32p. (J). (gr. 2-3). pap. 6.25 (978-1-4342-3056-0(2), 114656, Stone Arch Bks.) Capstone.

Melvin, Alice. The High Street. 2011. (ENG., Illus.). 52p. (J). (gr. -1-3). 15.95 (978-1-85437-943-6(7)) Tate Publishing, Ltd. GBR. Dist: Abrams, Inc.

Mills, Nathan & Okon, Jodi. Ava Goes Shopping, 1 vol. 2012. (Rosen Readers Ser.). (ENG., Illus.). 16p. (J). (gr. k-k). pap. 7.00 (978-1-4488-8658-6(9), bab11d6e-69c3-4322-9604-32b5f84127b2, Rosen Classroom) Rosen Publishing Group, Inc., The.

Mlawer, Teresa, tr. Cook It!/¡a Cocinar! Birkett, Georgie, illus. 2009. (Helping Hands English/Spanish Edition Ser.). (ENG.). 24p. (J). (gr. -1-k). pap. (978-1-84643-568-3(4)) Child's Play International Ltd.

Morgan, Beverly. Gregory Likes Saturdays: A Little Story about Being Lost in Wal-Mart. Brady, Jeannette, ed. l.t. ed. 2005. (Illus.). 27p. (J). 4.99 (978-0-9772109-1-6(X)) Joyful Noise.

Morris, Taylor. Blowout, 1. Higgins, Anne Keenan, illus. 2011. (Hello, Gorgeous! Ser.: 1). (ENG.). 224p. (J). (gr. 6-8). 18.69 (978-0-448-45526-6(9), Grosset & Dunlap) Penguin Publishing Group.

National Geographic Learning. Windows on Literacy Emergent (Social Studies: Economics/Government): New Clothes. 2007. (ENG., Illus.). 12p. (J). pap. 11.95 (978-0-7922-8947-0(1)) CENGAGE Learning.

Parker, Emma. The Butterfly on the Subway. 2010. (Illus.). pap. (978-1-877547-81-2(6)) First Edition Ltd.

Rallison, Janette. It's a Mall World after All. 2006. (ENG.). 230p. (YA). (gr. 6-8). 22.44 (978-0-8027-8853-5(X), 9780802788535) Walker & Co.

Raschka, Chris. New Shoes. 2018. (ENG., Illus.). 32p. (J). (gr. -1-3). 17.99 (978-0-06-265752-7(6), Greenwillow Bks.) HarperCollins Pubs.

Rylant, Cynthia. The Brownie & Pearl Collection: Brownie & Pearl Step Out; Brownie & Pearl Get Dolled up; Brownie & Pearl Grab a Bite; Brownie & Pearl See the Sights; Brownie & Pearl Go for a Spin; Brownie & Pearl Hit the Hay. Biggs, Brian, illus. 2016. (Brownie & Pearl Ser.). (ENG.). 144p. (J). (gr. -1-k). 12.99 (978-1-4814-8653-8(5), Simon Spotlight) Simon Spotlight.

—Brownie & Pearl See the Sights. Biggs, Brian, illus. 2010. (Brownie & Pearl Ser.). (ENG.). 24p. (J). (gr. -1-k). 16.99 (978-1-4169-8637-9(5), Beach Lane Bks.) Beach Lane Bks.

—Brownie & Pearl See the Sights: Ready-To-Read Pre-Level 1. Biggs, Brian, illus. 2013. (Brownie & Pearl Ser.). (ENG.). 24p. (J). (gr. -1-k). 17.99 (978-1-4424-8744-4(5)); pap. 4.99 (978-1-4424-8743-7(7)) Simon Spotlight. (Simon Spotlight).

Sadler, Marilyn & Bollen, Roger. Money, Money, Honey Bunny! 2006. (Bright & Early Books(R) Ser.). (ENG., Illus.). 36p. (J). (gr. -1-k). 9.99 (978-0-375-83370-0(6), Random Hse. Bks. for Young Readers) Random Hse. Children's Bks.

Sandlin, Pauline. Mannequins. 2011. 32p. pap. 21.99 (978-1-4568-2707-6(3)) Xlibris Corp.

Santillo, LuAnn. The Pig. Santillo, LuAnn, ed. 2003. (Half-Pint Kids Readers Ser.). (Illus.). 7p. (J). (gr. -1-1). pap. 1.00 (978-1-59256-064-6(4)) Half-Pint Kids, Inc.

Sebring, Ruthie. Charlie, Itty's Guinea Pig, 1 vol. 2010. 30p. 24.95 (978-1-4489-4391-3(4)) PublishAmerica, Inc.

Seibold, J. Otto. Lost Sloth. 2013. (Illus.). 32p. (J). 16.95 (978-1-938073-35-9(5), 17e71c47-97da-456c-be45-560119e3e943) McSweeney's Publishing.

Shopping with Dad, 6 vols., Pack. (gr. -1-2). 23.00 (978-0-7635-8991-2(8)) Rigby Education.

Souvenirs, 6 vols., Pack. (Literatura 2000 Ser.). (gr. 2-3). 33.00 (978-0-7635-0186-0(7)) Rigby Education.

Stockham, Jess, illus. Shopping! 2011. (Helping Hands Ser.). 24p. (J). (978-1-84643-412-9(2)) Child's Play International Ltd.

Tarcov, Susan. Raisins & Almonds: A Yiddish Lullaby. Sánchez, Sonia, illus. 2019. (ENG.). 32p. (J). (gr. -1-2). 17.99 (978-1-5415-2161-2(7), 68d48c45-8c0a-4a62-bf6b-1c30bbfe4af0, Kar-Ben Publishing) Lerner Publishing Group.

Thiel Annie. The Playdate Kids Dakota Gets Lost. 2007. 32p. 12.95 (978-1-933721-08-8(1)) Playdate Kids Publishing.

Thiel, Annie & Fanning, Tena. Dakota Gets Lost. Edwards, William M., illus. 2007. (Playdate Kids: Let's Be Friends! Ser.). 27p. (J). (gr. -1-3). per. 6.95 (978-1-933721-20-0(0)) Playdate Kids Publishing.

Thorp, Gloria J. & Ruotsala, Charity Aili. Anna's Hats: Anna has a hat for every Adventure. 2009. 40p. pap. 19.49 (978-1-4389-8967-9(9)) AuthorHouse.

Tice, Kimberly & Litvack, Venita. Lou Knows What to Do Supermarket, Vol. 1. Kerry, illus. 2017. (Lou Knows What to Do Ser.: 1). (ENG.). 23p. (J). (gr. -1-5). pap. 10.95 (978-1-944882-14-3(6)) Boys Town Pr.

Trent, Shanda. Farmers' Market Day. Dippold, Jane, illus. 2013. (ENG.). 32p. (J). (gr. -1-1). 12.95 (978-1-58925-115-1(6)) Tiger Tales.

Verdick, Elizabeth. On-The-Go Time. Heinlen, Marieka, illus. 2011. (Toddler Tools(r) Ser.). (ENG.). 26p. (J). (— 1). bds. 9.99 (978-1-57542-379-1(0), 23791) Free Spirit Publishing Inc.

Volker, Kerstin. Emma Goes Shopping. 2003. (Funny Friends Lift-and-Learn Bks.). 14p. (J). 5.99 (978-1-59384-021-1(7)) Parklane Publishing.

Webb, Sarah. Bridesmaid Blitz. 2012. (Ask Amy Green Ser.: 3). (ENG., Illus.). 320p. (YA). (gr. 7). pap. 6.99 (978-0-7636-5157-2(5)) Candlewick Pr.

West, Abby. The Adventures of Penny Ann & Alexa Jane. 2013. (ENG., Illus.). 28p. (gr. -1-4). pap. 13.95 (978-1-936205-33-2(5), P223205) Austin, Stephen F. State Univ. Pr.

Whitley-Kinzett, Sara. Grumpy Ted: The Teds Volume One. Ellams, Victoria, illus. 2009. 16p. pap. 10.65 (978-1-4251-0051-3(1)) Trafford Publishing.

Williams, Brenda. Lin Yi's Lantern: A Moon Festival Tale. Lacombe, Benjamin, illus. 2009. (ENG.). 32p. (J). (gr. -1-5). 16.99 (978-1-84686-147-5(0)) Barefoot Bks., Inc.

—Lin Yi's Lantern: A Moon Festival Tale. Tavares, Victor, illus. 2008. 32p. (J). (978-1-84686-148-2(9)) Barefoot Bks., Inc.

Williams, Shanica. Amy Goes Shopping for School. 2012. 16p. pap. 15.99 (978-1-4772-1360-5(0)) AuthorHouse.

Wilson, Karma. Mortimer's Christmas Manger. Chapman, Jane, illus. 2007. (ENG.). 40p. (J). (gr. -1-3). 9.99 (978-1-4169-5049-3(4), McElderry, Margaret K. Bks.) McElderry, Margaret K. Bks.

Wolfe, Frances. The Little Toy Shop. Wolfe, Frances, illus. 2008. (Illus.). 32p. (J). (gr. -1-2). 19.95 (978-0-88776-865-1(2), Tundra Bks.) Tundra Bks. CAN. Dist: Penguin Random Hse. LLC.

Wynne-Jones, Tim. Secret Agent Man Goes Shopping for Shoes. Won, Brian, illus. 2016. (ENG.). 32p. (J). (gr. -1-3). 16.99 (978-0-7636-7119-8(3)) Candlewick Pr.

Yanisko, Thomas. What You Eat It's up to You. Hoyes, Kerry, illus. 2012. 36p. pap. 9.99 (978-1-937260-26-2(7)) Sleepytown Pr.

SHORT STORIES

A., Khyrunnisa. Run, It's Butterfingers Again! 2017. (ENG.). 224p. (J). pap. 19.99 (978-0-14-333417-0(4), Puffin) Penguin Bks. India PVT, Ltd IND. Dist: Independent Pubs. Group.

A Lady. Tales from Ariosto: Retold for Children. 2007. pap. 28.95 (978-1-4304-5008-5(8)) Kessinger Publishing, LLC.

A Pastor. The Pearl Box: Containing One Hundred Beautiful Stories for Young People. 2017. (ENG., Illus.). (J). 22.95 (978-1-374-84170-3(6)); pap. 12.95 (978-1-374-84169-7(2)) Capital Communications, Inc.

A&C Black, A&C. The Secret Seven. 2017. (ENG.). 32p. (J). pap. 42.00 (978-1-4729-3393-5(1)) HarperCollins Pubs. Ltd. GBR. Dist: Independent Pubs. Group.

Abbate, Jason. Welcome to Xooxville. 2004. (YA). per. 12.95 (978-0-9760959-0-3(4)) Rarecity Pr.

Abbott, Jacob. Stories Told to Rollo's Cousin Lucy. 2005. pap. 22.95 (978-1-4179-5651-7(8)) Kessinger Publishing, LLC.

Abraham, Ametta. Miss Robbie's House. 2009. 64p. pap. 23.49 (978-1-4490-4571-5(5)) AuthorHouse.

Abraham, Rayna M. Just Imagine: Rayna Abraham's Creative Collection for Kids. 2011. 44p. pap. 16.59 (978-1-4634-1529-7(X)) AuthorHouse.

Abrefah, Nana K. My Amazing Short Stories & Questions. 2008. 60p. pap. 8.95 (978-0-595-51861-6(3)) iUniverse, Inc.

Abuhamda, Nasser. Short Stories. 2008. 48p. pap. 14.95 (978-1-59858-581-0(9)) Dog Ear Publishing, LLC.

—6 Tales of Adventure. 2009. 84p. pap. 14.95 (978-1-59858-833-0(8)) Dog Ear Publishing, LLC.

Acreman, Hayley. Found You Rabbit! Acreman, Hayley, illus. 2011. (ENG., Illus.). 34p. (J). (gr. k-2). pap. 9.95 (978-1-905762-87-3(9)) Parthian Bks. GBR. Dist: Independent Pubs. Group.

Adams II, Garry. The Bubble Gum Boy. 2008. (ENG.). 40p. pap. 19.99 (978-1-4343-7645-9(1)) AuthorHouse.

Adams, Jennifer. Edgar Gets Ready for Bed: a BabyLit(TM) Book: Inspired by Edgar Allan Poe's the Raven, 1 vol. Stucki, Ron, illus. 2014. (ENG.). 32p. (J). 16.99 (978-1-4236-3528-4(0)) Gibbs Smith, Publisher.

Adams, John Joseph, ed. Under the Moons of Mars: New Adventures on Barsoom. (ENG., Illus.). 368p. (YA). (gr. 7). 2013. pap. 9.99 (978-1-4424-2030-4(8)) 2012. 16.99 (978-1-4424-2029-8(4)) Simon & Schuster Bks. For Young Readers. (Simon & Schuster Bks. For Young Readers).

Adkinson, Gma Mary. Growing up with Princess Lizzy: Little Life Lessons. 2012. (ENG.). 50p. pap. 16.95 (978-1-4787-1993-9(1)) Outskirts Pr., Inc.

Adler, David A. The Day I Lost My Hampster: And Other True School Stories. 2006. 48p. (978-0-439-80289-5(X)) Scholastic, Inc.

Adler, Naomi. The Barefoot Book of Animal Tales. Hall, Amanda, illus. 2018. (ENG.). 80p. (J). (gr. 1-4). pap. 16.99 (978-1-78285-396-1(0)) Barefoot Bks., Inc.

Aesop, Aesop. The Aesop for Children. Winter, Milo, illus. 2013. 236p. pap. 9.97 (978-1-60386-613-2(2)) Rough Draft Printing.

Agnew, Kate. Would You Believe It? (ENG., Illus.). 128p. (J). pap. 7.50 (978-1-4052-0520-7(2)) Farshore GBR. Dist: Trafalgar Square Publishing.

Aguado, Bill & Newirth, Richard. Paint Me Like I Am: Teen Poems from WritersCorps. 2003. (ENG., Illus.). 144p. (YA). (gr. 8-18). pap. 8.99 (978-0-06-447264-7(7), HarperTeen) HarperCollins Pubs.

Aiken, Joan. A Necklace of Raindrops & Other Stories. Hawkes, Kevin, illus. 2003. 84p. (J). (gr. 1-5). 13.15 (978-0-7569-5686-8(2)) Perfection Learning Corp.

—Snow Horse & Other Stories. 2004. (978-0-7136-7654-9(X), A&C Black) Bloomsbury Publishing Plc.

Aitken, Amber. Perfect Match (the Cupid Company, Book 4), Book 4. 4th ed. 2011. (Cupid Company Ser.). (ENG.). 240p. (J). (gr. 4-6). pap. 9.99 (978-0-00-736263-9(3)) HarperCollins Pubs. Ltd. GBR. Dist: Independent Pubs. Group.

Akers, Martin, et al. Fran Grabs It - Stop! It's a Frog! - the Best Nest: BuildUp Unit 3 Lap Book. Palacios, Sara & Battuz, Christine, illus. 2015. (Build up Core Phonics Ser.). (J). (gr. 1). (978-1-4900-2602-2(9)) Benchmark Education Co.

Alam, Sarah H. Enchanting Fables. 2008. 48p. pap. 16.95 (978-1-60441-768-5(4)) America Star Bks.

Albee, Sarah & Stone, Jon. Sesame Street Little Golden Book Library 5-Book Boxed Set: My Name Is Elmo; Elmo Loves You; Elmo's Tricky Tongue Twisters; the Monster on the Bus; the Monster at the End of This Book, 5 vols. Smollin, Michael & Swanson, Maggie, illus. 2017. (Little Golden Book Ser.). (ENG.). 120p. (J). (-k). 24.95 (978-1-5247-2077-3(1), Golden Bks.) Random Hse. Children's Bks.

Albert, Beatrice. Adventure's Unlimited: Great Stories for Great Kids. 2009. 52p. (J). pap. 14.95 (978-1-4327-3224-0(2)) Outskirts Pr., Inc.

Alcott, Louisa. A Garland for Girls. 2006. pap. (978-1-4065-0587-0(0)) Dodo Pr.

—A Garland for Girls. l.t. ed. 2005. 376p. pap. (978-1-84637-049-6(3)) Echo Library.

—Kitty's Class Day. l.t. ed. 2005. 424p. pap. (978-1-84637-055-7(8)) Echo Library.

—Kitty's Class Day & Other Stories. 2005. 28.95 (978-1-4218-1485-8(4)); 268p. pap. 13.95 (978-1-4218-1585-5(0)) 1st World Publishing, Inc. (1st World Library - Literary Society).

—Kitty's Class Day & Other Stories. 2006. (ENG.). 208p. pap. 20.99 (978-1-4264-0876-2(5)) Creative Media Partners, LLC.

—Kitty's Class Day & Other Stories. 2006. pap. (978-1-4065-0588-7(9)) Dodo Pr.

—Kitty's Class Day, & Other Stories. 2013. 178p. (J). pap. 8.75 (978-1-61720-920-8(1)) Wilder Pubns., Corp.

—Kitty's Class Day & Other Stories. l.t. ed. 2006. 200p. pap. 21.99 (978-1-4264-0857-1(9)) Creative Media Partners, LLC.

—The Louisa Alcott Reader. l.t. ed. 2005. 228p. pap. (978-1-84637-058-8(2)) Echo Library.

—Silver Pitchers & Independence. 2011. 208p. pap. 14.95 (978-1-60664-548-2(X)) Rodgers, Alan Bks.

—Spinning-Wheel Stories. 2011. 202p. 27.95 (978-1-4638-9494-8(5)) Rodgers, Alan Bks.

Alemayehu, Tsehay. Bee-Come! A Collection of Short Stories. 2012. 58p. pap. 20.95 (978-1-4525-4816-6(1)) Balboa Pr.

Alexander, Lloyd. The Foundling: And Other Tales of Prydain. 6th rev. ed. 2006. (Chronicles of Prydain Ser.: 6). (ENG., Illus.). 112p. (J). (gr. 3-7). pap. 7.99 (978-0-8050-8053-7(8), 900038440) Square Fish.

Alfreda. Story Time Stories Without Rhyme. 2003. 21.95 *(978-0-913597-90-3(2))* Prosperity & Profits Unlimited, Distribution Services.

Allen, Nancy Kelly. Trouble in Troublesome Creek: A Troublesome Creek Kids Story. Crawford, K. Michael, illus. 2010. (ENG.). 32p. (J). (gr. -1-3). 16.95 *(978-1-933176-32-1(6))* Red Rock Pr., Inc.

Almond, David. Half a Creature from the Sea: A Life in Stories. Taylor, Eleanor, illus. 2015. (ENG.). 240p. (YA). (gr. 7). 16.99 *(978-0-7636-7877-7(5))* Candlewick Pr.

Alonso, Fernando. El Hombrecito Vestido de Gris. Wendell, Ulises, illus. 2003. (SPA.). 94p. (J). (gr. 3-5). pap. 8.95 *(978-968-19-0439-5(7))* Santillana USA Publishing Co., Inc.

Altes, Marta. No! 2011. (Child's Play Library). (Illus.). 32p. (J). *(978-1-84643-417-4(3))* Child's Play International Ltd.

Alvarez, Julia. De Como Tia Lola Termino Empezando Otra Vez (How Aunt Lola Ended up Starting over Spanish Edition) 2012. (Tia Lola Stories Ser.: 4). (SPA.). 192p. (J). (gr. 3-7). 7.99 *(978-0-307-93034-7(3)*, Yearling) Random Hse. Children's Bks.

Ambrose, Adrianne. Xoxo, Betty & Veronica: In Each Other's Shoes. 2011. (Archie Comics Ser.). (ENG.). 160p. (J). (gr. 4-6). 17.44 *(978-0-448-45712-3(1))* Penguin Young Readers Group.

Amerikaner, Susan, et al. Disney Princess Storybook Collection. 2015. (Illus.). 300p. (J). *(978-1-4847-5331-6(3)*, 1394934) Disney Publishing Worldwide.

Amery, H. Mini Stories from Around the World. rev. ed. 2013. (Mini Editions Ser.). 128p. (J). ring bd. 7.99 *(978-0-7945-3384-7(1)*, Usborne) EDC Publishing.

—Stories from Around the World. 2004. (Stories for Young Children Ser.). 128p. (J). 7.99 *(978-0-7945-0110-5(9)*, Usborne) EDC Publishing.

Amery, Heather. Little Book of First Stories. 2004. (Mini Storybooks Ser.). (ENG., Illus.). 128p. (J). 7.95 *(978-0-7945-0269-0(5)*, Usborne) EDC Publishing.

Amery, Heather & Cartwright, Stephen. Rusty's Train Ride. rev. ed. 2004. (Treasury of Farmyard Tales Ser.). 16p. (J). pap. 4.95 *(978-0-7945-0602-5(X))* EDC Publishing.

Ames, Arbour, et al. Harmonious Hearts 2016: Stories from the Young Author Challenge. Regan, Anne, ed. 2016. (Harmony Ink Press - Young Author Challenge Ser.: 3). (ENG., Illus.). 314p. (YA). pap. 17.99 *(978-1-63477-834-3(0)*, Harmony Ink Pr.) Dreamspinner Pr.

Amin, Karima, et al. The Adventures of Brer Rabbit & Friends. 2006. (ENG., Illus.). 64p. (J). (gr. 2-4). 22.44 *(978-0-7894-4925-2(0))* Dorling Kindersley Publishing, Inc.

Amnesty International Staff, ed. Free? Stories about Human Rights. 2010. (ENG., Illus.). 224p. (J). (gr. 6-8). 22.44 *(978-0-7636-4703-2(9))* Candlewick Pr.

Amos, Muriel & Olrun, Prudy. Animals of Nunivak Island. Amos, Muriel & Olrun, Prudy, illus. 2006. (Animal Story Collection Ser.). (Illus.). 16p. (J). (gr. 2-6). pap. 9.00 *(978-1-58084-238-9(0))* Lower Kuskokwim Schl. District.

Ana, Moh. Kookaburra Tales # 3: Laugh Not at Others. 2013. 16p. pap. 16.81 *(978-1-4669-3477-1(8))* Trafford Publishing.

Anaya, Hector. Cuenta Cuenta. Moreno, Sergio, illus. 2nd rev. ed. 2005. (Castillo de la Lectura Verde Ser.). (SPA & ENG.). 184p. (J). (gr. -1-7). pap. 7.95 *(978-970-20-0135-5(8))* Castillo, Ediciones, S. A. de C. V. MEX. Dist: Macmillan.

and Film Studio, Shanghai Animation & Tang, Sanmu. Three Monks. Ying, Wu, tr. from CHI. 2010. (Favorite Childrens Cartoons from China Ser.). (ENG., Illus.). 32p. (gr. -1-3). pap. 5.95 *(978-1-60220-973-2(1))* Shanghai Pr.

Andersen, Hans Christian. Hans Christian Andersen Tales. 2014. (Word Cloud Classics Ser.). (ENG., Illus.). 464p. pap. 14.99 *(978-1-62686-259-3(1)*, Canterbury Classics) Printers Row Publishing Group.

—Hans Christian Andersen's Fairy Tales. 2nd ed. 2010. (Puffin Classics Ser.). (Illus.). 224p. (J). (gr. 5-7). pap. 7.99 *(978-0-14-132901-7(7)*, Puffin Books) Penguin Young Readers Group.

Anderson, Claire. Talking to the Stars. 2009. 24p. pap. 12.99 *(978-1-4389-7268-8(7))* AuthorHouse.

Anderson, Hans Christian. Cuentos de Andersen. 2nd ed. 2003.Tr. of Stories from Han Andersen. (SPA., Illus.). 64p. *(978-84-392-8880-0(8)*, EV6475) Gaviota Ediciones ESP. Dist: Lectorum Pubns., Inc.

—Fairy Tales of Hans Christian Andersen. 2011. 892p. pap. 19.99 *(978-1-61382-020-9(8))* Simon & Brown.

—Hans Christian Andersen's Fairy Tales: An Illustrated Classic. Rackham, Arthur et al, illus. 2017. (Illustrated Classic Ser.). (ENG.). 260p. (J). 12.99 *(978-1-68412-031-4(4))* Readerlink Distribution Services, LLC.

—The Wild Swans & Other Tales. 2012. (Fairy Tales of Hans Christian Andersen Ser.). (ENG.). 152p. pap. 19.99 *(978-1-909438-12-5(X)*, Sovereign) Bollinger, Max GBR. Dist: Lightning Source UK, Ltd.

Anderson, Jennifer. Honey Creek Royalty. 2013. 246p. pap. 12.99 *(978-1-62237-148-8(8))* Turquoise Morning Pr.

Anderson, Mark A. Ma Ma, I'm Home, 1 vol. 2009. 48p. pap. 16.95 *(978-1-4489-9077-1(7))* America Star Bks.

Anderson, Matt & Durning, Tim. Cut the Rope: Strange Delivery. 2012. (ENG., Illus.). 104p. pap. 9.99 *(978-1-937676-04-9(8)*, 9781937676049) Ape Entertainment.

Anderson, Matt & Hutchins, Eric. White Picket Fences: Double Feature One-shot. 2008. (Illus.). 52p. (YA). pap. 6.95 *(978-0-9801314-9-9(9))* Ape Entertainment.

Anderson, Matt & Lambert, Chad. Kung Fu Panda Vol. 2: It's Elemental & Other Stories. 2012. (ENG., Illus.). 24p. pap., pap. 6.95 *(978-1-936340-56-9(9)*, 9781936340569) Ape Entertainment.

Anderson, Matthew. No Such Thing as the Real World. 2009. 8.99 *(978-0-06-147060-8(0))* HarperCollins Pubs.

Anderson, Max Elliot. Terror at Wolf Lake. 2004. (Tweener Press Adventure Ser.). (Illus.). 141p. (J). (gr. 4-7). per. 10.95 *(978-0-9729256-6-2(X)*, Tweener Pr.) Baker Trittin Pr.

Anderson, Phil. The Thomas Family Values. 2012. 84p. pap. 13.95 *(978-1-4772-2529-5(3))* AuthorHouse.

Anderson, Robert Gordon. HalfPast Seven Stories Illustrated Editi. 2006. pap. *(978-1-4065-0868-0(3))* Dodo Pr.

Anderson, Susannah. Susie. 2004. (ENG.). 60p. pap. 8.50 *(978-1-4116-2175-6(1))* Lulu Pr., Inc.

Andrews, Charlie J. Tales of Animals on Farmer Brown's Farm: Children Stories. 2007. 60p. per. 10.95 *(978-1-4327-0138-3(X))* Outskirts Pr., Inc.

Andrews, Jan. When Apples Grew Noses & White Horses Flew, 1 vol. Petričić, Dusan, illus. 2011. (ENG.). 72p. (J). (gr. 2-5). 16.95 *(978-0-88899-952-8(6))* Groundwood Bks. CAN. Dist: Publishers Group West (PGW).

Andrews, Jane & Hopkins, Louisa Parsons. The Seven Little Sisters Who Live on the Round Ball that Floats in the Air. 2004. reprint ed. pap. 21.95 *(978-1-4179-1646-7(X))* Kessinger Publishing, LLC.

Angel, Katharine Ann. Being Forgotten. 2012. (Illus.). 218p. pap. *(978-1-908098-45-0(7))* 2QT, Ltd. (Publishing).

Angelchild, P. Erotic Memoirs Volume 1. 2007. pap. *(978-1-84747-127-7(7))* Chipmunkapublishing.

Anholt, Catherine & Anholt, Laurence. Catherine & Laurence Anholt's Big Book of Little Children. Anholt, Catherine & Anholt, Laurence, illus. 2003. (ENG., Illus.). 80p. (J). (gr. -1-k). 15.99 *(978-0-7636-2210-7(9))* Candlewick Pr.

Anonymous. The Anonymous Diary Collection: Lucy in the Sky; Letting Ana Go; the Book of David. 2014. (Anonymous Diaries). (ENG., Illus.). 880p. (YA). (gr. 9). pap. 29.99 *(978-1-4814-1583-5(2)*, Simon Pulse) Simon Pulse.

Ansell, Liz. The Unforgettable Snow Lady: And Other Memorable Short Stories, Songs & Rhymes. 2012. (Illus.). 40p. (-18). pap. 22.88 *(978-1-4772-3533-1(7))* AuthorHouse.

Antologia Staff. El Libro de Oro de los Abuelos. 2004. (SPA.). 128p. *(978-980-257-274-8(8))* Ekare, Ediciones.

Anytime Stories. (Anytime Stories Ser.). 48p. (J). Vol 1. (Illus.). bds. *(978-2-7643-0177-7(4))* Vol. 2. *(978-2-7643-0178-4(2))* Vol. 3. (Illus.). bds. *(978-2-7643-0203-3(7))* Phidal Publishing, Inc./Editions Phidal, Inc.

Aperlo, Peter. The Unofficial Magnus Chase & the Gods of Asgard Companion: The Norse Heroes, Monsters & Myths Behind the Hit Series. 2015. (ENG., Illus.). 200p. (J). (gr. 2). pap. 12.95 *(978-1-61243-482-7(7))* Ulysses Pr.

Apple, Bonnie. The Karisma Tales. 2013. 142p. (gr. 4-6). 28.99 *(978-1-4525-7296-3(8))*; pap. 11.99 *(978-1-4525-7295-6(X))* Author Solutions, LLC. (Balboa Pr.).

Applehead, Zippy. You Are Who You Be. 2012. 28p. pap. 24.95 *(978-1-4626-6505-1(5))* America Star Bks.

Appleton, Victor. The Tom Swift Omnibus #1: Tom Swift & his Motor-Cycle, Tom Swift & His Motor-Boat, Tom Swift & His Airship. 2007. 292p. 24.95 *(978-1-60459-098-2(X))* Wilder Pubns., Corp.

—The Tom Swift Omnibus #2: Tom Swift & His Submarine Boat, Tom Swift & His Electric Runabout, Tom Swift & His Wireless Message. 2007. 296p. 24.95 *(978-1-60459-100-2(5))*; per. 12.99 *(978-1-60459-099-9(8))* Wilder Pubns., Corp.

Applin, Barbara & Simon, Veronica, eds. Treasure House 1: A Caribbean Anthology. 2006. (ENG., Illus.). 220p. (J). (gr. 3-5). per. 11.95 *(978-1-4050-3094-6(1))* Macmillan Caribbean GBR. Dist: Interlink Publishing Group, Inc.

Apps Ltd, Colossi. The Wild Bed Time Stories. 2011. 62p. pap. 12.95 *(978-1-4466-1546-1(4))* Lulu Pr., Inc.

árabe, Cuento popular. Ali Baba y Los Cuarenta Ladrones: Ali Baba & the Forty Thieves. 2004. (Troquelados Clasicos Ser.). (SPA.). 16p. (J). pap. 2.95 *(978-84-7864-732-3(5))* Combel Editorial, S.A. ESP. Dist: Independent Pubs. Group.

Arengo, Sue. Classic Tales: Thumbelina. Goulding, Celeste, illus. 2006. (ENG.). 24p. 5.50 *(978-0-19-422537-3(2))* Oxford Univ. Pr. GBR. Dist: Oxford Univ. Pr., Inc.

Arenstam, Peter. Nicholas, a New Hampshire Tale. Holman, Karen Busch, illus. 2015. (Nicholas Northeastern Ser.: 3). 158p. (J). (gr. k-7). pap. 8.95 *(978-1-938170-68-3(7)*, Mitten Pr.) Ann Arbor Editions LLC.

Armentrout, Jennifer L. Meet Cute: Some People Are Destined to Meet. 2019. (ENG.). 320p. (YA). (gr. 9). pap. 9.99 *(978-1-328-60428-6(4)*, 1731500, Clarion Bks.) HarperCollins Pubs.

Armentrout, Jennifer L., et al. Meet Cute. 2018. (ENG.). 320p. (YA). (gr. 9). 17.99 *(978-1-328-75987-0(3)*, 1679557, Clarion Bks.) HarperCollins Pubs.

Armstrong, Jennifer. Shattered: Stories of Children & War. 2003. (ENG.). 176p. (YA). (gr. 7). mass mkt. 6.99 *(978-0-440-23765-5(3)*, Laurel Leaf) Random Hse. Children's Bks.

Arnold, Caroline. Wiggle & Waggle. Peterson, Mary, illus. 2009. (ENG.). 48p. (J). (gr. k-3). pap. 6.99 *(978-1-58089-307-7(4))* Charlesbridge Publishing, Inc.

Arnold, Lisa Marie. Creative Short Stories for Smart Kids. 2008. 60p. pap. 21.99 *(978-1-4343-5515-7(2))* AuthorHouse.

Aronson, Marc, et al, eds. One Death, Nine Stories. 2014. (ENG.). 160p. (YA). (gr. 9). 16.99 *(978-0-7636-5285-2(7))* Candlewick Pr.

Artscroll Mesorah. The Best of Olomeinu: Stories for All Year 'Round: an Anthology of 20 Exciting, Inspiring & Beautifully Illustrating Stories for Young & Old (ArtScroll Youth) 2003. (ENG.). 136p. 13.99 *(978-1-57819-398-1(2)*, BO1H) Mesorah Pubns., Ltd.

Aryal, Aimee. Hello Hairy Dawg. Turnbull, Jesse, illus. 2004. (J). (gr. -1-3). 19.95 *(978-1-932888-04-1(7))* Amplify Publishing Group.

—Hello, Hook 'Em! Craig, Megan, illus. 2004. 24p. (J). (gr. -1-3). lib. bdg. 19.95 *(978-1-932888-10-2(1))* Amplify Publishing Group.

—Hello Joe Bruin! Perez, Gerry, illus. 2004. 24p. (J). 19.95 *(978-1-932888-15-7(2))* Amplify Publishing Group.

—Hello Mr. Wuf! Cooper, Blair, illus. 2004. 24p. (J). 19.95 *(978-1-932888-06-5(3))* Amplify Publishing Group.

—Hello Rameses! Cooper, Blair, illus. 2004. 24p. (J). 19.95 *(978-1-932888-17-1(9))* Amplify Publishing Group.

—Hello Smokey! Higgins, Krystal, illus. 2004. 22p. (J). 19.95 *(978-1-932888-09-6(8))* Amplify Publishing Group.

—Hello Tommy Trojan! Perez, Gerry, illus. 2004. 24p. (J). 19.95 *(978-1-932888-08-9(X))* Amplify Publishing Group.

—Howdy Reveille! Craig, Megan, illus. 2004. 24p. (J). 19.95 *(978-1-932888-18-8(7))* Amplify Publishing Group.

—Let's Go 49ers! 2008. (J). 14.95 *(978-1-932888-16-4(0))* Amplify Publishing Group.

—Let's Go Bears! 2008. (J). 14.95 *(978-1-932888-22-5(5))* Amplify Publishing Group.

Ashby, Gaylene. STORY TIME A Collection of Three Children's Stories. 2008. 28p. 14.95 *(978-1-4357-1929-3(8))* Lulu Pr., Inc.

Ashford, Kathy. Spencer's Birthday. 2009. 16p. pap. 24.95 *(978-1-60749-778-3(6))* America Star Bks.

Askew, Amanda. Sleeping Beauty. Rubio, Ayesha L., illus. 2018. (Once upon a Time ... Ser.). (ENG.). 24p. (J). (gr. -1-k). lib. bdg. 19.99 *(978-1-68297-299-1(2)*, a25caa47-7b5f-4539-9075-4745929ef85f) QEB Publishing Inc.

Atkinson, Ruth & Atkinson, Brett. Christmas Cutouts. Atkinson, Ruth & Atkinson, Brett, illus. (Illus.). (J). (gr. k-2). pap. *(978-1-876367-20-6(2))* Wizard Bks.

Attia, Stephan. Other Christmas Stories. 2009. 42p. pap. 19.68 *(978-0-557-11189-3(7))* Lulu Pr., Inc.

Audho, Gaitree. Moral Stories for Kids. 2011. (ENG.). 32p. pap. 12.77 *(978-1-4634-4709-0(4))* AuthorHouse.

Aulbach, Kathy. ABC's. 2008. 29p. 15.95 *(978-0-615-21180-0(1))* Flower Sprouts.

Ault, Kelly. Let's Sign, Baby! A Fun & Easy Way to Talk with Baby. Landry, Leo, illus. abr. ed. 2010. (ENG.). 40p. (J). (gr. k — 1). bds. 9.99 *(978-0-547-31596-6(1)*, 1415353, Clarion Bks.) HarperCollins Pubs.

Aunt Julie. Paddleduck! #2: Julie, Living in Texas. 2011. 56p. pap. *(978-1-4269-6656-9(3))* Trafford Publishing (UK) Ltd.

Autry, James A. & Autry, Rick. Everyday Virtues: Classic Tales to Read with Kids. Carlson, Mickey, illus. 2017. 195p. (J). pap. *(978-1-57312-971-8(2))* Smyth & Helwys Publishing, Inc.

Avalon-Pai, Phyllis. Children's Stories from Around the World. Arrott, Nancy, illus. 2008. 70p. pap. 9.95 *(978-0-9788283-8-7(0))* Acacia Publishing, Inc.

Avanti, Michele. GreeHee the Journey of Five: Tales of Tamoor Book One. 2008. (Illus.). 304p. (J). per. 14.99 *(978-0-9779590-4-4(X))* GreeHee Publishing.

Avi. The Most Important Thing: Stories about Sons, Fathers, & Grandfathers. (ENG.). 224p. (J). (gr. 5). 2019. pap. 8.99 *(978-1-5362-0883-2(3))* 2016. 16.99 *(978-0-7636-8111-1(3))* Candlewick Pr.

—Strange Happenings: Five Tales of Transformation. 2008. (ENG., Illus.). 160p. (J). (gr. 3-7). pap. 7.99 *(978-0-15-206461-7(3)*, 1199301, Clarion Bks.) HarperCollins Pubs.

—What Do Fish Have to Do with Anything? 2004. (ENG., Illus.). 208p. (J). (gr. 5-9). reprint ed. 8.99 *(978-0-7636-2319-7(9))* Candlewick Pr.

Ayagalria, Julia, et al. Animals of the River. Ayagalria, Julia et al, illus. 2006. (Animal Story Collection Ser.). 24p. (J). (gr. 2-6). pap. 9.00 *(978-1-58084-236-5(4))* Lower Kuskokwim Schl. District.

Azman, Hacer. The Adventures of Kyle. 2011. (ENG.). 96p. (J). (gr. k-1). 14.95 *(978-1-59784-231-0(1)*, Tughra Bks.) Blue Dome, Inc.

Azore, Barbara. Wanda & the Wild Hair. Graham, Georgia, illus. 2012. 32p. (J). (gr. -1-2). pap. 7.95 *(978-1-77049-306-3(9)*, Tundra Bks.) Tundra Bks. CAN. Dist: Penguin Random Hse. LLC.

Babbitt, Ellen C. Jataka Tales. 2012. 100p. *(978-1-78139-120-4(3))* Benediction Classics.

—Jataka Tales I & II. 2008. 80p. pap. 9.95 *(978-1-60459-517-8(5))* Wilder Pubns., Corp.

—More Jataka Tales. Young, Ellsworth, illus. 2008. 92p. pap. 7.95 *(978-1-59915-310-0(6))* Yesterday's Classics.

Babbitt, Ellen C. & Young, Ellsworth. The Monkey & the Crocodile: And Other Fables from the Jataka Tales of India. 2015. (ENG.). 192p. (gr. 1-6). pap. 8.99 *(978-0-486-79614-7(0)*, 796140) Dover Pubns., Inc.

Babbitt, Natalie. The Devil's Storybooks: Twenty Delightfully Wicked Stories. Babbitt, Natalie, illus. 2012. (ENG., Illus.). 224p. (J). (gr. 3-7). pap. 16.99 *(978-0-312-64158-0(3)*, 900077682) Square Fish.

Bach, Richard & Gardner, Sally. La Niña Más Pequeña del Mundo. Tapia, Sonia, tr. 2005. (Niños Mágicos Ser.).Tr. of One. (SPA & ENG., Illus.). 128p. (J). (gr. 2-4). pap. 7.95 *(978-84-666-1339-2(0))* Ediciones B ESP. Dist: Independent Pubs. Group.

Badger, Pearstina. Jessica's Journeys: Stories about Life's Lessons. 2006. 56p. pap. 16.95 *(978-1-4241-1576-1(0))* PublishAmerica, Inc.

Badoe, Adwoa. The Pot of Wisdom. Diakité, Baba Wagué, illus. 2008. (ENG.). 64p. (J). (gr. 1-2). pap. 14.95 *(978-0-88899-869-9(4))* Groundwood Bks. CAN. Dist: Publishers Group West (PGW).

Bailen, Mark & Bailen, Leaf. Earf. 2013. 48p. 16.75 *(978-0-9910809-0-8(4))* Splendid Benedict.

Bailer, Darice & Domínguez, Madelca. El Flautista de Hamelín. Vila Delclòs, Jordi, illus. 2007. (SPA & ENG.). 28p. (J). *(978-0-545-02961-2(9))* Scholastic, Inc.

Bailer, Darice, et al. El León y el Ratón. Subirana, Joan, illus. 2007. (SPA & ENG.). 28p. (J). *(978-0-545-02449-5(8))* Scholastic, Inc.

—El Pastorcito Mentiroso. Infante, Francesc, illus. 2007. (SPA & ENG.). 28p. (J). *(978-0-545-02960-5(0))* Scholastic, Inc.

Bailey, Carolyn Sherwin. Stories of Great Adventures. Burd, Clara M., illus. 2005. reprint ed. pap. 24.95 *(978-1-4179-0215-6(9))* Kessinger Publishing, LLC.

—Tell Me Another Story: The Book of Story Programs. 2017. (ENG., Illus.). (J). 25.95 *(978-1-374-84568-8(X))*; pap. 15.95 *(978-1-374-84567-1(1))* Capital Communications, Inc.

Bailey, Linda. If You Happen to Have a Dinosaur. Jack, Colin, illus. 2014. 40p. (J). (gr. -1-2). 17.99 *(978-1-77049-568-5(1)*, Tundra Bks.) Tundra Bks. CAN. Dist: Penguin Random Hse. LLC.

Bailey, Sherwin Carolyn. Tell Me Another Story. 2007. 224p. 42.99 *(978-1-4280-7529-0(1))*; per. 36.99 *(978-1-4280-7528-3(3))* IndyPublish.com.

Bakare, Rebecca. Short Stories by Rebecc. 2012. 54p. pap. 20.00 *(978-1-937911-26-3(8))* Heavenly Realm Publishing.

Bake a Cake & Other Stories: Individual Title Six-Pack. (Story Steps Ser.). (gr. k-2). 42.00 *(978-0-7635-9574-6(8))* Rigby Education.

Balcells, Jacqueline. El Archipielago de las Puntuadas. 2003. (SPA.). pap. *(978-956-13-1472-6(X)*, AB0859) Bello, Andres CHL. Dist: Lectorum Pubns., Inc.

Baldwin, James. Fifty Famous People. l.t. ed. 2006. (ENG.). 126p. pap. 19.99 *(978-1-4264-1427-5(7))* Creative Media Partners, LLC.

—Fifty Famous Stories Retold. 2007. 188p. 19.99 *(978-1-59986-708-3(7))* Filiquarian Publishing, LLC.

—Fifty Famous Stories Retold. 2009. 160p. 32.99 *(978-1-59547-545-9(1))* NuVision Pubns., LLC.

—Fifty Famous Stories Retold. 2008. 100p. pap. 9.50 *(978-1-60459-518-5(3))* Wilder Pubns., Corp.

—Fifty Famous Stories Retold. 2017. (ENG., Illus.). (J). 23.95 *(978-1-374-82000-5(8))* Capital Communications, Inc.

—Fifty Famous Stories Retold. 2018. (ENG.). (J). 180p. 39.95 *(978-0-344-06399-2(2))*; 180p. pap. 22.95 *(978-0-344-06398-5(4))*; (Illus.). 182p. 39.95 *(978-0-344-57737-6(6))*; (Illus.). 182p. pap. 22.95 *(978-0-344-57736-9(8))* Creative Media Partners, LLC.

—Fifty Famous Stories Retold. (ENG.). (J). 2019. 234p. pap. 18.99 *(978-1-6927-1227-3(6))* 2018. (Illus.). 182p. pap. 14.00 *(978-1-7917-3744-3(7))* Independently Published.

—Fifty Famous Stories Retold. 2020. (Mint Editions — Short Story Collections & Anthologies Ser.). (ENG.). 112p. pap. 7.99 *(978-1-5132-6482-0(6)*, West Margin Pr.) West Margin Pr.

—Fifty Famous Stories Retold. 2018. (ENG., Illus.). 100p. (J). 14.99 *(978-1-5154-3499-3(0))* Wilder Pubns., Corp.

Ball, Pauline E. Chubsey Tucker Tales. 2005. (Illus.). 98p. pap. *(978-1-84401-211-4(5))* Athena Pr.

Ballantyne, R. M. The Coxswain's Bride: Also Jack Frost & Sons; & A Double Rescue. 2007. (ENG.). 146p. pap. 18.99 *(978-1-4346-3664-5(X))* Creative Media Partners, LLC.

—The Lighthouse. 2006. pap. *(978-1-4065-0531-3(5))* Dodo Pr.

Ballard, George Anne. Read to Me! James, Melody A. & Arelys, Aguilar, illus. 2013. 60p. pap. 10.00 *(978-0-9855312-8-7(2))* Bolton Publishing LLC.

Bamford, Desmond Nicholas. Beekemose. 2012. (Illus.). 54p. (gr. 2-4). pap. 13.66 *(978-1-4685-7773-0(5))* AuthorHouse.

Bancks, Tristan. Mac Slater Hunts the Cool. 2010. (Mac Slater Hunts the Cool Ser.). (ENG.). 224p. (J). (gr. 3-7). 15.99 *(978-1-4169-8574-7(3)*, Simon & Schuster Bks. For Young Readers) Simon & Schuster Bks. For Young Readers.

Bandala, Luis Rodriguez. El Libro, el Escritor y Otros Cuentos. 2003. (SPA., Illus.). 184p. (YA). (gr. 5-12). 15.95 *(978-968-6966-18-3(8))* EDITER'S Publishing Hse. MEX. Dist: EDITER'S Publishing Hse.

Banghart, Tracy E. What the Sea Wants. Blum, Julia C., illus. 2006. 64p. (YA). kivar 16.00 *(978-0-9779753-0-3(4))* LizStar Bks.

Bansch, Helga. Odd Bird Out. 2011. (Gecko Press Titles Ser.). (ENG., Illus.). 32p. pap. 17.95 *(978-1-877467-08-0(1))* Gecko Pr. NZL. Dist: Lerner Publishing Group.

Barbauld, Anna. Little Stories for Children; Being Easy. 2004. reprint ed. pap. 20.95 *(978-0-7661-9037-5(4))* Kessinger Publishing, LLC.

Barbini, F. T. Tijaran Tales: White Child. 2011. 214p. pap. *(978-0-7552-1349-8(1))* Authors OnLine, Ltd.

Barbour, Ralph Henry. The New Boy at Hilltop & Other Stories. 2006. pap. *(978-1-4065-0779-9(2))* Dodo Pr.

Barker, Cicely Mary. The Girls' Book of Flower Fairies. 2008. (Flower Fairies Ser.). (ENG., Illus.). 208p. (J). (gr. -1-2). 25.00 *(978-0-7232-6273-2(X)*, Warne) Penguin Young Readers Group.

Barker, Henry, adapted by. Historical Adventure (a Connecticut Yankee in King Arthur's Court/ Around the World in 80 Days/ the Prisoner of Zenda), 1 vol. 2007. (Bank Street Graphic Novels Ser.). (ENG., Illus.). 56p. (gr. 3-3). lib. bdg. 33.67 *(978-0-8368-7927-8(9)*, 781cb54b-4250-4850-8448-ddc85b01602c) Stevens, Gareth Publishing LLLP.

Barker, Jane Valentine. Building Up. pap. 7.95 *(978-1-878611-07-9(0))* Silver Rim Pr.

Barkley, Roger C. Johnny Grasshopper. 2006. 52p. pap. 16.95 *(978-1-4241-0221-1(9))* PublishAmerica, Inc.

Barks, Carl, et al. Walt Disney's Comics & Stories #702. 2009. 64p. pap. 7.99 *(978-1-60360-092-7(2))* Gemstone Publishing, Inc.

—Walt Disney's Comics & Stories #704. 2009. 64p. pap. 7.99 *(978-1-60360-094-1(9))* Gemstone Publishing, Inc.

Barr, Robert. Dr. Barr's Tales: Stories of Katharine. 2007. 88p. per. 19.95 *(978-1-4241-7911-4(4))* America Star Bks.

Barrett, John F. The Stories of Jake. 2008. 64p. pap. 31.99 *(978-1-4363-2010-8(0))* Xlibris Corp.

Barrie, James Matthew. The Complete Adventures of Peter Pan Includes: The Little White Bird, Peter Pan in Kensington Gardens(Illustrated) & Peter. Rackham, Arthur & Bedford, F. D., illus. 2013. 326p. *(978-1-78139-361-1(3))* Benediction Classics.

Barron, Liz. Salcombe Seaside Fairies: Louise the Lobster Pot Fairy. 2009. (Illus.). 24p. pap. 11.49 *(978-1-4389-8525-1(8))* AuthorHouse.

Barrows, Annie & Blackall, Sophie. Ivy + Bean Take Care of the Babysitter. 2011. (Ivy & Bean Ser.). (ENG., Illus.). 128p. (J). (gr. 2-5). 31.36 *(978-1-59961-931-6(8)*, 10111, Chapter Bks.) Spotlight.

Barto, Linda "iLham", illus. Where the Ghost Camel Grins: Muslim Fables for Families of All Faiths. 2009. (ENG.). 119p. (gr. 5). 19.95 *(978-1-879402-24-9(6))* Tahrike Tarsile Quran, Inc.

BARWICK, Adam Mark. Three tales of Twaddle. 2008. (ENG.). 73p. pap. 12.50 *(978-1-4092-5181-1(0))* Lulu Pr., Inc.

Bassett, Jennifer. Oxford Bookworms Library: the Omega Files DS Short Stories: Level 1: 400-Word Vocabulary. 3rd ed. 2008. (ENG., Illus.). 64p. 11.00 *(978-0-19-478913-4(6))* Oxford Univ. Pr., Inc.

Bates, Robert L. Lopaka's Legends of Hawaii. 2008. 28p. pap. 19.95 *(978-1-4327-3655-2(8))* Outskirts Pr., Inc.

Batt, Tanya Robyn. The Barefoot Book of Faeries. Newey, Gail, illus. 2008. (ENG.). 64p. (J). (gr. -1-3). 15.99 *(978-1-84686-163-5(2))* Barefoot Bks., Inc.

Baum, L. Frank. American Fairy Tales. 2007. 112p. per. 9.95 *(978-1-60312-100-2(5))*; 22.95 *(978-1-60312-899-5(9))* Aegypan.

—Collected Short Stories of L. Frank Baum. 2006. (J). 29.95 *(978-1-930764-14-9(6))* International Wizard of Oz Club, The.

—Little Wizard Stories of Oz. Neill, John R., illus. 2011. (Dover Children's Classics Ser.). (ENG.). 160p. (J). (gr. 3-5). pap. 14.99 *(978-0-486-47644-5(8))* Dover Pubns., Inc.

—Little Wizard Stories of Oz. 2011. 80p. (gr. 3-18). 18.95 *(978-1-4638-9617-1(4))* Rodgers, Alan Bks.

—Tales of Mother Goose. 2009. 174p. (J). pap. *(978-1-934941-68-3(9))* Red & Black Pubs.

—The Tresury of Oz: The Wonderful Wizard of Oz, the Marvelous Land of Oz, Ozma of Oz, Dorothy & the Wizard in Oz, the Road to Oz, the Emerald City Of. 2007. 548p. per. 19.49 *(978-1-60459-029-6(7))* Wilder Pubns., Corp.

—7 Books In: L. Frank Baum's Original Oz Series, Volume 1 of 2. the Wonderful Wizard of Oz, the Marvelous Land of Oz, Ozma of Oz, Dorothy & the W. 2008. 820p. *(978-1-905921-02-7(0))* Shoes & Ships & Sealing Wax Ltd.

—7 Books In: L. Frank Baum's Oz Series, volume 1 of 2. the Wonderful Wizard of Oz, the Marvelous Land of Oz, Ozma of Oz, Dorothy & the Wizard In. 2008. 824p. pap. *(978-1-905921-01-0(2))* Shoes & Ships & Sealing Wax Ltd.

—8 Books In: L. Frank Baum's Original Oz Series, volume 2 of 2. Little Wizard Stories of Oz, Tik-Tok of Oz, the Scarecrow of Oz, Rinkitink in Oz, T. 2008. 764p. *(978-1-905921-03-4(9))* Shoes & Ships & Sealing Wax Ltd.

—8 Books In: L. Frank Baum's Oz Series, volume 2 of 2. Little Wizard Stories of Oz, Tik-Tok of Oz, the Scarecrow of Oz, Rinkitink in Oz, the Lost P. 2008. 812p. pap. *(978-1-905921-09-6(8))* Shoes & Ships & Sealing Wax Ltd.

Baum, L. Frank, et al. A Children's Treasury. 2007. 792p. per. 24.95 *(978-1-60459-011-1(4))* Wilder Pubns., Corp.

Baxter, Nicola. Bedtime Tales. Press, Jenny, illus. 2013. 80p. (J). (gr. -1-k). pap. 9.99 *(978-1-84322-952-0(8))* Anness Publishing GBR. Dist: National Bk. Network.

—Book of Five-Minute Farmyard Tales. Press, Jenny, illus. 2013. (ENG.). 80p. (J). (gr. -1-k). pap. 9.99 *(978-1-84322-953-7(6))* Anness Publishing GBR. Dist: National Bk. Network.

—A Book of Five-Minute Kitten Tales: A Treasury of over 35 Bedtime Stories. Press, Jenny, illus. 2013. 80p. (J). (gr. -1-12). pap. 9.99 *(978-1-84322-888-2(2))* Anness Publishing GBR. Dist: National Bk. Network.

—A Book of Five-Minute Teddy Bear Tales: A Treasury of over 35 Bedtime Stories. Press, Jenny, illus. 2013. (ENG.). 80p. (J). (gr. -1-12). pap. 9.99 *(978-1-84322-889-9(0))* Anness Publishing GBR. Dist: National Bk. Network.

—A Child's Treasury of Classic Stories: Charles Dickens, William Shakespeare, Oscar Wilde. Thorne, Jenny, illus. 2012. 240p. (J). (gr. 2-7). 18.99 *(978-1-84322-948-3(X))* Anness Publishing GBR. Dist: National Bk. Network.

—Classic Folk Tales: 80 Traditional Stories from Around the World. Langton, Roger, illus. 2013. (ENG.). 96p. (J). (gr. 7-12). pap. 9.99 *(978-1-84322-855-4(6))* Anness Publishing GBR. Dist: National Bk. Network.

—My Ballet Theatre: Peek Inside the 3-D Windows. Chaffey, Samantha, illus. 2014. (ENG.). 24p. (J). (gr. -1-12). 16.99 *(978-1-84322-949-0(8))*, Armadillo) Anness Publishing GBR. Dist: National Bk. Network.

—My Wonderful Treasury of Five-Minute Stories. Press, Jenny, illus. 2012. 256p. (J). (gr. k-4). 18.99 *(978-1-84322-805-9(X))* Anness Publishing GBR. Dist: National Bk. Network.

—Old MacDonald's: Barnyard Tales. Davis, Caroline, illus. 256p. (J). *(978-0-7525-8771-4(4))* Parragon Bk. Service Ltd.

—Princess Stories. Smith, Helen, illus. 2013. (ENG.). 80p. (J). (gr. k-4). pap. 9.99 *(978-1-84322-954-4(4))* Anness Publishing GBR. Dist: National Bk. Network.

—Tales from the Farmyard: 12 Stories of Grunting Pigs, Quacking Ducks, Clucking Hens, Neighing Horses, Bleating Sheep & Other Animals. Shuttleworth, Cathie, illus. 2013. (ENG.). 80p. (J). (gr. 1-8). pap. 9.99 *(978-1-84322-899-8(8))* Anness Publishing GBR. Dist: National Bk. Network.

—Tales from the Toy Box. Press, Jenny, illus. 2012. 80p. (J). (gr. k-4). pap. 9.99 *(978-1-84322-951-3(X))* Anness Publishing GBR. Dist: National Bk. Network.

—3-Minute Animal Stories. Everitt-Stewart, Andy, illus. 2013. (ENG.). 80p. (J). (gr. -1-k). pap. 9.99 *(978-1-84322-978-0(1)*, Armadillo) Anness Publishing GBR. Dist: National Bk. Network.

—3-Minute Sleepytime Stories. Siewart, Pauline, illus. 2013. (ENG.). 80p. (J). (gr. -1-3). pap. 9.99 *(978-1-84322-977-3(3)*, Armadillo) Anness Publishing GBR. Dist: National Bk. Network.

Baxter, Nicola, ed. Classic Stories: Charles Dickens, William Shakespeare & Oscar Wilde - A Treasury for Children. Thorne, Jenny, illus. 2015. 240p. (J). (gr. 4-7). 16.99 *(978-0-85723-756-9(X)*, Armadillo) Anness Publishing GBR. Dist: National Bk. Network.

—A Midsummer Night's Dream & Other Classic Tales of the Plays: Six Illustrated Stories from Shakespeare. Thorne, Jenny, illus. 2015. 80p. (J). (gr. 4-7). pap. 9.99 *(978-1-86147-466-7(0)*, Armadillo) Anness Publishing GBR. Dist: National Bk. Network.

Baxter, Nicola & Morton, Ken. A Storybook of Ugly Ogres & Terrible Trolls: Ten Fantastic Tales of Frightful Fun. 2013. (Illus.). 80p. (J). (gr. -1-12). pap. 9.99 *(978-1-84322-938-4(2)*, Armadillo) Anness Publishing GBR. Dist: National Bk. Network.

Baxter, Nicola & Siewert, Pauline. Sweet Dreams: Soothing Stories for Peaceful Bedtimes. 2012. (Illus.). 210p. (J). (gr. -1-12). pap. 7.99 *(978-1-84322-817-2(3)*, Armadillo) Anness Publishing GBR. Dist: National Bk. Network.

BBC. Doctor Who: Tales of Terror. 2018. (ENG., Illus.). 272p. (J). 16.99 *(978-1-4059-3003-1(9)*, 5b2dda25-4965-4f07-80c0-f2db1f01ba94) Penguin Bks., Ltd. GBR. Dist: Diamond Comic Distributors, Inc.

Beaudoin, Beau. Boetry. Beaudoin, Beau, illus. 2007. (Illus.). 40p. (J). per. 15.95 *(978-0-9788401-1-2(9))* Red Ink Pr.

Beckett, Bernard. Lester. 160p. (YA). (gr. 8-18). pap. *(978-1-877135-21-7(6)*, Longacre Pr.) Random Hse. New Zealand.

Beeson, J. K. Ali & Friends Adventures. 2010. 56p. pap. 10.49 *(978-1-4520-1509-5(0))* AuthorHouse.

Beifus, Ruth. Shlavim Classics 2-in-1 Vol. 1: The Best Reward & the Taste of Truth. 2009. 32p. 14.99 *(978-1-59826-329-9(3))* Feldheim Pubs.

—Shlavim Classics 2-in-1 Vol.2: Goodbye to Miri's Mess & Half a Cup of Water. 2009. 32p. 14.99 *(978-1-59826-330-5(7))* Feldheim Pubs.

Belanger, Kathleen. Cooldog's New Adventures. 2013. 78p. pap. 16.95 *(978-1-63004-207-3(2))* America Star Bks.

Bell, Aaron. Jak's Story. 2010. (ENG., Illus.). 96p. (YA). (gr. 4). pap. 10.99 *(978-1-55488-710-1(0))* Dundurn Pr. CAN. Dist: Publishers Group West (PGW).

Bell, Frank & Bowler, Colin. Panda Power. Seaman, Paul, illus. 2004. 24p. pap. 7.00 *(978-0-84161-084-9(4))* Ravette Publishing, Ltd. GBR. Dist: Parkwest Pubns., Inc.

Bell, Krista. No Strings. 2005. (Illus.). 159p. (J). (gr. -1-7). pap. *(978-0-7344-0626-2(6)*, Lothian Children's Bks.) Hachette Australia.

Bell, Lindzi. Sherlock Times Three, 1 vol. 2009. 62p. pap. 19.95 *(978-1-61582-028-3(0))* America Star Bks.

Bell, Shirley. Boys on the Make. 2007. 54p. 16.95 *(978-1-4241-6575-9(X))* America Star Bks.

Benintendi, Steve. Cyborg Mayhem. 2003. (Powermark Comics Ser.). (Illus.). 32p. (J). pap. 2.95 *(978-0-9705669-8-0(0))* PowerMark Productions.

—Face Off. 2003. (Powermark Comics Ser.). (Illus.). 32p. (J). pap. 2.95 *(978-0-9705669-4-2(8))* PowerMark Productions.

—Family Matter. 2003. (Powermark Comics Ser.). (Illus.). 32p. (J). pap. 2.95 *(978-0-9705669-7-3(2))* PowerMark Productions.

—Fang Shaw Revealed, Vol. 110. 2003. (Powermark Comics Ser.). (Illus.). 32p. (J). pap. 2.95 *(978-0-9705669-9-7(9))* PowerMark Productions.

—High & Mighty. 2003. (Powermark Comics Ser.). (Illus.). 32p. (J). pap. 2.95 *(978-0-9705669-6-6(4))* PowerMark Productions.

—They All Fall Down. 2003. (Powermark Comics Ser.). (Illus.). 32p. (J). pap. 2.95 *(978-0-9705669-5-9(6))* PowerMark Productions.

A Benji's Pup Set, 6 vols. 32p. (gr. 1-3). 37.50 *(978-0-322-00338-5(5))*; 31.50 incl. 5.25 hd *(978-0-7802-8045-8(8))* Wright Group/McGraw-Hill.

Bennet, Jill, et al. Cuentos de Terror, Vol. 2. (SPA.). (YA). 8.95 *(978-958-04-3393-4(3))* Norma S.A. COL. Dist: Distribuidora Norma, Inc.

Bennett, Bonnie. My Collection of Short Stories. 2012. 38p. 19.95 *(978-1-4626-7691-0(X))* America Star Bks.

Bennett, Jack. Tell Me a Story: A Collection of Short Stories. 2003. 68p. pap. *(978-1-894650-25-0(5))* Moose Enterprise.

Bennett, Ruth Elisabeth. Childhood Days: Stories for the Young & Young at Heart, 1 vol. 2009. 91p. pap. 19.95 *(978-1-4489-2904-7(0))* America Star Bks.

Bercowetz, Cynthia. Grandpa Herman's Petting Zoo. 2007. (Illus.). 48p. (J). per. 14.95 *(978-0-9708430-9-8(7))* Uitti, Daniel.

Berenstain, Jan & Berenstain, Stan. The Berenstain Bears' Big Bedtime Book. 2008. (Berenstain Bears Ser.). (ENG., Illus.). 48p. (J). (gr. -1-3). 13.99 *(978-0-06-057434-5(8)*, HarperFestival) HarperCollins Pubs.

Berenstain, Jan, et al. The Berenstain Bears' Big Bedtime Book. Berenstain, Stan & Jan, illus. 2011. (Berenstain Bears Ser.). (ENG.). 48p. (J). (gr. -1-3). pap. 7.99 *(978-0-06-057436-9(4)*, HarperCollins) HarperCollins Pubs.

Berenstain, Stan, et al. The Berenstain Bears' Big Bedtime Book. Berenstain, Jan & Berenstain, Mike, illus. 2008. (Berenstain Bears Ser.). 48p. (J). (gr. -1-3). 13.89 *(978-0-06-057435-2(6))* HarperCollins Pubs.

—My Favorite Berenstain Bears Stories: Learning to Read Box Set. Berenstain, Stan et al, illus. 2018. (I Can Read Level 1 Ser.). (ENG.). 160p. (J). (gr. -1-3). pap. 19.99 *(978-0-06-265459-5(4)*, HarperCollins) HarperCollins Pubs.

Beresford, Elisabeth. The Bigfoot Womble. (ENG., Illus.). 16p. pap. *(978-0-340-74673-8(4))* Hodder & Stoughton.

—The Great Womble Explorer. (ENG., Illus.). 16p. (J). (gr. k-6). pap. *(978-0-340-74675-2(0))* Hodder & Stoughton.

—The Invisible Womble. Price, Nick, illus. 2011. (ENG.). 112p. (J). (gr. 3-5). pap. *(978-1-4088-0834-4(X)*, 30799, Bloomsbury Children's Bks.) Bloomsbury Publishing Plc.

—The Wombles at Work. Price, Nick, illus. 2011. (ENG.). 256p. (J). (gr. 3-5). pap. *(978-1-4088-0836-8(6)*, 30801, Bloomsbury Children's Bks.) Bloomsbury Publishing Plc.

—The Wombles Go Round the World. Price, Nick, illus. 2011. (ENG.). 256p. (J). (gr. 3-5). pap. *(978-1-4088-0835-1(8)*, 30800, Bloomsbury Children's Bks.) Bloomsbury Publishing Plc.

—The Wombles to the Rescue. Price, Nick, illus. 2011. (ENG.). 192p. (J). (gr. 3-5). pap. *(978-1-4088-0838-2(2)*, 30803, Bloomsbury Children's Bks.) Bloomsbury Publishing Plc.

Bergida, Joanna. Wisdom from the Spring: A Collection of Short Storiesbrfrom the Class of 2010brCold Spring Harbor High School. 2007. 124p. per. 10.95 *(978-0-595-44281-2(1))* iUniverse, Inc.

Berocay, Roy. Babu. (SPA., Illus.). 60p. (J). (gr. 3-5). pap. 8.95 *(978-1-58105-634-1(6))* Santillana USA Publishing Co., Inc.

—Pateando Lunas. Soulier, Daniel, illus. 2003. (SPA.). 166p. (J). (gr. 3). pap. 12.95 *(978-9974-590-63-2(9))* Santillana S. A. URY. Dist: Santillana USA Publishing Co., Inc.

Best Bubble Blower. (J). (gr. 3-5). 75.00 *(978-0-669-13696-8(4))* Houghton Mifflin Harcourt School Pubs.

Beston, Henry. Chimney Farm Bedtime Stories. 2006. (Illus.). 80p. (J). pap. 13.95 *(978-0-942396-93-5(6))* Blackberry Maine.

Bettoni, Angela. More Adventures of Edmund & Martha. 2013. 194p. pap. *(978-0-9566421-1-0(X))* Angela Bettoni Publishing.

Between the Lions - Set of 5 Early Literacy Kits: Includes; Help!, Huff & Puff, Oh, Yes I Can!, Shooting Star & Zoop! Zoop!, 5 cass., 5 vols. 2005. (Between the Lions Ser.). 120p. (J). VHS 139.95 *(978-1-59375-295-8(4)*, WG38713) WGBH Boston Video.

Beverly, James. Seamus the Sheltie to the Rescue! 2011. 156p. pap. 14.95 *(978-1-933449-88-3(8))* Nightengale Pr.

Bevins, Pegi & Conan Doyle, Arthur. Sherlock Holmes. 2003. (Retold Classics Anthologies Ser.). (Illus.). 282p. (J). pap. 9.99 *(978-0-7891-5931-1(7))* Perfection Learning Corp.

Bibel, Philip. Tales of the Shtetl. 2004. (Illus.). 215p. per. 14.95 *(978-0-9634067-1-2(X))* Metchnikoff, Elie Memorial Library.

Bickel, Karla. Heart Petals on the Hearth: A Collection of Children's Stories. Bickel, Karla, illus. 2004. (Illus.). 64p. (J). (gr. -1-6). 20.00 *(978-1-891452-00-7(0))* Heart Arbor Bks.

—Heart Petals on the Hearth: A Collection of Children's Stories. 2004. (Illus.). 64p. (J). (gr. -1-6). pap. 16.00 *(978-1-891452-01-4(9))* Heart Arbor Bks.

Biedrzycki, David. Me & My Dragon. Biedrzycki, David, illus. 2011. (Me & My Dragon Ser.). (Illus.). 40p. (J). (gr. -1-3). pap. 7.95 *(978-1-58089-279-7(5))* Charlesbridge Publishing, Inc.

Bier, David & Bier, Seth. Bedtime with Rollo: The Nightspryte. 2009. (ENG., Illus.). 24p. 14.95 *(978-0-9677238-8-4(4)*, Sweet Dreams Pr.) Bier Brothers, Inc.

Bierce, Ambrose. An Occurrence at Owl Creek Bridge. 2010. (Creative Short Stories Ser.). (ENG.). 48p. (J). (gr. 5-8). 19.95 *(978-1-58341-922-9(5)*, 22124, Creative Education) Creative Co., The.

Big Book of R Carry-over Stories. 2004. per. 34.99 *(978-0-9760490-4-3(X))* Say It Right.

Big Davie. The Lady & Her Cat As Told by Bigdavie: A simple easy reading bedtime story that will leave children with delightful images while drifting off to S. 2009. (Illus.). 28p. pap. 12.49 *(978-1-4389-3124-1(7))* AuthorHouse.

Bildner, Phil. Busted. 2013. (ENG., Illus.). 256p. (YA). (gr. 9). pap. 16.99 *(978-1-4814-2171-3(9)*, Simon & Schuster Bks. For Young Readers) Simon & Schuster Bks. For Young Readers.

Billingsley, Morgan, et al. The Perfect Summer. 2015. (ENG., Illus.). 132p. (J). pap. 10.00 *(978-1-62517-871-8(9)*, Brown Girls Publishing) INscribe Digital.

Billingsley, ReShonda Tate. Drama Queens. 2010. (Good Girlz Ser.: 8). (ENG., Illus.). 244p. pap. 16.99 *(978-1-4391-5687-2(5)*, Gallery Bks.) Gallery Bks.

Billows, Denis. Down in Bluebell Wood. 2010. 164p. pap. 11.99 *(978-1-4490-8822-4(8))* AuthorHouse.

Binder, Betsy. The Wrinkled-at-the Knees Elephant & Other Tuneful Tales. Decenciere, Isabelle, illus. 2008. 28p. (J). pap. 19.95 incl. audio compact disk *(978-0-615-26652-7(5))* Velvet Pony Stories.

Binder, Mark. Genies, Giants & a Walrus. 2012. 132p. pap. 14.99 *(978-0-9824707-9-4(7))* Light Pubns.

Bingham, Frances. Bedtime Stories for the Inner Child: Reuniting with & Nurturing Your Inner Child. 2009. 68p. pap. 10.49 *(978-1-4389-3185-2(9))* AuthorHouse.

Bird, Betsy. Funny Girl: Funniest. Stories. Ever. 2018. (ENG., Illus.). 224p. (J). (gr. 3-7). 8.99 *(978-0-14-751783-8(4)*, Puffin Books) Penguin Young Readers Group.

—Funny Girl: Funniest. Stories. Ever. 2018. lib. bdg. 19.65 *(978-0-606-41309-1(X))* Turtleback.

Bird Song: The Little Stories of Manoosh & Baloosh. 2003. (J). mass mkt. *(978-1-932233-02-5(4))* Aurora Libris Corp.

Bishop, Barbara L. Children Today Around the U S A. Bishop, Barbara L., illus. 2008. (Illus.). 40p. pap. 13.95 *(978-1-934246-25-2(5))* Peppertree Pr., The.

Bishop, Michael. In the Wild Wood, 4 vols. Cloke, Rene, illus. 2012. (ENG.). 64p. (J). 4.95 *(978-1-84135-785-0(5))* Award Pubns. Ltd. GBR. Dist: Parkwest Pubns., Inc.

Black, & Still Beautiful. 2005. (YA). per. 6.95 *(978-0-9630951-3-8(7))* Karnak Co.

Black, Chuck. Lady Carliss & the Waters of Moorue. 2010. (Knights of Arrethtrae Ser.: 4). (ENG.). 208p. (YA). (gr. 5-7). pap. 9.99 *(978-1-60142-127-2(3)*, Multnomah Bks.) Crown Publishing Group, The.

Black, Holly. The Poison Eaters: And Other Stories. Black, Theo, illus. 2011. (ENG.). 224p. (YA). (gr. 9). pap. 12.99 *(978-1-4424-1232-3(1)*, McElderry, Margaret K. Bks.) McElderry, Margaret K. Bks.

—Zombies vs. Unicorns. 2012. lib. bdg. 22.10 *(978-0-606-23686-7(4))* Turtleback.

Black, Holly & Castellucci, Cecil, eds. Geektastic: Stories from the Nerd Herd. 2010. (ENG.). 432p. (J). (gr. 7-17). pap. 19.99 *(978-0-316-00810-5(9))* Little, Brown Bks. for Young Readers.

Black, Holly & Larbalestier, Justine, eds. Zombies vs. Unicorns. 2012. (ENG.). 432p. (YA). (gr. 9). pap. 12.99 *(978-1-4169-8954-7(4)*, McElderry, Margaret K. Bks.) McElderry, Margaret K. Bks.

Blackburn, Sheila M. Stewie Scraps & the Easy Rider. 2008. 72p. pap. *(978-1-903853-85-6(0))* Brilliant Pubns.

—Stewie Scraps & the Space Racer. 2008. 68p. pap. *(978-1-903853-84-9(2))* Brilliant Pubns.

—Stewie Scraps & the Super Sleigh. 2008. 72p. pap. *(978-1-903853-89-4(3))* Brilliant Pubns.

—Stewie Scraps & the Trolley Cart. 2008. 72p. pap. *(978-1-903853-88-7(5))* Brilliant Pubns.

Blackington, Debbie. Mama's Wish/Daughter's Wish. Sommer, Xiaolan, tr. from CHI. 2004. (Illus.). 48p. (J). 17.95 *(978-0-9760011-0-2(1))* Pebbleton Pr.

Blackman, Dorothy L. New York Patriots. Gulley, Martha, illus. 2007. (ENG.). v, 122p. (J). pap. *(978-1-59531-020-0(7))* North Country Bks., Inc.

Blackstone, Stella. Hip Shapes. Bell, Siobhan, illus. 2012. 24p. (J). (gr. -1-1). pap. 18.69 *(978-1-84686-762-0(2))* Barefoot Bks., Ltd. GBR. Dist: Children's Plus, Inc.

Blake, Quentin, illus. Charlie und die Schokoladenfabrik. (GER.). pap. 17.95 *(978-3-499-21211-6(0))* Rowohlt Taschenbuch Verlag GmbH DEU. Dist: Distribooks, Inc.

Blanco, Ms. Healing Hearts of Nature: Five Therapeutic Fables for Children. 2009. 52p. pap. 23.00 *(978-1-4490-1529-9(8))* AuthorHouse.

Blitz, Shmuel. Every Story Has a Soul. 2006. (ENG., Illus.). 47p. (J). 15.99 *(978-1-4226-0224-9(9))* Mesorah Pubns., Ltd.

Block, Francesca Lia. Blood Roses. 2008. 144p. (J). (gr. 9-18). 15.99 *(978-0-06-076384-8(1)*, Cotler, Joanna Books) HarperCollins Pubs.

Bloomfield, Susanne George & Reed, Eric Melvin, eds. Adventures in the West: Stories for Young Readers. 2007. (ENG., Illus.). 302p. (J). (gr. 3-7). pap. 19.95 *(978-0-8032-5974-4(3)*, BLOADX, Bison Bks.) Univ. of Nebraska Pr.

Blow, Wind, Blow! & Other Stories: Individual Title Six-Pack. (Story Steps Ser.). (gr. k-2). 42.00 *(978-0-7635-9586-9(1))* Rigby Education.

Blue Wolf & Friends Learning Adventure Package, 2 bks. 2004. (Illus.). 100p. lib. bdg. *(978-0-9758759-0-2(6))* Progressive Language, Inc.

Blume, Judy. Judy Blume Essentials (Boxed Set) Are You There God? It's Me, Margaret; Blubber; Deenie; Iggie's House; It's Not the End of the World; Then Again, Maybe I Won't; Starring Sally J. Freedman As Herself. 2014. (ENG., Illus.). 1616p. (J). (gr. 3-7). pap. 55.99 *(978-1-4814-3533-8(7)*, Atheneum Bks. for Young Readers) Simon & Schuster Children's Publishing.

—The Judy Blume Teen Collection (Boxed Set) Are You There God? It's Me, Margaret; Deenie; Forever; Then Again, Maybe I Won't; Tiger Eyes. 2014. (ENG., Illus.). 1056p. (YA). (gr. 9). pap. 54.99 *(978-1-4814-3534-5(5)*, Atheneum Bks. for Young Readers) Simon & Schuster Children's Publishing.

Blyton, Enid. The Adventure of the Secret Necklace. (Illus.). 84p. (J). pap. 7.99 *(978-0-7475-3211-8(7))* Bloomsbury Publishing Plc GBR. Dist: Trafalgar Square Publishing.

—The Boy Who Wanted a Dog. (Illus.). 91p. (J). pap. 7.99 *(978-0-7475-3213-2(3))* Bloomsbury Publishing Plc GBR. Dist: Trafalgar Square Publishing.

—The Children of St. Kidillin. (Illus.). 110p. (J). pap. 7.99 *(978-0-7475-3216-3(8))* Bloomsbury Publishing Plc GBR. Dist: Trafalgar Square Publishing.

—Enid Blyton Circus Stories. (Illus.). (J). 11.95 *(978-0-09-914131-0(0))* Penguin Random Hse. GBR. Dist: Trafalgar Square Publishing.

—Magic Snow Bird: And Other Stories. Hamilton, Dorothy, illus. 2013. (ENG.). 192p. (J). 9.95 *(978-1-84135-420-0(1))* Award Pubns. Ltd. GBR. Dist: Parkwest Pubns., Inc.

—Mr Meddle Stories. (ENG.). 240p. (J). pap. 5.95 *(978-0-09-965550-3(0))* Penguin Random Hse. GBR. Dist: Trafalgar Square Publishing.

—Mr Pink-Whistle's Party. 2nd ed. (Illus.). 111p. (J). pap. 7.99 *(978-0-7475-3853-0(0))* Bloomsbury Publishing Plc GBR. Dist: Trafalgar Square Publishing.

—The Secret of Cliff Castle. (Illus.). 117p. (J). pap. 7.99 *(978-0-7475-3214-9(1))* Bloomsbury Publishing Plc GBR. Dist: Trafalgar Square Publishing.

—The Secret of the Lost Necklace: 3 Great Adventure Stories. Biro, Val, illus. 2013. (ENG.). 272p. (J). 16.50 *(978-1-84135-587-0(9))* Award Pubns. Ltd. GBR. Dist: Parkwest Pubns., Inc.

—The Strange Umbrella: And Other Stories. Gregory, Sally, illus. 2013. 192p. (J). 9.95 *(978-1-84135-461-3(9))* Award Pubns. Ltd. GBR. Dist: Parkwest Pubns., Inc.

Blyton, Enid, et al. The Fairies' Shoemaker & Other Stories. 2013. (ENG., Illus.). 192p. (J). 9.99 *(978-1-84135-458-3(9))* Award Pubns. Ltd. GBR. Dist: Parkwest Pubns., Inc.

BMI Staff, compiled by. Fear Street Collection - Set, 98 vols. 2009. (YA). 114.81 *(978-1-60884-415-9(3))* BMI Educational Services.

Boatwright-Cook, Jane. The Skeleton Leaf Stories: Behind the Shutters. 2012. 124p. 23.99 *(978-1-4772-1346-9(5))*; pap. 14.95 *(978-1-4772-1347-6(3))* AuthorHouse.

Bock, Caroline. Lie: A Novel. 2011. (ENG.). 224p. (YA). (gr. 7-18). pap. 18.99 *(978-0-312-66832-7(5)*, 900071231, St. Martin's Griffin) St. Martin's Pr.

Boelter, Ashaki. Diaries of the Doomed. Boelter, Ashaki, illus. 2004. (Illus.). 88p. (YA). per. 6.95 *(978-0-9721067-4-0(X)*, Writing Wild & Crazy) Shakalot High Entertainment.

—Diaries of the Doomed 2: Fate of the Fatal. 2007. (Illus.). 114p. (J). per. 11.95 *(978-0-9796219-0-1(9)*, Writing Wild & Crazy) Shakalot High Entertainment.

Bogacki, Tomek. Mi Primer Jardin. 2003. (Picture Bks.). (SPA., Illus.). (J). *(978-970-690-649-6(5))* Planeta Mexicana Editorial S. A. de C. V.

Boie, Kirsten. King-Kong, Mi Mascota Secreta. (Torre de Papel Ser.) (SPA.). (J). (gr. 2). 7.95 *(978-958-04-1310-3(X))* Norma S.A. COL. Dist: Distribuidora Norma, Inc.

Bojunga, Lygia. La Cama. (SPA.). (J). *(978-958-04-6492-1(8))* Norma S.A. COL. Dist: Distribuidora Norma, Inc.

Boldt, Claudia. Uugghh! Boldt, Claudia, illus. 2011. (Child's Play Library). (Illus.). 32p. (J). (gr. 2-2). *(978-1-84643-372-6(X))* Child's Play International Ltd.

Bolt, Ranjit. The Hare & the Tortoise. Potter, Giselle, illus. 2006. (ENG.). 64p. (J). (gr. -1-3). 19.99 *(978-1-905236-54-1(9))* Barefoot Bks., Inc.

Bond, Alan. Tedoul. Swanson, Peter Joseph, illus. 2009. 28p. pap. 8.95 *(978-1-60076-137-9(2))* StoneGarden.net Publishing.

Bondanella Filutze, Ann M. On Gramma's Rocker: Animal Tales & Other Short Stories. 2013. 84p. pap. 27.95 *(978-1-4624-0498-8(7)*, Inspiring Voices) Author Solutions, LLC.

Bongiovanni, Debbie. It's All about Magic or Is It?, 1 vol. 2009. 55p. pap. 16.95 *(978-1-61546-875-1(7))* America Star Bks.

—Kindness Pays Off, 1 vol. 2010. 58p. pap. 16.95 *(978-1-4489-6320-1(6))* America Star Bks.

Bono, Elena & Bono, E. El Sombrero de Ramito. Brignole, Giancarla, tr. Bono, Elena, illus. rev. ed. 2006. (Fabulas De Familia Ser.). (SPA & ENG., Illus.). 32p. (J). (gr. k-4). pap. 6.95 *(978-970-20-0261-1(3))* Castillo, Ediciones, S. A. de C. V. MEX. Dist: Macmillan.

Booker, Carolyn. Mr. Green Squash Takes a Journey. 2005. (J). pap. 8.00 *(978-0-8059-6638-1(2))* Dorrance Publishing Co., Inc.

Borchini, Ernest. Three Stories about Jonathan, the Computer, & Little Kitty: Three Short Stories about a Boy & His Magic Cat. 2013. 36p. (gr. -1). pap. 15.49 *(978-1-4669-6636-9(X))* Trafford Publishing.

Borges, Jorge Luis. Breve Ant de Ctos Fantastico. (SPA.). pap. 11.95 *(978-950-07-1350-4(0))* Editorial Sudamericana S.A. ARG. Dist: Distribooks, Inc.

Borges, Jorge Luis, et al. Cuentos Latinoamericanos: Antologia. 2nd ed. 2003. (SPA., Illus.). 134p. (J). (gr. 8-12). 14.95 *(978-968-19-0319-0(6))* Aguilar, Altea, Taurus, Alfaguara, S.A. de C.V MEX. Dist: Santillana USA Publishing Co., Inc.

Bornemann, Elsa. Los Grendelines. Pez, illus. 2003.Tr. of Grendelines. (SPA.). 70p. (J). (gr. 3-5). pap. 11.95 *(978-950-511-244-9(0))* Alfaguara S.A. de Ediciones ARG. Dist: Santillana USA Publishing Co., Inc.

—El Nino Envuelto. Duforu, Sebastian, illus. 2003. (SPA.). 176p. (YA). (gr. 5-8). pap. 13.95 *(978-950-511-623-2(3))* Alfaguara S.A. de Ediciones ARG. Dist: Santillana USA Publishing Co., Inc.

—Socorro! 12 Cuentos para Caerse de Miedo. (SPA., Illus.). 192p. (J). (gr. 5-8). pap. 10.95 *(978-968-19-0549-1(0))* Santillana USA Publishing Co., Inc.

—Socorro Diez y Otros Cuentos.Tr. of Socorro Diez & Other Stories. (SPA.). (YA). (gr. 5-8). pap. 7.95 *(978-958-04-2776-6(3))* Norma S.A. COL. Dist: Distribuidora Norma, Inc.

Boudreau, Bobby A. Inspirational Stories for Spiritual Youth. 2010. 124p. 29.99 *(978-1-4490-8105-8(3))*; pap. 18.99 *(978-1-4490-8106-5(1))* AuthorHouse.

Bourne, Sylvia. Animal Tales. 2009. 49p. pap. 31.50 *(978-1-4452-1311-8(7))* Lulu Pr., Inc.

S

Bowden, Poona. Juno Wonders. 2009. (Illus.). (J). 15.99 *(978-0-9821737-0-1(9))* Elotos Pr., LLC.
—Juno¡¯s Dromen. 2009. (DUT., Illus.). (J). 15.99 *(978-0-9821737-1-8(7))* Elotos Pr., LLC.
Boyer, Allen B. Roberto's Bat. 2003. (Summit Books Ser.). (Illus.). 128p. (gr. 3-6). lib. bdg. 13.95 *(978-0-7569-1642-8(9))* Perfection Learning Corp.
Boyer, Allen B. & Hatala, Dan. Roberto's Bat. 2003. (Illus.). 128p. 6.95 *(978-0-7891-6149-9(4))* Perfection Learning Corp.
Boyle, T. C. The Human Fly & Other Stories. 2005. (ENG.). 192p. (YA). (gr. 7-7). 9.99 *(978-0-14-240363-1(6),* Speak) Penguin Young Readers Group.
Brackett, Leigh & Coppel, Jr., Alfred. Planet Stories - Summer 1949. 2008. 128p. (YA). pap. 14.95 *(978-1-59798-181-1(8))* Adventure Hse.
Bradshaw, John. Fun Campfire Ghost Stories. 2009. 114p. pap. 13.98 *(978-0-557-11729-1(1))* Lulu Pr., Inc.
—Fun campfire Stories. 2009. 132p. pap. 13.98 *(978-0-557-17897-1(5))* Lulu Pr., Inc.
—Fun campfire stories Anthology. 2009. (ENG.). 245p. pap. 19.98 *(978-0-557-18835-2(0))* Lulu Pr., Inc.
Bradshaw, Sara, et al. Nine Novels by Younger Americans. 2007. (ENG.). 864p. (J). (gr. 9). pap. 18.00 *(978-0-9770844-4-9(2))* 826 Valencia.
Brady, Karen. God Is Great: A Collection of 13 Story Book Poems. 1. I.t. ed. 2004. (Illus.). 20p. (J). 12.50 *(978-0-9754169-0-7(1))* Bradybooks.biz.
Brainard, Cecilia M., ed. Growing up Filipino: Stories for Young Adults. 2003. (Illus.). xv, 298p. (YA). per. 18.95 *(978-0-9719458-0-7(2))* PALH.
Brallier, Max. Beneath the Bed & Other Scary Stories: an Acorn Book (Mister Shivers #1), Vol. 1. Rubegni, Letizia, illus. 2019. (Mister Shivers Ser.: 1). (ENG.). 64p. (J). (gr. k-2). pap. 4.99 *(978-1-338-31853-1(5))* Scholastic, Inc.
—Beneath the Bed & Other Scary Stories: an Acorn Book (Mister Shivers #1) (Library Edition), Vol. 1. Rubegni, Letizia, illus. 2019. (Mister Shivers Ser.: 1). (ENG.). 64p. (J). (gr. k-2). 23.99 *(978-1-338-31854-8(3))* Scholastic, Inc.
—Galactic Hot Dogs Collection (Boxed Set) Galactic Hot Dogs 1; Galactic Hot Dogs 2; Galactic Hot Dogs 3. Maguire, Rachel & Kelley, Nichole, illus. 2017. (Galactic Hot Dogs Ser.). (ENG.). 912p. (J). (gr. 3-7). 41.99 *(978-1-4814-9802-9(9),* Aladdin) Simon & Schuster Children's Publishing.
Brandeis, Madeline. Shaun O'Day of Ireland. 2004. reprint ed. pap. 22.95 *(978-1-4179-2725-8(9))* Kessinger Publishing, LLC.
Braymer, Donna. The Adventures of Rowdy Raccoon. 2006. (J). audio compact disk 5.99 *(978-0-9766823-8-7(9))* Sable Creek Pr. LLC.
Breckon, Brett, illus. Dragon Days. 2004. (ENG.). 82p. 17.95 *(978-1-84323-301-5(0))* Beekman Bks., Inc.
Brennan, Sarah Rees & Clare, Cassandra. The Bane Chronicles. 2015. lib. bdg. 25.75 *(978-0-606-37862-8(6))* Turtleback.
Breshears, Alyce Park. Friends - a Collection of Stories. 2013. 88p. pap. 10.95 *(978-1-60414-682-0(6))* Fideli Publishing, Inc.
Brett, Jan, illus. Annie & the Wild Animals Book & CD. 2012. (ENG.). 32p. (J). (gr. -1-3). audio 10.99 *(978-0-547-85082-5(4),* 1501067, Clarion Bks.) HarperCollins Pubs.
Bridwell, Norman. Clifford Collection. Bridwell, Norman, illus. 2012. (ENG., Illus.). 192p. (J). (gr. -1-k). 12.99 *(978-0-545-45013-3(6))* Scholastic, Inc.
Bright, Belle. Crash, Bang, Boom, Zing. Bright, Michael, illus. 2009. 12p. pap. 24.95 *(978-1-60749-383-9(7))* America Star Bks.
Brindis, Laura. Cuentos Universales del Barroco a la Vanguardia. 2003. (SPA., Illus.). 224p. (YA). (gr. 7-18). *(978-968-6966-05-3(6))* EDITER'S Publishing Hse. MEX. Dist: EDITER'S Publishing Hse.
Brisley, Joyce Lankester. The Milly-Molly-Mandy Storybook. Brisley, Joyce Lankester, illus. 2019. (ENG., Illus.). 224p. (J). 15.99 *(978-0-7534-7471-6(9),* 900196716, Kingfisher) Roaring Brook Pr.
Broberg, Penelope Northrop. Sleuthy Gumshoe: The Remarkable Detective. 2011. 32p. (gr. -1). pap. 14.39 *(978-1-4567-6404-3(7))* AuthorHouse.
Broderick, Paula. The Quest: The First Toby & Sox Adventure. 2011. (ENG., Illus.). 160p. pap. *(978-1-84876-626-6(2))* Troubador Publishing Ltd.
Brodhead, Kimberly Renee. The Seedling: The Osarian Tales. 2008. 232p. pap. 24.95 *(978-1-60703-814-6(5))* America Star Bks.
Brodsky, Slava. Funny Children's Stories (in Russian - Smeshnye detskie Rasskazy) 2006. (RUS.). 144p. pap. 8.76 *(978-0-615-16120-4(0))* Manhattan Academia.
Bromfield, Val. If You Can't Sleep... & Other Stories. 2005. (ENG., Illus.). 48p. pap. *(978-1-84401-416-3(9))* Athena Pr.
Brooke, L. Leslie. The Story of the Three Little Pig & Other Shorts Works. I.t. ed. 2007. 70p. 18.99 *(978-1-4346-1999-0(0))* Creative Media Partners, LLC.
Brooks, Felicity & Litchfield, Jo. Tales from Littletown. 2004. (Usborne Easy Reading Bks.). (ENG., Illus.). 1p. (J). (gr. -1-3). 9.95 *(978-0-7460-3474-3(1))* EDC Publishing.
Brophy, Ann. Novus 3 & Me: Six Short Stories about Friendship. 2010. 44p. pap. 18.49 *(978-1-4490-7132-5(5))* AuthorHouse.
Brothers Grimm. Rapunzel & Other Tales: Includes the Ugly Duckling & the Boy Pirate. 2008. (J). 34.99 *(978-1-60514-832-8(6))* Findaway World, LLC.
Broutin, Christian & Delafosse, Claude. In the Jungle. Broutin, Christian, illus. 2013. (ENG., Illus.). 36p. (J). (gr. -1-k). spiral bd. 19.99 *(978-1-85103-417-8(X))* Moonlight Publishing, Ltd. GBR. Dist: Independent Pubs. Group.
Brouwer, Sigmund. Blazer Drive, 1 vol. 2007. (Orca Sports Ser.). (ENG.). 168p. (J). (gr. 4-7). per. 10.95 *(978-1-55143-717-0(1))* Orca Bk. Pubs. USA.
Brown, Abbie Farwell. Tales of the Red Children. 2006. pap. 20.95 *(978-1-4286-1602-8(0))* Kessinger Publishing, LLC.
Brown, Carron, ed. Beauty & the Beast & Jack & the Beanstalk: Two Tales & Their Histories, 1 vol. 2009. (World of Fairy Tales Ser.). (ENG., Illus.). 32p. (J). (gr. 1-2). lib. bdg. 27.27 *(978-1-60754-649-8(3),* 3079cb84-6d3c-43f2-97dd-d6322e622ae4, Windmill Bks.) Rosen Publishing Group, Inc., The.
—Cinderella & Aladdin: Two Tales & Their Histories, 1 vol. 2009. (World of Fairy Tales Ser.). (ENG., Illus.). 32p. (J). (gr. 1-2). pap. 11.55 *(978-1-60754-644-3(2),* 7d71cf35-ec17-42a7-8ead-0d0a31b5a40d); lib. bdg. 27.27 *(978-1-60754-643-6(4),* 10640e0c-5eb7-4d3a-a7c9-383eca662b1f) Rosen Publishing Group, Inc., The. (Windmill Bks.).
—Hansel & Gretel & the Pied Piper of Hamelin: Two Tales & Their Histories, 1 vol. 2009. (World of Fairy Tales Ser.). (ENG., Illus.). 32p. (J). (gr. 1-2). pap. 11.55 *(978-1-60754-647-4(7),* 50f28c21-5b2d-4816-a5d5-9a9c216f2b71); lib. bdg. 27.27 *(978-1-60754-646-7(9),* 78299961-bab8-4737-878a-ff17ffac108c) Rosen Publishing Group, Inc., The. (Windmill Bks.).
Brown, Craig. Mule Train Mail. Brown, Craig, illus. 2009. (ENG., Illus.). 36p. (J). (gr. -1-3). pap. 7.95 *(978-1-58089-188-2(8))* Charlesbridge Publishing, Inc.
Brown, Elizabeth. Collection of Children's Tales. 2006. 94p. pap. 16.95 *(978-1-4116-8022-7(7))* Lulu Pr., Inc.
Brown, Marc. Arthur & the Mystery of the Stolen Bike. 2012. (ENG., Illus.). 64p. (J). (gr. 1-4). pap. 5.99 *(978-0-316-13363-0(9))* Little, Brown Bks. for Young Readers.
Brown, Margaret Wise. A Baby's Gift: Goodnight Moon & the Runaway Bunny, 2 vols. Hurd, Clement, illus. 2022. (ENG.). 70p. (J). (gr. -1 — 1). pap. 15.99 *(978-0-694-01638-9(1),* HarperFestival) HarperCollins Pubs.
—Home for a Bunny: A Bunny Book for Kids. Williams, Garth, illus. 2012. (Little Golden Book Ser.). 24p. (J). (gr. k-k). 4.99 *(978-0-307-93009-5(2),* Golden Bks.) Random Hse. Children's Bks.
Brown, Paul. Still Another Time , Times Remembered. 2011. 128p. pap. 38.28 *(978-1-4670-2548-5(8))* AuthorHouse.
Brown, Paul Henry. Grandpa Still Remembers: Life Changing Stories for Kids of All Ages from a Missionary Kid in Africa. Deborah, Brown Armes, illus. 2013. 162p. pap. 14.95 *(978-1-61153-027-8(X))* Light Messages Publishing.
Brown, Roberta Simpson. Scared in School. 2005. (ENG.). 141p. (J). (gr. 6-9). pap. 8.95 *(978-0-87483-496-3(1))* August Hse. Pubs., Inc.
—The Walking Trees & Other Scary Stories. 2006. (ENG.). 140p. (J). (gr. 6-9). pap. 11.95 *(978-0-87483-143-6(1))* August Hse. Pubs., Inc.
Bruce, Ann Elizabeth. Inspire Your Spirit. 2007. 48p. per. *(978-1-897312-54-4(7))* Adlibbed Ltd.
Bruchac, Joseph. Flying with the Eagle, Racing the Great Bear: Tales from Native North America. 2011. (ENG., Illus.). 128p. (J). (gr. 3-9). pap. 12.95 *(978-1-55591-693-0(7))* Fulcrum Publishing.
Bruchac, Joseph, et al. Sports Shorts. 2007. (Illus.). 127p. (J). per. 4.99 *(978-1-58196-058-7(1),* Darby Creek) Lerner Publishing Group.
—Sports Shorts: An Anthology of Short Stories. 2005. (Illus.). 127p. (J). (gr. 4-7). 15.95 *(978-1-58196-040-2(9),* Darby Creek) Lerner Publishing Group.
Bryant, Sara Cone. Stories to Tell Children: Fifty-Four Stories with Some Suggestions for Telling. 2017. (ENG., Illus.). (J). 24.95 *(978-1-374-81610-7(8));* pap. 14.95 *(978-1-374-81609-1(4))* Capital Communications, Inc.
—Stories to Tell Children: Fifty-Four Stories with Some Suggestions for Telling. 2007. (ENG.). 186p. pap. 19.99 *(978-1-4346-0234-3(6))* Creative Media Partners, LLC.
Buchan, John. The Magic Walking Stick & Stories from the Arabian Nights. Soper, Vernon, illus. 2007. 336p. per. 19.95 *(978-0-9791702-8-7(1))* Capricorn Hse. Publishing.
Buckingham, Royce. Goblins! An Underearth Adventure. 2008. (ENG.). 240p. (J). (gr. 4-6). 21.19 *(978-0-399-25002-6(6))* Penguin Young Readers Group.
Bugs & Other Stories: Individual Title Six-Pack. (Story Steps Ser.). (gr. k-2). 48.00 *(978-0-7635-9616-3(7))* Rigby Education.
Bumpus, Tawanna. Tawanna's Children's Short Story Collections. 2005. (Illus.). 48p. (J). pap. 14.95 *(978-1-59800-007-8(1))* Outskirts Pr., Inc.
Bunting, Eve. Finn Mccool & the Great Fish. Pullen, Zachary, illus. 2010. (Myths, Legends, Fairy & Folktales Ser.). (ENG.). 32p. (J). (gr. 1-4). 16.95 *(978-1-58536-366-7(9),* 202151) Sleeping Bear Pr.
Burgess, Thornton W. Big Book of Animal Stories. 2011. (Dover Children's Classics Ser.). (ENG., Illus.). 272p. (J). (gr. 3-8). 9.95 *(978-0-486-41980-0(0),* 419800) Dover Pubns., Inc.
—Mother West Wind 'Where' Stories. 2009. 108p. 22.95 *(978-1-60664-597-0(8));* 104p. pap. 9.95 *(978-1-60664-326-6(6))* Rodgers, Alan Bks.
—Mother West Wind 'Why' Stories. 108p. (gr. -1-3). 2007. per. 9.95 *(978-1-60312-004-3(1))* 2006. 22.95 *(978-1-59818-467-9(9))* Aegypan.
—Mother West Wind's Children. Kerr, George, illus. 2013. (Dover Children's Classics Ser.). (ENG.). 144p. (J). (gr. 1-5). pap. 5.00 *(978-0-486-49724-2(0),* 497240) Dover Pubns., Inc.
—Old Mother West Wind. Kerr, George, illus. annot. ed. 2011. (Dover Children's Classics Ser.). (ENG.). 336p. (J). (gr. 1-5). 25.00 *(978-0-486-48051-0(8),* 480518) Dover Pubns., Inc.
—Old Mother West Wind. 2004. reprint ed. pap. 1.99 *(978-1-4192-3812-3(4));* pap. 15.95 *(978-1-4191-3812-6(X))* Kessinger Publishing, LLC.
—Old Mother West Wind. 2011. 110p. 23.95 *(978-1-4638-9554-9(2))* Rodgers, Alan Bks.
—Tales from the Storyteller's House. (J). 19.95 *(978-0-8488-0930-0(0))* Amereon Ltd.
—Thornton Burgess Five-Minute Bedtime Tales: From Old Mother West Wind's Library. Cady, Harrison, illus. 2011. (Dover Children's Classics Ser.). (ENG.). 128p. (J). (gr. 1-5). pap. 14.99 *(978-0-486-47111-2(X),* 47111X) Dover Pubns., Inc.
Burke, Ruth. Gowandale Adventure: And other stories for Boys. 2007. (Illus.). 96p. 9.00 *(978-1-84625-070-5(6))* DayOne Pubns. GBR. Dist: Send The Light Distribution LLC.
Burkhart, Jessica. Canterwood Crest Stable of Stories (Boxed Set) Take the Reins; Behind the Bit; Chasing Blue; Triple Fault. 2014. (Canterwood Crest Ser.). (ENG., Illus.). 1088p. (J). (gr. 4-8). pap. 31.99 *(978-1-4814-1474-6(7),* Aladdin) Simon & Schuster Children's Publishing.
Burleigh, Robert. Night Flight: Amelia Earhart Crosses the Atlantic. Minor, Wendell, illus. 2011. (ENG.). 40p. (J). (gr. -1-3). 19.99 *(978-1-4169-6733-0(8),* Simon & Schuster/Paula Wiseman Bks.) Simon & Schuster/Paula Wiseman Bks.
Burnett, Eric. 21st Century Voices. 2003. 210p. (YA). pap. 17.95 *(978-0-595-29649-1(1))* iUniverse, Inc.
Burnett, Frances. Esmeralda, Mère Giraud's Little Daughter, Little Saint Elizabeth & Other Stories: A Collection of Short Stories by Frances Hodgson Burnett. 2012. 378p. *(978-1-78139-164-8(5))* Benediction Classics.
Burnett, Roger J. & Burnett, Wilma J. Short Stories & Tall Tales. 2012. 104p. pap. 9.95 *(978-1-4759-5168-4(X))* iUniverse, Inc.
Burnham, Clara Louise. Jewel's Story Book. 2017. (ENG., Illus.). (J). 25.95 *(978-1-374-81424-0(5))* Capital Communications, Inc.
Burningham, John. John Burningham: Limited Edition. Burningham, John, illus. ltd. ed. 2009. (ENG., Illus.). 224p. (gr. 5-12). 70.00 *(978-0-7636-4434-5(X))* Candlewick Pr.
Burns, Dal. The Kookaburra & Other Stories. 2007. (ENG.). 76p. per. 16.95 *(978-1-4241-1770-3(4))* PublishAmerica, Inc.
Burrows, Terry. ¡Oh, No! Es Hipo! (SPA.). 78p. (J). (gr. k-2). *(978-968-5308-88-5(8),* Silver Dolphin en Español) Advanced Marketing, S. de R. L. de C. V.
Burt, Steve. Wicked Odd: Still More Stories to Chill the Heart. Hagerman, Jessica, illus. 2006. 144p. (gr. 5-18). pap. 14.95 *(978-0-9741407-2-8(4))* Burt, Steven E.
Burton, Bria & burton, brain. Lance & Ringo Tails: The Wild Adventures of a Dog & a Cat As Told by Their Human. 2013. 134p. pap. 9.99 *(978-1-939181-45-9(3))* Soul Attitude Press.
Burton, Tim. Melancholy Death of Oyster Boy, the-Holiday Ed: And Other Stories. 2008. (ENG., Illus.). 128p. (gr. 7-18). 19.95 *(978-0-06-052649-8(1),* Dey Street Bks.) HarperCollins Pubs.
Butler, Ellis Parker. Pigs Is Pigs & Other Favorites. 2004. reprint ed. pap. 20.95 *(978-1-4179-2471-4(3))* Kessinger Publishing, LLC.
Butler, Kynora. Knowing Is Believing in Reading: Facing Your Fears. 2007. 48p. per. 16.95 *(978-1-4241-7559-8(3))* America Star Bks.
Butler, Tom. My Childhood Stories. 2010. (ENG.). 103p. pap. *(978-0-557-26571-8(1))* Lulu Pr., Inc.
Butterworth, Nick. The Whisperer. Butterworth, Nick, illus. 2004. (ENG., Illus.). 32p. (J). *(978-0-00-712017-8(6))* HarperCollins Pubs.
Buyer, Robert & Coute, Ursula T. Family Work & Fun Through the Years: Four Stories about Children & Families Having Fun Working Together. 2013. 64p. (gr. 2-4). pap. 13.99 *(978-1-4624-0614-2(9),* Inspiring Voices) Author Solutions, LLC.
Buzzeo, Toni. No T. Rex in the Library. Yoshikawa, Sachiko, illus. 2010. (ENG.). 32p. (J). (gr. -1-3). 19.99 *(978-1-4169-3927-6(X),* McElderry, Margaret K. Bks.) McElderry, Margaret K. Bks.
Byers, Brian, illus. Noah's Babies Opposites & Offerings. 2005. 22p. (J). bds. 6.95 *(978-0-9746440-6-6(4))* Virtue Bks.
C., Brandi & Flanagan, Logan. City Mom Country Dad. 2009. pap. *(978-1-61584-398-5(1))* Independent Pub.
Caeden Goes to Daycare. 2004. (Illus.). 32p. (J). 5.95 *(978-0-9759321-1-7(X))* Rascal Treehouse Publishing.
Cagle, Erica. My Little Book of Stories. 2003. 40p. per. *(978-1-59196-418-6(0))* Instant Pub.
Caine, Rachel, pseud & Vincent, Rachel. Immortal: Love Stories with Bite. Cast, P.c., ed. 2009. (Illus.). 280p. (J). (gr. 9-12). pap. 8.95 *(978-1-933771-92-2(5))* BenBella Bks.
Calico Illustrated Classics, 12 vols., Set 3. Incl. Dracula. Stoker, Bram. Simon, Ute, illus. 38.50 *(978-1-61641-101-5(5),* 4009); Grimm's Fairy Tales. Grimm, Jacob & Grimm, Wilhelm K. Canga, C. B., illus. 38.50 *(978-1-61641-102-2(3),* 4011); Invisible Man. Wells, H. G. Fisher, Eric Scott, illus. 38.50 *(978-1-61641-103-9(1),* 4013); Journey to the Center of the Earth. Vern, Jules. Fisher, Eric Scott, illus. 38.50 *(978-1-61641-104-6(X),* 4015); Kidnapped. Stevenson, Robert Louis. Fisher, Eric Scott, illus. 38.50 *(978-1-61641-105-3(8),* 4017); Merry Adventures of Robin Hood. Pyle, Howard. Simon, Ute, illus. 38.50 *(978-1-61641-107-7(4),* 4021); Oliver Twist. Dickens, Charles. McWilliam, Howard, illus. 38.50 *(978-1-61641-106-0(6),* 4019); Secret Garden. Burnett, Frances. Simon, Ute, illus. 38.50 *(978-1-61641-108-4(2),* 4023); Sherlock Holmes & the Hound of the Baskervilles. Conan Doyle, Arthur. Caparó, Antonio Javier, illus. 38.50 *(978-1-61641-109-1(0),* 4025); War of the Worlds. Wells, H. G. Fisher, Eric Scott, illus. 38.50 *(978-1-61641-111-4(2),* 4029); White Fang. London, Jack. VanArsdale, Anthony, illus. 38.50 *(978-1-61641-112-1(0),* 4031); 20,000 Leagues under the Sea. Vern, Jules. Fisher, Eric Scott, illus. 38.50 *(978-1-61641-110-7(4),* 4027); (J). (gr. 2-5). (Calico Illustrated Classics Ser.: 12). (ENG.). 112p. 2011. Set lib. bdg. 462.00 *(978-1-61641-100-8(7),* 4007, Calico Chapter Bks.) ABDO Publishing Co.
Calico Illustrated Classics Set 4, 12 vols. 2011. (Calico Illustrated Classics Ser.: 12). (ENG., Illus.). 112p. (J). (gr. 2-5). 462.00 *(978-1-61641-609-6(2),* 4033, Calico Chapter Bks.) ABDO Publishing Co.
The Call of the Wild Guide. 16.47 *(978-0-13-425968-0(8))* Prentice Hall PTR.
Cam, Philip. Thinking Stories 3: Teacher Resource. (Illus.). 64p. tchr. ed. *(978-0-86806-633-2(8),* Hale & Iremonger) GHR Pr., The.
A Camel Called Bump-Along, 6 vols., Set B. 32p. (gr. 1-3). 31.50 *(978-0-7802-8049-6(0))* Wright Group/McGraw-Hill.
Campbell, Kathy. Down under Advent Calendar of Chrissy Stories: Great Activities for the 2013 Silly Season. 2013. 60p. pap. 23.95 *(978-1-4525-6540-8(6),* Balboa Pr.) Author Solutions, LLC.
Campos, Paula. The Turtle's Shell. Ortega, Macarena, illus. 2008.Tr. of tortuga Golosa. (J). pap. 14.95 *(978-0-9801147-5-1(6))* Jorge Pinto Bks.
Campus Confessions Sample Set: XO Ronette/Frenemies/Choices/Crush. 2013. (ENG.). (YA). (gr. 8-12). pap. 39.80 *(978-1-62250-787-0(8))* Saddleback Educational Publishing, Inc.
Caplan, Frank A. The Donkey Who Lost His Tail. 2010. (Illus.). 20p. 12.49 *(978-1-4520-2778-4(1))* AuthorHouse.
Caple, Kathy. Termite Tales: Brand New Readers. Caple, Kathy, illus. 2009. (Brand New Readers Ser.). (ENG., Illus.). 48p. (J). (gr. -1-3). pap. 6.99 *(978-0-7636-3901-3(X))* Candlewick Pr.
—Termite Trouble: Brand New Readers. Caple, Kathy, illus. 2005. (Brand New Readers Ser.). (ENG., Illus.). 32p. (J). (gr. -1-3). pap. 6.99 *(978-0-7636-2573-3(6))* Candlewick Pr.
Captain, Cliff. Fables by the Sea, 2 vols. 2005. 145p. (J). Vol. 1. pap. *(978-0-9766401-0-3(4))* Vol. 2. pap. *(978-0-9766401-1-0(2))* Aenor Trust, The.
Capucilli, Alyssa Satin. Biscuit's Neighborhood: 5 Fun-Filled Stories in 1 Box! Schories, Pat, illus. 2018. (My First I Can Read Ser.). (ENG.). 160p. (J). (gr. -1-3). pap. 19.99 *(978-0-06-268826-2(X),* HarperCollins) HarperCollins Pubs.
—Scat, Cat! Meisel, Paul, illus. 2010. (My First I Can Read Ser.). (ENG.). 32p. (J). (gr. -1 — 1). pap. 5.99 *(978-0-06-117756-9(3),* HarperCollins) HarperCollins Pubs.
Caracappa, Michael. Storybook: From Age Three to Young Teenager. 2012. 84p. 19.95 *(978-1-4626-6773-4(2))* America Star Bks.
Cardoso, Onelio Jorge. Caballito Blanco. 2003. (SPA.). 78p. *(978-84-85334-48-3(5),* LG0124) Lóguez Ediciones ESP. Dist: Lectorum Pubns., Inc.
Carey-Costa, Denise. A Tale of Three Tails. Sjostrom, Nicole & Iseminger, Jonathon, illus. 2009. 81p. 10.99 *(978-1-4251-8492-6(8))* Trafford Publishing.
Carle, Eric. The Eric Carle Mini Library (Boxed Set) A Storybook Gift Set. Carle, Eric, illus. 2009. (World of Eric Carle Ser.). (ENG., Illus.). 148p. (J). 14.99 *(978-1-4169-8516-7(6),* Little Simon) Little Simon.
—The Eric Carle Ready-To-Read Collection (Boxed Set) Have You Seen My Cat?; the Greedy Python; Pancakes, Pancakes!; Rooster Is off to See the World; a House for Hermit Crab; Walter the Baker. Carle, Eric, illus. 2014. (World of Eric Carle Ser.). (ENG., Illus.). 160p. (J). (gr. -1-2). pap. 15.99 *(978-1-4814-1632-0(4),* Simon Spotlight) Simon Spotlight.
—The Very Eric Carle Treasury. Carle, Eric, illus. 2017. (ENG., Illus.). 152p. (J). (-k). 35.00 *(978-1-5247-3992-8(8))* Penguin Young Readers Group.
Carlson, Lavelle. Can a Toucan Hoot Too? A Phonemic Awareness Tale, 10 vols. Adams, Lucas, illus. 2003. 32p. (J). (gr. -1-1). per. 16.95 *(978-0-9725803-0-4(1))* Children's Publishing.
Carlson, Lori Marie. Moccasin Thunder: American Indian Stories for Today. 2005. (ENG.). 176p. (YA). (gr. 8-18). 17.99 *(978-0-06-623957-6(5),* HarperCollins) HarperCollins Pubs.
Carlson, Melody. La Oveja Perdida. 2004.Tr. of Lost Lamb. 8.99 *(978-0-7899-1240-4(6))* Editorial Unilit.
Carmen Luisa. The Adventures of Cotin Mirel: Three Short Stories. 2012. 20p. pap. 10.95 *(978-1-4525-5161-6(8))* Balboa Pr.
Carmichael, Bruce. The Little Path by Shadow Mountain. 2003. (J). per. 10.95 *(978-1-58597-198-5(7))* Leathers Publishing.
Carolyn, Larsen. Grandmas 8 Special Stories for Little Boys. 2003. *(978-1-892354-87-7(X))* Educational Publishing Concepts, Inc.
Carpenter, Frances. Tales of a Korean Grandmother: 32 Traditional Tales from Korea. (Illus.). 318p. (J). (gr. 4-7). 2019. (ENG.). pap. 8.99 *(978-0-8048-5160-2(3))* 2017. pap. 9.95 *(978-0-8048-4920-3(X))* Tuttle Publishing.
Carrero, Jorge & Cody, William. Buffalo Bill. 2003. (Timeless Classics Ser.). (SPA., Illus.). 92p. (J). (gr. 5-8). pap. 12.95 *(978-84-204-5778-9(7))* Santillana USA Publishing Co., Inc.
Carroll, Lewis, pseud. AILICE'S AVENTURS IN WUNNERLAND. 2011. (GER., Illus.). 140p. pap. *(978-1-904808-64-0(6))* Evertype.
—Alice's Adventures in Wonderland & Other Stories. Tenniel, John, illus. 2013. (Leather-Bound Classics Ser.). (ENG.). 544p. lthr. 24.99 *(978-1-60710-933-4(6),* Canterbury Classics) Printers Row Publishing Group.
—LA AVENTURAS DE ALISIA EN LA PAIS DE MERVELIAS. 2012. (GER., Illus.). 136p. pap. *(978-1-904808-88-6(3))* Evertype.
—LES-AVENTURES D'ALICE O PEYIS DES MERVEY. 2012. (GER., Illus.). 150p. pap. *(978-1-904808-87-9(5))* Evertype.
Carroll, Lewis, pseud & Bué, Henri. Les Adventures D'Alice Au Pays des Merveilles. 2010. (FRE., Illus.). 138p. pap. *(978-1-904808-52-7(2))* Evertype.
Carroll, Lewis, pseud & Everson, Michael. Alice's Adventures in Wonderland: Retold in Words of One Syllable. 2010. (Illus.). 108p. pap. *(978-1-904808-44-2(1))* Evertype.
Carroll, Lewis, pseud & Roberts, Selyf. Anturiaethau Alys Yng Ngwlad Hud. 2010.Tr. of Alice in Wonderland. (WEL., Illus.). 126p. pap. *(978-1-904808-46-6(8))* Evertype.
Carroll, Lewis, pseud & Stowell, Brian. Contoyryssyn Ealish Ayns Cheer Ny Yindyssyn. 2010. (Illus.). 144p. pap. *(978-1-904808-48-0(4))* Evertype.
Carryl, Charles E. The Admiral's Caravan: A Tale Inspired by Lewis Carroll's Wonderland. 2011. 110p. pap. *(978-1-904808-66-4(2))* Evertype.
—Davy & the Goblin: Or, What Followed Reading 'Alice's Adventures in Wonderland' 2011. (Illus.). 128p. pap. *(978-1-904808-65-7(4))* Evertype.
Carson, Rae. The Girl of Fire & Thorns Stories. 2014. (Girl of Fire & Thorns Novella Ser.). (ENG., Illus.). 272p. (YA). (gr. 8). pap. 9.99 *(978-0-06-233433-6(6),* Greenwillow Bks.) HarperCollins Pubs.
Cart, Michael. Necessary Noise: Stories about Our Families As They Really Are. Noruzi, Charlotte, illus. 2006. (ENG.). 256p. (YA). (gr. 8-12). reprint ed. pap. 9.99 *(978-0-06-051437-2(X),* HarperTeen) HarperCollins Pubs.
Cart, Michael, ed. Love & Sex. 2003. (ENG.). 240p. (YA). (gr. 8). pap. 13.95 *(978-0-689-85668-6(7),* Simon Pulse) Simon Pulse.
Cart, Michael, et al. How Beautiful the Ordinary: Twelve Stories of Identity. 2009. (ENG.). 368p. (YA). (gr. 9-18). 17.99 *(978-0-06-115498-0(9),* HarperTeen) HarperCollins Pubs.
—Taking Aim: Power & Pain, Teens & Guns. 2016. (ENG.). 368p. (YA). (gr. 8). pap. 9.99 *(978-0-06-232736-9(4),* HarperTeen) HarperCollins Pubs.
Carter, Grant Matthew. The Disaster Caster. Morling, Donovan, illus. 2012. 38p. pap. 16.00 *(978-1-4349-8432-6(X),* RoseDog Bks.) Dorrance Publishing Co., Inc.

Carter-Johnson, Helen. Golden Memories of Childhood. 2012. 68p. pap. 10.00 *(978-0-9853814-0-0(X))* Professional Publishing Hse. LLC.

Cartwright, Stephen. Llittle Book of Train Stories. rev. ed. 2011. (Farmyard Tales Readers Ser.). 64p. (J). ring bd. 8.99 *(978-0-7945-3070-9(2),* Usborne) EDC Publishing.

Carvajal, Victor. Como un Salto de Campana. 2003. (Alfaguara Infantil y Juvenil Ser.). (SPA., Illus.). 143p. (J). (gr. 5-8). per. 10.95 *(978-956-270-001-6(1))* Santillana USA Publishing Co., Inc.

—Cuentatrapos. (Barco de Vapor). (SPA.). 120p. (YA). (gr. 5-8). *(978-84-348-1606-0(7),* SM0595) SM Ediciones.

Carver, Peter, ed. The Blue Jean Collection. 2007. (ENG.). 224p. mass mkt. 9.95 *(978-0-920633-94-6(3))* Thistledown Pr., Ltd. CAN. Dist: Univ. of Toronto Pr.

Carville, Declan. The Fairy Glen. (Illus.). 36p. pap. 7.95 *(978-0-9538222-3-2(0))* Discovery Pubns. GBR. Dist: Irish Bks. & Media, Inc.

Cassidy, Georgina M. The True Make Believe Story: TTMBS Collection. 2011. 64p. pap. 31.99 *(978-1-4628-6236-8(5))* Xlibris Corp.

Cast, Kristin, et al. Kisses from Hell. 2010. (ENG.). 272p. (YA). (gr. 9-18). pap. 10.99 *(978-0-06-195696-6(1),* HarperTeen) HarperCollins Pubs.

Castor, Harriet. The Incredible Present. Young, Norman, illus. 2004. (Usborne Young Reading: Series Two Ser.). 64p. (J). (gr. k-4). 8.99 *(978-0-7945-1785-4(4),* Usborne) EDC Publishing.

Cauvin, Raoul. Bluecoats - Greenhorn, Vol. 4. Lambil, Willy, illus. 4th ed. 2011. (Bluecoats Ser.: 4). 48p. (J). (gr. -1-12). pap. 11.95 *(978-1-84918-066-5(0))* CineBook GBR. Dist: National Bk. Network.

Caviezel, Giovanni. Little Bunny. Rigo, Laura, illus. 2010. (Look at Me Bks.). 10p. (J). (gr. -1-k). bds. 8.99 *(978-0-7641-6322-7(1))* Sourcebooks, Inc.

—Little Puppy. Rigo, Laura, illus. 2010. (Mini Look at Me Bks.). 10p. (J). (gr. -1 — 1). bds. 8.99 *(978-0-7641-6324-1(8))* Sourcebooks, Inc.

Cawthon, Scott. The Cliffs: an AFK Book (Five Nights at Freddy's: Fazbear Frights #7), 1 vol., Vol. 7. 2021. (Five Nights at Freddy's Ser.: 7). (ENG.). 224p. (YA). (gr. 7-7). pap. 9.99 *(978-1-338-70391-7(9))* Scholastic, Inc.

Cawthon, Scott, et al. Fazbear Frights Four Book Box Set: an AFK Book Series, 1 vol. 2020. (Five Nights at Freddy's Ser.). (ENG.). 1984p. (YA). (gr. 7-7). pap., pap., pap. 39.96 *(978-1-338-71580-4(1))* Scholastic, Inc.

—Step Closer: an AFK Book (Five Nights at Freddy's: Fazbear Frights #4), 1 vol. 2020. (Five Nights at Freddy's Ser.: 4). (ENG.). 224p. (YA). (gr. 7-7). pap. 9.99 *(978-1-338-57605-4(4))* Scholastic, Inc.

Celebrated A Staff. Story Parade: A Collection of Modern Stories for Boys & Girls. 2005. reprint ed. pap. 33.95 *(978-1-4191-1378-9(X))* Kessinger Publishing, LLC.

Cerebellum Corporation, prod. Willow Pond Storybook. 2011. cd-rom 39.95 *(978-1-61867-207-0(X))* Cerebellum Corp.

Cerpok, M. L. The Mobile Monk: A Zen Tale. Wagner, Gavin, illus. 2008. 73p. pap. 19.95 *(978-1-60610-138-4(2))* America Star Bks.

Challenger, Robert James. Grizzly's Home: And Other Northwest Coast Children's Stories, 1 vol. 2005. (ENG., Illus.). 48p. (J). (gr. 1-3). pap. 9.95 *(978-1-894384-94-0(6))* Heritage Hse. CAN. Dist: Orca Bk. Pubs. USA.

—Nature's Circle: And Other Northwest Coast Children's Stories, 1 vol. 2009. (ENG., Illus.). 48p. (J). (gr. 1-3). pap. 9.95 *(978-1-894384-77-3(6))* Heritage Hse. CAN. Dist: Orca Bk. Pubs. USA.

Chananie, Gloria. It's Story Time Grandm. 2009. 82p. pap. 19.95 *(978-1-4489-8091-8(7))* America Star Bks.

Chance, C. The Trepets Book Three Rabbit Race Day. Champion, Vanessa, illus. 2007. 112p. per. *(978-0-9551289-2-9(7),* Bumble Bks.) Dragonfly Bks. & Arts.

Channing, Blanche Mary. Zodiac Stories. 2006. pap. 30.95 *(978-1-4286-3675-0(7))* Kessinger Publishing, LLC.

Charles, Veronika Martenova. It's Not about the Apple! Easy-To-Read Wonder Tales. Parkins, David, illus. 2010. (Easy-To-Read Wonder Tales Ser.: 4). 64p. (J). (gr. k-3). pap. 5.95 *(978-0-88776-955-9(1),* Tundra Bks.) Tundra Bks. CAN. Dist: Penguin Random Hse. LLC.

—It's Not about the Crumbs! Easy-To-Read Wonder Tales. Parkins, David, illus. 2010. (Easy-To-Read Wonder Tales Ser.: 3). 64p. (J). (gr. k-3). pap. 5.99 *(978-0-88776-953-5(5),* Tundra Bks.) Tundra Bks. CAN. Dist: Penguin Random Hse. LLC.

—It's Not about the Hunter! Easy-To-Read Wonder Tales. Parkins, David, illus. 2010. (Easy-To-Read Wonder Tales Ser.: 1). 56p. (J). (gr. k-3). pap. 5.95 *(978-0-88776-948-1(9),* Tundra Bks.) Tundra Bks. CAN. Dist: Penguin Random Hse. LLC.

—It's Not about the Pumpkin! Easy-To-Read Wonder Tales. Parkins, David, illus. 2010. (Easy-To-Read Wonder Tales Ser.: 2). 64p. (J). (gr. k-3). pap. 5.95 *(978-0-88776-949-8(7),* Tundra Bks.) Tundra Bks. CAN. Dist: Penguin Random Hse. LLC.

—It's Not about the Rose! Easy-To-Read Wonder Tales. Parkins, David, illus. 2010. (Easy-To-Read Wonder Tales Ser.: 5). 64p. (J). (gr. k-3). pap. 5.95 *(978-0-88776-954-2(3),* Tundra Bks.) Tundra Bks. CAN. Dist: Penguin Random Hse. LLC.

Charlip, Remy & Joyner, Jerry. Thirteen. 2018. (ENG., Illus.). 32p. (J). (gr. k-4). 17.95 *(978-1-68137-230-3(4),* NYR Children's Collection) New York Review of Bks., Inc., The.

Chase, Anita, et al. Tundra Adventures. Chase, Anita et al, illus. 2006. (Adventure Story Collection Ser.). 28p. (J). (gr. 2-6). pap. 10.00 *(978-1-58084-254-9(2))* Lower Kuskokwim Schl. District.

Check, S. A., et al. Haunted Hijinks. Jourdan, Diego & Galligher, John, illus. 2019. (ENG.). 128p. (J). pap. 19.99 *(978-1-945205-17-0(2),* 569b79fc-c4dc-495f-80a1-cae5adb305ab) American Mythology Productions.

Cheyney, Arnold. Legends of Arts. 2007. 128p. pap. 14.95 *(978-1-59647-137-5(9))* Good Year Bks.

A Chicago Winds Set, 6 vols. 32p. (gr. 1-3). 26.50 *(978-0-7802-8047-2(4))* Wright Group/McGraw-Hill.

Chichester Clark, Emma. No Mas Besos! (SPA.). (J). 8.95 *(978-958-04-6884-4(2))* Norma S.A. COL. Dist: Distribuidora Norma, Inc.

Chidebelu-Eze/Dove Publishing, Chibueze / Obi. The Tales of Tortoise: Inspirational Stories of Wisdom. Newborne, David / F., illus. 2005. (ENG.). 76p. (J). 16.00 *(978-0-9766578-0-4(5))* Dove Publishing, Inc.

Chidley, Howard J. FiftyTwo Story Talks to Boys & Girls D. 2007. pap. *(978-1-4065-1446-9(2))* Dodo Pr.

Child, Lauren. I Am Really, Really Concentrating. 2008. (Charlie & Lola Ser.). (ENG.). 24p. (J). (gr. -1-k). mass mkt. 4.99 *(978-0-448-44905-0(6),* Grosset & Dunlap) Penguin Young Readers Group.

Child, Lydia Maria. The Magician's Show Box & Other Stories. 2007. (ENG.). 124p. per. *(978-1-4065-1354-7(7))* Dodo Pr.

—The Magician's Show Box & Other Stories. 2007. 88p. per. *(978-1-4068-4552-5(3))* Echo Library.

—The Magician's Show Box & Other Stories. 2004. reprint ed. pap. 19.95 *(978-1-4191-7122-2(4));* pap. 1.99 *(978-1-4192-7122-9(9))* Kessinger Publishing, LLC.

—The Magician's Show Box, & Other Stories by the Author of Rainbows for Children. 2006. 312p. per. 23.99 *(978-1-4255-2973-4(9))* Michigan Publishing.

Children of Appalachia. Teddy Bear Helps on the Farm. Children of Appalachia, illus. 2007. (Illus.). 64p. (J). per. 14.95 *(978-0-929915-73-9(9))* Headline Bks., Inc.

Childress, Story. The Old Codger, 1 vol. 2009. 23p. pap. 19.95 *(978-1-4489-2511-7(8))* PublishAmerica, Inc.

Chin, Oliver. Tales from the Chinese Zodiac: The 12 Year Box Set. 2017. (Tales from the Chinese Zodiac Ser.). (Illus.). 480p. (J). (gr. -1-3). pap. 179.95 *(978-1-59702-137-1(7))* Immedium.

Chisiya. Afrikan Lullaby: Folk Tales from Zimbabwe. 2012. (Illus.). 56p. pap. 31.99 *(978-1-4691-7174-6(0))* Xlibris Corp.

Choudhry, Fahima. The Snow Surprise. 2011. 24p. pap. 15.99 *(978-1-4653-4628-5(7))* Xlibris Corp.

Choyce, Lesley. Sudden Impact. 2006. (Orca Currents Ser.). 104p. (gr. 5-9). 19.95 *(978-0-7569-6876-2(3))* Perfection Learning Corp.

Christ at the Coffee Shop. 2004. lib. bdg. *(978-0-9747425-0-2(3),* 09747425) Tranquility Ranch Publishing.

Christ Legends & Other Stories. 2012. 204p. pap. *(978-1-84902-141-8(4))* Benediction Classics.

Christelow, Eileen. Five Little Monkeys Storybook Treasury. Christelow, Eileen, illus. 2009. (Five Little Monkeys Story Ser.). (ENG., Illus.). 192p. (J). (gr. -1-3). 12.99 *(978-0-547-23873-9(8),* 1084232, Clarion Bks.) HarperCollins Pubs.

Christensen, Gerda. Troll Peter Discovers the Bog-Woman's Secret & Other Stories. 2010. 40p. pap. 18.27 *(978-1-4251-8822-1(2))* Trafford Publishing.

—Troll Peter Finds A Treasure at the End of the Rainbow & Other Stories: Troll Peter's Adventures, Book 2. 2010. 36p. pap. 18.41 *(978-1-4269-3697-5(4))* Trafford Publishing.

Christian, Lmh. Stories from the Red Glass. 2008. 48p. pap. 14.95 *(978-0-9798154-9-2(5))* Living Waters Publishing Co.

Christie, Jackie. Wacky WaterSlide Wipeout. 2011. 28p. (gr. -1). pap. 16.09 *(978-1-4269-5821-2(8))* Trafford Publishing.

Christmas Is Coming. 2003. (J). 6.99 *(978-1-59384-012-9(8))* Parklane Publishing.

Church, Peggy Pond. The Pancake Stories: Cuentos Del Panqueque. Chilton, Noël, tr. Church, Elizabeth Comfort, illus. 2013. (ENG & SPA.). 96p. (J). 12.95 *(978-0-8263-5387-0(8),* P225290) Univ. of New Mexico Pr.

Civardi, Anne. Cambiarse de Casa. (SPA.). 16p. (J). 4.50 *(978-84-7655-125-7(8))* Plaza Joven, S.A. ESP. Dist: AIMS International Bks., Inc.

Claflin, Willy. Maynard Moose Tales. 2007. (J). 34.99 *(978-1-59895-864-5(X))* Findaway World, LLC.

Clairmont, Patsy. 5 Cheesy Stories: About Friendship, Bravery, Bullying, & More, 1 vol. Oeltjenbruns, Joni, illus. 2007. (Tails from the Pantry Ser.). (ENG.). 144p. (J). (gr. -1-2). 15.99 *(978-1-4003-1042-5(3),* Tommy Nelson) Nelson, Thomas Inc.

Clare, Cassandra, et al. The Bane Chronicles. Clare, Cassandra, ed. 2014. (Bane Chronicles Ser.). (ENG., Illus.). 528p. (YA). (gr. 9). 24.99 *(978-1-4424-9599-9(5),* McElderry, Margaret K. Bks.) McElderry, Margaret K. Bks.

Clark, Margery. The Poppy Seed Cakes: Illustrated by Maud & Miska Petersham. Petersham, Maud & Petersham, Miska, illus. 2013. (Everyman's Library Children's Classics Ser.). (ENG.). 160p. 26.95 *(978-0-375-71232-6(1),* Everyman's Library) Knopf Doubleday Publishing Group.

Clarke, J. Erskine. Chatterbox for 1927. 2005. pap. 30.95 *(978-1-4179-8685-9(9))* Kessinger Publishing, LLC.

—Chatterbox For 1928. 2005. reprint ed. pap. 30.95 *(978-1-4179-8686-6(7))* Kessinger Publishing, LLC.

Clasicos Argentinos. (Clasicos Juveniles Coleccion). (SPA.). (YA). (gr. 5-8). pap. *(978-950-11-1409-6(0),* SG7924) Sigmar ARG. Dist: Lectorum Pubns., Inc.

Clasicos de Amor. (Clasicos Juveniles Coleccion). (SPA.). (YA). (gr. 5-8). pap. *(978-950-11-1278-8(0),* SG4719) Sigmar ARG. Dist: Lectorum Pubns., Inc.

Clasicos de Animales. (Coleccion Clasicos Juveniles). (YA). (gr. 5-8). pap. *(978-950-11-1579-6(8),* SG1714) Sigmar ARG. Dist: Lectorum Pubns., Inc.

Clasicos de Humor. (Coleccion Clasicos Juveniles). (SPA.). (YA). (gr. 5-8). pap. *(978-950-11-1549-9(6),* SG30754) Sigmar ARG. Dist: Lectorum Pubns., Inc.

Clasicos para Sonar: Bambi, Mago de Oz, Pulgarcita, Sirenita (Libro Rosa) 2003. (SPA.). 84p. 18.95 *(978-84-305-9976-9(2))* Susaeta Ediciones, S.A. ESP. Dist: Giron Bks.

Clasicos para Sonar: Blancanieves, Gato C/Botas, Caperucita (Libro Rojo) 2003. (SPA.). 86p. 18.95 *(978-84-305-9975-2(4))* Susaeta Ediciones, S.A. ESP. Dist: Giron Bks.

Clasicos Para Sonar: Libro de la Selva, Casita Chocolate, Mago Merlin. 2003. (SPA.). 96p. 18.95 *(978-84-305-9974-5(6))* Susaeta Ediciones, S.A. ESP. Dist: Giron Bks.

Clasicos para Sonar: Pinocho, Bella y la Bestia, Alicia (Libro Verde) 2003. (SPA.). 82p. 18.95 *(978-84-305-9977-6(0))* Susaeta Ediciones, S.A. ESP. Dist: Giron Bks.

Class Trip, 6 vols., Set. 2009. (J). (gr. 2-5). lib. bdg. 179.70 *(978-1-58415-812-7(3))* Mitchell Lane Pubs.

Classic Characters of Little Golden Books: The Poky Little Puppy; Tootle; the Saggy Baggy Elephant; Tawny Scrawny Lion; Scuffy the Tugboat, 5 vols. 2010. (Little Golden Book Ser.). (ENG., Illus.). 24p. (J). (gr. -1-k). 24.95 *(978-0-375-85934-2(9),* Golden Bks.) Random Hse. Children's Bks.

Classic Children's Tales. 2005. (ENG.). 912p. pap. *(978-1-84022-063-6(5))* Wordsworth Editions, Ltd.

Clawson, Kimberly. Fun O' Licious. Bellomy, Gail, illus. 2007. (ENG.). 56p. per. 16.95 *(978-1-4241-5556-9(8))* America Star Bks.

Claybourne, Anna, retold by. Stories from Shakespeare. 2005. (Stories from Shakespeare Ser.). 192p. (J). 24.99 *(978-0-7945-0912-5(6),* Usborne) EDC Publishing.

Cleary, Beverly. Ramona Empieza el Curso. 2003. (Ramona Quimby Ser.).Tr. of Ramona Quimby, Age 8. (SPA.). 144p. (J). 9.95 *(978-84-239-8891-4(0))* Espasa Calpe, S.A. ESP. Dist: Planeta Publishing Corp.

—Ramona y Su Madre. 2003. (Ramona Quimby Ser.).Tr. of Ramona & Her Mother. (SPA.). 108p. (J). 9.95 *(978-84-239-9040-5(0))* Espasa Calpe, S.A. ESP. Dist: Planeta Publishing Corp.

Clements, Andrew. Andrew Clements' School Stories (Boxed Set) Frindle; Landry News; the Janitor's Boy; the School Story; a Week in the Woods; Lunch Money; Room One; No Talking; Lost & Found; Extra Credit. 2013. (ENG., Illus.). 1856p. (J). (gr. 3-7). pap. 79.99 *(978-1-4424-9386-5(0),* Atheneum Bks. for Young Readers) Simon & Schuster Children's Publishing.

—Head of the Class (Boxed Set) Frindle; the Landry News; the Janitor's Boy. Selznick, Brian, illus. 2007. (ENG.). 416p. (J). (gr. 3-7). pap. 23.99 *(978-1-4169-4974-9(7),* Atheneum Bks. for Young Readers) Simon & Schuster Children's Publishing.

Clements, Richmond. Turning Tiger Special Edition. Finbow, Alexander, ed. 2012. (Illus.). 56p. pap. 7.99 *(978-1-926914-87-9(2))* Arcana Studio, Inc.

Clendenin, Arlene M. & Clendenin, Bernard S. The Adventures of the Yellow Beak Bird & the Flying Cats: Yellow Beak Bird & the Flying Cats. 2013. 48p. pap. 11.99 *(978-0-9897662-1-0(7))* Clendenin Fine Art Concepts.

Clinton, Althea L. & Madsen, Eleanor. A Treasury of Bedtime Stories: More Than 40 Classic Tales for Sweet Dreams! Peat, Fern Bisel, illus. 2017. (Children's Classic Collections). (ENG.). 96p. (J). (gr. -1-3). 12.99 *(978-1-944686-07-9(X),* Racehorse Publishing) Skyhorse Publishing Co., Inc.

Cloyd, Suzy. Pippi's Silent Message: Adventures of Suzy Q & You Too. Barham, Timothy E., illus. 2012. 24p. 24.95 *(978-1-4512-7832-3(2))* America Star Bks.

Clynes, Kate. Ali Baba. Anstey, David, illus. 2005. (SWA & ENG.). 32p. (J). pap. *(978-1-84444-429-8(5))* Mantra Lingua.

Coates, Theresa. Imaginary Time of Life. 2007. 102p. pap. 10.95 *(978-0-7414-4067-9(9))* Infinity Publishing.

Cofer, Judith Ortiz. Animal Jamboree / La Fiesta de los Animales: Latino Folktales / Leyendas Latinas. Rosales-Yeomans, Natalia, tr. 2012. (SPA & ENG.). (J). pap. 9.95 *(978-1-55885-743-8(5),* Piñata Books) Arte Publico Pr.

—An Island Like You: Stories of the Barrio. 2011. 9.15 *(978-0-7848-3583-8(7),* Everbind) Marco Bk. Co.

—An Island Like You: Stories of the Barrio. 2009. 243p. 17.00 *(978-1-60686-446-3(7))* Perfection Learning Corp.

Cohen, Leslie, et al. Jewish Love Stories for Kids: An Anthology of Short Stories. 2005. (Jewish Stories for Kids Ser.). 232p. (J). 16.95 *(978-1-930143-45-6(1),* 3451); pap. 12.95 *(978-1-930143-46-3(X),* 346X) Simcha Media Group. (Devora Publishing).

Cohn, Marvin. Tell Me A Story Gramps. 2007. 52p. pap. 16.95 *(978-1-4241-5075-5(2))* America Star Bks.

Colbert, Larry C. Insights from an Out-of-Sight Guy. 2005. 111p. per. 20.00 *(978-0-9766329-0-0(X))* Driving Vision, Inc.

Cole, Babette. El libro de etiqueta de Lady Lupina. 2003. (Babette Cole Ser.). (SPA.). (J). 18.95 *(978-84-233-3337-0(X))* Ediciones Destino ESP. Dist: Planeta Publishing Corp.

Cole, Bob. Power Reading: Nail-Biters! 2. Morton, Vivian, illus. 2005. 94p. (J). (gr. 6-18). vinyl bd. 89.95 *(978-1-883186-25-8(0),* PPNB2) National Reading Styles Institute, Inc.

Coleman, Ryan S. The Wonderful World of Folli: Milly & Tilly. 2012. 24p. 24.95 *(978-1-4626-6759-8(7))* America Star Bks.

A Collection of Stories Inspired by My Grandchildren. 2005. (YA). per. *(978-1-59872-111-9(9))* Instant Pub.

Collier, Kevin Scott. Hope, the Angelfish. Collier, Kevin Scott, illus. 2008. (Illus.). 24p. pap. 10.95 *(978-1-933090-17-7(0))* Guardian Angel Publishing, Inc.

Collins, Bert McLemore. Excitement at Double B Acres. 2009. 52p. pap. 22.49 *(978-1-4389-8447-6(2))* AuthorHouse.

Collins, Ellen M. My Book: Fun Favorite Stories. 2010. 68p. pap. 26.99 *(978-1-4490-5236-2(3))* AuthorHouse.

Collins, Paul. A Tale of Two Squirrels. 2008. 104p. pap. 9.95 *(978-1-60693-204-9(7),* Eloquent Bks.) Strategic Book Publishing & Rights Agency (SBPRA).

Comeau, Ceara. Adventures of the Young & Curious. 2008. (ENG.). 136p. pap. 10.94 *(978-0-557-00914-5(6))* Lulu Pr., Inc.

Comella, Maria Angeles & Seix, Merce. Una Tarde con Joan Oro. (SPA., Illus.). (J). (gr. 2-4). *(978-84-261-3075-4(5),* JV8905) Juventud, Editorial ESP. Dist: Lectorum Pubns., Inc.

The Complete Gideon Trilogy (Boxed Set) The Time Travelers; the Time Thief; the Time Quake. 2014. (Gideon Trilogy Ser.). (ENG., Illus.). 1424p. (J). (gr. 5-9). pap. 29.99 *(978-1-4814-2613-8(3),* Simon & Schuster Bks. For Young Readers) Simon & Schuster Bks. For Young Readers.

Conan Doyle, Arthur. Adv of the Devils Foot. 2010. (Illus.). 254p. (J). pap. *(978-4-591-11698-2(0))* Fukuinkan Shoten.

—Sherlock Holmes. 2003. (Retold Ser.). (Illus.). 282p. (J). (gr. 7-18). 15.99 *(978-0-7569-1196-6(6))* Perfection Learning Corp.

Concordia International School Shanghai. Stories from Room 113: International Adventures. 2008. 304p. pap. 18.95 *(978-0-595-53090-8(7))* iUniverse, Inc.

Connell, Richard Edward. The Most Dangerous Game. 2010. (Creative Short Stories Ser.). (Illus.). 48p. (J). (gr. 5-18). 19.95 *(978-1-58341-920-5(9),* Creative Education) Creative Co., The.

Connolly, Brian A. Allegheny River Christmas & Other Stories. 2007. 56p. per. 20.95 *(978-1-58939-992-1(7))* Virtualbookworm.com Publishing, Inc.

Conrad, Perrin Cothran. The Ballad of the Shirley T & Other Stories. 2011. 80p. pap. 8.95 *(978-1-4620-5671-2(7))* iUniverse, Inc.

Constans, Gabriel. Skin of Lions. 2009. 63p. pap. 13.75 *(978-1-60695-014-2(2))* Cacoethes Publishing Hse., LLC.

Conteh, Gerald. I Still Believe in Santa. 2007. 188p. per. 14.95 *(978-1-60264-014-6(9))* Virtualbookworm.com Publishing, Inc.

Cook, Julia. Making Friends Is an Art! Barnes, Bridget, illus. 2012. (ENG.). 32p. (J). pap. 10.95 *(978-1-934490-30-3(X))* Boys Town Pr.

—Sorry, I Forgot to Ask! My Story about Asking Permission & Making an Apology! De Weerd, Kelsey, illus. 2012. (ENG.). 32p. 16.95 *(978-1-934490-29-7(6));*Volume 3. 31p. (J). pap. 10.95 *(978-1-934490-28-0(8))* Boys Town Pr.

Cooke, Flora J. Nature Myths & Stories for Little Chil. 2006. pap. 19.95 *(978-1-4254-9629-6(6))* Kessinger Publishing, LLC.

Cooling, Wendy, ed. Ten of the Best: School Stories with a Difference. 2009. (ENG., Illus.). 192p. pap. 7.99 *(978-0-00-713339-0(1),* HarperCollins Children's Bks.) HarperCollins Pubs. Ltd. GBR. Dist: HarperCollins Pubs.

Coppage, Merry Ann. Periwinkle Island. Venema, Lisa J. & Garland, Lynn Rockwell, illus. 2006. (ENG.). 84p. (gr. -1-3). per. 31.99 *(978-1-4259-1931-3(6))* AuthorHouse.

Coppard, A. E. Clorinda Walks in Heaven Stories. 2006. 220p. per. *(978-1-4067-9414-4(7),* Pomona Pr.) Read Bks.

Coppens, Katie. The Acadia Files: Book Two, Autumn Science, 1 vol. Hatam, Holly, illus. 2018. (Acadia Science Ser.: 2). (ENG.). 80p. (J). (gr. 4-7). 13.95 *(978-0-88448-604-6(4),* 884604) Tilbury Hse. Pubs.

Cornwell, Brendan W., illus. Aesop in Goudy. 2007. 48p. (J). 20.00 *(978-0-9711321-1-5(9))* Blue Tree LLC.

Coro, Edys. Edys' Collection of Short Tales. 2008. 64p. pap. 19.95 *(978-1-60672-856-7(3))* America Star Bks.

Cortázar, Julio. Todos Los Fuegos el Fuego. (SPA.). (J). 9.00 *(978-958-04-6757-1(9))* Norma S.A. COL. Dist: Distribuidora Norma, Inc.

Cortez, Sarah, ed. You Don't Have a Clue: Latino Mystery Stories for Teens. 2011. 320p. (YA). (gr. 6-18). pap. *(978-1-55885-692-9(7))* Arte Publico Pr.

Cortright, Angel. The Miss Adventure of Animals & Their Short Stories. 2013. 28p. pap. 24.95 *(978-1-62709-063-6(0))* America Star Bks.

Covey, Ken. The Adventures of a Little Boy Named Kenny. 2008. 68p. pap. 10.95 *(978-1-4327-3110-6(6))* Outskirts Pr., Inc.

Covey, Sean. The 7 Habits of Happy Kids. 2008. (Playaway Children Ser.). (J). (gr. -1-3). 39.99 *(978-1-60640-956-5(5))* Findaway World, LLC.

—The 7 Habits of Happy Kids Collection (Boxed Set) Just the Way I Am; When I Grow up; a Place for Everything; Sammy & the Pecan Pie; Lily & the Yucky Cookies; Sophie & the Perfect Poem; Goob & His Grandpa. Curtis, Stacy, illus. 2013. (7 Habits of Happy Kids Ser.). (ENG.). 224p. (J). (gr. -1-1). 55.99 *(978-1-4424-9617-0(7),* Simon & Schuster Bks. For Young Readers) Simon & Schuster Bks. For Young Readers.

Coville, Bruce. Aliens Ate My Homework Collection (Boxed Set) Aliens Ate My Homework; I Left My Sneakers in Dimension X; the Search for Snout; Aliens Stole My Body. Coville, Katherine, illus. 2018. (Rod Allbright & the Galactic Patrol Ser.). (ENG.). 848p. (J). (gr. 3-7). pap. 27.99 *(978-1-5344-1514-0(9),* Aladdin) Simon & Schuster Children's Publishing.

—Odds Are Good: An Oddly Enough & Odder Than Ever Omnibus. 2006. (ENG., Illus.). 352p. (YA). (gr. 7-12). pap. 16.95 *(978-0-15-205716-9(1),* 1197183, Clarion Bks.) HarperCollins Pubs.

Cowell, Cressida. How to Train Your Dragon Special Edition: With Brand New Short Stories! 2014. (How to Train Your Dragon Ser.: 1). (ENG., Illus.). 432p. (J). (gr. 3-7). pap. 10.00 *(978-0-316-40747-2(X))* Little, Brown Bks. for Young Readers.

Cowley, Joy. Friends: Snake & Lizard. 2011. (Gecko Press Titles Ser.). (ENG., Illus.). 144p. 16.95 *(978-1-877579-01-1(7))* Gecko Pr. NZL. Dist: Lerner Publishing Group.

—Mrs. Wishy-Washy's Tub. (Story Box Ser.). 8p. 20.95 *(978-0-7802-9365-6(7))* Wright Group/McGraw-Hill.

Cowsert, Sandra. The Continuing Adventures of Tammi & Her Dragon. 2007. 48p. per. 16.95 *(978-1-4241-8313-5(8))* America Star Bks.

Coxon, Rachel. A Collection of Children's Stories. 2005. (J). spiral bd. *(978-0-9761675-3-2(0))* Storybook Acres.

Coy, Steven. Sandwich: Short Stories & Screenplays by Steven Coy. Saia, Karla, ed. Vaughan, Jeremy, illus. 2003. 229p. (YA). per. 10.00 *(978-0-9743235-0-3(0))* Better Non Sequitur.

Craig-Gaddis, Lora. Elsie & Pooka Stories of the Sabbats & Seasons. 2008. 126p. pap. 43.18 *(978-0-557-01530-6(8))* Lulu Pr., Inc.

Craig, Lindsey. Dancing Feet! Brown, Marc, illus. 2012. 32p. (J). (gr. k-k). 6.99 *(978-0-307-93081-1(5),* Knopf Bks. for Young Readers) Random Hse. Children's Bks.

Craik, Dinah Maria Mulock. The Fairy Book: The Best Popular Stories Selected & Rendered Anew. 2017. (ENG., Illus.). (J). 27.95 *(978-1-374-91336-3(7))* Capital Communications, Inc.

—The Fairy Book: The Best Popular Stories Selected & Rendered Anew. 2016. (ENG., Illus.). (J). 27.95 *(978-1-358-35305-5(0))* Creative Media Partners, LLC.

Cranch, Christopher Pearse. Three Children's Novels by Christopher Pearse Cranch. Little, Greta D. & Myerson, Joel, eds. 2010. (ENG.). 200p. pap. 25.95 *(978-0-8203-3704-3(8),* 4325) Univ. of Georgia Pr.

Crane, Walter. The Walter Crane Storybook Collection. 2017. (Calla Editions Ser.). (ENG., Illus.). 128p. 25.00 *(978-1-60660-114-3(8),* 601148) Dover Pubns., Inc.

Craven, Georgina. Adventures & Rhymes with Grandmother. 2006. (Illus.). 76p. pap. *(978-1-84401-648-8(X))* Athena Pr.

Crenshaw, Mills. The Christmas of 45. 2010. 176p. pap. 11.99 *(978-1-59955-455-6(0))* Cedar Fort, Inc./CFI Distribution.

Cribbs, Randy, narrated by. Tales from the Oldest City: Selected Readings Vol 1. 2005. (YA). cd-rom 8.95 *(978-0-9725796-3-6(X))* River Pr.

Crockett, Tilly. The Crockett Tales for Children. 2009. (Illus.). 60p. pap. 10.49 *(978-1-4389-6154-5(5))* AuthorHouse.

Cronin, Doreen. A Barnyard Collection: Click, Clack, Moo & More. Lewin, Betsy, illus. 2010. (Click Clack Book Ser.). (ENG.). 128p. (J). (gr. -1-3). 19.99 *(978-1-4424-1263-7(1),*

Atheneum Bks. for Young Readers) Simon & Schuster Children's Publishing.
Cross, Linda B. Lines from Linda. l.t. ed. 2003. 104p. (YA). per. 7.00 *(978-0-9748591-2-5(5)*, MSP) Yetto Publishing Co.
Crouse, Judy M. A Cat's Tale: Peanut's Story. 2009. (ENG.). 28p. pap. 21.99 *(978-1-4415-5452-9(1))* Xlibris Corp.
Crowe, Robert L. Children's Stories for ALmost Everyone. l.t. ed. 2006. Orig. Title: Children's Stories for Adults. 92p. (J). per. *(978-0-9707173-8-2(5))* Consortium Publishing Co.
Cudjoe, Dzagbe. Tales My Ghanaian Grandmother Told Me. 2008. 52p. pap. 19.95 *(978-1-934925-87-4(X)*, Strategic Bk. Publishing) Strategic Book Publishing & Rights Agency (SBPRA).
Cuentecitos: El Pajaro Azul.Tr. of Little Stories: The Blue Bird. (SPA.). 12p. (J). 3.98 *(978-970-607-902-2(5))* Larousse, Ediciones, S. A. de C. V. MEX. Dist: Giron Bks.
Cuentos Egipcios. (SPA., Illus.). (YA). 11.95 *(978-84-7281-068-6(2)*, AF1068) Auriga, Ediciones S.A. ESP. Dist: Continental Bk. Co., Inc.
Cuentos, Mitos y Leyendas para Ninos de America Latina (Stories, Myths & Legends for Latin American Children) (SPA., Illus.). 72p. (J). 9.95 *(978-958-04-0957-1(9)*, NOR9609) Norma S.A. COL. Dist: Distribuidora Norma, Inc.
El Cuidado del Aire. (Colección Biblioteca Juvenil de Ecología). (SPA.). (YA). (gr. 5-8). pap. *(978-958-04-2406-2(3)*, 80424062) Norma S.A. COL. Dist: Lectorum Pubns., Inc.
Cumming, Hannah. The Cloud. Cumming, Hannah, illus. 2010. (Child's Play Library). (Illus.). 32p. (J). (gr. 1-2). pap. *(978-1-84643-343-6(6))* Child's Play International Ltd.
—The Lost Stars. Cumming, Hannah, illus. 2011. (Child's Play Library). (Illus.). 32p. (J). *(978-1-84643-416-7(5))* Child's Play International Ltd.
Cummings, Alicia. The Adventures of Jayda. 2010. 44p. pap. 16.99 *(978-1-4520-2564-3(9))* AuthorHouse.
Cunningham, Thelma. Lisa's Unforgettable Stories. 2011. (ENG.). 270p. (YA). pap. 141.99 *(978-1-4568-6746-1(6))* Xlibris Corp.
Curfew, Baron. Around the Houses. 2008. 48p. pap. *(978-1-84923-303-3(9))* YouWriteOn.
Currie, Robin. The Baby Bible ABCs, 1 vol. Basaluzzo, Constanza, illus. 2009. (Baby Bible Ser.). (ENG.). 48p. (J). bds. 12.99 *(978-1-4347-6542-0(3)*, 106166) Cook, David C.
Currier Brileya, Elizabeth. Grandma B. 's Bedtime Stories. 2006. 68p. (J). pap. 8.39 *(978-1-4116-9504-7(6))* Lulu Pr., Inc.
Curtiss, Phebe A. Christmas Stories & Legends. Curtiss, Phebe A., ed. 2011. 118p. 22.95 *(978-1-4638-9660-7(3))* Rodgers, Alan Bks.
Curtiss, Phebe A., compiled by. Christmas Stories & Legends. 2017. (ENG., Illus.). (YA). (gr. 7-12). pap. *(978-93-86367-98-3(X))* Alpha Editions.
Curtiss, Phebe A., ed. Christmas Stories & Legends. 2009. 120p. pap. 10.95 *(978-1-60664-397-6(5))* Rodgers, Alan Bks.
Cuxart, Bernardette, illus. Cuentame un Cuento, No. 4. (SPA.). 96p. (J). (gr. k-3). *(978-84-480-1602-9(5)*, TM8095) Timun Mas, Editorial S.A. ESP. Dist: Lectorum Pubns., Inc.
Cynthia, Rylant. Every Living Thing. 2014. (ENG.). 96p. (J). (gr. 5-9). 10.24 *(978-1-63245-336-5(3))* Lectorum Pubns., Inc.
Cyr, Joe. Magical Trees & Crayons: Great Stories. 2006. (Illus.). pap. 9.95 *(978-0-9778525-6-7(3))* Peppertree Pr., The.
—Two Happy Stories. Owen, Ramon, illus. 2007. 36p. per. 12.95 *(978-1-934246-73-3(5))* Peppertree Pr., The.
Czarnota, Lorna MacDonald. Medieval Tales: That Kids Can Read & Tell. 2009. (ENG., Illus.). 96p. (J). (gr. 3-7). pap. 14.95 *(978-0-87483-588-5(7))* August Hse. Pubs., Inc.
D C Thomson Staff, ed. Animals & You Annual 2004. 2003. (Illus.). 128p. (J). 9.95 *(978-0-85116-840-1(X))* Thomson, D.C. & Co., Ltd. GBR. Dist: APG Sales & Distribution Services.
—Bunty Annual for Girls 2004. 2003. (Illus.). 128p. (J). (gr. -1-4). *(978-0-85116-825-8(6))* Thomson, D.C. & Co., Ltd. GBR. Dist: APG Sales & Distribution Services.
Dade, Barbara A. Story Time with Grandm. 2008. 88p. pap. 41.99 *(978-1-4363-5325-0(4))* Xlibris Corp.
Dadey, Debbie. A Mermaid Tales Sparkling Collection (Boxed Set) Trouble at Trident Academy; Battle of the Best Friends; a Whale of a Tale; Danger in the Deep Blue Sea; the Lost Princess. Avakyan, Tatevik, illus. 2013. (Mermaid Tales Ser.). (ENG.). 592p. (J). (gr. 1-4). pap. 29.99 *(978-1-4814-0055-8(X)*, Aladdin) Simon & Schuster Children's Publishing.
Dahl, Michael. The Doll That Waved Goodbye: And Other Scary Tales. Bonet, Xavier, illus. 2015. (Michael Dahl's Really Scary Stories Ser.). (ENG.). 72p. (J). (gr. 1-3). lib. bdg. 25.32 *(978-1-4965-0595-8(6)*, 128708, Stone Arch Bks.) Capstone.
—Frightmares 2: More Scary Stories for the Fearless Reader. Bonet, Xavier, illus. 2016. (Michael Dahl's Really Scary Stories Ser.). (ENG.). 224p. (J). (gr. 1-3). pap., pap., pap. 8.95 *(978-1-4965-4136-9(7)*, 133386, Stone Arch Bks.) Capstone.
—The Phantom on the Phone & Other Scary Tales. Bonet, Xavier, illus. 2015. (Michael Dahl's Really Scary Stories Ser.). (ENG.). 72p. (J). (gr. 1-3). lib. bdg. 25.32 *(978-1-4965-0597-2(2)*, 128710, Stone Arch Bks.) Capstone.
—Zombie Cupcakes: And Other Scary Tales. Bonet, Xavier, illus. 2016. (Michael Dahl's Really Scary Stories Ser.). (ENG.). 72p. (J). (gr. 1-3). lib. bdg. 25.32 *(978-1-4965-3774-4(2)*, 133104, Stone Arch Bks.) Capstone.
Dahl, Roald. The Complete Adventures of Charlie & Mr. Willy Wonka. Blake, Quentin, illus. 2010. (ENG.). 336p. (J). (gr. 3-7). 11.99 *(978-0-14-241740-9(8)*, Puffin Books) Penguin Young Readers Group.
—Los Cretinos. Blake, Quentin, illus. 2005. (Infantil Ser.).Tr. of Twist. (SPA.). 106p. (gr. 3-5). per. 9.95 *(978-968-19-0559-0(8))* Santillana USA Publishing Co., Inc.
—The Missing Golden Ticket & Other Splendiferous Secrets. Blake, Quentin, illus. 2010. (ENG.). 128p. (J). (gr. 3-7). 7.99 *(978-0-14-241742-3(4)*, Puffin Books) Penguin Young Readers Group.
—The Umbrella Man & Other Stories. 2004. (ENG.). 288p. (YA). (gr. 7-18). pap. 10.99 *(978-0-14-240087-6(4)*, Speak) Penguin Young Readers Group.
Daisy & the Rabbit's Tail. 2017. (ENG., Illus.). 176p. (J). 9.00 *(978-1-78270-140-8(0))* Award Pubns. Ltd. GBR. Dist: Parkwest Pubns., Inc.
Dajani, Suad Farsakh. Grandma's Stories: A Collection of Six Children's Stories. 2013. 40p. 25.99 *(978-1-4808-0051-9(1))*; pap. 16.99 *(978-1-4808-0049-6(X))* Archway Publishing.
Daley, James. Great Horse Stories. 2010. (Dover Children's Classics Ser.). (ENG.). 240p. (J). (gr. 3-5). pap. 7.99 *(978-0-486-47669-8(3)*, 476693) Dover Pubns., Inc.
Daley, Michael J. Beach Socks, 1 vol. Corke, Estelle, illus. 2013. (ENG.). 10p. (J). bds. 6.99 *(978-1-59572-637-7(3))* Star Bright Bks., Inc.
d'Allancé, Mireille. What a Tantrum. 2005. (SPA., Illus.). 32p. (J). 15.99 *(978-84-8470-115-6(8))* Corimbo, Editorial S.L. ESP. Dist: Iaconi, Mariuccia Bk. Imports.
Dalton, Annie. The Cosmic Collection. 2008. (Mei Beeby Agent Angel Ser.). (ENG.). 496p. (J). (gr. 4-7). pap., pap., pap. 19.95 *(978-0-00-723308-3(6))* HarperCollins Pubs. Ltd. GBR. Dist: Independent Pubs. Group.
Damron, Dugan. Further Adventures of Old Shorty: Tales of a Midwest Country Boy, 1 vol. 2010. 112p. pap. 19.95 *(978-1-4489-5838-2(5))* America Star Bks.
—Old Shorty: Tales of a Midwestern Farm Boy, 1 vol. 2009. 51p. pap. 16.95 *(978-1-60813-651-3(5))* America Star Bks.
Daniels, Susan & Vincent, Seth. Student Bylines Vol. 1: Anthology. 2003. 184p. (YA). pap. 13.95 *(978-0-595-27133-7(2)*, Writer's Showcase Pr.) iUniverse, Inc.
Darby, Joel, et al. Milestones. Grant, Lisa, ed. Day, Linda S., illus. l.t. ed. 2004. 32p. (J). 12.95 *(978-0-9759579-0-5(2))* Denver Broncos.
Dasent, G. W. East o' the Sun & West o' the Moon. 2005. pap. 28.95 *(978-1-4179-0435-8(6))* Kessinger Publishing, LLC.
Datlow, Ellen & Windling, Terri. Teeth: Vampire Tales. 2011. (ENG.). 480p. (YA). (gr. 8-18). pap. 9.99 *(978-0-06-193514-5(X)*, HarperCollins) HarperCollins Pubs.
Dave, Grandpa. Children's Stories Iii. 2012. 104p. (gr. 2-4). pap. 11.79 *(978-1-4669-1829-0(2))* Trafford Publishing.
Davidson, Susanna. Treasury of Animal Stories. 2008. (Stories for Young Children Ser.). 96p. (J). 16.99 *(978-0-7945-2095-3(2)*, Usborne) EDC Publishing.
Davies, Helen Emanuel. Siff a Saff: A Straeon Eraill. Maclean, Andrew, illus. 2005. (WEL.). 64p. pap. *(978-0-86381-364-1(X))* Gwasg Carreg Gwalch.
Davies, Robert, adapted by. Lit a Shuck for Texas: Adapted Louis l'Amour Short Stories Series. 2003. (Adapted Louis L'Amour Short Stories Ser.). (Illus.). 56p. (YA). *(978-1-57035-983-5(0)*, 233LIT) Cambium Education, Inc.
—Merrano of the Dry Country: Adapted Louis l'Amour Short Story Series. 2003. (Adapted Louis L'Amour Short Stories Ser.). (Illus.). 60p. (J). *(978-1-57035-985-9(7)*, 233MERRANO) Cambium Education, Inc.
Davis, Anthony C. I Ain't Lying. 2008. 112p. pap. 19.95 *(978-1-60474-087-5(6))* America Star Bks.
Davis, Beneta. My Covers. 2008. 24p. pap. 24.95 *(978-1-60441-584-1(3))* America Star Bks.
Davis, Lowrey. Papa's Storybook. 2008. 116p. 19.99 *(978-1-60791-100-5(0))*; pap. 11.99 *(978-1-60791-099-2(3))* Salem Author Services.
Davis, Richard, Jr. The Red Cross Girl & Other Stories. 2004. reprint ed. pap. 1.99 *(978-1-4192-7996-6(3))* Kessinger Publishing, LLC.
Day, Ed D. Why Dogs Bark: & Other Tall Tales. Scott, Sarah C., illus. 2006. 50p. (J). per. 12.95 *(978-1-933002-20-0(4))* PublishingWorks.
A Day for JJ & Me Set B, 6 vols. 32p. (gr. 1-3). 31.50 *(978-0-7802-8050-2(4))* Wright Group/McGraw-Hill.
De Blumenthal, Verra X. K. Folk Tales from the Russian. 2008. 88p. pap. 8.95 *(978-1-60664-152-1(2))* Aegypan.
de Fontaine, Jean. Fables. (FRE.). 482p. pap. 9.95 *(978-2-266-12775-2(6))* Presses Pocket FRA. Dist: Distribooks, Inc.
de la Ramée, Louise. Bimbi. 2007. 84p. per. *(978-1-4068-3736-0(9))* Echo Library.
de la Ramée, Louise & Ouida. Bimbi. 2007. 152p. per. 13.95 *(978-1-60312-344-0(X))*; 24.95 *(978-1-60312-682-3(1))* Aegypan.
de Las Casas, Dianne. The Gigantic Sweet Potato, 1 vol. Gentry, Marita, illus. 2010. (ENG.). 32p. (J). (gr. k-3). 16.99 *(978-1-58980-755-6(3)*, Pelican Publishing) Arcadia Publishing.
De Lint, Charles. Waifs & Strays. 2004. (ENG.). 416p. (YA). (gr. 7-18). 8.99 *(978-0-14-240153-7(7)*, Firebird) Penguin Young Readers Group.
De Maupassant, Guy. Contes du jour et de la nuit, Level C. (FRE.). 282p. (YA). (gr. 7-12). 9.99 *(978-0-88436-989-9(7)*, 40303) EMC/Paradigm Publishing.
Dean - Eb - Tales of Betsy-May. 2007. *(978-0-603-56287-7(6))* Farshore.
DeAnda, Diane. The Monster in the Mattress & Other Stories: El Monstruo en el Colchón y Otros Cuentos. 2011. (SPA & ENG., Illus.). 90p. (J). (gr. 3-7). pap. 9.95 *(978-1-55885-693-6(5)*, Piñata Books) Arte Publico Pr.
Deborah Strandberg, Rebecca Reynolds and. Trammler Triplet Tales Advente #4 MYSTERIOUS ABBY. 2007. (ENG.). 113p. pap. 8.90 *(978-1-4357-0651-4(X))* Lulu Pr., Inc.
Deborah Wanda. Wanda's Wittle Wunders. 2009. 32p. pap. 14.49 *(978-1-4389-4862-1(X))* AuthorHouse.
Deegan, J. E. When I Was a Little Guy. 2008. 76p. pap. 19.95 *(978-1-60703-120-8(5))* America Star Bks.
Defreitas, Henrietta. Henratty Mortimer: The Meerville Myth. 2012. (Illus.). 84p. pap. 32.03 *(978-1-4772-3867-7(0))* AuthorHouse.
Dehm, Debbie. Animal Stories of the Desert. 2009. (Illus.). 41p. (J). pap. 20.95 *(978-1-4327-3461-9(X))* Outskirts Pr., Inc.
Deighton, Jo, adapted by. Ali Baba & the Forty Thieves: Traditional Stories:Cinderella: The Elves & the Shoemaker. (Scheherazade Presents Ser.: No. 11). (Illus.). 48p. (J). pap. *(978-1-85964-101-9(6)*, Ithaca Pr.) Garnet Publishing, Ltd.
—Bacbouc the Lazy Tailor: Traditional Stories:Beauty & the Beast: The Red Shoes. (Scheherazade Presents Ser.: No. 12). (Illus.). 48p. (J). pap. *(978-1-85964-102-6(4)*, Ithaca Pr.) Garnet Publishing, Ltd.
—The Fisherman & the Wicked Genie: Traditional Stories:The Shepherdess & the Chimney Sweep: Seven with One Blow. (Scheherazade Presents Ser.: No. 14). (Illus.). 48p. (J). pap. *(978-1-85964-104-0(0)*, Ithaca Pr.) Garnet Publishing, Ltd.
Del Amo, Montserrat. El Nudo. (SPA.). 94p. (YA). (gr. 5-8). *(978-84-261-1691-8(4)*, JV2941) Juventud, Editorial ESP. Dist: Lectorum Pubns., Inc.
Del Negro, Janice M. Passion & Poison: Tales of Shape-Shifters, Ghosts, & Spirited Women, 0 vols. Natale, Vince, illus. 2013. (ENG.). 64p. (YA). (gr. 7-12). pap. 9.99 *(978-1-4778-1685-1(2)*, 9781477816851, Skyscape) Amazon Publishing.
del Rio, Ana Maria. La Historia de Manu (Manu's Story) Cardemil, Carmen, illus. 2003. (Coleccion Derechos Del Nino Ser.). (SPA.). 32p. (J). (gr. 3-5). pap. 7.95 *(978-84-204-5845-8(7))* Santillana USA Publishing Co., Inc.
Delacre, Lulu. Salsa Stories. Delacre, Lulu, illus. 2012. (ENG., Illus.). 112p. (J). (gr. 2-5). pap. 6.99 *(978-0-545-43098-2(4)*, Scholastic Pr.) Scholastic, Inc.
—Us, in Progress: Short Stories about Young Latinos. Delacre, Lulu, illus. (ENG., Illus.). 256p. (J). (gr. 3-7). 2019. pap. 9.99 *(978-0-06-239215-2(8))* 2017. 18.99 *(978-0-06-239214-5(X))* HarperCollins Pubs. (HarperCollins).
DeLand, M. Maitland. The Great Katie Kate Offers Answers about Asthma. 2011. (Illus.). 32p. 14.95 *(978-1-60832-074-5(X))* Greenleaf Book Group.
DeLand, M. Maitland. Baby Santa & the Lost Letters. 2011. (Illus.). 36p. (J). 14.95 *(978-1-60832-194-0(0))* Greenleaf Book Group.
Delaney, Joseph. The Last Apprentice: a Coven of Witches. Arrasmith, Patrick, illus. (Last Apprentice Short Fiction Ser.: 2). (ENG.). 240p. (YA). (gr. 8). 2011. pap. 10.99 *(978-0-06-196040-6(3))* 2010. 16.99 *(978-0-06-196038-3(1))* HarperCollins Pubs. (Greenwillow Bks.).
Demi. The Pandas & Their Chopsticks: And Other Animal Stories. 2014. (Illus.). 28p. (J). (gr. k-2). 16.95 *(978-1-937786-16-8(1)*, Wisdom Tales) World Wisdom, Inc.
Denkhaus, Henry. Anna & the Magical Horse - Henry the Hobo - the Pond. 2013. (Illus.). 50p. pap. 8.99 *(978-1-4624-0734-7(X)*, Inspiring Voices) Author Solutions, LLC.
Deogratias Simba. The Mystery Door. 2005. (Illus.). 22p. pap. *(978-9987-417-21-6(3))* Mkuki na Nyoka Pubs. TZA. Dist: Michigan State Univ. Pr.
dePaola, Tomie. La Hermanita de Tommy. (Buenas Noches Ser.).Tr. of Baby Sister. (SPA.). (J). (gr. 1-3). pap. 7.95 *(978-958-04-4290-5(8))* Norma S.A. COL. Dist: Lectorum Pubns., Inc., Distribuidora Norma, Inc.
DeSantis, Debi. A Bunch of Giggles & Hugs. l.t. ed. 2005. (Illus.). 26p. (J). 12.95 *(978-0-9770043-0-0(9))* New Global Publishing.
Deseret Book Company Staff, contrib. by. A Story to Tell: The Classic Book of Virtues for Children. 2nd ed. 2004. 508p. (J). 16.95 *(978-1-59038-359-9(1))* Deseret Bk. Co.
Deskins, Charlotte H. Tales from Poplar Hollow. Allen, Dana K., illus. 2004. 104p. pap. *(978-0-9753671-1-7(0))* Shamus B. Publishing.
Diamond Head High Series Pack, Nos. 1-3. 12.95 *(978-1-57306-108-7(5))* Bess Pr., Inc.
Diaz, Gloria Cecilia. La Botella Azul. (SPA.). (J). 8.95 *(978-958-04-6489-1(8))* Norma S.A. COL. Dist: Distribuidora Norma, Inc.
Diaz Granados, Jose Luiz. Cuentos y Leyendas de Colombia. (Torre de Papel Ser.). (SPA.). (J). (gr. 4-18). 8.95 *(978-958-04-5127-3(3))* Norma S.A. COL. Dist: Distribuidora Norma, Inc.
DiCamillo, Kate. Francine Poulet Meets the Ghost Raccoon: Tales from Deckawoo Drive, Volume Two. Van Dusen, Chris, illus. 2016. (Tales from Deckawoo Drive Ser.: 2). (ENG.). 112p. (J). (gr. 1-4). pap. 6.99 *(978-0-7636-9088-5(0))* Candlewick Pr.
—Where Are You Going, Baby Lincoln? Tales from Deckawoo Drive, Volume Three. Van Dusen, Chris, illus. 2016. (Tales from Deckawoo Drive Ser.: 3). (ENG.). 112p. (J). (gr. 1-4). 14.99 *(978-0-7636-7311-6(0))* Candlewick Pr.
DiCicco, Sue. Five Classic Golden Book Tales. 2018. (Step into Reading Ser.). (Illus.). 160p. (J). (gr. -1-1). pap. 8.99 *(978-0-525-64516-0(0)*, Random Hse. Bks. for Young Readers) Random Hse. Children's Bks.
Dickens, Charles. Illustrated Stories from Dickens. Ablett, Barry, illus. 2010. (Illustrated Stories Ser.). 352p. (YA). (gr. 3-18). 19.99 *(978-0-7945-2628-3(4)*, Usborne) EDC Publishing.
—Oliver Twist & Other Classic Tales. Thorne, Jenny, illus. 2015. 80p. (J). (gr. -1-12). pap. 9.99 *(978-1-86147-408-7(3)*, Armadillo) Anness Publishing GBR. Dist: National Bk. Network.
Dickens, Charles, et al. Christmas Books & Stories. 2004. (YA). cd-rom, audio compact disk 25.00 *(978-0-917466-15-1(2))* Seltzer Bks.
Dickins, Rosie, retold by. Illustrated Stories from Shakespeare. 2014. (ENG., Illus.). 414p. (J). 19.99 *(978-0-7945-2997-0(6)*, Usborne) EDC Publishing.
Dickins, Rosie & Sims, Lesley. Aesop's Stories for Little Children. 2015. (Stories for Little Children Gift Bks.). (ENG.). 224p. (J). 19.99 *(978-0-7945-2307-7(2)*, Usborne) EDC Publishing.
Dickinson, Asa Don. Good Cheer Stories Every Child Should Know. 2017. (ENG., Illus.). (J). 25.95 *(978-1-374-84726-2(7))*; pap. 15.95 *(978-1-374-84725-5(9))* Capital Communications, Inc.
Dickinson, Asa Don & Dickinson, Helen Winslow, eds. Patriotic Stories Every Child Should Know. 2005. reprint ed. pap. 30.95 *(978-1-4179-0694-9(4))* Kessinger Publishing, LLC.
Dickinson, Asa Don & Skinner, Ada M. The Children's Book of Christmas Stories. 2004. reprint ed. pap. 24.95 *(978-1-4191-5657-1(8))*; pap. 1.99 *(978-1-4192-5657-8(2))* Kessinger Publishing, LLC.
Dickinson, Peter. Earth & Air: Tales of Elemental Creatures. 2012. (ENG.). 256p. (J). (gr. 4). pap. 14.95 *(978-1-61873-038-1(X)*, Big Mouth Hse.) Small Beer Pr.
Diffenderfer, David W. The Adventures of Boo & Fred. 2010. 58p. pap. 9.99 *(978-1-60911-966-9(5)*, Eloquent Bks.) Strategic Book Publishing & Rights Agency (SBPRA).
Dillingham Pierson, Clara. Among the Farmyard People. 2008. 112p. pap. 8.15 *(978-1-60459-505-5(1))* Wilder Pubns., Corp.
—Among the Forest People. 2008. 92p. pap. 8.15 *(978-1-60459-501-7(9))* Wilder Pubns., Corp.
—Among the Meadow People. 2008. 84p. pap. 8.15 *(978-1-60459-504-8(3))* Wilder Pubns., Corp.
—Among the Night People. 2008. 96p. pap. 8.15 *(978-1-60459-503-1(5))* Wilder Pubns., Corp.
—Among the Pond People. 2008. 96p. pap. 8.15 *(978-1-60459-502-4(7))* Wilder Pubns., Corp.
—Clara Dillingham Pierson's Complete among the People Series. 2008. 352p. pap. 19.99 *(978-1-60459-528-4(0))* Wilder Pubns., Corp.
Disney Book Club Staff. Pirates of the Caribbean - On Stranger Tides: Six Sea Chanties - An Original Graphic Novel Anthology. 2011. (ENG.). 128p. (YA). (gr. 8-18). pap. 10.99 *(978-1-4231-3320-9(X))* Disney Pr.
Disney Books. Disney Christmas Storybook Collection. 2014. (Storybook Collection). (ENG., Illus.). 304p. (J). (gr. -1-k). 16.99 *(978-1-4231-8450-8(5)*, Disney Press Books) Disney Publishing Worldwide.
—Disney Storybook Collection-3rd Edition. 2015. (Storybook Collection). (ENG., Illus.). 304p. (J). (gr. -1-k). 16.99 *(978-1-4847-1348-8(6)*, Disney Press Books) Disney Publishing Worldwide.
—Mickey's Christmas Storybook Treasury. 2017. (Storybook Treasury Ser.). (ENG., Illus.). 256p. (J). (gr. 1-3). 30.00 *(978-1-368-00256-1(0)*, Disney Press Books) Disney Publishing Worldwide.
—Scary Storybook Collection. 3rd ed. 2017. (Storybook Collection). (ENG., Illus.). 304p. (J). (gr. 1-3). 16.99 *(978-1-4847-3239-7(1)*, Disney Press Books) Disney Publishing Worldwide.
—5-Minute Racing Stories. 2017. (5-Minute Stories Ser.). (ENG., Illus.). 192p. (J). (gr. 1-3). 12.99 *(978-1-368-00075-8(4)*, Disney Press Books) Disney Publishing Worldwide.
Disney Princess Staff, adapted by. Princess Enchanted Palace: Storybook & Play Castle. 2010. (Playbox Ser.). (ENG., Illus.). 32p. (J). (gr. -1-2). bds. 19.99 *(978-0-7944-2035-2(4))* Reader's Digest Assn., Inc., The.
Disney Princess Super Activity Fun Storybook Collection. 2005. (J). *(978-1-59487-168-9(X))* Artist Studios, Ltd.
Disney Staff. Stories to Tell a Three Year Old. 2005. (J). pap. *(978-0-7868-4333-6(0))* Disney Pr.
Disney Storybook Collection. 2005. (J). *(978-1-59487-135-1(3))* Artist Studios, Ltd.
Doherty, Gillian. Stories of Wizards. Edwards, Linda, illus. 2008. (Stories for Young Children Ser.). 95p. (J). (gr. 1). 16.99 *(978-0-7945-1915-5(6)*, Usborne) EDC Publishing.
Donahue, Bill. Grandma Wentworth's Children's Storybooks, Volume One. 2007. 56p. per. 16.95 *(978-1-4241-3269-0(X))* PublishAmerica, Inc.
Doo, DooLee. 4D Stories. 2012. (ENG.). 130p. pap. 9.98 *(978-0-557-17618-2(2))* Lulu Pr., Inc.
Doodler, Todd H. Peas on Earth. 2012. (Illus.). 20p. (J). (gr. -1 — 1). 6.99 *(978-0-307-93088-0(2)*, Robin Corey Bks.) Random Hse. Children's Bks.
Dostoevsky, Fyodor. Fiodor Mijailovich Dostoievsky. Acosta, Patricia, illus. 2003. (Cajon de Cuentos Ser.). (SPA.). 223p. (J). (gr. 4-7). *(978-958-30-1027-9(8))* Panamericana Editorial.
Douglas, Kathleen. Johnny, the Unaware Angel. 2007. 108p. per. 19.95 *(978-1-4241-9939-6(5))* PublishAmerica, Inc.
Douglas, Rachel. "You're a Meany!" Drewes, Dan, illus. 2011. 13p. pap. 10.19 *(978-1-4567-8643-4(1))* AuthorHouse.
Dove, Trudy. The Bunnies. 2016. (ENG., Illus.). 119p. (J). pap. 13.95 *(978-1-78554-301-2(6)*, cd11b3eb-fbe0-429d-b593-f4e87c557324) Austin Macauley Pubs. Ltd. GBR. Dist: Baker & Taylor Publisher Services (BTPS).
Dovey, Belinda. Alphabet Adventures. 2012. 136p. pap. 71.99 *(978-1-4653-7250-5(4))* Xlibris Corp.
Dowley, T. El Viaje Maravilloso. 2003.Tr. of Amazing Escape. (SPA.). bds. 9.99 *(978-0-7899-1117-9(5))* Editorial Unilit.
Downie, David. Horrible Stories My Dad Told Me. Nanevych, Julia, tr. Seroya, Tea, illus. 2012. 44p. pap. *(978-1-922159-97-7(2))* Blue Peg Publishing.
Doyle, Christopher. Amazing Tales & Strange Stories of the Bible. 2009. 64p. (J). (gr. -1). 14.99 *(978-0-7586-1785-9(2))* Concordia Publishing Hse.
Doyle, William. Tell Me a Story Please: Read-Aloud Short Stories for Children & the Young at Heart. 2006. 116p. pap. 13.50 *(978-1-84426-387-5(8))* Upfront Publishing Ltd. GBR. Dist: Printondemand-worldwide.com.
Dozier, Kim. The Ear-Less Kingdom. Dozier, Ashlyn McCauley, illus. l.t. ed. 2003. (ENG.). 24p. (J). 7.50 *(978-0-9745839-1-4(X)*, Fun to Read Bks. with Royally Good Morals) MKADesigns.
—The Forgetful Princess. Dozier, Ashlyn McCauley, illus. 2nd l.t. ed. 2003. (ENG.). 24p. (J). 10.00 *(978-0-9745839-0-7(1)*, Fun to Read Bks. with Royally Good Morals) MKADesigns.
Draeger, Manuela. In the Time of the Blue Ball. Evenson, Brian & Evenson, Valerie, trs. 2011. (ENG.). 134p. pap. 16.00 *(978-0-9844693-3-8(8))* New York Review of Bks., Inc., The.
Dragonblood, A. The Whispering V: Children of the Others Collection. 2010. 84p. pap. 10.49 *(978-1-4520-3250-4(5))* AuthorHouse.
Dreissigacker Martin, Susan. Princess Stephanie Stories: The Road Trip & the New School. 2009. 32p. pap. 18.79 *(978-1-4389-1836-5(4))* AuthorHouse.
Dreser, Elena. El Secreto del Sauce. Diez, Dalia Alvarado, illus. 2003. (SPA.). 44p. (J). (gr. 3-5). pap. 6.95 *(978-968-19-0617-7(9))* Santillana USA Publishing Co., Inc.
Dube, Jasmine. Tu N'es Plus Seul, Nazaire. Daigle, Sylvie, illus. 2003. (Premier Roman Ser.). (FRE.). 64p. (J). (gr. 2-5). pap. *(978-2-89021-286-2(6))* Diffusion du livre Mirabel (DLM).
Dubois, Claude K. - Norac. QUIERO UN BESO. 2003. (SPA., Illus.). 15p. (J). (gr. -1-k). bds. 9.99 *(978-84-8470-104-0(2))* Corimbo, Editorial S.L. ESP. Dist: Lectorum Pubns., Inc.
—SOY UN CIELO. 2003. (SPA., Illus.). 15p. (J). (gr. -1-k). bds. 9.99 *(978-84-8470-105-7(0))* Corimbo, Editorial S.L. ESP. Dist: Lectorum Pubns., Inc.
Dubois, Marie. The Village Children, an Introduction to the Art of Painting Children & Their Stories. 2009. (FRE & ENG., Illus.). 120p. pap. 36.99 *(978-1-4343-7847-7(0))* AuthorHouse.

Dubrovin, Barbara. Fantasy Fair: Bright Stories of Imagination. Dubrovin, Barbara, illus. 2007. (Illus.). 128p. (J). pap. 17.50 *(978-0-9638339-6-9(0))* Storycraft Publishing.

Dubya, Jay. The Eighteen Story Gingerbread House. 2003. 172p. (J). 23.95 *(978-1-58909-176-4(0))*; pap. 15.95 *(978-1-58909-177-1(9))* Bookstand Publishing.

Duchene-Marshall, Michele A. Charley Finds A Family. Marshall, Alan David, ed. Ousley, Clayton Gerard, photos by. l.t. ed. 2004. Orig. Title: Charley finds a Home. (Illus.). 20p. (J). spiral bd. 10.00 *(978-0-9761675-2-5(2))* Storybook Acres.

Dudley, Sean. Who's Afraid of the Pumpkin Man??? 2009. 47p. pap. 10.01 *(978-0-557-12616-3(9))* Lulu Pr., Inc.

Duerksen, Carol, et al. Short Tales. 2012. (Illus.). 95p. (J). pap. *(978-0-9742716-4-4(0))* WillowSpring Downs.

Duey, K. & Bale, K. A. Salvados! Titanic. 2003. (Survival Ser.).Tr. of Survival! Titanic. (SPA.). (J). pap. 9.95 *(978-0-9715256-4-1(1))* Planeta Publishing Corp.

Dukes, Alicia. Ms. Mabel's Fables. 2010. 94p. pap. 42.20 *(978-0-557-31374-7(0))* Lulu Pr., Inc.

Dultz, Dorothy. Stories for Dreamers. Margolis, Al, illus. 2013. 68p. (J). pap. 9.95 *(978-1-61863-425-2(9))* Bookstand Publishing.

Duncan, Sharyn. The Mouse House & other Stories: You Are the Artist. 2004. 40p. (J). 9.95 *(978-1-933002-04-0(2))* PublishingWorks.

Dunsany, Taylor. The Little Witch Who Lost Her Broom & Other Stories. 2008. 48p. pap. 8.95 *(978-0-595-52506-5(7))* iUniverse, Inc.

Durán, Oscar Manuel. Mama Cuentame un Cuento. Durán, Ivy Adriana, ed. 2013. 146p. pap. 30.00 *(978-0-9886109-1-0(4))* duran, oscar.

Dyer-Groves, Beverly E. Spooky Nights on the Island. 2011. 64p. (gr. -1). pap. 11.99 *(978-1-4567-2040-7(6))* AuthorHouse.

Eastman, P. D., et al. The Big Purple Book of Beginner Books. 2012. (Beginner Books(R) Ser.). (ENG., Illus.). 288p. (J). (gr. -1-2). 16.99 *(978-0-307-97587-4(8)*, Random Hse. Bks. for Young Readers) Random Hse. Children's Bks.

EDCON Publishing Group Staff. Jack & the Beanstalk - The Stubborn Witch - Rapunzel - Betsy - The Magic Bus. l.t. ed. 2008. (Classic Children's Tales Ser.). 32p. (gr. k-4). pap. 8.95 *(978-1-55576-551-4(3))* EDCON Publishing Group.

—Little Toot - The Story of White Satin - Five Peas in a Pod - Rumpelstiltskin - The Little Magic Pot. l.t. ed. 2008. (Classic Children's Tales Ser.). 32p. (gr. k-4). pap. 8.95 *(978-1-55576-552-1(1))* EDCON Publishing Group.

—Surprise Pies - Snow White & Rose Red - The Emperor's New Clothes - The Three Bears - The Mixed up Family - A Valentine Story. l.t. ed. 2008. (Classic Children's Tales Ser.). 32p. (gr. k-4). pap. 8.95 *(978-1-55576-554-5(8))* EDCON Publishing Group.

Edgeworth, Maria. Moral Tales, by Maria Edgeworth Embellished with Original Designs, by Darley. 2006. 532p. per. 29.99 *(978-1-4255-5877-2(1))* Michigan Publishing.

—Parents Assistance or Stories for Child. 2006. 492p. (gr. 4-7). per. *(978-1-4067-9305-5(1)*, Hesperides Pr.) Read Bks.

—The Parent's Assistant; or, Stories for Children. 2007. 468p. (gr. 4-7). per. *(978-1-4065-1649-4(X))* Dodo Pr.

—Rosamond: With Other Tales. by Maria Edgeworth. 2006. 388p. per. 26.99 *(978-1-4255-4076-0(7))* Michigan Publishing.

Edgeworth, Maria & Anderson, Alexander. The Parent's Assistant; or, Stories for Children. 2016. (ENG., Illus.). (J). 25.95 *(978-1-358-39155-2(6))* Creative Media Partners, LLC.

Edgson, Alison, illus. The Magician's Apprentice. 2011. (Flip-Up Fairy Tales Ser.). 24p. (J). (gr. 2-2). *(978-1-84643-370-2(3))* Child's Play International Ltd.

Edward Eggleston. Queer Stories for Boys & Girls. 2007. 168p. per. 11.95 *(978-1-4218-3949-3(0)*, 1st World Library - Literary Society) 1st World Publishing, Inc.

Edwards, Garth & Statyuk, Max. Heroes of Mercy Hall. 2012. (Thorn Gate Trilogy Ser.). (ENG., Illus.). 112p. (gr. 4-6). pap. *(978-0-9567122-6-4(6))* Inside Pocket Publishing, Ltd.

Edwards, Jean E. Adventure Tales: For Kids Who Want to Become Better Readers. 2012. 102p. pap. 15.99 *(978-1-4771-4117-5(0))* Xlibris Corp.

Effie, Sandy. New Comings of What's Next. 2011. 32p. pap. 16.95 *(978-1-4626-0708-2(X))* America Star Bks.

Egan, Kate & Lane, Mike. The Incredible Twisting Arm, Bk. 2. Wight, Eric, illus. 2014. (Magic Shop Ser.: 2). (ENG.). 160p. (J). (gr. 2-4). pap. 7.99 *(978-1-250-04044-2(2)*, 900123920) Feiwel & Friends.

—The Vanishing Coin. Wight, Eric, illus. 2014. (Magic Shop Ser.: 1). (ENG.). 160p. (J). (gr. 2-4). pap. 9.99 *(978-1-250-04043-5(4)*, 900123919) Feiwel & Friends.

Egerton, George. Keynotes (Classic Reprint) 2015. (ENG., Illus.). 216p. (J). pap. 13.57 *(978-1-330-45466-4(9))* Forgotten Bks.

Eggleston, Margaret. Fireside Stories for Girls in Their Teen. 2005. pap. 20.95 *(978-1-885529-65-7(1))* Stevens Publishing.

Eggleton, Grace. Children's Stories My Mother Wrote. 2012. 96p. pap. 46.72 *(978-1-4797-3807-6(7))* Xlibris Corp.

Eghdam, Tara. My Little Mici. 2009. (Illus.). 24p. pap. 11.49 *(978-1-4389-8189-5(9))* AuthorHouse.

Ehrlich, Amy, ed. When I Was Your Age: Volumes I & II Vols. I & II: Original Stories about Growing Up. 2012. (ENG., Illus.). 352p. (J). (gr. 4-7). pap. 14.99 *(978-0-7636-5892-2(8))* Candlewick Pr.

El Wilson, Barbara. Sugarfootn' in the South with Brer' Rabbit: How Handclapping Got Started in the Church Sugarfootstrade; Tattle-Tales Series. Curry, Garrett A., illus. 2010. (ENG.). 24p. pap. 12.99 *(978-1-4520-3145-3(2))* AuthorHouse.

Eley, Kitt. Cindy Lou. 2013. 24p. pap. 24.95 *(978-1-4626-9367-2(9))* America Star Bks.

Eliotte, Lisa J. The Adventures of Derby Doodle. 2009. 640p. pap. 25.99 *(978-1-4389-3058-9(5))* AuthorHouse.

Elkins, Christy. Sir Stinks-A-Lot. 2011. (ENG.). 43p. pap. 12.00 *(978-0-557-34847-3(1))* Lulu Pr., Inc.

Elliott, Craig. Racer Buddies: Rematch at Richmond. 2005. (Racer Buddies Ser.). (Illus.). 40p. (J). (gr. -1-5). 12.95 *(978-0-9746445-1-6(X)*, 10000) Powerband, LLC.

Ellison, Harlan. Troublemakers: Stories by Harlan Ellison. 2009. 272p. pap. 13.95 *(978-0-7592-9198-0(5))* Open Road Integrated Media, Inc.

Elschner, Géraldine & Elschner, Géraldine. The Cat & the Bird: A Children's Book Inspired by Paul Klee. 2012. (Children's Books Inspired by Famous Artworks Ser.). (ENG., Illus.). 32p. (J). (gr. -1-3). 14.95 *(978-3-7913-7099-6(5))* Prestel Verlag GmbH & Co KG. DEU. Dist: Penguin Random Hse. LLC.

En la Corte del Rey Blas (In King Blas' Court) (SPA.). 24p. (J). 4.95 *(978-84-246-1629-8(4))* La Galera, S.A. Editorial ESP. Dist: AIMS International Bks., Inc.

The Enchanted Little Egg. 2017. (ENG., Illus.). 176p. (J). 9.00 *(978-1-78270-142-2(7))* Award Pubns. Ltd. GBR. Dist: Parkwest Pubns., Inc.

Ende, Michael. El Dragon y la Mariposa. De Horna, Luis, illus. 2003.Tr. of Der Lindwurm und der Schmetterling. (SPA.). 48p. (J). (gr. k-3). pap. 8.95 *(978-84-204-3710-1(7))* Santillana USA Publishing Co., Inc.

The Entire World of SH & CH Book of Stories. 2004. per. 34.99 *(978-0-9760490-2-9(3))* Say It Right.

Equipo Staff. Libro de la Selva y Cuatro Cuentos Mas.Tr. of Jungle Book & Four Tales More. (SPA.). 48p. (J). 16.48 *(978-84-305-9297-5(0))* Susaeta Ediciones, S.A. ESP. Dist: AIMS International Bks., Inc.

—Pinocho y Cuatro Cuentos Mas.Tr. of Piniccui & Four Tales More. (SPA.). 124p. (J). 16.48 *(978-84-305-9296-8(2))* Susaeta Ediciones, S.A. ESP. Dist: AIMS International Bks., Inc.

—365 Cuentos, uno para Cada Dia.Tr. of 365 Tales, One for Everyday. (SPA.). 304p. 29.98 *(978-84-305-2252-1(2))* Susaeta Ediciones, S.A. ESP. Dist: AIMS International Bks., Inc.

Erdrich, Lise. Bears Make Rock Soup & Other Stories, 1 vol. Fifield, Lisa, illus. 2014. (ENG.). 32p. (J). (gr. 3-5). pap. 11.95 *(978-0-89239-300-8(9)*, leelowcbp, Children's Book Press) Lee & Low Bks., Inc.

Ergun, Erol. The All-Merciful Master. 2009. (Beautiful Names of God Ser.). (ENG., Illus.). 128p. (J). (gr. 4-7). 14.95 *(978-1-59784-202-0(8)*, Tughra Bks.) Blue Dome, Inc.

Erickson, Arnold. Stories to Be Shared. 2006. 94p. (J). 40.00 *(978-0-9700108-3-4(4))* Creative Well, The.

Esopo. La Zorra Se Pasa de Lista. (Coleccion Fabulas y Cuentos Populares). (SPA.). 24p. (J). (gr. 2-4). *(978-84-246-1566-6(2)*, GL1066) La Galera, S.A. Editorial ESP. Dist: Lectorum Pubns., Inc.

Espinosa, Marta Catalina Vanni. Testigos 25 D - Y Mas. 2010. 56p. pap. 23.95 *(978-1-61764-285-2(1))* AuthorHouse.

Eureka! Stories of Amazing Discoveries. (Critical Reading Ser.). (YA). (gr. 6-12). pap. *(978-0-8092-1249-1(8))* Jamestown.

The Evangeline Nicholas Collection: 1 Each of 16. (gr. 1-3). tchr. ed., stu. ed. 91.50 *(978-0-322-00761-1(5))* Wright Group/McGraw-Hill.

The Evangeline Nicholas Collection: 1 Each of 6. (gr. 1-3). 199.50 *(978-0-7802-9517-9(X))* Wright Group/McGraw-Hill.

The Evangeline Nicholas Collection Set A: 6 Each of 8. (gr. 1-3). 222.50 *(978-0-7802-8056-4(3))* Wright Group/McGraw-Hill.

The Evangeline Nicholas Collection Set A,B: 6 Each of 16. (gr. 1-3). tchr. ed., stu. ed. 456.50 *(978-0-7802-9516-2(1))* Wright Group/McGraw-Hill.

The Evangeline Nicholas Collection Set B: 6 Each of 8. (gr. 1-3). stu. ed. 235.50 *(978-0-7802-8057-1(1))* Wright Group/McGraw-Hill.

Evans, Alwyn, et al. Monty's Tale. (Illus.). 16p. (J). pap. 7.49 *(978-1-86368-139-1(6))* Fremantle Pr. AUS. Dist: Independent Pubs. Group.

Evans, Florence Adéle. Alice's Adventures in Pictureland: A Tale Inspired by Lewis Carroll's Wonderland. 2011. (Illus.). 152p. pap. *(978-1-904808-63-3(8))* Evertype.

Evergreen, Nelson, illus. John Henry, Hammerin' Hero: The Graphic Novel. 2010. (Graphic Spin Ser.). (ENG.). 40p. (J). (gr. 3-6). pap. 5.95 *(978-1-4342-2265-7(9)*, 103128, Stone Arch Bks.) Capstone.

Ewing, Juliana Horatia. Brothers of Pity & Other Tales of Beasts & Men. 2017. (ENG., Illus.). (J). 23.95 *(978-1-374-96777-9(7))*; pap. 13.95 *(978-1-374-96776-2(9))* Capital Communications, Inc.

—Brothers of Pity & Other Tales of Beasts & Men. 2007. (Illus.). 168p. per. *(978-1-4065-2522-9(7))* Dodo Pr.

—The Brownies & Other Tales. 2007. 140p. per. *(978-1-4065-2523-6(5))* Dodo Pr.

—Mary's Meadow & Other Tales of Fields & Flowers. 2007. 152p. per. *(978-1-4065-2529-8(4))* Dodo Pr.

—Melchior's Dream & Other Tales. 2007. 176p. per. *(978-1-4065-2530-4(8))* Dodo Pr.

—Miscellanea. 2007. (Illus.). 212p. per. *(978-1-4065-2531-1(6))* Dodo Pr.

A Expressway Jewels Set, 6 vols. 32p. (gr. 1-3). 26.50 *(978-0-7802-8046-5(6))* Wright Group/McGraw-Hill.

Fabian, Ingrid. The Black Arabian Foal. 2011. (Illus.). 53p. pap. 15.95 *(978-1-84624-530-5(3))* Book Guild, Ltd. GBR. Dist: Trans-Atlantic Pubns., Inc.

Fables & Tall Tales (Gr. 3-4) 2003. (J). *(978-1-58232-072-4(1))* ECS Learning Systems, Inc.

Fabregat, Antonio-Manuel. Los Cuentos de Mi Escuela. (SPA.). 128p. (J). (gr. 4-6). *(978-84-216-1185-2(2)*, BU3866) Bruño, Editorial ESP. Dist: Lectorum Pubns., Inc.

Fabulas de Siempre. l.t. ed.Tr. of Traditional Fables. (SPA.). (J). 3.98 *(978-84-7630-901-8(5))* Selector, S.A. de C.V. MEX. Dist: Spanish Pubs., LLC.

Fafoutakis, Anne. Enchanted Talisman & Other Stories for Children of All Ages. 2004. 132p. pap. 13.50 *(978-1-84426-296-0(0))* Upfront Publishing Ltd. GBR. Dist: Printondemand-worldwide.com.

Faine, Edward Allan. More Little Ned Stories. 2003. 112p. (J). pap. 6.95 *(978-0-9716911-2-4(6))* IM Pr.

Falco, Joanna. Diana, the Angel, & the Holy Grail. 2007. 52p. (J). per. 8.95 *(978-0-595-45733-5(9))* iUniverse, Inc.

Falconi, María Inés. Hasta el Domingo. (Torre de Papel Ser.). (SPA.). (YA). (gr. 6-18). 8.95 *(978-958-04-2902-9(2))* Norma S.A. COL. Dist: Distribuidora Norma, Inc.

Falletta, Bernadette & Lewis, Maria. We Love to Read Stories & Songs. 2005. 27p. (J). 14.95 *(978-1-4116-4734-3(3))* Lulu Pr., Inc.

Falwell, Cathryn. Butterflies for Kiri, 1 vol. 2003. (ENG., Illus.). 32p. (J). (gr. k-3). pap. 11.95 *(978-1-60060-342-6(4)*, leelowbooks) Lee & Low Bks., Inc.

Family Stories: Jumbo Packs. (gr. k-2). 157.08 *(978-0-7362-0051-6(7))* CENGAGE Learning.

Farina von Buchwald, Martin & Prado Farina, Gabriela. The Joy of Giving. Avendano, Dolores, illus. Testino, Mario et al, photos by. 2005. 89p. (J). 18.00 *(978-0-9777266-0-8(6))* von Buchwald, Martin Farina.

Farley, Terri. Desert Dancer. 2003. (Phantom Stallion Ser.). (Illus.). 234p. (J). (gr. 5-9). 12.65 *(978-0-7569-3561-0(X))* Perfection Learning Corp.

Farnsworth-Simpson, Patricia Ann. Stories to Thrill & Delight. 2008. (ENG.). 142p. pap. 12.95 *(978-1-4357-3275-9(8))* Lulu Pr., Inc.

Farrant, Natasha. Eight Princesses & a Magic Mirror. Corry, Lydia, illus. 2020. (ENG.). 224p. (J). (gr. 4-7). 19.95 *(978-1-324-01556-7(X)*, 341556, Norton Young Readers) Norton, W. W. & Co., Inc.

Faul, Nicole. The Great Animal Race & Trap the Angry Elephant Finds a Friend. 2009. (Illus.). 44p. pap. 18.49 *(978-1-4389-3320-7(7))* AuthorHouse.

Faundez, Anne, ed. Little Red Riding Hood. 2004. (QEB Start Writing Ser.). (Illus.). 24p. (J). lib. bdg. 15.95 *(978-1-59566-020-6(8))* QEB Publishing Inc.

Fawbert, Malcolm. Tales from Thimble Hall Mrs Stopper's Bottle. 2010. (Illus.). 26p. pap. 12.00 *(978-1-60860-344-2(X)*, Strategic Bk. Publishing) Strategic Book Publishing & Rights Agency (SBPRA).

FeatherHill, Annaha. Little Britches. 2007. 76p. per. 19.95 *(978-1-4241-5303-9(4))* America Star Bks.

Ferrari, G. m. Lake, Sky, Dragonfly. 2009. 44p. pap. 16.99 *(978-1-4490-2895-4(0))* AuthorHouse.

Ferren, Stella. 5 Great Little Read-A-Loud Stories for Grandparents. 2009. 48p. pap. 11.49 *(978-1-4389-2625-4(1))* AuthorHouse.

Ferrier, Paul Eugene. Kavaldo & His Diamond Pills. Gettys, Katherine, illus. 2013. (ENG.). 72p. pap. 12.99 *(978-1-940395-07-4(0))* Yawn's Bks. & More, Inc.

Ferro, Beatriz. Arriba el Telon. (SPA.). (YA). 8.95 *(978-958-04-7263-6(7))* Norma S.A. COL. Dist: Distribuidora Norma, Inc.

Fiction Readers, 30, Set. 2013. (Book Collection). (SPA., Illus.). 20p. (gr. 1-1). 149.70 *(978-1-4938-0207-4(0))* Teacher Created Materials, Inc.

Fiedler, Christamaria. El Verano de los Animales. Kessler, Siglint, illus. 2003. (SPA.). 155p. (J). (gr. 5-8). 9.95 *(978-968-19-0706-8(X))* Aguilar, Altea, Taurus, Alfaguara, S.A. de C.V MEX. Dist: Santillana USA Publishing Co., Inc.

Field, Eugene. A Little Book of Profitable Tales. 2017. (ENG., Illus.). (J). 22.95 *(978-1-374-88634-6(3))*; pap. 12.95 *(978-1-374-88633-9(5))* Capital Communications, Inc.

—Profitable Tales. 2007. 308p. 29.95 *(978-1-4344-9217-3(6))*; per. 19.95 *(978-1-4344-9123-7(4))* Wildside Pr., LLC.

Fienberg, Anna & Fienberg, Barbara. Tashi & the Wicked Magician: And Other Stories. Kelly, Geoff & Gamble, Kim, illus. 2017. (Tashi Ser.). (ENG.). 96p. (J). (gr. k-3). pap. 10.99 *(978-1-76029-050-4(5))* Allen & Unwin AUS. Dist: Independent Pubs. Group.

Fiesta de Cuentos. (Coleccion Estrella). (SPA., Illus.). 64p. (J). 14.95 *(978-950-11-0016-7(2)*, SGM016) Sigmar ARG. Dist: Continental Bk. Co., Inc.

Filipek, Nina. Goldilocks & the Three Bears. O'Toole, Jeanette, illus. 2009. (Fairy Tale Firsts Ser.). 12p. (J). (gr. -1-k). bds. 11.40 *(978-1-60754-689-4(2))* Windmill Bks.

Filipi, Carmen. The Marvelous Fountain: And other stories my grandma told Me. Long, Dave, illus. 2007.Tr. of Fuente Maravillosa y otros cuentos que me conto mi Abuela. (ENG & SPA.). 55p. (J). per. 14.95 *(978-0-9797814-0-7(X))* Hispanic Institute of Social Issues.

First Stories (Gr. K-1) 2003. (J). *(978-1-58232-035-9(7))* ECS Learning Systems, Inc.

Fisher, Daniel, ed. 638 Potential Paper Cuts: 638 Pages of Stories by Sixth-Grade Students of Berkshire Middle School. 2008. (ENG.). 638p. pap. 11.00 *(978-1-4196-9572-8(X))* CreateSpace Independent Publishing Platform.

Fisher, Karin, adapted by. Fish, Fox, & Then Some: Seven Aesop's Fables Retold Using One-syllable Words for the Barton Reading & Spelling System. 2003. (J). pap. 7.95 *(978-0-9744343-1-5(0)*, SA-302) Bright Solutions for Dyslexia, LLC.

Fisher, Lillian M. Feathers in the Wind. 155p. (YA). (gr. 4-8). 9.99 *(978-0-88092-438-2(1))* Royal Fireworks Publishing Co.

Fitzer, Robin. Summer Stories. 2008. 45p. pap. 24.95 *(978-1-60563-742-6(4))* America Star Bks.

Fitzpatrick, Becca. The Complete Hush, Hush Saga (Boxed Set) Hush, Hush; Crescendo; Silence; Finale. 2013. (Hush, Hush Saga Ser.). (ENG., Illus.). 1824p. (YA). (gr. 9). pap. 55.99 *(978-1-4814-0084-8(3)*, Simon & Schuster Bks. For Young Readers) Simon & Schuster Bks. For Young Readers.

Flanagan, James. Stories Heard Around the Lunchroom. 2010. 96p. pap. 11.49 *(978-1-4490-8443-1(5))* AuthorHouse.

Flanagan, Jim. The School of Scary Stories. 2006. (Illus.). 125p. (J). per. 12.95 *(978-0-9766666-5-3(0))* Arcadian Hse.

Flanagan, John. The Battle for Skandia. 2009. (Ranger's Apprentice Ser.: 4). lib. bdg. 19.65 *(978-0-606-02208-8(2))* Turtleback.

Fleischman, Paul. Graven Images. Ibatoulline, Bagram, illus. 2005. (ENG.). 128p. (YA). (gr. 5-9). per. 8.99 *(978-0-7636-2984-7(7))* Candlewick Pr.

Flett, Julie. Wild Berries. 2013. (ENG., Illus.). 32p. (J). (gr. -1-3). 16.95 *(978-1-897476-89-5(2))* Simply Read Bks. CAN. Dist: Ingram Publisher Services.

Flickinger, Joie & Flickinger, Amanda. Clutch the Trucking Cat. 2007. 236p. per. 24.95 *(978-1-4241-9535-0(7))* America Star Bks.

Flint, Shamini. The Collected Diaries of a Sporting Superhero: Five Stories in One! Heinrich, Sally, illus. 2017. (Diary of A... Ser.). (ENG.). 512p. (J). (gr. 2-6). pap. 14.99 *(978-1-76029-345-1(8))* Allen & Unwin AUS. Dist: Independent Pubs. Group.

Flomper & the Flyaway Fairies. 2017. (ENG., Illus.). 176p. (J). 9.00 *(978-1-78270-144-6(3))* Award Pubns. Ltd. GBR. Dist: Parkwest Pubns., Inc.

Flor Ada, Alma & Campoy, F. Isabel. Una Semilla de Luz. Dávalos, Felipe, illus. 2003. (Coleccion Derechos Del Nino Ser.). (SPA.). 32p. (J). (gr. 3-5). pap. 7.95 *(978-84-204-5818-2(X))* Santillana USA Publishing Co., Inc.

Flynn, Ian. Mega Man 1: Let the Games Begin. Spaziante, Patrick 'Spaz', illus. 2011. (Mega Man Ser.: 1). (ENG.). 112p. (J). (gr. 4-7). pap. 11.95 *(978-1-879794-85-6(3))* Archie Comic Pubns., Inc.

Folk Tales of the West Lake. 2007. 72p. per. 11.95 *(978-1-59654-409-3(0))* Disruptive Publishing.

Foster, Cassandra. Do You Know Us? A Collection of Short Stories. 2006. (Illus.). 48p. (YA). per. 8.00 *(978-0-9778641-1-9(1))* Smith, Mildred C.

—A Good Story: A Collection of Short Short Stories. 2006. (Illus.). 37p. (YA). per. 8.00 *(978-0-9778641-0-2(3))* Smith, Mildred C.

Foth, Horst. Traumreisen. 2011. 120p. 26.50 *(978-1-4477-2150-5(0))* Lulu Pr., Inc.

Four Year Olds. Date not set. 96p. 7.98 *(978-0-7525-8710-3(2))* Parragon, Inc.

Francesca, Sieglinde De. A Donsy of Gnomes. 2009. pap. *(978-1-61623-243-6(9))* Independent Pub.

Frank, Church & Barnas, Aloura. The Epic Adventures of Whiz Grass & Poot Berry. 2011. 164p. (gr. -1). 22.99 *(978-1-4634-4525-6(3))*; pap. 11.99 *(978-1-4634-4524-9(5))* AuthorHouse.

Frankel, Valerie Estelle. Chelm for the Holidays. Wimmer, Sonja, illus. 2019. (ENG.). 72p. (J). (gr. 3-9). pap. 8.99 *(978-1-5415-5462-7(0)*, afdf6bb4-341d-400d-b5f2-173f45c6a355, Kar-Ben Publishing) Lerner Publishing Group.

Freedman, Bill. Boy Who Wanted to Marry His Dog. 2011. (ENG.). 50p. (J). pap. 14.99 *(978-1-926780-10-8(8)*, 6b517843-2115-4c84-b096-52a5214c28be) Key Publishing Hse., Inc., The CAN. Dist: Baker & Taylor Publisher Services (BTPS).

Freese, Thomas, reader. Fog Swirler & 11 Other Ghost Stories. 2006. (J). Pt. 1. cd-rom 13.95 *(978-0-9789511-0-8(7))*Pt. 2. cd-rom 13.95 *(978-0-9789511-1-5(5))*Pt. 3. cd-rom 13.95 *(978-0-9789511-2-2(3))* Illumination Pubns.

—Shaker Ghost Stories from Pleasant Hill, KY Audio Book/cd. 2006. (J). cd-rom 17.95 *(978-0-9789511-3-9(1))* Illumination Pubns.

French, Moira. The Swingewood Stories. 2009. 36p. pap. 16.99 *(978-1-4490-4777-1(7))* AuthorHouse.

Friederich, Uve. The World of Bridgett & Emily. Fitzpatrick, Meg & Ravenhill, John A., illus. 2004. 41p. (J). mass mkt. 8.95 *(978-0-9747532-4-9(6))* Taylor-Dth Publishing.

Friend, R. Time Out at Home. 2005. (Down on Friendly Acres Ser.: 2). (J). lib. bdg. *(978-0-9743627-4-8(3))*; pap. 6.95 *(978-0-9743627-1-7(9))* Sunflower Seeds Pr.

Friesen, Ray. Pirate Penguin vs Ninja Chicken Volume 1: Troublems with Frenemies. 2011. (Pirate Penguin vs Ninja Chicken Ser.: 1). (Illus.). 96p. (J). (gr. 4-7). 9.95 *(978-1-60309-071-1(1)*, 9781603090711) Top Shelf Productions.

Fruchter, Yaakov. Best of Olomeinu - Series 2: Stories for All Year 'Round. 2003. 136p. pap. 10.99 *(978-1-57819-399-8(0)*, BO1P) Mesorah Pubns., Ltd.

Fu, Shelley. Hoyi the Archer & other Classic Chinese Tales. Abboreno, Joseph F. & Fu, Sherwin, illus. 2005. 144p. (J). (gr. 4-8). reprint ed. 22.00 *(978-0-7567-9713-3(6))* DIANE Publishing Co.

Fuchs, Menucha. The Picky Eater & Other Stories. 2004. (Children's Learning Ser.: 20). (HEB., Illus.). 48p. (J). per. 4.95 *(978-1-932443-24-0(X)*, TPES) Judaica Pr., Inc., The.

Fuentes, Carlos. Aura. (SPA.). (YA). 8.00 *(978-958-04-6971-1(7))* Norma S.A. COL. Dist: Distribuidora Norma, Inc.

Fuertes, Gloria. Cuentos Para 365 Dias. 2003. (SPA.). 210p. 17.56 *(978-84-305-9282-1(2)*, SU2166) Susaeta Ediciones, S.A. ESP. Dist: Lectorum Pubns., Inc.

Fujikawa, Gyo. Sunny Books - Four-Favorite Tales, 4 bks., Set. Fujikawa, Gyo, illus. (Illus.). (J). (gr. -1). reprint ed. *(978-1-55987-042-9(7)*, Sunny Bks.) J B Communications, Inc.

Fun Short Stories on Values & Morals of Life. 2003. (Illus.). 90p. (YA). per. *(978-0-9742122-0-3(2))* Aunty Ems Boutique.

Furlong, Frank, illus. Pop Pop's Magic Chair. 2010. 24p. pap. 12.95 *(978-1-60844-658-2(1))* Dog Ear Publishing, LLC.

Furman, A. L., ed. Horse Stories: Young Readers. Geer, Charles, illus. 2011. 192p. 42.95 *(978-1-258-09836-0(9))* Literary Licensing, LLC.

—Pioneer Stories: Young Readers. Geer, Charles, illus. 2011. 190p. 42.95 *(978-1-258-09907-7(1))* Literary Licensing, LLC.

—Teenage Frontier Stories. Prezio, Victor, illus. 2011. 256p. 47.95 *(978-1-258-09865-0(2))* Literary Licensing, LLC.

The Furry Friends. 2005. (J). per. *(978-0-9664783-2-7(0))* Jacqueline Beverly Hills.

Fusek Peters, Andrew. Dingo Dog & the Billabong Storm. Wadham, Anna, illus. 2010. (Traditional Tales with a Twist Ser.). 32p. (J). (gr. -1-2). pap. incl. audio compact disk *(978-1-84643-350-4(9))* Child's Play International Ltd.

—The Talkative Tortoise. 2011. (Traditional Tales with a Twist Ser.). (Illus.). 32p. (J). *(978-1-84643-418-1(1))* Child's Play International Ltd.

Futch, Dorothy R. All about Life: A Collection of Children Stories. 2009. 40p. pap. 21.99 *(978-1-4415-2848-3(2))* Xlibris Corp.

Gaiman, Neil. M Is for Magic. Kristiansen, Teddy, illus. 272p. (J). (gr. 5-9). 2008. (ENG.). pap. 9.99 *(978-0-06-118647-9(3)*, HarperCollins) 2007. 16.99 *(978-0-06-118642-4(2))* HarperCollins Pubs.

—M Is for Magic. 2007. (Illus.). 151p. (J). (gr. 5-9). 60.00 *(978-1-59606-123-1(5))* Subterranean Pr.

—Unnatural Creatures: Stories Selected by Neil Gaiman. 2013. (ENG., Illus.). 480p. (YA). (gr. 8). 18.99 *(978-0-06-223629-6(6))*; pap. 12.99 *(978-0-06-223630-2(X))* HarperCollins Pubs. (HarperCollins).

—Unnatural Creatures: Stories Selected by Neil Gaiman. 2013. (Illus.). 462p. (YA). lib. bdg. 20.85 *(978-0-606-31804-4(6))* Turtleback.

Galjanic, Lisa. When Series 6 Volume Set, 6, 6. 2007. (Illus.). 100p. (J). 34.95 *(978-1-933532-06-6(8))* LSG Pubns.

Gall, Chris. Dinotrux. 2012. (Dinotrux Ser.: 1). (ENG., Illus.). 32p. (J). (gr. -1-3). pap. 8.99 *(978-0-316-13392-0(2))* Little, Brown Bks. for Young Readers.

S

Gallego García, Laura & Gallego García, Laura. El Valle de Los Lobos. 2004. (Ciclo el Valle de Los Lobos the Valley of the Wolves Cycle Ser.). (SPA., Illus.). 222p. (YA). 10.99 (*978-84-348-7361-2(3)*) SM Ediciones ESP. Dist: Lectorum Pubns., Inc.

Gallego, Laura, et al. La Leyenda Del Rey Errante. 2004. (SPA.). 224p. (YA). 7.99 (*978-84-348-8818-0(1)*) SM Ediciones ESP. Dist: Lectorum Pubns., Inc.

Gallo, Donald R. No Easy Answer. 2014. 17.50 (*978-1-63419-721-2(6)*) Perfection Learning Corp.

Gallo, Donald R., ed. First Crossing: Stories about Teen Immigrants. 2007. (ENG.). 240p. (YA). (gr. 7-12). per. 8.99 (*978-0-7636-3291-5(0)*) Candlewick Pr.

—On the Fringe: Stories. 2003. (Illus.). 240p. (YA). (gr. 7-7). 6.99 (*978-0-14-250026-2(7)*, Speak) Penguin Young Readers Group.

—Owning It: Stories about Teens with Disabilities. 2010. (ENG., Illus.). 224p. (YA). (gr. 7). mass mkt. 7.99 (*978-0-7636-4661-5(X)*) Candlewick Pr.

Galluzzi, Edward. Twelve upon a Time. Bocik, Adam, illus. 3rd ed. 2009. 298p. (J). pap. (*978-1-926585-69-7(0)*) CCB Publishing.

Galvin, Laura Gates & Luther, Jacqueline. Read-A-Picture Collection: First Stories for Family Reading. rev. ed. 2005. (Reading to Grow Ser.). (ENG., Illus.). 40p. (J). (gr. -1-3). 12.99 (*978-1-59069-449-7(X)*, 1A700) Studio Mouse LLC.

Ganz, Yaffa. Four in One: Four Favorites. Klineman, Harvey, illus. 2008. 24.99 (*978-1-59826-183-7(5)*) Feldheim Pubs.

Ganzer, Diane & St. Croix, Sammy. Adventures of a Kitten Named Raspberry & Other Tales. 2009. 176p. pap. 9.95 (*978-1-935105-30-5(2)*) Avid Readers Publishing Group.

García Márquez, Gabriel. Maria dos Prazeres. (SPA.). 28p. 10.50 (*978-958-04-5572-1(4)*) Norma S.A. COL. Dist: Distribuidora Norma, Inc.

Garfein, Stanley Joe. Tales of the Temple Mice. 2006. (Illus.). 92p. (J). 14.95 (*978-0-9787422-0-1(6)*) Garfein, Stanley.

Garn, Laura Aimee. Bella Basset Ballerina. Sokolova, Valerie, illus. 2006. 32p. (J). (gr. -1-3). 15.95 (*978-0-9759378-0-8(4)*) Pretty Please Pr., Inc.

Gartner, Hans & Poppel, Hans. Osito ILmpio y Osito Sucio. (SPA.). (J). 8.95 (*978-958-04-6257-6(7)*) Norma S.A. COL. Dist: Distribuidora Norma, Inc.

Gary R Kirby. Stories of Sunshine & Funtime of Wonder & Thunder of Mystery & Magic for the Young to Grow On. 2009. 404p. pap. 22.95 (*978-1-4401-8640-0(5)*) iUniverse, Inc.

Garza, Xavier. The Donkey Lady Fights la Llorona & Other Stories / la Señora Asno Se Enfrenta a la Llorona y Otros Cuentos. Álvarez, Mayra E., tr. from ENG. 2015. (ENG & SPA., Illus.). 144p. (J). (gr. 3-6). pap. 9.95 (*978-1-55885-816-9(4)*, Piñata Books) Arte Publico Pr.

—Kid Cyclone Fights Devil & Other Stories/Kid Ciclon Se Enfrenta a el Diablo y Otras Historias. Ventura, Gabriela Baeza, tr. from ENG. 2010. (ENG & SPA.). 64p. (J). (gr. 3-7). pap. 10.95 (*978-1-55885-599-1(8)*, Piñata Books) Arte Publico Pr.

Gatty, Alfred. Aunt Judy's Tales. 2007. 132p. per. (*978-1-4065-2814-5(5)*) Dodo Pr.

—The Fairy Godmothers & Other Tales. 2017. (ENG., Illus.). (J). (gr. 4-7). 22.95 (*978-1-374-97631-3(8)*) Capital Communications, Inc.

—The Fairy Godmothers & Other Tales. 2007. 120p. per. (*978-1-4065-2815-2(3)*) Dodo Pr.

—The Fairy Godmothers & Other Tales. 2007. 104p. (gr. 4-7). per. (*978-1-4068-0918-3(7)*) Echo Library.

Gatty, Margaret. The Fairy Godmothers, & Other Tales. 2016. (ENG., Illus.). (J). 23.95 (*978-1-358-19745-1(8)*) Creative Media Partners, LLC.

Gauthier, Bertrand. Les Jumeaux Bulle Series. Dumont, Daniel, illus. 2004. (FRE.). 64p. (J). (gr. 1-4). pap. (*978-2-89021-684-6(5)*) Diffusion du livre Mirabel (DLM).

Gauthier, Gilles & Derome, Pierre-Andre. Petit Chausson, Grande Babouche. 2003. (Premier Roman Ser.). 64p. (J). (gr. 2-5). pap. (*978-2-89021-308-1(0)*) Diffusion du livre Mirabel (DLM).

Gay, Michele. Leoncio's Adventures. 2013. 20p. pap. 17.99 (*978-1-4817-0427-4(3)*) AuthorHouse.

Gbala, Deswin R. Rock University: A Collection of Short Stories & Poems. Gbala, Deswin R., illus. Date not set. (Illus.). 51p. (Orig.). (J). (gr. 3-10). pap. 8.50 (*978-0-9650629-2-3(9)*) Coulee Region Pubns., Inc.

Geiger, Nina Friant. The Froblits of Round Pond. 2010. pap. 9.99 (*978-0-578-05331-8(4)*) Ingenuity 31 Inc.

Geis, Patricia. Paca Lamar. Geis, Patricia, illus. 2004. (Mi Ciudad Ser.). (SPA & ENG., Illus.). 24p. (J). (gr. -1-k). 6.95 (*978-84-7864-797-2(X)*) Combel Editorial, S.A. ESP. Dist: Independent Pubs. Group.

—Pascual Midón. Geis, Patricia, illus. 2004. (Mi Ciudad Ser.). (SPA & ENG., Illus.). 24p. (J). (gr. -1-k). 6.95 (*978-84-7864-799-6(6)*) Combel Editorial, S.A. ESP. Dist: Independent Pubs. Group.

—Pepa Pas. Geis, Patricia, illus. 2004. (Mi Ciudad Ser.). (SPA., Illus.). 24p. (J). (gr. -1-k). 6.95 (*978-84-7864-796-5(1)*) Combel Editorial, S.A. ESP. Dist: Independent Pubs. Group.

George E. Keely, Jr. The Happy Day Fable. 2010. 20p. pap. 10.00 (*978-1-4269-0064-8(3)*) Trafford Publishing.

Geras, Adèle, et al. War Girls: A Collection of First World War Stories Through the Eyes of Young Women. 2014. (ENG.). 288p. (YA). (gr. 7). pap. 15.99 (*978-1-78344-060-3(0)*) Andersen Pr. GBR. Dist: Independent Pubs. Group.

Gerovasiliou, Oreanthy. Yuri the Lion: Three Stories. 2010. (Illus.). 48p. pap. 13.00 (*978-1-60888-069-0(9)*) Nimble Bks. LLC.

Gershator, Phillis. Rata-Pata-scata-fata, 1 vol. Meade, Holly, illus. 2005. (ENG.). 32p. (J). (gr. -1-3). 5.95 (*978-1-932065-95-4(4)*); 15.95 (*978-1-932065-94-7(6)*) Star Bright Bks., Inc.

Giachetti, Julia & Benchmark Education Co. Staff. A Tail for a Tail - Cherokee Trickster Tales. 2014. (Text Connections Ser.). (J). (gr. 5). (*978-1-4900-1375-6(X)*) Benchmark Education Co.

Gibbons, Ted & Wilcox, S. Michael. Modern Fables. McCune, Mark, illus. 2010. (J). 14.99 (*978-1-59955-307-8(4)*) Cedar Fort, Inc./CFI Distribution.

Gibson, Sherri L. In the Mind of a Child: Children's Stories. 2013. 36p. pap. 24.95 (*978-1-62709-750-5(3)*) America Star Bks.

Gifford, P. S. Dr. Offig's Lessons from the Dark Side, Volume 1. 2008. (ENG.). 176p. (YA). pap. 10.95 (*978-0-9801506-2-9(0)*) BRP Publishing Group.

Giles, Lamar, ed. Fresh Ink: An Anthology. 2019. (Illus.). 224p. (YA). (gr. 7). pap. 11.99 (*978-1-5247-6631-3(3)*, Ember) Random Hse. Children's Bks.

Giles, Sophie. 365 Bedtime Stories. 2013. (ENG., Illus.). 224p. (J). 24.95 (*978-1-84135-614-3(X)*) Award Pubns. Ltd. GBR. Dist: Parkwest Pubns., Inc.

Gilliland, Tom. The Adventures of Archie Aardvark. 2012. 60p. pap. 10.00 (*978-1-4691-7957-5(1)*) Xlibris Corp.

Gilmore, Rachna. The Flute, 1 vol. Biswas, Pulak, illus. 2012. (ENG.). 32p. (J). (gr. -1-k). 16.95 (*978-1-896580-57-9(2)*) Tradewind Bks. CAN. Dist: Orca Bk. Pubs. USA.

Glaser, Shirley. The Alphazeds. Glaser, Milton, illus. 2005. 32p. (J). (gr. k-4). reprint ed. 20.00 (*978-0-7567-9367-8(X)*) DIANE Publishing Co.

Gleeson, Joseph M., illus. Just So Stories. 2013. 250p. pap. (*978-1-909302-29-7(5)*) Abela Publishing.

Glynn, Gower. Stories Told in the Wigwam. 2006. pap. 24.95 (*978-1-4254-9966-2(X)*) Kessinger Publishing, LLC.

Gmeyner, Elizabeth. The Key of the Kingdom: A Book of Stories & Poems for Children, 1 vol. Russell, Joyce, illus. 2004. (ENG.). 100p. (J). pap. 15.00 (*978-0-88010-549-1(6)*, Bell Pond Bks.) SteinerBooks, Inc.

Gogonya, Carol. The African Mermaid & Other Stories. 2011. 40p. pap. 32.70 (*978-1-4568-5416-4(X)*) Xlibris Corp.

Golda, Kata. Stories for Bedtime: A Keepsake Pocket & Tales to Cherish. 2011. (ENG.). 7p. (J). (gr. -1 — 1). 14.99 (*978-0-8118-7498-4(2)*) Chronicle Bks. LLC.

Golden Books. Eloise Wilkin Stories. Wilkin, Eloise, illus. 2005. 224p. (J). (gr. -1-2). 12.99 (*978-0-375-82928-4(8)*, Golden Bks.) Random Hse. Children's Bks.

—Little Golden Book Collection: Sleeptime Tales. 2006. (Illus.). 224p. (J). (gr. -1-2). 12.99 (*978-0-375-83848-4(1)*, Golden Bks.) Random Hse. Children's Bks.

—Nine Disney Classics (Disney Classic) Golden Books, illus. 2018. (Little Golden Book Ser.). (ENG., Illus.). 224p. (J). (-k). 12.99 (*978-0-7364-3788-2(6)*, Golden/Disney) Random Hse. Children's Bks.

Golden Books, illus. Disney Classics Little Golden Book Library (Disney Classic) Lady & the Tramp; 101 Dalmatians; the Lion King; Alice in Wonderland; the Jungle Book, 5 vols. 2013. (Little Golden Book Ser.). (ENG.). 24p. (J). (-k). 24.95 (*978-0-7364-3149-1(7)*, Golden/Disney) Random Hse. Children's Bks.

Golding, Jacqueline. Healing Stories: Picture Books for the Big & Small Changes in a Child's Life. 2006. (ENG.). 336p. per. 17.95 (*978-1-59077-097-9(8)*) Evans, M. & Co., Inc.

Gonzales Bertrand, Diane. There's a Name for This Feeling / Hay un Nombre para lo Que Siento. Baeza Ventura, Gabriela, tr. 2014. (ENG & SPA.). 72p. (J). pap. 10.95 (*978-1-55885-784-1(2)*, Piñata Books) Arte Publico Pr.

Gonzales, Felipe C. Little Folk Stories & Tales by Don Pablo: Bilingual Stories in Spanish & English = Chistes y Cuentos de Don Pablo: Cuentos Bilingües en Español e Inglés. 2010. (SPA & ENG.). (J). pap. 24.95 (*978-0-86534-772-4(7)*) Sunstone Pr.

Goodhart, Pippa. Ginny's Egg. (ENG., Illus.). 142p. (J). pap. 7.50 (*978-0-7497-4557-8(6)*) Farshore GBR. Dist: Trafalgar Square Publishing.

Goodman, Larry. The Cowboy & Other Stories. 2008. 36p. pap. 24.95 (*978-1-60813-546-2(2)*) America Star Bks.

Goodrich, C. C. Barnabee: At the Picnic. 2009. (Illus.). 32p. pap. 13.99 (*978-1-4389-8388-2(3)*) AuthorHouse.

—Barnabee: Goes Shopping. 2009. (Illus.). 32p. pap. 13.99 (*978-1-4389-9728-5(0)*) AuthorHouse.

—Barnabee: Goes to Work. 2009. (Illus.). 32p. pap. 13.99 (*978-1-4389-8461-2(8)*) AuthorHouse.

—Barnabee: In the Beehive. 2009. (Illus.). 24p. pap. 12.99 (*978-1-4389-7560-3(0)*) AuthorHouse.

—Barnabee: In the Meadow. 2009. (Illus.). 24p. pap. 12.99 (*978-1-4389-8389-9(1)*) AuthorHouse.

—Barnabee: Meets New Friends. 2009. (Illus.). 24p. pap. 12.99 (*978-1-4389-8390-5(5)*) AuthorHouse.

Gordon, Marie Elaina. My Grand-Mom Told Me... Book 1. 2006. 48p. pap. 16.95 (*978-1-4241-2655-2(X)*) America Star Bks.

—My Grand-Mom Told Me-down by the Sea. 2008. 108p. pap. 19.95 (*978-1-4241-9095-9(9)*) America Star Bks.

Gordon, Sylvia. Further Adventures of the Potty Wizard & His Cat, Muddles. 2009. (Illus.). 60p. pap. 10.49 (*978-1-4389-6819-3(1)*) AuthorHouse.

Gorey, Edward & Donnelly, James. Three Classic Children's Stories. 2010. (Illus.). 112p. (J). 17.95 (*978-0-7649-5546-4(2)*) Pomegranate Communications, Inc.

Gorman, Thomas. The Old Neighborhood. 2003. 77p. pap. 16.95 (*978-1-59286-514-7(3)*) PublishAmerica, Inc.

Gorrell, Nancy. Anna Banana. 2006. (ENG., Illus.). 96p. (J). (gr. -1-2). per. 6.99 (*978-1-84550-182-2(9)*, 8065ed6c-c535-43a1-adb7-b6b408153d87) Christian Focus Pubns. GBR. Dist: Baker & Taylor Publisher Services (BTPS).

Goscinny, René. The Bounty Hunter, Vol. 26. Morris Publishing Company Staff, illus. 2011. (Lucky Luke Ser.: 26). 48p. (J). (gr. -1-12). pap. 11.95 (*978-1-84918-059-7(8)*) CineBook GBR. Dist: National Bk. Network.

—Iznogoud - The Infamous, Vol. 7. Tabary, illus. 2011. (Iznogoud Ser.: 7). 48p. (J). (gr. -1-12). pap. 11.95 (*978-1-84918-074-0(1)*) CineBook GBR. Dist: National Bk. Network.

—Lucky Luke Versus Joss Jamon. Morris, illus. 27th ed. 2011. (Lucky Luke Ser.: 27). 48p. (J). (gr. -1-12). pap. 11.95 (*978-1-84918-071-9(7)*) CineBook GBR. Dist: National Bk. Network.

—Rockets to Stardom - Iznogoud, Vol. 8. Tabary, illus. 2011. (Iznogoud Ser.: 8). 48p. (J). (gr. -1-12). pap. 11.95 (*978-1-84918-092-4(X)*) CineBook GBR. Dist: National Bk. Network.

—The Stagecoach. Morris Publishing Company Staff, illus. 2011. (Lucky Luke Ser.: 25). 48p. (J). (gr. 3-17). pap. 11.95 (*978-1-84918-052-8(0)*) CineBook GBR. Dist: National Bk. Network.

Goscinny, René & Morris Publishing Company Staff. The Dalton Cousins. 2011. (Lucky Luke Ser.: 28). (Illus.). 48p. (J). (gr. -1-12). pap. 12.95 (*978-1-84918-076-4(8)*) CineBook GBR. Dist: National Bk. Network.

Goscinny, René & Uderzo, Albert. Bouclier Arverne. 21.95 (*978-2-01-210011-4(2)*) Hachette Groupe Livre FRA. Dist: Distribooks, Inc.

—Obelix et Compagnie. (FRE.). 21.95 (*978-2-01-210023-7(6)*) Hachette Groupe Livre FRA. Dist: Distribooks, Inc.

Gottfredson, Floyd, et al. Walt Disney's Comics & Stories #700. 2008. 80p. pap. 9.99 (*978-1-60360-057-6(4)*) Gemstone Publishing, Inc.

Gould, Terry. The Adventures of Sir Sniffsalot & His Friends. Proulx, Denis, illus. 2007. 48p. (gr. -1-3). pap. 15.99 (*978-0-9789057-3-6(3)*) Huntington Ludlow Media Group.

Graban, Virginia M. & Rasmussen, Jude. 3 Pigs Move On: Pigs on the Road, Pigs in Africa. 2005. (ENG.). 50p. pap. 15.99 (*978-1-4134-1508-7(3)*) Xlibris Corp.

Graham, Bob. Tales from the Waterhole. 2004. (Illus.). 64p. (J). (*978-0-7445-6593-5(6)*) Walker Bks., Ltd.

Grahame, Kenneth. Dream Days. Shepard, Ernest H., illus. 2004. reprint ed. pap. 21.95 (*978-1-4179-0979-7(X)*) Kessinger Publishing, LLC.

Grandpa Bob. The Dirty Nose Series. 2008. (ENG.). 284p. pap. 16.99 (*978-0-557-02079-9(4)*) Lulu Pr., Inc.

—The Dirty Nose Series - Olander. 2008. 284p. 33.86 (*978-1-4116-9246-6(2)*) Lulu Pr., Inc.

Grannan, Mary. Just Mary Reader: Mary Grannan Selected Stories. Hume, Margaret Anne, ed. 2006. (ENG., Illus.). 176p. (YA). pap. 24.99 (*978-1-55002-598-9(8)*) Dundurn Pr. CAN. Dist: Publishers Group West (PGW).

Granny's Favorite Tales. 2006. (Illus.). 156p. (J). per. 39.95 (*978-1-60002-098-8(4)*, 3915) Mountain Valley Publishing, LLC.

Grant, Joan Marshall. Redskin Morning & Other Stories. Lavers, Ralph, illus. 2010. (J). pap. (*978-1-59731-555-5(9)*) Perennis, Sophia.

—Scarlet Fish & Other Stories. Lavers, Ralph, illus. 2010. (J). pap. (*978-1-59731-554-8(0)*) Perennis, Sophia.

Grant, Susan. Tell Me a Story. Dall, Christopher M., illus. 2013. 56p. pap. (*978-1-4602-1356-8(4)*) FriesenPress.

Grasso, Lorraine. Short Stories, Tall Tales. 2011. 24p. pap. 15.99 (*978-1-4568-5491-1(7)*) Xlibris Corp.

Gratton, Tessa, et al. The Anatomy of Curiosity. 2018. (ENG.). 296p. (YA). (gr. 8-12). pap. 9.99 (*978-1-5415-1480-5(7)*, 2f5176c4-ec5f-4ae0-af03-2c9d17fb01e8, Carolrhoda Lab™) Lerner Publishing Group.

—The Curiosities: A Collection of Stories. 2014. (ENG.). 304p. (YA). (gr. 7-12). pap. 11.95 (*978-1-4677-1623-9(5)*, fc308abd-51e8-46a0-b22d-eb5831170362, Carolrhoda Lab™) Lerner Publishing Group.

Graves, Damien. The Deadly Catch. 2008. (Midnight Library). (Illus.). 170p. (J). (gr. 4-7). 13.65 (*978-0-7569-8824-1(1)*) Perfection Learning Corp.

—I Can See You. 2010. (Midnight Library Ser.). 160p. (J). 15.10 (*978-1-60686-248-3(0)*) Perfection Learning Corp.

Gray, Grandpa. The Land of the Three Elves: Inside the Curve of the River. 2013. (ENG.). 268p. (YA). pap. 14.95 (*978-1-4787-0314-3(8)*) Outskirts Pr., Inc.

Gray, Keith. Dead Trouble. (ENG., Illus.). 90p. (J). pap. 7.50 (*978-0-7497-4556-1(8)*) Farshore GBR. Dist: Trafalgar Square Publishing.

Grayson, Barry/Scott. Twisted Yarns: Bedtime Stories for Hip Kids. 2007. (Illus.). 40p. (J). pap. (*978-0-9774357-1-5(7)*) Grayson, Kate.

Great, Alex. Balkan Tales. 2009. 134p. pap. 18.36 (*978-1-4452-4363-4(6)*) Lulu Pr., Inc.

Great American Short Stories, 6 vols. 2004. (Great American Short Stories Ser.). (ENG.). 80p. (gr. 4-6). lib. bdg. 80.01 (*978-0-8368-4250-0(2)*, 6672476f-cfea-43e4-8953-949d25bd3dcf, Gareth Stevens Learning Library) Stevens, Gareth Publishing LLLP.

Great Books Foundation Staff, contrib. by. Junior Great Books. 2011. (J). (*978-1-933147-00-0(8)*) Great Bks. Foundation.

Green, John, et al. Let It Snow: Three Holiday Romances. 2008. (ENG.). 358p. (YA). (gr. 7-18). pap. 12.99 (*978-0-14-241214-5(7)*, Speak) Penguin Young Readers Group.

Green, Richard Lancelyn. The Adventures of Robin Hood. Terrazzini, Daniela Jaglenka, illus. 2010. (Puffin Classics Ser.). 336p. (J). (gr. 5-7). 16.99 (*978-0-14-133489-9(4)*, Puffin Books) Penguin Young Readers Group.

Greendyk, William, tr. from ENG. Las Doce Historias de la Tía Margarita. l.t. ed. 2004. Orig. Title: Aunt Margaret's Twelve Stories. (SPA.). 84p. (J). pap. 3.99 (*978-1-932789-00-3(6)*, X001N) Editorial Sendas Antiguas, LLC.

Greene, Janice. Blood & Basketball, 1 vol. unabr. ed. 2010. (Q Reads Ser.). (ENG.). 32p. (YA). (gr. 9-12). pap. 8.50 (*978-1-61651-213-2(X)*) Saddleback Educational Publishing, Inc.

—Breaking Point, 1 vol. unabr. ed. 2010. (Q Reads Ser.). (ENG.). 32p. (YA). (gr. 9-12). pap. 8.50 (*978-1-61651-199-9(0)*) Saddleback Educational Publishing, Inc.

—Outcast, 1 vol. unabr. ed. 2010. (Q Reads Ser.). (ENG.). 32p. (YA). (gr. 9-12). pap. 8.50 (*978-1-61651-201-9(6)*) Saddleback Educational Publishing, Inc.

Greene, Kimberly. My Sister's a Pop Star. 2011. (My Sister's a Pop Star Ser.). (ENG.). 277p. (J). (gr. 4-6). 18.69 (*978-0-7945-2899-7(6)*) EDC Publishing.

Gregg, Stacy. Riding Star, Book 3. 2011. (Pony Club Rivals Ser.: 3). (ENG.). 304p. (J). (gr. 4-7). pap. 7.99 (*978-0-00-733345-5(5)*, HarperCollins Children's Bks.) HarperCollins Pubs. Ltd. GBR. Dist: HarperCollins Pubs.

—Showjumpers, Book 2. 2010. (Pony Club Rivals Ser.: 2). (ENG.). 272p. (J). (gr. 4-7). pap. 7.99 (*978-0-00-733344-8(7)*, HarperCollins Children's Bks.) HarperCollins Pubs. Ltd. GBR. Dist: HarperCollins Pubs.

Gressett, William H., Jr. Nor all your Piety nor Wit... . 2005. (YA). per. 9.99 (*978-0-9765467-9-5(5)*) Creative Bk. Pubs.

Grethe, James. Weird & Wondrous Tales of Woodland Wyre. 2009. 60p. pap. 11.00 (*978-1-4269-1527-7(6)*) Trafford Publishing.

Grey, Erika. The Alphabet Bears: Spook-Tales Collection. Grey, Erika, illus. 2010. (Illus.). 127p. (YA). pap. 24.95 (*978-0-9790199-3-7(1)*) PeDante Pr.

Griffiths, Mark. Hanging on Every Word: 48 of the World's Greatest Stories, Retold for Reading Aloud, 1 vol. 2014. (ENG.). 224p. pap. 21.99 (*978-0-85721-506-2(X)*, de096ffb-0cb9-4a35-8f80-44075ebb7144, Monarch Bks.) Lion Hudson PLC GBR. Dist: Baker & Taylor Publisher Services (BTPS).

Grigorov, Yassen. Los Ángeles de la Guarda. 2003. (Los Especiales de A la Orilla Del Viento Ser.). (SPA.). 28p. (J). 9.99 (*978-968-16-7053-5(1)*) Fondo de Cultura Economica USA.

Grimes, Charles J. The Boys!, 1 vol. 2010. 186p. pap. 24.95 (*978-1-4489-5736-1(2)*) America Star Bks.

Grimly, Gris. Little Jordan Ray's Muddy Spud. Grimly, Gris, illus. 2005. (ENG., Illus.). 40p. pap. 19.95 (*978-0-9729388-6-0(9)*) Last Gasp of San Francisco.

Grimm. Bola de cristal. 2005. 24p. incl. cd-rom (*978-84-494-2897-5(1)*) Oceano Grupo Editoria, S.A.

—Tres pelos diablio. 2005. 24p. incl. audio compact disk (*978-84-494-2898-2(X)*) Oceano Grupo Editoria, S.A.

Grimm, Brothers. Hans in Luck: Seven Stories by the Brothers Grimm. Hoffmann, Felix, illus. 2017. (ENG.). 256p. (J). (gr. -1-3). 30.00 (*978-0-7358-4281-6(7)*) North-South Bks., Inc.

Grimm, Hermanos. El Caperucita Roja.Tr. of My First Library: Little Red Riding Hood. (SPA.). (J). 2.49 (*978-968-13-2470-4(6)*) Editorial Diana, S.A. MEX. Dist: Continental Bk. Co., Inc.

Grimm, Jacob. Cuentos de Grimm. Rackham, Arthur, illus. (Coleccion Cuentos Universales). (SPA.). 144p. (YA). (gr. 4-18). (*978-84-261-1098-5(3)*, JV30116) Juventud, Editorial ESP. Dist: Lectorum Pubns., Inc.

Grimm, Jacob & Grimm, Wilhelm K. Cuentos de Grimm.Tr. of Stories by Grimm. (SPA.). 144p. (J). (*978-84-261-0618-6(8)*) Juventud, Editorial.

—Cuentos de Grimm. (Coleccion Estrella).Tr. of Stories by Grimm. (SPA., Illus.). 64p. (J). 14.95 (*978-950-11-0015-0(4)*, SGM015) Sigmar ARG. Dist: Continental Bk. Co., Inc.

Gripari, Pierre. Le Gentil Petit Diable: Et Autres Contes de la Rue Broca. Rosado, Puig, illus. 2007. (Folio Junior Ser.). 142p. (J). per. (*978-2-07-061255-0(4)*) National Round Table on the Environment & the Economy (NRTEE)/Table ronde nationale sur l'environnement et l'economie (TRNEE).

Grizzell, Larry. The Star: A Christmas Song. 2006. (Illus.). 25p. (J). 19.95 (*978-0-9759542-2-5(9)*) Adventures Galore.

Gross, Jen & Hoch, Jen. A Visit up & down Wall Street. Gross, Margaret, illus. 2005. 32p. (J). 14.95 (*978-0-9760875-0-2(2)*) Harry & Stephanie Bks.

Gruber, Daveda. Red Barn & other Short Stories. 2010. 45p. pap. 19.50 (*978-0-557-41998-2(0)*) Lulu Pr., Inc.

—Tales of a Tiny Dog. 2010. (ENG.). 74p. pap. 29.50 (*978-0-557-43600-2(1)*) Lulu Pr., Inc.

Gruber, Michael. The Legend of the Brog. Gruber, Michael & Graves, Linda, illus. 2005. (J). per. 9.95 (*978-0-9770413-0-5(1)*) Gruber Enterprises.

Gruskin, Edward I. Roy Rogers: Robin Hood of the Range. Hess, Erwin L., illus. 2011. 420p. 54.95 (*978-1-258-04369-8(6)*) Literary Licensing, LLC.

Guardino, Dawn M. Nightmare Echoes: Short Scary Stories for Young Teens. 2003. 108p. 22.95 (*978-1-4107-8325-7(1)*); pap. 11.45 (*978-1-4107-8324-0(3)*) AuthorHouse.

Guerrero, Andres. La Noche. Guerrero, Andres, illus. 2003. (SPA., Illus.). 28p. (J). (gr. k-3). 7.95 (*978-84-204-4321-8(2)*) Santillana USA Publishing Co., Inc.

Guin, Anatoly. Smart Tales from Brainy the Cat. 2010. 84p. pap. 29.95 (*978-1-4327-6147-9(1)*) Outskirts Pr., Inc.

Gulliksen, Anne. A Boy from Nøtterøy. 2009. 108p. pap. 13.00 (*978-1-59858-939-9(3)*) Dog Ear Publishing, LLC.

Gump, Granny. The Giraffe Who Went to School. 2011. 48p. pap. 21.99 (*978-1-4568-5805-6(X)*) Xlibris Corp.

Guo, Jinsong. Touching Stories by Dr. Guo. 2004. pap. 10.00 (*978-0-8059-6606-0(4)*) Dorrance Publishing Co., Inc.

Gurney, Stella. Not so Silly Sausage. Million, Liz, illus. 2011. 32p. pap. (*978-1-84089-707-4(4)*) Zero to Ten, Ltd.

Gustafson, Scott. Classic Bedtime Stories. 2016. (ENG., Illus.). 84p. (J). (gr. k-3). 20.00 (*978-1-57965-760-4(5)*, 85760) Artisan.

Gustafson, Scott, illus. Cuentos y Cantos de Navidad. 2004. (ESP & SPA.). 98p. (YA). 12.98 (*978-1-4127-0628-5(9)*, 7137007) Phoenix International Publications, Inc.

Gutman, Dan. My Weird School Collection: Books 1 To 4, Bks. 1-4. Paillot, Jim, illus. 2010. (My Weird School Ser.). (ENG.). (J). (gr. 1-5). pap. 16.99 (*978-0-06-189489-3(3)*, HarperCollins) HarperCollins Pubs.

—My Weird School Daze 12-Book Box Set: Books 1-12, 12 vols. Paillot, Jim, illus. 2013. (My Weird School Daze Ser.). (ENG.). 500p. (J). (gr. 1-5). pap. 58.88 (*978-0-06-228891-2(1)*, HarperCollins) HarperCollins Pubs.

Guttiere, Benedicte. When Christmas Comes. 2011. (Funny Faces Ser.). (Illus.). 14p. bds. (*978-1-84089-710-4(4)*) Zero to Ten, Ltd.

Guy, Belinda. A First Aid Manual for Children: In the Form of Three Short Stories. 2012. (Illus.). 28p. pap. 21.35 (*978-1-4772-2671-1(0)*) AuthorHouse.

Guzaldo, Jessica. Murder & Betrayal DeFalco, Julie & Cowhey, Dennis R., eds. Cowhey, Dennis E., illus. 2003. 72p. (YA). (gr. 7-8). pap. 9.95 (*978-0-9642823-2-2(1)*) Key Answer Products, Inc.

Hachette Children's Group. The Pardoner's Tale. (ENG., Illus.). 48p. (*978-0-7502-3670-6(1)*) Hodder & Stoughton.

Haight, Travis. 2:30 AM: Wired on Coffee; Six Premium Blended (Not So) Shorts. 2007. 203p. pap. 13.95 (*978-1-4303-1004-4(9)*) Lulu Pr., Inc.

Hale, Shannon, et al. True Heroes: A Treasury of Modern-Day Fairy Tales Written by Best-Selling Authors. Diaz, Jonathan, ed. Diaz, Jonathan, photos by. 2015. (ENG., Illus.). 208p. (J). (gr. 3-6). 19.99 (*978-1-62972-103-3(4)*, 5140400, Shadow Mountain) Shadow Mountain Publishing.

Hall, Desis. Christmas in Jamaica & Other Stories. 2012. 64p. pap. (*978-1-908690-06-7(2)*) Abba Pr.

Hall, Jennie. The Viking Tales. 2008. 88p. pap. 8.15 (*978-1-60459-529-1(9)*) Wilder Pubns., Corp.

Hall, S.C. Turns of Fortune & Other Tales. 2007. (ENG.). 116p. per. (*978-1-4065-1586-2(8)*) Dodo Pr.

Halsey-Cody, J. E. Story Time. 2012. 110p. 29.99 (*978-1-4797-1401-8(1)*); pap. 19.99 (*978-1-4797-1400-1(3)*) Xlibris Corp.

Halsted, John David, ed. East of the Sun & West of the Moon & Other Moon Stories. 2012. (Illus.). 54p. pap. (*978-1-909302-02-0(3)*) Abela Publishing.

Hamilton, Seymour. The Laughing Princess. 2012. (ENG.). 146p. (J). pap. 7.99 (*978-1-937291-45-7(6)*) Acedrex Publishing.

Hamley, Dennis. Beautiful Games. Fenoughty, Charles, illus. 2004. 104p. per. *(978-1-904529-13-2(5)*, Back to Front) Solidus.
—Yule Logs. 2005. 96p. per. *(978-1-904529-17-0(8)*, Back to Front) Solidus.
Hammond, Meredith. The World According to Tiffany: The Airplane Trip. 2011. 28p. (gr. -1). pap. 12.03 *(978-1-4567-3150-2(5))* AuthorHouse.
Hampton, Sue. Aliens & Angels: Three Stories for Christmas. 2013. (ENG., Illus.). 96p. (J). pap. *(978-1-78228-315-7(3))* Pneuma Springs Publishing.
Handa, Nimret. Good Night Stories. 2004. (Illus.). 20p. (J). *(978-81-291-0373-4(7))* Rupa & Co.
Hannan, Peter. The Greatest Snowman in the World! Hannan, Peter, illus. 2010. (ENG., Illus.). 32p. (J). (gr. -1-3). 16.99 *(978-0-06-128480-9(7)*, HarperCollins) HarperCollins Pubs.
Hannigan, Katherine. True (... Sort Of) 2011. (ENG., Illus.). 368p. (J). (gr. 3-7). 16.99 *(978-0-06-196873-0(0)*, Greenwillow Bks.) HarperCollins Pubs.
Hanson, Martina D. & Benchmark Education Co. Staff. Analytical Arguments about Courage. 2014. (Text Connections Ser.). (J). (gr. 6). *(978-1-4900-1530-9(2))* Benchmark Education Co.
Harden, Perry Lee. The Percy Hargrove Stories: It's All Elementary. 2012. 160p. pap. 14.95 *(978-1-4772-2438-0(6))* AuthorHouse.
harkins, charles. Naptime Adventures of Luksi the Turtle. 2010. (ENG.). 174p. pap. 20.96 *(978-0-557-28695-9(6))* Lulu Pr., Inc.
Harman, Michael. El Loro y la Higuera. 2009. (SPA., Illus.). 32p. (J). (gr. -1-3). pap. 8.95 *(978-0-89800-431-1(4))* Dharma Publishing.
—The Parrot & the Fig Tree: A Story about Friendship & Respect for Nature. 2nd ed. 2009. (Jataka Tales Ser.). (Illus.). 32p. (J). (gr. -1-5). pap. 8.95 *(978-0-89800-430-4(6))* Dharma Publishing.
Harold & I. 2007. (ENG., Illus.). 291p. (J). (gr. 3-8). per. 13.99 *(978-0-7684-2432-4(1))* Send The Light Distribution LLC.
Harper, Eleanor. Honey & Harebell. 2010. 64p. pap. 11.95 *(978-0-9818092-7-4(8))* Illumina Publishing.
Harris, Christine. Four Tails: An Anthology of Four Tales for Children. 2011. (Illus.). 92p. (gr. -1). pap. 12.10 *(978-1-4520-7643-0(X))* AuthorHouse.
Harris, Joel Chandler. Told by Uncle Remus: New Stories of the. 2006. (Illus.). pap. 31.95 *(978-1-4254-9964-8(3))* Kessinger Publishing, LLC.
Harris, Kimberly Anne. Only in a Dream Series: Caught in a Web ~ the Trees Are My Friends~What Is All the Buzz About? 2012. 60p. pap. 24.99 *(978-1-4772-7005-9(1))* AuthorHouse.
Hartnett, Edith E. Once upon a Time. 2013. 168p. pap. 22.50 *(978-1-882260-22-5(8))* Calm Unity Pr.
Hartt-Sussman, Heather. Here Comes Hortense! Graham, Georgia, illus. 2012. 32p. (J). (gr. -1-1). 17.95 *(978-1-77049-221-9(6)*, Tundra Bks.) Tundra Bks. CAN. Dist: Penguin Random Hse. LLC.
Harvey, A. W. Llewellyn. Christmas Stories: For the Young & Young at Heart. 2012. 114p. (gr. -1). pap. 12.06 *(978-1-4669-5800-5(6))* Trafford Publishing.
Harvey, Irene J. William the Fairground Car. 2008. 116p. pap. 30.95 *(978-1-60693-210-0(1)*, Eloquent Bks.) Strategic Book Publishing & Rights Agency (SBPRA).
Hasling, Jack. The Little Rock & Other Stories: And Other Stories. Rogers, Denny, illus. 2003. (ENG.). 32p. (Orig.). (J). (gr. 1-6). pap. 9.95 *(978-1-878044-51-8(6)*, Wild Rose) Mayhaven Publishing, Inc.
—Salamander the Great! 2006. (Illus.). (J). per. 10.00 *(978-0-9786988-1-2(9))* Hazel Street Productions.
Hastings, Jacqueline. Jay's Tales. 2013. 70p. pap. *(978-1-909878-05-1(7))* Legend Pr.
Hasty, Shaudalon. My Body. 2003. pap. 12.00 *(978-0-8059-5968-0(8))* Dorrance Publishing Co., Inc.
Hawkins, Colin. Foxy Doesn't Feel Well. (Illus.). 23p. (J). pap. 8.99 *(978-0-00-664758-4(8)*, HarperCollins Children's Bks.) HarperCollins Pubs. Ltd. GBR. Dist: Trafalgar Square Publishing.
Hawley, Jim. Homer & Friends. 2012. 50p. pap. *(978-1-77097-709-9(0))* FriesenPress.
Hawthorn, P. Little Book of Bedtime Stories. 2004. (Mini Storybooks Ser.). (ENG., Illus.). 128p. (J). 7.95 *(978-0-7945-0268-3(7)*, Usborne) EDC Publishing.
Hawthorn, Phillip. Usborne Stories for Bedtime. Tyler, Jenny, ed. Cartwright, Stephen, illus. 2007. (Stories for Bedtime Ser.). 190p. (J). (gr. -1-3). 19.99 *(978-0-7945-1970-4(9)*, Usborne) EDC Publishing.
Hayashi, Leslie Ann. Fables Beneath the Rainbow. Bishop, Kathleen Wong, illus. 2005. 32p. (J). 14.95 *(978-1-56647-741-3(7)*, 477417) Mutual Publishing LLC.
Hayden, Gwendolen Lampshire. Mary Martha's Really Truly Stories: Book 3. 3rd ed. 2013. 130p. pap. 11.95 *(978-1-4796-0105-9(5))* TEACH Services, Inc.
Hayes, Joe. Juan Verdades: The Man Who Couldn't Tell a Lie / el Hombre Que No Sab�a Mentir, 1 vol. Fiedler, Joseph Daniel, illus. 2011.Tr. of Juan Verdades/The Man Who Couldn't Tell a Lie. (ENG.). 32p. (J). (gr. 2-5). pap. 11.95 *(978-1-933693-70-5(3)*, 23353382, Cinco Puntos Press) Lee & Low Bks., Inc.
—Watch Out for Clever Women! Cuidado con Las Mujeres Astutas, 1 vol. Hayes, Joe, tr. Hill, Vicki Trego, illus. 2019. (ENG.). 160p. (J). (gr. 3-6). 19.95 *(978-1-947627-00-0(7)*, 23353382, Cinco Puntos Press) Lee & Low Bks., Inc.
Hays, Helen Ashe. The Adventures of Prince Lazybones: And Other Stories. 2017. (ENG., Illus.). (J). 23.95 *(978-1-374-96199-9(X))*; pap. 13.95 *(978-1-374-96198-2(1))* Capital Communications, Inc.
Hearne, Betsy. The Canine Connection: Stories about Dogs & People. 2007. (ENG.). 128p. (YA). (gr. 7). pap. 8.95 *(978-1-4169-6817-7(2)*, Simon Pulse) Simon Pulse.
Hedley, Alistair, selected by. Read to Me Daddy. Date not set. (Read to Me Ser.). (Illus.). 192p. (J). 14.98 *(978-0-7525-9485-9(0))* Parragon, Inc.
Heer, Andrew De. Three African Short Stories for Young Readers: For Young Readers. 2011. 32p. pap. 21.99 *(978-1-4568-7973-0(1))* Xlibris Corp.
Hefferman, Danielle. Puppy Dog Tales. 2010. (Illus.). pap. *(978-0-9561590-5-2(2)*, Blue Cloud Pubns.) Black Leaf Publishing Group, The.
Heger, Bryan. Valor & Virtues from the Mind of a Child, 1 vol. 2009. 124p. pap. 19.95 *(978-1-60749-625-0(9))* America Star Bks.
Heichberger, Robert L. Tell Me A Story Grandpa. 2010. 56p. pap. 27.99 *(978-1-4520-1584-2(8))* AuthorHouse.
Heide, Florence Parry. Tales for the Perfect Child. Ruzzier, Sergio, illus. 2018. (ENG.). 112p. (J). (gr. 1-5). pap. 6.99 *(978-1-4814-6380-5(2))* Simon & Schuster Children's Publishing.
Heide, Florence Parry & Van Clief, Sylvia Worth. Fables You Shouldn't Pay Any Attention To. Ruzzier, Sergio, illus. 2017. (ENG.). 112p. (J). (gr. 1-5). 16.99 *(978-1-4814-6382-9(9))* Simon & Schuster Children's Publishing.
Heimdallson, Freydis, et al. Kindertales: Stories Old & New for the Children of the Folk. 2008. 100p. pap. 19.50 *(978-1-4357-2563-8(8))* Lulu Pr., Inc.
Heine, Helme. Cuentas de Elefante. 2003. (la Orilla Del Viento Ser.). (SPA.). 40p. (J). pap. 7.50 *(978-968-16-6423-7(X)*, 151) Fondo de Cultura Economica USA.
Henderson, Barbara. Down in Mr Brown's Garden. 2009. 40p. pap. 14.75 *(978-1-60860-703-7(8)*, Strategic Bk. Publishing) Strategic Book Publishing & Rights Agency (SBPRA).
Henderson, Mary Anne. The Adventures of Linda's Little Frog. 2004. 252p. 29.50 *(978-1-4184-1576-1(6))* AuthorHouse.
Henighan, Tom. The Boy from Left Field. 2012. (ENG.). 216p. (J). (gr. 5-5). pap. 12.99 *(978-1-4597-0060-4(0))* Dundurn Pr. CAN. Dist: Publishers Group West (PGW).
Henisz, Jerzy E. SOPHIE in PARIS & other Stories. 2009. (ENG.). 99p. pap. 9.46 *(978-0-557-09520-9(4))* Lulu Pr., Inc.
Henisz, Jerzy E. & Henisz, Sophie, illustrator. TEDDY BEAR who went on a Trip around the World & other Stories. 2006. (ENG.). 88p. (J). pap. *(978-0-615-13851-0(9))* Henisz, Jerzy E.
Henriquez, Cesar, illus. Jonathan's Colorful Campus Tour - University of Connecticut A-Z. 2004. (J). 9.99 *(978-1-933069-06-7(6))* Odd Duck Ink, Inc.
—Sebastian's Colorful Campus Tour - University of Miami A-Z. 2004. (J). 9.99 *(978-1-933069-05-0(8))* Odd Duck Ink, Inc.
Henry, Judy. Woodland Stories for Our Grandchildren. 2013. 40p. pap. 19.99 *(978-1-4669-7752-5(3))* Trafford Publishing.
Henry, O. & Escott, John. Oxford Bookworms Playscripts: One Thousand Dollars & Other Plays: Level 2: 700-Word Vocabulary. 2nd ed. 2008. (ENG., Illus.). 64p. 11.00 *(978-0-19-423520-4(3))* Oxford Univ. Pr., Inc.
Henry, O. & Gianni, Gary. The Gift of the Magi. (Classics Illustrated Ser.). (Illus.). 52p. (YA). pap. 4.95 *(978-1-57209-013-2(8))* Classics International Entertainment, Inc.
Henty, George. G. A. Henty Short Story Collection: Featuring: Sole Survivors, the Frontier Girl, the Ranch in the Valley, & on the Track, Vol. 1. 2004. (YA). pap. *(978-1-931587-34-1(5))* Preston-Speed Pubns.
—G. A. Henty Short Story Collecton (Deluxe Heirloom Edition) Featuring: Sole Survivors, the Frontier Girl, the Ranch in the Valley, & on the Track (Deluxe Heirloom Edition), Vol. 1. 2004. (YA). lib. bdg. *(978-1-931587-33-4(7))* Preston-Speed Pubns.
Herlihy, Matt & Clarke, Nzingha, selected by. Sweet Fancy Moses: Book 2. 2005. per. *(978-0-9767048-0-5(3))* Arts and Minds Studio Inc.
Herman, Carli. Good Graffiti Teen Talk on Tough Issues. 2009. 108p. pap. 10.00 *(978-0-578-01524-8(2))* Black Bart Bks.
La Hermanita; El Diente Molesto, 2 bks., Set. (Coleccion Chiquilines - Imagen y Sonido). (SPA.). (J). 15.95 incl. audio *(978-950-11-0627-5(6)*, SGM276) Sigmar ARG. Dist: Continental Bk. Co., Inc.
Herzog, Pearl. The Pink Dollhouse. 2008. 112p. 29.99 *(978-1-58330-797-7(4))* Feldheim Pubs.
Hester, Denia Lewis. Grandma Lenas Big Ol_Turnip. Urbanovic, Jackie, illus. 2005. (ENG.). 32p. (J). (gr. -1-3). 7.99 *(978-0-8075-3023-8(9)*, 807530239) Whitman, Albert & Co.
Hewling, Amy Megan. Wishes. 2010. (ENG.). 29p. *(978-1-907629-07-5(6))* ShieldCrest.
Higgins, M. G. Body Switch, 1 vol. 2014. (Red Rhino Ser.). (ENG.). 76p. (J). (gr. 4-7). pap. 9.95 *(978-1-62250-944-7(7))* Saddleback Educational Publishing, Inc.
—Flyer, 1 vol. 2014. (Red Rhino Ser.). (ENG.). 68p. (J). (gr. 4-7). pap. 9.95 *(978-1-62250-942-3(0))* Saddleback Educational Publishing, Inc.
Highstreet, Harry. Read Aloud Series. 2006. (ENG.). 134p. pap. 28.95 *(978-1-84728-641-3(0))* Lulu Pr., Inc.
Hildahl, Melita K. Life Is an Adventure with Ernie. 2008. 156p. per. 15.99 *(978-1-60477-139-8(9))* Salem Author Services.
Hill, Annemarie. Meaty Treats. 2012. 16p. pap. 15.41 *(978-1-4669-3118-3(3))* Trafford Publishing.
Hill, Clare. Granddad's Circus & Other Stories. 2004. 41p. pap. 19.95 *(978-1-4137-3647-2(5))* PublishAmerica, Inc.
Hill, Kathi Harper. The Christmas Closet & Other Works. 2012. (ENG.). 48p. 16.99 *(978-1-936815-58-6(3))* Yawn's Bks. & More, Inc.
Hillman, John E. Ancient Stories of the Hodj. 2012. (Illus.). 52p. pap. 27.45 *(978-1-4685-8215-4(1))* AuthorHouse.
Hilton, Charlotte. Adventure of the Pen Pot Pals. 2009. 36p. pap. 16.99 *(978-1-4389-4434-0(9))* AuthorHouse.
Hinckley, Betts. Mr Bumble. 2011. 24p. pap. 15.99 *(978-1-4568-9714-7(4))* Xlibris Corp.
Hines, Jerry E. Silly & Stinky Stories My Grandpa Tells. 2011. (ENG., Illus.). 144p. (J). (gr. 4-7). pap. 8.00 *(978-0-9831839-1-4(0))* Amber Skye Publishing LLC.
Hinojosa, Francisco. Ana, Verdad? Gedovius, Juan, illus. 2003. (Coleccion Derechos Del Nino Ser.). (SPA.). 32p. (J). (gr. 3-5). pap. 7.95 *(978-84-204-5824-3(4))* Santillana USA Publishing Co., Inc.
—Yanka, Yanka. Hinojosa, Francisco, illus. 2003. (SPA., Illus.). 44p. (J). (gr. k-3). pap. 10.95 *(978-968-19-0440-1(0))* Santillana USA Publishing Co., Inc.
Hinrichs, Tambra. Ryley's World, 1 vol. 2010. 28p. pap. 24.95 *(978-1-4489-6287-7(0))* PublishAmerica, Inc.
Hobbie, Holly. Gem. 2012. (ENG., Illus.). 32p. (J). (gr. -1-3). 16.99 *(978-0-316-20334-0(3))* Little, Brown Bks. for Young Readers.
Hobbs-Wyatt, Debz, ed. Wild N Free Too. 2013. 222p. pap. *(978-0-9568939-6-3(1))* Paws n Claws Publishing.
Hobby, Nathan. The Fur. 2004. 220p. (YA). pap. 16.50 *(978-1-920731-01-4(6))* Fremantle Pr. AUS. Dist: Independent Pubs. Group.
Hoberman, Mary Ann. Very Short Stories to Read Together. Emberley, Michael, illus. 2006. (You Read to Me, I'll Read to You Ser.: 1). (ENG.). 32p. (J). (gr. -1-3). pap. 8.99 *(978-0-316-01316-1(1))* Little, Brown Bks. for Young Readers.
—You Read to Me, I'll Read to You: Very Short Tall Tales to Read Together. Emberley, Michael, illus. 2019. (You Read to Me, I'll Read to You Ser.: 6). (ENG.). 32p. (J). (gr. -1-3). pap. 8.99 *(978-0-316-53140-5(5))* Little, Brown Bks. for Young Readers.
Hodgson, Julie. Miniature Horse Tales. 2005. 37p. (J). 15.00 *(978-1-4116-4144-0(2))* Lulu Pr., Inc.
Hoffmann, Heinrich. Slovenly Kate & Other Stories: From the Struwwelpeter Library. Hosemann, Theodor, illus. 2012. (Dover Children's Classics Ser.). (ENG.). 96p. (J). (gr. 3-5). pap. 12.99 *(978-0-486-49032-8(7)*, 490327) Dover Pubns., Inc.
Hogan, Robb Dragon. There Was a Time: A Journey into Black & White with Taz. 2003. (Illus.). 43p. 6.00 *(978-0-9742178-0-2(8))* TazTales.
Holden, Pam. Stone Soup, 1 vol. Hawley, Kelvin, illus. 2009. (Red Rocket Readers Ser.). (ENG.). 18p. (gr. 2-2). pap. *(978-1-877363-84-9(7))* Flying Start Bks.
Holland, Karen. The Garden Gang. 2010. (Illus.). 32p. pap. 12.99 *(978-1-4490-6532-4(5))* AuthorHouse.
Holling, Holling Clancy. Holling Clancy Holling's Stories from Many Lands. 2014. (ENG., Illus.). 144p. (J). (gr. 3-7). pap. 14.99 *(978-0-486-49634-4(1)*, 496341) Dover Pubns., Inc.
Holly, Julia. Mrs Winkler's Cure. Holly, Julia, illus. 2010. (Illus.). 214p. pap. 19.99 *(978-1-883376-45-1(9))* Stellium Pr.
Holm, Jennifer L. Full of Beans. 2018. lib. bdg. 18.40 *(978-0-606-40939-1(4))* Turtleback.
Hood, Karen Jean Matsko. Kids' Kindness Journal: A Daily Journal, bk. 9. Whispering Pine Press International, ed. Artistic Design Service Staff, illus. 2015. (Children's Journal Series). 160p. (J). spiral bd. 15.95 *(978-1-59649-416-9(6))* Whispering Pine Pr. International, Inc.
Hooten, K. J. Stories to Amuse the Kids, 1 vol. 2009. 47p. pap. 24.95 *(978-1-60749-730-1(1))* PublishAmerica, Inc.
Hooton, Margaret. The Laughing Pot & Other Stories: More Tales for All the Children of the World. 2013. 40p. pap. 16.95 *(978-1-4525-8601-4(2)*, Balboa Pr.) Author Solutions, LLC.
Hope, Kathleen. Jack Eagle the Pirate & Other Mysterious Tales. 2012. (Illus.). 48p. pap. 24.40 *(978-1-4678-9611-5(X))* AuthorHouse.
Hope, Laura Lee. The Bobbsey Twins: The First Fifteen Stories, Including Merry Days Indoors & Out, in the Country, at the Seashore, at School, at Snow Lodge, on A. 2013. 1080p. *(978-1-78139-372-7(9))* Benediction Classics.
Hopkins, William J. The Sandman: His House Stories (Yesterday's Classics) 2009. 136p. pap. 8.95 *(978-1-59915-304-9(1))* Yesterday's Classics.
—The Sandman: His Ship Stories (Yesterday's Classics) Horne, Diantha W., illus. 2009. 174p. pap. 9.95 *(978-1-59915-302-5(5))* Yesterday's Classics.
—The Sandman: More Farm Stories (Yesterday's Classics) Williamson, Ada Clendenin, illus. 2009. 150p. pap. 8.95 *(978-1-59915-301-8(7))* Yesterday's Classics.
Hopkinson, Deborah. Sky Boys: How They Built the Empire State Building. Ransome, James E., illus. 2012. 48p. (J). (gr. -1-3). pap. 8.99 *(978-0-375-86541-1(1)*, Dragonfly Bks.) Random Hse. Children's Bks.
Hopper, Celia. Violets. 2004. (YA). per. 8.99 *(978-0-9754818-7-5(8))* Creative Bk. Pubs.
Horowitz, Anthony. Alex Rider: Secret Weapon: Seven Untold Adventures from the Life of a Teenaged Spy. 2019. (Alex Rider Ser.: 12). (ENG., Illus.). 336p. (J). (gr. 5). 17.99 *(978-1-5247-3933-1(2)*, Philomel Bks.) Penguin Young Readers Group.
—Bloody Horowitz. 2011. (ENG.). 336p. (J). (gr. 5-18). 6.99 *(978-0-14-241874-1(9)*, Puffin Books) Penguin Young Readers Group.
Horvath, Polly. Todo Sobre una Wafle. Holguin, Magdalena, tr. Violi, Daniela, illus. 2006. (Coleccion Torre de Papel: Amarilla Ser.). (SPA.). 187p. (J). (gr. 4-7). per. 8.95 *(978-958-04-6495-2(2))* Norma S.A. COL. Dist: Distribuidora Norma, Inc.
Houselander, Caryll. Catholic Tales for Boys & Girls. 2003. Orig. Title: Terrible Farmer Timson (New York: Sheed & Ward, 1957). (Illus.). 160p. (J). pap. 11.95 *(978-1-928832-74-4(1))* Sophia Institute Pr.
Housman, Laurence. The Field of Clover. 2007. 108p. per. 9.95 *(978-1-60312-129-3(3))*; 22.95 *(978-1-60312-928-2(6))* Aegypan.
Housman, Laurence, ed. Moonshine & Clover. Housman, Clemence, illus. 2013. 236p. (J). pap. *(978-1-909302-25-9(2))* Abela Publishing.
Howard, A. G. Untamed (Splintered Series Companion) A Splintered Companion. 2016. (Splintered Ser.). (ENG., Illus.). 304p. (J). (gr. 8-17). pap. 9.95 *(978-1-4197-2203-5(4)*, 1128303, Amulet Bks.) Abrams, Inc.
Howard, Jim & Welsh-Howard, Paula. Tell Me, Tell Me, What You See. Knight, Vanessa, illus. 2009. 24p. (J). pap. *(978-1-926585-65-9(8)*, CCB Publishing) CCB Publishing.
Howe, James. Bunnicula in a Box (Boxed Set) Bunnicula; Howliday Inn; the Celery Stalks at Midnight; Nighty-Nightmare; Return to Howliday Inn; Bunnicula Strikes Again; Bunnicula Meets Edgar Allan Crow. Payne, C. F., illus. 2013. (Bunnicula & Friends Ser.). (ENG.). 1136p. (J). (gr. 3-7). pap. 55.99 *(978-1-4424-8521-1(3)*, Atheneum Bks. for Young Readers) Simon & Schuster Children's Publishing.
—The Color of Absence: 12 Stories about Loss & Hope. 2004. 238p. 17.00 *(978-0-7569-4097-3(4))* Perfection Learning Corp.
—Harold & Chester Stories. Date not set. (Bunnicula & Friends Ser.). (J). (gr. k-3). *(978-0-688-10298-2(0))*; lib. bdg. *(978-0-688-10299-9(9))* HarperCollins Pubs.
Howe, James, ed. The Color of Absence: 12 Stories about Loss & Hope. 2003. (ENG., Illus.). 256p. (YA). (gr. 7-18). pap. 9.99 *(978-0-689-85667-9(9)*, Atheneum Bks. for Young Readers) Simon & Schuster Children's Publishing.
—13: Thirteen Stories That Capture the Agony & Ecstasy of Being Thirteen. 2006. (ENG., Illus.). 288p. (YA). (gr. 7-12). pap. 10.99 *(978-1-4169-2684-9(4)*, Atheneum Bks. for Young Readers) Simon & Schuster Children's Publishing.
Howe, Kim, illus. American Life Series: Family, Teacher, Friend, 3 books. 2006. 80p. 19.95 *(978-1-59971-554-4(6))* Aardvark Global Publishing.
Howells, William D. Christmas Every Day & Other Stories. 2008. 68p. pap. 9.99 *(978-1-59547-634-0(2))* NuVision Pubns., LLC.
Howker, Janni. El Tejon de la Barca: Y Otras Historias. Tovar Cross, Juan Elias, tr. Janco, Tania, illus. 2003. (la Orilla del Viento Ser.). (SPA.). 160p. (J). per. *(978-968-16-6282-0(2))* Fondo de Cultura Economica.
Hronas, Georgia. Tell Us a Story, Grandma: More of Grandma's Orthodox Spiritual Stories. 2005. (ENG., Illus.). 114p. (gr. 3-7). pap. 13.95 *(978-1-880971-93-2(3))* Light & Life Publishing Co.
Hubbard, L. Ron, contrib. by. The Crossroads: Literature Guide for Teachers & Librarians, Based on Common Core ELA Standards for Classrooms 6-9. 2013. (Stories from the Golden Age Ser.). (ENG.). 35p. (gr. 6-9). pap., tchr. ed. 14.95 *(978-1-59212-810-5(6))* Galaxy Pr., LLC.
Huber, Randy. Of Heroes & Heroines. 2008. 48p. pap. 16.95 *(978-1-4241-5421-0(9))* America Star Bks.
Hughes, Shirley. An Evening at Alfie's. 2009. (Alfie Ser.). (Illus.). 32p. (J). (gr. k-k). pap. 12.99 *(978-1-86230-786-5(5)*, Red Fox) Random House Children's Books GBR. Dist: Independent Pubs. Group.
Hunt, Peter. The Fairy Penguin's Lesson & Other Tales. 2012. 44p. pap. 32.70 *(978-1-4797-4712-2(2))* Xlibris Corp.
Hunt, Zoe Paton. Azrael's Magical Moment. 2008. 24p. pap. 18.95 *(978-1-60693-070-0(2)*, Strategic Bk. Publishing) Strategic Book Publishing & Rights Agency (SBPRA).
Hunter, Erin. Tales from the Packs. 2015. (Survivors Ser.). (J). lib. bdg. 17.20 *(978-0-606-36959-6(7))* Turtleback.
—Warriors: the Untold Stories. McLoughlin, Wayne, illus. 2013. (Warriors Novella Ser.). (ENG.). 320p. (J). (gr. 3-7). pap. 9.99 *(978-0-06-223292-2(4)*, HarperCollins) HarperCollins Pubs.
Hunter, Roy. Larry the Bookworm Saves the Day. 2012. (ENG.). 131p. pap. 9.99 *(978-1-78035-453-8(3)*, Fastprint Publishing) Upfront Publishing Ltd. GBR. Dist: Printondemand-worldwide.com.
Hurrell, Dianne. Tom Burrows & Friends: Short Stories, Rhymes & Poems. 2010. (ENG., Illus.). 50p. pap. *(978-1-84748-782-7(3))* Athena Pr.
Hurt, John Washington, reader. Rabbit Ears World Tales. 2007. (J). 34.99 *(978-0-7393-7549-5(0))* Findaway World, LLC.
Hush Foundation. The Hush Treasure Book. 2015. (ENG., Illus.). 48p. (J). (gr. -1-5). 23.99 *(978-1-76011-279-0(8))* Allen & Unwin AUS. Dist: Independent Pubs. Group.
Hutchens, David. PageLand: A Story about Love & Sharing & Working Together. Gombert, Bobby, illus. 2004. (gr. 4-8). 14.99 *(978-0-8054-2726-4(0))* B&H Publishing Group.
Hutchinson, Emily, retold by. Edith Wharton, 1 vol. 2004. (Great American Short Stories Ser.). (ENG., Illus.). 80p. (gr. 4-6). lib. bdg. 26.67 *(978-0-8368-4256-2(1)*, 0c46dee0-8a79-4eef-ad5c-ff309b9e4c11, Gareth Stevens Learning Library) Stevens, Gareth Publishing LLLP.
—Nathaniel Hawthorne, 1 vol. 2004. (Great American Short Stories Ser.). (ENG., Illus.). 80p. (gr. 4-6). lib. bdg. 26.67 *(978-0-8368-4252-4(9)*, 7bd58e61-a59d-403d-9c43-845718f4279b, Gareth Stevens Learning Library) Stevens, Gareth Publishing LLLP.
A I am a Gypsy Pot Set, 6 vols. 32p. (gr. 1-3). 31.50 *(978-0-322-00336-1(9))*; 26.50 *(978-0-7802-8041-0(5))* Wright Group/McGraw-Hill.
I Never Want to go There Again. 2007. per. *(978-1-59916-217-1(2))* Printing Systems.
I Was a Tree Once. 2008. 272p. pap. 17.95 *(978-0-595-52197-5(5))* iUniverse, Inc.
I Write Short Stories by Kids for Kids. 2013. 336p. pap. 9.99 *(978-0-9854705-5-5(0))* LongTale Publishing, LLC.
Ibañez, Vincente Blasco & Lorente, Mariano J. Last Lion & Other Stories. 73p. (J). pap. 5.95 *(978-0-8283-1444-2(6))* Branden Bks.
Ihebereme, Chidozie . N. Dad Says Write. 2007. per. *(978-1-59872-954-2(3))* Instant Pub.
Ikpe, Ernest & Madge. African Stories about the Tortoise. 2011. 32p. pap. 17.00 *(978-1-4634-2726-9(3))* AuthorHouse.
Illustrated Fables from Around the World. 2017. (Illustrated Stories Ser.). (ENG.). (J). 19.99 *(978-0-7945-3944-3(0)*, Usborne) EDC Publishing.
Imagine This... Stories Inspired by Agriculture 2012: Stories Inspired by Agriculture 2012. 2013. (ENG., Illus.). 96p. (J). pap. 6.00 *(978-0-9850855-1-3(7))* California Foundation for Agriculture in the Classroom.
Infante, Begona. Takao Yo Soy de Japon (I'm from Japan) (SPA.). 32p. (J). 12.95 *(978-84-246-9402-9(3))* La Galera, S.A. Editorial ESP. Dist: AIMS International Bks., Inc.
Ingalls, Melodi J. Everyone Is Differphant. 2008. 20p. pap. 11.99 *(978-1-4389-1206-6(4))* AuthorHouse.
Ionescu, Angela C. Cuentos y Leyendas de Rumania. (Torre de Papel Ser.). (SPA.). (J). (gr. 4-18). 8.95 *(978-958-04-0781-2(9))* Norma S.A. COL. Dist: Distribuidora Norma, Inc.
Irvine, Patricia McCune. Haunted Pavilion: And Other Short Stories. 2003. 144p. 21.95 *(978-0-595-75249-2(7))* iUniverse, Inc.
Irving, Washington. The Legend of Sleepy Hollow & Other Stories. McKowen, Scott, illus. 2013. (Union Square Kids Unabridged Classics Ser.). 96p. (J). (gr. 5). 9.95 *(978-1-4549-0871-5(8))* Sterling Publishing Co., Inc.
—The Legend of Sleepy Hollow & Other Stories from the Sketch Book. 2006. (ENG., Illus.). 400p. (gr. 12-18). mass mkt. 8.95 *(978-0-451-53012-7(8)*, Signet) Penguin Publishing Group.
—The Legend of Sleepy Hollow & Rip Van Winkle, 1 vol. McWilliam, Howard, illus. 2010. (Calico Illustrated Classics Ser.). (ENG.). 112p. (J). (gr. 2-5). 38.50 *(978-1-60270-747-4(2)*, 3995, Calico Chapter Bks.) ABDO Publishing Co.
—Rip Van Winkle. 2010. (Creative Short Stories Ser.). (ENG., Illus.). 48p. (J). (gr. 5-8). 19.95 *(978-1-58341-923-6(3)*, 22125, Creative Education) Creative Co., The.
—Rip Van Winkle & Other Stories. 2011. (Puffin Classics Ser.). 208p. (J). (gr. 5-7). 7.99 *(978-0-14-133092-1(9)*, Puffin Books) Penguin Young Readers Group.
Isaacs, John. A Doggone Good Story. 2009. 30p. pap. 16.50 *(978-1-60693-471-5(6)*, Eloquent Bks.) Strategic Book Publishing & Rights Agency (SBPRA).

Isol. Secreto de Familia. 2003. (Los Primerisimos Ser.). (SPA.). 48p. (J). pap. 8.50 *(978-968-16-7046-7(9))* Fondo de Cultura Economica USA.

Itterman, Bert. Growing up with Grandpa. 2006. (illus.). 112p. pap. *(978-1-57579-330-6(X))* Pine Hill Pr.

Iturrondo, Angeles Molina. Pepitina. Guevara, Dennis Villanueva, illus. 2004. (Green Ser.). 24p. (J). *(978-1-57581-435-3(8))* Ediciones Santillana, Inc.

—Sapo Sapito Sapote. Umpierre, Migdalia, illus. 2004. (Green Ser.). 24p. (J). *(978-1-57581-440-7(4))* Ediciones Santillana, Inc.

Iturrondo, Angeles Molina & Iguina, Adriana. The Lost Sock. Ortiz Montanez, Nivea, illus. 2004. (Green Ser.). 24p. (J). *(978-1-57581-434-6(X))* Ediciones Santillana, Inc.

Iwamura, Kazuo & Yamashita, Haruo. Seven Little Mice Go to the Beach. 2012. (ENG., Illus.). 32p. (J). (gr. -1-1). 16.95 *(978-0-7358-4073-7(3))* North-South Bks., Inc.

Jacen, Kris, ed. Lost & Found. 2013. 430p. pap. 17.99 *(978-1-60820-866-1(4))* MLR Pr., LLC.

Jack In The Box Staff. Favorite Children's Stories by Jack in T. 2005. pap. 30.95 *(978-1-4179-8943-0(2))* Kessinger Publishing, LLC.

Jackson, Carolyn E. Tales from the Master. 2004. per. 12.95 *(978-0-9745866-2-5(5))* Innate Foundation Publishing.

Jackson, Ruth Montgomery. A Bit of Magic with Wee Willie & Double Trouble. 2011. 76p. pap. 27.50 *(978-1-4567-0050-8(2))* AuthorHouse.

Jacobs, Evan. Zombies! 2014. (Red Rhino Ser.). (J). lib. bdg. 18.40 *(978-0-606-36243-6(6))* Turtleback.

James, Jake. Jake s Short Stories. 2010. 64p. pap. 10.99 *(978-1-60957-640-0(3))* Salem Author Services.

Jamieson, Marianne & Benchmark Education Co. Staff. Analytical Arguments about Four Pioneers of Flight. 2014. (Text Connections Ser.). (J). (gr. 6). *(978-1-4900-1538-5(8))* Benchmark Education Co.

Jamiol, Paul. Bikers Are Animals: A Children's Book on Motorcycling. Habib, Linda, ed. 2009. 38p. pap. 14.95 *(978-1-60844-232-4(2))* Dog Ear Publishing, LLC.

Jansson, Tove. Tales from Moominvalley. Warburton, Thomas, tr. Jansson, Tove, illus. 2010. (Moomins Ser.: 6).Tr. of Osynliga Barnet. (ENG., Illus.). 192p. (J). (gr. 4-7). pap. 8.99 *(978-0-312-62542-9(1)*, 900066520) Square Fish.

Jasnoch, Dorothy. Frankie the Bunny: Helping the Birds. Korzeniowski, Samson O., ed. Jasnoch, Dorothy, illus. 2013. (Illus.). 28p. 17.99 *(978-1-937752-20-0(8))* Owl About Bks. Pubs.

—Frankie the Bunny: Mystery in the Forest. Korzeniowski, Samson O., ed. Jasnoch, Dorothy, illus. 2013. (Illus.). 32p. 17.99 *(978-1-937752-16-3(X))* Owl About Bks. Pubs.

—Frankie the Bunny: The Fall Scramble Begins. Korzeniowski, Samson O., ed. Jasnoch, Dorothy, illus. 2013. (Illus.). 28p. 17.99 *(978-1-937752-19-4(4))* Owl About Bks. Pubs.

—Frankie the Bunny: Woodland Warning. Korzeniowski, Samson O., ed. Jasnoch, Dorothy, illus. 2013. (Illus.). 28p. 17.99 *(978-1-937752-18-7(6))* Owl About Bks. Pubs.

—Frankie the Bunny: Woodland Warning. Korzeniowski, Samson, ed. Jasnoch, Dorothy, illus. 2012. (Illus.). 28p. pap. 12.99 *(978-1-937752-03-3(8))* Owl About Bks. Pubs.

—Frankie the Bunny Helping the Birds. Korzeniowski, Samson, ed. Jasnoch, Dorothy, illus. 2012. (ENG., Illus.). 28p. pap. 12.99 *(978-1-937752-05-7(4))* Owl About Bks. Pubs.

—Frankie the Bunny the Fall Scramble Begins. Korzeniowski, Samson, ed. Jasnoch, Dorothy, illus. 2012. (Illus.). 28p. pap. 12.99 *(978-1-937752-04-0(6))* Owl About Bks. Pubs.

Jay, Em. Once. 2009. 28p. pap. 12.50 *(978-1-4490-2662-2(1))* AuthorHouse.

Jeanmarie, Michele. Curiosity, Curiosity: Lost in an Array. 2008. 74p. pap. 19.95 *(978-1-60610-169-8(2))* America Star Bks.

Jeffers, Oliver. An Alphabet. Jeffers, Oliver, illus. 2017. (ENG., Illus.). 26p. (J). (— 1). bds. 9.99 *(978-0-399-54542-9(5)*, Philomel Bks.) Penguin Young Readers Group.

—Once upon an Alphabet: Short Stories for All the Letters. Jeffers, Oliver, illus. 2014. (ENG., Illus.). 112p. (J). (gr. -1-k). 26.99 *(978-0-399-16791-1(9)*, Philomel Bks.) Penguin Young Readers Group.

Jeffrey, Leonard J. Journeys of the Mind-Book. 2012. 140p. pap. 39.88 *(978-1-4669-3873-1(0))* Trafford Publishing.

—Journeys of the Mind-Book. 2011. 116p. (J). pap. *(978-1-4269-9333-6(1))* Trafford Publishing (UK) Ltd.

Jelloun, Tahar Ben. Papa, Que Es el Racismo? 2003.Tr. of Racism Explained to My Daughter. (SPA.). 92p. (J). (gr. 3-5). pap. 8.95 *(978-968-19-1014-3(1))* Santillana USA Publishing Co., Inc.

Jepson, Gill. Out of Time: The Secret of the Swan. 2011. (ENG.). 144p. pap. *(978-1-84876-612-9(2))* Troubador Publishing Ltd.

Jippes, Daan, et al. Walt Disney's Comics & Stories #703. 2009. 64p. pap. 7.99 *(978-1-60360-093-4(0))* Gemstone Publishing, Inc.

Jobling, Curtis. Max Helsing & the Thirteenth Curse. 2016. (Max Helsing: Monster Hunter Ser.: Vol. 1). (ENG.). 336p. (J). (gr. 5). 19.65 *(978-0-606-39334-8(X))* Turtleback.

Jocelyn, Marthe, ed. First Times: Stories Selected by Marthe Jocelyn. 2007. 200p. (J). (gr. 5-8). pap. 9.95 *(978-0-88776-777-7(X)*, Tundra Bks.) Tundra Bks. CAN. Dist: Penguin Random Hse. LLC.

Jocelyn, Marthe, selected by. Secrets: Stories Selected by Marthe Jocelyn. 2005. 184p. (J). (gr. 4-7). pap. 8.95 *(978-0-88776-723-4(0)*, Tundra Bks.) Tundra Bks. CAN. Dist: Penguin Random Hse. LLC.

Jocelyn, Marthe & Scrimger, Richard. Viminy Crowe's Comic Book. Dávila, Claudia, illus. 2014. 336p. (J). (gr. 4-7). 17.99 *(978-1-77049-479-4(0)*, Tundra Bks.) Tundra Bks. CAN. Dist: Penguin Random Hse. LLC.

Johnson, Alice W. & Warner, Allison H. Believe & You're There When Ammon Was a Missionary. Harston, Jerry, illus. 2010. (J). *(978-1-60641-247-3(7))* Deseret Bk. Co.

Johnson, Bud. Chirpy: Chirpy's First Time Flying. 2013. 32p. pap. 13.99 *(978-1-4525-6763-1(8))* Balboa Pr.

Johnson, James. Sugar & Spice. 2007. (Illus.). 48p. per. *(978-1-4065-3490-0(0))* Dodo Pr.

Johnson, James A. The Terror & the Talking Stick: Sundown Stories II. 2011. 56p. pap. 8.95 *(978-1-4502-8156-0(7))* iUniverse, Inc.

Johnson, Jane. Legends of the Shadow World: The Secret Country; the Shadow World; Dragon's Fire. Stower, Adam, illus. 2010. (ENG.). 1120p. (J). (gr. 3-7). pap. 14.99 *(978-1-4169-9082-6(8)*, Simon & Schuster Bks. For Young Readers) Simon & Schuster Bks. For Young Readers.

Johnson, Liliane & Dufton, Jo S. Children's Chillers & Thrillers. Bruhn, Joan Z., illus. 136p. (Orig.). (J). pap. 10.00 *(978-0-930069-04-9(8))* Jasmine Pr.

Johnson, Miri & Wachtel, Aleina, eds. 'Twas the Night Before... A Collection of Short Stories by Orchard Middle School Students. 2008. 212p. (YA). pap. 8.77 *(978-0-9663560-3-8(9)*, Orchard Pr.) Point Publishing.

Johnson, Rebecca. Juliet, Nearly a Vet Collection One: 4 Books in One. May, Kyla, illus. 2018. (Juliet, Nearly a Vet Ser.: 1). 384p. (J). (gr. 3-5). pap. 19.99 *(978-0-14-378691-7(1))* Random Hse. Australia AUS. Dist: Independent Pubs. Group.

—Juliet, Nearly a Vet, Collection Two, 4 Bks. May, Kyla, illus. 2018. (Juliet, Nearly a Vet Ser.: 2). 368p. (J). (gr. 3-5). pap. 16.99 *(978-0-14-378692-4(X))* Random Hse. Australia AUS. Dist: Independent Pubs. Group.

Johnson, Rossiter. Stories of Childhood. 2017. (ENG., Illus.). (J). 23.95 *(978-1-374-85332-4(1))*; pap. 13.95 *(978-1-374-85331-7(3))* Capital Communications, Inc.

Johnson, Rossiter, ed. Stories of Childhood. 2007. 164p. per. *(978-1-4065-3497-9(8))* Dodo Pr.

—Stories of Comedy. 2007. 168p. per. *(978-1-4065-3498-6(6))* Dodo Pr.

Johnson, Sally. Alfabeto Animal.Tr. of Animal Alphabet. (SPA., Illus.). (J). pap. 10.95 *(978-950-04-2009-9(0))* Emecé Editores S.A. ARG. Dist: Planeta Publishing Corp.

Johnson, Tammie D. Tammie's Tales: An ABC Cat Series Featuring Simon, the S Cat. 2004. (J). 14.95 *(978-1-58597-288-3(6))* Leathers Publishing.

Johnston, Annie Fellows. Mildred's Inheritance, Just Her Way & Ann's Own Way. Home, Diantha W., illus. 2007. 48p. per. *(978-1-4065-3515-0(X))* Dodo Pr.

Jones, Carl L. Aaron Burrd, the Paranoid Bird with Acute Acrophobi. Vicki, Jones, ed. 2008. 88p. pap. 16.00 *(978-0-9748266-2-2(6))* Grampa Jones's Publishing Co.

Jones, Carol. Lake of the Lost. 2005. (Illus.). 160p. pap. *(978-0-7344-0646-0(0)*, Lothian Children's Bks.) Hachette Australia.

Jones, Cynan. Three Tales. 2018. (ENG., Illus.). 48p. (J). 8.95 *(978-1-78562-233-5(1))* Gomer Pr. GBR. Dist: Casemate Pubs. & Bk. Distributors, LLC.

Jones, Diana Wynne. Unexpected Magic: Collected Stories. 2006. (ENG.). 608p. (J). (gr. 3-7). per. 7.99 *(978-0-06-055535-1(1)*, Greenwillow Bks.) HarperCollins Pubs.

Jones, Gareth P. Death or Ice Cream? 2017. (ENG.). 256p. (gr. 7). pap. 15.95 *(978-1-56792-610-1(X))* Godine, David R. Pub.

Jones, Karen. Stories from the Television Show Imagination Way. 2006. 10.00 *(978-0-8059-8195-7(0))* Dorrance Publishing Co., Inc.

Jones, Karen Lee. Giggle with Friends from Imagination Way. 2007. pap. 11.00 *(978-0-8059-8475-0(5))* Dorrance Publishing Co., Inc.

Jones, Marcia & Dadey, Debbie. Guys & Ghouls. Francis, Guy, illus. 2006. (Ghostville Elementary Ser.: Bk. 13). 81p. *(978-0-439-79402-2(1))* Scholastic, Inc.

Jones, Terry & Newman, Nanette. Bedtime Stories. Foreman, Michael, illus. 2007. (ENG.). 192p. (J). (gr. 2-4). pap. 16.99 *(978-1-84458-477-2(1))* Pavilion Bks. GBR. Dist: Independent Pubs. Group.

Jones, Vernon. Aesop's Fables. Rackham, Arthur, illus. 2007. 160p. (J). pap. 5.00 *(978-0-9788914-4-2(9))* Kahley, Glenn.

Jordan, Deloris. Dream Big: Michael Jordan & the Pursuit of Excellence. Root, Barry, illus. 2014. (ENG.). 32p. (J). (gr. -1-3). 8.99 *(978-1-4424-1270-5(4)*, Simon & Schuster/Paula Wiseman Bks.) Simon & Schuster/Paula Wiseman Bks.

José, Cañas Torregrosa. La cara de la inocencia. 2003. (Punto de Encuentro Ser.). (SPA.). 80p. (YA). (gr. 5-12). pap. 11.99 *(978-84-241-8072-0(0))* Everest Editora ESP. Dist: Lectorum Pubns., Inc.

José, F. Sionil. The Molave & the Orchid & Other Children's Stories. 2004. (Illus.). v, 37p. *(978-971-8845-40-0(2))* Solidaridad Publishing Hse.

Joseph, Lynn. El Color de Mis Palabras. 2004. (SPA., Illus.). (YA). pap. 8.99 *(978-1-930332-75-1(0))* Lectorum Pubns., Inc.

Joy Cowley Novels: Novel Set. (Joy Cowley Novels Ser.). 181p. (gr. 3-6). 16.50 *(978-0-7802-8509-5(3))* Wright Group/McGraw-Hill.

Juliao, David Sanchez. El País Más Hermoso del Mundo. 2012. (Torre de Papel Ser.). (SPA., Illus.). 146p. (gr. 3-5). pap. 11.99 *(978-958-04-0747-8(9))* Norma S.A. COL. Dist: Lectorum Pubns., Inc.

Juravel, Rabbi. A Journey with Rabbi Juravel: The Great Escape & Other Stories, Vol. 3. 2004. (Illus.). 252p. (J). 22.95 *(978-1-931681-63-6(5))* Israel Bookshop Pubns.

Kafer, Kathy & Benchmark Education Co. Staff. Analytical Arguments about Folklore. 2014. (Text Connections Ser.). (J). (gr. 6). *(978-1-4900-1522-4(1))* Benchmark Education Co.

Kalpish Ratna. Nyagrodha. Pandya, Yamini, illus. 2006. 287p. (J). *(978-0-670-04969-1(7)*, Puffin) Penguin Publishing Group.

Kandimba, V. T. Folktales from Zimbabwe: Short Stores. 2009. (Illus.). 56p. 24.99 *(978-1-4415-4281-6(7))* Xlibris Corp.

Kandimba, Vt. Folk Tales from Zimbabwe. 2009. 58p. pap. 15.99 *(978-1-4415-4280-9(9))* Xlibris Corp.

Kangira, Jairos. Creatures Great & Small: A Collection of Short Stories. 2005. vi, 114p. *(978-0-86922-786-2(6))* Mambo Pr.

Kanzler, Janine. Things Are Not As They Seem. 2004. 92p. (YA). 14.00 *(978-0-9759363-0-6(1))* Fernhouse Pr.

Kao, Sleepless, illus. Monchan's Bag. 2010. (ENG.). 36p. (J). (gr. -1-3). 16.95 *(978-1-897476-32-1(9))* Simply Read Bks. CAN. Dist: Ingram Publisher Services.

Karl, Jean E. The Turning Place: Stories of a Future Past. 2016. (ENG.). 224p. (YA). (gr. 5-8). pap. 7.99 *(978-0-486-80459-0(3)*, 804593) Dover Pubns., Inc.

Karlin, Ann Bell. Eight Bedtime Stories for Jewish Children. Mazo, Chaim, ed. 2012. 64p. pap. 11.95 *(978-1-936778-67-6(X))* Mazo Pubs.

Katz, Karen. Princess Baby. Katz, Karen, illus. 2012. (Princess Baby Ser.). (Illus.). 30p. (J). (gr. k-k). 7.99 *(978-0-307-93146-7(3)*, Schwartz & Wade Bks.) Random Hse. Children's Bks.

Kavanagh, Herminie Templeton. Darby O'Gill & the Crocks of Gold: And Other Irish Tales. Schluenderfritz, Ted, illus. 2003. ix, 155p. (J). pap. 14.95 *(978-1-928832-85-0(7))* Sophia Institute Pr.

Kay. Tiny Turtle's Holiday Sleeptime Stories Collection. 2010. 32p. pap. 14.99 *(978-1-4520-0687-1(3))* AuthorHouse.

Kaye, Danny. Danny Kaye's Stories from Far Away Places. Bevans Marks And Barrow, illus. 2011. 30p. 35.95 *(978-1-258-00232-9(9))* Literary Licensing, LLC.

—Danny Kaye's Stories from Many Lands. 2011. 32p. pap. 35.95 *(978-1-258-00179-7(9))* Literary Licensing, LLC.

Keary, Annie & Keary, Eliza. Tales of the Norse Warrior Gods: The Heroes of Asgard. Brock, C. E., illus. 2005. (ENG.). 272p. (gr. 3-7). per. 9.95 *(978-0-486-44053-8(2))* Dover Pubns., Inc.

Keaton, Skeet. The Adventures of Jd Losey. 2005. pap. 9.99 *(978-1-59781-353-2(2))* Salem Author Services.

Keenan, Sheila. Dogs of War: a Graphic Novel. Fox, Nathan, illus. 2013. (ENG.). 208p. (J). (gr. 3-7). pap. 14.99 *(978-0-545-12888-9(9)*, Graphix) Scholastic, Inc.

Keep Calm! Individual Title Six-Packs. (Bookweb Ser.). 32p. (gr. 4-18). 34.00 *(978-0-7635-3732-6(2))* Rigby Education.

Keith, Doug. The Storybook Prince. 2017. (Illus.). 40p. (J). 17.95 *(978-1-927018-75-0(7))* Simply Read Bks. CAN. Dist: Ingram Publisher Services.

Kellogg, Catherine Berry. The Moose Who Ate My Fort: Stories from Bella Sage. 2008. 36p. pap. 24.95 *(978-1-60441-696-1(3))* America Star Bks.

Kelly, L. Meme's Christmas Stories. 2005. pap. 16.95 *(978-1-4241-0026-2(7))* America Star Bks.

Kelly, Miles. Classic Stories. Kelly, Richard, ed. 2017. 512p. (J). pap. 23.95 *(978-1-78209-904-8(2))* Miles Kelly Publishing, Ltd. GBR. Dist: Parkwest Pubns., Inc.

—Horse & Pony Stories. Kelly, Richard, ed. 2017. (Illus.). 512p. (J). pap. 23.95 *(978-1-78617-077-4(9))* Miles Kelly Publishing, Ltd. GBR. Dist: Parkwest Pubns., Inc.

Kelly, Richard, ed. Illustrated Treasury of Bedtime Stories. Catling, Andy, illus. 2017. 384p. (J). 39.95 *(978-1-78209-987-1(5))* Miles Kelly Publishing, Ltd. GBR. Dist: Parkwest Pubns., Inc.

—Illustrated Treasury of Christmas Stories. Hinrichsen, Tamsin, illus. 2017. 384p. (J). 39.95 *(978-1-78209-988-8(3))* Miles Kelly Publishing, Ltd. GBR. Dist: Parkwest Pubns., Inc.

Kelsey, Avonelle. Grandma Says, 4 bks., Set. Kelsey, Avonelle, illus. (Series of Short Stories). (Illus.). 200p. (J). *(978-0-9640610-1-9(5))* Cheval International.

Kelsey, Juliet Grey. Nettie by the Sea Stories: Set I. 2010. 56p. pap. 23.99 *(978-1-4490-9452-2(X))* AuthorHouse.

Kemp, Dane. Imaginary Tales. 2011. 186p. pap. 24.95 *(978-1-4560-4686-6(1))* America Star Bks.

Kendall, Penny. Sleepy Baby. 2011. (Illus.). 14p. bds. *(978-1-84089-609-1(4))* Zero to Ten, Ltd.

—Socks. 2011. (Illus.). 14p. bds. *(978-1-84089-608-4(6))* Zero to Ten, Ltd.

Kenner, Crystal R. The King of All Tickle Bugs & Other Stories. 2011. (Illus.). 124p. (gr. -1). pap. 10.95 *(978-1-4502-9466-9(9))* iUniverse, Inc.

Kenrick, Joanna. Tears of a Friend. 2004. (Shades Ser.). 56p. (J). pap. *(978-0-237-52731-0(6))* Evans Brothers, Ltd.

Kerwin, Betsy. The Adventures of Floret the Woodland Fairy: The Adventures Begin. 2008. 44p. pap. 18.49 *(978-1-4343-9426-2(3))* AuthorHouse.

Kessler, Ramon Wilke. Treasure Trove of Pirate Stories: A Collection of Best Pirate Stories for Young People. Scott, A. O., illus. 2011. 294p. 48.95 *(978-1-258-05706-0(9))* Literary Licensing, LLC.

Keys, Demetria M. The Replacements. 2007. 68p. per. 7.95 *(978-1-4327-0649-4(7))* Outskirts Pr., Inc.

Keyser, Francois. Tiger Loses His Stripes. 2013. (ENG.). 24p. pap. 20.00 *(978-1-4669-9203-0(4))* Trafford Publishing.

Kibuishi, Kazu. Explorer (the Lost Islands #2) 2013. (Explorer Ser.). (ENG., Illus.). 128p. (J). (gr. 3-7). pap. 12.99 *(978-1-4197-0883-1(X)*, 1060103, Amulet Bks.) Abrams, Inc.

—The Mystery Boxes. 2012. (Explorer Ser.: 2). (YA). lib. bdg. 22.05 *(978-0-606-23820-5(4))* Turtleback.

Kibuishi, Kazu, ed. Explorer: The Mystery Boxes. 2012. (Explorer Ser.). (ENG., Illus.). 128p. (YA). (gr. 4-17). 19.95 *(978-1-4197-0010-1(3)*, 693501, Amulet Bks.) Abrams, Inc.

—Explorer (the Mystery Boxes #1) 2012. (Explorer Ser.). (ENG., Illus.). 128p. (gr. 4-17). pap. 12.99 *(978-1-4197-0009-5(X)*, 693503, Amulet Bks.) Abrams, Inc.

Kick, J. D. The Amazing Tale of Archie the Alligator. Just, John, illus. 2nd ed. 2003. (J). per. 12.95 *(978-1-929424-14-6(0)*, Owl Creek Farm Bks.) Owl Tree Pr.

Kiick, Lisa. Bailey & Friends. Stouch, Ryan, illus. 2008. 40p. pap. 14.95 *(978-1-59858-743-2(9))* Dog Ear Publishing, LLC.

Kilgore, Lee. The Mr. Munch Adventures: Six Short Stories, 1 vol. 2010. 73p. pap. 19.95 *(978-1-4489-2876-7(1))* America Star Bks.

Kim, Ja Youn. A Song of Pots. Kim, Seung Ae, tr. 2013. 98p. pap. 11.97 *(978-1-62212-984-3(9)*, Strategic Bk. Publishing) Strategic Book Publishing & Rights Agency (SBPRA).

Kimani, Kamande. Why the Hyena Has Short Hind Legs. Therrian, John, illus. 2011. 40p. pap. 24.95 *(978-1-4560-5468-7(6))* America Star Bks.

Kimmel, Eric A. & Kang, Setha. The Rolling Stone: And Other Read Aloud Stories. Kuon, Vuthy, illus. 2004. 36p. (J). (gr. k-6). 15.95 *(978-0-9651661-2-6(0))* Providence Publishing.

King, Ken. The Sunflower. Kearney, Jennifer, illus. 2008. 24p. (J). pap. 14.99 *(978-1-4343-8463-8(2))* AuthorHouse.

KING, R. O. N. S. A trilogy of magical Tales. 2010. 500p. pap. 26.95 *(978-1-4461-4016-1(4))* Lulu Pr., Inc.

Kinkade, Thomas. Disney Dreams Collection Thomas Kinkade Studios Disney Princess Coloring Poster. 2019. (ENG., Illus.). 42p. pap. 19.99 *(978-1-4494-9707-1(1))* Andrews McMeel Publishing.

Kinney, Scott. Kozmik. O'Reilly, Sean Patrick, ed. 2013. (Illus.). 78p. (J). pap. 14.95 *(978-1-927424-51-3(8))* Arcana Studio, Inc.

Kipling, Rudyard. Big Book of Just So Stories. Kelly, Richard, ed. 2017. (Illus.). 96p. (J). pap. 17.95 *(978-1-78617-016-3(7))* Miles Kelly Publishing, Ltd. GBR. Dist: Parkwest Pubns., Inc.

—A Collection of Rudyard Kipling's Just So Stories. 2004. (ENG., Illus.). 128p. (J). (gr. 2-4). 22.99 *(978-0-7636-2629-7(5))* Candlewick Pr.

—The Complete Children's Short Stories. 2005. (ENG., Illus.). 864p. pap. *(978-1-84022-057-5(0))* Wordsworth Editions, Ltd.

—The Jungle Books. 2004. (Barnes & Noble Classics Ser.). (ENG., Illus.). 432p. pap. 7.95 *(978-1-59308-109-6(X))* Barnes & Noble, Inc.

—The Jungle Books. 2013. (ENG.). 384p. (gr. 12). mass mkt. 5.95 *(978-0-451-41918-7(9)*, Signet) Penguin Publishing Group.

—Just So Stories. Kipling, Rudyard, illus. 2017. (Alma Junior Classics Ser.). (ENG., Illus.). 224p. (J). pap. 9.99 *(978-1-84749-637-9(7)*, 900184066, Alma Classics) Bloomsbury Publishing USA.

—Just So Stories. 2017. (ENG., Illus.). (J). (gr. 4-6). 27.99 *(978-1-366-55594-6(5))* Blurb, Inc.

—Just So Stories. 2015. (ENG., Illus.). (J). (gr. 4-6). 25.95 *(978-1-296-60798-2(4))*; 25.95 *(978-1-296-58896-0(3))* Creative Media Partners, LLC.

—Just So Stories. 2016. (ENG., Illus.). (J). (gr. 4). pap. *(978-1-911224-13-6(1))* Emma Stern Publishing.

—Just So Stories. 2009. (Oxford World's Classics Ser.). (ENG., Illus.). 304p. pap. 6.95 *(978-0-19-953860-7(3))* Oxford Univ. Pr., Inc.

—Just So Stories. Latimer, Alex, illus. 2008. (Puffin Classics Ser.). (ENG.). (J). (gr. 5). lib. bdg. 15.60 *(978-1-61383-686-6(4))* Perfection Learning Corp.

—Just So Stories. Bransom, Paul & Gleeson, J. M., illus. 2016. (ENG.). 256p. (J). (gr. 1-1). 16.99 *(978-1-944686-44-4(4)*, Racehorse Publishing) Skyhorse Publishing Co., Inc.

—Just So Stories. Gleeson, J. M. & Bransom, Paul, illus. 2009. 208p. pap. 9.95 *(978-1-59915-172-4(3))* Yesterday's Classics.

—Just So Stories Set: For Little Children. Date not set. (Illus.). 192p. (YA). (gr. 3-18). reprint ed. 7.95 *(978-1-56852-137-4(5)*, Konecky & Konecky) Konecky, William S. Assocs., Inc.

—Just So Stories Set: For Little Children. Salter, Safaya, illus. 2003. (Chrysalis Childrens Classics Ser.). 125p. (YA). pap. *(978-1-84365-036-2(3)*, Pavilion Children's Books) Pavilion Bks.

—Rikki-Tikki-Tavi & Toomai of the Elephants. 2008. (Unabridged Classics (in Audio) Ser.). (J). pap. 36.00 incl. audio compact disk *(978-1-58472-431-5(5)*, In Audio) Sound Room Pubs., Inc.

—Rudyard Kipling: The Complete Children's Short Stories. 2006. (Illus.). 854p. (J). (gr. 4-8). reprint ed. pap. 22.00 *(978-0-7567-9857-4(4))* DIANE Publishing Co.

Kirby, Matthew. Spider Stories. 2007. (ENG.). 242p. pap. 14.99 *(978-1-4196-6359-8(3))* CreateSpace Independent Publishing Platform.

Kirby, Stan. The Captain Awesome Collection (Boxed Set) A MI-TEE Boxed Set: Captain Awesome to the Rescue!; Captain Awesome vs. Nacho Cheese Man; Captain Awesome & the New Kid; Captain Awesome Takes a Dive. O'Connor, George, illus. 2013. (Captain Awesome Ser.). (ENG.). 512p. (J). (gr. k-4). pap. 23.99 *(978-1-4424-8977-6(4)*, Little Simon) Little Simon.

Kirkham, Tyler & Kirkham, Rian. My Best Friend's a Booger. O'Reilly, Sean Patrick, ed. 2012. (Illus.). 32p. pap. 6.95 *(978-1-926914-36-7(8))* Arcana Studio, Inc.

Kirkman, Robert. Super Dinosaur, Vol. 1. 2011. (ENG., illus.). 128p. (J). pap. 9.99 *(978-1-60706-420-6(0)*, cc7c7209-2e43-4ed4-99b7-594aca9b395b) Image Comics.

Kjelgaard, Jim. Eleven Novels by Jim Kjelgaard Including: The Spell of the White Sturgeon, the Lost Wagon, Trading Jeff & His Dog, Double. 2013. 1158p. *(978-1-78139-365-9(6))* Benediction Classics.

Klick, Kenn. Little Coyote Tales. 2007. 128p. pap. 12.95 *(978-0-615-16770-1(5))* BlueCougar Studios.

Kloepfer, John. The Zombie Chasers. Wolfhard, Steve, illus. 2011. (Zombie Chasers Ser.: 1). (ENG.). 224p. (J). (gr. 3-7). pap. 6.99 *(978-0-06-185306-7(2)*, HarperCollins) HarperCollins Pubs.

The Klondike Kid. 2005. (J). pap. *(978-1-60015-070-8(5))* Steps To Literacy, LLC.

Klutz Editors, contrib. by. Wishing Stars. (ENG.). 5.95 *(978-1-57054-560-3(X))* Klutz.

Koch, Claus. The Three Little Wolves & the Big Bad Boar. 2011. 68p. pap. 9.99 *(978-1-4520-5321-9(9))* AuthorHouse.

Kochalka, James. Dragon Puncher Book 2: Dragon Puncher Island. 2011. (Dragon Puncher Ser.: 2). (Illus.). 40p. (J). (gr. 1-3). 9.95 *(978-1-60309-085-8(1)*, 9781603090858) Top Shelf Productions.

Kola, Pamela, ed. East African How Stories. 2003. (Illus.). 48p. pap. *(978-9966-46-472-9(7))* Heinemann Kenya, Limited (East African Educational Publishers Ltd E.A.E.P.) KEN. Dist: Michigan State Univ. Pr.

—East African Why Stories. 2003. (Illus.). 48p. pap. *(978-9966-46-448-4(4))* Heinemann Kenya, Limited (East African Educational Publishers Ltd E.A.E.P.) KEN. Dist: Michigan State Univ. Pr.

Kondrchek, Jamie. A Day in the Life (Un Dia en la Vida), 4 vols., Set. Vega, Eida de la, tr. Rasemas, Joe, illus. Incl. My Favorite Time of Day (Mi Hora Preferida del Dia) lib. bdg. 25.70 *(978-1-58415-837-0(9))*; On My Way to School (De Camino a la Escuela) Rasemas, Joe. 25.70 *(978-1-58415-840-0(9))*; What Day Is It? (Que Dia Es Hoy?) Rasemas, Joe. 25.70 *(978-1-58415-838-7(7))*; What Should I Wear Today? (Que Ropa Me Pondre Hoy?) Rasemas, Joe. 25.70 *(978-1-58415-839-4(5))*; (Illus.). 32p. (J). (gr. -1-1). 2009. (ENG & SPA.). 2009. Set lib. bdg. 102.80 *(978-1-58415-844-8(1))* Mitchell Lane Pubs.

Koneitzko, Bryan. Avatar: the Last Airbender - the Lost Adventures. Gurihiru, illus. 2011. (Avatar: the Last Airbender Ser.). (ENG.). 240p. pap. 19.99 *(978-1-59582-748-7(X)*, Dark Horse Books) Dark Horse Comics.

Konigsburg, E. L. Altogether, One at a Time. Mayer, Mercer et al, illus. 3rd ed. 2008. (ENG.). 112p. (J). (gr. 3-7). pap. 6.99 *(978-1-4169-5501-6(1)*, Atheneum Bks. for Young Readers) Simon & Schuster Children's Publishing.

—The E. L. Konigsburg Newbery Collection: From the Mixed-Up Files of Mrs. Basil E. Frankweiler; Jennifer,

Hecate, Macbeth, William Mckinley, & Me, Elizabeth; the View from Saturday. 2013. (ENG., Illus.). 472p. (J). (gr. 3-7). pap. 26.99 *(978-1-4424-9743-6(2)*, Atheneum Bks. for Young Readers) Simon & Schuster Children's Publishing.
—Throwing Shadows. 2007. (ENG.). 176p. (J). (gr. 3-7). pap. 7.99 *(978-1-4169-4959-6(3)*, Atheneum Bks. for Young Readers) Simon & Schuster Children's Publishing.
Kopple, Deborah. A Spear of Golden Grass: Short Stories by Norwalk High School Honors English Students. 2010. 216p. (J). pap. 15.95 *(978-1-4502-1896-2(2))* iUniverse, Inc.
Kopple, Deborah, ed. Heads in the Ground: Short Stories by Norwalk High School Honor's English Students. 2008. 188p. pap. 13.95 *(978-0-595-50775-7(1))* iUniverse, Inc.
Korhonen, Kari, et al. Walt Disney's Comics & Stories #705. 2009. 64p. pap. 7.99 *(978-1-60360-095-8(7))* Gemstone Publishing, Inc.
Korman, Gordon. The Climb. 2012. (Everest Ser.: 2). lib. bdg. 17.20 *(978-0-606-23934-9(0))* Turtleback.
—The Contest. 2012. (Everest Ser.: 1). lib. bdg. 17.20 *(978-0-606-23933-2(2))* Turtleback.
Korté, Steven, adapted by. Growing Painz. 2017. (Illus.). 134p. (J). *(978-1-5182-4721-7(0))* Little Brown & Co.
Krahn, Fernando. Quien Ha Visto las Tijeras? 2004.Tr. of Who Has Seen the Scissors? (SPA., Illus.). (J). 20.99 *(978-84-8464-149-0(X))* Kalandraka Editora, S.L. ESP. Dist: Lectorum Pubns., Inc.
Krailing, Tessa. La Cabrita Revoltosa. (Club de las Mascotas Coleccion). (SPA.). 96p. (J). (gr. 3-5). *(978-84-88061-88-1(9))* Serres, Ediciones, S. L. ESP. Dist: Lectorum Pubns., Inc.
Krensky, Stephen. Anansi & the Box of Stories: [a West African Folktale]. Reeves, Jeni, illus. 2008. (On My Own Folklore Ser.). (ENG.). 48p. (J). (gr. 2-4). pap. 7.99 *(978-0-8225-6745-5(8)*, 981adfe3-9fdc-445c-811e-a22bb4bd7a2f, First Avenue Editions) Lerner Publishing Group.
—John Henry. Oldroyd, Mark, illus. 2007. (On My Own Folklore Ser.). (ENG.). 48p. (J). (gr. 2-4). per. 8.99 *(978-0-8225-6477-5(7)*, a768119c-8334-4843-953d-e0ea2784d85b, First Avenue Editions) Lerner Publishing Group.
—Paul Bunyan. Orback, Craig, illus. 2007. (On My Own Folklore Ser.). (ENG.). 48p. (J). (gr. 2-4). per. 7.99 *(978-0-8225-6479-9(3)*, bd620386-6b18-48ef-82bc-69b02315f5be, First Avenue Editions) Lerner Publishing Group.
Krensky, Stephen & Sarfatti, Esther. Arturo y la Carrera por la Lectura. 2004.Tr. of Arthur & the Race to Read. (SPA., Illus.). (J). pap. 4.95 *(978-1-930332-60-7(2))* Lectorum Pubns., Inc.
Krohn, Genendel. The Miracle of the Rock & other Stories: Timeless Tales from the Lives of Our Sages. Pelleg, Tirtsa, illus. 2003. 56p. (J). 14.99 *(978-1-58330-650-5(1))* Feldheim Pubs.
Kropp, Paul. El Lunatico y su Hermana Libertad. (SPA.). (YA). 9.95 *(978-958-04-4386-5(6))* Norma S.A. COL. Dist: Distribuidora Norma, Inc.
Krulik, Nancy. A Collection of Katie: Books 1-4. John and Wendy, illus. 2012. (Katie Kazoo, Switcheroo Ser.). 320p. (J). (gr. 2-4). pap. 8.99 *(978-0-448-46304-9(0)*, Grosset & Dunlap) Penguin Young Readers Group.
Kruse, Jan, et al. Walt Disney's Spring Fever Volume 3. 2009. 80p. pap. 9.99 *(978-1-60360-097-2(3))* Gemstone Publishing, Inc.
Kryzanowsky, Sari. Grandmother's Tales: Book One. 2008. 36p. pap. 17.99 *(978-1-4389-1630-9(2))* AuthorHouse.
Kuhn, Douglas Wolcik. Animals' Christmas Gift. Cimino, Nicole C., ed. 2011. 24p. pap. 24.95 *(978-1-4560-5244-7(6))* America Star Bks.
Kulkarni, Suresh. The Wise King & Other Stories. 2011. 44p. pap. 21.99 *(978-1-4535-0463-5(X))* Xlibris Corp.
Kunhardt, Dorothy. Now Open the Box. Kunhardt, Dorothy, illus. 2013. (Illus.). 60p. (J). (gr. -1-2). 16.95 *(978-1-59017-708-2(8)*, NYR Children's Collection) New York Review of Bks., Inc., The.
Kunze, Lauren & Onur, Rina. The Ivy. 2010. (Ivy Ser.: 1). (ENG.). 320p. (YA). (gr. 9-18). 16.99 *(978-0-06-196045-1(4)*, Greenwillow Bks.) HarperCollins Pubs.
Kuo, Julia. Everyone Eats. 2012. (ENG., Illus.). 22p. (J). (gr. -1). 9.95 *(978-1-897476-74-1(4))* Simply Read Bks. CAN. Dist: Ingram Publisher Services.
Kyber, Manfred. Fables & Fairytales to Delight All Ages: Books One to Three with 'Mantao the Jester King' 2009. (Illus.). 420p. *(978-1-84748-520-5(0))* Athena Pr.
Kyber, Manifred. Fables & Fairytales to Delight All Ages Book Two: Gossamer Kingdoms, 3 vols. 2007. (ENG., Illus.). 140p. per. *(978-1-84401-985-4(3))* Athena Pr.
Kyrja. Rupert's Tales: Making More Magick, 1 vol. Osborn, Tonia Bennington, illus. 2016. (ENG.). 56p. (J). (gr. -1-3). 16.99 *(978-0-7643-5124-2(9)*, 7401, Red Feather) Schiffer Publishing, Ltd.
LaBrant, Kenneth R. Uncle Kenny's Crazy Bedtime Stories. 2008. 73p. pap. 19.95 *(978-1-60563-602-3(9))* America Star Bks.
Lacasse, Michael. George & His Special New Friends. 2005. 48p. pap. 16.95 *(978-1-4137-8285-1(X))* PublishAmerica, Inc.
Lagerlöf, Selma. Christ Legends. 2004. pap. 14.95 *(978-0-8095-9388-0(2))*; 196p. 29.95 *(978-0-8095-9883-0(3))* Wildside Pr., LLC.
—Christ Legends: & Other Stories. 2010. 200p. pap. 44.50 *(978-1-4092-0934-8(2))* Lulu Pr., Inc.
Lago, Ángela. Juan Felizario Contento: El Rey de los Negocios. 2003. (Los Especiais de A la Orilla Del Viento Ser.). (SPA., Illus.). 32p. (J). (gr. 2-13). 14.99 *(978-968-16-7047-4(7))* Fondo de Cultura Economica USA.
Lagonegro, Melissa & Redbank, Tennant. Five Toy Tales. 2012. (Step into Reading - Level 1 Ser.). lib. bdg. 18.40 *(978-0-606-23853-3(0))* Turtleback.
Laird, Elizabeth. Where's Toto?/Donde esta Toto? Spanish/English Edition. Martin, Rosa Maria, tr. Ursell, Martin, illus. 2009. (Let's Read! Spanish-English Ser.). (ENG.). 31p. (J). (gr. k-3). 17.44 *(978-0-7641-4218-5(6)*, B.E.S. Publishing) Peterson's.
Lal, Ranjit. Caterpillar Who Went on a Diet & Other Stories. 2004. (ENG., Illus.). 194p. pap. 19.95 *(978-0-14-333593-1(6)*, Puffin) Penguin Publishing Group.
LaMaster, Melissa. Appaloosa Tales with a Christmas Spirit. 2006. 48p. pap. 16.95 *(978-1-4241-3153-2(7))* PublishAmerica, Inc.
Lamichhane, Shiva. Golden Ball in a Piggy Bank. 2012. 84p. pap. 17.95 *(978-1-62709-317-0(6))* America Star Bks.
Lampkins, Antonia. My First Book Collection. 2009. 16p. pap. 24.95 *(978-1-61546-538-5(3))* America Star Bks.
Lampshire Hayden, Gwendolen. Really Truly Stories #5/9. 2006. (Illus.). 130p. (YA). per. 12.95 *(978-1-57258-437-2(8)*, 945-6298) TEACH Services, Inc.
—Really Truly Stories #6/9. 2006. (Illus.). 128p. (YA). per. 11.95 *(978-1-57258-438-9(6)*, 945-6299) TEACH Services, Inc.
—Really Truly Stories #7/9. 2007. (Illus.). 126p. per. 11.95 *(978-1-57258-439-6(4)*, 945-6300) TEACH Services, Inc.
—Really Truly Stories #8/9. 2007. (Illus.). 126p. pap. 11.95 *(978-1-57258-440-2(8))* TEACH Services, Inc.
—Really Truly Stories #9/9. 2007. (Illus.). 125p. pap. 11.95 *(978-1-57258-441-9(6))* TEACH Services, Inc.
Lanagan, Margo. White Time. 2006. 224p. (YA). (gr. 7-18). lib. bdg. 16.89 *(978-0-06-074394-9(8))* HarperCollins Pubs.
Lancaster, Shannon E. Becky: The Budding Ballerina. 2008. 36p. pap. 15.99 *(978-1-4343-9860-4(9))* AuthorHouse.
Landen, Cynthia & Phillips, Lorrie. The Elson Readers, Primer. 2005. (ENG., Illus.). 120p. (J). (gr. -1-12). pap., tchr. ed. 16.99 *(978-1-890623-24-1(5))* Lost Classic Bks.
Lane Gross, Ila. Uncommon Tales Around the World: Global Understanding/Cultural Literacy. 2004. (Illus.). (YA). pap. 6.95 *(978-0-9713649-6-7(6))* L.E.A.P. (Learning through an Expanded Arts Program, Inc).
Lang, Andrew. Prince Ricardo of Pantouflia. 2006. (Illus.). pap. 24.95 *(978-1-4286-0645-6(9))* Kessinger Publishing, LLC.
—The Strange Story Book. 2006. pap. 31.95 *(978-1-4304-4181-6(X))* Kessinger Publishing, LLC.
—The Yellow Fairy Book. 2007. 396p. per. 15.95 *(978-1-4218-4502-9(4))*; 31.95 *(978-1-4218-4418-3(4))* 1st World Publishing, Inc. (1st World Library - Literary Society).
Lang, Andrew, ed. The Chronicles of Pantouflia: Prince Prigio; Prince Ricardo of Pantouflia. (J). 20.95 *(978-0-89190-088-7(8))* Amereon Ltd.
—The Red Book of Animal Stories 1899. Ford, Henry J., illus. 2004. reprint ed. pap. 34.95 *(978-1-4179-8249-3(7))* Kessinger Publishing, LLC.
Langston-George, Rebecca, et al. Encounter: Narrative Nonfiction Stories. 2018. (Encounter: Narrative Nonfiction Stories Ser.). (ENG.). (J). (gr. 3-7). 188.58 *(978-1-5435-1394-3(8)*, 27974, Capstone Pr.) Capstone.
Larned, W. T. & La Fontaine, Jean De. Reynard the Fox & Other Fables. Rae, John, illus. 2014. (ENG.). 96p. (J). (gr. 3-8). pap. 12.99 *(978-0-486-78197-6(6)*, 781976) Dover Pubns., Inc.
Larousse Mexico Staff, ed. Historias de Princesas y Hadas. 2008.Tr. of Princess & Fairy Stories. (ENG., Illus.). 35p. 9.95 *(978-970-22-1449-6(1))* Larousse, Ediciones, S. A. de C. V. MEX. Dist: Houghton Mifflin Harcourt Publishing Co.
Larsen, Angela Sage. Third Time's a Charm, Bk. 3. 2013. (Fifties Chix Ser.: 3). (ENG.). 200p. (YA). pap. 9.95 *(978-1-60746-155-5(2)*, Premiere) FastPrncil, Inc.
Larson, Mary Kay. Tales of Tillie Terwillie: Who Does Tillie Love? Larson, Wendi Sue, illus. 2012. (ENG.). 44p. pap. 21.99 *(978-1-4772-6643-4(7))* AuthorHouse.
Lauture, Mireille B. Loulou, Gason Vanyan! / Loulou, the Brave! 2012. 28p. pap. 16.99 *(978-1-4772-6348-8(9))* AuthorHouse.
—Mancy's Haitian Folktale Collection: Father Misery. Minckler, Kathleen L., illus. 2011. 24p. pap. 12.50 *(978-1-4634-3682-7(3))* AuthorHouse.
Lavarello, Jose Maria, illus. Cuentame un Cuento, No. 2. (SPA.). 366p. (J). (gr. k-3). *(978-84-480-1124-6(4)*, TM2346) Timun Mas, Editorial S.A. ESP. Dist: Lectorum Pubns., Inc.
Lawrence, D. Level 5: British & American Short Stories. 2nd ed. 2008. (ENG.). 88p. pap. 11.99 *(978-1-4058-8239-2(5))* Pearson Education.
Lawrence, Iain. The Giant-Slayer. 2012. 304p. (J). (gr. 3-7). 7.99 *(978-0-440-23971-0(0)*, Yearling) Random Hse. Children's Bks.
Lawrinson, Julia. Loz & Al. 2004. 148p. (Orig.). (J). pap. 13.50 *(978-1-920731-24-3(5))* Fremantle Pr. AUS. Dist: Independent Pubs. Group.
Lawson, Helen. The Spaceship Saga & Other Stories: Read a Play - Book 1. 2013. (ENG., Illus.). 60p. (J). (gr. -1-12). pap. 12.95 *(978-1-78099-357-7(9)*, Our Street Bks.) Hunt, John Publishing Ltd. GBR. Dist: National Bk. Network.
Lazewnik, Libby. The Burglar & Other Stories. 16.99 *(978-1-56871-307-6(X))* Targum Pr., Inc.
—Jumping in & Other Stories. 2009. (ENG., Illus.). 236p. (J). *(978-1-4226-0942-2(1))* Mesorah Pubns., Ltd.
Leal, Luis, compiled by. Cuentos Mexicanos - de los origenes a la Revolucion. 2007. (SPA.). 184p. (J). pap. 23.90 *(978-1-934768-04-4(9))* Stockcero, Inc.
Learning with Stories, 10 vols. 2017. (Learning with Stories Ser.). 24p. (ENG.). (gr. 1-1). 126.35 *(978-1-5081-6253-7(0)*, 3ba6eabe-b0af-48b4-8d8c-902496931a1d); (gr. 4-6). pap. 41.25 *(978-1-5081-6256-8(5))* Rosen Publishing Group, Inc., The. (PowerKids Pr.).
Leatham, Alan D. Four Cats, Five Monkeys, Absurd Birds & Other Fanciful Stuff. 2006. 108p. pap. 19.95 *(978-1-4241-0692-9(3))* America Star Bks.
Leavey, Peggy Dymond. Growing up Ivy. 2010. (ENG.). 256p. (YA). (gr. 4-8). pap. 10.99 *(978-1-55488-723-1(2))* Dundurn Pr. CAN. Dist: Publishers Group West (PGW).
Leavy, Una. The o'Brien Book of Irish Fairy Tales & Legends. Field, Susan, illus. 2012. (ENG.). 96p. (J). pap. 21.00 *(978-1-84717-313-3(6))* O'Brien Pr., Ltd., The IRL. Dist: Casemate Pubs. & Bk. Distributors, LLC.
Lederer, Susan. I Can Do That. Loehr, Jenny, illus. 2008. 28p. (J). per. 19.95 *(978-0-9789347-0-5(9))* Children's Publishing.
Lee, Anita Lynn. Kenny's Amazing Adventures. 2009. 36p. pap. 16.99 *(978-1-4490-1588-6(3))* AuthorHouse.
Lee, Carolyn A. My World & Me: The & Me Collection. 2010. 28p. 18.00 *(978-1-4269-4054-5(8))* Trafford Publishing.
Lee, Helen. Guide's Greatest Escape from Crime Stories. 2003. (Pathfinder Junior Book Club Ser.). 141p. (J). pap. 10.99 *(978-0-8280-1753-4(0)*, 79-967) Review & Herald Publishing Assn.
Lee, J. Marie. 4Teen Jellybean. 2003. 165p. (J). per. 19.95 *(978-1-59196-327-1(3))* Instant Pub.
Lee, Silver Ann. Amazing Bedtime Stories. 2010. 32p. pap. 19.99 *(978-1-4490-6094-7(3))* AuthorHouse.
Lee, Wan, et al. A Fish Wish - Lunch for Patch - Squid Twins: BuildUp Unit 4 Lap Book. Moor, Beka et al, illus. 2015. (Build up Core Phonics Ser.). (J). (gr. 1). *(978-1-4900-2603-9(7))* Benchmark Education Co.
Lees, Gemma. Smart Stories for Clever Kids. 2013. 44p. pap. *(978-1-84991-862-6(7))* Chipmunkapublishing.
Lefrancois, Viateur. Coureurs des Bois a Clark City. Arseneau, Philippe & Drouin, Julie Saint-Onge, illus. 2003. (Collection des 9 Ans: Vol. 32). (FRE.). 136p. 8.95 *(978-2-922565-69-0(6))* Editions de la Paix CAN. Dist: World of Reading, Ltd.
LeGrand, Hank, 3rd. Paddle Tail. Merrison, Stacy, illus. l.t. ed. 2004. 63p. (J). per. 7.95 *(978-1-59466-020-7(4)*, Growing Years) Port Town Publishing.
Lehti, Kauko. Beautiful Animal Stories for Good Children. 2009. 44p. pap. 18.00 *(978-1-60693-872-0(X)*, Strategic Bk. Publishing) Strategic Book Publishing & Rights Agency (SBPRA).
Leicester, Mal. Early Years Stories for the Foundation Stage: Ideas & Inspiration for Active Learning. 2006. (ENG., Illus.). 128p. per. 57.95 *(978-0-415-37603-7(3)*, RU76033) Routledge.
Lemonde, Connie. Short Stories: For the Young & Young at Heart. 2003. (YA). pap. 10.95 *(978-1-932303-81-0(2)*, Llumina Pr.) Aeon Publishing Inc.
Lenker, David "Papa". The Skin They're In. 2011. 28p. pap. 15.99 *(978-1-4568-7294-6(X))* Xlibris Corp.
Lenzi, Danielle E. My Search for Prince Charming's Normal Brother. 2011. 136p. pap. 25.70 *(978-1-4634-0446-8(8))*; (gr. 10-12). 33.70 *(978-1-4634-0445-1(X))* AuthorHouse.
Leppard, Lois Gladys. The Mandie Collection. (ENG.). (J). Bks. 16-20, Vol. 4. 2009. 608p. pap. 19.99 *(978-0-7642-0663-4(X))* Vol. 2. 2008. (Illus.). 576p. (gr. 3-8). pap. 17.99 *(978-0-7642-0538-5(2))* Bethany Hse. Pubs.
Lester, Helen & Munsinger, Lynn. Laugh-Along Lessons 5-Minute Stories. 2015. (Laugh-Along Lessons Ser.). (ENG., Illus.). 256p. (J). (gr. -1-3). 12.99 *(978-0-544-50392-2(9)*, 1604605, Clarion Bks.) HarperCollins Pubs.
Lester, R. A. Clearview Stories, 1 vol. 2009. 238p. pap. 19.95 *(978-1-61582-913-2(X))* PublishAmerica, Inc.
Let's Learn Aesop's Fables, 10 vols. 2017. (Let's Learn Aesop's Fables Ser.). 24p. (ENG.). (gr. 2-2). 131.35 *(978-1-4994-8272-0(8)*, 01d550e5-0105-4b57-a518-cfb16edd549b); (gr. 6-7). pap. 41.25 *(978-1-4994-8409-0(7))* Rosen Publishing Group, Inc., The. (Windmill Bks.).
Levine, Gussie. The Big Red Umbrella. 2010. 20p. 11.59 *(978-1-4269-4650-9(3))* Trafford Publishing.
Levithan, David. How They Met & Other Stories. 2009. (ENG.). 256p. (YA). (gr. 9). pap. 9.99 *(978-0-375-84323-5(X)*, Knopf Bks. for Young Readers) Random Hse. Children's Bks.
—21 Proms. 2015. lib. bdg. 20.85 *(978-0-606-36327-3(0))* Turtleback.
Lewis, Anne Margaret. Tears of Mother Bear. Fritz, Kathleen Cheney, illus. 2012. 32p. (J). (gr. -1-3). pap. 8.95 *(978-1-934133-62-0(0)*, Mackinac Island Press, Inc.) Charlesbridge Publishing, Inc.
Lewis, J. Patrick. The Wren & the Sparrow. Nayberg, Yevgenia, illus. 2015. (ENG.). 32p. (J). (gr. 3-6). E-Book 27.99 *(978-1-4677-6210-6(5)*, Kar-Ben Publishing) Lerner Publishing Group.
Lewman, David. Branch's Bunker Birthday (DreamWorks Trolls) Golden Books, illus. 2018. (Little Golden Book Ser.). 24p. (J). (-k). 4.99 *(978-1-5247-7260-4(7)*, Golden Bks.) Random Hse. Children's Bks.
—Chuckle & Cringe: SpongeBob's Book of Embarrassing Stories. 2007. (SpongeBob SquarePants Ser.). (ENG., Illus.). 48p. (J). (gr. 2-5). pap. 3.99 *(978-1-4169-4746-2(9)*, Simon Spotlight/Nickelodeon) Simon Spotlight/Nickelodeon.
Leyendas Americanas. (Coleccion Leyendas). (SPA., Illus.). 64p. (J). vinyl bd. 16.95 *(978-950-11-0133-1(9)*, SGM133) Sigmar ARG. Dist: Continental Bk. Co., Inc.
Leyendas Argentinas. (Coleccion Leyendas). (SPA., Illus.). 64p. (J). vinyl bd. 16.95 *(978-950-11-0132-4(0)*, SGM132) Sigmar ARG. Dist: Continental Bk. Co., Inc.
Leyendas Universales. (Coleccion Leyendas). (SPA., Illus.). 64p. (J). vinyl bd. 16.95 *(978-950-11-0002-0(2)*, SGM131) Sigmar ARG. Dist: Continental Bk. Co., Inc.
Li, Jian. The Water Dragon: A Chinese Legend - Retold in English & Chinese (Stories of the Chinese Zodiac) 2012. (Stories of the Chinese Zodiac Ser.). (Illus.). 42p. (gr. -1-3). 16.95 *(978-1-60220-978-7(2))* Shanghai Pr.
Li, Ma, et al. Chinese Fables & Folktales (II) Junjie, Cheng, illus. 2010. (ENG.). 48p. (J). (gr. -1-3). 16.95 *(978-1-60220-964-0(2))* Shanghai Pr.
Lias, Joe. The Wood Rats Dragging Their Long Tales. 2005. 183p. pap. 24.95 *(978-1-4137-5900-6(9))* America Star Bks.
Lichfield, Walter C. Fanciful Bear Stories for Small Kids & Factual Bear Stories for Big Kids. 2003. (Illus.). 84p. per. *(978-1-931456-47-0(X))* Athena Pr.
Liddiard, Merrilee. Fairy Friends: A Colors Primer, 1 vol. 2016. (Illus.). 22p. (J). bds. 9.99 *(978-1-4236-4531-3(6))* Gibbs Smith, Publisher.
Light, John. The Flower. Evans, Lisa, illus. 2011. (Child's Play Library). (ENG.). 32p. (J). *(978-1-84643-070-1(4))* Child's Play International Ltd.
Lilacs, Lotuses, & Ladybugs Set B, 6 vols. 32p. (gr. 1-3). 31.50 *(978-0-7802-8052-6(0))* Wright Group/McGraw-Hill.
Lim, Charlotte. Attack of the Swordfish & Other Singapore Tales: Text by Charlotte Lim: Illustrations by Alicia Tan Yen Ping: Creative Directing by Ruby Lim-Yang. 2005. (Illus.). 48p. *(978-981-05-3215-4(6))* National Heritage Board.
Linden, Joanne. Ben & Zip: Two Short Friends. Goldsmith, Tom, illus. 2014. (ENG.). 32p. (J). (gr. -1-k). 16.95 *(978-1-936261-28-4(6))* Flashlight Pr.
Lindop, Christine. Dolphin Readers 1. Jack the Hero. 2010. (ENG., Illus.). 20p. 5.00 *(978-0-19-440085-5(9))* Oxford Univ. Pr., Inc.
Lindop, Christine, retold by. Oxford Bookworms Library: the Long White Cloud: Stories from New Zealand: Level 3: 1000-Word Vocabulary. 3rd ed. 2008. (ENG., Illus.). 80p. 11.00 *(978-0-19-479139-7(4))* Oxford Univ. Pr., Inc.
Lindsay, Maud. More Mother Stories. Sanborn, F. C. & Railton, Fanny, illus. 2008. 160p. pap. 9.95 *(978-1-59915-168-7(5))* Yesterday's Classics.
Lindskoog, Kathryn & Hunsicker, Raneida Mack, eds. Faerie Gold: Treasures from the Lands of Enchantment. 2005. (Classics for Young Readers Ser.). 304p. (J). per. 11.99 *(978-0-87552-738-6(3))* P & R Publishing.
Lindstrom, Florence M. Meeting New Friends. 2nd ed. 2007. (Illus.). 185p. pap. 8.95 *(978-1-932971-00-2(9))* Christian Liberty Pr.
Linforth, Veda. More Toy Shop Tales. 2009. 124p. pap. 10.99 *(978-1-4389-0795-6(8))* AuthorHouse.
Link, Kelly. Pretty Monsters. 2010. (ENG., Illus.). 416p. (YA). (gr. 7-12). pap. 11.99 *(978-0-14-241672-3(X)*, Speak) Penguin Young Readers Group.
Link, Kelly & Grant, Gavin J., eds. Monstrous Affections: An Anthology of Beastly Tales. 2019. (ENG.). 480p. (J). (gr. 9). pap. 14.99 *(978-1-5362-0641-8(5))* Candlewick Pr.
—Monstrous Affections: an Anthology of Beastly Tales. 2014. (ENG., Illus.). 480p. (YA). (gr. 9). 22.99 *(978-0-7636-6473-2(1))* Candlewick Pr.
Linseman, Daniel. Shroobear's First Swim: Book I of the Shroobear Short Stories. 2008. 36p. pap. 15.49 *(978-1-4343-8252-8(4))* AuthorHouse.
Lionni, Leo. Pezzettino. 2012. (Illus.). 40p. (J). (gr. -1-3). pap. 8.99 *(978-0-307-92999-0(X)*, Dragonfly Bks.) Random Hse. Children's Bks.
Little Golden Book Daddy Stories. 2015. (Illus.). 80p. (J). (gr. -1-1). 6.99 *(978-0-553-49762-5(6)*, Golden Bks.) Random Hse. Children's Bks.
Little, Jean. Do Not Open until Christmas, 1 vol. 2014. (ENG.). 178p. (gr. 4-6). (J). 16.95 *(978-0-88995-527-1(1)*, a13af1bd-c89b-4698-b0ed-f34a7719a987); (YA). 16.95 *(978-0-88995-528-8(X)*, c569b713-6e9d-40aa-b979-8e029faa9539) Trifolium Bks., Inc. CAN. Dist: Firefly Bks., Ltd.
Lloyd, Jennifer. Ella's Umbrellas. Spires, Ashley, illus. 2010. (ENG.). 32p. (J). (gr. -1-3). 16.95 *(978-1-897476-23-9(X))* Simply Read Bks. CAN. Dist: Ingram Publisher Services.
Loewen, Nancy. The Other Side of the Fable. 2018. (Other Side of the Fable Ser.). (ENG.). 24p. (J). (gr. -1-3). 119.96 *(978-1-5158-2886-0(7)*, 28388, Picture Window Bks.) Capstone.
Loh-Hagan, Virginia. Tall Tale Stories. 2019. (Stone Circle Stories: Culture & Folktales Ser.). (ENG., Illus.). 32p. (J). (gr. 4-8). pap. 14.21 *(978-1-5341-4002-8(6)*, 212837); lib. bdg. 32.07 *(978-1-5341-4346-3(7)*, 212836) Cherry Lake Publishing. (45th Parallel Press).
Lohans, Alison. Picturing Alyssa. 2011. (ENG.). 216p. (J). (gr. 5-6). pap. 12.99 *(978-1-55488-925-9(1))* Dundurn Pr. CAN. Dist: Publishers Group West (PGW).
Loiske, Jennifer, et al. Tales of an Old Wizard. 2013. (ENG.). 116p. pap. 10.58 *(978-1-291-30601-9(3))* Lulu Pr., Inc.
Lombard, Ernest. Remember the Seagulls: A Modern Fable. 2004. (Illus.). 32p. (J). 3.95 *(978-0-9740473-0-0(9))* Pivotal Force.
Lombardi, Kristine & Disney Storybook Artists Staff. Disney Cars Carry along Treasury. 2010. (Carry along Bks.). (ENG., Illus.). 20p. (J). (gr. -1). bds. 14.99 *(978-0-7944-1947-9(X))* Reader's Digest Assn., Inc., The.
London, Jack. Brown Wolf & Other Stories. 2005. 156p. per. 13.95 *(978-1-59818-706-9(6))* Aegypan.
—The Faith of Men. 2019. (ENG.). 98p. (J). pap. 13.02 *(978-0-368-29103-6(0))* Blurb, Inc.
—The Faith of Men. 2018. (ENG., Illus.). (J). 160p. pap. 12.90 *(978-1-7903-4591-5(X))*; 108p. pap. 5.99 *(978-1-7241-6661-6(1))* Independently Published.
—Faith of Men. 2006. 116p. per. 9.95 *(978-1-59818-074-9(6))* Aegypan.
—Rumbo Oeste y Otros Cuentos. (Clasicos Juveniles Coleccion).Tr. of Short Stories. (SPA.). (YA). (gr. 5-8). pap. *(978-950-11-1331-0(0)*, SG2441) Sigmar ARG. Dist: Lectorum Pubns., Inc.
Long, Debbie. Short Stories with Imagination: The Imagination Series. 2004. 48p. (J). per. *(978-1-55306-820-4(3)*, Epic Pr.) Essence Publishing.
Long, Robert. Inside the Chrysanthemum: New Japanese Fables. 2006. (ENG.). 94p. pap. 53.30 *(978-1-4303-0543-9(6))* Lulu Pr., Inc.
Longo, Jason, illus. Otto's Colorful Campus Tour - Syracuse University A-Z. 2004. (J). 9.99 *(978-1-933069-04-3(X))* Odd Duck Ink, Inc.
Lopez- Jackson, Lillian. Eight 8 Short Stories for Children. 2011. 104p. pap. 37.66 *(978-1-4634-4672-7(1))* AuthorHouse.
Lopez, Bolivar. Z Finds a Kite. 2010. 32p. pap. 13.49 *(978-1-4490-8650-3(0))* AuthorHouse.
Lopez, Cheyene Montana. Blue Sky Rainbows: A Series of Children's Stories of the World of Dreams & Imaginations, 1 vol. 2009. 82p. pap. 16.95 *(978-1-61582-290-4(9))* PublishAmerica, Inc.
Lopez, Patricia A. Imaginations of Wonders, 1 vol. 2009. 128p. pap. 19.95 *(978-1-60813-276-8(5))* America Star Bks.
Lopez, Sabrina, et al. Disney Storybook Collection. 2015. (Illus.). 298p. (J). *(978-1-4847-5333-0(X))* Disney Publishing Worldwide.
Lord, Bruce & Richards, Elisabeth. Humpty Dumpty Was Pushed: And Other Cracked Tales. 2008. 196p. 24.95 *(978-0-595-71559-6(1))*; pap. 14.95 *(978-0-595-47691-6(0))* iUniverse, Inc.
Lord, Grant. Tales of Rex Riley Aged 10 & a Bit, It's A Dog's Life. 2009. 141p. pap. 12.95 *(978-1-4092-4782-1(1))* Lulu Pr., Inc.
Lore, Pittacus. I Am Number Four: the Lost Files: Hidden Enemy, Vol. 3. 2014. (Lorien Legacies: the Lost Files Ser.). (ENG.). 416p. (YA). (gr. 9). pap. 9.99 *(978-0-06-228768-7(0)*, HarperCollins) HarperCollins Pubs.
Lorenzo, Lucia Ann. Lucky, My Best Friend. 2012. 24p. pap. 17.99 *(978-1-4772-8087-4(1))* AuthorHouse.
Lorimer, Janet. Beasts, 1 vol. unabr. ed. 2010. (Q Reads Ser.). (ENG.). 32p. (YA). (gr. 9-12). pap. 8.50 *(978-1-61651-212-5(1))* Saddleback Educational Publishing, Inc.
—Ben Cody's Treasure, 1 vol. unabr. ed. 2010. (Q Reads Ser.). (ENG.). 32p. (YA). (gr. 9-12). pap. 8.50 *(978-1-61651-189-0(3))* Saddleback Educational Publishing, Inc.
—Danger on Ice, 1 vol. unabr. ed. 2010. (Q Reads Ser.). (ENG.). 32p. (YA). (gr. 9-12). pap. 8.50

S

(978-1-61651-179-1(6)) Saddleback Educational Publishing, Inc.
—Death Grip, 1 vol. unabr. ed. 2010. (Q Reads Ser.). (ENG.). 32p. (YA). (gr. 9-12). pap. 8.50 *(978-1-61651-200-2(8))* Saddleback Educational Publishing, Inc.
—Empty Eyes, 1 vol. unabr. ed. 2010. (Q Reads Ser.). (ENG.). 32p. (YA). (gr. 9-12). pap. 8.50 *(978-1-61651-180-7(X))* Saddleback Educational Publishing, Inc.
—Kula'i Street Knights, 1 vol. unabr. ed. 2010. (Q Reads Ser.). (ENG.). 32p. (YA). (gr. 9-12). pap. 8.50 *(978-1-61651-182-1(6))* Saddleback Educational Publishing, Inc.
Lotz, Dana R. Kids' Tales. 2008. 85p. pap. 19.95 *(978-1-60672-179-7(8))* America Star Bks.
Loughead, Deb & Shipley, Jocelyn. Cleavage: Breakaway Fiction for Real Girls, 1 vol. 2009. (ENG., Illus.). 192p. (YA). (gr. 7-11). pap. *(978-1-894549-76-9(7),* Sumach Pr.) Canadian Scholars.
Love, Katie. Fruit to Live By..., 1 vol. 2009. 62p. pap. 16.95 *(978-1-60836-122-9(5))* PublishAmerica, Inc.
Luba Folk Tales. 2005. (YA). 10.00 *(978-1-59872-207-9(7))* Instant Pub.
Lubar, David. Beware the Ninja Weenies: And Other Warped & Creepy Tales. 2013. (Weenies Stories Ser.). (ENG.). 192p. (J). (gr. 4-7). mass mkt. 6.99 *(978-0-7653-6879-9(X),* 900081102, Starscape) Doherty, Tom Assocs., LLC.
—Check Out the Library Weenies: And Other Warped & Creepy Tales. 2019. (Weenies Stories Ser.). (ENG.). 224p. (J). pap. 7.99 *(978-0-7653-9707-2(2),* 900180766, Starscape) Doherty, Tom Assocs., LLC.
—Curse of the Campfire Weenies: And Other Warped & Creepy Tales. 2008. (Weenies Stories Ser.). (ENG.). 208p. (J). (gr. 4-9). mass mkt. 5.99 *(978-0-7653-5771-7(2),* 900042665, Starscape) Doherty, Tom Assocs., LLC.
—Enter the Zombie. 2011. (Nathan Abercrombie, Accidental Zombie Ser.: 5). (ENG.). 192p. (J). (gr. 3-7). pap. 14.99 *(978-0-7653-2672-0(8),* 900066683, Starscape) Doherty, Tom Assocs., LLC.
—Invasion of the Road Weenies: And Other Warped & Creepy Tales. 2006. (Weenies Stories Ser.). (ENG.). 192p. (J). (gr. 4-7). mass mkt. 6.99 *(978-0-7653-5325-2(3),* 900031045, Starscape) Doherty, Tom Assocs., LLC.
—Lay Ups & Long Shots: Eight Short Stories. 2008. 128p. (YA). (gr. 5-8). 14.95 *(978-1-58196-078-5(6),* Darby Creek) Lerner Publishing Group.
Lucado, Max. A Max Lucado Children's Treasury: A Child's First Collection, 1 vol. 2007. (ENG., Illus.). 144p. (J). (gr. -1-3). 19.99 *(978-1-4003-1048-7(2),* Tommy Nelson) Nelson, Thomas Inc.
Lucan, Dawn. Daily Adventure Memories. 2010. (ENG.). 48p. pap. 16.95 *(978-0-557-53422-7(4))* Lulu Pr., Inc.
Lucas, Edward Verall. Forgotten Tales of Long Ago. 2006. (Illus.). pap. 36.95 *(978-1-4254-9801-6(9))* Kessinger Publishing, LLC.
Luftner, Kai. Lily Loves. Drews, Judith, illus. 2012. (ENG.). 32p. (J). (gr. -1-3). 16.95 *(978-1-897476-94-9(9))* Simply Read Bks. CAN. Dist: Ingram Publisher Services.
Lukacs, Krisztian. Bud & Barnie: 2 Tales. 2011. 38p. pap. 18.99 *(978-1-4475-9027-9(9))* Lulu Pr., Inc.
Luke, Pauline. Amber Pash on Pink. 2004. (Illus.). 160p. (Orig.). pap. *(978-0-7022-3428-6(1))* Univ. of Queensland Pr.
Luker, Penny. The Green Book. 2013. 68p. pap. *(978-0-9559896-3-6(9))* Bindon Bks.
Lupton, Hugh. The Story Tree. Fatus, Sophie, illus. 2009. (ENG.). 64p. (J). 19.99 *(978-1-84686-301-1(5))* Barefoot Bks., Inc.
—Tales of Wisdom & Wonder. Sharkey, Niamh, illus. 2006. 64p. (J). (gr. k-5). 15.99 *(978-1-905236-84-8(0))* Barefoot Bks., Inc.
Lyle-Soffe, Shari. The Misadventures of Rooter & Snuffle. Collier, Kevin Scott, illus. 2008. 20p. pap. 9.95 *(978-1-933090-88-7(X))* Guardian Angel Publishing, Inc.
—On the Go with Rooter & Snuffle. Collier, Kevin Scott, illus. 2008. 20p. pap. 9.95 *(978-1-933090-96-2(0))* Guardian Angel Publishing, Inc.
Lynch, Diane M., ed. Celebrate the Season! Twelve Short Stories for Advent & Christmas. 2010. (J). (gr. 3-6). pap. 7.95 *(978-0-8198-1585-9(3))* Pauline Bks. & Media.
—Family Ties: Thirteen Short Stories. 2010. 112p. (J). (gr. 4-7). pap. 7.95 *(978-0-8198-2688-6(X))* Pauline Bks. & Media.
—Now You're Cooking! Ten Short Stories with Recipes. 2009. (J). (gr. 4-7). pap. 7.95 *(978-0-8198-5167-3(1))* Pauline Bks. & Media.
Lynch, Katherine E. & Radclyffe, eds. OMGQueer. 2012. (ENG.). 264p. (J). (gr. 7). pap. 9.95 *(978-1-60282-682-3(X))* Bold Strokes Bks.
Lynch, P. J. Oscar Wilde Stories for Children. 2nd ed. 2006. (ENG., Illus.). 112p. (J). (gr. 2-4). pap. 7.99 *(978-0-340-89436-1(9))* Hachette Children's Group GBR. Dist: Hachette Bk. Group.
Lyons, Sarah. Fairy stories about sally & Mignonette. 2007. pap. 9.99 *(978-1-60034-860-0(2))* Salem Author Services.
Ma, Zheng & Li, Zheng. Chinese Fables & Folktales (I) She, Liu & Rujin, Ma, illus. 2010. (ENG.). 48p. (gr. -1-3). 16.95 *(978-1-60220-962-6(6))* Shanghai Pr.
—Chinese Fables & Folktales (II) Wei, Miao & Xianoqing, Pan, illus. 2010. (ENG.). 48p. (gr. -1-3). 16.95 *(978-1-60220-963-3(4))* Shanghai Pr.
—Stories Behind Chinese Idioms (I) Taxi, Su & Xiaoming, Wang, illus. 2010. (ENG.). 48p. (gr. 3-6). 16.95 *(978-1-60220-965-7(0))* Shanghai Pr.
—Stories Behind Chinese Idioms (III) She, Liu & Xiaoqing, Pan, illus. 2010. (ENG.). 48p. (gr. 3-6). 16.95 *(978-1-60220-967-1(7))* Shanghai Pr.
Maar, Paul. La Puerta Olvidada. (Torre de Papel Ser.). (SPA.). (J). (gr. 2). 7.95 *(978-958-04-1489-6(0))* Norma S.A. COL. Dist: Distribuidora Norma, Inc.
Mac Iver, Kathi. Ghosts of the Mining District. 2003. (Illus.). 60p. 9.95 *(978-0-9651272-1-9(4))* Columbine Pr.
Macaraeg, Diane. Last Meal. 2008. 132p. pap. *(978-3-639-03548-3(8))* AV Akademikerverlag GmbH & Co. KG.
Macaulay, David. Black & White: A Caldecott Award Winner. 2005. (ENG., Illus.). 32p. (J). (gr. -1-3). 8.99 *(978-0-618-63687-7(0),* 490567, Clarion Bks.) HarperCollins Pubs.
Macauley, Jo. Secrets & Spies, 1 vol. 2014. (Secrets & Spies Ser.). (ENG.). 224p. (J). (gr. 4-7). 83.97 *(978-1-4342-9618-4(0),* 22003, Stone Arch Bks.) Capstone.
MacDonald, George. George MacDonald's Fantasy Novels for Children Including: The Princess & the Goblin, the Princess & Curdie & at the Ba. 2013. 444p. *(978-1-78139-368-0(0))* Benediction Classics.
—The Light Princess & Other Fairy Stories. 2007. 102p. pap. 18.99 *(978-1-4346-1408-7(5))* Creative Media Partners, LLC.
—Stephen Archer & Other Tales. 2008. 212p. 26.95 *(978-1-60664-985-5(X))* Aegypan.
MacDonald, Margaret Read. Five-Minute Tales: More Stories to Read & Tell When Time Is Short. 2007. (ENG.). 160p. (J). (gr. -1-3). 24.95 *(978-0-87483-781-0(2))* August Hse. Pubs., Inc.
—Five Minute Tales: More Stories to Read & Tell When Time Is Short. 2007. (ENG.). 160p. (J). (gr. -1-3). per. 14.95 *(978-0-87483-782-7(0))* August Hse. Pubs., Inc.
MacGregor, Roy. Forever: The Annual Hockey Classic, 1 vol. Deines, Brian, illus. 2005. (ENG.). 64p. (J). (gr. 4-7). 19.95 *(978-0-88995-306-2(6),* 7dc812a6-0d6d-4bd3-806c-4138bc77301e) Red Deer Pr. CAN. Dist: Firefly Bks., Ltd.
MacHado, Ana Maria. Ah, Pajarita Si Yo Pudiera. (Torre de Papel Ser.). (SPA., Illus.). (J). 7.95 *(978-958-04-4526-5(5),* NR31207) Norma S.A. COL. Dist: Lectorum Pubns., Inc., Distribuidora Norma, Inc.
Machado, Ana Maria. Aunque Parezca Mentira. (SPA., Illus.). 64p. (J). 16.95 *(978-84-207-4412-4(3))* Grupo Anaya, S.A. ESP. Dist: Lectorum Pubns., Inc., Distribooks, Inc.
MacHado, Ana Maria. El Barbero y el Coronel. Coll, Ivar Da, illus.Tr. of Barber & the Colonel. (SPA.). (J). (gr. 2-3). 7.95 *(978-958-04-5035-1(8),* NR1718) Norma S.A. COL. Dist: Lectorum Pubns., Inc., Distribuidora Norma, Inc.
Mack, Karen. The Magical Adventures of Sun Beams. 2009. 42p. 31.99 *(978-1-4415-3636-5(1))* Xlibris Corp.
Mackall, Dandi Daley, et al. Troubled Times: the Great Depression: The Great Depression. Porfirio, Guy & Ellison, Chris, illus. 2014. (American Adventures Ser.). (ENG.). 80p. (J). (gr. 3-6). 6.99 *(978-1-58536-903-4(9),* 203552) Sleeping Bear Pr.
MacLachlan, Patricia. Your Moon, My Moon: A Grandmother's Words to a Faraway Child. Collier, Bryan, illus. 2011. (ENG.). 32p. (J). (gr. -1-3). 16.99 *(978-1-4169-7950-0(6),* Simon & Schuster Bks. For Young Readers) Simon & Schuster Bks. For Young Readers.
Maclean, Fiona. Death or Victory: Tales of the Clan Maclean. Turnbull, Brian, illus. 2011. 128p. (YA). pap. *(978-2-930583-06-8(1))* White & MacLean Publishing BEL. Dist: Gardners Bks. Ltd.
MacPhail, Cathy. Run, Zan, Run: Newly Rejacketed. 2011. (ENG.). 192p. (J). pap. *(978-1-4088-1733-9(0),* 31223, Bloomsbury Children's Bks.) Bloomsbury Publishing Plc.
Madden, Gloria. Grandmother's Bedtime Stories. 2005. 57p. pap. 16.95 *(978-1-4137-6489-5(4))* America Star Bks.
—Grandmothers Bedtime Stories. 2008. 68p. (gr. -1-7). pap. 10.49 *(978-1-4343-9201-5(5))* AuthorHouse.
—Grandmothers Bedtime Stories: Book 5. 2008. 144p. pap. 11.99 *(978-1-4343-9515-3(4))* AuthorHouse.
Mae, Darcie. Sammy & Robert Discover the Ocean, 1 vol. 2009. 39p. pap. 24.95 *(978-1-61546-827-0(7))* America Star Bks.
Magazine, Stories for Children. Best of Stories for Children Volume 1. 2009. 64p. pap. 26.95 *(978-0-557-02883-2(3))* Lulu Pr., Inc.
Maggiore, Angela T. Short Stories for Children. 2008. 428p. pap. 22.99 *(978-1-4343-3720-7(0))* AuthorHouse.
The Magical Singing Wood. 2017. (ENG., Illus.). 176p. (J). 9.00 *(978-1-78270-141-5(9))* Award Pubns. Ltd. GBR. Dist: Parkwest Pubns., Inc.
Magsamen, Sandra. Peep, Peep, I Love You! Magsamen, Sandra, illus. 2018. (ENG., Illus.). 10p. (J). (gr. -1 — 1). bds. 8.99 *(978-1-338-24314-7(4),* Cartwheel Bks.) Scholastic, Inc.
Maguire, Gregory. Leaping Beauty: And Other Animal Fairy Tales. Demarest, Chris L., illus. 2006. (ENG.). 224p. (J). (gr. 3-7). reprint ed. pap. 7.99 *(978-0-06-056419-3(9),* HarperCollins) HarperCollins Pubs.
Mahy, Margaret. Great Piratical Rumbustification & the Librarian & the Robbers. Blake, Quentin, illus. 2013. (ENG.). 64p. (J). pap. 8.95 *(978-1-56792-169-4(8))* Godine, David R. Pub.
—Shock Forest: And Other Stories. 2004. *(978-0-7136-7652-5(3),* A&C Black) Bloomsbury Publishing Plc.
Main Street Publishing, compiled by. The Talent among Us: Trail of Tales, Vol. 3. 2004. (ENG., Illus.). 142p. (YA). per. 14.00 *(978-0-9741294-2-6(9),* MSP) Yetto Publishing Co.
Making Words Count. 2007. pap. 8.95 *(978-0-9787472-1-3(6))* Ajoyin Publishing, Inc.
Maltby, Ethel H. My Animal Story Book: A Treasury of Sunshine Stories for Children. Richardson, Frederick, illus. 2004. reprint ed. pap. 15.95 *(978-1-4191-7300-4(6))* Kessinger Publishing, LLC.
Manary, Adria. More Mommy Magic: 506 Ways to Nurture Your Child. 2005. 257p. pap. 14.95 *(978-1-931643-65-8(2))* Seven Locks Pr.
Mandel, Muriel. A Donkey Reads, 1 vol. Letria, Andre, illus. 2011. (ENG.). 32p. (J). (gr. k-3). 16.95 *(978-1-59572-255-3(6));* pap. 6.95 *(978-1-59572-256-0(4))* Star Bright Bks., Inc.
Mannering, Rose. Roses: The Tales Trilogy, Book 1. 2016. (Tales Trilogy Ser.). (ENG.). 328p. (J). (gr. 6-6). pap. 9.99 *(978-1-63450-188-0(8),* Sky Pony Pr.) Skyhorse Publishing Co., Inc.
Manson, Beverlie, illus. Rapunzel. 2017. 24p. (J). (gr. -1-12). pap. 7.99 *(978-1-86147-827-6(5),* Armadillo) Anness Publishing GBR. Dist: National Bk. Network.
Mardinly, Berdan. Fresh Tarhana Soup: Story in English & in Turkish. 2008. (ENG & TUR., Illus.). 24p. (J). 8.75 *(978-0-9801675-4-2(X))* Robertson Publishing.
Mark, Jan. Eyes Wide Open. 2003. (ENG., Illus.). 105p. *(978-0-7136-7648-8(5),* A&C Black) Bloomsbury Publishing Plc.
Marlow, Herb. Sisters, Wild Dogs & Catfish Bait. Caffee, Julie, illus. 2005. 122p. (J). lib. bdg. 24.95 *(978-1-893595-45-3(5));* per. 16.95 *(978-1-893595-48-4(X))* Four Seasons Bks., Inc.
Marlow, Patricia. What Fairy Tales Are All About: Grandma's Stories. 2007. 94p. pap. 19.95 *(978-1-4241-6580-3(6))* America Star Bks.
Marr, Andrew. Creatures We Dream of Knowing: Stories of Our Life Together. 2011. 208p. 24.95 *(978-1-4502-8071-6(4));* pap. 14.95 *(978-1-4502-8070-9(6))* iUniverse, Inc.
Marr, Melissa. Faery Tales & Nightmares. 2013. (ENG.). 432p. (YA). (gr. 8-12). pap. 9.99 *(978-0-06-185273-2(2),* HarperCollins) HarperCollins Pubs.
Marr, Melissa, et al. Shards & Ashes. 2013. (ENG.). 384p. (YA). (gr. 8). pap. 9.99 *(978-0-06-209845-0(4),* HarperCollins) HarperCollins Pubs.
Marr Osb, Andrew. From Beyond to Here: Merendael's Gift & Other Stories. 2012. 320p. (gr. 4-6). 29.95 *(978-1-4759-3460-1(2));* pap. 19.95 *(978-1-4759-3458-8(0))* iUniverse, Inc.
Marshall, James. George & Martha: the Complete Stories of Two Best Friends Collector's Edition. collector's ed. 2008. (ENG., Illus.). 368p. (J). (gr. -1-3). 29.99 *(978-0-618-89195-5(1),* 559161, Clarion Bks.) HarperCollins Pubs.
Marston, Elsa. Figs & Fate: Stories about Growing up in the Arab World Today. 2005. (ENG.). 146p. (J). 22.50 *(978-0-8076-1551-5(X));* pap. 15.95 *(978-0-8076-1554-6(4))* Braziller, George Inc.
—Santa Claus in Baghdad & Other Stories about Teens in the Arab World. 2008. (ENG.). 216p. (gr. 3-7). pap. 15.95 *(978-0-253-22004-2(1),* 978-0-253-22004-2) Indiana Univ. Pr.
Marta, Karen, ed. Philippe Parreno & Johan Olander: Parade: A Book for Children. 2009. (ENG., Illus.). 36p. pap. 24.00 *(978-3-03764-048-7(0))* JRP Ringier Kunstverlag AG CHE. Dist: D.A.P./Distributed Art Pubs.
Martin, Ann M., ed. Because of Shoe & Other Dog Stories. 2013. (ENG., Illus.). 288p. (J). (gr. 3-7). pap. 8.99 *(978-1-250-02728-3(4),* 900098300) Square Fish.
Martin, Harvey. The Shaggy Dog Story Book. 2009. 108p. pap. 10.00 *(978-1-59858-932-0(6))* Dog Ear Publishing, LLC.
Martin, Kevin. Arnold Lobel Wrote Great Stories. 2017. (Text Connections Guided Close Reading Ser.). (J). (gr. 1). *(978-1-4900-1800-3(X))* Benchmark Education Co.
Martin, Kristina. Cozzi Dog Can't See. 2012. 40p. pap. 32.70 *(978-1-4771-3053-7(5))* Xlibris Corp.
Martins, E. V. Cookie Nana's Story Book: Featuring " Grumpy Granddad " 2009. (Illus.). 40p. pap. 16.99 *(978-1-4389-2325-3(2))* AuthorHouse.
Martzowka, John M. Quilt of Heroes. 2010. 56p. pap. 23.99 *(978-1-4520-6249-5(8))* AuthorHouse.
Maryann Pasda Diedwardo & Patricia J. Pasda. Pennsylvania Voices Book V: The Legacy of Allison. 2009. 64p. pap. 10.49 *(978-1-4389-4332-9(6))* AuthorHouse.
Masters, Anthony. Ghost Stories to Tell in the Dark. 2012. (ENG.). 92p. pap. *(978-1-4482-0501-1(8),* 146510, Bloomsbury Reader) Bloomsbury Publishing Plc.
Matheos, George P. Pure Magic. 2011. 156p. (gr. 2-4). 22.95 *(978-1-4620-1619-8(7));* pap. 12.95 *(978-1-4620-1617-4(0))* iUniverse, Inc.
Matthews, Annette. Mischievous Molly. 2006. (Illus.). x, 48p. pap. 13.00 *(978-1-4120-9693-5(6))* Trafford Publishing.
Matthews, Caitlín, et al. Fireside Stories: Tales for a Winter's Eve. 2007. (ENG., Illus.). 96p. (J). (gr. -1-5). 19.99 *(978-1-84686-065-2(2))* Barefoot Bks., Inc.
Matthews, Penny. The Nellie Stories: 4 Books in One. 2016. (Our Australian Girl Ser.). (Illus.). 480p. (J). (gr. 3-7). 24.99 *(978-0-670-07915-5(4))* Penguin Random Hse. AUS. Dist: Independent Pubs. Group.
Mawhinney, Art, illus. Dora & Diego to the Rescue! 2010. (Go, Diego, Go! Ser.). (ENG.). 48p. (J). pap. 5.99 *(978-1-4424-0660-5(7),* Simon Spotlight/Nickelodeon) Simon Spotlight/Nickelodeon.
Mawter, J. A. So Grotty! 5th ed. 2004. (So... Ser.: Bk. 5). (ENG., Illus.). 162p. (Orig.). (J). *(978-0-207-20007-6(6),* Angus & Robertson) HarperCollins Pubs. Australia.
Maxey, Ann. Country Style Oklahoma. 2005. (Illus.). 71p. (YA). per. 15.95 *(978-0-9771939-1-2(8),* 0001) New World Publishing.
May, Sophie. Dotty Dimple's Flyaway. 2018. (ENG., Illus.). 90p. (YA). (gr. 7-12). pap. *(978-93-5297-348-4(8))* Alpha Editions.
Mayer, Mercer. Fair Play. 2012. (Big Little Critter Ser.: 1). (ENG., Illus.). 98p. (J). 12.95 *(978-1-60746-763-2(1),* Premiere) FastPrncil, Inc.
—Helping Out. 2012. (Big Little Critter Ser.: 2). (ENG., Illus.). 96p. (J). 12.95 *(978-1-60746-071-8(8),* Premiere) FastPrncil, Inc.
Mayer, Mercer & Mayer, Gina. My Family: A Big Little Critter Book. 2013. (Big Little Critter Ser.: 2). (ENG., Illus.). 98p. (J). 12.95 *(978-1-60746-810-3(7),* Premiere) FastPrncil, Inc.
—On the Go. 2013. (Big Little Critter Ser.: 4). (ENG., Illus.). 96p. (J). 12.95 *(978-1-60746-983-4(9),* Premiere) FastPrncil, Inc.
—Staying Well. 2013. (Big Little Critter Ser.: 5). (ENG.). 96p. (J). 12.95 *(978-1-60746-732-8(1),* Premiere) FastPrncil, Inc.
Mazer, Anne & Particelli, Brice, eds. America Street: A Multicultural Anthology of Stories. 2019. (ENG.). 224p. (YA). (gr. 7-13). pap. 13.95 *(978-0-89255-491-1(6),* 255491) Persea Bks., Inc.
Mbalia, Kwame, ed. Black Boy Joy: 17 Stories Celebrating Black Boyhood. (J). (gr. 4-7). 2023. 336p. 8.99 *(978-0-593-37996-7(9),* Yearling) 2021. (Illus.). 320p. 17.99 *(978-0-593-37993-6(4),* Delacorte Bks. for Young Readers) 2021. (ENG., Illus.). 320p. lib. bdg. 19.99 *(978-0-593-37994-3(2),* Delacorte Bks. for Young Readers) Random Hse. Children's Bks.
McAllister, Angela. A World Full of Animal Stories: 50 Folk Tales & Legends, Volume 2. Aitch, illus. 2017. (World Full Of... Ser.: 2). (ENG.). 128p. (J). (gr. 1-4). 24.99 *(978-1-78603-045-0(4),* Frances Lincoln Children's Bks.) Quarto Publishing Group UK GBR. Dist: Hachette Bk. Group.
Mcauliffe, Timothy & McAuliffe, John Jobin. Snappy the Fox & Other Sleep Time Stories. 2008. 64p. pap. 18.95 *(978-1-4327-1934-0(3))* Outskirts Pr., Inc.
McBride-Smith, Barbara. Greek Myths, Western Style: Toga Tales with an Attitude. 2005. (ENG.). 128p. (J). (gr. 5-17). pap. 8.95 *(978-0-87483-617-2(4))* August Hse. Pubs., Inc.
McCall Smith, Alexander. El Arbol del Chicle Hinchable. (Raton de Biblioteca Coleccion). (SPA.). 128p. (J). (gr. 3). 7.95 *(978-84-88061-86-7(2))* Serres, Ediciones, S. L. ESP. Dist: Lectorum Pubns., Inc.
McCarthy, Bairbre. The Keeper of the Crock of Gold: Irish Leprechaun Tales. 2017. (ENG., Illus.). 96p. (J). 16.99 *(978-1-85635-564-3(0))* Mercier Pr., Ltd., The IRL. Dist: Casemate Pubs. & Bk. Distributors, LLC.
McCaughrean, Geraldine. Sky Ship & Other Stories. l.t. ed. 2004. *(978-0-7136-7653-2(1),* A&C Black) Bloomsbury Publishing Plc.
McCloskey, Robert. Make Way for Mccloskey. 2004. (Illus.). 144p. (J). (gr. k-3). 28.99 *(978-0-670-05934-8(X),* Viking Books for Young Readers) Penguin Young Readers Group.
McClure, Nikki. Apple. 2019. (ENG.). 30p. (J). (gr. -1-k). bds. 8.99 *(978-1-4197-3631-5(0),* 692110, Abrams Appleseed) Abrams, Inc.
McCluskey, J. E. Platypus Tales. 2009. 120p. pap. 14.95 *(978-1-4357-2635-2(9))* Lulu Pr., Inc.
Mccoshan, Duncan. Captain Fact's Creepy Crawly Adventure. 2004. (ENG., Illus.). 96p. (J). pap. *(978-1-4052-0834-5(1))* Farshore.
McDaniel, Lurlene. True Love: Three Novels. 2009. (ENG.). 672p. (YA). (gr. 7). pap. 10.99 *(978-0-375-86148-2(3),* Ember) Random Hse. Children's Bks.
Mcdonald, Megan. Julie Story Collection. Hunt, Robert, illus. 2007. 472p. pap. 29.95 *(978-1-59369-450-0(4))* American Girl Publishing, Inc.
McDonnell, Patrick. Hug Time. 2012. (ENG., Illus.). 30p. (J). (gr. -1 — 1). bds. 8.99 *(978-0-316-18295-9(8))* Little, Brown Bks. for Young Readers.
Mcduffee, William. Story Time with Grandpa Bill Collection. 2006. 50p. pap. 16.95 *(978-1-4241-4001-5(3))* America Star Bks.
McGill, Debora J. Faith Journeys with Hope & Love: Short Stories of Inspiration. 2011. (ENG.). 114p. pap. 19.99 *(978-1-4415-4203-8(5))* Xlibris Corp.
McGovern, Sheila. The Entire World of S & Z Book of Stories: 58 Targeted S & Z Pure Stories to Remediate Frontal & Lateral Lisps. l.t. ed. 2003. (Illus.). 148p. per. 34.99 *(978-0-9723457-5-0(2))* Say It Right.
McGrath, Barbara Barbieri. The Little Red Elf. Bonnet, Rosalinde, illus. 2010. (ENG.). 32p. (J). (gr. -1-2). pap. 7.95 *(978-1-58089-237-7(X))* Charlesbridge Publishing, Inc.
McGreal, Pat, et al. Walt Disney's Comics & Stories #701. 2009. 64p. pap. 7.99 *(978-1-60360-091-0(4))* Gemstone Publishing, Inc.
McHugh, Fiona. The Anne of Green Gables Story Book: Based on the Kevin Sullivan Film of Lucy Maud Montgomery's Classic Novel. 2004. (Illus.). 80p. (J). (gr. 4-8). reprint ed. 20.00 *(978-0-7567-8464-5(6))* DIANE Publishing Co.
McIntosh, Gavin. Hausaland Tales from the Nigerian Market Place. 2005. (Illus.). 98p. (J). (gr. 5-9). reprint ed. 22.00 *(978-0-7567-9714-0(4))* DIANE Publishing Co.
McKay, Jane. Tess & the Star Traveller. 2004. (Illus.). 96p. (Orig.). (J). pap. 8.95 *(978-1-920731-43-4(1))* Fremantle Pr. AUS. Dist: Independent Pubs. Group.
McKee, David. Elmer Sobre Zancos. 2003. (SPA., Illus.). 32p. (J). (gr. k-3). 12.95 *(978-84-372-2354-4(7))* Altea, Ediciones, S.A. - Grupo Santillana ESP. Dist: Santillana USA Publishing Co., Inc.
McKinley, Robin & Dickinson, Peter. Fire: Tales of Elemental Spirits. 2010. (ENG.). 304p. (gr. 12). 15.00 *(978-0-441-01919-9(6),* Ace) Penguin Publishing Group.
—Fire: Tales of Elemental Spirits. 2011. (ENG.). 320p. (YA). (gr. 7-18). 9.99 *(978-0-14-241945-8(1),* Firebird) Penguin Young Readers Group.
McKissack, Patricia. The Dark-Thirty: Southern Tales of the Supernatural. Pinkney, Brian, illus. 2022. 128p. (J). (gr. 3-7). 18.99 *(978-0-679-81863-2(4),* Knopf Bks. for Young Readers) Random Hse. Children's Bks.
—Porch Lies: Tales of Slicksters, Tricksters, & Other Wily Characters. Carrilho, Andre, illus. 2006. (ENG.). 160p. (J). (gr. 3-7). 19.99 *(978-0-375-83619-0(5),* Schwartz & Wade Bks.) Random Hse. Children's Bks.
McMann, Lisa. Gone. 2010. (Wake Ser.: Bk. 3). (ENG.). 224p. (YA). (gr. 9-18). 17.99 *(978-1-4169-7918-0(2),* Simon Pulse) Simon Pulse.
McNatt, Martha. Grandmother's Face in the Mirror. 2003. (YA). per. 14.00 *(978-0-9741294-0-2(2))* Yetto Publishing Co.
McQuinn, Anna. Lola Loves Stories. Beardshaw, Rosalind, illus. 2010. (Lola Reads Ser.: 2). (ENG.). 28p. (J). (gr. -1 — 1). pap. 7.99 *(978-1-58089-259-9(0))* Charlesbridge Publishing, Inc.
McSweeney's Books Staff. Noisy Outlaws, Unfriendly Blobs, & Some Other Things... That Aren't As Scary, Maybe, Depending on How You Feel about Lost Lands, Stray Cellphones, Creatures from the Sky, Parents Who Disappear in Peru, a Man Named Lars Farf, & One Other Story We Couldn't Quite Finish, So Maybe You Could Help Us Out. Thompson, Ted & Horowitz, Eli, eds. 2005. (ENG., Illus.). 208p. (J). (gr. 3-17). 22.00 *(978-1-932416-35-0(8),* 675ae53f-26cd-4417-8e9e-5987fd323bc0) McSweeney's Publishing.
Me, Myself, & I & Other Stories: Individual Title Six-Pack. (Story Steps Ser.). (gr. k-2). 48.00 *(978-0-7635-9813-6(5))* Rigby Education.
Medernach, T. K. On the High Seas. 2007. 104p. pap. 12.95 *(978-0-615-16040-5(9))* ThunderBolt Pubns.
Mehta, Shyam. Stories for Children. 2009. 68p. pap. 8.47 *(978-1-4092-8990-6(7))* Lulu Pr., Inc.
Melton, Lexi. Buck Toothed Charlie & Other Stories. 2010. 72p. pap. 34.99 *(978-1-4490-6183-8(4))* AuthorHouse.
Menix, Cinda. Tenbrook Farms. Menix, Cinda & McGuire, Bryan, illus. 2007. 67p. (J). (gr. 4-7). per. 23.99 *(978-1-59879-338-3(1))* Lifevest Publishing, Inc.
Menon, Geeta. Classic Collection: 22 Short Stories. Suman, Surendra, illus. 2005. 143p. (J). *(978-81-7011-970-8(7))* Children's Bk. Trust.
Menotti, Gian Carlo. Amahal y Los Tres Reyes. 2004. (Troquelados Clasicos Ser.). (SPA.). 16p. (J). pap. 2.95 *(978-84-7864-731-6(7))* Combel Editorial, S.A. ESP. Dist: Independent Pubs. Group.
Mercado, Nancy, ed. Every Man for Himself: Ten Short Stories about Being a Guy. 2007. (ENG., Illus.). 176p. (YA). (gr. 7-18). 6.99 *(978-0-14-240813-1(1),* Speak) Penguin Young Readers Group.

Mercer, Christa Blum. German War Child: Growing Up in World War II. 2004. (Illus.). 176p. pap. 14.95 *(978-1-893597-07-5(5))* A. Borough Bks.

Metal, Liana. Storytime. 2008. 33p. pap. 16.50 *(978-1-4092-2451-8(1))* Lulu Pr., Inc.

Metzger, Lois. Be Careful What You Wish For: Ten Stories about Wishes. 2007. 195p. (J). pap. *(978-0-439-93334-6(X))* Scholastic, Inc.

—Can You Keep a Secret? Ten Stories about Secrets. 2007. 156p. (J). *(978-0-439-88022-0(X))* Scholastic, Inc.

Meyer, Stephenie, et al. Prom Nights from Hell. 2010. (ENG.). 336p. (YA). (gr. 9). pap. 9.99 *(978-0-06-197600-1(8),* HarperTeen) HarperCollins Pubs.

Meza, Martin. Martin Mezas Story Time Three Short Stories, Vol. 1. 2007. 64p. pap. 14.21 *(978-1-4116-8486-7(9))* Lulu Pr., Inc.

—Martin Meza's story time Volume 5. 2007. 54p. pap. 25.95 *(978-0-615-16571-4(0))* Meza, Marti.

Mice & Other Stories: Individual Title Six-Pack. (Story Steps Ser.). (gr. k-2). 48.00 *(978-0-7635-9823-5(2))* Rigby Education.

Michael, Ted & Pultz, Josh. Starry-Eyed: 16 Stories That Steal the Spotlight. 2013. (ENG.). 400p. (YA). (gr. 7-17). pap. 19.99 *(978-0-7624-4949-1(7),* Running Pr. Kids) Running Pr.

Michael's Faith. 2004. (J). bds. 14.95 *(978-0-9741406-2-9(7),* 0138) Cranberry Quill Publishing Co.

Michel, Pauline. Haunted Childhoods. Spencer, Nigel, tr. 2006. (ENG.). 88p. pap. 19.95 *(978-1-894852-21-0(4))* Dundurn Pr. CAN. Dist: Publishers Group West (PGW).

—Haunted Childhoods. 2006. (ENG & FRE.). 94p. (J). *(978-2-89261-460-2(0))* X Y Z Publishing.

Milbourne, Anna, et al. Myths & Legends. 2007. 192p. (J). 22.99 *(978-0-7945-1451-8(0),* Usborne) EDC Publishing.

Miles Kelly Publishing, creator. Children's Classic Stories: Fairytales, Fables & Folktales. 2007. (Illus.). 512p. (J). pap. *(978-1-84236-384-3(0))* Miles Kelly Publishing, Ltd.

—Stories for Girls. 2007. (Illus.). 512p. (J). pap. *(978-1-84236-586-1(X))* Miles Kelly Publishing, Ltd.

Miles, Terry I. Gussie the Christmas Goose & Other Stories. 2007. (ENG.). 46p. per. 19.50 *(978-1-4343-1961-6(X))* AuthorHouse.

Miller, Bernice J. Bernice's Childrens Stories. 2010. 20p. pap. 10.49 *(978-1-4389-8498-8(7))* AuthorHouse.

Miller, J. Cris. Stories to Read to Children: The Pony & the Unicorn & 3 other Stories, 8 vols., Vol. 1. 2007. (Illus.). 80p. (J). 19.95 *(978-0-9725308-2-8(7))* Miller, J. Cris & Assocs.

Miller, Janet. Fox Tail Farms. 2011. 172p. pap. 19.95 *(978-1-257-85817-0(3))* Lulu Pr., Inc.

Miller, Lois. The Last Three Tall Tales. 2010. 72p. pap. 8.95 *(978-0-557-09181-2(0))* Lulu Pr., Inc.

Miller, Lois J. Three More Tall Tales. 2010. 93p. pap. 8.95 *(978-1-4357-4985-6(5))* Lulu Pr., Inc.

Miller, Michael Paul. Kid Tales. 2008. 103p. pap. 16.95 *(978-1-4357-0183-0(6))* Lulu Pr., Inc.

Miller, Moira. The Adventures of Hamish & Mirren: Magical Scottish Stories for Children, 20 vols. Hedderwick, Mairi, illus. 2015. 160p. (J). 9.95 *(978-1-78250-211-1(4),* Kelpies) Floris Bks. GBR. Dist: Consortium Bk. Sales & Distribution.

Milne, Alan Alexander. A Gallery of Children. Le Mair, Henriette Willebeek, illus. 2006. 79p. (J). (gr. k-4). reprint ed. 20.00 *(978-1-4223-5106-2(8))* DIANE Publishing Co.

Milroy, Jill & Milroy, Gladys. Eagle, Crow & Emu: Bird Stories. 2017. (Illus.). 88p. (J). (gr. 2-4). 9.95 *(978-1-925163-71-1(7))* Fremantle Pr. AUS. Dist: Independent Pubs. Group.

Mincher, Scott. The Blanket. 2009. 48p. pap. 15.99 *(978-1-4415-6632-4(5))* Xlibris Corp.

Mindel, Nissan. Eight Chanukah Tales. Toron, Eli & Graybar, Shmuel, illus. 2007. 78p. (J). 10.95 *(978-0-8266-0039-4(5))* Kehot Pubn. Society.

Mindy, Miss. Artist Sisters Vol. 2: Princess la la & the Little Bee - Teenie Weenie Tales. 2007. (ENG., Illus.). 64p. (J). (gr. 8-12). 30.00 *(978-0-9778949-7-0(5))* Baby Tattoo Bks.

Mirhady, Irandought. Thorn-Bush Boy: Pesare Tigh. Mirhady, Irandought, illus. 2004. Orig. Title: Pesare Tigh. (PEO., Illus.). 63p. (YA). per. *(978-0-9760323-0-4(9))* Mirhady, Farhad.

Miserius, Felicitatus. Terrible Tales: A the Absolutely, Positively, 100 Percent True Stories of Cinderella, Little Red Riding Hood, Those Three Greedy Pigs, Hairy Rapunzel. 2012. 106p. (-18). pap. 9.95 *(978-1-938908-20-0(1),* iUniverse Star) iUniverse, Inc.

Mitchell, Charlie. The Great M & M Caper. 2009. 82p. pap. 15.99 *(978-1-4415-2242-9(5))* Xlibris Corp.

Mitchell, Derrick Lee & Howard, Assuanta. Miyah & Koala's First Day. Mitchell, Derrick Lee, illus. 2012. (Illus.). 30p. 18.00 *(978-1-934947-69-2(5))* Asta Publications, LLC.

Mitchell, Laurence. Fish with Feet: From the Travels of Guppy Flynn, Book # 3. 2009. 32p. pap. 12.99 *(978-1-4389-5300-7(3))* AuthorHouse.

—Parents Don't Always Do the Right Things: Character Tales. 2009. 24p. pap. 12.00 *(978-1-4389-5407-3(7))* AuthorHouse.

Mitchell, Malinda. Spencer the Spring Chicken & Other Stories. Schandy, Rosita & Wooten, Neal, illus. 2007. 88p. pap. 23.95 *(978-0-9800675-0-7(2))* Mirror Publishing.

Mitchell, Stan R. Oskar Wins the Race. 2013. 28p. pap. 24.95 *(978-1-63000-407-1(3))* America Star Bks.

Molina, Maria Isabel. El Senor del Cero. Sole, Francisco, illus. 2003. (SPA.). 153p. (J). (gr. 5-8). pap. 10.95 *(978-968-19-0388-6(9))* Santillana USA Publishing Co., Inc.

Molina Tembourv, Pedro. No Encontrarás el Tíbet en un Mapa. 2004. (SPA., Illus.). 160p. (J). *(978-84-667-1418-1(9))* Grupo Anaya, S.A.

Molyneux, Caroline. A 1940 Christmas. 2012. 16p. pap. 15.99 *(978-1-4772-2899-9(3))* AuthorHouse.

momodu, oshiomowe. Tales by Moonlight. 2008. (ENG.). 33p. pap. 5.16 *(978-0-557-03777-3(8))* Lulu Pr., Inc.

Monical, Olivia R. The Forest of Thinks. Monical, Olivia R., illus. 2012. (ENG., Illus.). 28p. (J). pap. 10.95 *(978-1-57733-267-1(9),* Papillon Publishing) Blue Dolphin Publishing, Inc.

Monkman, Olga. Dos Perros y una Abuela. Calderon, Marcela, illus. 2003. (SPA.). 31p. (J). (gr. k-3). pap. 9.95 *(978-950-511-642-3(X))* Santillana USA Publishing Co., Inc.

—Lo Que Cuentan los Inuit. (SPA.). (YA). (gr. 4-18). pap. *(978-950-07-1845-5(6),* SA30064) Editorial Sudamericana S.A. ARG. Dist: Lectorum Pubns., Inc.

—Un Rey sin Corona. Sanchez, Javier G., illus. 2003. (SPA.). 39p. (J). (gr. k-3). pap. 7.95 *(978-950-511-368-2(4))* Santillana USA Publishing Co., Inc.

Montgomery, L. M. Akin to Anne: Tales of Other Orphans. (YA). 22.95 *(978-0-8488-2656-7(6))* Amereon Ltd.

—Along the Shore: Tales by the Sea. (YA). 22.95 *(978-0-8488-2655-0(8))* Amereon Ltd.

—Anne of Green Gables. Fiona Fox Staff, ed. 2012. (ENG., Illus.). 416p. (J). 15.00 *(978-1-84135-842-0(8))* Award Pubns. Ltd. GBR. Dist: Parkwest Pubns., Inc.

—The Anne of Green Gables Collection: Six Complete & Unabridged Novels in One Volume. 2013. 1140p. *(978-1-78139-344-4(3))* Benediction Classics.

Monti, Joe, ed. Diverse Energies: By 11 Speculative Fiction Authors, 1 vol. 2012. (ENG.). 368p. (YA). 19.95 *(978-1-60060-887-2(6),* Tu Bks.) Lee & Low Bks., Inc.

Moon, Jonny. The Beach Buoy, Book 5. 2011. (GUNK Aliens Ser.). (ENG., Illus.). 112p. (J). (gr. 2-4). 7.99 *(978-0-00-732616-7(5))* HarperCollins Pubs. Ltd. GBR. Dist: Independent Pubs. Group.

Moore, Stephanie Perry. Golden Spirit. 2006. (Carmen Browne Ser.: 3). (ENG.). 144p. (YA). (gr. 3-3). per. 6.99 *(978-0-8024-8169-6(8))* Moody Pubs.

Moral, Samantha Caballero Del. 100 Cuentos Clasicos. 2010. 512p. pap. *(978-607-404-198-9(9),* Silver Dolphin en Español) Advanced Marketing, S. de R. L. de C. V.

Morales, Alejandro. Little Nation & Other Stories. 2014. (ENG.). xxvi, 178p. (YA). pap. 17.95 *(978-1-55885-801-5(6))* Arte Publico Pr.

Morgan, Melissa J. The Complete First Summer: Books #1-4. 2009. (Camp Confidential Ser.: Nos. 1-4). 624p. (J). (gr. 3-7). pap. 16.99 *(978-0-448-45188-6(3),* Grosset & Dunlap) Penguin Young Readers Group.

Morgan, Robert. Bob Tales. Banton, Amy Renee, illus. 2003. 216p. (J). pap. 15.00 *(978-1-888562-06-4(4))* booksonnet.com.

Morgan, Winter. Martian Invasion: Tales of a Terrarian Warrior, Book Four. 2017. (ENG.). 112p. (J). (gr. 1-7). pap. 7.99 *(978-1-5107-2196-8(7),* Sky Pony Pr.) Skyhorse Publishing Co., Inc.

—Snow Fight: Tales of a Terrarian Warrior, Book Two. 2016. (ENG.). 112p. (J). (gr. 1-7). pap. 7.99 *(978-1-5107-1683-4(1),* Sky Pony Pr.) Skyhorse Publishing Co., Inc.

Moro, Robin, et al, illus. Read Aloud Spooky Stories. 2006. 320p. (J). (gr. 4-7). 15.98 *(978-0-7853-6338-5(6),* 7159100) Publications International, Ltd.

Morpurgo, Michael. The Kingfisher Book of Great Boy Stories: A Treasury of Classics from Children's Literature. 2006. (Illus.). 160p. (J). (gr. 4-8). reprint ed. 20.00 *(978-1-4223-5207-6(2))* DIANE Publishing Co.

—The Marble Crusher. 2012. (ENG., Illus.). 96p. (J). (gr. 2-4). pap. 6.99 *(978-1-4052-2924-1(1))* Farshore GBR. Dist: HarperCollins Pubs.

—The White Horse of Zennor. 2nd ed. 2017. (ENG.). 160p. (J). (gr. 4-7). pap. 7.99 *(978-1-4052-5675-9(3))* Farshore GBR. Dist: HarperCollins Pubs.

Morris, April. Eldon the Elephant. 2004. (J). lib. bdg. 25.95 *(978-1-893595-49-1(8))* Four Seasons Bks., Inc.

Morris, Elizabeth. The Quest for the Tellings. Troy, Michael, illus. 2012. 52p. (-18). pap. *(978-1-78222-055-8(0))* Paragon Publishing, Rothersthorpe.

Morris, Neil. African Myths, 1 vol. Kennedy, Graham & Sansom, Fiona, illus. 2009. (Myths from Many Lands Ser.). (ENG.). 48p. (YA). (gr. 5-5). 33.93 *(978-1-60754-215-5(3),* e846bf7c-4026-425b-bea4-6625f91de00a, Windmill Bks.) Rosen Publishing Group, Inc., The.

Morris Publishing Company Staff & Goscinny, René. The Daltons' Escape, Vol. 30. 2011. (Lucky Luke Ser.: 30). (Illus.). 48p. (J). (gr. -1-12). pap. 11.95 *(978-1-84918-091-7(1))* CineBook GBR. Dist: National Bk. Network.

Morrison, Jennifer. Beware of the Bull: Stories for the Young & the Incurably Eccentric. 2004. 90p. (YA). pap. 9.95 *(978-0-595-31054-8(0))* iUniverse, Inc.

Morrison, Toni & Morrison, Slade. Little Cloud & Lady Wind. Qualls, Sean, illus. 2010. (ENG.). 32p. (J). pap. 7.99 *(978-1-4169-8524-2(7),* Simon & Schuster Bks. For Young Readers) Simon & Schuster Bks. For Young Readers.

—Little Cloud & Lady Wind. Qualls, Sean, illus. 2010. (ENG.). 32p. (J). (gr. -1-3). 19.99 *(978-1-4169-8523-5(9),* Simon & Schuster/Paula Wiseman Bks.) Simon & Schuster/Paula Wiseman Bks.

—The Tortoise or the Hare. Cepeda, Joe, illus. 2010. (ENG.). 32p. (J). (gr. -1-3). 19.99 *(978-1-4169-8334-7(1),* Simon & Schuster/Paula Wiseman Bks.) Simon & Schuster/Paula Wiseman Bks.

Morrissette, Cora. Life Stories in the World of Fiction. 2009. 108p. 25.95 *(978-1-4327-3798-6(8))* Outskirts Pr., Inc.

Morse, William A. and & Morse, William A. And Dana Jo. Kurkle Kids: Spirit of America. 2009. 44p. pap. 16.99 *(978-1-4490-1009-6(1))* AuthorHouse.

Moseley, Tabitha. Pearl's Tales a Collection of Children's Stories. 2009. 92p. pap. 17.25 *(978-1-60860-670-2(8),* Strategic Bk. Publishing) Strategic Book Publishing & Rights Agency (SBPRA).

Moser, Erwin. Vicente, el Elefantito. (Buenas Noches Ser.). (SPA.). (J). (gr. k-3). 8.95 *(978-958-04-4903-4(1))* Norma S.A. COL. Dist: Distribuidora Norma, Inc.

Moss, J. P. The Kind Fairy Adventures: 3 Loving Fairy Tales from the Land of the Faye. 2010. (Illus.). 52p. pap. 22.99 *(978-1-4520-3868-1(6))* AuthorHouse.

Moss, Yvonne. The Butterfly Princess. 2011. 16p. (gr. -1). pap. 9.49 *(978-1-4567-4044-3(X))* AuthorHouse.

—Seasons Through the Eyes of A Child: The Snow, the Spring, the Summer, the Fall. 2010. 12p. pap. 9.49 *(978-1-4520-3757-8(4))* AuthorHouse.

Motalebi, Majede. Wise Animals 2. 2012. 56p. pap. 24.99 *(978-1-4772-1622-4(7))* AuthorHouse.

Mother Goose Staff & Studio Mouse Staff. Sugar & Spice, 6 Bks. 2005. (ENG., Illus.). 10p. (J). 12.95 *(978-1-59249-471-2(4),* 1D100) Soundprints.

Mourabiti, Hassan & Rosen, Lynn. Once upon a Time in Hunger Land. 2012. 48p. pap. 11.95 *(978-1-4772-0819-9(4))* AuthorHouse.

Mowat, Diane, retold by. Oxford Bookworms Library: a Pair of Ghostly Hands & Other Stories: Level 3: 1000-Word Vocabulary. 3rd ed. 2008. (ENG., Illus.). 80p. 11.00 *(978-0-19-479125-0(4))* Oxford Univ. Pr., Inc.

Mrs Molesworth & Molesworth, Mary Louisa S. The Thirteen Little Black Pigs & Other Stories. 2011. 66p. 16.95 *(978-1-4638-9845-8(2));* pap. 8.95 *(978-1-4638-0052-9(5))* Rodgers, Alan Bks.

Mueller, Sylvia Price. Barnyard Stories. 2003. 40p. pap. 9.00 *(978-0-8059-5939-0(4))* Dorrance Publishing Co., Inc.

Mullican, Norma Waldon & Zivney, Missy Mullican. A Collection of Squirrel Tales: Something to Crow About. 2009. 84p. pap. 10.99 *(978-1-60791-702-1(5))* Salem Author Services.

Mundy, Charlene & Chapline, Jo. David's Donkey Tales. 2007. (ENG.). 73p. pap. 12.50 *(978-0-615-16825-8(6))* Knee-High Adventures.

Muneefa. My Tales for Children. 2006. 90p. (J). pap. 13.95 *(978-1-58909-339-3(9))* Bookstand Publishing.

Munoz de Coronado, Martha, ed. Subidos de Tono: Cuentos de Amor. 2005. (SPA., Illus.). 253p. (J). pap. 14.95 *(978-9972-40-251-7(7))* Promocion Editorial Inca S.A., PEISA PER. Dist: Iaconi, Mariuccia Bk. Imports.

Munsch, Robert. Mortimer. Martchenko, Michael, illus. 10th ed. 2010. 24p. (J). (gr. -1). bds. 7.99 *(978-1-55451-228-7(X),* 9781554512287) Annick Pr., Ltd. CAN. Dist: Publishers Group West (PGW).

—Munsch Mini-Treasury One. Martchenko, Michael, illus. 5th ed. 2010. (Munsch for Kids Ser.). (ENG.). 144p. (J). (gr. -1-2). 18.95 *(978-1-55451-273-7(5),* 9781554512737) Annick Pr., Ltd. CAN. Dist: Publishers Group West (PGW).

—Munsch Mini-Treasury Two. Martchenko, Michael, illus. 4th ed. 2010. (Munsch for Kids Ser.). (ENG.). 136p. (J). (gr. -1-2). 18.95 *(978-1-55451-274-4(3),* 9781554512744) Annick Pr., Ltd. CAN. Dist: Publishers Group West (PGW).

Munsch, Robert & Martchenko, Michael. I Have to Go! Martchenko, Michael, illus. 8th ed. 2010. (ENG., Illus.). 24p. (J). (gr. -1-k). bds. 7.99 *(978-1-55451-253-9(0),* 9781554512539) Annick Pr., Ltd. CAN. Dist: Publishers Group West (PGW).

Munsch, Robert & McGraw, Sheila. Love You Forever. 2012. 18p. 29.95 *(978-1-59530-466-7(5))* Hallmark Card, Inc.

Munson, Weegie. The Tales of Weegie Munson. 2012. 44p. pap. 16.95 *(978-1-62709-684-3(1))* America Star Bks.

Murphy, Elspeth Campbell. God Makes It Right: Three Stories for Children Based on Favorite Bible Verses. Nelson, Jane E., illus. 72p. (J). *(978-1-55513-109-8(3))* Cook, David C.

Murphy, Lisa. Secret Smile. 2008. 52p. pap. 11.95 *(978-1-4092-2767-0(7))* Lulu Pr., Inc.

Murphy, Mary. Let's Go! 2005. (ENG., Illus.). 16p. (J). bds. 14.99 *(978-1-4052-1115-4(6))* Farshore GBR. Dist: Trafalgar Square Publishing.

Murphy, Stuart J. Freda Plans a Picnic. 2010. (I See I Learn Ser.: 2). (Illus.). 32p. (J). (gr. -1-k). 14.95 *(978-1-58089-456-2(9))* Charlesbridge Publishing, Inc.

—Good Job, Ajay! 2010. (I See I Learn Ser.: 3). (Illus.). 32p. (J). (gr. -1-k). 14.95 *(978-1-58089-454-8(2))* Charlesbridge Publishing, Inc.

Murray, Brendan. Tev on Home Turf. 2004. 192p. (YA). pap. 13.50 *(978-1-920731-33-5(4))* Fremantle Pr. AUS. Dist: Independent Pubs. Group.

Murray, George. The Tales of Molly Brand & MacNessie. 2008. 70p. pap. 14.95 *(978-1-4092-3724-2(9))* Lulu Pr., Inc.

Murray, Victoria Christopher. Veronique. 2009. (Divas Ser.). (ENG., Illus.). 257p. pap. 11.00 *(978-1-4165-6350-1(4),* Gallery Bks.) Gallery Bks.

Mwanamwalye, Crebby Ilishebo. Story Time. 2013. 52p. pap. 10.03 *(978-1-4669-9028-9(7))* Trafford Publishing.

My First Book of Christmas Stories. 2003. (J). 8.99 *(978-1-59384-014-3(4))* Parklane Publishing.

Myers, Tamar. Angels, Angels Everywhere. 2004. pap. 7.95 *(978-0-9747685-3-3(7))* Bella Rosa Bks.

Myers, Walter Dean. 145th Street: Short Stories. 2012. 208p. (YA). (gr. 7). pap. 11.99 *(978-0-307-97610-9(6),* Ember) Random Hse. Children's Bks.

Mysterious Chills & Thrills: 10 creepy, strange, adventurous short stories for kids to tickle the imagination. 2004. (J). per. 6.95 *(978-0-9749013-0-5(X))* LH Pubns. & Productions.

Nagel, Paula. Rollercoaster Series: Set. 2018. (Rollercoaster Ser.). (ENG., Illus.). 256p. (C). pap. 64.95 *(978-1-909301-80-1(9),* Y329888) Routledge.

Naidoo, Beverley. Out of Bounds: Seven Stories of Conflict & Hope. 2008. (ENG.). 208p. (J). (gr. 5). pap. 7.99 *(978-0-06-050801-2(9),* HarperCollins) HarperCollins Pubs.

Nambiar, Vinesh. Adventures in Human Values - Series 1: Courage, Kindness, Forgiveness, Teamwork, Compassion, Listening, Caring, Self-Confidence, Sharing. Lalmuanpuia Ralte, Albert, illus. 2007. (ENG.). (J). 25.00 *(978-0-9798986-0-0(9))* Human Values 4 Kids Foundation, The.

Napoli, Tony, retold by. Willa Cather, 1 vol. 2004. (Great American Short Stories Ser.). (ENG., Illus.). 80p. (gr. 4-6). lib. bdg. 26.67 *(978-0-8368-4251-7(0),* f487f442-81a5-4a21-b290-fc88056ee1c9, Gareth Stevens Learning Library) Stevens, Gareth Publishing LLLP.

Nappi, Frank. The Legend of Mickey Tussler: A Novel. 2012. (Mickey Tussler Ser.). (ENG.). 304p. (YA). (gr. 6-6). pap. 17.99 *(978-1-61608-658-9(0),* 608658, Sky Pony Pr.) Skyhorse Publishing Co., Inc.

—Sophomore Campaign: A Mickey Tussler Novel. 2012. (Mickey Tussler Ser.). (ENG.). 280p. (YA). (gr. 6-6). pap. 12.95 *(978-1-61608-663-3(7),* 608663, Sky Pony Pr.) Skyhorse Publishing Co., Inc.

Narváez, Concha López. El Fuego de los Pastores.Tr. of Shepherds' Fire. (SPA.). (YA). (gr. 5). pap. *(978-84-395-0902-8(2))* Espasa Calpe, S.A. ESP. Dist: Lectorum Pubns., Inc.

Nash, Scott. Shrunken Treasures: Literary Classics, Short, Sweet, & Silly. Nash, Scott, illus. 2016. (ENG., Illus.). 40p. (J). (gr. k-3). 15.99 *(978-0-7636-6972-0(5))* Candlewick Pr.

Nasir, Safia. Princess Neelam & Other Stories. 2005. 52p. *(978-91-21-51821-2(1)); (978-969-542-109-3(1))* Children Pubns.

Nass, Marcia & Campisi, Stephanie. Mini Mysteries & Kooky Spookies. Innes, Calvin, illus. 2007. 176p. per. 6.99 *(978-0-9795364-2-7(1))* Chowder Bay Bks.

National Wildlife Federation Staff. Ranger Rick's Story Book - Nature Tales from Ranger Rick Magazine. 2019. (Ranger Rick: Big Bks.). (Illus.). 128p. (J). (gr. -1-12). 26.95 *(978-1-63076-214-8(8))* Taylor Trade Publishing.

Naughton, Bill. The Goalkeeper's Revenge. 2012. (ENG.). 110p. (YA). pap. *(978-1-4482-0443-4(7),* 145965, Bloomsbury Reader) Bloomsbury Publishing Plc.

Nayeri, Daniel. Sasha & Puck & the Potion of Luck. Mak, Anneliese, illus. 2019. (Elixir Fixers Ser.: 1). (ENG.). 128p. (J). (gr. 1-5). 14.99 *(978-0-8075-7242-9(X),* 080757242X) Whitman, Albert & Co.

—Straw House, Wood House, Brick House, Blow: Four Novellas by Daniel Nayeri. 2011. (ENG., Illus.). 432p. (YA). (gr. 9). 19.99 *(978-0-7636-5526-6(0))* Candlewick Pr.

Nesbit, E. Beautiful Stories from Shakespeare. 2009. 116p. pap. 10.50 *(978-1-60459-575-8(2))* Wilder Pubns., Corp.

—The Book of Dragons. 2008. 108p. 23.95 *(978-1-60664-859-9(4));* (gr. 2-13). pap. 9.95 *(978-1-60664-106-4(9))* Aegypan.

—The Book of Dragons. 2018. (ENG., Illus.). 134p. (YA). (gr. 7-12). pap. *(978-93-5329-312-3(X))* Alpha Editions.

—The Book of Dragons. Fell, H. Granville & Millar, H. R., illus. unabr. ed. 2004. (Dover Children's Classics Ser.). (ENG.). 176p. (gr. 3-5). pap. 8.95 *(978-0-486-43648-7(9),* 436489) Dover Pubns., Inc.

—The Book of Dragons. (ENG.). (J). 2019. 114p. pap. 5.99 *(978-1-6976-2672-8(6))* 2019. 172p. pap. 12.99 *(978-1-0899-5915-1(X))* 2019. 172p. pap. 12.99 *(978-1-0830-5591-0(7))* 2019. 288p. pap. 19.99 *(978-1-0827-3393-2(8))* 2019. 172p. pap. 12.99 *(978-1-0708-9456-0(7))* 2018. (Illus.). 140p. pap. 12.99 *(978-1-7919-2711-0(4))* Independently Published.

—The Book of Dragons. 2017. (ENG.). 238p. (J). pap. *(978-81-8495-976-5(1))* Jaico Publishing Hse.

—Flehes an Hens Horn. Williams, Nicholas, tr. from ENG. Brock, Charles Edmund, illus. 2012. (COR.). 260p. pap. *(978-1-78201-003-6(3))* Evertype.

—The Magic World. 2006. 156p. (gr. -1-7). 24.95 *(978-1-59818-176-0(9))* Aegypan.

—Magic World. 2006. 156p. (gr. -1-7). per. 12.95 *(978-1-59818-966-7(2))* Aegypan.

—Pussy & Doggy Tales. 2011. 106p. 22.95 *(978-1-4638-9856-4(8));* pap. 9.95 *(978-1-4638-0127-4(0))* Rodgers, Alan Bks.

—The Rainbow & the Rose. l.t. ed. 2006. 124p. pap. *(978-1-84637-280-3(1))* Echo Library.

—The Seven Dragons & Other Stories. 2006. 140p. 24.95 *(978-1-59818-171-5(8))* Aegypan.

—Seven Dragons & Other Stories. 2006. 140p. per. 11.95 *(978-1-59818-964-3(6))* Aegypan.

—7 Books in 1 - "The Railway Children", "Five Children & It", "The Phoenix & the Carpet", "The Story of the Amulet", "The Story of the Treasure-Seekers", "The Would-Be-Goods" & "The Enchanted Castle" 2004. 472p. pap. *(978-0-9548401-0-5(0))* Shoes & Ships & Sealing Wax Ltd.

Nesbit, Edith. The Book of Dragons. 2019. (ENG.). (J). 276p. pap. 16.99 *(978-1-6967-8998-1(2));* 276p. pap. 12.99 *(978-1-6996-1569-0(1));* 276p. pap. 12.99 *(978-1-7018-0974-1(5));* 276p. pap. 16.99 *(978-1-6907-1428-6(X));* 280p. pap. 19.99 *(978-1-6932-1818-7(6));* 436p. pap. 25.99 *(978-1-6947-8845-0(8));* 112p. pap. 8.99 *(978-1-0867-3111-8(5));* 210p. pap. 13.99 *(978-1-0773-9445-2(4));* 278p. pap. 19.99 *(978-1-0779-9297-9(1));* 372p. pap. 24.99 *(978-1-0796-8686-9(X))* Independently Published.

Ness, Berthetta. Originals: Short Stories for Children. 2007. (YA). pap. *(978-1-57579-351-1(2))* Pine Hill Pr.

Neubert, Oliver. Chantel's Quest for the Silver Leaf. 2012. (Chantel's Quest Ser.). (ENG., Illus.). 200p. (J). (gr. 4-7). pap. 9.95 *(978-1-897476-43-7(4))* Simply Read Bks. CAN. Dist: Ingram Publisher Services.

New Burlington Books, creator. The Great Big Book of Bedtime Stories & Rhyme. 2008. (Illus.). 304p. (J). *(978-1-84538-882-9(8))* New Burlington Bks.

Newton-Kowalsky, Jacqueline. Itsy Bitsy Stories for Itsy Bitsy Tigers. 2012. 32p. pap. *(978-1-77097-138-7(6))* FriesenPress.

Nicholai, Rachel, et al. Bird Adventures. Nicholai, Rachel et al, illus. 2006. (Adventure Story Collection Ser.). 28p. (J). (gr. 2-6). pap. 10.00 *(978-1-58084-246-4(1))* Lower Kuskokwim Schl. District.

Nichols, C. D. Kids Courageous. 2010. 66p. pap. 9.99 *(978-1-60911-809-9(X),* Eloquent Bks.) Strategic Book Publishing & Rights Agency (SBPRA).

Nicholson, Nancy. Devotional Stories for Little Folks Too. 2007. (J). per. *(978-0-9771236-1-2(8))* For Little Folks.

Nick, Papa. Never Ending Stories. 2011. 44p. pap. 24.95 *(978-1-4626-3792-8(2))* America Star Bks.

—Never Ending Stories: Part Three. 2012. 48p. 24.95 *(978-1-4626-6243-2(9))* America Star Bks.

Nickel, Scott. Curse of the Red Scorpion, 1 vol. Harpster, Steve, illus. 2006. (Graphic Sparks Ser.). (ENG.). 40p. (J). (gr. 2-5). per. 5.95 *(978-1-59889-169-0(3),* 86492, Stone Arch Bks.) Capstone.

Nijkamp, Marieke. Unbroken: 13 Stories Starring Disabled Teens. 2018. (ENG.). 320p. (YA). 18.99 *(978-0-374-30650-2(8),* 900176128, Farrar, Straus & Giroux (BYR)) Farrar, Straus & Giroux.

Nikakhtar, Manijeh. Love & Joy. 2010. 65p. pap. 21.95 *(978-1-4327-4394-9(5))* Outskirts Pr., Inc.

Nikola-Lisa, W. La Alegriade Ser Tu Yo. 2004. (SPA., Illus.). (J). (gr. k-3). spiral bd. *(978-0-616-03093-6(2))* Canadian National Institute for the Blind/Institut National Canadien pour les Aveugles.

Nino, Jairo Anibal. El Quinto Viaje y Otras Historias del Nuevo Mundo. Isaza, Juanita, illus. 2004. (Literatura Juvenil (Panamericana Editorial) Ser.). (SPA.). 153p. (J). (gr. 4-7). pap. *(978-958-30-0573-2(8),* PV4381) Centro de Informacion y Desarrollo de la Comunicacion y la Literatura MEX. Dist: Lectorum Pubns., Inc.

Nite, Aluta. Folk Tales for Children's Enjoyment Book: Why & How Fables Number Two. 2011. 30p. pap. 16.95 *(978-1-4626-1033-4(1))* America Star Bks.

—Why & How Fables Number Three: Folk Tales for Children's Enjoyment Book 3. 2011. 40p. pap. 16.95 *(978-1-4626-2518-5(5))* America Star Bks.

Nix, Garth. Across the Wall: A Tale of the Abhorsen & Other Stories. 2006. (ENG.). 432p. (YA). (gr. 8-12). pap. 10.99 *(978-0-06-074715-2(3),* HarperTeen) HarperCollins Pubs.

S

—To Hold the Bridge. 2015. (ENG.). 416p. (YA). (gr. 8). 17.99 (978-0-06-229252-0(8), HarperCollins) HarperCollins Pubs.

Noel for Jeanne Marie. 2004. (Illus.). 34p. (J). mass mkt. 9.99 (978-0-9740599-5-2(1)) Omnibus Publishing.

Nolen, Jerdine. Big Jabe. Nelson, Kadir, illus. 2004. (gr. 1). 17.00 (978-0-7569-3184-1(3)) Perfection Learning Corp.

Norrie, Louise Rosalyn. The Adventures of Flat Cat. 2011. 144p. pap. 19.99 (978-1-4628-9396-6(1)) Xlibris Corp.

Northcott, Richard. Dolphin Readers 1. Meet Molly. 2010. (ENG., Illus.). 20p. 5.00 (978-0-19-440087-9(5)) Oxford Univ. Pr., Inc.

Nöstlinger, Christine. De Por Que a Franz le Dolio el Estomago. (Torre de Papel Ser.). (SPA.). (J). (gr. 2). 7.95 (978-958-04-1143-7(3)) Norma S.A. COL. Dist: Distribuidora Norma, Inc.

—Juanito Habichuela y Otros Cuentos. (Torre de Papel Ser.). (SPA.). (J). (gr. 4-18). 8.95 (978-958-04-4533-3(8)) Norma S.A. COL. Dist: Distribuidora Norma, Inc.

—Mas Historias de Franz. (Torre de Papel Ser.). (SPA.). (J). (gr. 2). 7.95 (978-958-04-1014-0(3)) Norma S.A. COL. Dist: Distribuidora Norma, Inc.

—Nuevas Historias de Franz en la Escuela. (Torre de Papel Ser.). (SPA.). (J). (gr. 2). 7.95 (978-958-04-1013-3(5)) Norma S.A. COL. Dist: Distribuidora Norma, Inc.

Novel Units. Edgar Allan Poe: A Collection of Stories Novel Units Student Packet. 2019. (ENG.). (YA). pap. 13.99 (978-1-58130-510-4(9), Novel Units, Inc.) Classroom Library Co.

Noyes, Deborah, ed. Sideshow: Ten Original Tales of Freaks, Illusionists & Other Matters Odd & Magical. 2009. (ENG., Illus.). 240p. (YA). (gr. 9-18). 16.99 (978-0-7636-3752-1(1)) Candlewick Pr.

Nyamnjoh, Francis B. Stories from Abakwa. 2007. (978-9956-558-00-1(1)) Langaa Research & Publishing Common Initiative Group CMR. Dist: Michigan State Univ. Pr.

Nye, Naomi Shihab. There Is No Long Distance Now: Very Short Stories. 2011. (ENG.). 208p. (YA). (gr. 8). 17.99 (978-0-06-201965-3(1), Greenwillow Bks.) HarperCollins Pubs.

Nyman, Mary. High School Stories: Short Takes from the Writers' Club. 2010. 64p. pap. 8.95 (978-1-4502-1585-5(8)) iUniverse, Inc.

Oates, Joyce Carol. Small Avalanches & Other Stories. 2003. 400p. (YA). 17.89 (978-0-06-001218-2(8), HarperTeen) HarperCollins Pubs.

O'Callaghan, G. The Eternals. 2007. 376p. per. (978-1-84693-055-3(3)) Best Global Publishing Ltd.

—Sorcerers Apprentice. 2007. 244p. per. (978-1-84693-024-9(3)) Best Global Publishing Ltd.

O'Connell, S. L. Short Stories to Tickle the Imagination. 2009. 48p. pap. 16.50 (978-1-60693-670-2(0), Eloquent Bks.) Strategic Book Publishing & Rights Agency (SBPRA).

O'Connor, Jane. Fancy Nancy: Nancy Clancy's Ultimate Chapter Book Quartet: Books 1 Through 4. Glasser, Robin Preiss, illus. 2015. (Nancy Clancy Ser.). (ENG.). 576p. (J). (gr. 1-5). 23.96 (978-0-06-242273-6(1), HarperCollins) HarperCollins Pubs.

—Fancy Nancy's Fabulous Fall Storybook Collection. Glasser, Robin Preiss, illus. 2014. (Fancy Nancy Ser.). (ENG.). 192p. (J). (gr. -1-3). bds. 12.99 (978-0-06-228884-4(9), HarperCollins) HarperCollins Pubs.

O'Dea, Rory & Benchmark Education Co. Staff. Books That Changed My Life. 2014. (Text Connections Ser.). (J). (gr. 5). (978-1-4900-1366-4(0)) Benchmark Education Co.

Odell, Carol. Once upon a Time in the Kitchen: Recipes & Tales from Classic Children's Stories. Pignataro, Anna, illus. 2010. (Myths, Legends, Fairy & Folktales Ser.). (ENG.). 48p. (J). (gr. 1-4). 12.95 (978-1-58536-518-0(1), 202208) Sleeping Bear Pr.

O'Dell, Patrick Timothy Wayne. Elvin. 2009. 58p. pap. 16.95 (978-1-61546-576-7(6)) America Star Bks.

Oduwole, Ben. The Flying Tortoise. 2009. 182p. pap. 43.50 (978-1-60693-611-5(5), Eloquent Bks.) Strategic Book Publishing & Rights Agency (SBPRA).

Oh, Ellen. Flying Lessons & Other Stories. 2019. (Penworthy Picks Middle School Ser.). (ENG.). 218p. (J). (gr. 4-5). 19.36 (978-1-64310-931-2(6)) Penworthy Co., LLC, The.

Oh, Ellen, ed. Flying Lessons & Other Stories. 2018. 240p. (J). (gr. 3-7). pap. 8.99 (978-1-101-93462-3(X), Yearling) Random Hse. Children's Bks.

Okeke-Ibezim, Felicia. African Folk Tales: Obiageli & Other Stories. 2006. (YA). per. 9.95 (978-0-9661598-7-5(X)) Orange County Publishing.

O'Kif, illus. No Somos Irrompibles (12 Cuentos de Chicos Enamorados) 2003. (SPA.). 143p. (J). (gr. 8-12). pap. 9.95 (978-950-511-243-2(2)) Santillana USA Publishing Co., Inc.

Okubo, Margaret. The Story of Angelo. 2005. (YA). per. 12.95 (978-0-9763686-2-5(5)) Rapha Publishing.

La Ola Gigante; El Primer Dia de Clases, 2 bks., Set. unabr. ed. (Coleccion Chiquilines - Imagen y Sonido). (SPA., Illus.). (J). 15.95 incl. audio (978-950-11-0626-8(8), SGM268) Sigmar ARG. Dist: Continental Bk. Co., Inc.

Olcott, Frances Jenkins. Good Stories for Great Holidays. l.t. ed. 2006. (ENG.). 324p. pap. 24.99 (978-1-4264-1125-0(1)) Creative Media Partners, LLC.

—Good Stories for Holidays. 2004. reprint ed. pap. 1.99 (978-1-4192-2211-5(2)); pap. 27.95 (978-1-4191-2211-8(8)) Kessinger Publishing, LLC.

Oldfield, Jenny. I'd Like a Little Word, Leonie! Child, Lauren, illus. (ENG.). 99p. (J). pap. 8.99 (978-0-340-78501-0(2)) Macmillan Pubs., Ltd. GBR. Dist: Trafalgar Square Publishing.

—Not Now, Nathan! Child, Lauren, illus. (ENG.). 107p. (J). pap. 7.99 (978-0-340-78502-7(0)) Macmillan Pubs., Ltd. GBR. Dist: Trafalgar Square Publishing.

—When Scott Got Lost No. 2. (ENG., Illus.). (J). mass mkt. 8.99 (978-0-340-85073-2(6)) Macmillan Pubs., Ltd. GBR. Dist: Trafalgar Square Publishing.

O'leary, Sara. When I Was Small. Morstad, Julie, illus. 2012. (ENG.). 32p. (J). (gr. -1-3). 16.95 (978-1-897476-38-3(8)) Simply Read Bks. CAN. Dist: Ingram Publisher Services.

Oliver, Chad. Far from This Earth & Other Stories. Olson, Priscilla, ed. Dennis, Jane, illus. 2003. (NESFA's Choice Ser.: 25). 480p. 24.00 (978-1-886778-48-1(5), NESFA Pr.) New England Science Fiction Assn., Inc.

—A Star Above It & Other Stories. Olson, Priscilla, ed. Dennis, Jane, illus. 2003. (NESFA's Choice Ser.: 24). 480p. 24.00 (978-1-886778-45-0(0), NESFA Pr.) New England Science Fiction Assn., Inc.

One Woman, One Hustle: Short Stories & Poems Inspired by Sheri J. Booker. 2003. per. 10.00 (978-0-9727776-0-5(1), Book Her Publications) Bk. Her Publishing.

O'Neill, Ian. Jimmy First & Destiny's Watch. 2011. 122p. pap. (978-0-7552-0675-9(4)) Authors OnLine, Ltd.

Ong, Gelyn. The Forest Fable. 2013. (Illus.). 54p. (J). (gr. -1-2). 19.99 (978-981-4408-56-1(5)) Marshall Cavendish International (Asia) Private Ltd. SGP. Dist: Independent Pubs. Group.

Opal, Paola, illus. Saffy & Ollie. 2012. (ENG.). 24p. (J). (gr. -1 — 1). bds. 7.95 (978-1-897476-69-7(8)) Simply Read Bks. CAN. Dist: Ingram Publisher Services.

Oppel, Kenneth. The Silverwing Collection (Boxed Set) Silverwing; Sunwing; Firewing. 2014. (Silverwing Trilogy Ser.). (ENG., Illus.). 896p. (J). (gr. 3-7). pap. 23.99 (978-1-4814-2725-8(3), Simon & Schuster Bks. For Young Readers) Simon & Schuster Bks. For Young Readers.

Oram, Hiawyn. Counting Leopard's Spots & other Stories. Warnes, Tim, illus. 2005. 96p. (J). (gr. k-4). reprint ed. 17.00 (978-0-7567-9252-7(5)) DIANE Publishing Co.

Orczy, Emmuska. Castles in the Air. 2008. 160p. 25.95 (978-1-60664-927-5(2)); pap. 14.95 (978-1-60664-047-0(X)) Aegypan.

—The Gallant Pimpernel - Unabridged - Lord Tony's Wife, the Way of the Scarlet Pimpernel, Sir Percy Leads the Band, the Triumph of the Scarlet Pimperne. 2012. 804p. (978-1-78139-227-0(7)) Benediction Classics.

Organ, Beryl E. Tiggy's World. 2010. 26p. pap. 15.99 (978-1-4500-7915-0(6)) Xlibris Corp.

Orme, David. Plague. 2004. (Shades Ser.). (ENG.). 58p. (J). pap. 7.99 (978-0-237-52729-7(4)) Evans Brothers, Ltd. GBR. Dist: Independent Pubs. Group.

Ormsby, Nathaniel Hosea. Timeless Tales of Anansi: Ancestral Realm of Africa. 2006. 108p. pap. 19.95 (978-1-4241-3396-3(3)) PublishAmerica, Inc.

Ortiz Cofer, Judith. An Island Like You: Stories of the Barrio. 2009. (ENG.). 256p. (J). (gr. 7-12). pap. 21.19 (978-0-545-13133-9(2)) Scholastic, Inc.

Ostendorf, Jenifer Wirth & Bisbee, Richard J. Worthwhile Family Tales. 2010. 160p. pap. 11.99 (978-1-4490-7605-4(X)) AuthorHouse.

O'Sullivan, Deirdre. Cousin Caleigh's Cartoons: And Other Stories, 1 vol. 2009. 97p. pap. 19.95 (978-1-60836-304-9(X)) America Star Bks.

Otenbaker, Audrey Lee. God's Jewel. 2009. 48p. (J). pap. 17.95 (978-1-4327-3340-7(0)) Outskirts Pr., Inc.

Our Lady of the Winding Sheets: The Cher'azade Series. 2006. (Cher'azade Ser.). (YA). 7.95 (978-0-9746669-2-1(0)) Franklin, J.E.

Outram, Evelyn. Sav & Josh O Lucky's Christmas Adventure & Magic Street. 2010. 56p. pap. 17.95 (978-1-60911-876-1(6), Eloquent Bks.) Strategic Book Publishing & Rights Agency (SBPRA).

Overell, J. J. The Dancing Flame. Lawrie, Robin, illus. 2003. (Overell Bks.). (ENG.). 128p. (C). per. 17.00 (978-0-7188-3036-6(9)) Lutherworth Pr., The GBR. Dist: ISD.

Owings, Jeff. Tiny Todd: Swooped Away. 2009. 20p. pap. 10.49 (978-1-4490-1214-4(0)) AuthorHouse.

—Tiny Todd: Tiny Todd's First Pet. 2009. 20p. pap. 10.49 (978-1-4490-1216-8(7)) AuthorHouse.

Ozaki, Yei. Warriors of Old Japan. 2007. 168p. per. 14.95 (978-1-59654-553-3(4)) Disruptive Publishing.

Padma, T. V. The Forbidden Temple: Stories from the Past. Vyas, Bhavana, illus. 2004. 95p. (J). (978-81-8146-041-7(3)) Tulika Pubs.

Pagan, Joseph. The Collection of Short Stories for Children & Young Adults. 2013. 136p. (gr. 2-4). 22.87 (978-1-4669-8462-2(7)); pap. 12.87 (978-1-4669-8463-9(5)) Trafford Publishing.

Page, Louise. Furballs' Fables. 2008. 100p. pap. 17.50 (978-1-4092-1068-9(5)) Lulu Pr., Inc.

Pajaroflor. 2003. (SPA.). pap. (978-956-13-1080-3(5), AB8005) Bello, Andres CHL. Dist: Lectorum Pubns., Inc.

Palahicky, Sophia. Kid's Reading Craze - a Collection of 20 Short Stories. 2013. 64p. pap. (978-1-4602-1576-0(1)) FriesenPress.

Palermo, Miguel Angel. Lo Que Cuentan los Onas. (SPA.). (YA). (gr. 4-18). pap. (978-950-07-1260-6(1), SA30066) Editorial Sudamericana S.A. ARG. Dist: Lectorum Pubns., Inc.

Paloma Sanllehi, David. UNA BUENA COSTUMBRE. 2003. (Caballo Alado Series-Al Galope Ser.). (SPA., Illus.). 24p. (J). (gr. k-2). pap. 5.95 (978-84-7864-671-5(X)) Combel Editorial, S.A. ESP. Dist: Independent Pubs. Group.

Panaitescu, Simona. The Unseen Paths of the Forest: 13 Tales about Love & Friendship. Moscal, Manuela, illus. 2012. (ENG.). 263p. pap. 14.95 (978-1-4327-7908-5(7)) Outskirts Pr., Inc.

Panman, Sandra & Panman, Richard. Short Stories. Panman, Sandra, ed. 5th ed. 2004. (Illus.). 192p. (YA). (gr. 7-12). reprint ed. pap. 23.95 (978-0-912813-32-5(6)) Active Learning Corp.

Pants & the Bully. 2004. (J). per. 7.99 (978-0-9755959-1-6(1)) Girl Named Pants, Inc., A.

Pants Feeds the Poor. 2004. (J). per. 7.99 (978-0-9755959-3-0(8)) Girl Named Pants, Inc., A.

Parker, Emma. Albert & the Dragon. 2010. (Illus.). 20p. pap. (978-1-877561-50-4(9)) First Edition Ltd.

—Bath Time. 2010. (Illus.). pap. (978-1-877547-83-6(2)) First Edition Ltd.

—Bill Hides Acorns. 2010. (Illus.). 24p. pap. (978-1-877561-33-7(9)) First Edition Ltd.

—Billy & the Deep Sea Monster. 2010. (Illus.). 20p. pap. (978-1-877561-57-3(6)) First Edition Ltd.

—Birthday Surprise. 2010. (Illus.). pap. (978-1-877547-85-0(9)) First Edition Ltd.

—The Butterfly on the Subway. 2010. (Illus.). pap. (978-1-877547-81-2(6)) First Edition Ltd.

—Can Your Dog? 2010. (Illus.). pap. (978-1-877547-96-6(4)) First Edition Ltd.

—Captain Gold. 2010. (Illus.). pap. (978-1-877561-26-9(6)) First Edition Ltd.

—The Carousel. 2010. (Illus.). 16p. pap. (978-1-877561-73-3(8)) First Edition Ltd.

—Cat on the High Seas. 2010. (Illus.). 16p. pap. (978-1-877561-75-7(4)) First Edition Ltd.

—Cecil the Caterpillar. 2010. (Illus.). pap. (978-1-877547-95-9(6)) First Edition Ltd.

—Delia Dynamite. 2010. (Illus.). 24p. pap. (978-1-877561-35-1(5)) First Edition Ltd.

—The Frog That Did Not Like Water. 2010. (Illus.). pap. (978-1-877547-93-5(X)) First Edition Ltd.

—The Fruity Girls. 2010. (Illus.). pap. (978-1-877561-11-5(8)) First Edition Ltd.

—The Lightning Game. 2010. (Illus.). 24p. pap. (978-1-877561-55-9(X)) First Edition Ltd.

—The Lucky Pearl. 2010. (Illus.). 20p. pap. (978-1-877561-18-4(5)) First Edition Ltd.

—Lulu & the Seed. 2010. (Illus.). pap. (978-1-877547-82-9(4)) First Edition Ltd.

—The Naughty Puppy. 2010. (Illus.). pap. (978-1-877547-89-8(1)) First Edition Ltd.

—The Not So Scary Scarecrow. 2010. (Illus.). pap. (978-1-877547-88-1(3)) First Edition Ltd.

—One Leg Ned. 2010. (Illus.). pap. (978-1-877561-12-2(6)) First Edition Ltd.

—Robot Tim. 2010. (Illus.). 20p. pap. (978-1-877561-54-2(1)) First Edition Ltd.

Parker, Emma & Renaud, Marguerite. Dragon Bowling. 2010. (Illus.). 24p. pap. (978-1-877561-82-5(7)) First Edition Ltd.

—Hedgehogs. 2010. (Illus.). 16p. pap. (978-1-877561-80-1(0)) First Edition Ltd.

—The Honey Bee Race. 2010. (Illus.). 16p. pap. (978-1-877561-78-8(9)) First Edition Ltd.

Parker, Natalie C., et al. Three Sides of a Heart: Stories about Love Triangles. (ENG.). 448p. (YA). (gr. 9). 2018. pap. 9.99 (978-0-06-242448-8(3)) 2017. 17.99 (978-0-06-242447-1(5)) HarperCollins Pubs. (HarperTeen).

Parker, Vic, compiled by. The Blind Men & the Elephant & Other Silly Stories, 1 vol. 2015. (Silly Stories Ser.). (ENG.). 40p. (J). (gr. 2-3). pap. 15.05 (978-1-4824-4195-6(0), e89bf5bb-3111-4697-a30a-b19914d2b94a) Stevens, Gareth Publishing LLLP.

—The Fish & the Hare & Other Silly Stories, 1 vol. 2015. (Silly Stories Ser.). (ENG.). 40p. (J). (gr. 2-3). pap. 15.05 (978-1-4824-4199-4(3), ab1e5772-9b68-4a07-ad79-1433bbf4329e) Stevens, Gareth Publishing LLLP.

—The Hare-Brained Crocodiles & Other Silly Stories, 1 vol. 2015. (Silly Stories Ser.). (ENG.). 40p. (J). (gr. 2-3). pap. 15.05 (978-1-4824-4202-1(7), ce434dd8-ca4a-4dc5-80ba-a76c09f9aff8) Stevens, Gareth Publishing LLLP.

—The Musicians of Bremen & Other Silly Stories, 1 vol. 2015. (Silly Stories Ser.). (ENG.). 40p. (J). (gr. 2-3). pap. 15.05 (978-1-4824-4207-6(8), 72908de5-c396-4c31-b7c3-2411d14bc812) Stevens, Gareth Publishing LLLP.

—The Open Road & Other Silly Stories, 1 vol. 2015. (Silly Stories Ser.). (ENG.). 40p. (J). (gr. 2-3). pap. 15.05 (978-1-4824-4211-3(6), c858f9e4-0059-4c82-bc29-f9a150d67478) Stevens, Gareth Publishing LLLP.

Parker, Vic, ed. The Demon with the Matted Hair & Other Stories, 1 vol. 2015. (Scary Fairy Tales Ser.). (ENG.). 40p. (J). (gr. 3-4). pap. 15.05 (978-1-4824-3073-8(8), 07a649e6-9b6a-4c17-bf45-a39b110bd5b3) Stevens, Gareth Publishing LLLP.

—The Goblin Pony & Other Stories, 1 vol. 2015. (Scary Fairy Tales Ser.). (ENG.). 40p. (J). (gr. 3-4). pap. 15.05 (978-1-4824-3077-6(0), b9a75ebd-0171-4623-b3dd-058c40ab0bab) Stevens, Gareth Publishing LLLP.

—Jack the Giant Killer & Other Stories, 1 vol. 2015. (Scary Fairy Tales Ser.). (ENG.). 40p. (J). (gr. 3-4). pap. 15.05 (978-1-4824-3081-3(9), 1f17aac1-aea3-4db6-8ce9-8c52f13fd66c) Stevens, Gareth Publishing LLLP.

—The Little Mermaid & Other Stories, 1 vol. 2015. (Scary Fairy Tales Ser.). (ENG.). 40p. (J). (gr. 3-4). pap. 15.05 (978-1-4824-3085-1(1), c9de130e-bb9f-45d8-a7f0-12317744645a) Stevens, Gareth Publishing LLLP.

—Little Red Riding Hood & Other Stories, 1 vol. 2015. (Scary Fairy Tales Ser.). (ENG., Illus.). 40p. (J). (gr. 3-4). pap. 15.05 (978-1-4824-3089-9(4), 00e00767-3b4e-4c9f-8e38-65e040b69076) Stevens, Gareth Publishing LLLP.

—The Ogre of Rashomon & Other Stories, 1 vol. 2015. (Scary Fairy Tales Ser.). (ENG.). 40p. (J). (gr. 3-4). pap. 15.05 (978-1-4824-3093-6(2), 512ce03d-a347-463f-aaf6-17d98262a169) Stevens, Gareth Publishing LLLP.

—The Prince & the Dragon & Other Stories, 1 vol. 2015. (Scary Fairy Tales Ser.). (ENG.). 40p. (J). (gr. 3-4). pap. 15.05 (978-1-4824-3097-4(5), 6de99058-98b4-4690-a573-0b875e271afe) Stevens, Gareth Publishing LLLP.

—The Rat Catcher & Other Stories, 1 vol. 2015. (Scary Fairy Tales Ser.). (ENG.). 40p. (J). (gr. 3-4). pap. 15.05 (978-1-4824-3101-8(7), d0d1dc09-527d-4ff7-a626-bd2d9e19c97e) Stevens, Gareth Publishing LLLP.

—The Snow Queen & Other Stories, 1 vol. 2015. (Scary Fairy Tales Ser.). (ENG.). 40p. (J). (gr. 3-4). pap. 15.05 (978-1-4824-3105-6(X), d31f6828-e3d9-4675-b186-264cccae340d) Stevens, Gareth Publishing LLLP.

—The Wicked Witch of the West & Other Stories, 1 vol. 2015. (Scary Fairy Tales Ser.). (ENG.). 40p. (J). (gr. 3-4). pap. 15.05 (978-1-4824-3109-4(2), 44f40ca1-160d-47f8-bc7c-7216c5551b2b) Stevens, Gareth Publishing LLLP.

Parragon Staff. Mickey Mouse: Adventure Tales & Stories. 2010. (Disney Diecut Classics). (Illus.). 72p. (J). (gr. -1-1). (978-1-4075-8937-4(7)) Parragon, Inc.

Parry, Rosanne. Second Fiddle. 2012. 240p. (J). (gr. 3-7). 6.99 (978-0-375-86166-6(1), Yearling) Random Hse. Children's Bks.

Pascal, Francine. Ambiente Hostil. Orig. Title: Out of Place. (SPA.). 128p. (J). 6.95 (978-84-272-3792-6(8)) Molino, Editorial ESP. Dist: AIMS International Bks., Inc.

—Cambios Oportunos.Tr. of Standing Out. (SPA.). 112p. (J). 6.95 (978-84-272-3795-7(2)) Molino, Editorial ESP. Dist: AIMS International Bks., Inc.

Pasquali, Elena. Two-Minute Bedtime Stories. Smee, Nicola, illus. 2010. (Two-Minute Stories Ser.). (ENG.). 48p. (J). (gr. -1-k). 12.99 (978-0-7459-6079-1(0)) Lion Hudson PLC GBR. Dist: Independent Pubs. Group.

Paterson, Andrew Barton 'Banjo'. Three Elephant Power & Other Stories. 2004. reprint ed. pap. 1.99 (978-1-4192-8979-8(9)); pap. 15.95 (978-1-4191-8979-1(4)) Kessinger Publishing, LLC.

Paterson, Judy. Scottish Folk Tales for Children. 2017. (Folk Tales for Children Ser.). (ENG., Illus.). 192p. (J). (gr. 2-4). pap. 16.99 (978-0-7509-6844-7(3)) History Pr. Ltd.,The GBR. Dist: Independent Pubs. Group.

Paterson, Katherine. A Stubborn Sweetness & Other Stories for the Christmas Season. 2013. (ENG.). 200p. 16.00 (978-0-664-23915-2(3), 0664239153) Westminster John Knox Pr.

Patten, William. Animal & Nature Stories Vol. 8: The Junior Classics. 2004. reprint ed. pap. 1.99 (978-1-4192-6805-2(8)) Kessinger Publishing, LLC.

Patterson, Horace. Ernie the Ermine. Parker, Jack, illus. 2007. 28p. per. 7.99 (978-1-58942-374-9(7)) R.H. Boyd Publishing Corp.

Paulitz, Kevin. A Letter from the Tooth Fairy. 2011. 28p. pap. 12.95 (978-1-4490-6671-0(2)) AuthorHouse.

Paulsen, Gary. The Gary Paulsen Collection (Boxed Set) Dancing Carl; Dogsong; Hatchet; Woodsong. 2013. (ENG., Illus.). 672p. (J). (gr. 3-7). pap. 33.99 (978-1-4424-9778-8(5), Simon & Schuster Bks. For Young Readers) Simon & Schuster Bks. For Young Readers.

—Paintings from the Cave: Three Novellas. 2012. (ENG.). 176p. (YA). (gr. 7-7). pap. 8.99 (978-0-553-49466-2(X), Ember) Random Hse. Children's Bks.

Paulsen, Gary, ed. Shelf Life: Stories by the Book. 2003. (ENG., Illus.). 192p. (J). (gr. 5-9). 18.99 (978-0-689-84180-4(9), Simon & Schuster Bks. For Young Readers) Simon & Schuster Bks. For Young Readers.

Pavlova, Chrisi É. da. Animal Stories from Green Lane Estate: Series Three. 2012. (ENG., Illus.). 254p. pap. 22.00 (978-1-78035-292-3(1), Fastprint Publishing) Upfront Publishing Ltd. GBR. Dist: Printondemand-worldwide.com.

Paws & Claws & Other Stories: Individual Title Six-Pack. (Story Steps Ser.). (gr. k-2). 42.00 (978-0-7635-9580-7(2)) Rigby Education.

Payton-Wright, Kaye. The Secret Wood. 2010. 28p. pap. 21.99 (978-1-4535-0321-8(8)) Xlibris Corp.

Pearce, Suzannah, ed. Five-Mintue Stories for Boys. 2014. (ENG., Illus.). 96p. (J). (978-1-74352-049-9(2)) Hinkler Bks. Pty, Ltd.

—Five-Minute Stories for Girls. 2014. (ENG., Illus.). 96p. (J). (978-1-74352-048-2(4)) Hinkler Bks. Pty, Ltd.

Peck, Richard. Past Perfect, Present Tense. (ENG., (J). 2004. Illus.). 177p. (gr. 6-8). 18.69 (978-0-8037-2998-8(7)) 2006. 192p. (gr. 3-7). reprint ed. 6.99 (978-0-14-240537-6(X), Puffin Books) Penguin Young Readers Group.

Peckham, Lori, ed. Guide's Greatest Animal Stories. 2006. 143p. (J). (gr. 5-9). per. 10.99 (978-0-8280-1944-6(4)) Review & Herald Publishing Assn.

—Guide's Greatest Funny Stories. 2014. (ENG.). 160p. (J). pap. 11.99 (978-0-8280-2778-6(1)) Review & Herald Publishing Assn.

—Guide's Greatest Mystery Stories. 2007. 155p. (J). per. 11.99 (978-0-8280-2038-1(8)) Review & Herald Publishing Assn.

Pedersen, Peggy A. Jasmine & the Magic Squirrel. 2008. 12p. pap. 24.95 (978-1-60474-052-3(3)) America Star Bks.

Pegler, Robin. Having Fun Together: A Collection of Children's Stories. 2010. 514p. pap. 23.95 (978-1-60693-817-1(7), Eloquent Bks.) Strategic Book Publishing & Rights Agency (SBPRA).

Peirce, Lincoln. Big Nate: Payback Time! 2019. (Big Nate Ser.: Vol. 20). (ENG., Illus.). (J). 178p. (gr. 3-6). 35.99 (978-1-5248-5126-2(4));Volume 20. 176p. pap. 11.99 (978-1-4494-9774-3(8)) Andrews McMeel Publishing.

—Big Nate: Payback Time! 2019. (Big Nate Ser.). (ENG.). 173p. (J). (gr. 4-5). 21.96 (978-0-87617-319-0(9)) Penworthy Co., LLC, The.

Pellicer López, Carlos. Juan y Sus Zapatos. 2003. (Los Especials de A la Orilla Del Viento Ser.). (SPA.). 20p. (J). 12.95 (978-968-16-7021-4(3)) Fondo de Cultura Economica USA.

Penick Phillips-Cermak, Mosetta. The Wishing Flower. 2007. 24p. 16.50 (978-0-615-15573-9(1)) PM Moon Pub., LLC.

Penn-Coughin, O. They're Coming for You: Scary Stories that Scream to be Read. 2009. (J). per. (978-0-9816836-0-7(6)) You Come Too Publishing.

The People on the Corner. 2003. pap. 15.00 (978-0-9740269-0-9(5)) Cyclops Pr.

Perelman, Helen. A Candy Fairies Sweet Collection (Boxed Set) Chocolate Dreams; Rainbow Swirl; Caramel Moon; Cool Mint. Waters, Erica-Jane, illus. 2013. (Candy Fairies Ser.). (ENG.). 512p. (J). (gr. 2-5). pap. 23.99 (978-1-4424-9390-2(9), Aladdin) Simon & Schuster Children's Publishing.

Perez, Vivian. Stolen Stories for My Nieces. 2007. (ENG.). 68p. per. 19.95 (978-1-4241-6679-4(9)) America Star Bks.

Perkins, Stephanie. My True Love Gave to Me: Twelve Holiday Stories. 2016. (ENG., Illus.). 336p. (YA). pap. 13.99 (978-1-250-05931-4(3), 900140423, St. Martin's Griffin) St. Martin's Pr.

—Summer Days & Summer Nights: Twelve Love Stories. 2017. (ENG.). 400p. (YA). pap. 17.99 (978-1-250-07913-8(6), 900154306, St. Martin's Griffin) St. Martin's Pr.

Perrault, Charles. Cuentos de Antano. (SPA.). 336p. (YA). (978-84-7525-123-3(4)) Ediciones Generales Anaya SA.

—Cuentos de Perrault.Tr. of Stories by Perrault. (SPA.). 128p. (J). 19.98 (978-84-305-8325-6(4)) Susaeta Ediciones, S.A. ESP. Dist: Giron Bks.

—Puffin Book of Five Minute Stories. (Illus.). 128p. (J). 24.95 (978-0-670-87680-8(1)) Penguin Publishing Group.

Perry, Glyn & Parry, Glyn. Invisible Girl. 2003. 160p. (YA). pap. 15.25 (978-1-920731-48-9(2)) Fremantle Pr. AUS. Dist: Independent Pubs. Group.

Pescetti, Luis Mariá. La Tarea Segun Natacha. O'Kif, illus. 2003. (Coleccion Derechos Del Nino Ser.). (SPA.). 32p. (J). (gr. 3-5). pap. 7.95 (978-84-204-5836-6(8)) Santillana USA Publishing Co., Inc.

Peszle, Brenda, et al. The Cranberry Tales. 2009. 40p. pap. 21.99 (978-1-4363-5925-2(2)) Xlibris Corp.

Pet Stories Set 2 800888, 3 vols. 2005. (J). pap. (978-1-59794-063-4(1)) Environments, Inc.

Pet Stories Set 800887, 3 vols. 2005. (J). pap. (978-1-59794-062-7(3)) Environments, Inc.

Petersen, David. Snowy Valentine. Petersen, David, illus. 2011. (ENG., Illus.). 32p. (J). (gr. -1-3). 14.99 (978-0-06-146378-5(7), HarperCollins) HarperCollins Pubs.

Peterson, Jay D. & Morgan, Collette A., eds. Sky Blue Water: Great Stories for Young Readers. 2016. (ENG.). 240p. 19.95 (978-0-8166-9876-9(7)) Univ. of Minnesota Pr.

Peterson, Jim. Kitten Tales. 2006. (ENG.). 76p. per. 16.95 (978-1-4241-4448-8(5)) PublishAmerica, Inc.

Peterson, Scott. The Ultimate Returns. 4th ed. 2009. (Spectrobes Ser.: No. 3). (ENG.). 144p. (J). (gr. 3-7). pap. 4.99 (978-1-4231-0811-5(6)) Disney Pr.

Petterson, Aline. El Papalote y el Nopal. Pacheco, Gabriel, illus. 2003. (SPA.). 34p. (J). (gr. 3-5). 15.95 (978-968-19-0750-1(7)) Santillana USA Publishing Co., Inc.

Petty, Kate. The Nightspinners. Smith, Mary Claire, illus. 2004. (ENG.). 32p. (J). pap. 8.99 (978-1-84255-105-9(1), Dolphin Paperbacks) Orion Publishing Group, Ltd. GBR. Dist: Trafalgar Square Publishing.

Peyo. The Smurfs #15: The Smurflings. 2013. (Smurfs Graphic Novels Ser.: 15). (ENG., Illus.). 56p. (J). (gr. 2-5). pap. 5.99 (978-1-59707-407-0(1), 900120422, Papercutz) Mad Cave Studios.

—The Smurfs #15: the Smurflings: The Smurflings, Vol. 15. 2013. (Smurfs Graphic Novels Ser.: 15). (ENG., Illus.). 56p. (J). (gr. 2-5). 10.99 (978-1-59707-408-7(X), 900120855, Papercutz) Mad Cave Studios.

Pfeiffer, Kathleen. Spartacus Sprout, Please Watch Out! 2011. (ENG.). 31p. 15.99 (978-1-257-50163-2(1)) Lulu Pr., Inc.

Philipson, Sandra J. Ollie's Monsters & Other Stories. Campbell, Jenny, illus. 2010. 48p. (J). pap. 10.95 (978-1-929821-09-9(3)) Chagrin River Publishing Co.

Phillips, Dee. Gladiator. 2014. (Yesterday's Voices Ser.). (YA). lib. bdg. 19.60 (978-0-606-35580-3(4)) Turtleback.

Phinn, Gervase. Royston Knapper: Return of the Rogue. Fisher, Chris, illus. 2005. (Child's Play Library - First Chapter Bks.). (ENG.). 126p. (J). (978-0-85953-024-8(8)) Child's Play International Ltd.

Phoenix International Staff, illus. Princess Sofia. 2013. (Play-A-Sound Ser.). (ENG.). 14p. (J). bds., bds. (978-1-4508-6822-8(3), 8877f18f-6f50-4b01-bcb0-36932429420b) Phoenix International Publications, Inc.

PI Kids. Disney: Baby Animal Stories 12 Board Books. The Disney Storybook Art Team, illus. 2011. (ENG.). 120p. (J). bds., bds., bds. 16.99 (978-1-4508-1571-0(5), 4194, PI Kids) Phoenix International Publications, Inc.

—Disney Junior Mickey Mouse Clubhouse: 12 Board Books. 2014. (ENG., Illus.). 120p. (J). bds., bds., bds. 16.99 (978-1-4127-6851-1(9), 4158, PI Kids) Phoenix International Publications, Inc.

—Disney: Me Reader 8 Book Disney Modern. 2011. (ENG.). 1p. (J). 34.99 (978-1-4508-2186-5(3), 1425, PI Kids) Phoenix International Publications, Inc.

Pierce, Tamora. Mastiff, 3. 2012. (Beka Cooper Ser.: Bk. 3). (ENG.). 608p. (J). (gr. 7-12). lib. bdg. 26.19 (978-0-375-91470-6(6)) Random Hse. Bks. for Young Readers.

—Tortall & Other Lands: a Collection of Tales. 2012. (ENG.). 400p. (YA). (gr. 7). pap. 10.99 (978-0-375-86633-3(7), Ember) Random Hse. Children's Bks.

La Pierna Lastimada, 2 bks., Set. (Coleccion Chiquilines - Imagen y Sonido). (SPA.). (J). 15.95 incl. audio (978-950-11-0625-1(X), SGM25X) Sigmar ARG. Dist: Continental Bk. Co., Inc.

Pinguilly, Yves. Contes et Legendes de Bretagne. pap. 14.95 (978-2-09-282237-1(3)) Nathan, Fernand FRA. Dist: Distribooks, Inc.

Pinkney, Andrea Davis. Bird in a Box. 2012. (ENG., Illus.). 288p. (J). (gr. 3-7). pap. 8.99 (978-0-316-07402-5(0)) Little, Brown Bks. for Young Readers.

Pinkney, Jerry. The Little Red Hen. Pinkney, Jerry, illus. 2006. (ENG., Illus.). 32p. (J). (gr. -1-3). 17.99 (978-0-8037-2935-3(9), Dial Bks) Penguin Young Readers Group.

Pirotta, Saviour. Around the World in 80 Tales. 2018. (ENG.). 176p. (J). 30.00 (978-0-7534-7508-9(1), 900203014, Kingfisher) Roaring Brook Pr.

Platt, Richard. A Question of Trust. 2018. (Visitor Ser.: Vol. 3). (ENG., Illus.). 222p. (YA). pap. (978-1-78222-603-1(6)) Paragon Publishing, Rothersthorpe.

Poe, Edgar Allan. Edgar Allan Poe's Tales of Mystery & Madness. Grimly, Gris, illus. 2004. (ENG.). 144p. (J). (gr. 6-9). 24.99 (978-0-689-84837-7(4), Atheneum Bks. for Young Readers) Simon & Schuster Children's Publishing.

Pombo, Rafael. Cuentos, Pombo Rafael. Acosta, Patricia, illus. (SPA.). 68p. (J). (gr. 2). pap. (978-958-30-0355-4(7), PV0862) Panamericana Editorial COL. Dist: Lectorum Pubns., Inc.

Ponti, Claude. Mi Valle. 2003. (SPA.). 46p. (978-84-95150-60-8(3)) Corimbo, Editorial S.L.

—La Tempestad. 2003. (SPA.). 32p. (978-84-95150-41-7(7)) Corimbo, Editorial S.L.

Porte, Barbara Ann. Beauty & the Serpent: Thirteen Tales of Unnatural Animals. Covey, Rosemary Feit, illus. 2008. (ENG.). 128p. (YA). (gr. 7). pap. 7.99 (978-1-4169-7579-3(9), Simon & Schuster/Paula Wiseman Bks.) Simon & Schuster/Paula Wiseman Bks.

Posadas, Carmen. Dorilda. 2nd ed. 2003. (SPA., Illus.). 127p. (J). (gr. 3-5). pap. 13.95 (978-84-204-5800-7(7)) Santillana USA Publishing Co., Inc.

Potter, Beatrix. Classic Tale of Peter Rabbit Hardcover: The Classic Edition by the New York Times Bestselling Illustrator, Charles Santore. 2013. (Charles Santore Children's Classics Ser.). (ENG., Illus.). 74p. (J). (gr. -1). 19.95 (978-1-60433-376-3(6), Applesauce Pr.) Cider Mill Pr. Bk. Pubs., LLC.

—The Complete Adventures of Peter Rabbit R/I. 2007. (Peter Rabbit Ser.). (ENG., Illus.). 80p. (J). (gr. -1-2). 17.99 (978-0-7232-5916-9(X), Warne) Penguin Young Readers Group.

—The Great Big Treasury of Beatrix Potter. 2007. (ENG.). 104p. pap. 18.99 (978-1-4264-3597-3(5)); 114p. pap. 19.99 (978-1-4264-3648-2(3)) Creative Media Partners, LLC.

—The Original Peter Rabbit Presentation Box 1-23 R/I, 23 vols., Set. 2006. (Peter Rabbit Ser.). (ENG., Illus.). 1388p. (J). (gr. -1-2). 170.00 (978-0-7232-5763-9(9), Warne) Penguin Young Readers Group.

Potter, Tina M. The Horse Story. 2005. 36p. (J). pap. 9.65 (978-1-4116-5761-8(6)) Lulu Pr., Inc.

Powell, Jillian. Hattie the Dancing Hippo. Dodson, Emma, illus. 2011. 32p. pap. (978-1-84089-709-8(0)) Zero to Ten, Ltd.

Power Reading: Power PAK. 2005. (Illus.). 80p. (J). (gr. 2-4). vinyl bd. 129.95 (978-1-883186-73-9(0), PPMX2-3); (gr. 4-5). vinyl bd. 129.95 (978-1-883186-72-2(2), PPMX4-5) National Reading Styles Institute, Inc.

Power Reading: Power PAK 4C. 2005. (Illus.). 80p. (J). (gr. 4-5). vinyl bd. 129.95 (978-1-883186-70-8(6), PPO4C) National Reading Styles Institute, Inc.

A Prairie Heart. 2007. (Illus.). (J). per. 19.95 (978-0-9793668-0-2(1)) Prairie Heart Publishing.

Pratchett, Terry. Dragons at Crumbling Castle: And Other Tales. Beech, Mark, illus. (ENG.). 352p. (J). (gr. 5-7). 2016. pap. 8.99 (978-0-544-81313-7(8), 1641909) 2015. 17.99 (978-0-544-46659-3(4), 1600657) HarperCollins Pubs. (Clarion Bks.).

Pray, Linda. Characters of the Dark. 2011. 36p. pap. 16.95 (978-1-4626-0329-9(7)) America Star Bks.

Preece, Mary Ellen Goble. The ABC Cousins & Fun from A to Z. 2007. (J). per. 12.00 (978-1-60458-005-1(4)) Instant Pub.

Preece, Phil. Nightmare Park. 2004. (Shades Ser.). 52p. (J). pap. (978-0-237-52730-3(8)) Evans Brothers, Ltd.

Preik, Christel D. Growing up Joyfully. 2012. 36p. pap. 15.49 (978-1-4669-0869-7(6)) Trafford Publishing.

—Sharing the Love. 2013. 36p. pap. 15.49 (978-1-4669-9975-6(6)) Trafford Publishing.

Press, Bothwell. Naughty Madge & Other Old-Fashioned Children's Stories. 2013. 120p. pap. 9.99 (978-0-9855353-0-8(X)) Bothwell Pr.

Prévert, Jacques. Contes pour enfants pas Sage. (FRE.). pap. 16.95 (978-2-07-053885-0(0)) Gallimard, Editions FRA. Dist: Distribooks, Inc.

Price, Kevin, ed. Fields of Wheat: And other Romance Stories. 2012. 200p. pap. (978-0-9872559-4-5(0), Crotchet Quaver) Logorythm.

Price, Margaret Evans, illus. & retold by. A Child's Book of Myths. Price, Margaret Evans, retold by. 2011. (Dover Read & Listen Ser.). (ENG.). 96p. (J). (gr. 3-8). pap. 14.99 incl. audio compact disk (978-0-486-48370-2(3), 483703) Dover Pubns., Inc.

Price, Roger & Stern, Leonard. Ad Lib Mad Libs: World's Greatest Word Game. 2011. (Mad Libs Ser.). 48p. (J). (gr. 3-7). pap. 4.99 (978-0-8431-9883-6(4), Mad Libs) Penguin Young Readers Group.

Price, Roger & Stern, Leonard, creators. Ninjas Mad Libs: World's Greatest Word Game. 2011. (Mad Libs Ser.). 48p. (J). (gr. 3-7). 5.99 (978-0-8431-9897-3(4), Mad Libs) Penguin Young Readers Group.

Price, Susan. Saga of Aslak. 2004. (Illus.). 96p. bds. 8.95 (978-0-7136-4076-2(6), A&C Black) Bloomsbury Publishing Plc GBR. Dist: Consortium Bk. Sales & Distribution.

Princess. Pula. 2005. (ENG.). 54p. pap. 20.99 (978-1-4134-8923-1(0)) Xlibris Corp.

Prindle House, creator. Mommy's Pleasures... Children's Treasures!, Volume 1. 2009. (Illus.). 51p. (J). (gr. -1-3). 14.95 (978-0-9759527-9-5(X)) Prindle Hse. Publishing Co.

Pritchett, Lee. The Tale of Greta Gumboot & Other Stories. 2010. (Illus.). 118p. pap. (978-1-84991-155-9(X)) Chipmunkapublishing.

Publications International Ltd. Staff. Little Treasuries Best Loved Children's Stories. 2007. 320p. (J). 12.98 (978-1-4127-8306-4(2)) Phoenix International Publications, Inc.

—Mother Goose Treasury. 2007. (Illus.). 316p. 15.98 (978-1-4127-8734-5(3)) Publications International, Ltd.

—Sweet Dreams Padded Treasury. 2013. 320p. (J). bds. (978-1-4127-6333-2(9), 1412763339) Phoenix International Publications, Inc.

Publications International Ltd. Staff, creator. Mother Goose. 2007. (Pop-up Treasury Ser.). (Illus.). 16p. (J). (gr. -1-3). 12.98 (978-1-4127-8833-5(1)) Publications International, Ltd.

—Thomas & Friends Musical Pop-up Treasury. 2007. (Thomas & Friends Ser.). (Illus.). 24p. (gr. -1). 15.98 (978-1-4127-9293-6(2)) Publications International, Ltd.

—Treasury of Best Loved Children's Stories. 2007. (Illus.). 320p. 15.98 (978-1-4127-8736-9(X)) Publications International, Ltd.

Publications International Ltd. Staff, ed. Bedtime Stories. 2010. (J). bds. 12.98 (978-0-7853-7921-8(5)) Phoenix International Publications, Inc.

—Cars: Starring Mater. 2010. 40p. (J). bds. 14.98 (978-1-60553-684-2(9)) Publications International, Ltd.

—Disney Princess: 26 Stories of Virtue. 2010. 12p. (J). 25.98 (978-1-60553-692-7(X)) Phoenix International Publications, Inc.

—Lights & Music Treasury 10Led Spa Disney Classics. 2009. 160p. 15.98 (978-1-4127-5454-5(2)) Phoenix International Publications, Inc.

—Musical Pop up Disney Princess. 2008. (SPA.). (J). 15.98 (978-1-4127-8980-6(X)) Publications International, Ltd.

—My 1st Libraries Disney Classics. 2011. 10p. (J). bds. 13.98 (978-1-4508-1029-6(2)) Phoenix International Publications, Inc.

—Once upon a Time. 2009. 24p. (J). bds. 17.98 (978-1-4127-5369-2(4), PIL Kids) Publications International, Ltd.

—Padded Treasury 160 Spa Sesame Street. 2009. 160p. 12.98 (978-1-4127-9548-7(6)) Phoenix International Publications, Inc.

—Play a Sound 10 Stories Winnie the Pooh. 2009. 24p. (J). 17.98 (978-1-4127-5370-8(8), PIL Kids) Publications International, Ltd.

—Puppy Learning. 2007. (J). 4.00 (978-1-4127-6959-4(0)) Publications International, Ltd.

—Really Useful Engines. 2010. 40p. (J). bds. 14.98 (978-1-60553-744-3(6)) Phoenix International Publications, Inc.

—Sesame Street: Good Night Stories. 2010. 40p. (J). bds. 14.98 (978-1-60553-861-7(2)) Phoenix International Publications, Inc.

—Stories to Grow on Spa Disney Classics. 2009. 40p. 9.98 (978-1-4127-1109-8(6)) Phoenix International Publications, Inc.

—Stories to Grow on Spa Mickey Mouse Clubhous. 2009. 40p. 9.98 (978-1-4127-1127-2(4), PIL Kids) Publications International, Ltd.

—Whats That Sound? 2009. 24p. (J). bds. 17.98 (978-1-4127-3974-0(8), PIL Kids) Publications International, Ltd.

—Winnie the Pooh. 2005. (J). 14.98 (978-1-4127-3470-7(3)) Publications International, Ltd.

Puckett, Gavin. Poppy the Police Horse: Fables from the Stables Book 4. Freeman, Tor, illus. 2018. (Fables from the Stables Ser.). (ENG.). 80p. 8.95 (978-0-571-33778-1(3), Faber & Faber Children's Bks.) Faber & Faber, Inc.

Puncel, Maria. Manana es Domingo y Otras Rimas Infantiles. Recio, Ricardo, illus. 2003. (SPA.). 32p. 4.95 (978-84-372-8021-9(4)) Altea, Ediciones, S.A. - Grupo Santillana ESP. Dist: Santillana USA Publishing Co., Inc.

—El Patio de Mi Casa y Otras Canciones Infantiles. Escrivá, Viví, illus. 2003. (SPA.). 32p. 4.95 (978-84-372-8018-9(4)) Altea, Ediciones, S.A. - Grupo Santillana ESP. Dist: Santillana USA Publishing Co., Inc.

—Yo Subia la Escalera y Otras Rimas Infantiles. Bayley, Nicola, illus. 2003. (SPA.). 24p. 4.95 (978-84-372-8015-8(X)) Altea, Ediciones, S.A. - Grupo Santillana ESP. Dist: Santillana USA Publishing Co., Inc.

Punter, Russell. Stories of Cowboys. Fiorin, Fabiano, illus. 2008. (Usborne Young Reading: Series One Ser.). 48p. (J). 8.99 (978-0-7945-1822-6(2), Usborne) EDC Publishing.

—Stories of Dinosaurs. Decker, Cynthia, illus. 2006. (Usborne Young Reading: Series One Ser.). 48p. (J). (gr. 2). lib. bdg. 13.99 (978-1-58086-940-9(8), Usborne) EDC Publishing.

—Stories of Santa. Webb, Philip, illus. 2006. (Young Reading Series 1 Gift Bks.). 48p. (J). 8.99 (978-0-7945-1476-1(6), Usborne) EDC Publishing.

Punter, Russell, retold by. Illustrated Stories from the Greek Myths. 2014. (ENG., Illus.). 350p. (J). 19.99 (978-0-7945-3237-6(3), Usborne) EDC Publishing.

Pushkin, Alexander, et al. Cuentos Clásicos Juveniles: Antología. Zuluaga, Conrado, ed. 2nd ed. 2003. (Serie Roja Anthologies Ser.). (SPA., Illus.). 124p. (YA). (gr. 8-12). pap. 12.95 (978-968-19-0320-6(X)) Santillana USA Publishing Co., Inc.

Puttock, Simon. Who's the Boss Rhinoceros? (ENG., Illus.). 32p. (J). pap. 8.99 (978-0-7497-4354-3(9)) Farshore GBR. Dist: Trafalgar Square Publishing.

Pyrtle Second Graders & Writers' Circle. Poetry & a Fifth Grade Cinderell: An Anthology from Nebraska. 2009. 60p. pap. 8.95 (978-0-595-53233-9(0)) iUniverse, Inc.

Quiroga, Horacio. Cuentos de la Selva. Vallejo, Esperanza, illus. 2004.Tr. of Jungle Stories. (SPA.). 186p. (YA). (gr. -1-7). pap. (978-958-30-0458-2(8)) Panamericana Editorial.

—Cuentos de la Selva. (Young Classics Ser.).Tr. of Jungle Stories. (SPA.). (J). (gr. 6-8). 5.60 (978-950-11-1268-9(3), SG8741) Sigmar ARG. Dist: Lectorum Pubns., Inc.

—Los Cuentos de Mis Hijos.Tr. of Stories of My Children. (SPA.). 104p. (YA). (gr. 5-8). 7.50 (978-84-204-4585-4(1)) Ediciones Alfaguara ESP. Dist: Lectorum Pubns., Inc.

R. Tatum, W. Brooks. Childrens Short Stories for the Soul. 2012. (ENG.). pap. 9.95 (978-1-4675-3658-5(X)) Independent Pub.

Rabbi David Cohen. Tell Me a Tale. 2005. (ENG., Illus.). 64p. (J). (978-1-4226-0018-4(1)) Mesorah Pubns., Ltd.

Rach, W. Dennis. The Goofy Principal at Silly School. 2007. (J). per. (978-0-9792579-0-2(5)) Rach, W. Dennis.

Rack, Charlene. The Adventures of Delaware Bear & Young Abraham Lincoln. 2011. 24p. (gr. -1). pap. 12.79 (978-1-4567-5619-2(2)) AuthorHouse.

Rackham, Arthur. A Fairy Book 1923. 2004. reprint ed. pap. 20.95 (978-1-4179-7656-0(X)) Kessinger Publishing, LLC.

Raichert, Lance, illus. Treasury of Values for Children. 2012. 159p. (J). (978-1-4508-3729-3(8)) Phoenix International Publications, Inc.

Ralph, Donna J. Critter Chronicles: Stories of Critters in a Colorado Wildlife Rehabilitator's Life. 2007. 200p. per. 16.95 (978-0-595-47858-3(1)) iUniverse, Inc.

Ramaswamy, Maya, illus. U Sier Lapalang: A Khasi Tale. 2005. (J). (978-81-89020-31-6(5)) Katha.

Ramoutar, Christine L. Tales from the Pine Forest. 2012. 108p. pap. 10.95 (978-1-4620-7030-5(2)) iUniverse, Inc.

Ramsnips, Tunder. The Hardly Boys. 2010. 196p. pap. 15.95 (978-0-557-38767-0(1)) Lulu Pr., Inc.

Random House. Nickelodeon 5-Minute Christmas Stories (Nickelodeon) Random House, illus. 2017. (ENG., Illus.). 160p. (J). (gr. -1-2). 12.99 (978-1-5247-6398-5(5), Random Hse. Bks. for Young Readers) Random Hse. Children's Bks.

—Six Magical Tales! (Shimmer & Shine) Random House, illus. 2018. (Step into Reading Ser.). (ENG., Illus.). 144p. (J). (gr. -1-1). pap. 8.99 (978-1-5247-7278-9(X), Random Hse. Bks. for Young Readers) Random Hse. Children's Bks.

—Trolls 5-Minute Stories (DreamWorks Trolls) Random House, illus. 2018. (ENG., Illus.). 160p. (J). (gr. -1-2). 12.99 (978-1-5247-7266-6(6), Random Hse. Bks. for Young Readers) Random Hse. Children's Bks.

Ranjalkar, Shreyans. My Sunny British Days - Stories for Children by a Child. 2013. (Illus.). 70p. pap. (978-1-78148-596-5(8)) Grosvenor Hse. Publishing Ltd.

Ransome, Arthur. Old Peter's Russian Tales. 2017. (ENG., Illus.). (J). pap. 20.95 (978-1-389-44200-1(4)) Blurb, Inc.

—Old Peter's Russian Tales. 2015. (ENG., Illus.). (J). 26.95 (978-1-298-52029-6(0)) Creative Media Partners, LLC.

Rao, Cheryl. Mixed Score: Ghost & Other Stories. 2004. 122p. 15.00 (978-81-291-0401-4(6)) Rupa & Co. IND. Dist: South Asia Bks.

Rasheed, Winona. Smiles & Frowns Through Animal Town's Storybook. 2008. 55p. pap. 13.70 (978-1-4357-4617-6(1)) Lulu Pr., Inc.

Raspe, Rudolf Erich. The Surprising Adventures of Baron Munchausen: Illustrated by Gustave Dore. Le Motteux, Pierre, tr. from GER. Dore, Gustave, illus. 2012. (Everyman's Library Children's Classics Ser.). (ENG.). 208p. 20.00 (978-0-307-96147-1(8), Everyman's Library) Knopf Doubleday Publishing Group.

Read to Me Mommy. Date not set. (Read to Me Ser.). 192p. (J). 14.98 (978-0-7525-9486-6(9)) Parragon, Inc.

Real, Stuart. The Cone Stories. 2007. 140p. per. 11.95 (978-0-9556755-0-8(2)) Lulu Pr., Inc.

Rebal, Tara. Sarah Sue Smith: A Crooked Wharf Adventure. 2010. 52p. pap. 22.49 (978-1-4520-7165-7(9)) AuthorHouse.

Rebmann, Charles. Christmas Stories from the Jersey Cape. 2003. 94p. pap. 9.95 (978-0-595-29692-7(0)) iUniverse, Inc.

Reeve, Elizabeth. Sassy: the short stories of being a service Dog. 2010. 35p. pap. 17.00 (978-0-557-39319-0(1)) Lulu Pr., Inc.

Reeve, Philip. Night Flights: a Mortal Engines Collection. McQue, Ian, illus. 2018. (Mortal Engines Ser.). (ENG.). 208p. (YA). (gr. 7-7). pap. 12.99 (978-1-338-28970-1(5), Scholastic Pr.) Scholastic, Inc.

Regan, Anne, ed. Harmonious Hearts. 2016. (ENG., Illus.). (YA). (gr. 9-12). 27.99 (978-1-63533-024-3(6), Harmony Ink Pr.) Dreamspinner Pr.

—Harmonious Hearts 2015. 2016. (ENG., Illus.). (YA). 24.99 (978-1-63533-025-0(4), Harmony Ink Pr.) Dreamspinner Pr.

—Harmonious Hearts 2016: Stories from the Young Author Challenge. 2017. (Harmony Ink Press - Young Author Challenge Ser.). (ENG., Illus.). (YA). 27.99 (978-1-64080-365-7(3), Harmony Ink Pr.) Dreamspinner Pr.

Reggie-Foster, Debbi. It's Cool to Be Me! Mini Stories about. 2006. 48p. pap. 16.95 (978-1-4241-4613-0(5)) PublishAmerica, Inc.

Regis, Tessa. The Hibiscus Conspiracies: Loss of Innocence. 2009. 116p. 20.95 (978-0-595-69133-3(1)); pap. 10.95 (978-0-595-44978-1(6)) iUniverse, Inc.

REID, D. H. Fantasies & Dreams. 2008. 208p. pap. 18.95 (978-0-557-01592-4(8)) Lulu Pr., Inc.

Reid, Rob. Wave Goodbye, 1 vol. Williams, Lorraine, illus. 2013. (ENG.). 24p. (J). (gr. -1-1). pap. 10.95 (978-1-60060-341-9(6), leelowbooks) Lee & Low Bks., Inc.

Reit, Seymour, adapted by. Great Stories of Courage (Call of the Wild/ Red Badge of Courage/ Treasure Island), 1 vol. 2007. (Bank Street Graphic Novels Ser.). (ENG., Illus.). 56p. (gr. 3-3). pap. 15.05 (978-0-8368-7933-9(3), 1d9f26ba-6299-4db8-beba-39136c4a82cb); lib. bdg. 33.67 (978-0-8368-7926-1(0), 274bb1bb-e14b-4dee-a0b6-7ae01714c828) Stevens, Gareth Publishing LLLP.

Relatos Escalofriantes. (SPA.). (YA). (gr. 5-8). pap. (978-956-13-1353-8(7), AB9026) Bello, Andres CHL. Dist: Lectorum Pubns., Inc.

Renee, Lindsey. What Kind of Fairy Is Merry Berry? 2010. (ENG., Illus.). 36p. (J). (gr. -1-1). 12.99 (978-0-8118-7685-8(3)) Chronicle Bks. LLC.

Renshaw, D. M. A Day to Remember. 2008. 100p. per. 23.95 (978-1-4327-0858-0(9)) Outskirts Pr., Inc.

Reviejo, Carlos & Reviejo, Carlos. Dejame Que te Cuente: Cincuenta Cuentos de Animales para Ninos. 2003. (SPA., Illus.). 212p. (978-84-348-7166-3(1), SM31147) SM Ediciones ESP. Dist: Lectorum Pubns., Inc.

Rey, H. A. Curious George Storybook Collection (CGTV) 2010. (Curious George Ser.). (ENG., Illus.). 208p. (J). (gr. -1-3). 13.99 (978-0-547-39631-6(7), 1427356, Clarion Bks.) HarperCollins Pubs.

—Curious George's 5-Minute Stories. 2013. (Curious George Ser.). (ENG., Illus.). 192p. (J). (gr. -1-3). 16.99 (978-0-544-10793-9(4), 1541117, Clarion Bks.) HarperCollins Pubs.

—A Treasury of Curious GeorgeColeccion de Oro Jorge el Curioso: Bilingual English-Spanish. 2011. (Curious George Ser.). (ENG., Illus.). 208p. (J). (gr. -1-3). 11.99 (978-0-547-52310-1(6), 1446149, Clarion Bks.) HarperCollins Pubs.

Rey, H. A. & Rey, Margret. Curious George Learns the Alphabet Book & CD, 1 vol. 2009. (Curious George Ser.). (ENG., Illus.). 80p. (J). (gr. -1-3). audio 10.99 (978-0-618-95966-2(1), 1021901, Clarion Bks.) HarperCollins Pubs.

—The H. A. Rey Treasury of Stories. 2015. (Dover Children's Classics Ser.). (ENG., Illus.). 112p. (J). (gr. 2-4). pap. 14.99 (978-0-486-78468-7(1), 784681) Dover Pubns., Inc.

Rey, Margret & Rey, H. A. Curious George at the Aquarium. 2014. (Curious George 8x8 Ser.). lib. bdg. 14.75 (978-1-4177-9792-9(4)) Turtleback.

Reyes, Yolanda. Los Anos Terribles. (SPA.). (YA). 9.95 (978-958-04-5633-9(X)) Norma S.A. COL. Dist: Distribuidora Norma, Inc.

—María de los Dinosaurios. 2011. (Torre de Papel Ser.). (SPA.). 94p. (gr. 2-4). pap. 11.99 (978-958-04-4277-6(0)) Norma S.A. COL. Dist: Lectorum Pubns., Inc.

Reynolds, Jason. Look Both Ways: A Tale Told in Ten Blocks. 2020. (ENG.). 240p. (gr. 7-12). 24.94 (978-1-5364-6605-8(0), Atheneum Bks. for Young Readers) Simon & Schuster Children's Publishing.

—Look Both Ways: A Tale Told in Ten Blocks. Nabaum, Alexander, illus. (ENG.). (J). (gr. 5-9). 2020. 240p. pap. 8.99 (978-1-4814-3829-2(8)) 2019. 208p. 17.99 (978-1-4814-3828-5(X)) Simon & Schuster Children's Publishing. (Atheneum/Caitlyn Dlouhy Books).

RH Disney. Princess Story Collection (Disney Princess) 2007. (Step into Reading Ser.). (ENG., Illus.). 160p. (J). (gr. k-3). pap. 7.99 (978-0-7364-2486-8(5), RH/Disney) Random Hse. Children's Bks.

Ricard, Anouk. Anna & Froga: Wanna Gumball? Wanna Gumball? Dascher, Helge, tr. 2012. (Anna & Froga Ser.). (ENG., Illus.). 40p. (J). (gr. k-4). 14.95 (978-1-77046-070-6(5), 900084353) Drawn & Quarterly Pubns. CAN. Dist: Macmillan.

Rice, David. Crazy Loco. 2008. 135p. 16.00 (978-0-7569-8951-4(5)) Perfection Learning Corp.

Rice, David & Garcia, Mike D. Heart-Shaped Cookies. 2011. (YA). pap. (978-1-931010-79-5(X)) Bilingual Pr./Editorial Bilingue.

Rice, David Talbot. Crazy Loco. 2003. (Illus.). 144p. (YA). (gr. 7-11). 8.99 (978-0-14-250056-9(9), Speak) Penguin Young Readers Group.
Rice, Dona Herwick. The North Wind & the Sun, 1 vol. rev. ed. 2008. (Reader's Theater Ser.). (ENG.). 24p. (gr. 1-3). pap. 8.99 (978-1-4333-0296-1(9)) Teacher Created Materials, Inc.
Rich, Susan. Half-Minute Horrors. 2011. (ENG., Illus.). 160p. (J). (gr. 5). pap. 6.99 (978-0-06-183381-6(9), HarperCollins) HarperCollins Pubs.
Richard Bellingham Edd. The Fables of Boris: Invitations to Meaningful Conversations. 2009. 280p. 27.95 (978-1-4401-6247-3(6)); pap. 17.95 (978-1-4401-6245-9(X)) iUniverse, Inc.
Richard, Martine. Chapeau, Camomille! Begin, Jean-Guy, illus. 2004. (Des 6 Ans Ser.). (FRE.). 64p. 7.95 (978-2-922565-96-6(3)) Editions de la Paix CAN. Dist: World of Reading, Ltd.
Richards, J. Danielle Jennson, Life Lessons of a Little Clown. 2006. 72p. per. 8.95 (978-1-59824-187-7(7)) E-BookTime LLC.
Richards, Justin. Licence to Fish, Book 3. 2011. (Agent Alfie Ser.). (ENG., Illus.). 176p. (J). (gr. 2-4). 6.99 (978-0-00-727359-1(2)) HarperCollins Pubs. Ltd. GBR. Dist: Independent Pubs. Group.
Richards, Laura Elizabeth Howe. Hildegarde's Neighbors. 2007. 92p. per. (978-1-4068-3864-0(0)) Echo Library.
Richards, Lisa. Family Short Stories Book. 2011. 44p. pap. 24.95 (978-1-4560-6711-3(7)) America Star Bks.
—Family Stories: A Collection of Short Stories by Lisa Richards, 1 vol. 2010. 52p. pap. 16.95 (978-1-4512-8988-6(X)) America Star Bks.
Richardson, Arleta. More Stories from Grandma's Attic. rev. ed. 2003. (Grandma's Attic Ser.). (Illus.). 144p. (J). pap. 6.99 (978-0-7814-3269-6(3), 0781432693) Cook, David C.
—Still More Stories from Grandma's Attic, 1. rev. ed. 2003. (Grandma's Attic Ser.). (Illus.). 144p. (J). (gr. 8-12). pap. 8.99 (978-0-7814-3270-2(7), 0781432707) Cook, David C.
—Treasures from Grandma. rev. ed. 2003. (Grandma's Attic Ser.). (Illus.). 144p. (J). (gr. 8-12). pap. 8.99 (978-0-7814-3271-9(5), 0781432715) Cook, David C.
Richmond, Beulah. Anancy & Friends: A Grandmother's Anancy Stories for Her Grandchildren. Brown, Clovis, illus. 2004. (ENG.). 52p. pap. 5.99 (978-976-8184-48-1(5)) Penguin Publishing Group.
Rider, John Russell. The Adventures of Acorn & Pinecone. 2010. 64p. pap. 25.95 (978-1-4520-8354-4(1)) AuthorHouse.
Ries, Lori. Aggie & Ben: Three Stories. Dormer, Frank W., illus. 2007. (Aggie & Ben Ser.). (ENG.). 48p. (J). (gr. -1-3). 5.95 (978-1-57091-649-6(7)) Charlesbridge Publishing, Inc.
—Aggie the Brave. Dormer, Frank W., illus. (Aggie & Ben Ser.). (ENG.). 48p. (J). (gr. -1-3). 2012. pap. 5.95 (978-1-57091-636-6(5)) 2010. 12.95 (978-1-57091-635-9(7)) Charlesbridge Publishing, Inc.
Riggs-Mayfield, Nellie. A Collection of Short Stories for Children. 2006. (J). per. 19.95 (978-1-59872-640-4(4)) Instant Pub.
Riggs, Ransom. Tales of the Peculiar. Davidson, Andrew, illus. (ENG.). (YA). (gr. 7). 2017. 208p. pap. 14.99 (978-0-399-53854-4(2), Penguin Books) 2016. 192p. 24.99 (978-0-399-53853-7(4), Dutton Books for Young Readers) Penguin Young Readers Group.
Rigo, Laura. Little Duckling. 2011. (Mini Look at Me Bks.). (Illus.). 10p. (J). bds. 8.99 (978-0-7641-6425-5(2)) Sourcebooks, Inc.
Rigo, Laura, illus. Little Chimp. 2011. (Mini Look at Me Bks.). 10p. (J). (gr. -1). bds. 7.99 (978-0-7641-6428-6(7)) Sourcebooks, Inc.
—Little Elephant. 2011. (Look at Me Bks.). 10p. (J). (gr. -1). bds. 8.99 (978-0-7641-6426-2(0)) Sourcebooks, Inc.
Riley, James. Story Thieves Complete Collection (Boxed Set) Story Thieves; the Stolen Chapters; Secret Origins; Pick the Plot; Worlds Apart. (Story Thieves Ser.). (ENG.). (J). (gr. 3-7). 2019. 2112p. pap. 43.99 (978-1-5344-4242-9(1)) 2018. (Illus.). 2032p. 89.99 (978-1-5344-1799-1(0)) Simon & Schuster Children's Publishing. (Aladdin).
Rinehart, J. D. Crown of Three Epic Collection Books 1-3 (Boxed Set) Crown of Three; the Lost Realm; a Kingdom Rises. 2018. (Crown of Three Ser.). (ENG., Illus.). 1376p. (J). (gr. 4-8). pap. 27.99 (978-1-5344-0032-0(X), Aladdin) Simon & Schuster Children's Publishing.
Riordan, Rick. The Cursed Carnival & Other Calamities: New Stories about Mythic Heroes. 2023. 464p. (J). (gr. 3-7). pap. 7.99 (978-1-368-07317-2(4), Rick Riordan Presents) Disney Publishing Worldwide.
—Rick Riordan Presents the Cursed Carnival & Other Calamities: New Stories about Mythic Heroes. 2021. (Illus.). 20p. (J). (gr. 3-7). 17.99 (978-1-368-07083-6(3), Riordan, Rick) Disney Publishing Worldwide.
—9 from the Nine Worlds-Magnus Chase & the Gods of Asgard. 2018. (Magnus Chase & the Gods of Asgard Ser.). (ENG., Illus.). 176p. (J). (gr. 3-7). 14.99 (978-1-368-02404-4(1), Disney-Hyperion) Disney Publishing Worldwide.
Rippel, Marie & LaTulippe, Renée. Heirloom Antics: A Collection of Short Stories. Goeddaeus, Donna & Panske, Andy, illus. 2014. 243p. (J). (978-1-935197-55-3(X)) All About Learning Pr.
Rippin, Sally. The Lina Stories. Masciullo, Lucia, illus. 2018. (Our Australian Girl Ser.). (ENG.). 480p. (J). (gr. 3-7). 19.99 (978-0-14-378377-0(7)) Random Hse. Australia AUS. Dist: Independent Pubs. Group.
Roberts, Emrys & Knipping, Rod. Dau Gymro Dewr: A Storïau Gwir Eraill. 2005. (WEL., Illus.). 72p. pap. (978-0-903131-17-9(X)) Urdd Gobaith Cymru.
Roberts, Nancy. Ghosts of the Wild West: Including Five Never-Before-published Stories. 2nd enl. ed. 2008. (ENG., Illus.). 120p. (gr. 3-7). pap. 17.99 (978-1-57003-732-0(9), P146721) Univ. of South Carolina Pr.
—Ghosts of the Wild West: Including Five Never-Before-published Stories. 2nd fac. ed. 2008. (ENG., Illus.). 120p. (gr. 3-7). 24.99 (978-1-57003-731-3(0), P146720) Univ. of South Carolina Pr.
Robinson, Hilary. Over the Moon. Abbott, Jane, illus. 2009. (Tadpoles Ser.). (ENG.). 24p. (J). (gr. k-2). pap. (978-0-7787-3899-2(X)); lib. bdg. (978-0-7787-3868-8(X)) Crabtree Publishing Co.
Robinson, Michelle. Bear Boar. Sim, David, illus. 2012. (ENG.). 12p. (J). (gr. -1-k). bds. (978-1-4088-1704-9(7), 38575, Bloomsbury Children's Bks.) Bloomsbury Publishing Plc.
Robinson, Ronnie D. Children Stories. 2nd ed. 2004. 112p. (YA). pap. 11.95 (978-0-7414-1439-7(2)) Infinity Publishing.
—Children's Stories. 2004. 134p. (YA). pap. 12.95 (978-0-7414-1438-0(4)) Infinity Publishing.
Robles, Eduardo. La Sombra Vegetal. 2005. (Ediciones Castillo Castillo Del Terror Ser.). (SPA.). 125p. (J). (gr. 4-7). per. 7.95 (978-970-20-0249-9(4)) Castillo, Ediciones, S. A. de C. V. MEX. Dist: Iaconi, Mariuccia Bk. Imports.
Rochman, Hazel & McCampbell, Darlene Z., eds. Who do you Think you Are? 2005. 176p. (YA). 23.00 (978-0-8446-7269-4(6), 3585) Smith, Peter Pub., Inc.
Rode, Linda & Moodie, Fiona. In the Never-Ever Wood. 2011. (ENG., Illus.). 240p. (978-0-624-04768-1(7)) NB Pubs. Ltd.
Rodriguez, Alfredo. Redfoot. O'Reilly, Sean Patrick, ed. 2011. (Illus.). 43p. pap. 8.95 (978-1-926914-59-6(7)) Arcana Studio, Inc.
Rodriguez, Elizabeth. Hannah's Ayuna. 2007. per. (978-1-59916-153-2(2)) Printing Systems.
—Hannah's Fast. 2006. per. (978-1-59916-144-0(3)) Printing Systems.
Rodriguez, Jason, ed. Colonial Comics: New England, 1620 ¿ 1750. 2014. (Colonial Comics Ser.). (ENG., Illus.). 208p. (gr. 4). pap. 29.95 (978-1-938486-30-2(7)) Fulcrum Publishing.
Roelofsen, Marjorie. Where Have All the Puppies Gone? A Sequel to SAM. 2010. 24p. pap. 14.00 (978-1-4490-6211-8(3)) AuthorHouse.
Rogers, Derek G. Monstrous Myths & Fabulous Fables. 2012. 184p. pap. (978-1-78176-741-2(6)) FeedARead.com.
Rogers, Roy. Roy Rogers & the Deadly Treasure. 2011. 286p. 48.95 (978-1-258-03926-4(5)) Literary Licensing, LLC.
Rojas, Emilio. Libro Mágico de los 101 Relatos para Niños: Fábulas, Cuentos y Leyendas. 2003. (SPA., Illus.). 224p. (YA). (gr. 5-18). 15.95 (978-968-6966-19-0(6)) EDITER'S Publishing Hse. MEX. Dist: EDITER'S Publishing Hse.
Rolón, Rebecca Alisa. Rebecca's Tales. 2007. 48p. pap. 16.95 (978-1-4241-9198-7(X)) America Star Bks.
Rolt, Molly. The Chocci-Croc & Other Stories. 2006. 64p. pap. (978-1-84401-890-1(3)) Athena Pr.
Romano, Elaine Ambrose. Gators & Taters: A Week of Bedtime Stories 2003. (Illus.). 64p. (J). pap. 9.95 (978-0-9728225-0-3(X)) Mill Park Publishing.
Romero Gutiérrez, Astrid. Cuentos de Angeles Para Ninos. 2011. (SPA., Illus.). 160p. (YA). (gr. -1-3). pap. (978-970-643-065-6(2)) Selector, S.A. de C.V.
Ronnholm, Ursula O. Mi Libro de Palabras, Oraciones y Cuentos. Deliz, Osdila O., ed. Montero, Miguel, illus. (SPA.). 100p. (J). (gr. k-6). pap. 7.00 (978-0-941911-02-3(0)) Two Way Bilingual, Inc.
A Rookie Reader Boxed Level B. 2004. (Rookie Reader Ser.). (ENG.). (J). (gr. -1-2). 9.95 (978-0-516-25001-4(9), Watts, Franklin) Scholastic Library Publishing.
Rookie Reader Boxed Set 2, Set. 2004. (Rookie Reader Ser.). (ENG.). (J). (gr. -1-2). 9.95 (978-0-516-25002-1(7), Watts, Franklin) Scholastic Library Publishing.
Rookie Reader Treasury: Wait Skates! & Other Funny Stories. 2009. (Rookie Reader Treasury Ser.). (ENG., Illus.). 128p. (J). 11.95 (978-0-531-20849-6(4), Children's Pr.) Scholastic Library Publishing.
Rosario Irish. Ensueño. 2010. 52p. pap. (978-1-4269-2489-7(5)) Trafford Publishing (UK) Ltd.
Rose, Lela. Truth in Stories for Children 4 Through 6. 2003. pap. 8.00 (978-0-8059-5923-9(8)) Dorrance Publishing Co., Inc.
Rose, Mary. Dolphin Readers 1. Little Helpers. International Edition. Wright, Craig, ed. 2010. (ENG., Illus.). 20p. 5.00 (978-0-19-440083-1(2)) Oxford Univ. Pr., Inc.
Rose, Simon. Time Camera, 1 vol. 2012. (ENG., Illus.). 96p. (J). (gr. 4-7). pap. 9.95 (978-1-896580-09-8(2)) Tradewind Bks. CAN. Dist: Orca Bk. Pubs. USA.
Rosen, Barry. Do You Know What a Stranger Is? Rosen, Barry & Bell, Greg, illus. 2003. 34p. (J). pap. 7.25 (978-0-9625593-4-1(2)) B.R. Publishing Co.
Rosenfeld, Dina. A Chanukah Story for Night Number Three. 2009. (Illus.). 32p. (J). 13.99 (978-1-929628-54-4(4)) Hachai Publishing.
Rosenthal, Amy Krouse. Little Books Boxed Set: Little Pea, Little Hoot, Little Oink: (Baby Board Books, Nursery Rhymes, Children's Book Sets, Nursery Books), 1 vol., Set. 2009. (Little Bks.). (ENG., Illus.). 80p. (J). (gr. -1 — 1). bds. 19.99 (978-0-8118-7054-2(5)) Chronicle Bks. LLC.
Rosero, Evelio. Teresita Cantaba. (SPA.). (J). (978-958-04-6491-4(X)) Norma S.A. COL. Dist: Distribuidora Norma, Inc.
Ross, Stewart. Dear Mum, I Miss You! Clark, Linda, illus. 54p. (J). (978-0-237-52318-3(3)) Evans Brothers, Ltd.
Ross, Tony. My Favourite Fairy Tales. Ross, Tony, illus. 2012. (ENG., Illus.). 96p. (J). (gr. -1-k). pap. 16.99 (978-1-84939-211-2(0)) Andersen Pr. GBR. Dist: Independent Pubs. Group.
—The Nights Before Christmas: 24 Classic Christmas Stories to Read Aloud. 2017. (ENG., Illus.). 240p. (J). (gr. 4-6). 26.99 (978-1-84939-580-9(2)) Andersen Pr. GBR. Dist: Independent Pubs. Group.
—Rizos de Oro y los Tres Osos: Little Books. 2003. (Nuevos Horizontes Ser.). (SPA., Illus.). 32p. (J). (gr. 3-5). pap. 5.95 (978-84-372-1575-4(7)) Santillana USA Publishing Co., Inc.
Rossbacher, John. From Father John's Story Book: Nine Fun Stories for Children & Grandchildren. 2010. 40p. pap. 23.99 (978-1-4520-7778-9(9)) AuthorHouse.
Rosseter, Patrick W. Grampa Pat's Little Animal Tales. 2005. 10.00 (978-0-8059-9797-2(0)) Dorrance Publishing Co., Inc.
Rothenberger, Charlene. Kara's Kapers with Katy Pillar. Rothenberger, Boyd & Bays, Gail, illus. 2006. 64p. per. 9.99 (978-0-9776260-6-9(7)) Bearhead Publishing, LLC.
Rounds, Harriet. The Magic Stairway, 1 vol. 2009. 48p. pap. 16.95 (978-1-60749-707-3(7)) America Star Bks.
Rousay II, Richard A. Choose the Right 'Walk with Alma' 2009. (ENG.). 94p. pap. 17.50 (978-0-557-13491-5(9)) Lulu Pr., Inc.
—Choose the Right! Walk with Ruth. 2009. 101p. pap. 17.50 (978-1-4092-5519-2(0)) Lulu Pr., Inc.
Rouse, W. H. D. The Giant Crab & Other Tales from Old Indi. 2011. 90p. 20.95 (978-1-4638-9898-4(3)) Rodgers, Alan Bks.
Rouse, W. H. D., ed. The Giant Crab & Other Tales from Old Indi. 2011. 90p. pap. 9.95 (978-1-4638-0139-7(4)) Rodgers, Alan Bks.
Rowe, John. Little Stories for Little People. 2013. 92p. pap. 25.95 (978-1-62516-542-8(0), Strategic Bk. Publishing) Strategic Book Publishing & Rights Agency (SBPRA).
Roxbee-Cox, Phil. Find the Teddy. Cartwright, Stephen, illus. 2004. (Rhyming Board Bks.). (ENG.). 1p. (J). (gr. -1-18). bds. 3.95 (978-0-7460-3825-3(9)) EDC Publishing.
Roxbee Cox, Phil. Phonics Stories for Young Readers, Vol. 2. 2009. (Phonics Readers Ser.). 96p. (J). 14.99 (978-0-7945-1887-5(7), Usborne) EDC Publishing.
Roxbee-Cox, Phil. Ted's Shed. 2004. (Easy Words to Read Ser.). (ENG., Illus.). 1p. (J). (gr. 1-18). pap. 6.95 (978-0-7460-4210-6(8)) EDC Publishing.
Roy, Alene Adele. The Legend of Dragonfly Pond: Book Three. 2010. (ENG.). 60p. pap. 23.99 (978-1-4490-0834-5(8)) AuthorHouse.
Roy Windham, Windham & Windham, Roy. Uncle Fuddy-Duddy & the Big Bad Bear. 2010. 28p. 16.09 (978-1-4269-3065-2(8)) Trafford Publishing.
Rsm Ma, Anne Frances Pulling. Tales from the Pumpkin Patch Spooky: Kitten Who Wanted to Fly. 2012. 24p. pap. 12.99 (978-1-4653-8747-9(1)) Xlibris Corp.
Ruben, Pamela J. Yenta the Chicken & Other Fowl Tales! Ruben, Anthony R., ed. 2004. (Illus.). 19p. (J). 12.95 (978-0-9764813-0-0(8)) Peppery Pr.
Rubin, Adam. The Human Kaboom. 2023. (ENG., Illus.). 416p. (J). (gr. 3-7). 18.99 (978-0-593-46239-3(4), G.P. Putnam's Sons Books for Young Readers) Penguin Young Readers Group.
—The Ice Cream Machine. (ENG., Illus.). (J). (gr. 3-7). 2023. 432p. 9.99 (978-0-593-32580-3(X)) 2022. 384p. 17.99 (978-0-593-32579-7(6)) Penguin Young Readers Group. (G.P. Putnam's Sons Books for Young Readers).
Ruffell, Ann & Orme, David. Treachery by Night. 2004. (Shades Ser.). (ENG.). 62p. (J). pap. (978-0-237-52728-0(6)) Evans Brothers, Ltd.
Ruffenach, Jessie E., et al. Learn along with Ashkii: First Grade Level 1. Whitethorne, Bahe, Jr., illus. 2003. (NAV & ENG.). 16p. (J). (gr. -1-3). pap. 7.95 (978-1-893354-41-8(5)) Salina Bookshelf Inc.
The Runaway Engine & Other Stories: Individual Title Six-Pack. (Story Steps Ser.). (gr. k-2). 48.00 (978-0-7635-9803-7(8)) Rigby Education.
Rupp, Dain Chistopher. The Greatest Saint Stories A-Z: (Book 1 of 2: A-M) 2008. 32p. per. 24.95 (978-1-60441-067-9(1)) America Star Bks.
Rushford, Betty. Best Buddies: And the Fruit of the Spirit. 2003. 41p. pap. 24.95 (978-1-59286-746-2(4)) America Star Bks.
Russell, Kitty, compiled by. Fairy Hearts & Charms: Stories of Yesteryear. 2012. (ENG.). 434p. 29.95 (978-1-937922-03-0(0)) Kittyco Pr.
—Fairy Lovely: Stories of Yesteryear. 2012. (ENG.). 416p. 29.95 (978-1-937922-04-7(9)) Kittyco Pr.
Russell, Rachel Renée. Dork Diaries Boxed Set (Books 4-6) Dork Diaries 4; Dork Diaries 5; Dork Diaries 6, Set. Russell, Rachel Renée, illus. 2013. (Dork Diaries: Nos. 4-6). (ENG., Illus.). 1056p. (J). (gr. 4-8). 41.99 (978-1-4424-9859-4(5), Aladdin) Simon & Schuster Children's Publishing.
—Tales from a Not-So-Dorky Drama Queen. 2015. (Dork Diaries: 9). lib. bdg. 25.75 (978-0-606-37316-6(0)) Turtleback.
Ruurs, Margriet & Gooderham, Andrew. Ms. Bee's magical bookcase. 2004. (Illus.). 32p. (J). pap. 8.95 (978-1-894601-10-8(6)) Chestnut Publishing Group CAN. Dist: Hushion Hse. Publishing, Ltd.
Ryan, Carrie, ed. Foretold: 14 Tales of Prophecy & Prediction. 2013. (ENG.). 368p. (YA). (gr. 7). pap. 10.99 (978-0-385-74130-9(8), Ember) Random Hse. Children's Bks.
S, Peter. 12 Minutes: So Short Stories. 2011. 28p. pap. 15.99 (978-1-4568-8841-1(2)) Xlibris Corp.
Saari, Danial. Tales with Tails: Bed Time Stories. 2012. (KAZ & ENG., Illus.). 68p. pap. 41.99 (978-1-4771-3252-4(X)) Xlibris Corp.
Sachs, Harley L. A Troll for Christmas & Other Stories. 2009. (ENG., Illus.). 240p. (J). pap. 14.99 (978-1-934841-80-8(3), Zumaya Thresholds) Zumaya Pubns. LLC.
Sadi. The Careless King & Other Stories. 2005. (Illus.). 64p. (J). (978-969-542-068-3(0)) Children Pubns.
Sadu, Itah & Condy, Roy. Christopher Changes His Name. (Tell Me a Story Ser.). (Illus.). 32p. (J). 12.99 (978-0-590-24670-5(4)) Scholastic, Inc.
Safari Stories. (My Animal Library). (Illus.). 10p. (J). (978-2-7643-0154-8(5)) Phidal Publishing, Inc./Editions Phidal, Inc.
Saffiedine, Amanda. Goodnight Sweet Baby: A Collection of Short Stories. 2009. 52p. pap. 22.49 (978-1-4490-0857-4(7)) AuthorHouse.
Saga-Whyte. Why the Naiads Dance: Book One of the Naiad Legends, 8 vols., Vol. 1. Saga-Whyte, illus. 2007. (Illus.). 25p. (J). (978-90-8885-018-9(6)) Saga-Whyte Pr.
Sakade, Florence. Japanese Children's Favorite Stories: Anniversary Edition. Kurosaki, Yoshisuke, illus. anniv. ed. 2014. (Favorite Children's Stories Ser.). 112p. (J). (gr. 3-8). 17.95 (978-4-8053-1260-5(2)) Tuttle Publishing.
Saldaña, René. Dancing with the Devil & Other Tales from Beyond / Bailando con el Diablo y Otros Cuentos del Más Allá. Baeza Ventura, Gabriela, tr. from ENG. 2012. (SPA & ENG.). (YA). pap. 9.95 (978-1-55885-744-5(3), Piñata Books) Arte Publico Pr.
Saldana, Theresa. The Almost Murder & Other Stories. 2008. (ENG.). 144p. (YA). (gr. 6-18). pap. 10.95 (978-1-55885-507-6(6), Piñata Books) Arte Publico Pr.
Saleff, Olga. Baba's Bedtime Stories. 2011. 64p. (gr. -1). pap. 25.48 (978-1-4567-6247-6(8)) AuthorHouse.
Salerno, Tony, et al. Tony Salerno's Good News Express. Thompson, Del et al, illus. 64p. (Orig.). (J). (gr. k-6). pap. (978-1-881597-00-1(8)) Magination.
Salsi, Lynn Sims. Young Ray Hicks: Learns the Jack Tales. 2005. (ENG., Illus.). 154p. (J). 16.00 (978-0-9706527-5-1(5)); pap. 8.00 (978-0-9706527-6-8(3)) Montville Pr.
The Salt Water Bath. 2004. (J). per. (978-1-57657-472-0(5)) Paradise Pr., Inc.
Sam, Kurutsi Dan'azumi. The Big Photograph of Sir Ahmadu Bello: And Other Short Stories for Children & Young Adults. 2013. 50p. pap. 10.97 (978-1-62212-440-4(5), Strategic Bk. Publishing) Strategic Book Publishing & Rights Agency (SBPRA).
Sam, Sam & Other Stories: Individual Title Six-Pack. (Story Steps Ser.). (gr. k-2). 48.00 (978-0-7635-9610-1(8)) Rigby Education.
Samson, Don. Teenage Aviation Stories. 2005. reprint ed. pap. 26.95 (978-1-4191-1624-7(X)) Kessinger Publishing, LLC.
San Souci, Robert D. Haunted Houses. Murphy, Kelly & Revoy, Antoine, illus. 2012. (Are You Scared Yet? Ser.). (ENG.). 304p. (J). (gr. 4-7). pap. 16.99 (978-0-312-55136-0(3), 900074422) Square Fish.
San Souci, Robert D. & San Souci, Daniel, illus. Sister Tricksters: Rollicking Tales of Clever Females. 2006. (ENG.). 70p. (J). (gr. 3-7). 19.95 (978-0-87483-791-9(X)) August Hse. Pubs., Inc.
Sánchez, Gloria. Siete Casas, Siete Brujas y un Huevo. 5th ed. 2005. (SPA., Illus.). 64p. (J). (gr. k-1). 6.95 (978-84-348-6003-2(1)) SM Ediciones ESP. Dist: Iaconi, Mariuccia Bk. Imports.
Sánchez, Haroldo & McCaughrean, Geraldine. Juegos de la Mente: La Vida de un Periodista Guatemalteco en 30 DÃ as. 2005. (Mythology Series Collection Mitos Ser.). (SPA., Illus.). 348p. (J). (gr. 2-3). 9.95 (978-84-348-9385-6(1)) SM Ediciones ESP. Dist: Iaconi, Mariuccia Bk. Imports.
Sand, Marc. Sheltered. 2003. (YA). per. 5.95 (978-0-9726764-0-3(6)) Sketch Publishing.
Sandage, Charley. I can tell you stories, if you gather round Big Book. 2005. (Illus.). (J). pap. (978-0-9794044-3-6(6)) Archeological Assessments, Inc.
Sandau, Carol E. 10 Puzzling Pieces. 2010. 80p. pap. 8.95 (978-1-4502-6244-6(9)) iUniverse, Inc.
Sandburg, Carl. Rootabaga Stories. (gr. 3-18). 2011. 126p. 24.95 (978-1-4638-9902-8(5)) 2009. 128p. pap. 10.95 (978-1-60664-425-6(4)) Rodgers, Alan Bks.
Sangster, Margaret Elizabeth. Holiday Stories for Young People. 2017. (ENG., Illus.). (J). 24.95 (978-1-374-93782-6(7)); pap. 14.95 (978-1-374-93781-9(9)) Capital Communications, Inc.
Sangster, Margaret Elizabeth, ed. Holiday Stories for Young People. 2007. 228p. per. (978-1-4065-3858-8(2)) Dodo Pr.
Sankey, Alice. Roy Rogers' Surprise for Donnie. Steel, John, illus. 2011. 32p. pap. 35.95 (978-1-258-03591-4(X)) Literary Licensing, LLC.
Sansone, V. K. A Tweens Book of Shorts. 2009. 32p. pap. 8.98 (978-0-557-06244-7(6)) Lulu Pr., Inc.
Santan. Good & Evil: The Princess & Devil. 2011. (Illus.). 64p. pap. 25.80 (978-1-4567-9683-9(6)) AuthorHouse.
Santore, Charles. Aesop's Fables: A Little Apple Classic. 2019. (Little Apple Bks.). (ENG., Illus.). 28p. (J). (gr. k). 4.99 (978-1-60433-923-9(3), Applesauce Pr.) Cider Mill Pr. Bk. Pubs., LLC.
—Aesop's Fables Hardcover: The Classic Edition by the New York Times Bestselling Illustrator, Charles Santore. 2018. (Charles Santore Children's Classics Ser.). (ENG., Illus.). 64p. (J). (gr. k-6). 19.95 (978-1-60433-810-2(5), Applesauce Pr.) Cider Mill Pr. Bk. Pubs., LLC.
Sargent, Dave & Sargent, Pat. Lizzy Lightning Bug/Lizzy la Luciérnaga, 10 vols., Vol. 17. Robinson, Laura, illus. 2004. (Learn to Read Ser.: 10).Tr. of Lizzy la Luciernaga. (ENG & SPA.). 18p. (J). (gr. k-2). lib. bdg. 20.95 (978-1-56763-993-3(3)) Ozark Publishing.
Sargent, Dave, et al. The Bundle Keeper: (Pawnee) Be Responsible, 20 vols., Vol. 18. Lenoir, Sue, illus. 2004. (Story Keeper Ser.: No. 18). 42p. (J). lib. bdg. 23.60 (978-1-56763-937-7(2)) Ozark Publishing.
Sargent, Pat L. Jaguar #8 (PB), 6 vols. 2007. (Barney the Bear Killer Ser.: 8). (YA). pap. 9.95 (978-1-59381-425-0(9)) Ozark Publishing.
Sastrias, Marta. Cuentos de Todo y de Nada. Martinez y Luis San Vicente, Enrique, illus. 2003. (SPA.). 82p. (J). (gr. 3-5). (978-968-19-0551-4(2)) Aguilar, Altea, Taurus, Alfaguara, S.A. de C.V.
Satchwell, Sm. Len Stories. 2012. (Illus.). 24p. pap. 19.82 (978-1-4685-0478-1(9)) AuthorHouse.
A Saturday Sandwiches Set, 6 vols. 32p. (gr. 1-3). 26.50 (978-0-7802-8043-4(1)) Wright Group/McGraw-Hill.
Satyajit, Ray. Unicorn Expedition & Other Stories. 2004. (ENG., Illus.). 248p. pap. 12.95 (978-0-14-333584-9(7), Puffin) Penguin Publishing Group.
Saunders. Saunders 2. Date not set. (J). 15.99 (978-0-380-97785-7(0)) HarperCollins Pubs.
Saunders, Helen B. Sweet Faces Story Book. 2004. Orig. Title: Sweet Faces. (Illus.). 29p. (J). 14.95 (978-0-9763143-0-1(4)) Happy Heart Kids Publishing.
Saunders, Jami Lynn. Feral: Book I of the Werecat Saga. 2011. 86p. (YA). pap. 4.99 (978-1-936307-15-9(4), 711Press) Vendera Publishing.
Sava, Scott Christian. Animal Crackers. 2011. (Illus.). 152p. pap. 11.99 (978-1-60010-619-4(6)) Idea & Design Works, LLC.
Sawyer, Debra D. Let Me Speak You A Secret. 2004. (YA). reprint ed. per. 16.00 (978-0-9761207-0-4(4)) DiaShah Pr., LLC.
Scaperrotta, Kirstyn. I Lost My Cracker to the Big Cheese: A Collection of Voices. 2003. 126p. (YA). pap. 10.95 (978-0-595-26478-0(6), Writers Club Pr.) iUniverse, Inc.
Schkolnik, Saul. Cuentos Ecologicos. Cardemil, Carmen, illus. 2nd ed. 2003. (la Orilla del Viento Ser.).Tr. of Ecological Tales. (SPA.). 56p. (J). (gr. 3-7). per. (978-968-16-4757-5(2), FC6400) Fondo de Cultura Economica MEX. Dist: Lectorum Pubns., Inc.
Scholastic, Inc. Staff. Adventure Collection, Bks. 9-16. 2018. (Pokémon Ser.). (ENG.). 96p. (J). (gr. 2-5). 39.92 (978-1-338-28400-3(2)) Scholastic, Inc.
Schonzeit, Miriam. The Sweetest Song & other Stories. 2006. 304p. (YA). 16.95 (978-1-932443-42-4(8), SWSH) Judaica Pr., Inc., The.
School, Waverly. Waverly Review: Spring 2003, Issue 1. 2003. 70p. (YA). pap. 8.95 (978-0-595-27691-2(1)) iUniverse, Inc.
Schraff, Anne. Black Widow Beauty, 1 vol. unabr. ed. 2010. (Q Reads Ser.). (ENG.). 32p. (YA). (gr. 9-12). pap. 8.50 (978-1-61651-178-4(8)) Saddleback Educational Publishing, Inc.

—Blackout, 1 vol. unabr. ed. 2010. (Q Reads Ser.). (ENG.). 32p. (YA). (gr. 9-12). pap. 8.50 *(978-1-61651-190-6(7))* Saddleback Educational Publishing, Inc.

Schulz, Kathy, et al. The Frog in the Pond & Other Animal Stories. Payne, Tom et al, illus. 2008. (Rookie Reader Treasury Ser.). (ENG.). 112p. (J). 11.95 *(978-0-531-21727-6(2),* Children's Pr.) Scholastic Library Publishing.

Scieszka, Jon. Race from a to Z, No. 4. Shannon, David et al, illus. 2014. (Jon Scieszka's Trucktown Ser.). (ENG.). 48p. (J). (gr. -1-3). 19.99 *(978-1-4169-4136-1(3),* Simon & Schuster Bks. For Young Readers) Simon & Schuster Bks. For Young Readers.

Scieszka, Jon, et al. Guys Read: Funny Business. 2010. (Guys Read Ser.: 1). (ENG., Illus.). 288p. (J). (gr. 3-7). 16.99 *(978-0-06-196374-2(7),* Waldon Pond Pr.) HarperCollins Pubs.

—Guys Read: Funny Business. 2010. (Guys Read Ser.: 1). (ENG., Illus.). 288p. (J). (gr. 3-7). pap. 7.99 *(978-0-06-196373-5(9),* Waldon Pond Pr.) HarperCollins Pubs.

—Guys Read: Heroes & Villains. 2017. (Guys Read Ser.: 7). (ENG., Illus.). 288p. (J). (gr. 3-7). pap. 7.99 *(978-0-06-238560-4(7),* Waldon Pond Pr.) HarperCollins Pubs.

—Guys Read: True Stories. 2014. (Guys Read Ser.: 5). (ENG.). 272p. (J). (gr. 3-7). pap. 7.99 *(978-0-06-196381-0(X),* Waldon Pond Pr.) HarperCollins Pubs.

Scollen, Chris. Busy Kids Sticker Storybook Goldilocks. 2008. (Illus.). 12p. (J). (gr. -1-3). pap. *(978-1-84610-641-5(9))* Make Believe Ideas.

—Busy Kids Sticker Storybook Little Mermaid. 2008. (Illus.). 12p. (J). (gr. -1-3). pap. *(978-1-84610-805-1(5))* Make Believe Ideas.

—Busy Kids Sticker Storybook Three Billy Goats. 2008. (Illus.). 12p. (J). (gr. -1-3). pap. *(978-1-84610-803-7(9))* Make Believe Ideas.

—Busy Kids Sticker Storybook Three Little Pigs. 2008. (Illus.). 12p. (J). (gr. -1-3). pap. *(978-1-84610-639-2(7))* Make Believe Ideas.

Scott-Branagan, Brownen. The Pandanuspeople. 2009. 32p. pap. 13.75 *(978-1-60860-006-9(8),* Strategic Bk. Publishing) Strategic Book Publishing & Rights Agency (SBPRA).

Scott, Dee Mary. The Adventures of Charles & Camilla Chinchilla. 2012. (ENG., Illus.). 46p. pap. 6.99 *(978-1-78035-389-0(8),* Fastprint Publishing) Upfront Publishing Ltd. GBR. Dist: Printondemand-worldwide.com.

Scott, Goeffrey. Fairy Tales for Adults. 2007. 116p. per. 19.95 *(978-1-4241-6532-2(6))* America Star Bks.

Scott, Robert. Shades of Monte Christo & Other Short Stories. 2004. (YA). per. 19.86 *(978-1-4116-0484-1(9))* Lulu Pr., Inc.

Scretching, Dorothy/Janis. Story Time with Princess Dorothy. Walters, Steve, ed. Brunot, Katerina, illus. 2012. 32p. (J). 20.00 *(978-0-9719767-4-0(0),* Crowned Warrior Publishing) Walters, Steve Ministries.

Seagull. 2004. (J). per. *(978-1-57657-457-7(1))* Paradise Pr., Inc.

Seals, Arthur. The Three Little Heroes: Book One of Kirk, Chelsea, & Samantha's Adventures. 2007. 84p. per. 8.95 *(978-0-595-44083-2(5))* iUniverse, Inc.

Seamons, Karen. Child of Virtue: SamiTales Relationship Series. 2012. (ENG.). 190p. 49.95 *(978-1-4327-8144-6(8))* Outskirts Pr., Inc.

Seeberger, Beverley, illus. Razzle Dazzler. 2007. (J). per. 15.00 *(978-0-9713589-8-0(2))* Ubavie's Gifts.

Seeger, Laura Vaccaro. Dog & Bear: Two Friends, Three Stories. Seeger, Laura Vaccaro, illus. 2012. (My Readers Ser.). (ENG., Illus.). 32p. (J). (gr. k-2). pap. 4.99 *(978-0-312-54799-8(4),* 900074326) Square Fish.

Segal, Lore. Tell Me a Mitzi. (Blue-Ribbon Listen-and-Read Ser.). (J). (gr. -1-2). pap. 5.95 incl. audio *(978-0-590-63063-4(6))* Scholastic, Inc.

Selena Who Speaks in Silence Set B, 6 vols. 32p. (gr. 1-3). 26.50 *(978-0-7802-8051-9(2));* 31.50 *(978-0-322-00939-4(1))* Wright Group/McGraw-Hill.

Selfors, Suzanne. Smells Like Treasure. 2012. (Smells Like Dog Ser.: 2). (ENG.). 432p. (J). (gr. 3-7). pap. 8.99 *(978-0-316-04402-8(4))* Little, Brown Bks. for Young Readers.

Senior, Suzy. Tales from Christmas Wood Activity Book. Grey, James Newman & Gray, James Newman, illus. 2016. (ENG.). 24p. (J). (gr. k-4). 7.99 *(978-0-7459-7694-5(8),* 3a3b5be8-0d7e-452e-a737-bf8f2414c2e3, Lion Books) Lion Hudson PLC GBR. Dist: Baker & Taylor Publisher Services (BTPS).

Sensenig, Janet Martin. Maria de Guatemala y Otras Historias. 2011. (SPA., Illus.). 233p. (J). *(978-0-7399-7767-5(9))* Rod & Staff Pubs., Inc.

—The Missing Bible: And Other Stories. 2003. (Sunbeam Ser.). (Illus.). 160p. (gr. -1-5). 6.40 *(978-0-7399-0341-4(1),* 2325) Rod & Staff Pubs., Inc.

Sente, Yves. The Sarcophagi of the Sixth Coninent, Pt. 1, Vol. 9. Juillard, André, illus. 2011. (Blake & Mortimer Ser.: 9). 64p. (J). (gr. -1-12). pap. 15.95 *(978-1-84918-067-2(9))* CineBook GBR. Dist: National Bk. Network.

Sente, Yves & Juillard, Andre. The Sarcophagi of the Sixth Continent, Pt. 2. 2011. (Blake & Mortimer Ser.: 10). (Illus.). 64p. pap. 15.95 *(978-1-84918-077-1(6))* CineBook GBR. Dist: National Bk. Network.

Serafin, Michael. 4 Seasons of Baghdad. 2007. (ENG.). 60p. per. 16.95 *(978-1-4241-2303-2(8))* PublishAmerica, Inc.

Serafin, Mike. 7 Stories from Baghdad. 2005. 50p. pap. 16.95 *(978-1-4137-8808-2(4))* PublishAmerica, Inc.

Serna, Ana. Cuentos y Recetas de la Abuela.Tr. of Tales & Recipes from Grandmother. (SPA.). 144p. (J). 19.98 *(978-84-305-7732-3(7))* Susaeta Ediciones, S.A. ESP. Dist: AIMS International Bks., Inc.

Sesame Street 5-Minute Stories (Sesame Street) 2017. (ENG., Illus.). 160p. (J). (gr. -1-2). 14.99 *(978-1-5247-1989-0(7),* Random Hse. Bks. for Young Readers) Random Hse. Children's Bks.

Seton, Ernest Thompson. Wild Animals I Have Known. 2009. 116p. pap. 9.50 *(978-1-60459-623-6(6))* Wilder Pubns., Corp.

Seuss. The Bippolo Seed & Other Lost Stories. 2011. (Classic Seuss Ser.). (ENG., Illus.). 72p. (J). (gr. k-4). 16.99 *(978-0-375-86435-3(0),* Random Hse. Bks. for Young Readers) Random Hse. Children's Bks.

—Horton & the Kwuggerbug & More Lost Stories. 2014. (Classic Seuss Ser.). (ENG., Illus.). 56p. (J). (gr. -1-3). 16.99 *(978-0-385-38298-4(7),* Random Hse. Bks. for Young Readers) Random Hse. Children's Bks.

Seuss, Dr. Gli Snicci e Altre Storie. pap. 24.95 *(978-88-09-02448-9(6))* Giunti Gruppo Editoriale ITA. Dist: Distribooks, Inc.

—Yoruga la Tortuga y Otros Cuentos, 1. Canetti, Yanitzia, tr. from ENG. 2008.Tr. of Yertle the Turtle & Other Stories. (SPA., Illus.). 76p. (J). (gr. 2-3). 15.99 *(978-1-933032-41-2(3))* Lectorum Pubns., Inc.

Sewell, Byron W. Alix's Adventures in Wonderland: Lewis Carroll's Nightmare. 2011. (Illus.). 130p. pap. *(978-1-904808-72-5(7))* Evertype.

Sewell, Kristin. A Collection of Seven Children's Stories. 2012. 80p. pap. 28.99 *(978-1-4685-3770-3(9))* AuthorHouse.

Shagam, Rodger. Stories from My Gramps. 2013. 76p. pap. 22.97 *(978-1-62516-161-1(1),* Strategic Bk. Publishing) Strategic Book Publishing & Rights Agency (SBPRA).

Shan, Darren, pseud. Vampire Destiny Trilogy: Books 10 - 12. 2005. (ENG.). 496p. pap., pap., pap. *(978-0-00-717959-6(6))* HarperCollins Pubs. Australia.

Shanddaramon. Pagan Stories for Children: A Fairy's First Year in the Forest of Songs. 2011. (ENG., Illus.). 146p. (J). pap. *(978-1-257-75438-0(6))* Astor Pr.

Shankman, Edward. The Cods of Cape Cod. 2009. (Shankman & O'Neill Ser.). (ENG., Illus.). 32p. (J). (gr. -1-3). 14.99 *(978-1-933212-78-4(0),* Commonwealth Editions) Applewood Bks.

Shanks Jr. A Father's Stories for His Children: A Christian Reader for Students Grades 5-9. 2006. pap. 9.99 *(978-1-59781-946-6(8))* Salem Author Services.

Sharkey, Niamh, illus. Tales of Wisdom & Wonder. 2005. (ENG.). 64p. (J). pap. *(978-1-84148-231-6(5))* Barefoot Bks., Inc.

Sharmat, Marjorie Weinman. Yo, el Gran Fercho. (Torre de Papel Ser.).Tr. of Nate the Great. (SPA.). (YA). 8.95 *(978-958-04-2599-1(X))* Norma S.A. COL. Dist: Distribuidora Norma, Inc.

Sharpe, Tess, et al. Toil & Trouble: 15 Tales of Women & Witchcraft. 2018. (ENG.). 416p. (YA). 18.99 *(978-1-335-01627-0(9),* Harlequin Teen) Harlequin Enterprises ULC CAN. Dist: HarperCollins Pubs.

Sharpless, Sheila M. Mystery on Bear's Island: A Short Adventure Novel for Girls Aged 8-11. 2012. 74p. 24.99 *(978-1-4691-3576-2(0));* pap. 15.99 *(978-1-4691-3575-5(2))* Xlibris Corp.

Shats, Marina. Nature Knows (Paperback) 2010. 24p. 21.50 *(978-0-557-32587-0(0))* Lulu Pr., Inc.

Shaw, Janet. Kirsten's Short Story Collection. Lewis, Kim & Graef, Renee, illus. 2006. (American Girls Collection). 213p. (J). (gr. 3-8). 12.95 *(978-1-59369-323-7(0))* American Girl Publishing, Inc.

Shaw, Nancy E. Sheep Blast Off! Apple, Margot, illus. 2011. (Sheep in a Jeep Ser.). (ENG.). 32p. (J). (gr. -1-3). pap. 6.99 *(978-0-547-52025-4(5),* 1445464, Clarion Bks.) HarperCollins Pubs.

Sheffield, Sherry Overton. Children's Choices: What Would YOU Do? 2005. (Illus.). 112p. (J). per. *(978-0-9772513-0-8(6),* 804-337-8915) Thumbs Up Pr.

Shephard, Esther. Paul Bunyan. Kent, Rockwell, illus. 2006. (ENG.). 256p. (J). (gr. 5-7). pap. 15.95 *(978-0-15-205857-9(5),* 1197592, Clarion Bks.) HarperCollins Pubs.

Shepherd, J. A., illus. Old Hendrik's Tales - 13 South African Folk Tales. 2013. 198p. pap. *(978-1-909302-15-0(5))* Abela Publishing.

Shepperson, Jacqueline. Martins of the Everglades. 2007. (ENG.). 152p. per. 24.95 *(978-1-4241-5446-3(4))* America Star Bks.

Shepperson, Jacqueline Ruth. The Blue Jay Tales. 2005. 89p. pap. 19.95 *(978-1-4137-3884-1(2))* America Star Bks.

Sherman, Harold Morrow. Flying Heels & Other Hockey Stories. 2011. 264p. 47.95 *(978-1-258-08063-1(X))* Literary Licensing, LLC.

Sherrard, Valerie. Testify. 2011. (ENG.). 144p. (YA). (gr. 8-12). pap. 9.99 *(978-1-55488-927-3(8),* 9781554889273) Dundurn Pr. CAN. Dist: Publishers Group West (PGW).

Sherwood, C. A. Aj's Easter Surprise. 2008. 56p. pap. 24.29 *(978-1-4343-7583-4(8))* AuthorHouse.

Shetty, Lalitha A. Tales of Toy World. Shetty, Lakshmi, illus. 2010. 48p. pap. 12.00 *(978-1-60911-157-1(5),* Eloquent Bks.) Strategic Book Publishing & Rights Agency (SBPRA).

Shewver, Margaret. Without a Trace & Other Stories. 2005. 91p. (YA). (gr. 6-12). pap. 17.95 *(978-0-936389-59-2(1))* Tudor Pubs., Inc.

Shiga, Jason. Meanwhile: Pick Any Path. 3,856 Story Possibilities. 2010. (ENG., Illus.). 80p. (J). (gr. 3-9). 17.99 *(978-0-8109-8423-3(7),* 665501, Amulet Bks.) Abrams, Inc.

Shoemaker, E. W. Mother Nature & the Tales of North Fork. 2009. 220p. pap. 18.75 *(978-1-4389-8604-3(1))* AuthorHouse.

Shoo, Shoo, Shoo! & Other Stories, 6 Packs. (Story Steps Ser.). (gr. k-2). 48.00 *(978-0-7635-9604-0(3))* Rigby Education.

Shoushen, Jin. Beijing Legends. Yang, Gladys, tr. 2007. (Illus.). 124p. per. 11.95 *(978-1-59654-392-8(2))* Disruptive Publishing.

Showstack, Richard. The Gift of the Magic: And Other Enchanting Character-Building Stories for Smart Teenage Girls Who Want to Grow up to Be Strong Women. Eric, Whitfield, illus. 2004. 156p. (YA). per. 14.95 *(978-1-888725-64-3(8),* BeachHouse Bks.) Science & Humanities Pr.

Shuff, Chrissi. The Dancing Tree & other Stories. 2010. (Illus.). 80p. pap. 28.99 *(978-1-4520-0054-1(9))* AuthorHouse.

Shusterman, Neal. UnBound: Stories from the Unwind World. (Unwind Dystology Ser.). (ENG.). (YA). (gr. 7). 2016. 336p. pap. 12.99 *(978-1-4814-5724-8(1))* 2015. (Illus.). 320p. 18.99 *(978-1-4814-5723-1(3))* Simon & Schuster Bks. For Young Readers. (Simon & Schuster Bks. For Young Readers).

—UnBound: Stories from the Unwind World. 2016. (Unwind Dystology Ser.). lib. bdg. 23.30 *(978-0-606-39748-3(5))* Turtleback.

Shuttleworth, Cathie, illus. Little Tales for Toddlers: 35 Stories about Adorable Teddy Bears, Puppies & Bunnies. 2013. (ENG.). 256p. (J). (gr. -1-12). pap. 14.99 *(978-1-84322-925-4(0))* Anness Publishing GBR. Dist: National Bk. Network.

Sibille, Lucinda. Dragon Swirl: Book II. 2009. 28p. pap. 14.95 *(978-1-4490-1057-7(1))* AuthorHouse.

—Dragon Swirl: Book III. 2009. 32p. pap. 14.95 *(978-1-4490-1072-0(5))* AuthorHouse.

—Dragon Swirl: Book IV. 2009. 32p. pap. 14.95 *(978-1-4490-1075-1(X))* AuthorHouse.

—Dragon Swirl: In the Beginning. 2009. 32p. pap. 14.95 *(978-1-4490-0965-6(4))* AuthorHouse.

Sidney, Margaret. Five Little Peppers Grown Up. 2008. 196p. (gr. -1-3). 26.95 *(978-1-60664-805-6(5))* Aegypan.

Sierra I Fabra, Jordi. La Asombrosa Historia del Viajero de las Estrellas. (SPA.). (YA). 8.95 *(978-958-04-6872-1(9))* Norma S.A. COL. Dist: Distribuidora Norma, Inc.

—El Niño Que Vivía en Las Estrellas. 2003. (SPA., Illus.). 102p. (J). 8.95 *(978-968-19-0557-6(1))* Aguilar, Altea, Taurus, Alfaguara, S.A. de C.V MEX. Dist: Santillana USA Publishing Co., Inc.

Silver, Connie. A Story Book for Beginning Readers. 2007. 124p. 20.95 *(978-0-595-70501-6(4));* per. 10.95 *(978-0-595-46524-8(2))* iUniverse, Inc.

Silver Dolphin en Español Editors. Disney Tesoro de Libros de Calcomanias, Volume 6, Vol. 6. 2005. (Disney Calcomanias Ser.). (SPA., Illus.). 96p. (J). (gr. -1). pap. *(978-970-718-245-5(8))* Advanced Marketing, S. de R. L. de C. V.

Silvestre, R. Quique lo Salvo y Otras Historias. (Raton de Biblioteca Coleccion). (SPA.). 139p. (J). (gr. 3-5). 7.95 *(978-84-88061-70-6(6))* Serres, Ediciones, S. L. ESP. Dist: Lectorum Pubns., Inc.

Simms, Donna A. The Hillsborough Tales. (Children's Book). (Illus.). 76p. (J). (gr. 4-7). *(978-0-942078-22-0(5))* Tanner, Ralph Assocs., Inc.

Simms, Laura. Stories to Nourish the Hearts of Our Children. Krizmanic, Tatjana, illus. 2013. 100p. pap. 19.99 *(978-0-9911692-1-4(2))* Simms, Laura Storyteller.

Simon & Schuster UK. Holiday Ha Ha Ha! 2018. (ENG.). 320p. (J). pap. 7.99 *(978-1-4711-4622-0(7),* Simon & Schuster Children's) Simon & Schuster, Ltd. GBR. Dist: Simon & Schuster, Inc.

Simon, Annette. Robot Zombie Frankenstein! Simon, Annette, illus. 2012. (ENG., Illus.). 40p. (J). (gr. -1-3). 16.99 *(978-0-7636-5124-4(9))* Candlewick Pr.

Simon, Francesca. Horrid Henry Rocks. Ross, Tony, illus. 2011. (Horrid Henry Ser.: 0). (ENG.). 112p. (J). (gr. 2-5). pap. 7.99 *(978-1-4022-5674-5(4),* 9781402256745, Sourcebooks Jabberwocky) Sourcebooks, Inc.

Simonds, William. Ella; or, Turning over a New Leaf by Walter Aimwell [Pseud.]. 2006. 292p. per. 23.99 *(978-1-4255-2794-5(9))* Michigan Publishing.

—Marcus; or, the Boy-Tamer by Walter Aimwell [Pseud.]. 2006. 336p. per. 23.99 *(978-1-4255-3348-9(5))* Michigan Publishing.

Simpson, Pat. A Compilation of Tales to Thrill & Chill. 2008. 103p. pap. 15.95 *(978-1-4357-2976-6(5))* Lulu Pr., Inc.

Sims, Anthony. Princess Zoe. 2012. (Illus.). 44p. pap. 24.40 *(978-1-4772-2365-9(7))* AuthorHouse.

Sims, Lesley. Delightful Illustrated Stories (was Illustrated Stories for Girls) 2015. (Illustrated Stories Ser.). (ENG.). 352p. (J). (gr. k-5). 19.99 *(978-0-7945-3541-4(0),* Usborne) EDC Publishing.

—Illustrated Classics Action & Adventure Stories for Young Readers. 2015. (Illustrated Stories Ser.). (ENG.). 384p. (J). (gr. k-5). 19.99 *(978-0-7945-3565-0(8),* Usborne) EDC Publishing.

—Illustrated Classics Enchanting Stories for Young Readers. 2015. (Illustrated Stories Ser.). (ENG.). 384p. (J). (gr. k-5). 19.99 *(978-0-7945-3532-2(1),* Usborne) EDC Publishing.

—Illustrated Classics for Children. 2015. (Illustrated Stories Ser.). (ENG.). 512p. (J). (gr. k-5). 21.99 *(978-0-7945-3106-5(7),* Usborne) EDC Publishing.

—Magical Stories for Little Children. 2012. (Picture Bks). 128p. (J). ring bd. 18.99 *(978-0-7945-2919-2(4),* Usborne) EDC Publishing.

Sims, Lesley & Stowell, Louie. Illustrated Stories for Boys. McNee, Ian, illus. 2007. (Usborne Illustrated Stories Ser.). 352p. (J). 19.99 *(978-0-7945-1420-4(0),* Usborne) EDC Publishing.

Simwenyi, Robbinson Namasaka. Death, the Only Gift, 1 vol. 2010. 66p. pap. 19.95 *(978-1-4489-4338-8(8))* America Star Bks.

Singer, Isaac Bashevis. Cuentos Judios de la Aldea de Chelm.Tr. of Zlateh the Goat & Other Stories. (SPA.). 62p. (J). 7.96 *(978-84-264-3404-3(5),* LM2595) Editorial Lumen ESP. Dist: Lectorum Pubns., Inc.

Singer, Marilyn, ed. Face Relations: 11 Stories about Seeing Beyond Color. (ENG., Illus.). 240p. (YA). (gr. 7). 2013. pap. 11.99 *(978-1-4424-9616-3(9))* 2004. 18.99 *(978-0-689-85637-2(7))* Simon & Schuster Bks. For Young Readers. (Simon & Schuster Bks. For Young Readers).

Singh, Jay. Once upon a Time in a Forest Far Away. 2009. 394p. pap. 33.12 *(978-1-4251-9122-1(3))* Trafford Publishing.

Singhose, Rose. Granny's Giggles. 2010. (ENG.). 35p. pap. 16.95 *(978-0-557-57269-4(X))* Lulu Pr., Inc.

—Granny's giggles book Three. 2010. 33p. pap. 16.95 *(978-0-557-59768-0(4))* Lulu Pr., Inc.

—Granny's giggles book Two. 2010. (ENG.). 35p. pap. 16.95 *(978-0-557-59182-4(1))* Lulu Pr., Inc.

Sirko, Teodora. Aesop's Fables. 2007. 36p. per. 17.95 *(978-1-84753-698-3(0))* Lulu Pr., Inc.

Slade, Arthur. Villainology: Fabulous Lives of the Big, the Bad, & the Wicked. Mah, Derek, illus. 2007. 96p. (J). (gr. 4-7). per. 9.95 *(978-0-88776-809-5(1),* Tundra Bks.) Tundra Bks. CAN. Dist: Penguin Random Hse. LLC.

Slim, Lillian, et al. Subsistence Adventures. Slim, Lillian et al, illus. 2006. (Adventure Story Collection Ser.). 28p. (J). (gr. 2-6). pap. 10.00 *(978-1-58084-252-5(6))* Lower Kuskokwim Schl. District.

Smith, Bethany. Hiding Sunrise. 2008. 130p. pap. 8.86 *(978-0-557-02630-2(X))* Lulu Pr., Inc.

Smith, Carol & Quest, Suzanne. Dr Daphne & Nurse Moira Stories. 2015. (ENG., Illus.). 44p. (J). mass mkt. 13.95 *(978-1-78455-086-8(8),* cc358c0f-4958-4871-960f-cb72f70c1e07) Austin Macauley Pubs. Ltd. GBR. Dist: Baker & Taylor Publisher Services (BTPS).

Smith, Cathy Jo. Seamus Mcseamus, an Irish Rover. 2005. (Illus.). 104p. per. 11.95 *(978-0-9766666-0-8(X))* Arcadian Hse.

Smith, Eric. Welcome Home. 2017. (ENG.). 352p. (YA). (gr. 9-12). pap. 11.99 *(978-1-63583-004-0(4),* 1635830044, Flux) North Star Editions.

Smith, Helen. A Day with Oaky & Other Stories for Small Children. 2017. (ENG., Illus.). 49p. (J). pap. 13.95 *(978-1-78554-601-3(5),* 20db7cc2-31c4-4f95-8ff4-aff9e1f8b273) Austin Macauley Pubs. Ltd. GBR. Dist: Baker & Taylor Publisher Services (BTPS).

Smith, Helene. Dreamstone. Guinard, Geraldine, illus. 2005. 80p. (YA). pap. 13.50 *(978-1-920731-63-2(6))* Fremantle Pr. AUS. Dist: Independent Pubs. Group.

Smith, Jeff & Sniegoski, Tom. Tall Tales: A Graphic Novel. Smith, Jeff, illus. 2010. (Bone Ser.).Tr. of (Bone Prequel). (ENG., Illus.). 128p. (J). (gr. 3-7). pap. 12.99 *(978-0-545-14096-6(X),* Graphix) Scholastic, Inc.

Smith, Molly. Border Breakdown: The Fall of the Berlin Wall. Opie, David, illus. 2010. (ENG.). 32p. (J). (gr. 1-6). 19.95 *(978-1-60727-125-3(7));* 9.95 *(978-1-60727-126-0(5));* 16.95 *(978-1-60727-123-9(0));* pap. 6.95 *(978-1-60727-124-6(9))* Soundprints.

Smith, Pamela Colman. Annancy Stories. 2006. (YA). reprint ed. pap. 19.99 *(978-0-9769612-2-2(9))* Darker Intentions Pr.

Smith, Roland, et al. N Is for Our Nation's Capital: A Washington DC Alphabet. Gibson, Barbara Leonard, illus. 2005. (Discover America State by State Ser.). (ENG.). 40p. (J). (gr. 1-3). 17.95 *(978-1-58536-148-9(8),* 202008) Sleeping Bear Pr.

Smith, Stephanie Harms. For Everything There Is a Season in God's Time. 2007. 84p. per. 11.99 *(978-1-60477-224-1(7))* Salem Author Services.

Smith, Valerie H. The Spirit Stories: A Series of Short Stories for Children. 2007. 64p. per. 8.95 *(978-1-59824-450-2(7))* E-BookTime LLC.

Smoot, Madeline, compiled by. Summer Shorts: A Short Story Collection. 2005. (ENG., Illus.). 360p. (J). (gr. 2-7). pap. 8.95 *(978-0-9769417-5-0(9))* Blooming Tree Pr.

Snow, Dorothea J. Roy Rogers' Favorite Western Stories. Ushler, John, illus. 2011. 250p. 46.95 *(978-1-258-04169-4(3))* Literary Licensing, LLC.

Sobol, Donald J. Encyclopedia Brown Keeps the Peace. 2008. (Encyclopedia Brown Ser.: 6). (ENG., Illus.). 96p. (J). (gr. 3-7). 6.99 *(978-0-14-240950-3(2),* Puffin Books) Penguin Young Readers Group.

Soffe, Caroline Dawn. Bluebell Wood. 2011. 166p. pap. 24.95 *(978-1-4560-5235-5(7))* America Star Bks.

Sohaili, Monira. Stories from Earth & Beyond: Enchanting & Inspirational Stories. 2006. (Illus.). 94p. per. 9.95 *(978-1-60002-044-5(5),* 2833) Mountain Valley Publishing, LLC.

Sohrabi, Behzad. The Legend of Sigh: A Collection of Fairy Tales. 2012. 76p. pap. 41.99 *(978-1-4771-1969-3(8))* Xlibris Corp.

Solomon, Jef. Right in My Own Neighborhood. 2008. (ENG.). 53p. pap. 15.50 *(978-0-557-05790-0(6))* Lulu Pr., Inc.

Solotareff, Gregoire. EDU, EL PEQUEÑO LOBO. 2003. (SPA.). 32p. 17.95 *(978-84-95150-44-8(1))* Corimbo, Editorial S.L. ESP. Dist: Distribooks, Inc.

—EDU, EL PETIT LLOP -CATALA-. 2003. (SPA.). 32p. *(978-84-95150-46-2(8))* Corimbo, Editorial S.L.

Somers, Dayle. Sergeant Steve's Station. 2012. 80p. pap. 42.05 *(978-1-4691-8096-0(0))* Xlibris Corp.

Somoskey, Rebecca. Say What? Kool Kids Stories from Appalachia. 2004. (J). 4.00 *(978-0-9768514-2-4(3))* Bearwallow Blessings Ministries.

Sones, Sonya. The Sonya Sones Collection: One of Those Hideous Books Where the Mother Dies; What My Mother Doesn't Know; What My Girlfriend Doesn't Know. 2013. (ENG., Illus.). 896p. (YA). (gr. 7). pap. 29.99 *(978-1-4424-9780-1(7),* Simon & Schuster Bks. For Young Readers) Simon & Schuster Bks. For Young Readers.

Soto, G., et al. Multicultural Collection. Byrd, S., illus. 2003. pap. 91.95 incl. audio *(978-0-87499-673-9(2))* Live Oak Media.

Soto, Gary. Facts of Life: Stories. 2012. (ENG.). 192p. (YA). (gr. 7-7). pap. 7.99 *(978-0-547-57734-0(6),* 1458543, Clarion Bks.) HarperCollins Pubs.

—Help Wanted: Stories. 2007. (ENG., Illus.). 240p. (YA). (gr. 7-12). pap. 8.99 *(978-0-15-205663-6(7),* 1197028, Clarion Bks.) HarperCollins Pubs.

—Local News: Stories. 2003. (ENG., Illus.). 160p. (J). (gr. 3-7). pap. 7.99 *(978-0-15-204695-8(X),* 252798, Clarion Bks.) HarperCollins Pubs.

—Petty Crimes. 2006. (ENG., Illus.). 176p. (J). (gr. 5-7). pap. 7.99 *(978-0-15-205437-3(5),* 1196362, Clarion Bks.) HarperCollins Pubs.

Spanos, Seva, retold by. Thumbelina's Song. 2004. (Treasure Tree Ser.). (Illus.). 32p. (J). *(978-0-7166-1601-6(7))* World Bk., Inc.

Speccy-Tacular AFL Stories. 2018. 288p. (J). (gr. 1-5). 15.99 *(978-0-14-378732-7(2))* Random Hse. Australia AUS. Dist: Independent Pubs. Group.

Speceal, Edetha. The Lost Egg & Other Stories. 2006. (Illus.). 144p. pap. *(978-1-84401-644-0(7))* Athena Pr.

A Spicy-Herby Day, 6 vols.; set. 32p. (gr. 1-3). 26.50 *(978-0-7802-8044-1(X))* Wright Group/McGraw-Hill.

Spohn, Bruce. Christmas Hope. 2011. 114p. pap. 19.95 *(978-1-4560-7541-5(1))* America Star Bks.

Spotswood, Jessica, ed. A Tyranny of Petticoats: 15 Stories of Belles, Bank Robbers & Other Badass Girls. (ENG.). 368p. (YA). (gr. 9). 2018. pap. 9.99 *(978-1-5362-0025-6(5))* 2016. 17.99 *(978-0-7636-7848-7(1))* Candlewick Pr.

Springett, Martin. Breakfast on a Dragon's Tail: And Other Book Bites. 2011. (ENG.). 32p. (J). *(978-1-55455-200-9(1))* Fitzhenry & Whiteside, Ltd.

Springham, James. Earth-n-Bones: Blue Things. 2006. 54p. pap. 16.95 *(978-1-4137-9738-1(5))* America Star Bks.

Spurr, Elizabeth. Happy Sparkling Halloween. Madden, Colleen, illus. 2010. (Sparkling Stories Ser.). (ENG.). 14p. (J).

S

(gr. k-k). bds. 5.95 *(978-1-4027-7138-5(X))* Sterling Publishing Co., Inc.

Spyri, Johanna. Moni, the Goat Boy & What Sami Sings with the Birds. 2006. 108p. per. 9.95 *(978-1-59818-472-3(5))* Aegypan.

Squeaky. 2004. (J). per. *(978-1-57657-352-5(4))* Paradise Pr., Inc.

St. Aubyn, Douglas. Caribbean Fables. 2007. 72p. pap. *(978-976-8054-72-2(7))* Paria Publishing Co., Ltd.

Staff, Gareth Editorial Staff, adapted by. The Doomed & the Dead, 1 vol. 2006. (Ghost Stories Ser.). (ENG., Illus.). 128p. (gr. 4-6). lib. bdg. 33.67 *(978-0-8368-6822-7(6)*, 0c46cdad-1391-45f8-ad66-8da66401084c, Gareth Stevens Learning Library) Stevens, Gareth Publishing LLLP.

Stagliano, Michael F. Wesley's Stories: Afterschool Adventures. 2008. 208p. 24.95 *(978-0-595-50215-8(6))*; pap. 14.95 *(978-0-595-50637-8(2))* iUniverse, Inc.

Stanek, Robert, pseud. Robert Stanek's Bugville Critters Storybook Treasury. 2008. (ENG., Illus.). 132p. (J). per. 24.95 *(978-1-57545-171-8(9))* RP Media.

—Robert Stanek's Bugville Critters Storybook Treasury Volume 2 (the Bugville Critters Storybook Collection, Volume 2), 4 vols., Vol. 2. 2008. (ENG., Illus.). 124p. (J). per. 24.95 *(978-1-57545-173-2(5))* RP Media.

—Student's Classroom Handbook for Robert Stanek's Magic Lands. 2005. (ENG.). 116p. (Orig.). pap. 14.00 *(978-1-57545-035-3(6)*, Ruin Mist Pubns.) RP Media.

Stanfield, Michael. Bucky & Becky - the Magic of Wigglepoo Mountain. 2009. 144p. pap. 14.96 *(978-0-557-02614-2(8))* Lulu Pr., Inc.

Stanley, John. Melvin Monster, Volume 3: The John Stanley Library, 3 vols. 2011. (John Stanley Library). (ENG., Illus.). 112p. 24.95 *(978-1-77046-030-0(6)*, 900072390) Drawn & Quarterly Pubns. CAN. Dist: Macmillan.

Stanwood, Jane. Squeak Jr's Short Stories: Comments & Information. 2008. 140p. pap. 12.95 *(978-1-4327-2819-9(9))* Outskirts Pr., Inc.

Stasse, Lisa M. The Uprising: The Forsaken Trilogy. 2014. (ENG., Illus.). 400p. (YA). (gr. 7). pap. 9.99 *(978-1-4424-3269-7(1)*, Simon & Schuster Bks. For Young Readers) Simon & Schuster Bks. For Young Readers.

Steadman, Pamela M. Hannah Savannah's Favorite Tales. 2005. 78p. (YA). per. 7.95 *(978-1-59196-854-2(2))* Instant Pub.

Steedman, Amy. In God's Garden (Yesterday's Classics) 2006. (J). per. 9.95 *(978-1-59915-032-1(8))* Yesterday's Classics.

—Our Island Saints (Yesterday's Classics) 2006. (J). per. 9.95 *(978-1-59915-031-4(X))* Yesterday's Classics.

Steel, Flora Annie. English Fairy Tales. 2017. (ENG., Illus.). (J). pap. 15.95 *(978-1-374-82021-0(0))* Capital Communications, Inc.

Steele, S. The Tell Me a Story Book. 2007. 116p. per. 13.99 *(978-1-4259-7993-5(9))* AuthorHouse.

Steps To Literacy Staff, compiled by. I Can Read: HFC004. 2005. (ENG., Illus.). (J). pap. *(978-1-59564-721-4(X))* Steps To Literacy, LLC.

Sternfeld, Nathan. Adventures with Rebbe Mendel. Pomerantz, Riva, tr. Bichman, David, illus. 230p. 21.99 *(978-1-58330-550-8(5))* Feldheim Pubs.

Steve Van Der Merwe. Policeman Bobby & Stinky. 2009. (Illus.). 24p. pap. 12.99 *(978-1-4389-6935-0(X))* AuthorHouse.

Stevenson, Charles. The Adventures of the Glo-Worm Family. 2012. (ENG., Illus.). 34p. pap. 9.99 *(978-1-78035-338-8(3)*, Fastprint Publishing) Upfront Publishing Ltd. GBR. Dist: Printondemand-worldwide.com.

Stevenson, Robert Louis. The Merry Men. 2004. 304p. pap. 14.95 *(978-1-59540-514-2(3)*, 1st World Library - Literary Society) 1st World Publishing, Inc.

Stevenson, Suçie, illus. Henry & Mudge Collector's Set (Boxed Set) Henry & Mudge; Henry & Mudge in Puddle Trouble; Henry & Mudge in the Green Time; Henry & Mudge under the Yellow Moon; Henry & Mudge in the Sparkle Days; Henry & Mudge & the Forever Sea. 2014. (Henry & Mudge Ser.). (ENG.). 280p. (J). (gr. k-2). pap. 17.99 *(978-1-4814-2147-8(6)*, Simon Spotlight) Simon Spotlight.

Stine, Faye. The Magic Forest: The Magic of Childhood. 2009. 117p. (J). pap. 10.95 *(978-1-4327-3617-0(5))* Outskirts Pr., Inc.

Stine, R. L. La Hora de Las Pesadillas. Batlles Vinn, Camila, tr. 2005. (Escritura desatada Ser.). (SPA.). 192p. (YA). 10.95 *(978-84-666-0020-0(5))* Ediciones B ESP. Dist: Independent Pubs. Group.

—Nightmare Hour TV Tie-In Edition. movie tie-in ed. 2011. (ENG.). 160p. (J). (gr. 3). pap. 7.99 *(978-0-06-210692-6(9)*, HarperCollins) HarperCollins Pubs.

—Temptation: Goodnight Kiss; Goodnight Kiss 2; "the Vampire Club" 2012. (ENG.). 416p. (YA). (gr. 7). pap. 11.99 *(978-1-4424-5068-4(1)*, Simon Pulse) Simon Pulse.

Stockham, Jess, illus. The Boy Who Cried Wolf. 2011. (Flip-Up Fairy Tales Ser.). 24p. (J). (gr. 2-2). *(978-1-84643-368-9(1))* Child's Play International Ltd.

—Dentist. 2011. (First Time Ser.). 24p. (J). (gr. 2-2). pap. *(978-1-84643-335-1(5))* Child's Play International Ltd.

—Doctor. 2011. (First Time Ser.). 24p. (J). (gr. 2-2). pap. *(978-1-84643-334-4(7))* Child's Play International Ltd.

—Hospital. 2011. (First Time Ser.). 24p. (J). (gr. 2-2). pap. *(978-1-84643-336-8(3))* Child's Play International Ltd.

—Moving Day! 2011. (Helping Hands Ser.). 24p. (J). *(978-1-84643-414-3(9))* Child's Play International Ltd.

—Recycling! 2011. (Helping Hands Ser.). 24p. (J). *(978-1-84643-415-0(7))* Child's Play International Ltd.

—Shopping! 2011. (Helping Hands Ser.). 24p. (J). *(978-1-84643-412-9(2))* Child's Play International Ltd.

—Vet. 2011. (First Time Ser.). 24p. (J). (gr. 2-2). pap. *(978-1-84643-337-5(1))* Child's Play International Ltd.

Stockton, Frank Richard. The Bee-Man of Orn & Other Fanciful Tales. 2007. (ENG.). 140p. pap. 18.99 *(978-1-4264-5788-3(X))* Creative Media Partners, LLC.

—John Gayther's Garden & the Stories Told Therein. 2008. 220p. 26.95 *(978-1-60664-746-2(6))* Rodgers, Alan Bks.

—The Lady or the Tiger. 2008. (Creative Short Stories Ser.). (Illus.). 32p. (J). lib. bdg. 28.50 *(978-1-58341-583-2(1)*, Creative Education) Creative Co., The.

Stokes, Brenda. Bella's Blessings. 2012. (ENG., Illus.). 50p. (J). (gr. -1-3). 17.95 *(978-1-897476-61-1(2))* Simply Read Bks. CAN. Dist: Ingram Publisher Services.

Stop! & Other Stories: Individual Title Six-Pack. (Story Steps Ser.). (gr. k-2). 42.00 *(978-0-7635-9592-0(6))* Rigby Education.

Stories & Fables from Around the World, 6 vols. 2016. (Stories & Fables from Around the World Ser.). 24p. (ENG.). (gr. 1-2). 78.81 *(978-1-4994-8118-1(7)*, 2c0aecdb-3229-452b-a835-b8f1ca5d1273); (gr. 2-1). pap. 24.75 *(978-1-4994-8128-0(4))* Rosen Publishing Group, Inc., The. (Windmill Bks.).

Stories from el Barrio. 2nd rev. ed. 2005. 135p. (YA). (gr. 9). per. 19.95 *(978-0-915117-11-6(8))* Freedom Voices Pubns.

Storm, Zed. Will Solvit & the Cannibal Cavemen. 2010. (Will Solvit Ser.: Bk. 5). (Illus.). 128p. (J). (gr. 1-7). pap. *(978-1-4075-8983-1(0))* Parragon, Inc.

—Will Solvit & the Deadly Gladiator. 2010. (Will Solvit Ser.: Bk. 6). (Illus.). 128p. (J). (gr. 1-7). pap. *(978-1-4075-8984-8(9))* Parragon, Inc.

—Will Solvit & the Dreaded Droids. 2010. (Will Solvit Ser.: Bk. 4). (Illus.). 128p. (J). (gr. 1-7). pap. *(978-1-4075-8980-0(6))* Parragon, Inc.

—Will Solvit & the Mission of Menace. 2010. (Will Solvit Ser.: Bk. 2). (Illus.). 128p. (J). (gr. 1-7). pap. *(978-1-4075-8981-7(4))* Parragon, Inc.

—Will Solvit & the Mummy's Curse. 2010. (Will Solvit Ser.: Bk. 3). (Illus.). 128p. (J). (gr. 1-7). pap. *(978-1-4075-8979-4(2))* Parragon, Inc.

—Will Solvit & the T-Rex Terror. 2010. (Will Solvit Ser.: Bk. 1). (Illus.). 128p. (J). (gr. 1-7). pap. *(978-1-4075-8982-4(2))* Parragon, Inc.

Stover, Anne Long. Cloudy. Spears, Ashley E., illus. 2005. 20p. (J). *(978-0-9762389-0-4(X))* Trent's Prints.

Stowe, Harriet. Betty's Bright Idea. 2006. pap. *(978-1-4068-3093-4(3))* Echo Library.

—The First Christmas of New England & O. 2006. 108p. per. 9.95 *(978-1-59818-758-8(9))* Aegypan.

Strasser, Todd. Nighttime: Too Dark to See. Cushman, Doug, illus. 2008. 79p. (J). *(978-0-439-80068-6(4))* Scholastic, Inc.

Strauss, Kevin. Loon & Moon: And Other Animal Stories. Scheibe, Nancy, illus. 2005. 48p. (J). (gr. 4-6). per. 12.95 *(978-0-9766264-3-5(8))* Raven Productions, Inc.

Strong, Abigail. Troggins Tales. 2010. 60p. pap. 34.95 *(978-1-4457-1581-0(3))* Lulu Pr., Inc.

Stuart, Elizabeth Billings. Delightful Stories for Children. 2013. (ENG., Illus.). 142p. (J). (gr. k-6). 26.95 *(978-0-911845-70-9(4)*, NP9070, Neumann Pr.) TAN Bks.

Students, Liberty Elementary School. Patriot Pages, Liberty Elementary School. 2010. 142p. pap. 12.95 *(978-1-936051-95-3(8))* Peppertree Pr., The.

Studio Mouse Staff. Puppy Dog Tails. 2005. (Read-Aloud Board Book Ser.). (ENG., Illus.). 12p. (J). (gr. -1-3). 12.95 *(978-1-59249-474-3(9)*, 1D101) Soundprints.

Sturt, M. Canterbury Pilgrims. 2007. pap. *(978-1-4068-3599-1(4))* Echo Library.

Stuve-Bodeen, Stephanie. Mama Elizabeti, Vol. 1. 2005. (Elizabeti Ser.). (ENG., Illus.). 32p. (J). (gr. -1-2). pap. 10.95 *(978-1-58430-236-0(4)*, leelowbooks) Lee & Low Bks., Inc.

Sullivan, Jean. The Blakely Field Stories. 2005. 58p. pap. 16.95 *(978-1-4137-8611-8(1))* PublishAmerica, Inc.

Summer & Winter: Individual Title Six-Packs. (Story Steps Ser.). (gr. k-2). 32.00 *(978-0-7635-9809-9(7))* Rigby Education.

Summer Sands, 6 vols., Set B. 32p. (gr. 1-3). 31.50 *(978-0-7802-8054-0(7))* Wright Group/McGraw-Hill.

Summers, Everette. Grandaddy's Short Stories. 2006. 48p. pap. 16.95 *(978-1-4241-2468-8(9))* PublishAmerica, Inc.

Suparna. The Science Playground: Fun with Science Concepts & Nature. 2009. (ENG.). 46p. pap. 24.99 *(978-1-4389-3466-2(1))* AuthorHouse.

Suresh, Shreyas. The Magic Lighthouse & other Stories. 2010. 49p. pap. 23.50 *(978-0-557-36448-0(5))* Lulu Pr., Inc.

The Surf Trilogy. 2003. (YA). per. 39.95 *(978-0-9640858-5-5(2))* Perelandra Publishing Co.

Surprise! Individual Title Six-Packs. (Story Steps Ser.). (gr. k-2). 32.00 *(978-0-7635-9605-7(1))* Rigby Education.

Surprises & Other Stories: Individual Title Six-Pack. (Story Steps Ser.). (gr. k-2). 48.00 *(978-0-7635-9818-1(6))* Rigby Education.

Surviving Southside, 6 vols., Set. Incl. Benito Runs. Fontes, Justine. lib. bdg. 27.99 *(978-0-7613-6151-0(0)*, 1e02666c-1414-4f2b-9c03-e05b4294b401); Shattered Star. Simon, Chaman. lib. bdg. 27.99 *(978-0-7613-6154-1(5)*, 1a8163e0-50cc-490f-9aa9-787901e7c8fd); 104p. (YA). (gr. 6-12). (Surviving Southside Ser.). (ENG.). 2011. Set lib. bdg. 335.16 *(978-0-7613-6148-0(0)*, Darby Creek) Lerner Publishing Group.

Sutcliff, Rosemary. Heather, Oak, & Olive: Three Stories. Ambrus, Victor, illus. 2015. (ENG.). 120p. (J). (gr. 3-6). pap. 11.95 *(978-1-58988-106-8(0))* Dry, Paul Bks., Inc.

Sutton, Kay. Nan & Grandad's Book of Short Stories. 2009. (Illus.). 52p. pap. 20.49 *(978-1-4490-0575-7(6))* AuthorHouse.

Swain, Gwenyth & Whelan, Gloria. Voices for Freedom. Geister, David et al, illus. 2013. (American Adventures Ser.). (ENG.). 72p. (J). (gr. 3-6). 6.99 *(978-1-58536-886-0(5)*, 202900) Sleeping Bear Pr.

Swan, Bill. Man-To-Man, 1 vol. 2009. (Lorimer Sports Stories Ser.). (ENG.). 144p. (J). (gr. 4-8). 16.95 *(978-1-55277-443-4(0)*, 443) James Lorimer & Co. Ltd., Pubs. CAN. Dist: Formac Lorimer Bks. Ltd.

Swan, Richard. The Listeners. 2009. (Illus.). 64p. pap. 10.49 *(978-1-4389-6224-5(X))* AuthorHouse.

Swanson, Maggie. Best-Loved Aesop's Fables Coloring Book. 2015. (Dover Classic Stories Coloring Book Ser.). (ENG.). 48p. (J). (gr. k-4). pap. 4.99 *(978-0-486-79747-2(3)*, 797473) Dover Pubns., Inc.

Sweeney, Samantha, et al. My First Farm Stories. Harry, Rebecca, illus. 2018. (ENG.). 44p. (J). (gr. -1-k). bds. 9.99 *(978-1-68010-544-5(2))* Tiger Tales.

Swenson, Dianne. An Ended Friendship: And Other Short Stories. 2006. (Fast Track Ser.). (Illus.). 98p. (YA). (gr. 8-12). lib. bdg. 12.25 *(978-0-8124-0632-0(X))* Perfection Learning Corp.

Swift, K. Marie. The Adventures of Jake & George: Jake Gets a New Brother. Paul, Kate, illus. 2010. 26p. pap. 11.75 *(978-1-60693-863-8(0)*, Eloquent Bks.) Strategic Book Publishing & Rights Agency (SBPRA).

Swindells, Robert. Doodlebug Alley. (ENG., Illus.). 56p. (J). pap. 6.99 *(978-0-7497-3860-0(X))* Farshore GBR. Dist: Trafalgar Square Publishing.

Swindells, Robert, et al. Cuentos de Terror. (SPA.). (YA). 8.95 *(978-958-04-3392-7(5))* Norma S.A. COL. Dist: Distribuidora Norma, Inc.

Szarka, Balazs. European Folk Tales. 2009. 60p. pap. 22.00 *(978-1-60860-432-6(2)*, Eloquent Bks.) Strategic Book Publishing & Rights Agency (SBPRA).

Tago, Anita. Traditional Stories from Binandere in Oro Province, Papua New Guinea. 2012. 44p. pap. *(978-9980-945-71-6(0))* Univ. of Papua New Guinea Pr.

Tagore, Rabindranath. He (Shey) Chaudhuri, Aparna, tr. 2007. (ENG., Illus.). 176p. (gr. 12-18). 19.95 *(978-0-14-310209-0(5)*, Penguin Global) Penguin Publishing Group.

Talbert, Marc. Doble o Nada. (Torre de Papel Ser.). (SPA.). (J). (gr. 4-18). 7.95 *(978-958-04-2384-3(9))* Norma S.A. COL. Dist: Distribuidora Norma, Inc.

Tales of Twinkle & Peeps. 2017. (ENG., Illus.). 176p. (J). 9.00 *(978-1-78270-145-3(1))* Award Pubns. Ltd. GBR. Dist: Parkwest Pubns., Inc.

Tamayo, Alex. Horizons Set 1, 5 books. Shea, Steve, ed. 2013. (Illus.). 48p. (YA). pap. 24.00 *(978-1-57128-809-7(0))* High Noon Bks.

Tan, Shaun. Lost & Found: Three by Shaun Tan. Tan, Shaun, illus. 2011. (ENG., Illus.). 128p. (J). (gr. 7-7). 24.99 *(978-0-545-22924-1(3)*, Levine, Arthur A. Bks.) Scholastic, Inc.

—Tales from Outer Suburbia. 2009. (J). pap. *(978-0-545-05588-8(1)*, Levine, Arthur A. Bks.) Scholastic, Inc.

—Tales from Outer Suburbia. Tan, Shaun, illus. 2009. (ENG., Illus.). 96p. (J). (gr. 7-18). 22.99 *(978-0-545-05587-1(3)*, Levine, Arthur A. Bks.) Scholastic, Inc.

—Tales from the Inner City. 2018. (ENG., Illus.). 224p. (J). (gr. 7-7). 24.99 *(978-1-338-29840-6(2)*, Levine, Arthur A. Bks.) Scholastic, Inc.

Taplin, Sam. Baby's Bedtime Storybook CV. 2011. (Baby Board Bks). 10p. (J). ring bd. 17.99 *(978-0-7945-3096-9(6)*, Usborne) EDC Publishing.

—Night-Night Stories. 2009. (Bedtime Board Books (with Bedtime Rhymes) Ser.). 12p. (J). bds. 12.99 *(978-0-7945-2364-0(1)*, Usborne) EDC Publishing.

—Sleepytime Stories. Chaira, Francesca di, illus. 2011. (Baby Board Books Ser.). 12p. (J). ring bd. 12.99 *(978-0-7945-3006-8(0)*, Usborne) EDC Publishing.

Tario, Francisco. Entre Nosches y Fantasmas. Esquivel, Isidro R., illus. 2016. (SPA.). 120p. (YA). 13.99 *(978-607-16-4268-4(X))* Fondo de Cultura Economica USA.

Tarkington, Booth. Beasley's Christmas Party. 2005. 76p. pap. 10.95 *(978-1-4218-0407-1(7)*, 1st World Library - Literary Society) 1st World Publishing, Inc.

—Beasley's Christmas Party. Clements, Ruth Sypherd, illus. 2004. reprint ed. pap. 15.95 *(978-1-4179-0186-9(1))* Kessinger Publishing, LLC.

—Beasley's Christmas Party. 2004. reprint ed. pap. 1.99 *(978-1-4192-0925-3(6))* Kessinger Publishing, LLC.

Tatulli, Mark. Desmond Pucket Makes Monster Magic. 2013. (Desmond Pucket Ser.: 1). (ENG.). 240p. (J). 13.99 *(978-1-4494-3548-6(3))* Andrews McMeel Publishing.

Tauiliili, Pemerika L. The Rat & the Bat: And Other Short Stories. 2009. 88p. pap. 16.99 *(978-1-4490-4389-6(5))*; pap. 32.49 *(978-1-4389-2700-8(2))* AuthorHouse.

Taylor, Catherine. Thirst, 1 vol. 2005. (ENG.). 224p. (YA). (gr. 7-9). per. 9.95 *(978-1-55005-107-0(5)*, 06aa09a4-4624-427c-bb70-e10f632699e3) éditeur, Annika Parance CAN. Dist: Firefly Bks., Ltd.

Taylor, Clifford. Taylor's Tales. 2004. 108p. 20.95 *(978-0-595-66558-7(6))* iUniverse, Inc.

Taylor-Gaines, Lonnetta. Fia & the Butterfly: 7 Stories for Character Education. 2005. 13.00 *(978-0-8059-9848-1(9))* Dorrance Publishing Co., Inc.

Taylor, Gaylia. George Crum & the Saratoga Chip, 1 vol. Morrison, Frank, illus. 2006. (ENG.). 32p. (J). (gr. 1-5). pap. 11.95 *(978-1-60060-656-4(3)*, leelowbooks) Lee & Low Bks., Inc.

Taylor, Kenneth N. Family-Time Bible in Pictures. 2007. (ENG., Illus.). 320p. (J). (gr. -1-1). 12.99 *(978-1-4143-1577-5(5)*, 4600434) Tyndale Hse. Pubs.

Taylor, Laini. Lips Touch: Three Times. Di Bartolo, Jim, illus. 2011. (ENG.). 288p. (YA). (gr. 7-7). pap. 14.99 *(978-0-545-05586-4(5)*, Levine, Arthur A. Bks.) Scholastic, Inc.

Taylor, R. W. The Curiosity of Sadie: A Collection of 35 Individual Stories about an Individual Little Girl & Her Puppy. 2011. 172p. (gr. 4-6). pap. 15.66 *(978-1-4567-8202-3(9))* AuthorHouse.

Taylor, Vincent. Cornbread Runs for Class President Griffin, Kasana & Griggs, Charles, eds. Latorre, Adolfo, illus. 2004. (Cornbread Ser.: 1). 96p. (J). per. 4.99 *(978-0-9704512-4-8(5))* TriEclipse, Inc.

Taylor, William. At the Big Red Rooster. 160p. (YA). (gr. 8-18). pap. *(978-1-877135-20-0(8)*, Longacre Pr.) Random Hse. New Zealand.

Tegen, Katherine. The Story of the Leprechaun. Lambert, Sally Anne, illus. 2011. (ENG.). 40p. (J). (gr. -1-3). 12.99 *(978-0-06-143086-2(2)*, HarperCollins) HarperCollins Pubs.

Tegen, Katherine Brown. The Story of the Leprechaun. Lambert, Sally Anne, illus. 2011. (J). lib. bdg. 14.89 *(978-0-06-143085-5(4))* HarperCollins Pubs.

Templeton Elementary Students. Tales from Templeton III. 2007. 108p. per. 15.95 *(978-0-9790446-6-3(9))* Pen & Publish, LLC.

Ten Little Ducks & Other Stories: Individual Title Six-Pack. (Story Steps Ser.). (gr. k-2). 48.00 *(978-0-7635-9798-6(8))* Rigby Education.

Terhune, Albert Payson. Buff, a Collie & Other Dog Stories. 2007. 348p. per. 18.95 *(978-1-59462-809-2(2)*, Bk. Jungle) Standard Publications, Inc.

Tesler, Ellen. Zeke in Central Park. 2010. 32p. pap. 12.99 *(978-1-4490-7211-7(9))* AuthorHouse.

Tetzlaff, Wendy Jo. A Girl Named Frannie. 2008. 28p. pap. 24.95 *(978-1-60703-055-3(1))* America Star Bks.

A These Old Rags Set, 6 vols. 32p. (gr. 1-3). 31.50 *(978-0-7802-8040-3(7))* Wright Group/McGraw-Hill.

Thomas, Amy Maude. Stories in My Eyes. 2011. 20p. pap. 7.99 *(978-1-936750-04-7(X))* Yorkshire Publishing Group.

Thomas, Gene. Tales from the Tree House. 2011. 112p. (gr. 10-12). 20.95 *(978-1-4620-1864-2(5))*; pap. 10.95 *(978-1-4620-1863-5(7))* iUniverse, Inc.

Thomas, Jatavius. Weird Things Happening at Southside Middle School: And Other Stories. 2010. 52p. pap. 8.95 *(978-1-4502-4049-9(6))* iUniverse, Inc.

Thomas, Rob & Macaya, Leopoldo. Doing Time: Notes from the Undergrad. 2018. (ENG.). 176p. (YA). (gr. 7). pap. 10.99 *(978-1-5344-3009-9(1)*, Simon & Schuster Bks. For Young Readers) Simon & Schuster Bks. For Young Readers.

Thomas, Teri. Bus 99, 1 vol. unabr. ed. 2010. (Q Reads Ser.). (ENG.). 32p. (YA). (gr. 9-12). pap. 8.50 *(978-1-61651-214-9(8))* Saddleback Educational Publishing, Inc.

Thomas, Terri & Greene, Janice. Dimes to Dollars, 1 vol. unabr. ed. 2010. (Q Reads Ser.). (ENG.). 32p. (YA). (gr. 9-12). pap. 8.50 *(978-1-61651-217-0(2))* Saddleback Educational Publishing, Inc.

Thomas the Tank Engine. 2012. *(978-0-7948-3764-8(6))* Farshore.

Thompson, Carol. Come to Me, My Chickadee! 2010. (Illus.). 24p. (J). pap. *(978-1-84643-188-3(3))* Child's Play International Ltd.

Thompson, Colin. The Floods Family Files. Thompson, Colin, illus. 2012. (Floods Ser.: 1). (ENG., Illus.). 32p. (J). (gr. 4-7). pap. 12.99 *(978-1-86471-942-0(7))* Random Hse. Australia AUS. Dist: Independent Pubs. Group.

Thompson, Susan A., et al. Mayan Folktales, Cuentos Folklóricos Mayas, 1 vol. 2007. (World Folklore Ser.). (ENG., Illus.). 236p. 60.00 *(978-1-59158-138-3(9)*, 900303856, Libraries Unlimited) Bloomsbury Publishing USA.

Thompson, Tolya L. Ingrown Tyrone. Brian, Harrold, illus. 2004. (Smarties Ser.: 4). 33p. (J). 16.00 *(978-0-9708296-2-7(0))* Savor Publishing Hse., Inc.

Thury, Fredrick H. Hoshmakaka. van Kampen, Vlasta, illus. 2003.Tr. of Last Straw. (SPA.). (J). (gr. 2-4). 13.56 *(978-84-8418-046-3(8))* Zendrera Zariquiey, Editorial ESP. Dist: Lectorum Pubns., Inc.

Tibbets, Albert B. Youth, Youth, Youth: Stories of Challenge, Confidence & Comradeship. Tibbets, Albert B., ed. 2011. 256p. 47.95 *(978-1-258-05880-7(4))* Literary Licensing, LLC.

Tiddle, Deanna Hessedal. Apartment Horse & Friends. 2003. 62p. (J). pap. 9.95 *(978-0-7414-1724-4(3))* Infinity Publishing.

TIG, Thomas. Illustrated Treasury of Classic Stories. Kelly, Richard, ed. 2017. (Illus.). 384p. (J). 39.95 *(978-1-78209-985-7(9))* Miles Kelly Publishing, Ltd. GBR. Dist: Parkwest Pubns., Inc.

Tillman, Nancy. You Are Loved Collection. Tillman, Nancy, illus. 2012. (ENG., Illus.). 96p. (J). (gr. k-1). 53.97 *(978-1-250-01135-0(3)*, 900084994) Feiwel & Friends.

Tingle, Tim & Moore, Doc. More Spooky Texas Tales. Benas, Jeanne, illus. 2010. (ENG.). 104p. (gr. 4-6). lib. bdg. 18.95 *(978-0-89672-700-7(9)*, P200878) Texas Tech Univ. Pr.

Tingle, Tim & Moore, James W. Spooky Texas Tales. Miller, Gina, illus. 2005. x, 85p. (J). pap. *(978-0-89672-566-9(9))* Texas Tech Univ. Pr.

Tokyopop and Art Impression Staff & Peymani, Christine. Skelanimals Vol. 1: It's a Wonderful Afterlife. 2011. (Illus.). 36p. 9.99 *(978-1-4278-3255-9(2))* TOKYOPOP, Inc.

Toler, Violet M. Churchmouse Tales: Puppet Plays, 10 vols., Vol. 2. Koefler, Leatha, illus. 2nd rev. ed. 2004. Orig. Title: "Puppet Plays, Adventures of Charlie & His Friends". (J). (gr. -1-6). pap. 10.95 *(978-0-9749749-1-0(9))* Wayside Pubns.

Tolstoy, Leo. The Lion & the Puppy: And Other Stories for Children. Riordan, James, tr. Sievert, Claus, illus. 2012. (ENG.). 76p. (J). (gr. 4-7). 16.95 *(978-1-61608-484-4(7)*, 608484, Sky Pony Pr.) Skyhorse Publishing Co., Inc.

Tomaselli, Mela. The Magic Pot: Folk Tales & Legends of the Giriama of Kenya. 2004. (Illus.). 80p. *(978-9966-21-950-3(1))* Paulines Pubns., Africa.

Tome. Spirou & Fantasio in New York. Janry, illus. 2011. (Spirou & Fantasio Ser.: 2). 48p. (J). (gr. 3-17). pap. 11.95 *(978-1-84918-054-2(7))* CineBook GBR. Dist: National Bk. Network.

A Tonka Tale. 2004. (J). *(978-0-9767179-1-1(3))* ABC Development, Inc.

Too-Tight Shoes, 6 vols. 2004. 32p. (gr. 1-3). 31.50 *(978-0-322-00337-8(7))* Wright Group/McGraw-Hill.

A Too-Tight Shoes Set, 6 vols. 32p. (gr. 1-3). 26.50 *(978-0-7802-8042-7(3))* Wright Group/McGraw-Hill.

La Tormenta de Truenos; Aventura en la Oscuridad, 2 bks., Set. (Coleccion Chiquilines - Imagen y Sonido). (SPA., Illus.). (J). 15.95 incl. audio *(978-950-11-0624-4(1)*, SGM241) Sigmar ARG. Dist: Continental Bk. Co., Inc.

Tormont Publications Inc., des. Perfect Presents, 20 bks. (Illus.). 40p. (J). vinyl bd. *(978-2-7641-1284-7(X))* Tormont Pubns.

Torres, Eliseo & Sawyer, Timothy L. Stories of Mexico's Independence Days & Other Bilingual Children's Fables. Ramirez, Herman, illus. 2005. (ENG.). 70p. (J). (gr. 3-7). pap. 16.95 *(978-0-8263-3886-0(0)*, P123362) Univ. of New Mexico Pr.

Torres, Mario. My Fun Wonderworld: Children's Stories Book, 1 vol. 2009. 74p. pap. 19.95 *(978-1-61582-704-6(8))* America Star Bks.

Tötemeyer, Andree-Jeanne. Under the Story Tree: Readathon Stories. 2005. (Illus.). 93p. *(978-99916-0-509-8(6))* Namibian Children's Bk. Forum.

Travesuras y Aventuras. 2003. (SPA.). pap. *(978-956-13-1045-2(7)*, AB8007) Bello, Andres CHL. Dist: Lectorum Pubns., Inc.

Treadwell, Harriette Taylor & Free, Margaret. The Primer. 2009. (Illus.). 118p. pap. *(978-1-904808-26-8(3))* Evertype.

El Trencito de los Cuentos. (Coleccion Estrella). (SPA., Illus.). 64p. (YA). 14.95 *(978-950-11-0018-1(9)*, SGM018) Sigmar ARG. Dist: Continental Bk. Co., Inc.

Las Tres Naranjas de la Vida. (Coleccion Fabulas y Cuentos Populares). (SPA.). (J). (gr. 2-4). *(978-84-246-1627-4(8)*, GL1107) La Galera, S.A. Editorial ESP. Dist: Lectorum Pubns., Inc.

Trilling, Richard J. Still More Stories of Stephanie & Friends: Volume 3 in the Stephanie Series. 2011. 72p. pap. 21.00 *(978-1-61204-546-7(4)*, Strategic Bk. Publishing) Strategic Book Publishing & Rights Agency (SBPRA).

Trinidad Joe. Santa's Key West Vacation. 2007. (Illus.). 80p. per. 12.95 *(978-0-9799474-0-7(5))* Seastory Pr.

Tripp, Valerie. Felicity Story Collection. Andreasen, Dan, illus. 2008. (ENG.). 404p. (J). 29.95 *(978-1-59369-452-4(0))* American Girl Publishing, Inc.

—Molly Story Collection. Backes, Nick, illus. 2004. (ENG.). 388p. 29.95 *(978-1-59369-458-6(X))* American Girl Publishing, Inc.

Trotter, Bob. Up the Wooden Hill: Bedtime Stories for Little Ones. Edgar, Barrie, illus. 2011. 98p. pap. 17.99 *(978-1-60976-139-4(1)*, Eloquent Bks.) Strategic Book Publishing & Rights Agency (SBPRA).

Trudell, Devin, illus. 3 Stories. Trudell, Devin, . 2007. (YA). 10.00 *(978-0-9794004-0-7(6))* Art Night Bks.

Truman, Dennay H. The Happy Endings. 2007. 65p. per. 8.95 *(978-1-59824-435-9(3))* E-BookTime LLC.

Tsaliovich, Anatoly. Of Wolves & Lambs & Others. Burke, Daniel, illus. 2005. 73p. (YA). pap. 12.99 *(978-0-9773816-0-9(9))* ATInternational Pubs.

Tulik, Alice, et al. Fishing Adventures. Tulik, Alice et al, illus. 2006. (Adventure Story Collection Ser.). 36p. (J). (gr. 2-6). pap. 12.00 *(978-1-58084-248-8(8))* Lower Kuskokwim Schl. District.

Turan, Kemal. Essence of Wisdom. 2011. 200p. (J). (gr. 7-10). pap. 13.95 *(978-1-59784-263-1(X)*, Tughra Bks.) Blue Dome, Inc.

Turner, Megan Whalen. Instead of Three Wishes: Magical Short Stories. 2006. (ENG.). 160p. (J). (gr. 5-9). per. 6.99 *(978-0-06-084231-4(8)*, Greenwillow Bks.) HarperCollins Pubs.

Turpin, Nick. Molly Is New. Raga, Silvia, illus. 2010. 32p. pap. *(978-1-84089-650-3(7))* Zero to Ten, Ltd.

Twain, Mark, pseud & Clemens, Samuel L. The Prince & the Pauper. 2013. (Works of Mark Twain). 425p. reprint ed. lthr. 79.00 *(978-0-7812-1120-8(4))* Reprint Services Corp.

Twain, Mark, pseud & Lawson, Jessica. The Tom Sawyer Collection: The Adventures of Tom Sawyer; the Adventures of Huckleberry Finn; the Actual & Truthful Adventures of Becky Thatcher. Bruno, Iacopo, illus. 2014. (ENG.). 944p. (J). (gr. 3-7). 52.99 *(978-1-4814-0536-2(5)*, Simon & Schuster Bks. For Young Readers) Simon & Schuster Bks. For Young Readers.

Tyler, Jenny. Animal Stories for Little Children. 2011. (Picture Books Ser.). 136p. (J). ring bd. 18.99 *(978-0-7945-2632-0(2)*, Usborne) EDC Publishing.

Tyler, Jenny & Doherty, Gillian, eds. Usborne Stories for Little Boys. 2008. (Picture Books Ser.). (Illus.). 135p. (J). (gr. -1-3). 18.99 *(978-0-7945-1973-5(3)*, Usborne) EDC Publishing.

Tyree, Omar R. 12 Brown Boys. 2008. 196p. (J). (gr. 3-7). pap. 9.95 *(978-1-933491-12-7(4))* Just Us Bks., Inc.

Tyson, Leigh Ann. Good Night, Little Dragons. 2012. (Little Golden Book Ser.). (Illus.). 24p. (J). (gr. k-k). 5.99 *(978-0-307-92957-0(4)*, Golden Bks.) Random Hse. Children's Bks.

Umezawa, Rui. Strange Light Afar: Tales of the Supernatural from Old Japan, 1 vol. Fujita, Mikiko, illus. 2015. (ENG.). 160p. (YA). (gr. 6). 18.95 *(978-1-55498-723-8(7))* Groundwood Bks. CAN. Dist: Publishers Group West (PGW).

Uncle Bernie. Michaels Adventures in the Land of Nod Book: Michaels Trip to Orange County. 2008. 32p. pap. 12.99 *(978-1-4389-1097-0(5))* AuthorHouse.

Under the Big Green Umbrella. 2008. (J). spiral bd. *(978-0-9793930-4-4(3))* Dandelion Publishing.

Ure, Jean. Is Anybody There? 2004. (ENG., Illus.). 192p. (J). (gr. 4-7). pap. 9.95 *(978-0-00-716136-2(0)*, HarperCollins Children's Bks.) HarperCollins Pubs. Ltd. GBR. Dist: HarperCollins Pubs.

Urish, J. D. The Adventures of Rex Bolton Volume 1. 2009. (ENG.). 60p. pap. 9.98 *(978-0-578-03676-2(2))* Jentmedia.

Urrea, Lourdes. Calle Secreto Numero 31. 2005. (Ediciones Castillo Castillo Del Terror Ser.). (SPA.). 119p. (J). (gr. 4-7). per. 7.95 *(978-970-20-0187-4(0))* Castillo, Ediciones, S. A. de C. V. MEX. Dist: Iaconi, Mariuccia Bk. Imports.

—Huellas en la Escalera. rev. ed. 2007. (Ediciones Castillo Castillo Del Terror Ser.). (SPA & ENG.). 120p. (J). (gr. 4-7). pap. 6.95 *(978-970-20-0243-7(5))* Castillo, Ediciones, S. A. de C. V. MEX. Dist: Macmillan.

—El Mago. rev. ed. 2003. (Ediciones Castillo Castillo Del Terror Ser.). (SPA & ENG.). 112p. (J). (gr. 2-6). pap. 6.95 *(978-970-20-0189-8(7))* Castillo, Ediciones, S. A. de C. V. MEX. Dist: Macmillan.

—El Nino de la Ventana. rev. ed. 2005. (Castillo del Terror Ser.). (SPA & ENG.). 312p. (J). (gr. -1-7). pap. 6.95 *(978-970-20-0188-1(9))* Castillo, Ediciones, S. A. de C. V. MEX. Dist: Macmillan.

—Vacaciones Mortales. rev. ed. 2007. (Ediciones Castillo Castillo Del Terror Ser.). (SPA & ENG.). 120p. (J). (gr. 6-9). pap. 6.95 *(978-970-20-0248-2(6))* Castillo, Ediciones, S. A. de C. V. MEX. Dist: Macmillan.

Urrea, Luis. Gruta Encantada. 2005. (Ediciones Castillo Castillo Del Terror Ser.). (SPA.). (J). (gr. 2-6). pap. 7.95 *(978-970-20-0244-4(3))* Castillo, Ediciones, S. A. de C. V. MEX. Dist: Iaconi, Mariuccia Bk. Imports.

Urrea, Luis Alberto & Urrea, Lourdes. Silencio en el Castillo. rev. ed. 2006. (Ediciones Castillo Castillo Del Terror Ser.). (SPA & ENG.). 116p. (J). (gr. 2-6). pap. 6.95 *(978-970-20-0247-5(8))* Castillo, Ediciones, S. A. de C. V. MEX. Dist: Macmillan.

V., Patti. My Na Na Stories. 2005. 18.00 *(978-0-8059-9806-1(3))* Dorrance Publishing Co., Inc.

Vallejo-Nagera, Alejandra. Cuanto me Quieren! Guerrero, Andres, illus. 2003. (SPA.). 23p. (J). (gr. k-1). 8.95 *(978-84-204-4951-7(2))* Santillana USA Publishing Co., Inc.

Van Allsburg, Chris. The Chronicles of Harris Burdick: Fourteen Amazing Authors Tell the Tales. 2011. (Playaway Young Adult Ser.). (ENG.). (J). (gr. 5-9). 69.99 *(978-1-4558-4373-2(3))* Findaway World, LLC.

Van Allsburg, Chris, et al. The Chronicles of Harris Burdick: Fourteen Amazing Authors Tell the Tales / with an Introduction by Lemony Snicket. Van Allsburg, Chris, illus. 2011. (ENG., Illus.). 208p. (J). (gr. 5-7). 25.99 *(978-0-547-54810-4(9)*, 1449313, Clarion Bks.) HarperCollins Pubs.

Van Horn, William, et al. Walt Disney's Comics. Clark, John, ed. 2006. (ENG., Illus.). 64p. Vol. 664. pap. 6.95 *(978-1-888472-17-2(0)*, 9781888472172) Vol. 667. pap. 6.95 *(978-1-888472-20-2(0)*, 9781888472202) Gemstone Publishing, Inc.

Vance, Elsbet, ed. & illus. Mistletoe Madness: A Short Story Collection. Vance, Elsbet, illus. 2004. (ENG.). 384p. (J). (gr. 1-5). pap. 8.95 *(978-0-9718348-2-8(2))* Blooming Tree Pr.

VanCe, Lilo. Once upon a Time & Other Stories. 2012. 52p. *(978-1-4602-0740-6(8))*; pap. *(978-1-4602-0738-3(6))* FriesenPress.

Vande Velde, Vivian. All Hallows' Eve: 13 Stories. 2010. (ENG., Illus.). 240p. (YA). (gr. 7). pap. 8.99 *(978-0-15-206473-0(7)*, 1199331, Clarion Bks.) HarperCollins Pubs.

—Curses, Inc. & Other Stories. 2007. (ENG., Illus.). 240p. (YA). (gr. 7-12). pap. 12.95 *(978-0-15-206107-4(X)*, 1198344, Clarion Bks.) HarperCollins Pubs.

—The Rumpelstiltskin Problem. 2013. (ENG.). 128p. (J). (gr. 5-7). pap. 5.99 *(978-0-544-10486-0(2)*, 1540795, Clarion Bks.) HarperCollins Pubs.

Various, illus. Let's Read with Dora! 2010. (Dora the Explorer Ser.). (ENG.). 144p. (J). (gr. -1-1). pap. 7.99 *(978-1-4169-9742-9(3)*, Simon Spotlight/Nickelodeon) Simon Spotlight/Nickelodeon.

Varonka, Steve. Hard Coal Times: Pennsylvania Anthracite Stories, Vol. 1. 2003. (Illus.). 40p. (J). 4.72 *(978-0-9709630-2-4(5))* Coal Hole Productions.

Vasco, Irene. El Dedo de Estefania y Otros Cuentos. 2003.Tr. of Estefania's Finger & Other Tales. (SPA., Illus.). 47p. (J). (gr. k-3). *(978-958-8061-54-2(7))* Distribuidora y Editora Aguilar, Altea, Taurus en el Sello Alfaguara S.A.

Vaz, Megan X. A Melody of Short Stories. 2011. 28p. pap. 12.03 *(978-1-4634-2651-4(8))* AuthorHouse.

Velvin, Ellen. Rataplan, a Rogue Elephant & Other Stories. 2007. 96p. per. *(978-1-4068-1627-3(2))* Echo Library.

Verma, Monika. My Storyland Animals. 2008. 29p. pap. 24.95 *(978-1-60563-010-6(1))* America Star Bks.

Vicente, Alidis. The Missing Chancleta & Other Top-Secret Cases / la Chancleta Perdida y Otros Casos Secretos. 2013. (SPA & ENG., Illus.). 64p. (J). pap. 9.95 *(978-1-55885-779-7(6)*, Piñata Books) Arte Publico Pr.

Vicente, Marta. La Cajita. 2004. (Los Especiales de A la Orilla Del Viento Ser.). (SPA., Illus.). 32p. (J). (gr. -1-7). 12.99 *(978-968-16-7181-5(3))* Fondo de Cultura Economica USA.

Villarreal, Carlos C. The Light Beneath the Shadow: Sharing God's Love with Your Child as You Read Together: A Bedtime Story Intended to Awaken Your Parental Christian Spirit. 2006. 48p. pap. 16.95 *(978-1-4241-1247-0(8))* PublishAmerica, Inc.

Villegas, Eduardo. El Baul de los Cuentos. (SPA.). (J). 7.98 *(978-970-643-159-2(4))* Selector, S.A. de C.V. MEX. Dist: Spanish Pubs., LLC.

Villnerve, Janice C. Mama Cat's Adventures in Child Training Presents No Whining! 2004. (Illus.). 32p. (J). lib. bdg. 14.95 *(978-0-9746013-0-4(6)*, 1230495) Paradigm Publishing.

Villoro, Carmen & Perez, Federico. Amarina y el Viejo Pesadilla y Otros Cuentos. (Torre de Papel Ser.). (SPA.). (J). (gr. 2). 7.95 *(978-958-04-3650-8(9))* Norma S.A. COL. Dist: Distribuidora Norma, Inc.

Vinson, Haley. Horizons Set 2, 5 books. Shea, Steve, ed. 2013. (Illus.). 48p. (YA). pap. 24.00 *(978-1-57128-815-8(5))* High Noon Bks.

Viorst, Judith. Earrings! Malone, Nola Langner, illus. 2010. (ENG.). 32p. (J). (gr. 1-5). 19.99 *(978-1-4424-1281-1(X)*, Atheneum Bks. for Young Readers) Simon & Schuster Children's Publishing.

Virtuous Short Stories of Fun & Prose. 2003. (Illus.). 90p. (YA). per. *(978-0-9742122-2-7(9))* Aunty Ems Boutique.

Vlashka, Vania. The Versaggi Brothers: Indigo Children are Here. 2011. 46p. (J). pap. 26.95 *(978-1-4327-6844-7(1))* Outskirts Pr., Inc.

Vogel, Kimberly. Sticks & Stones. 2013. (ENG.). 387p. pap. 20.00 *(978-1-300-65481-0(3))* Lulu Pr., Inc.

Voigt, Cynthia. Young Fredle. Yates, Louise, illus. 2012. 240p. (J). (gr. 3-7). 7.99 *(978-0-375-85787-4(7)*, Yearling) Random Hse. Children's Bks.

Volke, Gordon. The Big Posh Yacht. Bowler, Colin, illus. 2004. 24p. pap. 7.00 *(978-1-84161-116-7(6))* Ravette Publishing, Ltd. GBR. Dist: Parkwest Pubns., Inc.

—The Nasty Black Stuff. Bowler, Colin, illus. 2004. 24p. pap. 7.00 *(978-1-84161-119-8(0))* Ravette Publishing, Ltd. GBR. Dist: Parkwest Pubns., Inc.

—Old Grumpus & Other Stories. 2004. (Illus.). 91p. pap. 5.00 *(978-1-84161-035-1(6))* Ravette Publishing, Ltd. GBR. Dist: Parkwest Pubns., Inc.

—The Pirate's Gold. Bowler, Colin, illus. 2004. 24p. pap. 7.00 *(978-1-84161-117-4(4))* Ravette Publishing, Ltd. GBR. Dist: Parkwest Pubns., Inc.

—A Spider for Tea & Other Stories. 2004. (Illus.). 90p. pap. 5.00 *(978-1-84161-036-8(4))* Ravette Publishing, Ltd. GBR. Dist: Parkwest Pubns., Inc.

Volkov, Alexander. Tales of Magic Land 1. 2010. 360p. pap. 22.95 *(978-0-557-44825-8(5))* Lulu Pr., Inc.

von Eggers, Jennie, et al, creators. Times Tales. 2003. (J). spiral bd. 13.95 *(978-0-9762024-1-7(7))* Trigger Memory Co., LLC.

von Wielligh, G.R. Animal Tales: Volume 1, Vol. 1. Blankenaar, Dale, illus. 2012. (ENG.). 93p. pap. 12.00 *(978-1-86919-433-8(0))* Protea Boekhuis ZAF. Dist: Casemate Pubs. & Bk. Distributors, LLC.

—Animal Tales: Volume 2, Vol. 2. Blankenaar, Dale, illus. 2012. (ENG.). 93p. pap. 12.00 *(978-1-86919-504-5(3))* Protea Boekhuis ZAF. Dist: Casemate Pubs. & Bk. Distributors, LLC.

Wadsworth, Wallace. The Modern Story Book. Eger, Caroline Ruth, illus. 2010. (Dover Read & Listen Ser.). (ENG.). 112p. (J). (gr. 1-5). pap. 14.99 incl. audio compact disk *(978-0-486-47844-9(0))* Dover Pubns., Inc.

Wagner, Paul. Jock Jokes: And Other Stories. 2004. 236p. (YA). pap. 15.95 *(978-0-595-30757-9(4))* iUniverse, Inc.

Wake Up! Individual Title Six-Packs. (Story Steps Ser.). (gr. k-2). 29.00 *(978-0-7635-9581-4(0))* Rigby Education.

Walder, Chaim. Kids Speak, Vol. 4. 21.99 *(978-1-58330-442-6(8))* Feldheim Pubs.

Walker, Charmaine. Our Voices Through Writing. 2011. (ENG.). 65p. pap. 24.00 *(978-1-105-40141-1(3))* Lulu Pr., Inc.

Wall, Dorothy. The Complete Adventures of Blinky Bill. 2011. (Illus.). 442p. *(978-1-84902-571-3(1))* Benediction Classics.

Wallace, Karen. The Case of the Howling Armor. 2004. (Illus.). 47p. *(978-0-439-66552-0(3))* Scholastic, Inc.

Wallace, Rich. Sports Camp. 2012. 160p. (J). (gr. 4-7). 6.99 *(978-0-440-23993-2(1)*, Yearling) Random Hse. Children's Bks.

Walls, P. Abby: En busca del Tesoro. 2003. (Abby Ser.).Tr. of Abby: In Search of Treasure. pap. 6.99 *(978-0-7899-0968-8(5))* Editorial Unilit.

Walsh, Ann, ed. Beginnings: Stories of Canada's Past. 2005. (ENG., Illus.). 228p. (J). pap. 12.95 *(978-0-921870-87-6(6))* Ronsdale Pr. CAN. Dist: Literary Pr. Group of Canada.

Walsh, Maria Elena. Chaucha y Palito. Ink, Lancman, illus. 2003. (SPA.). 134p. (J). (gr. 5-8). pap. 11.95 *(978-950-511-615-7(2))* Santillana USA Publishing Co., Inc.

Walters, Catherine, et al. My Favorite Christmas Stories. 2015. (ENG.). 128p. (J). (gr. -1-2). 12.99 *(978-1-68010-200-0(1))* Tiger Tales.

Walther, William. A Collection of Fairy Tales: Volume One. 2007. (YA). per. 12.95 *(978-0-9795087-0-7(3))* Ctr. Stage Puppets.

Walton, Rick. Mini Mysteries 2: 20 More Tricky Tales to Untangle. Scheuer, Lauren, illus. 2006. 87p. (J). *(978-1-4156-6869-6(8)*, American Girl) American Girl Publishing, Inc.

Waltz, Michael. The Hen & I. 2012. (ENG.). pap. 15.00 *(978-1-4675-5236-3(4))* Independent Pub.

Ware, Shirley. Just Kids. 2006. 52p. pap. 16.95 *(978-1-4241-3194-5(4))* America Star Bks.

Warnasuriya, Chandrani. Favorite Folktales of Sri Lank. 2007. 108p. per. 19.95 *(978-1-4241-9965-5(4))* America Star Bks.

—Spooky Tales from the Orient: Tales of Ogres, Demons, Ghosts, Spells, Charms & the Enchanted, 1 vol. 2009. 167p. pap. 24.95 *(978-1-61546-978-9(8))* America Star Bks.

Warner, Rex. Men & Gods: Myths & Legends of the Ancient Greeks. Gorey, Edward, illus. 2008. 288p. 19.95 *(978-1-59017-263-6(9)*, NYRB Classics) New York Review of Bks., Inc., The.

Waters, Summer. Rising Star (Silver Dolphins, Book 7), Book 7. 2011. (Silver Dolphins Ser.). (ENG.). 176p. (J). (gr. 2-4). pap. 7.99 *(978-0-00-734812-1(6))* HarperCollins Pubs. Ltd. GBR. Dist: Independent Pubs. Group.

—Stormy Skies (Silver Dolphins, Book 8), Book 8. 2010. (Silver Dolphins Ser.: 8). (ENG.). 176p. (J). (gr. 2-4). pap. 7.99 *(978-0-00-734813-8(4)*, HarperCollins Children's Bks.) HarperCollins Pubs. Ltd. GBR. Dist: HarperCollins Pubs.

Watkins, Fred L. Sue, Mary & Charles, 1 vol. 2009. 127p. pap. 19.95 *(978-1-60749-110-1(9))* America Star Bks.

Watson, Margery. Ruffles & Danny or the Responsibility. 2005. pap. 22.95 *(978-1-4191-0387-2(3))* Kessinger Publishing, LLC.

Watson, Myrtle. Kite Flying in the Village: A Guyanese Girl's Story. 2011. 20p. 10.03 *(978-1-4520-8632-3(X))* AuthorHouse.

Watson, Viola. A Selection of Children's Short Stories. 2007. per. *(978-1-59581-349-7(7)*, Brentwood Christian Pr.) Brentwood Communications Group.

Wattley, Jason J. Anthology of Chaconia Creations. 2011. 24p. pap. 15.99 *(978-1-4568-7683-8(X))* Xlibris Corp.

Wax, Wendy A. Musica en Casa: Libro de Cuentos. de Alba, Arlette, tr. 2005. (Disney Princess Ser.). (SPA., Illus.). 38p. (J). (gr. -1-7). incl. audio compact disk *(978-970-718-289-9(X)*, Silver Dolphin en Español) Advanced Marketing, S. de R. L. de C. V.

Wealden House Staff. Soul-Fire. 2006. 132p. per. *(978-1-904529-18-7(6)*, Back to Front) Solidus.

Webb, Holly. The Missing Puppy & Other Tales. Williams, Sophy, illus. 2017. (Pet Rescue Adventures Ser.). (ENG.). 384p. (J). (gr. 1-4). pap. 10.99 *(978-1-68010-404-2(7))* Tiger Tales.

Webb, Mack Henry, Jr. Webb's Wondrous Tales Book 1. Webb, Celia, illus. 2006. 184p. (YA). per. 14.95 *(978-0-9779576-1-3(6))* Pilinut Pr., Inc.

Weed, Thurlow R. Camel Fables from the Sailors of the Sudan. 2004. 84p. pap. 15.95 *(978-0-7414-2229-3(8))* Infinity Publishing.

Weel, Rosalinda. Dream Clouds: Float Away with Seven Enchanting Children's Stories for Relaxation & Bedtime. 2012. 60p. pap. 23.99 *(978-1-4525-5860-8(4))* Balboa Pr.

Weinbrecht, William. Stories for Amand. 2009. 48p. pap. 15.50 *(978-1-60693-150-9(4)*, Eloquent Bks.) Strategic Book Publishing & Rights Agency (SBPRA).

Weis, Michael David. Diamond & the Fosters. Avant, Matthew, illus. 2013. 64p. 21.95 *(978-1-59663-635-4(1)*, Castle Keep Pr.) Rock, James A. & Co. Pubs.

Wells, Rosemary. Hungry Bunny Tales. 2012. (Max & Ruby Ser.). lib. bdg. 14.75 *(978-0-606-23658-4(9))* Turtleback.

Weninger, Brigitte. 24 Stories for Advent. Tharlet, Eve, illus. 2015. (ENG.). 120p. (J). (gr. -1-2). 19.95 *(978-0-7358-4229-8(9))* North-South Bks., Inc.

Wenke, Christine. Willa's Secret. 2005. 160p. (Orig.). pap. *(978-0-7344-0675-0(4)*, Lothian Children's Bks.) Hachette Australia.

Wernham, Sara. Phonic; Rainforests; Monster Party, 18 vols., Pack, Set. Maddison, Kevin & Wade, Sarah, illus. 2003. (ENG.). (J). pap. 37.50 *(978-1-84414-091-6(1)*, Jolly Learning) Jolly Learning, Ltd. GBR. Dist: American International Distribution Corp.

—Snakes; the Tree That Blinked; the Tree Billy Goats Gruff, 18 Bks., Pack. Maddison, Kevin & Stephen, Lib, illus. 2004. (ENG.). (J). pap. 42.00 *(978-1-84414-090-9(3)*, Jolly Learning) Jolly Learning, Ltd. GBR. Dist: American International Distribution Corp.

West, Denis. Sam of the Forest Railway. 2012. 66p. pap. 13.50 *(978-1-78035-361-6(8)*, Fastprint Publishing) Upfront Publishing Ltd. GBR. Dist: Printondemand-worldwide.com.

West, Hilary. The Secret Kingdom. 2013. 76p. pap. 17.95 *(978-1-62709-626-3(4))* America Star Bks.

West, Shawna Makala. Is There an Alligator at Kaipapau? 2004.Tr. of Aia Ka Alakeka Ma Kaipapau? (ENG & HAW.). (J). lib. bdg. 12.95 *(978-0-9760892-1-6(1)*, Ho'ulu Hou Project: Stories Told by Us) Na Kamalei Koolauloa Early Education Program.

What Do I Look Like? (Peek A Boo Pockets Ser.). 12p. (J). bds. *(978-2-7643-0106-7(5))* Phidal Publishing, Inc./Editions Phidal, Inc.

Whelan, Denise. In the Land of Six & Seven. 2010. 48p. 18.99 *(978-1-4520-3399-0(4))* AuthorHouse.

White, Elga Haymon. A Children's Adventure Duo: Thad the Sailor & Little Miss Lavendar. Freudiger, Victoria, ed. Bjornsen, Holly, illus. 2007. 130p. (J). per. 13.95 *(978-0-9785728-2-2(3))* Digi-Tall Media.

Whitler, Larry & MacBlane, Robin. The Gift of the Barking Frog. 2006. (ENG.). 572p. pap. 35.95 *(978-1-4116-1545-8(X))* Lulu Pr., Inc.

Who Does That? (Peek A Boo Pockets Ser.). 12p. (J). bds. *(978-2-89393-977-3(5))* Phidal Publishing, Inc./Editions Phidal, Inc.

Wicke, Ed. Wicked Tales. 2006. (ENG., Illus.). 156p. (J). per. 9.99 *(978-0-9677652-7-3(7)*, BlacknBlue Pr. UK) Blacknblue Pr.

Wicks, Krista. Mazie Moo & Her Clever Clouds, Wonderful Water & Silly Sunshine. 2012. 24p. pap. 12.45 *(978-1-4497-6901-7(2)*, WestBow Pr.) Author Solutions, LLC.

Wigger, Sherry. Scary Stories for Brave Kids, 1 vol. 2009. 73p. pap. 16.95 *(978-1-61582-308-6(5))* PublishAmerica, Inc.

Wiggin, Kate Douglas. The Bird's Christmas Carol. 2011. 88p. (gr. 4-7). 20.95 *(978-1-4638-9984-4(X))* Rodgers, Alan Bks.

—Homespun Tales. 2007. 240p. 26.95 *(978-1-60312-668-7(6))*; per. 14.95 *(978-1-60312-410-2(1))* Aegypan.

—The Village Watchtower. 2007. 108p. per. 9.95 *(978-1-60312-209-2(5))* Aegypan.

Wight, Eric. Frankie Pickle & the Pine Run 3000. Wight, Eric, illus. 2010. (Frankie Pickle Ser.). (ENG., Illus.). 96p. (J). (gr. 2-5). 10.99 *(978-1-4169-6485-8(1)*, Simon & Schuster Bks. For Young Readers) Simon & Schuster Bks. For Young Readers.

Wilberforce, Samuel. Agathos the Rocky Island & Other Sunday Stories & Parables. 2013. (ENG.). 236p. pap. 35.99 *(978-1-107-67169-0(8))* Cambridge Univ. Pr.

Wilbur's Wild Ride & Other Stories: Individual Title Six-Pack. (Story Steps Ser.). (gr. k-2). 42.00 *(978-0-7635-9598-2(5))* Rigby Education.

Wilde, Oscar. Cuentos de Oscar Wilde. (SPA.). (YA). 8.95 *(978-958-04-2378-2(4))* Norma S.A. COL. Dist: Distribuidora Norma, Inc.

—The Happy Prince. Russell, P. Craig, illus. 5th ed. 2012. (Fairy Tales of Oscar Wilde Ser.: 5). (ENG.). 32p. (J). (gr. 4-7). 16.99 *(978-1-56163-626-6(6))* NBM Publishing Co.

—The Happy Prince & Other Tales. Charles Robinson, illus. 2012. 84p. pap. 3.47 *(978-1-60386-460-2(1)*, Watchmaker Publishing) Wexford College Pr.

Wilde, Oscar. Oscar Wilde Stories for Children. 2023. (ENG.). 96p. (J). (gr. 4-6). pap. 17.99 ***(978-0-340-84171-6(0))*** Hachette Children's Group GBR. Dist: Hachette Bk. Group.

Wilkinson, Richard. Wilkinson Tales: A Collection of Holiday Short Stories for Young People. 2009. 80p. pap. 26.49 *(978-1-4490-0902-1(6))* AuthorHouse.

Wilkinson, Richard Fergus. Wilkinson Tales: A Collection of Adventure Short Stories for Young People. Murphy, Andrea, illus. 2010. 88p. pap. 27.49 *(978-1-4490-5489-2(7))* AuthorHouse.

Willems, Mo. Time to Sleep, Sheep the Sheep! Willems, Mo, illus. 2010. (ENG., Illus.). 32p. (J). (gr. -1-3). 12.99 *(978-0-06-172847-1(0))*; lib. bdg. 15.89 *(978-0-06-172848-8(9))* HarperCollins Pubs. (Balzer & Bray).

Williams, Ann. The Multifarious Adventures of Fred the Raindrop. 2005. 22p. (J). 8.00 *(978-1-4116-4175-4(2))* Lulu Pr., Inc.

Williams, Earnest L. The Invisible Cell: One Man's Story about Surviving in a Generation Lost in the Social Justice System. 2004. vi, 239p. (YA). per. 12.95 *(978-0-9745244-0-5(9))* William Works, Inc.

Williams, Jan. An Amazing Storytelling Cat. Peecock, Simon & McKissock, Charmaine, illus. 2013. 120p. pap. *(978-0-9568148-6-9(7))* Swift Publishing.

Williams, Marcia. The Elephant's Friend & Other Tales from Ancient India. Williams, Marcia, illus. 2014. (ENG., Illus.). 40p. (J). (gr. 1-4). 8.99 *(978-0-7636-7055-9(3))* Candlewick Pr.

Williams, Marie Sheppard. The Magic Stories. 2012. pap. 12.95 *(978-0-7414-7280-9(5))* Infinity Publishing.

Williams, Sandra. Look with Me. 2012. (Illus.). 40p. pap. 20.99 *(978-1-4772-1318-6(X))* AuthorHouse.

Williston, Teresa Peirce. Hindu Stories. Squire, Maud Hunt, illus. 2011. 110p. 39.95 *(978-1-258-02581-6(7))* Literary Licensing, LLC.

Wilson, Budge. Friendships. 2006. (ENG.). 224p. (YA). (gr. 7-18). 11.99 *(978-0-14-301766-0(7)*, Puffin Canada) PRH Canada Young Readers CAN. Dist: Penguin Random Hse. LLC.

—The Leaving, 1 vol. (ENG.). 176p. (J). mass mkt. 6.95 *(978-0-7736-7363-2(6))* Stoddart Kids CAN. Dist: Fitzhenry & Whiteside, Ltd.

Wilson, Essdale. Horses, Tigers & Neighbors. 2007. 160p. per. 24.95 *(978-1-4241-5811-9(7))* America Star Bks.

Wilson, Mary. Kopper "K" Kidds & Corky. 2003. per. *(978-1-59196-169-7(6))* Instant Pub.

Wilson, Pauline. Animal & Other Antics. 2004. (Illus.). 56p. pap. *(978-1-84401-313-5(8))* Athena Pr.

Wingate, Frank. Herman the Hedgehog: Bedtime Tales from the Woodland. 2009. (Illus.). 84p. pap. 10.49 *(978-1-4389-9134-4(7))* AuthorHouse.

Winkel, Andrew. Raceboy & Super Qwok Adventures. Brault, Christopher, illus. 2012. (ENG.). 356p. (J). pap. 16.00 *(978-0-9837905-1-8(5))* Hierophantasm.

Winners: Poems & Stories, 2003 Spring Writing Contest. 2003. (J). 5.00 *(978-0-9702646-2-6(3))*; (YA). 5.00 *(978-0-9702646-3-3(1))* New Sweden Pr.

Winter, Milo, illus. Aesop's Favorite Fables: More Than 130 Classic Fables for Children! 2017. (Children's Classic Collections). 112p. (J). (gr. k-3). 12.99 *(978-1-944686-08-6(8)*, Racehorse Publishing) Skyhorse Publishing Co., Inc.

Winter, Rosalind. The Mice of St Goran. 2010. 70p. pap. *(978-1-84923-461-0(2))* YouWriteOn.

Winters, John. Gramps' Children's Stories. 2007. (ENG.). 60p. pap. 6.96 *(978-1-4357-0038-3(4))* Lulu Pr., Inc.

Wise, Linda. Pearl's Gems. 2010. 96p. pap. 28.99 *(978-1-4520-1129-5(X))* AuthorHouse.

Wiseman, Eva. The Last Song. 2012. (Illus.). 232p. (YA). (gr. 7). 17.95 *(978-0-88776-979-5(9)*, Tundra Bks.) Tundra Bks. CAN. Dist: Penguin Random Hse. LLC.

Wittenbach, Jennie. Little Stories for Little Folks. 2011. 36p. pap. 21.99 *(978-1-4628-8818-4(6))* Xlibris Corp.
Wizard Academies I: The Heart of Darkness. 2006. 658p. pap. 24.96 *(978-1-4116-7787-6(0))* Lulu Pr., Inc.
Wolf, Ema. ¡Silencio, Niños! y Otros Cuentos. Pez, illus. 2019. (Torre de Papel Ser.).Tr. of Be Quiet Children & Other Stories. (SPA.). 112p. (J). (gr. 4-6). pap. 15.99 *(978-958-04-3927-1(3),* Norma) Norma S.A. COL. Dist: Distribuidora Norma, Inc.
Wolfe, Carolyn. The Bedtime of the Sky & Other Sleepy-Bye Stories. Mathis, Leslie, illus. 2010. 32p. pap. 11.25 *(978-1-935105-57-2(4))* Avid Readers Publishing Group.
Wolfe, Jaymie Stuart. Family Matters: Thirteen Short Stories. 2011. 126p. (J). pap. *(978-0-8198-2694-7(4))* Pauline Bks. & Media.
Wolos-Fonteno, Mary, et al. Tales with Tails: Animal Stories for Young People. Salaam, Kiini Ibura, ed. Wolos-Fonteno, Mary et al, illus. 2006. 168p. (YA). pap. 15.95 *(978-0-940938-43-4(X),* Pen & Rose Pr.) Harlin Jacque Pubns.
Wood, Carol. Grandma Carol's Book of Stories in Rhyme. 2009. (Illus.). 48p. pap. 19.49 *(978-1-4389-5413-4(1))* AuthorHouse.
Wood, Julie M. Learn to Read with Tug the Pup & Friends! Box Set 1: Levels Included: A-C, Set. Braun, Sebastien, illus. 2014. (My Very First I Can Read Ser.). (ENG.). 132p. (J). (gr. -1-3). pap. 14.99 *(978-0-06-226689-7(6),* HarperCollins) HarperCollins Pubs.
Wood, Maryrose. The Incorrigible Children of Ashton Place: The Mysterious Howling Howlin G, Bk. I. Klassen, Jon, illus. 2010. (Incorrigible Children of Ashton Place Ser.: 1). (ENG.). 272p. (J). (gr. 3-7). 16.99 *(978-0-06-179105-5(9),* Balzer & Bray) HarperCollins Pubs.
Wood, Maryrose & Klassen, Jon. The Incorrigible Children of Ashton Place: The Mysterious Howling. 2011. (Incorrigible Children of Ashton Place Ser.: Bk. 1). (ENG., Illus.). 288p. (J). (gr. 3-7). pap. 6.99 *(978-0-06-179110-9(5))* HarperCollins Pubs.
Wooden, John. Fiesta. Cornelison, Susan F., illus. 2007. (Coach John Wooden for Kids Ser.). 63p. (J). (gr. k-3). lib. bdg. 11.65 *(978-0-7569-7791-7(6));* pap., per. 4.99 *(978-0-7891-7187-0(2))* Perfection Learning Corp.
Wooden Soldier. 2004. (J). per. *(978-1-57657-383-9(4))* Paradise Pr., Inc.
Woods, Cindy Smith. Once Inside A Storybook... Good Morals in Short Stories to Encourage Correct Behavior in the Little Ones in Your Life. 2006. 59p. pap. 16.95 *(978-1-4241-2905-8(2))* America Star Bks.
Woody, Velma B. Branscum. Bandits, Bears, & Backaches: A Collection of Short Stories Based on Arkansas History. 2004. (ENG.). 78p. per. 15.00 *(978-0-9708574-2-2(X),* P145086) Butler Ctr. for Arkansas Studies.
World Peace, Metta & McBride, Heddrick. Metta's Bedtime Stories. Pax, H. H., illus. 2013. 36p. pap. 12.95 *(978-0-615-70075-5(6))* McBride, Heddrick.
Worwell. DOS ranas. 2004. (SPA., Illus.). 32p. (J). (gr. k-2). 20.99 *(978-84-261-3354-0(1))* Juventud, Editorial ESP. Dist: Lectorum Pubns., Inc.
Wray, Zoe, contrib. by. Usborne Illustrated Stories for Girls. 2007. (Usborne Illustrated Stories Ser.). (Illus.). 352p. (J). (gr. -1-3). 19.99 *(978-0-7945-1419-8(7),* Usborne) EDC Publishing.
Wrede, Patricia C. Book of Enchantments. 2005. (ENG., Illus.). 256p. (J). (gr. 5-7). pap. 14.95 *(978-0-15-205508-0(8),* 1196568, Clarion Bks.) HarperCollins Pubs.
Wright, Lloyd. Gramp's Variety of Stories. 2007. 200p. 24.95 *(978-0-595-71311-0(4));* per. 14.95 *(978-0-595-47731-9(3))* iUniverse, Inc.
—More Stories for Gramp's Little Friends. 2004. 180p. (J). 23.95 *(978-0-595-66836-6(4))* iUniverse, Inc.
—Stories for Gramp's Little Friends. 2004. 158p. (J). 22.95 *(978-0-595-66287-6(0));* pap. 12.95 *(978-0-595-31266-5(7))* iUniverse, Inc.
Wright, Sharrie. Wee Friends. 2011. (Illus.). 32p. (gr. -1). pap. 14.50 *(978-1-4567-7621-3(5))* AuthorHouse.
Wuest, Marcia. Twelve Things to Do at Age 12. 2009. (Readers for Teens Ser.). (ENG.). 26p. pap. 14.75 *(978-0-521-73733-3(8))* Cambridge Univ. Pr.
Yaber, Armando. Mariana Sale el Sol. 2005. (SPA.). (YA). per. 9.99 *(978-0-9765467-1-9(X))* Creative Bk. Pubs.
Yancey, Rick. The Monstrumologist Collection: The Monstrumologist; the Curse of the Wendigo; the Isle of Blood; the Final Descent. 2014. (Monstrumologist Ser.). (ENG., Illus.). 1808p. (YA). (gr. 9). pap. 51.99 *(978-1-4814-3012-8(2),* Simon & Schuster Bks. For Young Readers) Simon & Schuster Bks. For Young Readers.
Yang, Gladys. The Frog Rider & Other Folktales from Chin. 2008. 116p. 19.95 *(978-1-59654-569-4(0))* Disruptive Publishing.
Yates, Donnalyn. Let's Memorize States & Capitals Using Pictures & Stories. 2011. 128p. pap. 14.95 *(978-1-257-07566-9(7))* Lulu Pr., Inc.
Yeahpau, Thomas M. X-Indian Chronicles: The Book of Mausape. 2006. (ENG.). 240p. (YA). (gr. 9). 16.99 *(978-0-7636-2706-5(2))* Candlewick Pr.
The Year of Shadows. 2014. (ENG., Illus.). 416p. (J). (gr. 3-7). pap. 7.99 *(978-1-4424-4295-5(6),* Simon & Schuster Bks. For Young Readers) Simon & Schuster Bks. For Young Readers.
Yee, Paul. Tales from Gold Mountain, 1 vol. Ng, Simon, illus. 2011. (ENG.). 64p. (J). (gr. 1-2). pap. 14.95 *(978-1-55498-125-0(5))* Groundwood Bks. CAN. Dist: Publishers Group West (PGW).
Yee, Wong Herbert. Abracadabra! Magic with Mouse & Mole (Reader) 2010. (Mouse & Mole Story Ser.). (ENG., Illus.). 48p. (J). (gr. -1-3). pap. 4.99 *(978-0-547-40621-3(5),* 1428499, Clarion Bks.) HarperCollins Pubs.
Yellow Bananas, 11 bks. Incl. Amina's Blanket. Dunmore, Helen. Dainton, Paul, illus. lib. bdg. *(978-0-7787-0938-1(8));* Break in the Chain. d'Lacey, Chris. Carey, Joanna, illus. lib. bdg. 21.19 *(978-0-7787-0931-2(0));* Colly's Barn. Morpurgo, Michael. Andrew, Ian P., illus. lib. bdg. *(978-0-7787-0932-9(9));* Dragon Trouble. Lively, Penelope. Rowland, Andrew, illus. lib. bdg. *(978-0-7787-0941-1(8));* Fine Feathered Friend. Gavin, Jamila. Williams, Dan, illus. lib. bdg. *(978-0-7787-0939-8(6));* Jo-Jo the Melon Donkey. Morpurgo, Michael. Kerins, Tony, illus. lib. bdg. *(978-0-7787-0942-8(6));* Monster from Underground. Cross, Gillian. Priestley, Chris, illus. lib. bdg. *(978-0-7787-0935-0(3));* My Brother Bernadette. Wilson, Jacqueline. Roberts, David, illus. lib. bdg. *(978-0-7787-0940-4(X));* Soccer Star. Hardcastle, Michael. Cox, Ken, illus. lib. bdg. *(978-0-7787-0933-6(7));* Stranger from Somewhere in Time. McBratney, Sam. Chatterton, Martin & Chatterton, Ann, illus. lib. bdg. *(978-0-7787-0937-4(X));* Who's a Clever Girl? Impey, Rose & Ashe, Susan. Amstutz, Andre, illus. lib. bdg. *(978-0-7787-0930-5(2));* 48p. (J). (gr. 3-4). 2002. 2003. *(978-0-7787-0929-9(9))* Crabtree Publishing Co.
Yeoman, John. A Drink of Water. Blake, Quentin, illus. 2017. 64p. (J). (gr. 2-8). 14.95 *(978-0-500-65135-3(3),* 565135) Thames & Hudson.
Young, Judy & Scillian, Devin. Westward Journeys. Farnsworth, Bill et al, illus. 2013. (American Adventures Ser.). (ENG.). 96p. (J). (gr. 3-6). pap. 6.99 *(978-1-58536-860-0(1),* 202367) Sleeping Bear Pr.
Young, Larry. Astronauts in Trouble. 2003. (ENG., Illus.). (YA). pap. 16.95 *(978-1-932051-16-2(3),* 21e72934-f339-4201-af92-21d35703331a) A i T/Planet Lar.
Youngquist, D. M. Ghosts of Interstate 80. 2007. (ENG., Illus.). 180p. per. 9.95 *(978-1-57166-459-4(9))* Quixote Pr.
Youngs, Puma Wun. Dreamtime. 2010. 28p. pap. 13.99 *(978-1-4490-8378-6(1))* AuthorHouse.
Yourgrau, Barry. Nasty Book. 2005. (ENG.). 192p. (J). (gr. 5-9). 11.99 *(978-0-06-057978-4(1))* HarperCollins Pubs.
—NASTYbook. 2005. 192p. (J). (gr. k-9). lib. bdg. 13.89 *(978-0-06-057979-1(X))* HarperCollins Pubs.
Yoyo Books Staff. At Home: One Minute Goodnight Stories. 2004. 40p. bds. *(978-90-5843-583-5(0))* YoYo Bks.
—At School: One Minute Goodnight Stories. 2004. 40p. bds. *(978-90-5843-582-8(2))* YoYo Bks.
Yuki, Kaori. Godchild, Vol. 4. 2007. (GodChild Ser.: 4). (ENG., Illus.). 200p. pap. 8.99 *(978-1-4215-0478-0(2))* Viz Media.
Zakarin, Debra Mostow. First Fairytales. Fiore, Rob, illus. 2010. 10p. 9.95 *(978-1-60747-746-4(7),* Pickwick Pr.) Phoenix Bks., Inc.
Zemko Tetro, Maria, tr. from UKR. How the Animals Built their House & Other Stories. 2008. (Illus.). 40p. (J). 14.95 *(978-0-9797372-5-1(7))* Winter Light Bks., Inc.
Zimmerschied, P. Grampa Paul's Adventure Stories for Children. 2011. 112p. (gr. -1). 23.99 *(978-1-4634-2885-3(5));* pap. 13.99 *(978-1-4634-2883-9(9))* AuthorHouse.
Zipes, Jack, ed. & tr. Beauties, Beasts & Enchantment: Classic French Fairy Tales. Zipes, Jack. tr. 3rd ed. 2013. 610p. pap. *(978-1-86171-432-9(7))* Crescent Moon Publishing.
Zolotow, Charlotte. Hold My Hand: Five Stories of Love & Family. Thompson, Carol, illus. 2003. (ENG.). 64p. (gr. -1-k). 19.99 *(978-0-7868-0518-1(8))* Hyperion Pr.
Zondervan Staff. Story Early Elementary Curriculum: 31 Lessons, 1 vol. 2011. (Story Ser.). (ENG.). cd-rom 34.99 *(978-0-310-71921-2(6))* Zonderkidz.
—The Story for Kids: Later Elementary Curriculum - 31 Lessons, 1 vol. 2011. (Story Ser.). (ENG.). cd-rom 34.99 *(978-0-310-71922-9(4))* Zonderkidz.
—Story Preschool Curriculum: 31 Lessons, 1 vol. 2011. (Story Ser.). (ENG.). (J). cd-rom 34.99 *(978-0-310-71920-5(8))* Zonderkidz.
Zorro, Sephone. Growing Up: Home & School. Baxter, Rhea, illus. 2017. 144p. pap. 7.99 *(978-1-941429-55-6(6))* Handersen Publishing.
—Welcome. 2016. (Illus.). 133p. pap. 5.99 *(978-1-941429-33-4(5))* Handersen Publishing.
Zuill, Veronica M. E. Short Stories for Children Book. 2012. 28p. pap. 21.99 *(978-1-4771-4576-0(1))* Xlibris Corp.
Zullo, Allan. The Haunted Shortstop: True Ghostly Sports Stories. 2007. 128p. (J). pap. *(978-0-439-88618-5(X))* Scholastic, Inc.
Zuric, Vule. Orlovi Ponovo Lete: Nove Price o Magarecim Godinama. 2016. 202p. (J). *(978-86-521-2185-4(0))* Laguna.
Zwerger, Lisbeth, selected by. Aesop's Fables. 2006. (ENG., Illus.). 32p. (J). (gr. -1-3). 16.95 *(978-0-7358-2068-5(6))* North-South Bks., Inc.
3 Minutes Nursery Stories. (Illus.). 160p. (J). 9.98 *(978-0-7853-7821-1(9),* 7177000) Publications International, Ltd.
7 Cuentos para antes de Dormir.Tr. of 7 Bedtime Stories. (SPA.). (J). *(978-84-7773-016-3(4));* Vol. 2. *(978-84-7773-302-7(3));* Vol. 4. *(978-84-7773-017-0(2))* Grafalco, S.A.
101 Stories to Tell & Write. (Illus.). (J). (gr. 3-6). pap. *(978-1-876367-67-1(9))* Wizard Bks.
365 Fabulas.Tr. of 365 Fables. (SPA.). 208p. (J). *(978-84-7773-031-6(8))* Grafalco, S.A.
09' Young Writers Conf. Havana Elem. Words Have Wings. 2009. 32p. pap. 20.00 *(978-1-4490-5303-1(3))* AuthorHouse.

SHRIMPS

Cunningham, Kevin. Goby Fish & Pistol Shrimp. 2016. (21st Century Junior Library: Better Together Ser.). (ENG., Illus.). 24p. (J). (gr. 2-5). 29.21 *(978-1-63471-084-8(3),* 208415) Cherry Lake Publishing.
Plattner, Josh. Mantis Shrimp: Master of Punching, 1 vol. 2015. (Animal Superpowers Ser.). (ENG., Illus.). 24p. (J). (gr. k-3). 32.79 *(978-1-62403-736-8(4),* 17978, Super SandCastle) ABDO Publishing Co.
Schuetz, Kari. Goby Fish & Snapping Shrimp. 2019. (Animal Tag Teams Ser.). (ENG., Illus.). 24p. (J). (gr. k-3). lib. bdg. 26.95 *(978-1-62617-955-4(7),* Blastoff! Readers) Bellwether Media.
Sexton, Colleen. Shrimp. 2009. (Oceans Alive Ser.). (ENG., Illus.). 24p. (J). (gr. k-3). lib. bdg. 26.95 *(978-1-60014-252-9(4))* Bellwether Media.
—Shrimp. 2009. (Blastoff! Readers Ser.). (ENG., Illus.). 24p. (J). (gr. k-3). 20.00 *(978-0-531-21716-0(7),* Children's Pr.) Scholastic Library Publishing.
Shea, Therese. What Are Crustaceans?, 1 vol. 2016. (Let's Find Out! Marine Life Ser.). (ENG., Illus.). 32p. (J). (gr. 2-3). lib. bdg. 26.06 *(978-1-5081-0385-1(2),* b4d9f815-4032-46ca-a336-9fb396c57f77) Rosen Publishing Group, Inc., The.

SHRUBS

see also Landscape Gardening

Aldrich, William & Williamson, Don. Tree & Shrub Gardening for Illinois, 1 vol., Vol. 1. rev. ed. 2004. (ENG., Illus.). 352p. (gr. 4). pap. 18.95 *(978-1-55105-404-9(3),* 78116449-5f28-42de-b982-e75dedb9047c) Lone Pine Publishing USA.
Buckley, Arabella B. Trees & Shrubs. 2008. (Illus.). 88p. pap. 11.95 *(978-1-59915-275-2(4))* Yesterday's Classics.
De Medeiros, Michael. Chaparral. 2006. (J). 9.95 *(978-1-59036-439-0(2))* Weigl Pubs., Inc.
Tanem, Bob & Williamson, Don. Tree & Shrub Gardening for Northern California, 1 vol. rev. ed. 2003. (ENG., Illus.). 360p. (gr. 4). pap. 18.95 *(978-1-55105-275-5(X),* c3c657e4-5407-4355-b04b-f7bf0ec93f92) Lone Pine Publishing USA.
Wood, Tim & Beck, Alison. Tree & Shrub Gardening for Michigan, 1 vol. rev. ed. 2003. (ENG., Illus.). 352p. (gr. 4). pap. 18.95 *(978-1-55105-347-9(0),* 9d32c73f-cb05-4a97-b30a-b85221c344d0) Lone Pine Publishing USA.

SIAM

see Thailand

SIBERIA (RUSSIA)

Hautzig, Esther. The Endless Steppe: Growing up in Siberia. 2018. (ENG., Illus.). 256p. (J). (gr. 3-18). pap. 9.99 *(978-0-06-440577-5(X),* HarperCollins) HarperCollins Pubs.
Lengyel, Emil. Siberia. 2004. reprint ed. pap. 36.95 *(978-1-4191-0872-3(7))* Kessinger Publishing, LLC.
Sloan, Christopher. Baby Mammoth Mummy: Frozen in Time (Special Sales Edition) A Prehistoric Animal's Journey into the 21st Century. 2011. (ENG., Illus.). 48p. (J). (gr. 3-7). 17.95 *(978-1-4263-0865-9(5))* National Geographic Society.

SIBERIA (RUSSIA)—FICTION

Gregg, Stacy. The Diamond Horse. 2017. (ENG.). 272p. (J). 6.99 *(978-0-00-824384-5(0),* HarperCollins Children's Bks.) HarperCollins Pubs. Ltd. GBR. Dist: HarperCollins Pubs.
Ingram, W. J. Evelyn. Saint Crispin & Other Quaint Conceits. 2005. pap. 24.95 *(978-1-4179-6255-6(0))* Kessinger Publishing, LLC.
London, Jonathan. Little Lost Tiger, 0 vols. Spirin, Ilya, illus. 2012. (ENG.). 32p. (J). (gr. -1-3). 17.99 *(978-0-7614-6130-2(2),* 9780761461302, Two Lions) Amazon Publishing.
Mead, Richelle. Blood Promise. 2010. (Vampire Academy Ser.: 4). lib. bdg. 20.85 *(978-0-606-14565-7(6))* Turtleback.
—Blood Promise: A Vampire Academy Novel. 2010. (Vampire Academy Ser.: 4). (ENG.). 528p. (YA). (gr. 7-18). pap. 13.99 *(978-1-59514-310-5(6),* Razorbill) Penguin Young Readers Group.
PaleoJoe & Caszatt-Allen, Wendy. Mysterious Mammoths. 2008. (PaleoJoe's Dinosaur Detective Club Ser.). (Illus.). 200p. (J). (gr. 2-5). pap. 8.95 *(978-1-934133-43-9(4),* Mackinac Island Press, Inc.) Charlesbridge Publishing, Inc.
Popke, Suzanne L. The Adventures of Tolei Mergen. 2013. 36p. pap. 24.95 *(978-1-4626-8863-0(2))* America Star Bks.
Sepetys, Ruta. Ashes in the Snow (Movie Tie-In) 2018. (ENG.). 384p. (YA). (gr. 7). pap. 11.99 *(978-1-9848-3674-8(9),* Penguin Books) Penguin Young Readers Group.
—Between Shades of Gray. 2012. (ENG & JPN.). 398p. (YA). (gr. 7). pap. *(978-4-00-115651-5(2))* Iwanami Shoten.
—Between Shades of Gray. 2009. 10.36 *(978-0-7848-3779-5(1),* Everbind) Marco Bk. Co.
—Between Shades of Gray. (ENG., (YA). (gr. 7-18). 2012. Illus.). 384p. pap. 12.99 *(978-0-14-242059-1(X),* Penguin Books) 2011. 352p. 19.99 *(978-0-399-25412-3(9),* Philomel Bks.) Penguin Young Readers Group.
—Between Shades of Gray. l.t. ed. (ENG.). 2020. lib. bdg. 22.99 *(978-1-4328-7360-8(1))* 2011. 432p. (YA). 23.99 *(978-1-4104-4083-9(4))* Thorndike Pr.
—Between Shades of Gray. 2012. lib. bdg. 20.85 *(978-0-606-26089-3(7))* Turtleback.
Snell, Roy J. Triple Spies. 2017. (ENG., Illus.). (J). (gr. -1-7). 22.95 *(978-1-374-95345-1(8))* Capital Communications, Inc.
—Triple Spies. 2008. 112p. (gr. -1-7). 22.95 *(978-1-60664-743-1(1))* Rodgers, Alan Bks.
Spreng, Robert C. The Tahoe Tiger & the Lahontan Lion. 2008. 38p. pap. 14.50 *(978-0-557-02370-7(X))* Lulu Pr., Inc.
Young, H. M. (Hal). The huskies & the christmas Fawn. 2007. (ENG.). 56p. pap. 9.95 *(978-1-4357-0070-3(8))* Lulu Pr., Inc.

SIBLING RIVALRY—FICTION

Adams, Michelle Medlock & Adams, Michelle M. Sister for Sale!, 1 vol. Brooks, Karen Stormer, illus. 2007. (I Can Read! Ser.). (ENG.). 32p. (J). (gr. -1-1). pap. 4.99 *(978-0-310-71469-9(9))* Zonderkidz.
Al Shaikh, Latifa. I'm Still Waiting for that Chocolate. 2007. 52p. (YA). per. 8.95 *(978-0-595-42982-0(3))* iUniverse, Inc.
Alley, R. W., illus. Bratty Brothers & Selfish Sisters: All about Sibling Rivalry. 2007. (Elf-Help Books for Kids Ser.). 28p. (J). (gr. -1-3). per. 7.95 *(978-0-87029-404-4(0))* Abbey Pr.
Baldwin, Quinn. Crossover. 2010. (ENG.). 166p. pap. *(978-0-557-74844-0(5))* Lulu Pr., Inc.
Blabey, Aaron. The Brothers Quibble. Blabey, Aaron, illus. 2015. (Illus.). 32p. (J). (gr. k-3). 16.99 *(978-0-14-350706-2(0))* Random Hse. Australia AUS. Dist: Independent Pubs. Group.
Blume, Judy. The Pain & the Great One. Ohi, Debbie Ridpath, illus. 2014. (ENG.). 48p. (J). (gr. 1-5). pap. 5.99 *(978-1-4814-1145-5(4),* Atheneum Bks. for Young Readers) Simon & Schuster Children's Publishing.
—Soupy Saturdays with the Pain & the Great One. Stevenson, James, illus. (Pain & the Great One Ser.: 1). (ENG.). (J). 2009. 128p. (gr. 3-7). 7.99 *(978-0-440-42092-7(X),* Yearling) 2007. 108p. (gr. 2-4). lib. bdg. 18.69 *(978-0-385-90324-0(3),* Delacorte Pr.) Random Hse. Children's Bks.
—Superfudge. 2007.Tr. of Superfudge. (ENG.). 208p. (J). (gr. 3-7). 8.99 *(978-0-14-240880-3(8),* Puffin Books) Penguin Young Readers Group.
Boyd, Jeffery Allen. Wolf's Head Bay: The Journey Home. 2004. (ENG.). 392p. (YA). pap. 21.95 *(978-0-595-32230-5(1))* iUniverse, Inc.
Carkhuff, Denise. Mama's Heart Fits Two. 2015. (ENG., Illus.). 32p. (J). (gr. -1-2). 16.95 *(978-1-62634-222-4(9))* Greenleaf Book Group.
Chichester Clark, Emma. Mimi's Book of Opposites. Chichester Clark, Emma, illus. 2004. (Illus.). 24p. (J). 9.95 *(978-1-57091-574-1(1))* Charlesbridge Publishing, Inc.
Ciencin, Scott. Power at the Plate, 1 vol. Aburto, Jesus et al, illus. 2011. (Sports Illustrated Kids Graphic Novels Ser.). (ENG.). 56p. (J). (gr. 3-8). pap. 7.19 *(978-1-4342-3400-1(2),* 116413); lib. bdg. 26.65 *(978-1-4342-2239-8(X),* 103102) Capstone. (Stone Arch Bks.).
Dempsey, Sheena. Bye-Bye Baby Brother! 2013. (ENG., Illus.). 32p. (J). (gr. -1-2). 15.99 *(978-0-7636-6241-7(0))* Candlewick Pr.
Dungy, Tony & Dungy, Lauren. Go, Jade, Go! Ready-To-Read Level 2. Brantley-Newton, Vanessa, illus. 2013. (Tony & Lauren Dungy Ready-To-Reads Ser.). (ENG.). 32p. (J). (gr. k-2). 17.99 *(978-1-4424-5467-5(9));* pap. 3.99 *(978-1-4424-5466-8(0))* Simon Spotlight. (Simon Spotlight).
Forsyth, Christine. Two on One, 1 vol. 2005. (Lorimer Sports Stories Ser.: 83). (ENG.). 112p. (J). (gr. 4-8). 16.95 *(978-1-55028-901-5(2),* 901); 8.95 *(978-1-55028-900-8(4),* 900) James Lorimer & Co. Ltd., Pubs. CAN. Dist: Formac Lorimer Bks. Ltd.
Friedman, Laurie. Mallory vs. Max. Schmitz, Tamara, illus. 2006. (Mallory Ser.: 3). (ENG.). 160p. (J). (gr. 2-5). per. 7.99 *(978-1-57505-863-4(4),* a9938cdb-4867-42f6-9747-88b51dffd127, Darby Creek) Lerner Publishing Group.
Gaetz, Dayle Campbell. Spoiled Rotten, 1 vol. 2005. (Orca Currents Ser.). (ENG.). 128p. (J). (gr. 4-7). per. 9.95 *(978-1-55143-474-2(1))* Orca Bk. Pubs. USA.
Guest, Elissa Haden. Iris & Walter & Baby Rose. Davenier, Christine, illus. 2012. (Iris & Walter — Green Light Reader Ser.). lib. bdg. 13.55 *(978-0-606-26612-3(7))* Turtleback.
Gunn, Dusty M. Paul & Peter Possum. 2008. 20p. pap. 24.95 *(978-1-60474-503-0(7))* America Star Bks.
Henbit & the Roly-Poly. 2007. (J). *(978-0-9791982-2-9(4))* Pine Cone Pr.
Henbit & the Roly-Poly - Specially Formatted Edition. l.t. ed. 2007. (J). *(978-0-9791982-3-6(2))* Pine Cone Pr.
Henkes, Kevin. Julius, the Baby of the World. Henkes, Kevin, illus. 2003. (Illus.). (J). 28.95 incl. audio compact disk *(978-1-59112-518-1(9));* 25.95 incl. audio *(978-1-59112-250-0(3));* pap. 33.95 incl. audio *(978-1-59112-251-7(1));* pap. 35.95 incl. audio compact disk *(978-1-59112-523-5(5))* Live Oak Media.
Hinton, S. E. Tex. 2013. 224p. (YA). (gr. 7). pap. 10.99 *(978-0-385-37567-2(0),* Delacorte Pr.) Random Hse. Children's Bks.
Hughes, Mair Wynn & Davies, Tracy. Brawd Newydd. 2005. (WEL., Illus.). 15p. pap. *(978-0-86243-453-3(X))* Y Lolfa.
Hughes, Mark Peter. I Am the Wallpaper. 2007. (ENG.). 256p. (YA). (gr. 7-11). pap. 8.99 *(978-0-440-42046-0(6),* Delacorte Bks. for Young Readers) Random Hse. Children's Bks.
Jomo & Mata: Evaluation Guide. 2006. (J). *(978-1-55942-411-0(7))* Witcher Productions.
Kantorovitz, Sylvie. The Very Tiny Baby. Kantorovitz, Sylvie, illus. 2014. (Illus.). 240p. (J). (gr. -1-2). lib. bdg. 14.95 *(978-1-58089-445-6(3))* Charlesbridge Publishing, Inc.
—The Very Tiny Baby. 2014. (J). pap. *(978-1-58089-446-3(1))* Charlesbridge Publishing, Inc.
Koller, Jackie French & Koller. Horace the Horrible: A Knight Meets His Match, 1 vol. Urbanovic, Jackie, illus. 2003. (ENG.). 32p. (J). 16.95 *(978-0-7614-5150-1(1))* Marshall Cavendish Corp.
Lawson, Janet. The Alberts & Me. 2009. (J). *(978-0-15-205327-7(1))* Harcourt Trade Pubs.
Layne, Steven L. Share with Brother, 1 vol. Hoyt, Ard, illus. 2010. (ENG.). 32p. (J). (gr. k-3). 16.99 *(978-1-58980-860-7(6),* Pelican Publishing) Arcadia Publishing.
Li, Deborah, illus. Tricia & the Blue Cap. l.t. ed. 2003. 28p. (J). 7.95 net. *(978-0-9706654-5-4(8))* Sprite Pr.
Lynch, Jay. Mo & Jo Fighting Together Forever: Toon Books Level 3. Haspiel, Dean, illus. 2013. (Toon Ser.). (ENG.). 40p. (J). (gr. -1-3). pap. 4.99 *(978-1-935179-37-5(3),* Toon Books) Astra Publishing Hse.
MacCullough, Carolyn. Once a Witch. 2010. (ENG.). 320p. (YA). (gr. 7). pap. 17.99 *(978-0-547-41730-1(6),* 1430229, Clarion Bks.) HarperCollins Pubs.
—Once a Witch. 2009. (ENG.). 304p. (YA). (gr. 7-12). 24.94 *(978-0-547-22399-5(4))* Houghton Mifflin Harcourt Publishing Co.
MacKey, Cindy. My Sister Sophie. Tebbit, Jake, illus. 2013. 30p. pap. 12.99 *(978-0-9892699-9-5(X))* Cyrano Bks.
Mackey, Cindy. My Sister Sophie. 2017. (ENG., Illus.). (J). (gr. k-4). pap. 8.99 *(978-0-9990993-5-3(3))* Cyrano Bks.
Maddox, Jake. Blue Line Breakaway. Tiffany, Sean, illus. 2018. (Jake Maddox Sports Stories Ser.). (ENG.). 72p. (J). (gr. 3-6). pap. 5.95 *(978-1-4965-6319-4(0),* 138058, Stone Arch Bks.) Capstone.
Marychild, H. D. Skater Sister. 2013. (ENG.). 222p. (J). (gr. 5-12). pap. 9.52 *(978-0-9899964-9-5(2))* Small Wonder Publishing.
McAuslan, Fiona & Nicholson, Peter. The Resolving Sibling Rivalry Book. 2010. (Resolving Books Ser.). (ENG., Illus.). 88p. (J). pap. 9.95 *(978-1-84730-224-3(6))* Veritas Pubns. IRL. Dist: Casemate Pubs. & Bk. Distributors, LLC.
McNamee, Kevin. My Brother the Frog. Morris, Alexander, illus. 2011. 24p. 19.95 *(978-1-61633-167-2(4));* pap. 10.95 *(978-1-61633-159-7(3))* Guardian Angel Publishing, Inc.
Michels-Gualtieri, Akaela S. I Was Born to Be a Sister. Ramsey, Marcy Dunn, illus. 2005. (ENG.). 32p. (J). (gr. 4-7). 9.95 incl. lp *(978-1-930775-11-4(3))* Platypus Media, L.L.C.
Nooninals: Presents the New Baby. rev. ed. 2007. (Illus.). 40p. (J). per. 14.99 *(978-0-9796832-0-6(3))* Nooni Publishing.
Payton, Belle. May the Best Twin Win. 2015. (It Takes Two Ser.: 7). (ENG., Illus.). 160p. (J). (gr. 3-7). pap. 6.99 *(978-1-4814-3134-7(X),* Simon Spotlight) Simon Spotlight.
Pennypacker, Sara. Clementine & the Family Meeting. Frazee, Marla, illus. 2011. (Clementine Ser.: 5). (ENG.). 176p. (J). (gr. 1-5). 14.99 *(978-1-4231-2356-9(5))* Hyperion Pr.
—Clementine & the Family Meeting. Frazee, Marla, illus. 2012. (Clementine Ser.: 5). (ENG.). 176p. (J). (gr. 1-5). pap. 5.99 *(978-1-4231-2436-8(7))* Little, Brown Bks. for Young Readers.
Petruck, Rebecca. Steering Toward Normal. 2014. (ENG.). 336p. (J). (gr. 4-8). 16.95 *(978-1-4197-0732-2(9),* 1057501, Amulet Bks.) Abrams, Inc.
Phillips, Leigh Hope. Birthday Wishes. Fountain, John, illus. 2005. (J). pap. *(978-1-933156-10-1(4));* per. *(978-1-933156-03-3(1))* GSVQ Publishing. (VisionQuest Kids).

Poole, Philip. The Trouble with Time. 2012. (Illus.). 24p. pap. 19.82 *(978-1-4772-3459-4(4))* AuthorHouse.

Quay, Emma. Shrieking Violet. 2019. 32p. pap. 6.99 *(978-0-7333-3507-5(1))* ABC Bks. AUS. Dist: HarperCollins Pubs.

Rock, Brian. With All My Heart. Banta, Susan, illus. 2012. (ENG.). 24p. (J). *(978-1-58925-648-4(4))* Tiger Tales.

Schad, Kristine. Do You Love Me Best? Timmons, Gayle, illus. 2007. 40p. (J). lib. bdg. 23.95 *(978-1-58374-156-6(9))* Chicago Spectrum Pr.

Scott, Ann Herbert. On Mother's Lap/en Las Piernas de Mamá: Bilingual English-Spanish. Coalson, Glo, illus. 2007.Tr. of On Mother's Lap. (ENG.). 14p. (J). (gr. k — 1). bds. 5.95 *(978-0-618-75247-8(1)*, 100529, Clarion Bks.) HarperCollins Pubs.

Seif, Adam, creator. Tacos, Beans & Rice... the Episodes: From the Beginning. l.t. ed. 2006. (Illus.). 32p. (J). *(978-0-9719518-0-8(2))* Doodle Publishing.

Seitz, J. B. Freddy the Flea. 2009. 23p. pap. 24.95 *(978-1-60836-759-7(2))* America Star Bks.

Simmons, Cari & Burns, Laura J. Picture Perfect #5: All Together Now. Mingus, Cathi, illus. 2016. (Picture Perfect Ser.: 5). (ENG.). 192p. (J). (gr. 3-7). pap. 6.99 *(978-0-06-233676-7(2)*, HarperCollins) HarperCollins Pubs.

Simmons, Celeste. The Adventures of Booger Malone: Busted in the Backseat. 2007. (J). per. 10.95 *(978-0-9777041-2-5(2))* Third Dimension Publishing.

Simons, Joseph. Under a Living Sky, 1 vol. 2005. (Orca Young Readers Ser.). (ENG., Illus.). 112p. (J). (gr. 4-7). per. 5.95 *(978-1-55143-355-4(9))* Orca Bk. Pubs. USA.

Skinner, Daphne. Henry Lleva la Cuenta; Henry Keeps Score. 2008. pap. 34.95 *(978-1-58013-757-7(1))* Astra Publishing Hse.

Smith, Steven K. Brother Wars. 2017. (ENG.). 120p. (J). pap. 8.99 *(978-0-9861473-2-6(X))* MyBoys3 Pr.

Speed, Nakesha. Yucky Brother. 2006. pap. 16.95 *(978-1-4241-2040-6(3))* PublishAmerica, Inc.

Staniszewski, Anna. The Magic Mirror: a Branches Book (Once upon a Fairy Tale #1) Pamintuan, Macky, illus. 2019. (Once upon a Fairy Tale Ser.: 1). (ENG.). 96p. (J). (gr. 1-3). pap. 4.99 *(978-1-338-34971-9(6))* Scholastic, Inc.

Stine, R. L. Night of the Living Dummy (Classic Goosebumps #1) 2008. (Classic Goosebumps Ser.: 1). (ENG.). 160p. (J). (gr. 3-7). 7.99 *(978-0-545-03517-0(1)*, Scholastic Paperbacks) Scholastic, Inc.

Vega, Denise. Rock On: A Story of Guitars, Gigs, Girls, & a Brother (not Necessarily in That Order) 2013. (ENG., Illus.). 304p. (YA). (gr. 7-17). pap. 8.99 *(978-0-316-13309-8(4))* Little, Brown Bks. for Young Readers.

Wilson, Troy. Liam Takes a Stand. Holinaty, Josh, illus. 2017. (ENG.). 32p. (J). (gr. k-4). 16.95 *(978-1-77147-161-9(1))* Owlkids Bks. Inc. CAN. Dist: Publishers Group West (PGW).

SIBLINGS

Auld, Mary. Mi Hermano (My Brother), 1 vol. 2004. (Conoce la Familia (Meet the Family) Ser.). (SPA., Illus.). 24p. (gr. k-2). lib. bdg. 24.67 *(978-0-8368-3931-9(5)*, dcbaf077-2d15-4eeb-b7f6-06f1dc106053, Gareth Stevens Learning Library) Stevens, Gareth Publishing LLLP.

—My Brother, 1 vol. 2004. (Meet the Family Ser.). (ENG., Illus.). 24p. (J). (gr. k-2). 24.67 *(978-0-8368-3924-1(2)*, def9e0bf-3544-4a13-a297-e5d63239a054, Gareth Stevens Learning Library) Stevens, Gareth Publishing LLLP.

Barber, Nicola. A New Baby Arrives, 1 vol. (Big Day! Ser.). (ENG., Illus.). 24p. (J). (gr. 1-1). 2009. pap. 9.25 *(978-1-4358-2898-8(4)*, 1291898) 2008. lib. bdg. 26.27 *(978-1-4358-2842-1(9)*, 1291898) Rosen Publishing Group, Inc., The. (PowerKids Pr.).

Barber, Ronde & Barber, Tiki. Go Long! 2008. (Barber Game Time Bks.). (ENG.). 160p. (J). (gr. 3-7). 15.99 *(978-1-4169-3619-0(X)*, Simon & Schuster/Paula Wiseman Bks.) Simon & Schuster/Paula Wiseman Bks.

Barber, Tiki & Barber, Ronde. By My Brother's Side. Root, Barry, illus. 2004. (ENG.). 32p. (J). (gr. 1-5). 18.99 *(978-0-689-86559-6(7)*, Simon & Schuster/Paula Wiseman Bks.) Simon & Schuster/Paula Wiseman Bks.

—Game Day. Root, Barry, illus. 2005. (ENG.). 32p. (J). (gr. k-5). 19.99 *(978-1-4169-0093-1(4)*, Simon & Schuster/Paula Wiseman Bks.) Simon & Schuster/Paula Wiseman Bks.

—Kickoff! 2008. (Barber Game Time Bks.). (ENG.). 176p. (J). (gr. 3-7). pap. 7.99 *(978-1-4169-7080-4(0)*, Simon & Schuster/Paula Wiseman Bks.) Simon & Schuster/Paula Wiseman Bks.

—Teammates. Root, Barry, illus. 2006. (ENG.). 32p. (J). (gr. 1-5). 16.95 *(978-1-4169-2489-0(2)*, Simon & Schuster/Paula Wiseman Bks.) Simon & Schuster/Paula Wiseman Bks.

Berry, Joy. I Love Brothers & Sisters. Regan, Dana, illus. 2010. (Teach Me About Ser.). (ENG.). 20p. (J). (gr. k — 1). pap. 5.99 *(978-1-60577-002-4(7))* Berry, Joy Enterprises.

Bradex, Melissa A. Little Gregory. Crane, Eddie, illus. 2009. 32p. pap. 14.99 *(978-1-4490-3549-5(3))* AuthorHouse.

Crist, James J. & Verdick, Elizabeth. Siblings: You're Stuck with Each Other, So Stick Together. 2010. (Laugh & Learn(r) Ser.). (ENG., Illus.). 128p. (J). (gr. 3-7). pap. 10.99 *(978-1-57542-336-4(7)*, 23364) Free Spirit Publishing Inc.

Danzig, Dianne. Babies Don't Eat Pizza: A Big Kids' Book about Baby Brothers & Baby Sisters. Tilley, Debbie, illus. 2009. 32p. (J). (gr. -1-k). 18.99 *(978-0-525-47441-8(2)*, Dutton Books for Young Readers) Penguin Young Readers Group.

Dwight, Laura. Brothers & Sisters, 1 vol. (ENG., Illus.). 32p. (J). 2012. pap. 7.95 *(978-1-59572-364-2(1))* 2005. (gr. -1-3). 15.95 *(978-1-887734-80-6(5))* Star Bright Bks., Inc.

Dysinger, Stephen. William. Dysinger, Stephen, illus. 2007. (Illus.). 28p. (J). (gr. -1-3). per. 12.99 *(978-1-59879-297-3(0))* Lifevest Publishing, Inc.

Edwards, Dianna. It's Not Easy Being Patou - Book One. 2004. (J). *(978-0-9767756-1-4(1))* Patou Bks., LLC.

—Meet Patou. 2006. (J). pap. 29.95 *(978-0-9767756-0-7(3))* Patou Bks., LLC.

—When Niki Got Sick, Bk. 2. 2004. (J). *(978-0-9767756-2-1(X))* Patou Bks., LLC.

—Why Can't Everything Just Stay the Same? Book Three. 2004. (J). *(978-0-9767756-3-8(8))* Patou Bks., LLC.

Felix, Erica Lynn. Brother & Sisterly Love. 2011. 24p. pap. 24.95 *(978-1-4560-9726-4(1))* America Star Bks.

Ferguson, Addy. What to Do When Your Brother or Sister Is a Bully. 2014. (Stand up: Bullying Prevention Ser.). 24p. (J). (gr. k-3). pap. 49.50 *(978-1-4777-6621-7(9)*, PowerKids Pr.) Rosen Publishing Group, Inc., The.

Feuer, Bonnie. I Hear a Red Crayon: A Child's Perspective of Her Brother's Autism. Boemmels, Kayleigh, illus. l.t. ed. 2015. (ENG.). 36p. (gr. 3-12). 19.95 *(978-0-9825468-9-5(0))* Connecticut Pr., The.

Green, Tim. Football Hero. l.t. ed. 2008. (YA). 23.95 *(978-1-4104-1116-7(8))* Thorndike Pr.

Hale, Natalie. Oh, Brother! Growing up with a Special Needs Sibling. Sternberg, Kate, tr. Sternberg, Kate, illus. 2004. 48p. (J). pap. 9.95 *(978-1-59147-061-8(7)*, Magination Pr.) American Psychological Assn.

—Oh Brother! Growing up with a Special Needs Sibling. Sternberg, Kate, illus. 2004. (ENG.). 48p. (J). 14.95 *(978-1-59147-060-1(9)*, Magination Pr.) American Psychological Assn.

Harper, Hill. Letters to a Young Sister: DeFINE Your Destiny. 2009. 320p. (gr. 12-18). 18.00 *(978-1-59240-459-9(6)*, Avery) Penguin Publishing Group.

Hashey, Heather. I'm A Big Sister. Hashey, Kim, photos by. 2010. (Illus.). 16p. 8.49 *(978-1-4520-6293-8(5))* AuthorHouse.

Hewitt, Sally. Our New Baby. 2009. (Illus.). 32p. (J). 28.50 *(978-1-59920-232-7(8))* Black Rabbit Bks.

Jackson, Aariane R. & Lawhon, Leigh. Can You Hear Me Smiling? A Child Grieves a Sister. 2004. (ENG., Illus.). 40p. (J). pap. 9.95 *(978-0-87868-835-7(8)*, P544263, Child & Family Pr.) Child Welfare League of America, Inc.

Jamieson, Victoria & Mohamed, Omar. When Stars Are Scattered. Jamieson, Victoria & Geddy, Iman, illus. 2020. (ENG.). 264p. (J). (gr. 4-7). 22.99 *(978-0-525-55391-5(6))*; pap. 13.99 *(978-0-525-55390-8(8))* Penguin Young Readers Group. (Dial Bks).

Kane, Darlene. Missing Hannah: Based on a True Story of Sudden Infant Death. 2006. (ENG.). 58p. pap. 26.49 *(978-1-4259-0136-3(0))* AuthorHouse.

Kelly, Scott. My Journey to the Stars. Ceolin, André, illus. 2020. (ENG.). 48p. (J). (gr. k-3). pap. 8.99 *(978-0-593-12465-9(0)*, Dragonfly Bks.) Random Hse. Children's Bks.

—My Journey to the Stars (Step into Reading) Ceolin, André, illus. 2019. (Step into Reading Ser.). (ENG.). 48p. (J). (gr. k-3). pap. 5.99 *(978-1-5247-6380-0(2)*, Random Hse. Bks. for Young Readers) Random Hse. Children's Bks.

King Sprools, Wendy. Brothers Are Forever. 2011. 24p. pap. 7.99 *(978-0-88144-122-2(8))* Yorkshire Publishing Group.

Laff, Becky. Joseph the Dreamer. Laff, Becky, illus. 2016. (ENG., Illus.). 48p. (J). (gr. k-4). 17.99 *(978-1-4677-7845-9(1)*, 0ba032c2-b4b4-4b62-83f1-f362a8415f75, Kar-Ben Publishing) Lerner Publishing Group.

Langston-George, Rebecca. The Booth Brothers: Drama, Fame, & the Death of President Lincoln. 2017. (Encounter: Narrative Nonfiction Stories Ser.). (ENG., Illus.). 112p. (J). (gr. 3-7). lib. bdg. 31.32 *(978-1-5157-7338-2(8)*, 135667, Capstone Pr.) Capstone.

Loewen, Nancy & Skelley, Paula. Siblings, Curfews, & How to Deal: Questions & Answers about Family Life. Mora, Julissa, illus. 2015. (Girl Talk Ser.). (ENG.). 32p. (J). (gr. 3-9). lib. bdg. 28.65 *(978-1-4914-1858-1(3)*, 127295, Capstone Pr.) Capstone.

Mally, Sarah, et al. Making Brothers & Sisters Best Friends: How to Fight the Good Fight at Home. 2006. (ENG., Illus.). 272p. pap. 14.00 *(978-0-9719405-0-5(9))* Tomorrow's Forefathers, Inc.

McCormick, Patricia. Just Add One Chinese Sister (p) 2010. pap. 10.95 *(978-1-59078-772-4(2))* Highlights Pr., c/o Highlights for Children, Inc.

McKeon, Tess. Carried in Our Hearts. 2011. 52p. pap. 16.95 *(978-1-4560-8394-6(5))* America Star Bks.

Meyer, Donald & Vadasy, Patricia F. Living with a Brother or Sister with Special Needs: A Book for Sibs. 2nd exp. rev. ed. 2003. (ENG., Illus.). 144p. (C). (gr. -1-18). pap. 24.95 *(978-0-295-97547-4(4))* Univ. of Washington Pr.

Meyer, Donald J., ed. Sibling Slam Book. 2005. (ENG., Illus.). 186p. pap. 15.95 *(978-1-890627-52-2(6))* Woodbine Hse.

Mills, Lois. Three Together: Story of the Wright Brothers & Their Sister. Moyers, William, illus. 2011. 160p. 41.95 *(978-1-258-05968-2(1))* Literary Licensing, LLC.

Mullery Jr., Matthew W. Hanging Out with Happy Crackers, Fingers Baloo & Stinky Magoo: One Sunny Morning. 2008. 25p. pap. 24.95 *(978-1-60672-136-0(4))* America Star Bks.

Pacheco, Amanda J. Designer Genes. 2012. 28p. (-18). pap. 24.95 *(978-1-4626-5371-3(5))* America Star Bks.

Page, Robin. Sisters & Brothers: Sibling Relationships in the Animal World. 2012. lib. bdg. 18.40 *(978-0-606-23994-3(4))* Turtleback.

Poulin, Andreé. The Magic Clothesline. Arbona, Marion, illus. 2012. 32p. (J). pap. 9.95 *(978-1-4338-1195-1(2)*, Magination Pr.) American Psychological Assn.

Poulin, Andrée. The Magic Clothesline. Arbona, Marion, illus. 2012. 32p. (J). 14.95 *(978-1-4338-1194-4(4)*, Magination Pr.) American Psychological Assn.

Quattlebaum, Mary. Brother, Sister, Me & You. 2019. (Illus.). 32p. (J). (gr. -1-k). 16.99 *(978-1-4263-3290-6(4)*, National Geographic Kids) Disney Publishing Worldwide.

Raatma, Lucia. Brothers Are Part of a Family. 2017. (Our Families Ser.). (ENG.). 24p. (J). (gr. -1-2). lib. bdg. 22.65 *(978-1-5157-7461-7(9)*, 135807, Capstone Pr.) Capstone.

Raden, Tammy. Every Time I Want to Play, Brother & Sister Get in My Way. 2010. 24p. pap. 11.49 *(978-1-4490-5454-0(4))* AuthorHouse.

Rice, Earle. The Life & Times of the Brothers Custer: Galloping to Glory. 2008. (Profiles in American History Ser.). (Illus.). 48p. (J). (gr. 4-8). lib. bdg. 29.95 *(978-1-58415-665-9(1))* Mitchell Lane Pubs.

Rogers, Amy B. I Learn from My Brother & Sister, 1 vol. 2016. (Things I Learn Ser.). (ENG., Illus.). 24p. (J). (gr. 1-1). pap. 9.25 *(978-1-4994-2339-6(X)*, df3effe1-f8ba-4e62-a700-283efe3f17a7, PowerKids Pr.) Rosen Publishing Group, Inc., The.

Rusch, Elizabeth. Ready, Set ... Baby! Leng, Qin, illus. 2017. (ENG.). 32p. (J). (gr. -1-3). 17.99 *(978-0-544-47272-3(1)*, 1601681, Clarion Bks.) HarperCollins Pubs.

Schaefer, Lola M. Brothers: Revised Edition. rev. ed. 2008. (Families Ser.). (ENG., Illus.). 24p. (J). (gr. -1-2). per. 6.29 *(978-1-4296-1750-5(0)*, 94797) Capstone.

Sebastian, Emily. My Brothers & Sisters, 1 vol. 2010. (My Family Ser.). (ENG., Illus.). 24p. (J). (gr. 1-2). pap. 9.25 *(978-1-4488-1492-3(8)*, d7c1dd0f-9acb-449d-a3c9-a6ad4e6f9eea); lib. bdg. 26.27 *(978-1-4488-1463-3(4)*, decf8bef-eba3-463c-9971-01d5eeb0024f) Rosen Publishing Group, Inc., The. (PowerKids Pr.).

—My Brothers & Sisters: MIS Hermanos, 1 vol. 2010. (My Family / Mi Familia Ser.). (SPA & ENG., Illus.). 24p. (J). (gr. 1-2). lib. bdg. 26.27 *(978-1-4488-0718-5(2)*, 20aaea0a-bc8c-49e8-aac2-79ec9c3963a4) Rosen Publishing Group, Inc., The.

Shanta, N. D. He's My Brother. 2006. 24p. (J). 19.95 *(978-1-58909-380-5(1))* Bookstand Publishing.

Sheldon, Annette. Big Brother Now: A Story about Me & Our New Baby. Maizel, Karen, illus. 2008. 32p. (J). (gr. -1-1). (ENG.). 14.95 *(978-1-4338-0381-9(X))*; pap. 9.95 *(978-1-4338-0382-6(8))* American Psychological Assn. (Magination Pr.).

—Big Sister Now: A Story about Me & Our New Baby. Maizel, Karen, illus. 2005. 32p. (J). (gr. -1-1). per. 9.95 *(978-1-59147-244-5(X)*, Magination Pr.) American Psychological Assn.

Sheldon, Annette & Maizel, Karen. Big Sister Now: A Story about Me & Our New Baby. Maizel, Karen, illus. 2005. (ENG., Illus.). 32p. (J). (gr. -1-3). 14.95 *(978-1-59147-243-8(1)*, Magination Pr.) American Psychological Assn.

Skotko, Brian & Levine, Susan. Fasten Your Seatbelt: A Crash Course on down Syndrome for Brothers & Sisters. 2008. (ENG., Illus.). 192p. (J). (gr. 4-10). pap. 18.95 *(978-1-890627-86-7(0))* Woodbine Hse.

Smith, Brendan Powell. Joseph & the Colorful Coat: The Brick Bible for Kids. 2015. (Brick Bible for Kids Ser.). (ENG., Illus.). 32p. (J). (gr. -1-k). 12.99 *(978-1-63220-409-7(6)*, Sky Pony Pr.) Skyhorse Publishing Co., Inc.

Sussman, Elaine. The Boy Who Opened Our Eyes. Matsick, Anni, illus. 2017. 38p. (J). *(978-1-68265-353-1(6))* Sussman Sales Co.

Sutherland, Joe. The Broken Egg: A Story to Help Children Cope with the Loss of a Younger Sibling. Sutherland, Shailyn, illus. 2010. (ENG.). 24p. pap. 11.99 *(978-1-4490-8347-2(1))* AuthorHouse.

Telgemeier, Raina. Sisters. 2014. lib. bdg. 22.10 *(978-0-606-36038-8(7))* Turtleback.

—Sisters: a Graphic Novel. Telgemeier, Raina, illus. 2014. (ENG., Illus.). 208p. (J). (gr. 3-7). 24.99 *(978-0-545-54059-9(3)*, Graphix) Scholastic, Inc.

Tor, Seidler. Hermanos bajo cero. 2004. (Punto de Encuentro (Editorial Everest) Ser.). (SPA., Illus.). 118p. (J). (gr. 5-12). pap., pap. 11.99 *(978-84-241-8076-8(3))* Everest Editora ESP. Dist: Lectorum Pubns., Inc.

Vernick, Audrey. Brothers at Bat: The True Story of an Amazing All-Brother Baseball Team. Salerno, Steven, illus. 2012. (ENG.). 40p. (J). (gr. -1-3). 18.99 *(978-0-547-38557-0(9)*, 1425838, Clarion Bks.) HarperCollins Pubs.

Vitterito, Joseph A., 2nd. My Sister Is a Preemie: A Children's Guide to the NICU Experience. Chuzzlewit, Abraham R., illus. 2012. 30p. (J). (-18). pap. 15.99 *(978-0-9882940-9-7(5))* Bryson Taylor Publishing.

Webb, Jessica. A Simple Wish. 2009. 16p. pap. 10.95 *(978-1-4389-7899-4(5))* AuthorHouse.

Winchester, Elizabeth Siris & Siris-Winchester, Elizabeth. Sisters & Brothers: The Ultimate Guide to Understanding Your Siblings & Yourself. 2008. (Scholastic Choices Ser.). (ENG., Illus.). 112p. (J). (gr. 7-12). 27.00 *(978-0-531-13870-0(4)*, Children's Pr.) Scholastic Library Publishing.

Yoon, Salina. Duck, Duck, Porcupine! 2017. (J). lib. bdg. 16.00 *(978-0-606-40593-5(3))* Turtleback.

Zeavin, Carol & Silverbush, Rhona. New Baby! Davis, Jon, illus. 2020. 16p. (J). *(978-1-4338-3250-5(X)*, Magination Pr.) American Psychological Assn.

SIBLINGS—FICTION

Abbott, Jacob. Aunt Margaret; or, How John True Kept His Resolutions. 2013. 160p. pap. 19.95 *(978-1-4455-2937-0(8))* Research Pr.

Abdullah, Shaila. A Manual for Marco: Living, Learning, & Laughing with an Autistic Sibling. Tejpar, Iman, illus. 2015. (J). *(978-1-61599-248-5(0))* Loving Healing Pr., Inc.

Achatz, Eric. The Adventures of Ryan Alexander: The Great Space Chase. 2010. 52p. pap. 23.50 *(978-1-4269-3763-7(6))* Trafford Publishing.

Ackerman, Helen. Casper's Paper Caper. 2013. 36p. pap. 18.41 *(978-1-4669-7448-7(6))* Trafford Publishing.

Adamchuk, Rachelle G. Disappearance: The First Part of Trickery & Honest Deception. 2006. 169p. pap. 16.99 *(978-1-4120-8991-3(3))* Trafford Publishing.

Adam's Creations Publishing. Enchanted Fairyland: A Sphinx & Trevi Adventure. Bishop, Christina, illus. 2007. (ENG.). 30p. (J). 19.95 *(978-0-9785695-0-1(4))* Adam's Creations Publishing, LLC.

Adams, Jennifer. Edgar & the Tattle-Tale Heart: a BabyLit(TM) Book: Inspired by Edgar Allan Poe's the Tell-Tale Heart, 1 vol. Stucki, Ron, illus. 2014. (ENG.). 32p. (J). 16.99 *(978-1-4236-3766-0(6))* Gibbs Smith, Publisher.

—Edgar & the Tree House of Usher: Inspired by Edgar Allan Poe's the Fall of the House of Usher, 1 vol. Stucki, Ron, illus. (Edgar the Raven Ser.). (J). 2016. 22p. (— 1). bds. 9.99 *(978-1-4236-4493-4(X))* 2015. (ENG.). 32p. (gr. -1-k). 16.99 *(978-1-4236-4043-1(8))* Gibbs Smith, Publisher.

Adams, Michelle Medlock & Adams, Michelle M. Sister for Sale!, 1 vol. Brooks, Karen Stormer, illus. 2007. (I Can Read! Ser.). (ENG.). 32p. (J). (gr. -1-1). pap. 4.99 *(978-0-310-71469-9(9))* Zonderkidz.

Adams, Sheila Murphy. Beads, Bands, & a Brass Ring. 2011. 28p. pap. 14.95 *(978-1-4567-1550-2(X))* AuthorHouse.

Adderson, Caroline. Jasper John Dooley: Star of the Week. Clanton, Ben, illus. 2014. (Jasper John Dooley Ser.). (ENG.). 128p. (J). (gr. k-3). pap. 7.99 *(978-1-77138-119-2(1))* Kids Can Pr., Ltd. CAN. Dist: Hachette Bk. Group.

Adler, David A. Andy & Tamika. Hillenbrand, Will, illus. 2005. (Andy Russell Ser.: 2). (ENG.). 144p. (J). (gr. 1-4). pap. 7.99 *(978-0-15-205446-5(4)*, 1196390, Clarion Bks.) HarperCollins Pubs.

—Andy & Tamika. Hillenbrand, Will, illus. 2005. (Andy Russell Ser.: Bk. 2). 129p. 16.00 *(978-0-7569-4898-6(3))* Perfection Learning Corp.

Agha-Khan, Aliyar. Cyrus & Kaleo Go Rock Hunting. 2012. 32p. pap. 12.99 *(978-1-4634-1567-9(2))* AuthorHouse.

Ahdieh, Renée. Flame in the Mist. (Flame in the Mist Ser.: 1). (ENG.). (YA). (gr. 7). 2018. 448p. pap. 11.99 *(978-0-14-751387-8(1)*, Penguin Books) 2017. 416p. 17.99 *(978-0-399-17163-5(0)*, G.P. Putnam's Sons Books for Young Readers) Penguin Young Readers Group.

—Flame in the Mist. 2018. lib. bdg. 22.10 *(978-0-606-40878-3(9))* Turtleback.

—Smoke in the Sun. 2018. (Flame in the Mist Ser.: 2). (ENG.). 432p. (YA). (gr. 7). 18.99 *(978-1-5247-3814-3(X)*, G.P. Putnam's Sons Books for Young Readers) Penguin Young Readers Group.

Ahern, Dianne. Break-in at the Basilica: Adventures with Sister Philomena, Special Agent to the Pope. Larson, Katherine, illus. 2006. (J). *(978-0-9679437-8-7(7))* En Route Bks. & Media.

Aikins, Dave, illus. Big Sister Dora! 2005. (Dora the Explorer Ser.: Vol. 13). (ENG.). 24p. (J). pap. 3.99 *(978-0-689-87846-6(X)*, Simon Spotlight/Nickelodeon) Simon Spotlight/Nickelodeon.

Al Shaikh, Latifa. I'm Still Waiting for that Chocolate. 2007. 52p. (YA). per. 8.95 *(978-0-595-42982-0(3))* iUniverse, Inc.

Alarid, Carilyn & Markel, Marilyn. Talks All Day Has the Courage to Speak: Mimbres Children Learn Citizenship. Alarid, Carilyn & Markel, Marilyn, illus. 2006. (Illus.). 125p. (J). pap. 16.95 *(978-0-86534-470-9(1))* Sunstone Pr.

Alarid, Carilyn & Markel, Marilyn, illus. Runs Like the Wind Stops in Her Tracks: Mimbres Children Learn about Trustworthiness. 2016. 95p. (J). pap. *(978-1-63293-099-6(4))* Sunstone Pr.

Alborozo. And Then... Alborozo, illus. 2016. (Child's Play Library). (Illus.). 32p. (J). (ENG.). *(978-1-84643-696-3(6))*; pap. *(978-1-84643-695-6(8))* Child's Play International Ltd.

Alcock, Deborah. The King's Service: A Story of the Thirty Years' War. 2008. (Illus.). 183p. (YA). *(978-1-894666-06-0(2))* Inheritance Pubns.

Alexander, James W. Good - Better - Best: Classic Treatment of a Christian's Duty to the Poor. 2009. 224p. pap. 17.00 *(978-1-59925-143-1(4))* Solid Ground Christian Bks.

Alexander, Kwame. The Crossover. 2020. (ENG., Illus.). 218p. (J). (gr. 4-5). 24.19 *(978-1-64697-344-6(5))* Penworthy Co., LLC, The.

—The Crossover. 2014. lib. bdg. 29.40 *(978-0-606-37975-5(4))* Turtleback.

—The Crossover: A Newbery Award Winner. Anyabwile, Dawud, illus. (Crossover Ser.). (ENG.). (J). (gr. 3-7). 2019. 256p. pap. 10.99 *(978-0-544-93520-4(9)*, 1658124) 2014. 240p. 17.99 *(978-0-544-10771-7(3)*, 1540363) HarperCollins Pubs. (Clarion Bks.).

—El Crossover: Crossover (Spanish Edition), a Newbery Award Winner. Herrera, Juan Felipe, tr. Anyabwile, Dawud, illus. 2019. (Crossover Ser.). (SPA.). 256p. (J). (gr. 5-7). pap. 9.99 *(978-0-358-06473-2(2)*, 1743975, Clarion Bks.) HarperCollins Pubs.

Alexander, William. Goblin Secrets. (ENG., Illus.). (J). (gr. 3-7). 2013. 256p. pap. 7.99 *(978-1-4424-2727-3(2))* 2012. 240p. 19.99 *(978-1-4424-2726-6(4))* McElderry, Margaret K. Bks. (McElderry, Margaret K. Bks.).

Alfonsi, Alice. Freaked Out. 2004. 148p. (J). lib. bdg. 16.92 *(978-1-4242-0687-2(1))* Fitzgerald Bks.

Allen, Rachael. Taxonomy of Love. 2018. (ENG., Illus.). 336p. (J). (gr. 8-17). 17.99 *(978-1-4197-2541-8(6)*, 1185701, Amulet Bks.) Abrams, Inc.

Alley, R. W. Gretchen over the Beach. 2016. (ENG., Illus.). 32p. (J). (gr. -1-3). 14.99 *(978-0-547-90708-6(7)*, 1512358, Clarion Bks.) HarperCollins Pubs.

Alley, R. W., illus. Bratty Brothers & Selfish Sisters: All about Sibling Rivalry. 2007. (Elf-Help Books for Kids Ser.). 28p. (J). (gr. -1-3). per. 7.95 *(978-0-87029-404-4(0))* Abbey Pr.

Alston, B. B. Amari & the Great Game. (Supernatural Investigations Ser.). (ENG.). 432p. 2023. (gr. 4-7). 28.69 ***(978-1-5364-8191-4(2))*** 2023. (J). (gr. 3-7). pap. 10.99 ***(978-0-06-297520-1(X))*** 2022. (Illus.). (J). (gr. 3-7). 18.99 *(978-0-06-297519-5(6))* HarperCollins Pubs. (Balzer & Bray).

—Amari & the Night Brothers. (Supernatural Investigations Ser.: 1). (ENG.). 2022. 432p. (J). (gr. 3-7). pap. 11.99 *(978-0-06-297517-1(X))* 2021. (Illus.). 416p. (J). (gr. 3-7). 17.99 *(978-0-06-297516-4(1))*1. 2022. 432p. (gr. 4-7). 29.94 *(978-1-5364-7242-4(5))* HarperCollins Pubs. (Balzer & Bray).

Alston, B. B. Amari y Los Hermanos de la Noche / Amari & the Night Brothers. 2023. (Amari Ser.). (SPA.). 448p. (J). (gr. 4-7). pap. 14.95 ***(978-1-64473-875-7(9))*** Penguin Random House Grupo Editorial ESP. Dist: Penguin Random Hse. LLC.

Alward, Diane. Pedals & Promises: An Adventure Devotional for Kids. 2013. 86p. pap. 9.95 *(978-1-4908-0512-2(5)*, WestBow Pr.) Author Solutions, LLC.

Amery, H. & Cartwright, S. The Tournament. 2004. (First Stories Ser.). 16p. (J). pap. 4.95 *(978-0-7945-0520-2(1))*; lib. bdg. 12.95 *(978-1-58086-571-5(2))* EDC Publishing.

Anastasia off Her Rocker: Bk 4. 2015. (Anastasia Krupnik Story Ser.). (ENG., Illus.). 160p. (J). (gr. 5-7). pap. 8.99 *(978-0-544-43959-7(7)*, 1596853, Clarion Bks.) HarperCollins Pubs.

Andersen, C. B. The Book of Mormon Sleuth Vol. 3: The Hidden Path. 2003. ix, 214p. (J). pap. *(978-1-57008-988-6(4))* Deseret Bk. Co.

Anderson, Laurie Halse. New Beginnings, 13 vols., 13. 2012. (Vet Volunteers Ser.: 13). (ENG.). 192p. (J). (gr. 3-7). 7.99 *(978-0-14-241675-4(4)*, Puffin) Penguin Young Readers Group.

Anderson, Phil. The Thomas Family Values. 2012. 84p. pap. 13.95 *(978-1-4772-2529-5(3))* AuthorHouse.

Andrews, Jerome. The Initiation. 2006. 40p. pap. 8.50 *(978-1-4116-9167-4(9))* Lulu Pr., Inc.

Andrews, Jesse. Munmun. 2018. (ENG.). 416p. (YA). (gr. 9-17). 18.99 *(978-1-4197-2871-6(7)*, 1140101, Amulet Bks.) Abrams, Inc.

Andrews, Julie. The Little Grey Men: A Story for the Young in Heart. Watkins-Pitchford, Denys, illus. 2004. 304p. (J). 17.89 *(978-0-06-055449-1(5)*, Julie Andrews Collection) HarperCollins Pubs.

S

Andros, Camille. Charlotte the Scientist Is Squished. Farley, Brianne, illus. 2017. (Charlotte the Scientist Ser.). (ENG.). 40p. (J). (gr. -1-3). 17.99 *(978-0-544-78583-0(5)*, 1638581, Clarion Bks.) HarperCollins Pubs.

Ant Plays Bear. 9.95 *(978-1-59112-166-4(3))* Live Oak Media.

Antieau, Kim. Broken Moon. 2007. (ENG.). 192p. (YA). (gr. 9-12). 16.99 *(978-1-4169-1767-0(5)*, McElderry, Margaret K. Bks.) McElderry, Margaret K. Bks.

Apted, Violet. Tommy & Jacqui: Laughing with Kookaburras. 2011. 32p. pap. 13.00 *(978-1-61204-118-6(3)*, Eloquent Bks.) Strategic Book Publishing & Rights Agency (SBPRA).

Aragón, Carla, et al. Dance of the Eggshells: Baile de Los Cascarones. Aragon, Socorro, tr. Saville, Kathy Dee, illus. 2010. (ENG.). 32p. (J). (gr. 1). 18.95 *(978-0-8263-4770-1(3)*, P174638) Univ. of New Mexico Pr.

Arbuthnott, Gill. Chaos Quest, 52 vols. 2004. (Kelpies Ser.). (ENG.). 192p. 10.00 *(978-0-86315-459-1(X))* Floris Bks. GBR. Dist: SteinerBooks, Inc.

Arcos, Carrie. Out of Reach. (ENG., (YA). (gr. 9). 2013. Illus.). 272p. pap. 9.99 *(978-1-4424-4054-8(6))* 2012. 256p. 16.99 *(978-1-4424-4053-1(8))* Simon Pulse. (Simon Pulse).

—There Will Come a Time. 2014. (ENG., Illus.). 320p. (YA). (gr. 9). 17.99 *(978-1-4424-9585-2(5)*, Simon Pulse) Simon Pulse.

Aris, Mary. Bartholomew. 2010. 86p. pap. 36.95 *(978-1-4457-8958-3(2))*; pap. 36.50 *(978-1-4457-5351-5(0))* Lulu Pr., Inc.

Arnett, Mindee. Avalon. 2014. (Avalon Ser.: 1). (ENG.). 432p. (YA). (gr. 8). 17.99 *(978-0-06-223559-6(1)*, Balzer & Bray) HarperCollins Pubs.

—Polaris. 2015. (Avalon Ser.: 2). (ENG.). 432p. (YA). (gr. 8). 17.99 *(978-0-06-223562-6(1)*, Balzer & Bray) HarperCollins Pubs.

Arnold, David. The Strange Fascinations of Noah Hypnotik. 2019. 448p. (YA). (gr. 9). pap. 10.99 *(978-0-425-28887-0(0)*, Penguin Books) Penguin Young Readers Group.

Asch, Frank. Star Jumper: Journal of a Cardboard Genius. Asch, Frank, illus. 2006. (ENG., Illus.). 128p. (J). (gr. 2-5). 14.95 *(978-1-55337-886-0(5))* Kids Can Pr., Ltd. CAN. Dist: Hachette Bk. Group.

Ashburn, Boni. A Twin Is to Hug. 2019. (ENG., Illus.). 32p. (J). (gr. -1-1). 14.99 *(978-1-4197-3158-7(0)*, 1195301, Abrams Bks. for Young Readers) Abrams, Inc.

Ashley, Jonathan. Lily & Kosmo in Outer Outer Space. Ashley, Jonathan, illus. 2018. (ENG., Illus.). 208p. (J). (gr. 2-5). 16.99 *(978-1-5344-1364-1(2)*, Simon & Schuster Bks. For Young Readers) Simon & Schuster Bks. For Young Readers.

Ashton, Anna. Molly & Ben. 2007. (Illus.). 76p. per. *(978-1-84401-178-0(X))* Athena Pr.

Atinuke. B Is for Baby. Brooksbank, Angela, illus. 2019. (ENG.). 40p. (J). (gr. -1-2). 17.99 *(978-1-5362-0166-6(9))* Candlewick Pr.

Atkinson, Elizabeth. Lisa's Totally Unforgettable Winter. 2006. (ENG.). 56p. per. 16.95 *(978-1-4241-6249-9(1))* America Star Bks.

Atwood, Megan. Once upon a Winter. Andrewson, Natalie, illus. 2017. (Orchard Novel Ser.: 2). (ENG.). 240p. (J). (gr. 2-6). 12.99 *(978-1-4814-9049-8(4)*, Aladdin) Simon & Schuster Children's Publishing.

Auerbach, Annie. The Grosse Adventures: The Good, the Bad, & the Gassy, Vol. 1. Norton, Mike, illus. 2006. (Grosse Adventures Manga Ser.: 1). (ENG.). 96p. (J). (gr. 4-1). pap. 9.99 *(978-1-59816-049-9(4))* TOKYOPOP, Inc.

—The Grosse Adventures Vol. 3: Trouble at Twilight Cave, 1 vol. Nicholas, Jamar, illus. 2008. (Tokyopop Ser.). (ENG.). 96p. (J). (gr. 2-6). 32.79 *(978-1-59961-562-2(2)*, 14806, Graphic Novels) Spotlight.

Austin, Jamie Lea-Elizabeth. Reverie. 2012. 312p. 29.95 *(978-1-4626-6734-5(1))* PublishAmerica, Inc.

Authement, Louise. Diaries of the Fifth Grade Miseries. 2013. 68p. pap. 10.95 *(978-1-4327-9996-0(7))* Outskirts Pr., Inc.

Auxier, Jonathan. The Night Gardener. (ENG.). 2015. 384p. (YA). (gr. 3-7). pap. 9.99 *(978-1-4197-1531-0(3)*, 1076503) 2014. 368p. (J). (gr. 5-17). 19.99 *(978-1-4197-1144-2(X)*, 1076501, Amulet Bks.) Abrams, Inc.

—The Night Gardener. 2015. (J). lib. bdg. 19.60 *(978-0-606-36891-9(4))* Turtleback.

Avi & Vail, Rachel. Never Mind! 2005. (Twin Novels Ser.). 200p. (gr. 5-9). 16.00 *(978-0-7569-5667-7(6))* Perfection Learning Corp.

—Never Mind! A Twin Novel. 2005. (ENG.). 208p. (J). (gr. 5-18). reprint ed. pap. 6.99 *(978-0-06-054316-7(7)*, HarperCollins) HarperCollins Pubs.

Avraham, Kate Aver. What Will You Be, Sara Mee? O'Brien, Anne Sibley, illus. 2010. 32p. (J). (gr. -1-3). pap. 7.95 *(978-1-58089-211-7(6))* Charlesbridge Publishing, Inc.

Ayers, Linda. The Time Bridge Travelers & the Time Travel Station, 3 bks., Bk. 3. Ayers, Ryan, illus. Lt. ed. 2007. (Time Bridge Travelers Ser.: 3). 140p. (J). lib. bdg. 16.95 *(978-0-9786302-8-7(9))*; per. 7.95 *(978-0-9786302-7-0(0))* Blue Thistle Pr.

Babee says No. 2006. (YA). spiral bd. *(978-1-59872-479-0(7))* Instant Pub.

Bader, Arlys Elaine. The Adventures of Garth & Cloey. 2008. 40p. pap. 16.99 *(978-1-4389-2472-4(0))* AuthorHouse.

Baggott, Julianna. The Ever Breath. 2011. (ENG.). 240p. (J). (gr. 4-6). lib. bdg. 21.19 *(978-0-385-90676-0(5)*, Delacorte Pr.) Random Hse. Children's Bks.

Baghdasaryan, Rouzanna. The Dark. Morchiladze, Manana, illus. 2007. 32p. (J). (POL & ENG.). pap. 12.95 *(978-1-60195-096-3(9))*; (ARA & ENG.). pap. 12.95 *(978-1-60195-086-4(1))* International Step by Step Assn.

Bahk, Jane. Juna's Jar. Hoshino, Felicia, illus. 2015. (ENG.). 32p. (J). 17.95 *(978-1-60060-853-7(1)*, 9781600000000) Lee & Low Bks., Inc.

Bailey, J. L. Children's Gate. 2005. 292p. 21.95 *(978-1-58939-814-6(9))* Virtualbookworm.com Publishing, Inc.

Bailey, Kristin. Into the Nightfell Wood. 2018. (ENG.). 368p. (J). (gr. 3-7). 16.99 *(978-0-06-239860-4(1)*, Tegen, Katherine Bks) HarperCollins Pubs.

Bailey, Tressie. The Little Box Kittens meet Santa Claus. 2009. 37p. pap. 24.10 *(978-0-557-03196-6(2))* Lulu Pr., Inc.

Balcarcel, Rebecca. The Other Half of Happy: (Middle Grade Novel for Ages 9-12, Bilingual Tween Book) 2019. (ENG., Illus.). 332p. (J). (gr. 5-9). 16.99 *(978-1-4521-6998-9(5))* Chronicle Bks. LLC.

Ballantyne, R. M. Silver Lake. 2004. reprint ed. pap. 1.99 *(978-1-4192-4729-3(8))*; pap. 19.95 *(978-1-4191-4729-6(3))* Kessinger Publishing, LLC.

Banas, Danielle. The Supervillain & Me. 2019. (ENG.). 336p. (YA). pap. 20.99 *(978-1-250-30912-9(3)*, 900184401) Square Fish.

Bankert, Lisa. Operation: Oddball. Meyers, Nancy, illus. 2007. 100p. per. 5.99 *(978-0-9795364-0-3(5))* Chowder Bay Bks.

Banks, Jacqueline Turner. Egg-Drop Blues. 2003. (ENG.). 128p. (J). (gr. 5-7). pap. 10.95 *(978-0-618-25080-6(8)*, 481193, Clarion Bks.) HarperCollins Pubs.

Banks, Kate. Max's Words. 2011. (J). (gr. k-2). 29.95 *(978-0-545-04373-1(5))* Weston Woods Studios, Inc.

Banting, Celia. I only said I was telling the Truth. 2006. 240p. (YA). per. 14.99 *(978-0-9786648-4-8(1))* Wighita Pr.

Barber, Tiki & Barber, Ronde. End Zone. 2014. (Barber Game Time Bks.). (ENG., Illus.). 192p. (J). (gr. 3-7). pap. 7.99 *(978-1-4169-9098-7(4)*, Simon & Schuster/Paula Wiseman Bks.) Simon & Schuster/Paula Wiseman Bks.

—Red Zone. 2013. (Barber Game Time Bks.). (ENG., Illus.). 176p. (J). (gr. 3-7). pap. 7.99 *(978-1-4169-6861-0(X)*, Simon & Schuster/Paula Wiseman Bks.) Simon & Schuster/Paula Wiseman Bks.

—Wild Card. (Barber Game Time Bks.). (ENG.). 160p. (J). (gr. 3-7). 2012. pap. 7.99 *(978-1-4169-6859-7(8))* 2009. 15.99 *(978-1-4169-6858-0(X))* Simon & Schuster/Paula Wiseman Bks. (Simon & Schuster/Paula Wiseman Bks.).

Barbo, Maria S. The Rescue Mission (Pokémon Kalos: Scholastic Reader, Level 2) 2016. (Scholastic Reader, Level 2 Ser.: 1). (ENG.). 32p. (J). (gr. -1-3). pap. 5.99 *(978-1-338-11290-0(2))* Scholastic, Inc.

Barclay, Eric. Hiding Phil. 2013. (Illus.). (J). *(978-0-545-60456-7(7)*, Scholastic Pr.) Scholastic, Inc.

Barnaby, Hannah. Bad Guy. Yamada, Mike, illus. 2017. (ENG.). 32p. (J). (gr. -1-3). 17.99 *(978-1-4814-6010-1(2)*, Simon & Schuster Bks. For Young Readers) Simon & Schuster Bks. For Young Readers.

Barnacott, Anthony Royce. Permanoids of Chiion. 2009. 260p. 27.99 *(978-1-4389-3824-0(1))* AuthorHouse.

Barnes, Derrick D. Brand New School, Brave New Ruby (Ruby & the Booker Boys #1) Newton, Vanessa Brantley, illus. 2008. (Ruby & the Booker Boys Ser.: 1). (ENG.). 144p. (J). (gr. 2-5). pap. 5.99 *(978-0-545-01760-2(2)*, Scholastic Paperbacks) Scholastic, Inc.

—The Slumber Party Payback (Ruby & the Booker Boys #3). 3. Newton, Vanessa Brantley, illus. 2008. (Ruby & the Booker Boys Ser.: 3). (ENG.). 176p. (J). (gr. 2-5). pap. 5.99 *(978-0-545-01762-6(9))* Scholastic, Inc.

—Trivia Queen, Third Grade Supreme (Ruby & the Booker Boys #2) Newton, Vanessa Brantley, illus. 2008. (Ruby & the Booker Boys Ser.: 2). (ENG.). 144p. (J). (gr. 2-5). pap. 5.99 *(978-0-545-01761-9(0))* Scholastic, Inc.

Baron Cohen, H. V. The Story of Joe & His Magic Snout: An Operetta of Nursery Fairytales for 2 to 10 years Olds. 2009. 106p. pap. 19.27 *(978-1-4251-3582-9(X))* Trafford Publishing.

Barrett, Judith. Cloudy with a Chance of Meatballs. Barrett, Ron, illus. 2011. (Classic Board Bks.). (ENG.). 34p. (J). (gr. -1-k). bds. 8.99 *(978-1-4424-3023-5(0)*, Little Simon) Little Simon.

Barrett, Tracy. The Beast of Blackslope. 2011. (Sherlock Files Ser.: 2). (ENG., Illus.). 192p. (J). (gr. 3-7). pap. 9.99 *(978-0-312-65918-9(0)*, 900070505) Square Fish.

—The Case That Time Forgot. 3. 2011. (Sherlock Files Ser.: 3). (ENG., Illus.). 176p. (J). (gr. 4-6). pap. 10.99 *(978-0-312-56358-5(2)*, 900074759) Square Fish.

—Marabel & the Book of Fate. 2018. (Marabel Novel Ser.). (ENG.). 304p. (J). (gr. 3-7). 16.99 *(978-0-316-43399-0(3))* Little, Brown Bks. for Young Readers.

—The Missing Heir. 2012. (Sherlock Files Ser.: 4). (J). lib. bdg. 19.65 *(978-0-606-26131-9(1))* Turtleback.

—The 100-Year-Old Secret: The Sherlock Files Book One. 2010. (Sherlock Files Ser.: 1). (ENG., Illus.). 176p. (J). (gr. 3-7). pap. 8.99 *(978-0-312-60212-3(X)*, 900064227) Square Fish.

Barrowman, John & Barrowman, Carole. Conjuror. 2016. (Orion Chronicles Ser.). (ENG.). 320p. (YA). (gr. 7). 16.99 *(978-1-78185-637-6(0))* Head of Zeus GBR. Dist: Independent Pubs. Group.

Barrowman, John & Barrowman, Carole E. Bone Quill. 2014. (Hollow Earth Ser.). (ENG., Illus.). 304p. (J). (gr. 3-7). pap. 8.99 *(978-1-4424-8929-5(4)*, Aladdin) Simon & Schuster Children's Publishing.

Barrows, Marjorie. Little Duck. Myers, Marie Honre, illus. 2011. 50p. 35.95 *(978-1-258-08897-2(5))* Literary Licensing, LLC.

Barter, Catherine. Troublemakers. 2018. (ENG.). 360p. (YA). (gr. 7-12). 17.99 *(978-1-5124-7549-4(1)*, 6501f552-14c0-47e0-aa58-d3647a7e0d10, Carolrhoda Lab™) Lerner Publishing Group.

Bartone, Elisa. Peppe the Lamplighter. Lewin, Ted, illus. 2015. 32p. pap. 7.00 *(978-1-61003-612-2(3))* Center for the Collaborative Classroom.

Basir, A. As Told By: Sofie. 2006. 51p. pap. 16.95 *(978-1-4241-2030-7(6))* PublishAmerica, Inc.

Bass, Alexis. What's Broken Between Us. 2015. (ENG.). 304p. (YA). (gr. 9). 17.99 *(978-0-06-227535-6(6)*, HarperTeen) HarperCollins Pubs.

Bass, Ruth. Sarah's Daughter. 2007. 389p. (YA). (gr. 8-12). per. 14.95 *(978-0-9774053-4-3(6))* North River Pr. Publishing Corp., The.

Basye, Dale E. Blimpo Vol. 3: The Third Circle of Heck. Dob, Bob, illus. 2011. (Heck Ser.: 3). 464p. (J). (gr. 3-7). pap. 9.99 *(978-0-375-85677-8(3)*, Yearling) Random Hse. Children's Bks.

—Fibble: the Fourth Circle of Heck. Dob, Bob, illus. 2012. (Heck Ser.: 4). 384p. (J). (gr. 4-7). pap. 7.99 *(978-0-375-85679-2(X)*, Yearling) Random Hse. Children's Bks.

—Heck: Where the Bad Kids Go. Dob, Bob, illus. 2009. (Heck Ser.: 1). 304p. (J). (gr. 3-7). 6.99 *(978-0-375-84076-0(1)*, Yearling) Random Hse. Children's Bks.

—Precocia: the Sixth Circle of Heck. Dob, Bob, illus. 2013. (Heck Ser.: 6). 432p. (J). (gr. 3-7). 7.99 *(978-0-375-86807-8(0)*, Yearling) Random Hse. Children's Bks.

—Rapacia: the Second Circle of Heck. Dob, Bob, illus. 2010. (Heck Ser.: 2). 384p. (J). (gr. 3-7). pap. 7.99 *(978-0-375-84078-4(8)*, Yearling) Random Hse. Children's Bks.

—Snivel, 5. Dob, Bob, illus. 2013. (Heck Ser.). (ENG.). 448p. (J). (gr. 6-8). lib. bdg. 22.44 *(978-0-375-96834-1(2))* Random Hse. Bks. for Young Readers.

—Snivel: the Fifth Circle of Heck. Dob, Bob, illus. 2013. (Heck Ser.: 5). 448p. (J). (gr. 4-7). 8.99 *(978-0-375-86806-1(2)*, Yearling) Random Hse. Children's Bks.

Bateman, Anya. The Makeover of James Orville Wickenbee. 2007. 262p. (J). pap. *(978-1-59038-707-8(4))* Deseret Bk. Co.

Bates, Sonya Spreen. Thunder Creek Ranch, 1 vol. Charko, Kasia, illus. 2013. (Orca Echoes Ser.). (ENG.). 64p. (J). (gr. 1-3). pap. 7.95 *(978-1-4598-0112-7(1))* Orca Bk. Pubs. USA.

Batterson, Veronica Randolph. Billy's First Dance. 2010. (J). pap. 9.95 *(978-0-7414-5913-8(2))* Infinity Publishing.

Baucom, Ian. Through the Skylight. Gerard, Justin, illus. (ENG.). 400p. (J). (gr. 4-8). 2014. pap. 6.99 *(978-1-4424-8167-1(6))* 2013. 17.99 *(978-1-4169-1777-9(2))* Simon & Schuster Children's Publishing. (Atheneum Bks. for Young Readers).

Baugh, Ayana Sala. Loopiethotamus, the Chihuahua Who Thinks He Is a Hippopotamus Book: His Journey. 2011. 20p. pap. 14.99 *(978-1-4634-3437-3(5))* AuthorHouse.

Baum, Lonna. Monty the Menace: Understanding Differences. Messing, Dave, illus. 2012. (ENG.). 32p. (J). 16.95 *(978-0-9839373-0-2(3))* Baum & Baum, LLC.

Baumgart, Klaus. Laura's Secret. Waite, Judy, tr. from GER. 2003. (Illus.). 32p. (J). (gr. -1-2). tchr. ed. 16.95 *(978-1-58925-031-4(1))* Tiger Tales.

Bayard, Louis. Lucky Strikes. 2016. (ENG., Illus.). 320p. (YA). 29.99 *(978-1-62779-390-2(9)*, 900148815, Holt, Henry & Co. Bks. For Young Readers) Holt, Henry & Co.

—Lucky Strikes. 2017. (YA). lib. bdg. 20.85 *(978-0-606-39951-7(8))* Turtleback.

Bean, Raymond. The Curse of Mars. Vimislik, Matthew, illus. 2016. (Out of This World Ser.). (ENG.). 112p. (J). (gr. 2-5). lib. bdg. 32.65 *(978-1-4965-3615-0(0)*, 132831, Stone Arch Bks.) Capstone.

—First Family in Space. Vimislik, Matthew, illus. 2016. (Out of This World Ser.). (ENG.). 112p. (J). (gr. 2-5). lib. bdg. 32.65 *(978-1-4965-3617-4(7)*, 132833, Stone Arch Bks.) Capstone.

—Trouble on Venus. Vimislik, Matthew, illus. 2016. (Out of This World Ser.). (ENG.). 112p. (J). (gr. 2-5). lib. bdg. 32.65 *(978-1-4965-3614-3(2)*, 132830, Stone Arch Bks.) Capstone.

Beardslee, Nellie L. The Glenn's of Newberry Hills. 2008. 164p. pap. 24.95 *(978-1-60703-471-1(9))* America Star Bks.

Beam, Emily. Tumtum & Nutmeg: Adventures Beyond Nutmouse Hall. 2011. (Tumtum & Nutmeg Ser.: 1). (ENG., Illus.). 512p. (J). (gr. 3-7). pap. 14.99 *(978-0-316-07574-9(4))* Little, Brown Bks. for Young Readers.

—The Tumtum & Nutmeg: the Rose Cottage Adventures. Price, Nick, illus. 2013. (Tumtum & Nutmeg Ser.: 2). (ENG.). 416p. (J). (gr. 3-7). pap. 14.99 *(978-0-316-08598-4(7))* Little, Brown Bks. for Young Readers.

Beasley, David R. Canoe Trip. Milner, Elizabeth B., illus. 2006. 129p. (YA). per. 15.00 *(978-0-915317-21-9(4))* Davus Publishing.

Beaty, Andrea. Attack of the Fluffy Bunnies. 2012. (Fluffy Bunnies Ser.). (ENG.). 192p. (YA). (gr. 2-8). pap. 7.95 *(978-1-4197-0519-9(9)*, 670903, Amulet Bks.) Abrams, Inc.

—Cicada Summer. 2008. (ENG.). 176p. (J). (gr. 3-7). 16.95 *(978-0-8109-9472-0(0)*, 620501, Amulet Bks.) Abrams, Inc.

—Fluffy Bunnies 2: The Schnoz of Doom. Santat, Dan, illus. 2015. (Fluffy Bunnies Ser.). (ENG.). 192p. (J). (gr. 3-7). 12.95 *(978-1-4197-1051-3(6)*, 1068601, Amulet Bks.) Abrams, Inc.

—Secrets of the Cicada Summer. 2010. (ENG.). 176p. (YA). (gr. 3-7). pap. 8.99 *(978-0-8109-8419-6(9)*, 620503, Amulet Bks.) Abrams, Inc.

Beaufrand, M. J. Useless Bay. 2016. (ENG., Illus.). 240p. (YA). (gr. 8-17). 17.95 *(978-1-4197-2138-0(0)*, 1135401, Amulet Bks.) Abrams, Inc.

Beauty of the Broken. 2014. (ENG., Illus.). 368p. (YA). (gr. 9). 17.99 *(978-1-4814-0709-0(0)*, Simon Pulse) Simon Pulse.

Beifus, Ruth. Shlavim Classics 2-in-1 Vol.2: Goodbye to Miri's Mess & Half a Cup of Water. 2009. 32p. 14.99 *(978-1-59826-330-5(7))* Feldheim Pubs.

Bell, Jennifer. The Uncommoners #1: the Crooked Sixpence. 2017. (Uncommoners Ser.: 1). (ENG., Illus.). 320p. (J). (gr. 3-7). 16.99 *(978-0-553-49843-1(6)*, Crown Books For Young Readers) Random Hse. Children's Bks.

Bell, Lisa M. E. I Talked to Mom. 2013. 104p. pap. 9.99 *(978-1-60820-873-9(7))* MLR Pr., LLC.

Bell, William. Five Days of the Ghost, 1 vol. 2010. (ENG.). 208p. (J). (gr. 5-8). pap. 14.95 *(978-1-55455-152-1(8)*, e48d7118-e158-4846-ad46-2596604424ad) Fitzhenry & Whiteside, Ltd. CAN. Dist: Firefly Bks., Ltd.

Bellingham, Brenda. Lilly Babysits Her Brother, 1 vol. MacDonald, Clarke, illus. 2013. (Formac First Novels Ser.). (ENG.). 60p. (J). (gr. 2-3). 14.95 *(978-1-4595-0286-4(8)*, 0286); pap. 5.95 *(978-1-4595-0287-1(6)*, 0287) Formac Publishing Co., Ltd. CAN. Dist: Formac Lorimer Bks. Ltd.

Bemis, John Claude. The Nine Pound Hammer: Book 1 of the Clockwork Dark. 2010. (Clockwork Dark Ser.: 1). (ENG.). 384p. (J). (gr. 3-7). pap. 8.99 *(978-0-375-85565-8(3)*, Yearling) Random Hse. Children's Bks.

Benenfeld, Rikki. I Go to Eretz Yisroel. Benenfeld, Rikki, illus. 2017. (Toddler Experience Ser.). (ENG., Illus.). 28p. (J). 11.95 *(978-1-929628-92-6(7))* Hachai Publishing.

—I Go to the Dentist. Rosenfeld, Dina & Leverton, Yossi, eds. Bennenfeld, Rikki, illus. 2011. (Toddler Experience Ser.). (ENG.). 32p. (J). 11.99 *(978-1-929628-60-5(9))* Hachai Publishing.

—Let's Go Shopping. Benenfeld, Rikki, illus. 2005. (Toddler Experience Ser.). (ENG., Illus.). 24p. (J). 11.95 *(978-1-929628-20-9(X))* Hachai Publishing.

—Let's Go to the Park. 2015. (ENG., Illus.). 36p. (J). 11.99 *(978-1-929628-82-7(X))* Hachai Publishing.

Bennett, Holly. The Bonemender's Oath, 1 vol. 2006. (Bonemender Ser.: 2). (ENG.). 176p. (YA). (gr. 8-12). per. 9.95 *(978-1-55143-443-8(1))* Orca Bk. Pubs. USA.

Benway, Robin. Far from the Tree. (ENG.). (YA). (gr. 8). 2019. 400p. pap. 11.99 *(978-0-06-233063-5(2))* 2017. 384p. 17.99 *(978-0-06-233062-8(4))* HarperCollins Pubs. (HarperTeen).

Berenstain, Jan & Berenstain, Mike. The Berenstain Bears & Mama for Mayor! Berenstain, Jan & Berenstain, Mike, illus. 2012. (I Can Read Level 1 Ser.). (ENG., Illus.). 32p. (J). (gr. k-3). 16.99 *(978-0-06-207528-4(4)*, HarperCollins) HarperCollins Pubs.

—The Berenstain Bears & the Shaggy Little Pony. Berenstain, Jan & Berenstain, Mike, illus. 2011. (I Can Read Level 1 Ser.). (ENG., Illus.). 32p. (J). (gr. k-3). 16.99 *(978-0-06-168972-7(6))*; pap. 4.99 *(978-0-06-057419-2(4))* HarperCollins Pubs. (HarperCollins).

—The Berenstain Bears & the Tooth Fairy. Berenstain, Jan & Berenstain, Mike, illus. 2012. (Berenstain Bears Ser.). (ENG., Illus.). 24p. (J). (gr. -1-3). pap. 3.99 *(978-0-06-207549-9(7)*, HarperFestival) HarperCollins Pubs.

—The Berenstain Bears at the Aquarium. Berenstain, Jan & Berenstain, Mike, illus. 2012. (I Can Read Level 1 Ser.). (ENG., Illus.). 32p. (J). (gr. k-3). 16.99 *(978-0-06-207525-3(X))*; pap. 4.99 *(978-0-06-207524-6(1))* HarperCollins Pubs. (HarperCollins).

—The Berenstain Bears' Dinosaur Dig. Berenstain, Jan & Berenstain, Mike, illus. 2012. (Berenstain Bears Ser.). (ENG., Illus.). 24p. (J). (gr. -1-3). pap. 4.99 *(978-0-06-207548-2(9)*, HarperFestival) HarperCollins Pubs.

—The Berenstain Bears' Old-Fashioned Christmas: A Christmas Holiday Book for Kids. Berenstain, Jan, illus. 2012. (Berenstain Bears Ser.). (ENG.). 32p. (J). (gr. -1-3). 12.99 *(978-0-06-057443-7(7)*, HarperCollins) HarperCollins Pubs.

—The Berenstain Bears: Sick Days. Berenstain, Jan & Berenstain, Mike, illus. 2009. (Berenstain Bears Ser.). (ENG., Illus.). 32p. (J). (gr. -1-3). pap. 4.99 *(978-0-06-057392-8(9)*, HarperFestival) HarperCollins Pubs.

—The Berenstain Bears: We Love Our Mom! Berenstain, Jan & Berenstain, Mike, illus. 2012. (Berenstain Bears Ser.). (ENG., Illus.). 24p. (J). (gr. -1-3). pap. 4.99 *(978-0-06-207547-5(0)*, HarperFestival) HarperCollins Pubs.

—The Berenstain Bears: We Love Trucks! Berenstain, Jan & Berenstain, Mike, illus. 2013. (I Can Read Level 1 Ser.). (ENG., Illus.). 32p. (J). (gr. -1-3). 16.99 *(978-0-06-207536-9(5)*, HarperCollins) HarperCollins Pubs.

Berenstain, Jan & Berenstain, Stan. The Berenstain Bears Play T-Ball. Berenstain, Jan, illus. 2005. (I Can Read Level 1 Ser.). (ENG., Illus.). 32p. (J). (gr. k-3). 16.99 *(978-0-06-058337-8(1)*, HarperCollins) HarperCollins Pubs.

—The Berenstain Bears Play T Ball. 2004. (I Can Read Level 1 Ser.). (ENG., Illus.). 32p. (J). (gr. k-3). pap. 4.99 *(978-0-06-058338-5(X)*, HarperCollins) HarperCollins Pubs.

Berenstain, Jan, et al. The Berenstain Bears Go Back to School. Berenstain, Mike, illus. 2009. (Berenstain Bears Ser.). (ENG.). 32p. (J). (gr. -1-3). pap. 7.99 *(978-0-06-052675-7(0)*, HarperFestival) HarperCollins Pubs.

Berenstain, Mike. The Berenstain Bears & the Biggest Brag, 1 vol. 2014. (Berenstain Bears/Living Lights: a Faith Story Ser.). (ENG., Illus.). 24p. (J). pap. 3.99 *(978-0-310-73479-6(7))* Zonderkidz.

—The Berenstain Bears' Lemonade Stand. Berenstain, Mike, illus. 2014. (I Can Read Level 1 Ser.). (ENG., Illus.). 32p. (J). (gr. -1-3). 16.99 *(978-0-06-207545-1(4))*; pap. 4.99 *(978-0-06-207544-4(6))* HarperCollins Pubs. (HarperCollins).

—The Berenstain Bears' Lemonade Stand. 2014. (Berenstain Bears — I Can Read Ser.). (J). lib. bdg. 13.55 *(978-0-606-35072-3(1))* Turtleback.

—The Berenstain Bears Say "I'm Sorry!" 2015. (Berenstain Bears Ser.). (ENG., Illus.). 20p. (J). (gr. -1-k). bds. 7.99 *(978-0-8249-1954-2(8)*, Ideals Pubns.) Worthy Publishing.

Berenstain, Mike, et al. Sister Bear & the Golden Rule. 2017. (Illus.). 32p. (J). *(978-1-5182-4500-8(5))* Zonderkidz.

Berenstain, Stan & Berenstain, Jan. The Berenstain Bears Meet Santa Bear (Deluxe Edition) 2016. (First Time Books(R) Ser.). (Illus.). 32p. (J). (gr. -1-2). pap. 6.99 *(978-0-399-55767-5(9)*, Random Hse. Bks. for Young Readers) Random Hse. Children's Bks.

—The Berenstain Bears Play T-Ball. 2005. (Berenstain Bears Ser.). (Illus.). 32p. (J). 11.65 *(978-0-7569-5228-0(X))* Perfection Learning Corp.

Berenstain, Stan, et al. Do Not Fear, God Is Near, 1 vol. 2013. (I Can Read! / Berenstain Bears / Living Lights: a Faith Story Ser.). (ENG., Illus.). 32p. (J). pap. 5.99 *(978-0-310-72511-4(9))* Zonderkidz.

—God Loves You!, 1 vol. 2008. (Berenstain Bears/Living Lights: a Faith Story Ser.). (ENG., Illus.). 32p. (J). pap. 4.99 *(978-0-310-71250-3(5))* Zonderkidz.

Bergman, Mara. Snip Snap! What's That? Maland, Nick, illus. 2005. (ENG.). 32p. (J). (gr. -1-3). 17.99 *(978-0-06-077754-8(0)*, Greenwillow Bks.) HarperCollins Pubs.

Bergstrom, Sarah. Desert Dwellers Born by Fire: The First Book in the Paintbrush Saga. 2015. (ENG., Illus.). 312p. (J). (gr. -1-12). pap. 12.95 *(978-1-78279-587-2(1)*, Lodestone Bks.) Hunt, John Publishing Ltd. GBR. Dist: National Bk. Network.

Berlin, Eric. The Puzzling World of Winston Breen. (J). 2009. (Puzzling World of Winston Breen Ser.: 1). 256p. (gr. 3-7). pap. 7.99 *(978-0-14-241388-3(7)*, Puffin Books) 2007. (Puzzling World of Winston Breen Ser.). (ENG., Illus.). 215p. (gr. 4-6). 18.69 *(978-0-399-24693-7(2))* Penguin Young Readers Group.

Bermudez, Cyn. Taken Away, 1 vol. 2018. (Brothers Ser.). (ENG.). 88p. (YA). (gr. 2-3). 24.55 *(978-1-5383-8230-1(X)*, 64d26459-86cf-46ad-a761-3c76fa06bbab); pap. 14.85 *(978-1-5383-8229-5(6)*, c107d7b5-9fea-4acb-a690-0e18e5649a83) Enslow Publishing, LLC.

Bernard, Norah S. CLIVE & BRIE. 2007. (ENG.). 176p. (YA). per. *(978-0-615-15932-4(X))* HELORO Publishing Group.

Berneger, Marcia. A Dreidel in Time: A New Spin on an Old Tale. Castro, Beatriz, illus. 2019. (ENG.). 88p. (J). (gr. 3-7). 17.99 *(978-1-5415-4672-1(5)*, 192e3233-0d85-465d-9d2d-d3070039f409, Kar-Ben Publishing) Lerner Publishing Group.

Bernstein, Nina. Magic by the Book, 4 vols. unabr. ed. 2005. (J). 65.75 *(978-1-4193-3607-2(X)*, 42048) Recorded Bks., Inc.

Betancourt, Jeanne. Pony Mysteries #1: Penny & Pepper (Scholastic Reader, Level 3) Riley, Kellee, illus. 2011. (Scholastic Reader, Level 3 Ser.). (ENG.). 48p. (J). (gr. 1-3).

pap. 3.99 (978-0-545-11508-7(6), Cartwheel Bks.) Scholastic, Inc.

Bezek, Lyn. Ribbon the Border Collie: From Herder to Healer. 2008. (Illus.). 137p. (J). pap. 11.95 (978-1-932738-51-3(7)) Western Reflections Publishing Co.

Bingham, Laura. Älvor. 2009. 277p. (J). pap. 17.99 (978-1-59955-272-9(8)) Cedar Fort, Inc./CFI Distribution.

—Wings of Light. 2011. 240p. (J). pap. 15.99 (978-1-59955-492-1(5), Sweetwater Bks.) Cedar Fort, Inc./CFI Distribution.

Binns, B. A. Pull. 2010. 310p. (YA). (gr. 9-18). 16.95 (978-1-934813-43-0(5)) Westside Bks.

Birdsall, Jeanne. Flora's Very Windy Day. Phelan, Matt, illus. 2013. (ENG.). 32p. (J). (gr. -1-3). pap. 7.99 (978-0-547-99485-7(0), 1525240, Clarion Bks.) HarperCollins Pubs.

—The Penderwicks at Last. 2018. 256p. (J). (978-0-525-64458-3(X)) Knopf, Alfred A. Inc.

—The Penderwicks at Last. 2019. (Penderwicks Ser.: 5). 304p. (J). (gr. 3-7). 8.99 (978-0-385-75569-6(4), Yearling) Random Hse. Children's Bks.

Bitner, Pamela. A Brother-Sister Team. Poppen, Alex, illus. 2008. 16p. pap. 24.95 (978-1-60474-583-2(5)) America Star Bks.

Bitterman, Kevin. BD's Big Hit, 1 vol. 2009. (ENG.). 63p. pap. 19.95 (978-1-60836-366-7(X)) America Star Bks.

Black, Holly. White Cat. (Curse Workers Ser.: 1). (ENG.). (YA). (gr. 9). 2011. 336p. pap. 11.99 (978-1-4169-6397-4(9)) 2010. 320p. 17.99 (978-1-4169-6396-7(0)) McElderry, Margaret K. Bks. (McElderry, Margaret K. Bks.).

Black, Holly & DiTerlizzi, Tony. The Field Guide. DiTerlizzi, Tony, illus. movie tie-in ed. 2008. (Spiderwick Chronicles: 1). (ENG., Illus.). 128p. (J). (gr. 2-5). 10.99 (978-1-4169-5017-2(6), Simon & Schuster Bks. For Young Readers) Simon & Schuster Bks. For Young Readers.

—The Wrath of Mulgarath. l.t. ed. 2006. (Spiderwick Chronicles: Bk. 5). (Illus.). 183p. (J). (gr. 3-7). 23.95 (978-0-7862-8579-2(6)) Thorndike Pr.

Blackford, Ami. Quest for the Dragon Stone: A Duncan Family Adventure. Blackford, Ami, illus. 2006. (Illus.). 48p. (J). (gr. 3-7). 16.95 (978-1-60108-008-0(5), 1265253) Red Cygnet Pr.

—Quest for the Elfin Elixir: A Duncan Family Adventure Book 2. Blackford, Ami, illus. 2007. (Illus.). 79p. (J). (gr. 3-7). 16.95 (978-1-60108-021-9(2)) Red Cygnet Pr.

Blake, Ashley Herring. Girl Made of Stars. (ENG.). 304p. (YA). (gr. 9). 2019. pap. 9.99 (978-0-358-10822-1(5), 1748885) 2018. 17.99 (978-1-328-77823-9(1), 1681853) HarperCollins Pubs. (Clarion Bks.).

Blake-Garrett, Andrea. Las Aventuras de Izzy y Juju: Gemelos Detectives Investigadores (G. D. I.) 2012. 28p. pap. 19.99 (978-1-4772-2523-3(4)) AuthorHouse.

Blakemore, Megan Frazer. Good & Gone. 2017. (ENG.). 304p. (YA). (gr. 8). 17.99 (978-0-06-234842-5(6), HarperTeen) HarperCollins Pubs.

Bledsoe, Lucy Jane. Running Wild. 2019. 224p. (YA). (gr. 4-7). 17.99 (978-0-8234-4363-5(9), Margaret Ferguson Books) Holiday Hse., Inc.

Blevins, Wiley. Hansel & Gretel & the Haunted Hut. Cox, Steve, illus. 2016. (Scary Tales Retold Ser.). (ENG.). 24p. (J). (gr. k-3). pap. 6.99 (978-1-63440-097-8(6), 3901e723-1a08-42ee-a75c-16f968d8bfca); lib. bdg. 27.99 (978-1-63440-096-1(8), 5cfd02df-7edf-431d-873a-53668e90ccdf) Red Chair Pr.

Bliss, Bryan. No Parking at the End Times. 2015. (ENG.). 272p. (YA). (gr. 9). 17.99 (978-0-06-227541-7(0), Greenwillow Bks.) HarperCollins Pubs.

Blitt, Natalie. The Truth about Leaving. 2019. (ENG.). 304p. (YA). pap. 12.99 (978-1-948705-09-7(5)) Amberjack Publishing Co.

Block, Francesca Lia. Wasteland. 2003. (Illus.). 160p. (YA). 16.89 (978-0-06-028645-3(8), Cotler, Joanna Books) HarperCollins Pubs.

Bloor, Edward. Tangerine. 2007. (ENG.). 320p. (YA). (gr. 5-7). 18.00 (978-0-15-201246-5(X), 1189264, Clarion Bks.) HarperCollins Pubs.

Blount, Patty. Someone I Used to Know. 2018. (ENG.). 384p. (YA). (gr. 8-12). pap. 10.99 (978-1-4926-3281-8(3)) Sourcebooks, Inc.

Blume, Judy. Cool Zone with the Pain & the Great One. Stevenson, James, illus. 2009. (Pain & the Great One Ser.: 2). (ENG.). 128p. (J). (gr. 3-7). 5.99 (978-0-440-42093-4(8), Yearling) Random Hse. Children's Bks.

—Double Fudge. 2007. (ENG.). 240p. (J). (gr. 3-7). 8.99 (978-0-14-240878-0(6), Puffin Books) Penguin Young Readers Group.

—Double Fudge. 2004. (Fudge Ser.). 160p. (J). (gr. 3-7). pap. 36.00 incl. audio (978-0-8072-2036-8(1), Listening Library) Random Hse. Audio Publishing Group.

—Double Fudge. 2007. (Fudge Bks.: 5). lib. bdg. 18.40 (978-1-4177-8371-7(0)) Turtleback.

—Friend or Fiend? with the Pain & the Great One. Stevenson, James, illus. 2010. (Pain & the Great One Ser.: 4). (ENG.). 128p. (J). (gr. 3-7). 5.99 (978-0-440-42095-8(4), Yearling) Random Hse. Children's Bks.

—Fudge-A-Mania. 2007. (ENG.). 176p. (J). (gr. 3-7). 8.99 (978-0-14-240877-3(8), Puffin Books) Penguin Young Readers Group.

—Going, Going, Gone! with the Pain & the Great One. Stevenson, James, illus. 2010. (Pain & the Great One Ser.: 3). (ENG.). 128p. (J). (gr. 3-7). 5.99 (978-0-440-42094-1(6), Yearling) Random Hse. Children's Bks.

—Here's to You, Rachel Robinson. 2010. (ENG.). 208p. (J). (gr. 5). pap. 9.99 (978-0-385-73987-0(7), Delacorte Bks. for Young Readers) Random Hse. Children's Bks.

—The One in the Middle Is the Green Kangaroo. Ohi, Debbie Ridpath, illus. 2014. (ENG.). 48p. (J). (gr. 1-5). pap. 5.99 (978-1-4814-1131-8(4), Atheneum Bks. for Young Readers) Simon & Schuster Children's Publishing.

—The Pain & the Great One. Ohi, Debbie Ridpath, illus. 2014. (ENG.). 48p. (J). (gr. 1-5). pap. 5.99 (978-1-4814-1145-5(4), Atheneum Bks. for Young Readers) Simon & Schuster Children's Publishing.

—Soupy Saturdays with the Pain & the Great One. Stevenson, James, illus. (Pain & the Great One Ser.: 1). (ENG.). (J). 2009. 128p. (gr. 3-7). 7.99 (978-0-440-42092-7(X), Yearling) 2007. 108p. (gr. 2-4). lib. bdg. 18.69 (978-0-385-90324-0(3), Delacorte Pr.) Random Hse. Children's Bks.

—Superfudge. (Fudge Ser.).Tr. of Superfudge. 166p. (J). (gr. 2-4). pap. 4.99 (978-0-8072-1457-2(4), Listening Library) Random Hse. Audio Publishing Group.

—Superfudge. 2007. (Fudge Bks.: 3).Tr. of Superfudge. lib. bdg. 18.40 (978-1-4177-8843-9(7)) Turtleback.

—Tales of a Fourth Grade Nothing. 2009. 8.32 (978-0-7848-3046-8(0)); 8.32 (978-0-7848-0332-5(3)) Marco Bk. Co. (Everbind).

—Tales of a Fourth Grade Nothing. 2007. 17.00 (978-0-7569-7937-9(4)) 2004. (ENG.). 144p. (J). (gr. 3-7). 8.99 (978-0-425-19379-2(9), Berkley) Penguin Publishing Group.

—Tales of a Fourth Grade Nothing. 2007. (ENG.). 160p. (J). (gr. 3-7). 8.99 (978-0-14-240881-0(6), Puffin Books) Penguin Young Readers Group.

—Tales of a Fourth Grade Nothing. (Fudge Ser.). 120p. (J). (gr. 3-5). pap. 4.99 (978-0-8072-1496-1(5), Listening Library) Random Hse. Audio Publishing Group.

—Tales of a Fourth Grade Nothing. 2003. pap. (978-0-439-57779-3(9), Scholastic) Scholastic, Inc.

Blumenthal, Deborah. Don't Let the Peas Touch! Ering, Timothy Basil, illus. 2004. (J). (978-0-439-29733-2(8), Levine, Arthur A. Bks.) Scholastic, Inc.

Blumer, J. Michael. The Book of Broken Promises, Vol. 2. 2007. 280p. (YA). pap. 15.99 (978-1-59092-540-9(8)) Blue Forge Pr.

—The Book of Second Chances, Bk. 1. 2006. (Secret Books of Gabendoor Ser.). 284p. per. 14.99 (978-1-59092-317-7(0)) Blue Forge Pr.

Bo, Ben. Skullcrack. 2003. (ENG.). 168p. (YA). (gr. 5-12). pap. 6.95 (978-0-8225-3311-5(1)) Lerner Publishing Group.

Boat, Patty. A Disappointing Homecoming: (A Soldier's Story), 1 vol. 2009. 158p. pap. 24.95 (978-1-61546-997-0(4)) PublishAmerica, Inc.

Bogart, Jo Ellen. The Big Tree Gang. Griffiths, Dean, illus. 2005. 60p. (J). lib. bdg. 20.00 (978-1-4242-1251-4(0)) Fitzgerald Bks.

Boggs, Patdee. Island of Angels. 2006. 55p. pap. 16.95 (978-1-4241-3758-9(6)) PublishAmerica, Inc.

Bohannon, C. S. Spatula Boy: And the Secret of the Mysterious Old House. 2007. 52p. per. 16.95 (978-1-4241-6956-6(9)) America Star Bks.

Bolden, Tonya. Crossing Ebenezer Creek. (ENG.). 240p. (YA). 2018. pap. 10.99 (978-1-68119-699-2(9), 900182277, Bloomsbury Young Adult) 2017. 17.99 (978-1-59990-319-4(9), 900054246, Bloomsbury USA Childrens) Bloomsbury Publishing USA.

—Crossing Ebenezer Creek. 2018. (YA). lib. bdg. 22.10 (978-0-606-41078-6(3)) Turtleback.

Bollback, Anthony G. Capture of the Twin Dragon. 2012. 152p. pap. 8.99 (978-0-9849359-1-8(6)) Finding the Cause, LLC.

—Hijacked. 2012. 176p. pap. 8.99 (978-0-9849359-5-6(9)) Finding the Cause, LLC.

—Mystery of the Counterfeit Money. 2012. 170p. (gr. 4-7). pap. 8.99 (978-0-9849359-2-5(4)) Finding the Cause, LLC.

—Rescue at Cripple Creek. 2012. 178p. pap. 8.99 (978-0-9849359-3-2(2)) Finding the Cause, LLC.

—Smugglers in Hong Kong. 2012. 156p. pap. 8.99 (978-0-9849359-0-1(8)) Finding the Cause, LLC.

—The Tiger Shark Strikes Again. 2012. 172p. pap. 8.99 (978-0-9849359-4-9(0)) Finding the Cause, LLC.

Bollen, Christina. An Angel in My Garden, 1 vol. Matyuschenko, Tanya, illus. 2009. 47p. pap. 24.95 (978-1-60813-661-2(2)) America Star Bks.

Bond, Juliet C. Sam's Sister. Majewski, Dawn, illus. 2004. (J). 18.00 (978-0-944934-30-2(7)) Perspectives Pr., Inc.

Bonilla, Rocio. Little Bro, Big Sis. Bonilla, Rocio, illus. 2019. (ENG., Illus.). 56p. (J). (gr. -1-3). lib. bdg. 16.99 (978-1-62354-109-5(3)) Charlesbridge Publishing, Inc.

Bonk, John J. Madhattan Mystery. 2012. (ENG., Illus.). 304p. (J). (gr. 4-6). 22.44 (978-0-8027-2349-9(7), 9780802723499) Walker & Co.

Booth, Tom. Day at the Beach. Booth, Tom, illus. 2018. (Jeter Publishing Ser.). (ENG., Illus.). 40p. (J). (gr. -1-3). 19.99 (978-1-5344-1105-0(4), Aladdin) Simon & Schuster Children's Publishing.

Booty, Don V. Brave Little Starling. 2012. (ENG.). 24p. (J). pap. 19.95 (978-1-4327-9017-2(X)) Outskirts Pr., Inc.

Borden, Louise. Big Brothers Don't Take Naps. Dodd, Emma, illus. 2011. (ENG.). 32p. (J). (gr. -1-3). 19.99 (978-1-4169-5503-0(8), McElderry, Margaret K. Bks.) McElderry, Margaret K. Bks.

Boston, Ruth. Super Hero for A Day. 2007. 152p. per. 13.95 (978-1-4327-1427-7(9)) Outskirts Pr., Inc.

Bourgeois, Paulette. Franklin's Baby Sister. 2004. (Illus.). (J). (gr. k-3). spiral bd. (978-0-616-07219-6(8)); spiral bd. (978-0-616-07218-9(X)) Canadian National Institute for the Blind/Institut National Canadien pour les Aveugles.

—Franklin's Baby Sister. Clark, Brenda, illus. (Franklin Ser.). (ENG.). 32p. (J). (gr. -1-3). (978-1-55074-858-1(0)) Kids Can Pr., Ltd.

Bowen, Anne. When You Visit Grandma & Grandpa. Bogacki, Tomasz, tr. Bogacki, Tomasz, illus. 2004. (Carolrhoda Picture Books Ser.). 32p. (J). (gr. -1-3). 15.95 (978-1-57505-610-4(0)) Lerner Publishing Group.

Bowler, Tim. Frozen Fire. 2010. (ENG.). 352p. (YA). (gr. 7-18). 8.99 (978-0-14-241465-1(4), Speak) Penguin Young Readers Group.

Bowman, Andy. Pokey's Garden. Travis, Stephanie, illus. 26p. (J). (gr. k-5). pap. 6.95 (978-1-931650-08-3(X)); lib. bdg. 14.95 (978-1-931650-09-0(8)) Coastal Publishing Carolina, Inc.

Boyce, Frank Cottrell & Boyce, Frank Cottrell. Millions. 2004. (Illus.). 256p. (J). (gr. 3-18). 15.99 (978-0-06-073330-8(6)); lib. bdg. 16.89 (978-0-06-073331-5(4)) HarperCollins Pubs.

Bracegirdle, P. J. Fiendish Deeds. 2009. (Joy of Spooking Ser.: 1). (ENG.). 224p. (J). (gr. 3-7). pap. 5.99 (978-1-4169-3417-2(0), McElderry, Margaret K. Bks.) McElderry, Margaret K. Bks.

Braden, Ann. The Benefits of Being an Octopus. 2018. 256p. (J). (gr. 3-7). 16.99 (978-1-5107-3748-8(0), Sky Pony Pr.) Skyhorse Publishing Co., Inc.

Bradford, Michael. Button Hill, 1 vol. 2015. (ENG.). 264p. (J). (gr. 4-7). pap. 12.95 (978-1-4598-0755-6(3)) Orca Bk. Pubs. USA.

Bradley, Kimberly Brubaker. The War I Finally Won. (ENG.). (J). (gr. 4-7). 2018. 416p. 9.99 (978-0-14-751681-7(1), Puffin Books) 2017. 400p. 18.99 (978-0-525-42920-3(4), Dial Bks) Penguin Young Readers Group.

—The War That Saved My Life. (ENG.). (J). (gr. 4-7). 2016. 352p. 9.99 (978-0-14-751048-8(1), Puffin Books) 2015. 320p. 17.99 (978-0-8037-4081-5(6), Dial Bks) Penguin Young Readers Group.

—The War That Saved My Life. 2016. (J). lib. bdg. 19.65 (978-0-606-38843-6(5)) Turtleback.

Bradley, Natasha R. & Bradley, Jasmine N. Jessika's Diaries:Life's Not Fair. 2008. 132p. pap. 14.95 (978-0-615-21079-7(1)) On The Ball Publishing.

Branch, Dianne. Sydney Becomes a Big Sister. 2011. 24p. pap. 11.32 (978-1-4634-4093-0(6)) AuthorHouse.

Brandeis, Madeline. Mitz & Fritz of Germany. 2011. 164p. 41.95 (978-1-258-10138-1(6)) Literary Licensing, LLC.

Branson, Terri. Brother Dragon. Taylor, Chet, illus. 2004. (J). 18.99 (978-0-9755888-5-7(0)) Dragonfly Publishing, Inc.

Braun, Sebastien. Mayday Mouse. Braun, Sebastien, illus. 2017. (Child's Play Library). (ENG., Illus.). 32p. (J). (gr. k-3). (978-1-84643-759-5(8)) Child's Play International Ltd.

Bray, Pamela. The Day Lonyaie's Life Changed. 2008. 32p. pap. 24.95 (978-1-60474-859-8(1)) America Star Bks.

Breach, Jen. Clem Hetherington & the Ironwood Race. Holgate, Douglas, illus. 2018. (Clem Hetherington Ser.: 1). (ENG.). 208p. (J). (gr. 3-7). pap. 14.99 (978-0-545-81446-1(4), Graphix) Scholastic, Inc.

Break Away. 64p. (J). (gr. 6-12). pap. (978-0-8224-2391-1(X)) Globe Fearon Educational Publishing.

Breathed, Berkeley. Edwurd Fudwupper Fibbed Big. 2003. (ENG., Illus.). 40p. (J). (gr. 1-4). pap. 10.99 (978-0-316-14425-4(8)) Little, Brown Bks. for Young Readers.

Brenda Jenkins. Trick or Treat Every Night. 2012. 24p. 24.95 (978-1-4626-6055-1(X)) America Star Bks.

Brennan-Nelson, Denise. Leopold the Lion. Barshaw, Ruth McNally, illus. 2015. (ENG.). 32p. (J). (gr. 1-3). 16.99 (978-1-58536-828-0(8), 203951) Sleeping Bear Pr.

Brewer, Heather. The Cemetery Boys. 2016. (ENG.). 304p. (YA). (gr. 8). pap. 9.99 (978-0-06-230789-7(4), HarperTeen) HarperCollins Pubs.

—The Cemetery Boys. 2016. (YA). lib. bdg. 20.85 (978-0-606-38741-5(2)) Turtleback.

Brezenoff, Steve. The Absolute Value of -1. 2010. (Carolrhoda YA Ser.). (ENG.). 296p. (YA). (gr. 9-12). lib. bdg. 16.95 (978-0-7613-5417-8(4), Carolrhoda Bks.) Lerner Publishing Group.

Brian, Kate, pseud. Megan Meade's Guide to the Mcgowan Boys. 2006. (ENG.). 288p. (YA). (gr. 7-12). pap. 11.99 (978-1-4169-0031-3(4), Simon & Schuster Bks. For Young Readers) Simon & Schuster Bks. For Young Readers.

—Private. 2009. (Private Ser.: No. 1). (ENG.). 240p. (YA). pap. 9.99 (978-1-4169-9946-1(9), Simon & Schuster Bks. For Young Readers) Simon & Schuster Bks. For Young Readers.

Brightwood, Laura, illus. Ka-ulu the Strong. Brightwood, Laura, . 2006. (J). (978-0-9789871-3-8(6)) 3-C Institute for Social Development.

Brink, Carol Ryrie. Caddie Woodlawn. 2006. (ENG., Illus.). 288p. (J). (gr. 3-7). pap. 7.99 (978-1-4169-4028-9(6), Aladdin) Simon & Schuster Children's Publishing.

Brisebois, Ro. Sherlock & Elf: The Mystery of the Thicket Behind the Shed. 2008. 100p. pap. 12.99 (978-1-4343-9987-8(7)) AuthorHouse.

Brodien-Jones, Chris. The Dreamkeepers. 2009. (ENG.). 148p. (YA). (gr. 7). pap. 8.99 (978-1-4424-0221-8(0), Simon & Schuster Bks. For Young Readers) Simon & Schuster Bks. For Young Readers.

A Brother's Sin. 2008. 84p. pap. 9.95 (978-1-934335-21-5(5)) WordWright.biz, Inc.

Brown, Jeff. Invisible Stanley. Pamintuan, Macky, illus. 2009. (Flat Stanley Ser.). (ENG.). 112p. (J). (gr. 2-5). pap. 5.99 (978-0-06-009792-9(2), HarperCollins) HarperCollins Pubs.

—Invisible Stanley. 2009. (Flat Stanley Ser.: 4). (J). (gr. k-3). lib. bdg. 14.75 (978-0-613-68434-7(6)) Turtleback.

Brown, Jeffrey. Lucy & Andy Neanderthal. 2018. (Lucy & Andy Neanderthal Ser.: 1). (Illus.). 240p. (J). (gr. 3-7). pap. 7.99 (978-0-525-64397-5(4), Yearling) Random Hse. Children's Bks.

—Lucy & Andy Neanderthal. Brown, Jeffrey, illus. 2016. (Lucy & Andy Neanderthal Ser.: 1). (Illus.). 224p. (J). (gr. 3-7). 12.99 (978-0-385-38835-1(7), Crown Books For Young Readers) Random Hse. Children's Bks.

—The Stone Cold Age. 2018. (Lucy & Andy Neanderthal Ser.: 2). lib. bdg. 18.40 (978-0-606-40934-6(3)) Turtleback.

Brown, Linnet. Keep Your Eyes on the Goal. 2013. 48p. pap. (978-1-4602-1828-0(0)) FriesenPress.

Brown, Marc. Arthur & the Baby: A Classic Arthur Adventure. 2011. (Classic Arthur Adventure Ser.). (ENG., Illus.). 32p. (J). (gr. -1-3). pap. 8.99 (978-0-316-12905-3(4)) Little, Brown Bks. for Young Readers.

—Arthur in New York. 2008. (Step into Reading Ser.). (ENG., Illus.). 24p. (J). (gr. k-3). pap. 5.99 (978-0-375-82976-5(8), Random Hse. Bks. for Young Readers) Random Hse. Children's Bks.

—Arthur Turns Green. 2014. (ENG., Illus.). 32p. (J). (gr. 1-4). 7.99 (978-0-316-12923-7(2)) Little, Brown Bks. for Young Readers.

—Arthur Turns Green. 2014. (Arthur Adventures Ser.). (J). lib. bdg. 17.20 (978-0-606-34069-4(6)) Turtleback.

—Arthur's Classroom Fib. 2007. (Arthur Step into Reading Ser.). lib. bdg. 13.55 (978-1-4177-7281-0(6)) Turtleback.

—Arthur's Reading Trick. 2009. (Step into Reading Ser.). (ENG., Illus.). 24p. (J). (gr. k-3). pap. 4.99 (978-0-375-82977-2(6), Random Hse. Bks. for Young Readers) Random Hse. Children's Bks.

Brown, Marc & Sarfatti, Esther. D. W. y el Carne de Biblioteca. 2004.Tr. of D.W.'s Library Card. (ENG & SPA., Illus.). (J). pap. 6.95 (978-1-930332-47-8(5)) Lectorum Pubns., Inc.

Brown, Margery W. Baby Jesus Like My Brother. 2008. (Illus.). 32p. 6.95 (978-1-60349-000-9(0), Marimba Bks.) Just Us Bks., Inc.

Browne, Anthony. Hide & Seek. Browne, Anthony, illus. 2018. (ENG., Illus.). 32p. (J). (gr. -1-2). 17.99 (978-1-5362-0260-1(6)) Candlewick Pr.

Bruce, Mary Grant. Back to Billabong. l.t. ed. 2006. 200p. pap. 21.99 (978-1-4264-2197-6(4)) Creative Media Partners, LLC.

Bruneau M. D., Denise J. & Bruneau, Denise J. My Baby: Illustrations by MikeMotz. com. 2010. 28p. 13.99 (978-1-4490-8475-2(3)) AuthorHouse.

Bryon, Nathan. Rocket Says Look Up! Adeola, Dapo, illus. 2019. (Rocket Says... Ser.). (ENG.). 40p. (J). (gr. -1-2). 17.99 (978-1-9848-9442-7(0), Random Hse. Bks. for Young Readers) Random Hse. Children's Bks.

Buckley-Archer, Linda. The Time Quake, 3. 2009. (Gideon Trilogy Ser.: 3). (ENG.). 464p. (J). (gr. 5-9). 17.99 (978-1-4169-1529-4(X)) Simon & Schuster, Inc.

Buckley, Michael. The Inside Story. 2018. (Sisters Grimm Ser.: 8). (J). lib. bdg. 19.65 (978-0-606-41063-2(5)) Turtleback.

—The Problem Child. 2017. (Sisters Grimm Ser.: 3). (J). lib. bdg. 19.60 (978-0-606-39687-5(X)) Turtleback.

Bucky Badger A Children's Story: Becky Gets a Brother, 4 vols. l.t. ed. 2005. (Illus.). (J). 9.99 (978-0-9765510-0-3(4)) Badgerland Bks. LLC.

Budreau, Craig. Trail Map: Barton Creek Greenbelt — Loop 360 to Zilker Park. 2006. (J). per. 5.00 (978-1-932196-26-9(9)) WordWright.biz, Inc.

Bulion, Leslie. Uncharted Waters, 1 vol. 2009. 192p. (J). (gr. 3-7). pap. 7.95 (978-1-56145-485-3(0)) Peachtree Publishing Co. Inc.

Bumgarner, Sam. Little Sami's Silly Again, 1 vol. 2009. 32p. pap. 24.95 (978-1-60813-863-0(1)) America Star Bks.

—Silly Little Sami. 2008. 24p. pap. 24.95 (978-1-60474-260-2(7)) America Star Bks.

Bunting, Eve. A Sudden Silence. 2007. (ENG., Illus.). 144p. (YA). (gr. 7-12). pap. 7.99 (978-0-15-205868-5(0), 1197622, Clarion Bks.) HarperCollins Pubs.

Burch, Christian. The Manny Files. 2008. (Mix Ser.). (ENG.). 304p. (J). (gr. 4-8). pap. 14.99 (978-1-4169-5534-4(8), Aladdin) Simon & Schuster Children's Publishing.

Burg, Ann E. Serafina's Promise. 2015. (ENG.). 304p. (J). (gr. 3-7). pap. 7.99 (978-0-545-53567-0(0), Scholastic Pr.) Scholastic, Inc.

Burgess, Lisa Maria. Juma & Little Sungura. Gugu, Abdul M., illus. 2013. 32p. 19.95 (978-1-939604-06-4(0)); pap. 9.99 (978-1-939604-02-6(8)) Barranca Pr.

—Juma Cooks Chapati. Gugu, Abdul M., illus. 2013. 32p. 19.95 (978-1-939604-08-8(7)); pap. 9.99 (978-1-939604-04-0(4)) Barranca Pr.

—Juma on Safari. Gugu, Abdul M., illus. 2013. 32p. 19.95 (978-1-939604-07-1(9)); pap. 9.99 (978-1-939604-03-3(6)) Barranca Pr.

Burgess, Thornton W. The Christmas Reindeer. Chase, Rhoda, illus. 2013. (Dover Children's Classics Ser.). (ENG.). 152p. (J). (gr. k-3). pap. 5.99 (978-0-486-49153-0(6), 491536) Dover Pubns., Inc.

Burgis, Stephanie. Stolen Magic. (Kat, Incorrigible Ser.: 3). (ENG., Illus.). 400p. (J). (gr. 5-8). 2014. pap. 7.99 (978-1-4169-9452-7(1)) 2013. 17.99 (978-1-4169-9451-0(3), Atheneum Bks. for Young Readers) Simon & Schuster Children's Publishing.

Burnham, Molly B. Teddy Mars Book #1: Almost a World Record Breaker. Spencer, Trevor, illus. 2016. (Teddy Mars Ser.: 1). (ENG.). 240p. (J). (gr. 3-7). pap. 6.99 (978-0-06-227811-1(8), Tegen, Katherine Bks) HarperCollins Pubs.

—Teddy Mars Book #3: Almost an Outlaw. Spencer, Trevor, illus. 2018. (Teddy Mars Ser.: 3). (ENG.). 288p. (J). (gr. 3-7). pap. 6.99 (978-0-06-227818-0(5), Tegen, Katherine Bks) HarperCollins Pubs.

Burningham, John. There's Going to Be a Baby. Oxenbury, Helen, illus. 48p. (J). 2014. (ENG.). (-k). 9.99 (978-0-7636-7265-2(3)) 2010. (978-0-7445-4996-6(5)) 2010. (ENG.). (gr. -1-k). 16.99 (978-0-7636-4907-4(4)) Candlewick Pr.

Burns, Ian. Lissie Pendle. 2006. 196p. pap. 13.04 (978-1-4116-5491-4(9)) Lulu Pr., Inc.

But I Knew Better: Individual Title, 6 pack. (gr. k-1). 23.00 (978-0-7635-9033-8(9)) Rigby Education.

Butcher, Nicholas. The Hand above the Gate. 2008. 204p. pap. (978-1-84923-348-4(9)) YouWriteOn.

Byars, Betsy. The Summer of the Swans. 2008. (Puffin Modern Classics Ser.). (Illus.). 129p. (gr. 4). 16.00 (978-0-7569-8944-6(2)) Perfection Learning Corp.

—Summer of the Swans, the (Puffin Modern Classics) 2004. (Puffin Modern Classics Ser.). 144p. (J). (gr. 3-7). pap. 7.99 (978-0-14-240114-9(5), Puffin Books) Penguin Young Readers Group.

Caldwell, V. M. Runt: Story of a Boy. 2006. (ENG.). 208p. (J). (gr. 2-8). 16.95 (978-1-57131-662-2(0)); (gr. 3-7). per. 6.95 (978-1-57131-661-5(2)) Milkweed Editions.

Callahan, Susan. A New Way. 2012. 20p. pap. 17.99 (978-1-4772-4507-1(3)) AuthorHouse.

Callahan, Thera S. All Wrapped Up. Gordon, Mike, illus. 2003. (Rookie Readers Ser.). 32p. (J). 19.50 (978-0-516-22844-0(7), Children's Pr.) Scholastic Library Publishing.

—All Wrapped up (a Rookie Reader) Gordon, Mike, illus. 2004. (Rookie Reader Ser.). (ENG.). 32p. (J). (gr. k-2). pap. 4.95 (978-0-516-21949-3(9), Children's Pr.) Scholastic Library Publishing.

Calonita, Jen. Summer State of Mind. 2014. (ENG.). 256p. (YA). (gr. 7-17). pap. 10.00 (978-0-316-09115-2(4), Poppy) Little, Brown Bks. for Young Readers.

Candlewick Press. Peppa Pig & the Day at Snowy Mountain. 2014. (Peppa Pig Ser.). (ENG., Illus.). 32p. (J). (-k). 12.99 (978-0-7636-7455-7(9), Candlewick Entertainment) Candlewick Pr.

—Peppa Pig & the Lost Christmas List. Candlewick Press, illus. 2012. (Peppa Pig Ser.). (ENG., Illus.). 32p. (J). (gr. k-k). 12.99 (978-0-7636-6276-9(3), Candlewick Entertainment) Candlewick Pr.

Caputo, Kenneth. The Adventures of Jay & Tay: Our First Karate Class. 2011. 32p. pap. 14.99 (978-1-4567-1999-9(8)) AuthorHouse.

Caraballo, Samuel. My Big Sister / Mi Hermana Mayor. Muraida, Thelma, illus. 2012. (ENG & SPA.). (J). (gr. 3-8). 16.95 (978-1-55885-750-6(8), Piñata Books) Arte Publico Pr.

Carey, Janet Lee. Wenny Has Wings. 2004. (ENG.). 240p. (J). (gr. 3-7). reprint ed. pap. 11.99 (978-0-689-86759-0(X),

Atheneum Bks. for Young Readers) Simon & Schuster Children's Publishing.

Carlson, Melody. Playing with Fire. 2007. (Secret Life of Samantha Mcgregor Ser.: 3). (ENG.). 256p. (YA). (gr. 7-12). per. 12.99 (978-1-59052-694-1(5), Multnomah Bks.) Crown Publishing Group, The.

Carlson, Nancy. Harriet & Walt, 2nd Edition. rev. ed. 2004. (Nancy Carlson Picture Bks.). (ENG., Illus.). 32p. (J). (gr. k-2). 15.95 (978-1-57505-672-2(0), d27ad0a4-1b56-459c-8485-dc489735e32f, Carolrhoda Bks.) Lerner Publishing Group.

—I Don't Like to Read! Carlson, Nancy, illus. 2009. (ENG., Illus.). 32p. (J). (gr. k-2). pap. 8.99 (978-0-14-241451-4(4), Puffin Books) Penguin Young Readers Group.

—Louanne Pig in the Perfect Family. 2nd rev. ed. 2004. (Nancy Carlson's Neighborhood Ser.). (ENG., Illus.). 32p. (J). (gr. k-2). 15.95 (978-1-57505-611-1(9)) Lerner Publishing Group.

—Loudmouth George Earns His Allowance. Carlson, Nancy, illus. 2007. (ENG., Illus.). 32p. (J). (gr. k-2). 15.95 (978-0-8225-6560-4(9), Carolrhoda Bks.) Lerner Publishing Group.

Carmen, Martín Anguita. El primer día de colegio de David. 2008. (SPA., Illus.). 32p. (J). 10.99 (978-84-241-5790-6(7)) Everest Editora ESP. Dist: Lectorum Pubns., Inc.

Carpenter, Lynette Stutzman. My Brother, the Senator. 2010. 40p. pap. 16.95 (978-1-4497-0629-6(0), WestBow Pr.) Author Solutions, LLC.

Carr, C. Hanna's Way. 2011. (Illus.). 112p. 28.31 (978-1-4567-8179-8(0)); pap. 14.11 (978-1-4567-8178-1(2)) AuthorHouse.

Carroll, Emma. In Darkling Wood. 2018. (ENG.). 256p. (J). (gr. 5). 6.99 (978-0-399-55604-3(4), Yearling) Random Hse. Children's Bks.

Carroll, Katie L. Elixir Bound. 2013. 158p. pap. (978-1-77127-465-4(4)) MuseItUp Publishing.

Carter, Ally. Take the Key & Lock Her Up. 2018. (Embassy Row Ser.: 3). lib. bdg. 20.85 (978-0-606-41138-7(0)) Turtleback.

—Take the Key & Lock Her up (Embassy Row, Book 3) (Embassy Row Ser.: 3). (ENG.). (YA). (gr. 7). 2017. 336p. pap. 12.99 (978-0-545-65501-9(3)) 2016. 2p. audio compact disk 39.99 (978-0-545-81400-3(6)) Scholastic, Inc.

Carter, Dorothy. Wilhe'mina Miles: After the Stork Night. Stevenson, Harvey, illus. 2005. 30p. (J). (gr. k-4). reprint ed. 16.00 (978-0-7567-9421-7(8)) DIANE Publishing Co.

Carter, T. E. All We Could Have Been. 2020. (ENG.). 304p. (YA). pap. 18.99 (978-1-250-23354-7(2), 900188811) Square Fish.

Cartwheel: A Sequel to Double Eagle. 2013. (ENG.). 252p. (YA). 17.00 (978-0-9844460-3-2(6)) Bucking Horse Bks.

Carty, Hilda. Catventure. 2009. (Illus.). 40p. pap. 18.49 (978-1-4389-4659-7(7)) AuthorHouse.

Cascioli, Lucia. Shifters. 2011. 126p. 25.99 (978-1-257-86200-9(6)); pap. 9.99 (978-1-257-86197-2(2)) Lulu Pr., Inc.

Cassell, Jody. Where's Leon? Storybook & Reader's Guide CD-ROM, 1. Kristof Pincheira, Kyra, illus. l.t. ed. 2006. 48p. (J). lib. bdg. 17.95 (978-1-59494-013-2(4)) CPCC Pr.

Cast, P. C. & Cast, Kristin. Lost. unabr. ed. (House of Night Other World Ser.: 2). (ENG.). 2019. 416p. pap. 14.99 (978-1-9825-4647-2(6), PBahrs) 2018. 408p. (YA). 18.99 (978-1-5384-4074-2(1), HCahrs) Blackstone Audio, Inc.

Castilla, Julia Mercedes. Strange Parents. 2009. 144p. (J). (gr. 6-18). pap. 9.95 (978-1-55885-590-8(4), Piñata Books) Arte Publico Pr.

Castlemon, Harry. Sportsman's Club in the Saddle. 2006. pap. 30.95 (978-1-4286-5231-6(0)) Kessinger Publishing, LLC.

Caterer, Claire M. The Key & the Flame. (ENG.). (J). (gr. 3-7). 2015. 496p. pap. 7.99 (978-1-4424-5742-3(2)) 2013. 480p. 17.99 (978-1-4424-5741-6(4)) McElderry, Margaret K. Bks. (McElderry, Margaret K. Bks.).

Cayen, Alise. Patty Pom-Poms. 2009. 36p. pap. 16.50 (978-1-60693-685-6(9), Strategic Bk. Publishing) Strategic Book Publishing & Rights Agency (SBPRA).

Cena, John. Elbow Grease. McWilliam, Howard, illus. (Elbow Grease Ser.). (ENG.). (J). 2019. 34p. (— 1). bds. 8.99 (978-1-5247-7356-4(5)) 2018. 40p. (gr. -1-2). 17.99 (978-1-5247-7350-2(6)) 2018. 40p. (gr. -1-2). lib. bdg. 20.99 (978-1-5247-7351-9(4)) Random Hse. Children's Bks. (Random Hse. Bks. for Young Readers).

Cento, Nucci. Maverick & Miss Murphy at Rascal's Rescue Ranch. 2009. 48p. pap. 12.50 (978-1-60860-388-6(1), Eloquent Bks.) Strategic Book Publishing & Rights Agency (SBPRA).

Chandler, Ann. Kootenay Silver. 2010. (ENG.). 216p. (YA). (gr. 9). pap. 12.99 (978-1-55488-755-2(0)) Dundurn Pr. CAN. Dist: Publishers Group West (PGW).

Chappas, Bess. Kiki & the Red Shoes. Branam, Sandy, illus. 2007. (J). 17.99 (978-1-60131-012-5(9)) Big Tent Bks.

Charbonneau, Joelle. Dividing Eden. (YA). 2018. (ENG.). 432p. (gr. 8). pap. 9.99 (978-0-06-245385-3(8)) 2017. 336p. (978-0-06-267333-6(5)) 2017. 318p. (978-0-06-274088-5(1)) HarperCollins Pubs. (HarperTeen).

Charles, Norma. Chasing a Star. 2009. (ENG., Illus.). 182p. (YA). (gr. 5-8). pap. (978-1-55380-077-4(X)) Ronsdale Pr.

Cheaney, J. B. & Cheaney, Janie. The Middle of Somewhere. 2008. (ENG., Illus.). 224p. (J). (gr. 3-7). 7.99 (978-0-440-42165-8(9), Yearling) Random Hse. Children's Bks.

Chen, Da. Girl under a Red Moon: Growing up During China's Cultural Revolution (Scholastic Focus) 2019. (ENG., Illus.). 208p. (J). (gr. 3-7). 17.99 (978-1-338-26386-2(2), Scholastic Nonfiction) Scholastic, Inc.

Chew, Ruth. A Matter-Of-Fact Magic Book: No Such Thing As a Witch. 2013. (Matter-Of-Fact Magic Book Ser.). (Illus.). 128p. (J). (gr. 2-5). 5.99 (978-0-449-81562-5(5), Random Hse. Bks. for Young Readers) Random Hse. Children's Bks.

Chichester Clark, Emma. Mimi's Book of Opposites. Chichester Clark, Emma, illus. 2004. (Illus.). 24p. (J). 9.95 (978-1-57091-574-1(1)) Charlesbridge Publishing, Inc.

—My Baby Sister (Humber & Plum, Book 2), Book 2. Chichester Clark, Emma, illus. 2nd ed. 2009. (Humber & Plum Ser.: 2). (ENG., Illus.). 32p. (J). (gr. -1-k). 9.99 (978-0-00-727324-9(X), HarperCollins Children's Bks.) HarperCollins Pubs. Ltd. GBR. Dist: HarperCollins Pubs.

—Plum & Rabbit & Me (Humber & Plum, Book 3), Book 3. Chichester Clark, Emma, illus. 2010. (Humber & Plum Ser.: 3). (ENG., Illus.). 32p. (J). (gr. -1-k). pap. 9.99 (978-0-00-727325-6(8), HarperCollins Children's Bks.) HarperCollins Pubs. Ltd. GBR. Dist: HarperCollins Pubs.

Chick, Bryan. The Secret Zoo. 2010. (Secret Zoo Ser.: 1). (ENG.). 304p. (J). (gr. 3-7). 18.99 (978-0-06-198750-2(6), Greenwillow Bks.) HarperCollins Pubs.

Child, Lauren. But I Am an Alligator. 2008. (Charlie & Lola Ser.). (ENG.). 24p. (J). (gr. -1-k). mass mkt. 4.99 (978-0-448-44697-4(9), Grosset & Dunlap) Penguin Young Readers Group.

—Charlie & Lola: but Excuse Me That Is My Book. 2006. (Charlie & Lola Ser.). (ENG., Illus.). 32p. (J). (gr. -1-3). 17.99 (978-0-8037-3096-0(9), Dial Bks) Penguin Young Readers Group.

—I Absolutely Must Do Coloring Now or Painting or Drawing. 2006. (Charlie & Lola Ser.). (ENG., Illus.). 24p. (J). (gr. -1-k). 4.99 (978-0-448-44415-4(1), Grosset & Dunlap) Penguin Young Readers Group.

—I Am Going to Save a Panda! 2010. (Charlie & Lola Ser.). lib. bdg. 13.55 (978-0-606-10628-3(6)) Turtleback.

—I Am Too Absolutely Small for School. Child, Lauren, illus. (Charlie & Lola Ser.). (ENG., Illus.). 32p. (J). (gr. -1-2). 2004. 16.99 (978-0-7636-2403-3(9)) 2005. reprint ed. per. 9.99 (978-0-7636-2887-1(5)) Candlewick Pr.

—I Am Too Absolutely Small for School. 2007. (Charlie & Lola (Shang Yi Publishing) Ser.). (CHI., Illus.). (J). (978-957-762-437-6(5)) Hsin Yi Pubns.

—I Am Too Absolutely Small for School. Child, Lauren, illus. 2005. (ENG., Illus.). (J). (gr. -1-1). lib. bdg. 14.65 (978-0-7569-6495-5(4)) Perfection Learning Corp.

—I Can't Stop Hiccuping! 2010. (Charlie & Lola Ser.). lib. bdg. 13.55 (978-0-606-10629-0(4)) Turtleback.

—I Completely Must Do Drawing Now & Painting & Coloring. 2007. (Charlie & Lola Ser.). (ENG., Illus.). 24p. (J). (gr. -1-k). 5.99 (978-0-448-44560-1(3), Grosset & Dunlap) Penguin Young Readers Group.

—I Want to Be Much More Bigger Like You. 2008. (Charlie & Lola Ser.). (ENG., Illus.). 24p. (J). (gr. -1-k). mass mkt. 4.99 (978-0-448-44867-1(X), Grosset & Dunlap) Penguin Young Readers Group.

—I Will Never Not Ever Eat a Tomato. Child, Lauren, illus. 2003. (Charlie & Lola Ser.). (ENG., Illus.). 32p. (J). (gr. -1-3). reprint ed. 9.99 (978-0-7636-2180-3(3)) Candlewick Pr.

—I Will Never Not Ever Eat a Tomato. 2004. (Charlie & Lola Ser.). (Illus.). (gr. -1-3). 17.00 (978-0-7569-3178-0(9)) Perfection Learning Corp.

—I Will Never Not Ever Eat a Tomato. 2003. (Charlie & Lola Ser.). lib. bdg. 19.65 (978-0-613-69403-2(1)) Turtleback.

—I've Won, No I've Won, No I've Won. 2006. (Charlie & Lola Ser.). (ENG., Illus.). 32p. (J). (gr. -1-2). pap. 7.99 (978-0-448-44350-8(3), Grosset & Dunlap) Penguin Young Readers Group.

—My Wobbly Tooth Must Not Ever Never Fall Out. 2006. (Charlie & Lola Ser.). (ENG., Illus.). 32p. (J). (gr. -1-2). mass mkt. 6.99 (978-0-448-44255-6(8), Grosset & Dunlap) Penguin Young Readers Group.

—The New Small Person. Child, Lauren, illus. 2018. (ENG., Illus.). 32p. (J). (gr. -1-3). 8.99 (978-0-7636-9974-1(8)) Candlewick Pr.

—Sizzles Is Completely Not Here. 2007. (Illus.). 10p. (J). bds. (978-0-14-138337-8(2), Puffin) Penguin Publishing Group.

—Slightly Invisible. Child, Lauren, illus. 2011. (Charlie & Lola Ser.). (ENG., Illus.). 40p. (J). (gr. -1-2). 16.99 (978-0-7636-5347-7(0)) Candlewick Pr.

—You Can Be My Friend. 2007. (Charlie & Lola Ser.). (ENG., Illus.). 24p. (J). (gr. -1-k). mass mkt. 4.99 (978-0-448-44840-4(8), Grosset & Dunlap) Penguin Young Readers Group.

Child, Lauren, et al. Carys Blodyn, Dyma Fi. 2005. (WEL., Illus.). 32p. pap. (978-1-85596-670-3(0)) Dref Wen.

—Fydda i Byth Bythoedd yn Bwyta Tomato. 2005. (WEL., Illus.). 32p. pap. (978-1-85596-668-0(9)) Dref Wen.

Childs, Karin Alfelt. The Balm of Gilead. 2007. 356p. (YA). 15.95 (978-0-9748423-7-0(0)) Fountain Publishing.

Chin, Amanda. Chaff n' Skaffs: Mai & the Lost Moskivvy. Feldman, Luke, illus. 2009. (ENG.). 36p. (J). (gr. -1-3). 15.95 (978-1-59702-013-8(3)) Immedium.

Chin, Oliver. Timmy & Tammy's Train of Thought. McPherson, Heath, illus. 2007. (ENG.). 36p. (J). (gr. -1-3). 15.95 (978-1-59702-008-4(7)) Immedium.

Choldenko, Gennifer. Al Capone Does My Homework. 2014. (Tales from Alcatraz Ser.: 3). (ENG.). 240p. (J). (gr. 5). pap. 8.99 (978-0-14-242522-0(2), Puffin Books) Penguin Young Readers Group.

—Al Capone Does My Homework. 2014. (Tale from Alcatraz (Al Capone) Ser.: 3). lib. bdg. 18.40 (978-0-606-35714-2(9)) Turtleback.

—Al Capone Does My Shirts. (Tales from Alcatraz Ser.: 1). (ENG., Illus.). (J). (gr. 5-18). 2004. 240p. 17.99 (978-0-399-23861-1(1), G.P. Putnam's Sons Books for Young Readers) 2006. 288p. reprint ed. pap. 8.99 (978-0-14-240370-9(9), Puffin Books) Penguin Young Readers Group.

—Al Capone Does My Shirts. 2006. (Illus.). 317p. (J). (gr. 4-7). per. 10.95 (978-0-7862-8927-1(9)) Thorndike Pr.

—Al Capone Shines My Shoes. 2011. (Tales from Alcatraz Ser.: 2). (ENG.). 304p. (J). (gr. 5-18). 8.99 (978-0-14-241718-8(1), Puffin Books) Penguin Young Readers Group.

—Al Capone Shines My Shoes. 2011. (Tale from Alcatraz (Al Capone) Ser.: 2). lib. bdg. 18.40 (978-0-606-23072-8(6)) Turtleback.

—No Passengers Beyond This Point. 2011. (ENG., Illus.). 288p. (J). (gr. 6-8). 21.19 (978-0-8037-3534-7(0)) Penguin Young Readers Group.

—No Passengers Beyond This Point. 2012. lib. bdg. 17.20 (978-0-606-23637-9(6)) Turtleback.

—One-Third Nerd. Ceulemans, Églantine, illus. 2020. (ENG.). 224p. (J). (gr. 3-7). pap. 8.99 (978-1-5247-1891-6(2), Yearling) Random Hse. Children's Bks.

Choldenko, Gennifer, et al. No Passengers Beyond This Point. 2011. (Playaway Children Ser.). (J). 49.99 (978-1-61707-000-6(9)) Findaway World, LLC.

Christiansen, Rebecca. Maybe in Paris. 2017. (ENG.). 224p. (YA). (gr. 6-6). 16.99 (978-1-5107-0880-8(4), Sky Pony Pr.) Skyhorse Publishing Co., Inc.

Christie, Tory. Curious Mccarthy's Electric Ideas. Price, Mina, illus. 2017. (Curious Mccarthy Ser.). (ENG.). 112p. (J). (gr. 2-4). pap. 6.95 (978-1-5158-1648-5(6), 136303); lib. bdg. 25.32 (978-1-5158-1644-7(3), 136299) Capstone. (Picture Window Bks.).

—Curious Mccarthy's Family Chemistry. Price, Mina, illus. 2017. (Curious Mccarthy Ser.). (ENG.). 112p. (J). (gr. 2-4). pap. 6.95 (978-1-5158-1649-2(4), 136304); lib. bdg. 25.32 (978-1-5158-1645-4(1), 136300) Capstone. (Picture Window Bks.).

—Curious Mccarthy's Not-So-Perfect Pitch. Price, Mina, illus. 2017. (Curious Mccarthy Ser.). (ENG.). 112p. (J). (gr. 2-4). pap. 6.95 (978-1-5158-1647-8(8), 136302, Picture Window Bks.) Capstone.

—Curious Mccarthy's Power of Observation. Price, Mina, illus. 2017. (Curious Mccarthy Ser.). (ENG.). 112p. (J). (gr. 2-4). pap. 6.95 (978-1-5158-1650-8(8), 136305); lib. bdg. 25.32 (978-1-5158-1646-1(X), 136301) Capstone. (Picture Window Bks.).

Christopher, Danny. Putuguq & Kublu, 1 vol. Arijanto, Astrid, illus. 2017. (Putuguq & Kublu Ser.: 1). (ENG.). 40p. (J). (gr. 1-3). pap. 8.95 (978-1-77227-143-0(8)) Inhabit Media Inc. CAN. Dist: Consortium Bk. Sales & Distribution.

Christopher, Matt. The Great Quarterback Switch. 2008. (New Matt Christopher Sports Library). 144p. (J). (gr. 4-6). lib. bdg. 26.60 (978-1-59953-216-5(6)) Norwood Hse. Pr.

—Lacrosse Face-Off. 2006. (ENG.). 128p. (J). (gr. 3-7). per. 9.99 (978-0-316-79641-5(7)) Little, Brown Bks. for Young Readers.

—Snowboard Showdown. 2005. (Sports Classics IV Ser.). 167p. (J). lib. bdg. 15.00 (978-1-59054-770-0(5)) Fitzgerald Bks.

—Snowboard Showdown. l.t. ed. 2007. (New Matt Christopher Sports Library). 160p. (J). (gr. 4-6). lib. bdg. 26.60 (978-1-59953-109-0(7)) Norwood Hse. Pr.

Chronicle Books. My Big Evil Brother Packed My Lunch: 20+ Gross Lift-The-flaps (Kids Novelty Book, Children's Lift the Flaps Book, Sibling Rivalry Book) Watson, Laura, illus. 2019. (ENG.). 12p. (J). (gr. -1-3). 16.99 (978-1-4521-7089-3(4)) Chronicle Bks. LLC.

Chung, Arree. Ninja! Chung, Arree, illus. 2014. (Ninja! Ser.: 1). (ENG., Illus.). 40p. (J). (gr. -1-2). 18.99 (978-0-8050-9911-9(5), 900125303, Holt, Henry & Co. Bks. For Young Readers) Holt, Henry & Co.

Church, Alfred J. Three Greek Children. 2008. (Illus.). 160p. pap. 9.95 (978-1-59915-081-9(6)) Yesterday's Classics.

Church, Caroline Jayne. I Am a Big Sister. Church, Caroline Jayne, illus. 2015. (ENG., Illus.). 24p. (J). (gr. -1 — 1). 6.99 (978-0-545-68898-7(1), Cartwheel Bks.) Scholastic, Inc.

—I Am a Big Sister! / ¡Soy una Hermana Mayor! (Bilingual) (Bilingual Edition) Church, Caroline Jayne, illus. 2015.Tr. of ¡Soy una Hermana Mayor! (SPA., Illus.). 24p. (J). (gr. -1 — 1). 6.99 (978-0-545-84718-6(4), Scholastic en Espanol) Scholastic, Inc.

Ciraolo, Simona, illus. Whatever Happened to My Sister? 2015. (ENG.). 40p. (J). (gr. k-3). 17.95 (978-1-909263-52-9(4)) Flying Eye Bks. GBR. Dist: Penguin Random Hse. LLC.

Clarion Books, Clarion. Girl Power 5-Minute Stories. 2015. (5-Minute Stories Ser.). (ENG., Illus.). 224p. (J). (gr. -1-3). 12.99 (978-0-544-33925-5(8), 1584496, Clarion Bks.) HarperCollins Pubs.

Clark, Catherine. Frozen Rodeo. 2003. (ENG.). 304p. (YA). (gr. 8-18). 15.99 (978-0-06-009070-8(7)) HarperCollins Pubs.

Clark, Eleanor. Mary Elizabeth: Welcome to America. 2007. (Eleanor Ser.: Bk. 1). (Illus.). 187p. (J). (gr. 4-7). 14.99 (978-0-9753036-7-2(8)) HonorNet.

Clark, Isabelle. The Enchanted Forest of Hope. 2009. 44p. pap. 18.50 (978-1-4389-7781-2(6)) AuthorHouse.

Clark, Katherine. Seagull Sam. Huntington, Amy, illus. 2007. (ENG.). 32p. (J). (gr. -1-3). 15.95 (978-0-89272-715-5(2)) Down East Bks.

Clarke, Jane. G. E. M. Parsons, Garry, illus. 2008. (ENG.). 32p. (J). (gr. -1-k). pap. 9.95 (978-0-09-948012-9(3), Red Fox) Random House Children's Books GBR. Dist: Independent Pubs. Group.

Clarke, Judith. One Whole & Perfect Day. 2013. (ENG.). 248p. (YA). (gr. 8-12). pap. 9.95 (978-1-62091-025-2(X), Astra Young Readers) Astra Publishing Hse.

Claus, Rimana. I Want That! Moran, Lyn, illus. 2012. 36p. pap. 15.97 (978-1-61897-838-7(1), Strategic Bk. Publishing) Strategic Book Publishing & Rights Agency (SBPRA).

Clayton, Emma. The Whisper. 2012. 309p. (978-0-545-43365-5(7), Chicken Hse., The) Scholastic, Inc.

Cleary, Beverly. Ramona la Chinche. Palacios, Argentina, tr. Darling, Louis, illus. 2006. (Ramona Quimby Spanish Ser.: 2).Tr. of Ramona the Pest. (SPA.). 181p. (J). (gr. 4-7). lib. bdg. 16.00 (978-0-613-00464-0(7)) Turtleback.

—Ramona the Pest. (Ramona Quimby Ser.). (J). (gr. 3-5). Random House Publishing Group.

—Two Times the Fun. 2005. (ENG., Illus.). 96p. (J). (gr. -1-2). 16.99 (978-0-06-057921-0(8), HarperCollins) HarperCollins Pubs.

Cleaver, Vera & Cleaver, Bill. Donde Florecen los Lirios. (SPA.). 168p. (YA). (gr. 5-8). (978-84-204-3648-7(8), AF0285) Ediciones Alfaguara ESP. Dist: Lectorum Pubns., Inc.

Clements, Andrew. Troublemaker. Elliott, Mark, illus. 2011. (ENG.). 160p. (J). (gr. 3-7). lib. bdg. 18.99 (978-1-4169-4930-5(5), Atheneum Bks. for Young Readers) Simon & Schuster Children's Publishing.

C.M.M. A Life of Many Forms. 2012. 52p. pap. 16.95 (978-1-62709-318-7(4)) America Star Bks.

Coakley, Lena. Worlds of Ink & Shadow: A Novel of the Brontës. 2016. (ENG.). 352p. (J). (gr. 8-17). 17.95 (978-1-4197-1034-6(6), 1051801, Amulet Bks.) Abrams, Inc.

Coates, Jan L. Rocket Man, 1 vol. 2014. (ENG., Illus.). 120p. (J). (gr. 5-8). pap. 12.95 (978-0-88995-494-6(1), c430bc15-0a73-4cc5-a828-00c54e7ca2a4) Trifolium Bks., Inc. CAN. Dist: Firefly Bks., Ltd.

Cocca-Leffler, Maryann. Theo's Mood: A Book of Feelings. Cocca-Leffler, Maryann, illus. 2013. (ENG., Illus.). 24p. (J). (gr. -1-3). 17.99 (978-0-8075-7778-3(2), 807577782) Whitman, Albert & Co.

Codell, Esmé Raji. Vive la Paris. 2006. (ENG.). 224p. (J). (gr. 4-7). 15.99 (978-0-7868-5124-9(4)) Hyperion Pr.

Cody, Matthew. The Secrets of the Pied Piper 3: the Piper's Apprentice. 2017. (Secrets of the Pied Piper Ser.: 3). (ENG., Illus.). 288p. (J). (gr. 3-7). 16.99 (978-0-385-75530-6(9), Knopf Bks. for Young Readers) Random Hse. Children's Bks.

Coerr, Eleanor. Circus Day in Japan: Bilingual English & Japanese Text. Matsunari, Yumi, tr. Coerr, Eleanor, illus. 2016. (Illus.). 48p. (J). (gr. -1-3). 9.95 (978-0-8048-4743-8(6)) Tuttle Publishing.

Cohen, Miriam. My Big Brother, 1 vol. Himler, Ronald, illus. 2005. (ENG.). 32p. (J). 15.95 (978-1-59572-007-8(3)); pap. 6.95 (978-1-59572-158-7(4)) Star Bright Bks., Inc.

Cole, Joanna. I'm a Big Brother. 2010. (ENG., Illus.). 32p. (J). (gr. -1-3). pap. 7.99 (978-0-06-190065-5(6), HarperCollins) HarperCollins Pubs.

—I'm a Big Sister. Kightley, Rosalinda, illus. 2010. (ENG.). 32p. (J). (gr. -1-3). pap. 7.99 (978-0-06-190062-4(1), HarperCollins) HarperCollins Pubs.

—Soy un Hermano Mayor: I'm a Big Brother (Spanish Edition), 1 vol. Kightley, Rosalinda, illus. 2010. (SPA.). 32p. (J). (gr. -1-k). 7.99 (978-0-06-190066-2(4)) HarperCollins Español.

Colfer, Chris. An Author's Odyssey. 2016. (Land of Stories Ser.: 5). (ENG.). 496p. (J). (gr. 3-7). pap. 11.99 (978-0-316-27214-8(0)) Little, Brown Bks. for Young Readers.

—The Curvy Tree: A Tale from the Land of Stories. Dorman, Brandon, illus. 2015. (Land of Stories Ser.). (ENG.). 32p. (J). (gr. -1-3). 18.99 (978-0-316-40685-7(6)) Little, Brown Bks. for Young Readers.

—The Enchantress Returns. 2014. (Land of Stories Ser.: 2). (J). lib. bdg. 20.85 (978-0-606-37229-9(6)) Turtleback.

—A Grimm Warning. 2015. (Land of Stories Ser.: 3). (J). lib. bdg. 20.85 (978-0-606-37230-5(X)) Turtleback.

—The Land of Stories: a Grimm Warning. (Land of Stories Ser.: 3). (ENG.). (J). (gr. 3-7). 2015. 496p. pap. 9.99 (978-0-316-40682-6(1)) 2014. 480p. 19.99 (978-0-316-40681-9(3)) 2014. 768p. 50.99 (978-0-316-40964-3(2)) Little, Brown Bks. for Young Readers.

—The Land of Stories: an Author's Odyssey. (Land of Stories Ser.: 5). (ENG., Illus.). 464p. (J). (gr. 3-7). 2017. pap. 9.99 (978-0-316-38321-9(X)) 2016. 19.99 (978-0-316-38329-5(5)) Little, Brown Bks. for Young Readers.

—The Land of Stories: Beyond the Kingdoms. 2015. (Land of Stories Ser.: 4). (ENG., Illus.). (J). (gr. 3-7). 432p. 19.99 (978-0-316-40689-5(9)); 624p. 45.99 (978-0-316-33938-4(5)) Little, Brown Bks. for Young Readers.

—The Land of Stories: the Enchantress Returns. (Land of Stories Ser.: 2). (ENG.). (J). (gr. 3-7). 2014. 544p. pap. 9.99 (978-0-316-20155-1(3)) 2013. (Illus.). 528p. 19.99 (978-0-316-20154-4(5)) 2013. 832p. 52.99 (978-0-316-24235-6(7)) Little, Brown Bks. for Young Readers.

—The Land of Stories: the Wishing Spell. (Land of Stories Ser.: 1). (ENG., Illus.). (J). (gr. 3-7). 2013. 464p. pap. 9.99 (978-0-316-20156-8(1)) 2012. 448p. 19.99 (978-0-316-20157-5(X)) 2013. 672p. pap. 28.99 (978-0-316-24236-3(5)) Little, Brown Bks. for Young Readers.

—The Land of Stories: Worlds Collide. 2018. (Land of Stories Ser.: 6). (ENG.). 464p. (J). (gr. 3-7). pap. 9.99 (978-0-316-35588-9(7)) Little, Brown Bks. for Young Readers.

—The Wishing Spell. Dorman, Brandon, illus. 2012. 438p. (J). pap. (978-0-316-45393-6(5)) Little Brown & Co.

—The Wishing Spell. 2013. (Land of Stories Ser.: 1). (J). lib. bdg. 20.85 (978-0-606-31746-7(5)) Turtleback.

—Worlds Collide. Dorman, Brandon, illus. 2017. 434p. (J). (978-0-316-43920-6(7)) Little Brown & Co.

Colfer, Chris & Dorman, Brandon. The Land of Stories the Wishing Spell. 2013. pap. (978-0-545-64793-9(2)) Scholastic, Inc.

Collins, Carleen. Everyone Loves Chocolate. 2009. 60p. pap. 23.99 (978-1-4490-3049-0(1)) AuthorHouse.

Collins, Suzanne. Gregor & the Code of Claw. l.t. ed. 2007. (Underland Chronicles: Bk. 5). 413p. (YA). (gr. 8-12). 22.95 (978-0-7862-9696-5(8)) Thorndike Pr.

—Gregor & the Code of Claw (the Underland Chronicles #5) 2013. (Underland Chronicles Ser.: 5). (ENG., Illus.). 416p. (J). (gr. 4-7). pap. 7.99 (978-0-439-79144-1(8), Scholastic Paperbacks) Scholastic, Inc.

—Gregor & the Curse of the Warmbloods. 2006. (Underland Chronicles: Bk. 3). 358p. (gr. 4-7). 17.00 (978-0-7569-6766-6(X)) Perfection Learning Corp.

—Gregor & the Curse of the Warmbloods (the Underland Chronicles #3) 2013. (Underland Chronicles Ser.: 3). (ENG.). 368p. (J). (gr. 4-7). pap. 7.99 (978-0-439-65624-5(9), Scholastic Paperbacks) Scholastic, Inc.

—When Charlie McButton Lost Power. Lester, Mike, illus. 2009. 32p. 16.00 (978-1-60686-529-3(3)) Perfection Learning Corp.

—When Charlie Mcbutton Lost Power. Lester, Mike, illus. 2007. 32p. (J). (gr. -1-3). pap. 8.99 (978-0-14-240857-5(3), Puffin Books) Penguin Young Readers Group.

Columbus, Chris & Vizzini, Ned. House of Secrets. 2015. (House of Secrets Ser.: Vol. 1). (KOR.). 580p. (J). (978-89-491-7127-2(9)) Biryongso Publishing Co.

—House of Secrets. Call, Greg, illus. (House of Secrets Ser.: 1). (J). 2014. (ENG.). 512p. (gr. 3-7). pap. 7.99 (978-0-06-219247-9(7), Balzer & Bray) 2013. (ENG.). 496p. (gr. 3-7). 17.99 (978-0-06-219246-2(9), Balzer & Bray) 2013. 490p. (978-0-06-225964-6(4)) HarperCollins Pubs.

—House of Secrets. 2014. (House of Secrets Ser.: 1). (J). lib. bdg. 18.40 (978-0-606-35070-9(5)) Turtleback.

—House of Secrets: Battle of the Beasts. Call, Greg, illus. 2014. (House of Secrets Ser.: 2). (ENG.). 480p. (J). (gr. 3-7). 17.99 (978-0-06-219249-3(3), Balzer & Bray) HarperCollins Pubs.

Compestine, Ying Chang. The Story of Kites: Amazing Chinese Inventions. Xuan, YongSheng, illus. 2016. (Amazing Chinese Inventions Ser.). 40p. (J). (gr. -1-3). 15.95 (978-1-59702-122-7(9)) Immedium.

Condie, Catherine. Whirl of the Wheel. 2010. (ENG.). 107p. pap. 12.95 (978-1-4452-8648-8(3)) Lulu Pr., Inc.

Connelly, Neil. The Miracle Stealer. 2010. (ENG.). 240p. (J). (gr. 9-18). 17.99 *(978-0-545-13195-7(2)*, Levine, Arthur A. Bks.) Scholastic, Inc.

Conner, Sharon Landsberg. The Magnetizing Princess: A children's story that uses some of the most powerful tools available, to get more of what you Want. 2007. 56p. per. 8.95 *(978-0-595-44229-4(3))* iUniverse, Inc.

Connor, Leslie. Crunch. 2012. (ENG.). 336p. (J). (gr. 5). pap. 9.99 *(978-0-06-169234-5(4)*, Tegen, Katherine Bks) HarperCollins Pubs.

Connor, Patrick M. Tree House. 2011. 312p. pap. 29.95 *(978-1-4560-9578-9(1))* America Star Bks.

Conolan, Emily. Touch the Sun: the Freedom Finders. 2019. (Freedom Finders Ser.). (ENG., Illus.). 336p. (J). (gr. 4-8). pap. 10.99 *(978-1-76029-492-2(6))* Allen & Unwin AUS. Dist: Independent Pubs. Group.

Conrique, Samantha. The Pod-Poppers. 2007. (J). pap. 8.00 *(978-0-8059-7200-9(5))* Dorrance Publishing Co., Inc.

Cook, Deena & McIntosh, Cherie. Pinky & Peanut: The Adventure Begins. Scruggs, Trina, illus. 2007. 78p. (J). per. 4.99 *(978-0-9797020-0-6(3))* P & P Publishing LLC.

Cook, Julia. I Want to Be the Only Dog!, Volume 6. DuFalla, Anita, illus. 2015. (Building Relationships Ser.). (ENG.). 31p. (J). (gr. k-6). pap. 11.95 *(978-1-934490-86-0(5))* Boys Town Pr.

Cook, Sonya Correll. Quest for a Family Pet: The Adventures of Nique, Nick, & Nelle. Transou, Devora & Watkins, Karen, illus. 2008. (ENG.). 24p. pap. 11.49 *(978-1-4343-5043-5(6))* AuthorHouse.

Cook, Tina H. Lindsey & the Yellow Masterpiece. 2011. 36p. pap. 15.99 *(978-1-4634-0306-5(2))* AuthorHouse.

Cooke, Brandy. You Poked My Heart! Logan, Laura, illus. 2016. (ENG.). 16p. (J). (gr. -1-1). bds. 5.99 *(978-1-4998-0310-5(9))* Little Bee Books Inc.

Coolidge, Susan. Clover. 2005. (Illus.). 133p. pap. *(978-1-59569-026-5(3))* Mondial.

—What Katy Did. 2013. (ENG., Illus.). 200p. (J). 15.00 *(978-1-84135-843-7(6))* Award Pubns. Ltd. GBR. Dist: Parkwest Pubns., Inc.

—What Katy Did. Ledyard, Addie, illus. 2013. 132p. pap. *(978-1-909735-03-3(5))* Aziloth Bks.

—What Katy Did. 2012. 246p. pap. *(978-1-78139-262-1(5))* Benediction Classics.

—What Katy Did. 2017. (ENG., Illus.). (J). (gr. 4-6). pap. 9.90 *(978-1-366-50696-2(0))* Blurb, Inc.

—What Katy Did. 2016. (ENG., Illus.). (J). 26.95 *(978-1-359-87966-0(8))* 2015. (ENG., Illus.). (J). (gr. 2-4). 25.95 *(978-1-297-62709-5(1))* 2012. 302p. pap. 29.75 *(978-1-286-07372-8(3))* 2012. 300p. pap. 29.75 *(978-1-286-00091-5(2))* 2011. 290p. (gr. 3-7). pap. 28.75 *(978-1-179-65265-8(7))* 2010. (ENG.). 282p. (gr. 3-7). pap. 28.75 *(978-1-177-27477-7(9))* 2010. 302p. pap. 29.75 *(978-1-145-74830-9(9))* 2008. 164p. (gr. 4-7). 25.99 *(978-0-554-28634-1(3))* 2007. (ENG.). 144p. pap. 18.99 *(978-1-4346-5943-9(7))* 2007. (ENG.). 160p. pap. 21.99 *(978-1-4346-5944-6(5))* Creative Media Partners, LLC.

—What Katy Did. 2007. (ENG.). 148p. per. *(978-1-4065-1527-5(2))* Dodo Pr.

—What Katy Did. (Dover Children's Evergreen Classics Ser.). (ENG.). (J). 2018. 176p. pap. 5.99 *(978-0-486-82252-5(4)*, 822524) 2006. (Illus.). 160p. (gr. 3-8). per. 6.95 *(978-0-486-44760-5(X))* Dover Pubns., Inc.

—What Katy Did. 2007. (ENG.). 104p. per. *(978-1-4068-4855-7(7))* Echo Library.

—What Katy Did. 2010. (Illus.). 92p. (gr. 3-7). pap. 19.99 *(978-1-153-74507-9(0))* 2009. 104p. pap. 6.40 *(978-0-217-53637-0(9))* General Bks. LLC.

—What Katy Did. 2010. 132p. pap. *(978-1-4076-5115-6(3))* HardPr.

—What Katy Did. Ledyard, Addie, illus. 284p. 2010. 35.16 *(978-1-163-85079-4(9))* 2010. pap. 23.16 *(978-1-163-77965-1(2))* 2007. 43.95 *(978-0-548-53870-8(0))* 2007. per. 28.95 *(978-0-548-48700-6(6))* Kessinger Publishing, LLC.

—What Katy Did. 2017. (Virago Modern Classics,What Katy Did Ser.). (ENG.). 208p. (J). (gr. 4-6). 11.99 *(978-0-349-00959-9(7)*, Virago Press) Little, Brown Book Group Ltd. GBR. Dist: Hachette Bk. Group.

—What Katy Did. 2013. (Vintage Children's Classics Ser.). (Illus.). 256p. (J). (gr. 4-7). pap. 12.99 *(978-0-09-957312-8(1))* Penguin Random Hse. GBR. Dist: Independent Pubs. Group.

—What Katy Did. 2007. (ENG.). 192p. pap. 12.45 *(978-1-60424-403-8(8)*, Bk. Jungle) Standard Publications, Inc.

—What Katy Did. 144p. 2018. (ENG., Illus.). (J). 19.99 *(978-1-5154-3178-7(9))* 2010. pap. 4.99 *(978-1-61720-100-4(6))* Wilder Pubns., Corp.

—What Katy Did. 2011. 162p. (gr. 3-7). pap. *(978-3-8424-6664-7(1))* tredition Verlag.

—What Katy Did: Illustrated by Susan Hellard. Hellard, Susan, illus. 2016. (Alma Junior Classics Ser.). (ENG.). 246p. (J). pap. 9.99 *(978-1-84749-607-2(5)*, 331109) Alma Classics GBR. Dist: Bloomsbury Publishing Plc.

Coolidge, Susan & Ledyard, Addie. What Katy Did. 2010. (ENG.). 292p. pap. 28.75 *(978-1-172-34659-2(3))* Creative Media Partners, LLC.

Cooney, Caroline B. A Friend at Midnight. 2008. (ENG.). 192p. (YA). (gr. 7). pap. 8.99 *(978-0-385-73327-4(5)*, Delacorte Bks. for Young Readers) Random Hse. Children's Bks.

—If the Witness Lied. 2010. (ENG.). 224p. (YA). (gr. 7). pap. 8.99 *(978-0-385-73449-3(2)*, Ember) Random Hse. Children's Bks.

—The Terrorist. 2012. (ENG.). 144p. (YA). (gr. 7-12). pap. 6.99 *(978-1-4532-7467-5(7))* Open Road Integrated Media, Inc.

—The Voice on the Radio. 2012. (Face on the Milk Carton Ser.). 208p. (YA). (gr. 7). pap. 10.99 *(978-0-385-74240-5(1)*, Ember) Random Hse. Children's Bks.

—The Voice on the Radio. 2012. (Janie Bks.: 3). lib. bdg. 20.85 *(978-0-606-26369-6(1))* Turtleback.

—Whatever Happened to Janie? 2012. (Face on the Milk Carton Ser.). 224p. (YA). (gr. 7). pap. 10.99 *(978-0-385-74239-9(8)*, Ember) Random Hse. Children's Bks.

Cooper, Susan. The Dark Is Rising. 2009. 7.64 *(978-0-7848-2212-8(3)*, Everbind) Marco Bk. Co.

—The Dark Is Rising. 15.85 *(978-0-7569-8464-9(5))* Perfection Learning Corp.

—The Dark Is Rising. (Dark Is Rising Sequence Ser.). 244p. (YA). (gr. 5-18). pap. 4.99 *(978-0-8072-1533-3(3)*, Listening Library) Random Hse. Audio Publishing Group.

—Green Boy. 2003. (ENG., Illus.). 208p. (J). (gr. 4-7). pap. 7.99 *(978-0-689-84760-8(2)*, McElderry, Margaret K. Bks.) McElderry, Margaret K. Bks.

—Over Sea, under Stone. 2013. (Dark Is Rising Sequence Ser.: 1). (ENG., Illus.). 288p. (J). (gr. 3-7). 19.99 *(978-1-4424-9592-0(8)*, McElderry, Margaret K. Bks.) McElderry, Margaret K. Bks.

Corbett, Sue. 12 Again. 2007. 240p. (J). (gr. 5-18). 6.99 *(978-0-14-240729-5(1)*, Puffin Books) Penguin Young Readers Group.

Corlett, William. The Bridge in the Clouds. 2010. (Magician's House Quartet Ser.: 4). (ENG.). 352p. (YA). (gr. 5-8). pap. 15.99 *(978-1-4424-1412-9(X)*, Simon Pulse) Simon Pulse.

—The Door in the Tree. 2010. (Magician's House Quartet Ser.: 2). (ENG.). 304p. (YA). (gr. 5-8). pap. 13.99 *(978-1-4424-1414-3(6)*, Simon Pulse) Simon Pulse.

—The Steps up the Chimney. 2011. (Magician's House Quartet Ser.: 1). (ENG.). 288p. (YA). (gr. 7). pap. 13.99 *(978-1-4424-2935-2(6)*, Simon Pulse) Simon Pulse.

Corpi, Lucha. & National Geographic Learning Staff. Where Fireflies Dance: Ahi, Donde Bailan Las Luciernagas, 1 vol. Reisberg, Mira, illus. 2013. (ENG.). 32p. (J). (gr. k-2). pap. 12.95 *(978-0-89239-177-6(4)*, leelowcbp, Children's Book Press) Lee & Low Bks., Inc.

Corso, Erika. The Day You Came. Corso, Erika & Corso, Bertina, illus. 2006. (ENG.). 20p. (J). per. 12.95 *(978-1-59800-242-3(2))* Outskirts Pr., Inc.

Cory, Kim Delmar. Home to Mackinac: The Tale of Young Jack Murphy's Discovery of Loyalty, Family, & Forgiveness. Evans, Laura, illus. 2007. (ENG.). 175p. (J). (gr. 3-7). per. 9.95 *(978-0-911872-87-3(6))* Mackinac State Historic Parks.

—Tending Ben's Garden. 2009. 121p. (J). pap. *(978-0-88092-778-9(X))* Royal Fireworks Publishing Co.

Cosgrove, Stephen. Katy Didd Bigg: Standing up for Yourself. Arroyo, Fian, illus. 2004. (J). *(978-1-58804-378-8(9))* P C I Education.

Costa, T. L. Playing Tyler. 2013. (ENG.). 304p. (J). (gr. 9). pap. 9.99 *(978-1-908844-61-3(2)*, Strange Chemistry) Watkins Media Limited GBR. Dist: Penguin Random Hse. LLC.

Costello, David Hyde. Little Pig Joins the Band. Costello, David Hyde, illus. 2014. (Illus.). 32p. (J). (gr. -1-3). pap. 7.95 *(978-1-58089-265-0(5))* Charlesbridge Publishing, Inc.

—Little Pig Joins the Band. Costello, David Hyde, illus. 2012. (Illus.). 29.95 incl. audio compact disk *(978-1-4301-1139-9(9))* Live Oak Media.

—Little Pig Joins the Band. 2014. (ENG.). (J). (gr. -1-3). lib. bdg. 18.55 *(978-1-62765-428-9(3))* Perfection Learning Corp.

—Little Pig Saves the Ship. Costello, David Hyde, illus. 2017. (Illus.). 32p. (J). (gr. -1-2). 14.99 *(978-1-58089-715-0(0))* Charlesbridge Publishing, Inc.

Cotler, Steve. Cheesie Mack Is Running Like Crazy! Holgate, Douglas, illus. 2014. (Cheesie Mack Ser.: 3). 256p. (J). (gr. 3-7). pap. 7.99 *(978-0-307-97716-8(1)*, Yearling) Random Hse. Children's Bks.

Couloumbis, Audrey & Couloumbis, Akila. War Games. 2011. (ENG.). 240p. (J). (gr. 3-7). pap. 6.99 *(978-0-375-85629-7(3)*, Yearling) Random Hse. Children's Bks.

Coven, Wanda. Heidi Heckelbeck & the Snoopy Spy. Burris, Priscilla, illus. 2018. (Heidi Heckelbeck Ser.: 23). (ENG.). 128p. (J). (gr. k-4). 17.99 *(978-1-5344-1111-1(9))*; pap. 6.99 *(978-1-5344-1110-4(0))* Little Simon. (Little Simon).

Covey, Sean. Sammy & the Pecan Pie: Habit 4. Curtis, Stacy, illus. (7 Habits of Happy Kids Ser.: 4). (ENG.). 32p. (J). (gr. -1-1). 2018. 6.99 *(978-1-5344-1581-2(5))* 2013. 7.99 *(978-1-4424-7647-9(8))* Simon & Schuster Bks. For Young Readers. (Simon & Schuster Bks. For Young Readers).

—Sammy & the Pecan Pie: Habit 4 (Ready-To-Read Level 2) Curtis, Stacy, illus. 2019. (7 Habits of Happy Kids Ser.: 4). (ENG.). 32p. (J). (gr. k-2). 17.99 *(978-1-5344-4454-6(8))*; pap. 4.99 *(978-1-5344-4453-9(X))* Simon Spotlight. (Simon Spotlight).

Cowen-Fletcher, Jane. It Takes a Village. (J). (gr. 1-2). pap. *(978-0-590-46598-4(8))* Scholastic, Inc.

Cowley, Marjorie. The Golden Bull: A Mesopotamian Adventure. 2012. 224p. (J). (gr. 4-7). pap. 8.95 *(978-1-58089-182-0(9))* Charlesbridge Publishing, Inc.

Cowsar, Susan. The Magic Flower. 2013. 58p. pap. 10.99 *(978-1-62697-943-7(X))* Salem Author Services.

Coyle, Carmela Lavigna. Do Princesses Scrape Their Knees? 2006. (Do Princesses Ser.). (ENG., Illus.). 32p. (J). (gr. -1-2). 15.95 *(978-0-87358-909-3(2))* Cooper Square Publishing Llc.

Cozzo, Karole. How to Say I Love You Out Loud. 2015. (ENG.). 240p. (YA). (gr. 7). pap. 17.99 *(978-1-250-06359-5(0)*, 900142824) Feiwel & Friends.

Creech, Sharon. The Castle Corona. Diaz, David, illus. (J). 2013. (ENG.). 352p. (gr. 3-7). pap. 7.99 *(978-0-06-206395-3(2)*, HarperCollins) 2007. 336p. (gr. 4-7). lib. bdg. 19.89 *(978-0-06-084622-0(4)*, Cotler, Joanna Books) HarperCollins Pubs.

—Ruby Holler. 2012. (ENG.). 288p. (J). (gr. 3-7). pap. 7.99 *(978-0-06-056015-7(0)*, HarperCollins) HarperCollins Pubs.

—Ruby Holler. 2004. (Joanna Cotler Bks.). 310p. (gr. 3-7). 17.00 *(978-0-7569-1940-5(1))* Perfection Learning Corp.

—Ruby Holler. 2012. (J). (gr. 3-6). 17.20 *(978-0-613-86272-1(4))* Turtleback.

Crichton, Michael & Koepp, David. Jurassic Park. Holtsclaw, Josh, illus. 2018. (J). *(978-1-5444-0887-3(0)*, Golden Bks.) Random Hse. Children's Bks.

Croggon, Alison. The Singing: Book Four of Pellinor. 2017. (Pellinor Ser.). (ENG.). 496p. (J). (gr. 7). pap. 9.99 *(978-0-7636-9446-3(0))* Candlewick Pr.

Crook, M. J. Village on Crooked Hill. 2008. 168p. pap. 11.99 *(978-1-4389-0486-3(X))* AuthorHouse.

Crouch, Cheryl. Troo's Secret Clubhouse, 1 vol. Zimmer, Kevin, illus. 2011. (I Can Read! / Rainforest Friends Ser.). (ENG.). 32p. (J). (gr. -1-2). pap. 4.99 *(978-0-310-71809-3(0))* Zonderkidz.

Crow, Melinda Melton. Little Lizard's New Baby, 1 vol. Rowland, Andrew, illus. 2011. (Little Lizards Ser.). (ENG.). 32p. (J). (gr. -1-1). pap. 6.25 *(978-1-4342-3047-8(3)*, 114647, Stone Arch Bks.) Capstone.

Crum, Sally. Race to Moonrise Rev. Carlson, Eric S., illus. 2nd ed. 2006. 98p. (J). 12.95 *(978-1-932738-31-5(2))* Western Reflections Publishing Co.

Crumbaugh, David. The Primrose Kids. 2006. 81p. pap. 16.95 *(978-1-4241-3250-8(9))* PublishAmerica, Inc.

Crump, Fred, Jr. The Brave Toy Soldier. 2007. (Illus.). 32p. (J). 12.95 *(978-1-934056-20-2(0))* UMI (Urban Ministries, Inc.).

Crump Jr., Fred. The Brave Toy Soldier. 2007. (Illus.). 32p. (J). (gr. -1). pap. 9.95 *(978-1-932715-82-8(7))* UMI (Urban Ministries, Inc.).

Cumberland, Dale. Angel Trap. 2012. 166p. (-18). 22.95 *(978-1-4759-5601-6(0))*; pap. 12.95 *(978-1-4759-5599-6(5))* iUniverse, Inc.

Cummings, Priscilla. Beetle Boddiker, 1 vol. 2009. (ENG., Illus.). 30p. (J). (gr. -1-3). 13.95 *(978-0-87033-602-7(9)*, 3592, Cornell Maritime Pr./Tidewater Pubs.) Schiffer Publishing, Ltd.

Cumyn, Alan. The Secret Life of Owen Skye. 2nd ed. 2008. (ENG.). 176p. (J). (gr. 3-6). pap. 9.95 *(978-0-88899-867-5(8))* Groundwood Bks. CAN. Dist: Publishers Group West (PGW).

Currie, Colleen & Currie, David. Loving Baby Louie: Hope in the Midst of Grief. Streeter, Talena, illus. 2015. (ENG.). 54p. (J). 24.95 *(978-1-941447-44-4(9))* Emmaus Road Publishing.

Currinder, Michael. Running Full Tilt. 2017. 336p. (YA). (gr. 7). lib. bdg. 17.99 *(978-1-58089-802-7(5)*, Charlesbridge Teen) Charlesbridge Publishing, Inc.

Curtis, Christopher Paul. The Watsons Go to Birmingham — 1963. 2013. (ENG., Illus.). 224p. (J). (gr. 3-7). 8.99 *(978-0-385-38294-6(4)*, Yearling) Random Hse. Children's Bks.

—The Watsons Go to Birmingham 1963. 210p. (YA). (gr. 5-18). pap. 5.50 *(978-0-8072-8336-3(3))*; 2004. (J). (gr. 4-18). pap. 38.00 incl. audio *(978-0-8072-8335-6(5)*, YA166SP) Random Hse. Audio Publishing Group. (Listening Library).

Curtis, Christopher Paul & Vega, Eida de la. Los Watson Van a Birmingham - 1963. 2016. (SPA.). 200p. (J). (gr. 5-12). pap. 12.99 *(978-1-63245-640-3(0))* Lectorum Pubns., Inc.

Cusack, Dale. Gwen & the Dragon. 2007. (Illus.). 114p. pap. 9.95 *(978-1-4303-1080-8(4))* Lulu Pr., Inc.

Cushman, Jean, et al. Little Golden Book Mommy Stories. Wilkin, Eloise & Meisel, Paul, illus. 2015. 80p. (J). (-k). 7.99 *(978-0-385-39273-0(7)*, Golden Bks.) Random Hse. Children's Bks.

Cussler, Clive. The Adventures of Hotsy Totsy. 2011. (ENG., Illus.). 166p. (J). (gr. 3-7). 7.99 *(978-0-14-241873-4(0)*, Puffin Books) Penguin Young Readers Group.

Cuyler, Margery. Tick Tock Clock. Neubecker, Robert, illus. 2012. (My First I Can Read Ser.). (ENG.). 32p. (J). (gr. -1 — 1). pap. 4.99 *(978-0-06-136311-5(1)*, HarperCollins) HarperCollins Pubs.

Cuyler, Margery & Neubecker, Robert. Tick Tock Clock. 2012. (My First I Can Read Ser.). (ENG., Illus.). 32p. (J). (gr. -1 — 1). 16.99 *(978-0-06-136309-2(X)*, HarperCollins) HarperCollins Pubs.

Cyprus, Naomi. Sisters of Glass. (Sisters of Glass Ser.: 1). (ENG.). (J). (gr. 3-7). 2018. 400p. pap. 9.99 *(978-0-06-245849-0(3))* 2017. 384p. 16.99 *(978-0-06-245847-6(7))* HarperCollins Pubs. (HarperCollins).

Dafydd, Myrddin ap. Brwydr y Brodyr. 2005. (WEL.). 68p. pap. *(978-0-86381-906-3(0))* Gwasg Carreg Gwalch.

Dagg, Stephanie. The Big Brother. Clarke, Alan, illus. 2003. (Pandas Ser.: 24). (ENG.). 64p. (J). pap. 11.00 *(978-0-86278-779-0(3))* O'Brien Pr., Ltd., The IRL. Dist: Casemate Pubs. & Bk. Distributors, LLC.

Daher, Anita. Two Foot Punch, 1 vol. 2007. (Orca Sports Ser.). (ENG., Illus.). 176p. (J). (gr. 4-7). per. 10.95 *(978-1-55143-876-4(3))* Orca Bk. Pubs. USA.

Dahi, Khetam. The Mulberry Tree. 2013. 100p. (gr. -1). pap. 11.65 *(978-1-4669-8313-7(2))* Trafford Publishing.

Dahl, Michael. Fangs in the Mirror, 1 vol. Aime, Luigi, illus. 2012. (Dragonborn Ser.). (ENG.). 72p. (J). (gr. 4-8). pap. 7.10 *(978-1-4342-4255-6(2)*, 120316, Stone Arch Bks.) Capstone.

Dales, Cindy. Autumn's First Easter. 2009. 28p. pap. 12.99 *(978-1-4343-1433-8(2))* AuthorHouse.

Daley, James Ryan. Jesus Jackson. 2014. (ENG.). 288p. pap. 18.99 *(978-1-929345-06-9(2)*, Poisoned Pen Press) Sourcebooks, Inc.

Dallas, Sandra. Someplace to Call Home. (ENG., Illus.). 240p. (J). (gr. 3-6). 2020. pap. 9.99 *(978-1-58536-415-2(0)*, 204766) 2019. 15.95 *(978-1-58536-414-5(2)*, 204752) Sleeping Bear Pr.

Daly, Catherine. Double or Nothing: A Makers Story about 3D Printing. Lyon, Tammie, illus. 2018. (Makers Make It Work Ser.). 32p. (J). (gr. k-3). pap. 6.99 *(978-1-57565-989-3(1)*, 1b82b37e-f971-49a5-bd2a-c3b5e07aa673, Kane Press) Astra Publishing Hse.

Dana Kittendorf. Trail of Dreams. 2009. 136p. 21.95 *(978-1-4401-7787-3(2))*; pap. 11.95 *(978-1-4401-7785-9(6))* iUniverse, Inc.

Daniels, J. M. The Secret of the Little Dutch Doll. 2009. 68p. pap. 25.49 *(978-1-4343-9356-2(9))* AuthorHouse.

Danticat, Edwidge. Eight Days: a Story of Haiti. Delinois, Alix, illus. 2010. (ENG.). 32p. (J). (gr. k-1). 17.99 *(978-0-545-27849-2(X)*, Orchard Bks.) Scholastic, Inc.

D'Argenzio, Gertilyn Elinor. What Color Is Your Happiness? 2012. 24p. pap. 15.99 *(978-1-4669-1443-8(2))* Trafford Publishing.

Darrow, Sharon. Trash. 2006. (ENG.). 160p. (YA). (gr. 7-12). 16.99 *(978-0-7636-2624-2(4))* Candlewick Pr.

Dateno, Maria Grace. Braving the Storm, 6 vols., Vol. 2. Cunningham, Paul, illus. 2013. 70p. (J). pap. 5.95 *(978-0-8198-1204-9(8))* Pauline Bks. & Media.

—Courageous Quest. Cunningham, Paul, illus. 2014. 81p. (J). pap. 5.95 *(978-0-8198-1628-3(0))* Pauline Bks. & Media.

—Danger at Sea. Cunningham, Paul, illus. 2013. 80p. (J). pap. 5.95 *(978-0-8198-1891-1(7))* Pauline Bks. & Media.

—Discovery at Dawn. Cunningham, Paul, illus. 2014. (ENG.). 79p. (J). pap. 5.95 *(978-0-8198-1895-9(X))* Pauline Bks. & Media.

—Mystery of the Missing Jars. Cunningham, Paul, illus. 2014. 77p. (J). 5.95 *(978-0-8198-4922-9(7))* Pauline Bks. & Media.

—Shepherds to the Rescue, 6 vols., Vol. 1. Cunningham, Paul, illus. 2013. 71p. (J). pap. 5.95 *(978-0-8198-7251-7(2))* Pauline Bks. & Media.

Daunis, Marcia Prosco. Miller's Ben. 2008. 159p. pap. 24.95 *(978-1-60672-759-1(1))* America Star Bks.

David, Lawrence. To Catch a Clownosaurus. Gott, Barry, tr. Gott, Barry, illus. 2003. (Horace Splattly: Cupcaked Crusader Ser.). (ENG.). 150p. (J). (gr. 3-6). 17.44 *(978-0-525-47154-7(5))* Penguin Young Readers Group.

Daviddi, Evelyn. My Sister Makes Me Happy! My Sister Makes Me Mad! 2007. (ENG., Illus.). 32p. (J). (gr. 4-7). 10.95 *(978-1-59687-170-0(9))* IBks., Inc.

Davies, Jacqueline. The Bell Bandit. (Lemonade War Ser.: 3). (ENG., Illus.). 192p. (J). (gr. 3-7). 2022. pap. 9.99 *(978-0-544-02274-4(2)*, 1528495) 2012. 18.99 *(978-0-547-56737-2(5)*, 1455332) HarperCollins Pubs. (Clarion Bks.).

—The Bell Bandit. 2013. (Lemonade War Ser.: 3). lib. bdg. 18.40 *(978-0-606-31669-9(8))* Turtleback.

—The Candy Smash. 2022. (Lemonade War Ser.: 4). (ENG., Illus.). 240p. (J). (gr. 3-7). pap. 9.99 *(978-0-544-22500-8(7)*, 1563385, Clarion Bks.) HarperCollins Pubs.

—The Lemonade Crime. 2011. (Lemonade War Ser.: 2). (ENG., Illus.). 160p. (J). (gr. 3-7). 16.99 *(978-0-547-27967-1(1)*, 1411007, Clarion Bks.) HarperCollins Pubs.

—The Lemonade Crime. 2012. (Lemonade War Ser.: 2). lib. bdg. 18.40 *(978-0-606-24518-0(9))* Turtleback.

—The Lemonade War. (Lemonade War Ser.: 1). (ENG.). 192p. (J). (gr. 3-7). 2022. pap. 9.99 *(978-0-547-23765-7(0)*, 1083876) 2007. (Illus.). 18.99 *(978-0-618-75043-6(6)*, 511891) HarperCollins Pubs. (Clarion Bks.).

—The Magic Trap. 2014. (Lemonade War Ser.: 5). (ENG., Illus.). 272p. (J). (gr. 3-7). 18.99 *(978-0-544-05289-5(7)*, 1533150, Clarion Bks.) HarperCollins Pubs.

Davies, Katie. The Great Dog Disaster. Shaw, Hannah, illus. 2013. (Great Critter Capers Ser.). (ENG.). 208p. (J). (gr. 3-7). 12.99 *(978-1-4424-4517-8(3)*, Beach Lane Bks.) Beach Lane Bks.

Davies, Stephen. Outlaw. 2011. (ENG.). 304p. (YA). (gr. 7). 16.99 *(978-0-547-39017-8(3))* Houghton Mifflin Harcourt Publishing Co.

Davis, Catherine. Abby & Alex Feel Their Hearts' Little. 2006. 57p. pap. 16.95 *(978-1-4241-4586-7(4))* PublishAmerica, Inc.

Davis, Jacky. The Amazing Adventures of Bumblebee Boy. Soman, David, illus. 2011. (Ladybug Girl Ser.). 40p. (J). (gr. -1-k). 17.99 *(978-0-8037-3418-0(2)*, Dial Bks) Penguin Young Readers Group.

—Ladybug Girl. Soman, David, illus. 2008. (Ladybug Girl Ser.). 40p. (J). (gr. -1-k). 18.99 *(978-0-8037-3195-0(7)*, Dial Bks) Penguin Young Readers Group.

—Ladybug Girl: the Super Fun Edition. Soman, David, illus. 2015. (Ladybug Girl Ser.). 40p. (J). (-k). 18.99 *(978-1-101-99433-7(9)*, Dial Bks) Penguin Young Readers Group.

Davis, Rachel. My Life at Mapleleaf Cabin. 2nd ed. 2004. (YA). per. 10.00 *(978-0-9741176-8-3(4))* Wu Li Turtle Corp.

Davis, Samira And Edwina. Nikko & Sierra's Adventures: I Hate Knuckle Sandwiches. 2011. 24p. pap. 11.32 *(978-1-4634-0408-6(5))* AuthorHouse.

Davis, Tanita S. Happy Families. 2013. (ENG.). 240p. (YA). (gr. 7). pap. 9.99 *(978-0-375-87170-2(5)*, Ember) Random Hse. Children's Bks.

de Graaf, Anne. Son of a Gun. 2013. (ENG., Illus.). 125p. (J). (gr. 6-8). pap. 22.44 *(978-0-8028-5406-3(0))* Eerdmans, William B. Publishing Co.

De Haven, Tom. The Orphan's Tent. 2005. (Illus.). 192p. mass mkt. 5.99 *(978-0-7434-9772-5(4))* ibooks, Inc.

de la Peña, Matt. Carmela Full of Wishes. Robinson, Christian, illus. 2018. 40p. (J). (gr. -1-3). 18.99 *(978-0-399-54904-5(8)*, G.P. Putnam's Sons Books for Young Readers) Penguin Young Readers Group.

—Los Deseos de Carmela. Robinson, Christian, illus. 2018. 40p. (J). (gr. -1-3). 18.99 *(978-0-525-51870-9(3)*, G.P. Putnam's Sons Books for Young Readers) Penguin Young Readers Group.

—Milo Imagines the World. Robinson, Christian, illus. 2021. (ENG.). 40p. (J). (gr. -1-3). 18.99 *(978-0-399-54908-3(0)*, G.P. Putnam's Sons Books for Young Readers) Penguin Young Readers Group.

De La Peña, Matt. We Were Here. 2010. (ENG.). 368p. (YA). (gr. 8-12). lib. bdg. 26.19 *(978-0-385-90622-7(6))* Random House Publishing Group.

Dealey, Erin. Babies Come from Airports. Powell, Luciana Navarro, illus. 2018. (ENG.). 32p. (J). 12.99 *(978-1-61067-557-4(6))* Kane Miller.

—Goldie Locks Has Chicken Pox. 2004. (Illus.). (J). (gr. k-3). spiral bd. *(978-0-616-14573-9(X))*; spiral bd. *(978-0-616-14572-2(1))* Canadian National Institute for the Blind/Institut National Canadien pour les Aveugles.

—Goldie Locks Has Chicken Pox. Wakiyama, Hanako, illus. 2005. (ENG.). 40p. (J). (gr. -1-2). reprint ed. 8.99 *(978-0-689-87610-3(6)*, Aladdin) Simon & Schuster Children's Publishing.

Debono, Angelo. The Magic in You. 2011. 36p. pap. 13.95 *(978-1-61204-783-6(1)*, Strategic Bk. Publishing) Strategic Book Publishing & Rights Agency (SBPRA).

Decter, Nora. How Far We Go & How Fast, 1 vol. 2018. (ENG.). 264p. (YA). (gr. 8-12). pap. 14.95 *(978-1-4598-1688-6(9))* Orca Bk. Pubs. USA.

Dee, Barbara. Just Another Day in My Insanely Real Life. 2007. (Mix Ser.). (ENG.). 256p. (J). (gr. 4-8). pap. 8.99 *(978-1-4169-4739-4(6)*, Aladdin) Simon & Schuster Children's Publishing.

Deen, Natasha. Lark & the Diamond Caper, 1 vol. Cutler, Marcus, illus. 2017. (Orca Echoes Ser.: 2). (ENG.). 96p. (J). (gr. 1-3). pap. 7.95 *(978-1-4598-1400-4(2))* Orca Bk. Pubs. USA.

—Lark Takes a Bow, 1 vol. Cutler, Marcus, illus. 2018. (Orca Echoes Ser.: 3). (ENG.). 96p. (J). (gr. 1-3). pap. 7.95 *(978-1-4598-1715-9(X))* Orca Bk. Pubs. USA.

deGroat, Diane. Trick or Treat, Smell My Feet, 4 bks., Set. 2008. (J). (gr. -1-2). pap. 39.95 incl. audio compact disk *(978-1-4301-0428-5(7))*; pap. 37.95 incl. audio *(978-1-4301-0426-1(0))* Live Oak Media.

Deighton, Jo, adapted by. Codadad & His Brothers: Traditional Stories:The Grocer, the Student & the Elf: The Ugly Duckling. (Scheherezade Presents Ser.: No. 13). (Illus.). 48p. (J). pap. (978-1-85964-103-3(2), Ithaca Pr.) Garnet Publishing, Ltd.

Dekker, James C. Scum, 1 vol. 2008. (Orca Soundings Ser.). (ENG.). 112p. (YA). (gr. 8-12). pap. 9.95 (978-1-55143-924-2(7)) Orca Bk. Pubs. USA.

Delacre, Lulu. Rafi & Rosi. 2004. (Illus.). 64p. (J). lib. bdg. 13.85 (978-1-4242-0596-7(4)) Fitzgerald Bks.

—Rafi & Rosi. Delacre, Lulu, illus. 2005. (I Can Read Bks.). (Illus.). 64p. (J). (gr. k-3). pap. 3.99 (978-0-06-009897-1(X), Rayo) HarperCollins Pubs.

—Rafi & Rosi, 1 vol. 2016. (Rafi & Rosi Ser.). (ENG., Illus.). 64p. (J). (gr. k-3). pap. 11.95 (978-0-89239-379-4(3), leelowcbp) Lee & Low Bks., Inc.

—Rafi & Rosi, 1 vol. Delacre, Lulu, illus. 2016. (Rafi & Rosi Ser.). (ENG., Illus.). 64p. (J). (gr. k-3). pap. 11.95 (978-0-89239-377-0(7), leelowcbp) Lee & Low Bks., Inc.

—Rafi & Rosi: Music!, 1 vol. Delacre, Lulu, illus. 2019. (Rafi & Rosi Ser.). (ENG., Illus.). 64p. (J). (gr. 2-2). pap. 11.95 (978-0-89239-431-9(5), leelowcbp, Children's Book Press) Lee & Low Bks., Inc.

—Rafi & Rosi Pirates, 1 vol. 2017. (Rafi & Rosi Ser.). (ENG., Illus.). 64p. (J). (gr. k-3). 16.95 (978-0-89239-381-7(5), leelowcbp, Children's Book Press) Lee & Low Bks., Inc.

—Rafi y Rosi, 1 vol. Delacre, Lulu, illus. 2016. (Rafi & Rosi Ser.).Tr. of Rafi & Rosi. (SPA., Illus.). 64p. (J). (gr. k-3). pap. 10.95 (978-0-89239-378-7(5), leelowcbp) Lee & Low Bks., Inc.

—Rafi y Rosi Carnival, 1 vol. 2016. (Rafi & Rosi Ser.).Tr. of Rafi & Rosi Carnival. (SPA., Illus.). 64p. (J). (gr. k-3). pap. 11.95 (978-0-89239-380-0(7), leelowcbp) Lee & Low Bks., Inc.

—Rafi y Rosi ¡Música!, 1 vol. Delacre, Lulu, illus. 2019. (Rafi & Rosi Ser.). (SPA., Illus.). 64p. (J). (gr. k-3). pap. 10.95 (978-0-89239-432-6(3), leelowcbp, Children's Book Press) Lee & Low Bks., Inc.

—Rafi y Rosi ¡Piratas!, 1 vol. Delacre, Lulu, illus. 2017. (Rafi & Rosi Ser.). (SPA., Illus.). 64p. (J). (gr. k-3). 16.95 (978-0-89239-428-9(5), leelowcbp) Lee & Low Bks., Inc.

—Rafi y Rosi Piratas, 1 vol. 2017. (Rafi & Rosi Ser.). (SPA.). 64p. (J). (gr. k-3). pap. 11.95 (978-0-89239-382-4(3), leelowcbp) Lee & Low Bks., Inc.

Dempsey, Kristy. Superhero Instruction Manual. Fearing, Mark, illus. 2016. 40p. (J). (gr. k-3). 16.99 (978-0-385-75534-4(1), Knopf Bks. for Young Readers) Random Hse. Children's Bks.

Denise, Anika & Gomez, Lorena Alvarez. Starring Carmen! 2017. (ENG., Illus.). 32p. (J). (gr. k-2). 16.95 (978-1-4197-2321-6(9), 1143501, Abrams Bks. for Young Readers) Abrams, Inc.

Denise, Anika A. Bunny in the Middle. Denise, Christopher, illus. 2019. (ENG.). 40p. (J). 17.99 (978-1-250-12036-6(5), 900173006, Holt, Henry & Co. Bks. For Young Readers) Holt, Henry & Co.

DeNivo, Jennifer. Sneaky Sam. 2011. 24p. (gr. 1-2). pap. 12.79 (978-1-4567-5181-4(6)) AuthorHouse.

dePaola, Tomie. Meet the Barkers. dePaola, Tomie, illus. 2003. (Barker Twins Ser.). (Illus.). 32p. (J). (gr. -1-3). 7.99 (978-0-14-250083-5(6), Puffin Books) Penguin Young Readers Group.

—Meet the Barkers: Morgan & Moffat Go to School. 2005. (J). (gr. k-3). pap. 17.95 incl. audio (978-0-8045-6934-7(7), SAC6934) Spoken Arts, Inc.

Derby, Sally. Kyle's Island. 2014. 192p. (J). (gr. 5). pap. 7.95 (978-1-58089-317-6(1)) Charlesbridge Publishing, Inc.

deRubertis, Barbara. Oliver Otter's Own Office. Alley, R. W., illus. 2011. (Animal Antics A to Z Ser.). 32p. (J). pap. 45.32 (978-0-7613-7661-3(5)); (gr. -1-3). pap. 7.95 (978-1-57565-327-3(3), 419a901e-b7f6-4632-9be1-6d21f81440fe, Kane Press) Astra Publishing Hse.

deRubertis, Barbara & DeRubertis, Barbara. Oliver Otter's Own Office. Alley, R. W., illus. 2012. (Animal Antics A to Z Ser.). 32p. (J). (gr. 2 — 1). cd-rom 7.95 (978-1-57565-408-9(3)) Astra Publishing Hse.

Desai, Anita. The Village by the Sea. 2019. (ENG.). 276p. (J). (gr. 4-7). pap. 12.99 (978-1-68137-351-5(3), NYRB Kids) New York Review of Bks., Inc., The.

Dessen, Sarah. Saint Anything. 2016. (ENG.). 448p. (YA). (gr. 7). pap. 12.99 (978-0-14-751603-9(X), Speak) Penguin Young Readers Group.

—Saint Anything. 2016. lib. bdg. 22.10 (978-0-606-38833-7(8)) Turtleback.

DeVillers, Julia & Roy, Jennifer. Trading Faces. 2009. (Mix Ser.). (ENG., Illus.). 320p. (J). (gr. 4-8). pap. 7.99 (978-1-4169-6168-0(2), Aladdin) Simon & Schuster Children's Publishing.

D.G., Gigi. Cucumber Quest: the Doughnut Kingdom. 2017. (Cucumber Quest Ser.: 1). (ENG., Illus.). 192p. (J). pap. 14.99 (978-1-62672-832-5(1), 900175241, First Second Bks.) Roaring Brook Pr.

—Cucumber Quest: the Melody Kingdom. 2018. (Cucumber Quest Ser.: 3). (ENG., Illus.). 240p. (J). pap. 14.99 (978-1-62672-834-9(8), 900175251, First Second Bks.) Roaring Brook Pr.

—Cucumber Quest: the Ripple Kingdom. 2018. (Cucumber Quest Ser.: 2). (ENG., Illus.). 240p. (J). pap. 15.99 (978-1-62672-833-2(X), 900175246, First Second Bks.) Roaring Brook Pr.

Dicamillo, Kate. The Magician's Elephant. 2015. lib. bdg. 17.20 (978-0-606-37891-8(X)) Turtleback.

DiCamillo, Kate. The Magician's Elephant. Tanaka, Yoko, illus. (ENG.). (J). (gr. 3-7). 2015. 224p. pap. 8.99 (978-0-7636-8088-6(5)) 2009. 208p. 18.99 (978-0-7636-4410-9(2)) Candlewick Pr.

Dicamillo, Kate. The Magician's Elephant. l.t. ed. 2010. (ENG.). 242p. 23.95 (978-1-4104-2493-8(6)) Thorndike Pr.

—The Magician's Elephant. 2011. lib. bdg. 17.20 (978-0-606-15375-1(6)) Turtleback.

Dill, Margo L. Finding My Place: One Girl's Strength at Vicksburg. 2012. (ENG.). 202p. (J). pap. 8.95 (978-1-57249-408-4(5), White Mane Kids) White Mane Publishing Co., Inc.

Disney Press Staff. School's Out. 2010. 128p. pap. 4.99 (978-1-4231-2677-5(7)) Disney Pr.

DiTerlizzi, Tony & Black, Holly. The Ironwood Tree. l.t. ed. 2006. (Spiderwick Chronicles: Bk. 4). 90p. (YA). (gr. 2-18). 23.95 (978-0-7862-8583-9(4)) Thorndike Pr.

—Lucinda's Secret. l.t. ed. 2006. (Spiderwick Chronicles: Bk. 3). (Illus.). 142p. (J). (gr. 4-7). 23.95 (978-0-7862-8585-3(0)) Thorndike Pr.

DiVito, Anna. Annie Oakley Saves the Day. DiVito, Anna, illus. 2005. (Illus.). 32p. (J). lib. bdg. 15.00 (978-1-59054-939-1(2)) Fitzgerald Bks.

Dixon, Franklin W. The Bicycle Thief. Burroughs, Scott, illus. 2011. (Hardy Boys: the Secret Files Ser.: 6). (ENG.). 96p. (J). (gr. 1-4). pap. 5.99 (978-1-4169-9396-4(7), Aladdin) Simon & Schuster Children's Publishing.

—Burned, 6. 6th ed. 2005. (Hardy Boys (All New) Undercover Brothers Ser.: 6). (ENG., Illus.). 160p. (J). (gr. 3-7). pap. 5.99 (978-1-4169-0008-5(X)) Simon & Schuster, Inc.

—Deprivation House: Book One in the Murder House Trilogy. 22nd ed. 2008. (Hardy Boys (All New) Undercover Brothers Ser.: 22). (ENG., Illus.). 176p. (J). (gr. 3-7). pap. 6.99 (978-1-4169-6170-3(4), Aladdin) Simon & Schuster Children's Publishing.

—The Disappearance. 2019. (Hardy Boys Adventures Ser.: 18). (ENG.). 160p. (J). (gr. 3-7). 17.99 (978-1-5344-1489-1(4)); (Illus.). pap. 7.99 (978-1-5344-1488-4(6)) Simon & Schuster Children's Publishing. (Aladdin).

—Double Deception: Book Three in the Double Danger Trilogy, 27. 2009. (Hardy Boys (All New) Undercover Brothers Ser.: 27). (ENG.). 176p. (J). (gr. 3-7). pap. 6.99 (978-1-4169-6766-8(4)) Simon & Schuster, Inc.

—Double Down: Book Two in the Double Danger Trilogy, 26. 26th ed. 2008. (Hardy Boys (All New) Undercover Brothers Ser.: 26). (ENG.). 172p. (J). (gr. 3-7). pap. 7.99 (978-1-4169-7446-8(6)) Simon & Schuster, Inc.

—Dungeons & Detectives. 2019. (Hardy Boys Adventures Ser.: 19). (ENG., Illus.). 208p. (J). (gr. 3-7). pap. 6.99 (978-1-5344-2105-9(X), Simon & Schuster/Paula Wiseman Bks.) Simon & Schuster/Paula Wiseman Bks.

—Galaxy X: Book One in the Galaxy X Trilogy, Bk. 1. 2009. (Hardy Boys (All New) Undercover Brothers Ser.: 28). (ENG.). 160p. (J). (gr. 3-7). pap. 6.99 (978-1-4169-7801-5(1), Aladdin) Simon & Schuster Children's Publishing.

—The Gray Hunter's Revenge. 2018. (Hardy Boys Adventures Ser.: 17). (ENG., 144p. (J). (gr. 3-7). Illus.). 17.99 (978-1-5344-1151-7(8)); pap. 6.99 (978-1-5344-1150-0(X)) Simon & Schuster Children's Publishing. (Aladdin).

—Movie Menace: Book One in the Deathstalker Trilogy. 2011. (Hardy Boys (All New) Undercover Brothers Ser.: 37). (ENG.). 176p. (J). (gr. 3-7). pap. 5.99 (978-1-4424-0258-4(X), Aladdin) Simon & Schuster Children's Publishing.

—The Pirate Ghost. Gutierrez, Santy, illus. 2018. (Hardy Boys Clue Book Ser.: 7). (ENG.). 96p. (J). (gr. 1-4). 17.99 (978-1-4814-8873-0(2), Aladdin) Simon & Schuster Children's Publishing.

—Scavenger Hunt Heist. David, Matt, illus. 2017. (Hardy Boys Clue Book Ser.: 5). (ENG.). 96p. (J). (gr. 1-4). pap. 5.99 (978-1-4814-8516-6(4), Simon & Schuster/Paula Wiseman Bks.) Simon & Schuster/Paula Wiseman Bks.

—Typhoon Island, Vol. 180. 2003. (Hardy Boys Ser.: 180). (ENG., Illus.). 160p. (J). (gr. 3-7). pap. 5.99 (978-0-689-85884-0(1), Aladdin) Simon & Schuster Children's Publishing.

Dodge, Mary Mapes. Hans Brinker, or the Silver Skates. 2007. 308p. (gr. 3-7). 32.95 (978-1-4344-9309-5(1)); per. 19.95 (978-1-4344-9308-8(3)) Wildside Pr., LLC.

—Hans Brinker or the Silver Skates A Story of Life in Holland. Doggett, Allen B., illus. 2004. reprint ed. pap. 34.95 (978-1-4179-4127-8(8)) Kessinger Publishing, LLC.

—Hans Brinker, or, the Silver Skates (Dod. 2006. pap. (978-1-4065-0961-8(2)) Dodo Pr.

Doerrfeld, Cori. Maggie & Wendel: Imagine Everything! Doerrfeld, Cori, illus. 2016. (ENG., Illus.). 48p. (J). (gr. -1-3). 19.99 (978-1-4814-3974-9(X), Simon & Schuster Bks. For Young Readers) Simon & Schuster Bks. For Young Readers.

Dokey, Cameron. The World Above. 2010. (Once upon a Time Ser.). (ENG.). 208p. (YA). (gr. 7-18). pap. 6.99 (978-1-4424-0337-6(3), Simon Pulse) Simon Pulse.

Donaldson, Julia. The Giants & the Joneses. Swearingen, Greg, illus. 2008. (ENG.). 224p. (J). (gr. 4-6). pap. 15.99 (978-0-312-37961-2(7), 900050312) Square Fish.

Donegan, Noel & Donegan, Luz. The Sad Little Violin. 2013. (Magical Mozart & His Musical Ser.). (ENG.). 32p. (J). pap. 8.95 (978-1-84730-393-6(5)) Veritas Pubns. IRL. Dist: Casemate Pubs. & Bk. Distributors, LLC.

Donlon, Diane Youngblood. Tippee Tippee Tiptoe. Suhr, James W., illus. 2003. (J). 16.95 (978-0-9720427-0-3(9)) OLLY Publishing Co.

Donnelly, Rebecca. The Friendship Lie. 2019. (ENG., Illus.). 272p. (J). (gr. 4-7). 15.95 (978-1-68446-061-8(1), 140521, Capstone Editions) Capstone.

Donoghue, Emma. The Lotterys Plus One. l.t. ed. 2018. (ENG.). (J). lib. bdg. 22.99 (978-1-4328-4994-8(8)) Cengage Gale.

—The Lotterys Plus One. Hadilaksono, Caroline, illus. 2018. (ENG.). 336p. (J). (gr. 3-7). pap. 7.99 (978-0-545-92584-6(3)) Scholastic, Inc.

Dooley, Sarah. Free Verse. 2017. lib. bdg. 19.65 (978-0-606-39788-9(4)) Turtleback.

Dorato, A. P. Arthur, Donna, & the Magic Crown of Tiabora. 2006. pap. 24.95 (978-1-4137-8898-3(X)) PublishAmerica, Inc.

Dorisann. Blasting Ogres. 2012. 108p. (gr. 4-6). 20.95 (978-1-4759-2900-3(5)); pap. 10.95 (978-1-4759-2899-0(8)) iUniverse, Inc.

Dorris, Michael. Morning Girl. 2005. 80p. (J). (gr. 3-18). 20.50 (978-0-8446-7272-4(6), 3587) Smith, Peter Pub., Inc.

Dotlich, Rebecca Kai. You & Me. Reagan, Susan, illus. 2018. (ENG.). 14p. (J). (gr. -1-1). bds. 9.99 (978-1-56846-321-6(9), 19711, Creative Editions) Creative Co., The.

Doty, Linda. Hydrangea Hill: A New Home for Amy Manchester. 2008. 182p. pap. 24.95 (978-1-60610-840-6(9)) America Star Bks.

Dougherty, John. Stinkbomb & Ketchup-Face & the Badness of Badgers. Ricks, Sam, illus. 2018. (Stinkbomb & Ketchup-Face Ser.: 1). (ENG.). 160p. (J). (gr. 3-7). 7.99 (978-1-101-99663-8(3), Puffin Books) Penguin Young Readers Group.

—Stinkbomb & Ketchup-Face & the Quest for the Magic Porcupine. Ricks, Sam, illus. 2019. (Stinkbomb & Ketchup-Face Ser.: 2). (ENG.). 176p. (J). (gr. 3-7). 7.99 (978-1-101-99666-9(8), Puffin Books) Penguin Young Readers Group.

Dowd, Siobhan. The London Eye Mystery. 2009. (ENG.). 336p. (J). (gr. 3-7). 8.99 (978-0-385-75184-1(2), Yearling) Random Hse. Children's Bks.

—The London Eye Mystery. 2009. (London Eye Mystery Ser.: 1). lib. bdg. 18.40 (978-0-606-14413-1(7)) Turtleback.

Downham, Jenny. Unbecoming, 1 vol. (ENG.). 384p. (YA). (gr. 9-9). 2017. pap. 12.99 (978-1-338-16072-7(9)) 2016. 17.99 (978-0-545-90717-0(9)) Scholastic, Inc.

—You Against Me. 2012. (ENG.). 416p. (YA). (gr. 9). pap. 9.99 (978-0-385-75266-4(0), Ember) Random Hse. Children's Bks.

Doyle, Catherine. The Lost Tide Warriors. 2020. (Storm Keeper's Island Ser.: 2). (ENG.). 320p. (J). 16.99 (978-1-5476-0272-8(4), 900209549, Bloomsbury Children's Bks.) Bloomsbury Publishing USA.

—The Storm Keeper's Island. (Storm Keeper's Island Ser.: 1). (ENG.). (J). 2020. 336p. pap. 7.99 (978-1-5476-0253-7(8), 900210114) 2019. 304p. (gr. 3-6). E-Book 11.89 (978-1-5476-0011-3(X)) 2019. 320p. 16.99 (978-1-68119-959-7(9), 900194404) Bloomsbury Publishing USA. (Bloomsbury Children's Bks.).

Doyle McQuerry, Maureen. Between Before & After, 1 vol. 2019. (ENG., Illus.). 304p. (YA). pap. 9.99 (978-0-310-76728-2(8)) Blink.

Draper, Polly. Cry Wolff. 2007. 89p. (J). pap. (978-0-545-02570-6(2)) Scholastic, Inc.

Draper, Sharon M. Forged by Fire. 2013. (Hazelwood High Trilogy Ser.: 2). (ENG., Illus.). 176p. (YA). (gr. 7). pap. 10.99 (978-1-4424-8914-1(6), Atheneum Bks. for Young Readers) Simon & Schuster Children's Publishing.

—Forged by Fire. 2013. (Hazelwood High Trilogy Ser.: 2). lib. bdg. 20.85 (978-0-606-32333-8(3)) Turtleback.

Driscoll, Laura. A Mousy Mess. Melmon, Deborah, illus. 2014. (Mouse Math (r) Ser.). 32p. (J). (gr. -1-1). 22.60 (978-1-57565-646-5(9)) Astra Publishing Hse.

—A Mousy Mess. 2018. (Mouse Math Ser.). (ENG.). 32p. (J). (gr. -1-1). lib. bdg. 34.28 (978-1-4896-8295-6(3), AV2 by Weigl) Weigl Pubs., Inc.

—Super Specs. Gott, Barry, illus. 2005. (Math Matters Ser.). (ENG.). 32p. (J). (gr. k-2). pap. 5.95 (978-1-57565-145-3(9), b417abf4-0ea7-46ae-8105-656b1d62ddf0, Kane Press) Astra Publishing Hse.

Driscoll, Roger K. Echo Mccool, Outlaw Through Time. 2011. 190p. pap. (978-1-908105-26-4(7)) Grosvenor Hse. Publishing Ltd.

Dube, Jasmine. Gratelle au Bois Mordant. 2004. (FRE., Illus.). (J). (gr. -1-3). spiral bd. (978-0-616-01848-4(7)) Canadian National Institute for the Blind/Institut National Canadien pour les Aveugles.

Dubose, Sarah. Uncharted Waters. 2013. 440p. pap. (978-1-4596-6282-7(2)) ReadHowYouWant.com, Ltd.

Dubyn, Bj. The Thrilling & Dynamic Adventures of Barbara Ann, Her Kid Brother, Billy, Jr., & Manfred the Magnificent, Their Parrot. 2008. 104p. pap. 15.99 (978-1-4363-2652-0(4)) Xlibris Corp.

Duggan, Matt. The Royal Woods. 2018. (ENG., Illus.). 158p. (J). (gr. 4-7). pap. (978-0-9917115-7-4(2)) Duggan, Matt.

—The Royal Woods. 2010. (ENG., Illus.). 244p. (J). (gr. 4-7). pap. (978-1-55470-060-8(4)) Me to We.

Dumin, Jennifer. Wolfie & Freddie: the New Puppy. 2006. (ENG.). 44p. per. 22.65 (978-1-4257-0680-7(0)) Xlibris Corp.

Dunbar, Joyce. Tell Me Something Happy Before I Go to Sleep Lap Board Book. Gliori, Debi, illus. 2013. (Lullaby Lights Ser.). (ENG.). 24p. (J). (— 1). bds. 11.99 (978-0-547-94059-5(9), 1516931, Clarion Bks.) HarperCollins Pubs.

Dungy, Tony & Dungy, Lauren. Go, Jade, Go! Ready-To-Read Level 2. Brantley-Newton, Vanessa, illus. 2013. (Tony & Lauren Dungy Ready-To-Reads Ser.). (ENG.). 32p. (J). (gr. k-2). 17.99 (978-1-4424-5467-5(9)); pap. 3.99 (978-1-4424-5466-8(0)) Simon Spotlight. (Simon Spotlight).

Dunlop, Ed. Escape to Liechtenstein. 2003. (Young Refugees Ser.). 152p. (J). (gr. 3-7). per. 7.49 (978-1-59166-013-2(0)) BJU Pr.

—The Incredible Rescues. Halverson, Tom, illus. 2003. 166p. (J). (gr. 4-7). 7.49 (978-1-59166-012-5(2)) BJU Pr.

Dunmore, Helen. Ingo. (gr. 5). 2008. (Ingo Ser.: 1). (ENG.). 336p. (YA). per. 15.99 (978-0-06-081854-8(9), HarperTeen) 2006. 328p. (J). lib. bdg. 17.89 (978-0-06-081853-1(0)) HarperCollins Pubs.

—The Tide Knot. 2008. 330p. (J). 5.99 (978-0-06-081857-9(3)) HarperCollins Pubs.

Dunn, Joeming & Warner, Gertrude Chandler. The Lighthouse Mystery, 1 vol., Bk. 14. Dunn, Ben, illus. 2011. (Boxcar Children Graphic Novels Ser.). (ENG.). 32p. (J). (gr. 2-8). 32.79 (978-1-61641-122-0(8), 3684, Graphic Planet - Fiction) Magic Wagon.

—The Woodshed Mystery, 1 vol., Bk. 13. Dunn, Ben, illus. 2011. (Boxcar Children Graphic Novels Ser.). (ENG.). 32p. (J). (gr. 3-8). 32.79 (978-1-61641-121-3(X), 3683, Graphic Planet - Fiction) Magic Wagon.

Dunrea, Olivier. Gemma & Gus. Dunrea, Olivier, illus. 2017. (Gossie & Friends Ser.). (ENG., Illus.). 32p. (J). (gr. -1-3). pap. 5.99 (978-0-544-93722-2(8), 1658282, Clarion Bks.) HarperCollins Pubs.

—Gemma & Gus Board Book. Dunrea, Olivier, illus. 2016. (Gossie & Friends Ser.). (ENG., Illus.). 32p. (J). (— 1). bds. 7.99 (978-0-544-65647-5(4), 1622856, Clarion Bks.) HarperCollins Pubs.

Durand, Hallie. Just Desserts. Davenier, Christine, illus. 2011. (ENG.). 224p. (J). (gr. 2-5). pap. 5.99 (978-1-4169-6388-2(X), Atheneum Bks. for Young Readers) Simon & Schuster Children's Publishing.

—No Room for Dessert. Davenier, Christine, illus. 2012. (ENG.). 192p. (J). (gr. 2-5). pap. 6.99 (978-1-4424-0361-1(6), Atheneum Bks. for Young Readers) Simon & Schuster Children's Publishing.

Durfee, Jody Wind. Hadley-Hadley Benson. 2013. (ENG.). 144p. (J). pap. 11.99 (978-1-62108-151-7(6)) Covenant Communications, Inc.

Durrant, S. E. Little Bits of Sky. Harnett, Katie, illus. 2017. (ENG.). 208p. (J). (gr. 3-7). 16.95 (978-0-8234-3839-6(2)) Holiday Hse., Inc.

Dwyer, Cynthia. Can You See Me Now? Schuepbach, Lynnette, illus. 2006. 24p. (J). 12.95 (978-0-9677685-8-8(6)) Grannie Annie Family Story Celebration, The.

Dyer, Heather. The Girl with the Broken Wing. Bailey, Peter, illus. 2005. 147p. (J). (978-1-4156-3468-4(8)) Scholastic, Inc.

Dyer, Sarah. Princess for a Day: A Clementine & Mungo Story. Dyer, Sarah, illus. (Illus.). 32p. (J). (gr. -1-k). 2009. pap. 12.95 (978-0-7475-8891-7(0)) 2007. 22.95 (978-0-7475-8753-8(1)) Bloomsbury Publishing Plc GBR. Dist: Independent Pubs. Group.

Earhart, Kristin. Buttercup Mystery. Geddes, Serena, illus. 2015. (Marguerite Henry's Misty Inn Ser.: 2). (ENG.). 128p. (J). (gr. 2-5). pap. 6.99 (978-1-4814-1416-6(X), Aladdin) Simon & Schuster Children's Publishing.

—Finding Luck. Geddes, Serena, illus. 2016. (Marguerite Henry's Misty Inn Ser.: 4). (ENG.). 128p. (J). (gr. 2-5). pap. 6.99 (978-1-4814-1422-7(4), Aladdin) Simon & Schuster Children's Publishing.

—Runaway Pony. Geddes, Serena, illus. 2015. (Marguerite Henry's Misty Inn Ser.: 3). (ENG.). 128p. (J). (gr. 2-5). pap. 6.99 (978-1-4814-1419-7(4), Aladdin) Simon & Schuster Children's Publishing.

—Runaway Pony. 2015. (Marguerite Henry's Misty Inn Ser.: 3). lib. bdg. 16.00 (978-0-606-37835-2(9)) Turtleback.

—Welcome Home! Geddes, Serena, illus. 2015. (Marguerite Henry's Misty Inn Ser.: 1). (ENG.). 128p. (J). (gr. 2-5). 16.99 (978-1-4814-1414-2(3), Aladdin) Simon & Schuster Children's Publishing.

—Welcome Home! 2015. (Marguerite Henry's Misty Inn Ser.: 1). lib. bdg. 16.00 (978-0-606-37126-1(5)) Turtleback.

Earl, Cheri Pray & Williams, Carol Lynch. Secret in Pennsylvania. 2009. (J). (978-1-56145-477-8(X), Peachtree Junior) Peachtree Publishing Co. Inc.

Easley, Sean. The Hotel Between. 2018. (ENG., Illus.). 352p. (J). (gr. 4-7). 19.99 (978-1-5344-1697-0(8), Simon & Schuster Bks. For Young Readers) Simon & Schuster Bks. For Young Readers.

—The Key of Lost Things. 2020. (ENG.). 400p. (J). (gr. 4-7). pap. 8.99 (978-1-5344-3788-3(6), Simon & Schuster Bks. For Young Readers) Simon & Schuster Bks. For Young Readers.

Eastman, Brock. Hope. 2019. 509p. (J). pap. (978-1-59638-249-7(X)) P & R Publishing.

Eastman, Brock D. & Eastman, Brock. Taken. 2011. (Illus.). 315p. (J). pap. (978-1-59638-245-9(7)) P & R Publishing.

Eaton, Deborah. Canciones de Monstruos. Translations.com Staff, tr. from ENG. Handelman, Dorothy, photos by. 2007. (Lecturas para niños de verdad - Nivel 2 (Real Kids Readers - Level 2) Ser.).Tr. of Monster Songs. (SPA., Illus.). 32p. (gr. k-3). per. 5.95 (978-0-8225-7803-1(4)) Lerner Publishing Group.

Eaves, Victor Caleb. Vee's the Chapters of Expudict: Book One. 2008. 128p. pap. 12.00 (978-1-4389-3385-6(1)) AuthorHouse.

Eboch, Chris. The Riverboat Phantom. 2009. (Haunted Ser.). (ENG.). 192p. (J). (gr. 3-7). pap. 5.99 (978-1-4169-7549-6(7), Aladdin) Simon & Schuster Children's Publishing.

Eddy, Daniel. Walter's Tours in the East: Walter in Je. 2005. pap. 16.95 (978-1-59605-437-0(9), Cosimo Classics) Cosimo, Inc.

Edgren, David. The Serpent Scroll. 2009. 127p. (J). 11.99 (978-0-8163-2330-2(5)) Pacific Pr. Publishing Assn.

Edgren, Elizabeth. Little Tree's Mightiest Deed. Penk, Kathryn, illus. 2009. 36p. pap. 12.95 (978-1-59858-825-5(7)) Dog Ear Publishing, LLC.

Edvall, Lilian. The Rabbit Who Couldn't Find His Daddy. Gimbergsson, Sara, illus. 2006. 32p. (J). (gr. -1-3). 15.00 (978-91-29-66429-4(2)) R & S Bks. SWE. Dist: Macmillan.

Edwards, Felicity. The Spider King. 2012. 176p. pap. (978-1-78176-753-5(X)) FeedARead.com.

Edwards, Tanille & Edwards, Latoya. Jordan & Justine's Weekend Adventures Pts. 1-2: Plants. 2007. (SPA.). 32p. (J). (gr. k-3). 12.95 (978-0-9787302-3-9(2)) Fire Flies Entertainment, LLC.

Eggleston, George Cary. The Big Brother: A Story of Indian War. 2017. (ENG., Illus.). (J). 22.95 (978-1-374-93004-9(0)); pap. 12.95 (978-1-374-93003-2(2)) Capital Communications, Inc.

—The Big Brother: A Story of Indian War. 2007. (Illus.). 104p. per. (978-1-4065-2541-0(3)) Dodo Pr.

—The Big Brother: A Story of Indian War. 2017. (ENG., Illus.). (J). pap. (978-0-649-07400-6(9)) Trieste Publishing Pty Ltd.

Ehrmantraut, Brenda. I Want One Too! Short, Robbie, illus. 2003. (J). lib. bdg. 16.95 (978-0-9729833-1-0(7)); per. 9.95 (978-0-9729833-0-3(9)) Bubble Gum Pr.

Eisan, Daniel. The Lonely Peach. 2011. (Illus.). 48p. pap. 15.99 (978-1-4628-5634-3(9)) Xlibris Corp.

Ellery, Amanda. If I Had a Dragon. Ellery, Tom, illus. 2006. (ENG.). 40p. (J). (gr. -1-3). 19.99 (978-1-4169-0924-8(9), Simon & Schuster Bks. For Young Readers) Simon & Schuster Bks. For Young Readers.

Elliott, Rebecca. Eva & Baby Mo, 10. 2019. (Branches Early Ch Bks). (ENG.). 71p. (J). (gr. 2-3). 15.36 (978-0-87617-985-7(5)) Penworthy Co., LLC, The.

—Eva & Baby Mo: a Branches Book (Owl Diaries #10) Elliott, Rebecca, illus. 2019. (Owl Diaries: 10). (ENG., Illus.). 80p. (J). (gr. k-2). pap. 4.99 (978-1-338-29857-4(7)) Scholastic, Inc.

—Eva & Baby Mo: a Branches Book (Owl Diaries #10) (Library Edition), Vol. 10. Elliott, Rebecca, illus. 2019. (Owl Diaries: 10). (ENG., Illus.). 80p. (J). (gr. k-2). lib. bdg. 24.99 (978-1-338-29858-1(5)) Scholastic, Inc.

—Just Because. 2014. (ENG., Illus.). 12p. (J). (gr. k-2). bds. 6.99 (978-0-7459-6460-7(5), 2011181e-2b68-4ada-991c-9f5da2a12562, Lion Children's) Lion Hudson PLC GBR. Dist: Baker & Taylor Publisher Services (BTPS).

Ellis, Edward Sylvester. Through Forest & Fire. 2005. pap. 14.95 (978-1-59224-221-4(9)) Wildside Pr., LLC.

Ellis, Sarah. Big Ben. LaFave, Kim, illus. 2004. (J). (gr. -1-1). spiral bd. *(978-0-616-11108-6(8))*; spiral bd. *(978-0-616-11109-3(6))* Canadian National Institute for the Blind/Institut National Canadien pour les Aveugles.

Emerson, Kevin. The Shores Beyond Time. (Chronicle of the Dark Star Ser.: 3). (ENG.). 512p. (J). (gr. 3-7). 2020. pap. 8.99 *(978-0-06-230678-4(2))* 2019. 16.99 *(978-0-06-230677-7(4))* HarperCollins Pubs. (Walden Pond Pr.).

Emery, Joanna. Brothers of the Falls. Erickson, David, illus. 2004. (Adventures in America Ser.). (gr. 4). 14.95 *(978-1-893110-37-3(0))* Silver Moon Pr.

Emily, Katelyn. The Treasure-Trove Tales at the Gazebo. 2009. 120p. 18.95 *(978-1-59858-940-5(7))*; pap. 8.95 *(978-1-59858-855-2(9))* Dog Ear Publishing, LLC.

Encyclopaedia Britannica, Inc. Staff, compiled by. My Little Foster Sister. 2008. 49.95 *(978-1-59339-666-4(X))* Encyclopaedia Britannica, Inc.

Enderle, Dotti. Book 15: Rock & Roll!, 1 vol. 2014. (Ghost Detectors Ser.). (ENG., Illus.). 80p. (J). (gr. 2-5). lib. bdg. 35.64 *(978-1-62402-003-2(8)*, 8832, Calico Chapter Bks.) ABDO Publishing Co.

—Book 17: Grow a Ghost! 2014. (Ghost Detectors Set 3 Ser.). 80p. (J). (gr. 2-5). lib. bdg. 27.07 *(978-1-62402-005-6(4)*, Calico Chapter Bks) Magic Wagon.

—Grow a Ghost!, 1 vol. McWilliam, Howard, illus. 2015. (Ghost Detectors Ser.). (ENG.). 80p. (J). (gr. 2-5). 35.64 *(978-1-62402-100-8(X)*, 18142, Calico Chapter Bks.) ABDO Publishing Co.

Engle, Margarita. Forest World. 2017. (ENG., Illus.). 208p. (J). (gr. 5). 19.99 *(978-1-4814-9057-3(5)*, Atheneum Bks. for Young Readers) Simon & Schuster Children's Publishing.

—La Selva (Forest World) Romay, Alexis, tr. 2019. (SPA.). (J). (gr. 5). 224p. pap. 7.99 *(978-1-5344-2930-7(1))*; (Illus.). 208p. 17.99 *(978-1-5344-5107-0(2))* Simon & Schuster Children's Publishing. (Atheneum Bks. for Young Readers).

Engle, Margarita, et al. A Dog Named Haku: A Holiday Story from Nepal. Jeyaveeran, Ruth, illus. 2018. (ENG.). 32p. (J). (gr. k-3). 19.99 *(978-1-5124-3205-3(9)*, f7c55141-c8b7-4e5c-bd93-eb25853b9290, Millbrook Pr.) Lerner Publishing Group.

Enright, Elizabeth. Gone-Away Lake. Krush, Beth & Krush, Joe, illus. 2006. 256p. (J). (gr. 4-8). reprint ed. pap. 6.00 *(978-1-4223-5436-0(9))* DIANE Publishing Co.

—The Saturdays. Enright, Elizabeth, illus. 3rd ed. 2008. (Melendy Quartet Ser.: 1). (ENG., Illus.). 192p. (J). (gr. 3-7). per. 8.99 *(978-0-312-37598-0(0)*, 900048317) Square Fish.

—Then There Were Five. Enright, Elizabeth, illus. 3rd ed. 2008. (Melendy Quartet Ser.: 3). (ENG., Illus.). 272p. (J). (gr. 3-7). per. 14.99 *(978-0-312-37600-0(6)*, 900048319) Square Fish.

Enright, Robert D. Rising above the Storm Clouds: What It's Like to Forgive. Finney, Kathryn Kunz, illus. 2004. 32p. (J). (ENG.). 14.95 *(978-1-59147-075-5(7))*; pap. 9.95 *(978-1-59147-076-2(5))* American Psychological Assn. (Magination Pr.).

Ephron, Amy. Carnival Magic. 2019. (Other Side Ser.). (Illus.). 288p. (J). (gr. 3-7). 8.99 *(978-1-5247-4023-8(3)*, Puffin Books) Penguin Young Readers Group.

Erickson, Mary Ellen. Who Jinxed the CG Ranch? 2009. 196p. 24.95 *(978-1-4401-4218-5(1))*; pap. 14.95 *(978-1-4401-4216-1(5))* iUniverse, Inc.

Ernst, Lisa Campbell. Snow Surprise: A Winter & Holiday Book for Kids. Ernst, Lisa Campbell, illus. 2008. (ENG., Illus.). 24p. (J). (gr. k-2). pap. 4.99 *(978-0-15-206559-1(8)*, 1199534, Clarion Bks.) HarperCollins Pubs.

Ervin, Randy. Maycroft From 232nd. 2010. 150p. (J). pap. 10.00 *(978-0-578-05732-3(8))* Ervin, Randy.

Esbaum, Jill. How to Grow a Dinosaur. Boldt, Mike, illus. 2018. 40p. (J). (-k). 17.99 *(978-0-399-53910-7(7)*, Dial Bks) Penguin Young Readers Group.

Esche, Sandra. Sh! I've Got Something to Tell You. Davis, Karen, illus. 2005. (ENG.). 26p. (J). per. 13.99 *(978-1-4134-8324-6(0))* Xlibris Corp.

Esparza- Vela, Mary. You Can't Take the Dinosaur Home. Motz, Mike, illus. 2013. 16p. pap. 9.95 *(978-1-61633-364-5(2))* Guardian Angel Publishing, Inc.

Esther Cravens Schwalger. Not Too Close. Eve Cravens Nawahine, illus. 2009. 16p. pap. 8.49 *(978-1-4389-6987-9(2))* AuthorHouse.

Evan, Kelsey L. Starshine. 2013. 102p. pap. 19.95 *(978-1-63000-770-6(6))* PublishAmerica, Inc.

Evans, Rose-Marie. The Unexpected Adventure at East Haddam High. 2009. 80p. pap. 10.75 *(978-1-60860-182-0(X)*, Strategic Bk. Publishing) Strategic Book Publishing & Rights Agency (SBPRA).

Eve, Laure. The Curses: A Graces Novel. 2018. (ENG.). 336p. (YA). (gr. 8-17). 18.99 *(978-1-4197-2571-5(8)*, 1138201, Amulet Bks.) Abrams, Inc.

—Graces. 2016. (Graces Novel Ser.). (ENG.). 352p. (YA). (gr. 8-17). 18.95 *(978-1-4197-2123-6(2)*, 1138101, Amulet Bks.) Abrams, Inc.

Everheart, Chris. Three Chords & a Beat. 2015. (Tartan House Ser.). (ENG.). 96p. (J). (gr. 3-6). *(978-1-63235-058-9(0)*, 11685, 12-Story Library) Bookstaves, LLC.

Falk, Nick & Flowers, Tony. A Pterodactyl Stole My Homework: Saurus Street 2 (Large Print 16pt) 2013. 98p. pap. *(978-1-4596-5772-4(1))* ReadHowYouWant.com, Ltd.

Falwell, Cathryn. Mystery Vine. Falwell, Cathryn, illus. 2009. (Illus.). 32p. (J). lib. bdg. 17.89 *(978-0-06-177197-2(X)*, Greenwillow Bks.) HarperCollins Pubs.

Fantastik, B. Save the Sleepless Slumbernots! Valentine, M. K., illus. 2013. 32p. *(978-1-4602-2777-0(8))* FriesenPress.

Fantich, Susanna. A Cat's Tale. 2012. 210p. 33.99 *(978-1-4582-0527-8(4))*; pap. 15.99 *(978-1-4582-0525-4(8))* Author Solutions, LLC. (Abbott Pr.).

Farley, Grant. Bones of a Saint. 2021. 288p. (YA). (gr. 9). 18.99 *(978-1-64129-117-0(6)*, Soho Teen) Soho Pr., Inc.

Farmer, Nancy. The Sea of Trolls. (ENG., Illus.). 480p. 2006. (YA). (gr. 9-9). reprint ed. pap. 13.99 *(978-0-689-86746-0(8))*1. 2004. (J). (gr. 5-8). 21.99 *(978-0-689-86744-6(1))* Simon & Schuster Children's Publishing. (Atheneum Bks. for Young Readers).

Farnworth, Michael M. The Sinister Mr. Pickle & the Fickle He Got the Mcwickles Into. 2008. 40p. per. 24.95 *(978-1-60441-285-7(2))* America Star Bks.

Farrell, Bill. Walter's Pond: The True Story of Three Brothers Who Went Fishing for Trouble. Julich, Jenniffer, illus. 2008. 16p. 8.95 *(978-0-9797790-0-8(6))* Lower Lane Publishing LLC.

Faulkner, Matt. A Taste of Colored Water. Faulkner, Matt, illus. 2008. (ENG., Illus.). 48p. (J). (gr. 1-3). 18.99 *(978-1-4169-1629-1(6)*, Simon & Schuster Bks. For Young Readers) Simon & Schuster Bks. For Young Readers.

—A Taste of Colored Water. 2008. (YA). 29.95 incl. audio compact disk *(978-0-8045-4201-2(5))* Spoken Arts, Inc.

Faust, Jon. Helicopter Harry & the Copter Kids. 2016. (ENG., Illus.). (J). pap. 9.95 *(978-0-692-78184-5(6))* Mother Lode Pr. LLC.

Fearnley, Jan. Billy Tibble Moves Out! Fearnley, Jan, illus. 2006. (Illus.). 29p. (J). (gr. k-4). reprint ed. 16.00 *(978-1-4223-5557-2(8))* DIANE Publishing Co.

Feiffer, Kate. But I Wanted a Baby Brother! Goode, Diane, illus. 2010. (ENG.). 32p. (J). (gr. -1-3). 16.99 *(978-1-4169-3941-2(5)*, Simon & Schuster/Paula Wiseman Bks.) Simon & Schuster/Paula Wiseman Bks.

Fenner, Carol. Yolonda's Genius. unabr. ed. 2004. 211p. (J). (gr. 4-6). pap. 38.00 incl. audio *(978-0-8072-0462-7(5)*, Listening Library) Random Hse. Audio Publishing Group.

Fenwick, Nellie. Gracie & God's Great Ten: How One Girl Learned to Make Good Choices. 2012. 118p. (-18). pap. 17.99 *(978-0-9827627-8-3(X))* Port Hole Pubns.

Ferreri, Della Ross. Star of the Show. Weinstock, Tony, illus. 2009. (ENG.). 36p. (J). (gr. -1-3). 15.95 *(978-1-934860-03-8(4))* Shenanigan Bks.

Fields, T. S. Missing in the Mountains. 2008. (ENG., Illus.). 108p. (J). (gr. 4-7). pap. 8.95 *(978-0-87358-950-5(5))* Cooper Square Publishing Llc.

Finley, Mary Peace. Meadow Lark. 2003. (Santa Fe Trail Trilogy Ser.). (Illus.). 199p. (J). 15.95 *(978-0-86541-070-1(4))* Filter Pr., LLC.

Fiona Fox Staff, ed. The Railway Children. 2012. (ENG., Illus.). 64p. (J). 15.00 *(978-1-84135-840-6(1))* Award Pubns. Ltd. GBR. Dist: Parkwest Pubns., Inc.

Fiore, Kelly. Thicker Than Water. 2016. (ENG.). 320p. (YA). (gr. 9). 17.99 *(978-0-06-232473-3(X)*, HarperTeen) HarperCollins Pubs.

Fischel, Ana. The Twelve Quests - Book 4, Rapunzel's Hair. 2009. 158p. pap. *(978-1-84923-876-2(6))* YouWriteOn.

—The Twelve Quests - Book 6, the Enchanted Harp. 2009. 158p. pap. *(978-1-84923-878-6(2))* YouWriteOn.

Fishbone, Greg. The Penguins of Doom. 2007. (From the Desk of Septina Nash Ser.). (ENG., Illus.). 182p. (J). (gr. 2-7). 13.95 *(978-1-933831-03-9(0))* Blooming Tree Pr.

Fisher, Catherine. Darkhenge. 2006. 340p. (YA). (gr. 7-12). 15.99 *(978-0-06-078582-6(9))* HarperCollins Pubs.

Fitzgerald, John. Great Brain. 2006. 20.75 *(978-0-8446-7293-9(9))* Smith, Peter Pub., Inc.

Five Children & It. 2013. 58p. pap. 5.60 *(978-1-236-72792-3(4))* General Bks. LLC.

Five Children & It. 2010. (CAM.). 142p. pap. 10.95 *(978-1-4385-3539-5(2)*, Bk. Jungle) Standard Publications, Inc.

Flammer, JoAnn. The Last Wish. 2007. (ENG.). 80p. pap. 10.00 *(978-0-615-16197-6(9))* Flammer, Josephine.

Fleischman, Sid. The 13th Floor: A Ghost Story. Sis, Peter, illus. 2007. (ENG.). 240p. (J). (gr. 3-7). per. 7.99 *(978-0-06-134503-6(2)*, Greenwillow Bks.) HarperCollins Pubs.

Fletcher, Pamela. Who Is Freddy Farittle? 2011. 40p. pap. 16.99 *(978-1-4634-1086-5(7))* AuthorHouse.

Fletcher, Susan. Alphabet of Dreams. 2008. (ENG., Illus.). 432p. (YA). (gr. 7-12). mass mkt. 7.99 *(978-0-689-85152-0(9)*, Simon Pulse) Simon Pulse.

Flood, Tony. Jody Richards & the Secret Potion. 2nd ed. 2012. 146p. pap. *(978-0-9569682-9-6(5))* My Voice Publishing.

Flor Ada, Alma. Celebrate Christmas & Three Kings Day with Pablo & Carlitos. Torres, Walter, illus. 2006. (Cuentos para Celebrar / Stories to Celebrate Ser.). 30p. (J). (gr. k-6). per. 11.95 *(978-1-59820-136-9(0))* Santillana USA Publishing Co., Inc.

—Celebrate Hanukkah with Bubbe's Tales. Hayes, Joe & Franco, Sharon, trs. from SPA. Epelbaum, Mariano, illus. 2007. (Cuentos para Celebrar / Stories to Celebrate Ser.). 30p. (J). (gr. k-6). per. 11.95 *(978-1-59820-134-5(4))* Santillana USA Publishing Co., Inc.

Flores-Scott, Patrick. American Road Trip. 2019. (ENG.). 336p. (YA). pap. 10.99 *(978-1-250-21165-1(4)*, 900158804) Square Fish.

Flynn, M. H. The Shadow City Ghost Hunters Vol. 1: The Mystery of Mapleshade Manor. 2006. 48p. pap. 16.95 *(978-1-4241-2002-4(0))* PublishAmerica, Inc.

Foley, James. Brobot. 2018. (S. Tinker Inc Ser.). 112p. (J). (gr. 3-6). 6.99 *(978-1-925163-91-9(1))* Fremantle Pr. AUS. Dist: Independent Pubs. Group.

Forrester, Emma. Uncle Arthur's Art Studio. Nunn, Paul E., illus. 2008. (Spiderwick Chronicles). (ENG.). 48p. (J). (gr. 2-7). 10.99 *(978-1-4169-4955-8(0)*, Simon Scribbles) Simon Scribbles.

Forrester, Sandra. Leo & the Lesser Lion. 2011. (ENG.). 304p. (J). (gr. 9-12). lib. bdg. 21.19 *(978-0-375-95616-4(6)*, Knopf Bks. for Young Readers) Random Hse. Children's Bks.

Forte, Joseph. At the Window. 2013. 32p. pap. *(978-1-4602-2190-7(7))* FriesenPress.

Forte, Lauren. The Campout Challenge. 2018. (I Can Read! Level 2 Ser.). lib. bdg. 13.55 *(978-0-606-40851-6(7))* Turtleback.

Foster, Stewart. Bubble. 2017. (ENG., Illus.). 352p. (J). (gr. 3-5). 16.99 *(978-1-4814-8742-9(6)*, Simon & Schuster Bks. For Young Readers) Simon & Schuster Bks. For Young Readers.

Fox, Paula. Gus cara de piedra. (SPA.). 128p. (J). (gr. 3-5). *(978-84-279-3450-4(5)*, NG4694) Noguer y Caralt Editores, S. A. ESP. Dist: Lectorum Pubns., Inc.

Fragasso, Ruth Ann (Reichner). The Little Boy Who Ate Like a Bird. 2011. 16p. (gr. -1). 12.68 *(978-1-4269-6287-5(8))* Trafford Publishing.

Francois, Rose Darlie. Little Miss Daring Evelynne. 2009. (ENG.). 47p. pap. 19.10 *(978-0-557-07136-4(4))* Lulu Pr., Inc.

Frank, E. R. Wrecked. (ENG., (YA). 2015. Illus.). 336p. (gr. 9). pap. 10.99 *(978-1-4814-5137-6(5))* 2007. 256p. (gr. 7-12). pap. 9.99 *(978-0-689-87384-3(0))* Simon & Schuster Children's Publishing. (Atheneum Bks. for Young Readers).

Franklin, Kristine L. Dove Song. 2006. (ENG.). 192p. (J). (gr. 5-9). per. 5.99 *(978-0-7636-3219-9(8))* Candlewick Pr.

Franklin, Shirley A. Emma's Fantastique Word Play. 2009. 80p. pap. 8.95 *(978-1-4401-3824-9(9))* iUniverse, Inc.

Fraser, Kayo. Listen to Your Spirit: A Novel. 2019. (ENG., Illus.). 180p. (J). pap. *(978-1-937849-53-5(8))* Raven Publishing Inc. of Montana.

Fraser, Mary Ann. Heebie-Jeebie Jamboree. 2011. (ENG., Illus.). 32p. (J). (gr. -1-3). 15.95 *(978-1-59078-857-8(5)*, Astra Young Readers) Astra Publishing Hse.

Fraser, Mary Ann, illus. No Yeti Yet. 2015. (ENG.). 32p. (J). 16.99 *(978-1-4413-0855-9(5)*, 9781441308559) Peter Pauper Pr. Inc.

Frayre, A. R. Shannon Cabbage-Head. 2008. 33p. pap. 14.28 *(978-0-557-00442-3(X))* Lulu Pr., Inc.

Frazee, Marla. The Bossier Baby. Frazee, Marla, illus. 2016. (ENG., Illus.). 40p. (J). (gr. -1-3). 17.99 *(978-1-4814-7162-6(7)*, Beach Lane Bks.) Beach Lane Bks.

Frederick, Heather Vogel. Once upon a Toad. 2013. (ENG., Illus.). 288p. (J). (gr. 5-9). pap. 7.99 *(978-1-4169-8479-5(8)*, Simon & Schuster Bks. For Young Readers) Simon & Schuster Bks. For Young Readers.

—Once upon a Toad. 2012. (ENG., Illus.). 272p. (J). (gr. 5-9). 16.99 *(978-1-4169-8478-8(X))* Simon & Schuster, Inc.

French, Vivian. Mountain Mona: Band 09/Gold (Collins Big Cat) Fisher, Chris, illus. 2006. (Collins Big Cat Ser.). (ENG.). 24p. (J). (gr. 2-2). pap. 9.99 *(978-0-00-718700-3(9))* HarperCollins Pubs. Ltd. GBR. Dist: Independent Pubs. Group.

Friedland, Joyce, ed. Cool Zone with Pain & the Great One: Novel-Ties Study Guide. 2011. 29p. pap. 16.95 *(978-0-7675-4471-9(4))* Learning Links Inc.

Friedman, Laurie. High Five, Mallory! Kalis, Jennifer, illus. (Mallory Ser.: 26). (ENG.). 160p. (J). (gr. 2-5). 2016. E-Book 23.99 *(978-1-5124-0898-0(0)*, 9781512408980)No. 26. 2017. pap. 6.99 *(978-1-5124-5867-1(8)*, e77b2c75-4827-4a72-b6c0-96702204305a) Lerner Publishing Group. (Darby Creek).

—Mallory Mcdonald, Baby Expert, Bk. 22. Kalis, Jennifer, illus. 2015. (Mallory Ser.: Vol. 22). (ENG.). 152p. (J). (gr. 2-5). pap. 6.99 *(978-1-4677-0938-5(7)*, 4150cef3-b9b7-49f2-8c72-a14f5126eed4, Darby Creek) Lerner Publishing Group.

—Mallory Mcdonald, Super Snoop. Kalis, Jennifer, illus. 2013. (Mallory Ser.: 18). (ENG.). 152p. (J). (gr. 2-5). pap. 7.99 *(978-1-4677-0929-3(8)*, 9f0d8c1d-f5fc-4f9f-8ba3-9cfe7cb72a16, Darby Creek) Lerner Publishing Group.

Friedman, Robin. Nothing. 2008. (ENG.). 240p. (YA). (gr. 9-12). pap. 9.95 *(978-0-7387-1304-5(X)*, 073871304X, Flux) North Star Editions.

Friend, Ronda. R. Friend Swallows Her Pride. 2005. (Down on Friendly Acres Ser.: 1). (J). lib. bdg. *(978-0-9743627-3-1(5))* Sunflower Seeds Pr.

Friskey, Margaret. Surprise on Wheels. Patton, Lucia, illus. 2004. reprint ed. pap. 15.95 *(978-1-4191-1496-0(4))* Kessinger Publishing, LLC.

Frost, Libby. Princess Snowbelle & the Snow Games. 2018. (ENG., Illus.). 32p. (J). 16.99 *(978-1-5476-0025-0(X)*, 900195204, Bloomsbury Children's Bks.) Bloomsbury Publishing USA.

Frost, Robert Temple. Long Trip Home: Stand up Paddleboard Fantasy. 2013. 82p. pap. 10.95 *(978-1-62212-924-9(5)*, Strategic Bk. Publishing) Strategic Book Publishing & Rights Agency (SBPRA).

Fruchter, Jason, illus. The Baby Is Here! 2015. (Daniel Tiger's Neighborhood Ser.). (ENG.). 24p. (J). (gr. -1-2). pap. 4.99 *(978-1-4814-3013-5(0)*, Simon Spotlight) Simon Spotlight.

—Daniel Goes to the Playground. 2015. (Daniel Tiger's Neighborhood Ser.). (ENG.). 24p. (J). (gr. -1-2). pap. 3.99 *(978-1-4814-5198-7(7)*, Simon Spotlight) Simon Spotlight.

Fry, Jason. Edge of the Galaxy. 2014. 172p. (J). lib. bdg. 17.20 *(978-0-606-36536-9(2))* Turtleback.

—The Jupiter Pirates: Hunt for the Hydra. 2014. (Jupiter Pirates Ser.: 1). (ENG.). 272p. (J). (gr. 3-7). pap. 6.99 *(978-0-06-223021-8(2)*, HarperCollins) HarperCollins Pubs.

—Star Wars Rebels: Edge of the Galaxy. 2014. 172p. (J). *(978-1-4242-6295-3(X)*, Disney Lucasfilm Press) Disney Publishing Worldwide.

Fry, Jason & Weisman, Greg. Servants of the Empire. 2015. 171p. (J). *(978-1-4242-6297-7(6)*, Disney Lucasfilm Press) Disney Publishing Worldwide.

Fuchs-Rice, Dwayne. Shades of Ember. 2008. 456p. pap. 24.95 *(978-0-595-53315-2(9))* iUniverse, Inc.

Fuller, Rachel, illus. Look at Me! 2009. (New Baby Ser.). 12p. (J). (gr. -1). spiral bd. *(978-1-84643-278-1(2))* Child's Play International Ltd.

—My New Baby. 2009. (New Baby Ser.). 12p. (J). (gr. -1). spiral bd. *(978-1-84643-276-7(6))* Child's Play International Ltd.

Funari-Willever, Lisa. Theres A Kid under My Bed (Cj) 2008. 40p. 12.95 *(978-0-9760469-4-3(6))* Franklin Mason Pr.

Funaro, Gregory. Watch Hollow. Griffin, Matthew, illus. (Watch Hollow Ser.: 1). (ENG.). (J). (gr. 3-7). 2020. 272p. pap. 7.99 *(978-0-06-264346-9(0))* 2019. 256p. 16.99 *(978-0-06-264345-2(2))* HarperCollins Pubs. (HarperCollins).

Gaiman, Neil. The Day I Swapped My Dad for Two Goldfish. McKean, Dave, illus. 2004. (ENG.). 64p. (J). (gr. -1-3). 17.99 *(978-0-06-058701-7(6)*, HarperCollins) HarperCollins Pubs.

Gaither, Stefanie. Into the Abyss. (ENG.). 352p. (YA). (gr. 7). 2017. pap. 11.99 *(978-1-4814-4996-0(6))* 2016. (Illus.). 18.99 *(978-1-4814-4995-3(8))* Simon & Schuster Bks. For Young Readers. (Simon & Schuster Bks. For Young Readers).

Galvin, Laura. I Love My Sister. 2008. (ENG., Illus.). 16p. (J). (gr. -1-k). bds. 6.95 *(978-1-59249-867-3(1))* Soundprints.

Galvin, Laura Gates. I Love My Brother. Oughton, Taylor, illus. 2008. (ENG.). 16p. (J). (gr. -1-k). bds. 6.95 *(978-1-59249-866-6(3))* Soundprints.

—I Love My Sister. Oughton, Taylor et al, illus. 2011. (I Love My... Ser.). (ENG.). 16p. (gr. -1-k). 6.95 *(978-1-60727-311-0(X))* Soundprints.

Ganz, Yaffa. The Adventures of Jeremy & Heddy Levi. Katz, Avi, illus. 2005. 204p. (J). 16.95 *(978-1-930143-50-0(8)*, 3508); pap. 12.95 *(978-1-930143-51-7(6)*, 3516) Simcha Media Group. (Devora Publishing).

Garcia, Maria. Las Aventuras de Connie y Diego. 2004. (ENG & SPA., Illus.). (J). (gr. k-3). spiral bd. *(978-0-616-14605-7(1))* Canadian National Institute for the Blind/Institut National Canadien pour les Aveugles.

Garfield, Leon. The Complete Bostock & Harris. 2014. (ENG.). 336p. (J). (gr. 3-7). 17.95 *(978-1-59017-783-9(5)*, NYR Children's Collection) New York Review of Bks., Inc., The.

Garis, Howard R. The Curlytops & Their Playmates. 2009. 120p. 22.95 *(978-1-60664-610-6(9))*; pap. 10.95 *(978-1-60664-342-6(8))* Rodgers, Alan Bks.

—The Curlytops at Silver Lake. 2007. 260p. 29.95 *(978-1-4344-9207-4(9))*; per. 19.95 *(978-1-4344-9113-8(7))* Wildside Pr., LLC.

—The Curlytops on Star Island. 2018. (ENG., Illus.). 152p. (YA). (gr. 7-12). pap. *(978-93-5297-329-3(1))* Alpha Editions.

—The Curlytops on Star Island. 2009. 120p. 22.95 *(978-1-60664-611-3(7))*; pap. 10.95 *(978-1-60664-343-3(6))* Rodgers, Alan Bks.

—The Curlytops on Star Island; or, Camping Out with Grandpa. 2007. 164p. per. *(978-1-4065-2764-3(5))* Dodo Pr.

Garis, Howard Roger. The Curlytops at Uncle Franks Ranch. 2005. 192p. pap. 11.95 *(978-1-4218-1566-4(4)*, 1st World Library - Literary Society) 1st World Publishing, Inc.

—Daddy Takes Us Skating. 2007. 56p. per. *(978-1-4065-2765-0(3))* Dodo Pr.

—Daddy Takes Us to the Garden. 2007. (Illus.). 132p. per. *(978-1-4065-2766-7(1))* Dodo Pr.

Garner, Alan. The Weirdstone of Brisingamen: A Tale of Alderley. 2006. (ENG., Illus.). 288p. (J). (gr. 4-8). pap. 16.95 *(978-0-15-205636-0(X))* Houghton Mifflin Harcourt Publishing Co.

Garthwaite, Lynn D. Dirkle Smat Inside Mount Flatbottom. Howarth, Craig, illus. 2006. 48p. (J). pap. 9.95 *(978-1-59663-512-8(6)*, Castle Keep Pr.) Rock, James A. & Co. Pubs.

Gary, Meredith. Sometimes You Get What You Want. Brown, Lisa, illus. 2008. (ENG.). 32p. (J). (gr. -1 — 1). 17.99 *(978-0-06-114015-0(5)*, HarperCollins) HarperCollins Pubs.

Gaskin, Terri. Me & My Brother. 2010. 24p. 11.49 *(978-1-4520-5939-6(X))* AuthorHouse.

—Me & My Brother: Coloring Book. 2011. 24p. pap. 11.32 *(978-1-4567-6031-1(9))* AuthorHouse.

Gaskins, Terry & Treigle, Jimmy. The Very Big Storm: Created by Terry Gaskins Inspired by Jimmy Treigle. 2009. 28p. pap. 13.99 *(978-1-4389-4220-9(6))* AuthorHouse.

Gay, Marie-Louise. Buenos Días Samuel. 2004.Tr. of Good Morning Sam. (SPA.). (J). (gr. k-18). pap. 7.99 *(978-980-257-293-9(4))* Ekare, Ediciones VEN. Dist: Lectorum Pubns., Inc.

—Estela, Princesa de la Noche. 2nd ed. 2006.Tr. of Stella Princess of the Sky. (SPA., Illus.). 32p. (J). (gr. 1-2). 10.99 *(978-980-257-304-2(3)*, EK33231) Ekare, Ediciones VEN. Dist: Lectorum Pubns., Inc.

—Good Morning, Sam, 1 vol. 2003. (Stella & Sam Ser.: 1). (ENG., Illus.). 32p. (J). (gr. -1-k). 15.95 *(978-0-88899-528-5(8))* Groundwood Bks. CAN. Dist: Publishers Group West (PGW).

—Good Night, Sam, 1 vol. 2011. (Stella & Sam Ser.: 6). (ENG., Illus.). 32p. (J). (gr. -1-k). pap. 7.95 *(978-1-55498-116-8(6))* Groundwood Bks. CAN. Dist: Publishers Group West (PGW).

—Princess Pistachio, 1 vol. Homel, Jacob, tr. Gay, Marie-Louise, illus. 2015. (Princess Pistachio Ser.: 1). Orig. Title: Princesse Pistache. (ENG., Illus.). 48p. (J). (gr. k-3). 10.95 *(978-1-927485-69-9(X))* Pajama Pr. CAN. Dist: Publishers Group West (PGW).

—Read Me a Story, Stella, 1 vol. 2013. (Stella & Sam Ser.: 7). (ENG., Illus.). 32p. (J). (gr. -1-k). 16.95 *(978-1-55498-216-5(2))* Groundwood Bks. CAN. Dist: Publishers Group West (PGW).

—Stella - Fairy of the Forest. 2004. (Illus.). (J). (gr. -1-2). spiral bd. *(978-0-616-14580-7(2))*; spiral bd. *(978-0-616-14581-4(0))* Canadian National Institute for the Blind/Institut National Canadien pour les Aveugles.

—Stella, Fairy of the Forest, 1 vol. 2010. (Stella & Sam Ser.: 3). (ENG., Illus.). 32p. (J). (gr. -1-k). pap. 9.99 *(978-0-88899-993-1(3))* Groundwood Bks. CAN. Dist: Publishers Group West (PGW).

—Stella, Queen of the Snow. 2004. (J). (gr. -1-1). spiral bd. *(978-0-616-08493-9(5))* Canadian National Institute for the Blind/Institut National Canadien pour les Aveugles.

—Stella, Star of the Sea, 1 vol. (Illus.). 32p. (J). 2010. (Stella & Sam Ser.: 5). (gr. -1-k). pap. 9.99 *(978-0-88899-992-4(5))* 2004. (ENG., 7.95 *(978-0-88899-572-8(5))* Groundwood Bks. CAN. Dist: Publishers Group West (PGW).

Gennifer, Choldenko. Al Capone Does My Shirts. 2014. (ENG.). 240p. (J). (gr. 6-12). 12.24 *(978-1-63245-251-1(0))* Lectorum Pubns., Inc.

George, Jean Craighead, et al. Crowbar: The Smartest Bird in the World. Minor, Wendell, illus. 2021. (ENG.). 32p. (J). (gr. -1-3). 17.99 *(978-0-06-000257-2(3)*, Tegen, Katherine Bks) HarperCollins Pubs.

George, Jessica Day. Fridays with the Wizards. (Tuesdays at the Castle Ser.). (ENG.). 2017. 256p. (J). pap. 9.99 *(978-1-68119-204-8(7)*, 900162856) 2016. 240p. (YA). 16.99 *(978-1-61963-429-9(5)*, 900135951) Bloomsbury Publishing USA. (Bloomsbury USA Childrens).

—Thursdays with the Crown. (Tuesdays at the Castle Ser.). (ENG.). 2017. 240p. (J). pap. 8.99 *(978-1-68119-221-5(7)*, 900164100) 2014. 224p. (YA). (gr. 3-6). 16.99 *(978-1-61963-299-8(3)*, 900132430) Bloomsbury Publishing USA. (Bloomsbury USA Childrens).

George, K. Duck, Duck, Dinosaur: Perfect Pumpkin. Vidal, Oriol, illus. 2017. 32p. (J). *(978-1-5182-4363-9(0))* Harper & Row Ltd.

George, Kallie. Duck, Duck, Dinosaur: Snowy Surprise. Vidal, Oriol, illus. 2017. (My First I Can Read Ser.). (ENG.). 32p. (J). (gr. -1-3). 16.99 *(978-0-06-235319-1(5))*; pap. 5.99 *(978-0-06-235318-4(7))* HarperCollins Pubs. (HarperCollins).

—Duck, Duck, Dinosaur: Spring Smiles. Vidal, Oriol, illus. 2019. (My First I Can Read Ser.). (ENG.). 32p. (J). (gr. -1-3). 16.99 *(978-0-06-235322-1(5))*; pap. 4.99 *(978-0-06-235321-4(7))* HarperCollins Pubs. (HarperCollins).

Gerber, Lisa Ann. Elaina's Sleuthing Days, 1 vol. 2009. 60p. pap. 16.95 *(978-1-60749-623-6(2))* PublishAmerica, Inc.

S

Getachew, M. Sinziro. 2007. (ENG.). 32p. pap. 14.80 (978-1-4343-2961-5(5)) AuthorHouse.
Getzinger, Donna. Special. 2004. 108p. (J). pap. 7.95 (978-0-87714-530-1(X)) i-5 Publishing LLC.
Gewirtz, Adina Rishe. Blue Window. 2018. (ENG.). 576p. (J). (gr. 7). 18.99 (978-0-7636-6036-9(1)) Candlewick Pr.
—Zebra Forest. 208p. (J). (gr. 4-7). 2014. (Illus.). pap. 8.99 (978-0-7636-7166-2(5)) 2013. (ENG.). 15.99 (978-0-7636-6041-3(8)) Candlewick Pr.
Gidwitz, Adam. The Grimm Conclusion. 2014. (Grimm Ser.: 3). lib. bdg. 18.40 (978-0-606-36187-3(1)) Turtleback.
—A Tale Dark & Grimm. D'Andrade, Hugh, illus. 2011. (Tale Dark & Grimm Ser.). (ENG.). 288p. (J). (gr. 5-18). 8.99 (978-0-14-241967-0(2), Puffin Books) Penguin Young Readers Group.
—A Tale Dark & Grimm, 4 vols. (J). 55.75 (978-1-4498-6835-2(5)) Recorded Bks., Inc.
—A Tale Dark & Grimm. 2011. (Grimm Ser.: 1). lib. bdg. 18.40 (978-0-606-23144-2(7)) Turtleback.
Gidwitz, Adam, et al. A Tale Dark & Grimm. D'Andrade, Hugh, illus. 2010. (Tale Dark & Grimm Ser.). (ENG.). 272p. (J). (gr. 5-18). 17.99 (978-0-525-42334-8(6), Dutton Books for Young Readers) Penguin Young Readers Group.
Giff, Patricia Reilly. Gingersnap. 2014. (ENG.). 160p. (J). (gr. 3-7). 6.99 (978-0-440-42178-8(0), Yearling) Random Hse. Children's Bks.
—Nory Ryan's Song. 2004. 160p. (J). (gr. 4-7). pap. 36.00 incl. audio (978-0-8072-2093-1(0), Listening Library) Random Hse. Audio Publishing Group.
—Number One Kid. Bright, Alasdair, illus. 2010. (Zigzag Kids Ser.: 1). (ENG.). 80p. (J). (gr. 1-4). pap. 4.99 (978-0-553-49468-6(6), Yearling) Random Hse. Children's Bks.
—R My Name Is Rachel. 2012. (ENG.). 176p. (J). (gr. 4-7). pap. 6.99 (978-0-440-42176-4(4), Yearling) Random Hse. Children's Bks.
Gifford, Peggy. Moxy Maxwell Does Not Love Writing Thank-You Notes. Fisher, Valorie, illus. 2009. (Moxy Maxwell Ser.: 2). (ENG.). 192p. (J). (gr. 2-5). 6.99 (978-0-375-84343-3(4), Yearling) Random Hse. Children's Bks.
Gifford, Peggy Elizabeth. Moxy Maxwell Does Not Love Practicing the Piano: (But She Does Love Being in Recitals) Fisher, Valorie, illus. Fisher, Valorie, photos by. 2009. (Moxy Maxwell Ser.). (ENG.). 192p. (J). (gr. 4-6). lib. bdg. 21.19 (978-0-375-96688-0(9), Yearling) Random Hse. Children's Bks.
—Moxy Maxwell Does Not Love Writing Thank-You Notes. Fisher, Valorie, illus. Fisher, Valorie, photos by. 2008. (Moxy Maxwell Ser.). (ENG.). 176p. (J). (gr. 4-6). lib. bdg. 18.69 (978-0-375-94552-6(0), Yearling) Random Hse. Children's Bks.
Giles, Jeff. The Brink of Darkness. 2018. (Edge of Everything Ser.). (ENG.). 352p. (YA). 18.99 (978-1-61963-755-9(3), 900147530, Bloomsbury Young Adult) Bloomsbury Publishing USA.
Gill, Timothy. Flip & Fin: Super Sharks to the Rescue! 2016. (ENG., Illus.). 32p. (J). (gr. -1-3). 15.99 (978-0-06-224301-0(2), Greenwillow Bks.) HarperCollins Pubs.
Gillam, David. Gingertown. Gilliam, David, illus. 2012. 216p. (J). 29.99 (978-1-60131-122-1(2)) Big Tent Bks.
Gillmor, Don. Fabuleuse Melodie De. Gay, Marie-Louise, illus. 2013. (ENG.). 44p. (J). (gr. -1-k). 16.95 (978-2-923163-30-7(3)) La Montagne Secrete CAN. Dist: Independent Pubs. Group.
Giordano, Margaret A. The Bowditchers. 2006. 242p. per. 14.95 (978-1-59824-406-9(X)) E-BookTime LLC.
Giurco, Diane. The Adventures of Willy & Nilly. 2008. (Illus.). 32p. pap. 14.49 (978-1-4389-1134-2(3)) AuthorHouse.
Glaser, P. H. Chrystallia & the Source of Light. 2011. (Illus.). 196p. (J). 18.99 (978-1-60832-232-9(7)) Greenleaf Book Group.
Glatt, Lisa, et al. Abigail Iris: The One & Only. 2009. (Abigail Iris Ser.). (ENG., Illus.). 160p. (J). (gr. 4-6). 21.19 (978-0-8027-9782-7(2), 9780802797827) Walker & Co.
Glori, Debi. Where Did That Baby Come From? Glori, Debi, illus. 2005. (ENG., Illus.). 32p. (J). (gr. -1-3). 16.00 (978-0-15-205373-4(5), 1196178, Clarion Bks.) HarperCollins Pubs.
Glyn, Pamela. The green light in the Mountains. 2010. 32p. pap. 23.96 (978-1-4457-5153-5(4)) Lulu Pr., Inc.
Goelman, Ari. The Path of Names. 2013. (Illus.). 339p. (J). pap. (978-0-545-47431-3(0), Levine, Arthur A. Bks.) Scholastic, Inc.
Going, K. L. Bumpety, Dunkety, Thumpety-Thump! Shin, Simone, illus. 2017. (ENG.). 48p. (J). (gr. -1-k). 17.99 (978-1-4424-3414-1(7), Beach Lane Bks.) Beach Lane Bks.
Golant, Galina & Grant, Lisa. Play Checkers with Me. Golant, Evgenia, illus. 2003. 32p. (J). pap. 6.95 (978-1-932133-01-1(1)) Writers' Collective, The.
Goldman, Marcia. Lola & Tattletale Zeke. 2015. (Lola Ser.). (ENG., Illus.). 32p. (J). (gr. -1-k). 16.95 (978-1-939547-16-3(4), ae895ead-c77d-4056-ab1a-28e1c22a6bfc) Creston Bks.
Goldsberry, Booty. Scaredy-Cat, I'm Not. 2007. (ENG., Illus.). 40p. (gr. 4-7). pap. 9.95 (978-0-9792875-0-3(2)) Goldsberry, Booty.
Gonzalez Bertrand, Diane. The Ruiz Street Kids (Los Muchachos de la Calle Ruiz) Ventura, Gabriela Baeza, tr. 2006. (ENG & SPA., Illus.). (J). pap. 9.95 (978-1-55885-321-8(9), Piñata Books) Arte Publico Pr.
Gonzalez, Rafael. Cookie Boy! 2011. 20p. pap. 11.99 (978-1-4634-0324-9(0)) AuthorHouse.
Goobie, Beth. Jason's Why, 1 vol. 2012. (ENG.). 80p. (J). (gr. 4-6). pap. 8.95 (978-0-88995-484-7(4), 9c7bbc8b-0448-4e1b-911b-a87fc6d00ec2) Red Deer Pr. CAN. Dist: Firefly Bks., Ltd.
—Ni un Dia Más, 1 vol. 2009. (Spanish Soundings Ser.). Orig. Title: Kicked Out. (SPA.). 112p. (YA). (gr. 8-12). pap. 9.95 (978-1-55469-137-1(0)) Orca Bk. Pubs. USA.
Good Night, Little Brother: Individual Title Six-Packs. (Literatura 2000 Ser.). (gr. 1-2). 28.00 (978-0-7635-0090-0(9)) Rigby Education.
Goodhart, Pippa. Ginny's Egg. (ENG., Illus.). 142p. (J). pap. 7.50 (978-0-7497-4557-8(6)) Farshore GBR. Dist: Trafalgar Square Publishing.
Gorbachev, Valeri. The Best Cat. Gorbachev, Valeri, illus. 2010. (Illus.). 32p. (J). (gr. -1-2). 15.99 (978-0-7636-3675-3(4)) Candlewick Pr.
Gordon, David. The Ugly Truckling. Gordon, David, illus. 2004. (Illus.). 32p. (J). (gr. -1-2). lib. bdg. 16.89 (978-0-06-054601-4(8), Geringer, Laura Book) HarperCollins Pubs.
Gordon, Pauline C. The Adventures of the Droplet Twins. 2013. 136p. (978-1-4602-1343-8(2)); pap. (978-1-4602-1344-5(0)) FriesenPress.
Gorges, Julie A. Just Call Me Goody-Two-Shoes. 2006. 146p. (YA). per. 9.95 (978-0-9763274-1-7(4)) I.Form Ink, Publishing.
Gormally, Eleanor. The Little Flower Bulb: Helping Children Bereaved by Suicide. Loki, #VALUE! & Splink, illus. 2011. (ENG.). 32p. (J). (gr. -1-3). pap. 21.95 (978-1-84730-260-1(2)) Veritas Pubns. IRL. Dist: Casemate Pubs. & Bk. Distributors, LLC.
Gosling, Cherie & Disney Storybook Artists Staff. Mulan Is Loyal: Merida Is Brave. 2017. (Illus.). 24p. (J). (978-1-5379-5745-6(7)) Random Hse., Inc.
Gosling, Sharon. The Sapphire Cutlass. 2016. (Diamond Thief Ser.). (ENG.). 336p. (J). (gr. 9-12). 16.95 (978-1-63079-041-7(9), 131432, Switch Pr.) Capstone.
Gourlay, Candy. Tall Story. 2012. (ENG.). 304p. (J). (gr. 5). 8.99 (978-0-385-75233-6(4), Yearling) Random Hse. Children's Bks.
Grab, Daphne. Halftime. 2010. (J). (978-0-385-90693-7(5)); (978-0-385-73783-8(1)) Random House Publishing Group. (Delacorte Pr).
Grace, Amanda. No One Needs to Know. 2014. (ENG.). 240p. (YA). (gr. 9-12). pap. 9.99 (978-0-7387-3625-9(2), 0738736252, Flux) North Star Editions.
Grace, Hannah. The Popcorn MacHine. 2013. 56p. (978-1-4602-3282-8(8)) FriesenPress.
Grace, Kathleen. The Perfect Pug. 2011. 24p. pap. 24.95 (978-1-4512-7557-5(9)) America Star Bks.
Graff, Keir. The Phantom Tower. 2021. 288p. (J). (gr. 3-7). 8.99 (978-1-5247-3954-6(5), Puffin Books) Penguin Young Readers Group.
Graham, Bob. The Silver Button. Graham, Bob, illus. 2013. (ENG., Illus.). 32p. (J). (gr. -1-1). 16.99 (978-0-7636-6437-4(5)) Candlewick Pr.
—The Silver Button. Graham, Bob, illus. 2018. (ENG., Illus.). 32p. (J). (gr. -1-1). 7.99 (978-1-5362-0144-4(8)) Candlewick Pr.
Graham, Richard. Jack y el Monstruo. Varley, Susan, illus. (Cotton Cloud Ser.). (SPA.). 32p. (J). (gr. 1-3). (978-84-7722-680-2(6)) Timun Mas, Editorial S.A. ESP. Dist: Lectorum Pubns., Inc.
Grahame, Kenneth. The Golden Age. 2006. pap. (978-1-4068-3332-4(0)) Echo Library.
Grandma Bette. The Excellent Adventures of Max & Madison: Bedtime Stories for Youngsters. 2013. 32p. pap. 16.95 (978-1-4525-7264-2(X)); 36p. pap. 16.95 (978-1-4525-7270-3(4)); 32p. pap. 16.95 (978-1-4525-7268-0(2)); 32p. pap. 16.95 (978-1-4525-7266-6(6)) Author Solutions, LLC. (Balboa Pr.).
Grandpa Casey. Another Müsh-Mice Adventure: Florida Vacation, 1 vol. Brennan, Lisa, illus. 2009. 45p. pap. 24.95 (978-1-60813-329-1(X)) America Star Bks.
Grant, Tess. Flying in the Dark. 2013. 186p. pap. 10.99 (978-1-62237-167-9(4)) Turquoise Morning Pr.
Gratton, Tessa. Blood Magic. 2012. (Blood Journals). (ENG.). 416p. (YA). (gr. 8-12). lib. bdg. 26.19 (978-0-375-96733-7(8)) Random House Publishing Group.
—Blood Magic. 2011. 408p. (YA). pap. (978-0-375-86486-5(5)) Random Hse. Children's Bks.
Graves, Annie. Guinea Pig Killer, No. 4. McElhinney, Glenn, illus. 2015. (Nightmare Club Ser.: 4). (ENG.). 64p. (J). (gr. 2-5). pap. 6.99 (978-1-4677-6044-7(7), a4c5a6cf-c3ea-45c5-a529-d74e2b0a450b, Darby Creek) Lerner Publishing Group.
Graves, Kimberlee. I Have a New Baby Brother. 2017. (Learn-To-Read Ser.). (ENG., Illus.). (J). (gr. k-1). pap. 3.49 (978-1-68310-286-1(X)) Pacific Learning, Inc.
Graves, Susan Elaine. Lily the Lucky Ducky, 1 vol. 2010. 44p. 24.95 (978-1-4489-4433-0(3)) PublishAmerica, Inc.
Gray, Grandpa. The Land of the Three Elves Vol. 1: Beginnings. 2012. (ENG.). 317p. pap. 14.95 (978-1-4327-9551-1(1)) Outskirts Pr., Inc.
Green, D. L. Zeke Meeks vs the Gruesome Girls, 1 vol. Alves, Josh, illus. 2012. (Zeke Meeks Ser.). (ENG.). 128p. (J). (gr. 2-4). pap. 5.95 (978-1-4048-7221-9(3), 118073, Picture Window Bks.) Capstone.
—Zeke Meeks vs the No-Fun Fund-Raiser, 1 vol. Alves, Josh, illus. 2013. (Zeke Meeks Ser.). (ENG.). 128p. (J). (gr. 2-4). lib. bdg. 22.65 (978-1-4048-7640-8(5), 120159, Picture Window Bks.) Capstone.
—Zeke Meeks vs the Super Stressful Talent Show, 1 vol. Alves, Josh, illus. 2013. (Zeke Meeks Ser.). (ENG.). 128p. (J). (gr. 2-4). 8.95 (978-1-4048-8106-8(9), 121878, Picture Window Bks.) Capstone.
Green, Lucyna A. M., illus. Love You Little Brother. 2006. (J). (978-1-58669-185-1(6)); (978-1-58669-186-8(4)) Childcraft Education Corp.
Green, Paige. Family over Everything: A Novel. 2013. (ENG., Illus.). 216p. pap. 15.99 (978-1-59309-501-7(5), Strebor Bks.) Strebor Bks.
Green, Poppy. Looking for Winston. Bell, Jennifer A., illus. 2015. (Adventures of Sophie Mouse Ser.: 4). (ENG.). 128p. (J). (gr. k-4). pap. 6.99 (978-1-4814-3003-6(3), Little Simon) Little Simon.
—Looking for Winston. Bell, Jennifer A., illus. 2017. (Adventures of Sophie Mouse Ser.). (ENG.). 128p. (J). (gr. k-4). lib. bdg. 31.36 (978-1-5321-4113-3(0), 26986, Chapter Bks.) Spotlight.
Green, Tim. Deep Zone. 2012. (Football Genius Ser.: 5). (J). lib. bdg. 17.20 (978-0-606-26854-7(5)) Turtleback.
—Football Hero. (Football Genius Ser.: 2). (ENG.). (J). (gr. 3-7). 2009. 320p. pap. 9.99 (978-0-06-112276-7(9)) 2008. (Illus.). 304p. 16.99 (978-0-06-112274-3(2)) HarperCollins Pubs. (HarperCollins).
—Pinch Hit. 2013. (ENG.). 336p. (J). (gr. 3-7). pap. 9.99 (978-0-06-201247-0(9), HarperCollins) HarperCollins Pubs.
Greenburg, Dan. Secrets of Dripping Fang, Book Six: Attack of the Giant Octopus. Fischer, Scott M., illus. 2007. (Secrets of Dripping Fang Ser.: Bk. 6). (ENG.). 160p. (J). (gr. 3-7). 12.99 (978-0-15-206041-1(3), 1198144, Clarion Bks.) HarperCollins Pubs.
—Secrets of Dripping Fang, Book Three: The Vampire's Curse, Bk. 3. Fischer, Scott M., illus. 2006. (Secrets of Dripping Fang Ser.: Bk. 3). (ENG.). 144p. (J). (gr. 3-7). 12.99 (978-0-15-205469-4(3), 1196455, Clarion Bks.) HarperCollins Pubs.
—Secrets of Dripping Fang, Book Two: Treachery & Betrayal at Jolly Days. Fischer, Scott M., illus. 2006. (Secrets of Dripping Fang Ser.: Bk. 2). (ENG.). 144p. (J). (gr. 3-7). 12.99 (978-0-15-205463-2(4), 1196437, Clarion Bks.) HarperCollins Pubs.
Greene, Stephanie. Happy Birthday, Sophie Hartley. (ENG.). 128p. (J). (gr. 3-7). 2011. pap. 6.99 (978-0-547-55025-1(1), 1450235) 2010. 16.00 (978-0-547-25128-8(9), 1101533) HarperCollins Pubs. (Clarion Bks.).
Greenfield, Eloise. She Come Bringing Me That Little Baby Girl. Steptoe, John, illus. 2014. 32p. pap. 7.00 (978-1-61003-336-7(1)) Center for the Collaborative Classroom.
Greer, Hannah. The Castle Ivengless: The Velvet Bag Memoirs, Bk. 3. 2009. 145p. pap. 24.95 (978-1-60749-105-7(2)) America Star Bks.
—The Lighthouse Summer Greer, Tica, illus. 2009. 156p. pap. 24.95 (978-1-60813-493-9(8)) America Star Bks.
Gresh, Dannah. Danika's Totally Terrible Toss. 2008. (True Girl Fiction Ser.). (ENG., Illus.). 112p. pap. 7.99 (978-0-8024-8702-5(5)) Moody Pubs.
Gresh, Dannah & Mylin, Janet. Just Call Me Kate. 2008. (True Girl Fiction Ser.). (ENG., Illus.). 112p. pap. 7.99 (978-0-8024-8703-2(3)) Moody Pubs.
Greves, Julie, et al. Upside down & Backwards: A Sibling's Journey Through Childhood Cancer. 2014. (Illus.). 112p. (J). (978-1-4338-1637-6(7), Magination Pr.) American Psychological Assn.
Griffin, Adele. The Knaveheart's Curse: A Vampire Island Book. 2009. (Vampire Island Ser.: 2). (ENG.). 160p. (J). (gr. 3-7). 6.99 (978-0-14-241407-1(7), Puffin Books) Penguin Young Readers Group.
Griffin, Sarah Maria. Other Words for Smoke. 2019. (ENG.). 352p. (YA). (gr. 9). 17.99 (978-0-06-240891-4(7), Greenwillow Bks.) HarperCollins Pubs.
Grigsby, Cynthia. Hollow Creek: A Haunted Beginning, 01. 2006. 163p. (J). 14.95 (978-0-9786840-0-6(1)) Grigsby, Cynthia.
Grime, L. L. The Make up Story. 2007. 36p. 17.50 (978-1-4357-0585-2(8)) Lulu Pr., Inc.
Grimes, Nikki. The Road to Paris. 2008. (ENG.). 160p. (J). (gr. 3-7). 7.99 (978-0-14-241082-0(9), Puffin Books) Penguin Young Readers Group.
—The Road to Paris. 2008. 153p. (gr. 3-7). 17.00 (978-0-7569-8932-3(9)) Perfection Learning Corp.
Grindley, Sally. Hurricane Wills. 2007. 256p. (J). (gr. 4-7). pap. 8.95 (978-0-7475-9095-8(8)) Bloomsbury Publishing Plc GBR. Dist: Independent Pubs. Group.
Gritton, Steve. ... & Then I... 2007. (Illus.). (J). 17.95 (978-0-9795361-1-3(1)) Bad Frog Art/SMG Bks.
—The Trouble with Sisters & Robots. 2012. (Illus.). 32p. (J). 34.28 (978-1-61913-150-7(1)) Weigl Pubs., Inc.
Grosset & Dunlap. I Slightly Want to Go Home. 2011. (Charlie & Lola Ser.). (ENG., Illus.). 24p. (J). (gr. k-3). pap. 4.99 (978-0-448-45461-0(0), Grosset & Dunlap) Penguin Young Readers Group.
Grossman, Lev. The Silver Arrow. (ENG.). (J). (gr. 3-7). 2021. 272p. pap. 8.99 (978-0-316-53954-8(6)) 2020. (Illus.). 272p. 16.99 (978-0-316-53953-1(8)) 2020. (Illus.). 288p. 32.99 (978-0-316-54170-1(2)) Little, Brown Bks. for Young Readers.
—The Silver Arrow. 2022. (Penworthy Picks YA Fiction Ser.). (ENG., Illus.). 259p. (J). (gr. 4-5). 19.46 (978-1-68505-117-4(0)) Penworthy Co., LLC, The.
Groth, Darren. Munro vs. the Coyote, 1 vol. 2017. (ENG.). 288p. (YA). (gr. 8-12). 19.95 (978-1-4598-1409-7(6)) Orca Bk. Pubs. USA.
Grove, S. E. The Waning Age. 2019. 352p. (YA). (gr. 9). 18.99 (978-0-451-47985-3(8), Viking Books for Young Readers) Penguin Young Readers Group.
Guest, Elissa Haden. Iris & Walter & Baby Rose. Davenier, Christine, illus. 2012. (Iris & Walter Ser.). (ENG.). 44p. (J). (gr. 1-4). pap. 4.99 (978-0-547-85064-1(6), 1501049, Clarion Bks.) HarperCollins Pubs.
Guevara, Melva Vizcarrondo. My Grandma, My Hero. 2007. 58p. pap. 10.00 (978-0-8059-7296-2(X)) Dorrance Publishing Co., Inc.
Guiffre, William. The First Gift of Christmas. Baron, Cheri Ann, illus. 2008. 32p. (J). (gr. -1-3). pap. 9.95 (978-1-931650-33-5(0)) Guiffre Bk. Publishing.
Gundel, Jean. The Mystery Key at Camp Green Meadow. Robertson, R. H., illus. 2011. (J). pap. 14.95 (978-1-59571-730-6(7)) Word Association Pubs.
Gunderson, Jessica. Carrie & the Great Storm: A Galveston Hurricane Survival Story. Forsyth, Matt, illus. 2019. (Girls Survive Ser.). (ENG.). 112p. (J). (gr. 3-7). pap. 7.95 (978-1-4965-8447-2(3), 140972); lib. bdg. 26.65 (978-1-4965-8385-7(X), 140681) Capstone. (Stone Arch Bks.).
Gutierrez, Akemi. The Mummy & Other Adventures of Sam & Alice. 2005. (ENG., Illus.). 64p. (J). (gr. -1-3). 16.00 (978-0-618-50761-0(2), 560974, Clarion Bks.) HarperCollins Pubs.
Gutierrez-Haley, Lisa. The New Pet: Adventures of Hayden & Jace. 2011. 20p. pap. 24.95 (978-1-4626-1872-9(3)) America Star Bks.
—The Wiggly Tooth: Adventures of Hayden & Jace. 2011. 16p. pap. 24.95 (978-1-4626-1874-3(X)) America Star Bks.
Gutknecht, Allan. Don't Wear Polka-Dot Underwear with White Pants: (and Other Lessons I've Learned) Lewis, Stevie, illus. 2013. (ENG.). 160p. (J). (gr. 2-5). pap. 6.99 (978-1-4424-8392-7(X), Aladdin) Simon & Schuster Children's Publishing.
—Don't Wear Polka-Dot Underwear with White Pants: (and Other Lessons I've Learned) Lewis, Stevie, illus. 2013. (ENG.). 160p. (J). (gr. 2-5). 15.99 (978-1-4424-8393-4(8), Simon & Schuster/Paula Wiseman Bks.) Simon & Schuster/Paula Wiseman Bks.
Gutman, Dan. From Texas with Love. 2014. (Genius Files Ser.: 4). (J). lib. bdg. 17.20 (978-0-606-36462-1(5)) Turtleback.
—The Genius Files #2: Never Say Genius. 2012. (Genius Files Ser.: 2). (ENG.). (J). (gr. 3-7). 304p. pap. 6.99 (978-0-06-182769-3(X)); (Illus.). 288p. 16.99 (978-0-06-182767-9(3)) HarperCollins Pubs. (HarperCollins).
—The Genius Files #3: You Only Die Twice. 2013. (Genius Files Ser.: 3). (ENG.). (J). (gr. 3-7). 320p. pap. 7.99 (978-0-06-182772-3(X)); (Illus.). 304p. 16.99 (978-0-06-182770-9(3)) HarperCollins Pubs. (HarperCollins).
—The Genius Files #4: from Texas with Love. 2014. (Genius Files Ser.: 4). (ENG.). (J). (gr. 3-7). 304p. pap. 9.99 (978-0-06-182775-4(4)); (Illus.). 288p. 16.99 (978-0-06-182773-0(8)) HarperCollins Pubs. (HarperCollins).
—The Genius Files #5: License to Thrill. (Genius Files Ser.: 5). (ENG., 272p. (J). (gr. 3-7). 2016. Illus.). pap. 7.99 (978-0-06-223633-3(4)) 2015. 16.99 (978-0-06-223632-6(6)) HarperCollins Pubs. (HarperCollins).
—The Genius Files: Mission Unstoppable. 2011. (Genius Files Ser.: 1). (ENG.). 304p. (J). (gr. 3-7). pap. 7.99 (978-0-06-182766-2(5)); (Illus.). 16.99 (978-0-06-182764-8(9)) HarperCollins Pubs. (HarperCollins).
—Mission Unstoppable. 2011. (Genius Files Ser.: 1). (J). lib. bdg. 17.20 (978-0-606-23559-4(0)) Turtleback.
—Never Say Genius. 2012. (Genius Files Ser.: 2). (J). lib. bdg. 17.20 (978-0-606-27128-8(7)) Turtleback.
—You Only Die Twice. 2013. (Genius Files Ser.: 3). (J). lib. bdg. 17.20 (978-0-606-35043-3(8)) Turtleback.
Guy, Ginger Foglesong. Siesta: Bilingual English-Spanish. Moreno, Rene King, illus. 2005. (ENG.). 32p. (J). (gr. -1-k). 17.99 (978-0-06-056061-4(4), Greenwillow Bks.) HarperCollins Pubs.
—Siesta Board Book: Bilingual English-Spanish. Moreno, Rene King, illus. 2009. (ENG.). 34p. (J). (gr. -1 — 1). bds. 7.99 (978-0-06-168884-3(3)) HarperCollins Español.
Guzman, Raquel. The Adventures of Eliseo & Stefano: My Daddy Can Fly! Guzman, Jacob, illus. 2006. 28p. (J). 16.95 (978-0-9788332-0-6(1)) Images & Pages.
Haddix, Margaret Peterson. Among the Barons. 2004. (Shadow Children Ser.). 182p. (gr. 3-7). 17.00 (978-0-7569-3923-6(2)) Perfection Learning Corp.
—Among the Barons. (Shadow Children Ser.: 4). (ENG.). (J). (gr. 3-7). 2003. 192p. 18.99 (978-0-689-83906-1(5)) 2004. 208p. reprint ed. pap. 7.99 (978-0-689-83910-8(3)) Simon & Schuster Bks. For Young Readers. (Simon & Schuster Bks. For Young Readers).
—Children of Refuge. (Children of Exile Ser.: 2). (ENG.). (J). (gr. 5). 2018. 288p. pap. 7.99 (978-1-4424-5007-3(X)) 2017. (Illus.). 272p. 18.99 (978-1-4424-5006-6(1)) Simon & Schuster Bks. For Young Readers. (Simon & Schuster Bks. For Young Readers).
—Greystone Secrets #1: the Strangers. Lambelet, Anne, illus. (Greystone Secrets Ser.: 1). (ENG.). (J). (gr. 3-7). 2020. 432p. pap. 9.99 (978-0-06-283838-4(5)) 2019. 416p. 17.99 (978-0-06-283837-7(7)) 2019. 432p. E-Book (978-0-06-283839-1(3), 9780062838391) HarperCollins Pubs. (Tegen, Katherine Bks).
—Greystone Secrets #2: the Deceivers. (Greystone Secrets Ser.: 2). (ENG.). (J). (gr. 3-7). 2021. 464p. pap. 10.99 (978-0-06-283841-4(5)) 2020. (Illus.). 448p. 17.99 (978-0-06-283840-7(7)) HarperCollins Pubs. (Tegen, Katherine Bks).
—In over Their Heads. 2017. (Under Their Skin Ser.: 2). (ENG., Illus.). 320p. (J). (gr. 3-7). 18.99 (978-1-4814-1761-7(4), Simon & Schuster Bks. For Young Readers) Simon & Schuster Bks. For Young Readers.
—Redeemed. 2015. (Missing Ser.: 8). (ENG.). 416p. (J). (gr. 3-7). 19.99 (978-1-4424-9756-6(4), Simon & Schuster Bks. For Young Readers) Simon & Schuster Bks. For Young Readers.
—Redeemed. 2016. (Missing Ser.: 8). lib. bdg. 18.40 (978-0-606-39234-1(3)) Turtleback.
—Say What? Bernardin, James, illus. 2005. 91p. (J). 11.65 (978-0-7569-5465-9(7)) Perfection Learning Corp.
—Takeoffs & Landings. 2004. 201p. (gr. 5-9). 17.00 (978-0-7569-4255-7(1)) Perfection Learning Corp.
—Under Their Skin. 2016. (Under Their Skin Ser.: 1). (ENG., Illus.). 320p. (J). (gr. 3-7). 18.99 (978-1-4814-1758-7(4), Simon & Schuster Bks. For Young Readers) Simon & Schuster Bks. For Young Readers.
Haesche, Richard Paul, Sr. My Pet Dinosaur. 2007. (ENG.). 60p. (J). 6.99 (978-0-9800552-0-7(2)) Kreative X-Pressions Pubns.
Hahn, Mary Downing. All the Lovely Bad Ones: A Ghost Story 2009. (ENG.). 208p. (J). (gr. 3-7). pap. 7.99 (978-0-547-24878-3(4), 1100893, Clarion Bks.) HarperCollins Pubs.
—As Ever, Gordy. 2011. (ENG.). 192p. (J). (gr. 5-7). pap. 7.99 (978-0-547-54955-2(5), 1450108, Clarion Bks.) HarperCollins Pubs.
—Deep & Dark & Dangerous: A Ghost Story. 2007. (ENG.). 192p. (J). (gr. 5-7). 16.99 (978-0-618-66545-7(5), 100471, Clarion Bks.) HarperCollins Pubs.
—The Ghost of Crutchfield Hall. 2011. (ENG.). 160p. (J). (gr. 5-7). pap. 7.99 (978-0-547-57715-9(X), 1458473, Clarion Bks.) HarperCollins Pubs.
—Guest: A Changeling Tale. 2019. (ENG.). 224p. (J). (gr. 5-7). 16.99 (978-0-358-06731-3(6), 1744240, Clarion Bks.) HarperCollins Pubs.
—Hear the Wind Blow. 2017. (ENG.). 288p. (J). (gr. 5-7). pap. 7.99 (978-1-328-74092-2(7), 1677135, Clarion Bks.) HarperCollins Pubs.
—The Old Willis Place: A Ghost Story. 2007. (ENG.). 216p. (J). (gr. 5-7). pap. 7.99 (978-0-618-89741-4(0), 100589, Clarion Bks.) HarperCollins Pubs.
Haig, Matt. Shadow Forest. 2009. pap. 1.00 (978-1-4074-4391-1(7)) Recorded Bks., Inc.
Hairston, Kennard Lee. Rosie Bear Plays Baseball. 2009. 48p. pap. 19.49 (978-1-4389-7343-2(8)) AuthorHouse.
Haislip, Phyllis Hall. Lili's Gift: A Civil War Healer's Story. 2008. (ENG., Illus.). 204p. (J). pap. 8.95 (978-1-57249-392-6(5), White Mane Kids) White Mane Publishing Co., Inc.
Hajj, Sharon. Zula Blackburn & the Rising Sun Festival. 2012. 146p. 34.94 (978-1-105-79464-3(4)) Lulu.com GBR. Dist: Lulu Pr., Inc.

Hale, Bruce. Pirates of Underwhere. Hillman, Shane, illus. 2008. (Underwhere Ser.). 164p. (J). (gr. 3-7). lib. bdg. 16.89 (978-0-06-085128-6(7)) HarperCollins Pubs.

—Prince of Underwhere. Hillman, Shane, illus. 2009. (Underwhere Ser.: 1). (ENG.). 176p. (J). (gr. 3-7). pap. 5.99 (978-0-06-085126-2(0), HarperCollins) HarperCollins Pubs.

Haley, Jeannette. The Adventures of Zack & Mira. 2013. 116p. pap. 12.95 (978-0-9891683-0-4(1)) Hidden Manna Pubns.

Halpern, Julie. Into the Wild Nerd Yonder. 2011. (ENG.). 272p. (YA). (gr. 8-12). 17.99 (978-0-312-65307-1(7), 900069445) Square Fish.

Hamburg, Jennifer. Daniel Goes to the Playground. 2015. (Daniel Tiger's Neighborhood 8X8 Ser.). lib. bdg. 13.55 (978-0-606-38256-4(9)) Turtleback.

Hamilton, Pat. Peaches the Private Eye Poodle: The Missing Muffin Caper. 2008. 32p. pap. 13.50 (978-1-60693-277-3(2), Eloquent Bks.) Strategic Book Publishing & Rights Agency (SBPRA).

Hamilton-Sturdy, K. The Tree of Dreams. 2013. 138p. pap. (978-1-78299-683-5(4)) FeedARead.com.

Hamley, Dennis. The Ghosts Who Waited. 2005. 172p. (gr. -1-7). per. (978-1-904529-15-6(1), Back to Front) Solidus.

Han, Jenny. We'll Always Have Summer. 2011. (YA). 1.25 (978-1-4640-1977-7(0)) Recorded Bks., Inc.

—We'll Always Have Summer. (Summer I Turned Pretty Ser.). (ENG., Illus.). (YA). (gr. 7). 2012. 320p. pap. 11.99 (978-1-4169-9559-3(5)) 2011. 304p. 19.99 (978-1-4169-9558-6(7)) Simon & Schuster Bks. For Young Readers. (Simon & Schuster Bks. For Young Readers).

Hanif, Cristina. Logan & the Magic Tree. Stenton, Murray, illus. 2019. (J). (978-1-61599-422-9(X)) Loving Healing Pr., Inc.

Hanlon, Abby. Dory & the Real True Friend. 2016. (Dory Ser.: 2). lib. bdg. 18.40 (978-0-606-38846-7(X)) Turtleback.

—Dory Fantasmagory. (Dory Fantasmagory Ser.: 1). (ENG., Illus.). (J). (gr. 1-3). 2015. 176p. 7.99 (978-0-14-751067-9(8), Puffin Books) 2014. 160p. 16.99 (978-0-8037-4088-4(3), Dial Bks) Penguin Young Readers Group.

—Dory Fantasmagory. 2015. (Dory Ser.: 1). lib. bdg. 18.40 (978-0-606-36746-2(2)) Turtleback.

—Dory Fantasmagory: the Real True Friend. 2015. (Dory Fantasmagory Ser.: 2). (ENG., Illus.). 160p. (J). (gr. 1-3). 16.99 (978-0-525-42866-4(6), Dial Bks) Penguin Young Readers Group.

Hansel et Gretel.Tr. of Hansel & Gretel. (FRE.). 48p. pap. 12.95 incl. audio compact disk (978-2-89558-055-3(3)) Coffragants CAN. Dist: Penton Overseas, Inc.

Hapka, Cathy, pseud & Titlebaum, Ellen. How Not to Babysit Your Brother. Palen, Debbie, illus. 2005. (Step into Reading Ser.). 48p. (J). (gr. 2-4). pap. 4.99 (978-0-375-82856-0(7), Random Hse. Bks. for Young Readers) Random Hse. Children's Bks.

—How Not to Start Third Grade. Palen, Debbie, illus. 2007. (Step into Reading Ser.). 48p. (J). (gr. 2-4). pap. 5.99 (978-0-375-83904-7(6), Random Hse. Bks. for Young Readers) Random Hse. Children's Bks.

Hardesty, Ann A. Lucy's Trials in the Black Hills. 2009. 104p. pap. 10.99 (978-1-4490-5368-0(8)) AuthorHouse.

Harel, Moshe. Elf Prince. 2012. (ENG.). 258p. pap. (978-965-550-089-9(6)) Contento De Semrik.

Hargrave, Kiran Millwood. The Way Past Winter. 2020. (ENG., Illus.). 284p. (J). (gr. 5-10). 17.99 (978-1-4521-8155-4(1)) Chronicle Bks. LLC.

Hargreaves, Roger. Little Miss Whoops. 2008. (Mr. Men & Little Miss Ser.). (ENG., Illus.). 32p. (J). (gr. -1-2). mass mkt. 4.99 (978-0-8431-3350-9(3), Price Stern Sloan) Penguin Young Readers Group.

Harley, Bill. Dirty Joe, the Pirate: A True Story. Davis, Jack E., illus. 2008. (ENG.). 32p. (J). (gr. k-3). 17.99 (978-0-06-623780-0(7), HarperCollins) HarperCollins Pubs.

Harmon, Michael. Skate. 2008. 256p. (YA). (gr. 9). per. 7.99 (978-0-553-49510-2(0), Laurel Leaf) Random Hse. Children's Bks.

Harris, Donna. Ruff Life. 2011. 240p. pap. 17.99 (978-1-4567-5081-7(X)) AuthorHouse.

Harris, Dorothy Joan. Cameron & Me. 2004. (Illus.). (J). (gr. k-3). spiral bd. (978-0-616-01667-1(0)); spiral bd. (978-0-616-01668-8(9)) Canadian National Institute for the Blind/Institut National Canadien pour les Aveugles.

Harris, Robie H. Who's in My Family? All about Our Families. Westcott, Nadine Bernard, illus. 2012. (Let's Talk about You & Me Ser.). (ENG.). 40p. (J). (gr. -1-2). 17.99 (978-0-7636-3631-9(2)) Candlewick Pr.

Hartnett, Sonya. The Midnight Zoo. Offermann, Andrea, illus. 2018. (ENG.). 224p. (J). (gr. 5-9). pap. 8.99 (978-0-7636-6462-6(6)) Candlewick Pr.

—The Midnight Zoo. 2018. lib. bdg. 18.40 (978-0-606-40915-5(7)) Turtleback.

—Sadie & Ratz. James, Ann, illus. 2012. (ENG.). 64p. (J). (gr. k-3). 14.99 (978-0-7636-5315-6(2)) Candlewick Pr.

—Surrender. 2019. (ENG.). 256p. (J). (gr. 9). pap. 7.99 (978-1-5362-0644-9(X)) Candlewick Pr.

Harvey, Gwen. Esperanza Means Hope. Porfirio, Guy, illus. 2010. ix, 256p. (J). (978-0-910037-51-6(5)); pap. (978-0-910037-52-5(3)) Arizona Historical Society.

Harwood, Kelsey. Still Alive. 2012. 144p. pap. 9.99 (978-1-60820-746-6(3)) MLR Pr., LLC.

Hathorn, Libby. Incredibilia. Chapman, Gaye, illus. 2017. (ENG.). 40p. (J). (gr. -1-k). 19.99 (978-1-76012-525-7(3)) Little Hare Bks. AUS. Dist: Independent Pubs. Group.

Hausman, Michelle. Amelia's Eyes. 2010. (ENG.). 32p. pap. 15.95 (978-0-557-38618-5(7)) Lulu Pr., Inc.

Hautman, Pete. Slider. 288p. (J). (gr. 5-9). 2019. (ENG.). pap. 8.99 (978-1-5362-0432-2(3)) 2017. 17.99 (978-0-7636-9070-0(8)) Candlewick Pr.

Havill, Juanita. Flower Garden. O'Brien, Anne Sibley, illus. 2015. 32p. pap. 7.00 (978-1-61003-503-3(8)) Center for the Collaborative Classroom.

Hawes, Adrienne Hill. Moving Danielle. 2008. 22p. pap. 24.95 (978-1-4241-4977-3(0)) America Star Bks.

Hawkins-Walsh, Elizabeth & Pierson-Solis, Lennard. Katie's Premature Brother = el Hermano Prematuro de Katie. Blake, Anne Catharine, illus. 2006. (J). (978-1-56123-197-3(5)) Centering Corp.

Hawley, Mabel C. Four Little Blossoms & Their Winter Fun. 2007. 108p. per. (978-1-4065-4372-8(1)) Dodo Pr.

Hayes, Celeste. Cacao & the Jaded Orb: A Sphinx & Trevi Adventure. 2011. (Illus.). 62p. (J). pap. 22.95 (978-0-9785695-2-5(0)) Adam's Creations Publishing, LLC.

—Enchanted Fairyland: A Sphinx & Trevi Adventure. 2011. (Illus.). 30p. (J). pap. 19.95 (978-0-9785695-4-9(7)) Adam's Creations Publishing, LLC.

—The Puzzle Box of Nefertiti: A Sphinx & Trevi Adventure. Bishop, Christina, illus. 2011. 42p. (J). pap. 19.95 (978-0-9785695-3-2(9)) Adam's Creations Publishing, LLC.

Hayes, Christine. Mothman's Curse. 2016. (J). lib. bdg. 18.40 (978-0-606-39560-1(1)) Turtleback.

Hayes, Geoffrey. Benny & Penny in How to Say Goodbye: TOON Level 2. 2016. (Benny & Penny Ser.). (Illus.). 32p. (J). (gr. -1-3). 12.99 (978-1-935179-99-3(3), TOON Books) Astra Publishing Hse.

—Benny & Penny in Just Pretend, 1 vol. Hayes, Geoffrey, illus. 2013. (Toon Bks.). (ENG., Illus.). 36p. (J). (gr. 1-2). lib. bdg. 32.79 (978-1-61479-148-5(1), 14840) Spotlight.

—Benny & Penny in Just Pretend. 2013. (Toon Books Level 2 Ser.). lib. bdg. 14.75 (978-0-606-31597-5(7)) Turtleback.

—Benny & Penny in Just Pretend: Toon Books Level 2. Hayes, Geoffrey, illus. 2008. (Toon Ser.). (ENG., Illus.). 32p. (J). (gr. -1-3). 12.99 (978-0-9799238-0-7(8), TOON Books) Astra Publishing Hse.

—Benny & Penny in Lights Out: Toon Books Level 2. Hayes, Geoffrey, illus. 2012. (Toon Ser.). (ENG., Illus.). 32p. (J). (gr. -1-3). 12.99 (978-1-935179-20-7(9), Toon Books) Astra Publishing Hse.

—Benny & Penny in Lost & Found: Toon Books Level 2. Hayes, Geoffrey, illus. 2014. (Toon Ser.). (ENG., Illus.). 40p. (J). (gr. -1-3). 12.99 (978-1-935179-64-1(0), TOON Books) Astra Publishing Hse.

—Benny & Penny in the Big No-No! Toon Books Level 2. Hayes, Geoffrey, illus. (Toon Ser.). (ENG., Illus.). 32p. (J). (gr. -1-1). 2014. pap. 7.99 (978-1-935179-35-1(7)) 2009. 12.99 (978-0-9799238-9-0(1)) Astra Publishing Hse. (TOON Books).

—Benny & Penny in the Toy Breaker, 1 vol. Hayes, Geoffrey, illus. 2013. (Toon Bks.). (ENG., Illus.). 36p. (J). (gr. 1-2). lib. bdg. 32.79 (978-1-61479-149-2(X), 14841) Spotlight.

—Benny & Penny in the Toy Breaker. 2013. (Toon Books Level 2 Ser.). lib. bdg. 14.75 (978-0-606-31598-2(5)) Turtleback.

—Benny & Penny in the Toy Breaker: Toon Books Level 2. Hayes, Geoffrey, illus. 2010. (Toon Ser.). (ENG., Illus.). 32p. (J). (gr. -1-3). 12.95 (978-1-935179-07-8(1), Toon Books) Astra Publishing Hse.

Hayes, Sadie. The Social Code: A Novel. 2013. (Start-Up Ser.: 1). (ENG., Illus.). 320p. (YA). (gr. 7-12). pap. 22.99 (978-1-250-03565-3(1), 900121146, St. Martin's Griffin) St. Martin's Pr.

Haynes, Gibby. Me & Mr. Cigar. Haynes, Gibby, illus. 2020. (ENG., Illus.). 256p. (YA). (gr. 9). 18.99 (978-1-61695-812-1(X), Soho Teen) Soho Pr., Inc.

Hayward, Linda. Monster Bug. Palmisciano, Diane, illus. 2004. (Science Solves It! Ser.). (ENG.). 32p. (J). (gr. k-2). pap. 5.99 (978-1-57565-135-4(1), b7a409fd-180a-41bd-bd4f-8cd39a225f23, Kane Press) Astra Publishing Hse.

—Monster Bug. Palmisciano, Diane, illus. 2004. 32p. (J). lib. bdg. 20.00 (978-1-4242-1097-8(6)) Fitzgerald Bks.

—Monster Bug. Palmisciano, Diane, illus. 2004. (Science Solves It Ser.). 32p. (gr. -1-3). 15.00 (978-0-7569-4313-4(2)) Perfection Learning Corp.

Haywood, Carolyn. Here's a Penny. Haywood, Carolyn, illus. 2005. (ENG., Illus.). 160p. (J). (gr. 1-4). pap. 7.99 (978-0-15-205225-6(9), 1195745, Clarion Bks.) HarperCollins Pubs.

Head, Jean. Andrew's Christmas Dream. 2012. 28p. pap. 5.00 (978-1-937260-19-4(4)) Sleepytown Pr.

Headrick, Julianna. Our New Addition. Baker, David, illus. 2011. 28p. pap. 24.95 (978-1-4560-0933-5(8)) America Star Bks.

Hearne, Betsy. Wishes, Kisses, & Pigs. 2003. (ENG.). 144p. (J). (gr. 3-7). pap. 6.99 (978-0-689-86347-9(0), Simon & Schuster/Paula Wiseman Bks.) Simon & Schuster/Paula Wiseman Bks.

Heath, Paulette Powell. In the Mist. 2012. 24p. pap. 15.99 (978-1-4797-4354-4(2)) Xlibris Corp.

Heaton, Mark. Ruth Tells the Truth, 1 vol. 2006. (Neighborhood Readers Ser.). (ENG.). 16p. (gr. 1-2). pap. 6.50 (978-1-4042-7264-4(X), 1663cb73-ac8b-4eb1-97a8-8085faaae53e, Rosen Classroom) Rosen Publishing Group, Inc., The.

Hecht, Zalmy. My Very Own Letter. Judowitz, Chani, illus. 2016. (ENG.). 20p. (J). 11.95 (978-1-929628-89-6(7)) Hachai Publishing.

Hegg, Tom & Hanson, Warren. Peef & the Baby Sister. Hegg, Tom & Hanson, Warren, illus. 2006. (ENG., Illus.). 36p. (J). (gr. -1-3). 16.95 (978-0-931674-67-9(0), Waldman House Pr.) TRISTAN Publishing, Inc.

Heilprin Diehl, Jean. Three Little Beavers, 1 vol. Morrison, Cathy, illus. 2012. (ENG.). 32p. (J). (gr. -1-3). 17.95 (978-1-60718-524-6(5)); pap. 9.95 (978-1-60718-533-8(4)) Arbordale Publishing.

Helidoniotis, Kathy. Horse Mad Heroes. 2007. (ENG.). 274p. (J). (978-0-7322-8423-7(6)) HarperCollins Pubs. Australia.

—Horse Mad Western. 2008. (ENG.). 272p. (978-0-7322-8424-4(4)) HarperCollins Pubs. Australia.

Hellman, Charles. Adventures in SportsLand - the Tennis Bully (with accompanying CD) Tintilli, Robert, illus. 2008. (Adventures in SportsLand: the Bully Ser.). 32p. (J). (gr. -1-3). 19.95 (978-0-935938-32-6(X)) Stogo, Malcolm Assocs.

Helmer, Marilyn. Sharing Snowy, 1 vol. Charko, Kasia, illus. 2008. (Orca Echoes Ser.). (ENG.). 64p. (J). (gr. 1-3). pap. 6.95 (978-1-55469-021-3(8)) Orca Bk. Pubs. USA.

Hendershot, Eric. At Season's End. 2012. 164p. (YA). pap. 13.99 (978-1-59955-995-7(1)) Cedar Fort, Inc./CFI Distribution.

—A Horse for Christmas. 2012. (Illus.). 87p. (J). pap. 8.99 (978-1-4621-1078-0(9)) Cedar Fort, Inc./CFI Distribution.

Henderson, Leah. One Shadow on the Wall. (ENG.). 448p. (J). (gr. 3-7). 2018. pap. 8.99 (978-1-4814-6296-9(2)) 2017. (Illus.). 18.99 (978-1-4814-6295-2(4)) Simon & Schuster Children's Publishing. (Atheneum Bks. for Young Readers).

Hendry, Frances. Quest for a Queen: The Jackdaw. 2006. pap. (978-1-905665-05-1(9)) Pollinger In Print.

—Wee Malkie. l.t. ed. 2007. 240p. per. (978-1-905665-19-8(9)) Pollinger In Print.

Henkes, Kevin. Julius, el Rey de la Casa. 2017.Tr. of Julius, the Baby of the World. (SPA., Illus.). 31p. (J). pap. 9.99 (978-1-63245-668-7(0)) Lectorum Pubns., Inc.

Hennessey, M. G. The Echo Park Castaways. 2019. (ENG.). 208p. (J). (gr. 3-7). 16.99 (978-0-06-242769-4(5), HarperCollins) HarperCollins Pubs.

Hennessy, Claire. Afterwards. 2005. 188p. (YA). pap. (978-1-84223-207-1(X)) Poolbeg Pr.

Henry, Marguerite. Misty of Chincoteague. 2011. (CHI.). 165p. (J). (gr. 3-7). pap. (978-7-5434-8018-6(2)) Hebei Jiaoyu Chubanshe.

—Misty of Chincoteague. Dennis, Wesley, illus. 2007. 173p. (gr. 3-7). 17.00 (978-0-7569-8227-0(8)) Perfection Learning Corp.

—Misty of Chincoteague. Dennis, Wesley, illus. 60th ed. 2006. (ENG.). 176p. (J). (gr. 3-7). pap. 7.99 (978-1-4169-2783-9(2), Aladdin) Simon & Schuster Children's Publishing.

Henseleit, Jack. The Troll Heart, Volume 2. 2018. (Witching Hours Ser.: 2). (ENG., Illus.). 264p. (J). (gr. 2-4). pap. 15.99 (978-1-76012-926-2(7)) Hardie Grant Children?s Publishing AUS. Dist: Independent Pubs. Group.

—The Vampire Knife, Volume 1. 2017. (Witching Hours Ser.: 1). (ENG., Illus.). 240p. (J). (gr. 3-5). pap. 15.99 (978-1-76012-925-5(9)) Hardie Grant Children?s Publishing AUS. Dist: Independent Pubs. Group.

Hensley, Nathaniel. The Strange Tale of Hector & Hannah Crowe. 2015. (ENG.). 222p. (J). (gr. 8-18). 13.95 (978-1-937240-49-3(5)) Casa de Snapdragon LLC.

Herbertson, Lisa. Swimming Along. Kennedy, Catherine, illus. 2011. 26p. pap. 12.00 (978-1-60976-293-3(2), Eloquent Bks.) Strategic Book Publishing & Rights Agency (SBPRA).

Herman, Gail. Buried in the Backyard. Smath, Jerry, illus. 2003. (Science Solves It! Ser.). (ENG.). 32p. (J). (gr. k-2). pap. 5.99 (978-1-57565-126-2(2), 82a57d19-fce3-4036-91e0-c68e1229f1eb, Kane Press) Astra Publishing Hse.

—The Creeping Tide. Nez, John, illus. 2003. (Science Solves It! Ser.). (ENG.). 32p. (J). (gr. k-2). pap. 5.95 (978-1-57565-128-6(9), 0df45891-2536-4413-b0c3-a1f81d7cb5ea, Kane Press) Astra Publishing Hse.

—Enterrado en el Jardín: Buried in the Backyard. 2008. pap. 34.95 (978-1-58013-768-3(7)) Astra Publishing Hse.

Hermes, Patricia. Emma Dilemma & the Two Nannies, 0 vols. Carter, Abby, illus. 2012. (Emma Dilemma Ser.: 2). (ENG.). 126p. (J). (gr. 3-6). pap. 9.99 (978-0-7614-5835-7(2), 9780761458357, Two Lions) Amazon Publishing.

Herron, Carolivia, photos by & told to. Little Georgia & the Apples: A Retelling of Aunt Georgia's First Catalpa Tale Herron, Carolivia, told to. l.t. ed. 2004. (Illus.). 33p. (J). 10.00 (978-0-9760222-0-6(6), Catalpa01) Epicenter Literary Software.

Hervey, Cheston & Doane, Darren. Kill the Dragon, Get the Girl. 2017. 188p. (J). pap. (978-1-59128-188-7(1)) Canon Pr.

Heuiser Hill, Melanie. Giant Pumpkin Suite. 2017. (ENG.). 448p. (J). (gr. 4-7). 18.99 (978-0-7636-9155-4(0)) Candlewick Pr.

Hicks, Betty. Out of Order. 2007. (ENG.). 176p. (J). (gr. 3-7). pap. 15.99 (978-0-312-37355-9(4), 900045404) Square Fish.

Hicks, Deron R. Secrets of Shakespeare's Grave: The Shakespeare Mysteries, Book 1, Bk. 1. Geyer, Mark Edward, illus. 2013. (Shakespeare Mysteries Ser.: 1). (ENG.). 320p. (J). (gr. 3-7). pap. 7.99 (978-0-544-10504-1(4), 1540806, Clarion Bks.) HarperCollins Pubs.

Higgins, Jack & Richards, Justin. Death Run. 2009. (ENG.). 288p. (YA). (gr. 7-18). 8.99 (978-0-14-241475-0(1), Speak) Penguin Young Readers Group.

—First Strike. 2011. (Chance Twins Ser.: Bk. 4). (ENG.). 240p. (YA). (gr. 7-12). 24.94 (978-0-399-25240-2(1)) Penguin Young Readers Group.

—Sharp Shot. 2010. (ENG.). 240p. (YA). (gr. 7-18). 8.99 (978-0-14-241730-0(0), Speak) Penguin Young Readers Group.

—Sure Fire. 2008. (ENG.). 272p. (YA). (gr. 7-18). 8.99 (978-0-14-241213-8(9), Speak) Penguin Young Readers Group.

Higgins, M. G. Family Fix-It Plan. Taylor, Jo, illus. 2016. (Sibling Split Ser.). (ENG.). 112p. (J). (gr. 3-6). lib. bdg. 25.32 (978-1-4965-2590-1(6), 130719, Stone Arch Bks.) Capstone.

—The Impossible Wish. Taylor, Jo, illus. 2016. (Sibling Split Ser.). (ENG.). 112p. (J). (gr. 3-6). lib. bdg. 25.32 (978-1-4965-2593-2(0), 130722, Stone Arch Bks.) Capstone.

—Party of Nine. Taylor, Jo, illus. 2016. (Sibling Split Ser.). (ENG.). 112p. (J). (gr. 3-6). lib. bdg. 25.32 (978-1-4965-2592-5(2), 130721, Stone Arch Bks.) Capstone.

—Sibling Split, 4 vols. Taylor, Jo, illus. 2016. (Sibling Split Ser.). (ENG.). 112p. (J). (gr. 3-6). 106.60 (978-1-4965-2721-9(6), 24301, Stone Arch Bks.) Capstone.

—Trouble in the City. Taylor, Jo, illus. 2016. (Sibling Split Ser.). (ENG.). 112p. (J). (gr. 3-6). lib. bdg. 25.32 (978-1-4965-2591-8(4), 130720, Stone Arch Bks.) Capstone.

Higgins, Tiffany A. We've Seen Sant. Higgins, Clark L., illus. 2011. 26p. pap. 12.27 (978-1-61204-267-1(8), Eloquent Bks.) Strategic Book Publishing & Rights Agency (SBPRA).

Higginson, Sheila Sweeny. You're Getting a Baby Brother! Williams, Sam, illus. 2012. (ENG.). 24p. (J). (gr. -1-k). bds. 8.99 (978-1-4424-2021-2(9), Little Simon) Little Simon.

—You're Getting a Baby Sister! Williams, Sam, illus. 2012. (ENG.). 24p. (J). (gr. -1-k). bds. 8.99 (978-1-4424-2050-2(2), Little Simon) Little Simon.

Hill, C. J. Echo in Time. 2014. 387p. (YA). (978-0-06-212395-4(5)) HarperCollins Pubs.

Hill, Genita. My Very Special Brother. McCall, William L., illus. 2007. 40p. per. 24.95 (978-1-4241-8852-9(0)) America Star Bks.

Hill, Janet Muirhead. Kendall & Kyleah. Leonhard, Herb, illus. 2012. (J). pap. 14.00 (978-1-937849-05-4(8)) Raven Publishing Inc. of Montana.

Hill, Michelle M. Stanley. 2012. 12p. pap. 15.99 (978-1-4772-2923-1(X)) AuthorHouse.

Hill, Susanna Leonard. Not yet, Rose. Rutten, Nicole, illus. 2009. (ENG.). 34p. (J). (gr. -1-3). 16.50 (978-0-8028-5326-4(9), Eerdmans Bks For Young Readers) Eerdmans, William B. Publishing Co.

Hilton, Marilyn. Found Things. (ENG.). 240p. (J). (gr. 4-7). 2015. pap. 7.99 (978-1-4424-6088-1(1)) 2014. 16.99 (978-1-4424-6087-4(3)) Simon & Schuster Children's Publishing.

Hilton, N. E. The Spell. 2010. (Illus.). 216p. pap. 15.95 (978-1-4452-7791-2(3)) Lulu Pr., Inc.

Hilton, Nette. Sprite Downberry. 2008. (ENG.). 288p. (978-0-7322-8548-7(8)) HarperCollins Pubs. Australia.

Hinton, S. E. Rumble Fish. 2006. 21.50 (978-0-8446-7283-0(1)) Smith, Peter Pub., Inc.

—Rumble Fish. 2013. lib. bdg. 18.40 (978-0-606-35120-1(5)) Turtleback.

Hinton, Susan E. & E Hinton, Susan. La Ley de la Calle. 2015. (ENG & SPA., Illus.). 128p. (YA). pap. 13.95 (978-607-01-2325-2(5), Alfaguara) Santillana USA Publishing Co., Inc.

Hirsch, Andy. Varmints. 2016. (J). lib. bdg. 29.40 (978-0-606-39563-2(6)) Turtleback.

Hirsch, Jeff. The Darkest Path. 2013. (YA). pap. (978-0-545-51224-4(7), Scholastic Pr.) Scholastic, Inc.

Hirst, Daisy. I Do Not Like Books Anymore! Hirst, Daisy, illus. 2018. (ENG., Illus.). 40p. (J). (gr. -1-2). 17.99 (978-1-5362-0334-9(3)) Candlewick Pr.

Hoare, Pauline M. My Naughty Brother, David: And Other Stories. 2010. (Illus.). 124p. pap. 33.49 (978-1-4490-9696-0(4)) AuthorHouse.

Hoban, Russell. Best Friends for Frances. Hoban, Lillian, illus. 2009. (I Can Read Level 2 Ser.). (ENG.). 48p. (J). (gr. k-3). pap. 4.99 (978-0-06-083803-4(5), HarperCollins) HarperCollins Pubs.

—Harvey's Hideout. Hoban, Lillian, illus. 2018. (ENG.). 42p. (J). (gr. -1-3). 16.00 (978-0-87486-138-9(1)) Plough Publishing Hse.

—The Sorely Trying Day. Hoban, Lillian, illus. 2010. (ENG.). 48p. (J). (gr. -1-3). 14.95 (978-1-59017-343-5(0), NYR Children's Collection) New York Review of Bks., Inc., The.

Hobbs, Will. Jackie's Wild Seattle. (ENG.). 208p. (J). (gr. 5-18). 2004. pap. 6.99 (978-0-380-73311-8(0)) 2003. 19.99 (978-0-688-17474-3(4)) HarperCollins Pubs. (HarperCollins).

Hoberman, Mary Ann. The Seven Silly Eaters. Frazee, Marla, illus. 2004. (J). (gr. k-3). spiral bd. (978-0-616-14576-0(4)) Canadian National Institute for the Blind/Institut National Canadien pour les Aveugles.

Hodge, A. D. Bubbles & Boundaries. 2013. 32p. (978-1-4602-2858-6(8)) FriesenPress.

Hoena, Blake. Boy under the Bed. Bardin, Dave, illus. 2018. (Monster Heroes Ser.). (ENG.). 32p. (J). (gr. k-2). lib. bdg. 21.32 (978-1-4965-6414-6(6), 138261, Stone Arch Bks.) Capstone.

Holeman, Linda. Search of the Moon King's Daughter. 2003. 320p. (J). (gr. 5). pap. 10.95 (978-0-88776-609-1(9), Tundra Bks.) Tundra Bks. CAN. Dist: Penguin Random Hse. LLC.

Holland, Amy L. The Adventures of Bubba & Sis: Book One. 2009. 16p. pap. 8.49 (978-1-4389-5941-2(9)) AuthorHouse.

Holm, Jennifer L. Our Only May Amelia. 2019. (ENG., Illus.). 272p. (J). (gr. 3-7). pap. 9.99 (978-0-06-288177-9(9), HarperCollins) HarperCollins Pubs.

—Our Only May Amelia. unabr. ed. 2004. 253p. (J). (gr. 5-9). pap. 36.00 incl. audio (978-0-8072-8366-0(5), YA191SP, Listening Library) Random Hse. Audio Publishing Group.

—Swing It, Sunny: a Graphic Novel (Sunny #2) Holm, Matthew, illus. 2017. (Sunny Ser.: 2). (ENG.). 224p. (J). (gr. 3-7). 24.99 (978-0-545-74170-5(X)); pap. 12.99 (978-0-545-74172-9(6)) Scholastic, Inc. (Graphix).

—The Trouble with May Amelia. Gustavson, Adam, illus. (ENG.). 224p. (J). (gr. 3-7). 2012. pap. 5.99 (978-1-4169-1374-0(2))2. 2011. 17.99 (978-1-4169-1373-3(4)) Simon & Schuster Children's Publishing. (Atheneum Bks. for Young Readers).

Holman, T. A. Stop It, Tyrone! (Illus.). 42p. (J). (gr. k-4). pap. 7.50 (978-0-9660617-1-0(3)) PLEO.

Holub, Joan. Bed, Bats, & Beyond. Gallagher-Cole, Mernie, illus. 2010. (Darby Creek Exceptional Titles Ser.). (ENG.). 64p. (J). (gr. 1-3). pap. 6.95 (978-0-7613-6451-1(X)) Lerner Publishing Group.

Holub, Joan & Williams, Suzanne. Artemis the Loyal. 2013. (Goddess Girls Ser.: 7). (ENG., Illus.). 288p. (J). (gr. 3-7). 16.99 (978-1-4424-8594-5(9), Aladdin) Simon & Schuster Children's Publishing.

Hood, Ann. Crazy Horse: Brave Warrior, 5. Altmann, Scott, illus. 2013. (Treasure Chest: the Time-Traveling Adventures of the Robbins Twins Ser.: 5). (ENG.). 192p. (J). (gr. 4-6). 18.69 (978-0-448-45738-3(5)) Penguin Young Readers Group.

—Prince of Air, 4. Altmann, Scott & Zilber, Denis, illus. 2012. (Treasure Chest: the Time-Traveling Adventures of the Robbins Twins Ser.: 4). 208p. (J). (gr. 4-6). 21.19 (978-0-448-45474-0(2)) Penguin Young Readers Group.

Hooks, William H. Mr. Big Brother. Duke, Kate, illus. 2015. (ENG.). 34p. (J). pap. 11.95 (978-1-899694-58-7(7), ipicturebooks) ibooks, Inc.

Hope, Laura. Bunny Brown & His Sister Sue Giving A. 2006. pap. 14.95 (978-1-55742-655-0(4)) Wildside Pr., LLC.

Hope, Laura Lee. Bunny Brown & His Sister Sue. 2005. 188p. pap. 11.95 (978-1-4218-1165-9(0), 1st World Library - Literary Society) 1st World Publishing, Inc.

—Bunny Brown & his Sister Sue. 2005. 26.95 (978-1-4218-1065-2(4), 1st World Library - Literary Society) 1st World Publishing, Inc.

—Bunny Brown & his Sister Sue. 2007. (ENG.). 144p. pap. 18.99 (978-1-4264-1980-5(5)) Creative Media Partners, LLC.

—Bunny Brown & His Sister Sue. l.t. ed. 2007. (ENG.). 138p. pap. 19.99 (978-1-4264-2091-7(9)) Creative Media Partners, LLC.

—Bunny Brown & His Sister Sue & Their Shetland Pony. 2007. 204p. 27.95 (978-1-4218-3282-1(8)); per. 12.95 (978-1-4218-3382-8(4)) 1st World Publishing, Inc. (1st World Library - Literary Society).

S

—Bunny Brown & His Sister Sue at Aunt Lu's City Home. 2007. 184p. 25.96 *(978-1-4218-3886-1(9)*, 1st World Library - Literary Society) 1st World Publishing, Inc.
—Bunny Brown & His Sister Sue at Camp R. 2006. 26.95 *(978-1-4218-2972-2(X))*; pap. 11.95 *(978-1-4218-3072-8(8))* 1st World Publishing, Inc.
—Bunny Brown & His Sister Sue at Christmas Tree Cove. 2007. 176p. 27.95 *(978-1-4218-3887-8(7)*, 1st World Library - Literary Society) 1st World Publishing, Inc.
—Bunny Brown & His Sister Sue Giving A. 2006. 26.95 *(978-1-4218-2973-9(8))*; pap. 11.95 *(978-1-4218-3073-5(6))* 1st World Publishing, Inc.
—Bunny Brown & His Sister Sue in the Bi. 2006. 26.95 *(978-1-4218-2974-6(6))*; pap. 11.95 *(978-1-4218-3074-2(4))* 1st World Publishing, Inc.
—Bunny Brown & His Sister Sue Keeping S. 2006. 26.95 *(978-1-4218-2975-3(4))*; pap. 11.95 *(978-1-4218-3075-9(2))* 1st World Publishing, Inc.
—Bunny Brown & His Sister Sue on an Aut. 2006. 26.95 *(978-1-4218-2976-0(2))*; pap. 11.95 *(978-1-4218-3076-6(0))* 1st World Publishing, Inc.
—Bunny Brown & His Sister Sue on Grandpa's Farm. 2007. 192p. 26.95 *(978-1-4218-3283-8(6))*; per. 11.95 *(978-1-4218-3383-5(2))* 1st World Publishing, Inc. (1st World Library - Literary Society).
—Bunny Brown & His Sister Sue Playing C. 2006. 26.95 *(978-1-4218-2977-7(0))*; pap. 11.95 *(978-1-4218-3077-3(9))* 1st World Publishing, Inc.
—Freddie & Flossie. Pyle, Chuck, illus. 2005. (Bobbsey Twins Ser.). (ENG.). 32p. (J). (gr. -1-k). pap. 3.99 *(978-1-4169-0270-6(8)*, Simon Spotlight) Simon Spotlight.
—Freddie & Flossie. Pyle, Chuck, illus. 2006. (Bobbsey Twins Ser.). 32p. (J). (gr. -1-2). 22.78 *(978-1-59961-095-5(7))* Spotlight.
—Freddie & Flossie & Snap: Ready-To-Read Pre-Level 1. Pyle, Chuck, illus. 2005. (Bobbsey Twins Ser.). (ENG.). 32p. (J). (gr. -1-k). pap. 13.99 *(978-1-4169-0267-6(8)*, Simon Spotlight) Simon Spotlight.
—Freddie & Flossie & the Easter Egg Hunt. Downer, Maggie, illus. 2006. (Ready-To-Read Pre-Level 1 Ser.). (ENG.). 32p. (J). (gr. -1-1). 16.19 *(978-1-4169-1029-9(8))* Simon & Schuster, Inc.
—Freddie & Flossie & the Train Ride: Ready-To-Read Pre-Level 1. Pyle, Chuck, illus. 2005. (Bobbsey Twins Ser.). (ENG.). 32p. (J). (gr. -1-k). pap. 13.99 *(978-1-4169-0269-0(4)*, Simon Spotlight) Simon Spotlight.
—Freddie & Flossie at the Beach: Ready-To-Read Pre-Level 1. Pyle, Chuck, illus. 2005. (Bobbsey Twins Ser.). (ENG.). 32p. (J). (gr. -1-k). pap. 13.99 *(978-1-4169-0268-3(6)*, Simon Spotlight) Simon Spotlight.
—Six Little Bunkers at Cowboy Jack's. 2007. 180p. 25.96 *(978-1-4218-3888-5(5)*, 1st World Library - Literary Society) 1st World Publishing, Inc.
—Six Little Bunkers at Grandma Bell's. 2005. 26.95 *(978-1-4218-1066-9(2))*; 188p. pap. 11.95 *(978-1-4218-1166-6(9))* 1st World Publishing, Inc. (1st World Library - Literary Society).
—Six Little Bunkers at Grandpa Ford's. 2007. 188p. 25.96 *(978-1-4218-3889-2(3)*, 1st World Library - Literary Society) 1st World Publishing, Inc.
Hope, Lee Laura. Bunny Brown & His Sister Sue & Their Shetland Pony. 2007. 172p. 41.99 *(978-1-4280-7508-5(9))*; per. 35.99 *(978-1-4280-7514-6(3))* IndyPublish.com.
—Six Little Bunkers at Aunt Jo's. 2007. (ENG.). 144p. pap. 18.99 *(978-1-4346-3234-0(2))* Creative Media Partners, LLC.
—Six Little Bunkers at Aunt Jo's. 2007. 164p. 95.99 *(978-1-4280-7622-8(0))*; per. 89.99 *(978-1-4280-7620-4(4))* IndyPublish.com.
Hopkins, Ellen. Fallout. (Crank Trilogy Ser.). (ENG., (YA). (gr. 9). 2013. Illus.). 720p. pap. 14.99 *(978-1-4424-7180-1(8))* 2010. 672p. 18.99 *(978-1-4169-5009-7(5))* McElderry, Margaret K. Bks. (McElderry, Margaret K. Bks.).
Hopkinson, Nalo. The Chaos. (ENG., 256p. (YA). (gr. 9). 2013. Illus.). pap. 11.99 *(978-1-4424-5926-7(3))* 2012. 16.99 *(978-1-4169-5488-0(0))* McElderry, Margaret K. Bks. (McElderry, Margaret K. Bks.).
Horowitz, Anthony. South by Southeast. 2005. (Diamond Brothers Ser.). (ENG.). 160p. (J). (gr. 3-7). 6.99 *(978-0-14-240374-7(1)*, Puffin Books) Penguin Young Readers Group.
Horse, Harry. Little Rabbit's New Baby, 1 vol. 2016. (Little Rabbit Ser.). (ENG., Illus.). 32p. (J). (gr. -1-k). pap. 7.95 *(978-1-56145-915-5(1))* Peachtree Publishing Co. Inc.
—Little Rabbit's New Baby / Book & Doll Package. 2008. (Illus.). 32p. (J). (gr. k-1). pap. 22.90 *(978-1-56145-453-2(2))* Peachtree Publishing Co. Inc.
Horvath, Polly. My One Hundred Adventures. 2010. (My One Hundred Adventures Ser.: 1). (Illus.). 272p. (J). (gr. 3-7). 8.99 *(978-0-375-85526-9(2)*, Yearling) Random Hse. Children's Bks.
—The Trolls. 2008. (ENG.). 160p. (J). (gr. 4-7). pap. 14.99 *(978-0-312-38419-7(X)*, 900053320) Square Fish.
Howland, Ashley. The Homework Goblin. 2013. 24p. pap. 13.97 *(978-1-62516-301-1(0)*, Strategic Bk. Publishing) Strategic Book Publishing & Rights Agency (SBPRA).
Hughes, Alison. Hit the Ground Running, 1 vol. 2017. (ENG.). 216p. (YA). (gr. 8-12). pap. 14.95 *(978-1-4598-1544-5(0))* Orca Bk. Pubs. USA.
Hughes, Shirley. Alfie Gets in First. 2009. (Alfie Ser.). (Illus.). 32p. (J). (gr. -1-k). pap. 14.99 *(978-1-86230-783-4(0)*, Red Fox) Random House Children's Books GBR. Dist: Independent Pubs. Group.
—The Big Alfie & Annie Rose Storybook. Hughes, Shirley, illus. 2007. (Alfie Ser.). (Illus.). 64p. (J). (gr. -1-k). pap. 14.99 *(978-0-09-975030-7(9)*, Red Fox) Random House Children's Books GBR. Dist: Independent Pubs. Group.
Hulme-Cross, Benjamin. Grayfields. 2018. (Mission Alert Ser.). (ENG., Illus.). 72p. (J). (gr. 5-8). pap. 7.99 *(978-1-5415-2632-7(5)*, a52730cf-d72c-4750-9477-584023c33d5b, Darby Creek) Lerner Publishing Group.
—Island X. 2018. (Mission Alert Ser.). (ENG., Illus.). 72p. (J). (gr. 5-8). pap. 7.99 *(978-1-5415-2633-4(3)*, ac1afa40-f139-4730-918c-fb6bac75511b, Darby Creek) Lerner Publishing Group.
—Lab 101. 2018. (Mission Alert Ser.). (ENG., Illus.). 72p. (J). (gr. 5-8). pap. 7.99 *(978-1-5415-2634-1(1)*, e0aa8cce-4b5c-4c27-ab6d-9182c2e44a05); lib. bdg. 26.65 *(978-1-5415-2581-8(7)*, 8b70c8b2-a5c4-4888-8800-441922b9cd6b) Lerner Publishing Group. (Darby Creek).
—Viper Attack. 2018. (Mission Alert Ser.). (ENG., Illus.). 72p. (J). (gr. 5-8). pap. 7.99 *(978-1-5415-2635-8(X)*, 37ed1a29-87bb-4c86-8008-c787d7fb4c3f); lib. bdg. 26.65 *(978-1-5415-2582-5(5)*, 20dc948f-9702-402f-9a96-e489206343b6) Lerner Publishing Group. (Darby Creek).
Hulst, W. G. van de & Hulst, Willem G. van de, illus. The Basket. 2014. 48p. (J). *(978-1-928136-04-0(4))* Inheritance Pubns.
—Bruno the Bear. 2014. 48p. (J). *(978-1-928136-03-3(6))* Inheritance Pubns.
—Three Foolish Sisters. 2014. 48p. (J). *(978-1-928136-15-6(X))* Inheritance Pubns.
—Through the Thunderstorm. 2014. 48p. (J). *(978-1-928136-02-6(8))* Inheritance Pubns.
Hunt, Elizabeth Singer. Secret Agent Jack Stalwart: Book 6: the Pursuit of the Ivory Poachers: Kenya. 2008. (Secret Agent Jack Stalwart Ser.: 6). (ENG., Illus.). 144p. (J). (gr. 1-4). pap. 5.99 *(978-1-60286-021-6(1))* Hachette Bk. Group.
Hunter, Erin. Dark River. 2008. (Warriors: Power of Three Ser.: 2). (ENG.). 368p. (J). (gr. 3-7). pap. 6.99 *(978-0-06-089207-4(2))* HarperCollins Pubs.
—Eclipse. 2009. (Warriors: Power of Three Ser.: 4). (ENG., Illus.). 336p. (J). (gr. 3-7). pap. 7.99 *(978-0-06-089213-5(7))* HarperCollins Pubs.
—Long Shadows. 2009. (Warriors: Power of Three Ser.: 5). (ENG.). 352p. (J). (gr. 3-7). pap. 7.99 *(978-0-06-089216-6(1))* HarperCollins Pubs.
—Sunrise. 2010. (Warriors: Power of Three Ser.: 6). (ENG.). 368p. (J). (gr. 3-7). pap. 7.99 *(978-0-06-089219-7(6))* HarperCollins Pubs.
—Warriors: Power of Three #2: Dark River. 2007. (Warriors: Power of Three Ser.: 2). (ENG., Illus.). 352p. (J). (gr. 3-7). 16.99 *(978-0-06-089205-0(6)*, HarperCollins) HarperCollins Pubs.
—Warriors: Power of Three #3: Outcast. 2015. (Warriors: Power of Three Ser.: 3). (ENG.). 368p. (J). (gr. 3-7). pap. 9.99 *(978-0-06-236710-5(2)*, HarperCollins) HarperCollins Pubs.
—Warriors: Power of Three #4: Eclipse. 2015. (Warriors: Power of Three Ser.: 4). (ENG., Illus.). 368p. (J). (gr. 3-7). pap. 7.99 *(978-0-06-236711-2(0)*, HarperCollins) HarperCollins Pubs.
—Warriors: Power of Three #5: Long Shadows. 2008. (Warriors: Power of Three Ser.: 5). (ENG., Illus.). 336p. (J). (gr. 3-7). 16.99 *(978-0-06-089214-2(5)*, HarperCollins) HarperCollins Pubs.
—Warriors: Power of Three #1: the Sight. 2015. (Warriors: Power of Three Ser.: 1). (ENG.). 416p. (J). (gr. 3-7). pap. 7.99 *(978-0-06-236708-2(0)*, HarperCollins) HarperCollins Pubs.
—Warriors: Power of Three #2: Dark River. 2015. (Warriors: Power of Three Ser.: 2). (ENG.). 368p. (J). (gr. 3-7). pap. 9.99 *(978-0-06-236709-9(9)*, HarperCollins) HarperCollins Pubs.
—Warriors: Power of Three #3: Outcast. 2008. (Warriors: Power of Three Ser.: 3). (ENG., Illus.). 352p. (J). (gr. 3-7). 16.99 *(978-0-06-089208-1(0)*, HarperCollins) HarperCollins Pubs.
—Warriors: Power of Three #4: Eclipse. 2008. (Warriors: Power of Three Ser.: 4). (ENG., Illus.). 336p. (J). (gr. 3-7). 17.99 *(978-0-06-089211-1(0)*, HarperCollins) HarperCollins Pubs.
—Warriors: Power of Three #5: Long Shadows. 2015. (Warriors: Power of Three Ser.: 5). (ENG.). 368p. (J). (gr. 3-7). pap. 9.99 *(978-0-06-236712-9(9)*, HarperCollins) HarperCollins Pubs.
—Warriors: Power of Three #6: Sunrise. 6th ed. 2009. (Warriors: Power of Three Ser.: 6). (ENG., Illus.). 352p. (J). (gr. 3-7). 16.99 *(978-0-06-089217-3(X)*, HarperCollins) HarperCollins Pubs.
Hunter, R. C. Moon Kids. 2010. 64p. pap. 11.99 *(978-1-4490-7846-1(X))* AuthorHouse.
Hurst, Carol Otis. The Wrong One. 2003. (ENG.). 160p. (J). (gr. 5-7). tchr. ed. 15.00 *(978-0-618-27599-1(1)*, 588811, Clarion Bks.) HarperCollins Pubs.
Hurwitz, Johanna. Magical Monty. McGrory, Anik, illus. 2013. (Monty Ser.: 4). (ENG.). 112p. (J). (gr. k-4). pap. 5.99 *(978-0-7636-6457-2(X))* Candlewick Pr.
Hurwitz, Michele Weber. Ethan Marcus Makes His Mark. (ENG.). 272p. (J). (gr. 3-7). 2019. pap. 7.99 *(978-1-4814-8929-4(1))* 2018. (Illus.). 17.99 *(978-1-4814-8928-7(3))* Simon & Schuster Children's Publishing. (Aladdin).
—Ethan Marcus Stands Up. (ENG.). (J). (gr. 3-7). 2018. 288p. pap. 7.99 *(978-1-4814-8926-3(7))* 2017. (Illus.). 272p. 17.99 *(978-1-4814-8925-6(9))* Simon & Schuster Children's Publishing. (Aladdin).
Hutchins, Pat. Titch. 2014. 32p. pap. 7.00 *(978-1-61003-367-1(1))* Center for the Collaborative Classroom.
Huy, Barbara. Llamas Need Pajamas. 2012. 36p. pap. 15.49 *(978-1-4669-5752-7(2))* Trafford Publishing.
Hyde, Catherine Ryan. The Year of My Miraculous Reappearance. 2009. (ENG.). 240p. (YA). (gr. 7). pap. 10.99 *(978-0-375-83261-1(0)*, Knopf Bks. for Young Readers) Random Hse. Children's Bks.
Imfeld, Robert. Baylor's Guide to Dreadful Dreams. 2017. (ENG., Illus.). 320p. (J). (gr. 5-9). 16.99 *(978-1-4814-6639-4(9)*, Aladdin) Simon & Schuster Children's Publishing.
—A Guide to the Other Side. 2016. (Beyond Baylor Ser.: 1). (ENG., Illus.). 320p. (J). (gr. 5-9). 17.99 *(978-1-4814-6636-3(4)*, Aladdin) Simon & Schuster Children's Publishing.
Inches, Alison. Big Sister Dora! Aikins, Dave, illus. 2005. (Dora the Explorer Ser.: 13). 32p. (J). lib. bdg. 15.00 *(978-1-59054-790-8(X))* Fitzgerald Bks.
—Súper Bebés! Miller, Victoria, illus. 2006. (Dora la Exploradora Ser.). (SPA.). 24p. (J). (gr. -1-3). pap. 3.99 *(978-1-4169-2461-6(2)*, Libros Para Ninos) Libros Para Ninos.
Ingram, Fiona. The Secret of the Sacred Scarab. 2008. 272p. (gr. -1 — 1). 27.95 *(978-0-595-71977-8(5))*; pap. 17.95 *(978-0-595-45716-8(9))* iUniverse, Inc.
Interiano, Jeffrey. Critters of Forest City. 2006. pap. 10.00 *(978-1-4257-1721-6(7))* Xlibris Corp.
Iserles, Inbali, illus. The Taken. 2015. 252p. (J). pap. *(978-0-545-91869-5(3)*, Scholastic Pr.) Scholastic, Inc.
Island of Legends. 2014. (Unwanteds Ser.: 4). (ENG., Illus.). 496p. (J). (gr. 3-7). 19.99 *(978-1-4424-9328-5(3)*, Aladdin) Simon & Schuster Children's Publishing.
Jack, Keats Ezra. Peter's Chair. 2014. (ENG.). 40p. (J). (gr. k-k). 11.24 *(978-1-63245-276-4(6))* Lectorum Pubns., Inc.
Jacobson, Jennifer Richard. Paper Things. 2015. (ENG.). 384p. (J). (gr. 5). 17.99 *(978-0-7636-6323-0(9))* Candlewick Pr.
—Paper Things. 2017. (ENG.). (J). (gr. 5). lib. bdg. 19.65 *(978-0-606-39841-1(4))* Turtleback.
Jacques, Karen. Monsters Have My Brother. Cahanes, Erin, illus. 2015. (ENG.). (J). 16.95 *(978-1-59298-863-1(6))* Beaver's Pond Pr., Inc.
Jakubowski, Michele. The Grass Is Always Greener. Fekete, Hédi, illus. 2017. (Ashley Small & Ashlee Tall Ser.). (ENG.). 64p. (J). (gr. 1-3). pap. 4.95 *(978-1-5158-0016-3(4)*, Picture Window Bks.) Capstone.
—The Professor's Discovery. Pinelli, Amerigo, illus. 2016. (Sleuths of Somerville Ser.). (ENG.). 144p. (J). (gr. 4-6). lib. bdg. 25.99 *(978-1-4965-3177-3(9)*, 132216, Stone Arch Bks.) Capstone.
—The Professor's Discovery. Pinelli, Amerigo, illus. 2017. (Sleuths of Somerville Ser.). (ENG.). 144p. (J). (gr. 4-6). pap. 6.95 *(978-1-4965-3181-0(7)*, Stone Arch Bks.) Capstone.
—Tour of Trouble. Pinelli, Amerigo, illus. 2016. (Sleuths of Somerville Ser.). (ENG.). 144p. (J). (gr. 4-6). lib. bdg. 25.99 *(978-1-4965-3176-6(0)*, 132215, Stone Arch Bks.) Capstone.
—Tour of Trouble. Pinelli, Amerigo, illus. 2017. (Sleuths of Somerville Ser.). (ENG.). 144p. (J). (gr. 4-6). pap. 6.95 *(978-1-4965-3180-3(9)*, Stone Arch Bks.) Capstone.
Jamal L. O'Ettelle. Jayden & the Return of the Jalon Warriors. 2010. 120p. pap. 10.95 *(978-1-4502-0288-6(8))* iUniverse, Inc.
James, Brian. The Heights. 2009. (ENG.). 272p. (YA). (gr. 7-12). 22.44 *(978-0-312-60736-4(9))* Square Fish.
James, Richard E., III. Adventures of the Elements Vol. 3: Dangerous Games. Lyle, Maryann, ed. Welch, Chad, illus. 2004. 169p. (YA). (gr. 3-12). pap. 5.95 *(978-0-9675901-2-7(4))* Alchemy Creative, Inc.
Jamieson, Victoria & Mohamed, Omar. When Stars Are Scattered. Jamieson, Victoria & Geddy, Iman, illus. 2020. (ENG.). 264p. (J). (gr. 4-7). 22.99 *(978-0-525-55391-5(6))*; pap. 13.99 *(978-0-525-55390-8(8))* Penguin Young Readers Group. (Dial Bks).
Jane, Pamela. Milo & the Flapjack Fiasco! Johnson, Meredith, ed. Johnson, Meredith, tr. 2004. (Illus.). 32p. (J). 13.95 *(978-1-59336-113-6(0))*; pap. *(978-1-59336-114-3(9))* Mondo Publishing.
Janow, Jody. Eddie's Great Escape. 2010. 44p. pap. 19.99 *(978-1-4520-1764-8(6))* AuthorHouse.
Jantha, A. W. Hocus Pocus & the AllNew Sequel. 2018. (ENG., Illus.). 528p. (YA). (gr. 9-12). 12.99 *(978-1-368-02003-9(8)*, Disney-Hyperion) Disney Publishing Worldwide.
Jaramillo, Ann. La Linea: A Novel. 2008. (ENG.). 144p. (J). (gr. 5-9). pap. 8.99 *(978-0-312-37354-2(6)*, 900045403) Square Fish.
Jarrell, Robert. Sunday Afternoon Walk. 2012. 36p. pap. 24.95 *(978-1-4626-6620-1(5))* America Star Bks.
Javier's Sister - A Family's Struggle with Drug Addiction: One Day the Sun Will Shine Again Series. 2005. (J). pap. 16.95 *(978-0-9768827-8-7(7))* Prevention Through Puppetry, Inc.
Jeanmarie, Michele. Curiosity, Curiosity: Lost in an Array. 2008. 74p. pap. 19.95 *(978-1-60610-169-8(2))* America Star Bks.
Jenkins, Amanda. Mutant Bugs. 2005. (J). pap. *(978-1-4108-4219-0(3))* Benchmark Education Co.
Jenkins, Amanda & Benchmark Education Co., LLC. The Secret Life of Wally Smithers. Fagan, Martin, illus. 2014. (Text Connections Ser.). (J). (gr. 3). *(978-1-4509-9656-3(6))* Benchmark Education Co.
Jenkins, Emily. Lemonade in Winter: A Book about Two Kids Counting Money. Karas, G. Brian, illus. 2012. 40p. (J). (gr. -1-2). 18.99 *(978-0-375-85883-3(0)*, Schwartz & Wade Bks.) Random Hse. Children's Bks.
Jennings, Rashad. Arcade & the Golden Travel Guide, 1 vol. 2019. (Coin Slot Chronicles Ser.: 2). (ENG., Illus.). 240p. (J). 16.99 *(978-0-310-76743-5(1))* Zonderkidz.
Jennings, Sharon. The Bye-Bye Pie. 2004. (Illus.). (J). (gr. k-3). spiral bd. *(978-0-616-01684-8(0))* Canadian National Institute for the Blind/Institut National Canadien pour les Aveugles.
Jensen, Cordelia & Morrison, Laurie. Every Shiny Thing. (ENG.). (gr. 5-9). 2019. 384p. (YA). pap. 9.99 *(978-1-4197-3377-2(X)*, 1193803) 2018. 368p. (J). 16.99 *(978-1-4197-2864-8(4)*, 1193801) Abrams, Inc. (Amulet Bks.).
Jessell, Tim, illus. The Boardwalk Mystery. 2013. (Boxcar Children Mysteries Ser.: 131). (ENG.). 144p. (J). (gr. 2-5). pap. 6.99 *(978-0-8075-0803-9(9)*, 807508039);131. 15.99 *(978-0-8075-0802-2(0)*, 807508020) Random Hse. Children's Bks. (Random Hse. Bks. for Young Readers).
—The Boxcar Children Deluxe Hardcover Boxed Gift Set (#1-3). Set. 2013. (Boxcar Children Mysteries Ser.). (ENG.). 538p. (J). (gr. 2-5). lib. bdg., lib. bdg., lib. bdg. 45.00 *(978-0-8075-0864-0(0)*, 807508640, Random Hse. Bks. for Young Readers) Random Hse. Children's Bks.
—The Garden Thief. 2012. (Boxcar Children Mysteries Ser.: 130). (ENG.). 128p. (J). (gr. 2-5). 5.99 *(978-0-8075-2752-8(1)*, 807527521); 15.99 *(978-0-8075-2751-1(3)*, 807527513) Random Hse. Children's Bks. (Random Hse. Bks. for Young Readers).
—Mystery of the Fallen Treasure. 2013. (Boxcar Children Mysteries Ser.: 132). (ENG.). 128p. (J). (gr. 2-5). 15.99 *(978-0-8075-5508-8(8)*, 807555088); 5.99 *(978-0-8075-5506-4(1)*, 807555061) Random Hse. Children's Bks. (Random Hse. Bks. for Young Readers).
—The Mystery of the Stolen Snowboard. 2014. (Boxcar Children Mysteries Ser.: 134). (ENG.). 128p. (J). (gr. 2-5). 15.99 *(978-0-8075-8728-7(1)*, 807587281, Random Hse. Bks. for Young Readers) Random Hse. Children's Bks.
—The Mystery of the Wild West Bandit. 2014. (Boxcar Children Mysteries Ser.: 135). (ENG.). 128p. (J). (gr. 2-5). 15.99 *(978-0-8075-8725-6(7)*, 807587257, Random Hse. Bks. for Young Readers) Random Hse. Children's Bks.
—The Return of the Graveyard Ghost. 2013. (Boxcar Children Mysteries Ser.: 133). (ENG.). 128p. (J). (gr. 2-5). 5.99 *(978-0-8075-6936-8(4)*, 807569364); 15.99 *(978-0-8075-6935-1(6)*, 807569356) Random Hse. Children's Bks. (Random Hse. Bks. for Young Readers).
Jette, Sarah Marie. What the Wind Can Tell You, 1 vol. 2018. (ENG.). 200p. (J). pap. 14.95 *(978-1-944762-41-4(8)*, fc663e39-efc7-4487-a1c0-96325ef48495) Islandport Pr., Inc.
Johnson, Angela. Looking for Red. 2003. (ENG., Illus.). 128p. (YA). (gr. 7). pap. 7.99 *(978-0-689-86388-2(8)*, Simon Pulse) Simon Pulse.
Johnson, C. Homecoming. 2007. (Illus.). 64p. per. 10.00 *(978-1-4251-1358-2(3))* Trafford Publishing.
Johnson, Mo. Noah's Garden: When Someone You Love Is in the Hospital. Josse, Annabelle, illus. 2010. (ENG.). 32p. (J). (gr. -1-2). 15.99 *(978-0-7636-4782-7(9))* Candlewick Pr.
Johnson, Sandi. White Wolf at Dawn. Johnson, Britt, ed. Sturgen, Bobbi, illus. 2014. (ENG.). 30p. (J). (gr. k-5). pap. 12.99 *(978-1-929063-72-7(5)*, 171) Moons & Stars Publishing For Children.
Johnson, Terry Lynn. Avalanche! Orban, Jani, illus. 2018. (Survivor Diaries). (ENG.). 112p. (J). (gr. 1-5). pap. 6.99 *(978-1-328-51906-1(6)*, 1720632); 9.99 *(978-0-544-97039-7(X)*, 1662544) HarperCollins Pubs. (Clarion Bks.).
Johnson, William C. Little Tree. 2007. pap. 9.00 *(978-0-8059-8486-6(0))* Dorrance Publishing Co., Inc.
Johnston, James D. The Adventures of Lucas & Celi: Lucas Stows Away. 2009. 32p. pap. 12.99 *(978-1-4343-6372-5(4))* AuthorHouse.
Johnston, Tony. That Summer. Moser, Barry, illus. 2007. (ENG.). 32p. (J). (gr. 1-4). pap. 6.00 *(978-0-15-205856-2(7)*, 1197587, Clarion Bks.) HarperCollins Pubs.
Jonell, Lynne. Grasshopper Magic. Dorman, Brandon, illus. 2014. (Magical Mix-Ups Ser.: 3). (ENG.). 112p. (J). (gr. 1-4). pap. 4.99 *(978-0-307-93123-8(4)*, Random Hse. Bks. for Young Readers) Random Hse. Children's Bks.
Jones, C. B. Gone to the Buzzards. Green, Chris, illus. 2017. (Bog Hollow Boys Ser.). (ENG.). 72p. (J). (gr. 4-8). lib. bdg. 25.32 *(978-1-4965-4058-4(1)*, 133366, Stone Arch Bks.) Capstone.
Jones, Callie Carol Rodgers. Sweet Potato Pie. 2012. 20p. pap. 17.99 *(978-1-4685-6114-2(6))* AuthorHouse.
Jones, Chris. Cameron Jack & the Key to the Universe. 2010. (Illus.). 136p. pap. 10.99 *(978-1-4490-6547-8(3))* AuthorHouse.
Jones, Destry. What We Like. 2008. 16p. pap. 24.95 *(978-1-60474-364-7(6))* America Star Bks.
Jones, Erin. Tinfoil Crowns. 2019. (ENG.). 352p. (YA). (gr. 9-12). pap. 14.99 *(978-1-63583-032-3(X)*, 163583032X, Flux) North Star Editions.
Jones, Jen. Willow's Boy-Crazy Birthday. Franco, Paula, illus. 2014. (Sleepover Girls Ser.). (ENG.). 128p. (J). (gr. 3-5). lib. bdg. 22.65 *(978-1-4342-9757-0(8)*, 127105, Stone Arch Bks.) Capstone.
Jones, Kelly. Mama. Kewley, Ken, illus. 2004. 32p. (J). *(978-0-9745930-0-5(1))* Stunt Publishing.
Jones, Lisa A. The Black Dog. 2008. 20p. pap. 24.95 *(978-1-60474-960-1(1))* America Star Bks.
Jones, Michael. Finding Imagine Nation. 2007. (YA). per. 10.95 *(978-0-9789386-4-2(X))* Lucy Rose Publishing LLC.
Jones, Patrick. Taking Sides. 2015. (Locked Out Ser.). (ENG.). 104p. (YA). (gr. 6-12). lib. bdg. 27.99 *(978-1-4677-5800-0(0)*, 666c07ab-a572-44f0-a456-5017c9fe1267, Darby Creek) Lerner Publishing Group.
—Taking Sides. 2015. (Locked Out Ser.). (ENG.). 104p. (J). (gr. 6-12). E-Book 6.99 *(978-1-4677-7703-2(X)*, 9781467777032, Darby Creek) Lerner Publishing Group.
Jonsberg, Barry. Game Theory. 2017. (ENG.). 320p. (YA). (gr. 9). 13.99 *(978-1-76029-015-3(7))* Allen & Unwin AUS. Dist: Independent Pubs. Group.
Joosse, Barbara. I Love You the Purplest (Love Board Book, Sibling Book for Kids, Family Board Book) Whyte, Mary, illus. 2019. (ENG.). 24p. (J). (gr. -1 — 1). bds. 9.99 *(978-1-4521-7771-7(6))* Chronicle Bks. LLC.
Jordan, Brian. I Told You I Can Play! 2008. (Illus.). 32p. 6.95 *(978-1-60349-001-6(9)*, Marimba Bks.) Just Us Bks., Inc.
Jordan, Mark. Courage the Monkey. 2006. (Illus.). 40p. (J). 13.95 *(978-0-9717013-7-3(7))* Decere Publishing.
Joseph, Lynn. The Color of My Words. 2019. (ENG.). 160p. (J). (gr. 3-7). pap. 9.99 *(978-0-06-447204-3(3)*, HarperCollins) HarperCollins Pubs.
—Flowers in the Sky. 2013. (ENG.). 240p. (YA). (gr. 8). 17.99 *(978-0-06-029794-7(8)*, HarperTeen) HarperCollins Pubs.
Jougla, Frederic. Tricked on Halloween: Rina & Jax's Stories. Jougla, Karina, illus. l.t. ed. 2004. 36p. (J). bds. 14.99 *(978-0-9754287-0-2(5))* Imagery Pr.
Joyce, William. Rolie Polie Olie. Joyce, William, illus. 2017. (World of William Joyce Ser.). (ENG., Illus.). 48p. (J). (gr. -1-2). 17.99 *(978-1-4814-8957-7(7)*, Atheneum Bks. for Young Readers) Simon & Schuster Children's Publishing.
Judge, Chris. Tin. Judge, Chris, illus. 2014. (ENG., Illus.). 32p. (J). (gr. -1-3). 16.95 *(978-1-4677-5013-4(1)*, 7d268de1-6d20-40f4-aa73-6304cbae3041) Lerner Publishing Group.
Judge, Lita. Hoot & Peep. 2016. (Hoot & Peep Ser.). (ENG., Illus.). 40p. (J). (-k). 17.99 *(978-0-525-42837-4(2)*, Dial Bks) Penguin Young Readers Group.
Julie Shelton. World of Vampires Part 1: The Huntress. 2006. 49p. pap. 10.00 *(978-1-59926-998-6(8))* Xlibris Corp.
Kaaberbøl, Lene. Heartbreak Island. 2005. (W. I. T. C. H. Adventures Ser.: Bk. 3). (Illus.). 105p. (J). lib. bdg. 11.00 *(978-1-4242-0786-2(X))* Fitzgerald Bks.
Kaaberbol, Lene. The Serpent Gift. 3rd ed. 2007. (Shamer Chronicles Ser.: 3). Orig. Title: Slangens Gave. (ENG.). 384p. (J). (gr. 5-9). pap. 23.99 *(978-0-8050-8655-3(2)*, 900045311, Holt, Henry & Co. Bks. For Young Readers) Holt, Henry & Co.

Kadohata, Cynthia. Saucy. Raskin, Marianna, illus. (ENG.). (J). (gr. 3-7). 2021. 320p. pap. 8.99 *(978-1-4424-1279-8(8))* 2020. 304p. 17.99 *(978-1-4424-1278-1(X),* Atheneum/Caitlyn Dlouhy Books) Simon & Schuster Children's Publishing.
—The Thing about Luck. Kuo, Julia, illus. (ENG.). (J). (gr. 5-9). 2014. 304p. pap. 8.99 *(978-1-4424-7465-9(3),* Atheneum Bks. for Young Readers) 2013. 288p. 16.99 *(978-1-4169-1882-0(5))* Simon & Schuster Children's Publishing.
—The Thing about Luck. 2014. lib. bdg. 18.40 *(978-0-606-35798-2(X))* Turtleback.
Kalman, Maira. Hey Willy, See the Pyramids. 2017. (Illus.). 48p. (J). (gr. k-3). 18.95 *(978-1-68137-168-9(5),* NYR Children's Collection) New York Review of Bks., Inc., The.
Kalz, Jill. I Hate to Read: Beile Pepper. 2004. (Illus.). 32p. (J). pap. 9.95 *(978-0-89812-521-4(9),* Creative Paperbacks) Creative Co., The.
Kann, Victoria. Aqualicious. Kann, Victoria, illus. 2015. (ENG., Illus.). 40p. (J). (gr. -1-3). 18.99 *(978-0-06-233016-1(0),* HarperCollins) HarperCollins Pubs.
—Goldilicious. Kann, Victoria, illus. 2009. (ENG., Illus.). 40p. (J). (gr. k-3). 19.99 *(978-0-06-124408-7(2));* lib. bdg. 18.89 *(978-0-06-124409-4(0))* HarperCollins Pubs. (HarperCollins).
—Silverlicious. Kann, Victoria, illus. 2011. (ENG., Illus.). 40p. (J). (gr. k-3). 17.99 *(978-0-06-178123-0(1));* lib. bdg. 18.89 *(978-0-06-178124-7(X))* HarperCollins Pubs. (HarperCollins).
Kaplan, Bruce Eric. Meaniehead. Kaplan, Bruce Eric, illus. 2014. (ENG., Illus.). 40p. (J). (gr. -1-3). 17.99 *(978-1-4424-8542-6(6),* Simon & Schuster Bks. For Young Readers) Simon & Schuster Bks. For Young Readers.
—Monsters Eat Whiny Children. Kaplan, Bruce Eric, illus. 2010. (ENG., Illus.). 40p. (J). (gr. -1-3). 18.99 *(978-1-4169-8689-8(8),* Simon & Schuster Bks. For Young Readers) Simon & Schuster Bks. For Young Readers.
Karr, Kathleen. The 7th Knot. 1 vol. 2003. (ENG., Illus.). 300p. (J). 15.95 *(978-0-7614-5135-8(8))* Marshall Cavendish Corp.
Katcher, Brian. The Improbable Theory of Ana & Zak. 2016. (ENG.). 352p. (YA). (gr. 8). pap. 9.99 *(978-0-06-227278-2(0),* Tegen, Katherine Bks) HarperCollins Pubs.
Katschke, Judy. Home at Last. Geddes, Serena, illus. 2018. (Marguerite Henry's Misty Inn Ser.: 8). (ENG.). 144p. (J). (gr. 2-5). 17.99 *(978-1-4814-6995-1(9));* pap. 6.99 *(978-1-4814-6994-4(0))* Simon & Schuster Children's Publishing. (Aladdin).
Katz, Karen. Best-Ever Big Brother. 2006. (Illus.). 14p. (J). (gr. -1-k). 7.99 *(978-0-448-43914-3(X),* Grosset & Dunlap) Penguin Young Readers Group.
Kaufman, Amie. Elementals: Ice Wolves. Szabo, Levente, illus. 2019. (Elementals Ser.: 1). (ENG.). 368p. (J). (gr. 3-7). pap. 7.99 *(978-0-06-245799-8(3),* HarperCollins) HarperCollins Pubs.
—Elementals: Scorch Dragons. (Elementals Ser.: 2). (ENG.). (J). (gr. 3-7). 2020. 384p. pap. 9.99 *(978-0-06-245802-5(7))* 2019. (Illus.). 368p. 16.99 *(978-0-06-245801-8(9))* HarperCollins Pubs. (HarperCollins).
Keane, Claire. Little Big Girl. 2016. (Illus.). 32p. (J). (-k). 17.99 *(978-0-8037-3912-3(5),* Dial Bks) Penguin Young Readers Group.
Kear, Nicole C. The Fix-It Friends: Eyes on the Prize. Dockray, Tracy, illus. 2018. (Fix-It Friends Ser.: 5). (ENG.). 160p. (J). pap. 7.99 *(978-1-250-08672-3(8),* 900157583) Imprint IND. Dist: Macmillan.
—The Fix-It Friends: Sticks & Stones. Dockray, Tracy, illus. 2017. (Fix-It Friends Ser.: 2). (ENG.). 144p. (J). pap. 7.99 *(978-1-250-08586-3(1),* 900157366) Imprint IND. Dist: Macmillan.
—The Fix-It Friends: the Show Must Go On. Dockray, Tracy, illus. 2017. (Fix-It Friends Ser.: 3). (ENG.). 160p. (J). pap. 7.99 *(978-1-250-08668-6(X),* 900157576) Imprint IND. Dist: Macmillan.
—The Fix-It Friends: Wish You Were Here. Dockray, Tracy, illus. 2017. (Fix-It Friends Ser.: 4). (ENG.). 160p. (J). pap. 7.99 *(978-1-250-08670-9(1),* 900157581) Imprint IND. Dist: Macmillan.
Keats Curtis, Jennifer. Baby Owl's Rescue, 1 vol. Jacques, Laura, illus. 2009. (ENG.). 32p. (J). (gr. -1-3). 16.95 *(978-1-934359-95-2(5),* 9781934359952) Arbordale Publishing.
Keats, Ezra Jack. Peter's Chair. 2015. 40p. pap. 7.00 *(978-1-61003-534-7(8))* Center for the Collaborative Classroom.
—Peter's Chair. (J). (gr. -1-3). pap. 12.95 incl. audio Weston Woods Studios, Inc.
—Peter's Chair Board Book. 2006. (Illus.). 32p. (J). (gr. -1 — 1). bds. 7.99 *(978-0-670-06190-7(5),* Viking Books for Young Readers) Penguin Young Readers Group.
Keeling, Annie E. Andrew Golding A Tale of the Great Plague. 2004. reprint ed. pap. 15.95 *(978-1-4191-0694-1(5));* pap. 1.99 *(978-1-4192-0694-8(X))* Kessinger Publishing, LLC.
Keene, Carolyn. Strangers on a Train. 2013. (Nancy Drew Diaries: 2). (ENG.). 208p. (J). (gr. 3-7). pap. 7.99 *(978-1-4169-9073-4(9),* Aladdin) Simon & Schuster Children's Publishing.
Kehret, Peg. Abduction! 2006. (ENG.). 224p. (J). (gr. 5-18). 8.99 *(978-0-14-240617-5(1),* Puffin Books) Penguin Young Readers Group.
—Abduction! 2007. 215p. (gr. 3-7). 17.00 *(978-0-7569-8282-9(0))* Perfection Learning Corp.
—Escaping the Giant Wave. 2004. (ENG., Illus.). 160p. (J). (gr. 3-7). pap. 7.99 *(978-0-689-85273-2(8),* Aladdin) Simon & Schuster Children's Publishing.
Kellerman, Faye & Kellerman, Aliza. Prism. 2009. 272p. (YA). (gr. 7-18). lib. bdg. 17.89 *(978-0-06-168722-8(7),* HarperTeen) HarperCollins Pubs.
Kelly, Erin Entrada. We Dream of Space: A Newbery Honor Award Winner. 2020. (ENG., Illus.). 400p. (J). (gr. 3-7). 16.99 *(978-0-06-274730-3(4),* Greenwillow Bks.) HarperCollins Pubs.
Kemler, Nancy. Dragon Box: The Key to Magic. 2005. 108p. pap. 19.95 *(978-1-4137-8445-9(3))* America Star Bks.
Kennedy Center, The. Teddy Roosevelt & the Treasure of Ursa Major. Hoyt, Ard, illus. 2011. (ENG.). 128p. (J). (gr. 2-5). pap. 7.99 *(978-1-4169-4860-5(0),* Simon & Schuster Bks. For Young Readers) Simon & Schuster Bks. For Young Readers.
Kennedy, Pamela. A Sister for Matthew. 2008. (ENG., Illus.). 32p. (J). (gr. -1-3). 8.95 *(978-0-8249-5527-4(7),* 1256104, Ideals Pubns.) Worthy Publishing.
Kennemore, Tim. Alice's Shooting Star. 2009. (Illus.). 100p. (J). (gr. 2-6). 12.00 *(978-0-8028-5337-0(4),* Eerdmans Bks For Young Readers) Eerdmans, William B. Publishing Co.
Kent, Jaden. Ella & Owen 1: the Cave of Aaaaah! Doom! Bodnaruk, Iryna, illus. 2017. (Ella & Owen Ser.: 1). (ENG.). 112p. (J). (gr. k-3). pap. 5.99 *(978-1-4998-0368-6(0))* Little Bee Books Inc.
—Ella & Owen 10: the Dragon Games! Bodnaruk, Iryna, illus. 2018. (Ella & Owen Ser.: 10). (ENG.). 112p. (J). (gr. k-3). 16.99 *(978-1-4998-0617-5(5));* pap. 5.99 *(978-1-4998-0616-8(7))* Little Bee Books Inc.
—Ella & Owen 2: Attack of the Stinky Fish Monster! Bodnaruk, Iryna, illus. 2017. (Ella & Owen Ser.: 2). (ENG.). 112p. (J). (gr. k-3). pap. 5.99 *(978-1-4998-0369-3(9))* Little Bee Books Inc.
—Ella & Owen 5: the Great Troll Quest. Bodnaruk, Iryna, illus. 2017. (Ella & Owen Ser.: 5). (ENG.). 112p. (J). (gr. k-3). 16.99 *(978-1-4998-0474-4(1));* pap. 5.99 *(978-1-4998-0473-7(3))* Little Bee Books Inc.
—Ella & Owen 6: Dragon Spies! Bodnaruk, Iryna, illus. 2017. (Ella & Owen Ser.: 6). (ENG.). 112p. (J). (gr. k-3). 16.99 *(978-1-4998-0476-8(8));* pap. 5.99 *(978-1-4998-0475-1(X))* Little Bee Books Inc.
—Ella & Owen 7: Twin Trouble. Bodnaruk, Iryna, illus. 2018. (Ella & Owen Ser.: 7). (ENG.). 112p. (J). (gr. k-3). 16.99 *(978-1-4998-0611-3(6));* pap. 5.99 *(978-1-4998-0610-6(8))* Little Bee Books Inc.
—Ella & Owen 8: the Worst Pet. Bodnaruk, Iryna, illus. 2018. (Ella & Owen Ser.: 8). (ENG.). 112p. (J). (gr. k-3). 16.99 *(978-1-4998-0613-7(2));* pap. 5.99 *(978-1-4998-0612-0(4))* Little Bee Books Inc.
—Ella & Owen 9: Grumpy Goblins. Bodnaruk, Iryna, illus. 2018. (Ella & Owen Ser.: 9). (ENG.). 112p. (J). (gr. k-3). 16.99 *(978-1-4998-0615-1(9));* pap. 5.99 *(978-1-4998-0614-4(0))* Little Bee Books Inc.
Kent, Rose. Rocky Road. 2012. (ENG.). 304p. (J). (gr. 4-6). 21.19 *(978-0-375-86344-8(3),* Knopf Bks. for Young Readers); (gr. 3-7). 7.99 *(978-0-375-86345-5(1),* Yearling) Random Hse. Children's Bks.
KerascoUt, illus. Paul & Antoinette. 2016. (ENG.). 40p. (J). (gr. -1-3). 17.95 *(978-1-59270-196-4(5))* Enchanted Lion Bks., LLC.
Keyser, Amber J. The Way Back from Broken. (ENG.). 216p. (YA). (gr. 6-12). 2018. pap. 9.99 *(978-1-5415-1488-1(2),* 053f47d3-53bb-4099-bb59-532f84376fbd) 2015. E-Book 27.99 *(978-1-4677-8817-5(1))* Lerner Publishing Group. (Carolrhoda Lab™).
Kibuishi, Kazu. The Cloud Searchers. 3. 2018. (Amulet Ser.). (ENG.). 197p. (J). (gr. 4-5). 23.96 *(978-1-64310-257-3(5))* Penworthy Co., LLC, The.
—The Cloud Searchers. 2010. (Amulet Ser.: 3). lib. bdg. 24.50 *(978-0-606-15054-5(4))* Turtleback.
—The Cloud Searchers: a Graphic Novel (Amulet #3) 2015. (Amulet Ser.: 3). (ENG.). 208p. (J). (gr. 3-7). 24.99 *(978-0-545-20884-0(X),* Graphix) Scholastic, Inc.
—The Cloud Searchers: a Graphic Novel (Amulet #3) Kibuishi, Kazu, illus. 2010. (Amulet Ser.: 3). (ENG., Illus.). 208p. (J). (gr. 4-7). pap. 12.99 *(978-0-545-20885-7(8),* Graphix) Scholastic, Inc.
—Escape from Lucien. 6. 2018. (Amulet Ser.). (ENG.). 213p. (J). (gr. 4-5). 23.96 *(978-1-64310-260-3(5))* Penworthy Co., LLC, The.
—Escape from Lucien. 2014. (Amulet Ser.: 6). lib. bdg. 24.50 *(978-0-606-36039-5(5))* Turtleback.
—Escape from Lucien: a Graphic Novel (Amulet #6) Kibuishi, Kazu, illus. (Amulet Ser.: 6). (ENG., Illus.). 224p. (J). (gr. 3-7). 2015. 24.99 *(978-0-545-84899-2(7))* 6. 2014. pap. 12.99 *(978-0-545-43315-0(0))* Scholastic, Inc. (Graphix).
—Firelight. 7. 2018. (Amulet Ser.). (ENG.). 197p. (J). (gr. 4-5). 23.96 *(978-1-64310-261-0(3))* Penworthy Co., LLC, The.
—Firelight. 2016. (Amulet Ser.: 7). (ENG., Illus.). 224p. (J). (gr. 3-7). lib. bdg. 24.50 *(978-0-606-38070-6(1))* Turtleback.
—Firelight: a Graphic Novel (Amulet #7) Kibuishi, Kazu, illus. 2016. (Amulet Ser.: 7). (ENG., Illus.). 208p. (J). (gr. 3-7). 24.99 *(978-0-545-83966-2(1));* pap. 12.99 *(978-0-545-43316-7(9))* Scholastic, Inc. (Graphix).
—The Last Council. 4. 2018. (Amulet Ser.). (ENG.). 207p. (J). (gr. 4-5). 23.96 *(978-1-64310-258-0(3))* Penworthy Co., LLC, The.
—The Last Council. 2011. (Amulet Ser.: 4). lib. bdg. 24.50 *(978-0-606-23209-8(5))* Turtleback.
—The Last Council: a Graphic Novel (Amulet #4) 2015. (Amulet Ser.: 4). (ENG.). 224p. (J). (gr. 3-7). 24.99 *(978-0-545-20886-4(6),* Graphix) Scholastic, Inc.
—The Last Council: a Graphic Novel (Amulet #4) Kibuishi, Kazu, illus. 2011. (Amulet Ser.: 4). (ENG., Illus.). 224p. (J). (gr. 4-7). pap. 12.99 *(978-0-545-20887-1(4),* Graphix) Scholastic, Inc.
—Prince of the Elves. 5. 2018. (Amulet Ser.). (ENG.). 187p. (J). (gr. 4-5). 23.96 *(978-1-64310-259-7(1))* Penworthy Co., LLC, The.
—Prince of the Elves. 2012. (Amulet Ser.: 5). lib. bdg. 24.50 *(978-0-606-26499-0(X))* Turtleback.
—Prince of the Elves: a Graphic Novel (Amulet #5) Kibuishi, Kazu, illus. (Amulet Ser.: 5). (ENG.). 208p. (J). (gr. 3-7). 2015. 24.99 *(978-0-545-20888-8(2))* 2012. (Illus.). pap. 12.99 *(978-0-545-20889-5(0))* Scholastic, Inc. (Graphix).
—The Stonekeeper. 1. 2018. (Amulet Ser.). (ENG.). 185p. (J). (gr. 4-5). 23.96 *(978-1-64310-255-9(9))* Penworthy Co., LLC, The.
—The Stonekeeper. 2008. (Amulet Ser.: 1). (Illus.). 185p. lib. bdg. 24.50 *(978-1-4177-9712-7(6))* Turtleback.
—The Stonekeeper: a Graphic Novel (Amulet #1) Kibuishi, Kazu, illus. (Amulet Ser.: 1). (ENG., Illus.). 192p. (J). (gr. 3-7). 2015. 24.99 *(978-0-439-84680-6(3))* Vol. 1. 2008. pap. 12.99 *(978-0-439-84681-3(1))* Scholastic, Inc. (Graphix).
—The Stonekeeper's Curse. 2009. (Amulet Ser.: 2). lib. bdg. 24.50 *(978-0-606-10671-9(5))* Turtleback.
—The Stonekeeper's Curse: a Graphic Novel (Amulet #2) Kibuishi, Kazu, illus. (Amulet Ser.: 2). (ENG., Illus.). 224p. (J). 2015. (gr. 3-7). 24.99 *(978-0-439-84682-0(X))* 2009. (gr. 4-7). pap. 12.99 *(978-0-439-84683-7(8))* Scholastic, Inc. (Graphix).
—Supernova. 2018. (Amulet Ser.: 8). lib. bdg. 24.50 *(978-0-606-41498-2(3))* Turtleback.
—Supernova: a Graphic Novel (Amulet #8) 2018. (Amulet Ser.: 8). (ENG., Illus.). 208p. (J). (gr. 3-7). 24.99 *(978-0-545-85002-5(9));* pap. 12.99 *(978-0-545-82860-4(0))* Scholastic, Inc. (Graphix).
Kibuishi, Kazu, illus. Firelight. 2016. 197p. (J). *(978-1-4806-9909-0(8))* Baker & Taylor, CATS.
Kidd, Ronald. Undercover Kid: The Comic Book King. Sklar, Andy, illus. 2007. (All Aboard Mystery Reader Ser.). (ENG.). 48p. (J). pap. 3.99 *(978-0-448-44438-3(0),* Grosset & Dunlap) Penguin Publishing Group.
Kidwell, Justina. The Haunted Tree House, the Ghost Town, & the Dark Reaper: The Kent Boys' Adventures, 1 vol. 2009. 48p. pap. 16.95 *(978-1-60813-234-8(X))* America Star Bks.
Kim, Julie. Where's Halmoni? 2017. (Halmoni & Family Ser.). (Illus.). 96p. (J). (gr. k-4). 19.99 *(978-1-63217-077-4(9),* Little Bigfoot) Sasquatch Bks.
Kimble, Maggie T. Peep Learns to Sing. 2004. 21p. pap. 24.95 *(978-1-4137-2005-1(6))* PublishAmerica, Inc.
Kimmel, Elizabeth Cody. ParaNormaN. 2012. (ENG.). (J). (gr. 4-7). 64.99 *(978-1-61969-450-7(6))* Findaway World, LLC.
Kimmel, Eric A. Escape from Egypt. Stevanovic, Ivica, illus. 2015. (Scarlett & Sam Ser.). (ENG.). 168p. (J). (gr. 1-3). E-Book 23.99 *(978-1-4677-6207-6(5),* Kar-Ben Publishing) Lerner Publishing Group.
—Hank & Gertie: A Pioneer Hansel & Gretel Story. Penny, Mara, illus. 2018. (ENG.). 32p. (J). (gr. 1-3). 16.99 *(978-1-5132-6122-5(3),* West Winds Pr.) West Margin Pr.
—Search for the Shamir. Stevanovic, Ivica, illus. 2018. (Scarlett & Sam Ser.). (ENG.). 152p. (J). (gr. 1-3). pap. 6.99 *(978-1-5124-2938-1(4),* fa05c70d-97fc-4c41-af59-93be9cd9769f, Kar-Ben Publishing) Lerner Publishing Group.
King, Caro. Seven Sorcerers. (ENG.). 352p. (J). (gr. 3-7). 2012. pap. 6.99 *(978-1-4424-2043-4(X))* 2011. 15.99 *(978-1-4424-2042-7(1))* Simon & Schuster Children's Publishing. (Aladdin).
—Shadow Spell. 2012. (ENG.). 320p. (J). (gr. 3-7). pap. 6.99 *(978-1-4423-3908-8(X),* Aladdin) Simon & Schuster Children's Publishing.
—Shadow Spell. 2012. (ENG.). 320p. (J). (gr. 3-7). 15.99 *(978-1-4424-2045-8(6),* Simon & Schuster/Paula Wiseman Bks.) Simon & Schuster/Paula Wiseman Bks.
King, Juaness. The Prodigal's Quest. 2012. 54p. 19.95 *(978-1-4626-9042-8(4))* America Star Bks.
King, Lisa. Lurkey the Proud Turkey. 2013. 24p. pap. 24.95 *(978-1-63004-113-7(0))* America Star Bks.
Kingsbury, Karen & Russell, Tyler. Best Family Ever. 2019. (Baxter Family Children Story Ser.). (ENG., Illus.). 288p. (J). (gr. 3-7). 17.99 *(978-1-5344-1215-6(8),* Simon & Schuster Bks. For Young Readers) Simon & Schuster Bks. For Young Readers.
—Finding Home. 2020. (Baxter Family Children Story Ser.). (ENG., Illus.). 320p. (J). (gr. 3-7). 18.99 *(978-1-5344-1218-7(2),* Simon & Schuster Bks. For Young Readers) Simon & Schuster Bks. For Young Readers.
—Finding Home. 2021. (Baxter Family Children Story Ser.). (ENG.). 336p. (J). (gr. 3-7). pap. 8.99 *(978-1-5344-1219-4(0),* Simon & Schuster/Paula Wiseman Bks.) Simon & Schuster/Paula Wiseman Bks.
Kirby, Jessi. In Honor. (ENG., (YA). (gr. 9). 2013. Illus.). 256p. pap. 9.99 *(978-1-4424-1698-7(X))* 2012. 240p. 16.99 *(978-1-4424-1697-0(1))* Simon & Schuster Bks. For Young Readers. (Simon & Schuster Bks. For Young Readers).
Kirkham, Teresa. Tattie Tom. 2003. 27p. pap. 12.95 *(978-1-4137-0141-8(8))* America Star Bks.
Kirsch, R. A. The Big One: (A Bicycle Tale), 1 vol. 2009. 191p. pap. 24.95 *(978-1-60703-341-7(0))* PublishAmerica, Inc.
Kizer, Amber. A Matter of Days. 2016. (ENG.). 288p. (YA). (gr. 7). pap. 9.99 *(978-0-385-73974-0(5),* Ember) Random Hse. Children's Bks.
—A Matter of Days. 2016. lib. bdg. 20.85 *(978-0-606-38875-7(3))* Turtleback.
Kjersgaard, Carly. Muffins' New Beginning. 2009. 20p. pap. 10.95 *(978-1-4389-8001-0(9))* AuthorHouse.
Klassen, Barnett -. Sam y Leo cavan un hoyo. 2014. (SPA.). 44p. (gr. 1-3). 21.99 *(978-84-261-4091-3(2))* Juventud, Editorial ESP. Dist: Lectorum Pubns., Inc.
Klein, Abby. Camping Catastrophe! McKinley, John, illus. 2008. (Ready, Freddy! Ser.: Bk. 14). 95p. (J). (gr. -1-3). 11.65 *(978-0-7569-8837-1(3))* Perfection Learning Corp.
Kleven, Elisa. The Puddle Pail. Kleven, Elisa, illus. 2007. (Illus.). 32p. (J). (gr. -1-2). pap. 8.99 *(978-1-58246-206-6(2),* Tricycle Pr.) Random Hse. Children's Bks.
Kline, C. A. & Lauder, M. F. Halloween Night. 2012. 24p. pap. 17.99 *(978-1-4772-7417-0(0))* AuthorHouse.
Kling, Kevin. Big Little Mother. Monroe, Chris, illus. 2013. (ENG.). 32p. (J). (gr. -1-3). 17.95 *(978-0-87351-911-3(6),* Borealis Bk.) Minnesota Historical Society Pr.
Klingensmith, Ryan Lee & Klingensmith, Sherri Ann. Starlight Blue: A New Baby. Rollinger, Marsha, illus. 2012. 32p. pap. 24.95 *(978-1-4626-8219-5(7))* America Star Bks.
Knapman, Timothy. Time Now to Dream. Oxenbury, Helen, illus. 2017. (ENG.). 32p. (J). (gr. -1-2). 16.99 *(978-0-7636-9078-6(3))* Candlewick Pr.
Knecht, Eileen. Christine's Christmas Crib. 2009. 40p. pap. 18.49 *(978-1-4389-2265-2(5))* AuthorHouse.
Knight, Christopher. World Is Black & White. 2008. 459p. (YA). pap. 14.95 *(978-1-893699-97-7(8))* AudioCraft Publishing, Inc.
Knowles, Jo. Still a Work in Progress. 2019. (ENG.). 320p. (J). (gr. 5-9). pap. 7.99 *(978-1-5362-0737-8(3))* Candlewick Pr.
Knutsson, Catherine. Shadows Cast by Stars. 2013. (ENG., Illus.). 464p. (YA). (gr. 7). pap. 13.99 *(978-1-4424-0192-1(3),* Atheneum Bks. for Young Readers) Simon & Schuster Children's Publishing.
Koffsky, Ann. Judah Maccabee Goes to the Doctor: a Story for Hanukkah. Shipman, Talitha, illus. 2017. (ENG.). 32p. (J). 17.95 *(978-1-68115-522-7(2),* 57a5ddfc-cab2-49df-bc22-fafffeb5edf) Behrman Hse., Inc.
Koger, Danny K. The Misadventures of Carson & C J Crenshaw: In Search of the Book of Life. 2007. 184p. per. 13.95 *(978-0-595-42365-1(5))* iUniverse, Inc.
Kogler, Jennifer. The Otherworldlies. 2008. 400p. (J). lib. bdg. 17.89 *(978-0-06-073960-7(6));* (ENG.). (gr. 5-18). 16.99 *(978-0-06-073959-1(2))* HarperCollins Pubs. (Eos).
Kohlhepp, Michael. Within the Hearthstone: Book 1: the Trea. 2006. 127p. pap. 19.95 *(978-1-4241-3744-2(6))* PublishAmerica, Inc.
Kohlhepp, Michael G. Within the Hearthstone Book 2: The Fountain of Balance. 2007. (ENG.). 184p. per. 24.95 *(978-1-4241-4446-4(9))* PublishAmerica, Inc.
Konigsburg, E. L. Silent to the Bone. unabr. ed. 2004. (Middle Grade Cassette Librariestm Ser.). 272p. (J). (gr. 5-9). pap. 38.00 incl. audio *(978-0-8072-8741-5(5),* S YA 253 SP, Listening Library) Random Hse. Audio Publishing Group.
—Silent to the Bone. 2004. (ENG.). 272p. (YA). (gr. 7). mass mkt. 7.99 *(978-0-689-86715-6(8),* Simon Pulse) Simon Pulse.
Kopelke, Lisa. The Younger Brother's Survival Guide. Kopelke, Lisa, illus. 2006. (ENG., Illus.). 32p. (J). (gr. -1-3). 17.99 *(978-0-689-86249-6(0),* Simon & Schuster Bks. For Young Readers) Simon & Schuster Bks. For Young Readers.
Korman, Gordon. One False Note (the 39 Clues, Book 2), Volume 2. 2008. (39 Clues Ser.: 2). (ENG.). 176p. (J). (gr. 4-7). 13.99 *(978-0-545-06042-4(7))* Scholastic, Inc.
Korngold, Jamie. Sadie's Lag Ba'Omer Mystery. Fortenberry, Julie, illus. 2014. (ENG.). 32p. (J). (gr. -1-3). 9.99 *(978-0-7613-9048-0(0),* 034ad977-184b-4135-b7fb-d522d1bc86eb, Kar-Ben Publishing) Lerner Publishing Group.
Korngold, Jamie S. Mazel Tov! It's a Boy: Mazel Tov! It's a Girl. Finkelstein, Jeff, illus. Finkelstein, Jeff, photos by. 2015. (J). 6.99 *(978-1-4677-6206-9(7),* Kar-Ben Publishing) Lerner Publishing Group.
Krackow, Eric T. Have an Abominably Good Day, 1 vol. 2010. (ENG., Illus.). 64p. (J). (gr. -1-3). 16.99 *(978-0-7643-3496-2(4),* 3885) Schiffer Publishing, Ltd.
Kraft, Erik P. Lenny & Mel. Kraft, Erik P., illus. 2012. (Ready-For-Chapters Ser.). (ENG., Illus.). 64p. (J). (gr. 2-5). pap. 6.99 *(978-0-689-85891-8(4),* Aladdin) Simon & Schuster Children's Publishing.
—Lenny & Mel after-School Confidential. Kraft, Erik P., illus. 2012. (Lenny & Mel Ser.). (ENG., Illus.). 64p. (J). (gr. 2-5). pap. 6.99 *(978-1-4424-6314-1(7),* Simon & Schuster/Paula Wiseman Bks.) Simon & Schuster/Paula Wiseman Bks.
—Lenny & Mel's Summer Vacation. Kraft, Erik P., illus. 2012. (Ready-For-Chapters Ser.). (ENG., Illus.). 64p. (J). (gr. 2-5). pap. 6.99 *(978-0-689-86874-0(X),* Simon & Schuster/Paula Wiseman Bks.) Simon & Schuster/Paula Wiseman Bks.
Krawitz, Susan. Viva, Rose! 2017. (ENG.). 240p. (J). (gr. 5). 16.95 *(978-0-8234-3756-6(6))* Holiday Hse., Inc.
Kreilein, Debra. The Tombstone Treasure Mystery. 2013. 142p. pap. 12.99 *(978-1-62509-458-2(2))* Salem Author Services.
Krishnaswami, Uma. Bringing Asha Home, 1 vol. Akib, Jamel, illus. 2006. (ENG.). 32p. (J). (gr. -1-3). 16.95 *(978-1-58430-259-9(3));* pap. 11.95 *(978-1-62014-225-7(2),* leelowbooks) Lee & Low Bks., Inc.
Kropp, Paul. Against All Odds. Melanson, Matt, illus. 2012. (HIP Sr Ser.). (ENG.). 87p. (J). (gr. 7-12). 26.19 *(978-1-897039-06-9(9))* High Interest Publishing (HIP) CAN. Dist: Children's Plus, Inc.
Krull, Kathleen. How to Trick or Treat in Outer Space. Brewer, Paul, illus. 2004. (ENG.). 32p. (J). (gr. k-3). tchr. ed. 16.95 *(978-0-8234-1844-2(8))* Holiday Hse., Inc.
Kuchman, D. S. Krystal Steps: The Journey Begins. 2006. 57p. pap. 16.95 *(978-1-4241-5135-6(X))* America Star Bks.
Kuhlman, Evan. Great Ball of Light. Holmes, Jeremy, illus. 2015. (ENG.). 304p. (J). (gr. 5-9). 16.99 *(978-1-4169-6461-2(4))* Simon & Schuster Children's Publishing.
Kuhn, Douglas Wolcik. Uncle Kyle's Magic Kite. Kuhn, Douglas Wolcik, illus. 2012. (Illus.). 28p. pap. 24.95 *(978-1-4626-9699-4(6))* America Star Bks.
Kunkel, Mike. Brother vs. Brother!, 1 vol. 2014. (Billy Batson & the Magic of Shazam! Ser.). (ENG., Illus.). 32p. (J). (gr. 3-6). 22.60 *(978-1-4342-9228-5(2),* 125735, Stone Arch Bks.) Capstone.
—Magic Words!, 1 vol. 2014. (Billy Batson & the Magic of Shazam! Ser.). (ENG., Illus.). 32p. (J). (gr. 3-6). 22.60 *(978-1-4342-9209-4(6),* 125716, Stone Arch Bks.) Capstone.
—The World's Mightiest Mortal!, 1 vol. 2014. (Billy Batson & the Magic of Shazam! Ser.). (ENG., Illus.). 32p. (J). (gr. 3-6). 22.60 *(978-1-4342-9226-1(6),* 125733, Stone Arch Bks.) Capstone.
Kurtz, Jane. In the Small, Small Night. Isadora, Rachel, illus. 2005. (ENG.). 32p. (J). (gr. k-5). 17.99 *(978-0-06-623814-2(5),* Greenwillow Bks.) HarperCollins Pubs.
Kusugak, Michael & Munsch, Robert. A Promise Is a Promise. Krykorka, Vladyana, illus. 2019. (Classic Munsch Ser.). 32p. (J). (gr. k-2). 6.95 *(978-1-77321-293-7(1))* Annick Pr., Ltd. CAN. Dist: Publishers Group West (PGW).
Kviat, Hindy & Lefkowitz, Chaya. Yes I Can. Epstein, Len, illus. 2018. (ENG.). 28p. (J). 11.95 *(978-1-945560-05-7(3))* Hachai Publishing.
Lachenmeyer, Nathaniel. Eureka! Jack, Colin, illus. 2013. (J). *(978-0-8037-3514-9(6),* Dial) Penguin Publishing Group.
LaFleur, Suzanne. Listening for Lucca. 2015. (ENG.). 240p. (J). (gr. 4-7). pap. 8.99 *(978-0-307-98030-4(8),* Yearling) Random Hse. Children's Bks.
Lai, Thanhhà. Butterfly Yellow. 2019. (ENG.). 304p. (YA). (gr. 8). 17.99 *(978-0-06-222921-2(4),* HarperCollins) HarperCollins Pubs.
Lam, Maple. My Little Sister & Me. Lam, Maple, illus. 2016. (ENG., Illus.). 40p. (J). (gr. -1-3). 17.99 *(978-0-06-239697-6(8),* HarperCollins) HarperCollins Pubs.
Lambert, Roy. Lamb, the Hip Cat Daddy. 2005. per. 13.95 *(978-1-58909-253-2(8))* Bookstand Publishing.
Lanang, Vanessa. Whiteout. 2019. (To the Limit Ser.). (ENG.). 112p. (YA). (gr. 6-12). pap. 7.99 *(978-1-5415-4556-4(7),* 201b6a88-8b09-4d65-b8b4-68f5d8a9cd4c, Darby Creek) Lerner Publishing Group.
Landis, Mary M. Winter Days with the Treelo Triplets. 2012. (Illus.). 218p. (J). *(978-0-7399-2447-1(8))* Rod & Staff Pubs., Inc.
Lane, Jessica E. The Secret of the Swans. 2009. 52p. pap. 31.99 *(978-1-4415-5517-5(X))* Xlibris Corp.
Lang, Heidi. Wrong Way Summer. 2020. (ENG., Illus.). 288p. (J). (gr. 3-7). 16.99 *(978-1-4197-3693-3(0),* 1219301) Abrams, Inc.

S

Langdale, Mark Roland. Professor Doppelganger & the Fantastical Cloud Factory. 2012. 106p. pap. *(978-1-78003-267-2(6))* Pen Pr. Pubs., Ltd.

Langton, Jane. The Diamond in the Window. Blegvad, Erik, illus. 2018. (Hall Family Chronicles). xi, 245p. (J). pap. *(978-1-930900-93-6(7))* Purple Hse. Pr.

Lansdale, Joe R. All the Earth, Thrown to the Sky. 2012. (ENG.). 256p. (YA). (gr. 7). pap. 8.99 *(978-0-385-73932-0(X)*, Ember) Random Hse. Children's Bks.

LaReau, Kara. The Infamous Ratsos Are Not Afraid. Myers, Matt, illus. 2018. (Infamous Ratsos Ser.). (ENG.). 96p. (J). (gr. k-3). pap. 5.99 *(978-1-5362-0368-4(8))* Candlewick Pr.

Larsen, Andrew. A Squiggly Story. Lowery, Mike, illus. 2016. (ENG.). 32p. (J). (gr. -1-2). 18.99 *(978-1-77138-016-4(0))* Kids Can Pr., Ltd. CAN. Dist: Hachette Bk. Group.

Larson, Hope. Knife's Edge. 2018. (Four Points Ser.: 2). (J). lib. bdg. 24.50 *(978-0-606-41086-1(4))* Turtleback.

Larwood, Kieran. The Beasts of Grimheart. Wyatt, David, illus. 2019. (Longburrow Ser.). (ENG.). 272p. (J). (gr. 5-7). 16.99 *(978-1-328-69602-1(2)*, 1671320, Clarion Bks.) HarperCollins Pubs.

—The Five Realms: the Beasts of Grimheart. Wyatt, David, illus. 2019. (Five Realms Podkin One Ear Ser.). (ENG.). 320p. (J). (gr. 3-5). 15.95 *(978-0-571-32844-4(X)*, Faber & Faber Children's Bks.) Faber & Faber, Inc.

—The Gift of Dark Hollow. Wyatt, David, illus. 2018. (Longburrow Ser.). (ENG.). 272p. (J). (gr. 5-7). 16.99 *(978-1-328-69601-4(4)*, 1671318, Clarion Bks.) HarperCollins Pubs.

Laskin, Pamela L. Getting to Know You. 2003. (YA). 16.95 *(978-0-936389-92-9(3))* Tudor Pubs., Inc.

Lasky, Kathryn. A Voice in the Wind: A Starbuck Twins Mystery, Book Three. 2008. (ENG., Illus.). 272p. (J). (gr. 3-7). pap. 15.95 *(978-0-15-205875-3(3)*, 1197642, Clarion Bks.) HarperCollins Pubs.

Lassiter, Rhiannon. Void: Hex; Shadows; Ghosts. 2011. (ENG.). 688p. (YA). (gr. 7). pap. 9.99 *(978-1-4424-2929-1(1)*, Simon Pulse) Simon Pulse.

Latimer, Alex. Never Follow a Dinosaur, 1 vol. 2016. (ENG., Illus.). 32p. (J). (gr. -1-3). 16.95 *(978-1-56145-704-5(3))* Peachtree Publishing Co. Inc.

Laura Lee Hope. Bunny Brown & His Sister Sue at Aunt Lu's City Home. 2007. 184p. per. 11.95 *(978-1-4218-3986-8(5)*, 1st World Library - Literary Society) 1st World Publishing, Inc.

—Bunny Brown & His Sister Sue at Christmas Tree Cove. 2007. 176p. per. 12.95 *(978-1-4218-3987-5(3)*, 1st World Library - Literary Society) 1st World Publishing, Inc.

—Six Little Bunkers at Cowboy Jack's. 2007. 180p. per. 11.95 *(978-1-4218-3988-2(1)*, 1st World Library - Literary Society) 1st World Publishing, Inc.

—Six Little Bunkers at Grandpa Ford's. 2007. 188p. per. 11.95 *(978-1-4218-3989-9(X)*, 1st World Library - Literary Society) 1st World Publishing, Inc.

Laurie, Victoria. The Curse of Deadman's Forest. (ENG.). 432p. (J). 2011. (gr. 3-7). 8.99 *(978-0-440-42259-4(0)*, Yearling)2. 2010. (Oracles of Delphi Keep Ser.: No. 2). (gr. 6-8). lib. bdg. 22.44 *(978-0-385-90562-6(9)*, Delacorte Pr.) Random Hse. Children's Bks.

Lauterbach, B. L. Home-Grown Experiences. 2008. 68p. pap. 7.95 *(978-1-4327-2620-1(X))* Outskirts Pr., Inc.

Law, Ingrid. Savvy. 2011. 9.68 *(978-0-7848-3575-3(6)*, Everbind) Marco Bk. Co.

—Savvy. 2010. (Illus.). 368p. (J). (gr. 4-7). 9.99 *(978-0-14-241433-0(6)*, Puffin Books) Penguin Young Readers Group.

—Savvy. l.t. ed. 2011. (ENG.). 500p. 23.99 *(978-1-4104-3530-9(X))* Thorndike Pr.

—Savvy. 2010. lib. bdg. 18.40 *(978-0-606-14394-3(7))* Turtleback.

Lawrence, Antoinette & Lewis, Terry. I Remember. 2011. (ENG.). 29p. (J). pap. 12.95 *(978-1-4327-7342-7(9))* Outskirts Pr., Inc.

Lawson, Janet. The Alberts & Me. 2009. (J). *(978-0-15-205327-7(1))* Harcourt Trade Pubs.

Lawson, Richard. All We Can Do Is Wait. 2019. 288p. (YA). (gr. 7). pap. 9.99 *(978-0-448-49412-8(4)*, Razorbill) Penguin Young Readers Group.

Lay, Kathryn. The Substitutes: An Up2U Action Adventure, 1 vol. Calo, Marcos, illus. 2015. (Up2U Adventures Ser.). (ENG.). 80p. (J). (gr. 2-5). 35.64 *(978-1-62402-095-7(X)*, 17359, Calico Chapter Bks.) ABDO Publishing Co.

Laybourne, Emmy. Berserker. 2018. (Berserker Ser.: 1). (ENG.). 352p. (YA). pap. 10.99 *(978-1-250-18076-6(7)*, 900190256) Square Fish.

Layne, Steven L. Stay with Sister, 1 vol. Hoyt, Ard, illus. 2012. (ENG.). 32p. (J). (gr. k-3). 16.99 *(978-1-4556-1523-0(4)*, Pelican Publishing) Arcadia Publishing.

Layton, Neal. The Mammoth Academy. Layton, Neal, illus. 2010. (ENG., Illus.). 176p. (J). (gr. 4-6). 21.19 *(978-0-312-60882-8(9))* Square Fish.

Lazar, Tara. The Monstore. Burks, James, illus. 2013. (ENG.). 32p. (J). (gr. -1-2). 19.99 *(978-1-4424-2017-5(0)*, Aladdin) Simon & Schuster Children's Publishing.

LaZebnik, Claire. Things I Should Have Known. 2018. (ENG.). 320p. (YA). (gr. 7). pap. 9.99 *(978-1-328-86934-0(2)*, 1696699, Clarion Bks.) HarperCollins Pubs.

Lê, Minh. Lift. Santat, Dan, illus. 2020. (ENG.). 56p. (J). (gr. -1-3). 17.99 *(978-1-368-03692-4(9))* Little, Brown Bks. for Young Readers.

Leavitt, Lindsey. Commander in Cheese Super Special #1: Mouse Rushmore. Ford, A. G., illus. 2017. (Commander in Cheese Ser.: 1). 128p. (J). (gr. 2-5). 5.99 *(978-1-5247-2047-6(X)*, Random Hse. Bks. for Young Readers) Random Hse. Children's Bks.

Leder, Meg. Letting Go of Gravity. (ENG.). (YA). (gr. 7). 2019. 448p. pap. 12.99 *(978-1-5344-0317-8(5))* 2018. (Illus.). 432p. 19.99 *(978-1-5344-0316-1(7))* Simon Pulse. (Simon Pulse).

Lee, J. M. Shadows of the Dark Crystal #1. Froud, Brian, illus. 2016. (Jim Henson's the Dark Crystal Ser.: 1). 272p. (YA). (gr. 7). 17.99 *(978-0-448-48289-7(4)*, Grosset & Dunlap) Penguin Young Readers Group.

Lee, Mary Ellen. Danny & Life on Bluff Point: Blizzard of '95 revised Edition. 2009. 160p. (gr. 4-7). pap. 12.95 *(978-0-595-53308-4(6))* iUniverse, Inc.

Lee, Yoon. Dragon Pearl. 2019. (ENG.). 320p. lib. bdg. 18.80 *(978-1-6636-2730-8(4))* Perfection Learning Corp.

—Rick Riordan Presents Dragon Pearl (a Thousand Worlds Novel, Book 1) 2019. (ENG., Illus.). 320p. (J). (gr. 3-7). 16.99 *(978-1-368-01335-2(X)*, Riordan, Rick) Disney Publishing Worldwide.

—Rick Riordan Presents Dragon Pearl (a Thousand Worlds Novel Book 1) 2020. 320p. (J). (gr. 3-7). pap. 8.99 *(978-1-368-01474-8(7)*, Riordan, Rick) Disney Publishing Worldwide.

Lee, Yoon Ha. Dragon Pearl. 2020. (Thousand Worlds (Trade) Ser.). (ENG.). 320p. (gr. 4-7). 24.94 *(978-1-5364-6113-8(X)*, Riordan, Rick) Disney Pr.

—Dragon Pearl. 2019. 320p. 16.99 *(978-1-368-01519-6(0))* Disney Publishing Worldwide.

Leeuwen, Jean. Five Funny Bunnies: Three Bouncing Tales, 0 vols. Wilsdorf, Anne, illus. 2012. (ENG.). 40p. (J). (gr. -1-3). 17.99 *(978-0-7614-6114-2(0)*, 9780761461142, Two Lions) Amazon Publishing.

Leitich Smith, Greg. Chronal Engine. Henry, Blake, illus. 2013. (ENG.). 192p. (J). (gr. 5-7). pap. 6.99 *(978-0-544-02277-5(7)*, 1528498, Clarion Bks.) HarperCollins Pubs.

Leno, Katrina. The Lost & Found. 2016. (ENG.). 352p. (YA). (gr. 8). 17.99 *(978-0-06-223120-8(0)*, HarperTeen) HarperCollins Pubs.

Leo, Domenic. The Messengers: The Secret of the Orbs. 2007. 324p. per. 19.95 *(978-0-595-42668-3(9))* iUniverse, Inc.

Leonard, Marcia. Trae la Pelota, Tito. Handelman, Dorothy, photos by. 2005.Tr. of Get the Ball, Slim. (Illus.). 32p. (J). (ENG & SPA.). (gr. -1-1). pap. 4.99 *(978-0-8225-3293-4(X))*; (SPA., (gr. 1-1). per. 5.95 *(978-0-8225-3292-7(1)*, Ediciones Lerner) Lerner Publishing Group.

Lerangis, Peter. The Sword Thief (the 39 Clues, Book 3) 2009. (39 Clues Ser.: 3). (ENG.). 160p. (J). (gr. 4-7). 13.99 *(978-0-545-06043-1(5)*, Scholastic Pr.) Scholastic, Inc.

—The Sword Thief (the 39 Clues, Book 3) (Unabridged Edition), 1 vol. unabr. ed. 2009. (39 Clues Ser.: 3). (ENG.). 4p. (J). (gr. 4-7). audio compact disk 49.95 *(978-0-545-11949-8(9))* Scholastic, Inc.

Leslie, Emma. Glaucia the Greek Slave: A Tale of Athens in the First Century. Felter & Butterworth & Heath, illus. 2007. 308p. per. 14.95 *(978-1-934671-01-6(0))* Salem Ridge Press LLC.

Lester, Julius. When Dad Killed Mom. 2003. (YA). (gr. 7-12). mass mkt. 6.95 *(978-0-15-524698-0(4)*, Silver Whistle) Harcourt Trade Pubs.

—When Dad Killed Mom. 2003. (ENG.). 216p. (YA). (gr. 7-12). pap. 13.95 *(978-0-15-204698-9(4)*, 1194150, Clarion Bks.) HarperCollins Pubs.

Leuck, Laura. My Beastly Brother. Nash, Scott, illus. 2003. 32p. (J). (gr. -1-1). 16.89 *(978-0-06-029548-6(1))* HarperCollins Pubs.

Levin, Betty. Shoddy Cove. 2003. 208p. (J). (gr. 5-18). 15.99 *(978-0-06-052271-1(2))* HarperCollins Pubs.

Levithan, David. Are We There Yet? 2007. (ENG.). 224p. (YA). (gr. 7-12). per. 8.99 *(978-0-375-83956-6(9)*, Knopf Bks. for Young Readers) Random Hse. Children's Bks.

—The Mysterious Disappearance of Aidan S. (as Told to His Brother) 2021. (ENG.). 224p. (J). (gr. 3-7). 16.99 *(978-1-9848-4859-8(3)*, Knopf Bks. for Young Readers) Random Hse. Children's Bks.

Levitin, Sonia. Junkman's Daughter. Porfirio, Guy, illus. rev. ed. 2007. (Tales of Young Americans Ser.). (ENG.). 32p. (J). (gr. 1-4). 17.95 *(978-1-58536-315-5(4)*, 202119) Sleeping Bear Pr.

Lewis, Beverly. Cul-De-Sac Kids Collection Four: Books 19-24. 2018. (ENG.). 368p. (J). pap. 15.99 *(978-0-7642-3051-6(4))* Bethany Hse. Pubs.

—Cul-De-Sac Kids Collection One: Books 1-6. 2017. (ENG., Illus.). 352p. (J). pap. 14.99 *(978-0-7642-3048-6(4))* Bethany Hse. Pubs.

—Cul-De-Sac Kids Collection Three: Books 13-18. 2018. (ENG., Illus.). 368p. (J). pap. 14.99 *(978-0-7642-3050-9(6))* Bethany Hse. Pubs.

—Cul-De-Sac Kids Collection Two: Books 7-12. 2017. (ENG., Illus.). 352p. (J). pap. 13.99 *(978-0-7642-3049-3(2))* Bethany Hse. Pubs.

—In Jesse's Shoes: Appreciating Kids with Special Needs. Nikiel, Laura Gibbons, illus. 2007. (ENG.). 32p. (J). (gr. -1-4). 11.99 *(978-0-7642-0313-8(4))* Bethany Hse. Pubs.

Lewis, Richard. The Killing Sea. 2008. (ENG., Illus.). 256p. (J). (gr. 7-12). mass mkt. 8.99 *(978-1-4169-5372-2(8)*, Simon Pulse) Simon Pulse.

Liberts, Jennifer. Go, Go, Trucks! Yamada, Mike, illus. 2017. (Step into Reading Ser.). 32p. (J). (gr. -1-1). 5.99 *(978-0-399-54951-9(X)*, Random Hse. Bks. for Young Readers) Random Hse. Children's Bks.

Lien, Henry. Peasprout Chen, Future Legend of Skate & Sword. 2019. (Peasprout Chen Ser.: 1). (ENG., Illus.). 352p. (J). pap. 12.99 *(978-1-250-29436-4(3)*, 900187110) Square Fish.

Lincoln, James. The Rainbow Jars. Smith, Jacqui, illus. 2013. 28p. (J). pap. 14.95 *(978-1-60131-153-5(2)*, Castlebridge Bks.) Big Tent Bks.

Lindenbaum, Pija. Bridget & the Moose Brothers. Board, Kjersti, tr. from SWE. 2004. (Illus.). 32p. (J). 16.00 *(978-91-29-66046-3(7))* R & S Bks. SWE. Dist: Macmillan.

Lindgren, Astrid & Crampton, Patricia. The Red Bird. Tornqvist, Marit, illus. 2005. (J). 5.99 *(978-0-439-62797-9(4)*, Levine, Arthur A. Bks.) Scholastic, Inc.

Lindsay, Maud. Mother Stories. 2005. 25.95 *(978-1-4218-1492-6(7))*; 120p. pap. 10.95 *(978-1-4218-1592-3(3))* 1st World Publishing, Inc. (1st World Library - Literary Society).

Linehan, Jess Golden. Martin Mixed-Up at the Beach. 2011. (ENG., Illus.). 32p. (J). 15.95 *(978-0-615-45705-5(3))* Salty Pond Pubs.

Liparulo, Robert. Gatekeepers, 1 vol. 2009. (Dreamhouse Kings Ser.: 3). (ENG.). 320p. (YA). pap. 14.99 *(978-1-59554-729-3(0))* Nelson, Thomas Inc.

—Whirlwind, 1 vol. 2010. (Dreamhouse Kings Ser.: 5). (ENG.). 320p. (YA). pap. 14.99 *(978-1-59554-892-4(0))* Nelson, Thomas Inc.

Liphardt, Linda. Secret in the Old Barn. 2008. 116p. pap. 19.95 *(978-1-60703-615-9(0))* America Star Bks.

Lisle, Holly. Ruby Key, Bk. 1. 2008. 384p. (J). *(978-0-545-00013-0(0)*, Orchard Bks.) Scholastic, Inc.

Little, Jean. Emma's Strange Pet. 2004. (I Can Read Level 3 Ser.). (ENG., Illus.). 64p. (J). (gr. k-3). pap. 4.99 *(978-0-06-444259-6(4)*, HarperCollins) HarperCollins Pubs.

—Emma's Strange Pet. Plecas, Jennifer, illus. 2003. (I Can Read Bks.). 64p. (J). (gr. k-3). 15.99 *(978-0-06-028350-6(5))* HarperCollins Pubs.

Little, Jennifer. My Brother Is Such a Slob! 2013. 24p. pap. 24.95 *(978-1-63000-879-6(6))* America Star Bks.

Littlewood, Kathryn. Bite-Sized Magic. McGuire, Erin, illus. 2015. (Bliss Bakery Trilogy Ser.: 3). (ENG.). 432p. (J). (gr. 3-7). pap. 7.99 *(978-0-06-208427-9(5)*, Tegen, Katherine Bks) HarperCollins Pubs.

—Bliss. (Bliss Bakery Trilogy Ser.: 1). (ENG.). (J). (gr. 3-7). 2013. 400p. pap. 8.99 *(978-0-06-208424-8(0))* 2012. (Illus.). 384p. 16.99 *(978-0-06-208423-1(2))* HarperCollins Pubs. (Tegen, Katherine Bks).

Littman, Sarah Darer. Anything but Okay. 2019. (ENG.). 352p. (YA). (gr. 7-7). pap. 9.99 *(978-1-338-17758-9(3)*, Scholastic Paperbacks) Scholastic, Inc.

Lloyd-Jones, Sally. His Royal Highness, King Baby: A Terrible True Story. Roberts, David, illus. 2017. (ENG.). 48p. (J). (gr. -1-3). 16.99 *(978-0-7636-9793-8(1))* Candlewick Pr.

Loccisano, Rina. Baby Dario Eats His First Carrot. Baker, David, illus. 2012. 48p. pap. 24.95 *(978-1-4560-6100-5(3))* America Star Bks.

Loccisano, Rina Fuda. Little Rina Meets Baby Brother. Prouix, Denis, illus. 2011. 48p. pap. 24.95 *(978-1-4512-6299-5(X))* America Star Bks.

Locke, Katherine. The Spy with the Red Balloon. 2019. (Balloonmakers Ser.: 2). (ENG.). 368p. (YA). (gr. 8-12). pap. 9.99 *(978-0-8075-2938-6(9)*, 807529389) Whitman, Albert & Co.

Loewen, Ann E. Fast for My Feet. 2013. 176p. *(978-1-4602-3384-9(0))* FriesenPress.

Lohans, Alison. Waiting for the Sun, 1 vol. Mets, Marilyn & Ledwon, Peter, illus. 2006. (ENG.). 32p. (J). (gr. k-3). per. 6.95 *(978-0-88995-358-1(9)*, 58896360-c81f-4818-80ac-51128ad8241b) Red Deer Pr. CAN. Dist: Firefly Bks., Ltd.

London, Alex. Black Wings Beating. 2019. (Skybound Saga Ser.: 1). (ENG., Illus.). 448p. (YA). pap. 17.99 *(978-1-250-21148-4(4)*, 900177982) Square Fish.

London, C. Alexander. Mission Hindenburg (the 39 Clues: Doublecross, Book 2) 2018. (Follow Me Around... Ser.: 2). (ENG.). 192p. (J). (gr. 3-4). E-Book 27.00 *(978-0-545-76925-9(6))* Scholastic, Inc.

—We Are Not Eaten by Yaks. 2013. (Accidental Adventure Ser.: 1). 384p. (J). (gr. 3-7). pap. 8.99 *(978-0-14-242056-0(5)*, Puffin Books) Penguin Young Readers Group.

—We Dine with Cannibals. 2013. (Accidental Adventure Ser.: 2). 384p. (J). (gr. 3-7). pap. 7.99 *(978-0-14-242474-2(9)*, Puffin Books) Penguin Young Readers Group.

London, Jonathan. Froggy's Baby Sister. Remkiewicz, Frank, illus. 2005. (Froggy Ser.). (ENG.). 32p. (J). (gr. -1-k). pap. 7.99 *(978-0-14-240342-6(3)*, Puffin Books) Penguin Young Readers Group.

Long, Christopher E. & Warner, Gertrude Chandler. Tree House Mystery, 1 vol. Bloodworth, Mark, illus. 2010. (Boxcar Children Graphic Novels Ser.). (ENG.). 32p. (J). (gr. 3-8). 32.79 *(978-1-60270-716-0(2)*, 3677, Graphic Planet - Fiction) Magic Wagon.

The Long Legged Turtle. 2013. 44p. pap. 16.99 *(978-1-4808-0460-9(6))* Archway Publishing.

Long, Loren & Bildner, Phil. Blastin' the Blues. Long, Loren, illus. 2011. (Sluggers Ser.: 5). (ENG., Illus.). 448p. (J). (gr. 3-7). pap. 8.99 *(978-1-4169-1891-2(4)*, Simon & Schuster Bks. For Young Readers) Simon & Schuster Bks. For Young Readers.

—Home of the Brave. Long, Loren, illus. (Sluggers Ser.: 6). (ENG., Illus.). 336p. (J). (gr. 3-7). 2011. pap. 9.99 *(978-1-4169-1892-9(2))* 2010. 15.99 *(978-1-4169-1868-4(X))* Simon & Schuster Bks. For Young Readers. (Simon & Schuster Bks. For Young Readers).

—Magic in the Outfield. Long, Loren, illus. 2009. (Sluggers Ser.: 1). (ENG., Illus.). 160p. (J). (gr. 3-7). pap. 9.99 *(978-1-4169-1884-4(1)*, Simon & Schuster Bks. For Young Readers) Simon & Schuster Bks. For Young Readers.

—Water, Water Everywhere. Long, Loren, illus. (Sluggers Ser.: 4). (ENG., Illus.). (J). (gr. 3-7). 2010. 288p. pap. 9.99 *(978-1-4169-1890-5(6))* 2009. 272p. 14.99 *(978-1-4169-1866-0(3))* Simon & Schuster Bks. For Young Readers. (Simon & Schuster Bks. For Young Readers).

Longson, D. M. The Scunner. 2009. 32p. pap. 21.50 *(978-1-4092-6995-3(7))* Lulu Pr., Inc.

Look, Lenore. Alvin Ho: Allergic to Girls, School, & Other Scary Things. Pham, LeUyen, illus. 2009. (Alvin Ho Ser.: 1). (ENG.). 192p. (J). (gr. 1-4). 7.99 *(978-0-375-84930-5(0)*, Yearling) Random Hse. Children's Bks.

—Ruby Lu, Brave & True. Wilsdorf, Anne, illus. 2006. (Ruby Lu Ser.). 105p. (J). (gr. 1-5). 11.65 *(978-0-7569-6553-2(5))* Perfection Learning Corp.

Lopez Dekker, Anna. Everwhere. 2008. (ENG.). 137p. 31.95 *(978-1-4092-0318-6(2))* Lulu Pr., Inc.

Lord, Cynthia. Rules. 2007. (CHI.). 264p. (J). (gr. 4-7). pap. *(978-957-570-875-7(X))* Eastern Publishing Co., Ltd., The.

—Rules. 2009. 8.44 *(978-0-7848-2921-9(7)*, Everbind) Marco Bk. Co.

—Rules. 2008. (Illus.). 200p. (gr. 4-7). 17.00 *(978-0-7569-8283-6(9))* Perfection Learning Corp.

—Rules. (J). 2008. 77.49 *(978-1-4361-5837-4(0))* 2007. 220.75 *(978-1-4281-5209-0(1))* 2007. 87.75 *(978-1-4281-5214-4(8))* 2007. 74.75 *(978-1-4281-5208-3(3))* 2007. 89.75 *(978-1-4281-5212-0(1))* 2007. (SPA.). 72.75 *(978-1-4281-5210-6(5))* Recorded Bks., Inc.

—Rules. rev. l.t. ed. 2007. (Literacy Bridge Middle Reader Ser.). 191p. (J). (gr. 4-7). 23.95 *(978-0-7862-9559-3(7))* Thorndike Pr.

—Rules. 2008. lib. bdg. 17.20 *(978-1-4178-2956-9(7))* Turtleback.

—Rules (Scholastic Gold), 1 vol. (ENG.). (J). (gr. 4-7). 2008. 224p. pap. 8.99 *(978-0-439-44383-8(0)*, Scholastic Paperbacks) 2006. 208p. 19.99 *(978-0-439-44382-1(2)*, Scholastic Pr.) Scholastic, Inc.

Loving, Winifred "Oyoko". My Grandma Loves to Play. 2013. 28p. pap. 16.99 *(978-1-4669-7405-0(2))* Trafford Publishing.

Lowden, Stephanie. Time of the Eagle: A Story of an Ojibwe Winter. 2004. 128p. (J). pap. 12.00 *(978-1-883953-34-8(0))* Great Lakes Literary, LLC.

Lowden, Stephanie Golightly. Time of the Eagle: A Story of an Ojibwe Winter. 2006. 127p. (J). (gr. 3-7). 18.95 *(978-1-883953-38-6(3)*, Blue Horse Books) Great Lakes Literary, LLC.

Lowell, Susan. The Great Grand Canyon Time Train. Shroades, John / W., illus. 2011. 32p. (J). 15.95 *(978-1-933855-63-9(0))* Rio Nuevo Pubs.

Lowry, Brigid. Follow the Blue: A Novel. 2006. (ENG.). 208p. (YA). (gr. 8-12). pap. 18.99 *(978-0-312-34297-5(7)*, 900030648, St. Martin's Griffin) St. Martin's Pr.

Lowry, Lois. The Willoughbys. 2008. (Willoughbys Ser.). (ENG., Illus.). 176p. (J). (gr. 1-4). 17.99 *(978-0-618-97974-5(3)*, 1025183, Clarion Bks.) HarperCollins Pubs.

—The Willoughbys. 2010. (ENG.). 176p. (J). (gr. 3-7). 7.99 *(978-0-385-73776-0(9)*, Yearling) Random Hse. Children's Bks.

—The Willoughbys Return. 2020. (Willoughbys Ser.). (ENG.). 192p. (J). (gr. 3-7). 17.99 *(978-0-358-42389-8(9)*, 1792011, Clarion Bks.) HarperCollins Pubs.

Lu, Marie. The Kingdom of Back. 336p. (YA). (gr. 7). 2021. pap. 12.99 *(978-1-5247-3903-4(0)*, Penguin Books) 2020. (Illus.). 18.99 *(978-1-5247-3901-0(4)*, G.P. Putnam's Sons Books for Young Readers) Penguin Young Readers Group.

—The Kingdom of Back. 2019. (ENG.). 336p. lib. bdg. 22.80 *(978-1-6636-2728-5(2))* Perfection Learning Corp.

—Legend. aut. ltd. collector's ed. 2013. (Legend Trilogy: Bk. 1). (Illus.). 306p. (YA). mass mkt. 100.00 net. *(978-1-934267-38-7(4))* Gauntlet, Inc.

—Legend. 2011. (Legend Trilogy: Bk. 1). (ENG.). (YA). (gr. 8-12). 54.99 *(978-1-61657-044-6(X)*, Penguin AudioBooks) Penguin Publishing Group.

—Legend. (Legend Ser.: 1). (ENG.). (YA). (gr. 7). 2013. 352p. pap. 12.99 *(978-0-14-242207-6(X)*, Speak) 2011. 320p. 19.99 *(978-0-399-25675-2(X)*, G.P. Putnam's Sons Books for Young Readers) Penguin Young Readers Group.

—Legend. l.t. ed. 2012. (Legend Trilogy: Bk. 1). (ENG.). 394p. (J). (gr. 7-12). 23.99 *(978-1-4104-4606-0(9))* Thorndike Pr.

—Legend. (Legend Graphic Novels Ser.: 1). 2015. lib. bdg. 26.95 *(978-0-606-38424-7(3))* 2013. lib. bdg. 20.85 *(978-0-606-31701-6(5))* Turtleback.

Lubar, David. Curse of the Campfire Weenies: And Other Warped & Creepy Tales. 2008. (Weenies Stories Ser.). (ENG.). 208p. (J). (gr. 4-9). mass mkt. 5.99 *(978-0-7653-5771-7(2)*, 900042665, Starscape) Doherty, Tom Assocs., LLC.

—Sleeping Freshmen Never Lie. 2007. (ENG.). 288p. (YA). (gr. 7-18). 11.99 *(978-0-14-240780-6(1)*, Speak) Penguin Young Readers Group.

Lucado, Max. Itsy Bitsy Christmas: You're Never Too Little for His Love, 1 vol. 2013. (ENG., Illus.). 32p. (J). pap. 9.99 *(978-1-4003-2404-0(1))* Nelson, Thomas Inc.

Lucasfilm Book Group & Huddleston, Tom. The Darkness. 2017. (Star Wars Adventures in Wild Space Ser.: 4). (Illus.). 134p. (J). lib. bdg. 16.00 *(978-0-606-39962-3(3))* Turtleback.

Luchesi, Dennis. Benji Rabbit. 2013. 24p. pap. 24.95 *(978-1-62709-894-6(1))* America Star Bks.

Luciani, Brigitte. A Hubbub: Book 2, No. 2. Tharlet, Eve, illus. 2010. (Mr. Badger & Mrs. Fox Ser.: 2). (ENG.). 32p. (J). (gr. k-3). pap. 7.99 *(978-0-7613-5632-5(0)*, 16271d6f-0029-4813-9c24-d51cd664aca3, Graphic Universe™) Lerner Publishing Group.

—The Meeting: Book 1, No. 1. Tharlet, Eve, illus. 2010. (Mr. Badger & Mrs. Fox Ser.: 1). (ENG.). 32p. (J). (gr. k-3). pap. 7.99 *(978-0-7613-5631-8(2)*, 071a498b-43a0-413d-9653-5f39dd220232, Graphic Universe™) Lerner Publishing Group.

—Peace & Quiet: Book 4, No. 4. Tharlet, Eve, illus. 2012. (Mr. Badger & Mrs. Fox Ser.: 4). (ENG.). 32p. (J). (gr. k-3). pap. 7.99 *(978-0-8225-9163-4(4)*, c88a3e3a-49bd-4fd8-af9b-b8ad48fd6eb9, Graphic Universe™) Lerner Publishing Group.

—What a Team! Gauvin, Edward, tr. from FRE. Tharlet, Eve, illus. 2011. (Mr. Badger & Mrs. Fox Ser.: 3). (ENG.). 32p. (J). (gr. k-3). 25.26 *(978-0-7613-5627-1(4))* Lerner Publishing Group.

Luebbe, Tara & Cattie, Becky. Shark Nate-O. Duncan, Daniel, illus. 2018. (ENG.). 40p. (J). (gr. -1-3). 17.99 *(978-1-4998-0496-6(2))* Little Bee Books Inc.

Lukoff, Kyle. When Aidan Became a Brother, 1 vol. Juanita, Kaylani, illus. 2019. (ENG.). 32p. (J). (gr. -1-3). 19.95 *(978-1-62014-837-2(4)*, leelowbooks) Lee & Low Bks., Inc.

Luongo, Jane. Jake's First Word. Kelley, Patrick, illus. 2003. (Books for Young Learners). 16p. (J). 5.75 net. *(978-1-57274-258-1(5)*, 2456, Bks. for Young Learners) Owen, Richard C. Pubs., Inc.

Lupica, Mike. The Football Fiasco. 2018. (Zach & Zoe Mysteries Ser.: 3). (ENG., Illus.). 80p. (J). (gr. 1-4). 6.99 *(978-0-425-28943-3(5)*, Puffin Books); 14.99 *(978-0-425-28942-6(7)*, Philomel Bks.) Penguin Young Readers Group.

—The Half-Court Hero. 2018. (Zach & Zoe Mysteries Ser.: 2). (ENG., Illus.). 96p. (J). (gr. 1-4). 6.99 *(978-0-425-28940-2(0)*, Puffin Books) Penguin Young Readers Group.

—Heat. 2007. (ENG.). 256p. (J). (gr. 5-18). 8.99 *(978-0-14-240757-8(7)*, Puffin Books) Penguin Young Readers Group.

—Heat. 2007. 220p. (gr. 5-9). 18.00 *(978-0-7569-8131-0(X))* Perfection Learning Corp.

—The Hockey Rink Hunt. 2019. (Zach & Zoe Mysteries Ser.: 5). (ENG., Illus.). 80p. (J). (gr. 1-4). 14.99 *(978-0-425-28948-8(6)*, Philomel Bks.) Penguin Young Readers Group.

—Last Man Out. 2017. (ENG.). 272p. (J). (gr. 5). 8.99 *(978-0-14-751491-2(6)*, Puffin Books) Penguin Young Readers Group.

—The Missing Baseball. 2018. (Zach & Zoe Mysteries Ser.: 1). (ENG., Illus.). 80p. (J). (gr. 1-4). 6.99 *(978-0-425-28937-2(0)*, Puffin Books) Penguin Young Readers Group.

Luqman-Dawson, Amina. Freewater (Newbery & Coretta Scott King Award Winner) (ENG.). 416p. (J). (gr. 5-17). 2023. pap. 8.99 ***(978-0-316-05667-0(7))*** 2022. 16.99

(978-0-316-05661-8(8)) Little Brown & Co. (Jimmy Patterson).
Lynch, Chris. Angry Young Man. 2012. (ENG.). 192p. (YA). (gr. 7). pap. 10.99 *(978-1-4424-5419-4(9),* Simon & Schuster Bks. For Young Readers) Simon & Schuster Bks. For Young Readers.
—The Gravedigger's Cottage. 2004. (ENG.). 208p. (J). (gr. 7-18). 15.99 *(978-0-06-623940-8(0))* HarperCollins Pubs.
Lynn, Deidre. Treasure Delight: A Sweet Story about the Joy in Sharing. Morris, Jessica, illus. 2013. 36p. pap. 12.95 *(978-0-9893181-0-5(9))* LoveLight Media.
Lynn, Joseph. Color of My Words. 2014. (ENG.). 144p. (J). (gr. 5-12). 10.24 *(978-1-63245-277-1(4))* Lectorum Pubns., Inc.
Lyons, Maggie. Vin & Dorky Duet. 2012. 94p. pap. 9.95 *(978-1-61244-091-0(6))* Halo Publishing International.
Lyons-Reid, Nashika. My Brother the Superhero. 2008. 28p. pap. 15.99 *(978-1-4363-5941-2(4))* Xlibris Corp.
MacDonald, George. The History of Gutta-Percha Willie. 2006. 116p. per. 9.95 *(978-1-59818-578-2(0))* Aegypan.
—Ranald Bannermans Boyhood. 2006. 168p. per. 13.95 *(978-1-59818-238-5(2))* Aegypan.
MacDonald, Maryann. No Room for Francie. Richards, Virginia Helen, illus. 2010. 64p. (J). (gr. 1-3). pap. 6.95 *(978-0-8198-5168-0(X))* Pauline Bks. & Media.
MacDonald, Tom. Secret of the Tree: Marcus Speer's Ecosentinel. Stieber, Joel, illus. 2009. 300p. pap. 18.95 *(978-0-595-52402-0(8))* iUniverse, Inc.
Mack, Harry. The Treasure Mystery Clues. 2011. 70p. pap. 19.95 *(978-1-4626-2487-4(1))* America Star Bks.
Mack, Paulette. Cookout at Grandma's House: The Adventures of Mielle & Cheeky. 2006. (ENG., Illus.). 24p. per. 10.95 *(978-1-59800-998-9(2))* Outskirts Pr., Inc.
Mackall, Dandi Daley. Natalie Wants a Puppy, 1 vol. Blakeslee, Lys, illus. 2009. (That's Nat! Ser.: 6). (ENG.). 96p. (J). (gr. 1-4). pap. 4.99 *(978-0-310-71571-9(7))* Zonderkidz.
—The Silence of Murder. 2012. 336p. (YA). (gr. 9). pap. 10.99 *(978-0-375-87293-8(0),* Ember) Random Hse. Children's Bks.
—There's a Baby in There!, 0 vols. Whitt, Carlynn, illus. 2012. (ENG.). 32p. (J). (gr. -1-k). 16.99 *(978-0-7614-6191-3(4),* 9780761461913, Two Lions) Amazon Publishing.
MacKenzie, Carine. El Secreto de la Hermana Mayor, el Maria.Tr. of Big Sister's Secret. (SPA.). (J). 1.99 *(978-1-56063-700-4(5),* 497731) Editorial Unilit.
Mackler, Carolyn. Not If I Can Help It (Scholastic Gold) 2019. (ENG.). 240p. (J). (gr. 3-7). 16.99 *(978-0-545-70948-4(2),* Scholastic Pr.) Scholastic, Inc.
Maclachlan, Patricia. The Boxcar Children Beginning: the Aldens of Fair Meadow Farm. Jessell, Tim, illus. (Boxcar Children Mysteries Ser.). (ENG.). 144p. (J). (gr. 2-5). 2013. 7.99 *(978-0-8075-6617-6(9),* 807566179) 2012. 16.99 *(978-0-8075-6616-9(0),* 807566160) Random Hse. Children's Bks. (Random Hse. Bks. for Young Readers).
MacLachlan, Patricia. Fly Away. 2014. (ENG., Illus.). 128p. (J). (gr. 2). 15.99 *(978-1-4424-6008-9(3),* McElderry, Margaret K. Bks.) McElderry, Margaret K. Bks.
—The True Gift. Floca, Brian, illus. 2013. (ENG.). 112p. (J). (gr. 2-6). pap. 7.99 *(978-1-4424-8858-8(1),* Atheneum Bks. for Young Readers) Simon & Schuster Children's Publishing.
Maddox, Jake. Blue Line Breakaway. Tiffany, Sean, illus. 2018. (Jake Maddox Sports Stories Ser.). (ENG.). 72p. (J). (gr. 3-6). pap. 5.95 *(978-1-4965-6319-4(0),* 138058); lib. bdg. 25.99 *(978-1-4965-6317-0(4),* 138049) Capstone. (Stone Arch Bks.).
—Climbing Strong. 2019. (Jake Maddox JV Ser.). (ENG.). 96p. (J). (gr. 4-6). lib. bdg. 25.99 *(978-1-4965-7524-1(5),* 139146, Stone Arch Bks.) Capstone.
—Rookie Runner. 2018. (Jake Maddox JV Ser.). (ENG., Illus.). 96p. (J). (gr. 4-6). pap. 5.95 *(978-1-4965-6334-7(4),* 138064); lib. bdg. 25.99 *(978-1-4965-6332-3(8),* 138063) Capstone. (Stone Arch Bks.).
Maddox, Jake & Maddox, Jake. Cycling Champion, 1 vol. Garcia, Eduardo, illus. 2012. (Jake Maddox Sports Stories Ser.). (ENG.). 72p. (J). (gr. 3-6). pap. 5.95 *(978-1-4342-3904-4(7),* 118089); lib. bdg. 25.99 *(978-1-4342-3290-8(5),* 116253) Capstone. (Stone Arch Bks.).
Mader, Jan. My Brother Wants to Be Like Me. Palmer, Kate Salley, illus. l.t. ed. 2005. (ENG.). 16p. (gr. k-2). pap. 7.95 *(978-1-879835-27-6(4),* Kaeden Bks.) Kaeden Corp.
The Madrona Heroes Register: Echoes of the Past. 2013. (Illus.). 344p. pap. 12.43 *(978-0-9899905-4-7(0))* Atelier Mythologie.
Madrzak, Carole. The Arronna Crystal. 2012. 234p. pap. 24.95 *(978-1-4137-9968-2(X))* America Star Bks.
Magnin, Joyce. Jelly Bean Summer. 272p. (J). (gr. 3-7). 2018. pap. 7.99 *(978-1-4926-6084-2(1))* 2017. (ENG.). 16.99 *(978-1-4926-4672-3(5))* Sourcebooks, Inc.
Magoon, Kekla. Fire in the Streets. 2013. (ENG., Illus.). 352p. (J). (gr. 5-9). pap. 8.99 *(978-1-4424-2231-5(9),* Aladdin) Simon & Schuster Children's Publishing.
—The Rock & the River. 1. 2009. (ENG.). 304p. (J). (gr. 5-9). 19.99 *(978-1-4169-7582-3(9),* Aladdin) Simon & Schuster Children's Publishing.
Maher, Mickle Brandt. Master Stitchum & the Moon. Dousias, Spiro, illus. 2003. (J). 19.99 *(978-1-932188-01-1(0))* Bollix Bks.
Mahmoodian, Maryam. Muslim Teens In: Pitfalls & Pranks. 2008. (YA). per. 10.95 *(978-0-9793577-3-2(X))* Muslim Writers Publishing.
Mahoney, Jerry. My Rotten Stepbrother Ruined Cinderella. Bitskoff, Aleksei, illus. 2017. (My Rotten Stepbrother Ruined Fairy Tales Ser.). (ENG.). 160p. (J). (gr. 3-6). lib. bdg. 26.65 *(978-1-4965-4466-7(8),* 134771, Stone Arch Bks.) Capstone.
—My Rotten Stepbrother Ruined Snow White. Bitskoff, Aleksei, illus. 2017. (My Rotten Stepbrother Ruined Fairy Tales Ser.). (ENG.). 160p. (J). (gr. 3-6). pap. 8.95 *(978-1-4965-4467-4(6),* 134772); lib. bdg. 26.65 *(978-1-4965-4463-6(3),* 134768) Capstone. (Stone Arch Bks.).
—My Stupid Stepbrother Ruined Aladdin. Bitskoff, Aleksei, illus. 2017. (My Rotten Stepbrother Ruined Fairy Tales Ser.). (ENG.). 160p. (J). (gr. 3-6). lib. bdg. 26.65 *(978-1-4965-4464-3(1),* 134769, Stone Arch Bks.) Capstone.
—My Stupid Stepbrother Ruined Beauty & the Beast. Bitskoff, Aleksei, illus. 2017. (My Rotten Stepbrother Ruined Fairy Tales Ser.). (ENG.). 160p. (J). (gr. 3-6). lib. bdg. 26.65 *(978-1-4965-4465-0(X),* 134770, Stone Arch Bks.) Capstone.
Maier, Brenda. El Fuertecito Rojo (the Little Red Fort) Sánchez, Sonia, illus. 2018. (SPA.). 40p. (J). (gr. -1-3). pap. 4.99 *(978-1-338-26901-7(1),* Scholastic en Espanol) Scholastic, Inc.
—The Little Red Fort (Little Ruby's Big Ideas) Sánchez, Sonia, illus. 2018. (ENG.). 40p. (J). (gr. -1-3). 17.99 *(978-0-545-85919-6(0),* Scholastic Pr.) Scholastic, Inc.
Maier, Inger. Ben's Flying Flowers. Bogade, Maria, illus. 2012. 32p. (J). 14.95 *(978-1-4338-1133-3(2));* (ENG.). pap. 9.95 *(978-1-4338-1132-6(4))* American Psychological Assn. (Magination Pr.).
—When Lizzy Was Afraid of Trying New Things. Candon, Jennifer, illus. 2004. (ENG.). 32p. (J). 14.95 *(978-1-59147-170-7(2),* Magination Pr.) American Psychological Assn.
Maier, Inger M. When Lizzie Was Afraid: Of Trying New Things. Candon, Jennifer, illus. 2004. 32p. (J). pap. 9.95 *(978-1-59147-171-4(0),* Magination Pr.) American Psychological Assn.
Mair, J. Samia. The Great Race to Sycamore Street. 2013. (ENG., Illus.). 196p. (J). (gr. 3-6). pap. 12.99 *(978-1-84774-057-1(X))* Kube Publishing Ltd. GBR. Dist: Consortium Bk. Sales & Distribution.
Maisner, Heather & Stephenson, Kristina. It's My Turn! 2005. (First-Time Stories Ser.). (ENG., Illus.). 24p. (J). (gr. -1-1). pap. 16.19 *(978-0-7534-5740-5(7),* 9780753457405) Kingfisher Publications, plc GBR. Dist: Children's Plus, Inc.
Malcolm, Jahnna N. Pirate's Revenge. Comport, Sally Wern, illus. 2003. 77p. (J). *(978-1-931020-09-1(4))* HOP, LLC.
Malea. Princess Melia. 2007. 145p. (J). pap. 15.95 *(978-1-58909-367-6(4))* Bookstand Publishing.
Malison, Anna. Through Thick & Thin. 2006. (ENG.). 136p. per. *(978-1-897117-14-9(0))* Gospel Folio Pr.
Maltese, John. I Love You the Most. 2009. (ENG.). 33p. pap. 16.40 *(978-0-557-09465-3(8))* Lulu Pr., Inc.
Mammay, Judith. Knowing Joseph. (ENG., Illus.). 256p. (J). (gr. 2-7). 2009. pap. 8.95 *(978-1-933831-06-0(5))* 2008. 13.95 *(978-1-933831-05-3(7))* Blooming Tree Pr.
Mandarino, Gene. What's Autism? 2006. pap. 25.00 *(978-0-9786795-0-7(4))* Charlie's Gift.
Mangum, James A. & Spires, Sidney. The Fairy the Chupacabra & Those Marfa Lights: A West Texas Fable. Mangum, James A., illus. 2008. (Illus.). 32p. (J). 17.95 *(978-0-9798391-5-3(7))* Texas Bk. Pubs. Assn.
Manivong, Laura. Escaping the Tiger. 2010. (ENG.). 224p. (J). (gr. 5-18). 15.99 *(978-0-06-166177-8(5))* HarperCollins Pubs.
Mannering, Rose. The Spotty Dotty Daffodil. Straker, Bethany, illus. 2014. (ENG.). 32p. (J). (gr. -1-k). 16.95 *(978-1-62636-346-5(3),* Sky Pony Pr.) Skyhorse Publishing Co., Inc.
Mantchev, Lisa. Jinx & the Doom Fight Crime! Cotterill, Samantha, illus. 2018. (ENG.). 32p. (J). (gr. -1-3). 16.99 *(978-1-4814-6701-8(8),* Simon & Schuster/Paula Wiseman Bks.) Simon & Schuster/Paula Wiseman Bks.
Manushkin, Fran. Big Brothers Are the Best, 1 vol. Richards, Kirsten, illus. 2012. (Fiction Picture Bks.). (ENG.). 24p. (J). (gr. -1 — 1). 6.95 *(978-1-4048-7224-0(8),* 118098, Picture Window Bks.) Capstone.
—Big Sisters Are the Best, 1 vol. Richards, Kirsten, illus. 2012. (Fiction Picture Bks.). (ENG.). 24p. (J). (gr. -1 — 1). 6.95 *(978-1-4048-7225-7(6),* 118099, Picture Window Bks.) Capstone.
Marciniak, Christine. Lights, Camera, All! 2013. 232p. (J). pap. 13.99 *(978-1-61271-214-7(2))* Zumaya Pubns. LLC.
Maresca, Beth Anne, illus. Megan Owlet. 2015. (ENG.). 32p. (J). (gr. -1-k). 16.99 *(978-1-63220-404-2(5),* Sky Pony Pr.) Skyhorse Publishing Co., Inc.
Margaret I. Pascuzzo. Anton Finds a Treasure. Bicking, Judith, illus. 2008. (ENG.). 18p. pap. 12.00 *(978-1-4251-8683-8(1))* Trafford Publishing.
Margolis, Leslie. Girl's Best Friend. 2011. (Maggie Brooklyn Mystery Ser.). (ENG.). 288p. (J). (gr. 3-12). pap. 7.99 *(978-1-59990-690-4(2),* 900076050, Bloomsbury USA Childrens) Bloomsbury Publishing USA.
—Secrets at the Chocolate Mansion. 2014. (Maggie Brooklyn Mystery Ser.). (ENG.). 272p. (J). (gr. 3-6). pap. 7.99 *(978-1-61963-493-0(7),* 900138595, Bloomsbury USA Childrens) Bloomsbury Publishing USA.
—Vanishing Acts. 2013. (Maggie Brooklyn Mystery Ser.). (ENG.). 256p. (J). (gr. 3-6). pap. 7.99 *(978-1-59990-981-3(2),* 900096404, Bloomsbury USA Childrens) Bloomsbury Publishing USA.
Marinsky, Jane. Just Perfect. Marinsky, Jane, illus. 2012. (ENG., Illus.). 32p. (J). (gr. k). 16.95 *(978-1-56792-428-2(X))* Godine, David R. Pub.
Marmon, Jim. Alexander Barnaby Meadowlark. 2007. 132p. per. 19.95 *(978-1-4241-7662-5(X))* America Star Bks.
Marquess, Dana. Night of the Lighted Freedom - A Firefly Fantasy. 2006. (ENG., Illus.). 32p. (J). 19.95 *(978-1-932278-06-4(0))* Mayhaven Publishing, Inc.
Marquis, Michelle. Mikey & the Mysterious Door. 2008. 32p. pap. 14.99 *(978-1-4343-4823-4(7))* AuthorHouse.
Marr, Ella J. The Adventures of Curtis & Grammy. 2006. 57p. pap. 16.95 *(978-1-4241-4743-4(3))* PublishAmerica, Inc.
Marsden, Carolyn. The White Zone. 2012. (Exceptional Reading & Language Arts Titles for Intermediate Grades Ser.). (ENG.). 192p. (J). (gr. 4-8). 17.95 *(978-0-7613-7383-4(7),* Carolrhoda Bks.) Lerner Publishing Group.
Marsh, Carole. The Behemoth Blizzard Mystery. (Masters of Disasters Ser.). (Illus.). 118p. (J). (gr. 3-5). 2008. per. 5.99 *(978-0-635-06464-6(2))* 2007. 14.95 *(978-0-635-06467-7(7))* Gallopade International.
—The Colonial Caper Mystery at Williamsburg. 2009. (Real Kids, Real Places Ser.). (J). (gr. 2-9). lib. bdg. 18.99 *(978-0-635-06832-3(X));* (Illus.). 143p. (gr. 4-7). pap. 7.99 *(978-0-635-06826-2(5),* Marsh, Carole Bks.) Gallopade International.
—The Earthshaking Earthquake Mystery!, 1. 2009. (Carole Marsh's Masters of Disasters Ser.). (ENG., Illus.). 118p. (J). (gr. 3-6). 18.69 *(978-0-635-06339-7(5))* Gallopade International.
—The Ferocious Forest Fire Mystery. 2008. (Masters of Disasters Ser.). (Illus.). 118p. (J). (gr. 3-5). 14.95 *(978-0-635-06468-4(5));* 6. (ENG., (gr. 2-4). 18.69 *(978-0-635-06465-3(0))* Gallopade International.
—The Ghost of the Golden Gate Bridge. 2009. (Real Kids, Real Places Ser.). (Illus.). 146p. (J). lib. bdg. 18.99 *(978-0-635-07047-0(2),* Marsh, Carole Mysteries) Gallopade International.
—The Horrendous Hurricane Mystery. 2007. (Carole Marsh Mysteries Ser.). (Illus.). 118p. (J). (gr. 2-9). per. 7.99 *(978-0-635-06340-3(9))* Gallopade International.
—The Mystery at Fort Thunderbolt. 2007. (Pretty Darn Scary Mysteries Ser.). (Illus.). 113p. (YA). lib. bdg. 18.99 *(978-0-635-07021-0(9),* Marsh, Carole Mysteries) Gallopade International.
—The Mystery at Mount Vernon. Friedlander, Randolyn, illus. 2010. (Real Kids, Real Places Ser.). 32p. pap. 7.99 *(978-0-635-07444-7(3),* Marsh, Carole Mysteries) Gallopade International.
—The Mystery at Mount Vernon: Home of America's First President George Washington. 2010. (Real Kids, Real Places Ser.). (Illus.). 158p. (J). 18.99 *(978-0-635-07443-0(5),* Marsh, Carole Mysteries) Gallopade International.
—The Mystery at Yellowstone National Park. 2010. (Real Kids, Real Places Ser.). (Illus.). 158p. (J). 18.99 *(978-0-635-07437-9(0),* Marsh, Carole Mysteries) Gallopade International.
—The Mystery in Hawaii. Friedlander, Randolyn, illus. 2010. (Real Kids, Real Places Ser.). 32p. pap. 7.99 *(978-0-635-07447-8(8),* Marsh, Carole Mysteries) Gallopade International.
—The Mystery in Hawaii: The 50th State. 2010. (Real Kids, Real Places Ser.). (Illus.). 157p. (J). 18.99 *(978-0-635-07446-1(X),* Marsh, Carole Mysteries) Gallopade International.
—The Mystery in Las Vegas. 2009. (Real Kids, Real Places Ser.). (Illus.). 145p. (J). lib. bdg. 18.99 *(978-0-635-07045-6(6),* Marsh, Carole Mysteries) Gallopade International.
—The Mystery of the Graveyard of the Atlantic. 2009. (Real Kids, Real Places Ser.). (Illus.). 144p. (J). lib. bdg. 18.99 *(978-0-635-07046-3(4),* Marsh, Carole Mysteries) Gallopade International.
—The Mystery of the Haunted Ghost Town. 2009. (Real Kids, Real Places Ser.). 144p. (J). 18.99 *(978-0-635-07044-9(8),* Marsh, Carole Mysteries) Gallopade International.
—The Mystery on the Oregon Trail. 2010. (Real Kids, Real Places Ser.). (Illus.). 158p. (J). 18.99 *(978-0-635-07440-9(0),* Marsh, Carole Mysteries) Gallopade International.
—The Mystery on the Oregon Trail. Friedlander, Randolyn, illus. 2010. (Real Kids, Real Places Ser.). 32p. pap. 7.99 *(978-0-635-07441-6(9),* Marsh, Carole Mysteries) Gallopade International.
—The Secret of Eyesocket Island. 2009. (Pretty Darn Scary Mysteries Ser.). (Illus.). 113p. (J). lib. bdg. 18.99 *(978-0-635-07022-7(7),* Marsh, Carole Mysteries) Gallopade International.
—The Treacherous Tornado Mystery. 2007. (Masters of Disasters Ser.). (Illus.). 118p. (J). (gr. 2-9). 14.95 *(978-0-635-06394-6(8));* per. 5.99 *(978-0-635-06338-0(7))* Gallopade International.
—The Voracious Volcano Mystery. 2008. (Masters of Disasters Ser.). (Illus.). 118p. (J). (gr. 3-5). 14.95 *(978-0-635-06466-0(9));* per. 5.99 *(978-0-635-06463-9(4))* Gallopade International.
Marshall, Carly. The Babysitter & Little Mr. Trouble Maker. 2013. 24p. 24.95 *(978-1-63000-616-7(5));* pap. 24.95 *(978-1-63000-539-9(8))* America Star Bks.
Martens, Kara. The Two Missing Kids. 2008. 80p. pap. 11.49 *(978-1-4343-8696-0(1))* AuthorHouse.
Martin, Ann M. Mind Your Own Business, Kristy! (the Baby-Sitters Club #107) 2014. (39 Clues: Unstoppable Ser.: 107). (ENG.). 160p. (J). (gr. 3-7). E-Book 12.99 *(978-0-545-79315-5(7),* Scholastic Paperbacks) Scholastic, Inc.
Martin, Brian. The Lost Ring. McDonald, Kim, illus. 2007. 42p. (J). *(978-0-9798059-1-2(0))* Lunchbox Stories Inc.
Martin, C. L. Ducky Goes to the Dentist. 2013. 16p. pap. 24.95 *(978-1-62709-742-0(2))* America Star Bks.
Martin, David. Three Little Bears Play All Day: Brand New Readers. Gutierrez, Akemi, illus. 2010. (Brand New Readers Ser.). (ENG.). 48p. (J). (gr. -1-3). pap. 6.99 *(978-0-7636-4230-3(4))* Candlewick Pr.
Martin, Gary & Zondervan Bibles Staff. The Maiden of Thunder, 1 vol. Cariello, Sergio & Lanphear, Dave, illus. 2008. (Z Graphic Novels / Son of Samson Ser.). (ENG.). 160p. (J). (gr. 4-7). pap. 6.99 *(978-0-310-71281-7(5))* Zondervan.
Martin, Rafe. The Shark God. Shannon, David, illus. 2007. (Scholastic Bookshelf Ser.). (ENG.). 32p. (J). (gr. k-2). 18.69 *(978-0-590-39570-0(X))* Scholastic, Inc.
Maschari, Jennifer. The Remarkable Journey of Charlie Price. 2016. (ENG.). 304p. (J). (gr. 3-7). 16.99 *(978-0-06-238010-4(9),* Balzer & Bray) HarperCollins Pubs.
Masessa, Ed. Wandmaker. 2016. (ENG.). 336p. (J). (gr. 3-7). 12.99 *(978-0-545-86174-8(8),* Scholastic Pr.) Scholastic, Inc.
Mason, Aaron & Warr, Doug. Baffelgagging Blundernagging Brothers in the Curse of the Bog Frog. Walton, Jason, illus. 2008. (ENG.). 192p. (YA). 29.95 *(978-0-9800274-0-2(3))* Whirlwhim.
Mason, Craig. Turtle Games. Mason, Bergetta, illus. 2003. 32p. (J). 4.99 *(978-0-9729153-0-4(3))* 1 Sleeve Publishing.
Mason, Jane B. & Stephens, Sarah Hines. Play Dead, 1. 2013. (Dog & His Girl Mysteries Ser.). (ENG.). 208p. (J). (gr. 4-6). 18.69 *(978-0-545-43624-3(9))* Scholastic, Inc.
Masters, Susan Rowan. Night Journey to Vicksburg. Killcoyne, Hope L., ed. Smith, Duane A., illus. 2003. (Adventures in America Ser.). 74p. (J). (gr. 4). 14.95 *(978-1-893110-30-4(3))* Silver Moon Pr.
Mathieu, Jennifer. Afterward. 2017. (YA). lib. bdg. 20.85 *(978-0-606-40590-4(9))* Turtleback.
Matsakis, Cynthia. Sister Sun, Brother Storm. Silver, Jane, illus. 2012. 32p. 24.95 *(978-1-4575-0768-7(4))* Dog Ear Publishing, LLC.
Matson, Morgan. Save the Date. 2018. (ENG., Illus.). 432p. (YA). (gr. 7). 17.99 *(978-1-4814-0457-0(1),* Simon & Schuster Bks. For Young Readers) Simon & Schuster Bks. For Young Readers.
Matt and Dave, Matt and. Yuck's Pet Worm. Baines, Nigel, illus. 2013. (Yuck Ser.). (ENG.). 112p. (J). (gr. 2-5). pap. 6.99 *(978-1-4424-8149-7(8),* Simon & Schuster/Paula Wiseman Bks.) Simon & Schuster/Paula Wiseman Bks.
—Yuck's Robotic Butt Blast. Baines, Nigel, illus. 2013. (Yuck Ser.). (ENG.). 112p. (J). (gr. 2-5). 15.99 *(978-1-4424-8308-8(3));* pap. 4.99 *(978-1-4424-8309-5(1))* Simon & Schuster/Paula Wiseman Bks. (Simon & Schuster/Paula Wiseman Bks.).
Maxwell, John C. Sometimes You Win — Sometimes You Learn for Kids. Bjorkman, Steve, illus. 2016. (ENG.). 32p. (J). (gr. -1-3). 18.99 *(978-0-316-28408-0(4))* Little, Brown Bks. for Young Readers.
May, Eleanor. Albert Adds Up! Melmon, Deborah, illus. 2014. (Mouse Math (r) Ser.). 32p. (J). (gr. -1-1). 22.60 *(978-1-57565-744-8(9))* Astra Publishing Hse.
—Albert Adds Up! 2018. (Mouse Math Ser.). (ENG.). 32p. (J). (gr. -1-1). lib. bdg. 34.28 *(978-1-4896-8297-0(X),* AV2 by Weigl) Weigl Pubs., Inc.
—The Great Shape-up. 2008. pap. 34.95 *(978-1-58013-763-8(6))* Astra Publishing Hse.
—Keesha's Bright Idea. Wummer, Amy, illus. 2008. (Social Studies Connects Ser.). (ENG.). 32p. (J). (gr. 1-3). pap. 5.99 *(978-1-57565-273-3(0),* 3323200f-f322-464a-8b53-10c4aba531f6, Kane Press) Astra Publishing Hse.
—Keesha's Bright Idea. Wummer, Amy, illus. 2009. (Social Studies Connects (r) Ser.). (ENG.). (gr. 1-3). pap. 33.92 *(978-0-7613-4806-1(9))* Lerner Publishing Group.
May, Sophie. Dotty Dimple's Flyaway. 2018. (ENG., Illus.). 90p. (YA). (gr. 7-12). pap. *(978-93-5297-348-4(8))* Alpha Editions.
Mayer, Mercer. Bedtime Stories - Little Critter. Mayer, Mercer, illus. 2013. (Little Critter Ser.). (ENG., Illus.). 144p. (J). (gr. -1-3). pap. 11.99 *(978-0-06-223640-1(7),* HarperFestival) HarperCollins Pubs.
—Just a Little Too Little. 2012. (Little Critter Ser.). (Illus.). (J). lib. bdg. 13.55 *(978-0-606-23567-9(1))* Turtleback.
—Little Critter: It's Easter, Little Critter! An Easter & Springtime Book for Kids. Mayer, Mercer, illus. 2007. (Little Critter Ser.). (ENG., Illus.). 20p. (J). (gr. -1-1). pap. 6.99 *(978-0-06-053974-0(7),* HarperFestival) HarperCollins Pubs.
—Little Critter's Family Treasury. 2018. (Illus.). 176p. (J). (gr. -1-2). 9.99 *(978-1-5247-6619-1(4),* Random Hse. Bks. for Young Readers) Random Hse. Children's Bks.
Mayer, Mercer & Mayer, Gina. The New Potty (Little Critter) 2003. (Look-Look Ser.). (Illus.). 24p. (J). (-k). pap. 5.99 *(978-0-375-82631-3(9),* Random Hse. Bks. for Young Readers) Random Hse. Children's Bks.
Mazurick, Shannon K. Gemm: The Treasure Hunt with Griffin. 2012. 32p. pap. 19.99 *(978-1-4772-7740-9(4))* AuthorHouse.
Mbuthia, Waithira. My Sister's Wedding: A Story of Kenya. Karanja, Geoffrey Gacheru, illus. 2005. (Make Friends Around the World Ser.). (ENG.). 32p. (J). (gr. k-3). 19.95 *(978-1-56899-898-5(8),* BC8006); 15.95 *(978-1-56899-896-1(1),* B8006) Soundprints.
McCall Smith, Alexander. Max & Maddy & the Bursting Balloons Mystery. Pamintuan, Macky, illus. 2008. (Max & Maddy Ser.). (ENG.). 70p. (J). (gr. 3-6). 17.44 *(978-1-59990-035-3(1),* 9781599900353) Bloomsbury Publishing USA.
—Max & Maddy & the Chocolate Money Mystery. Pamintuan, Macky, illus. 2008. (Max & Maddy Ser.). (ENG.). 72p. (J). (gr. 3-6). 17.44 *(978-1-59990-036-0(X),* 9781599900360) Bloomsbury Publishing USA.
—School Ship Tobermory. 2016. (School Ship Tobermory Ser.: 1). (ENG., Illus.). 224p. (J). (gr. 3-7). 15.99 *(978-0-399-55261-8(8),* Delacorte Bks. for Young Readers) Random Hse. Children's Bks.
McCarthy, Andrew. Just Fly Away. 2018. (ENG.). 272p. (gr. 9-12). pap. 10.95 *(978-1-61620-800-4(7),* 73800) Algonquin Young Readers.
—Just Fly Away. 2018. lib. bdg. 22.05 *(978-0-606-40972-8(6))* Turtleback.
McCarty, Peter. Chloe. McCarty, Peter, illus. 2012. (ENG., Illus.). 40p. (J). (gr. -1-1). 16.99 *(978-0-06-114291-8(3),* Balzer & Bray) HarperCollins Pubs.
McClintock, Barbara. Adèle & Simon. McClintock, Barbara, illus. 2006. (Adele & Simon Ser.). (ENG., Illus.). 40p. (J). (gr. -1-3). 21.99 *(978-0-374-38044-1(9),* 900028406, Farrar, Straus & Giroux (BYR)) Farrar, Straus & Giroux.
McCLure, Beverly Stowe. Listen to the Ghost. 2005. 163p. (J). per. 16.95 *(978-1-933353-51-7(1),* Paladin Timeless) Twilight Times Bks.
McClure, Wendy. Wanderville. 2014. (Wanderville Ser.: 1). (ENG.). 240p. (J). (gr. 3-7). pap. 7.99 *(978-1-59514-701-1(2),* Razorbill) Penguin Young Readers Group.
Mccormick, Scott. Mr. Pants: It's Go Time! Lazzell, R. H., illus. 2015. (Mr. Pants Ser.: 1). 128p. (J). (gr. 1-3). 9.99 *(978-0-14-751710-4(9),* Puffin Books) Penguin Young Readers Group.
McCullough, Myrina D. Feet. Schafrath, Ty, illus. 2013. 28p. pap. 15.00 *(978-0-9847740-1-2(7))* Systems Group, Inc., The.
McCully, Emily Arnold. Sam & the Big Kids. McCully, Emily Arnold, illus. 2014. (I Like to Read Ser.). (ENG., Illus.). 24p. (J). (gr. -1-3). 7.99 *(978-0-8234-3060-4(X))* Holiday Hse., Inc.
McDaniel, Lurlene. Angels in Pink: Raina's Story. 2006. (Angels in Pink Ser.). (ENG.). 208p. (YA). (gr. 7-12). mass mkt. 6.99 *(978-0-440-23866-9(8),* Laurel Leaf) Random Hse. Children's Bks.
—Breathless. 2010. (ENG.). 176p. (YA). (gr. 7). mass mkt. 7.99 *(978-0-440-24016-7(6),* Delacorte Bks. for Young Readers) Random Hse. Children's Bks.
McDine, Donna M. Powder Monkey. Snider, Kc, illus. 2013. 24p. 19.95 *(978-1-61633-384-3(7));* pap. 10.95 *(978-1-61633-385-0(5))* Guardian Angel Publishing, Inc.
McDonald, Kirsten. The Big Rain, 1 vol. Meza, Erika, illus. 2015. (Carlos & Carmen Ser.). (ENG.). 32p. (J). (gr. k-3). 32.79 *(978-1-62402-137-4(9),* 19071, Calico Chapter Bks) Magic Wagon.

S

—The Costume Contest. Meza, Erika, illus. 2016. (Carlos & Carmen Ser.). (ENG.). 32p. (J). (gr. -1-3). lib. bdg. 32.79 (978-1-62402-182-4(4), 24543, Calico Chapter Bks) Magic Wagon.

—El Error Rico (the Yummy Mistake) Meza, Erika, illus. 2018. (Carlos & Carmen (Spanish Version) (Calico Kid) Ser.). (SPA.). 32p. (J). (gr. -1-3). lib. bdg. 32.79 (978-1-5321-3324-4(3), 28511, Calico Chapter Bks) Magic Wagon.

—El Fin de Semana Arenoso (the Sandy Weekend) Meza, Erika, illus. 2018. (Carlos & Carmen (Spanish Version) (Calico Kid) Ser.). (SPA.). 32p. (J). (gr. -1-3). lib. bdg. 32.79 (978-1-5321-3321-3(9), 28505, Calico Chapter Bks) Magic Wagon.

—The Fun Fort. Anaya, Fátima, illus. 2017. (Carlos & Carmen Ser.). (ENG.). 32p. (J). (gr. -1-3). lib. bdg. 32.79 (978-1-5321-3033-5(3), 27035, Calico Chapter Bks) Magic Wagon.

—The Green Surprise, 1 vol. Meza, Erika, illus. 2015. (Carlos & Carmen Ser.). (ENG.). 32p. (J). (gr. k-3). 32.79 (978-1-62402-138-1(7), 19073, Calico Chapter Bks) Magic Wagon.

—Las Ruedas Tambaleantes (the Wobbly Wheels) Meza, Erika, illus. 2018. (Carlos & Carmen (Spanish Version) (Calico Kid) Ser.). (SPA.). 32p. (J). (gr. -1-3). lib. bdg. 32.79 (978-1-5321-3323-7(5), 28509, Calico Chapter Bks) Magic Wagon.

—The Nighttime Noise, 1 vol. Meza, Erika, illus. 2015. (Carlos & Carmen Ser.). (ENG.). 32p. (J). (gr. k-3). 32.79 (978-1-62402-139-8(5), 19075, Calico Chapter Bks) Magic Wagon.

—The One-Tire House, 1 vol. Meza, Erika, illus. 2015. (Carlos & Carmen Ser.). (ENG.). 32p. (J). (gr. k-3). 32.79 (978-1-62402-140-4(9), 19077, Calico Chapter Bks) Magic Wagon.

—Over the Fence. Anaya, Fátima, illus. 2017. (Carlos & Carmen Ser.). (ENG.). 32p. (J). (gr. -1-3). lib. bdg. 32.79 (978-1-5321-3034-2(1), 27036, Calico Chapter Bks) Magic Wagon.

—The Perfect Piñatas. Meza, Erika, illus. 2016. (Carlos & Carmen Ser.). (ENG.). 32p. (J). (gr. -1-3). lib. bdg. 32.79 (978-1-62402-183-1(2), 24545, Calico Chapter Bks) Magic Wagon.

—The Pet Show Problem. Meza, Erika, illus. 2016. (Carlos & Carmen Ser.). (ENG.). 32p. (J). (gr. -1-3). lib. bdg. 32.79 (978-1-62402-184-8(0), 24547, Calico Chapter Bks) Magic Wagon.

—The Sandy Weekend, 1 vol. Meza, Erika, illus. 2016. (Carlos & Carmen Ser.). (ENG.). 32p. (J). (gr. -1-3). 32.79 (978-1-62402-142-8(5), 21551, Calico Chapter Bks) Magic Wagon.

—The Sparkly Night. Meza, Erika, illus. 2016. (Carlos & Carmen Ser.). (ENG.). 32p. (J). (gr. -1-3). lib. bdg. 32.79 (978-1-62402-185-5(9), 24549, Calico Chapter Bks) Magic Wagon.

—Tío Time, 1 vol. Meza, Erika, illus. 2016. (Carlos & Carmen Ser.). (ENG.). 32p. (J). (gr. -1-3). 32.79 (978-1-62402-143-5(3), 21553, Calico Chapter Bks) Magic Wagon.

—Too Many Valentines. Anaya, Fátima, illus. 2017. (Carlos & Carmen Ser.). (ENG.). 32p. (J). (gr. -1-3). lib. bdg. 32.79 (978-1-5321-3035-9(X), 27037, Calico Chapter Bks) Magic Wagon.

—Tooth Trouble. Anaya, Fátima, illus. 2017. (Carlos & Carmen Ser.). (ENG.). 32p. (J). (gr. -1-3). lib. bdg. 32.79 (978-1-5321-3036-6(8), 27038, Calico Chapter Bks) Magic Wagon.

—The Wobbly Wheels, 1 vol. Meza, Erika, illus. 2016. (Carlos & Carmen Ser.). (ENG.). 32p. (J). (gr. -1-3). 32.79 (978-1-62402-144-2(1), 21555, Calico Chapter Bks) Magic Wagon.

—The Yummy Mistake. Meza, Erika, illus. 2016. (Carlos & Carmen Ser.). (ENG.). 32p. (J). (gr. -1-3). lib. bdg. 32.79 (978-1-62402-145-9(X), 21557, Calico Chapter Bks) Magic Wagon.

Mcdonald, Megan. The Doctor Is In! 2010. (Judy Moody Ser.: 5). lib. bdg. 16.00 (978-0-606-12343-3(1)) Turtleback.

McDonald, Megan. Judy Moody & Friends: Judy Moody, Tooth Fairy. Madrid, Erwin, illus. 2017. (Judy Moody & Friends Ser.: 9). (ENG.). 64p. (J). (gr. -1-1). pap. 5.99 (978-0-7636-9168-4(2)) Candlewick Pr.

—Judy Moody & Friends: Stink Moody in Master of Disaster. Madrid, Erwin, illus. 2015. (Judy Moody & Friends Ser.: 5). (ENG.). 64p. (J). (gr. -1-1). 12.99 (978-0-7636-7218-8(1)) Candlewick Pr.

—Judy Moody & Stink: la Loca, Loca Búsqueda Del Tesoro / JM & Stink: the Mad, Mad, Mad, Mad Treasure Hunt. 2011. (Judy Moody & Stink Ser.). (SPA., Illus.). 144p. (J). (gr. 2-5). pap. 14.95 (978-1-61605-137-2(X), Alfaguara) Penguin Random House Grupo Editorial ESP. Dist: Penguin Random Hse. LLC.

—Judy Moody & Stink: the Mad, Mad, Mad, Mad Treasure Hunt. Reynolds, Peter H., illus. 2010. (Judy Moody & Stink Ser.: 2). (ENG.). 128p. (J). (gr. 1-4). pap. 7.99 (978-0-7636-4351-5(3)) Candlewick Pr.

—Judy Moody & Stink: the Wishbone Wish. Reynolds, Peter H., illus. 2015. (Judy Moody & Stink Ser.: 4). (ENG.). 128p. (J). (gr. 1-4). 14.99 (978-0-7636-7206-5(8)) Candlewick Pr.

—Judy Moody & the NOT Bummer Summer. Reynolds, Peter H., illus. 2018. (Judy Moody Ser.: 10). (ENG.). 208p. (J). (gr. 1-4). pap. 5.99 (978-1-5362-0084-3(0)) Candlewick Pr.

Mcdonald, Megan. Judy Moody & the Not Bummer Summer. 2012. (Judy Moody Ser.: 10). lib. bdg. 16.00 (978-0-606-23800-7(X)) Turtleback.

McDonald, Megan. The Judy Moody Double-Rare Collection: Books 4-6, 3 vols. Reynolds, Peter H., illus. 2019. (Judy Moody Ser.). (ENG.). 496p. (J). (gr. 1-4). pap. 17.97 (978-1-5362-0951-8(1)) Candlewick Pr.

—Judy Moody Gets Famous! Reynolds, Peter H., illus. 2010. (Judy Moody Ser.: 2). (ENG.). 144p. (J). (gr. 1-4). 16.99 (978-0-7636-4854-1(X)) Candlewick Pr.

Mcdonald, Megan. Judy Moody Gets Famous! 2010. (Judy Moody Ser.: 2). lib. bdg. 16.00 (978-0-606-12332-7(6)) Turtleback.

McDonald, Megan. Judy Moody, Girl Detective. Reynolds, Peter H., illus. 2018. (Judy Moody Ser.: 9). (ENG.). 192p. (J). (gr. 1-4). pap. 5.99 (978-1-5362-0079-9(4)) Candlewick Pr.

Mcdonald, Megan. Judy Moody, M. D. Reynolds, Peter H., illus. 2010. (Judy Moody Ser.: 5). (ENG.). 176p. (J). (gr. 1-4). 15.99 (978-0-7636-4862-6(0)) Candlewick Pr.

—Judy Moody Saves the World! Reynolds, Peter H., illus. 2004. (Judy Moody Ser.: Bk. 3). 144p. (J). (gr. 1-5). 13.65 (978-0-7569-2588-8(6)) Perfection Learning Corp.

McDonald, Megan. Judy Moody Saves the World! Reynolds, Peter H., illus. 2010. (Judy Moody Ser.: 3). (ENG.). 160p. (J). (gr. 1-4). 16.99 (978-0-7636-4860-2(4)) Candlewick Pr.

Mcdonald, Megan. Judy Moody Saves the World! 2010. (Judy Moody Ser.: 3). 144p. lib. bdg. 16.00 (978-0-606-12340-2(7)) Turtleback.

—The Mad, Mad, Mad, Mad Treasure Hunt. 2010. (Judy Moody & Stink Ser.: 2). lib. bdg. 18.40 (978-0-606-01311-6(3)) Turtleback.

—Stink. 2013. (Stink Ser.: 1). lib. bdg. 14.75 (978-0-606-31587-6(X)) Turtleback.

—Stink: The Incredible Shrinking Kid. Reynolds, Peter H., illus. 2010. (Stink Ser.: No. 1). (ENG.). 112p. (J). (gr. 1-5). 31.36 (978-1-59961-686-5(6), 13833, Chapter Bks.) Spotlight.

McDonald, Megan. Stink: The Incredible Shrinking Kid. Reynolds, Peter H., illus. 2013. (Stink Ser.: 1). (ENG.). 112p. (J). (gr. 1-4). 14.99 (978-0-7636-5388-9(3)) Candlewick Pr.

Mcdonald, Megan. The Wishbone Wish. Reynolds, Peter H., illus. 2016. (Judy Moody & Stink Ser.: 4). (ENG.). 116p. (J). (gr. 1-4). lib. bdg. 18.40 (978-0-606-39093-4(6)) Turtleback.

McDonald, Rae A. A Fishing Surprise. Kemly, Kathleen, illus. 2007. (ENG.). 32p. (J). (gr. -1-3). 16.95 (978-1-55971-977-3(X)) Cooper Square Publishing Llc.

Mcdoogle, Farrah. Olivia Says Good Night. 2016. (Olivia 8x8 Ser.). lib. bdg. 13.55 (978-0-606-39244-0(0)) Turtleback.

McDowell, Andrew. Beyond the Forest. 2007. 286p. pap. 16.95 (978-0-7414-4238-3(8)) Infinity Publishing.

McDunn, Gillian. Caterpillar Summer. (ENG.). (J). 2020. 320p. pap. 7.99 (978-1-5476-0314-5(3), 900211246) 2019. (Illus.). 304p. 16.99 (978-1-68119-743-2(X), 900184196) Bloomsbury Publishing USA. (Bloomsbury Children's Bks.).

McDunn, Rosemary. When Kids Dream & Trucks Fly. 2007. (ENG.). 52p. per. 12.99 (978-0-9792258-6-4(8)) Bezalel Bks.

Mcentire, Myra. Hourglass, 1. 2012. (Hourglass Ser.). (ENG.). 400p. (YA). (gr. 9-12). 26.19 (978-1-60684-144-0(0)) Farshore GBR. Dist: Children's Plus, Inc.

McFarlane, Brian. The Hockey Book. 11th ed. 2008. (Mitchell Brothers Ser.). (ENG.). 200p. (J). (gr. 3-7). per. (978-1-55168-312-6(1)) Magma.

—Season of Surprises. 9th ed. 2008. (Mitchell Brothers Ser.). (ENG.). 184p. (J). (gr. 3-7). pap. (978-1-55168-300-3(8)) Me to We.

McGeorge, Darby Q. Trickster Tre. 2012. 24p. pap. 9.95 (978-1-4575-0971-1(7)) Dog Ear Publishing, LLC.

McGhee, Alison. Dear Sister. Bluhm, Joe, illus. 2019. (ENG.). 192p. (J). (gr. 5). pap. 7.99 (978-1-4814-5143-7(X), Atheneum Bks. for Young Readers) Simon & Schuster Children's Publishing.

McGowan, Keith. The Witch's Guide to Cooking with Children: A Modern-Day Retelling of Hansel & Gretel, 1. Tanaka, Yoko, illus. 2011. (ENG.). 192p. (J). (gr. 4-6). pap. 12.99 (978-0-312-67486-1(4), 900072904) Square Fish.

McGowan, Maureen. Compliance, 0 vols. 2014. (Dust Chronicles Ser.: 2). (ENG.). 386p. (J). (gr. 7-12). pap. 9.99 (978-1-4778-1696-7(8), 9781477816967, Skyscape) Amazon Publishing.

—Deviants, 0 vols. 2012. (Dust Chronicles Ser.: 1). (ENG.). 322p. (YA). (gr. 7-12). pap. 9.99 (978-1-4778-1032-3(3), 9781477810323, Skyscape) Amazon Publishing.

—Glory, 0 vols. 2014. (Dust Chronicles Ser.: 3). (ENG.). 326p. (J). (gr. 7-12). pap. 9.99 (978-1-4778-4797-8(9), 9781477847978, Skyscape) Amazon Publishing.

McGrath, Alister. Chosen Ones, 1 vol. 2010. (Aedyn Chronicles Ser.). (ENG., Illus.). 208p. (J). (gr. 4-7). 14.99 (978-0-310-71812-3(0)) Zondervan.

McGugan, Jim. Bridge 6. 2004. (Illus.). (J). (gr. k-3). spiral bd. (978-0-616-01721-0(9)) Canadian National Institute for the Blind/Institut National Canadien pour les Aveugles.

McGuire, Sarah. The Flight of Swans. 2018. (ENG.). 448p. (J). (gr. 4-8). 18.99 (978-1-5124-4027-0(2), 9fb6e720-cb31-4131-933c-4199722cb62f, Carolrhoda Bks.) Lerner Publishing Group.

McIntosh, Will. Watchdog. 2019. (ENG.). 192p. (J). (gr. 5). 8.99 (978-1-5247-1387-4(2), Yearling) Random Hse. Children's Bks.

McKay, Hilary. Caddy Ever After. 2007. (ENG.). 240p. (J). (gr. 4-8). per. 7.99 (978-1-4169-0931-6(1), McElderry, Margaret K. Bks.) McElderry, Margaret K. Bks.

—Caddy's World. (ENG.). (J). (gr. 5-9). 2013. 288p. pap. 6.99 (978-1-4424-4106-4(2)) 2012. 272p. 16.99 (978-1-4424-4105-7(4)) McElderry, Margaret K. Bks. (McElderry, Margaret K. Bks.).

—Indigo's Star. 2006. (ENG.). 288p. (J). (gr. 3-7). reprint ed. per. 7.99 (978-1-4169-1403-7(X), McElderry, Margaret K. Bks.) McElderry, Margaret K. Bks.

—Permanent Rose. 2006. (ENG.). 256p. (J). (gr. 3-7). reprint ed. per. 8.99 (978-1-4169-2804-1(9), McElderry, Margaret K. Bks.) McElderry, Margaret K. Bks.

—Saffy's Angel. 2003. (ENG., Illus.). 256p. (J). (gr. 3-7). pap. 7.99 (978-0-689-84934-3(6), McElderry, Margaret K. Bks.) McElderry, Margaret K. Bks.

—Saffy's Angel. 2004. (Casson Family Ser.: Bk. 1). 160p. (J). (gr. 4-7). pap. 36.00 incl. audio (978-0-8072-2098-6(1), Listening Library) Random Hse. Audio Publishing Group.

McKernan, Victoria. The Devil's Paintbox, 1. 2010. (Devil's Paintbox Ser.). (ENG.). 368p. (J). (gr. 9-12). lib. bdg. 22.44 (978-0-375-93750-7(1)) Random House Publishing Group.

—The Devil's Paintbox. (ENG.). (YA). (gr. 9). 2013. 384p. pap. 9.99 (978-0-449-81655-4(9), Ember) 2010. 368p. mass mkt. 8.99 (978-0-440-23962-8(1), Laurel Leaf) Random Hse. Children's Bks.

McKernan, Wendy. The Thing I Say I Saw Last Night: A Christmas Story. Bzymek, Izabela, illus. 2011. 32p. (J). (978-0-9866204-0-9(8)); pap. (978-0-9866204-1-6(6)) Little Dragon Publishing.

McKinley, Ryan. The Pirate Bride. 2010. 105p. 21.95 (978-1-4327-5546-1(3)); (Illus.). pap. 14.95 (978-1-4327-5545-4(5)) Outskirts Pr., Inc.

McKissack, Patricia. The Home-Run King. 2009. (Scraps of Time Ser.). (ENG.). 112p. (J). (gr. 3-7). 7.99 (978-0-14-241459-0(X), Puffin Books) Penguin Young Readers Group.

McKy, Katie. Pumpkin Town! or, Nothing Is Better & Worse Than Pumpkins. Bernasconi, Pablo, illus. 2008. (ENG.). 32p. (J). (gr. -1-3). pap. 7.99 (978-0-547-18193-6(0), 1055964, Clarion Bks.) HarperCollins Pubs.

McMahan, Stephanie K. The Mystery of the Golden Rings. 2007. 140p. 21.95 (978-0-595-68451-9(3)); per. 11.95 (978-0-595-43998-0(5)) iUniverse, Inc.

McManis, Margaret. The Wild Texas Stampede!, 1 vol. Dupree, Bruce, illus. 2008. (ENG.). 32p. (J). (gr. 1-3). 16.99 (978-1-58980-568-2(2), Pelican Publishing) Arcadia Publishing.

McMann, Lisa. Dragon Bones. (Unwanteds Quests Ser.: 2). (ENG., Illus.). (J). (gr. 3-7). 2019. 432p. pap. 9.99 (978-1-4814-5685-2(7)) 2018. 416p. 19.99 (978-1-4814-5684-5(9)) Simon & Schuster Children's Publishing. (Aladdin).

—Dragon Captives. 2017. (Unwanteds Quests Ser.: 1). (ENG., Illus.). 432p. (J). (gr. 3-7). 19.99 (978-1-4814-5681-4(4), Simon & Schuster/Paula Wiseman Bks.) Simon & Schuster/Paula Wiseman Bks.

—Dragon Captives. 2018. (Unwanteds Quests Ser.: 1). lib. bdg. 18.40 (978-0-606-40846-2(0)) Turtleback.

—Dragon Curse. 2019. (Unwanteds Quests Ser.: 4). (ENG., Illus.). 432p. (J). (gr. 3-7). 18.99 (978-1-5344-1601-7(3), Simon & Schuster/Paula Wiseman Bks.) Simon & Schuster/Paula Wiseman Bks.

—Dragon Ghosts. 2019. (Unwanteds Quests Ser.: 3). (ENG., Illus.). 528p. (J). (gr. 3-7). 19.99 (978-1-5344-1598-0(X), Aladdin) Simon & Schuster Children's Publishing.

—Island of Dragons. 2017. (Unwanteds Ser.: 7). (ENG., Illus.). 544p. (J). (gr. 3-7). pap. 9.99 (978-1-4424-9338-4(0), Aladdin) Simon & Schuster Children's Publishing.

—Island of Shipwrecks. 2015. (Unwanteds Ser.: 5). (ENG., Illus.). 480p. (J). (gr. 3-7). pap. 9.99 (978-1-4424-9332-2(1), Aladdin) Simon & Schuster Children's Publishing.

—Island of Silence. 2013. (Unwanteds Ser.: 2). lib. bdg. 18.40 (978-0-606-32044-3(X)) Turtleback.

Mcmann, Lisa. Predator vs. Prey. 2018. (Going Wild Ser.: 2). (J). lib. bdg. 17.20 (978-0-606-41375-6(8)) Turtleback.

McMann, Lisa. The Unwanteds. 2011. (Unwanteds Ser.: Bk. 1). (J). 1.25 (978-1-4640-2489-4(8)) Recorded Bks., Inc.

—The Unwanteds. (Unwanteds Ser.: 1). (ENG., Illus.). (J). (gr. 3-7). 2012. 416p. pap. 8.99 (978-1-4424-0769-5(7)) 2011. 400p. 19.99 (978-1-4424-0768-8(9)) Simon & Schuster Children's Publishing. (Aladdin).

—The Unwanteds. 2012. (Unwanteds Ser.: 1). lib. bdg. 18.40 (978-0-606-26953-7(3)) Turtleback.

McManus, Karen M. Two Can Keep a Secret. 2019. (ENG.). 352p. lib. bdg. 21.80 (978-1-6636-2970-8(6)) Perfection Learning Corp.

—Two Can Keep a Secret. (ENG.). 352p. (YA). (gr. 9). 2021. pap. 12.99 (978-1-5247-1471-0(2), Ember) 2019. 19.99 (978-1-5247-1472-7(0), Delacorte Pr.) Random Hse. Children's Bks.

McMillan, Ernest. Psalms of Passion. 2006. 48p. pap. 8.95 (978-1-59800-224-9(4)) Outskirts Pr., Inc.

McMillion, Gloria. Whirlwinds Whirl Around. 2007. 136p. per. 11.95 (978-0-595-42248-7(9)) iUniverse, Inc.

McMullin, Perry. Fireflies. 2009. 20p. pap. 14.95 (978-1-4490-2730-8(X)) AuthorHouse.

McNamara, Margaret. The Three Little Aliens & the Big Bad Robot. Fearing, Mark, illus. 2011. (ENG.). 40p. (J). (gr. -1-3). 18.99 (978-0-375-86689-0(2)) Random Hse. Children's Bks.

McPhail, David. Sisters. McPhail, David, illus. 2003. (ENG., Illus.). 32p. (J). (gr. -1-3). 9.95 (978-0-15-204659-0(3), 1194040, Clarion Bks.) HarperCollins Pubs.

McQuerry, Maureen Doyle. Time Out of Time: Book One: Beyond the Door. (Time Out of Time Ser.). (ENG., Illus.). (J). 2015. 400p. (gr. 5-9). pap. 7.95 (978-1-4197-1493-1(7), 683303) 2014. 384p. (gr. 3-7). 16.95 (978-1-4197-1016-2(8), 683301) Abrams, Inc. (Amulet Bks.).

McQuinn, Anna. Lola le Lee Al Pequeno Leo. Beardshaw, Rosalind, illus. 2013. (Leo Can! Ser.: 3). 28p. (J). (-k). pap. 7.99 (978-1-58089-599-6(9)) Charlesbridge Publishing, Inc.

—Lola Reads to Leo. Beardshaw, Rosalind, illus. 2012. (Leo Can! Ser.: 3). (ENG.). 28p. (J). (-k). 16.99 (978-1-58089-403-6(8)); pap. 7.99 (978-1-58089-404-3(6)) Charlesbridge Publishing, Inc.

—Lola Reads to Leo. 2012. pap. 19.95 incl. audio compact disk (978-0-8045-4236-4(8)) Spoken Arts, Inc.

McQuinn, Anna, et al. Lola Reads to Leo: Lola le Lee Al Pequeño Leo. Beardshaw, Rosalind, illus. 2017. (SPA & ENG.). (J). pap. (978-1-63289-028-3(3)) Charlesbridge Publishing, Inc.

Mead, Alice. Junebug. 2009. (Junebug Ser.). (ENG.). 128p. (J). (gr. 3-7). pap. 7.99 (978-0-312-56126-0(1), 900058861) Square Fish.

Medearis, Angela Shelf. Lucy's Quiet Book. Ernst, Lisa Campbell, illus. 2004. (ENG.). 24p. (J). (gr. -1-3). pap. 5.99 (978-0-15-205143-3(0), 1195521, Clarion Bks.) HarperCollins Pubs.

—Lucy's Quiet Book. Ernst, Lisa Campbell, illus. 2004. (Green Light Readers Level 2 Ser.). (gr. k-2). 13.95 (978-0-7569-4310-3(8)) Perfection Learning Corp.

Meeks, Jane. Finding Home. 2011. 24p. pap. 15.99 (978-1-4653-6606-1(7)) Xlibris Corp.

Meierhenry, Mark, et al. The Mystery of the Maize. 2010. (Mystery Ser.). (ENG., Illus.). 44p. (J). 13.95 (978-0-9822749-1-0(2), P240880, South Dakota State Historical Society Pr.) South Dakota Historical Society Pr.

Mejias, John & Mejias, John, illus. The Hungry Brothers. 2009. (ENG.). 32p. (J). (gr. -1-2). 15.95 (978-0-9798841-1-5(X)) 4N Publishing LLC.

Meloy, Colin. Wildwood. Ellis, Carson, illus. (Wildwood Chronicles Ser.: 1). (ENG.). (J). (gr. 3). 2012. 576p. pap. 9.99 (978-0-06-202470-1(1)) 2011. 560p. 19.99 (978-0-06-202468-8(X)) HarperCollins Pubs. (Balzer & Bray).

—Wildwood. Ellis, Carson, illus. 2012. (Wildwood Chronicles Ser.: 1). (J). lib. bdg. 20.85 (978-0-606-26864-6(2)) Turtleback.

Mercer, Sienna. My Sister the Vampire #1: Switched. 2007. (My Sister the Vampire Ser.: 1). (ENG.). 208p. (J). (gr. 3-7). pap. 6.99 (978-0-06-087113-0(X), HarperCollins) HarperCollins Pubs.

Meroto, Tina. The Tooth Gnashing Witch. 2007. (ENG., Illus.). 48p. (J). 18.95 (978-84-96788-82-4(2)) OQO, Editora ESP. Dist: Baker & Taylor Bks.

Merry, Lindsay R. Dackshew Dragonfly. 2012. 24p. pap. 17.99 (978-1-4685-9885-8(6)) AuthorHouse.

Meserve, Jessica. Bedtime Without Arthur. Meserve, Jessica, illus. 2010. (ENG., Illus.). 32p. (J). (gr. -1-3). 16.95 (978-0-7613-5497-0(2), 8255c966-c581-4056-a251-c10096e0b470) Lerner Publishing Group.

Metikosh, Anne. Terra Incognita. 2005. (ENG., Illus.). 144p. (J). (gr. 3-9). pap., tchr. ed. 8.95 (978-0-921870-76-0(0)) Ronsdale Pr. CAN. Dist: Literary Pr. Group of Canada.

Meunier, Sylvain & Lapierre, Steeve. Graindsel et Bretel. Fil et, Julie, illus. 2004. (était une Fois Ser.). (FRE.). 24p. (J). (gr. -1). pap. (978-2-89021-699-0(3)) Diffusion du livre Mirabel (DLM).

Meyer, Franklyn E. Me & Caleb. fac. ed. 2015. 162p. reprint ed. 22.95 (978-1-62654-362-1(3)); (ENG.). pap. 16.95 (978-1-62654-361-4(5)) Echo Point Bks. & Media, LLC.

—Me & Caleb. Smith, Lawrence Beall, illus. 2006. (J). kivar 16.95 (978-0-9789388-0-2(1)) Hester Publishing.

—Me & Caleb Again. Liese, Charles, illus. 2006. (J). kivar 16.95 (978-0-9789388-1-9(X)) Hester Publishing.

Meyer, Karen Ruth. The Tiara Mystery. 2016. (ENG., Illus.). 154p. (J). pap. 10.99 (978-0-9974953-2-4(4)) Sable Creek Pr. LLC.

Michaels, Craig. Blackbeard's Treasure. 2008. (J). (978-0-936389-99-8(0)) Tudor Pubs., Inc.

Michaels, Joanna. Call Me Charly. Specht, Jessica, illus. 2012. 92p. pap. 10.95 (978-1-61493-102-7(X)) Peppertree Pr., The.

Michaels, Rune. Fix Me. 2011. (ENG., Illus.). 160p. (YA). (gr. 9). 16.99 (978-1-4169-5772-0(3), Atheneum Bks. for Young Readers) Simon & Schuster Children's Publishing.

—Genesis Alpha. 2007. (ENG.). 208p. (YA). (gr. 7-12). 23.80 (978-1-4287-4620-6(X), Followtbound) Follett School Solutions.

—Genesis Alpha. 2011. (ENG.). 224p. (YA). (gr. 7). pap. 10.99 (978-1-4169-6500-8(9), Atheneum Bks. for Young Readers) Simon & Schuster Children's Publishing.

Michels-Gualtieri, Zaydek G. I Was Born to Be a Brother. Liegey, Daniel, illus. 2005. 32p. (J). (gr. -1-3). 9.95 (978-1-930775-10-7(5)) Platypus Media, L.L.C.

Mignerey, Mary Buhs. If Dogs Could Talk: & Dogs Can Talk Two. 2007. 56p. per. 16.95 (978-1-4241-7675-5(1)) America Star Bks.

Milford, Kate. Bluecrowne: A Greenglass House Story. (Greenglass House Ser.). (ENG., Illus.). (J). (gr. 5-7). 2020. 288p. pap. 9.99 (978-0-358-09754-9(1), 1747616) 2018. 272p. 17.99 (978-1-328-46688-4(4), 1713526) HarperCollins Pubs. (Clarion Bks.).

Miller, Gary R. Taming Chaos: A Parable on Decision Making. 2017. (ENG.). 146p. (YA). pap. 14.95 (978-1-68350-060-5(1)) Morgan James Publishing.

Miller-Johnston, Renee. Courtney Logan Kennedy Presents Zoe. 2008. 76p. pap. 19.95 (978-1-60703-558-9(8)) America Star Bks.

Millet, Lydia. Pills & Starships. 2014. (ENG.). 256p. (YA). (gr. 7). 22.95 (978-1-61775-275-9(4), Black Sheep) Akashic Bks.

Milliner, Naomi. Super Jake & the King of Chaos. 2019. (ENG.). 288p. (J). (gr. 3-7). 16.99 (978-0-7624-6615-3(4), Running Pr. Kids) Running Pr.

Millner, Robert W. The Chicken Coop Gang. 2011. 130p. 29.99 (978-1-4568-5517-8(4)); pap. 19.99 (978-1-4568-5516-1(6)) Xlibris Corp.

Mills, Claudia. Write This Down. 2018. (ENG.). 272p. (J). pap. 13.99 (978-1-250-14391-4(8), 900180597) Square Fish.

Minich, Eric. Digger & the Search for Home. 2006. 48p. pap. 16.95 (978-1-4241-0321-8(5)) PublishAmerica, Inc.

Miraucourt, Christophe. Pirate Treasure. 2015. (Race Further with Reading Ser.). (ENG., Illus.). 48p. (J). (gr. 3-3). (978-0-7787-2031-7(4)) Crabtree Publishing Co.

Miyazaki, Hayao. Ponyo Film Comic, Vol. 1. movie tie-in ed. 2009. (Ponyo Film Comics Ser.: 1). (ENG., Illus.). 172p. (J). pap. 9.99 (978-1-4215-3077-2(5)) Viz Media.

—Ponyo Film Comic, Vol. 2. movie tie-in ed. 2009. (Ponyo Film Comics Ser.: 2). (ENG., Illus.). 152p. (J). pap. 9.99 (978-1-4215-3078-9(3)) Viz Media.

—Ponyo Film Comic, Vol. 3. movie tie-in ed. 2009. (Ponyo Film Comics Ser.: 3). (ENG., Illus.). 152p. (J). pap. 9.99 (978-1-4215-3079-6(1)) Viz Media.

—Ponyo Film Comic, Vol. 4. movie tie-in ed. 2009. (Ponyo Film Comics Ser.: 4). (ENG., Illus.). 168p. (J). pap. 9.99 (978-1-4215-3080-2(5)) Viz Media.

Mlawer, Teresa. If I Had a Dragon/Si Yo Tuviera un Dragon. Ellery, Tom & Ellery, Amanda, illus. 2006. (ENG & SPA.). (J). (gr. -1-3). per. 3.99 (978-1-933032-17-7(0)); 32p. (gr. 5-6). 12.99 (978-1-933032-16-0(2)) Lectorum Pubns., Inc.

Mlawer, Teresa, tr. Clean It!/¡a Limpiar! Birkett, Georgie, illus. 2009. (Helping Hands English/Spanish Edition Ser.). (ENG.). 24p. (J). (gr. -1-k). pap. (978-1-84643-569-0(2)) Child's Play International Ltd.

Mlynowski, Sarah. Beauty Queen (Whatever After #7) 2016. (Whatever After Ser.: 7). (ENG.). 176p. (J). (gr. 3-7). pap. 6.99 (978-0-545-74657-1(4), Scholastic Pr.) Scholastic, Inc.

—Cold As Ice (Whatever After #6) 2015. (Whatever After Ser.: 6). (ENG.). 176p. (J). (gr. 3-7). pap. 5.99 (978-0-545-62736-8(2), Scholastic Pr.) Scholastic, Inc.

—Dream on (Whatever After #4) 2014. (Whatever After Ser.: 4). (ENG.). 176p. (J). (gr. 3-7). pap. 5.99 (978-0-545-41572-9(1), Scholastic Paperbacks) Scholastic, Inc.

—Fairest of All (Whatever After #1) 2013. (Whatever After Ser.: 1). (ENG.). 176p. (J). (gr. 3-7). pap. 6.99 (978-0-545-48571-5(1), Scholastic Pr.) Scholastic, Inc.

—If the Shoe Fits. 2013. 176p. 14.99 (978-0-545-50465-2(1)) Scholastic, Inc.

—If the Shoe Fits (Whatever After #2) 2013. (Whatever After Ser.: 2). (ENG.). 176p. (J). (gr. 3-7). pap. 6.99 (978-0-545-41568-2(3), Scholastic Pr.) Scholastic, Inc.

—Sink or Swim. 2013. (Whatever After Ser.: No. 3). 165p. (J). (978-0-545-53316-4(3), Scholastic Pr.) Scholastic, Inc.

—Spill the Beans (Whatever After #13) 2019. (Whatever After Ser.: 13). (ENG.). 176p. (J). (gr. 3-7). 14.99 (978-1-338-16297-4(7), Scholastic Pr.) Scholastic, Inc.

—Two Peas in a Pod (Whatever After #11) (Whatever After Ser.: 11). (ENG.). 176p. (J). (gr. 3-7). 2019. pap. 6.99 (978-1-338-16291-2(8)) 2018. 14.99 (978-1-338-16289-9(6), Scholastic Pr.) Scholastic, Inc.

Moffett, Elzater. Tenan & Colleen: I Don't Want to Go to Bed. Thibodeaux, Rebecca, illus. 2010. 36p. 15.49 (978-1-4490-6633-8(X)) AuthorHouse.

—Tenan & Colleen: Who Is Harry? 2011. 36p. pap. 16.86 (978-1-4567-5378-8(9)) AuthorHouse.

Molesworth, Mary Louisa S. Grandmother Dear. 2008. 128p. 23.95 (978-1-60664-726-4(1)) Rodgers, Alan Bks.

—Peterkin. 2009. 128p. 23.95 (978-1-60664-659-5(1)); pap. 10.95 (978-1-60664-287-0(1)) Rodgers, Alan Bks.

—Robin Redbreast. 2011. 190p. 26.95 (978-1-4638-9847-2(9)); pap. 14.95 (978-1-4638-0123-6(8)) Rodgers, Alan Bks.

—The Tapestry Room. 2008. 116p. 22.95 (978-1-60664-990-9(6)) Aegypan.

Molitoris, Cathy. I've Got Music! McConnell, Sarah, illus. 2006. (J). (978-0-439-88620-8(1)) Scholastic, Inc.

Mollel, Tololwa. From the Lands of the Night, 1 vol. McCalla, Darrell, illus. 2013. (ENG.). 32p. (J). (gr. 2-5). 18.95 (978-0-88995-498-4(4), a210815f-8b9e-4199-8e3e-45c956d0931b) Trifolium Bks., Inc. CAN. Dist: Firefly Bks., Ltd.

Monette, Roz. Alex & the Enderson Brothers: Book One, bks. 3. 2nd ed. 2013. (ENG., Illus.). 162p. (YA). (gr. 7-7). pap. 12.95 (978-0-9835077-1-0(6)) Cedar Grove Publishing.

Monninger, Joseph. Wish. 2012. (ENG.). 208p. (YA). (gr. 7-12). lib. bdg. 24.94 (978-0-385-90788-0(5), Delacorte Pr.); pap. 8.99 (978-0-375-86213-7(7), Ember) Random Hse. Children's Bks.

Monson, Marianne. The Enchanted Tunnel Vol. 3: Journey to Jerusalem. Burr, Dan, illus. 2011. 85p. (YA). (gr. 3-6). pap. 7.99 (978-1-60908-068-6(8)) Deseret Bk. Co.

—The Enchanted Tunnel Vol. 4: Wandering in the Wilderness. Burr, Dan, illus. 2011. 85p. (YA). (gr. 3-6). pap. 7.99 (978-1-60908-069-3(6)) Deseret Bk. Co.

—Escape from Egypt. 2010. (Illus.). 85p. (J). (978-1-60641-670-9(7)) Deseret Bk. Co.

—Pioneer Puzzle. 2010. (Illus.). 84p. (J). (978-1-60641-669-3(3)) Deseret Bk. Co.

Montgomery, L. M. Rainbow Valley. 2018. (Anne of Green Gables: the Complete Collection: 7). (ENG.). 312p. (J). (gr. 6-12). 8.99 (978-1-78226-449-1(3), 285d3fc5-bfae-4f1e-8305-ef2973a53c9a) Sweet Cherry Publishing GBR. Dist: Baker & Taylor Publisher Services (BTPS).

—Rainbow Valley. 2018. (ENG., Illus.). 260p. (J). (gr. 4-6). 24.99 (978-1-5287-0641-4(2), Classic Bks. Library) The Editorium, LLC.

—Rainbow Valley. (ENG.). (J). (gr. 4-6). 2019. 504p. pap. 20.99 (978-1-7000-5609-2(3)) 2019. 504p. pap. 29.99 (978-1-6968-0671-8(2)) 2019. 504p. pap. 29.99 (978-1-6916-0284-1(1)) 2019. 504p. pap. 29.99 (978-1-6949-8132-5(0)) 2019. 358p. pap. 19.99 (978-1-0899-5686-0(X)) 2019. 360p. pap. 19.99 (978-1-0830-5096-0(6)) 2019. 360p. pap. 19.99 (978-1-0774-1069-5(7)) 2019. 360p. pap. 19.99 (978-1-0726-9469-4(7)) 2019. 360p. pap. 19.99 (978-1-0708-9450-8(8)) 2019. 344p. pap. 19.99 (978-1-0705-2885-4(4)) 2019. 470p. pap. 26.99 (978-1-0989-2756-1(7)) 2019. 506p. pap. 29.99 (978-1-0934-3846-8(0)) 2019. 474p. pap. 26.99 (978-1-0917-8168-9(0)) 2018. (Illus.). 226p. pap. 13.99 (978-1-7919-2259-7(7)) 2018. (Illus.). 450p. pap. 26.99 (978-1-7916-5635-5(8)) Independently Published.

—Rainbow Valley. 2019. (ENG.). 236p. (J). (gr. 4-6). pap. 27.99 (978-1-7077-9413-3(8)) Independently Published.

—Rainbow Valley. l.t. ed. 2007. (ENG.). 258p. pap. 23.99 (978-1-4346-5246-1(7)) Creative Media Partners, LLC.

Montgomery, Lucy Maud. Rainbow Valley. 2019. (ENG.). 450p. (J). pap. 27.99 (978-1-7992-9917-2(1)) Independently Published.

Moore, David Barclay. The Stars Beneath Our Feet. 2017. (ENG.). 304p. (J). (gr. 5). 17.99 (978-1-5247-0124-6(6), Knopf Bks. for Young Readers) Random Hse. Children's Bks.

Moore, Jodi. When a Dragon Moves in Again. McWilliam, Howard, illus. 2015. (When a Dragon Moves In Ser.). 32p. (J). (gr. k-2). 17.95 (978-1-936261-35-2(9)) Flashlight Pr.

Moore, Judith. Jessica the Furry Baroo. Brown, Karen, illus. 2007. 44p. per. 14.95 (978-1-59858-364-9(6)) Dog Ear Publishing, LLC.

Moore, Margaret & Moore, John Travers. The Three Tripps. Funk, Clotilde Embree, illus. 2011. 158p. 41.95 (978-1-258-08478-3(3)) Literary Licensing, LLC.

Moore, Stephanie Perry. Getting Home. 2018. (Attack on Earth Ser.). (ENG.). 104p. (YA). (gr. 6-12). pap. 7.99 (978-1-5415-2628-0(7), 6c7038c6-4bf9-4551-b3f6-a8e5fdd1c3f5); lib. bdg. 26.65 (978-1-5415-2575-7(2), 300dbd6a-844a-436f-b919-a2b2b67e6f26) Lerner Publishing Group. (Darby Creek).

Moraja, Melissa Perry. Madison & Ga: Tale of the Messed up Talent Show. 2013. 156p. pap. (978-0-9898293-1-1(6)) Roxby Media Ltd.

Morales, Yuyi. Niño Wrestles the World. Morales, Yuyi, illus. 2013. (ENG., Illus.). 40p. (J). (gr. -1-3). 19.99 (978-1-59643-604-6(2), 900065749) Roaring Brook Pr.

—Rudas: niño's Horrendous Hermanitas. 2018. (ENG., Illus.). 40p. (J). pap. 9.99 (978-1-250-14336-5(5), 900180500) Square Fish.

Morelli, Licia. The Lemonade Hurricane: A Story of Mindfulness & Meditation, 1 vol. Morris, Jennifer, illus. 2015. (ENG.). 32p. (J). (gr. -1-3). 17.95 (978-0-88448-396-0(7), 884396) Tilbury Hse. Pubs.

Morgan, Melissa J. A Fair to Remember #13. 2007. (Camp Confidential Ser.: 13). 160p. (J). (gr. 3-7). pap. 4.99 (978-0-448-44451-2(8), Grosset & Dunlap) Penguin Young Readers Group.

Morpurgo, Michael. Twist of Gold. 2004. (ENG.). 304p. (J). pap. 8.99 (978-0-7497-4687-2(4)) Farshore GBR. Dist: Trafalgar Square Publishing.

Morrel Disbrow, Corlyss. Ran's Upside-Down Day. 2012. 20p. pap. 24.95 (978-1-4626-8368-0(1)) America Star Bks.

Morris, Chad. Cragbridge Hall, Book 2: The Avatar Battle. 2014. (Cragbridge Hall Ser.: 2). (ENG., Illus.). 360p. (J). (gr. 3-9). 17.99 (978-1-60907-809-6(8), Shadow Mountain) Shadow Mountain Publishing.

—Cragbridge Hall, Book 3: The Impossible Race. 2015. (Cragbridge Hall Ser.: 3). (ENG., Illus.). 432p. (J). (gr. 3-9). 18.99 (978-1-60907-979-6(5), 5127575, Shadow Mountain) Shadow Mountain Publishing.

Morrissey, Dean & Krensky, Stephen. The Crimson Comet. Morrissey, Dean, illus. 2006. (Illus.). 32p. (J). (gr. k-4). 17.89 (978-0-06-008070-9(1)) HarperCollins Pubs.

Morse, William A. and & Morse, William A. And Dana Jo. Kurkle Kids: Spirit of America. 2009. 44p. pap. 16.99 (978-1-4490-1009-6(1)) AuthorHouse.

Mosby, Pamela. I'm So Angry. Brever, Amy, illus. 2013. 28p. pap. 7.99 (978-0-9886272-4-6(8)) Brothers N Publishing Corp.

Moskowitz, Hannah. Invincible Summer. 2011. (ENG.). 288p. (YA). (gr. 9-18). pap. 9.99 (978-1-4424-0751-0(4), Simon Pulse) Simon Pulse.

Moss, Christopher Hawthorne. Beloved Pilgrim. 2nd ed. (ENG., 2016. Illus.). (J). 29.99 (978-1-63477-939-5(8)) 2014. 304p. (YA). pap. 17.99 (978-1-62798-538-3(7)) Dreamspinner Pr. (Harmony Ink Pr.).

Mrozek, Elizabeth. The Fifth Chair. Mrozek, Elizabeth, illus. 2013. (Illus.). 38p. 19.95 (978-1-935766-80-3(5)) Windy City Pubs.

Muirhead, Maria. My Asthma Book. 2007. 72p. (J). (gr. 1-2). per. 11.95 (978-0-595-42925-7(4)) iUniverse, Inc.

Mull, Brandon. Champion of the Titan Games, vol. 4. 2020. (Dragonwatch Ser.: 4). (ENG., Illus.). 544p. (J). (gr. 5). 19.99 (978-1-62972-788-2(1), 5240661) Deseret Bk. Co.

—Champion of the Titan Games: A Fablehaven Adventure. 2021. (Dragonwatch Ser.: 4). (ENG., Illus.). 544p. (J). (gr. 3-8). pap. 9.99 (978-1-4814-8508-1(3), Aladdin) Simon & Schuster Children's Publishing.

—Fablehaven. 2006. (ENG., Illus.). 351p. (J). lib. bdg. 20.00 (978-1-4242-4831-5(0)) Fitzgerald Bks.

—Fablehaven. 2009. (SPA.). 306p. (YA). (gr. 5-8). 24.95 (978-84-9918-033-5(7)) Roca Editorial ESP. Dist: Spanish Pubs., LLC.

—Fablehaven. 2006. (Fablehaven Ser.: 1). (ENG., Illus.). 368p. (J). (gr. 3-7). 19.99 (978-1-59038-581-4(0), 4961111, Shadow Mountain) Shadow Mountain Publishing.

—Fablehaven. Dorman, Brandon, illus. 2007. (Fablehaven Ser.: 1). (ENG.). 384p. (J). (gr. 3-8). pap. 9.99 (978-1-4169-4720-2(5), Aladdin) Simon & Schuster Children's Publishing.

—Fablehaven. 2007. (Fablehaven Ser.: 01). lib. bdg. 18.40 (978-1-4177-9328-0(7)) Turtleback.

—Fablehaven: Las Llaves de la Prision de los Demonios. 2012. (SPA.). 466p. (YA). 24.95 (978-84-9918-438-8(3)) Roca Editorial ESP. Dist: Spanish Pubs., LLC.

—Fablehaven Complete Boxed Set: Rise of the Evening Star; Grip of the Shadow Plague; Secrets of the Dragon Sanctuary; Keys to the Demon Prison. 2010. (Fablehaven Ser.: Bks. 1-3). (ENG.). 2512p. (gr. 3-6). 99.99 (978-1-60641-832-1(7), 5046909, Shadow Mountain) Shadow Mountain Publishing.

—Fablehaven Complete Set (Boxed Set) Set: Fablehaven; Rise of the Evening Star; Grip of the Shadow Plague; Secrets of the Dragon Sanctuary; Keys to the Demon Prison. Dorman, Brandon, illus. 2011. (Fablehaven Ser.). (ENG.). 2512p. (J). (gr. 3-8). pap. 49.99 (978-1-4424-2977-2(1), Aladdin) Simon & Schuster Children's Publishing.

—Grip of the Shadow Plague. Dorman, Brandon, illus. 2008. (Fablehaven Ser.: 3). (ENG.). 480p. (J). (gr. 3-7). 19.99 (978-1-59038-898-3(4), 5004776, Shadow Mountain) Shadow Mountain Publishing.

—Keys to the Demon Prison. Dorman, Brandon, illus. 2011. (Fablehaven Ser.: 5). (ENG.). 640p. (J). (gr. 3-8). pap. 9.99 (978-1-4169-9029-1(1), Aladdin) Simon & Schuster Children's Publishing.

—Master of the Phantom Isle. 2019. (Dragonwatch Ser.: 3). (ENG., Illus.). 496p. (J). (gr. 5). 18.99 (978-1-62972-604-5(4), 5222032, Shadow Mountain) Deseret Bk. Co.

—Master of the Phantom Isle: A Fablehaven Adventure. 2020. (Dragonwatch Ser.: 3). (ENG., Illus.). 496p. (J). (gr. 3-8). pap. 9.99 (978-1-4814-8506-7(7), Aladdin) Simon & Schuster Children's Publishing.

—Rise of the Evening Star. Dorman, Brandon, illus. 2007. (Fablehaven Ser.: 2). (ENG.). 456p. (J). (gr. 3-7). 19.99 (978-1-59038-742-9(2), 4981432, Shadow Mountain) Shadow Mountain Publishing.

—Rise of the Evening Star. Dorman, Brandon, illus. 2008. (Fablehaven Ser.: 2). (ENG.). 480p. (J). (gr. 3-8). pap. 8.99 (978-1-4169-5770-6(7), Aladdin) Simon & Schuster Children's Publishing.

—Secrets of the Dragon Sanctuary. Dorman, Brandon, illus. 2010. (Fablehaven Ser.: 4). (ENG.). 560p. (J). (gr. 3-8). pap. 9.99 (978-1-4169-9028-4(3), Aladdin) Simon & Schuster Children's Publishing.

—Secrets of the Dragon Sanctuary. 2010. (Fablehaven Ser.: 4). lib. bdg. 19.65 (978-0-606-10685-6(5)) Turtleback.

Mullinax, Jerry. Enoree. 2009. (YA). pap. (978-0-88092-646-1(5)) Royal Fireworks Publishing Co.

Muñoz, Isabel. Eric & Julieta: Desastre en la Cocina / a Mess in the Kitchen (Bilingual) (Bilingual Edition) Mazali, Gustavo, illus. 2012. (Eric & Julieta Ser.). (SPA.). 24p. (J). (gr. -1-3). pap. 3.99 (978-0-545-35581-0(8), Scholastic en Espanol) Scholastic, Inc.

—Eric & Julieta: Es Mío / It's Mine (Bilingual) (Bilingual Edition) Mazali, Gustavo, illus. 2006. (Eric & Julieta Ser.).Tr. of It's Mine. (SPA.). 24p. (J). (gr. -1-3). pap. 3.99 (978-0-439-78370-5(4)) Scholastic, Inc.

—Just Like Mom. Mazali, Gustavo, illus. 2005. 22p. (J). pap. (978-0-439-78844-1(7)) Scholastic, Inc.

—Now, What? / ¿Ahora, Qué? (Eric & Julieta) (Bilingual) (Bilingual Edition) Mazali, Gustavo, illus. 2006. (Eric & Julieta Ser.). (SPA & ENG.). 24p. (J). (gr. -1-3). pap. 3.99 (978-0-439-78372-9(0)) Scholastic, Inc.

Murdoch, Patricia. Revelación, 1 vol. 2008. (Spanish Soundings Ser.). (SPA.). 112p. (YA). (gr. 8-12). pap. 9.95 (978-1-55469-053-4(6)) Orca Bk. Pubs. USA.

Murphy, Emily Bain. The Disappearances. (ENG.). 400p. (YA). (gr. 7). 2018. pap. 11.99 (978-1-328-90407-2(5), 1700752) 2017. 17.99 (978-0-544-87936-2(8), 1650974) HarperCollins Pubs. (Clarion Bks.).

—The Disappearances. 2018. lib. bdg. 20.85 (978-0-606-40998-8(X)) Turtleback.

Murphy, Patty. When I Grow Up. 2012. 24p. pap. 24.95 (978-1-4626-6441-2(5)) America Star Bks.

Murray, George. The Tales of Molly Brand & MacNessie. 2008. 70p. pap. 14.95 (978-1-4092-3724-2(9)) Lulu Pr., Inc.

Murray, Kirsty. Puddle Hunters. Blair, Karen, illus. 2019. (ENG.). 32p. (J). (gr. -1-1). 16.99 (978-1-76029-674-2(0)) Allen & Unwin AUS. Dist: Independent Pubs. Group.

Muschla, Gary Robert. The Sword & the Cross. 2009. (YA). pap. (978-0-88092-472-6(1)) Royal Fireworks Publishing Co.

Muscia, Marilena Carrubba. Misses Cowy to the Rescue. 2011. 24p. (gr. -1). 12.99 (978-1-4567-3582-1(9)) AuthorHouse.

Muth, Jon J. Addy's Cup of Sugar: Based on a Buddhist Story of Healing (a Stillwater & Friends Book) Muth, Jon J., illus. 2020. (ENG., Illus.). 32p. (J). (gr. -1-3). 17.99 (978-0-439-63428-1(8), Scholastic Pr.) Scholastic, Inc.

—Zen Ghosts (a Stillwater & Friends Book) Muth, Jon J., illus. 2010. (ENG., Illus.). 40p. (J). (gr. -1-3). 18.99 (978-0-439-63430-4(X), Scholastic Pr.) Scholastic, Inc.

—Zen Shorts, 1 vol. Muth, Jon J., illus. 2010. (ENG.). (J). (gr. -1-3). audio compact disk 18.99 (978-0-545-22760-5(7)) Scholastic, Inc.

—Zen Shorts (a Stillwater & Friends Book), 1 vol. Muth, Jon J., illus. 2005. (ENG., Illus.). 40p. (J). (gr. -1-3). 17.99 (978-0-439-33911-7(1), Scholastic Pr.) Scholastic, Inc.

—Zen Socks (a Stillwater & Friends Book) Muth, Jon J., illus. 2015. (ENG., Illus.). 40p. (J). (gr. -1-3). 17.99 (978-0-545-16669-0(1), Scholastic Pr.) Scholastic, Inc.

—Zen Ties (a Stillwater & Friends Book) Muth, Jon J., illus. 2008. (ENG., Illus.). 40p. (J). (gr. -1-3). 18.99 (978-0-439-63425-0(3), Scholastic Pr.) Scholastic, Inc.

My Baby Sister, Annie: Big Book. (Pebble Soup Explorations Ser.). 16p. (gr. -1-18). 31.00 (978-0-7578-1654-3(1)) Rigby Education.

My Baby Sister, Annie: Small Book. (Pebble Soup Explorations Ser.). 16p. (gr. -1-18). 5.00 (978-0-7578-1694-9(0)) Rigby Education.

Myers, Benjamin J. Blood Alchemy. 2010. (ENG.). 384p. (978-1-84255-641-2(X)) Orion Publishing Group, Ltd. GBR. Dist: Hachette Bk. Group.

Myers, Bill. The Chamber of Lies, 1 vol. 2009. (Elijah Project Ser.: 4). (ENG.). 128p. (J). (gr. 4-7). pap. 6.99 (978-0-310-71196-4(7)) Zonderkidz.

—The Enemy Closes In, 1 vol., 2. 2009. (Elijah Project Ser.). (ENG.). 128p. (J). (gr. 4-7). pap. 6.99 (978-0-310-71194-0(0)) Zonderkidz.

Myers, Bill & Riordan, James. On the Run, 1 vol., 1. 2009. (Elijah Project Ser.). (ENG.). 128p. (J). (gr. 4-7). pap. 4.99 (978-0-310-71193-3(2)) Zonderkidz.

Myers, Edward. Climb or Die. 2nd ed. 2016. 154p. (J). pap. (978-1-932727-12-8(4)) Montemayor Pr.

—Solos en la Montaña. 2016. (SPA.). 157p. (J). pap. (978-1-932727-18-0(3)) Montemayor Pr.

Myers, Walter Dean. A Star Is Born. 2012. (Cruisers Ser.: Bk. 3). 160p. (J). (978-0-439-91631-8(3)) Scholastic, Inc.

Myracle, Lauren. Friends of a Feather. Henry, Jed, illus. 2015. (Life of Ty Ser.: 3). (ENG.). 144p. (J). (gr. 1-4). 7.99 (978-0-14-242320-2(3), Puffin Books) Penguin Young Readers Group.

—Non-Random Acts of Kindness. Henry, Jed, illus. 2015. (Life of Ty Ser.: 2). (ENG.). 128p. (J). (gr. 1-4). 5.99 (978-0-14-242319-6(X), Puffin Books) Penguin Young Readers Group.

—Penguin Problems. 2014. (Life of Ty Ser.: 1). lib. bdg. 16.00 (978-0-606-34213-1(3)) Turtleback.

The Mystery of the Lion's Tail. 2014. (Greetings from Somewhere Ser.: 5). (ENG., Illus.). 128p. (J). (gr. -1-4). pap. 6.99 (978-1-4814-1464-7(X), Little Simon) Little Simon.

Mystery on Church Hill. 2013. 196p. (J). pap. 8.99 (978-0-9893414-3-1(7)) MyBoys3 Pr.

Na, An. Wait for Me. 2006. (ENG.). 176p. (J). (gr. 7-18). 22.44 (978-0-399-24275-5(9)) Penguin Young Readers Group.

Nadon, Yves. We Are Brothers. Claverie, Jean, illus. 2018. (ENG.). 32p. (J). (gr. 1-3). 18.99 (978-1-56846-292-9(1), 19676, Creative Editions) Creative Co., The.

Naidoo, Beverley. The Other Side of Truth. 2008. 252p. (gr. 5-9). 17.00 (978-0-7569-8941-5(8)) Perfection Learning Corp.

Napoli, Donna Jo. The Wishing Club: A Story about Fractions. Currey, Anna, illus. rev. ed. 2007. (ENG.). 32p. (J). (gr. 1-4). 18.99 (978-0-8050-7665-3(4), 900042104, Holt, Henry & Co. Bks. For Young Readers) Holt, Henry & Co.

Narsimhan, Mahtab. The Third Eye: Tara Trilogy. 2007. (Tara Trilogy Ser.: 1). (ENG.). 240p. (YA). (gr. 5-7). pap. 12.99 (978-1-55002-750-1(6), Boardwalk Bks.) Dundurn Pr. CAN. Dist: Ingram Publisher Services.

Nash, Andy. Marcus & His Monkey: For Kids Blessed with Popularity. 2010. (J). (978-0-8127-0452-5(5)) Autumn Hse. Publishing Co.

National Children's Book and Literacy Alliance Staff, contrib. by. The Exquisite Corpse Adventure. 2011. (ENG., Illus.). 288p. (J). (gr. 4-6). 22.44 (978-0-7636-5149-7(4)) Candlewick Pr.

Natl Children's Book & Literacy Alliance. The Exquisite Corpse Adventure. 2011. (ENG., Illus.). 288p. (J). (gr. 4-7). pap. 9.99 (978-0-7636-5773-4(5)) Candlewick Pr.

Naylor, Phyllis Reynolds. The Great Chicken Debacle, 0 vols. 2012. (ENG.). 114p. (J). (gr. 4-6). pap. 9.99 (978-0-7614-5148-8(X), 9780761451488, Two Lions) Amazon Publishing.

Neale, Jonathan. Lost at Sea. 2004. (ENG.). 112p. (J). (gr. 5-7). reprint ed. pap. 8.95 (978-0-618-43236-3(1), 491905, Clarion Bks.) HarperCollins Pubs.

Neenan, Colin. Thick. 2006. 126p. (YA). (gr. 7-16). per. 6.95 (978-0-9746481-9-4(1)) Brown Barn Bks.

Neil, Deanna. The Land of Curiosities (Book 2)) Lost in Yellowstone, 1872-1873. 2009. 320p. (J). pap. 12.95 (978-0-9798800-2-5(5)) EcoSeekers, The.

Neilsen, David. Beyond the Doors. 2017. 368p. (J). (gr. 3-7). 16.99 (978-1-101-93582-8(0), Crown Books For Young Readers) Random Hse. Children's Bks.

Nelson, Jandy. I'll Give You the Sun. 2015. (CHI.). 384p. (YA). (gr. 9). pap. (978-986-359-180-1(7)) Ecus Publishing Hse.

—I'll Give You the Sun. (ENG.). (YA). (gr. 9-12). 2015. 400p. pap. 11.99 (978-0-14-242576-3(1), Speak) 2014. 384p. 18.99 (978-0-8037-3496-8(4), Dial Bks) Penguin Young Readers Group.

—I'll Give You the Sun. 2015. (ENG.). 400p. (YA). (gr. 9). 21.30 (978-1-68065-512-4(4)) Perfection Learning Corp.

—I'll Give You the Sun. 2015. lib. bdg. 22.10 (978-0-606-37572-6(4)) Turtleback.

Nelson, S. D. The Star People: A Lakota Story. 2003. (ENG., Illus.). 40p. (J). (gr. -1-3). 19.99 (978-0-8109-4584-5(3)) Abrams, Inc.

Nelson, Theresa. Ruby Electric. 2004. 264p. (J). (gr. 5-7). 13.65 (978-0-7569-3530-6(X)) Perfection Learning Corp.

—Ruby Electric. 2004. (ENG.). 272p. (J). (gr. 5-7). reprint ed. pap. 12.99 (978-0-689-87146-7(5), Atheneum Bks. for Young Readers) Simon & Schuster Children's Publishing.

Nesbit, E. Five Children & IT. 2019. (ENG.). 296p. (YA). (gr. 7-12). pap. (978-0-359-90993-3(0)) Lulu Pr., Inc.

—Five Children & It. 2007. 192p. per. 12.95 (978-1-4218-3940-0(7)); (gr. 4-7). 27.95 (978-1-4218-3840-3(0)) 1st World Publishing, Inc. (1st World Library - Literary Society).

—Five Children & It. 2018. (ENG., Illus.). 190p. (YA). (gr. 7-12). pap. (978-93-5329-308-6(1)) Alpha Editions.

—Five Children & It. 207p. 20.95 (978-0-8488-2523-2(3)) Amereon Ltd.

—Five Children & It. 2013. 132p. pap. (978-1-908388-99-5(4)) Aziloth Bks.

—Five Children & It. Okstad, Ella, illus. 2017. (Alma Junior Classics Ser.). (ENG.). 160p. (J). pap. 10.00 (978-1-84749-636-2(9), 900184124, Alma Classics) Bloomsbury Publishing USA.

—Five Children & It. (gr. 4-6). 2011. 428p. pap. 35.75 (978-1-179-45023-0(X)) 2008. 200p. 25.99 (978-0-554-29413-1(3)) Creative Media Partners, LLC.

—Five Children & It. Millar, H. R., illus. l.t. ed. 2007. (ENG.). 198p. pap. 21.99 (978-1-4346-7587-3(4)) Creative Media Partners, LLC.

—Five Children & It. 2005. 96p. per. 4.95 (978-1-4209-2587-6(3)) Digireads.com Publishing.

—Five Children & It. Millar, H. R., illus. 2007. (ENG.). 204p. per. (978-1-4065-3077-3(8)) Dodo Pr.

—Five Children & It. 2017. (Dover Children's Evergreen Classics Ser.). (ENG., Illus.). 160p. (J). (gr. 3-8). pap. 4.00 (978-0-486-42366-1(2), 423662) Dover Pubns., Inc.

—Five Children & It. 2006. pap. (978-1-4068-3501-4(3)) 2005. 296p. pap. (978-1-84637-200-1(3)) Echo Library.

—Five Children & It. 2014. (ENG.). 240p. (J). pap. 7.00 (978-0-571-31476-8(7), Faber & Faber Children's Bks.) Faber & Faber, Inc.

—Five Children & It. 2010. 98p. pap. 19.99 (978-1-153-62213-4(0)) General Bks. LLC.

—Five Children & It. 2010. 144p. pap. (978-1-4076-4577-3(3)) HardPr.

—Five Children & It. (ENG.). 2019. 290p. (YA). (gr. 7-12). pap. 21.99 (978-1-6942-3886-3(5)) 2019. 122p. (YA). (gr. 7-12). pap. 5.99 (978-1-6953-5526-2(1)) 2019. 590p. (YA). (gr. 7-12). pap. 38.99 (978-1-0895-1495-4(6)) 2019. 284p. (YA). (gr. 7-12). pap. 16.99 (978-1-0899-6215-1(0)) 2019. 284p. (YA). (gr. 7-12). pap. 16.99 (978-1-0830-5922-2(X)) 2019. 574p. (YA). (gr. 7-12). pap. 38.99 (978-1-0825-4951-9(7)) 2019. 374p. (YA). (gr. 7-12). pap. 24.99 (978-1-0801-4237-8(1)) 2019. 284p. (YA). (gr. 7-12). pap. 16.99 (978-1-0774-1273-6(8)) 2019. 590p. (YA). (gr. 7-12). pap. 33.99 (978-1-0997-7213-9(3)) 2019. 392p. (YA). (gr. 7-12). pap. 22.99 (978-1-0989-2759-2(1)) 2019. 380p. (YA). (gr. 7-12). pap. 23.99 (978-1-0917-8106-1(0)) 2019. 408p. (YA). (gr. 7-12). pap. 24.99 (978-1-7965-5885-2(0)) 2018. (Illus.). 168p. (J). pap. 12.99 (978-1-7919-6814-4(7)) Independently Published.

—Five Children & It. 2010. 152p. pap. 17.56 (978-1-162-66290-9(5)) 2010. 152p. (gr. 3-7). 29.56 (978-1-169-26518-9(9)) 2010. 152p. 36.95 (978-1-161-43155-1(1)) 2004. reprint ed. pap. 21.95 (978-1-4191-1987-3(7)) 2004. reprint ed. pap. 1.99 (978-1-4192-1987-0(1)) Kessinger Publishing, LLC.

—Five Children & It. 2018. (ENG.). (J). 174p. (978-3-7340-4669-8(6)); 174p. pap. (978-3-7340-4668-1(8)); (Illus.). 130p. (978-3-7340-4531-8(2)); (Illus.). 130p. pap. (978-3-7340-4530-1(4)) Outlook Verlagsgesellschaft mbH.

—Five Children & It. Hische, Jessica, illus. 2013. (Penguin Drop Caps Ser.). 256p. (gr. 12). 30.00 (978-0-14-312466-5(8), Penguin Bks.) Penguin Publishing Group.

—Five Children & It. Nesbit, E., illus. 2004. (Illus.). 240p. (J). (gr. 5-18). 14.00 (978-0-14-303915-0(6), Penguin Classics) Penguin Publishing Group.

—Five Children & It. 2013. (Vintage Children's Classics Ser.). (ENG., Illus.). 272p. (J). (gr. 4-7). pap. 10.99 (978-0-09-957298-5(2)) Penguin Random Hse. GBR. Dist: Independent Pubs. Group.

—Five Children & It. 2008. (Puffin Classics Ser.). (Illus.). 272p. (J). (gr. 5-7). 7.99 (978-0-14-132161-5(X), Puffin Books) Penguin Young Readers Group.

—Five Children & It. 2005. (J). 1.25 (978-1-4025-4084-4(1)) Recorded Bks., Inc.

—Five Children & It. 2009. 128p. (gr. 4-7). pap. 4.95 (978-1-60459-692-2(9)) Wilder Pubns., Corp.

—Five Children & It. 2005. (ENG.). 29.95 (978-1-55742-510-2(8)); pap. 14.95 (978-1-55742-506-5(X)) Wildside Pr., LLC.

—Five Children & It. 2013. 160p. (978-3-8495-1928-5(7)) 2013. 160p. pap. (978-3-8495-0897-5(8)) 2011. 208p. pap. (978-3-8424-8390-3(2)) tredition Verlag.

—The House of Arden. 2006. 184p. (gr. 3-7). per. 14.95 (978-1-59818-967-4(0)); 26.95 (978-1-59818-181-4(5)) Aegypan.

—Level 2: the Railway Children. 2nd ed. 2008. (Pearson English Graded Readers Ser.). (ENG., Illus.). 48p. pap. 13.32 (978-1-4058-6964-5(X), Pearson ELT) Pearson Education.

—The Railway Children. 2007. 236p. per. 12.95 (978-1-4218-3945-5(8)); (ENG.). (gr. 4-7). 27.95 (978-1-4218-3845-8(1)) 1st World Publishing, Inc. (1st World Library - Literary Society).

—The Railway Children. 2006. (ENG.). 228p. (gr. 4-7). per. 14.95 (978-1-59818-933-9(6)); 26.95 (978-1-59818-179-1(3)) Aegypan.
—The Railway Children. 2013. 140p. pap. (978-1-908388-94-0(3)) Aziloth Bks.
—The Railway Children. 2008. (Illus.). 176p. (J). 8.99 (978-1-59166-924-1(3)) BJU Pr.
—The Railway Children. 2010. 146p. (gr. 4-7). pap. 8.95 (978-1-61104-337-2(9)) Cedar Lake Pubns.
—The Railway Children. Brock, C. E., illus. (YA). 14.95 (978-0-8118-4933-3(3)) Chronicle Bks. LLC.
—The Railway Children. 2012. (ENG.). 234p. pap. 14.99 (978-1-4812-4818-1(9)) CreateSpace Independent Publishing Platform.
—The Railway Children. 2008. 204p. (gr. 4-7). 24.99 (978-0-554-36009-6(8)); 27.99 (978-0-554-26706-7(3)) Creative Media Partners, LLC.
—The Railway Children. 2008. (gr. 4-7). pap. 5.99 (978-1-4209-3105-1(9)) Digireads.com Publishing.
—The Railway Children. Brock, C. E., illus. 2008. (ENG.). 248p. per. (978-1-4065-9815-5(1)) Dodo Pr.
—The Railway Children. 2007. (ENG.). 204p. per. (978-1-4065-3083-4(2)) Dodo Pr.
—The Railway Children. 2006. pap. (978-1-4068-3505-2(6)) 2005. 348p. pap. (978-1-84637-205-6(4)) Echo Library.
—The Railway Children. Brock, Charles Edmund, illus. 2012. 232p. pap. (978-1-78201-004-3(1)) Evertype.
—The Railway Children. 2010. (Illus.). 118p. pap. 19.99 (978-1-153-71841-7(3)) General Bks. LLC.
—The Railway Children. 2010. 184p. pap. (978-1-4076-1891-3(1)) HardPr.
—The Railway Children. (ENG.). (J). pap. (978-0-340-71497-3(2)) Hodder & Stoughton.
—The Railway Children. 2010. 194p. 30.36 (978-1-169-28328-2(4)) 2010. 194p. pap. 18.36 (978-1-162-70632-0(5)) 2010. 194p. 37.95 (978-1-161-47496-1(X)) 2004. reprint ed. pap. 1.99 (978-1-4192-7972-0(6)) 2004. reprint ed. pap. 22.95 (978-1-4191-7972-3(1)) Kessinger Publishing, LLC.
—The Railway Children. 2006. (Twelve-Point Ser.). lib. bdg. 25.00 (978-1-58287-399-2(2)); lib. bdg. 26.00 (978-1-58287-890-4(0)) North Bks.
—The Railway Children. unabr. ed. 2004. (Chrysalis Childrens Classics Ser.). (ENG., Illus.). 128p. (YA). pap. (978-1-84365-050-8(9), Pavilion Children's Books) Pavilion Bks.
—The Railway Children. 2nd ed. 2011. (Puffin Classics Ser.). (Illus.). 304p. (J). (gr. 5-7). pap. 8.99 (978-0-14-132160-8(1), Puffin Books) Penguin Young Readers Group.
—The Railway Children. 2004. (ENG.). 530p. (978-0-9548401-2-9(7)) Shoes & Ships & Sealing Wax Ltd.
—The Railway Children. 2009. 156p. (gr. 4-7). pap. 6.99 (978-1-60459-698-4(8)) Wilder Pubns., Corp.
—The Railway Children. 2011. 200p. (gr. 4-7). pap. (978-3-8424-4120-0(7)) tredition Verlag.
—Story of the Treasure Seekers. 2006. pap. (978-1-4068-3507-6(2)) Echo Library.
—The Story of the Treasure Seekers. 2009. 128p. (gr. 4-7). pap. 5.50 (978-1-60459-695-3(3)) Wilder Pubns., Corp.
—The Story of the Treasure Seekers: Being the Adventures of the Bastable Children in Search of A Fortune. Lt. ed. 2005. 288p. pap. (978-1-84637-207-0(0)) Echo Library.
Nesbit, E. & Treasures, Grandma's. Five Children & It. 2019. (ENG.). 180p. (YA). (gr. 7-12). (978-0-359-54872-9(5)); pap. (978-0-359-54847-7(4)) Lulu Pr., Inc.
Nesbit, Edith. Five Children & It. 2019. (ENG.). 180p. (J). pap. 9.99 (978-0-368-94992-0(3)) Blurb, Inc.
—Five Children & It. (ENG.). (J). 2019. 386p. pap. 39.99 (978-1-7068-6358-8(6)) 2019. 384p. pap. 15.99 (978-1-7018-0690-0(8)) 2019. 384p. pap. 15.99 (978-1-6996-1246-0(3)) 2019. 384p. pap. 22.99 (978-1-6967-8914-1(1)) 2019. 384p. pap. 22.99 (978-1-6949-5682-8(2)) 2019. 384p. pap. 22.99 (978-1-6907-1063-9(2)) 2019. 146p. pap. 11.99 (978-1-0891-0598-5(3)) 2019. 294p. pap. 19.99 (978-1-0723-4490-2(4)) 2019. 386p. pap. 22.99 (978-1-0704-5485-6(0)) 2019. 290p. pap. 18.99 (978-1-0704-9826-3(2)) 2019. 490p. pap. 26.99 (978-1-0968-8478-1(X)) 2019. 386p. pap. 25.99 (978-1-0936-9117-7(4)) 2019. 294p. pap. 16.99 (978-1-0934-3689-1(1)) 2018. 294p. pap. 20.99 (978-1-7313-2044-5(2)) 2018. (Illus.). 158p. pap. 13.22 (978-1-7294-5225-7(6)) 2018. (Illus.). 158p. pap. 13.22 (978-1-7294-5222-6(1)) 2018. (Illus.). 158p. pap. 13.22 (978-1-7294-5221-9(3)) 2018. (Illus.). 158p. pap. 13.22 (978-1-7294-5220-2(5)) Independently Published.
—The Railway Children. 2012. (Oxford Children's Classics Ser.). (ENG.). 240p. 9.95 (978-0-19-275819-4(5)) Oxford Univ. Pr., Inc.
—The Railway Children. 2013. (Vintage Children's Classics Ser.). 320p. (J). (gr. 4-7). pap. 10.99 (978-0-09-957299-2(0)) Penguin Random Hse. GBR. Dist: Independent Pubs. Group.
Nettrour, Nelani. Nunkey's Adventures Bk. 2: Birth of Reekey. 2006. (Illus.). 74p. (J). pap. 11.95 (978-1-932657-54-8(1)) Third Millennium Pubns.
Neubecker, Robert. Fall Is for School. Neubecker, Robert, illus. 2017. (ENG., Illus.). 32p. (J). (gr. -1-k). 17.99 (978-1-4847-3254-0(5)) Disney Pr.
Newman, John. Mimi. 2011. (ENG., Illus.). 192p. (J). (gr. 3-7). 15.99 (978-0-7636-5415-3(9)) Candlewick Pr.
Newman, Lesléa. Sparkle Boy, 1 vol. Mola, Maria, illus. 2017. (ENG.). 32p. (J). (gr. k-3). 18.95 (978-1-62014-285-1(6), leelowbooks) Lee & Low Bks., Inc.
Nielsen, Susin. Degrassi Junior High: Snake, 1 vol. 2006. (Degrassi Junior High Ser.). (ENG.). 184p. (YA). (gr. 5-10). 7.95 (978-1-55028-926-8(8), 926) James Lorimer & Co. Ltd., Pubs. CAN. Dist: Formac Lorimer Bks. Ltd.
Nikakhtar, Manijeh. Love & Joy. 2010. 65p. pap. 21.95 (978-1-4327-4394-9(5)) Outskirts Pr., Inc.
Nimmo, Jenny. The Box Boys & the Magic Shell. (Box Boys Ser.). (ENG., Illus.). 64p. (J). pap. (978-0-340-73290-8(3)) Hodder & Stoughton.
Noble, Trinka Hakes. The Last Brother: A Civil War Tale. Papp, Robert, illus. 2006. (Tales of Young Americans Ser.). (ENG.). 48p. (J). (gr. 1-4). 17.95 (978-1-58536-253-0(0), 202069) Sleeping Bear Pr.
—The Scarlet Stockings Spy. Papp, Robert, illus. 2004. (Tales of Young Americans Ser.). (ENG.). 48p. (J). (gr. 1-4). 16.95 (978-1-58536-230-1(1), 202055) Sleeping Bear Pr.
Noble, Trinka Hakes & Papp, Lisa. The Battles. Papp, Robert, illus. 2013. (American Adventures Ser.). (ENG.). 88p. (J). (gr. 3-6). pap. 9.99 (978-1-58536-861-7(X), 202368) Sleeping Bear Pr.
Noland, Charles. The Adventures of Drew & Ellie: The Daring Rescue. Moyer, Tom, illus. 2nd ed. 2006. 92p. (J). per. 7.95 (978-0-9789297-2-5(1)) TMD Enterprises.
Nolen, Jerdine. Block Party Surprise. Henninger, Michelle, illus. 2015. 41p. (J). (978-1-4806-8574-1(7)) Harcourt.
—Bradford Street Buddies: Block Party Surprise. Henninger, Michelle, illus. 2015. (ENG.). 48p. (J). (gr. 1-4). pap. 4.99 (978-0-544-35863-8(5), 1587297, Clarion Bks.) HarperCollins Pubs.
Noll, Amanda. Hey, That's MY Monster! McWilliam, Howard, illus. 2016. (I Need My Monster Ser.). 32p. (J). (gr. k-2). 17.95 (978-1-936261-37-6(5)) Flashlight Pr.
North, Ryan. How to Be a T. Rex. Lowery, Mike, illus. 2018. (ENG.). 32p. (J). (gr. -1-3). 17.99 (978-0-399-18624-0(7), Dial Bks) Penguin Young Readers Group.
Novak, Ali. My Life with the Walter Boys. (ENG.). (YA). 2019. 400p. (gr. 8-12). pap. 11.99 (978-1-7282-0547-2(6)) 2014. 368p. (gr. 7-12). pap. 10.99 (978-1-4022-9786-1(6), 9781402297861) Sourcebooks, Inc.
—The Heartbreakers. 2015. (Heartbreak Chronicles Ser.: 1). 336p. (YA). (gr. 6-12). pap. 12.99 (978-1-4926-1256-8(1), 9781492612568) Sourcebooks, Inc.
Novel Units. My Brother Sam Is Dead Novel Units Student Packet. 2019. (ENG.). (J). pap. 13.99 (978-1-56137-823-4(2), Novel Units, Inc.) Classroom Library Co.
—My Brother Sam Is Dead Novel Units Teacher Guide. 2019. (ENG.). (YA). pap. 12.99 (978-1-56137-380-2(X), Novel Units, Inc.) Classroom Library Co.
—Superfudge Novel Units Teacher Guide. 2019. (Fudge Ser.). (ENG.). (J). pap. 12.99 (978-1-56137-175-4(0), Novel Units, Inc.) Classroom Library Co.
Ntihemuka, Patty Froese. Hyacinth Doesn't Go to Jail: And, Hyacinth Doesn't Miss Christmas. 2009. (Illus.). 157p. (J). pap. 10.99 (978-0-8163-2372-2(0)) Pacific Pr. Publishing Assn.
Nugent, Matthew. Nightmares on Goose Rocks Beach in Kennebunkport, Maine: Book 4 of the Goose Rocks Tales. 2003. (Illus.). 204p. (J). per. 14.95 (978-0-9705812-3-5(8)) CBI Pr.
Numeroff, Laura. Beatrice Doesn't Want To. Munsinger, Lynn, illus. 2008. (ENG.). 32p. (J). (gr. -1-2). pap. 7.99 (978-0-7636-3843-6(9)) Candlewick Pr.
—What Brothers Do Best: (Big Brother Books for Kids, Brotherhood Books for Kids, Sibling Books for Kids) 2012. (What Brothers/Sisters Do Best Ser.). (ENG., Illus.). 20p. (J). (gr. -1 — 1). bds. 8.99 (978-1-4521-1073-8(5)) Chronicle Bks. LLC.
Nyaradi, J. A. Catching Santa. 2006. 140p. pap. 11.95 (978-0-7414-3462-3(8)) Infinity Publishing.
Nye, Bill & Mone, Gregory. Jack & the Geniuses: At the Bottom of the World. Iluzada, Nicholas, illus. (ENG.). (J). (gr. 3-7). 2018. 272p. pap. 8.99 (978-1-4197-3288-1(9), 1152603) 2017. 256p. 13.95 (978-1-4197-2303-2(0), 1152601, Amulet Bks.) Abrams, Inc.
—Lost in the Jungle: Jack & the Geniuses Book #3. Iluzada, Nicholas, illus. 2018. (Jack & the Geniuses Ser.). (ENG.). 288p. (J). (gr. 3-7). 13.99 (978-1-4197-2867-9(9), 1158101, Amulet Bks.) Abrams, Inc.
Nytra, David. The Secret of the Stone Frog. Nytra, David, illus. 2012. (ENG., Illus.). 8p. (J). (gr. 3-7). 16.99 (978-1-935179-18-4(7)) Astra Publishing Hse.
—Windmill Dragons: a Leah & Alan Adventure: A TOON Graphic. 2015. (Leah & Alan Adventures Ser.). (Illus.). 120p. (J). (gr. 3-7). 18.95 (978-1-935179-88-7(8), TOON Books) Astra Publishing Hse.
O'Brien, Anne Sibley. In the Shadow of the Sun. 2017. (ENG., Illus.). 336p. (YA). (gr. 3-7). 17.99 (978-0-545-90574-9(5), Levine, Arthur A. Bks.) Scholastic, Inc.
O'Connell, Jenny. Plan B. 2006. (ENG.). 288p. (YA). (gr. 9). pap. 18.99 (978-1-4165-2033-7(3), MTV Bks.) MTV Books.
O'Connor, Barbara. How to Steal a Dog: A Novel. 2009. (ENG.). 208p. (J). (gr. 3-7). pap. 7.99 (978-0-312-56112-3(1), 900058842) Square Fish.
O'Connor, Jane. Fancy Nancy: the Worst Secret Keeper Ever. Glasser, Robin Preiss, illus. 2016. (Fancy Nancy Ser.). (ENG.). 24p. (J). (gr. -1-3). pap. 4.99 (978-0-06-226960-7(7), HarperCollins) HarperCollins Pubs.
O'Coyne, James. Gravelle's Land of Horror. Whispering Pine Press International, Inc. Staff. ed. Baer, Brian, illus. 2007. (ENG.). 120p. (J). per. 9.95 (978-1-59649-604-0(5)) Whispering Pine Pr. International, Inc.
Ogaz, Nancy. Wishing on the Midnight Star: My Asperger Brother. 2003. 144p. (J). pap. 24.95 (978-1-84310-757-6(0), 695217) Kingsley, Jessica Pubs. GBR. Dist: Hachette UK Distribution.
Ogden, Charles. Frost Bites. Carton, Rick, illus. 2008. (Edgar & Ellen Nodyssey Ser.: 2). (ENG.). 192p. (J). (gr. 3-7). 23.99 (978-1-4169-5464-4(3), Simon & Schuster/Paula Wiseman Bks.) Simon & Schuster/Paula Wiseman Bks.
—Hot Air. Carton, Rick, illus. 2008. (Edgar & Ellen Nodyssey Ser.: 1). (ENG.). 192p. (J). (gr. 3-7). 9.99 (978-1-4169-5465-1(1), Aladdin) Simon & Schuster Children's Publishing.
—Nod's Limbs. Carton, Rick, illus. 2007. (Edgar & Ellen Ser.: 6). (ENG.). 224p. (J). (gr. 3-7). 24.99 (978-1-4169-1501-0(X), Simon & Schuster/Paula Wiseman Bks.) Simon & Schuster/Paula Wiseman Bks.
Oh, DaYun. We Are Brothers. Godeassi, Anna, illus. 2014. (MySELF Bookshelf Ser.). (ENG.). 32p. (J). (gr. k-2). pap. 11.94 (978-1-60357-692-5(4)) Norwood Hse. Pr.
O'Hair, Margaret. Twin to Twin. Courtin, Thierry, illus. 2003. (ENG.). 32p. (J). (gr. -1-3). 17.99 (978-0-689-84494-2(8), McElderry, Margaret K. Bks.) McElderry, Margaret K. Bks.
O'Hara, Mo. Jurassic Carp: My Big Fat Zombie Goldfish. Jagucki, Marek, illus. 2017. (My Big Fat Zombie Goldfish Ser.: 6). (ENG.). 224p. (J). pap. 6.99 (978-1-250-10260-7(X), 900163247) Square Fish.
Ohi, Ruth. Me & My Brother. 2007. (ENG., Illus.). 24p. (J). (gr. -1-k). 19.95 (978-1-55451-092-4(9), 9781554510924) Annick Pr., Ltd. CAN. Dist: Publishers Group West (PGW).
—Shh! My Brother's Napping. Ohi, Ruth, illus. 2017. (Illus.). 28p. (J). 11.99 (978-1-61067-552-9(5)) Kane Miller.
Older, Daniel José. Dactyl Hill Squad (Dactyl Hill Squad #1) (Dactyl Hill Squad Ser.: 1). (ENG.). (J). (gr. 3-7). 2019. 288p. pap. 6.99 (978-1-338-26882-9(1)) 2018. (Illus.). 272p. 16.99 (978-1-338-26881-2(3)) Scholastic, Inc. (Levine, Arthur A. Bks.).
Oldfield, Jenny. Sunny the Hero. (Home Farm Twins Ser.: No. 7). (ENG., Illus.). 120p. (J). pap. 7.99 (978-0-340-68990-5(0)) Hodder & Stoughton GBR. Dist: Trafalgar Square Publishing.
Olesen, Demetria Vassiliou. Lambyro. Forcada, Adiela & Giron, Elizabeth, illus. 2011. (ENG.). 32p. (J). 19.00 (978-0-615-47664-3(3)) Elissian Publishing Co.
Oliver, Helen. Ellen's First Swim. 2009. 32p. pap. 16.49 (978-1-4389-9828-2(7)) AuthorHouse.
Oliver, Lauren. The Spindlers. Bruno, Iacopo, illus. (ENG.). (J). (gr. 3-7). 2013. 272p. pap. 8.99 (978-0-06-197809-8(4)) 2012. 256p. 16.99 (978-0-06-197808-1(6)) HarperCollins Pubs. (HarperCollins).
Oliver, Lin. Attack of the Growling Eyeballs. Gilpin, Stephen, illus. 2009. (Who Shrunk Daniel Funk? Ser.: 1). (ENG.). 160p. (J). (gr. 3-7). pap. 7.99 (978-1-4169-0958-3(3), Simon & Schuster Bks. For Young Readers) Simon & Schuster Bks. For Young Readers.
—Double-Crossed #3. 2013. (Almost Identical Ser.: 3). 224p. (J). (gr. 3-7). pap. 7.99 (978-0-448-45193-0(X), Grosset & Dunlap) Penguin Young Readers Group.
—Double-Crossed #3 (HC), 3. 2013. (Almost Identical Ser.). (ENG.). 224p. (J). (gr. 4-6). 22.44 (978-0-448-46161-8(7)) Penguin Young Readers Group.
—Revenge of the Itty-Bitty Brothers. Gilpin, Stephen, illus. 2010. (Who Shrunk Daniel Funk? Ser.: 3). (ENG.). 176p. (J). (gr. 3-7). pap. 6.99 (978-1-4169-0962-0(1), Simon & Schuster Bks. For Young Readers) Simon & Schuster Bks. For Young Readers.
—Revenge of the Itty-Bitty Brothers, 3. Gilpin, Stephen, illus. 2009. (Who Shrunk Daniel Funk? Ser.: 3). (ENG.). 112p. (J). (gr. 2-4). 21.19 (978-1-4169-0961-3(3)) Simon & Schuster, Inc.
Olson, D. A. The Treasure Map. 2011. 36p. pap. 24.95 (978-1-4626-3655-6(1)) America Star Bks.
The One Hundredth Thing about Caroline. 2018. (Just the Tates! Ser.). (ENG.). 208p. (J). (gr. 5-7). pap. 7.99 (978-1-328-75057-0(4), 1678433, Clarion Bks.) HarperCollins Pubs.
One Tree Hill, No. 3. (YA). (978-0-439-71562-1(8)) Scholastic, Inc.
O'Neill, Alexis. Estela en el Mercado de Pulgas (Spanish Edition), 1 vol. 2005. (Illus.). 32p. (J). (SPA.). (gr. 1-4). pap. 12.95 (978-1-58430-246-9(1), leelowbooks); (ENG., (gr. -1-k). 16.95 (978-1-58430-245-2(3)) Lee & Low Bks., Inc.
O'Neill, Catharine. Annie & Simon: Banana Muffins & Other Stories. O'Neill, Catharine, illus. 2017. (ENG., Illus.). 64p. (J). (gr. k-3). 15.99 (978-0-7636-7498-4(2)) Candlewick Pr.
—Annie & Simon: the Sneeze & Other Stories: The Sneeze & Other Stories. O'Neill, Catharine, illus. 2013. (ENG., Illus.). 64p. (J). (gr. k-4). 15.99 (978-0-7636-4921-0(X)) Candlewick Pr.
Opel, Andrew. The Bobhouse: A Winnipesaukee Christmas. Hayes, Karel & Gorey, John, illus. 2017. (ENG.). 32p. (J). 19.95 (978-1-937721-45-9(0), Jetty Hse.) Randall, Peter E. Pub.
Opel, Andy. The Witches: A Winnipesaukee Adventure. Hayes, Karel, illus. 2011. (ENG.). 32p. (J). 19.95 (978-0-9828236-6-8(5), Jetty Hse.) Randall, Peter E. Pub.
Oppel, Kenneth. This Dark Endeavor: The Apprenticeship of Victor Frankenstein. 2011. (Apprenticeship of Victor Frankenstein Ser.: Bk. 1). (ENG.). (YA). (gr. 7-12). 64.99 (978-1-4558-2316-1(3)) Findaway World, LLC.
Optic, Oliver, pseud. Fighting for the Right. 2007. 136p. per. (978-1-4068-3635-6(4)) Echo Library.
—Taken by the Enemy. 2007. 132p. (gr. 4-7). per. (978-1-4068-4346-0(6)) Echo Library.
Oram, Hiawyn. Little Brother & the Cough. Rees, Mary, illus. (ENG.). 32p. (J). (gr. -1-1). (978-0-7112-0844-5(1)) ReiseArt Buchhandlung GmbH.
Orgill, Roxane. Go-Go Baby!, 1 vol. Salerno, Steven, tr. Salerno, Steven, illus. 2004. (ENG.). 32p. (J). 14.95 (978-0-7614-5157-0(9)) Marshall Cavendish Corp.
Orme, Helen. Brother Bother. 2008. (Siti's Sisters Ser.). (ENG., Illus.). 36p. pap. (978-1-84167-684-5(5)) Ransom Publishing Ltd.
—Party Time. 2008. (ENG., Illus.). 36p. pap. (978-1-84167-819-1(8)) Ransom Publishing Ltd.
Ormerod, Jan. The Baby Swap. Joyner, Andrew, illus. 2015. (ENG.). 32p. (J). (gr. -1-1). 16.99 (978-1-4814-1914-7(5), Little Simon) Little Simon.
Ortiz, Zirzeria. The Queen in Me & My Bumblebee. 2008. 48p. pap. 24.95 (978-1-60441-045-7(0)) America Star Bks.
O'Ryan, Ray. Operation Twin Trouble. Kraft, Jason, illus. 2015. (Galaxy Zack Ser.: 12). (ENG.). 128p. (J). (gr. k-4). pap. 5.99 (978-1-4814-4399-9(2), Little Simon) Little Simon.
Osborne Hale, Jennifer. Danny Blue! What Did You Do? 2009. 16p. pap. 9.95 (978-1-4490-1171-0(3)) AuthorHouse.
Osborne, Mary Pope. Abe Lincoln at Last! Murdocca, Sal, illus. 2013. (Magic Tree House (R) Merlin Mission Ser.: 19). 144p. (J). (gr. 2-5). 6.99 (978-0-375-86797-2(X), Random Hse. Bks. for Young Readers) Random Hse. Children's Bks.
—Abe Lincoln at Last! 2013. (Magic Tree House Merlin Missions Ser.: 19). lib. bdg. 16.00 (978-0-606-35563-6(4)) Turtleback.
—Blizzard of the Blue Moon. Murdocca, Sal, illus. 2007. (Magic Tree House (R) Merlin Mission Ser.: 8). 144p. (J). (gr. 2-5). 5.99 (978-0-375-83038-9(3), Random Hse. Bks. for Young Readers) Random Hse. Children's Bks.
—Carnival at Candlelight, Vol. 5. Murdocca, Sal, illus. 2006. (Magic Tree House (R) Merlin Mission Ser.: 5). 144p. (J). (gr. 2-5). 6.99 (978-0-375-83034-1(0), Random Hse. Bks. for Young Readers) Random Hse. Children's Bks.
—Christmas in Camelot. Murdocca, Sal, illus. 2009. (Magic Tree House (R) Merlin Mission Ser.: 1). 144p. (J). (gr. 2-5). 6.99 (978-0-375-85812-3(1), Random Hse. Bks. for Young Readers) Random Hse. Children's Bks.
—Christmas in Camelot. 2009. (Magic Tree House Merlin Missions Ser.: 1). lib. bdg. 16.00 (978-0-606-06386-9(2)) Turtleback.
—A Crazy Day with Cobras. Murdocca, Sal, illus. 2012. (Magic Tree House (R) Merlin Mission Ser.: 17). 144p. (J). (gr. 2-5). 5.99 (978-0-375-86795-8(3), Random Hse. Bks. for Young Readers) Random Hse. Children's Bks.
—A Crazy Day with Cobras. 2012. (Magic Tree House Merlin Missions Ser.: 17). lib. bdg. 16.00 (978-0-606-26997-1(5)) Turtleback.
—Dark Day in the Deep Sea. Murdocca, Sal, illus. 2009. (Magic Tree House (R) Merlin Mission Ser.: 11). 144p. (J). (gr. 2-5). 6.99 (978-0-375-83732-6(9), Random Hse. Bks. for Young Readers) Random Hse. Children's Bks.
—Dark Day in the Deep Sea. 2009. (Magic Tree House Merlin Missions Ser.: 11). lib. bdg. 16.00 (978-0-606-01778-7(X)) Turtleback.
—Dogs in the Dead of Night, Bk. 18. Murdocca, Sal, illus. 2013. (Magic Tree House (R) Merlin Mission Ser.: 18). 144p. (J). (gr. 2-5). 6.99 (978-0-375-86796-5(1), Random Hse. Bks. for Young Readers) Random Hse. Children's Bks.
—Dogs in the Dead of Night. 2013. (Magic Tree House Merlin Missions Ser.: 18). lib. bdg. 16.00 (978-0-606-31939-3(5)) Turtleback.
—Dragon of the Red Dawn. Murdocca, Sal, illus. 2008. (Magic Tree House (R) Merlin Mission Ser.: 9). 144p. (J). (gr. 2-5). 6.99 (978-0-375-83728-9(0), Random Hse. Bks. for Young Readers) Random Hse. Children's Bks.
—Eve of the Emperor Penguin. Murdocca, Sal, illus. 2009. (Magic Tree House (R) Merlin Mission Ser.: 12). (ENG.). 144p. (J). (gr. 2-5). 6.99 (978-0-375-83734-0(5), Random Hse. Bks. for Young Readers) Random Hse. Children's Bks.
—A Ghost Tale for Christmas Time. Murdocca, Sal, illus. 2012. (Magic Tree House (R) Merlin Mission Ser.: 16). 144p. (J). (gr. 2-5). pap. 6.99 (978-0-375-85653-2(6), Random Hse. Bks. for Young Readers) Random Hse. Children's Bks.
—A Ghost Tale for Christmas Time. 2012. (Magic Tree House Merlin Missions Ser.: 16). lib. bdg. 16.00 (978-0-606-26808-0(1)) Turtleback.
—A Good Night for Ghosts. 2010. (Magic Tree House Merlin Missions Ser.: No. 14). (Illus.). 157p. (J). pap. (978-4-8401-3411-8(1)) Fukuinkan Shoten.
—A Good Night for Ghosts. Murdocca, Sal, illus. 2011. (Magic Tree House (R) Merlin Mission Ser.: 14). 144p. (J). (gr. 2-5). 5.99 (978-0-375-85649-5(8), Random Hse. Bks. for Young Readers) Random Hse. Children's Bks.
—High Tide in Hawaii. Murdocca, Sal, illus. 2003. (Magic Tree House (R) Ser.: 28). 96p. (J). (gr. 1-4). pap. 6.99 (978-0-375-80616-2(4), Random Hse. Bks. for Young Readers) Random Hse. Children's Bks.
—High Tide in Hawaii. 2003. (Magic Tree House Ser.: 28). (gr. k-3). lib. bdg. 16.00 (978-0-613-62386-5(X)) Turtleback.
—Hurry up, Houdini! 2015. (Magic Tree House Merlin Missions Ser.: 22). lib. bdg. 16.00 (978-0-606-37718-8(2)) Turtleback.
—Leprechaun in Late Winter. Murdocca, Sal, illus. 2012. (Magic Tree House (R) Merlin Mission Ser.: 15). 144p. (J). (gr. 2-5). 6.99 (978-0-375-85651-8(X), Random Hse. Bks. for Young Readers) Random Hse. Children's Bks.
—Leprechaun in Late Winter. 2012. (Magic Tree House Merlin Missions Ser.: 15). lib. bdg. 16.00 (978-0-606-23860-1(3)) Turtleback.
—Monday with a Mad Genius. Murdocca, Sal, illus. 2009. (Magic Tree House (R) Merlin Mission Ser.: 10). 144p. (J). (gr. 2-5). 5.99 (978-0-375-83730-2(2), Random Hse. Bks. for Young Readers) Random Hse. Children's Bks.
—Monday with a Mad Genius. 2009. (Magic Tree House Merlin Missions Ser.: 10). lib. bdg. 16.00 (978-0-606-01777-0(1)) Turtleback.
—Moonlight on the Magic Flute, Bk. 13. Murdocca, Sal, illus. 2010. (Magic Tree House (R) Merlin Mission Ser.: 13). 144p. (J). (gr. 2-5). pap. 5.99 (978-0-375-85647-1(1), Random Hse. Bks. for Young Readers) Random Hse. Children's Bks.
—Navidad en Camelot. 2015. (Casa De árbol Ser.: 29). (SPA., Illus.). 144p. (J). (gr. 2-4). pap. 6.99 (978-1-63245-532-1(3)) Lectorum Pubns., Inc.
—Night of the New Magicians. Murdocca, Sal, illus. 2007. (Magic Tree House (R) Merlin Mission Ser.: 7). 144p. (J). (gr. 2-5). 6.99 (978-0-375-83036-5(7), Random Hse. Bks. for Young Readers) Random Hse. Children's Bks.
—Night of the New Magicians. 2007. (Magic Tree House Merlin Missions Ser.: 7). lib. bdg. 16.00 (978-1-4177-9108-8(X)) Turtleback.
—Night of the Ninth Dragon. Murdocca, Sal, illus. (Magic Tree House (R) Merlin Mission Ser.: 27). 144p. (J). (gr. 2-5). 2018. 6.99 (978-0-553-51092-8(4)) 2016. 13.99 (978-0-553-51089-8(4)) Random Hse. Children's Bks. (Random Hse. Bks. for Young Readers).
—A Perfect Time for Pandas, Bk. 20. Murdocca, Sal, illus. 2014. (Magic Tree House (R) Merlin Mission Ser.: 20). (ENG.). 144p. (J). (gr. 2-5). pap. 6.99 (978-0-375-86798-9(8), Random Hse. Bks. for Young Readers) Random Hse. Children's Bks.
—A Perfect Time for Pandas. 2014. (Magic Tree House Merlin Missions Ser.: 20). lib. bdg. 16.00 (978-0-606-35564-3(2)) Turtleback.
—Season of the Sandstorms. 2014. (Magic Tree House Merlin Missions Ser.: No. 6). 15.00 (978-1-63419-681-9(3)) Perfection Learning Corp.
—Season of the Sandstorms, Bk. 6. Murdocca, Sal, illus. 2006. (Magic Tree House (R) Merlin Mission Ser.: 6). 144p. (J). (gr. 2-5). 6.99 (978-0-375-83032-7(4), Random Hse. Bks. for Young Readers) Random Hse. Children's Bks.
—Shadow of the Shark. Murdocca, Sal, illus. 2017. (Magic Tree House (R) Merlin Mission Ser.: 25). 144p. (J). (gr. 2-5). 5.99 (978-0-553-51084-3(3), Random Hse. Bks. for Young Readers) Random Hse. Children's Bks.
—Soccer on Sunday. Murdocca, Sal, illus. 2016. (Magic Tree House (R) Merlin Mission Ser.: 24). 144p. (J). (gr. 2-5). 6.99 (978-0-307-98056-4(1), Random Hse. Bks. for Young Readers) Random Hse. Children's Bks.
—Stallion by Starlight. Murdocca, Sal, illus. 2014. (Magic Tree House (R) Merlin Mission Ser.: 21). 144p. (J). (gr. 2-5). pap. 5.99 (978-0-307-98044-1(8), Random Hse. Bks. for Young Readers) Random Hse. Children's Bks.
—Stallion by Starlight. 2014. (Magic Tree House Merlin Missions Ser.: 21). lib. bdg. 16.00 (978-0-606-36411-9(0)) Turtleback.

—Summer of the Sea Serpent, Bk. 3. Murdocca, Sal, illus. 2011. (Magic Tree House (R) Merlin Mission Ser.: 3). 144p. (J). (gr. 2-5). 6.99 *(978-0-375-86491-9(1),* Random Hse. Bks. for Young Readers) Random Hse. Children's Bks.

—El Verano de la Serpiente Marina. 2015. (Casa De árbol Ser.: 31). (SPA., Illus.). 144p. (J). (gr. 2-4). pap. 6.99 *(978-1-63245-534-5(X))* Lectorum Pubns., Inc.

Osborne, Mary Pope & PLC Editors Staff. Carnival at Candlelight. Murdocca, Sal, illus. 2006. (Magic Tree House Merlin Missions Ser.: No. 5). 105p. (gr. 2-6). 15.00 *(978-0-7569-6690-4(6))* Perfection Learning Corp.

Osborne, Mary Pope, et al. Carnaval a Media Luz. Murdocca, Sal, illus. 2016. (SPA.). 113p. (J). (gr. 2-4). pap. 6.99 *(978-1-63245-643-4(5))* Lectorum Pubns., Inc.

—Día Negro en el Fondo Del Mar. Murdocca, Sal, illus. 2018. (SPA.). 118p. (J). (gr. 2-4). pap. 6.99 *(978-1-63245-682-3(6))* Lectorum Pubns., Inc.

—El Dragon Del Amanecer Rojo. Murdocca, Sal, illus. 2018. (SPA.). 132p. (J). (gr. 2-4). pap. 6.99 *(978-1-63245-680-9(X))* Lectorum Pubns., Inc.

—La Estación de Las Tormentas de Arena. Murdocca, Sal, illus. 2016. (SPA.). 107p. (J). (gr. 2-4). pap. 5.99 *(978-1-63245-644-1(3))* Lectorum Pubns., Inc.

—Un Lunes con un Genio Loco. Murdocca, Sal, illus. 2018. (SPA.). 132p. (J). (gr. 2-4). pap. 6.99 *(978-1-63245-681-6(8))* Lectorum Pubns., Inc.

—Maremoto en Hawái. Murdocca, Sal, illus. 2014. (SPA.). 88p. (J). (gr. 2-4). pap. 6.99 *(978-1-933032-95-5(2))* Lectorum Pubns., Inc.

—La Noche de Los Nuevos Magos. Murdocca, Sal, illus. 2016. (SPA.). 111p. (J). (gr. 2-4). pap. 6.99 *(978-1-63245-645-8(1))* Lectorum Pubns., Inc.

—El Regalo Del Pingüino Emperador. Murdocca, Sal, illus. 2018. (SPA.). 118p. (J). (gr. 2-4). pap. 6.99 *(978-1-63245-683-0(4))* Lectorum Pubns., Inc.

—Tormenta de Nieve en Luna Azul. Murdocca, Sal, illus. 2016. (SPA.). (J). (gr. 2-4). pap. 6.99 *(978-1-63245-646-5(X))* Lectorum Pubns., Inc.

O'Shea, M.J. Cold Moon. 2nd ed. 2016. (ENG., Illus.). (J). 24.99 *(978-1-63477-954-8(1),* Harmony Ink Pr.) Dreamspinner Pr.

Ostrom, Melissa. The Beloved Wild. 2018. (ENG.). 320p. (YA). 29.99 *(978-1-250-13279-6(7),* 900177171) Feiwel & Friends.

O'Sullivan, Deirdre. Cousin Caleigh's Cartoons: And Other Stories, 1 vol. 2009. 97p. pap. 19.95 *(978-1-60836-304-9(X))* America Star Bks.

Oswald, Michael J. 3 Years Apart. 2006. 72p. pap. 11.95 *(978-0-7414-3108-0(4))* Infinity Publishing.

Ott, Alexandra. The Shadow Thieves. 2018. (Rules for Thieves Ser.: 2). (ENG., Illus.). 400p. (J). (gr. 3-7). 17.99 *(978-1-4814-7277-7(1),* Aladdin) Simon & Schuster Children's Publishing.

Owens, L. L. The Longest Car Ride Ever. Tolson, Scott, illus. 2004. 28p. *(978-1-57021-032-7(2))* Comprehensive Health Education Foundation.

Page, Nathan. The Montague Twins: the Witch's Hand: (a Graphic Novel) Shannon, Drew, illus. 2020. (Montague Twins Ser.: 1). 352p. (YA). (gr. 7). pap. 17.99 *(978-0-525-64677-8(9),* Knopf Bks. for Young Readers) Random Hse. Children's Bks.

Palmer, Deokie Savie. My Little Baby Sister & I, on a Cold Winter Day. 2007. 38p. 17.95 *(978-1-4303-2061-6(3))* Lulu Pr., Inc.

Palmer, Pamela. Horse of the Dawn. 2005. 89p. pap. 16.95 *(978-1-4137-9545-5(5))* PublishAmerica, Inc.

Panec, D. J. We Both Read - Changing Places. Elkerton, Andy, illus. 2017. (ENG.). 41p. (J). 9.95 *(978-1-60115-297-8(3))* Treasure Bay, Inc.

Papademetriou, Lisa. Chasing Normal. 2008. (ENG.). 193p. (J). (gr. 4-6). 18.69 *(978-1-4231-0341-7(6))* Hyperion Bks. for Children.

Papp, Robert, illus. The Amazing Mystery Show. 2010. (Boxcar Children Mysteries Ser.: 123). (ENG.). 128p. (J). (gr. 2-5). pap. 7.99 *(978-0-8075-0315-7(0),* 807503150);No. 123. 14.99 *(978-0-8075-0314-0(2),* 807503142) Random Hse. Children's Bks. (Random Hse. Bks. for Young Readers).

—The Clue in the Recycling Bin. 2011. (Boxcar Children Mysteries Ser.: 126). (ENG.). 128p. (J). (gr. 2-5). pap. 6.99 *(978-0-8075-1209-8(5),* 807512095); lib. bdg. 14.99 *(978-0-8075-1208-1(7),* 807512087) Random Hse. Children's Bks. (Random Hse. Bks. for Young Readers).

—The Ghost of the Chattering Bones. 2007. (Boxcar Children Ser.). 120p. 15.00 *(978-0-7569-7611-8(1))* Perfection Learning Corp.

—The Great Turkey Heist. 2011. (Boxcar Children Mysteries Ser.: 129). (ENG.). (J). (gr. 2-5). 144p. 6.99 *(978-0-8075-3051-1(4),* 807530514); 128p. lib. bdg. 14.99 *(978-0-8075-3050-4(6),* 807530506) Random Hse. Children's Bks. (Random Hse. Bks. for Young Readers).

—Monkey Trouble. 2011. (Boxcar Children Mysteries Ser.: 127). (ENG.). 128p. (J). (gr. 2-5). pap. 7.99 *(978-0-8075-5240-7(2),* 807552402); lib. bdg. 14.99 *(978-0-8075-5239-1(9),* 807552399) Random Hse. Children's Bks. (Random Hse. Bks. for Young Readers).

—Spooktacular Special. 2013. (Boxcar Children Mysteries Ser.). (ENG.). 400p. (J). (gr. 2-5). 9.99 *(978-0-8075-7605-2(0),* 807576050, Random Hse. Bks. for Young Readers) Random Hse. Children's Bks.

—The Spy Game. 2009. (Boxcar Children Mysteries Ser.: 118). (ENG.). 128p. (J). (gr. 2-5). 14.99 *(978-0-8075-7603-8(4),* 807576034, Random Hse. Bks. for Young Readers) Random Hse. Children's Bks.

—The Spy in the Bleachers. 2010. (Boxcar Children Mysteries Ser.: 122). (ENG.). 128p. (J). (gr. 2-5). 14.99 *(978-0-8075-7606-9(9),* 807576069);No. 122. pap. 6.99 *(978-0-8075-7607-6(7),* 807576077) Random Hse. Children's Bks. (Random Hse. Bks. for Young Readers).

—The Zombie Project. 2011. (Boxcar Children Mysteries Ser.: 128). (ENG.). 128p. (J). (gr. 2-5). 6.99 *(978-0-8075-9493-3(8),* 807594938); lib. bdg. 14.99 *(978-0-8075-9492-6(X),* 080759492X) Random Hse. Children's Bks. (Random Hse. Bks. for Young Readers).

Parcus, Stephanie, illus. Jupiter Storm. gif. ltd. ed. 2017. 256p. (J). (gr. 3-6). pap. 14.99 *(978-1-943169-31-3(4))* Plum Street Press.

Pardo, Juan. When the Morning Comes: A Mardi Gras Indian Story, 1 vol. Smith, Vernon, illus. 2019. (ENG.). 32p. (gr. -1-3). 19.99 *(978-1-4556-2439-3(X),* Pelican Publishing) Arcadia Publishing.

Paris, Harper. The Mystery Across the Secret Bridge. Calo, Marcos, illus. 2015. (Greetings from Somewhere Ser.: 7). (ENG.). 128p. (J). (gr. k-4). pap. 6.99 *(978-1-4814-2367-0(3),* Little Simon) Little Simon.

—The Mystery at the Coral Reef. Calo, Marcos, illus. 2015. (Greetings from Somewhere Ser.: 8). (ENG.). 128p. (J). (gr. k-4). pap. 6.99 *(978-1-4814-2370-0(3),* Little Simon) Little Simon.

—The Mystery in the Forbidden City. Calo, Marcos, illus. 2014. (Greetings from Somewhere Ser.: 4). (ENG.). 128p. (J). (gr. k-4). pap. 6.99 *(978-1-4814-0299-6(4),* Little Simon) Little Simon.

—The Mystery of the Gold Coin. Calo, Marcos, illus. 2014. (Greetings from Somewhere Ser.: 1). (ENG.). 128p. (J). (gr. k-4). pap. 5.99 *(978-1-4424-9718-4(1),* Little Simon) Little Simon.

—The Mystery of the Icy Paw Prints. Calo, Marcos, illus. 2015. (Greetings from Somewhere Ser.: 9). (ENG.). 128p. (J). (gr. k-4). pap. 5.99 *(978-1-4814-2373-1(8),* Little Simon) Little Simon.

—The Mystery of the Mosaic. Calo, Marcos, illus. 2014. (Greetings from Somewhere Ser.: 2). (ENG.). 128p. (J). (gr. k-2). pap. 6.99 *(978-1-4424-9721-4(1),* Little Simon) Little Simon.

—The Mystery of the Mosaic. Calo, Marcos, illus. 2014. (Greetings from Somewhere Ser.: Vol. 2). (ENG.). 115p. (J). (gr. k-2). lib. bdg. 16.80 *(978-1-62765-837-9(8))* Perfection Learning Corp.

—The Mystery of the Secret Society. Calo, Marcos, illus. 2016. (Greetings from Somewhere Ser.: 10). (ENG.). 128p. (J). (gr. k-4). pap. 5.99 *(978-1-4814-5171-0(5),* Little Simon) Little Simon.

—The Mystery of the Stolen Painting. Calo, Marcos, illus. 2014. (Greetings from Somewhere Ser.: 3). (ENG.). 128p. (J). (gr. k-4). pap. 6.99 *(978-1-4814-0296-5(X),* Little Simon) Little Simon.

—The Mystery of the Suspicious Spices. Calo, Marcos, illus. 2014. (Greetings from Somewhere Ser.: 6). (ENG.). 128p. (J). (gr. k-4). pap. 6.99 *(978-1-4814-1467-8(4),* Little Simon) Little Simon.

Park, Barbara. Junie B. Jones & a Little Monkey Business, Vol. 2. unabr. ed. 2004. (Junie B. Jones Ser.: Vol. 2). 68p. (J). (gr. k-3). pap. 17.00 incl. audio *(978-0-8072-0779-6(9),* LFTR 238 SP, Listening Library) Random Hse. Audio Publishing Group.

—Mick Harte Was Here. 88p. (J). (gr. 4-6). pap. 4.99 *(978-0-8072-1502-9(3),* Listening Library) Random Hse. Audio Publishing Group.

Park, Barbara, ed. Mick Harte Was Here. unabr. ed. 2004. (Middle Grade Cassette Librariestm Ser.). 88p. (J). (gr. 3-7). pap. 29.00 incl. audio *(978-0-8072-7797-3(5),* S YA 922 SP, Listening Library) Random Hse. Audio Publishing Group.

Parker, Glenn. The Shutout Girl. 2013. 152p. *(978-1-4602-1816-7(7));* pap. *(978-1-4602-1817-4(5))* FriesenPress.

Parramore, Helen. Maudie's Promise: A Girl on the Florida Frontier. 2008. 36p. pap. 20.99 *(978-1-4389-0226-5(3))* AuthorHouse.

Partis, Joanne. Stripe's Naughty Sister. 2003. (Picture Bks.). (Illus.). 32p. (J). (gr. -1-3). 15.95 *(978-0-87614-466-4(0),* Carolrhoda Bks.) Lerner Publishing Group.

Paterson, Katherine. The Same Stuff As Stars. 2015. (ENG.). 256p. (J). (gr. 5-7). pap. 7.99 *(978-0-544-54030-9(1),* 1608841, Clarion Bks.) HarperCollins Pubs.

—The Same Stuff as Stars. 2004. 270p. (gr. 3-7). 17.00 *(978-0-7569-2801-8(X))* Perfection Learning Corp.

Paton, Doug. Our Plane Is Down. Melanson, Matt, illus. 2004. (New Series Canada). 90p. (J). pap. *(978-1-897039-03-8(4))* High Interest Publishing (HIP).

Patricelli, Leslie. The Patterson Puppies & the Midnight Monster Party. Patricelli, Leslie, illus. 2010. (Patterson Puppies Ser.). (ENG., Illus.). 32p. (J). (gr. -1-k). 14.99 *(978-0-7636-3243-4(0))* Candlewick Pr.

Patron, Kristine Mary. An Artist? That's Me! 2013. 20p. (J). pap. 6.95 *(978-1-4327-8377-8(7))* Outskirts Pr., Inc.

Patterson, James. The Fire. 2011. (Playaway Children Ser.). (ENG.). (YA). (gr. 8-12). 59.99 *(978-1-61113-385-1(8))* Hachette Audio.

—The Gift. 2010. (Witch & Wizard Ser.: No. 2). (J). 59.99 *(978-1-60941-012-4(2))* Findaway World, LLC.

—The Gift. 2014. lthr. 79.00 *(978-1-62715-523-6(6))* Leatherbound Bestsellers.

—Maximum Ride Boxed Set #1. 2010. (ENG.). 1392p. (YA). (gr. 5-17). pap. 32.99 *(978-0-316-12825-4(2),* Jimmy Patterson) Little Brown & Co.

—Treasure Hunters: Quest for the City of Gold. Neufeld, Juliana, illus. 2018. (Treasure Hunters Ser.: 5). (ENG.). 384p. (J). (gr. 3-7). 14.99 *(978-0-316-34955-0(0),* Jimmy Patterson) Little Brown & Co.

—Witch & Wizard. 2014. lthr. 79.00 *(978-1-62715-529-8(5))* Leatherbound Bestsellers.

—Witch & Wizard. 2010. (Witch & Wizard Ser.: 1). (YA). lib. bdg. 20.85 *(978-0-606-15119-1(2))* Turtleback.

Patterson, James & Bergen, Julia. Middle School: Ultimate Showdown. 2014. (Middle School Ser.: 5). (ENG., Illus.). 256p. (J). (gr. 3-7). 13.99 *(978-0-316-32211-9(3),* Jimmy Patterson) Little Brown & Co.

Patterson, James & Charbonnet, Gabrielle. Witch & Wizard. (Witch & Wizard Ser.: 1). (ENG.). (J). (gr. 5-17). 2011. 368p. mass mkt. 8.99 *(978-0-446-56243-0(2))* 2010. 336p. pap. 11.99 *(978-0-316-03834-8(2))* 2009. 320p. 34.99 *(978-0-316-03624-5(2))* Little Brown & Co. (Jimmy Patterson).

—Witch & Wizard. 2011. (Witch & Wizard Ser.: 1). lib. bdg. 18.45 *(978-0-606-26452-5(3))* Turtleback.

Patterson, James & Dembowski, Jill. The Fire. (Witch & Wizard Ser.: 3). (ENG.). (YA). (gr. 5-17). 2013. 352p. mass mkt. 8.00 *(978-1-4555-2152-4(3))* 2011. 352p. 35.99 *(978-0-316-10190-5(7))* 2011. 448p. 30.99 *(978-0-316-19620-8(7))* Little Brown & Co. (Jimmy Patterson).

—The Fire. 2012. (Witch & Wizard Ser.: 3). (YA). lib. bdg. 20.85 *(978-0-606-26698-7(4))* Turtleback.

—The Kiss. 2013. (YA). (Witch & Wizard Ser.: 4). (ENG.). 368p. (gr. 7-17). 35.99 *(978-0-316-10191-2(5),* Jimmy Patterson); 357p. *(978-0-316-22640-0(8))* Little Brown & Co.

—The Kiss. 2013. (Witch & Wizard Ser.: 4). (YA). lib. bdg. 20.85 *(978-0-606-32281-2(7))* Turtleback.

Patterson, James & Grabenstein, Chris. Treasure Hunters. Neufeld, Juliana, illus. (Treasure Hunters Ser.: 1). (ENG.). 480p. (J). (gr. 3-7). 2015. pap. 9.99 *(978-0-316-20757-7(8))* 2013. 14.99 *(978-0-316-20756-0(X))* Little Brown & Co. (Jimmy Patterson).

—Treasure Hunters. 2015. (Treasure Hunters Ser.: 1). (J). lib. bdg. 18.45 *(978-0-606-37305-0(5))* Turtleback.

—Treasure Hunters: Danger down the Nile. Neufeld, Juliana, illus. (Treasure Hunters Ser.: 2). (ENG.). 480p. (J). (gr. 3-7). 2018. pap. 8.99 *(978-0-316-51510-8(8))* 2014. 14.99 *(978-0-316-37086-8(X))* Little Brown & Co. (Jimmy Patterson).

—Treasure Hunters: Peril at the Top of the World. Neufeld, Juliana, illus. 2016. (Treasure Hunters Ser.: 4). (ENG.). 384p. (J). (gr. 3-7). 14.99 *(978-0-316-34693-1(4),* Jimmy Patterson) Little Brown & Co.

—Treasure Hunters: Secret of the Forbidden City. Neufeld, Juliana, illus. 2015. (Treasure Hunters Ser.: 3). (ENG.). 448p. (J). (gr. 3-7). 14.99 *(978-0-316-28480-6(7),* Jimmy Patterson) Little Brown & Co.

Patterson, James & Paetro, Maxine. Confessions of a Murder Suspect. (YA). 2013. (Confessions Ser.: 1). (ENG.). 400p. (gr. 7-17). pap. 10.99 *(978-0-316-20700-3(4),* Jimmy Patterson) 2012. (Confessions Ser.: 1). (ENG.). 384p. (gr. 7-17). 19.99 *(978-0-316-20698-3(9),* Jimmy Patterson) 2012. 372p. 11.99 *(978-0-316-22641-7(6))* 2012. (Confessions Ser.: 1). (ENG.). 400p. (gr. 7-17). 36.99 *(978-0-316-22418-5(9),* Jimmy Patterson) Little Brown & Co.

—Confessions of a Murder Suspect. 2013. (Confessions Ser.: 1). lib. bdg. 20.85 *(978-0-606-32278-2(7))* Turtleback.

—Confessions: the Murder of an Angel. 2016. (Confessions Ser.: 4). (ENG.). 304p. (YA). (gr. 7-17). pap. 9.99 *(978-0-316-39218-1(9),* Jimmy Patterson) Little Brown & Co.

—Confessions: the Paris Mysteries. 2014. (Confessions Ser.: 3). (ENG.). (YA). (gr. 7-17). 320p. 33.99 *(978-0-316-37084-4(3));* 352p. 35.99 *(978-0-316-40963-6(4))* Little Brown & Co. (Jimmy Patterson).

—The Paris Mysteries. 2015. (Confessions Ser.: 3). (YA). lib. bdg. 20.85 *(978-0-606-37526-9(0))* Turtleback.

—The Private School Murders. 2014. (Confessions Ser.: 2). (YA). lib. bdg. 20.85 *(978-0-606-35945-0(1))* Turtleback.

Patterson, James & Papademetriou, Lisa. Middle School: Big Fat Liar. Swaab, Neil, illus. 2014. (Middle School Ser.: 3). (ENG.). 304p. (J). (gr. 3-7). 13.99 *(978-0-316-32203-4(2),* Jimmy Patterson) Little Brown & Co.

—Middle School: My Brother Is a Big, Fat Liar. Swaab, Neil, illus. 2013. (Middle School Ser.: 3). (ENG.). 304p. (J). (gr. 3-7). 33.99 *(978-0-316-20754-6(3),* Jimmy Patterson) Little Brown & Co.

Patterson, James & Raymond, Emily. The Lost. (YA). 2015. (Witch & Wizard Ser.: 5). (ENG.). 384p. (gr. 7-17). pap. 10.99 *(978-0-316-20774-4(8),* Jimmy Patterson) 2014. (Witch & Wizard Ser.: 5). (ENG.). 384p. (gr. 7-17). 36.99 *(978-0-316-20770-6(5),* Jimmy Patterson) 2014. 355p. *(978-0-316-24266-0(7))* 2014. (Witch & Wizard Ser.: 5). (ENG.). 480p. (gr. 7-17). 39.99 *(978-0-316-24002-4(8),* Jimmy Patterson) Little Brown & Co.

—The Lost. 2015. (Witch & Wizard Ser.: 5). (YA). lib. bdg. 20.85 *(978-0-606-37528-3(7))* Turtleback.

Patterson, James & Rust, Ned. The Gift. (Witch & Wizard Ser.: 2). (ENG.). (gr. 5-17). 2012. 352p. mass mkt. 7.99 *(978-0-446-56245-4(9))* 2011. 400p. pap. 10.99 *(978-0-316-03835-5(0))* 2010. 352p. 17.99 *(978-0-316-03625-2(0))* Little Brown & Co. (Jimmy Patterson).

—The Gift. 2012. (Witch & Wizard Ser.: 2). lib. bdg. 18.40 *(978-0-606-26451-8(5))* Turtleback.

Patterson, James & Tebbetts, Chris. Middle School: Born to Rock. Swaab, Neil, illus. 2019. (Middle School Ser.: 11). (ENG.). 320p. (J). (gr. 3-7). 14.99 *(978-0-316-34952-9(6),* Jimmy Patterson) Little Brown & Co.

Patterson, James, et al. Treasure Hunters. Neufeld, Juliana, illus. 2013. 451p. (J). *(978-0-316-24262-2(4))* Little Brown & Co.

Paul, Curtis Christopher. The Watsons Go to Birmingham 1963. 2014. (ENG.). 224p. (J). (gr. 12-12). 11.24 *(978-1-63245-108-8(5))* Lectorum Pubns., Inc.

Paul, Miranda. Mia Moves Out. Keiser, Paige, illus. 2018. 32p. (J). (gr. -1-2). 16.99 *(978-0-399-55332-5(0),* Knopf Bks. for Young Readers) Random Hse. Children's Bks.

Paulsen, Gary. Harris & Me. 2007. (ENG., Illus.). 176p. (J). (gr. 5-7). pap. 9.99 *(978-0-15-205880-7(X),* 1063431, Clarion Bks.) HarperCollins Pubs.

PC Treasures Staff, prod. Hansel & Gretel. 2007. (J). *(978-1-60072-030-7(7))* PC Treasures, Inc.

Peacock, L. A. Panic in Pompeii. Hale, Nathan, illus. 2011. 92p. (J). pap. *(978-0-545-34062-5(4))* Scholastic, Inc.

—Terror at Troy. Hale, Nathan, illus. 2012. 90p. (J). *(978-0-545-34063-2(2))* Scholastic, Inc.

Pearce, Jackson. Sweetly. 2012. (Fairy Tale Retelling Ser.). (ENG.). 336p. (YA). (gr. 10-17). pap. 17.99 *(978-0-316-06866-6(7))* Little, Brown Bks. for Young Readers.

Pearce, Jacqueline. The Truth about Rats (and Dogs), 1 vol. 2006. (ENG.). 160p. (J). (gr. 4-7). per. 7.95 *(978-1-55143-473-5(3))* Orca Bk. Pubs. USA.

Pearson, Ridley. Lock & Key: the Initiation. 2017. (Lock & Key Ser.: 1). (ENG.). 432p. (J). (gr. 3-7). pap. 9.99 *(978-0-06-239902-1(0),* HarperCollins) HarperCollins Pubs.

Pearson, Yvonne. Sadie Braves the Wilderness. Ritz, Karen, illus. 2017. (ENG.). 32p. (J). (gr. -1-2). 16.95 *(978-1-68134-038-8(0))* Minnesota Historical Society Pr.

Peck, Richard. Secrets at Sea. 2012. (ENG.). 272p. (J). (gr. 3-7). pap. 8.99 *(978-0-14-242183-3(9),* Puffin Books) Penguin Young Readers Group.

Peck, Robert Newton. Bro. 2004. (ENG.). 160p. (J). (gr. 7-18). 16.99 *(978-0-06-052974-1(1))* HarperCollins Pubs.

Pedley, Linda J. A Journey of Brothers. 2013. (Illus.). 96p. pap. *(978-0-9878319-7-2(6))* Dream Write Publishing, Ltd.

Peete, Holly Robinson & Peete, Ryan Elizabeth. My Brother Charlie. Evans, Shane, illus. 2010. (ENG.). 40p. (J). (gr. 1-5). 18.99 *(978-0-545-09466-5(6),* Scholastic Pr.) Scholastic, Inc.

Pelham, David. Sam's Sandwich. Pelham, David, illus. 2015. (ENG., Illus.). 24p. (J). (gr. -1-2). 14.99 *(978-0-7636-7808-1(2))* Candlewick Pr.

Pellowski, Anne & Sharpe, Roseanne. Stairstep Farm: Anna Rose's Story. 2011. (Latsch Valley Farm Ser.). (ENG., Illus.). 182p. (J). (gr. 3-4). pap. 12.95 *(978-1-932350-40-1(3))* Ignatius Pr.

Pennypacker, Sara. Clementine & the Family Meeting. Frazee, Marla, illus. 2011. (Clementine Ser.: 5). (ENG.). 176p. (J). (gr. 1-5). 14.99 *(978-1-4231-2356-9(5))* Hyperion Pr.

—Clementine & the Family Meeting. Frazee, Marla, illus. 2012. (Clementine Ser.: 5). (ENG.). 176p. (J). (gr. 1-5). pap. 5.99 *(978-1-4231-2436-8(7))* Little, Brown Bks. for Young Readers.

—Clementine & the Family Meeting. 2012. (Clementine Ser.: 5). (J). lib. bdg. 16.00 *(978-0-606-26093-0(5))* Turtleback.

Peppermint, Aurora. Beneath the Scales. 2016. (ENG., Illus.). (J). 24.99 *(978-1-63477-940-1(1),* Harmony Ink Pr.) Dreamspinner Pr.

Percival, Tom. The Magic Looking Glass. 2017. (Little Legends Ser.: 4). (ENG.). 192p. (J). (gr. 2-5). pap. 8.99 *(978-1-4926-4259-6(2),* Sourcebooks Jabberwocky) Sourcebooks, Inc.

Perkins, Mitali. Between Us & Abuela: A Family Story from the Border. Palacios, Sara, illus. 2019. (ENG.). 40p. (J). 18.99 *(978-0-374-30373-0(8),* 900157191, Farrar, Straus & Giroux (BYR)) Farrar, Straus & Giroux.

S

Perry, Jolene. The Next Door Boys. 2011. 266p. (YA). *(978-1-59955-910-0(2),* Bonneville Bks.) Cedar Fort, Inc./CFI Distribution.

Perry, Roseann. When Mama Said Yes. 2009. 36p. pap. 16.99 *(978-1-4490-5210-2(X))* AuthorHouse.

—When Mama Says No. 2009. 36p. pap. 16.99 *(978-1-4389-1938-6(7))* AuthorHouse.

Pertzborn, Cindy. How Do We Get to Heaven? 2012. 36p. pap. 16.95 *(978-1-4497-4585-1(7),* WestBow Pr.) Author Solutions, LLC.

Peschke, Marci. Dancing Queen, 1 vol. Mourning, Tuesday, illus. 2012. (Kylie Jean Ser.). (ENG.). 112p. (J). (gr. 1-3). lib. bdg. 22.65 *(978-1-4048-6798-7(8),* 116240, Picture Window Bks.) Capstone.

Peters, Anna. The Friendly Rubbish Monsters. 2011. 92p. pap. 10.00 *(978-1-60911-878-5(2),* Eloquent Bks.) Strategic Book Publishing & Rights Agency (SBPRA).

Peters, Julie Anne. Luna (National Book Award Finalist) 2006. (ENG.). 256p. (YA). (gr. 10-17). reprint ed. pap. 10.99 *(978-0-316-01127-3(4))* Little, Brown Bks. for Young Readers.

Petersen, Alicia. A Sparrow Alone. 2004. 154p. (YA). 8.99 *(978-1-59166-204-4(4))* BJU Pr.

Petersen, P. J. Wild River. 2013. 128p. (J). (gr. 4-7). 7.99 *(978-0-375-84624-3(7),* Yearling) Random Hse. Children's Bks.

Peterson, Andrew. North! or Be Eaten: The Wingfeather Saga Book 2. Sutphin, Joe, illus. 2020. (Wingfeather Saga Ser.: 2). (ENG.). 352p. (J). (gr. 3-7). 14.99 *(978-0-525-65357-8(0),* WaterBrook Pr.) Crown Publishing Group, The.

—On the Edge of the Dark Sea of Darkness: The Wingfeather Saga Book 1. Sutphin, Joe, illus. 2020. (Wingfeather Saga Ser.: 1). (ENG.). 304p. (J). (gr. 3-7). 14.99 *(978-0-525-65356-1(2),* WaterBrook Pr.) Crown Publishing Group, The.

Peterson Haddix, Margaret. El desafío final: The 39 Clues 10. 2013. (SPA.). 304p. (J). pap. 14.99 *(978-84-08-10876-4(X))* Noguer y Caralt Editores, S. A. ESP. Dist: Lectorum Pubns., Inc.

Peterson, John C. Adam Has No Brothers. 2009. 20p. pap. 10.99 *(978-1-4490-3207-4(9))* AuthorHouse.

Peterson, Will. Triskellion. 2008. (Triskellion Ser.: 1). (ENG., Illus.). 384p. (J). (gr. 9-12). 16.99 *(978-0-7636-3971-6(0))* Candlewick Pr.

—Triskellion 3: the Gathering. 2010. (Triskellion Ser.: 3). (ENG., Illus.). 384p. (J). (gr. 9-18). 16.99 *(978-0-7636-4847-3(7))* Candlewick Pr.

Petrlik, Andrea, illus. Hansel & Gretel. (Flip-Up Fairy Tales Ser.). 24p. (J). 2007. (gr. -1-2). *(978-1-84643-090-9(9))* 2006. (gr. 1-2). *(978-1-904550-73-0(8))* Child's Play International Ltd.

Pez, Alberto. Martes Peludo. Gleich, Jacky, illus. (SPA.). (J). 8.95 *(978-958-04-5092-4(7))* Norma S.A. COL. Dist: Distribuidora Norma, Inc.

Pfeffer, Susan Beth. The Dead & the Gone. 2010. (Life As We Knew It Ser.: 2). (ENG.). 336p. (YA). (gr. 7-12). pap. 9.99 *(978-0-547-25855-3(0),* 1402120, Clarion Bks.) HarperCollins Pubs.

—The Dead & the Gone. 2010. (Last Survivors Ser.: 2). 321p. lib. bdg. 19.65 *(978-0-606-14464-3(1))* Turtleback.

Pflugfelder, Bob & Hockensmith, Steve. Nick & Tesla's Secret Agent Gadget Battle: A Mystery with Spy Cameras, Code Wheels, & Other Gadgets You Can Build Yourself. 2014. (Nick & Tesla Ser.: 3). (Illus.). 256p. (J). (gr. 4-7). 12.95 *(978-1-59474-676-5(1))* Quirk Bks.

—Nick & Tesla's Special Effects Spectacular: A Mystery with Animatronics, Alien Makeup, Camera Gear, & Other Movie Magic You Can Make Yourself! 2015. (Nick & Tesla Ser.: 5). (Illus.). 256p. (J). (gr. 4-7). 12.95 *(978-1-59474-760-1(1))* Quirk Bks.

Phillips, Leigh Hope. Birthday Wishes. Fountain, John, illus. 2005. (J). pap. *(978-1-933156-10-1(4));* per. *(978-1-933156-03-3(1))* GSVQ Publishing. (VisionQuest Kids).

Phineas and Ferb. Phineas & Ferb Batter Up! 2010. pap. 5.99 *(978-1-4231-2408-5(1))* Disney Pr.

Pichon, Liz. TOM GATES: EXCUSAS PERFECTAS (Y OTRAS COSILLAS GENIALES) 2013. (SPA.). 346p. (J). pap. 21.99 *(978-84-216-8765-9(4))* Lectorum Pubns., Inc.

Pickett, Lanaya A. Walking with Angels. 2011. 192p. 23.95 *(978-1-4620-2306-6(1));* pap. 13.95 *(978-1-4620-2307-3(X))* iUniverse, Inc.

Pierce, Terry. Jack & Jill & T-Ball Bill. 2019. (Step into Reading Ser.). (ENG.). 32p. (J). (gr. k-1). 14.96 *(978-0-87617-966-6(9))* Penworthy Co., LLC, The.

—Jack & Jill & T-Ball Bill. DiCicco, Sue, illus. 2018. (Step into Reading Ser.). 32p. (J). (gr. -1-1). pap. 4.99

(978-1-5247-1413-0(5), Random Hse. Bks. for Young Readers) Random Hse. Children's Bks.

Pierpoint, Eric. The Last Ride of Caleb O'Toole. 2013. (ENG., Illus.). 304p. (J). (gr. 4-7). pap. 11.99 *(978-1-4022-8171-6(4)*, 9781402281716) Sourcebooks, Inc.

Pifferson Sisters, the. Zach & Lucy & the Museum of Natural Wonders: Ready-To-Read Level 3. Chambers, Mark, illus. 2016. (Zach & Lucy Ser.). (ENG.). 40p. (J). (gr. 1-3). pap. 4.99 *(978-1-4814-3935-0(9)*, Simon Spotlight) Simon Spotlight.

—Zach & Lucy & the Yoga Zoo: Ready-To-Read Level 3. Chambers, Mark, illus. 2016. (Zach & Lucy Ser.). (ENG.). 40p. (J). (gr. 1-3). pap. 4.99 *(978-1-4814-3938-1(3)*, Simon Spotlight) Simon Spotlight.

Pike, Kenneth & Stewart, Isaac. Jacob's Journal of Doom: Confessions of an Almost-Deacon. 2012. (Illus.). 196p. (J). 14.99 *(978-1-60907-016-8(X))* Deseret Bk. Co.

Pincus, Greg. The 14 Fibs of Gregory K. 2013. (ENG.). 240p. (J). (gr. 3-7). 17.99 *(978-0-439-91299-0(7)*, Levine, Arthur A. Bks.) Scholastic, Inc.

Pincus, Gregory K. The 14 Fibs of Gregory K. 2013. 226p. (J). pap. *(978-0-439-91300-3(4)*, Levine, Arthur A. Bks.) Scholastic, Inc.

Pingk, Rubin. Samurai Scarecrow: A Very Ninja Halloween. Pingk, Rubin, illus. 2018. (Samurai Holiday Ser.). (ENG., Illus.). 48p. (J). (gr. -1-3). 17.99 *(978-1-4814-3059-3(9)*, Simon & Schuster Bks. For Young Readers) Simon & Schuster Bks. For Young Readers.

Pisarik, Michael E. Loonhaunt. 2006. (J). per. 19.95 *(978-1-59872-600-8(5))* Instant Pub.

Pitchford, Dean. Captain Nobody. 2009. (ENG.). 208p. (J). (gr. 4-6). 21.19 *(978-0-399-25034-7(4))* Penguin Young Readers Group.

Plitt, Kay. Why Isn't Bobby Like Me, Mom? 2010. 32p. 14.75 *(978-1-4269-4038-5(6))* Trafford Publishing.

Plotkin, Andy. The Black Block Legend. 2007. 64p. per. 19.95 *(978-1-4241-9190-1(4))* America Star Bks.

Plozza, Shivaun. Frankie: A Novel. 2018. (ENG.). 352p. (YA). pap. 19.99 *(978-1-250-14300-6(4)*, 900180438) Flatiron Bks.

Pointon, Janet. A Matter of Choice. 2008. 82p. pap. 11.51 *(978-1-4092-3108-0(9))* Lulu Pr., Inc.

Polacco, Patricia. My Rotten Redheaded Older Brother. 2014. 40p. pap. 8.00 *(978-1-61003-358-9(2))* Center for the Collaborative Classroom.

—An Orange for Frankie. Polacco, Patricia, illus. 2004. (Illus.). 48p. (J). (gr. 1-4). 19.99 *(978-0-399-24302-8(X)*, Philomel Bks.) Penguin Young Readers Group.

—Rotten Richie & the Ultimate Dare. Polacco, Patricia, illus. 2006. (Illus.). 48p. (J). (gr. k-3). 18.99 *(978-0-399-24531-2(6)*, Philomel Bks.) Penguin Young Readers Group.

Pollock, Tom. This Story Is a Lie. 2019. (ENG.). 336p. (YA). (gr. 9). pap. 10.99 *(978-1-64129-032-6(3)*, Soho Teen) Soho Pr., Inc.

Poole, Richard. Jewel & Thorn. 2007. (Book of Lowmoor Ser.: 1). (ENG., Illus.). 400p. (J). (gr. 7-12). pap. 11.95 *(978-0-689-87290-7(9))* Simon & Schuster, Ltd. GBR. Dist: Simon & Schuster, Inc.

The Portal in the Park: By Cricket Casey, songs & audio book performed by Grandmaseter Melle Mel, features Lady Gaga, Included CD in Book. 2010. (Illus.). 132p. (J). mass mkt. 19.95 *(978-0-9786488-0-0(3))* SCOJO ENTERTAINMENT.

Potter, Ellen. The Kneebone Boy. 2011. (ENG.). 304p. (J). (gr. 4-7). pap. 17.99 *(978-0-312-67432-8(5)*, 900072847) Square Fish.

—Piper Green & the Fairy Tree, 1 vol. Leng, Qin, illus. 2015. (Piper Green & the Fairy Tree Ser.: 1). 112p. (J). (gr. 2-4). pap. 6.99 *(978-0-553-49926-1(2)*, dba7eb01-1f52-4f48-bc93-b0465825d4b4, Rosen Classroom) Random Hse. Children's Bks.

Poulin, Andrée. Monkey in the Mud, 1 vol. Eudes-Pascal, Élisabeth, illus. 2009. (Rainy Day Readers Ser.). (ENG.). 32p. (J). (gr. 1-2). 27.27 *(978-1-60754-370-1(2)*, 5131cf14-a2fd-4f18-8757-ace21e9c9915); pap. 11.55 *(978-1-60754-371-8(0)*, a3c27341-a9ae-467b-82ea-0094df091457) Rosen Publishing Group, Inc., The. (Windmill Bks.).

Powell, Gregg E. Goobadabers. Lea, Corinne, illus. 2011. 24p. pap. 24.95 *(978-1-4626-0734-1(9))* America Star Bks.

Power, Molly. Up & down with Lena Larocha. Carter, Barbara, illus. 2013. 169p. pap. 15.00 *(978-1-60571-176-8(4)*, Shires Press) Northshire Pr.

Pranali. The Secret Storybook. 2013. 64p. pap. 23.95 *(978-1-4828-0147-7(7))* Partridge Pub.

Preble, Joy. The Sweet Dead Life. 2014. (Sweet Dead Life Novel Ser.). (Illus.). 244p. (YA). (gr. 9). pap. 10.99 *(978-1-61695-368-3(3)*, Soho Teen) Soho Pr., Inc.

Preller, James. Blood Mountain. 2019. (ENG.). 240p. (J). 16.99 *(978-1-250-17485-7(6)*, 900189253) Feiwel & Friends.

Preston, Natasha. You Will Be Mine. 2018. (ENG., Illus.). 304p. (YA). (gr. 8-12). pap. 10.99 *(978-1-4926-5432-2(9))* Sourcebooks, Inc.

Price, Lissa. Starters. 2013. (Starters Ser.: 1). (ENG.). 384p. (YA). (gr. 7). pap. 10.99 *(978-0-385-74248-1(7)*, Ember) Random Hse. Children's Bks.

Priebe, Gigi. The Adventures of Henry Whiskers. Duncan, Daniel, illus. 2017. (Adventures of Henry Whiskers Ser.: 1). (ENG.). 160p. (J). (gr. 2-5). pap. 5.99 *(978-1-4814-6574-8(0)*, Simon & Schuster/Paula Wiseman Bks.) Simon & Schuster/Paula Wiseman Bks.

Pyros, Andrea. Pink Hair & Other Terrible Ideas. 2019. (ENG.). 256p. (J). (gr. 4-7). lib. bdg. 15.95 *(978-1-68446-028-1(X)*, 139700, Capstone Editions) Capstone.

Qualey, Marsha. Thin Ice. 2007. 214p. (YA). *(978-0-9793444-0-4(9))* Quercus Pr.

Quarles, Pamela. Jake & Josh Go Camping. Denison, Susan, illus. 2007. 40p. per. 14.00 *(978-1-59858-407-3(3))* Dog Ear Publishing, LLC.

Rae, Kimberly. Buying Samir. 2014. 147p. (YA). *(978-1-60682-952-3(1))* BJU Pr.

Railey, Shawna. The Messy Life of Blue. 2020. (ENG.). 240p. (J). (gr. 3-7). 16.99 *(978-1-4998-1025-7(3)*, Yellow Jacket) Bonnier Publishing USA.

Rainey. School Is Cool. Huggens, Karin, illus. 2004. (J). *(978-0-9666199-9-7(4))* DreamDog Pr.

Rallison, Janette. Just One Wish. 2009. (ENG.). 272p. (J). (gr. 7-12). 22.44 *(978-0-399-24618-0(5))* Penguin Young Readers Group.

Ramage, Rosalyn Rikel. The Graveyard: N/a. 2012. 184p. (gr. 4-6). pap. 11.88 *(978-1-4669-5033-7(1))* Trafford Publishing.

—The Windmill. 2013. 182p. (gr. 4-6). pap. 11.66 *(978-1-4907-0909-3(6))* Trafford Publishing.

Ramrattan Smith, Sherry & Smith, Benjamin Eric. Brothers: Best Friends Growing Up. 2010. 28p. pap. 14.95 *(978-1-4490-6339-9(X))* AuthorHouse.

Randolph, Joanne. Rose: a Flower's Story, 1 vol. 2009. (Nature Stories Ser.). (ENG., Illus.). 24p. (J). (gr. 1-2). pap. 9.15 *(978-1-60754-102-8(5)*, 6e56df0e-d448-45ab-b6f3-befca54da9af); lib. bdg. 27.27 *(978-1-60754-101-1(7)*, 87f4568d-22af-4789-8560-17dcb2322235) Rosen Publishing Group, Inc., The. (Windmill Bks.).

Ransom, Candice. Snow Day! 2019. (Step into Reading Ser.). (ENG.). 32p. (J). (gr. k-1). 14.96 *(978-0-87617-970-3(7))* Penworthy Co., LLC, The.

—Snow Day! Meza, Erika, illus. 2018. (Step into Reading Ser.). 32p. (J). (gr. -1-1). pap. 5.99 *(978-1-5247-2037-7(2)*, Random Hse. Bks. for Young Readers) Random Hse. Children's Bks.

Ransom, Marty. Our Father, Our Soldier, Our Hero. 2011. 36p. pap. 24.95 *(978-1-4626-1377-9(2))* America Star Bks.

Ransome, Arthur. Swallowdale. 2010. (Swallows & Amazons Ser.). (ENG., Illus.). 431p. (J). pap. 15.95 *(978-1-56792-421-3(2))* Godine, David R. Pub.

Rapp, Adam. Punkzilla. 2010. (ENG., Illus.). 256p. (YA). (gr. 9). pap. 7.99 *(978-0-7636-5297-5(0))* Candlewick Pr.

Rasheed, Winnona. Itchy Scratchy Spots. 2012. 56p. pap. 8.99 *(978-1-60820-727-5(7))* MLR Pr., LLC.

Rath, Tom & Reckmeyer, Mary. How Full Is Your Bucket? for Kids. Manning, Maurie J., illus. 2009. 32p. (J). (gr. -1-4). 17.95 *(978-1-59562-027-9(3))* Gallup Pr.

Raynor, Michelle. A Magical World. 2011. 20p. pap. 11.99 *(978-1-257-65025-5(4))* Lulu Pr., Inc.

Reagan, Jean. Always My Brother, 1 vol. Pollema-Cahill, Phyllis, illus. 2009. (ENG.). 32p. (J). (gr. 2-6). 16.95 *(978-0-88448-313-7(4)*, 884313) Tilbury Hse. Pubs.

Redmond, E. S. Bug Blonsky & His Very Long List of Don'ts. Redmond, E. S., illus. 2018. (ENG., Illus.). 80p. (J). (gr. 1-4). 15.99 *(978-0-7636-8935-3(1))* Candlewick Pr.

Reece, Colleen L. Wilderness Warriors. 2012. 114p. 18.95 *(978-1-61633-309-6(X))*; pap. 8.95 *(978-1-61633-310-2(3))* Guardian Angel Publishing, Inc.

Reed, T. K. Quasar & the Eye of the Serpent. 2009. 136p. 21.95 *(978-1-4401-2753-3(0))*; pap. 11.95 *(978-1-4401-2751-9(4))* iUniverse, Inc.

Rees Brennan, Sarah. The Demon's Covenant. 2010. (Demon's Lexicon Trilogy Ser.: 2). (ENG., Illus.). 448p. (YA). (gr. 9-18). 17.99 *(978-1-4169-6381-3(2)*, McElderry, Margaret K. Bks.) McElderry, Margaret K. Bks.

—The Demon's Lexicon. 2009. (Demon's Lexicon Trilogy Ser.: 1). (ENG., Illus.). 336p. (YA). (gr. 9-18). 18.99 *(978-1-4169-6379-0(0)*, McElderry, Margaret K. Bks.) McElderry, Margaret K. Bks.

Reeve, Penny. The Back Leg of a Goat. rev. ed. 2008. (Tania Abbey Adventure Ser.). (ENG., Illus.). 96p. (J). pap. 6.99 *(978-1-84550-340-6(6)*, 22e799f1-63ee-4400-99b8-cbf4a68f2655) Christian Focus Pubns. GBR. Dist: Baker & Taylor Publisher Services (BTPS).

Regan, Dian Curtis. Space Boy & His Dog. Neubecker, Robert, illus. 2015. (Space Boy Ser.). (ENG.). 32p. (J). (gr. -1-2). 16.95 *(978-1-59078-955-1(5)*, Astra Young Readers) Astra Publishing Hse.

—Space Boy & the Snow Monster. Neubecker, Robert, illus. 2017. (Space Boy Ser.). (ENG.). 32p. (J). (gr. -1-2). 17.95 *(978-1-59078-957-5(1)*, Astra Young Readers) Astra Publishing Hse.

—Space Boy & the Space Pirate. Neubecker, Robert, illus. 2016. (Space Boy Ser.). (ENG.). 40p. (J). (gr. -1-2). 16.95 *(978-1-59078-956-8(3)*, Astra Young Readers) Astra Publishing Hse.

Reid, Karlene & Reid, Mason. Me & My Big Brother. 2012. 32p. pap. 19.99 *(978-1-4685-2765-0(7))* AuthorHouse.

Reiss, Mike & Reiss, Mike. The Boy Who Wouldn't Share. Catrow, David, illus. 2008. (ENG.). 32p. (J). (gr. 1-3). 17.99 *(978-0-06-059132-8(3)*, HarperCollins) HarperCollins Pubs.

Repkin, Mark. Mommy Breastfeeds My Baby Brother/ Mama Amamanta A Mi Hermanito. Moneysmith, David, illus. 2011.Tr. of Mama Amamanta A Mi Hermanito. (SPA & ENG.). 24p. (J). pap. 9.99 *(978-0-9816538-1-5(2))* Istoria Hse.

Respondek, Kelly. Big Sister's Busy Day! 2010. 20p. 10.75 *(978-1-4520-6355-3(9))* AuthorHouse.

Reul, Sarah Lynne & Reul, Sarah Lynne. Allie All Along. 2018. (Illus.). 40p. (J). (gr. -1-2). 18.99 *(978-1-4549-2858-4(1))* Sterling Publishing Co., Inc.

Rex, Adam. Cold Cereal, 1. 2013. (Cold Cereal Saga Ser.: 1). (ENG.). 448p. (J). (gr. 3-7). pap. 7.99 *(978-0-06-206003-7(1)*, Balzer & Bray) HarperCollins Pubs.

Reynolds, Jason. As Brave As You. (ENG.). 432p. (J). (gr. 5). 2017. pap. 8.99 *(978-1-4814-1591-0(3)*, Atheneum Bks. for Young Readers) 2016. (Illus.). 19.99 *(978-1-4814-1590-3(5)*, Atheneum/Caitlyn Dlouhy Books) Simon & Schuster Children's Publishing.

—Long Way Down. 2022. (ENG.). 205p. (J). (gr. 6-8). 24.46 ***(978-1-68505-416-8(1))*** Penworthy Co., LLC, The.

—Long Way Down. (ENG., Illus.). (YA). (gr. 7). 2019. 336p. pap. 12.99 *(978-1-4814-3826-1(3)*, Atheneum Bks. for Young Readers) 2017. 320p. 19.99 *(978-1-4814-3825-4(5)*, Atheneum/Caitlyn Dlouhy Books) 2017. 320p. E-Book *(978-1-4814-3827-8(1)*, Atheneum/Caitlyn Dlouhy Books) Simon & Schuster Children's Publishing.

—When I Was the Greatest. 2014. (ENG., Illus.). 240p. (YA). (gr. 7). 19.99 *(978-1-4424-5947-2(6)*, Atheneum Bks. for Young Readers) Simon & Schuster Children's Publishing.

Reynolds Naylor, Phyllis. Alice in Blunderland. 2005. 200p. (J). (gr. 2-7). 13.65 *(978-0-7569-5075-0(9))* Perfection Learning Corp.

—Alice in Blunderland. 2012. (Alice Ser.). (ENG., Illus.). 240p. (J). (gr. 2-7). pap. 7.99 *(978-1-4424-4643-4(9)*, Atheneum Bks. for Young Readers) Simon & Schuster Children's Publishing.

—Boys in Control. 2005. (Boys Against Girls Ser.: No. 9). 143p. (J). (gr. 4-7). 13.65 *(978-0-7569-5094-1(5))* Perfection Learning Corp.

—Boys in Control. 2005. (Boy/Girl Battle Ser.: 9). 160p. (J). (gr. 3-7). 6.99 *(978-0-440-41681-4(7)*, Yearling) Random Hse. Children's Bks.

—The Boys Return. l.t. ed. 2003. (Boys Against Girls Ser.: No. 7). 170p. (J). 23.95 *(978-0-7862-5822-2(5))* Thorndike Pr.

—Boys Rock! 2007. (Boy/Girl Battle Ser.: 11). (ENG.). 144p. (J). (gr. 3-7). 5.99 *(978-0-440-41990-7(5)*, Yearling) Random Hse. Children's Bks.

—Girls Rule! 2006. (Boy/Girl Battle Ser.: 10). (ENG.). 160p. (J). (gr. 3-7). per. 6.99 *(978-0-440-41969-1(1)*, Yearling) Random Hse. Children's Bks.

—The Girls Take Over. 2004. (Boys Against Girls Ser.: No. 8). 146p. (J). (gr. 4-7). 13.65 *(978-0-7569-2804-9(4))* Perfection Learning Corp.

—I Like Him, He Likes Her: Alice Alone; Simply Alice; Patiently Alice. 2010. (Alice Ser.). (ENG.). 640p. (J). (gr. 7). pap. 12.99 *(978-1-4424-0978-1(9)*, Atheneum Bks. for Young Readers) Simon & Schuster Children's Publishing.

Reynolds, Paul A. Sydney & Simon: Full Steam Ahead! Reynolds, Peter H., illus. 2014. (Sydney & Simon Ser.: 1). (ENG.). 48p. (J). (gr. 1-4). 12.95 *(978-1-58089-675-7(8))* Charlesbridge Publishing, Inc.

—Sydney & Simon: to the Moon! Reynolds, Peter H., illus. 2017. (Sydney & Simon Ser.: 3). 48p. (J). (gr. 1-4). lib. bdg. 12.99 *(978-1-58089-679-5(0))* Charlesbridge Publishing, Inc.

Reynolds, Peter H. Ish. Reynolds, Peter H., illus. 2004. (Creatrilogy Ser.). (ENG., Illus.). 32p. (J). (gr. k-4). 15.00 *(978-0-7636-2344-9(X))* Candlewick Pr.

Ricchi, Brenda. The Grandchildren's Bible Journeys - the Creation Story. 2009. (ENG.). 36p. pap. 17.00 *(978-0-557-14903-2(7))* Lulu Pr., Inc.

Richard Richtmyer. A Bit of Magic: A Novel. 2009. 116p. pap. 10.95 *(978-1-4401-5565-9(8))* iUniverse, Inc.

Richardson, Deborra. Treasures at the Museum. 2011. (Illus.). 64p. (J). pap. 5.99 *(978-0-9824945-1-6(3))* Elevator Group, The.

Richmond, Marianne. Dear Sister: A Message of Love. 2008. (Illus.). 40p. (J). 15.95 *(978-1-934082-46-1(5)*, Marianne Richmond Studios, Inc.) Sourcebooks, Inc.

—You're a Big Brother. 2017. (Illus.). 32p. (J). (gr. -1-3). 10.99 *(978-1-4926-5049-2(8)*, 9781492650492, Sourcebooks Jabberwocky) Sourcebooks, Inc.

—You're a Big Sister. 2017. (Illus.). 32p. (J). (gr. -1-3). 10.99 *(978-1-4926-5051-5(X)*, 9781492650515, Sourcebooks Jabberwocky) Sourcebooks, Inc.

Rinaldi, Ann. Juliet's Moon. 2010. (ENG., Illus.). 256p. (YA). (gr. 7). pap. 14.99 *(978-0-547-25874-4(7)*, 1402328, Clarion Bks.) HarperCollins Pubs.

—Leigh Ann's Civil War. 2011. (Great Episodes Ser.). (ENG.). 320p. (YA). (gr. 7). pap. 17.99 *(978-0-547-54999-6(7)*, 1450168, Clarion Bks.) HarperCollins Pubs.

—My Vicksburg. 2011. (ENG.). 160p. (YA). (gr. 7). pap. 11.95 *(978-0-547-55000-8(6)*, 1450172, Clarion Bks.) HarperCollins Pubs.

Rinehart, J. D. The Lost Realm. 2017. (Crown of Three Ser.: 2). (ENG., Illus.). 512p. (J). (gr. 4-8). pap. 9.99 *(978-1-4814-2447-9(5)*, Aladdin) Simon & Schuster Children's Publishing.

Riordan, Rick. From the Kane Chronicles: Brooklyn House Magician's Manual-An Official Rick Riordan Companion Book: Your Guide to Egyptian Gods & Creatures, Glyphs & Spells, & More. 2018. (Kane Chronicles Ser.). (ENG., Illus.). 192p. (J). (gr. 3-7). 9.99 *(978-1-4847-8553-9(3)*, Disney-Hyperion) Disney Publishing Worldwide.

—Kane Chronicles, the, Book One: Red Pyramid: the Graphic Novel, the-Kane Chronicles, the, Book One, Bk. 1. 2012. (Kane Chronicles Ser.: 1). (ENG., Illus.). 192p. (J). (gr. 5-9). pap. 12.99 *(978-1-4231-5069-5(4)*, Disney-Hyperion) Disney Publishing Worldwide.

—Kane Chronicles, the, Book One: Red Pyramid, the-Kane Chronicles, the, Book One. 2010. (Kane Chronicles Ser.: 1). (ENG., Illus.). 528p. (J). (gr. 5-9). 19.99 *(978-1-4231-1338-6(1)*, Disney-Hyperion) Disney Publishing Worldwide.

—Kane Chronicles, the, Book One: Red Pyramid, the-The Kane Chronicles, Book One. 2018. (Kane Chronicles Ser.: 1). (ENG., Illus.). 576p. (J). (gr. 5-9). pap. 9.99 *(978-1-368-01358-1(9)*, Disney-Hyperion) Disney Publishing Worldwide.

—Kane Chronicles, the, Book Three: Serpent's Shadow: the Graphic Novel, the-Kane Chronicles, the, Book Three. 2017. (Kane Chronicles Ser.). (ENG., Illus.). 160p. (J). (gr. 5-9). 21.99 *(978-1-4847-8132-6(5))*; pap. 14.99 *(978-1-4847-8234-7(8))* Disney Publishing Worldwide. (Disney-Hyperion).

—Kane Chronicles, the, Book Three: Serpent's Shadow, the-Kane Chronicles, the, Book Three. 2018. (Kane Chronicles Ser.: 3). (ENG., Illus.). 496p. (J). (gr. 5-9). pap. 9.99 *(978-1-368-01357-4(0)*, Disney-Hyperion) Disney Publishing Worldwide.

—Kane Chronicles, the, Book Three: Serpent's Shadow, the-Kane Chronicles, the, Book Three, Bk. 3. 2012. (Kane Chronicles Ser.: 3). (ENG.). 416p. (J). (gr. 5-9). 19.99 *(978-1-4231-4057-3(5)*, Disney-Hyperion) Disney Publishing Worldwide.

—Kane Chronicles, the, Book Two: Throne of Fire, the-Kane Chronicles, the, Book Two. (Kane Chronicles Ser.: 2). (ENG.). (J). (gr. 5-9). 2018. Illus.). 528p. pap. 9.99 *(978-1-368-01359-8(7))*Bk. 2. 2011. 464p. 18.99 *(978-1-4231-4056-6(7))* Disney Publishing Worldwide. (Disney-Hyperion).

—The Red Pyramid. l.t. ed. 2018. (Kane Chronicles Ser.: 1). (ENG.). (J). pap. 15.99 *(978-1-4328-5029-6(6))* Cengage Gale.

—The Red Pyramid. 2009. (Kane Chronicles: Bk. 1). 11.04 *(978-0-7848-3733-7(3)*, Everbind) Marco Bk. Co.

—The Red Pyramid. 2012. 20.00 *(978-1-61383-660-6(0))* Perfection Learning Corp.

—The Red Pyramid. 2010. pap. *(978-0-545-40016-9(3))* Scholastic, Inc.

—The Red Pyramid. l.t. ed. 2010. (Kane Chronicles: Bk. 1). (ENG.). 671p. 23.95 *(978-1-4104-2536-2(3))* Thorndike Pr.

—The Red Pyramid. (Kane Chronicles Ser.: 1). (J). 2018. lib. bdg. 20.85 *(978-0-606-41205-6(0))* 2012. lib. bdg. 24.50 *(978-0-606-37510-8(4))* 2011. lib. bdg. 20.85 *(978-0-606-39216-7(5))* Turtleback.

—The Serpent's Shadow. 2012. 416p. *(978-0-14-133568-1(8)*, Puffin) Penguin Bks., Ltd.

—The Serpent's Shadow. l.t. ed. 2012. (Kane Chronicles: Bk. 3). (ENG.). 521p. (gr. 5-12). 23.99 *(978-1-4104-4789-0(8))* Thorndike Pr.

—The Serpent's Shadow. 2018. (Kane Chronicles Ser.: 3). (J). lib. bdg. 20.85 *(978-0-606-41206-3(9))* Turtleback.

—The Throne of Fire. l.t. ed. 2011. (Kane Chronicles Ser.: 2). (ENG.). 591p. lib. bdg. 23.99 *(978-1-4328-4405-9(9))* Cengage Gale.

—The Throne of Fire. 2011. (Kane Chronicles: Bk. 2). 452p. (J). pap. *(978-1-4231-5059-6(7))* Disney Pr.

—The Throne of Fire. 2nd ed. 2012. (ENG.). 464p. (YA). (gr. 5-9). pap. 9.99 *(978-1-4231-6703-7(1))* Hyperion Bks. for Children.

—The Throne of Fire. 2011. (Kane Chronicles: Bk. 2). (ENG., Illus.). 451p. 28.25 *(978-0-85757-231-8(8))*; 2nd ed. 554p. pap. *(978-0-14-133566-7(1))* Penguin Publishing Group. (Puffin).

—The Throne of Fire. l.t. ed. 2011. (Kane Chronicles: Bk. 2). (ENG.). 589p. 23.99 *(978-1-4104-3607-8(1))* Thorndike Pr.

—The Throne of Fire. (Kane Chronicles Graphic Novels Ser.: 2). 2015. lib. bdg. 24.50 *(978-0-606-37509-2(0))* 2018. (J). lib. bdg. 20.85 *(978-0-606-41204-9(2))* 2012. (J). lib. bdg. 20.85 *(978-0-606-39217-4(3))* Turtleback.

Riordan, Rick & Collar, Orpheus. Serpent's Shadow. 2017. (Kane Chronicles Graphic Novels Ser.: 3). (J). lib. bdg. 24.50 *(978-0-606-40604-8(2))* Turtleback.

Rizzo, Cynthia Marie. No No, Coco. 2008. 49p. pap. 16.95 *(978-1-60563-819-5(6))* America Star Bks.

Robert, Nadine. Elsie. Kastelic, Maja, illus. 2020. (ENG.). 40p. (J). (gr. -1-3). 16.99 *(978-1-4197-4072-5(5)*, 1303701, Abrams Bks. for Young Readers) Abrams, Inc.

(Robert Thompson), Pau Pau. Santa's Secret Helpers, 1 vol. 2009. 55p. pap. 16.95 *(978-1-60836-859-4(9))* America Star Bks.

Roberts, Willo Davis. Surviving Summer Vacation: How I Visited Yellowstone Park with the Terrible Rupes. 2015. (ENG., Illus.). 208p. (J). (gr. 3-7). pap. 6.99 *(978-1-4814-3718-9(6)*, Aladdin) Simon & Schuster Children's Publishing.

Robertson, Jacob Ryan. Far Away. 2012. 50p. (-18). pap. 15.99 *(978-1-4797-4679-8(7))* Xlibris Corp.

Robins, Eleanor. The Secret Message, 1 vol. unabr. ed. 2011. (Carter High Mysteries Ser.). (ENG.). 48p. (YA). (gr. 9-12). 9.75 *(978-1-61651-568-3(6))* Saddleback Educational Publishing, Inc.

Robinson, Barbara. The Best Christmas Pageant Ever. 2009. 8.32 *(978-0-7848-1246-4(2)*, Everbind) Marco Bk. Co.

—The Best Christmas Pageant Ever. 2005. (Illus.). 108p. (gr. 3-7). 16.00 *(978-0-7569-6531-0(4))* Perfection Learning Corp.

—The Best Christmas Pageant Ever. 2005. (J). 16.00 *(978-0-88103-998-6(5))* Turtleback.

—The Best Christmas Pageant Ever: A Christmas Holiday Book for Kids. 2005. (Best Ever Ser.). (ENG., Illus.). 128p. (J). (gr. 3-7). pap. 8.99 *(978-0-06-440275-0(4)*, HarperCollins) HarperCollins Pubs.

—The Best Christmas Pageant Ever (picture Book Edition) A Christmas Holiday Book for Kids. Cornell, Laura, illus. 2011. (ENG.). 40p. (J). (gr. -1-3). 17.99 *(978-0-06-089074-2(6)*, HarperCollins) HarperCollins Pubs.

—The Best Halloween Ever. 2006. (Illus.). 117p. (J). (gr. 3-7). 13.65 *(978-0-7569-6985-1(9))* Perfection Learning Corp.

Robinson, Craig & Mansbach, Adam. Jake the Fake Keeps It Real. Knight, Keith, illus. 2018. (Jake the Fake Ser.: 1). 160p. (J). (gr. 3-7). 7.99 *(978-0-553-52354-6(6)*, Yearling) Random Hse. Children's Bks.

Robinson, Gary. Little Brother of War. 2013. (PathFinders Ser.). (ENG.). 120p. (YA). (gr. 8-12). pap. 9.95 *(978-1-939053-02-2(1)*, 7th Generation) BPC.

Robinson, Jeanette. Blueberry Bunny. 2012. 32p. pap. 19.99 *(978-1-4685-6410-5(2))* AuthorHouse.

Robley Blake, Colleen. I Can't Wait till I'm Five. 2006. (J). 9.95 *(978-0-9767342-0-8(6))* Imaajinn This.

Rochkind, Pat. McGooster & Mcgyman Begin Their Adventures. Wozniak, Patricia A., illus. 2008. 144p. (J). (gr. 4-7). per. 12.95 *(978-0-9792430-1-1(7))* Wing Lane Pr.

Rocklin, Joanne. The Five Lives of Our Cat Zook. (ENG.). 240p. (J). (gr. 3-7). 2013. pap. 7.95 *(978-1-4197-0525-0(3)*, 687803) 2012. 17.95 *(978-1-4197-0192-4(4)*, 687801) Abrams, Inc. (Amulet Bks.).

Rockwell, Anne. Brendan & Belinda & the Slam Dunk! Meisel, Paul, illus. 2007. (Good Sports Ser.). 40p. (J). (gr. -1-1). 15.99 *(978-0-06-028443-5(9))* HarperCollins Pubs.

Rodda, Emily. The Silver Door. 2013. (Illus.). 278p. (J). pap. *(978-0-545-42993-1(5)*, Scholastic Pr.) Scholastic, Inc.

—The Third Door. 2013. (J). pap. *(978-0-545-42995-5(1)*, Scholastic Pr.) Scholastic, Inc.

Roddie, Shen. Baby Goes Too. Stojic, Manya, illus. 2003. 32p. (YA). *(978-1-85602-460-0(1)*, Pavilion Children's Books) Pavilion Bks.

Roddy, Lee. Eye of the Hurricane. 2007. (Ladd Family Adventure Ser.: Vol. 9). (Illus.). 161p. (J). (gr. 3-7). per. 7.99 *(978-0-88062-258-5(X))* Mott Media.

Rodkey, Geoff. The Tapper Twins Go to War (with Each Other) 2016. (Tapper Twins Ser.: 1). (ENG., Illus.). 240p. (J). (gr. 3-7). pap. 7.99 *(978-0-316-31597-5(4))* Little, Brown Bks. for Young Readers.

—The Tapper Twins Go Viral. 2017. (Tapper Twins Ser.: 4). (ENG., Illus.). 256p. (J). (gr. 3-7). 13.99 *(978-0-316-29784-4(4))* Little, Brown Bks. for Young Readers.

—The Tapper Twins Go Viral. 2018. (Tapper Twins Ser.: 4). (J). lib. bdg. 17.20 *(978-0-606-40992-6(0))* Turtleback.

—The Tapper Twins Run for President. 2016. (Tapper Twins Ser.: 3). (ENG., Illus.). 304p. (J). (gr. 3-7). 13.99 *(978-0-316-29785-1(2))* Little, Brown Bks. for Young Readers.

—The Tapper Twins Tear up New York. 2016. (Tapper Twins Ser.: 2). (ENG., Illus.). 288p. (J). (gr. 3-7). pap. 8.99 *(978-0-316-31601-9(6))* Little, Brown Bks. for Young Readers.

Rogers, Don. The Adventures of Shawn & Jeremy with Sister Nicole & the Hot Air Balloon: Volume Two. 2012. 24p. pap. 24.95 *(978-1-4626-7649-1(9))* America Star Bks.

Roland, Timothy. Monkey Me & the New Neighbor. 2014. (Monkey Me Ser.: 3). lib. bdg. 14.75 *(978-0-606-35360-1(7))* Turtleback.

—Monkey Me & the New Neighbor: a Branches Book (Monkey Me #3) Roland, Timothy, illus. 2014. (Monkey Me Ser.: 3). (ENG., Illus.). 96p. (J). (gr. 1-3). pap. 4.99 *(978-0-545-55984-3(7))* Scholastic, Inc.

—Monkey Me & the Pet Show. 2014. (Monkey Me Ser.: 2). lib. bdg. 14.75 *(978-0-606-35359-5(3))* Turtleback.

—Monkey Me & the Pet Show: a Branches Book (Monkey Me #2) Roland, Timothy, illus. 2014. (Monkey Me Ser.: 2). (ENG., Illus.). 96p. (J). (gr. 1-3). pap. 4.99 *(978-0-545-55980-5(4))* Scholastic, Inc.

—Monkey Me & the School Ghost. Roland, Timothy, illus. 2014. (Monkey Me Ser.: 4). (ENG., Illus.). 96p. (J). (gr. 1-3). pap. 4.99 *(978-0-545-55989-8(8))* Scholastic, Inc.

—Monkey Me & the School Ghost. 2014. (Monkey Me Ser.: 4). lib. bdg. 14.75 *(978-0-606-36053-1(0))* Turtleback.

Rollins, James. Jake Ransom & the Howling Sphinx. 2012. (Jake Ransom Ser.: 2). (ENG.). 160p. (J). (gr. 5). pap. 7.99 *(978-0-06-147384-5(7),* HarperCollins) HarperCollins Pubs.

—Jake Ransom & the Skull King's Shadow. (Jake Ransom Ser.: 1). (ENG.). (J). (gr. 5). 2010. 432p. pap. 7.99 *(978-0-06-147381-4(2))* 2009. 416p. 16.99 *(978-0-06-147379-1(0))* HarperCollins Pubs. (HarperCollins).

Romano, Ray. Raymie, Dickie, & the Bean: Why I Love & Hate My Brothers. Locke, Gary, illus. 2007. 30p. (J). 18.00 *(978-1-4223-6806-0(8))* DIANE Publishing Co.

Romero, Bernardita. Mummy, What's in Your Tummy? Romero, Bernardita, illus. 2020. (ENG., Illus.). 20p. (J). (gr. -1-k). bds. 8.99 *(978-1-78285-976-5(4))* Barefoot Bks., Inc.

Roop, Peter & Roop, Connie. An Eye for an Eye. 2004. 168p. (J). lib. bdg. 16.92 *(978-1-4242-0772-5(X))* Fitzgerald Bks.

Rorby, Ginny. How to Speak Dolphin. 2017. (ENG.). 272p. (J). (gr. 3-7). pap. 8.99 *(978-0-545-67607-6(X),* Scholastic Pr.) Scholastic, Inc.

Rosen, Chaya & Braverman, Rivkie. Our New Special Baby. 2013. *(978-1-59826-960-4(7))* Feldheim Pubs.

Rosen, Wendy & End, Jackie. Chicken Fingers, Mac & Cheese... Why Do You Always Have to Say Please? Tuck-Bernstein, Cheryl, illus. 2005. 32p. (J). 14.99 *(978-0-7666-1986-9(9))* Modern Publishing.

Rosenbaum, Andrea Warmflash. Hand in Hand. Shleifer, Maya, illus. 2018. (ENG.). 32p. (J). 17.95 *(978-1-68115-538-8(9),* 3447b1ea-4080-4d17-89e0-66a98406b7fd, Apples & Honey Pr.) Behrman Hse., Inc.

Rosenberg, Madelyn. How to Behave at a Tea Party. Ross, Heather, illus. 2014. (ENG.). 32p. (J). (gr. -1-3). 17.99 *(978-0-06-227926-2(2),* Tegen, Katherine Bks) HarperCollins Pubs.

Rosenblum, Gregg. Revolution 19. 2013. (Revolution 19 Ser.: 1). (ENG.). 272p. (YA). (gr. 8). 17.99 *(978-0-06-212595-8(8),* HarperTeen) HarperCollins Pubs.

Rosoff, Meg. Just in Case. 2008. (ENG.). 256p. (gr. 12-18). 14.00 *(978-0-452-28937-6(8),* Penguin Bks.) Penguin Publishing Group.

Ross, Sylvia. Lion Singer. Ross, Sylvia, illus. 2005. (Illus.). 33p. (J). (gr. 3-7). 12.95 *(978-1-59714-009-6(0),* Great Valley Bks.) Heyday.

Ross, Tony. I Want a Sister! Ross, Tony, illus. 2013. (ENG., Illus.). 32p. (J). (gr. -1-3). 16.95 *(978-1-4677-2047-2(X))* Andersen Pr. GBR. Dist: Lerner Publishing Group.

Roth, Veronica. Carve the Mark. 2017. (Carve the Mark Ser.: 1). (ENG.). (YA). (gr. 9). 512p. pap. 12.99 *(978-0-06-234864-7(7));* (Illus.). 480p. 22.99 *(978-0-06-234863-0(9))* HarperCollins Pubs. (Tegen, Katherine Bks).

—Carve the Mark. 2018. (YA). lib. bdg. 24.50 *(978-0-606-41030-4(9))* Turtleback.

—The Fates Divide. l.t. ed. 2018. (ENG.). 602p. (YA). lib. bdg. 24.99 *(978-1-4328-5197-2(7))* Cengage Gale.

—The Fates Divide. 2019. (Carve the Mark Ser.: 2). (ENG.). 480p. (YA). (gr. 9). pap. 14.99 *(978-0-06-242696-3(6))* 2018. (ENG.). 464p. (J). *(978-0-00-819220-4(0))* 2018. (Illus.). 443p. (J). *(978-0-06-284238-1(2))*Bk. 2. 2018. (Carve the Mark Ser.: 2). (ENG., Illus.). 464p. (YA). (gr. 9). 21.99 *(978-0-06-242695-6(8))* HarperCollins Pubs. (Tegen, Katherine Bks).

Rothchild, Erik. The Garden Adventures: The Mishaps of Martha & Matilda. Hief, Gina, illus. 2013. 44p. *(978-0-9883568-5-6(6))* Inkwell Books LLC.

Rothgery, Laura. My Brother's Heart. 2013. 26p. pap. 13.95 *(978-1-4497-8022-7(9),* WestBow Pr.) Author Solutions, LLC.

Rothstein, Evelyn. My Great Grandpa Dave. 2007. (J). per. 12.95 *(978-0-9786745-1-9(0))* Marble Hse. Editions.

Rouss, Sylvia A. Aaron's Bar Mitzvah. Dubois, Liz Goulet, tr. Dubois, Liz Goulet, illus. 2003. (J). 14.95 *(978-0-8246-0447-9(4))* David, Jonathan Pubs., Inc.

Rowe, Jeffrey. Gravity Falls:: Dipper & Mabel & the Curse of the Time Pirates' Treasure! A Select Your Own Choose-Venture! 2016. (ENG., Illus.). 288p. (J). (gr. 3-7). 12.99 *(978-1-4847-4668-4(6),* Disney Press Books) Disney Publishing Worldwide.

Rowley, Melissa. The Falcon Shield. 2009. (J). 6.99 *(978-1-60641-103-2(9))* Deseret Bk. Co.

Rowley, M'lin. The Silver Coat. 2009. (Knights of Right Ser.: Bk. 2). 71p. (J). (gr. 1-5). pap. 6.99 *(978-1-60641-104-9(7),* Shadow Mountain) Shadow Mountain Publishing.

Roy, Kasi. Elizabeth Dreams: And the Christmas House Clock. 2011. 96p. pap. 12.10 *(978-1-4520-1864-5(2))* AuthorHouse.

Roy, Ron. April Adventure. 2010. (Calendar Mysteries Ser.: 4). lib. bdg. 14.75 *(978-0-606-12465-2(9))* Turtleback.

—August Acrobat. 2012. (Calendar Mysteries Ser.: 8). lib. bdg. 14.75 *(978-0-606-26403-7(5))* Turtleback.

—Calendar Mysteries #1: January Joker. Gurney, John Steven, illus. 2009. (Calendar Mysteries Ser.: 1). 96p. (J). (gr. 1-4). 6.99 *(978-0-375-85661-7(7),* Random Hse. Bks. for Young Readers) Random Hse. Children's Bks.

—Calendar Mysteries #10: October Ogre. Gurney, John Steven, illus. 2013. (Calendar Mysteries Ser.: 10). 80p. (J). (gr. 1-4). 7.99 *(978-0-375-86888-7(7),* Random Hse. Bks. for Young Readers) Random Hse. Children's Bks.

—Calendar Mysteries #11: November Night. Gurney, John Steven, illus. 2014. (Calendar Mysteries Ser.: 11). 80p. (J). (gr. 1-4). 7.99 *(978-0-385-37165-0(9),* Random Hse. Bks. for Young Readers) Random Hse. Children's Bks.

—Calendar Mysteries #2: February Friend. Gurney, John Steven, illus. 2009. (Calendar Mysteries Ser.: 2). 80p. (J). (gr. 1-4). 6.99 *(978-0-375-85662-4(5),* Random Hse. Bks. for Young Readers) Random Hse. Children's Bks.

—Calendar Mysteries #3: March Mischief. Gurney, John Steven, illus. 2010. (Calendar Mysteries Ser.: 3). 80p. (J). (gr. 1-4). 6.99 *(978-0-375-85663-1(3),* Random Hse. Bks. for Young Readers) Random Hse. Children's Bks.

—Calendar Mysteries #4: April Adventure. Gurney, John Steven, illus. 2010. (Calendar Mysteries Ser.: 4). 80p. (J). (gr. 1-4). 6.99 *(978-0-375-86116-1(5),* Random Hse. Bks. for Young Readers) Random Hse. Children's Bks.

—Calendar Mysteries #5: May Magic. Gurney, John Steven, illus. 2011. (Calendar Mysteries Ser.: 5). 80p. (J). (gr. 1-4). 6.99 *(978-0-375-86111-6(4),* Random Hse. Bks. for Young Readers) Random Hse. Children's Bks.

—Calendar Mysteries #6: June Jam. Gurney, John Steven, illus. 2011. (Calendar Mysteries Ser.: 6). 80p. (J). (gr. 1-4). 6.99 *(978-0-375-86112-3(2),* Random Hse. Bks. for Young Readers) Random Hse. Children's Bks.

—Calendar Mysteries #7: July Jitters. Gurney, John Steven, illus. 2012. (Calendar Mysteries Ser.: 7). 80p. (J). (gr. 1-4). 7.99 *(978-0-375-86882-5(8),* Random Hse. Bks. for Young Readers) Random Hse. Children's Bks.

—Calendar Mysteries #8: August Acrobat. Gurney, John Steven, illus. 2012. (Calendar Mysteries Ser.: 8). 80p. (J). (gr. 1-4). 6.99 *(978-0-375-86886-3(0),* Random Hse. Bks. for Young Readers) Random Hse. Children's Bks.

—Calendar Mysteries #9: September Sneakers. Gurney, John Steven, illus. 2013. (Calendar Mysteries Ser.: 9). (ENG.). 80p. (J). (gr. 1-4). 7.99 *(978-0-375-86887-0(9),* Random Hse. Bks. for Young Readers) Random Hse. Children's Bks.

—July Jitters. 2012. (Calendar Mysteries Ser.: 7). lib. bdg. 14.75 *(978-0-606-26402-0(7))* Turtleback.

—June Jam. 6. Gurney, John, illus. 2011. (Calendar Mysteries Ser.). (ENG.). 80p. (J). (gr. 1-4). lib. bdg. 18.69 *(978-0-375-96112-0(7))* Random House Publishing Group.

—June Jam. 2011. (Calendar Mysteries Ser.: 6). lib. bdg. 14.75 *(978-0-606-16114-5(7))* Turtleback.

—March Mischief. 2010. (Calendar Mysteries Ser.: 3). lib. bdg. 14.75 *(978-0-606-12460-7(8))* Turtleback.

—October Ogre. 2013. (Calendar Mysteries Ser.: 10). lib. bdg. 14.75 *(978-0-606-32232-4(9))* Turtleback.

—September Sneakers. 2013. (Calendar Mysteries Ser.: 9). lib. bdg. 14.75 *(978-0-606-32231-7(0))* Turtleback.

Rozanski, Bonnie. Borderline. 2007. (ENG.). 208p. (YA). (gr. 10). pap. 22.95 *(978-0-88984-293-9(0))* Porcupine's Quill, Inc. CAN. Dist: Univ. of Toronto Pr.

Rubinacci, Mary Ellen. Srepsihw: The Land of Quiet? 2012. 36p. 19.95 *(978-1-4626-5872-5(5))* America Star Bks.

Ruby, Anne. Children of the Sea. Meier, Ty, illus. 2007. (YA). per. *(978-0-9787881-0-0(9))* Seachild.

Ruby, Laura. Bone Gap. (ENG.). 368p. (YA). (gr. 9). 2016. pap. 9.99 *(978-0-06-231762-9(8))* 2015. 17.99 *(978-0-06-231760-5(1))* HarperCollins Pubs. (Balzer & Bray).

—York: The Clockwork Ghost. 2019. (Illus.). 464p. (YA). *(978-0-06-293755-1(3),* Waldon Pond Pr.) HarperCollins Pubs.

—York: the Clockwork Ghost. 2019. (York Ser.: 2). (ENG., Illus.). 464p. (J). (gr. 3-7). 17.99 *(978-0-06-230696-8(0);* Waldon Pond Pr.) HarperCollins Pubs.

Ruelle, Karen Gray. Just in Time for New Year's! 2004. (ENG., Illus.). 32p. (J). tchr. ed. 14.95 *(978-0-8234-1841-1(3))* Holiday Hse., Inc.

—Mother's Day Mess. 2003. (ENG., Illus.). 32p. (J). (gr. k-3). tchr. ed. 14.95 *(978-0-8234-1773-5(5))* Holiday Hse., Inc.

Ruggieri, J. G. Weather Changes, Mountains Move, & Islands Disappear. 2012. 168p. pap. 15.00 *(978-0-9860300-0-0(7))* Alabaster Bk. Pub.

Ruskin, John. The King of the Golden River. 2004. reprint ed. pap. 1.99 *(978-1-4192-6821-2(X))* Kessinger Publishing, LLC.

—The King of the Golden River. Ghiuselev, Iassen, illus. 2005. (ENG.). 65p. (J). (gr. k). 19.95 *(978-1-894965-15-6(9))* Simply Read Bks. CAN. Dist: Ingram Publisher Services.

Russo, Marisabina. Peter Is Just a Baby. 2011. (ENG., Illus.). 32p. (J). 16.00 *(978-0-8028-5384-4(6),* Eerdmans Bks For Young Readers) Eerdmans, William B. Publishing Co.

—The Trouble with Baby. Russo, Marisabina, illus. 2003. (Illus.). 32p. (J). (gr. -1-18). 16.89 *(978-0-06-008925-2(3))* HarperCollins Pubs.

Ruth-Kilgore, Chanacee. Alphabet Soup. 2012. 108p. pap. 9.99 *(978-1-936453-13-9(4))* Bezalel Bks.

Ryan, Pam Muñoz. Becoming Naomi león (Scholastic Gold) 2005. (ENG.). 272p. (J). (gr. 4-7). reprint ed. per. 8.99 *(978-0-439-26997-1(0),* Scholastic Paperbacks) Scholastic, Inc.

—Tony Baloney: Buddy Trouble. Fotheringham, Ed, illus. 2013. 38p. (J). pap. *(978-0-545-48170-0(8))* Scholastic, Inc.

—Yo, Naomi León. 2005. (SPA.). 272p. (J). (gr. 4-7). pap. 8.99 *(978-0-439-75572-6(7),* Scholastic en Espanol) Scholastic, Inc.

Sage, Angie. Flyte. (Septimus Heap Ser.: 2). (J). 2009. 84.49 *(978-1-4361-5831-2(1))* 2008. 1.25 *(978-1-4193-9383-9(9))* 2006. 114.75 *(978-1-4193-9386-0(3))* 2006. 133.75 *(978-1-4193-9390-7(1))* 2006. 111.75 *(978-1-4193-9388-4(X))* 2006. 282.75 *(978-1-4193-9387-7(1))* 2006. 131.75 *(978-1-4193-9392-1(8))* Recorded Bks., Inc.

—Maximillian Fly. 2019. (ENG.). 384p. (J). (gr. 3-7). 16.99 *(978-0-06-257116-8(8),* Tegen, Katherine Bks) HarperCollins Pubs.

—Septimus Heap, Book Two: Flyte. Zug, Mark, illus. (Septimus Heap Ser.: 2). (ENG.). 544p. (J). (gr. 4-7). 2007. pap. 8.99 *(978-0-06-057736-0(3))* 2006. 17.99 *(978-0-06-057734-6(7))* HarperCollins Pubs. (Tegen, Katherine Bks).

Salom, Susie. Kyle Finds Her Way. 2016. (ENG.). 256p. (J). (gr. 5-9). 16.99 *(978-0-545-85266-1(8),* Levine, Arthur A. Bks.) Scholastic, Inc.

Same Day, Different Way! 2005. (J). pap. *(978-0-9769910-3-8(9))* Terrific Twins LLC.

Sammel, Rochelle. Tales of Two Mouse Brothers. 2008. 45p. pap. 24.95 *(978-1-4241-9798-9(8))* America Star Bks.

Samuel, Lynette M. Mommy's Hat. Capps, Leigh, illus. 2005. (J). per. *(978-0-9727703-3-0(X))* P.R.A. Publishing.

Sanchez, Helen. The Buddy Boys. 2008. 15p. pap. 24.95 *(978-1-60672-352-4(9))* America Star Bks.

Sanchez, Priscilla. Champ the Boxing Boxer. 2011. 12p. pap. 8.32 *(978-1-4634-7423-2(7))* AuthorHouse.

Sandau, Carol E. Prairie Patchwork. 2012. 88p. (gr. 4-6). pap. 9.95 *(978-1-4759-4807-3(7))* iUniverse, Inc.

Sanders-Wells, Linda. Maggie's Monkeys. Carter, Abby, illus. 2009. (ENG.). 32p. (J). (gr. -1-2). 16.99 *(978-0-7636-3326-4(7))* Candlewick Pr.

Sandford, John, pseud & Cook, Michele. Outrage (the Singular Menace, 2) 2016. (Singular Menace Ser.: 2). (ENG.). 336p. (YA). (gr. 9). pap. 10.99 *(978-0-385-75311-1(X),* Ember) Random Hse. Children's Bks.

—Rampage (the Singular Menace, 3) 2017. (Singular Menace Ser.: 3). (ENG.). 336p. (YA). (gr. 9). pap. 11.99 *(978-0-385-75315-9(2),* Ember) Random Hse. Children's Bks.

—Uncaged (the Singular Menace, 1) 2015. (Singular Menace Ser.: 1). (ENG.). 416p. (YA). (gr. 9). pap. 14.99 *(978-0-385-75305-0(5),* Ember) Random Hse. Children's Bks.

Sarn, Amélie & Trouillot, Virgile. The Argument, 1 vol. 2009. (Groove High Ser.). (ENG., Illus.). 112p. (YA). (gr. 5-5). 16.93 *(978-1-60754-538-5(1),* 7b9cf7f2-7a02-4e16-b9e7-eea7e9f9db9d); pap. 8.95 *(978-1-60754-539-2(X),* 6b530199-da9e-4374-ae69-247e6f35994f) Rosen Publishing Group, Inc., The. (Windmill Bks.).

Sarrasin, Alex. The Guardians of Neoegypti: Book One. 2007. 300p. per. 18.95 *(978-0-595-45710-6(X))* iUniverse, Inc.

Sarwari, Zohra. The Inheritance: A Journey to China (Book 1) 2013. 148p. pap. *(978-1-935948-30-8(X))* Roxby Media Ltd.

Satera, Diane. The Angel of Wild Springs: Jaiden & the Sacred Stones. 2010. 168p. 23.99 *(978-1-4520-3460-7(5));* pap. 11.99 *(978-1-4520-3461-4(3))* AuthorHouse.

Sateren, Shelley Swanson. Fearless Freddie. Melmon, Deborah, illus. 2015. (Adventures at Hound Hotel Ser.). (ENG.). 72p. (J). (gr. 1-3). lib. bdg. 25.32 *(978-1-4795-5898-8(2),* 127044, Picture Window Bks.) Capstone.

—Growling Gracie. Melmon, Deborah, illus. 2015. (Adventures at Hound Hotel Ser.). (ENG.). 72p. (J). (gr. 1-3). lib. bdg. 25.32 *(978-1-4795-5899-5(0),* 127045, Picture Window Bks.) Capstone.

—Homesick Herbie. Melmon, Deborah, illus. 2015. (Adventures at Hound Hotel Ser.). (ENG.). 72p. (J). (gr. 1-3). lib. bdg. 25.32 *(978-1-4795-5897-1(4),* 127043, Picture Window Bks.) Capstone.

—Mudball Molly. Melmon, Deborah, illus. 2015. (Adventures at Hound Hotel Ser.). (ENG.). 72p. (J). (gr. 1-3). lib. bdg. 25.32 *(978-1-4795-5900-8(8),* 127046, Picture Window Bks.) Capstone.

Saunders, Kate. The Whizz Pop Chocolate Shop. 2014. (ENG.). 304p. (J). (gr. 5). 7.99 *(978-0-385-74302-0(5),* Yearling) Random Hse. Children's Bks.

Saunders, Kate & Nesbit, E. Five Children on the Western Front. 2016. (J). *(978-0-553-49785-4(5),* Delacorte Pr) Random House Publishing Group.

Sava, Scott Christian. Magic Carpet. 2010. (Illus.). 110p. (J). pap. 11.99 *(978-1-60010-563-0(7))* Idea & Design Works, LLC.

Sawyer, Jacqueline. Little Racer Big Heart. 2012. 28p. pap. 16.95 *(978-1-62709-783-3(X))* America Star Bks.

Scampering Through Savannah. 2007. (YA). lib. bdg., act. bk. ed. *(978-0-9787589-2-9(7))* ON Words Publishing, LLC.

Schaaf, Ron. Tiger's Quest: Rounding Cape Horn. 2007. (J). *(978-0-9787555-0-8(2))* Hickory Tales Publishing.

Schaefer, Lola. One Special Day: A Story for Big Brothers & Sisters. Meserve, Jessica, illus. 2012. (ENG.). 40p. (J). (gr. -1-17). 17.99 *(978-1-4231-3760-3(4))* Little, Brown Bks. for Young Readers.

Schneider, Josh. Kid Amazing vs. the Blob. Schneider, Josh, illus. 2017. (ENG., Illus.). 32p. (J). (gr. -1-3). 16.99 *(978-0-544-80125-7(3),* 1640251, Clarion Bks.) HarperCollins Pubs.

—You'll Be Sorry. 2007. (ENG., Illus.). 32p. (J). (gr. -1-3). 15.00 *(978-0-618-81932-4(0),* 100554, Clarion Bks.) HarperCollins Pubs.

Schneider, Mical. Annie Quinn in America. 2003. (Adventures in Time Ser.). (Illus.). 252p. (J). (gr. 4-7). 15.95 *(978-1-57505-510-7(4),* Carolrhoda Bks.) Lerner Publishing Group.

Schnitzlein, Danny. Trick or Treat on Monster Street, 1 vol. Faulkner, Matt, illus. 2008. 32p. (J). (gr. -1-3). 16.95 *(978-1-56145-465-5(6))* Peachtree Publishing Co. Inc.

Scholastic. The Story of Peppa Pig (Peppa Pig) 2013. (ENG.). 32p. (J). (gr. -1-k). 8.99 *(978-0-545-46805-3(1))* Scholastic, Inc.

Scholastic, Inc. Staff. Night Creatures: A Lift-the-Flap Book. EOne, illus. 2018. (ENG.). 14p. (J). (gr. -1-k). bds. 10.99 *(978-1-338-22879-3(X))* Scholastic, Inc.

Schraff, Anne. Gingerbread Heart. 2008. 114p. (J). (gr. 4-7). 13.95 *(978-0-7569-8406-9(8))* Perfection Learning Corp.

—A Song to Sing. 2008. (Passages Ser.). 130p. (YA). (gr. 7-9). lib. bdg. 13.95 *(978-0-7569-8384-0(3))* Perfection Learning Corp.

—Under the Mushroom Cloud. 2008. (Passages to Adventure Ser.). 115p. (J). (gr. 4-6). lib. bdg. 13.95 *(978-0-7569-8399-4(1))* Perfection Learning Corp.

Schreiber, Ellen. Kissing Coffins. 2007. (Vampire Kisses Ser.: No. 2). (ENG.). 240p. (J). pap., pap. 5.99 *(978-0-06-077624-4(2),* HarperTeen) HarperCollins Pubs.

—Vampire Kisses 2: Kissing Coffins. 2005. (Vampire Kisses Ser.: 2). (ENG.). 176p. (YA). (gr. 8-18). 17.99 *(978-0-06-077622-0(6),* Tegen, Katherine Bks) HarperCollins Pubs.

—Vampire Kisses Boxed Set: Vampire Kisses; Kissing Coffins; Vampireville. 2008. (Vampire Kisses Ser.: Nos. 1-3). (J). pap. 15.99 *(978-0-06-169160-7(7),* HarperTeen) HarperCollins Pubs.

Schuster, Judith A. No Place to Call Home: Book Two-the Eddie Brewster Adventures. 2008. 196p. pap. 24.95 *(978-1-60563-559-0(6))* PublishAmerica, Inc.

Schwab, Victoria. New Beginnings. 2014. (Everyday Angel Ser.: No. 1). 195p. (J). pap. *(978-0-545-68443-9(9))* Scholastic, Inc.

Schwalbach, Pamela. The Happiest Day for Simeon & Sula. 2011. 28p. (gr. 4-6). pap. 15.00 *(978-1-4567-5062-6(3))* AuthorHouse.

Schwarz, S. L. Treasure at Lure Lake. 2016. (Illus.). 185p. (J). *(978-1-4621-2600-2(6))* Cedar Fort, Inc./CFI Distribution.

Scott, Dee Mary. The Adventures of Charles & Camilla Chinchilla. 2012. (ENG., Illus.). 46p. pap. 6.99 *(978-1-78035-389-0(8),* Fastprint Publishing) Upfront Publishing Ltd. GBR. Dist: Printondemand-worldwide.com.

Scott, Eric. Santa & the Cyberspace Plot. 2013. 114p. pap. 7.99 *(978-1-78333-397-4(9))* Acorn Bks.

Scott, Jonathan & Scott, Drew. Builder Brothers: Big Plans. Smith, Kim, illus. 2018. (Builder Brothers Ser.). (ENG.). 32p. (J). (gr. -1-3). 17.99 *(978-0-06-284662-4(0),* HarperCollins) HarperCollins Pubs.

Scott, Lisa Ann. Back on the Map. 2017. (ENG.). 320p. (J). (gr. 2-7). 15.99 *(978-1-5107-1353-6(0),* Sky Pony Pr.) Skyhorse Publishing Co., Inc.

Scott, Michael. The Alchemyst. 2009. (ENG., Illus.). 375p. (gr. 6-10). 19.00 *(978-1-60686-514-9(5))* Perfection Learning Corp.

—The Alchemyst. (Secrets of the Immortal Nicholas Flamel Ser.: 1). (ENG.). 400p. (YA). (gr. 7). 2008. pap. 11.99 *(978-0-385-73600-8(2),* Ember) 2007. (Illus.). 18.99 *(978-0-385-73357-1(7),* Delacorte Bks. for Young Readers) Random Hse. Children's Bks.

—The Enchantress. 2013. (Secrets of the Immortal Nicholas Flamel Ser.: 6). (ENG.). 528p. (YA). (gr. 7). pap. 10.99 *(978-0-385-73536-0(7),* Ember) Random Hse. Children's Bks.

—The Enchantress. 2013. (Secrets of the Immortal Nicholas Flamel Ser.: 6). lib. bdg. 22.10 *(978-0-606-31947-8(6))* Turtleback.

—The Magician. 2009. (Secrets of the Immortal Nicholas Flamel Ser.: 2). (ENG.). 496p. (YA). (gr. 7). pap. 11.99 *(978-0-385-73728-9(9),* Ember) Random Hse. Children's Bks.

—The Necromancer. 2011. (Secrets of the Immortal Nicholas Flamel Ser.: 4). (ENG.). 416p. (YA). (gr. 7). pap. 11.99 *(978-0-385-73532-2(4),* Ember) Random Hse. Children's Bks.

—The Necromancer. l.t. ed. 2010. (Secrets of the Immortal Nicholas Flamel Ser.). (ENG.). 690p. pap. 23.99 *(978-1-4104-2851-6(6))* Thorndike Pr.

—The Sorceress. 2010. (Secrets of the Immortal Nicholas Flamel Ser.: 3). (ENG.). 512p. (YA). (gr. 7-18). pap. 11.99 *(978-0-385-73530-8(8),* Ember) Random Hse. Children's Bks.

—The Sorceress. 2010. (Secrets of the Immortal Nicholas Flamel Ser.: 3). lib. bdg. 22.10 *(978-0-606-14133-8(2))* Turtleback.

—The Sorceress the Secrets of the Immortal Nicholas Flamel. l.t. ed. 2009. (Secrets of the Immortal Nicholas Flamel Ser.). (ENG.). 614p. (YA). 23.95 *(978-1-4104-2092-3(2))* Thorndike Pr.

—The Warlock. 2012. (Secrets of the Immortal Nicholas Flamel Ser.: 5). (ENG.). 400p. (YA). (gr. 7). pap. 11.99 *(978-0-385-73534-6(0),* Ember) Random Hse. Children's Bks.

—The Warlock. l.t. ed. 2011. (Secrets of the Immortal Nicholas Flamel Ser.). (ENG.). 545p. 23.99 *(978-1-4104-4157-7(1))* Thorndike Pr.

—The Warlock. 2012. (Secrets of the Immortal Nicholas Flamel Ser.: 5). lib. bdg. 22.10 *(978-0-606-26411-2(6))* Turtleback.

Scotton, Rob. Splat the Cat: Splat & the New Baby. Scotton, Rob, illus. 2018. (Splat the Cat Ser.). (ENG., Illus.). 40p. (J). (gr. -1-3). 17.99 *(978-0-06-213389-2(6),* HarperCollins) HarperCollins Pubs.

Sealls, Arthur. The Three Little Heroes: Book One of Kirk, Chelsea, & Samantha's Adventures. 2007. 84p. per. 8.95 *(978-0-595-44083-2(5))* iUniverse, Inc.

Sedgwick, Chantele. Love, Lucas. 2015. (Love, Lucas Novel Ser.: 1). (ENG.). 280p. (J). (gr. 6-6). 16.99 *(978-1-63220-417-2(7),* Sky Pony Pr.) Skyhorse Publishing Co., Inc.

Sedgwick, Marcus. She Is Not Invisible. 2015. (ENG.). 240p. (YA). (gr. 7). pap. 11.99 *(978-1-250-05698-6(5),* 900139107) Square Fish.

—Snowflake, AZ. 2019. (ENG.). 320p. (YA). (gr. 7-12). 18.95 *(978-1-324-00441-7(X),* 340441, Norton Young Readers) Norton, W. W. & Co., Inc.

Seidler, Tor. The Dulcimer Boy. Selznick, Brian, illus. 2003. 160p. (J). (gr. 3-7). lib. bdg. 16.89 *(978-0-06-623610-0(X))* HarperCollins Pubs.

—The Dulcimer Boy. Selznick, Brian, illus. 2004. 153p. (gr. 5-7). 17.00 *(978-0-7569-3520-7(2))* Perfection Learning Corp.

Seif, Adam, creator. Tacos, Beans & Rice... the Episodes: From the Beginning. l.t. ed. 2006. (Illus.). 32p. (J). *(978-0-9719518-0-8(2))* Doodle Publishing.

Seif, Adam/Jeffrey. Tacos, Beans & Rice Episode 2: Lights, Camera, Action! 2007. (Illus.). 32p. (J). per. 5.00 *(978-0-9719518-1-5(0))* Doodle Publishing.

Selfors, Suzanne. Smells Like Dog. 2011. (Smells Like Dog Ser.: 1). (ENG.). 384p. (J). (gr. 3-7). pap. 7.99 *(978-0-316-04397-7(4))* Little, Brown Bks. for Young Readers.

Sensenig, Janet Martin. The Missing Bible: And Other Stories. 2003. (Sunbeam Ser.). (Illus.). 160p. (gr. -1-5). 6.40 *(978-0-7399-0341-4(1),* 2325) Rod & Staff Pubs., Inc.

Service, Pamela F. Escape from Planet Yastol. Gorman, Mike, illus. (Way-Too-Real Aliens Ser.: 1). (ENG.). 112p. (J). (gr. 4-6). 2015. E-Book 53.32 *(978-1-4677-5960-1(0),* 9781467759601, Lerner Digital)No. 1. 2011. pap. 5.95 *(978-0-7613-7921-8(5),* Darby Creek) Lerner Publishing Group.

—The Not-So-Perfect Planet. Gorman, Mike, illus. (Way-Too-Real Aliens Ser.: 2). (ENG.). 120p. (J). (gr. 4-6). 2012. pap. 6.95 *(978-0-7613-7923-2(1),* Darby Creek) 2015. E-Book 53.32 *(978-1-4677-5961-8(9),* 9781467759618, Lerner Digital) Lerner Publishing Group.

—The Wizards of Wyrd World. Gorman, Mike, illus. 2015. (Way-Too-Real Aliens Ser.: 3). (ENG.). 112p. (J). (gr. 4-6).

S

E-Book 53.32 *(978-1-4677-5962-5(7)*, 9781467759625, Lerner Digital) Lerner Publishing Group.

Seuss, Dr. El Gato con Sombrero Viene de Nuevo! Canetti, Yanitzia, tr. from ENG. 2004.Tr. of Cat in the Hat Comes Back. (SPA., Illus.). 63p. (gr. -1-1). 8.99 *(978-1-930332-43-0(2))* Lectorum Pubns., Inc.

Seven, John. The Outlaw of Sherwood Forest, 1 vol. Hans, Stephanie, illus. 2014. (Time-Tripping Faradays Ser.). (ENG.). 192p. (J). (gr. 4-8). lib. bdg. 26.65 *(978-1-4342-9174-5(X)*, 125644, Stone Arch Bks.) Capstone.

Sevigny, Alisha. Summer Constellations. 2018. (ENG.). 264p. (J). (gr. 9-12). 17.99 *(978-1-77138-929-7(X))* Kids Can Pr., Ltd. CAN. Dist: Hachette Bk. Group.

Sévigny, Eric, illus. Caillou: Watches Rosie. rev. ed. 2008. (Playtime Ser.). (ENG.). 24p. (J). (gr. -1-1). pap. 4.95 *(978-2-89450-635-6(X))* Caillouet, Gerry.

Shannon, David. Grow up, David! Shannon, David, illus. 2018. (ENG., Illus.). 32p. (J). (gr. -1-k). 18.99 *(978-1-338-25097-8(3)*, Blue Sky Pr., The) Scholastic, Inc.

Sharing: Individual Title Six-Packs. (Literatura 2000 Ser.). (gr. k-1). 28.00 *(978-0-7635-0038-2(0))* Rigby Education.

Sharp, Cathy. The Boy with the Latch Key (Halfpenny Orphans, Book 4) 2018. (Halfpenny Orphans Ser.: 4). (ENG.). 416p. 12.99 *(978-0-00-827672-0(2)*, HarperCollins) HarperCollins Pubs.

Sharpe, Luke. Billy Sure Kid Entrepreneur & the Haywire Hovercraft. Ross, Graham, illus. 2016. (Billy Sure Kid Entrepreneur Ser.: 7). (ENG.). 160p. (J). (gr. 3-7). pap. 6.99 *(978-1-4814-6193-1(1)*, Simon Spotlight) Simon Spotlight.

Shaw, Dana Alton, III. My Friend Zundel. 2006. per. *(978-0-9791091-0-2(8))* Shaw, Dana.

Sheinmel, Courtney. Twinsanity. Bell, Jennifer A., illus. 2017. (Zacktastic Ser.). (ENG.). 272p. (J). (gr. 2-4). 11.99 *(978-1-58536-936-2(5)*, 204319); pap. 6.99 *(978-1-58536-937-9(3)*, 204333) Sleeping Bear Pr.

—Zacktastic. 2015. (Zacktastic Ser.). (ENG.). 272p. (J). (gr. 2-5). 11.99 *(978-1-58536-934-8(9)*, 203947) Sleeping Bear Pr.

Sheinmel, Courtney & Turetsky, Bianca. Magic on the Map #1: Let's Mooove! Lewis, Stevie, illus. 2019. (Magic on the Map Ser.: 1). 128p. (J). (gr. 2-5). 6.99 *(978-1-63565-166-9(2)*, Random Hse. Bks. for Young Readers) Random Hse. Children's Bks.

—Magic on the Map #2: the Show Must Go On. Lewis, Stevie, illus. 2019. (Magic on the Map Ser.: 2). 128p. (J). (gr. 2-5). 5.99 *(978-1-63565-169-0(7)*, Random Hse. Bks. for Young Readers) Random Hse. Children's Bks.

—Magic on the Map #3: Texas Treasure. 3. Lewis, Stevie, illus. 2020. (Magic on the Map Ser.: 3). 128p. (J). (gr. 2-5). 5.99 *(978-1-9848-9569-1(9)*, Random Hse. Bks. for Young Readers) Random Hse. Children's Bks.

Shepherd, Kat. The Gemini Mysteries: the Cat's Paw (the Gemini Mysteries Book 2) 2021. (Gemini Mysteries Ser.: 2). (ENG., Illus.). 304p. (J). (gr. 3-7). 16.99 *(978-1-4998-0810-0(0)*, Yellow Jacket) Bonnier Publishing USA.

Sheridan, Celi. Tolly & Maisie's Ghastly Adventure. 2011. (Illus.). 48p. (gr. -1). pap. 11.95 *(978-1-4670-0397-1(2))* AuthorHouse.

Sheriff, Jeanne. Walkabout Kid. 2013. 172p. pap. 12.95 *(978-1-4787-2130-7(8))* Outskirts Pr., Inc.

Sherrard, Valerie. Three Million Acres of Flame. 2007. (ENG.). 200p. (YA). pap. 12.99 *(978-1-55002-727-3(1))* Dundurn Pr. CAN. Dist: Publishers Group West (PGW).

Sherry, Maureen. Walls Within Walls. 2012. (ENG., Illus.). 368p. (J). (gr. 3-7). pap. 9.99 *(978-0-06-176703-6(4)*, Tegen, Katherine Bks) HarperCollins Pubs.

—Walls Within Walls. Stower, Adam, illus. 2010. (ENG.). 368p. (J). (gr. 3-7). 16.99 *(978-0-06-176700-5(X)*, Tegen, Katherine Bks) HarperCollins Pubs.

Sheth, Kashmira. Tiger in My Soup, 1 vol. Ebbeler, Jeffrey, illus. 32p. (J). (gr. -1-3). 2015. pap. 7.99 *(978-1-56145-890-5(2))* 2013. 15.95 *(978-1-56145-696-3(9))* Peachtree Publishing Co. Inc.

Shields, Gillian. The Littlest Bunny. Lovsin, Polona, illus. 2015. 32p. (J). *(978-1-4351-5967-9(5))* Barnes & Noble, Inc.

Shinoda, Anna. Learning Not to Drown. (ENG.). 352p. (YA). (gr. 9). 2019. pap. 11.99 *(978-1-5344-3948-1(X)*, Atheneum/Caitlyn Dlouhy Books) 2014. (Illus.). 17.99 *(978-1-4169-9393-3(2)*, Atheneum Bks. for Young Readers) Simon & Schuster Children's Publishing.

Shook, Karl. The Family Thing. 2004. 166p. (YA). pap. 12.95 *(978-0-595-31121-7(0))* iUniverse, Inc.

Shore, Diane Z. How to Drive Your Sister Crazy. Rankin, Laura, illus. 2008. (I Can Read Level 2 Ser.). (ENG.). 48p. (J). (gr. k-3). 16.99 *(978-0-06-052762-4(5)*, HarperCollins) HarperCollins Pubs.

—How to Drive Your Sister Crazy. Rankin, Laura, illus. 2012. (I Can Read! Level 2 Ser.). (J). lib. bdg. 13.55 *(978-0-606-26869-1(3))* Turtleback.

Short, Robbie, illus. I Want One Too! 2003. 32p. (J). lib. bdg. 12.95 *(978-0-9729833-2-7(5))* Bubble Gum Pr.

Shull, Megan. The Swap. 2014. (ENG.). 400p. (J). (gr. 5-9). 16.99 *(978-0-06-231169-6(7)*, Tegen, Katherine Bks) HarperCollins Pubs.

Shumaker, Heather. The Griffins of Castle Cary. 2019. (ENG., Illus.). 320p. (J). (gr. 3-7). 17.99 *(978-1-5344-3088-4(1)*, Simon & Schuster Bks. For Young Readers) Simon & Schuster Bks. For Young Readers.

Shurtliff, Liesl. Time Castaways #1: the Mona Lisa Key. (Time Castaways Ser.: 1). (ENG.). (J). (gr. 3-7). 2019. 416p. pap. 6.99 *(978-0-06-256816-8(7))* 2018. 400p. 16.99 *(978-0-06-256813-7(2))* HarperCollins Pubs. (Tegen, Katherine Bks).

Shusterman, Neal. Bruiser. 2010. (ENG.). 336p. (YA). (gr. 9-18). 17.99 *(978-0-06-113408-1(2)*, Quill Tree Bks.) HarperCollins Pubs.

—Full Tilt. 2003. (Neal Shusterman Collection). (ENG., Illus.). 201p. (YA). (gr. 7-12). 29.94 *(978-0-689-80374-1(5))* Simon & Schuster, Inc.

—Full Tilt. 2004. (ENG.). 208p. (YA). (gr. 7). mass mkt. 8.99 *(978-0-689-87325-6(5)*, Simon Pulse) Simon Pulse.

Shusterman, Neal & Shusterman, Jarrod. Dry. (ENG.). (YA). (gr. 7). 2019. 416p. pap. 12.99 *(978-1-4814-8197-7(5))* 2018. (Illus.). 400p. 19.99 *(978-1-4814-8196-0(7))* Simon & Schuster Bks. For Young Readers. (Simon & Schuster Bks. For Young Readers).

The Siblings Four. 2006. (J). *(978-0-9629124-6-7(8))* Floppinfish Publishing Co., Ltd.

Sicks, Linda. Nick's Holiday Celebration. Messing, Dave, illus. 2010. (Nick the Wise Old Cat Ser.: 4). (ENG.). 40p. (J). 18.95 *(978-1-936193-05-9(1)*, e96b6028-5d5f-4a23-88ae-2a103e07e55a) Nick The Cat, LLC.

Sidney, Margaret. Five Little Peppers Abroad. 2008. 212p. (gr. 4-7). 26.95 *(978-1-60664-996-1(5))*; per. 14.95 *(978-1-60312-546-8(9))* Aegypan.

—Five Little Peppers Abroad. 2017. (ENG., Illus.). (J). 25.95 *(978-1-374-90288-6(8))*; pap. 15.95 *(978-1-374-90287-9(X))* Capital Communications, Inc.

—Five Little Peppers & How They Grew. 2017. (ENG., Illus.). (J). 24.95 *(978-1-374-93472-6(0))*; pap. 14.95 *(978-1-374-93471-9(2))* Capital Communications, Inc.

—Five Little Peppers & How They Grew. 2006. (Dover Children's Classics Ser.). (ENG., Illus.). 224p. (J). (gr. 3-5). per. 9.95 *(978-0-486-45267-8(0)*. 452670) Dover Pubns., Inc.

—Polly Pepper's Book. 2011. 316p. 50.95 *(978-1-258-10539-6(X))* Literary Licensing, LLC.

Silberman, Shoshana. A Family Haggadah II, Vol. 2. Kahn, Katherine Janus, illus. l.t. ed. 2003. 64p. (J). pap. 6.95 *(978-1-58013-014-1(3)*, Kar-Ben Publishing) Lerner Publishing Group.

Sill, Cathryn. About Mollusks: A Guide for Children, 1 vol. Sill, John, illus. 2008. (About... Ser.: 9). 40p. (J). (gr. -1-2). pap. 7.95 *(978-1-56145-406-8(0))* Peachtree Publishing Co. Inc.

Silverman, Erica. Jack (Not Jackie) Hatam, Holly, illus. 2018. (ENG.). 40p. (J). (gr. -1-3). 17.99 *(978-1-4998-0731-8(7))* Little Bee Books Inc.

Silvey, Diane. Time of the Thunderbird. Mantha, John, illus. 2008. (ENG.). 88p. (J). (gr. 6-5). pap. 11.99 *(978-1-55002-792-1(1))* Dundurn Pr. CAN. Dist: Publishers Group West (PGW).

Simmons, Jane. Daisy & the Egg. 2005. (Daisy Ser.). (Illus.). 36p. (J). (gr. -1-1). (VIE, ENG, CHI, ARA & BEN.). pap. 11.95 *(978-1-84059-176-7(5))*; (ARA, ENG, VIE, CHI & BEN., pap. 11.95 *(978-1-84059-216-0(8))* Milet Publishing.

Simon, Charnan. Me Gusta Ganar! Translations.com Staff, tr. from ENG. Handelman, Dorothy, photos by. 2007. (Lecturas para niños de Verdad - Nivel 1 (Real Kids Readers - Level 1) Ser.).Tr. of I Like to Win! (SPA., Illus.). 32p. (J). (gr. k-2). per. 5.95 *(978-0-8225-7801-7(8)*, Ediciones Lerner) Lerner Publishing Group.

—Me Gusta Ganar; I Like to Win. 2008. pap. 34.95 *(978-0-8225-9499-4(4))* Lerner Publishing Group.

—Tressa the Musical Princess. Allen, Joy, illus. 2005. 25p. (J). *(978-1-58987-112-0(X))* Kindermusik International.

Simon, Coco. Emma: Sugar & Spice & Everything Nice. 2013. (Cupcake Diaries: 15). lib. bdg. 16.00 *(978-0-606-32052-8(0))* Turtleback.

—Emma All Stirred Up! (Cupcake Diaries: 7). (ENG., 160p. (J). (gr. 3-7). 2013. Illus.). 17.99 *(978-1-4424-8567-9(1))* 2012. pap. 6.99 *(978-1-4424-5078-3(9))* Simon Spotlight. (Simon Spotlight).

—Emma All Stirred Up! 2012. (Cupcake Diaries: 7). lib. bdg. 17.20 *(978-0-606-26309-2(8))* Turtleback.

—Emma Raining Cats & Dogs ... & Cupcakes! 2016. (Cupcake Diaries: 27). (ENG.. Illus.). 160p. (J). (gr. 3-7). pap. 7.99 *(978-1-4814-5524-4(9)*, Simon Spotlight) Simon Spotlight.

—Emma Raining Cats & Dogs... & Cupcakes! 2016. (Cupcake Diaries: 27). lib. bdg. 17.20 *(978-0-606-38251-9(8))* Turtleback.

Simon, Francesca. Horrid Henry. Ross, Tony, illus. 2009. (Horrid Henry Ser.: 0). (ENG.). 112p. (J). (gr. 2-5). pap. 7.99 *(978-1-4022-1775-3(7)*, 9781402217753, Sourcebooks Jabberwocky) Sourcebooks, Inc.

Simonds, William. Marcus; or, the Boy-Tamer by Walter Aimwell [Pseud.]. 2006. 336p. per. 23.99 *(978-1-4255-3348-9(5))* Michigan Publishing.

Simons, Paullina. Poppet Gets Two Big Brothers. 2015. (ENG., Illus.). 32p. (J). 17.99 *(978-0-00-811041-3(7)*, HarperCollins Children's Bks.) HarperCollins Pubs. Ltd. GBR. Dist: HarperCollins Pubs.

Singer, Marilyn. Tallulah's Solo. Boiger, Alexandra, illus. 2012. (Tallulah Ser.). (ENG.). 40p. (J). (gr. -1-3). 18.99 *(978-0-547-33004-4(9)*, 1417225, Clarion Bks.) HarperCollins Pubs.

Singleton, Clive. The City through the Clouds. 2006. 208p. pap. 13.99 *(978-1-4116-5982-7(1))* Lulu Pr., Inc.

Siobhan, Dowd. The London Eye Mystery. 2014. (ENG.). 336p. (J). (gr. 3-7). 12.24 *(978-1-63245-320-4(7))* Lectorum Pubns., Inc.

Siriano, A. M. Nod. 2010. 168p. pap. 14.95 *(978-0-557-26127-7(9))* Lulu Pr., Inc.

Sirowy, Alexandra. The Creeping. 2015. (ENG., Illus.). 400p. (YA). (gr. 7). 17.99 *(978-1-4814-1886-7(6))* Simon & Schuster Children's Publishing.

—The Telling. 2016. (ENG., Illus.). 400p. (YA). (gr. 7). 17.99 *(978-1-4814-1889-8(0)*, Simon & Schuster Bks. For Young Readers) Simon & Schuster Bks. For Young Readers.

Skead, Robert A. Patriots Redcoats & Spies, 1 vol. 2015. (American Revolutionary War Adventures Ser.). (ENG.). 192p. (J). 14.99 *(978-0-310-74841-0(0))* Zonderkidz.

Skinner, Daphne. Henry Lleva la Cuenta; Henry Keeps Score. 2008. pap. 34.95 *(978-1-58013-757-7(1))* Astra Publishing Hse.

Skogen, Jennifer. Shattered. 2017. (Survive Ser.). (ENG.). 192p. (YA). (gr. 5-12). lib. bdg. 31.42 *(978-1-68076-734-6(8)*, 25402, Epic Escape) EPIC Pr.

Skye, Evelyn. Circle of Shadows. 2019. (YA). (Circle of Shadows Ser.: 1). (ENG.). 480p. (gr. 8). pap. 10.99 *(978-0-06-264373-5(8))*; (Illus.). 464p. *(978-0-06-291540-5(1))*; (Circle of Shadows Ser.: 1). (ENG., Illus.). 464p. (gr. 8). 17.99 *(978-0-06-264372-8(X))* HarperCollins Pubs. (Balzer & Bray).

Slanina, Anne M. Baby Brother Goes to the Hospital. Agnew, Alicia, illus. 2007. (Adventures of Annie Mouse Ser.: Bk. 2). 28p. (J). 18.99 *(978-0-9793379-1-8(7))*; per. 9.99 *(978-0-9793379-0-1(9))* Annie Mouse Bks.

Smadja, Brigitte. Tarte aux Escargots. pap. 17.95 *(978-2-211-03633-7(3))* Archimede Editions FRA. Dist: Distribooks, Inc.

Smith, Amber. The Last to Let Go. 2018. (ENG.). 384p. (YA). (gr. 9). pap. 12.99 *(978-1-5344-2601-6(9))*; (Illus.). 17.99 *(978-1-4814-8073-4(1)*, McElderry, Margaret K. Bks.) McElderry, Margaret K. Bks.

Smith, Cheryl Jean. The Offering. 2006. (ENG.). 140p. per. 11.95 *(978-0-7414-3181-3(5))* Infinity Publishing.

Smith, Cynthia Leitich. Feral Pride. (Feral Ser.: 3). 304p. (YA). (gr. 9). 2018. pap. 7.99 *(978-1-5362-0367-7(X))* 2015. (ENG.). 17.99 *(978-0-7636-5911-0(8))* Candlewick Pr.

Smith, J. Albert. Goosey Green. 2011. 24p. pap. 24.95 *(978-1-4626-3392-0(7))* America Star Bks.

Smith, Jada. Touched by an Angel. 2009. 76p. pap. 13.95 *(978-1-4251-8552-7(5))* Trafford Publishing.

Smith, Jennifer E. The Storm Makers. Helquist, Brett, illus. 2013. (ENG.). 384p. (J). (gr. 3-7). pap. 19.99 *(978-0-316-17959-1(0))* Little, Brown Bks. for Young Readers.

Smith, L. J. The Fury & Dark Reunion. 2007. (Vampire Diaries: 3). (YA). lib. bdg. 20.85 *(978-0-606-07135-2(0))* Turtleback.

—Heart of Valor. 2008. (ENG.). 244p. (YA). pap. 11.99 *(978-1-4169-8966-0(8)*, Simon & Schuster Bks. For Young Readers) Simon & Schuster Bks. For Young Readers.

—Heart of Valor. 2010. (ENG.). 352p. (J). (gr. 3-7). pap. 7.99 *(978-1-4169-9841-9(1)*, Aladdin) Simon & Schuster Children's Publishing.

—The Night of the Solstice. 2010. (ENG.). 352p. (J). (gr. 3-7). pap. 7.99 *(978-1-4169-9840-2(3)*, Aladdin) Simon & Schuster Children's Publishing.

—The Vampire Diaries: the Fury & Dark Reunion, 2 vols. 2007. (Vampire Diaries: Nos. 3-4). (ENG.). 528p. (YA). (gr. 8-12). pap. 12.99 *(978-0-06-114098-3(8)*, HarperTeen) HarperCollins Pubs.

—The Vampire Diaries: the Hunters: Moonsong Vol. 9. 2013. (Vampire Diaries: the Hunters Ser.: 2). (ENG.). 416p. (YA). (gr. 9). pap. 10.99 *(978-0-06-201771-0(3)*, HarperTeen) HarperCollins Pubs.

—The Vampire Diaries: the Hunters: Phantom. (Vampire Diaries: the Hunters Ser.: 1). (ENG.). (YA). (gr. 9). 2012. 432p. pap. 10.99 *(978-0-06-201769-7(1))* 2011. 416p. 17.99 *(978-0-06-201768-0(3))* HarperCollins Pubs. (HarperTeen).

—The Vampire Diaries: the Return: Midnight. 2012. (Vampire Diaries: the Return Ser.: 3). (ENG.). 592p. (YA). (gr. 8). pap. 10.99 *(978-0-06-172086-4(0)*, HarperTeen) HarperCollins Pubs.

—The Vampire Diaries: the Return: Nightfall. 2010. (Vampire Diaries: the Return Ser.: 1). (ENG.). 608p. (YA). (gr. 8). pap. 11.99 *(978-0-06-172080-2(1)*, HarperTeen) HarperCollins Pubs.

—The Vampire Diaries: the Return: Shadow Souls. 2011. (Vampire Diaries: the Return Ser.: 2). (ENG.). 624p. (YA). (gr. 8). pap. 11.99 *(978-0-06-172083-3(6)*, HarperTeen) HarperCollins Pubs.

—The Vampire Diaries: the Struggle. 2010. (Vampire Diaries: 2). (ENG.). 304p. (YA). (gr. 8). mass mkt. 8.99 *(978-0-06-199076-2(0)*, HarperCollins) HarperCollins Pubs.

Smith, L. J. & Kevin Williamson & Julie Plec, Kevin Williamson. The Vampire Diaries: Stefan's Diaries #1: Origins No. 5. 2010. (Vampire Diaries: Stefan's Diaries: 1). (ENG.). 256p. (YA). (gr. 9-18). pap. 11.99 *(978-0-06-200393-5(3)*, HarperTeen) HarperCollins Pubs.

—The Vampire Diaries: Stefan's Diaries #5: the Asylum. 2012. (Vampire Diaries: Stefan's Diaries: 5). (ENG.). 256p. (YA). (gr. 9). pap. 11.99 *(978-0-06-211395-5(X)*, HarperTeen) HarperCollins Pubs.

Smith, L. J. & Smith, Tom. The Night of the Solstice. 2008. (ENG.). 244p. (YA). pap. 11.99 *(978-1-4169-8965-3(X)*, Simon & Schuster Bks. For Young Readers) Simon & Schuster Bks. For Young Readers.

Smith, Maggie. My Blue Bunny, Bubbit. Smith, Maggie, illus. 2014. (ENG., Illus.). 40p. (J). (gr. -1-3). 16.99 *(978-0-547-55861-5(9)*, 1453615, Clarion Bks.) HarperCollins Pubs.

Smith-Matheson, Shirlee. The Gambler's Daughter. 2nd ed. 2009. (ENG.). 144p. (YA). pap. 12.99 *(978-1-55002-718-1(2))* Dundurn Pr. CAN. Dist: Publishers Group West (PGW).

Smith, Nikki Shannon. Treasure Hunt. 2019. (Reality Show Ser.). (ENG.). 120p. (YA). (gr. 6-12). pap. 7.99 *(978-1-5415-4545-8(1)*, 86b165aa-f559-440e-812c-5e2c39f1c19f); 26.65 *(978-1-5415-4024-8(7)*, 71b1d250-8fbb-4bba-9b12-abaf5757d2e6) Lerner Publishing Group. (Darby Creek).

Smith, R. L. The Journals of Underwich: Book One. 2007. 253p. pap. 27.95 *(978-1-60441-490-5(1))* America Star Bks.

Smith, Roland. Cryptid Hunters. 2006. (ENG.). 352p. (J). (gr. 5-9). pap. 7.99 *(978-0-7868-5162-1(7))* Little, Brown Bks. for Young Readers.

—Independence Hall. (I, Q Ser.: Bk. 1). (ENG., 312p. (YA). (gr. 6-8). 2009. Illus.). 15.95 *(978-1-58536-468-8(1)*, 202188) 2008. pap. 12.99 *(978-1-58536-325-4(1)*, 202289) Sleeping Bear Pr.

Smith, Sasha Peyton. The Witch Haven. 2022. (ENG., Illus.). 464p. (YA). (gr. 9). pap. 13.99 *(978-1-5344-5439-2(X)*, Simon & Schuster Bks. For Young Readers) Simon & Schuster Bks. For Young Readers.

Smithwick, John W. Drift. 2012. 36p. pap. 13.95 *(978-1-61897-972-8(8)*, Strategic Bk. Publishing) Strategic Book Publishing & Rights Agency (SBPRA).

Smothers, Ethel Footman. Down in the Piney Woods. 2004. 128p. (J). pap. 7.00 *(978-0-8028-5248-9(3))* Eerdmans, William B. Publishing Co.

Snicket, Lemony, pseud. The Austere Academy. Helquist, Brett, illus. 2008. (Series of Unfortunate Events Ser.: Bk. 5). (ENG.). 240p. (J). (gr. 5-18). pap. 6.99 *(978-0-06-114634-3(X)*, Harper Trophy) HarperCollins Pubs.

—The Bad Beginning. 2007. (Ser. of Unfortunate Events Ser.: 1). (J). lib. bdg. 17.20 *(978-1-4177-8840-8(2))* Turtleback.

—The Bad Beginning or, Orphans! 2007. (Series of Unfortunate Events Ser.: 1). (ENG., Illus.). 176p. (J). (gr. 5-9). pap. 7.99 *(978-0-06-114630-5(7)*, HarperCollins) HarperCollins Pubs.

—The Grim Grotto. 2004. (Series of Unfortunate Events Ser.: 11). (ENG., Illus.). 352p. (J). (gr. 5-6). 13.99 *(978-0-06-441014-4(5)*, HarperCollins) HarperCollins Pubs.

—The Loathsome Library, Bks. 1-6. Helquist, Brett, illus. 2005. (Series of Unfortunate Events Ser.: Bks. 1-6). (J). (gr. 5). 65.00 *(978-0-06-083353-4(X))* HarperCollins Pubs.

—The Miserable Mill, 13 vols. Helquist, Brett, illus. 2008. (Series of Unfortunate Events Ser.: Bk. 4). (ENG.). 208p. (J). (gr. 5-18). pap. 6.99 *(978-0-06-114632-9(3)*, Harper Trophy) HarperCollins Pubs.

—A Series of Unfortunate Events #10: the Slippery Slope. Helquist, Brett & Kupperman, Michael, illus. 2003. (Series of Unfortunate Events Ser.: 10). (ENG.). 352p. (J). (gr. 5-6). 13.99 *(978-0-06-441013-7(7)*, HarperCollins) HarperCollins Pubs.

—A Series of Unfortunate Events #2: the Reptile Room. Helquist, Brett & Kupperman, Michael, illus. 2007. (Series of Unfortunate Events Ser.: 2). (ENG.). 192p. (J). (gr. 5-9). pap. 7.99 *(978-0-06-114631-2(5)*, HarperCollins) HarperCollins Pubs.

—A Series of Unfortunate Events Box: the Complete Wreck (Books 1-13), Bks. 1-13. Helquist, Brett, illus. 2006. (Series of Unfortunate Events Ser.: Bks. 1-13). (ENG.). (J). (gr. 5). 180.00 *(978-0-06-111906-4(7)*, HarperCollins) HarperCollins Pubs.

—A Series of Unfortunate Events Box: the Gloom Looms (Books 10-12), Bks. 10-12. Helquist, Brett, illus. 2005. (Series of Unfortunate Events Ser.: Bks. 10-12). (ENG.). (J). (gr. 5). 41.99 *(978-0-06-083909-3(0)*, HarperCollins) HarperCollins Pubs.

—The Slippery Slope. Helquist, Brett, illus. 2003. (Series of Unfortunate Events Ser.: Bk. 10). (YA). (gr. 5-18). 197.82 *(978-0-06-057743-8(6))*; 352p. (J). (gr. 3-6). lib. bdg. 15.89 *(978-0-06-029641-4(0))* HarperCollins Pubs.

—The Trouble Begins. Helquist, Brett, illus. movie tie-in ed. 2004. (Series of Unfortunate Events Ser.: Bks. 1-3). (J). 35.99 *(978-0-06-075773-1(6))* HarperCollins Pubs.

—The Wide Window or, Disappearance! 2007. (Series of Unfortunate Events Ser.: 3). (ENG., Illus.). 208p. (J). (gr. 5). pap. 7.99 *(978-0-06-114633-6(1)*, HarperCollins) HarperCollins Pubs.

Snyder, Laurel. Any Which Wall. Pham, LeUyen, illus. 256p. (J). 2010. (gr. 3-7). pap. 7.99 *(978-0-375-85561-0(0))* 2009. (ENG.). (gr. 6-8). lib. bdg. 21.19 *(978-0-375-95560-0(7))* Random Hse. Children's Bks. (Yearling).

—Charlie & Mouse: Book 1 (Classic Children's Book, Illustrated Books for Children) Hughes, Emily, illus. 2017. (Charlie & Mouse Ser.: 1). (ENG.). 48p. (J). 14.99 *(978-1-4521-3153-5(8))* Chronicle Bks. LLC.

—Charlie & Mouse Outdoors: Book 4 (Classic Children's Book, Beginning Chapter Book, Illustrated Books for Children), Bk. 4. Hughes, Emily, illus. 2020. (Charlie & Mouse Ser.: 4). (ENG.). 48p. (J). (gr. 1-4). 14.99 *(978-1-4521-7066-4(5))* Chronicle Bks. LLC.

Snyder, Rebecca. Two Hearts Are Better Than One. 2012. 174p. pap. 19.99 *(978-1-4797-5225-6(8))* Xlibris Corp.

Snyder, Zilpha Keatley. The Unseen. 2005. 199p. 16.00 *(978-0-7569-5670-7(6))* Perfection Learning Corp.

—William S. & the Great Escape. (ENG.). (J). (gr. 3-7). 2010. 240p. pap. 8.99 *(978-1-4169-6764-4(8))* 2009. 224p. 16.99 *(978-1-4169-6763-7(X))* Simon & Schuster Children's Publishing. (Atheneum Bks. for Young Readers).

—William's Midsummer Dreams. (ENG., (J). (gr. 3-7). 2012. Illus.). 240p. pap. 6.99 *(978-1-4424-1998-8(9))* 2011. 224p. 16.99 *(978-1-4424-1997-1(0))* Simon & Schuster Children's Publishing. (Atheneum Bks. for Young Readers).

Soileau, Hodges, illus. The Black Widow Spider Mystery. 2004. (Boxcar Children Special Ser.). 130p. (gr. 2-7). 15.50 *(978-0-7569-3266-4(1))* Perfection Learning Corp.

—The Comic Book Mystery. 2003. (Boxcar Children Ser.). 106p. (gr. 4-7). 15.00 *(978-0-7569-1611-4(9))* Perfection Learning Corp.

—The Great Shark Mystery. 2003. (Boxcar Children Special Ser.). 130p. (gr. 4-7). 15.50 *(978-0-7569-1616-9(X))* Perfection Learning Corp.

—The Mystery at Skeleton Point. 2003. (Boxcar Children Ser.). 120p. (gr. 4-7). 15.00 *(978-0-7569-1609-1(7))* Perfection Learning Corp.

Solomons, David. My Brother Is a Superhero. 2017. (ENG.). 320p. (J). (gr. 3-7). 9.99 *(978-0-14-751605-3(6)*, Puffin Books) Penguin Young Readers Group.

—My Brother Is a Superhero. 2017. lib. bdg. 18.40 *(978-0-606-39790-2(6))* Turtleback.

Soman, David. Three Bears in a Boat. 2014. (Illus.). 40p. (J). (gr. -1-k). 17.99 *(978-0-8037-3993-2(1)*, Dial Bks) Penguin Young Readers Group.

Sommer, Carl. You Move You Lose. James, Kennon, illus. 2014. (J). pap. *(978-1-57537-972-2(4))* Advance Publishing, Inc.

—You Move You Lose(El Que Se Mueva, Pierde) James, Kennon, illus. 2009. (Another Sommer-Time Story Bilingual Ser.). (SPA & ENG.). 48p. (J). lib. bdg. 16.95 *(978-1-57537-172-6(3))* Advance Publishing, Inc.

Sommers, Jackie Lea. Truest. 2015. (ENG.). 384p. (YA). (gr. 8). 17.99 *(978-0-06-234825-8(6)*, HarperCollins) HarperCollins Pubs.

Somper, Justin. Immortal War. 2013. (Vampirates Ser.: 6). (J). lib. bdg. 22.10 *(978-0-606-26696-3(8))* Turtleback.

—Vampirates: Black Heart. 2010. (Vampirates Ser.: 4). (ENG.). 512p. (J). (gr. 3-7). pap. 22.99 *(978-0-316-02088-6(5))* Little, Brown Bks. for Young Readers.

—Vampirates: Blood Captain. 2009. (Vampirates Ser.: 3). (ENG.). 592p. (J). (gr. 3-7). pap. 26.99 *(978-0-316-02086-2(9))* Little, Brown Bks. for Young Readers.

—Vampirates: Empire of Night. 2011. (Vampirates Ser.: 5). (ENG.). 512p. (J). (gr. 3-7). pap. 22.99 *(978-0-316-03323-7(5))* Little, Brown Bks. for Young Readers.

—Vampirates: Immortal War. 2013. (Vampirates Ser.: 6). (ENG.). 512p. (J). (gr. 3-7). pap. 23.99 *(978-0-316-03325-1(1))* Little, Brown Bks. for Young Readers.

Sonnenblick, Jordan. After Ever After. 2014. (ENG.). 272p. (YA). (gr. 7-7). pap. 10.99 *(978-0-545-72287-2(X))* Scholastic, Inc.

—Falling over Sideways. (ENG.). 272p. (YA). (gr. 7). 2017. pap. 10.99 *(978-0-545-86325-4(2))* 2016. 17.99 *(978-0-545-86324-7(4)*, Scholastic Pr.) Scholastic, Inc.
Soo, Kean. March Grand Prix: the Fast & the Furriest. Soo, Kean, illus. 2015. (March Grand Prix Ser.). (ENG., Illus.). 144p. (J). (gr. 3-6). pap., pap., pap. 14.95 *(978-1-62370-171-0(6)*, 126928, Capstone Young Readers) Capstone.
Soo, Kean, illus. The Great Desert Rally. 2015. (March Grand Prix Ser.). (ENG.). 48p. (J). (gr. 3-6). lib. bdg. 33.32 *(978-1-4342-9641-2(5)*, 126927, Capstone Young Readers) Capstone.
Sosna, Marvin. Brandon's Trail. 2006. 220p. per. 13.95 *(978-1-58939-875-7(0))* Virtualbookworm.com Publishing, Inc.
Spalding, Esta. Knock about with the Fitzgerald-Trouts. Smith, Sydney, illus. 2017. (ENG.). 320p. (J). (gr. 3-7). 16.99 *(978-0-316-29860-5(3))* Little, Brown Bks. for Young Readers.
Sparkes, Ali. Alligator Action, No. 14. Collins, Ross, illus. 2014. (S. W. I. T. C. H. Ser.: 14). (ENG.). 112p. (J). (gr. 2-5). lib. bdg. 27.99 *(978-1-4677-2117-2(4)*, a29ee350-23b8-409b-9c6f-f08687ada878, Darby Creek) Lerner Publishing Group.
—Frozen in Time. 2011. (ENG.). 320p. (J). (gr. 4-6). 22.44 *(978-1-60684-077-1(0))* Farshore GBR. Dist: Children's Plus, Inc.
Spence, Tom. Tough Day at the Plate. 2004. 39p. (J). (gr. -1-7). per. 5.95 *(978-1-59353-241-3(5))* Mountain Valley Publishing, LLC.
Sperring, Mark. Dino-Baby. Lloyd, Sam, illus. 2013. (ENG.). 32p. (J). (gr. -1-1). 14.99 *(978-1-61963-151-9(2)*, 900123359, Bloomsbury USA Childrens) Bloomsbury Publishing USA.
Sperry, John Lamont. Where Is Home? 2006. 136p. pap. 24.95 *(978-1-4241-1008-7(4))* PublishAmerica, Inc.
Spinelli, Eileen. Baby Loves You So Much! Wenzel, David, illus. 2008. (ENG.). 40p. (J). (gr. -1-3). 16.99 *(978-0-8249-5550-2(1)*, Ideals Pubns.) Worthy Publishing.
Spinelli, Jerry. Jake & Lily. 2012. (ENG.). 352p. (J). (gr. 3-7). 16.99 *(978-0-06-028135-9(9)*, Balzer & Bray) HarperCollins Pubs.
—Smiles to Go. 2009. (ENG.). 272p. (J). (gr. 5-8). pap. 7.99 *(978-0-06-447197-8(7)*, HarperCollins) HarperCollins Pubs.
Spires, Sharlene. The Grandsisters. 2010. 56p. pap. 15.99 *(978-1-4535-3004-7(5))* Xlibris Corp.
Spooner, Meagan. Shadowlark. 2013. (Skylark Trilogy Ser.). (ENG.). 336p. (YA). (gr. 7-12). E-Book 27.99 *(978-1-4677-1664-2(2)*, Carolrhoda Lab™) Lerner Publishing Group.
Spratt, R. A. The Adventures of Nanny Piggins. Santat, Dan, illus. 2012. (Nanny Piggins Ser.: 1). (ENG.). 272p. (J). (gr. 3-7). pap. 8.99 *(978-0-316-06818-5(7))* Little, Brown Bks. for Young Readers.
—Nanny Piggins & the Wicked Plan. 2013. (Nanny Piggins Ser.: 2). (ENG.). 320p. (J). (gr. 3-7). pap. 17.99 *(978-0-316-19922-3(2))* Little, Brown Bks. for Young Readers.
Springer, Nancy. The Boy on a Black Horse. 2010. (ENG.). 176p. (YA). (gr. 7). pap. 9.99 *(978-1-4424-1353-5(0)*, Atheneum Bks. for Young Readers) Simon & Schuster Children's Publishing.
—The Case of the Gypsy Good-Bye, 6 vols., 6. 2012. (Enola Holmes Mystery Ser.: 6). (ENG.). 176p. (J). (gr. 6-8). 18.69 *(978-0-399-25236-5(3))* Penguin Young Readers Group.
—Possessing Jessie. 2010. (ENG.). 128p. (YA). (gr. 7-18). pap. 16.95 *(978-0-8234-2259-3(3))* Holiday Hse., Inc.
Springham, James. Earth-n-Bones: Blue Things. 2006. 54p. pap. 16.95 *(978-1-4137-9738-1(5))* America Star Bks.
St John, Patricia. Other Kitten. 2007. (Illus.). 96p. pap. *(978-1-84427-290-7(7))* Scripture Union.
Stanley, Pauline. The Children & the Witches Magic. 2010. (Illus.). 48p. pap. 10.49 *(978-1-4490-9544-4(5))* AuthorHouse.
Stanton, Andy. Danny Mcgee Drinks the Sea. Layton, Neal, illus. 2017. (ENG.). 32p. (J). (gr. -1-3). 17.99 *(978-1-5247-1736-0(3)*, Schwartz & Wade Bks.) Random Hse. Children's Bks.
Starlight, Cyandria. Daydreams of a Little Girl. 2012. 18p. pap. 16.95 *(978-1-4626-6003-2(7))* America Star Bks.
Starrenburg, Hasko. The Queen's Orb. 2012. (Illus.). 144p. pap. 8.00 *(978-1-4349-8782-2(5)*, RoseDog Bks.) Dorrance Publishing Co., Inc.
Stead, Judy, illus. The Twelve Days of Christmas in North Carolina. 2017. (Twelve Days of Christmas in America Ser.). (ENG.). 22p. (J). (-k). bds. 7.95 *(978-1-4549-2285-8(0))* Sterling Publishing Co., Inc.
Steadman, A. F. Skandar & the Phantom Rider. 2023. (Illus.). (J). x, 484p. ***(978-1-6659-1277-8(4))***; (Skandar Ser.: 2). (ENG.). 496p. (gr. 3-7). 18.99 *(978-1-6659-1276-1(6))* Simon & Schuster Bks. For Young Readers. (Simon & Schuster Bks. For Young Readers).
Steele, Giselle. The off-Limits Watermelon Patch. 2006. (Illus.). 35p. (J). per. 12.95 *(978-0-9769949-0-9(9))* RJ Blackstone Ltd.
Steensland, Mark. Behind the Bookcase. Murphy, Kelly, illus. 2013. 288p. (J). (gr. 3-7). 6.99 *(978-0-385-74072-2(7)*, Yearling) Random Hse. Children's Bks.
Steinkraus, Kyla. Pastries with Pocahontas. Wood, Katie, illus. 2017. (Time Hop Sweets Shop Ser.). (ENG.). 32p. (gr. 1-3). 24.22 *(978-1-68342-330-0(5)*, 9781683423300) Rourke Educational Media.
Sternke, Kathy. Sh Sh Sh Let the Baby Sleep. Foster, Jack, illus. 2011. 20p. pap. 10.95 *(978-1-61633-156-6(9))* Guardian Angel Publishing, Inc.
Stenton, Murray, illus. My Brother Is Special: A Sibling with Cerebral Palsy. 2016. (J). pap. *(978-1-61599-309-3(6))* Loving Healing Pr., Inc.
Stephens, John. The Emerald Atlas. 2012. (Books of Beginning Ser.: 1). (ENG.). 464p. (J). (gr. 3-7). 10.99 *(978-0-375-87271-6(X)*, Yearling) Random Hse. Children's Bks.
—The Emerald Atlas. l.t. ed. 2012. (Books of Beginning Ser.). (ENG.). 547p. (J). (gr. 4-7). 23.99 *(978-1-4104-4234-5(9))* Thorndike Pr.
—The Fire Chronicle. 2012. (Illus.). 437p. (J). *(978-0-449-81015-6(1))* Knopf, Alfred A. Inc.
—The Fire Chronicle. 2013. (Books of Beginning Ser.: 2). (ENG., Illus.). 464p. (J). (gr. 3-7). 9.99 *(978-0-375-87272-3(8)*, Yearling) Random Hse. Children's Bks.
Steptoe, John. Baby Says. Steptoe, John, illus. 2018. (ENG., Illus.). 32p. (J). (gr. -1-4). 17.99 *(978-0-688-07423-4(5)*, HarperCollins) HarperCollins Pubs.
Stevenson, James. Peor Que Willy. (SPA., Illus.). (J). (gr. k-2). pap. *(978-84-348-1895-8(7)*, SM2858) SM Ediciones ESP. Dist: Lectorum Pubns., Inc.
Stevenson, Robin. Ben's Robot, 1 vol. Parkins, David, illus. 2010. (Orca Echoes Ser.). (ENG.). 64p. (J). (gr. 1-3). pap. 6.95 *(978-1-55469-153-1(2))* Orca Bk. Pubs. USA.
Stewart, A. W. Rooktime. 2010. 284p. pap. 15.49 *(978-1-4520-1460-9(4))* AuthorHouse.
Stiegemeyer, Julie. Under the Baobab Tree, 1 vol. Lewis, E. B., illus. 2012. (ENG.). 32p. (J). 16.99 *(978-0-310-72561-9(5))* Zonderkidz.
Stine, Fay. Star Ship Fantasy: The New Frontier of Space. 2008. 52p. pap. 10.95 *(978-1-4327-2703-1(6))* Outskirts Pr., Inc.
Stine, R. L. Attack of the Jack (Goosebumps SlappyWorld #2) 2017. (Goosebumps SlappyWorld Ser.: 2). (ENG.). 160p. (J). (gr. 3-7). pap. 7.99 *(978-1-338-06836-8(9)*, Scholastic Paperbacks) Scholastic, Inc.
—Escape from Shudder Mansion (Goosebumps SlappyWorld #5) 2018. (Goosebumps SlappyWorld Ser.: 5). (ENG.). 160p. (J). (gr. 3-7). pap. 6.99 *(978-1-338-22299-9(6)*, Scholastic Paperbacks) Scholastic, Inc.
—The Five Masks of Dr. Screem: Special Edition (Goosebumps Hall of Horrors #3), 1 vol. 2011. (Goosebumps Hall of Horrors Ser.: 3). (ENG.). 192p. (J). (gr. 3-7). pap. 7.99 *(978-0-545-28936-8(X)*, Scholastic Paperbacks) Scholastic, Inc.
—Here Comes the Shaggedy. 2016. (Goosebumps Most Wanted Ser.: 9). (Illus.). 140p. (J). lib. bdg. 17.20 *(978-0-606-38587-9(8))* Turtleback.
—Here Comes the Shaggedy (Goosebumps Most Wanted #9), Vol. 9. 2016. (Goosebumps Most Wanted Ser.: 9). (ENG., Illus.). 160p. (J). (gr. 3-7). pap. 6.99 *(978-0-545-82547-4(4)*, Scholastic Paperbacks) Scholastic, Inc.
—A Night in Terror Tower. 2009. (Goosebumps Ser.: 11). lib. bdg. 17.20 *(978-0-606-00240-0(5))* Turtleback.
—Please Do Not Feed the Weirdo, 4. 2018. (Goosebumps SlappyWorld Ser.). (ENG.). 160p. (J). (gr. 4-7). 22.44 *(978-1-5364-3367-8(5))* Scholastic, Inc.
—Please Do Not Feed the Weirdo. 2018. (Goosebumps SlappyWorld Ser.: 4). 135p. (J). lib. bdg. 18.40 *(978-0-606-41161-5(5))* Turtleback.
—Please Do Not Feed the Weirdo (Goosebumps SlappyWorld #4) 2018. (Goosebumps SlappyWorld Ser.: 4). (ENG.). 160p. (J). (gr. 3-7). pap. 7.99 *(978-1-338-06847-4(4)*, Scholastic Paperbacks) Scholastic, Inc.
—Slappy Birthday to You. 2017. 139p. (J). *(978-1-5182-4487-2(4))* Scholastic, Inc.
Stinson, Kathy. What Happened to Ivy, 1 vol. 2012. (ENG.). 120p. (YA). (gr. 7-10). pap. 11.95 *(978-1-926920-81-8(3))* Second Story Pr. CAN. Dist: Orca Bk. Pubs. USA.
Stohl, Margaret & Peterson, Lewis. Cats vs. Robots #1: This Is War. Peterson, Kay, illus. (ENG.). (J). (gr. 3-7). 2019. 336p. pap. 6.99 *(978-0-06-266571-3(5))* 2018. 320p. 16.99 *(978-0-06-266570-6(7))* HarperCollins Pubs. (Tegen, Katherine Bks).
Stokes, Phil. Phillip & Dickie. 2004. 384p. (YA). 28.95 *(978-0-9744360-0-5(3))* Da Wong Bks.
Stork, Francisco X. Disappeared. 2017. (ENG.). 336p. (YA). (gr. 7-7). 17.99 *(978-0-545-94447-2(3)*, Scholastic Pr.) Scholastic, Inc.
The Strange & Beautiful Sorrows of Ava Lavender. 2014. (ENG.). 320p. (YA). (gr. 9). E-Book 12.99 *(978-0-7636-7034-4(0)*, 28917) Candlewick Pr.
Strasnick, Lauren. Her & Me & You. (ENG.). 208p. (YA). (gr. 9). 2011. pap. 9.99 *(978-1-4169-8267-8(1))* 2010. 16.99 *(978-1-4169-8266-1(3))* Simon Pulse. (Simon Pulse).
Stratton, Allan. Chanda's Wars. 2009. (ENG.). 416p. (J). mass mkt. 7.99 *(978-0-06-155468-566-0(4)*, Harper Trophy) HarperCollins Pubs.
Streib, Sally. Octopus Encounter. 2007. (Illus.). 126p. (J). 6.97 *(978-0-8163-2210-7(4))* Pacific Pr. Publishing Assn.
Stretton, Hesba. Lost Gip. 2003. (Golden Inheritance Ser.: Vol. 7). (Illus.). 121p. (J). *(978-0-921100-93-5(0))* Inheritance Pubns.
Strickland, James R. Lincoln's Lost Papers. 2008. 131p. (J). pap. 11.95 *(978-0-7414-4601-5(4))* Infinity Publishing.
Stroud, Jonathan. Buried Fire. 2004. 332p. (J). pap. *(978-0-7868-5794-9(5))* Hyperion Bks., Inc.
Strungis, Elaine. Sammi & Danny Learn about Jupiter. 2012. 32p. pap. 14.50 *(978-1-4669-5411-3(6))* Trafford Publishing.
—Sammi & Danny Learn about Mercury. 2012. 28p. pap. 13.55 *(978-1-4669-5413-7(2))* Trafford Publishing.
—Sammi & Danny Learn about the Earth. 2012. 32p. pap. 14.50 *(978-1-4669-3731-4(9))* Trafford Publishing.
—Sammi & Danny Learn about Uranus. 2012. 32p. pap. 14.50 *(978-1-4669-6297-2(6))* Trafford Publishing.
—Sammi & Danny Learn about Venus. 2012. 32p. pap. 14.50 *(978-1-4669-3733-8(5))* Trafford Publishing.
Sturges, Philemon. I Love School! Halpern, Shari, illus. 2014. 32p. pap. 7.00 *(978-1-61003-329-9(9))* Center for the Collaborative Classroom.
—I Love School! Halpern, Shari, illus. 32p. (J). (gr. -1-1). 2004. lib. bdg. 14.89 *(978-0-06-009285-6(8))* 2006. (ENG.). reprint ed. pap. 9.99 *(978-0-06-009286-3(6)*, HarperCollins) HarperCollins Pubs.
Sturgill, Jean A. Bouncing Beaver Discovers God: A Drew's Animals Book. 2007. (ENG.). 30p. pap. 15.99 *(978-1-4196-7822-6(1))* CreateSpace Independent Publishing Platform.
Sullivan, Kathryn. Talking to Trees. 2017. (J). pap. *(978-1-61271-356-4(4))* Zumaya Pubns. LLC.
Sullivan, Laura L. Under the Green Hill, 1. 2010. (Green Hill Novels Ser.). (ENG.). 320p. (J). (gr. 4-6). 22.44 *(978-0-8050-8984-4(5)*, 9780805089844, Holt, Henry & Co.) Holt, Henry & Co.
—Under the Green Hill. 2011. (ENG.). 336p. (J). (gr. 4-8). pap. 17.99 *(978-0-312-55149-0(5)*, 900074427) Square Fish.
Sullivan-Ringe, Laurie. Noise in the Night. Matiuzzo, Nick, illus. 2008. 37p. pap. 24.95 *(978-1-60672-476-7(2))* America Star Bks.
Summers, Sherri Pankratz. Humpty Dumpty, Back Together Again? Pankratz, Justin, illus. 2003. 32p. (J). 8.95 *(978-0-9742637-1-7(0))* Pankratz Creations.
Surget, Alain. Escape from Veracruz. 2015. (Jolly Roger Ser.). (Illus.). 96p. (gr. 3-6). 28.50 *(978-1-909645-44-8(3))* Book Hse. GBR. Dist: Black Rabbit Bks.
—The Plumed Serpent's Gold. 2015. (Jolly Roger Ser.). (Illus.). 96p. (gr. 3-6). 28.50 *(978-1-909645-43-1(5))* Book Hse. GBR. Dist: Black Rabbit Bks.
—Shark Island. 2015. (Jolly Roger Ser.). (Illus.). 96p. (gr. 3-6). 28.50 *(978-1-909645-42-4(7))* Book Hse. GBR. Dist: Black Rabbit Bks.
Susie's Sister Has Food Allergy. 2004. (J). 5.00 *(978-1-882541-36-2(7))* Food Allergy & Anaphylaxis Network.
Sutton, Michelle. It's Not about Me. 2012. (Second Glances Ser.). (ENG.). 252p. pap. 12.99 *(978-0-9838836-9-2(6))* Sword of the Spirit Publishing.
Suzuma, Tabitha. Forbidden. (ENG.). 464p. (YA). (gr. 11). 2012. pap. 13.99 *(978-1-4424-1996-4(2))* 2011. 19.99 *(978-1-4424-1995-7(4))* Simon Pulse. (Simon Pulse).
Swanson, Matthew. The Real Mccoys. Behr, Robbi, illus. 2018. (Real Mccoys Ser.: 1). (ENG.). 352p. (J). pap. 7.99 *(978-1-250-09853-5(X)*, 900161849) Square Fish.
—The Real Mccoys: Wonder Undercover. Behr, Robbi, illus. 2019. (Real Mccoys Ser.: 3). (ENG.). 352p. (J). 16.99 *(978-1-250-30782-8(1)*, 900198140) Imprint IND. Dist: Macmillan.
Swanson Sateren, Shelley. Cool Crosby. Melmon, Deborah, illus. 2016. (Adventures at Hound Hotel Ser.). (ENG.). 72p. (J). (gr. 1-3). lib. bdg. 25.32 *(978-1-5158-0066-8(0)*, 131911, Picture Window Bks.) Capstone.
—Mighty Murphy. Melmon, Deborah, illus. 2016. (Adventures at Hound Hotel Ser.). (ENG.). 72p. (J). (gr. 1-3). lib. bdg. 25.32 *(978-1-5158-0067-5(9)*, 131916, Picture Window Bks.) Capstone.
—Stinky Stanley. Melmon, Deborah, illus. 2016. (Adventures at Hound Hotel Ser.). (ENG.). 72p. (J). (gr. 1-3). lib. bdg. 25.32 *(978-1-5158-0221-1(3)*, 132456, Picture Window Bks.) Capstone.
Swenson, Lynn. Rollie & Mollie: Disappearing Act. Baker, David, illus. 2012. 26p. 24.95 *(978-1-4626-5277-8(8))* America Star Bks.
Switcharound. 2018. (Just the Tates! Ser.). (ENG.). 160p. (J). (gr. 5-7). pap. 9.99 *(978-1-328-75087-7(6)*, 1678434, Clarion Bks.) HarperCollins Pubs.
Sybesma, Lila Jeanne Elliot. Yours: The Civil War, a Love Triangle, & the Steamboat Sultana. 2019. (Illus.). xiii, 307p. (YA). pap. *(978-0-87195-431-2(1))* Indiana Historical Society.
Taddonio, Lea. Book 3: First Fight. Price, Mina, illus. 2016. (Head over Heels Ser.). (ENG.). 48p. (J). (gr. 3-7). lib. bdg. 34.21 *(978-1-62402-194-7(8)*, 24567, Spellbound) Magic Wagon.
Tagert-Paul, Kimberley. God's Ten Promises: Helping Children Understand the Ten Commandments. 2010. (J). 12.99 *(978-0-8163-2379-1(8))* Pacific Pr. Publishing Assn.
Tahir, Sabaa. A Torch Against the Night. l.t. ed. 2016. (Ember in the Ashes Ser.: 2). (ENG.). (YA). (gr. 9-12). 22.99 *(978-1-4104-8925-8(6))* Cengage Gale.
—A Torch Against the Night. (Ember in the Ashes Ser.: 2). (ENG.). (YA). (gr. 9). 2017. 496p. pap. 12.99 *(978-1-101-99888-5(1))* 2016. (Illus.). 464p. 19.95 *(978-1-101-99887-8(3))* Penguin Young Readers Group. (Razorbill).
—A Torch Against the Night. 2017. (Ember in the Ashes Ser.: 2). lib. bdg. 23.30 *(978-0-606-40085-5(0))* Turtleback.
Taitano, Janice G. The Legend of Lutung. 2006. 260p. pap. 29.00 *(978-1-59752-482-7(4)*, Resource Pubns.(OR)) Wipf & Stock Pubs.
Talarico Msn, Karen M. My Hands. 2008. 36p. pap. 15.75 *(978-1-4389-3521-8(8))* AuthorHouse.
Tanaka, Shelley. Nobody Knows, 1 vol. 2012. (ENG., Illus.). 144p. (J). (gr. 4-5). 16.95 *(978-1-55498-140-3(9))* Groundwood Bks. CAN. Dist: Publishers Group West (PGW).
Tanguay, Dave. The Legacy of Mr. Banjo! Vaughns, Byron, illus. 2015. (Billy Batson & the Magic of Shazam! Ser.). (ENG.). 32p. (J). (gr. 3-6). lib. bdg. 22.60 *(978-1-4342-9746-4(2)*, 127078, Stone Arch Bks.) Capstone.
Tapia, Jeff. Hippomobile! 2013. (ENG., Illus.). 240p. (J). (gr. 5-7). 16.99 *(978-0-547-99548-9(2)*, 1525383, Clarion Bks.) HarperCollins Pubs.
Taylor, Bonnie Highsmith. Simon Can't Say Hippopotamus. Hornung, Phyllis, tr. Hornung, Phyllis, illus. 2003. 24p. (J). 14.95 *(978-1-59336-017-7(7))*; pap. *(978-1-59336-018-4(5))* Mondo Publishing.
Taylor, C. Brian. Atop the Tree Top: A Christmas Story. Butler, Sharon, illus. 2003. (J). 15.95 *(978-0-9747054-0-8(3))* Rilly Silly Bk. Co., The.
Taylor, Theodore & Taylor, Theodore. Ice Drift. 2006. (ENG., Illus.). 240p. (J). (gr. 3-7). pap. 7.99 *(978-0-15-205550-9(9)*, 1196692, Clarion Bks.) HarperCollins Pubs.
Taylor, Thomas. The Pets You Get. Reynolds, Adrian, illus. 2013. (ENG.). 32p. (J). (gr. -1-3). 16.95 *(978-1-4677-1143-2(8)*, 6b92e368-27d7-4535-bc74-f4d91d824681) Lerner Publishing Group.
Taylor, Vincent. Cornbread Has a Bad Habit. 2007. (Illus.). 96p. (J). pap. 4.99 *(978-0-9704512-5-5(3))* TriEclipse, Inc.
Teele, Elinor. The Mechanical Mind of John Coggin. 2016. (ENG., Illus.). 352p. (J). (gr. 3-7). 16.99 *(978-0-06-234510-3(9)*, Waldon Pond Pr.) HarperCollins Pubs.
Teitelbaum, Michael. The Ghost at the Grand Inn. 2015. (Cold Whispers Ser.). (ENG., Illus.). 32p. (J). (gr. 2-6). lib. bdg. 28.50 *(978-1-62724-808-2(0))* Bearport Publishing Co., Inc.
Telgemeier, Raina. Drama: a Graphic Novel. Telgemeier, Raina, illus. 2012. (ENG., Illus.). 240p. (J). (gr. 5-9). pap. 10.99 *(978-0-545-32699-5(0)*, Graphix) Scholastic, Inc.
—Drama: a Graphic Novel. Telgemeier, Raina, illus. 2012. (ENG., Illus.). 240p. (J). (gr. 5-9). 24.99 *(978-0-545-32698-8(2)*, Graphix) Scholastic, Inc.
Tellier, Derek. Anderson's Heat. 2016. (What's Your Dream? Ser.). (ENG., Illus.). 96p. (J). (gr. 4-6). lib. bdg. 25.99 *(978-1-4965-3441-5(7)*, 132559, Stone Arch Bks.) Capstone.
Terrell, Brandon. Phantom of the Library. Epelbaum, Mariano, illus. 2017. (Snoops, Inc Ser.). (ENG.). 112p. (J). (gr. 4-8). lib. bdg. 27.32 *(978-1-4965-5060-6(9)*, 135986, Stone Arch Bks.) Capstone.
—Science Fair Sabotage. Epelbaum, Mariano, illus. 2017. (Snoops, Inc Ser.). (ENG.). 112p. (J). (gr. 4-8). lib. bdg. 27.32 *(978-1-4965-4347-9(5)*, 134264, Stone Arch Bks.) Capstone.
—The Vanishing Treasure. Epelbaum, Mariano, illus. 2017. (Snoops, Inc Ser.). (ENG.). 112p. (J). (gr. 4-8). lib. bdg. 27.32 *(978-1-4965-4345-5(9)*, 134262, Stone Arch Bks.) Capstone.
Terry, Teri. Contagion. 2019. (Dark Matter Trilogy Ser.). (ENG.). 416p. (YA). (gr. 7). lib. bdg. 18.99 *(978-1-58089-989-5(7)*, Charlesbridge Teen) Charlesbridge Publishing, Inc.
—Deception. 2019. (Dark Matter Trilogy Ser.). (ENG., Illus.). 368p. (YA). (gr. 7). lib. bdg. 18.99 *(978-1-62354-106-4(9)*, Charlesbridge Teen) Charlesbridge Publishing, Inc.
Tesh, Jane & Klein-Higger, Joni. Land of Lost Socks: A Children's Musical. 2013. 24p. pap. 7.95 *(978-1-61633-397-3(9))* Guardian Angel Publishing, Inc.
Testa, Maggie. Olivia & Her Alien Brother. 2014. (Olivia 8x8 Ser.). lib. bdg. 13.55 *(978-0-606-35199-7(X))* Turtleback.
Tetzlaff, Wendy Jo. A Girl Named Frannie. 2008. 28p. pap. 24.95 *(978-1-60703-055-3(1))* America Star Bks.
Tharp, Barbara, et al. Tillena Lou's Day in the Sun. Denk, James, ed. Lewis, T., illus. 2nd ed. 2013. (My World & Me Ser.). (ENG.). 32p. (J). (gr. k-2). pap. *(978-1-888997-44-6(3)*, BioEd) Baylor College of Medicine.
Tharp, Tim. Badd. 2012. (ENG.). 320p. (YA). (gr. 9). pap. 9.99 *(978-0-375-86401-8(6)*, Ember) Random Hse. Children's Bks.
The Duda Family. The Adventures of Newo: Newo & Emma Visit Their Furry Friends. 2008. 28p. pap. 12.49 *(978-1-4343-9766-9(1))* AuthorHouse.
Theriault, Francis. Just Another Ghost Story: A critical thinking Novel. 2007. 68p. (J). per. 8.95 *(978-0-595-45258-3(2))* iUniverse, Inc.
Theule, Larissa. Born to Ride: A Story about Bicycle Face. Garrity-Riley, Kelsey, illus. 2019. (ENG.). 32p. (J). (gr. -1-3). 18.99 *(978-1-4197-3412-0(1)*, 1207001, Abrams Bks. for Young Readers) Abrams, Inc.
Thiel, Annie. Chloe's New Baby Brother. Marjoribanks, Karen & Edwards, William M., illus. 2006. (Playdate Kids Ser.). 32p. (J). (gr. -1-3). 14.95 *(978-1-933721-01-9(4))* Playdate Kids Publishing.
Thiel Annie. The Playdate Kids Chloe's New Baby Brother 2ED 2007. 2007. 32p. 12.95 *(978-1-933721-28-6(6))*; pap. 6.95 *(978-1-933721-24-8(3))* Playdate Kids Publishing.
Thomas, Charlie. I Need Glasses. Goldfinger, Jennifer P., illus. 2005. (Rookie Readers Ser.). (ENG.). 32p. (J). (gr. k-2). lib. bdg. 19.50 *(978-0-516-24863-9(4)*, Children's Pr.) Scholastic Library Publishing.
Thomas, Dee. Silly, Silly, Eggleton Egg: Meet the Egg's of Eggville. 2012. 28p. pap. 21.99 *(978-1-4771-5325-3(X))* Xlibris Corp.
Thomas, M. J. The Secret of the Hidden Scrolls: the Shepherd's Stone, Book 5. 2018. (Secret of the Hidden Scrolls Ser.: 5). (ENG., Illus.). 128p. (J). (gr. 1-4). pap. 6.99 *(978-0-8249-5691-2(5)*, Worthy Kids/Ideals) Worthy Publishing.
Thompson, Aiyana M. Miranda Fishhook: Makes a New Friend. 2010. 24p. 16.00 *(978-1-4520-2364-9(6))* AuthorHouse.
Thompson, Lauren. Mouse Loves Fall: Ready-To-Read Pre-Level 1. Erdogan, Buket, illus. 2018. (Mouse Ser.). (ENG.). 32p. (J). (gr. -1-k). 17.99 *(978-1-5344-2147-9(5))*; pap. 4.99 *(978-1-5344-2146-2(7))* Simon Spotlight. (Simon Spotlight).
—Mouse Loves Love: Ready-To-Read Pre-Level 1. Erdogan, Buket, illus. 2018. (Mouse Ser.). (ENG.). 32p. (J). (gr. -1-k). 17.99 *(978-1-5344-2150-9(5))*; pap. 4.99 *(978-1-5344-2149-3(1))* Simon Spotlight. (Simon Spotlight).
—Mouse Loves Summer: Ready-To-Read Pre-Level 1. Erdogan, Buket, illus. 2018. (Mouse Ser.). (ENG.). 32p. (J). (gr. -1-k). 17.99 *(978-1-5344-2057-1(6))*; pap. 4.99 *(978-1-5344-2056-4(8))* Simon Spotlight. (Simon Spotlight).
Thompson, Laurie. Be Gentle with Baby, 1 vol. 2010. 24p. 24.95 *(978-1-4489-3910-7(0))* PublishAmerica, Inc.
Thompson, Roger E., II. A Sister's Love: A Novel. 2007. 80p. per. 8.95 *(978-0-595-44549-3(7))* iUniverse, Inc.
Tiger Tales Staff, ed. & compiled by. Stories for Boys. Tiger Tales Staff, compiled by. 2015. (ENG.). 176p. (J). (gr. -1-3). 12.99 *(978-1-58925-535-7(6))* Tiger Tales.
Tilford, Michael. Reemie the Preemie. 2005. 22p. 8.72 *(978-1-4116-1394-2(5))* Lulu Pr., Inc.
To Be Perfectly Honest: A Novel Based on an Untrue Story. 2014. (ENG., Illus.). 496p. (YA). (gr. 7). pap. 11.99 *(978-0-689-87605-9(X)*, Simon & Schuster Bks. For Young Readers) Simon & Schuster Bks. For Young Readers.
Tobin, Richard K. Skating on Thick Ice. LeBlanc, Rebecca, ed. Chapman, Jesse, illus. 2013. 122p. (J). pap. 12.00 *(978-1-929882-96-0(3))* Biographical Publishing Co.
Tobin, Sophia. The Vanishing. 2018. (ENG.). 400p. pap. 16.99 *(978-1-4711-5162-0(X))* Simon & Schuster, Ltd. GBR. Dist: Simon & Schuster, Inc.
Todd, Anne. Teddy Powers: The Stone Keepers. 2012. 394p. pap. 13.99 *(978-1-938993-00-8(4))* Keogh, Anne.
Tolonen, Tuutikki. Monster Nanny. Silver, Annira, tr. Pitkanen, Pasi, illus. 2017. (ENG.). 304p. (J). (gr. 3-7). 16.99 *(978-0-544-94354-4(6)*, 1659015, Clarion Bks.) HarperCollins Pubs.
Tomasi-Dubois, Mary. Danger in the Jeweled City: A Matt & Heather Thriller. 2007. 188p. (YA). per. 15.95 *(978-0-9798633-5-6(X))* Robertson Publishing.
Toon Books, 6 vols., Set. 2013. (Toon Bks.: 10). (ENG.). 36p. (J). (gr. k-3). lib. bdg. 196.74 *(978-1-61479-147-8(3)*, 14839) Spotlight.
Treasure Quest Guide. 2004. pap. 5.99 *(978-1-56309-913-7(6))* Woman's Missionary Union.
Treyes, Jill. Brooke & Brandon Welcome Brandon. 2010. 28p. pap. 12.99 *(978-1-4389-1939-3(5))* AuthorHouse.

S

Triffo, Kahini H. Relentless Tears. 2011. 108p. (gr. 10-12). pap. 11.92 *(978-1-4269-6288-2(6))* Trafford Publishing.

Trillo, Carlos. Bird. Bobillo, Juan, illus. 2003. 48p. (YA). (gr. 11-18). 12.95 *(978-1-931724-22-7(9))* Diamond Select Toys & Collectibles.

Trimble, Tonya. Curiosity, with a Capital S. Enik, Ted, illus. 2011. 144p. (J). pap. 9.95 *(978-0-9816453-9-1(9))*; 16.95 *(978-0-9829421-5-4(X))* Tell Me Pr., LLC.

Trottier, Maxine. Three Songs for Courage. 2008. (ENG.). 328p. (YA). (gr. 9). pap. 10.95 *(978-0-88776-831-6(8)*, Tundra Bks.) Tundra Bks. CAN. Dist: Penguin Random Hse. LLC.

Troupe, Thomas Kingsley. Flight Down. 2016. (Tartan House Ser.). (ENG.). 96p. (J). (gr. 3-6). *(978-1-63235-161-6(7)*, 11892, 12-Story Library) Bookstaves, LLC.

Trueit, Trudi. Mom, There's a Dinosaur in Beeson's Lake. 2. Paillot, Jim, illus. 2010. (Secrets of a Lab Rat Ser.). (ENG.). 160p. (J). (gr. 3-7). 14.99 *(978-1-4169-7593-9(4))* Simon & Schuster, Inc.

—No Girls Allowed (Dogs Okay) Paillot, Jim, illus. 2010. (Secrets of a Lab Rat Ser.). (ENG.). 144p. (J). (gr. 3-7). pap. 5.99 *(978-1-4169-6111-6(9)*, Aladdin) Simon & Schuster Children's Publishing.

—No Girls Allowed (Dogs Okay) Paillot, Jim, illus. 2009. (Secrets of a Lab Rat Ser.). (ENG.). 128p. (J). (gr. 3-7). 14.99 *(978-1-4169-7592-2(6)*, Simon & Schuster/Paula Wiseman Bks.) Simon & Schuster/Paula Wiseman Bks.

Tuck, Justin. Home-Field Advantage. Rodriguez, Leonardo, illus. 2011. (ENG.). 40p. (J). (gr. -1-3). 16.99 *(978-1-4424-0369-7(1)*, Simon & Schuster Bks. For Young Readers) Simon & Schuster Bks. For Young Readers.

Turnbull, Elizabeth J. Janjak & Freda Go to the Iron Market. Turnbull, Wally R., tr. Jones, Mark, illus. 2013. 36p. pap. 12.95 *(978-1-61153-062-9(8))* Light Messages Publishing.

Tutor, Margaret. A Make-Do Christmas, 1 vol. 2009. 74p. pap. 19.95 *(978-1-4489-0849-3(3))* America Star Bks.

Two Lies & a Spy. 2014. (ENG., Illus.). 272p. (YA). (gr. 9). pap. 12.99 *(978-1-4424-8173-2(0)*, Simon & Schuster Bks. For Young Readers) Simon & Schuster Bks. For Young Readers.

Tyrrell, Melissa. Hansel & Gretel. McMullen, Nigel, illus. 2005. (Fairytale Friends Ser.). 12p. (J). bds. 5.95 *(978-1-58117-152-5(8)*, Intervisual/Piggy Toes) Bendon, Inc.

Uhlberg, Myron. Me & Mr. Mcgee. Sosa, Daniela, illus. 2020. (ENG.). 32p. (J). (gr. -1-3). 16.99 *(978-0-8075-5028-1(0)*, 807550280) Whitman, Albert & Co.

Umansky, Kaye. Clover Twig & the Perilous Path. Wright, Johanna, illus. 2013. (ENG.). 272p. (J). (gr. 3-7). pap. 15.99 *(978-1-250-02727-6(6)*, 900098299) Square Fish.

—Sophie in Charge. Currey, Anna, illus. 2005. 30p. (J). 9.95 *(978-1-56148-478-2(4)*, Good Bks.) Skyhorse Publishing Co., Inc.

Underwood, Deborah. Super Saurus & the Egg. Young, Ned, illus. 2018. (Super Saurus Ser.: 1). (ENG.). 40p. (J). (gr. -1-k). 16.99 *(978-1-4231-7569-8(7))* Little, Brown Bks. for Young Readers.

Underwood, Kim. The Wonderful World of Sparkle Girl & Doobins. Goldman, Garnet, illus. 2009. 48p. (J). pap. 16.95 *(978-0-89587-373-6(7)*, Blair) Carolina Wren Pr.

Ungerer, Tomi. Fog Island IBook. 2013. (ENG.). 48p. 5.99 *(978-0-7148-6777-9(2))* Phaidon Pr., Inc.

Urban, Linda. Mabel & Sam at Home: (Imagination Books for Kids, Children's Books about Creative Play) Hooper, Hadley, illus. 2018. (ENG.). 60p. (J). (gr. k-3). 17.99 *(978-1-4521-3996-8(2))* Chronicle Bks. LLC.

Vaid, Raj. The Case of the Holi Chocolate: The Super Sleuth - Mystery #1. 2011. 56p. pap. 9.99 *(978-1-4520-6903-6(4))* AuthorHouse.

Valente, Catherynne M. The Glass Town Game. Green, Rebecca, illus. (ENG.). (J). (gr. 5). 2018. 560p. pap. 9.99 *(978-1-4814-7697-3(1))* 2017. 544p. 17.99 *(978-1-4814-7696-6(3))* McElderry, Margaret K. Bks. (McElderry, Margaret K. Bks.).

—Glass Town Game. 2017. (ENG.). (J). (gr. 5). pap. 12.99 *(978-1-5344-1771-7(0))* Simon & Schuster.

Valente, Shannon. Trucks, Trains & Worm Brains. 2009. 16p. pap. 10.79 *(978-1-4389-5411-0(5))* AuthorHouse.

Van Allsburg, Chris. Probuditi! 2009. 30p. (J). 19.00 *(978-1-4379-6940-5(2))* DIANE Publishing Co.

—Probuditi! Van Allsburg, Chris, illus. 2006. (ENG., Illus.). 32p. (J). (gr. 1-4). 18.95 *(978-0-618-75502-8(0)*, 579489, Clarion Bks.) HarperCollins Pubs.

van Dam, Katrin. Come November. (ENG.). 384p. (YA). (gr. 7-7). 2020. pap. 10.99 *(978-1-338-26843-0(0))* 2018. 18.99 *(978-1-338-26842-3(2)*, Scholastic Pr.) Scholastic, Inc.

Van Dyne, Edith. Aunt Jane's Nieces at Millville. 2004. reprint ed. pap. 21.95 *(978-1-4191-0623-5(9))*; pap. 1.99 *(978-1-4192-0623-2(3))* Kessinger Publishing, LLC.

—Aunt Jane's Nieces in Society. 2004. reprint ed. pap. 20.95 *(978-1-4191-0824-2(7))*; pap. 1.99 *(978-1-4192-0824-9(1))* Kessinger Publishing, LLC.

—Aunt Jane's Nieces on Vacation. 2004. reprint ed. pap. 1.99 *(978-1-4192-0825-6(X))*; pap. 21.95 *(978-1-4191-0825-9(5))* Kessinger Publishing, LLC.

—Aunt Jane's Nieces Out West. 2004. reprint ed. pap. 21.95 *(978-1-4191-0826-6(3))*; pap. 1.99 *(978-1-4192-0826-3(8))* Kessinger Publishing, LLC.

Van Leeuwen, Jean. Cabin on Trouble Creek. 2008. (ENG.). 224p. (J). (gr. 3-7). 7.99 *(978-0-14-241164-3(7)*, Puffin Books) Penguin Young Readers Group.

Van, Muon Thi. Clever Little Witch. Yum, Hyewon, illus. 2019. (ENG.). 40p. (J). (gr. -1-1). 17.99 *(978-1-4814-8171-7(1))*; E-Book *(978-1-4814-8172-4(X))* McElderry, Margaret K. Bks. (McElderry, Margaret K. Bks.).

Van Stockum, Hilda. A Day on Skates: The Story of a Dutch Picnic. Van Stockum, Hilda, illus. 2007. (Illus.). 40p. (J). (gr. 1). 19.95 *(978-1-932350-18-0(7))* Bethlehem Bks.

Van Wright, Cornelius & Hu, Ying-Hwa, illus. I Told You I Can Play! 2006. (ENM.). 32p. (J). 16.95 *(978-1-933491-06-6(X))* Just Us Bks., Inc.

VanArsdale, Anthony, illus. The Shackleton Sabotage. 2017. (Boxcar Children Great Adventure Ser.: 4). (ENG.). 160p. (J). (gr. 2-5). 6.99 *(978-0-8075-0688-2(5)*, 807506885); 12.99 *(978-0-8075-0687-5(7)*, 807506877) Random Hse. Children's Bks. (Random Hse. Bks. for Young Readers).

Vande Velde, Vivian. There's a Dead Person Following My Sister Around. 2008. (ENG., Illus.). 160p. (J). (gr. 5-7). pap. 11.95 *(978-0-15-206467-9(2)*, 1199316, Clarion Bks.) HarperCollins Pubs.

Varlow, Scarlet. Blood & Cookies. Cotroneo, Marilisa, illus. 2019. (Creature Feature Ser.). (ENG.). 112p. (J). (gr. 2-5). lib. bdg. 38.50 *(978-1-5321-3496-8(7)*, 31911, Calico Chapter Bks.) ABDO Publishing Co.

Veissid, Jacqueline. Ruby's Sword. Zakimi, Paola, illus. 2019. (ENG.). 40p. (J). (gr. -1-k). 16.99 *(978-1-4521-6391-8(X))* Chronicle Bks. LLC.

Venable, Alan. The Man in the Iron Mask. 2007. (Classic Adventures Ser.). pap. 9.95 *(978-1-4105-0860-7(9))* Building Wings LLC.

—Take Me with You When You Go. Marshall, Laurie, illus. 2008. 112p. (J). 12.95 *(978-0-9777082-7-7(6))* One Monkey Bks.

Venkatraman, Padma. Climbing the Stairs. 2010. (ENG., Illus.). 254p. (YA). (gr. 7-18). 10.99 *(978-0-14-241490-3(5)*, Speak) Penguin Young Readers Group.

Ventrella, Kim. Skeleton Tree. (ENG.). 240p. (J). (gr. 3-7). 2018. pap. 7.99 *(978-1-338-04271-9(8))* 2017. 16.99 *(978-1-338-04270-2(X)*, Scholastic Pr.) Scholastic, Inc.

Ventrillo, James & Ventrillo, Nick. Rick & Bobo: Two Brothers. One a Genius. One Not, 4 vols. Kunardi, Marco, illus. 2009. 332p. (YA). pap. 13.95 *(978-0-615-28865-9(0))* Vanir Bks.

Verstraete, Majanka. The Doll Maker: Weirdville. I.t. ed. 2013. (ENG.). 86p. (gr. 2-6). pap. 9.95 *(978-1-62253-065-6(9))* Evolved Publishing.

Vilcoq, Marianne. Espero un Hermanito. (SPA.). 24p. (J). *(978-84-8470-013-5(5))* Corimbo, Editorial S.L. ESP. Dist: Lectorum Pubns., Inc.

Viorst, Judith. I'll Fix Anthony. Lobel, Arnold, illus. 2020. (ENG.). 32p. (J). (gr. -1-3). 17.99 *(978-1-5344-0481-6(3)*, Atheneum Bks. for Young Readers) Simon & Schuster Children's Publishing.

Vivat, Booki. Frazzled #3: Minor Incidents & Absolute Uncertainties. Vivat, Booki, illus. 2019. (ENG., Illus.). 224p. (J). (gr. 3-7). 13.99 *(978-0-06-239883-3(0)*, HarperCollins) HarperCollins Pubs.

Voigt, Cynthia. Dicey's Song. 2012. (Tillerman Cycle Ser.: 2). (ENG., Illus.). 256p. (YA). (gr. 7). 19.99 *(978-1-4424-5060-8(6))*; pap. 12.99 *(978-1-4424-2879-9(1))* Simon & Schuster Children's Publishing. (Atheneum Bks. for Young Readers).

—Dicey's Song. 2012. (Tillerman Ser.: 2). lib. bdg. 20.85 *(978-0-606-25260-7(6))* Turtleback.

—The Tale of Elske. 2015. (Tales of the Kingdom Ser.: 4). (ENG., Illus.). 368p. (YA). (gr. 7). 19.99 *(978-1-4814-2189-8(1)*, Atheneum Bks. for Young Readers) Simon & Schuster Children's Publishing.

Vrettos, Adrienne Maria. Skin. (ENG.). (YA). (gr. 7-12). 2007. 272p. pap. 12.99 *(978-1-4169-0656-8(8))* 2006. (Illus.). 240p. 16.95 *(978-1-4169-0655-1(X))* McElderry, Margaret K. Bks. (McElderry, Margaret K. Bks.).

W. Parents Are Lucky: They Don't Have to Do Chores. 2010. 24p. pap. 12.49 *(978-1-4520-7671-3(5))* AuthorHouse.

Wagner, Lori. Gateway of the Sun. 2007. 120p. pap. 9.95 *(978-0-9798627-2-4(8))* Affirming Faith.

Wait, Lea. Stopping to Home. 2003. (ENG.). 160p. (J). (gr. 3-7). pap. 8.99 *(978-0-689-83849-1(2)*, Simon & Schuster/Paula Wiseman Bks.) Simon & Schuster/Paula Wiseman Bks.

—Wintering Well. 2006. (ENG., Illus.). 192p. (J). (gr. 3-7). pap. 8.99 *(978-0-689-85647-1(4)*, McElderry, Margaret K. Bks.) McElderry, Margaret K. Bks.

Waldman, Neil. Al & Teddy. 2013. 48p. 17.95 *(978-0-615-72969-5(X))* Dream Yard Pr.

Walker, Courtney King. Chasing Midnight. 2016. 250p. (YA). pap. 16.99 *(978-1-4621-1763-5(5))* Cedar Fort, Inc./CFI Distribution.

Walker-Cox, Krysten. Amber's Metal Singlet. 2009. 48p. pap. 12.13 *(978-1-60860-316-9(4)*, Eloquent Bks.) Strategic Book Publishing & Rights Agency (SBPRA).

Walker-Renner, Christa. Santa's Magic. 2009. 20p. pap. 11.00 *(978-1-4389-8206-9(2))* AuthorHouse.

Walker, Sharon. Little Rose Grows. 2013. 24p. pap. 15.99 *(978-1-4797-6813-4(8))* Xlibris Corp.

Walker, Susan Eileen. Not Enough Time, 1 vol. 2010. 52p. pap. 16.95 *(978-1-4489-6196-6(X))* America Star Bks.

Wallace, Barbara Brooks. Secret in St. Something. 2003. (ENG., Illus.). 160p. (J). (gr. 3-7). pap. 9.95 *(978-0-689-85601-3(6)*, Aladdin) Simon & Schuster Children's Publishing.

Wallace, Bill. Snot Stew. McCue, Lisa, illus. 2nd ed. 2008. (ENG.). 96p. (J). (gr. 3-7). pap. 6.99 *(978-1-4169-5804-8(5)*, Aladdin) Simon & Schuster Children's Publishing.

Wallace, Karen. Wendy. 2005. 307p. (gr. 7-12). 17.00 *(978-0-7569-5658-5(7))* Perfection Learning Corp.

Wallace, Nancy Elizabeth. The Valentine Express, 0 vols. 2012. (ENG., Illus.). 32p. (J). (gr. -1-2). pap. 9.99 *(978-0-7614-5447-2(0)*, 9780761454472, Two Lions) Amazon Publishing.

Wallach, Tommy. Slow Burn. 2018. (Anchor & Sophia Ser.: 2). (ENG., Illus.). 416p. (YA). (gr. 9). 18.99 *(978-1-4814-6841-1(3)*, Simon & Schuster Bks. For Young Readers) Simon & Schuster Bks. For Young Readers.

Wallingford, Stephanie & Ryndens, Dawn. A Day at the Lake. Villnave, Erica Pelton, illus. 2013. (ENG.). 32p. (-k). pap. 10.95 *(978-1-938063-03-9(1)*, Mighty Media Kids) Mighty Media Pr.

Walls, Robert D. Tiny's Second-Grade Field Trip. 2010. 40p. 19.99 *(978-1-4490-9011-1(7))* AuthorHouse.

Walters, Eric. Walking Home. 2014. (ENG.). 304p. (J). (gr. 5). pap. 10.99 *(978-0-385-68157-5(7))* Doubleday Canada, Ltd. CAN. Dist: Penguin Random Hse. LLC.

Walton, Leslye. The Strange & Beautiful Sorrows of Ava Lavender. (ENG.). 320p. (YA). (gr. 9). 2015. pap. 12.99 *(978-0-7636-8027-5(3))* 2014. 17.99 *(978-0-7636-6566-1(5))* Candlewick Pr.

—The Strange & Beautiful Sorrows of Ava Lavender. 2015. lib. bdg. 19.65 *(978-0-606-36879-7(5))* Turtleback.

Ward, Caias. The Only Brother. 2008. (Cutting Edge Ser.). (ENG.). 200p. pap. *(978-1-84167-719-4(1))* Ransom Publishing Ltd.

Ward, Greta. Pinkie the Cat Gets a Baby Sister. 2007. (Illus.). 44p. (J). pap. 9.95 *(978-0-9798346-0-8(0))* P.M. Publishing.

Ward, Marcia. The Girl Who Found Her Voice. 2013. (ENG.). 276p. pap. 14.99 *(978-1-939927-28-6(5))* Telemachus Pr., LLC.

Wargin, Kathy-jo. Mitt & Minn's Illinois Adventure. Holman, Karen Busch, illus. 2007. (Mitt Midwest Ser.: 4). 144p. (J). (gr. k-7). 14.95 *(978-1-58726-306-4(8)*, Mitten Pr.) Ann Arbor Editions LLC.

Waring, Scott C. West's Time MacHine. 2007. 200p. 24.95 *(978-0-595-88775-0(9))*; per. 14.95 *(978-0-595-41887-9(2))* iUniverse, Inc.

Warner, Gertrude Chandler. The Box-Car Children. Gregory, Dorothy Lake, illus. 2020. (ENG.). 64p. (J). (gr. 2-5). pap. 6.99 *(978-1-4209-6966-5(8))* Digireads.com Publishing.

—The Box-Car Children. 2019. (ENG.). 70p. (J). (gr. 2-5). pap. 5.99 *(978-1-6777-0963-2(4))* Independently Published.

—The Box-Car Children. Gregory, Dorothy Lake, illus. 2019. (ENG.). 88p. (J). (gr. 1-5). 14.99 *(978-1-5154-4203-5(9))*; pap. 6.49 *(978-1-5154-4204-2(7))* Jorge Pinto Bks. (Illustrated Bks.).

—The Box-Car Children: The Original 1924 Edition. 2020. (ENG.). 160p. (J). (gr. 2-5). 14.99 *(978-0-486-83851-9(X)*, 83851X) Dover Pubns., Inc.

—The Boxcar Children. Deal, L. Kate, illus. 2020. (Boxcar Children Ser.). (ENG.). 160p. (J). (gr. 2-6). lib. bdg. 31.36 *(978-1-5321-4473-8(3)*, 35163, Chapter Bks.) Spotlight.

—The Boxcar Children Fully Illustrated Edition. Gilbert, Anne Yvonne & Powers, Gretchen Ellen, illus. 2017. (Boxcar Children Mysteries Ser.). (ENG.). 168p. (J). (gr. 2-5). 34.99 *(978-0-8075-0925-8(6)*, 807509256, Random Hse. Bks. for Young Readers) Random Hse. Children's Bks.

—The Haunted Cabin Mystery, 1 vol. Bloodworth, Mark, illus. 2010. (Boxcar Children Graphic Novels Ser.). (ENG.). 32p. (J). (gr. 3-8). 32.79 *(978-1-60270-717-7(0)*, 3678, Graphic Planet - Fiction) Magic Wagon.

—The Mystery of the Runaway Ghost. Soileau, Hodges, illus. 2004. (Boxcar Children Ser.). 135p. (J). 12.65 *(978-0-7569-3264-0(5))* Perfection Learning Corp.

—Snowbound Mystery, 1 vol. Dubisch, Mike, illus. 2010. (Boxcar Children Graphic Novels Ser.). (ENG.). 32p. (J). (gr. 3-8). 32.79 *(978-1-60270-715-3(4)*, 3676, Graphic Planet - Fiction) Magic Wagon.

Warner, Gertrude Chandler, creator. The Creature in Ogopogo Lake. 2006. (Boxcar Children Mysteries Ser.: 108). (ENG., Illus.). 128p. (J). (gr. 2-5). lib. bdg. 14.99 *(978-0-8075-1336-1(9)*, 807513369); per. 6.99 *(978-0-8075-1337-8(7)*, 807513377) Random Hse. Children's Bks. (Random Hse. Bks. for Young Readers).

—The Creepy Clues Special. 2017. (Boxcar Children Mysteries Ser.). (ENG., Illus.). 336p. (J). (gr. 2-5). pap. 9.99 *(978-0-8075-2848-8(X)*, 080752848X, Random Hse. Bks. for Young Readers) Random Hse. Children's Bks.

—The Ghost at the Drive-In Movie. 2008. (Boxcar Children Mysteries Ser.: 116). (ENG., Illus.). 128p. (J). (gr. 2-5). 14.99 *(978-0-8075-5577-4(0)*, 807555770, Random Hse. Bks. for Young Readers) Random Hse. Children's Bks.

—The Ghost-Hunting Special. 2015. (Boxcar Children Mysteries Ser.). (ENG., Illus.). 352p. (J). (gr. 2-5). 9.99 *(978-0-8075-2846-4(3)*, 807528463, Random Hse. Bks. for Young Readers) Random Hse. Children's Bks.

—The Ghost of the Chattering Bones. 2005. (Boxcar Children Mysteries Ser.: 102). (ENG., Illus.). 128p. (J). (gr. 2-5). pap. 6.99 *(978-0-8075-0874-9(8)*, 807508748, Random Hse. Bks. for Young Readers) Random Hse. Children's Bks.

—The Giant Yo-Yo Mystery. 2006. (Boxcar Children Mysteries Ser.: 107). (ENG., Illus.). 144p. (J). (gr. 2-5). per. 5.99 *(978-0-8075-0879-4(9)*, 807508799, Random Hse. Bks. for Young Readers) Random Hse. Children's Bks.

—The Great Detective Race. 2008. (Boxcar Children Mysteries Ser.: 115). (ENG., Illus.). 128p. (J). (gr. 2-5). 14.99 *(978-0-8075-5573-6(8)*, 807555738); pap. 5.99 *(978-0-8075-5574-3(6)*, 807555746) Random Hse. Children's Bks. (Random Hse. Bks. for Young Readers).

—The Haunted Legends Special. 2016. (Boxcar Children Mysteries Ser.). (ENG., Illus.). 368p. (J). (gr. 2-5). 9.99 *(978-0-8075-0724-7(5)*, 807507245, Random Hse. Bks. for Young Readers) Random Hse. Children's Bks.

—The Legend of the Irish Castle. 2016. (Boxcar Children Mysteries Ser.: 142). (ENG., Illus.). 128p. (J). (gr. 2-5). 15.99 *(978-0-8075-0705-6(9)*, 807507059, Random Hse. Bks. for Young Readers) Random Hse. Children's Bks.

—The Mystery of the Grinning Gargoyle. 2014. (Boxcar Children Mysteries Ser.: 137). (ENG., Illus.). 128p. (J). (gr. 2-5). pap. 5.99 *(978-0-8075-0893-0(4)*, 807508934, Random Hse. Bks. for Young Readers) Random Hse. Children's Bks.

—The Mystery of the Missing Pop Idol. 2015. (Boxcar Children Mysteries Ser.: 138). (ENG., Illus.). 128p. (J). (gr. 2-5). 15.99 *(978-0-8075-5605-4(X)*, 080755605X, Random Hse. Bks. for Young Readers) Random Hse. Children's Bks.

—The Mystery of the Soccer Snitch. 2014. (Boxcar Children Mysteries Ser.: 136). (ENG., Illus.). 128p. (J). (gr. 2-5). pap. 6.99 *(978-0-8075-0896-1(9)*, 807508969, Random Hse. Bks. for Young Readers) Random Hse. Children's Bks.

—The Mystery of the Stolen Dinosaur Bones. 2015. (Boxcar Children Mysteries Ser.: 139). (ENG., Illus.). 128p. (J). (gr. 2-5). 15.99 *(978-0-8075-5608-5(4)*, 807556084, Random Hse. Bks. for Young Readers) Random Hse. Children's Bks.

—The Rock 'n' Roll Mystery. 2006. (Boxcar Children Mysteries Ser.: 109). (ENG., Illus.). 128p. (J). (gr. 2-5). lib. bdg. 14.99 *(978-0-8075-7089-0(3)*, 807570893); per. 5.99 *(978-0-8075-7090-6(7)*, 807570907) Random Hse. Children's Bks. (Random Hse. Bks. for Young Readers).

—The Seattle Puzzle. 2007. (Boxcar Children Mysteries Ser.: 111). (ENG., Illus.). (J). (gr. 2-5). 128p. lib. bdg. 14.99 *(978-0-8075-5560-6(6)*, 807555606); 112p. per. 5.99 *(978-0-8075-5561-3(4)*, 807555614) Random Hse. Children's Bks. (Random Hse. Bks. for Young Readers).

—The Sword of the Silver Knight. 2005. (Boxcar Children Mysteries Ser.: 103). (ENG., Illus.). 128p. (J). (gr. 2-5). per. 6.99 *(978-0-8075-0876-3(4)*, 807508764, Random Hse. Bks. for Young Readers) Random Hse. Children's Bks.

—The Vanishing Passenger. 2006. (Boxcar Children Mysteries Ser.: 106). (ENG., Illus.). 112p. (J). (gr. 2-5). per. 7.99 *(978-0-8075-1067-4(X)*, 080751067X, Random Hse. Bks. for Young Readers) Random Hse. Children's Bks.

Warner, Michael N. The Titanic Game. Ordaz, Frank, illus. 2018. (ENG.). 208p. (J). pap. 11.95 *(978-0-9744446-2-8(6))* All About Kids Publishing.

Wass, Eliza. The Cresswell Plot. 2017. (ENG.). 288p. (YA). (gr. 9-17). pap. 9.99 *(978-1-4847-3253-3(7))* Hyperion Bks. for Children.

Waters, Tawni. Beauty of the Broken. 2014. 368p. 17.99 *(978-1-4814-1857-7(2))* Simon & Schuster, Inc.

Watson, Jude. Loot. 2015. (ENG.). 272p. (J). (gr. 3-7). pap. 8.99 *(978-0-545-46803-9(5)*, Scholastic Paperbacks) Scholastic, Inc.

—Mission Titanic (the 39 Clues: Doublecross, Book 1) 2014. (Geronimo Stilton Ser.: 1). (ENG.). 240p. (J). (gr. 2-5). E-Book 7.99 *(978-0-545-76918-1(3))* Scholastic, Inc.

Watson, Michael. Treasure, Trash, & Turtles. 2010. 24p. pap. 11.50 *(978-1-60911-500-5(7)*, Eloquent Bks.) Strategic Book Publishing & Rights Agency (SBPRA).

Watts, Frances. The Song of the Winns: the Spies of Gerander. 2013. (ENG., Illus.). 320p. (J). (gr. -1-2). 28.00 *(978-0-7624-4658-2(7)*, Running Pr. Kids) Running Pr.

Watts, Irene N. When the Bough Breaks. 2007. 152p. (YA). (gr. 7-7). pap. 9.95 *(978-0-88776-821-7(0)*, Tundra Bks.) Tundra Bks. CAN. Dist: Penguin Random Hse. LLC.

Weatherill, Cat. Wild Magic. 2008. (ENG., Illus.). 288p. (YA). (gr. 4-6). 21.19 *(978-0-8027-9799-5(7)*, 9780802797995) Walker & Co.

Webb, Robert N. We Were There at the Boston Tea Party. Ward, E. F., illus. 2013. (ENG.). 192p. (J). (gr. 3-8). pap. 9.99 *(978-0-486-49260-5(5)*, 492605) Dover Pubns., Inc.

Weber, Bob. Oh, Brother! Brat Attack! Stephens, Jay, illus. 2015. (ENG.). 176p. (J). pap. 9.99 *(978-1-4494-7225-2(7))* Andrews McMeel Publishing.

Weber, Jen Funk. Thimbletack's Activity Book. 2008. (Spiderwick Chronicles). (ENG., Illus.). 64p. (J). (gr. 2-7). pap. 4.99 *(978-1-4169-4954-1(2)*, Simon Scribbles) Simon Scribbles.

Weekes, Patrick. Feeder. 2018. (ENG., Illus.). 304p. (YA). (gr. 9). 17.99 *(978-1-5344-0016-0(8)*, McElderry, Margaret K. Bks.) McElderry, Margaret K. Bks.

Weeks, Sarah. Sophie Peterman Tells the Truth! Neubecker, Robert, illus. 2009. (ENG.). 32p. (J). (gr. -1-3). 19.99 *(978-1-4169-8686-7(3)*, Beach Lane Bks.) Beach Lane Bks.

Weinstein, Natalie. Katrina's New Room. Pluum, Ave, illus. 2004. (J). pap. 19.95 *(978-0-9749531-0-6(5))* Images For Presentation.

Weiss, Ellen & Friedman, Mel. The Stinky Giant. 2012. (Step into Reading Ser.). (Illus.). 48p. (J). (gr. k-3). pap. 5.99 *(978-0-375-86743-9(0)*, Random Hse. Bks. for Young Readers) Random Hse. Children's Bks.

—The Stinky Giant. Girasole, Alessia, illus. 2012. (Step into Reading Level 3 Ser.). lib. bdg. 13.55 *(978-0-606-23858-8(1))* Turtleback.

Welch, Jenna Evans. Love & Luck. (ENG.). (YA). (gr. 7). 2019. 336p. pap. 11.99 *(978-1-5344-0101-3(6))* 2018. (Illus.). 320p. 18.99 *(978-1-5344-0100-6(8))* Simon Pulse. (Simon Pulse).

Welch, Leah. Pretty on the Inside. 2007. (J). per. 10.00 *(978-1-59872-779-1(6))* Instant Pub.

Welch, Sheila. Waiting to Forget. 2011. 172p. (J). 18.95 *(978-1-60898-114-4(2))* namelos llc.

Welch, Sheila Kelly. Waiting to Forget. 2011. 172p. (J). pap. 9.95 *(978-1-60898-115-1(0))* namelos llc.

Wells, Carolyn. Marjorie's Maytime. 2007. (ENG.). 196p. per. 11.95 *(978-1-4218-3318-7(2))* 1st World Publishing, Inc.

Wells, Rosemary. Bunny Cakes (Edición en Español) Wells, Rosemary, illus. 2014. (Max & Ruby Ser.). (SPA., Illus.). 32p. (J). (gr. -1-k). 8.99 *(978-0-14-751586-5(6)*, Puffin Books) Penguin Young Readers Group.

—Bunny Party. 2003. (Max & Ruby Ser.). (Illus.). 32p. (J). (gr. -1-k). pap. 7.99 *(978-0-14-250162-7(X)*, Puffin Books) Penguin Young Readers Group.

—Max & Ruby Play School. 2003. (All Aboard Reading Ser.). (gr. -1-2). lib. bdg. 13.55 *(978-0-613-64064-0(0))* Turtleback.

—Max & Ruby's Bedtime Book. 2010. (Max & Ruby Ser.). (Illus.). 48p. (J). (gr. -1-k). 18.99 *(978-0-670-01141-4(X)*, Viking Books for Young Readers) Penguin Young Readers Group.

—Max & Ruby's Preschool Pranks. 2016. (Max & Ruby Ser.). (Illus.). 40p. (J). (-k). 17.99 *(978-0-670-78462-2(1)*, Viking Books for Young Readers) Penguin Young Readers Group.

—Max's Breakfast. 2004. (Max & Ruby Ser.). (ENG.). 12p. (J). (gr. 1 — 1). bds. 7.99 *(978-0-670-88712-5(9)*, Viking Books for Young Readers) Penguin Young Readers Group.

—Max's Bug. Grey, Andrew, illus. 2017. (Max & Ruby Ser.). 32p. (J). (gr. 1-2). pap. 5.99 *(978-0-515-15740-6(6)*, Penguin Young Readers) Penguin Young Readers Group.

—Max's Christmas. 2013. (Max & Ruby Ser.). (ENG.). 32p. (J). (gr. -1-k). 8.99 *(978-0-14-750947-5(5)*, Puffin Books) Penguin Young Readers Group.

—Max's Christmas. 2013. (Max Ruby Ser.). lib. bdg. 18.40 *(978-0-606-32139-6(X))* Turtleback.

—Max's Lunch. Grey, Andrew, illus. 2017. (Max & Ruby Ser.). 32p. (J). (gr. 1-2). pap. 4.99 *(978-0-515-15737-6(6)*, Penguin Young Readers) Penguin Young Readers Group.

—Ruby's Beauty Shop. Wells, Rosemary, illus. 2004. (Max & Ruby Ser.). (ENG., Illus.). 32p. (J). (gr. -1-k). pap. 8.99 *(978-0-14-240194-1(3)*, Puffin Books) Penguin Young Readers Group.

—Sporty Bunny Tales. 2014. (Max & Ruby Ser.). lib. bdg. 14.75 *(978-0-606-34464-7(0))* Turtleback.

Welvaert, Scott R. The Mosquito King: An Agate & Buck Adventure, 1 vol. Garvey, Brann, illus. 2007. (Agate & Buck Adventure Ser.). (ENG.). 112p. (J). (gr. 5-9). 26.65 *(978-1-59889-857-6(4)*, 94254, Stone Arch Bks.) Capstone.

—The Mosquito King: An Agate & Buck Adventure, 1 vol. Garvey, Brann, illus. 2008. (Vortex Bks.). (ENG.). 112p. (J). (gr. 2-3). pap. 6.95 *(978-1-59889-923-8(6)*, 94325, Stone Arch Bks.) Capstone.

Weninger, Brigitte. Davy Loves His Mommy. Tharlet, Eve, illus. 2014. (ENG.). 32p. (J). (gr. k-3). 15.95 *(978-0-7358-4164-2(0))* North-South Bks., Inc.

—Davy Loves the Baby. Tharlet, Eve, illus. 2015. (ENG.). 32p. (J). 15.95 *(978-0-7358-4210-6(8))* North-South Bks., Inc.

West, Kasie. On the Fence. 2014. (ENG.). 304p. (YA). (gr. 8). pap. 11.99 *(978-0-06-223567-1(2)*, HarperTeen) HarperCollins Pubs.

Weston, Anne. My Brother Needs a Boa, 1 vol. Nathan, Cheryl, illus. 2005. (ENG.). 32p. (J). (gr. -1-3). 15.95 *(978-1-932065-96-1(2))* Star Bright Bks., Inc.

Weston Woods Staff, creator. Casi. 2011. (SPA.). 29.95 *(978-0-439-90592-3(3))* Weston Woods Studios, Inc.
—Peter's Chair. 2011. 29.95 *(978-0-439-76006-5(2))* Weston Woods Studios, Inc.
Westover, Steve. Crater Lake: Battle for Wizard Island. 2012. pap. 14.99 *(978-1-59955-960-5(9))* Cedar Fort, Inc./CFI Distribution.
—Return of the Mystic Gray. 2013. 15.99 *(978-1-4621-1187-9(4))* Cedar Fort, Inc./CFI Distribution.
Whelan, Gloria. The Disappeared. 144p. (YA). (gr. 7-18). 2010. 6.99 *(978-0-14-241540-5(5),* Speak) 2008. (ENG.). 21.19 *(978-0-8037-3275-9(9))* Penguin Young Readers Group.
Whitaker, Alecia. The Way Back Home. 2016. (Wildflower Ser.: 3). (ENG.). 336p. (YA). (gr. 7-17). 17.99 *(978-0-316-25144-0(5),* Poppy) Little, Brown Bks. for Young Readers.
White, Amanda. Sand Sister. Morales, Yuyi, illus. 2004. (ENG.). 32p. (J). 16.99 *(978-1-84148-617-8(5))* Barefoot Bks., Inc.
White, J. A. The Thickety: Well of Witches. 2016. (Thickety Ser.: 3). (ENG., Illus.). 512p. (J). (gr. 5). 16.99 *(978-0-06-225732-1(3),* Tegen, Katherine Bks) HarperCollins Pubs.
—The Thickety #4: The Last Spell. Offermann, Andrea, illus. 2017. (Thickety Ser.: 4). (ENG.). 512p. (J). (gr. 5). 16.99 *(978-0-06-238139-2(3),* Tegen, Katherine Bks) HarperCollins Pubs.
—The Whispering Trees. Offermann, Andrea, illus. 2015. (Thickety Ser.: 2). (ENG.). 528p. (J). (gr. 5). 16.99 *(978-0-06-225729-1(3),* Tegen, Katherine Bks) HarperCollins Pubs.
White, Kathryn. El Hermanito de Ruby. Latimer, Miriam, illus. 2013. 32p. (J). pap. 8.99 *(978-1-78285-026-7(0))* Barefoot Bks., Inc.
—Ruby's Baby Brother. Latimer, Miriam, illus. 2013. 32p. (J). 16.99 *(978-1-84686-864-1(5));* (ENG.). (gr. -1-2). pap. 8.99 *(978-1-84686-950-1(1))* Barefoot Bks., Inc.
White, Tom. Lost in the Texas Desert. 2004. (Illus.). 132p. per. 7.95 *(978-0-9753611-0-8(4))* Arlington Pubns.
Whittemore, Jo. Odd Girl In. 2011. (Mix Ser.). (ENG.). 240p. (J). (gr. 4-8). pap. 8.99 *(978-1-4424-1284-2(4),* Aladdin) Simon & Schuster Children's Publishing.
Whitten, A. J. The Well. 2009. (ENG., Illus.). 336p. (YA). (gr. 7-18). pap. 18.95 *(978-0-547-23229-4(2),* 1082742, Clarion Bks.) HarperCollins Pubs.
Whybrow, Ian. Little Wolf's Diary of Daring Deeds. Ross, Tony, illus. (Middle Grade Fiction Ser.). 132p. (gr. 3-6). 2005. 14.95 *(978-1-57505-411-7(6))* 2003. (J). pap. 6.95 *(978-0-87614-536-4(5),* Carolrhoda Bks.) Lerner Publishing Group.
—Malicia para Principiantes: Una Aventura de Lobito y Apestosito. Quintana, Joela, tr. Ross, Tony, illus. 2005. (Libros Ilustrados (Picture Bks.)). (SPA.). 32p. (J). (gr. k-2). 16.95 *(978-0-8225-3211-8(5),* Ediciones Lerner) Lerner Publishing Group.
—That Naughty Meerkat! Parsons, Garry, illus. 2016. (ENG.). 32p. (J). *(978-0-00-813945-2(8),* HarperCollins Children's Bks.) HarperCollins Pubs. Ltd.
Whybrow, Ian & Ross, Tony. Badness for Beginners: A Little Wolf & Smellybreff Adventure. 2005. (Illus.). 32p. (J). (gr. -1-3). 16.95 *(978-1-57505-861-0(8),* Carolrhoda Bks.) Lerner Publishing Group.
Wiesner, David. Hurricane Book & Cd, 1 vol. 2008. (ENG., Illus.). 32p. (J). (gr. -1-3). audio compact disk 10.99 *(978-0-547-06433-8(0),* 1040022, Clarion Bks.) HarperCollins Pubs.
Wiggins, Bethany. Cured: A Stung Novel. 2015. (ENG.). 320p. (YA). (gr. 7). pap. 10.99 *(978-0-8027-3787-8(0),* 900139083, Bloomsbury USA Childrens) Bloomsbury Publishing USA.
Wildavsky, Rachel. The Secret of Rover. Caparo, Antonio, illus. 2015. (ENG.). 360p. (J). (gr. 4-8). pap. 7.95 *(978-1-4197-1968-4(8),* 681103, Amulet Bks.) Abrams, Inc.
Wildman, Dale. Nicholas Knows: Big Brother Nicholas Knows It All! Sisung, Peter, illus. 2006. 24p. (J). per. 2.99 *(978-1-59958-005-0(5))* Journey Stone Creations, LLC.
Wiles, Deborah. Countdown. (Sixties Trilogy Ser.). (ENG.). 400p. (J). (gr. 4-7). 2010. 21.99 *(978-0-545-10605-4(2),* Scholastic Pr.)1. 2013. pap. 9.99 *(978-0-545-10606-1(0),* Scholastic Paperbacks) Scholastic, Inc.
Williams, Alan. Archy the Flying Dolphin & the Vampire's Curse. 2007. pap. 15.38 *(978-1-4251-3151-7(4))* Trafford Publishing.
Williams, Annie Morris. Marianne's Secret Cousins. Oldham, Cindi, illus. 2005. (Family History Adventures for Young Readers Ser.: 2). 240p. (J). per. 10.00 *(978-0-9645272-8-7(6))* Field Stone Pubs.
Williams, Carol Lynch. Waiting. (ENG.). 352p. (YA). (gr. 9). 2013. pap. 9.99 *(978-1-4424-4354-9(5))* 2012. 16.99 *(978-1-4424-4353-2(7))* Simon & Schuster/Paula Wiseman Bks. (Simon & Schuster/Paula Wiseman Bks.).
Williams, Michael. Now Is the Time for Running. 2013. (ENG.). 240p. (YA). (gr. 7-17). pap. 10.99 *(978-0-316-07788-0(7))* Little, Brown Bks. for Young Readers.
Williams, Suzanne Morgan. Bull Rider. 2009. (ENG.). 256p. (YA). (gr. 7-8). 17.99 *(978-1-4169-6130-7(5))* Simon & Schuster, Inc.
Williams, Vera B. Amber Was Brave, Essie Was Smart. Williams, Vera B., illus. 2004. (ENG., Illus.). 72p. (J). (gr. 2-7). reprint ed. pap. 7.99 *(978-0-06-057182-5(9),* Greenwillow Bks.) HarperCollins Pubs.
Willson, Sarah. Do Not Wake Jake. Johnson, Meredith, illus. 2006. (Step-By-Step Readers Ser.). (J). *(978-1-59939-059-8(0),* Reader's Digest Young Families, Inc.) Studio Fun International.
—Pet Peeves. 2005. (Social Studies Connects Ser.). (Illus.). 32p. (J). (gr. 1-3). pap. 5.99 *(978-1-57565-149-1(1),* b2e53ab7-d45f-4ca7-b743-35182adb4c08, Kane Press) Astra Publishing Hse.
Wilson, Jodi L. When I Grow Up. Anderson, Kari A., illus. 32p. (Orig.). (J). (gr. 1-3). pap. 4.95 *(978-0-9628335-0-2(9))* Wilander Publishing Co.
Wilson, Mark A. The Legend of Crawley Creek. 2008. 104p. pap. 9.95 *(978-1-60693-423-4(6),* Eloquent Bks.) Strategic Book Publishing & Rights Agency (SBPRA).
Wilson, N. D. The Dragon's Tooth (Ashtown Burials #1) 2012. (Ashtown Burials Ser.: 1). (ENG.). 496p. (J). (gr. 3-7). 8.99 *(978-0-375-86396-7(6),* Yearling) Random Hse. Children's Bks.
Wilson, Shelliah. Samuel's Little Brother. 2005. 12p. 9.72 *(978-1-4116-4789-3(0))* Lulu Pr., Inc.
Winkler, Ashley & Winkler, Michael. One Good Quest Deserves Another: A Crown of Amaranth Story. 2009. 292p. 28.95 *(978-0-595-71039-3(5));* pap. 18.95 *(978-0-595-47365-6(2))* iUniverse, Inc.
Winkler, Henry & Oliver, Lin. Day of the Iguana. 2004. (Hank Zipzer Ser.: No. 3). 160p. (J). (gr. 2-6). pap. 29.00 incl. audio *(978-1-4000-9008-2(3),* Listening Library) Random Hse. Audio Publishing Group.
—Who Ordered This Baby? Definitely Not Me! 2007. (Hank Zipzer Ser.: No. 13). (Illus.). 152p. (gr. 4-7). 15.00 *(978-0-7569-8163-1(8))* Perfection Learning Corp.
Winter, Ariel S. One of a Kind. Hitch, David, illus. 2012. (ENG.). 32p. (J). (gr. -1-2). 15.99 *(978-1-4424-2016-8(2),* Aladdin) Simon & Schuster Children's Publishing.
Winthrop, Elizabeth. The Red-Hot Rattoons. Lewin, Betsy, illus. 2006. (ENG.). 224p. (J). (gr. 3-6). pap. 17.99 *(978-0-8050-7986-9(6),* 900034574, Holt, Henry & Co. Bks. For Young Readers) Holt, Henry & Co.
Wirth, Beverly. Flowers from Seeds: A Garden Parable. 2012. 40p. pap. 16.99 *(978-1-4624-0101-7(5),* Inspiring Voices) Author Solutions, LLC.
Wishinsky, Frieda. Please, Louise!, 1 vol. Gay, Marie-Louise, illus. 2007. (ENG.). 32p. (J). (gr. k-k). 17.95 *(978-0-88899-796-8(5))* Groundwood Bks. CAN. Dist: Publishers Group West (PGW).
Wissinger, Tamera Will. Gone Camping: A Novel in Verse. Cordell, Matthew, illus. 2017. (ENG.). 112p. (J). (gr. 1-4). 15.99 *(978-0-544-63873-0(5),* 1620560, Clarion Bks.) HarperCollins Pubs.
—Gone Fishing: A Novel in Verse. Cordell, Matthew, illus. 2015. (ENG.). 128p. (J). (gr. 1-4). pap. 6.99 *(978-0-544-43931-3(7),* 1596830, Clarion Bks.) HarperCollins Pubs.
Wizards of Waverly Place Insider's Guide. 2009. 128p. pap. 8.99 *(978-1-4231-2473-3(1))* Disney Pr.
Wodehouse, Pelham Grenville. Mike at Wrykyn. 2013. 189p. reprint ed. lthr. 69.00 *(978-0-7426-3265-3(2))* Classic Bks.
Wolf, Elaine. Camp. 2012. (ENG.). 256p. (YA). (gr. 6-6). 16.95 *(978-1-61608-657-2(2),* 608657, Sky Pony Pr.) Skyhorse Publishing Co., Inc.
Wood, Audrey. Balloonia. 2005. (Child's Play Library). (Illus.). 32p. (J). (gr. 1-2). pap. *(978-1-904550-49-5(5))* Child's Play International Ltd.
—Presto Change-O. 2005. (Child's Play Library). (Illus.). 32p. (J). pap. *(978-1-904550-52-5(5))* Child's Play International Ltd.
—Tooth Fairy. 2005. (Audrey Wood Bks.). (Illus.). 32p. (J). (gr. -1-1). pap. 24.94 *(978-0-85953-293-8(3))* Child's Play International Ltd. GBR. Dist: Children's Plus, Inc.
—Tooth Fairy. 2003. (ENG.). (J). (gr. -1-2). lib. bdg. 18.60 *(978-0-7569-6492-4(X))* Perfection Learning Corp.
—Tooth Fairy. 2003. (gr. -1-2). 18.40 *(978-0-613-76960-0(0))* Turtleback.
Woodcock, Fiona. Hello. Woodcock, Fiona, illus. 2019. (ENG., Illus.). 40p. (J). (gr. -1-3). 17.99 *(978-0-06-264456-5(4),* Greenwillow Bks.) HarperCollins Pubs.
—Look! 2018. (ENG., Illus.). 40p. (J). (gr. -1-3). 17.99 *(978-0-06-264455-8(6),* Greenwillow Bks.) HarperCollins Pubs.
Woodrow, Allan. The Pet War. 2015. (ENG.). 272p. (J). (gr. 3-7). pap. 8.99 *(978-0-545-51320-3(0),* Scholastic Paperbacks) Scholastic, Inc.
Woodrum, Margaret. The Christmas Tree Fort. Woodrum, Larry, illus. 2010. 32p. pap. 13.00 *(978-1-60911-329-2(2),* Eloquent Bks.) Strategic Book Publishing & Rights Agency (SBPRA).
Woodson, J. L. The Things I Could Tell You! Malone, Susan Mary et al, eds. collector's ed. 2003. 206p. pap. 14.95 *(978-0-9702699-6-6(X))* Macro Publishing Group.
Woodson, Jacqueline. Miracle's Boys. 2010. (ENG.). 176p. (J). (gr. 5-18). 8.99 *(978-0-14-241553-5(7),* Puffin Books) Penguin Young Readers Group.
—Peace, Locomotion. (ENG.). (J). 2010. 176p. (gr. 5-18). 8.99 *(978-0-14-241512-2(X),* Puffin Books) 2009. 144p. (gr. 4-6). 22.44 *(978-0-399-24655-5(X))* Penguin Young Readers Group.
—The Year We Learned to Fly. López, Rafael, illus. 2022. (ENG.). 32p. (J). (gr. k-3). 18.99 *(978-0-399-54553-5(0),* Nancy Paulsen Books) Penguin Young Readers Group.
Woodward, J. Howland. A Moment in Time. 2006. 55p. pap. 16.95 *(978-1-4241-1334-7(2))* America Star Bks.
Woollvin, Bethan. Hansel & Gretel. 2018. (ENG., Illus.). 32p. (J). (gr. k-4). 16.95 *(978-1-68263-073-0(0))* Peachtree Publishing Co. Inc.
Worrell, Maryellen. The Accidental Hero. 2008. 101p. pap. 19.95 *(978-1-60672-145-2(3))* America Star Bks.
Wozniak, Patricia. McGooster & Mcgyman Begin Their Adventures. 2008. (Illus.). 144p. (J). 16.95 *(978-0-9792430-0-4(9))* Wing Lane Pr.
Wrede, Patricia. Snow White & Rose Red. 2009. (ENG.). 288p. (YA). (gr. 7-18). 8.99 *(978-0-14-241121-6(3),* Firebird) Penguin Young Readers Group.
Wrench, Peter. The Night of the Round Stable. Holland, Ruth, illus. 2012. 174p. pap. *(978-1-908895-49-3(7))* FeedARead.com.
Wunsch, Emma. The Movie Version. 2016. (ENG.). 368p. (J). (gr. 9-17). 18.95 *(978-1-4197-1900-4(9),* 1121901, Amulet Bks.) Abrams, Inc.
Yaccarino, Dan. Where the Four Winds Blow. Yaccarino, Dan, illus. 2003. (Illus.). 104p. (J). 17.89 *(978-0-06-623627-8(4),* Cotler, Joanna Books) HarperCollins Pubs.
Yang, Belle. Always Come Home to Me. Yang, Belle, illus. 2007. (ENG., Illus.). 32p. (J). (gr. -1-3). 16.99 *(978-0-7636-2899-4(9))* Candlewick Pr.
Yang, Belle & Williams, Marcia. Archie's War: My Scrapbook of the First World War. Williams, Marcia, illus. 2007. (ENG., Illus.). 48p. (J). (gr. 3-7). 18.99 *(978-0-7636-3532-9(4))* Candlewick Pr.
Yasuda, Anita. Ghost Sounds, 1 vol. Harpster, Steve, illus. 2013. (Dino Detectives Ser.). (ENG.). 32p. (J). (gr. 1-2). pap. 5.95 *(978-1-4342-4831-2(3),* 121750); lib. bdg. 22.65 *(978-1-4342-4152-8(1),* 119896) Capstone. (Stone Arch Bks.).
—The Missing Trumpet, 1 vol. Harpster, Steve, illus. 2013. (Dino Detectives Ser.). (ENG.). 32p. (J). (gr. 1-2). pap. 5.95 *(978-1-4342-4832-9(1),* 121751, Stone Arch Bks.) Capstone.
Yates, Alexander. The Winter Place. 2015. (ENG., Illus.). 448p. (YA). (gr. 9). 17.99 *(978-1-4814-1981-9(1))* Simon & Schuster Children's Publishing.
Yavin, T. S. All-Star Season. 2006. 160p. (J). (gr. 3-7). lib. bdg. 15.95 *(978-1-58013-211-4(1),* Kar-Ben Publishing) Lerner Publishing Group.
Yazdani, Aliza. Protection: How far Would you go to Save a Brother? 2012. 84p. pap. 11.11 *(978-1-4669-0895-6(5))* Trafford Publishing.
The Year We Sailed the Sun. 2015. (ENG., Illus.). 432p. (J). (gr. 3-7). 17.99 *(978-0-689-85827-7(2),* Atheneum/Richard Jackson Bks.) Simon & Schuster Children's Publishing.
Yoo, David. The Detention Club. 2012. (ENG.). 304p. (J). (gr. 5). pap. 6.99 *(978-0-06-178380-7(3),* Balzer & Bray) HarperCollins Pubs.
Yoo, Paula. The Perfect Gift, 1 vol. Ng-Benitez, Shirley, illus. 2018. (Confetti Kids Ser.: 6). (ENG.). 32p. (J). (gr. k-2). 14.95 *(978-1-62014-567-8(7),* leelowbooks) Lee & Low Bks., Inc.
—The Perfect Gift (Confetti Kids), 1 vol. 2018. (Confetti Kids Ser.: 6). (ENG., Illus.). 32p. (J). (gr. k-2). pap. 10.95 *(978-1-62014-568-5(5),* leelowbooks) Lee & Low Bks., Inc.
Yoon, Salina. Penguin & Pumpkin. 2014. (Penguin Ser.). (ENG., Illus.). 40p. (J). (gr. -1-1). E-Book 6.39 *(978-0-8027-3770-0(6),* Bloomsbury USA Childrens) Bloomsbury Publishing USA.
Young, Adrienne. Sky in the Deep. (Sky & Sea Ser.: 1). (ENG.). (YA). 2019. 368p. pap. 11.99 *(978-1-250-16846-7(5),* 900187700) 2018. 352p. 18.99 *(978-1-250-16845-0(7),* 900187699) St. Martin's Pr. (Wednesday Bks.).
—Sky in the Deep. Lt. ed. 2020. (Sky & Sea Ser.: 1). (ENG.). lib. bdg. 22.99 *(978-1-4328-7818-4(2))* Thorndike Pr.
Young, Cybèle. A Few Bites, 1 vol. 2012. (ENG., Illus.). 48p. (J). (gr. k-2). 18.95 *(978-1-55498-295-0(2))* Groundwood Bks. CAN. Dist: Publishers Group West (PGW).
—A Few Blocks, 1 vol. 2011. (ENG., Illus.). 48p. (J). (gr. -1-2). 18.95 *(978-0-88899-995-5(X))* Groundwood Bks. CAN. Dist: Publishers Group West (PGW).
Young, Emma. She, Myself, & I. 2017. (ENG.). 336p. (YA). (gr. 8-17). 17.99 *(978-1-4197-2570-8(X),* 1169401, Amulet Bks.) Abrams, Inc.
Young, Jessica. Fin-Tastic Fashion. Sécheret, Jessica, illus. 2017. (Finley Flowers Ser.). (ENG.). 128p. (J). (gr. 1-3). lib. bdg. 25.32 *(978-1-4795-9804-5(6),* 133579, Picture Window Bks.) Capstone.
—Nature Calls. Sécheret, Jessica, illus. 2015. (Finley Flowers Ser.). (ENG.). 128p. (J). (gr. 1-3). 8.95 *(978-1-4795-5879-7(6),* 126923, Picture Window Bks.) Capstone.
—Pet-Rified. Sécheret, Jessica, illus. 2017. (Finley Flowers Ser.). (ENG.). 128p. (J). (gr. 1-3). lib. bdg. 25.32 *(978-1-4795-9805-2(4),* 133580, Picture Window Bks.) Capstone.
—Super Spooktacular. Sécheret, Jessica, illus. 2017. (Finley Flowers Ser.). (ENG.). 128p. (J). (gr. 1-3). lib. bdg. 25.32 *(978-1-4795-9807-6(0),* 133582, Picture Window Bks.) Capstone.
Young, Jessica & Spark, Sylvie. Finley Flowers Collection. Secheret, Jessica, illus. 2016. (Finley Flowers Ser.). (ENG.). 256p. (J). (gr. 1-3). 9.99 *(978-1-4795-9850-2(X),* 135049, Picture Window Bks.) Capstone.
Young, Judy. Digger & Daisy Go Camping. Sullivan, Dana, illus. 2019. (Digger & Daisy Ser.). (ENG.). 32p. (J). (gr. k-2). 9.99 *(978-1-5341-1022-9(4),* 204655); pap. 5.99 *(978-1-5341-1023-6(2),* 204663) Sleeping Bear Pr.
—Digger & Daisy Go on a Picnic. Sullivan, Dana, illus. 2014. (Digger & Daisy Ser.). (ENG.). 32p. (J). (gr. k-1). 9.99 *(978-1-58536-843-3(1),* 203006) Sleeping Bear Pr.
—Digger & Daisy Go to the City. Sullivan, Dana, illus. 2015. (Digger & Daisy Ser.). (ENG.). 32p. (J). (gr. k-2). pap. 4.99 *(978-1-58536-848-8(2),* 203821) Sleeping Bear Pr.
—Digger & Daisy Go to the Doctor. Sullivan, Dana, illus. 2014. (Digger & Daisy Ser.). (ENG.). 32p. (J). (gr. k-2). 9.99 *(978-1-58536-845-7(8),* 203674); pap. 5.99 *(978-1-58536-846-4(6),* 203728) Sleeping Bear Pr.
—Digger & Daisy Go to the Zoo. Sullivan, Dana, illus. 2013. (Digger & Daisy Ser.). (ENG.). 32p. (J). (gr. k-1). 9.99 *(978-1-58536-841-9(5),* 202897) Sleeping Bear Pr.
—Digger & Daisy Plant a Garden. Sullivan, Dana, illus. 2016. (Digger & Daisy Ser.). (ENG.). 32p. (J). (gr. k-2). 9.99 *(978-1-58536-931-7(4),* 204030) Sleeping Bear Pr.
—Digger et Daisy Vont Au Docteur (Digger & Daisy Go to the Doctor) Sullivan, Dana, illus. 2016. (Digger & Daisy Ser.). (FRE.). 32p. (J). (gr. k-2). 12.95 *(978-1-62753-949-4(2),* 204172) Sleeping Bear Pr.
—Digger y Daisy Van a la Ciudad (Digger & Daisy Go to the City) Sullivan, Dana, illus. 2016. (Digger & Daisy Ser.). (SPA.). 32p. (J). (gr. k-2). 9.99 *(978-1-62753-954-8(9),* 204177) Sleeping Bear Pr.
—Digger y Daisy Van Al Médico (Digger & Daisy Go to the Doctor) Sullivan, Dana, illus. 2016. (Digger & Daisy Ser.). (SPA.). 32p. (J). (gr. k-2). 9.99 *(978-1-62753-953-1(0),* 204176) Sleeping Bear Pr.
—Digger y Daisy Van Al Zoológico (Digger & Daisy Go to the Zoo) Sullivan, Dana, illus. 2016. (Digger & Daisy Ser.). (SPA.). 32p. (J). (gr. k-2). 9.99 *(978-1-62753-951-7(4),* 204174) Sleeping Bear Pr.
—Digger y Daisy Van de Picnic (Digger & Daisy Go on a Picnic) Sullivan, Dana, illus. 2016. (Digger & Daisy Ser.). (SPA.). 32p. (J). (gr. k-2). 9.99 *(978-1-62753-952-4(2),* 204175) Sleeping Bear Pr.
—Star in a Play. Sullivan, Dana, illus. 2015. (Digger & Daisy Ser.). (ENG.). 32p. (J). (gr. k-2). 9.99 *(978-1-58536-929-4(2),* 203950) Sleeping Bear Pr.
Young, Moira. Blood Red Road. (Dust Lands Ser.: 1). (ENG.). (YA). (gr. 9). 2012. 480p. pap. 12.99 *(978-1-4424-2999-4(2))* 2011. (Illus.). 464p. 17.99 *(978-1-4424-2998-7(4))* McElderry, Margaret K. Bks. (McElderry, Margaret K. Bks.).
—Blood Red Road, 9 vols. 2011. (YA). 122.75 *(978-1-4618-0629-5(1));* 286.75 *(978-1-4618-0634-9(8));* 1.25 *(978-1-4640-2632-4(7));* 120.75 *(978-1-4618-0633-2(X));* 120.75 *(978-1-4618-0630-1(5))* Recorded Bks., Inc.
—Raging Star. (Dust Lands Ser.: 3). (ENG., Illus.). 448p. (YA). (gr. 9). 2015. pap. 13.99 *(978-1-4424-3003-7(6))* 2014. 17.99 *(978-1-4424-3002-0(8))* McElderry, Margaret K. Bks. (McElderry, Margaret K. Bks.).
—Rebel Heart. (Dust Lands Ser.: 2). (ENG., Illus.). (YA). (gr. 9). 2013. 448p. pap. 13.99 *(978-1-4424-3001-3(X))* 2012. 432p. 17.99 *(978-1-4424-3000-6(1))* McElderry, Margaret K. Bks. (McElderry, Margaret K. Bks.).
Young, Suzanne. All in Pieces. (ENG.). (YA). (gr. 9). 2017. 288p. pap. 11.99 *(978-1-4814-1884-3(X))* 2016. (Illus.). 272p. 17.99 *(978-1-4814-1883-6(1))* Simon Pulse. (Simon Pulse).
—Hotel for the Lost. 2016. (ENG., Illus.). 304p. (YA). (gr. 9). pap. 10.99 *(978-1-4814-2301-4(0),* Simon Pulse) Simon Pulse.
—Hotel Ruby. 2015. (ENG., Illus.). 288p. (YA). (gr. 9). 17.99 *(978-1-4814-2300-7(2),* Simon Pulse) Simon Pulse.
Young, T. M. My Ten Cents. Victoria Washington and Carla Watts, ed. Cromwell, Danielle, illus. 2013. 24p. pap. 24.95 *(978-1-4626-5790-2(7))* America Star Bks.
Zafon, Carlos Ruiz. The Midnight Palace. 2012. (ENG.). 320p. (YA). (gr. 7-17). pap. 17.99 *(978-0-316-04474-5(1))* Little, Brown Bks. for Young Readers.
—The Prince of Mist. 2011. (ENG.). 256p. (YA). (gr. 7-17). pap., pap. 14.99 *(978-0-316-04480-6(6))* Little, Brown Bks. for Young Readers.
Zamenhof, Robert. The Adventures of Armadillo Baby & Annabelli. Baker, Sara, illus. 2013. 56p. pap. 9.29 *(978-0-615-80196-4(X))* RGZ Consulting.
Zarr, Sara. Gem & Dixie. 2018. (ENG.). 288p. (YA). (gr. 9). pap. 9.99 *(978-0-06-243461-6(6),* Balzer & Bray) HarperCollins Pubs.
—The Lucy Variations. 2014. (ENG.). 336p. (YA). (gr. 7-17). pap. 17.99 *(978-0-316-20500-9(1))* Little, Brown Bks. for Young Readers.
Zaugg, Sandra L. Secret of the Desert Lights: A Story about Following God's Laws. 2009. (J). pap. 9.99 *(978-0-8163-2294-7(5))* Pacific Pr. Publishing Assn.
Zerza, Safoora Z. Sophia V. Is Flower Girl. 2012. 24p. pap. 17.99 *(978-1-4685-5136-5(1))* AuthorHouse.
Zimmerman, Andrea & Clemesha, David. Digger Man. Zimmerman, Andrea, illus. 2007. (Digger Man Ser.: 1). (ENG., Illus.). 32p. (J). (gr. -1-k). pap. 8.99 *(978-0-8050-8203-6(4),* 900040876) Square Fish.
Zimmerman, Diana S. Kandide & the Secret of the Mists. Gadd, Maxine, illus. 2008. (Calabiyau Chronicles Ser.: Bk. 1). 296p. (YA). (gr. 5-18). 17.99 *(978-0-9794328-3-5(9));*Bk. 1. 290p. (J). (gr. 4-7). pap. 9.99 *(978-0-9794328-2-8(0))* Noesis Publishing.
Zindel, Paul. Loch. 2005. 209p. (YA). (gr. 7-12). 13.65 *(978-0-7569-6001-8(0))* Perfection Learning Corp.

SICILY (ITALY)—FICTION

Blasi, Kathleen McAlpin. A Name of Honor. Bowman, Leslie W., illus. 2006. (J). *(978-1-59336-692-6(2))* Mondo Publishing.
Grant, Michael. Silver Stars: A Front Lines Novel, Volume 2. 2017. (ENG., Illus.). 496p. (YA). pap. *(978-1-4052-8786-9(1))* HarperCollins Pubs.
Napoli, Donna Jo. The Wager. 2010. (ENG.). 272p. (YA). (gr. 7-12). 23.99 *(978-0-8050-8781-9(8),* 900050394, Holt, Henry & Co. Bks. For Young Readers) Holt, Henry & Co.
Williams, Annie Morris. Marianne's Secret Cousins. Oldham, Cindi, illus. 2005. (Family History Adventures for Young Readers Ser.: 2). 240p. (J). per. 10.00 *(978-0-9645272-8-7(6))* Field Stone Pubs.

SICK

see also Diseases; Mentally Ill

Carlson, Hannah. Addiction: The Brain Disease. 2010. (ENG., Illus.). 224p. (gr. 7-18). pap. 14.95 *(978-1-884158-35-3(8),* 03db31a0-ebf1-4ef8-b49f-db048b863aec) Bick Publishing Hse.
Chapeau, Chelsey. You Are Brave. Kriebel, Jacqueline, illus. 2017. 26p. pap. 11.99 *(978-1-943871-42-1(6))* Painted Gate Publishing.
Edwards, Dianna. Meet Patou. 2006. (J). pap. 29.95 *(978-0-9767756-0-7(3))* Patou Bks., LLC.
—When Niki Got Sick, Bk. 2. 2004. (J). *(978-0-9767756-2-1(X))* Patou Bks., LLC.
Fetty, Margaret. Seizure-Alert Dogs. 2009. (Dog Heroes Ser.). (Illus.). 32p. (YA). (gr. 2-5). lib. bdg. 28.50 *(978-1-59716-865-6(3))* Bearport Publishing Co., Inc.
Geis, Patricia. Let's Get Well! Folch, Sergio, illus. 2009. (Good Habits with Coco & Tula Ser.). 16p. (J). (gr. -1-k). bds. 11.40 *(978-1-60754-407-4(5))* Windmill Bks.
Jones, Viola & Wainwright, Tabitha. Living with an Illness in the Family, 1 vol., 1. 2015. (Family Issues & You Ser.). (ENG.). 48p. (J). (gr. 5-5). 33.47 *(978-1-4994-3693-8(5),* 0ac03678-b972-4725-a1bc-b88d0087a625, Rosen Central) Rosen Publishing Group, Inc., The.
Rocha, Toni L. Coping When Someone in Your Family Has Cancer. 2009. (Coping Ser.). 192p. (gr. 7-12). 63.90 *(978-1-61511-988-2(4))* Rosen Publishing Group, Inc., The.
Wainwright, Tabitha. You & an Illness in Your Family. 2009. (Family Matters Ser.). 48p. (gr. 5-8). 53.00 *(978-1-61512-477-0(2),* Rosen Reference) Rosen Publishing Group, Inc., The.

SICK—FICTION

Abbott, Roz. A Bump in the Road. Seltzer, Jerry Joe, illus. 2013. 26p. (J). 16.95 *(978-1-60131-179-5(6))* Big Tent Bks.
Alda, Arlene. Iris Has a Virus. Desimini, Lisa, illus. 2008. 24p. (J). (gr. -1-1). 18.95 *(978-0-88776-844-6(X),* Tundra Bks.) Tundra Bks. CAN. Dist: Penguin Random Hse. LLC.
Andros, Camille. Charlotte the Scientist Finds a Cure. Farley, Brianne, illus. 2019. (Charlotte the Scientist Ser.). (ENG.). 40p. (J). (gr. -1-3). 17.99 *(978-0-544-81376-2(6),* 1642033, Clarion Bks.) HarperCollins Pubs.
Appelt, Kathi. Mogie: The Heart of the House. Rosenthal, Marc, illus. 2014. (ENG.). 40p. (J). (gr. -1-3). 17.99 *(978-1-4424-8054-4(8),* Atheneum Bks. for Young Readers) Simon & Schuster Children's Publishing.
Archambault, Marc. Mommy Is Too Tired to Play. 2010. 32p. 18.97 *(978-0-557-23350-2(X))* Lulu Pr., Inc.
Archer, Dosh. Baaad Sheep. Archer, Dosh, illus. 2016. (Urgency Emergency! Ser.). (ENG., Illus.). 48p. (J). (gr. k-2). 12.99 *(978-0-8075-8349-4(9),* 807583499) Whitman, Albert & Co.

Avery, Lara. The Memory Book. (ENG.). (YA). 2017. 384p. (gr. 9-17). pap. 10.99 (978-0-316-28376-2(2)) 2016. 368p. (gr. 10-17). 17.99 (978-0-316-28374-8(6)) Little, Brown Bks. for Young Readers. (Poppy).

—The Memory Book. 2017. (YA). lib. bdg. 20.85 (978-0-606-39907-4(0)) Turtleback.

Avi. The Barn. 2014. (ENG.). 112p. (J). (gr. 3-7). pap. 7.99 (978-0-545-60744-5(2), Scholastic Paperbacks) Scholastic, Inc.

Banks, Steven. Spongebob Goes to the Doctor. Saunders, Zina, illus. 2005. 22p. (J). lib. bdg. 15.00 (978-1-4242-0976-7(5)) Fitzgerald Bks.

Basoff, Kathleen. Merdove Cove. 2008. 28p. pap. 14.95 (978-1-4389-2095-5(4)) AuthorHouse.

Beasley, Cassie. Circus Mirandus. 2016. (SPA.). 25.99 (978-84-246-5686-7(5)) La Galera, S.A. Editorial ESP. Dist: Lectorum Pubns., Inc.

—Circus Mirandus. 2016. (ENG., Illus.). 320p. (J). (gr. 4-7). pap. 8.99 (978-0-14-751554-4(8), Puffin Books) Penguin Young Readers Group.

—Circus Mirandus. l.t. ed. 2020. (ENG.). lib. bdg. 22.99 (978-1-4328-7834-4(4)) Thorndike Pr.

—Circus Mirandus. 2016. (ENG.). 304p. (J). (gr. 3-7). 19.65 (978-0-606-39311-9(0)) Turtleback.

Becker, Bonny. The Sniffles for Bear. Denton, Kady MacDonald, illus. 2019. (Bear & Mouse Ser.). (ENG.). 32p. (J). (gr. -1-2). 8.99 (978-0-7636-6539-5(8)) Candlewick Pr.

Beilenson, Evelyn. The Zoo Is Closed Today! Kennedy, Anne, illus. 2014. (ENG.). 32p. (J). 16.99 (978-1-4413-1526-7(8), bafefaaa-3ed9-4f39-af87-f94b55eddd8d) Peter Pauper Pr. Inc.

Bemelmans, Ludwig. Madeline: Edicion en Espanol. Anasal, Arshes, ed. 2005. (SPA., Illus.). 44p. (J). (gr. k-4). reprint ed. 16.00 (978-0-7567-8842-1(0)) DIANE Publishing Co.

Berry, Eileen M. Looking for Home. Manning, Maurie J., illus. 2006. 75p. (J). (gr. -1-3). per. (978-1-59166-493-2(4)) BJU Pr.

Blake, Kendare. Antigoddess. 2014. (Goddess War Ser.: 1). (ENG.). 352p. (YA). (gr. 7-12). pap. 18.99 (978-0-7653-3446-6(1), 900095865, Tor Teen) Doherty, Tom Assocs., LLC.

Blevins, Wiley. Ick's Bleh Day (Book 1), Bk. 1. Paillot, Jim, illus. 2017. (Funny Bone Books (tm) First Chapters — Ick & Crud Ser.). (ENG.). 32p. (J). (gr. k-2). pap. 6.99 (978-1-63440-188-3(3), 66fa8262-994a-4801-9698-cf6cc2832e89); lib. bdg. 19.99 (978-1-63440-185-2(9), 6e6ce89e-5171-4843-ab93-6f711d4f4a1c) Red Chair Pr.

Bowen, Cynthia Wiesner. Tamika & Grandpa Jake. 2007. 32p. per. 14.95 (978-1-4327-0642-5(X)) Outskirts Pr., Inc.

Branford, Anna. Violet Mackerel's Remarkable Recovery. Allen, Elanna, illus. 2013. (Violet Mackerel Ser.). (ENG.). 128p. (J). (gr. 1-5). pap. 5.99 (978-1-4424-3589-6(5), Atheneum Bks. for Young Readers) Simon & Schuster Children's Publishing.

—Violet Mackerel's Remarkable Recovery. Allen, Elanna, illus. 2013. (Violet Mackerel Ser.). (ENG.). 128p. (J). (gr. 1-5). 15.99 (978-1-4424-3588-9(7)) Simon & Schuster, Inc.

Carbone, Courtney. Dragon Pox! (Shimmer & Shine) Cartobaleno, illus. 2018. (Little Golden Book Ser.). (ENG.). 24p. (J). (-k). 4.99 (978-1-5247-6798-3(0), Golden Bks.) Random Hse. Children's Bks.

Carter, Candace. Sid's Surprise. Kim, Joung Un, illus. 2005. (Green Light Readers Level 1 Ser.). (gr. -1-3). 13.95 (978-0-7569-5242-6(5)) Perfection Learning Corp.

Castro, Anita. Two Hands to Hold. Wroth, Dean, illus. 2013. 32p. (J). pap. 10.49 (978-0-944727-57-7(3)); lib. bdg. 16.95 (978-0-944727-58-4(1)) Jason & Nordic Pubs. (Turtle Bks.).

Castrovilla, Selene. The Girl Next Door. 2010. 240p. (YA). (gr. 9-12). 16.95 (978-1-934813-15-7(X)) Westside Bks.

Cazet, Denys. Grandpa Spanielson's Chicken Pox Stories No. 1: The Octopus. Cazet, Denys, illus. 2005. (I Can Read Bks.). (Illus.). 48p. (J). (gr. -1-3). lib. bdg. 16.89 (978-0-06-051089-3(7)) HarperCollins Pubs.

—The Octopus. Cazet, Denys, illus. 2008. (Grandpa Spanielson's Chicken Pox Stories Ser.). (Illus.). (J). (gr. -1-3). pap. 16.95 incl. audio (978-1-4301-0455-1(4));Set. pap. 29.95 incl. audio (978-1-4301-0457-5(0));Set. pap. 31.95 incl. audio compact disk (978-1-4301-0460-5(0)) Live Oak Media.

Christopher, Matt. Slam Dunk. 2004. (ENG., Illus.). 128p. (J). (gr. 3-7). pap. 6.99 (978-0-316-60762-9(2)) Little, Brown Bks. for Young Readers.

Corchin, D. J. I Feel... Sick. 2020. (I Feel... Ser.). (Illus.). 56p. (J). (gr. -1-3). 14.99 (978-1-7282-1952-3(3)) Sourcebooks, Inc.

Cowan, Charlotte. Sadie's Sore Throat. Bratun, Katy, illus. 2007. (Dr. Hippo Ser.). (ENG.). 32p. (J). (gr. 3-7). 17.95 (978-0-9753516-4-2(8)) Hippocratic Pr., The.

Crutcher, Chris. Deadline. 2009. (ENG.). 336p. (YA). (gr. 9). pap. 10.99 (978-0-06-085091-3(4), Greenwillow Bks.) HarperCollins Pubs.

Cyrus, Kurt. Be a Good Dragon. Cyrus, Kurt, illus. 2018. (ENG., Illus.). 32p. (J). (gr. k-3). 16.99 (978-1-58536-383-4(9), 204395) Sleeping Bear Pr.

Davies, Katie. The Great Rabbit Rescue. Shaw, Hannah, illus. 2011. (Great Critter Capers Ser.). (ENG.). 224p. (J). (gr. 3-7). 12.99 (978-1-4424-2064-9(2), Beach Lane Bks.) Beach Lane Bks.

Day, Alexandra. Carl & the Sick Puppy. 2012. (My Readers: Level 1 Ser.). (J). lib. bdg. 13.55 (978-0-606-26121-0(4)) Turtleback.

De Kockere, Geert & Dom, An. Dragon Fire. van Hemeldonck, Tineke, illus. 2015. (ENG.). 32p. (J). (gr. -1-k). 16.99 (978-1-63220-599-5(8), Sky Pony Pr.) Skyhorse Publishing Co., Inc.

Dealey, Erin. Goldie Locks Has Chicken Pox. 2004. (Illus.). (J). (gr. k-3). spiral bd. (978-0-616-14572-2(1)); spiral bd. (978-0-616-14573-9(X)) Canadian National Institute for the Blind/Institut National Canadien pour les Aveugles.

—Goldie Locks Has Chicken Pox. Wakiyama, Hanako, illus. 2005. (ENG.). 40p. (J). (gr. -1-2). reprint ed. 8.99 (978-0-689-87610-3(6), Aladdin) Simon & Schuster Children's Publishing.

Dewdney, Anna. Llama Llama Home with Mama. 2011. (Llama Llama Ser.). (ENG., Illus.). 40p. (J). (gr. -1-k). 18.99 (978-0-670-01232-9(7), Viking Books for Young Readers) Penguin Young Readers Group.

DiTerlizzi, Tony & DiTerlizzi, Angela. Uh-Oh Sick! DiTerlizzi, Tony, illus. 2010. (Adventure of Meno Ser.: 4). (ENG., Illus.). 52p. (J). (gr. -1-k). 9.99 (978-1-4169-7153-5(X), Simon & Schuster Bks. For Young Readers) Simon & Schuster Bks. For Young Readers.

Duffield, Katy S. Aliens Get the Sniffles Too! Ahhh-Choo! Campbell, K. G., illus. 2017. (ENG.). 32p. (J). (gr. -1-2). 16.99 (978-0-7636-6502-9(9)) Candlewick Pr.

Duffy, Carol Ann. The Princess's Blankets. Hyde, Catherine, illus. 2009. (ENG.). 40p. (J). (gr. k-3). 18.99 (978-0-7636-4547-2(8), Templar) Candlewick Pr.

Estes, Don. Willy & Friends traveling through the Seasons: The continuing story of Willy the little fire Jeep. Glass, Eric, illus. 2006. (J). (978-1-883551-75-9(7), Maple Corners Press) Attic Studio Publishing Hse.

Fairy-Tale Flowers: Individual Title, 6 pack. (Story Steps Ser.). (gr. k-2). 23.00 (978-0-7635-9842-6(9)) Rigby Education.

Fenn, G. Manville. Brownsmith's Boy. 2008. 260p. pap. 15.95 (978-1-60664-154-5(9)) Aegypan.

Fontes, Justine. Jordan's Silly Sick Day. Lee, Jared, tr. Lee, Jared, illus. 2004. (Rookie Readers Ser.). 31p. (J). 19.50 (978-0-516-25897-3(4), Children's Pr.) Scholastic Library Publishing.

Friedman, Laurie. Happy New Year, Mallory! Kalis, Jennifer, illus. 2010. (Mallory Ser.: 12). (ENG.). 176p. (J). (gr. 2-5). pap. 7.99 (978-0-7613-3947-2(7), c930191f-8192-4d65-a9fd-492ff472642f, Darby Creek) Lerner Publishing Group.

—Happy New Year, Mallory! 12th rev. ed. 2010. pap. 33.92 (978-0-7613-6996-7(1)) Lerner Publishing Group.

Goldblatt, Mark. Finding the Worm (Twerp Sequel) 2016. (Twerp Ser.: 2). 368p. (J). (gr. 4-7). 7.99 (978-0-385-39111-5(0), Yearling) Random Hse. Children's Bks.

Grant, Michael. Plague. (Gone Ser.: 4). (ENG.). (YA). (gr. 8). 2014. 528p. pap. 12.99 (978-0-06-144914-7(8)) 2011. 512p. 17.99 (978-0-06-144912-3(1)) HarperCollins Pubs. (Tegen, Katherine Bks).

Gray, Kes. Daisy & the Trouble with Life. Parsons, Garry & Sharratt, Nick, illus. 2007. (Daisy Ser.: 12). (ENG.). 240p. (J). (gr. 2-4). pap. 11.95 (978-1-86230-167-2(0), Red Fox) Random House Children's Books GBR. Dist: Independent Pubs. Group.

Gray, Libba Moore. Miss Tizzy. Rowland, Jada, illus. 2014. 40p. pap. 8.00 (978-1-61003-356-5(6)) Center for the Collaborative Classroom.

Greenfield, Eloise. William & the Good Old Days. Date not set. (Illus.). 32p. (J). (gr. k-3). pap. 4.99 (978-0-06-443453-9(2)) HarperCollins Pubs.

Gregory, Dee. The Accidental Daughter: A Children's Story about Hope. 2008. 96p. pap. 10.49 (978-1-4389-3338-2(X)) AuthorHouse.

Greves, Julie, et al. Upside down & Backwards: A Sibling's Journey Through Childhood Cancer. 2014. (Illus.). 112p. (J). (978-1-4338-1637-6(7), Magination Pr.) American Psychological Assn.

Guest, Elissa Haden. Iris & Walter - The School Play. Davenier, Christine, illus. 2006. (Iris & Walter Ser.). 44p. (gr. 1-4). 15.95 (978-0-7569-6679-9(5)) Perfection Learning Corp.

Hannigan, Katherine. Ida B: ... & Her Plans to Maximize Fun, Avoid Disaster, & (Possibly) Save the World. 2004. (ENG.). 256p. (J). (gr. 4-18). 17.99 (978-0-06-073024-6(2), Greenwillow Bks.) HarperCollins Pubs.

—Ida B: ... And Her Plans to Maximize Fun, Avoid Disaster, & (Possibly) Save the World. 2004. 256p. (gr. 4-18). lib. bdg. 16.89 (978-0-06-073025-3(0)) HarperCollins Pubs.

—Ida B: ... & Her Plans to Maximize Fun, Avoid Disaster, & (Possibly) Save the World. 2011. (ENG.). 272p. (J). (gr. 5-9). reprint ed. pap. 7.99 (978-0-06-073026-0(9), Greenwillow Bks.) HarperCollins Pubs.

Harazin, S. A. Painless. 2015. (ENG.). 304p. (YA). (gr. 8-12). 16.99 (978-0-8075-6288-8(2), 807562882) Whitman, Albert & Co.

Harrison, Christy Gremore. Once upon A Monday. 2010. 40p. pap. 16.99 (978-1-4490-5854-8(X)) AuthorHouse.

Hayles, Marsha. Breathing Room. 2013. (ENG., Illus.). 272p. (J). (gr. 5-9). pap. 13.99 (978-1-250-03411-3(6), 900120581) Square Fish.

Headley, Maria Dahvana. Magonia. 2016. (Magonia Ser.: 1). (ENG.). 336p. (YA). (gr. 8). pap. 10.99 (978-0-06-232053-7(X), HarperCollins) HarperCollins Pubs.

Hest, Amy. Don't You Feel Well, Sam? Jeram, Anita, illus. 2007. (Sam Bks.). (ENG.). 32p. (J). (gr. -1-k). 5.99 (978-0-7636-2408-8(X)) Candlewick Pr.

Hill, Eric. Get Well Soon, Spot. 2017. (Spot Ser.). (ENG., Illus.). 12p. (J). (-k). bds. 6.99 (978-0-14-137242-6(7), Warne) Penguin Young Readers Group.

Hulst, W. G. van de & Hulst. Willem G. van de, illus. The Black Kitten. 2014. (J). (978-1-928136-07-1(9)) Inheritance Pubns.

—Bruno the Bear. 2014. 48p. (J). (978-1-928136-03-3(6)) Inheritance Pubns.

—The Secret in the Box. 2014. (J). (978-1-928136-17-0(6)) Inheritance Pubns.

Hurley, Tonya. Ghostgirl: Homecoming. 2010. (Ghostgirl Ser.: 2). (ENG.). 304p. (YA). (gr. 7-17). pap. 16.99 (978-0-316-08943-2(5)) Little, Brown Bks. for Young Readers.

Jensen, Patricia. I Am Sick. Hantel, Johanna, illus. 2005. (My First Reader Ser.). (ENG.). 32p. (J). (gr. k-1). lib. bdg. 18.50 (978-0-516-24878-3(2), Children's Pr.) Scholastic Library Publishing.

Jones, Frewin. Faerie Path #5: the Enchanted Quest. 2010. (Faerie Path Ser.: 5). (ENG.). 368p. (YA). (gr. 8-18). 16.99 (978-0-06-087158-1(X), HarperTeen) HarperCollins Pubs.

K/H (Pathways). Kindergarten Stepping Stones: Kindergarten the Bravest Dog Ever - The True Story of Balto Trade Book. rev. ed. 2010. (ENG.). 48p. pap. 9.00 (978-0-7575-8646-0(5)) Kendall Hunt Publishing Co.

Kann, Victoria. Pinkalicious & the Sick Day. Kann, Victoria, illus. 2015. (I Can Read Level 1 Ser.). (ENG., Illus.). 32p. (J). (gr. -1-3). 16.99 (978-0-06-224599-1(6), HarperCollins) HarperCollins Pubs.

—Pinkalicious: the Princess of Pink Slumber Party. Kann, Victoria, illus. 2012. (I Can Read Level 1 Ser.). (ENG., Illus.). 32p. (J). (gr. -1-3). 16.99 (978-0-06-198963-6(0), HarperCollins) HarperCollins Pubs.

Kann, Victoria, illus. Pinkalicious & the Sick Day. 2015. 30p. (J). (978-1-4806-8664-9(6)) Harper & Row Ltd.

Keeling, Annie E. Andrew Golding A Tale of the Great Plague. 2004. reprint ed. pap. 15.95 (978-1-4191-0694-1(5)); pap. 1.99 (978-1-4192-0694-8(X)) Kessinger Publishing, LLC.

Keller, Tae. When You Trap a Tiger. 2020. 304p. (J). (978-0-593-17534-7(4)) Random Hse., Inc.

—When You Trap a Tiger: (Newbery Medal Winner) (J). (gr. 3-7). 2023. 320p. pap. 8.99 (978-1-5247-1573-1(5), Yearling) 2020. (ENG.). 304p. 17.99 (978-1-5247-1570-0(0), Random Hse. Bks. for Young Readers) 2020. (ENG.). 304p. lib. bdg. 19.99 (978-1-5247-1571-7(9), Random Hse. Bks. for Young Readers) Random Hse. Children's Bks.

Kellogg, Elijah. The Young Shipbuilders of Elm Island by Rev Elijah Kellogg. 2006. 316p. per. 23.99 (978-1-4255-3063-1(X)) Michigan Publishing.

Ketteman, Helen. If Beaver Had a Fever, 0 vols. O'Malley, Kevin, illus. 2012. (ENG.). 32p. (J). (gr. -1-3). 16.99 (978-0-7614-5951-4(0), 9780761459514, Two Lions) Amazon Publishing.

Knights, Harry B. Angel's Star. 2006. (J). lib. bdg. 20.00 (978-0-9632248-8-0(3)) Synergetic Pubns., Inc.

Koertge, Ronald. Shakespeare Bats Cleanup. 2006. 116p. (gr. 7-12). 16.00 (978-0-7569-6571-6(3)) Perfection Learning Corp.

Krall, Dan. Sick Simon. Krall, Dan, illus. 2015. (ENG., Illus.). 48p. (J). (gr. -1-3). 18.99 (978-1-4424-9097-0(7), Simon & Schuster Bks. For Young Readers) Simon & Schuster Bks. For Young Readers.

Krulik, Nancy. Don't Sneeze! #2. Thomas, Louis, illus. 2017. (Kid from Planet Z Ser.: 2). 96p. (J). (gr. 1-3). 5.99 (978-0-451-53343-2(7), Grosset & Dunlap) Penguin Young Readers Group.

Lancett, Peter. The Dark Candle. 2007. (Dark Man Ser.). (ENG.). 36p. pap. (978-1-84167-603-6(9)) Ransom Publishing Ltd.

Lee, Jenny. Elvis & the Underdogs. Light, Kelly, illus. 2013. (Elvis & the Underdogs Ser.: 1). (ENG.). 304p. (J). (gr. 3-7). 16.99 (978-0-06-223554-1(0), Balzer & Bray) HarperCollins Pubs.

Lotto, Lisa Marie. Oh How We Feel When We Are Sick with the Flu: Oh the Things We See When We Go to the Park. 2008. 28p. pap. 13.99 (978-1-4343-6009-0(1)) AuthorHouse.

Lubar, David. Dunk. 2004. (ENG.). 272p. (YA). (gr. 7-18). reprint ed. pap. 9.99 (978-0-618-43909-6(9), 490005, Clarion Bks.) HarperCollins Pubs.

Maier, Inger. Ben's Flying Flowers. Bogade, Maria, illus. 2012. 32p. (J). 14.95 (978-1-4338-1133-3(2)); (ENG.). pap. 9.95 (978-1-4338-1132-6(4)) American Psychological Assn. (Magination Pr.).

Manushkin, Fran. Katie Woo Has the Flu, 1 vol. Lyon, Tammie, illus. 2011. (Katie Woo Ser.). (ENG.). 32p. (J). (gr. k-2). pap. 5.95 (978-1-4048-6854-0(2), 116435); lib. bdg. 21.32 (978-1-4048-6518-1(7), 114214) Capstone. (Picture Window Bks.).

Matas, Carol. Tales of a Reluctant Psychic: The Freak, Visions, & Far. 2009. (ENG.). 424p. (YA). (gr. 7-18). pap. (978-1-55470-203-9(8)) Me to We.

Matt and Dave, Matt and. Yuck's Fart Club. Baines, Nigel, illus. 2013. (Yuck Ser.). (ENG.). 112p. (J). (gr. 2-5). pap. 6.99 (978-1-4424-8152-7(8), Simon & Schuster/Paula Wiseman Bks.) Simon & Schuster/Paula Wiseman Bks.

Maurer, Shari. Change of Heart. 2010. 290p. (YA). 16.95 (978-1-934813-36-2(2)) Westside Bks.

Mayer, Mercer. Little Critter: Just a Little Sick. Mayer, Mercer, illus. 2009. (My First I Can Read Ser.). (ENG., Illus.). 32p. (J). (gr. -1-3). 16.99 (978-0-06-083556-9(7)); pap. 5.99 (978-0-06-083555-2(9)) HarperCollins Pubs. (HarperCollins).

Mcdonald, Megan. The Doctor Is In! 2010. (Judy Moody Ser.: 5). lib. bdg. 16.00 (978-0-606-12343-3(1)) Turtleback.

—Judy Moody, M. D. Reynolds, Peter H., illus. 2010. (Judy Moody Ser.: 5). (ENG.). 176p. (J). (gr. 1-4). 15.99 (978-0-7636-4862-6(0)) Candlewick Pr.

—Judy Moody, M. D. The Doctor Is In! 2018. (Judy Moody Ser.: 5). lib. bdg. 16.00 (978-0-606-41195-0(X)) Turtleback.

McGovern, Kate. Rules for 50/50 Chances: A Novel. 2015. (ENG.). 352p. (YA). (gr. 7). 17.99 (978-0-374-30158-3(1), 900140111, Farrar, Straus & Giroux (BYR)) Farrar, Straus & Giroux.

McKissack, Patricia C. & Moss, Onawumi Jean. Precious & the Boo Hag. Brooker, Kyrsten, illus. 2005. (ENG.). 40p. (J). (gr. -1-3). 19.99 (978-0-689-85194-0(4), Atheneum Bks. for Young Readers) Simon & Schuster Children's Publishing.

McPhail, David. Rick Is Sick. McPhail, David, illus. 2004. (Green Light Readers Ser.). (ENG., Illus.). 24p. (J). (gr. -1-3). pap. 5.99 (978-0-15-205092-4(2), 1195376, Clarion Bks.) HarperCollins Pubs.

—Rick Is Sick. 2004. (Green Light Readers Level 1 Ser.). 13.50 (978-0-613-97286-4(4)) Turtleback.

—Sick Day. 2013. (I Like to Read Ser.). (ENG.). 24p. (J). (gr. -1-3). pap. 7.99 (978-0-8234-2910-3(5)) Holiday Hse., Inc.

Michaels, Andie. ACHOO! ACHOO! I've Got the Flu. (ENG.). (J). 2021. pap. 14.95 (978-1-7330663-2-7(2)) 2019. 32p. 19.95 (978-1-7330663-0-3(6)) Mulberry Street Publishing.

Mikalatos, Matt. The Crescent Stone. 2018. (Sunlit Lands Ser.: 1). (ENG., Illus.). 448p. (YA). 24.99 (978-1-4964-3170-7(7), 20_31146, Wander) Tyndale Hse. Pubs.

—The Heartwood Crown. 2019. (Sunlit Lands Ser.: 2). (ENG., Illus.). 416p. (YA). pap. 15.99 (978-1-4964-3176-9(6), 20_31152, Wander) Tyndale Hse. Pubs.

Miller, Jennifer. Run, Rasputin, Run! Trials & Friendships (Book 2) 2006. (ENG., Illus.). 172p. per. 14.85 (978-1-4120-8494-9(6)) Trafford Publishing.

Milliner, Naomi. Super Jake & the King of Chaos. 2019. (ENG.). 288p. (J). (gr. 3-7). 16.99 (978-0-7624-6615-3(4), Running Pr. Kids) Running Pr.

Mills, Joyce C. Little Tree: A Story for Children with Serious Medical Illness. Sebern, Brian, illus. 2nd ed. 2003. 32p. (J). pap. 9.95 (978-1-59147-042-7(0)); 14.95 (978-1-59147-041-0(2)) American Psychological Assn. (Magination Pr.).

Moore, Helen H. The Secret of Willow Ridge: Gabe's Dad Finds Recovery. Blackford, John C., illus. 2010. (ENG.). 128p. (J). (gr. 3-7). pap. 12.95 (978-0-9818482-0-4(6)) Central Recovery Pr.

Moses, Shelia P. The Legend of Buddy Bush. 2005. (Illus.). 211p. (gr. 7-12). 17.00 (978-0-7569-5459-8(2)) Perfection Learning Corp.

—The Legend of Buddy Bush, 3 vols. unabr. ed. 2005. (YA). (gr. 3-7). 54.75 (978-1-4193-3575-4(8), 42043) Recorded Bks., Inc.

Mosier, Paul. Echo's Sister. 2018. (ENG., Illus.). 240p. (J). (gr. 3-7). 16.99 (978-0-06-245567-3(2), HarperCollins) HarperCollins Pubs.

Moss, John. The Girl in a Coma. 2016. 320p. (YA). pap. 18.99 (978-1-929345-24-3(0), Poisoned Pen Press) Sourcebooks, Inc.

Murphy, Jill. Mr. Large in Charge. Murphy, Jill, illus. 2007. (Large Family Ser.). (ENG., Illus.). 40p. (J). (gr. -1-3). 16.99 (978-0-7636-3504-6(9)) Candlewick Pr.

Murphy, Sally. Toppling. James, Rhian Nest, illus. 2012. (ENG.). 128p. (J). (gr. 3-7). 15.99 (978-0-7636-5921-9(5)) Candlewick Pr.

Nelid, Piper. Sick Visit, 1 vol., 1. 2015. (Rosen REAL Readers: STEM & STEAM Collection). (ENG.). 12p. (J). (gr. 1-2). pap. 6.33 (978-1-5081-1587-8(7), 958996eb-28f7-42bf-87ed-c98a009ca0da, Rosen Classroom) Rosen Publishing Group, Inc., The.

Nolan, Han. When We Were Saints. 2005. (ENG.). 312p. (YA). (gr. 7-12). pap. 15.95 (978-0-15-205322-2(0), 1196035, Clarion Bks.) HarperCollins Pubs.

O'Connor, Jane. Fancy Nancy: Bubbles, Bubbles, & More Bubbles! Glasser, Robin Preiss, illus. 2018. (I Can Read Level 1 Ser.). (ENG.). 32p. (J). (gr. -1-3). pap. 4.99 (978-0-06-237789-0(2), HarperCollins) HarperCollins Pubs.

Park, Barbara. Junie B. Jones #23: Shipwrecked, No. 23. Brunkus, Denise, illus. 2005. (Junie B. Jones Ser.: 23). (ENG.). 96p. (J). (gr. 1-4). mass mkt. 5.99 (978-0-375-82805-8(2), Random Hse. Bks. for Young Readers) Random Hse. Children's Bks.

Parr, Susan Sherwood. Christopher's Adventures: Chris Visits the Hospital, Vol. 2. Paraschiv, Doina, illus. 2nd alt. ed. 2013. (ENG.). 24p. (J). pap. 8.95 (978-0-9827998-8-8(8), Kid-E Bks.) Word Productions.

Parriera Jr., Jack. What to Do When Your Brother Is Sick. 2012. (ENG.). 32p. pap. 17.97 (978-1-105-47064-6(4)) Lulu Pr., Inc.

Perrin, Randy, et al. Time Like a River. 2004. 144p. (gr. 5-18). 14.95 (978-1-57143-061-8(X)) RDR Bks.

Porpora, Donnamarie. Grampa's Wings. 2013. 32p. pap. (978-1-4602-1366-7(1)) FriesenPress.

Powers, J. L. This Thing Called the Future, 1 vol. 2011. (ENG.). 208p. (YA). (gr. 9-12). 16.95 (978-1-933693-95-8(9), 23353382, Cinco Puntos Press) Lee & Low Bks., Inc.

Railsback, Lisa. Betti on the High Wire. 2011. (ENG.). 208p. (J). (gr. 4-6). 21.19 (978-0-8037-3388-6(7)) Penguin Young Readers Group.

Rakusin, Sudie. Dear Calla Roo... Love, Savannah Blue No. 2: A Letter about Getting Sick & Feeling Better. Rakusin, Sudie, illus. 2003. (Illus.). 32p. (J). (gr. -1-4). 16.95 (978-0-9664805-3-5(8)) Winged Willow Pr.

Reuterstrand, Siri. Ellis Goes to the Doctor. Wik, Jenny, illus. 2012. (ENG.). 24p. (J). (gr. -1-k). 12.95 (978-1-61608-662-6(9), 608662, Sky Pony Pr.) Skyhorse Publishing Co., Inc.

Riggs, Sandy. Nick Is Sick. Koeller, Carol, illus. 2006. (Barron's Reader's Clubhouse Level 1 Ser.). (ENG.). 24p. (J). (gr. k-3). 16.19 (978-0-7641-3284-1(9), B.E.S. Publishing) Peterson's.

Ritchie, Janet. Remember That I Love You. 2008. (ENG.). 40p. 18.99 (978-1-4389-3155-5(7)) AuthorHouse.

Rockliff, Mara. Chik Chak Shabbat. Brooker, Kyrsten, illus. 2016. (ENG.). 32p. (J). (gr. -1-2). 7.99 (978-0-7636-8895-0(9)) Candlewick Pr.

Rose, Naomi C. Tashi & the Tibetan Flower Care, 1 vol. 2016. (ENG.). 40p. (J). (gr. 1-6). 11.95 (978-1-62014-318-6(6), leelowbooks) Lee & Low Bks., Inc.

Rosenberry, Vera. When Vera Was Sick, 4 bks., Set. Rosenberry, Vera, illus. unabr. ed. 2006. (Picture Book Readalong Ser.). (Illus.). (J). (gr. -1-3). pap. 37.95 incl. audio (978-1-59519-652-1(8)); pap. 39.95 incl. audio compact disk (978-1-59519-653-8(6)) Live Oak Media.

Ross, Tony. I Feel Sick! Ross, Tony, illus. 2015. (ENG., Illus.). 32p. (J). (gr. -1-3). 16.99 (978-1-4677-5797-3(7)) Andersen Pr. GBR. Dist: Lerner Publishing Group.

—I Feel Sick! Ross, Tony, illus. 2015. (Little Princess Ser.). (ENG., Illus.). 32p. (J). (gr. -1-3). E-Book 27.99 (978-1-4677-5798-0(5)) Lerner Publishing Group.

Rouss, Sylvia A. Sammy Spider's First Mitzvah. Kahn, Katherine Janus, illus. 2014. (ENG.). 24p. (J). (gr. -1-3). 17.95 (978-1-4677-1947-6(1), a8861aa7-d249-435f-ac41-dc242b6e1326, Kar-Ben Publishing) Lerner Publishing Group.

Rowley, Deborah. The Miracle of the Wooden Shoes. 2008. 32p. (J). 18.95 (978-1-59038-990-4(5)) Deseret Bk. Co.

Rylant, Cynthia. Henry & Mudge Get the Cold Shivers. Stevenson, Suçie, illus. (Henry & Mudge Ser.). 9.95 (978-1-59112-290-6(2)) Live Oak Media.

—Mr. Putter & Tabby Catch the Cold. Howard, Arthur, illus. 2007. (Mr. Putter & Tabby Ser.). pap. 7.93 (978-1-4189-5220-4(6)) Houghton Mifflin Harcourt Trade & Reference Pubs.

—Mr. Putter & Tabby Catch the Cold. Howard, Arthur, illus. 2003. (Mr. Putter & Tabby Ser.). (gr. 1-4). 16.00 (978-0-7569-1514-8(7)) Perfection Learning Corp.

Salomon, Bob & Young, Rick. Beyond the Laces. 2015. (ENG., Illus.). (J). pap. 12.95 (978-1-4951-5694-6(X)) Independent Pub.

Sanschagrin, Joceline. Caillou at the Doctor. Brignaud, Pierre, illus. 3rd ed. 2013. (Step by Step Ser.). (ENG.). 24p. (J). (gr. -1-k). bds. 5.99 (978-2-89718-058-4(7)) Caillouet, Gerry.

Scholastic, Inc. Staff & Bermiss, Aamir Lee. I Hate to Be Sick! Wilson-Max, Ken, illus. 2004. (Just for You Ser.). (ENG.). 32p. (gr. k-3). pap. 3.99 (978-0-439-56877-7(3), Teaching Resources) Scholastic, Inc.

Scott, Laurian. Thisbe's Promise. Sharp, Kelley, illus. 2008. (ENG.). 32p. (J). 16.99 (978-0-9816642-0-0(2)) ETS Publishing.

Sedgwick, Chantele. Interlude. 2018. (Love, Lucas Novel Ser.: 3). (ENG.). 284p. (YA). (gr. 7-13). 16.99

The check digit for ISBN-10 appears in parentheses after the full ISBN-13

(978-1-5107-1515-8(0), Sky Pony Pr.) Skyhorse Publishing Co., Inc.
Sedgwick, Marcus. Snowflake, AZ. 2019. (ENG.). 320p. (YA). (gr. 7-12). 18.95 (978-1-324-00441-7(X), 340441, Norton Young Readers) Norton, W. W. & Co., Inc.
Sheils, B. Malone. Henry Has a Head Cold. 2010. 32p. 17.00 (978-1-4389-5326-7(7)) AuthorHouse.
Shepherd, Megan. The Secret Horses of Briar Hill. 2018. (ENG.). 240p. (J). (gr. 5). 9.99 (978-1-101-93978-9(8), Yearling) Random Hse. Children's Bks.
Simhaee, Rebeka. Avi's Choice: A Story about Bikur Cholim-Visiting the Sick. Hechter, Janice, illus. 2014. 35p. (J). (978-0-8266-0043-1(3)) Merkos L'Inyonei Chinuch.
Slade, Cheryl. Mummy Is Sick, but I Love You. 2019. (ENG.). 28p. 37.94 (978-1-9845-0474-6(6)); (Illus.). pap. 24.14 (978-1-9845-0473-9(8)) Xlibris Corp.
Slate, Joseph. Miss Bindergarten Stays Home from Kindergarten. Wolff, Ashley, illus. 2004. 40p. (J). (gr. -1-k). reprint ed. pap. 8.99 (978-0-14-230127-2(2), Puffin Books) Penguin Young Readers Group.
Sliwerski, Jessica Reid. Cancer Hates Kisses. Song, Mika, illus. 2017. 40p. (J). (-k). 18.99 (978-0-7352-2781-1(0), Dial Bks) Penguin Young Readers Group.
Sommers, Jackie Lea. Truest. 2015. (ENG.). 384p. (YA). (gr. 8). 17.99 (978-0-06-234825-8(6), HarperCollins) HarperCollins Pubs.
Sorell, Traci. Powwow Day. Goodnight, Madelyn, illus. 2022. 32p. (J). (gr. -1-3). lib. bdg. 17.99 (978-1-58089-948-2(X)) Charlesbridge Publishing, Inc.
Soto, Gary. Chato Goes Cruisin' Guevara, Susan, illus. 2008. (Chato Ser.). (J). 25.95 incl. audio (978-1-59519-906-5(3)) Live Oak Media.
—Chato Goes Cruisin' Guevara, Susan, illus. 2007. (Chato Ser.). (J). (gr. -1-3). 14.65 (978-0-7569-8147-1(6)) Perfection Learning Corp.
Stead, Philip C. A Sick Day for Amos McGee. Stead, Erin E., illus. 2010. (JPN.). 32p. (J). (gr. -1-1). (978-4-89572-814-0(5)) Hisakata-Child.
—A Sick Day for Amos McGee. 2012. (CHI.). (J). (gr. -1-1). (978-986-211-314-1(6)) Hsaio Lu Publishing Co., Ltd.
—A Sick Day for Amos Mcgee. Stead, Erin E., illus. (ENG.). (J). 2018. 34p. bds. 9.99 (978-1-250-17110-8(5), 900188204) 2010. 32p. (gr. -1-1). 18.99 (978-1-59643-402-8(3), 900051603) Roaring Brook Pr.
—A Sick Day for Amos Mcgee: 10th Anniversary Edition. Stead, Erin E., illus. 10th ed. 2019. (ENG.). 40p. (J). 29.99 (978-1-62672-105-0(X), 900136450) Roaring Brook Pr.
—A Sick Day for Amos Mcgee: Book & CD Storytime Set: Book & CD Storytime Set. Stead, Erin E., illus. 2017. (Macmillan Young Listeners Story Time Sets Ser.). (ENG.). 32p. (J). 12.99 (978-1-4272-8722-9(8), 900178665) Macmillan Audio.
Stockham, Jess, illus. Doctor. 2011. (First Time Ser.). 24p. (J). (gr. 2-2). pap. (978-1-84643-334-4(7)) Child's Play International Ltd.
—Hospital. 2011. (First Time Ser.). 24p. (J). (gr. 2-2). pap. (978-1-84643-336-8(3)) Child's Play International Ltd.
Tague, James E. The Krankel Family. 2008. 32p. pap. 21.99 (978-1-4363-7170-4(8)) Xlibris Corp.
Taylor-Butler, Christine. Ah-Choo. Koeller, Carol, illus. 2005. (My First Reader Ser.). (ENG.). 32p. (J). (gr. k-1). 18.50 (978-0-516-25175-2(9), Children's Pr.) Scholastic Library Publishing.
Thebo, Mimi. Dreaming the Bear. 2017. 169p. (YA). pap. (978-0-399-55753-8(9)) Earthscan Canada.
Thomas, Shelley Moore. Get Well, Good Knight. Plecas, Jennifer, illus. 2004. (Penguin Young Readers, Level 3 Ser.). 48p. (J). (gr. 1-3). 4.99 (978-0-14-240050-0(5), Penguin Young Readers) Penguin Young Readers Group.
—Get Well, Good Knight. Plecas, Jennifer, illus. 2004. (Easy-to-Read Ser.). 44p. (gr. k-3). 14.00 (978-0-7569-2923-7(7)) Perfection Learning Corp.
—Get Well, Good Knight. 2004. (Penguin Young Readers: Level 3 Ser.). 13.55 (978-0-613-97291-8(0)) Turtleback.
Tim Todd. The Town of Ill. 2009. 36p. pap. 18.99 (978-1-4389-2778-7(9)) AuthorHouse.
Weber, Lori. Tattoo Heaven, 1 vol. 2005. (Lorimer SideStreets Ser.). (ENG.). 168p. (YA). (gr. 9-12). 16.95 (978-1-55028-903-9(9), 903); 8.99 (978-1-55028-902-2(0), 13526657-8e5a-41db-be9d-fb80af7971e9) James Lorimer & Co. Ltd., Pubs. CAN. Dist: Formac Lorimer Bks. Ltd., Lerner Publishing Group.
Weston Woods Staff, creator. How Do Dinosaurs Get Well Soon? 2011. 29.95 (978-0-439-76689-0(3)); 38.75 (978-0-439-84622-6(6)); 18.95 (978-0-439-84621-9(8)) Weston Woods Studios, Inc.
When I Was Sick: Individual Title, 6 packs. (Literatura 2000 Ser.). (gr. 1-2). 28.00 (978-0-7635-0018-4(6)) Rigby Education.
Whitney, A. D. T. Patience Strong's Outings by Mrs a D T Whitney. 2006. 236p. per. 20.99 (978-1-4255-2007-6(3)) Michigan Publishing.
Wilson, Karma. Bear Feels Sick. Chapman, Jane, illus. 2012. (Bear Bks.). (ENG.). 34p. (J). (gr. -1-2). bds. 8.99 (978-1-4424-4093-7(7), Little Simon) Little Simon.
—Bear Feels Sick. Chapman, Jane, illus. 2007. (Bear Bks.). (ENG.). 40p. (J). (gr. -1-3). 19.99 (978-0-689-85985-4(6), McElderry, Margaret K. Bks.) McElderry, Margaret K. Bks.
Wilson, Rebekah. Grandmother's Hope Chest: Lucie's Snowflakes. l.t. ed. 2004. (Illus.). 80p. (J). 15.00 (978-1-59565-003-0(2)) Hope Chest Legacy, Inc.
Wylie, Sarah. All These Lives. 1 vol. 2012. (ENG.). 256p. (YA). (gr. 7-12). 24.99 (978-0-374-30208-5(1), 900072205, Farrar, Straus & Giroux (BYR)) Farrar, Straus & Giroux.
Yolen, Jane. How Do Dinosaurs Get Well Soon? Teague, Mark, illus. 2003. (ENG.). 40p. (J). (gr. -1-3). 18.99 (978-0-439-24100-7(6), Blue Sky Pr., The) Scholastic, Inc.
Yonge, Charlotte M. Little Lucy's Wonderful Globe. 2008. 152p. 36.95 (978-0-548-97272-4(9)) Kessinger Publishing, LLC.
Yonge, Charlotte Mary. Little Lucy's Wonderful Globe. 2016. (ENG., Illus.). (J). 22.95 (978-1-358-12109-8(5)) Creative Media Partners, LLC.
—Little Lucys Wonderful Globe. 2017. (ENG., Illus.). 78p. (J). (978-3-7326-1919-1(2)); pap. (978-3-7326-1918-4(4)) Klassik Literatur. ein Imprint der Salzwasser Verlag GmbH.
Young, Judy. Digger & Daisy Go to the Doctor. Sullivan, Dana, illus. 2014. (Digger & Daisy Ser.). (ENG.). 32p. (J). (gr. k-2). 9.99 (978-1-58536-845-7(8), 203674); pap. 5.99 (978-1-58536-846-4(6), 203728) Sleeping Bear Pr.
—Digger et Daisy Vont Au Docteur (Digger & Daisy Go to the Doctor) Sullivan, Dana, illus. 2016. (Digger & Daisy Ser.). (FRE.). 32p. (J). (gr. k-2). 12.95 (978-1-62753-949-4(2), 204172) Sleeping Bear Pr.
—Digger y Daisy Van Al Médico (Digger & Daisy Go to the Doctor) Sullivan, Dana, illus. 2016. (Digger & Daisy Ser.). (SPA.). 32p. (J). (gr. k-2). 9.99 (978-1-62753-953-1(0), 204176) Sleeping Bear Pr.
Youngberg, Norma R. Jungle Thorn. 2010. (Illus.). 132p. reprint ed. per. 11.95 (978-1-57258-157-9(3), 945-6024) TEACH Services, Inc.
Zaugg, Sandra L. A Prayer for Mother. 2005. (Illus.). 95p. (J). (978-0-8163-2056-1(X)) Pacific Pr. Pubns.

SIDEREAL SYSTEM
see Stars

SIERRA LEONE
DePrince, Michaela & Deprince, Elaine. Ballerina Dreams: from Orphan to Dancer (Step into Reading, Step 4) Morrison, Frank, illus. 2014. (Step into Reading Ser.). (ENG.). 48p. (J). (gr. 2-4). 5.99 (978-0-385-75515-3(5), Random Hse. Bks. for Young Readers) Random Hse. Children's Bks.
Fowler, Will. Counterterrorism in West Africa: The Most Dangerous SAS Assault, 1 vol. 2011. (Most Daring Raids in History Ser.). (ENG., Illus.). 64p. (YA). (gr. 7-7). lib. bdg. 37.13 (978-1-4488-1871-6(0), 22f33d10-ef04-408d-a5c0-1c6cf42079c8) Rosen Publishing Group, Inc., The.
Hasday, Judy L. Sierra Leone. 2012. (J). pap. (978-1-4222-2230-0(6)) Mason Crest.
—Sierra Leone. Rotberg, Robert I., ed. (Evolution of Africa's Major Nations Ser.). (Illus.). (J). 2012. 80p. (gr. 7). 22.95 (978-1-4222-2202-7(0)) 2009. 79p. (gr. 3-7). lib. bdg. 21.95 (978-1-4222-0092-6(2)) Mason Crest.
LeVert, Suzanne. Sierra Leone, 1 vol. 2007. (Cultures of the World (First Edition)(r) Ser.). (ENG., Illus.). 144p. (gr. 5-5). lib. bdg. 49.79 (978-0-7614-2334-8(6), 1dd7a85e-482a-4f1c-867e-77daa1383351) Cavendish Square Publishing LLC.

SIERRA LEONE—FICTION
Edinger, Monica. Africa Is My Home: A Child of the Amistad. Byrd, Robert, illus. 2015. (ENG.). 64p. (J). (gr. 5). pap. 9.99 (978-0-7636-7647-6(0)) Candlewick Pr.
Forde, Winston. Airborne Soldiers. 2010. (Illus.). 120p. 29.99 (978-1-4535-6451-6(9)) Xlibris Corp.

SIERRA NEVADA (CALIF. AND NEV.)
Harkins, Susan Sales & Harkins, William H. The Donner Party. 2008. (What's So Great About... ? Ser.). (Illus.). 32p. (J). (gr. 2-4). lib. bdg. 25.70 (978-1-58415-669-7(4)) Mitchell Lane Pubs.
Rajczak Nelson, Kristen. The Donner Party, 1 vol. 2015. (Doomed! Ser.). (ENG., Illus.). 32p. (J). (gr. 4-5). pap. 11.50 (978-1-4824-2928-2(4), b65c6e2c-00a0-43be-b0b6-56abfacb7c74) Stevens, Gareth Publishing LLLP.
Smith-Llera, Danielle. Stranded in the Sierra Nevada: The Story of the Donner Party. 2015. (Adventures on the American Frontier Ser.). (ENG., Illus.). 32p. (J). (gr. 3-6). pap. 7.95 (978-1-4914-4912-7(8), 128747, Capstone Pr.) Capstone.
Wadsworth, Ginger. Survival in the Snow. Orback, Craig, illus. 2011. 48p. (J). pap. 6.95 (978-0-7613-3941-0(8), First Avenue Editions) Lerner Publishing Group.

SIERRA NEVADA (CALIF. AND NEV.)—FICTION
Engle, Margarita. Mountain Dog. Ivanov, Aleksey & Olga, illus. 2014. (ENG.). 240p. (J). (gr. 3-7). pap. 13.99 (978-1-250-04424-2(3), 900128316) Square Fish.
Pryor, Bonnie. The Iron Dragon: The Courageous Story of Lee Chin, 1 vol. 2011. (Historical Fiction Adventures Ser.). (ENG., Illus.). 160p. (J). (gr. 3-5). 31.93 (978-0-7660-3389-4(9), 519a6a2e-bc8c-434a-847a-07470adaa637); pap. 13.88 (978-1-59845-215-0(0), 3f96b345-e985-4f22-a311-341cf9f481bc) Enslow Publishing, LLC.
Roddy, Lee. The City Bear's Adventures. 2008. (D. J. Dillon Adventure Ser.: No. 2). (J). 7.99 (978-0-88062-266-0(0)) Mott Media.
—Dooger, the Grasshopper Hound. 2008. (D. J. Dillon Adventure Ser.: No. 3). (J). 7.99 (978-0-88062-267-7(9)) Mott Media.
—The Ghost Dog of Stoney Ridge. 2008. (D. J. Dillon Adventure Ser.: No. 4). (J). 7.99 (978-0-88062-268-4(7)) Mott Media.
—The Hair-Pulling Bear Dog. 2008. (D. J. Dillon Adventure Ser.: No. 1). (J). 7.99 (978-0-88062-265-3(2)) Mott Media.
Shahan, Sherry. Death Mountain, 1 vol. 2007. 208p. (J). (gr. 5-9). pap. 8.95 (978-1-56145-428-0(1)) Peachtree Publishing Co. Inc.
Uncle Markie. Piglette & Bobo Join the Manscouts. 2003. (YA). ring bd. 9.95 (978-1-933129-05-1(0)) Studio 403.

SIGHT
see Vision

SIGN BOARDS
see Signs and Signboards

SIGN LANGUAGE
see also Indian Sign Language
Ace Academics, ed. Sign Language Pt. 1: A Whole Course in a Box!, 3 vols. 2007. (Exambusters Ser.: Part 1 of 3). (Illus.). 192p. (gr. 7-18). 12.95 (978-1-881374-95-4(5), Exambusters) Ace Academics, Inc.
Acredolo, Linda & Goodwyn, Susan. I Can Sign! Playtime. 2007. (Baby Signs (Ideals) Ser.). (ENG., Illus.). 12p. (gr. -1). 9.99 (978-0-8249-6708-6(9), Ideals Pubns.) Worthy Publishing.
Allen, Joy. Baby Signs: A Baby-Sized Introduction to Speaking with Sign Language. 2008. (Illus.). 16p. (J). (gr. -1 — 1). bds. 7.99 (978-0-8037-3193-6(0), Dial Bks) Penguin Young Readers Group.
Anthony, Michelle & Lindert, Reyna. Signing Smart: My First Signs. 2009. (Signing Smart Ser.). (ENG.). 14p. (J). (gr. -1 — 1). 7.99 (978-0-545-10924-6(8), Cartwheel Bks.) Scholastic, Inc.
Audia, John P. The Creation Story: In Words & Sign Language. Spohn, David, illus. 2007. (ENG.). 16p. (gr. 3-7). 9.95 (978-0-8146-3174-4(6)) Liturgical Pr.
Awareness & Caring - Sign Language, 10 bks. (J). lib. bdg. 175.50 (978-1-56674-912-1(3)) Forest Hse. Publishing Co., Inc.
Barfell, Judith A. Learn & Sign Funtime Beginnings. 2004. (Beginnings Ser.: Bk. 1). (Illus.). 40p. (J). per. 14.95 (978-0-9753717-1-8(1)) Learn & Sign Funtime Bks.
Barfell, Judy. Learn & Sign Funtime: The United States Presidents. 2005. (J). per. 29.90 (978-0-9753717-4-9(6)) Learn & Sign Funtime Bks.
Beginning Signs: Flip Charts. 2003. (J). spiral bd. 17.95 (978-1-930820-34-0(8)) Garlic Pr.
Campbell, Diana & Mosher, Nancy, eds. Everyday Signs for the Newborn Baby. Adilman, Katarzyna, illus. 2007. 20p. (J). bds. (978-0-9791059-0-6(0)) Dakitab, Inc.
Clay, Kathryn. The Kids' Guide to Sign Language, 1 vol. 2012. (Kids' Guides). (ENG., Illus.). 32p. (J). (gr. 3-9). lib. bdg. 28.65 (978-1-4296-8426-2(7), 118499, Capstone Pr.) Capstone.
—Signing at Home: Sign Language for Kids, 1 vol. Chewning, Randy, illus. 2013. (Time to Sign Ser.). (ENG.). 32p. (J). (gr. -1-2). 27.99 (978-1-62065-051-6(7), 120752) Capstone.
—Signing at School: Sign Language for Kids, 1 vol. Lucas, Margeaux, illus. 2013. (Time to Sign Ser.). (ENG.). 32p. (J). (gr. -1-2). 29.99 (978-1-62065-052-3(5), 120753) Capstone.
—Signing in My World: Sign Language for Kids, 1 vol. Griffo, Daniel, illus. 2013. (Time to Sign Ser.). (ENG.). 32p. (J). (gr. -1-2). 27.99 (978-1-62065-054-7(1), 120756) Capstone.
—Time to Sign: Sign Language for Kids, 1 vol. Reid, Michael et al, illus. 2013. (Time to Sign Ser.). (ENG.). 112p. (J). (gr. -1-2). pap., pap., pap. 8.95 (978-1-62065-687-7(6), 121684, Capstone Pr.) Capstone.
Clothes-Ropa Bilingual Board Book. 2008. (ENG & SPA.). (J). pap. 5.99 (978-0-9727886-9-4(7)) Osmosis, LLC.
Cooper, Teri. Meet Simple Signman: His quiet talk counting 1 Thru 10. 2011. 24p. 10.95 (978-1-4497-1137-5(5), WestBow Pr.) Author Solutions, LLC.
Dykema, Marjorie. Ella's Joy: Signs of Joy. Helsom, Geoff, illus. 2009. (ENG.). 32p. (J). 16.95 (978-0-615-31066-4(4)) One Coin Publishing, LLC.
Ehlke, Paul. Clouds: Science Information in American Sign Language: A Paws Science Adventure. 2003. (J). cd-rom 29.95 (978-0-9752933-2-4(X)) Institute for Disabilities Research & Training, Inc.
Everyday Signs for Bed Time. 2007. (J). bds. (978-0-9791059-2-0(7)) Dakitab, Inc.
Flodin, Mickey. The Kids' Pocket Signing Guide: The Simple Way to Learn to Sign Using Everyday Phrases. 2005. 192p. (gr. 5-9). 14.00 (978-0-399-53207-8(2), TarcherPerigee) Penguin Publishing Group.
—Signing for Kids: The Fun Way for Anyone to Learn American Sign Language, Expanded. rev. ed. 2007. (Illus.). 160p. (gr. 12-18). 17.00 (978-0-399-53320-4(6), TarcherPerigee) Penguin Publishing Group.
Gilmartin, Charles. Storybook Sign Language. 2008. 28p. pap. 13.95 (978-1-4327-2677-5(3)) Outskirts Pr., Inc.
Hack, Brittany. American Sign Language, Counting with Sea Creatures. 2012. 28p. pap. 24.95 (978-1-4626-8930-9(2)) America Star Bks.
Hall, Susan T. ABC Sign & Color: A Beginner's Book of American Sign Language. 2013. (Dover Kids Activity Bks.). (ENG.). 32p. (J). (gr. k-5). pap. 3.99 (978-0-486-49057-1(2), 490572) Dover Pubns., Inc.
Hay, John & Harwich, Mary Belle. Dancing Hands: Signs of Learning. Wapahi, Robert, illus. 2013. 78p. pap. 16.95 (978-0-9888972-0-5(2)) Scotland Gate, Inc.
Heller, Lora. Sign Language ABC. 2014. (Illus.). 28p. (J). (— 1). bds. 6.95 (978-1-4549-1145-6(X)) Sterling Publishing Co., Inc.
—Sign Language for Kids: A Fun & Easy Guide to American Sign Language. 2004. (Illus.). 96p. (J). (gr. k-7). 16.99 (978-1-4027-0672-1(3), 1233016) Sterling Publishing Co., Inc.
Holub, Joan. My First Book of Sign Language. Holub, Joan, illus. 2004. (ENG., Illus.). 32p. (J). (gr. -1-3). pap. 4.99 (978-0-439-63582-0(9)) Scholastic, Inc.
Jensema, Marissa, illus. ASL Songs for Kids - 1: With Songs in American Sign Language. 2003. (J). cd-rom 29.95 (978-0-9752933-1-7(1)) Institute for Disabilities Research & Training, Inc.
Kelley, Walter P. The "I Love You" Story. McGregor, Tony L., illus. 2004. (J). (978-0-9729569-4-9(8)) BuTo, Ltd. Co.
Kent, Deborah. What Is It Like to Be Deaf?, 1 vol. 2012. (Overcoming Barriers Ser.). (ENG., Illus.). 48p. (gr. 3-3). pap. 11.53 (978-1-4644-0154-1(3), dcfa943a-9e11-4a49-aee6-ef1eb32706b5, Enslow Elementary) Enslow Publishing, LLC.
—What Is Sign Language?, 1 vol. 2012. (Overcoming Barriers Ser.). (ENG.). 48p. (gr. 3-3). 27.93 (978-0-7660-3771-7(1), ceb5af79-dae6-4ba9-9d46-c525dc111b34); (Illus.). pap. 11.53 (978-1-4644-0156-5(X), f44c49f4-44b0-4086-9b37-8d01048fd83e) Enslow Publishing, LLC. (Enslow Elementary).
Kubler, Annie, illus. Itsy, Bitsy Spider: American Sign Language. 2005. (Sign & Singalong Ser.). (ENG.). 12p. (J). (gr. k-k). bds. (978-1-904550-43-3(6)) Child's Play International Ltd.
—Teddy Bear, Teddy Bear: American Sign Language. 2005. (Sign & Singalong Ser.). (ENG.). 12p. (J). (gr. k-1). bds. (978-1-904550-40-2(1)) Child's Play International Ltd.
—Twinkle, Twinkle, Little Star: American Sign Language. 2005. (Sign & Singalong Ser.). (ENG.). 12p. (J). (gr. k-k). bds. (978-1-904550-42-6(8)) Child's Play International Ltd.
Learn & Sign Funtime - Beginnings. 2007. (FRE.). (J). per. 14.95 (978-0-9753717-9-4(7)) Learn & Sign Funtime Bks.
Learn & Sign Funtime - Beginnings: British Edition. 2005. (J). per. (978-0-9753717-7-0(0)) Learn & Sign Funtime Bks.
Learn & Sign Funtime - Beginnings: Lakota Edition. 2007. Orig. Title: Learn & Sign Funtime. (SAI.). per. (978-0-9753717-8-7(9)) Learn & Sign Funtime Bks.
Learn & Sign Funtime - Haitian Edition: Beginnings. 2005. (CRP.). (J). per. 14.95 net. (978-0-9753717-6-3(2)) Learn & Sign Funtime Bks.
Learn & Sign Funtime: Beginnings. 4th ed. 2005. Orig. Title: Learn & Sign Funtime - Beginnings Third Edktion. (J). per. 14.95 (978-0-9753717-5-6(4)) Learn & Sign Funtime Bks.
Learn & Sign Funtime: Beginnings - Ausian. 3rd ed. 2004. per. 14.95 (978-0-9753717-3-2(8)) Learn & Sign Funtime Bks.
Lewis, Anthony, illus. Getting Ready: American Sign Language. 2006. (Sign About Ser.). (ENG.). 12p. (J). (gr. -1). bds. (978-1-84643-029-9(1)) Child's Play International Ltd.
—Going Out: American Sign Language. 2006. (Sign About Ser.). (ENG.). 12p. (J). (gr. -1). bds. (978-1-84643-032-9(1)) Child's Play International Ltd.
—Meal Time: American Sign Language. 2006. (Sign About Ser.). (ENG.). 12p. (J). (gr. -1). bds. (978-1-84643-030-5(5)) Child's Play International Ltd.
—Play Time: American Sign Language. 2006. (Sign About Ser.). (ENG.). 12p. (J). (gr. -1). bds. (978-1-84643-031-2(3)) Child's Play International Ltd.
Martin, Mabel. Talking with Hands. Witmer, Ruth, illus. 2007. (Little Jewel Book Ser.). 24p. (J). (gr. 2). pap. 2.70 (978-0-7399-2394-8(3)) Rod & Staff Pubs., Inc.
Neal, Vonda & Herbold, Marvin, compiled by. British Sign Language American Sign Language Translator. 2004. (YA). cd-rom 19.95 (978-0-9752933-8-6(9)) Institute for Disabilities Research & Training, Inc.
Sandviks HOP, Inc. Staff, ed. Hooked on Baby: Learn to Sign. 2008. 29.99 (978-1-62499-017-5(7)) HOP, LLC.
Scholastic. Sign Language: My First 100 Words. Nelson, Michiyo, illus. 2008. (ENG.). 32p. (J). (gr. -1-3). pap. 7.99 (978-0-545-05657-1(8), Cartwheel Bks.) Scholastic, Inc.
Scholastic Editors. Sign Language: My First 100 Words. Nelson, Michiyo, illus. 2008. 32p. (gr. -1-3). 17.00 (978-0-7569-8911-8(6)) Perfection Learning Corp.
Signing Time Flash Cards 5: ABC's. 2006. (J). 10.99 (978-1-933543-12-3(4)) Two Little Hands Productions LLC.
Signs & Symbols: Lessons & activities for children Ages 5-10. 2005. (J). pap. 14.95 (978-1-58459-268-6(0)) World Library Pubns.
Time to Sign. Time to Sign with Children Infant/Toddler: Time to Sign with Music Infant/Toddler. 2003. Orig. Title: Time to Sign with Music Infant/Toddler. (Illus.). 42p. per. 19.95 (978-0-9713666-0-2(8)) Time to Sign, Incorporated.
Two Little Hands, creator. Everyday Signs Board Book. 2007. (Signing Time! (Two Little Hands) Ser.). (Illus.). 30p. (J). (gr. -1-k). bds. (978-1-933543-02-4(7)) Two Little Hands Productions LLC.
—My First Signs Board Book. 2007. (Signing Time! (Two Little Hands) Ser.). (Illus.). 30p. (J). (gr. -1-k). bds. (978-1-933543-00-0(0)) Two Little Hands Productions LLC.
—Playtime Signs Board Book. 2007. (Signing Time! (Two Little Hands) Ser.). (Illus.). 30p. (J). (gr. -1-k). bds. (978-1-933543-01-7(9)) Two Little Hands Productions LLC.
Two Little Hands Productions, creator. Good Night, Alex & Leah. 2010. (ENG., Illus.). (J). (978-1-933543-73-4(6)) Two Little Hands Productions LLC.
—What Do You See Outside? 2010. (ENG., Illus.). (J). (978-1-933543-74-1(4)) Two Little Hands Productions LLC.
Two Little Hands Productions, prod. Board Book 4: Family, Feelings & Fun. 2010. (Illus.). (J). bds. (978-1-933543-49-9(3)) Two Little Hands Productions LLC.
—Board Book 5: ABC Signs. 2010. (Illus.). (J). bds. (978-1-933543-50-5(7)) Two Little Hands Productions LLC.
—Board Book 6: My Favorite Things. 2010. (Illus.). (J). bds. (978-1-933543-51-2(5)) Two Little Hands Productions LLC.
Vinopol, Corinne. Con-SIGN-tration 3: Computer Software Game in American Sign Language. 2003. (J). cd-rom 19.95 (978-0-9752933-6-2(2)) Institute for Disabilities Research & Training, Inc.
—Con-SIGN-tration 4: Computer Software Game in American Sign Language. 2003. (J). cd-rom (978-0-9752933-7-9(0)) Institute for Disabilities Research & Training, Inc.
—Spell Well: CD-ROM American Sign Language Spelling Game. 2003. (YA). cd-rom 19.95 (978-0-9752933-0-0(3)) Institute for Disabilities Research & Training, Inc.
Vinopol, Corinne & Bednarczyk, Angela. American Sign Language Clip & Create: Clip Art Software. 2003. (YA). cd-rom 34.95 (978-0-9752933-4-8(6)) Institute for Disabilities Research & Training, Inc.
Vinopol, Corinne K. American Sign Language Clip & Create 2. 2nd ed. 2004. cd-rom 34.95 (978-0-9760818-0-7(6)) Institute for Disabilities Research & Training, Inc.
Warner, Penny. Signing Fun: American Sign Language Vocabulary, Phrases, Games, & Activities. Gray, Paula, illus. 2006. (ENG.). 192p. (gr. 6-7). per. 27.00 (978-1-56368-292-6(3)) Gallaudet Univ. Pr.
Wyckoff, Edwin Brit. Sign Language Man: Thomas H. Gallaudet & His Incredible Work, 1 vol. 2010. (Genius at Work! Great Inventor Biographies Ser.). (ENG., Illus.). 32p. (gr. 3-3). lib. bdg. 26.60 (978-0-7660-3447-1(X), 2ce6028a-0fed-4805-8569-cb8f5cab6e58) Enslow Publishing, LLC.

SIGN LANGUAGE—FICTION
Brightwood, Laura, illus. Debate in Sign Language. Brightwood, Laura, . 2006. (J). (978-0-9779290-6-1(X)) 3-C Institute for Social Development.
Browne, Anthony. Little Beauty. Browne, Anthony, illus. 2010. (ENG., Illus.). 32p. (J). (gr. -1-2). pap. 8.99 (978-0-7636-4967-8(8)) Candlewick Pr.
—Little Beauty. 2010. lib. bdg. 17.20 (978-0-606-14714-9(4)) Turtleback.
Everyday Signs of Zoo Animals. 2007. (J). bds. (978-0-9791059-1-3(9)) Dakitab, Inc.
Ferris, Jean. Of Sound Mind. 2004. (ENG.). 224p. (YA). (gr. 7). reprint ed. pap. 11.99 (978-0-374-45584-2(8), 900022579, Farrar, Straus & Giroux (BYR)) Farrar, Straus & Giroux.
—Of Sound Mind. 2004. 215p. (YA). (gr. 7). 14.60 (978-0-7569-2970-1(9)) Perfection Learning Corp.
Fudge, Benjamin. Enrique Speaks with His Hands. Edmonson, Tim, illus. 2008. (ENG.). 32p. (J). (gr. -1-3). 16.95 (978-0-9800649-3-3(7)) Hilton Publishing Co.
Guest, Jacqueline. Secret Signs, 1 vol. 2006. (Orca Young Readers Ser.). (ENG., Illus.). 144p. (J). (gr. 4-7). per. 8.95 (978-1-55143-599-2(3)) Orca Bk. Pubs. USA.
Jordan, Sherryl. The Raging Quiet. 2018. (ENG.). 272p. (YA). (gr. 9-7). pap. 17.99 (978-1-5344-4119-4(0), Simon Pulse) Simon Pulse.
—The Raging Quiet. l.t. ed. 2005. 416p. 22.95 (978-0-7862-7313-3(5), Large Print Pr.) Thorndike Pr.

S

Kingsley, Linda Kurtz. Bringing up Sophie. Kingsley, Linda Kurtz, illus. 2010. (Illus.). 32p. (J). lib. bdg. 15.95 (978-0-944727-25-6(5), Turtle Bks.) Jason & Nordic Pubs.
—Bringing up Sophie. 2009. (Illus.). 32p. (J). pap. 9.95 (978-0-944727-24-9(7), Turtle Bks.) Jason & Nordic Pubs.
LeZotte, Ann Clare. Show Me a Sign (Show Me a Sign, Book 1), 1 vol., Vol. 1. (Show Me a Sign Ser.). (ENG.). (J). (gr. 3-7). 2021. 304p. pap. 8.99 (978-1-338-25582-9(7)) 2020. 288p. 18.99 (978-1-338-25581-2(9), Scholastic Pr.) Scholastic, Inc.
Martin, Kentrell. Shelly Goes to the Zoo. Rodriguez, Marc, illus. 2013. 32p. pap. 8.50 (978-0-9851845-1-3(5)) Shelly's Adventures LLC.
McCully, Emily Arnold. My Heart Glow: Alice Cogswell, Thomas Gallaudet, & the Birth of American Sign Language. McCully, Emily Arnold, illus. 2008. (ENG., Illus.). 40p. (gr. 1-4). 15.99 (978-1-4231-0028-7(X)) Hyperion Pr.
Roth, Judith L. & Rothshank, Brooke, illus. Julia's Words. 2008. (J). (gr. -1-3). pap. 12.99 (978-0-8361-9417-3(9)) Herald Pr.
Sawyer, Louise. Mother's Storybook Signs. 2004. (YA). Vol. 1. spiral bd. 19.95 (978-0-9719842-0-2(4)) Vol. 2. spiral bd. 19.95 (978-0-9719842-8-8(X)) Martin & Brothers.
Shelly's Outdoor Adventure. 2013. (ENG.). 28p. pap. 8.00 (978-0-9851845-0-6(7)) Shelly's Adventures LLC.
Uhlberg, Myron. The Printer, 1 vol. Sorensen, Henri, illus. 32p. (J). (gr. -1-3). 2009. pap. 8.99 (978-1-56145-483-9(4)) 2003. 16.95 (978-1-56145-221-7(1)) Peachtree Publishing Co. Inc.
Wemple, Sabrina. Gumby & Beanie. 2008. 32p. per. 13.95 (978-1-4327-0780-4(9)) Outskirts Pr., Inc.

SIGNALS AND SIGNALING

see also Flags; Radio

Cefrey, Holly. The Inventions of Martha Coston: Signal Flares That Save Sailors' Lives. 2009. (19th Century American Inventors Ser.). 24p. (gr. 2-3). 42.50 (978-1-60854-953-5(4), PowerKids Pr.) Rosen Publishing Group, Inc., The.
Jocelyn, Marthe. Which Way? Slaughter, Tom, illus. 2010. 24p. (J). (gr. k-k). 15.95 (978-0-88776-970-2(5), Tundra Bks.) Tundra Bks. CAN. Dist: Penguin Random Hse. LLC.
McNab, Chris. Survival in the Wilderness. 2015. (Illus.). 64p. (J). (978-1-4222-3081-7(3)) Mason Crest.
Wilson, Patrick. Surviving with Navigation & Signaling. Carney, John, ed. 2014. (Extreme Survival in the Military Ser.: 12). 64p. (J). (gr. 7-18). lib. bdg. 23.95 (978-1-4222-3093-0(7)) Mason Crest.
Woods, Michael & Woods, Mary B. Ancient Communication Technology: From Hieroglyphics to Scrolls. 2011. (Technology in Ancient Cultures Ser.). (ENG.). 96p. (gr. 6-12). lib. bdg. 31.93 (978-0-7613-6529-7(X)) Lerner Publishing Group.

SIGNERS OF THE DECLARATION OF INDEPENDENCE

see United States—Declaration of Independence

SIGNS (ADVERTISING)

see Signs and Signboards

SIGNS AND SIGNBOARDS

see also Posters

Benchmark Education Co., LLC. Safety Signs Big Book. 2014. (Shared Reading Foundations Ser.). (J). (gr. -1). (978-1-4509-9431-6(8)) Benchmark Education Co.
Byerly, Robbie & Kiley, Kieran. Look at the Signs. rev. ed. 2010. (1-3Y in My World Ser.). (ENG., Illus.). 16p. (J). (gr. k-1). pap. 8.00 (978-1-61541-461-1(4)) American Reading Co.
Gregory, Cam. Who Should Follow Signs? 2012. (Level F Ser.). (ENG., Illus.). 16p. (J). (gr. k-2). pap. 7.95 (978-1-927136-53-9(9), 19455) RiverStream Publishing.
Hill, Mary. Signs at the Airport. 2003. (Signs in My World Ser.). (ENG., Illus.). 24p. (J). 19.00 (978-0-516-24272-9(5), Children's Pr.) Scholastic Library Publishing.
—Signs at the Park. 2003. (Welcome Bks.). (ENG., Illus.). 24p. (J). (gr. -1-2). pap. 4.95 (978-0-516-24365-8(9), Children's Pr.) Scholastic Library Publishing.
—Signs at the Store. 2003. (Welcome Bks.). (ENG., Illus.). 24p. (J). (gr. -1-2). pap. 4.95 (978-0-516-24363-4(2), Children's Pr.) Scholastic Library Publishing.
—Welcome Books: Signs at the Airport. 2003. (Welcome Bks.). (ENG., Illus.). 24p. (J). (gr. -1-2). pap. 4.95 (978-0-516-24364-1(0), Children's Pr.) Scholastic Library Publishing.
Kessler, Leonard. Mr. Pine's Mixed-Up Signs: 55th Anniversary Edition. 55th ed. 2016. (Mr. Pine Ser.). (ENG., Illus.). 63p. (J). (gr. 1-4). pap. 8.99 (978-1-930900-92-9(9)) Purple Hse. Pr.
Leigh, Autumn. Signs on the Road: Learning to Identify the Four Basic Geometric Shapes, 1 vol. 2010. (Math for the REAL World Ser.). (ENG., Illus.). 8p. (gr. k-1). pap. 5.15 (978-0-8239-8857-0(0), f5253939-6466-46b7-a4e0-107d37c64b88) Rosen Publishing Group, Inc., The.
Macken, JoAnn Early. Road Signs. 2010. (My Community Ser.). (ENG.). 24p. (J). (gr. k-2). lib. bdg. 25.65 (978-1-60753-026-8(0), 17150) Amicus.
Milich, Zoran. City Signs. (ENG., Illus.). 32p. (J). (gr. -1-k). 2013. bds. 12.95 (978-1-55453-980-2(3)) 2005. pap. 7.99 (978-1-55337-748-1(6)) Kids Can Pr., Ltd. CAN. Dist: Hachette Bk. Group.
Tana, Hoban. I Read Signs. 2014. (ENG.). 32p. (J). (gr. k-3). 11.24 (978-1-63245-283-2(9)) Lectorum Pubns., Inc.

SIGNS AND SIGNBOARDS—FICTION

Armstrong, Jennifer. Once upon a Banana. Small, David, illus. (ENG.). 48p. (J). (gr. -1-3). 2013. 7.99 (978-0-689-85951-9(1)) 2006. 19.99 (978-0-689-84251-1(1)) Simon & Schuster/Paula Wiseman Bks. (Simon & Schuster/Paula Wiseman Bks.).
Bain, Michelle. The Adventures of Thumbs up Johnnie Zipp, Little Digit & the Happy Signs: Zipp, Little Digit & the Happy Signs. Lizana, Lorenzo, illus. 2007. (J). 14.95 (978-0-9795832-0-9(9)) Pixie Stuff LLC.
—Las aventuras de Juanito el Pulgarcito Zipp, Pequeño Dígito, las señales y las Señas: Zipp, Pequeño Dígito, las señales y las Señas. Lizana, Lorenzo, illus. 2007.Tr. of Zipp, Digit & the Happy Signs! (SPA.). 28p. (J). (978-0-9795832-3-0(3)) Pixie Stuff LLC.
Bell, Hilari. Crown of Earth. Willis, Drew, illus. 2010. (Shield, Sword, & Crown Ser.: 3). (ENG.). 272p. (J). (gr. 3-7). pap. 5.99 (978-1-4169-0599-8(5), Aladdin) Simon & Schuster Children's Publishing.
Blake, Christine & Lopez, Jill. Signs, Signs, Everywhere Signs. 2008. 32p. pap. 15.95 (978-1-4327-2523-5(8)) Outskirts Pr., Inc.
Doherty, Kathleen. Don't Feed the Bear. Wass, Chip, illus. 2018. 32p. (J). (gr. -1). 18.99 (978-1-4549-1979-7(5)) Sterling Publishing Co., Inc.
Kehret, Peg. Stolen Children. 2010. (ENG.). 176p. (J). (gr. 3-7). 7.99 (978-0-14-241513-9(8), Puffin Books) Penguin Young Readers Group.
Kondrchek, Jamie & Rasemas, Joe. On My Way to School (De Camino a la Escuela) Vega, Eida de la, tr. Rasemas, Joe, illus. 2009. (Day in the Life Ser.). (SPA & ENG., Illus.). 32p. (J). (gr. -1-1). 25.70 (978-1-58415-840-0(9)) Mitchell Lane Pubs.
Road Signs. 2005. (J). per. 9.95 (978-1-59352-179-0(0)) Christian Services Publishing.
Say, Allen. The Sign Painter. 2013. (ENG., Illus.). 32p. (J). (gr. -1-3). pap. 7.99 (978-0-544-10514-0(1), 1540812, Clarion Bks.) HarperCollins Pubs.

SIGNS AND SYMBOLS

see also Ciphers; Cryptography; Heraldry; Signals and Signaling; Symbolism

Avett, Harper. I See the Bald Eagle, 1 vol. 2016. (Symbols of Our Country Ser.). (ENG., Illus.). 24p. (J). (gr. 1-1). 25.27 (978-1-4994-3051-6(5), a3db218b-6feb-4300-b203-d74f77421f13); pap. 9.25 (978-1-4994-2763-9(8), ab19a3b5-7a21-46bf-886e-e3eaadee3ee8) Rosen Publishing Group, Inc., The. (PowerKids Pr.).
Benchmark Education Company. Symbols of the United States (Teacher Guide) 2005. (978-1-4108-4638-9(5)) Benchmark Education Co.
Bow, James. Secret Signs. 2013. (ENG.). 32p. (J). (978-0-7787-1125-4(0)); pap. (978-0-7787-1129-2(3)) Crabtree Publishing Co.
Brannon, Barbara. Discover Symbols of the United States. 2005. (J). pap. (978-1-4108-5144-4(3)) Benchmark Education Co.
Capstone Classroom & Stead, Tony. What's Your Symbol? 2017. (What's the Point? Reading & Writing Expository Text Ser.). (ENG., Illus.). 16p. (J). (gr. 1-1). pap. 6.95 (978-1-4966-0752-2(X), 132387, Capstone Classroom) Capstone.
Celebrate Freedom: Songs, Symbols, & Sayings of the United States. 2003. (Scott Foresman Social Study Ser.). (Illus.). 32p. (gr. k-2). (978-0-328-03672-1(2)); 48p. (gr. 3-6). (978-0-328-03674-5(9)) Addison-Wesley Educational Pubs., Inc. (Scott Foresman).
Cipriano, Jeri. Symbols of Our Country: Set Of 6. 2011. (Navigators Ser.). (J). pap. 44.00 net. (978-1-4108-5096-6(X)) Benchmark Education Co.
—Symbols of Our Country: Text Pairs. 2008. (Bridges/Navigators Ser.). (J). (gr. 3). 89.00 (978-1-4108-8373-5(6)) Benchmark Education Co.
Diaz-Cubero, Jose H. Practicas de Ortografia: 5 Grado. (SPA & ENG.). (J). (gr. 5). 9.95 (978-84-357-0125-9(5), CPR92) Ediciones y Distribuciones Codice, S.A. ESP. Dist: Continental Bk. Co., Inc.
Eldridge, Alison & Eldridge, Stephen. The Bald Eagle: An American Symbol, 1 vol. 2012. (All about American Symbols Ser.). (ENG.). 24p. (gr. -1-1). 25.27 (978-0-7660-4058-8(5), bdb3943a-3270-4779-8304-cb07dd5f2921); (Illus.). pap. 10.35 (978-1-4644-0047-6(4), 4ed07942-376d-42d7-af47-d9c11ddae246) Enslow Publishing, LLC. (Enslow Publishing).
—The Liberty Bell: An American Symbol, 1 vol. 2012. (All about American Symbols Ser.). (ENG.). 24p. (gr. -1-1). 25.27 (978-0-7660-4059-5(3), 0d12a906-9890-419d-a9e6-66d158e6537c, Enslow Publishing) Enslow Publishing, LLC.
Ferguson, Melissa. American Symbols: What You Need to Know. 2017. (Fact Files Ser.). (ENG.). 24p. (J). (gr. 1-3). lib. bdg. 27.99 (978-1-5157-8116-5(X), 136128, Capstone Pr.) Capstone.
Forest, Christopher. The Dollar Bill in Translation: What It Really Means. rev. ed. 2016. (Kids' Translations Ser.). (ENG.). 32p. (J). (gr. 3-6). pap. 8.10 (978-1-5157-6249-2(1), 135064, Capstone Pr.) Capstone.
Friesen, Helen Lepp. El Tío Sam. 2014. (SPA., Illus.). 24p. (J). (978-1-62127-625-8(2)) Weigl Pubs., Inc.
Goldsworthy, Kaite. Bald Eagle with Code. 2012. (AV2 American Icons Ser.). (ENG., Illus.). 24p. (J). pap. 12.95 (978-1-61913-300-6(8)); lib. bdg. 27.13 (978-1-61913-077-7(7)) Weigl Pubs., Inc. (AV2 by Weigl).
Hicks, Terry Allan. The Bald Eagle, 1 vol. 2007. (Symbols of America Ser.). (ENG., Illus.). 40p. (gr. 3-3). lib. bdg. 32.64 (978-0-7614-2133-7(5), 4cc77ac4-353f-4135-8229-fee1fad1bf3b) Cavendish Square Publishing LLC.
—Symbols of America Group 2, 12 vols., Set. Incl. Bald Eagle. lib. bdg. 32.64 (978-0-7614-2133-7(5), 4cc77ac4-353f-4135-8229-fee1fad1bf3b); Capitol. lib. bdg. 32.64 (978-0-7614-2132-0(7), 983498dc-4064-4d9b-a5fd-9541490d6e2c); Declaration of Independence. lib. bdg. 32.64 (978-0-7614-2135-1(1), b672c79b-ebcf-460a-bf6f-c79934c3be91); Ellis Island. lib. bdg. 32.64 (978-0-7614-2134-4(3), eadd5cdd-45bd-4dab-99b1-a60a5a76c2ba); Pledge of Allegiance. lib. bdg. 32.64 (978-0-7614-2136-8(X), 4f80c1f0-d3ea-4dd5-b747-5d88842745e5); Uncle Sam. lib. bdg. 32.64 (978-0-7614-2137-5(8), e6f9da10-1cd5-4edb-8cd5-0e9e233d21ec); (Illus.). 40p. (gr. 3-3). (Symbols of America Ser.). (ENG.). 2007. Set lib. bdg. 195.84 (978-0-7614-2130-6(0), b2a0354a-8705-48f9-b041-df7983c1050e, Cavendish Square) Cavendish Square Publishing LLC.
James, Trisha. Celebrating Texas: Patriotic Symbols & Landmarks, 1 vol. 2010. (Spotlight on Texas Ser.). (ENG., Illus.). 32p. (J). (gr. 3-4). pap. 11.75 (978-1-61532-484-2(4), 61edd9b1-91e6-4364-ad92-9834cf6a495e); lib. bdg. 28.93 (978-1-61532-486-6(0), 2f1ac580-4512-48ee-91b5-f030e002c736) Rosen Publishing Group, Inc., The.
Johnson, Etta. Symbols of the United States. 2005. (J). pap. (978-1-4108-4590-0(7)) Benchmark Education Co.
Keenan, Sheila. O, Say Can You See? America's Symbols, Landmarks, & Important Words. Boyajian, Ann, illus. 2007. (ENG.). 64p. (J). (gr. -1-3). pap. 7.99 (978-0-439-59360-1(3), Scholastic Nonfiction) Scholastic, Inc.
Keppeler, Jill. Betsy Ross Didn't Create the American Flag: Exposing Myths about U. S. Symbols, 1 vol. 2016. (Exposed! Myths about Early American History Ser.). (ENG., Illus.). 32p. (J). (gr. 2-3). pap. 11.50 (978-1-4824-5717-9(2), cf9181ec-aaf5-45d6-9da4-23975869c3a7) Stevens, Gareth Publishing LLLP.
Kishel, Ann-Marie. U. S. Symbols. 2007. (First Step Nonfiction - Government Ser.). (ENG., Illus.). 24p. (gr. k-2). lib. bdg. 23.93 (978-0-8225-6394-5(0), Lerner Pubns.) Lerner Publishing Group.
Kubler, Annie, illus. Baa, Baa, Black Sheep! American Sign Language. 2005. (Sign & Singalong Ser.). (ENG.). 12p. (J). (gr. k-1). bds. (978-1-904550-41-9(X)) Child's Play International Ltd.
—My First Signs: American Sign Language. 2005. (Baby Signing Ser.). (ENG.). 12p. (J). (gr. k-1). bds. (978-1-904550-39-6(8)) Child's Play International Ltd.
—My First Signs: Bsl. 2005. 12p. (J). spiral bd. (978-1-904550-04-4(5)) Child's Play International Ltd.
Lyons, Shelly. Signs in My Neighborhood. 2013. (My Neighborhood Ser.). (ENG.). 24p. (J). (gr. k-1). pap. 43.74 (978-1-62065-890-1(9), 19444); (Illus.). (gr. -1-2). pap. 7.29 (978-1-62065-889-5(5), 121806); (Illus.). (gr. -1-2). lib. bdg. 27.32 (978-1-62065-098-1(3), 120795) Capstone. (Capstone Pr.).
Machajewski, Sarah. Our Country's Symbols, 1 vol. 2012. (InfoMax Readers Ser.). (ENG., Illus.). 24p. (J). (gr. 1-1). pap. 8.25 (978-1-4488-8980-8(4), 4096fabd-54b7-4f3a-a45b-bf7d62a5cb87, Rosen Classroom) Rosen Publishing Group, Inc., The.
Marcovitz, Hal. The Bald Eagle. 2004. (American Symbols & Their Meanings Ser.). (Illus.). 48p. (J). (gr. 4-18). lib. bdg. 19.95 (978-1-59084-032-0(1)) Mason Crest.
—Bald Eagle: The Story of Our National Bird. Moreno, Barry, ed. 2014. (Patriotic Symbols of America Ser.: 20). 48p. (J). (gr. 4-18). 20.95 (978-1-4222-3120-3(8)) Mason Crest.
Mattern, Joanne. The Liberty Bell: History's Silent Witness. 2017. (Core Content Social Studies — Let's Celebrate America Ser.). (ENG., Illus.). 32p. (J). (gr. 2-5). pap. 8.99 (978-1-63440-235-4(9), 28ed5c3f-ee1c-4654-af96-f22535bc1256); lib. bdg. 26.65 (978-1-63440-225-5(1), 0b005936-2891-4184-8159-c5ba8f4d5d28) Red Chair Pr.
Miller, Heather. The 10 Most Outstanding American Symbols. 2008. 14.99 (978-1-55448-508-6(8)) Scholastic Library Publishing.
Mills, Nathan & Machajewski, Sarah. Symbols of the United States, 1 vol. 2012. (Rosen Readers Ser.). (ENG., Illus.). 24p. (J). (gr. 1-1). pap. 8.25 (978-1-4488-8761-3(5), 2abcb7ca-baa6-409b-8a02-9ef028a294de, Rosen Classroom) Rosen Publishing Group, Inc., The.
Monroe, Tyler. The Bald Eagle. 2013. (U. S. Symbols Ser.). (ENG.). 24p. (J). (gr. -1-2). 27.32 (978-1-4765-3089-5(0), 123066); pap. 7.95 (978-1-4765-3538-8(8), 123584) Capstone. (Capstone Pr.).
Moore, Elizabeth. All Kinds of Signs, 1 vol. 2011. (Wonder Readers Emergent Level Ser.). (ENG.). 8p. (gr. -1-1). (J). pap. 6.25 (978-1-4296-7837-7(2), 118150); pap. 35.94 (978-1-4296-8215-2(9)) Capstone. (Capstone Pr.).
Pearl, Norman. The Great Seal of the United States. Skeens, Matthew, illus. 2006. (American Symbols Ser.). (ENG.). 24p. (J). (gr. 1-3). lib. bdg. 27.32 (978-1-4048-2214-6(3), 92415); per. 9.95 (978-1-4048-2220-7(8), 93391) Capstone. (Picture Window Bks.).
Primary Sources of American Symbols, 10 vols. 2005. (Primary Sources of American Symbols Ser.). (ENG.). (J). (gr. 3-3). 131.35 (978-1-4042-3300-3(8), 3ec50e04-0122-4709-ae9c-c615a7906df0) Rosen Publishing Group, Inc., The.
Ruble, Eugene. Ancient Symbols, Artwork, Carvings & Alphabets. Burch, Lynda S., ed. 2009. 28p. pap. 10.95 (978-1-935137-90-0(5)) Guardian Angel Publishing, Inc.
Silate, Jennifer. The Bald Eagle. (Primary Sources of American Symbols Ser.). 24p. (gr. 3-3). 2009. 42.50 (978-1-60851-508-0(7), PowerKids Pr.) 2005. (ENG., Illus.). (J). lib. bdg. 26.27 (978-1-4042-2697-5(4), bea082d9-e5fb-4bab-816b-5b9ced1b0daf) Rosen Publishing Group, Inc., The.
Thames, Susan. Our American Symbols. 2006. (World Around Me Discovery Library). (Illus.). 24p. (J). (gr. 3-7). lib. bdg. 22.79 (978-1-59515-994-6(0)) Rourke Educational Media.
Traffic Signs Shape Book. 2016. (Illus.). 23p. (J). (978-0-87659-712-5(6)) Gryphon Hse., Inc.
Two Little Hands Productions, creator. Good Night, Alex & Leah. 2010. (ENG., Illus.). (J). (978-1-933543-73-4(6)) Two Little Hands Productions LLC.
—What Do You See Outside? 2010. (ENG., Illus.). (J). (978-1-933543-74-1(4)) Two Little Hands Productions LLC.
Yasuda, Anita. The 12 Most Amazing American Monuments & Symbols. 2015. (Amazing America Ser.). (ENG., Illus.). 32p. (J). (gr. 3-6). 32.80 (978-1-63235-009-1(2), 11548, 12-Story Library) Bookstaves, LLC.

SIKHISM

Barrow, Joy. Sikhism. 2003. (Illus.). lib. bdg. 28.50 (978-1-59389-134-3(2)) Chrysalis Education.
—Sikhism, 1 vol. 2005. (World Religions Ser.: 0). (ENG., Illus.). 58p. (YA). (gr. 6-10). pap. 8.95 (978-1-55285-652-9(6), 30f79ba9-185a-4c80-9e94-84cb50704289) Whitecap Bks., Ltd. CAN. Dist: Firefly Bks., Ltd.
Burton, Jennifer. Sikhism. 2017. (Illus.). 64p. (J). (978-1-4222-3821-9(0)) Mason Crest.
Dalton, Dave. Sikhism: Inderjeet's Story. 2013. (Our World of Faith Ser.). (Illus.). 32p. (J). (gr. 3-6). (978-1-84898-617-6(3), TickTock Books) Octopus Publishing Group.
Dicker, Katie & Perihar, Amar Singh. I Belong to the Sikh Faith, 1 vol. 2009. (I Belong Ser.). (ENG., Illus.). 24p. (J). (gr. 2-2). pap. 9.25 (978-1-4358-8626-1(7), 52e64880-aec2-49f8-9085-54281f49c61e, PowerKids Pr.); lib. bdg. 26.27 (978-1-4358-3036-3(9), 2026663b-f1c2-4fe6-8339-907c2d3bba8e) Rosen Publishing Group, Inc., The.
Elby, Tristan & McKain, Neil. World Religions: Hinduism, Buddhism & Sikhism. 2017. (ENG.). 120p. (J). (gr. 6-9). pap. 29.99 (978-0-00-822769-2(1)) HarperCollins Pubs. Ltd. GBR. Dist: Independent Pubs. Group.
Ganeri, Anita. The Guru Granth Sahib & Sikhism. 2003. 30p. (J). lib. bdg. 24.25 (978-1-58340-245-0(4)) Black Rabbit Bks.
—Sikh Festivals Throughout The Year. 2003. (Year of Festivals Ser.). (Illus.). 30p. lib. bdg. 24.25 (978-1-58340-374-7(4)) Black Rabbit Bks.
—Sikh Stories. Phillips, Rachael, illus. 2003. (Storyteller Ser.). 30p. (J). (978-0-237-52037-3(0)) Evans Brothers, Ltd.
Hawker, Frances & Bhatia, Mohini. Sikhism in India. Campbell, Bruce, photos by. 2009. (ENG., Illus.). 32p. (J). (gr. 3-6). (978-0-7787-5011-6(6)); pap. (978-0-7787-5028-4(0)) Crabtree Publishing Co.
Kaur, Harliv & Kaur, Jasmine, compiled by. My Gurmukhi Khajana: A Gurmat Based Primer. 2007. (ENG & PAN., Illus.). 43p. (J). pap. 13.00 (978-1-60411-000-5(7)) Sikh Research Institute.
Kaur-Singh, Kanwaljit. Sikhism. 2006. (QEB World of Faiths Ser.). (Illus.). 32p. (J). (gr. 3-6). lib. bdg. 27.10 (978-1-59566-211-8(1)) QEB Publishing Inc.
Kaur-Singh, Kanwaljit & Nason, Ruth. Visiting a Gurdwara. 2014. (Start up Religion Ser.). (Illus.). 32p. (J). (gr. -1-k). pap. 10.99 (978-0-237-54376-1(1)) Evans Brothers, Ltd. GBR. Dist: Independent Pubs. Group.
Marsico, Katie. Sikhism. 2017. (21st Century Skills Library: Global Citizens: World Religions Ser.). (ENG., Illus.). 32p. (J). (gr. 4-7). pap. 14.21 (978-1-63472-291-9(4), 209209) Cherry Lake Publishing.
McKain, Neil. Sikhism. 2017. (ENG., Illus.). 40p. (J). (gr. 6-9). pap. 15.95 (978-0-00-822774-6(8)) HarperCollins Pubs. Ltd. GBR. Dist: Independent Pubs. Group.
Regan, Michael. Understanding Sikhism. 2018. (Understanding World Religions & Beliefs Ser.). (ENG.). 112p. (J). (gr. 6-12). lib. bdg. 41.36 (978-1-5321-1429-8(X), 28840, Essential Library) ABDO Publishing Co.
Senker, Cath. My Sikh Year, 1 vol. 2007. (Year of Religious Festivals Ser.). (ENG., Illus.). 32p. (J). (gr. 3-3). lib. bdg. 28.93 (978-1-4042-3733-9(X), ff1bde32-cde0-4ef7-8e1e-347bdd11c6a0) Rosen Publishing Group, Inc., The.

SIKORSKY, IGOR IVANOVICH, 1889-1972

Wyckoff, Edwin Brit. Helicopter Man, 1 vol. 2010. (Genius at Work! Great Inventor Biographies Ser.). (ENG., Illus.). 32p. (J). (gr. 3-3). 26.60 (978-0-7660-3445-7(3), a26d4a57-effe-4485-9684-49021a91119c) Enslow Publishing, LLC.

SILK

see also Silkworms

Gleason, Carrie. The Biography of Silk, 1 vol. 2006. (How Did That Get Here? Ser.). (ENG., Illus.). 32p. (J). (gr. 4-7). pap. (978-0-7787-2523-7(5)); lib. bdg. (978-0-7787-2487-2(5)) Crabtree Publishing Co.

SILKWORMS

Jiang, Junjing. A Picture Book of Silk Weaving in Ancient China. Jiao, Bingzhen, illus. 2017. (978-1-62246-043-4(X)) Homa & Sekey Bks.
Kite, L. Patricia. Silkworms. 2008. 117p. (Orig.). pap. 14.95 (978-0-7414-4542-1(5)) Infinity Publishing.
Pfeffer, Wendy. Mysterious Spinners. Kim, Julie J., illus. 2005. 48p. (J). (978-1-59336-315-4(X)); pap. (978-1-59336-316-1(8)) Mondo Publishing.
Rice, Dona & Montgomery, Anne. Raising Silkworms. rev. ed. 2019. (Smithsonian: Informational Text Ser.). (ENG., Illus.). 24p. (J). (gr. 1-2). pap. 8.99 (978-1-4938-6648-9(6)) Teacher Created Materials, Inc.

SILVER

see also Money; Silversmithing

Belval, Brian. Silver. 2009. (Understanding the Elements of the Periodic Table Ser.). 48p. (gr. 6-6). 53.00 (978-1-60854-682-4(9), Rosen Reference) Rosen Publishing Group, Inc., The.
Perritano, John. Gold & Silver, Vol. 12. 2015. (North American Natural Resources Ser.). (Illus.). 64p. (J). (gr. 7). 23.95 (978-1-4222-3382-5(0)) Mason Crest.
Shea, Therese M. Silver, 1 vol., Vol. 1. 2013. (Rare & Precious Metals Ser.). (ENG.). 24p. (J). (gr. 2-3). 25.27 (978-1-4824-0509-5(1), 496f9c60-bec6-4647-b92e-4c072c5d4aee) Stevens, Gareth Publishing LLLP.
Toth, Henrietta. Silver, 1 vol. 2018. (Exploring the Elements Ser.). (ENG.). 48p. (gr. 6-6). 29.60 (978-0-7660-9926-5(1), 9e9c59ea-5f49-4aa2-8845-cc2d100a9999) Enslow Publishing, LLC.
Watt, Susan. Silver, 1 vol. 2003. (Elements Ser.). (ENG., Illus.). 32p. (gr. 4-4). 31.21 (978-0-7614-1464-3(9), ca46c5d9-4a64-4819-bbe1-a55bed6e27e3) Cavendish Square Publishing LLC.

SILVER MINES AND MINING—FICTION

Wallace, Rich. Double-Crossed at Cactus Flats: An Up2 U Western Adventure, 1 vol. Mitchell, Hazel, illus. 2013. (Up2U Adventures Ser.). (ENG.). 80p. (J). (gr. 2-5). lib. bdg. 35.64 (978-1-61641-966-0(0), 15215, Calico Chapter Bks.) ABDO Publishing Co.

SILVERSMITHING

see also Metal-Work

Mara, Wil. The Silversmith, 1 vol. 2011. (Colonial People Ser.). (ENG.). 48p. (gr. 4-4). 34.07 (978-0-7614-4804-4(7), b281651d-0b8b-491e-94d1-f1b43f638296) Cavendish Square Publishing LLC.

SIMPLE (FICTITIOUS CHARACTER)—FICTION

Hughes, Langston. Simple Speaks His Mind. (J). (gr. 5-6). reprint ed. lib. bdg. 22.95 (978-0-88411-061-3(3)) Amereon Ltd.

SIMPSON, O. J., 1947-

Blohm, Craig E. The O. J. Simpson Murder Trial, 1 vol. 2008. (Crime Scene Investigations Ser.). (ENG., Illus.). 104p. (gr. 7-7). lib. bdg. 42.03 (978-1-4205-0038-7(4), 73fed46b-f168-4dd6-adfa-8cf3fa02c260, Lucent Pr.) Greenhaven Publishing LLC.

SINGAPORE

Bosco, Don. Lion City Adventures: Explore Singapore, Learn Cool Stuff & Solve Mini-Mysteries. 2015. (ENG., Illus.). 80p. (J). pap. 16.95 (978-981-4634-34-2(4)) Marshall Cavendish International (Asia) Private Ltd. SGP. Dist: Independent Pubs. Group.
—Secrets of the Heartlands: Lion City Adventures. 2016. (Sherlock Hong Adventures Ser.: Volume 2). (ENG., Illus.).

96p. (J). pap. 16.95 *(978-981-4721-16-5(6))* Marshall Cavendish International (Asia) Private Ltd. SGP. Dist: Independent Pubs. Group.

Kummer, Patricia K. Singapore. 2003. (Enchantment of the World Ser.). (ENG., Illus.). 144p. (YA). (gr. 5-9). 39.00 *(978-0-516-22531-9(6))* Scholastic Library Publishing.

Meachen Rau, Dana. Singapore, 1 vol. 2004. (Discovering Cultures Ser.). (ENG., Illus.). 48p. (gr. 3-4). lib. bdg. 31.21 *(978-0-7614-1727-9(3),* 7d0fd50a-4f25-4f61-b562-f6e95d07ea5e) Cavendish Square Publishing LLC.

Owings, Lisa. Singapore. 2014. (Exploring Countries Ser.). (ENG., Illus.). 32p. (J). (gr. 3-7). lib. bdg. 27.95 *(978-1-60014-986-3(3),* Blastoff! Readers) Bellwether Media.

SINGAPORE—FICTION

Bidwell, Dafne. Danger Unlimited: Action, Mystery & Adventure. 2007. 244p. pap. 15.50 *(978-1-921064-89-0(7))* Fremantle Pr. AUS. Dist: Independent Pubs. Group.

Chan, Aletheia. Kody Chan: the Time Vortex. 2018. (ENG., Illus.). 126p. (J). pap. 13.77 *(978-1-5437-4639-6(X))* Partridge Pub.

Heidell, Valerie. Mirika's Story. 2006. (YA). per. 10.95 *(978-0-9774822-4-5(3))* Crosam Pr.

Irwin, Bindi & Kunz, Chris. Camouflage. 2011. (Bindi's Wildlife Adventures Ser.: 4). (ENG.). 112p. (J). (gr. 3-6). pap. 6.99 *(978-1-4022-5523-6(3),* Sourcebooks Jabberwocky) Sourcebooks, Inc.

Kok Hoong Derek, Wong. The Little Genius. 2007. 11p. 48.00 *(978-1-4303-1605-3(5))* Lulu Pr., Inc.

Lim, Andrew. Tales from the Kopitiam. 2009. (Paranormal Singapore Ser.: Vol. 4.). (ENG.). 1p. pap. 9.95 *(978-981-08-1081-8(4))* Monsoon Bks. Pte. Ltd. SGP. Dist: Tuttle Publishing.

Low, A. J. Sherlock Sam & the Ghostly Moans in Fort Canning: Book Two. Tan, Andrew, illus. 2016. (Sherlock Sam Ser.: 2). (ENG.). 120p. (J). pap. 7.99 *(978-1-4494-7788-2(7))* Andrews McMeel Publishing.

—Sherlock Sam & the Missing Heirloom in Katong: Book One. Tan, Andrew, illus. 2016. (Sherlock Sam Ser.: 1). (ENG.). 112p. (J). pap. 7.99 *(978-1-4494-7789-9(5))* Andrews McMeel Publishing.

—Sherlock Sam & the Sinister Letters in Bras Basah. Tan, Andrew, illus. 2017. (Sherlock Sam Ser.: 3). (ENG.). 144p. (J). pap. 7.99 *(978-1-4494-7975-6(8))* Andrews McMeel Publishing.

—Sherlock Sam & the Sinister Letters in Bras Basah. 2016. (Sherlock Sam Ser.: Vol. 3). (ENG., Illus.). 127p. (J). (gr. 2-6). 26.99 *(978-1-4494-8614-3(2))* Andrews McMeel Publishing.

Low, J. H. Lost in the Gardens. Low, J. H., illus. 2015. (ENG., Illus.). 48p. (J). 14.99 *(978-981-4677-10-3(8))* Marshall Cavendish International (Asia) Private Ltd. SGP. Dist: Independent Pubs. Group.

See, Ee Lin. My Kiasu Teenage Life in Singapore. 2005. (ENG., Illus.). 1p. per. 12.95 *(978-981-05-3016-7(1))* Monsoon Bks. Pte. Ltd. SGP. Dist: Tuttle Publishing.

Yunisa. Schoolaholic Princess 2: Romansa Singapura. 2008. 232p. pap. 14.88 *(978-1-4357-6044-8(1))* Lulu Pr., Inc.

—Schoolaholic Princess 3: Simfoni Cinta. 2008. 220p. pap. 14.88 *(978-1-4357-6045-5(X))* Lulu Pr., Inc.

SINGAPORE—HISTORY

Bankston, John. We Visit Singapore. 2014. (ENG., Illus.). 63p. (J). (gr. 4-8). lib. bdg. 33.95 *(978-1-61228-484-2(1))* Mitchell Lane Pubs.

Bosco, Don. Island of Legends. 2016. (ENG., Illus.). 96p. (J). pap. 16.95 *(978-981-4751-36-0(7))* Marshall Cavendish International (Asia) Private Ltd. SGP. Dist: Independent Pubs. Group.

Broadhead, Arp Raph. Mudley Explores Singapore: An Amazing Adventure into the Lion City. 2017. (ENG., Illus.). 64p. pap. 19.95 *(978-981-4721-95-0(6))* Marshall Cavendish International (Asia) Private Ltd. SGP. Dist: Independent Pubs. Group.

Daniels-Cowart, Catrina. Singapore. 2019. (Asian Countries Today Ser.). (Illus.). 96p. (J). (gr. 12). lib. bdg. 34.60 *(978-1-4222-4270-4(6))* Mason Crest.

Greathead, Helen. Lonely Planet Kids City Trails - Singapore 1. 2018. (Lonely Planet Kids Ser.). (ENG., Illus.). 88p. (J). (gr. 4-7). pap. 12.99 *(978-1-78701-483-1(5),* 5859) Lonely Planet Global Ltd. IRL. Dist: Hachette Bk. Group.

Klepeis, Alicia Z. Singapore, 1 vol. 2018. (Exploring World Cultures (First Edition) Ser.). (ENG.). 32p. (gr. 3-3). pap. 12.16 *(978-1-5026-4354-4(5),* 39d4187f-7d49-4c41-a336-9f1ba5091a6b) Cavendish Square Publishing LLC.

Layton, Lesley, et al. Singapore, 1 vol. 3rd rev. ed. 2012. (Cultures of the World (Third Edition)(r) Ser.). (ENG., Illus.). 144p. (gr. 5-5). 48.79 *(978-1-60870-787-4(3),* 5121f060-0ed3-4801-b236-0824e0c3d812) Cavendish Square Publishing LLC.

Lotlikar, Anita M. Goodnight Singapur. 2012. 28p. pap. 24.95 *(978-1-4626-9606-2(6))* America Star Bks.

Roydhouse, Sally. Find & Seek Singapore. 2015. (ENG., Illus.). 36p. (gr. -1-7). 24.95 *(978-1-939621-11-5(9))* ORO Editions.

SINGERS

Abdo, Kenny. Khalid. 2018. (Star Biographies Ser.). (ENG.). 24p. (J). (gr. 2-8). lib. bdg. 31.36 *(978-1-5321-2545-4(3),* 30099, Abdo Zoom-Fly) ABDO Publishing Co.

Adams, Colleen. Usher. (Stars in the Spotlight Ser.). 32p. (gr. 4-4). 2009. 47.90 *(978-1-60853-206-3(2),* PowerKids Pr.) 2006. (ENG., Illus.). (YA). lib. bdg. 28.93 *(978-1-4042-3516-8(7),* a2d57d65-57eb-4842-a167-dcd83a893ea1) Rosen Publishing Group, Inc., The.

Adams, Michelle. Katy Perry. 2011. (Blue Banner Biography Ser.). (Illus.). 32p. (YA). (gr. 4-7). lib. bdg. 25.70 *(978-1-61228-051-6(X))* Mitchell Lane Pubs.

Adams, Michelle Medlock. Jessica Simpson. 2007. (Blue Banner Biography Ser.). (Illus.). 32p. (YA). (gr. 4-7). lib. bdg. 25.70 *(978-1-58415-616-1(3))* Mitchell Lane Pubs.

Alagna, Magdalena. Billie Holiday. 2009. (Rock & Roll Hall of Famers Ser.). 112p. (gr. 5-8). 63.90 *(978-1-60852-468-6(X),* Rosen Reference) Rosen Publishing Group, Inc., The.

—Elvis Presley. 2009. (Rock & Roll Hall of Famers Ser.). 112p. (gr. 5-8). 63.90 *(978-1-60852-474-7(4),* Rosen Reference) Rosen Publishing Group, Inc., The.

Alexander, Lauren. Mad for Miley: An Unauthorized Biography. 2007. (Unauthorized Biographies Ser.). (ENG., Illus.). 128p. (J). (gr. 5-8). 17.44 *(978-0-8431-2684-6(1))* Penguin Young Readers Group.

Aloian, Molly. Lady Gaga. 2011. (ENG.). 32p. (J). pap. *(978-0-7787-7614-7(X));* (gr. 3-6). lib. bdg. *(978-0-7787-7609-3(3))* Crabtree Publishing Co.

Anderson, Sheila. Miley Cyrus: Music & TV Superstar, 1 vol. 2009. (Hot Celebrity Biographies Ser.). (ENG., Illus.). 48p. (gr. 5-7). lib. bdg. 27.93 *(978-0-7660-3213-2(2),* 3b4a59a3-91b9-4790-b7f4-cbed041c5934) Enslow Publishing, LLC.

Angel, Ann. Janis Joplin: Rise up Singing. 2010. (ENG., Illus.). 120p. (YA). (gr. 8-17). 24.95 *(978-0-8109-8349-6(4),* 641601, Amulet Bks.) Abrams, Inc.

Appleby, Alex. I Can Be a Singer, 1 vol. 2014. (When I Grow Up Ser.). (ENG.). 24p. (J). (gr. k-k). 24.27 *(978-1-4824-0757-0(4),* 00b4228d-dc9c-4203-8661-c2b1b2733129) Stevens, Gareth Publishing LLLP.

—Puedo Ser una Cantante / I Can Be a Singer, 1 vol. 2014. (Cuando Sea Grande / When I Grow Up Ser.). (SPA & ENG.). 24p. (J). (gr. k-k). 24.27 *(978-1-4824-0865-2(1),* e3727007-26fe-44f3-aeb2-089908983b35) Stevens, Gareth Publishing LLLP.

Aretha, David. Amy Winehouse: RandB, Jazz, & Soul Musician, 1 vol. 2012. (Lives Cut Short Set 2 Ser.). (ENG.). 112p. (YA). (gr. 6-12). 41.36 *(978-1-61783-483-7(1),* 11201, Essential Library) ABDO Publishing Co.

Azzarelli, Ally. Adele! Singing Sensation, 1 vol. 2013. (Sizzling Celebrities Ser.). (ENG.). 48p. (gr. 4-6). pap. 11.53 *(978-1-4644-0283-8(3),* dba8cb84-7e48-4f3f-9879-1cc2ebe63265); lib. bdg. 27.93 *(978-0-7660-4172-1(7),* 32789b9c-16b8-4a00-a215-f28852940b0a) Enslow Publishing, LLC.

—Justin Bieber: Teen Music Superstar, 1 vol. 2012. (Hot Celebrity Biographies Ser.). (ENG., Illus.). 48p. (gr. 5-7). pap. 11.53 *(978-1-59845-287-7(8),* a28e68af-65d2-4120-a2f9-58079db6af0e); lib. bdg. 27.93 *(978-0-7660-3873-8(4),* 35c2588d-b11b-4a47-9f97-d45e679ee90c) Enslow Publishing, LLC.

—Selena Gomez: Latina TV & Music Star, 1 vol. 2012. (Hot Celebrity Biographies Ser.). (ENG., Illus.). 48p. (gr. 5-7). pap. 11.53 *(978-1-59845-289-1(4),* 82d8106d-d7b3-4b34-8589-3b77a7b0dcbd) Enslow Publishing, LLC.

Bach, Greg. Ariana Grande. 2021. (Pop Music Stars Ser.: 5). (ENG.). 80p. (J). (gr. 7-12). 34.60 *(978-1-4222-4481-4(4))* Mason Crest.

Bailey, Diane. Miley Cyrus, 1 vol. 2011. (Megastars Ser.). (ENG., Illus.). 48p. (J). (gr. 5-5). pap. 12.75 *(978-1-4488-2259-1(9),* 93bdb6a4-9231-406f-8d4f-321d32390320); lib. bdg. 34.47 *(978-1-4358-3573-3(5),* 89cb6f5f-7cc9-47c7-89df-91d4b8cfb96c) Rosen Publishing Group, Inc., The. (Rosen Reference).

Baldwin, Garrett. The Justin Bieber Album. 2010. (ENG., Illus.). 64p. (gr. 3-11). pap. 12.95 *(978-0-85965-464-7(8))* Plexus Publishing, Ltd. GBR. Dist: Publishers Group West (PGW).

Bankston, John. Alicia Keys. 2004. (Blue Banner Biography Ser.). (Illus.). 32p. (J). lib. bdg. 25.70 *(978-1-58415-327-6(X))* Mitchell Lane Pubs.

—Christina Aguilera. 2004. (Blue Banner Biography Ser.). (Illus.). 32p. (J). lib. bdg. 25.70 *(978-1-58415-331-3(8))* Mitchell Lane Pubs.

—Missy Elliott: Hip-Hop Superstar. Lt. ed. 2004. (Blue Banner Biography Ser.). (Illus.). 32p. (J). (gr. 3-8). lib. bdg. 25.70 *(978-1-58415-219-4(2))* Mitchell Lane Pubs.

—What It's Like to Be Selena Gomez. 2012. (SPA.). (J). lib. bdg. 25.70 *(978-1-61228-321-0(7))* Mitchell Lane Pubs.

Barghoorn, Linda. Buffy Saint-Marie: Musician, Indigenous Icon, & Social Activist. 2018. (Remarkable Lives Revealed Ser.). (ENG.). 32p. (J). (gr. 3-3). *(978-0-7787-4709-3(3));* pap. *(978-0-7787-4715-4(8))* Crabtree Publishing Co.

—Harry Styles. 2018. (Superstars! Ser.). (ENG., Illus.). 32p. (J). (gr. 4-4). *(978-0-7787-4833-5(2));* pap. *(978-0-7787-4848-9(0))* Crabtree Publishing Co.

Bednar, Chuck. American Idol Profiles Index: Top Finalists from Each Season (82 Contestants) 2009. (Dream Big: American Idol Superstars Ser.). 64p. (YA). (gr. 5-18). pap. 9.95 *(978-1-4222-1593-7(8))* Mason Crest.

—Beyoncé. 2010. (Transcending Race in America Ser.). 64p. (YA). (gr. 4-8). lib. bdg. 22.95 *(978-1-4222-1607-1(1))* Mason Crest.

—David Archuleta. 2009. (Dream Big: American Idol Superstars Ser.). (Illus.). 64p. (J). (gr. 4-18). lib. bdg. 22.95 *(978-1-4222-1505-0(9));* (gr. 5-18). pap. 9.95 *(978-1-4222-1597-5(0))* Mason Crest.

—Kris Allen. 2009. (Dream Big: American Idol Superstars Ser.). (Illus.). 64p. (J). (gr. 5-18). pap. 9.95 *(978-1-4222-1596-8(2));* lib. bdg. 22.95 *(978-1-4222-1515-9(6))* Mason Crest.

Benson, Michael. Gloria Estefan. (Biography Ser.). (Illus.). 112p. (gr. 6-12). 2005. lib. bdg. 27.93 *(978-0-8225-4982-6(4))* 2003. (YA). pap. 7.95 *(978-0-8225-9692-9(X),* Carolrhoda Bks.) Lerner Publishing Group.

Betances, Maria. Selena Gomez: Superstar Singer & Actress, 1 vol. 2015. (Exceptional Latinos Ser.). (ENG., Illus.). 24p. (gr. 3-4). pap. 10.35 *(978-0-7660-6718-9(1),* 3cefe957-eb78-4199-b079-2bc3420c144c) Enslow Publishing, LLC.

Bezdecheck, Bethany. Missy Elliott. 2009. (Library of Hip-Hop Biographies Ser.). 48p. (gr. 5-5). 53.00 *(978-1-60853-697-9(1));* (ENG.). (J). lib. bdg. 34.47 *(978-1-4358-5056-9(4),* caf636e6-df40-42e3-83e2-0f2dc32fdc91); (ENG., Illus.). (J). pap. 12.75 *(978-1-4358-5442-0(X),* e743b4c5-b51e-484d-9878-90f72ae6709f) Rosen Publishing Group, Inc., The.

Bieber, Justin. Justin Bieber: Just Getting Started. (ENG., Illus.). 240p. *(978-0-00-744952-1(6))* HarperCollins Pubs. Ltd.

—Justin Bieber: First Step 2 Forever: My Story. 2010. (ENG., Illus.). 240p. (J). (gr. 3-7). 21.99 *(978-0-06-203974-3(1),* HarperCollins) HarperCollins Pubs.

—Justin Bieber: Just Getting Started. 2012. (ENG.). 240p. (J). (gr. 3-7). 21.99 *(978-0-06-220208-6(1),* HarperCollins) HarperCollins Pubs.

Big Buddy Pop Biographies, 12 vols. 2015. (Big Buddy Pop Biographies Ser.: 12). (ENG.). 32p. (J). (gr. 2-5). lib. bdg. 410.64 *(978-1-68078-051-2(4),* 19029, Big Buddy Bks.) ABDO Publishing Co.

Bingham, Hettie. Real-Life Stories: Gary Barlow. 2016. (Real-Life Stories Ser.). (ENG., Illus.). 32p. (J). (gr. 4-6). pap. 11.99 *(978-0-7502-8955-9(4),* Wayland) Hachette Children's Group GBR. Dist: Hachette Bk. Group.

Bloom, Ronny. Justin Bieber. 2011. (SPA.). 192p. (YA). 14.95 *(978-84-666-4680-2(9))* Ediciones B ESP. Dist: Spanish Pubs., LLC.

Bodden, Valerie. Rihanna. 2013. (Big Time Ser.). (ENG., Illus.). 24p. (J). (gr. 1-4). *(978-1-60818-479-8(X),* 21710, Creative Education) Creative Co., The.

—Selena Gomez. 2015. (Big Time Ser.). (ENG., Illus.). 24p. (J). (gr. 1-4). *(978-1-60818-498-9(6),* 21170, Creative Education) Creative Co., The.

Books, Triumph. Justin Bieber: Believe. 2012. (ENG.). 112p. (YA). (gr. 7). pap. 12.95 *(978-1-60078-792-8(4))* Triumph Bks.

Boone, Mary. Jennette McCurdy. 2010. (Robbie Reader Ser.). (Illus.). 32p. (J). (gr. 2-5). lib. bdg. 25.70 *(978-1-58415-900-1(6))* Mitchell Lane Pubs.

—Pink. 2009. (Blue Banner Biography Ser.). (Illus.). 32p. (YA). (gr. 4-7). lib. bdg. 25.70 *(978-1-58415-767-0(4))* Mitchell Lane Pubs.

—Vanessa Anne Hudgens. 2008. (Blue Banner Biography Ser.). (Illus.). 32p. (YA). (gr. 4-7). lib. bdg. 25.70 *(978-1-58415-672-7(4))* Mitchell Lane Pubs.

Boyd, Panchami. Beyonce, Vol. 11. 2018. (Hip-Hop & R & B: Culture, Music & Storytelling Ser.). (Illus.). 80p. (J). (gr. 7). lib. bdg. 33.27 *(978-1-4222-4177-6(7))* Mason Crest.

—Rihanna, Vol. 11. 2018. (Hip-Hop & R & B: Culture, Music & Storytelling Ser.). (Illus.). 80p. (J). (gr. 7). lib. bdg. 33.27 *(978-1-4222-4185-1(8))* Mason Crest.

—The Weeknd, Vol. 11. 2018. (Hip-Hop & R & B: Culture, Music & Storytelling Ser.). (Illus.). 80p. (J). (gr. 7). lib. bdg. 33.27 *(978-1-4222-4188-2(2))* Mason Crest.

Brian, Janeen. Meet... Nellie Melba. Murphy, Claire, illus. (J). 2017. 36p. (gr. 2). 15.99 *(978-0-14-378031-1(X))* 2016. 32p. (gr. k-2). 22.99 *(978-0-14-378029-8(8))* Random Hse. Australia AUS. Dist: Independent Pubs. Group.

Briere-Haquet, Alice. Nina. 2017. 40p. (J). (-2). 13.99 *(978-958-30-5461-7(5))* Panamericana Editorial COL. Dist: Lectorum Pubns., Inc.

Brière-Haquet, Alice. Nina: Jazz Legend & Civil-Rights Activist Nina Simone. Liance, Bruno, illus. 2017. (ENG.). 40p. (J). (gr. -1-3). lib. bdg. 16.99 *(978-1-58089-827-0(0))* Charlesbridge Publishing, Inc.

Briggs, John. Pete Seeger the People's Singer. 2015. (ENG., Illus.). 112p. (J). pap. 6.99 *(978-0-9905160-7-1(5))* Atombank Bks.

Broadwater, Andrea. The Life of Marian Anderson: Diva & Humanitarian, 1 vol. 2014. (Legendary African Americans Ser.). (ENG.). 96p. (gr. 6-6). 31.61 *(978-0-7660-6285-6(6),* 4a19d2c2-1a62-49db-b75c-b0ce87f523cd); pap. 13.88 *(978-0-7660-6286-3(4),* bdd66b39-cd24-4afa-b20a-151b0f688994) Enslow Publishing, LLC.

Brooks, Riley. Debby Ryan: Her Sweet Life! 2010. (Illus.). 32p. (J). pap. *(978-0-545-29637-3(4))* Scholastic, Inc.

—Willow Smith: Pop's Newest Princess. 2011. (Illus.). 46p. (J). pap. *(978-0-545-36887-2(1))* Scholastic, Inc.

Brown, Anne K. Gwen Stefani, 1 vol. 2009. (People in the News Ser.). (ENG., Illus.). 104p. (gr. 7-7). lib. bdg. 41.03 *(978-1-4205-0126-1(7),* b891cea2-1b2b-4f0c-bcde-ed3a11e1aeca, Lucent Pr.) Greenhaven Publishing LLC.

—Katy Perry, 1 vol. 2011. (People in the News Ser.). (ENG., Illus.). 112p. (gr. 7-7). lib. bdg. 41.03 *(978-1-4205-0609-9(9),* ad9b93fe-f707-4295-ae9f-0f3e4bc0b6b4, Lucent Pr.) Greenhaven Publishing LLC.

Brown, Monica. My Name Is Celia: The Life of Celia Cruz. López, Rafael, illus. 2004. Tr. of Me Llamo Celia - La Vida de Celia Cruz. (ENG.). 32p. (J). (gr. k-3). 15.95 *(978-0-87358-872-0(X))* Cooper Square Publishing Llc.

—My Name is Celia (Me Llamo Celia) The Life of Celia Cruz (La Vida de Celia Cruz) López, Rafael, illus. 2015. (ENG, MUL & SPA.). 32p. (J). (gr. k-3). pap. 7.95 *(978-1-58979-998-1(4))* Jaffe Book Solutions.

Brown, Risa. Day by Day with Carrie Underwood. 2014. (ENG., Illus.). 32p. (J). (gr. -1-2). 25.70 *(978-1-61228-631-0(3))* Mitchell Lane Pubs.

Burlingame, Jeff. Avril Lavigne: Celebrity with Heart, 1 vol. 2010. (Celebrities with Heart Ser.). (ENG.). 112p. (gr. 6-7). 35.93 *(978-0-7660-3407-5(0),* 31afa24d-73fc-4cdb-91a7-0e57482dbf41); (Illus.). pap. 13.88 *(978-1-59845-204-4(5),* 1cb08fbc-d1b7-4e16-b9cc-d1af6efb1d2d) Enslow Publishing, LLC.

—Demi! Latina Star Demi Lovato, 1 vol. 2013. (Sizzling Celebrities Ser.). (ENG.). 48p. (gr. 4-6). pap. 11.53 *(978-1-4644-0277-7(9),* 003aad0f-ed44-496e-9ef9-3803fb52ee68) Enslow Publishing, LLC.

Burns, Kylie. Carrie Underwood. 2013. (ENG., Illus.). 32p. (J). *(978-0-7787-0024-1(0));* pap. *(978-0-7787-0043-2(7))* Crabtree Publishing Co.

Caravantes, Peggy. Shawn Mendes: Pop Star. 2017. (Superstar Stories Ser.). (ENG.). 24p. (J). (gr. 3-6). lib. bdg. 32.79 *(978-1-5038-1997-9(3),* 211873) Child's World, Inc, The.

—Zendaya: Star Performer. 2017. (Superstar Stories Ser.). (ENG.). 24p. (J). (gr. 3-6). lib. bdg. 32.79 *(978-1-5038-2000-5(9),* 211876) Child's World, Inc, The.

Cartlidge, Cherese. Beyoncé, 1 vol. 2012. (People in the News Ser.). (ENG., Illus.). 112p. (gr. 7-7). lib. bdg. 41.03 *(978-1-4205-0752-2(4),* d17f8acb-0cdc-4155-a280-377c965cec18, Lucent Pr.) Greenhaven Publishing LLC.

—Jennifer Hudson, 1 vol. 2011. (People in the News Ser.). (ENG., Illus.). 96p. (gr. 7-7). lib. bdg. 41.03 *(978-1-4205-0607-5(2),* acf0d5fd-fe32-4165-a7c0-6407ff4c7800, Lucent Pr.) Greenhaven Publishing LLC.

Casapulla, Louise. Ashlee Simpson. 2005. (Pop People Ser.). (Illus.). 137p. (J). *(978-0-439-76581-7(1))* Scholastic, Inc.

Cefrey, Holly. Justin Timberlake. (Contemporary Musicians & Their Music Ser.). 48p. (gr. 6-6). 2009. 53.00 *(978-1-61511-938-7(8))* 2008. (ENG., Illus.). (J). lib. bdg. 34.47 *(978-1-4042-1815-4(7),* 7c833503-407e-469b-92c3-4737d69bda0c) 2008. (ENG., Illus.). pap. 12.75 *(978-1-4358-5123-8(4),* 5ee33313-2111-48ee-a47c-728401bf430f, Rosen Classroom) Rosen Publishing Group, Inc., The.

Chambers, Veronica. Celia Cruz, Queen of Salsa. Maren, Julie, illus. 2008. (J). (gr. -1-3). 28.95 incl. audio compact disk *(978-1-4301-0284-7(5));* 25.95 incl. audio *(978-1-4301-0281-6(0));* pap. 16.95 incl. audio *(978-1-4301-0280-9(2))* Live Oak Media.

—Celia Cruz, Queen of Salsa. Maren, Julie, illus. 2007. (ENG.). 40p. (J). (gr. k-3). pap. 8.99 *(978-0-14-240779-0(8),* Puffin Books) Penguin Young Readers Group.

—Celia Cruz, Queen of Salsa. Maren, Julie, illus. 2007. (gr. 2-5). 17.00 *(978-0-7569-8153-2(0))* Perfection Learning Corp.

Chandler, Michael. The Littlest Cowboy's Christmas, 2 vols. Jacobsen, Terry, illus. 2006. (ENG.). 32p. (J). (gr. k-3). 17.95 *(978-1-58980-381-7(7),* Pelican Publishing) Arcadia Publishing.

Collier Hillstrom, Laurie. Kelly Clarkson, 1 vol. 2007. (People in the News Ser.). (ENG., Illus.). 104p. (gr. 7-7). lib. bdg. 41.03 *(978-1-4205-0013-4(9),* d71e45fb-310b-4664-b0e1-a0cb286f120f, Lucent Pr.) Greenhaven Publishing LLC.

Coombs, Karen Mueller. Woody Guthrie: America's Folksinger. 2003. (Illus.). 120p. (J). pap. 8.95 *(978-0-8225-3750-2(8))* Lerner Publishing Group.

Cooper, Ilene. This Boy: The Early Lives of John Lennon & Paul Mccartney. 2023. (Illus.). 192p. (J). (gr. 5-9). 17.99 ***(978-0-451-47585-5(2),*** Viking Books for Young Readers) Penguin Young Readers Group.

Corporate Contributor. Selena Gomez. 2012. (ENG.). 32p. (J). *(978-0-7787-7617-8(4));* pap. *(978-0-7787-7630-7(1))* Crabtree Publishing Co.

Currie-McGhee, Leanne K. Miley Cyrus, 1 vol. 2009. (People in the News Ser.). (ENG., Illus.). 96p. (gr. 7-7). lib. bdg. 41.03 *(978-1-4205-0127-8(5),* f0dfa9b2-ad1a-4d5c-b086-431d9f15c363, Lucent Pr.) Greenhaven Publishing LLC.

Dann, Sarah. Beyoncé. 2013. (ENG., Illus.). 32p. (J). *(978-0-7787-0019-7(4))* Crabtree Publishing Co.

—Beyonce, 1 vol. 2013. (ENG., Illus.). 32p. (J). pap. *(978-0-7787-0039-5(9))* Crabtree Publishing Co.

Danziger, Meryl. Sing It! A Biography of Pete Seeger. 2016. (Illus.). 112p. (J). (gr. 3-7). 17.95 *(978-1-60980-655-2(7),* Triangle Square) Seven Stories Pr.

Davidson, Avelyn. Darren Criss, 1 vol. 2012. (Rising Stars Ser.). (ENG., Illus.). 32p. (gr. 1-1). 27.93 *(978-1-4339-7276-8(X),* 71c6be9c-0561-4be6-adee-9235259e36fb); pap. 11.50 *(978-1-4339-7277-5(8),* ea4526f6-804f-49a9-9a3a-02889787eeaa) Stevens, Gareth Publishing LLLP.

—KeKe Palmer, 1 vol. 2012. (Rising Stars Ser.). (ENG., Illus.). 32p. (J). (gr. 1-1). 27.93 *(978-1-4339-7287-4(5),* 19dd6a07-21c0-4cb6-8d9f-3d5c2c223f50); pap. 11.50 *(978-1-4339-7284-3(0),* 9c292b37-b419-48aa-8b25-ea140055e387) Stevens, Gareth Publishing LLLP.

Day, Holly. Shakira, 1 vol. 2007. (People in the News Ser.). (ENG., Illus.). 104p. (gr. 7-7). lib. bdg. 41.03 *(978-1-59018-974-0(4),* d6a0dedc-63a3-4123-9a86-86334f5c9ef0, Lucent Pr.) Greenhaven Publishing LLC.

De Medeiros, James. Justin Timberlake. 2008. (Remarkable People Ser.). (Illus.). 24p. (J). (gr. 4-6). pap. 8.95 *(978-1-59036-983-8(1));* lib. bdg. 24.45 *(978-1-59036-982-1(3))* Weigl Pubs., Inc.

Dougherty, Steve. Justin Timberlake. 2009. (Illus.). 112p. (J). *(978-0-531-23401-3(0),* Franklin Watts) Hachette Children's Group.

Dougherty, Terri. Justin Timberlake, 1 vol. 2008. (People in the News Ser.). (ENG., Illus.). 104p. (gr. 7-7). lib. bdg. 41.03 *(978-1-4205-0056-1(2),* 39716d2c-3241-4d87-8d41-751f6be1be9d, Lucent Pr.) Greenhaven Publishing LLC.

—Raven-Symoné. (Role Model Entertainers Ser.). (Illus.). 64p. (YA). 2010. (gr. 7-12). 22.95 *(978-1-4222-0508-2(8))* 2007. pap. 9.95 *(978-1-4222-0795-6(1))* Mason Crest.

Duggleby, John. Uh Huh! The Story of Ray Charles. 2005. (Modern Music Masters Ser.). (Illus.). 160p. (gr. 9-12). lib. bdg. 28.95 *(978-1-931798-65-5(6))* Reynolds, Morgan Inc.

Dylan, Penelope. Beyoncé, 1 vol. 2006. (Contemporary Musicians & Their Music Ser.). (ENG., Illus.). 48p. (YA). (gr. 6-6). lib. bdg. 34.47 *(978-1-4042-0712-7(0),* 692a6e02-0e47-4286-a81f-68f8cb3edca7, Rosen Reference) Rosen Publishing Group, Inc., The.

Dzidrums, Christine. Kelly Clarkson: Behind Her Hazel Eyes. 2013. 104p. pap. 9.99 *(978-1-938438-19-6(1))* Creative Media Publishing.

Earl, C. F. Alicia Keys. 2012. (J). pap. *(978-1-4222-2547-9(X));* (Illus.). 48p. (gr. 3-4). 19.95 *(978-1-4222-2521-9(6))* Mason Crest.

Earl, C. F. & Hill, Z. B. Rihanna. 2012. (Superstars of Hip-Hop Ser.). 48p. (J). (gr. 3-4). pap. 9.95 *(978-1-4222-2552-3(6));* (Illus.). 19.95 *(978-1-4222-2526-4(7))* Mason Crest.

Edge, Laura B. Hilary Duff: Celebrity with Heart, 1 vol. 2010. (Celebrities with Heart Ser.). (ENG., Illus.). 128p. (gr. 6-7). 35.93 *(978-0-7660-3404-4(6),* f8bfc7cb-0fe8-4ea5-acdd-901b92330a3e); pap. 13.88 *(978-1-59845-205-1(3),* d3a9e6ab-9378-42bb-b233-7e7ef8557987) Enslow Publishing, LLC.

Edwards, Laurie J. Rihanna, 1 vol. 2009. (People in the News Ser.). (ENG., Illus.). 104p. (gr. 7-7). lib. bdg. 41.03 *(978-1-4205-0129-2(1),*

S

be21a8d6-e3ab-45f4-bc74-495b41cc71f5, Lucent Pr.) Greenhaven Publishing LLC.

Ellison, Katie. Who Was Bob Marley? 2017. (Who Was... ? Ser.). lib. bdg. 16.00 (978-0-606-40115-9(6)) Turtleback.

Ellison, Katie & Who HQ. Who Was Bob Marley? Copeland, Gregory, illus. 2017. (Who Was? Ser.). 112p. (J). (gr. 3-7). 6.99 (978-0-448-48919-3(8), Penguin Workshop) Penguin Young Readers Group.

Erskine, Kathryn. Mama Africa! How Miriam Makeba Spread Hope with Her Song. Palmer, Charly, illus. 2017. (ENG.). 48p. (J). 18.99 (978-0-374-30301-3(0), 900152887, Farrar, Straus & Giroux (BYR)) Farrar, Straus & Giroux.

Etinde-Crompton, Charlotte & Crompton, Samuel Willard. Aretha Franklin: The Queen of Soul, 1 vol. 2019. (Celebrating Black Artists Ser.). (ENG.). 104p. (gr. 7-7). 38.93 (978-1-9785-0357-1(1), 6ead0d14-8960-4f46-b4ce-7e47f5dcc063) Enslow Publishing, LLC.

Figueroa, Acton. Julio Iglesias & Enrique Iglesias. 2009. (Famous Families Ser.). 48p. (gr. 5-5). 53.00 (978-1-61512-508-1(6)) Rosen Publishing Group, Inc., The.

Flores, Chris. Pharrell Williams: Singer & Songwriter, 1 vol. 2016. (Junior Biographies Ser.). (ENG.). 24p. (gr. 3-4). pap. 10.35 (978-0-7660-8192-5(3), 929a4e41-97a6-4274-9274-8bbcbc77ebf4) Enslow Publishing, LLC.

Ford, Carin T. Ray Charles: I Was Born with Music Inside Me, 1 vol. 2008. (African-American Biography Library). (ENG., Illus.). 128p. (gr. 6-7). lib. bdg. 35.93 (978-0-7660-2701-5(5), 9c2f4fd7-1db1-4b92-bb6e-76505244f384) Enslow Publishing, LLC.

Frank, Mary Kate. Carrie Underwood, 1 vol. 2009. (Today's Superstars Ser.). (ENG.). 48p. (J). (gr. 3-3). pap. 15.05 (978-1-4339-2377-7(7), 1096f238-965d-4a30-b64e-47509e74718f); lib. bdg. 34.60 (978-1-4339-2381-4(5), 8aa7767b-bab4-4edc-9317-b88d5fefedba) Stevens, Gareth Publishing LLLP.

—Rihanna, 1 vol. 2009. (Today's Superstars Ser.). (ENG.). 48p. (J). (gr. 3-3). pap. 15.05 (978-1-4339-2375-3(0), 9003a7c0-c7fa-46a6-8607-d3ab01fb6ebf); lib. bdg. 34.60 (978-1-4339-2379-1(3), 55fa66cf-23c2-4bee-9d44-9a9a42c642d0) Stevens, Gareth Publishing LLLP.

Franke, Amim. Julianne Hough, 1 vol. 2010. (Country Music Stars Ser.). (ENG.). 32p. (J). (gr. 1-1). pap. 11.50 (978-1-4339-3933-4(9), 975f373e-a92a-4511-91ca-c5bc577e1a9c); lib. bdg. 27.93 (978-1-4339-3932-7(0), df7fa4eb-2534-473e-9cbd-c51f5bea2eb1) Stevens, Gareth Publishing LLLP.

Franke, Livia. Kathleen Battle: American Soprano, 1 vol. 2010. (Inspiring Lives Ser.). (ENG., Illus.). 32p. (J). (gr. 1-1). pap. 11.50 (978-1-4339-3635-7(6), e2a04fd1-a147-4a8e-bd94-b77e16bef2f3); lib. bdg. 27.93 (978-1-4339-3634-0(8), f4a249ea-94dd-43a0-a7bc-1ae15f054f04) Stevens, Gareth Publishing LLLP.

Franks, Katie. Miley Cyrus. (Kid Stars! Ser.). 24p. (gr. 2-3). 2009. 42.50 (978-1-61513-885-2(4), PowerKids Pr.) 2008. (ENG.). pap. 10.40 (978-1-4042-4532-7(4), 6e0f5208-ad6e-4552-9480-e93909b22f49, Rosen Classroom) 2008. (ENG., Illus.). (J). lib. bdg. 26.27 (978-1-4042-4467-2(0), 900ab84a-0891-4fb7-8f15-64814bbe5ace, PowerKids Pr.) Rosen Publishing Group, Inc., The.

Freedman, Russell. The Voice That Challenged a Nation: A Newbery Honor Award Winner. 2011. (ENG., Illus.). 128p. (J). (gr. 5-7). pap. 11.99 (978-0-547-48034-3(2), 1439385, Clarion Bks.) HarperCollins Pubs.

Frisch, Aaron. Justin Bieber. 2013. (Big Time Ser.). (ENG., Illus.). 24p. (J). (gr. 1-4). 25.65 (978-1-60818-330-2(0), 21805, Creative Education) Creative Co., The.

—Katy Perry. 2013. (Big Time Ser.). (ENG., Illus.). 24p. (J). (gr. 1-4). 25.65 (978-1-60818-331-9(9), 21808, Creative Education) Creative Co., The.

—Lady Gaga. 2013. (Big Time Ser.). (ENG., Illus.). 24p. (J). (gr. 1-4). 25.65 (978-1-60818-332-6(7), 21811, Creative Education) Creative Co., The.

Gagne, Tammy. Adele. 2012. (Illus.). 32p. (J). lib. bdg. 25.70 (978-1-61228-314-2(4)) Mitchell Lane Pubs.

—Day by Day with Justin Bieber. 2011. (Day by Day with... Ser.). (Illus.). 32p. (J). (gr. -1-2). lib. bdg. 25.70 (978-1-58415-984-1(7)) Mitchell Lane Pubs.

—Debby Ryan. 2012. (Illus.). 32p. (J). lib. bdg. 25.70 (978-1-61228-332-6(2)) Mitchell Lane Pubs.

—Ed Sheeran. 2017. lib. bdg. 25.70 (978-1-68020-129-1(8)) Mitchell Lane Pubs.

—Kesha. 2011. (Blue Banner Biography Ser.). (Illus.). 32p. (YA). (gr. 4-7). lib. bdg. 25.70 (978-1-61228-052-3(8)) Mitchell Lane Pubs.

—The Weeknd. 2017. lib. bdg. 25.70 (978-1-68020-124-6(7)) Mitchell Lane Pubs.

Gaines, Ann Graham. Britney Spears. 2004. (Blue Banner Biography Ser.). (Illus.). 32p. (J). lib. bdg. 25.70 (978-1-58415-329-0(6)) Mitchell Lane Pubs.

Galaxy of Superstars. 2005. (Galaxy of Superstars Ser.). (gr. 6-12). 375.00 (978-0-7910-9145-6(7), Facts On File) Infobase Holdings, Inc.

Ganchy, Sally. Taylor Hicks. (Who's Your Idol? Ser.). 48p. (gr. 5-5). 2009. 53.00 (978-1-60854-789-0(2), Rosen Reference) 2008. (ENG., Illus.). (J). lib. bdg. 34.47 (978-1-4042-1368-5(6), e186c30a-6815-4f72-b76e-70f8f38c81d9) Rosen Publishing Group, Inc., The.

Gibson, Karen. What It's Like to Be Jennifer Lopez. de la Vega, Eida, tr. from ENG. 2011. (What It's Like to Be... = Que Se Sienta Al Ser... Ser.). (SPA., Illus.). 32p. (J). (gr. -1-2). lib. bdg. 25.70 (978-1-58415-990-2(1)) Mitchell Lane Pubs.

Gigliotti, Jim. Ariana Grande. 2018. (Amazing Americans: Pop Music Stars Ser.). (ENG.). 24p. (J). (gr. -1-3). lib. bdg. 26.99 (978-1-68402-458-2(7)) Bearport Publishing Co., Inc.

Gogerly, Liz. Justin Bieber. 2013. (ENG., Illus.). 32p. (J). 28.50 (978-1-59771-415-0(1), 1346767) Sea-To-Sea Pubns.

—Taylor Momsen. 2013. (ENG., Illus.). 32p. (J). 28.50 (978-1-59771-418-1(6)) Sea-To-Sea Pubns.

Golio, Gary. Strange Fruit: Billie Holiday & the Power of a Protest Song. Riley-Webb, Charlotte, illus. 2017. (ENG.). 40p. (J). (gr. 3-6). E-Book 30.65 (978-1-5124-2837-7(X), Millbrook Pr.) Lerner Publishing Group.

Goodall, Lian. Singing Towards the Future: The Story of Portia White. 2nd ed. 2008. (Stories of Canada Ser.: 6). (ENG.). 72p. (J). pap. 18.99 (978-1-894917-55-1(3), Napoleon & Co.) Dundurn Pr. CAN. Dist: Publishers Group West (PGW).

Gordon, Katherine. Michael Jackson: Ultimate Music Legend. 2010. (Illus.). 48p. (J). pap. 8.95 (978-0-7613-6002-5(6), Lerner Pubns.) Lerner Publishing Group.

Gosman, Gillian. Chris Colfer, 1 vol. 2012. (Kid Stars! Ser.). (ENG., Illus.). 24p. (J). (gr. 2-3). pap. 10.40 (978-1-4488-6347-1(3), df7bb87f-b786-4bbe-8235-0d04225df787); lib. bdg. 26.27 (978-1-4488-6193-4(4), fcebf361-da52-47dc-ae19-da9552291a50) Rosen Publishing Group, Inc., The. (PowerKids Pr.).

—Justin Bieber, 1 vol. 2012. (Kid Stars! Ser.). (ENG., Illus.). 24p. (J). (gr. 2-3). pap. 10.40 (978-1-4488-6339-6(2), 94bada5e-08ef-45ff-991a-b6f207f6af0b); lib. bdg. 26.27 (978-1-4488-6190-3(X), c376461a-7328-4630-a781-e09c82049389) Rosen Publishing Group, Inc., The. (PowerKids Pr.).

—Meaghan Jette Martin, 1 vol. 2012. (Kid Stars! Ser.). (ENG., Illus.). 24p. (J). (gr. 2-3). pap. 10.40 (978-1-4488-6343-3(0), f60f2ee2-cfb1-4373-b560-f4f74966b779); lib. bdg. 26.27 (978-1-4488-6192-7(6), ad57d72b-0a1a-44d1-9807-d74cb906f373) Rosen Publishing Group, Inc., The. (PowerKids Pr.).

Greenberger, Robert. Christina Aguilera. (Contemporary Musicians & Their Music Ser.). 48p. (gr. 6-6). 2009. 53.00 (978-1-61511-929-5(9)) 2008. (ENG., Illus.). (J). lib. bdg. 34.47 (978-1-4042-1816-1(5), 112a1446-e16a-4acd-b4d2-648afe0a87c5) 2008. (ENG., Illus.). pap. 12.75 (978-1-4358-5124-5(2), 5b5ddd5e-96c9-43cb-974f-fe04abea5bb7, Rosen Classroom) Rosen Publishing Group, Inc., The.

Greenfield, Eloise. Paul Robeson, 1 vol. 2009. (ENG., Illus.). 40p. (J). (gr. 3-6). pap. 12.95 (978-1-60060-262-7(2), leelowbooks) Lee & Low Bks., Inc.

—Paul Robeson. Ford, George, illus. 2009. (ENG.). 40p. (J). (gr. 1-6). 10.95 (978-1-60060-256-6(8)) Lee & Low Bks., Inc.

Griffin, Maeve. Ciara, 1 vol. 2012. (Hip-Hop Headliners Ser.). (ENG., Illus.). 32p. (J). (gr. 1-1). pap. 11.50 (978-1-4339-6602-6(6), e1e11617-60e1-489d-b027-4eb7e401864d); lib. bdg. 27.93 (978-1-4339-6600-2(X), 7b952833-1981-47cd-aed5-7f8c5fcb1a3c) Stevens, Gareth Publishing LLLP.

Griffiths, Katie. Beyoncé: Entertainment Industry Icon, 1 vol. 2017. (Leading Women Ser.). (ENG., Illus.). 112p. (YA). (gr. 7-7). 41.64 (978-1-5026-2705-6(1), ea49be16-bf57-49ea-879d-1ec72e415a89) Cavendish Square Publishing LLC.

—Rihanna. 2015. (Illus.). 48p. (J). lib. bdg. (978-1-62713-313-5(5)) Cavendish Square Publishing LLC.

Haldy, Emma E. Marian Anderson. Bane, Jeff, illus. 2016. (My Early Library: My Itty-Bitty Bio Ser.). (ENG.). 24p. (J). (gr. k-1). 30.64 (978-1-63471-023-7(1), 208172) Cherry Lake Publishing.

Hand. Westlife. (Illus.). 128p. (J). (978-1-85227-995-0(8), Virgin Books Limited) Ebury Publishing.

Harte, Harlee. I Justin Bieber. 2010. 144p. pap. 4.95 (978-1-60747-777-8(7), Pickwick Pr.) Phoenix Bks., Inc.

Heatley, Michael. Katy Perry. 2015. (Pop Icons Ser.). (Illus.). 64p. (J). (gr. 7). lib. bdg. 23.95 (978-1-4222-3248-4(4)) Mason Crest.

Heatley, Michael & Gent, Mike. Taylor Swift. 2015. (Pop Icons Ser.). (Illus.). 64p. (J). (gr. 7). lib. bdg. 23.95 (978-1-4222-3250-7(6)) Mason Crest.

Heos, Bridget. Lady Gaga, 1 vol. 2011. (Megastars Ser.). (ENG.). 48p. (YA). (gr. 5-5). pap. 12.75 (978-1-4488-2260-7(2), b3a02271-ccfc-4dd4-9957-47e990308885); (Illus.). lib. bdg. 34.47 (978-1-4358-3574-0(3), ac5215f1-d02d-4c52-9c46-dd59e686674f) Rosen Publishing Group, Inc., The.

—Rihanna, 1 vol. 2011. (Megastars Ser.). (ENG.). 48p. (YA). (gr. 5-5). pap. 12.75 (978-1-4488-2262-1(9), de6c4228-db6a-4786-91a3-ea13839e59db); (Illus.). lib. bdg. 34.47 (978-1-4358-3576-4(X), 36d91b06-06ef-4e73-8b43-42626cedf983) Rosen Publishing Group, Inc., The.

Herringshaw, DeAnn. Dorothy Dandridge: Singer & Actress, 1 vol. 2011. (Essential Lives Set 6 Ser.). (ENG., Illus.). 112p. (J). (gr. 6-12). lib. bdg. 41.36 (978-1-61714-779-1(6), 6723, Essential Library) ABDO Publishing Co.

Hill, Z. B. Beyoncé. 2012. (J). pap. (978-1-4222-2536-3(4)); (Illus.). 48p. (gr. 3-4). 19.95 (978-1-4222-2510-3(0)) Mason Crest.

—Ciara. 2012. (Superstars of Hip-Hop Ser.). (Illus.). 48p. (J). (gr. 3-4). 19.95 (978-1-4222-2513-4(5)) Mason Crest.

—Usher. 2012. (J). pap. (978-1-4222-2557-8(7)); (Illus.). 48p. (gr. 3-4). 19.95 (978-1-4222-2531-8(3)) Mason Crest.

Horn, Geoffrey M. Alicia Keys, 1 vol. 2005. (Today's Superstars Ser.). (ENG., Illus.). 32p. (gr. 3-3). lib. bdg. 34.60 (978-0-8368-4233-3(2), ec7853a4-e1ef-41a3-913d-364f4032e29d) Stevens, Gareth Publishing LLLP.

—Beyoncé, 1 vol. 2005. (Today's Superstars Ser.). (ENG., Illus.). 32p. (gr. 3-3). lib. bdg. 34.60 (978-0-8368-4230-2(8), 3f390ece-6d0d-4f70-992b-80b0dad45fb9) Stevens, Gareth Publishing LLLP.

Horning, Nicole. Lady Gaga: Born to Be a Star, 1 vol. 2019. (People in the News Ser.). (ENG.). 104p. (J). (gr. 7-7). pap. 20.99 (978-1-5345-6828-0(X), cf11e3cd-3c47-463f-8b1c-f0c471d1438f, Lucent Pr.) Greenhaven Publishing LLC.

Howse, Jennifer. Miley Cyrus. 2008. (Remarkable People Ser.). (Illus.). 24p. (J). (gr. 4-6). pap. 8.95 (978-1-59036-985-2(8)); lib. bdg. 24.45 (978-1-59036-984-5(X)) Weigl Pubs., Inc.

—Rihanna: Remarkable People. 2010. 25.70 (978-1-61690-151-6(9)); pap. 11.95 (978-1-61690-152-3(7)) Weigl Pubs., Inc. (AV2 by Weigl).

Hudd, Emily. Beyoncé. 2019. (Influential People Ser.). (ENG., Illus.). 32p. (J). (gr. 4-6). 30.65 (978-1-5435-7129-5(8), 140412) Capstone.

—Khalid. 2019. (Influential People Ser.). (ENG., Illus.). 32p. (J). (gr. 4-6). 30.65 (978-1-5435-7138-7(7), 140416) Capstone.

Hurst, Heidi. Jennifer Lopez. 2003. (People in the News Ser.). (Illus.). 112p. (J). 32.45 (978-1-59018-325-0(8), Lucent Bks.) Cengage Gale.

Isbell, Hannah. Rihanna: Pop Star, 1 vol. 2017. (Junior Biographies Ser.). (ENG.). 24p. (gr. 3-4). pap. 10.35 (978-0-7660-8783-5(2), c52056ae-18e9-49a6-ab8c-eddb72b4f45d); lib. bdg. 24.27 (978-0-7660-8674-6(7), dcc2e073-c3db-4af0-818c-cead5e85845b) Enslow Publishing, LLC.

Janic, Susan. Living the Dream: Hannah Montana & Miley Cyrus - The Unofficial Story. 2008. (ENG., Illus.). 144p. (J). (gr. 4-7). pap. 14.95 (978-1-55022-848-9(X), 18c76be9-2214-4b48-b6dc-44687670240b) ECW Pr. CAN. Dist: Baker & Taylor Publisher Services (BTPS).

Jeffery, Marika. Carrie Underwood. (Sharing the American Dream Ser.). 2009. 64p. (YA). (gr. 7-12). 22.95 (978-1-4222-0599-0(1)) 2008. (J). pap. 9.95 (978-1-4222-0764-2(1)) Mason Crest.

Jeffrey, Gary. Bob Marley: The Life of a Musical Legend, 1 vol. Riley, Terry, illus. 2006. (Graphic Nonfiction Biographies Ser.). (ENG.). 48p. (YA). (gr. 4-5). lib. bdg. 37.13 (978-1-4042-0854-4(2), 5d207acf-32f4-451c-baac-fa0ec9578448) Rosen Publishing Group, Inc., The.

Johns, Michael-Anne. School Cool. 2009. (Illus.). 48p. (J). (978-0-545-15901-2(6)) Scholastic, Inc.

Johnson, Robin. Katy Perry. 2011. (ENG.). 32p. (J). pap. (978-0-7787-7613-0(1)); (gr. 3-6). lib. bdg. (978-0-7787-7608-6(5)) Crabtree Publishing Co.

—Rihanna. 2013. (ENG., Illus.). 32p. (J). (978-0-7787-1051-6(3)); pap. (978-0-7787-1055-4(6)) Crabtree Publishing Co.

—Shawn Mendes. 2018. (Superstars! Ser.). (ENG., Illus.). 32p. (J). (gr. 4-4). (978-0-7787-4830-4(8)); pap. (978-0-7787-4845-8(6)) Crabtree Publishing Co.

Jordin Sparks. 2013. (Rising Stars Ser.). 32p. (J). (gr. 3-6). pap. 63.00 (978-1-4339-8983-4(2)) Stevens, Gareth Publishing LLLP.

Kaminsky, Kristy & Domboski, Brian. Ashlee & Jessica Simpson. 2008. (Pop Culture Ser.). (Illus.). 64p. (YA). (gr. 3-7). lib. bdg. 22.95 (978-1-4222-0208-1(9)) Mason Crest.

Kampff, Joseph. Beyoncé: Singer, Songwriter, & Actress, 1 vol. 2015. (Exceptional African Americans Ser.). (ENG., Illus.). 24p. (gr. 3-3). 24.27 (978-0-7660-7170-4(7), 56ec6e8a-3d72-46f0-a00d-33e3290429bc) Enslow Publishing, LLC.

Kawa, Katie & Cartlidge, Cherese. Taylor Swift: Superstar Singer, 1 vol. 2016. (People in the News Ser.). (ENG.). 104p. (J). (gr. 7-7). lib. bdg. 41.03 (978-1-5345-6025-3(4), ac227de1-650d-4244-a457-698940f8a45a, Lucent Pr.) Greenhaven Publishing LLC.

Kelley, True. Who Is Dolly Parton? 2014. (Who Is... ? Ser.). lib. bdg. 16.00 (978-0-606-34165-3(X)) Turtleback.

Kennon, Michou. Beyoncé, 1 vol. 2011. (Hip-Hop Headliners Ser.). (ENG., Illus.). 32p. (gr. 1-1). pap. 11.50 (978-1-4339-4789-6(7), ee1e7152-9d02-4fd4-bf05-4da3a1d5c0e1); (J). lib. bdg. 27.93 (978-1-4339-4788-9(9), 3f18dd4f-c807-4912-8fd6-6be85d5b19f8) Stevens, Gareth Publishing LLLP.

—Jordin Sparks, 1 vol. 2013. (Rising Stars Ser.). (ENG.). 32p. (J). (gr. 1-1). 27.93 (978-1-4339-8981-0(6), 288d8d95-0d9c-4550-ab47-07293d741549); pap. 11.50 (978-1-4339-8982-7(4), ce44b9e3-426b-408a-bebc-01d1b26f98bf) Stevens, Gareth Publishing LLLP.

Kjelle, Marylou Morano. Ashlee Simpson. 2005. (Blue Banner Biography Ser.). (Illus.). 32p. (J). (gr. 4-8). lib. bdg. 25.70 (978-1-58415-383-2(0)) Mitchell Lane Pubs.

—Jesse Mccartney. 2006. (Robbie Reader Ser.). (Illus.). 32p. (J). (gr. 2-5). lib. bdg. 25.70 (978-1-58415-500-3(0)) Mitchell Lane Pubs.

—Natasha Bedingfield. 2009. (Blue Banner Biography Ser.). (Illus.). 32p. (YA). (gr. 4-7). lib. bdg. 25.70 (978-1-58415-772-4(0)) Mitchell Lane Pubs.

Kreger-Boaz, Claire. Lady Gaga, 1 vol. 2011. (People in the News Ser.). (ENG.). 104p. (gr. 7-7). lib. bdg. 41.03 (978-1-4205-0426-2(6), bba85bf0-e97c-4b5e-ae3e-82c371ed9865, Lucent Pr.) Greenhaven Publishing LLC.

Krohn, Katherine. Biography Gwen Stefani. 2007. (Biography Ser.). (Illus.). 112p. (J). (gr. -1). lib. bdg. (978-0-8225-7157-5(9)) Twenty First Century Bks.

—Biography Shakira. 2007. (Biography Ser.). (Illus.). 112p. (J). (gr. -1). lib. bdg. 30.60 (978-0-8225-7159-9(5), Twenty-First Century Bks.) Lerner Publishing Group.

Krumenauer, Heidi. Harry Styles of One Direction: Harry Styles. 2014. (ENG.). 32p. (J). 25.70 (978-1-62469-008-2(4)) Purple Toad Publishing, Inc.

—Lady Gaga. 2010. (Blue Banner Biography Ser.). (Illus.). 32p. (YA). (gr. 4-7). lib. bdg. 25.70 (978-1-58415-904-9(9)) Mitchell Lane Pubs.

—Lorde. 2015. (ENG., Illus.). 32p. (J). 26.50 (978-1-62469-122-5(6)) Purple Toad Publishing, Inc.

—Rihanna. 2008. (Blue Banner Biography Ser.). (Illus.). 32p. (YA). (gr. 4-7). lib. bdg. 25.70 (978-1-58415-673-4(2)) Mitchell Lane Pubs.

—Sean Kingston. 2008. (Blue Banner Biography Ser.). (Illus.). 32p. (YA). (gr. 4-7). lib. bdg. 25.70 (978-1-58415-679-6(1)) Mitchell Lane Pubs.

La Bella, Laura. Carrie Underwood. (Who's Your Idol? Ser.). 48p. (gr. 5-5). 2009. 53.00 (978-1-60854-785-2(X), Rosen Reference) 2008. (ENG., Illus.). (J). lib. bdg. 34.47 (978-1-4042-1370-8(8), f2f18125-2c99-41d0-8b49-7603d1f67171) Rosen Publishing Group, Inc., The.

Lajiness, Katie. Adele. 2017. (Big Buddy Pop Biographies Set 2 Ser.). (ENG., Illus.). 32p. (J). (gr. 2-5). lib. bdg. 34.21 (978-1-5321-1057-3(X), 25690, Big Buddy Bks.) ABDO Publishing Co.

—Beyonce. 2017. (Big Buddy Pop Biographies Set 2 Ser.). (ENG., Illus.). 32p. (J). (gr. 2-5). lib. bdg. 34.21 (978-1-5321-1058-0(8), 25692, Big Buddy Bks.) ABDO Publishing Co.

—Blake Shelton. 2017. (Big Buddy Pop Biographies Set 2 Ser.). (ENG., Illus.). 32p. (J). (gr. 2-5). lib. bdg. 34.21 (978-1-5321-1063-4(4), 25702, Big Buddy Bks.) ABDO Publishing Co.

—Bruno Mars. 2017. (Big Buddy Pop Biographies Set 3 Ser.). (ENG.). 32p. (J). (gr. 2-5). lib. bdg. 34.21 (978-1-5321-1217-1(3), 27569, Big Buddy Bks.) ABDO Publishing Co.

—Calvin Harris. 2017. (Big Buddy Pop Biographies Set 3 Ser.). (ENG., Illus.). 32p. (J). (gr. 2-5). lib. bdg. 34.21 (978-1-5321-1215-7(7), 27567, Big Buddy Bks.) ABDO Publishing Co.

—Carrie Underwood. 2017. (Big Buddy Pop Biographies Set 2 Ser.). (ENG., Illus.). 32p. (J). (gr. 2-5). lib. bdg. 34.21 (978-1-5321-1064-1(2), 25704, Big Buddy Bks.) ABDO Publishing Co.

—Charlie Puth. 2018. (Big Buddy Pop Biographies Ser.). (ENG.). 32p. (J). (gr. 2-5). lib. bdg. 34.21 (978-1-5321-1802-9(3), 30650, Big Buddy Bks.) ABDO Publishing Co.

—Demi Lovato. 2017. (Big Buddy Pop Biographies Set 3 Ser.). (ENG.). 32p. (J). (gr. 2-5). lib. bdg. 34.21 (978-1-5321-1216-4(5), 27568, Big Buddy Bks.) ABDO Publishing Co.

—Ed Sheeran. 2017. (Big Buddy Pop Biographies Set 3 Ser.). (ENG.). 32p. (J). (gr. 2-5). lib. bdg. 34.21 (978-1-5321-1218-8(1), 27570, Big Buddy Bks.) ABDO Publishing Co.

—Justin Bieber. 2017. (Big Buddy Pop Biographies Set 2 Ser.). (ENG., Illus.). 32p. (J). (gr. 2-5). lib. bdg. 34.21 (978-1-5321-1059-7(6), 25694, Big Buddy Bks.) ABDO Publishing Co.

—Justin Timberlake, 1 vol. 2015. (Big Buddy Pop Biographies Ser.). (ENG., Illus.). 32p. (J). (gr. 2-5). 34.21 (978-1-68078-061-1(1), 19049, Big Buddy Bks.) ABDO Publishing Co.

—Katy Perry, 1 vol. 2015. (Big Buddy Pop Biographies Ser.). (ENG., Illus.). 32p. (J). (gr. 2-5). 34.21 (978-1-68078-057-4(3), 19041, Big Buddy Bks.) ABDO Publishing Co.

—Lady Gaga. 2017. (Big Buddy Pop Biographies Set 2 Ser.). (ENG., Illus.). 32p. (J). (gr. 2-5). lib. bdg. 34.21 (978-1-5321-1061-0(8), 25698, Big Buddy Bks.) ABDO Publishing Co.

—Meghan Trainor, 1 vol. 2015. (Big Buddy Pop Biographies Ser.). (ENG., Illus.). 32p. (J). (gr. 2-5). 34.21 (978-1-68078-062-8(X), 19051, Big Buddy Bks.) ABDO Publishing Co.

—Nick Jonas, 1 vol. 2015. (Big Buddy Pop Biographies Ser.). (ENG., Illus.). 32p. (J). (gr. 2-5). 34.21 (978-1-68078-053-6(0), 19033, Big Buddy Bks.) ABDO Publishing Co.

—Pharrell Williams, 1 vol. 2015. (Big Buddy Pop Biographies Ser.). (ENG., Illus.). 32p. (J). (gr. 2-5). 34.21 (978-1-68078-063-5(8), 19053, Big Buddy Bks.) ABDO Publishing Co.

—Rihanna. 2017. (Big Buddy Pop Biographies Set 2 Ser.). (ENG., Illus.). 32p. (J). (gr. 2-5). lib. bdg. 34.21 (978-1-5321-1062-7(6), 25700, Big Buddy Bks.) ABDO Publishing Co.

—Selena Gomez. 2017. (Big Buddy Pop Biographies Set 3 Ser.). (ENG., Illus.). 32p. (J). (gr. 2-5). lib. bdg. 34.21 (978-1-5321-1214-0(9), 27566, Big Buddy Bks.) ABDO Publishing Co.

—Zendaya. 2017. (Big Buddy Pop Biographies Set 3 Ser.). (ENG., Illus.). 32p. (J). (gr. 2-5). lib. bdg. 34.21 (978-1-5321-1220-1(3), 27572, Big Buddy Bks.) ABDO Publishing Co.

Latham, Donna. Norah Jones. (Sharing the American Dream Ser.). 64p. (YA). (gr. 7-12). 2009. 22.95 (978-1-4222-0590-7(8)) 2007. pap. 9.95 (978-1-4222-0751-2(X)) Mason Crest.

Lawlor, Michelle. Kelly Clarkson. (Pop Culture Ser.). (Illus.). 64p. (YA). (gr. 3-7). 2008. lib. bdg. 22.95 (978-1-4222-0199-2(6)) 2007. pap. 7.95 (978-1-4222-0353-8(0)) Mason Crest.

—Missy Elliot. 2008. (Hip-Hop Ser.). (Illus.). 64p. (YA). (gr. 7-12). lib. bdg. 22.95 (978-1-4222-0117-6(1)) Mason Crest.

Leavitt, Amie. Miley Cyrus. 2007. (Robbie Reader Ser.). (Illus.). 32p. (J). (gr. 2-5). lib. bdg. 25.70 (978-1-58415-590-4(6)) Mitchell Lane Pubs.

—Raven-Symone. 2007. (Robbie Reader Ser.). (Illus.). 32p. (YA). (gr. 2-5). lib. bdg. 25.70 (978-1-58415-593-5(0)) Mitchell Lane Pubs.

Leavitt, Amie Jane. Ciara. 2007. (Blue Banner Biography Ser.). (Illus.). 32p. (YA). (gr. 4-7). lib. bdg. 25.70 (978-1-58415-610-9(4)) Mitchell Lane Pubs.

—Day by Day with Miley Cyrus. 2010. (Randy's Corner Ser.). (Illus.). 32p. (J). (gr. -1-2). lib. bdg. 25.70 (978-1-58415-856-1(5)) Mitchell Lane Pubs.

—What It's Like to Be Miley Cyrus. Vega, Eida de la, tr. 2009. (What It's Like to Be/Que se Siente al Ser Ser.). (SPA & ENG., Illus.). 32p. (J). (gr. -1-2). lib. bdg. 25.70 (978-1-58415-841-7(7)) Mitchell Lane Pubs.

Lemmens, Mary Jo. Christina Aguilera. 2009. (Hip-Hop 2 Ser.). 64p. (YA). (gr. 7-12). lib. bdg. 22.95 (978-1-4222-0285-2(2)); (Illus.). (gr. 3-7). pap. 7.95 (978-1-4222-0348-4(4)) Mason Crest.

—Jennifer Lopez. 2009. (Hip Hop (Mason Crest Paperback) Ser.). (Illus.). 64p. (YA). (gr. 4-7). pap. 7.95 (978-1-4222-0347-7(6)) Mason Crest.

Lemmens, Maryjo. Jennifer Lopez. 2009. (Hip-Hop 2 Ser.). (Illus.). 64p. (J). (gr. 7-12). lib. bdg. 22.95 (978-1-4222-0296-8(8)) Mason Crest.

London, Martha. Daya. 2019. (Influential People Ser.). (ENG., Illus.). 32p. (J). (gr. 4-6). 28.65 (978-1-5435-7134-9(4), 140414) Capstone.

Lovato, Demi. Stay Strong. 2012. (ENG., Illus.). 272p. (YA). 24.99 (978-1-250-01310-1(0)) Feiwel & Friends.

Maccarry, Noel. Who Was Pete Seeger? 2017. (Who Was... ? Ser.). lib. bdg. 16.00 (978-0-606-40116-6(4)) Turtleback.

MacCarry, Noel & Who HQ. Who Was Pete Seeger? Marchesi, Stephen, illus. 2017. (Who Was? Ser.). 112p. (J).

(gr. 3-7). 5.99 (978-0-448-48475-4(7), Penguin Workshop) Penguin Young Readers Group.

MacDonald, Barry. Everything Real Justin Bieber Fans Should Know & Do. 2012. (ENG., Illus.). 192p. (J). (gr. 7). pap. 12.95 (978-1-60078-770-6(3)) Triumph Bks.

Maimone, Max Q. Justin Timberlake, 1 vol. 2011. (Hip-Hop Headliners Ser.). (ENG., Illus.). 32p. (J). (gr. 1-1). pap. 11.50 (978-1-4339-4801-5(X), fee2f63d-e4a0-49ed-a5f2-62c94024a5a6); lib. bdg. 27.93 (978-1-4339-4800-8(1), 40d6b74b-e6b2-42d1-9734-52b519879c9c) Stevens, Gareth Publishing LLLP.

Marcovitz, Hal. Elliott Yamin. 2009. (Dream Big: American Idol Superstars Ser.). 64p. (YA). (gr. 5-18). 22.95 (978-1-4222-1513-5(X)); pap. 9.95 (978-1-4222-1599-9(7)) Mason Crest.

—Jordin Sparks. 2009. (Dream Big: American Idol Superstars Ser.). 64p. (YA). (gr. 5-18). pap. 9.95 (978-1-4222-1602-6(0)); (Illus.). lib. bdg. 22.95 (978-1-4222-1511-1(3)) Mason Crest.

—Kellie Pickler. 2009. (Dream Big: American Idol Superstars Ser.). 64p. (YA). (gr. 5-18). pap. 9.95 (978-1-4222-1603-3(9)); lib. bdg. 22.95 (978-1-4222-1510-4(5)) Mason Crest.

Marquez, Heron. Latin Sensations. (Biography Ser.). (Illus.). 112p. (gr. 6-12). 2005. lib. bdg. 27.93 (978-0-8225-4993-2(X)) 2003. (YA). pap. 7.95 (978-0-8225-9695-0(4), Lerner Pubns.) Lerner Publishing Group.

Marvis, Barbara. Day by Day with Beyonce. 2010. (Randy's Corner Ser.). (Illus.). 32p. (J). (gr. -1-2). lib. bdg. 25.70 (978-1-58415-859-2(X)) Mitchell Lane Pubs.

Marvis, Barbara J. Selena. 2003. (Blue Banner Biography Ser.). (Illus.). 32p. (J). (gr. 3-8). lib. bdg. 25.70 (978-1-58415-226-2(5)) Mitchell Lane Pubs.

Mattern, Joanne. Jason Derulo. 2014. (Illus.). 32p. (J). 25.70 (978-1-61228-643-3(7)) Mitchell Lane Pubs.

—Jennifer Hudson. 2012. (Illus.). 32p. (J). (gr. 4-8). lib. bdg. 25.70 (978-1-61228-315-9(2)) Mitchell Lane Pubs.

—Keke Palmer. 2010. (Robbie Reader Ser.). (Illus.). 32p. (J). (gr. 2-5). lib. bdg. 25.70 (978-1-58415-896-7(4)) Mitchell Lane Pubs.

McConnell, Craig, ed. Theo Tams: Inside the Music. 2009. (ENG., Illus.). 48p. pap. 14.95 (978-1-894917-84-1(7), Napoleon & Co.) Dundurn Pr. CAN. Dist: Publishers Group West (PGW).

McDowell, Pamela. Adele. 2013. (J). (978-1-62127-389-9(X)) Weigl Pubs., Inc.

—Selena Gomez. 2012. (J). 27.13 (978-1-61913-588-8(4)); pap. 13.95 (978-1-61913-594-9(9)) Weigl Pubs., Inc.

Mckissack, Patricia & Mckissack, Fredrick. Marian Anderson: Amazing Opera Singer, 1 vol. 2013. (Famous African Americans Ser.). (ENG., Illus.). 24p. (gr. k-2). 25.27 (978-0-7660-4101-1(8), 0ff52f6d-e639-4005-bf7f-364572db9123); pap. 10.35 (978-1-4644-0202-9(7), 2a8cea21-2a90-4567-bf40-8b52cfc07aa4) Enslow Publishing, LLC. (Enslow Elementary).

—Paul Robeson: A Voice for Change, 1 vol. 2013. (Famous African Americans Ser.). (ENG.). 24p. (gr. k-2). pap. 10.35 (978-1-4644-0205-0(1), dc893b8a-0788-4dfc-ad53-35b11b21d047); (Illus.). 25.27 (978-0-7660-4107-3(7), 07716234-1468-4642-8459-5686579373a7) Enslow Publishing, LLC. (Enslow Elementary).

McNiven, Kelly. Carly Rae Jepsen. 2013. (ENG., Illus.). 32p. (J). (978-0-7787-0021-0(6)); pap. (978-0-7787-0042-5(9)) Crabtree Publishing Co.

McPhee, Edna. Kelly Clarkson: Music & Television Trailblazer, 1 vol. annot. ed. 2019. (People in the News Ser.). (ENG.). 104p. (gr. 7-7). pap. 20.99 (978-1-5345-6834-1(4), 436f04b7-a303-4f19-ad8b-0b628a9c02fe, Lucent Pr.) Greenhaven Publishing LLC.

McVeigh, Mark. Julio & Enrique Iglesias, 1 vol. 2004. (Famous Families Ser.). (ENG., Illus.). 48p. (J). (gr. 5-5). lib. bdg. 34.47 (978-1-4042-0260-3(9), bdddde79-f7cc-44f4-b26c-fc77979e5f95) Rosen Publishing Group, Inc., The.

Medina, Tony. I & I: Bob Marley. Watson, Jesse Joshua, illus. 2009. (ENG.). 48p. (J). (gr. 3-6). 19.95 (978-1-60060-257-3(6)) Lee & Low Bks., Inc.

—I & I Bob Marley, 1 vol. Watson, Jesse Joshua, illus. 2009. (ENG.). 48p. (J). (gr. 3-8). pap. 12.95 (978-1-62014-030-7(6), leelowbooks) Lee & Low Bks., Inc.

Meloy, Colin. The Golden Thread: A Song for Pete Seeger. 2018. (ENG., Illus.). 48p. (J). (gr. -1-3). 18.99 (978-0-06-236825-6(7), Balzer & Bray) HarperCollins Pubs.

Meltzer, Brad. I Am Dolly Parton. Eliopoulos, Christopher, illus. 2022. (Ordinary People Change the World Ser.). 40p. (J). (gr. k-4). 15.99 (978-0-593-40592-5(7), Dial Bks) Penguin Young Readers Group.

Menard, Valerie. Jennifer Lopez. 2003. (Blue Banner Biography Ser.). (Illus.). 32p. (J). (gr. 3-8). lib. bdg. 25.70 (978-1-58415-225-5(7)) Mitchell Lane Pubs.

Merwin, E. Beyoncé. 2018. (Amazing Americans: Pop Music Stars Ser.). (ENG.). 24p. (J). (gr. -1-3). lib. bdg. 26.99 (978-1-68402-678-4(4)) Bearport Publishing Co., Inc.

Merwin, E. & Roshell, Starshine. Lady Gaga. 2018. (Amazing Americans: Pop Music Stars Ser.). (ENG.). 24p. (J). (gr. -1-3). lib. bdg. 26.99 (978-1-68402-677-7(6)) Bearport Publishing Co., Inc.

Micklos, John & Micklos, John, Jr. Jennifer Hudson: A Biography of an American Music Idol, 1 vol. 2014. (African-American Icons Ser.). (ENG.). 104p. (J). (gr. 6-7). lib. bdg. 30.61 (978-0-7660-4233-9(2), bba0556c-ffee-480d-8fc8-d38eae03f808) Enslow Publishing, LLC.

Miller, Calvin Craig. Reggae Poet: The Story of Bob Marley. 2007. (Modern Music Masters Ser.). (Illus.). 128p. (YA). (gr. 9-18). lib. bdg. 27.95 (978-1-59935-071-4(8)) Reynolds, Morgan Inc.

Miller, Elaine Hobson. Nat King Cole: Unforgettable Musician. 2011. (Illus.). 104p. (J). (978-1-59421-070-9(5)) Seacoast Publishing, Inc.

Miller, Kat. I Love Miley Cyrus, 1 vol. 2010. (Fan Club Ser.). (ENG.). 24p. (J). (gr. 2-3). lib. bdg. 27.27 (978-1-61533-045-4(3), 92f3a020-cdfc-4f80-8536-1edf60b81606); (Illus.). pap. 9.15 (978-1-61533-046-1(1), 89b171ca-5617-441d-a14a-edc942640002) Rosen Publishing Group, Inc., The. (Windmill Bks.).

—I Love Taylor Swift, 1 vol. 2010. (Fan Club Ser.). (ENG.). 24p. (J). (gr. 2-3). lib. bdg. 27.27 (978-1-61533-051-5(8), 4b38f604-8508-4313-8545-8fefabce7c59); (Illus.). pap. 9.15 (978-1-61533-052-2(6), 6495b95f-37d2-49cd-b7a2-8f00c7268806) Rosen Publishing Group, Inc., The. (Windmill Bks.).

Mitchell, Susan. Jessica Simpson, 1 vol. 2007. (Today's Superstars Ser.). (ENG., Illus.). 32p. (gr. 3-3). lib. bdg. 34.60 (978-0-8368-8201-8(6), 03cb9233-afb7-4313-969c-88033d92bc68) Stevens, Gareth Publishing LLLP.

Mooney, Carla. Vanessa Hudgens. 2007. (Sharing the American Dream Ser.). 64p. (YA). (gr. 7-18). pap. 9.95 (978-1-4222-0749-9(8)) Mason Crest.

—Vanessa Hudgens/Carla Mooney. 2009. (Sharing the American Dream Ser.). 64p. (YA). (gr. 7-12). 22.95 (978-1-4222-0583-9(5)) Mason Crest.

Morganelli, Adrianna. Lorde. 2015. (Superstars! Ser.). (ENG., Illus.). 32p. (J). (gr. 4-4). (978-0-7787-8080-9(5)) Crabtree Publishing Co.

Morreale, Marie. Real Bios: Selena Gomez. 2015. (ENG., Illus.). 48p. pap. 7.95 (978-0-531-21663-7(2), Orchard Bks.) Scholastic, Inc.

Murcia, Rebecca Thatcher. Shakira. 2007. (Blue Banner Biography Ser.). (Illus.). 32p. (YA). (gr. 4-7). lib. bdg. 25.70 (978-1-58415-609-3(0)) Mitchell Lane Pubs.

Murphy, Maggie. Miley Cyrus: Rock Star, 1 vol. 2010. (Young & Famous Ser.). (ENG., Illus.). 24p. (J). (gr. 1-2). 26.27 (978-1-4488-0643-0(7), 956473f8-e7ee-43d7-9aeb-b0c0e055fe7c); pap. 9.85 (978-1-4488-1799-3(4), f0e8ec27-d6b2-42ac-a676-611f61c40f46, PowerKids Pr.) Rosen Publishing Group, Inc., The.

Murray, Laura K. Ariana Grande. 2016. (J). (978-1-60818-669-3(5), Creative Education) Creative Co., The.

Nagle, Jeanne. Jennifer Hudson, 1 vol. 2008. (Who's Your Idol? Ser.). (ENG., Illus.). 48p. (J). (gr. 5-5). lib. bdg. 34.47 (978-1-4042-1372-2(4), 3ef5c3a9-5cb6-43cd-88e3-ab4dc364f611) Rosen Publishing Group, Inc., The.

Neimark, Anne. There Ain't Nobody That Can Sing Like Me: The Life of Woody Guthrie. 2017. (ENG., Illus.). 128p. (J). (gr. 5-9). pap. 13.99 (978-1-5344-0950-7(5), Atheneum Bks. for Young Readers) Simon & Schuster Children's Publishing.

Nelson, Maria. Robert Pattinson, 1 vol. 2011. (Rising Stars Ser.). (ENG.). 32p. (J). (gr. 1-1). pap. 11.50 (978-1-4339-5900-4(3), 3d2bb9f6-8890-44ed-a1ce-72db276866a7); lib. bdg. 27.93 (978-1-4339-5898-4(8), 637ae504-22f8-4d7f-8afa-a7d6d8bbf68e) Stevens, Gareth Publishing LLLP.

—Selena Gomez, 1 vol. 2011. (Rising Stars Ser.). (ENG.). 32p. (J). (gr. 1-1). pap. 11.50 (978-1-4339-5904-2(6), 2c5c5057-e629-45c6-84d4-860dd98ede6c); lib. bdg. 27.93 (978-1-4339-5902-8(X), 31701f59-d212-4436-aeb7-5178202d41dc) Stevens, Gareth Publishing LLLP.

Neri, G. Hello, I'm Johnny Cash. Ford, A. G., illus. 2014. 40p. (J). (gr. 4-7). 17.99 (978-0-7636-6245-5(3)) Candlewick Pr.

Newroad, Adele. Carrie Underwood, 1 vol. 2010. (Country Music Stars Ser.). (ENG., Illus.). 32p. (J). (gr. 1-1). pap. 11.50 (978-1-4339-3602-9(X), dafe0ff8-f1e0-4127-81ab-6479199fec83); lib. bdg. 27.93 (978-1-4339-3601-2(1), 44937de3-3e1f-4fd3-8d41-39c3c68ec407) Stevens, Gareth Publishing LLLP.

O'Donnell, Jessica. Leontyne Price, 1 vol. 2010. (Inspiring Lives Ser.). (ENG.). 32p. (J). (gr. 1-1). lib. bdg. 27.93 (978-1-4339-3628-9(3), c7bfff22-3a05-4192-90f7-c55d145aa57b) Stevens, Gareth Publishing LLLP.

One Direction. Dare to Dream: Life As One Direction (100% Official) 2011. (ENG., Illus.). 288p. (YA). (gr. 7). 26.95 (978-0-00-744439-7(7)) HarperCollins Pubs. Ltd. GBR. Dist: Independent Pubs. Group.

One Direction, One. Dare to Dream: Life As One Direction (100% Official) 2012. (ENG., Illus.). 288p. pap. (978-0-00-748812-4(2), HarperCollins Children's Bks.) HarperCollins Pubs. Ltd.

Orgill, Roxane. Shout, Sister, Shout! Ten Girl Singers Who Shaped a Century. 2007. (ENG.). 160p. (YA). (gr. 7). pap. 12.95 (978-1-4169-6391-2(X), McElderry, Margaret K. Bks.) McElderry, Margaret K. Bks.

—Skit-Scat Raggedy Cat: Candlewick Biographies: Ella Fitzgerald. Qualls, Sean, illus. 2012. (Candlewick Biographies Ser.). (ENG.). 48p. (J). (gr. 3-7). pap. 5.99 (978-0-7636-6458-9(8)) Candlewick Pr.

Orr, Tamara. Emily Osment. 2009. (Robbie Reader Ser.). (Illus.). 32p. (YA). (gr. 2-5). lib. bdg. 25.70 (978-1-58415-755-7(0)) Mitchell Lane Pubs.

Orr, Tamra. Day by Day with Willow Smith. 2011. (Day by Day with... Ser.). (Illus.). 32p. (J). (gr. -1-2). lib. bdg. 25.70 (978-1-58415-983-4(9)) Mitchell Lane Pubs.

—Jordin Sparks. 2008. (Robbie Reader Ser.). (Illus.). 32p. (YA). (gr. 2-5). lib. bdg. 25.70 (978-1-58415-727-4(5)) Mitchell Lane Pubs.

Orr, Tamra B. Jamie Foxx. 2006. (Blue Banner Biography Ser.). (Illus.). 32p. (YA). (gr. 4-7). lib. bdg. 25.70 (978-1-58415-503-4(5)) Mitchell Lane Pubs.

—Jojo. 2007. (Blue Banner Biography Ser.). (Illus.). 32p. (YA). (gr. 4-7). lib. bdg. 25.70 (978-1-58415-615-4(5)) Mitchell Lane Pubs.

Oswald, Vanessa. Beyoncé: The Reign of Queen Bey, 1 vol. 2019. (People in the News Ser.). (ENG.). 104p. (gr. 7-7). 41.03 (978-1-5345-6706-1(2), ceb219ab-43d7-44dd-9418-8fb78b8bb7f2, Lucent Pr.) Greenhaven Publishing LLC.

—Katy Perry: Purposeful Pop Icon, 1 vol. 2018. (People in the News Ser.). (ENG.). 104p. (gr. 7-7). pap. 20.99 (978-1-5345-6323-0(7), c8c4229e-ba6c-46ab-8a1a-7fc3c704e658, Lucent Pr.) Greenhaven Publishing LLC.

Parish, James Robert. Gloria Estefan Singer: Singer. 2006. (Ferguson Career Biographies Ser.). (Illus.). 122p. (gr. 6-12). 25.00 (978-0-8160-5833-4(4), Ferguson Publishing Company) Infobase Holdings, Inc.

Parrish, Jacqueline. Beyoncé & Jay-Z, 1 vol. 2019. (Power Couples Ser.). (ENG.). 112p. (gr. 7-7). 38.80 (978-1-5081-8879-7(3), d7529c14-47a0-4568-822c-4b1ad02e73c5) Rosen Publishing Group, Inc., The.

Patrick, Chris. Beyoncé & Destiny's Child. 2005. (Illus.). 122p. (J). (978-0-439-80832-3(4)) Scholastic, Inc.

Peppas, Lynn. Demi Lovato. 2013. (ENG., Illus.). 32p. (J). (978-0-7787-1050-9(5)); pap. (978-0-7787-1054-7(8)) Crabtree Publishing Co.

—Justin Bieber, 1 vol. 2011. (ENG.). 32p. (J). pap. (978-0-7787-7612-3(3)); (gr. 3-6). lib. bdg. (978-0-7787-7607-9(7)) Crabtree Publishing Co.

—M. I. A. 2010. (Superstars! Ser.). (ENG., Illus.). 32p. (J). (gr. 3-6). lib. bdg. (978-0-7787-7249-1(7)) Crabtree Publishing Co.

—M.I.A., 1 vol. 2010. (Superstars! Ser.). (ENG., Illus.). 32p. (J). pap. (978-0-7787-7258-3(6)) Crabtree Publishing Co.

—Miley Cyrus. 2010. (Superstars! Ser.). (ENG.). 32p. (J). pap. (978-0-7787-7259-0(4)); (gr. 3-6). lib. bdg. (978-0-7787-7250-7(0)) Crabtree Publishing Co.

—Taylor Swift. 2010. (Superstars! Ser.). (ENG.). 32p. (J). pap. (978-0-7787-7261-3(6)) Crabtree Publishing Co.

—Zac Efron. 2010. (Superstars! Ser.). (ENG., Illus.). 32p. (J). pap. (978-0-7787-7263-7(2)) Crabtree Publishing Co.

Pettinella, Amy. Lady Gaga. 2015. (Illus.). 48p. (J). lib. bdg. (978-1-62713-322-7(4)) Cavendish Square Publishing LLC.

Pinkney, Andrea. Ella Fitzgerald: The Tale of a Vocal Virtuosa. Pinkney, Brian, illus. 2007. (Great Black Performers Ser.: 3). (ENG.). 32p. (J). (gr. 1-3). pap. 6.99 (978-0-7868-1416-9(0), Jump at the Sun) Hyperion Bks. for Children.

Rajczak Nelson, Kristen. Demi Lovato, 1 vol. 2011. (Rising Stars Ser.). (ENG., Illus.). 32p. (J). (gr. 1-1). pap. 11.50 (978-1-4339-5888-5(0), 8bb931d7-0305-4281-9345-eea788a4db0f); lib. bdg. 27.93 (978-1-4339-5886-1(4), 46045e94-9748-45e7-a751-2e16e8b50896) Stevens, Gareth Publishing LLLP.

—Ed Sheeran: Singer-Songwriter, 1 vol. 2018. (Junior Biographies Ser.). (ENG.). 24p. (gr. 3-4). 24.27 (978-0-7660-9727-8(7), 5672c608-83d6-409d-8903-75430b9efa9f) Enslow Publishing, LLC.

—Justin Bieber, 1 vol. 2011. (Rising Stars Ser.). (ENG., Illus.). 32p. (J). (gr. 1-1). pap. 11.50 (978-1-4339-5896-0(1), 7762dfe0-96ab-4d8b-8b0b-bbd8231c761c); lib. bdg. 27.93 (978-1-4339-5894-6(5), 80c5d330-d8a4-4bd5-98f1-5ba8fd425372) Stevens, Gareth Publishing LLLP.

Ransom, Candice. Maria von Trapp: Beyond the Sound of Music. 2003. 112p. (J). pap. 8.95 (978-0-8225-3749-6(4)) Lerner Publishing Group.

Rawson, Katherine. Vanessa Hudgens, 1 vol. 2009. (Kid Stars! Ser.). (ENG., Illus.). 24p. (J). (gr. 2-3). pap. 10.40 (978-1-4358-3408-8(9), 4ba8404e-c961-470b-b8df-41aa8464494b); lib. bdg. 26.27 (978-1-4042-8137-0(1), 6682b849-9bf7-43f1-8c20-019a4e441261) Rosen Publishing Group, Inc., The. (PowerKids Pr.).

Rector, Rebecca Kraft. Shawn Mendes: Singer-Songwriter, 1 vol. 2018. (Junior Biographies Ser.). (ENG.). 24p. (gr. 3-4). 24.27 (978-1-9785-0206-2(0), b89e3d6c-cbd5-4848-9a62-87e7722dfbca) Enslow Publishing, LLC.

Reich, Susanna. Stand up & Sing! Pete Seeger, Folk Music, & the Path to Justice. Gustavson, Adam, illus. 2017. (ENG.). 48p. (J). 17.99 (978-0-8027-3812-7(5), 900141410, Bloomsbury USA Childrens) Bloomsbury Publishing USA.

Reid, Jamie. Diana Krall. 2004. 224p. pap. 17.95 (978-1-894997-07-2(7)) Kingston Pr. CAN. Dist: SCB Distributors.

Reusser, Kayleen. Day by Day with Taylor Swift. 2010. (Randy's Corner Ser.). (Illus.). 32p. (J). (gr. -1-2). lib. bdg. 25.70 (978-1-58415-857-8(3)) Mitchell Lane Pubs.

—Leona Lewis. 2009. (Blue Banner Biography Ser.). (Illus.). 32p. (YA). (gr. 4-7). lib. bdg. 25.70 (978-1-58415-775-5(5)) Mitchell Lane Pubs.

—Selena Gomez. 2009. (Robbie Reader Ser.). (Illus.). 32p. (YA). (gr. 2-5). lib. bdg. 25.70 (978-1-58415-752-6(6)) Mitchell Lane Pubs.

Rice, Earle. Billie Holiday. 2012. (Illus.). 47p. (J). lib. bdg. 29.95 (978-1-61228-267-1(9)) Mitchell Lane Pubs.

Rivera, Ursula. Aretha Franklin. 2009. (Rock & Roll Hall of Famers Ser.). 112p. (gr. 5-8). 63.90 (978-1-60852-467-9(1), Rosen Reference) Rosen Publishing Group, Inc., The.

—The Supremes. 2009. (Rock & Roll Hall of Famers Ser.). 112p. (gr. 5-8). 63.90 (978-1-60852-479-2(5), Rosen Reference) Rosen Publishing Group, Inc., The.

Roberts, Russell. Alicia Keys: Singer-Songwriter, Musician, Actress, & Producer. 2012. (Transcending Race Ser.). 64p. (J). (gr. 5). 22.95 (978-1-4222-2727-5(8)) Mason Crest.

Robertson, Robbie, et al. Legends, Icons & Rebels: Music That Changed the World. 2016. (Illus.). 128p. (J). (gr. 4-7). pap. 18.99 (978-1-101-91868-5(3), Tundra Bks.) Tundra Bks. CAN. Dist: Penguin Random Hse. LLC.

Robeson, Susan. Grandpa Stops a War: A Paul Robeson Story. Brown, Rod, illus. 2019. 32p. (J). (gr. k-4). 17.95 (978-1-60980-882-2(7), Triangle Square) Seven Stories Pr.

Robson, David. Miley Cyrus. 2010. (Role Model Entertainers Ser.). (Illus.). 64p. (YA). (gr. 7-12). 22.95 (978-1-4222-0501-3(0)) Mason Crest.

Rodriguez, Patty & Stein, Ariana. Life of/la Vida de Celia, 1 vol. Reyes, Citlali, illus. 2018. (SPA.). 22p. (J). (gr. -1-k). bds. 9.99 (978-0-9861099-5-9(9)) Little Libros, LLC.

—The Life of/la Vida de Selena, 1 vol. Reyes, Citlali, illus. 2018. (SPA.). 22p. (J). (gr. -1-k). bds. 9.99 (978-0-9861099-9-7(1), Lil' Libros) Little Libros, LLC.

Rose, Elizabeth. Rihanna, 1 vol. 2012. (Hip-Hop Headliners Ser.). (ENG., Illus.). 32p. (J). (gr. 1-1). pap. 11.50 (978-1-4339-6618-7(2), 7b4af108-84b7-4ba8-8cfe-5222e87fde61); lib. bdg. 27.93 (978-1-4339-6616-3(6), 37d82bf5-526e-4f9a-be16-e54979882e2a) Stevens, Gareth Publishing LLLP.

Russell-Brown, Katheryn. A Voice Named Aretha. Freeman, Laura, illus. 2020. (ENG.). 40p. (J). 17.99 (978-1-68119-850-7(9), 900189371, Bloomsbury Children's Bks.) Bloomsbury Publishing USA.

Ryan, Pam Muñoz. When Marian Sang: The True Recital of Marian Anderson. Selznick, Brian, illus. pap. incl. audio compact disk (978-1-59112-949-3(4)); pap. 16.95 incl. audio (978-1-59112-943-1(5)); pap. 18.95 incl. audio compact disk (978-1-59112-947-9(8)); pap. incl. audio (978-1-59112-945-5(1)); 2004. (J). 28.95 incl. audio compact disk (978-1-59112-948-6(6)) Live Oak Media.

Saddleback Educational Publishing Staff. Beyonce. 2015. (Hip-Hop Biographies (Saddleback Publishing) Ser.). (YA). lib. bdg. 23.25 (978-0-606-36613-7(X)) Turtleback.

—Dr. Dre. 2015. (Hip-Hop Biographies (Saddleback Publishing) Ser.). (YA). lib. bdg. 23.25 (978-0-606-36614-4(8)) Turtleback.

—Pharrell Williams. 2015. (Hip-Hop Biographies (Saddleback Publishing) Ser.). (YA). lib. bdg. 23.25 (978-0-606-36616-8(4)) Turtleback.

—Rihanna. 2013. (Hip-Hop Biographies (Saddleback Publishing) Ser.). (YA). lib. bdg. 23.25 (978-0-606-31489-3(X)) Turtleback.

—Sean Combs. 2015. (Hip-Hop Biographies (Saddleback Publishing) Ser.). (YA). lib. bdg. 23.25 (978-0-606-36615-1(6)) Turtleback.

Santos, Rita. Alicia Keys: Singer-Songwriter, 1 vol. 2018. (Junior Biographies Ser.). (ENG.). 24p. (gr. 3-4). 24.27 (978-1-9785-0205-5(2), ee4a9889-71cf-487d-b124-44c8396e2be8) Enslow Publishing, LLC.

—Ariana Grande: Pop Star, 1 vol. 2018. (Junior Biographies Ser.). (ENG.). 24p. (gr. 3-4). 24.27 (978-0-7660-9723-0(4), a02c4f6d-5e94-4e73-af02-2ce1ea611755) Enslow Publishing, LLC.

—Camila Cabello: Cuban American Singer. 2019. (Junior Biographies Ser.). (ENG.). 24p. (gr. 3-4). 56.10 (978-1-9785-0881-1(6)) Enslow Publishing, LLC.

—Hailee Steinfeld: Actress & Singer, 1 vol. 2018. (Junior Biographies Ser.). (ENG.). 24p. (gr. 3-4). lib. bdg. 24.27 (978-1-9785-0208-6(7), 8fbe41c8-5b2b-4085-9912-1117602571fb) Enslow Publishing, LLC.

Sapet, Kerrily. Mariah Carey: Singer, Songwriter, Record Producer, Actress. 2009. (Transcending Race in America: Biographies of Biracial Achievers Ser.). 64p. (YA). (gr. 5-18). pap. 9.95 (978-1-4222-1627-9(6)) Mason Crest.

—Mariah Carey: Singer, Songwriter, Record Producer, & Actress. 2012. (Transcending Race Ser.). 64p. (J). (gr. 5). 22.95 (978-1-4222-2730-5(8)) Mason Crest.

Sawyer, Sarah. Avril Lavigne. (Contemporary Musicians & Their Music Ser.). 48p. (gr. 6-6). 2009. 53.00 (978-1-61511-923-3(X)) 2008. (ENG., Illus.). (J). lib. bdg. 34.47 (978-1-4042-1820-8(3), b65c61a5-7e73-49d6-bae8-66d53e9c99d8) 2008. (ENG., Illus.). pap. 12.75 (978-1-4358-5128-3(5), a11e91be-e51e-4fb7-8873-76b0388b7fda, Rosen Classroom) Rosen Publishing Group, Inc., The.

Scholl, Elizabeth. David Archuleta. 2009. (Robbie Reader Ser.). (Illus.). 32p. (YA). (gr. 2-5). lib. bdg. 25.70 (978-1-58415-758-8(5)) Mitchell Lane Pubs.

—Shontelle Layne. 2009. (Blue Banner Biography Ser.). (Illus.). 32p. (YA). (gr. 4-7). lib. bdg. 25.70 (978-1-58415-770-0(4)) Mitchell Lane Pubs.

Schroeder, Alan. Baby Flo: Florence Mills Lights up the Stage. Van Wright, Cornelius & Hu, Ying-Hwa, illus. 2012. (ENG.). 40p. (J). 18.95 (978-1-60060-410-2(2)) Lee & Low Bks., Inc.

Schubert, Leda. Listen: How Pete Seeger Got America Singing. Colon, Raul, illus. 2017. (ENG.). 40p. (J). 17.99 (978-1-62672-250-7(1), 900147273) Roaring Brook Pr.

Schuman, Michael A. Beyoncé: A Biography of a Legendary Singer, 1 vol. 2014. (African-American Icons Ser.). (ENG.). 112p. (gr. 6-7). lib. bdg. 30.61 (978-0-7660-4230-8(8), 4e11f61e-4a47-4641-b4c0-ee2508c62796) Enslow Publishing, LLC.

—Emma! Amazing Actress Emma Stone, 1 vol. 2013. (Sizzling Celebrities Ser.). (ENG.). 48p. (gr. 4-6). pap. 11.53 (978-1-4644-0175-6(6), 69e385f9-0a58-4937-b22d-b3fbe3f694ec); lib. bdg. 27.93 (978-0-7660-4113-4(1), b839e640-287b-4ab6-b39f-13289fbb8572) Enslow Publishing, LLC.

—Rihanna: Music Megastar, 1 vol. 2012. (Hot Celebrity Biographies Ser.). (ENG., Illus.). 48p. (gr. 5-7). pap. 11.53 (978-1-59845-285-3(1), f9c246b0-a422-405e-ad56-2b17ed1c8236); lib. bdg. 27.93 (978-0-7660-3871-4(8), 4fd1fd29-a826-4981-be4d-36109ce9931e) Enslow Publishing, LLC.

Schwartz, Heather E. Taylor Swift: Superstar Singer & Songwriter. 2019. (Gateway Biographies Ser.). (ENG., Illus.). 48p. (J). (gr. 4-8). 31.99 (978-1-5415-2885-7(9), bef4f13b-67d4-4169-bed1-7a4b2850fc21, Lerner Pubns.) Lerner Publishing Group.

Scott, Celicia. Mariah Carey. 2008. (Hip-Hop Ser.). (Illus.). 64p. (YA). (ENG.). (gr. 4-7). per. 7.95 (978-1-4222-0265-4(8)); (gr. 7-12). lib. bdg. 22.95 (978-1-4222-0114-5(7)) Mason Crest.

Seidman, David. Katharine Mcphee. (Who's Your Idol? Ser.). 48p. (gr. 5-5). 2009. 53.00 (978-1-60854-788-3(4), Rosen Reference) 2008. (ENG., Illus.). (J). lib. bdg. 34.47 (978-1-4042-1373-9(2), b3429c82-afc6-4b1a-8c6a-029513e2b215) Rosen Publishing Group, Inc., The.

Seigel, Rachel. Ed Sheeran. 2018. (Superstars! Ser.). (ENG., Illus.). 32p. (J). (gr. 4-4). (978-0-7787-4832-8(4)); pap. (978-0-7787-4847-2(2)) Crabtree Publishing Co.

Seven, John. Frankie Liked to Sing. Christy, Jana, illus. 2015. (ENG.). 32p. (J). (gr. -1-3). 16.95 (978-1-4197-1644-7(1), 1101801, Abrams Bks. for Young Readers) Abrams, Inc.

Shea, Abigail. Victoria Justice, 1 vol. 2013. (Rising Stars Ser.). (ENG.). 32p. (J). (gr. 1-1). pap. 11.50 (978-1-4339-8990-2(5), 7e012e0b-e99b-4ab4-970b-4e5536f44e9e); (Illus.). lib. bdg. 27.93 (978-1-4339-8989-6(1), 5b26cdce-6209-4f57-aa9f-cf7a6ff2fc51) Stevens, Gareth Publishing LLLP.

Shea, Mary Molly. Alicia Keys, 1 vol. 2011. (Hip-Hop Headliners Ser.). (ENG., Illus.). 32p. (gr. 1-1). pap. 11.50 (978-1-4339-4785-8(4), fd2058ad-7f71-4957-9395-180575e39eb2); (J). 27.93 (978-1-4339-4784-1(6), acb83c56-de2d-4634-b62d-0fc3f5992b68) Stevens, Gareth Publishing LLLP.

Shea, Therese M. Usher, 1 vol. 2011. (Hip-Hop Headliners Ser.). (ENG., Illus.). 32p. (gr. 1-1). pap. 11.50 (978-1-4339-4813-8(3), f9697ac7-bbc3-4e95-81ce-4087158155b2); (J). 27.93 (978-1-4339-4812-1(5), 0147663d-f70b-4386-b541-04fd20c28ecf) Stevens, Gareth Publishing LLLP.

—Zendaya: Actress & Singer, 1 vol. 2018. (Junior Biographies Ser.). (ENG.). 24p. (gr. 3-4). 24.27 (978-1-9785-0209-3(5), 49cc4396-c320-481f-9a23-ad342efb211d) Enslow Publishing, LLC.

Sheafer, Silvia Anne. Aretha Franklin: Motown Superstar, 1 vol. 2004. (African-American Biographies Ser.). (ENG., Illus.). 128p. (gr. 6-7). lib. bdg. 29.60 (978-0-89490-686-2(0), 8f92bc29-07fd-4f31-8f07-f4f4b3d6536e) Enslow Publishing, LLC.

Sherrard, Valerie. Vanessa Hudgens, 1 vol. 2010. (Superstars! Ser.). (ENG., Illus.). 32p. (J). pap. (978-0-7787-7262-0(4)); (gr. 3-6). lib. bdg. (978-0-7787-7253-8(5)) Crabtree Publishing Co.

Silvey, Anita. Let Your Voice Be Heard: The Life & Times of Pete Seeger. 2016. (ENG., Illus.). 112p. (J). (gr. 5-7). 17.99 (978-0-547-33012-9(X), 1417233, Clarion Bks.) HarperCollins Pubs.

Simone, Jacquelyn. Ciara. 2009. (Hip-Hop Ser.). (Illus.). 64p. (YA). pap. 7.95 (978-1-4222-0334-7(4)); (gr. 7-12). lib. bdg. 22.95 (978-1-4222-0286-9(0)) Mason Crest.

Sirota, Lyn. Pink, 1 vol. 2011. (Megastars Ser.). (ENG., Illus.). 48p. (YA). (gr. 5-5). 34.47 (978-1-4358-3577-1(8), d65a001e-d585-441a-ab57-3087a5179d18); pap. 12.75 (978-1-4488-2263-8(7), ddf4f35a-ae50-4788-abad-3b29dc06bc1c) Rosen Publishing Group, Inc., The. (Rosen Reference).

Sloate, Susan. Ray Charles: Find Another Way! 2006. (Defining Moments Ser.). (Illus.). 32p. (J). (gr. 2-5). lib. bdg. 28.50 (978-1-59716-267-8(1)) Bearport Publishing Co., Inc.

—Ray Charles: Young Musician. Henderson, Meryl, illus. 2007. (Childhood of Famous Americans Ser.). (ENG.). 176p. (J). (gr. 3-7). pap. 6.99 (978-1-4169-1437-2(4), Simon & Schuster/Paula Wiseman Bks.) Simon & Schuster/Paula Wiseman Bks.

Snyder, Gail. Brooke Knows Best. 2010. (Major Reality Shows Ser.). 48p. (YA). (gr. 7-18). lib. bdg. 19.95 (978-1-4222-1680-4(2)) Mason Crest.

—David Cook. 2009. (Dream Big: American Idol Superstars Ser.). (Illus.). 64p. (YA). (gr. 5-18). lib. bdg. 22.95 (978-1-4222-1507-4(5)) Mason Crest.

—Kelly Clarkson. 2009. (Dream Big: American Idol Superstars Ser.). 64p. (YA). (gr. 5-18). pap. 9.95 (978-1-4222-1604-0(7)); lib. bdg. 22.95 (978-1-4222-1506-7(7)) Mason Crest.

Sonneborn, Liz. Fantasia Barrino. (Who's Your Idol? Ser.). 48p. (gr. 5-5). 2009. 53.00 (978-1-60854-787-6(6), Rosen Reference) 2008. (ENG., Illus.). (J). lib. bdg. 34.47 (978-1-4042-1369-2(4), 812b2de0-e5d2-4997-b9e8-14cfa028f742) Rosen Publishing Group, Inc., The.

Spencer, Liv. The Miranda Cosgrove & iCarly Spectacular! Unofficial & Unstoppable. 2010. (ENG., Illus.). 142p. (J). (gr. 4-7). pap. 14.95 (978-1-55022-929-5(X), a320d589-d63c-4e2d-af5b-ec96858d718a) ECW Pr. CAN. Dist: Baker & Taylor Publisher Services (BTPS).

Sprinkel, Katy. Bieber Fever. 2011. (ENG., Illus.). 112p. (J). (gr. 7). pap. 12.95 (978-1-60078-634-1(0)) Triumph Bks.

Star Biographies. 2010. (Star Biographies Ser.). 32p. lib. bdg. 213.20 (978-1-4296-5883-6(5), Capstone Pr.) Capstone.

Stewart, Mark. Music Legends, 1 vol. 2009. (Ultimate 10: Entertainment Ser.). (ENG.). 48p. (gr. 3-3). (J). pap. 11.50 (978-1-4339-2213-8(4), 5545e1c1-8bf0-4979-828b-2c94ed101110); (YA). lib. bdg. 33.67 (978-0-8368-9165-2(1), 5f494f81-e911-4c16-8b2a-fb4ea4d5c341) Stevens, Gareth Publishing LLLP.

Strand, Jennifer. Taylor Swift. 2016. (Stars of Music Ser.). (ENG.). 24p. (J). (gr. -1-2). lib. bdg. 31.36 (978-1-68079-920-0(7), 24144, Abdo Zoom-Launch) ABDO Publishing Co.

Summers, Kimberly Dillon. Miley Cyrus: A Biography, 1 vol. 2009. (Greenwood Biographies Ser.). (ENG.). 180p. 43.00 (978-0-313-37847-8(9), 900301084, Bloomsbury Academic) Bloomsbury Publishing Plc GBR. Dist: Macmillan.

Superstars! Editors. Superstars! One Direction: Inside Their World. Superstars! Editors, ed. 2012. (ENG., Illus.). 128p. (J). (gr. 3-17). pap. 14.95 (978-1-60320-950-2(6), Liberty St.) Time Inc. Bks.

Sutcliffe, Jane. Marian Anderson. 2008. pap. 52.95 (978-0-8225-9394-2(7)) Lerner Publishing Group.

Terp, Gail. Demi Lovato. 2016. (Women Who Rock Ser.). (ENG., Illus.). 32p. (J). (gr. 4-6). 31.35 (978-1-68072-066-2(X), 10423, Bolt) Black Rabbit Bks.

Thatcher Murcia, Rebecca. What It's Like to Be Shakira. de la Vega, Eida, tr. from SPA. 2010. (What It's Like to Be/Que se Siente al Ser Ser.). (ENG & SPA., Illus.). 32p. (J). (gr. -1-2). lib. bdg. 25.70 (978-1-58415-851-6(4)) Mitchell Lane Pubs.

The Celebrities Arts Center. Beyonce Knowles, the Marvelous Queen. 2007. 76p. pap. 11.00 (978-0-9774483-9-5(8)) International Development Ctr.

Torres, Jennifer. Ashanti. 2005. (Blue Banner Biography Ser.). (Illus.). 32p. (J). lib. bdg. 25.70 (978-1-58415-378-8(4)) Mitchell Lane Pubs.

—Selena Gomez: Pop Singer & Actress, 1 vol. 2015. (Influential Latinos Ser.). (ENG., Illus.). 128p. (gr. 7-7). 38.93 (978-0-7660-6999-2(0), 864a3343-773c-4c52-ab74-9d6c8b441f1c) Enslow Publishing, LLC.

Torres, John. Usher. 2005. (Blue Banner Biography Ser.). (Illus.). 32p. (J). (gr. 4-8). lib. bdg. 25.70 (978-1-58415-379-5(2)) Mitchell Lane Pubs.

Torres, John Albert. Clay Aiken. 2004. (Blue Banner Biography Ser.). (Illus.). 32p. (J). (gr. 3-8). lib. bdg. 25.70 (978-1-58415-316-0(4)) Mitchell Lane Pubs.

Toyne, Jessica. Justin Bieber. 2015. (Pop Icons Ser.). (Illus.). 64p. (J). (gr. 7). lib. bdg. 23.95 (978-1-4222-3247-7(6)) Mason Crest.

Tracy, Kathleen. Aly & AJ. 2007. (Robbie Reader Ser.). (Illus.). 32p. (YA). (gr. 2-5). lib. bdg. 25.70 (978-1-58415-595-9(7)) Mitchell Lane Pubs.

—Avril Lavigne. 2004. (Uncharted, Unexplored & Unexplained Ser.). (Illus.). 32p. (J). (gr. 3-8). lib. bdg. 25.70 (978-1-58415-314-6(8)) Mitchell Lane Pubs.

—Bessie Smith. 2012. (J). lib. bdg. 29.95 (978-1-61228-271-8(7)) Mitchell Lane Pubs.

—Beyonce. 2004. (Blue Banner Biography Ser.). (Illus.). 32p. (J). (gr. 3-8). lib. bdg. 25.70 (978-1-58415-312-2(1)) Mitchell Lane Pubs.

—Carrie Underwood. 2005. (Blue Banner Biography Ser.). (Illus.). 32p. (J). (gr. 4-8). lib. bdg. 25.70 (978-1-58415-425-9(X)) Mitchell Lane Pubs.

—Justin Bieber. 2010. (Robbie Reader Ser.). (Illus.). 32p. (YA). (gr. 2-5). lib. bdg. 25.70 (978-1-58415-895-0(6)) Mitchell Lane Pubs.

—Justin Timberlake. 2007. (Blue Banner Biography Ser.). (Illus.). 32p. (YA). (gr. 4-7). lib. bdg. 25.70 (978-1-58415-611-6(2)) Mitchell Lane Pubs.

—Kelly Clarkson. 2006. (Blue Banner Biography Ser.). (Illus.). 32p. (YA). (gr. 4-7). lib. bdg. 25.70 (978-1-58415-518-8(3)) Mitchell Lane Pubs.

—Mariah Carey. 2006. (Blue Banner Biography Ser.). (Illus.). 32p. (YA). (gr. 4-7). lib. bdg. 25.70 (978-1-58415-516-4(7)) Mitchell Lane Pubs.

Triumph Books Staff. Austin Mahone: Startin' Something Spectacular. 2013. (ENG.). 112p. (J). (gr. 4-7). pap. 12.95 (978-1-60078-915-1(3)) Triumph Bks.

Troupe, Quincy. Little Stevie Wonder. Cohen, Lisa, illus. 2005. (ENG.). 32p. (J). (gr. -1-3). 18.00 (978-0-618-34060-6(2), 510518, Clarion Bks.) HarperCollins Pubs.

Turck, Mary C. Freedom Song: Young Voices & the Struggle for Civil Rights. 2008. (ENG., Illus.). 160p. (J). (gr. 4). pap. 18.95 (978-1-55652-773-9(X)) Chicago Review Pr., Inc.

Uschan, Michael V. Selena Gomez, 1 vol. 2014. (People in the News Ser.). (ENG.). 104p. (gr. 7-7). lib. bdg. 41.03 (978-1-4205-1213-7(7), 9cb1bde8-7132-4e86-81f1-d2fab7e247c4, Lucent Pr.) Greenhaven Publishing LLC.

Vaughan, Jenny. Selena Gomez - Teen Stars. 2013. (ENG., Illus.). 32p. (J). 28.50 (978-1-59771-417-4(8)) Sea-To-Sea Pubns.

Veirs, Laura. Libba: The Magnificent Musical Life of Elizabeth Cotten (Early Elementary Story Books, Children's Music Books, Biography Books for Kids) Fazlalizadeh, Tatyana, illus. 2018. (ENG.). 40p. (J). (gr. k-3). 17.99 (978-1-4521-4857-1(0)) Chronicle Bks. LLC.

Vetere, Lori. Pharrell, Vol. 11. 2018. (Hip-Hop & R & B: Culture, Music & Storytelling Ser.). (Illus.). 80p. (J). (gr. 7). lib. bdg. 33.27 (978-1-4222-4183-7(1)) Mason Crest.

Victoria Justice. 2013. (Rising Stars Ser.). 32p. (J). (gr. 3-6). pap. 63.00 (978-1-4339-8991-9(3)) Stevens, Gareth Publishing LLLP.

Waters, Rosa. Ashanti. 2008. (Hip-Hop Ser.). (Illus.). 64p. (YA). (gr. 3-7). lib. bdg. 22.95 (978-1-4222-0111-4(2)); per. 7.95 (978-1-4222-0263-0(1)) Mason Crest.

—Bob Marley & the Wailers. (Pop Rock Ser.). (Illus.). 64p. (YA). 2008. (gr. 7-18). lib. bdg. 22.95 (978-1-4222-0192-3(9)) 2007. pap. 7.95 (978-1-4222-0317-0(4)) Mason Crest.

Watson, Renée. Harlem's Little Blackbird: The Story of Florence Mills. Robinson, Christian, illus. 2012. 40p. (J). (gr. -1-2). 17.99 (978-0-375-86973-0(5), Random Hse. Bks. for Young Readers) Random Hse. Children's Bks.

Watson, Stephanie. Prince: Musical Icon. 2016. (Lives Cut Short Ser.). (ENG., Illus.). 112p. (J). (gr. 6-12). lib. bdg. 41.36 (978-1-68078-364-3(5), 23216, Essential Library) ABDO Publishing Co.

Weatherford, Carole Boston. The Legendary Miss Lena Horne. Zunon, Elizabeth, illus. 2017. (ENG.). 48p. (J). (gr. -1-3). 17.99 (978-1-4814-6824-4(3)) Simon & Schuster Children's Publishing.

Weber, Terri. Alicia Keys. 2004. (J). pap. (978-1-932724-29-5(X)); lib. bdg. (978-1-932724-28-8(1)) Panda Publishing, L.L.C. (Bios for Kids).

Weber, Terri Smith. Dixie Chicks. 2004. (J). lib. bdg. (978-0-9740180-1-0(5), Bios for Kids) Panda Publishing, L.L.C.

—Jennifer Lopez: Living the Dream. 2004. (J). pap. (978-1-932724-21-9(4)); lib. bdg. (978-1-932724-20-2(6)) Panda Publishing, L.L.C. (Bios for Kids).

—Jennifer Lopez: Realizando Los Suenos. 2003. (SPA.). (J). pap. (978-0-9740180-4-1(X)); lib. bdg. (978-0-9740180-3-4(1)) Panda Publishing, L.L.C. (Bios for Kids).

—Shakira: Following Her Heart. 2004. (SPA.). (J). pap. (978-1-932724-05-9(2)); lib. bdg. (978-1-932724-04-2(4)) Panda Publishing, L.L.C. (Bios for Kids).

Webster, Christine. Beyonce Knowles. 2005. (Great African American Women for Kids Ser.). (Illus.). 24p. (J). (gr. 2-3). lib. bdg. 24.45 (978-1-59036-331-7(0)) Weigl Pubs., Inc.

Wells, Peggy Sue. Fergie. 2007. (Blue Banner Biography Ser.). (Illus.). 32p. (YA). (gr. 4-7). lib. bdg. 25.70 (978-1-58415-521-8(3)) Mitchell Lane Pubs.

Weston Woods Staff, creator. Ella Fitzgerald. 2011. 18.95 (978-0-545-02761-8(6)); 38.75 (978-0-545-02763-2(2)) Weston Woods Studios, Inc.

Wheeler, Jill C. Jennifer Lopez. 2003. (Star Tracks Ser.). (Illus.). 64p. (J). (gr. 3-8). lib. bdg. 27.07 (978-1-57765-770-5(5)) ABDO Publishing Co.

—Kelly Clarkson. 2003. (Young Profiles Ser.). (Illus.). 32p. (J). (gr. k-6). 27.07 (978-1-57765-994-5(5)) ABDO Publishing Co.

—Madonna. 2003. (Star Tracks Ser.). (Illus.). 64p. (gr. 3-8). lib. bdg. 27.07 (978-1-57765-768-2(3), Abdo & Daughters) ABDO Publishing Co.

Whiting, Jim. Mandy Moore. (Pop Culture Ser.). (Illus.). 64p. (YA). (gr. 3-7). 2008. lib. bdg. 22.95 (978-1-4222-0207-4(0)) 2007. pap. 7.95 (978-1-4222-0362-0(X)) Mason Crest.

Wilcox, Christine. Justin Bieber, 1 vol. 2013. (People in the News Ser.). (ENG., Illus.). 96p. (gr. 7-7). lib. bdg. 41.03 (978-1-4205-0756-0(7), 5564123d-8ab4-4a6e-b2c9-c6f22d23d414, Lucent Pr.) Greenhaven Publishing LLC.

Williams, Zella. Selena Gomez: Actress & Singer, 1 vol. 2010. (Hispanic Headliners Ser.). (ENG., Illus.). 24p. (J). (gr. 2-3). pap. 9.25 (978-1-4488-1482-4(0), 1ba6db8c-bec1-4cdd-a508-43507abd6b16); lib. bdg. 26.27 (978-1-4488-1458-9(8), 1311e5b0-ff67-40b6-b462-4bf7050f1987) Rosen Publishing Group, Inc., The. (PowerKids Pr.).

—Selena Gomez: Actress & Singer - Actriz y Cantante, 1 vol. 2010. (Hispanic Headliners / Hispanos en Las Noticias Ser.). (ENG & SPA.). 24p. (J). (gr. 2-3). lib. bdg. 26.27 (978-1-4488-0715-4(8), 15a4913c-b0e3-4c4e-8d4e-75ac2ec5e994) Rosen Publishing Group, Inc., The.

—Shakira: Star Singer, 1 vol. 2010. (Hispanic Headliners Ser.). (ENG.). 24p. (J). (gr. 2-3). pap. 9.25 (978-1-4488-1480-0(4), ddc78bf0-e43e-4a50-8ffb-288391671e1b); lib. bdg. 26.27 (978-1-4488-1457-2(X), fb1a05d7-e0b5-4a93-ad2a-cdd3c7b85e39) Rosen Publishing Group, Inc., The. (PowerKids Pr.).

—Shakira: Star Singer - Estrella de la Canción, 1 vol. 2010. (Hispanic Headliners / Hispanos en Las Noticias Ser.). (SPA & ENG.). 24p. (J). (gr. 2-3). lib. bdg. 26.27 (978-1-4488-0714-7(X), 03c78672-66a9-4ec6-95ec-308d75bcbb7c) Rosen Publishing Group, Inc., The.

Worth, Richard. Christina Aguilera: Pop Singer, 1 vol. 2015. (Influential Latinos Ser.). (ENG., Illus.). 128p. (gr. 7-8). lib. bdg. 38.93 (978-0-7660-7180-3(4), ece5027f-82db-4fd8-be3d-4687e861807e) Enslow Publishing, LLC.

Wright, David K. The Life of Paul Robeson: Actor, Singer, Political Activist, 1 vol. 2014. (Legendary African Americans Ser.). (ENG.). 96p. (gr. 6-7). 31.61 (978-0-7660-6157-6(4), 6f8e9895-253b-47ce-b998-cc41b66e00f4); (Illus.). (J). pap. 13.88 (978-0-7660-6158-3(2), 616d3255-1d32-439e-928c-494ed21749e3) Enslow Publishing, LLC.

Yasuda, Anita. Justin Bieber. 2011. 24p. (YA). (gr. 2-4). (978-1-77071-647-6(5)); pap. (978-1-77071-651-3(3)) Weigl Educational Pubs. Ltd.

—Justin Bieber. 2011. (J). (gr. 4-6). pap. 12.95 (978-1-61690-672-6(3), AV2 by Weigl); (Illus.). 24p. (YA). (gr. 3-6). 27.13 (978-1-61690-667-2(7)) Weigl Pubs., Inc.

—Justin Bieber: Ma Vie. Karvonen, Tanjah, tr. from ENG. 2011. (FRE., Illus.). 24p. (YA). (gr. 2-4). (978-1-77071-432-8(4)) Weigl Educational Pubs. Ltd.

—Lady Gaga. 2012. (J). (978-1-61913-753-0(4)); pap. (978-1-61913-754-7(2)) Weigl Pubs., Inc.

—Miranda Cosgrove. 2011. (J). (gr. 4-6). pap. 12.95 (978-1-61690-673-3(1), AV2 by Weigl); (Illus.). 24p. (YA). (gr. 3-6). 27.13 (978-1-61690-668-9(5)) Weigl Pubs., Inc.

—Nikki Yanofsky. 2011. 24p. (YA). (gr. 2-4). pap. (978-1-77071-652-0(1)) Weigl Educational Pubs. Ltd.

—Nikki Yanofsky: Ma Vie. Karvonen, Tanjah, tr. from ENG. 2011. (FRE., Illus.). 24p. (YA). (gr. 2-4). (978-1-77071-433-5(2)) Weigl Educational Pubs. Ltd.

—Taylor Swift. 2010. (Remarkable People Ser.). (Illus.). 24p. (J). (gr. 4-6). pap. 11.95 (978-1-61690-158-5(6)); lib. bdg. 25.70 (978-1-61690-157-8(8)) Weigl Pubs., Inc.

Ziegler, Mackenzie. Kenzie's Rules for Life: How to Be Happy, Healthy, & Dance to Your Own Beat. 2018. (ENG., Illus.). 256p. 17.99 (978-1-5011-8357-7(5), Gallery Bks.) Gallery Bks.

SINGERS—FICTION

Anastasiu, Heather & Brown, Anne Greenwood. Girl Last Seen. 2016. (ENG.). 272p. (YA). (gr. 8-12). 16.99 (978-0-8075-8140-7(2), 807581402); pap. 9.99 (978-0-8075-8141-4(0), 807581410) Whitman, Albert & Co.

Bach, Mette. Charming. 2019. (Lorimer Real Love Ser.). (ENG.). 176p. (YA). (gr. 9-12). lib. bdg. 27.99 (978-1-4594-1389-4(X), 64a3b812-9ec1-4656-93c1-1bf43a1f2fe8) James Lorimer & Co. Ltd., Pubs. CAN. Dist: Lerner Publishing Group.

Cass, Kiera. The Selection 4-Book Box Set: The Selection, the Elite, the One, the Heir. 2016. (Selection Ser.). (ENG.). 1456p. (YA). (gr. 8). pap. 39.96 (978-0-06-242440-2(8), HarperTeen) HarperCollins Pubs.

Collard, Claire. Footpaths on the Sea. 2015. (ENG., Illus.). 292p. (J). pap. (978-1-78222-420-4(3)) Paragon Publishing, Rothersthorpe.

Denman, K. L. Stuff We All Get, 1 vol. 2011. (Orca Currents Ser.). (ENG.). 128p. (J). (gr. 4-7). pap. 9.95 (978-1-55469-820-2(0)); lib. bdg. 16.95 (978-1-55469-821-9(9)) Orca Bk. Pubs. USA.

Dimopoulos, Elaine. Material Girls. 2016. (ENG.). 336p. (YA). (gr. 9). pap. 8.99 (978-0-544-67173-7(2), 1625822, Clarion Bks.) HarperCollins Pubs.

Flinn, Alex. Diva. 2013. (ENG.). 304p. (YA). (gr. 9). pap. 9.99 (978-0-06-212434-0(X), HarperTeen) HarperCollins Pubs.

Frosting & Friendship. 2014. (ENG., Illus.). 240p. (J). (gr. 3-7). pap. 7.99 (978-1-4424-7397-3(5), Aladdin) Simon & Schuster Children's Publishing.

Geiger, A. V. Tell Me No Lies. 2018. (Follow Me Back Ser.: 2). 336p. (YA). (gr. 8-12). pap. 10.99 (978-1-4926-4825-3(6)) Sourcebooks, Inc.

Goo, Maurene. Somewhere Only We Know. 2019. (ENG.). 336p. (YA). 17.99 (978-0-374-31057-8(2), 900193167, Farrar, Straus & Giroux (BYR)) Farrar, Straus & Giroux.

—Somewhere Only We Know. 2020. (ENG.). 336p. (YA). pap. 10.99 (978-1-250-25078-0(1), 900193168) Square Fish.

Graham, Sabrina Depina. Breanna & Amber: Help Each Other Achieve Their Dreams (Christian Version) 2012. 92p. 19.99 (978-1-4691-6411-3(6)); pap. 12.99 (978-1-4691-6410-6(8)) Xlibris Corp.

Greene, Kimberly. Fame Game & Me. 2011. (My Sister's a Pop Star Ser.). (ENG.). 320p. (J). (gr. 4-6). 17.44 (978-0-7945-2900-0(3)) EDC Publishing.

—My Life on TV. 2011. (My Sister's a Pop Star Ser.). (ENG.). 320p. (J). (gr. 6-8). 18.69 (978-0-7945-2901-7(1)) EDC Publishing.

Harmon, Michael. Brutal. 2011. 240p. (YA). (gr. 9). pap. 8.99 (978-0-440-23995-6(8), Knopf Bks. for Young Readers) Random Hse. Children's Bks.

Hertz, Kellen. Tenney Shares the Stage. 2017. 189p. (J). (978-1-338-16722-1(7)) Scholastic, Inc.

Hopkins, Cathy. The Princess of Pop. 2012. (Truth or Dare Ser.). (ENG.). 224p. (YA). (gr. 7). pap. 10.99 (978-1-4424-6057-7(1), Simon Pulse) Simon Pulse.

Hurley, Jeanette Clinger. The Crystal Prince: Love Is the Only Way. 2010. (Illus.). 77p. pap. 32.95 (978-0-578-03963-3(X)) Outskirts Pr., Inc.

Jones, Harmony. Girl vs. Boy Band: The Right Track. 2016. (ENG.). 240p. (J). 16.99 (978-1-61963-947-8(5), 900152788, Bloomsbury USA Childrens) Bloomsbury Publishing USA.

—The High Note (Girl vs Boy Band 2) The High Note. 2017. (ENG.). 240p. (J). 16.99 (978-1-61963-949-2(1), 900152779, Bloomsbury USA Childrens) Bloomsbury Publishing USA.

Kadence, Sam. Evolution. 2013. 230p. pap. 14.99 (978-1-62380-410-7(8), Harmony Ink Pr.) Dreamspinner Pr.

—Evolution [Library Edition]. 2013. 230p. pap. 14.99 (978-1-62380-924-9(X), Harmony Ink Pr.) Dreamspinner Pr.

Karpes, H. R. Morris ... the Downside-Up Bat. 2013. (ENG., Illus.). 32p. (J). (gr. -1-k). 11.95 (978-1-62087-987-0(5), 620987, Sky Pony Pr.) Skyhorse Publishing Co., Inc.

Keene, Carolyn. Springtime Crime. Francis, Peter, illus. 2018. (Nancy Drew Clue Book Ser.: 9). (ENG.). 112p. (J). (gr. 1-4). 16.99 (978-1-4814-9954-5(8)); pap. 5.99 (978-1-4814-9953-8(X)) Simon & Schuster Children's Publishing. (Aladdin).

Ketchum, Liza. The Life Fantastic: A Novel in Three Acts. 2017. (ENG.). 256p. (YA). 17.99 (978-1-4405-9876-0(2), Simon Pulse) Simon Pulse.

Levy, Marianne. Katie Cox Goes Viral. 2017. (ENG.). 368p. (J). (gr. 5-9). pap. 12.99 (978-1-4926-4250-3(9), 9781492642503) Sourcebooks, Inc.

—Katie Cox vs. the Boy Band. 2018. (ENG.). 336p. (J). (gr. 5-9). pap. 7.99 (978-1-4926-4608-2(3)) Sourcebooks, Inc.

Lord, Emery. Open Road Summer. 2018. (ENG.). 368p. (YA). pap. 10.99 (978-1-68119-593-3(3), 900179020, Bloomsbury USA Childrens) Bloomsbury Publishing USA.

MacLachlan, Patricia. Just Dance. (ENG.). 128p. (J). (gr. 2). 2018. pap. 7.99 (978-1-4814-7253-1(4)) 2017. (Illus.). 15.99 (978-1-4814-7252-4(6)) McElderry, Margaret K. Bks. (McElderry, Margaret K. Bks.).

Mancuso, Rudy. How to Be Famous in Six Seconds. 2016. (YA). pap. (978-1-5011-2767-0(5), Keywords Press) Atria Bks.

Marko, Cyndi. Bok! Bok! Boom! 2014. (Kung Pow Chicken Ser.: 2). lib. bdg. 14.75 (978-0-606-35357-1(7)) Turtleback.

McKay, Sindy. We Both Read-The Ruby Rose Show. Johnson, Meredith, illus. 2010. (We Both Read Ser.). 44p. (J). (gr. k-3). pap. 5.99 (978-1-60115-246-6(9)) Treasure Bay, Inc.

Nall, Gail. Out of Tune. 2017. (Mix Ser.). (ENG.). 352p. (J). (gr. 4-8). pap. 7.99 (978-1-4814-5816-0(7), Aladdin) Simon & Schuster Children's Publishing.

—Out of Tune. 2016. (Mix Ser.). (ENG., Illus.). 336p. (J). (gr. 4-9). 17.99 (978-1-4814-5817-7(5), Simon & Schuster/Paula Wiseman Bks.) Simon & Schuster/Paula Wiseman Bks.

Novak, Ali. The Heartbreakers. 2015. (Heartbreak Chronicles Ser.: 1). 336p. (YA). (gr. 6-12). pap. 12.99 (978-1-4926-1256-8(1), 9781492612568) Sourcebooks, Inc.

Olsen, Sylvia. Molly's Promise, 1 vol. 2013. (Orca Young Readers Ser.). (ENG.). 136p. (J). (gr. 4-7). pap. 7.95 (978-1-4598-0277-3(2)) Orca Bk. Pubs. USA.

Philbin, Joanna. The Daughters Take the Stage. 2011. (Daughters Ser.: 3). (ENG.). 304p. (YA). (gr. 7-17). pap. 16.99 (978-0-316-04908-5(5), Poppy) Little, Brown Bks. for Young Readers.

Prendergast, Gabrielle. The Frail Days, 1 vol. 2015. (Orca Limelights Ser.). (ENG.). 128p. (J). (gr. 4-7). pap. 9.95 (978-1-4598-0464-7(3)) Orca Bk. Pubs. USA.

—Pinch Me, 1 vol. 2017. (Orca Soundings Ser.). (ENG.). 144p. (YA). (gr. 8-12). pap. 9.95 (978-1-4598-1364-9(2)) Orca Bk. Pubs. USA.

Rippin, Sally. Scary Solo. Spartels, Stephanie, illus. 2013. (ENG.). 48p. (J). pap. 4.99 (978-1-61067-122-4(8)) Kane Miller.

Rosner, Gillian, tr. The Phantom of the Opera: Based on the Novel by Gaston Leroux. Druvert, Hélène, illus. 2016. (ENG.). 40p. (J). (gr. k-2). 19.95 (978-1-4197-2086-4(4), 1648901, Abrams Bks. for Young Readers) Abrams, Inc.

Rudnick, Paul. It's All Your Fault. (ENG.). 304p. (YA). (gr. 9-9). 2017. pap. 10.99 (978-0-545-46429-1(3)) 2016. 19.99 (978-0-545-46428-4(5), Scholastic Pr.) Scholastic, Inc.

Ryan, Tom. Big Time, 1 vol. 2014. (Orca Limelights Ser.). (ENG.). 144p. (J). (gr. 4-7). pap. 9.95 (978-1-4598-0461-6(9)) Orca Bk. Pubs. USA.

Ryder, Chloe. Princess Ponies 8: a Singing Star. 2015. (Princess Ponies Ser.). (ENG., Illus.). 128p. (J). (gr. 2-4). pap. 5.99 (978-1-61963-567-8(4), 900140704, Bloomsbury USA Childrens) Bloomsbury Publishing USA.

SaBerre, Kristen. A Noble Cause. 2018. (Suddenly Royal Ser.). (ENG.). 112p. (YA). (gr. 6-12). pap. 7.99 (978-1-5415-2639-6(2), 38f3af7a-8598-4396-82c0-6ccb288be95c); lib. bdg. 26.65 (978-1-5415-2569-6(8), eef4bf2d-fdad-48be-b43c-f1e8c406a1fb) Lerner Publishing Group. (Darby Creek).

Schraff, Anne. Facing It, 1 vol. 2013. (Urban Underground Ser.). (ENG.). 194p. (YA). (gr. 9-12). pap. 11.95 (978-1-62250-045-1(8)) Saddleback Educational Publishing, Inc.

Schraff, Anne E. Facing It. 2013. (Urban Underground — Harriet Tubman High School Ser.). (YA). lib. bdg. 20.80 (978-0-606-31583-8(7)) Turtleback.

Shine, Joe. Bobby Sky: Boy Band or Die. 2019. 288p. (YA). (gr. 9). 10.99 (978-1-61695-851-0(0), Soho Teen) Soho Pr., Inc.

Snowe, Olivia. The Glass Voice, 1 vol. Lamoreaux, Michelle, illus. 2014. (Twicetold Tales Ser.). (ENG.). 128p. (J). (gr. 3-6). 25.32 (978-1-4342-9148-6(0), 125596, Stone Arch Bks.) Capstone.

Storm, Tallia & Courtenay, Lucy. Pop Girl. 2017. 314p. (J). (978-1-338-16024-6(9)) Scholastic, Inc.

Supplee, Suzanne. Somebody Everybody Listens To. 2011. 288p. (YA). (gr. 7-12). 8.99 (978-0-14-241886-4(2), Speak) Penguin Young Readers Group.

The check digit for ISBN-10 appears in parentheses after the full ISBN-13

Teitelbaum, Michael. The Secret of the Tragic Theater. 2015. (Cold Whispers Ser.). (ENG., Illus.). 32p. (J). (gr. 2-6). lib. bdg. 28.50 (978-1-62724-809-9(9)) Bearport Publishing Co., Inc.

Warne, Jude. The It Factor. 2017. (Crushing Ser.). (ENG.). 192p. (YA). (gr. 5-12). lib. bdg. 31.42 (978-1-68076-718-6(6), 25384, Epic Escape) EPIC Pr.

Warner, Gertrude Chandler, creator. The Mystery of the Missing Pop Idol. 2015. (Boxcar Children Mysteries Ser.: 138). (ENG., Illus.). 128p. (J). (gr. 2-5). 15.99 (978-0-8075-5605-4(X), 080755605X, Random Hse. Bks. for Young Readers) Random Hse. Children's Bks.

Winter, Jonah. Jazz Age Josephine: Dancer, Singer — Who's That, Who? Why, That's MISS Josephine Baker, to You! Priceman, Marjorie, illus. 2012. (ENG.). 40p. (J). (gr. -1-3). 19.99 (978-1-4169-6123-9(2), Atheneum Bks. for Young Readers) Simon & Schuster Children's Publishing.

SINGING

see also Voice

Appleby, Alex. Puedo Ser una Cantante / I Can Be a Singer, 1 vol. 2014. (Cuando Sea Grande / When I Grow Up Ser.). (SPA & ENG.). 24p. (J). (gr. k-k). 24.27 (978-1-4824-0865-2(1), e3727007-26fe-44f3-aeb2-089908983b35) Stevens, Gareth Publishing LLLP.

Beall, Pamela Conn & Nipp, Susan Hagen. Wee Sing & Move. Klein, Nancy & Guida, Liisa, illus. 2009. (Wee Sing Ser.). 64p. (J). (gr. -1-2). 10.99 (978-0-8431-8959-9(2), Price Stern Sloan) Penguin Young Readers Group.

Brewer, Mike & Harris, Paul. Improve Your Sight-Singing! Elementary Low / Medium Treble. 2003. (Faber Edition Ser.). (ENG.). 40p. (gr. 1-5). pap. 9.99 (978-0-571-51766-4(8)) Faber & Faber, Ltd. GBR. Dist: Alfred Publishing Co., Inc.

Emerson, Roger. Sing 6-7-8! Fifty Ways to Improve Your Elementary or Middle School Choir. 2008. (ENG.). 96p. pap. 12.99 (978-1-4234-5479-3(0), 08747950) Leonard, Hal Corp.

Feierabend, John M. The Book of Pitch Exploration: Can Your Voice Do This? 2004. (First Steps in Music Ser.). (ENG.). 33p. (J). pap. 11.95 (978-1-57999-242-2(0)); (Illus.). (gr. -1-2). pap. 12.95 (978-1-57999-265-1(X), G-5276) G I A Pubns., Inc.

Greenhalgh, Zoe. Music & Singing in the Early Years: A Guide to Singing with Young Children. 2018. (ENG., Illus.). 106p. (C). pap. 29.95 (978-1-138-23323-2(4), Y309041) Routledge.

Howard, Elisabeth. ABCs of Vocal Harmony: Music Reading, Ear Training. rev. ed. 2004. (Illus.). 124p. per. 29.95 (978-0-934419-01-7(9)) Vocal Power Inc.

Jacobs, Ruth Krehbiel, ed. Collected Notes on Children's Choirs: Compiled from the Choristers' Guild Letters of September, 1949 to June 1954. 2011. 244p. 46.95 (978-1-258-01814-6(4)) Literary Licensing, LLC.

Johnson, Anne, et al. Songbooks - Shukalaka Shake: Songs for a Young Child's Day, 1 vol. 2011. (Songbooks Ser.). (ENG., Illus.). 64p. (J). pap. 24.95 incl. audio compact disk (978-1-4081-4657-6(6)) HarperCollins Pubs. Ltd. GBR. Dist: Independent Pubs. Group.

Kain, Roger. Xtreme Vocals. 2005. (Illus.). 80p. audio compact disk 11.95 (978-1-84492-034-1(8)) Sanctuary Publishing, Ltd. GBR. Dist: Leonard, Hal Corp.

Landau, Elaine. Is Singing for You? 2010. (Ready to Make Music Ser.). (ENG.). 40p. (gr. 4-6). lib. bdg. 27.93 (978-0-7613-5427-7(1), Lerner Pubns.) Lerner Publishing Group.

Leck, Henry H., et al. Creating Artistry Through Choral Excellence. 2009. (978-1-4234-3711-6(X)) Leonard, Hal Corp.

Nunn, Daniel. Voices, 1 vol. 2011. (Instruments & Music Ser.). (ENG.). 24p. (J). (gr. -1-1). 25.32 (978-1-4329-5061-3(4), 115115, Heinemann) Capstone.

Raposo, Joe. Sing. Lichtenheld, Tom, illus. 2013. (ENG.). 40p. (J). (gr. -1-3). 16.99 (978-0-8050-9071-0(1), 900061330, Holt, Henry & Co. Bks. For Young Readers) Holt, Henry & Co.

Ross, Mary H. Primary Partners Singing Fun. Guymon-King, Jennette, illus. 2004. (978-1-59156-793-6(9)) Covenant Communications.

Ross, Melanie H. & Guymon-King. Super Little Singers. 2004. pap. 12.95 (978-1-59156-163-7(9)); cd-rom 12.95 (978-1-59156-164-4(7)) Covenant Communications, Inc.

Sieling, Peter. Folk Songs. 2004. (North American Folklore Ser.). (Illus.). 112p. (J). (gr. 7-18). lib. bdg. 22.95 (978-1-59084-344-4(4)) Mason Crest.

Storey, Rita. The Voice & Singing. 2010. (J). 28.50 (978-1-59920-216-7(6)) Black Rabbit Bks.

Stultz, Marie. Innocent Sounds: Building Choral Tone & Artistry with the Beginning Treble Voice. 2007. pap. 22.95 (978-0-944529-44-7(5)) Morning Star Music Pubs.

—Innocent Sounds, Book II: Building Choral Tone & Artistry in Your Children's Choir. 2008. 240p. per. (978-0-944529-45-4(3)) Morning Star Music Pubs.

Terry, Charles L. Sing Mama's Boy Sing. 2012. (ENG.). (J). pap. (978-1-4675-1270-1(2)) Independent Pub.

Turck, Mary C. Freedom Song: Young Voices & the Struggle for Civil Rights. 2008. (ENG., Illus.). 160p. (J). (gr. 4). pap. 18.95 (978-1-55652-773-9(X)) Chicago Review Pr., Inc.

VanVoorst, Jenny Fretland. El Canto. 2016. (El Estudio del Artista (Artist's Studio)).Tr. of Singing. (SPA.). 24p. (J). (gr. k-2). lib. bdg. 25.65 (978-1-62031-321-3(9), Bullfrog Bks.) Jump! Inc.

—Singing. 2016. (Artist's Studio Ser.). (Illus.). 24p. (J). (gr. k-2). lib. bdg. 25.65 (978-1-62031-285-8(9), Bullfrog Bks.) Jump! Inc.

SINGING—FICTION

Ambatchew, Daniel. Mimi Mystery. 2012. (Illus.). 39p. pap. 10.95 (978-9988-647-83-4(2)) Sub-Saharan Pubs. & Traders GHA. Dist: African Bks. Collective, Ltd.

Andrews, Julie & Hamilton, Emma Walton. The Very Fairy Princess Sparkles in the Snow. Davenier, Christine, illus. 2013. (Very Fairy Princess Ser.). (ENG.). 32p. (J). (gr. -1-3). 18.00 (978-0-316-21963-1(0)) Little, Brown Bks. for Young Readers.

Arnold, Karen. Leaper Joins the Choir. 2011. 28p. pap. 15.99 (978-1-4568-6535-1(8)) Xlibris Corp.

Baker, Georgette. Cantemos Chiquitos, No. 2. (SPA., Illus.). (J). (gr. k-12). pap. 12.95 incl. audio (978-0-9623930-2-0(9), TAL002) Cantemos-bilingual bks. and music.

Ballantyne, R. M. Red Rooney: Or, the Last of the Crew. 2007. (R. M. Ballantyne Collection). (Illus.). 408p. 22.00 (978-1-934554-08-1(1)) Vision Forum, Inc., The.

Bardhan-Quallen, Sudipta. Purrmaids #5: a Star Purr-Formance. Wu, Vivien, illus. 2019. (Purrmaids Ser.: 5). (ENG.). 96p. (J). (gr. 1-4). 6.99 (978-0-525-64634-1(5), Random Hse. Bks. for Young Readers) Random Hse. Children's Bks.

Barkley, Callie. Ellie's Lovely Idea. Riti, Marsha, illus. 2013. (Critter Club Ser.: 6). (ENG.). 128p. (J). (gr. k-4). 17.99 (978-1-4424-8219-7(2)); pap. 6.99 (978-1-4424-8218-0(4)) Little Simon. (Little Simon).

—Ellie's Lovely Idea. 2013. (Critter Club Ser.: 6). (J). lib. bdg. 16.00 (978-0-606-32321-5(X)) Turtleback.

Barton, Suzanne. The Sleepy Songbird. 2016. (ENG., Illus.). 32p. (J). 16.99 (978-0-8027-3648-2(3), 9780802736482, Bloomsbury USA Childrens) Bloomsbury Publishing USA.

Birdsall, Jeanne. The Penderwicks in Spring. 2015. (Penderwicks Ser.: 4). (ENG.). 352p. (J). (gr. 3-7). 16.99 (978-0-375-87077-4(6), Knopf Bks. for Young Readers) Random Hse. Children's Bks.

Bradley, Kimberly Brubaker. For Freedom: The Story of a French Spy. 2005. 181p. 16.00 (978-0-7569-5091-0(0)) Perfection Learning Corp.

—For Freedom: The Story of a French Spy. 2005. (ENG.). 192p. (YA). (gr. 7-9). mass mkt. 8.99 (978-0-440-41831-3(3), Laurel Leaf) Random Hse. Children's Bks.

Brian, Janeen. Cat-Astrophe at the Opera, 1 vol. rev. ed. 2013. (Literary Text Ser.). (ENG., Illus.). 28p. (J). (gr. 2-3). pap. 10.99 (978-1-4333-5597-4(3)) Teacher Created Materials, Inc.

—Cat-Astrpohe at the Opera. rev. ed. 2013. (Literary Text Ser.). (ENG., Illus.). 28p. (J). (gr. 2-3). lib. bdg. 19.96 (978-1-4807-1719-0(3)) Teacher Created Materials, Inc.

Brightwood, Laura, illus. I Am A Frog. Brightwood, Laura, . 2007. (J). DVD (978-1-934409-02-2(2)) 3-C Institute for Social Development.

Brouillard, Anne. The Bathtub Prima Donna. Brouillard, Anne, illus. 2004. (Illus.). 24p. (J). (gr. k-4). reprint ed. 13.00 (978-0-7567-7755-5(0)) DIANE Publishing Co.

Brown, Deborah. Here to Save the Day. 2012. 28p. pap. 24.95 (978-1-4626-0387-9(4)) America Star Bks.

Carmichael, Leslie. Lyranel's Song. (Illus.). 288p. (J). 2007. (ENG.). (gr. 2-7). pap. 8.95 (978-0-9718348-6-6(5)) 2005. 16.95 (978-0-9718348-5-9(7)) Blooming Tree Pr.

Chapman, Jason. Who's That Singing? A Pull-The-Tab Book. Chapman, Jason, illus. 2010. (ENG., Illus.). 12p. (J). (gr. -1-1). bds. 9.99 (978-1-4169-8736-9(3), Little Simon) Little Simon.

Chewins, Hayley. The Turnaway Girls. 2018. (ENG.). 272p. (J). (gr. 5-9). 16.99 (978-0-7636-9792-1(3)) Candlewick Pr.

Conkling, Neil & Philip, Hilda. A Bird's Way of Singing. Date not set. (J). 12.95 (978-0-8050-4795-0(6), Holt, Henry & Co. Bks. For Young Readers) Holt, Henry & Co.

Cowley, Joy. Big Bear & Little Bear: Singing. Lam, Amy, illus. 2013. (ENG.). 8p. pap. (978-1-927186-25-1(0), Joy Cowley Club) Flying Start Bks.

Cox, Tiffany. Amy, the Frog Who Loved to Sing. 2006. 9.00 (978-0-8059-8806-2(8)) Dorrance Publishing Co., Inc.

Cronin, Doreen. Dooby Dooby Moo. Lewin, Betsy, illus. 2010. (Click Clack Book Ser.). (ENG.). 40p. (J). (gr. -1-k). bds. 7.99 (978-1-4424-0890-6(1), Little Simon) Little Simon.

—Dooby Dooby Moo. Lewin, Betsy, illus. 2006. (Click Clack Book Ser.). (ENG.). 40p. (J). (gr. -1-3). 19.99 (978-0-689-84507-9(3), Atheneum Bks. for Young Readers) Simon & Schuster Children's Publishing.

—Dooby Dooby Moo, 1 vol. Lewin, Betsy, illus. 2006. (Doreen Cronin: Click-Clack & More Ser.). (ENG.). 40p. (J). (gr. k-5). lib. bdg. 31.36 (978-1-59961-423-6(5), 5423, Picture Bk.) Spotlight.

—Dooby Dooby Moo. Lewin, Betsy, illus. 2011. (J). (gr. -1-3). 29.95 (978-0-545-04281-9(X)) Weston Woods Studios, Inc.

Crossley-Holland, Kevin. Crossing to Paradise. 2008. (Illus.). 339p. (J). pap. (978-0-545-05868-1(6), Levine, Arthur A. Bks.) Scholastic, Inc.

De Gasztold, Carmen B. & Godden, Rumer. The Creatures' Choir. (FRE., Illus.). (J). (gr. 3-8). 29.95 (978-0-8288-9331-2(4), F140841) French & European Pubns., Inc.

Dean, James, illus. I Love My White Shoes. 2010. (Pete the Cat Ser.). (J). lib. bdg. (978-0-06-107623-7(6)) HarperCollins Pubs.

Deedy, Carmen Agra. The Rooster Who Would Not Be Quiet! Yelchin, Eugene, illus. 2017. (ENG.). 48p. (J). (gr. -1-3). 18.99 (978-0-545-72288-9(8), Scholastic Pr.) Scholastic, Inc.

Dixon, Franklin. Top Ten Ways to Die. 2006. 169p. (J). lib. bdg. 16.92 (978-1-4242-0390-1(2)) Fitzgerald Bks.

Edwards, Antonio. Script the Strong Ant. 2011. 32p. pap. 15.99 (978-1-4634-2201-1(6)) AuthorHouse.

Flaxman, Jessica & Hall, Kirsten. Who Says? Becker, Wayne, illus. 2003. (My First Reader Ser.). (ENG.). 32p. (J). 18.50 (978-0-516-22958-4(3), Children's Pr.) Scholastic Library Publishing.

Flinn, Alex. Diva. 2006. 263p. (YA). (gr. 7-12). 16.99 (978-0-06-056843-6(7)); lib. bdg. 18.89 (978-0-06-056845-0(3)) HarperCollins Pubs. (HarperTeen).

Frost, Libby. Princess Snowbelle. 2017. (ENG., Illus.). 32p. (J). 16.99 (978-1-68119-690-9(5), 900182161, Bloomsbury USA Childrens) Bloomsbury Publishing USA.

Geller, Beverly. Ellies Shabbat Surprise. 2008. (ENG.). 32p. 13.95 (978-965-229-390-9(3)) Gefen Publishing Hse., Ltd ISR. Dist: Gefen Bks.

Geras, Adèle & Geras, Adèle. Pictures of the Night: The Egerton Hall Novels, Volume Three. 2005. (ENG.). 192p. (YA). (gr. 7-12). pap. 11.95 (978-0-15-205543-1(6), 1196670, Clarion Bks.) HarperCollins Pubs.

Graham, D. A. The Right Note. 2019. (Reality Show Ser.). (ENG.). 112p. (YA). (gr. 6-12). 26.65 (978-1-5415-4025-5(5), 8be9b624-d5a9-4a1f-916d-efd82d827d4e, Darby Creek) Lerner Publishing Group.

Grant, Ruthie. Oh, No! Fancy-Free Amy Gets Bad News. de la Rosa, Jingo, illus. 2012. (ENG.). 24p. pap. 13.99 (978-1-4634-4700-7(0)) AuthorHouse.

Greenfield, Amy Butler. Chantress Alchemy. 2015. (Chantress Ser.). (ENG., Illus.). 368p. (YA). (gr. 7). pap. 10.99 (978-1-4424-5708-9(2), McElderry, Margaret K. Bks.) McElderry, Margaret K. Bks.

Gunderson, Jessica. Desastre en el Musical. Aparicio Publishing LLC, Aparicio Publishing, tr. Cho, Sumin, illus. 2020. (Drama en la Secundaria Ser.). (SPA.). 64p. (J). (gr. 3-6). pap. 6.95 (978-1-4965-9318-4(9), 142348); lib. bdg. 25.99 (978-1-4965-9163-0(1), 142080) Capstone. (Stone Arch Bks.).

—The School Musical Meltdown. Cho, Sumin, illus. 2018. (Junior High Drama Ser.). (ENG.). 64p. (J). (gr. 3-6). 25.99 (978-1-4965-4711-8(X), 135225, Stone Arch Bks.) Capstone.

Gutknecht, Allison. Sing Like Nobody's Listening. 2018. (Mix Ser.). (ENG.). 256p. (J). (gr. 4-8). 18.99 (978-1-4814-7157-2(0)); (Illus.). pap. 7.99 (978-1-4814-7156-5(2)) Simon & Schuster Children's Publishing. (Aladdin).

HB Staff. The Little Chicks Sing. 97th ed. 2003. (Signatures Ser.). (gr. 1-18). pap. 16.50 (978-0-15-308159-0(7)) Harcourt Schl. Pubs.

Hendricks, Brenda K. What's Better Than That, Seren Dippity? Hendricks, Brenda K., illus. 2013. (Illus.). 32p. pap. 9.99 (978-0-9826582-4-6(9)) Two Small Fish Pubns.

Holmes, Lynda. Spring Cleaning. 2006. 55p. pap. 16.95 (978-1-4241-4324-5(1)) PublishAmerica, Inc.

Holt, Kimberly Willis. Dear Hank Williams. 2016. (J). lib. bdg. 18.40 (978-0-606-38551-0(7)) Turtleback.

Hopgood, Tim, illus. Singing in the Rain. 2017. (ENG.). 32p. (J). 18.99 (978-1-250-12770-9(X), 900175515, Holt, Henry & Co. Bks. For Young Readers) Holt, Henry & Co.

Howe, James. Horace & Morris Join the Chorus (but What about Dolores?) Walrod, Amy, illus. 2006. (J). pap. 44.95 incl. audio compact disk (978-1-59112-909-7(5)); pap. incl. audio (978-1-59112-449-8(2)) Live Oak Media.

Hudson, Cheryl. Songs I Love to Sing. 2009. 24p. 5.95 (978-1-60349-032-0(9), Marimba Bks.) Just Us Bks., Inc.

Inman, Robert. The Christmas Bus. Baskin, Lyle, illus. 2006. 77p. 19.95 (978-0-9760963-6-8(6)) Novello Festival Pr.

Jeong, SoYun. Lulu the Shy Piglet. Orsolini, Laura, illus. rev. ed. 2014. (MySELF Bookshelf Ser.). (ENG.). 32p. (J). (gr. k-2). pap. 11.94 (978-1-60357-654-3(1)); lib. bdg. 25.27 (978-1-59953-645-3(5)) Norwood Hse. Pr.

Joachimowski, Paula L. Swamp Band Lullaby. 2007. (J). per. 12.99 (978-1-59879-211-9(3)) Lifevest Publishing, Inc.

Jules, Jacqueline. Cantante Súper Estrella. Smith, Kim, illus. 2018. (Sofia Martinez en Español Ser.). (SPA.). 32p. (J). (gr. k-2). lib. bdg. 21.32 (978-1-5158-2452-7(7), 137555, Picture Window Bks.) Capstone.

—Singing Superstar. Smith, Kim, illus. 2016. (Sofia Martinez Ser.). (ENG.). 32p. (J). (gr. k-2). lib. bdg. 21.32 (978-1-4795-8716-2(8), 131110, Picture Window Bks.) Capstone.

Keane, Sarah. Cuckoo, Cuckoo: A Folktale from Mexico, 1 vol. rev. ed. 2013. (Literary Text Ser.). (ENG., Illus.). 24p. (J). (gr. 1-3). pap. 8.99 (978-1-4333-5526-4(4)) Teacher Created Materials, Inc.

Kemnitz, Dianna. Sing with Jack. 2012. 38p. 24.95 (978-1-4626-5656-1(0)) America Star Bks.

Killian, Brandon. The Seesaw Book. 2011. 20p. 12.90 (978-1-4567-4163-1(2)) AuthorHouse.

Lacamara, Laura. Floating on Mama's Song. Morales, Yuyi, illus. 2010. (ENG.). 32p. (J). (gr. -1-2). 17.99 (978-0-06-084368-7(3), Tegen, Katherine Bks) HarperCollins Pubs.

Levine, Gail Carson. Fairest. (J). (gr. 3-7). 2012. (ENG.). 352p. pap. 7.99 (978-0-06-073410-7(8), HarperCollins) 2006. 326p. lib. bdg. 18.89 (978-0-06-073409-1(4)) HarperCollins Pubs.

—Fairest. l.t. rev. ed. 2007. (Literacy Bridge Young Adult Ser.). 349p. (J). (gr. 3-7). 23.95 (978-0-7862-9270-7(9)) Thorndike Pr.

Little Tommy Tucker: 6 Small Books. (gr. k-2). 23.00 (978-0-7635-8502-0(5)) Rigby Education.

Litwin, Eric. The Nuts: Sing & Dance in Your Polka-Dot Pants. Magoon, Scott, illus. 2015. (ENG.). 32p. (J). (gr. -1-3). 18.99 (978-0-316-32250-8(4)) Little, Brown Bks. for Young Readers.

—Pete the Cat & His Four Groovy Buttons. 2013. (CHI & ENG.). (J). (gr. -1-2). (978-957-570-982-2(9)) Eastern Publishing Co., Ltd., The.

Litwin, Eric, ed. Rocking in My School Shoes. 2011. (978-0-545-50106-4(7)) Scholastic, Inc.

Litwin, Eric & Dean, James. I Love My White Shoes. 2010. (Pete the Cat Ser.). pap. (978-0-545-41966-6(2)) Scholastic, Inc.

Litwin, Eric & Dean, Kimberly. Pete the Cat & His Four Groovy Buttons. Dean, James, illus. 2012. (Pete the Cat Ser.). (ENG.). 40p. (J). (gr. -1-2). 19.99 (978-0-06-211058-9(6)); lib. bdg. 18.89 (978-0-06-211059-6(4)) HarperCollins Pubs. (HarperCollins).

—Pete the Cat: I Love My White Shoes. Dean, James, illus. 2010. (Pete the Cat Ser.). (ENG.). 40p. (J). (gr. -1-3). 19.99 (978-0-06-190622-0(0)); lib. bdg. 21.89 (978-0-06-190623-7(9)) HarperCollins Pubs. (HarperCollins).

—Pete the Cat: Rocking in My School Shoes: A Back to School Book for Kids. Dean, James, illus. 2011. (Pete the Cat Ser.). (ENG.). 40p. (J). (gr. -1-3). 19.99 (978-0-06-191024-1(4)); lib. bdg. 17.89 (978-0-06-191025-8(2)) HarperCollins Pubs. (HarperCollins).

Loftin, Nikki. Nightingale's Nest. 2015. 272p. (J). (gr. 3-7). pap. 8.99 (978-1-59514-623-6(7), Razorbill) Penguin Young Readers Group.

Lou, Cindy, illus. & text. The King of Ing Wants to Sing. Lou, Cindy, text. 2008. (J). 12.00 (978-1-935332-00-8(7)) Kite Tales Publishing.

The Magical Singing Wood. 2017. (ENG., Illus.). 176p. (J). 9.00 (978-1-78270-141-5(9)) Award Pubns. Ltd. GBR. Dist: Parkwest Pubns., Inc.

Mandell, Sherri. The Elephant in the Sukkah. Kuman, Ivana, illus. 2019. (ENG.). 32p. (J). (gr. -1-2). 17.99 (978-1-5415-2212-1(5), 74932875-71e9-4511-bcc7-4c7c08af1988); pap. 7.99 (978-1-5415-2213-8(3), 6f257079-ee4c-48b2-872c-f747f0da82da) Lerner Publishing Group. (Kar-Ben Publishing).

Matheson, Anne. I Love to Sing. Cutting, David A., illus. 2014. (ENG.). 32p. (J). (gr. 1-5). 7.99 (978-1-4867-0001-1(2)) Flowerpot Children's Pr. Inc. CAN. Dist: Cardinal Pubs. Group.

Meadows, Daisy. Alyssa the Star-Spotter Fairy. 2013. (Rainbow Magic — the Superstar Fairies Ser.: 6). lib. bdg. 14.75 (978-0-606-31518-0(7)) Turtleback.

—Frankie the Makeup Fairy. 2013. (Rainbow Magic — the Superstar Fairies Ser.: 5). lib. bdg. 14.75 (978-0-606-31517-3(9)) Turtleback.

—Jessie the Lyrics Fairy. 2013. (Rainbow Magic — the Superstar Fairies Ser.: 1). lib. bdg. 14.75 (978-0-606-31513-5(6)) Turtleback.

Millner, Denene. Early Sunday Morning. Brantley-Newton, Vanessa, illus. 2020. (ENG.). 40p. (J). (gr. -1-3). 18.99 (978-1-5344-7653-0(9)) Simon & Schuster, Inc.

Mills, Claudia. Mason Dixon: Fourth-Grade Disasters. Francis, Guy, illus. 2012. (Mason Dixon Ser.: 2). 176p. (J). (gr. 4-7). 6.99 (978-0-375-87275-4(2), Yearling) Random Hse. Children's Bks.

Mitchell, Margaree King. When Grandmama Sings. Ransome, James, illus. 2012. (ENG.). 40p. (J). (gr. k-4). 16.99 (978-0-688-17563-4(5), HarperCollins) HarperCollins Pubs.

Moore, Stephanie Perry. Turn up for Real, No. 3. 2014. (Sharp Sisters Ser.: 3). (ENG.). 168p. (YA). (gr. 6-12). pap. 7.95 (978-1-4677-4490-4(5), de59dd5f-2ef4-4a9e-8592-cfe9541a147a, Darby Creek) Lerner Publishing Group.

Negroni, Jay. Emerald's Flight, 1 vol. 2008. (ENG.). 29p. pap. 24.95 (978-1-60672-863-5(6)) America Star Bks.

Parker, Emma. Karaoke Colin. 2010. (Illus.). 20p. pap. (978-1-877561-34-4(7)) First Edition Ltd.

Paul, Bette. Nurses: Nikki, Barbara & Nick. 2007. 488p. per. (978-1-905665-44-0(X)) Pollinger In Print.

Payne, C. C. Something to Sing About. 2008. (ENG.). 167p. (J). (gr. 4-7). pap. 8.50 (978-0-8028-5344-8(7)) Eerdmans, William B. Publishing Co.

Peschke, Marci. Singing Queen, 1 vol. Mourning, Tuesday, illus. 2012. (Kylie Jean Ser.). (ENG.). 112p. (J). (gr. 1-3). lib. bdg. 22.65 (978-1-4048-6800-7(3), 116242, Picture Window Bks.) Capstone.

Publications International Ltd. Staff, ed. Mickey Mouse Clubhouse: Colors: Sing & Learn. 2010. 12p. (J). bds. 10.98 (978-1-4127-1729-8(9)) Publications International, Ltd.

—Sesame Street: Sing with Elmo, Let's Sing! & Wake up, Elmo! 2011. (J). bds. 14.98 (978-1-4508-0627-5(9)) Phoenix International Publications, Inc.

—9 Button Record Song Dora Superstar. 2011. 18p. 19.98 (978-1-4508-1913-8(3)) Phoenix International Publications, Inc.

Rippin, Sally. The Scary Solo. Spartels, Stephanie, illus. 2012. (Hey Jack! Ser.). (ENG.). 43p. (J). (978-1-61067-136-1(8)) Kane Miller.

Ryan, Tom. Big Time, 1 vol. 2014. (Orca Limelights Ser.). (ENG.). 144p. (J). (gr. 4-7). pap. 9.95 (978-1-4598-0461-6(9)) Orca Bk. Pubs. USA.

Sandusky, Thomas. The Frogs Stopped Singing. 2011. pap. 8.95 (978-0-7414-6450-7(0)) Infinity Publishing.

Santillo, LuAnn. The King. Santillo, LuAnn, ed. 2003. (Half-Pint Kids Readers Ser.). (Illus.). 7p. (J). (gr. -1-1). pap. 1.00 (978-1-59256-050-9(4)) Half-Pint Kids, Inc.

Sewer, Anecia. Why Transfer Day, Anyway? Samuel, Karen, illus. 2007. 16p. (J). 15.99 (978-0-9752986-0-2(7)) Research Institute Pr., The.

Sharpe, Luke. Billy Sure Kid Entrepreneur Is NOT a SINGER! Ross, Graham, illus. 2016. (Billy Sure Kid Entrepreneur Ser.: 9). (ENG.). 160p. (J). (gr. 3-7). pap. 6.99 (978-1-4814-6895-4(2), Simon Spotlight) Simon Spotlight.

Simon, Charnan. Shattered Star. (Surviving Southside Ser.). (ENG.). 104p. (YA). (gr. 6-12). 2011. pap. 7.95 (978-0-7613-6168-8(5), 1ed5f678-1d5d-404f-8a8f-49150e157d71, Darby Creek) 2011. lib. bdg. 27.99 (978-0-7613-6154-1(5), 1a8163e0-50cc-490f-9aa9-787901e7c8fd, Darby Creek) 2015. E-Book 53.32 (978-1-4677-6011-9(0), 9781467760119, Lerner Digital) Lerner Publishing Group.

Snowe, Olivia. The Glass Voice, 1 vol. Lamoreaux, Michelle, illus. 2014. (Twicetold Tales Ser.). (ENG.). 128p. (J). (gr. 3-6). 25.32 (978-1-4342-9148-6(0), 125596, Stone Arch Bks.) Capstone.

Spyri, Johanna. How Wiseli Was Provided For. 2006. 108p. per. 9.95 (978-1-59818-473-0(3)) Aegypan.

Stalling-Patton, Deborah. Shypoodle: Getting to Know You. 2009. 40p. pap. 17.99 (978-1-4389-3899-8(3)) AuthorHouse.

Struyk-Bonn, Chris. Nice Girls Endure. 2016. (ENG.). 256p. (YA). (gr. 9-12). 16.95 (978-1-63079-047-9(8), 131502, Switch Pr.) Capstone.

Tanemura, Arina. Full Moon, Vol. 6 Vol. 6, 7 vols. 2006. (Full Moon Ser.: 6). (ENG., Illus.). 168p. pap. 9.99 (978-1-4215-0397-4(2)) Viz Media.

Tanner, Lian. Battlesong: Book Three in the Icebreaker Trilogy. 2018. (Icebreaker Trilogy Ser.: 3). (ENG.). 304p. (J). pap. 15.99 (978-1-250-15871-0(0), 900185527) Square Fish.

Taylor, Helen. Kakapo Dance. 2019. 14p. (J). (— 1). bds. 10.99 (978-0-14-377222-4(8)) Penguin Group New Zealand, Ltd. NZL. Dist: Independent Pubs. Group.

Thomas Nelson Publishing Staff. The Pirates Who Don't Do Anything - Veggietales Movie: Squawk-Along Songs & Games. 2008. (Adventures in Odyssey Activity Pack Ser.). 48p. (J). pap. 12.99 (978-1-4003-1235-1(3)) Nelson, Thomas Inc.

Thompson, Carol. Sing. Thompson, Carol, illus. 2018. (Amazing Me! Ser.: 4). (Illus.). 12p. (J). (gr. k-k). spiral bd. (978-1-84643-962-9(0)) Child's Play International Ltd.

Van Dusen, Chris. Hattie & Hudson. Van Dusen, Chris, illus. 2017. (ENG., Illus.). 40p. (J). (gr. -1-3). 17.99 (978-0-7636-6545-6(2)) Candlewick Pr.

Walker, Anna. I Love to Sing. Walker, Anna, illus. 2011. (ENG., Illus.). 32p. (J). (gr. -1-1). 9.99 (978-1-4169-8322-4(8), Simon & Schuster Bks. For Young Readers) Simon & Schuster Bks. For Young Readers.

Walker, Sally M. Freedom Song: The Story of Henry Box Brown. Qualls, Sean, illus. 2012. (ENG.). 40p. (J). (gr. -1-3). 18.99 (978-0-06-058310-1(X), HarperCollins) HarperCollins Pubs.

Weinheimer, Kim, illus. & as told by. The Bear Song. Weinheimer, Kim, as told by. 2012. 24p. pap. 9.95 *(978-1-935752-30-1(8))* Bryce Cullen Publishing.

Wells, Tina. Mackenzie Blue, 1. 2013. (Mackenzie Blue Ser.: 1). (ENG.). 224p. (J). (gr. 3-7). pap. 6.99 *(978-0-06-158310-0(3),* HarperCollins) HarperCollins Pubs.

West, Tracey. Song of the Poison Dragon. 2016. (Dragon Masters Ser.: 5). lib. bdg. 14.75 *(978-0-606-38808-5(7))* Turtleback.

—Song of the Poison Dragon: a Branches Book (Dragon Masters #5) Jones, Damien, illus. 2016. (Dragon Masters Ser.: 5). (ENG.). 96p. (J). (gr. 1-3). pap. 4.99 *(978-0-545-91387-4(X))* Scholastic, Inc.

—Song of the Poison Dragon: a Branches Book (Dragon Masters #5) (Library Edition) Jones, Damien, illus. 2016. (Dragon Masters Ser.: 5). (ENG.). 96p. (J). (gr. 1-3). 15.99 *(978-0-545-91388-1(8))* Scholastic, Inc.

Winston, Sherri. The Sweetest Sound. 2018. (ENG.). 288p. (J). (gr. 3-7). pap. 7.99 *(978-0-316-30293-7(7))* Little, Brown Bks. for Young Readers.

Woodward, Caroline. Singing Away the Dark. Morstad, Julie, illus. 2017. 44p. (J). (gr. -1-3). 16.95 *(978-1-77229-019-6(X))* Simply Read Bks. CAN. Dist: Ingram Publisher Services.

Wooster, Devin Ann. Sing It Out (Barbie in Rock 'n Royals) 2015. (Step into Reading Ser.). (ENG., Illus.). 24p. (J). (gr. -1-1). 4.99 *(978-0-553-52438-3(0),* Random Hse. Bks. for Young Readers) Random Hse. Children's Bks.

Wright, Bil. When the Black Girl Sings. 2009. (ENG.). 272p. (YA). (gr. 7). mass mkt. 7.99 *(978-1-4169-4003-6(0),* Simon Pulse) Simon Pulse.

Zimmer, Frank. Bird Singing Contest. 2008. 28p. pap. 13.99 *(978-1-4343-7971-9(X))* AuthorHouse.

Zion, Gene. Harry & the Lady Next Door. Graham, Margaret Bloy, illus. 2003. (I Can Read Level 1 Ser.). (ENG.). 64p. (J). (gr. -1-3). pap. 4.99 *(978-0-06-444008-0(7),* HarperCollins) HarperCollins Pubs.

—Harry & the Lady Next Door. Graham, Margaret Bloy, illus. 2004. (I Can Read Bks.). 64p. (gr. -1-3). 14.00 *(978-0-7569-3087-5(1))* Perfection Learning Corp.

—Harry & the Lady Next Door. 2003. (I Can Read! Level 1 Ser.). (J). (gr. k-3). lib. bdg. 13.55 *(978-0-8085-2612-4(X))* Turtleback.

SINGING GAMES

Albrecht, Sally K., et al. Rhythm All Around: 10 Rhythmic Songs for Singing & Learning (Teacher's Handbook) 2007. (ENG.). 72p. pap. 29.95 *(978-0-7390-4643-2(8))* Alfred Publishing Co., Inc.

Baxter, Nicola. Head, Shoulders, Knees & Toes & Other Action Rhymes. Buckingham, Gabriella, illus. 2013. 16p. (J). (gr. -1-6). bds. 7.99 *(978-1-84322-829-5(7),* Armadillo) Anness Publishing GBR. Dist: National Bk. Network.

Beausoliel, Loyan & Wells, Leah. Games That Sing: 25 Activities to Keep Children on Their Toes. 2011. (Illus.). 52p. pap. 16.95 incl. audio compact disk *(978-1-4291-2116-3(5))* Heritage Music Pr.

Court, Shirley, et al. Singing Sherlock Vol. 2: The Complete Singing Resorce for Primary Schools. 2004. (ENG.). 88p. pap. 79.00 incl. audio compact disk *(978-0-85162-353-5(0),* 48012149) Leonard, Hal Corp.

Key Porter Books, creator. Music Play: Inspired Ways to Explore Music. rev. ed. 2007. (Gymboree Play & Music Ser.). (ENG., Illus.). 36p. (J). (gr. -1-2). bds. *(978-1-55263-964-1(9))* Magma.

Kubler, Annie. Head, Shoulders, Knees & Toes. (Illus.). 10p. (J). 2004. (ENG & GUJ.). bds. *(978-1-84444-150-1(4))* 2004. (ENG & PAN., bds. *(978-1-84444-151-8(2))* 2004. (ENG & POR., bds. *(978-1-84444-152-5(0))* 2004. (ENG & SOM., bds. *(978-1-84444-153-2(9))* 2004. (ENG & SPA., bds. *(978-1-84444-154-9(7))* 2004. (ENG & TAM., bds. *(978-1-84444-155-6(5))* 2004. (ENG & TUR., bds. *(978-1-84444-156-3(3))* 2004. (FRE & ENG., bds. *(978-1-84444-149-5(0))* 2004. (ENG & PER., bds. *(978-1-84444-148-8(2))* 2004. (ENG & CHI., bds. *(978-1-84444-147-1(4))* 2004. (ENG & ARA., bds. *(978-1-84444-145-7(8))* 2004. (ENG & ALB., bds. *(978-1-84444-144-0(X))* 2003. (BEN & ENG., bds. *(978-1-84444-146-4(6))* Mantra Lingua.

Kubler, Annie, illus. The Wheels on the Bus Go Round & Round. 2003. (Classic Books with Holes 8x8 Ser.). (ENG.). 16p. (J). *(978-0-85953-136-8(8))* Child's Play International Ltd.

Warhola, James. If You're Happy & You Know It. Geist, Ken, ed. Warhola, James, illus. 2007. (ENG., Illus.). 32p. (J). (gr. -1-k). 16.99 *(978-0-439-72766-2(9),* Orchard Bks.) Scholastic, Inc.

SINGLE-PARENT FAMILIES

Apel, Melanie Ann. Let's Talk about Living with Your Single Dad. 2009. (Let's Talk Library). 24p. (gr. 2-3). 42.50 *(978-1-60853-445-6(6),* PowerKids Pr.) Rosen Publishing Group, Inc., The.

Hadley, Margie. Looking Back in the Mirror. 2013. 36p. pap. 16.95 *(978-1-63004-529-6(2))* America Star Bks.

Haerens, Margaret, ed. Single-Parent Families, 1 vol. 2016. (Opposing Viewpoints Ser.). (ENG.). 272p. (gr. 10-12). 50.43 *(978-0-7377-7528-0(9),* aca83608-4acd-44ee-b6d1-7e8524c24e96); pap. 34.80 *(978-0-7377-7529-7(7),* 445b4629-f5b3-45f5-bb0b-64d4f59d8976) Greenhaven Publishing LLC. (Greenhaven Publishing).

Herbert, Denis & Silver, Joanne. Complément éducatif: Mon Enfance Lilloise Racontée à Ma Fille: Récits D'antan (1950 à 1955) 2010. *(978-0-9819417-4-5(5))* Beach Lloyd Pubs., LLC.

Levete, Sarah. The Hidden Story of Family Breakups, 1 vol., 1. 2013. (Undercover Story Ser.). (ENG.). 48p. (J). (gr. 5-5). 34.41 *(978-1-4777-2801-7(5),* 150c29c4-31d0-4ef5-b91f-7a8a0862dfa5, Rosen Reference) Rosen Publishing Group, Inc., The.

—Taking Action Against Family Breakups, 1 vol. 2009. (Taking Action Ser.). (ENG.). 48p. (YA). (gr. 5-6). pap. 12.75 *(978-1-61532-311-1(2),* e52c35ba-08d7-430a-beec-71edbca54dcf, Rosen Reference); lib. bdg. 34.47 *(978-1-61532-310-4(4),* 9960207d-3ce6-4764-9648-6e42d5be17f8) Rosen Publishing Group, Inc., The.

Levins, Sandra. Was It the Chocolate Pudding? A Story for Little Kids about Divorce. Langdo, Bryan, illus. 2005. 40p. (J). (gr. -1-3). per. 9.95 *(978-1-59147-309-1(8),* Magination Pr.) American Psychological Assn.

Nielsen, Susin. Word Nerd. 2008. (ENG.). 256p. (J). (gr. 4-7). 18.95 *(978-0-88776-875-0(X),* Tundra Bks.) Tundra Bks. CAN. Dist: Penguin Random Hse. LLC.

Poole, H. W. Single-Parent Families, Vol. 12. 2016. (Families Today Ser.). (Illus.). 48p. (J). (gr. 5). 20.95 *(978-1-4222-3623-9(4))* Mason Crest.

Schuette, Sarah L. Single-Parent Families, 1 vol. 2010. (My Family Ser.). (ENG.). 24p. (J). (gr. -1-2). pap. 6.29 *(978-1-4296-4838-7(4),* 112818); (gr. -1-2). lib. bdg. 24.65 *(978-1-4296-3980-4(6),* 102589); (gr. k-1). pap. 38.74 *(978-1-4296-5160-8(1),* 15192, Pebble) Capstone.

Simons, Rae. Single Parents. 2010. (Changing Face of Modern Families Ser.). (Illus.). 64p. (YA). (gr. 6-18). 22.95 *(978-1-4222-1493-0(1))* Mason Crest.

Tomories, K. G. Someone Special for You to Know. 2010. 28p. pap. 13.99 *(978-1-4389-9651-6(9))* AuthorHouse.

Tsioumanis, Marina. Mum & Dad Are Separating: A Practical Resource for Separating Families & Family Therapy Professionals, 2 vols. 2017. (ENG., Illus.). 176p. (C). pap. 51.95 *(978-0-86388-669-0(8),* Y329910) Routledge.

SINGLE-PARENT FAMILIES—FICTION

Acampora, Paul. Confusion Is Nothing New. 2018. (ENG.). 192p. (J). (gr. 3-7). 16.99 *(978-1-338-20999-0(X),* Scholastic Pr.) Scholastic, Inc.

—Rachel Spinelli Punched Me in the Face. 2013. (ENG.). 192p. (J). (gr. 8-12). pap. 14.99 *(978-1-250-01669-0(X),* 900087083) Square Fish.

Aceves, Fred. The Closest I've Come. (ENG.). (YA). (gr. 9). 2020. 336p. pap. 11.99 *(978-0-06-248854-1(6))* 2017. 320p. 17.99 *(978-0-06-248853-4(8))* HarperCollins Pubs. (HarperTeen).

Allen, Kate. The Line Tender. 2019. (Illus.). 384p. (J). (gr. 5). 17.99 *(978-0-7352-3160-3(5),* Dutton Books for Young Readers) Penguin Young Readers Group.

Almond, David. My Name Is Mina. 2012. (ENG.). 304p. (J). (gr. 6-8). 21.19 *(978-0-375-98964-3(1),* Yearling) Random Hse. Children's Bks.

Amato, Mary. Guitar Notes. 2014. (ENG., Illus.). 320p. (YA). (gr. 7-12). pap. 10.99 *(978-1-60684-503-5(9),* 012af6c8-2b15-4576-82cf-476ac42f8d26, Carolrhoda Lab™) Lerner Publishing Group.

—Invisible Lines. Caparó, Antonio Javier, illus. 2011. (ENG.). 336p. (gr. 4-6). lib. bdg. 22.44 *(978-1-60684-043-6(6))* Farshore GBR. Dist: Children's Plus, Inc.

Arnold, Elana K. Infandous. 2015. (ENG.). 200p. (YA). (gr. 8-12). 18.99 *(978-1-4677-3849-1(2),* 5f116506-df41-46d9-aaec-833557c7c676, Carolrhoda Lab™) Lerner Publishing Group.

Atkinson, Elizabeth. I, Emma Freke. 2012. (ENG.). 240p. (J). (gr. 4-7). 10.99 *(978-0-7613-8500-4(2),* 4c09ccbf-9456-48aa-8415-47bb3cfd891b, Carolrhoda Bks.) Lerner Publishing Group.

Baragrey, Wen Jane. What Goes Up. 2018. 224p. (J). (gr. 3-7). 16.99 *(978-1-5247-6581-1(3),* Random Hse. Bks. for Young Readers) Random Hse. Children's Bks.

Barnholdt, Lauren. Girl Meets Ghost. 2013. (Girl Meets Ghost Ser.: 1). (ENG.). 240p. (J). (gr. 4-9). pap. 7.99 *(978-1-4424-2146-2(0),* Aladdin) Simon & Schuster Children's Publishing.

Barrett, Tracy. Freefall Summer. 2018. 272p. (J). (gr. 7). lib. bdg. 17.99 *(978-1-58089-801-0(7),* Charlesbridge Teen) Charlesbridge Publishing, Inc.

Bauer, Joan. Close to Famous. 2012. (ENG.). 272p. (J). (gr. 5-8). 8.99 *(978-0-14-242017-1(4),* Puffin Books) Penguin Young Readers Group.

Benwell, Sarah. The Last Leaves Falling. 2015. (ENG., Illus.). 368p. (YA). (gr. 9). 17.99 *(978-1-4814-3065-4(3))* Simon & Schuster Children's Publishing.

Binns, Barbara. Courage. 2018. (ENG.). 368p. (J). (gr. 3-7). 16.99 *(978-0-06-256165-7(0),* HarperCollins) HarperCollins Pubs.

Birdsall, Jeanne. The Penderwicks: A Summer Tale of Four Sisters, Two Rabbits, & a Very Interesting Boy. (Penderwicks Ser.: 1). (ENG.). (J). (gr. 3-7). 2007. 288p. 8.99 *(978-0-440-42047-7(4),* Yearling) 2005. 272p. 17.99 *(978-0-375-83143-0(6),* Knopf Bks. for Young Readers) Random Hse. Children's Bks.

—The Penderwicks: A Summer Tale of Four Sisters, Two Rabbits & a Very Interesting Boy. 2007. (Penderwicks (Hardback) Ser.). 262p. (gr. 3-7). 18.00 *(978-0-7569-7798-6(3))* Perfection Learning Corp.

—The Penderwicks: A Summer Tale of Four Sisters, Two Rabbits, & a Very Interesting Boy. 2007. (Penderwicks Ser.: 1). (Illus.). 262p. (gr. 4-7). lib. bdg. 18.40 *(978-1-4177-7275-9(1))* Turtleback.

—The Penderwicks: A Summer Tale of Four Sisters, Two Rabbits & a Very Interesting Boy. 2009. 8.80 *(978-0-7848-2826-7(1),* Everbind) Marco Bk. Co.

—The Penderwicks: A Summer Tale of Four Sisters, Two Rabbits & a Very Interesting Boy. Lt. ed. 2006. (Penderwick Ser.). 304p. (J). (gr. 3-7). 23.95 *(978-0-7862-8897-7(3))* Thorndike Pr.

—The Penderwicks in Spring. 2015. (Penderwicks Ser.: 4). (ENG.). 352p. (J). (gr. 3-7). 16.99 *(978-0-375-87077-4(6),* Knopf Bks. for Young Readers) Random Hse. Children's Bks.

—The Penderwicks on Gardam Street. 2011. (Playaway Children Ser.). (J). (gr. 3-6). 44.99 *(978-1-61707-435-6(7))* Findaway World, LLC.

—The Penderwicks on Gardam Street. 2010. (Penderwicks Ser.: 2). (ENG.). 336p. (J). (gr. 3-7). 8.99 *(978-0-440-42203-7(5),* Yearling) Random Hse. Children's Bks.

—The Penderwicks on Gardam Street. 2010. (Penderwicks Ser.: 2). lib. bdg. 18.40 *(978-0-606-14418-6(8))* Turtleback.

Black, Chuck. Rise of the Fallen: Wars of the Realm, Book 2. 2015. (Wars of the Realm Ser.: 2). (ENG.). 320p. (YA). (gr. 7). pap. 13.00 *(978-1-60142-504-1(X),* Multnomah Bks.) Crown Publishing Group, The.

Black, Holly & DiTerlizzi, Tony. The Field Guide. DiTerlizzi, Tony, illus. movie tie-in ed. 2008. (Spiderwick Chronicles: 1). (ENG., Illus.). 128p. (J). (gr. 2-5). 10.99 *(978-1-4169-5017-2(6),* Simon & Schuster Bks. For Young Readers) Simon & Schuster Bks. For Young Readers.

Blecher, Jennifer. Out of Place. Liddiard, Merrilee, illus. 2019. (ENG.). 304p. (J). (gr. 3-7). 16.99 *(978-0-06-274859-1(9),* Greenwillow Bks.) HarperCollins Pubs.

Bledsoe, Lucy Jane. Running Wild. 2019. 224p. (YA). (gr. 4-7). 17.99 *(978-0-8234-4363-5(9),* Margaret Ferguson Books) Holiday Hse., Inc.

Blejwas, Emily. Like Nothing Amazing Ever Happened. 2020. (ENG.). 224p. (J). (gr. 4-7). 19.99 *(978-1-9848-4849-9(6),* Delacorte Bks. for Young Readers) Random Hse. Children's Bks.

Blitt, Natalie. The Truth about Leaving. 2019. (ENG.). 304p. (YA). pap. 12.99 *(978-1-948705-09-7(5))* Amberjack Publishing Co.

Bodeen, S. A. The Gardener. 2011. (ENG.). 256p. (YA). (gr. 7-12). pap. 11.99 *(978-0-312-65942-4(3),* 900070540) Square Fish.

Bryant, Jen. Kaleidoscope Eyes. 2010. 272p. (J). (gr. 3-7). 7.99 *(978-0-440-42190-0(X),* Yearling) Random Hse. Children's Bks.

Caletti, Deb. The Fortunes of Indigo Skye. (ENG.). (YA). (gr. 7). 2009. 320p. pap. 9.99 *(978-1-4169-1008-4(5))* 2008. 304p. 15.99 *(978-1-4169-1007-7(7))* Simon Pulse. (Simon Pulse).

Callender, Kacen. This Is Kind of an Epic Love Story. 2019. (ENG.). 304p. (YA). (gr. 9). pap. 10.99 *(978-0-06-282023-5(0),* Balzer & Bray) HarperCollins Pubs.

Callender, Kheryn. This Is Kind of an Epic Love Story. 2018. (ENG.). 304p. (YA). (gr. 9). 17.99 *(978-0-06-282022-8(2),* Balzer & Bray) HarperCollins Pubs.

Chen, Justina. Nothing but the Truth (and a Few White Lies) 2007. (Justina Chen Novel Ser.). (ENG.). 256p. (J). (gr. 7-17). per. 15.99 *(978-0-316-01131-0(2))* Little, Brown Bks. for Young Readers.

Cherry, Alison. Ella Unleashed. 2018. (ENG., Illus.). 208p. (J). (gr. 3-7). 17.99 *(978-1-5344-1212-5(3),* Aladdin) Simon & Schuster Children's Publishing.

Citra, Becky. Duke's Den, 1 vol. 2016. (ENG.). 208p. (J). (gr. 4-7). pap. 10.95 *(978-1-4598-0901-7(7))* Orca Bk. Pubs. USA.

Cline-Ransome, Lesa. Finding Langston. (Finding Langston Trilogy Ser.). 112p. (J). (gr. 3-7). 2020. pap. 7.99 *(978-0-8234-4582-0(8))* 2018. 16.99 *(978-0-8234-3960-7(7))* Holiday Hse., Inc.

Cochrane, Mick. Fitz. 2013. (ENG.). 192p. (YA). (gr. 7). pap. 8.99 *(978-0-375-84611-3(5),* Ember) Random Hse. Children's Bks.

Colbert, Brandy. Finding Yvonne. 2018. (ENG.). 288p. (YA). (gr. 9-17). 17.99 *(978-0-316-34905-5(4))* Little, Brown Bks. for Young Readers.

Collins, Amberly & Collins, Brandilyn. Final Touch, 1 vol. 2010. (Rayne Tour Ser.). (ENG.). 224p. (YA). (gr. 8-11). pap. 9.99 *(978-0-310-71933-5(X))* Zondervan.

Conway, Celeste. The Goodbye Time. 2011. (ENG.). 112p. (J). (gr. 2-4). lib. bdg. 18.69 *(978-0-385-90540-4(8),* Delacorte Pr.) Random Hse. Children's Bks.

Coolidge, Susan. What Katy Did. 2013. (ENG., Illus.). 200p. (J). 15.00 *(978-1-84135-843-7(6))* Award Pubns. Ltd. GBR. Dist: Parkwest Pubns., Inc.

—What Katy Did. 2012. 246p. pap. *(978-1-78139-262-1(5))* Benediction Classics.

—What Katy Did. 2017. (ENG., Illus.). (J). (gr. 4-6). pap. 9.90 *(978-1-366-50696-2(0))* Blurb, Inc.

—What Katy Did. 2016. (ENG., Illus.). (J). 26.95 *(978-1-359-87966-0(8))* 2015. (ENG., Illus.). (J). (gr. 2-4). 25.95 *(978-1-297-62709-5(1))* 2012. 300p. pap. 29.75 *(978-1-286-00091-5(2))* 2012. 302p. pap. 29.75 *(978-1-286-07372-8(3))* 2011. 290p. (gr. 3-7). pap. 28.75 *(978-1-179-65265-8(7))* 2010. (ENG.). 282p. (gr. 3-7). pap. 28.75 *(978-1-177-27477-7(9))* 2010. 302p. pap. 29.75 *(978-1-145-74830-9(9))* 2008. 164p. (gr. 4-7). 25.99 *(978-0-554-28634-1(3))* 2007. (ENG.). 144p. pap. 18.99 *(978-1-4346-5943-9(7))* 2007. (ENG.). 160p. pap. 21.99 *(978-1-4346-5944-6(5))* Creative Media Partners, LLC.

—What Katy Did. 2007. (ENG.). 148p. per. *(978-1-4065-1527-5(2))* Dodo Pr.

—What Katy Did. (Dover Children's Evergreen Classics Ser.). (ENG.). (J). 2018. 176p. pap. 5.99 *(978-0-486-82252-5(4),* 822524) 2006. (Illus.). 160p. (gr. 3-8). per. 6.95 *(978-0-486-44760-5(X))* Dover Pubns., Inc.

—What Katy Did. 2007. (ENG.). 104p. per. *(978-1-4068-4855-7(7))* Echo Library.

—What Katy Did. 2010. (Illus.). 92p. (gr. 3-7). pap. 19.99 *(978-1-153-74507-9(0))* 2009. 104p. pap. 6.40 *(978-0-217-53637-0(9))* General Bks. LLC.

—What Katy Did. 2010. 132p. pap. *(978-1-4076-5115-6(3))* HardPr.

—What Katy Did. Ledyard, Addie, illus. 284p. 2010. 35.16 *(978-1-163-85079-4(9))* 2010. pap. 23.16 *(978-1-163-77965-1(2))* 2007. 43.95 *(978-0-548-53870-8(0))* 2007. per. 28.95 *(978-0-548-48700-6(6))* Kessinger Publishing, LLC.

—What Katy Did. 2013. (Vintage Children's Classics Ser.). (Illus.). 256p. (J). (gr. 4-7). pap. 12.99 *(978-0-09-957312-8(1))* Penguin Random Hse. GBR. Dist: Independent Pubs. Group.

—What Katy Did. 2007. (ENG.). 192p. pap. 12.45 *(978-1-60424-403-8(8),* Bk. Jungle) Standard Publications, Inc.

—What Katy Did. 144p. 2018. (ENG., Illus.). (J). 19.99 *(978-1-5154-3178-7(9))* 2010. pap. 4.99 *(978-1-61720-100-4(6))* Wilder Pubns., Corp.

—What Katy Did. 2011. 162p. (gr. 3-7). pap. *(978-3-8424-6664-7(1))* tredition Verlag.

—What Katy Did: Illustrated by Susan Hellard. Hellard, Susan, illus. 2016. (Alma Junior Classics Ser.). (ENG.). 246p. (J). pap. 9.99 *(978-1-84749-607-2(5),* 331109) Alma Classics GBR. Dist: Bloomsbury Publishing Plc.

Coolidge, Susan & Ledyard, Addie. What Katy Did. 2010. (ENG.). 292p. pap. 28.75 *(978-1-172-34659-2(3))* Creative Media Partners, LLC.

Cotugno, Katie. How to Love. (ENG.). 416p. (YA). (gr. 9). 2020. pap. 10.99 *(978-0-06-296394-9(5))* 2015. pap. 9.99 *(978-0-06-221636-6(8))* HarperCollins Pubs. (Balzer & Bray).

Couloumbis, Audrey. Jake. 2011. (ENG.). 176p. (J). (gr. 3-7). pap. 6.99 *(978-0-375-85631-0(5),* Yearling) Random Hse. Children's Bks.

Courgeon, Remi. Feather. Bedrick, Claudia Zoe, tr. 2017. (ENG., Illus.). 36p. (J). (gr. k-4). 17.95 *(978-1-59270-210-7(4))* Enchanted Lion Bks., LLC.

Creedle, Laura. The Love Letters of Abelard & Lily. (ENG.). 352p. (YA). (gr. 7). 2019. pap. 10.99 *(978-1-328-60366-1(0),* 1732073) 2017. 17.99 *(978-0-544-93205-0(6),* 1658576) HarperCollins Pubs. (Clarion Bks.).

Curtin, Ann. Dreamcatcher. 2015. 201p. (YA). *(978-1-61271-246-8(0))* Zumaya Pubns. LLC.

Davis, Terrance. Mom & Me. 2012. 24p. (-18). pap. 24.95 *(978-1-4626-9502-7(7))* America Star Bks.

Day, Karen. A Million Miles from Boston. 2012. (ENG.). 224p. (J). (gr. 4-6). lib. bdg. 21.19 *(978-0-385-90763-7(X),* Lamb, Wendy Bks.) Random Hse. Children's Bks.

Dee, Barbara. Just Another Day in My Insanely Real Life. 2007. (Mix Ser.). (ENG.). 256p. (J). (gr. 4-8). pap. 8.99 *(978-1-4169-4739-4(6),* Aladdin) Simon & Schuster Children's Publishing.

—Maybe He Just Likes You. 2019. (ENG., Illus.). 304p. (J). (gr. 4-8). 19.99 *(978-1-5344-3237-6(X),* Simon & Schuster/Paula Wiseman Bks.) Simon & Schuster/Paula Wiseman Bks.

Dellaira, Ava. In Search of Us. 2020. (ENG.). 416p. (YA). pap. 10.99 *(978-1-250-29461-6(4),* 900163346) Square Fish.

Deriso, Christine Hurley. Talia Talk. 2009. 184p. (J). pap. *(978-0-375-84496-6(1),* Delacorte Pr) Random House Publishing Group.

Detweiler, Katelyn. The Undoing of Thistle Tate. 2019. (ENG.). 272p. (YA). (gr. 9). 17.99 *(978-0-8234-4239-3(X),* Margaret Ferguson Books) Holiday Hse., Inc.

Deuker, Carl. Runner. 2007. (ENG.). 224p. (YA). (gr. 7-12). pap. 15.99 *(978-0-618-73505-1(4),* 410112, Clarion Bks.) HarperCollins Pubs.

Doyle McQuerry, Maureen. Between Before & After, 1 vol. 2019. (ENG., Illus.). 304p. (YA). pap. 9.99 *(978-0-310-76728-2(8))* Blink.

Easton, Kelly. To Be Mona. 2008. (ENG.). 224p. (YA). (gr. 7). 16.99 *(978-1-4169-0054-2(3),* McElderry, Margaret K. Bks.) McElderry, Margaret K. Bks.

Eulberg, Elizabeth. Past Perfect Life. 2019. (ENG.). 336p. (YA). 18.99 *(978-1-5476-0092-2(6),* 900198456, Bloomsbury Young Adult) Bloomsbury Publishing USA.

Falkoff, Michelle. Questions I Want to Ask You. 2018. (ENG.). 320p. (YA). (gr. 9). 17.99 *(978-0-06-268023-5(4),* HarperCollins) HarperCollins Pubs.

Farish, Terry. Either the Beginning or the End of the World. 2015. (ENG.). 200p. (YA). (gr. 8-12). 18.99 *(978-1-4677-7483-3(9),* b2cbce4f-14d6-4326-9b41-74047d9506c0); E-Book 29.32 *(978-1-4677-8813-7(9))* Lerner Publishing Group. (Carolrhoda Lab™).

Fenn, Jennifer. Flight Risk: A Novel. 2017. (ENG.). 384p. (YA). 21.99 *(978-1-62672-760-1(0),* 900172860) Roaring Brook Pr.

Ferguson, Alane. The Angel of Death. 2008. (Forensic Mystery Ser.). 258p. 17.00 *(978-0-7569-8929-3(9))* Perfection Learning Corp.

Ferruolo, Jeanne Zulick. Ruby in the Sky. 2020. (ENG.). 320p. (J). pap. 9.99 *(978-1-250-23329-5(1),* 900188386) Square Fish.

Fogelin, Adrian. The Real Question, 1 vol. 2009. 256p. (YA). (gr. 7-9). pap. 7.95 *(978-1-56145-501-0(6))* Peachtree Publishing Co. Inc.

Frank, Lucy. Lucky Stars. 2014. (ENG.). 304p. (J). (gr. 5-9). pap. 14.99 *(978-1-4814-2901-6(9),* Atheneum Bks. for Young Readers) Simon & Schuster Children's Publishing.

Friend, Natasha. For Keeps. 2011. (YA). (ENG.). 256p. (gr. 8-12). 22.44 *(978-0-670-01190-2(8));* 272p. (gr. 7-18). 7.99 *(978-0-14-241846-8(3),* Speak) Penguin Young Readers Group.

Fuqua, Jonathon Scott. The Reappearance of Sam Webber. 2010. (ENG.). 250p. (J). pap. 12.95 *(978-1-890862-60-2(6),* cb4b7efc-fa7c-4a12-9a81-b27771d1d626) Bancroft Pr.

Gantos, Jack. Joey Pigza Swallowed the Key. 2009. 8.30 *(978-0-7848-3764-1(3));* 8.32 *(978-0-7848-1771-1(5))* Marco Bk. Co. (Everbind).

—Joey Pigza Swallowed the Key. unabr. ed. 2004. (Joey Pigza Ser.: Bk. 1). 154p. (J). (gr. 5-9). pap. 29.00 incl. audio *(978-0-8072-8166-6(2),* YA120SP, Listening Library) Random Hse. Audio Publishing Group.

—Joey Pigza Swallowed the Key. 2007. (Joey Pigza Ser.: 1). (J). 1.25 *(978-1-4193-6006-0(X))* Recorded Bks., Inc.

—Joey Pigza Swallowed the Key. 2014. (Joey Pigza Ser.: 1). (ENG.). 176p. (J). (gr. 5-9). pap. 7.99 *(978-1-250-06168-3(7),* 900142030) Square Fish.

—Joey Pigza Swallowed the Key. 2014. (Joey Pigza Ser.: 1). (J). lib. bdg. 18.40 *(978-0-606-23019-3(X))* Turtleback.

Gemeinhart, Dan. The Remarkable Journey of Coyote Sunrise. 2019. (Coyote Sunrise Ser.). (ENG.). 352p. (J). 16.99 *(978-1-250-19670-5(1),* 900194230, Holt, Henry & Co. Bks. For Young Readers) Holt, Henry & Co.

Gervay, Susanne. Being Jack. Wilcox, Cathy, illus. (J). 2016. (ENG.). 192p. pap. 5.99 *(978-1-61067-379-2(4))* 2015. 167p. *(978-1-61067-455-3(3))* Kane Miller.

Gibaldi, Lauren. This Tiny Perfect World. 2019. (ENG.). 320p. (YA). (gr. 8). pap. 10.99 *(978-0-06-249008-7(7),* HarperTeen) HarperCollins Pubs.

Gilbert, Melissa. Daisy & Josephine. Kuo, Julia, illus. 2014. (ENG.). 32p. (J). (gr. -1-3). 17.99 *(978-1-4424-4578-9(5),* Simon & Schuster/Paula Wiseman Bks.) Simon & Schuster/Paula Wiseman Bks.

Glasgow, Kathleen. How to Make Friends with the Dark. (ENG.). (YA). (gr. 9). 2020. 448p. pap. 12.99 *(978-1-101-93478-4(6),* Ember) 2019. 432p. 18.99 *(978-1-101-93475-3(1),* Delacorte Pr.) 2019. 432p. lib. bdg. 21.99 *(978-1-101-93477-7(8),* Delacorte Pr.) Random Hse. Children's Bks.

Goldstein, Meredith. Chemistry Lessons. 2018. (ENG.). 256p. (YA). (gr. 7). 17.99 *(978-1-328-76464-5(8),* 1681106, Clarion Bks.) HarperCollins Pubs.

Goode, John. Going the Distance. (YA). 2016. (ENG., Illus.). (gr. 8-12). 24.99 *(978-1-63533-020-5(3),* Harmony Ink Pr.) 2015. 190p. lib. bdg. *(978-1-63216-620-3(8))* Dreamspinner Pr.

Grabenstein, J. J. & Grabenstein, Chris. Shine! 2019. (Illus.). 224p. (J). (gr. 3-7). 16.99 *(978-1-5247-1766-7(5),* Random Hse. Bks. for Young Readers) Random Hse. Children's Bks.

Graff, Keir. The Phantom Tower. 2021. 288p. (J). (gr. 3-7). 8.99 *(978-1-5247-3954-6(5),* Puffin Books) Penguin Young Readers Group.
Green, Julia. Hunter's Heart. 2007. 264p. (YA). (gr. 7-12). 16.95 *(978-0-7613-9493-8(1),* Carolrhoda Bks.) Lerner Publishing Group.
Green, Tim. The Big Time. 2010. (Football Genius Ser.: 4). (ENG.). 288p. (J). (gr. 3-7). 16.99 *(978-0-06-168619-1(0),* HarperCollins) HarperCollins Pubs.
—The Big Time: A Football Genius Novel. 2011. (Football Genius Ser.: 4). (ENG.). 304p. (J). (gr. 3-7). pap. 7.99 *(978-0-06-168621-4(2),* HarperCollins) HarperCollins Pubs.
Griffin, Paul. Saving Marty. 2018. (ENG.). 224p. (J). (gr. 5-9). 8.99 *(978-0-399-53908-4(5),* Puffin Books) Penguin Young Readers Group.
Grindele, Jenny. Josh, the Jock of High School. 2005. 48p. pap. 16.95 *(978-1-4137-6950-0(0))* America Star Bks.
Grindley, Sally. Bravo, Max! Ross, Tony, illus. 2007. (ENG.). 160p. (J). (gr. 1-4). pap. 8.99 *(978-1-4169-3645-9(9),* Simon & Schuster/Paula Wiseman Bks.) Simon & Schuster/Paula Wiseman Bks.
Hahn, Mary Downing. Witch Catcher. 2011. (ENG.). 240p. (J). (gr. 5-7). pap. 7.99 *(978-0-547-57714-2(1),* 1458462, Clarion Bks.) HarperCollins Pubs.
Halse, Leif. The Boys from Vangen: Vangsgutane. Huntrods, Alexander Knud, tr. Nilssen, Jens R., illus. 2009. (ENG & NNO.). 176p. (J). 19.95 *(978-0-9760541-5-3(9))* Astri My Astri Publishing.
Hand, Cynthia. Unearthly. 2011. (Unearthly Ser.: 1). (ENG.). 464p. (YA). (gr. 8). pap. 9.99 *(978-0-06-199617-7(3),* HarperTeen) HarperCollins Pubs.
Harrell, Mary. The Mythmaker. 2018. (YA). pap. *(978-1-63051-500-3(0));* (ENG., Illus.). 148p. (J). pap. 14.95 *(978-1-63051-503-4(5))* Chiron Pubns.
Hayes, Christine. Mothman's Curse. 2016. (J). lib. bdg. 18.40 *(978-0-606-39560-1(1))* Turtleback.
Horvath, Polly. My One Hundred Adventures. 2010. (My One Hundred Adventures Ser.: 1). (Illus.). 272p. (J). (gr. 3-7). 8.99 *(978-0-375-85526-9(2),* Yearling) Random Hse. Children's Bks.
Howard, J. J. That Time I Joined the Circus. 2013. (ENG.). 272p. (YA). (gr. 7). 17.99 *(978-0-545-43381-5(9))* Scholastic, Inc.
Howe, James. Also Known As Elvis. 2015. (Misfits Ser.). (ENG., Illus.). 304p. (J). (gr. 5-9). pap. 8.99 *(978-1-4424-4511-6(4))* Simon & Schuster Children's Publishing.
Hughes, Shirley. The Christmas Eve Ghost. Hughes, Shirley, illus. 2010. (ENG., Illus.). 32p. (J). (gr. -1-3). 15.99 *(978-0-7636-4472-7(2))* Candlewick Pr.
Jayne, Hannah. The Escape. 2015. (ENG., Illus.). 256p. (YA). (gr. 8-12). pap. 10.99 *(978-1-4926-1654-2(0),* 9781492616542) Sourcebooks, Inc.
Jones, Jen. Lissa & the Fund-Raising Funk: #3, 1 vol. (Team Cheer Ser.). (ENG.). 112p. (J). (gr. 4-6). 2012. pap. 7.19 *(978-1-4342-4251-8(X),* 120309)No. 3. 2011. lib. bdg. 25.32 *(978-1-4342-2996-0(3),* 114389) Capstone. (Stone Arch Bks.).
Jukes, Mavis. The New Kid. (ENG.). 288p. (J). (gr. 4-6). 2013. lib. bdg. 21.19 *(978-0-375-95879-3(7),* Knopf Bks. for Young Readers) 2012. 7.99 *(978-0-375-85367-8(7),* Yearling) Random Hse. Children's Bks.
Kadohata, Cynthia. Checked. Zorat, Maurizio, illus. 2018. (ENG.). 416p. (J). (gr. 5-9). 17.99 *(978-1-4814-4661-7(4),* Atheneum/Caitlyn Dlouhy Books) Simon & Schuster Children's Publishing.
Kanady, Mary Ellen Murdock. Mommy & Me. 2008. (Illus.). 32p. (J). pap. 8.00 *(978-0-8059-7728-8(7))* Dorrance Publishing Co., Inc.
Karre, Elizabeth. All You Are. 2014. (Gift Ser.). (ENG.). 120p. (YA). (gr. 6-12). pap. 7.95 *(978-1-4677-4477-5(8),* eb718cc1-6713-4a48-b567-548e6a7ebfcf, Darby Creek) Lerner Publishing Group.
Katcher, Brian. Almost Perfect. 2010. 368p. (YA). (gr. 9). pap. 10.99 *(978-0-385-73665-7(7),* Delacorte Bks. for Young Readers) Random Hse. Children's Bks.
Kent, Rose. Rocky Road. 2012. (ENG.). 304p. (J). (gr. 4-6). 21.19 *(978-0-375-86344-8(3),* Knopf Bks. for Young Readers) Random Hse. Children's Bks.
Kenyon, Sherrilyn. The Dark-Hunters: Infinity, Vol. 1, Vol. 1. 2013. (Dark-Hunters Ser.: 1). (ENG., Illus.). 240p. (gr. 11-17). 13.00 *(978-0-316-19053-4(5),* Yen Pr.) Yen Pr. LLC.
—Infinity: Chronicles of Nick. 2011. (Chronicles of Nick Ser.: 1). (ENG.). 480p. (YA). (gr. 7-18). pap. 14.00 *(978-0-312-60304-5(5),* 900064303, St. Martin's Griffin) St. Martin's Pr.
Kinsey-Warnock, Natalie. Lumber Camp Library. Bernardin, James, illus. 2003. (ENG.). 96p. (J). (gr. 2-5). pap. 4.99 *(978-0-06-444292-3(6),* HarperCollins) HarperCollins Pubs.
Kleinman, Estelle. The Penderwicks: A Study Guide. Friedland, Joyce & Kessler, Rikki, eds. 2008. (Novel-Ties Ser.). (Illus.). 39p. pap. 16.95 *(978-0-7675-1488-0(2))* Learning Links Inc.
Krovatin, Christopher. Venomous. Yates, Kelly, illus. 2011. (ENG.). 336p. (YA). (gr. 8). pap. 8.99 *(978-1-4424-1298-9(4),* Atheneum Bks. for Young Readers) Simon & Schuster Children's Publishing.
Kurzweil, Allen. Leon & the Spitting Image. Bertholf, Bret, illus. (ENG.). 320p. (J). (gr. 3-18). 2005. pap. 7.99 *(978-0-06-053932-0(1),* Greenwillow Bks.) 2003. 16.99 *(978-0-06-053930-6(5))* HarperCollins Pubs.
Kyi, Tanya Lloyd. Anywhere but Here. 2013. (ENG., Illus.). 320p. (YA). (gr. 9). 17.99 *(978-1-4424-8070-4(X));* pap. 9.99 *(978-1-4424-8069-8(6))* Simon Pulse. (Simon Pulse).
Lacont'e. Overcoming Obstacles. 2012. 28p. 19.95 *(978-1-4626-7076-5(8))* America Star Bks.
Lai, Remy. Pie in the Sky. Lai, Remy, illus. 2019. (ENG., Illus.). 384p. (J). 21.99 *(978-1-250-31409-3(7),* 900199487); pap. 14.99 *(978-1-250-31410-9(0),* 900199488) Holt, Henry & Co. (Holt, Henry & Co. Bks. For Young Readers).
Lang, Heidi. Wrong Way Summer. 2020. (ENG., Illus.). 288p. (J). (gr. 3-7). 16.99 *(978-1-4197-3693-3(0),* 1219301) Abrams, Inc.
Lange, Erin Jade. Dead Ends. 2013. (ENG.). 304p. E-Book 7.99 *(978-1-61963-081-9(8),* Bloomsbury USA Childrens) Bloomsbury Publishing USA.
Larsen, Jen. Future Perfect. 2015. (ENG.). 320p. (YA). (gr. 8-12). 17.99 *(978-0-06-232123-7(4),* HarperTeen) HarperCollins Pubs.
Lauture, Mireille B. Mancy's Haitian Folktale Collection: Father Misery. Minckler, Kathleen L., illus. 2011. 24p. pap. 12.50 *(978-1-4634-3682-7(3))* AuthorHouse.
Lean, Sarah. A Dog Called Homeless. 2012. (ENG.). 208p. (J). (gr. 3-7). 16.99 *(978-0-06-212220-9(7),* Tegen, Katherine Bks) HarperCollins Pubs.
Leonard, Connie King. Sleeping in My Jeans. 2018. (ENG.). 240p. (YA). pap. 16.00 *(978-1-947845-00-8(4))* Ooligan Pr.
Levy, Janice. Totally Uncool. Monroe, Chris, illus. 2003. (Picture Bks.). 32p. (J). (gr. -1-3). reprint ed. 6.95 *(978-1-57505-555-8(4),* Carolrhoda Bks.) Lerner Publishing Group.
Lindelauf, Benny. Nine Open Arms. Nieuwenhuizen, John, tr. 2014. (ENG., Illus.). 264p. (J). (gr. 3). 16.95 *(978-1-59270-146-9(9))* Enchanted Lion Bks., LLC.
Lloyd, Natalie. A Snicker of Magic. 2015. lib. bdg. 17.20 *(978-0-606-37089-9(7))* Turtleback.
—A Snicker of Magic (Scholastic Gold) 2015. (ENG.). 336p. (J). (gr. 3-7). pap. 7.99 *(978-0-545-55273-8(7),* Scholastic Pr.) Scholastic, Inc.
—A Snicker of Magic (Scholastic Gold) (Unabridged Edition), 2 vols. unabr. ed. 2014. (ENG.). 2p. (J). (gr. 3-7). audio compact disk 34.99 *(978-0-545-70679-7(3))* Scholastic, Inc.
Lloyd, Natalie, et al. A Snicker of Magic. 2014. (ENG.). mass mkt. *(978-0-545-68447-7(1))* Scholastic, Inc.
Loewen, Iris. My Mom Is So Unusual, 1 vol. Pakarnyk, Alan, illus. 2015. (ENG.). 32p. (J). pap. 7.95 *(978-0-919143-37-1(7),* f4e06253-2f7e-4a91-92df-1b390d7510ec) Pemmican Pubns., Inc. CAN. Dist: Firefly Bks., Ltd.
Luciani, Brigitte. The Meeting: Book 1. No. 1. Tharlet, Eve, illus. 2010. (Mr. Badger & Mrs. Fox Ser.: 1). (ENG.). 32p. (J). (gr. k-3). pap. 7.99 *(978-0-7613-5631-8(2),* 071a498b-43a0-413d-9653-5f39dd220232, Graphic Universe™) Lerner Publishing Group.
Lupica, Mike. Batting Order. (ENG.). (J). (gr. 3-7). 2020. 320p. pap. 8.99 *(978-1-5344-2156-1(4))* 2019. (Illus.). 304p. 19.99 *(978-1-5344-2155-4(6))* Simon & Schuster Bks. For Young Readers. (Simon & Schuster Bks. For Young Readers).
Lyga, Barry. Bang. 2018. (ENG.). 304p. (YA). (gr. 7-17). pap. 16.99 *(978-0-316-31551-7(6))* Little, Brown Bks. for Young Readers.
—Hero-Type. 2009. (ENG.). 312p. (YA). (gr. 7). pap. 17.99 *(978-0-547-24877-6(6),* 1100781, Clarion Bks.) HarperCollins Pubs.
Lynch, Chris. Angry Young Man. 2012. (ENG.). 192p. (YA). (gr. 7). pap. 10.99 *(978-1-4424-5419-4(9),* Simon & Schuster Bks. For Young Readers) Simon & Schuster Bks. For Young Readers.
Lyne, Jennifer H. Catch Rider. 2014. (ENG.). 288p. (YA). (gr. 7). pap. 8.99 *(978-0-544-30182-5(X),* 1577488, Clarion Bks.) HarperCollins Pubs.
Lyon, George Ella. Sonny's House of Spies. 2007. (ENG.). 304p. (J). (gr. 6-9). pap. 14.95 *(978-1-4169-6815-3(6),* Simon & Schuster/Paula Wiseman Bks.) Simon & Schuster/Paula Wiseman Bks.
Maddox, Jake. Snowboard Struggle. 2016. (Jake Maddox JV Ser.). (ENG., Illus.). 96p. (J). (gr. 4-6). lib. bdg. 26.65 *(978-1-4965-3980-9(X),* 133203, Stone Arch Bks.) Capstone.
—Tae Kwon Do Clash. 2016. (Jake Maddox JV Ser.). (ENG., Illus.). 96p. (J). (gr. 4-6). lib. bdg. 26.65 *(978-1-4965-3981-6(8),* 133204, Stone Arch Bks.) Capstone.
Madonia, Kristen-Paige. Fingerprints of You. (ENG., Illus.). 272p. (YA). (gr. 9). 2013. pap. 9.99 *(978-1-4424-2921-5(6))* 2012. 16.99 *(978-1-4424-2920-8(8))* Simon & Schuster Bks. For Young Readers. (Simon & Schuster Bks. For Young Readers).
Maldonado, Torrey. Secret Saturdays. 2012. (ENG.). 208p. (YA). (gr. 5-18). 7.99 *(978-0-14-241747-8(5),* Puffin Books) Penguin Young Readers Group.
—Secret Saturdays. 2012. lib. bdg. 18.40 *(978-0-606-23645-4(7))* Turtleback.
Mankell, Henning. A Bridge to the Stars. 2009. (Joel Gustafsson Ser.: No. 1). (ENG.). 176p. (YA). (gr. 7). pap. 7.99 *(978-0-440-24042-6(5),* Delacorte Bks. for Young Readers) Random Hse. Children's Bks.
—When the Snow Fell. 2011. (Joel Gustafsson Ser.: No. 3). (ENG.). 256p. (YA). (gr. 7). pap. 8.99 *(978-0-440-24044-0(1),* Delacorte Bks. for Young Readers) Random Hse. Children's Bks.
Manning, Matthew K. Operation Copycat. Douglas, Allen, illus. 2018. (Drone Academy Ser.). (ENG.). 112p. (J). (gr. 4-8). lib. bdg. 27.32 *(978-1-4965-6075-9(2),* 137497, Stone Arch Bks.) Capstone.
Mason, David. Davey McGravy. Silverstein, Grant, illus. 2015. (ENG.). 120p. (J). (gr. k). pap. 14.95 *(978-1-58988-099-3(4))* Dry, Paul Bks., Inc.
McClintock, Norah. Watch Me, 1 vol. 2008. (Orca Currents Ser.). (ENG.). 128p. (J). (gr. 4-7). pap. 9.95 *(978-1-55469-039-8(0))* Orca Bk. Pubs. USA.
McDaniel, Lurlene. Prey. (ENG.). 208p. (YA). 2010. (gr. 7). mass mkt. 7.99 *(978-0-440-24015-0(8),* Laurel Leaf) 2008. (gr. 9-12). lib. bdg. 21.19 *(978-0-385-90457-5(6),* Delacorte Pr.) Random Hse. Children's Bks.
McDunn, Gillian. Caterpillar Summer. (ENG.). (J). 2020. 320p. pap. 7.99 *(978-1-5476-0314-5(3),* 900211246) 2019. (Illus.). 304p. 16.99 *(978-1-68119-743-2(X),* 900184196) Bloomsbury Publishing USA. (Bloomsbury Children's Bks.).
McGhee, Alison. What I Leave Behind. (ENG.). (YA). (gr. 9). 2019. 224p. pap. 11.99 *(978-1-4814-7657-7(2))* 2018. (Illus.). 208p. 18.99 *(978-1-4814-7656-0(4))* Simon & Schuster Children's Publishing. (Atheneum Bks. for Young Readers).
McNish, Cliff. Breathe: A Ghost Story. 2006. (ENG.). 264p. (J). (gr. 4-8). lib. bdg. 15.95 *(978-0-8225-6443-0(2),* Carolrhoda Bks.) Lerner Publishing Group.
Mead, Alice. Junebug. 2009. (Junebug Ser.). (ENG.). 128p. (J). (gr. 3-7). pap. 7.99 *(978-0-312-56126-0(1),* 900058861) Square Fish.
—Junebug in Trouble. 2003. (ENG., Illus.). 144p. (J). (gr. 3-7). 5.99 *(978-0-440-41937-2(9),* Yearling) Random Hse. Children's Bks.
Messner, Kate. The Exact Location of Home. (ENG.). (J). 2018. 272p. pap. 8.99 *(978-1-68119-898-9(3),* 900191676, Bloomsbury Children's Bks.) 2017. 256p. 16.99 *(978-1-68119-548-3(8),* 900177288, Bloomsbury USA Childrens) Bloomsbury Publishing USA.
Michaels, Rune. Nobel Genes. (ENG., (YA). (gr. 7). 2011. Illus.). 208p. pap. 8.99 *(978-1-4424-2401-2(X))* 2010. 192p. 16.99 *(978-1-4169-1259-0(2))* Simon & Schuster Children's Publishing. (Atheneum Bks. for Young Readers).
Mills, Claudia. Being Teddy Roosevelt: A Boy, a President & a Plan. Alley, R. W., illus. 2012. (ENG.). 112p. (J). (gr. 2-5). pap. 16.99 *(978-0-312-64018-7(8),* 900077669) Square Fish.
Mills, Wendy. Positively Beautiful. 2016. (ENG.). 368p. (YA). pap. 9.99 *(978-1-68119-025-9(7),* 9781681190259, Bloomsbury USA Childrens) Bloomsbury Publishing USA.
Mohr, L. C. Krumbuckets. Musheno, Erica, illus. 2007. (ENG.). 144p. (J). (gr. 2-7). 13.95 *(978-0-9769417-6-7(7))* Blooming Tree Pr.
Monninger, Joseph. Game Change. 2019. (ENG.). 240p. (YA). (gr. 9). pap. 15.99 *(978-1-328-59586-7(2),* 1730760, Clarion Bks.) HarperCollins Pubs.
—Whippoorwill. 2016. (ENG.). 288p. (YA). (gr. 7). pap. 9.99 *(978-0-544-81356-4(1),* 1641957, Clarion Bks.) HarperCollins Pubs.
—Wish. 2012. (ENG.). 208p. (YA). (gr. 7-12). lib. bdg. 24.94 *(978-0-385-90788-0(5),* Delacorte Pr.); pap. 8.99 *(978-0-375-86213-7(7),* Ember) Random Hse. Children's Bks.
Morphew, Chris. The Man in the Shadows, Volume 1. 2017. (Phoenix Files Ser.: 1). (ENG.). 512p. (YA). (gr. 7). pap. 13.95 *(978-1-76012-425-0(7))* Hardie Grant Children?s Publishing AUS. Dist: Independent Pubs. Group.
Morpurgo, Michael. Private Peaceful. 2006. 18.00 *(978-0-7569-6630-0(2))* Perfection Learning Corp.
—Private Peaceful. 2006. (YA). 1.25 *(978-1-4193-2976-0(6))* Recorded Bks., Inc.
—Private Peaceful. 2006. (ENG., Illus.). 224p. (J). (gr. 7-12). per. 8.99 *(978-0-439-63653-7(1),* Scholastic Paperbacks) Scholastic, Inc.
—Snakes & Ladders. Wilson, Anne, illus. 2006. (Yellow Bananas Ser.). (ENG.). 48p. (J). (gr. -1-3). lib. bdg. *(978-0-7787-0952-7(3))* Crabtree Publishing Co.
Morton-Shaw, Christine. The Hunt for the Seventh. 2009. (ENG.). 288p. (J). (gr. 5). pap. 7.99 *(978-0-06-072824-3(8),* Tegen, Katherine Bks) HarperCollins Pubs.
Mullin, Mike. Surface Tension. 2018. (ENG.). 424p. (YA). (gr. 8-12). 17.99 *(978-1-939100-16-0(X))* Tanglewood Pr.
Murdock, Kita Helmetag. Future Flash. 2014. (ENG.). 208p. (J). (gr. 2-7). 12.95 *(978-1-62873-822-3(7),* Sky Pony Pr.) Skyhorse Publishing Co., Inc.
Nelson, Theresa. Ruby Electric. 2004. 264p. (J). (gr. 5-7). 13.65 *(978-0-7569-3530-6(X))* Perfection Learning Corp.
—Ruby Electric. 2004. (ENG.). 272p. (J). (gr. 5-7). reprint ed. pap. 12.99 *(978-0-689-87146-7(5),* Atheneum Bks. for Young Readers) Simon & Schuster Children's Publishing.
Ness, Patrick. A Monster Calls: Inspired by an Idea from Siobhan Dowd. Kay, Jim, illus. (ENG.). 224p. (YA). (gr. 7). 2013. pap. 12.00 *(978-0-7636-6065-9(5))* 2011. 22.99 *(978-0-7636-5559-4(7))* Candlewick Pr.
—A Monster Calls: Inspired by an Idea from Siobhan Dowd. 2011. (Playaway Children Ser.). (YA). (gr. 7-12). 54.99 *(978-1-4558-4499-9(3))* Findaway World, LLC.
—A Monster Calls: Inspired by an Idea from Siobhan Dowd. 2013. lib. bdg. 23.30 *(978-0-606-31603-3(5))* Turtleback.
—A Monster Calls: a Novel (Movie Tie-In) Inspired by an Idea from Siobhan Dowd. 2016. (ENG.). 240p. (YA). (gr. 7). pap. 9.99 *(978-0-7636-9215-5(8))* Candlewick Pr.
Newman, John. Mimi. 2011. (ENG., Illus.). 192p. (J). (gr. 3-7). 15.99 *(978-0-7636-5415-3(9))* Candlewick Pr.
Nielsen, Susin. Word Nerd. 2010. (ENG.). 264p. (J). (gr. 4-7). pap. 12.95 *(978-0-88776-990-0(X),* Tundra Bks.) Tundra Bks. CAN. Dist: Penguin Random Hse. LLC.
Olson, Justin. Earth to Charlie. 2019. (ENG., Illus.). 288p. (YA). (gr. 7). 18.99 *(978-1-5344-1952-0(7),* Simon & Schuster Bks. For Young Readers) Simon & Schuster Bks. For Young Readers.
Patrick, Cat. The Originals. (ENG.). (YA). (gr. 7-17). 2014. 320p. pap. 10.00 *(978-0-316-21945-7(2))* 2013. 304p. 18.00 *(978-0-316-21943-3(6))* Little, Brown Bks. for Young Readers.
Pearsall, Shelley. All Shook Up. 2009. 272p. (J). (gr. 3-7). 7.99 *(978-0-440-42139-9(X),* Yearling) Random Hse. Children's Bks.
Penn, Farrah. Twelve Steps to Normal. 2018. (ENG.). 384p. (YA). (gr. 8-17). 17.99 *(978-0-316-47160-2(7),* Jimmy Patterson) Little Brown & Co.
Perry, Hailey. On the Move. 2010. 188p. pap. 12.00 *(978-1-60844-428-1(7))* Dog Ear Publishing, LLC.
Philbin, Joanna. The Daughters Break the Rules. 2011. (Daughters Ser.: 2). (ENG.). 304p. (YA). (gr. 7-17). pap., pap. 16.99 *(978-0-316-04905-4(0),* Poppy) Little, Brown Bks. for Young Readers.
Philippe, Ben. The Field Guide to the North American Teenager. (ENG.). 384p. (YA). (gr. 8). 2020. pap. 11.99 *(978-0-06-282412-7(0))* 2019. 18.99 *(978-0-06-282411-0(2))* HarperCollins Pubs. (Balzer & Bray).
Pimentel, Sandy. The Boy with Two Homes. 2011. (ENG.). 32p. pap. 21.99 *(978-1-4568-3620-7(X))* Xlibris Corp.
Pitchford, Dean. The Big One-Oh. 2009. 208p. (J). (gr. 3-7). 7.99 *(978-0-14-241292-3(9),* Puffin Books) Penguin Young Readers Group.
Polacco, Patricia. Something about Hensley's. Polacco, Patricia, illus. 2006. (Illus.). 48p. (J). (gr. -1-3). 18.99 *(978-0-399-24538-1(3),* Philomel Bks.) Penguin Young Readers Group.
Presley, Daniel & Polders, Claire. A Whale in Paris. McGuire, Erin, illus. (ENG.). 256p. (J). (gr. 5). 2019. pap. 7.99 *(978-1-5344-1916-2(0))* 2018. 17.99 *(978-1-5344-1915-5(2))* Simon & Schuster Children's Publishing. (Atheneum Bks. for Young Readers).
Pyros, Andrea. Pink Hair & Other Terrible Ideas. 2019. (ENG.). 256p. (J). (gr. 4-7). lib. bdg. 15.95 *(978-1-68446-028-1(X),* 139700, Capstone Editions) Capstone.
Quattlebaum, Mary. Jackson Jones & the Curse of the Outlaw Rose. 2008. (Jackson Jones Ser.). (ENG.). 112p. (J). (gr. 3-7). 5.99 *(978-0-440-42138-2(1),* Yearling) Random Hse. Children's Bks.
Railey, Shawna. The Messy Life of Blue. 2020. (ENG.). 240p. (J). (gr. 3-7). 16.99 *(978-1-4998-1025-7(3),* Yellow Jacket) Bonnier Publishing USA.
Rapp, Adam. The Children & the Wolves. 2012. (ENG., Illus.). 160p. (YA). (gr. 9). 16.99 *(978-0-7636-5337-8(3))* Candlewick Pr.
Reichs, Kathy. Code: A Virals Novel. 2013. (Virals Ser.: 3). (ENG.). 432p. (J). (gr. 5). pap. 11.99 *(978-1-59514-572-7(9),* Puffin Books) Penguin Young Readers Group.
—Virals. 2014. lthr. 79.00 *(978-1-62715-582-3(1))* Leatherbound Bestsellers.
—Virals. 2011. (Virals Ser.: 1). (ENG.). 480p. (J). (gr. 5-18). 11.99 *(978-1-59514-426-3(9),* Puffin Books) Penguin Young Readers Group.
—Virals. 2011. 20.00 *(978-1-61383-226-4(5))* Perfection Learning Corp.
Reichs, Kathy & Reichs, Brendan. Code. 2013. (Virals Ser.: 3). lib. bdg. 19.65 *(978-0-606-32140-2(3))* Turtleback.
—Virals. 2011. (Virals Ser.: 1). lib. bdg. 20.85 *(978-0-606-23069-8(6))* Turtleback.
Reinhardt, Dana. The Summer I Learned to Fly. 2012. (ENG.). 224p. (YA). (gr. 7). pap. 8.99 *(978-0-385-73955-9(9),* Ember) Random Hse. Children's Bks.
Resau, Laura. The Indigo Notebook. 2010. (Notebook Ser.: 1). 336p. (YA). (gr. 7). pap. 9.99 *(978-0-375-84524-6(0),* Ember) Random Hse. Children's Bks.
—The Ruby Notebook. 2012. (Notebook Ser.). 384p. (YA). (gr. 7). pap. 9.99 *(978-0-375-84525-3(9),* Ember) Random Hse. Children's Bks.
Reynolds Naylor, Phyllis. Alice in April. 2011. (Alice Ser.: 5). (ENG.). 192p. (J). (gr. 5-9). pap. 7.99 *(978-1-4424-2757-0(4),* Atheneum Bks. for Young Readers) Simon & Schuster Children's Publishing.
—Alice In-Between. 2011. (Alice Ser.: 6). (ENG.). 192p. (J). (gr. 5-9). pap. 7.99 *(978-1-4424-2758-7(2),* Atheneum Bks. for Young Readers) Simon & Schuster Children's Publishing.
—Alice In-Between. 2008. (Alice McKinley Ser.: No. 6). (ENG.). 176p. (J). pap. 5.99 *(978-1-4169-6770-5(2),* Simon & Schuster/Paula Wiseman Bks.) Simon & Schuster/Paula Wiseman Bks.
—Alice in Blunderland. 2005. 200p. (J). (gr. 2-7). 13.65 *(978-0-7569-5075-0(9))* Perfection Learning Corp.
—Alice in Blunderland. 2012. (Alice Ser.). (ENG., Illus.). 240p. (J). (gr. 2-7). pap. 7.99 *(978-1-4424-4643-4(9),* Atheneum Bks. for Young Readers) Simon & Schuster Children's Publishing.
—Alice in Lace. 2009. (Alice McKinley Ser.: No. 8). (ENG.). 160p. (J). pap. 7.99 *(978-1-4169-7543-4(8),* Simon & Schuster/Paula Wiseman Bks.) Simon & Schuster/Paula Wiseman Bks.
—Alice in Rapture, Sort Of. 2011. (Alice Ser.: 2). (ENG.). 208p. (J). (gr. 5-9). pap. 7.99 *(978-1-4424-2362-6(5),* Atheneum Bks. for Young Readers) Simon & Schuster Children's Publishing.
—Alice on the Outside. 2012. (Alice Ser.: 11). (ENG., Illus.). 208p. (J). (gr. 5-9). pap. 7.99 *(978-1-4424-3495-0(3),* Atheneum Bks. for Young Readers) Simon & Schuster Children's Publishing.
—Alice the Brave. 2011. (Alice Ser.: 7). (ENG., Illus.). 176p. (J). (gr. 5-9). pap. 7.99 *(978-1-4424-2851-5(1))* Simon & Schuster, Inc.
—I Like Him, He Likes Her: Alice Alone; Simply Alice; Patiently Alice. 2010. (Alice Ser.). (ENG.). 640p. (J). (gr. 7). pap. 12.99 *(978-1-4424-0978-1(9),* Atheneum Bks. for Young Readers) Simon & Schuster Children's Publishing.
—Lovingly Alice. 2004. (Alice Bks.). 166p. (J). (gr. 4-6). 13.65 *(978-0-7569-6604-1(3))* Perfection Learning Corp.
—Lovingly Alice. 2006. (Alice Ser.). (ENG., Illus.). 176p. (J). (gr. 4-7). pap. 5.99 *(978-0-689-84400-3(X),* Atheneum Bks. for Young Readers) Simon & Schuster Children's Publishing.
—Outrageously Alice. 2011. (Alice Ser.: 9). (ENG., Illus.). 176p. (J). (gr. 5-9). pap. 7.99 *(978-1-4424-2853-9(8),* Atheneum Bks. for Young Readers) Simon & Schuster Children's Publishing.
—Reluctantly Alice. 2011. (Alice Ser.: 3). (ENG.). 240p. (J). (gr. 5-9). pap. 7.99 *(978-1-4424-2361-9(7),* Atheneum Bks. for Young Readers) Simon & Schuster Children's Publishing.
—Reluctantly Alice. 2008. (Alice McKinley Ser.: No. 3). (ENG.). 208p. (J). pap. 5.99 *(978-1-4169-5876-5(2),* Simon & Schuster/Paula Wiseman Bks.) Simon & Schuster/Paula Wiseman Bks.
—Starting with Alice. 2004. (Alice Bks.). 181p. (J). (gr. 4-7). 12.65 *(978-0-7569-2940-4(7))* Perfection Learning Corp.
—Starting with Alice. 2012. (Alice Ser.). (ENG., Illus.). 224p. (J). (gr. 2-7). pap. 7.99 *(978-1-4424-4642-7(0),* Atheneum Bks. for Young Readers) Simon & Schuster Children's Publishing.
Roberts, Barbara Carroll. Nikki on the Line. 2019. (ENG.). 336p. (J). (gr. 3-7). 16.99 *(978-0-316-52190-1(6))* Little, Brown Bks. for Young Readers.
Roberts, Willo Davis. Megan's Island. 2016. (ENG., Illus.). 288p. (J). (gr. 3-7). pap. 7.99 *(978-1-4814-4907-6(9),* Aladdin) Simon & Schuster Children's Publishing.
Rue, Nancy. You Can't Sit with Us, 1 vol. 2014. (Mean Girl Makeover Ser.: 2). (ENG.). 224p. (J). pap. 9.99 *(978-1-4003-2371-5(1),* Tommy Nelson) Nelson, Thomas Inc.
Rue, Nancy N. Lucy Out of Bounds, 1 vol. 2016. (Faithgirlz / a Lucy Novel Ser.: 2). (ENG.). 224p. (J). pap. 7.99 *(978-0-310-75505-0(0))* Zonderkidz.
Rylant, Cynthia. A Kindness. Date not set. (Sky Bks.). 104p. pap. 54.75 *(978-0-582-08106-2(8))* Addison-Wesley Longman, Ltd. GBR. Dist: Trans-Atlantic Pubns., Inc.
Sanders, Scott Loring. Gray Baby. 2009. (ENG.). 336p. (YA). (gr. 7-18). 17.00 *(978-0-547-07661-4(4),* 1042029, Clarion Bks.) HarperCollins Pubs.
Sarno, Melissa. Just under the Clouds. 2019. (ENG.). 256p. (J). (gr. 3-7). pap. 8.99 *(978-1-5247-2011-7(9),* Yearling) Random Hse. Children's Bks.
Savage, Melissa. Lemons. 2018. (ENG.). 320p. (J). (gr. 3-7). 8.99 *(978-1-5247-0015-7(0),* Yearling) Random Hse. Children's Bks.
Schindler, Holly. Feral. 2014. (ENG.). 432p. (YA). (gr. 8). 17.99 *(978-0-06-222020-2(9),* HarperTeen) HarperCollins Pubs.

S

Schwartz, Virginia Frances. Messenger, 1 vol. 2005. (ENG., Illus.). 282p. (YA). (gr. 7-9). per. 9.95 *(978-1-55041-946-7(3),* ec9648c9-fdf2-48e9-94ca-1dab3ad48b17) Fitzhenry & Whiteside, Ltd. CAN. Dist: Firefly Bks., Ltd.
Sevigny, Alisha. Summer Constellations. 2018. (ENG.). 264p. (J). (gr. 9-12). pap. 10.99 *(978-1-5253-0043-1(1))* Kids Can Pr., Ltd. CAN. Dist: Hachette Bk. Group.
Shea, John & Harmon, Michael B. A Kid from Southie. 2011. 240p. (YA). (gr. 9-18). 16.95 *(978-1-934813-53-9(2))* Westside Bks.
Shearer, Alex. Sea Legs. 2006. (ENG.). 320p. (J). (gr. 5-9). per. 17.99 *(978-0-689-87144-3(9),* Simon & Schuster/Paula Wiseman Bks.) Simon & Schuster/Paula Wiseman Bks.
Shofner, Corabel. Almost Paradise. 2018. (ENG.). 304p. (J). pap. 19.99 *(978-1-250-15858-1(3),* 900157543) Square Fish.
—Almost Paradise. 2018. (J). lib. bdg. 18.40 *(978-0-606-41107-3(0))* Turtleback.
Shull, Megan. The Swap. (ENG.). 400p. (J). (gr. 5-9). 2016. pap. 7.99 *(978-0-06-231170-2(0))* 2014. 16.99 *(978-0-06-231169-6(7))* HarperCollins Pubs. (Tegen, Katherine Bks).
Sidney, Margaret. Five Little Peppers & How They Grew. 2017. (ENG., Illus.). (J). 24.95 *(978-1-374-93472-6(0));* pap. 14.95 *(978-1-374-93471-9(2))* Capital Communications, Inc.
—Five Little Peppers & How They Grew. 2006. (Dover Children's Classics Ser.). (ENG., Illus.). 224p. (J). (gr. 3-5). per. 9.95 *(978-0-486-45267-8(0),* 452670) Dover Pubns., Inc.
Sizer, Ralph Robuck. Rashad & Rameen. 2011. 26p. pap. 16.95 *(978-1-4560-6459-4(2))* America Star Bks.
Skovron, Jon. Struts & Frets. 2011. (ENG.). 288p. (YA). (gr. 8-17). pap. 7.95 *(978-1-4197-0028-6(6),* 657403, Amulet Bks.) Abrams, Inc.
Sommer, Carl. Dare to Dream! Martinez, Jorge et al, illus. 2007. (Another Sommer-Time Story Ser.). (ENG.). 48p. (J). (gr. -1-3). 16.95 incl. audio compact disk *(978-1-57537-523-6(0))* Advance Publishing, Inc.
Sosna-Spear, Quinn. The Remarkable Inventions of Walter Mortinson. 2019. (ENG., Illus.). 336p. (J). (gr. 3-7). 17.99 *(978-1-5344-2080-9(0),* Simon & Schuster Bks. For Young Readers) Simon & Schuster Bks. For Young Readers.
Spencer, Octavia. The Case of the Time-Capsule Bandit. To, Vivienne, illus. 2013. (Randi Rhodes, Ninja Detective Ser.: 1). (ENG.). 224p. (J). (gr. 3-7). 16.99 *(978-1-4424-7681-3(8),* Simon & Schuster Bks. For Young Readers) Simon & Schuster Bks. For Young Readers.
Spinelli, Eileen. Birdie. 2019. (ENG., Illus.). 208p. (J). *(978-0-8028-5513-8(X),* Eerdmans Bks For Young Readers) Eerdmans, William B. Publishing Co.
Stampler, Ann Redisch. Afterparty. 2013. (ENG., Illus.). 416p. (YA). (gr. 9). 17.99 *(978-1-4424-2324-4(2),* Simon Pulse) Simon Pulse.
Staniszewski, Anna. Dirt Diary. 2014. (Dirt Diary Ser.: 1). 256p. (J). (gr. 5-9). pap. 11.99 *(978-1-4022-8636-0(8),* 9781402286360) Sourcebooks, Inc.
—The Gossip File. 2015. (Dirt Diary Ser.: 3). 224p. (J). (gr. 5-9). pap. 9.99 *(978-1-4926-0463-1(1),* 9781492604631) Sourcebooks, Inc.
—The Prank List. 2014. (Dirt Diary Ser.: 2). 256p. (J). (gr. 5-9). pap. 11.99 *(978-1-4022-8639-1(2),* 9781402286391) Sourcebooks, Inc.
Stevens, Court. The June Boys, 1 vol. 2020. (ENG., Illus.). (YA). 384p. pap. 12.99 *(978-0-7852-2194-4(8));* 368p. 18.99 *(978-0-7852-2190-6(5))* Nelson, Thomas Inc.
Tan, Amy Rebecca. A Kind of Paradise. 2019. (ENG.). 304p. (J). (gr. 3-7). 16.99 *(978-0-06-279541-0(4),* HarperCollins) HarperCollins Pubs.
Thiel Annie. The Playdate Kids Cosmos' Mom & Dad are Moving Apart 2ED 2007. 2007. 32p. 12.95 *(978-1-933721-31-6(6));* pap. 6.95 *(978-1-933721-27-9(8))* Playdate Kids Publishing.
Thompson, Lauren. A Christmas Gift for Mama. Burke, Jim, illus. 2003. (J). pap. 16.95 *(978-0-590-30726-0(6))* Scholastic, Inc.
Thompson, T. D. Flight of the Wild Geese, 1 vol. 2015. (ENG.). 32p. (YA). (gr. 7-11). mass mkt. 14.95 *(978-1-894717-51-9(1),* 1a4f1a32-712f-41ae-bb4b-643400df8d1e) Pemmican Pubns., Inc. CAN. Dist: Firefly Bks., Ltd.
To Be Perfectly Honest: A Novel Based on an Untrue Story. 2014. (ENG., Illus.). 496p. (YA). (gr. 7). pap. 11.99 *(978-0-689-87605-9(X),* Simon & Schuster Bks. For Young Readers) Simon & Schuster Bks. For Young Readers.
Toliver, Wendy. Lifted. 2010. (ENG.). 352p. (YA). (gr. 9-18). pap. 9.99 *(978-1-4169-9048-2(8),* Simon Pulse) Simon Pulse.
Ullman, Barb Bentler. Whistle Bright Magic: A Nutfolk Tale. 2010. 224p. (J). (gr. 3-7). 16.99 *(978-0-06-188286-9(0))* HarperCollins Pubs.
Verdi, Jessica. And She Was. 2018. (ENG.). 368p. (YA). (gr. 9). 18.99 *(978-1-338-15053-7(7),* Scholastic Pr.) Scholastic, Inc.
—What You Left Behind. 2015. (ENG.). 368p. (YA). (gr. 8-12). pap. 9.99 *(978-1-4926-0874-5(2))* Sourcebooks, Inc.
Vrettos, Adrienne Maria. Sight. 2008. (ENG.). 272p. (YA). (gr. 7). pap. 8.99 *(978-1-4169-0658-2(4),* McElderry, Margaret K. Bks.) McElderry, Margaret K. Bks.
—Sight. 2007. (ENG., Illus.). 254p. (YA). (gr. 7-12). 21.19 *(978-1-4169-0657-5(6))* Simon & Schuster, Inc.
Warner, Sally. Only Emma. Harper, Jamie, illus. 2006. (Emma Ser.: 1). (ENG.). 144p. (J). (gr. 3-7). 6.99 *(978-0-14-240711-0(9),* Puffin Books) Penguin Young Readers Group.
Wells, Rosemary. On the Blue Comet. Ibatoulline, Bagram, illus. (ENG.). 336p. (J). (gr. 5). 2012. pap. 9.99 *(978-0-7636-5815-1(4))* 2010. 16.99 *(978-0-7636-3722-4(X))* Candlewick Pr.
West, Kasie. The Distance Between Us. 2013. (ENG.). 320p. (YA). (gr. 8). pap. 9.99 *(978-0-06-223565-7(6),* HarperTeen) HarperCollins Pubs.
—On the Fence. 2014. (ENG.). 304p. (YA). (gr. 8). pap. 11.99 *(978-0-06-223567-1(2),* HarperTeen) HarperCollins Pubs.
Weyn, Suzanne. Snapstreak: How My Friends Saved My (Social) Life. 2018. (ENG., Illus.). 192p. (J). (gr. 5-7). 14.99 *(978-1-328-71346-9(6),* 1673599, Clarion Bks.) HarperCollins Pubs.
Wheeler, Eliza. Home in the Woods. Wheeler, Eliza, illus. 2019. (Illus.). 40p. (J). (gr. k-3). 18.99 *(978-0-399-16290-9(9),* Nancy Paulsen Books) Penguin Young Readers Group.
Williams-Garcia, Rita. Clayton Byrd Goes Underground. 2019. (Penworthy Picks Middle School Ser.). (ENG.). 166p. (J). (gr. 4-5). 18.49 *(978-1-64310-913-8(8))* Penworthy Co., LLC, The.
Williams, Laura E. Slant. 2008. (ENG.). 160p. (J). (gr. 2-8). pap. 6.95 *(978-1-57131-682-0(5))* Milkweed Editions.
Willis, Meredith Sue. Meli's Way. 2015. 178p. (YA). *(978-1-932727-15-9(9))* Montemayor Pr.
Wolf, Jennifer Shaw. Dead Girls Don't Lie. 2013. (ENG.). 304p. E-Book 7.99 *(978-0-8027-3450-1(2),* Bloomsbury USA Childrens) Bloomsbury Publishing USA.
Wolff, Virginia Euwer. Make Lemonade. unabr. ed. 2004. (Make Lemonade Trilogy: No. 1). 200p. (J). (gr. 7-18). pap. 36.00 incl. audio *(978-0-8072-0793-2(4),* S YA 348 SP, Listening Library) Random Hse. Audio Publishing Group.
—Make Lemonade: A Novel. 2006. (ENG.). 208p. (YA). (gr. 5-9). pap. 9.99 *(978-0-8050-8070-4(8),* 900038834) Square Fish.
—True Believer. 2004. (Make Lemonade Trilogy: No. 2). 272p. (J). (gr. 7-18). pap. 38.00 incl. audio *(978-0-8072-2283-6(6),* Listening Library) Random Hse. Audio Publishing Group.
Woodson, Jacqueline. Pecan Pie Baby. Blackall, Sophie, illus. 2013. (ENG.). 32p. (J). (gr. k-3). 8.99 *(978-0-14-751128-7(3),* Puffin Books) Penguin Young Readers Group.
Wright, Bil. Putting Makeup on the Fat Boy. (ENG., 240p. (YA). (gr. 7). 2012. Illus.). pap. 12.99 *(978-1-4169-4004-3(9))* 2011. 19.99 *(978-1-4169-3996-2(2))* Simon & Schuster Bks. For Young Readers. (Simon & Schuster Bks. For Young Readers).
Zaugg, Sandra L. Secret of the Yellow Van: A Book about Dealing with Loss. 2008. (J). pap. 8.99 *(978-0-8163-2246-6(5))* Pacific Pr. Publishing Assn.

SISTERS

Auld, Mary. Mi Hermana (My Sister), 1 vol. 2004. (Conoce la Familia (Meet the Family) Ser.). (SPA., Illus.). 24p. (gr. k-2). lib. bdg. 24.67 *(978-0-8368-3930-2(7),* 77757a0b-a436-4666-82a3-f01e51b0dd7e, Gareth Stevens Learning Library) Stevens, Gareth Publishing LLLP.
—My Sister, 1 vol. 2004. (Meet the Family Ser.). (ENG., Illus.). 24p. (gr. k-2). lib. bdg. 24.67 *(978-0-8368-3928-9(5),* 45dfef4e-2034-4b16-a2b8-e8368f58394c, Gareth Stevens Learning Library) Stevens, Gareth Publishing LLLP.
Gamble, Adam & Jasper, Mark. Good Night Little Sister. Stevenson, Harvey, illus. 2016. (Good Night Our World Ser.). (ENG.). 20p. (J). (— 1). bds. 9.95 *(978-1-60219-506-6(4))* Good Night Bks.
Hannula, Kate. Forever, Jewel. 2011. (Illus.). 32p. (J). pap. 13.95 *(978-1-4497-2381-1(0),* WestBow Pr.) Author Solutions, LLC.
Litchfield, Jo, illus. Baby Sister Look & Say. 2008. (Look & Say Board Bks). 12p. (J). bds. 7.99 *(978-0-7945-2102-8(9),* Usborne) EDC Publishing.
Miller, Sarah. The Miracle & Tragedy of the Dionne Quintuplets. 2019. (Illus.). 320p. (YA). (gr. 7). 18.99 *(978-1-5247-1381-2(3));* (ENG., 20.99 *(978-1-5247-1382-9(1),* Schwartz & Wade Bks.) Random Hse. Children's Bks.
Mqp, creator. Sisters Make the Best Friends. 2005. 96p. 9.95 *(978-1-84601-014-9(4))* M Q Pubns.
Olsen, Mary-Kate & Olsen, Ashley. The Ultimate Guide to Mary-Kate & Ashley. 2004. (Illus.). 93p. *(978-0-00-718136-0(1))* HarperCollins Pubs. Australia.
Powell, Jillian. My New Sister. 2012. (New Beginnings Ser.). (ENG., Illus.). 24p. (J). (gr. k-3). 21.25 *(978-1-4488-6634-2(0),* PowerKids Pr.) Rosen Publishing Group, Inc., The.
Raatma, Lucia. Sisters Are Part of a Family. 2017. (Our Families Ser.). (ENG., Illus.). 24p. (J). (gr. -1-2). lib. bdg. 22.65 *(978-1-5157-7460-0(0),* 135806, Capstone Pr.) Capstone.
Schaefer, Lola M. Sisters: Revised Edition. rev. ed. 2008. (Families Ser.). (ENG., Illus.). 24p. (J). (gr. -1-2). per. 6.29 *(978-1-4296-1757-4(8),* 94804) Capstone.
Townes-Richards, Carolyn. Nothing Like Christine: Living Through Literature with Aunt Curly's Collection. 2009. (ENG.). 90p. pap. 18.99 *(978-1-4251-1129-8(7))* Trafford Publishing.
Whelahan, Marlene Verno. My Best Friend's Sister... A True Story. 2010. 20p. 12.99 *(978-1-4389-8729-3(3))* AuthorHouse.

SISTERS—FICTION

Abel, Cheyanne. It's Better by Far, When You Are Who You Are. 2012. 24p. pap. 17.99 *(978-1-4685-7492-0(2))* AuthorHouse.
Abrams, Kelsey. Buddy Blues: An Emily Story. Tejido, Jomike, illus. 2019. (Second Chance Ranch Set 2 Ser.). (ENG.). 120p. (J). (gr. 3-4). pap. 7.99 *(978-1-63163-252-5(3),* 1631632523); lib. bdg. 27.13 *(978-1-63163-251-8(5),* 1631632515) North Star Editions. (Jolly Fish Pr.).
—Llama Drama: A Grace Story. Tejido, Jomike, illus. 2019. (Second Chance Ranch Set 2 Ser.). (ENG.). 120p. (J). (gr. 3-4). pap. 7.99 *(978-1-63163-264-8(7),* 1631632647); lib. bdg. 27.13 *(978-1-63163-263-1(9),* 1631632639) North Star Editions. (Jolly Fish Pr.).
—Taking Chances. Tejido, Jomike, illus. 2018. (Second Chance Ranch Ser.). (ENG.). 120p. (J). (gr. 3-4). pap. 7.99 *(978-1-63163-149-8(7),* 1631631497, Jolly Fish Pr.) North Star Editions.
—Taking Chances: A Grace Story. Tejido, Jomike, illus. 2018. (Second Chance Ranch Ser.). (ENG.). 120p. (J). (gr. 3-4). lib. bdg. 27.13 *(978-1-63163-148-1(9),* 1631631489, Jolly Fish Pr.) North Star Editions.
Adachi, Mitsuru. Cross Game, Vol. 2. 2011. (Cross Game Ser.: 2). (ENG., Illus.). 376p. pap. 14.99 *(978-1-4215-3766-5(4))* Viz Media.
—Cross Game, Vol. 4. 2011. (Cross Game Ser.: 4). (ENG., Illus.). 376p. pap. 14.99 *(978-1-4215-3768-9(0))* Viz Media.
The Adventure's of Prissy & Missy "Sleepwalk Affair" 2nd ed. 2009. (Illus.). (J). 15.95 *(978-0-615-28905-2(3))* House of the Guilded Scribe.
Afterglow. 2014. (ENG., Illus.). 336p. (YA). (gr. 9). pap. 11.99 *(978-1-4424-5038-7(X),* Simon & Schuster Bks. For Young Readers) Simon & Schuster Bks. For Young Readers.
Ahn, Flora, illus. Two's a Crowd. 2018. 119p. (J). *(978-1-338-27713-5(8),* Scholastic Pr.) Scholastic, Inc.
Alcott, Louisa. Little Women. Dunn, Robert, illus. 2013. 46p. (J). *(978-1-4351-4813-0(4))* Barnes & Noble, Inc.
—Little Women. 2007. 264p. (YA). 11.95 *(978-1-933486-01-7(5))* Core Knowledge Foundation.
—Little Women. unabr. ed. 2004. (Chrysalis Childrens Classics Ser.). (Illus.). 190p. (YA). pap. *(978-1-84365-049-2(5),* Pavilion Children's Books) Pavilion Bks.
—Little Women. 2013. (Works of Louisa May Alcott). 451p. reprint ed. lthr. 79.00 *(978-0-7812-1627-2(3))* Reprint Services Corp.
—Little Women. 2008. (Puffin Classics Ser.). (gr. k-3). lib. bdg. 19.65 *(978-0-613-86261-5(9))* Turtleback.
—Little Women: Bring the Classics to Life. 2008. (Bring the Classics to Life Ser.). (Illus.). 72p. (gr. 1-12). pap., act. bk. ed. 10.95 *(978-1-55576-047-2(3),* EDCTR-103B) EDCON Publishing Group.
—Little Women: With a Discussion of Family. Lauter, Richard, illus. 2003. (Values in Action Illustrated Classics Ser.). 191p. (J). *(978-1-59203-032-3(7))* Learning Challenge, Inc.
—A Modern Cinderella. l.t. ed. 2005. 224p. pap. *(978-1-84637-050-2(7))* Echo Library.
—Modern Cinderella or the Little Old Shoe. 2006. pap. 44.99 *(978-1-4219-8892-4(5))* IndyPublish.com.
—Mujercitas.Tr. of Little Women. (SPA., Illus.). 192p. (YA). 11.95 *(978-84-7281-101-0(8),* AF1101) Auriga, Ediciones S.A. ESP. Dist: Continental Bk. Co., Inc.
—Mujercitas. 2004.Tr. of Little Women. (SPA.). lib. bdg. *(978-1-4135-2067-5(7))* El Cid Editor Incorporated.
—Mujercitas. (Coleccion Estrella).Tr. of Little Women. (SPA., Illus.). 64p. (J). 14.95 *(978-950-11-0010-5(3),* SGM010) Sigmar ARG. Dist: Continental Bk. Co., Inc.
Alcott, Louisa & Lacey, Mike. Little Women, 1 vol. 2011. (Calico Illustrated Classics Ser.: No. 4). (ENG., Illus.). 112p. (J). (gr. 2-5). 38.50 *(978-1-61641-617-1(3),* 4049, Calico Chapter Bks.) ABDO Publishing Co.
Alcott, Louisa May. Classic Starts(r): Little Women. Corvino, Lucy, illus. 2005. (Classic Starts(r) Ser.). 160p. (J). (gr. 2-4). 6.95 *(978-1-4027-1236-4(7))* Sterling Publishing Co., Inc.
—Little Women. 2013. (Vintage Children's Classics Ser.). (Illus.). 432p. (J). (gr. 4-7). pap. 10.99 *(978-0-09-957296-1(6))* Penguin Random Hse. GBR. Dist: Independent Pubs. Group.
Alegria, Malin. Border Town #2: Quince Clash. 2012. (Border Town Ser.). (ENG.). 192p. (J). (gr. 7). pap. 5.99 *(978-0-545-40241-5(7),* Scholastic Paperbacks) Scholastic, Inc.
Alender, Katie. As Dead As It Gets. 2013. (Bad Girls Don't Die Ser.: 3). (ENG.). 448p. (J). (gr. 5-9). pap. 9.99 *(978-1-4231-3778-8(7))* Hyperion Pr.
—Bad Girls Don't Die. 2010. (Bad Girls Don't Die Ser.: 1). (ENG.). 352p. (YA). (gr. 9-17). pap. 10.99 *(978-1-4231-0877-1(9))* Little, Brown Bks. for Young Readers.
—From Bad to Cursed. 2012. (Bad Girls Don't Die Ser.: 2). (ENG.). 448p. (YA). (gr. 5-9). pap. 11.99 *(978-1-4231-3777-1(9))* Hyperion Pr.
Alexander, Goldie. Body & Soul. 2003. 236p. pap. *(978-0-9578735-9-9(X))* IAD Pr.
Alexander, Heather. The Case of the Tattooed Cat. 2003. (New Adventures of Mary-Kate & Ashley Ser.). (Illus.). 83p. (J). (gr. 1-5). 12.65 *(978-0-7569-5351-5(0))* Perfection Learning Corp.
Alexander, K. R. The Collector. 2019. (Penworthy Picks YA Fiction Ser.). (ENG.). 217p. (J). (gr. 4-5). 17.59 *(978-0-87617-662-7(7))* Penworthy Co., LLC, The.
—The Collector. 2018. (ENG.). 224p. (J). (gr. 4-7). pap. 7.99 *(978-1-338-21224-2(9),* Scholastic Pr.) Scholastic, Inc.
Allen, Elise & Stanford, Halle. Jim Henson's Enchanted Sisters: Autumn's Secret Gift. 2014. (Enchanted Sisters Ser.). (ENG., Illus.). 128p. (J). (gr. 2-4). pap. 5.99 *(978-1-61963-254-7(3),* 900131787, Bloomsbury USA Childrens) Bloomsbury Publishing USA.
—Winter's Flurry Adventure. Pooler, Paige, illus. 2014. (Enchanted Sisters Ser.: 2). (YA). lib. bdg. 16.00 *(978-0-606-36217-7(7))* Turtleback.
Alpine, Rachele. A Void the Size of the World. 2017. (ENG., Illus.). 368p. (YA). (gr. 9). 17.99 *(978-1-4814-8571-5(7),* Simon Pulse) Simon Pulse.
Alvarez, Julia. How the Garcia Girls Lost Their Accents. 2011. 13.46 *(978-0-7848-3532-6(2),* Everbind) Marco Bk. Co.
Amato, Carol J. The Lost Treasure of the Golden Sun. 2005. 172p. (J). *(978-0-9713756-3-5(1))* Stargazer Publishing Co.
—The Secret of Blackhurst Manor. 2017. (ENG.). 232p. (J). pap. 9.95 *(978-1-933277-02-8(5))* Stargazer Publishing Co.
Amirkhan, Michele. Princess Elian's Quest. 2008. 112p. 20.95 *(978-0-595-50870-9(7));* pap. 10.95 *(978-0-595-51400-7(6))* iUniverse, Inc.
An, Na. Wait for Me. 2017. (ENG., Illus.). (YA). (gr. 7). 192p. 19.99 *(978-1-4814-4242-8(2));* 208p. pap. 10.99 *(978-1-4814-4243-5(0))* Simon & Schuster Children's Publishing. (Atheneum/Caitlyn Dlouhy Books).
Anderson, E. V. The Many Lives of Lilith Lane, 0 vols. unabr. ed. 2012. (ENG.). 162p. (J). (gr. 7-12). pap. 14.95 *(978-1-61109-792-4(4),* 9781611097924, Skyscape) Amazon Publishing.
Anderson, Lynda & Bennett, Melanie. The Micro Meanies. 2008. 180p. pap. *(978-0-9783204-7-8(6))* Aaspirations.
Anderson, Paris. The Sisters Kennington. 2004. 140p. (J). per. 16.00 *(978-1-58982-195-8(5),* Millennial Mind Publishing) American Bk. Publishing Group.
Anderson, Rachael. Los Mejores Amigos. McNicholas, Shelagh, illus. 2003. (SPA.). 120p. (J). (gr. 3-5). 9.95 *(978-84-204-4377-5(8))* Ediciones Alfaguara ESP. Dist: Santillana USA Publishing Co., Inc.
Ando, Natsumi. Arisa 1. 2012. (Arisa Ser.: 1). (Illus.). 208p. (gr. 8-12). pap. 10.99 *(978-1-61262-335-1(2))* Kodansha America, Inc.
Andracki, Zenon. Dear Ashley: A Middle Grade Novel. 2006. (ENG.). 84p. per. 19.95 *(978-1-4241-6168-3(1))* America Star Bks.
Andrews, Jane. Each & All: The Seven Little Sisters Prove Their Sisterhood (Yesterday's Classics) 2009. 120p. pap. 8.95 *(978-1-59915-308-7(4))* Yesterday's Classics.
—Seven Little Sisters Who Live on the Rou. 2006. (Illus.). pap. *(978-1-4065-0858-1(6))* Dodo Pr.
—Young Reader's Series: The seven little sisters who live on the round ball that floats in the Air. 2008. 152p. pap. 14.95 *(978-1-60444-020-1(1))* IndoEuropeanPublishing.com.
Andrews, Jane & Hopkins, Louisa Parsons. The Seven Little Sisters Who Live on the Round Ball that Floats in the Air. 2004. reprint ed. pap. 21.95 *(978-1-4179-1646-7(X))* Kessinger Publishing, LLC.
Andrews-McKinney, Joyce. Jentle & Jewel Fix Things Andrews-McKinney, Joyce, illus. l.t. ed. 2006. (Illus.). 17p. (J). pap. 8.00 *(978-0-9728975-4-9(2))* JA-M Pubs., LLC.
Anna, Jennifer. The Best Thing: An Almost True Story of Ladybugs & Sisters. 2007. (Illus.). 64p. (Orig.). (J). pap. 14.99 *(978-1-59092-154-8(2))* Blue Forge Pr.
App, Linda Hoogeveen. Emma Pearl, Flower Girl. 2012. 34p. pap. 16.95 *(978-1-4497-6619-1(6),* WestBow Pr.) Author Solutions, LLC.
Appelt, Kathi & Alison Mcghee. Maybe a Fox. 2017. lib. bdg. 18.40 *(978-0-606-39744-5(2))* Turtleback.
Appelt, Kathi & McGhee, Alison. Maybe a Fox. 2016. (ENG., Illus.). 272p. (J). (gr. 5-9). 18.99 *(978-1-4424-8242-5(7),* Atheneum/Caitlyn Dlouhy Books) Simon & Schuster Children's Publishing.
Applegate, Katherine & Grant, Michael. The Islanders: Volume 2 Vol. 2: Nina Won't Tell & Ben's in Love. 2015. (Islanders Ser.: 2). (ENG.). 464p. (YA). (gr. 8). pap. 9.99 *(978-0-06-234078-8(6),* HarperTeen) HarperCollins Pubs.
Arenella, Betsy Bottino. Isabelle's Dream: A Story & Activity Book for a Child's Grief Journey. Henderson, Dana, illus. 2007. 64p. (gr. -1-3). per. 7.95 *(978-0-9675532-9-0(6))* Quality of Life Publishing Co.
Aristophane. The Zabime Sisters. Madden, Matt, tr. Aristophane, illus. 2010. (ENG., Illus.). 96p. (YA). (gr. 7-18). pap. 17.99 *(978-1-59643-638-1(7),* 900068446, First Second Bks.) Roaring Brook Pr.
Armstrong, Ashley Sage-Taylor. The Adventures of Starlight & Sunny: Book Four in the Adventures of Starlight & Sunny Series, ?Princesses Don't Need a Job !? How to Be an Indepen. 2013. 52p. pap. *(978-1-927863-02-2(3))* Armstrong, Ashley.
—The Adventures of Starlight & Sunny: Building a Dream , How to Focus & Make Your Dreams Come to Life, with Positive Conscious Morals. Picture Boo. 2013. 52p. pap. *(978-1-927863-04-6(X))* Armstrong, Ashley.
—The Adventures of Starlight & Sunny: I Am Me ! Who Are You?, How to Find Good Quality Friends & Stand up for One Another, with Positive Morals, Pi. 2013. 52p. pap. *(978-1-927863-00-8(7))* Armstrong, Ashley.
Armstrong, Kelley. Sea of Shadows. (Age of Legends Trilogy Ser.: 1). (ENG.). (YA). (gr. 8). 2015. 432p. pap. 9.99 *(978-0-06-207125-5(4))* 2014. 416p. 17.99 *(978-0-06-207124-8(6))* HarperCollins Pubs. (HarperCollins).
—Sea of Shadows. 2015. (Age of Legends Ser.: 1). (YA). lib. bdg. 20.85 *(978-0-606-36511-6(7))* Turtleback.
Asch, Sheila. Katy's Time. 2007. 184p. pap. 16.95 *(978-1-84753-333-3(7))* Lulu Pr., Inc.
Ashby, Gaylene. STORY TIME A Collection of Three Children's Stories. 2008. 28p. 14.95 *(978-1-4357-1929-3(8))* Lulu Pr., Inc.
Austen, Jane. Sense & Sensibility. 2011. (ENG.). 464p. (YA). (gr. 8). pap. 8.99 *(978-0-06-201563-1(X),* HarperTeen) HarperCollins Pubs.
—Sense & Sensibility. Kronheimer, Ann, illus. 2013. (Jane Austen Ser.). (ENG.). 64p. pap. 7.95 *(978-1-906230-11-1(0))* Real Reads Ltd. GBR. Dist: Casemate Pubs. & Bk. Distributors, LLC.
Austen, Jane. & Fisher, Eric Scott. Pride & Prejudice: Lit for Little Hands, 1 vol. 2011. (Calico Illustrated Classics Ser.: No. 4). (ENG., Illus.). 112p. (J). (gr. 2-5). 38.50 *(978-1-61641-619-5(X),* 4053, Calico Chapter Bks.) ABDO Publishing Co.
Banghart, Tracy. Grace & Fury. 2019. (Grace & Fury Ser.: 1). (ENG.). 336p. (YA). (gr. 9-17). pap. 10.99 *(978-0-316-47142-8(9))* Little, Brown Bks. for Young Readers.
Banks, Lynne Reid. Angela & Diabola. 163p. (J). (gr. 4-6). pap. 4.50 *(978-0-8072-1515-9(5),* Listening Library) Random Hse. Audio Publishing Group.
Baratz-Logsted, Lauren. Annie's Adventures. 2008. (Sisters Eight Ser.: 1). (ENG., Illus.). 144p. (J). (gr. 1-4). pap. 6.99 *(978-0-547-05338-7(X),* 1036248, Clarion Bks.) HarperCollins Pubs.
—Durinda's Dangers. 2008. (Sisters Eight Ser.: 2). (ENG., Illus.). 128p. (J). (gr. 1-4). pap. 6.99 *(978-0-547-05339-4(8),* 1036249, Clarion Bks.) HarperCollins Pubs.
—Durinda's Dangers, 2. Weber, Lisa K., illus. 2008. (Sisters 8 Ser.: 2). (ENG.). 128p. (J). (gr. 2-4). 18.69 *(978-0-547-13347-8(2))* Houghton Mifflin Harcourt Publishing Co.
—The Final Battle... for Now Bk. 9. 2012. (Sisters Eight Ser.: 9). (ENG., Illus.). 160p. (J). (gr. 1-4). pap. 6.99 *(978-0-547-55441-9(9),* 1452177, Clarion Bks.) HarperCollins Pubs.
—Georgia's Greatness. 2009. (Sisters Eight Ser.: 3). (ENG., Illus.). 128p. (J). (gr. 1-4). pap. 7.99 *(978-0-547-05340-0(1),* 1036250, Clarion Bks.) HarperCollins Pubs.
—Petal's Problems. 2010. (Sisters Eight Ser.: 6). (ENG., Illus.). 144p. (J). (gr. 1-4). pap. 6.99 *(978-0-547-33403-5(6),* 1417756, Clarion Bks.) HarperCollins Pubs.
—Petal's Problems, 6. 2010. (Sisters 8 Ser.: 6). (ENG., Illus.). 144p. (J). (gr. 2-4). 18.69 *(978-0-547-33402-8(8))* Houghton Mifflin Harcourt Publishing Co.
—Rebecca's Rashness, Bk. 7. 2011. (Sisters Eight Ser.: 7). (ENG., Illus.). 144p. (J). (gr. 1-4). pap. 6.99 *(978-0-547-55434-1(6),* 1452145, Clarion Bks.) HarperCollins Pubs.
Baratz-Logsted, Lauren & Logsted, Jackie. Marcia's Madness. Weber, Lisa K., illus. 2010. (Sisters Eight Ser.: 5). (ENG.). 128p. (J). (gr. 1-4). pap. 6.99 *(978-0-547-32864-5(8),* 1416978, Clarion Bks.) HarperCollins Pubs.
Baratz-Logsted, Lauren, et al. Marcia's Madness, 5. Weber, Lisa K., illus. 2010. (Sisters 8 Ser.: 5). (ENG.). 128p. (J). (gr. 2-4). 18.69 *(978-0-547-33401-1(X))* Houghton Mifflin Harcourt Publishing Co.
Barden, Stephanie. Cinderella Smith. Goode, Diane, illus. 2011. (Cinderella Smith Ser.: 1). (ENG.). 160p. (J). (gr. 3-7). 16.99 *(978-0-06-196423-7(9),* HarperCollins) HarperCollins Pubs.

Barkley, Callie. Amy Meets Her Stepsister. Riti, Marsha, illus. 2013. (Critter Club Ser.: 5). (ENG.). 128p. (J). (gr. k-2). 17.99 *(978-1-4424-8216-6(8))*; pap. 6.99 *(978-1-4424-8215-9(X))* Little Simon. (Little Simon).
—Amy Meets Her Stepsister. 2013. (Critter Club Ser.: 5). lib. bdg. 16.00 *(978-0-606-32320-8(1))* Turtleback.
—Marion Takes Charge. Riti, Marsha, illus. 2015. (Critter Club Ser.: 12). (ENG.). 128p. (J). (gr. k-4). pap. 5.99 *(978-1-4814-2408-0(4),* Little Simon) Little Simon.
Barnes, Jennifer Lynn. The Fixer. 2016. (ENG.). 400p. (YA). pap. 11.99 *(978-1-61963-598-2(4),* 900141877, Bloomsbury USA Childrens) Bloomsbury Publishing USA.
Barnholdt, Lauren. Fake Me a Match. 2012. (Mix Ser.). (ENG.). 304p. (J). (gr. 4-8). pap. 6.99 *(978-1-4424-2259-9(9),* Aladdin) Simon & Schuster Children's Publishing.
Barraclough, Lindsey. Long Lankin. 2014. (ENG.). 464p. (YA). (gr. 7). pap. 9.99 *(978-0-7636-6937-9(7))* Candlewick Pr.
Barrows, Annie. Ivy + Bean Take Care of the Babysitter. Blackall, Sophie, illus. 2007. (Ivy & Bean Ser.: Bk. 4). (ENG.). pap., tchr. ed. *(978-0-8118-8667-3(0))* Chronicle Bks. LLC.
—Ivy & Bean One Big Happy Family (Book 11) Blackall, Sophie, illus. 2018. (Ivy & Bean Ser.: 11). (ENG.). 124p. (J). (gr. 1-4). 14.99 *(978-1-4521-6400-7(2))* Chronicle Bks. LLC.
—Ivy & Bean Take Care of the Babysitter: Book 4, Volume 4. Blackall, Sophie, illus. 2008. (Ivy & Bean Ser.: IVYB). (ENG.). 128p. (J). (gr. 1-5). pap. 5.99 *(978-0-8118-6584-5(3))* Chronicle Bks. LLC.
—Magic in the Mix. 2015. (ENG.). 288p. (YA). (gr. 3-6). pap. 8.99 *(978-1-61963-798-6(7),* 900148899, Bloomsbury USA Childrens) Bloomsbury Publishing USA.
Barrows, Annie & Blackall, Sophie. Ivy + Bean Take Care of the Babysitter. 2011. (Ivy & Bean Ser.). (ENG., Illus.). 128p. (J). (gr. 2-5). 31.36 *(978-1-59961-931-6(8),* 10111, Chapter Bks.) Spotlight.
Bashford, Taryn. The Harper Effect. 2018. (ENG.). 408p. (YA). (gr. 8-8). 17.99 *(978-1-5107-2665-9(9),* Sky Pony Pr.) Skyhorse Publishing Co., Inc.
Bassett-Giehtbrock, Dianne. Sissy & Me. 2011. 16p. pap. 8.99 *(978-1-4567-6943-7(X))* AuthorHouse.
Batanda, Jackee Budesta. The Blue Marble. 2005. (Illus.). 44p. pap. *(978-9988-550-89-9(8))* Sub-Saharan Pubs. & Traders GHA. Dist: Michigan State Univ. Pr.
Bateman, Rachel. Someone Else's Summer. 2018. (ENG.). 336p. (YA). (gr. 8-17). pap. 17.99 *(978-0-7624-6505-7(0),* Running Pr. Kids) Running Pr.
Bath, K. P. Flip Side. 2009. (YA). 16.99 *(978-0-316-03836-2(9))* Little Brown & Co.
Bauer, Joan. Raising Lumie. 2020. (ENG.). 288p. (J). (gr. 5). 16.99 *(978-0-593-11320-2(9),* Viking Books for Young Readers) Penguin Young Readers Group.
Bauer, Marion Dane. The Red Ghost. Ferguson, Peter, illus. 2009. (Stepping Stone Book(TM) Ser.). 96p. (J). (gr. 1-4). 4.99 *(978-0-375-84082-1(6),* Random Hse. Bks. for Young Readers) Random Hse. Children's Bks.
Bauman, Beth Ann. Rosie & Skate. 2011. (ENG.). 224p. (YA). (gr. 9). pap. 8.99 *(978-0-385-73736-4(X),* Ember) Random Hse. Children's Bks.
Bayerl, Katie. A Psalm for Lost Girls. 2018. 368p. (YA). (gr. 7). pap. 10.99 *(978-0-399-54527-6(1),* Speak) Penguin Young Readers Group.
Beamish, Diane. Amy's Silent World. 2006. 24p. 10.25 *(978-1-4116-5759-5(4))* Lulu Pr., Inc.
Behrens, Rebecca. The Last Grand Adventure. (ENG.). (J). (gr. 3-7). 2019. 352p. pap. 8.99 *(978-1-4814-9693-3(X))* 2018. (Illus.). 336p. 17.99 *(978-1-4814-9692-6(1))* Simon & Schuster Children's Publishing. (Aladdin).
Bell, G. F. Angel Wings & S'Mores. 2008. 152p. 29.99 *(978-1-4257-7491-2(1))*; pap. 19.99 *(978-1-4257-7489-9(X))* Xlibris Corp.
Belton-Terrell, Alice F. Kailah & Lyndsey: Sharing Spaces. 2008. 24p. pap. 11.49 *(978-1-4389-3726-7(1))* AuthorHouse.
Bemelmans, Ludwig. The Golden Basket. 2016. (ENG., Illus.). 96p. (J). (gr. 1-5). pap. 9.99 *(978-0-486-80717-1(7))* Dover Pubns., Inc.
Benevenia, Rose. Dolly & Babe. Benevenia, Rose, illus. l.t. ed. 2004. (Illus.). 9p. (J). (gr. k-2). pap. 9.00 *(978-0-9729044-0-7(9))* Cabbage Patch Pr.
Benko, Kamilla. Fire in the Star. 2020. (Unicorn Quest Ser.). (ENG., Illus.). 384p. (J). 16.99 *(978-1-68119-249-9(7),* 900164375, Bloomsbury Children's Bks.) Bloomsbury Publishing USA.
—Secret in the Stone. (Unicorn Quest Ser.). (ENG.). (J). 2020. 352p. pap. 8.99 *(978-1-5476-0310-7(0),* 900211266) 2019. (Illus.). 336p. 16.99 *(978-1-68119-247-5(0),* 900164378) Bloomsbury Publishing USA. (Bloomsbury Children's Bks.).
—The Unicorn Quest. (Unicorn Quest Ser.). (ENG.). 336p. (J). 2019. pap. 8.99 *(978-1-68119-983-2(1),* 900194729, Bloomsbury Children's Bks.) 2018. 16.99 *(978-1-68119-245-1(4),* 900164376, Bloomsbury USA Childrens) Bloomsbury Publishing USA.
Bennett, James W. & Bennett, James. Faith Wish. 2003. (ENG.). 160p. (J). (gr. 7-18). tchr. ed. 16.95 *(978-0-8234-1778-0(6))* Holiday Hse., Inc.
Bennett, Sophia. The Look. 2013. (ENG.). 336p. (YA). (gr. 7). 17.99 *(978-0-545-46438-3(2))*; (J). *(978-0-545-46439-0(0))* Scholastic, Inc. (Chicken Hse., The).
Bennett, Veronica. Cassandra's Sister. 2007. (ENG., Illus.). 240p. (YA). (gr. 7-12). 15.99 *(978-0-7636-3464-3(6))* Candlewick Pr.
Benway, Robin. The Extraordinary Secrets of April, May, & June. 2011. (ENG.). 288p. (YA). (gr. 7-12). 24.94 *(978-1-59514-286-3(X))* Penguin Young Readers Group.
Berg, Deva Jean. A Tail of Two Sisters. Berg, Deva Jean, illus. 2013. (Illus.). 26p. pap. 9.95 *(978-1-939790-07-1(7))* Lorian Assn., The.
Bergmeier-Johnson. Ya Ya's Boom Booms. 2005. (ENG.). 32p. per. 18.00 *(978-1-4184-8826-0(7))* AuthorHouse.
Berten, Jinny Powers & Holt, Norah. Littsie of Cincinnati. 2003. (Illus.). 125p. (J). per. 9.95 *(978-0-9724421-0-7(3))* Fountain Square Publishing.
Berube, Amelinda. Here There Are Monsters. 2019. (ENG., Illus.). 352p. (YA). (gr. 8-12). pap. 10.99 *(978-1-4926-7101-5(0))* Sourcebooks, Inc.
Best Sisters Ever! 2016. (Illus.). (J). *(978-1-5182-2655-7(8))* Random Hse., Inc.
Beynon, Veronica. My Sister Has Autism & That's Okay. 2013. 24p. pap. *(978-1-4602-2066-5(8))* FriesenPress.
Bial, Raymond. Shadow Island: A Tale of Lake Superior. 2006. 172p. (J). (gr. 3-7). 18.95 *(978-1-883953-37-9(5))*; per. 12.95 *(978-1-883953-36-2(7))* Great Lakes Literary, LLC. (Blue Horse Books).
Big Little Sister. 2003. per. *(978-0-9740182-1-8(X))* HuntForMo Creations.
Billingsley, Franny. Chime. 2011. (Playaway Young Adult Ser.). (YA). 59.99 *(978-1-61707-143-0(9))* Findaway World, LLC.
—Chime. 2012. (ENG.). 320p. (YA). (gr. 7-12). 26.19 *(978-0-8037-3552-1(9),* Dial) Penguin Publishing Group.
—Chime. 2012. (ENG.). 384p. (YA). (gr. 7-18). 8.99 *(978-0-14-242092-8(1),* Speak) Penguin Young Readers Group.
Birdsall, Jeanne. The Penderwicks: A Summer Tale of Four Sisters, Two Rabbits, & a Very Interesting Boy. (Penderwicks Ser.: 1). (ENG.). (J). (gr. 3-7). 2007. 288p. 8.99 *(978-0-440-42047-7(4),* Yearling) 2005. 272p. 17.99 *(978-0-375-83143-0(6),* Knopf Bks. for Young Readers) Random Hse. Children's Bks.
—The Penderwicks: A Summer Tale of Four Sisters, Two Rabbits & a Very Interesting Boy. 2007. (Penderwicks (Hardback) Ser.). 262p. (gr. 3-7). 18.00 *(978-0-7569-7798-6(3))* Perfection Learning Corp.
—The Penderwicks: A Summer Tale of Four Sisters, Two Rabbits, & a Very Interesting Boy. 2007. (Penderwicks Ser.: 1). (Illus.). 262p. (gr. 4-7). lib. bdg. 18.40 *(978-1-4177-7275-9(1))* Turtleback.
—The Penderwicks: A Summer Tale of Four Sisters, Two Rabbits & a Very Interesting Boy. 2009. 8.80 *(978-0-7848-2826-7(1),* Everbind) Marco Bk. Co.
—The Penderwicks: A Summer Tale of Four Sisters, Two Rabbits & a Very Interesting Boy. l.t. ed. 2006. (Penderwick Ser.). 304p. (J). (gr. 3-7). 23.95 *(978-0-7862-8897-7(3))* Thorndike Pr.
—The Penderwicks at Point Mouette. 2011. (Playaway Children Ser.). (J). (gr. k). 44.99 *(978-1-61707-434-9(9))* Findaway World, LLC.
—The Penderwicks at Point Mouette. (Penderwicks Ser.: 3). (ENG.). (J). (gr. 3-7). 2012. 320p. 8.99 *(978-0-375-85135-3(6),* Yearling) 2011. 304p. 16.99 *(978-0-375-85851-2(2),* Knopf Bks. for Young Readers) Random Hse. Children's Bks.
—The Penderwicks on Gardam Street. 2011. (Playaway Children Ser.). (J). (gr. 3-6). 44.99 *(978-1-61707-435-6(7))* Findaway World, LLC.
—The Penderwicks on Gardam Street. 2010. (Penderwicks Ser.: 2). (ENG.). 336p. (J). (gr. 3-7). 8.99 *(978-0-440-42203-7(5),* Yearling) Random Hse. Children's Bks.
—The Penderwicks on Gardam Street. 2010. (Penderwicks Ser.: 2). lib. bdg. 18.40 *(978-0-606-14418-6(8))* Turtleback.
Bishop, Jenn. The Distance to Home. 2017. 240p. (J). (gr. 3-7). 7.99 *(978-1-101-93874-4(9),* Yearling) Random Hse. Children's Bks.
Bitner, Amanda Marie. Baby Sister. 2012. 28p. pap. 24.95 *(978-1-4626-8684-1(2))* America Star Bks.
Black, Holly. The Cruel Prince. 2023. (YA). 45.00 *(978-1-955876-16-2(9))* LitJoy Crate.
—The Cruel Prince. 2018. (Folk of the Air Ser.: 1). (ENG.). (YA). (gr. 9-17). 416p. pap. 12.99 *(978-0-316-31031-4(X))*; (Illus.). 384p. 19.99 *(978-0-316-31027-7(1))* Little, Brown Bks. for Young Readers.
—The Queen of Nothing. (Folk of the Air Ser.: 3). (ENG., Illus.). (YA). (gr. 9-17). 2020. 336p. pap. 12.99 *(978-0-316-31037-6(9))* 2019. 320p. 19.99 *(978-0-316-31042-0(5))* Little, Brown Bks. for Young Readers.
—The Wicked King. 2022. (ENG.). (YA). 45.00 *(978-1-955876-17-9(7))* LitJoy Crate.
—The Wicked King. (Folk of the Air Ser.: 2). (ENG., Illus.). (J). (gr. 9-17). 2020. 368p. pap. 12.99 *(978-0-316-31032-1(8))* 2019. 336p. 19.99 *(978-0-316-31035-2(2))* Little, Brown Bks. for Young Readers.
Black, Sonia W. Jumping the Broom. Van Wright, Cornelius & Hu, Ying-Hwa, illus. 2004. 32p. (J). lib. bdg. 15.00 *(978-1-4242-0234-8(5))* Fitzgerald Bks.
Black, Yelena. Dance of Shadows. 2014. (Dance of Shadows Ser.). (ENG., Illus.). 384p. (YA). (gr. 7). pap. 9.99 *(978-1-61963-185-4(7),* 900125810, Bloomsbury USA Childrens) Bloomsbury Publishing USA.
Blackman, S. A. A Smickamookum Drinks Belly. Gubitosi, Lillian, illus. 2003. 32p. (J). (gr. -1-k). 16.95 incl. audio *(978-1-929409-02-0(8))* Blade Publishing.
Blake, Kendare. One Dark Throne. (YA). 2019. (Three Dark Crowns Ser.: 2). (ENG.). 480p. (gr. 9). pap. 12.99 *(978-0-06-238547-5(X),* Quill Tree Bks.) 2017. (Three Dark Crowns Ser.: 2). (ENG., Illus.). 464p. (gr. 9). 18.99 *(978-0-06-238546-8(1),* Quill Tree Bks.) 2017. (Illus.). 448p. *(978-0-06-274764-8(9),* HarperTeen) 2017. (Illus.). 448p. *(978-0-06-269730-1(7),* HarperTeen) 2017. (Illus.). 448p. *(978-0-06-269935-0(0),* HarperTeen) 2017. (Illus.). 448p. *(978-0-06-269045-6(0),* HarperTeen) 2017. (Illus.). 448p. *(978-0-06-279729-2(8),* HarperTeen) HarperCollins Pubs.
—Three Dark Crowns. (Three Dark Crowns Ser.: 1). (ENG.). (YA). (gr. 9). 2018. 432p. pap. 15.99 *(978-0-06-238544-4(5))* 2016. (Illus.). 416p. 17.99 *(978-0-06-238543-7(7))* HarperCollins Pubs. (Quill Tree Bks.).
—Three Dark Crowns. 2018. (YA). lib. bdg. 22.10 *(978-0-606-40404-4(X))* Turtleback.
—Two Dark Reigns. 2018. (Three Dark Crowns Ser.: 3). (ENG., Illus.). 464p. (YA). (gr. 9). 18.99 *(978-0-06-268614-5(3),* Quill Tree Bks.) HarperCollins Pubs.
—Two Dark Reigns: Three Dark Crowns Book 3. 2018. (ENG., Illus.). 432p. (J). *(978-1-5098-7649-5(9),* HarperTeen) HarperCollins Pubs.
Blume, Lesley M. M. Cornelia & the Audacious Escapades of the Somerset Sisters. 2008. 272p. (J). (gr. 3-7). 8.99 *(978-0-440-42110-8(1),* Yearling) Random Hse. Children's Bks.
Bohrer, Maddie. Penny's Penny Puzzle. 2010. 24p. pap. 11.49 *(978-1-4490-6477-8(9))* AuthorHouse.
Boling, Katharine. January 1905: a Novel. 2006. (ENG., Illus.). 192p. (J). (gr. 5-7). pap. 11.99 *(978-0-15-205121-1(X),* 1195464, Clarion Bks.) HarperCollins Pubs.
Bonnett-Rampersaud, Louise. Bubble & Squeak, 1 vol. Banta, Susan, illus. 2006. (ENG.). 24p. (J). (gr. -1-2). 14.99 *(978-0-7614-5310-9(5))* Marshall Cavendish Corp.
Boricchio, Frances. A Box of Red Dominos. 2010. 28p. pap. 12.49 *(978-1-4520-5946-4(2))* AuthorHouse.
Bosworth, Jennifer. The Killing Jar. 2016. (ENG.). 352p. (YA). 34.99 *(978-0-374-34137-4(0),* 900126267, Farrar, Straus & Giroux (BYR)) Farrar, Straus & Giroux.
Bourgeois, Paulette. Benjamin et Sa Petite Soeur. 2004.Tr. of Franklin's Baby Sister. (FRE., Illus.). (J). (gr. k-3). spiral bd. *(978-0-616-14597-5(7))* Canadian National Institute for the Blind/Institut National Canadien pour les Aveugles.
Bowe, Julie. Formula for Friends. 2015. (Victoria Torres, Unfortunately Average Ser.). (ENG., Illus.). 160p. (J). (gr. 4-8). pap. 5.95 *(978-1-4965-0539-2(5),* 128611, Stone Arch Bks.) Capstone.
Boza, Eduardo Robles. Mi Amigo Tiene Hermanita (My Friend Has a Little Sister) (SPA.). (J). 4.95 *(978-968-419-844-9(2))* Grijalbo, Editorial MEX. Dist: AIMS International Bks., Inc.
Bradford, Arthur. Benny's Brigade. Hanawalt, Lisa, illus. 2012. (ENG.). 48p. (J). 19.95 *(978-1-936365-61-6(8),* d90f3ed6-666e-4056-88ba-efe956ba2f74) McSweeney's Publishing.
Bradley, James. The Silent Invasion: the Change Trilogy 1. 2017. (Change Trilogy Ser.: 1). (ENG.). 300p. (YA). (gr. 7). 7.95 *(978-1-74354-989-6(X),* Pan) Pan Macmillan Australia Pty, Ltd. AUS. Dist: Independent Pubs. Group.
Bradley, Kimberly Brubaker. Fighting Words. 2020. (ENG.). 272p. (J). (gr. 5-7). 17.99 *(978-1-9848-1568-2(7),* Dial Bks) Penguin Young Readers Group.
Brendler, Carol. The Two Mutch Sisters. Brown, Lisa, illus. 2018. (ENG.). 40p. (J). (gr. -1-3). 18.99 *(978-0-544-43074-7(3),* 1595749, Clarion Bks.) HarperCollins Pubs.
Brewer, Zac. The Blood Between Us. 2017. (ENG.). 304p. (YA). (gr. 8). pap. 9.99 *(978-0-06-230792-7(4),* HarperTeen) HarperCollins Pubs.
Bright, J. E. Splat the Cat & the Big Secret. 2018. 24p. (J). 13.89 *(978-1-64310-115-6(3))* Penworthy Co., LLC, The.
Brogle, Jennifer. The Adventures of Jennifer & Sherry: Summertime. 2013. 60p. pap. 25.36 *(978-1-4669-7560-6(1))* Trafford Publishing.
Brown, Mia. Goodnight Joy! Abdullah, Tariq, illus. 2010. 20p. 12.49 *(978-1-4520-1492-0(2))* AuthorHouse.
Bruneau M. D., Denise J. & Bruneau, Denise J. My Baby: Illustrations by MikeMotz. com. 2010. 28p. 13.99 *(978-1-4490-8475-2(3))* AuthorHouse.
Bryan, Barbara. Starfish, Seashells, Coral & Gems. 2010. 47p. (J). pap. 27.95 *(978-1-4327-6265-0(6))*; pap. 21.95 *(978-1-4327-6009-0(2))* Outskirts Pr., Inc.
Bryant, Ann. She's No Angel. 2005. (Step-Chain Ser.). 190p. (J). pap. 4.95 *(978-1-894222-75-4(X))* Lobster Pr. CAN. Dist: Univ. of Toronto Pr.
Bryson, Karen Mueller. The Incredibly Awesome Adventures of Puggie Liddel, the Graphic Novel. Tisdel, L. L, illus. 2013. 108p. pap. *(978-1-927384-09-1(5))* Zeta Comics.
Buckley, Michael. The Council of Mirrors. (Sisters Grimm Ser.: 9). 2018. lib. bdg. 19.65 *(978-0-606-41062-5(7))* 2013. (J). lib. bdg. 18.40 *(978-0-606-31650-7(7))* Turtleback.
—The Council of Mirrors (the Sisters Grimm #9) 10th Anniversary Edition. 10th ed. 2018. (Sisters Grimm Ser.). (ENG., Illus.). 304p. (J). (gr. 3-7). pap. 9.99 *(978-1-4197-2009-3(0),* 696406, Amulet Bks.) Abrams, Inc.
—The Everafter War. 2018. (Sisters Grimm Ser.: 7). (J). lib. bdg. 19.65 *(978-0-606-41064-9(3))* Turtleback.
—The Fairy-Tale Detectives. (Sisters Grimm Ser.: 1). (J). 2008. 81.45 *(978-1-4361-0398-5(3))* 2007. 214.75 *(978-1-4193-6197-5(X))* 2007. 1.25 *(978-1-4193-6193-7(7))* 2006. 71.75 *(978-1-4193-6198-2(8))* 2006. 86.75 *(978-1-4193-8749-4(9))* 2006. 74.75 *(978-1-4193-6196-8(1))* 2006. 89.75 *(978-1-4193-8747-0(2))* Recorded Bks., Inc.
—The Fairy-Tale Detectives: And the Unusual Suspects. Ferguson, Peter, illus. 2012. 580p. (J). *(978-1-4351-4487-3(2),* Amulet Bks.) Abrams, Inc.
—The Fairy-Tale Detectives (the Sisters Grimm #1) 10th Anniversary Edition. 10th anniv. ed. 2017. (Sisters Grimm Ser.). (ENG., Illus.). 288p. (J). (gr. 3-7). pap. 9.99 *(978-1-4197-2005-5(8),* 580406) Abrams, Inc.
—The Inside Story, 6 vols. 2010. (Sisters Grimm Ser.: 8). (J). 89.75 *(978-1-4498-1969-9(9))*; 72.75 *(978-1-4498-1967-5(2))*; 219.75 *(978-1-4498-1966-8(4))*; 87.75 *(978-1-4498-1971-2(0))*; 1.25 *(978-1-4498-1973-6(7))* Recorded Bks., Inc.
—The Inside Story (the Sisters Grimm #8) 10th Anniversary Edition. 10th ed. 2018. (Sisters Grimm Ser.). (ENG., Illus.). 240p. (J). (gr. 3-7). pap. 9.99 *(978-1-4197-2006-2(6),* 660306, Amulet Bks.) Abrams, Inc.
—The Problem Child: The Sisters Grimm. 2007. (Sisters Grimm Ser.: 3). (YA). lib. bdg. 18.40 *(978-1-4178-0733-8(4))* Turtleback.
—The Problem Child (the Sisters Grimm #3) 10th Anniversary Edition. Ferguson, Peter, illus. 10th ed. 2017. (Sisters Grimm Ser.). (ENG.). 288p. (J). (gr. 3-7). pap. 9.99 *(978-1-4197-2004-8(X),* 580606, Amulet Bks.) Abrams, Inc.
—The Unusual Suspects. 2006. (Sisters Grimm Ser.: Bk. 2). 1.00 *(978-1-4237-8623-8(8))* Recorded Bks., Inc.
—The Unusual Suspects. (Sisters Grimm Ser.: 2). (J). 2017. lib. bdg. 19.60 *(978-0-606-39686-8(1))* 2007. lib. bdg. 18.40 *(978-1-4178-0732-1(6))* Turtleback.
—The Unusual Suspects (the Sisters Grimm #2) 10th Anniversary Edition. Ferguson, Peter, illus. 10th anniv. ed. 2017. (Sisters Grimm Ser.). (ENG.). 288p. (J). (gr. 3-7). pap. 8.95 *(978-1-4197-2008-6(2),* 580506, Amulet Bks.) Abrams, Inc.
—A Very Grimm Guide. Ferguson, Peter, illus. 2012. (Sisters Grimm Ser.). (ENG.). 128p. (J). (gr. 3-7). 17.99 *(978-1-4197-0201-3(7),* 1019601, Amulet Bks.) Abrams, Inc.
Buehrlen, M. G. The Untimely Deaths of Alex Wayfare. 2016. (ENG.). 232p. (YA). pap. 15.99 *(978-1-68230-058-9(7),* Diversion Bks.) Diversion Publishing Corp.
Burbank, Vivian. My Grandma's Playhouse. 2010. 29p. (J). pap. 17.95 *(978-1-4327-5112-8(3))* Outskirts Pr., Inc.
Burgis, Stephanie. Kat, Incorrigible. 2012. (Kat, Incorrigible Ser.: 1). (ENG., Illus.). 320p. (J). (gr. 5-9). pap. 8.99 *(978-1-4169-9448-0(3),* Atheneum Bks. for Young Readers) Simon & Schuster Children's Publishing.
—Kat, Incorrigible, 1. 2011. (Kat, Incorrigible Ser.: 1). (ENG., Illus.). 304p. (J). (gr. 5-9). 16.99 *(978-1-4169-9447-3(5))* Simon & Schuster, Inc.
—The Princess Who Flew with Dragons. 2019. (Dragon Heart Ser.: 3). (ENG.). 224p. (J). 16.99 *(978-1-5476-0207-0(4),* 900203278, Bloomsbury Children's Bks.) Bloomsbury Publishing USA.
—Renegade Magic, 2. 2012. (Kat, Incorrigible Ser.: 2). (ENG., Illus.). 336p. (J). (gr. 5-9). 16.99 *(978-1-4169-9449-7(1),* Atheneum Bks. for Young Readers) Simon & Schuster Children's Publishing.
Burkhart, Alma J. If You Could See Her Smile. Burns, Sandra, illus. 2013. 24p. pap. 8.99 *(978-1-938768-32-3(9))* Gypsy Pubns.
Burns, Jane. My Sister's My Teacher! 2017. (ENG.). 182p. (J). pap. 14.95 *(978-1-78612-482-1(3),* aab81ec6-e7a5-4641-b583-7cdbe7df8e23) Austin Macauley Pubs. Ltd. GBR. Dist: Baker & Taylor Publisher Services (BTPS).
Busath, Isabelle & Thordsen, Isabella. Isabelle & Isabella's Little Book of Rules. Burris, Priscilla, illus. 2013. (ENG.). 120p. (J). (gr. -1-7). 12.99 *(978-1-4424-9980-5(X),* Simon Spotlight) Simon Spotlight.
Busby, Cylin. The Stranger Game. (ENG.). 288p. (YA). (gr. 8). 2018. pap. 9.99 *(978-0-06-235461-7(2))* 2016. 17.99 *(978-0-06-235460-0(4))* HarperCollins Pubs. (Balzer & Bray).
Bush Hager, Jenna & Bush, Barbara Pierce. Sisters First. Kaulitzki, Ramona, illus. 2019. (ENG.). 40p. (J). (gr. -1-3). 18.99 *(978-0-316-53478-9(1))* Little, Brown Bks. for Young Readers.
—The Superpower Sisterhood. Wojciechowski, Cyndi, illus. 2022. (ENG.). 40p. (J). (gr. -1-3). 18.99 *(978-0-316-62844-0(1))* Little, Brown Bks. for Young Readers.
Bush, Rosetta Bowman. My Name Is Violet. 2013. 20p. pap. 24.95 *(978-1-63000-515-3(0))* America Star Bks.
Busheri, Devora. My Sister Is Sleeping. Kichka, Michel, illus. 2020. (ENG.). 24p. (J). (gr. -1-2). 17.99 *(978-1-5415-4244-0(4),* a29a9ff7-3e01-4694-bf05-694ee5c133be, Kar-Ben Publishing) Lerner Publishing Group.
Butcher, Nancy, et al. It's Snow Problem, 3 vols. 2003. (ENG., Illus.). 112p. *(978-0-00-714466-2(0),* HarperCollins Children's Bks.) HarperCollins Pubs. Ltd.
—Two for the Road. 2003. (ENG., Illus.). 112p. *(978-0-00-714463-1(6),* HarperCollins Children's Bks.) HarperCollins Pubs. Ltd.
Butler, Dori Hillestad. Yes, I Know the Monkey Man, 1 vol. 2018. 224p. (J). (gr. 5-9). pap. 7.95 *(978-1-68263-060-0(9))* Peachtree Publishing Co. Inc.
By Kaleena Ma. Glasses for Me? Oh No! Dawn Phillips, illus. 2009. 40p. pap. 18.49 *(978-1-4389-5418-9(2))* AuthorHouse.
Byars, Betsy. The Golly Sisters Go West. Truesdell, Sue, illus. 2003. (I Can Read Level 3 Ser.). (ENG.). 64p. (J). (gr. k-3). pap. 4.99 *(978-0-06-444132-2(6),* HarperCollins) HarperCollins Pubs.
—Keeper of the Doves. 2004. (Illus.). 128p. (J). (gr. 3-7). reprint ed. 7.99 *(978-0-14-240063-0(7),* Puffin Books) Penguin Young Readers Group.
Byars, Betsy & Byars, B. The Golly Sisters Go West. 2003. (I Can Read! Level 3 Ser.). (J). (gr. k-3). lib. bdg. 13.55 *(978-0-8335-4709-5(7))* Turtleback.
Byrne, Elizabeth. The Grave Keepers. 2017. (ENG.). 320p. (YA). (gr. 8). 17.99 *(978-0-06-248475-8(3),* HarperTeen) HarperCollins Pubs.
Caletti, Deb. The Six Rules of Maybe. 2011. (ENG.). 352p. (YA). (gr. 7). pap. 12.99 *(978-1-4169-7971-5(9),* Simon Pulse) Simon Pulse.
Callaghan, Cindy. Lost in London. 2013. (Mix Ser.). (ENG., Illus.). 240p. (J). (gr. 4-8). pap. 7.99 *(978-1-4424-6653-1(7),* Aladdin) Simon & Schuster Children's Publishing.
Calonita, Jen. The Grass Is Always Greener. 2014. (Belles Ser.: 3). (ENG.). 320p. (YA). (gr. 7-17). pap. 10.00 *(978-0-316-09109-1(X),* Poppy) Little, Brown Bks. for Young Readers.
—Tricked. 2018. (Fairy Tale Reform School Ser.: 3). lib. bdg. 18.40 *(978-0-606-40515-7(1))* Turtleback.
—Winter White. 2013. (Belles Ser.: 2). (ENG.). 384p. (YA). (gr. 7-17). pap. 19.99 *(978-0-316-09118-3(9),* Poppy) Little, Brown Bks. for Young Readers.
Cameron, Ann. The Secret Life of Amanda K. Woods. 2014. (ENG.). 208p. (J). (gr. 5-9). pap. 14.99 *(978-1-250-04419-8(7),* 900128307) Square Fish.
Candelario, Margo. Looking to the Clouds for Daddy. Craft, Jerry, illus. 2009. (J). *(978-0-9820221-7-7(4))* Hunter, Karen Media.
Cannon, Deborah. The Pirate Vortex: Elizabeth Latimer, Pirate Hunter. 2009. 260p. pap. 20.00 *(978-1-4269-0532-2(7))* Trafford Publishing.
Cannon, Sarah. Oddity. 2019. (ENG.). 320p. (J). pap. 7.99 *(978-1-250-17906-7(8),* 900174055) Square Fish.
Cantor, Jillian. The September Sisters. 2009. (ENG.). 368p. (YA). (gr. 8-18). 16.99 *(978-0-06-168648-1(4),* HarperTeen) HarperCollins Pubs.
Capucilli, Alyssa Satin. Hannah Is a Big Sister. Stott, Dorothy, illus. 2014. (Hannah & Henry Ser.). 32p. (J). (gr. -1-k). 5.99 *(978-0-7641-6750-8(2))* Sourcebooks, Inc.
—Katy Duck, Big Sister. Cole, Henry, illus. 2007. (ENG.). 14p. (J). (gr. -1-k). bds. 7.99 *(978-1-4169-4209-2(2),* Little Simon) Little Simon.
Caring, Angela. Becoming Bryn. 2013. (ENG.). 297p. (YA). (gr. 7). pap. 11.95 *(978-1-935089-66-7(8))* Acacia Publishing, Inc.
Carkhuff, Denise. Mama's Heart Fits Two. 2015. (ENG., Illus.). 32p. (J). (gr. -1-2). 16.95 *(978-1-62634-222-4(9))* Greenleaf Book Group.
Carvalho, Marcela. Three Sisters, Three Weddings, & One Dress. 2010. (ENG.). 36p. pap. 24.94 *(978-0-557-52962-9(X))* Lulu Pr., Inc.
Carvell, Marlene. Sweetgrass Basket. 2005. 256p. (J). (gr. 5-6). 17.99 *(978-0-525-47547-7(8),* Dutton Books for Young Readers) Penguin Young Readers Group.
The Case of the Secret Box. 2007. 56p. pap. 7.75 *(978-0-8341-2268-8(X),* 083-412-288X) Beacon Hill Pr. of Kansas City.
Castellucci, Cecil. The Year of the Beasts. Powell, Nate, illus. 2014. (ENG.). 208p. (YA). (gr. 7-12). pap. 14.99 *(978-1-250-05076-2(6),* 900134147) Square Fish.

S

Castle, Amber. Spell Sisters: Olivia the Otter Sister. Hall, Mary, illus. 2013. (ENG.). 160p. (J). (gr. 2-4). pap. 7.99 *(978-0-85707-253-5(6),* Simon & Schuster Children's) Simon & Schuster, Ltd. GBR. Dist: Simon & Schuster, Inc.

Castle, Jennifer. Butterfly Wishes 1: the Wishing Wings. 2017. (Butterfly Wishes Ser.). (ENG., Illus.). 128p. (J). 15.99 *(978-1-68119-491-2(0),* 9781681194912, Bloomsbury USA Childrens) Bloomsbury Publishing USA.

—Butterfly Wishes 2: Tiger Streak's Tale. 2017. (Butterfly Wishes Ser.). (ENG.). 128p. (J). pap. 5.99 *(978-1-68119-373-1(6),* 900171778, Bloomsbury USA Childrens) Bloomsbury Publishing USA.

—Butterfly Wishes 3: Blue Rain's Adventure. 2018. (Butterfly Wishes Ser.). (ENG., Illus.). 128p. (J). 16.99 *(978-1-68119-691-6(3),* 900182258); pap. 5.99 *(978-1-68119-375-5(2),* 900171781) Bloomsbury Publishing USA. (Bloomsbury USA Childrens).

Castleman, Virginia. Sara Lost & Found. 2016. (ENG., Illus.). 320p. (J). (gr. 3-7). 16.99 *(978-1-4814-3871-1(9),* Aladdin) Simon & Schuster Children's Publishing.

Castner, K. D. Daughters of Ruin. 2017. (ENG.). 320p. (YA). (gr. 9). pap. 11.99 *(978-1-4814-3666-3(X),* McElderry, Margaret K. Bks.) McElderry, Margaret K. Bks.

Cattie, Becky & Luebbe, Tara. I Used to Be Famous. Lew-Vriethoff, Joanne, illus. 2019. (ENG.). 32p. (J). (gr. -1-3). 16.99 *(978-0-8075-3443-4(9),* 807534439) Whitman, Albert & Co.

Cecil, Lauren. Lalaloopsy: Cinder Slippers & the Grand Ball. Hill, Prescott, illus. 2013. (Lalaloopsy Ser.). (ENG.). 24p. (J). (gr. -1-3). pap. 3.99 *(978-0-545-47769-7(7))* Scholastic, Inc.

Chan, Queenie. The Dreaming Collection. 2010. (ENG., Illus.). 576p. pap. 19.99 *(978-1-4278-1871-3(1))* TOKYOPOP, Inc.

Chandler, Elizabeth. Dark Secrets 2 No. 2: No Time to Die; the Deep End of Fear. 2010. (Dark Secrets Ser.: 2). (ENG.). 624p. (YA). (gr. 7). pap. 9.99 *(978-1-4169-9462-6(9),* Simon Pulse) Simon Pulse.

Chankhamma, Shari. The Sisters' Luck. 2010. (ENG., Illus.). 144p. (YA). pap. 12.95 *(978-1-59362-190-2(6),* 7ad4c114-07c1-44ee-a74e-6f5f42969ae6) Slave Labor Bks.

Chapman, Brenda. Where Trouble Leads: A Jennifer Bannon Mystery. 2007. (Jennifer Bannon Mystery Ser.: 3). (ENG., Illus.). 136p. (YA). (gr. 5-18). per. 9.95 *(978-1-894917-44-5(8),* Napoleon & Co.) Dundurn Pr. CAN. Dist: Publishers Group West (PGW).

Chapman, Elsie. Along the Indigo. 2018. (ENG.). 392p. (gr. 8-17). 17.99 *(978-1-4197-2531-9(9),* Amulet Bks.) Abrams, Inc.

Chen, Justina. Lovely, Dark, & Deep. 2018. (ENG.). 352p. (YA). (gr. 7-7). 18.99 *(978-1-338-13406-3(X),* Levine, Arthur A. Bks.) Scholastic, Inc.

Cherry, Alison. She's the Liar. 2019. (ENG.). 208p. (J). (gr. 3-7). 17.99 *(978-1-338-30614-9(6),* Scholastic Pr.) Scholastic, Inc.

Child, Lauren. Slightly Invisible. Child, Lauren, illus. 2016. (Charlie & Lola Ser.). (ENG., Illus.). 40p. (J). (gr. -1-3). 19.65 *(978-0-606-39107-8(X))* Turtleback.

Childs, Tera Lynn. Goddess Boot Camp. 2010. (ENG.). 272p. (YA). (gr. 7-18). pap. 7.99 *(978-0-14-241665-5(7),* Speak) Penguin Young Readers Group.

—Sweet Legacy. 2013. (Sweet Venom Ser.: 3). (ENG.). 384p. (YA). (gr. 8). 17.99 *(978-0-06-200185-6(X),* Tegen, Katherine Bks) HarperCollins Pubs.

—Sweet Shadows. (Sweet Venom Ser.: 2). (ENG.). (YA). (gr. 8). 2013. 352p. pap. 9.99 *(978-0-06-200184-9(1))* 2012. 336p. 17.99 *(978-0-06-200183-2(3))* HarperCollins Pubs. (Tegen, Katherine Bks).

—Sweet Venom. 2012. (Sweet Venom Ser.: 1). (ENG.). 384p. (YA). (gr. 8). pap. 9.99 *(978-0-06-200182-5(5),* Tegen, Katherine Bks) HarperCollins Pubs.

Chokshi, Roshani. Aru Shah & the City of Gold: A Pandava Novel Book 4. l.t. ed. 2021. (Pandava Novel Ser.: 4). (ENG.). lib. bdg. 22.99 *(978-1-4328-8689-9(4))* Thorndike Pr.

—Rick Riordan Presents Aru Shah & the City of Gold: A Pandava Novel Book 4. 2021. (Pandava Ser.: 4). (ENG.). 400p. (J). (gr. 3-7). 16.99 *(978-1-368-01386-4(4),* Riordan, Rick) Disney Publishing Worldwide.

—Rick Riordan Presents Aru Shah & the City of Gold (a Pandava Novel, Book 4) A Pandava Novel Book 4. 2022. (Pandava Ser.: 4). (ENG.). 416p. (J). (gr. 3-7). pap. 8.99 *(978-1-368-02358-0(4),* Riordan, Rick) Disney Publishing Worldwide.

Chou, Joey, illus. Olaf's Frozen Adventure. 2017. (J). *(978-1-5379-5893-4(3),* Golden Bks.) Random Hse. Children's Bks.

Church, Caroline Jayne. I Am a Big Sister. Church, Caroline Jayne, illus. 2015. (ENG., Illus.). 24p. (J). (gr. -1 — 1). 6.99 *(978-0-545-68898-7(1),* Cartwheel Bks.) Scholastic, Inc.

—I Am a Big Sister! / ¡Soy una Hermana Mayor! (Bilingual) (Bilingual Edition) Church, Caroline Jayne, illus. 2015.Tr. of ¡Soy una Hermana Mayor! (SPA., Illus.). 24p. (J). (gr. -1 — 1). 6.99 *(978-0-545-84718-6(4),* Scholastic en Espanol) Scholastic, Inc.

Clare, Mimi St. The Fairbluffs of Pennington Island. 2013. 36p. pap. 12.99 *(978-1-935986-49-2(X))* Liberty University Press.

Clark-Elliott, Mary. The Day Ms. Qualbaum Came to Visit. 2013. 44p. pap. 20.72 *(978-1-4907-0921-5(5))* Trafford Publishing.

Clarke, Cat. The Lost & the Found. 2016. (ENG.). 368p. (YA). (gr. 9). 17.99 *(978-1-101-93204-9(X),* Crown Books For Young Readers) Random Hse. Children's Bks.

Cleary, Beverly. Beezus & Ramona. Rogers, Jacqueline, illus. 2020. (Ramona Ser.: 1). (ENG.). 208p. (J). (gr. 3-7). 17.99 *(978-0-688-21076-2(7));* pap. 7.99 *(978-0-380-70918-2(X))* HarperCollins Pubs. (HarperCollins).

—Beezus & Ramona. 2011. 9.01 *(978-0-7848-3570-8(5),* Everbind) Marco Bk. Co.

—Beezus & Ramona. (Ramona Quimby Ser.). 142p. (J). (gr. 3-5). pap. 4.99 *(978-0-8072-1441-1(8),* Listening Library) Random Hse. Audio Publishing Group.

—Beezus & Ramona. Darling, Louis, illus. (gr. 3-5). pap. *(978-0-545-24980-5(5))* Scholastic, Inc.

—Beezus & Ramona. (Ramona Quimby Ser.: 1). (J). 2013. lib. bdg. 17.20 *(978-0-88103-289-5(1))* 2010. lib. bdg. 16.00 *(978-0-606-15072-9(2))* Turtleback.

—Beezus & Ramona Movie Tie-In Edition. Rogers, Jacqueline, illus. movie tie-in ed. 2010. (Ramona Ser.: 1). (ENG.). 208p. (J). (gr. 3-7). pap. 5.99 *(978-0-06-191461-4(4),* HarperFestival) HarperCollins Pubs.

—The Complete 8-Book Ramona Collection: Beezus & Ramona, Ramona & Her Father, Ramona & Her Mother, Ramona Quimby, Age 8, Ramona Forever, Ramona the Brave, Ramona the Pest, Ramona's World. Rogers, Jacqueline, illus. 2020. (Ramona Ser.). (ENG.). 1728p. (J). (gr. 3-7). pap. 63.92 *(978-0-06-196090-1(X),* HarperCollins) HarperCollins Pubs.

—The Ramona 4-Book Collection, Volume 1 Vol. 1: Beezus & Ramona, Ramona & Her Father, Ramona the Brave, Ramona the Pest, Vol. 1. Rogers, Jacqueline, illus. 2020. (Ramona Ser.). (ENG.). 848p. (J). (gr. 3-7). pap. 31.96 *(978-0-06-124647-0(6),* HarperCollins) HarperCollins Pubs.

—The Ramona 4-Book Collection, Volume 2 Vol. 2: Ramona & Her Mother, Ramona Quimby, Age 8; Ramona Forever; Ramona's World. Rogers, Jacqueline, illus. 2020. (Ramona Ser.). (ENG.). 880p. (J). (gr. 3-7). pap. 31.96 *(978-0-06-124648-7(4),* HarperCollins) HarperCollins Pubs.

—Sister of the Bride. 2007. (ENG., Illus.). 272p. (J). (gr. 5-18). pap. 9.99 *(978-0-380-72807-7(9),* HarperCollins) HarperCollins Pubs.

Clement, Emily. Thea Stilton & the Hollywood Hoax. Pellizzari, Barbara & Balleello, Chiara, illus. 2015. 159p. (J). *(978-1-5182-1175-1(5))* Scholastic, Inc.

—Thea Stilton & the Tropical Treasure. Cairoli, Valeria et al, illus. 2015. 157p. (J). *(978-1-4806-9889-5(X))* Scholastic, Inc.

Clement-Moore, Rosemary. Texas Gothic. 2012. (ENG.). 416p. (YA). (gr. 9). pap. 10.99 *(978-0-385-73694-7(0),* Ember) Random Hse. Children's Bks.

Cleverly, Sophie. The Curse in the Candlelight: a Scarlet & Ivy Mystery. 2019. (ENG.). 384p. (J). 7.99 *(978-0-00-830822-3(5),* HarperCollins Children's Bks.) HarperCollins Pubs. Ltd. GBR. Dist: HarperCollins Pubs.

—The Dance in the Dark. 2018. (Scarlet & Ivy Ser.: 3). (ENG.). 320p. (J). (gr. 5-8). pap. 7.99 *(978-1-4926-3409-6(3))* Sourcebooks, Inc.

—The Last Secret: a Scarlet & Ivy Mystery. 2019. (ENG.). 320p. (J). 7.99 *(978-0-00-830823-0(3),* HarperCollins Children's Bks.) HarperCollins Pubs. Ltd. GBR. Dist: HarperCollins Pubs.

—The Lights under the Lake: a Scarlet & Ivy Mystery. 2018. (ENG.). 304p. (J). 7.99 *(978-0-00-830821-6(7),* HarperCollins Children's Bks.) HarperCollins Pubs. Ltd. GBR. Dist: HarperCollins Pubs.

—The Lost Twin. 2017. (Scarlet & Ivy Ser.: 1). (ENG.). 320p. (J). (gr. 5-8). 7.99 *(978-1-4926-4792-8(6),* 9781492647928) Sourcebooks, Inc.

—The Whispers in the Walls. 2017. (Scarlet & Ivy Ser.: 2). (ENG.). 288p. (J). (gr. 5-8). pap. 12.99 *(978-1-4926-3406-5(9),* 9781492634065) Sourcebooks, Inc.

Cochrane, Ian. Shian & the Corryvreckan. 2013. (Illus.). 96p. pap. *(978-1-909465-09-1(7))* Cloister Hse. Pr., The.

Cocks, Heather & Morgan, Jessica. Spoiled. 2012. (ENG.). 384p. (YA). (gr. 10-17). pap. 19.99 *(978-0-316-09827-4(2),* Poppy) Little, Brown Bks. for Young Readers.

Cohen, Jeff. Eva & Sadie & the Best Classroom EVER! Allen, Elanna, illus. 2015. (ENG.). 32p. (J). (gr. -1-3). 17.99 *(978-0-06-224938-8(X),* HarperCollins) HarperCollins Pubs.

Cohen, Paula Marantz. Beatrice Bunson's Guide to Romeo & Juliet. 2016. (ENG.). 223p. (YA). (gr. 4-9). pap. 11.95 *(978-1-58988-105-1(2))* Dry, Paul Bks., Inc.

Cole, Joanna. Soy una Hermana Mayor: I'm a Big Sister (Spanish Edition), 1 vol. Kightley, Rosalinda, illus. 2010.Tr. of I am a Big Sister. (SPA.). 32p. (J). (gr. -1-k). 7.99 *(978-0-06-190063-1(X))* HarperCollins Español.

Cole, Penelope Anne. Magical Mea. Collier, Kevin, illus. 2013. 24p. 19.95 *(978-1-61633-394-2(4));* pap. 10.95 *(978-1-61633-395-9(2))* Guardian Angel Publishing, Inc.

Coleman, K. R. Off Course. 2020. (Road Trip Ser.). (ENG.). 112p. (YA). (gr. 6-12). 26.65 *(978-1-5415-5688-1(7),* 9357fa30-bd0d-473d-a077-2f69a92d5727, Darby Creek) Lerner Publishing Group.

Collins, Rudy. Vanessa Owens & the Bond of Sisterhood. 2011. 106p. pap. 19.95 *(978-1-4560-7873-7(9))* America Star Bks.

Coman, Carolyn. The Memory Bank. Shepperson, Rob, illus. 2010. 263p. (J). pap. *(978-0-545-21067-6(4),* Levine, Arthur A. Bks.) Scholastic, Inc.

Condie, Ally. Atlantia. 2015. (ENG.). 320p. (YA). (gr. 7). pap. 10.99 *(978-0-14-751065-5(1),* Speak) Penguin Young Readers Group.

—Atlantia. 2015. lib. bdg. 22.10 *(978-0-606-37576-4(7))* Turtleback.

—Being Sixteen. 2010. 249p. (YA). *(978-1-60641-233-6(7))* Deseret Bk. Co.

Cone, Carl. There's a Season for All. Cone, Carl, illus. 2008. (ENG., Illus.). pap. 14.95 *(978-0-9801555-6-3(8))* Argus Enterprises International, Inc.

Connis, Dave. The Temptation of Adam: A Novel. 2017. (ENG.). 352p. (gr. 9-13). 16.99 *(978-1-5107-0730-6(1),* Sky Pony Pr.) Skyhorse Publishing Co., Inc.

Cook, Eileen. Fourth Grade Fairy, 1. 2011. (Fourth Grade Fairy Ser.: 1). (ENG.). 176p. (J). (gr. 3-7). pap. 7.99 *(978-1-4169-9811-2(X),* Aladdin) Simon & Schuster Children's Publishing.

Cook, Kajsa. Discoveries in the Shriver Family Attic: How a Woman & Her Children Dealt with the Battle of Gettysburg. 2009. (Illus.). 122p. (J). (gr. 4-8). pap. 8.95 *(978-1-57249-398-8(4),* White Mane Kids) White Mane Publishing Co., Inc.

Coolidge, Susan. Clover. 2017. (ENG., Illus.). (J). 23.95 *(978-1-374-96593-5(6))* Capital Communications, Inc.

—Clover. 2016. (ENG., Illus.). (J). 26.95 *(978-1-359-71234-9(8))* Creative Media Partners, LLC.

—What Katy Did at School. 2016. (ENG., Illus.). (J). 26.95 *(978-1-358-88715-4(2))* Creative Media Partners, LLC.

—What Katy Did at School. 2007. (ENG.). 108p. per. *(978-1-4068-4853-3(0))* Echo Library.

—What Katy Did at School. 2006. (ENG.). 180p. per. 8.95 *(978-1-59462-472-8(0),* 508, Bk. Jungle) Standard Publications, Inc.

—What Katy Did at School. 2004. reprint ed. pap. 20.95 *(978-1-4191-9354-5(6));* pap. 1.99 *(978-1-4192-9354-2(0))* Kessinger Publishing, LLC.

Coon, Kelly. Gravemaidens. 416p. (YA). (gr. 9). 2020. pap. 11.99 *(978-0-525-64784-3(3),* Ember) 2019. (ENG.). lib. bdg. 21.99 *(978-0-525-64785-0(6),* Delacorte Pr.) Random Hse. Children's Bks.

Coonan, Candace N. The Darkest Hour: Tales from Fadreama: Book 1. 2012. 328p. (gr. 4-6). pap. 19.11 *(978-1-4669-3565-5(0))* Trafford Publishing.

Cooney, Caroline B. Three Black Swans. 2012. (ENG.). 288p. (YA). (gr. 7). pap. 9.99 *(978-0-385-73868-2(4),* Ember) Random Hse. Children's Bks.

Cordell, Evie & Cordell, Ryan. Two Girls Want a Puppy. Lam, Maple, illus. 2015. (ENG.). 32p. (J). (gr. -1-3). 17.99 *(978-0-06-229261-2(7),* HarperCollins) HarperCollins Pubs.

Coster, Charles. Flemish Legends. 2005. pap. 15.50 *(978-1-59605-351-9(8),* Cosimo Classics) Cosimo, Inc.

Couloumbis, Audrey. Getting near to Baby. unabr. ed. 2004. 211p. (J). (gr. 5-9). pap. 36.00 incl. audio *(978-0-8072-8876-4(4),* LYA 287 SP, Listening Library) Random Hse. Audio Publishing Group.

—The Misadventures of Maude March: Or Trouble Rides a Fast Horse. 2007. (Illus.). 295p. (gr. 3-7). 18.00 *(978-0-7569-7770-2(3))* Perfection Learning Corp.

Courtney, Nadine Jolie. Romancing the Throne. 2017. (ENG.). 400p. (YA). (gr. 8). 17.99 *(978-0-06-240662-0(0),* Tegen, Katherine Bks) HarperCollins Pubs.

Craig, Erin A. House of Salt & Sorrows. (Sisters of the Salt Ser.). 416p. (YA). (gr. 7). 2020. pap. 12.99 *(978-1-9848-3195-8(X),* Ember) 2019. (ENG.). 21.99 *(978-1-9848-3193-4(3),* Delacorte Pr.) 2019. 19.99 *(978-1-9848-3192-7(5),* Delacorte Pr.) Random Hse. Children's Bks.

Crispin, Paula. I'm Getting a Baby Sister? 2004. 23p. pap. 24.95 *(978-1-4137-3380-8(8))* PublishAmerica, Inc.

Cross, Kady. Sisters of Salt & Iron. 2016. (Sisters of Blood & Spirit Ser.: 2). (ENG.). 352p. (YA). 18.99 *(978-0-373-21176-0(7),* Harlequin Teen) Harlequin Enterprises ULC CAN. Dist: HarperCollins Pubs.

Cross, Mimi. Shining Sea, 0 vols. 2016. (ENG.). 432p. (YA). (gr. 9-12). pap. 9.99 *(978-1-5039-3553-2(1),* 9781503935532, Skyscape) Amazon Publishing.

Crossan, Sarah. One. 2015. (ENG.). 400p. (YA). (gr. 8). 17.99 *(978-0-06-211875-2(7),* Greenwillow Bks.) HarperCollins Pubs.

Crowder, Melanie. A Nearer Moon. 2019. (Penworthy Picks Middle School Ser.). (ENG.). 160p. (J). (gr. 4-5). 18.96 *(978-1-64310-941-1(3))* Penworthy Co., LLC, The.

—A Nearer Moon. (ENG., Illus.). (J). (gr. 3-7). 2016. 176p. pap. 7.99 *(978-1-4814-4149-0(3),* Atheneum Bks. for Young Readers) 2015. 160p. 16.99 *(978-1-4814-4148-3(5))* Simon & Schuster Children's Publishing.

—A Nearer Moon. 2016. (ENG.). 176p. (J). (gr. 3-7). 18.40 *(978-0-606-39238-9(6))* Turtleback.

Cuasay, Alison Taimangio. Tasi & Matina: The Story of the First Clown Fish. 2010. 28p. pap. 12.99 *(978-1-4520-6672-1(8))* AuthorHouse.

Culbertson, Jan E. The Legend of Dunsmoor Manor. 2006. 88p. pap. 13.95 *(978-1-58909-348-5(8))* Bookstand Publishing.

—The Legend of the Lost Tiki. 2006. 95p. (YA). pap. 13.95 *(978-1-58909-315-7(1))* Bookstand Publishing.

Culwell, Lori. The Dirt. 2011. (ENG.). 208p. (YA). pap. 11.95 *(978-1-935961-36-9(5),* Booktrope Editions) Booktrope.

Cushing, Mims. The Sleepover Surprise. Phillips, Alan, illus. 2010. 24p. pap. 12.95 *(978-1-936343-01-0(0))* Peppertree Pr., The.

Cyprus, Naomi. Sisters of Glass. (Sisters of Glass Ser.: 1). (ENG.). (J). (gr. 3-7). 2018. 400p. pap. 9.99 *(978-0-06-245849-0(3))* 2017. 384p. 16.99 *(978-0-06-245847-6(7))* HarperCollins Pubs. (HarperCollins).

Dadey, Debbie. A Tale of Two Sisters. Avakyan, Tatevik, illus. 2015. (Mermaid Tales Ser.: 10). (ENG.). 128p. (J). (gr. 1-4). 17.99 *(978-1-4814-0258-3(7));* pap. 6.99 *(978-1-4814-0257-6(9))* Simon & Schuster Children's Publishing. (Aladdin).

Dalton, Michelle. Fifteenth Summer. 2013. (ENG.). 272p. (YA). (gr. 7). 17.99 *(978-1-4424-7267-9(7));* (Illus.). pap. 11.99 *(978-1-4424-7266-2(9))* Simon Pulse. (Simon Pulse).

Dalton, R. M. The Sisters' Story: The Legend of Queen Brighton & Sister Jasmine. 2012. 146p. 46.72 *(978-1-4771-4886-0(8));* pap. 28.03 *(978-1-4771-4885-3(X))* Xlibris Corp.

Daniels, W. J. The Empress Academy: The Secret of Glittershine. 2009. 144p. pap. 16.95 *(978-1-4327-2335-4(9))* Outskirts Pr., Inc.

Danna, Natasha. Any Two Can Be Twindollicious. Dye, Jerel, illus. 2013. 32p. (J). 17.95 *(978-1-60131-154-2(0),* Castlebridge Bks.) Big Tent Bks.

Darlison, Aleesah. Quinn's Riddles. Brailsford, Jill, illus. 2017. (Unicorn Riders Ser.). (ENG.). 112p. (J). (gr. 3-5). pap. 5.95 *(978-1-4795-6552-8(0),* 128542, Picture Window Bks.) Capstone.

—Quinn's Truth. Brailsford, Jill, illus. 2017. (Unicorn Riders Ser.). (ENG.). 112p. (J). (gr. 3-5). pap. 5.95 *(978-1-4795-6556-6(3),* 128546, Picture Window Bks.) Capstone.

Dasilva, D. Mom Has Left & Gone to Vegas. Craig, Dan, illus. 2008. 32p. pap. 19.95 *(978-1-59858-603-9(3))* Dog Ear Publishing, LLC.

Davis, Lisa Selin. Lost Stars. 2017. (ENG.). 288p. (YA). (gr. 9). pap. 9.99 *(978-1-328-78731-6(1),* 1684477, Clarion Bks.) HarperCollins Pubs.

Davis, Tanita S. Mare's War. 2011. (ENG.). 352p. (YA). (gr. 7). pap. 12.99 *(978-0-375-85077-6(5),* Knopf Bks. for Young Readers) Random Hse. Children's Bks.

Dawn, Sasha. Blink. 2018. (ENG.). 344p. (YA). (gr. 8-12). 17.99 *(978-1-5124-3977-9(0),* df9a5d50-6f73-45f3-8467-9620d5e1b05f, Carolrhoda Lab™) Lerner Publishing Group.

De Lint, Charles. Seven Wild Sisters: A Modern Fairy Tale. Vess, Charles, illus. 2014. (ENG.). 272p. (J). (gr. 3-7). 18.00 *(978-0-316-05356-3(2))* Little, Brown Bks. for Young Readers.

Deiss, A. The Sullivan Girls & the Mystery of Moonhouse. 2003. 104p. (Orig.). pap. 9.95 *(978-0-595-29580-7(0))* iUniverse, Inc.

Dematteis, Heidi Gestvang. Sisters Are Forever. 2012. 20p. (-18). pap. 24.95 *(978-1-4626-8791-6(1))* America Star Bks.

Demonia, Lori. Leah's Voice. 2013. 28p. 16.95 *(978-1-61244-240-2(4))* Halo Publishing International.

—Leah's Voice. Turchan, Monique, illus. 2012. 28p. pap. 12.95 *(978-1-61244-089-7(4))* Halo Publishing International.

Depken, Kristen L. Barbie Let's Plant a Garden! 2018. (Illus.). 24p. (J). *(978-1-5444-0240-6(6))* Random Hse., Inc.

—Happy Birthday to You! Aikins, Dave, illus. 2018. 24p. (J). *(978-1-5444-0156-0(6))* Random Hse., Inc.

—Happy Birthday to You! (Shimmer & Shine) Aikins, Dave, illus. 2018. (Step into Reading Ser.). (ENG.). 24p. (J). (gr. -1-1). pap. 5.99 *(978-1-5247-6799-0(9),* Random Hse. Bks. for Young Readers) Random Hse. Children's Bks.

—Let's Build a Snowman! 2017. (Illus.). 24p. (J). *(978-1-5182-5209-9(5))* Random Hse., Inc.

—Let's Build a Snowman! (Barbie) Dynamo Limited, illus. 2017. (Step into Reading Ser.). (ENG.). 24p. (J). (gr. -1-1). pap. 5.99 *(978-1-5247-6480-7(9),* Random Hse. Bks. for Young Readers) Random Hse. Children's Bks.

—Let's Plant a Garden! (Barbie) 2018. (Step into Reading Ser.). (ENG., Illus.). 24p. (J). (gr. -1-1). pap. 5.99 *(978-1-5247-6683-6(9),* Random Hse. Bks. for Young Readers) Random Hse. Children's Bks.

—Winter Wishes! Aikins, Dave, illus. 2017. 23p. (J). *(978-1-5182-5212-9(5))* Random Hse., Inc.

DeVillers, Julia & Roy, Jennifer. Double Feature. 2012. (Mix Ser.). (ENG.). (J). (gr. 4-8). 288p. pap. 7.99 *(978-1-4424-3403-5(1));* 272p. 16.99 *(978-1-4424-3402-8(3))* Simon & Schuster Children's Publishing. (Aladdin).

—Take Two. 2010. (Mix Ser.). (ENG.). 304p. (J). (gr. 4-8). pap. 8.99 *(978-1-4169-6731-6(1),* Aladdin) Simon & Schuster Children's Publishing.

—Times Squared. 2011. (Mix Ser.). (ENG.). (J). (gr. 4-8). 272p. pap. 8.99 *(978-1-4169-6732-3(X));* 240p. 16.99 *(978-1-4169-7532-8(2))* Simon & Schuster Children's Publishing. (Aladdin).

—Trading Faces. 2008. (Mix Ser.). (ENG.). 304p. (J). (gr. 4-8). 16.99 *(978-1-4169-7531-1(4),* Simon & Schuster/Paula Wiseman Bks.) Simon & Schuster/Paula Wiseman Bks.

—Triple Trouble. 2014. (Mix Ser.). (ENG., Illus.). 240p. (J). (gr. 4-8). pap. 7.99 *(978-1-4424-3406-6(6),* Aladdin) Simon & Schuster Children's Publishing.

Devlin, Calla. Tell Me Something Real. 2016. (ENG., Illus.). 304p. (YA). (gr. 9). 17.99 *(978-1-4814-6115-3(X),* Atheneum Bks. for Young Readers) Simon & Schuster Children's Publishing.

Dhami, Narinder. Bindi Babes. 2005. (Bindi Babes Ser.: 1). (ENG.). 192p. (J). (gr. 3-7). reprint ed. 6.99 *(978-0-440-42019-4(9),* Yearling) Random Hse. Children's Bks.

Dhami, Narinder & Dhami, Narinder. Bhangra Babes. 2006. (Bindi Babes Ser.). (ENG.). 185p. (J). (gr. 4-6). 18.69 *(978-0-440-42106-1(3))* Random House Publishing Group.

DiCamillo, Kate. Where Are You Going, Baby Lincoln? Tales from Deckawoo Drive, Volume Three. Van Dusen, Chris, illus. 2017. (Tales from Deckawoo Drive Ser.: 3). (ENG.). 112p. (J). (gr. 1-4). pap. 6.99 *(978-0-7636-9758-7(3))* Candlewick Pr.

Dillon, Elena. Breathe. 2013. 190p. pap. 9.99 *(978-0-9886353-2-6(1))* Dillon, Elena.

Disney. Frozen Cinestory, Volume 1. 2014. lib. bdg. 26.95 *(978-0-606-36645-8(8))* Turtleback.

Disney Books. Frozen ReadAlong Storybook & CD. 2013. (Read-Along Storybook & CD Ser.). (ENG., Illus.). 32p. (J). (gr. -1-k). pap. 6.99 *(978-1-4231-7064-8(4),* Disney Press Books) Disney Publishing Worldwide.

Disney Editors. Frozen. 2013. lib. bdg. 14.75 *(978-0-606-32207-2(8))* Turtleback.

—Frozen - Anna's Icy Adventure. 2013. lib. bdg. 14.75 *(978-0-606-32206-5(X))* Turtleback.

Dodd, Anne. Angel of Winter. 2017. (ENG., Illus.). (J). pap. 8.95 *(978-1-947247-00-0(X))* Yorkshire Publishing Group.

Donnelly, Jennifer. Stepsister. (ENG.). (YA). 2020. 368p. (gr. 8-12). pap. 10.99 *(978-1-338-26847-8(3))* 2019. 352p. (gr. 7-7). 17.99 *(978-1-338-26846-1(5),* Scholastic Pr.) Scholastic, Inc.

Dooley, Sarah. Ashes to Asheville. 2017. 256p. (J). (gr. 5). 16.99 *(978-0-399-16504-7(5),* G.P. Putnam's Sons Books for Young Readers) Penguin Young Readers Group.

Dower, Laura. Maggie's Magic Chocolate Moon. Lazuli, Lilly, illus. 2016. (Dessert Diaries). (ENG.). 160p. (J). (gr. 4-8). pap. 5.95 *(978-1-4965-4141-3(3),* 133429, Stone Arch Bks.) Capstone.

Doyle, Marissa. Bewitching Season. 2009. (ENG.). 368p. (YA). (gr. 9-12). 24.94 *(978-0-312-59695-8(2),* 9780312596958) Square Fish.

Drake, Raelyn. Picking up Speed. 2018. (Superhuman Ser.). (ENG.). 104p. (YA). (gr. 6-12). pap. 7.99 *(978-1-5415-1050-0(X),* a3c8eb1b-eecb-4d50-a140-ef741d3cd510); 25.32 *(978-1-5124-9831-8(9),* 0d62eed7-3333-4987-81f2-288feafcf1dd) Lerner Publishing Group. (Darby Creek).

Driscoll, Laura. We Are Twins. 2012. (Penguin Young Readers: Level 1 Ser.). lib. bdg. 13.55 *(978-0-606-26641-3(0))* Turtleback.

Duble, Kathleen Benner. The Sacrifice. 2007. (ENG.). 224p. (J). (gr. 5-9). pap. 8.99 *(978-0-689-87651-6(3),* McElderry, Margaret K. Bks.) McElderry, Margaret K. Bks.

DuJardin, Rosamond. Practically Seventeen: A Tobey Heydon Story. 2003. (YA). per. 12.95 *(978-1-930009-68-4(2),* 800-691-7779) Image Cascade Publishing.

Dunkle, Clare B. The Hollow Kingdom: Book I — the Hollow Kingdom Trilogy. 2006. (Hollow Kingdom Trilogy Ser.: 1). (ENG.). 240p. (J). (gr. 6-9). reprint ed. pap. 16.99 *(978-0-8050-8108-4(9),* 900039576, Holt, Henry & Co. Bks. For Young Readers) Holt, Henry & Co.

Durnil, Lari. A Tale of Two Sisters. 2009. (J). pap. 11.89 *(978-0-88144-455-1(3),* Total Publishing & Media) Yorkshire Publishing Group.

Durst, Sarah Beth. Journey Across the Hidden Islands. 2017. (ENG., Illus.). 352p. (J). (gr. 5-7). 16.99 *(978-0-544-70679-8(X),* 1628641, Clarion Bks.) HarperCollins Pubs.

Dzidrums, Christine. Fair Youth: Emylee of Forest Springs. Lopez, Lyle & Dzidrums, Joseph, illus. 2012. (ENG.). 120p. (YA). pap. 9.99 *(978-1-938438-05-9(1))* Creative Media Publishing.

Eaddy, Susan. Poppy's Best Babies. Bonnet, Rosalinde, illus. 2018. 40p. (J). (gr. k-3). 15.99 *(978-1-58089-770-9(3))* Charlesbridge Publishing, Inc.

Edmonds, Lin. Patric the Pony & the Shining Star. 2010. 36p. pap. 17.49 *(978-1-4520-7389-7(9))* AuthorHouse.

Eiselein, Gregory, et al. Little Women. 2003. (Norton Critical Editions Ser.: 0). (ENG., Illus.). 688p. (C). pap. 13.00 *(978-0-393-97614-4(9)*, 97614) Norton, W. W. & Co., Inc.

Ele, Delores. Horse Bones: The Adventures of Daisy & Maisy. 2012. 56p. pap. 15.99 *(978-1-4771-4113-7(8))* Xlibris Corp.

Elizabeth's Story 1848. 2014. (Secrets of the Manor Ser.: 3). (ENG., Illus.). 160p. (J). (gr. 3-7). pap. 7.99 *(978-1-4814-1840-9(8)*, Simon Spotlight) Simon Spotlight.

Elliott, Kate, pseud. Court of Fives. 2016. (Court of Fives Ser.: 1). (ENG., Illus.). 464p. (YA). (gr. 7-17). pap. 12.99 *(978-0-316-36430-0(4))* Little, Brown Bks. for Young Readers.

Ellis, Ann Dee. You May Already Be a Winner. 2017. 352p. (J). (gr. 5-9). 16.99 *(978-1-101-99385-9(5)*, Dial Bks) Penguin Young Readers Group.

—You May Already Be a Winner. 2018. lib. bdg. 19.65 *(978-0-606-41307-7(3))* Turtleback.

Ellis, Marvie. Keisha's Doors Bk. 1: An Autism Story. l.t. ed. 2005.Tr. of Las Puertas de Keisha. (SPA., Illus.). 32p. (J). per. 16.95 *(978-1-933319-00-1(3))* Speech Kids Texas Pr.

Elliston, Beth. A Baby Book as told by ME! the Big Sister. 2009. (ENG.). 32p. pap. 14.95 *(978-0-557-07646-8(3))* Lulu Pr., Inc.

Erlbaum, Janice. Let Me Fix That for You. 2020. (ENG.). 304p. (J). pap. 12.99 *(978-1-250-25030-8(7)*, 900184341) Square Fish.

Ernshaw, Shea. The Wicked Deep. (ENG.). (YA). (gr. 9). 2019. 336p. pap. 12.99 *(978-1-4814-9735-0(9))* 2018. (Illus.). 320p. 19.99 *(978-1-4814-9734-3(0))* Simon Pulse. (Simon Pulse).

Esparra, Lydia. Heaven Is All Around You. Esparra, Veronica, illus. 2012. 28p. pap. 12.95 *(978-1-61244-071-2(1))* Halo Publishing International.

Estelle, Carrie. Molly Loves Her Sister. 2011. 20p. pap. 11.00 *(978-1-4567-6425-8(X))* AuthorHouse.

Falls the Shadow. 2014. (ENG., Illus.). 352p. (YA). (gr. 7). 18.99 *(978-1-4424-9753-5(X)*, Simon & Schuster Bks. For Young Readers) Simon & Schuster Bks. For Young Readers.

Farley, Brianne. Secret Tree Fort. Farley, Brianne, illus. 2016. (ENG., Illus.). 32p. (J). (gr. -1-3). 16.99 *(978-0-7636-6297-4(6))* Candlewick Pr.

Farley, Robin. Mia & the Big Sister Ballet. 2012. (My First I Can Read Ser.). (ENG., Illus.). 32p. (J). (gr. -1-3). pap. 5.99 *(978-0-06-173307-9(5)*, HarperCollins) HarperCollins Pubs.

—Mia & the Big Sister Ballet. 2012. (Mia I Can Read Bks.). (J). lib. bdg. 13.55 *(978-0-606-26282-8(2))* Turtleback.

—Mia & the Tiny Toe Shoes. 2012. (Mia I Can Read Bks.). (J). lib. bdg. 13.55 *(978-0-606-26863-9(4))* Turtleback.

Farshtey, Greg. Way of the Ninja. 2012. (LEGO Ninjago Ser.). (ENG.). 32p. (J). (gr. 1-3). pap. 3.99 *(978-0-545-40113-5(5))* Scholastic, Inc.

Fawcett, Heather. Even the Darkest Stars. (Even the Darkest Stars Ser.: 1). (ENG.). (YA). (gr. 8). 2018. 448p. pap. 9.99 *(978-0-06-246339-5(X))* 2017. 432p. 17.99 *(978-0-06-246338-8(1))* HarperCollins Pubs. (Balzer & Bray).

Fellure, Kathy Boyd. Mr Snowman Ate Our Picnic Lunch. 2010. (ENG.). 36p. pap. 16.95 *(978-0-557-79684-7(9))* Lulu Pr., Inc.

Fernandez, Alexa. Darn Baby! 2012. (ENG.). 18p. 15.00 *(978-1-105-89540-1(8))* Lulu Pr., Inc.

Fiedler, Lisa & Wallach, Anya. Curtain Up. 2015. (Stagestruck Ser.). (ENG.). 256p. (J). (gr. 4-7). 11.99 *(978-1-58536-923-2(3)*, 203816) Sleeping Bear Pr.

Figley, Marty Rhodes. The Schoolchildren's Blizzard. Haas, Shelly O., illus. 2004. (On My Own History Ser.). (ENG.). 48p. (J). (gr. 2-4). pap. 8.99 *(978-1-57505-619-7(4)*, a675f403-7243-488e-ad5b-fbd615d20ef5, First Avenue Editions) Lerner Publishing Group.

Finnegan, Marco. Lizard in a Zoot Suit. Finnegan, Marco, illus. 2020. (ENG., Illus.). 144p. (YA). (gr. 7-12). 31.99 *(978-1-5415-2365-4(2)*, a6f85d3f-7999-47b7-b6d3-96fccb4d533f, Graphic Universe™) Lerner Publishing Group.

Fisher, Valorie. My Big Sister. 2003. (ENG., Illus.). 40p. (J). (gr. -1-3). 17.99 *(978-0-689-85479-8(X)*, Atheneum Bks. for Young Readers) Simon & Schuster Children's Publishing.

Flannigan, Liz. Cara & the Wizard, 2 vols. Docampo, Valeria, illus. 2013. (Magic Stories Ser.). 48p. (J). (gr. 1-4). pap. 8.99 *(978-1-84686-780-4(0))* Barefoot Bks., Inc.

Flood, Nancy Bo. Soldier Sister, Fly Home. Begay, Shonto, illus. 2016. 176p. (J). (gr. 5). lib. bdg. 16.95 *(978-1-58089-702-0(9))* Charlesbridge Publishing, Inc.

Foggo, Cheryl. I Have Been in Danger, 1 vol. 2005. (In the Same Boat Ser.: No. 3). (ENG., Illus.). 184p. (J). (gr. 4-6). pap. 7.95 *(978-1-55050-185-8(2))* Coteau Bks. CAN. Dist: Fitzhenry & Whiteside, Ltd.

Ford, Adam B. The Six Sisters & Their Flying Carpets. 2017. (ENG., Illus.). (J). (gr. k-2). pap. 10.95 *(978-0-9794104-7-5(9))* H Bar Pr.

—The Six Sisters & Their Flying Carpets. Abbott, Kristin, illus. 2012. 34p. (-18). 20.95 *(978-0-9794104-6-8(0))* H Bar Pr.

France, Emily. Zen & Gone. 2019. (ENG.). 1p. (YA). (gr. 9). pap. 10.99 *(978-1-64129-031-9(5)*, Soho Teen) Soho Pr., Inc.

Frankel, Jordana. The Isle. 2016. (ENG.). 384p. (YA). (gr. 8). 17.99 *(978-0-06-209537-4(4)*, Tegen, Katherine Bks) HarperCollins Pubs.

—The Ward. 2016. (ENG.). 496p. (YA). (gr. 8). pap. 9.99 *(978-0-06-209535-0(8)*, Tegen, Katherine Bks) HarperCollins Pubs.

Frazier, Sundee T. The Other Half of My Heart. 2011. 304p. (J). (gr. 3-7). 8.99 *(978-0-440-24006-8(9)*, Yearling) Random Hse. Children's Bks.

Frazier, Sundee Tucker. The Other Half of My Heart. 2011. (ENG.). 304p. (J). (gr. 4-6). lib. bdg. 21.19 *(978-0-385-90446-9(0)*, Delacorte Pr.) Random Hse. Children's Bks.

Freeman, Martha. The Case of the Diamond Dog Collar, 2. 2nd ed. 2012. (First Kids Mysteries Ser.: 2). (ENG.). 144p. (J). (gr. 2-4). 21.19 *(978-0-8234-2337-8(9))* Holiday Hse., Inc.

—The Case of the Rock 'N' Roll Dog, 1. 2012. (First Kids Mysteries Ser.: 1). (ENG., Illus.). 128p. (J). (gr. 2-4). 21.19 *(978-0-8234-2267-8(4))* Holiday Hse., Inc.

Freymann-Weyr, Garret. Stay with Me. 2007. (ENG.). 320p. (YA). (gr. 9-12). pap. 17.99 *(978-0-618-88404-9(1)*, 487146, Clarion Bks.) HarperCollins Pubs.

Friedman, Aimee. Two Summers. 2016. (ENG.). 368p. (YA). (gr. 7). 17.99 *(978-0-545-51807-9(5))* Scholastic, Inc.

Friedman, Robin. The Importance of Wings. 2017. 176p. (J). (gr. 5). pap. 7.99 *(978-1-58089-331-2(7))* Charlesbridge Publishing, Inc.

Friedmann, Patty. Taken Away. 2010. (ENG.). 427p. (J). (gr. 6). pap. 18.95 *(978-0-9845318-2-0(3))* Tiny Stachel Pr.

Friend, Natasha. Perfect. 2004. (ENG.). 232p. (J). pap. 10.00 *(978-1-57131-651-6(5))* Milkweed Editions.

Frillman, K. Country Stars: The Road Less Traveled. 2007. 348p. per. 21.95 *(978-1-4303-1234-5(3))* Lulu Pr., Inc.

Funk, Constance J. Holy as Thou. 2009. (Illus.). 400p. pap. 22.00 *(978-1-933002-66-8(2))* PublishingWorks.

Gabriel, Nat. Bubble Trouble. Nez, John, illus. 2004. 32p. (J). lib. bdg. 20.00 *(978-1-4242-1085-5(2))* Fitzgerald Bks.

—Bubble Trouble. Nez, John, illus. 2004. (Science Solves It Ser.). 32p. (gr. -1-3). 15.00 *(978-0-7569-4286-1(1))* Perfection Learning Corp.

Galvin, Laura Gates & Studio Mouse Editorial. Cinderella: Dreams Do Come True. 2008. (ENG., Illus.). 36p. (J). (gr. -1). 7.99 *(978-1-59069-436-7(8))* Studio Mouse LLC.

Gamache, Line. Hello, Me Pretty. Cochrane, KerryAnn, tr. 2007. (ENG., Illus.). 64p. per. 15.00 *(978-1-894994-23-1(X))* Conundrum Pr. CAN. Dist: Consortium Bk. Sales & Distribution.

Garber, Stephanie. Caraval. l.t. ed. 2017. (Caraval Ser.). (ENG.). 510p. 24.95 *(978-1-4328-4221-5(8))* Cengage Gale.

—Caraval. (ENG.). (YA). 2018. (Caraval Ser.: 1). 448p. pap. 11.99 *(978-1-250-09526-8(3)*, 900160654) 2017. (gr. 8-12). pap. 11.99 *(978-1-250-14149-1(4))* 2017. (Caraval Ser.: 1). 416p. 18.99 *(978-1-250-09525-1(5)*, 900160653) Flatiron Bks.

—Caraval. 2018. (YA). lib. bdg. 22.10 *(978-0-606-41093-9(7))* Turtleback.

—Finale. 2019. (Illus.). 478p. (YA). *(978-1-250-23197-0(3))* St. Martin's Pr.

—Finale: A Caraval Novel. 2019. (Caraval Ser.: 3). (ENG., Illus.). 496p. (YA). 19.99 *(978-1-250-15766-9(8)*, 900185295) Flatiron Bks.

—Legendary. 2018. (CHI.). (YA). (gr. 8-12). pap. *(978-986-235-684-5(7))* Faces Pubns.

—Legendary. 2018. (Caraval Ser.). (ENG., Illus.). 495p. (YA). (gr. 8-13). pap. 11.99 *(978-1-250-19222-6(6))* Flatiron Bks.

—Legendary. 2018. (Illus.). 451p. (YA). *(978-1-250-30127-7(0))*; *(978-1-250-30129-1(7))* St. Martin's Pr.

—Legendary: A Caraval Novel. (Caraval Ser.: 2). (ENG., Illus.). (YA). 2019. 512p. pap. 11.99 *(978-1-250-09532-9(8)*, 900160660) 2018. 464p. 19.99 *(978-1-250-09531-2(X)*, 900160659) Flatiron Bks.

Garber, Stephanie & Davies, Rhys. Finale. 2019. (Illus.). 478p. (YA). *(978-1-250-24386-7(6))* St. Martin's Pr.

Garcia McCall, Guadalupe. Summer of the Mariposas. 2012. (ENG.). (YA). 352p. 19.95 *(978-1-60060-900-8(7))*; 384p. (gr. 6-13). pap. 15.95 *(978-1-62014-010-9(1)*, leelowtu) Lee & Low Bks., Inc. (Tu Bks.).

Gardner, Lyn. Into the Woods. Grey, Mini, illus. 2009. (Eden Sisters Ser.). (ENG.). 448p. (J). (gr. 3-7). 8.99 *(978-0-440-42223-5(X)*, Yearling) Random Hse. Children's Bks.

—Out of the Woods. 2011. (Eden Sisters Ser.). (ENG., Illus.). 368p. (J). (gr. 3-7). 8.99 *(978-0-385-75226-8(1)*, Yearling) Random Hse. Children's Bks.

Garoche, Camille. The Snow Rabbit. 2015. (Illus.). 56p. (J). (gr. -1-3). 16.95 *(978-1-59270-181-0(7))* Enchanted Lion Bks., LLC.

Gartlan, Daniel. Poor Hannah. 2012. 24p. pap. 24.95 *(978-1-4626-6030-8(4))* America Star Bks.

Gaydos, Nora. I'M a New Big Sister. Gutierrez, Akemi, illus. 2010. (ENG.). 30p. (J). (gr. -1-17). 6.99 *(978-1-60169-009-8(6))* Innovative Kids.

Gayle, Amber. On the Naive but Honorable Self-Determination of Teenage Girls: My Evil Twin Sister No. 5. 2004. 228p. (YA). pap. 6.00 *(978-0-9712972-8-9(2))* Evil Twin Pubns.

Gee, Randi. Goldfish & Poodle. 2010. 32p. pap. 15.50 *(978-0-557-52979-7(4))* Lulu Pr., Inc.

Gibbs, Lynne. Molly Mouse Is Shy: A Story of Shyness, 1 vol. Mitchell, Missy, illus. 2009. (Let's Grow Together Ser.). (ENG.). 32p. (J). (gr. k-1). pap. 11.55 *(978-1-60754-761-7(9)*, 6aac5f9c-dab3-409a-95c2-a45eaeb14dcd); lib. bdg. 27.27 *(978-1-60754-756-3(2)*, 2e202d76-3c52-42a4-b9bb-002ce24a3c6d) Rosen Publishing Group, Inc., The. (Windmill Bks.).

Gill, Shelley. Prickly Rose. Love, Judy, illus. 2014. 32p. (J). (gr. -1-3). pap. 7.99 *(978-1-57091-357-0(9))* Charlesbridge Publishing, Inc.

Gliori, Debi. Witch Baby & Me on Stage. 2011. (Illus.). 336p. (J). (gr. 2-4). pap. 7.99 *(978-0-552-55679-8(3))* Transworld Publishers Ltd. GBR. Dist: Independent Pubs. Group.

Godbersen, Anna. The Luxe, Rumors, & Envy, Set, Bks. 1-3. 2009. (Luxe Ser.). (YA). (gr. 9). pap. 24.99 *(978-0-06-192118-6(1))* HarperCollins Pubs.

Godwin, Jane. Falling from Grace. 2007. (ENG.). 204p. (J). (gr. 6-12). 16.95 *(978-0-8234-2105-3(8))* Holiday Hse., Inc.

Golf, Cali. Umkhuba: The Journal. 2011. 36p. (gr. -1). pap. 19.95 *(978-1-4520-4128-5(8))* AuthorHouse.

Goodell, Mary. The Chicken Pox Puppy: Kate & Jen's Daily Adventures. Goodell, Mary, illus. 2007. (Illus.). 29p. (J). per. 11.99 *(978-1-59879-382-6(9))* Lifevest Publishing, Inc.

Goodlett, Ellen. Rule. 2019. (Rule Ser.: 1). (ENG.). 400p. (YA). (gr. 9-17). pap. 10.99 *(978-0-316-51529-0(9))* Little, Brown Bks. for Young Readers.

Goodman, Leandria D. Firecracker, Firecracker, Boom, Boom, Boom!, 1 vol. 2009. 21p. pap. 24.95 *(978-1-60749-475-1(2))* America Star Bks.

Gow, Kailin. Diary of a Discount Donna: A Fashion Fables Book: A Novel. 2005. 274p. (YA). per. 10.95 *(978-1-59748-858-7(5))* Sparklesoup LLC.

—The Stoker Sisters. 2010. 266p. (YA). pap. *(978-1-59748-947-8(6))* Sparklesoup LLC.

Grady, Karen. It's Not My Fault, She Started It. 2005. (Illus.). (J). *(978-1-59975-127-6(5))* Independent Pub.

Graham, Bob. April & Esme Tooth Fairies. Graham, Bob, illus. 2013. (ENG., Illus.). 40p. (J). (gr. k-4). 7.99 *(978-0-7636-6347-6(6))* Candlewick Pr.

Grainger, A. J. The Sisterhood. 2019. (ENG., Illus.). 304p. (YA). (gr. 7). 18.99 *(978-1-4814-2906-1(X)*, Simon & Schuster Bks. For Young Readers) Simon & Schuster Bks. For Young Readers.

Grant, Natalie. Miracle in Music City, 1 vol. 2016. (Faithgirlz / Glimmer Girls Ser.: 3). (ENG.). 208p. (J). pap. 8.99 *(978-0-310-75250-9(7))* Zonderkidz.

Gray, Louise. Izzy the Invisible. Anderson, Laura Ellen, illus. 2016. (ENG.). 144p. (J). (gr. 2-4). pap. 8.99 *(978-1-84812-509-4(7))* Bonnier Publishing GBR. Dist: Independent Pubs. Group.

Gray, Mila. Come Back to Me. 2015. (ENG., Illus.). 352p. (YA). (gr. 11). 17.99 *(978-1-4814-3965-7(0)*, Simon Pulse) Simon Pulse.

Green, D. L. Kaitlyn & the Competition. 2016. (Babysitter Chronicles Ser.). (ENG.). 160p. (J). (gr. 4-7). pap. 6.95 *(978-1-4914-8861-4(1)*, 131486, Stone Arch Bks.) Capstone.

—Sparkling Jewel: a Branches Book (Silver Pony Ranch #1) Wallis, Emily, illus. 2015. (Silver Pony Ranch Ser.: 1). (ENG.). 96p. (J). (gr. 1-3). pap. 5.99 *(978-0-545-79765-8(9))* Scholastic, Inc.

Green, Holly G. Don't Slam the Door. Scott, Sarah Chamberlin, illus. 2005. (ENG.). 39p. (J). (gr. 2-7). 19.95 *(978-0-9744803-7-4(1))* PublishingWorks.

Greene, Janice. The Plot, 1 vol. unabr. ed. 2010. (Q Reads Ser.). (ENG.). 32p. (YA). (gr. 9-12). pap. 8.50 *(978-1-61651-204-0(0))* Saddleback Educational Publishing, Inc.

Greene, Kimberly. My Life on TV. 2011. (My Sister's a Pop Star Ser.). (ENG.). 320p. (J). (gr. 6-8). 18.69 *(978-0-7945-2901-7(1))* EDC Publishing.

Greenwood, R. L. A Visit to the Kingdom of Camelot. 2013. 62p. (gr. 2-2). pap. 8.95 *(978-1-4759-8097-4(3))* iUniverse, Inc.

Gregory, Kristiana. My Darlin' Clementine. 2009. (ENG.). 192p. (J). (gr. 5-18). 16.95 *(978-0-8234-2198-5(8))* Holiday Hse., Inc.

Griffin, Adele. Where I Want to Be. (ENG.). (YA). (gr. 7-12). 2011. 150p. 22.44 *(978-0-399-23783-6(6))* 2007. 176p. 8.99 *(978-0-14-240948-0(0)*, Speak) Penguin Young Readers Group.

Grimm, Brothers. Mother Holly. Watts, Bernadette, illus. 2016. (ENG.). 32p. 17.95 *(978-0-7358-4267-0(1))* North-South Bks., Inc.

Grimm, Jacob & Grimm, Wilhelm K. Hut in the Forest, 20 vols. Lawson, Polly, tr. Stietencron, Bettina, illus. 2007. (Grimm's Fairy Tales Ser.). (ENG.). 28p. (J). *(978-0-86315-615-1(0))* Floris Bks.

Grinti, Mike & Grinti, Rachel. Claws. 2012. (J). *(978-0-545-43314-3(2)*, Chicken Hse., The) Scholastic, Inc.

Grossman, Bill. My Little Sister Hugged an Ape. Hawkes, Kevin, illus. 2008. (ENG.). 40p. (J). (gr. -1-2). pap. 7.99 *(978-0-385-73660-2(6)*, Dragonfly Bks.) Random Hse. Children's Bks.

Guess, Bob. Hey Mister, How's Your Sister? 2009. 40p. pap. 16.99 *(978-1-4389-7041-7(2))* AuthorHouse.

Guest, Elissa Haden. Iris & Walter & Baby Rose. Davenier, Christine, illus. 2012. (Iris & Walter — Green Light Reader Ser.). lib. bdg. 13.55 *(978-0-606-26612-3(7))* Turtleback.

—Iris & Walter: Lost & Found. Davenier, Christine, illus. 2014. (Iris & Walter Ser.). (ENG.). 44p. (J). (gr. 1-4). pap. 4.99 *(978-0-544-22789-7(1)*, 1563719, Clarion Bks.) HarperCollins Pubs.

Gurtler, Janet. I'm Not Her. 2011. (ENG.). 304p. (YA). (gr. 7-12). pap. 12.99 *(978-1-4022-5636-3(1)*, 9781402256363) Sourcebooks, Inc.

Half Baked Sistas-in the Beginning. 2004. 242p. (YA). lib. bdg. 12.99 *(978-0-9761819-0-3(8)*, 002) Smart Publishing.

Hall, Angela Marie. Priscilla Pennybrook: Hello World, I Have Arrived!, 1 vol. 2009. 55p. pap. 16.95 *(978-1-61582-899-9(0))* America Star Bks.

Hall, Kirsten. Hide-and-Seek: All about Location. Luedecke, Bev, illus. 2005. (Beastieville Ser.). (ENG.). 32p. (J). (gr. k-1). pap. 3.95 *(978-0-516-25519-4(3)*, Children's Pr.) Scholastic Library Publishing.

Hallinan, P. K. Sisters Forever. 2014. (ENG., Illus.). 22p. (J). bds. 7.99 *(978-0-8249-1921-4(1)*, Ideals Pubns.) Worthy Publishing.

Halstead, Jayce N. The True Legend of White Crow: Adventures of the Fudge Sisters. Twomey-Lange, Marianna, photos by. 2004. (Illus.). 80p. (J). per. 7.95 *(978-0-9749046-3-4(5))* Aarow Pr.

Hamilton, Laura, reader. Sheila Rae, the Brave. 2003. (Illus.). (J). (gr. -1-2). 28.95 incl. audio compact disk *(978-1-59112-550-1(2))* Live Oak Media.

Han, Jenny. Always & Forever, Lara Jean. 2018. (To All the Boys I've Loved Before Ser.: 3). (ENG., Illus.). 336p. (YA). (gr. 7). pap. 10.99 *(978-1-4814-3049-4(1)*, Simon & Schuster Bks. For Young Readers) Simon & Schuster Bks. For Young Readers.

—P. S. I Still Love You. (To All the Boys I've Loved Before Ser.: 2). (ENG., 352p. (YA). (gr. 7). 2015. Illus.). 19.99 *(978-1-4424-2673-3(X))* 2015. (Illus.). E-Book *(978-1-4424-2675-7(6))* 2019. pap. 10.99 *(978-1-5344-6926-6(5))* Simon & Schuster Bks. For Young Readers. (Simon & Schuster Bks. For Young Readers).

—P. S. I Still Love You. 2017. (To All the Boys I've Loved Before Ser.: 2). (ENG.). 352p. (YA). (gr. 7). pap. 10.99 *(978-1-4424-2674-0(8))* Simon & Schuster Children's Publishing.

—P.S. I Still Love You. 2018. (CHI.). (YA). (gr. 7). pap. *(978-957-10-7723-9(2))* Sharp Point Publishing Co., Ltd.

—P.S. I Still Love You. 2015. (ENG.). (YA). (gr. 7). pap. 10.99 *(978-1-4814-4471-2(9))* Simon & Schuster.

—To All the Boys I've Loved Before. (To All the Boys I've Loved Before Ser.: 1). (ENG., (YA). (gr. 7-10). 2016. Illus.). 384p. pap. 12.99 *(978-1-4424-2671-9(3))* 2014. (Illus.). 368p. 19.99 *(978-1-4424-2670-2(5))* 2018. 384p. pap. 12.99 *(978-1-5344-3837-8(8))* Simon & Schuster Bks. For Young Readers. (Simon & Schuster Bks. For Young Readers).

—To All the Boys I've Loved Before. 2016. lib. bdg. 22.10 *(978-0-606-38270-0(4))* Turtleback.

—The to All the Boys I've Loved Before Collection (Boxed Set) To All the Boys I've Loved Before; P. S. I Still Love You; Always & Forever, Lara Jean. 2017. (To All the Boys I've Loved Before Ser.). (ENG., Illus.). 1056p. (YA). (gr. 7). 53.99 *(978-1-4814-9536-3(4)*, Simon & Schuster Bks. For Young Readers) Simon & Schuster Bks. For Young Readers.

Han, Xuemei. Brave Little Mongolian Sisters. Han, Xuemei, illus. 2007. (Illus.). (J). pap. 12.99 *(978-0-9763168-7-9(0))* DigitalKu.

Hannigan, Katherine. Gwendolyn Grace. Hannigan, Katherine, illus. 2015. (ENG., Illus.). 32p. (J). (gr. -1-3). 17.99 *(978-0-06-234519-6(2)*, Greenwillow Bks.) HarperCollins Pubs.

Hansen, Brandy A. Madd Maddox: Sister for Sale. 2012. 16p. pap. 17.99 *(978-1-4685-5969-9(9))* AuthorHouse.

Hardegree, Maureen. Haint She Sweet. 2013. 206p. (YA). pap. 12.95 *(978-1-61194-325-2(6)*, Bell Bridge Bks.) BelleBks., Inc.

Hardinge, Frances. Gullstruck Island. 2018. (ENG.). 480p. (gr. 7-17). pap. 10.99 *(978-1-4197-3149-5(1)*, 1248003, Amulet Bks.) Abrams, Inc.

—The Lost Conspiracy. 2009. 576p. (J). (gr. 5). lib. bdg. 17.89 *(978-0-06-088042-2(2))*; 16.99 *(978-0-06-088041-5(4))* HarperCollins Pubs.

Hardy, Janice. The Healing Wars: Book II: Blue Fire. (Healing Wars Ser.: II). (ENG.). (J). (gr. 5). 2011. 400p. pap. 7.99 *(978-0-06-174744-1(0))*Bk. 2. 2010. 384p. 16.99 *(978-0-06-174741-0(6))* HarperCollins Pubs. (Balzer & Bray).

—The Shifter. 2009. (Healing Wars Ser.). 384p. (J). (gr. 5-18). lib. bdg. 17.89 *(978-0-06-176177-5(X))* HarperCollins Pubs.

Harris, Meena. Kamala & Maya's Big Idea. González, Ana Ramírez, illus. 2020. (ENG.). 32p. (J). (gr. -1-3). 18.99 *(978-0-06-293740-7(5)*, Balzer & Bray) HarperCollins Pubs.

Harris, Teresa E. The Perfect Place. 2014. (ENG.). 272p. (J). (gr. 5-7). 17.99 *(978-0-547-25519-4(5)*, 1388242, Clarion Bks.) HarperCollins Pubs.

Hasbro. Gift of Maud Pie. 2016. (Passport to Reading Level 2 Ser.). (J). lib. bdg. 13.55 *(978-0-606-39194-8(0))* Turtleback.

Hathaway, Jill. Impostor. 2013. (Slide Ser.: 2). (ENG.). 272p. (YA). (gr. 9). 17.99 *(978-0-06-207798-1(8)*, Balzer & Bray) HarperCollins Pubs.

—Slide, 1. 2013. (Slide Ser.: 1). (ENG.). 272p. (YA). (gr. 9-12). pap. 9.99 *(978-0-06-207796-7(1)*, Balzer & Bray) HarperCollins Pubs.

Haydu, Corey Ann. Eventown. 2019. (ENG.). 336p. (J). (gr. 3-7). 16.99 *(978-0-06-268980-1(0)*, Tegen, Katherine Bks) HarperCollins Pubs.

Hayes, Joe. Don't Say a Word, MamÃ¡ - No Digas Nada, MamÃ¡, 1 vol. Valencia, Esau Andrade, illus. 2013. (ENG.). 40p. (J). (gr. -1-3). pap. 12.95 *(978-1-935955-45-0(4)*, 23353382, Cinco Puntos Press) Lee & Low Bks., Inc.

HB Staff. My Sister Is My Friend. 97th ed. 2003. (First-Place Reading Ser.). (gr. 1-18). pap., suppl. ed. 16.50 *(978-0-15-308128-6(7))* Harcourt Schl. Pubs.

Hearn, Julie. The Minister's Daughter. 2006. (ENG.). 272p. (YA). (gr. 7-12). pap. 7.99 *(978-0-689-87691-2(2)*, Atheneum Bks. for Young Readers) Simon & Schuster Children's Publishing.

Heathfield, Lisa. Flight of a Starling. 2019. (ENG.). 264p. (YA). (gr. 7-12). 18.99 *(978-1-5415-2611-2(2)*, 45cf4905-0d6c-4c69-84fe-8d1265f6dccf, Carolrhoda Lab™) Lerner Publishing Group.

Hebert, Marie-Francine. This Side of the Sky, 1 vol. Ouriou, Susan, tr. 2006. (ENG.). 112p. (YA). (gr. 9-18). per. 6.95 *(978-0-88995-369-7(4)*, 6769f377-a38f-45b0-b953-5cf946544e52) Trifolium Bks., Inc. CAN. Dist: Firefly Bks., Ltd.

Heckman, Ashley. The Last Three Words. 2013. 104p. pap. *(978-1-77130-651-5(3))* Evernight Publishing.

Heim, Alastair. No Tooting at Tea. Not, Sara, illus. 2017. (ENG.). 40p. (J). (gr. -1-3). 17.99 *(978-0-544-77474-2(4)*, 1637141, Clarion Bks.) HarperCollins Pubs.

Heine, Theresa & Barefoot Books Staff. Chandra's Magic Light. Gueyfier, Judith, illus. 2013. (J). 16.99 *(978-1-84686-493-3(3))* Barefoot Bks., Inc.

Heller, Maryellen. My Big Sister's First Day of School. Soman, David, illus. 2009. (J). *(978-0-8037-3246-9(5)*, Dial) Penguin Publishing Group.

Henbit & the Roly-Poly. 2007. (J). *(978-0-9791982-2-9(4))* Pine Cone Pr.

Henbit & the Roly-Poly - Specially Formatted Edition. l.t. ed. 2007. (J). *(978-0-9791982-3-6(2))* Pine Cone Pr.

Henkes, Kevin. Sheila Rae, the Brave. Henkes, Kevin, illus. (Illus.). 9.95 *(978-1-59112-865-6(X))* Live Oak Media.

Henning, Ann. Cow Patty Patti. 2004. 47p. pap. 24.95 *(978-1-4137-3456-0(1))* PublishAmerica, Inc.

Heredia, Maria Fernanda. Por Si No Te Lo He Dicho. 2003. (SPA., Illus.). 24p. (J). (gr. 3-5). 15.95 *(978-9978-07-467-1(8))* Santillana USA Publishing Co., Inc.

Herman, Gail. Flower Girl. Billin-Frye, Paige, illus. 2012. (Penguin Young Readers: Level 3 Ser.: Level 2). (ENG.). 48p. (J). (gr. 1-3). 16.19 *(978-0-448-41108-8(3))* Penguin Young Readers Group.

Hershey, Mary. My Big Sister Is So Bossy She Says You Can't Read This Book. 2006. (Illus.). 176p. (J). (gr. 3-7). per. 6.99 *(978-0-553-48797-8(3)*, Yearling) Random Hse. Children's Bks.

Hesse, Karen. Wish on a Unicorn. 2009. (ENG.). 128p. (J). (gr. 3-7). pap. 16.99 *(978-0-312-37611-6(1)*, 9780312376116) Square Fish.

Hidden. 2014. (ENG., Illus.). 384p. (YA). (gr. 7). 17.99 *(978-1-4424-8300-2(8)*, Simon & Schuster/Paula Wiseman Bks.) Simon & Schuster/Paula Wiseman Bks.

Higgins, M. G. Falling Out of Place, 1 vol. 2012. (Gravel Road Ser.). (ENG.). 144p. (YA). (gr. 9-12). pap. 11.95 *(978-1-62250-021-5(0))* Saddleback Educational Publishing, Inc.

—Falling Out of Place. 2013. (Gravel Road Ser.). (YA). lib. bdg. 20.80 *(978-0-606-26963-6(0))* Turtleback.

Higginson, Sheila Sweeny. You're Getting a Baby Sister! Williams, Sam, illus. 2012. (ENG.). 24p. (J). (gr. -1-k). bds. 8.99 *(978-1-4424-2050-2(2)*, Little Simon) Little Simon.

Hill, C. J. Echo in Time. 2014. 387p. (YA). *(978-0-06-212395-4(5))* HarperCollins Pubs.

Hillyer, Lexa. Winter Glass. 2019. (Spindle Fire Ser.: 2). (ENG.). 352p. (YA). (gr. 9). pap. 9.99 *(978-0-06-244091-4(8),* HarperTeen) HarperCollins Pubs.
Ho, Joanna. Eyes That Kiss in the Corners. Ho, Dung, illus. 2021. (ENG.). 40p. (J). (gr. -1-3). 17.99 *(978-0-06-291562-7(2),* HarperCollins) HarperCollins Pubs.
Hoang, Melanie Rowland. The Gift. 2011. 32p. pap. 13.95 *(978-1-4525-3524-1(8))* Get Published.
Hoban, Russell. A Baby Sister for Frances. 2011. (I Can Read Level 2 Ser.). (ENG., Illus.). 48p. (J). (gr. k-3). 16.99 *(978-0-06-083804-1(3),* HarperCollins) HarperCollins Pubs.
—Best Friends for Frances. Hoban, Lillian, illus. 2016. (ENG.). 32p. (J). (gr. -1-3). pap. 5.99 *(978-0-06-239244-2(1),* HarperFestival) HarperCollins Pubs.
Hocking, Amanda. Wake. 2013. (Watersong Novel Ser.: 1). (ENG.). 320p. (YA). (gr. 7). pap. 23.99 *(978-1-250-00564-9(7),* 900080965, St. Martin's Griffin) St. Martin's Pr.
Hodgson, Mona. The Princess Twins & the Puppy, 1 vol. 2015. (I Can Read! / Princess Twins Ser.). (ENG., Illus.). 32p. (J). pap. 4.99 *(978-0-310-75064-2(4))* Zonderkidz.
—The Princess Twins Play in the Garden, 1 vol. 2015. (I Can Read! / Princess Twins Ser.). (ENG., Illus.). 32p. (J). pap. 4.99 *(978-0-310-75050-5(4))* Zonderkidz.
Hoena, Blake. The Horrible Hex. Bardin, Dave, illus. 2018. (Monster Heroes Ser.). (ENG.). 32p. (J). (gr. k-2). lib. bdg. 21.32 *(978-1-4965-6413-9(8),* 138260, Stone Arch Bks.) Capstone.
—Witch's Brew. Bardin, Dave, illus. 2016. (Monster Heroes Ser.). (ENG.). 32p. (J). (gr. k-2). lib. bdg. 21.32 *(978-1-4965-3756-0(4),* 133082, Stone Arch Bks.) Capstone.
Hofmeister, Alan, et al. Sis in a Mess. (Reading for All Learners Ser.). (Illus.). (J). pap. *(978-1-56861-091-7(2))* Swift Learning Resources.
—Sis in the Well. (Reading for All Learners Ser.). (Illus.). (J). pap. *(978-1-56861-098-6(X))* Swift Learning Resources.
Holder, Nancy, et al. Crusade. (Crusade Ser.). (ENG.). (YA). (gr. 9). 2011. 496p. pap. 9.99 *(978-1-4169-9803-7(9))* 2010. 480p. 16.99 *(978-1-4169-9802-0(0))* Simon Pulse. (Simon Pulse).
—Vanquished. 2012. (Crusade Ser.). (ENG.). 496p. (YA). (gr. 9). 16.99 *(978-1-4169-9806-8(3));* pap. 9.99 *(978-1-4169-9807-5(1))* Simon Pulse. (Simon Pulse).
Holstein, Ima. A Dragons Daydream. 2011. 24p. pap. 12.99 *(978-1-4634-0430-7(1))* AuthorHouse.
Holt, Kimberly Willis. Piper Reed, Clubhouse Queen. Davenier, Christine, illus. 2011. (Piper Reed Ser.: 2). (ENG.). 160p. (J). (gr. 3-6). 15.99 *(978-0-8050-9431-2(8),* 900076845, Holt, Henry & Co. Bks. For Young Readers) Holt, Henry & Co.
—Piper Reed, Clubhouse Queen. Davenier, Christine, illus. 2011. (Piper Reed Ser.: 2). (ENG.). 176p. (J). (gr. 3-6). pap. 9.99 *(978-0-312-61676-2(7),* 900076846) Square Fish.
—Piper Reed, Navy Brat. Davenier, Christine, illus. 2011. (Piper Reed Ser.: 1). (ENG.). 176p. (J). (gr. 3-6). pap. 9.99 *(978-0-312-62548-1(0),* 900077153) Square Fish.
—Piper Reed, Rodeo Star. Davenier, Christine, illus. 2012. (Piper Reed Ser.: 5). (ENG.). 176p. (J). (gr. 3-6). pap. 9.99 *(978-1-250-00409-3(8),* 900080156) Square Fish.
Holub, Joan & Williams, Suzanne. Cinderella Stays Late. 2014. (Grimmtastic Girls Ser.: 1). lib. bdg. 16.00 *(978-0-606-35395-3(X))* Turtleback.
Holyoak, Kathleen & Summers, Sherry. Flowers in Heaven. 2009. 32p. pap. 14.49 *(978-1-4389-4607-8(4))* AuthorHouse.
Homberg, Ruth. Across the Sea (Disney Frozen) RH Disney, illus. 2016. (Step into Reading Ser.). (ENG.). 24p. (J). (gr. -1-1). 5.99 *(978-0-7364-3398-3(8),* RH/Disney) Random Hse. Children's Bks.
Hood, Ann. Jude Banks, Superhero. 2021. (Illus.). 320p. (J). (gr. 3-7). 16.99 *(978-0-593-09407-5(7),* Penguin Workshop) Penguin Young Readers Group.
Hood, Kim. Plain Jane: When Does Being Stuck Become ... Unstuck? 2016. (ENG., Illus.). 304p. (J). 15.00 *(978-1-84717-784-1(0))* O'Brien Pr., Ltd., The IRL. Dist: Dufour Editions, Inc.
Hopkins, Ellen. Identical. (ENG.). (YA). (gr. 9-18). 2010. 592p. pap. 14.99 *(978-1-4169-5006-6(0))* 2008. 576p. 24.99 *(978-1-4169-5005-9(2))* McElderry, Margaret K. Bks. (McElderry, Margaret K. Bks.).
—Smoke. (ENG., Illus.). (YA). (gr. 9). 2015. 576p. pap. 14.99 *(978-1-4169-8329-3(5))* 2013. 560p. 21.99 *(978-1-4169-8328-6(7))* McElderry, Margaret K. Bks. (McElderry, Margaret K. Bks.).
Hopkins, K. C. The Night the Spirits Danced. 2008. 115p. pap. 15.00 *(978-0-615-23929-3(3))* Hopkins, KC.
Horowitz, Nancy Ellis. Nicely Dunn & the Lost Little Sister. 2009. 88p. pap. 30.49 *(978-1-4389-3011-4(9))* AuthorHouse.
Horrocks, Anita. What They Don't Know. braille ed. 2003. (J). (gr. 2). spiral bd. *(978-0-616-15267-6(1))* Canadian National Institute for the Blind/Institut National Canadien pour les Aveugles.
Hostetter, Joyce Moyer. Drive. 2018. (Bakers Mountain Stories Ser.). (Illus.). 352p. (J). (gr. 5-9). 18.95 *(978-1-62979-865-3(7),* Calkins Creek) Highlights Pr., c/o Highlights for Children, Inc.
Howland, Leila. The Brightest Stars of Summer. 2017. (Silver Sisters Ser.: 2). (ENG.). 384p. (J). (gr. 3-7). pap. 6.99 *(978-0-06-231873-2(X),* HarperCollins) HarperCollins Pubs.
—The Silver Moon of Summer. (Silver Sisters Ser.: 3). (ENG.). 304p. (J). (gr. 3-7). 2018. pap. 6.99 *(978-0-06-231876-3(4))* 2017. (Illus.). 16.99 *(978-0-06-231875-6(6))* HarperCollins Pubs. (HarperCollins).
Howson, Imogen. Linked. 2014. (ENG., Illus.). 384p. (YA). (gr. 7). pap. 9.99 *(978-1-4424-4660-1(9),* Simon & Schuster Bks. For Young Readers) Simon & Schuster Bks. For Young Readers.
—Unravel. 2014. (ENG., Illus.). 480p. (YA). (gr. 7). 17.99 *(978-1-4424-4658-8(7),* Simon & Schuster Bks. For Young Readers) Simon & Schuster Bks. For Young Readers.
Hudson, Katura J. I'm a Big Sister Now. 2009. 32p. pap. 6.95 *(978-1-60349-022-1(1),* Marimba Bks.) Just Us Bks., Inc.
Hulst, W. G. van de & Hulst, Willem G. van de, illus. The Woods Beyond the Wall. 2017. (J). *(978-1-928136-08-8(7))* Inheritance Pubns.
Human, Deborah. Pinky Promise. 2009. 40p. (J). pap. 11.99 *(978-0-9818374-0-6(9))* Writing Bench LLC., The.
Hummel, Jim. Imagination: On Planet Hic-Cup. 2013. 36p. pap. 15.49 *(978-1-4669-8903-0(3))* Trafford Publishing.
Hunt, Tiffani "Paradise". Glamorous 5: In the City of Garden Valley. 2012. 24p. pap. 17.99 *(978-1-4772-7922-9(9))* AuthorHouse.
Hunter, Jana. Trick or Treat (the Sleepover Club) 2010. (Sleepover Club Ser.). (ENG., Illus.). 112p. (J). (gr. 2-6). pap. 6.99 *(978-0-00-727254-9(5),* HarperCollins Children's Bks.) HarperCollins Pubs. Ltd. GBR. Dist: HarperCollins Pubs.
Hurley, Tonya. Ghostgirl: Homecoming. 2010. (Ghostgirl Ser.: 2). (ENG.). 304p. (YA). (gr. 7-17). pap. 16.99 *(978-0-316-08943-2(5))* Little, Brown Bks. for Young Readers.
Hurwitz, Johanna. The Two & Only Kelly Twins. Mourning, Tuesday, illus. 2018. (ENG.). 96p. (J). (gr. 1-4). pap. 4.99 *(978-1-5362-0050-8(6))* Candlewick Pr.
Hutton, Clare. Emma Moves In, 1. 2018. (American Girl Contemporary Ser.). (ENG.). 188p. (J). (gr. 4-5). 16.96 *(978-1-64310-229-0(X))* Penworthy Co., LLC, The.
Hyde, E. A. Watson. Little Sisters to the Camp Fire Girls. 2004. reprint ed. pap. 15.95 *(978-1-4179-9442-7(8))* Kessinger Publishing, LLC.
Iorillo, Kristin. The Wacko Baby. 2011. 28p. pap. 15.99 *(978-1-4628-5792-0(2))* Xlibris Corp.
Ireland, Justina. Scream Site. 2018. (ENG.). 264p. (YA). (gr. 7-12). 15.95 *(978-1-63079-102-5(4),* 138468, Capstone Editions) Capstone.
Isbell, Tom. The Capture. 2016. (Prey Trilogy Ser.: 2). (ENG.). 448p. (YA). (gr. 8). 17.99 *(978-0-06-221605-2(8),* HarperTeen) HarperCollins Pubs.
—The Prey. 2015. (Prey Trilogy Ser.: 1). (ENG.). 416p. (YA). (gr. 8). 17.99 *(978-0-06-221601-4(5),* HarperTeen) HarperCollins Pubs.
Ius, Dawn. Overdrive. (ENG.). (YA). (gr. 9). 2017. 368p. pap. 10.99 *(978-1-4814-3945-9(6))* 2016. (Illus.). 352p. 17.99 *(978-1-4814-3944-2(8))* Simon Pulse. (Simon Pulse).
Jacobson, Jennifer Richard. This Is MY Room! (No Tigers Allowed) Neonakis, Alexandria, illus. 2019. (ENG.). 48p. (J). (gr. -1-3). 17.99 *(978-1-5344-0211-9(X),* Simon & Schuster Bks. For Young Readers) Simon & Schuster Bks. For Young Readers.
Jaden, Denise. Losing Faith. 2010. (ENG.). 400p. (YA). (gr. 9-18). pap. 9.99 *(978-1-4169-9609-5(5),* Simon Pulse) Simon Pulse.
—Never Enough. 2012. (ENG.). 400p. (YA). (gr. 9). pap. 9.99 *(978-1-4424-2907-9(0),* Simon Pulse) Simon Pulse.
Jasper, Elizabeth. The Golden Cuckoo. 2013. 102p. (J). pap. *(978-1-78299-195-3(6))* FeedARead.com.
Jefferson, Jewell E. I'm Going to Be A Big Sister! 2008. 20p. 12.25 *(978-1-4357-0907-2(1))* Lulu Pr., Inc.
Jenkins, Carla LaVern. The Disappearance of Mrs. Brown: A Jenkins Girl Mystery. 2010. 72p. 23.55 *(978-1-4269-4537-3(X));* pap. 13.55 *(978-1-4251-6659-5(8))* Trafford Publishing.
Jiya, Tapiwa. The Epic of Goz. 2008. 144p. pap. 11.99 *(978-1-4343-5730-4(9))* AuthorHouse.
Jocelyn, Marthe. Mable Riley: A Reliable Record of Humdrum, Peril, & Romance. 2007. 279p. (gr. 4-7). 17.00 *(978-0-7569-8183-9(2))* Perfection Learning Corp.
—Would You. 2008. (ENG.). 176p. (J). (gr. 4-7). 19.99 *(978-0-88776-816-3(4),* Tundra Bks.) Tundra Bks. CAN. Dist: Penguin Random Hse. LLC.
Johnson, Angela. A Cool Moonlight. 2005. (ENG.). 144p. (J). (gr. 3-7). reprint ed. 6.99 *(978-0-14-240284-9(2),* Puffin Books) Penguin Young Readers Group.
Johnson, Janie, compiled by. Up from the Cotton Fields. 2003. 114p. per. 29.95 net. *(978-0-9718254-8-2(3))* Printsbury.
Johnson, Maureen. The Key to the Golden Firebird. 2004. (ENG.). 304p. (J). (gr. 7-18). 15.99 *(978-0-06-054138-5(5))* HarperCollins Pubs.
Johnson, Michael E. Barley & Betsy: Journey #1 A cat & dog's great adventure to the Mall. Atchley, Kendra, illus. 2011. 36p. pap. 24.95 *(978-1-4560-4077-2(4))* America Star Bks.
Johnson, Young, et al. Princess Hope & the Hidden Treasure, 1 vol. Aranda, Omar, illus. 2012. (I Can Read! / Princess Parables Ser.). (ENG.). 32p. (J). pap. 4.99 *(978-0-310-73250-1(6))* Zonderkidz.
Johnston, Carol Shaw. Lily & Sophie: Sisters & Best Friends. 2010. (ENG.). 65p. pap. 26.99 *(978-0-557-35894-6(9))* Lulu Pr., Inc.
Johnston, Julie. A Very Fine Line. 2006. 208p. (YA). (gr. 7). 18.95 *(978-0-88776-746-3(X),* Tundra Bks.) Tundra Bks. CAN. Dist: Penguin Random Hse. LLC.
Jones, Patrick. On Guard. 2016. (Bounce Ser.). (ENG.). 104p. (YA). (gr. 6-12). lib. bdg. 26.65 *(978-1-5124-1123-2(X),* ff83faaa-d129-49fb-825f-23e38ebf8ec2, Darby Creek) Lerner Publishing Group.
Jordan, Apple, adapted by. The Right Track. 2017. (Illus.). 24p. (J). *(978-1-5182-3645-7(6))* Random Hse., Inc.
Jordan, Sophie. Firelight. (Firelight Ser.: 1). (ENG.). (YA). (gr. 8). 2011. 352p. pap. 9.99 *(978-0-06-193509-1(3))* 2010. 336p. 16.99 *(978-0-06-193508-4(5))* HarperCollins Pubs. (HarperCollins).
Jules, Jacqueline. Lío de Caléndulas. Smith, Kim, illus. 2018. (Sofia Martinez en Español Ser.). (SPA.). 32p. (J). (gr. k-2). lib. bdg. 21.32 *(978-1-5158-2447-3(0),* 137550, Picture Window Bks.) Capstone.
—Lista para la Foto. Smith, Kim, illus. 2018. (Sofia Martinez en Español Ser.). (SPA.). 32p. (J). (gr. k-2). lib. bdg. 21.32 *(978-1-5158-2449-7(7),* 137552, Picture Window Bks.) Capstone.
—The Marigold Mess. Smith, Kim, illus. 2015. (Sofia Martinez Ser.). (ENG.). 32p. (J). (gr. k-2). lib. bdg. 21.32 *(978-1-4795-5776-9(5),* 126808, Picture Window Bks.) Capstone.
—The Missing Mouse. Smith, Kim, illus. 2015. (Sofia Martinez Ser.). (ENG.). 32p. (J). (gr. k-2). lib. bdg. 21.32 *(978-1-4795-5774-5(9),* 126806, Picture Window Bks.) Capstone.
—Picture Perfect. Smith, Kim, illus. 2015. (Sofia Martinez Ser.). (ENG.). 32p. (J). (gr. k-2). lib. bdg. 21.32 *(978-1-4795-5773-8(0),* 126805, Picture Window Bks.) Capstone.
Julius, Jessica. A New Reindeer Friend. 2015. lib. bdg. 13.55 *(978-0-606-36680-9(6))* Turtleback.
—A New Reindeer Friend (Disney Frozen) RH Disney, illus. 2015. (Little Golden Book Ser.). (ENG.). 24p. (J). (-k). 5.99 *(978-0-7364-3351-8(1),* Golden/Disney) Random Hse. Children's Bks.
Juwayriyah, Umm & Ayed, Juwayriyah. Hind's Hands: A Story about Autism. Apple, Emma, illus. 2013. 16p. (J). pap. 6.00 *(978-1-935437-76-5(3),* As Sabr Pubns.) Imago Pr.
Kadohata, Cynthia. Kira-Kira. (ENG., Illus.). (J). (gr. 5-9). 2004. 256p. 19.99 *(978-0-689-85639-6(3))* 2006. 272p. reprint ed. pap. 8.99 *(978-0-689-85640-2(7))* Simon & Schuster Children's Publishing. (Atheneum Bks. for Young Readers).
—Outside Beauty. (ENG.). (YA). (gr. 7). 2009. 288p. pap. 8.99 *(978-1-4169-9818-1(7))* 2008. (Illus.). 272p. 16.99 *(978-0-689-86575-6(9))* Simon & Schuster Children's Publishing. (Atheneum Bks. for Young Readers).
Kain, Jamie. The Good Sister: A Novel. 2015. (ENG.). 304p. (YA). (gr. 9-12). pap. 22.99 *(978-1-250-04774-8(9),* 900132217, St. Martin's Griffin) St. Martin's Pr.
Kato, Shakila Maria Inviolata & Kato, Sharifa Maria Inviolata. The Adventures by the Magic Bicycle. 2012. 134p. 24.95 *(978-1-4137-5716-3(2))* America Star Bks.
Katschke, Judy, et al. Bye-Bye Boyfriend, 3 vols. 2003. (ENG., Illus.). 112p. *(978-0-00-714467-9(9),* HarperCollins Children's Bks.) HarperCollins Pubs. Ltd.
Katz, Bebe Weinberg. Princess Claudia & the Freckles. 2007. 48p. per. 16.95 *(978-1-4241-6446-2(X))* America Star Bks.
Katz, Karen. Best-Ever Big Sister. 2006. (Illus.). 14p. (J). (gr. -1-k). 7.99 *(978-0-448-43915-0(8),* Grosset & Dunlap) Penguin Young Readers Group.
Kauffman, Christopher G. Faith's Star. Jenkins, Jacqueline, illus. 2011. 32p. pap. 24.95 *(978-1-4560-9584-0(6))* America Star Bks.
Kaupp, Rosemarie. The Amberella Tales: Amberella in the City. 2012. 120p. (gr. 4-6). 22.33 *(978-1-4669-0594-8(8));* pap. 12.33 *(978-1-4669-0595-5(6))* Trafford Publishing.
Kawashita, Mizuki. Ichigo 100% Sweet Little Sister, Vol. 7. (JPN., Illus.). 180p. (YA). pap. *(978-4-08-873518-4(8))* Shuei-Sha.
Kay, Susan. Abby & Gabby Tales. 2009. 16p. pap. 9.99 *(978-1-4389-6467-6(6))* AuthorHouse.
Keats, Israel. Behind the Screen. 2018. (Mason Falls Mysteries Ser.). (ENG.). 104p. (YA). (gr. 6-12). pap. 7.99 *(978-1-5415-0115-7(2),* eedc1df0-a0a3-4b02-be8a-d39f3b9a36f5); lib. bdg. 25.32 *(978-1-5415-0114-0(4),* 62d3269f-d719-4e8f-8994-08e18fd459df) Lerner Publishing Group. (Darby Creek).
Kehret, Peg. Runaway Twin. 2011. (ENG.). 208p. (J). (gr. 5-18). 8.99 *(978-0-14-241849-9(8),* Puffin Books) Penguin Young Readers Group.
Keller, Tae. When You Trap a Tiger. 2020. 304p. (J). *(978-0-593-17534-7(4))* Random Hse., Inc.
—When You Trap a Tiger: (Newbery Medal Winner) (J). (gr. 3-7). 2023. 320p. pap. 8.99 *(978-1-5247-1573-1(5),* Yearling) 2020. (ENG.). 304p. 17.99 *(978-1-5247-1570-0(0),* Random Hse. Bks. for Young Readers) 2020. (ENG.). 304p. lib. bdg. 19.99 *(978-1-5247-1571-7(9),* Random Hse. Bks. for Young Readers) Random Hse. Children's Bks.
Kelley, Jane. The Girl Behind the Glass. 2012. (ENG.). 192p. (J). (gr. 4-7). pap. 6.99 *(978-0-375-86219-9(6),* Yearling) Random Hse. Children's Bks.
Kelly, Erin Entrada. Hello, Universe. Roxas, Isabel, illus. 2018. (ENG.). 320p. (J). (gr. 3-7). 8.99 *(978-0-06-287750-5(X),* Greenwillow Bks.) HarperCollins Pubs.
—Hello, Universe. 2018. lib. bdg. 17.20 *(978-0-606-41021-2(X))* Turtleback.
—Hello, Universe: A Newbery Award Winner. Roxas, Isabel, illus. (ENG.). (J). (gr. 3-7). 2020. 352p. pap. 9.99 *(978-0-06-241416-8(X))* 2017. 320p. 16.99 *(978-0-06-241415-1(1))* HarperCollins Pubs. (Greenwillow Bks.).
—The Land of Forgotten Girls. (ENG.). (J). (gr. 3-7). 2017. 320p. pap. 9.99 *(978-0-06-223865-8(5))* 2016. 304p. 16.99 *(978-0-06-223864-1(7))* HarperCollins Pubs. (Greenwillow Bks.).
Kelly, J. M. Speed of Life. 2016. (ENG.). 352p. (YA). (gr. 9). 17.99 *(978-0-544-74782-1(8),* 1633256, Clarion Bks.) HarperCollins Pubs.
Kennedy, A. L. Uncle Shawn & Bill & the Almost Entirely Unplanned Adventure. Correll, Gemma, illus. 2018. (ENG.). 192p. (J). pap. 5.99 *(978-1-61067-740-0(4))* Kane Miller.
Kerry, Mary. Saving the Scrolls. 2003. 159p. (J). (gr. 4-7). 16.95 *(978-1-888842-30-2(X))* Absey & Co.
Khan, Rukhsana. Big Red Lollipop. Blackall, Sophie, illus. 2010. (ENG.). 40p. (J). (gr. -1-3). 18.99 *(978-0-670-06287-4(1),* Viking Books for Young Readers) Penguin Young Readers Group.
Kiernan, Kristy. Catching Genius. 2007. (ENG.). 384p. (gr. 12-18). 16.00 *(978-0-425-21435-0(4),* Berkley) Penguin Publishing Group.
Kilgus, Walter C. Bess Takes a Ride. Howarth, Craig, illus. 2008. (ENG.). 36p. pap. 17.49 *(978-1-4257-8807-0(6))* Xlibris Corp.
King, Amy Sarig. The Year We Fell from Space (Scholastic Gold) 2021. (ENG.). 288p. (J). (gr. 3-7). pap. 7.99 *(978-1-338-23645-3(8))* Scholastic, Inc.
Kingsley Troupe, Thomas. A Starlet's Shadow. Ivy, Maggie, illus. 2019. (Haunted States of America Set 2 Ser.). (ENG.). 136p. (J). (gr. 3-4). pap. 7.99 *(978-1-63163-360-7(0),* 1631633600); lib. bdg. 27.13 *(978-1-63163-359-1(7),* 1631633597) North Star Editions. (Jolly Fish Pr.).
Kleinman, Estelle. The Penderwicks: A Study Guide. Friedland, Joyce & Kessler, Rikki, eds. 2008. (Novel-Ties Ser.). (Illus.). 39p. pap. 16.95 *(978-0-7675-1488-0(2))* Learning Links Inc.
Knight, Karsten. Afterglow. 2013. (ENG., Illus.). 336p. (YA). (gr. 9). 17.99 *(978-1-4424-5037-0(1),* Simon & Schuster Bks. For Young Readers) Simon & Schuster Bks. For Young Readers.
—Embers & Echoes. (ENG.). (YA). (gr. 9). 2013. Illus.). 496p. pap. 9.99 *(978-1-4424-5035-6(5))* 2012. 480p. 16.99 *(978-1-4424-5030-1(4))* Simon & Schuster Bks. For Young Readers. (Simon & Schuster Bks. For Young Readers).
—Wildefire. 2011. (ENG.). 400p. (YA). (gr. 9-18). 16.99 *(978-1-4424-2117-2(7),* Simon & Schuster Bks. For Young Readers) Simon & Schuster Bks. For Young Readers.
Knudsen, Michelle. The Case of Vampire Vivian. Wummer, Amy, illus. 2003. (Science Solves It! Ser.). (ENG.). 32p. (J). (gr. 1-3). pap. 5.99 *(978-1-57565-127-9(0),* 2c9530f1-72fd-49cf-9a9e-9544a676ab37, Kane Press) Astra Publishing Hse.
—El Caso de Vivian la Vampira. Wummer, Amy, illus. 2008. (Science Solves It! en Espanol Ser.). (SPA.). 32p. (J). (gr. -1-3). pap. 5.95 *(978-1-57565-277-1(3))* Astra Publishing Hse.
—El Caso de Vivian la Vampira (the Case of Vampire Vivian) Wummer, Amy, illus. 2009. (Science Solves It! (r) en Espanol Ser.). (SPA.). (gr. 1-3). pap. 33.92 *(978-0-7613-4800-9(X))* Lerner Publishing Group.
Kokias, Kerri. Snow Sisters! White, Teagan, illus. 2018. 32p. (J). (gr. -1-2). 18.99 *(978-1-101-93883-6(8),* Knopf Bks. for Young Readers) Random Hse. Children's Bks.
Korba, Joanna. Cindy Eller Plays Ball: A Modern-Day Cinderella Tale. 2006. (J). pap. *(978-1-4108-6164-1(3))* Benchmark Education Co.
Korngold, Jamie S. Mazel Tov! It's a Boy: Mazel Tov! It's a Girl. Finkelstein, Jeff, illus. Finkelstein, Jeff, photos by. 2015. (J). 6.99 *(978-1-4677-6206-9(7),* Kar-Ben Publishing) Lerner Publishing Group.
—Sadie's Sukkah Breakfast. Fortenberry, Julie, illus. 2011. (Sukkot & Simchat Torah Ser.). (ENG.). 24p. (J). (gr. -1-1). lib. bdg. 16.95 *(978-0-7613-5647-9(9),* Kar-Ben Publishing) Lerner Publishing Group.
Kraus, Joanna H. A Night of Tamales & Roses. Caravela, Elena, illus. 2007. (ENG.). 32p. (J). (gr. -1-3). 15.95 *(978-0-9726614-4-7(1))* Shenanigan Bks.
Kuipers, Alice. Polly Diamond & the Magic Book: Book 1. Toledano, Diana, illus. 2018. (Polly Diamond Ser.). (ENG.). 160p. (J). (gr. 1-4). 14.99 *(978-1-4521-5232-5(2))* Chronicle Bks. LLC.
—Polly Diamond & the Magic Book: Book 1 (Book Series for Elementary School Kids, Children's Chapter Book for Bookworms) Toledano, Diana, illus. 2019. (Polly Diamond Ser.). (ENG.). 112p. (J). (gr. 1-4). pap. 6.99 *(978-1-4521-8221-6(3))* Chronicle Bks. LLC.
Kurilovitch, Mike. Silly Sisters. 2012. 32p. pap. 18.48 *(978-1-4772-6011-1(0))* AuthorHouse.
Kurtagich, Dawn. And the Trees Crept In. 2017. (ENG.). 368p. (YA). (gr. 10-17). pap. 9.99 *(978-0-316-29871-1(9))* Little, Brown Bks. for Young Readers.
Kvasnosky, Laura McGee. The Runaways. 2007. (Zelda & Ivy Ser.). (Illus.). 42p. (J). (gr. -1-3). 12.65 *(978-0-7569-8140-2(9))* Perfection Learning Corp.
—Zelda & Ivy & the Boy Next Door. Kvasnosky, Laura McGee, illus. 2014. (Candlewick Sparks Ser.). (ENG., Illus.). 40p. (J). (gr. k-4). pap. 5.99 *(978-0-7636-7182-2(7))* Candlewick Pr.
—Zelda & Ivy: Keeping Secrets: Candlewick Sparks. Kvasnosky, Laura McGee, illus. 2013. (Candlewick Sparks Ser.). (ENG., Illus.). 48p. (J). (gr. k-4). pap. 5.99 *(978-0-7636-6636-1(X))* Candlewick Pr.
—Zelda & Ivy: the Big Picture: Candlewick Sparks. Kvasnosky, Laura McGee, illus. 2013. (Candlewick Sparks Ser.). (ENG., Illus.). 48p. (J). (gr. k-4). pap. 5.99 *(978-0-7636-6637-8(8))* Candlewick Pr.
—Zelda & Ivy: the Runaways: Candlewick Sparks. Kvasnosky, Laura McGee, illus. 2013. (Candlewick Sparks Ser.). (ENG., Illus.). 48p. (J). (gr. k-4). pap. 5.99 *(978-0-7636-6635-4(1))* Candlewick Pr.
LaFleur, Suzanne. Counting to Perfect. 2018. (ENG.). 208p. (J). (gr. 3-7). 16.99 *(978-1-5247-7179-9(1));* lib. bdg. 19.99 *(978-1-5247-7180-5(5))* Random Hse. Children's Bks. (Lamb, Wendy Bks.).
LaFleur, Suzanne M. Counting to Perfect. 2018. 197p. (J). pap. *(978-1-5247-7182-9(1),* Delacorte Pr) Random House Publishing Group.
Lagonegro, Melissa. Frozen - A Tale of Two Sisters. 2013. (Disney Princess Step into Reading Ser.). lib. bdg. 13.55 *(978-0-606-32205-8(1))* Turtleback.
Lagonegro, Melissa, adapted by. Ghost Hunt! 2018. (Illus.). 22p. (J). *(978-1-5490-4049-8(9))* Random Hse., Inc.
Lake, Donna C. The Big Sister. 2011. 24p. pap. 15.99 *(978-1-4628-5250-5(5))* Xlibris Corp.
Lane, Dakota. Orpheus Obsession. 2005. (Illus.). 288p. (J). lib. bdg. 17.89 *(978-0-06-074174-7(0),* HarperTeen) HarperCollins Pubs.
—The Orpheus Obsession. 2008. (ENG., Illus.). 288p. (YA). (gr. 9). pap. 8.99 *(978-0-06-074175-4(9),* HarperTeen) HarperCollins Pubs.
Langer, Dana. Siren Sisters. 2017. (ENG., Illus.). 256p. (J). (gr. 4-8). 17.99 *(978-1-4814-6686-8(0),* Simon & Schuster/Paula Wiseman Bks.) Simon & Schuster/Paula Wiseman Bks.
LaReau, Kara. Flight of the Bluebird (the Unintentional Adventures of the Bland Sisters Book 3) Hill, Jen, illus. 2019. (ENG.). 224p. (J). (gr. 3-7). 14.99 *(978-1-4197-3144-0(0),* 1139501, Amulet Bks.) Abrams, Inc.
—The Jolly Regina (the Unintentional Adventures of the Bland Sisters Book 1) Hill, Jen, illus. 2018. (Unintentional Adventures of the Bland Sisters Ser.). (ENG.). 184p. (J). (gr. 3-7). pap. 7.99 *(978-1-4197-2605-7(6),* 1138303, Amulet Bks.) Abrams, Inc.
—The Uncanny Express (the Unintentional Adventures of the Bland Sisters Book 2) Hill, Jen, illus. 2018. (Unintentional Adventures of the Bland Sisters Ser.). (ENG.). (J). (gr. 3-7). 184p. pap. 7.99 *(978-1-4197-3204-1(8),* 1139403); 176p. 14.99 *(978-1-4197-2568-5(8),* 1139401) Abrams, Inc. (Amulet Bks.).
—Unintentional Adventures of the Bland Sisters: The Jolly Regina. Hill, Jen, illus. 2017. (ENG.). 176p. (J). (gr. 3-7). 14.95 *(978-1-4197-2136-6(4),* 1138301, Amulet Bks.) Abrams, Inc.
Larsen, Kirsten. Tara Pays Up! Billin-Frye, Paige, illus. 2006. (Social Studies Connects Ser.). (ENG.). 32p. (J). (gr. 1-3). pap. 5.99 *(978-1-57565-187-3(4),* e51c2255-355d-4b78-9cb1-61348fb0f40a, Kane Press) Astra Publishing Hse.
Las dos Hermanas: Lap Book. (Pebble Soup Exploraciones Ser.). (SPA.). 16p. (gr. -1-18). 21.00 *(978-0-7578-1692-5(4))* Rigby Education.
Las dos Hermanas: Small Book. (Pebble Soup Exploraciones Ser.). (SPA.). 16p. (gr. -1-18). 5.00 *(978-0-7578-1732-8(7))* Rigby Education.
Lasser, Jon & Foster-Lasser, Sage. Grow Kind. 2020. (Illus.). 32p. (J). *(978-1-4338-3050-1(7),* Magination Pr.) American Psychological Assn.

Lauren, Ruth. Prisoner of Ice & Snow. 2017. (ENG.). 288p. (J). 16.99 *(978-1-68119-131-7(8)*, 900159799, Bloomsbury USA Childrens) Bloomsbury Publishing USA.

Lauter, Richard, illus. Little Women. (Young Collector's Illustrated Classics Ser.). 192p. (J). 9.95 *(978-1-56156-371-5(4))* Kidsbooks, LLC.

Lavender, William. Aftershocks. 2006. (ENG., Illus.). 352p. (YA). (gr. 7-12). 17.00 *(978-0-15-205882-1(6)*, 1197660, Clarion Bks.) HarperCollins Pubs.

LaZebnik, Claire. Epic Fail. 2011. (ENG.). 304p. (YA). (gr. 8-18). pap. 9.99 *(978-0-06-192126-1(2)*, HarperTeen) HarperCollins Pubs.

—Things I Should Have Known. 2017. (ENG.). 320p. (YA). (gr. 7). 17.99 *(978-0-544-82969-5(7)*, 1644035, Clarion Bks.) HarperCollins Pubs.

Lemon, Sarah Nicole. Valley Girls. 2018. (ENG., Illus.). 400p. (gr. 7-17). 18.99 *(978-1-4197-2964-5(0)*, 1218701, Amulet Bks.) Abrams, Inc.

Leonard, Connie King. Sleeping in My Jeans. 2018. (ENG.). 240p. (YA). pap. 16.00 *(978-1-947845-00-8(4))* Ooligan Pr.

Leprechaun, Seamus T. The o'Shea Chronicles. 2013. 312p. pap. *(978-1-78407-190-5(0))* FeedARead.com.

Levine, Gail Carson. The Two Princesses of Bamarre. (J). 2012. (ENG.). 272p. (gr. 3-7). pap. 9.99 *(978-0-06-440966-7(X)*, HarperCollins) 2004. (Illus.). 304p. (gr. 7-18). reprint ed. pap. 6.99 *(978-0-06-057580-9(8))* HarperCollins Pubs.

Levinson, Robin K. Miriam's Journey: Discovering a New World. 2006. (Illus.). 64p. (J). per. 12.00 *(978-0-9773673-0-6(4))* Gali Girls, Inc.

Levy, Janice. Flip-Flop & the Absolutely Awful New Baby, 1 vol. Madden, Colleen M., illus. 2011. (Flip-Flop Adventure Ser.). (ENG.). 32p. (J). (gr. -1-4). 32.79 *(978-1-61641-651-5(3)*, 7768, Looking Glass Library) Magic Wagon.

Lieurance, Suzanne. The Locket: Surviving the Triangle Shirtwaist Fire, 1 vol. 2008. (Historical Fiction Adventures Ser.). (ENG., Illus.). 160p. (J). (gr. 3-5). lib. bdg. 31.93 *(978-0-7660-2928-6(X)*, 22662cfe-5ae4-4ede-affa-913d7a92d0d5) Enslow Publishing, LLC.

Lilly-Lolly Little-Legs: Individual Title, 6 packs. (Literatura 2000 Ser.). (gr. 1-2). 28.00 *(978-0-7635-0095-5(X))* Rigby Education.

Lin, Cindy. The Twelve. 2019. (ENG.). 384p. (J). (gr. 3-7). 16.99 *(978-0-06-282127-0(X)*, HarperCollins) HarperCollins Pubs.

Lin, Grace. Ling & Ting: Not Exactly the Same! 2011. (Passport to Reading Level 3 Ser.). (ENG.). 48p. (J). (gr. 1-4). pap. 4.99 *(978-0-316-02453-2(8))* Little, Brown Bks. for Young Readers.

—Ling & Ting Share a Birthday. 2014. (ENG.). 48p. (J). (gr. 1-4). pap. 4.99 *(978-0-316-18404-5(7))* Little, Brown Bks. for Young Readers.

—Ling & Ting Share a Birthday. 2014. (Passport to Reading Level 3 Ser.). (J). lib. bdg. 14.75 *(978-0-606-35932-0(X))* Turtleback.

—Ling & Ting: Together in All Weather. 2016. (ENG.). 48p. (J). (gr. 1-4). pap. 4.99 *(978-0-316-33548-5(7))* Little, Brown Bks. for Young Readers.

Lindman. Flicka, Ricka, Dicka & the Little Dog. Lindman, illus. 2013. (Flicka, Ricka, Dicka Ser.). (ENG., Illus.). 32p. (J). (gr. -1-3). 9.99 *(978-0-8075-2509-8(X)*, 080752509X) Whitman, Albert & Co.

—Flicka, Ricka, Dicka & the New Dotted Dresses. Lindman, illus. 2012. (Flicka, Ricka, Dicka Ser.). (ENG., Illus.). 32p. (J). (gr. -1-3). 9.99 *(978-0-8075-2484-8(0)*, 807524840) Whitman, Albert & Co.

—Flicka, Ricka, Dicka & the Strawberries. Lindman, illus. 2013. (Flicka, Ricka, Dicka Ser.). (ENG., Illus.). 32p. (J). (gr. -1-3). 9.99 *(978-0-8075-2512-8(X)*, 080752512X) Whitman, Albert & Co.

—Flicka, Ricka, Dicka & the Three Kittens. Lindman, illus. 2013. (Flicka, Ricka, Dicka Ser.). (ENG., Illus.). 32p. (J). (gr. -1-3). 9.99 *(978-0-8075-2515-9(4)*, 807525154) Whitman, Albert & Co.

—Flicka, Ricka, Dicka & Their New Skates. Lindman, illus. 2011. (Flicka, Ricka, Dicka Ser.). (ENG., Illus.). 32p. (J). (gr. -1-3). 9.99 *(978-0-8075-2491-6(3)*, 807524913) Whitman, Albert & Co.

—Flicka, Ricka, Dicka Bake a Cake. Lindman, illus. 2013. (Flicka, Ricka, Dicka Ser.). (ENG., Illus.). 32p. (J). (gr. -1-3). 9.99 *(978-0-8075-2506-7(5)*, 807525065) Whitman, Albert & Co.

—Flicka, Ricka, Dicka Go to Market. Lindman, illus. 2012. (Flicka, Ricka, Dicka Ser.). (ENG., Illus.). 32p. (J). (gr. -1-3). 9.99 *(978-0-8075-2478-7(6)*, 807524786) Whitman, Albert & Co.

Liniers. The Big Wet Balloon: Toon Books Level 2. Liniers, illus. 2013. (ENG., Illus.). 32p. (J). (gr. -1-3). 12.99 *(978-1-935179-32-0(2)*, TOON Books) Astra Publishing Hse.

—The Big Wet Balloon/ el Globo Grande y Mojado: Toon Books Level 2. Liniers, illus. 2013. (ENG., Illus.). 32p. (J). (gr. -1-3). pap. 7.99 *(978-1-935179-39-9(X)*, Toon Books) Astra Publishing Hse.

—Wildflowers: Special Gift Edition. 2021. (ENG., Illus.). 40p. (J). (gr. 1-4). 16.99 *(978-1-943145-54-6(7)*, Toon Books) Astra Publishing Hse.

—Wildflowers: TOON Level 2. 2021. (ENG., Illus.). 40p. (J). (gr. 1-4). 12.99 *(978-1-943145-53-9(9)*, Toon Books) Astra Publishing Hse.

Liniers, illus. The Big Wet Balloon/el Globo Grande y Mojado: Toon Books Level 2. 2013. (SPA.). 32p. (J). (gr. -1-3). 12.95 *(978-1-935179-40-5(3)*, Toon Books) Candlewick Pr.

Linko, Gina. Flower Moon. 2018. (ENG.). 256p. (J). (gr. 4-8). 15.99 *(978-1-5107-2274-3(2)*, Sky Pony Pr.) Skyhorse Publishing Co., Inc.

Lispi, Robert. Buddy Hawk: Story of Buddy Hawk. 2005. (J). pap. 8.00 *(978-0-8059-6602-2(1))* Dorrance Publishing Co., Inc.

Little, Ashley. The New Normal, 1 vol. 2013. (ENG.). 232p. (YA). (gr. 8-12). pap. 12.95 *(978-1-4598-0074-8(5))* Orca Bk. Pubs. USA.

Little Reader Digital Storybook: Cinderella. 2005. (J). cd-rom 8.99 *(978-0-9767657-7-6(2))* Mullings Media.

Littman, Sarah Darer. Backlash. 2015. (ENG.). 336p. (YA). (gr. 7). 17.99 *(978-0-545-65126-4(3)*, Scholastic Pr.) Scholastic, Inc.

Livan, Paco. WHAT A SNOUT! 2007. (ENG., Illus.). 48p. (J). 18.95 *(978-84-96788-87-9(3))* OQO, Editora ESP. Dist: Baker & Taylor Bks.

Lloyd-Jones, Sally. How to Be a Baby ... by Me, the Big Sister. Heap, Sue, illus. (ENG.). 40p. (J). (gr. -1-3). 2011. pap. 7.99 *(978-0-375-87388-1(0))* 2007. 16.99 *(978-0-375-83843-9(0))* Random Hse. Children's Bks. (Schwartz & Wade Bks.).

—How to Be a Baby... by Me, the Big Sister. Heap, Sue, illus. 2011. (How to Ser.). (ENG.). 40p. (J). (gr. -1-1). 21.19 *(978-0-375-93843-6(5)*, Dragonfly Bks.) Random Hse. Children's Bks.

Lopez, Diana. Choke. 2012. (ENG.). 240p. (YA). (gr. 7-7). 17.99 *(978-0-545-41822-5(4))* Scholastic, Inc.

Lopez, Silvia. Just Right Family: An Adoption Story. Chen, Ziyue, illus. 2018. (ENG.). 32p. (J). (gr. -1-3). 16.99 *(978-0-8075-4082-4(X)*, 080754082X) Whitman, Albert & Co.

Lopuszynski, Barbara. Angel & Brie. 2013. (ENG.). 246p. (YA). pap. 14.95 *(978-1-4787-0886-5(7))* Outskirts Pr., Inc.

Lovelady, W. f. The Adventures of Johnny Saturday: Back to the Drawing Board. 2012. 76p. pap. 12.95 *(978-1-4685-5286-7(4))* AuthorHouse.

Lowrey, Becky. Chirps. 2004. 45p. pap. 24.95 *(978-1-4137-2984-9(3))* PublishAmerica, Inc.

Lysiak, Hilde & Lysiak, Matthew. Bear on the Loose!: a Branches Book (Hilde Cracks the Case #2) Lew-Vriethoff, Joanne, illus. 2nd ed. 2017. (Hilde Cracks the Case Ser.: 2). (ENG.). 96p. (J). (gr. 1-3). pap. 6.99 *(978-1-338-14158-0(9))* Scholastic, Inc.

—Bear on the Loose!: a Branches Book (Hilde Cracks the Case #2) (Library Edition) Lew-Vriethoff, Joanne, illus. 2nd ed. 2017. (Hilde Cracks the Case Ser.: 2). (ENG.). 80p. (J). (gr. 1-3). lib. bdg. 15.99 *(978-1-338-14159-7(7))* Scholastic, Inc.

Maccoll, Michaela & Nichols, Rosemary. Rory's Promise. 2014. (Hidden Histories Ser.). (ENG.). 288p. (J). (gr. 4-7). 16.95 *(978-1-62091-623-0(1)*, Calkins Creek) Highlights Pr., c/o Highlights for Children, Inc.

MacDonald, Betty. Nancy & Plum. GrandPre, Mary, illus. 2011. 240p. (J). (gr. 3-7). 7.99 *(978-0-375-85986-1(1)*, Yearling) Random Hse. Children's Bks.

MacGregor, Doug. The Incredible Tongue Twister That Swallowed My Sister: Another Santa Story by Doug MacGregor. MacGregor, Doug, illus. ltd. ed. 2006. (Illus.). 40p. (J). per. *(978-0-9654843-5-0(1))* MacGregor, Doug.

MacHoka, Rebecca. The Dog Sisters: One Missing Sister. 2010. 36p. pap. 15.49 *(978-1-4490-8306-9(4))* AuthorHouse.

MacIntyre, R. P. Revved. 2006. (ENG.). 220p. pap. 12.95 *(978-1-894345-46-0(0))* Thistledown Pr., Ltd. CAN. Dist: Univ. of Toronto Pr.

Mackall, Dandi Daley. Please Reply! 2004. 128p. (J). pap. 5.99 *(978-1-4003-0328-1(1))* Nelson, Thomas Inc.

MacKey, Cindy. My Sister Sophie. Tebbit, Jake, illus. 2013. 30p. pap. 12.99 *(978-0-9892699-9-5(X))* Cyrano Bks.

Mackey, Cindy. My Sister Sophie. 2017. (ENG., Illus.). (J). (gr. k-4). pap. 8.99 *(978-0-9990993-5-3(3))* Cyrano Bks.

Maddox, Jake. Rebound Time, 1 vol. Wood, Katie, illus. 2013. (Jake Maddox Girl Sports Stories Ser.). (ENG.). 72p. (J). (gr. 3-6). pap. 5.95 *(978-1-4342-4202-0(1)*, 120260); lib. bdg. 25.32 *(978-1-4342-4013-2(4)*, 118394) Capstone. (Stone Arch Bks.).

—Spinning Away. 2017. (Jake Maddox JV Girls Ser.). (ENG., Illus.). 96p. (J). (gr. 4-8). lib. bdg. 26.65 *(978-1-4965-4927-3(9)*, 135824, Stone Arch Bks.) Capstone.

—Striker's Sister. Wood, Katie, illus. 2018. (Jake Maddox Girl Sports Stories Ser.). (ENG.). 72p. (J). (gr. 3-6). lib. bdg. 25.32 *(978-1-4965-6355-2(7)*, 138071, Stone Arch Bks.) Capstone.

Madison, Alan. Velma Gratch & the Way Cool Butterfly. Hawkes, Kevin, illus. 2012. 40p. (J). (gr. -1-3). pap. 8.99 *(978-0-307-97804-2(4)*, Schwartz & Wade Bks.) Random Hse. Children's Bks.

Magor, Dianne M. Ed. Lauren's Wish. 2012. 32p. (-18). pap. 21.99 *(978-1-4691-3986-9(3))* Xlibris Corp.

Mahoney, Tammy. Eddie the Eagle Learns to Fly. 2012. 24p. pap. 19.99 *(978-1-4772-1747-4(9))* AuthorHouse.

Maizel, Rebecca. Between Us & the Moon. 2015. (ENG.). 384p. (YA). (gr. 9). 17.99 *(978-0-06-232761-1(5)*, HarperTeen) HarperCollins Pubs.

Maloney, Brenna. Philomena's New Glasses. 2017. (Illus.). 40p. (J). (gr. -1-1). 17.99 *(978-0-425-28814-6(5)*, Viking Books for Young Readers) Penguin Young Readers Group.

Man-Kong, Mary. My Visit to the Doctor. Riley, Kellee, illus. 2017. (J). *(978-1-5182-2648-9(5))* Random Hse., Inc.

Mann, Jennifer Ann. Sunny Sweet Can So Get Lost. 2015. (Sunny Sweet Ser.). (ENG., Illus.). 208p. (YA). (gr. 3-6). 15.99 *(978-1-61963-505-0(4)*, 900138708, Bloomsbury USA Childrens) Bloomsbury Publishing USA.

—Sunny Sweet Is So Dead Meat. 2015. (Sunny Sweet Ser.). (ENG., Illus.). 208p. (YA). (gr. 3-6). pap. 6.99 *(978-1-61963-563-0(1)*, 900140700, Bloomsbury USA Childrens) Bloomsbury Publishing USA.

—Sunny Sweet Is So Not Scary. 2015. (Sunny Sweet Ser.). (ENG.). 192p. (YA). (gr. 3-6). 15.99 *(978-1-61963-507-4(0)*, 900138710, Bloomsbury USA Childrens) Bloomsbury Publishing USA.

Mantchev, Lisa. Sister Day! Sánchez, Sonia & Sánchez, Sonia, illus. 2017. (ENG.). 32p. (J). (gr. -1-3). 17.99 *(978-1-4814-3795-0(X)*, Simon & Schuster Bks. For Young Readers) Simon & Schuster Bks. For Young Readers.

Manushkin, Fran. Big Sisters Are the Best, 1 vol. Richards, Kirsten, illus. 2012. (Fiction Picture Bks.). (ENG.). 24p. (J). (gr. -1 — 1). 6.95 *(978-1-4048-7225-7(6)*, 118099, Picture Window Bks.) Capstone.

Marconi, Martina. Birthday Wishes, 1 vol. 2010. 20p. pap. 24.95 *(978-1-4489-6067-5(3))* PublishAmerica, Inc.

Marillier, Juliet. Cybele's Secret. 2011. (Wildwood Dancing Ser.: 2). (ENG.). 448p. (YA). (gr. 7). pap. 9.99 *(978-0-553-49486-0(4)*, Knopf Bks. for Young Readers) Random Hse. Children's Bks.

—Wildwood Dancing. 2008. (Wildwood Dancing Ser.: 1). (ENG.). 432p. (YA). (gr. 7). pap. 16.99 *(978-0-375-84474-4(0)*, Knopf Bks. for Young Readers) Random Hse. Children's Bks.

Marina, Budhos. Ask Me No Questions. 2014. (ENG.). 176p. (YA). (gr. 7-12). 14.24 *(978-1-63245-300-6(2))* Lectorum Pubns., Inc.

Marlow, Herb. Sisters, Wild Dogs & Catfish Bait. Caffee, Julie, illus. 2005. 122p. (J). lib. bdg. 24.95 *(978-1-893595-45-3(5))*; per. 16.95 *(978-1-893595-48-4(X))* Four Seasons Bks., Inc.

Marshall, Carly. The Babysitter & Little Miss Bossy. 2013. 26p. 24.95 *(978-1-63000-618-1(1))*; 28p. pap. 24.95 *(978-1-63000-541-2(X))* America Star Bks.

Martin, Ann M. Abby's un-Valentine (the Baby-Sitters Club #127) A Geronimo Stilton Adventure. 2011. (Thea Stilton Ser.: 127). (ENG.). 160p. (J). (gr. 2-5). E-Book 8.99 *(978-0-545-87475-5(0)*, Scholastic Paperbacks) Scholastic, Inc.

—Best Friends. 2008. (Illus.). 195p. (J). pap. *(978-0-545-05062-3(6))* Scholastic, Inc.

—Needle & Thread. 2007. (Main Street Ser.). (Illus.). 205p. (J). (gr. 4-7). 14.65 *(978-0-7569-8328-4(2))* Perfection Learning Corp.

—Needle & Thread. Andreasen, Dan, illus. 2007. 205p. (J). pap. *(978-0-545-03660-3(7))* Scholastic, Inc.

—The Secret Book Club. 2008. (Main Street Ser.). (Illus.). 212p. (J). (gr. 4-7). 14.65 *(978-0-7569-8823-4(3))* Perfection Learning Corp.

—Ten Good & Bad Things about My Life (So Far) 2013. (ENG.). 288p. (J). (gr. 4-7). pap. 8.99 *(978-1-250-03413-7(2)*, 900120583) Square Fish.

—Ten Rules for Living with My Sister. 2012. (ENG.). 256p. (J). (gr. 4-7). pap. 11.99 *(978-1-250-01021-6(7)*, 900084758) Square Fish.

—Tis the Season. 2007. (Main Street Ser.). (Illus.). 195p. (J). (gr. 4-7). 14.65 *(978-0-7569-8327-7(4))* Perfection Learning Corp.

—Welcome to Camden Falls. 2007. (Main Street Ser.). (Illus.). 174p. (J). (gr. 4-7). 14.65 *(978-0-7569-8326-0(6))* Perfection Learning Corp.

Martin, Ann M. & Martin Ann, M. Claudia & Mean Janine. Telgemeier, Raina, illus. 2016. (Baby-Sitters Club Graphix Ser.: 4). (ENG.). 176p. (J). (gr. 3-7). lib. bdg. 22.10 *(978-0-606-38056-0(6))* Turtleback.

Martin, Emily Winfield. Snow & Rose. (Illus.). 224p. (J). (gr. 3-7). 2019. pap. 9.99 *(978-0-553-53821-2(7)*, Yearling) 2017. 17.99 *(978-0-553-53818-2(7)*, Random Hse. Bks. for Young Readers) Random Hse. Children's Bks.

Martin, Jacqueline Briggs. The Finest Horse in Town. Gaber, Susan, illus. 2016. (ENG.). (J). pap. 8.99 *(978-1-930900-82-0(1))* Purple Hse. Pr.

Martinez, Jessica. The Space Between Us. (ENG., (YA). (gr. 9). 2013. Illus.). 416p. pap. 9.99 *(978-1-4424-2056-4(1))* 2012. 400p. 16.99 *(978-1-4424-2055-7(3))* Simon Pulse. (Simon Pulse).

Marychild, H. D. Skater Sister. 2013. (ENG.). 222p. (J). (gr. 5-12). pap. 9.52 *(978-0-9899964-9-5(2))* Small Wonder Publishing.

Mason-Black, Jennifer. Devil & the Bluebird. 2016. (ENG.). 336p. (J). (gr. 8-17). 17.95 *(978-1-4197-2000-0(7)*, 1135901, Amulet Bks.) Abrams, Inc.

Mason, Lizzy. The Art of Losing. 2019. 336p. (YA). *(978-1-64129-104-0(4))* Soho Pr., Inc.

Matthews, Elli. Surprising Katie on Halloween. Written by Elli Matthews; Illustrated by, illus. 2011. 24p. pap. 24.95 *(978-1-4560-7486-9(5))* America Star Bks.

Matthews, L. S. Lexi. 2008. 200p. (J). pap. *(978-0-385-73575-9(8)*, Delacorte Pr) Random House Publishing Group.

Matute, Ana María. El Polizón del Ulises. (SPA.). 126p. (YA). (gr. 5-18). 10.36 *(978-84-264-3022-9(8)*, LM0588) Editorial Lumen ESP. Dist: Lectorum Pubns., Inc.

May, Sophie. Little Prudy's Dotty Dimple. 2018. (ENG., Illus.). 76p. (YA). (gr. 7-12). pap. *(978-93-5297-349-1(6))* Alpha Editions.

Mayfield, Marilee Joy. The Tiny Adventures of Big Sister & Little Sister: A Hearts-Beared Book. 2004. 48p. (J). lib. bdg. 19.95 *(978-0-9659222-2-7(7))* Leaping Antelope Productions.

Mazer, Anne. Mabel Strikes a Chord, 4. Brown, Bill, illus. 2008. (Sister Magic Ser.). (ENG.). 86p. (J). (gr. 3-6). 17.44 *(978-0-439-87249-2(9))* Scholastic, Inc.

Mazer, Norma Fox. The Missing Girl. 2010. (ENG.). 304p. (YA). (gr. 8-12). pap. 9.99 *(978-0-06-447365-1(1)*, HarperTeen) HarperCollins Pubs.

—Ten Ways to Make My Sister Disappear. (ENG.). 160p. (J). (gr. 4-6). 2012. 21.19 *(978-0-439-83984-6(X))* 2007. 16.99 *(978-0-439-83983-9(1))* Scholastic, Inc. (Levine, Arthur A. Bks.).

—Ten Ways to Make My Sister Disappear. l.t. ed. 2008. (Thorndike Literacy Bridge Ser.). 207p. (J). (gr. 4-7). 22.95 *(978-1-4104-0510-4(9))* Thorndike Pr.

McCafferty, Megan. Bumped. 2012. (Bumped Ser.: 1). (ENG.). 352p. (YA). (gr. 9). pap. 9.99 *(978-0-06-196275-2(9)*, Balzer & Bray) HarperCollins Pubs.

—Jessica Darling's It List: The (Totally Not) Guaranteed Guide to Popularity, Prettiness & Perfection. 2014. (Jessica Darling's It List Ser.: 1). (ENG.). 240p. (J). (gr. 3-7). pap. 14.99 *(978-0-316-24498-5(8)*, Poppy) Little, Brown Bks. for Young Readers.

—Thumped. 2013. (Bumped Ser.: 2). (ENG.). 304p. (YA). (gr. 8). pap. 8.99 *(978-0-06-196277-6(5)*, Balzer & Bray) HarperCollins Pubs.

McCall, Guadalupe García. El Verano de Las Mariposas, 1 vol. Bowles, David, tr. 2018. Orig. Title: Summer of the Mariposas. (SPA.). 384p. (YA). (gr. 6-12). pap. 16.95 *(978-1-62014-786-3(6)*, leelowtu, Tu Bks.) Lee & Low Bks., Inc.

McCartney, Tania. Peas in a Pod. Snerling, Tina, illus. 2015. (ENG.). 32p. (J). (gr. -1-2). 17.95 *(978-1-921966-71-2(8))* Exisle Publishing Pty Ltd. AUS. Dist: Two Rivers Distribution.

McCombie, Karen. Candy Girl. 2012. (Stoke Books Titles Ser.). 64p. (J). (gr. 5-8). pap. 7.95 *(978-1-78112-012-5(9))*; lib. bdg. 22.60 *(978-1-78112-011-8(0))* Stoke Bks.

—In Sarah's Shadow. 2003. (ENG.). 224p. (J). pap. *(978-0-00-712680-4(8)*, Flamingo) HarperCollins Pubs. Ltd. GBR. Dist: HarperCollins Pubs.

McCormack, Caren McNelly. The Fiesta Dress: A Quinceanera Tale, 0 vols. Aviles, Martha, illus. 2012. (ENG.). 42p. (J). (gr. -1-3). pap. 9.99 *(978-0-7614-6236-1(8)*, 9780761462361, Two Lions) Amazon Publishing.

McDaniel, Lurlene. The End of Forever. 2013. (Erin Bennett Ser.). (ENG.). 320p. (YA). (gr. 7). pap. 8.99 *(978-0-385-74380-8(7)*, Ember) Random Hse. Children's Bks.

McDonald, Abby. Jane Austen Goes to Hollywood. 2013. (ENG.). 336p. (YA). (gr. 9). 17.99 *(978-0-7636-5508-2(2))* Candlewick Pr.

Mcdonald, Megan. Cloudy with a Chance of Boys. 2011. (Sisters Club Ser.: 3). (Illus.). 272p. (J). (gr. 3-7). 15.99 *(978-0-7636-4615-8(6))* Candlewick Pr.

McDonald, Megan. The Sisters Club. 2008. (Sisters Club Ser.: 1). (ENG., Illus.). 208p. (J). (gr. 3-7). pap. 7.99 *(978-0-7636-3251-9(1))* Candlewick Pr.

Mcdonald, Megan. The Sisters Club. 2008. (Sisters Club Ser.: 1). lib. bdg. 16.00 *(978-1-4178-1785-6(2))* Turtleback.

McDonald, Megan. The Sisters Club: Cloudy with a Chance of Boys. 2012. (Sisters Club Ser.: 3). (ENG., Illus.). 272p. (J). (gr. 3-7). pap. 6.99 *(978-0-7636-5577-8(5))* Candlewick Pr.

—The Sisters Club: Rule of Three. (Sisters Club Ser.: 2). (ENG., Illus.). 240p. (J). (gr. 3-7). 2010. pap. 7.99 *(978-0-7636-4830-5(2))* 2009. 15.99 *(978-0-7636-4153-5(7))* Candlewick Pr.

McDowell, Kara. Just for Clicks. 2019. (ENG.). 250p. (YA). pap. 12.99 *(978-1-948705-19-6(2))* Amberjack Publishing Co.

Mcelfresh, Lynn. Strong Deaf. 2012. 130p. 18.95 *(978-1-60898-126-7(6))*; pap. 9.95 *(978-1-60898-127-4(4))* namelos llc.

McGhee, Alison. All Rivers Flow to the Sea. 2005. (ENG.). 176p. (YA). (gr. 9-12). 15.99 *(978-0-7636-2591-7(4))* Candlewick Pr.

—The Sweetest Witch Around. Bliss, Harry, illus. 2014. (ENG.). 32p. (J). (gr. -1-3). 15.99 *(978-1-4424-7833-6(0)*, Simon & Schuster/Paula Wiseman Bks.) Simon & Schuster/Paula Wiseman Bks.

McGowan, Patricia. House of Friends. 2012. 242p. 46.95 *(978-1-258-23494-2(7))*; pap. 31.95 *(978-1-258-24543-6(4))* Literary Licensing, LLC.

McKay, Hilary. The Exiles. 2007. (ENG.). 208p. (J). (gr. 4-7). pap. 12.95 *(978-1-4169-6728-6(1)*, McElderry, Margaret K. Bks.) McElderry, Margaret K. Bks.

—The Exiles at Home. 2007. (ENG.). 208p. (J). (gr. 3-7). pap. 12.95 *(978-1-4169-6729-3(X)*, McElderry, Margaret K. Bks.) McElderry, Margaret K. Bks.

—The Exiles in Love. 2007. (ENG., Illus.). 176p. (J). (gr. 3-7). pap. 9.95 *(978-1-4169-6797-2(4)*, McElderry, Margaret K. Bks.) McElderry, Margaret K. Bks.

Mckee, Jessica. Piddle Diddle Stuck in the Middle. 2010. (Illus.). 24p. (J). pap. *(978-0-9867017-0-2(X))* Little Black Dog Publishing.

McKinley, Robin. Beauty: A Retelling of Beauty & the Beast. 2018. (ENG.). 320p. (J). (gr. 3-7). pap. 7.99 *(978-0-06-280345-0(X)*, Greenwillow Bks.) HarperCollins Pubs.

McKissack, Patricia C. The All-I'll-Ever-Want Christmas Doll. Pinkney, Jerry, illus. 2007. (ENG.). 40p. (J). (gr. -1-3). 17.99 *(978-0-375-83759-3(0)*, Schwartz & Wade Bks.) Random Hse. Children's Bks.

—What Is Given from the Heart. Harrison, April, illus. 2019. 40p. (J). (gr. -1-3). 17.99 *(978-0-375-83615-2(2)*, Schwartz & Wade Bks.) Random Hse. Children's Bks.

McKnight, Gillian. To Catch a Prince. 2010. (ENG.). 240p. (YA). (gr. 7). pap. 11.99 *(978-1-4424-2718-1(3)*, Simon Pulse) Simon Pulse.

McLaughlin, Dawn L. Two Tickets to Heaven, Please! 2009. 48p. pap. 16.25 *(978-1-60693-061-8(3)*, Eloquent Bks.) Strategic Book Publishing & Rights Agency (SBPRA).

McLemore, Anna-Marie. Blanca & Roja. 2020. (ENG.). 400p. (YA). pap. 14.99 *(978-1-250-21163-7(8)*, 900186385) Square Fish.

—When the Moon Was Ours: A Novel. 2018. (ENG.). 288p. (YA). pap. 10.99 *(978-1-250-16010-2(3)*, 900185827, Wednesday Bks.) St. Martin's Pr.

McNally, Janet. The Looking Glass. 2018. (ENG., Illus.). 336p. (YA). (gr. 8). 17.99 *(978-0-06-243627-6(9)*, HarperTeen) HarperCollins Pubs.

McNamara, Margaret. The Fairy Bell Sisters #1: Sylva & the Fairy Ball. Denos, Julia, illus. 2013. (Fairy Bell Sisters Ser.: 1). (ENG.). 128p. (J). (gr. 1-5). 15.99 *(978-0-06-222802-4(1))*; pap. 4.99 *(978-0-06-222801-7(3))* HarperCollins Pubs. (Balzer & Bray).

—The Fairy Bell Sisters #2: Rosy & the Secret Friend. Denos, Julia, illus. 2013. (Fairy Bell Sisters Ser.: 2). (ENG.). 128p. (J). (gr. 1-5). pap. 4.99 *(978-0-06-222804-8(8)*, Balzer & Bray) HarperCollins Pubs.

—The Fairy Bell Sisters #3: Golden at the Fancy-Dress Party No. 3. Denos, Julia, illus. 2013. (Fairy Bell Sisters Ser.: 3). (ENG.). 144p. (J). (gr. 1-5). pap. 4.99 *(978-0-06-222807-9(2)*, Balzer & Bray) HarperCollins Pubs.

—The Fairy Bell Sisters #4: Clara & the Magical Charms. Denos, Julia, illus. 2013. (Fairy Bell Sisters Ser.: 4). (ENG.). 128p. (J). (gr. 1-5). pap. 4.99 *(978-0-06-222810-9(2)*, Balzer & Bray) HarperCollins Pubs.

—The Fairy Bell Sisters #6: Christmas Fairy Magic. Collingridge, Catharine, illus. 2014. (Fairy Bell Sisters Ser.: 6). (ENG.). 144p. (J). (gr. 1-5). pap. 4.99 *(978-0-06-226723-8(X)*, Balzer & Bray) HarperCollins Pubs.

—Golden at the Fancy-Dress Party. 2013. (Fairy Bell Sisters Ser.: 3). (J). lib. bdg. 14.75 *(978-0-606-32154-9(3))* Turtleback.

—Rosy & the Secret Friend. 2013. (Fairy Bell Sisters Ser.: 2). (J). lib. bdg. 14.75 *(978-0-606-31797-9(X))* Turtleback.

—Sylva & the Fairy Ball. 2013. (Fairy Bell Sisters Ser.: 1). (J). lib. bdg. 14.75 *(978-0-606-31796-2(1))* Turtleback.

McPhail, David. Sisters. McPhail, David, illus. 2010. (ENG., Illus.). 28p. (J). (gr. -1 — 1). bds. 7.99 *(978-0-547-48087-9(3)*, 1439407, Clarion Bks.) HarperCollins Pubs.

McPhail, J. A. Dawn of Day. Battis, Gwen, illus. 2012. 200p. pap. 10.99 *(978-0-9851196-1-4(6))* Rowe Publishing.

McTighe, Carolyn. The Sakura Tree, 1 vol. Brownlee, Karen, illus. 2007. (ENG.). 32p. (J). (gr. k-3). 15.95 *(978-0-88995-354-3(6)*, e343120d-f345-4018-a057-25b04d214bff) Red Deer Pr. CAN. Dist: Firefly Bks., Ltd.

McVoy, Terra Elan. Being Friends with Boys. 2013. (ENG., Illus.). 384p. (YA). (gr. 9). pap. 10.99 *(978-1-4424-2160-8(6)*, Simon Pulse) Simon Pulse.

S

—The Summer of Firsts & Lasts. 2011. (ENG.). 432p. (YA). (gr. 9-18). 16.99 *(978-1-4424-0213-3(X),* Simon Pulse) Simon Pulse.

Mcwherter, Barbara. Oliver & His Mountain Climbing Adventures. McWherter, Shelley, illus. 2012. 34p. 24.95 *(978-1-4626-7601-9(4))* America Star Bks.

Mendle, Jane. My Ultimate Sister Disaster: A Novel. 2010. (ENG.). 208p. (YA). (gr. 7-18). pap. 18.99 *(978-0-312-36904-0(2),* 900042729, St. Martin's Griffin) St. Martin's Pr.

Mendoza, Jessica & Mendoza, Alana. There's No Base Like Home, 1 vol. McNally Barshaw, Ruth, illus. 2018. (ENG.). 240p. (J). (gr. 3-7). 18.95 *(978-1-62014-588-3(X),* leelowtu, Tu Bks.) Lee & Low Bks., Inc.

Mercer, Sienna. My Sister the Vampire #2: Fangtastic! 2007. (My Sister the Vampire Ser.: 2). (ENG.). 208p. (J). (gr. 3-7). per. 6.99 *(978-0-06-087115-4(6),* HarperCollins) HarperCollins Pubs.

Meredith, Christina. Kiss Crush Collide. 2012. (ENG.). 320p. (YA). (gr. 9). pap. 9.99 *(978-0-06-206225-3(5),* Greenwillow Bks.) HarperCollins Pubs.

Messer, Celeste M. The Ghost of Piper's Landing. Hoeffner, Deb, illus. 2004. 82-92p. 4.95 *(978-0-9702171-7-2(X))* AshleyAlan Enterprises.

Meyer, Shawna Rae. When the Baby-Sitter Comes. 2011. 28p. pap. 14.95 *(978-1-4567-3808-2(9))* AuthorHouse.

Michels-Gualtieri, Akaela S. I Was Born to Be a Sister. Ramsey, Marcy Dunn, illus. 2005. (ENG.). 32p. (J). (gr. 4-7). 9.95 incl. lp *(978-1-930775-11-4(3))* Platypus Media, L.L.C.

Mikaelsen, Ben. Tree Girl. 2005. (ENG.). 240p. (YA). (gr. 8). pap. 11.99 *(978-0-06-009006-7(5),* HarperTeen) HarperCollins Pubs.

Miller, Barnabas, et al. 7 Souls. 2011. (ENG.). 384p. (J). (gr. 9-12). 26.19 *(978-0-385-73673-2(8),* Delacorte Pr.) Random Hse. Children's Bks.

Miller, Sarah. The Lost Crown. (ENG., Illus.). 448p. (YA). (gr. 7). 2012. pap. 12.99 *(978-1-4169-8341-5(4))* 2011. 17.99 *(978-1-4169-8340-8(6))* Simon & Schuster Children's Publishing. (Atheneum Bks. for Young Readers).

Miller, Stefne & Madison, Bailee. Losing Brave, 1 vol. 2018. (ENG.). 352p. (YA). 17.99 *(978-0-310-76054-2(2))* Blink.

Millner, Denene & Miller, Mitzi. If Only You Knew, Bk. 2. 2008. (Hotlanta Ser.: 2). (ENG.). 254p. (J). (gr. 7-18). 24.94 *(978-0-545-00309-4(1))* Scholastic, Inc.

Mills, Tessa L. The Adventures of Avery & Cali. 2007. 60p. per. 16.95 *(978-1-4241-7982-4(3))* America Star Bks.

Mindy, Miss. Artist Sisters Vol. 2: Princess la la & the Little Bee - Teenie Weenie Tales. 2007. (ENG., Illus.). 64p. (J). (gr. 8-12). 30.00 *(978-0-9778949-7-0(5))* Baby Tattoo Bks.

Mitchell, Carolann. The Song of the Snow. 2011. 68p. (gr. 4-6). pap. 8.95 *(978-0-595-46609-2(5))* iUniverse, Inc.

Mittal, Anjali. The Convent Rules. 2009. (Illus.). 80p. pap. 10.49 *(978-1-4389-8575-6(4))* AuthorHouse.

Miyazaki, Hayao. My Neighbor Totoro Picture Book: New Edition. 2013. (My Neighbor Totoro Picture Book (New Edition) Ser.). (ENG., Illus.). 112p. (J). 19.99 *(978-1-4215-6122-6(0))* Viz Media.

Mlynowski, Sarah. Spells & Sleeping Bags. 2008. (Magic in Manhattan Ser.: 3). (ENG.). 320p. (YA). (gr. 7-12). pap. 8.99 *(978-0-385-73388-5(7),* Delacorte Pr.) Random Hse. Children's Bks.

Mlynowski, Sarah & Rigaud, Debbie. The Sister Switch (Best Wishes #2) Vee, Maxine, illus. 2023. (Best Wishes Ser.). (ENG.). 192p. (J). (gr. 3-7). 15.99 *(978-1-338-62828-9(3),* Scholastic Pr.) Scholastic, Inc.

Moderow, Hannah. Lily's Mountain. 2017. (ENG., Illus.). 192p. (J). (gr. 5-7). 16.99 *(978-0-544-97800-3(5),* 1663727, Clarion Bks.) HarperCollins Pubs.

Moore, Mykela. Meet the Super Sisters. Garrett, Myers, illus. 2013. (J). 9.99 *(978-0-9852746-9-6(7))* Hope of Vision Publishing.

Moore, Stephanie Perry. Better Than Picture Perfect, No. 2. 2014. (Sharp Sisters Ser.: 2). (ENG.). 160p. (YA). (gr. 6-12). pap. 7.95 *(978-1-4677-4486-7(7),* add2aaa3-7821-4781-9f47-582ec3843188, Darby Creek) Lerner Publishing Group.

—Icing on the Cake, No. 5. 2014. (Sharp Sisters Ser.: 5). (ENG.). 160p. (YA). (gr. 6-12). pap. 7.95 *(978-1-4677-4487-4(5),* 29998c09-e540-4b5a-8fc4-8602f7f158b6); lib. bdg. 27.99 *(978-1-4677-3728-9(3),* f405893c-9260-48ce-94ea-f4ca879855dc) Lerner Publishing Group. (Darby Creek).

—Truth & Nothing But, No. 4. 2014. (Sharp Sisters Ser.: 4). (ENG.). 160p. (YA). (gr. 6-12). pap. 7.95 *(978-1-4677-4489-8(1),* 5499bf15-c234-411b-a0b7-7f09c055b2b2, Darby Creek) Lerner Publishing Group.

—Turn up for Real, No. 3. 2014. (Sharp Sisters Ser.: 3). (ENG.). 168p. (YA). (gr. 6-12). pap. 7.95 *(978-1-4677-4490-4(5),* de59dd5f-2ef4-4a9e-8592-cfe9541a147a, Darby Creek) Lerner Publishing Group.

Morah, Chizoba. The Anderson Twins. 2007. 76p. per. 19.95 *(978-1-60441-015-0(9))* America Star Bks.

Morgan, C. M. Silver Doorway #6: The Alchemist's Girl. 2008. 108p. pap. 6.99 *(978-0-9771005-2-1(9))* Sabledrake Enterprises.

Morris, David. My Twins First Christmas. 2008. (Illus.). 24p. (J). pap. 14.95 *(978-0-9799885-0-9(0))* New Year Publishing.

Morris, Lynn. Don't eat your Broccoli! Mettler, Joe, illus. 2007. 32p. (J). per. 6.95 *(978-0-9755548-2-1(4))* Log Cabin Bks.

Morris, Paris. My Twins First Halloween. 2008. (J). pap. 12.95 *(978-0-9760095-9-7(5))* New Year Publishing.

Morris, Paris & Florzak, Douglas. My Twins First Birthday. 2010. (ENG., Illus.). 24p. (J). pap. 12.95 *(978-0-9760095-8-0(7))* New Year Publishing.

Moss, Marissa. Amelia's 6th-Grade Notebook. Moss, Marissa, illus. 2005. (Amelia Ser.). (ENG., Illus.). 80p. (J). (gr. 4-7). 14.99 *(978-0-689-87040-8(X),* Simon & Schuster/Paula Wiseman Bks.) Simon & Schuster/Paula Wiseman Bks.

—Amelia's Are-We-There-Yet Longest Ever Car Trip. Moss, Marissa, illus. (Amelia Ser.). (ENG., Illus.). 40p. (J). (gr. 2-5). 2012. pap. 8.99 *(978-1-4169-1287-3(8))* 2006. 14.99 *(978-1-4169-0906-4(0))* Simon & Schuster/Paula Wiseman Bks. (Simon & Schuster/Paula Wiseman Bks.).

—Amelia's Longest, Biggest, Most-Fights-Ever Family Reunion. Moss, Marissa, illus. 2006. (Amelia Ser.). (ENG., Illus.). 80p. (J). (gr. 4-7). 12.99 *(978-0-689-87447-5(2),* Simon & Schuster/Paula Wiseman Bks.) Simon & Schuster/Paula Wiseman Bks.

—Amelia's Most Unforgettable Embarrassing Moments. Moss, Marissa, illus. 2005. (Amelia Ser.). (ENG., Illus.). 80p. (J). (gr. 4-7). 14.99 *(978-0-689-87041-5(8),* Simon & Schuster/Paula Wiseman Bks.) Simon & Schuster/Paula Wiseman Bks.

—Amelia's Notebook. Moss, Marissa, illus. 2006. (Amelia Ser.). (ENG., Illus.). (J). 5.99 *(978-1-4169-1286-6(X));* 40p. (gr. 2-5). 14.99 *(978-1-4169-0905-7(2))* Simon & Schuster/Paula Wiseman Bks. (Simon & Schuster/Paula Wiseman Bks.).

—Amelia's Summer Survival Guide: Amelia's Longest, Biggest, Most-Fights-Ever Family Reunion; Amelia's Itchy-Twitchy, Lovey-Dovey Summer at Camp Mosquito. Moss, Marissa, illus. 2011. (Amelia Ser.). (ENG., Illus.). 160p. (J). (gr. 5-8). 12.99 *(978-1-4424-2331-2(5),* Simon & Schuster/Paula Wiseman Bks.) Simon & Schuster/Paula Wiseman Bks.

Moulton, Erin E. Flutter: The Story of Four Sisters & an Incredible Journey. 2012. (ENG.). 224p. (J). (gr. 3-7). pap. 6.99 *(978-0-14-242133-8(2),* Puffin Books) Penguin Young Readers Group.

—Tracing Stars. 2013. (ENG.). 256p. (J). (gr. 3-7). pap. 6.99 *(978-0-14-242653-1(9),* Puffin Books) Penguin Young Readers Group.

Mowry, Tia & Mowry, Tamera. Twintuition: Double Cross. 2018. (Twintuition Ser.: 4). (ENG.). 208p. (J). (gr. 3-7). 16.99 *(978-0-06-237295-6(5),* HarperCollins) HarperCollins Pubs.

—Twintuition: Double Dare. (Twintuition Ser.: 3). (ENG.). (J). (gr. 3-7). 2018. 224p. pap. 6.99 *(978-0-06-237293-2(9))* 2017. 208p. 16.99 *(978-0-06-237292-5(0))* HarperCollins Pubs. (HarperCollins).

—Twintuition: Double Vision. 2015. (Twintuition Ser.: 1). (ENG.). 208p. (J). (gr. 3-7). 16.99 *(978-0-06-237286-4(6),* HarperCollins) HarperCollins Pubs.

Muhammad, Ibtihaj. The Proudest Blue: A Story of Hijab & Family. Aly, Hatem, illus. 2019. (ENG.). 40p. (J). (gr. -1-3). 17.99 *(978-0-316-51900-7(6))* Little, Brown Bks. for Young Readers.

Murdoch, Emily. If You Find Me: A Novel. 2014. (ENG.). 288p. (YA). (gr. 7). pap. 12.99 *(978-1-250-03327-7(6),* 900096076, St. Martin's Griffin) St. Martin's Pr.

Musgrove, Marianne. Forget-me-not Fairies Story Collection. MacCarthy, Patricia, illus. 2013. (ENG.). 192p. (J). (gr. -1-3). *(978-1-74308-536-3(2))* Hinkler Bks. Pty, Ltd.

My Sister Jess: Set C Individual Title Six-Packs. (Supersonic Phonics Ser.). (gr. k-3). 29.00 *(978-0-7635-0546-2(3))* Rigby Education.

Myracle, Lauren. The Backward Season. (Wishing Day Ser.: 3). (ENG.). 304p. (J). (gr. 3-7). 2019. pap. 6.99 *(978-0-06-234213-3(4))* 2018. 16.99 *(978-0-06-234212-6(6))* HarperCollins Pubs. (Tegen, Katherine Bks).

Nagai, Mariko. Under the Broken Sky. 2019. (ENG., Illus.). 304p. (J). 17.99 *(978-1-250-15921-2(0),* 900185614, Holt, Henry & Co. Bks. For Young Readers) Holt, Henry & Co.

Nahall Nikoo Fells. Drowning in the Mainstream: Confessions of a Sister. 2010. 284p. 27.95 *(978-1-4502-0552-8(6))* iUniverse, Inc.

Nash, Ronza R. The Chocolate Wonders: The Adventures of Lila & Lester. 2011. 36p. pap. 16.86 *(978-1-4634-1619-5(9))* AuthorHouse.

Nazarian, Leslie. Orelda & Corelda's Ocean Voyage. 2007. 52p. (J). 15.94 *(978-1-4116-2373-6(8))* Lulu Pr., Inc.

Neasi, Barbara J. Just Like Me. Hantel, Johanna, illus. 2011. (Rookie Ready to Learn — All about Me! Ser.). 40p. (J). (gr. -1-k). lib. bdg. 25.00 *(978-0-531-26371-6(1),* Children's Pr.) Scholastic Library Publishing.

—Just Like Me (Rookie Ready to Learn - All about Me!) Hantel, Johanna, illus. 2011. (Rookie Ready to Learn Ser.). (ENG.). 40p. (J). (gr. -1-k). pap. 5.95 *(978-0-531-26676-2(1),* Children's Pr.) Scholastic Library Publishing.

Nefflen, Marjorie E. My Big Sister Knows... 2012. 32p. pap. 10.95 *(978-1-4626-8879-1(9));* 30p. 24.95 *(978-1-62709-509-9(8))* America Star Bks.

Nelson, Jandy. The Sky Is Everywhere. 2011. (ENG.). 320p. (YA). (gr. 9-18). 9.99 *(978-0-14-241780-5(7),* Speak) Penguin Young Readers Group.

—The Sky Is Everywhere. 2011. (ENG., Illus.). 275p. (gr. 9-12). 19.00 *(978-1-61383-223-3(0))* Perfection Learning Corp.

Nicholls, Sally. Season of Secrets. 2011. 225p. (J). pap. *(978-0-545-21826-9(8),* Levine, Arthur A. Bks.) Scholastic, Inc.

Nichols, Lori. Maple. Nichols, Lori, illus. (Illus.). 32p. (J). 2019. (— 1). bds. 8.99 *(978-1-9848-1298-8(X))* 2014. (gr. -1-k). 17.99 *(978-0-399-16085-1(X))* Penguin Young Readers Group. (Nancy Paulsen Books).

—Maple & Willow Together. Nichols, Lori, illus. 2014. (Illus.). 32p. (J). (gr. -1-k). 17.99 *(978-0-399-16283-1(6),* Nancy Paulsen Books) Penguin Young Readers Group.

—Maple & Willow's Christmas Tree. Nichols, Lori, illus. 2016. (Illus.). 32p. (J). (-k). 17.99 *(978-0-399-16756-0(0),* Nancy Paulsen Books) Penguin Young Readers Group.

Night, P. J. The House Next Door. 2013. (You're Invited to a Creepover Ser.: 16). (ENG., Illus.). 160p. (J). (gr. 3-7). pap. 6.99 *(978-1-4424-8233-3(8),* Simon Spotlight) Simon Spotlight.

—Together Forever. 2012. (You're Invited to a Creepover Ser.: 8). (ENG.). 160p. (J). (gr. 3-7). pap. 6.99 *(978-1-4424-5159-9(9),* Simon Spotlight) Simon Spotlight.

Nix, Garth. Frogkisser! 2019. (ENG.). 384p. (YA). (gr. 7-7). pap. 12.99 *(978-1-338-05209-1(8))* Scholastic, Inc.

Noland, Charles. The Adventures of Drew & Ellie: The Magical Dress. Baker, Sherri, illus. 2006. (J). *(978-0-9789297-1-8(3));* 2nd rev. ed. 84p. per. 7.95 *(978-0-9789297-0-1(5))* TMD Enterprises.

Noonan, Rosalind, et al. The Love Factor. 2003. (ENG., Illus.). 128p. *(978-0-00-714454-9(7),* HarperCollins Children's Bks.) HarperCollins Pubs. Ltd.

Nöstlinger, Christine. Por Favor, Vuelve a Casa.Tr. of Please, Come Back Home. (SPA.). 176p. (YA). (gr. 7-9). 9.95 *(978-958-04-2379-9(2),* 10266266) Norma S.A. COL. Dist: Distribuidora Norma, Inc.

Novak, Ali. The Heartbreakers. 2015. (Heartbreak Chronicles Ser.: 1). 336p. (YA). (gr. 6-12). pap. 12.99 *(978-1-4926-1256-8(1),* 9781492612568) Sourcebooks, Inc.

Numeroff, Laura. What Sisters Do Best: (Big Sister Books for Kids, Sisterhood Books for Kids, Sibling Books for Kids) Munsinger, Lynn, illus. 2012. (What Brothers/Sisters Do Best Ser.). (ENG.). 20p. (J). (gr. -1 — 1). bds. 7.99 *(978-1-4521-1074-5(3))* Chronicle Bks. LLC.

Numeroff, Laura Joffe. The Chicken Sisters. Collicott, Sharleen, illus. abr. ed. 2003. (J). (gr. -1-2). 28.95 incl. audio compact disk *(978-1-59112-533-4(2))* Live Oak Media.

Nusom, Jacqueline. My Little Sister & Me. 2006. 12p. (J). 8.47 *(978-1-4116-7352-6(2))* Lulu Pr., Inc.

Nyikos, Stacy. Dragon Wishes. 2008. (ENG.). 256p. (J). (gr. 2-7). 16.95 *(978-1-933831-11-4(1))* Blooming Tree Pr.

Oaks, Tina. Sister Trap, No. 2. 2003. (Stepsisters Ser.). (ENG.). (J). pap. 2.50 *(978-0-590-40903-2(4))* Scholastic, Inc.

O'Brien, Thomas E. The Magic of Finbar. 2011. 68p. pap. 19.95 *(978-1-4560-4235-6(1))* America Star Bks.

O'Connor, Jane. Fancy Nancy & the Fabulous Fashion Boutique. Glasser, Robin Preiss, illus. 2010. (Fancy Nancy Ser.). (ENG.). 32p. (J). (gr. -1-3). 17.99 *(978-0-06-123592-4(X));* lib. bdg. 18.89 *(978-0-06-123593-1(8))* HarperCollins Pubs. (HarperCollins).

—Fancy Nancy: Fanciest Doll in the Universe. Glasser, Robin Preiss, illus. 2013. (Fancy Nancy Ser.). (ENG.). 32p. (J). (gr. -1-3). 17.99 *(978-0-06-170384-3(2));* lib. bdg. 18.89 *(978-0-06-170385-0(0))* HarperCollins Pubs. (HarperCollins).

—Fancy Nancy: Jojo & Daddy Bake a Cake. Glasser, Robin Preiss, illus. 2017. (My First I Can Read Ser.). (ENG.). 32p. (J). (gr. -1-3). 16.99 *(978-0-06-237802-6(3));* pap. 4.99 *(978-0-06-237801-9(5))* HarperCollins Pubs. (HarperCollins).

—Fancy Nancy: Saturday Night Sleepover. Glasser, Robin Preiss, illus. 2016. (Fancy Nancy Ser.). (ENG.). 32p. (J). (gr. -1-3). 17.99 *(978-0-06-226985-0(2),* HarperCollins) HarperCollins Pubs.

—Lulu & the Witch Baby. Sinclair, Bella, illus. 2014. (I Can Read Level 2 Ser.). (ENG.). 48p. (J). (gr. -1-3). pap. 4.99 *(978-0-06-230516-9(6),* HarperCollins) HarperCollins Pubs.

O'Connor, Jane & Glasser, Robin Preiss. Fancy Nancy: Stellar Stargazer. 2011. (Fancy Nancy Ser.). (ENG., Illus.). 32p. (J). (gr. -1-2). 13.99 *(978-0-06-191523-9(8),* HarperCollins) HarperCollins Pubs.

Odierno, Lisa. Kitten & Her Sister. 2009. (ENG.). 16p. (J). 6.95 *(978-1-60727-000-3(5))* Soundprints.

Olaizola, José Luis. Mi Hermana Gabriela. (SPA., Illus.). 120p. (YA). (gr. 5-8). *(978-84-207-3065-3(3),* GS4005) Grupo Anaya, S.A. ESP. Dist: Lectorum Pubns., Inc.

Olena Rudge. The Adventures of Sophie & Katia in the Enchanted Forest. 2013. 220p. pap. *(978-3-85438-685-8(0))* united p.c. Verlag.

Oliver, Lauren. Vanishing Girls. (ENG.). (YA). (gr. 9). 2016. 384p. pap. 11.99 *(978-0-06-222411-8(5))* 2015. 368p. 18.99 *(978-0-06-222410-1(7))* HarperCollins Pubs. (HarperCollins).

—Vanishing Girls. 2016. (YA). lib. bdg. 20.85 *(978-0-606-38171-0(6))* Turtleback.

Olsen, Mary-Kate & Olsen, Ashley. Dare to Scare. 2005. (ENG., Illus.). 112p. *(978-0-00-715887-4(4))* HarperCollins Pubs. Australia.

—Love-Set-Match. 2005. (ENG., Illus.). 112p. *(978-0-00-715885-0(8))* HarperCollins Pubs. Australia.

—Santa Girls, 3 vols. 2005. (ENG., Illus.). 112p. *(978-0-00-715888-1(2))* HarperCollins Pubs. Australia.

—Winner Take All. 2003. (ENG., Illus.). 112p. *(978-0-00-714471-6(7),* HarperCollins Children's Bks.) HarperCollins Pubs. Ltd.

Olson, Norah. Twisted Fate. 2016. (ENG.). 288p. (YA). (gr. 8). pap. 9.99 *(978-0-06-227206-5(3),* Tegen, Katherine Bks) HarperCollins Pubs.

Omara, Charlotte. My Scary First Day of School. 2012. 26p. 24.95 *(978-1-4626-7652-1(9))* America Star Bks.

Onyebuchi, Tochi. War Girls. 2019. (ENG.). 464p. (YA). (gr. 7). 18.99 *(978-0-451-48167-2(4),* Razorbill) Penguin Young Readers Group.

Orante, Ann-Jeanette P. Best Sisters for Life... 2007. (ENG., Illus.). 36p. (J). per. 11.95 *(978-1-59800-972-9(9))* Outskirts Pr., Inc.

Orgel, Doris. Sarah's Room. Sendak, Maurice, illus. 2005. 47p. (J). (gr. k-4). reprint ed. 15.00 *(978-0-7567-9683-9(0))* DIANE Publishing Co.

Orr, Wendy. The Princess & Her Panther. Stringer, Lauren, illus. 2010. (ENG.). 40p. (J). (gr. -1-3). 16.99 *(978-1-4169-9780-1(6),* Beach Lane Bks.) Beach Lane Bks.

O'Ryan, Ray. Operation Twin Trouble. Kraft, Jason, illus. 2015. (Galaxy Zack Ser.: 12). (ENG.). 128p. (J). (gr. k-4). pap. 5.99 *(978-1-4814-4399-9(2),* Little Simon) Little Simon.

Otten, Charlotte F. Home in a Wilderness Fort: Copper Harbor 1844. 2006. (Illus.). 232p. (J). (gr. 2-7). per. 14.95 *(978-0-9766104-5-8(0))* Arbutus Pr.

Pagratis, Maggie. My Sister the Bee. 2004. 29p. (J). per. 16.68 *(978-1-4116-1098-9(9))* Lulu Pr., Inc.

Palmer, Iva-Marie. The Summers, 0 vols. 2014. (ENG.). 272p. (YA). (gr. 10-12). pap. 9.99 *(978-1-4778-2730-7(7),* 9781477827307, Skyscape) Amazon Publishing.

Palmer, Robin. Girl vs. Superstar, 1. 2010. (Yours Truly, Lucy B. Parker Ser.: 1). 224p. (J). (gr. 6-8). 21.19 *(978-0-14-241500-9(6))* Penguin Young Readers Group.

—Yours Truly, Lucy B. Parker: Take My Advice: Book 4, 4 vols., 4. 2012. (Yours Truly, Lucy B. Parker Ser.: 4). 224p. (J). (gr. 6-8). 21.19 *(978-0-14-241503-0(0))* Penguin Young Readers Group.

Palmieri, Kathryn & Palmieri, Patricia. GYPSY McPHEE: The New Kid in Town. 2011. (Illus.). 40p. (J). pap. 12.95 *(978-1-58909-750-6(5))* Bookstand Publishing.

Pandanas, Ms L. A. The Slinky Luminescence: Two Plus Who? 2013. 84p. pap. *(978-0-9870702-9-6(0))* Reed, Laura.

Pandora. Ankh: Conquering the Seven Deadly Sins. 2013. 100p. pap. 10.95 *(978-1-62212-908-9(3),* Strategic Bk. Publishing) Strategic Book Publishing & Rights Agency (SBPRA).

The Paper Pup. 2004. 39p. pap. 24.95 *(978-1-4137-3012-8(4))* PublishAmerica, Inc.

Parker, Emma & Renaud, Marguerite. Who Took My Things? 2010. (Illus.). 20p. pap. *(978-1-877561-76-4(2))* First Edition Ltd.

Parr, todd. The Sister Book. 2018. (ENG., Illus.). 32p. (J). (gr. -1-1). 14.99 *(978-0-316-26520-1(9))* Little, Brown Bks. for Young Readers.

Paterson, Katherine. Jacob Have I Loved: A Newbery Award Winner. 2020. (ENG.). 272p. (YA). (gr. 8-8). pap. 7.99 *(978-0-06-440368-9(8),* HarperCollins) HarperCollins Pubs.

Patrick, Cat. The Originals. (ENG.). (YA). (gr. 7-17). 2014. 320p. pap. 10.00 *(978-0-316-21945-7(2))* 2013. 304p. 18.00 *(978-0-316-21943-3(6))* Little, Brown Bks. for Young Readers.

Patron, Susan. Maybe Yes, Maybe No, Maybe Maybe. Halpin, Abigail, illus. 2009. (ENG.). 128p. (J). (gr. 3-5). pap. 5.99 *(978-1-4169-6176-5(3),* Atheneum Bks. for Young Readers) Simon & Schuster Children's Publishing.

Patterson, James. Crazy House. 2019. (Crazy House Ser.: 1). (ENG.). 352p. mass mkt. 8.99 *(978-1-5387-1406-5(X))* Grand Central Publishing.

—Crazy House. 2018. (Crazy House Ser.: 1). (ENG.). 384p. (YA). (gr. 9-17). pap. 9.99 *(978-0-316-51499-6(3),* Jimmy Patterson) Little Brown & Co.

Patterson, James & Grabenstein, Chris. Katt vs. Dogg. López, Anuki, illus. (ENG.). (J). (gr. 3-7). 2021. (Katt vs. Dogg Ser.: 1). 336p. pap. 8.99 *(978-0-316-39712-4(1))* 2019. 320p. 13.99 *(978-0-316-41156-1(6))* Little Brown & Co. (Jimmy Patterson).

Patterson, Valerie O. The Other Side of Blue. 2011. (ENG.). 240p. (YA). (gr. 7). pap. 13.99 *(978-0-547-55215-6(7),* 1450660, Clarion Bks.) HarperCollins Pubs.

Paty, Miss. May's Wild Walk: Book 1, No. 1. 2017. (Whiskers Sisters Ser.: Vol. 1). (ENG., Illus.). (J). (gr. k-3). 48p. pap. 9.99 *(978-1-5124-5416-1(8),* 50c90cd3-06ee-4009-9034-b8940cb182ee); 40p. 26.65 *(978-1-5124-2527-7(3),* 51faf95d-2d03-48bc-863c-b963be703835) Lerner Publishing Group. (Graphic Universe™).

—The Mystery of the Tree Stump Ghost: Book 2. 2018. (Whiskers Sisters Ser.). (ENG., Illus.). (J). (gr. k-3). Bk. 2. 48p. pap. 9.99 *(978-1-5415-1045-6(3),* fd30a799-5e30-44ba-94f8-87e9549a58bf)No. 2. 40p. 26.65 *(978-1-5124-2528-4(1),* 0e4f01e7-88e0-4f26-b068-a65d6dca2270) Lerner Publishing Group. (Graphic Universe™).

Pau Preto, Nicki. Crown of Feathers. 2019. (Crown of Feathers Ser.). (ENG., Illus.). 496p. (YA). (gr. 7). 21.99 *(978-1-5344-2462-3(8),* Simon Pulse) Simon Pulse.

Paulits, John. Philip & the Case of the Mistaken Identity & Philip & the Baby. 2007. (ENG.). 150p. (YA). pap. 10.95 *(978-1-59705-897-1(1))* Wings ePress, Inc.

Payton, Belle. Two Cool for School. 2014. (It Takes Two Ser.: 2). (ENG., Illus.). 160p. (J). (gr. 3-7). 16.99 *(978-1-4814-0645-1(0),* Simon Spotlight) Simon Spotlight.

—A Whole New Ball Game. 2014. (It Takes Two Ser.: 1). (ENG., Illus.). 160p. (J). (gr. 3-7). pap. 7.99 *(978-1-4814-0641-3(8),* Simon Spotlight) Simon Spotlight.

Pearce, Jackson. Fathomless. 2013. (Fairy Tale Retelling Ser.). (ENG.). 320p. (YA). (gr. 10-17). pap. 8.99 *(978-0-316-20777-5(2))* Little, Brown Bks. for Young Readers.

—Sisters Red. 2011. (Fairy Tale Retelling Ser.). (ENG.). 352p. (YA). (gr. 10-17). pap. 18.99 *(978-0-316-06867-3(5))* Little, Brown Bks. for Young Readers.

Pearson, Mary E. Generous Me. Krejca, Gary, illus. 2011. (Rookie Ready to Learn — All about Me! Ser.). 40p. (J). (gr. -1-k). lib. bdg. 25.00 *(978-0-531-26427-0(0));* (ENG.). pap. 5.95 *(978-0-531-26652-6(4))* Scholastic Library Publishing. (Children's Pr.).

Perez, Marlene. Dead Is Just a Rumor. 2010. (Dead Is Ser.: 4). lib. bdg. 18.40 *(978-0-606-14958-7(9))* Turtleback.

—Dead Is Not an Option. 2011. (Dead Is Ser.: 5). (ENG.). 256p. (YA). (gr. 7-18). pap. 7.99 *(978-0-547-34593-2(3),* 1419607, Clarion Bks.) HarperCollins Pubs.

Perez, Melissa E. Adventures of Camron, Tiffany & Lydi. 2011. 24p. pap. 24.95 *(978-1-4626-3724-9(8))* America Star Bks.

Perkins, Lynne Rae. Secret Sisters of the Salty Sea. Perkins, Lynne Rae, illus. 2019. (ENG., Illus.). 256p. (J). (gr. 3-7). pap. 6.99 *(978-0-06-249967-7(X),* Greenwillow Bks.) HarperCollins Pubs.

—Secret Sisters of the Salty Sea. 2018. (ENG., Illus.). 240p. (J). (gr. 3-7). 16.99 *(978-0-06-249966-0(1),* Greenwillow Bks.) HarperCollins Pubs.

Perkins, Mitali. Secret Keeper. (ENG.). 240p. (YA). (gr. 7). 2010. pap. 8.99 *(978-0-440-23955-0(9),* Ember) 2009. (Illus.). lib. bdg. 22.44 *(978-0-385-90356-1(1),* Delacorte Pr.) Random Hse. Children's Bks.

Perkyns, Dorothy. Bridget's Black '47. 2009. (ENG.). 160p. (J). (gr. 5-18). pap. 12.99 *(978-1-55488-400-1(4))* Dundurn Pr. CAN. Dist: Publishers Group West (PGW).

Peters, Julie Anne. Rage: a Love Story. 2010. 304p. (YA). (gr. 9). pap. 9.99 *(978-0-375-84411-9(2),* Knopf Bks. for Young Readers) Random Hse. Children's Bks.

Peterson, Jeanne Whitehouse. Don't Forget Winona. Root, Kimberly Bulcken, illus. 2004. 32p. (J). (gr. -1-3). lib. bdg. 15.89 *(978-0-06-027198-5(1))* HarperCollins Pubs.

Petro-Roy, Jen. P. S. I Miss You. 2023. (ENG.). 336p. (J). pap. 8.99 *(978-1-250-29430-2(4),* 900174212) Square Fish.

Petrone, Epp. Anna's Teeth. Maiste, Piia, illus. 2013. 94p. pap. *(978-9949-511-27-3(5))* Petrone Print.

Pham, LeUyen. Big Sister, Little Sister. Pham, LeUyen, illus. 2005. (ENG., Illus.). 40p. (J). (gr. -1-3). 17.99 *(978-0-7868-5182-9(1))* Little, Brown Bks. for Young Readers.

Phillips, Helen. Here Where the Sunbeams Are Green. 2013. (ENG.). 304p. (J). (gr. 5). 7.99 *(978-0-307-93145-0(5),* Yearling) Random Hse. Children's Bks.

Pichon, L. Tom Gates: Excellent Excuses (and Other Good Stuff) Pichon, L., illus. 2015. (Tom Gates Ser.: 2). (ENG., Illus.). 352p. (J). (gr. 3-7). 12.99 *(978-0-7636-7474-8(5))* Candlewick Pr.

Pichon, Liz. Excellent Excuses (and Other Good Stuff) 2016. (Brilliant World of Tom Gates Ser.: 2). lib. bdg. 18.40 *(978-0-606-37941-0(X))* Turtleback.

Pilon, Laura. Just Like My Little Sister. 2013. 24p. pap. 17.99 *(978-1-4817-0562-2(8))* AuthorHouse.

Pilumeli, Tanya. The Dragonfly Keeper. 2008. 264p. (J). per. 12.95 *(978-0-9801396-0-0(0))* FAVA Pr.

Pixley, Marcella. Freak: A Novel. 2013. (ENG.). 160p. (YA). (gr. 7-10). pap. 14.99 (978-1-250-02742-9(X), 900098314) Square Fish.

Plum, Amy. Die for Me. (Die for Me Ser.: 1). (ENG.). (YA). (gr. 9). 2012. 368p. pap. 8.99 (978-0-06-200402-4(6)) 2011. 352p. 17.99 (978-0-06-200401-7(8)) HarperCollins Pubs. (HarperTeen).

Podos, Rebecca. The Wise & the Wicked. 2019. (ENG.). 368p. (YA). (gr. 9). 17.99 (978-0-06-269902-2(4), Balzer & Bray) HarperCollins Pubs.

Popovic, Lana. Wicked Like a Wildfire. (ENG.). (YA). (gr. 9). 2018. 432p. 10.99 (978-0-06-243684-9(8)) 2017. 416p. 17.99 (978-0-06-243683-2(X)) HarperCollins Pubs. (Tegen, Katherine Bks).

Posner-Sanchez, Andrea. A Frozen Christmas (Disney Frozen) RH Disney, illus. 2015. (ENG.). 12p. (J). (gr. -1 — 1). bds. 8.99 (978-0-7364-3479-9(8), RH/Disney) Random Hse. Children's Bks.

Potter, Giselle. Tell Me What to Dream About. Potter, Giselle, illus. 2015. (Illus.). 40p. (J). (gr. -1-2). 17.99 (978-0-385-37423-1(2), Schwartz & Wade Bks.) Random Hse. Children's Bks.

Powell, Joyce. The Greatest Marriage Ever. Schacher, Tracey, illus. 2011. 26p. pap. 11.95 (978-1-4575-0215-6(1)) Dog Ear Publishing, LLC.

Powell, Pamela. La Patrulla de las Tortugas. 2003. (SPA., Illus.). 190p. (YA). (gr. 5-8). (978-84-236-3791-1(3), ED1183) Edebé ESP. Dist: Lectorum Pubns., Inc.

Preble, Joy. Finding Paris. 2015. (ENG.). 272p. (YA). (gr. 9). 17.99 (978-0-06-232130-5(7), Balzer & Bray) HarperCollins Pubs.

Psanis, Maria. I Love My Sister but Sometimes I Don't. 2013. 70p. pap. 14.99 (978-1-4817-0846-3(5)) AuthorHouse.

Pyles, Mary Kay. Rise & Shine Rosie. 2013. 134p. pap. 11.95 (978-0-9887836-9-0(X)) Taylor and Seale Publishing.

Quartey, Esme. Life with My Sister ChanSadiefay Thompso. 2006. 64p. per. 8.95 (978-0-595-39224-7(5)) iUniverse, Inc.

Quay, Emma. Shrieking Violet. 2019. 32p. pap. 6.99 (978-0-7333-3507-5(1)) ABC Bks. AUS. Dist: HarperCollins Pubs.

Racaniello, P. Emilia & Emma Say Please. 2011. 20p. pap. 9.99 (978-1-257-65455-0(1)) Lulu Pr., Inc.

—Emilia & Emma Say Sorry. 2012. 20p. pap. 9.99 (978-1-257-63118-6(7)) Lulu Pr., Inc.

—Emilia & Emma Say Thank You. 2012. 20p. pap. 9.99 (978-1-257-63119-3(5)) Lulu Pr., Inc.

Raether, Erin F. When Auntie Angie Left for Iraq & Remi Came to Stay. 2008. 15p. pap. 24.95 (978-1-4241-8735-5(4)) America Star Bks.

Raghbeer, Anjali. Rescue by Design. Modak, Tejas, illus. 2012. (Art Tales from India Ser.). (ENG.). 24p. (J). 14.95 (978-81-8328-194-2(X)) Wisdom Tree IND. Dist: SCB Distributors.

Raheb, Donna. The Adventures of Henrietta Ham. 2007. 32p. per. 14.95 (978-1-4327-0142-0(8)) Outskirts Pr., Inc.

Rahim, Rahimah. The Trunk. 2012. 64p. pap. (978-1-78176-715-3(7)) FeedARead.com.

Rallison, Janette. My Fair Godmother. 2009. (ENG.). 384p. (J). (gr. 6-8). 21.19 (978-0-8027-9780-3(6), 900051897) Walker & Co.

Ramée, Lisa Moore. A Good Kind of Trouble. 2019. (ENG.). 368p. (J). (gr. 3-7). 16.99 (978-0-06-283668-7(4), Balzer & Bray) HarperCollins Pubs.

Ramos, Ramona J. A Summer with Kaitlyn & Lexi. 2011. 48p. pap. 16.95 (978-1-4626-1890-3(1)) America Star Bks.

Random House. Meet Shimmer & Shine! (Shimmer & Shine) Cardona, Jose Maria, illus. 2016. (Step into Reading Ser.). (ENG.). 24p. (J). (gr. -1-1). 4.99 (978-0-553-52203-7(5), Random Hse. Bks. for Young Readers) Random Hse. Children's Bks.

Raven, Margot Theis. America's White Table. Benny, Mike, illus. 2005. (ENG.). 32p. (J). (gr. 1-4). 16.95 (978-1-58536-216-5(6), 202046) Sleeping Bear Pr.

Raye, Marianna & Raye, Daniel. Olis & the Big Outside. 2011. (Illus.). 32p. pap. 14.09 (978-1-4567-7157-7(4)) AuthorHouse.

Reavis, Vicky 'A' Blevins. The Night Before Christmas. 2013. 72p. pap. 17.95 (978-1-4241-2838-9(2)) America Star Bks.

Redman, Kati. Kate & the Fairy. 2010. 32p. pap. 7.50 (978-0-557-60891-1(0)) Lulu Pr., Inc.

Redmond, Zelie. The Adventures of Sister Regina Marie: Sister Finds a Friend. Redmond, Zelie, . 2005. (J). per. 6.95 (978-0-9774345-0-3(8)) Joy of my Youth Pubns., The.

Reeves, Dia. Slice of Cherry. 2011. (ENG.). (YA). (gr. 9). 528p. pap. 14.99 (978-1-4169-8621-8(9)); 512p. 16.99 (978-1-4169-8620-1(0)) Simon Pulse. (Simon Pulse).

Renninson, Lou. Frontalknutschen. pap. 17.95 (978-3-570-30008-4(0)) Bertelsman, Verlagsgruppe C. GmbH DEU. Dist: Distribooks, Inc.

Restivo, Andrea E. Arabella & the Perilous Pantheon. 2010. 28p. pap. 12.99 (978-1-60693-790-7(1), Strategic Bk. Publishing) Strategic Book Publishing & Rights Agency (SBPRA).

Reynolds Naylor, Phyllis. The Boys Return. 2003. (Boys Against Girls Ser.: No. 7). 132p. (gr. 4-7). 16.00 (978-0-7569-1381-6(0)) Perfection Learning Corp.

—The Girls Take Over. 2004. (Boy/Girl Battle Ser.: 8). 160p. (J). (gr. 3-7). 6.99 (978-0-440-41678-4(7), Yearling) Random Hse. Children's Bks.

—Who Won the War? 2008. (Boy/Girl Battle Ser.: 12). (ENG.). 160p. (J). (gr. 3-7). 5.99 (978-0-440-41991-4(3), Yearling) Random Hse. Children's Bks.

RH Disney. Frozen Story Collection (Disney Frozen) RH Disney, illus. 2015. (Step into Reading Ser.). (ENG., Illus.). 160p. (J). (gr. -1-2). pap. 8.99 (978-0-7364-3435-5(6), RH/Disney) Random Hse. Children's Bks.

Rice, Luanne. Pretend She's Here. 2019. (ENG.). 352p. (YA). (gr. 7-7). 18.99 (978-1-338-29850-5(X), Scholastic Pr.) Scholastic, Inc.

—The Secret Language of Sisters. 2016. (ENG.). 352p. (YA). (gr. 7). 18.99 (978-0-545-83955-6(6)) Scholastic, Inc.

Rice, Philippa. Sister BFFs. 2018. (ENG., Illus.). 144p. 14.99 (978-1-4494-8935-9(4)) Andrews McMeel Publishing.

Rippin, Sally. The Big Sister: Billie B. Brown. 2014. (ENG., Illus.). 48p. (J). pap. 4.99 (978-1-61067-184-2(8)) Kane Miller.

Rivers, Karen. Finding Ruby Starling. 2014. (ENG.). 304p. (J). (gr. 5-9). 17.99 (978-0-545-53479-6(8), Levine, Arthur A. Bks.) Scholastic, Inc.

Rizzo, Cynthia. Julie & the Unicorn 2. 2004. 55p. pap. 16.95 (978-1-4137-4841-3(4)) America Star Bks.

Roberts, D. W. Pep Squad Mysteries Book 1: Cavern in the Hills. 2009. (ENG.). 103p. pap. 8.99 (978-0-557-05513-5(X)) Lulu Pr., Inc.

—Pep Squad Mysteries Book 2:the Haunting of Townsand Hall. 2008. (ENG.). 101p. pap. 8.95 (978-0-557-05289-9(0)) Lulu Pr., Inc.

Roberts, Dw. Pep Squad Mysteries Book: Cavern in the Hills. 2008. (ENG., Illus.). 67p. pap. 9.96 (978-0-557-02446-9(3)) Lulu Pr., Inc.

Roberts McKinnon, Hannah. The Properties of Water. 2010. (ENG.). 176p. (YA). (gr. 5-9). 28.99 (978-0-374-36145-7(2), 900049781, Farrar, Straus & Giroux (BYR)) Farrar, Straus & Giroux.

Roberts, Willo Davis. The One Left Behind. 2007. (ENG., Illus.). 144p. (J). (gr. 3-7). pap. 8.99 (978-0-689-85083-7(2), Aladdin) Simon & Schuster Children's Publishing.

Robinson, A. M. Vampire Crush. 2010. (ENG.). 416p. (YA). (gr. 8-18). pap. 8.99 (978-0-06-198971-1(1), HarperTeen) HarperCollins Pubs.

Robinson, Kathleen Marie. Snowflake Sandwiches. 2007. 15p. pap. 24.95 (978-1-4241-8620-4(X)) America Star Bks.

Robinson, Kelley. Naming: Book One of the Magic of Io Series. Curtiss, Melody, illus. 2013. 138p. pap. 8.95 (978-0-9745865-1-9(X), SarahRose Children's Bks.) SarahRose Publishing.

Robinson, Kerby Mae. Give 'N Go. 2010. 84p. pap. 8.95 (978-1-4502-5075-7(0)) iUniverse, Inc.

Rodda, Emily. The Sister of the South, 4. McBride, Marc, illus. 2005. (Dragons of Deltora Ser.: 4). (ENG.). 205p. (J). (gr. 5-8). 17.44 (978-0-439-63376-5(1)) Scholastic, Inc.

Roorda, Julie. Wings of a Bee, 1 vol. 2008. (ENG., Illus.). 224p. (YA). (gr. 7-11). pap. (978-1-894549-68-4(6), Sumach Pr.) Canadian Scholars.

Rosenthal, Amy Krouse. Little Miss, Big Sis. Reynolds, Peter H., illus. 2015. (ENG.). 40p. (J). (gr. -1-3). 19.99 (978-0-06-230203-8(5), HarperCollins) HarperCollins Pubs.

Rosinsky, Lisa. Inevitable & Only. 2017. (ENG.). 276p. (J). (gr. 7). 17.95 (978-1-62979-817-2(7), Astra Young Readers) Astra Publishing Hse.

Rotellar, Carlos. Little Red Monster: Tales of Monica. 2009. 24p. pap. 11.49 (978-1-4490-2812-1(8)) AuthorHouse.

Rothberg, Abraham. Pinocchio's Sister: A Feminist Fable. 2005. 159p. pap. 11.95 (978-1-4116-4347-5(X)) Lulu Pr., Inc.

Rozevskis, Diana. Crystal Waters & on to North America. 2013. (Illus.). 280p. pap. (978-1-78299-851-8(9)) FeedARead.com.

Rubiano, Brittany. Frozen: Anna Loves Elsa. 2015. (ENG., Illus.). 14p. (J). (gr. -1-k). bds. 9.99 (978-1-4847-2470-5(4), Disney Press Books) Disney Publishing Worldwide.

Rubino, Tony. Who Ate the Brownies. 2013. 28p. pap. 24.95 (978-1-63004-481-7(4)) America Star Bks.

Rushton, Abbie. Consumed. 2017. (ENG.). 352p. (YA). 11.99 (978-0-349-00203-3(7), Atom Books) Little, Brown Book Group Ltd. GBR. Dist: Hachette Bk. Group.

Russon, Penni. The Endsister. 2018. (ENG., Illus.). 256p. (J). (gr. 6-9). pap. 14.99 (978-1-74175-065-2(2)) Allen & Unwin AUS. Dist: Independent Pubs. Group.

Ryan, Amy Kathleen. Zen & Xander Undone. 2011. (ENG.). 228p. (YA). (gr. 9). pap. 13.99 (978-0-547-55030-5(8), 1450239, Clarion Bks.) HarperCollins Pubs.

S., Lisa Hamilton Ed. The Tale of the Talking Trees: The Tale of the Talking Trees a Story of Suspense & Surprise. 2012. 32p. pap. 21.99 (978-1-4691-7846-2(X)) Xlibris Corp.

Saddlewick, A. B. Monstrous Maud: Big Fright. 2017. (ENG., Illus.). 128p. (J). (gr. 1-5). pap. 7.99 (978-1-5107-1698-8(X), Sky Pony Pr.) Skyhorse Publishing Co., Inc.

Salemi, Dianne. We Hear the Dead. 2010. 448p. (YA). (gr. 7-12). pap. 14.99 (978-1-4022-3092-9(3)) Sourcebooks, Inc.

Salisbury, Linda G. No Sisters Sisters Club: A Bailey Fish Adventure. Grotke, Christopher A., illus. 2005. 188p. (J). per. 8.95 (978-1-881539-40-7(7)) Tabby Hse. Bks.

Sánchez, Erika L. I Am Not Your Perfect Mexican Daughter. 2019. (ENG.). lib. bdg. 22.80 (978-1-6636-2193-1(4)) Perfection Learning Corp.

—I Am Not Your Perfect Mexican Daughter. (ENG.). (YA). (gr. 9). 2019. 368p. pap. 12.99 (978-1-5247-0051-5(7), Ember) 2017. 352p. 19.99 (978-1-5247-0048-5(7), Knopf Bks. for Young Readers) Random Hse. Children's Bks.

Sanderson, Ruth. Rose Red & Snow White. Sanderson, Ruth, illus. 2015. (Ruth Sanderson Collection). (ENG., Illus.). 32p. (J). (gr. 2-3). pap. 7.95 (978-1-56656-934-7(6), Crocodile Bks.) Interlink Publishing Group, Inc.

Santillo, LuAnn. Jane. Santillo, LuAnn, ed. 2003. (Half-Pint Kids Readers Ser.). (Illus.). 7p. (J). (gr. -1-1). pap. 1.00 (978-1-59256-099-8(7)) Half-Pint Kids, Inc.

Santopolo, Jill. All That Glitters. 2014. (Sparkle Spa Ser.: 1). (ENG., Illus.). 128p. (J). (gr. 2-5). pap. 6.99 (978-1-4424-7380-5(0), Aladdin) Simon & Schuster Children's Publishing.

—Bad News Nails. 2015. (Sparkle Spa Ser.: 5). (ENG., Illus.). 128p. (J). (gr. 2-5). pap. 5.99 (978-1-4814-2384-7(3), Aladdin) Simon & Schuster Children's Publishing.

—Bling It On! 2015. (Sparkle Spa Ser.: 7). (ENG., Illus.). 112p. (J). (gr. 2-5). pap. 5.99 (978-1-4814-2390-8(8), Aladdin) Simon & Schuster Children's Publishing.

—Fashion Disaster. 2016. (Sparkle Spa Ser.: 9). (ENG., Illus.). 96p. (J). (gr. 2-5). pap. 5.99 (978-1-4814-6391-1(8), Aladdin) Simon & Schuster Children's Publishing.

—Fashion Disaster. 2016. (Sparkle Spa Ser.: 9). (ENG., Illus.). 96p. (J). (gr. 2-5). 16.99 (978-1-4814-6392-8(6), Simon & Schuster/Paula Wiseman Bks.) Simon & Schuster/Paula Wiseman Bks.

—Glam Opening! Mingus, Cathi, illus. 2017. (Sparkle Spa Ser.: 10). (ENG.). 112p. (J). (gr. 2-5). pap. 5.99 (978-1-4814-6395-9(0), Aladdin) Simon & Schuster Children's Publishing.

—A Picture-Perfect Mess. 2015. (Sparkle Spa Ser.: 6). (ENG., Illus.). 112p. (J). (gr. 2-5). pap. 6.99 (978-1-4814-2387-8(8), Aladdin) Simon & Schuster Children's Publishing.

—Purple Nails & Puppy Tails. 2014. (Sparkle Spa Ser.: 2). (ENG., Illus.). 128p. (J). (gr. 2-5). pap. 5.99 (978-1-4424-7383-6(5), Aladdin) Simon & Schuster Children's Publishing.

—Sparkle Spa 4-Books-In-1! All That Glitters; Purple Nails & Puppy Tails; Makeover Magic; True Colors. 2016. (Sparkle Spa Ser.). (ENG., Illus.). 496p. (J). (gr. 2-5). 14.99 (978-1-4814-7594-5(0), Aladdin) Simon & Schuster Children's Publishing.

—True Colors. 2014. (Sparkle Spa Ser.: 4). (ENG., Illus.). 128p. (J). (gr. 2-5). pap. 5.99 (978-1-4424-7389-8(4), Aladdin) Simon & Schuster Children's Publishing.

—True Colors. 2014. (Sparkle Spa Ser.: 4). (ENG., Illus.). 128p. (J). (gr. 2-5). 16.99 (978-1-4424-7390-4(8), Simon & Schuster/Paula Wiseman Bks.) Simon & Schuster/Paula Wiseman Bks.

—Wedding Bell Blues. 2016. (Sparkle Spa Ser.: 8). (ENG., Illus.). 112p. (J). (gr. 2-5). pap. 5.99 (978-1-4814-2393-9(2), Aladdin) Simon & Schuster Children's Publishing.

Sarno, Melissa. Just under the Clouds. 2019. (ENG.). 256p. (J). (gr. 3-7). pap. 8.99 (978-1-5247-2011-7(9), Yearling) Random Hse. Children's Bks.

Sattler, Jennifer. Dollop & Mrs. Fabulous. 2019. (ENG., Illus.). 32p. (J). (gr. -1-2). lib. bdg. 20.99 (978-0-399-55336-3(3), Knopf Bks. for Young Readers) Random Hse. Children's Bks.

Savage, Kim. Beautiful Broken Girls. 2018. (ENG.). 352p. (YA). pap. 14.99 (978-1-250-14416-4(7), 900180623) Square Fish.

Saxon, Victoria. Frozen (Disney Frozen) Lee, Grace & Cagol, Andrea, illus. 2015. (Little Golden Book Ser.). (ENG.). 24p. (J). (-k). 5.99 (978-0-7364-3471-3(2), Golden/Disney) Random Hse. Children's Bks.

Scattergood, Augusta. Glory Be. 2014. (ENG.). 208p. (J). (gr. 4-7). pap. 7.99 (978-0-545-33181-4(1), Scholastic Pr.) Scholastic, Inc.

Schaefer, Laura. Littler Women: A Modern Retelling. 2017. (ENG., Illus.). 224p. (J). (gr. 3-7). 16.99 (978-1-4814-8761-0(2), Simon & Schuster/Paula Wiseman Bks.) Simon & Schuster/Paula Wiseman Bks.

Schmidt, Tiffany. Bookish Boyfriends. 2018. (ENG.). 272p. (gr. 8-17). pap. 9.99 (978-1-4197-2860-0(1), 1199603, Amulet Bks.) Abrams, Inc.

—Boy Next Story: A Bookish Boyfriends Novel. 2019. (ENG., Illus.). 272p. (gr. 7-17). pap. 9.99 (978-1-4197-3436-6(9), 1210203, Amulet Bks.) Abrams, Inc.

Schrefer, Eliot. The Deadly Sister. 2010. (ENG.). 320p. (J). (gr. 7-18). 17.99 (978-0-545-16574-7(1), Scholastic Pr.) Scholastic, Inc.

—The Lost Rainforest: Mez's Magic. 2018. (Illus.). 368p. (J). (978-0-06-283959-6(4), Tegen, Katherine Bks) HarperCollins Pubs.

—The Lost Rainforest #1: Mez's Magic. Dziubak, Emilia, illus. 2018. (ENG.). (J). (gr. 3-7). 384p. pap. 6.99 (978-0-06-249113-8(X)); 368p. 16.99 (978-0-06-249107-7(5)) HarperCollins Pubs. (Tegen, Katherine Bks).

Schroeder, Lisa. Sealed with a Secret. 2016. (ENG.). 224p. (J). (gr. 3-7). 16.99 (978-0-545-90734-7(9), Scholastic Pr.) Scholastic, Inc.

Schumacher, Julie. Black Box. 2008. (ENG.). 176p. (YA). (gr. 7-12). lib. bdg. 22.44 (978-0-385-90523-7(8)) Random House Publishing Group.

—Black Box. 2010. (ENG.). 176p. (YA). (gr. 7-18). pap. 7.99 (978-0-440-24064-8(6), Delacorte Bks. for Young Readers) Random Hse. Children's Bks.

Schwabach, Karen. The Hope Chest. 2010. 288p. (J). (gr. 3-7). 8.99 (978-0-375-84096-8(6), Yearling) Random Hse. Children's Bks.

Schwartz, Corey Rosen. Twinderella, a Fractioned Fairy Tale. Marcero, Deborah, illus. 2017. 32p. (J). (gr. -1-3). 17.99 (978-0-399-17633-3(0), G.P. Putnam's Sons Books for Young Readers) Penguin Young Readers Group.

Schwarzenegger Pratt, Katherine. Good Night, Sister. Fleming, Lucy, illus. 2023. 32p. (J). (gr. -1-2). 18.99 (978-0-593-38581-4(0), Penguin Workshop) Penguin Young Readers Group.

Schwemm, Diane. The Year I Turned Sixteen: Rose, Daisy, Laurel, Lily. 2010. (ENG.). 720p. (YA). (gr. 7). pap. 12.99 (978-1-4169-8597-6(2), Simon Pulse) Simon Pulse.

Scott, Elizabeth. Between Here & Forever. 2012. (ENG.). 272p. (YA). (gr. 9). pap. 9.99 (978-1-4169-9485-5(8), Simon Pulse) Simon Pulse.

Scott, Gwen. Blackberry Junction. Baker, David, illus. 2011. 28p. pap. 24.95 (978-1-4560-0951-9(6)) America Star Bks.

Sedgwick, Chantele. Interlude. 2018. (Love, Lucas Novel Ser.: 3). (ENG.). 284p. (YA). (gr. 7-13). 16.99 (978-1-5107-1515-8(0), Sky Pony Pr.) Skyhorse Publishing Co., Inc.

Seewald, Jacqueline. Clair's Curse. 2004. 228p. (YA). per. 22.00 (978-1-58982-191-0(2), Bedside Bks.) American Bk. Publishing Group.

Sgarlato, Dawn. Big Sister. 2012. 24p. pap. 17.99 (978-1-4685-9426-3(5)) AuthorHouse.

Shakespeare, Nancy. Benjamin the Bear Gets a Sister. Clouette, Katie, illus. 2013. (Benjamin the Bear Ser.). (ENG.). (J). (gr. -1-3). 14.95 (978-1-62086-316-9(2)) Amplify Publishing Group.

Shanker, Tarun & Zekas, Kelly. These Vicious Masks. 2016. (These Vicious Masks Ser.: 1). (ENG.). 320p. (YA). pap. 15.99 (978-1-250-07389-1(8), 900150894) Feiwel & Friends.

Shaw, J. D. The Secrets of Loon Lake. 2010. (ENG.). 338p. (J). (gr. 5). pap. 16.95 (978-0-9845318-0-6(7)) Tiny Stachel Pr.

Shaw, Natalie. A Guide to Being a Big Sister. 2014. (Olivia 8x8 Ser.). lib. bdg. 16.00 (978-0-606-35761-6(0)) Turtleback.

Shay, Kenley. Prommy Meets Her Match: An Unofficial Story for Shopkins Collectors. 2015. (Unofficial Shopkins Collectors Ser.). (ENG.). 112p. (J). (gr. 1-7). pap. 7.99 (978-1-5107-0374-2(8), Sky Pony Pr.) Skyhorse Publishing Co., Inc.

Shear, Dani. The Foodie Club. Weinstein, Holly, illus. 2013. (ENG.). 50p. (J). 16.99 (978-1-61053-027-9(6)) Blackbird Bks.

Shepard, Sara. Hide & Seek. 2012. (Lying Game Ser.: Bk. 4). 289p. (YA). 9.99 (978-0-06-219369-8(4), HarperTeen) HarperCollins Pubs.

—The Lying Game. (Lying Game Ser.: 1). (ENG.). (YA). (gr. 9-18). 2010. 320p. 17.99 (978-0-06-186970-9(8))1. 2011. 336p. pap. 11.99 (978-0-06-186971-6(6)) HarperCollins Pubs. (HarperTeen).

—The Lying Game. 2011. (Lying Game (Quality) Ser.: Vol. 1). (ENG.). (YA). (gr. 9). lib. bdg. 20.60 (978-1-61383-667-5(8)) Perfection Learning Corp.

—The Lying Game #2: Never Have I Ever. (Lying Game Ser.: 2). (ENG.). (YA). (gr. 9). 2012. 336p. pap. 10.99 (978-0-06-186973-0(2)) 2011. 320p. 16.99 (978-0-06-186972-3(4)) HarperCollins Pubs. (HarperTeen).

—The Lying Game #3: Two Truths & a Lie. (Lying Game Ser.: 3). (ENG.). (YA). (gr. 9). 2013. 320p. pap. 10.99 (978-0-06-186975-4(9)) 2012. 304p. 17.99 (978-0-06-186974-7(0)) HarperCollins Pubs. (HarperTeen).

—The Lying Game #4: Hide & Seek. 2013. (Lying Game Ser.: 4). (ENG.). 320p. (YA). (gr. 9). pap. 10.99 (978-0-06-186977-8(5), HarperTeen) HarperCollins Pubs.

—The Lying Game #6: Seven Minutes in Heaven. 2014. (Lying Game Ser.: 6). (ENG.). 400p. (YA). (gr. 9). pap. 11.99 (978-0-06-212823-2(X), HarperTeen) HarperCollins Pubs.

Sherri L. Berner. Healthy Fun with Benjamin & Jasmine: ABCs of the Human Body. Michael A. Cicchetti, illus. 2009. 32p. pap. 12.99 (978-1-4343-8297-9(4)) AuthorHouse.

Shields, Brooke. Welcome to Your World, Baby. Doerrfeld, Cori, illus. 2008. 32p. (J). (gr. -1-3). lib. bdg. 17.89 (978-0-06-125312-6(X)) HarperCollins Pubs.

Shore, Diane Z. How to Drive Your Sister Crazy. Rankin, Laura, illus. 2012. (I Can Read Level 2 Ser.). (ENG.). 48p. (J). (gr. k-3). pap. 5.99 (978-0-06-052764-8(1), HarperCollins) HarperCollins Pubs.

Shu, Sammy. There's a Season for All. Cone, Carl, illus. 2006. 54p. (J). (gr. -1-3). 16.95 (978-0-9778211-0-5(2), Raynestorm Bks.) Silver Rose Publishing.

Sidwell, Beth. Zack the Zombie. 2012. 24p. pap. 15.99 (978-1-4797-0962-5(X)) Xlibris Corp.

Simoneau, Shelly. The Cows Came Running & the Horses Did Too! 2011. 28p. pap. 14.99 (978-1-4567-3107-6(6)) AuthorHouse.

Simukka, Salla & Witesman, Owen. As White As Snow. 2017. (YA). pap. (978-1-5247-1348-5(1)) Bantam Doubleday Dell Large Print Group, Inc.

Skrypuch, Marsha Forchuk. Making Bombs for Hitler. 2019. (ENG.). 240p. (J). (gr. 3-7). pap. 8.99 (978-1-338-31283-6(9)) Scholastic, Inc.

Slaughter, Kristi. Emma & Allie. Hanks, Carol, illus. 2009. 28p. pap. 12.49 (978-1-4389-9812-1(0)) AuthorHouse.

Smith, Debora Ann Baker. The Magnificent Fairy Party. 2010. (Illus.). 30p. pap. 13.00 (978-1-60911-404-6(3), Eloquent Bks.) Strategic Book Publishing & Rights Agency (SBPRA).

Smith, Evelyn. Seven Sisters at Queen Anne's. Coller, H., illus. 2013. 162p. pap. (978-1-909423-07-7(6)) Bks. to Treasure.

Smith, John D. H. The Whale Whisperers, 1 vol. Smith, Anne, illus. 2009. 17p. pap. 24.95 (978-1-60749-211-5(3)) America Star Bks.

Smith, Roland. Kitty Hawk. 2012. (I, Q Ser.: Bk. 3). (ENG., Illus.). 240p. (YA). (gr. 6-8). pap. 9.99 (978-1-58536-604-0(8), 202326);Bk. 3. lib. bdg. 16.99 (978-1-58536-605-7(6), 202327) Sleeping Bear Pr.

Smith, Sherwood. The Emerald Wand of Oz. Stout, William, illus. 2007. 262p. (J). 17.00 (978-1-4223-6710-0(X)) DIANE Publishing Co.

Snow, Maya. Blade's Edge. 2009. 245p. (J). lib. bdg. 17.89 (978-0-06-124391-2(4)) HarperCollins Pubs.

—Sisters of the Sword. 2008. (Sisters of the Sword Ser.). (J). (gr. 5-18). 288p. 16.99 (978-0-06-124387-5(6)); 275p. lib. bdg. 17.89 (978-0-06-124388-2(4)) HarperCollins Pubs.

Soderberg, Erin. The Quirks & the Quirkalicious Birthday. 2015. (Quirks Ser.). (ENG., Illus.). 208p. (J). (gr. 3-6). 13.99 (978-1-61963-370-4(1), 9781619633704, Bloomsbury USA Childrens) Bloomsbury Publishing USA.

Solomon, Rachel Lynn. You'll Miss Me When I'm Gone. 2018. (ENG., Illus.). 384p. (YA). (gr. 9). 19.99 (978-1-4814-9773-2(1), Simon Pulse) Simon Pulse.

Soontornvat, Christina. The Changelings. 2017. (Changelings Ser.: 1). (ENG.). 304p. (J). (gr. 5-8). pap. 8.99 (978-1-4926-4795-9(0)) Sourcebooks, Inc.

Spangler, Paula Jeanne. Abigail's Christmas ~ Christmas Mom Reveals A Newborn. 2004. 17p. (J). pap. 14.08 (978-1-4116-1045-3(8)) Lulu Pr., Inc.

The Sparkle Spa Shimmering Collection Books 1-4 (Glittery Nail Stickers Inside!) (Boxed Set) All That Glitters; Purple Nails & Puppy Tails; Makeover Magic; True Colors. 2014. (Sparkle Spa Ser.). (ENG., Illus.). 512p. (J). (gr. 2-5). pap. 23.99 (978-1-4814-1658-0(8), Aladdin) Simon & Schuster Children's Publishing.

Spieller, Lauren. She's the Worst. 2020. (ENG.). 288p. (YA). (gr. 9). pap. 12.99 (978-1-5344-3659-6(6), Simon & Schuster Bks. For Young Readers) Simon & Schuster Bks. For Young Readers.

Spirn, Michele Sobel. The Bridges in Edinburgh. 2004. (Going to Ser.). 144p. (J). pap. 6.95 (978-1-893577-11-4(2)) Four Corners Publishing Co., Inc.

Spotswood, Jessica. Born Wicked. 2013. (Cahill Witch Chronicles Ser.: 1). (ENG.). 352p. (YA). (gr. 7). pap. 10.99 (978-0-14-242187-1(1), Speak) Penguin Young Readers Group.

—Born Wicked. 2013. lib. bdg. 22.10 (978-0-606-26729-8(8)) Turtleback.

—The Last Summer of the Garrett Girls. 2018. 368p. (YA). (gr. 8-12). pap. 10.99 (978-1-4926-2219-2(2)) Sourcebooks, Inc.

St. John, Wylly Folk. The Ghost Next Door. Hyman, Trina Schart, illus. 2019. 184p. (J). pap. (978-1-948959-08-7(9)) Purple Hse. Pr.

Stadelmann, Amy Marie. Olive & Beatrix: The Super-Smelly Moldy Blob, Vol. 2. Stadelmann, Amy Marie, illus. 2016. (Olive & Beatrix Ser.: 2). (ENG., Illus.). 80p. (J). (gr. k-2). 15.99 (978-0-545-81485-0(5)) Scholastic, Inc.

Staniszewski, Anna. The Magic Mirror: a Branches Book (Once upon a Fairy Tale #1) Pamintuan, Macky, illus. 2019. (Once upon a Fairy Tale Ser.: 1). (ENG.). 96p. (J). (gr. 1-3). pap. 4.99 (978-1-338-34971-9(6)) Scholastic, Inc.

Stella, Lennon & Stella, Maisy. In the Waves. Bjorkman, Steve, illus. 2015. (ENG.). 40p. (J). (gr. -1-3). 17.99 (978-0-06-235939-1(8), HarperCollins) HarperCollins Pubs.

Stern, Jacqueline. Mystery of the Whispering Walls. 2004. (J). 148p. pap. (978-1-57168-844-6(7)); (Hollow Tree Mystery Ser.: Bk. 6). (Illus.). v, 142p. (978-1-57168-850-7(1), Eakin Pr.) Eakin Pr.

S

Stevenson, Robin. Record Breaker, 1 vol. 2013. (ENG.). 152p. (J). (gr. 4-7). pap. 9.95 *(978-1-55469-959-9(2))* Orca Bk. Pubs. USA.

Stewart, Nancy. One Pelican at a Time: A Story of the Gulf Oil Spill. Bell, Samantha, illus. 2011. 26p. (J). 19.95 *(978-1-61633-138-2(0))*; pap. 11.95 *(978-1-61633-139-9(9))* Guardian Angel Publishing, Inc.

Stilton, Thea. The Secret of the Fairies (Thea Stilton: Special Edition #2) A Geronimo Stilton Adventure. 2018. (True Book (Relaunch) Ser.). (ENG.). 320p. (J). (gr. 3-5). E-Book 7.95 *(978-0-545-55688-0(0)*, Scholastic Paperbacks) Scholastic, Inc.

—Thea Stilton & the Dragon's Code (Thea Stilton #1) A Geronimo Stilton Adventure. 2009. (Thea Stilton Ser.: 1). (ENG., Illus.). 176p. (J). (gr. 2-5). pap. 8.99 *(978-0-545-10367-1(3)*, Scholastic Paperbacks) Scholastic, Inc.

—Thea Stilton & the Frozen Fiasco. 2017. (Thea Stilton Ser.: 25). lib. bdg. 19.65 *(978-0-606-40181-4(4))* Turtleback.

—Thea Stilton & the Hollywood Hoax. 2016. (Thea Stilton Ser.: 23). lib. bdg. 18.40 *(978-0-606-38799-6(4))* Turtleback.

—Thea Stilton & the Journey to the Lion's Den. 2013. (Thea Stilton Ser.: 17). lib. bdg. 19.65 *(978-0-606-32382-6(1))* Turtleback.

—Thea Stilton & the Legend of the Fire Flowers. 2013. (Thea Stilton Ser.: 15). lib. bdg. 19.65 *(978-0-606-32000-9(8))* Turtleback.

—Thea Stilton & the Missing Myth. 2014. (Thea Stilton Ser.: 20). lib. bdg. 19.65 *(978-0-606-36058-6(1))* Turtleback.

—Thea Stilton & the Mountain of Fire (Thea Stilton #2) A Geronimo Stilton Adventure. 2009. (Thea Stilton Ser.: 2). (ENG., Illus.). 176p. (J). (gr. 2-5). pap. 8.99 *(978-0-545-15060-6(4)*, Scholastic Paperbacks) Scholastic, Inc.

—Thea Stilton & the Mystery on the Orient Express. 2012. (Thea Stilton Ser.: 13). lib. bdg. 19.65 *(978-0-606-26757-1(3))* Turtleback.

—Thea Stilton & the Mystery on the Orient Express (Thea Stilton #13) A Geronimo Stilton Adventure. 2012. (Thea Stilton Ser.: 13). (ENG., Illus.). 176p. (J). (gr. 2-5). pap. 8.99 *(978-0-545-34105-9(1)*, Scholastic Paperbacks) Scholastic, Inc.

—Thea Stilton & the Spanish Dance Mission (Thea Stilton #16) A Geronimo Stilton Adventure. 2018. (True Book (Relaunch) Ser.: 16). (ENG.). 176p. (J). (gr. 3-5). E-Book 7.95 *(978-0-545-55685-9(6)*, Scholastic Paperbacks) Scholastic, Inc.

—Thea Stilton: Big Trouble in the Big Apple (Thea Stilton #8) A Geronimo Stilton Adventure, Volume 8. 2011. (Thea Stilton Ser.: 8). (ENG., Illus.). 176p. (J). (gr. 2-5). pap. 8.99 *(978-0-545-22775-9(5)*, Scholastic Paperbacks) Scholastic, Inc.

Stine, Megan, et al. Girl Talk. 2003. (ENG., Illus.). 128p. *(978-0-00-714453-2(9)*, HarperCollins Children's Bks.) HarperCollins Pubs. Ltd.

—Sealed with a Kiss. 2003. (ENG., Illus.). 112p. *(978-0-00-714461-7(X)*, HarperCollins Children's Bks.) HarperCollins Pubs. Ltd.

—Surprise, Surprise! 2003. (ENG., Illus.). 112p. *(978-0-00-714462-4(8)*, HarperCollins Children's Bks.) HarperCollins Pubs. Ltd.

—War of the Wardrobes. 2003. (ENG., Illus.). 112p. *(978-0-00-714468-6(7)*, HarperCollins Children's Bks.) HarperCollins Pubs. Ltd.

Stine, R. L. Dangerous Girls. 2003. 256p. (J). 111.92 *(978-0-06-056909-9(3))*; 111.92 *(978-0-06-056910-5(7))*; (ENG., Illus.). (gr. 7-18). 13.99 *(978-0-06-053080-8(4))* HarperCollins Pubs.

—First Evil. 2011. (Fear Street Cheerleaders Ser.: 1). (ENG.). 176p. (YA). (gr. 9). pap. 9.99 *(978-1-4424-3086-0(9)*, Simon Pulse) Simon Pulse.

Stone, Phoebe. Paris for Two. 2016. (J). (ENG.). 272p. (gr. 3-7). 16.99 *(978-0-545-44362-3(8))*; 257p. *(978-1-338-04510-9(5))* Scholastic, Inc. (Levine, Arthur A. Bks.).

Stork, Francisco X. Irises. 2012. 288p. (YA). pap. *(978-0-545-15136-8(8)*, Levine, Arthur A. Bks.) Scholastic, Inc.

Suguitan, Jazel A. We're Moving?! Shari Tucker's Wacky World #1. 2010. 124p. 20.95 *(978-1-4502-6874-5(9))*; pap. 10.95 *(978-1-4502-6871-4(4))* iUniverse, Inc.

Sullivan, Laura L. Delusion. 2014. (ENG.). 352p. (YA). (gr. 7). pap. 18.99 *(978-0-544-10478-5(1)*, 1540787, Clarion Bks.) HarperCollins Pubs.

Suma, Nova Ren. Imaginary Girls. 2012. (ENG.). 352p. (YA). (gr. 9-18). pap. 8.99 *(978-0-14-242143-7(X)*, Speak) Penguin Young Readers Group.

Summers, Courtney. Sadie. 2018. (ENG.). 320p. (YA). 18.99 *(978-1-250-10571-4(4)*, 900164264, Wednesday Bks.) St. Martin's Pr.

—Sadie. 2019. (SPA.). 344p. (YA). pap. 18.99 *(978-607-8614-62-2(2))* V&R Editoras.

—Sadie: A Novel. 2020. (ENG.). 336p. (YA). pap. 11.99 *(978-1-250-26713-9(7)*, 900211700, Wednesday Bks.) St. Martin's Pr.

Sumner, Bea. Sisters Three: Scary's Not a Part of Me. 2007. (J). pap. *(978-0-9787375-0-4(4))* Sisters Three Publishing Inc.

Szymona, Marlene L. My Sister Beth's Pink Birthday. Battuz, Christine, illus. 2014. 32p. (J). pap. *(978-1-4338-1655-0(5)*, Magination Pr.) American Psychological Assn.

—My Sister Beth's Pink Birthday: A Story about Sibling Relationships. Battuz, Christine, illus. 2014. 32p. (J). *(978-1-4338-1654-3(7)*, Magination Pr.) American Psychological Assn.

Tada, Joni Eareckson & Jensen, Steve. The Mission Adventure. 2005. (Darcy & Friends Ser.). 143p. (gr. 3-6). pap. 5.99 *(978-1-58134-257-4(8)*, Crossway Bibles) Crossway.

Talhah, Abu & Books, Greenbird. My Sister Saarah. Fowler, Claire, illus. 2013. 30p. pap. *(978-0-9576379-6-2(9))* Greenbird Bks.

Tansil-Mitchell, Angela. Kimmie C Sunshine: When Mommy & Daddy Loses Their Jobs. 2011. 24p. pap. 13.79 *(978-1-4567-5666-6(4))* AuthorHouse.

Taranta, Mary. Shimmer & Burn. 2018. (ENG.). 352p. (YA). (gr. 9). pap. 11.99 *(978-1-4814-7200-5(3)*, McElderry, Margaret K. Bks.) McElderry, Margaret K. Bks.

—Splendor & Spark. (ENG.). 336p. (YA). (gr. 9). 2019. pap. 12.99 *(978-1-4814-7203-6(8))* 2018. (Illus.). 18.99 *(978-1-4814-7202-9(X))* McElderry, Margaret K. Bks. (McElderry, Margaret K. Bks.).

Tate, Nikki. Fallout, 1 vol. 2011. (Orca Soundings Ser.). (ENG.). 168p. (YA). (gr. 8-12). pap. 9.95 *(978-1-55469-272-9(5))*; lib. bdg. 16.95 *(978-1-55469-976-6(2))* Orca Bk. Pubs. USA.

Taylor, Cora. Finding Melissa, 1 vol. 2013. (ENG.). 184p. (J). (gr. 6-10). pap. 12.95 *(978-1-55455-274-0(5)*, 270cb0c0-5f1b-47d2-a33e-2aea755f76ae) éditeur, Annika Parance CAN. Dist: Firefly Bks., Ltd.

Taylor, Jessica. A Map for Wrecked Girls. 2018. lib. bdg. 22.10 *(978-0-606-41318-3(9))* Turtleback.

Taylor, Laini. Muse of Nightmares. LitJoy Crate et al, illus. 2021. (YA). 59.99 *(978-1-7350633-8-6(X))* LitJoy Crate.

—Muse of Nightmares. (Strange the Dreamer Ser.: 2). (ENG.). (YA). (gr. 9-17). 2019. 544p. pap. 12.99 *(978-0-316-34169-1(X))* 2018. 528p. 19.99 *(978-0-316-34171-4(1))* Little, Brown Bks. for Young Readers.

Taylor, Sydney. All-Of-a-Kind Family Uptown. 2014. (ENG.). 200p. (J). (gr. 3). pap. 12.95 *(978-1-939601-17-9(7))* Ig Publishing, Inc.

Telgemeier, Raina. Ghosts: a Graphic Novel. Telgemeier, Raina, illus. 2016. (ENG., Illus.). 256p. (J). (gr. 3-7). 24.99 *(978-0-545-54061-2(5)*, Graphix) Scholastic, Inc.

Terry, Teri. The Book of Lies. 2017. (ENG.). 384p. (YA). (gr. 7). 17.99 *(978-0-544-90048-6(0)*, 1654927, Clarion Bks.) HarperCollins Pubs.

Thame, Val. Witches in Deed. I.t. ed. 2007. 100p. per. *(978-1-905665-25-9(3))* Pollinger In Print.

Thomas, Kara. The Darkest Corners. 2017. 352p. (YA). (gr. 9). pap. 9.99 *(978-0-553-52148-1(9)*, Ember) Random Hse. Children's Bks.

Thompson, Lauren. Little Quack's ABC's. Anderson, Derek, illus. 2010. (Super Chubbies Ser.). (ENG.). 26p. (J). (gr. -1 — 1). bds. 5.99 *(978-1-4169-6091-1(0)*, Little Simon) Little Simon.

Thor, Annika. A Faraway Island. Schenck, Linda, tr. 2011. (Faraway Island Ser.: 1). 256p. (J). (gr. 3-7). 7.99 *(978-0-375-84495-9(3)*, Yearling) Random Hse. Children's Bks.

Thornburgh, Blair. Ordinary Girls. 2019. (ENG.). 368p. (YA). (gr. 8). 17.99 *(978-0-06-244781-4(5)*, HarperTeen) HarperCollins Pubs.

Thornton, M. H. Kylee & Lexie: Mystery of the Gholdees. 2010. 64p. pap. 10.99 *(978-1-4269-3713-2(X))* Trafford Publishing.

Tillworth, Mary. Leah's Dream Dollhouse (Shimmer & Shine) Yum, Heekyoung & Aikins, Dave, illus. 2016. (Pictureback(R) Ser.). (ENG.). 16p. (J). (gr. -1-2). 4.99 *(978-1-101-93249-0(X)*, Random Hse. Bks. for Young Readers) Random Hse. Children's Bks.

Tims, Laura. Please Don't Tell. 2016. (ENG.). 336p. (YA). (gr. 8). 17.99 *(978-0-06-231732-2(6)*, HarperTeen) HarperCollins Pubs.

Torras, Meri. Mi Hermana Aixa. Valverde, Mikel, illus. (SPA.). 120p. (J). (gr. 3-5). *(978-84-246-5915-8(5)*, GL6491) La Galera, S.A. Editorial ESP. Dist: Lectorum Pubns., Inc.

Torres, Jennifer. The Fresh New Face of Griselda. 2019. (ENG., Illus.). 256p. (J). (gr. 3-7). 31.99 *(978-0-316-45260-1(2))* Little, Brown Bks. for Young Readers.

Trionfo, Nikki. Shatter. 2017. 346p. (YA). pap. 18.99 *(978-1-4621-2013-0(X)*, Horizon Pubs.) Cedar Fort, Inc./CFI Distribution.

Tripp, Valerie. Nellie's Promise. England, Tamara, ed. Andreasen, Dan, illus. 2004. (American Girls Collection: Samantha Stories Ser.). (ENG.). 96p. (J). (gr. 2-4). pap. 18.69 *(978-1-58485-890-4(7))* American Girl Publishing, Inc.

Troulis, Jennifer. Penelope & Priscilla: And the Enchanted House of Whispers. 2nd ed. 2004. (Illus.). 229p. per. 13.95 *(978-0-9768602-0-4(1))* Twin Monkeys Pr.

Troupe, Thomas Kingsley. Darling Doll. Faber, Rudy, illus. 2016. (Hauntiques Ser.). (ENG.). 128p. (J). (gr. 4-6). lib. bdg. 25.32 *(978-1-4965-3548-1(0)*, 132657, Stone Arch Bks.) Capstone.

—Ghostly Goalie. Faber, Rudy, illus. 2016. (Hauntiques Ser.). (ENG.). 128p. (J). (gr. 4-6). lib. bdg. 25.32 *(978-1-4965-3544-3(8)*, 132654, Stone Arch Bks.) Capstone.

Trueit, Trudi. The Sister Solution. 2015. (Mix Ser.). (ENG., Illus.). 240p. (J). (gr. 4-8). pap. 7.99 *(978-1-4814-3239-9(7)*, Aladdin) Simon & Schuster Children's Publishing.

Tucker, Kathy. The Seven Chinese Sisters. Lin, Grace, illus. 2003. (ENG.). 32p. (J). (gr. -1-3). per. 8.99 *(978-0-8075-7310-5(8)*, 807573108) Whitman, Albert & Co.

Tupper Ling, Nancy. My Sister, Alicia May. Bersani, Shennen, illus. 2009. (ENG.). 32p. (J). (gr. k-2). 16.95 *(978-0-9792035-9-6(7))* Pleasant St. Pr.

Turner, Diane. Tangle-Leina? I'll Tangle-Leina Them. Mason, Roberta Black, illus. 2008. 48p. pap. 24.95 *(978-1-60563-586-6(3))* America Star Bks.

Turner, Suzy. The Ghost of Josiah Grimshaw: A Morgan Sisters Novel. 2013. 286p. pap. *(978-989-97348-6-9(1))* Turner, Suzanne.

The Two Sisters: Lap Book. (Pebble Soup Explorations Ser.). (SPA.). 16p. (gr. -1-18). 21.00 *(978-0-7578-1668-0(1))* Rigby Education.

The Two Sisters: Small Book. (Pebble Soup Explorations Ser.). (SPA.). 16p. (gr. -1-18). 5.00 *(978-0-7578-1708-3(4))* Rigby Education.

Two Sisters Circle. The Lady of the Lane. 2013. 116p. pap. 19.95 *(978-1-63004-330-8(3))* America Star Bks.

Tym, Kate. Time to Share. 2008. (Manners Ser.). (Illus.). 24p. (J). (gr. -1-1). lib. bdg. 16.95 *(978-1-59566-591-1(9))* QEB Publishing Inc.

Ultman, Suzy, illus. Masha & Her Sisters: (Russian Doll Board Books, Children's Activity Books, Interactive Kids Books) 2017. (ENG.). 10p. (J). bds. 9.99 *(978-1-4521-5159-5(8))* Chronicle Bks. LLC.

Ure, Jean. Boys Beware. 2011. (ENG., Illus.). 192p. (gr. 4-7). pap. 7.99 *(978-0-00-716138-6(7)*, HarperCollins Children's Bks.) HarperCollins Pubs. Ltd. GBR. Dist: HarperCollins Pubs.

—Love & Kisses. 2009. (ENG.). 192p. (J). (gr. 4-7). pap. 9.99 *(978-0-00-728172-5(2)*, HarperCollins Children's Bks.) HarperCollins Pubs. Ltd. GBR. Dist: HarperCollins Pubs.

Vail, Rachel. Brilliant. 2011. (Avery Sisters Trilogy Ser.: 3). (ENG., Illus.). 256p. (YA). (gr. 8-12). pap. 9.99 *(978-0-06-089051-3(7)*, HarperTeen) HarperCollins Pubs.

Varveris, Ariana Eleni. The Adventures of Magic Island: Book I-Welcome to Magic Island. 2012. 122p. (gr. 2-2). pap. 9.95 *(978-1-4620-5751-1(9))* iUniverse, Inc.

Veit, Kimberly Michelle. To Be Thirteen. 2006. 57p. pap. 16.95 *(978-1-4241-1392-7(X))* PublishAmerica, Inc.

Villanueva, Gail D. My Fate According to the Butterfly. 2019. (ENG.). 240p. (J). (gr. 3-7). 17.99 *(978-1-338-31050-4(X)*, Scholastic Pr.) Scholastic, Inc.

Villasante, Alexandra. The Grief Keeper. 2019. (ENG.). 320p. (YA). (gr. 7). 17.99 *(978-0-525-51402-2(3)*, G.P. Putnam's Sons Books for Young Readers) Penguin Young Readers Group.

Viorst, Judith. Lulu Is Getting a Sister: (Who WANTS Her? Who NEEDS Her?) Cornell, Kevin, illus. (Lulu Ser.). (ENG.). 192p. (J). (gr. 1-5). 2019. pap. 8.99 *(978-1-4814-7191-6(0))* 2018. 16.99 *(978-1-4814-7190-9(2))* Simon & Schuster.

Vitello, Suzy. The Moment Before. 2014. (ENG.). 216p. (YA). pap. 12.99 *(978-1-62681-167-6(9)*, Diversion Bks.) Diversion Publishing Corp.

Voudrie, Krista. Sisters of Destiny. 2011. 96p. pap. 19.95 *(978-1-4560-5636-0(0))* America Star Bks.

Wait for Me. 2007. 169p. (gr. 4-7). 18.00 *(978-0-7569-7959-1(5))* Perfection Learning Corp.

Wakefield, Vikki. In-Between Days. 2016. (ENG., Illus.). 352p. (YA). (gr. 9). 17.99 *(978-1-4424-8656-0(2)*, Simon & Schuster Bks. For Young Readers) Simon & Schuster Bks. For Young Readers.

Waldman, Alan/A. Erica from America & the Start of the Gang of Four. Scobie, Andrea, illus. 2013. 44p. pap. *(978-0-9840514-2-7(2))* Roxby Media Ltd.

Wallace, Kali. The Memory Trees. 2017. (ENG.). 432p. (YA). (gr. 9). 17.99 *(978-0-06-236623-8(8)*, Tegen, Katherine Bks) HarperCollins Pubs.

Wallace, Lizzie. My Sister's Turning into a Monster. 2011. (Illus.). 20p. 10.96 *(978-1-4520-9930-9(8))* AuthorHouse.

Walters, Nicole Y. Charis: A Journey to Pandora's Jar. Conard, Vincent, illus. 2013. 214p. 32.95 *(978-1-62015-318-5(1)*, Booktrope Editions) Booktrope.

Ward, Dan. Meet the Boomer Sisters. 2006. 131p. pap. 13.95 *(978-1-4116-6927-7(4))* Lulu Pr., Inc.

Ward, Marcia. The Girl Who Found Her Voice. 2013. (ENG.). 276p. pap. 14.99 *(978-1-939927-28-6(5))* Telemachus Pr., LLC.

Waters, Fiona. Faithful Sister. (Illus.). 94p. (J). pap. 10.99 *(978-0-7475-4704-4(1))* Bloomsbury Publishing Plc GBR. Dist: Trafalgar Square Publishing.

Watkins, Steve. Juvie. 2013. (ENG.). 320p. (YA). (gr. 9). 17.99 *(978-0-7636-5509-9(0))* Candlewick Pr.

Watson, Renee. This Side of Home. 2015. (ENG.). 336p. (YA). (gr. 7). 18.99 *(978-1-59990-668-3(6)*, 900074806, Bloomsbury USA Childrens) Bloomsbury Publishing USA.

Weaver, Susan. My Goofy Girls. 2007. 24p. per. 24.95 *(978-1-4241-8933-5(0))* America Star Bks.

Weber, Lori. Klepto, 1 vol. 2004. (Lorimer SideStreets Ser.). (ENG.). 160p. (YA). (gr. 9-12). 8.99 *(978-1-55028-836-0(9)*, b20dc03d-4ed9-46db-9f5b-ee3d8c7b0a79); 16.95 *(978-1-55028-837-7(7)*, 837) James Lorimer & Co. Ltd., Pubs. CAN. Dist: Lerner Publishing Group, Formac Lorimer Bks. Ltd.

Wees, Alyssa. The Waking Forest. 2019. 304p. (YA). (gr. 7). 17.99 *(978-0-525-58116-1(2)*, Delacorte Pr.) Random Hse. Children's Bks.

Weingarten, Lynn. Wherever Nina Lies (Point Paperbacks) 2018. (ENG.). 272p. (YA). (gr. 7-7). pap. 9.99 *(978-1-338-29178-0(5))* Scholastic, Inc.

Weisenberg, Marit. Select. (Select Ser.: 1). (YA). (gr. 9). 2018. 384p. pap. 10.99 *(978-1-58089-895-9(5))* 2017. 352p. lib. bdg. 17.99 *(978-1-58089-806-5(8))* Charlesbridge Publishing, Inc. (Charlesbridge Teen).

Welch, Lester. Last Summer. 2004. 12.95 *(978-1-930252-96-7(X))* PageFree Publishing, Inc.

Wesley, Valerie Wilson. How to Almost Ruin Your School Play. 2005. (Illus.). 105p. (J). lib. bdg. 15.00 *(978-1-4242-0645-2(6))* Fitzgerald Bks.

West, Carly Anne. The Murmurings. (ENG.). 384p. (YA). (gr. 9). 2014. Illus.). pap. 13.99 *(978-1-4424-4180-4(1))* 2013. 16.99 *(978-1-4424-4179-8(8))* Simon Pulse. (Simon Pulse).

Westerfeld, Scott. Impostors, 1 vol. (Impostors Ser.). (ENG.). 416p. (YA). (gr. 7-7). 2021. 12.99 *(978-1-338-75790-3(3))* 2018. 18.99 *(978-1-338-15151-0(7)*, Scholastic Pr.) Scholastic, Inc.

Weston, Carol. Ava & Pip. 2015. (Ava & Pip Ser.: 1). (ENG.). 224p. (J). (gr. 5-7). pap. 10.99 *(978-1-4926-0183-8(7))* Sourcebooks, Inc.

Wexler, Django. Ship of Smoke & Steel. 2020. (Wells of Sorcery Trilogy Ser.: 1). (ENG., Illus.). 368p. (YA). pap. 18.99 *(978-0-7653-9725-6(0)*, 900181138, Tor Teen) Doherty, Tom Assocs., LLC.

Weymouth, Laura E. The Light Between Worlds. (ENG.). (YA). (gr. 8). 2019. 384p. pap. 10.99 *(978-0-06-269688-5(2))* 2018. 368p. 17.99 *(978-0-06-269687-8(4))* HarperCollins Pubs. (HarperTeen).

Weyn, Suzanne. The Night Dance: A Retelling of "the Twelve Dancing Princesses" 2008. (Once upon a Time Ser.). (ENG., Illus.). 224p. (YA). (gr. 7). mass mkt. 8.99 *(978-1-4169-6132-1(1)*, Simon Pulse) Simon Pulse.

White, Kiersten. Mind Games. 2013. (Mind Games Ser.: 1). (ENG.). 304p. (YA). (gr. 8). pap. 9.99 *(978-0-06-213532-2(5)*, HarperTeen) HarperCollins Pubs.

Whitten, A. J. The Cellar. 2011. (ENG.). 288p. (YA). (gr. 7-18). pap. 16.99 *(978-0-547-23253-9(5)*, 1082798, Clarion Bks.) HarperCollins Pubs.

Wiebe, Trina. Lizards Don't Wear Lip Gloss. Sarrazin, Marisol, illus. 2004. (Abby & Tess Pet-Sitters Ser.). 91p. 15.95 *(978-0-7569-3425-5(7))* Perfection Learning Corp.

Wild, Ailsa. Squishy Taylor & a Question of Trust. 2018. (Squishy Taylor Ser.). (ENG., Illus.). 128p. (J). (gr. 2-4). pap. 6.95 *(978-1-5158-1971-4(X)*, 136642, Picture Window Bks.) Capstone.

—Squishy Taylor & the Bonus Sisters. 2018. (Squishy Taylor Ser.). (ENG., Illus.). 128p. (J). (gr. 2-4). pap. 6.95 *(978-1-5158-1972-1(8)*, 136643, Picture Window Bks.) Capstone.

—Squishy Taylor & the Mess Makers. 2018. (Squishy Taylor Ser.). (ENG., Illus.). 128p. (J). (gr. 2-4). pap. 6.95 *(978-1-5158-1973-8(6)*, 136645, Picture Window Bks.) Capstone.

—Squishy Taylor & the Vase That Wasn't. 2018. (Squishy Taylor Ser.). (ENG., Illus.). 128p. (J). (gr. 2-4). pap. 6.95 *(978-1-5158-1974-5(4)*, 136644, Picture Window Bks.) Capstone.

Wild, Alisa. Squishy Taylor & a Question of Trust. Wood, Ben, illus. 2017. (Squishy Taylor Ser.). (ENG.). 128p. (J). (gr. 2-4). lib. bdg. 25.32 *(978-1-5158-1955-4(8)*, 136638, Picture Window Bks.) Capstone.

—Squishy Taylor & the Bonus Sisters. Wood, Ben, illus. 2017. (Squishy Taylor Ser.). (ENG.). 128p. (J). (gr. 2-4). lib. bdg. 25.32 *(978-1-5158-1956-1(6)*, 136639, Picture Window Bks.) Capstone.

—Squishy Taylor & the Mess-Makers. Wood, Ben, illus. 2017. (Squishy Taylor Ser.). (ENG.). 128p. (J). (gr. 2-4). lib. bdg. 25.32 *(978-1-5158-1957-8(4)*, 136640, Picture Window Bks.) Capstone.

—Squishy Taylor & the Vase That Wasn't. Wood, Ben, illus. 2017. (Squishy Taylor Ser.). (ENG.). 128p. (J). (gr. 2-4). lib. bdg. 25.32 *(978-1-5158-1958-5(2)*, 136641, Picture Window Bks.) Capstone.

Wilde, Fran. Riverland. 2019. (ENG., Illus.). 352p. (YA). (gr. 5-9). 17.99 *(978-1-4197-3372-7(9)*, 1256101, Amulet Bks.) Abrams, Inc.

Wilder, Laura Ingalls. Pioneer Sisters. 2017. (Little House Chapter Book Ser.: 2). (ENG., Illus.). 112p. (J). (gr. 1-5). pap. 6.99 *(978-0-06-237710-4(8)*, HarperCollins) HarperCollins Pubs.

Wilder, Vickie. The Umbrella. 2013. 24p. pap. 11.97 *(978-1-62212-534-0(7)*, Strategic Bk. Publishing) Strategic Book Publishing & Rights Agency (SBPRA).

Wiley, Melissa. Beyond the Heather Hills. Graef, Renee, illus. 2003. (Little House Ser.). 189p. (J). (gr. 3-7). 14.65 *(978-0-7569-3467-5(2))* Perfection Learning Corp.

Wilhite, Becca. Bright Blue Miracle. 2009. 176p. (J). pap. 8.99 *(978-1-60641-031-8(8)*, Shadow Mountain) Shadow Mountain Publishing.

Willard, Eliza, et al. Love Is in the Air. 2004. (ENG.). 128p. *(978-0-00-718094-3(2))* HarperCollins Pubs. Australia.

Williams, Carol Lynch. Glimpse. (ENG., (YA). (gr. 9). 2012. Illus.). 512p. pap. 13.99 *(978-1-4169-9731-3(8))* 2010. 496p. 16.99 *(978-1-4169-9730-6(X))* Simon & Schuster/Paula Wiseman Bks. (Simon & Schuster/Paula Wiseman Bks.).

Williams-Garcia, Rita. Gone Crazy in Alabama. (ENG.). (J). (gr. 3-7). 2016. 320p. pap. 8.99 *(978-0-06-221589-5(2))* 2015. (Illus.). 304p. 16.99 *(978-0-06-221587-1(6))* HarperCollins Pubs. (Quill Tree Bks.).

—One Crazy Summer. 2009. (KOR.). 272p. (J). pap. *(978-89-7199-494-8(0))* Dolbegae Publishing Co.

—One Crazy Summer. 2011. (ENG.). 240p. (J). (gr. 3-7). pap. 9.99 *(978-0-06-076090-8(7)*, Quill Tree Bks.) HarperCollins Pubs.

—One Crazy Summer. (J). 2011. 1.25 *(978-1-4498-2201-9(0))* 2010. 69.75 *(978-1-4498-2197-5(9))* 2010. 67.75 *(978-1-4498-2199-9(5))* Recorded Bks., Inc.

—One Crazy Summer. 2011. (J). lib. bdg. 17.20 *(978-0-606-23555-6(8))* Turtleback.

—One Crazy Summer: A Newbery Honor Award Winner. 2010. (ENG.). 224p. (J). (gr. 3-7). 18.99 *(978-0-06-076088-5(5))*; lib. bdg. 16.89 *(978-0-06-076089-2(3))* HarperCollins Pubs. (Quill Tree Bks.).

—P. S. Be Eleven. 2015. (ENG.). 304p. (J). (gr. 3-7). pap. 8.99 *(978-0-06-193864-1(5)*, Quill Tree Bks.) HarperCollins Pubs.

Williams, Venus & Williams, Serena. SisterTales 2. 2010. (gr. 5-9). *(978-0-618-44915-6(9))* Houghton Mifflin Harcourt Trade & Reference Pubs.

Willis, S. J. The Wishwasher. 2011. 128p. (gr. 4-6). pap. 13.32 *(978-1-4567-8751-6(9))* AuthorHouse.

Willis, Wren. Why Is My Name September? 2005. 155p. pap. 11.39 *(978-1-4116-6534-7(1))* Lulu Pr., Inc.

Winn, Sheridan. The Sprite Sisters: Magic at Drysdale's School (Vol 7) Winn, Christopher, illus. 2013. 256p. pap. *(978-0-9574231-2-1(8))* Winn, Sheridan.

Wishinsky, Frieda. Maggie Can't Wait, 1 vol. Griffiths, Dean, illus. 2009. (ENG.). 32p. (J). (gr. -1-1). 17.95 *(978-1-55455-103-3(X)*, b93c1bd4-e847-4eb4-a342-031efc5ebcf4) Fitzhenry & Whiteside, Ltd. CAN. Dist: Firefly Bks., Ltd.

Witek, Jo. Hello in There! A Big Sister's Book of Waiting. 2013. (Growing Hearts Ser.). (ENG., Illus.). 28p. (J). (gr. -1 — 1). 18.99 *(978-1-4197-0371-3(4)*, 1037007, Abrams Appleseed) Abrams, Inc.

Wojton, Roxane. My Mommy & Me & Baby Makes Three. 2012. (ENG., Illus.). 38p. pap. 19.99 *(978-1-105-06616-0(9))* Lulu Pr., Inc.

Wong, Karine. Don't Sit on Her! 2013. 44p. pap. 21.99 *(978-1-4797-6912-4(6))* Xlibris Corp.

Woods, Brenda. The Red Rose Box. 2003. (Illus.). 144p. (J). (gr. 3-7). 5.99 *(978-0-14-250151-1(4)*, Puffin Books) Penguin Young Readers Group.

Wright, Betty Ren. The Dollhouse Murders (35th Anniversary Edition) Nickolls, Leo, illus. 35th ed. 2019. 160p. (J). (gr. 3-7). pap. 8.99 *(978-0-8234-3984-3(4))* Holiday Hse., Inc.

—The Dollhouse Murders (35th Anniversary Edition) 35th ed. 2018. 160p. (J). (gr. 3-7). 17.99 *(978-0-8234-4030-6(3))* Holiday Hse., Inc.

Wulf, Linda Press. The Night of the Burning. 2007. 224p. pap. *(978-0-7475-9051-4(6))* Bloomsbury Publishing Plc.

Wylie, Sarah. All These Lives, 1 vol. 2012. (ENG.). 256p. (YA). (gr. 7-12). 24.99 *(978-0-374-30208-5(1)*, 900072205, Farrar, Straus & Giroux (BYR)) Farrar, Straus & Giroux.

Yeh, Kat. The Truth about Twinkie Pie. 2015. (ENG.). 352p. (J). E-Book *(978-0-316-23671-3(3))* Little Brown & Co.

Yost, Beth. The Mysterious Sock Caper. 2007. 20p. per. 10.95 *(978-1-4327-1242-6(X))* Outskirts Pr., Inc.

Young, Judy. A Book for Black-Eyed Susan. Ettlinger, Doris, illus. 2011. (Tales of Young Americans Ser.). (ENG.). 32p. (J). (gr. 1-4). lib. bdg. 16.95 *(978-1-58536-463-3(0)*, 202185) Sleeping Bear Pr.

Yu, Brenna Burns. Hazel & Twig: the Birthday Fortune. Yu, Brenna Burns, illus. 2018. (Hazel & Twig Ser.). (ENG., Illus.).

40p. (J). (gr. -1-2). 15.99 *(978-0-7636-8970-4(X))* Candlewick Pr.

Yum, Hyewon. The Twins' Blanket. Yum, Hyewon, illus. 2011. (ENG., Illus.). 40p. (J). (gr. -1-1). 19.99 *(978-0-374-37972-8(6)*, 900068267, Farrar, Straus & Giroux (BYR)) Farrar, Straus & Giroux.

Yusuf, Hanna S. & Day, Cansarra. Katie Mcchoir. 2010. 80p. pap. 10.49 *(978-1-4490-7378-7(6))* AuthorHouse.

Zahler, Diane. Sleeping Beauty's Daughters. 2013. 216p. (J). lib. bdg. *(978-0-06-200497-0(2))* Harper & Row Ltd.

—The Thirteenth Princess. 2011. (ENG.). 272p. (J). (gr. 3-7). pap. 6.99 *(978-0-06-182500-2(X)*, HarperCollins) HarperCollins Pubs.

Zemach, Margot & Zemach, Kaethe, illus. Eating up Gladys. 2005. (J). *(978-0-439-66491-2(8)*, Levine, Arthur A. Bks.) Scholastic, Inc.

Zenk, Molly. Hyperion Keats. 2013. 134p. pap. 5.49 *(978-0-9895262-5-8(9))* Highland Pr.

Zhang, Kat. Echoes of Us. 2015. (Hybrid Chronicles Ser.: 3). (ENG.). 368p. (YA). (gr. 8). pap. 10.99 *(978-0-06-211494-5(8)*, HarperCollins) HarperCollins Pubs.

—What's Left of Me. 2013. (Hybrid Chronicles Ser.: 1). (ENG.). 368p. (YA). (gr. 8). pap. 10.99 *(978-0-06-211488-4(3)*, HarperCollins) HarperCollins Pubs.

Ziegler, Jennifer. Revenge of the Angels. 2015. (Brewster Triplets Ser.). (ENG.). 256p. (J). (gr. 3-7). 16.99 *(978-0-545-83899-3(1)*, Scholastic Pr.) Scholastic, Inc.

—Revenge of the Angels: a Wish Novel (the Brewster Triplets) 2017. (Brewster Triplets Ser.). (ENG.). 256p. (J). (gr. 3-7). pap. 6.99 *(978-0-545-83902-0(5)*, Scholastic Pr.) Scholastic, Inc.

—Revenge of the Teacher's Pets. 2018. (ENG.). 256p. (J). (gr. 3-7). 16.99 *(978-1-338-09123-6(9)*, Scholastic Pr.) Scholastic, Inc.

—Sass & Serendipity. 2012. 384p. (YA). (gr. 7-12). (ENG.). lib. bdg. 26.19 *(978-0-385-90762-0(1)*, Delacorte Pr.); pap. 9.99 *(978-0-375-85964-9(0)*, Ember) Random Hse. Children's Bks.

Zimmer, Tracie Vaughn. Sketches from a Spy Tree. Glass, Andrew, illus. 2005. (ENG.). 64p. (J). (gr. 5-7). 16.00 *(978-0-618-23479-0(9)*, 111177, Clarion Bks.) HarperCollins Pubs.

Zimmerman, Mary Joyce. Just Four. 2005. (Illus.). 32p. (J). (gr. -1-5). 2.70 *(978-0-7399-2340-5(4)*, 2779) Rod & Staff Pubs., Inc.

Zink, Michelle. Circle of Fire. 2012. (Prophecy of the Sisters Ser.: 3). (ENG.). 368p. (YA). (gr. 7-17). pap. 19.99 *(978-0-316-03446-3(0))* Little, Brown Bks. for Young Readers.

—Guardian of the Gate. 2011. (Prophecy of the Sisters Ser.: 2). (ENG.). 368p. (YA). (gr. 7-17). pap. 18.99 *(978-0-316-02740-3(5))* Little, Brown Bks. for Young Readers.

—Prophecy of the Sisters. 2010. (Prophecy of the Sisters Ser.: 1). (ENG.). 368p. (YA). (gr. 7-17). pap. 18.99 *(978-0-316-02741-0(3))* Little, Brown Bks. for Young Readers.

SISTERS (IN RELIGIOUS ORDERS, CONGREGATIONS, ETC.)

see Nuns

SITTING BULL, 1831-1890

Abnett, Dan. Sitting Bull & the Battle of the Little Bighorn. (Jr. Graphic Biographies Ser.). (ENG.). 24p. (gr. 2-3). 2009. (J). 47.90 *(978-1-61513-822-7(6)*, PowerKids Pr.) 2006. (Illus.). (J). lib. bdg. 28.93 *(978-1-4042-3394-2(6)*, f0e34536-71fb-4966-826f-56f539643bb7) 2006. (Illus.). pap. 10.60 *(978-1-4042-2147-5(6)*, a9929d73-f261-48e9-ae0a-ace8c3e521bc, PowerKids Pr.) Rosen Publishing Group, Inc., The.

—Toro Sentado y la Batalla de Little Bighorn, 1 vol. 2009. (Historietas Juveniles: Biografías (Jr. Graphic Biographies) Ser.). (SPA., Illus.). 24p. (gr. 2-3). (J). 28.93 *(978-1-4358-8562-2(7)*, 2879172c-3b85-4fcd-aa7a-41f6781a356c); pap. 10.60 *(978-1-4358-3318-0(X)*, 643c8a66-07a0-409b-938a-c5a86c6e7064) Rosen Publishing Group, Inc., The.

Bailey, Gerry & Foster, Karen. Sitting Bull's Tomahawk. Radford, Karen & Noyes, Leighton, illus. 2008. (Stories of Great People Ser.). (ENG.). 40p. (J). (gr. 3-8). pap. *(978-0-7787-3714-8(4))*; lib. bdg. *(978-0-7787-3692-9(X))* Crabtree Publishing Co.

Collard, Sneed B., III. Sitting Bull, 1 vol. 2010. (American Heroes Ser.). (ENG.). 48p. (gr. 3-3). 32.64 *(978-0-7614-4059-8(3)*, d331b804-8748-40a1-a55d-cc9e79408f93) Cavendish Square Publishing LLC.

Collier, James Lincoln. Sitting Bull You Never Knew. Copeland, Greg, illus. 2004. (You Never Knew Ser.). (ENG.). 80p. (J). (gr. 4-6). pap. 6.95 *(978-0-516-25836-2(2)*, Children's Pr.) Scholastic Library Publishing.

Davis, Kenneth C. Don't Know Much about Sitting Bull Sitting Bull, Vol. 2. 2003. (Don't Know Much About Ser.). (Illus.). 144p. (J). (gr. 3-7). 16.89 *(978-0-06-028818-1(3))* HarperCollins Pubs.

DeFord, Diane. Chief Sitting Bull. 2009. pap. 13.25 *(978-1-60559-070-7(3))* Hameray Publishing Group, Inc.

Evento, Susan. Sitting Bull. 2005. (Rookie Biographies Ser.). (ENG., Illus.). 32p. (J). (gr. 1-2). pap. 4.95 *(978-0-516-25829-4(X)*, Children's Pr.) Scholastic Library Publishing.

Hayhurst, Chris. Sitting Bull, 1 vol. 2003. (Primary Sources of Famous People in American History Ser.). (ENG., Illus.). 32p. (gr. 3-4). lib. bdg. 29.13 *(978-0-8239-4120-9(5)*, 539eb5eb-40bd-43e1-8372-399501b1c6f3, Rosen Reference) Rosen Publishing Group, Inc., The.

—Sitting Bull: Sioux Chief = Toro Sentado: Jefe Sioux, 1 vol. de la Vega, Eida, tr. 2003. (Famous People in American History / Grandes Personajes en la Historia de Los Estados Unidos Ser.). (ENG & SPA., Illus.). 32p. (gr. 2-3). lib. bdg. 29.13 *(978-0-8239-4168-1(X)*, 7c2b3e50-df9d-4b60-95e9-904698643800, Editorial Buenas Letras) Rosen Publishing Group, Inc., The.

—Sitting Bull: Sioux War Chief. 2009. (Primary Sources of Famous People in American History Ser.). 32p. (gr. 2-3). 47.90 *(978-1-60851-724-4(1))* Rosen Publishing Group, Inc., The.

—Sitting Bull / Toro Sentado: Sioux War Chief / Jefe Sioux. 2009. (Famous People in American History/Grandes personajes en la historia de los Estados Unidos Ser.). (SPA.). 32p. (gr. 2-3). 47.90 *(978-1-61512-555-5(8)*, Editorial Buenas Letras) Rosen Publishing Group, Inc., The.

—Toro Sentado: Jefe sioux (Sitting Bull: Sioux War Chief) 2009. (Grandes personajes en la historia de los Estados Unidos (Famous People in American History) Ser.). (SPA.). 32p. (gr. 2-3). 47.90 *(978-1-61512-809-9(3)*, Editorial Buenas Letras) Rosen Publishing Group, Inc., The.

Jeffrey, Gary. Sitting Bull: The Life of a Lakota Chief. 2009. (Graphic Nonfiction Biographies Ser.). (ENG.). 48p. (YA). (gr. 4-5). 58.50 *(978-1-61513-027-6(6)*, Rosen Reference) Rosen Publishing Group, Inc., The.

Jeffrey, Gary & Petty, Kate. Sitting Bull: The Life of a Lakota Sioux Chief, 1 vol. 2005. (Graphic Nonfiction Biographies Ser.). (ENG., Illus.). 48p. (YA). (gr. 4-6). lib. bdg. 37.13 *(978-1-4042-0247-4(1)*, 9175d2ac-487b-4e78-831d-01c6d6e70097) Rosen Publishing Group, Inc., The.

LaPlante, Walter. Sitting Bull, 1 vol. 2015. (Native American Heroes Ser.). (ENG., Illus.). 24p. (J). (gr. 1-2). 24.27 *(978-1-4824-2702-8(8)*, 5c8ad679-caff-48f7-857c-ac24e787c709) Stevens, Gareth Publishing LLLP.

Mapua, Jeff. Sitting Bull, 1 vol., 1. 2015. (Britannica Beginner Bios Ser.). (ENG., Illus.). 32p. (J). (gr. 2-3). pap. 13.90 *(978-1-5081-0062-1(4)*, 126be1f2-b54a-447b-9f5f-6fd2ef0dbddc, Britannica Educational Publishing) Rosen Publishing Group, Inc., The.

Marsh, Carole. Sitting Bull. 2003. 12p. (gr. k-4). 2.95 *(978-0-635-02378-0(4))* Gallopade International.

McDonnell, Julia. Sitting Bull in His Own Words. 2014. (Eyewitness to History Ser.). 32p. (J). (gr. 4-6). pap. 63.00 *(978-1-4824-1223-9(3))* Stevens, Gareth Publishing LLLP.

McLeese, Don. Sitting Bull. 2003. (Native American Legends Ser.). (Illus.). 32p. (J). lib. bdg. 28.50 *(978-1-58952-730-0(5))* Rourke Educational Media.

Minor, Wendell. Sitting Bull Remembers. Date not set. 32p. (J). (gr. -1-3). 15.99 *(978-0-06-029153-2(2))*; pap. 5.99 *(978-0-06-443725-7(6))*; lib. bdg. 16.89 *(978-0-06-029154-9(0))* HarperCollins Pubs.

Nelson, S. D. Sitting Bull: Lakota Warrior & Defender of His People. 2015. (ENG., Illus.). 64p. (J). (gr. 3-7). 20.99 *(978-1-4197-0731-5(0)*, 1057301, Abrams Bks. for Young Readers) Abrams, Inc.

Roxburgh, Ellis. Sitting Bull vs. George Armstrong Custer: The Battle of the Little Bighorn, 1 vol. 2015. (History's Greatest Rivals Ser.). (ENG., Illus.). 48p. (J). (gr. 6-8). pap. 15.05 *(978-1-4824-4235-9(3)*, aa50f84d-c548-4b07-b750-1ecf1f5453f1) Stevens, Gareth Publishing LLLP.

Rucker, Jeffrey A. La Historia de Toro Sentado, 1 vol. Gonzalez, Tomas, tr. 2003. (Reading Room Collection: Spanish Ser.).Tr. of Story of Sitting Bull. (SPA., Illus.). 24p. (J). (gr. 2-2). lib. bdg. 26.27 *(978-0-8239-6516-8(3)*, e311da95-8fe2-4a14-b218-5be545f4fbb9, Editorial Buenas Letras) Rosen Publishing Group, Inc., The.

—La historia de Toro Sentado (the Story of Sitting Bull) 2009. (Reading Room Collection: Spanish Ser.). (SPA.). 24p. (gr. 3-4). 42.50 *(978-1-60854-178-2(9)*, Editorial Buenas Letras) Rosen Publishing Group, Inc., The.

—The Story of Sitting Bull. (Reading Room Collection 2 Ser.). 24p. (gr. 3-4). 2009. 42.50 *(978-1-60851-998-9(8)*, PowerKids Pr.) 2003. (ENG.). 43.95 *(978-0-8239-8731-3(0))* Rosen Publishing Group, Inc., The.

Sanford, William R. Hunkpapa Lakota Chief Sitting Bull, 1 vol. 2013. (Native American Chiefs & Warriors Ser.). (ENG., Illus.). 48p. (gr. 5-7). lib. bdg. 25.27 *(978-0-7660-4097-7(6)*, 01439197-4907-4648-b855-91378a6c060e) Enslow Publishing, LLC.

Shaffer, Jody Jensen. Sitting Bull: Eagles Cannot Be Crows. rev. ed. 2017. (Social Studies: Informational Text Ser.). (ENG., Illus.). 32p. (gr. 4-8). pap. 11.99 *(978-1-4938-3800-4(8))* Teacher Created Materials, Inc.

Silate, Jennifer. Seeing the Future: The Final Vision of Sitting Bull. (Great Moments in American History Ser.). 32p. (gr. 3-3). 2009. 47.90 *(978-1-61513-150-1(7))* 2003. (ENG., Illus.). (J). lib. bdg. 29.13 *(978-0-8239-4384-5(4)*, b8e3d943-207a-4e4d-8e97-524798406eb0, Rosen Reference) Rosen Publishing Group, Inc., The.

Sitting Bull. 2010. (ENG., Illus.). 128p. (gr. 6-12). 35.00 *(978-1-60413-527-5(1)*, P179303, Facts On File) Infobase Holdings, Inc.

Spinner, Stephanie. Who Was Sitting Bull? 2014. (Who Was... ? Ser.). lib. bdg. 16.00 *(978-0-606-36179-8(0))* Turtleback.

Spinner, Stephanie & Who HQ. Who Was Sitting Bull? Eldridge, Jim, illus. 2014. (Who Was? Ser.). 112p. (J). (gr. 3-7). 6.99 *(978-0-448-47965-1(6)*, Penguin Workshop) Penguin Young Readers Group.

Weil, Ann. Sitting Bull, 1 vol. 2012. (American Biographies Ser.). (ENG.). 48p. (gr. 4-6). (J). lib. bdg. 35.32 *(978-1-4329-6449-8(6)*, 119048); pap. 9.95 *(978-1-4329-6460-3(7)*, 119057) Capstone. (Heinemann).

SIX DAY WAR, 1967

see Israel-Arab War, 1967

SIZE AND SHAPE

ABDO Publishing Company Staff & Gaarder-Juntti, Oona. Shapes Everywhere, 6 vols. 2013. (Shapes Everywhere Ser.: 6). (ENG.). 24p. (J). (gr. k-4). lib. bdg. 196.74 *(978-1-61783-410-3(6)*, 13324, Super SandCastle) ABDO Publishing Co.

ABDO Publishing Company Staff & Hanson, Anders. 3-D Shapes, 1 vol. 2007. (3-D Shapes Ser.: 6). (ENG.). 24p. (J). (gr. -1-3). lib. bdg. 29.93 *(978-1-59928-885-7(0)*, 2169, SandCastle) ABDO Publishing Co.

Aboff, Marcie. If You Were a Polygon, 1 vol. Dillard, Sarah, illus. 2009. (Math Fun Ser.). (ENG.). 24p. (J). (gr. 2-4). pap. 7.95 *(978-1-4048-5692-9(7)*, 102272, Picture Window Bks.) Capstone.

Adams, Colleen. Carlos's Cubby, 1 vol. 2006. (Neighborhood Readers Ser.). (ENG.). 12p. (gr. k-1). pap. 5.90 *(978-1-4042-5756-6(X)*, 3c5474f7-ad14-4199-827d-1071ebfedd74, Rosen Classroom) Rosen Publishing Group, Inc., The.

Adler, David A. Triangles. Miller, Edward, illus. 2015. (ENG.). 32p. (J). (gr. 1-4). 8.99 *(978-0-8234-3305-6(6))* Holiday Hse., Inc.

Aigner-Clark, Julie. Asomate y Ve Las Figuras. Zaidi, Nadeem, illus. 2004. (Baby Einstein Ser.). (SPA.). 16p. (J). bds. *(978-970-718-151-9(6)*, Silver Dolphin en Español) Advanced Marketing, S. de R. L. de C. V.

Alaina, Maria. Shapes, 1 vol. 2011. (Wonder Readers Early Level Ser.). (ENG.). 16p. (gr. -1-1). (J). pap. 6.25 *(978-1-4296-7810-0(0)*, 117982); pap. 35.94 *(978-1-4296-8145-2(4))* Capstone. (Capstone Pr.).

—Shapes in the City, 1 vol. 2011. (Wonder Readers Early Level Ser.). (ENG.). 16p. (gr. -1-1). (J). pap. 6.25 *(978-1-4296-7811-7(9)*, 117983); pap. 35.94 *(978-1-4296-8147-6(0)*, Capstone Pr.) Capstone.

Albers, Josef. Squares & Other Shapes: With Josef Albers. 2016. (ENG., Illus.). 30p. (gr. -1 — 1). bds. 12.95 *(978-0-7148-7256-8(3))* Phaidon Pr., Inc.

Alexander, Emmett. Formas / Sort It by Shape, 1 vol. de la Vega, Eida, tr. 2015. (Vamos a Agrupar Por... / Sort It Out! Ser.). (ENG & SPA., Illus.). 24p. (J). (gr. k-1). lib. bdg. 24.27 *(978-1-4824-3217-6(X)*, 66e72416-9096-4985-aff6-6b3fdf019074) Stevens, Gareth Publishing LLLP.

Alvarez, Lourdes M. My First Book Shapes. Brooks, David, illus. 2005. (My First Book Ser.). 9p. (J). (gr. -1-1). bds. 3.95 *(978-1-933050-11-9(X))* Sweetwater Pr.

Amery, Heather. What's Happening on the Farm? Cartwright, Stephen, illus. rev. ed. 2006. (What's Happening? Ser.). 32p. (J). (gr. -1-3). 5.99 *(978-0-7945-1288-0(7)*, Usborne) EDC Publishing.

Anderson, Graylin. Seeing the Shapes + Drawing the Shapes = Drawing the Object. 2008. (ENG.). 32p. pap. 11.99 *(978-1-4196-9609-1(2))* CreateSpace Independent Publishing Platform.

Anderson, James. Around Home. rev. ed. 2011. (Mathematics in the Real World Ser.). (ENG.). 32p. (gr. k-1). pap. 9.99 *(978-1-4333-3439-9(9))* Teacher Created Materials, Inc.

—Around Town. rev. ed. 2011. (Mathematics in the Real World Ser.). (ENG.). 32p. (gr. k-1). pap. 9.99 *(978-1-4333-3438-2(0))* Teacher Created Materials, Inc.

Anderson, Jill. Finding Shapes with Sebastian Pig & Friends at the Museum, 1 vol. 2009. (Math Fun with Sebastian Pig & Friends! Ser.). (ENG., Illus.). 32p. (gr. k-2). (J). lib. bdg. 26.60 *(978-0-7660-3363-4(5)*, fdb92957-f7c6-490d-8983-6b0f1f8b1a87); pap. 10.35 *(978-0-7660-5981-8(2)*, 083ce63e-b9e8-40a1-877b-7e066ff37aef, Enslow Elementary) Enslow Publishing, LLC.

Anderson, Lynne. Rocket Ship Shapes. 2011. (Early Connections Ser.). (J). *(978-1-61672-596-9(6))* Benchmark Education Co.

Armadillo Press. Dog & Friends! A Box of Exciting Picture Books, 6 vols. 2017. (ENG., Illus.). 54p. (J). (gr. -1-12). bds. 14.99 *(978-1-86147-640-1(X)*, Armadillo) Anness Publishing GBR. Dist: National Bk. Network.

Arps, Melissa. Shapes. 2006. (Illus.). (J). *(978-0-7364-2383-0(4))* Random Hse., Inc.

Ashley, Michele. Who Has Ears Like These? 2012. (Level C Ser.). (ENG., Illus.). 16p. (J). (gr. k-2). pap. 7.95 *(978-1-927136-27-0(X)*, 19450) RiverStream Publishing.

Avery, Logan. Art & Culture. 2018. (Mathematics in the Real World Ser.). (ENG., Illus.). 20p. (J). (gr. k-1). 8.99 *(978-1-4258-5629-8(2))* Teacher Created Materials, Inc.

—Arte y Cultura: Figuras. rev. ed. 2019. (Mathematics in the Real World Ser.). (SPA., Illus.). 20p. (J). (gr. k-1). 8.99 *(978-1-4258-2836-3(1))* Teacher Created Materials, Inc.

—Engineering Marvels: Birdhouses. 2018. (Mathematics in the Real World Ser.). (ENG., Illus.). 20p. (J). (gr. k-1). 8.99 *(978-1-4258-5630-4(6))* Teacher Created Materials, Inc.

—Ingeniería Asombrosa: Figuras. rev. ed. 2019. (Mathematics in the Real World Ser.). (SPA.). 20p. (J). (gr. k-1). 8.99 *(978-1-4258-2837-0(X))* Teacher Created Materials, Inc.

—Juguetes: Partición de Figuras. rev. ed. 2019. (Mathematics in the Real World Ser.). (SPA., Illus.). 24p. (J). (gr. 1-2). pap. 9.99 *(978-1-4258-2857-8(4))* Teacher Created Materials, Inc.

Avery, Sebastian. The School Garden: Reason with Shapes & Their Attributes, 1 vol. 2014. (Rosen Math Readers Ser.). (ENG.). 24p. (J). (gr. 3-3). pap. 8.25 *(978-1-4777-4875-6(X)*, 93bad9e9-8338-4711-8339-7154d2f1b08c, Rosen Classroom) Rosen Publishing Group, Inc., The.

Avett, Harper. Go Fly a Kite! Reason with Shapes & Their Attributes, 1 vol. 2014. (Rosen Math Readers Ser.). (ENG., Illus.). 24p. (J). (gr. 3-3). pap. 8.25 *(978-1-4777-4881-7(4)*, 004fdc4a-3d91-422d-9cb6-38d30bb743b4, Rosen Classroom) Rosen Publishing Group, Inc., The.

AZ Books, creator. What Shape? 2012. (Smarty Ser.). (ENG., Illus.). 10p. (J). (gr. -1 — 1). 9.95 *(978-1-61889-247-8(9))* AZ Bks. LLC.

AZ Books Staff. Colors & Shapes. Petrovskaya, Olga, ed. 2012. (Matching Game Ser.). (ENG.). 18p. (J). (gr. -1-k). spiral bd. 4.95 *(978-1-61889-201-0(0))* AZ Bks. LLC.

—Find a Pair. Petrovskaya, Olga, ed. 2012. (Matching Game Ser.). (ENG.). 18p. (J). (gr. -1-k). spiral bd. 4.95 *(978-1-61889-009-2(3))* AZ Bks. LLC.

—Shapes. Slusar, Julia, ed. 2012. (Pull It Out Ser.). (ENG.). 10p. (J). (— 1). 7.95 *(978-1-61889-194-5(4))* AZ Bks. LLC.

Baker, Ella. Big & Small, 1 vol. 2012. (InfoMax Readers Ser.). (ENG., Illus.). 16p. (J). (gr. k-k). pap. 7.00 *(978-1-4488-8875-7(1)*, 2c59ecb8-0ab7-4825-9fb6-0eb5ae0bebb3, Rosen Classroom) Rosen Publishing Group, Inc., The.

Barradas, Michele. Rainbow of Shapes: Learn shapes & Colors. 2008. 20p. pap. 15.95 *(978-1-4389-0177-0(1))* AuthorHouse.

Bartowski, Amy. Shapes at the Store: Identify & Describe Shapes. 2013. (InfoMax Math Readers Ser.). (ENG.). 16p. (J). (gr. k-1). pap. 42.00 *(978-1-4777-1974-9(1))*; (Illus.). pap. 7.00 *(978-1-4777-1973-2(3)*, d5bb1654-c839-4cc9-9a38-be92101c6087) Rosen Publishing Group, Inc., The. (Rosen Classroom).

Begin Smart Books Staff, contrib. by. What Shapes Do You See? 2010. (Illus.). 14p. (J). bds. *(978-1-60906-005-3(9))* Begin Smart LLC.

Believe It Or Not!, Ripleys, compiled by. Ripley's Believe It or Not! It's a Circle: But Not Just a Circle! 2018. (Little Bks.: 3). (ENG., Illus.). 20p. (J). bds. 6.99 *(978-1-60991-211-6(X))* Ripley Entertainment, Inc.

Belinda, Gallagher. Learn to Write - Colours & Shapes. Kelly, Richard, ed. 2017. 14p. (J). pap. 5.95 *(978-1-78209-629-0(9))* Miles Kelly Publishing, Ltd. GBR. Dist: Parkwest Pubns., Inc.

Benchmark Education Company, compiled by. Insects Measure up! & ¡Vamos a Medir Insectos! 2005. (J). 62.00 net. *(978-1-4108-4496-5(X))* Benchmark Education Co.

Benchmark Education Company, LLC Staff, compiled by. Patterns & Shapes. 2006. (J). 265.00 *(978-1-4108-7049-0(9))* Benchmark Education Co.

—Patterns & Shapes: Theme Set. 2006. (J). 274.00 *(978-1-4108-7075-9(8))*; 147.00 *(978-1-4108-7092-6(8))* Benchmark Education Co.

Benduhn, Tea. What Is Shape? 2009. (Get Art Smart Ser.). (ENG., Illus.). 24p. (J). (gr. k-4). lib. bdg. *(978-0-7787-5125-0(2))*; (gr. 1-2). pap. *(978-0-7787-5139-7(2))* Crabtree Publishing Co.

Bennett, Elizabeth. Safari Patterns. 2014. (Illus.). (J). pap. *(978-0-545-61305-7(1))* Scholastic, Inc.

Benton, Linda. I See Patterns. 2017. (Learn-To-Read Ser.). (ENG., Illus.). (J). (gr. k-2). pap. 3.49 *(978-1-68310-218-2(5))* Pacific Learning, Inc.

Berger, Melvin & Berger, Gilda. Supersize Animals. 2015. (Scholastic Reader Level 2 Ser.). lib. bdg. 13.55 *(978-0-606-37756-0(5))* Turtleback.

Berger, Samantha & Chanko, Pamela. Big & Little. 2013. (Illus.). 14p. (J). *(978-0-439-69937-2(1))* Scholastic, Inc.

Best, Arthur. Shape, Size, & Volume, 1 vol. 2018. (Properties of Matter Ser.). (ENG.). 24p. (J). (gr. 1-1). pap. 9.22 *(978-1-5026-4246-2(8)*, 77a61e86-677e-41a8-b282-ff9734880d60) Cavendish Square Publishing LLC.

Bienik, Stella. Sculpting with Clay: Reason with Shapes & Their Attributes, 1 vol. 2014. (Math Masters: Geometry Ser.). (ENG.). 24p. (J). (gr. 2-2). 25.27 *(978-1-4777-6444-2(5)*, f73197c7-b598-4bb2-a986-fe9f997baa26); pap. 8.25 *(978-1-4777-4906-7(3)*, ac5ccb34-644b-4532-acef-b1883fe2aea4) Rosen Publishing Group, Inc., The. (Rosen Classroom).

BIG [Capstone Sole Source]. 2010. (Big Ser.). 24p. lib. bdg. 215.91 *(978-1-4296-5846-1(0)*, Capstone Pr.) Capstone.

Big KeyBoard IR. 2017. (My First KeyBDs Ser.). (ENG.). (J). spiral bd. 24.99 *(978-0-7945-3933-7(5)*, Usborne) EDC Publishing.

Bixley, Donovan. My First Board Book: Shapes. 2022. (My First Board Book Ser.). (ENG., Illus.). 24p. (J). (gr. -1-k). bds. 13.99 *(978-1-86971-347-8(8))* Hachette New Zealand NZL. Dist: Hachette Bk. Group.

Blaisdell, Molly. If You Were a Quadrilateral, 1 vol. Carabelli, Francesca, illus. 2009. (Math Fun Ser.). (ENG.). 24p. (J). (gr. 2-4). pap. 7.95 *(978-1-4048-5690-5(0)*, 102271, Picture Window Bks.) Capstone.

Bluemel Oldfield, Dawn. Patterns at the Seashore. 2014. (Math Blast!: Seeing Patterns All Around Ser.). (ENG.). 32p. (J). (gr. -1-3). lib. bdg. 28.50 *(978-1-62724-335-3(6))* Bearport Publishing Co., Inc.

Blyton, Enid, et al. My First Colours & Shapes. 2013. (ENG., Illus.). 20p. (J). bds. 11.50 *(978-1-84135-760-7(X))* Award Pubns. Ltd. GBR. Dist: Parkwest Pubns., Inc.

Bogart, Jo Ellen. Big & Small, Room for All. Newland, Gillian, illus. 2017. 30p. (J). (— 1). bds. 8.99 *(978-0-14-319893-2(9)*, Tundra Bks.) Tundra Bks. CAN. Dist: Penguin Random Hse. LLC.

Bolam, Emily. Rookie Preschool: My First Rookie Reader: It's Circle Time! Shapes. 2009. (Rookie Preschool Ser.). (ENG.). 24p. (J). (gr. -1). 23.00 *(978-0-531-24401-2(6))* Scholastic Library Publishing.

Boothroyd, Jennifer. Combining Shapes. 2007. (First Step Nonfiction — Early Math Ser.). (ENG., Illus.). 8p. (J). (gr. k-2). pap. 5.99 *(978-0-8225-6831-5(4)*, 464a6a5b-2543-4ec5-a5fd-a82288e1eddd) Lerner Publishing Group.

—Cone. 2008. pap. 22.95 *(978-0-8225-9364-5(5))* Lerner Publishing Group.

—Patterns. 2007. (First Step Nonfiction — Early Math Ser.). (ENG., Illus.). 8p. (J). (gr. k-2). pap. 5.99 *(978-0-8225-6829-2(2)*, d0696bf6-8f86-44a8-b063-f5c4b6161b85) Lerner Publishing Group.

Braidich, Victoria. Animals on the Farm: Learning to Compare Size, 1 vol. 2010. (Math for the REAL World Ser.). (ENG.). 12p. (gr. 1-2). pap. 5.90 *(978-0-8239-8847-1(3)*, 67fd2ff5-4ab8-4f9f-be27-8997ef68d3de, Rosen Classroom) Rosen Publishing Group, Inc., The.

—Shapes at Home: Learning to Recognize Basic Geometric Shapes, 1 vol. 2010. (Math for the REAL World Ser.). (ENG.). 12p. (gr. 1-2). pap. 5.90 *(978-0-8239-8863-1(5)*, 708eec44-6c1c-4d02-ac1c-55dc27784d2f, Rosen Classroom) Rosen Publishing Group, Inc., The.

Brighter Child, compiled by. Colors & Shapes. 2006. (ENG., Illus.). 54p. (gr. -1-1). 2.99 *(978-0-7696-4689-3(1)*, 0769646891, Brighter Child) Carson-Dellosa Publishing, LLC.

Brocket, Jane. Circles, Stars, & Squares: Looking for Shapes. Brocket, Jane, photos by. 2012. (Jane Brocket's Clever Concepts Ser.). (ENG., Illus.). 32p. (J). (gr. -1-2). lib. bdg. 26.65 *(978-0-7613-4611-1(2)*, 61ad0bc1-7fa7-4bde-9b0e-33f270089087, Millbrook Pr.) Lerner Publishing Group.

—Spotty, Stripy, Swirly: What Are Patterns? Brocket, Jane, photos by. 2012. (Jane Brocket's Clever Concepts Ser.). (ENG., Illus.). 32p. (J). (gr. -1-2). lib. bdg. 26.65 *(978-0-7613-4613-5(9)*, 015e6d6c-62ee-4587-9e50-9d63b73b73e6, Millbrook Pr.) Lerner Publishing Group.

Brooks, Felicity. First Shapes. Litchfield, Jo, illus. MMStudios, photos by. 2007. (Usborne Look & Say Ser.). 12p. (J). (gr. -1-k). bds. 14.99 *(978-0-7945-1450-1(2)*, Usborne) EDC Publishing.

—Usborne Shapes Jigsaw Book. 2008. (Usborne Jigsaw Bks.). (Illus.). 12p. (J). (gr. -1-3). bds. 9.99 *(978-0-7945-2046-5(4)*, Usborne) EDC Publishing.

Brown, Margery W. Afro-Bets Book of Shapes. Blair, Culverson & Simpson, Howard, illus. 2nd ed. 2004. (Afro-Bets Ser.).

S

24p. (J). (gr. -1-1). pap. 3.95 *(978-0-940975-58-3(0),* Sankofa Bks.) Just Us Bks., Inc.
Brundle, Joanna. The Scale of Animals. 2020. (Illus.). 24p. (J). *(978-0-7787-7653-6(0))* Crabtree Publishing Co.
Buchanan, Theodore. Fractals. 2nd rev. ed. 2017. (TIME(r): Informational Text Ser.). (ENG., Illus.). 48p. (gr. 6-8). pap. 13.99 *(978-1-4938-3626-0(9))* Teacher Created Materials, Inc.
Budney, Blossom. What Is Round?, 1 vol. Bobri, Vladimir, illus. 2018. 32p. (J). 20.00 *(978-1-85124-481-2(6))* Bodleian Library GBR. Dist: Chicago Distribution Ctr.
Budnick, Madeleine. Hello, Círculos! Shapes in English y Espanol. 2013. (ArteKids Ser.). (ENG., Illus.). 16p. (J). (gr. k-k). bds. 7.95 *(978-1-59534-140-2(4))* Trinity Univ. Pr.
Bullard, Lisa. Big & Small [Scholastic]: An Animal Opposites Book. 2009. (Animal Opposites Ser.). 32p. (gr. 1-2). pap. 1.00 *(978-1-4296-4230-9(0),* Capstone Pr.) Capstone.
Burke, Zoe. Lines & Triangles & Squares, Oh My! Hall, Carey, illus. 2017. 24p. (J). bds. 10.95 *(978-0-7649-7864-7(0),* POMEGRANATE KIDS) Pomegranate Communications, Inc.
Burton, Margie, et al. Bigger Than? Smaller Than? 2011. (Early Connections Ser.). (J). *(978-1-61672-249-4(5))* Benchmark Education Co.
—The Guessing Jar. 2011. (Early Connections Ser.). (J). *(978-1-61672-541-9(9))* Benchmark Education Co.
—Looking for Shapes. 2011. (Early Connections Ser.). (J). *(978-1-61672-498-6(6))* Benchmark Education Co.
—What Comes Next? & ¿Qué Sigue? 6 English, 6 Spanish Adaptations. 2011. (J). spiral bd. 75.00 net. *(978-1-4108-5628-9(3))* Benchmark Education Co.
Butler, Roberta. Making Shapes. Moon, Jo, illus. 2006. (Making... Ser.). 14p. (J). (gr. -1-3). bds. 7.95 *(978-1-57791-250-7(0))* Brighter Minds Children's Publishing.
Caillou: Colors & Shapes. 2003. 32p. pap., wbk. ed. 14.95 incl. cd-rom *(978-1-57791-029-9(X))* Brighter Minds Children's Publishing.
Canavan, Thomas. Shapes & Symmetry: 50 Math Super Puzzles, 1 vol. 2011. (Math Standards Workout Ser.). (ENG., Illus.). 48p. (YA). (gr. 5-5). pap. 12.75 *(978-1-4488-6683-0(9),* 2b0eec55-5545-4658-a254-4a03e92130c9, Rosen Reference) Rosen Publishing Group, Inc., The.
Candel, Arianna. Las Formas. Rovira, Francesc, illus. 2004. (Osito Estudiante / Little Bear's Firsts Ser.).Tr. of Shapes. (SPA.). 36p. (J). (gr. k-3). 21.19 *(978-0-7641-2995-7(3),* B.E.S. Publishing) Peterson's.
Canetti, Yanitzia. Colorful Shapes/Figuras de Colores: A World of Color. 2010. (SPA & ENG.). 24p. (J). pap. 6.99 *(978-1-59835-278-8(4),* BrickHouse Education) Cambridge BrickHouse, Inc.
Carle, Eric. My Very First Book of Shapes. Carle, Eric, illus. 2005. (ENG., Illus.). 20p. (J). (gr. -1 — 1). bds. 6.99 *(978-0-399-24387-5(9))* Penguin Young Readers Group.
Carr, Aaron. Formas. 2013. (SPA.). (J). *(978-1-62127-613-5(9))* Weigl Pubs., Inc.
—Grandes y Pequeño. 2012. (SPA.). (J). *(978-1-61913-205-4(2))* Weigl Pubs., Inc.
—Shapes. 2012. (Science Kids Ser.). (ENG., Illus.). 24p. (J). (gr. -1-1). pap. 12.95 *(978-1-61913-307-5(5));* lib. bdg. 27.13 *(978-1-61913-084-5(X))* Weigl Pubs., Inc. (AV2 by Weigl).
Carroll, Danielle. Tiling with Shapes. 2005. (Yellow Umbrella Fluent Level Ser.). (ENG., Illus.). 16p. (gr. k-1). pap. 35.70 *(978-0-7368-5323-1(5),* Capstone Pr.) Capstone.
Carrow, Ian. Jackson's Surprise Party, 1 vol. 2013. (InfoMax Math Readers Ser.). (ENG.). 24p. (J). (gr. 1-1). pap. 8.25 *(978-1-4777-2204-6(1),* b092930f-1454-4742-afe4-720115f691c2, Rosen Classroom) Rosen Publishing Group, Inc., The.
—Jackson's Surprise Party: Shapes & Their Attributes. 2013. (InfoMax Math Readers Ser.). (ENG.). 24p. (J). (gr. 1-2). pap. 49.50 *(978-1-4777-2205-3(X),* Rosen Classroom) Rosen Publishing Group, Inc., The.
Carson-Dellosa Publishing Staff. Shapes, Grades PK - K. 2010. (Home Workbooks Ser.: 18). (ENG.). 64p. (gr. -1-k). pap. 4.49 *(978-1-60418-764-9(6),* 104333) Carson-Dellosa Publishing, LLC.
Cartogna, Eileen. Jobs Around Town: Learning to Sort & Classify, 1 vol. (Math for the REAL World Ser.). (ENG., Illus.). 8p. (gr. k-1). 2009. pap. 5.15 *(978-0-8239-8910-2(0),* 46186454-1f29-4ea0-a646-f19141e6c3cc) 2004. 29.95 *(978-0-8239-7629-4(7))* Rosen Publishing Group, Inc., The.
Cartonia, Lucia. What Shape Is It?, 1 vol. 2008. (Real Life Readers Ser.). (ENG.). 8p. (gr. k-1). pap. 5.15 *(978-1-4042-7985-8(7),* 37ff6634-74c9-430f-b580-d25e3bd993c9, Rosen Classroom) Rosen Publishing Group, Inc., The.
Chabbert, Ingrid & Beal, Marjorie. In Shape. 2017. (ENG., Illus.). 18p. (J). bds. 14.95 *(978-1-58423-656-6(6),* 09094aad-6275-4fc3-a2e0-63b4c11cd321) Gingko Pr., Inc.
Chapman, Joan. Heavy & Light: Learning to Compare Weights of Objects, 1 vol. 2010. (Math for the REAL World Ser.). (ENG., Illus.). 8p. (gr. k-1). pap. 5.15 *(978-0-8239-8844-0(9),* d813d4e2-b543-4c4e-97a3-f529b5258d53) Rosen Publishing Group, Inc., The.
Chedru, Delphine. Who's the Biggest? 2018. (ENG., Illus.). 32p. (J). (gr. -1-k). 12.95 *(978-0-500-65149-0(3),* 565149) Thames & Hudson.
Christian, Cheryl. What's in My Toybox? Spanish/English, 1 vol. Ericsson, Annie Beth, illus. 2009. (ENG.). 32p. (J). bds. 6.25 *(978-1-59572-179-2(7))* Star Bright Bks., Inc.
Clark Sawyer, J. Patterns in the City. 2015. (J). lib. bdg. 28.50 *(978-1-62724-336-0(4))* Bearport Publishing Co., Inc.
—Patterns in the Park. 2015. (J). lib. bdg. 28.50 *(978-1-62724-339-1(9))* Bearport Publishing Co., Inc.
Cleary, Brian P. Windows, Rings, & Grapes — a Look at Different Shapes. Gable, Brian, illus. (Math Is CATegorical (r) Ser.). (ENG.). 32p. (J). (gr. k-3). 2011. pap. 8.99 *(978-1-58013-846-8(2),* a4b8f86d-5fcc-4209-ab97-c3d86163a16c) 2009. 16.95 *(978-0-8225-7879-6(4),* 3346d996-66b4-4020-8faf-7a53aa9d556a) Lerner Publishing Group. (Millbrook Pr.).
—Windows, Rings, & Grapes - A Look at Different Shapes. Gable, Brian, illus. 2011. (Math Is CATegorical Ser.). pap. 39.62 *(978-0-7613-8360-4(3),* Millbrook Pr.) Lerner Publishing Group.
Clement, Rod. Counting on Frank, 1 vol. 2019. (Counting on Frank Ser.). (ENG.). 32p. (J). (gr. 1-3). pap. 10.50 *(978-1-5382-4973-4(1))* Stevens, Gareth Publishing LLLP.
Cocagne, Marie-Pascale. The Big Book of Shapes. Stevens-Marzo, Bridget, illus. 2009. (ENG.). 60p. (J). (gr. -1-3). 15.95 *(978-1-85437-851-4(1))* Tate Publishing, Ltd. GBR. Dist: Abrams, Inc.
Cohen, Marina. 3-D Shapes. 2010. (My Path to Math Ser.). (ENG.). 24p. (J). (gr. k-3). *(978-0-7787-6779-4(5));* pap. *(978-0-7787-6788-6(4))* Crabtree Publishing Co.
Coirault, Christine, illus. My First Book of Learning. 2009. (J). *(978-1-74089-930-7(X))* Fog City Pr.
Colors & Shapes. rev. ed. 2007. (ENG., Illus.). 28p. (J). (gr. -1-1). 16.99 *(978-1-59069-505-0(4),* 1C1000) Studio Mouse LLC.
Connelly, Neil O. Shapes. Thornburgh, Rebecca, illus. 10p. (J). (gr. -1). bds. 3.95 *(978-1-58989-002-2(7))* Thurman Hse., LLC.
Cornell, Kari. Goldilocks & the Three Pancakes: A Story of Shapes, Numbers, & Friendship. Sevig, Kirsten, illus. 2016. 32p. (J). pap. *(978-0-87659-706-4(1))* Gryphon Hse., Inc.
Coss, Lauren. Let's Sort by Size. 2014. (21st Century Basic Skills Library: Sorting Ser.). (ENG., Illus.). 24p. (J). (gr. k-3). 26.35 *(978-1-63137-635-1(7),* 205323) Cherry Lake Publishing.
—Let's Sort Shapes. 2014. (21st Century Basic Skills Library: Sorting Ser.). (ENG., Illus.). 24p. (J). (gr. k-3). 26.35 *(978-1-63137-632-0(2),* 205311) Cherry Lake Publishing.
Cox, Tracey M. Shaping up the Year. Bell, Samantha, illus. 2009. 24p. pap. 10.95 *(978-1-935137-73-3(5))* Guardian Angel Publishing, Inc.
Cuxart, Bernadette. Modeling Clay with 3 Basic Shapes: Model More Than 40 Animals with Teardrops, Balls, & Worms. 2016. (ENG., Illus.). 96p. (J). (gr. 2-7). pap. 12.99 *(978-1-4380-0908-7(9))* Sourcebooks, Inc.
Dale, Jay. I Am Big. Gulliver, Amanda, illus. 2012. (Engage Literacy Magenta Ser.). (ENG.). 16p. (J). (gr. k-2). pap. 36.94 *(978-1-4296-8875-8(0),* 18333); pap. 6.99 *(978-1-4296-8874-1(2),* 119940) Capstone. (Capstone Pr.).
Danielson, Christopher. Which One Doesn't Belong? 2019. (ENG.). 36p. (J). (gr. k-1). 17.96 *(978-1-64310-948-0(0))* Penworthy Co., LLC, The.
—Which One Doesn't Belong? A Shapes Book. 2016. (ENG., Illus.). 36p. (gr. k-12). stu. ed. 20.00 *(978-1-62531-060-4(3))* Stenhouse Pubs.
—Which One Doesn't Belong? Playing with Shapes. 2019. (Illus.). 40p. (J). (gr. -1-3). lib. bdg. 15.99 *(978-1-58089-944-4(7))* Charlesbridge Publishing, Inc.
Davis, Bela. Diseños en el Parque. 2018. (¡Diseños Divertidos! (Patterns Are Fun!) Ser.).Tr. of Patterns at the Park. (SPA.). 24p. (J). (gr. -1-2). lib. bdg. 31.36 *(978-1-5321-8374-4(7),* 29941, Abdo Kids) ABDO Publishing Co.
—Diseños en la Escuela. 2018. (¡Diseños Divertidos! (Patterns Are Fun!) Ser.).Tr. of Patterns at School. (SPA.). 24p. (J). (gr. -1-2). lib. bdg. 31.36 *(978-1-5321-8373-7(9),* 29939, Abdo Kids) ABDO Publishing Co.
—Patterns at School. 2018. (Patterns Are Fun! Ser.). (ENG., Illus.). 24p. (J). (gr. -1-2). lib. bdg. 31.36 *(978-1-5321-0793-1(5),* 28147, Abdo Kids) ABDO Publishing Co.
—Patterns at the Park. 2018. (Patterns Are Fun! Ser.). (ENG., Illus.). 24p. (J). (gr. -1-2). lib. bdg. 31.36 *(978-1-5321-0794-8(3),* 28149, Abdo Kids) ABDO Publishing Co.
de Alba, Laura, tr. Caritas Felices. 2007. (Disney Winnie the Pooh (SilverDolphin) Ser.). (Illus.). 8p. (J). (gr. -1). bds. *(978-970-718-391-9(8),* Silver Dolphin en Español) Advanced Marketing, S. de R. L. de C. V.
de Klerk, Roger, illus. Foxy Learns Colors, 1 vol. 2009. (Foxy Learns Ser.). (ENG.). 16p. (J). pap. 4.95 *(978-1-59496-181-6(6))* Teora USA LLC.
—Foxy Learns Shapes, 1 vol. 2009. (Foxy Learns Ser.). (ENG.). 16p. (J). pap. 4.95 *(978-1-59496-179-3(4))* Teora USA LLC.
—Foxy Learns to Add, 1 vol. 2009. (Foxy Learns Ser.). (ENG.). 16p. (J). pap. 4.95 *(978-1-59496-178-6(6))* Teora USA LLC.
Deen, Marilyn. Taking Shape, 1 vol. 2011. (Wonder Readers Fluent Level Ser.). (ENG.). 16p. (gr. -1-2). (J). pap. 6.25 *(978-1-4296-7936-7(0),* 118268); pap. 35.94 *(978-1-4296-8165-0(9))* Capstone. (Capstone Pr.).
—Tiling Shapes. 2011. (Wonder Readers Fluent Level Ser.). (ENG.). 16p. (gr. -1-2). pap. 35.94 *(978-1-4296-8188-9(8),* Capstone Pr.) Capstone.
Del Moral, S., tr. Formas. 2006. (Disney Learning (Silver Dolphin en Espanol) Ser.). (Illus.). 22p. (J). (gr. -1). *(978-970-718-429-9(9),* Silver Dolphin en Español) Advanced Marketing, S. de R. L. de C. V.
Del Moral, Susana. El Juego de las Formas. Zaidi, Nadeem, illus. 2005. (Baby Einstein: Libros de Carton Ser.). (SPA.). 6p. (J). (gr. -1). bds. *(978-970-718-303-2(9),* Silver Dolphin en Español) Advanced Marketing, S. de R. L. de C. V.
Demitri, Alyssa. I See Shapes, 1 vol. 2012. (InfoMax Readers Ser.). (ENG., Illus.). 16p. (J). (gr. k-k). pap. 7.00 *(978-1-4488-8637-1(6),* 1f5edae7-4519-4d53-b986-e3788743a0c2, Rosen Classroom) Rosen Publishing Group, Inc., The.
Deneux, Xavier. TouchThinkLearn: Shapes. 2014. (Touch Think Learn Ser.). (ENG., Illus.). 20p. (J). (gr. -1 — 1). bds. 15.99 *(978-1-4521-1727-0(6))* Chronicle Bks. LLC.
Dicmas, Courtney. Shapes. Dicmas, Courtney, illus. 2017. (Wild! Concepts Ser.: 4). (Illus.). 14p. (J). spiral bd. *(978-1-84643-994-0(9))* Child's Play International Ltd.
Dilkes, D. H. I See Circles, 1 vol. 2010. (All about Shapes Ser.). (ENG., Illus.). 24p. (-1). pap. 10.35 *(978-1-59845-150-4(2),* 10b01976-a6d6-4051-b6bd-9ccfe79b22ea, Enslow Publishing) Enslow Publishing, LLC.
—I See Ovals, 1 vol. 2010. (All about Shapes Ser.). (ENG., Illus.). 24p. (gr. -1-1). lib. bdg. 25.27 *(978-0-7660-3800-4(9),* f0f62aa2-54b2-41b7-bc6d-36f9989ddf51, Enslow Publishing) Enslow Publishing, LLC.
—I See Rectangles, 1 vol. 2010. (All about Shapes Ser.). (ENG., Illus.). 24p. (-1). pap. 10.35 *(978-1-59845-152-8(9),* 20952685-74b3-4107-8285-5b773de4b53d); (gr. -1-1). lib. bdg. 25.27 *(978-0-7660-3801-1(7),* 61e2f5c5-1a2a-4469-b11e-88f0993a2a49) Enslow Publishing, LLC. (Enslow Publishing).
—I See Squares, 1 vol. 2010. (All about Shapes Ser.). (ENG., Illus.). 24p. (-1). pap. 10.35 *(978-1-59845-153-5(7),* a28e566c-f936-4893-9245-65426e88849f); (gr. -1-1). lib. bdg. 25.27 *(978-0-7660-3802-8(5),* 0aad2095-fc0f-49bb-aabd-fa174abbbb32) Enslow Publishing, LLC. (Enslow Publishing).
—I See Stars, 1 vol. 2010. (All about Shapes Ser.). (ENG., Illus.). 24p. (-1). pap. 10.35 *(978-1-59845-154-2(5),* 4c0acc72-671d-4ddf-9f0b-4edeac0244b6); (gr. -1-1). lib. bdg. 25.27 *(978-0-7660-3803-5(3),* 82b68912-a7d0-43ac-acbd-70969cf17239) Enslow Publishing, LLC. (Enslow Publishing).
—I See Triangles, 1 vol. 2010. (All about Shapes Ser.). (ENG., Illus.). 24p. (-1). pap. 10.35 *(978-1-59845-155-9(3),* 4e4b1a07-9e95-4d7f-b33b-67d149774f99); (gr. -1-1). lib. bdg. 25.27 *(978-0-7660-3804-2(1),* d7224264-a77c-4de2-b4d6-4cf4b7182f14) Enslow Publishing, LLC. (Enslow Publishing).
Dingles, Molly. Crescent Kitchen. Brodie, Neale, illus. 2006. (Community of Shapes Ser.). (J). *(978-1-59646-049-2(0))* Dingles & Co.
—Crescent Kitchen: Cocina de Medialuna. Brodie, Neale, illus. 2006. (ENG & SPA.). (J). 21.65 *(978-1-59646-050-8(4))* Dingles & Co.
—Diamond Downhill. Dobson, Len, illus. 2005. (Community of Shapes Ser.). 32p. (J). pap. 10.95 *(978-1-59646-240-3(X));* lib. bdg. 21.65 *(978-1-59646-043-0(1));* per. 10.95 *(978-1-59646-241-0(8))* Dingles & Co.
—Diamond Downhill/Cuesta abajo en forma de Rombo. Dobson, Len, illus. 2005. (Community of Shapes Ser.).Tr. of Cuesta abajo en forma de Rombo. (ENG & SPA.). 32p. (J). pap. 10.95 *(978-1-59646-242-7(6));* lib. bdg. 20.65 *(978-1-59646-044-7(X));* per. 10.95 *(978-1-59646-243-4(4))* Dingles & Co.
—Oval Opera. Brodie, Neale, illus. 2006. (Community of Shapes Ser.). 29p. (J). *(978-1-59646-047-8(4))* Dingles & Co.
—Oval Opera: Ópera de óvalos. Brodie, Neale, illus. 2006. (SPA & ENG.). (J). *(978-1-59646-048-5(2))* Dingles & Co.
—Rectangle Ranch. Dobson, Len, illus. 2005. (Community of Shapes Ser.). 32p. (J). pap. 10.95 *(978-1-59646-244-1(2));* lib. bdg. 21.65 *(978-1-59646-035-5(0));* per. 10.95 *(978-1-59646-245-8(0))* Dingles & Co.
—Rectangle Ranch/Rancho Rectangular. Dobson, Len, illus. 2005. (Community of Shapes Ser.).Tr. of Rancho Rectangular. (ENG & SPA.). 32p. (J). pap. 10.95 *(978-1-59646-246-5(9));* lib. bdg. 20.65 *(978-1-59646-036-2(9));* per. 10.95 *(978-1-59646-247-2(7))* Dingles & Co.
—Seaside Circles. Brodie, Neale, illus. 2006. (Community of Shapes Ser.). 32p. (J). pap. 10.95 *(978-1-59646-256-4(6));* lib. bdg. 21.65 *(978-1-59646-033-1(4));* per. 10.95 *(978-1-59646-257-1(4))* Dingles & Co.
—Seaside Circles/Círculos a la orilla del Mar. Brodie, Neale, illus. 2006. (Community of Shapes Ser.).Tr. of Círculos a la orilla del Mar. (ENG & SPA.). 32p. (J). pap. 10.95 *(978-1-59646-258-8(2));* lib. bdg. 21.65 *(978-1-59646-034-8(2))* Dingles & Co.
—Seaside Circles/Círculos a la orilla del Mar. Brodie, Neal, illus. 2006. (Community of Shapes Ser.).Tr. of Círculos a la orilla del Mar. (ENG & SPA.). 32p. (J). per. 10.95 *(978-1-59646-259-5(0))* Dingles & Co.
—Star Ship. Brodie, Neale, illus. 2006. (Community of Shapes Ser.). 29p. (J). *(978-1-59646-039-3(3))* Dingles & Co.
—Star Ship: Barco de Estrellas. Brodie, Neale, illus. 2006. (SPA & ENG.). (J). *(978-1-59646-040-9(7))* Dingles & Co.
—Sweet Hearts. Brodie, Neale, illus. 2006. (Community of Shapes Ser.). (J). *(978-1-59646-037-9(7))* Dingles & Co.
—Sweet Hearts: Dulce Corazón. Brodie, Neale, illus. 2006. (SPA & ENG.). (J). *(978-1-59646-038-6(5))* Dingles & Co.
—Town Squares. Brodie, Neale, illus. 2006. (Community of Shapes Ser.). 32p. (J). pap. 10.95 *(978-1-59646-264-9(7));* lib. bdg. 21.65 *(978-1-59646-041-6(5));* per. 10.95 *(978-1-59646-265-6(5))* Dingles & Co.
—Town Squares/Cuadrados en la Plaza. Brodie, Neale, illus. 2006. (Community of Shapes Ser.).Tr. of Cuadrados en la Plaza. (ENG & SPA.). 32p. (J). pap. 10.95 *(978-1-59646-266-3(3));* lib. bdg. 21.65 *(978-1-59646-042-3(3));* per. 10.95 *(978-1-59646-267-0(1))* Dingles & Co.
—Triangle Trail: Sendero de Triángulos. 2005. (ENG & SPA., Illus.). 32p. (J). lib. bdg. 21.65 *(978-1-59646-046-1(6))* Dingles & Co.
Disney Books. Disney Parks Presents: It's a Small World: Shapes! 2018. (Disney Parks Presents Ser.). (ENG., Illus.). 20p. (J). (gr. -1 — 1). bds. 7.99 *(978-1-368-03930-7(8),* Disney Press Books) Disney Publishing Worldwide.
Disney Staff, contrib. by. Write, Slide & Learn Disney Mickey Mouse Clubhouse: Colors & Shapes. 2011. (Disney Write, Slide & Learn Ser.). 12p. (J). 9.99 *(978-1-74183-850-3(9))* Hinkler Bks. Pty, Ltd. AUS. Dist: Ideals Pubns.
DK. DK Braille: Shapes. 2016. (DK Braille Bks.). (ENG., Illus.). 18p. (J). (-k). bds. 16.99 *(978-1-4654-3612-2(X),* DK Children) Dorling Kindersley Publishing, Inc.
—My First Shapes. 2017. (My First Board Bks.). (ENG., Illus.). 36p. (J). (— 1). bds. 6.99 *(978-1-4654-6082-0(9),* DK Children) Dorling Kindersley Publishing, Inc.
—My First Touch & Feel Picture Cards: Colors & Shapes. 2018. (My First Board Bks.). (ENG.). 17p. (J). (— 1). 12.99 *(978-1-4654-6816-1(1),* DK Children) Dorling Kindersley Publishing, Inc.
Does It Belong? 2003. (Preschool Ser.). (ENG.). (J). cd-rom 19.99 *(978-1-58947-903-6(3))* School Zone Publishing Co.
Domiano, Gloria. Ship Shapes: Identify & Describe Shapes. 2013. (Rosen Math Readers Ser.). (ENG.). 16p. (J). (gr. k-1). pap. 42.00 *(978-1-4777-1666-3(1));* (Illus.). pap. 7.00 *(978-1-4777-1665-6(3),* 009e772f-1da8-472c-9149-9c657f2b92ae) Rosen Publishing Group, Inc., The. (Rosen Classroom).
Dorling Kindersley Publishing Staff. Shapes. 2008. (Gymboree Play & Music Ser.). (ENG., Illus.). 24p. (J). (gr. -1). bds. *(978-1-55470-040-0(0))* Me to We.
Draze, Dianne. Attribute Block - Thinking Activities - Sequences. 2005. (ENG.). 32p. pap. 9.95 *(978-1-59363-053-9(0))* Prufrock Pr.
Dudley, Linda S. Aunt Linda's Shape Book. Neal, Jill Faith, illus. 2007. (ENG.). 32p. per. 24.95 *(978-1-4241-8618-1(8))* America Star Bks.
Eagan, Mary. Alexee's Animals from A-Z, 1 vol. King, Cheryl, illus. 2010. 30p. 24.95 *(978-1-4489-3967-1(4))* PublishAmerica, Inc.
Earle, Erin. Surprise Party!, 1 vol. 2013. (Core Math Skills: Measurement & Geometry Ser.). (ENG.). 24p. (J). (gr. 1-1). 26.27 *(978-1-4777-2230-5(0),* 197d47e7-4295-4b0f-9749-a6984070f523); pap. 8.25 *(978-1-4777-2103-2(7),* a7525908-95f3-4f8f-9414-17bdf4f66b68) Rosen Publishing Group, Inc., The. (Rosen Classroom).
—Surprise Party! Shapes & Their Attributes. 2013. (Rosen Math Readers Ser.). (ENG.). 24p. (J). (gr. 1-2). pap. 49.50 *(978-1-4777-2104-9(5),* Rosen Classroom) Rosen Publishing Group, Inc., The.
Eck, Kristin. Shapes in My House. 2004. (Look-And-Learn Books). (Illus.). (J). lib. bdg. 8.95 *(978-1-4042-2699-9(0),* PowerKids Pr.) Rosen Publishing Group, Inc., The.
Editorial Staff, Gareth. I Know Big & Small, 1 vol. 2005. (I'm Ready for Math Ser.). (ENG., Illus.). 16p. (gr. k-1). pap. 6.30 *(978-0-8368-6479-3(4),* 86df821c-dd7d-463a-aa7f-883645438b37, Weekly Reader Leveled Readers) Stevens, Gareth Publishing LLLP.
—I Know Big & Small / Grande y Pequeño, 1 vol. 2005. (I'm Ready for Math / Ya Puedo Aprender Matemáticas Ser.). (ENG & SPA., Illus.). 16p. (gr. k-1). pap. 6.30 *(978-0-8368-6489-2(1),* 882fe47c-8818-465c-a1fd-c28e67b892b7, Weekly Reader Leveled Readers) Stevens, Gareth Publishing LLLP.
—I Know Shapes / Las Figuras, 1 vol. 2005. (I'm Ready for Math / Ya Puedo Aprender Matemáticas Ser.). (ENG & SPA., Illus.). 16p. (gr. k-1). pap. 6.30 *(978-0-8368-6492-2(1),* 8bfcb1fc-28f5-4645-953c-593b59988876, Weekly Reader Leveled Readers) Stevens, Gareth Publishing LLLP.
Ellis, Belinda. Baby See-A-Shape Things That Go! 2005. (Baby See a Shape Ser.). (Illus.). 10p. (gr. -1 — 1). bds. *(978-1-84610-022-2(4))* Make Believe Ideas.
Emberley, Ed. The Wing on a Flea. 2015. (ENG., Illus.). 48p. 17.95 *(978-1-62326-058-3(2))* AMMO Bks., LLC.
Evanson, Ashley. Paris: A Book of Shapes. Evanson, Ashley, illus. 2015. (Hello, World Ser.). (Illus.). 16p. (J). (— 1). bds. 7.99 *(978-0-448-48915-5(5),* Penguin Workshop) Penguin Young Readers Group.
Falk, Liane. Spots. 2009. 24p. pap. 13.50 *(978-1-4389-8724-8(2))* AuthorHouse.
Feldman, Jean. Highway Letters, Numbers & Shapes: PreK-1. 2010. 80p. pap. 22.99 *(978-1-61601-036-2(3))* Creative Teaching Pr., Inc.
Felix, Rebecca. Patterns at School. 2015. (21st Century Basic Skills Library: Patterns All Around Ser.). (ENG., Illus.). 24p. (J). (gr. k-3). pap. 12.79 *(978-1-63188-934-9(6),* 205997) Cherry Lake Publishing.
Fish, Simon. Silly Shapes. 2012. (ENG.). (J). pap. *(978-1-4675-0898-8(5))* Independent Pub.
Flatt, Lizann. Shaping up Summer. Barron, Ashley, illus. 2018. (Math in Nature Ser.: 4). (ENG.). 32p. (J). (gr. k-4). pap. 8.95 *(978-1-77147-163-3(8))* Owlkids Bks. Inc. CAN. Dist: Publishers Group West (PGW).
—Sorting Through Spring. Barron, Ashley, illus. 2018. (Math in Nature Ser.: 2). (ENG.). 32p. (J). (gr. 1-4). pap. 8.95 *(978-1-77147-153-4(0))* Owlkids Bks. Inc. CAN. Dist: Publishers Group West (PGW).
Flowerpot Press Staff, contrib. by. Sockheadz: Shapes. 2013. (ENG., Illus.). 20p. (J). (gr. -1-k). 6.99 *(978-1-77093-596-9(7))* Flowerpot Children's Pr. Inc. CAN. Dist: Cardinal Pubs. Group.
Formas. (Coleccion Mi Primer Libro). (SPA., Illus.). (J). 13.95 *(978-84-207-3781-2(X),* ANY877) Grupo Anaya, S.A. ESP. Dist: Continental Bk. Co., Inc.
Formas. (Coleccion Libritos Acordeon). (SPA., Illus.). 10p. (J). pap. 5.50 *(978-950-11-0793-7(0),* SGM930) Sigmar ARG. Dist: Continental Bk. Co., Inc.
Formas (Shapes) (SPA.). (J). 6.95 *(978-968-419-056-6(5))* Grijalbo, Editorial MEX. Dist: AIMS International Bks., Inc.
Formas y Colores. (Coleccion Picaros Peluchines). (SPA.). (J). 5.50 *(978-950-11-0400-4(1),* SGM400) Sigmar ARG. Dist: Continental Bk. Co., Inc.
Forte, Imogene. Ready to Learn Shapes & Colors. 2003. (Illus.). 64p. per. 7.95 *(978-0-86530-593-9(5))* Incentive Pubns., Inc.
Fretland VanVoorst, Jenny. Las Formas en la Ciudad. 2015.Tr. of Shapes in the City. (SPA., Illus.). 24p. (J). lib. bdg. *(978-1-62031-246-9(8),* Bullfrog Bks.) Jump! Inc.
—Las Formas en la Escuela. 2015.Tr. of Shapes at School. (SPA., Illus.). 24p. (J). lib. bdg. *(978-1-62031-248-3(4),* Bullfrog Bks.) Jump! Inc.
—Las Formas en la Playa. 2015.Tr. of Shapes by the Sea. (SPA., Illus.). 24p. (J). lib. bdg. *(978-1-62031-249-0(2),* Bullfrog Bks.) Jump! Inc.
—Shapes at School. 2015. (Illus.). 24p. (J). lib. bdg. *(978-1-62031-203-2(4),* Bullfrog Bks.) Jump! Inc.
—Shapes by the Sea. 2015. (Illus.). 24p. (J). lib. bdg. *(978-1-62031-202-5(6),* Bullfrog Bks.) Jump! Inc.
—Shapes in the City. 2015. (Illus.). 24p. (J). lib. bdg. *(978-1-62031-200-1(X),* Bullfrog Bks.) Jump! Inc.
—Shapes on the Farm. 2015. 24p. (J). lib. bdg. *(978-1-62031-201-8(8),* Bullfrog Bks.) Jump! Inc.
Fried, Miriam. My Jelly Bean Book. 2005. (Illus.). (J). *(978-1-57400-049-8(7))* Data Trace Publishing, Co.
Gaarder-Juntti, Oona. Shapes at Home, 1 vol. 2013. (Shapes Everywhere Ser.). (ENG.). 24p. (J). (gr. k-4). lib. bdg. 32.79 *(978-1-61783-411-0(4),* 13326, Super SandCastle) ABDO Publishing Co.
—Shapes at School, 1 vol. 2013. (Shapes Everywhere Ser.). (ENG.). 24p. (J). (gr. k-4). lib. bdg. 32.79 *(978-1-61783-412-7(2),* 13328, Super SandCastle) ABDO Publishing Co.
—Shapes in Food, 1 vol. 2013. (Shapes Everywhere Ser.). (ENG.). 24p. (J). (gr. k-4). lib. bdg. 32.79 *(978-1-61783-413-4(0),* 13330, Super SandCastle) ABDO Publishing Co.
—Shapes in Nature, 1 vol. 2013. (Shapes Everywhere Ser.). (ENG.). 24p. (J). (gr. k-4). lib. bdg. 32.79 *(978-1-61783-414-1(9),* 13332, Super SandCastle) ABDO Publishing Co.

—Shapes in Sports, 1 vol. 2013. (Shapes Everywhere Ser.). (ENG.). 24p. (J). (gr. k-4). lib. bdg. 32.79 *(978-1-61783-415-8(7)*, 13334, Super SandCastle) ABDO Publishing Co.
—Shapes on a Farm, 1 vol. 2013. (Shapes Everywhere Ser.). (ENG.). 24p. (J). (gr. k-4). lib. bdg. 32.79 *(978-1-61783-416-5(5)*, 13336, Super SandCastle) ABDO Publishing Co.
Galvin, Laura Gates. Peep's Shapes. 2006. (Peep & the Big Wide World Ser.). (ENG., Illus.). 24p. (J). (gr. -1-k). 15.99 *(978-1-59249-521-4(4)*, 1C304) Soundprints.
George, Chris. I Want Pizza, 1 vol. 2017. (Early Concepts Ser.). (ENG.). 24p. (gr. 1-1). pap. 9.25 *(978-1-5081-6213-1(1)*, 63f4089d-71ec-408c-a4d4-b3db515063ad, PowerKids Pr.) Rosen Publishing Group, Inc., The.
Gerstein, Sherry. Imagination Vacation: A Color-Foil Shapes Book. Bennett, Andy, illus. 2006. 14p. (J). (gr. -1-3). bds. 6.95 *(978-1-57791-261-3(6))* Brighter Minds Children's Publishing.
Ghigna, Charles. Shapes Are Everywhere! Jatkowska, Ag, illus. 2013. 24p. (J). pap. *(978-1-4795-1929-3(4)*, Picture Window Bks.) Capstone.
Giles, Angela & Award, Anna. Patterns. 2017. (Illus.). 10p. (J). bds. 9.00 *(978-1-909763-45-6(4))* Award Pubns. Ltd. GBR. Dist: Parkwest Pubns., Inc.
Giles, Angela & Picthall, Chez. Colours & Shapes. Calver, Paul, illus. 2015. (ENG.). 6p. (J). bds. 9.99 *(978-1-909763-42-5(X))* Award Pubns. Ltd. GBR. Dist: Parkwest Pubns., Inc.
Ginsburg, Herbert P., et al. Favorite Shapes. 2003. (Illus.). 9.95 *(978-0-7690-3043-2(2))* Seymour, Dale Pubns.
Giulieri, Anne. Here Is a Robot. 2012. (Engage Literacy Magenta Ser.). (ENG.). 16p. (J). (gr. k-2). pap. 36.94 *(978-1-4296-8849-9(1)*, 18320); (Illus.). pap. 6.99 *(978-1-4296-8848-2(3)*, 119927) Capstone. (Capstone Pr.).
—Look at the Picture. 2012. (Engage Literacy Magenta Ser.). (ENG.). 16p. (J). (gr. k-2). pap. 36.94 *(978-1-4296-8859-8(9)*, 18325); (Illus.). pap. 6.99 *(978-1-4296-8858-1(0)*, 119932) Capstone. (Capstone Pr.).
Glaser, Byron & Higashi, Sandra. Zolocolor! Doodling Between Black & White. Glaser, Byron & Higashi, Sandra, illus. 2011. (ENG., Illus.). 96p. (J). 7.99 *(978-1-4424-2261-2(0)*, Little Simon) Little Simon.
Gobo, creator. Little Learners Ready to Read & Write. 2007. (Magnix Little Learners Ser.). (Illus.). 40p. (J). (gr. -1-3). 14.95 *(978-1-932915-44-0(3))* Sandvik Innovations, LLC.
Gordon, Sharon. Big, Small, 1 vol. (Just the Opposite Ser.). (ENG.). 24p. (gr. k-1). 2008. pap. 9.23 *(978-0-7614-3279-1(5)*, 00295524-dc0a-4408-b591-c5b591e86b01) 2003. (Illus.). lib. bdg. 25.50 *(978-0-7614-1568-8(8)*, b36c3d15-7970-4bd8-8e73-342bf4c70321) Cavendish Square Publishing LLC.
—Grande, Pequeno / Big, Small, 1 vol. 2008. (Exactamente lo Opuesto / Just the Opposite Ser.). (ENG & SPA., Illus.). 24p. (gr. k-1). lib. bdg. 25.50 *(978-0-7614-2445-1(8)*, c7e50626-85f5-4c65-948e-adb87f3dfcc2) Cavendish Square Publishing LLC.
Gould, Jane. In the Garden. rev. ed. 2011. (Mathematics in the Real World Ser.). 32p. (gr. k-1). pap. 9.99 *(978-1-4333-3431-3(3))* Teacher Created Materials, Inc.
Greathouse, Lisa. Farm Animals: Classifying & Sorting. rev. ed. 2011. (Mathematics in the Real World Ser.). (ENG.). 32p. (gr. k-1). pap. 9.99 *(978-1-4333-3442-9(9))* Teacher Created Materials, Inc.
—Games Are Fun. rev. ed. 2011. (Mathematics in the Real World Ser.). (ENG.). 32p. (gr. k-1). pap. 9.99 *(978-1-4333-3437-5(2))* Teacher Created Materials, Inc.
—Recess Time: Patterns. rev. ed. 2011. (Mathematics in the Real World Ser.). (ENG.). 32p. (gr. k-1). pap. 9.99 *(978-1-4333-3436-8(4))* Teacher Created Materials, Inc.
—Wild Animals, Level K. rev. ed. 2011. (Mathematics in the Real World Ser.). (ENG.). 32p. (gr. k-1). pap. 9.99 *(978-1-4333-3443-6(7))* Teacher Created Materials, Inc.
Gunzi, Christiane. Las Formas. 2004. (My Very First Look At Ser.). (SPA., Illus.). 24p. (J). (gr. -1-k). pap. 5.95 *(978-1-58728-431-1(6))* Cooper Square Publishing Llc.
Gunzl, Christiane. Shapes. 2014. (ENG., Illus.). 20p. pap. 8.95 *(978-1-907604-25-6(1))* Award Pubns. Ltd. GBR. Dist: Parkwest Pubns., Inc.
Haas, Kristin. The Shape Family Babies, 1 vol. Bersani, Shennen, illus. 2014. (ENG.). 32p. (J). (gr. -1-3). 17.95 *(978-1-62855-211-9(5))* Arbordale Publishing.
—The Shape Family Babies: Spanish, 1 vol. Bersani, Shennen, illus. 2014.Tr. of Shape Family Babies. (SPA.). 32p. (J). (gr. k-1). pap. 11.95 *(978-1-62855-229-4(8)*, 7549eeb9-cd18-4d9e-85a8-4759621d2e4f) Arbordale Publishing.
Haley, Charly. Ella Goes to the Park: A Book about Shapes. 2018. (My Day Readers Ser.). (ENG.). 24p. (J). (gr. -1-2). lib. bdg. 32.79 *(978-1-5038-2487-4(X)*, 212353) Child's World, Inc, The.
Hamilton, Laura. Cones, 1 vol. Mitter, Kathryn, illus. 2012. (Everyday 3-D Shapes Ser.). (ENG.). 24p. (J). (gr. -1-2). lib. bdg. 31.36 *(978-1-61641-872-4(9)*, 6867, Looking Glass Library) Magic Wagon.
—Cubes, 1 vol. Mitter, Kathryn, illus. 2012. (Everyday 3-D Shapes Ser.). (ENG.). 24p. (J). (gr. -1-2). lib. bdg. 31.36 *(978-1-61641-873-1(7)*, 6869, Looking Glass Library) Magic Wagon.
—Cylinders, 1 vol. Mitter, Kathryn, illus. 2012. (Everyday 3-D Shapes Ser.). (ENG.). 24p. (J). (gr. -1-2). lib. bdg. 31.36 *(978-1-61641-874-8(5)*, 6871, Looking Glass Library) Magic Wagon.
—Prisms, 1 vol. Mitter, Kathryn, illus. 2012. (Everyday 3-D Shapes Ser.). (ENG.). 24p. (J). (gr. -1-2). lib. bdg. 31.36 *(978-1-61641-875-5(3)*, 6873, Looking Glass Library) Magic Wagon.
—Pyramids, 1 vol. Mitter, Kathryn, illus. 2012. (Everyday 3-D Shapes Ser.). (ENG.). 24p. (J). (gr. -1-2). lib. bdg. 31.36 *(978-1-61641-876-2(1)*, 6875, Looking Glass Library) Magic Wagon.
—Spheres, 1 vol. Mitter, Kathryn, illus. 2012. (Everyday 3-D Shapes Ser.). (ENG.). 24p. (J). (gr. -1-2). lib. bdg. 31.36 *(978-1-61641-877-9(X)*, 6877, Looking Glass Library) Magic Wagon.
Harcourt, creator. I Know Shapes: Math Concept Reader. 2007. (Illus.). (J). pap. 31.53 *(978-0-15-379896-2(3))* Houghton Mifflin Harcourt School Pubs.
Harmon, Minnie P. Golden's Shapes & Colors. 2011. 36p. pap. 21.99 *(978-1-4628-6253-5(5))* Xlibris Corp.
Harris, Beatrice. We Love Cones!, 1 vol. 2018. (Our Favorite Shapes Ser.). (ENG.). 24p. (gr. k-k). 24.27 *(978-1-5382-2867-8(X)*, 1e1ed6bf-cbc7-461e-bdac-ae0a2bed38f0) Stevens, Gareth Publishing LLLP.
—We Love Cubes!, 1 vol. 2018. (Our Favorite Shapes Ser.). (ENG.). 24p. (gr. k-k). 24.27 *(978-1-5382-2868-5(8)*, 0e8026fa-daca-4ab1-8d3e-04e49c2e29b2) Stevens, Gareth Publishing LLLP.
—We Love Cylinders!, 1 vol. 2018. (Our Favorite Shapes Ser.). (ENG.). 24p. (gr. k-k). 24.27 *(978-1-5382-2869-2(6)*, c5cd5be3-19a9-48ce-bc92-c38bb525ac5d) Stevens, Gareth Publishing LLLP.
—We Love Diamonds!, 1 vol. 2017. (Our Favorite Shapes Ser.). (ENG.). 24p. (J). (gr. k-k). pap. 9.15 *(978-1-5382-0989-9(6)*, 7b6fe216-ae8b-4411-8085-34c74917e5f9) Stevens, Gareth Publishing LLLP.
—We Love Ovals!, 1 vol. 2017. (Our Favorite Shapes Ser.). (ENG.). 24p. (J). (gr. k-k). pap. 9.15 *(978-1-5382-0993-6(4)*, 34e8a2fa-55c4-4b2d-8df6-08d80773874a) Stevens, Gareth Publishing LLLP.
Harrison, Lorraine. Flat Shapes, Solid Shapes: Identify & Describe Shapes. 2013. (Rosen Math Readers Ser.). (ENG.). 16p. (J). (gr. k-1). pap. 42.00 *(978-1-4777-1615-1(7))*; (Illus.). pap. 7.00 *(978-1-4777-1614-4(9)*, 829165f7-bab5-4623-afd9-5052b7ee27b2) Rosen Publishing Group, Inc., The. (Rosen Classroom).
Harvey, Jayne. Busy Bugs: A Book about Patterns. Adnet, Bernard, illus. 2003. (Penguin Young Readers, Level 2 Ser.: Level 1). 32p. (J). (gr. 1-2). pap. 4.99 *(978-0-448-43159-8(9)*, Penguin Young Readers) Penguin Young Readers Group.
Heinze, Monica Bacon. A Day with Shapes. Dow, S. B., illus. 2004. (J). *(978-0-9761710-0-3(7))* Paisley Publishing.
Helenek, Sophie. My First Book SHAPES: GOLD Mom's Choice Awards Recipient. 2014. (My First Book Ser.). (ENG., Illus.). 16p. (J). (gr. -1 — 1). bds. 5.99 *(978-0-9894505-1-5(1))* Nursery Bks.
Herbst, Kailee. Who's Short? Who's Tall? Learning to Compare Heights, 1 vol. 2010. (Math for the REAL World Ser.). (ENG., Illus.). 8p. (gr. k-1). pap. 5.15 *(978-0-8239-8856-3(2)*, 9f1eaf25-636a-4b38-8a04-42b66ab68df5) Rosen Publishing Group, Inc., The.
Hewitt, Angie. Colors & Shapes: Touch-And-Trace Early Learning Fun! 2017. (Little Groovers Ser.). (ENG., Illus.). 12p. (J). (— 1). bds. 7.99 *(978-1-5107-0837-2(5)*, Sky Pony Pr.) Skyhorse Publishing Co., Inc.
Hicks, Barbara Jean. I Like Colors. Prap, Lila, illus. 2006. 24p. (J). (gr. -1-3). 9.95 *(978-1-58925-057-4(5))* Tiger Tales.
Holden, Arianne. It's Fun to Learn about Shapes: A Busy Picture Book Full of Fabulous Facts & Things to Do! 2016. (Illus.). 32p. (J). (gr. -1-12). 9.99 *(978-1-86147-709-5(0)*, Armadillo) Anness Publishing GBR. Dist: National Bk. Network.
Holden, Pam. Show Me a Shape, 1 vol. Cooper, Jenny, illus. 2009. (Red Rocket Readers Ser.). (ENG.). 16p. (gr. -1-1). pap. *(978-1-877363-27-6(8)*, Red Rocket Readers) Flying Start Bks.
—Show Me a Shape - BIG BOOK, 1 vol. Cooper, Jenny, illus. 2016. (ENG.). 16p. (-1). pap. *(978-1-77654-160-7(X)*, Red Rocket Readers) Flying Start Bks.
Howells, Tania. Starring Shapes! Howells, Tania, illus. 2015. (ENG., Illus.). 24p. (J). (gr. -1-2). 15.95 *(978-1-55453-743-3(6))* Kids Can Pr., Ltd. CAN. Dist: Hachette Bk. Group.
Hubbard, Ben. Top 10 Biggest. 2010. (Crabtree Contact Ser.). (ENG., Illus.). 32p. (J). (gr. 3-6). lib. bdg. *(978-0-7787-7487-7(2)*, 1308100) Crabtree Publishing Co.
—Top 10 Longest. 2010. (ENG., Illus.). 32p. (J). pap. *(978-0-7787-7510-2(0))*; lib. bdg. *(978-0-7787-7489-1(9))* Crabtree Publishing Co.
—Top 10 Smallest. 2010. (ENG., Illus.). 32p. (J). lib. bdg. *(978-0-7787-7491-4(0))* Crabtree Publishing Co.
Hughes, Mónica. Shapes: Band 01A/Pink a (Collins Big Cat) 2006. (Collins Big Cat Ser.). (ENG., Illus.). 16p. (J). (gr. -1-k). pap. 6.99 *(978-0-00-718649-5(5))* HarperCollins Pubs. Ltd. GBR. Dist: Independent Pubs. Group.
Hughes, Tom. Tall & Short, 1 vol. 2016. (All about Opposites Ser.). (ENG., Illus.). 24p. (gr. k-1). pap. 10.35 *(978-0-7660-8078-2(1)*, 18d911c9-e234-488b-8fd3-2e13d5b296f0) Enslow Publishing, LLC.
—Tight & Loose, 1 vol. 2016. (All about Opposites Ser.). (ENG., Illus.). 24p. (gr. k-1). pap. 10.35 *(978-0-7660-8116-1(8)*, 7f258722-5854-4fa3-9a20-7d895836c511) Enslow Publishing, LLC.
—Wide & Narrow, 1 vol. 2016. (All about Opposites Ser.). (ENG., Illus.). 24p. (gr. k-1). pap. 10.35 *(978-0-7660-8117-8(6)*, 92dc0cf5-7c59-4c64-862d-1ea6a5ea7892) Enslow Publishing, LLC.
Hunt, Darleen L. Samantha Visits Grandpa Geo: Shapes. Komarck, Michael, illus. 2003. (Sherman's Math Corner Ser.). (J). (gr. -1-3). *(978-1-929591-01-5(2))* Reading Rock, Inc.
Hunt, Janie. Shapes. Chrystall, Claire, illus. 2003. (Busy Finger Ser.). 10p. (J). bds. 10.95 *(978-1-57145-938-1(3)*, Silver Dolphin Bks.) Readerlink Distribution Services, LLC.
I Know My Shapes. 2005. (J). pap., stu. ed. 19.95 *(978-1-58970-699-6(4))* Lakeshore Learning Materials.
I Know My Shapes! Big Book Series. 2005. (J). pap. 49.95 *(978-1-58970-698-9(6))* Lakeshore Learning Materials.
Ikids Staff. Shapes. Larranaga, Ana Martin, illus. 2009. (ENG.). 12p. (J). (gr. -1 — 1). bds. 5.99 *(978-1-58476-937-8(8))* Innovative Kids.
—Soft Shapes: Dinosaurs (Baby's First Book + Puzzle) Ski, Jenn, illus. 2010. (ENG.). 8p. (J). (gr. -1 — 1). 10.99 *(978-1-60169-043-2(6))* Innovative Kids.
—Soft Shapes: Trucks (Baby's First Book + Puzzle) Ski, Jenn, illus. 2010. (ENG.). 8p. (J). (gr. -1 — 1). 10.99 *(978-1-60169-044-9(4))* Innovative Kids.
Imperato, Teresa. Trick or Treat! A Halloween Shapes Book. Winston, Jeannie, illus. 2005. 12p. (J). 7.95 *(978-1-58117-325-3(3)*, Intervisual/Piggy Toes) Bendon, Inc.
Innovative Kids Staff. Shapes - Soft Shapes. 2010. (ENG.). 8p. (J). (gr. -1 — 1). 10.99 *(978-1-58476-961-3(0))* Innovative Kids.
Innovative Kids Staff, creator. Soft Shapes - Animals. 2010. (ENG.). 8p. (J). (gr. -1 — 1). 10.99 *(978-1-58476-964-4(5))* Innovative Kids.
—Soft Shapes - Colors. 2010. (ENG.). 8p. (J). (gr. -1 — 1). 10.99 *(978-1-58476-963-7(7))* Innovative Kids.
—Soft Shapes - Counting. 2010. (ENG.). 8p. (J). (gr. -1 — 1). 10.99 *(978-1-58476-962-0(9))* Innovative Kids.
James, Trisha. We Love Prisms!, 1 vol. 2018. (Our Favorite Shapes Ser.). (ENG.). 24p. (gr. k-k). 24.27 *(978-1-5382-2870-8(X)*, 1d6c2e7d-84ac-4a27-bcaa-6dc577b59235) Stevens, Gareth Publishing LLLP.
—We Love Pyramids!, 1 vol. 2018. (Our Favorite Shapes Ser.). (ENG.). 24p. (gr. k-k). 24.27 *(978-1-5382-2871-5(8)*, ab184fc3-41ed-4d00-9c07-e3deb7244a07) Stevens, Gareth Publishing LLLP.
—We Love Spheres!, 1 vol. 2018. (Our Favorite Shapes Ser.). (ENG.). 24p. (gr. k-k). 24.27 *(978-1-5382-2872-2(6)*, 75e0c9fa-56ca-4f5c-8745-e610e14babfd) Stevens, Gareth Publishing LLLP.
Jaramillo, Gloria. Busy Kids' Colors, Shapes & Sizes. Poirier, Nadine, illus. 2008. (Busy Kids Ser.). 36p. (J). (gr. -1-k). bds. 12.99 *(978-2-7641-1677-7(2))* Gardner Pubns.
Jeffries, Joyce. Long & Short, 1 vol. 2013. (Dinosaur School Ser.). (ENG., Illus.). 24p. (gr. k-k). 25.27 *(978-1-4339-8095-4(9)*, 356f2a75-b6db-4c49-8409-ae2a2632b448); pap. 9.15 *(978-1-4339-8096-1(7)*, 2b5c1f5f-24bc-45f7-b42a-9320efd5935e) Stevens, Gareth Publishing LLLP.
—Shapes at School: Identify & Describe Shapes. 2013. (Rosen Math Readers Ser.). (ENG.). 16p. (J). (gr. k-1). pap. 42.00 *(978-1-4777-1588-8(6))*; (Illus.). pap. 7.00 *(978-1-4777-1587-1(8)*, cdde6fe1-fedf-4181-8dc0-84012927b2bf) Rosen Publishing Group, Inc., The. (Rosen Classroom).
Jenkins, Pete. Shapes in Nature. 2018. (I Know Ser.). (ENG., Illus.). 16p. (gr. -1-2). pap. 9.95 *(978-1-64156-227-0(7)*, 9781641562270) Rourke Educational Media.
Jocelyn, Marthe. One Some Many. Slaughter, Tom, illus. 2006. 16p. (J). (gr. k-k). 7.95 *(978-0-88776-789-0(3)*, Tundra Bks.) Tundra Bks. CAN. Dist: Penguin Random Hse. LLC.
—Over Under. Slaughter, Tom, illus. 2005. 24p. (J). (gr. k-k). 15.99 *(978-0-88776-708-1(7)*, Tundra Bks.) Tundra Bks. CAN. Dist: Penguin Random Hse. LLC.
Johanson, Sarah Margaret. Caillou: Parade of Shapes. Sévigny, Eric, illus. 2012. (Puzzle Bks.). (ENG.). 18p. (J). (gr. -1-1). bds. 12.95 *(978-2-89450-839-8(5))* Caillouet, Gerry.
Johnson, Jinny & Woods, Michael. How Big Is a Whale? (Illus.). (J). pap. 18.99 *(978-0-590-24629-3(1))* Scholastic, Inc.
Jones, Otis. Geonopolis, the Shapely City of Geometry. 2003. (ENG., Illus.). 21p. (J). *(978-0-9744123-0-6(9))* Jeb Cool Kids Entertainment, Inc.
Jones, Tammy. Look at the Shapes. 2009. (Sight Word Readers Set A Ser.). (J). 3.49 net. *(978-1-60719-152-0(0))* Newmark Learning LLC.
—What Has Stripes? 2009. (Sight Word Readers Set A Ser.). (J). 3.49 net. *(978-1-60719-151-3(2))* Newmark Learning LLC.
Jordan, Christopher. Hockey Shapes. 2010. (My First NHL Bks.). (ENG., Illus.). 30p. (J). (gr. -1). bds. *(978-1-55168-370-6(9))* Me to We.
—Hockey Shapes. 2011. (My First NHL Book Ser.). (ENG., Illus.). 30p. (J). (-k). bds. 8.99 *(978-1-77049-321-6(2))* Tundra Bks. CAN. Dist: Random Hse., Inc.
Joyce, Jeffrey. Pablo's Paper Crafts, 1 vol. 2013. (Core Math Skills: Measurement & Geometry Ser.). (ENG., Illus.). 24p. (J). (gr. 1-1). 26.27 *(978-1-4777-2232-9(7)*, 59244322-8ca8-46fd-8514-889cc88a51d2, Rosen Classroom) Rosen Publishing Group, Inc., The.
—Pablo's Paper Crafts: Shapes & Their Attributes, 1 vol. 2013. (Rosen Math Readers Ser.). (ENG., Illus.). 24p. (J). (gr. 1-1). pap. 8.25 *(978-1-4777-2049-3(9)*, 093e049e-a4d1-494c-ab81-dbbfe48fd228); pap. 49.50 *(978-1-4777-2050-9(2)*, 1359255) Rosen Publishing Group, Inc., The. (Rosen Classroom).
Kalman, Bobbie. ¿Es Grande O Pequeño? 2008. (SPA.). 24p. (J). pap. *(978-0-7787-8733-4(8))* Crabtree Publishing Co.
—How Does It Look? 2007. (Looking at Nature Ser.). (ENG., Illus.). 24p. (J). (gr. -1-2). pap. *(978-0-7787-3335-5(1))*; lib. bdg. *(978-0-7787-3315-7(7))* Crabtree Publishing Co.
—Is It Big or Small?, 1 vol. 2007. (Looking at Nature Ser.). (ENG., Illus.). 24p. (J). (gr. -1-2). pap. *(978-0-7787-3336-2(X))* Crabtree Publishing Co.
—My Big & Small Pets. 2010. (My World Ser.). (ENG., Illus.). 16p. (J). (gr. k-2). *(978-0-7787-9426-4(1))*; pap. *(978-0-7787-9470-7(9))* Crabtree Publishing Co.
—My Toys Have Shapes. 2010. (ENG., Illus.). 16p. (J). (gr. k-2). *(978-0-7787-9413-4(X))*; pap. *(978-0-7787-9457-8(1))* Crabtree Publishing Co.
—¿Qué Aspecto Tiene? 2008. (SPA.). 24p. (J). pap. *(978-0-7787-8732-7(X))* Crabtree Publishing Co.
—¿Qué forma Tiene? 2008. (SPA & ENG., Illus.). 24p. (J). lib. bdg. *(978-0-7787-8726-0(1))* Crabtree Publishing Co.
—¿Qué Forma Tiene? 2008. (SPA & ENG., Illus.). 24p. (J). pap. *(978-0-7787-8737-2(0))* Crabtree Publishing Co.
—¿Qué Sigue? 2008. (SPA.). 24p. (J). pap. *(978-0-7787-8736-5(2))* Crabtree Publishing Co.
—What Shape Is It? 2007. (Looking at Nature Ser.). (ENG., Illus.). 24p. (J). (gr. -1-2). pap. *(978-0-7787-3340-9(8))* Crabtree Publishing Co.
Katirgis, Jane. Big & Little, 1 vol. 2011. (All about Opposites Ser.). (ENG., Illus.). 24p. (gr. -1-1). pap. 10.35 *(978-1-59845-263-1(0)*, 39add510-cb02-4eb7-a1d5-df937438332f); lib. bdg. 25.27 *(978-0-7660-3911-7(0)*, 4d9ae2c1-22fc-4afb-b9ea-fc4c97749968) Enslow Publishing, LLC. (Enslow Publishing).
—Tall & Short, 1 vol. 2011. (All about Opposites Ser.). (ENG., Illus.). 24p. (gr. -1-1). pap. 10.35 *(978-1-59845-261-7(4)*, 391f7971-182c-4e4d-8ea7-45616864c273, Enslow Publishing) Enslow Publishing, LLC.
Katz, David Bar. DC Super Heroes Colors, Shapes & More! 2012. (DC Super Heroes Ser.). (ENG.). 20p. (J). (gr. -1 — 1). bds. 9.99 *(978-1-935703-73-0(0))* Downtown Bookworks.
Katz, Karen. Baby's Shapes. Katz, Karen, illus. 2010. (ENG., Illus.). 14p. (J). (gr. -1 — 1). bds. 7.99 *(978-1-4169-9824-2(1)*, Little Simon) Little Simon.
Kenah, Katharine. Big Beasts. 2006. (Extreme Readers: Level 1 Ser.). (Illus.). 32p. (gr. -1-3). 13.95 *(978-0-7569-6839-7(9))* Perfection Learning Corp.
Kenison, Misti, illus. The Tiny Traveler: Egypt: A Book of Shapes. 2015. (ENG.). 24p. (J). (— 1). bds. 5.95 *(978-1-62914-607-2(2)*, Sky Pony Pr.) Skyhorse Publishing Co., Inc.
King, Zelda. Try it with Triangles: Learning to Put Triangles Together to Form Other Shapes. 2004. (Math Big Booksm Ser.). (ENG.). 16p. (gr. 2-3). 37.95 *(978-0-8239-7641-6(6))* Rosen Publishing Group, Inc., The.
Kompelein, Tracy. Lets Compare, If You Dare!, 1 vol. 2007. (Math Made Fun Ser.). (Illus.). 24p. (J). (gr. k-3). lib. bdg. 24.21 *(978-1-59928-537-5(1)*, SandCastle) ABDO Publishing Co.
Kompelien, Tracy. I See a Pattern, What Can I Learn?, 1 vol. 2007. (Math Made Fun Ser.). (Illus.). 24p. (J). (gr. k-3). lib. bdg. 24.21 *(978-1-59928-533-7(9)*, SandCastle) ABDO Publishing Co.
—2-D Shapes Are Behind the Drapes!, 1 vol. 2007. (Math Made Fun Ser.). (Illus.). 24p. (J). (gr. k-3). lib. bdg. 24.21 *(978-1-59928-507-8(X)*, SandCastle) ABDO Publishing Co.
—3-D Shapes Are Like Green Grapes!, 1 vol. 2007. (Math Made Fun Ser.). (Illus.). 24p. (J). (gr. k-3). lib. bdg. 24.21 *(978-1-59928-509-2(6)*, SandCastle) ABDO Publishing Co.
Kumon. Let's Cut Paper, 4 vols. 2005. (Kumon First Steps Workbooks Ser.). (ENG., Illus.). 40p. (J). (gr. -1). pap. 5.95 *(978-1-933241-14-2(4))* Kumon Publishing North America, Inc.
Lady Bird Johnson Wildflower Center Staff, Lady Bird Johnson, compiled by. Exploring the Native Plant World Pre-K-K: Patterns & Shapes. 2004. 44p. (J). pap. 14.95 *(978-1-57168-680-0(0)*, Eakin Pr.) Eakin Pr.
Lafette, Jordan. Kites: Shapes in the Air: Reason with Shapes & Their Attributes, 1 vol. 2014. (InfoMax Math Readers Ser.). (ENG.). 24p. (J). (gr. 3-3). pap. 8.25 *(978-1-4777-4582-3(3)*, e296efa3-8d3c-43fa-83a1-cae4da4cd6e2, Rosen Classroom) Rosen Publishing Group, Inc., The.
Lamb, Stacey. Shapes Sticker Book. Lamb, Stacey, illus. 2009. (Sticker Bks). (Illus.). 16p. (J). pap. 6.99 *(978-0-7945-2501-9(6)*, Usborne) EDC Publishing.
Lawrence, Elizabeth K. I See Circles, 1 vol. 2014. (Shapes! Ser.). (ENG.). 24p. (gr. 1-1). pap. 9.23 *(978-1-5026-0263-3(6)*, 108816a7-acbd-41ae-b94b-d07fce1d5956) Cavendish Square Publishing LLC.
—I See Ovals, 1 vol. 2014. (Shapes! Ser.). (ENG.). 24p. (gr. 1-1). 25.93 *(978-1-5026-0264-0(4)*, dd82618a-de74-4cbf-9166-40c7074d3f3a) Cavendish Square Publishing LLC.
—I See Rectangles, 1 vol. 2014. (Shapes! Ser.). (ENG.). 24p. (gr. 1-1). pap. 9.23 *(978-1-5026-0259-6(8)*, e0350f11-cc94-4330-b50c-e559ceb6444b) Cavendish Square Publishing LLC.
Leach, John. Figuras en Alimentos: Figuras Bidimensionales. rev. ed. 2019. (Mathematics in the Real World Ser.). (SPA.). 24p. (J). (gr. 1-2). pap. 9.99 *(978-1-4258-2854-7(X))* Teacher Created Materials, Inc.
—Fun & Games: Food Shapes: 2-D Shapes (Grade 1) 2018. (Mathematics in the Real World Ser.). (ENG., Illus.). 24p. (J). (gr. 1-2). pap. 9.99 *(978-1-4258-5692-2(6))* Teacher Created Materials, Inc.
Learning Company Books Staff, ed. Reader Rabbit Fun with Paint: Shapes. 2004. (Illus.). 32p. (J). pap. *(978-0-7630-7739-6(9))* Magma.
Lee, Anna. The Menu of Shapes: A Delightful Learning Adventure in English & Mandarin Chinese. Lee, Anna, illus. 2021. (ENG, CHI & CMN.). (J). 15.99 *(978-1-7367889-1-2(4))*; pap. *(978-1-7367889-0-5(6))* Lee, Anna.
Leech, Bonnie Coulter. Circles & Spheres, 1 vol. 2006. (Exploring Shapes Ser.). (ENG., Illus.). 24p. (J). (gr. 2-3). lib. bdg. 26.27 *(978-1-4042-3494-9(2)*, 996627ec-88d9-4e95-a5a5-eaa3ca7a4e9c, PowerKids Pr.) Rosen Publishing Group, Inc., The.
—Triangles. (Exploring Shapes Ser.). 24p. (gr. 2-3). 2009. 42.50 *(978-1-61512-376-6(8))* 2006. (ENG., Illus.). (J). lib. bdg. 26.27 *(978-1-4042-3495-6(0)*, b871d719-3dbd-4116-87c6-da2fbda8c890) Rosen Publishing Group, Inc., The. (PowerKids Pr.).
Leigh, Autumn. Signs on the Road: Learning to Identify the Four Basic Geometric Shapes, 1 vol. 2010. (Math for the REAL World Ser.). (ENG., Illus.). 8p. (gr. k-1). pap. 5.15 *(978-0-8239-8857-0(0)*, f5253939-6466-46b7-a4e0-107d37c64b88) Rosen Publishing Group, Inc., The.
Leonard, Barry, ed. Squishy Shapes: Dinosaurs. 2005. (Illus.). 10p. (J). (gr. -1-2). reprint ed. 13.00 *(978-0-7567-8529-1(4))* DIANE Publishing Co.
LernerClassroom Editors. First Step Nonfiction-Shapes Set II Teaching Guide. 2009. pap. 7.95 *(978-0-8225-6885-8(3))* Lerner Publishing Group.
Let's Draw with Shapes: Set 1, 8 vols. 2003. (Let's Draw with Shapes / Vamos a Dibujar con Figuras Ser.).Tr. of Vamos a Dibujar con Figuras. (ENG & SPA., Illus.). 24p. (gr. k-1). lib. bdg. 105.08 *(978-1-4042-7530-0(4)*, 7e9d5638-d924-4648-adb6-d6d221ea7569, Editorial Buenas Letras) Rosen Publishing Group, Inc., The.
Let's Draw with Shapes: Set 2, 4 vols. 2004. (Let's Draw with Shapes / Vamos a Dibujar con Figuras Ser.).Tr. of Vamos a dibujar con figuras Set 2. (ENG & SPA., Illus.). (J). (gr. k-1). 52.54 *(978-1-4042-7560-7(6)*, 5127f832-9b59-4f29-9b68-b63218fa1afb, Editorial Buenas Letras); 157.62 *(978-1-4042-2947-1(7)*,

S

87f11b11-2e2b-4fd4-ad25-571f4df3329a, Powerstart Pr.) Rosen Publishing Group, Inc., The.

El Libro de Contar de los Chocolates M & M's Brand. 2004. 32p. (J). pap. 6.95 *(978-1-57091-370-9(6))* Charlesbridge Publishing, Inc.

Linda, Winder. Glitter: My First Book of Shapes Numbers Colors & the Alphabet Gods Way. 2003. *(978-1-892354-85-3(3))* Educational Publishing Concepts, Inc.

Line & Circle. 2004. (Illus.). 24p. (J). (CHI & ENG.). *(978-1-84444-004-7(4))*; (ENG & POR., *(978-1-84444-014-6(1))* Mantra Lingua.

Lionni, Leo. Pezzettino. Lionni, Leo, illus. 2006. (Illus.). 40p. (J). (gr. -1-3). lib. bdg. 17.99 *(978-0-394-93156-2(4)*, Pantheon) Knopf Doubleday Publishing Group.

Little, Richard. I Know Flat & Solid Shapes, 1 vol. 2018. (What I Know Ser.). (ENG.). 24p. (gr. k-k). 24.27 *(978-1-5382-1734-4(1)*, f69eb507-3dff-4b6d-8688-8c35eb048651) Stevens, Gareth Publishing LLLP.

Llewellyn, Claire. It's Fun to Learn about Sizes: A Busy Picture Book Full of Fabulous Facts & Things to Do! 2016. (Illus.). 32p. (J). (gr. -1-12). 9.99 *(978-1-86147-761-3(9)*, Armadillo) Anness Publishing GBR. Dist: National Bk. Network.

Long, Dorian. What Are Polygons? Reason with Shapes & Their Attributes, 1 vol. 2014. (Math Masters: Geometry Ser.). (ENG.). 24p. (J). (gr. 2-2). 25.27 *(978-1-4777-6409-1(7)*, 49d7ac19-5b85-4c09-9152-80745582f82f, Rosen Classroom) Rosen Publishing Group, Inc., The.

Lorenz Books Staff, creator. Patterns, 12 vols. 2006. (Learn-A-Word Picture Bks.). (ENG., Illus.). 12p. (J). (gr. -1-k). bds. 6.99 *(978-0-7548-1460-3(2))* Anness Publishing GBR. Dist: National Bk. Network.

Loughrey, Anita. Cirles. 2011. (ENG., Illus.). 24p. (J). pap. 8.95 *(978-1-77092-003-3(X))* Saunders Bk. Co. CAN. Dist: RiverStream Publishing.

—Rectangles. 2011. (ENG., Illus.). 24p. (J). pap. 8.95 *(978-1-77092-004-0(8))* Saunders Bk. Co. CAN. Dist: RiverStream Publishing.

—Squares. 2011. (ENG., Illus.). 24p. (J). pap. 8.95 *(978-1-77092-005-7(6))* Saunders Bk. Co. CAN. Dist: RiverStream Publishing.

—Triangles. 2011. (ENG., Illus.). 24p. (J). pap. 8.95 *(978-1-77092-006-4(4))* Saunders Bk. Co. CAN. Dist: RiverStream Publishing.

Lowery, Lawrence F. Look & See. 2nd ed. 2004. (J). per. *(978-0-9762724-9-6(0))* Educational Research & Applications, LLC.

Lucarelli, Marco. Finding Shapes at the Fair: Identify & Describe Shapes. 2013. (InfoMax Math Readers Ser.). (ENG.). 16p. (J). (gr. k-1). pap. 42.00 *(978-1-4777-1956-5(3))*; (Illus.). pap. 7.00 *(978-1-4777-1955-8(5)*, 60d287d3-d51b-457c-bca7-50c23547daac) Rosen Publishing Group, Inc., The. (Rosen Classroom).

Lucas, Bruce. Drawing Shapes: Shapes & Their Attributes, 1 vol. 2013. (InfoMax Math Readers Ser.). (ENG.). 24p. (J). (gr. 1-1). pap. 8.25 *(978-1-4777-2148-3(7)*, a04b493e-cd92-4236-8b76-e4145afe35f2); pap. 49.50 *(978-1-4777-2149-0(5))* Rosen Publishing Group, Inc., The. (Rosen Classroom).

Lunis, Natalie. Pet-Sized Dinos. 2008. (Dino Times Trivia Ser.). (Illus.). 24p. (J). (gr. k-3). lib. bdg. 26.99 *(978-1-59716-710-9(X))* Bearport Publishing Co., Inc.

MacDonald, Suse. Dino Shapes. MacDonald, Suse, illus. 2014. (ENG., Illus.). 20p. (J). (gr. -1-2). bds. 9.99 *(978-1-4814-0093-0(2)*, Little Simon) Little Simon.

Maderna, Victoria. Look & Find Shapes to Color. 2011. (Dover Kids Activity Bks.). (ENG.). 48p. (J). (gr. -1-2). pap. 4.99 *(978-0-486-47991-0(9)*, 479919) Dover Pubns., Inc.

Maile, Ruby. Shapes. 2008. (Discovering & Exploring Science Ser.). (Illus.). 16p. (J). (gr. -1-3). lib. bdg. 12.95 *(978-0-7569-8255-3(3))* Perfection Learning Corp.

Maisano, Lucy. Who Thought Learning Could be Fun: The Fun Book. 2011. 84p. pap. 13.99 *(978-1-4567-3678-1(7))* AuthorHouse.

Mamada, Mineko. Which Is Round? Which Is Bigger? Mamada, Mineko, illus. 2013. (ENG., Illus.). 24p. (J). (gr. -1-1). 16.95 *(978-1-55453-973-4(0))* Kids Can Pr., Ltd. CAN. Dist: Hachette Bk. Group.

Markovics, Joyce L. Patterns in the Desert. 2014. (Math Blast!: Seeing Patterns All Around Ser.). (ENG.). 32p. (J). (gr. -1-3). lib. bdg. 28.50 *(978-1-62724-337-7(2))* Bearport Publishing Co., Inc.

—Patterns in the Jungle. 2014. (Math Blast!: Seeing Patterns All Around Ser.). (ENG.). 32p. (J). (gr. -1-3). lib. bdg. 28.50 *(978-1-62724-338-4(0))* Bearport Publishing Co., Inc.

Marqina, Mignon. Shapes & Me: A Flip & Learn Book. I.t. ed. 2006. (Illus.). 32p. (J). lib. bdg. *(978-1-934190-05-0(5))* Ocean Front Bk. Publishing, Inc.

Martin, Dayna. Shapes. 2018. (J). pap. *(978-1-4896-9654-0(7)*, AV2 by Weigl) Weigl Pubs., Inc.

—Sizes. 2018. (Illus.). 32p. (J). *(978-1-4896-9641-0(5)*, AV2 by Weigl) Weigl Pubs., Inc.

Maruda, Trotsky. Line & Circle. 2004. (J). (ENG & RUS.). *(978-1-84444-015-3(X))*; (FRE & ENG., Illus.). 24p. *(978-1-84444-007-8(9))*; (ENG & GER., Illus.). 24p. *(978-1-84444-008-5(7))*; (ENG & POL., Illus.). 24p. *(978-1-84444-013-9(3))*; (Illus.). 24p. *(978-1-84444-010-8(9))*; (ENG & KUR., Illus.). 24p. *(978-1-84444-011-5(7))* Mantra Lingua.

—Line & Circle. Maruda, Trotsky, illus. 2004. (Illus.). 32p. (J). (ALB & ENG.). pap. *(978-1-84444-000-9(1))*; (BEN & ENG., pap. *(978-1-84444-003-0(6))*; (CZE & ENG., pap. *(978-1-84444-005-4(2))*; (ENG & PER., pap. *(978-1-84444-006-1(0))*; (PAN & ENG., pap. *(978-1-84444-012-2(5))*; (SER & ENG., pap. *(978-1-84444-016-0(8))*; (SOM & ENG., pap. *(978-1-84444-017-7(6))*; (ENG & TUR., pap. *(978-1-84444-019-1(2))*; (URD & ENG., pap. *(978-1-84444-020-7(6))*; (VIE & ENG., pap. *(978-1-84444-021-4(4))*; (ARA & ENG., pap. *(978-1-84444-002-3(8))* Mantra Lingua.

Marudu, Trotsky. Line & Circle. 2004. (GUJ & ENG., Illus.). 32p. (J). pap. *(978-1-84444-009-2(5))* Mantra Lingua.

Max and Sid, illus. Learning. 2016. (What Can You Spot? Ser.). (ENG.). 18p. (J). (gr. -1 — 1). bds. 7.99 *(978-1-4998-0270-2(6))* Little Bee Books Inc.

McAneney, Caitlin. Quadrilaterals in Art: Reason with Shapes & Their Attributes, 1 vol. 2014. (Rosen Math Readers Ser.). (ENG.). 24p. (J). (gr. 3-3). pap. 8.25 *(978-1-4777-4878-7(4)*, 296f03de-7a48-4b7f-92da-71b9cfb58956, PowerKids Pr.) Rosen Publishing Group, Inc., The.

McCallister, Wendy. Shapes: 4 Friends Lost. 2004. (Illus.). 32p. (J). (gr. -1-18). 14.99 *(978-1-59094-004-4(0)*, Top Shelf) Jawbone Publishing Corp.

McMahon Brett. Baby Read Patterns. 2009. (Illus.). 1p. (J). 4.95 *(978-1-921073-57-1(8))* New Holland Pubs. Pty. Ltd. AUS. Dist: Tuttle Publishing.

Meachen Rau, Dana. Bookworms: The Shape of the World, 6 bks., Set. Incl. Circles. lib. bdg. 25.50 *(978-0-7614-2280-8(3)*, f926c67c-a845-4b13-992f-7f4bcae914a4); Many-Sided Shapes. lib. bdg. 25.50 *(978-0-7614-2279-2(X)*, bede390e-589f-45b6-943c-dee4aa969706); Ovals. lib. bdg. 25.50 *(978-0-7614-2281-5(1)*, befa603b-1f04-4f46-8846-5a3314978499); Rectangles. lib. bdg. 25.50 *(978-0-7614-2282-2(X)*, 664c9884-97a3-4c04-b1dd-1903f92656a6); Squares. lib. bdg. 25.50 *(978-0-7614-2284-6(6)*, f4f924d8-f5bf-4f30-86c1-938b343874cd); Triangles. lib. bdg. 25.50 *(978-0-7614-2286-0(2)*, 80ad03e7-e005-42d9-b81d-80461fd8d8f9); (Illus.). 24p. (gr. k-1). 2007. (Bookworms: the Shape of the World Ser.). 2006. lib. bdg. *(978-0-7614-2278-5(1)*, Cavendish Square) Cavendish Square Publishing LLC.

—Many-Sided Shapes, 1 vol. 2007. (Shape of the World Ser.). (ENG., Illus.). 24p. (gr. k-1). lib. bdg. 25.50 *(978-0-7614-2279-2(X)*, bede390e-589f-45b6-943c-dee4aa969706) Cavendish Square Publishing LLC.

Meet the Shapes Lift the Flap Book. 2005. (J). bds. 9.99 *(978-0-9770215-0-5(5))* Preschool Prep Co.

Menon, Radhika. Line & Circle. Marudu, Trotsky, illus. 2004. (ENG & SPA.). 24p. (J). *(978-1-84444-018-4(4))* Mantra Lingua.

Meyers, Nancy. Doodles Shapes. Meyers, Nancy, illus. 2012. (Doodles Ser.). (ENG., Illus.). 64p. (J). (gr. k-5). pap. 7.95 *(978-1-61608-668-8(8)*, 608668, Sky Pony Pr.) Skyhorse Publishing Co., Inc.

Micklethwait, Lucy. I Spy Shapes in Art. 2004. (ENG., Illus.). 40p. (J). (gr. -1-3). 19.99 *(978-0-06-073193-9(1)*, Greenwillow Bks.) HarperCollins Pubs.

Miles Kelly Staff. Sizes: Let's Learn. Nilsen, Anna, ed. 2003. (Let's Learn Ser.). (Illus.). 20p. (J). 7.95 *(978-1-84236-140-5(6))* Miles Kelly Publishing, Ltd. GBR. Dist: Independent Pubs. Group.

Miles Kelly Staff & Nilsen, Anna. Shapes: Let's Learn. 2003. (Let's Learn Ser.). (Illus.). 20p. (J). 7.95 *(978-1-84236-016-3(7))* Miles Kelly Publishing, Ltd. GBR. Dist: Independent Pubs. Group.

Mills, Nathan & Flynn, Wesley. Big or Small?, 1 vol. 2012. (Rosen Readers Ser.). (ENG., Illus.). 16p. (J). (gr. k-k). pap. 7.00 *(978-1-4488-8640-1(6)*, d81fe992-1c68-4561-82b8-27b32d554f2a, Rosen Classroom) Rosen Publishing Group, Inc., The.

Mills, Nathan & Star, Pat. Describe It: Size, Shape, & Color, 1 vol. 2012. (Rosen Readers Ser.). (ENG., Illus.). 16p. (J). (gr. k-k). pap. 7.00 *(978-1-4488-8755-2(0)*, 946e5aa9-78df-485e-a7f6-735a2570843b, Rosen Classroom) Rosen Publishing Group, Inc., The.

Mills, Nathan & Worthy, Shanya. Shapes, 1 vol. 2012. (Rosen Readers Ser.). (ENG., Illus.). 16p. (J). (gr. k-k). pap. 7.00 *(978-1-4488-8634-0(1)*, ced723aa-f5d4-4158-a48d-57f9f039b093, Rosen Classroom) Rosen Publishing Group, Inc., The.

Minden, Cecilia. Shapes Everywhere. 2010. (21st Century Basic Skills Library: Measurements Ser.). (ENG., Illus.). 24p. (gr. k-3). lib. bdg. 26.35 *(978-1-60279-850-2(8)*, 200566) Cherry Lake Publishing.

Mitchell, Susan K. Biggest vs. Smallest Amazing Mammals, 1 vol. 2010. (Biggest vs. Smallest Animals Ser.). (ENG., Illus.). 24p. (gr. k-2). 25.27 *(978-0-7660-3582-9(4)*, e3c16631-3421-42a2-b5d5-c2b032ef6570, Enslow Elementary) Enslow Publishing, LLC.

—Biggest vs. Smallest Creepy, Crawly Creatures, 1 vol. 2010. (Biggest vs. Smallest Animals Ser.). (ENG., Illus.). 24p. (gr. k-2). 25.27 *(978-0-7660-3581-2(6)*, 4e77b2a2-6e9d-4810-a5ff-98770a3c0885, Enslow Elementary) Enslow Publishing, LLC.

—Biggest vs. Smallest Incredible Insects, 1 vol. 2010. (Biggest vs. Smallest Animals Ser.). (ENG., Illus.). 24p. (gr. k-2). 25.27 *(978-0-7660-3583-6(2)*, 01c451ca-d641-4eed-92da-fafa4a5f5ead, Enslow Elementary) Enslow Publishing, LLC.

—Biggest vs. Smallest Sea Creatures, 1 vol. 2010. (Biggest vs. Smallest Animals Ser.). (ENG., Illus.). 24p. (gr. k-2). 25.27 *(978-0-7660-3580-5(8)*, b870c237-3a34-4d45-82c2-5f3439953602, Enslow Elementary) Enslow Publishing, LLC.

—Biggest vs. Smallest Slimy, Scaly Creatures, 1 vol. 2010. (Biggest vs. Smallest Animals Ser.). (ENG., Illus.). 24p. (gr. k-2). 25.27 *(978-0-7660-3579-9(4)*, 590d0b31-fc15-43e8-9759-5783ae81f371, Enslow Elementary) Enslow Publishing, LLC.

—Biggest vs. Smallest Things with Wings, 1 vol. 2010. (Biggest vs. Smallest Animals Ser.). (ENG., Illus.). 24p. (gr. k-2). 25.27 *(978-0-7660-3578-2(6)*, 7f7567d6-b8e9-4028-9317-1f79b3ca91bb, Enslow Elementary) Enslow Publishing, LLC.

Mitten, Luana K. Three Dimensional Shapes: Cones. 2008. (Concepts Ser.). (Illus.). 24p. (J). (gr. -1-k). lib. bdg. 22.79 *(978-1-60472-415-8(3))* Rourke Educational Media.

Montague-Smith, Ann. Sizes & Shapes. 2004. (QEB Start Math Ser.). (Illus.). 24p. (J). Vol. 1. lib. bdg. 15.95 *(978-1-59566-026-8(7))* Vol. 2. lib. bdg. 15.95 *(978-1-59566-030-5(5))* QEB Publishing Inc.

Montgomery, Anne. Finding the Right Container. rev. ed. 2019. (Smithsonian: Informational Text Ser.). (ENG., Illus.). 20p. (J). (gr. k-1). 7.99 *(978-1-4938-6640-3(0))* Teacher Created Materials, Inc.

Moore, Cassandra. Shape/Color Master. 2007. (Illus.). 75p. (J). spiral bd. 12.95 *(978-1-886297-30-2(4))* Omega Publishing Hse.

Morganelli, Adrianna. Building with Shapes. 2019. (Full STEAM Ahead! - Math Matters Ser.). (Illus.). 24p. (J). (gr. 1-1). *(978-0-7787-6231-7(9))*; pap. *(978-0-7787-6292-8(0))* Crabtree Publishing Co.

Murphy, Stuart J. A House for Birdie. Miller, Edward, illus. 2004. (MathStart 1 Ser.). (ENG.). 40p. (J). (gr. -1). pap. 6.99 *(978-0-06-052353-4(0)*, HarperCollins) HarperCollins Pubs.

My Big Box of Colors, Shapes, & Numbers: Contains Twenty Beautifully Illustrated Board Books. (Illus.). (J). bds. *(978-1-904613-80-0(2))* O'Mara, Michael Bks., Ltd.

My First Book of Shapes. 2003. (J). 41.70 *(978-0-590-66408-0(5))* Scholastic, Inc.

Nancy Giorgio-Kupiec. Nanje's Imagination or Is It ? 2009. 20p. pap. 10.49 *(978-1-4389-7068-4(4))* AuthorHouse.

Napier, Angi. Bible Baby: Shapes. 2012. 28p. 24.95 *(978-1-4626-5633-2(1))* America Star Bks.

National Geographic Kids. National Geographic Kids Look & Learn: Shapes! 2012. (Look & Learn Ser.). (Illus.). 24p. (J). (gr. -1-k). bds. 6.99 *(978-1-4263-1042-3(0)*, National Geographic Kids) Disney Publishing Worldwide.

National Geographic Learning. Reading Expeditions (Science: Math Behind the Science): Sizing up Shapes. 2007. (ENG., Illus.). 24p. (J). pap. 15.95 *(978-0-7922-4589-6(X))* CENGAGE Learning.

National Geographic Society (U.S.) Staff, contrib. by. Shapes! 2013. (Illus.). (J). *(978-0-545-62212-7(3))* Scholastic, Inc.

Neave, Rosie. Colors & Shapes, 1 vol. 2018. (My Book Of Ser.). (ENG.). 24p. (gr. k-1). 26.27 *(978-1-5081-9595-5(1)*, 58ffe21a-7bec-44ce-bbbc-a0b6cef216de, Windmill Bks.) Rosen Publishing Group, Inc., The.

Norma Staff, ed. Formas. 2005. 14p. *(978-958-04-8070-9(2))* Norma S.A.

Nouvion, Judith. Shapes. 2015. (Picture This Ser.). (ENG., Illus.). 40p. (J). (gr. -1-3). bds. 7.99 *(978-0-544-51830-8(6)*, 1606228, Clarion Bks.) HarperCollins Pubs.

Nunn, Daniel. Animals Big & Small, 1 vol. 2012. (Math Every Day Ser.). (ENG., Illus.). 24p. (gr. -1-k). pap. 9.95 *(978-1-4329-5738-4(4)*, 117387, Raintree) Capstone.

Nunn, Daniel & Rissman, Rebecca. Patterns Outside, 1 vol. 2012. (Math Every Day Ser.). (ENG.). 24p. (gr. -1-k). pap. 9.95 *(978-1-4329-5736-0(8)*, 117385, Raintree) Capstone.

—Shapes Around Us, 1 vol. 2012. (Math Every Day Ser.). (ENG.). 24p. (gr. -1-k). pap. 9.95 *(978-1-4329-5737-7(6)*, 117386, Raintree) Capstone.

Nussbaum, Ben. Tracing Shapes. rev. ed. 2005. (Trace & Learn Ser.). (ENG., Illus.). 28p. (J). (gr. -1-3). 16.49 *(978-1-59069-445-9(7)*, 1A600) Studio Mouse LLC.

Omary, Rachel, illus. Shapes & Colors in Dari. 2004. 5p. (J). spiral bd. 14.95 *(978-0-9740535-7-8(0))* Knight Publishing.

—Shapes & Colors in Farsi. I.t. ed. 2004. 5p. (J). spiral bd. 14.95 *(978-0-9740535-6-1(2))* Knight Publishing.

—Shapes & Colors in Pashto. I.t. ed. 2004. 5p. (J). spiral bd. 14.95 *(978-0-9740535-8-5(9))* Knight Publishing.

Owen, Ruth. Top 10 Tallest. 2010. (Crabtree Contact Ser.). (ENG., Illus.). 32p. (J). (gr. 3-6). pap. *(978-0-7787-7513-3(5))*; lib. bdg. *(978-0-7787-7492-1(9))* Crabtree Publishing Co.

Oxley, Kathy. Meet the Shapes. Rosario, Sherwin, illus. 2nd ed. 2005. (J). 7.99 *(978-0-9770215-1-2(3))* Preschool Prep Co.

Pagni, Gianpaolo. Gianpaolo Pagni: Double Face. 2010. (ENG., Illus.). 40p. pap. 27.00 *(978-88-7570-218-2(7))* Corraini ITA. Dist: D.A.P./Distributed Art Pubs.

Parker, Steve. In Focus: Big Beasts. 2018. (In Focus Ser.). (ENG.). 64p. (J). 17.99 *(978-0-7534-7428-0(X)*, 900187151); (Illus.). pap. 12.99 *(978-0-7534-7429-7(8)*, 900187152) Roaring Brook Pr. (Kingfisher).

Penn, M. W. 2 Lines. Firos, Daphne, illus. 2011. (ENG.). 32p. (J). pap. 11.95 *(978-0-9840425-0-0(4))* MathWord Pr., LLC.

Penton Overseas, Inc. Staff. Colors, Shapes & Sizes. abr. ed. 2003. (J). (gr. -1-3). 12.99 incl. audio, cd-rom *(978-1-894677-24-0(2))* Kidzup Productions.

Perritano, John. Start the Game: Geometry in Sports. 2013. (IMath Ser.). (Illus.). 32p. (J). (gr. 3-4). lib. bdg. 22.60 *(978-1-59953-563-0(7))* Norwood Hse. Pr.

Peterson, Ingela, illus. Ellie & Pinky's Pop-Up Shapes. 2003. (First Concepts Ser.). 10p. (J). 7.95 *(978-1-58117-184-6(6)*, Intervisual/Piggy Toes) Bendon, Inc.

Phidal Publishing Staff, ed. Shapes. (Turn & Learn Ser.). 12p. (J). *(978-2-7643-0078-7(6))* Phidal Publishing, Inc./Editions Phidal, Inc.

Phillips, Dee. Big Zoo. 2009. (Flip Flap Fun Bks.). (ENG.). 5p. (J). (gr. -1-k). bds. 5.95 *(978-1-84696-086-4(X)*, TickTock Books) Octopus Publishing Group GBR. Dist: Independent Pubs. Group.

Phillips, Sarah & Tattam, Mark. Shapes. 2005. (Baby See a Shape Ser.). (Illus.). 12p. (gr. -1-k). bds. *(978-1-905051-90-8(5))* Make Believe Ideas.

Picthall, Chez, creator. Flip Flaps Shapes. 2014. (ENG., Illus.). 32p. 10.00 *(978-1-906572-80-8(1))* Award Pubns. Ltd. GBR. Dist: Parkwest Pubns., Inc.

Picthall, Chez, des. Hearts & Stars. 2015. (Illus.). 10p. (J). bds. 9.99 *(978-1-909763-05-0(5))* Award Pubns. Ltd. GBR. Dist: Parkwest Pubns., Inc.

Piddock, Claire. Slides, Flips, & Turns. 2010. (ENG., Illus.). 24p. (J). *(978-0-7787-5251-6(8))*; pap. *(978-0-7787-5298-1(4))* Crabtree Publishing Co.

Pluckrose, Henry. Shape (Math Counts: Updated Editions) 2018. (Math Counts, New & Updated Ser.). (ENG., Illus.). 32p. (J). (gr. k-3). pap. 5.95 *(978-0-531-13520-4(9)*, Children's Pr.) Scholastic Library Publishing.

—Shape (Math Counts: Updated Editions) (Library Edition) 2018. (Math Counts, New & Updated Ser.). (ENG., Illus.). 32p. (J). (gr. k-3). lib. bdg. 25.00 *(978-0-531-17511-8(1)*, Children's Pr.) Scholastic Library Publishing.

—What Shape Is It? 2006. (Let's Explore, Maths Set Ser.). (Illus.). 32p. (J). (gr. -1-3). lib. bdg. 27.10 *(978-1-59771-039-8(3))* Sea-To-Sea Pubns.

—What Size Is It? 2006. (Let's Explore, Maths Set Ser.). (Illus.). 32p. (J). (gr. -1-3). lib. bdg. 27.10 *(978-1-59771-040-4(7))* Sea-To-Sea Pubns.

Price, Justine. The Class Mural: Reason with Shapes & Their Attributes, 1 vol. 2014. (Math Masters: Geometry Ser.). (ENG.). 24p. (J). (gr. 2-2). 25.27 *(978-1-4777-6443-5(7)*, d12b707a-690b-4f54-9fe9-23b7b9dd1133); pap. 8.25 *(978-1-4777-4903-6(9)*, 2ccbc0d2-baeb-4c72-8223-458ff05c4e96) Rosen Publishing Group, Inc., The. (Rosen Classroom).

Priddy, Roger. Big Board Books Colors, ABC, Numbers. 2008. (First 100 Ser.). (ENG.). 14p. (J). (gr. -1 — 1). bds. 9.99 *(978-0-312-50219-5(2)*, 900052985) St. Martin's Pr.

—First 100 Padded: Numbers, Colors, Shapes. 2011. (First 100 Ser.). (ENG., Illus.). 24p. (J). (gr. -1 — 1). bds. 5.99 *(978-0-312-51081-7(0)*, 900075562) St. Martin's Pr.

—Hello Baby: Words: A High-Contrast Board Book. 2013. (Hello Baby Ser.). (ENG., Illus.). 16p. (J). (gr. -1 — 1). bds. 5.99 *(978-0-312-51598-0(7)*, 900118661) St. Martin's Pr.

—Sticker Early Learning: Shapes: With Reusable Stickers. 2016. (Sticker Early Learning Ser.). (ENG., Illus.). 24p. (J). pap. 4.99 *(978-0-312-52015-1(8)*, 900156573) St. Martin's Pr.

Princess Adjepong. My First Shapes & Numbers Colouring Book. 2013. 52p. pap. 27.45 *(978-1-4817-9519-7(8))* AuthorHouse.

Professor Q's Chinese-English Language Books: Xing Zhuàng - Shapes. 2006. (J). *(978-0-9743359-4-0(0))* Murdock Publishing Co.

Publications International Ltd. Staff, ed. Baby's Shapes. 2010. 18p. (J). bds. 7.98 *(978-1-60553-963-8(5))*; (Illus.). bds. 7.98 *(978-1-60553-965-2(1))* Phoenix International Publications, Inc.

—My Shapes Book. 2011. 32p. (J). bds. *(978-1-4508-1023-4(3))* Publications International, Ltd.

Pugliano-Martin, Carol. Building with Shapes. 2004. (Shared Connections Ser.). (J). pap., instr.'s gde. ed. 27.00 *(978-1-4108-1613-9(3))* Benchmark Education Co.

—Building with Shapes: Small Book. 2004. (Shared Connections Ser.). (J). pap. *(978-1-4108-1637-5(0))* Benchmark Education Co.

QEB Start Math Book Stores Edition: Sizes & Shapes - Book 1. 2006. (J). per. *(978-1-59566-273-6(1))* QEB Publishing Inc.

QEB Start Math Book Stores Edition: Sizes & Shapes Book 2. 2006. (J). per. *(978-1-59566-277-4(4))* QEB Publishing Inc.

Ranchetti, Sebastiano. Shapes in Animals, 1 vol. 2008. (Learn with Animals Ser.). (ENG., Illus.). 24p. (gr. k-1). pap. 9.15 *(978-0-8368-8829-4(4)*, 40d3eeb4-617e-429c-805a-9e153fa157f1); lib. bdg. 24.67 *(978-0-8368-8824-9(3)*, b922b994-4e32-42d2-a96e-6de84745d3d7) Stevens, Gareth Publishing LLLP. (Weekly Reader Leveled Readers).

—Shapes in Animals / Figuras en Los Animales, 1 vol. 2008. (Learn with Animals / Aprende con Los Animales Ser.). (SPA & ENG.). 24p. (gr. k-1). pap. 9.15 *(978-0-8368-9045-7(0)*, 32c15be9-1a29-417a-80c5-622b6ffa4dac); (Illus.). lib. bdg. 24.67 *(978-0-8368-9040-2(X)*, 9cefb7dc-c9fc-4864-be25-95a73b437a89) Stevens, Gareth Publishing LLLP. (Weekly Reader Leveled Readers).

Randolph, Joanne. Let's Draw a Bird with Shapes. 2009. (Let's Draw with Shapes Ser.). 24p. (gr. k-k). 42.50 *(978-1-61514-203-3(7)*, PowerKids Pr.) Rosen Publishing Group, Inc., The.

—Let's Draw a Bird with Shapes, 1 vol. Muschinske, Emily, illus. 2004. (Let's Draw with Shapes Ser.). (ENG.). 24p. (J). (gr. k-k). lib. bdg. 26.27 *(978-1-4042-2792-7(X)*, 3c785bb8-297b-42cd-9c0a-36ad14b28b11, PowerKids Pr.) Rosen Publishing Group, Inc., The.

—Let's Draw a Bird with Shapes: Vamos a Dibujar un Ave Usando Figuras, 1 vol. Muschinske, Emily, illus. 2004. (Let's Draw with Shapes / Vamos a Dibujar con Figuras Ser.). (ENG & SPA.). 24p. (J). (gr. k-1). 26.27 *(978-1-4042-7555-3(X)*, 753d2b23-d0f0-4127-a1c9-98d953e0baa6) Rosen Publishing Group, Inc., The.

—Let's Draw a Bird with Shapes/Vamos a dibujar un ave usando Figuras. 2009. (Let's Draw with Shapes / Vamos a dibujar con figuras Ser.). (ENG & SPA.). 24p. (gr. k-1). 42.50 *(978-1-61514-214-9(2)*, Editorial Buenas Letras) Rosen Publishing Group, Inc., The.

Ranson, Erin. Magnetic Playtime Shapes. Parry, Jo, illus. 2007. (Magnetic Playtime Shapes Ser.). 10p. (J). (gr. -1-3). *(978-1-84666-363-5(6)*, Tide Mill Pr.) Top That! Publishing PLC.

Rau, Dana Meachen. A Star in My Orange: Looking for Nature's Shapes. 2006. (ENG., Illus.). 32p. (J). (gr. k-2). pap. 8.99 *(978-0-8225-5992-4(7)*, 1a7a4fdc-0e50-4e33-8d7d-306bfded4a2e, First Avenue Editions) Lerner Publishing Group.

Rebman, Nick. What Is Biggest? A Book about Sizes. 2016. (Concept Fun Ser.). (ENG.). 16p. (J). (gr. -1-2). 29.93 *(978-1-5038-0766-2(5)*, 210614) Child's World, Inc, The.

—Which Is the Circle? A Book about Shapes. 2016. (Concept Fun Ser.). (ENG.). 16p. (J). (gr. -1-2). 29.93 *(978-1-5038-0765-5(7)*, 210613) Child's World, Inc, The.

Reisberg, Joanne Anderson. Zachary Zormer: Shape Transformer. Hohn, David, illus. 2006. (Charlesbridge Math Adventures Ser.). (ENG.). 32p. (J). (gr. 2-5). per. 7.95 *(978-1-57091-876-6(7))* Charlesbridge Publishing, Inc.

Rice, Dona. Aventuras de Viaje: Figuras Bidimensionales. rev. ed. 2019. (Mathematics in the Real World Ser.). (SPA.). 20p. (J). (gr. k-1). 8.99 *(978-1-4258-2834-9(5))* Teacher Created Materials, Inc.

Rice, Dona Herweck. Big & Little, 1 vol. 2nd rev. ed. (TIME for KIDS(r): Informational Text Ser.). (ENG., 12p. (gr. k-1). 2013. Illus.). (J). lib. bdg. 15.96 *(978-1-4807-1004-7(0))* 2011. 7.99 *(978-1-4333-3565-5(4))* Teacher Created Materials, Inc.

—Figuras. 2nd rev. ed. 2011. (TIME for KIDS(r): Informational Text Ser.). (SPA.). 12p. (gr. k-1). 7.99 *(978-1-4333-4406-0(8))* Teacher Created Materials, Inc.

—Grande y Pequeño. 2nd rev. ed. 2011. (TIME for KIDS(r): Informational Text Ser.). (SPA.). 12p. (gr. k-1). 7.99 *(978-1-4333-4404-6(1))* Teacher Created Materials, Inc.

—Shapes, 1 vol. 2nd rev. ed. (TIME for KIDS(r): Informational Text Ser.). (ENG., 12p. (gr. k-1). 2014. Illus.). (J). lib. bdg. 15.96 *(978-1-4807-1006-1(7))* 2011. 7.99 *(978-1-4333-3567-9(0))* Teacher Created Materials, Inc.

—Travel Adventures: Camping. 2018. (Mathematics in the Real World Ser.). (ENG., Illus.). 20p. (J). (gr. k-1). 8.99 *(978-1-4258-5627-4(6))* Teacher Created Materials, Inc.

—Use Your Math Mind: Describe It. 2nd rev. ed. 2015. (TIME for KIDS(r): Informational Text Ser.). (ENG., Illus.). 12p. (gr.

-1-k). 7.99 *(978-1-4938-2142-6(3))* Teacher Created Materials, Inc.
Rigby Education Staff. Discovery World Yel Sizes. (Discovery World Ser.). (Illus.). 12p. (gr. k-1). 23.00 *(978-0-7635-2695-5(9))* Rigby Education.
—Little & Big. (Illus.). 8p. (J). bds. 3.95 *(978-0-7635-6467-4(2),* 764672C99) Rigby Education.
Rigol, Francesc, illus. Dan & Din Learn Shapes. 2009. (Learning with Dan & Din Ser.). 12p. (J). (gr. -1-k). bds. 11.40 *(978-1-60754-400-5(8))* Windmill Bks.
Riley, Matt. Making Shapes: Analyze, Compare, Create, & Compose Shapes. 2013. (Rosen Math Readers Ser.). (ENG.). 16p. (J). (gr. k-1). pap. 42.00 *(978-1-4777-1657-1(2));* (Illus.). pap. 7.00 *(978-1-4777-1656-4(4),* 374b7f0b-0e91-4d15-aada-5ef3bf0cb07a) Rosen Publishing Group, Inc., The. (Rosen Classroom).
Ripley's Believe It or Not Editors. Expect the Unexpected: Larger than Life. 2010. (Ripley's Remarkable & Unexpected Ser.). 36p. (J). (gr. 3-18). lib. bdg. 19.95 *(978-1-4222-2023-8(0))* Mason Crest.
Rivera, Sheila. Is It Big or Little? 2005. (First Step Nonfiction — Properties of Matter Ser.). (ENG., Illus.). 8p. (J). (gr. k-2). pap. 5.99 *(978-0-8225-5406-6(2),* 73d53d14-c37d-4d4a-9cbf-3bf486f15321) Lerner Publishing Group.
Robbins, Karen S. Think Circles! A Lift-The-Flap Counting, Color, & Shape Book, 1 vol. 2017. (ENG., Illus.). 24p. (J). bds. 12.99 *(978-0-7643-5382-6(9),* 9780764353826) Schiffer Publishing, Ltd.
—Think Squares! A Lift-The-Flap Counting, Color, & Shape Book, 1 vol. 2017. (ENG., Illus.). 24p. (J). bds. 12.99 *(978-0-7643-5383-3(7),* 9780764353833) Schiffer Publishing, Ltd.
—Think Triangles! A Lift-The-Flap Counting, Color, & Shape Book, 1 vol. 2017. (ENG., Illus.). 24p. (J). bds. 12.99 *(978-0-7643-5381-9(0),* 9780764353819) Schiffer Publishing, Ltd.
Rodriguez, Patty & Stein, Ariana. Cuauhtemoc: Shapes/Formas, 1 vol. Reyes, Citlali, illus. 2018.Tr. of Spanish. (SPA.). 22p. (J). (gr. -1-k). bds. 9.99 *(978-0-9861099-3-5(2))* Little Libros, LLC.
Rosenthal-Gazit, Roni. On Shapes & More. 2007. (J). per. 7.99 *(978-0-9792800-0-9(1))* StoryTime World Publishing Hse.
Ross, Tony. Figuras. 2006. (Little Princess Ser.).Tr. of Shapes. (SPA.). (J). (gr. -1-k). bds. 7.95 *(978-968-19-1486-8(4),* AT33280) Lectorum Pubns., Inc.
Rossiter, Brienna. Tall & Short. 2019. (Opposites Ser.). (ENG., Illus.). 16p. (J). (gr. k-1). 25.64 *(978-1-64185-351-4(4),* 1641853514, Focus Readers) North Star Editions.
Rozines Roy, Jennifer & Roy, Gregory. Shapes in Transportation, 1 vol. (Math All Around Ser.). (ENG., Illus.). 32p. (gr. 2-2). 2008. pap. 9.23 *(978-0-7614-3387-3(2),* 6f295ceb-6ea9-4f86-ac9a-86411c9ee12d) 2007. lib. bdg. 32.64 *(978-0-7614-2265-5(X),* 3ce6ec45-cd78-4dc2-bf97-36b786ae4847) Cavendish Square Publishing LLC.
Santillana & Dorling Kindersley Publishing Staff. Figuras. (Ensename Ser.). (SPA., Illus.). 16p. (J). (gr. -1-k). bds. 6.95 *(978-1-58986-327-9(5))* Santillana USA Publishing Co., Inc.
—Tamanos. (Ensename Ser.). (SPA., Illus.). 16p. (J). (gr. -1-k). bds. 6.95 *(978-1-58986-328-6(3))* Santillana USA Publishing Co., Inc.
Sargent, Brian. Grandfather's Shape Story. 2006. (Rookie Read-About Math Ser.). (ENG., Illus.). 32p. (J). (gr. -1-3). 20.50 *(978-0-516-29919-8(0),* Children's Pr.) Scholastic Library Publishing.
Saviola, Ava. Dinosaur Shapes, 1 vol. 2012. (Dinosaur School Ser.). (ENG., Illus.). 24p. (J). (gr. k-k). pap. 9.15 *(978-1-4339-7148-8(8),* a1ab8958-cb5c-491a-8f05-08d24e215544); lib. bdg. 25.27 *(978-1-4339-7147-1(X),* a5a3aac4-d9fe-4710-b447-70bb3db559ab) Stevens, Gareth Publishing LLLP.
Scholastic. Do You See Shapes? (Rookie Toddler) 2010. (Rookie Toddler Ser.). (ENG.). 14p. (J). (gr. -1 — 1). bds. 6.95 *(978-0-531-25234-5(5),* Children's Pr.) Scholastic Library Publishing.
—My First Book of Shapes: Scholastic Early Learners (My First) 2017. (Scholastic Early Learners Ser.). (ENG.). 14p. (J). (gr. -1 — 1). bds. 6.99 *(978-1-338-16151-9(2),* Cartwheel Bks.) Scholastic, Inc.
Scholastic, Inc. Staff. Shapes at Home. 2015. (Rookie Toddler(r) Ser.). (ENG.). 12p. (J). bds. 6.95 *(978-0-531-20573-0(8))* Scholastic Library Publishing.
Scholastic, Inc. Staff, contrib. by. I Am Bigger Than... 2014. (Rookie Toddler(r) Ser.). (ENG., Illus.). 12p. (J). bds. 6.95 *(978-0-531-20492-4(8))* Scholastic Library Publishing.
Scholastic, Inc. Staff, ed. Secret Shapes. (Changing Picture Bks.). (Illus.). (J). pap. 9.99 *(978-0-590-24644-6(5))* Scholastic, Inc.
School Zone Publishing. Same or Different. 2003. (Preschool Ser.). (ENG.). (J). cd-rom 19.99 *(978-1-58947-902-9(5))* School Zone Publishing Co.
School Zone Publishing Company Staff. Colors & Shapes. 2018. (ENG.). 64p. (J). (gr. -1-k). pap., wbk. ed. 4.49 *(978-1-58947-357-7(4),* fc4c4f3d-83db-438e-a1fa-cc7c625d7ab5) School Zone Publishing Co.
School Zone Staff. Bilingual Colors, Shapes & More, 56 vols. 2019. (SPA.). (J). 3.49 *(978-1-58947-988-3(2),* e7dc55fd-ac2a-491b-83e0-6d7f90da9899) School Zone Publishing Co.
Schuette, Sarah L. Figuras Geométricas/Shapes. 2012. (Figuras Geométricas/Shapes Ser.). (MUL.). 32p. (gr. 1-2). pap. 190.80 *(978-1-4296-8537-5(9),* Capstone Pr.) Capstone.
Schuh, Mari. The Crayola (r) Shapes Book. 2017. (Crayola (r) Concepts Ser.). (ENG., Illus.). 24p. (J). (gr. -1-3). 29.32 *(978-1-5124-3284-8(9),* f572ef58-5a72-432d-8286-ade5a7a21e68, Lerner Pubns.) Lerner Publishing Group.
—The World's Biggest Mammals. 2015. (Illus.). 24p. (J). lib. bdg. *(978-1-62031-204-9(2))* Jump! Inc.
Schumacher, Bev. Patterns. 2007.Tr. of Los Disenos. 20p. (J). lib. bdg. 9.95 *(978-0-9768706-3-0(0))* Learning Props.
—Shape Land. 2004.Tr. of Figuralandia. (ENG.). 20p. (J). lib. bdg. 9.95 *(978-0-9741549-8-5(9))* Learning Props.
—Shapeland / Figuralandia. 2004.Tr. of Figuralandia. (SPA.). 20p. lib. bdg. 9.95 *(978-0-9741549-2-3(X))* Learning Props.
—What Color Is It? / de Que Color Es? 2004. (SPA & CHI., Illus.). 20p. (J). lib. bdg. 9.95 *(978-0-9741549-0-9(3))* Learning Props.
Sesame Street Staff, creator. Sesame Street: Early Learning Boxed Set. 2011. 72p. (J). bds. 12.99 *(978-1-60745-237-9(5))* Flying Frog Pubs.
Shapes. (Sparkly Board Bks.). (Illus.). (J). bds. *(978-1-84239-256-0(5))* Alligator Bks. Ltd.
Shapes. 2003. (Illus.). 12p. 5.95 *(978-0-7548-0378-2(3),* Lorenz Bks.) Anness Publishing GBR. Dist: National Bk. Network.
Shapes. 2004. 12p. (J). bds. 3.99 *(978-1-85997-814-6(2))* Byeway Bks.
Shapes. 2003. (J). per. *(978-1-57657-915-2(8));* per. *(978-1-57657-917-6(4))* Paradise Pr., Inc.
Shapes. Date not set. (Illus.). 16p. (J). 2.98 *(978-0-7525-9454-5(0))* Parragon, Inc.
Shapes. 2003. (Preschool Ser.). (ENG.). (J). cd-rom 19.99 *(978-1-58947-904-3(1))* School Zone Publishing Co.
Shapes! (Shapes! Ser.). (ENG.). 24p. (J). (gr. 1-1). 2015. 49.32 *(978-1-5026-0331-9(4))* 2014. lib. bdg. 155.58 *(978-1-5026-0314-2(4),* fc3bda96-a34b-4301-8405-48fee04c2ecf) Cavendish Square Publishing LLC. (Cavendish Square).
Shapes, Vol. 4. (Early Intervention Levels Ser.). 3.85 *(978-1-56334-972-0(8))* CENGAGE Learning.
Shapes All Around. 2010. (Shapes Around Town Ser.). 32p. lib. bdg. 155.94 *(978-1-4048-6221-0(8),* Picture Window Bks.) Capstone.
Shapes anc colors shaped layer Book. 2006. (J). bds. 4.99 *(978-1-934004-08-1(1))* Byeway Bks.
Shapes Are Fun!, 6 vols. 2015. (Shapes Are Fun! Ser.: 6). (ENG.). 24p. (J). (gr. -1-2). lib. bdg. 188.16 *(978-1-68080-141-5(4),* 19452, Abdo Kids) ABDO Publishing Co.
Shapes in My World: Big Book: Level F. (Visions Ser.). 8p. 20.95 *(978-0-322-00629-4(5))* Wright Group/McGraw-Hill.
Sharman, Lydia. The Amazing Book of Shapes. (Illus.). 40p. (J). pap. 18.95 *(978-0-590-24306-3(3))* Scholastic, Inc.
Shepard, Daniel. Solid Shapes. 2005. (Yellow Umbrella Fluent Level Ser.). (ENG.). 16p. (gr. k-1). pap. 35.70 *(978-0-7368-5319-4(7),* Capstone Pr.) Capstone.
Shepherd, Jodie. The Crayola (r) Comparing Sizes Book. 2017. (Crayola (r) Concepts Ser.). (ENG., Illus.). 24p. (J). (gr. -1-3). 29.32 *(978-1-5124-3289-3(X),* 371c731e-20e4-4be1-b0e8-82ead72c2079, Lerner Pubns.) Lerner Publishing Group.
Shulman, Mark. My Square Breakfast. Milne, Bill, photos by. 2006. (Illus.). 10p. (J). (gr. k-4). reprint ed. 6.00 *(978-1-4223-5710-1(4))* DIANE Publishing Co.
Sidman, Joyce. Round. Yoo, Taeeun, illus. 2017. (ENG.). 32p. (J). (gr. -1-3). 17.99 *(978-0-544-38761-4(9),* 1592445, Clarion Bks.) HarperCollins Pubs.
Siwanowicz, Igor. Animals up Close: Zoom in on the World's Most Incredible Creatures. 2014. (Illus.). 96p. (J). *(978-1-4351-5620-3(X))* Barnes & Noble, Inc.
Sizes: Individual Title Six-Packs. (Discovery World Ser.). 12p. (gr. k-1). 28.00 *(978-0-7635-8447-4(9))* Rigby Education.
Sizes & Shapes. 2005. (J). Bk. 1. per. 8.95 *(978-1-59566-155-5(7))*Bk. 2. per. 8.95 *(978-1-59566-159-3(X))* QEB Publishing Inc.
Slaughter, Tom. One, Two, Three. 2003. (Illus.). 24p. (J). (gr. k-k). 12.95 *(978-0-88776-664-0(1),* Tundra Bks.) Tundra Bks. CAN. Dist: Penguin Random Hse. LLC.
Smith, Carrie. Finding Shapes: Lap Book. 2009. (My First Reader's Theater Set B Ser.). (J). 28.00 *(978-1-4108-8542-5(9))* Benchmark Education Co.
Smith, Mary Lou. I See Squares, 1 vol. 2014. (Shapes! Ser.). (ENG.). 24p. (J). (gr. 1-1). 25.93 *(978-1-5026-0260-2(1),* 04786462-979a-48d9-add7-266eef92473d) Cavendish Square Publishing LLC.
Smith, Mary-Lou. I See Stars, 1 vol. 2014. (Shapes! Ser.). (ENG.). 24p. (J). (gr. 1-1). 25.93 *(978-1-5026-0271-8(7),* 9f2b726f-1ccb-4399-828b-16f1b42a2f6e) Cavendish Square Publishing LLC.
Smith, Mary Lou. I See Triangles. 2015. (J). pap. *(978-1-62713-511-5(1))* Musa Publishing.
Smith, Sian. Big & Small, 1 vol. 2014. (Opposites Ser.). (ENG.). 24p. (J). (gr. -1-1). pap. 5.99 *(978-1-4846-0332-1(X),* 126421, Heinemann) Capstone.
Snozek, Lee Anne. Terrific Triangles. 2010. (Dover Design Coloring Bks.). (ENG., Illus.). 32p. (gr. 3-8). pap. 3.99 *(978-0-486-47678-0(2))* Dover Pubns., Inc.
Sosa, Maritza, concept. Formas - Shapes. 2006. (ENG & SPA.). (J). bds. 5.99 *(978-1-934113-02-8(6))* Little Cubans, LLC.
Stadler, Charlotte. Building a Castle. 2011. (Early Connections Ser.). (J). *(978-1-61672-628-7(8))* Benchmark Education Co.
Staff, Gareth Editorial Staff. I Know Big & Small, 1 vol. 2005. (I'm Ready for Math Ser.). (ENG., Illus.). 16p. (gr. k-1). lib. bdg. 21.67 *(978-0-8368-6474-8(3),* f371cd78-5490-4b9f-93a7-c6c1f40533df, Weekly Reader Leveled Readers) Stevens, Gareth Publishing LLLP.
—I Know Shapes / Las Figuras, 1 vol. 2005. (I'm Ready for Math / Ya Puedo Aprender Matemáticas Ser.). (ENG & SPA., Illus.). 16p. (gr. k-1). lib. bdg. 21.67 *(978-0-8368-6487-8(5),* f6c01122-ab72-4dfd-9ffd-f5f4bd39ea33, Weekly Reader Leveled Readers) Stevens, Gareth Publishing LLLP.
Stanley, Joseph. Is It Flat or Is It Solid? Identify & Describe Shapes. 2013. (InfoMax Math Readers Ser.). (ENG.). 16p. (J). (gr. k-1). pap. 42.00 *(978-1-4777-2001-1(4));* (Illus.). pap. 7.00 *(978-1-4777-2000-4(6),* ea48f495-127b-4dc3-ba7b-b0cfe0201749) Rosen Publishing Group, Inc., The. (Rosen Classroom).
Steck-Vaughn Staff. Early Math: Shapes, 10 Pack. 2005. pap. 29.95 *(978-1-4190-0344-8(5))* Steck-Vaughn.
—Early Math Set 1: Shapes. 2005. pap. 2.99 *(978-1-4190-0320-2(8))* Steck-Vaughn.
—Head for Home: Colors & Shapes. 2004. (Illus.). pap. *(978-0-7398-8554-3(5))* Steck-Vaughn.
—Super Sizes! 2003. pap. 4.10 *(978-0-7398-7658-9(9))* Steck-Vaughn.
Steffora, Tracey. Shapes in the Kitchen, 1 vol. 2011. (Math Around Us Ser.). (ENG.). 24p. (J). (gr. -1-1). pap. 6.29 *(978-1-4329-4930-3(6),* 114832, Heinemann) Capstone.
Stich, Tim. Paper Crafts: Shapes & Their Attributes, 1 vol. 2013. (InfoMax Math Readers Ser.). (ENG.). 24p. (J). (gr. 1-1). pap. 8.25 *(978-1-4777-2142-1(8),* 099f569e-7cee-4f8b-8576-6f45ec8355ca); pap. 49.50 *(978-1-4777-2143-8(6))* Rosen Publishing Group, Inc., The. (Rosen Classroom).
Studio Mouse. Princess Colors & Shapes Pack. 2003. (ENG., Illus.). 36p. (J). (gr. -1-3). 12.99 *(978-1-59069-366-7(3),* 1A501) Studio Mouse LLC.
Studio Mouse, creator. Princess Shapes. 2004. (Early Learning Ser.). (ENG., Illus.). 36p. (J). (gr. -1-3). 12.99 *(978-1-59069-369-8(8),* 1A103) Studio Mouse LLC.
Sugimoto, Nao. 100 Shapes. 2010. (ENG., Illus.). 45p. (gr. k). spiral bd. 12.95 *(978-1-934734-45-2(4))* Seven Footer Pr.
Tagel, Peggy, illus. On the Go. 2003. (Squishy Shapes Ser.). 10p. (J). 12.95 *(978-1-57145-739-4(9),* Silver Dolphin Bks.) Readerlink Distribution Services, LLC.
Teis, Kyra. Look!, 1 vol. 2005. (ENG., Illus.). 16p. (J). (gr. -1). bds. 6.95 *(978-1-59572-022-1(7))* Star Bright Bks., Inc.
Thong, Roseanne Greenfield. Round Is a Tortilla: A Book of Shapes. 2015. (J). lib. bdg. 18.40 *(978-0-606-37442-2(6))* Turtleback.
Thornton, Geoffrey. What's Wrong? Visual Adventures in Critical Thinking. 2007. 32p. per. 19.95 *(978-1-59858-296-3(8))* Dog Ear Publishing, LLC.
Ticktock Media, Ltd. Staff. Favorite Foods: Colors & Shapes. 2008. (Tab Bks.). (ENG.). 10p. (J). (gr. -1-k). bds. 4.95 *(978-1-84696-821-1(6),* TickTock Books) Octopus Publishing Group GBR. Dist: Independent Pubs. Group.
—Friendly Dinosaurs. 2009. (Dinosaur Shape Bks.). (ENG.). 10p. (J). (gr. -1-k). bds. 5.95 *(978-1-84696-833-4(X),* TickTock Books) Octopus Publishing Group GBR. Dist: Independent Pubs. Group.
—Hungry Dinosaurs. 2009. (Dinosaur Shape Bks.). (ENG.). 10p. (J). (gr. -1-k). bds. 5.95 *(978-1-84696-834-1(8),* TickTock Books) Octopus Publishing Group GBR. Dist: Independent Pubs. Group.
Top That! Kids, creator. Magnetic Play + Learn Shapes. 2005. (Magnetic Play & Learn Ser.). (Illus.). 12p. (J). (gr. -1-3). bds. *(978-1-84510-048-3(4))* Top That! Publishing PLC.
Traffic Signs Shape Book. 2016. (Illus.). 23p. (J). *(978-0-87659-712-5(6))* Gryphon Hse., Inc.
Tuxworth, Nicola. Patterns: Learn-a-Word Book. 2016. (Illus.). 20p. (J). (gr. -1-12). bds. 6.99 *(978-1-86147-462-9(8),* Armadillo) Anness Publishing GBR. Dist: National Bk. Network.
Twine, Alice. My Favorite Book of Shapes. 2008. (Board Bks.). (Illus.). 14p. (J). (gr. -1-k). bds. 11.95 *(978-1-4042-4255-5(4))* Rosen Publishing Group, Inc., The.
Tyler, Madeline. Monster Patterns. Li, Amy, illus. 2020. (Monster Math Ser.). (ENG.). 24p. (J). (gr. -1-2). pap. 7.99 *(978-1-5415-8921-6(1),* 23c9a3ae-08b6-46a4-b87a-3bbc8b8a2062); lib. bdg. 26.65 *(978-1-5415-7929-3(1),* 83c9bb97-b340-449a-9d97-abbebb659144) Lerner Publishing Group. (Lerner Pubns.).
—Monster Shapes. Li, Amy, illus. 2020. (Monster Math Ser.). (ENG.). 24p. (J). (gr. -1-2). pap. 7.99 *(978-1-5415-8922-3(X),* 55b1a377-1fa8-48eb-9ddb-23b493d06833); lib. bdg. 26.65 *(978-1-5415-7930-9(5),* 3093a34c-8570-404b-bd7c-ec814354854e) Lerner Publishing Group. (Lerner Pubns.).
Walter, Jackie. My First Maths: What Shape Is It? 2018. (My First Maths Ser.). (ENG., Illus.). 24p. (J). (gr. -1-1). pap. 8.99 *(978-1-4451-5750-4(0),* Franklin Watts) Hachette Children's Group GBR. Dist: Hachette Bk. Group.
Watson, Hannah. Lift-The-Flap Sizes & Measuring. 2017. (Lift-The-Flap Board Bks.). (ENG.). 16p. 13.99 *(978-0-7945-4039-5(2),* Usborne) EDC Publishing.
Weakland, Mark. Hockey Shapes, 1 vol. 2013. (SI Kids Rookie Bks.). (ENG., Illus.). 32p. (J). (gr. -1-2). 27.99 *(978-1-4765-0225-0(0),* Capstone Pr.) Capstone.
Wells, Robert E. Is a Blue Whale the Biggest Thing There Is? 2012. (J). 34.28 *(978-1-61913-116-3(1))* Weigl Pubs., Inc.
—What's Smaller Than a Pygmy Shrew? 2012. (J). *(978-1-61913-158-3(7))* Weigl Pubs., Inc.
Welzen, Jon. I Know Shapes, 1 vol. 2016. (What I Know Ser.). (ENG., Illus.). 24p. (J). (gr. k-k). pap. 9.15 *(978-1-4824-5478-9(5),* b619b4a7-3d18-4a02-b0c2-c7cf7caeac76) Stevens, Gareth Publishing LLLP.
Winn, Michael. The Shape People. 2008. 28p. pap. 24.95 *(978-1-60474-544-3(4))* America Star Bks.
Winslow, Jeremy. Hours of Coloring Fun with Shapes & Patterns. 2011. 182p. 30.99 *(978-1-4568-8227-3(9));* pap. 20.99 *(978-1-4568-8226-6(0))* Xlibris Corp.
Wise the Turtle Counts to Tenb & Shapes. 2003. 3.99 *(978-0-915960-05-7(2))* Ebon Research Systems Publishing, LLC.
Wojick, Luke. I Can Draw Shapes, 1 vol. 2013. (Core Math Skills: Measurement & Geometry Ser.). (ENG., Illus.). 24p. (J). (gr. 1-1). 26.27 *(978-1-4777-2231-2(9),* 4b4445a0-5f9d-42bc-8492-2db561c1eb25); pap. 8.25 *(978-1-4777-2055-4(3),* 7ea84c8f-7d5f-41c0-92b5-c4d523c3abca) Rosen Publishing Group, Inc., The. (Rosen Classroom).
—I Can Draw Shapes: Shapes & Their Attributes. 2013. (Rosen Math Readers Ser.). (ENG., Illus.). 24p. (J). (gr. 1-2). pap. 49.50 *(978-1-4777-2056-1(1),* Rosen Classroom) Rosen Publishing Group, Inc., The.
Woodhull, Anne. Shapes. Rotner, Shelley, photos by. 2020. (Illus.). 32p. (J). (-k). 17.99 *(978-0-8234-4638-4(7))* Holiday Hse., Inc.
Wooster, Devin Ann. Big Dinosaur, Little Dinosaur. 2016. (Step into Reading - Level 1 Ser.). lib. bdg. 14.75 *(978-0-606-38479-7(0))* Turtleback.
World Book, Inc. Staff, contrib. by. Fun with Shapes. 2011. (J). *(978-0-7166-0229-3(6))* World Bk., Inc.
The World of Eric Carle My Shapes Activity Kit. 2007. (J). 16.99 *(978-0-9794445-3-1(5))* Loew-Cornell, Inc.
Yates, Gene. The Snake Shapes Book. 2004. (Illus.). 14p. (J). *(978-1-58865-155-6(X))* Kidsbooks, LLC.
Yates, Gene, illus. The Snake Shapes Book. 2006. (J). *(978-1-58865-365-9(X))* Kidsbooks, LLC.
Yegoryan, Kristina & Yegoryan, Rubik. I Know Digits & Shapes. 2009. 108p. pap. 33.49 *(978-1-4389-5444-8(1))* AuthorHouse.
Your Baby Can Learn! Shapes, Vol. 1. 2007. (J). 7.95 *(978-1-931026-13-0(0))* Infant Learning Co., The.
Zaidi, Nadeem, illus. Formas: Libro con Ventanas. 2007. (Baby Einstein Ser.). 5p. (J). (gr. -1). *(978-970-718-468-8(X),* Silver Dolphin en Español) Advanced Marketing, S. de R. L. de C. V.
Zuckerman, Rory. Shapely Sleepy Sheep. Roos, Maryn, illus. 2004. (J). bds. 12.95 *(978-0-9749305-2-7(0))* Castle Pacific Publishing.
—Shapely Sleepy Sheep. Roos, Maryn, illus. 2007. (Sleepy Sheep Ser.). (J). (gr. -1). bds. 7.95 incl. audio compact disk *(978-0-9796393-4-0(4))* Little Lion Pr.
Zuravicky, Orli. Exploring Pyramids Around the World: Making Models of Geometric Solids, 1 vol. 2003. (PowerMath: Proficiency Ser.). (ENG., Illus.). 32p. (J). (gr. 4-5). lib. bdg. 28.93 *(978-0-8239-8992-8(5),* 5b92d1b2-80fa-4330-b2d9-d9049261cd92, PowerKids Pr.) Rosen Publishing Group, Inc., The.

SIZE AND SHAPE—FICTION

Adler, David A. Don't Throw It to Mo! 2016. (Penguin Young Readers Level 2 Ser.). lib. bdg. 13.55 *(978-0-606-38852-8(4))* Turtleback.
—Pass the Ball, Mo! 2019. (Penguin Young Readers Ser.). (ENG.). 29p. (J). (gr. k-1). 14.89 *(978-0-87617-760-0(7))* Penworthy Co., LLC, The.
Albee, Sarah. Kidoozle Kids & the Great Shape Rescue! 2004. (Illus.). 12p. bds. 9.95 *(978-1-932915-02-0(8))* Sandvik Publishing.
Auerbach, Adam. The Three Vikings. Auerbach, Adam, illus. 2019. (ENG., Illus.). 40p. (J). 21.99 *(978-1-62779-601-9(0),* 900156502, Holt, Henry & Co. Bks. For Young Readers) Holt, Henry & Co.
Baldwin, Kevin. Beetle Dan & the Big Purple Slide: A Beetle Dan Story. 2006. (ENG., Illus.). 32p. (J). (gr. -1-2). 14.99 *(978-1-59185-921-5(2),* 9212, Creation Hse.) Charisma Media.
Barchers, Suzanne I. How Big Is Kip?, 1 vol. rev. ed. 2011. (Phonics Ser.). (ENG., Illus.). 16p. (gr. k-1). 6.99 *(978-1-4333-2410-9(5))* Teacher Created Materials, Inc.
Barnett, Mac. Circle. Klassen, Jon, illus. (Shapes Trilogy Ser.: 3). (ENG.). 48p. (J). (gr. k-4). 2023. 9.99 *(978-1-5362-2877-9(X))* 2019. 15.99 *(978-0-7636-9608-5(0))* Candlewick Pr.
—Square. Klassen, Jon, illus. (Shapes Trilogy Ser.: 2). (ENG.). (J). (gr. k-4). 2023. 40p. 9.99 *(978-1-5362-2876-2(1))* 2018. 48p. 15.99 *(978-0-7636-9607-8(2))* Candlewick Pr.
—Square. 2018. (KOR.). (J). *(978-89-527-8665-4(3))* Sigongsa Co., Ltd.
—Square. 2018. (CHI.). (J). *(978-986-440-224-3(2))* Viking International Co., Ltd.
—Triangle. Klassen, Jon, illus. 2017. (Shapes Trilogy Ser.). (ENG.). 48p. (J). (gr. k-4). 15.99 *(978-0-7636-9603-0(X))* Candlewick Pr.
Bauer, Joan. Stand Tall. 2005. (ENG.). 192p. (YA). (gr. 7-7). pap. 9.99 *(978-0-14-240427-0(6),* Speak) Penguin Young Readers Group.
Baxter, Nicola. Shapes. Siewert, Pauline, illus. 2021. 5p. (J). (gr. -1-12). bds. 2.99 *(978-1-84322-782-3(7),* Armadillo) Anness Publishing GBR. Dist: National Bk. Network.
Bedford, David. Big Bears Can! Hansen, Gaby, illus. 2007. (Storytime Board Bks.). 16p. (J). (gr. -1-k). bds. 6.95 *(978-1-58925-826-6(6))* Tiger Tales.
Bedford, David & Worthington, Leonie. Big. 2006. (Illus.). 16p. pap. *(978-1-921049-22-4(7))* Little Hare Bks. AUS. Dist: HarperCollins Pubs. Australia.
Bellisario, Gina. Mighty Pet Sitter. von Innerebner, Jessika, illus. 2018. (Ellie Ultra Ser.). (ENG.). 128p. (J). (gr. 1-3). lib. bdg. 25.99 *(978-1-4965-5238-9(5),* 136263, Stone Arch Bks.) Capstone.
Benjamin, A. H. I'm Taller Than You! O'Kif, illus. 2008. (Tadpoles Ser.). (ENG.). 24p. (J). (gr. -1-3). lib. bdg. *(978-0-7787-3854-1(X))* Crabtree Publishing Co.
Bentley, Jonathan. Little Big. 2015. (ENG., Illus.). 32p. (J). 16.00 *(978-0-8028-5462-9(1),* Eerdmans Bks For Young Readers) Eerdmans, William B. Publishing Co.
Berlin, Ethan T. The Hugely-Wugely Spider. Edwards, Karl Newsom, illus. 2018. (ENG.). 40p. (J). 18.99 *(978-0-374-30616-8(8),* 900174319, Farrar, Straus & Giroux (BYR)) Farrar, Straus & Giroux.
Bessen, Luc. Arthur & the Minimoys. Sowchek, Ellen, tr. from FRE. 2005. (ENG.). 240p. (J). 15.99 *(978-0-06-059623-1(6))* HarperCollins Pubs.
Besson, Luc. Arthur & the Forbidden City. Sowchek, Ellen, tr. 2006. (ENG., Illus.). 192p. (J). (gr. 3-7). pap., pap. 5.99 *(978-0-06-059628-6(7),* Harper Trophy) HarperCollins Pubs.
—Arthur & the Forbidden City. 2005. (ENG., Illus.). 192p. (J). 15.99 *(978-0-06-059626-2(0))* HarperCollins Pubs.
—Arthur & the Minimoys. 2005. (Illus.). 240p. (J). lib. bdg. 16.89 *(978-0-06-059624-8(4))* HarperCollins Pubs.
Bingham, Kelly. Circle, Square, Moose. Zelinsky, Paul O., illus. 2014. (ENG.). 48p. (J). (gr. -1-3). 17.99 *(978-0-06-229003-8(7),* Greenwillow Bks.) HarperCollins Pubs.
Birkhead, Jennifer. Peeping Through the Low, Green Grass. 2011. 28p. pap. 12.03 *(978-1-4490-5490-8(0))* AuthorHouse.
Blackstone, Stella. Bear in a Square / Oso en un Cuadrado. Harter, Debbie, illus. 2009. (Bear Ser.). (ENG.). 24p. (J). (gr. -1-1). pap. 8.99 *(978-1-84686-387-5(2))* Barefoot Bks., Inc.
—Ship Shapes. Bell, Siobhan, illus. (J). 2008. (ENG.). 24p. (gr. -1-k). bds. 8.99 *(978-1-84686-157-4(8))* 2006. *(978-1-4156-6474-2(9))* Barefoot Bks., Inc.
—Ship Shapes. 2012. lib. bdg. 17.20 *(978-0-606-23826-7(3))* Turtleback.
Boldt, Mike. Colors Versus Shapes. 2014. (ENG., Illus.). 40p. (J). (gr. -1-3). 16.99 *(978-0-06-210303-1(2),* HarperCollins) HarperCollins Pubs.
Bova, Della L. The Adventures of Pono: A Puppy Dog's Tale. 2011. 24p. pap. 11.49 *(978-1-4490-7354-1(9))* AuthorHouse.
Bowen, Fred. Full Court Fever, 1 vol. rev. ed. 2009. (Fred Bowen Sports Story Ser.: 6). (Illus.). 103p. (J). (gr. 2-6). pap. 6.95 *(978-1-56145-508-9(3))* Peachtree Publishing Co. Inc.
Bowman, Crystal. Little David Sings for the King, 1 vol. Hartung, Susan Kathleen, illus. 2010. (I Can Read! / Little

S

David Ser.). (ENG.). 32p. (J). pap. 4.99 *(978-0-310-71711-9(6))* Zonderkidz.

Boxes, 6 Pack. (Literatura 2000 Ser.). (gr. 1-2). 28.00 *(978-0-7635-0122-8(0))* Rigby Education.

Braun, Sebastien. Toot & Pop! Braun, Sebastien, illus. 2012. (ENG., Illus.). 32p. (J). (gr. -1-2). 12.99 *(978-0-06-207750-9(3)*, HarperCollins) HarperCollins Pubs.

Brexel, Bernadette. Gloria's Triangles, 1 vol. 2015. (Rosen REAL Readers: STEM & STEAM Collection). (ENG.). 8p. (gr. k-1). pap. 5.46 *(978-1-4994-9535-5(8)*, 3984e411-d404-412f-b439-b9c9202af015, Rosen Classroom) Rosen Publishing Group, Inc., The.

Bridwell, Norman. Clifford Makes the Team (Scholastic Reader, Level 1) Bridwell, Norman, illus. 2011. (Scholastic Reader, Level 1 Ser.). (ENG., Illus.). 32p. (J). (gr. -1-1). pap. 3.99 *(978-0-545-23141-1(8))* Scholastic, Inc.

Brière-Haquet, Alice. ONE Very Big Bear. Philipponneau, Olivier & Enjary, Raphaële, illus. 2016. (ENG.). 32p. (J). (gr. -1-k). 14.95 *(978-1-4197-2117-5(8)*, 1120001, Abrams Appleseed) Abrams, Inc.

Bright, Paul. The Hole Story. Ingman, Bruce, illus. 2017. (Andersen Press Picture Bks.). (ENG.). 32p. (gr. -1-3). 35.99 *(978-1-5124-3972-4(X))* Lerner Publishing Group.

Bunting, Eve. Little Yellow Truck. Zimmer, Kevin, illus. 2019. (ENG.). 32p. (J). (gr. k-3). 16.99 *(978-1-58536-407-7(X)*, 204649) Sleeping Bear Pr.

Carle, Eric. My First Busy Book. Carle, Eric, illus. 2015. (World of Eric Carle Ser.). (ENG., Illus.). 12p. (J). (gr. -1). bds. 16.99 *(978-1-4814-5791-0(8)*, Little Simon) Little Simon.

Carlson, Nancy. ¡Piensa en Grande! 2005. (Libros Ilustrados (Picture Bks.)). (SPA., Illus.). 32p. (J). (gr. k-2). lib. bdg. 15.95 *(978-0-8225-3192-0(5)*, Ediciones Lerner) Lerner Publishing Group.

—Think Big! 2005. (Illus.). 28p. (J). (gr. -1-3). 15.95 *(978-1-57505-622-7(4)*, Carolrhoda Bks.) Lerner Publishing Group.

Cha, Hanna. Tiny Feet Between the Mountains. Cha, Hanna, illus. 2019. (ENG., Illus.). 40p. (J). (gr. -1-3). 17.99 *(978-1-5344-2992-5(1)*, Simon & Schuster Bks. For Young Readers) Simon & Schuster Bks. For Young Readers.

Chaconas, Dori. Short & Tall. McCue, Lisa, illus. 2006. (Penguin Young Readers: Level 3 Ser.: 2). (ENG.). 32p. (J). (gr. 1-3). 16.19 *(978-0-670-05985-0(4)*, Viking) Penguin Publishing Group.

—Short & Tall No. 2, 2 vols. McCue, Lisa, illus. 2010. (Cork & Fuzz Ser.: 2). 32p. (J). (gr. 1-3). mass mkt. 4.99 *(978-0-14-241594-8(4)*, Penguin Young Readers) Penguin Young Readers Group.

Child, Lauren. I Want to Be Much More Bigger Like You. 2008. (Charlie & Lola Ser.). (ENG., Illus.). 24p. (J). (gr. -1-k). mass mkt. 4.99 *(978-0-448-44867-1(X)*, Grosset & Dunlap) Penguin Young Readers Group.

Clay III, J. Percy. Sampson's Pumpkin Playhouse. 2012. 30p. 24.95 *(978-1-4626-7226-4(4))* America Star Bks.

Cole, Henry. Big Bug. Cole, Henry, illus. 2018. (Classic Board Bks.). (ENG., Illus.). 28p. (J). (gr. -1 — 1). bds. 7.99 *(978-1-5344-1690-1(0)*, Little Simon) Little Simon.

—Big Bug. Cole, Henry, illus. 2014. (ENG., Illus.). 32p. (J). (gr. -1-2). 18.99 *(978-1-4424-9897-6(8)*, Little Simon) Little Simon.

Conn, Marla. I See Shapes, Dear Dragon, 10 vols. David Schimmell, illus. 2019. (Dear Dragon Developing Readers Ser.). (ENG.). 24p. (J). (gr. k-k). pap. 11.94 *(978-1-68404-321-7(2))* Norwood Hse. Pr.

Costello, David Hyde. Little Pig Joins the Band. Costello, David Hyde, illus. 2014. (Illus.). 32p. (J). (gr. -1-3). pap. 7.95 *(978-1-58089-265-0(5))* Charlesbridge Publishing, Inc.

—Little Pig Joins the Band. 2014. (ENG.). (J). (gr. -1-3). lib. bdg. 18.55 *(978-1-62765-428-9(3))* Perfection Learning Corp.

Coulton, Mia. Danny's Favorite Shapes. Coulton, Mia, photos by. 2004. (ENG., Illus.). pap. *(978-0-9746475-4-8(3))* Maryruth Bks., Inc.

Coville, Bruce. Jeremy Thatcher, Dragon Hatcher: A Magic Shop Book. Lippincott, Gary A., illus. 20th ed. 2007. (Magic Shop Book Ser.: 2). (ENG.). 176p. (J). (gr. 5-7). pap. 7.99 *(978-0-15-206252-1(1)*, 1198750, Clarion Bks.) HarperCollins Pubs.

Crews, Donald. Diez Puntos Negros: Ten Black Dots (Spanish Edition), 1 vol. Crews, Donald, illus. 2009. (SPA., Illus.). 32p. (J). (gr. -1-3). 17.99 *(978-0-06-177138-5(4))* HarperCollins Español.

—Ten Black Dots. 2010. (ENG., Illus.). 32p. (J). (gr. -1-3). bds. 8.99 *(978-0-06-185779-9(3)*, Greenwillow Bks.) HarperCollins Pubs.

Curato, Mike. Little Elliot, Big City. Curato, Mike, illus. 2014. (Little Elliot Ser.: 1). (ENG., Illus.). 40p. (J). (gr. -1-3). 18.99 *(978-0-8050-9825-9(9)*, 900121237, Holt, Henry & Co. Bks. For Young Readers) Holt, Henry & Co.

—Little Elliot, Fall Friends. Curato, Mike, illus. 2017. (Little Elliot Ser.: 4). (ENG., Illus.). 40p. (J). 18.99 *(978-1-62779-640-8(1)*, 900157312, Holt, Henry & Co. Bks. For Young Readers) Holt, Henry & Co.

Dahl, Roald. Esio Trot. 2009. 8.32 *(978-0-7848-2293-7(X)*, Everbind) Marco Bk. Co.

—Esio Trot. Blake, Quentin, illus. 2009. (ENG.). 96p. (J). (gr. 3-7). 7.99 *(978-0-14-241382-1(8)*, Puffin Books) Penguin Young Readers Group.

—Esio Trot. 2004. (CHI.). (J). pap. 11.70 *(978-957-574-477-9(2))* Youth Cultural Publishing Co. CHN. Dist: Chinasprout, Inc.

Dale, Katie. Thumbelina Thinks Big! 2016. (ENG., Illus.). 32p. (J). *(978-0-7787-2473-5(5))* Crabtree Publishing Co.

d'Aulaire, Ingri, et al. Too Big. 2008. (Illus.). 40p. (J). (gr. k-k). 16.95 *(978-1-59017-291-9(4)*, NYR Children's Collection) New York Review of Bks., Inc., The.

David, Lawrence. The Terror of the Pink Dodo Balloons. Gott, Barry, illus. 2003. (Horace Splattly Ser.). 153p. (J). (gr. 4-7). 12.65 *(978-0-7569-2816-2(8))* Perfection Learning Corp.

Daywalt, Drew. Happy Easter from the Crayons. Jeffers, Oliver, illus. 2023. (ENG.). 32p. (J). (gr. -1-3). 9.99 *(978-0-593-62105-9(0)*, Philomel Bks.) Penguin Young Readers Group.

Delle Donne, Elena. Elle of the Ball. 2019. (Hoops Ser.: 1). (ENG., Illus.). 176p. (J). (gr. 3-7). pap. 7.99 *(978-1-5344-1232-3(8)*, Simon & Schuster Bks. For Young Readers) Simon & Schuster Bks. For Young Readers.

DeStefano, Anthony. Little Star. 2013. (ENG., Illus.). 36p. (J). (gr. k-3). 15.99 *(978-0-7369-5859-2(2)*, 6958592) Harvest Hse. Pubs.

Diaz, Neibaliz. Laura y Su Caja de Sorpresas. 2007. (SPA.). 48p. 14.95 *(978-0-8477-0452-1(1))* Univ. of Puerto Rico Pr.

Dodd, Emma. Dog & Friends: Shapes. 2017. (Illus.). 12p. (J). (gr. -1-12). bds. 9.99 *(978-1-86147-844-3(5)*, Armadillo) Anness Publishing GBR. Dist: National Bk. Network.

Donahue, Laurie. Mr. Blue a Job for You. Bryan, Hintz, illus. 2010. 32p. (J). 15.95 *(978-0-9799116-2-0(1))* LifeSong Pubs.

Donnio, Sylviane. I'd Really Like to Eat a Child. 2012. (ENG., Illus.). 32p. (J). (gr. -1-2). pap. 7.99 *(978-0-307-93008-8(4)*, Dragonfly Bks.) Random Hse. Children's Bks.

—I'd Really Like to Eat a Child. 2012. lib. bdg. 18.40 *(978-0-606-23845-8(X))* Turtleback.

Dougherty, Brandi. The Littlest Elf. Richards, Kirsten, illus. 2012. (Littlest Ser.). (ENG.). 24p. (J). (gr. -1-k). pap. 4.99 *(978-0-545-43654-0(0)*, Cartwheel Bks.) Scholastic, Inc.

—The Littlest Elf. Richards, Kirsten, illus. 2012. (J). pap. *(978-0-545-48978-2(4)*, WestBow Pr.) Scholastic, Inc.

—The Littlest Pilgrim. Richards, Kirsten, illus. 2008. (Littlest Ser.). (ENG.). 32p. (J). (gr. -1-k). pap. 3.99 *(978-0-545-05372-3(2)*, Cartwheel Bks.) Scholastic, Inc.

Dull, Dennis Stanley. Baby Basics & Beyond: ABC's, 123's & Shapes. Dull, Dennis Stanley, illus. 2nd ed. 2004. (Illus.). (J). *(978-0-9717475-4-8(7))* Laurel Valley Graphics, Inc.

Duvall, Sheila Marie. I See Fun. 2009. 16p. pap. 8.75 *(978-1-4389-4963-5(4))* AuthorHouse.

Dyer, Nick. Little Things. Pousette, Kelly, illus. 2019. (ENG.). 32p. (J). 16.99 *(978-1-4413-2859-5(9)*, 257f1e78-ecf3-4255-97cb-b94cb912f40a) Peter Pauper Pr. Inc.

Emberley, Rebecca. The Lion & the Mice. Emberley, Ed, illus. 2012. (I Like to Read Ser.). (ENG.). 24p. (J). (gr. -1-3). pap. 7.99 *(978-0-8234-2641-6(6))* Holiday Hse., Inc.

Emma Treehouse Ltd. My Friends. Davis, Caroline, illus. 2007. (Easy Flaps Ser.). 10p. (J). (gr. -1). bds. 6.95 *(978-1-58925-823-5(1))* Tiger Tales.

Enderle, Dotti. Clawed! An Up2U Horror Adventure, 1 vol. To, Vivienne, illus. 2013. (Up2U Adventures Ser.). (ENG.). 80p. (J). (gr. 2-5). lib. bdg. 35.64 *(978-1-61641-965-3(2)*, 15213, Calico Chapter Bks.) ABDO Publishing Co.

Evans, Cordelia. So Many Shapes! 2016. (Yo Gabba Gabba! Ser.). (ENG., Illus.). 24p. (J). (gr. -1-1). 16.19 *(978-1-4844-8404-3(5)*, Simon Spotlight) Simon & Schuster Children's Publishing.

Findlay, Lisa. Gulliver in Lilliput. Caparo, Antonio Javier, illus. 2010. (Step into Reading Ser.). 48p. (J). (gr. k-3). pap. 4.99 *(978-0-375-86585-5(3)*, Random Hse. Bks. for Young Readers) Random Hse. Children's Bks.

Findlay, Lisa & Swift, Jonathan. Gulliver in Lilliput. Caparó, Antonio Javier, illus. 2010. (Step into Reading: Step 3 Ser.). (ENG.). 48p. (J). (gr. k-2). lib. bdg. 16.19 *(978-0-375-96585-2(8))* Random Hse. Bks. for Young Readers.

Fisher, Doris. Happy Birthday to Whooo?, 1 vol. Downey, Lisa, illus. 2006. (ENG.). 32p. (J). (gr. -1-3). 15.95 *(978-0-9768823-1-2(0))*; pap. 8.95 *(978-1-934359-06-8(8))* Arbordale Publishing.

Fleming, Denise. Go, Shapes, Go! Fleming, Denise, illus. 2014. (ENG., Illus.). 40p. (J). (gr. -1-3). 18.99 *(978-1-4424-8240-1(0)*, Beach Lane Bks.) Beach Lane Bks.

Flory, Neil. The Short Giraffe. 2015. (Illus.). 24p. (J). *(978-1-4896-3885-4(7))* Weigl Pubs., Inc.

Fontes, Justine. Black Meets White. Waring, Geoff, illus. 2005. (ENG.). 24p. (J). (— 1). 12.99 *(978-0-7636-1933-6(7))* Candlewick Pr.

Foxley, Janet. Muncle Trogg. 2012. (J). *(978-0-545-37801-7(X))* Scholastic, Inc.

Friedman, Mel, et al. Un Castillo para Gatitos. Adams, Lynn, illus. 2008. (SPA.). (J). *(978-1-57565-275-7(7))* Astra Publishing Hse.

Galvin, Laura. Pooh & Friends Colors & Shapes. 2008. (ENG.). 24p. (J). (gr. -1). 4.99 *(978-1-59069-736-8(7))* Studio Mouse LLC.

Galvin, Laura Gates. Mickey Mouse Clubhouse Fun with Numbers & Shapes. 2008. (ENG.). 20p. (J). (gr. -1-3). 9.99 *(978-1-59069-655-2(7))* Studio Mouse LLC.

Garland, Michael. Hooray José!, 1 vol. Garland, Michael, illus. 2007. (ENG., Illus.). 32p. (J). (gr. -1-3). 16.99 *(978-0-7614-5345-1(8))* Marshall Cavendish Corp.

Garner, Albert. The Adventures of Dimi. 2013. (ENG.). 48p. (J). 24.95 *(978-1-4787-1677-8(0))* Outskirts Pr., Inc.

Gillespie, Jane. Diving for Shapes in Hawaii: An Identification Book for Keiki. Bosgra, Johann, illus. 2004. (ENG.). 20p. (J). bds. 8.95 *(978-1-933067-04-9(7))* Beachhouse Publishing, LLC.

Goldberg, Ella, ed. Simple Shapes. 2013. (Matching Pictures Ser.). (ENG.). 20p. (J). (gr. -1-k). bds. 5.95 *(978-1-61889-311-6(4))* AZ Bks. LLC.

Gomi, Taro. Little Boat: (Taro Gomi Kids Book, Board Book for Toddlers, Children's Boat Book) 2018. (Taro Gomi by Chronicle Bks.). (ENG., Illus.). 22p. (J). (gr. -1 — 1). bds. 6.99 *(978-1-4521-6301-7(4))* Chronicle Bks. LLC.

Gourlay, Candy. Tall Story. 2012. (ENG.). 304p. (J). (gr. 5). 8.99 *(978-0-385-75233-6(4)*, Yearling) Random Hse. Children's Bks.

Graham, Elspeth. Sandwich that Jack Made. Mould, Chris, illus. 2004. (ENG.). 24p. (J). lib. bdg. 23.65 *(978-1-59646-698-2(7))* Dingles & Co.

Granhold, Adriana. Mattie Knowsmath & the Great Shape Hunt. 2012. 32p. pap. 24.95 *(978-1-4626-7202-8(7))* America Star Bks.

Gravett, Emily. Blue Chameleon. Gravett, Emily, illus. 2011. (ENG., Illus.). 32p. (J). (gr. -1-1). 16.99 *(978-1-4424-1958-2(X)*, Simon & Schuster Bks. For Young Readers) Simon & Schuster Bks. For Young Readers.

Greban, Tanguy. Sarah So Small. Greban, Quentin, illus. 2004. 32p. (J). 16.95 *(978-0-689-03594-4(2)*, Milk & Cookies) ibooks, Inc.

Green, Judy. The Little Blue Octopus. 2009. 28p. pap. 21.99 *(978-1-4415-3393-7(1))* Xlibris Corp.

Greenburg, J. C. Andrew Lost #16: in Uncle Al, No. 16. Gerardi, Jan, illus. 2007. (Andrew Lost Ser.: 16). (ENG.). 96p. (J). (gr. 1-4). 4.99 *(978-0-375-83565-0(2)*, Random Hse. Bks. for Young Readers) Random Hse. Children's Bks.

—Andrew Lost #18: with the Frogs. Gerardi, Jan, illus. 2008. (Andrew Lost Ser.: 18). (ENG.). 96p. (J). (gr. 1-4). 6.99 *(978-0-375-84668-7(9)*, Random Hse. Bks. for Young Readers) Random Hse. Children's Bks.

—With the Frogs, 18. Gerardi, Jan, illus. 2008. (Andrew Lost Ser.: No. 18). (ENG.). 86p. (J). (gr. 3-6). lib. bdg. 16.19 *(978-0-375-94668-4(3))* Random House Publishing Group.

Guettier, Nancy. Jude's Moon. Walsh, Tina, illus. 2014. (ENG.). 32p. (J). (gr. -1-4). pap. 9.95 *(978-1-61448-964-1(5))* Morgan James Publishing.

Hale, Bruce. Danny & the Dinosaur: Too Tall. Cutting, David, illus. 2015. 29p. (J). *(978-1-4806-8575-8(5))* Harper & Row Ltd.

Hall, Kirsten. Tug-of-War: All about Balance. Luedecke, Bev, illus. 2004. (Beastieville Ser.). 31p. (J). 19.50 *(978-0-516-22899-0(4)*, Children's Pr.) Scholastic Library Publishing.

Hall, Michael. Perfect Square. Hall, Michael, illus. 2011. (ENG., Illus.). 40p. (J). (gr. -1-k). 17.99 *(978-0-06-191513-0(0)*, Greenwillow Bks.) HarperCollins Pubs.

Hansen, Dustin. Tiny-Raptor Pack Attack. 2018. (Microsaurs Ser.: 2). (J). lib. bdg. 17.20 *(978-0-606-41108-0(9))* Turtleback.

Hanson, Warren. Grandpa Has a Great Big Face. Elliott, Mark, illus. 2006. 32p. (J). (gr. -1-3). 17.89 *(978-0-06-078776-9(7)*, Geringer, Laura Book) HarperCollins Pubs.

Hanton, Sophie. Shapes on the Farm. 2009. (Mag-NUT-Tics! Ser.). (Illus.). (J). bds. 9.99 *(978-1-934650-74-5(9))* Just For Kids Pr., LLC.

Hartmann, Annabelle. As Big As a Mountain. 2003. (ENG., Illus.). 32p. (YA). *(978-1-84365-001-0(0)*, Pavilion Children's Books) Pavilion Bks.

Have You Seen Joe?, Pk. 6. (gr. -1-2). 23.00 *(978-0-7635-8800-7(8))* Rigby Education.

Hawkes, Kevin. The Wicked Big Toddlah. 2010. 40p. (J). (gr. -1-2). pap. 7.99 *(978-0-440-41788-0(0)*, Dragonfly Bks.) Random Hse. Children's Bks.

Henry, Steve. Here Is Big Bunny. 2017. (I Like to Read Ser.). (ENG.). 32p. (J). (gr. -1-3). 4.99 *(978-0-8234-3885-3(6))*; 7.99 *(978-0-8234-3774-0(4))* Holiday Hse., Inc.

Henson, Tara. The Littlest Blue Jay. 2011. 24p. pap. 15.99 *(978-1-4568-7956-3(1))* Xlibris Corp.

Herman, R. A. The Littlest Christmas Tree. Rogers, Jacqueline, illus. 2007. (ENG.). 32p. (J). (gr. -1-3). pap. 3.99 *(978-0-439-54007-0(0))* Scholastic, Inc.

—Pal Saves the Day. Ogden, Betina, illus. 2004. (Pal the Pony Ser.). 32p. (J). pap. *(978-0-439-64985-8(4))*; pap. *(978-0-439-57746-5(2))* Scholastic, Inc.

Hillert, Margaret. Dear Dragon's Fun with Shapes. Schimmell, David, illus. 2015. (BeginningtoRead Ser.). 32p. (J). (-2). lib. bdg. 22.60 *(978-1-59953-544-9(0))* Norwood Hse. Pr.

—Dear Dragon's Fun with Shapes. David Schimmell, illus. 2012. (Beginning-To-Read Ser.). (ENG.). 32p. (J). (gr. k-2). pap. 13.26 *(978-1-60357-447-1(6))* Norwood Hse. Pr.

—I Like Things. (J). 4.95 *(978-0-87895-683-8(2))* Modern Curriculum Pr.

—I Like Things. Hopkins, Jeff, illus. 2016. (BeginningtoRead Ser.). (ENG.). 32p. (J). (gr. 1-2). 22.60 *(978-1-59953-817-4(2))* Norwood Hse. Pr.

—Pulgarcito. Yu-Mei Han, illus. 2018. (Beginning-To-Read Ser.).Tr. of Tom Thumb. (SPA.). 32p. (J). (gr. k-2). pap. 13.26 *(978-1-68404-244-9(5))* Norwood Hse. Pr.

—Pulgarcito. Jack Pullan & Han, Yu-Mei, illus. 2017. (BeginningtoRead Ser.).Tr. of Tom Thumb. (ENG & SPA.). 32p. (J). (-2). pap. 11.94 *(978-1-68404-052-0(3))* Norwood Hse. Pr.

—¿Qué Tengo en el Bolsillo, Querido Dragón? Fernandez, Queta, tr. from ENG. Schimmell, David, illus. 2014. (BeginningtoRead Ser.).Tr. of What's in My Pocket, Dear Dragon? (ENG & SPA.). 32p. (J). (-2). lib. bdg. 22.60 *(978-1-59953-611-8(0))* Norwood Hse. Pr.

—What's in My Pocket, Dear Dragon? Schimmell, David, illus. 2014. (BeginningtoRead Ser.). (ENG.). 32p. (J). (-2). lib. bdg. 22.60 *(978-1-59953-579-1(3))* Norwood Hse. Pr.

—What's in My Pocket, Dear Dragon? David Schimmell, illus. 2013. (Beginning-To-Read Ser.). (ENG.). 32p. (J). (gr. k-2). pap. 13.26 *(978-1-60357-415-0(8))* Norwood Hse. Pr.

Hillert, Margaret, et al. Pulgarcito. Han, Yu-Mei, illus. 2018. (BeginningtoRead Ser.).Tr. of Tom Thumb. (SPA.). 32p. (J). (gr. -1-2). lib. bdg. 22.60 *(978-1-59953-960-7(8))* Norwood Hse. Pr.

Hoefler, Kate. Great Big Things. Klocek, Noah, illus. 2017. (ENG.). 40p. (J). (gr. -1-3). 17.99 *(978-0-544-77477-3(9)*, 1637144, Clarion Bks.) HarperCollins Pubs.

Holub, Joan. Itty Bitty Kitty. Burks, James, illus. 2015. (ENG.). 32p. (J). (gr. -1-3). 17.99 *(978-0-06-232219-7(2)*, HarperCollins) HarperCollins Pubs.

—Itty Bitty Kitty & the Rainy Play Day. Burks, James, illus. 2016. (ENG.). 32p. (J). (gr. -1-3). 17.99 *(978-0-06-232220-3(6)*, HarperCollins) HarperCollins Pubs.

Hopgood, Tim. Walter's Wonderful Web: A First Book about Shapes. 2016. (ENG., Illus.). 32p. (J). 18.99 *(978-0-374-30352-5(5)*, 900156325, Farrar, Straus & Giroux (BYR)) Farrar, Straus & Giroux.

Hopper, Ada. Invasion of the Insects. Ricks, Sam, illus. 2017. (DATA Set Ser.: 6). (ENG.). 128p. (J). (gr. -1-4). 17.99 *(978-1-4814-7117-6(1)*, Little Simon) Little Simon.

Howe, James. Brontorina. Cecil, Randy, illus. (ENG.). 32p. (J). (gr. -1-3). 2013. 7.99 *(978-0-7636-5323-1(3))* 2010. 17.99 *(978-0-7636-4437-6(4))* Candlewick Pr.

—Brontorina. 2013. lib. bdg. 17.20 *(978-0-606-31600-2(0))* Turtleback.

Hutchins, Pat. Titch. 2014. 32p. pap. 7.00 *(978-1-61003-367-1(1))* Center for the Collaborative Classroom.

Inches, Alison. I'm Not Little! Thomas, Glenn, illus. 2017. (ENG.). 32p. (J). (gr. -1-3). 16.99 *(978-1-4998-0377-8(X))* Little Bee Books Inc.

Jensen, Joel, et al. Tiny Hamster Is a Giant Monster. 2015. (ENG., Illus.). 32p. (J). (gr. -1-3). 17.99 *(978-1-4814-5110-9(3)*, Simon & Schuster Bks. For Young Readers) Simon & Schuster Bks. For Young Readers.

Joyce, William. George Shrinks. Joyce, William, illus. 2017. (World of William Joyce Ser.). (ENG., Illus.). 40p. (J). (gr. -1-3). 17.99 *(978-1-4814-8953-9(4)*, Atheneum/Caitlyn Dlouhy Books) Simon & Schuster Children's Publishing.

Kanninen, Barbara. Circle Rolls. 2018. (ENG., Illus.). 32p. (gr. -1-k). 16.95 *(978-0-7148-7630-6(5))* Phaidon Pr., Inc.

Keane, Claire. Little Big Girl. 2016. (Illus.). 32p. (J). (-k). 17.99 *(978-0-8037-3912-3(5)*, Dial Bks) Penguin Young Readers Group.

Klimo, Kate. Twinky the Dinky Dog. Fleming, Michael, illus. 2013. (Step into Reading Ser.). 48p. (J). (gr. k-3). pap. 5.99 *(978-0-307-97667-3(X)*, Random Hse. Bks. for Young Readers) Random Hse. Children's Bks.

Kling, Kevin. Big Little Brother. Monroe, Chris, illus. 2011. (ENG.). 48p. (J). (gr. -1-2). 17.95 *(978-0-87351-844-4(6)*, Borealis Bk.) Minnesota Historical Society Pr.

Krajenbrink Hulin, Yvonne. My Magic Box of Shapes. 2013. 28p. pap. 11.99 *(978-0-9794133-7-7(0))* Holst Bks.

Kranz, Linda. One Yellow Fish. 2016. (Illus.). 24p. (J). (gr. -1-12). 6.95 *(978-1-63076-246-9(6))* Muddy Boots Pr.

Krauss, Ruth. Big & Little. Szilagyi, Mary, illus. 2003. (J). pap. 12.95 *(978-0-590-40698-7(1))* Scholastic, Inc.

Ladrillo, Antonio. This Way, That Way. 2017. (ENG., Illus.). 24p. (J). (gr. -1-1). 12.95 *(978-1-84976-451-3(4))* Tate Publishing, Ltd. GBR. Dist: Hachette Bk. Group.

Lane, Alison Hoffman. Uncle Arnel & the Awful, Angry Alligator. 2009. (Uncle Arnel Ser.). (Illus.). 32p. (J). 15.95 *(978-1-58980-645-0(X)*, Pelican Publishing) Arcadia Publishing.

Latimer, Miriam. Shrinking Sam. Latimer, Miriam, illus. 2007. (Illus.). 32p. (J). (gr. -1-3). 16.99 *(978-1-84686-038-6(5))* Barefoot Bks., Inc.

Law, Felicia. Shapes. Knight, Paula, illus. 2015. (Patchwork Ser.). (ENG.). 24p. (J). (gr. k-3). lib. bdg. 22.60 *(978-1-59953-714-6(1))* Norwood Hse. Pr.

—Size. Knight, Paula, illus. 2015. (Patchwork Ser.). (ENG.). 24p. (J). (gr. k-3). pap. 11.94 *(978-1-60357-803-5(X))*; lib. bdg. 22.60 *(978-1-59953-713-9(3))* Norwood Hse. Pr.

Law, Felicia & Way, Steve. Crocodile Teeth: Geometric Shapes in Action, 1 vol. Spoor, Mike, illus. 2009. (Mandrill Mountain Math Mysteries Ser.). (ENG.). 32p. (J). (gr. 2-3). 27.27 *(978-1-60754-816-4(X)*, f316fc20-91e6-4a71-a59a-55448d4523ab); pap. 11.55 *(978-1-60754-821-8(6)*, d64648f7-9081-4d51-9365-aff6071b54489) Rosen Publishing Group, Inc., The. (Windmill Bks.).

Lawson, Robert. The Fabulous Flight. 2018. (ENG., Illus.). 160p. (gr. 3-7). pap. 12.95 *(978-0-486-82332-4(6)*, 823326) Dover Pubns., Inc.

Lee, Lori K. Bonnie the Honeybee & the Case of the Butterfly Blues. 2011. (ENG., Illus.). 30p. (J). 12.95 *(978-0-9828689-6-6(0)*, BQB Publishing) Boutique of Quality Books Publishing Co., Inc.

Leigh, Autumn. Spots & Stripes, 1 vol. 2005. (Rosen REAL Readers Ser.). (ENG.). 8p. (gr. k-1). pap. 5.15 *(978-0-8239-6335-5(7)*, a16394d0-46d2-4456-864b-23101daab771, Rosen Classroom) Rosen Publishing Group, Inc., The.

Lichtenheld, Tom. Cloudette. Lichtenheld, Tom, illus. 2011. (ENG., Illus.). 40p. (J). (gr. -1-2). 19.99 *(978-0-8050-8776-5(1)*, 900050160, Holt, Henry & Co. Bks. For Young Readers) Holt, Henry & Co.

Light, Steven. Have You Seen My Monster? Light, Steve, illus. 2015. (ENG.). 48p. (J). (-k). 16.99 *(978-0-7636-7513-4(X))* Candlewick Pr.

Litwin, Eric. The Nuts: Keep Rolling! Magoon, Scott, illus. 2017. (ENG.). 32p. (J). (gr. -1-3). 18.99 *(978-0-316-32251-5(2))* Little, Brown Bks. for Young Readers.

Loughran, Kelley. A Crab Called Mouse. 2006. (Illus.). (J). (gr. -1-3). pap. 9.50 *(978-0-9787995-2-6(6))* High-Pitched Hum Inc.

Love, Pamela. Dos pies suben, dos pies Bajan: Two Feet up, Two Feet Down. Chapman, Lynne, illus. 2005. (Rookie Reader Español Ser.). 32p. (gr. k-2). 19.50 *(978-0-516-25252-0(6)*, Children's Pr.) Scholastic Library Publishing.

MacDonald, Suse. Shape by Shape. MacDonald, Suse, illus. 2009. (ENG., Illus.). 24p. (J). (gr. -1-3). 17.99 *(978-1-4169-7147-4(5)*, Little Simon) Little Simon.

Malone, Marianne. The Secret of the Key: a Sixty-Eight Rooms Adventure. 2015. (Sixty-Eight Rooms Adventures Ser.: 4). (ENG., Illus.). 256p. (J). (gr. 3-7). 8.99 *(978-0-307-97724-3(2)*, Yearling) Random Hse. Children's Bks.

—The Sixty-Eight Rooms, 1. Triplett, Gina & Call, Greg, illus. 2011. (Sixty-Eight Rooms Adventures Ser.). (ENG.). 288p. (J). (gr. 4-6). lib. bdg. 22.44 *(978-0-375-95710-9(3))* Random House Publishing Group.

—The Sixty-Eight Rooms. Call, Greg, illus. 2011. (Sixty-Eight Rooms Adventures Ser.: 1). (ENG.). 288p. (J). (gr. 3-7). pap. 9.99 *(978-0-375-85711-9(7)*, Yearling) Random Hse. Children's Bks.

—Stealing Magic, 2. Call, Greg, illus. 2013. (Sixty-Eight Rooms Adventures Ser.). (ENG.). 272p. (J). (gr. 4-6). lib. bdg. 21.19 *(978-0-375-96819-8(9)*, Yearling) Random Hse. Children's Bks.

—Stealing Magic: a Sixty-Eight Rooms Adventure. Call, Greg, illus. 2013. (Sixty-Eight Rooms Adventures Ser.: 2). (ENG.). 272p. (J). (gr. 3-7). pap. 9.99 *(978-0-375-86790-3(2)*, Yearling) Random Hse. Children's Bks.

Mann, Elizabeth. Little Man: A Novel. 2014. (ENG., Illus.). 208p. (J). (gr. 5-7). 18.95 *(978-1-931414-49-4(1)*, 38f69c8a-89d2-4d48-aaba-c6ec00ff1c92) Mikaya Pr.

Mara, Nichole. All Aboard! (an Abrams Extend-A-Book) Let's Ride a Train. Kolb, Andrew, illus. 2017. (Abrams Extend-A-Book Ser.). (ENG.). 10p. (J). (gr. -1 — 1). bds. 9.95 *(978-1-4197-2567-8(X)*, 1180210, Abrams Appleseed) Abrams, Inc.

Marie, Lynne. The Star in the Christmas Play. Hussey, Lorna, illus. 2018. 32p. (J). 16.99 *(978-1-5064-3813-9(X)*, Beaming Books) 1517 Media.

Martin, Emily Winfield. The Littlest Family's Big Day. (ENG., Illus.). (J). 2018. 38p. (— 1). bds. 8.99 *(978-0-525-57867-3(6))* 2016. 36p. (gr. -1-2). 17.99 *(978-0-553-51101-7(7))* Random Hse. Children's Bks. (Random Hse. Bks. for Young Readers).

May, Eleanor. Albert's Bigger Than Big Idea. 2018. (Mouse Math Ser.). (ENG.). 32p. (J). (gr. -1-1). lib. bdg. 34.28 *(978-1-4896-8309-0(7)*, AV2 by Weigl) Weigl Pubs., Inc.

—Albert's BIGGER Than Big Idea. Melmon, Deborah, illus. 2013. (Mouse Math Ser.). 32p. (J). (gr. -1-1). pap. 7.99

(978-1-57565-522-2(5), d6fbf856-4964-472b-bcd8-64f9d26d0cbd, Kane Press) Astra Publishing Hse.
—Mice on Ice. Melmon, Deborah, illus. 2013. (Mouse Math Ser.). 32p. (J). (gr. -1-1). 22.60 *(978-1-57565-527-7(6))*; pap. 7.99 *(978-1-57565-528-4(4),* 2a9ca53b-ef64-4466-beb6-a3300c56f275, Kane Press) Astra Publishing Hse.
Mayer, Mercer. Just Big Enough. 2013. (Little Critter Ser.). (J). lib. bdg. 13.55 *(978-0-606-31809-9(7))* Turtleback.
—When I Get Bigger. 2014. 24p. pap. 4.00 *(978-1-61003-373-2(6))* Center for the Collaborative Classroom.
McAllister, Angela. Samson, the Mighty Flea! Reed, Nathan, illus. 2017. (ENG.). 40p. (J). (gr. -1-3). 17.99 *(978-1-5124-8123-5(8),* a0c4f002-7596-4d37-9408-342e40ab22f0) Lerner Publishing Group.
McClure, Brian D. The Raindrop. 2006. (Illus.). 36p. (J). 14.95 *(978-1-933426-01-3(2))* Universal Flag Publishing.
McCully, Emily Arnold. Sam & the Big Kids. McCully, Emily Arnold, illus. 2014. (I Like to Read Ser.). (ENG., Illus.). 24p. (J). (gr. -1-3). 7.99 *(978-0-8234-3060-4(X))* Holiday Hse., Inc.
McDonald, Jill. Shapes: A Play-with-Me BK. McDonald, Jill, illus. 2007. (ENG., Illus.). 10p. bds. 6.95 *(978-1-58117-604-9(X),* Intervisual/Piggy Toes) Bendon, Inc.
Mcdonald, Megan. Stink. 2013. (Stink Ser.: 1). lib. bdg. 14.75 *(978-0-606-31587-6(X))* Turtleback.
—Stink: The Incredible Shrinking Kid. Reynolds, Peter H., illus. 2010. (Stink Ser.: No. 1). (ENG.). 112p. (J). (gr. 1-5). 31.36 *(978-1-59961-686-5(6),* 13833, Chapter Bks.) Spotlight.
McDonald, Megan. Stink: The Incredible Shrinking Kid. Reynolds, Peter H., illus. 2013. (Stink Ser.: 1). (ENG.). 112p. (J). (gr. 1-4). 14.99 *(978-0-7636-6388-9(3))* Candlewick Pr.
McGrath, Barbara Barbieri. Teddy Bear Counting. Nihoff, Tim, illus. 2010. (McGrath Math Ser.: 1). (ENG.). 32p. (J). (gr. -1-2). pap. 7.95 *(978-1-58089-216-2(7))* Charlesbridge Publishing, Inc.
McNamara, Margaret. How Many Seeds in a Pumpkin? (Mr. Tiffin's Classroom Series) Karas, G. Brian, illus. 2007. (Mr. Tiffin's Classroom Ser.). (ENG.). 40p. (J). (gr. -1-2). 17.99 *(978-0-375-84014-2(1),* Schwartz & Wade Bks.) Random Hse. Children's Bks.
Mead, David. Noah's Babies Shapes & Sharing. Byers, Brian, illus. 2005. 22p. (J). bds. 6.95 *(978-0-9746440-5-9(6))* Virtue Bks.
Meddaugh, Susan. Just Teenie. 2006. (ENG., Illus.). 32p. (J). (gr. -1-3). 16.00 *(978-0-618-68565-3(0),* 591422, Clarion Bks.) HarperCollins Pubs.
Membrino, Anna. Big Shark, Little Shark. Budgen, Tim, illus. 2017. (Step into Reading Ser.). 32p. (J). (gr. -1-1). pap. 5.99 *(978-0-399-55728-6(8),* Random Hse. Bks. for Young Readers) Random Hse. Children's Bks.
Montgomery, Ross. Max & the Millions. 2018. 265p. (J). pap. *(978-1-5247-1887-9(4))* Earthscan Canada.
—Max & the Millions. 2018. (ENG.). 272p. (J). (gr. 3-7). 16.99 *(978-1-5247-1884-8(X),* Lamb, Wendy Bks.) Random Hse. Children's Bks.
Morris, Suzanne. A Trapezoid Is Not a Dinosaur! Morris, Suzanne, illus. 2019. (Illus.). 32p. (J). (gr. k-3). pap. 7.99 *(978-1-58089-580-4(8))* Charlesbridge Publishing, Inc.
Mould, Chris. The Great Drain Escape. Mould, Chris, illus. 2018. (Pocket Pirates Ser.: 2). (ENG., Illus.). 144p. (J). (gr. 1-4). 17.99 *(978-1-4814-9118-1(0))*; pap. 6.99 *(978-1-4814-9117-4(2))* Simon & Schuster Children's Publishing. (Aladdin).
Mueller, Doris. Small One's Adventure. Fulton, Parker, illus. 2004. 32p. (J). (gr. k-5). 16.95 *(978-0-9710278-1-7(1))* All About Kids Publishing.
Mullican, Judy & Crowell, Knox. Caillou Finds Shapes. Gillen, Lisa P., illus. l.t. ed. 2005. (HRL Board Book Ser.). (J). (gr. -1-k). bds. 10.95 *(978-1-57332-312-3(8),* HighReach Learning, Incorporated) Carson-Dellosa Publishing, LLC.
Munsch, Robert. Marilou Casse-Cou. 2004.Tr. of Up, Up, Down. (FRE., Illus.). (J). (gr. k-3). spiral bd. *(978-0-616-11144-4(4))* Canadian National Institute for the Blind/Institut National Canadien pour les Aveugles.
My Daddy Is a Giant. 2004. (J). (ENG & TAG.). *(978-1-84444-508-0(9))*; (ENG & SPA.). *(978-1-84444-520-2(8))*; (ENG & SOM.). *(978-1-84444-519-6(4))*; (ENG & POR.). *(978-1-84444-517-2(8))*; (ENG & POL.). *(978-1-84444-516-5(X))*; (ENG & PAN.). *(978-1-84444-515-8(1))*; (ENG & KUR.). *(978-1-84444-514-1(3))*; (ALB & ENG.). *(978-1-84444-499-1(6))*; (ARA & ENG.). *(978-1-84444-501-1(1))*; (CHI & ENG.). *(978-1-84444-504-2(6))*; (ENG & PER.). *(978-1-84444-506-6(2))*; (ENG & FRE.). *(978-1-84444-507-3(0))*; (ENG & GUJ.). *(978-1-84444-509-7(7))*; (ENG & HIN.). *(978-1-84444-510-3(0))*; (ENG & ITA.). *(978-1-84444-511-0(9))*; (ENG & JPN.). *(978-1-84444-512-7(7))*; (ENG & URD.). *(978-1-84444-523-3(2))*; (ENG & TUR.). *(978-1-84444-522-6(4))*; (ENG & TAM.). *(978-1-84444-521-9(6))*; (CRO & ENG.). *(978-1-84444-505-9(4))* Mantra Lingua.
Nash, Margaret. Sammy's Secret. Axworthy, Anni, illus. 2008. (Tadpoles Ser.). (ENG.). 24p. (J). (gr. -1-3). pap. *(978-0-7787-3894-7(9))*; lib. bdg. *(978-0-7787-3863-3(9))* Crabtree Publishing Co.
Neal, Christopher Silas. Animal Shapes. 2018. (Christopher Silas Neal Ser.). (ENG., Illus.). 40p. (J). (gr. -1-1). bds. 12.99 *(978-1-4998-0534-5(9))* Little Bee Books Inc.
Nolen, Jerdine. Hewitt Anderson's Great Big Life. Nelson, Kadir, illus. (ENG.). 40p. (J). (gr. k-3). 2013. 8.99 *(978-1-4424-6035-5(0))* 2005. 19.99 *(978-0-689-86866-5(9))* Simon & Schuster/Paula Wiseman Bks. (Simon & Schuster/Paula Wiseman Bks.).
Norac, Carl. My Daddy Is a Giant. 2005. (J). (ENG & VIE.). 16.95 *(978-1-84444-524-0(0))*; (ENG & RUS.). 16.95 *(978-1-84444-518-9(6))*; (ENG & KOR.). 16.95 *(978-1-84444-513-4(5))*; (BEN & ENG.). 16.95 *(978-1-84444-502-8(X))*; (CHI & ENG.). 16.95 *(978-1-84444-503-5(8))* Mantra Lingua GBR. Dist: Chinasprout, Inc.
Ofelia, Dumas Lachtman. Big Enough Bastante Grande. Enrique, Sanchez, illus. 2008. 32p. (J). pap. 7.95 *(978-1-55885-239-6(5))* Arte Publico Pr.
O'leary, Sara. When You Were Small. Morstad, Julie, illus. 2006. (ENG.). 32p. (J). (gr. -1-3). 16.95 *(978-1-894965-36-1(1))* Simply Read Bks. CAN. Dist: Ingram Publisher Services.
Oliver, Lin. Attack of the Growling Eyeballs. Gilpin, Stephen, illus. 2009. (Who Shrunk Daniel Funk? Ser.: 1). (ENG.). 160p. (J). (gr. 3-7). pap. 7.99 *(978-1-4169-0958-3(3),* Simon & Schuster Bks. For Young Readers) Simon & Schuster Bks. For Young Readers.
—Escape of the Mini-Mummy. Gilpin, Stephen, illus. 2009. (Who Shrunk Daniel Funk? Ser.: 2). (ENG.). 160p. (J). (gr. 3-7). pap. 8.99 *(978-1-4169-0960-6(5),* Simon & Schuster Bks. For Young Readers) Simon & Schuster Bks. For Young Readers.
—Revenge of the Itty-Bitty Brothers. Gilpin, Stephen, illus. 2010. (Who Shrunk Daniel Funk? Ser.: 3). (ENG.). 176p. (J). (gr. 3-7). pap. 6.99 *(978-1-4169-0962-0(1),* Simon & Schuster Bks. For Young Readers) Simon & Schuster Bks. For Young Readers.
—Revenge of the Itty-Bitty Brothers, 3. Gilpin, Stephen, illus. 2009. (Who Shrunk Daniel Funk? Ser.: 3). (ENG.). 112p. (J). (gr. 2-4). 21.19 *(978-1-4169-0961-3(3))* Simon & Schuster, Inc.
—Secret of the Super-Small Superstar. Gilpin, Stephen, illus. 2010. (Who Shrunk Daniel Funk? Ser.: 4). (ENG.). 160p. (J). (gr. 3-7). 14.99 *(978-1-4169-0963-7(X),* Simon & Schuster Bks. For Young Readers) Simon & Schuster Bks. For Young Readers.
Olsen, Jan Z. Mat Man on the Go. Delaney, Molly, illus. 2010. (ENG.). stu. ed. 13.75 *(978-1-934825-39-6(5))* Handwriting Without Tears.
Owens, Robert. The Littlest Warrior. 2008. 32p. pap. 24.95 *(978-1-4241-9156-7(4))* America Star Bks.
Panec, D. J. We Both Read - Changing Places. Elkerton, Andy, illus. 2017. (ENG.). 41p. (J). 9.95 *(978-1-60115-297-8(3))* Treasure Bay, Inc.
Paton Walsh, Jill. A Parcel of Patterns. 137p. (YA). (gr. 7-18). pap. 3.95 *(978-0-8072-1485-5(X),* Listening Library) Random Hse. Audio Publishing Group.
Patricelli, Leslie. Bigger! Bigger! Patricelli, Leslie, illus. 2018. (ENG., Illus.). 32p. (J). (-k). 15.99 *(978-0-7636-7930-9(5))* Candlewick Pr.
—Silencio Ruido. Rozarena, P., tr. Patricelli, Leslie, illus. 2003. (SPA., Illus.). 25p. (J). (gr. -1-k). bds. 7.95 *(978-970-29-0987-3(2))* Santillana USA Publishing Co., Inc.
Paul, Chris. Long Shot: Never Too Small to Dream Big. Morrison, Frank, illus. 2009. (ENG.). 32p. (J). (gr. -1-3). 19.99 *(978-1-4169-5079-0(6),* Simon & Schuster Bks. For Young Readers) Simon & Schuster Bks. For Young Readers.
Percival, Tom. Ravi's Roar. 2020. (Big Bright Feelings Ser.). (ENG., Illus.). 32p. (J). 18.99 *(978-1-5476-0300-8(3),* 900211008, Bloomsbury Children's Bks.) Bloomsbury Publishing USA.
Perkins, Al. The Nose Book. Mathieu, Joe, illus. 2003. (Bright & Early Board Books(TM) Ser.). (ENG.). 24p. (J). (— 1). bds. 5.99 *(978-0-375-82493-7(6),* Random Hse. Bks. for Young Readers) Random Hse. Children's Bks.
Perry, Gina. Small. 2017. (ENG., Illus.). 40p. (J). (gr. -1-3). 17.99 *(978-1-4998-0401-0(6))* Little Bee Books Inc.
Petty, Dev. I Don't Want to Be a Frog. Boldt, Mike, illus. 2018. (J). (ENG.). 32p. (gr. -1-2). pap. 8.99 *(978-1-9848-5208-3(6),* Dragonfly Bks.); 26p. (— 1). bds. 8.99 *(978-0-525-57950-2(8),* Doubleday Bks. for Young Readers) Random Hse. Children's Bks.
—I Don't Want to Be Big. Boldt, Mike, illus. 2016. 32p. (J). (gr. -1-2). 16.99 *(978-1-101-93920-8(6),* Doubleday Bks. for Young Readers) Random Hse. Children's Bks.
Pfister, Marcus. Penguin Pete. 2013. (Penguin Pete Ser.). (ENG., Illus.). 32p. (J). (gr. -1-3). 16.95 *(978-0-7358-4118-5(7))* North-South Bks., Inc.
Pitino, Donna Marie. Too-Tall Tina. Woodruff, Liza, illus. 2005. (Math Matters Ser.). 32p. (J). (gr. k-2). pap. 5.95 *(978-1-57565-150-7(5),* ab8f34ba-7005-4f87-9d67-ed858dd707cd, Kane Press) Astra Publishing Hse.
Platt, Randall. Professor Renoir's Collection of Oddities, Curiosities, & Delights. 2019. (ENG.). 416p. (J). (gr. 3). 16.99 *(978-0-06-264334-6(7),* HarperCollins) HarperCollins Pubs.
Plourde, Lynn. Maxi's Secrets: (or, What You Can Learn from a Dog) 2017. 272p. (J). (gr. 5). 8.99 *(978-0-399-54568-9(9),* Puffin Books) Penguin Young Readers Group.
Pollack, Pam & Belviso, Meg. Gallinas de Aqui para Alla: Chickens on the Move. 2008. pap. 34.95 *(978-1-58013-784-3(9))* Astra Publishing Hse.
Potter, Beatrix. Peter Rabbit Rainbow Shapes & Colors. Potter, Beatrix, illus. 2006. (Peter Rabbit Seedlings Ser.). (ENG., Illus.). 10p. (J). (gr. k-18). bds. 5.99 *(978-0-7232-5722-6(1),* Puffin) Penguin Publishing Group.
Powell, Richard. What's in the Box? Martín Larrañaga, Ana, illus. 2004. (Ana's Mini Movers Ser.). 12p. (J). 5.95 *(978-1-58925-742-9(1))* Tiger Tales.
Pratchett, Terry. The Carpet People. 2015. (ENG., Illus.). 304p. (J). (gr. 2-5). pap. 8.99 *(978-0-544-43954-2(6),* 1596848, Clarion Bks.) HarperCollins Pubs.
Publications International Ltd. Staff, ed. Shapes Wipe off Learning Board. 2011. 1p. (J). bds. *(978-1-4508-1432-4(8))* Publications International, Ltd.
Quinn, Susan. The Littlest Dragon. Jatkowska, Ag, illus. 2016. (J). *(978-1-4351-6573-1(X))* Barnes & Noble, Inc.
Rayner, Catherine. Ernest, the Moose Who Doesn't Fit. Rayner, Catherine, illus. 2010. (ENG., Illus.). 32p. (J). (gr. -1-1). 19.99 *(978-0-374-32217-5(1),* 900065793, Farrar, Straus & Giroux (BYR)) Farrar, Straus & Giroux.
Reasoner, Charles. Shapes at the Beach. Pitt, Sarah, illus. 2009. (3D Board Bks.). 12p. (J). (gr. -1-k). bds. 9.99 *(978-1-934650-36-3(6))* Just For Kids Pr., LLC.
—Shapes for Lunch! 2009. (Bite Bks.). (Illus.). (J). bds. 7.99 *(978-1-934650-16-5(1))* Just For Kids Pr., LLC.
Reid, Camilla. Lulu Loves Shapes. Busby, Ailie, illus. 2015. (Lulu Ser.). (ENG.). 12p. (J). (gr. -1-1). bds. *(978-1-4088-4958-3(5),* 233927, Bloomsbury Children's Bks.) Bloomsbury Publishing Plc.
RH Disney. Shapes, Colors, Counting & More! (Disney/Pixar Cars), 4 vols. RH Disney, illus. 2013. (ENG., Illus.). 48p. (J). (gr. -1-2). bds. 10.99 *(978-0-7364-3105-7(5),* RH/Disney) Random Hse. Children's Bks.
Richmond, Lori. Pax & Blue. Richmond, Lori, illus. 2017. (ENG., Illus.). 32p. (J). (gr. -1-3). 17.99 *(978-1-4814-5132-1(4),* Simon & Schuster/Paula Wiseman Bks.) Simon & Schuster/Paula Wiseman Bks.
Riggs, Kate. Shapes All Around. Devernay, Laëtitia, illus. 2018. (ENG.). 14p. (J). (gr. -1-k). bds. 8.99 *(978-1-56846-317-9(0),* 19651, Creative Editions) Creative Co., The.
Rinker, Sherri Duskey. Bulldozer's Shapes: Goodnight, Goodnight, Construction Site (Kids Construction Books, Goodnight Books for Toddlers) Long, Ethan, illus. 2019. (Goodnight, Goodnight Construction Site Ser.). (ENG.). 20p. (J). (gr. -1 — 1). bds. 6.99 *(978-1-4521-5321-6(3))* Chronicle Bks. LLC.
—Tiny & the Big Dig. Myers, Matt, illus. 2018. (ENG.). 32p. (J). (gr. -1-k). 16.99 *(978-0-545-90429-2(3),* Scholastic Pr.) Scholastic, Inc.
Rizvi, Sobia. Zebra Stripes. 2011. 24p. pap. 15.99 *(978-1-4653-4618-6(X))* Xlibris Corp.
Rockliff, Mara. Al lado de una Hormiga: Next to an Ant. Constantin, Pascale, illus. 2005. (Rookie Reader Español Ser.). (ENG & SPA.). 24p. (J). (gr. k-2). 19.50 *(978-0-516-25251-3(8),* Children's Pr.) Scholastic Library Publishing.
Roddie, Shen. You're Too Small! Lavis, Steve, illus. 2004. 32p. (J). 6.95 *(978-1-58925-385-8(X))*; tchr. ed. 15.95 *(978-1-58925-038-3(9))* Tiger Tales.
Root, Andrew. Hamsters Don't Fight Fires! Ollen, Jessica, illus. 2017. (ENG.). 40p. (J). (gr. -1-3). 17.99 *(978-0-06-245294-8(0),* HarperCollins) HarperCollins Pubs.
Rørvik, Bjø F. The Little Paintbrush. Hansen, Thore, illus. 2014. (ENG.). 32p. (J). (gr. -1-k). 12.95 *(978-1-62087-996-2(4),* 620996, Sky Pony Pr.) Skyhorse Publishing Co., Inc.
Rumph-Geddis, Ashlye V. Tori Finds Shapes All Around. 2007. (Illus.). 12p. (J). 9.45 *(978-0-9792934-0-5(5))* Ashlye V. Enterprises, LLC.
Sagerman, Evan. Giraffe Rescue Company. Chou, Joey, illus. 2016. (J). *(978-1-4424-1366-5(2))* Simon & Schuster Children's Publishing.
Salzano, Tammi. One Sunny Day. 2013. pap. *(978-0-545-53655-4(3))* Scholastic, Inc.
Sasso, Sandy Eisenberg. The Story of And: The Little Word That Changed the World. Rothenberg, Joani Keller, illus. 2019. (ENG.). 40p. (J). (gr. -1-2). 18.00 *(978-1-947888-05-0(6),* 1947888056, Flyaway Bks.) Westminster John Knox Pr.
Schafer, Milton. I'm Big! Lew-Vriethoff, Joanne, illus. 2006. (J). *(978-1-4156-8150-3(3),* Dial) Penguin Publishing Group.
Schoonmaker, Elizabeth. Square Cat. Schoonmaker, Elizabeth, illus. 2011. (ENG., Illus.). 32p. (J). (gr. -1-3). 19.99 *(978-1-4424-0619-3(4),* Aladdin) Simon & Schuster Children's Publishing.
Schreiber, Joe. Lenny Cyrus, School Virus. Smith, Matt, illus. 2014. (ENG.). 288p. (J). (gr. 5-7). pap. 16.99 *(978-0-544-33628-5(3),* 1584174, Clarion Bks.) HarperCollins Pubs.
Sheena, Roberts & Roberts, Sheena. We All Go Traveling By. Siobhan, Bell, illus. 2003. (ENG.). 24p. (J). pap. 6.99 *(978-1-84148-595-9(0))* Barefoot Bks., Inc.
Sherry, Kevin. I'm the Biggest Thing in the Ocean! (J). (gr. -1 — 1). 2010. 28p. bds. 8.99 *(978-0-8037-3529-3(4))* 2007. (ENG., Illus.). 32p. 18.99 *(978-0-8037-3192-9(2))* Penguin Young Readers Group. (Dial Bks).
Shulman, Mark. Big Cat. Chambers, Sally, illus. 2004. 8p. (J). bds. 6.95 *(978-1-58925-737-5(5))* Tiger Tales.
Silver Dolphin Staff, creator. Disney Caritas Felices: Dumbo. 2007. (Illus.). 8p. (J). (gr. -1). bds. *(978-970-718-394-0(2),* Silver Dolphin en Español) Advanced Marketing, S. de R. L. de C. V.
Simon, Charnan. Pumpkin Fever. Bryan-Hunt, Jan, illus. 2011. (Rookie Ready to Learn Ser.). 40p. (J). (ENG.). pap. 5.95 *(978-0-531-26803-2(9))*; (gr. -1-k). lib. bdg. 23.00 *(978-0-531-25643-5(X))* Scholastic Library Publishing. (Children's Pr.).
Simon, Coco. Alexis: The Icing on the Cupcake. 2014. (Cupcake Diaries: 20). lib. bdg. 17.20 *(978-0-606-35786-9(6))* Turtleback.
—Alexis the Icing on the Cupcake. 2014. (Cupcake Diaries: 20). (ENG., Illus.). 160p. (J). (gr. 3-7). pap. 7.99 *(978-1-4814-0468-6(7),* Simon Spotlight) Simon Spotlight.
Simson, Dana. Shapes. 2003. (Dana Simson Chunky Books Ser.). 10p. (J). bds. 2.95 *(978-1-74047-257-9(8))* Book Co. Publishing Pty, Ltd., The AUS. Dist: Penton Overseas, Inc.
Sloan, Holly Goldberg. Short. (ENG.). (J). (gr. 3-7). 2018. 320p. 9.99 *(978-0-399-18622-6(0),* Puffin Books) 2017. 304p. 17.99 *(978-0-399-18621-9(2),* Dial Bks) Penguin Young Readers Group.
—Short. 2018. lib. bdg. 19.65 *(978-0-606-40875-2(4))* Turtleback.
Snyder, Zilpha Keatley. The Treasures of Weatherby. 2008. (ENG.). 240p. (J). (gr. 3-7). pap. 8.99 *(978-1-4169-1399-3(8),* Atheneum Bks. for Young Readers) Simon & Schuster Children's Publishing.
Stein, Peter. Toys Galore. Staake, Bob, illus. 2013. (ENG.). 32p. (J). (gr. -1-3). 17.99 *(978-0-7636-6254-7(2))* Candlewick Pr.
Studio Mouse Staff. Sesame Street Colors & Shapes. 2008. (ENG.). 36p. (J). (gr. -1). 12.99 *(978-1-59069-741-2(3))* Studio Mouse LLC.
Tagel, Peggy, illus. Animal Safari. 2003. (Squishy Shapes Ser.). 10p. (J). 12.95 *(978-1-57145-741-7(0),* Silver Dolphin Bks.) Readerlink Distribution Services, LLC.
—Dinosaurs. 2003. (Squishy Shapes Ser.). 10p. (J). 12.95 *(978-1-57145-740-0(2),* Silver Dolphin Bks.) Readerlink Distribution Services, LLC.
Thompson, Lauren. Little Chick. Butler, John, illus. 2014. (ENG.). 30p. (J). (gr. -1-3). bds. 5.99 *(978-1-4424-9311-7(9),* Little Simon) Little Simon.
—Little Chick. Butler, John, illus. 2014. (J). *(978-1-4351-5351-6(0),* Simon & Schuster Bks. For Young Readers) Simon & Schuster Bks. For Young Readers.
—Wee Little Chick. Butler, John, illus. 2008. (Wee Little Ser.). (ENG.). 32p. (J). (gr. -1-3). 19.99 *(978-1-4169-3468-4(5),* Simon & Schuster Bks. For Young Readers) Simon & Schuster Bks. For Young Readers.
Thong, Roseanne. Round Is a Tortilla: A Book of Shapes. Parra, John, illus. 2015. (Latino Book of Concepts Ser.). (ENG.). 40p. (J). (gr. -1-k). 7.99 *(978-1-4521-4568-6(7))* Chronicle Bks. LLC.
Thong, Roseanne Greenfield. Round Is a Mooncake: A Book of Shapes. 2014. (Multicultural Shapes & Colors Ser.). (Illus.). 40p. (J). lib. bdg. 28.50 *(978-1-60753-564-5(5))* Amicus Learning.
—Round Is a Tortilla: A Book of Shapes. 2014. (Multicultural Shapes & Colors Ser.). (Illus.). 40p. (J). lib. bdg. 28.50 *(978-1-60753-566-9(1))* Amicus Learning.
Top That! Playtime Shapes (large Version) Parry, Jo, illus. 2007. 10p. (J). (gr. -1). *(978-1-84666-555-4(8),* Tide Mill Pr.) Top That! Publishing PLC.
Townsend, Stephanie Z. Not Too Small at All: A Mouse Tale. Looney, Bill, illus. 2008. (ENG.). 30p. (J). (gr. -1). 13.99 *(978-0-89051-524-2(7),* Master Books) New Leaf Publishing Group.
Tresselt, Alvin. The Smallest Elephant in the World. Glaser, Milton, illus. 2019. (ENG.). 40p. (J). 16.95 *(978-1-59270-261-9(9))* Enchanted Lion Bks., LLC.
Tuttle, Sarah Grace. Spot, Spike, Spiral. Nerlove, Miriam, illus. 2019. (ENG.). 28p. (J). (gr. -1-k). bds. 8.99 *(978-1-56846-333-9(2),* 18672, Creative Editions) Creative Co., The.
Tuxworth, Nicola. Shapes. 2015. (Illus.). 20p. (J). (gr. -1-12). bds. 6.99 *(978-1-86147-648-7(5),* Armadillo) Anness Publishing GBR. Dist: National Bk. Network.
Van Fleet, Matthew. Tails. 2017. (ENG., Illus.). 20p. (J). (— 1). bds. 14.99 *(978-1-328-88685-9(9),* 1699384, Clarion Bks.) HarperCollins Pubs.
Verdick, Elizabeth. Small Walt. Rosenthal, Marc, illus. 2017. (ENG.). 40p. (J). (gr. -1-3). 17.99 *(978-1-4814-4845-1(5),* Simon & Schuster Bks. For Young Readers) Simon & Schuster Bks. For Young Readers.
Vere, Ed. Everyone's Little. 2003. (ENG., Illus.). 12p. (J). bds. 6.95 *(978-0-333-78039-8(6))* Macmillan Pubs., Ltd. GBR. Dist: Trafalgar Square Publishing.
Watt, Fiona. Taller & Shorter. 2017. (Taller & Shorter Ser.). (ENG.). 10p. 9.99 *(978-0-7945-4041-8(4),* Usborne) EDC Publishing.
Weiland, Peter. So Big yet So Small. Coffey, Kevin, illus. 2012. (J). 14.95 *(978-1-937406-16-5(4))* Amplify Publishing Group.
Weinberg, Steven. You Must Be This Tall. Weinberg, Steven, illus. 2016. (ENG., Illus.). 40p. (J). (gr. -1-3). 17.99 *(978-1-4814-2981-8(7),* McElderry, Margaret K. Bks.) McElderry, Margaret K. Bks.
Weston Woods Staff, creator. The Caterpillar & the Polliwog. 2011. 38.75 *(978-0-439-73154-6(2))*; 18.95 *(978-0-439-73152-2(6))* Weston Woods Studios, Inc.
Wiede, Matt, illus. Star, Circle, Baylor: A Little Bear Shapes Book, 5460 vols. 2013. (Big Bear Bks.). (ENG.). 18p. (J). (gr. 17). bds. 9.95 *(978-1-60258-979-7(8))* Baylor Univ. Pr.
Willis, Jeanne. Cottonball Colin. Ross, Tony, illus. 2008. 26p. (J). (gr. -1-4). 16.00 *(978-0-8028-5331-8(5),* Eerdmans Bks For Young Readers) Eerdmans, William B. Publishing Co.
Wilson, Barbara E. Small Enough Tall Enough. Gospodinov, George, illus. 2012. 46p. pap. 14.95 *(978-0-9838964-0-1(2))* Simply Silly Stories.
Wilson, Zachary. A Circle in the Sky. Adinolfi, JoAnn, illus. (Rookie Ready to Learn Ser.). (ENG.). (J). 2011. 40p. pap. 5.95 *(978-0-531-26746-2(6))* 2006. 32p. lib. bdg. 19.50 *(978-0-531-12570-0(X))* Scholastic Library Publishing. (Children's Pr.).
—Rookie Ready to Learn en Español: un Círculo en el Cielo. Adinolfi, JoAnn, illus. 2011. (Rookie Ready to Learn Español Ser.). Orig. Title: Rookie Ready to Learn: a Circle in the Sky. (SPA.). 40p. (J). pap. 5.95 *(978-0-531-26791-2(1),* Children's Pr.) Scholastic Library Publishing.
Wilson, Zachary & Adinolfi, JoAnn. Un Circulo en el Cielo. Adinolfi, JoAnn, illus. 2011. (Rookie Ready to Learn Español Ser.). (SPA., Illus.). 40p. (J). lib. bdg. 23.00 *(978-0-531-26123-1(9),* Children's Pr.) Scholastic Library Publishing.
Winters, Kay. The Teeny Tiny Ghost & the Monster, Vol. 3. Munsinger, Lynn, illus. 2004. (ENG.). 32p. (J). (gr. -1-3). 14.99 *(978-0-06-028884-6(1))* HarperCollins Pubs.
Wynne-Jones, Tim. I'll Make You Small. (J). pap. 4.95 *(978-0-88899-105-8(3))*; pap. 15.95 *(978-0-88899-045-7(6))* Groundwood Bks. CAN. Dist: Publishers Group West (PGW).
Yates, Gene. What Can Simon Be? 2005. (Illus.). (J). *(978-1-58865-284-3(X))* Kidsbooks, LLC.
Yates, Gene & Frank, Thomas. What Can Simon Be? Yates, Gene, illus. 2006. (Illus.). (J). *(978-1-58865-366-6(8))* Kidsbooks, LLC.
YoYo. Forms, Colors, & Opposites. 2005. 40p. bds. *(978-90-5843-888-1(0))* YoYo Bks.

SKATEBOARDING

Abdo, Kenny. Skateboarding. 2017. (Action Sports (Fly!) Ser.). (ENG., Illus.). 24p. (J). (gr. 2-8). lib. bdg. 31.36 *(978-1-5321-2094-7(X),* 26777, Abdo Zoom-Fly) ABDO Publishing Co.
Adamson, Thomas K. Big Air Skateboarding. 2015. (Extreme Sports Ser.). (ENG., Illus.). 24p. (J). (gr. 3-7). lib. bdg. 26.95 *(978-1-62617-272-2(2),* Epic Bks.) Bellwether Media.
—Skateboarding Street Style. 2015. (Extreme Sports Ser.). (ENG., Illus.). 24p. (J). (gr. 3-7). lib. bdg. 26.95 *(978-1-62617-277-7(3),* Epic Bks.) Bellwether Media.
Arcy, Sean & Marshall, Phillip. Freestyle Skateboarding Tricks: Flat Ground, Rails, Transitions. 2010. (ENG., Illus.). 128p. pap. 14.95 *(978-1-55407-666-6(8),* 3ff2a304-1d0f-40a5-be05-f279ae117032) Firefly Bks., Ltd.
Arnold, Quinn M. Skateboards. 2019. (Seedlings: on the Go Ser.). (ENG.). 24p. (J). (gr. -1-1). pap. 8.99 *(978-1-62832-735-9(9),* 19133, Creative Paperbacks) Creative Co., The.
Beal, Becky. Skateboarding: The Ultimate Guide, 1 vol. 2013. (Greenwood Guides to Extreme Sports Ser.). (ENG., Illus.). 176p. (C). 45.00 *(978-0-313-38112-6(7),* 789881, Greenwood) Bloomsbury Publishing USA.
Becker, Helaine. Skateboarding Science. 2008. (Sports Science Ser.). (ENG., Illus.). 32p. (J). (gr. 4-6). pap. *(978-0-7787-4553-2(8))*; lib. bdg. *(978-0-7787-4536-5(8))* Crabtree Publishing Co.
Blaine, Victor. Mi Monopatín / My Skateboard, 1 vol. 2014. (¡Mírame, Ahí Voy! / Watch Me Go! Ser.). (ENG & SPA.,

S

Illus.). 24p. (J). (gr. 1-2). 25.27 *(978-1-4994-0278-0(3),* ac62cf03-a467-4ee5-ae80-97e49b2ff82b, PowerKids Pr.) Rosen Publishing Group, Inc., The.

—Mis Patines de Ruedas / My Skates, 1 vol. 2014. (¡Mírame, Ahí Voy! / Watch Me Go! Ser.). (ENG & SPA., Illus.). 24p. (J). (gr. 1-2). 25.27 *(978-1-4994-0280-3(5),* 7b5fdce9-3a95-4c3e-95e2-b898c9c1bcfb, PowerKids Pr.) Rosen Publishing Group, Inc., The.

—My Ripstik, 1 vol. 2014. (Watch Me Go! Ser.). (ENG., Illus.). 24p. (J). (gr. 1-2). lib. bdg. 25.27 *(978-1-4994-0251-3(1),* 02a68cea-e01f-4691-b5bb-6d898f8b9a6d, PowerKids Pr.) Rosen Publishing Group, Inc., The.

—My Skateboard, 1 vol. 2014. (Watch Me Go! Ser.). (ENG., Illus.). 24p. (J). (gr. 1-2). lib. bdg. 25.27 *(978-1-4994-0252-0(X),* 96517a9f-561e-44ff-9fb1-22ce5b057996, PowerKids Pr.) Rosen Publishing Group, Inc., The.

Blomquist, Christopher. Skateboarding in the X Games. 2009. (Kid's Guide to the X Games Ser.). 24p. (gr. 3-3). 42.50 *(978-1-61511-210-4(3),* PowerKids Pr.) Rosen Publishing Group, Inc., The.

Bowman, Chris. Vert Skateboarding. 2016. (Extreme Sports Ser.). (ENG., Illus.). 24p. (J). (gr. 3-7). lib. bdg. 26.95 *(978-1-62617-354-5(0),* Epic Bks.) Bellwether Media.

Bradley, Michael. Tony Hawk, 1 vol. 2006. (All-Stars Ser.). (ENG., Illus.). 48p. (gr. 4-4). 34.07 *(978-0-7614-1759-0(1),* fa4082aa-4e1a-41b1-8af4-d8e868ff8cfd) Cavendish Square Publishing LLC.

Braun, Eric. Tony Hawk. 2004. (Amazing Athletes Ser.). (Illus.). 32p. (J). (ENG.). (gr. 2-5). pap. 7.95 *(978-0-8225-3686-4(2),* 56c3f644-deee-4790-bcdf-7b830ce5096a); (gr. 3-4). lib. bdg. 23.93 *(978-0-8225-1367-4(6))* Lerner Publishing Group.

Bussiere, Desireé. Skateboarding by the Numbers, 1 vol. 2013. (Sports by the Numbers Ser.). (ENG.). 24p. (J). (gr. k-3). lib. bdg. 29.93 *(978-1-61783-845-3(4),* 13704, SandCastle) ABDO Publishing Co.

Carr, Aaron. Skateboard. 2013. (ENG & SPA.). (J). *(978-1-62127-631-9(7))* Weigl Pubs., Inc.

—Skateboarding. (Illus.). 24p. (J). 2013. *(978-1-61913-512-3(4),* 1345813) 2012. (ENG., pap. 12.95 *(978-1-61913-518-5(3),* AV2 by Weigl) Weigl Pubs., Inc.

Casil, Amy Sterling. Tony Hawk: Skateboard Mogul, 1 vol. 2009. (Super Skateboarding Ser.). (ENG., Illus.). 48p. (gr. 5-8). (J). pap. 12.75 *(978-1-4358-5391-1(1),* e4090b1b-10d9-47cd-9321-8950e192cf35); (YA). lib. bdg. 34.47 *(978-1-4358-5047-7(5),* 16515748-a265-4496-9a7b-b8cd335e5797) Rosen Publishing Group, Inc., The.

Castellano, Peter. Longboard Skateboarding, 1 vol. 2015. (Daredevil Sports Ser.). (ENG., Illus.). 32p. (J). (gr. 1-1). pap. 11.50 *(978-1-4824-2972-5(1),* cf24479f-781d-49e4-9fd9-121426e38954); lib. bdg. 28.27 *(978-1-4824-2978-7(0),* ba786974-688c-42dc-b32d-58fe450f89e6) Stevens, Gareth Publishing LLLP.

Cefrey, Holly. Competitive Skateboarding. 2009. (Super Skateboarding Ser.). 48p. (gr. 5-8). 53.00 *(978-1-60853-207-0(0),* Rosen Reference); (ENG., Illus.). (YA). lib. bdg. 34.47 *(978-1-4358-5050-7(5),* c460ad1e-e842-41d7-83d0-e3446fcfade2) Rosen Publishing Group, Inc., The.

Cobb, Allan B. Skating the X-Games, 1 vol. 2009. (Super Skateboarding Ser.). (ENG., Illus.). 48p. (gr. 5-8). (J). pap. 12.75 *(978-1-4358-5392-8(X),* d489aa89-5cd0-42a1-a493-96d6a3095cc4); (YA). lib. bdg. 34.47 *(978-1-4358-5048-4(3),* 07f1db9a-3a12-43b7-a7f4-9602a8be4f01) Rosen Publishing Group, Inc., The.

—Skating the X Games. 2009. (Super Skateboarding Ser.). 48p. (gr. 5-8). 53.00 *(978-1-60853-213-1(5),* Rosen Reference) Rosen Publishing Group, Inc., The.

Craats, Rennay. Skateboarding. (J). 2013. 27.13 *(978-1-62127-319-6(9))* 2013. pap. 12.95 *(978-1-62127-324-0(5))* 2009. 24p. (gr. 3-5). pap. 8.95 *(978-1-60596-121-7(3))* 2009. (Illus.). 24p. (gr. 3-5). lib. bdg. 24.45 *(978-1-60596-120-0(5))* Weigl Pubs., Inc.

Crabtree Editors & Winters, Jaime. Shred It Skateboarding. 2012. (Sports Starters Ser.). (ENG., Illus.). 32p. (J). (gr. 1-4). lib. bdg. *(978-0-7787-3151-1(0))* Crabtree Publishing Co.

Crossingham, John. Extreme Skateboarding. 2003. (Extreme Sports - No Limits Ser.). (ENG., Illus.). 32p. (J). (gr. 3). pap. *(978-0-7787-1714-0(3))* Crabtree Publishing Co.

—Patinetas en Acción. 2005. (Deportes en Acción Ser.). (SPA., Illus.). 32p. (J). lib. bdg. *(978-0-7787-8574-3(2))* Crabtree Publishing Co.

David, Jack. Big Air Skateboarding. 2007. (Action Sports Ser.). (ENG., Illus.). 24p. (J). (gr. 3-7). lib. bdg. 26.95 *(978-1-60014-121-8(8))* Bellwether Media.

Davies, Monika. The Art & Science of Skateboarding. rev. ed. 2018. (Smithsonian: Informational Text Ser.). (ENG., Illus.). 32p. (J). (gr. 4-8). pap. 11.99 *(978-1-4938-6717-2(2))* Teacher Created Materials, Inc.

Enz, Tammy. Engineering a Totally Rad Skateboard with Max Axiom, Super Scientist. Pop Art Studios, illus. 2013. (Graphic Science & Engineering in Action Ser.). (ENG.). 32p. (J). (gr. 3-4). pap. 49.60 *(978-1-62065-704-1(X),* 19301); pap. 8.10 *(978-1-62065-703-4(1),* 121699) Capstone. (Capstone Pr.).

Fandel, Jennifer. Skateboarding. 2007. (Active Sports Ser.). (ENG., Illus.). 24p. (J). (gr. 1-4). lib. bdg. 24.25 *(978-1-58341-469-9(X),* 22079, Creative Education) Creative Co., The.

Fitzpatrick, Jim. Skateboarding. 2008. (21st Century Skills Innovation Library: Innovation in Sports Ser.). (ENG., Illus.). 32p. (gr. 4-8). lib. bdg. 32.07 *(978-1-60279-259-3(3),* 200033) Cherry Lake Publishing.

Gifford, Clive & Dorling Kindersley Publishing Staff. Skateboarding. 2006. (ENG., Illus.). 64p. (J). (gr. 5-12). pap. 9.99 *(978-0-7566-2074-5(0),* DK Children) Dorling Kindersley Publishing, Inc.

Greathouse, Lisa. Bicicletas y Tablas. rev. ed. 2010. (Science: Informational Text Ser.). (SPA., Illus.). 32p. (gr. 3-5). pap. 11.99 *(978-1-4333-2146-7(7))* Teacher Created Materials, Inc.

Greene, Edgar. Tony Hawk. 2003. (Sports Heroes & Legends Ser.). (Illus.). 103p. (J). *(978-0-7607-3216-8(7))* Barnes & Noble, Inc.

Hamilton, John. Skateboarding. 2014. (Action Sports Ser.). (ENG., Illus.). 32p. (J). (gr. 3-9). lib. bdg. 32.79 *(978-1-62403-443-5(8),* 1161, Abdo & Daughters) ABDO Publishing Co.

Hocing, Justin. Skateboard Design & Construction: How Your Board Gets Built. 2009. (Power Skateboarding Ser.). 24p. (gr. 3-4). 42.50 *(978-1-60851-339-0(4),* PowerKids Pr.) Rosen Publishing Group, Inc., The.

Hocking, Justin. Dream Builders: The World's Best Skate Park Creators. 2009. (Skateboarder's Guide to Skate Parks, Half-Pipes, Bowls, & Obstacles Ser.). 48p. (gr. 5-8). 53.00 *(978-1-60854-229-1(7),* Rosen Reference) Rosen Publishing Group, Inc., The.

—Off the Wall: A Skateboarder's Guide to Riding Bowls & Pools. (Skateboarder's Guide to Skate Parks, Half-Pipes, Bowls, & Obstacles Ser.). 48p. (gr. 5-8). 2009. 53.00 *(978-1-60854-230-7(0),* Rosen Reference) 2004. (ENG., Illus.). (J). lib. bdg. 34.47 *(978-1-4042-0339-6(7),* b2cb4910-cb84-4b36-b1f2-4fb8422732b1) Rosen Publishing Group, Inc., The.

—Rippin' Ramps: A Skateboarder's Guide to Riding Half-Pipes. 2009. (Skateboarder's Guide to Skate Parks, Half-Pipes, Bowls, & Obstacles Ser.). 48p. (gr. 5-8). 53.00 *(978-1-60854-231-4(9),* Rosen Reference) Rosen Publishing Group, Inc., The.

—Rippin' Ramps: A Skateboarder's Guide to Riding Halfpipes, 1 vol. 2004. (Skateboarder's Guide to Skate Parks, Half-Pipes, Bowls, & Obstacles Ser.). (ENG., Illus.). 48p. (J). (gr. 5-8). lib. bdg. 34.47 *(978-1-4042-0340-2(0),* db74af8e-233c-4d28-8428-547d4b5dc91d) Rosen Publishing Group, Inc., The.

—Skate Parks, 1 vol. 2005. (Power Skateboarding Ser.). (ENG., Illus.). 24p. (J). (gr. 3-4). lib. bdg. 26.27 *(978-1-4042-3047-7(5),* 739e139f-2d9d-43c2-9f67-c3509d0b1179, PowerKids Pr.) Rosen Publishing Group, Inc., The.

—Skateboarding Competitions, 1 vol. 2005. (Power Skateboarding Ser.). (ENG., Illus.). 24p. (gr. 3-4). lib. bdg. 26.27 *(978-1-4042-3052-1(1),* dbefe916-b3aa-4000-81ee-25beef0656ec, PowerKids Pr.) Rosen Publishing Group, Inc., The.

—Skateboarding Design & Construction: How Your Board Gets Built, 1 vol. 2005. (Power Skateboarding Ser.). (ENG., Illus.). 24p. (J). (gr. 3-4). lib. bdg. 26.27 *(978-1-4042-3048-4(3),* 5afdda37-5424-4fcd-8d2d-245c88149584, PowerKids Pr.) Rosen Publishing Group, Inc., The.

—Skateboarding Half-Pipes, Ramps, & Obstacles, 1 vol. 2005. (Power Skateboarding Ser.). (ENG., Illus.). 24p. (gr. 3-4). lib. bdg. 26.27 *(978-1-4042-3051-4(3),* 3f2ce72d-3765-4993-9bcb-f50f7f80479b, PowerKids Pr.) Rosen Publishing Group, Inc., The.

—Skateboarding Half-pipes, Ramps, & Obstacles. 2009. (Power Skateboarding Ser.). 24p. (gr. 3-4). 42.50 *(978-1-60851-341-3(6),* PowerKids Pr.) Rosen Publishing Group, Inc., The.

—Taking Action: How to Get Your City to Build a Public Skatepark, 1 vol. 2004. (Skateboarder's Guide to Skate Parks, Half-Pipes, Bowls, & Obstacles Ser.). (ENG., Illus.). 48p. (J). (gr. 5-8). lib. bdg. 34.47 *(978-1-4042-0341-9(9),* bc305443-ae0e-4aa1-9764-ba66f490a013) Rosen Publishing Group, Inc., The.

—The World's Greatest Skate Parks, 1 vol. 2009. (Super Skateboarding Ser.). (ENG.). 48p. (gr. 5-8). (YA). lib. bdg. 34.47 *(978-1-4358-5046-0(7),* e754452a-d965-41ee-a1ec-f6624f9ce277); (Illus.). (J). pap. 12.75 *(978-1-4358-5390-4(3),* d49f373b-bec7-4300-a2fd-0951b8040140) Rosen Publishing Group, Inc., The.

Hocking, Justin & Michalski, Peter. Riding Bowls & Pools, 1 vol. 2016. (Skateboarding Tips & Tricks Ser.). (ENG.). 48p. (J). (gr. 5-5). pap. 12.75 *(978-1-4777-8866-0(2),* af7e853c-1c2f-4b43-962d-6d665088ad54, Rosen Reference) Rosen Publishing Group, Inc., The.

—Riding Half-Pipes, 1 vol. 2016. (Skateboarding Tips & Tricks Ser.). (ENG.). 48p. (J). (gr. 5-5). pap. 12.75 *(978-1-4777-8878-3(6),* 8eab20da-216d-43fe-9cba-6e381bcdb6fd, Rosen Reference) Rosen Publishing Group, Inc., The.

Holden, Pam. Let's Go Riding. 1 vol. 2015. (ENG., Illus.). 16p. (-1). pap. *(978-1-77654-114-0(6),* Red Rocket Readers) Flying Start Bks.

Horsley, Andrew. How to Improve at Skateboarding. 2009. (How to Improve at... Ser.). (ENG., Illus.). 48p. (J). (gr. 4-8). lib. bdg. *(978-0-7787-3575-5(3))* Crabtree Publishing Co.

Horsley, Andy. Skateboarding. 2008. (ENG., Illus.). 32p. (J). (gr. 5-9). lib. bdg. *(978-0-7787-3771-1(3))* Crabtree Publishing Co.

—Skateboarding, 1 vol. 2012. (To the Limit Ser.). (ENG., Illus.). 32p. (J). (gr. 3-6). pap. 11.00 *(978-1-4488-7068-4(2),* dc236d60-c3f7-45f0-91cd-0b37d52344f7); lib. bdg. 28.93 *(978-1-4488-7029-5(1),* 9bf8e7e7-2ad3-43a6-8fe5-bc8d6d655431) Rosen Publishing Group, Inc., The. (PowerKids Pr.).

Kamberg, Mary-Lane. Longboarding, 1 vol. 2016. (Skateboarding Tips & Tricks Ser.). (ENG.). 48p. (J). (gr. 5-5). pap. 12.75 *(978-1-4777-8863-9(8),* 7197badc-36d9-4674-b824-cee9204fe29a, Rosen Reference) Rosen Publishing Group, Inc., The.

Kennedy, Mike. Tony Hawk, 1 vol. 2009. (People We Should Know (Second Series) Ser.). (ENG.). 48p. (J). (gr. 3-5). pap. 11.50 *(978-1-4339-2191-9(X),* 50efe211-bfe9-4ae6-a322-b0117570e90b); lib. bdg. 33.67 *(978-1-4339-1952-7(4),* 449999e6-f670-459d-8244-b2820381bce2) Stevens, Gareth Publishing LLLP. (Gareth Stevens Learning Library).

Kesselring, Susan. On Wheels. 2018. (J). pap. *(978-1-4896-9972-5(4),* AV2 by Weigl) Weigl Pubs., Inc.

Kjelle, Marylou Morano. Extreme Skateboarding with Paul Rodriquez JR. 2006. (Extreme Sports Ser.). (Illus.). 32p. (J). (gr. 1-4). lib. bdg. 25.70 *(978-1-58415-489-1(6))* Mitchell Lane Pubs.

Knutson, Jeff. The Business of Skateboarding: From Board to Boardroom, 1 vol. 2009. (Super Skateboarding Ser.). (ENG., Illus.). 48p. (YA). (gr. 5-8). lib. bdg. 34.47 *(978-1-4358-5051-4(3),* 267ac0be-f0a8-44e8-b4a3-5e36210fc9a3) Rosen Publishing Group, Inc., The.

Knutson, Jeffrey. The Business of Skateboarding: From Board to Boardroom. 2009. (Super Skateboarding Ser.). 48p. (gr. 5-8). 53.00 *(978-1-60853-216-2(X),* Rosen Reference) Rosen Publishing Group, Inc., The.

Lakin, Patricia. Skateboards. 2017. (Made by Hand Ser.: 1). (ENG., Illus.). 32p. (J). (gr. 3-7). 17.99 *(978-1-4814-4833-8(1),* Simon & Schuster/Paula Wiseman Bks.) Simon & Schuster/Paula Wiseman Bks.

Loh-Hagan, Virginia. Extreme Ice Cross Downhill. 2016. (Nailed It! Ser.). (ENG., Illus.). 32p. (J). (gr. 4-8). 32.07 *(978-1-63470-486-1(X),* 207675) Cherry Lake Publishing.

—Extreme Skateboarding. 2015. (Nailed It! Ser.). (ENG., Illus.). 32p. (J). (gr. 4-8). 32.07 *(978-1-63470-015-3(5),* 206732) Cherry Lake Publishing.

Lovitt, Chip. Skate Parks: On a Roll! 2003. (ENG., Illus.). 32p. (J). (gr. 6-8). pap. 7.97 net. *(978-0-7652-3274-8(X),* Celebration Pr.) Savvas Learning Co.

Lucent Books, ed. Skateboarding. 2014. (Science Behind Sports Ser.). (ENG.). 112p. (gr. 7-10). lib. bdg. 37.45 *(978-1-4205-1211-3(0),* Lucent Bks.) Cengage Gale.

MacDonald, Margaret. Scooters & Skates. 2011. (Learn-Abouts Ser.). (Illus.). 16p. (J). pap. 7.95 *(978-1-59920-650-9(1))* Black Rabbit Bks.

Mahaney, Ian. Tony Hawk: Skateboarding Champ, 1 vol. 2004. (Extreme Sports Biographies Ser.). (ENG., Illus.). 24p. (J). (gr. 3-4). 26.27 *(978-1-4042-2747-7(4),* 927bcbbf-3613-42cd-a44c-4a1b742f9194, PowerKids Pr.) Rosen Publishing Group, Inc., The.

Mahaney, Ian F. Tony Hawk: Skateboarding Champion. 2009. (Extreme Sports Biographies Ser.). 24p. (gr. 3-4). 42.50 *(978-1-61512-472-5(1),* PowerKids Pr.) Rosen Publishing Group, Inc., The.

Marsh, James. Super.Activ Skateboarding. (ENG., Illus.). 128p. (YA). pap. 8.99 *(978-0-340-79160-8(8))* Hodder & Stoughton GBR. Dist: Trafalgar Square Publishing.

McClellan, Ray. Skateboarding. 2010. (My First Sports Ser.). (ENG., Illus.). 24p. (J). (gr. 2-5). lib. bdg. 26.95 *(978-1-60014-462-2(4),* Blastoff! Readers) Bellwether Media.

Michalski, Peter & Hocking, Justin. Riding Street Courses, 1 vol. 2016. (Skateboarding Tips & Tricks Ser.). (ENG.). 48p. (J). (gr. 5-5). pap. 12.75 *(978-1-4777-8874-5(3),* d4f639c8-ad51-4e47-9056-cc004826447c, Rosen Reference) Rosen Publishing Group, Inc., The.

Miller, Raymond H. Tony Hawk. 2004. (Stars of Sport Ser.). (ENG., Illus.). 48p. (J). 27.50 *(978-0-7377-1568-2(5),* Greenhaven Pr., Inc.) Cengage Gale.

Murdico, Suzanne J. Street Luge & Dirtboarding. 2009. (World of Skateboarding Ser.). 48p. (gr. 5-8). 53.00 *(978-1-60854-316-8(1),* Rosen Reference) Rosen Publishing Group, Inc., The.

Murdico, Suzanne J. & Michalski, Peter. Street Luge & Dirtboarding, 1 vol. 2016. (Skateboarding Tips & Tricks Ser.). (ENG.). 48p. (J). (gr. 5-5). pap. 12.75 *(978-1-4777-8870-7(0),* 0fb09519-4967-432d-8219-03cbed31c86a, Rosen Reference) Rosen Publishing Group, Inc., The.

Noll, Rhyn. Skateboarding: Past — Present — Future, 1 vol. 2003. (ENG., Illus.). 192p. (gr. 10-13). pap. 29.95 *(978-0-7643-1845-0(4),* 1851) Schiffer Publishing, Ltd.

Otfinoski, Steven. Extreme Skateboarding, 1 vol. 2013. (Sports on the Edge Ser.). (ENG.). 48p. (gr. 4-4). pap. 13.93 *(978-1-62712-131-6(5),* 2388feef-eee7-49f3-a95f-1141940fbec0); (Illus.). 32.64 *(978-1-60870-221-3(9),* 5a8704ce-fdbc-42dc-b035-4a14e6ba536c) Cavendish Square Publishing LLC.

Perez, Marlene. Skateboarding. 2004. (Shared Connections Ser.). (J). pap. *(978-1-4108-1636-8(2));* pap., instr.'s gde. ed. 27.00 *(978-1-4108-1612-2(5))* Benchmark Education Co.

Powell, Ben. Skateboarding. 2003. (Extreme Sports Ser.). (ENG., Illus.). 32p. (gr. 3-6). lib. bdg. 22.60 *(978-0-8225-1241-7(6))* Lerner Publishing Group.

Rajczak, Kristen. Skateboarding, 1 vol. 2015. (Sports to the Extreme Ser.). (ENG., Illus.). 48p. (J). (gr. 5-6). 33.47 *(978-1-4994-3569-6(X),* 7ace7d50-ece0-4ac6-a07c-2e05cefb858d, Rosen Central) Rosen Publishing Group, Inc., The.

Rosenberg, Aaron & Michalski, Peter. Advanced Skateboarding, 1 vol. 2016. (Skateboarding Tips & Tricks Ser.). (ENG., Illus.). 48p. (J). (gr. 5-5). pap. 12.75 *(978-1-4777-8859-2(X),* 8baff582-8f6a-4d7b-bc88-083a66c8986c, Rosen Reference) Rosen Publishing Group, Inc., The.

Sandler, Michael. Gnarly Skateboarders. 2009. (X-Moves Ser.). (Illus.). 24p. (J). (gr. 2-5). lib. bdg. 26.99 *(978-1-59716-950-9(1))* Bearport Publishing Co., Inc.

Segovia, Patty. Skate Girls. 2016. (Illus.). 32p. (J). *(978-1-4896-4783-2(X))* Weigl Pubs., Inc.

Segovia, Patty & Meredith Books Staff. On the Edge Skateboarding/on the Edge Snowboarding: Tips & Tricks from Six of the Coolest Skateboarders/Tips & Tricks from Six of the Coolest Snowboarders. 2008. (On the Edge Ser.). (Illus.). 48p. (YA). (gr. 8-12). per. 6.99 *(978-0-696-23980-9(9))* Meredith Bks.

Sheen, Barbara. Tony Hawk, 1 vol. 2007. (People in the News Ser.). (ENG., Illus.). 104p. (gr. 7-7). lib. bdg. 41.03 *(978-1-4205-0016-5(3),* 86c09256-3dc7-4ce2-85c3-8c0165f3dbf0, Lucent Pr.) Greenhaven Publishing LLC.

Skateboarding Tips & Tricks, 12 vols. 2016. (Skateboarding Tips & Tricks Ser.). 48p. (gr. 5-5). (ENG.). 200.82 *(978-1-4994-3840-6(0),* a470dc36-95dc-463a-a67e-7a9698348eb6); pap. 70.50 *(978-1-4777-8984-1(7))* Rosen Publishing Group, Inc., The. (Rosen Central).

Smith, Terri Smith. Tony Hawk: Flying High. 2003. (J). pap. *(978-1-932724-01-1(X),* Bios for Kids) Panda Publishing, L.L.C.

Sterling Casil, Amy. Tony Hawk: Skateboard Mogul. 2009. (Super Skateboarding Ser.). 48p. (gr. 5-8). 53.00 *(978-1-60853-219-3(4),* Rosen Reference) Rosen Publishing Group, Inc., The.

Stewart, Mark. One Wild Ride: The Life of Skateboarding Superstar Tony Hawk. 2003. (Illus.). 64p. (gr. 6-18). pap. 9.95 *(978-0-7613-1689-3(2),* Twenty-First Century Bks.) Lerner Publishing Group.

Streissguth, Thomas. Skateboard Vert. 2008. (Action Sports Ser.). (ENG., Illus.). 24p. (J). (gr. 3-7). lib. bdg. 26.95 *(978-1-60014-141-6(2))* Bellwether Media.

—Skateboarding Street Style. 2008. (Action Sports Ser.). (ENG., Illus.). 24p. (J). (gr. 3-7). lib. bdg. 26.95 *(978-1-60014-142-3(0))* Bellwether Media.

Super Skateboarding, 12 vols., Set. Incl. Business of Skateboarding: From Board to Boardroom. Knutson, Jeff. (Illus.). lib. bdg. 34.47 *(978-1-4358-5051-4(3),* 267ac0be-f0a8-44e8-b4a3-5e36210fc9a3); Competitive Skateboarding. Cefrey, Holly. (Illus.). lib. bdg. 34.47 *(978-1-4358-5050-7(5),* c460ad1e-e842-41d7-83d0-e3446fcfade2); Skateboarding Today & Tomorrow. Hasan, Heather. (Illus.). lib. bdg. 34.47 *(978-1-4358-5049-1(1),* 592d022c-2065-43a6-bff6-2410dd7756a7); Skating the X-Games. Cobb, Allan B. (Illus.). lib. bdg. 34.47 *(978-1-4358-5048-4(3),* 07f1db9a-3a12-43b7-a7f4-9602a8be4f01); Tony Hawk: Skateboard Mogul. Casil, Amy Sterling. (Illus.). lib. bdg. 34.47 *(978-1-4358-5047-7(5),* 16515748-a265-4496-9a7b-b8cd335e5797); World's Greatest Skate Parks. Hocking, Justin. lib. bdg. 34.47 *(978-1-4358-5046-0(7),* e754452a-d965-41ee-a1ec-f6624f9ce277); 48p. (YA). (gr. 5-8). 2009. (Super Skateboarding Ser.). (ENG.). 2008. Set lib. bdg. 206.82 *(978-1-4358-5216-7(8),* 6d55a30c-7cb8-41a5-ac17-59835081943c) Rosen Publishing Group, Inc., The.

Teller, Jackson. Skateboarding. 2012. (Adrenaline Rush Ser.). (Illus.). 32p. (gr. 4-7). lib. bdg. 31.35 *(978-1-59920-685-1(4))* Black Rabbit Bks.

Weber, Terri Smith. Tony Hawk: Flying High. 2003. (J). lib. bdg. *(978-1-932724-00-4(1),* Bios for Kids) Panda Publishing, L.L.C.

Weigl Publishers Staff & Craats, Rennay. For the Love of Skateboarding. Nault, Jennifer & Turner, Kara, eds. 2003. (For the Love of Sports Ser.). (Illus.). 24p. (J). pap. 8.95 *(978-1-59036-070-5(2))* Weigl Pubs., Inc.

Whiting, Jim. Skateboarding. 2018. (Odysseys in Extreme Sports Ser.). (ENG.). 80p. (J). (gr. 7-10). *(978-1-60818-694-5(6),* 19878, Creative Education) Creative Co., The.

Willet, Edward. Skateboarding: Techniques & Tricks. 2009. (Rad Sports: Techniques & Tricks Ser.). 48p. (gr. 5-8). 53.00 *(978-1-60851-937-8(6),* Rosen Reference) Rosen Publishing Group, Inc., The.

Wingate, Brian. Tony Hawk: Skateboarding Champion. 2009. (World of Skateboarding Ser.). 48p. (gr. 5-8). 53.00 *(978-1-60854-320-5(X),* Rosen Reference) Rosen Publishing Group, Inc., The.

Winters, Jaime. Shred It Skateboarding, 1 vol. 2012. (ENG., Illus.). 32p. (J). pap. *(978-0-7787-3162-7(6))* Crabtree Publishing Co.

Wiseman, Blaine. Skateboarding. 2015. (J). *(978-1-5105-0004-4(9))* SmartBook Media, Inc.

—Skateboarding. 2020. (J). *(978-1-7911-1836-5(4),* AV2 by Weigl) Weigl Pubs., Inc.

—Skateboarding: X Games. 2008. (Extreme Ser.). (Illus.). 32p. (J). (gr. 4-6). pap. 9.95 *(978-1-59036-913-5(0));* lib. bdg. 26.00 *(978-1-59036-912-8(2))* Weigl Pubs., Inc.

SKATEBOARDING—FICTION

Barwin, Steven. Sk8er, 1 vol. 2007. (Lorimer Sports Stories Ser.). (ENG., 128p. (J). (gr. 4-8). Illus.). 16.95 *(978-1-55028-985-5(3),* 985); 8.95 *(978-1-55028-983-1(7),* 983) James Lorimer & Co. Ltd., Pubs. CAN. Dist: Formac Lorimer Bks. Ltd.

Berend, Janet Eoff. True Vert. 2016. (ENG.). 128p. (J). (gr. 5-10). pap. 12.95 *(978-1-62124-024-2(X))* Breakaway Bks.

—Vertical. 2012. (ENG.). 160p. (J). (gr. 5-10). pap. 12.95 *(978-1-891369-98-8(9))* Breakaway Bks.

Birle, Pete. Locals Only. 2013. (Av2 Audio Chapter Bks.). (ENG.). 121p. (J). 27.13 *(978-1-62127-985-3(5),* AV2 by Weigl) Weigl Pubs., Inc.

Carlson, Nancy. Arnie & the Skateboard Gang. Carlson, Nancy, illus. 2012. (Nancy Carlson Picture Bks). (Illus.). 32p. (J). (gr. k-2). 56.72 *(978-0-7613-9303-0(X),* Carolrhoda Bks.) Lerner Publishing Group.

Chapman, Megan Joy. Lion Heart & Alessio Book 2: Mission, Peace, Patience, Kindness. 2014. (Lion Heart & Alessio Ser.: 2). (ENG.). 192p. (J). (gr. 3-7). pap. 11.99 *(978-1-62136-755-0(X),* Creation Hse.) Charisma Media.

Choyce, Lesley. Skate Freak, 1 vol. 2008. (Orca Currents Ser.). (ENG.). (J). 128p. (gr. 4-7). pap. 9.95 *(978-1-55469-042-8(0));* 108p. (gr. 6-8). 26.19 *(978-1-55469-043-5(9))* Orca Bk. Pubs. USA.

—Smoke & Mirrors. 2004. (ENG.). 200p. (YA). (gr. 7). pap. 8.99 *(978-1-55002-534-7(1))* Dundurn Pr. CAN. Dist: Publishers Group West (PGW).

Christopher, Matt. The Extreme Team: into Danger Zone. 6th ed. 2004. (Extreme Team Ser.: 6). (ENG., Illus.). 64p. (J). (gr. 1-4). pap. 8.99 *(978-0-316-76267-0(9))* Little, Brown Bks. for Young Readers.

—The Extreme Team: Skateboard Moves. Leonard, David, illus. 2018. (Matt Christopher Sports Readers Ser.). (ENG.). 32p. (J). (gr. 1-4). lib. bdg. 31.36 *(978-1-5321-4257-4(9),* 31057) Spotlight.

—Skateboard Tough. 2007. (New Matt Christopher Sports Library). 167p. (J). (gr. 4-6). lib. bdg. 26.60 *(978-1-59953-115-1(1))* Norwood Hse. Pr.

Cowan, Brad V. Skinner's Banks, 1 vol. 2013. (Seven Stair Crew Ser.). (ENG., Illus.). 160p. (J). (gr. 4-6). pap. 12.95 *(978-1-4594-0522-6(6),* eb280d38-d295-4c0d-9fd1-39ab4d486e4f) James Lorimer & Co. Ltd., Pubs. CAN. Dist: Lerner Publishing Group.

—Street Kings, 1 vol. 2013. (Seven Stair Crew Ser.). (ENG.). 136p. (J). (gr. 4-6). 12.95 *(978-1-4594-0450-2(5),* eb0678ea-4338-4a13-a05e-cccadfde4177) James Lorimer & Co. Ltd., Pubs. CAN. Dist: Lerner Publishing Group.

Dixon, Franklin. Stolen Identity. 2018. (Hardy Boys Adventures Ser.: 16). (ENG.). 144p. (J). (gr. 3-7). 17.99 *(978-1-4814-9967-5(X),* Aladdin) Simon & Schuster Children's Publishing.

Dixon, Franklin W. A Skateboard Cat-Astrophe. David, Matt, illus. 2017. (Hardy Boys Clue Book Ser.: 6). (ENG.). 96p. (J).

(gr. 1-4). 17.99 (978-1-4814-8870-9(8)); pap. 5.99 (978-1-4814-8869-3(4)) Simon & Schuster Children's Publishing. (Aladdin).

—Stolen Identity. 2018. (Hardy Boys Adventures Ser.: 16). (ENG., Illus.). 144p. (J). (gr. 3-7). pap. 6.99 (978-1-4814-9966-8(1), Aladdin) Simon & Schuster Children's Publishing.

Doeden, Matt. Shaun White. 2006. (Amazing Athletes Ser.). (Illus.). 32p. (J). (gr. 2-5). pap. 6.95 (978-0-8225-6841-4(1), First Avenue Editions) Lerner Publishing Group.

Drake, Raelyn. Stretched Too Thin. 2018. (Superhuman Ser.). (ENG.). 104p. (YA). (gr. 6-12). pap. 7.99 (978-1-5415-1051-7(8), 7b316d00-ddf6-4bc7-a371-64e4105cfd9c); 25.32 (978-1-5124-9828-8(9), 61a90da5-40ed-4b55-a7d6-e17b21ef522c) Lerner Publishing Group. (Darby Creek).

Dufresne, Michèle. Little Dinosaur's Skateboard. 2005. (Georgie Giraffe Set 1 Ser.). (J). pap. 7.33 (978-1-932570-42-7(X)) Pioneer Valley Bks.

Emberley, Rebecca. Mice on Ice. Emberley, Ed, illus. 2013. (I Like to Read Ser.). (ENG.). 24p. (J). (gr. -1-3). pap. 7.99 (978-0-8234-2908-0(3)) Holiday Hse., Inc.

Faber, Toni Tuso. The Poodle Tales: Book Five. Rudd, Benton, illus. 2013. 24p. 16.99 (978-0-9892711-0-3(2)); pap. 10.99 (978-0-9892711-1-0(0)) Mindstir Media.

Fein, Eric. Skateboard Breakdown, 1 vol. Sandoval, Gerardo, illus. 2010. (Sports Illustrated Kids Graphic Novels Ser.). (ENG.). 56p. (J). (gr. 3-8). 26.65 (978-1-4342-2011-0(7), 102775); pap. 7.19 (978-1-4342-2785-0(5), 114052) Capstone. (Stone Arch Bks.).

Free Wheelin' Coloring/Activity Book (English) 2005. (Illus.). (J). 2.99 (978-0-9770455-7-0(9)) Mighty Kids Media.

Harmon, Michael. Under the Bridge. 2013. (ENG.). 272p. (YA). (gr. 9). pap. 8.99 (978-0-375-85930-4(6), Ember) Random Hse. Children's Bks.

Hornby, Nick. Slam. 2009. (JPN.). 444p. (YA). (978-4-8340-2418-0(0)) Fukuinkan Shoten.

—Slam. (ENG.). 320p. (gr. 12). 2009. 17.00 (978-1-59448-471-1(6)) 2008. 15.00 (978-1-59448-345-5(0)) Penguin Publishing Group. (Riverhead Bks.).

Hurd, Thacher. Bad Frogs. Hurd, Thacher, illus. 2009. (ENG., Illus.). 40p. (J). (gr. -1-2). 15.99 (978-0-7636-3253-3(8)) Candlewick Pr.

Jenkins, Emily. The Little Bit Scary People. Boiger, Alexandra, illus. 2008. (ENG.). 32p. (gr. -1-1). 16.99 (978-1-4231-0075-1(1)) Hyperion Pr.

Kovalkova-McKenna, Svetlana & McKenna, Alexandra. The Fairy Book. 2009. 52p. pap. 7.58 (978-0-557-06160-0(1)) Lulu Pr., Inc.

Krebs, Patricia, illus. On Your Mark, Get Set, Go! 2009. 32p. (J). 16.95 (978-0-9796380-1-5(1)) Three Wishes Publishing Co.

Maddox, Jake. Board Battle. Aburto, Jesus, illus. 2013. (Jake Maddox Sports Stories Ser.). (ENG.). 72p. (J). (gr. 2-3). pap. 35.70 (978-1-4342-6235-6(9), 20040); (gr. 3-6). pap. 5.95 (978-1-4342-6208-0(1), 123506); (gr. 3-6). lib. bdg. 25.99 (978-1-4342-5975-2(7), 122932) Capstone. (Stone Arch Bks.).

—Board Rebel. Tiffany, Sean, illus. 2007. (Jake Maddox Sports Stories Ser.). (ENG.). 72p. (J). (gr. 3-6). pap. 5.95 (978-1-59889-414-1(5), 93561); lib. bdg. 25.99 (978-1-59889-319-9(X), 93515) Capstone. (Stone Arch Bks.).

—Longboard Letdown. Wood, Katie, illus. 2017. (Jake Maddox Girl Sports Stories Ser.). (ENG.). 72p. (J). (gr. 3-6). lib. bdg. 25.32 (978-1-4965-4972-3(4), 135864, Stone Arch Bks.) Capstone.

—El Rebelde de la Patineta, 1 vol. Heck, Claudia, tr. Tiffany, Sean, illus. 2012. (Jake Maddox en Español Ser.). (SPA.). 72p. (J). (gr. 3-6). 25.32 (978-1-4342-3816-0(4), 117505, Stone Arch Bks.) Capstone.

—Skate Park Challenge, 1 vol. Tiffany, Sean, illus. 2006. (Jake Maddox Sports Stories Ser.). (ENG.). 72p. (J). (gr. 3-6). 25.99 (978-1-59889-064-8(6), 86535, Stone Arch Bks.) Capstone.

—Skateboard Idol. 2016. (Jake Maddox JV Ser.). (ENG., Illus.). 96p. (J). (gr. 4-6). lib. bdg. 26.65 (978-1-4965-2631-1(7), 131193, Stone Arch Bks.) Capstone.

—Skateboard Save, 1 vol. Tiffany, Sean, illus. 2008. (Jake Maddox Sports Stories Ser.). (ENG.). 72p. (J). (gr. 3-6). pap. 5.95 (978-1-4342-0871-2(0), 95232, Stone Arch Bks.) Capstone.

—Skateboard Struggle, 1 vol. Tiffany, Sean, illus. 2011. (Jake Maddox Sports Stories Ser.). (ENG.). 72p. (J). (gr. 3-6). lib. bdg. 25.99 (978-1-4342-2987-8(4), 114283, Stone Arch Bks.) Capstone.

—Skatepark Challenge. Tiffany, Sean, illus. 2010. (Jake Maddox Sports Story Ser.). 72p. pap. 0.60 (978-1-4342-3207-6(7), Stone Arch Bks.) Capstone.

—Skaters Feroces. Aparicio Publishing LLC, Aparicio Publishing, tr. Muñiz, Berenice, illus. 2020. (Jake Maddox Novelas Gráficas Ser.). (SPA.). 72p. (J). (gr. 3-8). pap. 6.95 (978-1-4965-9314-6(6), 142344); lib. bdg. 27.99 (978-1-4965-9179-1(8), 142088) Capstone. (Stone Arch Bks.).

—Strange Boarders. Muñiz, Berenice, illus. 2018. (Jake Maddox Graphic Novels Ser.). (ENG.). 72p. (J). (gr. 3-8). pap. 6.95 (978-1-4965-6050-6(7), 137431); lib. bdg. 27.99 (978-1-4965-6046-9(9), 137427) Capstone. (Stone Arch Bks.).

Nelson, Blake. Paranoid Park. 2008. (ENG.). 192p. (YA). (gr. 7-18). 6.99 (978-0-14-241156-8(6), Puffin Books) Penguin Young Readers Group.

Pavey, Stephen. Free RollinApos. 2005. pap. 24.95 (978-1-4137-0890-5(0)) PublishAmerica, Inc.

Phillips, Dee. Grind, 1 vol. unabr. ed. 2010. (Right Now! Ser.). (ENG., Illus.). 45p. (YA). (gr. 9-12). pap. 10.75 (978-1-61651-250-7(4)) Saddleback Educational Publishing, Inc.

Sommer, Isabell & Reinhardt, Swen. CHIP CHIPS JAM - 4: Der Schatz in der Elbe. 2010. 86p. pap. (978-3-8391-0219-0(7)) Books on Demand GmbH.

Stevens, Eric. Skateboard Sonar, 1 vol. Sandoval, Gerardo, illus. 2010. (Sports Illustrated Kids Graphic Novels Ser.). (ENG.). 56p. (J). (gr. 3-8). 26.65 (978-1-4342-1910-7(0), 102369); pap. 7.19 (978-1-4342-2295-4(0), 103164) Capstone. (Stone Arch Bks.).

Stoudemire, Amar'e. Home Court. 2012. (STAT: Standing Tall & Talented Ser.: 1). lib. bdg. 16.00 (978-0-606-26169-2(9)) Turtleback.

Strange, Jason. Text 4 Revenge, 1 vol. Parks, Phil & Dal Lago, Alberto, illus. 2011. (Jason Strange Ser.). (ENG.). 72p. (J). (gr. 3-6). pap. 6.25 (978-1-4342-3432-2(0), 116453, Stone Arch Bks.) Capstone.

—Text 4 Revenge, 1 vol. Dal Lago, Alberto, illus. 2011. (Jason Strange Ser.). (ENG.). 72p. (J). (gr. 3-6). lib. bdg. 25.32 (978-1-4342-3233-5(6), 116205, Stone Arch Bks.) Capstone.

Suen, Anastasia. Skate Trick: A Robot & Rico Story, 1 vol. Laughead, Michael, illus. 2009. (Robot & Rico Ser.). (ENG.). 32p. (J). (gr. 1-2). pap. 6.25 (978-1-4342-1750-9(7), 102222, Stone Arch Bks.) Capstone.

Teitelbaum, Michael. Tricked Out, 6 vols., 6. Zalme, Ron, illus. 2009. (Backyard Sports Ser.: 6). (ENG.). 80p. (J). (gr. k-3). 16.19 (978-0-448-45072-8(0)) Penguin Young Readers Group.

Terrell, Brandon. Above. Cano, Fernando, illus. 2013. (Tony Hawk: Live2Skate Ser.). (ENG.). 72p. (gr. 3-4). pap. 35.70 (978-1-4342-6266-0(9), Stone Arch Bks.) Capstone.

Thompson, Vinny. Vinny & Bud. 2009. 64p. pap. 11.99 (978-1-4490-2551-9(X)) AuthorHouse.

Tony Hawk: Live2Skate. 2013. (Tony Hawk: Live2Skate Ser.). (ENG.). 72p. (gr. 3-4). pap. 142.80 (978-1-4342-6304-9(5)); (gr. 4-5). pap. 23.80 (978-1-4342-6225-7(1)) Capstone. (Stone Arch Bks.).

Walters, Eric. A Fond la Planche!, 1 vol. 2010. (Orca Soundings en Français Ser.). (FRE.). 136p. (YA). (gr. 8-12). pap. 9.95 (978-1-55469-373-3(X)) Orca Bk. Pubs. USA.

Warner, Sally. EllRay Jakes & the Beanstalk. Biggs, Brian, illus. 2013. (EllRay Jakes Ser.: 5). (ENG.). 144p. (J). (gr. 1-3). pap. 6.99 (978-0-14-242359-2(9), Puffin Books) Penguin Young Readers Group.

—EllRay Jakes & the Beanstalk. 2013. (EllRay Jakes Ser.: 5). lib. bdg. 16.00 (978-0-606-32137-2(3)) Turtleback.

Yasuda, Anita. I've Got the No-Skateboard Blues, 1 vol. Santillan, Jorge H., illus. 2012. (Sports Illustrated Kids Victory School Superstars Ser.). (ENG.). 56p. (J). (gr. 1-3). pap. 5.95 (978-1-4342-3866-5(0), 118048); lib. bdg. 26.65 (978-1-4342-2244-2(6), 103107) Capstone. (Stone Arch Bks.).

SKATING

Bix, Jasper. Let's Go Ice-Skating!, 1 vol. 2015. (Winter Fun Ser.). (ENG.). 24p. (J). (gr. k-k). lib. bdg. 24.27 (978-1-4824-3757-7(0), cdbced88-cac5-4cfc-8f20-1ca155239f71); (Illus.). pap. 9.15 (978-1-4824-3755-3(4), 249f71a3-6a4f-4de2-9122-794cc9c854a0) Stevens, Gareth Publishing LLLP.

—Let's Go Sledding!, 1 vol. 2015. (Winter Fun Ser.). (ENG.). 24p. (J). (gr. k-k). lib. bdg. 24.27 (978-1-4824-3761-4(9), 2c594532-52b5-4366-8d2e-af1d1157ab60) Stevens, Gareth Publishing LLLP.

Blaine, Victor. My Skates, 1 vol. 2014. (Watch Me Go! Ser.). (ENG., Illus.). 24p. (J). (gr. 1-2). lib. bdg. 25.27 (978-1-4994-0254-4(6), 274c5c89-99f0-4064-bd0c-9b7e907c7ac4, PowerKids Pr.) Rosen Publishing Group, Inc., The.

Browning, Kurt. A Is for Axel: An Ice Skating Alphabet. Rose, Melanie, illus. 2015. (Av2 Fiction Readalong 2016 Ser.). (ENG.). (J). (gr. 1-4). lib. bdg. 34.28 (978-1-4896-3732-1(X), AV2 by Weigl) Weigl Pubs., Inc.

—A Is for Axel: An Ice Skating Alphabet. Rose, Melanie, illus. rev. ed. 2005. (Sports Alphabet Ser.). (ENG.). 40p. (J). (gr. 1-4). 17.95 (978-1-58536-280-6(8), 202091) Sleeping Bear Pr.

Challen, Paul. Spin It Figure Skating, 1 vol. 2010. (ENG., Illus.). 32p. (J). pap. (978-0-7787-3178-8(2), 1308270); lib. bdg. (978-0-7787-3146-7(4), 1308270) Crabtree Publishing Co.

Cham, Stephanie. Michelle Kwan. 2018. (Great Asian Americans Ser.). (ENG., Illus.). 24p. (J). (gr. -1-2). lib. bdg. 27.32 (978-1-5157-9958-0(1), 136956, Capstone Pr.) Capstone.

Chen, Karen. Finding the Edge: My Life on the Ice. 2017. (ENG., Illus.). 224p. (J). (gr. 3-7). 17.99 (978-0-06-282268-0(3), HarperCollins) HarperCollins Pubs.

Cohen, Sasha. Sasha Cohen: Autobiography of a Champion Figure Skater. Goedeken, Kathy, illus. 2005. (ENG.). 192p. (J). (gr. 3-18). pap. 9.99 (978-0-06-072489-4(7)) HarperCollins Pubs.

Dzidrums, Christine. Yuna Kim: Ice Queen. Rendon, Leah, ed. Dzidrums, Joseph et al, photos by. 2011. (Skate Stars Ser.: Vol. 2). (Illus.). 72p. (YA). pap. 10.99 (978-0-9826435-9-4(4)) Creative Media Publishing.

Dzidrums, Christine & Rendon, Leah. Joannie Rochette: Canadian Ice Princess. Allison, Elizabeth, ed. Adeff, Jay & Mittan, J. Barry, photos by. 2nd exp. rev. ed. 2010. (Skate Stars Ser.: Vol. 1). (Illus.). 100p. (YA). pap. 12.99 (978-0-9826435-0-1(0)) Creative Media Publishing.

Farbs, C. Olympic Ice Skating. 2009. (Great Moments in Olympic History Ser.). 48p. (gr. 5-6). 53.00 (978-1-61513-161-7(2), Rosen Reference) Rosen Publishing Group, Inc., The.

First Sticker Book Ice Skating. 2017. (First Sticker Bks.). (ENG.). (J). pap. 6.99 (978-0-7945-3875-0(4), Usborne) EDC Publishing.

Freese, Joan. Play-by-Play Figure Skating. King, Andy, illus. King, Andy, photos by. 2004. (Play-by-Play Ser.). 80p. (J). (gr. 4-8). lib. bdg. 23.93 (978-0-8225-3934-6(9)) Lerner Publishing Group.

Gaetz, Dayle. Catriona le May Doan: La Plus Rapide des Patineuses. 2004. (FRE., Illus.). (J). (978-2-7650-0745-6(4)) Les Editions de la Cheneliere, Inc.

Goodridge, Catherine. Michelle Kwan & Michelle Kwan (Spanish) 6 English, 6 Spanish Adaptations. 2011. (ENG & SPA.). (J). 79.00 net. (978-1-4108-5659-3(3)) Benchmark Education Co.

—Michelle Kwan (Spanish) 2011. (SPA.). (J). pap. 40.00 net. (978-1-4108-2428-8(4), A24284) Benchmark Education Co.

Gustaitis, Joseph. Figure Skating. 2009. (Winter Olympic Sports Ser.). (ENG., Illus.). 32p. (J). (gr. 3-6). lib. bdg. (978-0-7787-4022-3(6)) Crabtree Publishing Co.

—Speed Skating. 2009. (Winter Olympic Sports Ser.). (ENG., Illus.). 32p. (J). (gr. 3-6). lib. bdg. (978-0-7787-4027-8(7)) Crabtree Publishing Co.

Heller, Alyson. Let's Go Skating! Ready-To-Read Level 1. Björkman, Steve & Björkman, Steve, illus. 2009. (After-School Sports Club Ser.). (ENG.). 32p. (J). (gr. -1-1). pap. 4.99 (978-1-4169-9411-4(4), Simon Spotlight) Simon Spotlight.

Hill, Anne E. Sasha Cohen. 2008. (ENG.). (gr. 5-12). pap. 56.72 (978-0-8225-9400-0(5)) Lerner Publishing Group.

Hughes, Morgan. Ice Skating. 2005. (Junior Sports Ser.). (Illus.). 32p. (gr. 2-4). 19.95 (978-1-59515-192-6(3)) Rourke Educational Media.

Kirkpatrick, Rob. Tara Lipinski: Super Ice-Skater. 2009. (Great Record Breakers in Sports Ser.). 24p. (gr. 3-3). 42.50 (978-1-61513-191-4(4), PowerKids Pr.) Rosen Publishing Group, Inc., The.

Labrecque, Ellen. Figure Skating. 2018. (21st Century Skills Library: Global Citizens: Olympic Sports Ser.). (ENG.). 32p. (J). (gr. 4-7). pap. 14.21 (978-1-5341-0855-4(6), 210784); (Illus.). lib. bdg. 32.07 (978-1-5341-0756-4(8), 210783) Cherry Lake Publishing.

—The Science of a Triple Axel. 2015. (21st Century Skills Library: Full-Speed Sports Ser.). (ENG., Illus.). 32p. (J). (gr. 4-7). 32.07 (978-1-63362-587-7(7), 206532) Cherry Lake Publishing.

—Speed Skating. 2018. (21st Century Skills Library: Global Citizens: Olympic Sports Ser.). (ENG., Illus.). 32p. (J). (gr. 4-7). pap. 14.21 (978-1-5341-0854-7(8), 210780); lib. bdg. 32.07 (978-1-5341-0755-7(X), 210779) Cherry Lake Publishing.

MacKay, Jennifer. Figure Skating, 1 vol. 2012. (Science Behind Sports Ser.). (ENG.). 104p. (gr. 7-7). 41.03 (978-1-4205-0784-3(2), 89a608a1-6dfe-44a2-9a7f-ad09f598fd3d, Lucent Pr.) Greenhaven Publishing LLC.

Marsico, Katie. Speed Skating. 2008. (21st Century Skills Library: Real World Math Ser.). (ENG.). 32p. (gr. 4-8). lib. bdg. 32.07 (978-1-60279-250-0(X), 200128) Cherry Lake Publishing.

McDougall, Chros. Girls Play to Win Figure Skating. 2010. (Girls Play to Win Ser.). 64p. (J). (gr. 3-6). lib. bdg. 27.93 (978-1-59953-389-6(8)) Norwood Hse. Pr.

Michalski, Pete & Moncrief, Kathryn M. Figure Skating: Girls Rocking It, 1 vol., 1. 2015. (Title IX Rocks! Ser.). (ENG.). 64p. (J). (gr. 6-6). 36.13 (978-1-5081-7033-4(9), 7810b3b2-4591-4b7d-a561-e42ca8315d0c, Rosen Young Adult) Rosen Publishing Group, Inc., The.

Miller, Raymond H. Michelle Kwan. 2003. (Stars of Sports Ser.). (ENG., Illus.). 48p. (J). 27.50 (978-0-7377-1540-8(5), Greenhaven Pr., Inc.) Cengage Gale.

Pettiford, Rebecca. Zamboni Ice Resurfacers. 2017. (Mighty Machines in Action Ser.). (ENG., Illus.). 24p. (J). (gr. k-3). lib. bdg. 26.95 (978-1-62617-634-8(5), Blastoff! Readers) Bellwether Media.

Publications International Ltd. Staff, ed. Teenage Ninja Turtles: Skateboard Heroes! 2014. 12p. (J). bds. 12.98 (978-1-4508-8453-2(9), 5b3a6351-f0d0-4a36-b0d1-c89677f0352a) Phoenix International Publications, Inc.

Ruscoe, Michael. Skating to Spelling Success, 1 vol. 2009. (Grammar All-Stars: Writing Tools Ser.). (ENG.). 32p. (J). (gr. 2-4). pap. 11.50 (978-1-4339-2137-7(5), 9ee053ce-4d92-4b9f-b255-72dded519768); lib. bdg. 28.67 (978-1-4339-1944-2(3), b3faba62-22ed-443f-ace8-3f17aafbe71f) Stevens, Gareth Publishing LLLP. (Gareth Stevens Learning Library).

Sandler, Michael. Ice Skating: The Incredible Michelle Kwan. 2006. (Upsets & Comebacks Ser.). (Illus.). 32p. (J). (gr. 3-6). lib. bdg. 28.50 (978-1-59716-252-4(3)) Bearport Publishing Co., Inc.

Schuh, Mari. Figure Skating. 2019. (Spot Sports Ser.). (ENG.). 16p. (J). (gr. -1-2). lib. bdg. (978-1-68151-650-9(0), 10782) Amicus.

Schulte, Mary E. Synchronized Skating. 2017. (Figure Skating Ser.). (ENG., Illus.). 32p. (J). (gr. 3-9). lib. bdg. 28.65 (978-1-5157-8186-8(0), 136157, Capstone Pr.) Capstone.

Schwartz, Heather E. Pairs Skating. 2017. (Figure Skating Ser.). (ENG., Illus.). 32p. (J). (gr. 3-9). lib. bdg. 28.65 (978-1-5157-8187-5(9), 136158, Capstone Pr.) Capstone.

—Singles Skating. 2017. (Figure Skating Ser.). (ENG., Illus.). 32p. (J). (gr. 3-9). lib. bdg. 28.65 (978-1-5157-8188-2(7), 136159, Capstone Pr.) Capstone.

Streeter, Michael. Ice Skating. 2005. (Sports Injuries Ser.). (Illus.). 64p. (YA). lib. bdg. 19.95 (978-1-59084-635-3(4)) Mason Crest.

Suen, Anastasia. La Historia Del Patinaje Artistico, 1 vol. 2003. (Historia de Los Deportes (Sports History) Ser.). (SPA., Illus.). 24p. (J). (gr. 2-2). lib. bdg. 26.27 (978-0-8239-6872-5(3), 8a9faafc-8d8c-4f1b-89e6-b216f64c8cf4) Rosen Publishing Group, Inc., The.

—La historia del patinaje artístico (the Story of Figure Skating) 2009. (Historia de los deportes (Sports History) Ser.). (SPA.). 24p. (gr. 2-2). 42.50 (978-1-61513-314-7(3), Editorial Buenas Letras) Rosen Publishing Group, Inc., The.

Throp, Claire, et al. Figure Skating. 2017. (Figure Skating Ser.). (ENG.). 32p. (J). (gr. 3-9). 122.60 (978-1-5157-8202-5(6), 27016, Capstone Pr.) Capstone.

Uschan, Michael V. Apolo Anton Ohno, 1 vol. 2011. (People in the News Ser.). (ENG.). 104p. (gr. 7-7). lib. bdg. 41.03 (978-1-4205-0603-7(X), bc32c909-9283-4f7c-8a7f-916efddff23c, Lucent Pr.) Greenhaven Publishing LLC.

Ventura, Marne. Stem in Figure Skating. 2017. (STEM in Sports Ser.). (ENG., Illus.). 48p. (J). (gr. 3-6). lib. bdg. 34.21 (978-1-5321-1349-9(8), 27647, SportsZone) ABDO Publishing Co.

Viña, Rose. Ice Breaker: How Mabel Fairbanks Changed Figure Skating. Almon, Claire, illus. 2019. (She Made History Ser.). (ENG.). 32p. (J). (gr. -1-3). 16.99 (978-0-8075-3496-0(X), 080753496X) Whitman, Albert & Co.

Waxman, Laura Hamilton. Figure Skating. 2017. (Winter Olympic Sports Ser.). (ENG.). 32p. (J). (gr. 2-5). 20.95 (978-1-68151-148-1(7), 14692) Amicus.

—Speed Skating. 2017. (Winter Olympic Sports Ser.). (ENG., Illus.). 32p. (J). (gr. 2-5). 20.95 (978-1-68151-153-5(3), 14696) Amicus.

—Winter Olympic Sports: Figure Skating. 2017. (Winter Olympic Sports Ser.). (ENG.). 32p. (J). (gr. 2-5). pap. 9.99 (978-1-68152-179-4(2), 14811) Amicus.

—Winter Olympic Sports: Speed Skating. 2017. (Winter Olympic Sports Ser.). (ENG., Illus.). 32p. (J). (gr. 2-5). pap. 9.99 (978-1-68152-184-8(9), 14815) Amicus.

Weyn, Suzanne, adapted by. Ice Princess. 2005. (Illus.). 124p. (J). pap. (978-0-439-74552-9(7)) Scholastic, Inc.

Where Is Kate's Skate? KinderReaders Individual Title Six-Packs. (Kinderstarters Ser.). 8p. (gr. -1-1). 21.00 (978-0-7635-8644-7(7)) Rigby Education.

Wood, Alix. You Can Be an Ice-Skater, 1 vol., Vol. 1. 2013. (Let's Get Moving! Ser.). (ENG., Illus.). 32p. (J). (gr. 3-4). 29.27 (978-1-4824-0283-4(1), 47975ab0-48af-40cc-b27f-b07486d7ad53) Stevens, Gareth Publishing LLLP.

SKATING—FICTION

Allen, Kenny. A Great Day to Skate, 1 vol. 2006. (Neighborhood Readers Ser.). (ENG.). 8p. (gr. 1-2). pap. 5.15 (978-1-4042-6819-7(7), 2c234750-98f6-4792-a959-89e7affe33e5, Rosen Classroom) Rosen Publishing Group, Inc., The.

Alma, Ann. Skateway to Freedom. 2nd ed. 2008. (ENG.). 136p. (YA). (gr. 5-8). pap. 11.99 (978-1-55002-719-8(0)) Dundurn Pr. CAN. Dist: Publishers Group West (PGW).

Bailey, Linda. The Best Figure Skater in the Whole Wide World. 2004. (Illus.). (J). (gr. k-3). spiral bd. (978-0-616-11094-2(4)); spiral bd. (978-0-616-11093-5(6)) Canadian National Institute for the Blind/Institut National Canadien pour les Aveugles.

Barragan, Sophia & Barragan, Ivy. Susana Banana the Fantastic Figure Skater. 2008. 32p. pap. 12.99 (978-1-4389-0169-5(0)) AuthorHouse.

Bentley, Sue. Sparkling Skates. 2014. (Magic Puppy Ser.: 13). lib. bdg. 14.75 (978-0-606-35685-5(1)) Turtleback.

Biggs, Brian. Everything Goes: Henry Goes Skating. Biggs, Brian & Abbott, Simon, illus. 2012. (My First I Can Read Ser.). (ENG.). 32p. (J). (gr. -1-3). 16.99 (978-0-06-195821-2(2)); pap. 4.99 (978-0-06-195820-5(4)) HarperCollins Pubs. (HarperCollins).

—Henry Goes Skating. Abbott, Simon, illus. 2012. (My First I Can Read Ser.). (J). lib. bdg. 13.55 (978-0-606-26852-3(9)) Turtleback.

Brown, Jeff. Flat Stanley: on Ice. Pamintuan, Macky, illus. 2015. (I Can Read Level 2 Ser.). (ENG.). 32p. (J). (gr. -1-3). pap. 5.99 (978-0-06-218981-3(6), HarperCollins) HarperCollins Pubs.

Carlson, Nancy. Snowden. Carlson, Nancy, illus. 2012. (Nancy Carlson Picture Bks). (Illus.). 32p. (J). (gr. k-2). 56.72 (978-0-7613-9307-8(2), Carolrhoda Bks.) Lerner Publishing Group.

Christopher, Matt. Snowboard Maverick. 2005. (Sports Classics IV Ser.). 156p. (J). lib. bdg. 15.00 (978-1-59054-769-4(1)) Fitzgerald Bks.

Clark, Catherine. Frozen Rodeo. 2003. (ENG.). 304p. (YA). (gr. 8-18). 15.99 (978-0-06-009070-8(7)) HarperCollins Pubs.

Dodge, Mary Mapes. Hans Brinker, or the Silver Skates. 2007. 308p. (gr. 3-7). 32.95 (978-1-4344-9309-5(1)); per. 19.95 (978-1-4344-9308-8(3)) Wildside Pr., LLC.

—Hans Brinker or the Silver Skates A Story of Life in Holland. Doggett, Allen B., illus. 2004. reprint ed. pap. 34.95 (978-1-4179-4127-8(8)) Kessinger Publishing, LLC.

—Hans Brinker; or, the Silver Skates (Dod. 2006. pap. (978-1-4065-0961-8(2)) Dodo Pr.

—The Silver Skates. Bailey, Peter, illus. 2019. (Alma Junior Classics Ser.). (ENG.). 320p. (J). pap. 11.00 (978-1-84749-720-8(9), 900200636, Alma Classics) Bloomsbury Publishing USA.

Eulberg, Elizabeth. The Great Shelby Holmes & the Coldest Case. 2018. (ENG., Illus.). 224p. (J). 16.99 (978-1-68119-057-0(5), 900157430, Bloomsbury Children's Bks.) Bloomsbury Publishing USA.

Fisch, Sarah. Skating with Friends. Durk, Jim, illus. 2007. (Little Red Reader Ser.). (J). pap. (978-0-439-90898-6(1)) Scholastic, Inc.

Flynn, Pat. Alex Jackson: Closing Out. 2003. 168p. (J). pap. (978-0-7022-3353-1(6)) Univ. of Queensland Pr.

Freitas, Donna. Gold Medal Winter. 2017. (ENG.). 336p. (J). (gr. 5-9). pap. 7.99 (978-0-545-64378-8(3), Scholastic Pr.) Scholastic, Inc.

Garis, Howard R. Daddy Takes Us Skating. 2018. (ENG., Illus.). 52p. (YA). (gr. 7-12). pap. (978-93-5297-330-9(5)) Alpha Editions.

Garis, Howard Roger. Daddy Takes Us Skating. 2004. reprint ed. pap. 15.95 (978-1-4191-1489-2(1)); pap. 1.99 (978-1-4192-1489-9(6)) Kessinger Publishing, LLC.

Gassman, Julie. Skating Is Hard When You're Homesick, 1 vol. Santillan, Jorge, illus. 2011. (Sports Illustrated Kids Victory School Superstars Ser.). (ENG.). 56p. (J). (gr. 1-3). pap. 5.95 (978-1-4342-3398-1(7), 116411); lib. bdg. 26.65 (978-1-4342-2237-4(3), 103099) Capstone. (Stone Arch Bks.).

Gibson, Sylvia Scott. Ricky the Skating Worm & Friends, 1 vol. Gibson, Gregory V., illus. 2009. 21p. pap. 24.95 (978-1-60836-473-2(9)) America Star Bks.

Harvey, John. My New Skates, 1 vol. 2006. (Neighborhood Readers Ser.). (ENG.). 16p. (gr. 1-2). pap. 6.50 (978-1-4042-7172-2(4), e7690410-2446-4a69-9818-2000b054a2f2, Rosen Classroom) Rosen Publishing Group, Inc., The.

Hawley, Mabel C. Four Little Blossoms Through the Holidays. 2005. pap. 22.95 (978-1-4179-9003-0(1)) Kessinger Publishing, LLC.

Hope, Lee Laura. The Outdoor Girls in a Winter Camp or Glorious Days on Skates & Ice Boats. 2007. 156p. 41.99 (978-1-4280-7498-9(8)); per. 35.99 (978-1-4280-7509-2(7)) IndyPublish.com.

Houran, Lori Haskins. Flat Stanley on Ice. Pamintuan, Macky, illus. 2015. 29p. (J). (978-1-4242-6418-6(9)) HarperCollins Pubs.

Hutchins, Hazel. Skate, Robyn, Skate. Cathcart, Yvonne, illus. 2004. 57p. (J). lib. bdg. 12.00 (978-1-4242-1244-6(8)) Fitzgerald Bks.

—Skate, Robyn, Skate, 1 vol. Cathcart, Yvonne, illus. 2004. (Formac First Novels Ser.: 30). (ENG.). 64p. (J). (gr. 1-5). 4.95 *(978-0-88780-626-1(0)*, 626); 14.95 *(978-0-88780-627-8(9)*, 627) Formac Publishing Co., Ltd. CAN. Dist: Formac Lorimer Bks. Ltd.

Idle, Molly. Flora & the Penguin. 2014. (Flora & Friends Ser.). (ENG., Illus.). 40p. (J). (gr. -1-k). 16.99 *(978-1-4521-2891-7(X))* Chronicle Bks. LLC.

Jewel, Judy. Sole Shoes: Nate the Skate in Search of His Mate. 2005. 19.95 *(978-0-9767066-0-1(1))* Dunamis Development.

Keller, Holly. Pearl's New Skates. Keller, Holly, illus. 2005. (Illus.). 24p. (J). lib. bdg. 17.89 *(978-0-06-056281-6(1))* HarperCollins Pubs.

Kovalski, Maryann. Omar on Ice. 2004. (J). (gr. k-3). spiral bd. *(978-0-616-01691-6(3))*; spiral bd. *(978-0-616-01690-9(5))* Canadian National Institute for the Blind/Institut National Canadien pour les Aveugles.

Krulik, Nancy. 'Snot Funny! 2015. (George Brown, Class Clown Ser.: 14). lib. bdg. 14.75 *(978-0-606-36584-0(2))* Turtleback.

LEVEL 1 WONDER WHEELS PREPACK [News Group]. 2013. (Wonder Wheels Ser.). (ENG.). pap. 94.80 *(978-1-4342-9031-1(X)*, Stone Arch Bks.) Capstone.

Lewis, Beverly. Girls Only! 2008. (Girls Only (Go!) Ser.: Vols. 5-8). (ENG.). (J). (gr. 4-7). 510p. pap. 20.00 *(978-0-7642-0462-3(9))*;Vols. 1-4. 512p. pap. 21.00 *(978-0-7642-0461-6(0))* Bethany Hse. Pubs.

Lien, Henry. Peasprout Chen, Future Legend of Skate & Sword. 2019. (Peasprout Chen Ser.: 1). (ENG., Illus.). 352p. (J). pap. 12.99 *(978-1-250-29436-4(3)*, 900187110) Square Fish.

Manning, Matthew K. Strong. 2013. (Tony Hawk: Live2Skate Ser.). (ENG.). 72p. (gr. 3-4). pap. 35.70 *(978-1-4342-6269-1(3)*, Stone Arch Bks.) Capstone.

Marychild, H. D. Skater Sister. 2013. (ENG.). 222p. (J). (gr. 5-12). pap. 9.52 *(978-0-9899964-9-5(2))* Small Wonder Publishing.

May, Eleanor. Mice on Ice. Melmon, Deborah, illus. 2013. (Mouse Math Ser.). 32p. (J). (gr. -1-1). 22.60 *(978-1-57565-527-7(6))*; pap. 7.99 *(978-1-57565-528-4(4)*, 2a9ca53b-ef64-4466-beb6-a3300c56f275, Kane Press) Astra Publishing Hse.

McBride, Susan Carro. Katrina & the Magic Skates. 2011. 32p. pap. 21.99 *(978-1-4500-0730-6(9))* Xlibris Corp.

McClatchy, Lisa. Eloise Skates! Ready-To-Read Level 1. Lyon, Tammie, illus. 2008. (Eloise Ser.). (ENG.). 32p. (J). (gr. -1-1). pap. 4.99 *(978-1-4169-6406-3(1))* Simon & Schuster, Inc.

Morrill, Lauren. Being Sloane Jacobs. 2015. (ENG.). 352p. (YA). (gr. 7). pap. 9.99 *(978-0-385-74180-4(4)*, Ember) Random Hse. Children's Bks.

Mun-Ensor, Michelle. The Faithful Christmas. 2011. 28p. pap. 24.95 *(978-1-4560-7077-9(0))* America Star Bks.

Nall, Gail. Breaking the Ice. 2015. (Mix Ser.). (ENG., Illus.). 320p. (J). (gr. 3-7). 16.99 *(978-1-4814-1911-6(0)*, Aladdin) Simon & Schuster Children's Publishing.

Ockler, Sarah. Bittersweet. 2012. (ENG.). (YA). (gr. 9). 400p. pap. 9.99 *(978-1-4424-3036-5(2))*; 384p. 16.99 *(978-1-4424-3035-8(4))* Simon Pulse. (Simon Pulse).

O'Neill, Jacquie, illus. Figure Skating. 2010. (Sticker Stories Ser.). (ENG.). 16p. (J). (gr. -1-k). pap. 5.99 *(978-0-448-45343-9(6)*, Grosset & Dunlap) Penguin Publishing Group.

Paulsen, Gary. Dancing Carl. 2007. (ENG.). 112p. (J). (gr. 5-9). pap. 8.99 *(978-1-4169-3938-2(5)*, Simon & Schuster Bks. For Young Readers) Simon & Schuster Bks. For Young Readers.

Perkins, Stephanie. Lola & the Boy Next Door. 2013. 368p. (YA). (gr. 9). pap. 12.99 *(978-0-14-242201-4(0)*, Speak) Penguin Young Readers Group.

Polak, Monique. Scarred, 1 vol. (Lorimer SideStreets Ser.). (ENG.). 168p. (YA). (gr. 9-12). 2011. 8.99 *(978-1-55028-964-0(0)*, 85e5c948-30d7-4a0d-96a8-bb89caa35af9) 2007. 16.95 *(978-1-55028-965-7(9)*, 965) James Lorimer & Co. Ltd., Pubs. CAN. Dist: Lerner Publishing Group, Formac Lorimer Bks. Ltd.

Sandrey, Alexander & Sellers, Carolyn. Cold Weather Bro's Arctic Adventure. 2012. 36p. 17.95 *(978-1-4575-1701-3(9))* Dog Ear Publishing, LLC.

Sass, A. J. Ana on the Edge. 2020. (ENG.). 384p. (J). (gr. 3-7). 16.99 *(978-0-316-45861-0(9))* Little, Brown Bks. for Young Readers.

Shaw, Mary. Brady Brady & the Super Skater, 11 vols. Temple, Chuck, illus. l.t. ed. 2005. 32p. (J). per. *(978-1-897169-06-3(X))* Brady Brady, Inc.

Shen, E. L. The Comeback: A Figure Skating Novel. 2021. (ENG., Illus.). 272p. (J). 16.99 *(978-0-374-31379-1(2)*, 900221649, Farrar, Straus & Giroux (BYR)) Farrar, Straus & Giroux.

Silvestro, Annie. Mice Skating. White, Teagan, illus. 2017. (Mice Skating Ser.: 1). 32p. (J). (gr. -1). 17.99 *(978-1-4549-1632-1(X))* Sterling Publishing Co., Inc.

Singer, Marilyn. Tallulah's Ice Skates: A Winter & Holiday Book for Kids. Boiger, Alexandra, illus. 2018. (Tallulah Ser.). (ENG.). 48p. (J). (gr. -1-3). 17.99 *(978-0-544-59692-4(7)*, 1615570, Clarion Bks.) HarperCollins Pubs.

Sparks, Megan. Boot Camp Blues, 1 vol. 2014. (Roller Girls Ser.). (ENG.). 256p. (YA). (gr. 8-10). 12.95 *(978-1-62370-057-7(4)*, 124413, Capstone Young Readers) Capstone.

—In a Jam, 1 vol. 2014. (Roller Girls Ser.). (ENG.). 256p. (YA). (gr. 8-10). 12.95 *(978-1-62370-058-4(2)*, 124414, Capstone Young Readers) Capstone.

Staunton, Ted. Morgan on Ice, 1 vol. Slavin, Bill, illus. 2013. (Formac First Novels Ser.). (ENG.). 56p. (J). (gr. 2-3). 14.95 *(978-1-4595-0289-5(2)*, 0289) Formac Publishing Co., Ltd. CAN. Dist: Formac Lorimer Bks. Ltd.

Stilton, Thea. Thea Stilton & the Lost Letters. 2015. (Thea Stilton Ser.: 21). (Illus.). 159p. (J). lib. bdg. 18.40 *(978-0-606-37061-5(7))* Turtleback.

—Thea Stilton Mouseford Academy #10: A Dream on Ice. 2016. (Illus.). 128p. (J). *(978-0-545-91797-1(2))* Scholastic, Inc.

Turcotte, Michael. Colours Made in Heaven, 1 vol. Turcotte, Derek, illus. 2009. 13p. pap. 24.95 *(978-1-60836-316-2(3))* America Star Bks.

Van Stockum, Hilda. A Day on Skates: The Story of a Dutch Picnic. Van Stockum, Hilda, illus. 2007. (Illus.). 40p. (J). (gr. 1). 19.95 *(978-1-932350-18-0(7))* Bethlehem Bks.

Vaughan, Garth. Tommy's New Block Skates PB, 1 vol. Smith, David Preston, illus. 2007. (ENG.). 36p. (J). (gr. 1-3). pap. 12.95 *(978-1-55109-620-9(X)*, 1d8ca434-d869-49ba-aaa1-01ecef613a79) Nimbus Publishing, Ltd. CAN. Dist: Baker & Taylor Publisher Services (BTPS).

Warren, George A. The Banner Boy Scouts on a Tour. 2017. (ENG., Illus.). 256p. (J). pap. *(978-93-86874-78-8(4))* Alpha Editions.

—The Banner Boy Scouts on a Tour. 2005. pap. 30.95 *(978-1-885529-38-1(4))* Stevens Publishing.

Wisler, Joelle. Ariana Gold. 2016. (What's Your Dream? Ser.). (ENG., Illus.). 96p. (J). (gr. 4-6). lib. bdg. 25.99 *(978-1-4965-3442-2(5)*, 132564, Stone Arch Bks.) Capstone.

Withers, Pam. Skater Stuntboys, 1 vol. 2005. (Take It to the Xtreme Ser.: 4). (ENG.). 198p. (YA). (gr. 7-10). pap. 6.95 *(978-1-55285-647-5(X)*, 3d5a6d3b-c6a9-4bcc-885d-eabc5a2eeb3d) Whitecap Bks., Ltd. CAN. Dist: Firefly Bks., Ltd.

Yamaguchi, Kristi. Dream Big, Little Pig! Bowers, Tim, illus. 32p. (J). (gr. -1-3). 2022. 7.99 *(978-1-7282-5259-9(8))* 2011. 16.99 *(978-1-4022-5275-4(7))* Sourcebooks, Inc. (Sourcebooks Jabberwocky).

—It's a Big World, Little Pig! Bowers, Tim, illus. 32p. (J). (gr. -1-3). 2022. 7.99 *(978-1-7282-5260-5(1))* 2012. 16.99 *(978-1-4022-6644-7(8))* Sourcebooks, Inc. (Sourcebooks Jabberwocky).

SKELETON

Arnau, Eduard. Nuestra Arquitectura Osea. (Mundo Invisible Ser.). (SPA., Illus.). (YA). (gr. 5-8). pap. 8.00 *(978-958-04-3227-2(9))* Norma S.A. COL. Dist: Lectorum Pubns., Inc., Distribuidora Norma, Inc.

—Nuestra Arquitectura Osea. (SPA.). 88p. (J). 10.00 *(978-84-342-1739-3(2))* Parramon Ediciones S.A. ESP. Dist: Distribuidora Norma, Inc.

Arnold, Caroline. El sistema osec (the Skeletal System) 2007. (Libros Sobre el Cuerpo Humano para Madrugadores Ser.). (Illus.). 48p. (J). (gr. -1-3). per. 8.95 *(978-0-8225-6648-9(6))* Lerner Publishing Group.

—The Skeletal System. 2005. (Early Bird Body Systems Ser.). (Illus.). 48p. (J). (gr. 2-4). lib. bdg. 25.26 *(978-0-8225-5140-9(3))* Lerner Publishing Group.

—Skeletal System. 2005. (Early Bird Body Systems Ser.). (ENG., Illus.). 48p. (gr. 2-5). pap. 7.95 *(978-0-8225-2523-3(2)*, Lerner Pubns.) Lerner Publishing Group.

Autumn Publishing Staff, illus. My Skeleton. 2004. (Wall Charts Ser.). (J). pap. 4.99 *(978-1-85997-268-7(3))* Byeway Bks.

Balkan, Gabrielle. Book of Bones: 10 Record-Breaking Animals. 2017. (ENG., Illus.). 48p. (gr. -1-4). 19.95 *(978-0-7148-7512-5(0))* Phaidon Pr., Inc.

Beevor, Lucy. Understanding Our Skeleton. 2017. (Brains, Body, Bones! Ser.). (ENG., Illus.). 32p. (J). (gr. 3-6). lib. bdg. 33.32 *(978-1-4109-8578-1(4)*, 134419, Raintree) Capstone.

Benchmark Education Company. Your Skeleton (Teacher Guide) 2005. *(978-1-4108-4643-3(1))* Benchmark Education Co.

Bounford, Trevor. The Skeleton. 2005. (Glow in the Dark Ser.). 24p. (J). *(978-1-902626-74-1(5))* Red Bird Publishing.

Brannon, Barbara. Discover Your Skeleton. 2005. (J). pap. *(978-1-4108-5135-2(4))* Benchmark Education Co.

Build a Skeleton. 2004. (J). per. 7.99 *(978-1-932855-16-6(5))* becker&mayer! books.

Cumbaa, Stephen. The Bones Book & Skeleton. 2nd ed. 2006. (ENG., Illus.). 64p. (J). (gr. 1-7). 19.95 *(978-0-7611-4218-8(5)*, 14218) Workman Publishing Co., Inc.

Domnauer, Teresa. The Skeletal System. 2003. (Illus.). 24p. (J). lib. bdg. 21.35 *(978-1-58340-311-2(6))* Black Rabbit Bks.

Edmunds, Kate, illus. Dry Bones. 2007. (Classic Books with Holes Board Book Ser.). (J). 14p. (gr. -1-1). spiral bd. *(978-1-84643-112-8(3))*; 16p. (gr. 1-1). pap. *(978-1-84643-108-1(5))* Child's Play International Ltd.

Emminizer, Theresa. 20 Fun Facts about the Skeletal System, 1 vol. 2018. (Fun Fact File: Body Systems Ser.). (ENG.). 32p. (gr. 2-3). lib. bdg. 20.95 *(978-1-5382-2926-2(9)*, 659261a6-2c04-4737-a617-906a8e1027e3) Stevens, Gareth Publishing LLLP.

Gilbert, Laura. The Skeletal System. 2009. (Insider's Guide to the Body Ser.). 48p. (gr. 5-8). 53.00 *(978-1-61513-586-8(3)*, Rosen Reference) Rosen Publishing Group, Inc., The.

Green, Emily & Manolis, Kay. The Skeletal System. 2009. (Body Systems Ser.). (ENG., Illus.). 24p. (J). (gr. 2-5). lib. bdg. 26.95 *(978-1-60014-247-5(8))* Bellwether Media.

Gross, Ruth Belov & Björkman, Steve. A Book about Your Skeleton. (Hello Reader! Ser.). (FRE., Illus.). 42p. (J). pap. 5.99 *(978-0-590-16005-6(2))* Scholastic, Inc.

Haywood, Karen Diane. Skeletal System, 1 vol. 2009. (Amazing Human Body Ser.). (ENG.). 80p. (gr. 6-6). lib. bdg. 36.93 *(978-0-7614-3056-8(3)*, 572cb514-e264-41f1-9fcb-50dbf485fc83) Cavendish Square Publishing LLC.

Hewitt, Sally. My Bones. 2012. (My Body Ser.). (ENG., Illus.). 24p. (gr. k-4). pap. 7.95 *(978-1-926853-95-6(4))* Saunders Bk. Co. CAN. Dist: RiverStream Publishing.

Houghton, Gillian. Bones: The Skeletal System. 2009. (Body Works Ser.). 24p. (gr. 2-3). 42.50 *(978-1-61511-642-3(7)*, PowerKids Pr.) Rosen Publishing Group, Inc., The.

—The Skeletal System, 1 vol. 2006. (Human Body: a Closer Look Ser.). (ENG., Illus.). 24p. (gr. 2-3). pap. 9.25 *(978-1-4042-2182-6(4)*, 8b9ca4b6-f795-4c7b-866e-e49f37bf588c, PowerKids Pr.) Rosen Publishing Group, Inc., The.

Levine, Sara. Bone by Bone: Comparing Animal Skeletons. Spookytooth, T. S., illus. 2013. (Animal by Animal Ser.). (ENG.). 32p. (J). (gr. k-4). lib. bdg. 26.65 *(978-0-7613-8464-9(2)*, d7e9149c-36bf-4343-8afa-4f3ef8e7daf9, Millbrook Pr.) Lerner Publishing Group.

Loria, Laura. The Bones in Your Body, 1 vol. 2014. (Let's Find Out! the Human Body Ser.). (ENG.). 32p. (J). (gr. 2-3). 26.06 *(978-1-62275-624-7(X)*, d21edbac-0734-4ac6-bfdb-090a86d46aa9, Britannica Educational Publishing) Rosen Publishing Group, Inc., The.

Lowell, Barbara. El Sistema Esquelético. 2018. (Asombroso Cuerpo Humano Ser.). (SPA., Illus.). 32p. (J). (gr. 4-6). lib. bdg. *(978-1-68072-962-7(4)*, 12435, Bolt) Black Rabbit Bks.

—The Skeletal System. 2018. (Amazing Human Body Ser.). (ENG.). 32p. (gr. 2-7). 9.95 *(978-1-68072-686-2(2))*; (Illus.). (J). (gr. 4-6). lib. bdg. *(978-1-68072-392-2(8)*, 23162); (J). (gr. 4-6). pap. 9.99 *(978-1-64466-239-7(6)*, 12211) Black Rabbit Bks. (Bolt).

—Le Système Squelettique. 2018. (incroyable Corps Humain Ser.). (FRE.). 32p. (J). (gr. 4-6). *(978-1-77092-446-8(9)*, 12443, Bolt) Black Rabbit Bks.

Lundgren, Julie K. Skeletons & Exoskeletons. 2012. (My Science Library). (ENG.). 24p. (gr. 3-4). pap. 8.95 *(978-1-61810-221-8(4)*, 9781618102218) Rourke Educational Media.

Maestro, Betsy. What Is a Skeleton? Date not set. 40p. (J). (gr. -1-1). 15.99 *(978-0-06-029006-1(4))*; pap. 4.99 *(978-0-06-445215-1(8))*; lib. bdg. 16.89 *(978-0-06-029007-8(2))* HarperCollins Pubs.

Manolis, Kay. The Skeletal System. 2009. (Blastoff! Readers Ser.). (ENG., Illus.). 24p. (J). (gr. k-3). 20.00 *(978-0-531-21706-1(X)*, Children's Pr.) Scholastic Library Publishing.

Mason, Paul. Your Strong Skeleton & Amazing Muscular System. 2015. (Your Brilliant Body! Ser.). (ENG., Illus.). 32p. (J). (gr. 4-5). lib. bdg. *(978-0-7787-2208-3(2))* Crabtree Publishing Co.

Meachen Rau, Dana. My Bones & Muscles, 1 vol. 2008. (What's Inside Me? Ser.). (ENG.). 32p. (gr. 1-2). pap. 9.23 *(978-0-7614-3351-4(1)*, 9219fa8c-2f94-41ca-96fa-2c317d7f3bbe) Cavendish Square Publishing LLC.

Naughton, Diane. Bones: And the Stories They Tell, 1 vol. 2014. (ENG., Illus.). 28p. (J). pap., E-Book, E-Book 9.50 *(978-1-107-67054-9(3))* Cambridge Univ. Pr.

Nettleton, Pamela Hill. Bend & Stretch: Learning about Your Bones & Muscles. Shipe, Becky, illus. 2004. (Amazing Body Ser.). (ENG.). 24p. (J). (gr. k-3). per. 8.95 *(978-1-4048-0507-1(9)*, 92578, Picture Window Bks.) Capstone.

Our Skeleton, 6 vols. (Sunshinetm Science Ser.). 24p. (gr. 1-2). 31.50 *(978-0-7802-0299-3(6))* Wright Group/McGraw-Hill.

Parsons, Michelle Hyde. Your Skeleton. 2005. (J). pap. *(978-1-4108-4595-5(8))* Benchmark Education Co.

Pettiford, Rebecca. The Skeletal System. 2019. (Your Body Systems Ser.). (ENG., Illus.). 24p. (J). (gr. k-3). pap. 7.99 *(978-1-61891-756-0(0)*, 12313, Blastoff! Readers) Bellwether Media.

Rose, Simon. Bones: All about the Skeletal System. 2017. (Illus.). 32p. (J). *(978-1-5105-0899-6(6))* SmartBook Media, Inc.

—Skeletal System. (J). 2018. (Illus.). 32p. *(978-1-4896-9931-2(7)*, AV2 by Weigl) 2014. *(978-1-4896-1182-6(7))* Weigl Pubs., Inc.

Rotner, Shelley. Body Bones. 2014. pap. *(978-0-8234-3249-3(1))* Holiday Hse., Inc.

Rushworth, Gary. Body Systems: Set of 6: Skeletal & Muscular. 2011. (Navigators Ser.). (J). pap. *(978-1-4108-5085-0(4))* Benchmark Education Co.

Rustad, Martha E. H. My Skeletal System: A 4D Book. 2018. (My Body Systems Ser.). (ENG., Illus.). 24p. (J). (gr. -1-2). lib. bdg. 29.32 *(978-1-9771-0019-1(8)*, 138172, Capstone Pr.) Capstone.

Shea, Therese. Using Your Bones. 2019. (Investigate the Human Body Ser.). (ENG.). 24p. (gr. 2-2). 59.70 *(978-1-9785-1298-6(8))* Enslow Publishing, LLC.

Snedden, Robert. Understanding Muscles & the Skeleton, 1 vol. (Understanding the Human Body Ser.). (ENG., Illus.). 48p. (YA). (gr. 7-7). 2010. lib. bdg. 34.47 *(978-1-4358-9686-4(6)*, 43dd2b46-c1a0-4de8-aec6-785a19ef64d7) 2009. pap. 12.75 *(978-1-4358-9692-5(0)*, c7adbc1c-a769-4c3d-a8da-04a203785f77) Rosen Publishing Group, Inc., The. (Rosen Reference).

Spilsbury, Louise & Spilsbury, Richard. The Science of the Skeleton & Muscles. 2017. (Flowchart Smart Ser.). 48p. (gr. 4-5). pap. 84.30 *(978-1-5382-0686-7(2))* Stevens, Gareth Publishing LLLP.

Thames, Susan. Our Skeleton. 2007. (ENG., Illus.). 24p. (gr. k-1). 28.50 *(978-1-60472-113-3(8))* Rourke Educational Media.

Thornburgh, Blair. Skulls! Campbell, Scott, illus. 2019. (ENG.). 40p. (J). (gr. -1-3). 18.99 *(978-1-5344-1400-6(2))* Simon & Schuster Children's Publishing.

Williams, Ben. Look Inside: Your Skeleton & Muscles, 1 vol. 2nd rev. ed. 2013. (TIME for KIDS(r): Informational Text Ser.). (ENG., Illus.). 28p. (J). (gr. 2-3). lib. bdg. 23.96 *(978-1-4807-1056-6(3))* Teacher Created Materials, Inc.

—Your Skeleton & Muscles, 1 vol. 2nd rev. ed. 2011. (TIME for KIDS(r): Informational Text Ser.). (ENG.). 28p. (gr. 2-3). pap. 10.99 *(978-1-4333-3635-5(9))* Teacher Created Materials, Inc.

Wood, Lily. Skeletons. 2011. (Scholastic Reader: Level 2 Ser.). (ENG.). 32p. (J). (gr. k-2). 16.19 *(978-0-545-33148-7(X))* Scholastic, Inc.

World Book, Inc. Staff, contrib. by. The Skeletal System/The Muscular System. 2006. (World Book's Human Body Works). (Illus.). 48p. (J). *(978-0-7166-4426-2(6))* World Bk., Inc.

Yancey, Diane. Body Farms, 1 vol. 2009. (Crime Scene Investigations Ser.). (ENG., Illus.). 112p. (gr. 7-7). lib. bdg. 37.08 *(978-1-4205-0106-3(2)*, 75af6c68-8356-42f5-aa2b-a326915a636d, Lucent Pr.) Greenhaven Publishing LLC.

SKETCHING

see Drawing

SKIING

see Skis and Skiing

SKIN

Andrus, Aubre. Gloss, Floss, & Wash: DIY Crafts & Recipes for a Fresh Face & Teeth. 2017. (DIY Day Spa Ser.). (ENG., Illus.). 48p. (J). (gr. 4-8). lib. bdg. 31.99 *(978-1-5157-3447-5(1)*, 133425, Capstone Pr.) Capstone.

Anton, Carrie. The Skin & Nails Book: Care & Keeping Advice for Girls. Masse, Josee, illus. 2018. (American Girl(r) Wellbeing Ser.). (ENG.). 64p. (J). pap. 9.99 *(978-1-68337-106-9(2))* American Girl Publishing, Inc.

Berger, Melvin & Berger, Gilda. Your Skin. 2005. (Illus.). pap. *(978-0-439-77372-0(5))* Scholastic, Inc.

Boothroyd, Jennifer. Skin. 2011. (First Step Nonfiction — Body Coverings Ser.). (gr. k-2). (ENG., Illus.). 24p. (J). pap. 6.99 *(978-0-7613-7831-0(6)*, df45f95f-434f-43db-8378-49ef45383743); pap. 33.92 *(978-0-7613-8611-7(4))*; (ENG., Illus.). 24p. lib. bdg. 23.93 *(978-0-7613-5789-6(0))* Lerner Publishing Group.

Bozzo, Linda. Amazing Animal Skin. (Creature Features Ser.). 24p. (gr. 2-3). 2009. 42.50 *(978-1-61512-067-3(X))* 2008. (ENG., Illus.). (J). lib. bdg. 26.27 *(978-1-4042-4168-8(X)*, 8a98cb2b-f9b3-4a79-aee2-57461e5c862e) Rosen Publishing Group, Inc., The. (PowerKids Pr.).

Brown, Jonatha A. Animal Skin & Fur, 1 vol. 2006. (Why Animals Look Different Ser.). (ENG., Illus.). 24p. (gr. 2-4). pap. 9.15 *(978-0-8368-6867-8(6)*, cf2edd2e-0a86-41ac-afb8-b8dd0d29a685); lib. bdg. 24.67 *(978-0-8368-6862-3(5)*, 2bab389b-6f5e-4908-978e-9f8c4b0fe8f6) Stevens, Gareth Publishing LLLP. (Weekly Reader Leveled Readers).

—La Piel y el Pelo de Los Animales (Animal Skin & Fur), 1 vol. 2006. (En Qué Se Diferencian Los Animales (Why Animals Look Different) Ser.). (SPA., Illus.). 24p. (J). (gr. 2-4). lib. bdg. 24.67 *(978-0-8368-7415-0(3)*, 69d9c034-0cb3-4f43-83f3-a959826224be, Weekly Reader Leveled Readers) Stevens, Gareth Publishing LLLP.

Buckmaster, Marjorie L. Skin Cancer, 1 vol. 2008. (Health Alert Ser.). (ENG., Illus.). 64p. (gr. 4-4). lib. bdg. 35.50 *(978-0-7614-2703-2(1)*, 2965129b-7dc6-4acd-b58c-0dc82531fd6b) Cavendish Square Publishing LLC.

Butt, Kyle. Amazing Skin: Designed by God. 2016. (Illus.). 32p. (J). pap. *(978-1-60063-108-5(8))* Apologetics Pr., Inc.

Cardenas, Ernesto A. Textures. 2009. 23.95 *(978-1-60698-047-7(5))*; pap. 4.95 *(978-1-60698-045-3(9))* Milo Educational Bks. & Resources.

Caster, Shannon. Skin, 1 vol. 2010. (Human Body: a Closer Look Ser.). (ENG., Illus.). 24p. (gr. 2-3). pap. 9.25 *(978-1-4358-9822-6(2)*, 250c3836-c60f-4956-bfe8-831b43de8955, PowerKids Pr.); (YA). lib. bdg. 26.27 *(978-1-4358-9367-2(0)*, 800175e9-aaa6-4381-b425-14d39a0913a3) Rosen Publishing Group, Inc., The.

Ceasar, Jennifer. Everything You Need to Know about Acne. 2009. (Need to Know Library). 64p. (gr. 5-5). 58.50 *(978-1-60854-051-8(0))* Rosen Publishing Group, Inc., The.

Chang, Heidi. The Skin on Your Body, 1 vol. 2014. (Let's Find Out! the Human Body Ser.). (ENG.). 32p. (J). (gr. 2-3). 26.06 *(978-1-62275-644-5(4)*, 65bf5023-1670-455e-b071-52819e4e26ba, Britannica Educational Publishing) Rosen Publishing Group, Inc., The.

Cobb, Vicki. Your Body Battles A Skinned Knee. 2009. pap. 40.95 *(978-0-7613-4620-3(1))* Lerner Publishing Group.

Croy, Anita. Scary Skin Care, 1 vol. 2018. (Bizarre History of Beauty Ser.). (ENG.). 48p. (gr. 5-6). lib. bdg. 33.60 *(978-1-5382-2685-8(5)*, c9d8a110-ce4a-4207-b02a-0109d9e66901) Stevens, Gareth Publishing LLLP.

Donovan, Sandy. Stay Clear! What You Should Know about Skin Care. Desrocher, Jack, illus. 2008. (Health Zone Ser.). (ENG.). 64p. (gr. 4-7). lib. bdg. 30.60 *(978-0-8225-7550-4(7))* Lerner Publishing Group.

Dudley Gold, Susan. Learning about the Musculoskeletal System & the Skin, 1 vol. 2013. (Learning about the Human Body Systems Ser.). (ENG.). 48p. (gr. 5-6). 27.93 *(978-0-7660-4159-2(X)*, 189b57fb-5102-4272-b561-4f90cb67bb8e); pap. 11.53 *(978-1-4644-0239-5(6)*, 8c2b45ec-e122-4714-9833-e0780f72f12e) Enslow Publishing, LLC.

Faulk, Michelle. The Case of the Flesh-Eating Bacteria: Annie Biotica Solves Skin Disease Crimes, 1 vol. 2013. (Body System Disease Investigations Ser.). (ENG.). 48p. (gr. 5-6). lib. bdg. 27.93 *(978-0-7660-3945-2(5)*, adaeb3b9-ea4a-4256-8929-bbe8831084c4) Enslow Publishing, LLC.

Faulkner, Nicholas & Spalding, Frank. Tattoo Removal, 1 vol. 2018. (Body Arts: the History of Tattooing & Body Modification Ser.). (ENG.). 64p. (gr. 7-7). 36.13 *(978-1-5081-8079-1(2)*, 0f67ef13-a588-49ac-b46c-08ad5e83fd84) Rosen Publishing Group, Inc., The.

Garstecki, Julia. Make Your Own Fake Skin. 24p. (J). 2019. (Illus.). pap. *(978-1-68072-758-6(3))* 2018. (ENG.). (gr. 1-3). pap. 8.99 *(978-1-64466-311-0(2)*, 12539, Hi Jinx) 2018. (ENG., Illus.). (gr. 4-6). lib. bdg. 28.50 *(978-1-68072-622-0(6)*, 12538, Hi Jinx) Black Rabbit Bks.

Harrison, Emma. From Head to Toe: The Girls' Life Guide to Taking Care of You. Montagna, Frank, illus. 2004. 124p. (J). *(978-0-439-44983-0(9))* Scholastic, Inc.

Holland, Mary. Animal Skins. 2020. (ENG., Illus.). 32p. (J). pap. 9.95 *(978-1-64351-340-9(0))* Arbordale Publishing.

Jaworski, Sabrina K. & Chehoski, Robert. Skin Care, 1 vol. 2011. (Girls' Health Ser.). (ENG.). 48p. (YA). (gr. 5-6). lib. bdg. 34.47 *(978-1-4488-4574-3(2)*, beabd2ed-ed7c-4a3e-85af-37bc560c4616) Rosen Publishing Group, Inc., The.

Jenkins, Pete. Skin. Quintanilla, Hazel, illus. 2017. (I See, I Saw Ser.). (ENG.). 24p. (gr. -1-2). 28.50 *(978-1-68342-310-2(0)*, 9781683423102); pap. 9.95 *(978-1-68342-406-2(9)*, 9781683424062) Rourke Educational Media.

Kirk, Bill. The Skin We're In: The Sum of Our Parts Series. Ruble, Eugene, illus. 2012. 24p. pap. 10.95 *(978-1-61633-296-9(4))* Guardian Angel Publishing, Inc.

Kissinger, Katie. All the Colors We Are/Todos Los Colores de Nuestra Piel: The Story of How We Get Our Skin Color/la Historia de Por Qué Tenemos Diferentes Colores de Piel. 2014. (ENG., Illus.). 32p. (J). (gr. -1-5). 19.95 *(978-1-60554-079-5(X))* Redleaf Pr.

Klingel, Cynthia & Noyed, Robert B. Skin, 1 vol. 2010. (Let's Read about Our Bodies (Second Edition) Ser.). (ENG., Illus.). 24p. (gr. k-2). pap. 9.15 *(978-1-4339-3375-2(6)*,

1d406892-af7e-4222-b782-8ac08fc49cae); (J). lib. bdg. 24.67 *(978-1-4339-3374-5(8),* d0d25068-b7a9-47ea-80a9-0d88a5dc66e2) Stevens, Gareth Publishing LLLP.
—Skin / la Piel, 1 vol. 2010. (Let's Read about Our Bodies / Hablemos Del Cuerpo Humano Ser.). (SPA & ENG., Illus.). 24p. (gr. k-2). pap. 9.15 *(978-1-4339-3751-4(4),* 43c38744-5a3e-4bc3-b245-9b7602f2ee99); (J). lib. bdg. 24.67 *(978-1-4339-3750-7(6),* a79cc109-3cba-41c1-a978-597de8cb9d6c) Stevens, Gareth Publishing LLLP.
Klosterman, Lorrie. Skin, 1 vol. 2009. (Amazing Human Body Ser.). (ENG.). 80p. (gr. 6-6). lib. bdg. 36.93 *(978-0-7614-3057-5(1),* b37298d7-40c8-420d-b576-46927fce5bc7) Cavendish Square Publishing LLC.
Labella, Susan. Chameleons & Other Animals with Amazing Skin. 2005. (Scholastic News Nonfiction Readers Ser.). (ENG., Illus.). 24p. (J). (gr. 1-2). lib. bdg. 22.00 *(978-0-516-24925-4(8))* Scholastic Library Publishing.
Leed, Percy. Skin & Hair (a Sickening Augmented Reality Experience) 2020. (Gross Human Body in Action: Augmented Reality Ser.). (ENG., Illus.). 32p. (J). (gr. 3-5). 31.99 *(978-1-5415-9807-2(5),* 8fd632c4-c973-491d-971a-25810373ac4b, Lerner Pubns.) Lerner Publishing Group.
Marsico, Katie. I Get Sunburned. 2015. (Tell Me Why Library). (ENG., Illus.). 24p. (gr. 2-5). pap. 12.79 *(978-1-63362-034-6(4),* 205893) Cherry Lake Publishing.
Meachen Rau, Dana. My Skin, 1 vol. (Bookworms: My Body Ser.). (ENG.). 2013. 24p. (gr. 2-2). pap. 9.23 *(978-1-62712-036-4(X),* dac29e5e-2f7c-48eb-b60c-b4e45a7c831e) 2008. 32p. (gr. 1-2). pap. 9.23 *(978-0-7614-3356-9(2),* 08e7a39e-03d3-4a04-954e-07360b443c18) 2006. (Illus.). 32p. (gr. 1-2). 25.50 *(978-0-7614-1778-1(8),* d69d84f5-7e94-4370-8949-ebf5400bb5de) 2nd ed. 2013. 24p. (gr. 1-2). 24.07 *(978-1-60870-436-1(X),* bbfede4a-fb5a-46c2-8f94-c96fb46620c4) Cavendish Square Publishing LLC.
—La Piel / My Skin, 1 vol. 2008. (Qué Hay Dentro de Mí? / What's Inside Me? Ser.). (ENG & SPA., Illus.). 32p. (gr. 1-2). lib. bdg. 25.50 *(978-0-7614-2484-0(9),* ea5cba0b-4b0e-45e6-bedc-2d496b71a7d5) Cavendish Square Publishing LLC.
—La Piel (My Skin), 1 vol. 2008. (Qué Hay Dentro de Mí? (What's Inside Me?) Ser.). (SPA., Illus.). 32p. (gr. 1-2). lib. bdg. 25.50 *(978-0-7614-2406-2(7),* 8c4879c4-9b7c-4a59-ab5c-5181a8602b74) Cavendish Square Publishing LLC.
Miller, Derek. Shells, Scales, & Skin, 1 vol. 2018. (Animal Structures Ser.). (ENG.). 24p. (gr. 1-1). 25.93 *(978-1-5026-4251-6(4),* fe62fd7d-93f9-4029-bd0e-aa8b56ea43b0) Cavendish Square Publishing LLC.
My Skin: Big Book: Level E. (Wonder Worldtm Ser.). 16p. 26.50 *(978-0-7802-3475-8(8))* Wright Group/McGraw-Hill.
My Skin: Level E, 6 vols. (Wonder Worldtm Ser.). 16p. 29.95 *(978-0-7802-1229-9(0))* Wright Group/McGraw-Hill.
The Nervous System/The Senses/The Skin. 2006. (World Book's Human Body Works). (Illus.). 48p. (J). *(978-0-7166-4430-9(4))* World Bk., Inc.
Ollhoff, Jim. The Skin. 2012. (J). *(978-1-61783-257-4(X))* ABDO Publishing Co.
René, Ellen. Investigating Why Animals Shed Their Skin. (Science Detectives Ser.). 24p. (gr. 2-3). 2009. 42.50 *(978-1-60853-015-1(9),* PowerKids Pr.) 2008. (ENG., Illus.). (J). lib. bdg. 26.27 *(978-1-4042-4486-3(7),* 10a5c22d-9297-437a-a16d-b398794582df) Rosen Publishing Group, Inc., The.
Rice, Dona Herweck. Always Growing. 2nd rev. ed. 2015. (TIME for KIDS(r): Informational Text Ser.). (ENG., Illus.). 12p. (gr. -1-k). 7.99 *(978-1-4938-2060-3(5))* Teacher Created Materials, Inc.
Rissman, Rebecca. Makeup & Skin Hacks: Your Skin Situations Solved! 2017. (Beauty Hacks Ser.). (ENG., Illus.). 48p. (J). (gr. 4-8). lib. bdg. 31.99 *(978-1-5157-6828-9(7),* 135360, Capstone Pr.) Capstone.
Settel, Joanne. Your Amazing Skin from Outside In. Timmons, Bonnie, illus. 2018. (Your Amazing Body Bks.). (ENG.). 96p. (J). (gr. 3-7). 18.99 *(978-1-4814-2205-5(7))* Simon & Schuster Children's Publishing.
ShackletonCaroline. SKIN UPPER INTERMEDIATE BOOK WITH ONLINE ACCESS, 1 vol. 2014. (ENG., Illus.). 28p. (J). pap., E-Book, E-Book 9.50 *(978-1-107-64189-1(6))* Cambridge Univ. Pr.
Sheen, Barbara. Acne. 2007. (Diseases & Disorders Ser.). (ENG., Illus.). 96p. (J). 32.45 *(978-1-59018-345-8(2),* Lucent Bks.) Cengage Gale.
Silverstein, Virginia & Silverstein Nunn, Laura. Handy Health Guide to Burns & Blisters, 1 vol. 2013. (Handy Health Guides). (ENG.). 48p. (gr. 5-6). pap. 11.53 *(978-1-4644-0487-0(9),* 34d79567-fe09-4261-b356-7afb36a13a61) Enslow Publishing, LLC.
Smith, Sian. Staying Safe in the Sun, 1 vol. 2012. (Take Care of Yourself! Ser.). (ENG.). 24p. (gr. -1-1). (J). 25.32 *(978-1-4329-6712-3(6),* 119342); pap. 6.29 *(978-1-4329-6719-2(3),* 119348) Capstone. (Heinemann).
Stewart, Melissa. Here We Grow: The Secrets of Hair & Nails, 1 vol. Hamlin, Janet, illus. 2011. (Gross & Goofy Body Ser.). (ENG.). 48p. (gr. 3-3). 32.64 *(978-0-7614-4172-4(7),* 52d37d59-bbac-413a-a45c-26f32a7fece1) Cavendish Square Publishing LLC.
—The Skin You're In! The Secrets of Skin, 1 vol. Hamlin, Janet, illus. 2011. (Gross & Goofy Body Ser.). (ENG.). 48p. (gr. 3-3). 32.64 *(978-0-7614-4169-4(7),* 95bf90c6-8499-473b-8316-896e6e3ac35c) Cavendish Square Publishing LLC.
Swan Miller, Sara. Skin, 1 vol. 2008. (All Kinds Of... Ser.). (ENG., Illus.). 48p. (gr. 4-4). lib. bdg. 32.64 *(978-0-7614-2713-1(9),* 030735fa-c79d-49b9-814c-1e4967a7d423) Cavendish Square Publishing LLC.
Turnbull, Stephanie. Beauty Blitz. 2016. (Sleepover Secrets Ser.). 24p. (gr. 2-6). 28.50 *(978-1-62588-376-6(5),* Smart Apple Media) Black Rabbit Bks.
Tyler, Madeline. Why Do I Itch? 2018. (Why Do I? Ser.). (Illus.). 24p. (J). (gr. 3-4). *(978-0-7787-5143-4(0))* Crabtree Publishing Co.
Wittenstein, Barry. The Boo-Boos That Changed the World: A True Story about an Accidental Invention (Really!) Hsu, Chris, illus. 2018. 32p. (J). (gr. -1-3). lib. bdg. 17.99 *(978-1-58089-745-7(2))* Charlesbridge Publishing, Inc.

SKIN, COLOR OF

see Human Skin Color

SKIN—DISEASES

Abramovitz, Melissa. Lupus, 1 vol. 2007. (Diseases & Disorders Ser.). (ENG., Illus.). 96p. (gr. 7-7). lib. bdg. 41.53 *(978-1-59018-999-3(X),* 9aac9f22-d359-4372-af2b-2aa3b53d87e8, Lucent Pr.) Greenhaven Publishing LLC.
Cobb, Vicki. Your Body Battles a Skinned Knee. Harris, Andrew, illus. Kunkel, Dennis, photos by. 2009. (Body Battles Ser.). (ENG.). 32p. (gr. 2-5). lib. bdg. 25.26 *(978-0-8225-6814-8(4))* Lerner Publishing Group.
Donovan, Sandy. Stay Clear! What You Should Know about Skin Care. 2009. pap. 52.95 *(978-0-7613-4686-9(4))* Lerner Publishing Group.
Egan, Tracie. Skin Cancer: Current & Emerging Trends in Detection & Treatment. 2009. (Cancer & Modern Science Ser.). 64p. (gr. 5-5). 58.50 *(978-1-61511-788-8(1))* Rosen Publishing Group, Inc., The.
Faulk, Michelle. The Case of the Flesh-Eating Bacteria: Annie Biotica Solves Skin Disease Crimes, 1 vol. 2013. (Body System Disease Investigations Ser.). (ENG.). 48p. (gr. 5-6). pap. 11.53 *(978-1-4644-0224-1(6),* ddf1882a-4ea5-407d-ab65-4398a8051a20) Enslow Publishing, LLC.
Fromer, Liza & Gerstein, Francine. My Itchy Body. Weissmann, Joe, illus. 2012. (Body Works). 24p. (J). (gr. 1-4). 12.95 *(978-1-77049-311-7(5),* Tundra Bks.) Tundra Bks. CAN. Dist: Penguin Random Hse. LLC.
Landau, Elaine. Burns, 1 vol. 2011. (Head-To-Toe Health Ser.). (ENG.). 32p. (J). (gr. 2-2). 31.21 *(978-0-7614-4832-7(2),* acb31693-2564-4ff9-943c-c33ffa4f7489) Cavendish Square Publishing LLC.
—Rashes, 1 vol. 2011. (Head-To-Toe Health Ser.). (ENG.). 32p. (J). (gr. 2-2). 31.21 *(978-0-7614-4835-8(7),* 4d3e7ad4-41f7-46b4-ae08-c41d0c908ce0) Cavendish Square Publishing LLC.
—Warts, 1 vol. 2011. (Head-To-Toe Health Ser.). (ENG.). 32p. (J). (gr. 2-2). 31.21 *(978-0-7614-4836-5(5),* d53bcefb-ff94-472c-9315-cceeee3d22a8) Cavendish Square Publishing LLC.
Lew, Kristi & Lewandowski, Laura C. Itch & Ooze: Gross Stuff on Your Skin. Slack, Michael H., illus. 2009. (Gross Body Science Ser.). (ENG.). 48p. (gr. 3-5). lib. bdg. 29.27 *(978-0-8225-8963-1(X))* Lerner Publishing Group.
Mitchell Haugen, Hayley, ed. Lupus, 1 vol. 2010. (Perspectives on Diseases & Disorders Ser.). (ENG., Illus.). 136p. (gr. 10-12). 45.93 *(978-0-7377-4789-8(7),* 168b3a2f-f660-4e18-94eb-528395e81b8c, Greenhaven Publishing) Greenhaven Publishing LLC.
Royston, Angela. Head Lice. 2009. (How's Your Health? Ser.). (J). (gr. 1-4). 28.50 *(978-1-59920-218-1(2))* Black Rabbit Bks.
San-Joyz, Naweko. Acne Messages: Crack the Code of Your Zits & Say Goodbye to Acne. 2004. (Illus.). 224p. (YA). per. 14.99 *(978-0-9749122-0-2(4))* Noixia's Reading Circle.
Sanchez, Anita. Itch! Everything You Didn't Want to Know about What Makes You Scratch. Ford, Gilbert, illus. 2018. (ENG.). 80p. (J). (gr. 3-7). 17.99 *(978-0-544-81101-0(1),* 1641759, Clarion Bks.) HarperCollins Pubs.
Sheen, Barbara. Acne. 2007. (Diseases & Disorders Ser.). (ENG., Illus.). 96p. (J). 32.45 *(978-1-59018-345-8(2),* Lucent Bks.) Cengage Gale.
Silverstein, Alvin, et al. Handy Health Guide to Burns & Blisters, 1 vol. 2013. (Handy Health Guides). (ENG.). 48p. (gr. 5-6). lib. bdg. 27.93 *(978-0-7660-4272-8(3),* 6e4528a2-0191-4602-9e52-7281d416d998) Enslow Publishing, LLC.
Simons, Rae. Healthy Skin. McDonnell, Mary Ann & Forman, Sara, eds. 2013. (Young Adult's Guide to the Science of Health Ser.: 15). 128p. (J). (gr. 7-18). 24.95 *(978-1-4222-2812-8(6))* Mason Crest.
Woolf, Alex. The Science of Acne & Warts: the Itchy Truth about Skin (the Science of the Body) 2017. (Science Of... Ser.). (ENG., Illus.). 40p. (J). (gr. 3). pap. 9.95 *(978-0-531-23236-1(0),* Watts, Franklin) Scholastic Library Publishing.
—The Science of Acne & Warts: the Itchy Truth about Skin (the Science of the Body) (Library Edition) 2017. (Science Of... Ser.). (ENG., Illus.). 32p. (J). (gr. 3). lib. bdg. 29.00 *(978-0-531-23141-8(0),* Watts, Franklin) Scholastic Library Publishing.

SKIN DIVING

Here are entered works on free diving with the use of mask, fins, and snorkel. Works on free diving with the use of a self-contained underwater breathing apparatus are entered under Scuba Diving.

see also Underwater Exploration

Dessen, Maci. Let's Go Snorkeling! Use Place Value Understanding, 1 vol. 2014. (Rosen Math Readers Ser.). (ENG.). 24p. (J). (gr. 3-3). pap. 8.25 *(978-1-4777-4938-8(1),* 26966a10-3115-47d8-8850-09ce66334c7c, Rosen Classroom) Rosen Publishing Group, Inc., The.
Ralphs, Matt. Space Jump: Band 11 Lime/Band 17 Diamond (Collins Big Cat Progress) 2014. (Collins Big Cat Progress Ser.). (ENG., Illus.). 32p. (J). (gr. 5-6). pap. 10.99 *(978-0-00-751938-5(9))* HarperCollins Pubs. Ltd. GBR. Dist: Independent Pubs. Group.
Rickard, Stephen. Free Dive. 2008. (321 Go! Ser.). (ENG., Illus.). 36p. pap. *(978-1-84167-782-8(5))* Ransom Publishing Ltd.

SKIN DIVING—FICTION

Alexander, Sarah. The Art of Not Breathing. 2017. (ENG.). 288p. (YA). (gr. 9). pap. 9.99 *(978-0-544-93687-4(6),* 1658695, Clarion Bks.) HarperCollins Pubs.
Somper, Justin. Dead Deep. 2009. pap. 1.00 *(978-1-4074-4559-5(6))* Recorded Bks., Inc.

SKINS

see Hides and Skins

SKIS AND SKIING

Abramovitz, Melissa. Skiing, 1 vol. 2014. (Science Behind Sports Ser.). (ENG., Illus.). 120p. (gr. 7-7). lib. bdg. 41.03 *(978-1-4205-1155-0(6),* 4adae9a8-ded1-46c2-b289-d551c5568a73, Lucent Pr.) Greenhaven Publishing LLC.
Bailey, Ellen. Katya's Gold: What Will Her Dreams Cost? 2008. (ENG.). 123p. (J). (gr. 4-9). pap. 10.99 *(978-0-8280-2335-1(2))* Review & Herald Publishing Assn.
Bowman, Chris. Ski Patroller. 2014. (Dangerous Jobs Ser.). (ENG., Illus.). 24p. (J). (gr. 3-7). lib. bdg. 26.95 *(978-1-62617-113-8(0),* Torque Bks.) Bellwether Media.
Braun, Eric. Lindsey Vonn. 2017. (Sports All-Stars (Lerner (tm) Sports) Ser.). (ENG., Illus.). 32p. (J). (gr. 2-5). 29.32 *(978-1-5124-2580-2(X),* 0c534438-90da-41c3-8f84-fabc1a245444); E-Book 42.65 *(978-1-5124-3785-0(9),* 9781512437850); E-Book 42.65 *(978-1-5124-2825-4(6));* E-Book 6.99 *(978-1-5124-3786-7(7),* 9781512437867) Lerner Publishing Group. (Lerner Pubns.).
Burns, Kylie. Biathlon, Cross Country, Ski Jumping, & Nordic Combined. 2009. (Winter Olympic Sports Ser.). (ENG., Illus.). 32p. (J). (gr. 3-6). lib. bdg. *(978-0-7787-4021-6(8));* (gr. 4-6). pap. *(978-0-7787-4040-7(4))* Crabtree Publishing Co.
Carr, Aaron. Esquí. 2013. (Deportes de Moda Ser.). (SPA., Illus.). 24p. (J). (gr. k-2). lib. bdg. 27.13 *(978-1-62127-633-3(3),* AV2 by Weigl) Weigl Pubs., Inc.
—Skiing. (Illus.). (J). 2013. 32p. *(978-1-61913-514-7(0))* 2012. (ENG., 24p. pap. 12.95 *(978-1-61913-520-8(5),* AV2 by Weigl) Weigl Pubs., Inc.
Champion, Neil. Wild Snow: Skiing & Snowboarding. 2013. (Illus.). 32p. (J). lib. bdg. *(978-1-59920-808-4(3))* Black Rabbit Bks.
Crossingham, John & Kalman, Bobbie. Skiing in Action, 1 vol. 2004. (Sports in Action Ser.). (ENG., Illus.). 32p. (J). pap. *(978-0-7787-0357-0(6));* lib. bdg. *(978-0-7787-0337-2(1))* Crabtree Publishing Co.
Dann, Sarah. Lindsey Vonn. 2013. (ENG., Illus.). 32p. (J). *(978-0-7787-0025-8(9));* pap. *(978-0-7787-0067-8(4))* Crabtree Publishing Co.
Edwards Phillips, H. On a Jet Ski, 1 vol. 2014. (Life in the Fast Lane Ser.). (ENG., Illus.). 48p. (gr. 4-4). 33.07 *(978-1-62713-046-2(2),* 52a52908-6f5e-4059-8b71-8ec6a1bf1ca5) Cavendish Square Publishing LLC.
Gifford, Clive. Get Outdoors: Skiing. 2016. (Get Outdoors Ser.). (ENG., Illus.). 32p. (J). (gr. 4-6). pap. 11.99 *(978-0-7502-8894-1(9),* Wayland) Hachette Children's Group GBR. Dist: Hachette Bk. Group.
—Skiing, 1 vol. 2011. (Get Outdoors Ser.). (ENG., Illus.). 32p. (J). (gr. 4-4). lib. bdg. 28.93 *(978-1-4488-3298-9(5),* d983e71e-01bc-4c11-84b5-60209056c339, PowerKids Pr.) Rosen Publishing Group, Inc., The.
Labrecque, Ellen. Alpine Skiing. 2018. (21st Century Skills Library: Global Citizens: Olympic Sports Ser.). (ENG., Illus.). 32p. (J). (gr. 4-7). pap. 14.21 *(978-1-5341-0849-3(1),* 210760); lib. bdg. 32.07 *(978-1-5341-0750-2(9),* 210759) Cherry Lake Publishing.
Loh-Hagan, Virginia. Extreme Downhill Ski Racing. 2016. (Nailed It! Ser.). (ENG., Illus.). 32p. (J). (gr. 4-8). 32.07 *(978-1-63471-092-3(4),* 208479, 45th Parallel Press) Cherry Lake Publishing.
—Extreme Snow Skiing. 2015. (Nailed It! Ser.). (ENG., Illus.). 32p. (J). (gr. 4-8). 32.07 *(978-1-63470-017-7(1),* 206740) Cherry Lake Publishing.
MacAulay, Kelley & Kalman, Bobbie. Extreme Skiing, 1 vol. 2006. (Extreme Sports No Limits! Ser.). (ENG., Illus.). 32p. (J). (gr. 3-7). pap. *(978-0-7787-1728-7(3),* 1253447); lib. bdg. *(978-0-7787-1682-2(1),* 1253447) Crabtree Publishing Co.
Mattern, Joanne. Bernie Mac. 2006. (Blue Banner Biography Ser.). (Illus.). 32p. (J). (gr. 3-7). lib. bdg. 25.70 *(978-1-58415-488-4(8))* Mitchell Lane Pubs.
Nagelhout, Ryan. Lindsey Vonn, 1 vol. 2016. (Sports MVPs Ser.). (ENG.). 24p. (J). (gr. 1-2). 24.27 *(978-1-4824-4641-8(3),* b4a856d3-ddf8-4923-a0d2-8cdd3b1ad67f) Stevens, Gareth Publishing LLLP.
Schindler, John. Extreme Skiing, 1 vol. 2004. (Extreme Sports Ser.). (ENG., Illus.). 24p. (gr. 2-4). pap. 9.15 *(978-0-8368-4546-4(3),* 2baffd4b-e27d-4d73-a003-b32de5e63b95); lib. bdg. 25.67 *(978-0-8368-4539-6(0),* 13b8193f-2a71-441b-b4cf-b7c5b325e6b8) Stevens, Gareth Publishing LLLP. (Gareth Stevens Learning Library).
SchreyerKarmel. TRAGEDY ON THE SLOPES UPPER INTERMEDIATE BOOK WITH ONLINE ACCESS, 1 vol. 2014. (ENG., Illus.). 28p. pap., E-Book 9.50 *(978-1-107-62159-6(3))* Cambridge Univ. Pr.
Teitelbaum, Michael. Skiing. 2007. (21st Century Skills Library: Healthy for Life Ser.). (ENG., Illus.). 32p. (gr. 4-8). lib. bdg. 32.07 *(978-1-60279-015-5(9),* 200034) Cherry Lake Publishing.
Tomljanovic, Tatiana. Skiing. 2015. (J). *(978-1-5105-0006-8(5))* SmartBook Media, Inc.
—Skiing. 2020. (J). *(978-1-7911-1840-2(2),* AV2 by Weigl) Weigl Pubs., Inc.
—Skiing: X Games. 2008. (Extreme Ser.). (Illus.). 32p. (J). (gr. 4-6). pap. 9.95 *(978-1-59036-919-7(X));* lib. bdg. 26.00 *(978-1-59036-918-0(1))* Weigl Pubs., Inc.
Waxman, Laura Hamilton. Skiing. 2017. (Winter Olympic Sports Ser.). (ENG.). 32p. (J). (gr. 1-4). 20.95 *(978-1-68151-151-1(7),* Amicus High Interest) Amicus Learning.
—Winter Olympic Sports: Skiing. 2017. (Winter Olympic Sports Ser.). (ENG.). 32p. (J). (gr. 2-5). pap. 9.99 *(978-1-68152-182-4(2),* 14813) Amicus.
Yomtov, Nel. The Science of a Carve Turn. 2015. (21st Century Skills Library: Full-Speed Sports Ser.). (ENG., Illus.). 32p. (J). (gr. 4-7). 32.07 *(978-1-63362-580-8(X),* 206504) Cherry Lake Publishing.
Zweig, Eric. Crazy Canucks: The Uphill Battle of Canada's Downhill Ski Team, 1 vol. 2008. (Lorimer Recordbooks Ser.). (ENG., Illus.). 144p. (gr. 8-12). 9.95 *(978-1-55277-019-1(2),* 019); 16.95 *(978-1-55277-020-7(6))* James Lorimer & Co. Ltd., Pubs. CAN. Dist: Formac Lorimer Bks. Ltd., Casemate Pubs. & Bk. Distributors, LLC.

SKIS AND SKIING—FICTION

Balaban, Mariah. Scooby-Doo & the Scary Snowman, 1 vol. Sur, Duendes Del, illus. 2011. (Scooby-Doo! Ser.: No. 2). (ENG.). 24p. (J). (gr. k-4). lib. bdg. 31.36 *(978-1-59961-869-2(9),* 13247, Picture Bk.) Spotlight.
Blackburn, Sheila M. Stewie Scraps & the Super Sleigh. 2008. 72p. pap. *(978-1-903853-89-4(3))* Brilliant Pubns.
Bryant, Louella. Two Tracks in the Snow. Fargo, Todd, illus. I.t. ed. 2004. (Turtle Bks.). 32p. (J). lib. bdg. 15.95 *(978-0-944727-46-1(8));* per. 9.95 *(978-0-944727-45-4(X))* Jason & Nordic Pubs. (Turtle Bks.).
Butcher, Nancy, et al. It's Snow Problem, 3 vols. 2003. (ENG., Illus.). 112p. *(978-0-00-714466-2(0),* HarperCollins Children's Bks.) HarperCollins Pubs. Ltd.
Crossingham, John & Kalman, Bobbie. Le Ski Alpin. Briere, Marie-Josee, tr. from ENG. 2007. (Sans Limites Ser.). (FRE., Illus.). 32p. (J). pap. 9.95 *(978-2-89579-167-6(8))* Bayard Canada Livres CAN. Dist: Crabtree Publishing Co.
Curious George Snowy Day. 2007. (Curious George Ser.). (ENG., Illus.). 24p. (J). (gr. -1-3). 4.99 *(978-0-618-80043-8(3),* 489784, Clarion Bks.) HarperCollins Pubs.
Daly, Catherine. The Ghost of Christmas Past. 2012. 162p. (J). *(978-0-545-48422-0(7))* Scholastic, Inc.
Dixon, Franklin. Water-Ski Wipeout. David, Matt, illus. 2016. (Hardy Boys Clue Book Ser.: 3). (ENG.). 96p. (J). (gr. 1-4). 16.99 *(978-1-4814-5056-0(5),* Simon & Schuster/Paula Wiseman Bks.) Simon & Schuster/Paula Wiseman Bks.
Dower, Laura. Give Me a Break. 2004. 166p. (J). lib. bdg. 16.92 *(978-1-4242-0649-0(9))* Fitzgerald Bks.
Elbee, Viviane. Teach Your Giraffe to Ski. Gowdy, Danni, illus. 2018. (ENG.). 32p. (J). (gr. -1-3). 16.99 *(978-0-8075-7767-7(7),* 807577677) Whitman, Albert & Co.
Feldkamp, Jim And Cate. The Adventures of Tommy & Clara on Mount Catherine. 2008. 32p. pap. 14.49 *(978-1-4389-1366-7(4))* AuthorHouse.
Fields, T. S. Missing in the Mountains. 2008. (ENG., Illus.). 108p. (J). (gr. 4-7). pap. 8.95 *(978-0-87358-950-5(5))* Cooper Square Publishing Llc.
Fincher, Cecilia. Chandra's Adventure. 2012. 28p. pap. 19.99 *(978-1-4772-0137-4(8))* AuthorHouse.
Flood, Heather. Snowwhere. 2006. (ENG.). 268p. pap. 19.48 *(978-1-84728-391-7(8))* Lulu Pr., Inc.
Friedman, Laurie. A Twist of Fate. Shaloshvili, Natasha, illus. 2016. (Mostly Miserable Life of April Sinclair Ser.: 7). (ENG.). 168p. (J). (gr. 5-9). E-Book 27.99 *(978-1-5124-0899-7(9),* Darby Creek) Lerner Publishing Group.
Gehrke, William & Gehrke, Dolores. Sonia's Choice. 2011. 28p. pap. 15.99 *(978-1-4634-0825-1(0))* AuthorHouse.
Giacomoni, Carol A. I can ski despite these Ducky feet on Me. 2010. 24p. 14.95 *(978-1-4269-3187-1(5))* Trafford Publishing.
Gibbs, Stuart. Spy Ski School. (Spy School Ser.). (ENG.). (J). (gr. 3-7). 2017. 384p. pap. 8.99 *(978-1-4814-4563-4(4))* 2016. (Illus.). 368p. 18.99 *(978-1-4814-4562-7(6))* Simon & Schuster Bks. For Young Readers. (Simon & Schuster Bks. For Young Readers).
Gregory, Matt. To Announce at a Later Date. 2005. (Illus.). 36p. (J). 20.00 *(978-0-9766442-0-0(7))* Gregory, Charles Matthew.
High Escape (Ski Racing) 64p. (YA). (gr. 6-12). pap. 10.95 *(978-0-8224-6478-5(0))* Globe Fearon Educational Publishing.
Imagine This, James Robert. Individual Title, 6 packs. (Action Packs Ser.). 120p. (gr. 3-5). 44.00 *(978-0-7635-8418-4(5))* Rigby Education.
Jacks, C. S. The Adventures of Pisten Billy: Pisten Billy Makes the Grade! 2010. 32p. pap. 12.99 *(978-1-4520-6624-0(8))* AuthorHouse.
Jay, Basil. The Adventures of Twig. 2011. (Illus.). 120p. pap. 32.90 *(978-1-4567-8631-1(8))* AuthorHouse.
Jones, Melanie Davis. I Can Ski! 2004. (Rookie Reader Skill Set Ser.). (ENG., Illus.). 32p. (J). (gr. k-2). pap. 4.95 *(978-0-516-27901-5(7),* Children's Pr.) Scholastic Library Publishing.
—I Can Ski! Boles, Terry, illus. 2003. (Rookie Readers Ser.). 32p. (J). 19.50 *(978-0-516-22878-5(1),* Children's Pr.) Scholastic Library Publishing.
Keene, Carolyn. A Nancy Drew Christmas. 2018. (Nancy Drew Diaries). (ENG., Illus.). 352p. (J). (gr. 3-7). 18.99 *(978-1-5344-3164-5(0),* Aladdin) Simon & Schuster Children's Publishing.
—Ski School Sneak. Pamintuan, Macky, illus. 11th ed. 2007. (Nancy Drew & the Clue Crew Ser.: 11). (ENG.). 96p. (J). (gr. 1-4). pap. 5.99 *(978-1-4169-4936-7(4),* Aladdin) Simon & Schuster Children's Publishing.
Leblanc, Louise. Leo's Skiing Surprise. Prud'homme, Jules, illus. 2007. (Formac First Novels Ser.). (ENG.). 64p. (J). (gr. 2-5). 14.95 *(978-0-88780-738-1(0),* 738) Formac Publishing Co., Ltd. CAN. Dist: Formac Lorimer Bks. Ltd.
Lemke, Donald. Zinc Alloy: the Invincible Boy-Bot. 2012. (Zinc Alloy Ser.). (ENG.). 128p. (J). (gr. 2-5). pap., pap., pap. 8.95 *(978-1-4342-4597-7(7),* 120572, Stone Arch Bks.) Capstone.
Lewis, Beverly. Girls Only! 2008. (Girls Only (Go!) Ser.: Vols. 5-8). (ENG.). (J). (gr. 4-7). 510p. pap. 20.00 *(978-0-7642-0462-3(9));*Vols. 1-4. 512p. pap. 21.00 *(978-0-7642-0461-6(0))* Bethany Hse. Pubs.
Linkowski, Tami Leli. Lynn Was a Cow Who Could Ski. 2008. 20p. pap. 24.95 *(978-1-4241-9626-5(4))* America Star Bks.
Lorenz Guest, Donna. The Enchanted Ride. 2009. 32p. pap. 14.99 *(978-1-4389-8116-1(3))* AuthorHouse.
Mead, Richelle. Frostbite: A Vampire Academy Novel. 2008. (Vampire Academy Ser.: 2). 336p. (YA). (gr. 7-18). pap. 12.99 *(978-1-59514-175-0(8),* Razorbill) Penguin Young Readers Group.
Meister, Cari. Buzz Beaker & the Speed Secret. McGuire, Bill, illus. 2010. (Buzz Beaker Bks.). (ENG.). 32p. (J). (gr. 2-3). pap. 6.25 *(978-1-4342-2798-0(7),* 114065, Stone Arch Bks.) Capstone.
Morrison, Janet Love. Radar the Rescue Dog. 2013. 40p. pap. *(978-1-4602-2575-2(9))* FriesenPress.
Nielsen, Gwyn English. Torey the Turkey Goes Skiing. 2003. (Illus.). 24p. (Orig.). (gr. -1-4). pap. 5.99 *(978-0-9660726-0-0(X))* C.G.S. Pr.

S

Oceanak, Karla. Hotdogger. Spanjer, Kendra, illus. 2013. (Aldo Zelnick Comic Novel Ser.: 8). (ENG.). 160p. (J). (gr. 3-7). 12.95 *(978-1-934649-37-4(6))* Bailiwick Pr.

Osorio, Rick. The Great Adventure of Sally Rock & el Lobo. 2007. (ENG.). 96p. per. 19.95 *(978-1-4241-5869-0(9))* America Star Bks.

O'Sullivan, Joanne. Between Two Skies. (ENG.). 272p. (gr. 7). 2019. (J). pap. 7.99 *(978-1-5362-0638-8(5))* 2017. (YA). 16.99 *(978-0-7636-9034-2(1))* Candlewick Pr.

Parker, Emma. The Snowman Olympics. 2010. (Illus.). 20p. pap. *(978-1-877561-36-8(3))* First Edition Ltd.

Parker, John. Chaos Mountain. 2007. 96p. (YA). pap. *(978-1-4207-0734-2(5))* Sundance/Newbridge Educational Publishing.

Pogo the Clown. The Great Blue Sky: Harley's Great Adventures. Miller, Richard D., illus. 2005. (J). 12.95 *(978-0-9755253-6-4(0))* Chilric Pubns.

Ray, J. Hamilton. Squirrels on Skis. Lemaître, Pascal, illus. 2013. (Beginner Books(R) Ser.). 64p. (J). (gr. -1-2). 9.99 *(978-0-449-81081-1(X),* Random Hse. Bks. for Young Readers) Random Hse. Children's Bks.

Rueda, Claudia. Bunny Slopes: (Winter Books for Kids, Snow Children's Books, Skiing Books for Kids) 2016. (Bunny Interactive Picture Bks.). (ENG., Illus.). 60p. (J). (gr. -1-k). 16.99 *(978-1-4521-4197-8(5))* Chronicle Bks. LLC.

Seuling, Barbara. Robert & the Great Escape. Brewer, Paul, illus. 2003. (Robert Bks.). (ENG.). 120p. (J). 15.95 *(978-0-8126-2700-8(8))* Cricket Bks.

Skiing: KinderConcepts Individual Title Six-Packs. (Kinderstarters Ser.). 8p. (gr. -1-1). 21.00 *(978-0-7635-8718-5(4))* Rigby Education.

Smith, Alex T. Claude on the Slopes, 1 vol. 2016. (Claude Ser.: 4). (ENG., Illus.). 96p. (J). (gr. 2-4). pap. 7.95 *(978-1-56145-923-0(2))* Peachtree Publishing Co. Inc.

Terrell, Brandon. Race down the Slopes. 2015. (Game On! Ser.). (ENG.). 80p. (J). (gr. 3-6). *(978-1-63235-050-3(5),* 11661, 12-Story Library) Bookstaves, LLC.

Van Dusen, Chris. Learning to Ski with Mr. Magee: (Read Aloud Books, Series Books for Kids, Books for Early Readers) 2010. (Mr. Magee Ser.). (ENG., Illus.). 36p. (J). (gr. -1-3). 16.99 *(978-0-8118-7495-3(8))* Chronicle Bks. LLC.

Weinmann, Julianne. The Mis-Adventures of Frissue the Tissue. 2005. (ENG.). 57p. (J). pap. 15.69 *(978-1-4116-5310-8(6))* Lulu Pr., Inc.

Wells, Helen. Cherry Ames, Ski Nurse Mystery. 2007. (Cherry Ames Nurse Stories Ser.). 224p. (J). (gr. 3-7). 14.95 *(978-0-8261-0437-3(1))* Springer Publishing Co., Inc.

Wilshire, Florence A. They're all from the Skies. 2005. 82p. pap. 24.95 *(978-1-4116-3892-1(1))* Lulu Pr., Inc.

Withers, Pam. Peak Survival, 1 vol. 2003. (Take It to the Xtreme Ser.: 2). (ENG.). 176p. (YA). (gr. 7-11). pap. 6.95 *(978-1-55285-530-0(9),* 53bcb917-f83f-4bc4-ac0f-e24e853fb1e7) Whitecap Bks., Ltd. CAN. Dist: Firefly Bks., Ltd.

SKULL

see Brain

SKUNKS

Bekkering, Annalise. Skunks. 2007. (Backyard Animals Ser.). (Illus.). 24p. (J). (gr. -1-3). lib. bdg. 24.45 *(978-1-59036-685-1(9))* Weigl Pubs., Inc.

—Skunks. Hudak, Heather C., ed. 2007. (Backyard Animals Ser.). (Illus.). 24p. (J). (gr. -1-3). pap. 8.95 *(978-1-59036-686-8(7))* Weigl Pubs., Inc.

Bodden, Valerie. Skunks. 2016. (Amazing Animals Ser.). (ENG., Illus.). 24p. (J). (gr. 1-3). pap. 10.99 *(978-1-62832-220-0(9),* 20441, Creative Paperbacks); 28.50 *(978-1-60818-614-3(8),* 20443, Creative Education) Creative Co., The.

Bogue, Gary. Is That a Skunk? Todd, Chuck, illus. 2018. (ENG.). 40p. (J). 16.00 *(978-1-59714-399-8(5))* Heyday.

Borgert-Spaniol, Megan. Baby Skunks. 2017. (Super Cute! Ser.). (ENG., Illus.). 24p. (J). (gr. k-3). lib. bdg. 26.95 *(978-1-62617-547-1(0),* Blastoff! Readers) Bellwether Media.

Bowman, Chris. Striped Skunks. 2016. (North American Animals Ser.). (ENG., Illus.). 24p. (J). (gr. k-3). lib. bdg. 26.95 *(978-1-62617-338-5(9),* Blastoff! Readers) Bellwether Media.

Campbell, Sam. Sweet Sue's Adventures. Fox, Charles Philip, photos by. 2010. (Illus.). 119p. (J). reprint ed. pap. 10.95 *(978-1-57258-210-1(3))* TEACH Services, Inc.

Caswell, Deanna. Baby Skunks. 2020. (J). pap. *(978-1-62310-067-4(4))* Black Rabbit Bks.

Dieker, Wendy Strobel. Skunks. (Spot Backyard Animals Ser.). (ENG., Illus.). 16p. (J). (gr. -1-2). 2018. pap. 7.99 *(978-1-68152-221-0(7),* 14752) 2017. 17.95 *(978-1-68151-096-5(0),* 14633) Amicus.

—El Zorrillo (Skunks) 2017. (Spot Backyard Animals Ser.). (ENG & SPA.). 16p. (J). (gr. k-3). 17.95 *(978-1-68151-276-1(9),* Amicus Readers) Amicus Learning.

Gish, Melissa. Living Wild: Skunks. 2014. (Living Wild Ser.). (ENG., Illus.). 48p. (J). (gr. 4-7). pap. 12.00 *(978-0-89812-843-7(9),* 21644, Creative Paperbacks) Creative Co., The.

—Skunks. 2013. (Illus.). 46p. (J). 35.65 *(978-1-60818-290-9(8),* Creative Education) Creative Co., The.

Gonzales, Doreen. Skunks in the Dark, 1 vol. 2009. (Creatures of the Night Ser.). (ENG.). 24p. (gr. 2-3). (YA). pap. 9.25 *(978-1-4358-3255-8(8),* 0402b2a2-b77d-48ba-a733-abb8e581de40); (Illus.). (J). 26.27 *(978-1-4042-8099-1(5),* b242b6cc-fbe6-4a73-a876-3deb7468d028) Rosen Publishing Group, Inc., The.

Gray, Susan H. Skunks Smell Bad. 2015. (Tell Me Why Library). (ENG., Illus.). 24p. (gr. 2-5). 29.21 *(978-1-63188-999-8(0),* 205908) Cherry Lake Publishing.

Green, Emily. Skunks. 2010. (Backyard Wildlife Ser.). (ENG., Illus.). 24p. (J). (gr. k-3). lib. bdg. 26.95 *(978-1-60014-445-5(4),* Blastoff! Readers) Bellwether Media.

Heckt, Jackie. Skunks, 1 vol. 2016. (Creatures of the Forest Habitat Ser.). (ENG.). 24p. (J). (gr. 3-3). pap. 9.25 *(978-1-4994-2716-5(6),* 606d512f-dd92-4d63-8ec3-bdce3492b9fc, PowerKids Pr.) Rosen Publishing Group, Inc., The.

Hildebrand, Cody. How the Skunk Earned His Stripes: A Pet Parent's Guide to Having a Skunk in the Family. 2004. (YA). 14.95 *(978-0-9753729-0-6(4))* Hildebrand, Betty.

Jobes, Cecily. Watch Out for Skunks!, 1 vol., 1. 2015. (Wild Backyard Animals Ser.). (ENG., Illus.). 24p. (J). (gr. 3-4). pap. 9.25 *(978-1-5081-4267-6(X),* e1109b46-27f2-4c79-8643-85404688b1f1, PowerKids Pr.) Rosen Publishing Group, Inc., The.

Krueger, Carol. Smelly Skunks. 2004. (Rigby Sails Early Ser.). (ENG., Illus.). 16p. (gr. 1-2). pap. 6.95 *(978-0-7578-9955-3(2))* Houghton Mifflin Harcourt Publishing Co.

Markle, Sandra. Los Zorrillos (Skunks) 2009. (SPA.). pap. 46.95 *(978-0-7613-4722-4(4))* Lerner Publishing Group.

—Skunks. 2008. (Animal Prey Ser.). (Illus.). 39p. (J). (gr. 3-7). per. 7.95 *(978-0-8225-6440-9(8),* First Avenue Editions); pap. 46.95 *(978-0-8225-9324-9(6))* Lerner Publishing Group.

—Los Zorrillos. Translations.com Staff, tr. from ENG. 2008. (Animales Presa (Animal Prey) Ser.). (SPA.). 40p. (gr. 3-6). 25.26 *(978-0-7613-3899-4(3))* Lerner Publishing Group.

—Los Zorrillos (Skunks) 2008. 40p. (J). pap. 7.95 *(978-0-7613-3903-8(5),* Ediciones Lerner) Lerner Publishing Group.

Mattern, Joanne. Skunks Are Night Animals, 1 vol. 2007. (Night Animals Ser.). (ENG., Illus.). 24p. (gr. 1-3). lib. bdg. 24.67 *(978-0-8368-7850-9(7),* e34b6f34-185a-4c0b-bbd3-48a3603252c8, Weekly Reader Leveled Readers) Stevens, Gareth Publishing LLLP.

—Skunks Are Night Animals / Los Zorrillos Son Animales Nocturnos, 1 vol. 2007. (Night Animals / Animales Nocturnos Ser.). (SPA & ENG., Illus.). 24p. (gr. 1-3). pap. 9.15 *(978-0-8368-8054-0(4),* 357931ff-5635-4d71-aa3f-aae6647fd955); lib. bdg. 24.67 *(978-0-8368-8047-2(1),* 39a2d7d6-4617-4917-9f6b-f628c960977b) Stevens, Gareth Publishing LLLP. (Weekly Reader Leveled Readers).

McGill, Jordan. Skunks. 2011. (J). *(978-1-61690-580-4(8));* 27.13 *(978-1-61690-934-5(X))* Weigl Pubs., Inc.

—Zorrillos. 2012. (SPA.). (J). *(978-1-61913-196-5(X))* Weigl Pubs., Inc.

Moore Niver, Heather. Skunks after Dark, 1 vol. 2015. (Animals of the Night Ser.). (ENG.). 32p. (gr. 3-3). pap. 11.52 *(978-0-7660-7358-6(0),* 1b584ff8-ad6a-4259-8c75-93247bbe09c9); (Illus.). lib. bdg. 26.93 *(978-0-7660-7360-9(2),* f64660af-6f7e-4442-949e-acf2c1e67a69) Enslow Publishing, LLC.

Nelson, Kristin L. Spraying Skunks. 2003. (Pull Ahead Bks.). (Illus.). 32p. (J). 22.60 *(978-0-8225-4670-2(1),* Lerner Pubns.) Lerner Publishing Group.

Nichols, Catherine. Smelly Skunks. (Gross-Out Defenses Ser.). 24p. (J). (gr. k-3). 2018. (ENG.). 7.99 *(978-1-64280-075-3(9))* 2008. (Illus.). lib. bdg. 21.28 *(978-1-59716-716-1(9),* 1284316) Bearport Publishing Co., Inc.

Otfinoski, Steven. Skunks, 1 vol. 2009. (Animals, Animals Ser.). (ENG.). 48p. (gr. 5-5). lib. bdg. 32.64 *(978-0-7614-2929-6(8),* a81a73cf-f2d0-4cac-8571-174ff5fdb731) Cavendish Square Publishing LLC.

Owen, Ruth. Skunk Kits. 2011. (Wild Baby Animals Ser.). 24p. (J). (gr. k-3). lib. bdg. 25.65 *(978-1-61772-161-8(1));* lib. bdg., E-Book 39.93 *(978-1-61772-243-1(X))* Bearport Publishing Co., Inc.

Pallotta, Jerry. Jaguar vs. Skunk. Bolster, Rob, illus. 2017. 32p. (J). *(978-1-338-20629-6(X))* Scholastic, Inc.

Roza, Greg. Phew! The Skunk & Other Stinky Animals, 1 vol. 2011. (Armed & Dangerous Ser.). (ENG., Illus.). 24p. (gr. 2-3). (J). pap. 9.25 *(978-1-4488-2682-7(9),* 1bc4547b-a390-40f0-afe2-0dba9aa375b4, PowerKids Pr.); (YA). lib. bdg. 26.27 *(978-1-4488-2549-3(0),* dc52edcd-df80-4dd0-b922-de3c814d45a3) Rosen Publishing Group, Inc., The.

Schuh, Mari. Skunks. 2017. (Black & White Animals Ser.). (ENG., Illus.). 24p. (J). (gr. -1-2). lib. bdg. 22.65 *(978-1-5157-3622-6(9),* 133603, Pebble) Capstone.

—Skunks. 2015. (My First Animal Library). (Illus.). 24p. (J). (gr. k-2). lib. bdg. 25.65 *(978-1-62031-291-9(3),* Bullfrog Bks.) Jump! Inc.

Shoemaker, Kate. Skunk Stench, 1 vol. 2014. (Nature's Grossest Ser.). (ENG., Illus.). 24p. (J). (gr. 1-2). 24.27 *(978-1-4824-1851-4(7),* 3bada02e-0e57-42b4-873c-2c131de11a59) Stevens, Gareth Publishing LLLP.

SKUNKS—FICTION

Amato, Mary. Sniff a Skunk! Jenkins, Ward, illus. 2015. (Good Crooks Ser.: 3). (ENG.). 128p. (J). (gr. 2-4). E-Book 22.65 *(978-1-5124-0169-1(2),* Darby Creek) Lerner Publishing Group.

Arnold, Elana K. Bat & the End of Everything. Santoso, Charles, illus. 2019. (Bat Ser.: 3). (ENG.). 192p. (J). (gr. 1-5). 16.99 *(978-0-06-279844-2(8),* Walden Pond Pr.) HarperCollins Pubs.

Barnett, Mac. The Skunk: A Picture Book. McDonnell, Patrick, illus. 2015. (ENG.). 40p. (J). (gr. -1-3). 18.99 *(978-1-59643-966-5(1),* 900126271) Roaring Brook Pr.

Beckstedt, Cynthia M. The Great Smoky Mountain Skunk Adventure, 1 vol. 2009. 28p. pap. 24.95 *(978-1-60836-034-5(2))* America Star Bks.

Burgess, Thornton W. The Adventures of Jimmy Skunk. 112p. 2008. per. 9.95 *(978-1-60312-416-4(0))* 2007. 22.95 *(978-1-60312-594-9(9))* Aegypan.

—The Adventures of Jimmy Skunk. (J). 18.95 *(978-0-8488-0384-1(1))* Amereon Ltd.

—The Adventures of Jimmy Skunk. 2016. (ENG., Illus.). (J). 22.95 *(978-1-358-39350-1(8))* Creative Media Partners, LLC.

—The Adventures of Jimmy Skunk. 2011. 110p. 23.95 *(978-1-4638-9560-0(7))* Rodgers, Alan Bks.

Calvani, Mayra. Humberto, the Bookworm Hamster. Grady, Kit, illus. 2009. 20p. pap. 10.95 *(978-1-935137-92-4(1))* Guardian Angel Publishing, Inc.

Choyce, Lesley. Skunks for Breakfast, 1 vol. Jones, Brenda, illus. 2nd ed. 2019. (ENG.). 32p. (J). pap. 8.95 *(978-1-77108-785-8(4),* 9773be3f-a054-4a67-b957-8cb99300e93b) Nimbus Publishing, Ltd. CAN. Dist: Baker & Taylor Publisher Services (BTPS).

Covey, Sean. Lily & the Yucky Cookies: Habit 5. Curtis, Stacy, illus. (7 Habits of Happy Kids Ser.: 5). (ENG.). 32p. (J). (gr. -1-1). 2018. 6.99 *(978-1-5344-1582-9(3))* 2013. 7.99 *(978-1-4424-7649-3(4))* Simon & Schuster Bks. For Young Readers. (Simon & Schuster Bks. For Young Readers).

—Lily & the Yucky Cookies: Habit 5 (Ready-To-Read Level 2) Curtis, Stacy, illus. 2020. (7 Habits of Happy Kids Ser.: 5). (ENG.). 32p. (J). (gr. k-2). 17.99 *(978-1-5344-4457-7(2));* pap. 4.99 *(978-1-5344-4456-0(4))* Simon Spotlight. (Simon Spotlight).

Crenshaw, Glenda. Friends of the Enchanted Forest: How they Save Christmas. 2011. 28p. pap. 15.47 *(978-1-4520-0512-6(5))* AuthorHouse.

Cretney, Brian. Tooter's Stinky Wish, 1 vol. Collins, Peggy, illus. 2011. (Tell Me More Storybook Ser.). (ENG.). 32p. (J). (gr. k-2). 18.95 *(978-1-55455-165-1(X),* fd62d527-5e0e-47e6-a80f-450bf77d5068) Trifolium Bks., Inc. CAN. Dist: Firefly Bks., Ltd.

Deak, Gloria. The Kissing Skunks. Nathan, Cheryl, illus. 2006. 40p. (J). (gr. -1). 16.95 *(978-1-932065-46-6(6))* Star Bright Bks., Inc.

DeLuise, Dom & Carter, Derek. Pouch Potato. 2007. 33p. pap. 9.95 *(978-0-9717952-0-4(7))* Bacchus Bks.

Derubertis, Barbara. Sammy Skunk's Super Sniffer. Alley, R. W., illus. 2011. (Animal Antics A to Z Set III Ser.). pap. 45.32 *(978-0-7613-8428-1(6))* Astra Publishing Hse.

deRubertis, Barbara. Sammy Skunk's Super Sniffer. Alley, R. W., illus. 2011. (Animal Antics a to Z Ser.). 32p. (J). (gr. -1-3). pap. 7.95 *(978-1-57565-344-0(3),* 16bcbd5e-f8d1-4d8e-aeb0-6d16e78957fc, Kane Press) Astra Publishing Hse.

deRubertis, Barbara & DeRubertis, Barbara. Sammy Skunk's Super Sniffer. Alley, R. W., illus. 2012. (Animal Antics A to Z Ser.). 32p. (J). (gr. 2 — 1). cd-rom 7.95 *(978-1-57565-412-6(1))* Astra Publishing Hse.

Dyan, Penelope. There's a Skunk in My Trunk. Dyan, Penelope, illus. 2012. (Illus.). 34p. pap. 11.95 *(978-1-61477-045-9(X))* Bellissima Publishing, LLC.

Erickson, John. The Case of the Perfect Dog. Holmes, Gerald L., illus. 2012. 127p. (J). *(978-1-59188-259-6(1))* Maverick Bks.

—The Case of the Perfect Dog. Holmes, Gerald L., illus. 2012. (Hank the Cowdog (Quality) Ser.). (ENG.). 127p. (J). (gr. 3-6). pap. 5.99 *(978-1-59188-159-9(5))* Maverick Bks., Inc.

—The Case of the Secret Weapon. Holmes, Gerald L., illus. 2011. (Hank the Cowdog Ser.). (ENG.). 125p. (J). (gr. 3-6). pap. 5.99 *(978-1-59188-155-1(2))* Maverick Bks., Inc.

Fabrizio, Anthony. The Last Forest, 1 vol. 2009. 64p. pap. 19.95 *(978-1-61546-861-4(7))* America Star Bks.

Hamilton, Elizabeth L. Stinky Skunk's Self-Control. 2004. (Character Critters Ser.: No. 4). (Illus.). 32p. (J). (gr. -1-3). per. 5.95 *(978-0-9713749-6-6(1),* Character-in-Action) Quiet Impact, Inc.

Hayes, Joe. The Lovesick Skunk, 1 vol. Castro L., Antonio, illus. (ENG.). 32p. (J). (gr. k-7). 2016. 7.95 *(978-1-941026-04-5(4),* 8d7d164e-2331-4b4d-9c16-177daac6c8e2) 2010. 16.95 *(978-1-933693-81-1(9),* 41f5c7d6-6dd6-4b56-af34-fe1790e53e54) Lee & Low Bks., Inc. (Cinco Puntos Press).

Hillenbrand, Will. All for a Dime! A Bear & Mole Story. (Bear & Mole Ser.: 4). (ENG.). 32p. (J). (gr. -1-k). 2016. 7.99 *(978-0-8234-3684-2(5))* 2015. (Illus.). 16.95 *(978-0-8234-2946-2(6))* Holiday Hse., Inc.

Kelly, Jacqueline. Skunked!: Calpurnia Tate, Girl Vet. White, Teagan & Meyer, Jennifer L., illus. 2016. (Calpurnia Tate, Girl Vet Ser.: 1). (ENG.). 112p. (J). 15.99 *(978-1-62779-868-6(4),* 900161279, Holt, Henry & Co. Bks. For Young Readers) Holt, Henry & Co.

—Skunked!: Calpurnia Tate, Girl Vet. White, Teagan & Meyer, Jennifer L., illus. 2017. (Calpurnia Tate, Girl Vet Ser.: 1). (ENG.). 128p. (J). pap. 6.99 *(978-1-250-12944-4(3),* 900161280) Square Fish.

Mack, Jeff. Who Needs a Bath? Mack, Jeff, illus. 2015. (ENG., Illus.). 40p. (J). (gr. -1-3). 17.99 *(978-0-06-222028-8(4),* HarperCollins) HarperCollins Pubs.

—Who Wants a Hug? 2015. (ENG., Illus.). 40p. (J). (gr. -1-3). 17.99 *(978-0-06-222026-4(8),* HarperCollins) HarperCollins Pubs.

Martin, Anne E. Midnight Kitties. 2007. (Illus.). 35p. (J). per. 13.99 *(978-1-59879-245-4(8))* Lifevest Publishing, Inc.

Masterson, Josephine. A Smelly Surprise, 1 vol. 2015. (Rosen REAL Readers: STEM & STEAM Collection). (ENG.). 8p. (gr. k-1). pap. 5.46 *(978-1-4994-9485-3(8),* 1abcb23e-18a3-4b66-a7a8-1bae082b9f41, Rosen Classroom) Rosen Publishing Group, Inc., The.

Montileaux, Donald F. & Gay, Agnes. Muskrat & Skunk / Sinkpe Na Maka: A Lakota Drum Story. 2018. (ENG & DAK., Illus.). 32p. (J). 19.95 *(978-1-941813-16-4(X),* P559865) South Dakota Historical Society Pr.

Nanette. Buddy & Muddy: The Twin Brown Skunks. 2004. (J). 12.95 *(978-0-9741269-5-1(0))* St. Bernard Publishing, LLC.

Pate, Ginger. Would You Invite a Skunk to Your Wedding? Blanski, Maribeth, illus. 2009. 32p. (J). 16.95 *(978-1-880851-73-9(3))* Greene Bark Pr., Inc.

Penn, Audrey. A Kiss Goodbye. Gibson, Barbara, illus. 2007. (Kissing Hand Ser.). (ENG.). 32p. (J). (gr. -1-3). 16.99 *(978-1-933718-04-0(8))* Tanglewood Pr.

—Sassafras. Harper, Ruth, illus. 2006. (ENG.). 32p. (J). (gr. -1-3). 16.95 *(978-1-933718-03-3(X))* Tanglewood Pr.

Pochocki, Ethel. The Blessing of the Beasts. Moser, Barry, illus. 2014. (ENG.). 40p. (J). (gr. -1). pap. 19.99 *(978-1-61261-582-0(1))* Paraclete Pr., Inc.

Sargent, Dave. Finding Sammy #1 (PB), 10 vols. 2007. (Little Stinker Ser.: 1). (J). pap. 10.95 *(978-1-59381-274-4(4))* Ozark Publishing.

—I Named Him Sammy #7, 10 vols. 2007. (Little Stinker Ser.: 7). (J). lib. bdg. 23.60 *(978-1-59381-291-1(4))* Ozark Publishing.

—I Named Him Sammy #7 (PB), 10 vols. 2007. (Little Stinker Ser.: 7). (J). pap. 10.95 *(978-1-59381-292-8(2))* Ozark Publishing.

Sargent, Dave & Sargent, Pat. Sammy Skunk: I'm a Little Stinker, 56 vols., Vol. 9. Huff, Jeane, illus. 2nd rev. ed. 2003. (Animal Pride Ser.: 9). 42p. (J). lib. bdg. 20.95 *(978-1-56763-775-5(2))* Ozark Publishing.

Schmid, Paul. A Pet for Petunia. 2011. (J). lib. bdg. 14.89 *(978-0-06-196332-2(1))* HarperCollins Pubs.

—A Pet for Petunia. Schmid, Paul, illus. 2011. (ENG., Illus.). 40p. (J). (gr. -1-2). 12.99 *(978-0-06-196331-5(3),* HarperCollins) HarperCollins Pubs.

Service, Pamela F. Stinker's Return. 2018. (ENG.). 96p. (gr. 2-5). pap. 6.99 *(978-0-486-81887-0(X))* Dover Pubns., Inc.

Shaskan, Trisha Speed. Punk Skunks. Shaskan, Stephen, illus. 2016. (ENG.). 40p. (J). (gr. -1-3). 17.99 *(978-0-06-236396-1(4),* HarperCollins) HarperCollins Pubs.

Stauffacher, Sue. Animal Rescue Team: Special Delivery! Lamont, Priscilla, illus. 2011. (Animal Rescue Team Ser.: 2). 176p. (J). (gr. 3-7). 6.99 *(978-0-375-85132-2(1),* Yearling) Random Hse. Children's Bks.

Thomas, Jan. The Easter Bunny's Assistant. 2012. (ENG., Illus.). 40p. (J). (gr. -1-3). 12.99 *(978-0-06-169286-4(7),* HarperCollins) HarperCollins Pubs.

Timberlake, Amy. Skunk & Badger (Skunk & Badger 1) Klassen, Jon, illus. 2020. (Skunk & Badger Ser.: 1). (ENG.). 136p. (J). (gr. 3-7). 18.95 *(978-1-64375-005-7(4),* 74005) Algonquin Young Readers.

Weiss, Dylan. Sebastian's Tale: A Skunk Tales Trilogy Book. 2016. (J). *(978-1-943267-16-3(2))* Red Engine Pr.

Wilhelm, Hans. Noodles & the Bully. 2012. (Illus.). (J). *(978-0-545-34499-9(9))* Scholastic, Inc.

Yardi, Robin. The Midnight War of Mateo Martinez. 2018. (ENG.). 184p. (J). (gr. 3-6). pap. 9.99 *(978-1-5415-1483-6(1),* db266dd5-e965-4980-9ce2-73d5fa151b04, Carolrhoda Bks.) Lerner Publishing Group.

SKY DIVING

see Skydiving

SKYDIVING

Goldish, Meish. Skydiving Dogs. 2014. (Dog Heroes Ser.). (Illus.). 32p. (J). (gr. 2-7). lib. bdg. 28.50 *(978-1-62724-087-1(X))* Bearport Publishing Co., Inc.

Gordon, Nick. Smoke Jumper. 2012. (Dangerous Jobs Ser.). (ENG., Illus.). 24p. (J). (gr. 3-7). lib. bdg. 26.95 *(978-1-60014-781-4(X),* Torque Bks.) Bellwether Media.

Harris, Tim. Triumphs of Human Flight: From Wingsuits to Parachutes. 2018. (Feats of Flight Ser.). (ENG., Illus.). 32p. (J). (gr. 3-6). 27.99 *(978-1-5415-0096-9(2),* 9f12d1f5-e0c4-4765-948e-03b8dde7bd92, Hungry Tomato (r)) Lerner Publishing Group.

Kennedy, Robert. Would You Dare Go Skydiving?, 1 vol. 2016. (Would You Dare? Ser.). (ENG.). 32p. (J). (gr. 1-2). pap. 11.50 *(978-1-4824-5818-3(7),* 807c28b2-3d98-4347-a5bb-8549ba00231e) Stevens, Gareth Publishing LLLP.

Loh-Hagan, Virginia. Extreme Skydiving. 2015. (Nailed It! Ser.). (ENG., Illus.). 32p. (J). (gr. 4-8). 32.07 *(978-1-63470-021-4(X),* 206736) Cherry Lake Publishing.

McFee, Shane. Skydiving. (Living on the Edge Ser.). 24p. (gr. 2-3). 2009. 42.50 *(978-1-61514-299-6(1),* PowerKids Pr.) 2008. (ENG., Illus.). (J). lib. bdg. 26.27 *(978-1-4042-4215-9(5),* 0519e49b-13d1-4e33-bb9b-759340b306ae) Rosen Publishing Group, Inc., The.

Montana, Jack. Parachute Regiment. 2010. (Special Forces Ser.). 64p. (YA). (gr. 7-18). lib. bdg. 22.95 *(978-1-4222-1845-7(7))* Mason Crest.

Mooney, Carla. Skydiving, 1 vol. 2015. (Sports to the Extreme Ser.). (ENG., Illus.). 48p. (J). (gr. 5-6). 33.47 *(978-1-4994-3577-1(0),* d023042d-b325-41eb-8f81-0bd0a3df6b32, Rosen Central) Rosen Publishing Group, Inc., The.

Moore Niver, Heather. Skydiving, 1 vol. 2013. (Thrill Seekers Ser.). (ENG., Illus.). 32p. (J). (gr. 3-4). 29.27 *(978-1-4339-9916-1(1),* 6ae9189c-2945-4e23-8b2e-3a27493d40c7) Stevens, Gareth Publishing LLLP.

Norman, Tony. Skydiving, 1 vol. 2005. (Action Sports Ser.). (ENG., Illus.). 32p. (gr. 3-5). lib. bdg. 28.67 *(978-0-8368-6369-7(0),* f9be4d63-daaa-4260-9e43-786efee3aee7, Gareth Stevens Learning Library) Stevens, Gareth Publishing LLLP.

Orr, Tamra B. Extreme Skysurfing, 1 vol. 2013. (Sports on the Edge Ser.). (ENG.). 48p. (gr. 4-4). pap. 13.93 *(978-1-62712-136-1(6),* 6a5da2b5-a99a-4a42-9ab4-f5b3592f1867) Cavendish Square Publishing LLC.

Rickard, Stephen. Sky Dive. 2008. (321 Go! Ser.). (ENG., Illus.). 36p. pap. *(978-1-84167-785-9(X))* Ransom Publishing Ltd.

Schindler, John. Skydiving, 1 vol. 2004. (Extreme Sports Ser.). (ENG., Illus.). 24p. (J). (gr. 2-4). pap. 9.15 *(978-0-8368-4550-1(1),* 7e333c7e-fee9-432e-9f7d-6704d6af0a72); lib. bdg. 25.67 *(978-0-8368-4543-3(9),* 278f044b-7761-40dc-83ee-f24046cd4ca0) Stevens, Gareth Publishing LLLP. (Gareth Stevens Learning Library).

Whiting, Jim. Skydiving. 2018. (Odysseys in Extreme Sports Ser.). (ENG.). 80p. (J). (gr. 7-10). *(978-1-60818-695-2(4),* 19879, Creative Education) Creative Co., The.

SKYDIVING—FICTION

Barrett, Tracy. Freefall Summer. 2018. 272p. (J). (gr. 7). lib. bdg. 17.99 *(978-1-58089-801-0(7),* Charlesbridge Teen) Charlesbridge Publishing, Inc.

Clark, Tracy. Mirage. 2017. (ENG.). 272p. (YA). (gr. 9). pap. 9.99 *(978-0-544-93727-7(9),* 1658700, Clarion Bks.) HarperCollins Pubs.

Stadler, John. Three Cheers for Hippo!, 1 vol. 2006. (ENG., Illus.). 32p. (J). (gr. -1-3). reprint ed. pap. 5.95 *(978-1-59572-046-7(4))* Star Bright Bks., Inc.

Starfall Education. Sky Ride. Starfall Education, ed. 2004. (ENG., Illus.). 8p. (J). pap. *(978-1-59577-008-0(9))* Starfall Education.

SKYSCRAPERS

Barker, Geoff. Incredible Skyscrapers. 2010. (Superstructures Ser.). 32p. (YA). (gr. 4-7). 28.50 *(978-1-60753-133-3(X))* Amicus Learning.

Barker, Geoff P. Incredible Skyscrapers. 2012. (What's in My Food Ser.). (Illus.). 32p. (gr. 1-4). lib. bdg. 27.10 *(978-1-59920-419-2(3))* Black Rabbit Bks.

Bernhardt, Carolyn. Engineer It! Skyscraper Projects. 2017. (Super Simple Engineering Projects Ser.). (ENG., Illus.). 32p. (J). (gr. k-4). lib. bdg. 34.21 *(978-1-5321-1126-6(6),* 25828, Super SandCastle) ABDO Publishing Co.

Bowman, Chris. Skyscrapers. 2018. (Everyday Engineering Ser.). (ENG., Illus.). 24p. (J). (gr. k-3). lib. bdg. 26.95 (978-1-62617-825-0(9), Blastoff! Readers) Bellwether Media.

Britton, Tamara L. The Empire State Building. 2005. (Symbols, Landmarks, & Monuments Set 3 Ser.: Set III). (Illus.). 32p. (gr. k-6). 27.07 (978-1-59197-834-3(3), Checkerboard Library) ABDO Publishing Co.

—The World Trade Center. 2003. (Symbols, Landmarks & Monuments Set 1 Ser.). 32p. (gr. k-6). 27.07 (978-1-57765-850-4(7), Checkerboard Library) ABDO Publishing Co.

Burns, Kylie. A Skyscraper Reaches Up. 2017. (Be an Engineer! Designing to Solve Problems Ser.). 24p. (J). (gr. 2-2). (978-0-7787-2904-4(4)) Crabtree Publishing Co.

Curlee, Lynn. Skyscraper. 2007. (ENG., Illus.). 48p. (J). (gr. 3-7). 19.99 (978-0-689-84489-8(1), Atheneum Bks. for Young Readers) Simon & Schuster Children's Publishing.

Currie, Stephen. The Tallest Building. 2003. (Extreme Places Ser.). (ENG., Illus.). 48p. (J). (gr. 3-5). 27.50 (978-0-7377-1374-9(7), Kidhaven) Cengage Gale.

Diemer, Lauren. Sears Tower. 2009. (Structural Wonders Ser.). (Illus.). 32p. (J). (gr. 4-6). 9.95 (978-1-60596-139-2(6)); lib. bdg. 26.00 (978-1-60596-138-5(8)) Weigl Pubs., Inc.

Dittmer, Lori. Empire State Building. 2019. (Landmarks of America Ser.). (ENG.). 24p. (J). (gr. 1-4). pap. 8.99 (978-1-62832-686-4(7), 18962, Creative Paperbacks) Creative Co., The.

—The Empire State Building. 2019. (Landmarks of America Ser.). (ENG.). 24p. (J). (gr. 1-4). (978-1-64026-123-5(0), 18961, Creative Education) Creative Co., The.

—Space Needle. 2019. (Landmarks of America Ser.). (ENG.). 24p. (J). (gr. 1-4). pap. 8.99 (978-1-62832-691-8(3), 18982, Creative Paperbacks) Creative Co., The.

Finger, Brad. 13 Skyscrapers Children Should Know, 1 vol. 2016. (13 Children Should Know Ser.). (ENG., Illus.). 48p. (J). (gr. 3-7). 14.95 (978-3-7913-7251-8(3)) Prestel Verlag GmbH & Co KG. DEU. Dist: Penguin Random Hse. LLC.

Franchino, Vicky. How Did They Build That? Skyscraper. 2009. (Community Connections: How Did They Build That? Ser.). (ENG.). 24p. (gr. 2-5). lib. bdg. 29.21 (978-1-60279-485-6(5), 200258) Cherry Lake Publishing.

Goldish, Meish. One-World Trade Center. 2018. (American Places: from Vision to Reality Ser.). (ENG.). 32p. (J). (gr. 2-7). lib. bdg. 19.95 (978-1-68402-435-3(8)) Bearport Publishing Co., Inc.

—Spectacular Skyscrapers. 2011. (So Big Compared to What? Ser.). 24p. (YA). (gr. 1-4). lib. bdg. 26.99 (978-1-61772-303-2(7)) Bearport Publishing Co., Inc.

Hardyman, Robyn. Skyscrapers, 1 vol. 2016. (Engineering Eurekas Ser.). (ENG.). 32p. (J). (gr. 3-4). pap. 11.00 (978-1-4994-3105-6(8), c9f0a86c-54ec-46ea-b968-eece435c8ca8, PowerKids Pr.) Rosen Publishing Group, Inc., The.

Hayes, Amy. Building Bridges & Roads: Civil Engineers, 1 vol., 1. 2015. (Engineers Rule! Ser.). (ENG., Illus.). 32p. (J). (gr. 4-5). pap. 12.75 (978-1-5081-4532-5(6), 1dad5ae6-3e6f-4007-91be-d9c5b4340235, PowerKids Pr.) Rosen Publishing Group, Inc., The.

Holland, Gini. The Empire State Building: How It Was Built & How It Is Used. 2004. (Illus.). 48p. (J). (gr. 4-8). reprint ed. 15.00 (978-0-7567-7718-0(6)) DIANE Publishing Co.

Hurley, Jorey. Skyscraper. Hurley, Jorey, illus. 2019. (ENG., Illus.). 40p. (J). (gr. -1-2). 17.99 (978-1-4814-7001-8(9), Simon & Schuster/Paula Wiseman Bks.) Simon & Schuster/Paula Wiseman Bks.

Hurley, Michael. The World's Most Amazing Skyscrapers, 1 vol. 2011. (Landmark Top Tens Ser.). (ENG., Illus.). 32p. (J). (gr. 3-5). pap. 8.29 (978-1-4109-4253-1(8), 115805, Raintree) Capstone.

Joseph, Leonard. Rascacielos: Por dentro y por fuera (Skyscrapers: Inside & Out) 2009. (Tecnología: Mapas para el Futuro Ser.). (SPA.). 48p. (gr. 4-4). 53.00 (978-1-60853-288-9(7), Editorial Buenas Letras) Rosen Publishing Group, Inc., The.

—Skyscrapers: Inside & Out. 2009. (Technology: Blueprints of the Future Ser.). 48p. (gr. 4-4). 53.00 (978-1-60853-284-1(4)) Rosen Publishing Group, Inc., The.

Kallen, Stuart. Burj Khalifa: The Tallest Tower in the World. 2014. (Great Idea Ser.). (ENG.). 48p. (J). (gr. 4-6). pap. 13.26 (978-1-60357-578-2(2)) Norwood Hse. Pr.

Kallen, Stuart A. Burj Khalifa: The Tallest Tower in the World. 2014. (Great Idea Ser.). (ENG.). 48p. (J). (gr. 4-6). lib. bdg. 26.60 (978-1-59953-598-2(X)) Norwood Hse. Pr.

Kenney, Karen Latchana. Building a Skyscraper. 2018. (Sequence Amazing Structures Ser.). (ENG.). 32p. (J). (gr. 2-5). pap. 9.99 (978-1-68152-351-4(5), 15166); lib. bdg. (978-1-68151-431-4(1), 15160) Amicus.

Koll, Hilary & Mills, Steve. Using Math to Build a Skyscraper, 1 vol. 2006. (Mathworks! Ser.). (ENG., Illus.). 32p. (gr. 3-5). lib. bdg. 28.67 (978-0-8368-6764-0(5), e094c3b7-2641-4555-973a-9726d3ab9994, Gareth Stevens Learning Library) Stevens, Gareth Publishing LLLP.

Latham, Donna. Skyscrapers: Investigate Feats of Engineering with 25 Projects. Christensen, Andrew, illus. 2013. (Build It Yourself Ser.). (ENG.). 128p. (J). (gr. 3-7). pap. 16.95 (978-1-61930-193-1(8), f5fac4f4-ff92-4deb-a860-82fce4fc086a) Nomad Pr.

Lee, Michelle. Burj Khalifa. 2015. (How Did They Build That? Ser.). (ENG., Illus.). 32p. (gr. 3-8). 27.99 (978-1-62920-557-1(5)) Scobre Pr. Corp.

Loh-Hagan, Virginia. Skyscrapers. 2017. (21st Century Junior Library: Extraordinary Engineering Ser.). (ENG., Illus.). 24p. (J). (gr. 2-5). lib. bdg. 29.21 (978-1-63472-165-3(9), 209232) Cherry Lake Publishing.

Malam, John. You Wouldn't Want to Be a Skyscraper Builder! 2009. (You Wouldn't Want To Ser.). lib. bdg. 20.80 (978-0-606-04274-1(1)) Turtleback.

Markovics, Joyce L. Shiny & Soaring: What Am I? 2018. (American Place Puzzlers Ser.). (ENG.). 24p. (J). (gr. -1-3). lib. bdg. 17.95 (978-1-68402-483-4(8)) Bearport Publishing Co., Inc.

—Tall & Sleek: What Am I? 2018. (American Place Puzzlers Ser.). (ENG.). 24p. (J). (gr. -1-3). lib. bdg. 17.95 (978-1-68402-479-7(X)) Bearport Publishing Co., Inc.

Marsico, Katie. A a True Book - Engineering Wonders (NEW SUBSET): Skyscrapers. 2016. (True Book(tm) — Engineering Wonders Ser.). (ENG., Illus.). 48p. (J). pap. 6.95 (978-0-531-22273-7(X), Children's Pr.) Scholastic Library Publishing.

McCarthy, Cecilia Pinto. Engineering Burj Khalifa. 2017. (Building by Design Set 2 Ser.). (ENG., Illus.). 48p. (J). (gr. 4-8). lib. bdg. 35.64 (978-1-5321-1371-0(4), 27669) ABDO Publishing Co.

Meachen Rau, Dana. Bookworms: The Inside Story, 12 vols., Set. Incl. Castle. lib. bdg. 25.50 (978-0-7614-2272-3(2), adab9f74-2818-438e-ba0f-67058d410319); Igloo. lib. bdg. 25.50 (978-0-7614-2273-0(0), b4264f9e-e40b-4791-87cc-23c1251e18a5); Log Cabin. lib. bdg. 25.50 (978-0-7614-2274-7(9), 0eb1f358-eb38-4d47-8e2b-9fc2cb65a564); Pyramid. lib. bdg. 25.50 (978-0-7614-2275-4(7), 10863ddc-9eee-46aa-abac-fc1eac1dec26); Skyscraper. lib. bdg. 25.50 (978-0-7614-2276-1(5), 21c7e684-e08a-4a1d-ba8f-a7294f9995c3); Tepee. lib. bdg. 25.50 (978-0-7614-2277-8(3), 36db5006-1580-4f2f-8b71-a10cc6b6c655); (Illus.). 32p. (gr. k-1). (Inside Story Ser.). (ENG.). 2007. Set lib. bdg. 153.00 (978-0-7614-2271-6(4), 26d3d7dd-7d58-4920-aa34-ec2e62335409, Cavendish Square) Cavendish Square Publishing LLC.

—Skyscraper, 1 vol. (Inside Story Ser.). (ENG.). 32p. (gr. k-1). 2008. pap. 9.23 (978-0-7614-3303-3(1), 7ec5b6b9-d54c-416e-9201-31f45c8adc60) 2007. (Illus.). lib. bdg. 25.50 (978-0-7614-2276-1(5), 21c7e684-e08a-4a1d-ba8f-a7294f9995c3) Cavendish Square Publishing LLC.

Monsman, Stacy. Engineering Marvels: Stand-Out Skyscrapers: Area (Grade 3) 2017. (Mathematics in the Real World Ser.). (ENG., Illus.). 32p. (gr. 3-4). pap. 11.99 (978-1-4807-5810-0(8)) Teacher Created Materials, Inc.

Murray, Julie. One World Trade Center. 2018. (Super Structures Ser.). (ENG., Illus.). 24p. (J). (gr. k-4). lib. bdg. 31.36 (978-1-5321-2312-2(4), 28391, Abdo Zoom-Dash) ABDO Publishing Co.

—The Shard. 2018. (Super Structures Ser.). (ENG., Illus.). 24p. (J). (gr. k-4). lib. bdg. 31.36 (978-1-5321-2313-9(2), 28393, Abdo Zoom-Dash) ABDO Publishing Co.

—Space Needle. 2018. (Super Structures Ser.). (ENG., Illus.). 24p. (J). (gr. k-4). lib. bdg. 31.36 (978-1-5321-2314-6(0), 28395, Abdo Zoom-Dash) ABDO Publishing Co.

Nagelhout, Ryan. Gareth's Guide to Building a Skyscraper, 1 vol. 2018. (Gareth Guides to an Extraordinary Life Ser.). (ENG.). 32p. (gr. 4-5). 29.60 (978-1-5382-2055-9(5), 5ce56764-b9ab-4209-b365-cc281b6bee67) Stevens, Gareth Publishing LLLP.

—The Unofficial Guide to Building Skyscrapers in Minecraft, 1 vol. 2018. (STEM Projects in Minecraft(r) Ser.). (ENG.). 24p. (gr. 3-3). 25.27 (978-1-5081-6937-6(3), baa521fc-97c7-4e8c-8ee2-cc3886f56155, PowerKids Pr.) Rosen Publishing Group, Inc., The.

Newland, Sonya. Extraordinary Skyscrapers: The Science of How & Why They Were Built. 2018. (Exceptional Engineering Ser.). (ENG., Illus.). 32p. (J). (gr. 3-6). lib. bdg. 27.99 (978-1-5435-2906-7(2), 138504, Capstone Pr.) Capstone.

O'Connor, Jim. What Were the Twin Towers? 2018. (ENG.). (J). (gr. 3-7). pap. (978-1-338-10028-0(9)) Penguin Canada.

Oxlade, Chris. Skyscrapers 3 Explorers. 2017. (Cambridge Reading Adventures Ser.). (ENG., Illus.). 32p. pap. 8.60 (978-1-108-41189-9(4)) Cambridge Univ. Pr.

Perish, Patrick. Skyscraper Builder. 2015. (Dangerous Jobs Ser.). (ENG., Illus.). 24p. (J). (gr. 3-7). lib. bdg. 26.95 (978-1-62617-197-8(1), Torque Bks.) Bellwether Media.

Pettiford, Rebecca. Skyscrapers. 2015. (Illus.). 24p. (J). lib. bdg. (978-1-62031-210-0(7)) Jump! Inc.

Phillips, Cynthia & Priwer, Shana. Skyscrapers & High Rises. 2014. (ENG., Illus.). 112p. (C). (gr. 6-18). lib. bdg. 180.00 (978-0-7656-8121-8(8), Y183566) Routledge.

Polinsky, Paige V. Skyscrapers. 2017. (Engineering Super Structures Ser.). (ENG., Illus.). 24p. (J). (gr. -1-3). lib. bdg. 29.93 (978-1-5321-1105-1(3), 25786, SandCastle) ABDO Publishing Co.

Romero, Libby. National Geographic Readers: Skyscrapers (Level 3) 2017. (Readers Ser.). (Illus.). 48p. (J). (gr. 3-7). pap. 4.99 (978-1-4263-2681-3(5), National Geographic Kids) Disney Publishing Worldwide.

Schmermund, Elizabeth. Skyscrapers! With 25 Science Projects for Kids. Crosier, Mike, illus. 2018. (Explore Your World Ser.). 96p. (J). (gr. 3-5). 19.95 (978-1-61930-651-6(4), 914c7a1c-ae93-45e5-8e58-2f11e2c6ec1f) Nomad Pr.

Scremin, Lauren. The 10 Most Amazing Skyscrapers. 2007. (J). 14.99 (978-1-55448-480-5(4)) Scholastic Library Publishing.

Shea, Therese M. How a Skyscraper Is Built, 1 vol. 2015. (Engineering Our World Ser.). (ENG.). 24p. (J). (gr. 2-3). pap. 9.15 (978-1-4824-3935-9(2), 27994aab-e68f-47a4-841f-a6cf0914365e) Stevens, Gareth Publishing LLLP.

Spielman, Madison. Build It: Skyscrapers, 1 vol. 2nd rev. ed. 2011. (TIME for KIDS(r): Informational Text Ser.). (ENG.). 28p. (gr. 2-3). pap. 9.99 (978-1-4333-3620-1(0)) Teacher Created Materials, Inc.

Spray, Sally. Awesome Engineering Skyscrapers. 2018. (Awesome Engineering Ser.). (ENG.). 32p. (J). (gr. 3-6). lib. bdg. 27.99 (978-1-5435-1333-2(6), 137763, Capstone Pr.) Capstone.

Stefoff, Rebecca. Building Skyscrapers, 1 vol. 2015. (Great Engineering Ser.). (ENG.). 32p. (gr. 3-3). 30.21 (978-1-5026-0607-5(0), 302b428f-06af-46f1-81a9-b623eeac7a8e) Cavendish Square Publishing LLC.

Stern, Steven L. Building Green-Scrapers. 2009. (Going Green Ser.). (Illus.). 32p. (YA). (gr. 3-6). lib. bdg. 28.50 (978-1-59716-962-2(5)) Bearport Publishing Co., Inc.

Thomas, Mark. The Petronas Twin Towers: World's Tallest Buildings. 2009. (Record-Breaking Structures Ser.). 24p. (gr. 1-2). 42.50 (978-1-60852-457-0(4), PowerKids Pr.) Rosen Publishing Group, Inc., The.

—Las Torres Gemelas Petronas: Los Edificios Más Altos del Mundo (The Petronas Twin Towers: World'S Tallest Building) 2009. (Estructuras extraordinarias (Record-Breaking Structures) Ser.). (SPA.). 24p. (gr. 1-2). 42.50 (978-1-61512-314-8(8), Editorial Buenas Letras) Rosen Publishing Group, Inc., The.

Wolny, Philip. High Risk Construction Work: Life Building Skyscrapers, Bridges, & Tunnels, 1 vol. 2008. (Extreme Careers Ser.). (ENG., Illus.). 64p. (YA). (gr. 5-5). lib. bdg. 37.13 (978-1-4042-1789-8(4), 0960af74-fa6b-4f71-aea5-51c5e2f3c888) Rosen Publishing Group, Inc., The.

—High-Risk Construction Work: Life Building Skyscrapers, Bridges, & Tunnels. 2009. (Extreme Careers Ser.). 64p. (gr. 5-5). 58.50 (978-1-61512-397-1(0), Rosen Reference) Rosen Publishing Group, Inc., The.

—21st-Century Skyscrapers, 1 vol. 2018. (Feats of 21st-Century Engineering Ser.). (ENG.). 48p. (gr. 4-4). 29.60 (978-0-7660-9703-2(X), cedc9fb0-b01e-4c72-8f98-c5bc6356688b) Enslow Publishing, LLC.

SKYSCRAPERS—FICTION

Hopkinson, Deborah. Sky Boys: How They Built the Empire State Building. Ransome, James E., illus. 2012. lib. bdg. 18.40 (978-0-606-23847-2(6)) Turtleback.

McGee, Katharine. The Towering Sky. (Thousandth Floor Ser.: 3). (ENG.). 464p. (YA). (gr. 8). 2019. pap. 11.99 (978-0-06-241866-1(1)) 2018. 18.99 (978-0-06-241865-4(3)) HarperCollins Pubs. (HarperCollins).

Skyscrapers & Farms. 2005. (J). per. 5.00 (978-1-59872-020-4(1)) Instant Pub.

SKYWALKER, ANAKIN (FICTITIOUS CHARACTER)—FICTION

see Vader, Darth (Fictitious Character)—Fiction

SKYWALKER, LUKE (FICTITIOUS CHARACTER)—FICTION

Aaron, Jason. Skywalker Strikes. Cassaday, John & Martin, Laura, illus. 2016. (Star Wars: Skywalker Strikes Ser.). (ENG.). (J). (gr. 6-12). 24p. lib. bdg. 31.36 (978-1-61479-530-8(4), 21430); 24p. lib. bdg. 31.36 (978-1-61479-532-2(0), 21432); Vol. 1. 32p. lib. bdg. 31.36 (978-1-61479-527-8(4), 21427); Vol. 2. 24p. lib. bdg. 31.36 (978-1-61479-528-5(2), 21428); Vol. 3. 24p. lib. bdg. 31.36 (978-1-61479-529-2(0), 21429); Vol. 5. 24p. lib. bdg. 31.36 (978-1-61479-531-5(2), 21431) Spotlight. (Graphic Novels).

—Vader down: Volume 1. Deodato, Mike & Martin, Laura, illus. 2016. (Star Wars: Vader Down Ser.). (ENG.). 36p. (J). (gr. 6-12). lib. bdg. 31.36 (978-1-61479-561-2(4), 24395, Graphic Novels) Spotlight.

—Vader down: Volume 3. Deodato, Mike & Martin, Laura, illus. 2016. (Star Wars: Vader Down Ser.). (ENG.). 24p. (J). (gr. 6-12). lib. bdg. 31.36 (978-1-61479-563-6(0), 24397, Graphic Novels) Spotlight.

—Vader down: Volume 5. Deodato, Mike & Martin, Laura, illus. 2016. (Star Wars: Vader Down Ser.). (ENG.). 24p. (J). (gr. 6-12). lib. bdg. 31.36 (978-1-61479-565-0(7), 24399, Graphic Novels) Spotlight.

Beecroft, Simon. DK Readers L1: Star Wars: Luke Skywalker's Amazing Story. 2008. (DK Readers Level 1 Ser.). (ENG.). 32p. (J). (gr. k-2). pap. 4.99 (978-0-7566-4518-2(2), DK Children) Dorling Kindersley Publishing, Inc.

Cohee, Ron, illus. Return of the Jedi. 2015. (J). (978-1-4806-9362-3(6), Golden Bks.) Random Hse. Children's Bks.

Disney Book Group. Trapped in the Death Star! 2016. (Star Wars: World of Reading Ser.). (Illus.). 30p. (J). lib. bdg. 14.75 (978-0-606-39174-0(6)) Turtleback.

DK. Star Wars the Rise of Skywalker Amazing Sticker Adventures. 2019. (Ultimate Sticker Collection). (ENG.). 72p. (J). (gr. k-2). pap. 12.99 (978-1-4654-7904-4(X), DK Children) Dorling Kindersley Publishing, Inc.

Gillen, Kieron. Vader down: Volume 4. Larroca, Salvador & Delgado, Edgar, illus. 2016. (Star Wars: Vader Down Ser.). (ENG.). 24p. (J). (gr. 6-12). lib. bdg. 31.36 (978-1-61479-564-3(9), 24398, Graphic Novels) Spotlight.

—Vader down: Volume 6. Larroca, Salvador & Delgado, Edgar, illus. 2016. (Star Wars: Vader Down Ser.). (ENG.). 24p. (J). (gr. 6-12). lib. bdg. 31.36 (978-1-61479-566-7(5), 24400, Graphic Novels) Spotlight.

Hibbert, Clare. DK Readers L1: Star Wars: Tatooine Adventures. 2011. (DK Readers Level 1 Ser.). (ENG.). 48p. (J). (gr. k-4). 4.99 (978-0-7566-7128-0(0), DK Children) Dorling Kindersley Publishing, Inc.

King, Trey. Death Star Battle. 2016. (Illus.). 30p. (J). (978-1-4806-9628-0(5), Disney Lucasfilm Press) Disney Publishing Worldwide.

Landers, Ace. Empire Strikes Out. 2013. (LEGO Star Wars Chapter Bks.). lib. bdg. 14.75 (978-0-606-31554-8(3)) Turtleback.

Lucas Film Book Group. Trouble on Tatooine. 2017. (Star Wars: World of Reading Ser.). (J). lib. bdg. 14.75 (978-0-606-39963-0(1)) Turtleback.

Lucasfilm Press, Lucasfilm. 5-Minute Star Wars Stories Strike Back. 2017. (Illus.). 20p. (J). (gr. 1-3). 12.99 (978-1-368-00351-3(6), Disney Lucasfilm Press) Disney Publishing Worldwide.

Saunders, Catherine. The Jedi & the Force. 2014. (Illus.). 144p. (J). (978-1-4351-5416-2(9)) Dorling Kindersley Publishing, Inc.

Scott, Cavan. Star Wars: A Luke & Leia Adventure. Charretier, Elsa, illus. 2018. 137p. (J). (978-1-5444-1928-2(7), Disney Lucasfilm Press) Disney Publishing Worldwide.

—Star Wars: a Luke & Leia Adventure: A Choose Your Destiny Chapter Book. 2018. (Choose Your Destiny Chapter Book Ser.). (ENG., Illus.). 144p. (J). (gr. 1-3). pap. 5.99 (978-1-368-02424-2(6), Disney Lucasfilm Press) Disney Publishing Worldwide.

Siglain, Michael. Use the Force! Roux, Stéphane, illus. 2017. (World of Reading Level 2 (Leveled Readers) Ser.). (ENG.). 32p. (J). (gr. k-3). 31.36 (978-1-5321-4065-5(7), 25436) Spotlight.

Smith, Geof. Star Wars: Return of the Jedi (Star Wars) Cohee, Ron, illus. 2015. (Little Golden Book Ser.). (ENG.). 24p. (J). (-k). 5.99 (978-0-7364-3548-2(4), Golden Bks.) Random Hse. Children's Bks.

Wang, Jack & Wang, Holman. Star Wars Epic Yarns: Return of the Jedi. 2015. (ENG., Illus.). 24p. (J). (gr. -1 — 1). 9.95 (978-1-4521-3500-7(2)) Chronicle Bks. LLC.

Watson, Jude. The Desperate Mission. 2005. (Star Wars Ser.: No. 1). 168p. (J). lib. bdg. 20.00 (978-1-4242-0774-9(6)) Fitzgerald Bks.

Windham, Ryder. A New Hope: The Life of Luke Skywalker. 2009. 208p. (J). (978-0-545-16177-0(0)) Scholastic, Inc.

SLAVE TRADE

Alexander, richard. The Transatlantic Slave Trade: The Forced Migration of Africans to America (1607-1830), 1 vol., 1. 2015. (Spotlight on Immigration & Migration Ser.). (ENG., Illus.). 24p. (J). (gr. 4-5). pap. 11.00 (978-1-5081-4100-6(2), c13da223-d783-4a35-be11-1d9ba0da1f08, PowerKids Pr.) Rosen Publishing Group, Inc., The.

Allman, Toney. The Transatlantic Slave Trade, 1 vol. 2009. (World History Ser.). (ENG., Illus.). 104p. (gr. 7-7). 41.53 (978-1-4205-0132-2(1), a6e19cf4-0484-4db8-bbd1-97f8d8c7df09, Lucent Pr.) Greenhaven Publishing LLC.

Amistad 2nd Edition 2009: Freedom Is not given, it Is a Birthright. 2009. (My Ancestors — My Heroes Ser.: Vol. 9). (ENG., Illus.). 86p. (J). (gr. 3-4). incl. cd-rom (978-1-893091-08-5(2), My Ancestors, My Heroes) Parker-Wallace Publishing Co., LLC.

Aretha, David. The Middle Passage. 2014. xvi, 585p. (J). (978-1-59935-408-8(X)) Reynolds, Morgan Inc.

Baumann, Susan K. The Middle Passage & the Revolt on the Amistad, 1 vol. 2013. (Jr. Graphic African American History Ser.). (Illus.). 24p. (J). (ENG.). (gr. 2-3). pap. 11.60 (978-1-4777-1447-8(2), f54c224b-1452-4485-858a-99f75c1acd30); (ENG., (gr. 2-3). lib. bdg. 28.93 (978-1-4777-1311-2(5), a874e2bf-b504-42a3-9403-71e32fdb6a9a); (gr. 3-6). pap. 63.60 (978-1-4777-1448-5(0)) Rosen Publishing Group, Inc., The. (PowerKids Pr.).

Cottman, Michael H. Shackles from the Deep: Tracing the Path of a Sunken Slave Ship, a Bitter Past, & a Rich Legacy. 2017. 128p. (J). (gr. 5-9). 17.99 (978-1-4263-2663-9(7), National Geographic Kids) Disney Publishing Worldwide.

Eisen Azarian, Melissa. The Amistad Mutiny: From the Court Case to the Movie, 1 vol. 2010. (Famous Court Cases That Became Movies Ser.). (ENG., Illus.). 128p. (J). (gr. 6-7). lib. bdg. 35.93 (978-0-7660-3054-1(7), 08c9b0cf-2581-4e47-9d4f-8a1cf7a1aad5) Enslow Publishing, LLC.

Haskins, James & Benson Haskins, Kathleen. Africa: A Look Back, 1 vol. 2007. (Drama of African-American History Ser.). (ENG., Illus.). 80p. (J). (gr. 6-6). lib. bdg. 38.36 (978-0-7614-2148-1(3), 1c1cd1b9-2063-462a-943d-5d55457363e9) Cavendish Square Publishing LLC.

Hatt, Christine. The African-American Slave Trade. 2003. (Questioning History Ser.). (J). lib. bdg. 28.50 (978-1-58340-265-8(9)) Black Rabbit Bks.

Keller, Kristin Thoennes. The Slave Trade in Early America. rev. ed. 2016. (Colonial America Ser.). (ENG.). 48p. (J). (gr. 3-9). pap. 8.19 (978-1-5157-5192-2(9), 134716) Capstone.

Littlejohn, Randy. A Timeline of the Slave Trade in America. (Timelines of American History Ser.). 32p. (gr. 4-4). 2009. 47.90 (978-1-60854-390-8(0)) 2004. (ENG., Illus.). lib. bdg. 29.13 (978-0-8239-4540-5(5), 1c308b4c-e4e3-4c4a-a616-f859bdc46cca) Rosen Publishing Group, Inc., The. (Rosen Reference).

Mann, Charles. 1493 for Young People: From Columbus's Voyage to Globalization. 2016. (For Young People Ser.). (Illus.). 416p. (J). (gr. 7). pap. 22.95 (978-1-60980-663-7(8), Triangle Square) Seven Stories Pr.

McAneney, Caitie. Aboard the Amistad, 1 vol. 2019. (History on the High Seas Ser.). (ENG.). 24p. (J). (gr. 2-3). pap. 9.15 (978-1-5382-3790-8(3), 13bfb77a-c055-44f8-aaa3-db6037088fef) Stevens, Gareth Publishing LLLP.

Nardo, Don. The Atlantic Slave Trade, 1 vol. 2007. (Lucent Library of Black History Ser.). (ENG., Illus.). 104p. (gr. 7-7). lib. bdg. 41.03 (978-1-4205-0007-3(4), de99408b-5d64-48ef-8125-db14a314f232, Lucent Pr.) Greenhaven Publishing LLC.

Saidian, Siyavush. The Transatlantic Slave Trade: Slavery Comes to the New World, 1 vol. 2017. (Lucent Library of Black History Ser.). (ENG.). 104p. (YA). (gr. 7-7). 41.03 (978-1-5345-6237-0(0), 88b6f1af-88c1-4698-a107-5dde433942eb); pap. 20.99 (978-1-5345-6299-8(0), 3b904e0f-a21c-433b-993b-0307ee119110) Greenhaven Publishing LLC. (Lucent Pr.).

Sharp, S. Pearl & Schomp, Virginia. The Slave Trade & the Middle Passage, 1 vol. 2007. (Drama of African-American History Ser.). (ENG., Illus.). 80p. (gr. 6-6). lib. bdg. 38.36 (978-0-7614-2176-4(9), 54b03cf0-3993-459b-8d39-1da98298bb58) Cavendish Square Publishing LLC.

Toler, Pamela. Transatlantic Slave Networks, 1 vol. 2017. (Routes of Cross-Cultural Exchange Ser.). (ENG.). 96p. (YA). (gr. 8-8). 44.50 (978-1-5026-2696-7(9), a14f0e3a-12c2-4903-90c6-256641978d23) Cavendish Square Publishing LLC.

SLAVERY

Africans in America: America's Journey Through Slavery. 2004. (gr. 7-18). tchr. ed. 19.95 incl. VHS, cd-rom (978-1-57807-195-1(X), WG665) WGBH Boston Video.

Aronson, Marc & Budhos, Marina. Sugar Changed the World: A Story of Magic, Spice, Slavery, Freedom, & Science. 2010. (ENG., Illus.). 176p. (YA). (gr. 7-18). 21.99 (978-0-618-57492-6(1), 100422, Clarion Bks.) HarperCollins Pubs.

Berlatsky, Noah, ed. Slavery & Human Trafficking, 1 vol. 2016. (Opposing Viewpoints Ser.). (ENG.). 216p. (gr. 10-12). 50.43 (978-0-7377-7530-3(0), eacb9cee-5861-401d-9748-46fc57688982, Greenhaven Publishing) Greenhaven Publishing LLC.

Brindell Fradin, Dennis. The Underground Railroad, 1 vol. 2009. (Turning Points in U. S. History Ser.). (ENG.). 48p. (gr. 4-4). lib. bdg. 34.07 (978-0-7614-3014-8(8), 9dc92785-4a3d-4835-bf07-5679dd35196f) Cavendish Square Publishing LLC.

Brownell, Richard. The Civil War: The Fall of the Confederacy & the End of Slavery. 2005. (History's Great Defeats Ser.). (ENG., Illus.). 109p. (YA). (gr. 7-10). lib. bdg. 30.85 (978-1-59018-429-5(7), Lucent Bks.) Cengage Gale.

Buell, Tonya. Slavery in America: A Primary Source History of the Intolerable Practice of Slavery. 2009. (Primary Sources in

American History Ser.). 64p. (gr. 5-8). 58.50 (978-1-60851-491-5(9)) Rosen Publishing Group, Inc., The.

Burchard, Peter. Frederick Douglass: For the Great Family of Man. 2007. (ENG., Illus.). 240p. (YA). (gr. 7). pap. 13.95 (978-1-4169-6752-1(4), Atheneum Bks. for Young Readers) Simon & Schuster Children's Publishing.

Caravantes, Peggy. Escaping Slavery. 2018. (Great Escapes in History Ser.). (ENG.). 32p. (J). (gr. 3-6). lib. bdg. 35.64 (978-1-5038-2530-7(2), 212349, MOMENTUM) Child's World, Inc, The.

Cheng, Andrea. Etched in Clay: The Life of Dave, Enslaved Potter & Poet. Cheng, Andrea, illus. 2013. (ENG., Illus.). 146p. (J). 17.95 (978-1-60060-451-5(X)) Lee & Low Bks., Inc.

A Child's Anti-Slavery Book. 2004. reprint ed. pap. 1.99 (978-1-4192-0040-3(2)); pap. 15.95 (978-1-4191-0040-6(8)) Kessinger Publishing, LLC.

A Child's Anti-Slavery Book. 2008. 72p. pap. 7.95 (978-1-60597-847-5(7), Bk. Jungle) Standard Publications, Inc.

Cline-Ransome, Lesa. Words Set Me Free: The Story of Young Frederick Douglass. Ransome, James E., illus. 2011. (ENG.). 32p. (J). (gr. k-4). 19.99 (978-1-4169-5903-8(3), Simon & Schuster/Paula Wiseman Bks.) Simon & Schuster/Paula Wiseman Bks.

Courtauld, Sarah. The Story of Slavery. 2008. (Usborne Young Reading: Series Three Ser.). (Illus.). 60p. (J). 8.99 (978-0-7945-1895-0(8), Usborne) EDC Publishing.

Currie, Stephen. A Peculiar Institution: Slavery in the Plantation South. 2005. (Lucent Library of Black History). (ENG., Illus.). 112p. (J). (gr. 7-10). lib. bdg. 33.45 (978-1-59018-704-3(0), Lucent Bks.) Cengage Gale.

Eisen Azarian, Melissa. The Amistad Mutiny: From the Court Case to the Movie, 1 vol. 2010. (Famous Court Cases That Became Movies Ser.). (ENG., Illus.). 128p. (J). (gr. 6-7). lib. bdg. 35.93 (978-0-7660-3054-1(7), 08c9b0cf-2581-4e47-9d4f-8a1cf7a1aad5) Enslow Publishing, LLC.

Frederick Douglass. 2018. (J). (978-0-7166-2280-2(7)) World Bk., Inc.

Gale Research Inc. Unlocking Current Issues: Race & the Law. 2018. (Unlocking Current Issues Ser.). (ENG., Illus.). 240p. 51.00 (978-1-4103-8096-8(3)) Cengage Gale.

Ganeri, Anita. Harriet Tubman: The Life of an African-American Abolitionist, 1 vol. Shone, Rob, illus. 2004. (Graphic Nonfiction Biographies Ser.). (ENG.). 48p. (gr. 4-6). pap. 14.05 (978-1-4042-5172-4(3), c18f7686-5d5e-4423-a6ef-da0119694c22) Rosen Publishing Group, Inc., The.

Gateway Christian Academy (Fort Lauderdale, Fla.) Staff & Juvenile Collection Staff, contrib. by. Letters from Minty: An Imaginative Look into the Life & Thoughts of a Young Harriet Tubman. 2016. (Illus.). 31p. (J). (978-1-338-13424-7(8)) Scholastic, Inc.

Gregory, Josh. Frederick Douglass. 2015. (ENG., Illus.). 48p. (J). lib. bdg. (978-0-531-21597-5(0), Orchard Bks.) Scholastic, Inc.

Hoffman, Kurt. Young Heroes, a Learner's Guide to Changing the World: Abolish Slavery Edition. 2012. (978-0-9865555-5-8(X)); pap. (978-0-9865555-6-5(8)) Brighter Bks. Publishing Hse.

House, Catherine. Voices Against Slavery: Ten Christians Who Spoke Out for Freedom. rev. ed. 2006. (ENG.). 160p. (J). per. 7.99 (978-1-84550-145-7(4), 1ff9ba16-21ee-4af4-97ec-2c2ada65c8d2) Christian Focus Pubns. GBR. Dist: Baker & Taylor Publisher Services (BTPS).

Huey, Lois Miner. Forgotten Bones: Uncovering a Slave Cemetery. 2015. (ENG., Illus.). 56p. (J). (gr. 4-8). E-Book 46.65 (978-1-4677-6300-4(4), Millbrook Pr.) Lerner Publishing Group.

Jacobs Altman, Linda. The Story of Slavery & Abolition in United States History, 1 vol. 2014. (In United States History Ser.). (ENG.). 96p. (gr. 5-5). 31.61 (978-0-7660-6330-3(5), d0ce5d31-9c90-4cd9-b6e0-5bac66be9619) Enslow Publishing, LLC.

King, Wilma. Children of the Emancipation. 2005. (Picture the American Past Ser.). (Illus.). 48p. (J). (gr. 2-5). 22.60 (978-1-57505-396-7(9)) Lerner Publishing Group.

Kramer, Barbara. National Geographic Readers: Frederick Douglass (Level 2) 2017. (Readers Bios Ser.). (Illus.). 32p. (J). (gr. 1-3). pap. 4.99 (978-1-4263-2756-8(0), National Geographic Kids) Disney Publishing Worldwide.

Landau, Elaine. The Underground Railroad: Would You Help Them Escape?, 1 vol. 2014. (What Would You Do? Ser.). (ENG., Illus.). 48p. (gr. 3-3). 27.93 (978-0-7660-4225-4(1), 5f3aaa1d-72e8-444b-833a-bd13daeb04dc) Enslow Publishing, LLC.

Levin, Judy. A Timeline of the Abolitionist Movement. (Timelines of American History Ser.). 32p. (gr. 4-4). 2009. 47.90 (978-1-60854-381-6(1)) 2004. (ENG., Illus.). (J). lib. bdg. 29.13 (978-0-8239-4537-5(5), 0cb0a0cb-2bb0-4cc2-a53f-cd87d0c86654) Rosen Publishing Group, Inc., The. (Rosen Reference).

Linde, Barbara M. Slavery in North America, 1 vol. 2016. (American History Ser.). (ENG.). 104p. (YA). (gr. 7-7). lib. bdg. 41.03 (978-1-5345-6060-4(2), 358e6e30-a76c-4a64-9beb-7569b232bfe0, Lucent Pr.) Greenhaven Publishing LLC.

Littlejohn, Randy. A Timeline of the Slave Trade in America, 1 vol. 2004. (Timelines of American History Ser.). (ENG., Illus.). 32p. (gr. 4-4). lib. bdg. 29.13 (978-0-8239-4540-5(5), 1c308b4c-e4e3-4c4a-a616-f859bdc46cca, Rosen Reference) Rosen Publishing Group, Inc., The.

Llanas, Sheila Griffin. The Underground Railroad: A History Perspectives Book. 2013. (Perspectives Library). (ENG., Illus.). 32p. (J). (gr. 4-8). pap. 14.21 (978-1-62431-499-5(6), 202814) Cherry Lake Publishing.

Maloof, Torrey. True Life: Frederick Douglass. 2nd rev. ed. 2017. (TIME(r): Informational Text Ser.). (ENG., Illus.). 48p. (gr. 7-8). pap. 13.99 (978-1-4938-3634-5(X)) Teacher Created Materials, Inc.

Marcovitz, Hal. The History of Slavery. 2014. (Understanding World History Ser.). (ENG., Illus.). 96p. (J). lib. bdg. (978-1-60152-742-4(X)) ReferencePoint Pr., Inc.

Mckissack, Patricia & Mckissack, Fredrick. Carter G. Woodson: Black History Pioneer, 1 vol. 2013. (Famous African Americans Ser.). (ENG.). 24p. (gr. k-2). pap. 10.35 (978-1-4644-0195-4(0), 95b9c3c7-6c85-48b9-8055-2bd45d164715, Enslow Elementary) Enslow Publishing, LLC.

—Frederick Douglass: Fighter Against Slavery, 1 vol. 2013. (Famous African Americans Ser.). (ENG.). 24p. (gr. k-2). pap. 10.35 (978-1-4644-0196-1(9), dcc5b08d-3be4-4932-b752-9c1b8c1a042b, Enslow Elementary) Enslow Publishing, LLC.

Moore, Cathy. Ellen Craft's Escape from Slavery. 2010. pap. 56.72 (978-0-7613-6925-7(2)) Lerner Publishing Group.

Morley, Jacqueline. Be a Sumerian Slave! A Life of Hard Labor You'd Rather Avoid. Antram, David, illus. 2007. (You Wouldn't Want to... Ser.). (ENG.). 32p. (J). (gr. 4-7). 29.00 (978-0-531-18728-9(4), Watts, Franklin) Scholastic Library Publishing.

Myers, Walter Dean. Frederick Douglass: the Lion Who Wrote History. Cooper, Floyd, illus. 2017. (ENG.). 40p. (J). (gr. -1-3). 17.99 (978-0-06-027709-3(2), Quill Tree Bks.) HarperCollins Pubs.

Nardo, Don. Debates on the Slave Trade. 2018. (Debates in History Ser.). (ENG.). 80p. (YA). (gr. 6-12). 39.93 (978-1-68282-373-6(3)) ReferencePoint Pr., Inc.

—Slavery Through Ages, 1 vol. 2014. (World History Ser.). (ENG., Illus.). 104p. (gr. 7-7). lib. bdg. 41.53 (978-1-4205-0860-4(1), 565cf8a9-f1e1-44a5-9976-ca2474a35e70, Lucent Pr.) Greenhaven Publishing LLC.

Nelson, Kadir. Heart & Soul: The Story of America & African Americans. Nelson, Kadir, illus. 2013. (ENG., Illus.). 112p. (J). (gr. 1-5). pap. 9.99 (978-0-06-173079-5(3), Balzer & Bray) HarperCollins Pubs.

—Heart & Soul: The Story of America & African Americans. 2013. (J). lib. bdg. 19.65 (978-0-606-35050-1(0)) Turtleback.

Raatma, Lucia. The Underground Railroad. 2011. (Cornerstones of Freedom, Third Ser.). (Illus.). 64p. (J). lib. bdg. 30.00 (978-0-531-25043-3(1), Children's Pr.) Scholastic Library Publishing.

Rausch, Monica. Harriet Tubman, 1 vol. 2007. (Great Americans Ser.). (ENG.). 24p. (J). (gr. 2-4). pap. 9.15 (978-0-8368-7693-2(8), 4353d179-8f76-4e6a-a060-e37e98de4633); (Illus.). lib. bdg. 24.67 (978-0-8368-7686-4(5), 71172d49-c35b-42d9-9142-6c544f8c12fc) Stevens, Gareth Publishing LLLP. (Weekly Reader Leveled Readers).

Rikson, Paule. Daily Life on a Southern Plantation 1853. 2004. (Illus.). 48p. (J). (gr. 4-8). reprint ed. 17.00 (978-0-7567-7709-8(7)) DIANE Publishing Co.

Roop, Peter & Roop, Connie. Who Conducted the Underground Railroad? And Other Questions about the Path to Freedom. 2008. (Illus.). 44p. (J). pap. (978-0-439-02524-9(9)) Scholastic, Inc.

Saidian, Siyavush. The Transatlantic Slave Trade: Slavery Comes to the New World, 1 vol. 2017. (Lucent Library of Black History Ser.). (ENG.). 104p. (YA). (gr. 7-7). pap. 20.99 (978-1-5345-6299-8(0), 3b904e0f-a21c-433b-993b-0307ee119110, Lucent Pr.) Greenhaven Publishing LLC.

Schraff, Anne. John Brown: We Came to Free the Slaves, 1 vol. 2008. (Americans: the Spirit of a Nation Ser.). (ENG., Illus.). 128p. (gr. 5-6). lib. bdg. 35.93 (978-0-7660-3355-9(4), 4d2d0bf1-4734-41ec-b384-c08076340bc5) Enslow Publishing, LLC.

Sepahban, Lois. 12 Questions about Slave Narratives. 2017. (Examining Primary Sources Ser.). (ENG., Illus.). 32p. (J). (gr. 3-6). 32.80 (978-1-63235-287-3(7), 11756, 12-Story Library) Bookstaves, LLC.

Sharp, S. Pearl & Schomp, Virginia. The Slave Trade & the Middle Passage, 1 vol. 2007. (Drama of African-American History Ser.). (ENG., Illus.). 80p. (gr. 6-6). lib. bdg. 38.36 (978-0-7614-2176-4(9), 54b03cf0-3993-459b-8d39-1da98298bb58) Cavendish Square Publishing LLC.

Shea, Nicole. Frederick Douglass in His Own Words, 1 vol., Vol. 1. 2014. (Eyewitness to History Ser.). (ENG.). 32p. (J). (gr. 4-5). pap. 11.50 (978-1-4824-3288-6(9), 1867b109-3ac3-49a9-a2e7-df4bd2f57a4d) Stevens, Gareth Publishing LLLP.

Shone, Rob & Ganeri, Anita. Harriet Tubman: The Life of an African-American Abolitionist, 1 vol. 2004. (Graphic Nonfiction Biographies Ser.). (ENG., Illus.). 48p. (J). (gr. 4-6). lib. bdg. 37.13 (978-1-4042-0245-0(5), ba8a5d50-aee5-4c2c-802b-2ead9f0d0c2a) Rosen Publishing Group, Inc., The.

Slavery in the Nineteenth Century. (YA). (gr. 5-8). spiral bd., tchr.'s planning gde. ed. 13.00 (978-0-382-40935-6(3)) Cobblestone Publishing Co.

Stein, R. Conrad. Escaping Slavery on the Underground Railroad, 1 vol. 2008. (From Many Cultures, One History Ser.). (ENG., Illus.). 128p. (gr. 5-6). lib. bdg. 35.93 (978-0-7660-2799-2(6), 6824421d-86d0-4c2b-880d-c9848439e5d1) Enslow Publishing, LLC.

Stoltman, Joan. Frederick Douglass, 1 vol. 2018. (Heroes of Black History Ser.). (ENG.). 32p. (J). (gr. 3-4). 28.27 (978-1-5382-3017-6(8), 33c38884-7b1c-4e56-b1e8-f6f62f920719) Stevens, Gareth Publishing LLLP.

Vander Hook, Sue. Frederick Douglass: Fugitive Slave & Abolitionist, 1 vol. 2010. (Essential Lives Set 5 Ser.). (ENG., Illus.). 112p. (YA). (gr. 6-12). lib. bdg. 41.36 (978-1-61613-513-3(1), 6709, Essential Library) ABDO Publishing Co.

Vasil Biscontini, Tracey & Sparling, Rebecca, eds. Amendment XIII: Abolishing Slavery, 1 vol. 2008. (Constitutional Amendments: Beyond the Bill of Rights Ser.). (ENG., Illus.). 200p. (gr. 10-12). lib. bdg. 44.83 (978-0-7377-4122-3(8), 762c21d1-ad6d-4cf7-88ac-a22fa832bbb2, Greenhaven Publishing) Greenhaven Publishing LLC.

Watkins, Richard. Slavery: Bondage throughout History. Watkins, Richard, photos by. 2006. (Illus.). 136p. (J). (gr. 4-8). reprint ed. 18.00 (978-1-4223-5333-2(8)) DIANE Publishing Co.

Whitman Blair, Margaret. Liberty or Death: The Surprising Story of Runaway Slaves Who Sided with the British During the American Revolution (Large Print 16pt) l.t. ed. 2013. 122p. pap. (978-1-4596-6716-7(6)) ReadHowYouWant.com, Ltd.

Willen, Janet & Gann, Marjorie. Speak a Word for Freedom: Women Against Slavery. 2015. (Illus.). 216p. (YA). (gr. 7). 21.99 (978-1-77049-651-4(3), Tundra Bks.) Tundra Bks. CAN. Dist: Penguin Random Hse. LLC.

Wilson, Camilla. Frederick Douglass: A Voice for Freedom in the 1800s. 2003. (Scholastic Biography Ser.). (Illus.). 90p. (J). pap. (978-0-439-38082-9(0)) Scholastic, Inc.

Wolny, Philip. The Underground Railroad: A Primary Source History of the Journey to Freedom. 2009. (Primary Sources in American History Ser.). 64p. (gr. 5-8). 58.50 (978-1-60851-505-9(2)) Rosen Publishing Group, Inc., The.

SLAVERY—FICTION

Amnesty International, ed. Free? Stories about Human Rights. 2010. (ENG., Illus.). 224p. (J). (gr. 5-18). pap. 9.99 (978-0-7636-4926-5(0)) Candlewick Pr.

Anderson, Laurie Halse. Ashes. (Seeds of America Trilogy Ser.: Bk. 3). (ENG., Illus.). (J). (gr. 5). 2017. 320p. pap. 8.99 (978-1-4169-6147-5(X)) 2016. 304p. 19.99 (978-1-4169-6146-8(1), Atheneum/Caitlyn Dlouhy Books) Simon & Schuster Children's Publishing.

—Chains. (Seeds of America Trilogy Ser.). (ENG., Illus.). (J). (gr. 5-9). 2010. 336p. pap. 8.99 (978-1-4169-0586-8(3)) 2008. 320p. 19.99 (978-1-4169-0585-1(5)) Simon & Schuster Children's Publishing. (Atheneum Bks. for Young Readers).

—Forge. (Seeds of America Trilogy Ser.). (ENG., Illus.). (J). (gr. 5-9). 2012. 320p. pap. 8.99 (978-1-4169-6145-1(3)) 2010. 304p. 19.99 (978-1-4169-6144-4(5)) Simon & Schuster Children's Publishing. (Atheneum Bks. for Young Readers).

Anderson, M. T. The Astonishing Life of Octavian Nothing, Traitor to the Nation, Volume I: The Pox Party, Vol. 1. 2008. (ENG., Illus.). 384p. (YA). (gr. 9-12). pap. 13.99 (978-0-7636-3679-1(7)) Candlewick Pr.

Anderson, Matthew. The Astonishing Life of Octavian Nothing, Traitor to the Nation, Volume I: The Pox Party. 2009. (Astonishing Life of Octavian Nothing, Traitor to the Nation Ser.: Vol. 1). 11.94 (978-0-7848-1900-5(9), Everbind) Marco Bk. Co.

—The Astonishing Life of Octavian Nothing, Traitor to the Nation, Volume I: The Pox Party. 2011. 22.00 (978-1-60686-925-3(6)) Perfection Learning Corp.

—The Astonishing Life of Octavian Nothing, Traitor to the Nation, Volume I: The Pox Party. l.t. ed. 2020. (ENG.). pap. 15.99 (978-1-4328-7401-8(2)) Thorndike Pr.

—The Astonishing Life of Octavian Nothing, Traitor to the Nation, Volume II: The Kingdom on the Waves. 2009. (ENG., Illus.). 592p. (YA). (gr. 9). pap. 12.99 (978-0-7636-4626-4(1)) Candlewick Pr.

—The Astonishing Life of Octavian Nothing, Traitor to the Nation, Volume II: The Kingdom on the Waves. 2011. 24.00 (978-1-60686-926-0(4)) Perfection Learning Corp.

Appelt, Kathi. Angel Thieves. (ENG.). 336p. (YA). (gr. 9). 2020. pap. 11.99 (978-1-4423-3966-8(7), Atheneum Bks. for Young Readers) 2019. 18.99 (978-1-4424-2109-7(6), Atheneum/Caitlyn Dlouhy Books) Simon & Schuster Children's Publishing.

Armand, Glenda. Love Twelve Miles Long, 1 vol. Bootman, Colin, illus. (ENG.). 32p. (J). 2015. (gr. 1-6). pap. 11.95 (978-1-62014-254-7(6), leelowbooks) 2013. 17.95 (978-1-60060-245-0(2)) Lee & Low Bks., Inc.

Avi. Something Upstairs. 2010. (ENG.). 144p. (J). (gr. 4-7). 9.99 (978-0-545-21491-9(2), Scholastic Pr.) Scholastic, Inc.

—Something Upstairs. 2010. lib. bdg. 16.00 (978-0-606-14682-1(2)) Turtleback.

Bachorz, Pam. Drought. 2011. (ENG.). 400p. (YA). (gr. 7-12). 17.99 (978-1-60684-016-0(9), 287c1b93-a51d-4c11-892e-c61df04d0ed9, Carolrhoda Lab™) Lerner Publishing Group.

Ballard, Allen. Where Im Bound. 2006. pap. 18.95 (978-0-595-39856-0(1), Backinprint.com) iUniverse, Inc.

Bannen, Megan. The Bird & the Blade. (ENG.). 432p. (YA). (gr. 8). 2019. pap. 9.99 (978-0-06-267416-6(1)) 2018. (Illus.). 17.99 (978-0-06-267415-9(3)) HarperCollins Pubs. (Balzer & Bray).

Barbieri, Kara. White Stag: A Permafrost Novel. 2019. (ENG.). 368p. (YA). pap. (978-1-250-22619-8(8), Wednesday Bks.) St. Martin's Pr.

Bauer Mueller, Pamela. Neptune's Honor: A Story of Loyalty & Love. 2005. (ENG., Illus.). 195p. (YA). (gr. 6). pap. 11.99 (978-0-9685097-5-3(4)) Pinata Publishing CAN. Dist: Independent Pubs. Group.

Booth, Bradley. Plagues in the Palace. 2006. 159p. (J). 10.99 (978-0-8163-2143-8(4)) Pacific Pr. Publishing Assn.

Boston Weatherford, Carole. Freedom in Congo Square. Christie, R. Gregory, illus. 2016. (ENG.). 40p. (J). (gr. -1-3). 17.99 (978-1-4998-0103-3(3)) Little Bee Books Inc.

Bradbury, Jennifer. River Runs Deep. 2015. (ENG., Illus.). 336p. (J). (gr. 4-8). 17.99 (978-1-4424-6824-5(6), Atheneum Bks. for Young Readers) Simon & Schuster Children's Publishing.

Brill, Marlene Targ. Allen Jay & the Undergound Railroad, 4 bks., Set. Porter, Janice Lee, illus. 2007. (Readalongs for Beginning Readers Ser.). (J). (gr. 1-3). pap. 37.95 incl. audio (978-1-59519-947-8(0)) Live Oak Media.

—The Underground Railroad Adventure of Allen Jay, Antislavery Activist. Hammond, Ted & Carbajal, Richard Pimentel, illus. 2011. (History's Kid Heroes Set III Ser.). pap. 51.02 (978-0-7613-8622-3(X), Graphic Universe™) Lerner Publishing Group.

Brook, Harry, retold by. Kidnapped. 2004. (Paperback Classics Ser.). 144p. (J). lib. bdg. 12.95 (978-1-58086-640-8(9), Usborne) EDC Publishing.

Brown, Marc. D. W. the Big Boss. 2005. (ENG., Illus.). 24p. (J). (gr. -1-1). per. 3.99 (978-0-316-73395-3(4)) Little, Brown Bks. for Young Readers.

Broyles, Anne. Priscilla & the Hollyhocks. Alter, Anna, illus. 2019. 32p. (J). (gr. 1-4). pap. 7.99 (978-1-57091-676-2(4)) Charlesbridge Publishing, Inc.

Bryan, Ashley. Freedom over Me: Eleven Slaves, Their Lives & Dreams Brought to Life by Ashley Bryan. Bryan, Ashley, illus. 2016. (ENG., Illus.). 56p. (J). (gr. 4-6). 17.99 (978-1-4814-5690-6(3), Atheneum/Caitlyn Dlouhy Books) Simon & Schuster Children's Publishing.

Bugtime Adventures - Blessing in Disguise. 2005. (J). 3.95 (978-1-933262-26-0(5)) Santa Fe Communications, Inc.

Burg, Ann & Burg, Ann E. Unbound. 2018. (ENG.). 352p. (J). (gr. 3-7). pap. 8.99 (978-1-338-28208-5(5), Scholastic Pr.) Scholastic, Inc.

C. Larene Hall. Martha's Freedom Train. 2009. 100p. pap. 10.49 (978-1-4389-7977-9(0)) AuthorHouse.

Carbone, Elisa. Stealing Freedom. 2003. (EMC Masterpiece Series Access Editions). (Illus.). xix, 284p. (J). 12.99 (978-0-8219-2507-2(5)) EMC/Paradigm Publishing.

Carter, Noni. Good Fortune. 2011. (ENG.). 496p. (YA). (gr. 7). pap. 12.99 (978-1-4169-8481-8(X), Simon & Schuster Bks. For Young Readers) Simon & Schuster Bks. For Young Readers.

—Good Fortune. 2010. (ENG.). 496p. (YA). (gr. 7-6). 16.99 (978-1-4169-8480-1(1)) Simon & Schuster, Inc.

Chimombo, S. The Bird Boy's Song. 2004. 96p. pap. (978-99908-48-07-6(6)) Wasi Pubns. ZWE. Dist: Michigan State Univ. Pr.

Chiu, Harry. Enve Lopt Unfolded. 2007. 268p. per. 17.95 (978-0-595-44707-7(4)) iUniverse, Inc.

Cline-Ransome, Lesa. Light in the Darkness: A Story about How Slaves Learned in Secret. Ransome, James E., illus. 2013. (ENG.). 40p. (J). (gr. -1-3). 18.99 (978-1-4231-3495-4(8)) Little, Brown Bks. for Young Readers.

Cohen, Deborah Bodin. Nachshon, Who Was Afraid to Swim: A Passover Story. Silver, Jago, illus. 2008. (Passover Ser.). (ENG.). 32p. (J). (gr. -1-3). 17.95 (978-0-8225-8764-4(5), Kar-Ben Publishing) Lerner Publishing Group.

Cooper, Floyd. Juneteenth for Mazie. Cooper, Floyd, illus. 2015. (ENG., Illus.). 40p. (J). (gr. 1-4). lib. bdg. 25.32 (978-1-4795-5819-3(2), 126912, Picture Window Bks.) Capstone.

Cuate, Melodie A. Journey to Galveston. 2014. (Mr. Barrington's Mysterious Trunk Ser.). (ENG., Illus.). 192p. (J). 18.95 (978-0-89672-852-3(8)) Texas Tech Univ. Pr.

Curry, Kenneth. The Legend of the Dancing Trees: An African American Folk Tale. 2007. 111p. (J). per. 14.95 (978-0-9798364-0-4(9)) Curry Brothers Publishing Group.

Curry, Kenneth, et al. The Legend of the Dancing Tees Teachers Resource: The Legend of the Dancing Trees. 2007.Tr. of Teachers Resource. per. 19.95 (978-0-9798364-1-1(7)) Curry Brothers Publishing Group.

Curtis, Christopher Paul. Elijah of Buxton (Scholastic Gold), 1 vol. (ENG.). (J). (gr. 4-7). 2009. 368p. pap. 7.99 (978-0-439-02345-0(9), Scholastic Paperbacks) 2007. 352p. 19.99 (978-0-439-02344-3(0), Scholastic Pr.) Scholastic, Inc.

—The Journey of Little Charlie. 2018. (ENG.). 256p. (J). (gr. 4-7). 19.99 (978-0-545-15666-0(1), Scholastic Pr.) Scholastic, Inc.

Curtis, Christopher Paul & Vega, Eida de la. El Viaje de Charlie. 2019. (SPA.). (J). 12.99 (978-1-63245-697-7(4)) Lectorum Pubns., Inc.

Dauphin, Lili. I Will Fly Again: The Restavek. 2007. 284p. 29.95 (978-0-9748329-9-9(5)); per. 18.95 (978-0-9748329-8-2(7)) MiraQuest.

Downey, Glen. Gladiators. 2007. (Illus.). 48p. (J). lib. bdg. 23.08 (978-1-4242-1627-7(3)) Fitzgerald Bks.

Draper, Sharon M. Copper Sun. 2014. (ENG.). 336p. (YA). 14.24 (978-1-63245-110-1(7)) Lectorum Pubns., Inc.

—Copper Sun. 2011. 11.04 (978-0-7848-3373-5(7), Everbind) Marco Bk. Co.

—Copper Sun. (ENG.). (YA). 2008. 336p. (gr. 9-12). pap. 12.99 (978-1-4169-5348-7(5)) 2006. 320p. (gr. 8-18). 19.99 (978-0-689-82181-3(6)) Simon & Schuster Children's Publishing. (Atheneum Bks. for Young Readers).

—Copper Sun. l.t. ed. 2006. 358p. (YA). (gr. 8-18). 22.95 (978-0-7862-8948-6(1)) Thorndike Pr.

—Copper Sun. 2008. 316p. lib. bdg. 22.10 (978-1-4177-9702-8(9)) Turtleback.

Dublin, Anne. A Cage Without Bars, 1 vol. 2018. (ENG.). 154p. (J). (gr. 5-8). pap. 11.95 (978-1-77260-069-8(5)) Second Story Pr. CAN. Dist: Orca Bk. Pubs. USA.

Durango, Julia. The Walls of Cartagena. Pohrt, Tom, illus. 2008. (ENG.). 160p. (J). (gr. 3-7). 19.99 (978-1-4169-4102-6(9), Simon & Schuster Bks. For Young Readers) Simon & Schuster Bks. For Young Readers.

Dyer, Mary E. Secret Whispers. 2008. 99p. pap. 19.95 (978-1-60610-261-9(3)) America Star Bks.

Elliott, L. M. Annie, Between the States. 2006. (ENG.). 544p. (YA). (gr. 8-12). per. 10.99 (978-0-06-001213-7(7), Tegen, Katherine Bks) 2004. (Illus.). 496p. (J). (gr. 7-18). 16.99 (978-0-06-001211-3(0)) HarperCollins Pubs.

Engle, Margarita. Lion Island: Cuba's Warrior of Words. (ENG.). (J). (gr. 5). 2017. 192p. pap. 7.99 (978-1-4814-6113-9(3)) 2016. (Illus.). 176p. 16.99 (978-1-4814-6112-2(5), Atheneum Bks. for Young Readers) Simon & Schuster Children's Publishing.

Esenwa, Anthony. Jaja, King of Opobo. 2009. (Illus.). 24p. pap. 11.49 (978-1-4389-5886-6(2)) AuthorHouse.

Evans, Freddi Williams. Hush Harbor: Praying in Secret. Banks, Erin, illus. 2008. (ENG.). 32p. (J). (gr. k-3). 16.95 (978-0-8225-7965-6(0), Carolrhoda Bks.) Lerner Publishing Group.

Ewing, Amy. The Black Key. 2017. (Lone City Trilogy Ser.: 3). (ENG.). 304p. (YA). (gr. 9). pap. 10.99 (978-0-06-223585-5(0), HarperTeen) 2016. (Lone City Trilogy Ser.: 3). (ENG.). 304p. (YA). (gr. 9). 17.99 (978-0-06-223584-8(2), HarperTeen) 2016. 295p. (J). (978-0-06-256581-5(8)) HarperCollins Pubs.

—The Jewel. (Lone City Trilogy Ser.: 1). (ENG.). (YA). (gr. 9). 2015. 400p. pap. 10.99 (978-0-06-223578-7(8)) 2014. 368p. 17.99 (978-0-06-223579-4(6)) HarperCollins Pubs. (HarperTeen).

—The White Rose. 2016. (Lone City Trilogy Ser.: 2). (ENG.). 336p. (YA). (gr. 9). pap. 10.99 (978-0-06-223582-4(6), HarperTeen) 2015. (Lone City Trilogy Ser.: 2). (ENG.). 320p. (YA). (gr. 9). 17.99 (978-0-06-223581-7(8), HarperTeen) 2015. 320p. pap. 17.99 (978-0-06-241475-5(5)) HarperCollins Pubs.

Finotti, M. C. The Treasure of Amelia Island. (Florida Historical Fiction for Youth Ser.). (Illus.). (J). (gr. -1-12). 2012. 104p. pap. 8.95 (978-1-56164-536-7(2)) 2008. (ENG., 97p. 14.95 (978-1-56164-416-2(1)) Pineapple Pr., Inc.

Fleischman, Sid. The Whipping Boy: A Newbery Award Winner. Sis, Peter, illus. 2003. (ENG.). 96p. (J). (gr. 3-8). pap. 8.99 (978-0-06-052122-6(8), Greenwillow Bks.) HarperCollins Pubs.

Fleischner, Jennifer. Nobody's Boy. 2006. (ENG., Illus.). 112p. (gr. 4). per. 12.95 *(978-1-883982-58-4(8))* Missouri Historical Society Pr.

Fox, Paula. The Slave Dancer. unabr. ed. 2004. 152p. (J). (gr. 5-9). pap. 38.00 incl. audio *(978-0-8072-0458-0(7)*, Listening Library) Random Hse. Audio Publishing Group.

Frank, Pat. Little Warriors. 2008. 88p. pap. 8.95 *(978-1-60594-158-5(1)*, Llumina Pr.) Aeon Publishing Inc.

Fraser, Kayo. Listen to Your Spirit: A Novel. 2019. (ENG., Illus.). 180p. (J). pap. *(978-1-937849-53-5(8))* Raven Publishing Inc. of Montana.

Friesner, Esther. Spirit's Chosen. 2014. (Princesses of Myth Ser.). (ENG., Illus.). 512p. (YA). (gr. 7). pap. 10.99 *(978-0-375-87316-4(3)*, Ember) Random Hse. Children's Bks.

Gaillard, Frye. Go South to Freedom. Rush, Anne Kent, illus. 2016. (ENG.). 72p. (J). 17.95 *(978-1-58838-316-7(4)*, 8799, NewSouth Bks.) NewSouth, Inc.

Gaines, Ernest J. The Autobiography of Miss Jane Pittman: And Related Readings. 2006. (McDougal Littell Literature Connections Ser.). (ENG.). 384p. (gr. 6-8). 16.90 *(978-0-395-86993-2(5)*, 2-70829) Great Source Education Group, Inc.

Gary, Paulsen. Nightjohn. 2014. (ENG.). 112p. (YA). 11.24 *(978-1-63245-096-8(8))* Lectorum Pubns., Inc.

Gaughen, A. C. Imprison the Sky. (Elementae Ser.). (ENG.). 432p. (YA). 2020. pap. 10.99 *(978-1-68119-116-4(4)*, 900159233) 2019. (Illus.). 18.99 *(978-1-68119-114-0(8)*, 900159230) Bloomsbury Publishing USA. (Bloomsbury Young Adult).

Gayle, Sharon Shavers. Emma's Escape: A Story of America's Underground Railroad. Velasquez, Eric, illus. 3rd ed. 2003. (Soundprints' Read-and-Discover Ser.). (ENG.). 48p. (J). (gr. -1-3). pap. 3.95 *(978-1-59249-021-9(2)*, S2009) Soundprints.

Gee, Maurice. Gool, 1 vol. 2012. (Salt Trilogy Ser.: 2). (ENG.). 240p. (YA). (gr. 8-12). pap. 12.95 *(978-1-4598-0196-7(2))* Orca Bk. Pubs. USA.

—Salt, 1 vol., 1. 2011. (Salt Trilogy Ser.: 1). (ENG., Illus.). 272p. (YA). (gr. 8-12). 12.95 *(978-1-55469-369-6(1))* Orca Bk. Pubs. USA.

Gibney, Shannon. Dream Country. 2019. (ENG., Illus.). 368p. (YA). (gr. 9). pap. 10.99 *(978-0-7352-3168-9(0)*, Penguin Books) Penguin Young Readers Group.

Gilfert, Shirley Tankersley. The Other Side of Jordan: A Story of the Underground Railroad. 2007. 140p. 21.95 *(978-0-595-70289-3(9))*; per. 11.95 *(978-0-595-46274-2(X))* iUniverse, Inc.

Golding, Julia. Cat among the Pigeons, 2. 2006. (Cat Royal Adventure Ser.: 2). (ENG.). 400p. (J). (gr. 6-8). 22.44 *(978-0-312-60215-4(4)*, 900064230) Square Fish.

Gordon, Bonnie J. Escape from Goshen. 2012. (ENG.). (J). pap. 10.00 *(978-1-4675-1915-1(4))* Independent Pub.

Grimes, Nikki. Chasing Freedom: the Life Journeys of Harriet Tubman & Susan B. Anthony, Inspired by Historical Facts. Wood, Michele, illus. 2015. (ENG.). 56p. (J). (gr. 1-5). 21.99 *(978-0-439-79338-4(6)*, Orchard Bks.) Scholastic, Inc.

Guzman, Lila & Guzman, Rick. Lorenzo's Secret Mission. 2005. 153p. (gr. 4-7). 19.95 *(978-0-7569-5599-1(8))* Perfection Learning Corp.

Hahn, Mary Downing. Promises to the Dead. 2009. (ENG.). 208p. (J). (gr. 5-7). pap. 7.99 *(978-0-547-25838-6(0)*, 1402071, Clarion Bks.) HarperCollins Pubs.

Haislip, Phyllis Hall. Between the Lines: A Revolutionary War Slave's Journey to Freedom. 2012. (ENG., Illus.). 190p. (J). pap. 8.95 *(978-1-57249-409-1(3)*, White Mane Kids) White Mane Publishing Co., Inc.

—Lottie's Courage: A Contraband Slave's Story. 2003. (Illus.). 120p. (J). pap. 7.95 *(978-1-57249-311-7(9)*, White Mane Kids) White Mane Publishing Co., Inc.

Halse Anderson, Laurie. Ashes. l.t. ed. 2017. (Seeds of America Ser.: 3). (ENG.). 410p. 22.99 *(978-1-4104-9607-2(4))* Cengage Gale.

—Chains. l.t. ed. 2017. (Seeds of America Ser.). (ENG.). 442p. 22.99 *(978-1-4104-9917-2(0))* Cengage Gale.

—Chains. 2014. (Seeds of America Trilogy). (ENG.). 336p. (J). 12.24 *(978-1-63245-094-4(1))* Lectorum Pubns., Inc.

—Chains. 2009. 9.00 *(978-0-7848-3678-1(7)*, Everbind) Marco Bk. Co.

—Chains. l.t. ed. 2009. (ENG.). 390p. (YA). 23.95 *(978-1-4104-1425-0(6))* Thorndike Pr.

—Chains. 2010. (Seeds of America Trilogy Ser.: 1). lib. bdg. 19.65 *(978-0-606-14520-6(6))* Turtleback.

—Forge. l.t. ed. 2017. (Seeds of America Ser.). (ENG.). 418p. 22.99 *(978-1-4104-9918-9(9))* Cengage Gale.

—Forge. 2012. 18.00 *(978-1-61383-316-2(4))* Perfection Learning Corp.

—Forge. 2012. (Seeds of America Trilogy Ser.: 2). lib. bdg. 18.40 *(978-0-606-23680-5(5))* Turtleback.

Hamilton, Virginia. The People Could Fly: the Picture Book. Dillon, Leo & Dillon, Diane, illus. movie tie-in ed. 2004. 32p. (J). (gr. -1-3). 18.99 *(978-0-375-82405-0(7)*, Knopf Bks. for Young Readers) Random Hse. Children's Bks.

Hannah-Jones, Nikole & Watson, Renée. The 1619 Project: Born on the Water. Smith, Nikkolas, illus. 2021. 48p. (J). (gr. 2-5). 18.99 *(978-0-593-30735-9(6)*, Kokila) Penguin Young Readers Group.

Hart, Alison. Horse Diaries #2: Bell's Star. Sanderson, Ruth, illus. 2009. (Horse Diaries: 2). 144p. (J). (gr. 3-7). pap. 7.99 *(978-0-375-85204-6(2)*, Random Hse. Bks. for Young Readers) Random Hse. Children's Bks.

Hawke, Rosanne. Spirit of a Mountain Wolf, 1 vol. 2014. (Scarlet Voyage Ser.). (ENG., Illus.). 216p. (YA). (gr. 9-10). pap. 13.88 *(978-1-62324-034-9(4)*, 751f42df-3bc6-4b75-8ba8-9edc9b34e0b9) Enslow Publishing, LLC.

Haynes, Betsy. Cowslip. 2008. (J). (gr. 4-7). 22.50 *(978-0-8446-6244-2(5))* Smith, Peter Pub., Inc.

Helgerson, Joseph. Crows & Cards. 2010. (ENG.). 352p. (J). (gr. 3-7). pap. 19.99 *(978-0-547-33909-2(7)*, 1418456, Clarion Bks.) HarperCollins Pubs.

Helget, Nicole. Wonder at the Edge of the World. 2015. (ENG., Illus.). 384p. (J). (gr. 3-7). 17.00 *(978-0-316-24510-4(0))* Little, Brown Bks. for Young Readers.

Helwani, Najiyah Diana. Sophia's Journal: Time Warp 1857. 2008. (YA). per. *(978-0-9793577-2-5(1))* Muslim Writers Publishing.

Herwick Rice, Dona & Isecke, Harriet. The Sojourner Truth Story, 1 vol. rev. ed. 2009. (Reader's Theater Ser.). (ENG.). 32p. (gr. 3-8). pap. 11.99 *(978-1-4333-0544-3(5))* Teacher Created Materials, Inc.

Hicks, Clifford B. Alvin Fernald's Incredible Buried Treasure. Bradfield, Roger, illus. 2009. (J). 17.95 *(978-1-930900-43-1(0))* Purple Hse. Pr.

Higgins, Joanna. Waiting for the Queen: A Novel of Early America. 2013. (ENG.). 256p. (J). (gr. 4-10). 16.95 *(978-1-57131-700-1(7))* Milkweed Editions.

Hopkinson, Deborah. From Slave to Soldier: Based on a True Civil War Story (Ready-To-Read Level 3) Floca, Brian, illus. (Ready-To-Read Ser.). (ENG.). 48p. (J). (gr. 1-3). 2007. pap. 4.99 *(978-0-689-83966-5(9))* 2005. 16.99 *(978-0-689-83965-8(0))* Simon Spotlight. (Simon Spotlight).

—Our Kansas Home. Faricy, Patrick, illus. 2003. (Prairie Skies Ser.). 69p. (J). 11.65 *(978-0-7569-3448-4(6))* Perfection Learning Corp.

—Sweet Clara & the Freedom Quilt. Ransome, James, illus. 25th ed. 2018. 40p. (J). (gr. -1-2). 16.99 *(978-0-679-82311-7(5)*, Knopf Bks. for Young Readers) Random Hse. Children's Bks.

—Under the Quilt of Night. Ransome, James E., illus. 2005. (gr. k-5). 18.00 *(978-0-7569-5077-4(5))* Perfection Learning Corp.

Hubbs, M. E. The Secret of Wattensaw Bayou. Lyndon, Tracy S., illus. 2013. 170p. pap. 12.95 *(978-1-934610-76-3(3))* Bluewater Pubns.

Hulme, Lucy V. Passages, 1 bk. Redpath, Dale, illus. 2005. 40p. (J). 7.95 *(978-0-9769854-0-2(3)*, 001) Combs-Hulme Publishing.

Hurmence, Belinda. A Girl Called Boy. 2006. (ENG.). 176p. (J). (gr. 5-7). pap. 12.95 *(978-0-618-68925-5(7)*, 100474, Clarion Bks.) HarperCollins Pubs.

Hush: An Irish Princess' Tale. 2014. (ENG., Illus.). 336p. (YA). (gr. 7). pap. 11.99 *(978-1-4424-9496-1(4)*, Simon & Schuster/Paula Wiseman Bks.) Simon & Schuster/Paula Wiseman Bks.

Jacques, Brian. Voyage of Slaves. 2007. (Castaways of the Flying Dutchman Ser.: 3). (ENG.). 320p. (gr. 12-18). 7.99 *(978-0-441-01528-3(X)*, Ace) Penguin Publishing Group.

Jameson, Bernadette. The Boy Who Played His Way to Freedom. 2012. 80p. pap. 12.95 *(978-1-4710-6968-0(0))* Lulu Pr., Inc.

Johnson, Lois Walfrid. The Raider's Promise. 2006. (Viking Quest Ser.: 5). (ENG., Illus.). 304p. (J). (gr. 3-3). per. 10.99 *(978-0-8024-3116-5(X))* Moody Pubs.

Jones, Joyce Elaine. For Such a Journey. 2005. (J). 5.99 *(978-0-9766559-0-9(X))* Treorca Pr.

Jones, Vernon. Aesop's Fables. Rackham, Arthur, illus. 2007. 160p. (J). pap. 5.00 *(978-0-9788914-4-2(9))* Kahley, Glenn.

Kendall, Jane. Horse Diaries #9: Tennessee Rose. Sheckels, Astrid, illus. 2012. (Horse Diaries: 9). (ENG.). 160p. (J). (gr. 3-7). pap. 7.99 *(978-0-375-87006-4(7)*, Random Hse. Bks. for Young Readers) Random Hse. Children's Bks.

Kenney, Rebecca. Where I Belong. 2008. (J). 8.99 *(978-1-59166-873-2(5))* BJU Pr.

Kirkpatrick, Katherine. Escape Across the Wide Sea. 2004. (ENG., Illus.). 224p. (J). (gr. 4-6). tchr. ed. 17.95 *(978-0-8234-1854-1(5))* Holiday Hse., Inc.

Kliever, S. I. A Slave's Quest. 2011. 284p. pap. *(978-1-77069-178-0(2))* Word Alive Pr.

Lawrence, Caroline. The Dolphins of Laurentum. 2005. (Roman Mysteries Ser.). (Illus.). 161p. (J). (gr. 6-9). 13.65 *(978-0-7569-6538-9(1))* Perfection Learning Corp.

—The Pirates of Pompeii. 2004. (Roman Mysteries Ser.). (Illus.). 159p. (J). (gr. 3-7). 13.65 *(978-0-7569-5938-8(1))* Perfection Learning Corp.

Lee, Stacey. Under a Painted Sky. 2016. lib. bdg. 22.10 *(978-0-606-38391-2(3))* Turtleback.

Leslie, Emma. From Bondage to Freedom: A Tale of the Times of Mohammed. Symmons, Sheeres, illus. 2007. 308p. 24.95 *(978-1-934671-10-8(X))* Salem Ridge Press LLC.

—Glaucia the Greek Slave: A Tale of Athens in the First Century. Felter & Butterworth & Heath, illus. 2007. 308p. per. 14.95 *(978-1-934671-01-6(0))* Salem Ridge Press LLC.

—Gytha's Message: A Tale of Saxon England. Staniland, C., illus. 2007. 256p. 22.95 *(978-1-934671-11-5(8))* Salem Ridge Press LLC.

LeSourd, Nancy. Escape on the Underground Railroad, 1 vol. 2008. (Liberty Letters Ser.). (ENG.). 224p. (J). pap. 7.99 *(978-0-310-71391-3(9))* Zonderkidz.

—Secrets of Civil War Spies, 1 vol. 2008. (Liberty Letters Ser.). (ENG.). 224p. (J). pap. 7.99 *(978-0-310-71390-6(0))* Zonderkidz.

Lester, Julius. Day of Tears (Coretta Scott King Author Honor Title) 2007. (ENG., Illus.). 192p. (J). (gr. 5-9). pap. 9.99 *(978-1-4231-0409-4(9))* Little, Brown Bks. for Young Readers.

Letters from a Slave Girl. 2011. 8.32 *(978-0-7848-3635-4(3)*, Everbind) Marco Bk. Co.

Levine, Ellen. Henry's Freedom Box, 1 vol. Nelson, Kadir, illus. 2007. (ENG.). 40p. (J). (gr. -1-3). 18.99 *(978-0-439-77733-9(X)*, Scholastic Pr.) Scholastic, Inc.

—Henry's Freedom Box: A True Story from the Underground Railroad. Nelson, Kadir, illus. 2011. (J). (gr. 2-5). 29.95 *(978-0-545-13455-2(2))* Weston Woods Studios, Inc.

Luqman-Dawson, Amina. Freewater (Newbery & Coretta Scott King Award Winner) (ENG.). 416p. (J). (gr. 5-17). 2023. pap. 8.99 ***(978-0-316-05667-0(7))*** 2022. 16.99 *(978-0-316-05661-8(8))* Little Brown & Co. (Jimmy Patterson).

Lyons, Kelly Starling. Ellen's Broom. Minter, Daniel, illus. 2012. (ENG.). 32p. (J). (gr. k-3). 17.99 *(978-0-399-25003-3(4)*, G.P. Putnam's Sons Books for Young Readers) Penguin Young Readers Group.

—Hope's Gift. Tate, Don, illus. 2012. 32p. (J). (gr. 1-3). 17.99 *(978-0-399-16001-1(9)*, G.P. Putnam's Sons Books for Young Readers) Penguin Young Readers Group.

Lyons, Mary E. Letters from a Slave Boy: The Story of Joseph Jacobs. 2009. (ENG.). 208p. (YA). (gr. 7). mass mkt. 7.99 *(978-0-689-87868-8(0)*, Simon Pulse) Simon Pulse.

—Letters from a Slave Girl: The Story of Harriet Jacobs. 2008. (Illus.). 175p. (gr. 7-12). 16.00 *(978-0-7569-8474-8(2))* Perfection Learning Corp.

—Letters from a Slave Girl: The Story of Harriet Jacobs. 2007. (ENG., Illus.). 192p. (YA). (gr. 7). mass mkt. 7.99 *(978-1-4169-3637-4(8)*, Simon Pulse) Simon Pulse.

—The Poison Place. 2007. (ENG.). 160p. (YA). (gr. 7). pap. 9.99 *(978-1-4169-6842-9(3)*, Simon & Schuster/Paula Wiseman Bks.) Simon & Schuster/Paula Wiseman Bks.

Maccoll, Michaela & Nichols, Rosemary. Freedom's Price. 2015. (Hidden Histories Ser.). (ENG., Illus.). 288p. (J). (gr. 4-7). 17.95 *(978-1-62091-624-7(X)*, Calkins Creek) Highlights Pr., c/o Highlights for Children, Inc.

MacHado, Ana Maria. Del Otro Lado Hay Secretos. (SPA.). pap. 11.95 *(978-950-07-2221-6(6))* Editorial Sudamericana S.A. ARG. Dist: Distribooks, Inc.

Machado, Ana Maria. Until the Day Arrives, 1 vol. Springer, Jane, tr. from POR. 2014. (ENG.). 152p. (J). (gr. 5-8). 16.95 *(978-1-55498-455-8(6))* Groundwood Bks. CAN. Dist: Publishers Group West (PGW).

Malaspina, Ann. The People Could Fly: An African-American Folktale. Otero, Sole, illus. 2013. (Folktales from Around the World Ser.). (ENG.). 24p. (J). (gr. k-3). 32.79 *(978-1-62323-617-5(7)*, 206385) Child's World, Inc, The.

Marlow, Susan K. Andrea Carter & the San Francisco Smugglers, 1 vol. 2019. (Circle C Adventures Ser.: 4). 144p. pap. 8.99 *(978-0-8254-4503-3(5))* Kregel Pubns.

Marrone, Amanda. Only the Stars Know Her Name: Salem's Lost Story of Tituba's Daughter. 2019. (ENG.). 304p. (J). (gr. 4-9). 16.99 *(978-1-4998-0890-2(9)*, Yellow Jacket) Bonnier Publishing USA.

Marshall, G. Skies of Dawn. 2007. 160p. per. 12.95 *(978-0-595-42946-2(7))* iUniverse, Inc.

Masters, Susan Rowan. Night Journey to Vicksburg. Killcoyne, Hope L., ed. Smith, Duane A., illus. 2003. (Adventures in America Ser.). 74p. (J). (gr. 4). 14.95 *(978-1-893110-30-4(3))* Silver Moon Pr.

McCormick, Patricia. Sold. 2011. 10.36 *(978-0-7848-3420-6(2)*, Everbind) Marco Bk. Co.

—Sold. 2008. 263p. (J). (gr. 7-12). 19.65 *(978-1-4178-1810-5(7))* Turtleback.

—Sold (National Book Award Finalist) 2008. (ENG.). 272p. (J). (gr. 5-9). pap. 11.99 *(978-0-7868-5172-0(4))* Little, Brown Bks. for Young Readers.

McDougal-Littell Publishing Staff. Literature Connections English: I, Juan de Pareja. 2004. (McDougal Littell Literature Connections Ser.). (ENG.). 224p. (gr. 7-7). 16.90 *(978-0-395-77531-8(0)*, 2-80100) Great Source Education Group, Inc.

McKissack, Patricia C. A Picture of Freedom (Dear America) 2011. (Dear America Ser.). (ENG.). 240p. (J). (gr. 3-9). 14.99 *(978-0-545-24253-0(3)*, Scholastic Pr.) Scholastic, Inc.

McMann, Lisa. The Trap Door. 2015. (Infinity Ring Ser.: 3). lib. bdg. 17.20 *(978-0-606-37788-1(3))* Turtleback.

McMullan, Margaret. How I Found the Strong. 2006. (ENG.). 144p. (YA). (gr. 7-12). reprint ed. mass mkt. 6.99 *(978-0-553-49492-1(9)*, Laurel Leaf) Random Hse. Children's Bks.

Meloy, Alice McFeely. As the Crow Flies: Preface to Gettysburg: the Enemy Is Here! 2012. 106p. (J). pap. 8.95 *(978-1-57249-411-4(5)*, White Mane Kids) White Mane Publishing Co., Inc.

Meltzer, Milton. Underground Man. 2006. (ENG.). 288p. (J). (gr. 5-7). pap. 15.99 *(978-0-15-205524-0(X)*, 1196611, Clarion Bks.) HarperCollins Pubs.

Moody Publishing Staff & Lawton, Wendy G. Freedom's Pen: A Story Based on the Life of Freed Slave & Author Phillis Wheatley 2009. (Daughters of the Faith Ser.). (ENG.). 144p. (gr. 3-3). pap. 8.99 *(978-0-8024-7639-5(2))* Moody Pubs.

Morris, J. & J. Little Black Pearl. 2010. 80p. pap. *(978-1-905553-51-8(X))* BookPublishingWorld.

Moses, Shelia P. The Baptism. 2008. (ENG., Illus.). 144p. (J). (gr. 5-9). pap. 7.99 *(978-1-4169-5833-8(9)*, McElderry, Margaret K. Bks.) McElderry, Margaret K. Bks.

Moses, Tammy. The Prophecy. 2006. 288p. per. 19.99 *(978-1-58169-194-8(7))* Genesis Communications, Inc.

Mosley, Walter. 47. 2006. (ENG., Illus.). 272p. (J). (gr. 7-17). reprint ed. per. 11.99 *(978-0-316-01635-3(7))* Little, Brown Bks. for Young Readers.

Moulder, Holly. Eyes of the Calusa. 2007. 111p. (J). pap. 8.95 *(978-0-9790405-0-4(7))* White Pelican Pr.

Mull, Brandon. Champion of the Titan Games, vol. 4. 2020. (Dragonwatch Ser.: 4). (ENG., Illus.). 544p. (J). (gr. 5). 19.99 *(978-1-62972-788-2(1)*, 5240661) Deseret Bk. Co.

—Champion of the Titan Games: A Fablehaven Adventure. 2021. (Dragonwatch Ser.: 4). (ENG., Illus.). 544p. (J). (gr. 3-8). pap. 9.99 *(978-1-4814-8508-1(3)*, Aladdin) Simon & Schuster Children's Publishing.

Murray, Maturin. The Circassian Slave. 2009. 116p. 23.95 *(978-1-60664-664-9(8))*; pap. 9.95 *(978-1-60664-292-4(8))* Rodgers, Alan Bks.

Mussi, Sarah. The Door of No Return. (ENG.). 400p. (YA). (gr. 7). 2009. pap. 10.99 *(978-1-4169-6825-2(3))* 2008. 17.99 *(978-1-4169-1550-8(8))* McElderry, Margaret K. Bks. (McElderry, Margaret K. Bks.).

Myers, Walter Dean. The Glory Field. 2008. (ENG.). 400p. (J). (gr. 7). pap. 9.99 *(978-0-545-05575-8(X)*, Scholastic Paperbacks) Scholastic, Inc.

Napoli, Donna Jo. Hush: An Irish Princess' Tale. 2007. (ENG., Illus.). 340p. (YA). (gr. 7-12). 18.69 *(978-0-689-86176-5(1))* Simon & Schuster, Inc.

Nelson, Marilyn. Pemba's Song. 2008. (ENG.). 112p. (J). (gr. 7-7). 16.99 *(978-0-545-02076-3(X)*, Scholastic Pr.) Scholastic, Inc.

Nelson, Vaunda Micheaux. Almost to Freedom. Bootman, Colin, illus. 2003. (ENG.). 40p. (J). (gr. k-3). 19.99 *(978-1-57505-342-4(X)*, be180074-5c10-415a-9c04-ab11908ca27f, Carolrhoda Bks.) Lerner Publishing Group.

Nibali, Ellen Cook. Secret of St. Nicholas. 2010. 32p. 16.95 *(978-0-9818154-1-1(3))* Fairland Bks.

Nielsen, Jennifer A. Wrath of the Storm (Mark of the Thief, Book 3) 2017. (Mark of the Thief Ser.: 3). (ENG.). 352p. (J). (gr. 4-7). 16.99 *(978-0-545-56207-2(4)*, Scholastic Pr.) Scholastic, Inc.

Nixon, Joan Lowery. Caesar's Story, 1759. 2004. (J). *(978-0-87935-199-1(3))* Colonial Williamsburg Foundation.

—Will's Story, 1771. 2004. (J). *(978-0-87935-226-4(4))* Colonial Williamsburg Foundation.

Noël, Alyson. Shimmer. 2011. pap. *(978-0-545-39923-4(8))* Scholastic, Inc.

—Shimmer. 2011. (Riley Bloom Ser.: 2). (J). lib. bdg. 20.85 *(978-0-606-21683-8(9))* Turtleback.

Nolen, Jerdine. Big Jabe. Nelson, Kadir, illus. 2003. (ENG.). 32p. (J). (gr. k-5). pap. 7.99 *(978-0-06-054061-6(3)*, Amistad) HarperCollins Pubs.

—Big Jabe. Nelson, Kadir, illus. 2004. (gr. 1). 17.00 *(978-0-7569-3184-1(3))* Perfection Learning Corp.

—Calico Girl. 2019. (Penworthy Picks Middle School Ser.). (ENG.). 164p. (J). (gr. 4-5). 20.36 *(978-1-64310-939-8(1))* Penworthy Co., LLC, The.

—Calico Girl. (ENG.). (J). (gr. 3-7). 2018. 208p. pap. 8.99 *(978-1-4814-5982-2(1))* 2017. (Illus.). 192p. 18.99 *(978-1-4814-5981-5(3))* Simon & Schuster/Paula Wiseman Bks. (Simon & Schuster/Paula Wiseman Bks.).

—Calico Girl. 2018. lib. bdg. 18.40 *(978-0-606-40837-0(1))* Turtleback.

—Eliza's Freedom Road: An Underground Railroad Diary. Strickland, Shadra, illus. 2011. (ENG.). 160p. (J). (gr. 3-7). 19.99 *(978-1-4169-5814-7(2)*, Simon & Schuster/Paula Wiseman Bks.) Simon & Schuster/Paula Wiseman Bks.

North, Julian. State of Order. 2017. (ENG.). 344p. (YA). pap. *(978-0-9992658-0-2(6))* Plebeian Media.

Novel Units. The Slave Dancer Novel Units Teacher Guide. 2019. (ENG.). (YA). pap. 12.99 *(978-1-56137-133-4(5)*, Novel Units, Inc.) Classroom Library Co.

O'Callaghan, G. Slave Prince. 2007. 172p. per. *(978-1-84693-031-7(6))* Best Global Publishing Ltd.

O'Maley, Elizabeth. By Freedom's Light. 2009. 188p. (J). 15.95 *(978-0-87195-273-8(4))*; pap. 7.95 *(978-0-87195-274-5(2))* Indiana Historical Society.

Optic, Oliver, pseud. Watch & Wait; or, the Young Fugitives a Story for Young People by Oliver Optic [Pseud]. 2006. 284p. per. 23.99 *(978-1-4255-2683-2(7))* Michigan Publishing.

Oron, Judie. Cry of the Giraffe. 2010. (ENG., Illus.). 208p. (YA). (gr. 9-12). pap. 12.95 *(978-1-55451-271-3(9)*, 9781554512713) Annick Pr., Ltd. CAN. Dist: Publishers Group West (PGW).

Orzechowski, Shawneen. Midnight Journey: Running for Freedom on the Underground Railroad. 2006. 112p. (J). (gr. 3-7). per. 8.95 *(978-1-57249-379-7(8)*, White Mane Kids) White Mane Publishing Co., Inc.

Pace, Lorenzo. Jalani & the Lock, 1 vol. 2015. (African American Quartet Ser.). (ENG.). 48p. (J). (gr. 2-3). 32.93 *(978-1-4777-9277-3(5)*, 4e4751ae-76a9-41ad-b729-747fc4dcea42, Windmill Bks.) Rosen Publishing Group, Inc., The.

Paul, Curtis Christopher. Elías de Buxton. 2008. (SPA.). 368p. (gr. 6-12). pap. 12.99 *(978-84-441-4101-5(1))* Everest Editora ESP. Dist: Lectorum Pubns., Inc.

Paulsen, Gary. The Legend of Bass Reeves. 2008. (ENG., Illus.). 160p. (YA). (gr. 7-9). mass mkt. 7.99 *(978-0-553-49429-7(5)*, Laurel Leaf) Random Hse. Children's Bks.

—Nightjohn: El Esclavo Que Me Enseno a Leer. 2003. (SPA., Illus.). 72p. (YA). (gr. 5-8). *(978-84-8453-003-9(5)*, PT2562) Ediciones del Bronce ESP. Dist: Lectorum Pubns., Inc.

Pearsall, Shelley. Trouble Don't Last. 2003. (ENG.). 256p. (J). (gr. 3-7). reprint ed. 7.99 *(978-0-440-41811-5(9)*, Yearling) Random Hse. Children's Bks.

Peet, Mal. The Penalty. 2016. (ENG.). 272p. (J). (gr. 7). pap. 8.99 *(978-0-7636-8747-2(2))* Candlewick Pr.

Phillips, Dee. Runaway. 2014. (Yesterday's Voices Ser.). (YA). lib. bdg. 19.60 *(978-0-606-35584-1(7))* Turtleback.

Pinkney, Andrea. Sojourner Truth's Step-Stomp Stride. Pinkney, Brian, illus. 2009. (ENG.). 32p. (J). (gr. 1-3). 18.99 *(978-0-7868-0767-3(9)*, Jump at the Sun) Hyperion Bks. for Children.

Platt, Christine. Summer in Savannah. Sordo, Sharon, illus. 2018. (Ana & Andrew Ser.). (ENG.). 32p. (J). (gr. -1-3). lib. bdg. 32.79 *(978-1-5321-3354-1(5)*, 31131, Calico Chapter Bks) Magic Wagon.

Platt, Richard. Roman Diary: The Journal of Iliona, a Young Slave. Parkins, David, illus. 2014. (ENG.). 128p. (J). (gr. 4-7). pap. 7.99 *(978-0-7636-7053-5(7))* Candlewick Pr.

Polacco, Patricia. January's Sparrow. Polacco, Patricia, illus. 2009. (Illus.). 96p. (J). (gr. 3-7). 23.99 *(978-0-399-25077-4(8)*, Philomel Bks.) Penguin Young Readers Group.

Polisar, Barry Louis. Stolen Man: The Story of the Amistad Rebellion. Clark, David, illus. 2007. (ENG.). 32p. (J). (gr. 2-6). per. 7.95 *(978-0-938663-50-8(X)*, a59aafb4-6286-4277-bbda-93dd15fe3126) Rainbow Morning Music Alternatives.

Porter, Janice Lee, illus. Allen Jay & the Underground Railroad, 4 bks., Set. 2006. (Readalongs for Beginning Readers Ser.). (J). (gr. 2-5). pap. 39.95 incl. audio compact disk *(978-1-59519-951-5(9))* Live Oak Media.

Raasch, Sara. Frost Like Night. (Snow Like Ashes Ser.: 3). (ENG.). (YA). (gr. 9). 2017. 512p. pap. 10.99 *(978-0-06-228699-4(4))* 2016. (Illus.). 496p. 17.99 *(978-0-06-228698-7(6))* HarperCollins Pubs. (Balzer & Bray).

—Ice Like Fire. (Illus.). (YA). 2016. (Snow Like Ashes Ser.: 2). (ENG.). 512p. (gr. 9). pap. 9.99 *(978-0-06-228696-3(X)*, Balzer & Bray) 2015. (Snow Like Ashes Ser.: 2). (ENG., 496p. (gr. 9-12). 17.99 *(978-0-06-228695-6(1)*, Balzer & Bray) 2015. 496p. pap. *(978-0-06-242793-9(8))* HarperCollins Pubs.

—Snow Like Ashes. (Snow Like Ashes Ser.: 1). (ENG., Illus.). (YA). (gr. 9). 2015. 448p. pap. 15.99 *(978-0-06-228693-2(5))* 2014. 432p. 17.99 *(978-0-06-228692-5(7))* HarperCollins Pubs. (Balzer & Bray).

Ransome, James E. The Bell Rang. Ransome, James E., illus. 2019. (ENG., Illus.). 40p. (J). (gr. -1-3). 17.99 *(978-1-4424-2113-4(4)*, Atheneum/Caitlyn Dlouhy Books) Simon & Schuster Children's Publishing.

Raven, Margot Theis. Night Boat to Freedom. Lewis, E. B., illus. 2008. (ENG.). 40p. (J). (gr. 1-4). pap. 10.99 *(978-0-312-55018-9(9)*, 900055951) Square Fish.

Reed, Jennifer. Hadi's Journey. 2003. 110p. pap. 10.95 *(978-0-595-29375-9(1))* iUniverse, Inc.

Reed, Stephanie. The Light Across the River, 1 vol. 2008. (Illus.). 216p. (J). (gr. 4-7). pap. 10.99 *(978-0-8254-3574-4(9))* Kregel Pubns.

Rees, Celia. Pirates! The True & Remarkable Adventures of Minerva Sharpe & Nancy Kington, Female Pirates. 2005.

(Illus.). 379p. (YA). (gr. 9-12). 16.60 *(978-0-7569-6304-0(4))* Perfection Learning Corp.

Riley, Lehman, et al. The Adventures of Papa Lemon's Little Wanderers Bk. 2: The Dangerous Escape from Slavery. 2005. 52p. pap. 5.99 *(978-0-9760523-1-9(8))* Matter of Africa America Time.

Rinaldi, Ann. Come Juneteenth. 2007. (Great Episodes Ser.). (ENG., Illus.). 256p. (J). (gr. 6-8). 21.19 *(978-0-15-205947-7(4))* Harcourt Children's Bks.

—Come Juneteenth. 2009. (Great Episodes Ser.). (ENG., Illus.). 256p. (YA). (gr. 7). pap. 7.99 *(978-0-15-206392-4(7),* 1099019, Clarion Bks.) HarperCollins Pubs.

—Hang a Thousand Trees with Ribbons: The Story of Phillis Wheatley. 2005. (Great Episodes Ser.). 336p. (gr. 5-9). 18.00 *(978-0-7569-5018-7(X))* Perfection Learning Corp.

—The Letter Writer. 2008. (Great Episodes Ser.). (ENG., Illus.). 224p. (YA). (gr. 7-12). 22.44 *(978-0-15-206402-0(8))* Harcourt Children's Bks.

—Taking Liberty: The Story of Oney Judge, George Washington's Runaway Slave. 2004. (ENG., Illus.). 272p. (YA). (gr. 7). mass mkt. 8.99 *(978-0-689-85188-9(X),* Simon Pulse) Simon Pulse.

—An Unlikely Friendship: A Novel of Mary Todd Lincoln & Elizabeth Keckley. 2008. (Great Episodes Ser.). (ENG., Illus.). 256p. (J). (gr. 5-7). pap. 7.99 *(978-0-15-206398-6(6),* 1199153, Clarion Bks.) HarperCollins Pubs.

Robbins, Dean. Two Friends: Susan B. Anthony & Frederick Douglass. Qualls, Sean & Alko, Selina, illus. 2016. (ENG.). 32p. (J). (gr. -1-3). 17.99 *(978-0-545-39996-8(3),* Orchard Bks.) Scholastic, Inc.

Roop, Peter. Lead Us to Freedom, Harriet Tubman! 2006. (Illus.). 58p. (J). pap. *(978-0-439-79255-4(X))* Scholastic, Inc.

Rosen, Michael J. A School for Pompey Walker. 2012. (ENG.). (J). pap. *(978-1-4675-1412-5(8))* Independent Pub.

Rubenstein, Dan. Railroad of Courage. 2017. (ENG.). 162p. pap. 11.95 *(978-1-55380-514-4(3))* Ronsdale Pr. CAN. Dist: SPD-Small Pr. Distribution.

Russell, Krista. Chasing the Nightbird. 192p. (J). (gr. 5-9). 2018. pap. 7.95 *(978-1-68263-065-5(X))* 2011. 15.95 *(978-1-56145-597-3(0))* Peachtree Publishing Co. Inc.

Sánchez-Korrol, Virginia. Feminist & Abolitionist: The Story of Emilia Casanova. 2013. (ENG.). 248p. (YA). pap. 12.95 *(978-1-55885-765-0(6),* Piñata Books) Arte Publico Pr.

Schraff, Anne. The Burning of the Valley. 2008. (Passages to History Ser.). 115p. (J). (gr. 4-6). lib. bdg. 13.95 *(978-0-7569-8400-7(9))* Perfection Learning Corp.

—Freedom Knows No Color. 2008. (Passages to History Ser.). 118p. (J). lib. bdg. 13.95 *(978-0-7569-8392-5(4))*; (YA). (gr. 7-12). pap. 8.50 *(978-0-7891-7567-0(3))* Perfection Learning Corp.

Schwabach, Karen. The Storm Before Atlanta. 2011. 320p. (J). (gr. 3-7). pap. 7.99 *(978-0-375-85867-3(9),* Yearling) Random Hse. Children's Bks.

Sewell, Helen & Coatsworth, Elizabeth. The White Horse. 2005. (ENG., Illus.). 169p. (J). (gr. 3-4). per. 11.95 *(978-1-883937-86-7(8))* Ignatius Pr.

Shan, Darren, pseud. The Thin Executioner. 2011. (ENG.). 512p. (YA). (gr. 10-17). pap. 23.99 *(978-0-316-07864-1(6))* Little, Brown Bks. for Young Readers.

Shazak. Out of Egypt. 2007. 104p. 24.99 *(978-1-930925-11-3(5))* Feldheim Pubs.

Simmons, Kristen. The Glass Arrow. 2016. (ENG.). 352p. (YA). pap. 18.99 *(978-0-7653-3664-4(2),* 900121071, Tor Teen) Doherty, Tom Assocs., LLC.

Simon, T. R. Zora & Me: the Cursed Ground. 2018. (Zora & Me Ser.). (ENG.). 272p. (J). (gr. 5-9). 16.99 *(978-0-7636-4301-0(7))* Candlewick Pr.

Skrypuch, Marsha Forchuk. The War Below. 2018. (ENG.). 256p. (J). (gr. 3-7). 17.99 *(978-1-338-23302-5(5),* Scholastic Pr.) Scholastic, Inc.

Smith, Nikki Shannon. Charlotte Spies for Justice: A Civil War Survival Story. Trunfio, Alessia, illus. 2019. (Girls Survive Ser.). (ENG.). 112p. (J). (gr. 3-7). pap. 7.95 *(978-1-4965-8446-5(5),* 140971); E-Book 4.95 *(978-1-4965-8389-5(2),* 186555) Capstone. (Stone Arch Bks.).

Smolik, Jane Petrlik. Currents. 2015. (Illus.). 336p. (J). (gr. 4-7). lib. bdg. 16.95 *(978-1-58089-648-1(0))* Charlesbridge Publishing, Inc.

Soentpiet, Chris K. & McGill, Alice. Molly Bannaky. 2009. (ENG., Illus.). 32p. (J). (gr. -1-3). pap. 9.99 *(978-0-547-07676-8(2),* 1042032, Clarion Bks.) HarperCollins Pubs.

Squier, Robert, illus. Follow the Drinking Gourd: An Underground Railroad Story, 1 vol. 2012. (Night Sky Stories Ser.). (ENG.). 24p. (J). (gr. 2-4). pap. 8.95 *(978-1-4048-7714-6(2),* 120446, Picture Window Bks.) Capstone.

Stewart, A. W. Rooktime. 2010. 284p. pap. 15.49 *(978-1-4520-1460-9(4))* AuthorHouse.

Stockton, Frank Richard. Ting-a-Ling Tales. 2008. 88p. pap. 8.95 *(978-1-60664-056-2(9))* Aegypan.

Stowe, Harriet. Uncle Tom's Cabin Vol. 1: Or, Life among the Lowly. Solimene, Laura, ed. 2008. (Bring the Classics to Life Ser.). (Illus.). 72p. (gr. 1-12). pap., act. bk. ed. 10.95 *(978-1-55576-323-7(5),* EDCTR-108B) EDCON Publishing Group.

—Uncle Toms Cabin Young Folks Edition Ill. 2006. pap. *(978-1-4065-1077-5(7))* Dodo Pr.

Strohmeier, Lenice. Mingo, 1 vol. Farnsworth, Bill, illus. 2003. (ENG.). 32p. (J). 16.95 *(978-0-7614-5111-2(0))* Marshall Cavendish Corp.

Stroud, Bettye. The Patchwork Path: A Quilt Map to Freedom. Bennett, Erin Susanne, illus. 2007. (ENG.). 32p. (J). (gr. k-3). pap. 7.99 *(978-0-7636-3519-0(7))* Candlewick Pr.

Sutcliff, Rosemary. The Mark of the Horse Lord. 2015. (Rediscovered Classics Ser.: 21). (ENG.). 296p. (YA). (gr. 7). pap. 12.95 *(978-1-61373-154-3(X))* Chicago Review Pr., Inc.

Swain, Gwenyth & Whelan, Gloria. Voices for Freedom. Geister, David et al, illus. 2013. (American Adventures Ser.). (ENG.). 72p. (J). (gr. 3-6). 6.99 *(978-1-58536-886-0(5),* 202900) Sleeping Bear Pr.

The Sword, the Ring, & the Parchment. 2006. (J). per. 7.99 *(978-0-9785523-0-5(X))* Cross & Crown Publishing.

Tingle, Tim. Crossing Bok Chitto: A Choctaw Tale of Friendship & Freedom, 1 vol. Bridges, Jeanne Rorex, illus. 2008. (ENG.). 40p. (J). (gr. 1-7). pap. 12.95 *(978-1-933693-20-0(7),* 23353382, Cinco Puntos Press) Lee & Low Bks., Inc.

—Stone River Crossing, 1 vol. 2019. (ENG., Illus.). 336p. (J). (gr. 3-7). 20.95 *(978-1-62014-823-5(4),* leelowtu, Tu Bks.) Lee & Low Bks., Inc.

Towell, Ann. Grease Town. 2010. 240p. (YA). (gr. 7-9). 17.95 *(978-0-88776-983-2(7),* Tundra Bks.) Tundra Bks. CAN. Dist: Penguin Random Hse. LLC.

Turner, Diane D. My Name Is Oney Judge. Massey, Cal, illus. 2010. (J). pap. *(978-0-88378-321-4(5))* Third World Press.

Turner, Glennette Tilley. Running for Our Lives. 2004. (J). pap. 7.95 *(978-0-938990-06-2(3))* Newman Educational Publishing Co.

Turner, Megan Whalen. Thick As Thieves. (Queen's Thief Ser.: 5). (ENG.). (YA). (gr. 8). 2018. 384p. pap. 11.99 *(978-0-06-256826-7(4))* 2017. 352p. 17.99 *(978-0-06-256824-3(8))* HarperCollins Pubs. (Greenwillow Bks.).

Twain, Mark, pseud. The Adventures of Huckleberry Finn. (Coleccion Clasicos de la Juventud). (SPA., Illus.). 192p. (J). 12.95 *(978-84-7189-027-6(5),* ORT313) Ortells, Alfredo Editorial S.L. ESP. Dist: Continental Bk. Co., Inc.

—The Adventures of Huckleberry Finn. 2008. (Puffin Classics Ser.). 386p. (gr. 3-7). lib. bdg. 16.00 *(978-0-613-63913-2(8))* Turtleback.

—The Adventures of Huckleberry Finn: With a Discussion of Friendship. Lauter, Richard, tr. Lauter, Richard, illus. 2003. (Values in Action Illustrated Classics Ser.). (J). *(978-1-59203-042-2(4))* Learning Challenge, Inc.

—Classic Starts(r): the Adventures of Huckleberry Finn: Retold from the Mark Twain Original. Andreasen, Dan, illus. 2006. (Classic Starts(r) Ser.). 160p. (J). (gr. 2-4). 7.99 *(978-1-4027-2499-2(3))* Sterling Publishing Co., Inc.

Vande Velde, Vivian. There's a Dead Person Following My Sister Around. 2008. (ENG., Illus.). 160p. (J). (gr. 5-7). pap. 11.95 *(978-0-15-206467-9(2),* 1199316, Clarion Bks.) HarperCollins Pubs.

Verne, Jules. Dick Sand. Munro, George, tr. 2008. 296p. 29.95 *(978-1-60664-752-3(0))* Rodgers, Alan Bks.

—Dick Sands: The Boy Captain. ELLEN E. FREWER, tr. 2007. (ENG.). 298p. pap. 21.99 *(978-1-4264-3403-7(0)),* Creative Media Partners, LLC.

—Dick Sands: The Boy Captain. Frewer, Ellen E., tr. Lt. ed. 2007. (ENG.). 328p. pap. 24.99 *(978-1-4264-3453-2(7))* Creative Media Partners, LLC.

Voigt, Cynthia. The Tale of Birle. 2015. (Tales of the Kingdom Ser.: 2). (ENG., Illus.). 416p. (YA). (gr. 7). 19.99 *(978-1-4424-8356-9(3),* Atheneum Bks. for Young Readers) Simon & Schuster Children's Publishing.

Wait, Lea. Seaward Born. 2004. (ENG., Illus.). 160p. (J). (gr. 3-7). pap. 8.99 *(978-0-689-84860-5(9),* McElderry, Margaret K. Bks.) McElderry, Margaret K. Bks.

Walker, Sally M. Freedom Song: The Story of Henry Box Brown. Qualls, Sean, illus. 2012. (ENG.). 40p. (J). (gr. -1-3). 18.99 *(978-0-06-058310-1(X),* HarperCollins) HarperCollins Pubs.

Walter, Mildred Pitts. Alec's Primer. Johnson, Larry, illus. 2005. (ENG.). 32p. (J). (gr. -1-3). 15.95 *(978-0-916718-20-6(4))* Vermont Folklife Ctr.

Ward, David. Beneath the Mask: The Grassland Trilogy: Book Two, Bk. 2. 2008. (ENG.). 272p. (YA). (gr. 5-17). 16.95 *(978-0-8109-7074-8(0),* 6255, Amulet Bks.) Abrams, Inc.

Warner, Susan. Daisy in the Field. 2017. (ENG., Illus.). (J). 26.95 *(978-1-374-97071-7(9))* Capital Communications, Inc.

Warner, Susan & Wetherell, Elizabeth. Daisy in the Field. 2011. 272p. 29.95 *(978-1-4638-9964-6(5))*; pap. 16.95 *(978-1-4638-0163-2(7))* Rodgers, Alan Bks.

Warren, Bertie. Sammie's Journey to Freedom. 2006. (ENG.). 52p. per. 16.95 *(978-1-4241-5142-4(2))* America Star Bks.

Weston Woods Staff, creator. Henry's Freedom Box. 2011. 18.95 *(978-0-545-31402-2(X))*; 38.75 *(978-0-545-31403-9(8))* Weston Woods Studios, Inc.

Westrick, Anne. Brotherhood. 2014. 384p. (J). (gr. 5). pap. 8.99 *(978-0-14-242237-3(1),* Puffin Books) Penguin Young Readers Group.

Whelan, Gloria. The Listeners. Benny, Mike, illus. 2009. (Tales of Young Americans Ser.). (ENG.). 40p. (J). (gr. 1-4). 18.99 *(978-1-58536-419-0(3),* 202154) Sleeping Bear Pr.

Wilson, Diane Lee. Black Storm Comin' 2006. (ENG.). 240p. (J). (gr. 5-9). pap. 8.99 *(978-0-689-87138-2(4),* McElderry, Margaret K. Bks.) McElderry, Margaret K. Bks.

—Black Storm Comin' 2006. (Illus.). 291p. (gr. 5-9). 17.00 *(978-0-7569-6908-0(5))* Perfection Learning Corp.

Wisler, G. Clifton. Caleb's Choice. 2004. 154p. (gr. 5-9). 16.00 *(978-0-7569-4090-4(7))* Perfection Learning Corp.

Woods, Brenda. My Name Is Sally Little Song. (J). 2007. 192p. (gr. 3-7). 7.99 *(978-0-14-240943-5(X),* Puffin Books) 2006. (ENG.). 182p. (gr. 4-6). 18.69 *(978-0-399-24312-7(7))* Penguin Young Readers Group.

—My Name Is Sally Little Song. 2007. (Illus.). 182p. (gr. 2-7). 17.00 *(978-0-7569-8156-3(5))* Perfection Learning Corp.

Woodson, Jacqueline. Show Way. Talbott, Hudson, illus. 2005. (ENG.). 48p. (J). (gr. -1-3). 18.99 *(978-0-399-23749-2(6),* G.P. Putnam's Sons Books for Young Readers) Penguin Young Readers Group.

Wyeth, Sharon Dennis. Message in the Sky Bk. 3: Corey's Underground Railroad Diary. 2003. (My America Ser.). (ENG.). 112p. (J). 10.95 *(978-0-439-37057-8(4),* Scholastic Pr.) Scholastic, Inc.

SLAVERY—UNITED STATES

see also Abolitionists; Slave Trade; Southern States—History; Underground Railroad

Abnett, Dan. Harriet Tubman & the Underground Railroad, 1 vol. 2006. (Jr. Graphic Biographies Ser.). (ENG., Illus.). 24p. (J). (gr. 2-3). pap. 10.60 *(978-1-4042-2146-8(8),* 1e1e4fac-305d-4a55-a5ea-272406655f1b, PowerKids Pr.); lib. bdg. 28.93 *(978-1-4042-3393-5(8),* faf3f8b3-291f-45bf-a467-b7772adb82ea) Rosen Publishing Group, Inc., The.

—Harriet Tubman y el Ferrocarril Clandestino, 1 vol. 2009. (Historietas Juveniles: Biografías (Jr. Graphic Biographies) Ser.). (SPA., Illus.). 24p. (J). (gr. 2-3). 28.93 *(978-1-4358-8563-9(5),* 23c71f0e-1635-4a3c-be35-311206bd48c0); pap. 10.60 *(978-1-4358-3320-3(1),* c5f7e9e3-e763-46ae-87d5-410dd4478a6b) Rosen Publishing Group, Inc., The.

Agard, Sandra A. Trailblazers: Harriet Tubman: A Journey to Freedom. 2019. (Trailblazers Ser.). (ENG., Illus.). 192p. (J). (gr. 3-7). 7.99 *(978-0-593-12407-9(3))*; lib. bdg. 12.99 *(978-0-593-12408-6(1))* Random Hse. Children's Bks. (Random Hse. Bks. for Young Readers).

Allen, Thomas B. Harriet Tubman, Secret Agent: How Daring Slaves & Free Blacks Spied for the Union During the Civil War. 2008. (Illus.). 192p. (J). (gr. 5-9). 5.95 *(978-1-4263-0401-9(3),* National Geographic Kids) Disney Publishing Worldwide.

Anderson, Dale. The Causes of the Civil War, 1 vol. 2004. (World Almanac(r) Library of the Civil War Ser.). (ENG., Illus.). 48p. (gr. 5-8). pap. 15.05 *(978-0-8368-5590-6(6),* ae885cb8-42d8-49e0-b9ca-32f9a28d4d37); lib. bdg. 33.67 *(978-0-8368-5581-4(7),* 88052b64-ee89-4168-9b03-c8645b27670f) Stevens, Gareth Publishing LLLP. (Gareth Stevens Secondary Library).

Anthony, David H. Freedom: Life after Slavery, 1 vol. rev. ed. 2011. (Social Studies: Informational Text Ser.). (ENG.). 32p. (gr. 4-8). pap. 11.99 *(978-1-4333-1521-3(1))* Teacher Created Materials, Inc.

Apte, Sunita & Hess, Debra. Amistad: Fight for Freedom. 2007. (Read on! Special Edition: Level RA Ser.). (Illus.). 23p. pap. 18.51 *(978-1-4190-3507-4(X))* Steck-Vaughn.

Arato, Rona. Working for Freedom: The Story of Josiah Henson. 2009. (Stories of Canada Ser.: 13). (ENG., Illus.). 88p. (J). (gr. 4-18). 18.95 *(978-1-894917-50-6(2),* Napoleon & Co.) Dundurn Pr. CAN. Dist: Publishers Group West (PGW).

Aretha, David. Sabotage, Sedition, & Sundry Acts of Rebellion. 2014. (J). *(978-1-59935-406-4(3))* Reynolds, Morgan Inc.

Arnéz, Lynda. My Journey on the Underground Railroad, 1 vol. 2015. (My Place in History Ser.). (ENG., Illus.). 24p. (J). (gr. 2-3). 24.27 *(978-1-4824-3997-7(2),* 0db0d968-c6f2-4dac-bd95-9eb248fbb175); pap. 9.15 *(978-1-4824-4010-2(5),* 8a49b461-5176-463b-bfa9-0d362da284d1) Stevens, Gareth Publishing LLLP.

Ashby, Ruth. The Underground Railroad. 2016. (Civil War Chronicles Ser.: Vol. 1). (ENG., Illus.). 48p. (J). (gr. 4-6). pap. 23.95 *(978-1-59687-515-9(1),* ipicturebooks) ibooks, Inc.

Beckett, Leslie. Abolitionists & Human Rights: Fighting for Emancipation, 1 vol. 2016. (Spotlight on American History Ser.). (ENG.). 24p. (J). (gr. 4-6). 27.93 *(978-1-5081-4937-8(2),* 44df7110-5d05-4ad1-ac95-2fd92a184641, PowerKids Pr.) Rosen Publishing Group, Inc., The.

Bennett, Doraine. Harriet Tubman. 2012. (Illus.). 24p. (J). *(978-1-935884-44-6(1))* State Standards Publishing, LLC.

Bjornlund, Lydia D. Women in Colonial America. 2003. (Women in History Ser.). (ENG., Illus.). 112p. (J). 33.45 *(978-1-59018-470-7(X),* Lucent Bks.) Cengage Gale.

Bolden, Tonya. Facing Frederick: The Life of Frederick Douglass, a Monumental American Man. 2018. (ENG., Illus.). 208p. (J). (gr. 5-9). 19.99 *(978-1-4197-2546-3(7),* 1161101, Abrams Bks. for Young Readers) Abrams, Inc.

—No Small Potatoes: Junius G. Groves & His Kingdom in Kansas. Tate, Don, illus. 2018. 40p. (J). (gr. -1-3). 18.99 *(978-0-385-75276-3(8),* Knopf Bks. for Young Readers) Random Hse. Children's Bks.

Bolte, Mari. Flight to Freedom! Nickolas Flux & the Underground Railroad, 1 vol. Simmons, Mark, illus. 2014. (Nickolas Flux History Chronicles Ser.). (ENG.). 32p. (J). (gr. 3-9). lib. bdg. 31.32 *(978-1-4914-0254-2(7),* 125809) Capstone.

Brill, Marlene Targ. Allen Jay Y el Ferrocarril Subterraneo: Allen Jay & the Underground Railroad. 2008. pap. 40.95 *(978-0-8225-9679-0(2))* Lerner Publishing Group.

Brindell Fradin, Dennis. The Emancipation Proclamation, 1 vol. 2008. (Turning Points in U. S. History Ser.). (ENG., Illus.). 48p. (J). (gr. 4-4). lib. bdg. 34.07 *(978-0-7614-2038-5(X),* e0c254de-5d25-4baf-bfe6-f3f40a5f3650) Cavendish Square Publishing LLC.

—The Underground Railroad, 1 vol. 2012. (Great Escapes Ser.). (ENG.). 80p. (gr. 6-6). 36.93 *(978-1-60870-476-7(9),* 6bfe942d-9f47-4295-a9b2-e50357064da3) Cavendish Square Publishing LLC.

Brooks-Simon, Barbara. Escape to Freedom: The Underground Railroad Adventures of Callie & William. 2004. (I Am American Ser.). (Illus.). 40p. (J). (gr. 3-7). pap. 6.99 *(978-0-7922-6551-1(3),* National Geographic Kids) Disney Publishing Worldwide.

Brown, Susan Taylor. Robert Smalls Sails to Freedom. Marshall, Felicia, illus. 2006. (On My Own History Ser.). 48p. (J). (gr. 3-7). pap. 6.95 *(978-0-8225-6051-7(8),* First Avenue Editions) Lerner Publishing Group.

Buell, Tonya. Slavery in America, 1 vol. 2004. (Primary Sources in American History Ser.). (ENG., Illus.). 64p. (gr. 5-8). lib. bdg. 37.13 *(978-0-8239-4513-9(8),* 1de7226b-52cd-4e89-a83c-8022ab2474a9, Rosen Reference) Rosen Publishing Group, Inc., The.

Burgan, Michael. African Americans in the Thirteen Colonies. 2013. (Cornerstones of Freedom™, Third Ser.). (ENG., Illus.). 64p. (J). lib. bdg. 30.00 *(978-0-531-23600-0(5))* Scholastic Library Publishing.

Byers, Ann. The Emancipation Proclamation, 1 vol. 2018. (America's Most Important Documents: Inquiry into Historical Sources Ser.). (ENG.). 64p. (J). (gr. 6-6). lib. bdg. 37.36 *(978-1-5026-3598-3(4),* 7f22fdda-24b7-47c9-8648-ab69c99a32a1) Cavendish Square Publishing LLC.

Campbell, Ciara. Slavery in America, 1 vol. 2015. (African American Experience: from Slavery to the Presidency Ser.). (ENG., Illus.). 80p. (J). (gr. 7-8). 35.47 *(978-1-68048-036-8(7),* e51b3af4-a76c-4d4d-a6d4-ba1732d9eac7, Britannica Educational Publishing) Rosen Publishing Group, Inc., The.

Campbell, Ciara, ed. Slavery in America, 4 vols. 2015. (African American Experience: from Slavery to the Presidency Ser.). (ENG.). 80p. (YA). (gr. 7-8). 70.94 *(978-1-68048-037-5(5),* b949c965-ddf2-48c5-8ce3-bb882fcfcada, Britannica Educational Publishing) Rosen Publishing Group, Inc., The.

Carlson-Berne, Emma. Face of Freedom: How the Photos of Frederick Douglass Celebrated Racial Equality. 2017. (Captured History Ser.). (ENG., Illus.). 64p. (J). (gr. 5-9). lib. bdg. 35.32 *(978-0-7565-5617-4(1),* 135802, Compass Point Bks.) Capstone.

Carosella, Melissa. The Fight for Freedom: Ending Slavery in America. rev. ed. 2011. (Social Studies: Informational Text Ser.). (ENG., Illus.). 32p. (J). (gr. 4-8). pap. 11.99 *(978-1-4333-1519-0(X))* Teacher Created Materials, Inc.

—Frederick Douglass: Líder Del Movimiento Abolicionista. rev. ed. 2019. (Social Studies: Informational Text Ser.). (SPA., Illus.). 32p. (J). (gr. 4-8). pap. 11.99 *(978-1-64290-120-7(2))* Teacher Created Materials, Inc.

Cartlidge, Cherese. Reparations for Slavery, 1 vol. 2007. (Lucent Library of Black History Ser.). (ENG., Illus.). 104p. (gr. 7-7). lib. bdg. 41.03 *(978-1-59018-868-2(3),* edff4443-4bec-4021-8b21-1880401ea62b, Lucent Pr.) Greenhaven Publishing LLC.

Cary, Lorene. Free! Great Escapes from Slavery on the Underground Railroad. 2011. (J). pap. 15.00 *(978-0-9819560-3-9(3))* New City Community Pr.

Child, Lydia Maria. The Duty of Disobedience to the Fugitive Slave Act. 2007. (ENG.). 48p. per. *(978-1-4065-1352-3(0))* Dodo Pr.

Chipley Slavicek, Louise. Harriet Tubman & the Underground Railroad, 1 vol. 2006. (Lucent Library of Black History Ser.). (ENG., Illus.). 104p. (gr. 7-7). lib. bdg. 36.43 *(978-1-59018-927-6(2),* 57368502-a57f-4f41-a791-2010e42c49f1, Lucent Pr.) Greenhaven Publishing LLC.

Clark, Willow. The True Story of the Emancipation Proclamation, 1 vol. 2013. (What Really Happened? Ser.). (ENG., Illus.). 24p. (J). (gr. 2-3). 26.27 *(978-1-4488-9695-0(9),* ed9c49fd-1083-41ae-b071-1a993beabfb5); pap. 9.25 *(978-1-4488-9848-0(X),* f7848aa6-8a09-463b-b38a-5f880afeb521) Rosen Publishing Group, Inc., The. (PowerKids Pr.).

Clinton, Catherine. When Harriet Met Sojourner. Evans, Shane W., illus. 2007. (ENG.). 32p. (J). (gr. k-3). 16.99 *(978-0-06-050425-0(0),* Tegen, Katherine Bks) HarperCollins Pubs.

Cloud-Tapper, Suzanne. Views on Slavery: In the Words of Enslaved Africans, Merchants, Owners, & Abolitionists, 1 vol. 2016. (Slavery & Slave Resistance Ser.). (ENG., Illus.). 128p. (gr. 6-6). 38.93 *(978-0-7660-7553-5(2),* fd69db0c-d592-4faa-97e9-ae4f836e9c50) Enslow Publishing, LLC.

Collard, Sneed B., III. Phillis Wheatley, 1 vol. 2010. (American Heroes Ser.). (ENG., Illus.). 48p. (gr. 3-3). 32.64 *(978-0-7614-4057-4(7),* b5aabf94-bd02-4815-9f30-a3d8be34143b) Cavendish Square Publishing LLC.

Conkling, Winifred. Passenger on the Pearl: The True Story of Emily Edmonson's Flight from Slavery. 2016. (ENG., Illus.). 176p. (YA). (gr. 7-10). pap. 10.95 *(978-1-61620-550-8(4),* 73550) Algonquin Young Readers.

Cooke, Tim. Causes of the War, 1 vol. 2012. (American Civil War: the Right Answer Ser.). (ENG., Illus.). 48p. (J). (gr. 6-8). pap. 15.05 *(978-1-4339-7536-3(X),* 824013a5-fd98-4be7-821d-1e0bb4a86e23); lib. bdg. 34.60 *(978-1-4339-7535-6(1),* 35413caa-60d4-4e41-aea4-43d818cb473d) Stevens, Gareth Publishing LLLP.

—Causes of the War: 1860-1861. 2012. (Civil War Highlights Ser.). (Illus.). 48p. (gr. 5-12). lib. bdg. 37.10 *(978-1-59920-813-8(X))* Black Rabbit Bks.

Corrick, James A. The Civil War & Emancipation, 1 vol. 2007. (Lucent Library of Black History Ser.). (ENG., Illus.). 104p. (J). (gr. 7-7). lib. bdg. 41.03 *(978-1-4205-0008-0(2),* e49d4f5d-f292-4497-87e1-8cd18b6c3b79, Lucent Pr.) Greenhaven Publishing LLC.

Currie, Stephen. Escapes from Slavery. 2003. (Great Escapes Ser.). (ENG., Illus.). 112p. (J). 30.85 *(978-1-59018-276-5(6),* Lucent Bks.) Cengage Gale.

—The Quest for Freedom: The Abolitionist Movement. 2005. (Lucent Library of Black History). (ENG., Illus.). 112p. (YA). (gr. 7-10). lib. bdg. 33.45 *(978-1-59018-703-6(2),* Lucent Bks.) Cengage Gale.

Davis, Kenneth C. In the Shadow of Liberty: The Hidden History of Slavery, Four Presidents, & Five Black Lives. 2019. (ENG., Illus.). 304p. (J). pap. 12.99 *(978-1-250-14411-9(6),* 900180617) Square Fish.

De Medeiros, James. Slavery. (Illus.). (J). 2013. 47p. *(978-1-62127-195-6(1))* 2013. 47p. pap. *(978-1-62127-201-4(X))* 2008. 48p. (gr. 5-8). pap. 10.95 *(978-1-59036-875-6(4))* 2008. 48p. (gr. 5-8). lib. bdg. 29.05 *(978-1-59036-874-9(6))* Weigl Pubs., Inc.

DeFord, Diane. Harriet Tubman. 2009. pap. 13.25 *(978-1-60559-061-5(4))* Hameray Publishing Group, Inc.

Deiters, Erika & Deiters, Jim. The African Community in America. 2003. (J). lib. bdg. *(978-1-58417-032-7(8))* Lake Street Pubs.

Devereaux Jordan, Anne & Schomp, Virginia. Slavery & Resistance, 1 vol. 2007. (Drama of African-American History Ser.). (ENG., Illus.). 80p. (J). (gr. 6-6). lib. bdg. 38.36 *(978-0-7614-2178-8(5),* 4fb9f4af-0981-4ebf-ae63-bf2b8438c5bc) Cavendish Square Publishing LLC.

Doak, Robin S. Phillis Wheatley: The Inspiring Life Story of the American Poet. 2016. (Inspiring Stories Ser.). (ENG., Illus.). 112p. (J). (gr. 5-7). lib. bdg. 38.65 *(978-0-7565-5166-7(8),* 128794, Compass Point Bks.) Capstone.

Dodge Cummings, Judy. The Underground Railroad: Navigate the Journey from Slavery to Freedom. Casteel, Tom, illus. 2017. (Build It Yourself Ser.). (ENG.). 128p. (J). (gr. 4-7). 22.95 *(978-1-61930-486-4(4),* e3d6f9a9-2860-4192-b376-74bb2cb1fe44); pap. 17.95 *(978-1-61930-490-1(2),* d95113fe-daff-4a4f-b949-a7dd29f0b56c) Nomad Pr.

Dudley Gold, Susan. The Missouri Compromise, 1 vol. 2011. (Landmark Legislation Ser.). (ENG.). 128p. (YA). (gr. 8-8). 42.64 *(978-1-60870-041-7(0),* 183c9afd-ef50-4b45-ad79-61237b1a486d) Cavendish Square Publishing LLC.

—United States V. Amistad: Slave Ship Mutiny, 1 vol. 2007. (Supreme Court Milestones Ser.). (ENG., Illus.). 128p. (J). (gr. 8-8). lib. bdg. 45.50 *(978-0-7614-2143-6(2),* 37ed5658-e209-4386-81f8-e545b2d42868) Cavendish Square Publishing LLC.

Dunbar, Erica Armstrong & Van Cleve, Kathleen. Never Caught, the Story of Ona Judge: George & Martha

Washington's Courageous Slave Who Dared to Run Away; Young Readers Edition. 2019. (ENG., Illus.). 272p. (J). (gr. 4-8). 19.99 (978-1-5344-1617-8(X), Aladdin) Simon & Schuster Children's Publishing.

Dunn, Joe. The Underground Railroad, 1 vol. 2007. (Graphic History Ser.). (ENG., Illus.). 32p. (J). (gr. 3-8). 32.79 (978-1-60270-080-2(X), 9046, Graphic Planet - Fiction) Magic Wagon.

Durst Johnson, Claudia, ed. Slavery & Racism in the Narrative Life of Frederick Douglass, 1 vol. 2014. (Social Issues in Literature Ser.). (ENG., Illus.). 136p. (J). (gr. 10-12). lib. bdg. 48.03 (978-0-7377-6986-9(6), c9d95ed9-36ea-46a1-a8f0-c489aa03dd0f, Greenhaven Publishing) Greenhaven Publishing LLC.

Edison, Erin. Harriet Tubman, 1 vol. 2013. (Great Women in History Ser.). (ENG.). 24p. (J). (gr. -1-2). pap. 6.29 (978-1-62065-859-8(3), 121792); (gr. k-1). pap. 37.74 (978-1-62065-860-4(7), 19427, Pebble) Capstone.

The Emancipation Proclamation & the End of Slavery in America, 1 vol. 2014. (Celebration of the Civil Rights Movement Ser.). (ENG., Illus.). 80p. (J). (gr. 6-6). 37.47 (978-1-4777-7749-7(0), 20d82c0d-2d59-4140-9fc1-adf790e79e4c) Rosen Publishing Group, Inc., The.

Erickson, Paul. Daily Life on a Southern Plantation. Gabbey, Terry, illus. Slingsby, Miki, photos by. 2006. 48p. (J). (gr. 2-5). reprint ed. pap. 8.00 (978-1-4223-5727-9(9)) DIANE Publishing Co.

Feinstein, Stephen & Taylor, Charlotte. Harriet Tubman: Hero of the Underground Railroad, 1 vol. 2015. (Exceptional African Americans Ser.). (ENG., Illus.). 24p. (J). (gr. 3-4). 24.27 (978-0-7660-7128-5(6), cf2c9f02-bc5b-4c9a-8a5b-0b63839c3f25) Enslow Publishing, LLC.

Figley, Marty Rhodes. Washington Is Burning. Orback, Craig, illus. 2007. (On My Own History Ser.). (ENG.). 48p. (J). (gr. 2-4). per. 8.99 (978-0-8225-6050-0(X), 220511bf-9018-498f-8ff3-a73d591dfbeb, First Avenue Editions) Lerner Publishing Group.

Finegan, Jeffrey E., Sr. Colonel Washington & Me: George Washington, His Slave William Lee & Their Incredible Journey Together. Nikolopoulos, Stephanie, ed. 2012. (ENG., Illus.). 32p. (J). 16.95 (978-0-9852819-0-8(1)) Seigle Bks.

Ford, Carin T. The Emancipation Proclamation, Lincoln, & Slavery Through Primary Sources, 1 vol. 2013. (Civil War Through Primary Sources Ser.). (ENG.). 48p. (gr. 4-6). pap. 11.53 (978-1-4644-0187-9(X), 39a9f8dc-63ab-4b9b-94df-bb3af9d021ae); (Illus.). (J). lib. bdg. 27.93 (978-0-7660-4129-5(8), b2263e7e-8ce7-4531-a353-b06b36d2fe69) Enslow Publishing, LLC.

—The Underground Railroad & Slavery Through Primary Sources, 1 vol. 2013. (Civil War Through Primary Sources Ser.). (ENG.). 48p. (gr. 4-6). pap. 11.53 (978-1-4644-0185-5(3), cf8e5917-daa9-4221-aab6-93e96218af39); lib. bdg. 27.93 (978-0-7660-4127-1(1), a9f3a436-595a-4fd6-aa17-0fcf3ef94920) Enslow Publishing, LLC.

A Forgotten History: The Slave Trade & Slavery in New England, 2. 2005. (Illus.). 104p. (YA). pap. (978-1-891306-86-0(3)) Choices Program, Brown Univ.

Goldy-Brown, Sarah. Reparations for Slavery: The Fight for Compensation, 1 vol. annot. ed. 2017. (Lucent Library of Black History Ser.). (ENG.). 104p. (YA). (gr. 7-7). pap. 20.99 (978-1-5345-6297-4(4), 27efb4be-dd9e-422e-a98d-08c4c1a41fff); lib. bdg. 41.03 (978-1-5345-6233-2(8), 4d494be3-6c71-4b78-a184-f139fcb2e011) Greenhaven Publishing LLC. (Lucent Pr.).

Grack, Rachel. Juneteenth. 2018. (Celebrating Holidays Ser.). (ENG., Illus.). 24p. (J). (gr. k-3). lib. bdg. 26.95 (978-1-62617-788-8(0), Blastoff! Readers) Bellwether Media.

Grady, Cynthia. Like a Bird: The Art of the American Slave Song. Wood, Michele, illus. 2016. (ENG.). 40p. (J). (gr. 3-6). E-Book 30.65 (978-1-5124-0889-8(1), Millbrook Pr.) Lerner Publishing Group.

Hall, Shyima. Hidden Girl: The True Story of a Modern-Day Child Slave. 2014. (ENG., Illus.). 240p. (YA). (gr. 9). 19.99 (978-1-4424-8168-8(4), Simon & Schuster Bks. For Young Readers) Simon & Schuster Bks. For Young Readers.

Hansen, Joyce & McGowan, Gary. Freedom Roads: Searching for the Underground Railroad. Ransome, James, illus. 2003. (ENG.). 166p. (J). (gr. 5-9). 18.95 (978-0-8126-2673-5(7)) Cricket Bks.

Harasymiw, Therese. Freedom by Force: The History of Slave Rebellions, 1 vol. 2017. (Lucent Library of Black History Ser.). (ENG.). 104p. (J). (gr. 7-7). lib. bdg. 41.03 (978-1-5345-6235-6(4), 47ab6440-8f55-4888-abcb-735f3a12d10e, Lucent Pr.) Greenhaven Publishing LLC.

Harris, Duchess & Wyskowski, Lindsay. Oney Ona Judge: Escape from Slavery & the President's House. 2018. (Freedom's Promise Ser.). (ENG., Illus.). 48p. (J). (gr. 4-8). lib. bdg. 35.64 (978-1-5321-1773-2(6), 30834) ABDO Publishing Co.

Haskins, James & Benson Haskins, Kathleen. Africa: A Look Back, 1 vol. 2007. (Drama of African-American History Ser.). (ENG., Illus.). 80p. (J). (gr. 6-6). lib. bdg. 38.36 (978-0-7614-2148-1(3), 1c1cd1b9-2063-462a-943d-5d55457363e9) Cavendish Square Publishing LLC.

Hatt, Christine. The African-American Slave Trade. 2003. (Questioning History Ser.). (J). lib. bdg. 28.50 (978-1-58340-265-8(9)) Black Rabbit Bks.

Herda, D. J. The Dred Scott Case: Slavery & Citizenship, 1 vol. rev. ed. 2010. (Landmark Supreme Court Cases, Gold Edition Ser.). (ENG., Illus.). 104p. (gr. 6-7). 35.93 (978-0-7660-3427-3(5), 93b18d2b-b363-4fc5-b99b-7b1b87095065) Enslow Publishing, LLC.

—Slavery & Citizenship: The Dred Scott Case, 1 vol. 2016. (U. S. Supreme Court Landmark Cases Ser.). (ENG., Illus.). 128p. (J). (gr. 7-7). 38.93 (978-0-7660-8426-1(4), ffcb8d36-7c36-4d76-8da3-8ca5072dc032) Enslow Publishing, LLC.

Herschbach, Elisabeth. Slavery & the Missouri Compromise. 2018. (Expansion of Our Nation Ser.). (ENG., Illus.). 32p. (J). (gr. 3-5). pap. 9.95 (978-1-63517-987-3(4), 1635179874); lib. bdg. 31.35 (978-1-63517-886-9(X), 163517886X) North Star Editions. (Focus Readers).

—Slavery & the Missouri Compromise. 2018. (Illus.). 32p. (J). pap. (978-1-4896-9887-2(6), AV2 by Weigl) Weigl Pubs., Inc.

Hicks, Kyra E. Martha Ann's Quilt for Queen Victoria. Fodi, Lee Edward, illus. 2006. 28p. (J). (gr. -1-3). 16.95 (978-1-933285-59-7(1)) Brown Books Publishing Group.

Hill, Laban Carrick. Dave the Potter: Artist, Poet, Slave. 2012. (CHI, ENG & JPN., Illus.). 42p. (J). (978-4-89572-839-3(0)) Mitsumura Kyouiku Tosho Co., Ltd.

—Dave the Potter (Caldecott Honor Book) Artist, Poet, Slave. Collier, Bryan, illus. 2010. (ENG.). 40p. (J). (gr. -1-3). 19.99 (978-0-316-10731-0(X)) Little, Brown Bks. for Young Readers.

Hill, Laban Carrik. Dave the Potter: Artist, Poet, Slave. 2011. (J). (978-1-4618-1706-2(4)) Recorded Bks., Inc.

Hohn, Nadia L. Harriet Tubman: Freedom Fighter. Mazali, Gustavo, illus. 2018. (I Can Read Level 2 Ser.). (ENG.). 32p. (J). (gr. -1-3). 16.99 (978-0-06-243285-8(0)); pap. 4.99 (978-0-06-243284-1(2)) HarperCollins Pubs. (HarperCollins).

Holzer, Harold. Lincoln: How Abraham Lincoln Ended Slavery in America: a Companion Book for Young Readers to the Steven Spielberg Film. 2013. (ENG., Illus.). 240p. pap. 7.99 (978-0-06-226511-1(3), Newmarket for It Bks.) HarperCollins Pubs.

—Lincoln: How Abraham Lincoln Ended Slavery in America: A Companion Book for Young Readers to the Steven Spielberg Film. 2012. (ENG., Illus.). 240p. 16.99 (978-0-06-226509-8(1), Newmarket for It Bks.) HarperCollins Pubs.

Hooks, Gwendolyn. Ona Judge Outwits the Washingtons: An Enslaved Woman Fights for Freedom. Agoussoye, Simone, illus. 2019. (ENG.). 40p. (J). (gr. 3-6). 18.95 (978-1-5435-1280-9(1), 137745, Capstone Editions) Capstone.

Hopper, Whitney. Slavery in the United States: "The Abominable Trade", 1 vol. 2016. (Spotlight on American History Ser.). (ENG., Illus.). 24p. (J). (gr. 4-6). 27.93 (978-1-5081-4940-8(2), 7cde20e2-767c-49f6-95be-a37165bee0ca, PowerKids Pr.) Rosen Publishing Group, Inc., The.

Howell, Brian. U.S. Growth & Change in the 19th Century. 2011. (Explorer Library: Language Arts Explorer Ser.). (ENG.). 32p. (gr. 4-8). pap. 14.21 (978-1-61080-290-1(X), 201213) Cherry Lake Publishing.

—US Growth & Change in the 19th Century. 2011. (Explorer Library: Language Arts Explorer Ser.). (ENG., Illus.). 32p. (gr. 4-8). lib. bdg. 32.07 (978-1-61080-202-4(0), 201180) Cherry Lake Publishing.

Howse, Jennifer. Reconstruction. 2013. (Illus.). 48p. (J). (978-1-62127-194-9(3)); pap. (978-1-62127-200-7(1)) Weigl Pubs., Inc.

Hudson, Wade. The Underground Railroad. 2005. (Cornerstones of Freedom Ser.). (ENG., Illus.). 48p. (J). (gr. 4-6). 26.00 (978-0-516-23630-8(X), Children's Pr.) Scholastic Library Publishing.

Hurt, Avery Elizabeth. Frederick Douglass: Abolitionist & Writer. 2018. (J). pap. (978-1-5026-4068-0(6)) Musa Publishing.

Jacobs Altman, Linda. The Story of Slavery & Abolition in United States History, 1 vol. 2014. (In United States History Ser.). (ENG.). 96p. (gr. 5-5). pap. 13.88 (978-0-7660-6331-0(3), 17ea487c-4aac-4c97-8c6f-4160ba5f6fc9) Enslow Publishing, LLC.

Jarrow, Jesse. Phillis Wheatley: African American Poet / Poeta Afroamericana. 2009. (Famous People in American History/Grandes personajes en la historia de los Estados Unidos Ser.). (ENG & SPA.). 32p. (gr. 2-3). 47.90 (978-1-61512-554-8(X), Editorial Buenas Letras) Rosen Publishing Group, Inc., The.

—Phillis Wheatley: Poeta afroamericana (Phillis Wheatley: African American Poet) 2009. (Grandes personajes en la historia de los Estados Unidos (Famous People in American History) Ser.). (SPA.). 32p. (gr. 2-3). 47.90 (978-1-61512-807-5(7), Editorial Buenas Letras) Rosen Publishing Group, Inc., The.

Jones, Lynda. Mrs. Lincoln's Dressmaker: The Unlikely Friendship of Elizabeth Keckley & Mary Todd Lincoln. 2009. (Illus.). 80p. (J). (gr. 5-9). 18.95 (978-1-4263-0377-7(7), National Geographic Kids) Disney Publishing Worldwide.

Jopp, Kelsey. John Brown & the Harpers Ferry Raid. 2020. (Civil War Ser.). (ENG., Illus.). 48p. (J). (gr. 5-6). 34.21 (978-1-64493-082-3(X), 164493082X, Focus Readers) North Star Editions.

Kamma, Anne. If You Lived When There Was Slavery in America. Johnson, Pamela, illus. 2004. (If You Lived Ser.). 63p. (J). 14.65 (978-0-7569-3016-5(2)) Perfection Learning Corp.

—If You Lived When There Was Slavery in America. Johnson, Pamela, illus. 2004. (If You... Ser.). (ENG.). 64p. (J). (gr. 2-5). pap. 6.99 (978-0-439-56706-0(8)) Scholastic, Inc.

Kawa, Katie. Slavery Wasn't Only in the South: Exposing Myths about the Civil War, 1 vol. 2019. (Exposed! More Myths about American History Ser.). (ENG.). 32p. (gr. 2-3). pap. 11.50 (978-1-5382-3754-0(7), 85774fa5-adde-4413-acf7-8701cefd0381) Stevens, Gareth Publishing LLLP.

Kent, Jacqueline C. Phillis Wheatley. 2003. (Women of the Revolution Ser.). (J). pap. (978-1-58417-089-1(1)); lib. bdg. (978-1-58417-026-6(3)) Lake Street Pubs.

Kiely Miller, Barbara. Frederick Douglass, 1 vol. 2007. (Great Americans Ser.). (Illus.). 24p. (J). (gr. 2-4). (ENG.). pap. 9.15 (978-0-8368-8322-0(5), cec7cdfc-8a06-4de5-befe-4cfa4efd716d); (SPA., pap. 9.15 (978-0-8368-8335-0(7), 66cd4101-8489-4463-b0c8-0774211efac0); (SPA., lib. bdg. 24.67 (978-0-8368-8328-2(4), a9c1cfc5-b917-49ea-99fb-b321f4985ef6); (ENG., lib. bdg. 24.67 (978-0-8368-8315-2(2), 6766fb17-e159-4d91-8538-2492f4a05b78) Stevens, Gareth Publishing LLLP. (Weekly Reader Leveled Readers).

Kimmel, Allison Crotzer. A Primary Source History of Slavery in the United States. 2015. (Primary Source History Ser.). (ENG., Illus.). 32p. (J). (gr. 3-6). lib. bdg. 27.99 (978-1-4914-1839-0(7), 127276, Capstone Pr.) Capstone.

Knudsen, Shannon. When Were the First Slaves Set Free During the Civil War? And Other Questions about the Emancipation Proclamation. 2010. (Six Questions of American History Ser.). (ENG., Illus.). 48p. (J). (gr. 4-6). pap. 11.99 (978-0-7613-6121-3(9), 439921d9-9f33-4651-8e71-fe9a4cd4c225); lib. bdg. 30.65 (978-1-58013-670-9(2), 5021e694-5f71-402d-8d11-6438e13df8bb, Lerner Pubns.) Lerner Publishing Group.

Landau, Elaine. The Emancipation Proclamation: Would You Do What Lincoln Did?, 1 vol. 2008. (What Would You Do? Ser.). (ENG., Illus.). 48p. (gr. 3-3). (J). lib. bdg. 27.93 (978-0-7660-2899-9(2), 39c1ee83-f4bc-4608-8499-383b6829d109); pap. 11.53 (978-1-59845-194-8(4), ecefcba4-d07c-4bb8-83db-4ac89f6f1c78) Enslow Publishing, LLC. (Enslow Elementary).

—Fleeing to Freedom on the Underground Railroad: The Courageous Slaves, Agents, & Conductors. 2006. (People's History Ser.). (ENG., Illus.). 88p. (gr. 5-12). lib. bdg. 33.26 (978-0-8225-3490-7(8)) Lerner Publishing Group.

Lanier, Wendy & Nelson, Robin. What Was the Missouri Compromise? And Other Questions about the Struggle over Slavery. 2012. (Start to Finish, Second Series: Nature's Cycles Ser.). (ENG.). 48p. (gr. k-3). pap. 39.62 (978-0-7613-9293-4(9)) Lerner Publishing Group.

Lanier, Wendy Hinote. What Was the Missouri Compromise? And Other Questions about the Struggle over Slavery. 2012. (Six Questions of American History Ser.). (ENG., Illus.). 48p. (J). (gr. 4-6). pap. 11.99 (978-0-7613-8565-3(7), 33f0adec-f615-4d33-a027-8dd0fb8b729f); lib. bdg. 30.65 (978-0-7613-5331-7(3), a2fb97b4-b354-4c72-a24a-4306e916a70a, Lerner Pubns.) Lerner Publishing Group.

Lantier, Patricia. Harriet Tubman: Conductor on the Underground Railroad, 1 vol. 2009. (Voices for Freedom Ser.). (ENG., Illus.). 64p. (J). (gr. 5-8). pap. (978-0-7787-4838-0(3)); lib. bdg. (978-0-7787-4822-9(7)) Crabtree Publishing Co.

Leavitt, Amie Jane. Harriet Tubman. 2007. (What's So Great About... ? Ser.). (Illus.). 32p. (J). (gr. 2-4). lib. bdg. 25.70 (978-1-58415-577-5(9)) Mitchell Lane Pubs.

Lester, Julius. To Be a Slave. Feelings, Tom, illus. 2005. (Puffin Modern Classics Ser.). 176p. (J). (gr. 3-7). 8.99 (978-0-14-240386-0(5), Puffin Books) Penguin Young Readers Group.

Levin, Judy. A Timeline of the Abolitionist Movement, 1 vol. 2004. (Timelines of American History Ser.). (ENG., Illus.). 32p. (J). (gr. 4-4). lib. bdg. 29.13 (978-0-8239-4537-5(5), 0cb0a0cb-2bb0-4cc2-a53f-cd87d0c86654, Rosen Reference) Rosen Publishing Group, Inc., The.

Levy, Debbie. Slaves on a Southern Plantation. 2004. (Daily Life Ser.). (ENG., Illus.). 48p. (J). 27.50 (978-0-7377-1827-0(7), Greenhaven Pr., Inc.) Cengage Gale.

Levy, Janey. Juneteenth: Celebrating the End of Slavery. 2009. (Reading Room Collection 2 Ser.). 24p. (gr. 3-4). 42.50 (978-1-60851-976-7(7), PowerKids Pr.) Rosen Publishing Group, Inc., The.

Linde, Barbara M. Slavery in Early America, 1 vol. 2011. (Story of America Ser.). (ENG., Illus.). 32p. (J). (gr. 4-5). lib. bdg. 29.27 (978-1-4339-4776-6(5), cd1c573c-1c64-42b1-b3ea-2a3c83e1ba4d, Gareth Stevens Learning Library) Stevens, Gareth Publishing LLLP.

Littlejohn, Randy. A Timeline of the Slave Trade in America. (Timelines of American History Ser.). 32p. (gr. 4-4). 2009. 47.90 (978-1-60854-390-8(0)) 2004. (ENG., Illus.). lib. bdg. 29.13 (978-0-8239-4540-5(5), 1c308b4c-e4e3-4c4a-a616-f859bdc46cca) Rosen Publishing Group, Inc., The. (Rosen Reference).

Llanas, Sheila Griffin. The Underground Railroad: A History Perspectives Book. 2013. (Perspectives Library). (ENG., Illus.). 32p. (J). (gr. 4-8). 32.07 (978-1-62431-423-0(6), 202812) Cherry Lake Publishing.

Lynch, Seth. The Emancipation Proclamation, 1 vol. 2018. (Look at U. S. History Ser.). (ENG.). 32p. (J). (gr. 2-2). 28.27 (978-1-5382-2119-8(5), 6585d053-970a-4d85-9432-f4efcb166780) Stevens, Gareth Publishing LLLP.

Marlowe, Sam. Learning about Dedication from the Life of Frederick Douglass. 2009. (Character Building Book Ser.). 24p. (gr. 2-3). 42.50 (978-1-60854-970-2(4), PowerKids Pr.) Rosen Publishing Group, Inc., The.

McClafferty, Carla Killough. Buried Lives: The Enslaved People of George Washington's Mount Vernon. 2018. (ENG., Illus.). 168p. (J). (gr. 5-7). 24.99 (978-0-8234-3697-2(7)) Holiday Hse., Inc.

McConaghy, Lorraine & Bentley, Judy. Free Boy: A True Story of Slave & Master. 2013. (V Ethel Willis White Bks.). (ENG., Illus.). 112p. (J). pap. 18.95 (978-0-295-99271-6(9)) Univ. of Washington Pr.

McDonough, Yona Zeldis. Who Was Harriet Tubman? 2004. (ENG., Illus.). 106p. (J). lib. bdg. 13.00 (978-1-4242-2135-6(8)) Dingles & Co.

—Who Was Harriet Tubman? Harrison, Nancy, illus. 2003. (Who Was... ? Ser.). 106p. (gr. 4-7). 15.00 (978-0-7569-1590-2(2)) Perfection Learning Corp.

McDonough, Yona Zeldis & Who HQ. Who Was Harriet Tubman? Harrison, Nancy, illus. 2019. (Who Was? Ser.). 112p. (J). (gr. 3-7). 5.99 (978-0-593-09722-9(X)); 15.99 (978-0-593-09723-6(8)) Penguin Young Readers Group. (Penguin Workshop).

McDougal-Littell Publishing Staff, contrib. by. A Nation Dividing 1800-1860. 2004. (Stories in History Ser.). (Illus.). 176p. (gr. 6-12). 13.32 (978-0-618-14222-4(3), 2-00242) Holt McDougal.

McKinney, Louise Chessi. The Journey to Freedom on the Underground Railroad. 2006. (ENG.). 32p. pap. 14.99 (978-1-4257-2304-0(7)) Xlibris Corp.

Mckissack, Patricia & Mckissack, Fredrick. Frederick Douglass: Fighter Against Slavery, 1 vol. 2013. (Famous African Americans Ser.). (ENG., Illus.). 24p. (gr. k-2). 25.27 (978-0-7660-4098-4(4), 119432c1-b3c2-4bd9-a960-5bce9bdb12f1, Enslow Elementary) Enslow Publishing, LLC.

McKissack, Patricia C. & McKissack, Fredrick L., Jr. Hard Labor: The First African Americans 1619. Fiedler, Joseph Daniel, illus. 2004. (Milestone Ser.). (ENG.). 64p. (J). (gr. 2-5). pap. 6.99 (978-0-689-86149-9(4), Simon & Schuster/Paula Wiseman Bks.) Simon & Schuster/Paula Wiseman Bks.

McLendon, Jacquelyn. Phillis Wheatley: A Revolutionary Poet. 2009. (Library of American Lives & Times Ser.). 112p. (gr. 5-5). 69.20 (978-1-60853-499-9(5)) Rosen Publishing Group, Inc., The.

McNeese, Tim. Dred Scott V. Sandford. 2006. (Great Supreme Court Decisions Ser.). (ENG., Illus.). 120p. (J). (gr. 5-9). lib. bdg. 32.95 (978-0-7910-9236-1(4), P114570, Facts On File) Infobase Holdings, Inc.

Meltzer, Brad. I Am Harriet Tubman. Eliopoulos, Christopher, illus. 2018. (Ordinary People Change the World Ser.). 40p. (J). (gr. k-4). 16.99 (978-0-7352-2871-9(X), Dial Bks) Penguin Young Readers Group.

Meriwether, Louise & Green, Jonathan. The Freedom Ship of Robert Smalls. 2018. (Young Palmetto Bks.). (ENG., Illus.). 32p. (J). 19.99 (978-1-61117-855-5(X), P568005) Univ. of South Carolina Pr.

Metz, Lorijo. El Movimiento Abolicionista / the Abolitionist Movement, 1 vol., 1. Beullens-Maoui, Nathalie, ed. 2013. (¡Celebremos la Libertad! / Let's Celebrate Freedom! Ser.). (SPA & ENG., Illus.). 24p. (J). (gr. 3-3). 26.27 (978-1-4777-3249-6(7), 75f9d84d-956e-4a99-9f2d-1740495f98e4, PowerKids Pr.) Rosen Publishing Group, Inc., The.

Moore, Cathy. Ellen Craft's Escape from Slavery. Braught, Mark, illus. 2010. (History Speaks: Picture Books Plus Reader's Theater Ser.). (ENG.). 48p. (gr. 2-4). (J). lib. bdg. 27.93 (978-0-7613-5875-6(7), Millbrook Pr.); pap. 9.95 (978-0-7613-6672-0(5)) Lerner Publishing Group.

Moriarty, J. T. Phillis Wheatley: African American Poet. 2009. (Primary Sources of Famous People in American History Ser.). 32p. (gr. 2-3). 47.90 (978-1-60851-717-6(9)) Rosen Publishing Group, Inc., The.

Morlock, Jeremy. Abolitionists & Slave Owners. 2019. (Opponents in American History Ser.). (ENG., Illus.). 32p. (J). (gr. 4-5). 60.00 (978-1-5383-4539-9(0), PowerKids Pr.) Rosen Publishing Group, Inc., The.

Morretta, Alison. John Brown: Armed Abolitionist, 1 vol. 2018. (Hero or Villain? Claims & Counterclaims Ser.). (ENG.). 112p. (YA). (gr. 8-8). lib. bdg. 45.93 (978-1-5026-3520-4(8), 974225df-4747-47c6-848c-ef5bfe691eff) Cavendish Square Publishing LLC.

—Slavery & Citizenship: Dred Scott V. Sandford, 1 vol. 2018. (Courting History Ser.). (ENG.). 64p. (gr. 6-6). lib. bdg. 37.36 (978-1-5026-3595-2(X), fbb21ed7-2481-454e-9750-4a44116b212a) Cavendish Square Publishing LLC.

—Slavery in Colonial America, 1 vol. 2017. (Primary Sources of Colonial America Ser.). (ENG.). 64p. (gr. 6-6). 35.93 (978-1-5026-3142-8(3), bc93833b-66e8-40f8-953f-8f6770f58450); pap. 16.28 (978-1-5026-3460-3(0), be73a4fc-1b87-4e14-a3b5-46fdee9e5059) Cavendish Square Publishing LLC.

Naden, Corinne & Flum Galvin, Irene. Dred Scott: Person or Property?, 1 vol. 2006. (Supreme Court Milestones Ser.). (ENG., Illus.). 128p. (J). (gr. 8-8). 45.50 (978-0-7614-1841-2(5), c0c31031-3114-488f-83a3-2d4a01460e85) Cavendish Square Publishing LLC.

National Geographic Learning. Reading Expeditions (Social Studies: People Who Changed America): the Anti-Slavery Movement. 2007. (Rise & Shine Ser.). (ENG.). 40p. pap. 21.95 (978-0-7922-8622-6(7)) National Geographic School Publishing, Inc.

—Reading Expeditions (Social Studies: Voices from America's Past): the Underground Railroad. 2007. (Nonfiction Reading & Writing Workshops Ser.). (ENG., Illus.). 40p. (J). pap. 21.95 (978-0-7922-4549-0(0)) National Geographic School Publishing, Inc.

Nelson, Drew & Nelson, Vaunda Micheaux. Juneteenth. Schroder, Mark, illus. 2006. (On My Own Holidays Ser.). (ENG.). 48p. (J). (gr. 2-4). per. 8.99 (978-0-8225-5974-0(9), b01ab1ed-2881-461d-b67a-64e6fc3464a0, First Avenue Editions) Lerner Publishing Group.

Norwich, Grace. I Am Harriet Tubman. Simon, Ute, illus. 2013. 127p. (J). (978-0-545-61344-6(2)) Scholastic, Inc.

—I Am Harriet Tubman (I Am #6) Simon, Ute, illus. 2013. (I Am Ser.: 6). (ENG.). 128p. (J). (gr. 3-5). pap. 5.99 (978-0-545-48436-7(7), Scholastic Paperbacks) Scholastic, Inc.

Otfinoski, Steven. From Fugitive to Freedom: The Story of the Underground Railroad. 2017. (Tangled History Ser.). (ENG., Illus.). 112p. (J). (gr. 3-9). lib. bdg. 32.65 (978-1-5157-3604-2(0), 133594, Capstone Pr.) Capstone.

Owens, Tom. Traveling on the Freedom Machines of the Transportation Age. 2003. (Reading Essentials in Social Studies). (Illus.). 40p. pap. 8.00 (978-0-7891-5873-4(6)) Perfection Learning Corp.

Paley, Caitlyn. Slave Narratives & the Writings of Freedmen, 1 vol. 2015. (Primary Sources of the Abolitionist Movement Ser.). (ENG., Illus.). 64p. (J). (gr. 6-6). 35.93 (978-1-5026-0524-5(4), dc581257-57ac-4cb3-a224-fbd8556214ec) Cavendish Square Publishing LLC.

Patterson, Marie. Slavery in America, 1 vol. rev. ed. 2005. (Social Studies: Informational Text Ser.). (ENG.). 24p. (gr. 4-8). pap. 10.99 (978-0-7439-8911-4(2)) Teacher Created Materials, Inc.

Peppas, Lynn. Juneteenth. 2010. (Celebrations in My World Ser.). (ENG., Illus.). 32p. (J). (gr. k-3). (978-0-7787-4928-8(2)); pap. (978-0-7787-4935-6(5)) Crabtree Publishing Co.

Perrin, Pat & Coleman, Wim. The Mystery of the Vanishing Slaves. 2004. (Cover-To-Cover Books). (Illus.). 64p. (J). (gr. 4-7). lib. bdg. 17.95 (978-0-7569-1041-9(2)) Perfection Learning Corp.

Perritano, John. Free at Last! How the Freeing of the Slaves Changed American History. 2008. (Graphic America Ser.). (ENG., Illus.). 32p. (J). (gr. 3-6). pap. (978-0-7787-4212-8(1)); lib. bdg. (978-0-7787-4185-5(0)) Crabtree Publishing Co.

Porterfield, Jason. Frederick Douglass: Abolitionist & Fighter for Equality, 1 vol. 2017. (Britannica Beginner Bios Ser.). (ENG.). 32p. (J). (gr. 2-3). pap. 13.90 *(978-1-68048-802-9(3),* 8eaee0ce-f673-4150-831c-71c61eefb1ba, Britannica Educational Publishing) Rosen Publishing Group, Inc., The.

Press, David P. Abraham Lincoln: The Great Emancipator. 2013. (ENG., Illus.). 64p. (J). *(978-0-7787-1061-5(0));* pap. *(978-0-7787-1064-6(5))* Crabtree Publishing Co.

Rappaport, Doreen. No More! Stories & Songs of Slave Resistance. Evans, Shane W., illus. 2005. (ENG.). 64p. (J). (gr. 4-7). reprint ed. pap. 9.99 *(978-0-7636-2876-5(X))* Candlewick Pr.

Ratliff, Thomas. You Wouldn't Want to Be a Civil War Soldier! A War You'D Rather Not Fight. 2013. (You Wouldn't Want To Ser.). lib. bdg. 20.80 *(978-0-606-31627-9(2))* Turtleback.

Rausch, Monica. Harriet Tubman, 1 vol. 2007. (Grandes Personajes (Great Americans) Ser.). (SPA & ENG., Illus.). 24p. (J). (gr. 2-4). lib. bdg. 24.67 *(978-0-8368-7985-8(6),* 37c3334d-c56d-49f8-a22f-710f4fba4f8b) Stevens, Gareth Publishing LLLP.

Rosen, Daniel. Dred Scott & the Supreme Court: Set Of 6. 2011. (Navigators Ser.). (J). pap. 48.00 net. *(978-1-4108-6258-7(5))* Benchmark Education Co.

Roxburgh, Ellis. Nat Turner's Slave Rebellion. 2017. (Rebellions, Revolts, & Uprisings Ser.). 48p. (gr. 5-5). pap. 84.30 *(978-1-5382-0753-6(2))* Stevens, Gareth Publishing LLLP.

Roza, Greg. Guide My Pen: The Poems of Phillis Wheatley, 1 vol. 2003. (Great Moments in American History Ser.). (ENG., Illus.). 32p. (J). (gr. 3-4). lib. bdg. 29.13 *(978-0-8239-4381-4(X),* 893e7e99-5c63-4123-9adb-02e4e0b7c4c9, Rosen Reference) Rosen Publishing Group, Inc., The.

Ruffin, Frances E. Sally Hemings. 2009. (American Legends Ser.). 24p. (gr. 3-3). 42.50 *(978-1-61511-386-6(X),* PowerKids Pr.) Rosen Publishing Group, Inc., The.

Russo, Kristin J. Viewpoints on the Underground Railroad. 2018. (Perspectives Library: Viewpoints & Perspectives Ser.). (ENG., Illus.). 48p. (J). (gr. 5-8). lib. bdg. 39.21 *(978-1-5341-2969-6(3),* 211920) Cherry Lake Publishing.

Saidian, Siyavush. The Transatlantic Slave Trade: Slavery Comes to the New World, 1 vol. 2017. (Lucent Library of Black History Ser.). (ENG.). 104p. (YA). (gr. 7-7). 41.03 *(978-1-5345-6237-0(0),* 88b6f1af-88c1-4698-a107-5dde433942eb, Lucent Pr.) Greenhaven Publishing LLC.

Sawyer, Kem Knapp. Harriet Tubman. 2010. (DK Biography Ser.). (ENG., Illus.). 128p. (J). (gr. 5-8). 18.69 *(978-0-7566-5807-6(1))* Dorling Kindersley Publishing, Inc.

Schmid, Katie Kelley. Nat Turner & Slave Life on a Southern Plantation, 1 vol. 2013. (Jr. Graphic African American History Ser.). (Illus.). 24p. (J). (ENG.). (gr. 2-3). pap. 11.60 *(978-1-4777-1453-9(7),* 8bc536b5-87fd-4812-ba81-35b2ae4fa79e); (ENG., (gr. 2-3). lib. bdg. 28.93 *(978-1-4777-1314-3(X),* 92a828d3-4636-48db-8581-fb3bf864f169); (gr. 3-6). pap. 63.60 *(978-1-4777-1454-6(5))* Rosen Publishing Group, Inc., The. (PowerKids Pr.).

Sebree, Chet'la & Sirimarco, Elizabeth. Historical Sources on Slavery, 1 vol. 2019. (America's Story Ser.). (ENG.). 144p. (gr. 8-8). pap. 22.16 *(978-1-5026-4066-4(4),* 5ef36569-555b-449e-8a10-32a7d45ab5c4) Cavendish Square Publishing LLC.

Shea, Therese M. The African Burial Ground, 1 vol. 2016. (Hidden History Ser.). (ENG., Illus.). 32p. (J). (gr. 4-5). pap. 11.50 *(978-1-4824-5787-2(3),* 819cc515-201f-4a11-9ab1-b6c2dbbb160a) Stevens, Gareth Publishing LLLP.

Sherman, Pat. Ben & the Emancipation Proclamation. Cooper, Floyd, illus. 2009. (ENG.). 32p. (J). (gr. 3-7). 17.00 *(978-0-8028-5319-6(6),* Eerdmans Bks For Young Readers) Eerdmans, William B. Publishing Co.

Sirimarco, Elizabeth. The Time of Slavery, 1 vol. 2007. (American Voices From Ser.). (ENG., Illus.). 160p. (gr. 6-6). lib. bdg. 41.21 *(978-0-7614-2169-6(6),* 807c3378-871d-4140-afb9-5d2454c00e63) Cavendish Square Publishing LLC.

Skog, Jason. The Dred Scott Decision. 2006. (We the People: Civil War Era Ser.). (ENG., Illus.). 48p. (gr. 5-6). 7.95 *(978-0-7565-2038-0(X),* Compass Point Bks.) Capstone.

Slavery: Analyzing Visual Primary Sources. 2006. cd-rom 59.95 net. *(978-1-56004-262-4(1))* Social Studies Schl. Service.

Slavery & Slave Resistance, 12 vols. 2016. (Slavery & Slave Resistance Ser.). (ENG.). 128p. (gr. 6-6). lib. bdg. 233.58 *(978-0-7660-7504-7(4),* faaf8cbd-367d-4a99-96ef-5ecf8693a1da) Enslow Publishing, LLC.

Smith, Jr, Charles R. Brick by Brick. 2012. (ENG., Illus.). 32p. (J). (gr. -1-3). 17.99 *(978-0-06-192082-0(7),* Amistad) HarperCollins Pubs.

Smith, Charles R., Jr. Brick by Brick. Cooper, Floyd, illus. 2015. (ENG.). 32p. (J). (gr. -1-3). pap. 8.99 *(978-0-06-192084-4(3),* Amistad) HarperCollins Pubs.

—Brick by Brick. 2015. (J). lib. bdg. 17.20 *(978-0-606-37371-5(3))* Turtleback.

Smith, Maximilian. The History of Juneteenth, 1 vol. 2015. (History of Our Holidays Ser.). (ENG.). 24p. (J). (gr. 1-2). pap. 9.15 *(978-1-4824-3894-9(1),* ad53d1d3-110c-43ce-b7ee-c0c883f856b5) Stevens, Gareth Publishing LLLP.

Stearns, Dan. Harriet Tubman & the Underground Railroad, 1 vol. 2005. (In the Footsteps of American Heroes Ser.). (ENG., Illus.). 64p. (J). (gr. 5-8). lib. bdg. 36.67 *(978-0-8368-6428-1(X),* 0c93b9fc-79bf-476e-a6cc-85a9c820bfac, Gareth Stevens Secondary Library) Stevens, Gareth Publishing LLLP.

Stein, R. Conrad. Harriet Tubman: On My Underground Railroad I Never Ran My Train off the Track, 1 vol. 2008. (Americans: the Spirit of a Nation Ser.). (ENG., Illus.). 128p. (J). (gr. 5-6). lib. bdg. 35.93 *(978-0-7660-3481-5(X),* f1675bad-1c07-4b76-adc6-eb89aa02c903) Enslow Publishing, LLC.

Sterling, Dorothy. Forever Free: The Story of the Emancipation Proclamation. Crichlow, Ernest, illus. 2012. 216p. 44.95 *(978-1-258-25034-8(9));* pap. 29.95 *(978-1-258-25547-3(2))* Literary Licensing, LLC.

Stoltman, Joan. Did the Abolition Movement Abolish Slavery?, 1 vol. 2018. (Key Questions in American History Ser.). (ENG.). 32p. (gr. 4-5). 29.27 *(978-1-5081-6750-1(8),* 5f824fcc-3a71-479f-8519-58adb3b1021c, PowerKids Pr.) Rosen Publishing Group, Inc., The.

Sullivan, Laura. The Colonial Slave Family, 1 vol. 2015. (Colonial People Ser.). (ENG., Illus.). 48p. (gr. 4-4). 34.07 *(978-1-5026-0486-6(8),* 27404ad0-e6b7-49b2-9a9a-3dd69d10d871) Cavendish Square Publishing LLC.

Susienka, Kristen. Frederick Douglass, 1 vol. 2019. (African American Leaders of Courage Ser.). (ENG.). 24p. (J). (gr. 1-2). pap. 9.25 *(978-1-7253-0834-3(7),* 5db88bbf-a07c-4b5f-97b8-907dda7a0163, PowerKids Pr.) Rosen Publishing Group, Inc., The.

Sutherland, Jonathan. Slavery & the Abolition Movement. 2017. (Civil War Ser.: Vol. 5). (ENG., Illus.). 79p. (J). (gr. 7-12). 24.95 *(978-1-4222-3883-7(0))* Mason Crest.

Tate, Don. William Still & His Freedom Stories: The Father of the Underground Railroad. 2020. (Illus.). 40p. (J). (gr. 1-4). 18.99 *(978-1-56145-935-3(6))* Peachtree Publishing Co. Inc.

Taylor, Charlotte. Phillis Wheatley: Colonial African-American Poet, 1 vol. 2015. (Exceptional African Americans Ser.). (ENG., Illus.). 24p. (J). (gr. 3-3). 24.27 *(978-0-7660-7326-5(2),* 4a41e8fd-059b-4d93-9146-095434763890) Enslow Publishing, LLC.

Taylor, Yuval, ed. Growing up in Slavery: Stories of Young Slaves As Told by Themselves. 2007. (ENG., Illus.). 256p. (J). (gr. 9). pap. 16.99 *(978-1-55652-635-0(0))* Chicago Review Pr., Inc.

Thomas, Paul. Olaudah Equiano: from Slavery to Freedom: Band 15/Emerald (Collins Big Cat) Ambrus, Victor, illus. 2007. (Collins Big Cat Ser.). (ENG.). 48p. (J). (gr. 3-4). pap. 11.99 *(978-0-00-723096-9(6))* HarperCollins Pubs. Ltd. GBR. Dist: Independent Pubs. Group.

Thomas, William David. William Lloyd Garrison: A Radical Voice Against Slavery, 1 vol. 2009. (Voices for Freedom Ser.). (ENG.). 64p. (J). (gr. 5-8). pap. *(978-0-7787-4841-0(3));* lib. bdg. *(978-0-7787-4825-0(1))* Crabtree Publishing Co.

Thompson, Michael D. Working on the Dock of the Bay: Labor & Enterprise in an Antebellum Southern Port. 2018. (ENG., Illus.). 296p. (J). pap. 31.99 *(978-1-61117-857-9(6),* P568034) Univ. of South Carolina Pr.

Trumbauer, Lisa. Abraham Lincoln & the Civil War. rev. ed. 2016. (Life in the Time Of Ser.). (ENG.). 32p. (J). (gr. 1-3). pap. 8.29 *(978-1-4846-3822-4(0),* 134722, Heinemann) Capstone.

Turner, Glennette Tilley. Fort Mose: And the Story of the Man Who Built the First Free Black Settlement in Colonial America. 2010. (ENG., Illus.). 48p. (J). (gr. 3-7). 18.95 *(978-0-8109-4056-7(6),* 652801) Abrams, Inc.

Uhl, Xina M. & Buell, Tonya. A Primary Source Investigation of Slavery, 1 vol. 2018. (Uncovering American History Ser.). (ENG.). 64p. (gr. 6-6). pap. 13.95 *(978-1-5081-8408-9(9),* 910491eb-2281-4972-acec-6910024d6dd0, Rosen Reference) Rosen Publishing Group, Inc., The.

Underwood, Deborah. Nat Love. 2008. (History Maker Biographies Ser.). (ENG., Illus.). 48p. (J). (gr. 3-6). lib. bdg. 27.93 *(978-0-8225-7171-1(4),* Lerner Pubns.) Lerner Publishing Group.

Uschan, Michael V. The Civil Rights Movement, 1 vol. 2010. (American History Ser.). (ENG.). 128p. (gr. 7-7). 41.03 *(978-1-4205-0261-9(1),* b4cb94dc-a14b-4853-9b95-77c46af42b7d, Lucent Pr.) Greenhaven Publishing LLC.

Waxman, Laura Hamilton. How Did Slaves Find a Route to Freedom? And Other Questions about the Underground Railroad. 2011. (Six Questions of American History Ser.). (ENG.). 48p. (gr. 4-6). pap. 56.72 *(978-0-7613-7641-5(0));* (Illus.). (J). lib. bdg. 30.65 *(978-0-7613-5229-7(5),* c97e1afb-3b6e-49d9-bb44-63d8c24cf045, Lerner Pubns.) Lerner Publishing Group.

Weatherford, Carole Boston. The Beatitudes: From Slavery to Civil Rights. Ladwig, Tim, illus. 2009. (ENG.). 36p. (J). (gr. 3-7). 17.00 *(978-0-8028-5352-3(8),* Eerdmans Bks For Young Readers) Eerdmans, William B. Publishing Co.

Wells-Cole, Catherine. Slavery & the Forging of Early America. 2014. (J). *(978-1-59935-410-1(1))* Reynolds, Morgan Inc.

White, Arisa & Atkins, Laura. Biddy Mason Speaks Up. Freeman, Laura, illus. 2019. (Fighting for Justice Ser.: 2). (ENG.). 112p. (J). 18.00 *(978-1-59714-403-2(7))* Heyday.

Winter, Jonah. My Name Is James Madison Hemings. Widener, Terry, illus. 2016. (ENG.). 40p. (J). (gr. k-4). 17.99 *(978-0-385-38342-4(8),* Schwartz & Wade Bks.) Random Hse. Children's Bks.

Winters, Kay. Voices from the Underground Railroad. Day, Larry, illus. 2018. 48p. (J). (gr. 2-4). 18.99 *(978-0-8037-4092-1(1),* Dial Bks) Penguin Young Readers Group.

Woelfle, Gretchen. Mumbet's Declaration of Independence. Delinois, Alix, illus. 2014. (ENG.). 32p. (J). (gr. 1-4). 19.99 *(978-0-7613-6589-1(3),* 67deb318-9dc6-42ef-9909-b3bfab8d493f, Carolrhoda Bks.) Lerner Publishing Group.

Wolny, Philip. The Underground Railroad: A Primary Source History of the Journey to Freedom, 1 vol. 2004. (Primary Sources in American History Ser.). (ENG., Illus.). 64p. (J). (gr. 5-8). lib. bdg. 37.13 *(978-0-8239-4008-0(X),* 9edec6a4-1163-41a6-b9ed-75ecfb826a0e, Rosen Reference) Rosen Publishing Group, Inc., The.

5,000 Miles to Freedom: Ellen & William Craft's Flight from Slavery. Lt. ed. 2013. 202p. pap. *(978-1-4596-6713-6(1))* ReadHowYouWant.com, Ltd.

SLAVERY—UNITED STATES—POETRY

Alexander, richard. The Transatlantic Slave Trade: The Forced Migration of Africans to America (1607-1830), 1 vol., 1. 2015. (Spotlight on Immigration & Migration Ser.). (ENG., Illus.). 24p. (J). (gr. 4-5). pap. 11.00 *(978-1-5081-4100-6(2),* c13da223-d783-4a35-be11-1d9ba0da1f08, PowerKids Pr.) Rosen Publishing Group, Inc., The.

Engle, Margarita. The Poet Slave of Cuba: A Biography of Juan Francisco Manzano. Qualls, Sean, illus. 2011. (SPA.). 208p. (YA). (gr. 7-12). pap. 10.99 *(978-0-312-65928-8(8),* 900070514) Square Fish.

Hinton, KaaVonia. To Preserve the Union: Causes & Effects of the Missouri Compromise, 1 vol. 2013. (Cause & Effect Ser.). (ENG.). 32p. (J). (gr. 3-6). 27.99 *(978-1-4765-0238-0(2),* 122292); pap. 8.95 *(978-1-4765-3404-6(7),* 123535) Capstone.

McLeese, Don. Phillis Wheatley. 2004. (Heroes of the American Revolution Ser.). (Illus.). 32p. (J). (gr. -1 — 1). pap. 5.95 *(978-1-59515-320-3(9))* Rourke Educational Media.

Moriarty, J. T. Phillis Wheatley: African American Poet = Poeta Afroamericana, 1 vol. 2003. (Famous People in American History / Grandes Personajes en la Historia de Los Estados Unidos Ser.). (ENG & SPA., Illus.). 32p. (J). (gr. 3-4). lib. bdg. 29.13 *(978-0-8239-4167-4(1),* d6c50ca0-35d0-44e5-b6e3-2c186c5b8a60, Editorial Buenas Letras) Rosen Publishing Group, Inc., The.

Rissman, Rebecca. Slavery in the United States, 1 vol. 2014. (African-American History Ser.). (ENG.). 48p. (J). (gr. 4-8). 35.64 *(978-1-62403-148-9(X),* 1177) ABDO Publishing Co.

Schraff, Anne. The Life of Frederick Douglass: Speaking Out Against Slavery, 1 vol. 2014. (Legendary African Americans Ser.). (ENG.). 96p. (gr. 6-7). 31.61 *(978-0-7660-6132-3(9),* 6401201b-beaa-4a45-97e2-a99b8230aed7) Enslow Publishing, LLC.

SLAVS—UNITED STATES

Brindell Fradin, Dennis. The Underground Railroad, 1 vol. 2009. (Turning Points in U. S. History Ser.). (ENG.). 48p. (gr. 4-4). lib. bdg. 34.07 *(978-0-7614-3014-8(8),* 9dc92785-4a3d-4835-bf07-5679dd35196f) Cavendish Square Publishing LLC.

SLEEP

see also Dreams

Aida, Arlene. The Book of ZZZs. 2009. (Illus.). 16p. (J). (gr. k-k). 7.95 *(978-0-88776-906-1(3),* Tundra Bks.) Tundra Bks. CAN. Dist: Penguin Random Hse. LLC.

Barraclough, Sue. Sleep & Rest. 2012. (Healthy Habits Ser.). (ENG., Illus.). 24p. (gr. 1-3). lib. bdg. 24.25 *(978-1-59771-309-2(0))* Sea-To-Sea Pubns.

Beck, Isabel L., et al. Trophies Kindergarten: I Nap. 2003. (Trophies Ser.). (gr. k-6). 13.80 *(978-0-15-329528-7(7))* Harcourt Schl. Pubs.

Berger, Melvin & Berger, Gilda. Go to Sleep. 2007. (Illus.). 32p. (J). pap. *(978-0-439-02450-1(1))* Scholastic, Inc.

Berry, Joy. I Love Bedtime. Regan, Dana, illus. 2010. (Teach Me About Ser.). (ENG.). 20p. (J). (gr. k — 1). pap. 5.99 *(978-1-60577-004-8(3))* Berry, Joy Enterprises.

—Teach Me about Bedtime. 2009. (ENG.). 40p. (J). (gr. k — 1). bds. 7.95 *(978-1-60577-010-9(8))* Berry, Joy Enterprises.

Bonnett-Rampersaud, Louise. How Do You Sleep?, 0 vols. Kest, Kristin, illus. 2013. (ENG.). 32p. (J). (gr. -1-1). pap. 9.99 *(978-1-4778-1669-1(0),* 9781477816691, Two Lions) Amazon Publishing.

Christelis, Paul. Sleep Easy: A Mindfulness Guide to Getting a Good Night's Sleep. Paganelli, Elisa, illus. 2018. (Everyday Mindfulness Ser.). (ENG.). 32p. (J). (gr. k-4). 16.99 *(978-1-63198-334-4(2),* 83344) Free Spirit Publishing Inc.

Colligan, L. H. Sleep Disorders, 1 vol. 2009. (Health Alert Ser.). (ENG.). 64p. (gr. 4-4). lib. bdg. 35.50 *(978-0-7614-2913-5(1),* e5e5a659-1b11-4cd2-874a-5e39d58be2cb) Cavendish Square Publishing LLC.

Currie-McGhee, L. K. What Are Sleep Disorders? 2015. (ENG., Illus.). 80p. (J). lib. bdg. *(978-1-60152-930-5(9))* ReferencePoint Pr., Inc.

Esherick, Joan. Drug Therapy & Sleep Disorders. 2003. (Psychiatric Disorders: Drugs & Psychology for the Mind & Bod Ser.). (Illus.). 126p. (YA). (gr. 7). pap. 14.95 *(978-1-4222-0400-9(6))* Mason Crest.

—Sleep Deprivation & Its Consequences. Bridgemohan, Carolyn & Forman, Sara, eds. 2013. (Young Adult's Guide to the Science of Health Ser.). (Illus.). 128p. (J). (gr. 7-18). pap. 14.95 *(978-1-4222-3003-9(1))* Mason Crest.

Esherick, Joan, frwd. Drug Therapy & Sleep Disorders. 2004. (Encyclopedia of Psychiatric Drugs & Their Disorders Ser.). (Illus.). 128p. (YA). lib. bdg. 24.95 *(978-1-59084-576-9(5))* Mason Crest.

Feeney, Kathy. Sleep Well: Why You Need to Rest. 2004. (Your Health Ser.). (ENG., Illus.). 24p. (J). (gr. 2-4). per. 7.45 *(978-0-7368-4452-9(X),* 90845, Capstone Pr.) Capstone.

Feldman, Eve B. Animals Don't Wear Pajamas: A Book about Sleeping. 2004. (Illus.). 32p. (J). pap. 16.95 *(978-0-9764957-0-3(8))* Saturn International.

Furstinger, Nancy. How Do Dolphins Sleep? 2018. (Crazy Animal Facts Ser.). (ENG., Illus.). 32p. (J). (gr. 4-6). lib. bdg. 28.65 *(978-1-5435-4118-2(6),* 139072, Capstone Pr.) Capstone.

Gaestel, Tiffany & Benchmark Education Co. Staff. The Science of Sleep & Dreams. 2014. (Text Connections Ser.). (J). (gr. 5). *(978-1-4900-1381-7(4))* Benchmark Education Co.

Gaston, P. J. How Do You Know When It's Time to Go to Bed? Gaston, Carter J., illus. 2008. (ENG.). 28p. (J). 10.00 *(978-0-9675574-2-7(9))* "How Do You Know".

Gates, Mariam. Sweet Dreams: Bedtime Visualizations for Kids. 2019. (ENG., Illus.). 32p. (J). 17.95 *(978-1-68364-170-4(1),* 900220892) Sounds True, Inc.

Gelb, John. Power Nap Kit. 2003. (YA). 34.95 *(978-0-9742002-0-0(4))* At Peace Media, LLC.

Gleisner, Jenna Lee. My Body Needs Rest. 2014. (Healthy Me Ser.). (ENG., Illus.). 24p. (J). (gr. 1-4). lib. bdg. 27.10 *(978-1-60753-588-1(2),* 15963) Amicus.

Harris, Brooke. Are You Sleeping? Oliver, Mark, illus. 2010. (Rising Readers Ser.). (J). 3.49 *(978-1-60719-685-3(9))* Newmark Learning LLC.

La Hora de Dormir, 6 Packs. (Chiquilibros Ser.). (SPA.). (gr. k-1). 23.00 *(978-0-7635-8597-6(1))* Rigby Education.

Hughes, Susan. Nap Time. 2017. (ENG., Illus.). 14p. (J). (gr. -1). bds. 7.99 *(978-1-55451-949-1(7))* Annick Pr., Ltd. CAN. Dist: Publishers Group West (PGW).

Janisch, Heinz. Good Night Giants. Bansch, Helga, illus. 2011. 32p. (J). (gr. -1-3). pap. 9.95 *(978-1-4338-0951-4(6));* pap. 14.95 *(978-1-4338-0950-7(8))* American Psychological Assn. (Magination Pr.).

Johnson, Marion. Caillou, What's That Noise. CINAR Corporation Staff, illus. 2004. (Clubhouse Usa Ser.). (ENG.). 24p. (J). pap. 3.95 *(978-2-89450-489-5(6))* Ellipsis Pr.

Kocienda, Genevieve. Do Not Disturb: the Importance of Sleep High Beginning Book with Online Access, 1 vol. 2014. (ENG., Illus.). 24p. pap., E-Book, E-Book 9.50 *(978-1-107-64682-7(0))* Cambridge Univ. Pr.

Légaré, Gisèle & L'Heureux. Good Night! Brignaud, Pierre, illus. 2006. (Hand in Hand Ser.). (ENG.). 24p. (J). (gr. -1-k). 5.95 *(978-2-89450-588-5(4))* Caillouet, Gerry.

Légaré, Gisèle & L'Heureux, Christine. Caillou: Good Night! Sleep Well: Nighttime. Brignaud, Pierre, illus. 2017. (Caillou's Essentials Ser.). (ENG.). 24p. (J). (gr. -1-k). bds. 7.99 *(978-2-89718-357-8(8))* Caillouet, Gerry.

Maerov, Jeff. Boca Buddies. Can't We Just Say Goodnight? 2012. 40p. pap. 11.99 *(978-0-578-11402-6(X))* Maerov, Jeffrey.

Mahjouri. The Science of Sleep. Mahjouri, illus. 2014. (ENG., Illus.). pap. 9.99 *(978-1-941006-04-7(3))* SoGo Creation.

Maile, Ruby. When Do You Sleep? 2012. (Level E Ser.). (ENG., Illus.). 16p. (J). (gr. k-2). pap. 7.95 *(978-1-927136-40-9(7),* 19434) RiverStream Publishing.

Marcus, Mary Brophy. Sleep Disorders. 2009. (Psychological Disorders Ser.). (ENG., Illus.). 128p. (gr. 7-12). 37.50 *(978-1-60413-085-0(7),* P159431, Facts On File) Infobase Holdings, Inc.

Marsico, Katie. Get a Good Night's Sleep! 2015. (21st Century Junior Library: Your Healthy Body Ser.). (ENG., Illus.). 24p. (gr. 2-5). 29.21 *(978-1-63188-988-2(5),* 205864) Cherry Lake Publishing.

—Sleep Well! Bane, Jeff, illus. 2019. (My Early Library: My Healthy Habits Ser.). (ENG.). 24p. (J). (gr. k-1). pap. 12.79 *(978-1-5341-3936-7(2),* 212573); lib. bdg. 30.64 *(978-1-5341-4280-0(0),* 212572) Cherry Lake Publishing.

McAneney, Caitie. Freaky Stories While You Sleep, 1 vol. 2016. (Freaky True Science Ser.). (ENG., Illus.). 32p. (J). (gr. 4-5). pap. 11.50 *(978-1-4824-4851-1(3),* e84f85df-e8ac-4d82-b98f-af2cdb52bb59) Stevens, Gareth Publishing LLLP.

Moriarty, Susie. Mmmmmm My Blankie. 2012. 20p. pap. 13.77 *(978-1-4269-6573-9(7))* Trafford Publishing.

Peterkin, Allan D. National Geographic Kids Dream Journal. 2019. 144p. (J). (gr. 3-7). 12.99 *(978-1-4263-3326-2(9),* National Geographic Kids) Disney Publishing Worldwide.

Peterson, Judy Monroe. Frequently Asked Questions about Sleep & Sleep Deprivation, 1 vol. 2010. (FAQ: Teen Life Ser.). (ENG., Illus.). 64p. (YA). (gr. 5-6). lib. bdg. 37.13 *(978-1-4358-3512-2(3),* 3b6e314f-2528-452d-ac35-f7cb5b69fe54) Rosen Publishing Group, Inc., The.

Poole, H. W. Sleep Disorders, Vol. 13. Walters, Anne S., ed. 2015. (Mental Illnesses & Disorders: Awareness & Understanding Ser.). (Illus.). 48p. (J). (gr. 5). 20.95 *(978-1-4222-3376-4(6))* Mason Crest.

Royston, Angela. Why Do I Sleep? 2012. (My Body Ser.). (ENG., Illus.). 24p. (gr. k-4). pap. 7.95 *(978-1-77092-001-9(3))* Saunders Bk. Co. CAN. Dist: RiverStream Publishing.

Silverstein, Alvin, et al. Handy Health Guide to Better Sleep, 1 vol. 2013. (Handy Health Guides). (ENG.). 48p. (gr. 5-6). lib. bdg. 27.93 *(978-0-7660-4278-0(2),* dc4ea26b-2934-410b-a218-83448c430619) Enslow Publishing, LLC.

Silverstein, Virginia & Silverstein Nunn, Laura. Handy Health Guide to Better Sleep, 1 vol. 2013. (Handy Health Guides). (ENG.). 48p. (gr. 5-6). pap. 11.53 *(978-1-4644-0499-3(2),* 2bb4ae0e-679c-4947-82e9-579df1587f82) Enslow Publishing, LLC.

Sjonger, Rebecca. You Need Rest to Be at Your Best! 2015. (Healthy Habits for a Lifetime Ser.). (ENG., Illus.). 24p. (J). (gr. 2-2). *(978-0-7787-1881-9(6))* Crabtree Publishing Co.

Sleeping: Individual Title Six-Packs. (Literatura 2000 Ser.). (gr. 1-2). 28.00 *(978-0-7635-0113-6(1))* Rigby Education.

Snedden, Robert. Sleep, Dreams, & Your Brain, 1 vol. 2018. (What Goes on Inside Your Brain? Ser.). (ENG.). 48p. (gr. 4-5). pap. 15.05 *(978-1-5382-3554-6(4),* 2484f590-51cd-45fa-8a21-c2a605d71865) Stevens, Gareth Publishing LLLP.

Studio Mouse & Studio Mouse. My First Sleepover. rev. ed. 2007. (Carry Tune Ser.). (ENG., Illus.). 24p. (J). 4.99 *(978-1-59069-607-1(7))* Studio Mouse LLC.

Tompkins, Michael A. & Thompson, Monique A. The Insomnia Workbook for Teens: Skills to Help You Stop Stressing & Start Sleeping Better. 2018. (ENG.). 176p. (YA). (gr. 6-12). pap. 23.95 *(978-1-68403-124-5(9),* 41245, Instant Help Books) New Harbinger Pubns.

Treisman, Karen. Neon the Ninja Activity Book for Children Who Struggle with Sleep & Nightmares: A Therapeutic Story with Creative Activities for Children Aged 5-10. 2018. (Therapeutic Treasures Collection). 128p. (C). pap. 29.95 *(978-1-78592-550-4(4),* 696881) Kingsley, Jessica Pubs. GBR. Dist: Hachette UK Distribution.

Vallejo-Nagera, Alejandra. No Tengo Sueno! Guerrero, Andres, illus. (SPA.). 31p. (J). (gr. k-1). 8.95 *(978-1-58986-546-4(4))* Santillana USA Publishing Co., Inc.

Verdick, Elizabeth & Lisovskis, Marjorie. Rest: A Board Book about Bedtime. 2014. (Happy Healthy Baby(r) Ser.). (ENG., Illus.). 24p. (J). (— 1). bds. 7.99 *(978-1-57542-427-9(4))* Free Spirit Publishing Inc.

Zolotow, Charlotte. Sleepy Book. Date not set. (ENG.). 40p. (J). (gr. -1-3). pap. 5.99 *(978-0-06-443737-0(X))* HarperCollins Pubs.

SLEEP—FICTION

Ackerley, Sarah. Patrick the Somnambulist. Ackerley, Sarah, illus. 2008. (ENG., Illus.). 32p. (J). (gr. -1 — 1). 14.95 *(978-1-933831-07-7(3))* Blooming Tree Pr.

Albee, Sarah. Time for Bed, Elmo! (Sesame Street) Swanson, Maggie, illus. 2014. (Little Golden Book Ser.). (ENG.). 24p. (J). (-k). 5.99 *(978-0-385-37138-4(1),* Golden Bks.) Random Hse. Children's Bks.

Ambrosio, Michael. It Takes a Lot of Love. Awes, Jennifer, illus. 2007. 32p. (J). 14.95 *(978-0-9716085-4-2(7))* LionX Publishing.

Amen, Daniel. Time for Bed, Sleepyhead: The Falling Asleep Book, 1 vol. Yerrill, Gail, illus. 2016. (ENG.). 32p. (J). 16.99 *(978-0-310-75822-8(X))* Zonderkidz.

Arant, Bruce. Simpson's Sheep Just Want to Sleep! 2017. (ENG., Illus.). 32p. (J). 16.99 *(978-1-4413-2429-0(1),* d1d43977-002e-4650-9006-9d38e13ced02) Peter Pauper Pr. Inc.

Arnold, Marsha Diane. Baby Animals Take a Nap. Tildes, Phyllis Limbacher, illus. 2017. 10p. (J). (— 1). bds. 6.99 *(978-1-58089-539-2(5))* Charlesbridge Publishing, Inc.
Ashby, Gaylene. STORY TIME A Collection of Three Children's Stories. 2008. 28p. 14.95 *(978-1-4357-1929-3(8))* Lulu Pr., Inc.
Baker, Ken. Cow Can't Sleep. Gray, Steve, illus. 2018. (ENG.). 25p. (J). (gr. -1-3). pap. 9.99 *(978-1-5420-9205-0(1),* 9781542092050, Two Lions) Amazon Publishing.
—Cow Can't Sleep, 0 vols. Gray, Steve, illus. 2012. (ENG.). 24p. (J). (gr. -1-3). 12.99 *(978-0-7614-6198-2(1),* 9780761461982, Two Lions) Amazon Publishing.
Balog, Cyn. Sleepless. 2010. (ENG.). 240p. (YA). (gr. 7-12). 22.44 *(978-0-385-73848-4(X))* Random House Publishing Group.
Barchers, Suzanne I. Dad Wants a Nap, 1 vol. rev. ed. 2011. (Phonics Ser.). (ENG., Illus.). 16p. (gr. k-1). 6.99 *(978-1-4333-2407-9(5))* Teacher Created Materials, Inc.
—Pete Has Fast Feet, 1 vol. rev. ed. 2011. (Phonics Ser.). (ENG., Illus.). 16p. (gr. k-2). 6.99 *(978-1-4333-2915-9(8))* Teacher Created Materials, Inc.
Benchmark Education Co., LLC. Mr. Jitters & the Sleep Machine Big Book. 2014. (Shared Reading Foundations Ser.). (J). (gr. -1). *(978-1-4509-9435-4(0))* Benchmark Education Co.
—One Frosty Night at the Farm Big Book. 2014. (Shared Reading Foundations Ser.). (J). (gr. -1). *(978-1-4509-9443-9(1))* Benchmark Education Co.
Bergren, Lisa Tawn. God Gave Us Sleep. Bryant, Laura J., illus. 2015. (ENG.). 40p. (J). (gr. -1-2). 11.99 *(978-1-60142-663-5(1),* WaterBrook Pr.) Crown Publishing Group, The.
Berry, Ron & Sharp, Chris. It's Bedtime. Sharp, Chris & Currant, Gary, illus. 2003. (It's Time to Ser.). (ENG.). 14p. (J). (gr. -1-k). bds. 6.95 *(978-1-891100-61-1(0))* Smart Kidz Media, Inc.
Blair, Eric. Sleeping Beauty: A Retelling of the Grimm's Fairy Tale, 1 vol. Ouren, Todd, illus. 2011. (My First Classic Story Ser.). (ENG.). 32p. (J). (gr. k-3). pap. 7.10 *(978-1-4048-7360-5(0),* 118576, Picture Window Bks.) Capstone.
Blomgren, Jennifer. Where Do I Sleep? A Pacific Northwest Lullaby. Gabriel, Andrea, illus. 2015. (ENG.). 22p. (J). (— 1). bds. 10.99 *(978-1-63217-019-4(1),* Little Bigfoot) Sasquatch Bks.
Bonnell, Kris. Where Can Louis Sleep? 2007. (J). pap. 5.95 *(978-1-933727-57-8(8))* Reading Reading Bks., LLC.
Bonnett-Rampersaud, Louise. How Do You Sleep?, 1 vol. Kest, Kristin, illus. 2008. (ENG.). 34p. (J). (gr. -1). 6.99 *(978-0-7614-5449-6(7))* Marshall Cavendish Corp.
A Book of Sleep. 2011. (ENG.). 24p. (J). (gr. k — 1). bds. 6.99 *(978-0-375-86618-0(3),* Knopf Bks. for Young Readers) Random Hse. Children's Bks.
Boynton, Sandra. The Going to Bed Book. Boynton, Sandra, illus. 2006. (ENG., Illus.). 14p. (J). bds. 12.95 *(978-1-4169-2794-5(8),* Little Simon) Little Simon.
Boza, Eduardo Robles. Mi Amiga No Qiere Dormir.Tr. of My Friend Doesn't Want to Sleep. (SPA.). (J). 4.95 *(978-970-05-0130-7(2))* Grijalbo, Editorial MEX. Dist: AIMS International Bks., Inc.
Bradford, Wade. There's a Dinosaur on the 13th Floor. Hawkes, Kevin, illus. 2018. (ENG.). 40p. (J). (gr. -1-3). 17.99 *(978-0-7636-8665-9(4))* Candlewick Pr.
Brannock, Martha Lee. Teddy Bear Too-Too. 2007. 28p. per. 18.65 *(978-1-4257-4143-3(6))* Xlibris Corp.
Braun, Sebastien. Back to Bed, Ed! 2010. (ENG., Illus.). 32p. (J). (gr. -1-k). 16.95 *(978-1-56145-518-8(0))* Peachtree Publishing Co. Inc.
Bray, Libba. Lair of Dreams: A Diviners Novel. 2015. (Diviners Ser.: 2). (ENG.). 624p. (YA). (gr. 7-17). E-Book 45.00 *(978-0-316-36488-1(6))* Little, Brown Bks. for Young Readers.
Brewer, Elly. Jerry & the Jannans. 2006. 320p. (J). (gr. 4-7). pap. 11.99 *(978-0-7475-8213-7(0))* Bloomsbury Publishing Plc GBR. Dist: Independent Pubs. Group.
Brown, Marc, illus. Monkey: Not Ready for Bedtime. 2017. (J). pap. *(978-0-399-55782-8(2))* Knopf, Alfred A. Inc.
Brown, Margaret Wise. Margaret Wise Brown's the Whispering Rabbit. Won, Annie, illus. 2017. (J). *(978-1-5182-2278-8(1),* Golden Bks.) Random Hse. Children's Bks.
Burlingham, Abigail. All Grown Up, 1 vol. Everitt-Stewart, Andy, illus. 2009. (Stories to Grow With Ser.). (ENG.). 24p. (J). (gr. 1-2). 27.27 *(978-1-60754-469-2(5),* 9a1658ce-e9e3-4679-8f17-ee20181e6304); pap. 9.15 *(978-1-60754-470-8(9),* 8d0efe7a-0bcb-4991-805f-c28dc359e4b2) Rosen Publishing Group, Inc., The. (Windmill Bks.).
Cabral, Jeane. Good Night Little Moo. Howarth, Daniel, illus. 2007. (Night Light Book Ser.). 10p. (gr. -1-k). *(978-1-84666-128-0(5),* Tide Mill Pr.) Top That! Publishing PLC.
Camacho, Celi C. Bedtime for Meaghan. 2008. 33p. pap. 24.95 *(978-1-60563-527-9(8))* America Star Bks.
Chacon, Dulce. LA VOZ DORMIDA. 2005. (SPA., Illus.). 384p. pap. 22.95 *(978-84-204-6438-1(4),* AF13909, Alfaguara) Santillana USA Publishing Co., Inc.
Chadha, Radhika & Kuriyan, Priya. I'm So Sleepy. 2004. (Illus.). 24p. (J). *(978-81-8146-033-2(2))* Tulika Pubs.
Chapman, Jason. Who's That Snoring? A Pull-The-Tab Bedtime Book. Chapman, Jason, illus. 2010. (ENG., Illus.). 12p. (J). (gr. -1-1). bds. 9.99 *(978-1-4169-8937-0(4),* Little Simon) Little Simon.
Cheever, Karen J. The Tuck-In: (a Child's Event) 2012. 24p. (-18). pap. 17.99 *(978-1-4772-7546-7(0))* AuthorHouse.
Chriscoe, Sharon. Fire Truck Dreams. Mottram, Dave, illus. 2018. (ENG.). 32p. (J). (gr. -1-3). 17.99 *(978-0-7624-6285-8(X),* Running Pr. Kids) Running Pr.
—Race Car Dreams. Mottram, Dave, illus. 2016. (ENG.). 32p. (J). (gr. -1 — 1). 17.99 *(978-0-7624-5964-3(6),* Running Pr. Kids) Running Pr.
Christine Battuz, Christine, illus. Goodnight, Sleepy Animals: A Nightlight Book. 2016. (Nightlight Book Ser.). 14p. (J). (gr. -1-k). 12.99 *(978-2-89718-338-7(1),* CrackBoom! Bks.) Chouette Publishing CAN. Dist: Publishers Group West (PGW).
Claflin, Willy. The Little Moose Who Couldn't Go to Sleep. Stimson, James, illus. 2014. (ENG.). 36p. 18.95 *(978-1-939160-67-6(7))* August Hse. Pubs., Inc.
Cook, Sally. Good Night Pillow Fight. Date not set. (Illus.). (J). pap. 5.99 *(978-0-06-205932-1(7))* HarperCollins Pubs.
Cornell, Kevin. Go to Sleep, Monster! Cornell, Kevin, illus. 2016. (ENG., Illus.). 32p. (J). (gr. -1-3). 17.99 *(978-0-06-234915-6(5),* Balzer & Bray) HarperCollins Pubs.
Cosgrove, Stephen. Good Night, Wheedle. James, Robin, illus. 2016. 20p. (J). (— 1). bds. 9.99 *(978-1-63217-075-0(2),* Little Bigfoot) Sasquatch Bks.
—Wheedle on the Needle. James, Robin, illus. 2009. (ENG.). 32p. (J). (gr. -1-2). 18.99 *(978-1-57061-628-0(0),* Little Bigfoot) Sasquatch Bks.
Cottrell, Stephen. The Sleepy Shepherd: A Timeless Retelling of the Christmas Story. Hagan, Chris, illus. 2018. (ENG.). 48p. (J). pap. 14.99 *(978-0-281-07802-8(5),* d3c4ce1e-9bfe-4b68-810f-58e524ae21e4) SPCK Publishing GBR. Dist: Baker & Taylor Publisher Services (BTPS).
Cowlard, Irene. Moriarty's Dream. 2007. (Illus.). 52p. per. *(978-1-84748-062-0(4))* Athena Pr.
Cox, Phil Roxbee. Sam Sheep Can't Sleep. Tyler, Jenny, ed. Cartwright, Stephen, illus. rev. ed. 2006. (Usborne Phonics Bks.). 16p. (J). (gr. -1-k). 6.99 *(978-0-7945-1508-9(8),* Usborne) EDC Publishing.
Creech, Natalee. When Day Is Done. Dunn, Robert, illus. 2019. 32p. (J). (gr. -1-k). 16.99 *(978-1-5064-4772-8(4),* Beaming Books) 1517 Media.
Cronin, Doreen. Click, Clack, Peep! 2019. (Ready-To-Read Ser.). (ENG.). 37p. (J). (gr. k-1). 13.96 *(978-0-87617-991-8(X))* Penworthy Co., LLC, The.
—Click, Clack, Peep! Lewin, Betsy, illus. 2015. (Click Clack Book Ser.). (ENG.). 40p. (J). (gr. -1-3). 17.99 *(978-1-4814-2411-0(4))* Simon & Schuster Children's Publishing.
—Click, Clack, Peep!/Ready-To-Read Level 2. Lewin, Betsy, illus. 2019. (Click Clack Book Ser.). (ENG.). 40p. (J). (gr. k-2). 17.99 *(978-1-5344-1386-3(3));* pap. 4.99 *(978-1-5344-1385-6(5))* Simon Spotlight. (Simon Spotlight).
Cushing, Mims. The Sleepover Surprise. Phillips, Alan, illus. 2010. 24p. pap. 12.95 *(978-1-936343-01-0(0))* Peppertree Pr., The.
Dahl, Michael. Nap Time for Kitty, 1 vol. Vidal, Oriol, illus. 2011. (Hello Genius Ser.). (ENG.). 20p. (J). (gr. -1 — 1). bds. 7.99 *(978-1-4048-5216-7(6),* 95516, Picture Window Bks.) Capstone.
Daniels, Kristine. Floyd & the Mysterious Night Time Noise. 2011. (Illus.). 34p. pap. 18.00 *(978-1-4575-0141-8(4))* Dog Ear Publishing, LLC.
Daniels, Linda. A Friend Called Glen. 2011. 28p. pap. 16.09 *(978-1-4269-4848-0(4))* Trafford Publishing.
De Mouy, Iris. Naptime, 1 vol. Tanaka, Shelley, tr. 2014. (ENG., Illus.). 28p. (J). (gr. -1-k). 16.95 *(978-1-55498-487-9(4))* Groundwood Bks. CAN. Dist: Publishers Group West (PGW).
Dennis, Jen. Snoozy Sam. 2013. 42p. pap. *(978-1-922204-78-3(1))* Vivid Publishing.
Derubertis, Barbara. Zachary Zebra's Zippity Zooming. Alley, R. W., illus. 2011. (Animal Antics A to Z Set III Ser.). pap. 45.32 *(978-0-7613-8435-9(9))* Astra Publishing Hse.
deRubertis, Barbara. Zachary Zebra's Zippity Zooming. Alley, R. W., illus. 2011. (Animal Antics A to Z Ser.). 32p. (J). (gr. -1-3). pap. 7.95 *(978-1-57565-351-8(6),* c1ec6b17-d95a-42d6-8f11-06c8d8f9765c, Kane Press) Astra Publishing Hse.
deRubertis, Barbara & DeRubertis, Barbara. Zachary Zebra's Zippity Zooming. Alley, R. W., illus. 2012. (Animal Antics A to Z Ser.). 32p. (J). (gr. 2 — 1). cd-rom 7.95 *(978-1-57565-419-5(9))* Astra Publishing Hse.
Diesen, Deborah. The Pout-Pout Fish & the Can't-Sleep Blues. Hanna, Dan, illus. 2018. (Pout-Pout Fish Adventure Ser.). (ENG.). 32p. (J). 18.99 *(978-0-374-30403-4(3),* 900158633, Farrar, Straus & Giroux (BYR)) Farrar, Straus & Giroux.
DK. Pop-Up Peekaboo! I Love You. 2018. (Pop-Up Peekaboo! Ser.). (ENG., Illus.). 12p. (J). (— 1). bds. 12.99 *(978-1-4654-6526-9(X),* DK Children) Dorling Kindersley Publishing, Inc.
Dufresne, Michèle. Sleep Tight Spaceboy: Spaceboy Set 1. 2003. (Spaceboy Set 1 Ser.). (J). pap. 7.33 *(978-1-932570-02-1(0))* Pioneer Valley Bks.
Dunbar, Joyce. Tell Me Something Happy Before I Go to Sleep Padded Board Book. Gliori, Debi, illus. 2018. (Lullaby Lights Ser.). (ENG.). 24p. (J). (— 1). bds. 8.99 *(978-1-328-91068-4(7),* 1701812, Clarion Bks.) HarperCollins Pubs.
Duskey Rinker, Sherri. It's So Quiet: A Not-Quite-Going-To-Bed Book. Fucile, Tony, illus. 2021. (ENG.). 56p. (J). (gr. -1-k). 17.99 *(978-1-4521-4544-0(X))* Chronicle Bks. LLC.
Ehrlin, Carl-Johan Forssén. The Little Elephant Who Wants to Fall Asleep: A New Way of Getting Children to Sleep. Hanson, Sydney, illus. 2016. (ENG.). 40p. (J). (gr. -1-2). 16.99 *(978-0-399-55423-0(8),* Crown Books For Young Readers) Random Hse. Children's Bks.
Eulate, Ana. Little Cloud Lamb. Brokenbrow, Jon, tr. Carretero, Mónica, illus. 2011. (Light (Cuento de Luz) Ser.). 28p. (J). (gr. 1-3). 14.95 *(978-84-938240-2-0(X))* Cuento de Luz SL ESP. Dist: Publishers Group West (PGW).
Fahy, Thomas. Sleepless. 2010. (ENG.). 224p. (YA). (gr. 7). pap. 8.99 *(978-1-4169-5902-1(5),* Simon & Schuster Bks. For Young Readers) Simon & Schuster Bks. For Young Readers.
—Sleepless. 2009. (ENG.). 224p. (YA). (gr. 7-12). 15.99 *(978-1-4169-5901-4(7))* Simon & Schuster, Inc.
Fehrenbach, Heather. Go to Sleep Dinosaurs. 2011. 36p. pap. 15.99 *(978-1-4567-6302-2(4))* AuthorHouse.
Finney, Shad. Princess Nap. 2008. 28p. pap. 15.99 *(978-1-4363-2119-8(0))* Xlibris Corp.
Flam, Chanie. Good Night. (Goldie Gold Board Book Ser.: Vol. 6). (Illus.). (J). (gr. -1-1). bds. 4.95 *(978-1-58330-030-5(9))* Feldheim Pubs.
Fleuriel, Allison. Are You Done Sleeping? 2006. (J). pap. 16.00 *(978-0-8059-7115-6(7))* Dorrance Publishing Co., Inc.
Fourie, Amanda. Daddy Bird's Lousy Night. 2013. 20p. pap. 15.29 *(978-1-4669-9145-3(3))* Trafford Publishing.
Fox, Mem & Horacek, Judy. Where Is the Green Sheep? Horacek, Judy, illus. 2004. (ENG., Illus.). 32p. (J). (gr. -1-3). 17.99 *(978-0-15-204907-2(X),* 1194817, Clarion Bks.) HarperCollins Pubs.
—Where Is the Green Sheep? Padded Board Book. Horacek, Judy, illus. 2019. (ENG., Illus.). 32p. (J). (— 1). bds. 8.99 *(978-1-328-48266-2(9),* 1715797, Clarion Bks.) HarperCollins Pubs.
Fraley, Patty. Fear at Night: To Matthew. 2011. 24p. (gr. -1). pap. 12.79 *(978-1-4567-5555-3(2))* AuthorHouse.
Frampton, David. The Whole Night Through. Frampton, David, illus. Date not set. (Illus.). 32p. (J). (gr. -1-1). pap. 5.99 *(978-0-06-443652-6(7))* HarperCollins Pubs.
—The Whole Night Through: A Lullaby. Frampton, David, illus. 2004. (Illus.). 30p. (J). (gr. k-4). reprint ed. *(978-0-7567-7723-4(2))* DIANE Publishing Co.
Ganges, Montse. Cooper, King of Cushion Island, 1 vol. Urberuaga, Emilio, illus. 2009. (Cooper Ser.). (ENG.). 24p. (J). (gr. 1-1). pap. 9.15 *(978-1-60754-243-8(9),* 4c0a7c1e-fc98-4df3-8810-ae1c62a2a847); lib. bdg. 27.27 *(978-1-60754-242-1(0),* a4404dac-cc88-4587-b950-004bd45c6f42) Rosen Publishing Group, Inc., The. (Windmill Bks.).
Gates, Mysti. Noises in the Night. Steward, Brian, photos by. 2009. (ENG.). 52p. pap. 22.99 *(978-1-4389-4359-6(8))* AuthorHouse.
Geis, Patricia. Let's Go to Sleep! Folch, Sergio, illus. 2009. (Good Habits with Coco & Tula Ser.). 16p. (J). (gr. -1-k). bds. 11.40 *(978-1-60754-408-1(3))* Windmill Bks.
Gershator, Phillis. Time for a Nap. Walker, David, illus. 2018. (Snuggle Time Stories Ser.: 9). 22p. (J). (— 1). bds. 7.95 *(978-1-4549-3130-0(2))* Sterling Publishing Co., Inc.
Glass, Timothy. Sleepytown Beagles Penny's 4th of July. Mikle, Toby, illus. 2006. 24p. (J). per. 15.95 *(978-1-888461-10-7(1));* 16.95 *(978-1-888461-11-4(X))* Islewest Publishing.
Golden Books. Sleepy Bunny (Pat the Bunny) Cloth Book. 2003. (Cloth Book Ser.). (ENG., Illus.). 8p. (J). (gr. -1 — 1). 16.99 *(978-0-375-82531-6(2),* Golden Bks.) Random Hse. Children's Bks.
Graux, Amélie. I Love to Sleep: Deluxe Touch-And-Feel. Graux, Amélie, illus. deluxe ed. 2012. (ENG., Illus.). 12p. (J). (gr. k — 1). bds. 9.99 *(978-0-547-84843-3(9),* 1500672, Clarion Bks.) HarperCollins Pubs.
Graves, Kimberlee. I Can't Sleep. 2017. (Learn-To-Read Ser.). (ENG., Illus.). (J). (gr. -1-3). pap. 3.49 *(978-1-68310-185-7(5))* Pacific Learning, Inc.
Graves, Sue. Night, Night. 2009. (ENG., Illus.). 24p. (J). pap. *(978-0-7787-3898-5(1));* lib. bdg. *(978-0-7787-3867-1(1))* Crabtree Publishing Co.
Greenway, Bethany. Waikiki Lullaby. America, illus. 2009. (ENG.). 20p. (J). (gr. -1-1). bds. 7.95 *(978-1-933067-30-8(6))* Beachhouse Publishing, LLC.
Gribel, Christiane & Orlando. No Voy a Dormir/I Am Not Going to Sleep. Gribel, Christiane & Orlando, illus. 2009. (ENG & SPA., Illus.). 40p. (J). (gr. -1-1). pap. 7.99 *(978-1-933032-51-1(0))* Lectorum Pubns., Inc.
Grover, Neha Lamba. Shaurya's Adventures. 2010. 43p. pap. 17.40 *(978-0-557-12636-1(3))* Lulu Pr., Inc.
Guiffre, William. The Wrong Side of the Bed. Baron, Cheri Ann, illus. 2008. 32p. (J). (gr. -1-3). pap. 9.95 *(978-1-931650-34-2(9))* Guiffre Bk. Publishing.
Gutierrez, Rochelle. Dear Monster. 2010. 16p. pap. 8.95 *(978-1-4490-7281-0(X))* AuthorHouse.
Guy, Ginger Foglesong. Siesta: Bilingual English-Spanish. Moreno, Rene King, illus. 2005. (ENG.). 32p. (J). (gr. -1-k). 17.99 *(978-0-06-056061-4(4),* Greenwillow Bks.) HarperCollins Pubs.
—Siesta Board Book: Bilingual English-Spanish. Moreno, Rene King, illus. 2009. (ENG.). 34p. (J). (gr. -1 — 1). bds. 7.99 *(978-0-06-168884-3(3))* HarperCollins Español.
Halpern, Jake & Kujawinski, Peter. World's End, 2. 2012. (Dormia Ser.). (ENG., Illus.). 496p. (J). (gr. 4-6). 22.44 *(978-0-547-48037-4(7))* Houghton Mifflin Harcourt Publishing Co.
Hamilton, Covette J. Begethie Wenferd Meets King Tut. 2012. 32p. pap. *(978-1-77097-189-9(0))* FriesenPress.
Hamm, Diane Johnston. Rock-A-Bye Farm. Natchev, Alexi, illus. 2008. (ENG.). 32p. (J). (gr. -1 — 1). bds. 8.99 *(978-1-4169-3621-3(1),* Little Simon) Little Simon.
Harder, Christopher. It's Tough to Nap on a Turtle. Harder, Rolf, illus. 2008. (ENG.). 11p. (J). (gr. -1-k). bds. 5.95 *(978-0-9726614-9-2(2))* Shenanigan Bks.
Harshman, Marc. All the Way to Morning. Dávalos, Felipe, illus. 2006. (J). per. 7.95 *(978-1-891852-49-7(3))* Quarrier Pr.
Heine, Helme. Wunderbare Reise Durch Die Na. 12.95 *(978-3-7876-9528-7(1))* Middelhauve Verlags GmbH DEU. Dist: Distribooks, Inc.
Henry, Jed. Good Night, Mouse! Henry, Jed, illus. 2013. (ENG., Illus.). 32p. (J). (gr. -1-3). 16.99 *(978-0-547-98156-7(2),* 1523510, Clarion Bks.) HarperCollins Pubs.
Hest, Amy. Charley's First Night. Oxenbury, Helen, illus. 2012. (ENG.). 32p. (J). (gr. -1-2). 15.99 *(978-0-7636-4055-2(7))* Candlewick Pr.
Higgins, Gladys. Goodnight, Charlie. 2005. 18.00 *(978-0-8059-8116-2(0))* Dorrance Publishing Co., Inc.
Hillard, Shirley. Who's Not Asleep? 2004. (Illus.). 24p. (J). 15.95 *(978-1-933014-31-9(8))* Mamoo Hse.
Hillenbrand, Will. Spring Is Here: A Bear & Mole Story. 2012. (Bear & Mole Ser.: 1). (ENG., Illus.). 32p. (J). (-k). pap. 7.99 *(978-0-8234-2431-3(6))* Holiday Hse., Inc.
Hilton, Jennifer & McCurry, Kristen. Sleep Tight Tonight: A Book about Bedtime. Rimmington, Natasha, illus. 2018. (Frolic First Faith Ser.). 22p. (J). (gr. -1 — 1). bds. 6.99 *(978-1-5064-3969-3(1),* Sparkhouse Family) 1517 Media.
Hinman, Bobbie. The Knot Fairy. Bridgeman, Kristi, illus. 2010. (ENG.). 32p. (J). (gr. -1-1). 16.95 *(978-0-9786791-0-1(5))* Best Fairy Bks.
Hiris, Monica. Sleepy Polar Bear. Harston, Jerry, illus. l.t. ed. 2006. (ENG.). 24p. (gr. k-2). pap. 8.95 *(978-1-57874-072-7(X),* Kaeden Bks.) Kaeden Corp.
Holub, Joan. Bed, Bats, & Beyond. Gallagher-Cole, Mernie, illus. 2010. (Darby Creek Exceptional Titles Ser.). (ENG.). 64p. (J). (gr. 1-3). pap. 6.95 *(978-0-7613-6451-1(X))* Lerner Publishing Group.
Howatt, Sandra J. Sleepyheads. Wan, Joyce, illus. 2014. (ENG.). 32p. (J). (gr. -1-3). 17.99 *(978-1-4424-2266-7(1),* Beach Lane Bks.) Beach Lane Bks.
Hutchins, Pat. Good-Night, Owl! Hutchins, Pat, illus. 2015. (Classic Board Bks.). (ENG., Illus.). 34p. (J). (gr. -1 — 1). bds. 8.99 *(978-1-4814-4424-8(7),* Little Simon) Little Simon.
Ira Sleeps Over. 2005. (J). *(978-1-59564-973-7(5))* Steps To Literacy, LLC.
Iriyama, Satoshi. Good Night, Chirp. 2015. (Chirp the Chick Ser.). (ENG., Illus.). 36p. (J). (— 1). 8.99 *(978-0-544-35994-9(1),* 1587557, Clarion Bks.) HarperCollins Pubs.
Irving, Washington. & Busch, Jeffrey. Rip Van Winkle. (Classics Illustrated Ser.). (Illus.). 52p. (YA). pap. 4.95 *(978-1-57209-009-5(X))* Classics International Entertainment, Inc.
Jam, Teddy. Night Cars, 1 vol. Beddows, Eric, illus. 2006. (ENG.). 32p. (J). (gr. k — 1). bds. 9.95 *(978-0-88899-748-7(5))* Groundwood Bks. CAN. Dist: Publishers Group West (PGW).
—This New Baby, 1 vol. Johnson, Virginia, illus. 2011. (ENG.). 22p. (J). (gr. -1 — 1). bds. 8.95 *(978-1-55498-088-8(7))* Groundwood Bks. CAN. Dist: Publishers Group West (PGW).
James, Lincoln. Sal Sleeps In, 1 vol. 2006. (Neighborhood Readers Ser.). (ENG.). 8p. (gr. k-1). pap. 5.15 *(978-1-4042-5780-1(2),* 3ccfab18-4749-4780-93d3-fc4b7a34c502, Rosen Classroom) Rosen Publishing Group, Inc., The.
Jarvis. Lazy Dave. 2015. (ENG., Illus.). 32p. (J). (gr. -1-3). 17.99 *(978-0-06-235598-0(8),* HarperCollins) HarperCollins Pubs.
Jefferson, Coretta Carte. Cranky Christopher. 2013. 20p. pap. 24.95 *(978-1-4626-9671-0(6))* America Star Bks.
Jennings, Patrick. Hissy Fitz. Austin, Michael Allen, illus. 2015. (ENG.). 128p. (J). (gr. 2-4). E-Book 27.99 *(978-1-5124-0137-0(4),* Carolrhoda Bks.) Lerner Publishing Group.
Jepsen, D. R. Fred's Exciting Night. 2008. 20p. pap. 24.95 *(978-1-60813-547-9(0))* America Star Bks.
Johnson, Linda & Hodges, Quae. 21st Century Parables: A Child's Book. 2006. 48p. pap. 14.95 *(978-1-60145-071-5(0))* Booklocker.com, Inc.
Johnson, Mariana Ruiz. While You Are Sleeping: (Bedtime Books for Kids, Wordless Bedtime Stories for Kids) 2018. (ENG., Illus.). 36p. (J). (gr. -1-k). 16.99 *(978-1-4521-6599-8(8))* Chronicle Bks. LLC.
Johnstone, G. L. Sleep Tight Nancy... 2012. (Illus.). 12p. pap. 18.30 *(978-1-4772-1517-3(4))* AuthorHouse.
Kalman, Maira. Hey Willy, See the Pyramids. 2017. (Illus.). 48p. (J). (gr. k-3). 18.95 *(978-1-68137-168-9(5),* NYR Children's Collection) New York Review of Bks., Inc., The.
Kang, Anna. Will You Help Me Fall Asleep? Weyant, Christopher, illus. 2018. (ENG.). 40p. (J). (gr. -1-3). 17.99 *(978-0-06-239685-3(4),* HarperCollins) HarperCollins Pubs.
Kapoor, Natalya. My Favorite Time of Day. 2013. 12p. pap. 12.99 *(978-1-4772-8344-8(7))* AuthorHouse.
Kay, Devora. The Sleep Sheep Story. 2012. (ENG.). pap. *(978-1-4675-4640-9(2))* Independent Pub.
Keselman, Gabriela. Marc Just Couldn't Sleep. Villamuza, Noemi, illus. 2007. (ENG.). 32p. (J). (gr. -1-k). pap. 5.99 *(978-1-929132-91-1(3))* Kane Miller.
Kitamura, Satoshi. When Sheep Can't Sleep (Cuando los Borregos no Pueden Dormir) (SPA.). (J). (gr. 1-6). 19.95 *(978-84-372-6605-3(X))* Santillana USA Publishing Co., Inc.
Kite, Justin. Even Tigers Need to Sleep. 2012. 24p. pap. 28.03 *(978-1-4691-8880-5(5))* Xlibris Corp.
Kitzing, Constanze V. Are You Sleeping? Kitzing, Constanze V., illus. 2018. (ENG., Illus.). 32p. (J). (gr. -1-k). 9.99 *(978-1-78285-395-4(2))* Barefoot Bks., Inc.
Koniver, Laura. Together We Sleep. 2012. 54p. pap. 16.99 *(978-1-937848-01-9(9))* Do Life Right, Inc.
Kopczynski, Megan. Anastasia Rose Sleeps in Her Own Room, 1 vol. Stasiuk, Max, illus. 2010. 26p. pap. 24.95 *(978-1-4489-4923-6(8))* PublishAmerica, Inc.
Krauss, Ruth. Goodnight Goodnight Sleepyhead. Dyer, Jane, illus. 2004. 32p. (J). (gr. -1-1). lib. bdg. 16.89 *(978-0-06-028895-2(7))* HarperCollins Pubs.
—Goodnight Goodnight Sleepyhead Board Book. Dyer, Jane, illus. 2007. (ENG.). 32p. (J). (gr. -1-3). bds. 7.99 *(978-0-694-01501-6(6),* HarperFestival) HarperCollins Pubs.
Kuskin, Karla. The Lullaway of Rockabye. Date not set. 32p. (J). (gr. -1-18). 14.89 *(978-0-06-027716-1(5))* HarperCollins Pubs.
Kwaymullina, Ezekiel & Morgan, Sally. We All Sleep. (Illus.). (J). 2019. 24p. bds. 9.95 *(978-1-925591-53-8(0))* 2017. 32p. (gr. -1-1). 12.99 *(978-1-925163-18-6(0))* Fremantle Pr. AUS. Dist: Independent Pubs. Group.
Langford, Jane. Hero. Vince, Dawn, illus. 2005. (ENG.). 24p. (J). lib. bdg. 23.65 *(978-1-59646-720-0(7))* Dingles & Co.
Lester, Helen. Boris & the Worrisome Wakies. Munsinger, Lynn, illus. 2017. (ENG.). 32p. (J). (gr. -1-3). 16.99 *(978-0-544-64094-8(2),* 1620832, Clarion Bks.) HarperCollins Pubs.
Lewis, Anne Margaret. Sleeping Bear: The Legend. Grant, Sarah, illus. 2007. 36p. (J). (gr. -1-2). 16.95 *(978-1-934133-15-6(9),* Mackinac Island Press, Inc.) Charlesbridge Publishing, Inc.
Logue, Mary. Sleep Like a Tiger: A Caldecott Honor Award Winner. Zagarenski, Pamela, illus. 2012. (ENG.). 40p. (J). (gr. -1-3). 17.99 *(978-0-547-64102-7(8),* 1469620, Clarion Bks.) HarperCollins Pubs.
Long, Ethan. One Drowsy Dragon. 2010. (Illus.). (J). *(978-0-545-23412-2(3),* Orchard Bks.) Scholastic, Inc.
Lujan Ed.D., Nan. The Snoozles. Montgomery, Samantha, illus. 2012. 20p. pap. 24.95 *(978-1-4626-8831-9(4))* America Star Bks.
Lum, Misha Anne. Sleepy Time, Baby Mine, 1 vol. 2010. 18p. 24.95 *(978-1-60749-202-3(4))* PublishAmerica, Inc.
Luning, Barbara. The Quilted Zoo. 2008. 28p. pap. 15.99 *(978-1-4363-1778-8(9))* Xlibris Corp.
Lyon, Tammie Speer, illus. Now I Lay Me down to Sleep. 2006. 8p. (J). bds. 10.95 *(978-1-57791-211-8(X))* Brighter Minds Children's Publishing.
Mackall, Deborah. What Happens When I'm Asleep? Mackall, Debbie, illus. 2008. (ENG.). 32p. (J). (gr. -1-k). 15.95 *(978-0-9762273-1-1(2))* Dimensions in Media, Inc.
MacLean, Craig. Where Does a Giraffe Go to Bed? 2020. (ENG.). 32p. pap. 6.99 *(978-1-4607-5228-9(7),* HarperCollins) HarperCollins Pubs.

S

MacLeod, Jennifer Tzivia. Fast Asleep in a Little Village in Israel. Beeke, Tiphanie, illus. 2018. (ENG.). 32p. (J). 17.95 *(978-1-68115-539-5(7),* 73160a0c-1e6a-4190-81ea-4157ce5b2e5a, Apples & Honey Pr.) Behrman Hse., Inc.

Madel, Dan. Cracker the Cat, Almost Caught. 2008. 24p. pap. 24.95 *(978-1-4241-9252-6(8))* America Star Bks.

Magic Moon Dreams. 2003. (J). 11.95 *(978-0-89610-767-0(1))* Island Heritage Publishing.

Mahr, Frank J. I Can Sleep Alone. Mistrey, Dawn Bourdeau, illus. 2013. 34p. pap. 6.99 *(978-1-4575-1895-9(3))* Dog Ear Publishing, LLC.

Marchini, Tracy. Chicken Wants a Nap. Felix, Monique, illus. 2017. 24p. (J). (gr. 1-3). 17.99 *(978-1-56846-308-7(1),* 20169, Creative Editions) Creative Co., The.

Markes, Julie. Shhhhh! Everybody's Sleeping. Parkins, David, illus. 32p. (J). (gr. -1-1). 2005. lib. bdg. 16.89 *(978-0-06-053791-3(4))* 2004. (ENG.). 16.99 *(978-0-06-053790-6(6),* HarperCollins) HarperCollins Pubs.

Marks, Allison & Marks, Wayne. Og's Ark. Peluso, Martina, illus. 2016. (ENG.). 32p. (J). (gr. -1-3). 17.99 *(978-1-4677-6149-9(4),* 2b0d9617-d05e-45c2-82e3-1faaa703679e, Kar-Ben Publishing) Lerner Publishing Group.

Marsh, Richard Phillip. Mattress People Go to Bear Park. 2009. 44p. pap. 10.95 *(978-1-935125-39-6(7))* Robertson Publishing.

Marshall, Linda Elovitz. Good Night, Wind: A Yiddish Folktale. Dolivieux, Maelle, illus. 2019. 32p. (J). (gr. -1-3). 18.99 *(978-0-8234-3788-7(4))* Holiday Hse., Inc.

Marx, Patricia. Now I Will Never Go to Sleep. Date not set. (Illus.). (J). 14.99 *(978-0-06-027483-2(2));* 15.89 *(978-0-06-027482-5(4))* HarperCollins Pubs.

Massie, Diane Redfield. The Baby Beebee Bird. Kellogg, Steven, illus. 2003. (ENG.). 32p. (J). (gr. -1-1). pap. 7.99 *(978-0-06-051784-7(0),* HarperCollins) HarperCollins Pubs.

McCourt, Lisa. Goodnight, Stinky Face. Moore, Cyd, illus. 2016. (ENG.). 32p. (J). (— 1). bds. 7.99 *(978-0-545-90592-3(3),* Cartwheel Bks.) Scholastic, Inc.

McOmber, Rachel B., ed. McOmber Phonics Storybooks: Snores & More. rev. ed. (Illus.). (J). *(978-0-944991-59-6(9))* Swift Learning Resources.

Meadows, Michelle. Hibernation Station. Cyrus, Kurt, illus. 2010. (ENG.). 40p. (J). (gr. -1-3). 18.99 *(978-1-4169-3788-3(9),* Simon & Schuster Bks. For Young Readers) Simon & Schuster Bks. For Young Readers.

Merkel, Tara & Monahan, Ryan. The Thunderstorm. 2007. 20p. per. 11.00 *(978-1-4343-0585-5(6))* AuthorHouse.

Michaels, Kat. Gentle Is the Night. 2008. (J). 15.95 *(978-0-9745052-7-5(7))* Tree Of Life Publishing.

Michelin, Linda. Henry's Night. Johnson, D. B., illus. 2019. (Henry Book Ser.). (ENG.). 32p. (J). (gr. -1-3). pap. 7.99 *(978-0-358-11208-2(7),* 1749867, Clarion Bks.) HarperCollins Pubs.

Miles, David W., creator. But First, We Nap: A Little Book about Nap Time. 2018. (ENG., Illus.). 16p. (J). (gr. -1-k). bds. 9.99 *(978-1-64170-017-7(3),* 550017) Familius LLC.

Miller, Pat Zietlow. Wide-Awake Bear. Kim, Jean, illus. 2018. (ENG.). 40p. (J). (gr. -1-3). 17.99 *(978-0-06-235603-1(8),* HarperCollins) HarperCollins Pubs.

Milligan, Domino. The Sandman. Spiller, Michael, illus. 2008. 16p. pap. 24.95 *(978-1-60703-728-6(9))* America Star Bks.

Morales, Yuyi. Little Night / Nochecita. 2016. (SPA.). (J). lib. bdg. 18.40 *(978-0-606-38443-8(X))* Turtleback.

Morris, Kerry Nicole. The Baby Who Just... WON't Sleep! Parker's Story. 2004. 35p. pap. 24.95 *(978-1-4137-3724-0(2))* PublishAmerica, Inc.

Mortimer, Anne. Bunny's Easter Egg. 2010. (ENG., Illus.). 32p. (J). (gr. -1-2). 12.99 *(978-0-06-136664-2(1),* Tegen, Katherine Bks) HarperCollins Pubs.

Moulton, Eugena. The Age of Merrik: The Anointing. 2007. 200p. 24.95 *(978-0-595-67899-0(8));* per. 14.95 *(978-0-595-41367-6(6))* iUniverse, Inc.

Muldrow, Diane. How Do Giraffes Take Naps? Walker, David M., illus. 2016. (Little Golden Book Ser.). 24p. (J). (gr. -1-k). 5.99 *(978-0-553-51333-2(8),* Golden Bks.) Random Hse. Children's Bks.

Mumford, Martha. Hop Little Bunnies. 2020. (Bunny Adventures Ser.). (ENG., Illus.). 24p. (J). 17.99 *(978-1-5476-0268-1(6),* 900209360, Bloomsbury Children's Bks.) Bloomsbury Publishing USA.

Muñoz, Isabel. Eric & Julieta: Es Mío / It's Mine (Bilingual) (Bilingual Edition) Mazali, Gustavo, illus. 2006. (Eric & Julieta Ser.). Tr. of It's Mine. (SPA.). 24p. (J). (gr. -1-3). pap. 3.99 *(978-0-439-78370-5(4))* Scholastic, Inc.

Munsch, Robert. 50 below Zero. Martchenko, Michael, illus. 2019. (Classic Munsch Ser.). 24p. (J). 19.95 *(978-1-77321-101-5(3));* pap. 6.95 *(978-1-77321-100-8(5))* Annick Pr., Ltd. CAN. Dist: Publishers Group West (PGW).

Murray, Marjorie Dennis. Don't Wake up the Bear!, 0 vols. Wittmann, Patricia, illus. unabr. ed. 2013. (ENG.). 34p. (J). (gr. -1-2). per. 9.99 *(978-0-7614-5330-7(X),* 9780761453307, Two Lions) Amazon Publishing.

Nastanlieva, Vanya. Mo & Beau. 2015. (Illus.). 36p. (J). (gr. -1-3). 15.95 *(978-1-927018-63-7(3))* Simply Read Bks. CAN. Dist: Ingram Publisher Services.

Neubeck, Jon. The Quest. 2009. 47p. pap. 23.10 *(978-0-557-07108-1(9))* Lulu Pr., Inc.

Niner, Holly L. No More Noisy Nights. 2017. (ENG., Illus.). (J). (gr. k-2). 7.99 *(978-1-936261-96-3(0))* Flashlight Pr.

—No More Noisy Nights. Wolek, Guy, illus. 2017. (ENG.). 32p. (J). (gr. k-2). 17.95 *(978-1-936261-93-2(6))* Flashlight Pr.

North, Laura. The Princess & the Frozen Peas. Dreidemy, Joelle, illus. 2014. (Tadpoles: Fairytale Twists Ser.). (ENG.). 32p. (J). (gr. 1-2). *(978-0-7787-0446-1(7));* pap. *(978-0-7787-0481-2(5))* Crabtree Publishing Co.

Noullet, Georgette. Bed Hog, 0 vols. Slonim, David, illus. 2012. (ENG.). 24p. (J). (gr. -1-2). 12.99 *(978-0-7614-5823-4(9),* 9780761458234, Two Lions) Amazon Publishing.

O'Connor, Jane. Every Day Is Earth Day. 2010. (Fancy Nancy - I Can Read! Ser.). (J). lib. bdg. 13.55 *(978-0-606-12294-8(X))* Turtleback.

—Fancy Nancy & the Late, Late, LATE Night. Glasser, Robin Preiss, illus. 2010. (Fancy Nancy Ser.). (ENG.). 24p. (J). (gr. -1-3). pap. 4.99 *(978-0-06-170377-5(X),* HarperFestival) HarperCollins Pubs.

—Fancy Nancy & the Late, Late, Late Night. 2010. (Fancy Nancy Picture Bks.). (J). lib. bdg. 13.55 *(978-0-606-12312-9(1))* Turtleback.

Ohanesian, Diane. Snuggle down Deep. Bornoff, Emily, illus. 2018. (ENG.). 32p. (J). (gr. -1-3). 16.99 *(978-1-4998-0651-9(5))* Little Bee Books Inc.

Ohi, Ruth. Shh! My Brother's Napping. Ohi, Ruth, illus. 2017. (Illus.). 28p. (J). 11.99 *(978-1-61067-552-9(5))* Kane Miller.

Oppenheim, Joanne. Wake up, Baby! Lynn, Sweat, illus. 2015. (ENG.). 34p. (J). pap. 11.95 *(978-1-899694-56-3(0),* ipicturebooks) ibooks, Inc.

Owen, Dan. Ellen. 2006. (ENG.). 35p. (J). pap. 11.99 *(978-1-4116-9069-1(9))* Lulu Pr., Inc.

Paiva, Teresa & Pinto, Helena Rebelo. Mein Freund, der Schlaf. 2011. (FRE.). 60p. (gr. 1-2). pap. 14.95 *(978-1-4567-8991-6(0))* AuthorHouse.

—My Friend, Sleep. 2011. (Illus.). 68p. pap. 35.25 *(978-1-4567-8990-9(2));* 60p. (gr. 1-2). pap. 14.95 *(978-1-4567-8952-7(X))* AuthorHouse.

Palfreman-Bunker, Claire. Can Kittens Take a Catnap? Relf, Adam, illus. 2007. (J). pap. *(978-0-545-02595-9(8))* Scholastic, Inc.

Paniagua, Kelly. Bedtime for Sarah Sullivan. Warrick, Jessica, illus. 2012. 36p. (J). 13.95 *(978-1-60131-119-1(2));* pap. 10.95 *(978-1-60131-120-7(6))* Big Tent Bks. (Castlebridge Bks.).

Pappas, Diane H. & Covey, Richard D. Why I Need My Sleep. Estrada, Ric, illus. 2007. (J). pap. *(978-0-545-01427-4(1))* Scholastic, Inc.

Parker, Amy. Night Night, Sleepytown, 1 vol. Allyn, Virginia, illus. 2018. (Night Night Ser.). (ENG.). 20p. (J). bds. 9.99 *(978-1-4003-1003-6(2),* Tommy Nelson) Nelson, Thomas Inc.

Parry, Jo. Sleep, Little Pup. Parry, Jo, illus. 2017. (Story Corner Ser.). (ENG., Illus.). 24p. (J). (gr. -1-k). lib. bdg. 19.99 *(978-1-68297-183-3(X),* bb617383-c35d-4db3-9614-b0dc5129f56c) QEB Publishing Inc.

Partridge, Helen L. Blinky: The Bear Who Wouldn't Hibernate. 2008. 32p. per. 24.95 *(978-1-4241-9261-8(7))* America Star Bks.

Penelope Panda's Shooting Star. 2008. (Illus.). 32p. (J). (gr. k-3). pap. 14.99 *(978-0-9717290-3-2(4))* Adrema Pr.

Pierce, Barbara A. The Game That Sam Plays. 2018. (ENG., Illus.). 24p. (J). 20.99 *(978-1-948304-72-6(4));* pap. 9.99 *(978-1-948304-71-9(6))* PageTurner: Pr. & Media.

Pilkey, Dav. The Paperboy. 2015. 32p. pap. 7.00 *(978-1-61003-556-9(9))* Center for the Collaborative Classroom.

Price, Mathew. Gatito. Goldman, Judy, tr. Kemp, Moira, illus. 2010. (SPA & ENG.). 10p. bds. 5.99 *(978-1-935021-99-5(0))* Price, Mathew Ltd.

Price, Rebecca. Toby & the Flood, 70 vols. 2008. (ENG., Illus.). 32p. (J). pap. *(978-0-86315-635-9(5))* Floris Bks.

Price, Tom, illus. Champion Sleeper. 2008. 32p. (J). pap. 9.95 *(978-0-9748226-1-7(2))* Murphy's Bone Publishing.

Publications International Ltd. Staff, ed. Sleepy Baby. 2011. 8p. (J). bds. 7.98 *(978-1-4508-1241-2(4))* Publications International, Ltd.

Quintart, Natalie. Mama Bear. Blanchart, Stephanie, illus. 2005. (Tiger Tales Ser.). 32p. (J). (gr. -1-2). 6.95 *(978-1-58925-394-0(9))* Tiger Tales.

Raab, Brigitte. Mama, I Can't Sleep. Otten, Manuela, illus. 2012. (ENG.). 32p. (J). (gr. -1-k). 16.95 *(978-1-61608-965-8(2),* 608965, Sky Pony Pr.) Skyhorse Publishing Co., Inc.

Radzinski, Kandy. Where to Sleep. Radzinski, Kandy, illus. (ENG., Illus.). (J). (gr. 1-4). 2010. 22p. bds. 9.95 *(978-1-58536-535-7(1),* 202321) 2009. 32p. 15.95 *(978-1-58536-436-7(3),* 202164) Sleeping Bear Pr.

Remsburg, Rebecca. Night, Night, Knight, 1 vol. 2009. 19p. pap. 24.95 *(978-1-60836-942-3(0))* America Star Bks.

Renee, Sherry. Bye Bye Bed-Dy: Andrew Gets a Big Boy Bed. 2012. 20p. pap. 17.99 *(978-1-4685-7498-2(1))* AuthorHouse.

Reyes, Yolanda. Una Cama para Tres. Coll, Ivar Da, illus. 2004. (SPA.). 36p. (J). (gr. k-3). 14.95 *(978-958-704-055-5(4))* Santillana USA Publishing Co., Inc.

Roash, Riki. Mom, I Can Sleep in My Bed Tonight! 2013. 24p. pap. 24.95 *(978-1-4626-8255-3(3))* America Star Bks.

Robbins, Maria Polushkin. Mother, Mother, I Want Another. Goodell, Jon, illus. 2005. (ENG.). 32p. (J). (gr. -1-1). lib. bdg. 21.19 *(978-0-375-92588-7(0))* Random House Publishing Group.

Rock, Michelle L. Nighttime Adventures Counting Sheep. Longmore, Nickolai, illus. 2006. 32p. (J). 3.99 net. *(978-0-9771700-1-2(2))* Mystic Arts, LLC.

Rothstein, Nancy H. & Gilpin, Stephen. My Daddy Snores. 2006. (Illus.). (J). pap. *(978-0-439-87142-6(5))* Scholastic, Inc.

Rowe, Thereza. Mister Pip. 2016. (ENG., Illus.). 32p. (J). (gr. -1-k). 16.95 *(978-1-84976-382-0(8),* 1648201) Tate Publishing, Ltd. GBR. Dist: Abrams, Inc.

Runion, Laura K. Sleepy Faces in Sleeping Places. 2012. 28p. pap. 16.10 *(978-1-4669-4020-8(4))* Trafford Publishing.

Samarrippas, Gloria. In Search for Lucky's Lost Toys. 2006. 17.00 *(978-0-8059-7329-7(X))* Dorrance Publishing Co., Inc.

Sapp, Karen. Rookie Preschool: Rookie Learn about Nauture: Who Is Sleeping? 2009. (Rookie Preschool-NEW Ser.). (ENG.). 24p. (J). pap. 6.95 *(978-0-531-24586-6(1));* (gr. -1). lib. bdg. 23.00 *(978-0-531-24411-1(3))* Scholastic Library Publishing. (Children's Pr.).

Schmidt, Hans-Christian. Are You Sleeping Little One? Német, Andrea, illus. 2012. (ENG.). 18p. (J). (gr. k-k). 6.95 *(978-0-7892-1120-0(3),* 791120, Abbeville Kids) Abbeville Pr., Inc.

Schneider, Dianna. Rocky Ford Stories: Sleepytime at Rocky Ford. 2012. 42p. pap. 17.45 *(978-1-4525-5310-8(6))* Balboa Pr.

Scotton, Rob. Russell the Sheep. Scotton, Rob, illus. (ENG., Illus.). (J). (gr. -1-3). 2015. 32p. pap. 6.99 *(978-0-06-239243-5(3),* HarperFestival) 2011. 32p. pap. 6.99 *(978-0-06-059850-1(6))* 2007. 16p. 9.99 *(978-0-06-128434-2(3))* 2005. 32p. 17.99 *(978-0-06-059848-8(4),* HarperCollins) HarperCollins Pubs.

—Russell the Sheep Board Book. Scotton, Rob, illus. 2009. (ENG., Illus.). 32p. (J). (gr. -1-3). bds. 7.99 *(978-0-06-170996-8(4),* HarperFestival) HarperCollins Pubs.

Scribens, Sunny. Baby Dream / Soñando con Bebé. 2019. (ENG., Illus.). 16p. (J). (gr. -1-k). bds. 7.99 *(978-1-78285-737-2(0))* Barefoot Bks., Inc.

Seuss. Dr. Seuss's Sleep Softly Book. 2012. (Dr. Seuss Nursery Collection). (ENG., Illus.). 12p. (J). (gr. -1 — 1). 11.99 *(978-0-375-87003-3(2),* Random Hse. Bks. for Young Readers) Random Hse. Children's Bks.

Shapely Sleepy Sheep. 2005. (J). bds. 7.95 *(978-0-9749305-6-5(3))* Castle Pacific Publishing.

Sharmat, Mitchell. Berkley, the Terrible Sleeper: Ready-To-Read Level 2. Kurilla, Renée & Kurilla, Renée, illus. 2015. (Ready-To-Read Ser.). (ENG.). 32p. (J). (gr. k-2). pap. 3.99 *(978-1-4814-3832-2(8),* Simon Spotlight) Simon Spotlight.

Smith, Carrie. Little Bo Peep. Abbott, Jason, illus. 2010. (Rising Readers Ser.). (J). 3.49 *(978-1-60719-700-3(6))* Newmark Learning LLC.

Star, Nancy. Mystery of the Snow Day Bigfoot. Bernardin, James, illus. 2005. (Calendar Club Mysteries Ser.: Vol. 3). 77p. (J). pap. 3.95 *(978-0-439-67262-7(7))* Scholastic, Inc.

Sullivan, Mary. Up on Bob. 2020. (ENG., Illus.). 40p. (J). (gr. -1-3). 17.99 *(978-1-328-99471-4(6),* 1710823, Clarion Bks.) HarperCollins Pubs.

Teckentrup, Britta. Don't Wake up the Tiger. Teckentrup, Britta, illus. 2016. (ENG., Illus.). 30p. (J). (-k). 18.99 *(978-0-7636-8996-4(3))* Candlewick Pr.

—Sleep Tight Little Bear. 2014. (ENG., Illus.). 40p. (J). (gr. -1-2). 17.95 *(978-0-7358-4180-2(2))* North-South Bks., Inc.

Ted in a Red Bed Kid Kit. 2004. (Kid Kits Ser.). (Illus.). 10p. (J). bds. 9.95 *(978-1-58086-404-6(X))* EDC Publishing.

Tetri, Emily. Tiger vs. Nightmare. Tetri, Emily, illus. 2018. (ENG., Illus.). 64p. (J). 18.99 *(978-1-62672-535-5(7),* 900160471, First Second Bks.) Roaring Brook Pr.

Theobald, Joseph. When Arthur Wouldn't Sleep: Band 06/Orange (Collins Big Cat) Theobald, Joseph, illus. 2006. (Collins Big Cat Ser.). (ENG., Illus.). 24p. (J). (gr. 2-2). pap. 8.99 *(978-0-00-718688-4(6))* HarperCollins Pubs. Ltd. GBR. Dist: Independent Pubs. Group.

Thompson, Lauren. Little Quack's Bedtime. Anderson, Derek, illus. 2009. (Classic Board Bks.). (ENG.). 34p. (J). (gr. -1-k). bds. 8.99 *(978-1-4169-6873-3(3),* Little Simon) Little Simon.

Tillman, Nancy & Metaxas, Eric. It's Time to Sleep, My Love. Tillman, Nancy, illus. 2008. (ENG., Illus.). 32p. (J). (gr. -1 — 1). 17.99 *(978-0-312-38371-8(1),* 900053023) Feiwel & Friends.

Topper, Wendy. Where's the Pacifier? 2008. 8p. pap. 24.95 *(978-1-60563-823-2(4))* America Star Bks.

Torrel, Wendy. GUARDIAN of DREAMS (1st Edition) Klingbeil, Kendall, illus. l.t. ed. 2004. 32p. (J). 14.95 *(978-0-9746890-0-5(9));* pap. 10.95 *(978-0-9746890-1-2(7))* White Tulip Publishing.

Toshiley. The Sponge & the River of Sleepiness. 2009. 24p. pap. 13.50 *(978-1-60860-562-0(0),* Eloquent Bks.) Strategic Book Publishing & Rights Agency (SBPRA).

Trasler, Janee. Bedtime for Chickies: An Easter & Springtime Book for Kids. Trasler, Janee, illus. 2014. (Chickies Ser.). (ENG., Illus.). 24p. (J). (gr. -1 — 1). bds. 8.99 *(978-0-06-227468-7(6),* HarperFestival) HarperCollins Pubs.

Tremblay, Carole. Floop in the Dark, 1 vol. Beshwaty, Steve, illus. 2009. (Floop Ser.). (ENG.). 24p. (J). (gr. -1-k). 27.27 *(978-1-60754-341-1(9),* f9f994d3-11e5-46ab-b443-f75e57a42e33, Windmill Bks.) Rosen Publishing Group, Inc., The.

Valério, Geraldo, illus. Go to Sleep, Gecko! A Balinese Folktale. 2015. (ENG.). 32p. (J). (gr. -1-3). pap. 8.95 *(978-1-939160-92-8(8))* August Hse. Pubs., Inc.

Van Genechten, Guido. The Big Sleep Book. 2008. (ENG.). 20p. (J). (gr. k — 1). bds. 12.95 *(978-1-60537-012-5(6))* Clavis Publishing.

Vere, Ed. A Dormir, Monstruos! 2012. (SPA.). 32p. (J). (gr. -1-1). pap. 21.99 *(978-84-261-3890-3(X))* Juventud, Editorial ESP. Dist: Lectorum Pubns., Inc.

—Everyone's Sleepy. 2003. (ENG., Illus.). 12p. (J). 8.99 *(978-0-333-78038-1(8))* Macmillan Pubs., Ltd. GBR. Dist: Trafalgar Square Publishing.

Vien, Ashley. Justin Fights Sleep. Stenton, Murray, illus. 2018. (J). pap. *(978-1-61599-376-5(2)); (978-1-61599-383-3(5))* Loving Healing Pr., Inc.

Volker, Kerstin. Suzie Goes to Sleep. 2003. (Funny Friends Lift-and-Learn Bks.). (Illus.). 14p. (J). 5.99 *(978-1-59384-024-2(1))* Parklane Publishing.

Walker, Nan. The Midnight Kid. 2007. (Science Solves It! Ser.). (Illus.). 32p. (J). (gr. 1-3). pap. 5.99 *(978-1-57565-238-2(2),* 9aafbad2-27d1-4006-8c94-b8ac863c628e, Kane Press) Astra Publishing Hse.

Watt, F. Felices Suenos! 2004. (Mundo del Pequenin Ser.). Tr. of Baby's Bedtime. (SPA., Illus.). 16p. (YA). (gr. -1-18). pap. 4.95 *(978-0-7460-3869-7(0))* EDC Publishing.

Watt, Mélanie & Watt, Mélanie. Scaredy Squirrel at Night. Watt, Mélanie & Watt, Mélanie, illus. 2009. (Scaredy Squirrel Ser.). (ENG., Illus.). 32p. (J). (gr. -1-3). 16.99 *(978-1-55453-288-9(4))* Kids Can Pr., Ltd. CAN. Dist: Hachette Bk. Group.

Weir, Jaime L. Out of Bed. 2008. 20p. pap. 24.95 *(978-1-60474-363-0(8))* America Star Bks.

Wells, Rosemary. Max's Bedtime. 2003. (Max & Ruby Ser.). (ENG.). 12p. (J). (gr. -1 — 1). bds. 7.99 *(978-0-670-88710-1(2),* Viking Books for Young Readers) Penguin Young Readers Group.

Weston Woods Staff, creator. The Napping House. 2011. 29.95 *(978-0-439-72863-8(0))* Weston Woods Studios, Inc.

Wheeler, Lisa. Babies Can Sleep Anywhere. Búzio, Carolina, illus. 2019. (ENG.). 22p. (J). (gr. -1 — 1). bds. 7.99 *(978-1-4197-3492-2(X),* 1166810, Abrams Appleseed) Abrams, Inc.

—Babies Can Sleep Anywhere. Buzio, Carolina, illus. 2017. (ENG.). 32p. (J). (gr. -1-k). 14.95 *(978-1-4197-2536-4(X),* 1166801, Abrams Appleseed) Abrams, Inc.

—Even Monsters Need to Sleep. 2017. (ENG., Illus.). 32p. (J). (gr. -1-3). 17.99 *(978-0-06-236640-5(8),* Balzer & Bray) HarperCollins Pubs.

Willems, Mo. I Will Take a Nap!-An Elephant & Piggie Book. 2015. (Elephant & Piggie Book Ser.: 23). (ENG., Illus.). 64p. (J). (gr. 1-3). 9.99 *(978-1-4847-1630-4(2),* Hyperion Books for Children) Disney Publishing Worldwide.

Williams, Annik. Mr. Mole's Day Off: With Goodnight Little Birdie. 2010. 20p. 15.78 *(978-1-4520-3756-1(6))* AuthorHouse.

Williams, Becky. Good Night Little Piggy. Howarth, Daniel, illus. 2007. (Night Light Book Ser.). 10p. (gr. -1-k). bds. *(978-1-84666-129-7(3),* Tide Mill Pr.) Top That! Publishing PLC.

Wilson, Karma. Bear Stays up for Christmas. Chapman, Jane, illus. 2011. (Bear Bks.). (ENG.). 34p. (J). (gr. -1 — 1). bds. 8.99 *(978-1-4424-2790-7(6),* Little Simon) Little Simon.

Wood, Audrey. The Full Moon at the Napping House. Wood, Don, illus. 2015. (ENG.). 32p. (J). (gr. -1-3). 17.99 *(978-0-544-30832-9(8),* 1581566, Clarion Bks.) HarperCollins Pubs.

—The Napping House. Wood, Don, illus. 25th ed. 2009. (ENG.). 32p. (J). (gr. -1-3). 18.99 *(978-0-15-256708-8(9),* 1099017, Clarion Bks.) HarperCollins Pubs.

—The Napping House/la Casa Adormecida: Bilingual English-Spanish. Wood, Don, illus. 2012. (ENG.). 32p. (J). (gr. -1 — 1). bds. 7.99 *(978-0-547-71920-7(5),* 1481835, Clarion Bks.) HarperCollins Pubs.

Written By Tori Velle; Illustrated By Al. Tia Tot Rules! Aguila, Alicia del, illus. 2011. 44p. pap. 24.95 *(978-1-4241-7833-9(9))* America Star Bks.

Yisrael, A'mon. Mr. Jerry's Nap. 2005. (Illus.). 9p. (J). 8.99 *(978-0-9772424-0-5(4))* Yisrael, Sean Publishing Co.

Zaibak, Bushra. I am Not Afraid. 2007. (Illus.). 37p. (J). mass mkt. *(978-0-9787849-7-3(9))* Lucent Interpretations, LLC.

SLEEPING BEAUTY (FICTITIOUS CHARACTER)—FICTION

Amery, H. & Cartwright, S. Sleeping Beauty. 2004. (First Stories Ser.). 16p. (J). pap. 4.95 *(978-0-7945-0604-9(6))* EDC Publishing.

AZ Books Staff. Sleeping Beauty. Zyl, Olga, ed. 2012. (Classic Fairy Tales Ser.). (ENG.). 10p. (J). (gr. -1-k). bds. 9.95 *(978-1-61889-006-1(9))* AZ Bks. LLC.

Baker, Sara, illus. Ready to Read Sleeping Beauty. 2007. (Ready to Read Ser.). 31p. (J). (gr. k-2). *(978-1-84610-441-1(6))* Make Believe Ideas.

Barella, Laura, illus. Sleeping Beauty. 2009. (Flip-Up Fairy Tales Ser.). 24p. (J). (gr. -1-2). pap. *(978-1-84643-252-1(9))* Child's Play International Ltd.

Braswell, Liz. Once upon a Dream: A Twisted Tale. 2017. (Twisted Tale Ser.). (YA). lib. bdg. 20.85 *(978-0-606-39935-7(6))* Turtleback.

—Once upon a Dream-A Twisted Tale. 2017. (Twisted Tale Ser.). (ENG.). 464p. (YA). (gr. 7-12). pap. 10.99 *(978-1-4847-0730-2(3),* Disney Press Books) Disney Publishing Worldwide.

Brown, Carron, ed. Sleeping Beauty & Snow White & the Seven Dwarfs: Two Tales & Their Histories, 1 vol. 2009. (World of Fairy Tales Ser.). (ENG., Illus.). 32p. (J). (gr. 1-2). pap. 11.55 *(978-1-60754-635-1(3),* 85434d31-dc86-4f19-899e-add68306efa8); lib. bdg. 27.27 *(978-1-60754-634-4(5),* 210ba78f-6bda-4b3c-8798-3c1d39b6a67c) Rosen Publishing Group, Inc., The. (Windmill Bks.).

Carney, Larry, adapted by. Sleeping Beauty. 2009. (ENG., Illus.). 24p. (J). 6.95 *(978-1-60072-116-8(8))* PC Treasures, Inc.

Cartwright, Stephen, illus. Sleeping Beauty. 2006. (First Stories Sticker Bks.). 16p. (J). (gr. -1-3). pap. 6.99 *(978-0-7945-1313-9(1),* Usborne) EDC Publishing.

Davies, Kate & Award, Anna. The Sleeping Beauty. 2017. (ENG., Illus.). 24p. (J). pap. 6.00 *(978-1-84135-968-7(8))* Award Pubns. Ltd. GBR. Dist: Parkwest Pubns., Inc.

Disney Staff. The Sleeping Beauty. (FRE.). 96p. (J). (gr. k-5). pap. 9.95 *(978-0-7859-8854-0(8))* French & European Pubns., Inc.

Dulac, Edmund, illus. The Sleeping Beauty & Other Fairy Tales. 2011. (Calla Editions Ser.). (ENG.). 208p. 35.00 *(978-1-60660-019-1(2))* Dover Pubns., Inc.

Fairy Tales- Sleeping Beauty. 2005. (J). bds. *(978-1-4194-0042-1(8))* Paradise Pr., Inc.

Fear, Sharon, retold by. Sleeping Beauty. 2004. (Treasure Tree Ser.). (Illus.). 32p. (J). *(978-0-7166-1605-4(X))* World Bk., Inc.

Gaiman, Neil. The Sleeper & the Spindle. Riddell, Chris, illus. (ENG.). (YA). (gr. 8). 2019. 72p. pap. 10.99 *(978-0-06-239825-3(3))* 2015. 64p. 19.99 *(978-0-06-239824-6(5))* HarperCollins Pubs. (HarperCollins).

Gibb, Sarah, illus. Sleeping Beauty: Based on the Original Story by the Brothers Grimm. 2015. (ENG.). 32p. (J). (gr. -1-3). 16.99 *(978-0-8075-7351-8(5),* 807573515) Whitman, Albert & Co.

Gilani, Fawzia. Sleeping Beauty: An Islamic Tale. Davis, Jacqui, illus. 2018. (Islamic Fairy Tales Ser.). (ENG.). 40p. (J). (gr. 5-8). 14.00 *(978-0-86037-597-5(8))* Kube Publishing Ltd. GBR. Dist: Consortium Bk. Sales & Distribution.

Heapy, Teresa. Very Little Sleeping Beauty. Heap, Sue, illus. 2016. (Very Little Ser.). (ENG.). 32p. (J). (gr. -1-3). 16.99 *(978-0-544-28279-7(5),* 1570975, Clarion Bks.) HarperCollins Pubs.

Leonard, Barry, ed. Sleeping Beauty. 2003. (Illus.). 12p. (J). (gr. k-4). reprint ed. 17.00 *(978-0-7567-6865-2(9))* DIANE Publishing Co.

Lewis, Jan, illus. First Fairy Tales: Sleeping Beauty. 2013. (ENG.). 24p. (J). (gr. -1-k). bds. 6.99 *(978-1-86147-338-7(9),* Armadillo) Anness Publishing GBR. Dist: National Bk. Network.

Man-Kong, Mary. Sleeping Beauty. 2014. (Disney Princess Step into Reading Ser.). lib. bdg. 13.55 *(978-0-606-36001-2(8))* Turtleback.

—Sleeping Beauty Step into Reading (Disney Princess) RH Disney, illus. 2014. (Step into Reading Ser.). (ENG.). 32p. (J). (gr. -1-1). 5.99 *(978-0-7364-3226-9(4),* RH/Disney) Random Hse. Children's Bks.

Mass, Wendy. Sleeping Beauty: The One Who Took the Really Long Nap. 2012. (Twice upon a Time Ser.: 2). lib. bdg. 17.20 *(978-0-606-26530-0(9))* Turtleback.

—Sleeping Beauty, the One Who Took the Really Long Nap: a Wish Novel (Twice upon a Time #2) 2018. (Twice upon a Time Ser.: 2). (ENG.). 176p. (J). (gr. 3-7). pap. 7.99 *(978-0-439-79658-3(X),* Scholastic Pr.) Scholastic, Inc.

McGowan, Maureen. Sleeping Beauty: Vampire Slayer. 2010. 320p. pap. 8.95 *(978-1-60747-779-2(3)*, Pickwick Pr.) Phoenix Bks., Inc.

Ottolenghi, Carol. Sleeping Beauty. 2009. (Brighter Child Keepsake Story Ser.). (ENG.). 32p. (gr. k-2). 16.19 *(978-0-7696-5866-7(0))* School Specialty, Incorporated.

Scollen, Chris. Busy Kids Sticker Storybook Sleeping Beauty. 2008. (Illus.). 12p. (J). (gr. -1-3). pap. *(978-1-84610-807-5(1))* Make Believe Ideas.

Sleeping Beauty. (Read-Along Ser.). (J). 7.99 incl. audio *(978-1-55723-010-2(2))* Walt Disney Records.

Susaeta, Equipo. La bella durmiente - Sleeping beauty. 2011. (Cuentos Bilingües Ser.). (SPA & ENG.). 34p. (J). (gr. k-2). 8.99 *(978-84-305-2453-2(3))* Susaeta Ediciones, S.A. ESP. Dist: Independent Pubs. Group.

Taplin, Sam. Sleeping Beauty. 2008. (First Fairytales Look & Say Ser.). 12p. (J). (gr. -1). bds. 9.99 *(978-0-7945-2200-1(9)*, Usborne) EDC Publishing.

TBC. Peek Inside a Fairytale Sleeping Beauty. 2017. (Peek Inside Board Bks.). (ENG.). 14p. (J). 14.99 *(978-0-7945-4037-1(6)*, Usborne) EDC Publishing.

Teitelbaum, Michael. Sleeping Beauty (Disney Princess) Dias, Ron, illus. 2004. (Little Golden Book Ser.). (ENG.). 24p. (J). (gr. -1-k). 5.99 *(978-0-7364-2198-0(X)*, Golden/Disney) Random Hse. Children's Bks.

Umansky, Kaye. Sleeping Beauty. 2003. (Plays & Play Collections). (Illus.). 48p. (J). pap. 15.00 *(978-0-7136-5371-7(X)*, A&C Black) Bloomsbury Publishing Plc GBR. Dist: Players Pr., Inc.

Underwood, Deborah. Reading Beauty: (Empowering Books, Early Elementary Story Books, Stories for Kids, Bedtime Stories for Girls) 2019. (Future Fairy Tales Ser.). (ENG., Illus.). 44p. (J). (gr. -1-k). 17.99 *(978-1-4521-7129-6(7))* Chronicle Bks. LLC.

Valentino, Serena. Mistress of All Evil-Villains, Book 4. 2017. (Villains Ser.: 4). (ENG.). 320p. (YA). (gr. 7-12). 17.99 *(978-1-368-00901-0(8)*, Disney Press Books) Disney Publishing Worldwide.

Zahler, Diane. Sleeping Beauty's Daughters. 2013. (ENG.). 224p. (J). (gr. 3-7). 16.99 *(978-0-06-200496-3(4)*, HarperCollins) HarperCollins Pubs.

SLEEPOVERS

Brown, Jennifer. It's Time for a Sleepover, 1 vol. 2017. (It's Time Ser.). (ENG.). 24p. (J). (gr. 1-1). 25.27 *(978-1-5081-6365-7(0)*, ce2a4ba3-8dda-4dda-bfbd-11821fb4dc3b, PowerKids Pr.) Rosen Publishing Group, Inc., The.

Hurley, Jo. Slumber-Ific! Great Sleepover Ideas for You & Your Friends. Morley, Taia, illus. 2007. 63p. (J). *(978-0-439-02015-2(8))* Scholastic, Inc.

Loh-Hagan, Virginia. Bloody Mary. 2017. (Urban Legends: Don't Read Alone! Ser.). (ENG., Illus.). 32p. (J). (gr. 4-8). lib. bdg. 32.07 *(978-1-63472-895-9(5)*, 210006, 45th Parallel Press) Cherry Lake Publishing.

Nicholson, Sue. Sleepover. 2003. (Wicked Wallets Ser.). (Illus.). 96p. (YA). pap. *(978-1-84347-061-8(6)*, Pavilion Children's Books) Pavilion Bks.

Olsen, Mary-Kate & Olsen, Ashley. Mary-Kate & Ashley Yearbook. 2005. (Illus.). 96p. *(978-0-00-720729-9(8))* HarperCollins Pubs. Australia.

—Sleepover Party Mini Box. 2005. 32p. *(978-0-00-719585-5(0))* HarperCollins Pubs. Australia.

Rober, Harold. Having a Sleepover. 2017. (Bumba Books (r) — Fun Firsts Ser.). (ENG., Illus.). 24p. (J). (gr. -1-1). 26.65 *(978-1-5124-2555-0(9)*, 567fec16-66dd-465c-9b63-27d7ade18843); E-Book 39.99 *(978-1-5124-2751-6(9))*; E-Book 39.99 *(978-1-5124-3683-9(6)*, 9781512436839); E-Book 4.99 *(978-1-5124-3684-6(4)*, 9781512436846) Lerner Publishing Group. (Lerner Pubns.).

Ross, Kathy. Girlfriends' Get-Together Craft Book. Bosch, Nicole in den, illus. 2007. (Girl Crafts Ser.). (ENG.). 48p. (gr. 2-5). pap. 7.95 *(978-0-7613-9465-5(6)*, First Avenue Editions) Lerner Publishing Group.

—Girlfriends' Get-Together Craft Book. In Den Bosch, Nicole, illus. 2007. (Girl Crafts Ser.). (ENG.). 48p. (gr. 2-5). lib. bdg. 26.60 *(978-0-7613-3408-8(4)*, Millbrook Pr.) Lerner Publishing Group.

Ventura, Marne. A Girl's Guide to the Perfect Sleepover. 2017. (Go-To Guides). (ENG., Illus.). 32p. (J). (gr. 3-9). lib. bdg. 28.65 *(978-1-5157-3663-9(6)*, 133648, Capstone Pr.) Capstone.

SLEEPOVERS—FICTION

Allen, Elise & Stanford, Halle. Spring's Sparkle Sleepover. Pooler, Paige, illus. 2015. (Enchanted Sisters Ser.: 3). (J). lib. bdg. 16.00 *(978-0-606-36218-4(5))* Turtleback.

Barker, Henry. It Came from Outer Space. Gott, Barry, illus. 2003. (Science Solves It! Ser.). (ENG.). 32p. (J). (gr. 1-3). pap. 5.99 *(978-1-57565-122-4(X)*, 37a9b6ce-3e44-4ec8-9e17-fda1872c5c53, Kane Press) Astra Publishing Hse.

—Vino Del Espacio (It Came from Outer Space) Gott, Barry, illus. 2009. (Science Solves It! (r) en Espanol Ser.). (SPA.). (gr. 1-3). pap. 33.92 *(978-1-58013-771-3(7))* Lerner Publishing Group.

Barkley, Callie. Liz at Marigold Lake. Riti, Marsha, illus. 2014. (Critter Club Ser.: 7). (ENG.). 128p. (J). (gr. k-4). pap. 5.99 *(978-1-4424-9525-8(1)*, Little Simon) Little Simon.

—Liz at Marigold Lake. 2014. (Critter Club Ser.: 7). lib. bdg. 16.00 *(978-0-606-35445-5(X))* Turtleback.

—Liz's Night at the Museum. Bishop, Tracy, illus. 2016. (Critter Club Ser.: 15). (ENG.). 128p. (J). (gr. k-4). pap. 6.99 *(978-1-4814-7164-0(3)*, Little Simon) Little Simon.

Barnaby, Hannah. There's Something about Sam. Wilsdorf, Anne, illus. 2020. (ENG.). 32p. (J). (gr. -1-3). 17.99 *(978-1-328-76680-9(2)*, 1680919, Clarion Bks.) HarperCollins Pubs.

Beck, Scott. Monster Sleepover! 2009. (ENG., Illus.). 32p. (J). (gr. k-2). 15.95 *(978-0-8109-4059-8(0)*, 601001, Abrams Bks. for Young Readers) Abrams, Inc.

Becker, Bonny. A Bedtime for Bear. Denton, Kady MacDonald, illus. 2010. (J). *(978-0-7636-5364-4(0))* Candlewick Pr.

Bell, Cece. Rabbit & Robot. 2014. (Candlewick Sparks Ser.). lib. bdg. 13.55 *(978-0-606-35169-0(8))* Turtleback.

—Rabbit & Robot: The Sleepover. Bell, Cece, illus. 2014. (Candlewick Sparks Ser.). (ENG., Illus.). 56p. (J). (gr. k-4). pap. 5.99 *(978-0-7636-6875-4(3))* Candlewick Pr.

Bellisario, Gina. Super Spooked. von Innerebner, Jessika, illus. 2018. (Ellie Ultra Ser.). (ENG.). 128p. (J). (gr. 1-3). lib. bdg. 25.99 *(978-1-4965-6512-9(6)*, 138517, Stone Arch Bks.) Capstone.

Benenfeld, Rikki. I Go Visiting. 2007. (Toddler Experience Ser.). (ENG., Illus.). 32p. (J). (gr. -1-k). 11.99 *(978-1-929628-33-9(1))* Hachai Publishing.

Berenstain, Jan & Berenstain, Mike. The Berenstain Bears' Sleepover. Berenstain, Jan & Berenstain, Mike, illus. 2008. (I Can Read Level 1 Ser.). (ENG., Illus.). 32p. (J). (gr. k-3). 16.99 *(978-0-06-168974-1(2)*, HarperCollins) HarperCollins Pubs.

Bergen, Lara Rice & Bergen, Lara. Dora's Sleepover. Miller, Victoria, illus. 2006. (Dora the Explorer Ser.: 12). (ENG.). 24p. (J). (gr. -1-1). pap. 3.99 *(978-1-4169-1508-9(7)*, Simon Spotlight/Nickelodeon) Simon Spotlight/Nickelodeon.

Bliss, Emily. Unicorn Princesses 8: Feather's Flight. Hanson, Sydney, illus. 2018. (Unicorn Princesses Ser.: 8). (ENG.). 128p. (J). 16.99 *(978-1-68119-930-6(0)*, 900192387); pap. 5.99 *(978-1-68119-929-0(7)*, 900192375) Bloomsbury Publishing USA. (Bloomsbury Children's Bks.).

Bramsen, Carin. Sleepover Duck! Bramsen, Carin, illus. 2018. (Illus.). 40p. (J). (gr. -1-2). 17.99 *(978-0-385-38417-9(3)*, Random Hse. Bks. for Young Readers) Random Hse. Children's Bks.

Brody, Jessica. A Dragon in the Castle? 2018. (Illus.). 94p. (J). *(978-1-5444-2142-1(7))* Disney Publishing Worldwide.

—A Dragon in the Castle?, 2. 2019. (Lego Disney Princess Ch Bks). (ENG., Illus.). 96p. (J). (gr. 2-4). 16.79 *(978-1-64310-791-2(7))* Penworthy Co., LLC, The.

Brosgol, Vera. Be Prepared. 2018. (ENG., Illus.). 256p. (J). 26.99 *(978-1-62672-444-0(X)*, 900157563); pap. 14.99 *(978-1-62672-445-7(8)*, 900157564) Roaring Brook Pr. (First Second Bks.).

—Be Prepared. 2018. (Illus.). 244p. (J). lib. bdg. 24.50 *(978-0-606-41104-2(6))* Turtleback.

Butler, Dori Hillestad. The Case of the School Ghost. 2013. (Buddy Files Ser.: 6). lib. bdg. 16.00 *(978-0-606-31843-3(7))* Turtleback.

Capucilli, Alyssa Satin. Biscuit's First Sleepover. Schories, Pat, illus. 2008. (Biscuit Ser.). (ENG.). 24p. (J). (gr. -1-1). 5.99 *(978-0-06-112842-4(2)*, HarperFestival) HarperCollins Pubs.

Carroll, Jody. Mitsy Morgan: Six Monkeys Past Midnight. 2010. 44p. pap. 18.75 *(978-1-4520-0796-0(9))* AuthorHouse.

Castor, Harriet. Dance Off. 2009. (Sleepover Club Ser.). (ENG.). 144p. (J). (gr. 2-6). pap. 6.99 *(978-0-00-726492-6(5))* HarperCollins Pubs. Ltd. GBR. Dist: Independent Pubs. Group.

—Hit the Beach! (the Sleepover Club) 2010. (Sleepover Club Ser.). (ENG.). 128p. (J). (gr. 2-6). pap. 6.99 *(978-0-00-727256-3(1)*, HarperCollins Children's Bks.) HarperCollins Pubs. Ltd. GBR. Dist: HarperCollins Pubs.

Churchman, Jennifer & Churchman, John. The SheepOver. (Sweet Pea & Friends Ser.: 1). (ENG., Illus.). (J). (gr. -1 — 1). 2017. 24p. bds. 7.99 *(978-0-316-27355-8(4))* 2015. 44p. 17.99 *(978-0-316-27356-5(2))* Little, Brown Bks. for Young Readers.

Cousins, Lucy. Maisy Goes on a Sleepover. Cousins, Lucy, illus. 2016. (Maisy First Experiences Ser.). (ENG., Illus.). 32p. (gr. -1-2). 17.20 *(978-0-606-39089-7(8))* Turtleback.

Coven, Wanda. Heidi Heckelbeck Might Be Afraid of the Dark. Burris, Priscilla, illus. 2015. (Heidi Heckelbeck Ser.: 15). (ENG.). 128p. (J). (gr. k-4). pap. 6.99 *(978-1-4814-4627-3(4)*, Little Simon) Little Simon.

Cummings, Fiona. TV Stars! (the Sleepover Club) 2011. (Sleepover Club Ser.). (ENG.). 144p. (gr. 2-6). pap. 7.99 *(978-0-00-726493-3(3)*, HarperCollins Children's Bks.) HarperCollins Pubs. Ltd. GBR. Dist: HarperCollins Pubs.

Dean, James. Pete the Cat's Train Trip. 2015. (Pete the Cat I Can Read Ser.). (J). lib. bdg. 13.55 *(978-0-606-36967-1(8))* Turtleback.

Dean, James & Dean, Kimberly. Pete the Cat & the Bedtime Blues. Dean, James, illus. 2015. (Pete the Cat Ser.). (ENG., Illus.). 40p. (J). (gr. -1-3). 18.99 *(978-0-06-230430-8(5))*; lib. bdg. 18.89 *(978-0-06-230431-5(3))* HarperCollins Pubs. (HarperCollins).

—Pete the Cat & the Bedtime Blues. Dean, James, illus. 2023. (Pete the Cat Ser.). (ENG., Illus.). 40p. (J). (gr. -1-3). pap. 8.99 *(978-0-06-230432-2(1)*, HarperCollins) HarperCollins Pubs.

Denton, P. J. Girls Against Boys. Denos, Julia, illus. 2013. (Sleepover Squad Ser.: 7). (ENG.). 96p. (J). (gr. 1-4). pap. 4.99 *(978-1-4169-5933-5(5)*, Simon & Schuster/Paula Wiseman Bks.) Simon & Schuster/Paula Wiseman Bks.

Dewdney, Anna. Llama Llama Gram & Grandpa. (Llama Llama Ser.). (Illus.). (J). (— 1). 2020. (ENG.). 36p. bds. 9.99 *(978-0-593-11775-0(1))* 2015. 40p. bds. 18.99 *(978-0-670-01396-8(X))* Penguin Young Readers Group. (Viking Books for Young Readers).

Edwards, Helen L. Clara's Imagination. Doggett, Al, illus. 2005. 19.95 *(978-0-9765414-0-0(8))* Bad Publishing.

Edwards, Pamela Duncan. Dinosaur Sleepover. Allwright, Deborah, illus. 2013. (J). *(978-1-4351-4923-6(8))* Barnes & Noble, Inc.

Elliott, Rebecca. Eva's Big Sleepover, 9. 2019. (Branches Early Ch Bks). (ENG.). 72p. (J). (gr. 2-3). 15.36 *(978-0-87617-987-1(1))* Penworthy Co., LLC, The.

—Eva's Big Sleepover. 2018. (Owl Diaries — Branches Ser.: 9). lib. bdg. 14.75 *(978-0-606-41508-8(4))* Turtleback.

—Eva's Big Sleepover: a Branches Book (Owl Diaries #9) Elliott, Rebecca, illus. 2018. (Owl Diaries: 9). (ENG., Illus.). 80p. (J). (gr. k-2). pap. 4.99 *(978-1-338-16306-3(X))* Scholastic, Inc.

—Eva's Big Sleepover: a Branches Book (Owl Diaries #9) (Library Edition), Vol. 9. Elliott, Rebecca, illus. 2018. (Owl Diaries: 9). (ENG., Illus.). 80p. (J). (gr. k-2). lib. bdg. 24.99 *(978-1-338-16307-0(8))* Scholastic, Inc.

Ellis, Sarah. Ben over Night, 1 vol. LaFave, Kim, illus. 2005. (ENG.). 32p. (J). (gr. -1-1). 10.95 *(978-1-55041-807-1(6)*, 0e84cead-52c1-40e8-bd0e-975d5935d88e) Fitzhenry & Whiteside, Ltd. CAN. Dist: Firefly Bks., Ltd.

Epstein, Robin. Choose or Lose: How to Pick a Winner. 2005. (Groovy Girls Sleepover Club Ser.: Vol. 5). 60p. (J). *(978-0-439-65793-8(8))* Scholastic, Inc.

—Pranks a Lot: The Girls vs. the Boys. 2005. (Groovy Girls Sleepover Club Ser.: Vol. 2). (Illus.). 58p. (J). pap. *(978-0-439-65790-7(3))* Scholastic, Inc.

Feuti, Norm. Let's Have a Sleepover!: an Acorn Book (Hello, Hedgehog! #2) Feuti, Norm, illus. 2019. (Hello, Hedgehog! Ser.: 2). (ENG., Illus.). 48p. (J). (gr. -1-1). pap. 4.99 *(978-1-338-28141-5(0))* Scholastic, Inc.

Fisch, Sholly & Hagan, Merrill. But Games Can Never Hurt Me & Sleep Over. Corona, Jorge, illus. 2019. (DC Teen Titans Go! Ser.). (ENG.). 32p. (J). (gr. 2-6). lib. bdg. 21.93 *(978-1-4965-7998-0(4)*, 139829, Stone Arch Bks.) Capstone.

Friedman, Laurie. Mallory's Super Sleepover. Kalis, Jennifer, illus. (Mallory Ser.: 16). (ENG.). 160p. (J). (gr. 2-5). 2012. pap. 7.99 *(978-1-4677-0209-6(9)*, 869ca9fe-ce75-45b6-9716-311e54cd8c12)No. 16. 2011. 15.95 *(978-0-8225-8887-0(0))* Lerner Publishing Group. (Darby Creek).

Fruchter, Jason, illus. Daniel's First Sleepover. 2015. (Daniel Tiger's Neighborhood Ser.). (ENG.). 24p. (J). (gr. -1-2). pap. 4.99 *(978-1-4814-2893-4(4)*, Simon Spotlight) Simon Spotlight.

Galante, Cecilia. Little Wings #2: Be Brave, Willa Bean! Valiant, Kristi, illus. 2011. (Little Wings Ser.: 2). 112p. (J). (gr. 1-4). 4.99 *(978-0-375-86948-8(4)*, Random Hse. Bks. for Young Readers) Random Hse. Children's Bks.

Giglio, Judy. The Tapping Tale. Cepeda, Joe, illus. 2003. (Green Light Readers Level 1 Ser.). (ENG.). 24p. (J). (gr. -1-3). pap. 4.99 *(978-0-15-204852-5(9)*, 1194651, Clarion Bks.) HarperCollins Pubs.

Grosset & Dunlap. I Slightly Want to Go Home. 2011. (Charlie & Lola Ser.). (ENG., Illus.). 24p. (J). (gr. k-3). pap. 4.99 *(978-0-448-45461-0(0)*, Grosset & Dunlap) Penguin Young Readers Group.

Guest, Elissa Haden. Iris & Walter, the Sleepover. Davenier, Christine, illus. 2006. (Iris & Walter Ser.). 44p. (gr. 1-4). 15.95 *(978-0-7569-6681-2(7))* Perfection Learning Corp.

—Iris & Walter: the Sleepover. Davenier, Christine, illus. alt. ed. 2012. (Iris & Walter Ser.). (ENG.). 44p. (J). (gr. 1-4). pap. 4.99 *(978-0-547-74556-5(7)*, 1486269, Clarion Bks.) HarperCollins Pubs.

—The Sleepover. 2012. (Iris & Walter — Green Light Reader Ser.). lib. bdg. 13.55 *(978-0-606-24266-0(X))* Turtleback.

Haave, Meghan. Christopher's Night at Grandma & Grandpa's. 2012. 32p. (J). 9.95 *(978-1-59530-458-2(4))* Hallmark Card, Inc.

Hale, Bruce. Clark the Shark. 2016. (Clark the Shark: I Can Read Level 1 Ser.). (J). lib. bdg. 13.55 *(978-0-606-38774-3(9))* Turtleback.

—Clark the Shark: Afraid of the Dark. Francis, Guy, illus. 2015. (Clark the Shark Ser.). (ENG.). 32p. (J). (gr. -1-3). 18.99 *(978-0-06-237450-9(8)*, HarperCollins) HarperCollins Pubs.

HarperCollins Publishers Ltd. Staff. A My Little Pony. 2003. 115.84 *(978-0-06-056197-0(1))* HarperCollins Pubs.

Hartley, Susan. Jake's Sleepover. 2011. (Early Connections Ser.). (J). *(978-1-61672-583-9(4))* Benchmark Education Co.

—Jake's Sleepover: Set Of 6. 2011. (Early Connections Ser.). (J). pap. 37.00 net. *(978-1-4108-1090-8(9))* Benchmark Education Co.

Hopkins, Cathy. Mates, Dates, & Sleepover Secrets. 2010. (Mates, Dates Ser.). (ENG.). 208p. (YA). (gr. 7). pap. 10.99 *(978-1-4424-1421-1(9)*, Simon Pulse) Simon Pulse.

Hunter, Jana. Trick or Treat (the Sleepover Club) 2010. (Sleepover Club Ser.). (ENG., Illus.). 112p. (J). (gr. 2-6). pap. 6.99 *(978-0-00-727254-9(5)*, HarperCollins Children's Bks.) HarperCollins Pubs. Ltd. GBR. Dist: HarperCollins Pubs.

Impey, Rose. Best Friends! (the Sleepover Club) 2008. (Sleepover Club Ser.). (ENG., Illus.). 128p. (gr. 2-6). pap. 6.99 *(978-0-00-726494-0(1)*, HarperCollins Children's Bks.) HarperCollins Pubs. Ltd. GBR. Dist: HarperCollins Pubs.

Jakubowski, Michele. Sleepover. Fekete, Hédi, illus. (Ashley Small & Ashlee Tall Ser.). (ENG.). 64p. (J). (gr. 1-3). 2017. pap. 4.95 *(978-1-5158-0015-6(6))* 2016. lib. bdg. 20.65 *(978-1-5158-0011-8(3)*, 131848) Capstone. (Picture Window Bks.).

Jones, Jen. Maren's New Family. Franco, Paula, illus. 2015. (Sleepover Girls Ser.). (ENG.). 128p. (J). (gr. 3-5). lib. bdg. 22.65 *(978-1-4965-0540-8(9)*, 128612, Stone Arch Bks.) Capstone.

Joyner, Andrew. Boris Sees the Light: a Branches Book (Boris #4) Joyner, Andrew, illus. 2013. (Boris Ser.: 4). (ENG.). 80p. (J). (gr. k-2). pap. 5.99 *(978-0-545-48454-1(5))* Scholastic, Inc.

Kane, Kim. The NOT-MUCH Sleepover Starring Ginger Green, Volume 2. Davis, Jon, illus. 2019. (Ginger Green Ser.: 2). (ENG.). 144p. (J). (gr. k-2). pap. 8.99 *(978-1-76050-106-8(9))* Hardie Grant Children?s Publishing AUS. Dist: Independent Pubs. Group.

Kann, Victoria. Pinkalicious: the Princess of Pink Slumber Party. Kann, Victoria, illus. 2012. (I Can Read Level 1 Ser.). (ENG., Illus.). 32p. (J). (gr. -1-3). 16.99 *(978-0-06-198963-6(0)*, HarperCollins) HarperCollins Pubs.

—The Princess of Pink Slumber Party. 2012. (Pinkalicious I Can Read Ser.). (J). lib. bdg. 13.55 *(978-0-606-23581-5(7))* Turtleback.

Keene, Carolyn. The Nancy Drew & the Clue Crew Collection (Boxed Set) Sleepover Sleuths; Scream for Ice Cream; Pony Problems; the Cinderella Ballet Mystery; Case of the Sneaky Snowman. Pamintuan, Macky, illus. 2014. (Nancy Drew & the Clue Crew Ser.). (ENG.). 480p. (J). (gr. 1-4). pap. 29.99 *(978-1-4814-1472-2(0)*, Aladdin) Simon & Schuster Children's Publishing.

—Sleepover Sleuths, 1. Pamintuan, Macky, illus. 2006. (Nancy Drew & the Clue Crew Ser.: 1). (ENG.). 96p. (J). (gr. 1-4). pap. 5.99 *(978-1-4169-1255-2(X))* Simon & Schuster, Inc.

Kellie, Kerrie. The Sleep over Adventure. 2011. 20p. pap. 24.95 *(978-1-4560-6884-4(9))* America Star Bks.

Lagonegro, Melissa, adapted by. Ghost Hunt! 2018. (Illus.). 22p. (J). *(978-1-5490-4049-8(9))* Random Hse., Inc.

Lang, Suzanne. Grumpy Monkey up All Night. Lang, Max, illus. 2020. (Grumpy Monkey Ser.). (ENG.). 32p. (J). (gr. -1-2). 21.99 *(978-0-593-11976-1(2)*, Random Hse. Bks. for Young Readers); 18.99 *(978-0-593-11975-4(4))*; E-Book *(978-0-593-11977-8(0)*, Random Hse. Bks. for Young Readers) Random Hse. Children's Bks.

London, Jonathan. Froggy's Sleepover. Remkiewicz, Frank, illus. 2007. (Froggy Ser.). 32p. (J). (gr. -1-k). pap. 7.99 *(978-0-14-240750-9(X)*, Puffin Books) Penguin Young Readers Group.

Long, Kathy. Christopher SAT Straight up in Bed. Cantor, Patricia, illus. 2013. (ENG.). 40p. (J). 16.00 *(978-0-8028-5359-2(5)*, Eerdmans Bks For Young Readers) Eerdmans, William B. Publishing Co.

Long, Melinda & Wyrick, Monica. Art Smart, Science Detective: The Case of the Sliding Spaceship. 2018. (Young Palmetto Bks.). (ENG., Illus.). 64p. pap. 12.99 *(978-1-61117-935-4(1)*, P599510) Univ. of South Carolina Pr.

Lozano, Neal. Can God See Me in the Dark? Hatke, Ben, illus. 2007. (ENG.). 32p. (J). 16.95 *(978-1-883551-45-2(5)*, Maple Corners Press) Attic Studio Publishing Hse.

Mabry, Sheri. The Kid & the Chameleon Sleepover (the Kid & the Chameleon: Time to Read, Level 3) Stone, Joanie, illus. 2019. (Time to Read Ser.). (ENG.). 48p. (J). (gr. k-2). 12.99 *(978-0-8075-4180-7(X)*, 080754180X) Whitman, Albert & Co.

MacDonald, Anne Louise. The Memory Stone, 1 vol. Ouellet, Joanne, illus. 2003. (ENG.). 24p. (J). (gr. -1-3). 7.95 *(978-1-55109-442-7(8)*, c738446c-270f-4f3c-a624-276c51fa4a3b) Nimbus Publishing, Ltd. CAN. Dist: Baker & Taylor Publisher Services (BTPS).

Maed, Mary Ann Graziani. Filled to Capacity. 2008. 56p. pap. 24.50 *(978-0-615-16077-1(8))* Wishing Star Children's Bks.

Malone, Jen. The Sleepover. (Mix Ser.). (ENG., Illus.). (J). (gr. 4-8). 2017. 256p. pap. 7.99 *(978-1-4814-5260-1(6))* 2016. 240p. 17.99 *(978-1-4814-5261-8(4))* Simon & Schuster Children's Publishing. (Aladdin).

Mann, Jennifer Ann. Sunny Sweet Is So Not Scary. 2015. (Sunny Sweet Ser.). (ENG.). 192p. (YA). (gr. 3-6). 15.99 *(978-1-61963-507-4(0)*, 900138710, Bloomsbury USA Childrens) Bloomsbury Publishing USA.

Manushkin, Fran. Katie's Spooky Sleepover. Lyon, Tammie, illus. 2016. (Katie Woo Ser.). (ENG.). 32p. (J). (gr. k-2). lib. bdg. 21.32 *(978-1-4795-9640-9(X)*, 131859, Picture Window Bks.) Capstone.

—A Nervous Night, 1 vol. Lyon, Tammie, illus. 2010. (Katie Woo Ser.). (ENG.). 32p. (J). (gr. k-2). pap. 5.95 *(978-1-4048-6060-5(6)*, 103150); lib. bdg. 21.32 *(978-1-4048-5725-4(7)*, 102302) Capstone. (Picture Window Bks.).

McAuley, Rowan. Sleep-Over!, 5. Oswald, Ash, illus. 2008. (Go Girl! Ser.: 2). (ENG.). 85p. (J). (gr. 1-3). 16.19 *(978-0-312-34641-6(7)*, 9780312346416, Feiwel & Friends) Feiwel & Friends.

Mcdonald, Megan. Stink & the Shark Sleepover. Reynolds, Peter H., illus. 2019. (Stink Ser.). (ENG.). 168p. (J). (gr. 1-5). lib. bdg. 31.36 *(978-1-5321-4333-5(8)*, 31863, Chapter Bks.) Spotlight.

McDonald, Megan. Stink & the Shark Sleepover. Reynolds, Peter, illus. 2014. (Stink Ser.: 9). (ENG.). 176p. (J). (gr. 1-4). 14.99 *(978-0-7636-6474-9(X))* Candlewick Pr.

Mcdonald, Megan. Stink & the Shark Sleepover. 2015. (Stink Ser.: 9). lib. bdg. 14.75 *(978-0-606-36859-9(0))* Turtleback.

McDonnell, Patrick. Thank You & Good Night. (ENG., Illus.). (J). (gr. -1 — 1). 2018. 24p. bds. 8.99 *(978-0-316-33799-1(4))* 2015. 40p. 15.99 *(978-0-316-33801-1(X))* Little, Brown Bks. for Young Readers.

McFarlane, Susannah. In the Dark. 2015. 122p. (J). *(978-1-61067-445-4(6))* Kane Miller.

McPhail, David. The Blue Door, 1 vol. 2003. (First Flight Level 2 Ser.). (ENG., Illus.). 32p. (J). (gr. -1-1). pap. 4.95 *(978-1-55041-802-6(5)*, e00e64fc-e139-4123-a087-796c57062883) Fitzhenry & Whiteside, Ltd. CAN. Dist: Firefly Bks., Ltd.

Meddaugh, Susan. Campfire Stories. 2013. (Martha Speaks Ser.). (ENG., Illus.). 96p. (J). (gr. 1-4). pap. 5.99 *(978-0-547-97021-9(8))* Houghton Mifflin Harcourt Publishing Co.

—Martha Speaks: Campfire Stories (Chapter Book) 2013. (Martha Speaks Ser.). (ENG., Illus.). 96p. (J). (gr. 1-4). 14.99 *(978-0-547-97024-0(2))* Houghton Mifflin Harcourt Publishing Co.

Melling, David. Hugless Douglas & the Big Sleepover. 2013. (ENG., Illus.). 32p. (J). *(978-1-58925-116-8(4))* Tiger Tales.

Morrissey, Dean & Krensky, Stephen. The Monster Trap. Morrissey, Dean, illus. 2004. (Illus.). 40p. (J). lib. bdg. 17.89 *(978-0-06-052499-9(5))* HarperCollins Pubs.

Mullins, Julie. The Sleepover. Foye, Lloyd, illus. 2005. (Girlz Rock! Ser.). (J). pap. *(978-1-59336-707-7(4))* Mondo Publishing.

Night, P. J. Best Friends Forever. (You're Invited to a Creepover Ser.: 6). (ENG.). 160p. (J). (gr. 3-7). 2018. 17.99 *(978-1-5344-3169-0(1))* 2012. pap. 6.99 *(978-1-4424-4150-7(X))* Simon Spotlight. (Simon Spotlight).

—Best Friends Forever. 2012. (Creepover Ser.: 6). lib. bdg. 17.20 *(978-0-606-26336-8(5))* Turtleback.

—Is She for Real? 2012. (You're Invited to a Creepover Ser.: 7). (ENG.). 160p. (J). (gr. 3-7). pap. 6.99 *(978-1-4424-5056-1(8)*, Simon Spotlight) Simon Spotlight.

—Is She for Real? 2012. (Creepover Ser.: 7). lib. bdg. 17.20 *(978-0-606-26340-5(3))* Turtleback.

—It Spells Z-O-M-B-I-e! 2017. (You're Invited to a Creepover Ser.: 22). (ENG., Illus.). 160p. (J). (gr. 3-7). pap. 7.99 *(978-1-5344-0082-5(6)*, Simon Spotlight) Simon Spotlight.

—It Spells Z-O-M-B-I-E! 2017. 138p. (J). *(978-1-5182-4688-3(5)*, Simon Spotlight) Simon Spotlight.

—Ready for a Scare? (You're Invited to a Creepover Ser.: 3). (ENG.). 160p. (J). (gr. 3-7). 2018. 17.99 *(978-1-5344-2109-7(2))* 2011. pap. 7.99 *(978-1-4424-2903-1(8))* Simon Spotlight. (Simon Spotlight).

—Ready for a Scare?, 1 vol. 2013. (You're Invited to a Creepover Ser.). (ENG.). 160p. (J). (gr. 3-6). lib. bdg. 31.36 *(978-1-61479-062-4(0)*, 15850, Chapter Bks.) Spotlight.

—Ready for a Scare? 2011. (Creepover Ser.: 3). lib. bdg. 17.20 *(978-0-606-23747-5(X))* Turtleback.

—The Show Must Go On! 2011. (You're Invited to a Creepover Ser.: 4). (ENG.). 160p. (J). (gr. 3-7). pap. 6.99 *(978-1-4424-2905-5(4)*, Simon Spotlight) Simon Spotlight.

—The Show Must Go On! 2011. (Creepover Ser.: 4). lib. bdg. 16.00 *(978-0-606-23748-2(8))* Turtleback.

—There's Something Out There. (You're Invited to a Creepover Ser.: 5). (ENG.). 160p. (J). (gr. 3-7). 2018. 17.99 *(978-1-5344-3168-3(3))* 2011. pap. 6.99 *(978-1-4424-4148-4(8))* Simon Spotlight. (Simon Spotlight).

S

O'Connor, Jane. Fancy Nancy: Saturday Night Sleepover. Glasser, Robin Preiss, illus. 2016. (Fancy Nancy Ser.). (ENG.). 32p. (J). (gr. -1-3). 17.99 *(978-0-06-226985-0(2),* HarperCollins) HarperCollins Pubs.

Orme, Helen. Sleepover. 2008. (Siti's Sisters Ser.). (ENG., Illus.). 36p. pap. *(978-1-84167-741-5(8))* Ransom Publishing Ltd.

Oxley, Jennifer & Aronson, Billy. Peg + Cat: the Sleepover. 2018. (Peg + Cat Ser.). (ENG.). 24p. (J). (gr. -1-2). 5.99 *(978-1-5362-0345-5(9),* Candlewick Entertainment) Candlewick Pr.

Pace, Anne Marie. Vampirina Ballerina Hosts a Sleepover-Vampirina Ballerina. 2013. (Vampirina Ser.: 2). (ENG., Illus.). 40p. (J). (gr. -1-k). 16.99 *(978-1-4231-7570-4(0),* Disney-Hyperion) Disney Publishing Worldwide.

Parish, Herman. Amelia Bedelia Sleeps Over. 2012. (I Can Read Level 1 Ser.). (ENG., Illus.). 32p. (J). (gr. -1-3). 16.99 *(978-0-06-209524-4(2),* Greenwillow Bks.) HarperCollins Pubs.

—Amelia Bedelia Sleeps Over. Avril, Lynne, illus. 2012. (I Can Read Level 1 Ser.). (ENG.). 32p. (J). (gr. -1-3). pap. 5.99 *(978-0-06-209523-7(4),* Greenwillow Bks.) HarperCollins Pubs.

—Amelia Bedelia Sleeps Over. 2012. (Amelia Bedelia: I Can Read! Ser.). (J). lib. bdg. 13.55 *(978-0-606-26849-3(9))* Turtleback.

Penn, Audrey. Chester Raccoon & the Almost Perfect Sleepover. Gibson, Barbara, illus. 2017. (Kissing Hand Ser.). (ENG.). 32p. (J). (gr. -1-3). 16.95 *(978-1-939100-11-5(9))* Tanglewood Pr.

Perl, Erica S. Aces Wild. 2015. (ENG.). 224p. (J). (gr. 3-7). 7.99 *(978-0-307-93173-3(0),* Yearling) Random Hse. Children's Bks.

Peschke, Marci. Party Queen, 1 vol. Mourning, Tuesday, illus. 2013. (Kylie Jean Ser.). (ENG.). 112p. (J). (gr. 1-3). lib. bdg. 22.65 *(978-1-4048-7582-1(4),* 119874, Picture Window Bks.) Capstone.

Pinkwater, Daniel & Pinkwater, Daniel M. Sleepover Larry, 0 vols. Pinkwater, Jill, illus. 2013. (ENG.). 34p. (J). (gr. -1-3). pap. 9.99 *(978-1-4778-4765-7(0),* 9781477847657, Two Lions) Amazon Publishing.

Pinkwater, Daniel M. Sleepover Larry. 2007. (Illus.). 32p. 16.99 *(978-0-7614-5335-2(0))* Marshall Cavendish Corp.

Punter, Russell. Llamas in Pajamas. 2015. (Phonics Readers (no Flaps) Ser.). (ENG.). 24p. (J). pap. 6.99 *(978-0-7945-2739-6(6),* Usborne) EDC Publishing.

Regan, Dian. The Snow Blew Inn. Cushman, Doug, illus. 2011. (ENG.). 32p. (J). 16.95 *(978-0-8234-2351-4(4))* Holiday Hse., Inc.

Reuterstrand, Siri. Ellis Is Scared of the Dark. Wik, Jenny, illus. 2012. (ENG.). 24p. (J). (gr. -1-k). 12.95 *(978-1-61608-667-1(X),* 608667, Sky Pony Pr.) Skyhorse Publishing Co., Inc.

Rey, H. A. Curious George & the Sleepover. 2017. (Curious George Ser.). (ENG., Illus.). 24p. (J). (gr. -1-3). 14.99 *(978-0-544-76346-3(7),* 1635106, Clarion Bks.) HarperCollins Pubs.

Rippin, Sally. The Worst Sleepover: Hey Jack! 2014. (ENG., Illus.). 48p. (J). pap. 4.99 *(978-1-61067-185-9(6))* Kane Miller.

Rissi, Anica Mrose. Anna, Banana, & the Sleepover Secret. Kuo, Cassey, illus. 2018. (Anna, Banana Ser.: 7). (ENG.). 128p. (J). (gr. 1-5). 17.99 *(978-1-5344-1719-9(2));* pap. 5.99 *(978-1-5344-1718-2(4))* Simon & Schuster Bks. For Young Readers. (Simon & Schuster Bks. For Young Readers).

Roy, Ron. Colossal Fossil. 2018. (to Z Mysteries Ser.). lib. bdg. 16.00 *(978-0-606-40922-3(X))* Turtleback.

Rylant, Cynthia. Annie & Snowball & the Grandmother Night. 2013. (Annie & Snowball Ready-To-Read Ser.). lib. bdg. 13.55 *(978-0-606-35183-6(3))* Turtleback.

—Annie & Snowball & the Grandmother Night: Ready-To-Read Level 2. Stevenson, Suçie & Stevenson, Suçie, illus. (Annie & Snowball Ser.: 12). (ENG.). 40p. (J). (gr. k-2). 2013. pap. 4.99 *(978-1-4169-7204-4(8))* 2012. 17.99 *(978-1-4169-7203-7(X))* Simon Spotlight. (Simon Spotlight).

—Henry & Mudge & the Big Sleepover. Stevenson, Suçie, illus. 2007. (Henry & Mudge Ser.). 40p. (gr. k-2). lib. bdg. 14.00 *(978-0-7569-8117-4(4))* Perfection Learning Corp.

—Henry & Mudge & the Big Sleepover. Stevenson, Suçie, illus. 2007. (Henry & Mudge Ready-To-Read Ser.: 28). 40p. (gr. -1-3). lib. bdg. 13.55 *(978-1-4177-8140-9(8))* Turtleback.

—Henry & Mudge & the Big Sleepover: Ready-To-Read Level 2. Stevenson, Suçie et al, illus. 2006. (Henry & Mudge Ser.: 28). (ENG.). 40p. (J). (gr. k-2). 17.99 *(978-0-689-81171-5(3),* Simon Spotlight) Simon Spotlight.

—Henry & Mudge & the Big Sleepover: Ready-To-Read Level 2, Bk. 28. Stevenson, Suçie & Stevenson, Suçie, illus. 2007. (Henry & Mudge Ser.: 28). (ENG.). 40p. (J). (gr. k-2). pap. 4.99 *(978-0-689-83451-6(9),* Simon Spotlight) Simon Spotlight.

Santomero, Angela C. Daniel's First Sleepover. 2015. (Daniel Tiger's Neighborhood 8X8 Ser.). lib. bdg. 13.55 *(978-0-606-36315-0(7))* Turtleback.

Scholastic Editors. La Primera Fiesta de Pijamas de Peppa (Peppa's First Sleepover) 2016. (Peppa Pig 8X8 Ser.). (ENG & SPA., Illus.). 24p. (J). (gr. -1-k). 13.55 *(978-0-606-39159-7(2))* Turtleback.

Scholastic, Inc. Staff & Ladybird Books Staff. Peppa's First Sleepover. 2014. (Peppa Pig 8X8 Ser.). lib. bdg. 13.55 *(978-0-606-36374-7(2))* Turtleback.

Selfors, Suzanne. Wish upon a Sleepover. 2019. (ENG.). 240p. (J). pap. 7.99 *(978-1-250-30874-0(7),* 900165707) Square Fish.

Sesame Street Staff & Studio Mouse Staff. Learning Fun. 2008. (ENG.). 60p. (J). 4.99 *(978-1-59069-671-2(9))* Studio Mouse LLC.

Sheinmel, Courtney. Stella Batts Scaredy Cat. Bell, Jennifer A., illus. 2016. (Stella Batts Ser.). (ENG.). 160p. (J). (gr. 1-3). 9.99 *(978-1-58536-919-5(5),* 204026) Sleeping Bear Pr.

Siamon, Sharon. Haunted Hotel Sleepover, Bk. 3. (ENG., Illus.). 152p. (J). pap. 8.99 *(978-0-340-67278-5(1))* Hodder & Stoughton GBR. Dist: Trafalgar Square Publishing.

—Lost Attic, Bk. 6. (ENG., Illus.). 137p. (J). pap. 8.99 *(978-0-340-70905-4(7))* Hodder & Stoughton GBR. Dist: Trafalgar Square Publishing.

—Sleepover: Secret Room. (ENG., Illus.). 137p. (J). pap. *(978-0-340-67276-1(5))* Hodder & Stoughton.

Stanek, Robert, pseud. The Bugville Critters Have a Sleepover. 2008. (ENG.). 28p. (J). per. 9.99 *(978-1-57545-146-6(8))* RP Media.

—Have a Sleepover. 2008. (ENG., Illus.). 28p. (J). pap. 5.29 *(978-1-57545-189-3(1))* RP Media.

Stierle, Cynthia. Diego in the Dark: Being Brave at Night. Maher, Alex, illus. 2008. (Go, Diego, Go! Ser.). (ENG.). 16p. (J). (gr. -1-2). pap. 6.99 *(978-1-4169-5935-9(1),* Simon Spotlight/Nickelodeon) Simon Spotlight/Nickelodeon.

Thaler, Mike. New Year's Eve Sleepover from the Black Lagoon, 1 vol. Lee, Jared, illus. 2014. (Black Lagoon Adventures Ser.). (ENG.). 64p. (J). (gr. 2-6). lib. bdg. 31.36 *(978-1-61479-204-8(6),* 3613, Chapter Bks.) Spotlight.

Ventura, Marne. Edgy Estella Aces the Sleepover Party. Trinidad, Leo, illus. 2016. (Worry Warriors Ser.). (ENG.). 96p. (J). (gr. 2-4). lib. bdg. 25.99 *(978-1-4965-3610-5(X),* 132816, Stone Arch Bks.) Capstone.

Viselman, Kenn. The Surprise. 2003. 32p. pap. 3.99 *(978-0-06-054839-1(8),* Harper Entertainment) HarperCollins Pubs.

Waber, Bernard. Quique Duerme Fuera de Casa. Mlawer, Teresa, tr. 2003. (SPA., Illus.). (J). (gr. k-2). pap. *(978-968-6579-15-4(X),* SI6510) Sistemas Tecnicos de Edicion, S.A. de C.V. MEX. Dist: Lectorum Pubns., Inc.

Warner, Sally. Absolutely Alfie & the Worst Best Sleepover. Malone, Shearry, illus. 2018. (Absolutely Alfie Ser.: 3). (ENG.). 144p. (J). (gr. 1-3). 5.99 *(978-1-101-99994-3(2),* Puffin Books); 14.99 *(978-1-101-99992-9(6),* Viking Books for Young Readers) Penguin Young Readers Group.

—Absolutely Alfie & the Worst Best Sleepover. 2018. (Absolutely Alfie Ser.: 3). lib. bdg. 16.00 *(978-0-606-40884-4(3))* Turtleback.

White, Kathryn. Ruby's Sleepover. Latimer, Miriam, illus. (ENG.). 32p. (J). 2013. (gr. -1-2). pap. 8.99 *(978-1-84686-758-3(4))* 2012. 16.99 *(978-1-84686-593-0(X))* Barefoot Bks., Inc.

Willems, Mo. Time to Sleep, Sheep the Sheep! Willems, Mo, illus. 2010. (ENG., Illus.). 32p. (J). (gr. -1-3). 12.99 *(978-0-06-172847-1(0));* lib. bdg. 15.89 *(978-0-06-172848-8(9))* HarperCollins Pubs. (Balzer & Bray).

Winthrop, Elizabeth. Squashed in the Middle. Cummins, Pat, illus. 2008. (J). (gr. k-4). 28.95 incl. audio compact disk *(978-1-4301-0443-8(0));* 25.95 incl. audio *(978-1-4301-0440-7(6))* Live Oak Media.

SLEIGHT OF HAND

see Magic

SLESSOR, MARY MITCHELL, 1848-1915

Jay, Ruth Johnson. Mary Slessor: Missionary to Calabar. 2006. (Illus.). 143p. (J). *(978-1-56265-077-3(7))* Accelerated Christian Education, Inc.

Kelly, Terri B. Mary Slessor: Missionary Mother. 2014. (Illus.). 164p. (J). *(978-1-60682-630-0(1))* BJU Pr.

SLOTHS

Beer, Julie. Sharks vs. Sloths. 2019. (Illus.). 64p. (J). (gr. 1-3). 17.99 *(978-1-4263-3523-5(7),* National Geographic Kids) Disney Publishing Worldwide.

Bell, Samantha S. Sloths Are Awesome. 2018. (Animals Are Awesome Ser.). (ENG., Illus.). 32p. (J). (gr. 3-6). 32.80 *(978-1-63235-439-6(X),* 13817, 12-Story Library) Bookstaves, LLC.

Bodden, Valerie. Sloths. 2018. (Amazing Animals Ser.). (ENG., Illus.). 24p. (J). (gr. 1-3). pap. 10.99 *(978-1-62832-499-0(6),* 19656, Creative Paperbacks); *(978-1-60818-883-3(3),* 19658, Creative Education) Creative Co., The.

Borgert-Spaniol, Megan. Sloths. 2015. (Animal Safari Ser.). (ENG., Illus.). 24p. (J). (gr. k-3). lib. bdg. 26.95 *(978-1-62617-214-2(5),* Blastoff! Readers) Bellwether Media.

Bozzo, Linda. How Sloths Grow Up, 1 vol. 2019. (Animals Growing Up Ser.). (ENG.). 24p. (gr. 1-2). pap. 10.35 *(978-1-9785-1241-2(4),* 75cac777-782e-4e52-94c8-45c94fe86763) Enslow Publishing, LLC.

Buller, Laura. Sloths. 2019. (Illus.). 48p. (J). *(978-1-5444-3235-9(6))* Dorling Kindersley Publishing, Inc.

Clark, Willow. Three-Toed Sloths, 1 vol. 2012. (Up a Tree Ser.). (ENG., Illus.). 24p. (J). (gr. 2-3). pap. 9.25 *(978-1-4488-6331-0(7),* dea3ab90-646e-4d0e-8a23-ed6cfd492767, PowerKids Pr.); lib. bdg. 26.27 *(978-1-4488-6186-6(1),* 1e0b9d9e-3ea8-49b0-b16e-4869570e3c26) Rosen Publishing Group, Inc., The.

Cooke, Lucy. A Little Book of Sloth. Cooke, Lucy, photos by. 2013. (ENG., Illus.). 64p. (J). (gr. k). 18.99 *(978-1-4424-4557-4(2),* McElderry, Margaret K. Bks.) McElderry, Margaret K. Bks.

DK. Sloths. 2019. (ENG., Illus.). 48p. (J). *(978-0-241-37926-4(1))* Dorling Kindersley Publishing, Inc.

Furstinger, Nancy. How Do Sloths Poop? 2018. (Crazy Animal Facts Ser.). (ENG., Illus.). 32p. (J). (gr. 4-6). lib. bdg. 28.65 *(978-1-5435-4117-5(8),* 139071, Capstone Pr.) Capstone.

Gish, Melissa. Sloths. (Living Wild Ser.). (ENG., Illus.). 48p. (J). (gr. 4-7). 2017. pap. 12.00 *(978-1-62832-305-4(1),* 20626, Creative Paperbacks) 2016. *(978-1-60818-709-6(8),* 20628, Creative Education) Creative Co., The.

Goecke, Michael P. Giant Ground Sloth, 1 vol. 2003. (Prehistoric Animals Ser.). (ENG.). 24p. (gr. k-4). 25.65 *(978-1-57765-968-6(6),* Buddy Bks.) ABDO Publishing Co.

Guidone, Julie. Sloths, 1 vol. 2009. (Animals That Live in the Rain Forest Ser.). (ENG.). 24p. (J). (gr. 1-1). pap. 9.15 *(978-1-4339-0108-9(0),* ed775a1f-9cff-4d2a-808e-f1a3b75b66b2); lib. bdg. 25.27 *(978-1-4339-0026-6(2),* 1e760ff5-200e-4603-9ee3-1bda1e103e2e) Stevens, Gareth Publishing LLLP. (Weekly Reader Leveled Readers).

—Sloths / Perezosos, 1 vol. 2009. (Animals That Live in the Rain Forest / Animales de la Selva Ser.). (SPA & ENG.). 24p. (J). (gr. 1-1). pap. 9.15 *(978-1-4339-0115-7(3),* c87ee7e4-18c2-4dda-8cb5-db90190a5af1); lib. bdg. 25.27 *(978-1-4339-0065-5(3),* 7d0f5f66-cde4-4f70-b38a-f1953546dded) Stevens, Gareth Publishing LLLP. (Weekly Reader Leveled Readers).

Jeffrey, Gary. Giant Sloth. 2017. (Graphic Prehistoric Animals Ser.). (ENG., Illus.). 32p. (J). (gr. 5-8). lib. bdg. 31.35 *(978-1-62588-409-1(5),* 19278, Smart Apple Media) Black Rabbit Bks.

Lang, Aubrey. Baby Sloth, 1 vol. Lynch, Wayne, photos by. 2004. (Nature Babies Ser.). (ENG., Illus.). 36p. (J). (gr. k-3). pap. 7.95 *(978-1-55041-827-9(0),* a9a62cab-c605-4971-a51a-a7b258b18c5d) Trifolium Bks., Inc. CAN. Dist: Firefly Bks., Ltd.

Lunis, Natalie. Three-Toed Sloths: Green Mammals. 2010. (Disappearing Acts Ser.). (Illus.). 24p. (J). (gr. k-3). lib. bdg. 26.99 *(978-1-936087-42-6(1))* Bearport Publishing Co., Inc.

Lynette, Rachel. Three-Toed Sloths. 2013. (Jungle Babies of the Amazon Rain Forest Ser.). 24p. (J). (gr. -1-3). lib. bdg. 25.65 *(978-1-61772-756-6(3))* Bearport Publishing Co., Inc.

McDonnell, Julia . Being a Sloth, 1 vol. 2013. (Can You Imagine? Ser.). (ENG.). 32p. (gr. 2-3). pap. 11.50 *(978-1-4824-3274-9(9),* b108051a-34fd-4d15-ba0e-ab633b330413) Rosen Publishing Group, Inc., The.

McDonnell, Julia. Being a Sloth, 1 vol., Vol. 1. 2013. (Can You Imagine? Ser.). (ENG., Illus.). 32p. (J). (gr. 2-3). 27.92 *(978-1-4824-0099-1(5),* cfd8f419-df9d-49c9-9737-111c03a46f05) Stevens, Gareth Publishing LLLP.

Miller, Sara Swan. Sloths. (Paws & Claws Ser.). 24p. (gr. 2-3). 2009. 42.50 *(978-1-60851-154-9(5))* 2008. (ENG., Illus.). (J). lib. bdg. 26.27 *(978-1-4042-4166-4(3),* 09fc4634-e4bc-45d2-a5d0-a3dfad7a2019) Rosen Publishing Group, Inc., The. (PowerKids Pr.).

Murray, Julie. Sloths. 2016. (I Like Animals! Set 2 Ser.). (ENG., Illus.). 24p. (J). (gr. -1-2). lib. bdg. 31.36 *(978-1-68080-909-1(1),* 23293, Abdo Kids) ABDO Publishing Co.

Paige, Joy. The Sloth: World's Slowest Mammal. 2009. (Record-Breaking Animals Ser.). 24p. (gr. 1-1). 42.50 *(978-1-60852-443-3(4),* PowerKids Pr.) Rosen Publishing Group, Inc., The.

—The Sloth / el Perezoso: The World's Slowest Mammal / el mamífero más lento del Mundo. 2009. (Record-Breaking Animals / Campeones del mundo animal Ser.). (ENG & SPA.). 24p. (gr. 1-1). 42.50 *(978-1-60852-449-5(3),* Editorial Buenas Letras) Rosen Publishing Group, Inc., The.

—The Sloth: The World's Slowest Mammal: El Perezoso: El Mamifero Mas Lento Del Mundo, 1 vol. 2003. (Record-Breaking Animals / Campeones Del Mundo Animal Ser.). (SPA & ENG., Illus.). 24p. (J). (gr. 1-1). lib. bdg. 26.27 *(978-0-8239-6893-0(6),* 2b0af767-eea4-40b9-86da-1acb93495fad) Rosen Publishing Group, Inc., The.

Piehl, Janet. Let's Look at Sloths. 2010. (Lightning Bolt Books (r) — Animal Close-Ups Ser.). (ENG., Illus.). 32p. (J). (gr. 1-3). pap. 9.99 *(978-0-7613-6042-1(5),* 0db812b5-0eb0-4264-9fcd-f96401fe176b); pap. 45.32 *(978-0-7613-6979-0(1))* Lerner Publishing Group.

Rafferty, John P., ed. Rats, Bats, & Xenarthrans, 4 vols. 2011. (Britannica Guide to Predators & Prey Ser.). (ENG., Illus.). 256p. (YA). (gr. 10-10). 110.58 *(978-1-61530-456-1(8),* ef0d386b-6fc9-4143-8fda-139d9c03565c) Rosen Publishing Group, Inc., The.

Ryndak, Rob. Sloths, 1 vol. 2014. (Jungle Animals Ser.). (ENG., Illus.). 24p. (J). (gr. k-k). 24.27 *(978-1-4824-1760-9(X),* a21c480d-5260-45dd-9dcf-439c78816b9e) Stevens, Gareth Publishing LLLP.

Schuetz, Kari. Baby Sloths. 2013. (Super Cute! Ser.). (ENG., Illus.). 24p. (J). (gr. k-3). lib. bdg. 26.95 *(978-1-60014-933-7(2),* Blastoff! Readers) Bellwether Media.

Schuh, Mari. Sloths. 2014. (Illus.). 24p. (J). lib. bdg. 25.65 *(978-1-62031-112-7(7),* Bullfrog Bks.) Jump! Inc.

Stewart, Melissa. Sloths. 2005. (Nature Watch Ser.). (Illus.). 48p. (J). (gr. 3-7). lib. bdg. 25.26 *(978-1-57505-577-0(5),* Carolrhoda Bks.) Lerner Publishing Group.

Storm, Marysa. Sloths. 2020. (Awesome Animal Lives Ser.). (ENG.). 24p. (J). (gr. k-3). lib. bdg. *(978-1-62310-155-8(7),* 14414, Bolt Jr.) Black Rabbit Bks.

Terp, Gail. Sloths. 2017. (Wild Animal Kingdom Ser.). (ENG.). (J). (gr. 4-7). pap. 9.95 *(978-1-68072-490-5(8));* 32p. pap. 9.99 *(978-1-64466-227-4(2),* 11507); (Illus.). 32p. lib. bdg. *(978-1-68072-193-5(3),* 10569) Black Rabbit Bks. (Bolt).

Windsor, Jo. An Upside down Life: Early Level Satellite Individual Title Six-Packs. (Sails Literacy Ser.). 16p. (gr. 1-2). 27.00 *(978-0-7578-2937-6(6))* Rigby Education.

SLOTHS—FICTION

Carle, Eric. "Slowly, Slowly, Slowly," Said the Sloth. Carle, Eric, illus. 2007. (Illus.). (gr. -1-3). 18.00 *(978-0-7569-8002-3(X))* Perfection Learning Corp.

—Slowly, Slowly, Slowly, Said the Sloth. Carle, Eric, illus. 2007. (ENG., Illus.). 32p. (J). (gr. -1-2). pap. 7.99 *(978-0-14-240847-6(6))* Penguin Young Readers Group.

—"Slowly, Slowly, Slowly," Said the Sloth. 2007. 18.40 *(978-1-4177-7475-3(4))* Turtleback.

Carminati, Chiara. Smile, Breathe, & Go Slowly: Slumby the Sloth Goes to School. Angaramo, Roberta, illus. 2020. 40p. (J). (gr. -1-2). 18.99 *(978-0-8234-4246-1(2))* Holiday Hse., Inc.

Clarke, Jane. Plodney Creeper, Supersloth. 2006. (Blue Bananas Ser.). (ENG., Illus.). 48p. (J). (gr. -1-3). lib. bdg. *(978-0-7787-0850-6(0))* Crabtree Publishing Co.

Kimmelman, Leslie. Bat & Sloth Hang Around (Bat & Sloth: Time to Read, Level 2) Braun, Seb, illus. 2020. (Time to Read Ser.). (ENG.). 32p. (J). (gr. k-2). 12.99 *(978-0-8075-0585-4(4),* 807505854) Whitman, Albert & Co.

—Bat & Sloth Lost & Found (Bat & Sloth: Time to Read, Level 2) Braun, Seb, illus. 2020. (Time to Read Ser.). (ENG.). 32p. (J). (gr. k-2). 12.99 *(978-0-8075-0586-1(2),* 807505862) Whitman, Albert & Co.

Lee, Bonnie. Go Go Sadie. Taylor, Erin, illus. 2011. 46p. 24.00 *(978-1-4349-8679-5(9),* RoseDog Bks.) Dorrance Publishing Co., Inc.

Lehrhaupt, Adam. Sloth Went. Shum, Benson, illus. 2020. (ENG.). 32p. (J). 17.99 *(978-1-5476-0245-2(7),* 900207573, Bloomsbury Children's Bks.) Bloomsbury Publishing USA.

Luper, Eric. The Risky Rescue (Key Hunters #6) 2017. (Key Hunters Ser.: 6). (ENG., Illus.). 128p. (J). (gr. 2-5). pap. 5.99 *(978-1-338-21229-7(X),* Scholastic Paperbacks) Scholastic, Inc.

McKenzie, Heath. Archie: No Ordinary Sloth. 2020. (Archie Ser.: 1). (ENG.). 32p. (J). (gr. -1-k). pap. 9.99 *(978-1-76040-972-2(3))* Hardie Grant Children?s Publishing AUS. Dist: Independent Pubs. Group.

Miles, David W., creator. But First, We Nap: A Little Book about Nap Time. 2018. (ENG., Illus.). 16p. (J). (gr. -1-k). bds. 9.99 *(978-1-64170-017-7(3),* 550017) Familius LLC.

Murray, Andrew. The Very Sleepy Sloth. Tickle, Jack, tr. Tickle, Jack, illus. 2003. 32p. (J). tchr. ed. 15.95 *(978-1-58925-033-8(8))* Tiger Tales.

Preston-Gannon, Frann. Sloth Slept On. 2019. (ENG.). 30p. (J). (gr. -1). bds. 7.95 *(978-1-4549-3449-3(2))* Sterling Publishing Co., Inc.

Seibold, J. Otto. Lost Sloth. 2013. (Illus.). 32p. (J). 16.95 *(978-1-938073-35-9(5),* 17e71c47-97da-456c-be45-560119e3e943) McSweeney's Publishing.

Venable, Colleen AF. Amy the Red Panda Is Writing the Best Story in the World. Chan, Ruth, illus. 2017. (ENG.). 40p. (J). (gr. -1-3). 17.99 *(978-0-06-233848-8(X),* Greenwillow Bks.) HarperCollins Pubs.

—Mervin the Sloth Is about to Do the Best Thing in the World. Chan, Ruth, illus. 2016. (ENG.). 40p. (J). (gr. -1-3). 17.99 *(978-0-06-233847-1(1),* Greenwillow Bks.) HarperCollins Pubs.

Wild, Margaret. The Sloth Who Slowed Us Down. To, Vivienne, illus. 2018. (ENG.). 32p. (J). (gr. -1-2). 16.99 *(978-1-4197-3195-2(5),* 1248101, Abrams Bks. for Young Readers) Abrams, Inc.

Willan, Alex. Jasper & Ollie. 2019. (Illus.). 40p. (J). (gr. -1-2). 18.99 *(978-0-525-64521-4(7),* Doubleday Bks. for Young Readers) Random Hse. Children's Bks.

SLUMBER SONGS

see Lullabies

SLUMS

see Housing

SMALL ARMS

see Firearms

SMALL BUSINESS

Bea Is for Business: The Party Planning Venture. 2014. (ENG., Illus.). 35p. (J). 9.99 *(978-0-9893403-2-8(5))* Bea is for Business.

Bernstein, Daryl. Better Than a Lemonade Stand! Small Business Ideas for Kids. Husberg, Rob, illus. 2012. (ENG.). 224p. (J). (gr. 4-9). pap. 14.99 *(978-1-58270-330-5(2))* Aladdin/Beyond Words.

Bochner, Arthur, et al. New Totally Awesome Business Book for Kids: Revised Edition. 3rd rev. ed. 2007. (New Totally Awesome Ser.: 2). (ENG., Illus.). 192p. (gr. 7-9). per. 15.99 *(978-1-55704-757-1(X),* William Morrow Paperbacks) HarperCollins Pubs.

Earl, C. F. Building a Business in the Virtual World. Madrian, Brigitte, ed. 2013. (Young Adult Library of Small Business & Finance Ser.: 10). 64p. (J). (gr. 7-18). 22.95 *(978-1-4222-2913-2(0));* (Illus.). pap. 12.95 *(978-1-4222-2980-4(7))* Mason Crest.

—Business Funding & Finances. Madrian, Brigitte, ed. 2013. (Young Adult Library of Small Business & Finance Ser.: 10). 64p. (J). (gr. 7-18). 22.95 *(978-1-4222-2915-6(7))* Mason Crest.

—Marketing Your Business. Madrian, Brigitte, ed. 2013. (Young Adult Library of Small Business & Finance Ser.: 10). 64p. (J). (gr. 7-18). 22.95 *(978-1-4222-2919-4(X))* Mason Crest.

—What Does It Mean to Be an Entrepreneur? Madrian, Brigitte, ed. 2013. (Young Adult Library of Small Business & Finance Ser.: 10). 64p. (J). (gr. 7-18). 22.95 *(978-1-4222-2922-4(X))* Mason Crest.

Fischer, James. Keeping Your Business Organized: Time Management & Workflow. Madrian, Brigitte, ed. 2013. (Young Adult Library of Small Business & Finance Ser.: 10). 64p. (J). (gr. 7-18). 22.95 *(978-1-4222-2917-0(3));* (Illus.). pap. 12.95 *(978-1-4222-2982-8(3))* Mason Crest.

—Starting a Business: Creating a Plan. 2013. (J). *(978-1-4222-2912-5(2))* Mason Crest.

—Starting a Business: Creating a Plan. Madrian, Brigitte, ed. 2013. (Young Adult Library of Small Business & Finance Ser.). 64p. (J). (gr. 7-18). pap. 12.95 *(978-1-4222-2984-2(X));* 22.95 *(978-1-4222-2920-0(3))* Mason Crest.

Hobson Gormer, Jennifer J. Kidceo: Amazing Kids Share Their Success in Business. 2017. (ENG., Illus.). 184p. (J). (gr. 4-6). pap. 19.99 *(978-0-9988802-3-5(X))* Gormer, Jennifer Hobson.

Hyde, Natalie. What Is Entrepreneurship? 2016. (Your Start-Up Starts Now! a Guide to Entrepreneurship Ser.). (ENG., Illus.). 48p. (J). (gr. 5-9). *(978-0-7787-2758-3(0));* pap. *(978-0-7787-2766-8(1))* Crabtree Publishing Co.

Kahan, Alex. Entrepreneurship: Create Your Own Business. Crosier, Mike, illus. 2014. (Build It Yourself Ser.). (ENG.). 128p. (J). (gr. 3-7). pap. 17.95 *(978-1-61930-265-5(9),* a1c4aebc-8ac2-40ea-83df-0c4092cd3405) Nomad Pr.

Larsen, Becca. Buying & Selling, 1 vol. 2013. (Rosen Readers Ser.). (ENG.). 24p. (J). (gr. 2-2). pap. 8.25 *(978-1-4777-2260-2(2),* 9cea1a72-defe-4498-a75f-18b20c8ccff3); pap. 49.50 *(978-1-4777-2261-9(0))* Rosen Publishing Group, Inc., The. (Rosen Classroom).

Mariotti, Steve. Entrepreneurship: How to Start & Operate a Small Business. 2005. (YA). pap., stu. ed. 15.00 *(978-1-890859-19-0(2));* (gr. 9-12). tchr. ed. 46.95 *(978-1-890859-21-3(4));* (gr. 9-12). pap. 79.95 *(978-1-890859-20-6(6));* (gr. 9-12). trans. 15.00 *(978-1-890859-23-7(0))* National Foundation for Teaching Entrepreneurship, The.

—How to Start & Operate a Small Business: Exam View Text Bank - CD. 2005. (YA). (gr. 9-12). pap. incl. cd-rom *(978-1-890859-24-4(9))* National Foundation for Teaching Entrepreneurship, The.

Meinking, Mary. Start Your Crafting Business. 2017. (Build Your Business Ser.). (ENG., Illus.). 32p. (J). (gr. 3-9). lib. bdg. 28.65 *(978-1-5157-6690-2(X),* 135252, Capstone Pr.) Capstone.

Minden, Cecilia. Starting Your Own Business. (21st Century Skills Library: Real World Math Ser.). (ENG., Illus.). 32p. (gr. 4-7). 2015. (J). 32.07 *(978-1-63362-576-1(1),* 206488) 2009. lib. bdg. 32.07 *(978-1-60279-313-2(1),* 200209) Cherry Lake Publishing.

Mooney, Carla. Starting a Business: Have Fun & Make Money. 2010. (Creative Adventure Guides). 48p. (J). (gr. 3-6). 26.60 *(978-1-59953-386-5(3))* Norwood Hse. Pr.

Offord, Alexander. What Is Environmental Entrepreneurship? 2016. (Your Start-Up Starts Now! a Guide to Entrepreneurship Ser.). (ENG., Illus.). 48p. (J). (gr. 5-9). *(978-0-7787-2756-9(4))*; pap. *(978-0-7787-2764-4(5))* Crabtree Publishing Co.

Ruffin, Frances E. Let's Have a Bake Sale: Calculating Profit & Unit Cost, 1 vol. 2010. (Math for the REAL World Ser.). (ENG., Illus.). 24p. (gr. 3-4). pap. 8.25 *(978-0-8239-8893-8(7),* fa375125-9655-49d9-a189-2e4223c37adb, PowerKids Pr.) Rosen Publishing Group, Inc., The.

Snyder, Gail. Teen Guide to Starting a Business. 2016. (ENG.). 64p. (J). (gr. 5-12). lib. bdg. *(978-1-68282-088-9(2))* ReferencePoint Pr., Inc.

Thompson, Helen. Business & the Government: Law & Taxes. Madrian, Brigitte, ed. 2013. (Young Adult Library of Small Business & Finance Ser.: 10). 64p. (J). (gr. 7-18). 22.95 *(978-1-4222-2916-3(5))* Mason Crest.

—Managing Employees. Madrian, Brigitte, ed. 2013. (Young Adult Library of Small Business & Finance Ser.: 10). 64p. (J). (gr. 7-18). 22.95 *(978-1-4222-2918-7(1))* Mason Crest.

Ulmer, Mikaila. Bee Fearless: Dream Like a Kid. 2020. (ENG., Illus.). 240p. (J). (gr. 5). 17.99 *(978-1-9848-1508-8(3),* G.P. Putnam's Sons Books for Young Readers) Penguin Young Readers Group.

SMALLS, ROBERT, 1839-1915

Brown, Susan Taylor. Robert Smalls Sails to Freedom. Marshall, Felicia, illus. 2006. (On My Own History Ser.). 48p. (J). (gr. 3-7). pap. 6.95 *(978-0-8225-6051-7(8),* First Avenue Editions); (ENG.). (gr. 2-4). lib. bdg. 25.26 *(978-1-57505-872-6(3))* Lerner Publishing Group.

Halfmann, Janet. Seven Miles to Freedom: The Robert Smalls Story, 1 vol. Smith, Duane, illus. 2008. 40p. (J). (gr. 1-6). (ENG.). pap. 12.95 *(978-1-60060-986-2(4),* leelowbooks); 17.95 *(978-1-60060-232-0(0))* Lee & Low Bks., Inc.

Jones-Radgowski, Jehan. The Escape of Robert Smalls: A Daring Voyage Out of Slavery. Kang, Poppy, illus. 2019. (ENG.). 40p. (J). (gr. 3-6). 18.95 *(978-1-5435-1281-6(X),* 137747, Capstone Editions) Capstone.

Meriwether, Louise & Green, Jonathan. The Freedom Ship of Robert Smalls. 2018. (Young Palmetto Bks.). (ENG., Illus.). 32p. (J). 19.99 *(978-1-61117-855-5(X),* P568005) Univ. of South Carolina Pr.

Thompson, Michael D. Working on the Dock of the Bay: Labor & Enterprise in an Antebellum Southern Port. 2018. (ENG., Illus.). 296p. (J). pap. 31.99 *(978-1-61117-857-9(6),* P568034) Univ. of South Carolina Pr.

SMELL

Aloian, Molly. What Is Smell? 2013. (ENG., Illus.). 24p. (J). *(978-0-7787-0971-8(X))*; (gr. 1-2). pap. *(978-0-7787-0999-2(X))* Crabtree Publishing Co.

Appleby, Alex. What I Smell, 1 vol. 2014. (My Five Senses Ser.). (ENG.). 24p. (J). (gr. k-k). 24.27 *(978-1-4824-0813-3(9),* 482ee750-d1df-44bc-b53b-c8ab9e786947); pap. 9.15 *(978-1-4824-0814-0(7),* 5c2fb743-023e-42b3-ac04-ecaecd2885f1) Stevens, Gareth Publishing LLLP.

Barraclough, Sue. What Can I Smell? 2005. (J). *(978-1-4034-7079-9(0))*; (ENG.). 32p. pap. *(978-1-4034-7085-0(5))* Steck-Vaughn.

Beaumont, Susanna & Baby Senses Staff. Smell. 2005. (Baby Senses Ser.). (Illus.). 12p. (gr. -1-k). bds. *(978-1-905051-49-6(2))* Make Believe Ideas.

Bellamy, Adam. What's That Smell?, 1 vol. 2017. (All about My Senses Ser.). (ENG.). 24p. (gr. k-1). lib. bdg. 24.27 *(978-0-7660-8607-4(0),* a6b1ff3a-84cd-4d1d-b401-31739f184159) Enslow Publishing, LLC.

Braun, Eric. Awesome, Disgusting, Unusual Facts about Everything Stinky, Squishy, & Slimy. 24p. (J). 2019. (Illus.). pap. *(978-1-68072-752-4(4))* 2018. (ENG.). (gr. 4-6). pap. 8.99 *(978-1-64466-305-9(8),* 12515, Hi Jinx) 2018. (ENG., Illus.). (gr. 4-6). lib. bdg. 28.50 *(978-1-68072-610-7(2),* 12514, Hi Jinx) Black Rabbit Bks.

—Beurk! le Livre Différent et Fascinant Sur Tout Ce Qui Pue, Qui Est Mou et Gluant. 2018. (Notre Monde: dégoûtant Mais Génial! Ser.). (FRE.). 24p. (J). (gr. 4-6). *(978-1-77092-454-3(X),* 12583, Hi Jinx) Black Rabbit Bks.

Carr, Aaron. El Olfato. 2013. (Mis Sentidos Ser.). (SPA., Illus.). 24p. (J). (gr. 3-7). lib. bdg. 27.13 *(978-1-62127-579-4(5),* AV2 by Weigl) Weigl Pubs., Inc.

Casado, Dami & Casado, Alicia. El Olfato. 2005. (Sentidos y Algo Más). (SPA & ESP.). 16p. 8.99 *(978-84-272-6413-7(5))* Molino, Editorial ESP. Dist: Santillana USA Publishing Co., Inc.

Castaldo, Nancy. Sniffer Dogs: How Dogs (and Their Noses) Save the World. 2014. (ENG., Illus.). 160p. (J). (gr. 5-7). 16.99 *(978-0-544-08893-1(X),* 1537764, Clarion Bks.) HarperCollins Pubs.

Cleland, Joann. I Smell, Sing & Read. 2010. (Our Five Senses Sing & Read Ser.). (Illus.). 24p. (J). (gr. -1-k). 22.79 *(978-1-61590-287-3(2))* Rourke Educational Media.

Cucini, Sara & Gillespie, Katie. Smell. 2018. (Illus.). 24p. (J). *(978-1-4896-5695-7(2),* AV2 by Weigl) Weigl Pubs., Inc.

Douglas, Lloyd G. My Nose. 2004. (Welcome Books: My Body Ser.). (ENG.). 24p. (J). (gr. k-3). 17.44 *(978-0-516-24063-3(3),* Children's Pr.) Scholastic Library Publishing.

Durrie, Karen. Smell. 2012. (J). *(978-1-61913-311-2(3))*; pap. *(978-1-61913-316-7(4))* Weigl Pubs., Inc.

Enslow, Brian. My Nose, 1 vol. 2010. (All about My Body Ser.). (ENG., Illus.). 24p. (-1). pap. 10.35 *(978-1-59845-170-2(7),* 2c622098-842f-48b2-a94b-84c0b670c747); (gr. -1-1). 25.27 *(978-0-7660-3814-1(9),* 4ca97102-660b-48fc-a966-e8b236a761c0) Enslow Publishing, LLC. (Enslow Publishing).

Equipo Staff. El Olfato. (Coleccion Mundo Maravilloso). (SPA., Illus.). 38p. (J). (gr. 2-4). *(978-84-348-4778-1(7),* OL2004) SM Ediciones.

Furgang, Kathy. My Nose. 2009. (My Body Ser.). 24p. (gr. 3-3). 42.50 *(978-1-61514-691-8(1),* PowerKids Pr.) Rosen Publishing Group, Inc., The.

Ganeri, Anita. Smell. 2013. (Senses Ser.). (Illus.). 24p. (gr. k-3). 28.50 *(978-1-59920-853-4(9))* Black Rabbit Bks.

Hall, Kirsten. Animal Smell, 1 vol. 2005. (Animals & Their Senses Ser.). (ENG., Illus.). 24p. (J). (gr. k-2). pap. 9.15 *(978-0-8368-4810-6(1),* 1cb235ee-6c16-4a91-aa14-d32752ede90d); lib. bdg. 24.67 *(978-0-8368-4804-5(7),* 051c24bf-bd54-46c2-b1ca-2d23f9b91421) Stevens, Gareth Publishing LLLP. (Weekly Reader Leveled Readers).

—Animal Smell / el Olfato en Los Animales, 1 vol. 2005. (Animals & Their Senses / Los Sentidos de Los Animales Ser.). (ENG & SPA., Illus.). 24p. (J). (gr. k-2). lib. bdg. 24.67 *(978-0-8368-4816-8(0),* d81bcaff-f2a2-43b9-ad94-a798c33a60e0, Weekly Reader Leveled Readers) Stevens, Gareth Publishing LLLP.

Hamdan, Russell. Your Nose, 1 vol. 2018. (Your Amazing Body! Ser.). (ENG.). 24p. (gr. k-k). 24.27 *(978-1-5382-1824-2(0),* 59d7d22e-6151-4e39-82e3-a4662e8148bb) Stevens, Gareth Publishing LLLP.

Hanel, Rachael. Smell. 2003. 24p. (J). lib. bdg. 21.35 *(978-1-58340-306-8(X))* Black Rabbit Bks.

Hewitt, Sally. Smell It! 2008. (Let's Start Science Ser.). (ENG., Illus.). 24p. (J). (gr. 3-7). pap. *(978-0-7787-4060-5(9))* Crabtree Publishing Co.

Issa, Joanna. What Can I Smell?, 1 vol. 2014. (These Are My Senses Ser.). (ENG., Illus.). 24p. (J). (gr. -1-1). pap. 5.99 *(978-1-4846-0434-2(2),* 126590, Heinemann) Capstone.

Jenkins, Steve. Stinkiest! 20 Smelly Animals. Jenkins, Steve, illus. 2018. (Extreme Animals Ser.). (ENG., Illus.). 40p. (J). (gr. -1-3). pap. 5.99 *(978-1-328-84197-1(9),* 1691822, Clarion Bks.) HarperCollins Pubs.

Kay, Edward. Stinky Science: Why the Smelliest Smells Smell So Smelly. Shiell, Mike, illus. 2019. (ENG.). 44p. (J). (gr. 3-7). 17.99 *(978-1-77138-382-0(8))* Kids Can Pr., Ltd. CAN. Dist: Hachette Bk. Group.

Klepeis, Alicia Z. How Animals Smell, 1 vol. 2018. (Science of Senses Ser.). (ENG.). 32p. (gr. 3-3). pap. 11.58 *(978-1-5026-4208-0(5),* 9b13e895-4f4e-4687-b708-6791b75408df) Cavendish Square Publishing LLC.

Koontz, Robin. Sniffs & Stinks: How Animals Use Odor to Survive, 1 vol. 2012. (Amazing Animal Skills Ser.). (ENG., Illus.). 48p. (J). (gr. 4-4). 32.64 *(978-0-7614-4908-9(6),* d0941631-6a3c-49de-bfd6-86d5c957539e) Cavendish Square Publishing LLC.

Kubler, Annie, illus. What Can I Smell? 2011. (Small Senses Ser.). 12p. (J). spiral bd. *(978-1-84643-376-4(2))* Child's Play International Ltd.

Kurtz, John. The World Around Us! Smelling. 2011. (Dover Science for Kids Coloring Bks.). (ENG.). 32p. (J). (gr. k-3). pap. 4.99 *(978-0-486-48036-7(4),* 480364) Dover Pubns., Inc.

Llewellyn, Claire. Smelling & Tasting. 2005. (I Know That! Ser.). (Illus.). 24p. (J). (gr. 1-3). lib. bdg. 22.80 *(978-1-932889-49-9(3))* Sea-To-Sea Pubns.

Lowery, Lawrence F. Fragrant As a Flower. 2017. (I Wonder Why Ser.). (ENG., Illus.). 36p. (J). (gr. k-2). pap. 13.99 *(978-1-68140-353-3(6),* P531926) National Science Teachers Assn.

Match Game Staff. Smelly Scented Memory Game. 2005. pap. 19.95 *(978-0-9762524-3-6(0))* Gimme Gimme Toys & Games, Inc.

Meachen Rau, Dana. Sniff, Sniff [Scholastic]: A Book about Smell. Peterson, Rick, illus. 2010. (Amazing Body: the Five Senses Ser.). 24p. pap. 0.56 *(978-1-4048-6542-6(X),* Picture Window Bks.) Capstone.

Milet Publishing Staff. My Bilingual Book - Smell, 1 vol. 2014. (My Bilingual Book Ser.). (ENG & CHI., Illus.). 24p. (J). (gr. -1-k). 9.95 *(978-1-84059-806-3(9))* Milet Publishing.

—My Bilingual Book-Smell, 1 vol. 2014. (My Bilingual Book Ser.). (ENG., Illus.). 24p. (J). (gr. -1-k). 9.95 *(978-1-84059-811-7(5))* Milet Publishing.

—My Bilingual Book-Smell (English-Arabic), 1 vol. 2014. (My Bilingual Book Ser.). (ENG & ARA., Illus.). 24p. (J). (gr. -1-k). 9.95 *(978-1-84059-804-9(2))* Milet Publishing.

—My Bilingual Book-Smell (English-Bengali), 1 vol. 2014. (My Bilingual Book Ser.). (ENG & BEN., Illus.). 24p. (J). (gr. -1-k). 9.95 *(978-1-84059-805-6(0))* Milet Publishing.

—My Bilingual Book-Smell (English-Farsi), 1 vol. 2014. (My Bilingual Book Ser.). (ENG., Illus.). 24p. (J). (gr. -1-k). 9.95 *(978-1-84059-807-0(7))* Milet Publishing.

—My Bilingual Book-Smell (English-Italian), 1 vol. 2014. (My Bilingual Book Ser.). (ENG & ITA., Illus.). 24p. (J). (gr. -1-k). 9.95 *(978-1-84059-810-0(7))* Milet Publishing.

—My Bilingual Book-Smell (English-Polish), 1 vol. 2014. (My Bilingual Book Ser.). (ENG & POR., Illus.). 24p. (J). (gr. -1-k). 9.95 *(978-1-84059-812-4(3))* Milet Publishing.

—My Bilingual Book-Smell (English-Russian), 1 vol. 2014. (My Bilingual Book Ser.). (ENG & RUS., Illus.). 24p. (J). (gr. -1-k). 9.95 *(978-1-84059-814-8(X))* Milet Publishing.

—My Bilingual Book-Smell (English-Somali), 1 vol. 2014. (My Bilingual Book Ser.). (ENG., Illus.). 24p. (J). (gr. -1-k). 9.95 *(978-1-84059-815-5(8))* Milet Publishing.

—My Bilingual Book-Smell (English-Turkish), 1 vol. 2014. (My Bilingual Book Ser.). (ENG., Illus.). 24p. (J). (gr. -1-k). 9.95 *(978-1-84059-817-9(4))* Milet Publishing.

—My Bilingual Book-Smell (English-Urdu), 1 vol. 2014. (My Bilingual Book Ser.). (ENG., Illus.). 24p. (J). (gr. -1-k). 9.95 *(978-1-84059-818-6(2))* Milet Publishing.

—My Bilingual Book-Smell (English-Vietnamese), 1 vol. 2014. (My Bilingual Book Ser.). (ENG., Illus.). 24p. (J). (gr. -1-k). 9.95 *(978-1-84059-819-3(0))* Milet Publishing.

—Smell / Das Riechen, 1 vol. 2014. (My Bilingual Book Ser.). (ENG & GER., Illus.). 24p. (J). (gr. -1-k). 9.95 *(978-1-84059-809-4(3))* Milet Publishing.

—Smell (English-French), 1 vol. 2014. (My Bilingual Book Ser.). (ENG & FRE., Illus.). 24p. (J). (gr. -1-k). 9.95 *(978-1-84059-808-7(5))* Milet Publishing.

—Smell O olfato, 1 vol. 2014. (My Bilingual Book Ser.). (ENG & POR., Illus.). 24p. (J). (gr. -1-k). 9.95 *(978-1-84059-813-1(1))* Milet Publishing.

Miller, Connie Colwell. The Stinkiest Animals. 2011. (Extreme Animals Ser.). (ENG.). 24p. (gr. k-1). pap. 41.70 *(978-1-4296-6380-9(4),* Capstone Pr.) Capstone.

Mlawer, Teresa, tr. What Do I Smell? / ¿Qué Huelo? Kubler, Annie, illus. 2015. (Small Senses Bilingual Ser.: 5). (ENG.). 12p. (J). bds. *(978-1-84643-723-6(7))* Child's Play International Ltd.

Mooney, Carla. The Gross Science of Bad Smells, 1 vol. 2018. (Way Gross Science Ser.). (ENG.). 48p. (gr. 5-5). 33.47 *(978-1-5081-8165-1(9),* 19f6370d-713e-4ef1-9ea3-4db692391d21, Rosen Reference) Rosen Publishing Group, Inc., The.

Morgan, Sally. How Smell Works. 2010. (Our Senses Ser.). 24p. (J). (gr. k-2). pap. 8.25 *(978-1-61532-561-0(1),* PowerKids Pr.); (ENG., Illus.). (gr. 1-1). lib. bdg. 26.27 *(978-1-61532-554-2(9),* 78b672e1-e74a-47ec-93d3-42663ce91ff6) Rosen Publishing Group, Inc., The.

Murphy, Patricia J. Smell. 2003. (True Book: Health Ser.). (ENG., Illus.). 48p. (J). (gr. 3-5). 18.69 *(978-0-516-22598-2(7))* Scholastic Library Publishing.

Murray, Julie. I Can Smell, 1 vol. 2015. (Senses Ser.). (ENG., Illus.). 24p. (J). (gr. -1-2). 31.36 *(978-1-62970-927-7(1),* 18312, Abdo Kids) ABDO Publishing Co.

Nelson, Robin. El Olfato. Translations.com Staff, tr. from ENG. 2006. (Mi Primer Paso Al Mundo Real - Los Sentidos (First Step Nonfiction - Senses) Ser.). (SPA., Illus.). 24p. (gr. k-2). lib. bdg. 23.93 *(978-0-8225-6223-8(5),* Ediciones Lerner) Lerner Publishing Group.

—El Olfato (Smelling) 2006. (Mi Primer Paso al Mundo Real Ser.). (Illus.). 23p. (J). (gr. -1-3). per. 5.95 *(978-0-8225-6546-8(3),* Ediciones Lerner) Lerner Publishing Group.

Owings, Lisa. Smelling. 2018. (Five Senses Ser.). (ENG., Illus.). 24p. (J). (gr. k-3). lib. bdg. 26.95 *(978-1-62617-770-3(8),* Blastoff! Readers) Bellwether Media.

Patent, Dorothy Hinshaw. Super Sniffers: Dog Detectives on the Job. 2014. (ENG., Illus.). 48p. (J). (gr. 2-4). 17.99 *(978-0-8027-3618-5(1),* 900123873, Bloomsbury USA Childrens) Bloomsbury Publishing USA.

Qamaruddin, Rizwana. Allah Gave Me a Nose to Smell. Stratford, Stevan, illus. 2015. (ENG.). 32p. (J). 8.95 *(978-0-86037-333-9(9))* Kube Publishing Ltd. GBR. Dist: Consortium Bk. Sales & Distribution.

Randolph, Joanne. Whose Nose Is This? 2009. (Animal Clues Ser.). 24p. (gr. 1-1). 42.50 *(978-1-61511-433-7(5),* PowerKids Pr.) Rosen Publishing Group, Inc., The.

—Whose Nose Is This? / ¿de quién es esta Nariz? 2009. (Animal Clues / ¿Adivina de Quién Es? Ser.). (ENG & SPA.). 24p. (gr. 1-1). 42.50 *(978-1-61511-439-9(4),* Editorial Buenas Letras) Rosen Publishing Group, Inc., The.

Ransom, Candice. Let's Explore the Sense of Smell. 2020. (Bumba Books (r) — Discover Your Senses Ser.). (ENG., Illus.). 24p. (J). (gr. -1-1). 26.65 *(978-1-5415-7686-5(1),* eb4866fa-ce6f-46e4-bfec-c5387bfc1b01, Lerner Pubns.) Lerner Publishing Group.

Reade, Clara. El Olfato / Smell, 1 vol., 1. De La Vega, Eida, ed. 2014. (Tus Cinco Sentidos y Tu Sexto Sentido / Your Five Senses & Your Sixth Sense Ser.). (SPA & ENG.). 24p. (J). (gr. 1-2). 26.27 *(978-1-4777-3277-9(2),* 57303549-19dd-44cd-a57b-2b57ac0c361a, PowerKids Pr.) Rosen Publishing Group, Inc., The.

—Smell, 1 vol., 1. 2014. (Your Five Senses & Your Sixth Sense Ser.). (ENG.). 24p. (J). (gr. 1-2). 26.27 *(978-1-4777-2857-4(0),* 4c75a7d6-bd24-441f-be4e-2f9645328314, PowerKids Pr.) Rosen Publishing Group, Inc., The.

Rustad, Martha E. H. Smelling. 2014. (Illus.). 24p. (J). lib. bdg. 25.65 *(978-1-62031-117-2(8),* Bullfrog Bks.) Jump! Inc.

Rybolt, Leah M. & Rybolt, Thomas R. Smelly Science Fair Projects, 1 vol. 2015. (Prize-Winning Science Fair Projects Ser.). (ENG.). 128p. (gr. 7-7). lib. bdg. 38.93 *(978-0-7660-7022-6(0),* a75e5cd0-58a2-4208-8c96-c743084731c3) Enslow Publishing, LLC.

Sarkisian, K. You Need Your Nose: Learning the N Sound. 2009. (PowerPhonics Ser.). 24p. (gr. 1-1). 39.90 *(978-1-60851-482-3(X),* PowerKids Pr.) Rosen Publishing Group, Inc., The.

Schuh, Mari. The Sense of Smell. 2007. (Senses Ser.). (ENG., Illus.). 24p. (J). (gr. 2-5). lib. bdg. 26.95 *(978-1-60014-072-3(6))* Bellwether Media.

Smeldit, H. W. Farts in the Wild: A Spotter's Guide. 2012. (ENG., Illus.). 24p. (J). (gr. -1-17). 16.99 *(978-1-4521-0631-1(2))* Chronicle Bks. LLC.

Spiro, Ruth. Baby Loves the Five Senses: Smell! Chan, Irene, illus. 2020. (Baby Loves Science Ser.). 20p. (J). (— 1). bds. 8.99 *(978-1-62354-153-8(0))* Charlesbridge Publishing, Inc.

Stewart, Melissa. Nifty Noses up Close, 1 vol. 2012. (Animal Bodies up Close Ser.). (ENG.). 24p. (gr. k-2). 25.27 *(978-0-7660-3892-9(0),* 364bbb47-306a-40f3-b399-439dc8ccfed9, Enslow Elementary) Enslow Publishing, LLC.

Tekiela, Stan. Snouts & Sniffers, 1 vol. 2013. (Adventure Boardbook Ser.). (ENG.). 22p. (J). (gr. -1-k). bds. 8.95 *(978-1-59193-426-4(5),* Adventure Pubns.) AdventureKEEN.

Towne, Isobel & Viegas, Jennifer. The Mouth & Nose in 3D, 1 vol. 2015. (Human Body In 3D Ser.). (ENG., Illus.). 64p. (J). (gr. 5-6). 36.13 *(978-1-4994-3609-9(2),* 94cbb7ae-01e1-49cc-911a-c1b9aef10b63, Rosen Central) Rosen Publishing Group, Inc., The.

Tyler, Jenny & Hawthorn, P. Who's Making That Smell? rev. ed. 2004. (Illus.). 16p. (J). (gr. 1-18). pap. 7.95 *(978-0-7945-0523-3(6))* EDC Publishing.

Wearing, Judy. Smell. 2009. (World of Wonder Ser.). (Illus.). 24p. (J). (gr. 2-4). pap. 8.95 *(978-1-60596-061-6(6))*; lib. bdg. 24.45 *(978-1-60596-060-9(8))* Weigl Pubs., Inc.

Weiss, Ellen. The Sense of Smell. 2009. (True Bks.). (ENG.). 48p. (J). pap. 6.95 *(978-0-531-21834-1(1),* Children's Pr.) Scholastic Library Publishing.

Woodward, Kay. Smell, 1 vol. 2004. (Our Senses Ser.). (ENG., Illus.). 24p. (gr. 1-3). lib. bdg. 25.67 *(978-0-8368-4408-5(4),* 979448b4-699f-4fec-9735-50a17657269b, Gareth Stevens Learning Library) Stevens, Gareth Publishing LLLP.

Wright, Frankie. Smell. 2016. (Illus.). 16p. (J). pap. *(978-1-338-03052-5(3))* Scholastic, Inc.

SMELL—FICTION

Beaty, Andrea. Fluffy Bunnies 2: The Schnoz of Doom. 2016. (ENG., Illus.). 208p. (J). (gr. 3-7). pap. 7.95 *(978-1-4197-1942-4(4),* 1068603, Amulet Bks.) Abrams, Inc.

—Fluffy Bunnies 2: The Schnoz of Doom. Santat, Dan, illus. 2015. (Fluffy Bunnies Ser.). (ENG.). 192p. (J). (gr. 3-7). 12.95 *(978-1-4197-1051-3(6),* 1068601, Amulet Bks.) Abrams, Inc.

Chartrand, Lili. The Smelly Story of Hazel the Weasel, 1 vol. Eid, Jean-Paul, illus. 2009. (Rainy Day Readers Ser.). (ENG.). 32p. (J). (gr. 1-2). 27.27 *(978-1-60754-379-4(6),* 1a0dac32-12f0-49c2-800c-cfed51f6cb4b); pap. 11.55 *(978-1-60754-380-0(X),* 088407fe-92c8-48f5-8fe7-7550f159d1ea) Rosen Publishing Group, Inc., The. (Windmill Bks.).

Cook, Sherry & Johnson, Terri. Nosey Nina, 26 vols. Kuhn, Jesse, illus. l.t. ed. 2006. (Quirkles — Exploring Phonics through Science Ser.: 14). 32p. (J). 7.99 *(978-1-933815-13-8(2),* Quirkles, The) Creative 3, LLC.

DeBord, Tina Ballon. Smell My Elephant. DeBord, Kim Jackson, illus. 2017. (ENG.). 32p. (J). (gr. k-3). 16.99 *(978-1-58536-992-8(6),* 204235) Sleeping Bear Pr.

Derubertis, Barbara. Sammy Skunk's Super Sniffer. Alley, R. W., illus. 2011. (Animal Antics A to Z Set III Ser.). pap. 45.32 *(978-0-7613-8428-1(6))* Astra Publishing Hse.

deRubertis, Barbara. Sammy Skunk's Super Sniffer. Alley, R. W., illus. 2011. (Animal Antics a to Z Ser.). 32p. (J). (gr. -1-3). pap. 7.95 *(978-1-57565-344-0(3),* 16bcbd5e-f8d1-4d8e-aeb0-6d16e78957fc, Kane Press) Astra Publishing Hse.

deRubertis, Barbara & DeRubertis, Barbara. Sammy Skunk's Super Sniffer. Alley, R. W., illus. 2012. (Animal Antics A to Z Ser.). 32p. (J). (gr. 2 — 1). cd-rom 7.95 *(978-1-57565-412-6(1))* Astra Publishing Hse.

Gabbitas, Jay. A Smell in the Air. 2011. (Illus.). 20p. (gr. 2-4). pap. 12.12 *(978-1-4520-3220-7(3))* AuthorHouse.

Gates, Laura. A Very Good Smell. 2006. (ENG., Illus.). 28p. (J). (gr. -1-3). pap. 2.99 *(978-1-59249-552-8(4))* Soundprints.

Hyde, Margaret. Mo Smells the Ballpark. Chaudhary, Aman, illus. 2014. (ENG.). 24p. (J). (gr. -1-k). 14.95 *(978-1-62873-668-7(2),* Sky Pony Pr.) Skyhorse Publishing Co., Inc.

Isadora, Rachel. I Hear a Pickle: And Smell, See, Touch, & Taste It, Too! Isadora, Rachel, illus. (Illus.). (J). (— 1). 2017. 30p. bds. 8.99 *(978-1-5247-3958-4(8))* 2016. 32p. 17.99 *(978-0-399-16049-3(3))* Penguin Young Readers Group. (Nancy Paulsen Books).

Lubar, David. The Big Stink. 2010. (Nathan Abercrombie, Accidental Zombie Ser.: 4). (ENG.). 176p. (J). (gr. 3-7). pap. 13.99 *(978-0-7653-2510-5(1),* 900063903, Starscape) Doherty, Tom Assocs., LLC.

Mcdonald, Megan. Stink & the World's Worst Super-Stinky Sneakers. Reynolds, Peter H., illus. 2010. (Stink Ser.: No. 3). (ENG.). 144p. (J). (gr. 1-5). 31.36 *(978-1-59961-685-8(8),* 13832, Chapter Bks.) Spotlight.

—Stink & the World's Worst Super-Stinky Sneakers. 2013. (Stink Ser.: 3). lib. bdg. 14.75 *(978-0-606-31589-0(6))* Turtleback.

McDonald, Megan. Stink & the World's Worst Super-Stinky Sneakers, Bk. 3. Reynolds, Peter H., illus. 2013. (Stink Ser.: 3). (ENG.). 144p. (J). (gr. 1-4). 14.99 *(978-0-7636-6390-2(5))* Candlewick Pr.

—Stink It Up! A Guide to the Gross, the Bad, & the Smelly. Reynolds, Peter H., illus. 2013. (Stink Ser.). (ENG.). 128p. (J). (gr. 1-4). pap. 5.99 *(978-0-7636-5942-4(8))* Candlewick Pr.

Meddaugh, Susan. Martha Speaks: Martha Stinks! (Reader) 2013. (Martha Speaks Ser.). (ENG., Illus.). 24p. (J). (gr. -1-3). 12.99 *(978-0-544-09662-2(2))* Houghton Mifflin Harcourt Publishing Co.

—Martha Stinks! 2013. (Martha Speaks Ser.). (ENG., Illus.). 24p. (J). (gr. -1-3). pap. 3.99 *(978-0-544-10012-1(3))* Houghton Mifflin Harcourt Publishing Co.

Meisel, Peter. Stinky Spike & the Royal Rescue. Meisel, Paul, illus. 2018. (Read & Bloom Ser.). (ENG.). 80p. (J). pap. 7.99 *(978-1-61963-886-0(X),* 900150927, Bloomsbury Children's Bks.) Bloomsbury Publishing USA.

Munsch, Robert. Smelly Socks. 2005. 15.00 *(978-0-7569-5139-9(9))* Perfection Learning Corp.

Nash, Sarah. Smelly Blanket, 1 vol. Everitt-Stewart, Andy, illus. 2009. (Stories to Grow With Ser.). (ENG.). 24p. (J). (gr. 1-2). 27.27 *(978-1-60754-466-1(0),* cbdea808-5bc2-4355-887c-42b3b889c5f7); pap. 9.15 *(978-1-60754-467-8(9),* 077e479a-b278-4b3c-8673-332cb6ac52a4) Rosen Publishing Group, Inc., The. (Windmill Bks.).

Rubinstein, Elana. Once upon an Apple Cake: a Rosh Hashanah Story. Naalchigar, Jennifer, illus. 2019. (Saralee Siegel Ser.: 1). (ENG.). 112p. (J). 16.95 *(978-1-68115-549-4(4),* 2d23f6b0-2647-46dc-b5fa-b78fbf8c47a8, Apples & Honey Pr.) Behrman Hse., Inc.

Sias, Ryan. Sniff! Sniff! 2015. (ENG., Illus.). 32p. (J). (gr. -1-2). 14.95 *(978-1-4197-1490-0(2),* 1088901) Abrams, Inc.

Taylor, Alastair. Mr. Blewitt's Nose. 2005. (J). (gr. k-3). 16.00 *(978-0-618-58111-5(1))* Houghton Mifflin Harcourt Trade & Reference Pubs.

Tyler, Jenny & Hawthorn, Phillip. Who's Making That Smell? Cartwright, Stephen, illus. 2007. (Luxury Flap Bks). 16p. (J). (gr. -1-3). 9.99 *(978-0-7945-1696-3(3),* Usborne) EDC Publishing.

Urey, Gary. Super Schnoz & the Gates of Smell. Long, Ethan, illus. (Super Schnoz Ser.: 1). (ENG.). 160p. (J). (gr. 3-7). 2015. pap. 6.99 *(978-0-8075-7560-4(7),* 807575607) 2013. 14.99 *(978-0-8075-7555-0(0),* 807575550) Whitman, Albert & Co.

—Super Schnoz & the Invasion of the Snore Snatchers. Frawley, Keith, illus. 2014. (Super Schnoz Ser.: 2). (ENG.). 160p. (J). (gr. 3-7). 14.99 *(978-0-8075-7557-4(7),* 807575577) Whitman, Albert & Co.

Young, Judy. Digger & Daisy Go on a Picnic. Sullivan, Dana, illus. 2014. (Digger & Daisy Ser.). (ENG.). 32p. (J). (gr. k-1). 9.99 *(978-1-58536-843-3(1),* 203006) Sleeping Bear Pr.

—Digger y Daisy Van de Picnic (Digger & Daisy Go on a Picnic) Sullivan, Dana, illus. 2016. (Digger & Daisy Ser.). (SPA.). 32p. (J). (gr. k-2). 9.99 *(978-1-62753-952-4(2),* 204175) Sleeping Bear Pr.

SMITH, BESSIE, 1898-1937

Tracy, Kathleen. Bessie Smith. 2012. (J). lib. bdg. 29.95 *(978-1-61228-271-8(7))* Mitchell Lane Pubs.

SMITH, JEDEDIAH STRONG, 1799-1831

Maynard, Charles W. Jedediah Smith: Mountain Man of the American West. 2009. (Famous Explorers of the American West Ser.). 24p. (gr. 3-4). 42.50 *(978-1-61512-501-2(9),* PowerKids Pr.) Rosen Publishing Group, Inc., The.

SMITH, JOHN, 1580-1631

Adams, Colleen. Pocahontas. 2009. (Reading Room Collection 1 Ser.). 16p. (gr. 2-3). 37.50 *(978-1-60851-949-1(X),* PowerKids Pr.) Rosen Publishing Group, Inc., The.

—Pocahontas: The Life of an Indian Princess, 1 vol. 2005. (Reading Room Collection 1 Ser.). (ENG., Illus.). 16p. (J). (gr. 2-3). lib. bdg. 22.27 *(978-1-4042-3348-5(2),* 9742d742-8b33-4c42-acaf-7741d03ed4f6) Rosen Publishing Group, Inc., The.

—The True Story of Pocahontas. (What Really Happened? Ser.). 24p. (gr. 2-3). 2009. 42.50 *(978-1-60854-765-4(5),* PowerKids Pr.) 2008. (ENG., Illus.). (J). lib. bdg. 26.27 *(978-1-4042-4475-7(1),* f0084636-13eb-497c-aee5-c454b0859aa2) Rosen Publishing Group, Inc., The.

Benge, Janet & Benge, Geoff. Heroes of History - John Smith: A Foothold in the New World. 2006. (Heroes of History Ser.). (ENG., Illus.). 224p. (YA). (gr. 3-7). pap. 11.99 *(978-1-932096-36-1(1))* Emerald Bks.

Bruchac, Joseph. Pocahontas. 2005. (ENG., Illus.). 192p. (YA). (gr. 7-12). pap. 7.99 *(978-0-15-205465-6(0),* 1196444, Clarion Bks.) HarperCollins Pubs.

—Pocahontas. 2005. (Illus.). 173p. (gr. 7). 15.95 *(978-0-7569-5604-2(8))* Perfection Learning Corp.

Edison, Erin. Pocahontas, 1 vol. 2013. (Great Women in History Ser.). (ENG.). 24p. (J). (gr. -1-2). lib. bdg. 24.65 *(978-1-62065-074-5(6),* 120776) Capstone.

Harkins, Susan Sales & Harkins, William H. Pochantas. 2008. (What's So Great About... ? Ser.). (Illus.). 32p. (J). (gr. 2-4). lib. bdg. 25.70 *(978-1-58415-682-6(1))* Mitchell Lane Pubs.

Jones, Rebecca C. Captain John Smith's Big & Beautiful Bay, 1 vol. 2011. (ENG., Illus.). 32p. (gr. 3-6). 14.99 *(978-0-7643-3869-4(2),* 4273, Schiffer Publishing Ltd) Schiffer Publishing, Ltd.

Loker, Aleck. Fearless Captain: The Adventures of John Smith. 2006. (Founders of the Republic Ser.). (Illus.). 176p. (J). (gr. 6-12). lib. bdg. 26.95 *(978-1-931798-83-9(4))* Reynolds, Morgan Inc.

Nagle, Jeanne. Pocahontas: Facilitating Exchange Between the Powhatan & the Jamestown Settlers, 1 vol. 2017. (Women Who Changed History Ser.). (ENG., Illus.). 48p. (J). (gr. 6-7). pap. 15.05 *(978-1-68048-653-7(5),* f27feb14-1c67-4feb-a53f-db24e1cfb8b5, Britannica Educational Publishing) Rosen Publishing Group, Inc., The.

Sita, Lisa. Pocahontas: The Powhatan Culture & the Jamestown Colony. (Library of American Lives & Times Ser.). 112p. (gr. 5-5). 2009. 69.20 *(978-1-60853-500-2(2))* 2004. (ENG., Illus.). (J). lib. bdg. 38.27 *(978-1-4042-2653-1(2),* 0630cc02-b680-457c-b3b0-922753babdca) Rosen Publishing Group, Inc., The.

SMITH, JOHN, 1580-1631—FICTION

Ransom, Candice. Sam Collier & the Founding of Jamestown. Archambault, Matthew, illus. 2006. (On My Own History Ser.). 48p. (J). (gr. 1-2). 25.26 *(978-1-57505-874-0(X),* Millbrook Pr.) Lerner Publishing Group.

Smith, Andrea P. Pocahontas & John Smith. (Illus.). 24p. (J). 2012. 63.60 *(978-1-4488-5219-2(6))* 2011. (ENG., (gr. 2-3). pap. 11.60 *(978-1-4488-5218-5(8),* b60ab931-cd98-4c6a-8e80-ee5088d5964a) 2011. (ENG., (gr. 2-3). lib. bdg. 28.93 *(978-1-4488-5190-4(4),* 7856ab38-7648-4ab9-abab-e8472a2624c3) Rosen Publishing Group, Inc., The. (PowerKids Pr.).

SMITH, JOSEPH, JR., 1805-1844

Bagley, Val Chadwick. Joseph's First Vision. 2005. (Illus.). (J). *(978-1-59156-996-1(6))* Covenant Communications.

Lasater, Amy. This Is the Hill. Gerber, Patric, illus. 2005. (J). *(978-1-59156-720-2(3))* Covenant Communications.

Passey, Marion. My Tiny Book of Joseph Smith. 2004. (Illus.). (J). 5.95 *(978-1-59038-243-1(9))* Deseret Bk. Co.

Perry, David Earl, retold by. Joseph Smith, a Sacred Story. 2005. (Illus.). 149p. (J). per. *(978-0-941518-51-2(5))* Perry Enterprises.

Turley, Richard & Littke, Lael. Stories from the Life of Joseph Smith. 2008. 192p. pap. 16.95 *(978-1-60641-080-6(6))* Deseret Bk. Co.

Turley, Richard E. & Littke, Lael. Stories from the Life of Joseph Smith. 2003. (Illus.). viii, 184p. (J). *(978-1-57008-915-2(9))* Deseret Bk. Co.

SMITHSONIAN INSTITUTION

Britton, Tamara L. The Smithsonian Institution. 2004. (Symbols, Landmarks, & Monuments Set 2 Ser.). 32p. (gr. k-6). 27.07 *(978-1-59197-521-2(2),* Checkerboard Library) ABDO Publishing Co.

Smith, Roland & Smith, Marie. S Is for Smithsonian: America's Museum Alphabet. Frankenhuyzen, Gijsbert van, illus. 2010. (Science Alphabet Ser.). (ENG.). 32p. (J). (gr. 1-4). 17.95 *(978-1-58536-314-8(6),* 202118) Sleeping Bear Pr.

SMITHSONIAN INSTITUTION—FICTION

Messner, Kate. Capture the Flag, 1. 2013. (ENG.). 240p. (J). (gr. 3-7). pap. 8.99 *(978-0-545-41974-1(3),* Scholastic Paperbacks) Scholastic, Inc.

SMOKING

see also Tobacco Habit

Allen, John. Teens & Vaping. 2019. (ENG.). 80p. (YA). (gr. 6-12). 41.27 *(978-1-68282-755-0(0))* ReferencePoint Pr., Inc.

Bass, Elissa. E-Cigarettes: The Risks of Addictive Nicotine & Toxic Chemicals, 1 vol. 2015. (Dangerous Drugs Ser.). (ENG.). 64p. (gr. 6-6). lib. bdg. 35.93 *(978-1-5026-0564-1(3),* 31bde2c4-39a2-4ff8-ad01-375840aa458d) Cavendish Square Publishing LLC.

Chandler, Matt. Understanding Tobacco. 2019. (21st Century Skills Library: Upfront Health Ser.). (ENG., Illus.). 32p. (J). (gr. 4-8). pap. 14.21 *(978-1-5341-5087-4(0),* 213655); lib. bdg. 32.07 *(978-1-5341-4801-7(9),* 213654) Cherry Lake Publishing.

Chastain, Zachary. Tobacco: Through the Smoke Screen. Henningfield, Jack E., ed. 2012. (Illicit & Misused Drugs Ser.). 128p. (J). (gr. 7). 24.95 *(978-1-4222-2442-7(2));* pap. 14.95 *(978-1-4222-2461-8(9))* Mason Crest.

Cornell, Kari A. E-Cigarettes & Their Dangers. 2019. (Drugs & Their Dangers Ser.). (ENG.). 80p. (YA). (gr. 6-12). 41.27 *(978-1-68282-705-5(4),* BrightPoint Pr.) ReferencePoint Pr., Inc.

Crozrock. Dr Crozrock Says Don't Smoke! 2010. 12p. pap. 8.49 *(978-1-4490-8163-8(0))* AuthorHouse.

Egendorf, Laura K., ed. Smoking, 1 vol. 2007. (Issues That Concern You Ser.). (ENG., Illus.). 136p. (gr. 7-10). lib. bdg. 43.63 *(978-0-7377-2420-2(X),* e8c9280a-4970-4781-b760-912ac3724835, Greenhaven Publishing) Greenhaven Publishing LLC.

Esherick, Joan. No More Butts: Kicking the Tobacco Habit. 2008. (J). pap. 26.95 *(978-1-4222-1330-8(7))* Mason Crest.

—Smoking-Related Health Issues. McDonnell, Mary Ann & Forman, Sara, eds. 2013. (Young Adult's Guide to the Science of Health Ser.: 15). 128p. (J). (gr. 7-18). 24.95 *(978-1-4222-2816-6(9))* Mason Crest.

Espejo, Roman, ed. Teen Smoking, 1 vol. 2014. (At Issue Ser.). (ENG.). 104p. (gr. 10-12). pap. 28.80 *(978-0-7377-6867-1(3),* 9fca11cf-8dcd-460d-bc6f-ecfb6b493d48); lib. bdg. 41.03 *(978-0-7377-6866-4(5),* 11253c92-6b99-4404-ad74-937b2a4247e7) Greenhaven Publishing LLC. (Greenhaven Publishing).

—Tobacco & Smoking, 1 vol. (Opposing Viewpoints Ser.). (ENG., Illus.). (gr. 10-12). 2015. 248p. 50.43 *(978-0-7377-7294-4(8),* 2b083b8f-45c5-44be-adf2-da51c3043318) 2014. 168p. lib. bdg. 43.63 *(978-0-7377-6405-5(8),* d28c4b71-48f9-436e-a48c-cd5d21af5177) Greenhaven Publishing LLC. (Greenhaven Publishing).

Evans, Lesli. But All My Friends Smoke: Cigarettes & Peer Pressure. 2009. (Illus.). 112p. (J). pap. 26.95 *(978-1-4222-1327-8(7),* 1291217) Mason Crest.

Gordon, Sherri Mabry. Everything You Need to Know about Smoking, Vaping, & Your Health, 1 vol. 2018. (Need to Know Library). (ENG.). 64p. (gr. 6-6). pap. 13.95 *(978-1-5081-8351-8(1),* 012a7052-942c-425c-9de7-01bc82a54666, Rosen Young Adult) Rosen Publishing Group, Inc., The.

Holt, Rinehart and Winston Staff. Decisions for Health Blue, Chptr. 14: Tobacco, 4th ed. 2004. (YA). pap. 11.20 *(978-0-03-068048-9(4))* Holt McDougal.

Hunter, David. But Smoking Makes Me Happy: The Link Between Nicotine & Depression. 2009. (Tobacco: the Deadly Drug Ser.). (Illus.). 112p. (YA). (gr. 7-12). 26.95 *(978-1-4222-0244-9(5));* (J). pap. 26.95 *(978-1-4222-1335-3(8))* Mason Crest.

Jaime, Everett. Baby Don't Smoke. Brown, Eliot R., illus. 2012. (ENG.). 40p. (YA). pap. 9.95 *(978-1-935826-20-0(4))* Kalindi Pr.

Jones, David C. One Person to Another: Smoking, Chewing Tobacco & Young Peopole. l.t. ed. 2003. 20p. (YA). 4.00 *(978-1-878400-17-8(7))* Dolphin Publishing.

Karpan, Andrew, ed. Vaping, 1 vol. 2019. (At Issue Ser.). (ENG.). 128p. (gr. 10-12). pap. 28.80 *(978-1-5345-0513-1(X),* d1861875-05c1-4727-ba76-83209a6fa943) Greenhaven Publishing LLC.

Keyishan, Elizabeth. Todo lo que necesitas saber sobre el cigarillo (Everything You Need to Know about Smoking) 2009. (Todo lo que necesitas (the Need to Know Library) Ser.). (SPA.). 64p. (gr. 6-6). 58.50 *(978-1-60854-407-3(9),* Editorial Buenas Letras) Rosen Publishing Group, Inc., The.

Keyishian, Elizabeth. Everything You Need to Know about Smoking. 2009. (Need to Know Library). 64p. (gr. 5-5). 58.50 *(978-1-60854-086-0(3))* Rosen Publishing Group, Inc., The.

—Smoking, 1 vol. rev. ed. 2003. (Need to Know Library (1994-2004) Ser.). (ENG., Illus.). 64p. (J). (gr. 5-5). lib. bdg. 37.13 *(978-0-8239-4092-9(6),* 99252132-b6f2-4c6d-bf79-63a05e89f907) Rosen Publishing Group, Inc., The.

Krajnik, Elizabeth. Why Is Smoking Bad for Me?, 1 vol. 2018. (Help Me Understand Ser.). (ENG., Illus.). 24p. (J). (gr. 3-3). 25.27 *(978-1-5081-6730-3(3),* 14eb5581-7f2e-4c6a-ab9f-826f78ee6f0e, PowerKids Pr.) Rosen Publishing Group, Inc., The.

Landau, Elaine. Cigarettes. 2003. (Watts Library). (ENG.). 64p. (J). (gr. 5-7). pap. 8.95 *(978-0-531-16666-6(X),* Watts, Franklin) Scholastic Library Publishing.

LeVert, Suzanne. The Facts about Nicotine, 1 vol. 2007. (Facts about Drugs Ser.). (ENG., Illus.). 128p. (gr. 6-6). lib. bdg. 45.50 *(978-0-7614-2244-0(7),* 0265ed30-e887-407a-afda-da8a28d67173) Cavendish Square Publishing LLC.

Malaspina, Ann. False Images, Deadly Promises: Smoking & the Media. 2007. (Tobacco: the Deadly Drug Ser.). (Illus.). 112p. (YA). pap. 12.95 *(978-1-4222-0812-0(5))* Mason Crest.

marcovitz, hal. Should Smoking Be Banned? 2012. (Illus.). 96p. (J). lib. bdg. *(978-1-60152-462-1(5))* ReferencePoint Pr., Inc.

Mason, Paul. Know the Facts about Drinking & Smoking. 2009. (J). 70.50 *(978-1-4353-5463-5(2),* Rosen Reference); (ENG.). 48p. (YA). (gr. 5-6). pap. 12.75 *(978-1-4358-5462-8(4),* 9f74385e-5423-4c2a-ad5b-60043b320a85, Rosen Reference); (ENG., Illus.). 48p. (YA). (gr. 5-6). lib. bdg. 34.47 *(978-1-4358-5339-3(3),* ac847bdd-b18b-4c77-a0e0-bf83a0a39684) Rosen Publishing Group, Inc., The.

McCormick, Anita Louise. Vaping, 1 vol. 2019. (Facts & Fiction about Drugs Ser.). (ENG.). 48p. (gr. 4-5). pap. 12.75 *(978-1-7253-4769-4(5),* d9e9f3eb-d67d-4633-899f-e95d16244ec7) Rosen Publishing Group, Inc., The.

Meinking, Mary. Cash Crop to Cash Cow: The History of Tobacco & Smoking in America. 2007. (Tobacco: the Deadly Drug Ser.). (Illus.). 112p. (YA). pap. 12.95 *(978-1-4222-0811-3(7))* Mason Crest.

Merino, Noël, ed. Smoking, 1 vol. 2010. (Introducing Issues with Opposing Viewpoints Ser.). (ENG.). 144p. (gr. 7-10). 43.63 *(978-0-7377-5101-7(0),* 9a1c204c-5469-40fa-a518-758bc27329f0, Greenhaven Publishing) Greenhaven Publishing LLC.

Mooney, Carla. Addicted to e-Cigarettes & Vaping. 2019. (Addicted Ser.). (ENG.). 80p. (YA). (gr. 6-12). 41.27 *(978-1-68282-567-9(1))* ReferencePoint Pr., Inc.

Paris, Stephanie. Straight Talk: Smoking, 1 vol. 2nd rev. ed. (TIME for KIDS(r): Informational Text Ser.). (ENG., Illus.). 48p. (gr. 4-5). 2013. (J). lib. bdg. 29.96 *(978-1-4807-1110-5(1))* 2012. pap. 13.99 *(978-1-4333-4858-7(6))* Teacher Created Materials, Inc.

Parks, Peggy J. The Dangers of E-Cigarettes. 2016. (ENG.). 80p. (J). (gr. 5-12). *(978-1-68282-014-8(9))* ReferencePoint Pr., Inc.

—Smoking. rev. ed. 2014. (Matters of Opinion Ser.). (ENG.). 64p. (J). (gr. 4-6). pap. 14.60 *(978-1-60357-582-9(0));* lib. bdg. 27.93 *(978-1-59953-602-6(1))* Norwood Hse. Pr.

Reimer, Jackie. No Thanks, but I'd Love to Dance! Choosing to Live Smoke Free. Reimer, Jackie, illus. 2010. (ENG., Illus.). 32p. (J). (gr. 2-4). 14.95 *(978-1-60443-027-1(3))* American Cancer Society, Inc.

Sharp, Katie John. Smokeless Tobacco: Not a Safe Alternative. 2009. (Illus.). 112p. (J). pap. 26.95 *(978-1-4222-1332-2(3),* 1291227) Mason Crest.

Smoking. 2008. (Current Controversies Ser.). (Illus.). 176-240p. (gr. 10-12). 36.20 *(978-0-7377-3293-1(8));* pap. 24.95 *(978-0-7377-3294-8(6))* Cengage Gale. (Greenhaven Pr., Inc.).

Stewart, Gail B. Ripped from the Headlines: Smoking. 2007. (Ripped from the Headlines Ser.). (J). (gr. 7-12). 23.95 *(978-1-60217-017-9(7))* Erickson Pr.

Stollers, Veronica & Keyishian, Elizabeth. Frequently Asked Questions about Smoking, 1 vol. 2011. (FAQ: Teen Life Ser.). (ENG.). 64p. (J). (gr. 5-6). lib. bdg. 37.13 *(978-1-4488-4631-3(5),* 4007b9e8-1579-4c56-8ba1-730efad04c56) Rosen Publishing Group, Inc., The.

Synder, Gail. Teens & Smoking. 2015. (Illus.). 80p. (J). *(978-1-60152-918-3(X))* ReferencePoint Pr., Inc.

Thomas, Amy N. Burning Money: The Cost of Smoking. (Tobacco: the Deadly Drug Ser.). (Illus.). 112p. 2009. (YA). (gr. 7-12). 26.95 *(978-1-4222-0242-5(9))* 2009. (J). pap. 26.95 *(978-1-4222-1326-1(9))* 2007. (YA). (gr. 3-7). pap. 12.95 *(978-1-4222-0808-3(7))* Mason Crest.

Wagner, Heather Lehr. Nicotine. 2003. (Drugs: the Straight Facts Ser.). (ENG., Illus.). 112p. (gr. 9-13). 30.00 *(978-0-7910-7264-6(9),* P113780, Facts On File) Infobase Holdings, Inc.

Walker, Ida. Addiction in America: Society, Psychology & Heredity. 2012. (Illus.). 128p. (J). *(978-1-4222-2424-3(4));* *(978-1-4222-2443-4(0))* Mason Crest.

SMOKING—FICTION

Baker, Susan F. Don't Smoke, Daddy. 2008. 27p. 30.95 *(978-1-4357-2127-2(6))* Lulu Pr., Inc.

Gosselin, Kim. Smoking Stinks!! Buttner, Thom, illus. 2nd ed. 2009. (Substance Free Kids Ser.). 30p. (J). (gr. -1-3). pap. 16.95 *(978-1-891383-20-5(5))* JayJo Bks., LLC.

Hankins, M. Lil' Mikie Tells It Like It is. 2007. 20p. per. 24.95 *(978-1-4137-0168-5(X))* America Star Bks.

MacGregor, Doug, creator. Ochre the Smoker: A fantastic Fable. 2007. (Illus.). 48p. (J). per. 14.95 *(978-0-9654843-2-9(7))* MacGregor, Doug.

Maria Muirhead. Smoking = Problems: Flora-Lee's Journal. 2010. 56p. pap. 8.95 *(978-1-4502-0645-7(X))* iUniverse, Inc.

McDaniel, Carren. Fresh Air Friends: The Dangers of Secondhand Smoke. 2012. (ENG.). 33p. (J). pap. 14.95 *(978-1-4327-9818-5(9))* Outskirts Pr., Inc.

Proctor, Darrell. The Cigarette Monster. 2006. (J). pap. 8.00 *(978-0-8059-6790-6(7))* Dorrance Publishing Co., Inc.

Thuma, Chris. Cigarette Sue. 2008. 24p. per. 12.95 *(978-1-59858-561-2(4))* Dog Ear Publishing, LLC.

The Tobacco Temptation. (J). 39.50 *(978-1-56230-082-1(2))* Syndistar, Inc.

SMUGGLING

Nichols, Katherine. Deep Water. 2017. (Simon True Ser.). (ENG., Illus.). 288p. (YA). (gr. 9). pap. 12.99 *(978-1-4814-8106-9(1),* Simon Pulse) Simon Pulse.

SMUGGLING—FICTION

Aldridge, Janet. The Meadow-Brook Girls by the Sea, or Th. 2006. pap. *(978-1-4065-0693-8(1))* Dodo Pr.

Anderson, Sandra. Rockcliffe. 2007. 156p. per. 8.95 *(978-1-59800-893-7(5))* Outskirts Pr., Inc.

Baker, Mary. Christmas Annie. 2009. 70p. pap. 7.96 *(978-0-557-17289-4(6))* Lulu Pr., Inc.

Balliett, Blue. Hold Fast. 2015. (ENG.). 288p. (J). (gr. 3-7). pap. 8.99 *(978-0-545-29989-3(6),* Scholastic Paperbacks) Scholastic, Inc.

Barnett, Mac. Danger Goes Berserk. Myers, Matt, illus. (Brixton Brothers Ser.: 4). (ENG.). 256p. (J). (gr. 3-7). 2013. pap. 8.99 *(978-1-4424-3978-8(5))* 2012. 17.99 *(978-1-4424-3977-1(7))* Simon & Schuster Bks. For Young Readers. (Simon & Schuster Bks. For Young Readers).

Benjamin, Ruth. The Mysterious Lighthouse of Chelton. 2006. (ENG.). 160p. (J). 14.95 *(978-1-932443-57-8(6))* Judaica Pr., Inc., The.

Bollback, Anthony G. Smugglers in Hong Kong. 2012. 156p. pap. 8.99 *(978-0-9849359-0-1(8))* Finding the Cause, LLC.

Chamberlain, Penny. Chasing the Moon, 1 vol. 2007. (ENG.). 252p. (J). (gr. 4-7). per. 8.95 *(978-1-55039-157-2(7))* Sono Nis Pr. CAN. Dist: Orca Bk. Pubs. USA.

Decary, Marie. Adam et le Raton Dessinateur. Beshwathy, Steve, illus. 2004. (Premier Roman Ser.). (FRE.). 64p. (J). (gr. 1-4). pap. *(978-2-89021-643-3(8))* Diffusion du livre Mirabel (DLM).

—Adam's Tropical Adventure. Beshwaty, Steve, illus. 2005. 54p. (J). lib. bdg. 12.00 *(978-1-4242-1202-6(2))* Fitzgerald Bks.

Deuker, Carl. Runner. 2007. (ENG.). 224p. (YA). (gr. 7-12). pap. 15.99 *(978-0-618-73505-1(4),* 410112, Clarion Bks.) HarperCollins Pubs.

Falkner, J. Meade. Moonfleet. 2018. (Dover Children's Evergreen Classics Ser.). (ENG.). 288p. (gr. 2-6). pap. 5.99 *(978-0-486-82878-7(6),* 828786) Dover Pubns., Inc.

Falkner, John Meade. Moonfleet: A Classic Tale of Smuggling. Marks, Alan, illus. 2007. (Young Reading Series 3 Gift Bks). 63p. (J). (gr. 4-7). 8.99 *(978-0-7945-1906-3(7),* Usborne) EDC Publishing.

Fitzpatrick, Deb. Spectacular Spencer Gray The. 2017. (Spencer Gray Ser.). (Illus.). 168p. (J). (gr. 3-7). 9.99 *(978-1-925164-67-1(5))* Fremantle Pr. AUS. Dist: Independent Pubs. Group.

Furtney, Charles S. Tryconnel: An Antebellum Adventure along the C & O Canal. 2004. (Illus.). iii, 156p. (J). pap. *(978-0-9711835-3-7(8))* Local History Co., The.

Grant, Myrna. Ivan & the Secret in the Suitcase. 2006. (Flamingo Fiction 9-13s Ser.). (ENG., Illus.). 144p. (J). (gr. 4-7). per. 6.99 *(978-1-84550-136-5(5),* 90cf7cab-dea4-49c0-a1e1-347bc14e92d3) Christian Focus Pubns. GBR. Dist: Baker & Taylor Publisher Services (BTPS).

Harvey, M. A. The Scorpion Secret: Dare to Take the Test. 2004. (Illus.). 128p. (J). pap. *(978-1-84458-050-7(4),* Pavilion Children's Books) Pavilion Bks.

Holmes, Victoria. Rider in the Dark: An Epic Horse Story. 2004. (Illus.). 320p. (J). (gr. 5-18). (ENG.). 15.99 *(978-0-06-052025-0(6));* lib. bdg. 16.89 *(978-0-06-052026-7(4))* HarperCollins Pubs.

Inspector Grub & the Fizzer-X Spy: Individual Title Six-Packs. (Bookweb Ser.). 32p. (gr. 5-18). 34.00 *(978-0-7635-3786-9(1))* Rigby Education.

Jorgensen, Norman. Smuggler's Curse. 2017. 356p. (J). (gr. 4-7). 8.95 *(978-1-925164-19-0(5))* Fremantle Pr. AUS. Dist: Independent Pubs. Group.

Korman, Gordon. Escape. 2008. (Island (Playaway Audio) Ser.). (J). 34.99 *(978-1-60514-854-0(7))* Findaway World, LLC.

Mezrich, Ben & Mezrich, Tonya. Charlie Numbers & the Woolly Mammoth. 2020. (Charlie Numbers Adventures Ser.). (ENG.). 192p. (J). (gr. 3-7). pap. 8.99 *(978-1-5344-4101-9(8),* Simon & Schuster Bks. For Young Readers) Simon & Schuster Bks. For Young Readers.

Milford, Kate. Ghosts of Greenglass House: A Greenglass House Story. (Greenglass House Ser.). (ENG., Illus.). (J). (gr. 5-7). 2018. 480p. pap. 9.99 *(978-1-328-59442-6(4),* 1730255) 2017. 464p. 17.99 *(978-0-544-99146-0(X),* 1666502) HarperCollins Pubs. (Clarion Bks.).

Morgan, Nicola. The Highwayman's Curse. 2009. (J). *(978-0-7636-4066-8(2))* Candlewick Pr.

Mowat, Farley. The Black Joke. 2009. (ENG.). 192p. pap. 9.95 *(978-0-7710-6469-2(1),* Emblem Editions) McClelland & Stewart CAN. Dist: Random Hse., Inc.

Nielsen, Jennifer A. Words on Fire. 2019. (ENG.). 336p. (J). (gr. 3-7). 17.99 *(978-1-338-27547-6(X),* Scholastic Pr.) Scholastic, Inc.

Prins, Piet. The Haunted Castle. 2006. (Illus.). 139p. (J). pap. *(978-1-894666-44-2(5))* Inheritance Pubns.

Service, Pamela F. Camp Alien. 2010. pap. 33.92 *(978-0-7613-6955-4(4))* Lerner Publishing Group.

Sherman, M. Zachary. Heart of the Enemy, 1 vol. Cage, Josef, illus. 2012. (Bloodlines Ser.). (ENG.). 88p. (J). (gr. 4-8). lib. bdg. 27.32 *(978-1-4342-3767-5(2),* 117028, Stone Arch Bks.) Capstone.

Stem, Jacqueline. The Ghosts of Goliad. 2003. iii, 165p. (J). 17.95 *(978-1-57168-785-2(8),* Eakin Pr.) Eakin Pr.

Striker, Fran. Lone Ranger Traps Smugglers. (J). 21.95 *(978-0-8488-1183-9(6))* Amereon Ltd.

Taranta, Mary. Shimmer & Burn. 2018. (ENG.). 352p. (YA). (gr. 9). pap. 11.99 *(978-1-4814-7200-5(3),* McElderry, Margaret K. Bks.) McElderry, Margaret K. Bks.

Wells, Helen. Cherry Ames Jungle Nurse. 2007. (Cherry Ames Nurse Stories Ser.). 224p. (J). (gr. 3-7). 14.95 *(978-0-8261-0433-5(9))* Springer Publishing Co., Inc.

—Cherry Ames, Ski Nurse Mystery. 2007. (Cherry Ames Nurse Stories Ser.). 224p. (J). (gr. 3-7). 14.95 *(978-0-8261-0437-3(1))* Springer Publishing Co., Inc.

SMURFS (FICTITIOUS CHARACTERS)—FICTION

Delporte, Yvan & Peyo. The Smurfs #1: The Purple Smurfs. 2010. (Smurfs Graphic Novels Ser.: 1). (ENG., Illus.). 56p. (J). (gr. 2-5). pap. 6.99 *(978-1-59707-206-9(0),* 900070208);No. 1. 12.99 *(978-1-59707-207-6(9),* 900070209) Mad Cave Studios. (Papercutz).

—The Smurfs #2: The Smurfs & the Magic Flute. 2010. (Smurfs Graphic Novels Ser.: 2). (ENG., Illus.). 64p. (J). (gr. 2-5). pap. 5.99 *(978-1-59707-208-3(7),* 900070210, Papercutz) Mad Cave Studios.

Gos. The Smurfs #7: The Astrosmurf. 2011. (Smurfs Graphic Novels Ser.: 7). (ENG., Illus.). 56p. (J). (gr. 2-5). pap. 5.99 *(978-1-59707-250-2(8),* 900075394, Papercutz) Mad Cave Studios.

—The Smurfs #8: the Smurf Apprentice: The Smurf Apprentice, Vol. 8. 2011. (Smurfs Graphic Novels Ser.: 8). (ENG., Illus.). 56p. (J). (gr. 2-5). 10.99 *(978-1-59707-280-9(X),* 900078894, Papercutz) Mad Cave Studios.

Gos & Delporte, Yvan. The Smurfs #6: Smurfs & the Howlibird: The Smurfs & the Howlibird, Vol. 6. 2011. (Smurfs Graphic Novels Ser.: 6). (ENG., Illus.). 56p. (J). (gr. 2-5). pap. 5.99 *(978-1-59707-260-1(5),* 900075410, Papercutz) Mad Cave Studios.

—The Smurfs #6: Smurfs & the Howlibird: The Smurfs & the Howlibird, Vol. 6. 2011. (Smurfs Graphic Novels Ser.: 6). (ENG., Illus.). 56p. (J). (gr. 2-5). 10.99 *(978-1-59707-261-8(3),* 900075411, Papercutz) Mad Cave Studios.

Peyo. The Smurf Championship Games. 2012. (Simon & Schuster Ready-To-Read Level 2 Ser.). lib. bdg. 13.55 *(978-0-606-26363-4(2))* Turtleback.

—The Smurfs #10: the Return of Smurfette: The Return of the Smurfette, Vol. 10. 2012. (Smurfs Graphic Novels Ser.: 10). (ENG., Illus.). 56p. (J). (gr. 2-5). pap. 5.99 *(978-1-59707-292-2(3),* 900080869, Papercutz) Mad Cave Studios.

—The Smurfs #12: Smurf Versus Smurf. 2012. (Smurfs Graphic Novels Ser.: 12). (ENG., Illus.). 56p. (J). (gr. 2-5). 10.99 *(978-1-59707-321-9(0),* 900085168, Papercutz) Mad Cave Studios.

—The Smurfs #14: the Baby Smurf: The Baby Smurf, Vol. 14. 2013. (Smurfs Graphic Novels Ser.: 14). (ENG., Illus.). 56p. (J). (gr. 1-5). 10.99 *(978-1-59707-382-0(2),* 900118001, Papercutz) Mad Cave Studios.

—The Smurfs #15: The Smurflings. 2013. (Smurfs Graphic Novels Ser.: 15). (ENG., Illus.). 56p. (J). (gr. 2-5). pap. 5.99 *(978-1-59707-407-0(1),* 900120422, Papercutz) Mad Cave Studios.

—The Smurfs #15: the Smurflings: The Smurflings, Vol. 15. 2013. (Smurfs Graphic Novels Ser.: 15). (ENG., Illus.). 56p. (J). (gr. 2-5). 10.99 *(978-1-59707-408-7(X),* 900120855, Papercutz) Mad Cave Studios.

—The Smurfs #16: the Aerosmurf: The Aerosmurf, Vol. 16. 2013. (Smurfs Graphic Novels Ser.: 16). (ENG., Illus.). 56p. (J). (gr. 2-5). 10.99 *(978-1-59707-427-8(6)*, 900120844); pap. 5.99 *(978-1-59707-426-1(8)*, 900120843) Mad Cave Studios. (Papercutz).

—The Smurfs Anthology #2. 2013. (Smurfs Anthology Ser.: 2). (ENG., Illus.). 192p. (J). (gr. 6-5). 19.99 *(978-1-59707-445-2(4)*, 900123332, Papercutz) Mad Cave Studios.

—The Smurfs Christmas. 2013. (Smurfs Graphic Novels Ser.). (ENG., Illus.). 56p. (J). (gr. 2-5). 10.99 *(978-1-59707-452-0(7)*, 900123339); pap. 5.99 *(978-1-59707-451-3(9)*, 900123338) Mad Cave Studios. (Papercutz).

—The Smurfs Graphic Novels Boxed Set: Vol. #10-12. 2013. (Smurfs Graphic Novels Ser.). (ENG., Illus.). 168p. (J). (gr. 2-5). pap. 17.99 *(978-1-59707-386-8(5)*, 900117999, Papercutz) Mad Cave Studios.

Peyo & Delporte, Yvan. The Smurfs #11: the Smurf Olympics: The Smurf Olympics, Vol. 11. 2012. (Smurfs Graphic Novels Ser.: 11). (ENG., Illus.). 56p. (J). (gr. 2-4). 10.99 *(978-1-59707-302-8(4)*, 900080979, Papercutz) Mad Cave Studios.

—The Smurfs #13: Smurf Soup. 2012. (Smurfs Graphic Novels Ser.: 13). (ENG., Illus.). 56p. (J). (gr. 1-6). pap. 5.99 *(978-1-59707-358-5(X)*, 900087559, Papercutz) Mad Cave Studios.

—The Smurfs #13: Smurf Soup: Smurf Soup, Vol. 13. 2012. (Smurfs Graphic Novels Ser.: 13). (ENG., Illus.). 56p. (J). (gr. 1-6). 10.99 *(978-1-59707-359-2(8)*, 900087560, Papercutz) Mad Cave Studios.

—The Smurfs Graphic Novels Boxed Set: Vol. #1 - 3, 3 Vols., Vol. 1. 2011. (Smurfs Graphic Novels Ser.). (ENG., Illus.). 184p. (J). (gr. 2-5). pap. 17.99 *(978-1-59707-273-1(7)*, 900078889, Papercutz) Mad Cave Studios.

—The Smurfs Graphic Novels Boxed Set: Vol. #4-6, Set, Vols. 4-6. 2012. (Smurfs Graphic Novels Ser.). (ENG., Illus.). 184p. (J). (gr. 2-5). pap. 17.99 *(978-1-59707-306-6(7)*, 900080977, Papercutz) Mad Cave Studios.

—The Smurfs Graphic Novels Boxed Set: Vol. #7-9. 2012. (Smurfs Graphic Novels Ser.). (ENG., Illus.). 168p. (J). (gr. 2-5). pap. 17.99 *(978-1-59707-340-0(7)*, 900087540, Papercutz) Mad Cave Studios.

Publications International Ltd. Staff, ed. The Smurfs Large Play a Sound. 2011. 24p. (J). 14.98 *(978-1-60553-403-9(X))* Phoenix International Publications, Inc.

SNAILS

Alessi, Jolene. Zombie Snails, 1 vol. 2015. (Zombie Animals: Parasites Take Control! Ser.). (ENG., Illus.). 24p. (J). (gr. 2-3). pap. 9.15 *(978-1-4824-2848-3(2)*, 53ae166c-5875-4ef5-b90a-110e1ddf5263) Stevens, Gareth Publishing LLLP.

Allen, Judy. Are You a Snail? Humphries, Tudor, illus. 2003. (Backyard Bks.). (ENG.). 31p. (J). (gr. k-3). pap. 7.99 *(978-0-7534-5604-0(4)*, 900052552, Kingfisher) Roaring Brook Pr.

Appleton-Smith, Laura & Blackaby, Susan. Keeping Track of Snail Facts. 2014. (Book to Remember Ser.). (ENG., Illus.). 26p. (J). pap. 8.95 *(978-1-60541-148-4(5)*, Books To Remember) Flyleaf Publishing.

Baxter, Bethany. Conches. 2013. (Awesome Armored Animals Ser.). 24p. (J). (gr. k-5). pap. 49.50 *(978-1-4777-0965-8(7))*; (ENG.). (gr. 2-3). 26.27 *(978-1-4777-0796-8(4)*, f6879602-10aa-4162-95fb-c2e781dfa3eb); (ENG.). (gr. 2-3). pap. 9.25 *(978-1-4777-0964-1(9)*, 8afc3ea6-ccae-4361-8d24-843136e7cc00) Rosen Publishing Group, Inc., The. (PowerKids Pr.).

Cain, Marie Mowery. Slow Slugs & Snails. 2013. (Big Books, Red Ser.). (ENG & SPA., Illus.). 16p. pap. 33.00 *(978-1-59246-221-6(9))* Big Books, by George!

Campbell, Sarah C. Wolfsnail: A Backyard Predator. Campbell, Sarah C. & Campbell, Richard P., photos by. 2008. (ENG., Illus.). 32p. (J). (gr. k-2). 17.95 *(978-1-59078-554-6(1)*, Astra Young Readers) Astra Publishing Hse.

Clark, Willow & Rockwood, Leigh. Snails Are Gross!, 1 vol. 2010. (Creepy Crawlies Ser.). (ENG., Illus.). 24p. (J). (gr. 2-3). pap. 9.25 *(978-1-4488-1359-9(X)*, 118d63a2-55fe-4053-80f9-338fe444c2ce, PowerKids Pr.); lib. bdg. 26.27 *(978-1-4488-0699-7(2)*, ea88bdf1-452d-4663-8008-c9971926158d) Rosen Publishing Group, Inc., The.

Dellaccio, Tanya. Raising Snails, 1 vol. 2019. (Unusual Farm Animals Ser.). (ENG.). 24p. (gr. 2-3). pap. 9.25 *(978-1-7253-0914-2(9)*, eb407871-0838-4891-895c-98ac515fdcb2, PowerKids Pr.) Rosen Publishing Group, Inc., The.

Fredericks, Anthony D. In One Tidepool: Crabs, Snails, & Salty Tails. DiRubbio, Jennifer, illus. 2004. (Sharing Nature with Children Book Ser.). 32p. (J). (gr. -1-2). 16.95 *(978-1-58469-039-9(9))* Take Heart Pubns.

Gaertner, Meg. Snails. 2019. (Pond Animals Ser.). (ENG., Illus.). 24p. (J). (gr. 1-1). pap. 8.95 *(978-1-64185-581-5(9)*, 1641855819) North Star Editions.

—Snails. 2018. (Pond Animals Ser.). (ENG., Illus.). 24p. (J). (gr. k-3). lib. bdg. 31.36 *(978-1-5321-6210-7(3)*, 30203, Pop! Cody Koala) Pop!

Gates, Margo. Snails. 2013. (Backyard Wildlife Ser.). (ENG., Illus.). 24p. (J). (gr. k-3). lib. bdg. 26.95 *(978-1-60014-920-7(0)*, Blastoff! Readers) Bellwether Media.

Gray, Susan H. Giant African Snail. 2008. (21st Century Skills Library: Animal Invaders Ser.). (ENG., Illus.). 32p. (gr. 4-8). lib. bdg. 32.07 *(978-1-60279-241-8(0)*, 200115) Cherry Lake Publishing.

How Snails Live: 6 Each of 1 Student Book, 6 vols. (Sunshinetm Science Ser.). 24p. (gr. 1-2). 41.95 *(978-0-7802-2702-6(6))* Wright Group/McGraw-Hill.

How Snails Live: Big Book. (Sunshinetm Science Ser.). 24p. (gr. 1-2). 37.50 *(978-0-7802-2785-9(9))* Wright Group/McGraw-Hill.

How Snails Protect Themselves: 6 Each of 1 Student Book, 6 vols. (Sunshinetm Science Ser.). 24p. (gr. 1-2). 41.95 *(978-0-7802-2704-0(2))* Wright Group/McGraw-Hill.

How Snails Protect Themselves: Big Book. (Sunshinetm Science Ser.). 24p. (gr. 1-2). 37.50 *(978-0-7802-2786-6(7))* Wright Group/McGraw-Hill.

Jacobs, Liza. Snails. 2003. (Wild Wild World Ser.). (Illus.). 24p. (J). 22.45 *(978-1-4103-0034-8(X)*, Blackbirch Pr., Inc.) Cengage Gale.

Jones, Tammy. At the Shore. 2009. (Sight Word Readers Set A Ser.). (J). 3.49 net. *(978-1-60719-137-7(7))* Newmark Learning LLC.

Legg, Gerald. Minibeasts. 2008. (Hot Topics Ser.). (Illus.). 32p. (J). (gr. 3-7). *(978-1-84239-936-1(5))* Alligator Bks. Ltd.

The Life Cycle of a Snail. (Sunshinetm Science Ser.). 24p. (gr. 1-2). 37.50 *(978-0-7802-2784-2(0))* Wright Group/McGraw-Hill.

The Life Cycle of a Snail: 6 Each of 1 Student Book, 6 vols. (Sunshinetm Science Ser.). 24p. (gr. 1-2). 41.95 *(978-0-7802-2700-2(X))* Wright Group/McGraw-Hill.

McCloskey, Kevin. Snails Are Just My Speed! TOON Level 1. 2018. (Giggle & Learn Ser.). (Illus.). 40p. (J). (gr. k-1). 12.99 *(978-1-943145-27-0(X)*, TOON Books) Astra Publishing Hse.

Popova, Maria. The Snail with the Right Heart: A True Story. Zhu, Ping, illus. 2021. 56p. (J). (gr. 2-6). 18.95 *(978-1-59270-349-4(6))* Enchanted Lion Bks., LLC.

Ross, Michael Elsohn. Snailology. Erickson, Darren, illus. Grogan, Brian, photos by. 2003. (Backyard Buddies Ser.). 48p. (YA). (gr. 3-5). 6.95 *(978-1-57505-437-7(X)*, Carolrhoda Bks.) Lerner Publishing Group.

The Snail Trail. 2004. 10p. (J). bds. 5.99 *(978-1-85997-875-7(4))* Byeway Bks.

Snails Sets: 1 Each of 3 Big Books. (Sunshinetm Science Ser.). (gr. 1-2). 111.50 *(978-0-7802-2822-1(7))* Wright Group/McGraw-Hill.

Snails Sets: 1 Each of 3 Student Books. (Sunshinetm Science Ser.). (gr. 1-2). 20.95 *(978-0-7802-2823-8(5))* Wright Group/McGraw-Hill.

Strain Trueit, Trudi. Slugs, Snails, & Worms, 1 vol. 2013. (Backyard Safari Ser.). (ENG.). 32p. (gr. 3-3). 31.21 *(978-1-60870-247-3(2)*, 8efd9e6f-7a42-4131-8c18-b405c5b18cd2); pap. 11.58 *(978-1-62712-030-2(0)*, 19a27dfb-191e-4634-a652-c7279b71561f) Cavendish Square Publishing LLC.

Waxman, Laura Hamilton. Let's Look at Snails. 2009. (Lightning Bolt Books (r) — Animal Close-Ups Ser.). (ENG., Illus.). 32p. (J). (gr. 1-3). pap. 9.99 *(978-1-58013-865-9(9)*, 418805c5-0c9e-418c-b114-fca22aa23a4f) Lerner Publishing Group.

—Slimy Snails. 2016. (First Step Nonfiction — Backyard Critters Ser.). (ENG., Illus.). 24p. (J). (gr. k-2). 23.99 *(978-1-5124-0879-9(4)*, d3c7be9a-6977-4185-8a6b-8bae1535afb8); E-Book 35.99 *(978-1-5124-1003-7(9))* Lerner Publishing Group. (Lerner Pubns.).

White, Nancy. Creeping Land Snails. 2009. (No Backbone! Ser.). (Illus.). 24p. (J). (gr. k-3). lib. bdg. 26.99 *(978-1-59716-753-6(3))* Bearport Publishing Co., Inc.

Williams, Susie. Snails. Tolson, Hannah, illus. 2020. 32p. (J). *(978-0-7787-7388-7(4))* Crabtree Publishing Co.

Woodward, John. Snail. 2010. (Garden Minibeasts up Close Ser.). 32p. (gr. 2-4). 30.00 *(978-1-60413-900-6(5)*, Chelsea Clubhse.) Infobase Holdings, Inc.

SNAILS—FICTION

Adkins, Laura. Ordinary Oscar. Hearn, Sam, illus. 2010. (ENG.). 32p. (J). (gr. -1-2). 15.95 *(978-1-58925-085-7(0))*; (gr. k-2). pap. 7.95 *(978-1-58925-418-3(X))* Tiger Tales.

Ana, Moh. Kookaburra Tales # 3: Laugh Not at Others. 2013. 16p. pap. 16.81 *(978-1-4669-3477-1(8))* Trafford Publishing.

Anderson, Hans Christian. IceMaiden & Other Tales. 2006. pap. *(978-1-4068-0421-8(5))* Echo Library.

Aspesi, Carol. The Tale of the Snail. 2008. 25p. pap. 24.95 *(978-1-60672-794-2(X))* America Star Bks.

Avi. A Beginning, a Muddle, & an End: The Right Way to Write Writing. Tusa, Tricia, illus. 2008. (ENG.). 176p. (J). (gr. 3-7). 14.95 *(978-0-15-205555-4(X)*, 1196706, Clarion Bks.) HarperCollins Pubs.

—The End of the Beginning: Being the Adventures of a Small Snail (and an Even Smaller Ant) Tusa, Tricia, illus. 2008. (ENG.). 144p. (J). (gr. 3-7). pap. 7.99 *(978-0-15-205532-5(0)*, 1196636, Clarion Bks.) HarperCollins Pubs.

Berger, Samantha. Snail Mail. Patton, Julia, illus. 2018. (ENG.). 32p. (J). (gr. -1-3). 17.99 *(978-0-7624-6251-3(5)*, Running Pr. Kids) Running Pr.

Brewin, Barbara. Sidney Snail's Wonderful World of Adventure. 2009. (Illus.). 32p. pap. 14.49 *(978-1-4389-4100-4(5))* AuthorHouse.

Bridges, Sonya. A Snail's Pace. 2011. 28p. pap. 11.32 *(978-1-4634-2752-8(2))* AuthorHouse.

Brown, Ruth. Snail Trail. Brown, Ruth, illus. 2013. (ENG., Illus.). 20p. (J). (gr. -1-k). 12.99 *(978-1-84939-252-5(8))* Andersen Pr. GBR. Dist: Independent Pubs. Group.

Carlton, Glenis. Four Snails & an Umbrella. 2016. (ENG., Illus.). 22p. (J). 23.95 *(978-1-78612-332-9(0)*, 6c37e2f4-5144-43d4-8c65-5bd5a8655cd9) Austin Macauley Pubs. Ltd. GBR. Dist: Baker & Taylor Publisher Services (BTPS).

Cazet, Denys. Snail & Slug. Cazet, Denys, illus. 2016. (ENG., Illus.). 32p. (J). (gr. -1-3). 17.99 *(978-1-4814-4506-1(5)*, Atheneum/Richard Jackson Bks.) Simon & Schuster Children's Publishing.

Chojnowski, Bryan. Muffin Time: Origins. 2005. 98p. pap. 25.01 *(978-1-4116-4440-3(9))* Lulu Pr., Inc.

Crowl, Janice. Kili & the Singing Snails. Orme, Harinani, illus. 2011. (J). 16.95 *(978-1-58178-104-5(0))* Bishop Museum Pr.

d'Lacey, Chris. The Snail Patrol. Reeve, Philip, illus. 2005. 123p. (J). (gr. 2-5). per. 5.95 *(978-1-903015-30-8(8))* Barn Owl Bks, London GBR. Dist: Independent Pubs. Group.

Donaldson, Julia. The Snail & the Whale. 2004. (ENG., Illus.). 32p. (J). (gr. -1-2). 18.99 *(978-0-8037-2922-3(7)*, Dial Bks) Penguin Young Readers Group.

—The Snail & the Whale. Scheffler, Axel, illus. 2006. (ENG.). 32p. (J). (gr. -1-2). reprint ed. pap. 8.99 *(978-0-14-240580-2(9)*, Puffin Books) Penguin Young Readers Group.

Ferry, Ann. Gusty the Cloud & Streakie the Snail. Swope, Brenda, illus. 2011. 28p. pap. 24.95 *(978-1-4560-0928-1(1))* America Star Bks.

Flowers, Natasha. Sammy the Snail. 2006. 10.00 *(978-0-8059-9158-1(1))* Dorrance Publishing Co., Inc.

Freedman, Deborah. The Story of Fish & Snail. 3rd ed. 2013. (Illus.). 40p. (J). (gr. -1-k). 17.99 *(978-0-670-78489-9(3)*, Viking Books for Young Readers) Penguin Young Readers Group.

George, Lindsay Barrett. The Secret. George, Lindsay Barrett, illus. 2005. (Illus.). 32p. (J). 16.89 *(978-0-06-029600-1(3))* HarperCollins Pubs.

Gram, Golden. Gail the Snail: A Holiday Tale. 2008. 20p. pap. 11.95 *(978-1-59858-848-4(6))* Dog Ear Publishing, LLC.

—Gail the Snail: Goes on Vacation. 2008. 20p. pap. 11.95 *(978-1-59858-860-6(5))* Dog Ear Publishing, LLC.

—Gail the Snail: How I Met Gail. 2007. 16p. per. 10.95 *(978-1-59858-430-1(8))* Dog Ear Publishing, LLC.

—Gail the Snail: Night Owl. 2008. 20p. pap. 11.95 *(978-1-59858-859-0(1))* Dog Ear Publishing, LLC.

—Gail the Snail: Snailing Around. 2007. 20p. per. 11.95 *(978-1-59858-435-6(9))* Dog Ear Publishing, LLC.

Hazen, Lynn E. The Amazing Trail of Seymour Snail. Cushman, Doug, illus. 2009. (ENG.). 64p. (J). (gr. 1-4). 17.99 *(978-0-8050-8698-0(6)*, 900048258, Holt, Henry & Co. Bks. For Young Readers) Holt, Henry & Co.

Hendra, Sue & Linnet, Paul. Norman the Slug with the Silly Shell. Hendra, Sue, illus. 2017. (ENG., Illus.). 32p. (J). (gr. -1-3). 15.99 *(978-1-4814-9032-0(X)*, Aladdin) Simon & Schuster Children's Publishing.

Henry, Kristina. The Fish Tank, 1 vol. 2011. (ENG., Illus.). 48p. (J). (gr. -1-3). 16.99 *(978-0-7643-3706-2(8)*, 4066, Schiffer Publishing Ltd) Schiffer Publishing, Ltd.

Holladay, Shirley. Gail the Snail. 2009. 28p. pap. 14.99 *(978-1-4389-8744-6(7))* AuthorHouse.

Howe, Tina Field. Snailsworth, a slow litte Story. Howe, Tina Field, illus. 2007. (Illus.). 24p. (J). per. 12.95 *(978-0-9768585-3-9(3))* Howe, Tina Field.

Howells, Angela. The Tails of Victoria Way. 2009. (Illus.). 32p. pap. 12.99 *(978-1-4490-4432-9(8))* AuthorHouse.

Hughes, Christina Margaret Ann. Lucy & Her Unusual Pet. 2008. (Illus.). 64p. per. *(978-1-84748-238-9(4))* Athena Pr.

Hyde, Margaret E. DreddieLocks & the Three Slugs. Parker, Curtis, illus. 2003. 36p. (J). lib. bdg. 16.95 *(978-1-888108-07-1(X))* Budding Artists, Inc.

Karre, Nancy. On Herman's Pond. 2005. 8.00 *(978-1-933281-00-1(6)*, 2267) Battle Creek Area Mathematics & Science Ctr.

Krensky, Stephen. My Home Is Better Than Yours! Hobai, Ioana, illus. 2017. (J). *(978-0-7680-8415-3(6))* SAE Intl.

Kügler, Tina. Snail & Worm: Three Stories about Two Friends. (Snail & Worm Ser.). (ENG., Illus.). 32p. (J). (gr. -1-3). 2019. pap. 6.99 *(978-1-328-59645-1(1)*, 1730707) 2016. 16.99 *(978-0-544-49412-1(1)*, 1604088) HarperCollins Pubs. (Clarion Bks.).

—Snail & Worm Again: Three Stories about Two Friends. 2017. (Snail & Worm Ser.). (ENG., Illus.). 32p. (J). (gr. -1-3). 16.99 *(978-0-544-79249-4(1)*, 1639349, Clarion Bks.) HarperCollins Pubs.

Lecher, Doris. A New House for Charlie. 2014. (ENG., Illus.). 28p. (J). (gr. -1-k). 16.95 *(978-1-62873-814-8(6)*, Sky Pony Pr.) Skyhorse Publishing Co., Inc.

Lee, Laura. Snail Race at Penny's Place. 2009. 24p. pap. 11.99 *(978-1-4389-9958-6(5))* AuthorHouse.

Lstarte, Sam the Slug. 2012. 30p. (J). pap. 10.99 *(978-0-9830686-4-8(X))* Capital Apple Pr.

Lustig, Lindsey Beth. Snail's Trail. 2008. 21p. pap. 24.95 *(978-1-60610-310-4(5))* America Star Bks.

May, Eleanor. Albert's Amazing Snail. Melmon, Deborah, illus. 2012. (Mouse Math Ser.). 32p. (J). (gr. -1-1). (ENG.). 22.60 *(978-1-57565-448-5(2))*; pap. 7.99 *(978-1-57565-442-3(3)*, 66896184-54ad-4084-ae2c-c88e04a215c0, Kane Press) Astra Publishing Hse.

—Albert's Amazing Snail. 2018. (Mouse Math Ser.). (ENG.). 32p. (J). (gr. -1-1). lib. bdg. 34.28 *(978-1-4896-8307-6(0)*, AV2 by Weigl) Weigl Pubs., Inc.

McKirdy, Mark. The Garden Party. 2004. 19p. (J). pap. 13.95 *(978-1-4116-1847-3(5))* Lulu Pr., Inc.

Miranda, Conchita. Yago's Heartbeat. Brokenbrow, Jon, tr. Carretero, Mónica, illus. 2011. (Light (Cuento de Luz) Ser.). 42p. (J). (gr. k-3). 15.95 *(978-84-938240-3-7(8))* Cuento de Luz SL ESP. Dist: Publishers Group West (PGW).

Moh Ana. Kookaburra Tales # 4: Lighten My Path, Brighten My Heart. 2013. 16p. pap. 16.81 *(978-1-4669-9129-3(1))* Trafford Publishing.

Nath, D. Smith. She, the Tale of a Sail. 30p. (J). (gr. k-2). pap. 5.95 *(978-1-886134-03-4(0))* Miraculous Fingerprints Pubs.

New Home for Snail. 2003. (Daisy Board Books Ser.). 10p. (J). bds. 9.95 *(978-0-7525-8299-3(2))* Parragon, Inc.

Nicholson, Devon, et al. Fundi the Snail. 2008. 48p. pap. 26.50 *(978-1-4357-1551-6(9))* Lulu Pr., Inc.

Niddrie, June. Sweetpea & His Friends. 2010. 36p. pap. 17.30 *(978-0-557-31853-7(X))* Lulu Pr., Inc.

Ostrow, Kim. The Great Snail Race. Bond, Clint & Clark, Andy, illus. 2005. (SpongeBob SquarePants Ser.: No. 6). 22p. (J). lib. bdg. 15.00 *(978-1-59054-830-1(2))* Fitzgerald Bks.

Parker, Emma. Sam the Traveling Snail. 2010. (Illus.). pap. *(978-1-877561-19-1(3))* First Edition Ltd.

Paul, Ann Whitford. Snail's Good Night. Litzinger, Rosanne, illus. 2008. (Holiday House Readers: Level 1 Ser.). (ENG.). 32p. (J). (gr. -1-3). 14.95 *(978-0-8234-1912-8(6))* Holiday Hse., Inc.

Pearson, Susan. Slugger, 0 vols. Slonim, David, illus. 2013. (ENG.). 32p. (J). (gr. -1-2). 14.99 *(978-1-4778-1641-7(0)*, 9781477816417, Two Lions) Amazon Publishing.

—Slugs in Love, 0 vols. O'Malley, Kevin, illus. 2012. (ENG.). 34p. (J). (gr. -1-3). pap. 7.99 *(978-0-7614-6248-4(1)*, 9780761462484, Two Lions) Amazon Publishing.

Peterson, Mary. Snail Has Lunch. Peterson, Mary, illus. 2016. (Pix Ser.). (ENG., Illus.). 64p. (J). (gr. 1-4). 12.99 *(978-1-4814-5302-8(5)*, Aladdin) Simon & Schuster Children's Publishing.

Porter, Marylyn Kight. Speedy the Snail & His New Family. 2006. 10.00 *(978-0-8059-9134-5(4))* Dorrance Publishing Co., Inc.

Punter, Russell & MacKinnon, Mairi. Snail Brings the Mail. Blunt, Fred, illus. 2014. (Usborne Phonics Readers Ser.). (ENG.). (J). pap. 6.99 *(978-0-7945-3369-4(8)*, Usborne) EDC Publishing.

Rempt, Fiona. Snail's Birthday Wish. Smit, Noelle, illus. 2007. (ENG.). 32p. (J). (gr. -1-1). 14.95 *(978-1-905417-52-0(7))* Boxer Bks., Ltd. GBR. Dist: Sterling Publishing Co., Inc.

Rigby Education Staff. Animals Say... (Sails Literacy Ser.). (Illus.). 16p. (gr. 2-3). 27.00 *(978-0-7635-9943-0(3)*, 699433C99) Rigby Education.

Rinne, Teresa & Dillon, Preston. Snail Tails: Let's Play Ball! 2009. 40p. pap. 16.99 *(978-1-4389-7076-9(5))* AuthorHouse.

Rooks, Jo. Sophie's Shell. 2019. (Illus.). 32p. (J). *(978-1-4338-3089-1(2)*, Magination Pr.) American Psychological Assn.

Russell, Philip. A Sunny Day for Snails. 2011. 24p. pap. 15.99 *(978-1-4628-2950-7(3))* Xlibris Corp.

Santillo, LuAnn. Bee. Santillo, LuAnn, ed. 2003. (Half-Pint Kids Readers Ser.). (Illus.). 7p. (J). (gr. -1-1). pap. *(978-1-59256-108-7(X))* Half-Pint Kids, Inc.

—Snail. Santillo, LuAnn, ed. 2003. (Half-Pint Kids Readers Ser.). (Illus.). 7p. (J). (gr. -1-1). pap. 1.00 *(978-1-59256-106-3(3))* Half-Pint Kids, Inc.

Santos, Dennis. Earl the Pearl. 2007. 28p. per. 10.95 *(978-1-59526-833-4(2)*, Llumina Kids) Aeon Publishing Inc.

Shaw, Natalie. Get Your Shell On. 2013. (Simon & Schuster Ready-To-Read Level 1 Ser.). lib. bdg. 13.55 *(978-0-606-32058-0(X))* Turtleback.

The Shy Snail. 2003. (J). per. *(978-1-57657-937-4(9))* Paradise Pr., Inc.

Slater, Dashka. Escargot. Hanson, Sydney, illus. 2017. (Escargot Ser.). (ENG.). 40p. (J). 18.99 *(978-0-374-30281-8(2)*, 900151640, Farrar, Straus & Giroux (BYR)) Farrar, Straus & Giroux.

S

Stadler, John. Snail Saves the Day, 1 vol. 2006. (ENG., Illus.). 32p. (J). (gr. -1-3). reprint ed. pap. 5.95 *(978-1-59572-045-0(6))* Star Bright Bks., Inc.

Stewart, Dorothy. It's Hard to Hurry When You're a Snail, 1 vol. Taylor, Thomas, illus. 2009. 32p. (J). 14.95 *(978-0-8254-7838-3(3)*, Lion Children's) Lion Hudson PLC GBR. Dist: Kregel Pubns.

Stokholm, Susan Mary. Between a Shadow & the Moon. 2010. (ENG.). 264p. pap. 14.49 *(978-1-4520-1752-5(2))* AuthorHouse.

Strack, Beth. Sammy the Snail's Bright Ideas. 2013. 32p. pap. 9.99 *(978-0-9898991-0-9(1))* Strack, Beth.

Strickland, A. W. The Adventures of Ralph & Elmer This Potato Is for You. 2012. 38p. pap. 14.95 *(978-0-9820649-9-3(3))* Andromeda Pr.

Tafoya, Jody. Sammy: A Day in the Life of a Snail. 2012. 24p. pap. 24.95 *(978-1-62709-389-7(3))* America Star Bks.

Ticktock Media, Ltd. Staff. In the Garden with the Hungry Little Snail. 2009. (Touch & Feel Fun Ser.). (ENG.). 10p. (J). (gr. k — 1). bds. 5.95 *(978-1-84696-810-5(0)*, TickTock Books) Octopus Publishing Group GBR. Dist: Independent Pubs. Group.

Twiss, Jill. The Someone New. Keller, E. G., illus. 2019. (ENG.). 32p. (J). (gr. -1-3). 18.99 *(978-0-06-293374-4(4)*, HarperCollins) HarperCollins Pubs.

Ungerer, Tomi. Snail, Where Are You? 2015. (ENG., Illus.). 32p. (gr. -1-k). 14.95 *(978-0-7148-6799-1(3))* Phaidon Pr., Inc.

Volta, A. Patulous, the Different Caterpillar. 2008. (Illus.). 28p. (J). 17.99 *(978-0-9711040-6-6(X))* Working Parents, LLC.

Waring, Geoff. Oscar & the Snail: A Book about Things That We Use. Waring, Geoff, illus. (Start with Science Ser.). (ENG., Illus.). 32p. (J). (gr. -1-3). 2011. pap. 6.99 *(978-0-7636-5303-3(9))* 2009. 14.99 *(978-0-7636-4039-2(5))* Candlewick Pr.

Wenger, Shaunda. Caterpillar Can't Wait! 2006. (Early Explorers Ser.). (J). pap. *(978-1-4108-6101-6(5))* Benchmark Education Co.

Woodford, Pamela. Sortof the Snail. 2013. (Brighter Little Minds Ser.). (ENG., Illus.). 18p. (J). 10.95 *(978-1-871305-83-8(7))* Orpen Pr. IRL. Dist: Dufour Editions, Inc.

SNAKES

Adamson, Thomas K. Anaconda vs. Jaguar. 2020. (Animal Battles Ser.). (ENG.). 24p. (J). (gr. 3-7). lib. bdg. 26.95 *(978-1-64487-155-3(6)*, Torque Bks.) Bellwether Media.

Albertson, Al. Cottonmouths. 2019. (North American Animals Ser.). (ENG., Illus.). 24p. (J). (gr. k-3). lib. bdg. 26.95 *(978-1-62617-983-7(2)*, Blastoff! Readers) Bellwether Media.

Alinsky, Shelby. National Geographic Readers: Slither, Snake! 2015. (Readers Ser.). (Illus.). 24p. (J). (gr. -1-k). pap. 4.99 *(978-1-4263-1955-6(X)*, National Geographic Kids) Disney Publishing Worldwide.

—Slither, Snake! (1 Hardcover/1 CD) 2017. (National Geographic Kids Ser.). (ENG.). (J). 29.95 *(978-1-4301-2657-7(4))* Live Oak Media.

—Slither, Snake! (1 Paperback/1 CD) 2017. (National Geographic Kids Ser.). (ENG.). (J). pap. 19.95 *(978-1-4301-2656-0(6))* Live Oak Media.

—Slither, Snake! (4 Paperbacks/1 CD) 2017. (National Geographic Kids Ser.). (ENG.). (J). pap. 31.95 *(978-1-4301-2658-4(2))* Live Oak Media.

Allyn, Daisy. Python, 1 vol. 2011. (Killer Snakes Ser.). (ENG., Illus.). 24p. (J). (gr. 2-2). lib. bdg. 25.27 *(978-1-4339-4559-5(2)*, 7958905b-92e4-4f9c-9c35-8cd53b677248) Stevens, Gareth Publishing LLLP.

—Python / Pitón, 1 vol. 2011. (Killer Snakes / Serpientes Asesinas Ser.). (SPA & ENG., Illus.). 24p. (J). (gr. 2-2). 25.27 *(978-1-4339-4563-2(0)*, 159bcc4b-9adc-4b09-bd86-5677400a7ca1) Stevens, Gareth Publishing LLLP.

Amazing Snakes, 10 vols. 2014. (Amazing Snakes Ser.). 24p. (J). (gr. 3-3). (ENG.). 126.35 *(978-1-4777-6512-8(3)*, c5c9e01e-3633-4c64-a38a-5b80e1182f33); pap. 41.25 *(978-1-4777-7211-9(1))* Rosen Publishing Group, Inc., The. (PowerKids Pr.).

Arnold, Tedd. Fly Guy Presents: Snakes (Scholastic Reader, Level 2) Arnold, Tedd, illus. 2016. (Scholastic Reader, Level 2 Ser.). (ENG., Illus.). 32p. (J). (gr. k-2). pap. 4.99 *(978-0-545-85188-6(2))* Scholastic, Inc.

Arnold, Tedd, illus. Fly Guy Presents: Snakes. 2016. (J). *(978-1-5182-0352-7(3))* Scholastic, Inc.

Austen, Amy. Pythons, 1 vol. 2016. (Snakes on the Hunt Ser.). (ENG., Illus.). 24p. (J). (gr. 3-3). pap. 9.25 *(978-1-4994-2198-9(2)*, a70b17f8-8437-4a17-a0b2-c04305bd5a34, PowerKids Pr.) Rosen Publishing Group, Inc., The.

Avery, Sebastian. Anacondas, 1 vol. 2016. (Snakes on the Hunt Ser.). (ENG.). 24p. (J). (gr. 3-3). pap. 9.25 *(978-1-4994-2190-3(7),* 9e4a8db0-32d2-4125-bf6c-220e8e147ed8, PowerKids Pr.) Rosen Publishing Group, Inc., The.

Barnes, J. Lou. 101 Facts about Snakes, 1 vol. 2004. (101 Facts about Predators Ser.). (ENG., Illus.). 32p. (gr. 2-4). lib. bdg. 28.67 *(978-0-8368-4040-7(2),* 0853007d-82e5-4c4e-b19b-4a5c050d52af, Gareth Stevens Learning Library) Stevens, Gareth Publishing LLLP.

Barr, Brady & Zoehfeld, Kathleen Weidner. National Geographic Kids Chapters: Scrapes with Snakes! True Stories of Adventures with Animals. 2015. (NGK Chapters Ser.). 112p. (J). (gr. 3-7). pap. 5.99 *(978-1-4263-1914-3(2),* National Geographic Kids) Disney Publishing Worldwide.

Barraclough, Susan. Snakes & Reptiles: The Scariest Cold-Blooded Creatures on Earth. 2008. (Illus.). 192p. (J). *(978-1-4351-0774-8(8))* Barnes & Noble, Inc.

Believe It Or Not, Ripley's, compiled by. Ripley Twists: Snakes & Reptiles. 2015. (Twist Ser.: 14). (ENG., Illus.). 48p. (J). 12.95 *(978-1-60991-141-6(5))* Ripley Entertainment, Inc.

Believe It Or Not!, Ripleys, compiled by. Ripley Twists PB: Snakes & Reptiles. 2018. (Twist Ser.: 14). (ENG.). 48p. (J). pap. 7.99 *(978-1-60991-233-8(0))* Ripley Entertainment, Inc.

Bell, Samantha. Anaconda. 2015. (21st Century Skills Library: Exploring Our Rainforests Ser.). (ENG., Illus.). 32p. (gr. 3-6). 32.07 *(978-1-63188-973-8(7),* 205804) Cherry Lake Publishing.

Berger, Melvin & Berger, Gilda. A Snake Grows Up. 2008. (Illus.). 32p. (J). *(978-0-439-02526-3(5))* Scholastic, Inc.

Bishop, Nic. Nic Bishop: Snakes. Bishop, Nic, illus. 2012. (ENG., Illus.). 48p. (J). (gr. -1-3). 19.99 *(978-0-545-20638-9(3),* Scholastic Nonfiction) Scholastic, Inc.

—Snakes. 2016. (Illus.). 31p. (J). *(978-0-545-95529-4(7))* Scholastic, Inc.

Blake, Kevin. Deadly Snake Bite! 2018. (Envenomators Ser.). (ENG., Illus.). 24p. (J). (gr. 2-7). 19.45 *(978-1-68402-655-5(5))* Bearport Publishing Co., Inc.

—Guam's Brown Tree Snakes: Hanging Out. 2015. (They Don't Belong: Tracking Invasive Species Ser.). (ENG., Illus.). 32p. (J). (gr. 2-7). lib. bdg. 28.50 *(978-1-62724-830-3(7))* Bearport Publishing Co., Inc.

Blazeman, Christopher. Snakes up Close, 1 vol. 2nd rev. ed. 2011. (TIME for KIDS(r): Informational Text Ser.). (ENG.). 28p. (gr. 2-3). pap. 8.99 *(978-1-4333-3618-8(9))* Teacher Created Materials, Inc.

Blobaum, Cindy. Awesome Snake Science! 40 Activities for Learning about Snakes. 2012. (Young Naturalists Ser.: 2). (ENG., Illus.). 128p. (J). (gr. 4-6). pap. 16.99 *(978-1-56976-807-5(2))* Chicago Review Pr., Inc.

Boa Constrictor: Killer King of the Jungle. 2013. (Top of the Food Chain Ser.). 32p. (J). (gr. k-5). pap. 60.00 *(978-1-61533-800-9(4),* PowerKids Pr.) Rosen Publishing Group, Inc., The.

Bodden, Valerie. Snake. 2014. (Grow with Me Ser.). (ENG.). 32p. (J). (gr. 3-6). pap. 9.99 *(978-0-89812-992-2(3),* 21342, Creative Paperbacks); (Illus.). *(978-1-60818-406-4(4),* 21341, Creative Education) Creative Co., The.

—Snakes. (J). (gr. 1-17). 2011. (ENG.). 24p. pap. 5.99 *(978-1-926722-28-3(0),* Creative Paperbacks) 2010. (ENG.). 24p. 16.95 *(978-1-58341-813-0(X),* 23062, Creative Education) 2009. 24.25 *(978-1-58341-724-9(9),* Creative Education) Creative Co., The.

Books Are Fun 8 Title Animal Lives Set: Snakes. 2006. (J). *(978-1-59566-306-1(1))* QEB Publishing Inc.

Bowman, Chris. Gaboon Vipers. 2014. (Amazing Snakes! Ser.). (ENG.). 24p. (J). (gr. 3-7). 26.95 *(978-1-62617-123-7(8),* Epic Bks.) Bellwether Media.

—Inland Taipans. 2014. (Amazing Snakes! Ser.). (ENG.). 24p. (J). (gr. 3-7). 26.95 *(978-1-62617-124-4(6),* Epic Bks.) Bellwether Media.

—Rainbow Boas. 2014. (Amazing Snakes! Ser.). (ENG.). 24p. (J). (gr. 3-7). 26.95 *(978-1-62617-125-1(4),* Epic Bks.) Bellwether Media.

—Western Diamondback Rattlesnakes. 2014. (Amazing Snakes! Ser.). (ENG.). 24p. (J). (gr. 3-7). 26.95 *(978-1-62617-126-8(2),* Epic Bks.) Bellwether Media.

Bozzo, Linda. How Snakes Grow Up, 1 vol. 2019. (Animals Growing Up Ser.). (ENG.). 24p. (gr. 1-2). pap. 10.35 *(978-1-9785-1245-0(7),* b69d2f08-d08c-4695-8a9c-daac7c327d7b) Enslow Publishing, LLC.

Braidich, Victoria. Copperhead, 1 vol. 2011. (Killer Snakes Ser.). (ENG.). 24p. (J). (gr. 2-2). pap. 9.15 *(978-1-4339-5629-4(2),* 0af1b30b-6b95-4a3a-be7a-d2ddcd9361db); lib. bdg. 25.27 *(978-1-4339-5627-0(6),* a13dfa5c-501d-4c56-95ce-43a9a5eafdcd) Stevens, Gareth Publishing LLLP.

—Copperhead / Serpiente Cabeza de Cobre, 1 vol. 2011. (Killer Snakes / Serpientes Asesinas Ser.). (SPA & ENG., Illus.). 24p. (J). (gr. 2-2). 25.27 *(978-1-4339-5631-7(4),* 3787025c-ec65-4ed9-89f6-82fd0171cfa5) Stevens, Gareth Publishing LLLP.

Burke, Juliet. Anaconda, 1 vol. 2011. (Killer Snakes Ser.). (ENG., Illus.). 24p. (J). (gr. 2-2). 25.27 *(978-1-4339-4523-6(1),* 685bebcc-fe03-411f-9a40-6910fdec6c99); pap. 9.15 *(978-1-4339-4524-3(X),* 35be0d6a-05b2-467a-a0e4-f544e35d624f) Stevens, Gareth Publishing LLLP.

—Anaconda / Anaconda, 1 vol. 2011. (Killer Snakes / Serpientes Asesinas Ser.). (ENG & SPA., Illus.). 24p. (J). (gr. 2-2). 25.27 *(978-1-4339-4527-4(4),* e2936b7e-dcac-4b89-9ee9-67af4e400793) Stevens, Gareth Publishing LLLP.

Byars, Betsy. The Moon & I. 2014. 112p. pap. 6.00 *(978-1-61003-379-4(5))* Center for the Collaborative Classroom.

Calhoun, Kelly. Deslizadores Furtivos. 2016. (Adivina (Guess What) Ser.). (SPA., Illus.). 24p. (J). (gr. k-2). pap. 12.79 *(978-1-63471-468-6(7),* 208872) Cherry Lake Publishing.

—Reptadores Furtivos (Slinky Sliders) Serpiente de Cascabel (Rattlesnake) 2016. (Adivina (Guess What) Ser.). (SPA., Illus.). 24p. (J). (gr. k-2). 30.64 *(978-1-63471-452-5(0),* 208871) Cherry Lake Publishing.

—Slinky Sliders: Rattlesnake. 2015. (Guess What Ser.). (ENG., Illus.). 24p. (J). (gr. k-2). pap. 12.79 *(978-1-63362-721-5(7),* 206697) Cherry Lake Publishing.

Campbell, Jonathan A. & Lamar, William W. The Venomous Reptiles of the Western Hemisphere, 2 vols. 2004. (ENG., Illus.). 528p. (gr. 17). 184.95 *(978-0-8014-4141-7(2),* 978-0-8014-4141-7, Comstock Publishing Assocs.) Cornell Univ. Pr.

Canasi, Brittany. Green Anaconda. 2018. (World's Coolest Snakes Ser.). (ENG., Illus.). 32p. (gr. 4-8). lib. bdg. 32.79 *(978-1-64156-486-1(5),* 9781641564861) Rourke Educational Media.

Carraway, Rose. Slithering Snakes, 1 vol. 2012. (Pet Corner Ser.). (ENG., Illus.). 24p. (J). (gr. k-k). pap. 9.15 *(978-1-4339-6303-2(5),* 9fcd5eaf-ff5d-459e-853e-da7bd85612a8); lib. bdg. 25.27 *(978-1-4339-6301-8(9),* 6d0fe6d8-2634-4256-ac5f-5f405e629b40) Stevens, Gareth Publishing LLLP.

—Slithering Snakes / Serpientes Resbaladizas, 1 vol. 2012. (Pet Corner / Rincón de Las Mascotas Ser.). (SPA & ENG.). 24p. (J). (gr. k-k). lib. bdg. 25.27 *(978-1-4339-6645-3(X),* 7f28b1c0-6bf7-497a-8128-6298b83294c1) Stevens, Gareth Publishing LLLP.

Cheng, Christopher. Python. Jackson, Mark, illus. 2016. (Read & Wonder Ser.). (ENG.). 32p. (J). (gr. k-3). 8.99 *(978-0-7636-8773-1(1))* Candlewick Pr.

Christiansen, Per. Constrictor Snakes, 1 vol. 2008. (Nature's Monsters: Reptiles & Amphibians Ser.). (ENG., Illus.). 32p. (YA). (gr. 3-5). lib. bdg. 28.67 *(978-0-8368-9220-8(8),* 1bc53228-af8b-4e09-83ff-9ebb3dc8f233) Stevens, Gareth Publishing LLLP.

Ciletti, Barbara. Burmese Pythons. 2016. (Invasive Species Takeover Ser.). (ENG.). 32p. (J). (gr. 4-6). pap. 9.99 *(978-1-64466-144-4(6),* 10278); (Illus.). 31.35 *(978-1-68072-017-4(1),* 10277) Black Rabbit Bks. (Bolt).

Clark Sawyer, J. Las Serpientes de Cascabel de Bandas. 2014. (¿a dónde Van en Invierno? Ser.). (SPA.). 24p. (J). (gr. -1-3). lib. bdg. 26.99 *(978-1-62724-460-2(3))* Bearport Publishing Co., Inc.

—Timber Rattlesnakes. 2015. (Illus.). 24p. (J). lib. bdg. 26.99 *(978-1-62724-318-6(6))* Bearport Publishing Co., Inc.

Clark, Willow. Burmese Pythons, 1 vol. 2012. (Animals of Asia Ser.). (ENG., Illus.). 24p. (J). (gr. 2-3). 26.27 *(978-1-4488-7418-7(1),* 6a884a3d-6ad0-4b75-87af-b8d08e7a96a9); pap. 9.25 *(978-1-4488-7491-0(2),* 8828a3b3-04b8-43a6-a91c-d46b5ff78d19) Rosen Publishing Group, Inc., The. (PowerKids Pr.).

—Green Tree Pythons, 1 vol. 2012. (Up a Tree Ser.). (ENG., Illus.). 24p. (J). (gr. 2-3). pap. 9.25 *(978-1-4488-6333-4(3),* fe3dc781-34a8-495d-bb56-605e23ecd6fb, PowerKids Pr.); lib. bdg. 26.27 *(978-1-4488-6187-3(X),* b1d753c0-9793-453e-af41-6019497ce276) Rosen Publishing Group, Inc., The.

—Rattlesnake!, 1 vol. 2010. (Animal Danger Zone Ser.). (ENG.). 24p. (J). (gr. 2-3). lib. bdg. 27.27 *(978-1-60754-958-1(1),* c84cc4be-ab83-435e-8bb9-5e1edcd5073e); (Illus.). pap. 9.15 *(978-1-60754-970-3(0),* b952d0f2-1e7c-434c-90b6-b842167da3f1) Rosen Publishing Group, Inc., The. (Windmill Bks.).

Clausen-Grace, Nicki. Anacondas. 2018. (Wild Animal Kingdom (Continuation) Ser.). (ENG.). 32p. (gr. 2-7). 9.95 *(978-1-68072-733-3(8));* (J). (gr. 4-6). pap. 9.99 *(978-1-64466-286-1(8),* 12397); (J). (gr. 4-6). lib. bdg. *(978-1-68072-439-4(8),* 12396) Black Rabbit Bks. (Bolt).

Cleave, Andrew. Snakes & Reptiles - Pb: A Portrait of the Animal World. 2013. (Portrait of the Animal World Ser.). (Illus.). 80p. pap. 9.95 *(978-1-59764-318-4(1))* New Line Bks.

Coates, Jennifer. Snakes. (J). 2009. (Illus.). 112p. 14.95 *(978-1-932904-41-3(7))* 2008. *(978-1-932904-33-8(6))* Eldorado Ink.

Corwin, Jeff. Snake-Tacular. Pascoe, Elaine, ed. 2003. (Jeff Corwin Experience Ser.). (J). 23.70 *(978-1-4103-0205-2(9));* 9.95 *(978-1-4103-0206-9(7))* Cengage Gale. (Blackbirch Pr., Inc.).

—Snakes. 2009. (All Aboard Reading: Station Stop 3 Ser.). (ENG.). 48p. (J). (gr. 2-4). 16.19 *(978-0-448-45177-0(8))* Penguin Young Readers Group.

—The World of Snakes. 2014. (Wildlife & Nature Identification Ser.). (ENG., Illus.). 12p. (J). (gr. -1-12). 7.95 *(978-1-58355-850-8(0))* Waterford Pr., Inc.

Craats, Rennay. Caring for Your Snake. (Caring for Your Pet Ser.). (Illus.). 32p. (J). 2005. (gr. 4-7). per. 9.95 *(978-1-59036-216-7(0))* 2004. lib. bdg. 26.00 *(978-1-59036-196-2(2))* Weigl Pubs., Inc.

—Snake. 2010. pap. 9.95 *(978-1-61690-083-0(0));* 32p. (J). (gr. 3-5). lib. bdg. 27.13 *(978-1-61690-082-3(2))* Weigl Pubs., Inc.

Crossingham, John & Kalman, Bobbie. The Life Cycle of a Snake, 1 vol. 2003. (Life Cycle Ser.). (ENG., Illus.). 32p. (J). (gr. 3-4). pap. *(978-0-7787-0690-8(7));* lib. bdg. *(978-0-7787-0660-1(5))* Crabtree Publishing Co.

—Les Serpents. 2006. (Petit Monde Vivant Ser.). (FRE., Illus.). 32p. (J). (gr. k-6). pap. 9.95 *(978-2-89579-100-3(7))* Bayard Canada Livres CAN. Dist: Crabtree Publishing Co.

Las Culebras, 6 vols., Vol. 2. (Explorers. Exploradores Nonfiction Sets Ser.). (SPA.). 32p. (gr. 3-6). 44.95 *(978-0-7699-0639-3(7))* Shortland Pubns. (U. S. A.) Inc.

Cunningham, Malta. How Do Snakes Poop? 2018. (Crazy Animal Facts Ser.). (ENG., Illus.). 32p. (J). (gr. 4-6). lib. bdg. 28.65 *(978-1-5435-4115-1(1),* 139069, Capstone Pr.) Capstone.

De Medeiros, James. Anacondas. 2008. (Amazing Animals Ser.). (Illus.). 24p. (J). (gr. 2-4). pap. 8.95 *(978-1-59036-961-6(0),* 1290899); lib. bdg. 24.45 *(978-1-59036-960-9(2),* 1290899) Weigl Pubs., Inc.

Dennard, Deborah. Snakes. Dewey, Jennifer Owings, illus. 2003. (Our Wild World Ser.). (ENG.). 48p. (J). (gr. 2-5). pap. 7.95 *(978-1-55971-855-4(2))* Cooper Square Publishing Llc.

Dibble, Traci. Cobras. 2011. (Predator Animals Ser.). 16p. pap. 39.62 *(978-1-61541-368-3(5))* American Reading Co.

—Cobras. Dibble, Traci, illus. 2011. (1-3Y Wild Animals Ser.). (ENG., Illus.). 16p. (J). (gr. k-2). pap. 9.60 *(978-1-61541-367-6(7))* American Reading Co.

Dibble, Traci & Sánchez, Lucía M. Cobras. 2011. (2Y Animales Depredadores Ser.). (SPA.). 16p. (J). (gr. k-2). pap. 9.60 *(978-1-61541-369-0(3))* American Reading Co.

DK & Woodward, John. Everything You Need to Know about Snakes. 2013. (Everything You Need to Know Ser.). (ENG.). 80p. (J). (gr. 2-5). 15.99 *(978-1-4654-0246-2(2),* DK Children) Dorling Kindersley Publishing, Inc.

Donovan, Sandy. A Snake in Its Burrow. 2003. (Where Do Animals Live? Ser.). (J). pap. *(978-1-58417-193-5(6));* lib. bdg. *(978-1-58417-192-8(8))* Lake Street Pubs.

Dorisi-Winget, Dianna. Pythons. 2011. (Wild about Snakes Ser.). (ENG.). 32p. (gr. 3-4). pap. 47.70 *(978-1-4296-7288-7(9),* Capstone Pr.) Capstone.

Dufresne, Michèle. Snakes: Nonfiction Yellow Set. 2007. (Nonfiction Collection). (ENG.). (J). pap. 8.00 *(978-1-60343-010-4(5))* Pioneer Valley Bks.

Duhaime, Darla. Snakes. 2017. (Reptiles! Ser.). (ENG.). 24p. (gr. -1-1). pap. 9.95 *(978-1-68342-198-6(1),* 9781683421986) Rourke Educational Media.

Dunn, Mary R. Copperheads, 1 vol. 2013. (Snakes Ser.). (ENG., Illus.). 24p. (J). (gr. -1-2). lib. bdg. 27.32 *(978-1-4765-2071-1(2),* 122805, Capstone Pr.) Capstone.

—Garter Snakes, 1 vol. 2013. (Snakes Ser.). (ENG.). 24p. (J). (gr. -1-2). lib. bdg. 27.32 *(978-1-4765-2072-8(0),* 122806, Capstone Pr.) Capstone.

—Rattlesnakes, 1 vol. 2013. (Snakes Ser.). (ENG.). 24p. (J). (gr. -1-2). lib. bdg. 27.32 *(978-1-4765-2085-8(2),* 122808, Capstone Pr.) Capstone.

Dussling, Jennifer. DK Readers L2: Slinky, Scaly Snakes. 2011. (DK Readers Level 2 Ser.). (ENG.). 32p. (J). (gr. 1-3). 4.99 *(978-0-7566-7587-5(1),* DK Children) Dorling Kindersley Publishing, Inc.

Early Macken, JoAnn. Rattlesnakes, 1 vol. (Animals That Live in the Desert (First Edition) Ser.). (ENG., 24p. (gr. 1-1). 2005. Illus.). pap. 9.15 *(978-0-8368-4836-6(5),* bf34c244-783f-4ff1-a830-c299090a211c) 2nd rev. ed. 2009. (J). pap. 9.15 *(978-1-4339-2451-4(X),* ec788c75-eea1-45fc-a67f-56a7ecee8bb4) 2nd rev. ed. 2009. (J). lib. bdg. 25.27 *(978-1-4339-2150-6(2),* a6b7ce83-583d-4fdc-a5f1-37f1e55543e5) Stevens, Gareth Publishing LLLP. (Weekly Reader Leveled Readers).

—Rattlesnakes / Serpientes de Cascabel, 1 vol. 2nd rev. ed. 2009. (Animals That Live in the Desert / Animales Del Desierto (Second Edition) Ser.). (SPA & ENG.). 24p. (J). (gr. 1-1). pap. 9.15 *(978-1-4339-2459-0(5),* 50dea247-9f06-45b8-be05-bbc763384601, Weekly Reader Leveled Readers); lib. bdg. 25.27 *(978-1-4339-2133-9(2),* 8aec0b38-50eb-4361-8f75-4b74b524c5a4) Stevens, Gareth Publishing LLLP.

—Snakes / Las Serpientes, 1 vol. 2004. (Animals I See at the Zoo / Animales Que Veo en el Zoológico Ser.). (SPA & ENG., Illus.). 24p. (gr. k-2). lib. bdg. 24.67 *(978-0-8368-4385-9(1),* bfa64dbb-b788-41c4-89c9-0104bfe2c2d7) Stevens, Gareth Publishing LLLP.

Editors of Kingfisher. It's All about... Slithering Snakes: Everything You Want to Know about Snakes in One Amazing Book. 2017. (It's All About... Ser.). (ENG.). 32p. (J). pap. 5.99 *(978-0-7534-7369-6(0),* 900178395, Kingfisher) Roaring Brook Pr.

Feldman, Heather. Copperheads. (Really Wild Life of Animals Ser.). 24p. (gr. 3-4). 2009. 42.50 *(978-1-60854-185-0(1))* 2003. (ENG., Illus.). (J). lib. bdg. 26.27 *(978-0-8239-6721-6(2),* 5addae2d-6e47-4064-8607-2766b220ce66) Rosen Publishing Group, Inc., The. (PowerKids Pr.).

—Coral Snakes. (Really Wild Life of Animals Ser.). 24p. (gr. 3-4). 2009. 42.50 *(978-1-60854-186-7(X))* 2003. (ENG., Illus.). (J). lib. bdg. 26.27 *(978-0-8239-6719-3(0),* 552c5968-8a28-458e-bd49-9bdfe037890c) Rosen Publishing Group, Inc., The. (PowerKids Pr.).

—King Snakes. (Really Wild Life of Animals Ser.). 24p. (gr. 3-4). 2009. 42.50 *(978-1-60854-195-9(9))* 2003. (ENG., Illus.). (J). lib. bdg. 26.27 *(978-0-8239-6723-0(9),* 4fa9bc48-fe0a-420b-bee2-d9f8830e6ba6) Rosen Publishing Group, Inc., The. (PowerKids Pr.).

—Milk Snakes. (Really Wild Life of Animals Ser.). 24p. (gr. 3-4). 2009. 42.50 *(978-1-60854-200-0(9))* 2003. (ENG.). (J). lib. bdg. 26.27 *(978-0-8239-6720-9(4),* 9490e195-e9b1-41b8-bb51-7230df4cb4de) Rosen Publishing Group, Inc., The. (PowerKids Pr.).

Fiedler, Julie. Boas. (Scary Snakes Ser.). 24p. (gr. 2-3). 2009. 42.50 *(978-1-60852-986-5(X),* PowerKids Pr.) 2007. (ENG., Illus.). (J). lib. bdg. 26.27 *(978-1-4042-3836-7(0),* 9ec27abb-0ac0-4bd1-b59b-d231ae9cdbfe) Rosen Publishing Group, Inc., The.

—Cobras. (Scary Snakes Ser.). 24p. (gr. 2-3). 2009. 42.50 *(978-1-60852-987-2(8))* 2007. (ENG., Illus.). (J). lib. bdg. 26.27 *(978-1-4042-3837-4(9),* beee7b9c-0657-41b7-b255-b810e6916a92) Rosen Publishing Group, Inc., The. (PowerKids Pr.).

—Mambas. (Scary Snakes Ser.). 24p. (gr. 2-3). 2009. 42.50 *(978-1-60852-988-9(6),* PowerKids Pr.) 2007. (ENG., Illus.). (YA). lib. bdg. 26.27 *(978-1-4042-3838-1(7),* 7efd949c-9946-4520-8c57-c74ffe4a97d7) Rosen Publishing Group, Inc., The.

—Pythons. (Scary Snakes Ser.). 24p. (gr. 2-3). 2009. 42.50 *(978-1-60852-989-6(4),* PowerKids Pr.) 2007. (ENG., Illus.). (J). lib. bdg. 26.27 *(978-1-4042-3835-0(2),* 0f32a1a9-9152-4846-abac-ed5d5a130ac1) Rosen Publishing Group, Inc., The.

—Rattlesnakes. (Scary Snakes Ser.). 24p. (gr. 2-3). 2009. 42.50 *(978-1-60852-990-2(8),* PowerKids Pr.) 2007. (ENG., Illus.). (YA). lib. bdg. 26.27 *(978-1-4042-3834-3(4),* b34b7e56-5176-421a-9019-cba1ab0d1ec0) Rosen Publishing Group, Inc., The.

—Vipers. (Scary Snakes Ser.). 24p. (gr. 2-3). 2009. 42.50 *(978-1-60852-991-9(6),* PowerKids Pr.) 2007. (ENG., Illus.). (YA). lib. bdg. 26.27 *(978-1-4042-3833-6(6),* e167c767-df8b-44cf-8988-125774f81962) Rosen Publishing Group, Inc., The.

Figorito, Juliet. Banded Sea Snake, 1 vol. 2011. (Killer Snakes Ser.). (ENG.). 24p. (J). (gr. 2-2). pap. 9.15 *(978-1-4339-5623-2(3),* dca91a45-b799-472a-af9f-067d90747455); lib. bdg. 25.27 *(978-1-4339-5621-8(7),* 0e2c1809-0aac-4642-b241-1f359c5d27f0) Stevens, Gareth Publishing LLLP.

—Banded Sea Snake / Serpiente Marina Rayada, 1 vol. 2011. (Killer Snakes / Serpientes Asesinas Ser.). (SPA & ENG., Illus.). 24p. (J). (gr. 2-2). lib. bdg. 25.27 *(978-1-4339-5625-6(X),* 24527e10-9bc2-47c6-88bd-4fb6f1587372) Stevens, Gareth Publishing LLLP.

Frazel, Ellen. Bull Snakes. 2011. (Snakes Alive Ser.). (ENG., Illus.). 24p. (J). (gr. k-3). lib. bdg. 26.95 *(978-1-60014-613-8(9),* Blastoff! Readers) Bellwether Media.

—Kraits. 2011. (Snakes Alive Ser.). (ENG., Illus.). 24p. (J). (gr. k-3). lib. bdg. 26.95 *(978-1-60014-614-5(7),* Blastoff! Readers) Bellwether Media.

—Tiger Snakes. 2011. (Snakes Alive Ser.). (ENG., Illus.). 24p. (J). (gr. k-3). lib. bdg. 26.95 *(978-1-60014-615-2(5),* Blastoff! Readers) Bellwether Media.

Gallagher, Debbie. Snakes, 1 vol. 2010. (Zoo Animals Ser.). (ENG.). 32p. (gr. 2-2). lib. bdg. 21.27 *(978-0-7614-4749-8(0),* 5cd43b20-2cda-4486-b087-4ba770fe0ef9) Cavendish Square Publishing LLC.

Gambino, Karlie. Cottonmouth, 1 vol. 2011. (Killer Snakes Ser.). (ENG., Illus.). 24p. (J). (gr. 2-2). pap. 9.15 *(978-1-4339-5640-9(3),* 7c3553a8-f078-4e7e-a837-e01e8de62b97); lib. bdg. 25.27 *(978-1-4339-5638-6(1),* 623938d7-647a-4f59-ba34-aae6d6497370) Stevens, Gareth Publishing LLLP.

—Cottonmouth / Serpiente Boca de Algodón, 1 vol. 2011. (Killer Snakes / Serpientes Asesinas Ser.). (SPA & ENG., Illus.). 24p. (J). (gr. 2-2). lib. bdg. 25.27 *(978-1-4339-5642-3(X),* 7752cebb-26bc-45b2-80a6-27ad335fdd8d) Stevens, Gareth Publishing LLLP.

Gangemi, Angelo. Black Mamba, 1 vol. 2011. (Killer Snakes Ser.). (ENG., Illus.). 24p. (J). (gr. 2-2). pap. 9.15 *(978-1-4339-4530-4(4),* f3c15b14-96c2-4b2f-86b4-305931b8b8d6); lib. bdg. 25.27 *(978-1-4339-4529-8(0),* c639b18b-a58d-4503-b61d-7495b4844e1a) Stevens, Gareth Publishing LLLP.

—Black Mamba / Mamba Negra, 1 vol. 2011. (Killer Snakes / Serpientes Asesinas Ser.). (ENG & SPA., Illus.). 24p. (J). (gr. 2-2). 25.27 *(978-1-4339-4533-5(9),* b82b6d70-bf9b-4d3d-b9dc-7750e84facb9) Stevens, Gareth Publishing LLLP.

George, Gale. Sea Snakes, 1 vol. 2016. (Snakes on the Hunt Ser.). (ENG.). 24p. (J). (gr. 3-3). pap. 9.25 *(978-1-4994-2206-1(7),* 042fd11e-d488-4bc0-a8df-9c294f2657a2, PowerKids Pr.) Rosen Publishing Group, Inc., The.

GIANT ANACONDA & OTHER CRYPTIDS. 2010. (ENG., Illus.). 112p. (gr. 5-8). 32.95 *(978-0-7910-9782-3(X),* P179190, Facts On File) Infobase Holdings, Inc.

Gibbons, Gail & Gibbons, Gail. Snakes. 2010. (ENG., Illus.). 32p. (J). (gr. -1-3). pap. 7.99 *(978-0-8234-2300-2(X))* Holiday Hse., Inc.

Gillespie, Katie. A Rattlesnake's World. 2018. (Illus.). 24p. (J). *(978-1-4896-5686-5(3),* AV2 by Weigl) Weigl Pubs., Inc.

Gish, Melissa. Snakes. 2017. (X-Books: Predators Ser.). (ENG., Illus.). 32p. (J). (gr. 3-6). *(978-1-60818-822-2(1),* 20399, Creative Education) Creative Co., The.

—X-Books: Snakes. 2017. (X-Bks.). (ENG., Illus.). 32p. (J). (gr. 3-7). pap. 9.99 *(978-1-62832-425-9(2),* 20400, Creative Paperbacks) Creative Co., The.

Goldish, Meish. Reticulated Python: The World's Longest Snake. 2010. (More SuperSized! Ser.). (Illus.). 24p. (J). (gr. k-3). lib. bdg. 26.99 *(978-1-936087-30-3(8))* Bearport Publishing Co., Inc.

Golkar, Golriz. Anacondas. 2018. (Rain Forest Animals Ser.). (ENG., Illus.). 24p. (J). (gr. 1-1). pap. 8.95 *(978-1-63517-819-7(3),* 1635178193) North Star Editions.

—Anacondas. 2018. (Rain Forest Animals (Cody Koala) Ser.). (ENG., Illus.). 24p. (J). (gr. k-3). lib. bdg. 31.36 *(978-1-5321-6024-0(0),* 28680, Pop! Cody Koala) Pop!

Grack, Rachel. Anacondas. 2019. (Animals of the Rain Forest Ser.). (ENG., Illus.). 24p. (J). (gr. k-3). lib. bdg. 26.95 *(978-1-62617-947-9(6),* Blastoff! Readers) Bellwether Media.

Graham, Audry. Boa Constrictor, 1 vol. 2011. (Killer Snakes Ser.). (ENG., Illus.). 24p. (J). (gr. 2-2). 25.27 *(978-1-4339-4535-9(5),* 8a79077f-87b8-42f2-a962-8f951930140a); pap. 9.15 *(978-1-4339-4536-6(3),* d5c8e76d-3a6a-425d-8844-b46ed0488ab9) Stevens, Gareth Publishing LLLP.

—Boa Constrictor / Boa Constrictora, 1 vol. 2011. (Killer Snakes / Serpientes Asesinas Ser.). (SPA & ENG., Illus.). 24p. (J). (gr. 2-2). 25.27 *(978-1-4339-4539-7(8),* e35d2cff-8bf7-4815-9bb7-6f5dbb567794) Stevens, Gareth Publishing LLLP.

Graham, Chris. So Many Snakes. (Rosen Real Readers Big Bookstm Ser.). (ENG., Illus.). 12p. (gr. 1-2). 2006. 33.50 *(978-1-4042-6214-0(8))* 2005. pap. 5.90 *(978-0-8239-8197-7(5),* 0de2054f-9df9-4d28-b7da-d7981a08c8a3) Rosen Publishing Group, Inc., The.

Gray, Leon. King Cobra: The World's Longest Venomous Snake. 2013. (Even More SuperSized! Ser.). 24p. (J). (gr. k-3). lib. bdg. 26.99 *(978-1-61772-732-0(6))* Bearport Publishing Co., Inc.

Gray, Susan H. Snakes Shed Their Skin. 2015. (Tell Me Why Library). (ENG., Illus.). 24p. (J). (gr. 2-5). 29.21 *(978-1-63362-616-4(4),* 206648) Cherry Lake Publishing.

Green, Emily. Snakes. 2010. (Backyard Wildlife Ser.). (ENG., Illus.). 24p. (J). (gr. k-3). lib. bdg. 26.95 *(978-1-60014-446-2(2),* Blastoff! Readers) Bellwether Media.

Green, Jen. Snakes. 2010. (Amazing Animal Hunters Ser.). (ENG., Illus.). 32p. (J). (gr. 3-5). pap. 8.95 *(978-1-926722-51-1(5),* 17202); lib. bdg. 28.50 *(978-1-60753-047-3(3),* 17201) Amicus.

Gregory, Helen. All about Snakes & Lizards, 1 vol. 2011. (Wonder Readers Fluent Level Ser.). (ENG.). 16p. (gr. -1-1). (J). pap. 6.25 *(978-1-4296-7796-7(1),* 117968); pap. 35.94 *(978-1-4296-8068-4(7))* Capstone. (Capstone Pr.).

Gregory, Josh. Nature's Children: Rattlesnakes. 2015. (ENG.). 48p. (J). pap. 6.95 *(978-0-531-21186-1(X),* Orchard Bks.) Scholastic Library Publishing.

Guidone, Julie. Snakes, 1 vol. 2009. (Animals That Live in the Rain Forest Ser.). (ENG.). 24p. (gr. 1-1). (J). lib. bdg. 25.27 *(978-1-4339-0027-3(0),* b1abb875-5cf3-4160-a1f7-5463d4c84d9d); pap. 9.15 *(978-1-4339-0109-6(9),* 20095e1d-00e9-472a-a2ce-3fc6ade8a2b8) Stevens, Gareth Publishing LLLP. (Weekly Reader Leveled Readers).

—Snakes / Serpientes, 1 vol. 2009. (Animals That Live in the Rain Forest / Animales de la Selva Ser.). (SPA & ENG.). 24p. (gr. 1-1). pap. 9.15 *(978-1-4339-0116-4(1),* bd4056b2-a241-439d-a7c4-0b547fc34657); lib. bdg. 25.27 *(978-1-4339-0066-2(1),* c7aef450-598d-49b0-977d-e41158b78d35) Stevens, Gareth Publishing LLLP. (Weekly Reader Leveled Readers).

Gunzi, Christiane. My Best Book of Snakes. 2020. (Best Book Of Ser.). (ENG.). 32p. (J). pap. 7.99 *(978-0-7534-7538-6(3),* 900211378, Kingfisher) Roaring Brook Pr.

Hamilton, S. L. Anacondas. 2018. (Xtreme Snakes Ser.). (ENG., Illus.). 32p. (J). (gr. 3-9). lib. bdg. 32.79 *(978-1-5321-1599-8(7),* 28774, Abdo & Daughters) ABDO Publishing Co.

—Cobras. 2018. (Xtreme Snakes Ser.). (ENG., Illus.). 32p. (J). (gr. 3-9). lib. bdg. 32.79 *(978-1-5321-1600-1(4),* 28776, Abdo & Daughters) ABDO Publishing Co.

—Copperheads. 2018. (Xtreme Snakes Ser.). (ENG., Illus.). 32p. (J). (gr. 3-9). lib. bdg. 32.79 *(978-1-5321-1601-8(2),* 28778, Abdo & Daughters) ABDO Publishing Co.

—Mambas. 2018. (Xtreme Snakes Ser.). (ENG., Illus.). 32p. (J). (gr. 3-9). lib. bdg. 32.79 *(978-1-5321-1602-5(0),* 28780, Abdo & Daughters) ABDO Publishing Co.

—Pythons. 2018. (Xtreme Snakes Ser.). (ENG., Illus.). 32p. (J). (gr. 3-9). lib. bdg. 32.79 *(978-1-5321-1603-2(9),* 28782, Abdo & Daughters) ABDO Publishing Co.

—Rattlesnakes. 2018. (Xtreme Snakes Ser.). (ENG., Illus.). 32p. (J). (gr. 3-9). lib. bdg. 32.79 *(978-1-5321-1604-9(7),* 28784, Abdo & Daughters) ABDO Publishing Co.

—Snakes. 2010. (Xtreme Predators Ser.). (ENG.). 32p. (J). (gr. 3-9). lib. bdg. 32.79 *(978-1-60453-994-3(1),* 15732, Abdo & Daughters) ABDO Publishing Co.

Hamilton, Sue. Bitten by a Rattlesnake, 1 vol. 2010. (Close Encounters of the Wild Kind Ser.). (ENG.). 32p. (J). (gr. 5-9). 32.79 *(978-1-60453-930-1(5),* 310, Abdo & Daughters) ABDO Publishing Co.

Hansen, Grace. Green Anacondas, 1 vol. 2016. (Super Species Ser.). (ENG., Illus.). 24p. (J). (gr. -1-2). lib. bdg. 32.79 *(978-1-68080-546-8(0),* 21372, Abdo Kids) ABDO Publishing Co.

—Snakes, 1 vol. 2014. (Reptiles (Abdo Kids) Ser.). (ENG.). 24p. (J). (gr. -1-2). lib. bdg. 32.79 *(978-1-62970-061-8(4),* 1614, Abdo Kids) ABDO Publishing Co.

Hardyman, Robyn. Snakes. 2008. (World of Animals Ser.). (ENG.). 32p. (J). (gr. 2-4). 31.35 *(978-1-933834-32-0(3),* 16826) Brown Bear Bks.

Harris, Terrell. Nonvenomous Snakes, 1 vol. 2010. (Slimy, Scaly, Deadly Reptiles & Amphibians Ser.). (ENG., Illus.). 32p. (J). (gr. 3-4). pap. 11.50 *(978-1-4339-3433-9(7),* 842720f5-caa2-46ce-9f55-b7a0f1c3495c); lib. bdg. 28.67 *(978-1-4339-3432-2(9),* a288c10b-fe8a-4bb5-b663-5fcdaa5d54bc) Stevens, Gareth Publishing LLLP. (Gareth Stevens Learning Library).

—Venomous Snakes, 1 vol. 2010. (Slimy, Scaly, Deadly Reptiles & Amphibians Ser.). (ENG., Illus.). 32p. (J). (gr. 3-4). pap. 11.50 *(978-1-4339-3430-8(2),* bb30d726-4506-4004-9718-7515d6af9d0c); lib. bdg. 28.67 *(978-1-4339-3429-2(9),* c6407d40-cd4e-46d5-bb30-31bd0cfdd8a3) Stevens, Gareth Publishing LLLP. (Gareth Stevens Learning Library).

Harris, Tim. Snakes. 2008. (Nature's Children Ser.). (Illus.). 52p. (J). *(978-0-7172-6244-1(8))* Grolier, Ltd.

Harrison, Paul. Snakes. (Up Close Ser.). 24p. (gr. 3-3). 2009. 47.90 *(978-1-60854-703-6(5))* 2006. (ENG., Illus.). (J). lib. bdg. 28.93 *(978-1-4042-3764-3(X),* ba1eb754-45b8-4dd1-bf8b-9b52cdd717eb) Rosen Publishing Group, Inc., The. (PowerKids Pr.).

Hart, Joyce. Snakes, 1 vol. 2009. (Great Pets Ser.). (ENG.). 48p. (gr. 3-3). lib. bdg. 32.64 *(978-0-7614-2996-8(4),* cbcd11b0-5a23-44bc-a513-3a076c8f5d8f) Cavendish Square Publishing LLC.

Heos, Bridget. Do You Really Want a Snake? Longhi, Katya, illus. 2015. (Do You Really Want a Pet? Ser.). (ENG.). 24p. (J). (gr. 1-4). lib. bdg. 19.95 *(978-1-60753-751-9(6),* 15281) Amicus.

Herrington, Lisa M. It's a Good Thing There Are Snakes (Rookie Read-About Science: It's a Good Thing...) 2014. (Rookie Read-About Science Ser.). (ENG.). 32p. (J). (gr. 1-2). pap. 5.95 *(978-0-531-22833-3(9),* Children's Pr.) Scholastic Library Publishing.

—Rookie Read-About Science: It's a Good Thing There Are Snakes (Library Edition) 2014. (Rookie Read-About(tm) Science — It's a Good Thing... Ser.). (ENG.). 32p. (J). lib. bdg. 25.00 *(978-0-531-22361-1(2))* Scholastic Library Publishing.

Hibbert, Clare. If You Were a Snake. 2013. (If You Were A... Ser.). 32p. (gr. 2-5). 31.35 *(978-1-59920-963-0(2))* Black Rabbit Bks.

Higgins, Melissa. Anacondas, 1 vol. 2013. (Snakes Ser.). (ENG.). 24p. (J). (gr. -1-2). lib. bdg. 27.32 *(978-1-4765-2066-7(6),* 122802, Capstone Pr.) Capstone.

—Cobras, 1 vol. 2013. (Snakes Ser.). (ENG., Illus.). 24p. (J). (gr. -1-2). lib. bdg. 27.32 *(978-1-4765-2070-4(4),* 122804, Capstone Pr.) Capstone.

Hileman, Jane & Taylor, Trace. Rattlesnakes. 2013. (Animal Behaviors Ser.). (ENG.). 32p. (J). (gr. k-2). pap. 8.00 *(978-1-61541-249-5(2))* American Reading Co.

Hinton, Kerry. Pythons. 2009. (Really Wild Life of Animals Ser.). 24p. (gr. 3-4). 42.50 *(978-1-60854-207-9(6),* PowerKids Pr.) Rosen Publishing Group, Inc., The.

Hirsch, Rebecca E. King Cobras: Hooded Venomous Reptiles. 2015. (Comparing Animal Traits Ser.). (ENG., Illus.). 32p. (J). (gr. 2-4). 26.65 *(978-1-4677-7983-8(0),* 7389e990-5d96-4f06-a2f1-bb1f8d8e6522, Lerner Pubns.) Lerner Publishing Group.

Hirschmann, Kris. Deadliest Snakes. 2016. (ENG.). 80p. (J). (gr. 5-12). *(978-1-68282-056-8(4))* ReferencePoint Pr., Inc.

Hofer, Charles C. Snakebite! Antivenom & a Global Health Crisis. 2018. (ENG., Illus.). 104p. (YA). (gr. 6-12). 37.32 *(978-1-5124-8373-4(7),* 355e5a84-7f5a-44b4-938d-9709d29fae6a, Twenty-First Century Bks.) Lerner Publishing Group.

Hoff, Mary. Snakes. 2006. (Wild World of Animals Ser.). (Illus.). 31p. (J). (gr. 3-5). 18.95 *(978-1-58341-436-1(3),* Creative Education) Creative Co., The.

Hoffmeister, Noelle. Amazing Animals: Venomous Snakes: Fractions & Decimals (Grade 4) 2017. (Mathematics in the Real World Ser.). (ENG., Illus.). 32p. (gr. 4-5). pap. 11.99 *(978-1-4258-5557-4(1))* Teacher Created Materials, Inc.

Holmes, Parker. Amazing Snakes of the Northeast, 1 vol. 2014. (Amazing Snakes Ser.). (ENG., Illus.). 24p. (J). (gr. 3-3). 25.27 *(978-1-4777-6487-9(9),* 3da766bb-d51b-487c-8a31-6723df69a43d, PowerKids Pr.) Rosen Publishing Group, Inc., The.

—Amazing Snakes of the Northwest, 1 vol. 2014. (Amazing Snakes Ser.). (ENG., Illus.). 24p. (J). (gr. 3-3). 25.27 *(978-1-4777-6507-4(7),* 9f49225d-95e9-4043-9f95-c82c66d72424, PowerKids Pr.) Rosen Publishing Group, Inc., The.

—Amazing Snakes of the Southeast, 1 vol. 2014. (Amazing Snakes Ser.). (ENG., Illus.). 24p. (J). (gr. 3-3). 25.27 *(978-1-4777-6496-1(8),* 4894daa7-53fb-4092-a6ac-5d9a8c678483, PowerKids Pr.) Rosen Publishing Group, Inc., The.

—Amazing Snakes of the Southwest & West Coast, 1 vol. 2014. (Amazing Snakes Ser.). (ENG., Illus.). 24p. (J). (gr. 3-3). pap. 9.25 *(978-1-4777-6503-6(4),* 3c2b5392-5c7e-4477-8d62-456b0b82e1ce, PowerKids Pr.) Rosen Publishing Group, Inc., The.

—Pythons on the Hunt. 2017. (Searchlight Books (tm) — Predators Ser.). (ENG., Illus.). 32p. (J). (gr. 3-5). lib. bdg. 30.65 *(978-1-5124-3396-8(9),* 3d5b89d5-e776-475a-8477-e98576be272d, Lerner Pubns.) Lerner Publishing Group.

Holub, Joan. Why Do Snakes Hiss? And Other Questions about Snakes, Lizards, & Turtles. DiVito, Anna, illus. 2004. (Penguin Young Readers, Level 3 Ser.). 48p. (J). (gr. 1-3). mass mkt. 4.99 *(978-0-14-240105-7(6),* Penguin Young Readers) Penguin Young Readers Group.

Honders, Jamie. Coral Snake, 1 vol. 2011. (Killer Snakes Ser.). (ENG.). 24p. (J). (gr. 2-2). pap. 9.15 *(978-1-4339-5634-8(9),* 01089e15-f328-40d3-8d10-4ffd0611a5bd); lib. bdg. 25.27 *(978-1-4339-5632-4(2),* 659b1681-5897-48a0-a34c-cf228c00eef2) Stevens, Gareth Publishing LLLP.

Howard, Melanie A. Copperheads. 2012. (Wild about Snakes Ser.). (ENG.). 32p. (gr. 3-4). pap. 47.70 *(978-1-4296-8513-9(1),* Capstone Pr.) Capstone.

—Corn Snakes. 2012. (Wild about Snakes Ser.). (ENG.). 32p. (gr. 3-4). pap. 47.70 *(978-1-4296-8514-6(X),* Capstone Pr.) Capstone.

—Wild about Snakes. 2012. (Wild about Snakes Ser.). (ENG.). 32p. (gr. 3-4). pap. 477.00 *(978-1-4296-8516-0(6),* Capstone Pr.) Capstone.

Huggins-Cooper, Lynn. Slithering Snakes. 2006. (Killer Nature! Ser.). (Illus.). 32p. (J). (gr. 4-7). lib. bdg. 28.50 *(978-1-58340-934-3(3),* 1262609) Black Rabbit Bks.

Humphrey, Natalie. 20 Fun Facts about Rattlesnakes, 1 vol. 2020. (Fun Fact File: North American Animals Ser.). (ENG.). 32p. (gr. 2-3). pap. 11.50 *(978-1-5382-5752-4(1),* b15c5767-c895-4eef-9ae6-cc930f35dfec) Stevens, Gareth Publishing LLLP.

Jackson, Tom. Deadly Snakes, 1 vol. 2010. (Dangerous Animals Ser.). (ENG., Illus.). 32p. (gr. 2-4). (J). pap. 11.50 *(978-1-4339-4041-5(8),* ac2b13f1-220b-4b7d-ace6-41728a3bb6c5, Gareth Stevens Learning Library); (YA). lib. bdg. 29.27 *(978-1-4339-4040-8(X),* 2c9953a3-b0f6-4202-b90c-e79470f35050) Stevens, Gareth Publishing LLLP.

—Inside the Mind of a Deadly Cobra, 1 vol. 2012. (Animal Instincts Ser.). (ENG., Illus.). 32p. (J). (gr. 3-3). pap. 11.00 *(978-1-4488-7076-9(3),* 89d4c6e6-dc3d-460f-bc49-e53fcc4d9bf9); lib. bdg. 28.93 *(978-1-4488-7033-2(X),* 3659dfb1-7499-4abb-8507-78fc8680ac01) Rosen Publishing Group, Inc., The. (PowerKids Pr.).

—Snake Bite. 2008. (ENG., Illus.). 32p. (J). (gr. 5-9). pap. *(978-0-7787-3794-0(2))* Crabtree Publishing Co.

James, Lincoln. Death Adder, 1 vol. 2011. (Killer Snakes Ser.). (ENG., Illus.). 24p. (J). (gr. 2-2). 25.27 *(978-1-4339-4541-0(X),* 2300fecc-0024-48c0-9e85-5738e2c710d7); pap. 9.15 *(978-1-4339-4542-7(8),* 9575c2bb-e2df-42c2-b287-ca395ef3bc2c) Stevens, Gareth Publishing LLLP.

—Death Adder / Víboras de la Muerte, 1 vol. 2011. (Killer Snakes / Serpientes Asesinas Ser.). (ENG & SPA., Illus.). 24p. (J). (gr. 2-2). 25.27 *(978-1-4339-4545-8(2),* 864610b2-da39-4a99-b2e7-4eba4dac26f8) Stevens, Gareth Publishing LLLP.

Johnson, Rebecca. Super Snakes, 1 vol. 2017. (Reptile Adventures Ser.). (ENG.). 24p. (J). (gr. 1-2). 26.27 *(978-1-5081-9357-9(6),* fc6bd2db-b4fa-4f18-868b-fd1c84e5ab37); pap. 9.25 *(978-1-5081-9361-6(4),* e049b54c-16a2-4e1a-bbc6-b31473c762c4) Rosen Publishing Group, Inc., The. (Windmill Bks.).

Johnson, Sylvia A. Cobras. 2007. (Nature Watch Ser.). (ENG., Illus.). 48p. (gr. 4-8). lib. bdg. 27.93 *(978-1-57505-871-9(5),* Lerner Pubns.) Lerner Publishing Group.

Jones, Cede. King Cobra, 1 vol. 2011. (Killer Snakes Ser.). (ENG., Illus.). 24p. (J). (gr. 2-2). lib. bdg. 25.27 *(978-1-4339-4553-3(3),* e6f98fa5-58a2-4384-a768-ce1a19addd72) Stevens, Gareth Publishing LLLP.

—King Cobra / Cobra Real, 1 vol. 2011. (Killer Snakes / Serpientes Asesinas Ser.). (ENG & SPA., Illus.). 24p. (J). (gr. 2-2). 25.27 *(978-1-4339-4557-1(6),* 74d99ce9-d9a9-4bc2-991c-858fae19489b) Stevens, Gareth Publishing LLLP.

Jones, Charles M. Superlong Anacondas, 1 vol. 2017. (Great Big Animals Ser.). (ENG.). 24p. (J). (gr. k-k). pap. 9.15 *(978-1-5382-0915-8(2),* 23a353c1-8dc0-48ab-8763-0e1dcac295f9); lib. bdg. 25.27 *(978-1-5382-0917-2(9),* 715b7663-3110-4bcc-958c-dbd0088cb08d) Stevens, Gareth Publishing LLLP.

Jordan, Apple. Guess Who Bites, 1 vol. 2nd rev. ed. 2012. (Guess Who? Ser.). (ENG., Illus.). 32p. (gr. k-1). 24.07 *(978-1-60870-428-6(9),* 02ae256c-2692-45c3-9c58-f44aa50d107e) Cavendish Square Publishing LLC.

Killer Snakes, 16 vols., Set. Incl. Anaconda. Burke, Juliet. 25.27 *(978-1-4339-4523-6(1),* 685bebcc-fe03-411f-9a40-6910fdec6c99); Black Mamba. Gangemi, Angelo. lib. bdg. 25.27 *(978-1-4339-4529-8(0),* c639b18b-a58d-4503-b61d-7495b4844e1a); Boa Constrictor. Graham, Audry. 25.27 *(978-1-4339-4535-9(5),* 8a79077f-87b8-42f2-a962-8f951930140a); Death Adder. James, Lincoln. 25.27 *(978-1-4339-4541-0(X),* 2300fecc-0024-48c0-9e85-5738e2c710d7); Diamondback Rattlesnake. Leigh, Autumn. lib. bdg. 25.27 *(978-1-4339-4547-2(9),* 81d2b11d-f72d-41ab-8064-70b415b45db9); King Cobra. Jones, Cede. lib. bdg. 25.27 *(978-1-4339-4553-3(3),* e6f98fa5-58a2-4384-a768-ce1a19addd72); Python. Allyn, Daisy. lib. bdg. 25.27 *(978-1-4339-4559-5(2),* 7958905b-92e4-4f9c-9c35-8cd53b677248); Taipan. Worthy, Shanya. lib. bdg. 25.27 *(978-1-4339-4565-6(7),* a0a9819a-5903-4156-b25f-8e66446d8bf1); (J). (gr. 2-2). (Killer Snakes Ser.). (ENG., Illus.). 24p. 2011. Set lib. bdg. 202.16 *(978-1-4339-4953-1(9),* ee0f5b0c-266e-4dd7-ba08-b0f003d545fd) Stevens, Gareth Publishing LLLP.

Kim, Carol. Pit Viper. 2018. (World's Coolest Snakes Ser.). (ENG., Illus.). 32p. (gr. 4-8). lib. bdg. 32.79 *(978-1-64156-482-3(2),* 9781641564823) Rourke Educational Media.

Klepeis, Alicia. The Boomslang Snake. 2017. (Toxic Creatures Ser.). 32p. (gr. 3-3). pap. 63.48 *(978-1-5026-2581-6(4),* Cavendish Square) Cavendish Square Publishing LLC.

Klepeis, Alicia Z. Snakes Are Awesome. 2018. (Animals Are Awesome Ser.). (ENG., Illus.). 32p. (J). (gr. 3-6). 32.80 *(978-1-63235-440-2(3),* 13818, 12-Story Library) Bookstaves, LLC.

Lanser, Amanda. Boa Constrictor Paperback. 2013. (Great Predators Ser.). (ENG., Illus.). 48p. (J). (gr. 4-8). pap. 18.50 *(978-1-62403-010-9(6),* 10786) ABDO Publishing Co.

Lawrence, Ellen. Cottonmouth. 2016. (Swamp Things: Animal Life in a Wetland Ser.). (ENG.). 24p. (J). (gr. -1-3). 26.99 *(978-1-944102-52-4(3))* Bearport Publishing Co., Inc.

—Green Anaconda. 2016. (Apex Predators of the Amazon Rain Forest Ser.). (ENG., Illus.). 24p. (J). (gr. -1-3). 26.99 *(978-1-68402-031-7(X))* Bearport Publishing Co., Inc.

—A Snake's Life. 2012. (Animal Diaries: Life Cycles Ser.). 24p. (J). (gr. -1-3). lib. bdg. 26.99 *(978-1-61772-416-9(5))* Bearport Publishing Co., Inc.

Leigh, Autumn. Diamondback Rattlesnake, 1 vol. 2011. (Killer Snakes Ser.). (ENG., Illus.). 24p. (J). (gr. 2-2). pap. 9.15 *(978-1-4339-4548-9(7),* ab4673ea-db81-499f-8c91-e51ee620618b); lib. bdg. 25.27 *(978-1-4339-4547-2(9),* 81d2b11d-f72d-41ab-8064-70b415b45db9) Stevens, Gareth Publishing LLLP.

—Diamondback Rattlesnake / Cascabel Diamantada, 1 vol. 2011. (Killer Snakes / Serpientes Asesinas Ser.). (ENG & SPA., Illus.). 24p. (J). (gr. 2-2). 25.27 *(978-1-4339-4551-9(7),* f6fb432b-2949-476a-bdfa-090405f970e1) Stevens, Gareth Publishing LLLP.

Linde, Barbara M. Snakes Are Not Pets!, 1 vol. 2013. (When Pets Attack! Ser.). (Illus.). 32p. (J). (gr. 3-4). (ENG.). 29.27 *(978-1-4339-9298-8(1),* f9e659de-fa0b-49f0-8978-37d6333e3a4e); pap. 63.00 *(978-1-4339-9300-8(7))* Stevens, Gareth Publishing LLLP.

Lukeman, Noah. Do Snakes Wear Socks? 2015. (ENG., Illus.). 24p. (J). pap. 5.99 *(978-1-63291-413-2(1))* Morgan Rice Bks.

Lynch, Michelle & Taylor, Trace. Cobras. Taylor, Trace, illus. 2015. (2G Predator Animals Ser.). (ENG., Illus.). 24p. (J). (gr. k-2). pap. 8.00 *(978-1-61541-504-5(1))* American Reading Co.

Lynch, Seth. Snakes at the Zoo, 1 vol. 2019. (Zoo Animals Ser.). (ENG.). 24p. (gr. k-k). pap. 9.15 *(978-1-5382-3946-9(9),* e761849a-de6b-44ea-a255-292b30a3a695) Stevens, Gareth Publishing LLLP.

Lynette, Rachel. Anacondas, 1 vol. 2013. (Monsters of the Animal Kingdom Ser.). (ENG., Illus.). 24p. (J). (gr. 2-3). pap. 9.25 *(978-1-4488-9719-3(X),* 02d6a6a9-9601-4ee8-88cd-6ec5f37568c1); lib. bdg. 26.27 *(978-1-4488-9631-8(2),* e46dc170-8205-403c-b7a8-2162c9004b68) Rosen Publishing Group, Inc., The. (PowerKids Pr.).

MacLaine, James. Snakes. Parker, Paul & Moor, Becka, illus. 2014. (Usborne Beginners Ser.). (ENG.). 32p. (J). (gr. 1-4). 4.99 *(978-0-7945-2686-3(1),* Usborne) EDC Publishing.

Macleod, Steve. Anacondas. 2011. (J). *(978-1-61690-755-6(X)); (978-1-61690-762-4(2))* Weigl Pubs., Inc.

Markle, Sandra. Rattlesnakes. 2009. (Animal Predators Ser.). (ENG., Illus.). 40p. (J). (gr. 3-6). 26.65 *(978-1-58013-539-9(0),* 35021226-750f-493f-9a4b-50df3b419125, Lerner Pubns.) Lerner Publishing Group.

—Snakes: Biggest! Littlest! Mcdonald, Joe, photos by. 2011. (Biggest! Littlest! Ser.). (ENG., Illus.). 32p. (J). (gr. k-2). pap. 10.95 *(978-1-59078-874-5(5),* Astra Young Readers) Astra Publishing Hse.

Marsico, Katie. King Cobras. 2013. (Nature's Children Ser.). (ENG.). 48p. (J). pap. 6.95 *(978-0-531-24304-6(4),* Children's Pr.) Scholastic Library Publishing.

McDonald, Mary Ann. Boas. 2015. (Animals of the Rain Forest Ser.). (ENG.). 24p. (J). (gr. 2-5). 32.79 *(978-1-63143-701-4(1),* 208515) Child's World, Inc, The.

McDonnell, Mary Rose. Sorting with Snakes, 1 vol. 2013. (Animal Math Ser.). (ENG.). 24p. (J). (gr. 1-2). 25.27 *(978-1-4339-9328-2(7),* 67bc28f8-0d19-4fbb-8d9c-e1064f7d6a5d) Stevens, Gareth Publishing LLLP.

McFadden, Jesse. Watch Out for Rattlesnakes!, 1 vol., 1. 2015. (Wild Backyard Animals Ser.). (ENG., Illus.). 24p. (J). (gr. 3-4). pap. 9.25 *(978-1-5081-4263-8(7),* 6c91a5d2-b6a9-42d4-a9da-d9c215006a9b, PowerKids Pr.) Rosen Publishing Group, Inc., The.

Meachen Rau, Dana. Guess Who Hisses, 1 vol. 2009. (Guess Who? Ser.). (ENG.). 32p. (gr. k-1). pap. 9.23 *(978-0-7614-3553-2(0),* 6b3bb1f3-6265-4ba4-a098-fa5fd28e44a6) Cavendish Square Publishing LLC.

Meadows, Graham & Vial, Claire. Introducing Snakes. 2004. (ENG., Illus.). 24p. (J). (gr. 2-3). pap. 7.47 net. *(978-0-7685-1637-1(4),* Dominie Elementary) Savvas Learning Co.

Meister, Cari. Pythons. 2015. (Illus.). 24p. (J). lib. bdg. *(978-1-62031-198-1(4),* Bullfrog Bks.) Jump! Inc.

Mitchell, Melanie. Snakes. 2003. (First Step Nonfiction — Animal Life Cycles Ser.). (ENG., Illus.). 24p. (J). (gr. k-2). pap. 6.99 *(978-0-8225-4607-8(8),* 455aef9f-1edf-4d53-a2a0-47259fe5b6a1) Lerner Publishing Group.

Mitchell, Melanie S. Snakes. 2005. (First Step Nonfiction Ser.). (Illus.). 24p. (gr. k-2). lib. bdg. 17.27 *(978-0-8225-4606-1(X))* Lerner Publishing Group.

Morgan, Sally. Lizards & Snakes. 2012. (Pets Plus Ser.). 32p. (gr. 3-6). lib. bdg. 31.35 *(978-1-59920-704-9(4))* Black Rabbit Bks.

Mulks, Mitchell. Zonata: The California Mountain Kingsnake. Merker, Gerold, photos by. 2004. (Illus.). 64p. pap. 15.95 *(978-0-9760770-0-8(0))* LM Digital.

Munro, Roxie. Slithery Snakes, 0 vols. Munro, Roxie, illus. 2013. (ENG.). 40p. (J). (gr. 1-5). 17.99 *(978-1-4778-1658-5(5),* 9781477816585, Two Lions) Amazon Publishing.

Murray, Julie. Black Mambas. 2017. (Slithering Snakes Ser.). (ENG., Illus.). 24p. (J). (gr. k-4). lib. bdg. 31.36 *(978-1-5321-2071-8(0),* 26754, Abdo Zoom-Dash) ABDO Publishing Co.

—Boomslangs. 2017. (Slithering Snakes Ser.). (ENG., Illus.). 24p. (J). (gr. k-4). lib. bdg. 31.36 *(978-1-5321-2072-5(9),* 26755, Abdo Zoom-Dash) ABDO Publishing Co.

—Copperheads. 2019. (Animal Kingdom Ser.). (ENG., Illus.). 32p. (J). (gr. 2-5). lib. bdg. 34.21 *(978-1-5321-1624-7(1),* 32359, Big Buddy Bks.) ABDO Publishing Co.

—Gaboon Vipers. 2017. (Slithering Snakes Ser.). (ENG., Illus.). 24p. (J). (gr. k-4). lib. bdg. 31.36 *(978-1-5321-2073-2(7),* 26756, Abdo Zoom-Dash) ABDO Publishing Co.

—King Cobras. (Animal Kingdom Ser.). (ENG., Illus.). (J). 2019. 32p. (gr. 2-5). lib. bdg. 34.21 *(978-1-5321-1642-1(X),* 32395, Big Buddy Bks.) 2017. 24p. (gr. k-4). lib. bdg. 31.36 *(978-1-5321-2074-9(5),* 26757, Abdo Zoom-Dash) ABDO Publishing Co.

—Pythons. 2019. (Animal Kingdom Ser.). (ENG.). 32p. (J). (gr. 2-5). lib. bdg. 34.21 *(978-1-5321-1650-6(0),* 32411, Big Buddy Bks.) ABDO Publishing Co.

—Rattlesnakes. (Animal Kingdom Ser.). (ENG.). (J). 2019. 32p. (gr. 2-5). lib. bdg. 34.21 *(978-1-5321-1651-3(9),* 32413, Big Buddy Bks.) 2017. (Illus.). 24p. (gr. k-4). lib. bdg. 31.36 *(978-1-5321-2075-6(3),* 26758, Abdo Zoom-Dash) ABDO Publishing Co.

—Tiger Snakes. 2017. (Slithering Snakes Ser.). (ENG., Illus.). 24p. (J). (gr. k-4). lib. bdg. 31.36 *(978-1-5321-2076-3(1),* 26759, Abdo Zoom-Dash) ABDO Publishing Co.

National Geographic Editors. Creepy Crawly Collection. 2012. lib. bdg. 18.40 *(978-0-606-26822-6(7))* Turtleback.

Nichols, Catherine. Emerald Boas: Rain Forest Undercover. 2010. (Disappearing Acts Ser.). (Illus.). 24p. (J). (gr. k-3). lib. bdg. 26.99 *(978-1-936087-41-9(3))* Bearport Publishing Co., Inc.

Oachs, Emily Rose. Burmese Pythons. 2014. (Amazing Snakes! Ser.). (ENG., Illus.). 24p. (J). (gr. 3-7). lib. bdg. 26.95 *(978-1-62617-089-6(4),* Epic Bks.) Bellwether Media.

—Green Anacondas. 2014. (Amazing Snakes! Ser.). (ENG., Illus.). 24p. (J). (gr. 3-7). lib. bdg. 26.95 *(978-1-62617-093-3(2),* Epic Bks.) Bellwether Media.

—Spitting Cobras. 2014. (Amazing Snakes! Ser.). (ENG., Illus.). 24p. (J). (gr. 3-7). lib. bdg. 26.95 *(978-1-62617-095-7(9),* Epic Bks.) Bellwether Media.

O'Donnell, Jessica. Egyptian Cobra, 1 vol. 2011. (Killer Snakes Ser.). (ENG., Illus.). 24p. (J). (gr. 2-2). pap. 9.15 *(978-1-4339-5645-4(4),* 1f436c11-212d-43cf-bf99-d59d4f7e2c18); lib. bdg. 25.27 *(978-1-4339-5643-0(8),* 0973e6ef-88cd-4bad-be83-2ef8e1175442) Stevens, Gareth Publishing LLLP.

—Egyptian Cobra / Cobra Egipcia, 1 vol. 2011. (Killer Snakes / Serpientes Asesinas Ser.). (SPA & ENG., Illus.). 24p. (J). (gr. 2-2). 25.27 *(978-1-4339-5647-8(0),* 77509c2c-bf71-4284-a985-d430a591d4b0) Stevens, Gareth Publishing LLLP.

O'Donnell, Kerri. Snakes of the World: Learning to Use Inches & Feet to Measure an Object, 1 vol. 2010. (Math for the REAL World Ser.). (ENG.). 16p. (gr. 2-3). pap. 7.05 *(978-0-8239-8874-7(0),* 4fd2d959-fad1-4ea7-87fe-2b2735328351, Rosen Classroom) Rosen Publishing Group, Inc., The.

O'Hare, Ted. Boas. 2005. (Amazing Snakes Discovery Library Ser.). (Illus.). 24p. (gr. 1-4). 14.95 *(978-1-59515-143-8(5))* Rourke Educational Media.

Ohare, Ted. Boas. Rourke Publishing Staff, ed. 2009. 24p. (J). pap. 3.99 *(978-0-8249-5147-4(6),* Ideals Pubns.) Worthy Publishing.

O'Hare, Ted. Cobras. 2005. (Amazing Snakes Discovery Library Ser.). (Illus.). 24p. (J). (gr. 1-4). 14.95 *(978-1-59515-144-5(3))* Rourke Educational Media.

Ohare, Ted. Cobras. Rourke Publishing Staff, ed. 2009. 24p. (J). pap. 3.99 *(978-0-8249-5148-1(4),* Ideals Pubns.) Worthy Publishing.

O'Hare, Ted. Copperheads. 2005. (Amazing Snakes Discovery Library Ser.). (Illus.). 24p. (gr. 1-4). 14.95 *(978-1-59515-145-2(1))* Rourke Educational Media.

—Coral Snakes. 2005. (Amazing Snakes Discovery Library). (Illus.). 24p. (gr. 1-4). 14.95 *(978-1-59515-142-1(7))* Rourke Educational Media.

—Mambas. 2005. (Amazing Snakes Discovery Library Ser.). (Illus.). 24p. (gr. 1-4). 14.95 *(978-1-59515-147-6(8))* Rourke Educational Media.

—Pythons. 2005. (Amazing Snakes Discovery Library Ser.). (Illus.). 24p. (gr. 1-4). 14.95 *(978-1-59515-148-3(6))* Rourke Educational Media.

Ohare, Ted. Rattlesnakes. Rourke Publishing Staff, ed. 2009. 24p. (J). pap. 3.99 *(978-0-8249-5146-7(6)*, Ideals Pubns.) Worthy Publishing.

Orr, Tamra B. Reticulated Python. 2015. (21st Century Skills Library: Exploring Our Rainforests Ser.). (ENG., Illus.). 32p. (gr. 3-6). 32.07 *(978-1-63188-979-0(6)*, 205828) Cherry Lake Publishing.

Osborne, Mary Pope & Boyce, Natalie Pope. Snakes & Other Reptiles: A Nonfiction Companion to Magic Tree House Merlin Mission #17: a Crazy Day with Cobras. Murdocca, Sal, illus. 2011. (Magic Tree House (R) Fact Tracker Ser.: 23). 128p. (J). (gr. 2-5). 6.99 *(978-0-375-86011-9(8)*, Random Hse. Bks. for Young Readers) Random Hse. Children's Bks.

O'Shaughnessy, Ruth. Snakes after Dark, 1 vol. 2015. (Animals of the Night Ser.). (ENG.). 32p. (gr. 3-4). pap. 11.52 *(978-0-7660-6766-0(1)*, ba5a2650-d6f9-49cd-9c02-8d21b49d54c4); (Illus.). 26.93 *(978-0-7660-6768-4(8)*, 43c9ee6d-d368-49a5-9dcf-9bf4e029386b) Enslow Publishing, LLC.

Owings, Lisa. The Black Mamba. 2013. (Nature's Deadliest Ser.). (ENG., Illus.). 24p. (J). (gr. 3-8). lib. bdg. 27.95 *(978-1-60014-877-4(8)*, Pilot Bks.) Bellwether Media.

—The King Cobra. 2012. (Nature's Deadliest Ser.). (ENG., Illus.). 24p. (J). (gr. 3-8). lib. bdg. 27.95 *(978-1-60014-743-2(7)*, Pilot Bks.) Bellwether Media.

—Snake Attack. 2012. (Animal Attacks Ser.). (ENG., Illus.). 24p. (J). (gr. 3-7). lib. bdg. 26.95 *(978-1-60014-791-3(7)*, Torque Bks.) Bellwether Media.

Pallotta, Jerry. Komodo Dragon vs. King Cobra (Who Would Win?) Bolster, Rob, illus. 2016. (Who Would Win? Ser.). (ENG.). 32p. (J). (gr. 1-3). pap. 3.99 *(978-0-545-30171-8(8))* Scholastic, Inc.

Perish, Patrick. Sidewinders. 2019. (Animals of the Desert Ser.). (ENG., Illus.). 24p. (J). (gr. k-3). lib. bdg. 26.95 *(978-1-62617-924-0(7)*, Blastoff! Readers) Bellwether Media.

Petrie, Kristin. Garter Snakes, 1 vol. 2015. (Backyard Animals Ser.). (ENG.). 32p. (J). (gr. 3-6). 32.79 *(978-1-62403-660-6(0)*, 16818, Checkerboard Library) ABDO Publishing Co.

Phillips, Dee. Green Tree Python. 2013. (Science Slam: Treed-Animal Life in the Trees Ser.). 24p. (J). (gr. -1-3). lib. bdg. 26.99 *(978-1-61772-909-6(4))* Bearport Publishing Co., Inc.

Pressberg, Dava. Vipers, 1 vol. 2016. (Snakes on the Hunt Ser.). (ENG., Illus.). 24p. (J). (gr. 3-3). pap. 9.25 *(978-1-4994-2210-8(5)*, d8f3bb52-7739-4b52-a2cb-01371aa20b2a, PowerKids Pr.) Rosen Publishing Group, Inc., The.

Pringle, Laurence. Snakes! Strange & Wonderful. Henderson, Meryl Learnihan, illus. 2009. (Strange & Wonderful Ser.). (ENG.). 32p. (J). (gr. 2-5). pap. 9.95 *(978-1-59078-744-1(7)*, Astra Young Readers) Astra Publishing Hse.

Raatma, Lucia. How Do We Live Together? Snakes. 2010. (Community Connections: How Do We Live Together? Ser.). (ENG., Illus.). 24p. (gr. 2-5). lib. bdg. 29.21 *(978-1-60279-620-1(3)*, 200331) Cherry Lake Publishing.

—Pythons. 2012. (Nature's Children Ser.). (ENG., Illus.). 48p. (J). pap. 6.95 *(978-0-531-25482-0(8))*; lib. bdg. 28.00 *(978-0-531-26837-7(3))* Scholastic Library Publishing.

Rajczak, Kristen. How Snakes & Other Animals Taste the Air, 1 vol. 2015. (Superior Animal Senses Ser.). (ENG., Illus.). 24p. (J). (gr. 3-4). pap. 9.25 *(978-1-4994-0995-6(8)*, 02837a1d-a1c3-46f9-b600-653fe26203b3, PowerKids Pr.) Rosen Publishing Group, Inc., The.

Rake, Jody Sullivan. Pythons. 2010. (African Animals Ser.). (ENG.). 24p. (gr. k-1). pap. 41.70 *(978-1-4296-5084-7(2)*, Capstone Pr.) Capstone.

Randolph, Joanne. Snakes. (Classroom Pets Ser.). 24p. (gr. 2-3). 2009. 42.50 *(978-1-61511-859-5(4))* 2006. (ENG., Illus.). (J). lib. bdg. 26.27 *(978-1-4042-3679-0(1)*, a3440aa5-262a-4d5b-bd82-05bd08f7de04) Rosen Publishing Group, Inc., The. (PowerKids Pr.).

Rathburn, Betsy. Diamondback Rattlesnakes. 2017. (North American Animals Ser.). (ENG., Illus.). 24p. (J). (gr. k-3). lib. bdg. 26.95 *(978-1-62617-637-9(X)*, Blastoff! Readers) Bellwether Media.

Raum, Elizabeth. Anacondas. 2013. (Snakes Ser.). (ENG.). 32p. (J). (gr. 2-5). lib. bdg. 28.50 *(978-1-60753-371-9(5)*, 16342) Amicus.

—Boa Constrictors. 2013. (Snakes Ser.). (ENG.). 32p. (J). (gr. 2-5). lib. bdg. 28.50 *(978-1-60753-372-6(3)*, 16343) Amicus.

—Cobras. 2013. (Snakes Ser.). (ENG.). 32p. (J). (gr. 2-5). lib. bdg. 28.50 *(978-1-60753-373-3(1)*, 16344) Amicus.

—Garter Snakes. 2013. (Snakes Ser.). (ENG.). 32p. (J). (gr. 2-5). lib. bdg. 28.50 *(978-1-60753-374-0(X)*, 16345) Amicus.

—Pythons. 2013. (Snakes Ser.). (ENG.). 32p. (J). (gr. 2-5). lib. bdg. 28.50 *(978-1-60753-375-7(8)*, 16346) Amicus.

—Rattlesnakes. 2013. (Snakes Ser.). (ENG.). 32p. (J). (gr. 2-5). lib. bdg. 28.50 *(978-1-60753-376-4(6)*, 16347) Amicus.

Reher, Matt. My Pet Snake. 2017. (1G Domestic Animals Ser.). (ENG., Illus.). 24p. (J). pap. 9.60 *(978-1-64053-190-1(4)*, ARC Pr. Bks.) American Reading Co.

Reynolds, Shaye. Rattlesnakes, 1 vol. 2016. (Snakes on the Hunt Ser.). (ENG., Illus.). 24p. (J). (gr. 3-3). pap. 9.25 *(978-1-4994-2202-3(4)*, 39c60a35-a11e-4e21-a6b7-fb5140d74b5e, PowerKids Pr.) Rosen Publishing Group, Inc., The.

Ricciuti, Edward R. Adivina Quién Silba / Guess Who Hisses, 1 vol. 2009. (Adivina Quién / Guess Who? Ser.). (ENG & SPA.). 32p. (gr. k-2). 25.50 *(978-0-7614-2883-1(6)*, d7d9a8aa-b4d6-45a3-ba57-84c92ad6a8d3) Cavendish Square Publishing LLC.

—Adivina Quién Silba (Guess Who Hisses), 1 vol. 2009. (Adivina Quién (Guess Who?) Ser.). (SPA.). 32p. (gr. k-2). 25.50 *(978-0-7614-2866-4(6)*, 1d2caa26-7844-46dc-95ac-3720c503870b) Cavendish Square Publishing LLC.

—Guess Who Hisses, 1 vol. 2006. (Guess Who? Ser.). (ENG., Illus.). 32p. (gr. k-1). 25.50 *(978-0-7614-1767-5(2)*, db5bb11e-4cdd-434e-895f-f7a1e59f9699) Cavendish Square Publishing LLC.

Riggs, Kate. Seedlings: Snakes. 2014. (Seedlings Ser.). (ENG.). 24p. (J). (gr. -1-k). pap. 9.99 *(978-0-89812-888-8(9)*, 21683, Creative Paperbacks) Creative Co., The.

—Snakes. 2013. (Seedlings Ser.). (ENG.). 24p. (J). (gr. -1-k). 25.65 *(978-1-60818-343-2(2)*, 21682, Creative Education) Creative Co., The.

Rothaus, Don P. Pythons. 2015. (Animals of the Rain Forest Ser.). (ENG.). 24p. (J). (gr. 2-5). 32.79 *(978-1-63143-751-9(8)*, 208580) Child's World, Inc, The.

Roza, Greg. Poison! The Spitting Cobra & Other Venomous Animals, 1 vol. 2011. (Armed & Dangerous Ser.). (ENG., Illus.). 24p. (gr. 2-3). (J). pap. 9.25 *(978-1-4488-2684-1(5)*, 2603ea83-75fd-46b8-8817-31ba958cf8b1, PowerKids Pr.); (YA). lib. bdg. 26.27 *(978-1-4488-2550-9(4)*, 4835aa33-5722-41a3-8ce0-dae1e89c9262) Rosen Publishing Group, Inc., The.

Rudenko, Dennis. Cobras, 1 vol. 2016. (Snakes on the Hunt Ser.). (ENG., Illus.). 24p. (J). (gr. 3-3). pap. 9.25 *(978-1-4994-2194-1(X)*, 5f639297-fbf0-4ee3-b9f6-bc11b1b13097, PowerKids Pr.) Rosen Publishing Group, Inc., The.

Rudy, Lisa Jo. Snakes! 2005. 32p. (J). lib. bdg. 13.85 *(978-1-4242-0861-6(0))* Fitzgerald Bks.

Sabelko, Rebecca. Common Garter Snakes. 2019. (North American Animals Ser.). (ENG., Illus.). 24p. (J). (gr. k-3). lib. bdg. 26.95 *(978-1-62617-910-3(7)*, Blastoff! Readers) Bellwether Media.

Schafer, Susan. Snakes, 1 vol. 2003. (Perfect Pets Ser.). (ENG., Illus.). 32p. (gr. 3-5). 31.21 *(978-0-7614-1396-7(0)*, 74170754-e115-4687-a773-236e7eb284e2) Cavendish Square Publishing LLC.

Schuh, Mari. Snakes. 2019. (Spot Backyard Animals Ser.). (ENG.). 16p. (J). (gr. -1-2). lib. bdg. *(978-1-68151-549-6(0)*, 14510) Amicus.

Schwartz, David M. Green Snake. Kuhn, Dwight, photos by. (Life Cycles Ser.). (Illus.). 16p. (J). (gr. 1-3). pap. 2.99 *(978-1-57471-557-6(7)*, 3067) Creative Teaching Pr., Inc.

Scott, L. K. Snakes. Mangiat, Jeff, illus. 2008. (ENG.). 24p. (J). (gr. 3-18). 19.95 *(978-1-58117-799-2(2)*, Intervisual/Piggy Toes) Bendon, Inc.

Sexton, Colleen. Anacondas. 2010. (Snakes Alive Ser.). (ENG., Illus.). 24p. (J). (gr. k-3). lib. bdg. 26.95 *(978-1-60014-313-7(X)*, Blastoff! Readers) Bellwether Media.

—Boa Constrictors. 2010. (Snakes Alive Ser.). (ENG., Illus.). 24p. (J). (gr. k-3). lib. bdg. 26.95 *(978-1-60014-314-4(8)*, Blastoff! Readers) Bellwether Media.

—Cobras. 2010. (Snakes Alive Ser.). (ENG., Illus.). 24p. (J). (gr. k-3). lib. bdg. 26.95 *(978-1-60014-315-1(6)*, Blastoff! Readers) Bellwether Media.

—Copperheads. 2010. (Snakes Alive Ser.). (ENG., Illus.). 24p. (J). (gr. k-3). lib. bdg. 26.95 *(978-1-60014-453-0(5)*, Blastoff! Readers) Bellwether Media.

—Coral Snakes. 2010. (Snakes Alive Ser.). (ENG., Illus.). 24p. (J). (gr. k-3). lib. bdg. 26.95 *(978-1-60014-316-8(4)*, Blastoff! Readers) Bellwether Media.

—Cottonmouths. 2010. (Snakes Alive Ser.). (ENG., Illus.). 24p. (J). (gr. k-3). lib. bdg. 26.95 *(978-1-60014-454-7(3)*, Blastoff! Readers) Bellwether Media.

—Mambas. 2010. (Snakes Alive Ser.). (ENG., Illus.). 24p. (J). (gr. k-3). lib. bdg. 26.95 *(978-1-60014-317-5(2)*, Blastoff! Readers) Bellwether Media.

—Pythons. 2010. (Snakes Alive Ser.). (ENG., Illus.). 24p. (J). (gr. k-3). lib. bdg. 26.95 *(978-1-60014-318-2(0)*, Blastoff! Readers) Bellwether Media.

—Rat Snakes. 2010. (Snakes Alive Ser.). (ENG., Illus.). 24p. (J). (gr. k-3). lib. bdg. 26.95 *(978-1-60014-455-4(1)*, Blastoff! Readers) Bellwether Media.

—Rattlesnakes. 2010. (Snakes Alive Ser.). (ENG., Illus.). 24p. (J). (gr. k-3). lib. bdg. 26.95 *(978-1-60014-319-9(9)*, Blastoff! Readers) Bellwether Media.

—Sea Snakes. 2010. (Snakes Alive Ser.). (ENG., Illus.). 24p. (J). (gr. k-3). lib. bdg. 26.95 *(978-1-60014-320-5(2)*, Blastoff! Readers) Bellwether Media.

—Sidewinders. 2010. (Snakes Alive Ser.). (ENG., Illus.). 24p. (J). (gr. k-3). lib. bdg. 26.95 *(978-1-60014-456-1(X)*, Blastoff! Readers) Bellwether Media.

Shaffer, Lindsay. Sea Snakes. 2020. (Animals of the Coral Reef Ser.). (ENG.). 24p. (J). (gr. k-3). lib. bdg. 26.95 *(978-1-64487-134-8(3)*, Blastoff! Readers) Bellwether Media.

Shea, Therese. Snakes. (Big Bad Biters Ser.). 24p. (gr. 2-3). 2009. 42.50 *(978-1-61511-564-8(1)*, PowerKids Pr.) 2006. (ENG., Illus.). (J). lib. bdg. 26.27 *(978-1-4042-3520-5(5)*, f43c7e43-cc16-407c-add3-e3cf9eefce4c) Rosen Publishing Group, Inc., The.

Sheikh-Miller, Jonathan. Snakes. 2004. (Discovery Program Ser.). (SPA., Illus.). 64p. (J). (gr. 2-18). pap. 8.95 *(978-0-7945-0004-7(8)*, Usborne); lib. bdg. 16.95 *(978-1-58086-344-5(2))* EDC Publishing.

Sheikh-Miller, Jonathan. Snakes II. 2010. (Discovery Nature Ser.). 64p. (J). 8.99 *(978-0-7945-2240-7(8)*, Usborne) EDC Publishing.

Silverman, Buffy. Gliding Garter Snakes. 2006. (Pull Ahead Bks.). (Illus.). 32p. (J). (gr. 3-7). lib. bdg. 22.60 *(978-0-8225-6043-2(7)*, Lerner Pubns.) Lerner Publishing Group.

Silverstein, Alvin, et al. Boas & Pythons: Cool Pets!, 1 vol. 2012. (Far-Out & Unusual Pets Ser.). (ENG., Illus.). 48p. (gr. 3-3). 27.93 *(978-0-7660-3878-3(5)*, 88b54025-586d-452d-b348-7bcba32b25c8); pap. 11.53 *(978-1-4644-0129-9(2)*, 7dbbf2f2-ad1c-48d5-9fe2-570fbc050858) Enslow Publishing, LLC. (Enslow Elementary).

Simon, Seymour. Poisonous Snakes. Downey, William, illus. 2012. (Dover Children's Science Bks.). (ENG.). 80p. (J). (gr. 3-5). pap. 5.99 *(978-0-486-48470-9(X)*, 48470X) Dover Pubns., Inc.

—Snakes. 2007. (ENG., Illus.). 32p. (J). (gr. k-4). pap. 7.99 *(978-0-06-114095-2(3)*, HarperCollins) HarperCollins Pubs.

Singer, Marilyn. Venom. 2007. (Junior Library Guild Selection Ser.). (Illus.). 96p. (J). (gr. 4-7). 19.95 *(978-1-58196-043-3(3)*, Darby Creek) Lerner Publishing Group.

Smith, Molly. Green Anaconda: The World's Heaviest Snake. (SuperSized! Ser.). 24p. (J). (gr. k-3). 2016. (ENG.). pap. 7.99 *(978-1-944998-38-7(1))* 2007. (Illus.). lib. bdg. 26.99 *(978-1-59716-391-0(0)*, 1265936) Bearport Publishing Co., Inc.

The Snake: Individual Title Six-Packs. (Sails Literacy Ser.). 16p. (gr. k-18). 27.00 *(978-0-7635-4429-4(9))* Rigby Education.

Snake Animals in Wild Series. 2003. (J). pap. 2.50 *(978-0-590-44625-9(8))* Scholastic, Inc.

Snakes! (Creatures Corner Ser.). 16p. (J). *(978-2-7643-0124-1(3))* Phidal Publishing, Inc./Editions Phidal, Inc.

Snakes. (Eyes on Nature Ser.). 32p. (J). (gr. 1). pap. *(978-1-882210-58-9(1))* Action Publishing, Inc.

Snakes: Level N, 6 vols. (Wonder Worldtm Ser.). 48p. 34.95 *(978-0-7802-4601-0(2))* Wright Group/McGraw-Hill.

Snakes: Level P, 6 vols., Vol. 2. (Explorers Ser.). 32p. (gr. 3-6). 44.95 *(978-0-7699-0603-4(6))* Shortland Pubns. (U. S. A.) Inc.

Snakes Discovery Library, 5 bks. (J). (gr. 1-4). Set I. lib. bdg. 111.60 *(978-0-86592-954-8(8))*Set II. lib. bdg. 111.60 *(978-0-86592-243-3(8))* Rourke Enterprises, Inc.

Snakes on the Hunt, 12 vols. 2016. (Snakes on the Hunt Ser.). 24p. (gr. 3-3). (ENG.). 151.62 *(978-1-4994-1918-4(X)*, 77f08438-34b6-4a4d-a925-1b9051372e03); pap. 49.50 *(978-1-4994-2458-4(2))* Rosen Publishing Group, Inc., The. (PowerKids Pr.).

Somervill, Barbara A. Brown Treesnake. 2008. (21st Century Skills Library: Animal Invaders Ser.). (ENG., Illus.). 32p. (gr. 4-8). lib. bdg. 32.07 *(978-1-60279-239-5(9)*, 200114) Cherry Lake Publishing.

—Python. 2010. (21st Century Skills Library: Animal Invaders Ser.). (ENG., Illus.). 32p. (gr. 4-8). lib. bdg. 32.07 *(978-1-60279-629-4(7)*, 200335) Cherry Lake Publishing.

Spilsbury, Louise. Boa Constrictor, 1 vol. 2013. (Top of the Food Chain Ser.). (ENG.). 32p. (J). (gr. 2-3). 29.92 *(978-1-61533-741-5(5)*, e9cb147d-04cf-45c2-be07-d84437fd359e); pap. 11.00 *(978-1-61533-799-6(7)*, 5a0c8cdd-7c86-4087-b047-c62ba8ac67ca) Rosen Publishing Group, Inc., The. (PowerKids Pr.).

Sprott, Gary. King Cobra. 2018. (World's Coolest Snakes Ser.). (ENG., Illus.). 32p. (gr. 4-8). pap. 9.95 *(978-1-64156-609-4(4)*, 9781641566094) Rourke Educational Media.

—Western Diamondback Rattlesnake. 2018. (World's Coolest Snakes Ser.). (ENG., Illus.). 32p. (gr. 4-8). lib. bdg. 32.79 *(978-1-64156-485-4(7)*, 9781641564854) Rourke Educational Media.

Statts, Leo. Anacondas. 2016. (Rain Forest Animals Ser.). (ENG.). 24p. (J). (gr. -1-2). 49.94 *(978-1-68079-360-4(8)*, 22981, Abdo Zoom-Launch) ABDO Publishing Co.

—Cobras. 2016. (Desert Animals Ser.). (ENG.). 24p. (J). (gr. -1-2). 49.94 *(978-1-68079-348-2(9)*, 22969, Abdo Zoom-Launch) ABDO Publishing Co.

—Rattlesnakes. 2016. (Desert Animals Ser.). (ENG.). 24p. (J). (gr. -1-2). 49.94 *(978-1-68079-351-2(9)*, 22972, Abdo Zoom-Launch) ABDO Publishing Co.

Stewart, Melissa. National Geographic Readers: Snakes! 2009. (Readers Ser.). (Illus.). 32p. (J). (gr. 1-3). 5.99 *(978-1-4263-0428-6(5)*, National Geographic Kids); (ENG., lib. bdg. 14.90 *(978-1-4263-0429-3(3)*, National Geographic Children's Bks.) Disney Publishing Worldwide.

Stone, Tanya Lee. Snakes. 2003. (Wild Wild World Ser.). 24p. (YA). 24.94 *(978-1-56711-823-0(2)*, Blackbirch Pr., Inc.) Cengage Gale.

Sweazey, Davy. Ball Pythons. 2014. (Amazing Snakes! Ser.). (ENG., Illus.). 24p. (J). (gr. 3-7). lib. bdg. 26.95 *(978-1-62617-088-9(6)*, Epic Bks.) Bellwether Media.

—Bush Vipers. 2014. (Amazing Snakes! Ser.). (ENG., Illus.). 24p. (J). (gr. 3-7). lib. bdg. 26.95 *(978-1-62617-090-2(8)*, Epic Bks.) Bellwether Media.

—Death Adders. 2014. (Amazing Snakes! Ser.). (ENG., Illus.). 24p. (J). (gr. 3-7). lib. bdg. 26.95 *(978-1-62617-091-9(6)*, Epic Bks.) Bellwether Media.

—King Cobras. 2014. (Amazing Snakes! Ser.). (ENG., Illus.). 24p. (J). (gr. 3-7). lib. bdg. 26.95 *(978-1-62617-094-0(0)*, Epic Bks.) Bellwether Media.

Taylor, Barbara. Exploring Nature - Amazing Snakes: An Exciting Insight into the Weird & Wonderful World of Snakes & How They Live, with 190 Pictures. 2013. (ENG., Illus.). 64p. (J). (gr. 3-7). 12.99 *(978-1-84322-736-6(3))* Anness Publishing GBR. Dist: National Bk. Network.

—Snakes. 2010. (Remarkable Man & Beast Ser.). (Illus.). 48p. (J). (gr. 3-18). lib. bdg. 19.95 *(978-1-4222-1975-1(5))* Mason Crest.

Taylor, Trace & Lynch, Michelle. Cobras. 2011. (ARC Press / Power 100 - Predator Animals Ser.). pap. 45.32 *(978-1-61541-505-2(X))* American Reading Co.

Terp, Gail. Boa Constrictors. 2021. (Slithering Snakes Ser.). (ENG.). 32p. (J). (gr. 4-6). *(978-1-62310-271-5(5)*, 13364, Bolt) Black Rabbit Bks.

—Cobras. 2021. (Slithering Snakes Ser.). (ENG.). 32p. (J). (gr. 4-6). *(978-1-62310-272-2(3)*, 13368, Bolt) Black Rabbit Bks.

—Copperheads. 2021. (Slithering Snakes Ser.). (ENG.). 32p. (J). (gr. 4-6). *(978-1-62310-273-9(1)*, 13372, Bolt) Black Rabbit Bks.

—Pythons. 2021. (Slithering Snakes Ser.). (ENG.). 32p. (J). (gr. 4-6). *(978-1-62310-274-6(X)*, 13376, Bolt) Black Rabbit Bks.

—Rattlesnakes. 2021. (Slithering Snakes Ser.). (ENG.). 32p. (J). (gr. 4-6). *(978-1-62310-275-3(8)*, 13380, Bolt) Black Rabbit Bks.

—Sea Snakes. 2022. (Super Sea Creatures Ser.). (ENG.). 32p. (J). (gr. 4-6). *(978-1-62310-286-9(3)*, 13472, Bolt) Black Rabbit Bks.

Thatcher, Henry. Pythons & Garter Snakes, 1 vol., 1. 2014. (Big Animals, Small Animals Ser.). (ENG.). 32p. (J). (gr. 2-3). 28.93 *(978-1-4777-6110-6(1)*, 8c99d199-dc64-4e17-bda4-2cfe5c886245, PowerKids Pr.) Rosen Publishing Group, Inc., The.

Thomas, Isabel. Slinky's Guide to Caring for Your Snake, 1 vol. Peterson, Rick, illus. 2014. (Pets' Guides). (ENG.). 32p. (J). (gr. 1-3). 29.99 *(978-1-4846-0263-8(3)*, 126314); pap. 7.99 *(978-1-4846-0270-6(6)*, 126320) Capstone. (Heinemann).

Thomson, Sarah L. Amazing Snakes! 2006. (I Can Read Level 2 Ser.). (ENG., Illus.). 32p. (J). (gr. k-3). pap. 5.99 *(978-0-06-054464-5(3)*, HarperCollins) HarperCollins Pubs.

Troller, Leah. Look at the Snakes. 2015. (1-3Y Animals Ser.). (ENG., Illus.). 16p. (J). pap. 9.60 *(978-1-63437-595-5(5))* American Reading Co.

Turnbull, Stephanie. Snake. 2015. (Big Beasts Ser.). (ENG., Illus.). 24p. (J). (gr. 1-4). 28.50 *(978-1-62588-171-7(1)*, 17286) Black Rabbit Bks.

—Snake. 2015. (ENG., Illus.). 24p. (J). pap. 8.95 *(978-1-77092-219-8(9))* RiverStream Publishing.

Wallach, Van. Una Cobra Al Descubierto. 2007. (Al Descubierto Ser.). (Illus.). 16p. (J). (gr. 3-7). *(978-970-718-497-8(3)*, Silver Dolphin en Español) Advanced Marketing, S. de R. L. de C. V.

Weakland, Mark. Scooby-Doo! an Addition Mystery: The Case of the Angry Adder, 1 vol. Gross, Scott, illus. 2014. (Solve It with Scooby-Doo!: Math Ser.). (ENG.). 24p. (J). (gr. k-2). lib. bdg. 28.65 *(978-1-4914-1539-9(8)*, 126793, Capstone Pr.) Capstone.

Wechsler, Doug. Garter Snakes. 2009. (Really Wild Life of Animals Ser.). 24p. (gr. 3-4). 42.50 *(978-1-60854-192-8(4)*, PowerKids Pr.) Rosen Publishing Group, Inc., The.

—Rattlesnakes. 2009. (Really Wild Life of Animals Ser.). 24p. (gr. 3-4). 42.50 *(978-1-60854-206-4(4)*, PowerKids Pr.) Rosen Publishing Group, Inc., The.

Weingarten, E. T. I See a Snake, 1 vol. 2018. (In My Backyard Ser.). (ENG.). 24p. (gr. k-k). 25.27 *(978-1-5382-2874-6(2)*, ab1e63b4-d206-48a6-9ff9-4894b8227de8) Stevens, Gareth Publishing LLLP.

Wexo, John Bonnett. Serpientes. Rountree, Monica, tr. 2003. (Zoobooks Ser.). Orig. Title: Snakes. (SPA., Illus.). 24p. (J). (gr. 1-7). lib. bdg. 15.95 *(978-1-888153-83-5(0))* National Wildlife Federation.

—Snakes. rev. ed. 2003. (Illus.). 24p. 10.95 *(978-1-888153-96-5(2)*, Zoo Bks.) National Wildlife Federation.

White, Nancy. Black Mambas: Sudden Death! 2009. (Fangs Ser.). (Illus.). 24p. (YA). (gr. 1-4). lib. bdg. 26.99 *(978-1-59716-766-6(5))* Bearport Publishing Co., Inc.

—Coral Snakes: Beware the Colors! 2009. (Fangs Ser.). (Illus.). 24p. (YA). (gr. 1-4). lib. bdg. 26.99 *(978-1-59716-763-5(0))* Bearport Publishing Co., Inc.

—Death Adders: Super Deadly! 2009. (Fangs Ser.). (Illus.). 24p. (J). (gr. 1-4). lib. bdg. 26.99 *(978-1-59716-764-2(9))* Bearport Publishing Co., Inc.

—Diamondback Rattlers: America's Most Venomous Snakes! (Fangs Ser.). 24p. (gr. 1-6). 2016. (ENG.). (J). pap. 7.99 *(978-1-944998-65-3(9))* 2009. (Illus.). (YA). lib. bdg. 26.99 *(978-1-59716-765-9(7))* Bearport Publishing Co., Inc.

—Fer-De-Lance: Master Killer! 2009. (Fangs Ser.). (Illus.). 24p. (J). (gr. 1-4). lib. bdg. 26.99 *(978-1-59716-769-7(X)*, 1292401) Bearport Publishing Co., Inc.

—King Cobras: The Biggest Venomous Snakes of All! 2009. (Fangs Ser.). (Illus.). 24p. (J). (gr. 1-4). lib. bdg. 26.99 *(978-1-59716-767-3(3))* Bearport Publishing Co., Inc.

Whiting, Jim. Care for a Pet Snake. 2007. (How to Convince Your Parents You Can ... Ser.). (Illus.). 32p. (YA). (gr. 1-4). lib. bdg. 25.70 *(978-1-58415-604-8(X))* Mitchell Lane Pubs.

Wild about Snakes. 2011. (Wild about Snakes Ser.). (ENG.). 32p. (gr. 3-4). pap. 381.60 *(978-1-4296-7290-0(0))*; pap. 190.80 *(978-1-4296-6427-1(4))* Capstone. (Capstone Pr.).

Wilhelm, Doug. Snake Invasion. Semionov, Vladimir, illus. 2016. (ENG.). 144p. (J). (gr. 4-8). pap. 6.99 *(978-1-937133-52-8(4))* Chooseco LLC.

Willebrandt, Avery. Spitting Cobra, 1 vol. 2011. (Killer Snakes Ser.). (ENG., Illus.). 24p. (J). (gr. 2-2). pap. 9.15 *(978-1-4339-5651-5(9)*, 0afa13f1-d5bd-4b88-b54c-464097d57b99); lib. bdg. 25.27 *(978-1-4339-5649-2(7)*, 5437ca9a-22c4-4f40-9c40-2c964d521398) Stevens, Gareth Publishing LLLP.

—Spitting Cobra / Cobra Escupidora, 1 vol. 2011. (Killer Snakes / Serpientes Asesinas Ser.). (SPA & ENG., Illus.). 24p. (J). (gr. 2-2). 25.27 *(978-1-4339-5653-9(5)*, 0f806a1e-4a76-4ca2-8eeb-9932043bb898) Stevens, Gareth Publishing LLLP.

Wilsdon, Christina. Snakes, 1 vol. (Amazing Animals Ser.). (ENG.). 48p. (gr. 3-5). 2009. pap. 11.50 *(978-1-4339-2019-6(0)*, 267f2ebf-90eb-417c-9e0c-d05795a5ac68, Gareth Stevens Learning Library) 2008. (YA). lib. bdg. 30.67 *(978-0-8368-9102-7(3)*, f961300e-a9eb-4cfa-9d16-7a4f9fa4a538) Stevens, Gareth Publishing LLLP.

—Snakes. 2007. (J). *(978-1-59939-137-3(6)*, Reader's Digest Young Families, Inc.) Studio Fun International.

Wimmer, Teresa. Snakes. 2009. (Living Wild Ser.). (Illus.). 48p. (J). 22.95 *(978-1-58341-743-0(5)*, Creative Education) Creative Co., The.

Wood, Selina. Snakes. 2009. (Extreme Pets Ser.). (YA). (gr. 4-7). 28.50 *(978-1-59920-233-4(6))* Black Rabbit Bks.

Worthy, Shanya. Taipan, 1 vol. 2011. (Killer Snakes Ser.). (ENG., Illus.). 24p. (J). (gr. 2-2). pap. 9.15 *(978-1-4339-4566-3(5)*, 3432a1bf-fe05-4579-a0c5-5a32ba158810); lib. bdg. 25.27 *(978-1-4339-4565-6(7)*, a0a9819a-5903-4156-b25f-8e66446d8bf1) Stevens, Gareth Publishing LLLP.

—Taipan / Taipán, 1 vol. 2011. (Killer Snakes / Serpientes Asesinas Ser.). (ENG & SPA., Illus.). 24p. (J). (gr. 2-2). 25.27 *(978-1-4339-4569-4(X)*, 330acabc-5668-4512-b1f3-197ada04cef6) Stevens, Gareth Publishing LLLP.

Yates, Gene, illus. The Snake Shapes Book. 2006. (J). *(978-1-58865-365-9(X))* Kidsbooks, LLC.

Young, Phil. The Best Book on Northern Brown Snakes. 2010. 49p. pap. 23.98 *(978-0-557-43753-5(9))* Lulu Pr., Inc.

SNAKES—FICTION

Adler, David A. Cam Jansen: the Scary Snake Mystery #17. Natti, Susanna, illus. 2005. (Cam Jansen Ser.: 17). (ENG.). 64p. (J). (gr. 2-5). 5.99 *(978-0-14-240288-7(5)*, Puffin Books) Penguin Young Readers Group.

Aidinoff, Elsie V. The Garden. 2005. (ENG.). 416p. (J). (gr. 9). pap. 6.99 *(978-0-06-055607-5(2)*, HarperTeen) HarperCollins Pubs.

Aldous, Huxley. The Crows of Pearblossom. (J). 15.95 *(978-0-89190-167-9(1))* Amereon Ltd.

Ata, Te. Baby Rattlesnake, 1 vol. Reisberg, Mira, illus. 2006. (ENG.). 32p. (J). (gr. k-3). pap. 10.95 *(978-0-89239-216-2(9)*, leelowcbp) Lee & Low Bks., Inc.

—Baby Rattlesnake / Viborita de Cascabel, 1 vol. Alarcón, Francisco X., tr. Reisberg, Mira, illus. 2013. (ENG.). 32p. (J).

(gr. k-3). pap. 11.95 (978-0-89239-188-2(X), leelowcbp) Lee & Low Bks., Inc.

Ata, Te, et al. Baby Rattlesnake. Reisberg, Mira, illus. 2013. (ENG.). 32p. (J). (gr. -1-18). pap. 9.95 (978-0-89239-049-6(2)) Lee & Low Bks., Inc.

Atwater-Rhodes, Amelia. Falcondance: The Kiesha'ra: Volume Three. 2007. (Kiesha'ra Ser.: Bk. 3). (ENG.). 208p. (YA). (gr. 7-12). per. 7.99 (978-0-440-23885-0(4), Delacorte Pr.) Random Hse. Children's Bks.

—Snakecharm: The Kiesha'ra: Volume Two. 2007. (Kiesha'ra Ser.: Bk. 2). (ENG.). 176p. (YA). (gr. 7-12). per. 7.99 (978-0-385-73493-6(X), Delacorte Pr.) Random Hse. Children's Bks.

—Wolfcry. 2008. (Kiesha'ra Ser.: Bk. 4). (ENG.). 208p. (YA). (gr. 9-12). pap. 7.99 (978-0-440-23886-7(2), Delacorte Pr.) Random Hse. Children's Bks.

Bagley, Conor. Ziggy McFinster's Nantucket Adventure. Bernard Westcott, Nadine, illus. 2008. (ENG.). 40p. (J). (gr. -1-3). 16.95 (978-1-56625-315-4(2)) Bonus Bks., Inc.

Bapiraju Gandham. The Wizard of Ants. 2010. 88p. pap. 33.48 (978-1-4269-1940-4(9)) Trafford Publishing.

Beeson, Jan. Mysterious World of the Puffins the Treasure Hunt Book 1. 2013. 74p. pap. 19.99 (978-0-9890482-0-0(9)) Beeson, Jan.

Bellingham, Brenda. Lilly & the Snakes. MacDonald, Clarke, illus. 2007. (Formac First Novels Ser.: 37). (ENG.). 64p. (J). (gr. 2-5). 14.95 (978-0-88780-727-5(5), 727); 4.95 (978-0-88780-723-7(2), 723) Formac Publishing Co., Ltd. CAN. Dist: Formac Lorimer Bks. Ltd.

Bernstrom, Daniel. One Day in the Eucalyptus, Eucalyptus Tree. Wenzel, Brendan, illus. 2016. (ENG.). 32p. (J). (gr. -1-3). 17.99 (978-0-06-235485-3(X), HarperCollins) HarperCollins Pubs.

Brennan, Sarah. The Tale of Sybil Snake. Harrison, Harry, illus. 2012. (ENG.). 32p. (J). (978-1-937160-53-1(X)) Auspicious Times.

Buckley, Richard. The Foolish Tortoise: Book & CD. Carle, Eric, illus. 2013. (World of Eric Carle Ser.). (ENG.). 24p. (J). (gr. -1-3). pap. 10.99 (978-1-4424-6638-8(3), Little Simon) Little Simon.

—The Greedy Python. Carle, Eric, illus. 2009. (World of Eric Carle Ser.). (ENG.). 24p. (J). (gr. -1-k). bds. 8.99 (978-1-4169-8290-6(6), Little Simon) Little Simon.

—The Greedy Python. 2012. (Eric Carle Ready-To-Read Ser.). lib. bdg. 13.55 (978-0-606-26357-3(8)) Turtleback.

—The Greedy Python: Lap Edition. Carle, Eric, illus. 2013. (World of Eric Carle Ser.). (ENG.). 24p. (J). (gr. -1-k). bds. 12.99 (978-1-4424-8991-2(X), Little Simon) Little Simon.

—The Greedy Python/Ready-To-Read Level 1. Carle, Eric, illus. 2012. (World of Eric Carle Ser.). (ENG.). 24p. (J). (gr. -1-1). 17.99 (978-1-4424-4577-2(7), Simon Spotlight) Simon Spotlight.

Burton, Thomas. Bluey & Dingo's Outback Adventure. 2011. 40p. 15.66 (978-1-4567-7006-8(3)) AuthorHouse.

Byrd, Betty. They Call Me Pharaoh. 2008. 20p. pap. 24.95 (978-1-60563-008-3(X)) America Star Bks.

Cannon. VERDI - català. 2003. (SPA., Illus.). 48p. (J). (gr. 1-3). (978-84-261-3042-6(9), JV7591) Juventud, Editorial ESP. Dist: Lectorum Pubns., Inc.

Cannon, Janell. Verdi. pap. 24.95 (978-85-325-1343-4(3)) Rocco, Editora, Ltda BRA. Dist: Distribooks, Inc.

Carter, Candace. Sid's Surprise. Kim, Joung Un, illus. 2005. (Green Light Readers Level 1 Ser.). (ENG.). 32p. (J). (gr. -1-3). pap. 4.99 (978-0-15-205182-2(1), 1195629, Clarion Bks.) HarperCollins Pubs.

—Sid's Surprise. Kim, Joung Un, illus. 2005. (Green Light Readers Level 1 Ser.). (gr. -1-3). 13.95 (978-0-7569-5242-6(5)) Perfection Learning Corp.

Chin, Oliver, ed. The Year of the Snake: Tales from the Chinese Zodiac. Wood, Jennifer, illus. 2012. (Tales from the Chinese Zodiac Ser.: 8). (ENG.). 36p. (J). (gr. -1-3). 15.95 (978-1-59702-038-1(9)) Immedium.

Clark, Jeanne B. The Second Encounter: With the Snake Named Bully. 2012. 40p. pap. 24.99 (978-1-4772-1568-5(9)) AuthorHouse.

Clarke, Ella. The Snake's Diary by Little Yellow, 1 vol. rev. ed. 2013. (Literary Text Ser.). (ENG., Illus.). 24p. (gr. 2-3). pap. 7.99 (978-1-4333-5531-8(0)) Teacher Created Materials, Inc.

Condi-Babich, Kris. 4Cam. us. 2004. 71p. pap. 19.95 (978-1-4137-2241-3(5)) America Star Bks.

Cook, Beatrice. A Journey with the Spider & Snake to Arizona. Campis, Adrian, Jr., illus. 2007. (J). 14.95 (978-0-9795867-0-5(4)) Travel America Bks.

Cook, Sherry & Johnson, Terri. Susie Sound, 26. Kuhn, Jesse, illus. l.t. ed. 2006. 32p. (J). 7.99 (978-1-933815-18-3(3), Quirkles, The) Creative 3, LLC.

Cote, Jenny. The Ark, the Reed & the Fire Cloud: The Amazing Tales of Max & Liz Book One, 2 bks, Bk 1. 2008. (Amazing Tales of Max & Liz Ser.: 1). (ENG., Illus.). 432p. (J). (gr. 5-11). pap. 16.99 (978-0-89957-198-0(0), Living Ink Bks.) AMG Pubs.

Cotton, Peter B. When Jungle Jim Comes to Visit Fred the Snake. Lemaire, Bonnie, illus. 2013. 48p. 24.95 (978-0-9883370-4-6(5)) Fig & The Vine, LLC, The.

Coudakpo, Agrey Emile A. The Malignant & a Malignant One & Half: The Story of the Baby Frog & the Vicious Viper. 2013. 44p. pap. 20.72 (978-1-4669-8247-5(0)) Trafford Publishing.

Cowley, Joy. Friends: Snake & Lizard. 2011. (Gecko Press Titles Ser.). (ENG., Illus.). 144p. 16.95 (978-1-877579-01-1(7)) Gecko Pr. NZL. Dist: Lerner Publishing Group.

Dale, Jay. Where Is Carl the Corn Snake? Alder, Charlie, illus. 2012. (Engage Literacy Green Ser.). (ENG.). 16p. (J). (gr. k-2). pap. 36.94 (978-1-4296-8995-3(1), 18394); pap. 6.99 (978-1-4296-8994-6(3), 120003) Capstone. (Capstone Pr.).

Darlene, Cannon. Dollygal, Peacock, & the Serpent. Mathis, Leslie, illus. 2011. 108p. pap. 19.95 (978-1-61286-001-5(X)) Avid Readers Publishing Group.

Davey, Keith Peter. Squeaks Narrow Squeaks. Frost, Justine, illus. 2009. 32p. pap. 14.62 (978-1-4120-4402-8(2)) Trafford Publishing.

Davies, Nicola. I (Don't) Like Snakes. Lozano, Luciano, illus. 2018. (Read & Wonder Ser.). (ENG.). 32p. (J). (gr. k-4). 7.99 (978-1-5362-0323-3(8)) Candlewick Pr.

De Lint, Charles. The Cats of Tanglewood Forest. 2014. (J). lib. bdg. 22.10 (978-0-606-36532-1(X)) Turtleback.

Degman-Reed, Ruth. Blake the Snake Had a Bellyache. 2011. 24p. (gr. -1). pap. 12.79 (978-1-4520-9652-0(X)) AuthorHouse.

Dixon, Franklin W. The Great Escape. Burroughs, Scott, illus. 2015. (Hardy Boys: the Secret Files Ser.: 17). (ENG.). 112p. (J). (gr. 1-4). pap. 5.99 (978-1-4814-2267-3(7), Aladdin) Simon & Schuster Children's Publishing.

Downie, David. David & Jacko. Tatsi, Andreanna, tr. Seroya, Tea, illus. 2012. 52p. pap. (978-1-922159-24-3(7)); pap. (978-1-922159-15-1(8)) Blue Peg Publishing.

—David & Jacko. Ivanova, Kalina, tr. Seroya, Tea, illus. 2012. 52p. pap. (978-1-922159-01-4(8)) Blue Peg Publishing.

—David & Jacko. Seroya, Tea, illus. 2012. 52p. pap. (978-1-922159-99-1(9)) Blue Peg Publishing.

Downing, Johnette. Why the Oyster Has the Pearl, 1 vol. Hill, Bethanne, illus. 2011. (ENG.). 32p. (J). (gr. k-3). 16.99 (978-1-4556-1460-8(2), Pelican Publishing) Arcadia Publishing.

Duckers, John. The Amazing Adventures of the Silly Six. 2013. (Illus.). 188p. pap. (978-1-78148-626-9(3)) Grosvenor Hse. Publishing Ltd.

Dunlap, Jim. Sam Snake Says. Holland, Kathy, illus. 2008. 35p. pap. 24.95 (978-1-60672-709-6(5)) America Star Bks.

Dyckman, Ame. Huggy the Python Hugs Too Hard. Griffiths, Alex G., illus. 2018. (Wee Beasties Ser.). (ENG.). 22p. (J). (gr. -1-k). bds. 8.99 (978-1-5344-1080-0(5), Little Simon) Little Simon.

Eagle, Golden. It's Good to Shed Your Skin (Snake Medicine) l.t. ed. 2004. (Illus.). 20p. (J). per. 12.99 (978-1-932338-38-6(1)) Lifevest Publishing, Inc.

Estes-Hill, Katrina. My Imagination. Kwong, Alvina, illus. 2007. 32p. (J). (gr. -1-2). 15.95 (978-0-9745715-6-0(3)) KRBY Creations, LLC.

Ferrara, Gin. I'm Not Afraid of Snakes. 2009. (ENG.). 39p. pap. 22.95 (978-0-557-15979-6(2)) Lulu Pr., Inc.

Fewer, Patrick W. Sammy the Snow Snake: A Halloween Haunting Yukon Style. 2009. 24p. pap. 11.49 (978-1-4490-2075-0(5)) AuthorHouse.

—Sammy the Snow Snake: Christmas Rain. 2008. (ENG.). 28p. 12.49 (978-1-4389-4283-4(4)) AuthorHouse.

Fitzpatrick-Hale-Herself, Donna Marie. Snake & Mouse: Ryan's birthday Tea. 2011. (Illus.). 44p. pap. 17.04 (978-1-4567-8590-1(7)) AuthorHouse.

Fletcher, Perry. Why Snakes Don't Have Legs. 2008. 44p. pap. 24.95 (978-1-60474-973-1(3)) America Star Bks.

Foltyn, Sue. Mayzeemioletu. 2009. 12p. pap. 9.95 (978-1-4490-2244-0(8)) AuthorHouse.

Forde, Catherine. Slippy. 2012. (Stoke Books Titles Ser.). 72p. (J). (gr. 5-8). pap. 45.32 (978-0-7613-9223-1(8)); pap. 7.95 (978-1-78112-032-3(3)); lib. bdg. 22.60 (978-1-78112-031-6(5)) Stoke Bks.

Fowler, Lisa. Snakes & Stones. (ENG.). (J). (gr. 2-7). 2018. 296p. pap. 8.99 (978-1-5107-3554-5(2)) 2016. 240p. 15.99 (978-1-5107-1031-3(0)) Skyhorse Publishing Co., Inc. (Sky Pony Pr.).

Funk, Lynda. The Snake, the Humming Bird & Me. 2013. 44p. pap. 19.99 (978-1-4685-3329-3(0)) AuthorHouse.

Giff, Patricia Reilly. Watch Out! Man-Eating Snake. 79p. (J). (gr. 1-2). pap. 3.99 (978-0-8072-1281-3(4), Listening Library) Random Hse. Audio Publishing Group.

Goss, Jamie. The Snake Without a Hiss, 1 vol. 2010. 36p. pap. 24.95 (978-1-4489-4446-0(5)) PublishAmerica, Inc.

Graham, Bobby G. Jake the Snake. 2010. 24p. pap. 16.95 (978-1-4497-0568-8(5), WestBow Pr.) Author Solutions, LLC.

Greedy Python, 1 vol. 2012. (Your Reading Path Ser.). (ENG., Illus.). 24p. (J). (gr. 3-3). pap. (978-1-4424-4576-5(9), 747e8978-ed66-4776-a205-3d260273a01b, Rosen Classroom) Rosen Publishing Group, Inc., The.

Green, Poppy. Forget-Me-Not Lake. Bell, Jennifer A., illus. 2015. (Adventures of Sophie Mouse Ser.: 3). (ENG.). 128p. (J). (gr. k-4). 17.99 (978-1-4814-3000-5(9), Little Simon) Little Simon.

—Forget-Me-Not Lake. Bell, Jennifer A., illus. 2017. (Adventures of Sophie Mouse Ser.). (ENG.). 128p. (J). (gr. k-4). lib. bdg. 31.36 (978-1-5321-4112-6(2), 26985, Chapter Bks.) Spotlight.

—A New Friend. Bell, Jennifer A., illus. 2015. (Adventures of Sophie Mouse Ser.: 1). (ENG.). 128p. (J). (gr. k-4). pap. 6.99 (978-1-4814-2832-3(2), Little Simon) Little Simon.

Greenburg, Dan. Secrets of Dripping Fang, Book Eight: When Bad Snakes Attack Good Children. Fischer, Scott M., illus. 2007. (Secrets of Dripping Fang Ser.: Bk. 8). (ENG.). 144p. (J). (gr. 3-7). 11.99 (978-0-15-206056-5(1), 1198190, Clarion Bks.) HarperCollins Pubs.

Greene, Joshua M. Kaliya, Serpent King: New Edition. rev. ed. 2012. (ENG., Illus.). 24p. (gr. -1). 14.99 (978-1-60887-148-3(7)) Mandala Publishing.

Grover, Kuloa A. Charlie the Snake. 2012. 32p. pap. 19.99 (978-1-4685-5568-4(5)) AuthorHouse.

Guillain, Charlotte. Rumplesnakeskin, 1 vol. Beacon, Dawn, illus. 2014. (Animal Fairy Tales Ser.). (ENG.). 24p. (J). (gr. -1-2). lib. bdg. 23.99 (978-1-4109-6111-2(7), 124738, Raintree) Capstone.

Gutman, Dan. My Weird School: Class Pet Mess! Paillot, Jim, illus. 2017. (I Can Read Level 2 Ser.). (ENG.). 32p. (J). (gr. -1-3). pap. 4.99 (978-0-06-236746-4(3), HarperCollins) HarperCollins Pubs.

Halfmann, Janet. Garter Snake at Willow Creek Lane. Wertheim, Anne, illus. 2011. (ENG.). 32p. (J). (gr. k-4). 19.95 (978-1-60727-206-9(7)); pap. 8.95 (978-1-60727-208-3(3)) Soundprints.

Haussinger, D. & Hassinger, Peter W. Susanna the Snake. Date not set. (ENG.). 320p. (YA). (gr. 7-18). pap. 5.99 (978-0-06-447212-8(4)) HarperCollins Pubs.

Hayes, Joe. The Gum Chewing Rattler, Vol .1. Castro L., Antonio, illus. 2008. (ENG.). 32p. (J). (gr. k-6). pap. 11.95 (978-1-933693-19-4(3), 23353382, Cinco Puntos Press) Lee & Low Bks., Inc.

—My Pet Rattlesnake. 2014. (ENG., Illus.). 32p. (J). (gr. k-4). 16.95 (978-1-935955-61-0(6), 23353382, Cinco Puntos Press) Lee & Low Bks., Inc.

—My Pet Rattlesnake, 1 vol. L., Antonio Castro, illus. 2014. (ENG.). 32p. (J). (gr. k-4). pap. 11.95 (978-1-935955-62-7(4), 23353382, Cinco Puntos Press) Lee & Low Bks., Inc.

Hiiasen, Carl. Hoot. 2014. 17.00 (978-1-63419-707-6(0)) Perfection Learning Corp.

Hill, Michelle M. Stanley. 2012. 12p. pap. 15.99 (978-1-4772-2923-1(X)) AuthorHouse.

Himes, John. Everyone Is Special. 2012. 24p. pap. 24.95 (978-1-4626-7462-6(3)) America Star Bks.

Hobson, Joseph. The Snake River Adventures: Floating the Snake. 2012. 88p. pap. 10.95 (978-1-938223-04-4(7)) Salem Author Services.

Hoenecke, Karen. Snake Hunts for Lunch. Drzewiecki, Paul, illus. l.t. ed. 2005. (ENG.). 12p. (gr. k-2). pap. 7.95 (978-1-57874-006-2(1), Kaeden Bks.) Kaeden Corp.

Hsia, Pei Chen. The Little Dumpling. 2012. 82p. pap. 19.95 (978-1-4626-8041-2(0)) America Star Bks.

Jackson, Barry E. Danny Diamondback. Jackson, Barry E., illus. 2008. (Illus.). 40p. (J). (gr. k-2). lib. bdg. 17.89 (978-0-06-113185-1(7)) HarperCollins Pubs.

Jake the Snake: Set D Individual Title, 6 Packs. (Supersonic Phonics Ser.). (gr. k-3). 29.00 (978-0-7635-0550-9(1)) Rigby Education.

Jamesson, Christine. The Adventures of Samantha the Black Racer Snake. 2005. (ENG.). 28p. per. 18.00 (978-1-4208-1873-4(2)) AuthorHouse.

Jarman, Julia. Class Two at the Zoo. Chapman, Lynne, illus. 2007. (Carolrhoda Picture Bks.). (ENG.). 32p. (J). (gr. k-2). 16.95 (978-0-8225-7132-2(3), Carolrhoda Bks.) Lerner Publishing Group.

Jennings, Patrick. We Can't All Be Rattlesnakes. (J). 2011. (ENG.). 144p. (gr. 3-7). pap. 9.99 (978-0-06-082117-3(5), HarperCollins) 2009. 121p. lib. bdg. 16.89 (978-0-06-082116-6(7)) HarperCollins Pubs.

Jones, C. B. The Cats' Meow. Green, Chris, illus. 2017. (Bog Hollow Boys Ser.). (ENG.). 72p. (J). (gr. 4-8). lib. bdg. 25.32 (978-1-4965-4057-7(3), 133365, Stone Arch Bks.) Capstone.

—Kiss of the Snake. Green, Chris, illus. 2017. (Bog Hollow Boys Ser.). (ENG.). 72p. (J). (gr. 4-8). lib. bdg. 25.32 (978-1-4965-4056-0(5), 133364, Stone Arch Bks.) Capstone.

Josephine Breglia. The Adventures of Poke Sa' Baar. 2012. 28p. pap. 24.95 (978-1-4626-8820-3(9)) America Star Bks.

Jostand, Jeffrey Jay. Sedrick the Snake. Llamas, Kristin, illus. 2008. 32p. pap. 24.95 (978-1-4241-9944-0(1)) America Star Bks.

Kidd, Jessica A. Zachary Zoom. 2009. 28p. pap. 12.25 (978-1-60860-502-6(7), Eloquent Bks.) Strategic Book Publishing & Rights Agency (SBPRA).

Kimmel, Eric A. Why the Snake Crawls on Its Belly. Davis, Allen, illus. 2005. 32p. (J). (gr. 1-4). 14.95 (978-1-930143-20-3(6), Devora Publishing) Simcha Media Group.

Kimura, Ken. 999 Frogs & a Little Brother. Murakami, Yasunari, illus. 2015. (ENG.). 40p. (J). (gr. -1-2). 17.95 (978-0-7358-4202-1(7)) North-South Bks., Inc.

Kipling, Rudyard & Pinkney, Jerry. Rikki-Tikki-Tavi. 2004. (Illus.). (gr. -1-3). 17.00 (978-0-7569-3250-3(5)) Perfection Learning Corp.

Klemer, Amy Wade. The Scary Snake Monster. 2003. (Illus.). 16p. (J). pap. 8.00 (978-0-9729216-1-9(3)) ABCDMoon Publishing.

Krepela, Rebecca. Vernon, Drake & Chomp. 2013. 20p. pap. 24.95 (978-1-62709-841-0(0)) America Star Bks.

Krulik, Nancy. Free the Worms! John & Wendy, illus. 2008. (Katie Kazoo, Switcheroo Ser.). 78p. (J). 11.65 (978-0-7569-8807-4(1)) Perfection Learning Corp.

Lane, Leonie. Fork Tongue Freimon. 2006. 164p. per. (978-1-84667-009-1(8)) Derwent Pr., The.

Lawrence, Cherry. David & the Blue Racer. 2006. 53p. pap. 16.95 (978-1-4241-3339-0(4)) PublishAmerica, Inc.

Little, Lorna. The Mark of the Wagarl. Lyndon, Janice, illus. 2004. 28p. (J). (978-1-875641-97-0(1)) Magabala Bks.

Lumry, Amanda & Hurwitz, Laura. Operation Orangutan. 2007. (Adventures of Riley (Unnumberd) Ser.). (Illus.). 36p. (J). (gr. -1-3). 18.95 (978-0-9748411-7-5(X)) Eaglemont Pr.

Maelor, Gwawr, et al. Neli Neidr. 2005. (WEL., Illus.). 12p. pap. (978-1-85644-839-0(8)) CAA.

Marchetti, Dave. Nestle's Big Adventure. 2012. 28p. pap. 21.99 (978-1-4691-4672-0(X)) Xlibris Corp.

Marsh, Carole. The Mystery at Rattlesnake Ridge. 2014. (Wildlife Mysteries Ser.). (ENG., Illus.). 158p. (J). (gr. 2-9). pap. 7.99 (978-0-635-11188-3(8), Marsh, Carole Bks.) Gallopade International.

McBrayer, Cassidy. You Can, Toucan! You Can. 2008. 20p. pap. 15.95 (978-1-4327-1132-0(6)) Outskirts Pr., Inc.

McGuire, Leslie. We Read Phonics-If I Had a Snake. Johnson, Meredith, illus. 2010. (We Read Phonics Ser.). 32p. (J). (gr. 1-5). 9.95 (978-1-60115-333-3(3)); pap. 4.99 (978-1-60115-334-0(1)) Treasure Bay, Inc.

Meister, Cari. Clues in the Attic, 1 vol. Simard, Rémy, illus. 2010. (My First Graphic Novel Ser.). (ENG.). 32p. (J). (gr. k-2). pap. 6.25 (978-1-4342-2283-1(7), 103151, Stone Arch Bks.) Capstone.

Miller, Scott. Prairie Whispers. 2006. 99p. pap. 16.95 (978-1-4241-4790-8(5)) PublishAmerica, Inc.

Minz-Kammer, Koda. Pinpot Tiger & the Lost Monkey. 2008. (ENG.). 54p. pap. 20.00 (978-0-557-01646-4(0)) Lulu Pr., Inc.

Montgomery Gibson, Jane. Jake the Fake Snake. Montgomery Gibson, Jane, illus. 2005. (Illus.). (J). bds. 8.99 (978-1-4183-0026-5(8)) Christ Inspired, Inc.

Morpurgo, Michael. Snakes & Ladders. Wilson, Anne, illus. 2006. (Yellow Bananas Ser.). (ENG.). 48p. (J). (gr. -1-3). lib. bdg. (978-0-7787-0952-7(3)) Crabtree Publishing Co.

Mullarkey, Lisa. Carly. Franco, Paula, illus. (Chicas Poni (Pony Girls) Ser.).Tr. of Carly. 112p. (J). 2016. (SPA.). (gr. 1-4). lib. bdg. 38.50 (978-1-61479-621-3(1), 25052) 2015. (ENG.). (gr. 2-5). 38.50 (978-1-62402-127-5(1), 19375) ABDO Publishing Co. (Calico Chapter Bks.).

Nelson, Sean. Bungles Does the Bunny Op. 2012. 36p. pap. 16.95 (978-1-4575-1106-6(1)) Dog Ear Publishing, LLC.

Newton-Kowalsky, Jacqueline. Itsy Bitsy Stories for Itsy Bitsy Tigers. 2012. 32p. pap. (978-1-77097-138-7(6)) FriesenPress.

Noble, Trinka Hakes. Jimmy's Boa & the Bungee Jump Slam Dunk. Kellogg, Steven, illus. 2005. 28p. (gr. -1-3). 16.00 (978-0-7569-5765-0(6)) Perfection Learning Corp.

Noruziaan, Bahman. The Lonely Snake: Stories of Inspector Rabbit. 2013. 20p. pap. 13.77 (978-1-4669-8678-7(6)) Trafford Publishing.

Parker, Emma. Square Sidney. 2010. 16p. pap. (978-1-877561-31-3(2)) First Edition Ltd.

Partee, Andrea. Jed, the Boy, the Snake & the Window. 2007. 160p. 30.99 (978-1-4257-6401-2(0)); per. 20.99 (978-1-4257-6399-2(5)) Xlibris Corp.

Perry, Marie/Fritz. Cecil's New Year's Eve Tail. Perry, Marie/Fritz, illus. 2007. (Illus.). 32p. (J). lib. bdg. (978-0-9755675-2-4(7)) Buttonweed Pr., L.L.C.

Provencher, Rose-Marie. Slithery Jake. Carter, Abby, illus. 2004. (ENG.). 32p. (J). 15.99 (978-0-06-623820-3(X)) HarperCollins Pubs.

Rhiger, Tenna. The Story about How the Spotted Wobblepig Got Its Spots. 2012. 40p. pap. (978-1-84903-152-3(5)) Schiel & Denver Publishing Ltd.

Ricchi, Brenda. The Grandchildren's Bible Journey-the Big Fall. 2010. (ENG.). 34p. pap. 15.51 (978-0-557-38645-1(4)) Lulu Pr., Inc.

Riordan, Rick. Kane Chronicles, the Book Three: Serpent's Shadow, the-Kane Chronicles, the Book Three. 2018. (Kane Chronicles Ser.: 3). (ENG., Illus.). 496p. (J). (gr. 5-9). pap. 9.99 (978-1-368-01357-4(0), Disney-Hyperion) Disney Publishing Worldwide.

Ripes, Laura. The Spaghetti-Slurping Sewer Serpent, 0 vols. Zenz, Aaron, illus. 2012. (ENG.). 32p. (J). (gr. -1-3). 16.99 (978-0-7614-6101-2(9), 9780761461012, Two Lions) Amazon Publishing.

Rogers, Kelly. Buyer Beware, 1 vol. Peterschmidt, Betsy, illus. 2016. (Rm. 201 Ser.). (ENG.). 48p. (J). (gr. 3-7). lib. bdg. 34.21 (978-1-62402-167-1(0), 21581, Spellbound) Magic Wagon.

Rose, Chloe Gayle & Rose, Tammy Marie. The Snake That Eats Cake. 2012. 28p. pap. 24.95 (978-1-4626-9882-0(4)) America Star Bks.

Sande, Hans. Snake in the Grass. Vetleseter, Tonje, tr. from NOR. Moursund, Gry, illus. 2008. 40p. (J). (gr. -1-1). 16.95 (978-0-9815761-0-7(9)) Mackenzie Smiles, LLC.

Sargent, Dave & Sargent, Pat. Young Redi: Friendship!, Vol. 3. Woodward, Elaine, illus. 2003. (Young Animal Pride Ser.: 3). 24p. (J). pap. 10.95 (978-1-56763-868-4(6)); lib. bdg. 20.95 (978-1-56763-867-7(8)) Ozark Publishing.

Schleuning, Todd & Schleuning, Cheryl. The Misphits: Story of Snake. Vene, Alessandro, illus. 2013. (ENG.). (J). (gr. -1-3). 15.95 (978-1-62086-302-2(2)) Amplify Publishing Group.

Scholastic, Inc. Staff & West, Tracey. Snake Attack! 2012. (LEGO Ninjago Chapter Bks.: 5). lib. bdg. 14.75 (978-0-606-26770-0(0)) Turtleback.

Schraff, Anne. Something Dreadful down Below, 1 vol. unabr. ed. 2010. (Q Reads Ser.). (ENG.). 32p. (YA). (gr. 9-12). pap. 8.50 (978-1-61651-205-7(9)) Saddleback Educational Publishing, Inc.

Schwartz, Jean. The Snake with a Bellyache. Fisher, Todd, illus. 2007. 20p. per. 10.95 (978-1-934246-41-2(7)) Peppertree Pr., The.

Seuling, Barbara. Robert & the Great Escape. Brewer, Paul, illus. 2003. (Robert Bks.). (ENG.). 120p. (J). 15.95 (978-0-8126-2700-8(8)) Cricket Bks.

Sharp, Kevin. The Amazing Adventures of Ted Shuttle: Book One. 2012. (Illus.). 24p. pap. 19.82 (978-1-4772-4286-5(4)) AuthorHouse.

Shepherd, Donna J. Sully's Topsy Tale. Collier, Kevin Scott, illus. 2010. 20p. pap. 10.95 (978-1-61633-047-7(3)) Guardian Angel Publishing, Inc.

Shi, Charleston. The Quest of the Phoenix: Book 3, Rage of the Serpents. 2010. 188p. pap. 14.95 (978-1-60844-403-8(1)) Dog Ear Publishing, LLC.

Slider-Baker, Belinda. Lost Stripes, Please Return. 2008. 32p. pap. 24.95 (978-1-60813-075-7(4)) America Star Bks.

Smiley, Mark. A Journey Far Away. 2006. 164p. pap. 13.95 (978-1-59526-494-7(9)) Aeon Publishing Inc.

Snake's Reward: Individual Title Six-Packs. (Story Steps Ser.). (gr. k-2). 32.00 (978-0-7635-9821-1(6)) Rigby Education.

Snicket, Lemony, pseud. Le Laboratoire aux Serpents. 24.95 (978-2-09-211034-8(9)) Nathan, Fernand FRA. Dist: Distribooks, Inc.

Snyder, Susan E. Shivers & Shakes. 2006. (Illus.). 31p. (J). (gr. k-2). 9.95 (978-0-9767163-5-8(6)) Kotzig Publishing, Inc.

Spohn, Kate. Turtle & Snake's Day at the Beach. Spohn, Kate, illus. 2004. (Penguin Young Readers, Level 2 Ser.). (Illus.). 32p. (J). (gr. 1-2). mass mkt. 4.99 (978-0-14-240157-6(9), Penguin Young Readers) Penguin Young Readers Group.

—Turtle & Snake's Day at the Beach. Spohn, Kate, illus. 2004. (Puffin Easy-to-Read Ser.). (Illus.). 32p. (gr. k-3). 14.00 (978-0-7569-2826-1(5)) Perfection Learning Corp.

—Turtle & Snake's Spooky Halloween. Spohn, Kate, illus. 2003. (Easy-to-Read Ser.). (Illus.). 32p. (J). (gr. -1-3). 11.65 (978-0-7569-1949-8(5)) Perfection Learning Corp.

Standish, Joyce, ed. The Adventures of Ryan Lincoln. Cooper, Nicole, illus. 2012. 46p. (J). pap. 10.00 (978-0-9716244-5-0(3)) TLS Publishing.

Stengel, Joyce. St. Patrick & the Three Brave Mice, 1 vol. Leonhard, Herb, illus. 2009. (ENG.). 32p. (J). (gr. k-3). 16.99 (978-1-58980-663-4(8), Pelican Publishing) Arcadia Publishing.

Stepp, Shirley. Santa Lost His Cell Phone. 2012. 24p. 24.95 (978-1-4626-5479-6(7)) America Star Bks.

Storad, Conrad J. Rattlesnake Rules. Jensen, Nathaniel P., illus. 2012. (ENG.). 40p. (J). (gr. 1-4). pap. 10.50 (978-1-58985-211-2(7), Story Monsters Pr.) Story Monsters LLC.

Stycznski, Gary. The Animals of Greenback Valley: The Magic Card. 2009. 32p. pap. 24.95 (978-1-59858-930-6(X)) Dog Ear Publishing, LLC.

Suen, Anastasia. A Great Idea? An Up2U Character Education Adventure, 1 vol. Dippold, Jane, illus. 2015. (Up2U Adventures Ser.). (ENG.). 80p. (J). (gr. 2-5). 35.64 (978-1-62402-093-3(3), 17355, Calico Chapter Bks.) ABDO Publishing Co.

Sussman, Michael. Duckworth, the Difficult Child. Sardà, Júlia, illus. 2019. (ENG.). 40p. (J). (gr. -1-3). 17.99 (978-1-5344-0512-7(7)) Simon & Schuster Children's Publishing.

Taylor, Melissa Utz. Sneaky Snake. 2011. 24p. (gr. 1-2). pap. 14.99 (978-1-4567-5518-8(8)) AuthorHouse.

Top That, ed. Revolving Nursery Rhymes. 2008. 12p. (978-1-84666-573-8(6), Tide Mill Pr.) Top That! Publishing PLC.

—Sammy the Snake. 2008. (Story Book Ser.). 18p. (J). (gr. -1). *(978-1-84666-541-7(8)*, Tide Mill Pr.) Top That! Publishing PLC.

Trevethan, Glenn A. The Adventures of Sammi Snake: Sammi's Coat. 2012. 24p. pap. 13.97 *(978-1-61897-926-1(4)*, Strategic Bk. Publishing) Strategic Book Publishing & Rights Agency (SBPRA).

Turner, Nicci. Milky's Story, 1 vol. 2010. 18p. pap. 24.95 *(978-1-4489-6808-4(9))* PublishAmerica, Inc.

Twinem, Neecy. Baby Snake's Shapes. 2004. (New Board Book Ser.).Tr. of Las formas de Bebe Serpiente. (ENG., Illus.). 12p. (J). (gr. -1-k). bds. 5.95 *(978-0-87358-850-8(9))*; bds. 6.95 *(978-0-87358-866-9(5))* Cooper Square Publishing Llc.

van Arsdale, Peternelle. The Cold Is in Her Bones. (ENG.). (YA). (gr. 7). 2020. 304p. pap. 11.99 *(978-1-4814-8845-7(7))* 2019. (Illus.). 288p. 18.99 *(978-1-4814-8844-0(9))* McElderry, Margaret K. Bks. (McElderry, Margaret K. Bks.).

Velle, Tori. Jake the Snake. 2009. 40p. pap. 16.99 *(978-1-4490-4431-2(X))* AuthorHouse.

Virginia H. Lasher. The Secret of Crooked Creek. 2006. 58p. 20.00 *(978-1-59926-625-1(3))*; pap. 10.00 *(978-1-4134-9728-1(4))* Xlibris Corp.

Walker, Cheryl. Black Snake, King Snake. 2003. 7p. (J). pap. 1.50 *(978-0-9726326-2-1(X))* TechArts International LLC.

Walters, Eric. Ricky. 2011. (ENG.). 238p. (J). (gr. 5-7). pap. 9.95 *(978-1-55455-121-7(8)*, 5ab2257a-79a4-4920-8a0c-2f3a783d7c18) Fitzhenry & Whiteside, Ltd. CAN. Dist: Firefly Bks., Ltd.

Warner, Michael N. Tales to Make You Scream for Your Momma. Warner, Robert, illus. 2018. 208p. (J). pap. 11.95 *(978-0-9963756-1-0(9))* All About Kids Publishing.

Weigl Publishers, creator. The Snake & His Tail: How Can You Support Your Team? 2013. (AV2 Animated Storytime Ser.: Vol. 19). (ENG., Illus.). 32p. (J). (gr. -1-3). lib. bdg. 29.99 *(978-1-62127-923-5(5)*, AV2 by Weigl) Weigl Pubs., Inc.

Welsh, Mary Reddick. Sammy, the Little Green Snake Who Wanted to Fly. Welsh, Mary Reddick, illus. 2011. (Illus.). 26p. pap. 11.95 *(978-1-936411-09-2(1))* YBK Pubs., Inc.

West, Tracey. Rise of the Snakes. 2012. (Ninjago Readers Ser.: 4). lib. bdg. 13.55 *(978-0-606-26556-0(2))* Turtleback.

—Snake Attack!, Bk. 5. 2012. (LEGO Ninjago Ser.). (ENG.). 80p. (J). (gr. 2-5). pap. 4.99 *(978-0-545-46518-2(4))* Scholastic, Inc.

Weston, Anne. My Brother Needs a Boa, 1 vol. Nathan, Cheryl, illus. 2005. (ENG.). 32p. (J). (gr. -1-3). 15.95 *(978-1-932065-96-1(2))* Star Bright Bks., Inc.

Weston Woods Staff, creator. Crictor. 2011. 38.75 *(978-0-545-23361-3(5))*; 18.95 *(978-0-545-23360-6(7))* Weston Woods Studios, Inc.

—Rikki-Tikki-Tavi. 2011. 38.75 *(978-0-439-72979-6(3))*; 18.95 *(978-0-439-72977-2(7))* Weston Woods Studios, Inc.

Wheeler, J. D. Gummery & Lubber. 2008. 56p. pap. 16.95 *(978-1-60563-432-6(8))* America Star Bks.

Whitmore, Gary. Prince Luna & the Space Dreamers. 2011. (ENG.). 204p. pap. 8.50 *(978-1-4565-8438-2(3))* CreateSpace Independent Publishing Platform.

Wildsmith, Brian. Jungle Party, 1 vol. Wildsmith, Brian, illus. 2006. (ENG., Illus.). 32p. (J). pap. 6.95 *(978-1-59572-053-5(7))*; (gr. -1-3). 17.95 *(978-1-59572-052-8(9))* Star Bright Bks., Inc.

Willems, Mo. Can I Play Too? 2012. (Elephant & Piggie Bks.). (CHI & JPN.). (J). (gr. -1-3). pap. *(978-986-189-329-7(6))* Grimm Cultural Ent., Co., Ltd.

—Can I Play Too?-An Elephant & Piggie Book. 2010. (Elephant & Piggie Book Ser.). (ENG., Illus.). 64p. (J). (gr. -1-k). 9.99 *(978-1-4231-1991-3(6)*. Hyperion Books for Children) Disney Publishing Worldwide.

Willis, Jeanne. Be Gentle, Python! Birchall, Mark, illus. 2005. (Picture Bks.). 28p. (J). (gr. k-2). 7.95 *(978-1-57505-508-4(2))* Lerner Publishing Group.

Wilson-Timmons, Karen. Agha the Eight-Mile Monster. Dubois, Marie Thérèse, illus. rev. ed. 2012. (ENG.). 32p. (J). (gr. -1). 16.99 *(978-1-60887-124-7(X))* Mandala Publishing.

Winkler, Henry & Oliver, Lin. Fake Snakes & Weird Wizards #4. Garrett, Scott, illus. 2015. (Here's Hank Ser.: 4). (ENG.). 128p. (J). (gr. 1-3). 6.99 *(978-0-448-48252-1(5)*, Penguin Workshop) Penguin Young Readers Group.

Yates, Gene. What Can Simon Be? 2005. (Illus.). (J). *(978-1-58865-284-3(X))* Kidsbooks, LLC.

Yates, Gene & Frank, Thomas. What Can Simon Be? Yates, Gene, illus. 2006. (Illus.). (J). *(978-1-58865-366-6(8))* Kidsbooks, LLC.

Yoon, Salina. Opposnakes: A Lift-The-Flap Book about Opposites. Yoon, Salina, illus. 2009. (ENG., Illus.). 16p. (J). (gr. -1-1). 14.99 *(978-1-4169-7875-6(5)*, Little Simon) Little Simon.

SNOOPY (FICTITIOUS CHARACTER)—FICTION

Publications International Ltd. Staff, ed. Look & Find: Snoopy. 2013. 24p. (J). (gr. 1-3). 7.99 *(978-1-4127-1722-9(1)*, 6273d751-5dbd-41ad-a19f-1ef74baf570f) Phoenix International Publications, Inc.

Schulz, Charles. Alles Peanuts. Herbst, Gabriele & Rolle, Ekkehard, trs. from ENG. (Snoopy & die Peanuts Ser.: Vol. 26). (GER., Illus.). 96p. (J). pap. *(978-3-8105-1871-2(9))* Kruger, Wolfgang Verlag, GmbH DEU. Dist: International Bk. Import Service, Inc.

—Allzeit Bereit. Herbst, Gabriele & Rolle, Ekkehard, trs. from ENG. (Snoopy & die Peanuts Ser.: Vol. 35). (GER., Illus.). 96p. (J). pap. *(978-3-8105-1891-0(3))* Kruger, Wolfgang Verlag, GmbH DEU. Dist: International Bk. Import Service, Inc.

— An der Langen Leine. Herbst, Gabriele & Rolle, Ekkehard, trs. from ENG. (Snoopy & die Peanuts Ser.: Vol. 30). (GER., Illus.). 96p. (J). pap. *(978-3-8105-1880-4(8))* Kruger, Wolfgang Verlag, GmbH DEU. Dist: International Bk. Import Service, Inc.

—Auf den Hund Gekommen. Herbst, Gabriele & Rolle, Ekkehard, trs. from ENG. (Snoopy & die Peanuts Ser.: Vol. 34). (GER., Illus.). 96p. (J). pap. *(978-3-8105-1888-0(3))* Kruger, Wolfgang Verlag, GmbH DEU. Dist: International Bk. Import Service, Inc.

—Den Wind im Ruecken. Herbst, Gabriele & Rolle, Ekkehard, trs. from ENG. (Snoopy & die Peanuts Ser.: Vol. 6). (GER., Illus.). 96p. (J). pap. *(978-3-8105-1819-4(0))* Kruger, Wolfgang Verlag, GmbH DEU. Dist: International Bk. Import Service, Inc.

—Einfach Genial. Herbst, Gabriele & Rolle, Ekkehard, trs. from ENG. (Snoopy & die Peanuts Ser.: Vol. 31). (GER., Illus.). 96p. (J). pap. *(978-3-8105-1881-1(6))* Kruger, Wolfgang Verlag, GmbH DEU. Dist: International Bk. Import Service, Inc.

—Einfach Unschlagbar. Herbst, Gabriele & Rolle, Ekkehard, trs. from ENG. (Snoopy & die Peanuts Ser.: Vol. 1). (GER., Illus.). 96p. (J). pap. *(978-3-8105-1811-8(5))* Kruger, Wolfgang Verlag, GmbH DEU. Dist: International Bk. Import Service, Inc.

—Grundlos Gluecklich. Herbst, Gabriele & Rolle, Ekkehard, trs. from ENG. (Snoopy & die Peanuts Ser.: Vol. 37). (GER., Illus.). 96p. (J). pap. *(978-3-8105-1893-4(X))* Kruger, Wolfgang Verlag, GmbH DEU. Dist: International Bk. Import Service, Inc.

—Gut Aufgelegt. Herbst, Gabriele & Rolle, Ekkehard, trs. from ENG. (Snoopy & die Peanuts Ser.: Vol. 12). (GER., Illus.). 96p. (J). pap. *(978-3-8105-1828-6(X))* Kruger, Wolfgang Verlag, GmbH DEU. Dist: International Bk. Import Service, Inc.

—Herzlich Unverschaemt. Herbst, Gabriele & Rolle, Ekkehard, trs. from ENG. (Snoopy & die Peanuts Ser.: Vol. 9). (GER., Illus.). 128p. (J). pap. *(978-3-8105-1823-1(9))* Kruger, Wolfgang Verlag, GmbH DEU. Dist: International Bk. Import Service, Inc.

—Himmel & Hoelle. Herbst, Gabriele & Rolle, Ekkehard, trs. from ENG. (Snoopy & die Peanuts Ser.: Vol. 23). (GER., Illus.). 96p. (J). pap. *(978-3-8105-1867-5(0))* Kruger, Wolfgang Verlag, GmbH DEU. Dist: International Bk. Import Service, Inc.

—Hoch die Tassen. Herbst, Gabriele & Rolle, Ekkehard, trs. from ENG. (Snoopy & die Peanuts Ser.: Vol. 36). (GER., Illus.). 96p. (J). pap. *(978-3-8105-1892-7(1))* Kruger, Wolfgang Verlag, GmbH DEU. Dist: International Bk. Import Service, Inc.

—Immer Dabei. Herbst, Gabriele & Rolle, Ekkehard, trs. from ENG. (Snoopy & die Peanuts Ser.: Vol. 27). (GER., Illus.). 96p. (J). pap. *(978-3-8105-1872-9(7))* Kruger, Wolfgang Verlag, GmbH DEU. Dist: International Bk. Import Service, Inc.

—Kaum zu Bremsen. Rolle, Ekkehard, tr. from ENG. (Snoopy & die Peanuts Ser.: Vol. 11). (GER., Illus.). 128p. (J). pap. *(978-3-8105-1827-9(1))* Kruger, Wolfgang Verlag, GmbH DEU. Dist: International Bk. Import Service, Inc.

—Pfoten Hoch! Herbst, Gabriele & Rolle, Ekkehard, trs. from ENG. (Snoopy & die Peanuts Ser.: Vol. 33). (GER., Illus.). 96p. (J). pap. *(978-3-8105-1887-3(5))* Kruger, Wolfgang Verlag, GmbH DEU. Dist: International Bk. Import Service, Inc.

—Schwer in Fahrt. Herbst, Gabriele & Rolle, Ekkehard, trs. from ENG. (Snoopy & die Peanuts Ser.: Vol. 7). (GER., Illus.). 128p. (J). pap. *(978-3-8105-1820-0(4))* Kruger, Wolfgang Verlag, GmbH DEU. Dist: International Bk. Import Service, Inc.

—Voll auf die Schnauze. Herbst, Gabriele & Rolle, Ekkehard, trs. from ENG. (Snoopy & die Peanuts Ser.: Vol. 32). (GER., Illus.). 96p. (J). pap. *(978-3-8105-1886-6(7))* Kruger, Wolfgang Verlag, GmbH DEU. Dist: International Bk. Import Service, Inc.

—Voll im Griff. Herbst, Gabriele & Rolle, Ekkehard, trs. from ENG. (Snoopy & die Peanuts Ser.: Vol. 13). (GER., Illus.). 128p. (J). pap. *(978-3-8105-1829-3(8))* Kruger, Wolfgang Verlag, GmbH DEU. Dist: International Bk. Import Service, Inc.

Schulz, Charles M. It's the Easter Beagle, Charlie Brown. Scott, Vicki, illus. 2016. (Peanuts Ser.). (ENG.). 32p. (J). (gr. -1). 7.99 *(978-1-4814-6159-7(1)*, Simon Spotlight) Simon Spotlight.

—It's the Great Pumpkin, Charlie Brown: with Sound & Music. 2012. (ENG., Illus.). 48p. (J). (gr. -1-3). 19.95 *(978-0-7624-4606-3(4)*, Running Pr. Kids) Running Pr.

—Snoopy: Cowabunga! A PEANUTS Collection. 2013. (Peanuts Kids Ser.: 1). (ENG., Illus.). 224p. (J). 11.99 *(978-1-4494-5079-3(2))* Andrews McMeel Publishing.

—Snoopy's Thanksgiving. 2014. (Peanuts Seasonal Collection: 0). (ENG., Illus.). 64p. (J). (gr. 1-12). 9.99 *(978-1-60699-778-9(5)*, 699778) Fantagraphics Bks.

Schulz, Charles M., creator. Peanuts: Be Brave: Peanuts Wisdom to Carry You Through. 2013. (ENG., Illus.). 72p. (J). (gr. -1-17). 7.95 *(978-0-7624-4861-6(X)*, Running Pr. Kids) Running Pr.

SNORKELING

see Skin Diving

SNOW

Alvarez García, Gloria. La nieve-juego de leer. 2005. (El Juego de Leer Ser.). (SPA.). 6p. 9.95 *(978-84-272-6681-0(2))* Molino, Editorial ESP. Dist: Distribooks, Inc.

Appleby, Alex. It's Snowing!, 1 vol. 2013. (What's the Weather? Ser.). 24p. (J). (gr. k-k). (ENG.). 25.27 *(978-1-4339-9400-5(3)*, a6105c64-914b-4df2-8023-527dbb5b97ea); (ENG.). pap. 9.15 *(978-1-4339-9401-2(1)*, 9dee1de7-57db-4d52-ad1f-83321d0ea882); pap. 48.90 *(978-1-4339-9402-9(X))* Stevens, Gareth Publishing LLLP.

—It's Snowing! / ¡Está Nevando!, 1 vol. 2013. (What's the Weather? / ¿Qué Tiempo Hace? Ser.). (SPA & ENG., Illus.). 24p. (J). (gr. k-k). 25.27 *(978-1-4339-9458-6(5)*, 0c42ee97-da26-4587-9e9b-e13f5c79f888) Stevens, Gareth Publishing LLLP.

Bauer, Marion Dane. Snow: Ready-To-Read Level 1. Wallace, John, illus. 2003. (Weather Ready-To-Reads Ser.). (ENG.). 32p. (J). (gr. -1-1). pap. 4.99 *(978-0-689-85437-8(4)*, Simon Spotlight) Simon Spotlight.

Berger, Melvin & Berger, Gilda. Snowflakes Are Falling. 2010. (Illus.). 16p. (J). *(978-0-545-16082-7(0))* Scholastic, Inc.

Bix, Jasper. Building a Snowman, 1 vol. 2015. (Winter Fun Ser.). (ENG., Illus.). 24p. (J). (gr. k-k). pap. 9.15 *(978-1-4824-3747-8(3)*, e3e6475b-741b-4afe-b903-4fd8d54fb335) Stevens, Gareth Publishing LLLP.

Bobek, Joanne R. A Day at Pond Snow. 2011. 16p. 8.47 *(978-1-4567-1706-3(5))* AuthorHouse.

Bodden, Valerie. Our Wonderful Weather: Snow. 2014. (Our Wonderful Weather Ser.). (ENG., Illus.). 24p. (J). (gr. 4-7). pap. 9.99 *(978-0-89812-921-2(4)*, 22268, Creative Paperbacks) Creative Co., The.

—Snow. 2012. (Our Wonderful Weather Ser.). (ENG.). 24p. (J). (gr. 1-4). 25.65 *(978-1-60818-148-3(0)*, 22263, Creative Education) Creative Co., The.

Boyett, Suzi. Let's Read about Snow, 1 vol. 2007. (Let's Read about Weather Ser.). (ENG., Illus.). 12p. (gr. k-1). lib. bdg. 17.67 *(978-0-8368-7806-6(X)*, 8446ee61-df99-4f0f-a2a9-841c13b20e53, Weekly Reader Leveled Readers) Stevens, Gareth Publishing LLLP.

—Nieva (Let's Read about Snow), 1 vol. 2007. (¿Qué Tiempo Hace? (Let's Read about Weather) Ser.). (SPA., Illus.). 12p. (J). (gr. k-1). pap. 5.10 *(978-0-8368-8119-6(2)*, b81ea23f-fc30-4ff7-84a3-dc67ecd09832, Weekly Reader Leveled Readers); lib. bdg. 17.67 *(978-0-8368-8114-1(1)*, 32ac75d2-62b5-48f3-9e48-7838537e05f3) Stevens, Gareth Publishing LLLP.

Brinker, Spencer. A Snowy Day. 2018. (Weather Watch Ser.). (ENG., Illus.). 16p. (J). (gr. -1-1). 6.99 *(978-1-64280-136-1(4))* Bearport Publishing Co., Inc.

Brown, Tammy. What Is Snow? 2018. (I Know Ser.). (ENG., Illus.). 16p. (gr. -1-2). lib. bdg. 28.50 *(978-1-64156-170-9(X)*, 9781641561709) Rourke Educational Media.

Bundey, Nikki. Snow & People. 2005. (Science of Weather Ser.). (Illus.). 32p. (gr. 4-6). lib. bdg. 21.27 *(978-1-57505-496-4(5))* Lerner Publishing Group.

—Snow & the Earth. 2005. (Science of Weather Ser.). (Illus.). 32p. (gr. 4-6). lib. bdg. 21.27 *(978-1-57505-471-1(X))* Lerner Publishing Group.

Cassino, Mark. The Story of Snow: The Science of Winter's Wonder. 2017. (ENG., Illus.). 36p. (J). (gr. k-3). 7.99 *(978-1-4521-6436-6(3))* Chronicle Bks. LLC.

Cox Cannons, Helen. Snow, 1 vol. 2014. (Weather Wise Ser.). (ENG., Illus.). 24p. (J). (gr. -1-1). pap. 5.99 *(978-1-4846-0556-1(X)*, 126647, Heinemann) Capstone.

D'Aubuisson, Elisabeth. Snowy Days, 1 vol. 2006. (What's the Weather? Ser.). (ENG., Illus.). 24p. (J). (gr. 2-3). lib. bdg. 26.27 *(978-1-4042-3684-4(8)*, 83c99a91-7552-4051-ad32-e2c62d68eb2d, PowerKids Pr.) Rosen Publishing Group, Inc., The.

d'Aubuisson, Elisabeth. Snowy Days. 2009. (What's the Weather? Ser.). 24p. (gr. 2-3). 42.50 *(978-1-60854-776-0(0)*, PowerKids Pr.) Rosen Publishing Group, Inc., The.

Davies, Monika. Blizzards, 1 vol. 2020. (Force of Nature Ser.). (ENG.). 48p. (gr. 4-5). pap. 12.71 *(978-1-9785-1836-0(6)*, a4ab9f39-4884-4f03-aa44-83599681a2d7) Enslow Publishing, LLC.

deMarin, Layne. Too Much Snow! 2011. (Wonder Readers Fluent Level Ser.). (ENG.). 16p. (gr. -1-2). pap. 35.94 *(978-1-4296-8192-6(6)*, Capstone Pr.) Capstone.

—Too Much Snow. 2011. (Wonder Readers Fluent Level Ser.). (ENG.). 16p. (J). (gr. -1-2). pap. 6.25 *(978-1-4296-7944-2(1)*, 118276, Capstone Pr.) Capstone.

Donaldson, Chelsea. Snow. 2014. (Illus.). (J). *(978-0-545-61736-9(7))* Scholastic, Inc.

Doubleday Entertainment USA - Weather Watch: Snow. 2006. (J). per. 7.95 *(978-1-59566-232-3(4))* QEB Publishing Inc.

Doudna, Kelly. It Is Snowing, 1 vol. 2003. (Weather Ser.). (ENG., Illus.). 24p. (J). (gr. k-3). lib. bdg. 24.21 *(978-1-57765-775-0(6)*, SandCastle) ABDO Publishing Co.

Drake, Jane & Love, Ann. Snow Amazing: Cool Facts & Warm Tales. Thurman, Mark, illus. 2004. 80p. (J). (gr. 4-7). 19.95 *(978-0-88776-670-1(6)*, Tundra Bks.) Tundra Bks. CAN. Dist: Penguin Random Hse. LLC.

Edison, Erin. Snow, 1 vol. 2011. (Weather Basics Ser.). (ENG.). 24p. (J). (gr. -1-2). pap. 7.29 *(978-1-4296-7080-7(0)*, 116756); (gr. -1-2). lib. bdg. 27.32 *(978-1-4296-6059-4(7)*, 114994); (gr. k-1). pap. 43.74 *(978-1-4296-7086-9(X)*, 16679) Capstone. (Capstone Pr.).

Felix, Rebecca. How's the Weather in Winter? 2014. (21st Century Basic Skills Library: Let's Look at Winter Ser.). (ENG., Illus.). 24p. (J). (gr. k-3). 26.35 *(978-1-63137-605-4(5)*, 205203) Cherry Lake Publishing.

—We See Snowflakes in Winter. 2014. (21st Century Basic Skills Library: Let's Look at Winter Ser.). (ENG., Illus.). 24p. (J). (gr. k-3). 26.35 *(978-1-63137-612-2(8)*, 205231) Cherry Lake Publishing.

Gamble, Adam & Jasper, Mark. Good Night Snow. 2016. (Good Night Our World Ser.). (ENG., Illus.). 20p. (J). (— 1). bds. 9.95 *(978-1-60219-412-0(2))* Good Night Bks.

Ganeri, Anita. Snow, 1 vol. 2004. (Weather Around You Ser.). (ENG., Illus.). 24p. (gr. 2-4). lib. bdg. 24.67 *(978-0-8368-4300-2(2)*, 6920881a-6642-48da-8506-f6fd2fd4b1fd, Weekly Reader Leveled Readers) Stevens, Gareth Publishing LLLP.

Gardner, Kate. Snow Falls. Scott, Brandon James, illus. 2020. (ENG.). 32p. (J). (gr. -1-2). 17.99 *(978-1-101-91921-7(3)*, Tundra Bks.) Tundra Bks. CAN. Dist: Penguin Random Hse. LLC.

Gates, Margo. Snow Day. Engell, Mette, illus. 2019. (Let's Look at Weather (Pull Ahead Readers — Fiction) Ser.). (ENG.). 16p. (J). (gr. -1-1). pap. 8.99 *(978-1-5415-7318-5(8)*, 0e67d03d-5f6e-47d6-958a-7bd616429ee0, Lerner Pubns.) Lerner Publishing Group.

Greene, Carol. Snow Joe. Sharp, Paul, illus. 2011. (Rookie Ready to Learn Ser.). 40p. (J). (ENG.). pap. 5.95 *(978-0-531-26804-9(7))*; (gr. -1-k). lib. bdg. 23.00 *(978-0-531-25644-2(8))* Scholastic Library Publishing. (Children's Pr.).

Hansen, Grace. Snow, 1 vol. 2015. (Weather Ser.). (ENG., Illus.). 24p. (J). (gr. -1-2). 32.79 *(978-1-62970-933-8(6)*, 18324, Abdo Kids) ABDO Publishing Co.

Hardyman, Robyn. Snow & Blizzards, 1 vol. 2010. (Weatherwise Ser.). (ENG.). 32p. (gr. 4-4). (J). pap. 11.60 *(978-1-61532-276-3(0)*, 2d8ff99c-cf67-4dd0-ab0d-11cdede007be, PowerKids Pr.); (Illus.). (YA). lib. bdg. 30.27 *(978-1-61532-264-0(7)*, fbb7146e-10e9-4997-905e-daed24d6bd1f) Rosen Publishing Group, Inc., The.

Helget, Nicole. Snow. 2006. (My First Look at Weather Ser.). (Illus.). 24p. (J). (gr. -1-3). lib. bdg. 15.95 *(978-1-58341-451-4(7)*, Creative Education) Creative Co., The.

Herriges, Ann. Snow. 2006. (Weather Ser.). (ENG., Illus.). 24p. (J). (gr. k-3). lib. bdg. 26.95 *(978-1-60014-029-7(7))* Bellwether Media.

—Snow. 2011. (Blastoff! Readers Ser.). 24p. (J). pap. 5.95 *(978-0-531-27623-5(6)*, Children's Pr.) Scholastic Library Publishing.

Lawrence, Ellen. How Are Rain, Snow, & Hail Alike? 2018. (Weather Wise Ser.). (ENG.). 24p. (J). (gr. -1-3). 7.99 *(978-1-64280-089-0(9))* Bearport Publishing Co., Inc.

Lee, Sally. Snowy Weather: A 4D Book. 2018. (All Kinds of Weather Ser.). (ENG., Illus.). 24p. (J). (gr. -1-2). lib. bdg. 24.65 *(978-1-9771-0186-0(0)*, 138712, Pebble) Capstone.

Libbrecht, Kenneth. The Secret Life of a Snowflake: An up-Close Look at the Art & Science of Snowflakes. 2010. (ENG., Illus.). 48p. (J). (gr. 1-9). 19.99 *(978-0-7603-3676-2(8)*, 0760336768, Voyageur Pr.) Quarto Publishing Group USA.

Lindeen, Mary. Winter! 2015. (BeginningtoRead Ser.). (ENG., Illus.). 32p. (J). (gr. k-2). lib. bdg. 22.60 *(978-1-59953-682-8(X))* Norwood Hse. Pr.

Manolis, Kay. Blizzards. 2008. (Extreme Weather Ser.). (ENG., Illus.). 24p. (J). (gr. 2-5). lib. bdg. 26.95 *(978-1-60014-183-6(8))* Bellwether Media.

Martin, Jacqueline Briggs. Snowflake Bentley. 2004. (Illus.). (J). (gr. -1-3). spiral bd. *(978-0-616-01714-2(6))* Canadian National Institute for the Blind/Institut National Canadien pour les Aveugles.

Masterson, Josephine. We Can Build a Snowman, 1 vol. 2015. (Rosen REAL Readers: STEM & STEAM Collection). (ENG.). 8p. (gr. k-1). pap. 5.46 *(978-1-4994-9736-6(9)*, 5bd40111-ac66-43d0-800b-b80b2ef5da73, Rosen Classroom) Rosen Publishing Group, Inc., The.

McAuliffe, Bill. Snow. (X-Books: Weather Ser.). (ENG., (J). 2017. Illus.). 32p. (gr. 3-6). pap. 9.99 *(978-1-62832-429-7(5)*, 20412, Creative Paperbacks) 2017. (Illus.). 32p. (gr. 3-6). *(978-1-60818-826-0(4)*, 20411, Creative Education) 2010. 48p. (gr. 5-8). lib. bdg. 23.95 *(978-1-58341-929-8(2)*, 22285) Creative Co., The.

McNeil, Niki, et al. HOCPP 1136 Let it Snow. 2006. spiral bd. 14.00 *(978-1-60308-136-8(4))* In the Hands of a Child.

Nelson, John. Polar Ice Caps in Danger: Expedition to Antarctica. (Jr. Graphic Environmental Dangers Ser.). (ENG.). 24p. (J). 2008. 47.90 *(978-1-61532-097-4(0))* 2007. (Illus.). (gr. 4-4). lib. bdg. 28.93 *(978-1-4042-4227-2(9)*, ac33ec7f-2b80-47c4-8b97-183a208ca330) Rosen Publishing Group, Inc., The. (PowerKids Pr.).

Nelson, John & Obregón, José María. Casquetes Polares en Riesgo: Expedición a la Antártida, 1 vol. 2009. (Historietas Juveniles: Peligros Del Medioambiente (Jr. Graphic Environmental Dangers) Ser.). (SPA., Illus.). 24p. (gr. 4-4). pap. 10.60 *(978-1-4358-8475-5(2)*, c74f3921-6cd2-4472-a45a-e67eb6168d38); (YA). lib. bdg. 28.93 *(978-1-4358-8474-8(4)*, d42799de-cdae-4607-b338-bee86145a376) Rosen Publishing Group, Inc., The.

Nelson, Robin. Un Dia Nevado. Translations.com Staff, tr. from ENG. 2006. (Mi Primer Paso Al Mundo Real - el Estado Del Tiempo (First Step Nonfiction - Weather) Ser.). (SPA., Illus.). 24p. (gr. k-2). lib. bdg. 23.93 *(978-0-8225-6212-2(X)*, Ediciones Lerner) Lerner Publishing Group.

—Un Día nevado (A Snowy Day) 2006. (Mi Primer Paso al Mundo Real Ser.). (Illus.). 23p. (J). (gr. -1-3). per. 5.95 *(978-0-8225-6551-2(X)*, Ediciones Lerner) Lerner Publishing Group.

—Snowy. (First Step Nonfiction — Kinds of Weather Ser.). (ENG., Illus.). 8p. (J). (gr. k-2). 2005. pap. 5.99 *(978-0-8225-5366-3(X)*, 0451f643-9ab3-431b-82e1-3de7817c404a) 2015. E-Book 23.99 *(978-1-5124-1038-9(1))* Lerner Publishing Group.

Orr, Tamra B. It Snows. 2015. (Tell Me Why Library). (ENG., Illus.). 24p. (gr. 2-5). 29.21 *(978-1-63188-998-1(2)*, 205904) Cherry Lake Publishing.

Peters, Elisa. It's Snow! (Everyday Wonders Ser.). 24p. (gr. 1-1). 2009. 42.50 *(978-1-61512-326-1(1)*, PowerKids Pr.) 2008. (ENG., Illus.). (J). lib. bdg. 26.27 *(978-1-4042-4462-7(X)*, 377d17d4-1105-479d-a16c-b0d999181715) Rosen Publishing Group, Inc., The.

—It's Snow! La Nieve!, 1 vol. 2008. (Everyday Wonders / Maravillas de Todos Los Días Ser.). (SPA & ENG.). 24p. (J). (gr. 1-1). lib. bdg. 26.27 *(978-1-4358-2527-7(6)*, 999f0bd4-d515-4722-9d85-2d79000abeba) Rosen Publishing Group, Inc., The.

—It's Snow! / ¡la Nieve! 2009. (Everyday Wonders / Maravillas de todos los días Ser.). (ENG & SPA.). 24p. (gr. 1-1). 42.50 *(978-1-61512-332-2(6)*, Editorial Buenas Letras) Rosen Publishing Group, Inc., The.

Peters, Katie. The Snow Is Fun. 2019. (Let's Look at Weather (Pull Ahead Readers — Nonfiction) Ser.). (ENG., Illus.). 16p. (J). (gr. -1-1). 27.99 *(978-1-5415-5834-2(0)*, fdb38069-7912-4d3b-8906-a7d49ade9a12, Lerner Pubns.) Lerner Publishing Group.

—Winter Fun. 2019. (Seasons All Around Me (Pull Ahead Readers — Nonfiction) Ser.). (ENG., Illus.). 16p. (J). (gr. -1-1). pap. 8.99 *(978-1-5415-7347-5(1)*, eeaed2e3-0b79-4877-9525-e3ae86394391); lib. bdg. 27.99 *(978-1-5415-5869-4(3)*, 177f8cda-46f2-4478-9683-55e02492ae7c) Lerner Publishing Group. (Lerner Pubns.).

Pettiford, Rebecca. Snowplows. 2017. (Mighty Machines in Action Ser.). (ENG., Illus.). 24p. (J). (gr. k-3). lib. bdg. 26.95 *(978-1-62617-633-1(7)*, Blastoff! Readers) Bellwether Media.

Purslow, Frances. Precipitation. 2015. (Illus.). 24p. (J). *(978-1-5105-0054-9(5))*; pap. *(978-1-5105-0286-4(6))* SmartBook Media, Inc.

Rain, Snow, & Hail: Individual Title Six-Packs. (Discovery World Ser.). 16p. (gr. 1-2). 28.00 *(978-0-7635-8466-5(5))* Rigby Education.

Rao, Joe. The Cool Story Behind Snow: Ready-To-Read Level 3. Downey, Dagney, illus. 2015. (Science of Fun Stuff Ser.). (ENG.). 48p. (J). (gr. 1-3). pap. 4.99 *(978-1-4814-4413-2(1)*, Simon Spotlight) Simon Spotlight.

Rau, Dana Meachen. Building Snow Forts. 2012. (How-To Library). (ENG., Illus.). 32p. (gr. 3-6). (J). pap. 14.21 *(978-1-61080-643-5(3)*, 202253); 32.07 *(978-1-61080-469-1(4)*, 202079) Cherry Lake Publishing.

Rice, Dona & Otterman, Joseph. Studying Snowflakes. rev. ed. 2019. (Smithsonian: Informational Text Ser.). (ENG., Illus.). 24p. (J). (gr. 1-2). pap. 8.99 *(978-1-4938-6659-5(1))* Teacher Created Materials, Inc.

Ring, Susan. Snow, 6 vols., Set. 2005. (Yellow Umbrella Fluent Level Ser.). (ENG., Illus.). 16p. (gr. k-1). pap. 35.70 *(978-0-7368-5297-5(2)*, Capstone Pr.) Capstone.

Rockwell, Anne. The First Snowfall. 2014. (ENG., Illus.). 24p. (J). (gr. -1-3). 14.99 *(978-1-4814-1135-6(7),* Aladdin) Simon & Schuster Children's Publishing.

Rossiter, Brienna. Snow. 2019. (Weather Ser.). (ENG., Illus.). 16p. (J). (gr. k-1). 25.64 *(978-1-64185-791-8(9),* 1641857919, Focus Readers) North Star Editions.

Rustad, Martha E. H. Today Is a Snowy Day. 2017. (What Is the Weather Today? Ser.). (ENG., Illus.). 24p. (J). (gr. -1-2). lib. bdg. 24.65 *(978-1-5157-4919-6(3),* 134535); (gr. k-2). pap. 6.29 *(978-1-4966-0942-7(5),* 134529) Capstone. (Pebble).

—100 Snowflakes: A Winter Counting Book. 2016. (1, 2, 3 Count with Me Ser.). (ENG., Illus.). 24p. (J). (gr. k-2). pap. 8.99 *(978-1-68152-109-1(1),* 15520) Amicus.

—100 Snowflakes: A Winter Counting Book. 2016. (1, 2, 3 Count with Me Ser.). (ENG., Illus.). 24p. (J). (gr. k-3). 20.95 *(978-1-60753-918-6(7))* Amicus Learning.

Ruth, Angie. My Adventure in the Snow. 2006. 44p. (J). 8.99 *(978-1-59092-435-8(5))* Blue Forge Pr.

Sayre, April Pulley. Best in Snow. 2016. (Weather Walks Ser.). (ENG., Illus.). 40p. (J). (gr. -1-3). 18.99 *(978-1-4814-5916-7(3),* Beach Lane Bks.) Beach Lane Bks.

Schuh, Mari. What Are Blizzards? 2019. (Wicked Weather Ser.). (ENG., Illus.). 24p. (J). (gr. -1-2). lib. bdg. 22.65 *(978-1-9771-0329-1(4),* 139320, Pebble) Capstone.

Shaw, Gina. Curious about Snow. 2016. (Smithsonian Ser.). (Illus.). 32p. (J). (gr. 1-3). bds. 4.99 *(978-0-448-49018-2(8),* Grosset & Dunlap) Penguin Young Readers Group.

Silverman, Maida. Snow Search Dogs. 2005. (Dog Heroes Ser.). 32p. (J). lib. bdg. 28.50 *(978-1-59716-017-9(2))* Bearport Publishing Co., Inc.

Snow, Virginia. Winter Walk, 1 vol. 2014. (ENG., Illus.). 32p. (J). 16.99 *(978-1-4236-3747-9(X))* Gibbs Smith, Publisher.

Snow, Virginia B. Winter Walk, 1 vol. 2019. (ENG.). 32p. (J). (gr. -1-3). 8.99 *(978-1-4236-5392-9(0))* Gibbs Smith, Publisher.

Sommers, Michael A. Antarctic Melting: The Disappearing Antarctic Ice Cap. 2009. (Extreme Environmental Threats Ser.). 64p. (gr. 6-6). 58.50 *(978-1-61512-423-7(3))* Rosen Publishing Group, Inc., The.

Stewart, Melissa. Under the Snow, 1 vol. Bergum, Constance R., illus. 2019. 32p. (J). (gr. -1-3). pap. 7.99 *(978-1-68263-125-6(7))* Peachtree Publishing Co. Inc.

Strain Trueit, Trudi. Snowy Days, 1 vol. 2010. (Weather Watch Ser.). (ENG.). 24p. (gr. k-1). 25.50 *(978-0-7614-4015-4(1),* 37d50e00-b4f3-46cf-b80a-0fd7560d4c9c) Cavendish Square Publishing LLC.

Sturm, Matthew. Apun: The Arctic Snow. 2nd ed. 2009. (ENG., Illus.). 44p. (J). pap. 13.95 *(978-1-60223-069-9(2))* Univ. of Alaska Pr.

Taylor, Clif. Snowflake. Whitmire, Anna, illus. 2010. (J). *(978-1-886769-97-7(4))* Gold Leaf Pr.

Urmston, Kathleen & Evans, Karen. Snowflakes. Kaeden Corp. Staff, ed. Graves, Dennis, illus. 2006. (ENG.). 12p. (gr. k-1). pap. 7.95 *(978-1-879835-01-6(0),* Kaeden Bks.) Kaeden Corp.

Waldman, Neil. The Snowflake: A Water Cycle Story. 2003. (ENG., Illus.). 32p. (J). (gr. k-3). 19.99 *(978-0-7613-2347-1(3),* cb9049f0-a49e-43fd-9e10-b7e9a93f3543, Millbrook Pr.) Lerner Publishing Group.

Weston Woods Staff, creator. Snowflake Bentley. 2011. 18.95 *(978-0-545-31414-5(3));* 38.75 *(978-0-545-31415-2(1))* Weston Woods Studios, Inc.

Williams, Judith. How Come It's Snowing?, 1 vol. 2014. (How Does Weather Happen? Ser.). (ENG.). 24p. (gr. k-1). pap. 10.35 *(978-0-7660-6386-0(0),* 51dbce44-dd7b-48ef-9b4c-cb12b767a16c); lib. bdg. 24.27 *(978-0-7660-6385-3(2),* e1202889-4903-4c65-90f3-f35b7452f16c) Enslow Publishing, LLC. (Enslow Elementary).

—¿Por Qué Está Nevando? / Why Is It Snowing?, 1 vol. 2010. (Me Gusta el Clima / I Like Weather! Ser.). (SPA & ENG.). 24p. (gr. k-2). 25.27 *(978-0-7660-3239-2(6),* d0dd92d9-8523-4c2a-9236-dcd62a1dc5e5, Enslow Elementary) Enslow Publishing, LLC.

Yomtov, Nelson. Polar Ice Caps in Danger: Expedition to Antarctica, 1 vol. 2007. (Jr. Graphic Environmental Dangers Ser.). (ENG., Illus.). 24p. (gr. 4-4). pap. 10.60 *(978-1-4042-4594-5(4),* 2e1f3a08-4e95-453e-a8e8-627d55881d9f, PowerKids Pr.) Rosen Publishing Group, Inc., The.

Zuehlke, Jeffrey. Snowplows. 2006. (Pull Ahead Books-Mighty Movers Ser.). (ENG., Illus.). 32p. (gr. k-3). lib. bdg. 22.60 *(978-0-8225-6009-8(7),* Lerner Pubns.) Lerner Publishing Group.

SNOW—FICTION

Adams, Colleen. Jugando en la nieve (Playing in the Snow) 2007. (Lecturas del barrio (Neighborhood Readers) Ser.). (SPA.). 8p. 29.95 *(978-1-4042-7064-0(7),* Rosen Classroom) Rosen Publishing Group, Inc., The.

—Playing in the Snow. (Neighborhood Readers Ser.). (ENG.). 8p. 2007. 29.95 *(978-1-4042-7059-6(0))* 2006. pap. 5.15 *(978-1-4042-5657-6(1),* 4320a7bb-8d68-4736-8d92-88b1d246c4d7) Rosen Publishing Group, Inc., The. (Rosen Classroom).

Aikins, Dave, illus. Dora Saves the Snow Princess. 2008. (Dora the Explorer Ser.: 27). (ENG.). 24p. (J). (gr. -1-2). pap. 3.99 *(978-1-4169-5866-6(5),* Simon Spotlight/Nickelodeon) Simon Spotlight/Nickelodeon.

Ailes, Mark Cusco. The Snow Dargles: Book Two: the Chronicles of Weekland. 2010. 244p. pap. 16.95 *(978-1-4327-5223-1(5))* Outskirts Pr., Inc.

Albrecht, Sally K., et al. Snow Way Out! a Vacation in Winter's Wonderland: A Mini-Musical for Unison & 2-Part Voices (Teacher's Handbook) 2009. (ENG.). 68p. pap. 34.99 *(978-0-7390-5835-0(5))* Alfred Publishing Co., Inc.

Alexander, Annette M. Snow Magic & the Sad Little Christmas Tree. 2011. (Illus.). 32p. 14.66 *(978-1-4567-7182-9(5))* AuthorHouse.

Allen, J. J. Hello Kitty's Fun Friend Day! 2003. (Illus.). 32p. (J). pap. *(978-0-439-44917-5(0))* Scholastic, Inc.

Anderson, H. C. La Reine des Neiges. (FRE.). pap. 16.95 *(978-2-07-051630-8(X))* Gallimard, Editions FRA. Dist: Distribooks, Inc.

Arena, Jen. 100 Snowmen, 0 vols. Gilpin, Stephen, illus. 2013. (ENG.). 24p. (J). (gr. k-3). 14.99 *(978-1-4778-4703-9(0),* 9781477847039, Two Lions) Amazon Publishing.

Arnold, Marsha Diane. Waiting for Snow. Liwska, Renata, illus. 2016. (ENG.). 32p. (J). (gr. -1-3). 14.99 *(978-0-544-41687-1(2),* 1594762, Clarion Bks.) HarperCollins Pubs.

August, Elaine. It Only Snows in Brooklyn. 2012. 30p. 24.95 *(978-1-4626-9438-9(1));* 32p. pap. 24.95 *(978-1-4626-7588-3(3))* America Star Bks.

Baccalario, Pierdomenico., et al. The Story of Snowflake & Inkdrop. 2015. (ENG., Illus.). 56p. (J). (gr. -1-3). 22.95 *(978-1-59270-186-5(8))* Enchanted Lion Bks., LLC.

Balaban, Mariah. Scooby-Doo & the Scary Snowman, 1 vol. Sur, Duendes Del, illus. 2011. (Scooby-Doo! Ser.: No. 2). (ENG.). 24p. (J). (gr. k-4). lib. bdg. 31.36 *(978-1-59961-869-2(9),* 13247, Picture Bk.) Spotlight.

Barner. Snow. (J). 16.95 *(978-0-8118-4171-9(5))* Chronicle Bks. LLC.

Bauer, Dane. Snow. Wallace, John, illus. 2005. 32p. (J). lib. bdg. 15.00 *(978-1-59054-934-6(1))* Fitzgerald Bks.

Bean, Jonathan. Big Snow. Bean, Jonathan, illus. 2013. (ENG., Illus.). 32p. (J). (gr. -1-1). 17.99 *(978-0-374-30696-0(6),* 900087739, Farrar, Straus & Giroux (BYR)) Farrar, Straus & Giroux.

Bedford, David. Bedtime for Little Bears. Pedler, Caroline, illus. 2018. (ENG.). 16p. (J). (— 1). bds. 9.99 *(978-1-5107-3620-7(4),* Sky Pony Pr.) Skyhorse Publishing Co., Inc.

Bell, Jake. Freezer Burned, 2. Giarrusso, Chris, illus. 2010. (Amazing Adventures of Nate Banks Ser.: 2). (ENG.). 176p. (J). (gr. 4-6). 18.69 *(978-0-545-15670-7(X))* Scholastic, Inc.

Bentley, Sue. Winter Wonderland. 2013. (Magic Ponies Ser.: 5). lib. bdg. 16.00 *(978-0-606-32118-1(7))* Turtleback.

Berenstain, Mike. The Berenstain Bears & the Christmas Angel, 1 vol. 2016. (Berenstain Bears/Living Lights: a Faith Story Ser.). (ENG., Illus.). 24p. (J). pap. 4.99 *(978-0-310-74924-0(7))* Zonderkidz.

Berger, Carin. A Perfect Day. Berger, Carin, illus. 2012. (ENG., Illus.). 40p. (J). (gr. -1-3). 16.99 *(978-0-06-201580-8(X),* Greenwillow Bks.) HarperCollins Pubs.

Bianchi, John. Snowed in at Pokeweed Public School. (Illus.). 24p. (J). (gr. 1-5). *(978-1-894323-34-5(3))* Pokeweed Pr.

Biggs, Brian. Henry Goes Skating. Abbott, Simon, illus. 2012. (My First I Can Read Ser.). (J). lib. bdg. 13.55 *(978-0-606-26852-3(9))* Turtleback.

Bildner, Phil. Turkey Bowl. 2008. (ENG., Illus.). 32p. (J). (gr. k-3). 19.99 *(978-0-689-87896-1(6),* Simon & Schuster Bks. For Young Readers) Simon & Schuster Bks. For Young Readers.

Bishop, Celeste. It's Snowing, 1 vol. 2016. (What's the Weather Like? Ser.). (ENG.). 24p. (gr. 1-1). pap. 9.25 *(978-1-4994-2355-6(1),* a43d408e-545f-4680-baaa-b80d0ddc7c23, PowerKids Pr.) Rosen Publishing Group, Inc., The.

Blackstone, Stella. Cleo in the Snow. Mockford, Caroline, illus. 2013. 24p. (J). pap. 6.99 *(978-1-78285-055-7(4));* bds. 6.99 *(978-1-78285-054-0(6))* Barefoot Bks., Inc.

Blanca Nieves - (Estrella de Mar) 2003. (SPA., Illus.). 16p. 2.95 *(978-968-855-185-1(6))* Suromex, Ediciones, S.A. MEX. Dist: Giron Bks.

Bledsoe, Lucy Jane. Tracks in the Snow. 2019. 192p. (J). (gr. 3-7). pap. 7.99 *(978-0-8234-4449-6(X))* Holiday Hse., Inc.

Blitt, Natalie. Snow One Like You. 2017. 258p. (J). pap. *(978-1-338-17474-8(6))* Scholastic, Inc.

Blizzard: Colorado 1886. 2014. (Survivors Ser.). (ENG., Illus.). 160p. (J). (gr. 3-7). pap. 7.99 *(978-1-4814-0969-8(7),* Aladdin) Simon & Schuster Children's Publishing.

Bonnell, Kris. The White, White Snow. 2007. (J). pap. 5.95 *(978-1-933727-44-8(6))* Reading Reading Bks., LLC.

Boynton, Sandra. Merry Christmas, Little Pookie. Boynton, Sandra, illus. 2018. (Little Pookie Ser.). (ENG., Illus.). 18p. (J). (gr. -1-k). bds. 6.99 *(978-1-5344-3724-1(X))* Simon & Schuster, Inc.

Brege, K. B. Abominable Snowman A Frozen Nightmare! 2009. (Mick Morris Myth Solver Ser.: No. 5). (Illus.). 156p. (J). pap. 6.99 *(978-0-9774119-4-8(X))* Team B Creative LLC.

Bright, Rachel. Snowflake in My Pocket. Rong, Yu, illus. 2017. 32p. (J). 12.99 *(978-1-61067-551-2(7))* Kane Miller.

Brooke, S. The Snow Diamond: the Fourth Journey, 1 vol. 2010. 180p. pap. 24.95 *(978-1-4512-1383-6(2))* America Star Bks.

Brothers Grimm. Snow White & Rose Red: A Grimms' Fairy Tale, 1 vol. Marshall, Denise, illus. 2008. (ENG.). 28p. (J). 17.95 *(978-0-88010-591-0(7),* Bell Pond Bks.) SteinerBooks, Inc.

Brown, Gina Bates. Zen & Bodhi's Snowy Day. Hinder, Sarah Jane, illus. 2014. (ENG.). 24p. (J). 15.95 *(978-1-61429-165-7(9))* Wisdom Pubns.

Brown, Jeff. The Intrepid Canadian Expedition. 2009. (Flat Stanley's Worldwide Adventures Ser.: 4). (J). lib. bdg. 14.75 *(978-0-606-10068-7(7))* Turtleback.

Brown, Marc. Arthur & the Big Snow. Brown, Marc, illus. 2005. (ENG., Illus.). 32p. (J). (gr. -1-1). per. 3.99 *(978-0-316-05770-7(3))* Little, Brown Bks. for Young Readers.

Bruel, Nick. Bad Kitty Does Not Like Snow. 2016. (Bad Kitty Picture Bks.). (ENG.). 24p. (J). (gr. -1-k). 14.75 *(978-0-606-39296-9(3))* Turtleback.

—Bad Kitty Does Not Like Snow: Includes Stickers. 2016. (Bad Kitty Ser.). (ENG., Illus.). 24p. (J). pap. 5.99 *(978-1-62672-581-2(0),* 900162178) Roaring Brook Pr.

Bruss, Deborah. Good Morning, Snowplow! Johnson, Steve & Fancher, Lou, illus. 2018. (ENG.). 32p. (J). (gr. -1 — 1). 17.99 *(978-1-338-08949-3(8),* Levine, Arthur A. Bks.) Scholastic, Inc.

Bryant, Megan E. My Snow Globe: a Sparkly Peek-Through Story. Iwai, Melissa, illus. 2016. (ENG.). 10p. (J). (gr. -1). bds. 7.99 *(978-0-545-92176-3(7),* Cartwheel Bks.) Scholastic, Inc.

Buehner, Caralyn. Snowmen All Year. Buehner, Mark, illus. 2010. 32p. (J). (gr. -1-2). 17.99 *(978-0-8037-3383-1(6),* Dial Bks) Penguin Young Readers Group.

—Snowmen at Night. 2004. (Illus.). 26p. (J). (gr. -1 — 1). bds. 8.99 *(978-0-8037-3041-0(1),* Dial Bks) Penguin Young Readers Group.

Burton, Virginia Lee. Katy & the Big Snow Book & Cd: A Winter & Holiday Book for Kids, 1 vol. 2009. (ENG., Illus.). 40p. (J). (gr. -1-3). audio 10.99 *(978-0-547-25264-3(1),* 1271216, Clarion Bks.) HarperCollins Pubs.

Butler, M. Christina. The First Snow. Endersby, Frank, illus. 2012. (J). *(978-1-4351-4320-3(5))* Barnes & Noble, Inc.

Butler, M. Christina & Endersby, Frank. The First Snow. 2018. (ENG.). 24p. (J). (gr. -1-1). bds. 9.99 *(978-1-68099-427-8(1),* Good Bks.) Skyhorse Publishing Co., Inc.

—The First Snow - Choice Edition. 2018. (ENG.). 24p. (J). (gr. -1-1). bds. 9.99 *(978-1-68099-424-7(7),* Good Bks.) Skyhorse Publishing Co., Inc.

Butterworth, Nick. One Snowy Night. Butterworth, Nick, illus. 2007. (ENG., Illus.). 32p. (J). 24.00 *(978-0-00-725942-7(5))* HarperCollins Pubs. Ltd. GBR. Dist: Independent Pubs. Group.

Candlewick Press. Peppa Pig & the Day at Snowy Mountain. 2014. (Peppa Pig Ser.). (ENG., Illus.). 32p. (J). (-k). 12.99 *(978-0-7636-7455-7(9),* Candlewick Entertainment) Candlewick Pr.

Capozzi, Suzy. Frosty the Snowman Big Golden Book (Frosty the Snowman) Laguna, Fabio & Cagol, Andrea, illus. 2014. (Big Golden Book Ser.). (ENG.). 48p. (J). (gr. -1-2). 10.99 *(978-0-385-38877-1(2),* Golden Bks.) Random Hse. Children's Bks.

Carbone, Courtney. Snow Day! 2014. (Step into Reading Level 2 Ser.). lib. bdg. 13.55 *(978-0-606-36009-8(3))* Turtleback.

—Snow Day! (Frosty the Snowman) Random House, illus. 2014. (Step into Reading Ser.). (ENG.). 32p. (J). (gr. -1-1). 4.99 *(978-0-385-38726-2(1),* Random Hse. Bks. for Young Readers) Random Hse. Children's Bks.

Carey, Catherine Elaine. The Colorful & Playful Animal Friends, 1 vol. 2009. 73p. pap. 16.95 *(978-1-60749-480-5(9))* PublishAmerica, Inc.

Carle, Eric. Dream Snow. Carle, Eric, illus. 2015. (Illus.). 22p. (J). (gr. -1 — 1). bds. 9.99 *(978-0-399-17314-1(5))* Penguin Young Readers Group.

Carlson, Claudia. Avi & the Snowy Day. Decker, C. B., illus. 2017. (ENG.). 32p. (J). 9.95 *(978-1-68115-528-9(1),* 6363aae9-476f-492a-a905-b7d889214a40) Behrman Hse., Inc.

Carlson, Nancy. Harriet & Walt, 2nd Edition. rev. ed. 2004. (Nancy Carlson Picture Bks.). (ENG., Illus.). 32p. (J). (gr. k-2). 15.95 *(978-1-57505-672-2(0),* d27ad0a4-1b56-459c-8485-dc489735e32f, Carolrhoda Bks.) Lerner Publishing Group.

—Take Time to Relax! Carlson, Nancy, illus. 2012. (Nancy Carlson Picture Bks). (Illus.). 32p. (J). (gr. k-2). 56.72 *(978-0-7613-9304-7(8),* Carolrhoda Bks.) Lerner Publishing Group.

Carter, David A. A Snowy Day in Bugland! Ready-To-Read Level 1. Carter, David A., illus. 2012. (David Carter's Bugs Ser.). (ENG., Illus.). 24p. (J). (gr. -1-1). 17.99 *(978-1-4424-3895-8(9));* pap. 3.99 *(978-1-4424-3894-1(0))* Simon Spotlight. (Simon Spotlight).

Chang, Mi-Kyoung. Mina's White Canvas. Yi, Hyon-Ju, illus. 2015. (ENG.). 38p. (J). 17.99 *(978-1-4413-1826-8(7),* 0c6f777b-887d-44cf-babd-93b24358c92e) Peter Pauper Pr. Inc.

Chelsea, David. Snow Angel. Chelsea, David, illus. 2016. (Illus.). 112p. (J). (gr. 3-7). pap. 9.99 *(978-1-61655-940-3(3))* Dark Horse Comics.

Christopher, Matt. Snowboard Maverick. 2007. (New Matt Christopher Sports Library). 152p. (J). (gr. 4-6). lib. bdg. 26.60 *(978-1-59953-116-8(X))* Norwood Hse. Pr.

—Snowboard Showdown. l.t. ed. 2007. (New Matt Christopher Sports Library). 160p. (J). (gr. 4-6). lib. bdg. 26.60 *(978-1-59953-109-0(7))* Norwood Hse. Pr.

Chronicle Books & ImageBooks. Snow Baby: Finger Puppet Book. 2011. (Little Finger Puppet Board Bks.). (ENG.). 12p. (J). (gr. -1 — 1). 6.99 *(978-1-4521-0220-7(1))* Chronicle Bks. LLC.

Chronicle Books, Chronicle & ImageBooks. Little Snowman: Finger Puppet Book: (Finger Puppet Book for Toddlers & Babies, Baby Books for First Year, Animal Finger Puppets) 2008. (Little Finger Puppet Board Bks.). (ENG., Illus.). 12p. (J). (gr. -1 — 1). bds. 7.99 *(978-0-8118-6356-8(5))* Chronicle Bks. LLC.

Colandro, Lucille. There Was a Cold Lady Who Swallowed Some Snow! Lee, Jared, illus. (J). 2003. (ENG.). 32p. (gr. -1-3). pap. 6.99 *(978-0-439-56703-9(3))* 2003. 32p. (gr. k-3). pap. 5.95 *(978-0-439-47109-1(5),* Cartwheel Bks.) 2006. (ENG.). (gr. -1-3). pap. 9.99 incl. audio compact disk *(978-0-439-89556-9(1))* Scholastic, Inc.

—There Was a Cold Lady Who Swallowed Some Snow! (a Board Book) Lee, Jared, illus. 2017. (ENG.). 32p. (J). (— 1). bds. 6.99 *(978-1-338-15187-9(8),* Cartwheel Bks.) Scholastic, Inc.

Coleman, Roger. The Pope & the Snowman: A Christmas Tale. Becker, Richard, illus. 2009. (ENG.). 108p. 23.99 *(978-1-4490-1128-4(4));* pap. 12.49 *(978-1-4490-1127-7(6))* AuthorHouse.

Cordell, Matthew. Wolf in the Snow. 2017. (ENG., Illus.). 48p. (J). 18.99 *(978-1-250-07636-6(6),* 900152144) Feiwel & Friends.

—Wolf in the Snow. 2018. (CHI.). (gr. -1-1). *(978-986-189-861-2(1))* Grimm Cultural Ent., Co., Ltd.

Costa, Deborah Da. Snow in Jerusalem. Hu, Ying-Hwa & Wright, Cornelius Van, illus. 2008. (ENG.). 32p. (J). (gr. -1-3). 6.99 *(978-0-8075-7525-3(9),* 807575259) Whitman, Albert & Co.

Courtin, Thierry. T choupi fait un bonhomme De. 13.95 *(978-2-09-202037-1(4))* Nathan, Fernand FRA. Dist: Distribooks, Inc.

Crow, Melinda Melton. Snow Trouble, 1 vol. Rooney, Veronica, illus. 2009. (Truck Buddies Ser.). (ENG.). 32p. (J). (gr. -1-1). pap. 6.25 *(978-1-4342-1755-4(8),* 102227, Stone Arch Bks.) Capstone.

Cummings, Phil. Touch the Moon. Tulloch, Coral, illus. 2019. (ENG.). 32p. (J). (gr. 1). 19.99 *(978-1-76052-365-7(8),* A&U Children's) Allen & Unwin AUS. Dist: Independent Pubs. Group.

Cummings, Troy. Flurry of the Snombies. 2015. (Notebook of Doom Ser.: 7). (ENG., Illus.). 96p. (J). (gr. 1-3). 15.99 *(978-0-545-79551-7(6))* Scholastic, Inc.

—Flurry of the Snombies. 2015. (Notebook of Doom Ser.: 7). lib. bdg. 14.75 *(978-0-606-36340-2(8))* Turtleback.

—Flurry of the Snombies: a Branches Book (the Notebook of Doom #7) Cummings, Troy, illus. 2015. (Notebook of Doom Ser.: 7). (ENG., Illus.). 96p. (J). (gr. 1-3). pap. 5.99 *(978-0-545-79550-0(8))* Scholastic, Inc.

Curious George Snowy Day. 2007. (Curious George Ser.). (ENG., Illus.). 24p. (J). (gr. -1-3). 4.99 *(978-0-618-80043-8(3),* 489784, Clarion Bks.) HarperCollins Pubs.

Cuyler, Margery. The Christmas Snowman. Westerman, Johanna, illus. 2011. (ENG.). 32p. (J). (gr. k-3). 12.95 *(978-1-61608-483-7(9),* 608483, Sky Pony Pr.) Skyhorse Publishing Co., Inc.

Davis, Jacky. Ladybug Girl & the Big Snow. Soman, David, illus. 2013. (Ladybug Girl Ser.). 40p. (J). (gr. -1-k). 18.99 *(978-0-8037-3583-5(9),* Dial Bks) Penguin Young Readers Group.

Day, Alexandra. Carl's Snowy Afternoon. Day, Alexandra, illus. 2009. (Carl Ser.). (ENG., Illus.). 32p. (J). (gr. -1-1). 13.99 *(978-0-374-31086-8(6),* 900042212, Farrar, Straus & Giroux (BYR)) Farrar, Straus & Giroux.

De La Cour, Gary, illus. & creator. Counting in the Snow. De La Cour, Gary, creator. gif. ed. 2005. 10p. (J). bds. 9.99 *(978-1-57791-186-9(5))* Brighter Minds Children's Publishing.

de la Mare, Walter. Snow. Rabei, Carolina, illus. 2018. (Four Seasons of Walter de la Mare Ser.). (ENG.). 16p. bds. 7.95 *(978-0-571-33713-2(9),* Faber & Faber Children's Bks.) Faber & Faber, Inc.

Dean, James. Snow Daze. Dean, James, illus. 2016. (Pete the Cat I Can Read Ser.). (ENG., Illus.). 32p. (J). (gr. -1-3). lib. bdg. 13.55 *(978-0-606-39264-8(5))* Turtleback.

Dean, James, illus. Pete the Cat: Snow Daze. 2016. (I Can Read Book: My First Ser.). (ENG.). 32p. (J). (gr. -1-1). 17.44 *(978-1-4844-9513-1(6))* HarperCollins Pubs.

Dean, James & Dean, Kimberly. Pete the Cat: Snow Daze: A Winter & Holiday Book for Kids. Dean, James, illus. 2016. (My First I Can Read Ser.). (ENG., Illus.). 32p. (J). (gr. -1-3). 17.99 *(978-0-06-240425-1(3),* HarperCollins) HarperCollins Pubs.

deGroat, Diane. Jingle Bells, Homework Smells. deGroat, Diane, illus. 2008. (Illus.). (J). (gr. -1-3). pap. 16.95 incl. audio *(978-1-4301-0419-3(8))* Live Oak Media.

Delsol, Wendy. Frost. (ENG., Illus.). 384p. (YA). (gr. 7). 2012. pap. 8.99 *(978-0-7636-6249-3(6))* 2011. 15.99 *(978-0-7636-5386-6(1))* Candlewick Pr.

dePaola, Tomie. Andy & Sandy & the First Snow. dePaola, Tomie, illus. (Andy & Sandy Book Ser.). (ENG., Illus.). 32p. (J). (gr. -1-3). 2018. 5.99 *(978-1-5344-1374-0(X))* 2016. 9.99 *(978-1-4814-4159-9(0))* Simon & Schuster Bks. For Young Readers. (Simon & Schuster Bks. For Young Readers).

Depken, Kristen L. Let's Build a Snowman! 2017. (Illus.). 24p. (J). *(978-1-5182-5209-9(5))* Random Hse., Inc.

—Let's Build a Snowman! (Barbie) Dynamo Limited, illus. 2017. (Step into Reading Ser.). (ENG.). 24p. (J). (gr. -1-1). pap. 5.99 *(978-1-5247-6480-7(9),* Random Hse. Bks. for Young Readers) Random Hse. Children's Bks.

—The Shy Little Kitten's Christmas. DiCicco, Sue, illus. 2018. (Step into Reading Ser.). 32p. (J). (gr. -1-1). pap. 4.99 *(978-1-5247-6809-6(X),* Random Hse. Bks. for Young Readers) Random Hse. Children's Bks.

DePrisco, Dorothea. Snowbear's Winter Day: A Winter Wonder Book. Fehlau, Dagmar, illus. 2005. 18p. (J). (gr. -1). 9.95 *(978-1-58117-133-4(1),* Intervisual/Piggy Toes) Bendon, Inc.

Dillemuth, Julie. Camilla, Cartographer. Wood, Laura, illus. 2019. (ENG.). 32p. (J). *(978-1-4338-3033-4(7),* Magination Pr.) American Psychological Assn.

Disney Books. Disney First Tales: Disney Frozen Do You Want a Hug? 2016. (ENG., Illus.). 64p. (J). (gr. 1-3). 10.99 *(978-1-4847-8775-5(7),* Disney Press Books) Disney Publishing Worldwide.

—Frozen ReadAlong Storybook & CD. 2013. (Read-Along Storybook & CD Ser.). (ENG., Illus.). 32p. (J). (gr. -1-k). pap. 6.99 *(978-1-4231-7064-8(4),* Disney Press Books) Disney Publishing Worldwide.

—Olaf's Frozen Adventure: Olaf's Journey: A Light-Up Board Book. 2017. (Light-Up Board Book Ser.). (ENG., Illus.). 10p. (J). (gr. -1-k). bds. 12.99 *(978-1-368-00674-3(4),* Disney Press Books) Disney Publishing Worldwide.

Disney Editors. Frozen. 2013. lib. bdg. 14.75 *(978-0-606-32207-2(8))* Turtleback.

—Frozen - Anna's Icy Adventure. 2013. lib. bdg. 14.75 *(978-0-606-32206-5(X))* Turtleback.

DiVito, Anna. Annie Oakley Saves the Day. DiVito, Anna, illus. 2005. (Illus.). 32p. (J). lib. bdg. 15.00 *(978-1-59054-939-1(2))* Fitzgerald Bks.

Doi, Kaya. Chirri & Chirra, the Snowy Day. Kaneko, Yuki, tr. 2017. (Chirri & Chirra Ser.: 3). (Illus.). 36p. (J). (gr. -1-3). 16.95 *(978-1-59270-203-9(1))* Enchanted Lion Bks., LLC.

Dooley, Norah. Everybody Serves Soup. Thornton, Peter J., illus. 2004. (Picture Bks.). 40p. (J). (gr. -1-3). 15.95 *(978-1-57505-422-3(1));* (ENG.). (gr. k-3). per. 7.99 *(978-1-57505-791-0(3),* b119f586-7af5-4945-872e-c5e57cd069ee, First Avenue Editions) Lerner Publishing Group.

Downey, Glen. Ice Journey. Brucker, Glenn, illus. 2007. 48p. (J). lib. bdg. 23.08 *(978-1-4242-1618-5(4))* Fitzgerald Bks.

Downey, Tika. The Biggest Snowball, 1 vol. 2006. (Neighborhood Readers Ser.). (ENG.). 16p. (gr. 1-2). pap. 6.50 *(978-1-4042-7200-2(3),* 1472f103-c896-4209-bcf6-3bdf00fadd22, Rosen Classroom) Rosen Publishing Group, Inc., The.

—Tracks in the Snow, 1 vol. 2006. (Neighborhood Readers Ser.). (ENG.). 16p. (gr. 1-2). pap. 6.50 *(978-1-4042-7180-7(5),* 510446d8-1f90-41d2-ac8b-45d75e748255, Rosen Classroom) Rosen Publishing Group, Inc., The.

Drake, Paula. How to Make a Snow Day: The Official Rules & Regulations. 2011. 28p. (gr. -1). pap. 15.00 *(978-1-4567-1830-5(4))* AuthorHouse.

Drummond, Ree. Charlie the Ranch Dog: Charlie's New Friend. deGroat, Diane, illus. 2014. (I Can Read Level 1 Ser.). (ENG.). 32p. (J). (gr. -1-3). 16.99 *(978-0-06-221915-2(4));* pap. 4.99 *(978-0-06-221914-5(6))* HarperCollins Pubs. (HarperCollins).

—Charlie's Snow Day. 2013. (I Can Read! Level 1 Ser.). (J). lib. bdg. 13.55 *(978-0-606-32161-7(6))* Turtleback.

S

Dufresne, Michèle. Fun in the Snow: Bella & Rosie Yellow Set. 2003. (Bella & Rosie Set 1 Ser.). (J). pap. 7.67 *(978-1-932570-13-7(6))* Pioneer Valley Bks.

—Gilbert in the Snow. 2005. (Gilbert the Pig Chapter Ser.). (J). pap. 7.67 *(978-1-58453-297-2(1))* Pioneer Valley Bks.

Dunham, Wendy. Winter Snow Fun: God Gives Us Friends When We're Ready for Adventure. 2018. (Tales of Buttercup Grove Ser.). (ENG., Illus.). 64p. (J). (gr. -1-2). 12.99 *(978-0-7369-7207-9(2)*, 6972079) Harvest Hse. Pubs.

Dunshee, Gloria Fjare. Will & the Magic Snowman. 2010. 32p. pap. 11.95 *(978-0-9828231-1-8(8))* WillGo Pr.

Echols, Jennifer. The Ex Games. 2011. (Romantic Comedies Ser.). (ENG.). 240p. (YA). (gr. 7). pap. 11.99 *(978-1-4424-3083-9(4)*, Simon Pulse) Simon Pulse.

Edwards, Richard. We Love the Snow. Wallace, John, illus. 2015. (ENG.). 32p. (J). (gr. -1-3). 7.99 *(978-1-85733-719-8(0))* Lerner Publishing Group.

Ehlert, Lois. Snowballs. 2004. (Illus.). (gr. -1-3). 17.00 *(978-0-7569-4243-4(8))* Perfection Learning Corp.

Emerson, Alice B. Ruth Fielding at Snow Camp: Or, Lost in the Backwoods. 2017. (ENG., Illus.). (J). pap. 12.95 *(978-1-374-90179-7(2))* Capital Communications, Inc.

Ernst, Lisa Campbell. Snow Surprise: A Winter & Holiday Book for Kids. Ernst, Lisa Campbell, illus. 2008. (ENG., Illus.). 24p. (J). (gr. k-2). pap. 4.99 *(978-0-15-206559-1(8)*, 1199534, Clarion Bks.) HarperCollins Pubs.

Farley, Robin. Mia: The Snow Day Ballet. 2014. (Mia Ser.). (ENG., Illus.). 24p. (J). (gr. -1-k). pap. 4.99 *(978-0-06-210015-3(7)*, HarperFestival) HarperCollins Pubs.

Flodin, Louise E. Sherman the Frog Meets the Snow Princess. l.t. ed. 2006. (Illus.). 24p. (J). (gr. -1-3). 15.95 *(978-0-9745052-5-1(0)*, 1) Tree Of Life Publishing.

Ford, Bernette. First Snow. Braun, Sébastien, illus. 2005. 32p. (J). *(978-0-9547373-3-7(4))* Boxer Bks., Ltd.

—First Snow. Braun, Sébastien, illus. 2018. (ENG.). 28p. (J). (gr. -1-1). bds. 7.95 *(978-1-910716-63-2(4))* Boxer Bks., Ltd. GBR. Dist: Sterling Publishing Co., Inc.

Foster, Ron, illus. I Like Snow! 2006. 28p. (J). (gr. -1-3). *(978-1-929039-37-1(9))* Ambassador Bks., Inc.

French, Vivian. The Snow Dragon. Fisher, Chris, illus. 2003. 32p. (J). pap. 11.99 *(978-0-552-54595-2(3))* Transworld Publishers Ltd. GBR. Dist: Trafalgar Square Publishing.

Friend, Larry. Icy the Iceberg. Makis, Sidney, illus. 2008. 28p. pap. 13.95 *(978-1-4327-3777-1(5))* Outskirts Pr., Inc.

Frost, Libby. Princess Snowbelle. 2017. (ENG., Illus.). 32p. (J). 16.99 *(978-1-68119-690-9(5)*, 900182161, Bloomsbury USA Childrens) Bloomsbury Publishing USA.

Garoche, Camille. The Snow Rabbit. 2015. (Illus.). 56p. (J). (gr. -1-3). 16.95 *(978-1-59270-181-0(7))* Enchanted Lion Bks., LLC.

Gay, Marie-Louise. Stella, Queen of the Snow. 2004. (J). (gr. -1-1). spiral bd. *(978-0-616-08493-9(5))* Canadian National Institute for the Blind/Institut National Canadien pour les Aveugles.

—Stella, Reine des Neiges. 2004.Tr. of Stella, Queen of the Snow. (FRE., Illus.). (J). (gr. k-3). spiral bd. *(978-0-616-14596-8(9))* Canadian National Institute for the Blind/Institut National Canadien pour les Aveugles.

Gay, Marie-Louise, illus. Stella, Queen of the Snow. braille ed. 2004. (J). (gr. -1-1). spiral bd. *(978-0-616-08492-2(7))* Canadian National Institute for the Blind/Institut National Canadien pour les Aveugles.

George, Jean Craighead. Snowboard Twist. Minor, Wendell, illus. 2004. (Outdoor Adventures Ser.). (ENG.). 32p. (J). 15.99 *(978-0-06-050595-0(8))* HarperCollins Pubs.

George, Joshua. I'm Just a Little Snowman. Green, Barry, illus. 2017. (Googley-Eye Bks.). (ENG.). 12p. (J). (gr. -1-k). bds. 7.99 *(978-1-78700-079-7(6))* Top That! Publishing PLC GBR. Dist: Independent Pubs. Group.

—In My Little Snowman Bed. Gulliver, Amanda, illus. 2017. (In My Bed Bks.). (ENG.). 24p. (J). (gr. -1-k). bds. 9.99 *(978-1-78700-080-3(X))* Top That! Publishing PLC GBR. Dist: Independent Pubs. Group.

George, Kallie. Duck, Duck, Dinosaur: Snowy Surprise. Vidal, Oriol, illus. 2017. (My First I Can Read Ser.). (ENG.). 32p. (J). (gr. -1-3). 16.99 *(978-0-06-235319-1(5))*; pap. 5.99 *(978-0-06-235318-4(7))* HarperCollins Pubs. (HarperCollins).

Ghigna, Charles. Snow Wonder. Woolf, Julia, illus. 2008. (Step into Reading Ser.: Vol. 2). 24p. (J). (gr. -1-1). 4.99 *(978-0-375-85586-3(6)*, Random Hse. Bks. for Young Readers) Random Hse. Children's Bks.

Giff, Patricia Reilly. The Sneaky Snow Fox (Fiercely & Friends) (Library Edition) Palmisciano, Diane, illus. 2012. (Fiercely & Friends Ser.). (ENG.). 40p. (J). (gr. k-2). 22.99 *(978-0-545-43378-5(9)*, Orchard Bks.) Scholastic, Inc.

Gilman, Grace. Dixie & the Best Day Ever. 2014. (I Can Read Level 1 Ser.). (ENG., Illus.). 32p. (J). (gr. -1-3). pap. 4.99 *(978-0-06-208659-4(6)*, HarperCollins) HarperCollins Pubs.

Gilman, Phoebe. Jillian Jiggs & the Great Big Snow. 2004. (Illus.). (J). (gr. k-3). spiral bd. *(978-0-616-14582-1(9))*; spiral bd. *(978-0-616-14583-8(7))* Canadian National Institute for the Blind/Institut National Canadien pour les Aveugles.

Goggins, Jean. The Adventures of Boo & Koty: Snow. 2009. 36p. pap. 21.99 *(978-1-4415-4670-8(7))* Xlibris Corp.

Golden Books. Snow Wonder! (Frosty the Snowman) Golden Books, illus. 2013. (ENG., Illus.). 128p. (J). (gr. -1-2). pap. 7.99 *(978-0-385-37179-7(9)*, Golden Bks.) Random Hse. Children's Bks.

Gorbachev, Valeri. Pizza-Pie Snowman. 2018. (Illus.). 40p. (J). (gr. -1-3). pap. 8.99 *(978-0-8234-4040-5(0))* Holiday Hse., Inc.

Gore, Leonid. Danny's First Snow. Gore, Leonid, illus. 2007. (ENG., Illus.). 40p. (J). (gr. -1-3). 19.99 *(978-1-4169-1330-6(0)*, Atheneum Bks. for Young Readers) Simon & Schuster Children's Publishing.

Gosier, Phil. Snow Beast Comes to Play. Gosier, Phil, illus. 2017. (ENG., Illus.). 32p. (J). 17.99 *(978-1-62672-519-5(5)*, 9781626725195) Roaring Brook Pr.

Graber, Mark. The Brave Little Explorer. Graber, Jack, illus. 2015. (ENG.). (J). 16.99 *(978-0-692-43867-1(X))* JourneytimeBks.

Grandma Sue. Bubba the Bear. 2010. 12p. pap. 8.49 *(978-1-4490-1813-9(0))* AuthorHouse.

Gravett, Emily. Bear & Hare Snow! Gravett, Emily, illus. 2015. (Bear & Hare Ser.). (ENG., Illus.). 32p. (J). (gr. -1-3). 16.99 *(978-1-4814-4514-6(6)*, Simon & Schuster Bks. For Young Readers) Simon & Schuster Bks. For Young Readers.

Grizzell, Larry. What Would You Like to Do Today? Fun in the Snow. 2006. (Illus.). 30p. (J). 16.95 *(978-0-9759542-1-8(0))* Adventures Galore.

Grogan, John. Marley: Snow Dog Marley: A Winter & Holiday Book for Kids. Cowdrey, Richard, illus. 2010. (I Can Read Level 2 Ser.). (ENG.). 32p. (J). (gr. k-3). pap. 4.99 *(978-0-06-185392-0(5)*, HarperCollins) HarperCollins Pubs.

Hader, Berta and Elmer. The Big Snow & Other Stories: A Treasury of Caldecott Award Winning Tales. 2015. (ENG., Illus.). 160p. (J). (gr. 1-4). pap. 14.99 *(978-0-486-78163-1(1)*, 781631) Dover Pubns., Inc.

Hall, Kirsten. The Big Sled Race. Burnett, Lindy, illus. 2003. (Hello Reader! Ser.). (J). pap. 3.99 *(978-0-439-32104-4(2))* Scholastic, Inc.

Hamilton, Pamela Greenhalgh. Snow Day. 2011. 34p. (J). pap. 18.95 *(978-1-4327-5743-4(1))* Outskirts Pr., Inc.

Hanson, Bonnie Compton. Lost on Monster Mountain. 2004. (Ponytail Girls Ser.). (Illus.). 208p. (J). pap. 7.99 *(978-1-58411-031-6(7)*, Legacy Pr.) Rainbow Pubs. & Legacy Pr.

Harper, Lee & Harper, Lee. Snow! Snow! Snow! Harper, Lee & Harper, Lee, illus. 2009. (ENG., Illus.). 40p. (J). (gr. -1-3). 19.99 *(978-1-4169-8454-2(2)*, Simon & Schuster/Paula Wiseman Bks.) Simon & Schuster/Paula Wiseman Bks.

Harris, Shelly J. A Snowman's Love, 1 vol. 2009. 19p. pap. 24.95 *(978-1-60836-708-5(8))* America Star Bks.

Harrison, Paula. The Snow Jewel. 2013. (Rescue Princesses Ser.: 5). lib. bdg. 14.75 *(978-0-606-32372-7(4))* Turtleback.

Heigh, Stephen. The Snowman in the Moon. Burton, Kevin, ed. Heigh, Stephen, illus. 2005. (Illus.). 28p. (J). (gr. -1-3). 16.95 *(978-0-9745715-5-3(5))* KRBY Creations, LLC.

Heinz, Brian J. A Coming of Winter in the Adirondacks. Healy, Maggie, illus. 2011. (ENG.). 32p. (J). 19.95 *(978-1-59531-038-5(X))* North Country Bks., Inc.

Hendry, Diana. The Very Snowy Christmas. Chapman, Jane, illus. (J). 2013. (ENG.). 16p. (gr. -1-k). bds. 8.95 *(978-1-58925-617-0(4))* 2007. 32p. pap. 6.95 *(978-1-58925-406-0(6))* 2005. 32p. (gr. -1-2). 15.95 *(978-1-58925-051-2(6))* Tiger Tales.

Hest, Amy. The Reader, 0 vols. Castillo, Lauren, illus. 2012. (ENG.). 32p. (J). (gr. -1-3). 16.99 *(978-0-7614-6184-5(1)*, 9780761461845, Two Lions) Amazon Publishing.

Higginson, Sheila Sweeny. Chilly Catches a Cold. 2013. (Doc Mcstuffins 8X8 Ser.). (J). lib. bdg. 13.55 *(978-0-606-35109-6(4))* Turtleback.

Hileman, Jane & Pitt, Marilyn. Snow Dog. Bianchi, John, illus. 2011. (Power 50 - Potato Chip Bks). 12p. pap. 33.92 *(978-1-61541-298-3(0))* American Reading Co.

Hillenbrand, Will. Snowman's Story, 0 vols. 2014. (ENG., Illus.). 32p. (J). (gr. -1-2). 16.99 *(978-1-4778-4787-9(1)*, 9781477847879, Two Lions) Amazon Publishing.

Hillert, Margaret. I Did It, Dear Dragon. Schimmell, David, illus. 2009. (BeginningtoRead Ser.). 32p. (J). (gr. k-2). lib. bdg. 22.60 *(978-1-59953-295-0(6))* Norwood Hse. Pr.

—The Snow Baby. Laura Krushak-Green, illus. 21st ed. 2016. (Beginning-To-Read Ser.). (ENG.). 32p. (J). (gr. k-2). pap. 13.26 *(978-1-60357-945-2(1))* Norwood Hse. Pr.

—The Snow Baby. Krushak-Green, Laura, illus. 21st ed. 2016. (BeginningtoRead Ser.). (ENG.). 32p. (J). (gr. 1-2). 22.60 *(978-1-59953-804-4(0))* Norwood Hse. Pr.

Hills, Tad. Duck & Goose, It's Time for Christmas! Hills, Tad, illus. 2010. (Duck & Goose Ser.). (Illus.). 22p. (J). (gr. -1 — 1). 7.99 *(978-0-375-86484-1(9))* Random Hse. Children's Bks.

Hoffman, Don. A Very Special Snowflake. Dakins, Todd, illus. 2nd ed. 2016. (ENG.). 28p. (J). (gr. -1-k). pap. 3.99 *(978-1-943154-01-2(5))* Peek-A-Boo Publishing.

Holub, Joan. Snow Day! A Winter Tale (Ready-To-Read Pre-Level 1) Terry, Will, illus. 2008. (Ant Hill Ser.). (ENG.). 24p. (J). (gr. -1-k). pap. 4.99 *(978-1-4169-5135-3(0)*, Simon Spotlight) Simon Spotlight.

Howard, Kate. Snowball Trouble. Gilpin, Stephen, illus. 2015. (ANG.). 40p. (J). pap. *(978-0-545-75839-0(4))* Scholastic, Inc.

Howell, Gail L. Sarah & the Blue Sled: Sarah's World (Series) 2010. 32p. pap. 12.99 *(978-1-4389-7597-9(X))* AuthorHouse.

Howell, Gill. Snow King. Cann, Helen, illus. 2005. (ENG.). 24p. (J). lib. bdg. 23.65 *(978-1-59646-742-2(8))* Dingles & Co.

Hulst, W. G. van de & Hulst, Willem G. van de, illus. Footprints in the Snow. 2014. (J). *(978-1-928136-13-2(3))* Inheritance Pubns.

Hutchins, Hazel J. Ben's Snow Song: A Winter Picnic. 2004. (Illus.). (J). (gr. k-3). spiral bd. *(978-0-616-01677-0(8))* Canadian National Institute for the Blind/Institut National Canadien pour les Aveugles.

Isadora, Rachel. Mr. Moon. Date not set. (J). 15.99 *(978-0-06-029821-0(9))*; lib. bdg. 16.89 *(978-0-06-029822-7(7))* HarperCollins Pubs.

Jack, Keats Ezra. The Snowy Day. 2014. (ENG.). 40p. (J). (gr. 3-7). 12.24 *(978-1-63245-154-5(9))* Lectorum Pubns., Inc.

Jackson, Laura Gower. The Snowman & the Magic Eyeglasses. 2010. 24p. 11.99 *(978-1-4520-3544-4(X))* AuthorHouse.

Jackson, Richard. Snow Scene. Vaccaro Seeger, Laura, illus. 2017. (ENG.). 40p. (J). 17.99 *(978-1-62672-680-2(9)*, 900170475) Roaring Brook Pr.

Jakubowski, Michele. Snowy Blast. Waters, Erica-Jane, illus. 2014. (Perfectly Poppy Ser.). (ENG.). 32p. (J). (gr. k-2). lib. bdg. 22.65 *(978-1-4795-2283-5(X)*, 124318, Picture Window Bks.) Capstone.

James, Lauren & Kisloski, Carolyn. Building a Snowman. de Polonia, Nina, illus. 2017. (Play Time Ser.). (ENG.). 24p. (gr. -1-2). pap. 9.95 *(978-1-68342-784-1(X)*, 9781683427841) Rourke Educational Media.

Jeannine & Egan, Jennifer. Jack the Brave Conquers the Snow. 2012. 44p. pap. 21.99 *(978-1-4797-1713-2(4))* Xlibris Corp.

Jenkins, Barbie. The Legend of the Christmas Kiss. 2010. (ENG.). 32p. pap. 11.99 *(978-1-4391-9623-6(0)*, Howard Bks.) Howard Bks.

Jenkins, Emily. Toys Meet Snow: Being the Wintertime Adventures of a Curious Stuffed Buffalo, a Sensitive Plush Stingray, & a Book-Loving Rubber Ball. Zelinsky, Paul O., illus. 2015. 40p. (J). (gr. -1-2). 17.99 *(978-0-385-37330-2(9)*, Schwartz & Wade Bks.) Random Hse. Children's Bks.

Johnson, Andi. Hailey Snowstorm. 2004. (Illus.). 16p. 9.00 *(978-1-84161-113-6(1))* Ravette Publishing, Ltd. GBR. Dist: Parkwest Pubns., Inc.

Johnson, Christine. Deep in Alaska. Johnson, Gary R., illus. 2013. (ENG.). 42p. pap. 13.95 *(978-1-60223-215-0(6))* Univ. of Alaska Pr.

Johnson, Crockett. Time for Spring. Johnson, Crockett, illus. 2016. (ENG., Illus.). 40p. (J). (gr. -1-3). 14.99 *(978-0-06-243033-5(5)*, HarperCollins) HarperCollins Pubs.

Joyce, William. Snowie Rolie. Joyce, William, illus. 2017. (World of William Joyce Ser.). (ENG., Illus.). 40p. (J). (gr. -1-2). 17.99 *(978-1-4814-8967-6(4)*, Atheneum Bks. for Young Readers) Simon & Schuster Children's Publishing.

K/H (Pathways). Kindergarten Stepping Stones: Kindergarten the Bravest Dog Ever - The True Story of Balto Trade Book. rev. ed. 2010. (ENG.). 48p. pap. 9.00 *(978-0-7575-8646-0(5))* Kendall Hunt Publishing Co.

Kann, Victoria. Pinkalicious & the Snow Globe. 2015. (Pinkalicious Ser.). (J). lib. bdg. 14.75 *(978-0-606-37641-9(0))* Turtleback.

—Pinkalicious & the Snow Globe: A Winter & Holiday Book for Kids. Kann, Victoria, illus. 2015. (Pinkalicious Ser.). (ENG., Illus.). 24p. (J). (gr. -1-3). pap. 5.99 *(978-0-06-224588-5(0)*, HarperFestival) HarperCollins Pubs.

Kauflin, Chris. Smiletown's Big Snow Day. 2006. (J). per. 14.95 *(978-0-9785132-0-7(7)*, Smiletown Bks.) Smile-a-Lot, LLP.

Keats, Ezra Jack. The Snowy Day. 2012. 32p. (J). (gr. -1 — 1). bds. 13.99 *(978-0-670-01325-8(0)*, Viking Books for Young Readers) Penguin Young Readers Group.

—The Snowy Day: 50th Anniversary Edition. 50th anniv. ed. 2011. 48p. (J). (gr. k-3). 19.99 *(978-0-670-01270-1(X)*, Viking Books for Young Readers) Penguin Young Readers Group.

Kessler, Kathryn. Marvin Discovers Snow. 2010. 36p. (J). pap. 15.77 *(978-1-4520-0590-4(7))* AuthorHouse.

Keyes, Diane. Spirit of the Snowpeople. Stevens, Helen, illus. 2008. (ENG.). 32p. (J). (gr. -1-3). 15.95 *(978-0-89272-710-0(1))* Down East Bks.

Kim, Sang-Keun. Little Mole's Wish. 2019. (Illus.). 40p. (J). (gr. -1-2). 17.99 *(978-0-525-58134-5(0)*, Schwartz & Wade Bks.) Random Hse. Children's Bks.

Kirby, Stan. Captain Awesome Has the Best Snow Day Ever? O'Connor, George, illus. 2016. (Captain Awesome Ser.: 18). (ENG.). 128p. (J). (gr. k-4). 17.99 *(978-1-4814-7816-8(8)*, Little Simon) Little Simon.

Kleyn, Diana & Beeke, Joel R. How God Used a Snowdrift. rev. ed. 2013. (Building on the Rock Ser.). (ENG., Illus.). 176p. (J). pap. 8.99 *(978-1-85792-817-4(2)*, cba4a9ca-6757-4eaf-8b54-b1a1926a786f, CF4Kids) Christian Focus Pubns. GBR. Dist: Baker & Taylor Publisher Services (BTPS).

Kneen, Maggie. The Christmas Surprise. Kneen, Maggie, illus. 2006. (Illus.). 18p. (J). (gr. k-4). reprint ed. 16.00 *(978-0-7567-9837-6(X))* DIANE Publishing Co.

Knudsen, Michelle. Winter Is for Snowflakes. Denise & Fernando, illus. 2003. (Please Read to Me Ser.). (ENG.). 24p. (J). (gr. -1-1). 16.19 *(978-0-375-82215-5(1))* Random House Publishing Group.

Koehler, Lora. The Little Snowplow. Parker, Jake, illus. (ENG.). (J). 2022. 32p. (gr. -1-2). 7.99 *(978-1-5362-2777-2(3))* 2018. 30p. (— 1). bds. 8.99 *(978-1-5362-0340-0(8))* 2015. 32p. (gr. -1-2). 17.99 *(978-0-7636-7074-0(X))* Candlewick Pr.

Kokias, Kerri. Snow Sisters! White, Teagan, illus. 2018. 32p. (J). (gr. -1-2). 18.99 *(978-1-101-93883-6(8)*, Knopf Bks. for Young Readers) Random Hse. Children's Bks.

Korda, Lerryn. Millions of Snow. Korda, Lerryn, illus. 2010. (Playtime with Little Nye Ser.). (ENG., Illus.). 32p. (J). (— 1). 8.99 *(978-0-7636-4651-6(2))* Candlewick Pr.

Krackow, Eric T. Bill the Snowman, 1 vol. 2009. (ENG., Illus.). 64p. (J). (gr. -1-3). 16.99 *(978-0-7643-3219-7(8)*, 3573) Schiffer Publishing, Ltd.

—Have an Abominably Good Day, 1 vol. 2010. (ENG., Illus.). 64p. (J). (gr. -1-3). 16.99 *(978-0-7643-3496-2(4)*, 3885) Schiffer Publishing, Ltd.

Kreder Sr., Edward G. & Kreder, Mary Ellen DeLuca. Sparkle's Journey. Vanden Berg, Myra, illus. 2013. 32p. pap. 5.99 *(978-0-9913232-0-3(3))* Kreder, Mary Ellen DeLuca.

LaBree Stute, Lela. The Sunnyset Pugs. 2010. 34p. pap. 19.99 *(978-0-557-41751-3(1))* Lulu Pr., Inc.

Lagonegro, Melissa. Frozen - A Tale of Two Sisters. 2013. (Disney Princess Step into Reading Ser.). lib. bdg. 13.55 *(978-0-606-32205-8(1))* Turtleback.

Lakin, Patricia. Max & Mo Make a Snowman: Ready-To-Read Level 1. Floca, Brian, illus. 2007. (Max & Mo Ser.). (ENG.). 32p. (J). (gr. -1-1). pap. 4.99 *(978-1-4169-2537-8(6)*, Simon Spotlight) Simon Spotlight.

Lamerton, Todd. A Tale from Flurryville: The Berg's Big Surprise. 2003. 28p. 7.61 *(978-0-7575-0655-0(0))* Kendall Hunt Publishing Co.

Laminack, Lester L. Snow Day!, 1 vol. Gustavson, Adam, illus. 2007. 32p. (J). (gr. -1-3). 17.99 *(978-1-56145-418-1(4))* Peachtree Publishing Co. Inc.

Laughing Elephant Staff, ed. The Truth about Snow People. 2005. (Classic Children's Bks.). (ENG., Illus.). 32p. (J). (gr. -1-3). 17.95 *(978-1-59583-052-4(9)*, 9781595830524) Laughing Elephant.

Lawler, Janet. Snowzilla, 0 vols. Haley, Amanda, illus. 2012. (ENG.). 32p. (J). (gr. -1-3). 16.99 *(978-0-7614-6188-3(4)*, 9780761461883, Two Lions) Amazon Publishing.

Lê, Christine & Lê, Michel, illus. The Hawai'i Snowman. 2008. (J). 14.95 *(978-1-56647-879-3(0))* Mutual Publishing LLC.

Lecis, Alessandro. I Am Not Little Red Riding Hood. Wolfsgruber, Linda, illus. 2013. (ENG.). 32p. (J). (gr. -1-1). 16.95 *(978-1-62087-985-6(9)*, 620985, Sky Pony Pr.) Skyhorse Publishing Co., Inc.

Lin, Grace. A Big Bed for Little Snow. 2019. (ENG., Illus.). 40p. (J). (gr. -1-3). 18.99 *(978-0-316-47836-6(9))* Little, Brown Bks. for Young Readers.

Linkowski, Tami Leli. Lynn Was a Cow Who Could Ski. 2008. 20p. pap. 24.95 *(978-1-4241-9626-5(4))* America Star Bks.

Little Bee Books. My Snowman Book. 2015. (ENG., Illus.). 12p. (J). (gr. -1 — 1). bds. 5.99 *(978-1-4998-0130-9(0))* Little Bee Books Inc.

London, Jonathan. Little Fox in the Snow. Miyares, Daniel, illus. 2018. (ENG.). 40p. (J). (gr. -1-3). 16.99 *(978-0-7636-8814-1(2))* Candlewick Pr.

Louise, Martha. Why Kings & Queens Don't Wear Crowns. Sevig-Fajardo, Mari Elise, tr. from NOR. Nyhus, Svein, illus. 2005. Orig. Title: Hvorfor de kongelige ikke har krone på Hodet. 32p. (J). 17.95 *(978-1-57534-037-1(2)*, CSC 100) Skandisk, Inc.

Maclachlan, Patricia. Snowflakes Fall. Kellogg, Steven, illus. 2013. 32p. (J). (gr. -1-2). 17.99 *(978-0-385-37693-8(6))* Random Hse. Children's Bks.

Macnaughton, Tina. One Snowy Rescue. 2015. (ENG.). pap. *(978-0-545-92909-7(1))* Scholastic, Inc.

Majestic's Search. 2004. (J). *(978-0-615-12544-2(1))* Jadenaila Publishing.

Mancusi, Mari. Golden Girl. 2015. (Mix Ser.). (ENG., Illus.). 336p. (J). (gr. 4-8). pap. 7.99 *(978-1-4814-3762-2(3)*, Aladdin) Simon & Schuster Children's Publishing.

Manushkin, Fran. Pedro Keeps His Cool. Lyon, Tammie, illus. 2019. (Pedro Ser.). (ENG.). 32p. (J). (gr. k-2). pap. 5.95 *(978-1-5158-4564-5(8)*, 141152); lib. bdg. 21.32 *(978-1-5158-4451-8(X)*, 140566) Capstone. (Picture Window Bks.).

—Pedro No Pierde la Calma. Aparicio Publishing LLC, Aparicio Publishing, tr. Lyon, Tammie, illus. 2020. (Pedro en Español Ser.).Tr. of Pedro Keeps His Cool. (SPA.). 32p. (J). (gr. k-2). pap. 5.95 *(978-1-5158-5725-9(5)*, 142093); lib. bdg. 21.32 *(978-1-5158-5723-5(9)*, 142090) Capstone. (Picture Window Bks.).

Marie, Charity. Jason, Lizzy & the Snowman Village: Jason & Lizzy's Legendary Adventures Book 1. 2013. (ENG., Illus.). 132p. (J). 19.99 *(978-0-9859601-1-7(6))* Texas Pride Publishing.

Markey, Kevin. Wall Ball. 2011. (ENG.). 208p. (J). (gr. 3-7). pap. 7.99 *(978-0-06-115223-8(4)*, HarperCollins) HarperCollins Pubs.

Marsoli, Lisa Ann & Bridwell, Norman. The Snow Dog. Haefele, Steve, illus. 2004. (Big Red Reader Ser.). (J). pap. *(978-0-439-58559-0(7))* Scholastic, Inc.

Martin, David. Peep & Ducky It's Snowing! Walker, David, illus. 2018. (Peep & Ducky Ser.). 32p. (J). (— 1). 14.99 *(978-0-7636-9433-3(9))* Candlewick Pr.

Mason, Jane B. & Stephens, Sarah Hines. Snowfall Surprise. 2009. (Candy Apple Ser.: 21). (ENG.). 144p. (J). (gr. 3-7). 5.99 *(978-0-545-10067-0(4)*, Scholastic Paperbacks) Scholastic, Inc.

May, Eleanor. Let's Go, Snow! Pillo, Cary, illus. 2017. (Math Matters Ser.). 32p. (J). (gr. k-4). pap. 5.99 *(978-1-57565-807-0(0)*, c10b9d6d-d8c6-494f-882f-04311f6945c8, Kane Press) Astra Publishing Hse.

—Let's Go, Snow! Temperature Measurement. Pillo, Cary, illus. 2017. (Math Matters (r) Ser.). (ENG.). 32p. (J). (gr. k-3). E-Book 23.99 *(978-1-57565-808-7(9))* Astra Publishing Hse.

May, Kyla. Pug's Snow Day: a Branches Book (Diary of a Pug #2) (Library Edition) May, Kyla, illus. 2019. (Diary of a Pug Ser.: 2). (ENG., Illus.). 80p. (J). (gr. k-2). 24.99 *(978-1-338-53007-0(0))* Scholastic, Inc.

Mayer, Mercer. Little Critter: Just a Snowman: A Winter & Holiday Book for Kids. Mayer, Mercer, illus. 2004. (Little Critter Ser.). (ENG., Illus.). 24p. (J). (gr. -1-2). pap. 4.99 *(978-0-06-053947-4(X)*, HarperFestival) HarperCollins Pubs.

Mazer, Harry. Snow Bound. 144p. (YA). (gr. 7-18). pap. 4.99 *(978-0-8072-1367-4(5)*, Listening Library) Random Hse. Audio Publishing Group.

McCarty, Peter. First Snow. McCarty, Peter, illus. 2015. (ENG., Illus.). 40p. (J). (gr. -1-3). 16.99 *(978-0-06-218996-7(4)*, Balzer & Bray) HarperCollins Pubs.

McClatchy, Lisa. Eloise & the Snowman, 1 vol. Lyon, Tammie, illus. 2015. (Kay Thompson's Eloise Ser.). (ENG.). 32p. (J). (gr. -1-2). 31.36 *(978-1-61479-402-8(2)*, 18187) Spotlight.

—Eloise & the Snowman: Ready-To-Read Level 1. Lyon, Tammie, illus. 2006. (Eloise Ser.). (ENG.). 32p. (J). (gr. -1-1). pap. 4.99 *(978-0-689-87451-2(0)*, Simon Spotlight) Simon Spotlight.

McCully, Emily Arnold. First Snow. McCully, Emily Arnold, illus. 2003. (ENG., Illus.). 32p. (J). (gr. -1-3). 17.99 *(978-0-06-623852-4(8)*, HarperCollins) HarperCollins Pubs.

McDaniels, Preston. A Perfect Snowman. McDaniels, Preston, illus. 2007. (ENG., Illus.). 40p. (J). (gr. -1-3). 18.99 *(978-1-4169-1026-8(3)*, Simon & Schuster Bks. For Young Readers) Simon & Schuster Bks. For Young Readers.

McDonald, Kirsten. Tío Time, 1 vol. Meza, Erika, illus. 2016. (Carlos & Carmen Ser.). (ENG.). 32p. (J). (gr. -1-3). 32.79 *(978-1-62402-143-5(3)*, 21553, Calico Chapter Bks) Magic Wagon.

McGhee, Alison. Making a Friend. Rosenthal, Marc, illus. 2011. (ENG.). 40p. (J). (gr. -1-3). 16.99 *(978-1-4169-8998-1(6)*, Atheneum Bks. for Young Readers) Simon & Schuster Children's Publishing.

McKee, David. Elmer in the Snow. McKee, David, illus. 2004. (Elmer Bks.). (Illus.). 32p. (J). 9.99 *(978-0-06-075240-8(8))* HarperCollins Pubs.

Meister, Cari. Snorp on the Slopes, 1 vol. Messner, Dennis, illus. 2010. (Monster Friends Ser.). (ENG.). 32p. (J). (gr. 2-3). lib. bdg. 22.65 *(978-1-4342-1873-5(2)*, 102333, Stone Arch Bks.) Capstone.

Meschenmoser, Sebastian. Waiting for Winter. 2015. (ENG., Illus.). 58p. (J). (gr. k-3). 10.99 *(978-1-61067-435-5(9))* Kane Miller.

Messner, Kate. Over & under the Snow. Neal, Christopher Silas, illus. 2014. (Over & Under Ser.). (ENG.). 44p. (J). (gr. -1-3). 8.99 *(978-1-4521-3646-2(7))* Chronicle Bks. LLC.

Metzger, Steve. The Little Snowflake. Wellington, Monica, illus. 2003. (J). *(978-0-439-55656-9(2))* Scholastic, Inc.

Milbourne, Anna. The Snowy Day. Temporin, Elena, illus. 2007. (J). *(978-0-439-88988-9(X))* Scholastic, Inc.

Mills, Charles. Storm on Shadow Mountain. 2003. 127p. (J). 7.99 *(978-0-8163-1993-0(6))* Pacific Pr. Publishing Assn.

Milway, Alex. Operation Robot Storm: The Mythical 9th Division. 2013. (ENG., Illus.). 224p. (J). pap. 5.99 *(978-1-61067-074-6(4))* Kane Miller.

Milz, Cynthia A. Waiting for the Last Leaf to Fall. 2008. 20p. per. 24.95 *(978-1-4241-8965-6(9))* America Star Bks.

Mitchell, Robin & Steedman, Judith. Snowy & Chinook. 2005. (ENG., Illus.). 22p. (J). (gr. -1-3). 15.95 *(978-0-9688768-9-3(7))* Simply Read Bks. CAN. Dist: Ingram Publisher Services.

Mitchell, Sherry. Snowy Days. 2012. 20p. pap. 17.99 *(978-1-4685-8086-0(8))* AuthorHouse.

Mozelle, Shirley. Zack's Alligator & the First Snow. 2011. (I Can Read Level 2 Ser.). (ENG., Illus.). 32p. (J). (gr. k-3). pap.

4.99 *(978-0-06-147372-2(3)*, HarperCollins) HarperCollins Pubs.

Myers, Bernice. Dog Meets Dog. 2020. (I Like to Read Ser.). (Illus.). 32p. (J). (gr. -1-3). 15.99 *(978-0-8234-4451-9(1))* Holiday Hse., Inc.

Nakagawa, Masafumi. Dr. Mouse's Mission. Perry, Mia Lynn, tr. Yamawaki, Yuriko, illus. 2007. (R. I. C. Story Chest Ser.). 27p. (J). (gr. -1-1). 14.95 incl. audio compact disk *(978-1-74126-051-9(5))* R.I.C. Pubns. AUS. Dist: SCB Distributors.

Nelson, Steve & Rollins, Jack. Frosty the Snowman. Williams, Sam, illus. 2013. (ENG.). 16p. (J). (gr. -1-k). bds. 9.99 *(978-0-545-45005-8(5)*, Cartwheel Bks.) Scholastic, Inc.

Neubecker, Robert. Winter Is for Snow. 2020. (ENG., Illus.). 30p. (J). (gr. -1 — 1). bds. 7.99 *(978-1-368-04543-8(X))* Hyperion Bks. for Children.

Night, P. J. Ready for a Scare? (You're Invited to a Creepover Ser.: 3). (ENG.). 160p. (J). (gr. 3-7). 2018. 17.99 *(978-1-5344-2109-7(2))* 2011. ppr. 7.99 *(978-1-4424-2903-1(8))* Simon Spotlight. (Simon Spotlight).

—Ready for a Scare?, 1 vol. 2013. (You're Invited to a Creepover Ser.). (ENG.). 160p. (J). (gr. 3-6). lib. bdg. 31.36 *(978-1-61479-062-4(0)*, 15850, Chapter Bks.) Spotlight.

—Ready for a Scare? 2011. (Creepover Ser.: 3). lib. bdg. 17.20 *(978-0-606-23747-5(X))* Turtleback.

Nolan, Allia Zobel. God's Winter Wonderland. Mitchell, Melanie, illus. 2006. 10p. (J). bds. 8.99 *(978-0-8254-5526-1(X))* Kregel Pubns.

Novel Units. Snow Treasure Novel Units Teacher Guide. 2019. (ENG.). (J). pap. 12.99 *(978-1-56137-285-0(4)*, Novel Units, Inc.) Classroom Library Co.

—The Snowy Day Novel Units Teacher Guide. 2019. (ENG.). (J). pap., wbk. ed. 12.99 *(978-1-56137-476-2(8)*, Novel Units, Inc.) Classroom Library Co.

O'Connell, Matthew J. The Adventures of Rick Cliff: The Almost Great Penguin Race. 2004. 80p. (J). pap. 6.95 *(978-1-932560-66-4(1)*, Llumina Pr.) Aeon Publishing Inc.

O'Connor, Jane. Fancy Nancy - There's No Day Like a Snow Day. 2012. (Fancy Nancy Picture Bks.). (J). lib. bdg. 14.75 *(978-0-606-26857-8(X))* Turtleback.

—Fancy Nancy: There's No Day Like a Snow Day: A Winter & Holiday Book for Kids. Glasser, Robin Preiss, illus. 2012. (Fancy Nancy Ser.). (ENG.). 24p. (J). (gr. -1-3). pap. 4.99 *(978-0-06-208629-7(4)*, HarperFestival) HarperCollins Pubs.

—The Snow Globe Family. Schindler, S. D., illus. 2008. 40p. (J). (gr. 1-3). pap. 8.99 *(978-0-14-241242-8(2)*, Puffin Books) Penguin Young Readers Group.

O'Malley, Kevin. Straight to the Pole. 2004. (Illus.). 32p. (J). (gr. -1-3). 16.85 *(978-0-8027-8868-9(8))* Walker & Co.

O'Neill, Jacquie, illus. Figure Skating. 2010. (Sticker Stories Ser.). (ENG.). 16p. (J). (gr. -1-k). pap. 5.99 *(978-0-448-45343-9(6)*, Grosset & Dunlap) Penguin Publishing Group.

Ori, Anthony. Snow Makes a Snowman. 2008. 24p. pap. 24.95 *(978-1-60703-308-0(9))* America Star Bks.

O'Ryan, Ray. A Green Christmas! Jack, Colin, illus. 2013. (Galaxy Zack Ser.: 6). (ENG.). 128p. (J). (gr. k-2). 17.99 *(978-1-4424-8225-8(7))*; pap. 6.99 *(978-1-4424-8224-1(9))*; pap. 6.99 *(978-1-4424-8224-1(9))* Little Simon. (Little Simon).

—A Green Christmas! 2013. (Galaxy Zack Ser.: 6). lib. bdg. 14.75 *(978-0-606-35185-0(X))* Turtleback.

Pace, Anne Marie. Vampirina in the Snow-A Vampirina Ballerina Book. 2018. (Vampirina Ser.: 4). (ENG., Illus.). 40p. (J). (gr. -1-k). 17.99 *(978-1-368-02318-4(5)*, Disney-Hyperion) Disney Publishing Worldwide.

Parenteau, Shirley. Bears in the Snow. Walker, David, illus. 2016. (Bears on Chairs Ser.). 32p. (J). (-k). 15.99 *(978-0-7636-8148-7(2))* Candlewick Pr.

Parisi, Anthony. Baby Harp Seal's Snowy Day. 2010. (ENG.). 16p. (J). (gr. -1). 6.95 *(978-1-60727-136-9(2))* Soundprints.

Parker, Emma. The Magic Snow Globe. 2010. (Illus.). pap. *(978-1-877561-30-6(4))* First Edition Ltd.

Parker, Sydney. Scoop That Snow! Shannon, David et al, illus. 2009. (Jon Scieszka's Trucktown Ser.). (ENG.). 12p. (J). (gr. -1-k). 7.99 *(978-1-4169-4182-8(7)*, Little Simon) Little Simon.

Parker, Vic, ed. The Snow Queen & Other Stories, 1 vol. 2015. (Scary Fairy Tales Ser.). (ENG.). 40p. (J). (gr. 3-4). pap. 15.05 *(978-1-4824-3105-6(X)*, d31f6828-e3d9-4675-b186-264cccae340d) Stevens, Gareth Publishing LLLP.

Parvensky Barwell, Catherine A. Tommi's First Snowfall, 4 vols. 2006. (Illus.). 32p. (J). *(978-0-9774409-1-7(5)*, TL002) ILT Publishing.

Payne, Liane. The Snowy Day. 2007. (ENG., Illus.). 32p. (J). *(978-1-55168-317-1(2))* Fenn, H. B. & Co., Ltd.

Pendziwol, Jean E. Once upon a Northern Night, 1 vol. Arsenault, Isabelle, illus. 2013. (ENG.). 36p. (J). (gr. k-2). 17.95 *(978-1-55498-138-0(7))* Groundwood Bks. CAN. Dist: Publishers Group West (PGW).

Perkins, Lynne Rae. Snow Music. Perkins, Lynne Rae, illus. 2003. (Illus.). 40p. (J). lib. bdg. 16.89 *(978-0-06-623958-3(3))* HarperCollins Pubs.

—Snow Music. 2003. (ENG., Illus.). 40p. (J). (gr. -1-3). 17.99 *(978-0-06-623956-9(7)*, Greenwillow Bks.) HarperCollins Pubs.

Perkins, Nicole D. I Wish for Snow. Ogene, Chuma C., illus. 2005. (J). per. 19.95 *(978-0-9755566-0-3(6))* Azreal Publishing Co.

PI Kids. Disney Frozen: Sing-Along Songs! Piano Book. 2015. (ENG.). 12p. (J). bds. 21.99 *(978-1-4508-9139-4(X)*, 1688, PI Kids) Phoenix International Publications, Inc.

Pil, et al. Frosty the Snowman. McGee, Warner, illus. 2011. (J). *(978-1-4508-2604-4(0))* Publications International, Ltd.

Pingk, Rubin. Samurai Santa: A Very Ninja Christmas. Pingk, Rubin, illus. 2015. (Samurai Holiday Ser.). (ENG., Illus.). 40p. (J). (gr. -1-3). 17.99 *(978-1-4814-3057-9(2)*, Simon & Schuster Bks. For Young Readers) Simon & Schuster Bks. For Young Readers.

Pitt, Marilyn & Sanchez, Lucia M. La Nevada: Snow Dog. Bianchi, John, illus. 2011. (poder de 50 - Libros papas fritas Ser.). (SPA.). 12p. pap. 33.92 *(978-1-61541-439-0(8))* American Reading Co.

Plourde, Lynn. The Blizzard Wizard. Aardema, John, illus. 2010. (ENG.). 32p. (J). (gr. -1-3). 16.95 *(978-0-89272-789-6(6))* Down East Bks.

Potvin, James E. The Adventures of Forest the Ferret: Forest's First Snowfall & Forest's Cottage. 2007. 32p. per. 13.95 *(978-1-4327-0556-5(3))* Outskirts Pr., Inc.

Prince, April Jones. Snowy Race. Davenier, Christine, illus. 2019. 40p. (J). (gr. -1-2). 18.99 *(978-0-8234-4141-9(5)*, Margaret Ferguson Books) Holiday Hse., Inc.

Pugiano-Martin, Carol & Bridwell, Norman. The Snow Champion. Haefele, Steve, illus. 2006. (Big Red Reader Ser.). (J). *(978-0-439-80845-3(6))* Scholastic, Inc.

Ragland, Jean. I Want to Be A Snowman. 2011. 24p. (gr. 1-2). 11.95 *(978-1-4567-1140-5(7))* AuthorHouse.

Random House. Thomas & the Snowy Tracks (Thomas & Friends) 2017. (Pictureback(R) Ser.). (ENG., Illus.). 16p. (J). (gr. -1-2). pap. 5.99 *(978-1-5247-1958-6(7)*, Random Hse. Bks. for Young Readers) Random Hse. Children's Bks.

Ransom, Candice. Snow Day! 2019. (Step into Reading Ser.). (ENG.). 32p. (J). (gr. k-1). 14.96 *(978-0-87617-970-3(7))* Penworthy Co., LLC, The.

—Snow Day! Meza, Erika, illus. 2018. (Step into Reading Ser.). 32p. (J). (gr. -1-1). pap. 5.99 *(978-1-5247-2037-7(2)*, Random Hse. Bks. for Young Readers) Random Hse. Children's Bks.

Regan, Dian Curtis. Space Boy & the Snow Monster. Neubecker, Robert, illus. 2017. (Space Boy Ser.). (ENG.). 32p. (J). (gr. -1-2). 17.95 *(978-1-59078-957-5(1)*, Astra Young Readers) Astra Publishing Hse.

Rey and others, Rey and. Start Your Engines 5-Minute Stories. 2014. (5-Minute Stories Ser.). (ENG., Illus.). 224p. (J). (gr. -1-3). 12.99 *(978-0-544-15881-8(4)*, 1550258, Clarion Bks.) HarperCollins Pubs.

RH Disney. Frozen Story Collection (Disney Frozen) RH Disney, illus. 2015. (Step into Reading Ser.). (ENG., Illus.). 160p. (J). (gr. -1-2). pap. 8.99 *(978-0-7364-3435-5(6)*, RH/Disney) Random Hse. Children's Bks.

—Sparkle Magic! (Disney Frozen) RH Disney, illus. 2015. (Pictureback(R) Ser.). (ENG., Illus.). 16p. (J). (gr. -1-2). 5.99 *(978-0-7364-3366-2(X)*, RH/Disney) Random Hse. Children's Bks.

Richards, Stephen J. The Twins First Snow. 2010. 28p. pap. 13.99 *(978-1-4490-8853-8(8))* AuthorHouse.

Robbins, James L. Aristotle & Burgoo & the Ditto-Flake-Flu. 2012. 44p. pap. 21.99 *(978-1-4771-3551-8(0))* Xlibris Corp.

Robinson, Kathleen Marie. Snowflake Sandwiches. 2007. 15p. pap. 24.95 *(978-1-4241-8620-4(X))* America Star Bks.

Rocco, John. Blizzard. Rocco, John, illus. 2014. (ENG., Illus.). 40p. (J). (gr. -1-k). 18.99 *(978-1-4231-7865-1(3))* Little, Brown Bks. for Young Readers.

Rockwell, Anne. The First Snowfall. Rockwell, Harlow, illus. 2016. (ENG.). 24p. (J). (gr. -1-3). 7.99 *(978-1-4814-1136-3(5)*, Aladdin) Simon & Schuster Children's Publishing.

Rohmann, Eric. A Kitten Tale. 2012. 32p. (J). (gr. -1-2). pap. 8.99 *(978-0-307-97774-8(9)*, Dragonfly Bks.) Random Hse. Children's Bks.

Roode, Daniel. Little Bea & the Snowy Day. Roode, Daniel, illus. 2011. (ENG., Illus.). 32p. (J). (gr. -1-k). 12.99 *(978-0-06-199395-4(6)*, Greenwillow Bks.) HarperCollins Pubs.

Root, Phyllis. Snowy Sunday. Craig, Helen, illus. 2015. (ENG.). 24p. (J). (-k). 14.99 *(978-0-7636-3627-2(4))* Candlewick Pr.

Rosen, Robert. Our Snowy Day. Curzon, Brett, illus. 2017. (Seasons Around Me Ser.). (ENG.). 24p. (gr. -1-2). pap. 9.95 *(978-1-68342-797-1(1)*, 9781683427971) Rourke Educational Media.

Ross, Tony. I Want Snow! Ross, Tony, illus. 2017. (Little Princess Ser.). (ENG., Illus.). 32p. (J). (gr. -1-3). 17.99 *(978-1-5124-8125-9(4)*, e250c5be-8fca-4986-a652-4f29ea729961) Lerner Publishing Group.

Rylant, Cynthia. Annie & Snowball & the Wedding Day. 2015. (Annie & Snowball Ready-To-Read Ser.). lib. bdg. 13.55 *(978-0-606-36310-5(5))* Turtleback.

—Snow: A Winter & Holiday Book for Kids. Stringer, Lauren, illus. (ENG.). 40p. (J). (gr. -1-3). 2017. pap. 8.99 *(978-1-328-74055-7(2)*, 1677027) 2008. 17.99 *(978-0-15-205303-1(4)*, 1195978) HarperCollins Pubs. (Clarion Bks.).

Sabuda, Robert, illus. Winter in White: Winter in White. 2007. (ENG.). 18p. (J). (gr. -1-3). 17.99 *(978-0-689-85365-4(3)*, Little Simon) Little Simon.

Saddleback Educational Publishing Staff, ed. Blizzard, 1 vol. unabr. ed. 2011. (Heights Ser.). (ENG.). 50p. (gr. 4-8). 9.75 *(978-1-61651-623-9(2))* Saddleback Educational Publishing, Inc.

Sakai, Komako. The Snow Day. 2009. (J). pap. *(978-0-545-01322-2(4)*, Levine, Arthur A. Bks.) Scholastic, Inc.

Salmieri, Daniel. Bear & Wolf. 2018. (Illus.). 48p. (J). (gr. -1-3). 17.95 *(978-1-59270-238-1(4))* Enchanted Lion Bks., LLC.

Sams, Carl R. First Snow in the Woods. Stoick, Jean, photos by. 2007. (ENG., Illus.). 49p. (J). (gr. -1-3). 19.95 *(978-0-9770108-6-8(4))* Sams, II, Carl R. Photography, Inc.

Sander, Sonia, adapted by. Dragon's Snowy Day. 2005. (Scholastic Reader Ser.). (Illus.). 32p. (J). pap. *(978-0-439-80163-8(X))* Scholastic, Inc.

Sattler, Jennifer. Bundle Up. Sattler, Jennifer, illus. 2018. (ENG., Illus.). 22p. (J). (gr. -1-k). bds. 7.99 *(978-1-5341-1002-1(X)*, 204582) Sleeping Bear Pr.

Sauers, Joey. How to Make a Snowman. 2012. 24p. pap. 15.99 *(978-1-4691-7780-9(3))* Xlibris Corp.

Schaffer, Jacqueline. Porsha & the Great Snowmen Adventure. 2009. 36p. pap. 15.99 *(978-1-4490-5421-2(8))* AuthorHouse.

Schertle, Alice. All You Need for a Snowman: A Winter & Holiday Book for Kids. Lavallee, Barbara, illus. 2007. (ENG.). 32p. (J). (gr. -1-3). pap. 7.99 *(978-0-15-206115-9(0)*, 1198369, Clarion Bks.) HarperCollins Pubs.

Schneider, Antonie. Snow for Everyone! Chang, Pei-Yu, illus. 2019. (ENG.). 32p. (J). (gr. -1-2). 17.95 *(978-0-7358-4320-2(1))* North-South Bks., Inc.

Scieszka, Jon. Snow Trucking! Ready-To-Read Level 1. Gordon, David et al, illus. 2008. (Jon Scieszka's Trucktown Ser.). (ENG.). 24p. (J). (gr. -1-1). pap. 4.99 *(978-1-4169-4140-8(1)*, Simon Spotlight) Simon Spotlight.

Scotton, Rob. Blow, Snow, Blow. 2013. (Splat the Cat: I Can Read Ser.). (J). lib. bdg. 13.55 *(978-0-606-32160-0(8))* Turtleback.

Scraper, Katherine. Max's Job. 2006. (Early Explorers Ser.). (J). pap. *(978-1-4108-6035-4(3))* Benchmark Education Co.

Shaw, Gina. Waiting for Snow. Barton, Patrice, illus. 2010. 48p. (J). pap. *(978-0-545-24385-8(8))* Scholastic, Inc.

Shea, Christine. Las Aventuras de Max, el Camión Volteador: El Mejor Día de Nieve! = the Adventures of Max the Dump Truck: The Greatest Snow Day Ever! Chase, Michelle B. & Chase, Tanor R., illus. 2007. (ENG & SPA.). (J). *(978-1-933002-01-9(8))* PublishingWorks.

Shopping for Snowflakes. (J). pap. 13.75 *(978-0-8136-3403-6(2))* Modern Curriculum Pr.

Shulevitz, Uri. Snow. 2004. (J). (gr. k-3). spiral bd. *(978-0-616-01781-4(2))* Canadian National Institute for the Blind/Institut National Canadien pour les Aveugles.

—Snow, 1 vol. Shulevitz, Uri, illus. 2012. (ENG., Illus.). 34p. (J). (gr. -1-2). bds. 7.99 *(978-0-374-37093-0(1)*, 900078982, Farrar, Straus & Giroux (BYR)) Farrar, Straus & Giroux.

—Snow. Shulevitz, Uri, illus. 2004. (ENG., Illus.). 32p. (J). (gr. -1-2). reprint ed. pap. 8.99 *(978-0-374-46862-0(1)*, 900024515) Square Fish.

—Snow Storytime Set. Shulevitz, Uri, illus. unabr. ed. 2013. (Macmillan Young Listeners Story Time Sets Ser.). (ENG., Illus.). (J). 12.99 *(978-1-4272-4370-6(0)*, 900135924) Macmillan Audio.

Sidman, Joyce. Before Morning. Krommes, Beth, illus. 2016. (ENG.). 48p. (J). (gr. -1-3). 17.99 *(978-0-547-97917-5(7)*, 1523509, Clarion Bks.) HarperCollins Pubs.

Simon, Francesca. Horrid Henry & the Abominable Snowman. Ross, Tony, illus. 2010. (Horrid Henry Ser.: 0). (ENG.). 112p. (J). (gr. 2-5). pap. 7.99 *(978-1-4022-4256-4(5)*, 9781402242564, Sourcebooks Jabberwocky) Sourcebooks, Inc.

Slater, Jean M. Wonderful Snow! Slater, Jean M., illus. 2003. (Illus.). 9p. (J). bds. 16.00 *(978-0-9743149-1-4(9))* Slater Software, Inc.

Slayton, Fran Cannon. Snowball Moon. Bishop, Tracy, illus. (ENG.). (J). (gr. -1-k). 2019. 26p. bds. 7.99 *(978-1-4998-0991-6(3))* 2017. 32p. 16.99 *(978-1-4998-0495-9(4))* Little Bee Books Inc.

Slusser, Janet S. Smokey & the Big Snow. 2003. (Illus.). 32p. (J). per. 15.95 *(978-0-9745171-0-0(0))* RiverCreek Bks., Inc.

Snow X-mas. 2004. (J). per. *(978-1-57657-384-6(2))* Paradise Pr., Inc.

Snyder, Donna. Rose & Rosey. 2008. 16p. pap. 24.95 *(978-1-60441-618-3(1))* America Star Bks.

Solomon, Harry. The Day Silver Snowed. Solomon, Harry, illus. 2009. (Illus.). 112p. 80.00 *(978-0-9630376-1-9(7))* Figure 8 Pr.

Spurr, Elizabeth. In the Snow, 1 vol. Oliphant, Manelle, illus. 2017. (In the Weather Ser.). 22p. (J). (gr. -1 — 1). bds. 6.99 *(978-1-56145-855-4(4))* Peachtree Publishing Co. Inc.

Stead, Philip C. Samson in the Snow. 2016. (ENG., Illus.). 40p. (J). 17.99 *(978-1-62672-182-1(3)*, 900143664) Roaring Brook Pr.

Steers, Billy. Tractor Mac Saves Christmas. 24p. (J). 9.95 *(978-1-59445-461-5(2))* Dogs in Hats Children's Publishing Co.

—Tractor Mac Saves Christmas. 2015. (Tractor Mac Ser.). (ENG., Illus.). 32p. (J). (gr. -1-2). 9.99 *(978-0-374-30112-5(3)*, 900138390, Farrar, Straus & Giroux (BYR)) Farrar, Straus & Giroux.

Steig, William. Brave Irene: A Picture Book. Steig, William, illus. 2011. (ENG., Illus.). 32p. (J). (gr. -1-3). pap. 8.99 *(978-0-312-56422-3(8)*, 900074775) Square Fish.

Stoick, Jean & Sams, Carl R., photos by. Stranger in the Woods. 2010. (ENG., Illus.). 48p. 21.95 *(978-0-9827625-0-9(X))* Sams, II, Carl R. Photography, Inc.

Stones, Yvonne. Olivia's Magical Moment. 2010. 36p. pap. 16.99 *(978-1-4490-8045-7(6))* AuthorHouse.

Suen, Anastasia. Snow Games: A Robot & Rico Story. Laughead, Michael, illus. 2010. (Robot & Rico Ser.). (ENG.). 32p. (J). (gr. 1-2). pap. 6.25 *(978-1-4342-2302-9(7)*, 103171); lib. bdg. 22.65 *(978-1-4342-1869-8(4)*, 102326) Capstone. (Stone Arch Bks.).

Sullivan, Kate. On Linden Square. Sullivan, Kate, illus. 2013. (ENG., Illus.). 40p. (J). (gr. 1-3). 15.99 *(978-1-58536-832-7(6)*, 202894) Sleeping Bear Pr.

Swanson Sateren, Shelley. Max & Zoe at School, 1 vol. Sullivan, Mary, illus. 2013. (Max & Zoe Ser.). (ENG.). 32p. (J). (gr. k-2). pap. 5.19 *(978-1-4048-8059-7(3)*, 121735, Picture Window Bks.) Capstone.

Taylor, Mark. Henry the Explorer. Booth, Graham, illus. 2011. (J). 18.95 *(978-1-930900-48-6(1))* Purple Hse. Pr.

Thaler, Mike. The Snow Day from the Black Lagoon. Lee, Jared, illus. 2008. 63p. (J). pap. *(978-0-545-01766-4(1))* Scholastic, Inc.

The Series, Superdaddies. Superdaddies; the Series, Presents: Daddy, I Broke My Snowball! 2009. 32p. pap. 14.49 *(978-1-4490-2632-5(X))* AuthorHouse.

Thomas, Peggy. Snow Dance. 1 vol. Fackiam, Paul, illus. 2008. (ENG.). 32p. (J). (gr. 1-3). 16.99 *(978-1-58980-478-4(3)*, Pelican Publishing) Arcadia Publishing.

Thompson, Carol. Snow. Thompson, Carol, illus. 2014. (Whatever the Weather Ser.). (Illus.). 12p. (J). (gr. k-k). spiral bd. *(978-1-84643-681-9(8))* Child's Play International Ltd.

Thompson, Lauren. Mouse Loves Snow. 2018. (Ready-To-Read Ser.). (ENG.). 32p. (J). (gr. -1-1). 13.89 *(978-1-64310-618-2(X))* Penworthy Co., LLC, The.

—Mouse Loves Snow: Ready-To-Read Pre-Level 1. Erdogan, Buket, illus. 2017. (Mouse Ser.). (ENG.). 32p. (J). (gr. -1-k). 17.99 *(978-1-5344-0182-2(2))*; pap. 4.99 *(978-1-5344-0181-5(4))* Simon Spotlight. (Simon Spotlight).

—Mouse's First Snow. Erdogan, Buket, illus. 2011. (Classic Board Bks.). (ENG.). 34p. (J). (gr. -1 — 1). bds. 7.99 *(978-1-4424-2651-1(9)*, Little Simon) Little Simon.

—Mouse's First Snow. Erdogan, Buket, illus. 2005. (ENG.). 32p. (J). (gr. -1-3). 19.99 *(978-0-689-85836-9(1)*, Simon & Schuster Bks. For Young Readers) Simon & Schuster Bks. For Young Readers.

Thomson, Sarah L. Imagine a Night. Gonsalves, Rob, illus. 2003. (Imagine A... Ser.). (ENG.). 40p. (J). (gr. -1-3). 19.99 *(978-0-689-85218-3(5)*, Atheneum Bks. for Young Readers) Simon & Schuster Children's Publishing.

Tiger Tales. Ten Sparkly Snowflakes: Twinkly Countdown Fun! Julian, Russell, illus. 2017. (ENG.). 26p. (J). (gr. -1-k). mass mkt. 4.99 *(978-1-68010-413-4(6))* Tiger Tales.

Tyrell, Melissa. Hurray for Snow! Patrick, Tom, illus. enl. ed. 2005. (ENG.). 10p. (J). (gr. -1-3). 4.95 *(978-1-58117-118-1(8)*, Intervisual/Piggy Toes) Bendon, Inc.

Tyrrell, Colm. Snow Day. 2015. (Illus.). 32p. (J). *(978-1-5182-0102-8(4))* Disney Publishing Worldwide.

Uhlberg, Myron. Flying over Brooklyn, 1 vol. Fitzgerald, Gerald, illus. 2003. 32p. (J). (gr. -1-3). pap. 7.95 *(978-1-56145-294-1(7))* Peachtree Publishing Co. Inc.

Usher, Sam. Snow. Usher, Sam, illus. 2015. (Seasons Quartet Ser.). (ENG., Illus.). 40p. (J). (gr. -1-2). 16.99 *(978-0-7636-7958-3(5)*, Templar) Candlewick Pr.

Viau, Nancy. First Snow. Shipman, Talitha, illus. 2018. (ENG.). 32p. (J). (gr. -1-3). 16.99 *(978-0-8075-2440-4(9)*, 807524409) Whitman, Albert & Co.

Villanueva, Pedro. Chronicle of a New Kid. 2017. (Text Connections Guided Close Reading Ser.). (J). (gr. 1). *(978-1-4900-1825-6(5))* Benchmark Education Co.

von Olfers, Sibylle. The Story of the Snow Children, 44 vols. 2005. (Illus.). 24p. (J). 17.95 *(978-0-86315-499-7(9))* Floris Bks. GBR. Dist: Consortium Bk. Sales & Distribution.

Wallace, Sharolyn. The Adventures of Bruce, Ben & Gerry: The Surprise. 2013. 24p. pap. 17.99 *(978-1-4772-9489-5(9))* AuthorHouse.

Ward, Nick. Tinyrannosaurus & the Bigfootosaurus. 2015. (ENG., Illus.). 24p. (J). (gr. -1-3). 7.99 *(978-1-85733-734-1(4))* Lerner Publishing Group.

Wasserman, Robin. Scooby-Doo & the Snow Monster Scare, 1 vol. Sur, Duendes del, illus. 2016. (Scooby-Doo Early Reading Adventures Ser.). (ENG.). 24p. (J). (gr. -1-2). lib. bdg. 31.36 *(978-1-61479-473-8(1)*, 21386) Spotlight.

Watt, Fiona. That's Not My Snowman. Wells, Rachel, illus. 2006. (Usborne Touchy-Feely Board Bks.). 10p. (J). (gr. -1). bds. 9.99 *(978-0-7945-1414-3(6)*, Usborne) EDC Publishing.

—That's Not My Snowman. rev. ed. 2011. (Touchy-Feely Board Bks). 10p. (J). ring bd. 8.99 *(978-0-7945-3120-1(2)*, Usborne) EDC Publishing.

Weinshall Liberman, Judith. Ice Cream Snow. 2012. (Illus.). 34p. (J). 18.99 *(978-1-4575-1578-1(4))* Dog Ear Publishing, LLC.

Wells, Erica. Diamonds in the Snow: A Story about the Magic of Snow. 2010. 24p. pap. 16.99 *(978-1-4490-4969-0(9))* AuthorHouse.

Weston Woods Staff, creator. The Snowy Day. 2004. 29.95 *(978-1-55592-853-7(6))* Weston Woods Studios, Inc.

Wetterer, Margaret K. & Wetterer, Charles M. The Snow Walker. Young, Mary O'Keefe, illus. unabr. ed. (Historical Fiction Ser.). (J). (gr. 1-6). 24.95 incl. audio *(978-0-87499-394-3(6))* Live Oak Media.

White, S.D. Sing along with the Santa Claus That Never Saw a Child. 2008. 20p. pap. 12.89 *(978-1-4389-0305-7(7))* AuthorHouse.

Williams, Rozanne Lanczak. Tess Builds a Snowman. Maio, Barbara & Faulkner, Stacey, eds. Harris, Jenny B., illus. 2006. (J). per. 6.99 *(978-1-59198-337-8(1))* Creative Teaching Pr., Inc.

Williams, Teresa Ann. Friends of Wildwood, 1 vol. 2009. 48p. pap. 16.95 *(978-1-4489-9419-9(5))* America Star Bks.

Wilson, CeCe. Snow: Snow Much Fun!, 1 vol. 2015. (Rosen REAL Readers: STEM & STEAM Collection). (ENG.). 8p. (gr. k-1). pap. 5.46 *(978-1-4994-9551-5(X)*, bad94dab-5784-49d5-9552-b7bd9f1609dc, Rosen Classroom) Rosen Publishing Group, Inc., The.

Wing, Natasha. The Night Before the Snow Day. Wummer, Amy, illus. 2016. (Night Before Ser.). 32p. (J). (-k). pap. 4.99 *(978-0-399-53942-8(5)*, Grosset & Dunlap) Penguin Young Readers Group.

—The Night Before the Snow Day. Wummer, Amy, illus. 2016. (Night Before Ser.). (ENG.). 32p. (J). (gr. -1-1). 14.75 *(978-0-606-39315-7(3))* Turtleback.

Wood, David. The Toy Cupboard. Fowler, Richard, illus. 2005. 14p. (J). (gr. -1-3). 14.95 *(978-1-58117-103-7(X)*, Intervisual/Piggy Toes) Bendon, Inc.

Wood, Francis. The SnowPeople. Larsen, Dan, illus. 2003. 96p. (YA). per. 14.95 *(978-0-9746372-0-4(3))* Tip-Of-The-Moon Publishing Co.

Wozniak, Paul. Stranded in a Snowstorm! Webber, Mike, illus. 2014. 82p. pap. 11.95 *(978-1-63047-173-6(9))* Morgan James Publishing.

Xiong, Kim, illus. Paper Horse. 2008. (ENG & CHI.). 37p. (J). 18.95 *(978-1-60603-003-5(5))* Better Chinese LLC.

Yee, Wong Herbert. Mouse & Mole, a Winter Wonderland: A Winter & Holiday Book for Kids. Yee, Wong Herbert, illus. 2011. (Mouse & Mole Story Ser.). (ENG., Illus.). 48p. (J). (gr. 1-4). pap. 4.99 *(978-0-547-57697-8(8)*, 1458451, Clarion Bks.) HarperCollins Pubs.

—Tracks in the Snow. Yee, Wong Herbert, illus. 2007. (ENG., Illus.). 32p. (J). (gr. -1-1). per. 8.99 *(978-0-312-37134-0(9)*, 900044562) Square Fish.

Yeomans, Ellen. Some Snow Is... Offermann, Andrea, illus. 2019. 32p. (J). (gr. -1-3). 17.99 *(978-0-399-54754-6(1)*, G.P. Putnam's Sons Books for Young Readers) Penguin Young Readers Group.

Yerxa, Leo. Last Leaf First Snowflake to Fall. Yerxa, Leo, illus. (Illus.). (J). 16.95 *(978-0-88899-183-6(5))* Groundwood Bks. CAN. Dist: Publishers Group West (PGW).

Yildirim, Rabia. Wind, Rain & Snow. 2013. (ENG., Illus.). 53p. (J). (gr. k-1). pap. 9.95 *(978-1-59784-284-6(2)*, Tughra Bks.) Blue Dome, Inc.

Young, Francis Kerr. The Paperweight. Steele, Andrew & Clement, Devyn, illus. 2008. 39p. pap. 24.95 *(978-1-60610-034-9(3))* America Star Bks.

Ziegler, Argentina Palacios, tr. Dora y la Princesa de la Nieve (Dora Saves the Snow Princess) Aikins, Dave, illus. 2008. (Dora la Exploradora Ser.). (SPA.). 24p. (J). (gr. -1-2). pap. 3.99 *(978-1-4169-5870-3(3)*, Libros Para Ninos) Libros Para Ninos.

SNOWBOARDING

Abdo, Kenny. Snowboarding. 2017. (Action Sports (Fly!) Ser.). (ENG., Illus.). 24p. (J). (gr. 2-8). lib. bdg. 31.36 *(978-1-5321-2096-1(6)*, 26779, Abdo Zoom-Fly) ABDO Publishing Co.

Adamson, Thomas K. Big Air Snowboarding. 2016. (Extreme Sports Ser.). (ENG., Illus.). 24p. (J). (gr. 3-7). lib. bdg. 26.95 *(978-1-62617-351-4(6)*, Epic Bks.) Bellwether Media.

—Snowboarding Slopestyle. 2016. (Extreme Sports Ser.). (ENG., Illus.). 24p. (J). (gr. 3-7). lib. bdg. 26.95 *(978-1-62617-353-8(2)*, Epic Bks.) Bellwether Media.

S

Barr, Matt & Moran, Chris. Snowboarding. 2003. (Extreme Sports Ser.). (ENG., Illus.). 32p. (gr. 3-6). lib. bdg. 22.60 *(978-0-8225-1242-4(4))* Lerner Publishing Group.

Benjamin, Daniel. Extreme Snowboarding, 1 vol. 2012. (Sports on the Edge Ser.). (ENG.). 48p. (gr. 4-4). 32.64 *(978-1-60870-229-9(4),* 8b989832-3665-42e9-b5c3-927bd6864052) Cavendish Square Publishing LLC.

Brouwer, Sigmund. Snowboarding . . . to the Extreme: Rippin' 2004. (Illus.). 60p. (YA). pap. 3.99 *(978-1-55305-011-7(8))* Cygnet Publishing Group, Inc./Coolreading.com CAN. Dist: Orca Bk. Pubs. USA.

Carr, Aaron. Snowboard. 2013. (ENG & SPA.). (J). *(978-1-62127-635-7(X))* Weigl Pubs., Inc.

—Snowboarding. (Illus.). (J). 2013. 32p. *(978-1-61913-513-0(2))* 2012. (ENG., 24p. pap. 12.95 *(978-1-61913-519-2(1),* AV2 by Weigl) Weigl Pubs., Inc.

Champion, Neil. Wild Snow: Skiing & Snowboarding. 2013. (Illus.). 32p. (J). lib. bdg. *(978-1-59920-808-4(3))* Black Rabbit Bks.

Craats, Rennay. Snowboarding. 2007. (Outdoor Adventures (Weigl Hardcover) Ser.). (Illus.). 24p. (J) (gr. 4-7). lib. bdg. 24.45 *(978-1-59036-687-5(5))*; per. 8.95 *(978-1-59036-688-2(3))* Weigl Pubs., Inc.

Crabtree Editors & Winters, Jaime. Carve It Snowboarding. 2012. (Sports Starters Ser.). (ENG., Illus.). 32p. (J). (gr. 1-4). lib. bdg. *(978-0-7787-3148-1(0))* Crabtree Publishing Co.

Doeden, Matt. Shaun White. 2006. (Amazing Athletes Ser.). (Illus.). 32p. (J). (gr. 2-5). lib. bdg. 23.93 *(978-0-8225-6840-7(3),* Lerner Pubns.) Lerner Publishing Group.

—Shaun White, 2nd Edition. 2nd rev. ed. 2012. (Amazing Athletes Ser.). (ENG., Illus.). 32p. (J). (gr. 2-5). pap. 7.95 *(978-0-7613-9067-1(7),* 7d1285d1-659d-4f04-8025-b2ba4549ca7e) Lerner Publishing Group.

—Shaun White (Revised Edition) 2012. (Amazing Athletes Ser.). 32p. (J). (gr. 2-5). pap. 45.32 *(978-0-7613-9139-5(8))* Lerner Publishing Group.

Dufresne, Michèle. Snowboarding: Nonfiction Orange Set. 2007. (Nonfiction Collection). (J). pap. 8.00 *(978-1-932570-99-1(3))* Pioneer Valley Bks.

Endres, Hollie. Snowboarding. 2007. (Action Sports Ser.). (ENG., Illus.). 24p. (J). (gr. 3-7). lib. bdg. 26.95 *(978-1-60014-128-7(5))* Bellwether Media.

Fandel, Jennifer. Snowboarding. 2007. (Active Sports Ser.). (Illus.). 24p. (J). (gr. -1-3). lib. bdg. 24.25 *(978-1-58341-470-5(3),* Creative Education) Creative Co., The.

Figorito, Marcus. Friction & Gravity: Snowboarding Science. (Science Scope Ser.). 32p. (gr. 5-5). 2009. 47.90 *(978-1-60853-053-3(1))* 2009. (ENG.). (J). lib. bdg. 28.93 *(978-1-4358-2995-4(6),* f370f919-cc72-48d7-b754-cc1652c020b6) 2008. (ENG., Illus.). (J). pap. 10.00 *(978-1-4358-0185-1(7),* 1ebbccf1-c38d-4e02-bcf4-fa7b73e94767) Rosen Publishing Group, Inc., The. (PowerKids Pr.).

Fitzpatrick, Jim. Snowboarding. 2008. (21st Century Skills Innovation Library: Innovation in Sports Ser.). (ENG., Illus.). 32p. (gr. 4-8). lib. bdg. 32.07 *(978-1-60279-260-9(7),* 200035); lib. bdg. 32.07 *(978-1-60279-018-6(3),* 200202) Cherry Lake Publishing.

Gustaitis, Joseph. Snowboard. 2009. (Winter Olympic Sports Ser.). (ENG., Illus.). 32p. (J). (gr. 3-6). lib. bdg. *(978-0-7787-4026-1(9))* Crabtree Publishing Co.

Hamilton, John. Snowboarding. 2014. (Action Sports Ser.). (ENG.). 32p. (J). (gr. 3-9). lib. bdg. 32.79 *(978-1-62403-444-2(6),* 1163, Abdo & Daughters) ABDO Publishing Co.

Hansen, Grace. Mikaela Shiffrin. 2018. (Olympic Biographies Ser.). (ENG., Illus.). 24p. (J). (gr. -1-2). lib. bdg. 32.79 *(978-1-5321-8144-3(2),* 29774, Abdo Kids) ABDO Publishing Co.

—Red Gerard. 2018. (Olympic Biographies Ser.). (ENG., Illus.). 24p. (J). (gr. -1-2). lib. bdg. 32.79 *(978-1-5321-8145-0(0),* 29776, Abdo Kids) ABDO Publishing Co.

—Shaun White. 2018. (Olympic Biographies Ser.). (ENG., Illus.). 24p. (J). (gr. -1-2). lib. bdg. 32.79 *(978-1-5321-8146-7(9),* 29778, Abdo Kids) ABDO Publishing Co.

Hantula, Richard. Science at Work in Snowboarding, 1 vol. 2012. (Sports Science Ser.). (ENG., Illus.). 32p. (gr. 5-5). 31.21 *(978-1-60870-590-0(0),* b05c251f-239a-4c4e-8fca-343df2eff231) Cavendish Square Publishing LLC.

Hedlund, Stephanie F. Snowboarding. 2003. (X-Treme Sports Ser.). 32p. (J). (gr. k-6). 27.07 *(978-1-57765-929-7(5),* Checkerboard Library) ABDO Publishing Co.

Herman, Gail. Snowboarding Similes & Metaphors, 1 vol. 2009. (Grammar All-Stars: Writing Tools Ser.). (ENG.). 32p. (J). (gr. 2-4). pap. 11.50 *(978-1-4339-2138-4(3),* cafad19b-84fc-4d83-9bb7-3fa19be5c95a); lib. bdg. 28.67 *(978-1-4339-1945-9(1),* 6dbbf281-05d0-45b5-8d61-7d64374b86da) Stevens, Gareth Publishing LLLP. (Gareth Stevens Learning Library).

Hewson, Anthony K. Shaun White. 2018. (Olympic Stars Ser.). (ENG., Illus.). 32p. (J). (gr. 3-9). lib. bdg. 32.79 *(978-1-5321-1609-4(8),* 29802, SportsZone) ABDO Publishing Co.

Iguchi, Bryan. Jovenes Aficionados al Snowboard (The Young Snowboarder) (SPA.). 38p. (YA). (gr. 2-18). 18.36 *(978-84-272-4970-7(5))* Molino, Editorial ESP. Dist: Lectorum Pubns., Inc.

Kalman, Bobbie & MacAulay, Kelley. Extreme Snowboarding. 2003. (Extreme Sports - No Limits Ser.). (ENG., Illus.). 32p. (J). pap. *(978-0-7787-1718-8(6))*; lib. bdg. *(978-0-7787-1672-3(4))* Crabtree Publishing Co.

Kennedy, Mike. Shaun White, 1 vol. 2009. (Today's Superstars Ser.). (ENG.). 48p. (J). (gr. 3-3). pap. 15.05 *(978-1-4339-2161-2(8),* 01a42eed-0da3-4739-97d5-a574479f2d90); lib. bdg. 34.60 *(978-1-4339-1968-8(0),* dcff15b6-57d1-4950-ab8d-614c1b378bfe) Stevens, Gareth Publishing LLLP.

Labrecque, Ellen. Snowboarding. 2018. (21st Century Skills Library: Global Citizens: Olympic Sports Ser.). (ENG.). 32p. (J). (gr. 4-7). pap. 14.21 *(978-1-5341-0848-6(3),* 210756); (Illus.). lib. bdg. 32.07 *(978-1-5341-0749-6(5),* 210755) Cherry Lake Publishing.

Loh-Hagan, Virginia. Extreme Snowboarding. 2015. (Nailed It! Ser.). (ENG., Illus.). 32p. (J). (gr. 4-8). 32.07 *(978-1-63470-018-4(X),* 206744) Cherry Lake Publishing.

Lurie, Jon. Play-by-Play Snowboarding. 2004. (Play-by-Play Ser.). (Illus.). 80p. (J). (gr. 4-8). lib. bdg. 23.93 *(978-0-8225-3937-7(3))* Lerner Publishing Group.

—Play-by-Play Snowboarding. Clarke, Jimmy, photos by. 2003. (Play-by-Play Ser.). (Illus.). 80p. (J). (gr. 5-18). pap. 7.95 *(978-0-8225-9881-7(7))* Lerner Publishing Group.

Mahaney, Ian F. Kevin Jones: Snowboarding Champion, 1 vol. 2004. (Extreme Sports Biographies Ser.). (ENG., Illus.). 24p. (J). (gr. 3-4). 26.27 *(978-1-4042-2745-3(8),* c839ecb5-b812-4541-b24f-83b1287cfb95, PowerKids Pr.) Rosen Publishing Group, Inc., The.

Mason, Paul. Snowboarding, 1 vol. 2012. (To the Limit Ser.). (ENG., Illus.). 32p. (J). (gr. 3-6). pap. 11.00 *(978-1-4488-7131-5(X),* 0af9c059-1e64-40d2-bf35-87eb57897daa); lib. bdg. 28.93 *(978-1-4488-7130-8(1),* 40297831-7325-4cfe-b5cb-5b1f2712c37e) Rosen Publishing Group, Inc., The. (PowerKids Pr.).

McClellan, Ray. Snowboarding. 2010. (My First Sports Ser.). (ENG., Illus.). 24p. (J). (gr. 2-5). lib. bdg. 26.95 *(978-1-60014-463-9(2),* Blastoff! Readers) Bellwether Media.

McKinney, Donna B. Stem in Snowboarding. 2017. (STEM in Sports Ser.). (ENG., Illus.). 48p. (J). (gr. 3-6). lib. bdg. 34.21 *(978-1-5321-1352-9(8),* 27650, SportsZone) ABDO Publishing Co.

Murdico, Suzanne J. Snowboarding: Techniques & Tricks. 2009. (Rad Sports: Techniques & Tricks Ser.). 48p. (gr. 5-8). 53.00 *(978-1-60851-938-5(4),* Rosen Reference) Rosen Publishing Group, Inc., The.

O'Neal, Claire. Extreme Snowboarding with Lindsey Jacobelis. 2007. (Extreme Sports Ser.). (Illus.). 32p. (J). (gr. 1-4). lib. bdg. 25.70 *(978-1-58415-598-0(1))* Mitchell Lane Pubs.

Price, Karen. Red Gerard. 2018. (Olympic Stars Ser.). (ENG., Illus.). 32p. (J). (gr. 3-9). lib. bdg. 32.79 *(978-1-5321-1606-3(3),* 29796, SportsZone) ABDO Publishing Co.

Raum, Elizabeth. Chloe Kim. 2017. (Pro Sports Biographies Ser.). (ENG., Illus.). 24p. (J). (gr. 1-4). lib. bdg. 20.95 *(978-1-68151-134-4(7),* 14678) Amicus.

—Pro Sports Biographies: Chloe Kim. 2017. (Pro Sports Biographies Ser.). (ENG., Illus.). 24p. (J). (gr. 1-3). pap. 9.99 *(978-1-68152-165-7(2),* 14797) Amicus.

Sandler, Michael. Cool Snowboarders. 2009. (X-Moves Ser.). (Illus.). 24p. (YA). (gr. 2-5). lib. bdg. 26.99 *(978-1-59716-949-3(8))* Bearport Publishing Co., Inc.

Schuh, Mari. Snowboarding. 2019. (Spot Sports Ser.). (ENG.). 16p. (J). (gr. -1-1). pap. 7.99 *(978-1-68152-438-2(4),* 11024); lib. bdg. *(978-1-68151-652-3(7),* 10784) Amicus.

Schweitzer, Karen. Shaun White. 2010. (Modern Role Models Ser.). (Illus.). 64p. (YA). (gr. 7-12). lib. bdg. 22.95 *(978-1-4222-0493-1(6))* Mason Crest.

Segovia, Patty & Meredith Books Staff. On the Edge Skateboarding/on the Edge Snowboarding: Tips & Tricks from Six of the Coolest Skateboarders/Tips & Tricks from Six of the Coolest Snowboarders. 2008. (On the Edge Ser.). (Illus.). 48p. (YA). (gr. 8-12). per. 6.99 *(978-0-696-23980-9(9))* Meredith Bks.

Slade, Suzanne. Let's Go Snowboarding. (Adventures Outdoors Ser.). 32p. (gr. 4-5). 2009. 47.90 *(978-1-61511-272-2(3))* 2006. (ENG., Illus.). (J). lib. bdg. 28.93 *(978-1-4042-3648-6(1),* c8062675-0524-4653-bf8b-76323721e916) Rosen Publishing Group, Inc., The. (PowerKids Pr.).

Thorpe, Yvonne. Snowboarding. 2012. (Adrenaline Rush Ser.). (Illus.). 32p. (gr. 4-7). lib. bdg. 31.35 *(978-1-59920-686-8(2))* Black Rabbit Bks.

Waxman, Laura Hamilton. Snowboarding. 2017. (Winter Olympic Sports Ser.). (ENG., Illus.). 32p. (J). (gr. 2-5). lib. bdg. 20.95 *(978-1-68151-152-8(5),* 14695) Amicus.

—Winter Olympic Sports: Snowboarding. 2017. (Winter Olympic Sports Ser.). (ENG., Illus.). 32p. (J). (gr. 2-5). pap. 9.99 *(978-1-68152-183-1(0),* 14814) Amicus.

Weinstein, Anna. Kevin Jones: Snowboarding Superstar. 2009. (Extreme Sports Biographies Ser.). 64p. (gr. 3-4). 58.50 *(978-1-61512-466-4(7),* Rosen Reference) Rosen Publishing Group, Inc., The.

—Kevin Jones, Snowboarding Superstar, 1 vol. 2004. (Extreme Sports Biographies Ser.). (ENG., Illus.). 64p. (J). (gr. 5-8). lib. bdg. 37.13 *(978-1-4042-0068-5(1),* b59c6b07-5c3a-4d0c-89a5-3bf81b57892e) Rosen Publishing Group, Inc., The.

Whiting, Jim. Snowboarding. 2018. (Odysseys in Extreme Sports Ser.). (ENG.). 80p. (J). (gr. 7-10). *(978-1-60818-696-9(2),* 19880, Creative Education) Creative Co., The.

Winters, Jaime. Carve It Snowboarding. 2012. (ENG., Illus.). 32p. (J). pap. *(978-0-7787-3159-7(6))* Crabtree Publishing Co.

Wiseman, Blaine. Shaun White. 2010. (Remarkable People Ser.). (Illus.). 24p. (J). (gr. 4-6). pap. 11.95 *(978-1-60596-998-5(2))*; lib. bdg. 25.70 *(978-1-60596-997-8(4))* Weigl Pubs., Inc.

—Snowboarding. 2015. (J). *(978-1-5105-0008-2(1))* SmartBook Media, Inc.

—Snowboarding: X Games. 2008. (Extreme Ser.). (Illus.). 32p. (J). (gr. 4-6). pap. 9.95 *(978-1-59036-921-0(1))*; lib. bdg. 26.00 *(978-1-59036-920-3(3))* Weigl Pubs., Inc.

Woods, Bob. Snowboarding, 1 vol. 2003. (Extreme Sports Ser.). (ENG., Illus.). 24p. (gr. 2-4). lib. bdg. 25.67 *(978-0-8368-3725-4(8),* 6bb21f20-f8ad-4c2c-b740-e4b6f75ae3fa, Gareth Stevens Learning Library) Stevens, Gareth Publishing LLLP.

Young, Jeff. Shaun White. 2008. (Xtreme Athletes Ser.). (Illus.). 112p. (YA). (gr. 7-12). lib. bdg. 27.95 *(978-1-59935-081-3(5))* Reynolds, Morgan Inc.

SNOWMOBILES

Arnold, Quinn M. Snowmobiles. 2019. (Seedlings: on the Go Ser.). (ENG.). 24p. (J). (gr. -1-1). pap. 8.99 *(978-1-62832-736-6(7),* 19136, Creative Paperbacks) Creative Co., The.

Older, Jules. Snowmobile: Bombardier's Dream Machine. Lauritano, Michael, illus. 2012. 64p. (J). (gr. 3-7). 14.95 *(978-1-58089-334-3(1))*; pap. 6.95 *(978-1-58089-335-0(X))* Charlesbridge Publishing, Inc.

Sommers, Michael A. Snowmobiling: Have Fun, Be Smart. 2009. (Explore the Outdoors Ser.). 64p. (gr. 5-5). 58.50 *(978-1-61512-344-5(X))* Rosen Publishing Group, Inc., The.

Von Finn, Denny. Snowmobiles. 2009. (Torque Ser.). (ENG.). 24p. (J). (gr. 3-7). 20.00 *(978-0-531-21739-9(6),* Children's Pr.) Scholastic Library Publishing.

Wiseman, Blaine. Snowmobiling. 2009. (Extreme Ser.). (Illus.). 32p. (J). (gr. 4-6). pap. 9.95 *(978-1-60596-135-4(3))*; lib. bdg. 26.00 *(978-1-60596-134-7(5))* Weigl Pubs., Inc.

Woods, Bob. Racing Snowmobiles, 1 vol. 2017. (Speed Racers Ser.). (ENG.). 48p. (gr. 6-6). 29.60 *(978-0-7660-9272-3(0),* 7b7f62f1-c371-4e88-85a8-05686b0eb88a) Enslow Publishing, LLC.

Zahensky, Kenneth & Sommers, Michael A. Snowmobiling, 1 vol., 1. 2015. (Outdoor Living Ser.). (ENG., Illus.). 64p. (J). (gr. 6-6). 36.13 *(978-1-4994-6229-6(8),* c9ce5223-6714-4c08-8fe5-b619adad34b8, Rosen Young Adult) Rosen Publishing Group, Inc., The.

SOAP

Best, B. J. Fat to Soap, 1 vol. 2016. (How It Is Made Ser.). (ENG., Illus.). 24p. (gr. 1-1). pap. 9.22 *(978-1-5026-2122-1(3),* 02716463-5ca2-473e-b605-7949c49f2371) Cavendish Square Publishing LLC.

Editors of Klutz. Make Your Own Soap. 2017. (ENG.). 36p. (J). (gr. k-7). 21.99 *(978-1-338-10645-9(7))* Klutz.

Shores, Erika L. How to Make Bubbles: A 4D Book. rev. ed. 2018. (Hands-On Science Fun Ser.). (ENG., Illus.). 24p. (J). (gr. -1-2). lib. bdg. 29.32 *(978-1-5435-0947-2(9),* 137654, Capstone Pr.) Capstone.

Tocci, Salvatore. Experiments with Soap. 2003. (True Bks.). (ENG.). 48p. (gr. 3-5). pap. 6.95 *(978-0-516-27466-9(X),* Children's Pr.) Scholastic Library Publishing.

Woolf, Alex. You Wouldn't Want to Live Without Soap! 2015. (You Wouldn't Want to Live Without Ser.). lib. bdg. 20.80 *(978-0-606-37473-6(6))* Turtleback.

SOAP BOX DERBIES—FICTION

Holm, Jennifer L. & Holm, Matthew. Burns Rubber. 2010. (Babymouse Ser.: 12). lib. bdg. 17.20 *(978-0-606-07025-6(7))* Turtleback.

SOAP CARVING

see Soap Sculpture

SOAP SCULPTURE

Asher, Melissa. Toys, Blocks & Cars, Oh My, 1 vol. 2009. 56p. pap. 16.95 *(978-1-4489-1959-8(2))* America Star Bks.

SOARING (AERONAUTICS)

see Gliding and Soaring

SOCCER

Abdo, Kenny. History of Soccer. 2019. (History of Sports Ser.). (ENG., Illus.). 24p. (J). (gr. 2-8). lib. bdg. 31.36 *(978-1-5321-2742-7(1),* 31691, Abdo Zoom-Fly) ABDO Publishing Co.

—Neymar. 2018. (Sports Biographies Ser.). (ENG., Illus.). 24p. (J). (gr. 2-8). lib. bdg. 31.36 *(978-1-5321-2480-8(5),* 28433, Abdo Zoom-Fly) ABDO Publishing Co.

Adamson, Thomas K. Soccer. 2019. (Let's Play Sports! Ser.). (ENG., Illus.). 24p. (J). (gr. k-3). lib. bdg. 26.95 *(978-1-64487-002-0(9),* Blastoff! Readers) Bellwether Media.

—Soccer Records. 2018. (Incredible Sports Records Ser.). (ENG., Illus.). 32p. (J). (gr. 3-8). pap. 8.99 *(978-1-61891-316-6(6),* 12111, Blastoff! Discovery) Bellwether Media.

Alaníz, Eduardo Martínez. Hugo Sanchez. 2012. (Superstars of Soccer SPANISH Ser.). (SPA.). 32p. (J). (gr. 4). 19.95 *(978-1-4222-2615-5(8))* Mason Crest.

—Hugo Sanchez. 2012. (Superstars of Soccer ENGLISH Ser.). (Illus.). 32p. (J). (gr. 4). 19.95 *(978-1-4222-2668-1(9))* Mason Crest.

Alexander, Heather. U. S. Women's Soccer: Go for Gold! 2016. (Penguin Young Readers, Level 4 Ser.). (Illus.). 32p. (J). (gr. 3-4). pap. 5.99 *(978-0-399-54223-7(X),* Penguin Young Readers) Penguin Young Readers Group.

Anness Publishing Staff. The Step-by-Step Training Manual of Soccer Skills & Techniques. 2011. (Illus.). 192p. (J). (gr. -1-12). pap. 9.99 *(978-1-84322-771-7(1))* Anness Publishing GBR. Dist: National Bk. Network.

Arnold. Fifa Latin America. 2005. (J). pap. 2.50 *(978-0-00-638306-2(8))* HarperCollins Pubs.

Arturo Miranda Bravo, Jorge. Andres Guardado. 2012. (Superstars of Soccer ENGLISH Ser.). 32p. (J). (gr. 4). 19.95 *(978-1-4222-2666-7(2))*; (SPA., Illus.). 19.95 *(978-1-4222-2613-1(1))* Mason Crest.

Avise, Jonathan. Champions League Legends. 2018. (Super Soccer Ser.). (ENG., Illus.). 32p. (J). (gr. 3-6). lib. bdg. 32.79 *(978-1-5321-1743-5(4),* 30774, SportsZone) ABDO Publishing Co.

—FC Barcelona. 2017. (Europe's Best Soccer Clubs Ser.). (ENG., Illus.). 48p. (J). (gr. 3-6). lib. bdg. 34.21 *(978-1-5321-1131-0(2),* 25838, SportsZone) ABDO Publishing Co.

—Great Soccer Debates. 2018. (Great Sports Debates Ser.). (ENG., Illus.). 48p. (J). (gr. 3-6). lib. bdg. 34.21 *(978-1-5321-1446-5(X),* 29034, SportsZone) ABDO Publishing Co.

—Lionel Messi vs. Pelé. 2017. (Versus Ser.). (ENG., Illus.). 32p. (J). (gr. 3-6). lib. bdg. 32.79 *(978-1-5321-1356-7(0),* 27654, SportsZone) ABDO Publishing Co.

Bader, Bonnie. What Is the World Cup? 2018. (What Is... . ? Ser.). lib. bdg. 16.00 *(978-0-606-40890-5(8))* Turtleback.

Bader, Bonnie & Who HQ. What Is the World Cup? Marchesi, Stephen, illus. 2018. (What Was? Ser.). 112p. (J). (gr. 3-7). 7.99 *(978-0-515-15821-2(6),* Penguin Workshop) Penguin Young Readers Group.

Bage, Grant. The Story of Football: Band 17/Diamond (Collins Big Cat) 2016. (Collins Big Cat Ser.). (ENG.). 56p. (J). (gr. 5-6). pap. 11.99 *(978-0-00-816398-3(7))* HarperCollins Pubs. Ltd. GBR. Dist: Independent Pubs. Group.

Bailey, Diane. Great Moments in World Cup History, 1 vol. 2009. (World Soccer Bks.). (ENG., Illus.). 64p. (YA). (gr. 5-5). lib. bdg. 37.13 *(978-1-4358-9139-5(2),* 8954287c-690e-490c-84c9-30a94adec6bf, Rosen Reference) Rosen Publishing Group, Inc., The.

Bankston, John. Abby Wambach. 2013. (ENG.). 32p. (gr. 4-8). lib. bdg. 25.70 *(978-1-61228-465-1(5))* Mitchell Lane Pubs.

Barker, Geoff, et al. Soccer Star: Find Out How Your Favorite Soccer Players Made It! 2012. (Celeb Ser.). (ENG., Illus.). 32p. (gr. 4-6). lib. bdg. 28.50 *(978-1-59771-334-4(1))* Sea-To-Sea Pubns.

Barth, Katrin & Zempel, Ullrich, trs. from GER. Learning Soccer. 2004. (Illus.). 136p. pap. 14.95 *(978-1-84126-130-0(0))* Meyer & Meyer Sport, Ltd. GBR. Dist: Lewis International, Inc.

—Training Soccer. 2004. (Illus.). 152p. pap. 14.95 *(978-1-84126-131-7(9))* Meyer & Meyer Sport, Ltd. GBR. Dist: Lewis International, Inc.

Battista, Brianna. Cristiano Ronaldo, 1 vol. 2018. (Soccer Stars Ser.). (ENG., Illus.). 24p. (J). (gr. 3-3). 25.27 *(978-1-5383-4348-7(7),* e31fbe2a-fc1d-49c6-8738-ccfb3161365b, PowerKids Pr.) Rosen Publishing Group, Inc., The.

—Luis Suárez, 1 vol. 2018. (Soccer Stars Ser.). (ENG.). 24p. (J). (gr. 3-3). 25.27 *(978-1-5383-4351-7(7),* aeaf56de-bfb6-4d5a-94c3-e085d816d428, PowerKids Pr.) Rosen Publishing Group, Inc., The.

Bellos, Alex & Lyttleton, Ben. Soccer School Season 1: Where Soccer Explains (Rules) the World. Gerrell, Spike, illus. (Soccer School Ser.: 1). (ENG.). 208p. (J). (gr. 2-5). 2019. pap. 7.99 *(978-1-5362-0835-1(3))* 2018. 15.99 *(978-1-5362-0435-3(8))* Candlewick Pr.

—Soccer School Season 2: Where Soccer Explains (Saves) the World. Gerrell, Spike, illus. 2018. (Soccer School Ser.: 2). (ENG.). 208p. (J). (gr. 2-5). 15.99 *(978-1-5362-0436-0(6))* Candlewick Pr.

Besley, Adrian. Zlatan Ibrahimovic: The Ultimate Fan Book. 2017. (Y Ser.). (ENG., Illus.). 64p. (gr. 4). pap. 9.95 *(978-1-78097-934-2(7))* Carlton Bks., Ltd. GBR. Dist: Two Rivers Distribution.

Bielby, Paul. Simply the Best: 500 Football Tips for Youngsters. 2011. (ENG.). 260p. pap. 12.95 *(978-1-84358-350-9(X))* Blake, John Publishing, Ltd. GBR. Dist: Independent Pubs. Group.

Bishop, Amanda. Soccer Superstars: The Best of the Best. 2013. (ENG., Illus.). 32p. (J). *(978-0-7787-0243-6(X))*; pap. *(978-0-7787-0252-8(9))* Crabtree Publishing Co.

—Winning Big: World & Euro Cup Soccer. 2013. (ENG., Illus.). 32p. (J). *(978-0-7787-0245-0(6))*; pap. *(978-0-7787-0253-5(7))* Crabtree Publishing Co.

Bjorklund, Ruth. Neymar: Superstar Striker, 1 vol. 2019. (At the Top of Their Game Ser.). (ENG.). 112p. (gr. 9-9). pap. 20.99 *(978-1-5026-5100-6(9),* 070640b0-d2ce-4760-bc64-3b9374a65362) Cavendish Square Publishing LLC.

Bodden, Valerie. Soccer. 2016. (Making the Play Ser.). (ENG., Illus.). 24p. (J). (gr. 1-4). lib. bdg. 9.99 *(978-1-60818-657-0(1),* 20492, Creative Education) Creative Co., The.

Borth, Teddy. Futbol Americano: Grandes Momentos, Récords y Datos (Spanish Version) 2016. (Grandes Deportes (Great Sports) Ser.). (SPA., Illus.). 24p. (J). (gr. -1-2). lib. bdg. 32.79 *(978-1-68080-736-3(6),* 22634, Abdo Kids) ABDO Publishing Co.

—Soccer: Great Moments, Records, & Facts, 1 vol. 2015. (Great Sports Ser.). (ENG., Illus.). 24p. (J). (gr. -1-2). lib. bdg. 32.79 *(978-1-62970-692-4(2),* 16710, Abdo Kids) ABDO Publishing Co.

Bratton, Deboral B. & Bratton, Ashley D. Record-a-Sport Soccer Sport Organizer. Bratton, Deboral B. & Bratton, Ashley D., eds. 2003. (Illus.). (gr. 1-18). 18.95 *(978-1-931746-04-5(4))* Sport Your Stuff Corp.

Brown, Jonatha A. Soccer, 1 vol. 2004. (My Favorite Sport Ser.). (ENG., Illus.). 24p. (gr. 2-4). lib. bdg. 24.67 *(978-0-8368-4341-5(X),* ff17151e-ee9a-4b1e-b5c7-1e6895fc8f3b, Weekly Reader Leveled Readers) Stevens, Gareth Publishing LLLP.

Brown, Monica. Pele, King of Soccer/Pele, el Rey Del Futbol. Gutierrez, Rudy, illus. 2017. (ENG.). 40p. (J). (gr. -1-3). pap. 9.99 *(978-0-06-122780-6(3))* HarperCollins Español.

—Pele, King of Soccer/Pele, el Rey Del Futbol: Bilingual English-Spanish. Gutierrez, Rudy, illus. 2008. (ENG.). 40p. (J). (gr. -1-3). 18.99 *(978-0-06-122779-0(X))* HarperCollins Español.

Buckley, James, Jr. & Who HQ. Who Was Pelé? Thomson, Andrew, illus. 2018. (Who Was? Ser.). 112p. (J). (gr. 3-7). 6.99 *(978-0-399-54261-9(2),* Penguin Workshop) Penguin Young Readers Group.

Buckley, Jim. Soccer. 2008. (21st Century Skills Innovation Library: Innovation in Sports Ser.). (ENG., Illus.). 32p. (gr. 4-8). lib. bdg. 32.07 *(978-1-60279-261-6(5),* 200123) Cherry Lake Publishing.

Buckley, Jr., James. It's a Numbers Game! Soccer: The Math Behind the Perfect Goal, the Game-Winning Save, & So Much More! 2020. (It's a Numbers Game! Ser.). (ENG., Illus.). 128p. (J). (gr. 3-7). 14.99 *(978-1-4263-3923-3(2),* National Geographic Kids) Disney Publishing Worldwide.

Buckley, Jr, James. It's a Numbers Game! Soccer: The Math Behind the Perfect Goal, the Game-Winning Save, & So Much More! 2020. (It's a Numbers Game! Ser.). (ENG.). 128p. (J). (gr. 3-7). 24.90 *(978-1-4263-3924-0(0),* National Geographic Kids) Disney Publishing Worldwide.

Burdett, Benjamin. Julie Ertz, 1 vol. 2018. (Soccer Stars Ser.). (ENG.). 24p. (J). (gr. 3-3). 25.27 *(978-1-5383-4349-4(5),* e3255336-ded3-40ee-b590-e607c40d6324, PowerKids Pr.) Rosen Publishing Group, Inc., The.

Burdick, Mason. Soccer, 1 vol. 2012. (On the Team Ser.). (ENG., Illus.). 24p. (J). (gr. 2-3). pap. 9.15 *(978-1-4339-6454-1(6),* 0e10dc91-7f7e-4f5b-a7ad-e30439482945); lib. bdg. 25.27 *(978-1-4339-6452-7(X),* 4cb7a588-eac3-499c-91b0-d2246749bfcf) Stevens, Gareth Publishing LLLP. (Gareth Stevens Learning Library).

Burlingame, Jeff. Soccer Star Andrés Iniesta, 1 vol. 2014. (Goal! Latin Stars of Soccer Ser.). (ENG.). 48p. (gr. 4-6). 30.60 *(978-1-62285-225-3(7),* 3b051035-4e7a-4654-a84d-87db84d10948); pap. 11.53 *(978-1-62285-226-0(5),* 282a18fb-01d9-4055-b47a-3b5abe7264f2) Enslow Publishing, LLC.

—Soccer Star Kaká, 1 vol. 2014. (Goal! Latin Stars of Soccer Ser.). (ENG.). 48p. (gr. 4-6). 30.60 *(978-1-62285-230-7(3),* 344cc6e8-dbe2-4f90-a6fb-a835b4cc0693); pap. 11.53 *(978-1-62285-231-4(1),* 173f477a-13c2-4ada-bad5-fad803b01605) Enslow Publishing, LLC.

Burshtein, Karen. Lionel Messi: Soccer's Top Scorer, 1 vol. 2015. (Living Legends of Sports Ser.). (ENG.). 48p. (J). (gr. 5-6). pap. 15.05 *(978-1-68048-130-3(4),* 7c915d59-ac6d-4fa0-a76a-63ac162c1155); (illus.). 28.41 *(978-1-68048-129-7(0),* ab31414f-a24b-4b07-812b-ff970d71d006) Rosen Publishing Group, Inc., The. (Britannica Educational Publishing).

Capucilli, Alyssa Satin. My First Soccer Game: A Book with Foldout Pages. Jensen, Leyah, photos by. 2011. (My First Ser.). (ENG., Illus.). 14p. (J). (gr. -1-k). 9.99 *(978-1-4424-2747-1(7),* Little Simon) Little Simon.

—My First Soccer Game: Ready-To-Read Pre-Level 1. Jensen, Leyah, photos by. 2016. (My First Ser.). (ENG., Illus.). 32p. (J). (gr. -1-k). pap. 4.99 *(978-1-4814-6185-6(0),* Simon Spotlight) Simon Spotlight.

Carlson-Berne, Emma. What a Kick: How a Clutch World Cup Win Propelled Women's Soccer. 2016. (Captured History Sports Ser.). (ENG., Illus.). 64p. (J). (gr. 5-9). lib. bdg. 35.32 *(978-0-7565-5293-0(1),* 130888, Compass Point Bks.) Capstone.

Carothers, Thomas. Great Moments in Olympic Soccer. (Super Soccer Ser.). (ENG., Illus.). 32p. (J). 2019. (gr. 4-4). pap. 9.95 *(978-1-64185-626-3(2),* 1641856262) 2018. (gr. 3-5). lib. bdg. 32.79 *(978-1-5321-1744-2(2),* 30776) ABDO Publishing Co. (SportsZone).

—Juventus FC. 2017. (Europe's Best Soccer Clubs Ser.). (ENG., Illus.). 48p. (J). (gr. 3-6). lib. bdg. 34.21 *(978-1-5321-1134-1(7),* 25844, SportsZone) ABDO Publishing Co.

—Pro Soccer Upsets. 2020. (Sports' Wildest Upsets (Lerner (tm) Sports) Ser.). (ENG., Illus.). 32p. (J). (gr. 2-5). 29.32 *(978-1-5415-7713-8(2),* 1539af49-77fb-44d6-ab64-f876940485a9, Lerner Pubns.) Lerner Publishing Group.

—Women's World Cup Heroes. 2018. (Super Soccer Ser.). (ENG., Illus.). 32p. (J). (gr. 3-6). lib. bdg. 32.79 *(978-1-5321-1747-3(7),* 30782, SportsZone) ABDO Publishing Co.

Castillo, Rodolfo Iguaran. Freddy Rincon. 2012. (Superstars of Soccer ENGLISH Ser.). (ENG., Illus.). 32p. (J). (gr. 4-7). lib. bdg. 19.95 *(978-1-4222-2662-9(X))* Mason Crest.

Chacoff, Juan Domingo. Carlos Valderrama. 2012. (Superstars of Soccer ENGLISH Ser.). (ENG., Illus.). 32p. (J). (gr. 4-7). lib. bdg. 19.95 *(978-1-4222-2661-2(1))* Mason Crest.

Chalk, Gary & Sutherland, Jon. Avon United. 2005. (Football Fantasy S. Ser.). (ENG., Illus.). 304p. 9.50 *(978-1-84046-622-5(7))* Icon Bks., Ltd. GBR. Dist: Publishers Group Canada.

—Clyde Rovers. 2005. (Football Fantasy S. Ser.). (ENG., Illus.). 272p. 9.50 *(978-1-84046-621-8(9))* Icon Bks., Ltd. GBR. Dist: Publishers Group Canada.

—Tyne Athletic - 4-3-3. 2004. (Football Fantasy S. Ser.). (ENG., Illus.). 272p. pap. 9.50 *(978-1-84046-596-9(4),* Wizard Books) Icon Bks., Ltd. GBR. Dist: Publishers Group Canada.

Christopher, Matt. Great Americans in Sports: Mia Hamm. 2015. (ENG., Illus.). 192p. (J). (gr. 3-7). pap. 12.99 *(978-0-316-26101-2(7))* Little, Brown Bks. for Young Readers.

—World Cup: An Action-Packed Look at Soccer's Biggest Competition. rev. ed. 2018. (ENG.). 192p. (J). (gr. 3-7). pap. 6.99 *(978-0-316-48487-9(3))* Little, Brown Bks. for Young Readers.

Cline-Ransome, Lesa. Young Pele: Soccer's First Star. Ransome, James E., illus. (ENG.). 40p. (J). (gr. -1-4). 2012. lib. bdg. 22.44 *(978-0-375-93599-2(1))* 2011. pap. 8.99 *(978-0-375-87156-6(X))* Random Hse. Children's Bks. (Dragonfly Bks.).

Contro, Arturo. Cristiano Ronaldo. 2009. (World Soccer Stars / Estrellas del fútbol mundial Ser.). (ENG & SPA.). 24p. (gr. 2-2). 42.50 *(978-1-60854-839-2(2),* Editorial Buenas Letras) Rosen Publishing Group, Inc., The.

—Gianluigi Buffon. 2009. (World Soccer Stars / Estrellas del fútbol mundial Ser.). (ENG & SPA.). 24p. (gr. 2-2). 42.50 *(978-1-60854-844-6(9),* Editorial Buenas Letras) Rosen Publishing Group, Inc., The.

—Gianluigi Buffon, 1 vol. Benson, Megan, tr. 2008. (World Soccer Stars / Estrellas Del Fútbol Mundial Ser.). (SPA & ENG., Illus.). 24p. (J). (gr. 2-2). lib. bdg. 26.27 *(978-1-4042-7668-0(8),* f6bc9999-9c62-4d5f-b759-0b9a080256f3) Rosen Publishing Group, Inc., The.

—Landon Donovan. 2009. (World Soccer Stars / Estrellas del fútbol mundial Ser.). (ENG & SPA.). 24p. (gr. 2-2). 42.50 *(978-1-60854-847-7(3),* Editorial Buenas Letras) Rosen Publishing Group, Inc., The.

—Landon Donovan, 1 vol. Benson, Megan, tr. 2008. (World Soccer Stars / Estrellas Del Fútbol Mundial Ser.). (SPA & ENG., Illus.). 24p. (J). (gr. 2-2). lib. bdg. 26.27 *(978-1-4042-7666-6(1),* afb00a3b-138e-462c-bc34-f2d6500b3bbd) Rosen Publishing Group, Inc., The.

—Rafael Marquez. 2009. (World Soccer Stars / Estrellas del fútbol mundial Ser.). (ENG & SPA.). 24p. (gr. 2-2). 42.50 *(978-1-60854-849-1(X),* Editorial Buenas Letras) Rosen Publishing Group, Inc., The.

—Rafael Marquez, 1 vol. Benson, Megan, tr. 2008. (World Soccer Stars / Estrellas Del Fútbol Mundial Ser.). (SPA & ENG., Illus.). 24p. (J). (gr. 2-2). lib. bdg. 26.27 *(978-1-4042-7667-3(X),* 532df3a4-41c1-41d6-a62e-5a6aa686ccbc) Rosen Publishing Group, Inc., The.

Cook, Malcolm. 101 Youth Soccer Drills for 12 to 16 Year Olds. 2003. (Illus.). 128p. (YA). pap. 14.95 *(978-1-890946-23-4(0))* Reedswain, Inc.

Crats, Rennay & Rediger, Pat. For the Love of Soccer. Kissock, Heather, ed. 2003. (For the Love of Sports Ser.). (Illus.). 24p. (J). pap. 8.95 *(978-1-59036-069-9(9))* Weigl Pubs., Inc.

Crowther, Robert. Soccer: Facts & Stats & the World Cup & Superstars: A Pop-up Book. Crowther, Robert, illus. 2004. (Illus.). 14p. (J). (gr. 2-8). reprint ed. 18.00 *(978-0-7567-7368-7(7))* DIANE Publishing Co.

Czeskleba, Abby. Cool Soccer Facts. Saunders-Smith, Gail, illus. 2011. (Cool Sports Facts Ser.). (ENG.). 24p. (gr. k-1). pap. 41.70 *(978-1-4296-7397-6(4),* Capstone Pr.) Capstone.

Dann, Sarah. Play Like a Pro: Soccer Skills & Drills. 2013. (ENG., Illus.). 32p. (J). *(978-0-7787-0241-2(3));* pap. *(978-0-7787-0250-4(2))* Crabtree Publishing Co.

D'Arcy, Sean. Freestyle Soccer Street Moves: Tricks, Stepovers, Passes. 2009. (ENG., Illus.). 128p. pap. 14.95 *(978-1-55407-583-6(1),* b06ed2d2-e35c-4ee3-80e9-03a897f59ba4) Firefly Bks., Ltd.

Derr, Aaron. Soccer: An Introduction to Being a Good Sport. Angle, Scott, illus. 2017. (Start Smart (tm) — Sports Ser.). (ENG.). 32p. (J). (gr. k-3). lib. bdg. 26.65 *(978-1-63440-132-6(8),* 4deb42b2-9fb8-4ecc-a3cf-b20fa8b78e5a); E-Book 39.99 *(978-1-63440-144-9(1))* Red Chair Pr.

Doeden, Matt. Cristiano Ronaldo. 2017. (Sports All-Stars (Lerner (tm) Sports) Ser.). (ENG., Illus.). 32p. (J). (gr. 2-5). 29.32 *(978-1-5124-2582-6(6),* 53b49520-6467-4fa1-913f-f0b594de0e5c); E-Book 42.65 *(978-1-5124-3782-9(4),* 9781512437829); E-Book 6.99 *(978-1-5124-3783-6(2),* 9781512437836) Lerner Publishing Group. (Lerner Pubns.).

—The World Cup: Soccer's Global Championship. 2018. (Spectacular Sports Ser.). (ENG., Illus.). 64p. (J). (gr. 5-8). 34.65 *(978-1-5124-2755-4(1),* 1a388e36-9fb6-4bb8-bddb-99b8bbd151c4, Millbrook Pr.) Lerner Publishing Group.

—The World's Greatest Soccer Players. 2010. (World's Greatest Sports Stars (Sports Illustrated for Kids) Ser.). (ENG.). 32p. (gr. 2-3). pap. 53.70 *(978-1-4296-5105-9(9))* Capstone.

Dolphin, Colleen. Soccer by the Numbers, 1 vol. 2010. (Team Sports by the Numbers Ser.). (ENG.). 24p. (J). (gr. k-3). lib. bdg. 29.93 *(978-1-60453-771-0(X),* 14684, SandCastle) ABDO Publishing Co.

Donaldson, Chelsea. Christine Sinclair, 1 vol. 2014. (Canadian Biographies Ser.). (ENG., Illus.). 24p. (J). (gr. -1-2). 27.32 *(978-1-4914-1959-5(8),* 127372, Capstone Pr.) Capstone.

Douglas, Peter. Soccer: Breaking Away on the Pitch. 2017. (Preparing for Game Day Ser.: Vol. 10). (ENG., Illus.). 79p. (J). (gr. 7-12). 24.95 *(978-1-4222-3919-3(5))* Mason Crest.

Downing, Erin. For Soccer-Crazy Girls Only. 2014. (ENG., Illus.). 160p. (J). (gr. 2-5). 16.99 *(978-1-250-04709-0(9),* 900131933) Feiwel & Friends.

Doyle, Brian. Cristiano Ronaldo: World-Beater, 1 vol. 2017. (At the Top of Their Game Ser.). (ENG., Illus.). 112p. (YA). (gr. 9-9). 44.50 *(978-1-5026-2834-3(1),* 730b1f8e-7d23-4d47-b918-eb6586a770e8) Cavendish Square Publishing LLC.

duopress labs. Messi: Superstar. 2016. (Illus.). 140p. (J). (gr. 3-7). pap. 14.99 *(978-1-938093-57-9(7),* 809357) Duo Pr. LLC.

Durrie, Karen. Al Fútbol. 2012. (J). *(978-1-61913-203-0(6))* Weigl Pubs., Inc.

—Soccer. 2011. (J). 27.13 *(978-1-61690-942-0(0));* *(978-1-61690-588-0(3))* Weigl Pubs., Inc.

Edom, Helen & Osborne, Mike. Starting Soccer. Young, Norman, illus. 2006. (First Skills Ser.). 32p. (J). (gr. k-3). lib. bdg. 12.99 *(978-1-58086-907-2(6),* Usborne) EDC Publishing.

Ejaz, Khadija. Lionel Messi. 2013. (ENG.). 32p. (gr. 4-8). lib. bdg. 25.70 *(978-1-61228-467-5(1))* Mitchell Lane Pubs.

Elzaurdia, Paco. Cuauhtemoc Blanco. 2012. (Superstars of Soccer SPANISH Ser.). (Illus.). 32p. (J). (gr. 4). (SPA.). 19.95 *(978-1-4222-2614-8(X));* 19.95 *(978-1-4222-2667-4(0))* Mason Crest.

—Rafael Marquez. 32p. (J). 2013. (Illus.). *(978-1-4222-2594-3(1))* 2012. (SPA.). (gr. 4). 19.95 *(978-1-4222-2598-1(4))* 2012. (Illus.). (gr. 4). 19.95 *(978-1-4222-2651-3(4))* Mason Crest.

England World Cup Junior Companion: Everything You Need to Know about the 2006 World Cup. 2006. (ENG., Illus.). 48p. (J). pap. 8.99 *(978-0-00-721698-7(X),* HarperCollins Children's Bks.) HarperCollins Pubs. Ltd. GBR. Dist: Independent Pubs. Group.

Ertz, Julie. Chase Your Dreams: How Soccer Taught Me Strength, Perseverance, & Leadership. 2019. (ENG.). 176p. (J). (gr. 2-7). 16.99 *(978-0-7369-7932-0(8),* 6979320) Harvest Hse. Pubs.

Falk, Laine. Let's Talk Soccer. 2008. (Scholastic News Nonfiction Readers Ser.). (ENG., Illus.). 24p. (J). (gr. k-1). lib. bdg. 22.00 *(978-0-531-13830-4(5),* Children's Pr.) Scholastic Library Publishing.

Faulkner, Nicholas & Sherman, Josepha. Soccer: Girls Rocking It, 1 vol., 1. 2015. (Title IX Rocks! Ser.). (ENG., Illus.). 64p. (J). (gr. 6-6). 36.13 *(978-1-5081-7039-6(8),* d36418db-7752-49a8-b0d1-9130ac65bbf7, Rosen Young Adult) Rosen Publishing Group, Inc., The.

Feldman, Heather. Mia Hamm: Soccer Superstar. 2009. (Sports Superstars Ser.). 24p. (gr. 1-1). 42.50 *(978-1-60853-180-6(5),* PowerKids Pr.) Rosen Publishing Group, Inc., The.

—Mia Hamm: Soccer/Soccer Superstar/Superestrella del Fútbol. 2009. (Superstars of Sports/Superestrellas del deporte Ser.). (ENG & SPA.). 24p. (gr. 1-2). 42.50 *(978-1-60853-240-7(2),* Editorial Buenas Letras) Rosen Publishing Group, Inc., The.

—Mia Hamm: Superestrella del Fútbol Soccer (Soccer Superstar. 2009. (Superestrellas del Deporte (Superstars of Sports) Ser.). (SPA.). 24p. (gr. 1-2). 42.50 *(978-1-60853-228-5(3),* Editorial Buenas Letras) Rosen Publishing Group, Inc., The.

Fischer, David. Cristiano Ronaldo: International Soccer Star, 1 vol. 2018. (Influential Lives Ser.). (ENG.). 128p. (gr. 7-7). 40.27 *(978-0-7660-9205-1(4),* 7bee6757-e708-4971-b86e-4126e204bff4) Enslow Publishing, LLC.

Fishman, Jon M. Neymar. 2018. (Sports All-Stars (Lerner (tm) Sports) Ser.). (ENG., Illus.). 32p. (J). (gr. 2-5). pap. 9.99 *(978-1-5415-2805-5(0),* 491fb12b-6dc8-4769-bfb6-78f123fb4054); lib. bdg. 29.32 *(978-1-5415-2459-0(4),* e780c0f5-5713-458d-881d-7303d0705c36, Lerner Pubns.) Lerner Publishing Group.

—Soccer Superstar Cristiano Ronaldo. 2020. (J). *(978-1-5415-5564-8(3))* Lerner Publishing Group.

—Soccer Superstar Lionel Messi. 2019. (Bumba Books (r) — Sports Superstars Ser.). (ENG., Illus.). 24p. (J). (gr. -1-1). lib. bdg. 26.65 *(978-1-5415-7673-5(X),* c4159219-66ab-4b43-916b-a637325c9ce8, Lerner Pubns.) Lerner Publishing Group.

—Soccer's G. O. A. T. Pelé, Lionel Messi, & More. 2019. (Sports' Greatest of All Time (Lerner (tm) Sports) Ser.). (ENG., Illus.). 32p. (J). (gr. 2-5). 30.65 *(978-1-5415-5600-3(3),* a986f891-88e2-4aef-b0fd-3b0dca613fd7); pap. 9.99 *(978-1-5415-7445-8(1),* 9364a458-bb62-4c70-9d40-23ebef43f59c) Lerner Publishing Group. (Lerner Pubns.).

—Tim Howard. 2015. (Amazing Athletes Ser.). (ENG., Illus.). 32p. (J). (gr. 2-5). lib. bdg. 26.65 *(978-1-4677-5746-1(2),* 0e8b6c03-208d-49a3-a920-f42a9d99b8d9, Lerner Pubns.) Lerner Publishing Group.

Flynn, Brendan. Soccer Time! 2016. (Bumba Books (r) — Sports Time! Ser.). (ENG., Illus.). 24p. (J). (gr. -1-1). 26.65 *(978-1-5124-1934-4(9),* 573753d7-9ed3-4c98-824c-f5393ab83b25, Lerner Pubns.) Lerner Publishing Group.

—Superstars of the World Cup. 2018. (Sports' Greatest Superstars Ser.). (ENG., Illus.). 24p. (J). (gr. 1-1). pap. 8.95 *(978-1-63517-830-2(4),* 1635178304) North Star Editions.

—Superstars of the World Cup. 2018. (Sports' Greatest Superstars Ser.). (ENG., Illus.). 24p. (J). (gr. k-3). lib. bdg. 31.36 *(978-1-5321-6035-6(6),* 28702, Pop! Cody Koala) Pop!

Forest, Christopher. Play Soccer Like a Pro: Key Skills & Tips. 2010. (Play Like the Pros (Sports Illustrated for Kids) Ser.). (ENG.). 32p. (J). (gr. 3-4). pap. 43.14 *(978-1-4296-5956-7(4),* 15686); pap. 7.19 *(978-1-4296-5647-4(6),* 114138); lib. bdg. 27.32 *(978-1-4296-4827-1(9),* 103353) Capstone.

Gagne, Tammy. Day by Day with Mia Hamm. 2012. (J). lib. bdg. 25.70 *(978-1-61228-327-2(6))* Mitchell Lane Pubs.

—Hope Solo. 2014. (Illus.). 32p. (J). 25.70 *(978-1-61228-642-6(9))* Mitchell Lane Pubs.

Gaspar, Joe. What Is Soccer?, 1 vol. 2018. (Let's Find Out! Sports Ser.). (ENG.). 32p. (gr. 2-3). 26.06 *(978-1-5383-0476-1(7),* c8ed0e25-44ad-428d-81c5-2752020364e7, Britannica Educational Publishing) Rosen Publishing Group, Inc., The.

Gatto, Kimberly. Lionel Messi: A Soccer Star Who Cares, 1 vol. 2014. (Sports Stars Who Care Ser.). (ENG.). 48p. (gr. 3-3). pap. 11.53 *(978-1-4644-0543-3(3),* bee01a14-30f9-4d23-885b-f3b11790c510, Enslow Elementary); (Illus.). 27.93 *(978-0-7660-4299-5(5),* 08475c51-df1f-4517-a61a-3b4f172ff020) Enslow Publishing, LLC.

Gibbons, Alan. Read on - Being Rooney. 2014. (Read On Ser.). (ENG., Illus.). 160p. (J). (gr. 5). 9.99 *(978-0-00-748894-0(7))* HarperCollins Pubs. Ltd. GBR. Dist: Independent Pubs. Group.

Gifford, Clive. The Business of Soccer, 1 vol. 2010. (Spotlight on Soccer Ser.). (ENG., Illus.). 32p. (J). (gr. 4-4). lib. bdg. 28.93 *(978-1-61532-610-5(3),* ad527812-64a8-49c0-af76-80174ab0235b, PowerKids Pr.) Rosen Publishing Group, Inc., The.

—The Inside Story of Soccer, 1 vol. 2011. (Sports World Ser.). (ENG.). 48p. (YA). (gr. 5-5). lib. bdg. 34.47 *(978-1-4488-4847-8(4),* 2b122029-70a6-441c-9787-e80c09287e8d) Rosen Publishing Group, Inc., The.

—The Inside Story of World Cup Soccer, 1 vol. 2011. (Sports World Ser.). (ENG.). 48p. (YA). (gr. 5-5). lib. bdg. 34.47 *(978-1-4488-4849-2(0),* 5fd42e70-cafa-4df2-bbce-f847afaae2ff) Rosen Publishing Group, Inc., The.

—The Kingfisher Soccer Encyclopedia. 2020. (Kingfisher Encyclopedias Ser.). (ENG.). 144p. (J). 19.99 *(978-0-7534-7546-1(4),* 900211425, Kingfisher) Roaring Brook Pr.

—So You Think You Know David Beckham? 2003. (ENG.). 128p. (J). pap. 9.99 *(978-0-340-87765-4(0))* Hodder & Stoughton GBR. Dist: Trafalgar Square Publishing.

—Soccer, 1 vol. 2010. (Tell Me about Sports Ser.). (ENG.). 32p. (gr. 4-4). 31.21 *(978-0-7614-4460-2(2),* 26d87a40-55f5-48a2-b4dd-69753ed9635c) Cavendish Square Publishing LLC.

—Soccer, 1 vol. 2008. (Personal Best Ser.). (ENG., Illus.). 32p. (YA). (gr. 4-4). lib. bdg. 30.27 *(978-1-4042-4441-2(7),* 68a6a9bd-a44c-4aaf-b9db-2f6726939f1b) Rosen Publishing Group, Inc., The.

—Soccer: The Ultimate Guide to the Beautiful Game. 2020. (ENG.). 96p. (J). pap. 9.99 *(978-0-7534-7547-8(2),* 900211426, Kingfisher) Roaring Brook Pr.

—Soccer Legends. 2009. (ENG., Illus.). 32p. (J). (gr. 4-7). lib. bdg. *(978-0-7787-3777-3(2))* Crabtree Publishing Co.

—Soccer Rules & Regulations, 1 vol. 2010. (Spotlight on Soccer Ser.). (ENG., Illus.). 32p. (J). (gr. 4-4). lib. bdg. 28.93 *(978-1-61532-608-2(1),* 7477ee96-faa9-48b5-a57c-c75ac7d7b24c, PowerKids Pr.) Rosen Publishing Group, Inc., The.

—Teamwork in Soccer, 1 vol. 2010. (Spotlight on Soccer Ser.). (ENG., Illus.). 32p. (J). (gr. 4-4). lib. bdg. 28.93 *(978-1-61532-609-9(X),* 0067f2e5-de79-4757-9c00-0c368a18f13d, PowerKids Pr.) Rosen Publishing Group, Inc., The.

Gifford, Clive & Phillips, Dee. Soccer World Cup. 2009. (ENG., Illus.). 32p. (J). (gr. 4-7). lib. bdg. *(978-0-7787-3778-0(0))* Crabtree Publishing Co.

Gilles, Renae & Rylands, Warren. Soccer. 2019. (Illus.). 24p. (J). *(978-1-4896-8034-1(9),* AV2 by Weigl) Weigl Pubs., Inc.

Gitlin, Marty. Neymar: Soccer Superstar, 1 vol. 2018. (Living Legends of Sports Ser.). (ENG.). 48p. (gr. 5-6). 28.41 *(978-1-5383-0214-9(4),* 95ed20c4-cae3-4052-a867-72014ab4dcb6, Britannica Educational Publishing) Rosen Publishing Group, Inc., The.

—Soccer Star Robinho, 1 vol. 2014. (Goal! Latin Stars of Soccer Ser.). (ENG.). 48p. (gr. 4-6). 30.60 *(978-1-62285-216-1(8),* 9e06e6ef-ef22-4143-9b7b-21a719ef9652) Enslow Publishing, LLC.

Glaser, Jason. David Beckham. (Sports Idols Ser.). 24p. (gr. 2-3). 2009. 42.50 *(978-1-60853-141-7(4),* PowerKids Pr.) 2007. (ENG., Illus.). (J). lib. bdg. 26.27 *(978-1-4042-4182-4(5),* 69f8a4f3-d5ee-445b-9c76-095c4618132b) Rosen Publishing Group, Inc., The.

Goldsworthy, Steve. Soccer. 2011. (J). (gr. 4-6). pap. 13.95 *(978-1-61690-704-4(5),* AV2 by Weigl); (Illus.). 32p. (YA). (gr. 2-5). 28.55 *(978-1-61690-699-3(5))* Weigl Pubs., Inc.

Goodstein, Madeline. Goal! Science Projects with Soccer, 1 vol. 2009. (Score! Sports Science Projects Ser.). (ENG., Illus.). 104p. (gr. 5-6). lib. bdg. 35.93 *(978-0-7660-3106-7(3),* 4e2da253-e69d-416f-a848-a59dec36c85f) Enslow Publishing, LLC.

Grady, Daniel John. Diego Forlan. 2012. (Superstars of Soccer ENGLISH Ser.). (ENG., Illus.). 32p. (J). (gr. 4-7). lib. bdg. 19.95 *(978-1-4222-2665-0(4))* Mason Crest.

—Mario Yepes. 2012. (Superstars of Soccer ENGLISH Ser.). (ENG., Illus.). 32p. (J). (gr. 4-7). lib. bdg. 19.95 *(978-1-4222-2664-3(6))* Mason Crest.

Greathouse, Lisa. Count Me In! Soccer Tournament, 1 vol. 2nd rev. ed. 2011. (TIME for KIDS(r): Informational Text Ser.). (ENG.). 28p. (gr. 2-3). pap. 10.99 *(978-1-4333-3638-6(3))* Teacher Created Materials, Inc.

Greder, Andy. Behind the Scenes Soccer. 2019. (Inside the Sport (Lerner (tm) Sports) Ser.). (ENG., Illus.). 32p. (J). (gr. 2-5). pap. 8.99 *(978-1-5415-7439-7(7),* dec98802-8678-4bf4-a990-651130c1d1f1); lib. bdg. 29.32 *(978-1-5415-5607-2(0),* f7e0361d-f484-4fe7-bd7e-38cbf03a556f) Lerner Publishing Group. (Lerner Pubns.).

Group/McGraw-Hill, Wright. SoCer: Level I, 6 vols. (Take Twostm Ser.). 16p. 29.95 *(978-0-322-08970-9(0))* Wright Group/McGraw-Hill.

Haley, Charly. Jake Goes to Soccer Practice: A Book about Telling Time. 2018. (My Day Readers Ser.). (ENG.). 24p. (J). (gr. -1-2). lib. bdg. 32.79 *(978-1-5038-2491-1(8),* 212357) Child's World, Inc, The.

Hamm, Mia, et al. Mia Hamm. 2015. (Quotes from the Greatest Athletes Ser.). (ENG., Illus.). 24p. (J). lib. bdg. 12.95 *(978-1-4896-3365-1(0));* lib. bdg. 28.55 *(978-1-4896-3364-4(2))* Weigl Pubs., Inc. (AV2 by Weigl).

Hammelef, Danielle S. First Source to Soccer: Rules, Equipment, & Key Playing Tips. 2017. (First Sports Source Ser.). (ENG., Illus.). 24p. (J). (gr. 1-3). lib. bdg. 27.99 *(978-1-5157-6946-0(1),* 135420, Capstone Pr.) Capstone.

—Top Soccer Tips. 2017. (Top Sports Tips Ser.). (ENG., Illus.). 32p. (J). (gr. 3-9). lib. bdg. 28.65 *(978-1-5157-4722-2(0),* 134357, Capstone Pr.) Capstone.

Hantula, Richard. Science at Work in Soccer, 1 vol. 2012. (Sports Science Ser.). (ENG., Illus.). 32p. (gr. 5-5). 31.21 *(978-1-60870-591-7(9),* d3228d60-012c-4dd1-b500-64e8212a2270) Cavendish Square Publishing LLC.

HarperCollins Children's Books, creator. England the Facts Sticker Book: All the Facts, All the Stats, All the Stickers! 2006. (ENG., Illus.). 32p. (J). pap. 8.99 *(978-0-00-721695-6(5),* HarperCollins Children's Bks.) HarperCollins Pubs. Ltd. GBR. Dist: Independent Pubs. Group.

HarperCollins UK Staff. England World Cup Dream Team: Live Your Own World Cup Dream! 2006. (ENG., Illus.). 6p. (J). pap. 8.99 *(978-0-00-721696-3(3),* HarperCollins Children's Bks.) HarperCollins Pubs. Ltd. GBR. Dist: Independent Pubs. Group.

Havelka, Jacqueline. STEM in Soccer. 2019. (Connecting STEM & Sports Ser.). (Illus.). 80p. (J). (gr. 12). lib. bdg. 34.60 *(978-1-4222-4337-4(0))* Mason Crest.

Haw, Jennie. Score! The Story of Soccer. 2013. (ENG., Illus.). 32p. (J). *(978-0-7787-0242-9(1));* pap. *(978-0-7787-0251-1(0))* Crabtree Publishing Co.

Hellebuyck, Adam & Deimel, Laura. FIFA World Cup. 2019. (21st Century Skills Library: Global Citizens: Sports Ser.). (ENG., Illus.). 32p. (J). (gr. 4-7). pap. 14.21 *(978-1-5341-5033-1(1),* 213439); lib. bdg. 32.07 *(978-1-5341-4747-8(0),* 213438) Cherry Lake Publishing.

Henderson, Brien. FC Barcelona, 1 vol. 2020. (Soccer's Greatest Clubs Ser.). (ENG.). 64p. (J). (gr. 5-5). pap. 16.28 *(978-1-5026-5258-4(7),* cb30256a-bb6a-49e0-ae97-54b4c12f7b35) Cavendish Square Publishing LLC.

Herzog, Brad. K Is for Kick: A Soccer Alphabet. Rose, Melanie, illus. rev. ed. (Sports Alphabet Ser.). (ENG.). 40p. (J). (gr. 1-4). 2006. pap. 7.95 *(978-1-58536-339-1(1),* 202302) 2003. 16.95 *(978-1-58536-130-4(5),* 201992) Sleeping Bear Pr.

—K Is for Kick: A Soccer Alphabet. Rose, Melanie, illus. 2015. (Av2 Fiction Readalong 2016 Ser.). (ENG.). (J). (gr. 1-4). lib. bdg. 34.28 *(978-1-4896-3756-7(7),* AV2 by Weigl) Weigl Pubs., Inc.

—Little Soccer. Bowles, Doug, illus. 2011. (Little Sports Ser.). (ENG.). 20p. (J). (gr. -1-1). bds. 7.95 *(978-1-58536-197-7(6),* 202248) Sleeping Bear Pr.

Hileman, Jesse & Reher, Matt. Soccer vs Football. 2012. (2R Sports Ser.). (ENG., Illus.). 36p. (J). pap. 8.00 *(978-1-64053-101-7(7),* ARC Pr. Bks.) American Reading Co.

Hoena, Blake. National Geographic Kids Everything Soccer: Score Tons of Photos, Facts, & Fun. 2014. (National Geographic Kids Everything Ser.). (ENG., Illus.). 64p. (J). (gr. 3-7). pap. 12.99 *(978-1-4263-1713-2(1),* National Geographic Kids) Disney Publishing Worldwide.

—Soccer. 2015. (J). lib. bdg. 25.65 *(978-1-62031-181-3(X),* Bullfrog Bks.) Jump! Inc.

Hollar, Sherman. Soccer & Its Greatest Players, 1 vol. 2011. (Inside Sports Ser.). (ENG., Illus.). 96p. (J). (gr. 6-6). lib. bdg. 35.29 *(978-1-61530-516-2(5),* 5a66b6ec-ca48-4919-8b39-ca0dda66f3dd) Rosen Publishing Group, Inc., The.

Hood, Susan & Somhiran, Pathana. Titan & the Wild Boars: The True Cave Rescue of the Thai Soccer Team. Phumiruk, Dow, illus. 2019. (ENG.). 48p. (J). (gr. -1-3). 19.99 *(978-0-06-290772-1(7),* HarperCollins) HarperCollins Pubs.

Howard, Tim. The Keeper: the Unguarded Story of Tim Howard Young Readers' Edition. (ENG.). 288p. (J). (gr. 3-7). 2015. pap. 9.99 *(978-0-06-238758-5(8))* 2014. (Illus.). 16.99 *(978-0-06-238755-4(3))* HarperCollins Pubs. (HarperCollins).

S

Hughes, Morgan. Soccer. 2005. (Junior Sports Ser.). (Illus.). 32p. (gr. 2-4). 19.95 (978-1-59515-187-2(7)) Rourke Educational Media.

Hyde, Natalie. Soccer Science. 2008. (Sports Science Ser.). (ENG., Illus.). 32p. (J). (gr. 4-6). pap. (978-0-7787-4554-9(6)) Crabtree Publishing Co.

James, Ryan. Soccer. 2016. (Game on! Psyched for Sports Ser.). (ENG.). 32p. (gr. 3-9). 32.79 (978-1-68191-753-5(X), 9781681917535) Rourke Educational Media.

Jankowski, Emily. Soccer's Greatest Records, 1 vol. 2014. (Greatest Records in Sports Ser.). (ENG.). 32p. (J). (gr. 4-5). pap. 11.00 (978-1-4994-0001-4(2), 81eee212-d51d-4475-8da7-a0104ec6e7c8); (Illus.). lib. bdg. 27.93 (978-1-4994-0000-7(4), a4342385-c928-47be-b82e-90e7a959361e) Rosen Publishing Group, Inc., The. (PowerKids Pr.).

Jökulsson, Illugi. Before They Were Stars: How Messi, Alex Morgan, & Other Soccer Greats Rose to the Top. 2019. (World Soccer Legends Ser.: 0). (ENG., Illus.). 64p. (J). (gr. 1-8). 14.95 (978-0-7892-1327-3(3), 791327, Abbeville Kids) Abbeville Pr., Inc.

—Neymar. 2015. (World Soccer Legends Ser.: 8). (ENG., Illus.). 64p. (J). (gr. 1). 13.95 (978-0-7892-1227-6(7), 791227, Abbeville Kids) Abbeville Pr., Inc.

—Stars of All Time. 2017. (World Soccer Legends Ser.: 0). (ENG.). 64p. (J). (gr. 1). 15.95 (978-0-7892-1295-5(1), 791295, Abbeville Kids) Abbeville Pr., Inc.

—Stars of Women's Soccer. 2nd ed. 2018. (ENG., Illus.). 64p. (J). (gr. 1-11). 14.95 (978-0-7892-1305-1(2), 791305, Abbeville Kids) Abbeville Pr., Inc.

—Stars of World Soccer: 2nd Edition. 2nd ed. 2018. (ENG., Illus.). 64p. (J). (gr. 1-1). 14.95 (978-0-7892-1316-7(8), 791316, Abbeville Kids) Abbeville Pr., Inc.

—The World?s Greatest Clubs. 2019. (ENG.). 64p. (J). (gr. 1). 14.95 (978-0-7892-1353-2(2), 791353, Abbeville Kids) Abbeville Pr., Inc.

Jökulsson, Illugi & Jökulsson, Illugi. James Rodriguez. 2015. (ENG., Illus.). 64p. (J). (gr. 1). 13.95 (978-0-7892-1237-5(4), 1395706, Abbeville Kids) Abbeville Pr., Inc.

—Messi: Second Edition. 2nd ed. 2015. (World Soccer Legends Ser.: 6). (ENG., Illus.). 64p. (J). (gr. 1). 14.95 (978-0-7892-1225-2(0), 791225, Abbeville Kids) Abbeville Pr., Inc.

Jones, Jeremy V. The Keeper: The Tim Howard Story. 2010. (ZonderKidz Biography Ser.). (ENG.). 128p. (J). (gr. 4-7). pap. 6.99 (978-0-310-72004-1(4)) Zonderkidz.

—Toward the Goal: The Kaká Story, 1 vol. 2010. (Zonderkids Biographies Ser.). (ENG.). 128p. (J). (gr. 5-8). 21.19 (978-0-310-72003-4(6)) Zonderkidz.

—Toward the Goal, Revised Edition: The Kaka Story, 1 vol. rev. ed. 2014. (ZonderKidz Biography Ser.). (ENG.). 160p. (J). pap. 7.99 (978-0-310-73840-4(7)) Zonderkidz.

Kajumulo, Alex. Soccer Monster: Mwalimu Wa Soca. 2012. (ENG.). pap. 8.95 (978-1-4675-1671-6(6)) Independent Pub.

Kalman, Bobbie & Crossingham, John. Fútbol para Patear. 2008.Tr. of Kick It Soccer. (SPA.). 32p. (J). pap. (978-0-7787-8647-4(1)) Crabtree Publishing Co.

—Kick It Soccer. 2007. (Sports Starters Ser.). (ENG., Illus.). 32p. (J). (gr. 3-7). lib. bdg. (978-0-7787-3138-2(3)); (gr. -1-3). pap. (978-0-7787-3170-2(7)) Crabtree Publishing Co.

Kane, Bryce. Superstars of Women's Soccer. 2019. (J). (978-1-4222-4212-4(9)); Vol. 4. (Illus.). 80p. (gr. 12). lib. bdg. 33.27 (978-1-4222-4213-1(7)) Mason Crest.

—Top Teams in Women's Soccer, Vol. 4. 2019. (Women's Soccer Today Ser.). (Illus.). 80p. (J). (gr. 12). lib. bdg. 33.27 (978-1-4222-4214-8(5)) Mason Crest.

Karpovich, Todd. Manchester United. 2017. (Europe's Best Soccer Clubs Ser.). (ENG.). 48p. (J). (gr. 3-6). lib. bdg. 34.21 (978-1-5321-1135-8(5), 25846, SportsZone) ABDO Publishing Co.

Kassouf, Jeff. Girls Play to Win Soccer. 2011. (Girls Play to Win Ser.). 64p. (J). (gr. 3-6). lib. bdg. 27.93 (978-1-59953-464-0(9)) Norwood Hse. Pr.

Kelley, K. C. Top 10 Soccer Superstars. 2018. (Top 10 in Sports Ser.). (ENG.). 24p. (J). (gr. 2-5). lib. bdg. 32.79 (978-1-5038-2723-3(2), 212556) Child's World, Inc, The.

Kennedy, Mike & Stewart, Mark. Soccer in Africa. 2011. (Smart about Soccer Ser.). 24p. (J). (gr. k-3). lib. bdg. 22.60 (978-1-59953-441-1(X)) Norwood Hse. Pr.

—Soccer in Asia. 2011. (Smart about Soccer Ser.). 24p. (J). (gr. k-3). lib. bdg. 22.60 (978-1-59953-448-0(7)) Norwood Hse. Pr.

—Soccer in Eastern Europe. 2011. (Smart about Soccer Ser.). 24p. (J). (gr. k-3). lib. bdg. 22.60 (978-1-59953-445-9(2)) Norwood Hse. Pr.

—Soccer in South America. 2011. (Smart about Soccer Ser.). 24p. (J). (gr. k-3). lib. bdg. 22.60 (978-1-59953-446-6(0)) Norwood Hse. Pr.

—Soccer in the British Isles. 2011. (Smart about Soccer Ser.). 24p. (J). (gr. k-3). lib. bdg. 22.60 (978-1-59953-442-8(8)) Norwood Hse. Pr.

—Soccer in Western Europe. 2011. (Smart about Soccer Ser.). 24p. (J). (gr. k-3). lib. bdg. 22.60 (978-1-59953-447-3(9)) Norwood Hse. Pr.

Killion, Ann. Champions of Women's Soccer. 2019. 276p. (J). (gr. 3-7). 8.99 (978-0-399-54903-8(X), Puffin Books) Penguin Young Readers Group.

Kirkpatrick, Rob. Alexi Lalas: Sensación del Fútbol Soccer (Soccer Sensation) 2009. (Grandes Idolos (Hot Shots) Ser.). 24p. (gr. 1-1). 42.50 (978-1-61512-733-7(X), Editorial Buenas Letras) Rosen Publishing Group, Inc., The.

—Alexi Lalas: Soccer Sensation / Sensación del Fútbol Soccer. 2009. (Hot Shots/Grandes idolos Ser.). (SPA.). 24p. (gr. 1-1). 42.50 (978-1-61513-411-3(5), Editorial Buenas Letras) Rosen Publishing Group, Inc., The.

—Cobi Jones: Estrella del Fútbol Soccer (Soccer Star) 2009. (Grandes Idolos (Hot Shots) Ser.). (SPA.). 24p. (gr. 1-1). 42.50 (978-1-61512-734-4(8), Editorial Buenas Letras) Rosen Publishing Group, Inc., The.

—Cobi Jones: Soccer Star / Estrella del Fútbol Soccer. 2009. (Hot Shots/Grandes idolos Ser.). (ENG & SPA.). 24p. (gr. 1-1). 42.50 (978-1-61513-412-0(3), Editorial Buenas Letras) Rosen Publishing Group, Inc., The.

—Mia Hamm: Soccer Star. 2009. (Great Record Breakers in Sports Ser.). 24p. (gr. 3-3). 42.50 (978-1-61513-189-1(2), PowerKids Pr.) Rosen Publishing Group, Inc., The.

Kortemeier, Todd. AC Milan. 2017. (Europe's Best Soccer Clubs Ser.). (ENG., Illus.). 48p. (J). (gr. 3-6). lib. bdg. 34.21 (978-1-5321-1129-7(0), 25834, SportsZone) ABDO Publishing Co.

—Cristiano Ronaldo: Soccer Star. 2018. (Biggest Names in Sports Set 2 Ser.). (ENG., Illus.). 32p. (J). (gr. 3-5). pap. 9.95 (978-1-63517-560-8(7), 1635175607); lib. bdg. 31.35 (978-1-63517-488-5(0), 1635174880) North Star Editions. (Focus Readers).

—Kylian Mbappé: Soccer Star. 2019. (Illus.). 32p. (J). (978-1-64185-436-8(7)); (ENG., (gr. 3-5). pap. 9.95 (978-1-64185-378-1(6), 1641853786); (ENG., (gr. 3-5). lib. bdg. 31.35 (978-1-64185-320-0(4), 1641853204) North Star Editions. (Focus Readers).

—Make Me the Best Soccer Player. 2016. (Make Me the Best Athlete Ser.). (ENG., Illus.). 48p. (J). (gr. 4-6). lib. bdg. 34.21 (978-1-68078-491-6(9), 23791, SportsZone) ABDO Publishing Co.

—Real Madrid Cf. 2017. (Europe's Best Soccer Clubs Ser.). (ENG.). 48p. (J). (gr. 3-6). lib. bdg. 34.21 (978-1-5321-1136-5(3), 25848, SportsZone) ABDO Publishing Co.

—Superstars of World Soccer. 2016. (Pro Sports Superstars Ser.). (ENG., Illus.). 24p. (J). (gr. 1-4). lib. bdg. 20.95 (978-1-60753-942-1(X), 15672) Amicus.

—Total Soccer. 2016. (Total Sports Ser.). (ENG., Illus.). 64p. (J). (gr. 3-6). lib. bdg. 35.64 (978-1-68078-507-4(9), 23837, SportsZone) ABDO Publishing Co.

Laínez, René Colato. Juguemos Al Futbol y Al Football!/Let's Play Futbol & Football! 2014. (ENG & SPA., Illus.). 31p. (J). (gr. -1-2). 16.00 (978-0-88272-328-0(6), Alfaguara) Santillana USA Publishing Co., Inc.

Lindeen, Mary. Let's Play Soccer. 2015. (Beginning-To-Read Ser.). (ENG., Illus.). 32p. (J). (gr. k-2). pap. 13.26 (978-1-60357-743-4(2)); lib. bdg. 22.60 (978-1-59953-683-5(8)) Norwood Hse. Pr.

Littlejohn, James & Shipley, Matthew. G Is for Golazo: The Ultimate Soccer Alphabet. 2019. (ABC to MVP Ser.: 2). (ENG., Illus.). 32p. (J). (gr. -1-k). 17.95 (978-1-62937-671-4(X)) Triumph Bks.

Logothetis, Paul. Cristiano Ronaldo: International Soccer Star. 2015. (Playmakers Ser.). (ENG., Illus.). 32p. (J). (gr. 2-5). 32.79 (978-1-62403-841-9(7), 18052, SportsZone) ABDO Publishing Co.

—Lionel Messi: Soccer Sensation. 2015. (Playmakers Ser.). (ENG., Illus.). 32p. (J). (gr. 2-5). 32.79 (978-1-62403-839-6(5), 18048, SportsZone) ABDO Publishing Co.

Lozano, Gustavo Vazquez, et al. Luis Suarez. 2012. (Superstars of Soccer SPANISH Ser.). (SPA., Illus.). 32p. (J). (gr. 4-7). lib. bdg. 19.95 (978-1-4222-2603-2(4)) Mason Crest.

Luke, Andrew. Making the Final 32. 2018. (J). (978-1-4222-3949-0(7)) Mason Crest.

—Soccer, Vol. 13. 2016. (Inside the World of Sports Ser.: Vol. 13). (ENG., Illus.). 80p. (J). (gr. 7-12). 24.95 (978-1-4222-3465-5(7)) Mason Crest.

—U. S. Women's Team, Vol. 4. 2019. (Women's Soccer Today Ser.). (Illus.). 80p. (J). (gr. 12). lib. bdg. 33.27 (978-1-4222-4215-5(3)) Mason Crest.

MacDonald, Margaret. Rules on the Soccer Field. 2011. (Learn-Abouts Ser.). (Illus.). 16p. (J). pap. 7.95 (978-1-59920-616-5(1)) Black Rabbit Bks.

Machajewski, David. Lionel Messi, 1 vol. 2018. (Soccer Stars Ser.). (ENG., Illus.). 24p. (J). (gr. 3-3). 25.27 (978-1-5383-4350-0(9), f3b731d9-3854-40f0-8831-a2516cf5483e, PowerKids Pr.) Rosen Publishing Group, Inc., The.

Machajewski, Sarah. Neymar, 1 vol. 2018. (Soccer Stars Ser.). (ENG.). 24p. (J). (gr. 3-3). 25.27 (978-1-5383-4353-1(3), bcccd662-4cbb-4821-93a1-c634df1ef998, PowerKids Pr.) Rosen Publishing Group, Inc., The.

Mahaney, Ian F. The Math of Soccer, 1 vol. 2011. (Sports Math Ser.). (J). (ENG.). 24p. (gr. 2-3). pap. 9.25 (978-1-4488-2700-8(0), ba6dcc75-3c13-4e25-aa4c-cc173552fe78, PowerKids Pr.); (ENG.). 24p. (gr. 2-3). lib. bdg. 26.27 (978-1-4488-2557-8(1), 84dfcfcc-a4a2-4f5f-8c94-f5a928ab118f); 49.50 (978-1-4488-2701-5(9), PowerKids Pr.) Rosen Publishing Group, Inc., The.

Mahoney, Emily Jankowski. The Science of Soccer, 1 vol. 2015. (Sports Science Ser.). (ENG., Illus.). 32p. (J). (gr. 4-5). pap. 11.00 (978-1-4994-1071-6(9), 6f094458-8651-45c7-b462-43585d4d17ed, PowerKids Pr.) Rosen Publishing Group, Inc., The.

Mara, Wil. Soccer. 2012. (Rookie Read-about Ser.). (ENG., Illus.). 32p. (J). pap. 5.95 (978-0-531-20927-1(X)); (gr. -1-1). lib. bdg. 18.69 (978-0-531-20858-8(3)) Scholastic Library Publishing. (Children's Pr.).

Marquardt, Meg. Stem in Soccer. 2017. (STEM in Sports Ser.). (ENG., Illus.). 48p. (J). (gr. 3-6). lib. bdg. 34.21 (978-1-5321-1353-6(6), 27651, SportsZone) ABDO Publishing Co.

Marthaler, Jon. Arsenal FC. 2017. (Europe's Best Soccer Clubs Ser.). (ENG., Illus.). 48p. (J). (gr. 3-6). lib. bdg. 34.21 (978-1-5321-1130-3(4), 25836, SportsZone) ABDO Publishing Co.

—FC Bayern Munich. 2017. (Europe's Best Soccer Clubs Ser.). (ENG.). 48p. (J). (gr. 3-6). lib. bdg. 34.21 (978-1-5321-1132-7(0), 25840, SportsZone) ABDO Publishing Co.

—Ultimate Soccer Road Trip. 2018. (Ultimate Sports Road Trips Ser.). (ENG., Illus.). 48p. (J). (gr. 3-6). lib. bdg. 34.21 (978-1-5321-1757-2(4), 30802, SportsZone) ABDO Publishing Co.

—US Men's Professional Soccer. 2018. (Super Soccer Ser.). (ENG., Illus.). 32p. (J). (gr. 3-6). lib. bdg. 32.79 (978-1-5321-1745-9(0), 30778, SportsZone) ABDO Publishing Co.

—US Women's Professional Soccer. 2018. (Super Soccer Ser.). (ENG., Illus.). 32p. (J). (gr. 3-6). lib. bdg. 32.79 (978-1-5321-1746-6(9), 30780, SportsZone) ABDO Publishing Co.

Martínez Alaníz, Eduardo. Hugo Sanchez. 2013. (Illus.). 32p. (J). (978-1-4222-2647-6(6)) Mason Crest.

Mason, Paul. Strange but True!: Football. 2019. (Strange but True! Ser.). (ENG., Illus.). 32p. (J). (gr. 3-5). pap. 11.99 (978-1-4451-5721-4(7), Franklin Watts) Hachette Children's Group GBR. Dist: Hachette Bk. Group.

—The Unofficial Guide to the World Cup. 2018. (ENG., Illus.). 32p. (J). (gr. 4-6). 16.99 (978-1-4451-5598-2(2), Franklin Watts) Hachette Children's Group GBR. Dist: Hachette Bk. Group.

Mason, Paul & Eason, Sarah. Street Soccer. 2011. (On the Radar: Sports Ser.). (ENG., Illus.). 32p. (gr. 4-8). lib. bdg. 26.60 (978-0-7613-7760-3(3)) Lerner Publishing Group.

Mattern, Joanne. Brian Mcbride. 2005. (No Hands Allowed Ser.). (Illus.). 32p. (J). (gr. 2-4). lib. bdg. 25.70 (978-1-58415-389-4(X)) Mitchell Lane Pubs.

—I Know Soccer. 2013. (21st Century Basic Skills Library: I Know Sports Ser.). (ENG., Illus.). 24p. (J). (gr. k-3). 26.35 (978-1-62431-402-5(3), 202728); pap. 12.79 (978-1-62431-478-0(3), 202730) Cherry Lake Publishing.

May, Pete. Players. 2014. (Illus.). 32p. (J). (978-1-62588-133-5(9)) Black Rabbit Bks.

—Teams. 2014. (Illus.). 32p. (J). (978-1-62588-134-2(7)) Black Rabbit Bks.

McCollum, Sean. Full STEAM Soccer: Science, Technology, Engineering, Arts, & Mathematics of the Game. 2018. (Full STEAM Sports Ser.). (ENG., Illus.). 32p. (J). (gr. 3-6). lib. bdg. 27.99 (978-1-5435-3040-7(0), 138624, Capstone Pr.) Capstone.

McDougall, Chros. Best Soccer Players of All Time, 1 vol. 2015. (Sports' Best Ever Ser.). (ENG., Illus.). 64p. (J). (gr. 3-6). lib. bdg. 35.64 (978-1-62403-621-7(X), 17319, SportsZone) ABDO Publishing Co.

—Soccer, 1 vol. 2012. (Best Sport Ever Ser.). (ENG.). 64p. (J). (gr. 4-6). 35.64 (978-1-61783-146-1(8), 3505, SportsZone) ABDO Publishing Co.

McFee, Shane. Let's Play Soccer. (Let's Get Active Ser.). 24p. (gr. 2-3). 2009. 42.50 (978-1-61514-255-2(X)) 2008. (ENG., Illus.). (J). lib. bdg. 26.27 (978-1-4042-4191-6(4), 55b963a2-acac-46bd-9337-c144062710e9) Rosen Publishing Group, Inc., The. (PowerKids Pr.).

McGrath, Barbara Barbieri & Alderman, Peter. Soccer Counts! (El Fútbol Cuenta!) Estrada, Pau, illus. 2011. (SPA & ENG.). 32p. (J). (gr. -1-3). 22.44 (978-1-57091-795-0(7)) Charlesbridge Publishing, Inc.

McIntosh, J. S. Soccer. 2010. (Getting the Edge Ser.). 96p. (YA). lib. bdg. 24.95 (978-1-4222-1739-9(6)) Mason Crest.

McKinney, Donna B. Excelling in Soccer. 2019. (Teen Guide to Sports Ser.). (ENG.). 80p. (J). (gr. 6-12). 41.27 (978-1-68282-703-1(8)) ReferencePoint Pr., Inc.

—Women in Soccer. 2020. (She's Got Game Ser.). (ENG., Illus.). 32p. (J). (gr. 3-5). pap. 9.95 (978-1-64493-141-7(9), 1644931419); lib. bdg. 31.35 (978-1-64493-062-5(5), 1644930625) North Star Editions. (Focus Readers).

Mikoley, Kate. Soccer: Stats, Facts, & Figures, 1 vol. 2017. (Do Math with Sports Stats! Ser.). (ENG.). 32p. (J). (gr. 3-4). pap. 11.50 (978-1-5382-1145-8(9), ea84b6e1-3311-44d5-853f-82e531264a9e); lib. bdg. 28.27 (978-1-5382-1147-2(5), bcf517fa-673b-4d8d-afae-2e86370c1317) Stevens, Gareth Publishing LLLP.

Miller, Calvin Craig. David Beckham. 2008. (Xtreme Athletes Ser.). (Illus.). 100p. (J). (gr. 5-13). lib. bdg. 27.95 (978-1-59935-082-0(3)) Reynolds, Morgan Inc.

Miller, Derek. FC Bayern Munich, 1 vol. 2019. (Soccer's Greatest Clubs Ser.). (ENG.). 64p. (gr. 5-5). pap. 16.28 (978-1-5026-5276-8(5), e8f14f8d-ffaf-428e-8515-098c9b2c9907) Cavendish Square Publishing LLC.

Mills, Andrea & Mills, Andrea. The Soccer Book. 2016. (ENG., Illus.). 64p. (J). (gr. 4-7). pap. 12.95 (978-1-77085-729-2(X), bc0aa10e-5f43-441c-9552-0936f1cc6f33) Firefly Bks., Ltd.

Minden, Cecilia. Buzz Plays Soccer. 2018. (Little Blossom Stories Ser.). (ENG.). 16p. (J). (gr. -1-2). pap. 11.36 (978-1-5341-2863-7(8), 211510, Cherry Blossom Press) Cherry Lake Publishing.

—Soccer. 2008. (21st Century Skills Library: Real World Math Ser.). (ENG., Illus.). 32p. (gr. 4-8). lib. bdg. 32.07 (978-1-60279-244-9(5), 200195) Cherry Lake Publishing.

Mitchell Lane Publishers Inc. Staff. A Robbie Reader-No Hands Allowed, 13 vols. 2007. (No Hands Allowed Ser.). (Illus.). (J). lib. bdg. 334.10 (978-1-58415-602-4(3)) Mitchell Lane Pubs.

Morey, Allan & Hoena, Blake. The World Cup. 2018. (Sports Championships Ser.). (ENG., Illus.). 24p. (J). (gr. 3-7). pap. 7.99 (978-1-61891-487-3(1), 12140, Torque Bks.) Bellwether Media.

Morgan, Alex. Breakaway: Beyond the Goal. 2015. (ENG., Illus.). 320p. (YA). (gr. 7). 17.99 (978-1-4814-5107-9(3), Simon & Schuster Bks. For Young Readers) Simon & Schuster Bks. For Young Readers.

Morreale, Marie. Real Bios: Lionel Messi (Library Edition) 2016. (Real Bios Ser.). (ENG.). 48p. (J). lib. bdg. 29.00 (978-0-531-22379-6(5), Children's Pr.) Scholastic Library Publishing.

Moussavi, Sam. Soccer Underdog Stories. 2018. (Underdog Sports Stories Ser.). (ENG., Illus.). 48p. (J). (gr. 5-8). lib. bdg. 34.21 (978-1-5321-1764-0(7), 30816, SportsZone) ABDO Publishing Co.

—World Cup Heroes. 2018. (Super Soccer Ser.). (ENG., Illus.). 32p. (J). (gr. 3-6). lib. bdg. 32.79 (978-1-5321-1748-0(5), 30784, SportsZone) ABDO Publishing Co.

Murcia, Rebecca Thatcher. Ronaldinho. 2007. (No Hands Allowed Ser.). (Illus.). 32p. (J). (gr. 2-4). lib. bdg. 25.70 (978-1-58415-600-0(7)) Mitchell Lane Pubs.

—What It's Like to Be Kaka. de la Vega, Eida, tr. 2011. (What It's Like to Be... = Que Se Sienta Al Ser... Ser.). (ENG & SPA., Illus.). 32p. (J). (gr. -1-2). lib. bdg. 25.70 (978-1-58415-989-6(8)) Mitchell Lane Pubs.

Murray, Julie. Soccer. 2017. (Sports How To Ser.). (ENG., Illus.). 24p. (J). (gr. -1-2). lib. bdg. 31.36 (978-1-5321-0416-9(2), 26542, Abdo Kids) ABDO Publishing Co.

Murray, Laura K. Alex Morgan. 2016. (Big Time Ser.). (ENG., Illus.). 24p. (J). (gr. 1-3). (978-1-60818-667-9(9), 20776, Creative Education) Creative Co., The.

—Cristiano Ronaldo. 2016. (Big Time Ser.). (ENG., Illus.). 24p. (J). (gr. 1-3). (978-1-60818-670-9(9), 20787, Creative Education) Creative Co., The.

Murray, Stuart A. P. Score with Soccer Math, 1 vol. 2013. (Score with Sports Math Ser.). (ENG.). 48p. (gr. 3-3). pap. 11.53 (978-1-4644-0289-0(2), 3d09a7c7-0302-46ed-b448-be58d32533fb); lib. bdg. 27.93 (978-0-7660-4175-2(1), 2827d9d4-177f-463e-8eb7-0bcb0443bc43) Enslow Publishing, LLC. (Enslow Elementary).

Nagelhout, Ryan. Abby Wambach, 1 vol. 2016. (Sports MVPs Ser.). (ENG., Illus.). 24p. (J). (gr. 1-2). 24.27 (978-1-4824-4639-5(1), d9ec0017-f0e3-46f9-8aef-ac521cb9030f) Stevens, Gareth Publishing LLLP.

—I Love Soccer, 1 vol. 2014. (My Favorite Sports Ser.). (ENG., Illus.). 24p. (J). (gr. k-k). 24.27 (978-1-4824-0734-1(5), e60d651e-5424-46a3-858a-30e86188c3e6) Stevens, Gareth Publishing LLLP.

—Me Encanta el Fútbol / I Love Soccer, 1 vol. 2014. (Mis Deportes Favoritos / My Favorite Sports Ser.). (SPA & ENG.). 24p. (J). (gr. k-k). 24.27 (978-1-4824-0855-3(4), 5317a4ee-5373-4244-b525-03f92f088913) Stevens, Gareth Publishing LLLP.

—Soccer: Who Does What?, 1 vol. 2017. (Sports: What's Your Position? Ser.). (ENG.). 32p. (gr. 3-4). pap. 11.50 (978-1-5382-0413-9(4), c20b7685-74ad-40f3-bd36-8871f06a6cc9) Stevens, Gareth Publishing LLLP.

—Talk Like a Soccer Player, 1 vol. 2016. (Let's Talk Sports! Ser.). (ENG.). 32p. (J). (gr. 2-3). pap. 11.50 (978-1-4824-5712-4(1), f783cd43-6825-4d71-8029-a230ba2744a6) Stevens, Gareth Publishing LLLP.

—20 Fun Facts about Soccer, 1 vol. 2015. (Fun Fact File: Sports! Ser.). (ENG., Illus.). 32p. (J). (gr. 2-3). lib. bdg. 20.95 (978-1-4824-3982-3(4), a9b98b6f-3822-4aeb-848b-3bf71cd58645) Stevens, Gareth Publishing LLLP.

Nelson, Robin. From Plastic to Soccer Ball. 2014. (Start to Finish, Second Ser.). (ENG., Illus.). 24p. (J). (gr. k-3). pap. 7.99 (978-1-4677-4562-8(6), 3ad5d938-0e23-42c9-92b3-dfa40334b682) Lerner Publishing Group.

—Soccer Is Fun! 2013. (First Step Nonfiction — Sports Are Fun! Ser.). (ENG., Illus.). 24p. (J). (gr. k-2). pap. 6.99 (978-1-4677-1538-6(7), 783db1a1-7fdb-47a2-b514-a428c26908a4) Lerner Publishing Group.

Nixon, James. Defending & Goaltending. 2011. (Soccer File Ser.). 32p. (gr. 4-7). lib. bdg. 31.35 (978-1-59920-527-4(0)) Black Rabbit Bks.

—Passing & Dribbling. 2011. (Soccer File Ser.). 32p. (gr. 4-7). lib. bdg. 31.35 (978-1-59920-528-1(9)) Black Rabbit Bks.

—Rules of the Game. Humphrey, Bobby, photos by. 2011. (Soccer File Ser.). (Illus.). 32p. (gr. 4-7). lib. bdg. 31.35 (978-1-59920-529-8(7)) Black Rabbit Bks.

No Hands Allowed: Stories for Kids Who Love Soccer, 7 bks., Set. Incl. Brandi Chastain. Adams, Michelle Medlock. (gr. 1-4). lib. bdg. 25.70 (978-1-58415-390-0(3)); Brian Mcbride. Mattern, Joanne. (gr. 2-4). lib. bdg. 25.70 (978-1-58415-389-4(X)); DaMarcus Beasley: Soccer Star Sensation. Smalley, Carol Parenzan. (gr. 1-4). lib. bdg. 25.70 (978-1-58415-387-0(3)); David Beckham. Murcia, Rebecca Thatcher. (gr. 1-4). lib. bdg. 25.70 (978-1-58415-384-9(9)); Freddy Adu. Murcia, Rebecca Thatcher. (gr. 1-4). lib. bdg. 25.70 (978-1-58415-385-6(7)); Josh Wolff: Three-Team Player. Kjelle, Marylou Morano. (gr. 2-4). lib. bdg. 25.70 (978-1-58415-388-7(1)); Landon Donovan. Murcia, Rebecca Thatcher. (gr. 1-4). lib. bdg. 25.70 (978-1-58415-386-3(5)); 32p. (J). 2005. (Robbie Reader Ser.). (Illus.). 2005. Set lib. bdg. 118.65 (978-1-58415-413-6(6)) Mitchell Lane Pubs.

Obregón, José María. Argentina, 1 vol. 2009. (Great National Soccer Teams / Grandes Selecciones Del Fútbol Mundial Ser.). (SPA & ENG.). 24p. (gr. 2-3). pap. 8.25 (978-1-4358-2495-9(4), d4bb3ecd-0d37-44ce-9069-3aa5b49f46fe, PowerKids Pr.) Rosen Publishing Group, Inc., The.

—Argentina, 1 vol. Benson, Megan, tr. 2009. (Great National Soccer Teams / Grandes Selecciones Del Fútbol Mundial Ser.). (SPA & ENG., Illus.). 24p. (J). (gr. 2-3). lib. bdg. 26.27 (978-1-4042-8088-5(X), bbe38097-296e-4233-a0ce-4a851ec43639) Rosen Publishing Group, Inc., The.

—Brazil: Brasil, 1 vol. 2009. (Great National Soccer Teams / Grandes Selecciones Del Fútbol Mundial Ser.). (SPA & ENG., Illus.). 24p. (gr. 2-3). lib. bdg. 26.27 (978-1-4042-8085-4(5), 5cb3a3fe-197e-4316-8f3d-26a3b0ea6072) Rosen Publishing Group, Inc., The.

—Brazil - Brasil, Vol. 1. 2009. (Great National Soccer Teams / Grandes Selecciones Del Fútbol Mundial Ser.). (SPA & ENG.). 24p. (gr. 2-3). pap. 8.25 (978-1-4358-2489-8(X), dd3f4353-8724-4d0d-b339-cecb5df93a4e, PowerKids Pr.) Rosen Publishing Group, Inc., The.

—Cuauhtémoc Blanco. 2009. (World Soccer Stars / Estrellas del fútbol mundial Ser.). 24p. (gr. 2-2). (ENG & SPA.). 42.50 (978-1-60854-840-8(6), Editorial Buenas Letras); (SPA & ENG., Illus.). (J). lib. bdg. 26.27 (978-1-4358-2731-8(7), f122bf04-473b-4bed-8ba2-a529eaf32dbb) Rosen Publishing Group, Inc., The.

Obregon, Jose Maria. David Beckham. 2009. (World Soccer Stars / Estrellas del fútbol mundial Ser.). (ENG & SPA.). 24p. (gr. 2-2). 42.50 (978-1-60854-841-5(4), Editorial Buenas Letras) Rosen Publishing Group, Inc., The.

Obregón, José María. Didier Drogba, 1 vol. 2009. (World Soccer Stars / Estrellas Del Fútbol Mundial Ser.). (SPA & ENG.). 24p. (J). (gr. 2-2). lib. bdg. 26.27 (978-1-4358-2967-1(0), f78733f0-c4a5-4929-9c23-86128b92906c) Rosen Publishing Group, Inc., The.

—England: Inglaterra, 1 vol. Benson, Megan, tr. 2009. (Great National Soccer Teams / Grandes Selecciones Del Fútbol Mundial Ser.). (SPA & ENG., Illus.). 24p. (J). (gr. 2-3). lib. bdg. 26.27 (978-1-4042-8089-2(8), 95511bd3-70a2-421d-a235-4c5d230aedec) Rosen Publishing Group, Inc., The.

—England/Inglaterra, 1 vol. 2009. (Great National Soccer Teams / Grandes Selecciones Del Fútbol Mundial Ser.). (SPA & ENG.). 24p. (gr. 2-3). pap. 8.25 (978-1-4358-3235-0(3),

65f0064b-6c13-4232-a8f5-84a66bc84e81, PowerKids Pr.) Rosen Publishing Group, Inc., The.

—Freddy Adu, 1 vol. 2009. (World Soccer Stars / Estrellas Del Fútbol Mundial Ser.). (SPA & ENG., Illus.). 24p. (J). (gr. 2-2). lib. bdg. 26.27 (978-1-4358-2730-1(9), 4771c84f-07fd-41b8-92de-b40238df6d29) Rosen Publishing Group, Inc., The.

—Germany: Alemania, 1 vol. Benson, Megan, tr. 2009. (Great National Soccer Teams / Grandes Selecciones Del Fútbol Mundial Ser.). (SPA & ENG., Illus.). 24p. (J). (gr. 2-3). lib. bdg. 26.27 (978-1-4042-8087-8(1), fd0af989-1aaf-4588-a07f-86a4641db82e) Rosen Publishing Group, Inc., The.

—Germany/Alemania, 1 vol. 2009. (Great National Soccer Teams / Grandes Selecciones Del Fútbol Mundial Ser.). (SPA & ENG.). 24p. (gr. 2-3). pap. 8.25 (978-1-4358-2493-5(8), 61882394-7a7b-42a3-adb9-91527be0594c) Rosen Publishing Group, Inc., The.

—Italy: Italia, 1 vol. Benson, Megan, tr. 2009. (Great National Soccer Teams / Grandes Selecciones Del Fútbol Mundial Ser.). (SPA & ENG., Illus.). 24p. (J). (gr. 2-3). lib. bdg. 26.27 (978-1-4042-8086-1(3), ebe197bc-41d3-4f5d-97ff-907b70a22704) Rosen Publishing Group, Inc., The.

—Italy/Italia, 1 vol. 2009. (Great National Soccer Teams / Grandes Selecciones Del Fútbol Mundial Ser.). (SPA & ENG.). 24p. (gr. 2-3). pap. 8.25 (978-1-4358-2491-1(1), d93479b4-5ec5-4dd6-bd56-a08c442e3458, PowerKids Pr.) Rosen Publishing Group, Inc., The.

—Juan Pablo Ángel. 2009. (World Soccer Stars / Estrellas del fútbol mundial Ser.). 24p. (gr. 2-2). (ENG & SPA.). 42.50 (978-1-60854-845-3(7), Editorial Buenas Letras); (SPA & ENG.). (J). lib. bdg. 26.27 (978-1-4358-2732-5(5), 159f9b8a-4c5b-475a-b511-c556816e4af2) Rosen Publishing Group, Inc., The.

—Kaká. 2009. (World Soccer Stars / Estrellas del fútbol mundial Ser.). 24p. (gr. 2-2). (ENG & SPA.). 42.50 (978-1-60854-846-0(5), Editorial Buenas Letras); (SPA & ENG.). (J). lib. bdg. 26.27 (978-1-4358-2733-2(3), cf31fb27-2358-485d-941e-fdcb90422598) Rosen Publishing Group, Inc., The.

—Lionel Messi. 2009. (World Soccer Stars / Estrellas del fútbol mundial Ser.). 24p. (gr. 2-2). (ENG & SPA.). 42.50 (978-1-60854-848-4(1), Editorial Buenas Letras); (SPA & ENG.). (J). lib. bdg. 26.27 (978-1-4358-2729-5(5), 5d74bda6-09db-4b82-b6e7-08a46bb83f8a) Rosen Publishing Group, Inc., The.

—Mexico - México, Vol. 1. 2009. (Great National Soccer Teams / Grandes Selecciones Del Fútbol Mundial Ser.). (SPA & ENG.). 24p. (J). (gr. 2-3). pap. 8.25 (978-1-4358-2498-0(9), 22c8536d-35c9-444e-8682-bd1e2228ae3b, PowerKids Pr.) Rosen Publishing Group, Inc., The.

—Mexico/México, 1 vol. Benson, Megan, tr. 2009. (Great National Soccer Teams / Grandes Selecciones Del Fútbol Mundial Ser.). (SPA & ENG., Illus.). 24p. (J). (gr. 2-3). lib. bdg. 26.27 (978-1-4358-2497-3(0), 11495e57-a0c4-426b-a369-376960f13c41) Rosen Publishing Group, Inc., The.

—Mexico/México. 2009. (SPA & ENG.). (J). 49.50 (978-1-4358-3234-3(5), PowerKids Pr.) Rosen Publishing Group, Inc., The.

Obregon, Jose Maria. Ronaldhino. 2009. (World Soccer Stars / Estrellas del fútbol mundial Ser.). (ENG & SPA.). 24p. (gr. 2-2). 42.50 (978-1-60854-850-7(3), Editorial Buenas Letras) Rosen Publishing Group, Inc., The.

—Ronaldinho, 1 vol. Benson, Megan, tr. 2008. (World Soccer Stars / Estrellas Del Fútbol Mundial Ser.). (SPA & ENG., Illus.). 24p. (J). (gr. 2-2). lib. bdg. 26.27 (978-1-4042-7664-2(5), ef5f93e3-27be-4f40-9f57-c81d80a33876) Rosen Publishing Group, Inc., The.

Oldfield, Matt. Carragher: From the Playground to the Pitch. 2017. (Ultimate Sports Heroes Ser.). (ENG.). 176p. (J). (gr. 4-8). pap. 9.99 (978-1-78606-463-9(4)) Blake, John Publishing, Ltd. GBR. Dist: Independent Pubs. Group.

—Coutinho: From the Playground to the Pitch. 2017. (Ultimate Football Heroes Ser.). (ENG.). 176p. (J). (gr. 4-8). pap. 9.99 (978-1-78606-462-2(6)) Blake, John Publishing, Ltd. GBR. Dist: Independent Pubs. Group.

Oldfield, Matt & Oldfield, Tom. Luis Suarez: el Pistolero. 2016. (ENG., Illus.). 160p. (J). (gr. 4-7). pap. 8.99 (978-1-78606-012-9(4)) Blake, John Publishing, Ltd. GBR. Dist: Independent Pubs. Group.

Oldfield, Tom & Oldfield, Matt. Raheem Sterling: Red Lightning. 2016. (ENG.). 160p. (J). (gr. 4-7). pap. 8.99 (978-1-78418-646-3(5), Dino Books) Blake, John Publishing, Ltd. GBR. Dist: Independent Pubs. Group.

—Steven Gerrard. 2017. (ENG.). 160p. (J). (gr. 4-7). pap. 9.99 (978-1-78606-219-2(4)) Blake, John Publishing, Ltd. GBR. Dist: Independent Pubs. Group.

—Wayne Rooney: Captain of England. 2016. (ENG.). 160p. (J). (gr. 4-7). pap. 8.99 (978-1-78418-647-0(3)) Blake, John Publishing, Ltd. GBR. Dist: Independent Pubs. Group.

—Zinedine Zidane: One of the Greats. 2017. (Ultimate Football Heroes Ser.). (ENG.). 176p. (J). (gr. 4-8). pap. 9.99 (978-1-78606-461-5(8)) Blake, John Publishing, Ltd. GBR. Dist: Independent Pubs. Group.

Orme, David. Football. 2007. (Trailblazers Ser.). (ENG., Illus.). 36p. (J). (gr. -1-3). pap. (978-1-84167-425-4(7)) Ransom Publishing Ltd.

Orr, Tamra B. Abby Wambach. 2007. (No Hands Allowed Ser.). (Illus.). 32p. (J). (gr. 2-4). lib. bdg. 25.70 (978-1-58415-601-7(5)) Mitchell Lane Pubs.

Osborne, Mary Pope & Boyce, Natalie Pope. Soccer. 2014. (Magic Tree House Fact Tracker Ser.: 29). lib. bdg. 17.20 (978-0-606-36016-6(6)) Turtleback.

—Soccer: A Nonfiction Companion to Magic Tree House Merlin Mission #24: Soccer on Sunday. Murdocca, Sal, illus. 2014. (Magic Tree House (R) Fact Tracker Ser.: 29). 128p. (J). (gr. 2-5). 6.99 (978-0-385-38629-6(X), Random Hse. Bks. for Young Readers) Random Hse. Children's Bks.

Otten, Jack. Futbol, 1 vol. 2003. (Entrenamiento Deportivo (Sports Training) Ser.). (SPA., Illus.). 24p. (J). (gr. 1-2). lib. bdg. 26.27 (978-0-8239-6850-3(2), 8b4a7856-1bd8-4223-8329-e8dad6836231) Rosen Publishing Group, Inc., The.

—Fútbol (Soccer) 2009. (Entrenamiento deportivo (Sports Training) Ser.). (SPA.). 24p. (gr. 1-2). 42.50 (978-1-61512-269-1(9), Editorial Buenas Letras) Rosen Publishing Group, Inc., The.

—Soccer. 2009. (Sports Training Ser.). 24p. (gr. 1-2). 42.50 (978-1-60853-188-2(0), PowerKids Pr.) Rosen Publishing Group, Inc., The.

Page, Jason. Basketball, Soccer, & Other Ball Games. 2008. (Olympic Sports Ser.). (ENG., Illus.). 32p. (J). (gr. 4-7). pap. (978-0-7787-4029-2(3)); lib. bdg. (978-0-7787-4012-4(9)) Crabtree Publishing Co.

—El Futbol. 2004. (Club Deportivo Ser.).Tr. of Soccer. (SPA., Illus.). 32p. (J). (gr. 3-6). 9.95 (978-1-58728-398-7(0), Two-Can Publishing) T&N Children's Publishing.

Parrish, Charles & Nauright, John. Soccer Around the World: A Cultural Guide to the World's Favorite Sport, 1 vol. 2014. (ENG., Illus.). 432p. (C). 108.00 (978-1-61069-302-8(7), 826559) ABC-CLIO, LLC.

Part, Michael. Cristiano Ronaldo: The Rise of a Winner. 2017. (ENG., Illus.). (J). pap. 7.75 (978-1-938591-55-6(0)) Sole Bks.

—The Flea: The Amazing Story of Leo Messi. 2017. (ENG., Illus.). (J). pap. 7.75 (978-1-938591-53-2(4)) Sole Bks.

Pearl, Melissa Sherman & Sherman, David A. FUNDaFIELD: Charities Started by Kids! 2017. (Community Connections: How Do They Help? Ser.). (ENG., Illus.). 24p. (J). (gr. 2-5). lib. bdg. 29.21 (978-1-63472-843-0(2), 209798) Cherry Lake Publishing.

Pendleton, Ken. David Beckham. 2007. (Sports Heroes & Legends Ser.). (Illus.). 106p. (YA). (gr. 7-12). lib. bdg. 30.60 (978-0-8225-7161-2(7)) Twenty First Century Bks.

Pendleton, Ken & Savage, Jeff. David Beckham. 2008. (Sports Heroes & Legends Ser.). (ENG.). (gr. 5-12). pap. 56.72 (978-1-57505-993-8(2)) Lerner Publishing Group.

Peterson, Megan Cooley. Equipos de Fútbol Del Mundo. 2017. (En la Cancha Ser.). (SPA., Illus.). 32p. (J). (gr. 4-6). lib. bdg. (978-1-68072-569-8(6), 10599, Bolt) Black Rabbit Bks.

—Las Estrellas Del Fútbol Femenino. 2017. (En la Cancha Ser.). (SPA.). 32p. (J). (gr. 4-6). lib. bdg. (978-1-68072-571-1(8), 10603, Bolt) Black Rabbit Bks.

—Las Estrellas Del Fútbol Masculino. 2017. (En la Cancha Ser.). (SPA., Illus.). 32p. (J). (gr. 4-6). lib. bdg. (978-1-68072-570-4(X), 10601, Bolt) Black Rabbit Bks.

—Las Reglas Del Fútbol. 2018. (SPA.). 32p. (J). lib. bdg. (978-1-68072-567-4(X)) Black Rabbit Bks.

—Los Grandes Momentos Del Fútbol. 2018. (SPA., Illus.). 31p. (J). lib. bdg. (978-1-68072-568-1(8)) Black Rabbit Bks.

—Récords Mundiales de Fútbol. 2017. (En la Cancha Ser.). (SPA.). 32p. (J). (gr. 4-6). lib. bdg. (978-1-68072-572-8(6), 10605, Bolt) Black Rabbit Bks.

—Soccer Rules! 2017. (On the Pitch Ser.). (ENG.). 32p. (gr. 2-7). 9.95 (978-1-68072-465-3(7)); (J). (gr. 4-6). pap. 9.99 (978-1-64466-202-1(7), 11458); (Illus.). (J). (gr. 4-6). lib. bdg. (978-1-68072-168-3(2), 10520) Black Rabbit Bks. (Bolt).

—Soccer Teams from Around the World. 2017. (On the Pitch Ser.). (ENG.). 32p. (gr. 2-7). 9.95 (978-1-68072-467-7(3)); (J). (gr. 4-6). pap. 9.99 (978-1-64466-204-5(3), 11462); (Illus.). (J). (gr. 4-6). lib. bdg. (978-1-68072-170-6(4), 10524) Black Rabbit Bks. (Bolt).

—Soccer's Biggest Moments. 2017. (On the Pitch Ser.). (ENG.). 32p. (gr. 2-7). 9.95 (978-1-68072-466-0(5)); (J). (gr. 4-6). pap. 9.99 (978-1-64466-203-8(5), 11460); (Illus.). (J). (gr. 4-6). lib. bdg. (978-1-68072-169-0(0), 10522) Black Rabbit Bks. (Bolt).

—Stars of Men's Soccer. 2017. (On the Pitch Ser.). (ENG.). 32p. (gr. 2-7). 9.95 (978-1-68072-468-4(1)); (J). (gr. 4-6). pap. 9.99 (978-1-64466-205-2(1), 11464); (Illus.). (J). (gr. 4-6). lib. bdg. (978-1-68072-171-3(2), 10526) Black Rabbit Bks. (Bolt).

—Stars of Women's Soccer. 2017. (On the Pitch Ser.). (ENG.). 32p. (gr. 2-7). 9.95 (978-1-68072-469-1(X)); (J). (gr. 4-6). pap. 9.99 (978-1-64466-206-9(X), 11466); (Illus.). (J). (gr. 4-6). lib. bdg. (978-1-68072-172-0(0), 10528) Black Rabbit Bks. (Bolt).

—Wacky Soccer Trivia: Fun Facts for Every Fan. 2016. (Wacky Sports Trivia Ser.). (ENG., Illus.). 32p. (J). (gr. 3-9). lib. bdg. 28.65 (978-1-5157-1996-0(0), 132652, Capstone Pr.) Capstone.

—World Soccer Records. 2017. (On the Pitch Ser.). (ENG.). 32p. (gr. 2-7). 9.95 (978-1-68072-470-7(3)); (J). (gr. 4-6). pap. 9.99 (978-1-64466-207-6(8), 11468); (Illus.). (J). (gr. 4-6). lib. bdg. (978-1-68072-173-7(9), 10530) Black Rabbit Bks. (Bolt).

Porter, Esther. Abby Wambach. 2016. (Women in Sports Ser.). (ENG., Illus.). 24p. (J). (gr. -1-2). lib. bdg. 27.32 (978-1-4914-7974-2(4), 130470, Capstone Pr.) Capstone.

Porterfield, Jason. Cristiano Ronaldo: Soccer Champion, 1 vol. 2018. (Living Legends of Sports Ser.). (ENG.). 48p. (gr. 5-6). lib. bdg. 28.41 (978-1-5383-0217-0(9), 8ddffa29-963e-46ec-9eca-356d2dafcf12, Britannica Educational Publishing) Rosen Publishing Group, Inc., The.

Poulton, J. Alexander. World's Greatest Soccer Players: Today's Hottest Superstars, 1 vol. rev. ed. 2006. (ENG., Illus.). 144p. per. 9.95 (978-0-9737681-9-0(3), e2937a9f-754a-41b0-ba6e-b7a2fef9e1d5, OverTime Bks.) Editions de la Montagne Verte, Inc. CAN. Dist: Lone Pine Publishing USA.

Powell, Elizabeth. Math at the Game, 1 vol. 2016. (Math Is Everywhere! Ser.). (ENG., Illus.). 24p. (J). (gr. k-k). pap. 9.15 (978-1-4824-5482-6(3), 4652185f-1c89-482e-92b7-fdd158c0c06f) Stevens, Gareth Publishing LLLP.

Puck & Stollberg, Jon. Totally Epic, True & Wacky Soccer Facts & Stories. 2017. (Illus.). 156p. (J). (gr. 3-7). pap. 12.95 (978-1-938093-81-4(X)) Duo Pr. LLC.

Raum, Elizabeth. Carli Lloyd. 2017. (Pro Sports Biographies Ser.). (ENG.). 24p. (J). (gr. 1-4). 20.95 (978-1-68151-132-0(0), 14677) Amicus.

—Pro Sports Biographies: Carli Lloyd. 2017. (Pro Sports Biographies Ser.). (ENG.). 24p. (J). (gr. 1-3). pap. 9.99 (978-1-68152-163-3(6), 14796) Amicus.

Rausch, David. Major League Soccer. 2014. (Major League Sports Ser.). (ENG.). 24p. (J). (gr. 3-7). 26.95 (978-1-62617-134-3(3), Epic Bks.) Bellwether Media.

Rebman, Nick. Soccer. 2018. (Sports Ser.). (ENG., Illus.). 16p. (J). (gr. k-1). pap. 7.95 (978-1-64185-024-7(8), 1641850248); lib. bdg. 25.64 (978-1-63517-922-4(X), 163517922X) North Star Editions. (Focus Readers).

Rediger, Pat. Soccer. (For the Love of Sports Ser.). 24p. (J). 2019. (ENG.). (gr. 3-6). pap. 12.95 (978-1-7911-0570-9(X)) 2019. (ENG., Illus.). (gr. 3-6). lib. bdg. 28.55 (978-1-7911-0026-1(0)) 2009. (gr. 3-5). pap. 8.95 (978-1-60596-125-5(6)) 2009. (Illus.). lib. bdg. 24.45 (978-1-60596-124-8(8)) Weigl Pubs., Inc.

Rice, Dona Herweck. Soccer or Basketball (Grade 1) 2018. (See Me Read! Everyday Words Ser.). (ENG., Illus.). 12p. (J). (gr. k-1). 6.99 (978-1-4938-9863-3(9)) Teacher Created Materials, Inc.

Riner, Dax. Pelé. 2010. (Sports Heroes & Legends Ser.). (ENG., Illus.). 120p. (J). (gr. 5-12). lib. bdg. 30.60 (978-0-7613-5368-3(2)) Lerner Publishing Group.

Robinson, Sacha. My Soccer Journal. 2015. (ENG., Illus.). 46p. (J). pap. (978-1-78222-419-8(X)) Paragon Publishing, Rothersthorpe.

Robinson, Tom. David Beckham: Soccer's Superstar, 1 vol. 2008. (People to Know Today Ser.). (ENG., Illus.). 112p. (gr. 6-7). lib. bdg. 35.93 (978-0-7660-3110-4(1), 32a4a6d2-f5ad-49af-ba25-883a6daf7e03) Enslow Publishing, LLC.

Rogers, Amy B. Soccer: Science on the Pitch, 1 vol. 2017. (Science Behind Sports Ser.). (ENG.). 104p. (gr. 7-7). lib. bdg. 41.03 (978-1-5345-6115-1(3), a384ae81-4e55-4a14-aa80-e75eeef33c64, Lucent Pr.) Greenhaven Publishing LLC.

Roland, James. The Science & Technology of Soccer. 2019. (Science & Technology of Sports Ser.). (ENG.). 80p. (J). (gr. 6-12). 41.27 (978-1-68282-655-3(4)) ReferencePoint Pr., Inc.

Roseborough, Elizabeth. Women's Soccer on the Rise, Vol. 4. 2019. (Women's Soccer Today Ser.). (Illus.). 80p. (J). (gr. 12). lib. bdg. 33.27 (978-1-4222-4216-2(1)) Mason Crest.

Roselius, J. Chris. David Beckham: Gifted & Giving Soccer Star, 1 vol. 2010. (Sports Stars Who Give Back Ser.). (ENG., Illus.). 128p. (gr. 5-6). lib. bdg. 35.93 (978-0-7660-3587-4(5), e2f976aa-b6d9-4695-8418-0e59441985d5) Enslow Publishing, LLC.

—Soccer Skills: How to Play Like a Pro, 1 vol. 2008. (How to Play Like a Pro Ser.). (ENG., Illus.). 48p. (gr. 5-7). lib. bdg. 27.93 (978-0-7660-3206-4(X), 5bc9c813-881b-4126-bb29-c97663baccb8) Enslow Publishing, LLC.

Ross, Dev. We Both Read-Soccer! Wenzel, David, illus. 2010. 44p. (J). 9.95 (978-1-60115-239-8(6)); pap. 5.99 (978-1-60115-240-4(X)) Treasure Bay, Inc.

Roth, B. A. David Beckham: Born to Play. 2007. (All Aboard Reading Station Stop 3 Collection). (Illus.). 48p. (gr. 1-3). 14.00 (978-0-7569-8918-7(3)) Perfection Learning Corp.

Roytman, Arkady. The Soccer Coloring Book. 2016. (Dover Sports Coloring Bks.). (ENG.). 32p. (J). (gr. 2-5). pap. 3.99 (978-0-486-80481-1(X), 80481X) Dover Pubns., Inc.

Roza, Greg. David Beckham: Soccer Superstar, 1 vol. 2005. (Content-Area Literacy Collections). (ENG.). 24p. (gr. 3-4). pap. 8.85 (978-1-4042-5539-5(7), 99fa87a3-9916-4b2c-938e-b53666aa775a) Rosen Publishing Group, Inc., The.

Rumaner, Marc. Let's Play Soccer! Incl. 2 1/2 " Soccer Ball. (Illus.). 12p. (J). (gr. -1-1). bds. (978-1-56021-373-4(6), 220) W.J. Fantasy, Inc.

Sabino, David. Breakaway: Ready-To-Read Level 2. Fiadzigbey, Setor, illus. 2019. (Game Day Ser.). (ENG.). 40p. (J). (gr. k-2). 17.99 (978-1-5344-3935-1(8)); pap. 4.99 (978-1-5344-3934-4(X)) Simon Spotlight. (Simon Spotlight).

Sad, Elizabeth Levy & Eliaszevich, Esteban. Gonzalo Higuain. 2012. (Superstars of Soccer ENGLISH Ser.). (ENG., Illus.). 32p. (J). (gr. 4-7). lib. bdg. 19.95 (978-1-4222-2649-0(2)) Mason Crest.

—Luis Amaranto Perea. 2012. (Superstars of Soccer ENGLISH Ser.). (ENG., Illus.). 32p. (J). (gr. 4-7). lib. bdg. 19.95 (978-1-4222-2654-4(9)) Mason Crest.

—Radamel Falcao. 2012. (Superstars of Soccer ENGLISH Ser.). (ENG., Illus.). 32p. (J). (gr. 4-7). lib. bdg. 19.95 (978-1-4222-2653-7(0)) Mason Crest.

Sandler, Michael. Soccer: The Amazing U. S. World Cup Team. 2006. (Upsets & Comebacks Ser.). (Illus.). 32p. (J). (gr. 3-6). lib. bdg. 28.50 (978-1-59716-169-5(1)) Bearport Publishing Co., Inc.

Savage, Jeff. David Beckham. 2008. (Amazing Athletes Ser.). (Illus.). 32p. (J). (gr. -1). per. 6.95 (978-0-8225-8975-4(3), First Avenue Editions); (Illus.). 32p. (YA). (gr. 2-5). lib. bdg. 23.93 (978-0-8225-8834-4(X)); pap. 40.95 (978-0-8225-9491-8(9)) Lerner Publishing Group.

—Freddy Adu. 2006. (Amazing Athletes Ser.). (Illus.). 32p. (J). (gr. 2-5). pap. 6.95 (978-0-8225-3595-9(5), First Avenue Editions) Lerner Publishing Group.

—La Galaxy: Soccer Champions. 2018. (Champion Soccer Clubs Ser.). (ENG., Illus.). 32p. (J). (gr. 2-5). 27.99 (978-1-5415-1989-3(2), 5f8e2819-fc5f-4e53-81b7-a371f4e76728, Lerner Pubns.) Lerner Publishing Group.

—Manchester United: Soccer Champions. 2018. (Champion Soccer Clubs Ser.). (ENG., Illus.). 32p. (J). (gr. 2-5). lib. bdg. 27.99 (978-1-5415-1987-9(6), e518ec36-2ae7-4e64-9eed-325032c9ae7d, Lerner Pubns.) Lerner Publishing Group.

—Soccer Super Stats. 2017. (Pro Sports Stats (Alternator Books (r)) Ser.). (ENG., Illus.). 32p. (J). (gr. 3-6). 29.32 (978-1-5124-3409-5(4), 0f1aaf01-feda-489c-916e-1a88da930ad9, Lerner Pubns.) Lerner Publishing Group.

—Top 25 Soccer Skills, Tips, & Tricks, 1 vol. 2012. (Top 25 Sports Skills, Tips, & Tricks Ser.). (ENG., Illus.). 48p. (gr. 4-6). pap. 11.53 (978-1-59845-359-1(9), df9a9d3c-3389-4d15-9510-f10c70f509a8); lib. bdg. 27.93 (978-0-7660-3860-8(2), eb7d8d08-8f79-469a-a307-49771dcc1a04) Enslow Publishing, LLC.

Schalter, Ty. Soccer for Fun & Fitness, 1 vol. 2019. (Sports for Fun & Fitness Ser.). (ENG.). 32p. (gr. 3-3). pap. 11.53 (978-1-9785-1345-7(3), 35dc5cef-5e44-447b-8617-788d065d14b6) Enslow Publishing, LLC.

Scheff, Matt. Alex Morgan: Soccer Star. 2019. (Biggest Names in Sports Set 4 Ser.). (ENG., Illus.). 32p. (J). (gr. 3-5). pap. 9.95 (978-1-64185-380-4(8), 1641853808); lib. bdg. 31.35 (978-1-64185-322-4(0), 1641853220) North Star Editions. (Focus Readers).

Schuh, Mari. Soccer. (Spot Ser.). (ENG., Illus.). 16p. (J). (gr. -1-1). 2018. pap. 7.99 (978-1-68152-208-1(X), 14739) 2017. 17.95 (978-1-68151-089-7(8), 14620) Amicus.

Schwartz, Heather E. Carli Lloyd: Soccer Star. 2018. (Women Sports Stars Ser.). (ENG., Illus.). 32p. (J). (gr. 3-9). lib. bdg. 28.65 (978-1-5157-9710-4(4), 136858, Capstone Pr.) Capstone.

Seidel, Jeff. Chelsea FC. 2017. (Europe's Best Soccer Clubs Ser.). (ENG., Illus.). 48p. (J). (gr. 3-6). lib. bdg. 34.21 (978-1-5321-1133-4(9), 25842, SportsZone) ABDO Publishing Co.

Seigerman, David. Becky Sauerbrunn. 2017. (Real Sports Content Network Presents Ser.). (ENG.). 128p. (J). (gr. 3-7). 17.99 (978-1-4814-8217-2(3)); (Illus.). pap. 7.99 (978-1-4814-8216-5(5)) Simon & Schuster Children's Publishing. (Aladdin).

Shaabneh, Nevien. Mohamed Salah: Get to Know the Soccer Superstar. 2019. (People You Should Know Ser.). (ENG., Illus.). 32p. (J). (gr. 3-6). pap. 7.95 (978-1-5435-7467-8(X), 140907); lib. bdg. 27.99 (978-1-5435-7185-1(9), 140436) Capstone.

Shea, Therese. Soccer Stars. Shea, Therese, illus. 2007. (Sports Stars Ser.). (ENG., Illus.). 48p. (J). (gr. 4-7). pap. 6.95 (978-0-531-18705-0(5)) Scholastic Library Publishing.

Sheaffer, C. H. Soccer Heart: A Story & Guide for the Friendly Contender. 2010. (Illus.). 168p. (978-0-9840922-0-8(X)) SilverBrown Bks.

Shoup, Kate. Lionel Messi: Legendary Soccer Player, 1 vol. 2019. (At the Top of Their Game Ser.). (ENG.). 112p. (gr. 9-9). pap. 20.99 (978-1-5026-5116-7(5), 33aee108-2644-4423-a8c0-2a993671fd1e) Cavendish Square Publishing LLC.

—Paris Saint-Germain FC, 1 vol. 2019. (Soccer's Greatest Clubs Ser.). (ENG.). 64p. (gr. 5-5). pap. 16.28 (978-1-5026-5285-0(4), 31644f96-9d42-4617-af99-b7b6407956a3) Cavendish Square Publishing LLC.

—Real Madrid CF, 1 vol. 2019. (Soccer's Greatest Clubs Ser.). (ENG.). 64p. (J). (gr. 5-5). pap. 16.28 (978-1-5026-5261-4(7), 8425b07b-748b-485b-9017-5e748e6db3c2) Cavendish Square Publishing LLC.

Simon, Eddy. Pelé: The King of Soccer. Brascaglia, Vincent, illus. 2017. (ENG.). 144p. (J). pap. 16.99 (978-1-62672-755-7(4), 900172778, First Second Bks.) Roaring Brook Pr.

Skinner, J. E. U. S. Women's National Soccer Team. 2018. (21st Century Skills Library: Sports Unite Us Ser.). (ENG., Illus.). 32p. (J). (gr. 3-6). lib. bdg. 32.07 (978-1-5341-2964-1(2), 211900) Cherry Lake Publishing.

Slenzak, Miller. I Can Be a Soccer Player, 1 vol. 2018. (I Can Be Anything! Ser.). (ENG.). 24p. (gr. k-k). 24.27 (978-1-5382-1768-9(6), 1312fb1e-5f56-4f52-b3ce-7e579f9658a7) Stevens, Gareth Publishing LLLP.

Small, Cathleen. Manchester United FC, 1 vol. 2019. (Soccer's Greatest Clubs Ser.). (ENG.). 64p. (gr. 5-5). pap. 16.28 (978-1-5026-5264-5(1), b60b03d4-5a3d-4faf-99c6-227a49574863) Cavendish Square Publishing LLC.

—Soccer, 1 vol. 2018. (Mind vs Muscle: the Psychology of Sports Ser.). (ENG.). 48p. (gr. 5-6). pap. 15.05 (978-1-5382-2538-7(7), 015e3e97-cbf3-4ce0-a71e-4c89f200a91a) Stevens, Gareth Publishing LLLP.

Soccer: Level 30. 2003. 31.95 (978-0-673-57967-6(0)) Celebration Pr.

Soccer Smarts, 8 vols. 2017. (Soccer Smarts Ser.). 32p. (ENG.). (gr. 3-3). 111.72 (978-1-4994-3403-3(0), 3a3585ac-7b92-4c55-b309-42d21d60c94e); (gr. 8-8). pap. 40.00 (978-1-4994-3498-9(7)) Rosen Publishing Group, Inc., The. (PowerKids Pr.).

Sommers, Annie Leah. Great National Soccer Teams, 1 vol. 2010. (World Soccer Bks.). (ENG., Illus.). 64p. (YA). (gr. 5-5). lib. bdg. 37.13 (978-1-4358-9138-8(4), 114d9c49-1b2d-4002-98e9-020db89da664, Rosen Reference) Rosen Publishing Group, Inc., The.

Sosa, Carlos. Lionel Messi. 2012. (Superstars of Soccer ENGLISH Ser.). (ENG., Illus.). 32p. (J). (gr. 4-7). lib. bdg. 19.95 (978-1-4222-2659-9(X)) Mason Crest.

Sports Illustrated for Kids Editors. My First Book of Soccer: Mostly Everything Explained about the Game. 2017. (ENG., Illus.). 48p. (J). (gr. -1-1). 11.99 (978-1-68330-002-1(5)) Sports Illustrated For Kids.

St. John, Warren. Outcasts United: The Story of a Refugee Soccer Team That Changed a Town. 2013. 240p. (YA). (gr. 7). pap. 10.99 (978-0-385-74195-8(2), Ember) Random Hse. Children's Bks.

Stewart, Mark. A. C. Milan. 2017. (First Touch Soccer Ser.). (ENG., Illus.). 24p. (J). (gr. k-3). 23.93 (978-1-59953-855-6(5)) Norwood Hse. Pr.

—Arsenal F. C. 2017. (First Touch Soccer Ser.). (ENG., Illus.). 24p. (J). (gr. k-3). 23.93 (978-1-59953-856-3(3)) Norwood Hse. Pr.

—C. A. River Plate. 2017. (First Touch Soccer Ser.). (ENG., Illus.). 24p. (J). (gr. k-3). 23.93 (978-1-59953-867-9(9)) Norwood Hse. Pr.

—Chelsea F. C. 2017. (First Touch Soccer Ser.). (ENG., Illus.). 24p. (J). (gr. k-3). 23.93 (978-1-59953-858-7(X)) Norwood Hse. Pr.

—F. C. Barcelona. 2017. (First Touch Soccer Ser.). (ENG.). 24p. (J). (gr. k-3). 23.93 (978-1-59953-859-4(8)) Norwood Hse. Pr.

—F. C. Bayern Munich. 2017. (First Touch Soccer Ser.). (ENG., Illus.). 24p. (J). (gr. k-3). 23.93 (978-1-59953-857-0(1)) Norwood Hse. Pr.

—Houston Dynamo. 2017. (First Touch Soccer Ser.). (ENG., Illus.). 24p. (J). (gr. k-3). 23.93 (978-1-59953-863-1(6)) Norwood Hse. Pr.

—Los Angeles Galaxy. 2017. (First Touch Soccer Ser.). (ENG., Illus.). 24p. (J). (gr. k-3). 23.93 (978-1-59953-864-8(4)) Norwood Hse. Pr.

—Manchester United. 2017. (First Touch Soccer Ser.). (ENG., Illus.). 24p. (J). (gr. k-3). 23.93 (978-1-59953-860-0(1)) Norwood Hse. Pr.

—New York Red Bulls. 2017. (First Touch Soccer Ser.). (ENG., Illus.). 24p. (J). (gr. k-3). 23.93 (978-1-59953-865-5(2)) Norwood Hse. Pr.

—Paris Saint-Germain. 2017. (First Touch Soccer Ser.). (ENG., Illus.). 24p. (J). (gr. k-3). 23.93 (978-1-59953-861-7(X)) Norwood Hse. Pr.

—Portland Timbers. 2017. (First Touch Soccer Ser.). (ENG., Illus.). 24p. (J). (gr. k-3). 23.93 (978-1-59953-866-2(0)) Norwood Hse. Pr.

—Real Madrid C. F. 2017. (First Touch Soccer Ser.). (ENG., Illus.). 24p. (J). (gr. k-3). 23.93 (978-1-59953-862-4(8)) Norwood Hse. Pr.

—São Paulo F. C. 2017. (First Touch Soccer Ser.). (ENG., Illus.). 24p. (J). (gr. k-3). 23.93 (978-1-59953-868-6(7)) Norwood Hse. Pr.

—Seattle Sounders F. C. 2017. (First Touch Soccer Ser.). (ENG., Illus.). 24p. (J). (gr. k-3). 23.93 (978-1-59953-869-3(5)) Norwood Hse. Pr.

—Toronto F. C. 2017. (First Touch Soccer Ser.). (ENG., Illus.). 24p. (J). (gr. k-3). 23.93 (978-1-59953-870-9(9)) Norwood Hse. Pr.

—The World Cup. Kennedy, Mike, ed. 2003. (Watts History of Sports Ser.). (ENG., Illus.). 96p. (J). 34.50 (978-0-531-11957-0(2)) Scholastic Library Publishing.

Stone, Lynn M. Goalies. 2007. (Playmakers (High Interest) Ser.). (Illus.). 24p. (YA). (gr. 3-6). lib. bdg. 27.07 (978-1-60044-593-4(4)) Rourke Educational Media.

—Strikers. 2007. (Playmakers (High Interest) Ser.). (Illus.). 24p. (YA). (gr. 3-6). lib. bdg. 27.07 (978-1-60044-598-9(5)) Rourke Educational Media.

Suen, Anastasia. La historia del fútbol (the Story of Soccer) 2009. (Historia de los deportes (Sports History) Ser.). (SPA.). 24p. (gr. 2-2). 42.50 (978-1-61513-311-6(9), Editorial Buenas Letras) Rosen Publishing Group, Inc., The.

—The Story of Soccer. 2009. (Sports History Ser.). 24p. (gr. 2-2). 42.50 (978-1-60853-139-4(2), PowerKids Pr.) Rosen Publishing Group, Inc., The.

Sullivan, George. All about Soccer. 2005. (Illus.). 122p. (J). (gr. 4-8). reprint ed. pap. 10.00 (978-0-7567-9750-8(0)) DIANE Publishing Co.

Sutherland, Adam. Soccer Stars, 1 vol. 2012. (Celebrity Secrets Ser.). (ENG., Illus.). 24p. (J). (gr. 5-6). pap. 9.25 (978-1-4488-7086-8(0), 2607d305-7ed4-4a98-ac1b-074c9b273f90); lib. bdg. 26.27 (978-1-4488-7038-7(0), b3fb7826-dc2c-4152-b9e7-f4fa1b8f4409) Rosen Publishing Group, Inc., The. (PowerKids Pr.).

Swope, Bob. Teach'n Beginning Offensive Soccer Drills, Plays, Strategies, & Games Free Flow Handbook. 2013. 96p. pap. 19.95 (978-0-9911151-2-9(0)) Jacobob Pr., LLC.

Taylor, Trace. Soccer. Taylor, Trace, illus. 2009. (2G Sports Ser.). (ENG., Illus.). 16p. (J). (gr. k-2). pap. 9.60 (978-1-59301-878-8(9)) American Reading Co.

Teixeira, Thiago Jorge. Neymar. 2012. (Superstars of Soccer ENGLISH Ser.). (ENG., Illus.). 32p. (J). (gr. 4-7). lib. bdg. 19.95 (978-1-4222-2648-3(4)) Mason Crest.

Terrell, Brandon. Soccer Showdown: U. S. Women's Stunning 1999 World Cup Win. Garcia, Eduardo, illus. 2019. (Greatest Sports Moments Ser.). (ENG.). 32p. (J). (gr. 3-9). pap. 7.95 (978-1-5435-4222-6(0), 139120); lib. bdg. 31.32 (978-1-5435-4220-2(4), 139118) Capstone.

Thatcher Murcia, Rebecca. What Its Like to Be Marta Vieira. de la Vega, Eida, tr. 2010. (What It's Like to Be/Que se Siente al Ser Ser.). (ENG & SPA., Illus.). 32p. (J). (gr. -1-2). lib. bdg. 25.70 (978-1-58415-852-3(2)) Mitchell Lane Pubs.

Thomas, Mark. The Maracana: World's Largest Soccer Stadium. 2009. (Record-Breaking Structures Ser.). 24p. (gr. 1-2). 42.50 (978-1-60852-456-3(6), PowerKids Pr.) Rosen Publishing Group, Inc., The.

Torres, John A. Cristiano Ronaldo: Champion Soccer Star, 1 vol. 2017. (Sports Star Champions Ser.). (ENG.). 48p. (gr. 5-6). lib. bdg. 29.60 (978-0-7660-8688-3(7), e8c03239-ad53-44e6-8c61-64774db5f07a) Enslow Publishing, LLC.

—Lionel Messi: Top-Scoring Soccer Star, 1 vol. 2015. (Influential Latinos Ser.). (ENG.). 128p. (gr. 7-8). 38.93 (978-0-7660-7260-2(6), 36b8615d-70ae-4a99-9c7b-97d859458543) Enslow Publishing, LLC.

—Neymar: Champion Soccer Star, 1 vol. 2017. (Sports Star Champions Ser.). (ENG.). 48p. (gr. 5-6). pap. 12.70 (978-0-7660-8757-6(3), 39854981-c891-4f43-ace0-b96269ad1bbc); lib. bdg. 29.60 (978-0-7660-8694-4(1), d3203d5f-9c69-421a-b6a5-4d0d9c785a00) Enslow Publishing, LLC.

—Soccer Star Cristiano Ronaldo, 1 vol. 2014. (Goal! Latin Stars of Soccer Ser.). (ENG.). 48p. (gr. 4-6). 30.60 (978-1-62285-222-2(2), c2c70be1-411e-4860-821e-483cf75a58fb) Enslow Publishing, LLC.

—Soccer Star Lionel Messi, 1 vol. 2014. (Goal! Latin Stars of Soccer Ser.). (ENG.). 48p. (gr. 4-6). 30.60 (978-1-62285-221-5(4), 427fa743-98da-4553-b025-ee82f93b8fff) Enslow Publishing, LLC.

—Soccer Star Ronaldinho, 1 vol. 2014. (Goal! Latin Stars of Soccer Ser.). (ENG.). 48p. (gr. 4-6). 30.60 (978-1-62285-223-9(0), 8b6b8cc2-18fd-47a7-93a5-ddea11edbaf2) Enslow Publishing, LLC.

Trollinger, Patsi B. Thrill in The 'Ville. Thompson, Elizabeth, illus. 2012. 128p. (J). pap. 6.99 (978-0-9836106-1-8(4)) Benjamin Pr.

Trusdell, Brian. Neymar: Soccer Superstar. 2017. (Playmakers Set 6 Ser.). (ENG., Illus.). 32p. (J). (gr. 2-6). lib. bdg. 32.79 (978-1-5321-1150-1(9), 25876, SportsZone) ABDO Publishing Co.

—12 Reasons to Love Soccer. 2018. (Sports Report). (ENG., Illus.). 32p. (J). (gr. 3-6). 32.80 (978-1-63235-430-3(6), 13793, 12-Story Library) Bookstaves, LLC.

Turner, Tracy. Soccer Stars. 2015. (Head-To-Head Ser.). (ENG., Illus.). 24p. (gr. 3-8). 28.50 (978-1-62588-154-0(1)) Black Rabbit Bks.

Uschan, Michael V. David Beckham, 1 vol. 2008. (People in the News Ser.). (ENG., Illus.). 112p. (gr. 7-7). lib. bdg. 41.03 (978-1-4205-0054-7(6), 97f25fba-e220-42e2-b30c-36dbb6bca64e, Lucent Pr.) Greenhaven Publishing LLC.

Valay, Ana Patricia. Giovani Dos Santos. 2012. (Superstars of Soccer SPANISH Ser.). 32p. (J). (gr. 4). (SPA.). 19.95 (978-1-4222-2597-4(6)); (ENG., Illus.). lib. bdg. 19.95 (978-1-4222-2650-6(6)) Mason Crest.

Valay, Ana Patricia & Sandoval, Ana Valay. Arnoldo Iguaran. 2012. (Superstars of Soccer ENGLISH Ser.). (ENG., Illus.). 32p. (J). (gr. 4-7). lib. bdg. 19.95 (978-1-4222-2663-6(8)) Mason Crest.

Vazquez, Gustavo & Vargas, Fredrico. Chicharito Hernndez. 2012. (Superstars of Soccer ENGLISH Ser.). (Illus.). 32p. (J). (gr. 4). 19.95 (978-1-4222-2660-5(3)) Mason Crest.

Vazquez-Lozano, Gustavo. Ivan Cordoba. 2012. (Superstars of Soccer ENGLISH Ser.). (ENG., Illus.). 32p. (J). (gr. 4-7). lib. bdg. 19.95 (978-1-4222-2652-0(2)) Mason Crest.

Vazquez-Lozano, Gustavo & Benard, Federico Vargas. Luis Suarez. 2012. (Superstars of Soccer ENGLISH Ser.). (ENG., Illus.). 32p. (J). (gr. 4-7). lib. bdg. 19.95 (978-1-4222-2656-8(5)) Mason Crest.

Velázquez de León, Mauricio. Top Soccer Tournaments Around the World, 1 vol. 2009. (World Soccer Bks.). (ENG., Illus.). 64p. (YA). (gr. 5-5). lib. bdg. 37.13 (978-1-4358-9140-1(6), a9b9801e-dbe8-452d-8f55-aad9d7113d78, Rosen Reference) Rosen Publishing Group, Inc., The.

—20 Soccer Legends, 1 vol. 2010. (World Soccer Bks.). (ENG., Illus.). 64p. (YA). (gr. 5-5). lib. bdg. 37.13 (978-1-4358-9136-4(8), 64593dbc-9d22-4ae5-88ff-4e950d308951, Rosen Reference) Rosen Publishing Group, Inc., The.

Waddell, Martin. Football Spy: Band 13/Topaz. Keylock, Andy & Veres, Laszlo, illus. 2007. (Collins Big Cat Ser.). (ENG.). 40p. (J). (gr. 2-3). pap. 10.99 (978-0-00-723086-0(9)) HarperCollins Pubs. Ltd. GBR. Dist: Independent Pubs. Group.

Walker, Niki & Dann, Sarah. Fútbol en Acción. 2005. (Deportes en Accion Ser.). (SPA., Illus.). 32p. (J). (gr. 6-9). pap. (978-0-7787-8616-0(1)) Crabtree Publishing Co.

—Le Soccer. Briere, Marie-Josee, tr. from ENG. rev. ed. 2007. (Sans Limites Ser.). (FRE., Illus.). 32p. (J). (gr. 1-7). pap. 9.95 (978-2-89579-124-9(4)) Bayard Canada Livres CAN. Dist: Crabtree Publishing Co.

Wambach, Abby. Forward: My Story Young Readers' Edition. (ENG.). 224p. (J). (gr. 3-7). 2017. pap. 7.99 (978-0-06-245793-6(4)) 2016. 16.99 (978-0-06-245792-9(6)) HarperCollins Pubs. (HarperCollins).

Wandersman, Aldo. Ronaldinho. 2012. (Superstars of Soccer SPANISH Ser.). (Illus.). 32p. (J). (gr. 4). (SPA.). 19.95 (978-1-4222-2604-9(2)); (ENG., lib. bdg. 19.95 (978-1-4222-2657-5(3)) Mason Crest.

—Ronaldo. 2012. (Superstars of Soccer ENGLISH Ser.). (ENG., Illus.). 32p. (J). (gr. 4-7). lib. bdg. 19.95 (978-1-4222-2658-2(1)) Mason Crest.

Ward, Adam. Motson's National Obsession: The Greatest Football Trivia Book Ever. 2004. (Illus.). 200p. (978-1-86074-601-7(2)) Sanctuary Publishing, Ltd.

Watson, Galadriel. David Beckham. 2007. (Remarkable People Ser.). (Illus.). 24p. (J). (gr. 3-7). pap. 8.95 (978-1-59036-642-4(5)) Weigl Pubs., Inc.

Watson, Galadriel Findlay. David Beckham. 2007. (Remarkable People Ser.). (Illus.). 24p. (J). (gr. 3-7). lib. bdg. 24.45 (978-1-59036-641-7(7)) Weigl Pubs., Inc.

Watson, Stephanie. The Science Behind Soccer, Volleyball, Cycling, & Other Popular Sports. 2016. (Science of the Summer Olympics Ser.). (ENG., Illus.). 32p. (J). (gr. 3-9). lib. bdg. 28.65 (978-1-4914-8160-8(9), 130639, Capstone Pr.) Capstone.

Wendorff, Anne. Soccer. 2009. (My First Sports Ser.). (ENG., Illus.). 24p. (J). (gr. 2-5). lib. bdg. 26.95 (978-1-60014-329-8(6), Blastoff! Readers) Bellwether Media.

Wetzel, Dan. Epic Athletes: Alex Morgan. Thomas, Cory, illus. 2020. (Epic Athletes Ser.: 2). (ENG.). 176p. (J). pap. 8.99 (978-1-250-25071-1(4), 900195184) Square Fish.

Wheeler, Jill C. David Beckham. 2007. (Awesome Athletes Set 4 Ser.). (Illus.). 32p. (gr. 4-7). 27.07 (978-1-59928-304-3(2), Checkerboard Library) ABDO Publishing Co.

Whitfield, David. World Cup. (We Are the Champions Ser.). (J). 2019. (ENG.). 32p. (gr. 4-7). pap. 13.95 (978-1-7911-0583-9(1)) 2019. (ENG., Illus.). 32p. (gr. 4-7). lib. bdg. 29.99 (978-1-7911-0050-6(3)) 2012. (978-1-61913-062-3(9)) 2012. pap. (978-1-61913-624-3(4)) 2007. (Illus.). 32p. (gr. 4-7). lib. bdg. 26.00 (978-1-59036-695-0(6)) 2007. (Illus.). 32p. (gr. 4-7). per. 9.95 (978-1-59036-696-7(4)) Weigl Pubs., Inc.

—The World Cup. 2017. (Illus.). 32p. (J). (978-1-5105-0858-3(9)) Lightbox, The.

Whiting, Jim. AC Milan. 2016. (J). (978-1-56660-846-6(5), Creative Education); (ENG.). 24p. (gr. 1-3). pap. 9.99 (978-1-62832-352-8(3), 20755, Creative Paperbacks); (ENG.). 48p. (gr. 4-7). pap. 12.00 (978-1-62832-195-1(4), 21055, Creative Paperbacks) Creative Co., The.

—Bayern Munich. (Soccer Stars Ser.). (ENG., (J). 2016. Illus.). 24p. (gr. 1-3). (978-1-60818-800-0(0), 20760, Creative Education) 2016. 48p. (gr. 4-7). pap. 12.00 (978-1-62832-192-0(X), 21046, Creative Paperbacks) 2015. (Illus.). 48p. (gr. 4-7). (978-1-60818-587-0(7), 21045, Creative Education) Creative Co., The.

—Boca Juniors. 2018. (Soccer Champions Ser.). (ENG.). 48p. (J). (gr. 3-6). (978-1-60818-977-9(5), 19965, Creative Education); pap. 12.00 (978-1-62832-604-8(2), 19971, Creative Paperbacks) Creative Co., The.

—David Beckham. 2012. (Role Model Athletes Ser.). 64p. (J). (gr. 7). 22.95 (978-1-4222-2708-4(1)) Mason Crest.

—FC Barcelona. (Soccer Stars Ser.). (ENG., (J). 2016. Illus.). 24p. (gr. 1-3). (978-1-60818-801-7(9), 20763, Creative Education) 2016. 48p. (gr. 4-7). pap. 12.00 (978-1-62832-191-3(1), 21043, Creative Paperbacks) 2015. (Illus.). 48p. (gr. 4-7). (978-1-60818-586-3(9), 21042, Creative Education) Creative Co., The.

—Flamengo. 2018. (Soccer Champions Ser.). (ENG.). 48p. (J). (gr. 3-6). (978-1-60818-979-3(1), 19967, Creative Education); pap. 12.00 (978-1-62832-606-2(9), 19972, Creative Paperbacks) Creative Co., The.

—La Galaxy. 2018. (Soccer Champions Ser.). (ENG.). 48p. (J). (gr. 3-6). pap. 12.00 (978-1-62832-607-9(7), 19973, Creative Paperbacks) Creative Co., The.

—LA Galaxy. 2018. (Soccer Champions Ser.). (ENG.). 48p. (J). (gr. 3-6). (978-1-60818-980-9(5), 19968, Creative Education) Creative Co., The.

—Liverpool FC. 2015. (Soccer Champions Ser.). (ENG., Illus.). 48p. (J). (gr. 4-7). (978-1-60818-588-7(5), 21048, Creative Education) Creative Co., The.

—Manchester United. (Soccer Stars Ser.). (ENG., (J). 2016. Illus.). 24p. (gr. 1-3). (978-1-60818-803-1(5), 20769, Creative Education) 2016. 48p. (gr. 4-7). pap. 12.00 (978-1-62832-194-4(6), 21052, Creative Paperbacks) 2015. (Illus.). 48p. (gr. 4-7). (978-1-60818-589-4(3), 21051, Creative Education) Creative Co., The.

—Real Madrid. 2015. (Soccer Champions Ser.). (ENG., Illus.). 48p. (J). (gr. 4-7). (978-1-60818-591-7(5), 21057, Creative Education) Creative Co., The.

—River Plate. 2018. (Soccer Champions Ser.). (ENG.). 48p. (J). (gr. 3-6). (978-1-60818-978-6(3), 19966, Creative Education); pap. 12.00 (978-1-62832-605-5(0), 19974, Creative Paperbacks) Creative Co., The.

—Santos FC. 2018. (Soccer Champions Ser.). (ENG.). 48p. (J). (gr. 3-6). (978-1-60818-981-6(3), 19969, Creative Education); pap. 12.00 (978-1-62832-608-6(5), 19975, Creative Paperbacks) Creative Co., The.

—Seattle Sounders FC. 2018. (Soccer Champions Ser.). (ENG.). 48p. (J). (gr. 3-6). (978-1-60818-982-3(1), 19970, Creative Education); pap. 12.00 (978-1-62832-609-3(3), 19976, Creative Paperbacks) Creative Co., The.

Williams, Cinthia Louise. The Flippin' Soccer Guide. 2003. (Illus.). 40p. (YA). 14.95 (978-0-9742500-0-7(7)) Flippin' Bks. LLC.

Williams, Heather. Soccer: A Guide for Players & Fans. 2019. (Sports Zone Ser.). (ENG., Illus.). 32p. (J). (gr. 3-6). pap. 7.95 (978-1-5435-7461-6(0), 140901); lib. bdg. 27.99 (978-1-5435-7429-6(7), 140714) Capstone.

Wingate, Brian. Soccer: Rules, Tips, Strategy, & Safety. (Sports from Coast to Coast Ser.). 48p. (gr. 6-6). 2009. 53.00 (978-1-60853-129-5(5), Rosen Reference) 2007. (ENG., Illus.). (J). lib. bdg. 34.47 (978-1-4042-0995-4(6), 1f7842d4-8c2f-4ff3-b8d4-c01a7f337b6c) Rosen Publishing Group, Inc., The.

Wiseman, Blaine. Soccer. 2010. (Record Breakers Ser.). (Illus.). 24p. (YA). (gr. 3-6). lib. bdg. 27.13 (978-1-61690-106-6(3)); (J). (gr. 4-6). pap. 12.95 (978-1-61690-107-3(1)) Weigl Pubs., Inc.

Woods, Mark & Owen, Ruth. Goal! 2010. (Top Score Maths Ser.). (Illus.). 32p. pap. (978-0-237-54279-5(X)) Evans Brothers, Ltd.

—Goal! Soccer Facts & Stats, 1 vol. 2011. (Top Score Math Ser.). (ENG., Illus.). 32p. (J). (gr. 4-5). lib. bdg. 29.27 (978-1-4339-5015-5(4), 8b988238-466a-4044-9a40-5d1ad3ae6974) Stevens, Gareth Publishing LLLP.

Woods, P. Improve Your Soccer Skills. 2004. (Superskills Ser.). (Illus.). 48p. (YA). (gr. 6-10). lib. bdg. 13.95 (978-0-88110-296-3(2)) EDC Publishing.

Woods, Sadie. It's Time for the Soccer Game, 1 vol. 2017. (Let's Tell Time Ser.). (ENG., Illus.). 24p. (J). (gr. 1-1). 25.27 (978-1-5081-5727-4(8), 5055753c-f6e5-48fe-8669-c681efe6d2fa, PowerKids Pr.) Rosen Publishing Group, Inc., The.

World Soccer Books, 8 vols., Set. Incl. Great Moments in World Cup History. Bailey, Diane. 2009. lib. bdg. 37.13 (978-1-4358-9139-5(2), 8954287c-690e-490c-84c9-30a94adec6bf, Rosen Reference); Great National Soccer Teams. Sommers, Annie Leah. 2010. lib. bdg. 37.13 (978-1-4358-9138-8(4), 114d9c49-1b2d-4002-98e9-020db89da664, Rosen Reference); Top Soccer Tournaments Around the World. Velázquez de León, Mauricio. 2009. lib. bdg. 37.13 (978-1-4358-9140-1(6), a9b9801e-dbe8-452d-8f55-aad9d7113d78, Rosen Reference); 20 Soccer Legends. Velázquez de León, Mauricio. 2010. lib. bdg. 37.13 (978-1-4358-9136-4(8), 64593dbc-9d22-4ae5-88ff-4e950d308951, Rosen Reference); 20 Soccer Superstars. Velázquez de León, Mauricio. 2010. lib. bdg. 37.13 (978-1-4358-9137-1(6), 05aa07bb-9362-49bf-a37e-f434f6939bf6); (YA). (gr. 5-5). (World Soccer Bks.). (ENG., Illus.). 64p. 2009. Set lib. bdg. 148.52 (978-1-4358-9141-8(4), 9febe5e8-ff2f-492a-ba9f-abac6ee326dc, Rosen Reference) Rosen Publishing Group, Inc., The.

Young-Brown, Fiona. Chelsea FC, 1 vol. 2019. (Soccer's Greatest Clubs Ser.). (ENG.). 64p. (gr. 5-5). pap. 16.28 (978-1-5026-5267-6(6), 7274b7ab-c5bd-41e3-b38f-8e9a49810bdf) Cavendish Square Publishing LLC.

Zweig, Eric. Absolute Expert: Soccer. 2018. (Absolute Expert Ser.). (Illus.). 112p. (J). (gr. 3-7). 14.99 (978-1-4263-3008-7(1)); (ENG., lib. bdg. 24.90 (978-1-4263-3009-4(X)) Disney Publishing Worldwide. (National Geographic Kids).

SOCCER—FICTION

Alexander, Kwame. Booked. (Crossover Ser.). (ENG.). (J). (gr. 5-7). 2019. 336p. pap. 9.99 (978-1-328-59630-7(3), 1731272) 2016. 320p. 16.99 (978-0-544-57098-6(7), 1612557) HarperCollins Pubs. (Clarion Bks.).

—Booked. 2016. lib. bdg. 29.40 (978-0-606-37992-2(4)) Turtleback.

Andrews, Phil. Own Goals. (ENG.). 320p. (J). pap. 16.95 (978-0-340-74821-3(4)) Hodder & Stoughton GBR. Dist: Trafalgar Square Publishing.

Arena, Felice & Kettle, Phil. Park Soccer. Gordon, Gus, illus. 2004. (J). (978-1-59336-366-6(4)) Mondo Publishing.

Battista, Brianna. I Want to Be a Referee, 1 vol. 2018. (What Do I Want to Be? Ser.). (ENG.). 24p. (gr. 1-1). 25.27 (978-1-5383-3003-6(2), 3910c6fe-6d27-4062-b153-7fa94d0e3984); pap. 9.25 (978-1-5383-3005-0(9), 0a560a34-3809-455d-a19c-ed4b62858761) Rosen Publishing Group, Inc., The. (PowerKids Pr.).

Beck, Adrian. Boot It. 2018. (Champion Charlies Ser.: 2). (ENG., Illus.). 144p. (J). (gr. 2-6). 13.99 (978-0-14-379126-3(5)) Random Hse. Australia AUS. Dist: Independent Pubs. Group.

—The Champion Charlies 4: The Grand Finale. 2018. (Champion Charlies Ser.: 4). (ENG.). 176p. (J). (gr. k-2). 15.99 (978-0-14-379130-0(3)) Random Hse. Australia AUS. Dist: Independent Pubs. Group.

—Knockout Cup. 2018. (Champion Charlies Ser.: 3). (ENG., Illus.). 176p. (J). (gr. k-2). 15.99 (978-0-14-379128-7(1)) Random Hse. Australia AUS. Dist: Independent Pubs. Group.

—Mix-Up. 2018. (Champion Charlies Ser.: 1). (Illus.). 176p. (J). (gr. 2-6). 13.99 (978-0-14-379124-9(9)) Random Hse. Australia AUS. Dist: Independent Pubs. Group.

Bedford, David. Soccer Camp. Brumpton, Keith, illus. 3rd ed. 2004. 80p. (978-1-877003-45-5(X)) Little Hare Bks. AUS. Dist: HarperCollins Pubs. Australia.

—The Soccer Machine, 1. Brumpton, Keith, illus. 2006. (Team Ser.). (ENG.). 68p. (J). (gr. 3-6). 17.44 (978-1-933605-00-5(6)) Kane Miller.

—The Soccer Machine. Brumpton, Keith, illus. 2003. 80p. (978-1-877003-26-4(3)) Little Hare Bks. AUS. Dist: HarperCollins Pubs. Australia.

—The Team Bind-up. 2007. (Illus.). 227p. (978-1-921272-04-2(X)) Little Hare Bks. AUS. Dist: HarperCollins Pubs. Australia.

—Top of the League. Brumpton, Keith, illus. 2nd ed. 2003. 80p. (978-1-877003-30-1(1)) Little Hare Bks. AUS. Dist: HarperCollins Pubs. Australia.

Benson, Donna. Spotlight on the Cupcakes: The Cupcakes Club #3. 2008. (ENG.). 115p. (J). pap. 7.95 (978-0-9799159-2-5(9)) Pink Lemonade, LLC.

Berenstain, Jan, et al. The Berenstain Bears Play a Good Game, 1 vol. 2009. (Berenstain Bears/Living Lights: a Faith Story Ser.). (ENG., Illus.). 32p. (J). (gr. -1-2). pap. 4.99 (978-0-310-71252-7(1)) Zonderkidz.

Berenstain, Mike. We Love Soccer! 2016. (Berenstain Bears — I Can Read Ser.). (J). lib. bdg. 13.55 (978-0-606-38123-9(6)) Turtleback.

Berenstain, Stan, et al. The Berenstain Bears Play a Fair Game, 1 vol. 2018. (I Can Read! / Berenstain Bears / Living Lights: a Faith Story Ser.). (ENG., Illus.). 32p. (J). pap. 4.99 (978-0-310-76024-5(0)) Zonderkidz.

Berg, Dorlisa H. Fat Freddy Gets Fit. 2012. 158p. pap. 19.99 (978-1-4797-6309-2(8)) Xlibris Corp.

Berry, Andrea. Goalie: The Dynamite Diaries. 2003. 144p. (YA). pap. 11.95 (978-0-595-27678-3(4)) iUniverse, Inc.

Bildner, Phil. The Soccer Fence: A Story of Friendship, Hope, & Apartheid in South Africa. Watson, Jesse Joshua, illus. 2014. 40p. (J). (gr. 1-3). 18.99 (978-0-399-24790-3(4), G.P. Putnam's Sons Books for Young Readers) Penguin Young Readers Group.

Blackburn, Sheila M. Football Crazy: Sam's Football Stories - Set a, Book 1. 2015. (ENG., Illus.). 34p. pap. (978-1-903853-01-6(X)) Brilliant Pubns.

Bloor, Edward. Tangerine. (ENG.). 320p. (gr. 5-7). 2007. (YA). 18.00 (978-0-15-201246-5(X), 1189264) 2006. (Illus.). (J). pap. 9.99 (978-0-15-205780-0(3), 252998) HarperCollins Pubs. (Clarion Bks.).

Boelts, Maribeth. El Futbol Me Hace Feliz (Happy Like Soccer) Castillo, Lauren, illus. 2016. (ENG & SPA.). 32p. (J). (gr. k-4). 17.20 (978-0-606-39111-5(8)) Turtleback.

—Happy Like Soccer. Castillo, Lauren, illus. 2014. (ENG.). 32p. (J). (gr. k-4). pap. 7.99 (978-0-7636-7049-8(9)) Candlewick Pr.

Bosco, Don & Boo, Benedict. Superkicks: Dare to Dream. 2018. (ENG.). 1p. (J). (gr. k-2). pap. 12.95 (978-981-4794-49-7(X)) Marshall Cavendish International (Asia) Private Ltd. SGP. Dist: Independent Pubs. Group.

—Superkicks: Time to Play. 2017. (ENG., Illus.). 88p. (J). (gr. 2-4). pap. 12.95 (978-981-4771-41-2(4)) Marshall Cavendish International (Asia) Private Ltd. SGP. Dist: Independent Pubs. Group.

Bossley, Michele Martin. Kicker, 1 vol. 2007. (Orca Sports Ser.). (ENG.). 152p. (J). (gr. 4-8). per. 10.95 (978-1-55143-706-4(6)) Orca Bk. Pubs. USA.

Bowen, Fred. Go for the Goal!, 1 vol. 2012. (Fred Bowen Sports Story Ser.: 17). 128p. (J). (gr. 2-6). pap. 6.99 (978-1-56145-632-1(2)) Peachtree Publishing Co. Inc.

—Out of Bounds, 1 vol. 2015. (Fred Bowen Sports Story Ser.: 20). 144p. (J). (gr. 2-6). pap. 6.95 (978-1-56145-894-3(5)) Peachtree Publishing Co. Inc.

—Soccer Team Upset, 1 vol. 2009. (Fred Bowen Sports Story Ser.: 10). 128p. (J). (gr. 2-6). pap. 6.99 (978-1-56145-495-2(8)) Peachtree Publishing Co. Inc.

Brenda Seabrooke. Jerry on the Line. 2010. 132p. pap. 10.95 (978-1-4401-8766-7(5)) iUniverse, Inc.

Bryant, Anne. The Fantasy Soccer Wall. 2015. (Race Further with Reading Ser.). (ENG., Illus.). 48p. (J). (gr. 3-3). (978-0-7787-2061-4(6)) Crabtree Publishing Co.

Burton, Margie, et al. New Soccer Nets. 2011. (Early Connections Ser.). (J). (978-1-61672-529-7(X)) Benchmark Education Co.

Carey, Becky. Wilma Goes to the Hospital. 2007. (Illus.). (J). 9.95 (978-0-9791331-0-7(6)) Carey, Rebecca.

Carlson-Berne, Emma. Under Pressure. 2013. (Counterattack Ser.). (ENG.). 104p. (YA). (gr. 6-12). pap. 7.95 (978-1-4677-0718-3(X), a24134f3-ade8-4ba8-a4d0-709bb61425e1); lib. bdg. 27.99 (978-1-4677-0303-1(6), b0cbbeaf-429b-4c39-a3d0-609184a04d33) Lerner Publishing Group. (Darby Creek).

Carman, Patrick. The Walnut Cup. James, Steve, illus. 2009. (Elliot's Park Ser.: Bk. 3). 80p. (J). (gr. 1-5). 8.99 (978-0-545-01932-3(X), Orchard Bks.) Scholastic, Inc.

Carmona, Adela. The Boy Who Could See. Chapman, Robert E., illus. 2008. 32p. pap. 24.95 (978-1-60672-697-6(8)) PublishAmerica, Inc.

Carr, Patrick W. The Legend's Granddaughter: Not Quite Super, Book 1. Dabbs, Douglas, illus. 2007. 281p. (J). pap. (978-0-9793168-0-7(4)) NQSBks.

Chambers, Sally, et al. Waldo'n Ennill y Dydd. 2005. (WEL., Illus.). 32p. pap. (978-1-85596-658-1(1)) Dref Wen.

Childs, Rob. Keeper's Ball. Sheppard, Kate, illus. 2005. (Corgi Pups Ser.). (ENG.). 64p. (J). pap. 7.50 (978-0-552-55030-7(2)) Transworld Publishers Ltd. GBR. Dist: Independent Pubs. Group.

Choat, Beth. Soccerland, 0 vols. 2012. (International Sports Academy Ser.: 0). (ENG., Illus.). 242p. (YA). (gr. 7-12). pap.

8.99 (978-0-7614-6249-1(X), 9780761462491, Skyscape) Amazon Publishing.

Choyce, Lesley. Sudden Impact. 2006. (Orca Currents Ser.). 104p. (gr. 5-9). 19.95 (978-0-7569-6876-2(3)) Perfection Learning Corp.

Chrisotpher, Matt. Top Wing. 2005. (Sports Classics III Ser.). 154p. (J). lib. bdg. 15.00 (978-1-59054-776-2(4)) Fitzgerald Bks.

Christopher, Matt. Comeback Challenge. 2008. (New Matt Christopher Sports Library). 160p. (J). (gr. 4-6). lib. bdg. 26.60 (978-1-59953-211-0(5)) Norwood Hse. Pr.

—Heads Up. Vasconcellos, Daniel, illus. 2003. (Soccer Cats Ser.: Bk. 6). 54p. (J). (gr. 1-4). 12.65 (978-0-7569-3904-5(6)) Perfection Learning Corp.

—Soccer 'Cats: Heads Up! 6th ed. 2003. (ENG., Illus.). 64p. (J). (gr. 1-4). pap. 8.99 (978-0-316-16497-9(6)) Little, Brown Bks. for Young Readers.

—Soccer 'Cats: Kick It! Vasconcellos, Daniel, illus. 2003. (ENG.). 64p. (J). (gr. 1-4). pap. 8.99 (978-0-316-73808-8(5)) Little, Brown Bks. for Young Readers.

—Soccer 'Cats: Master of Disaster. Vasconcellos, Daniel, illus. 2003. (ENG.). 64p. (J). (gr. 1-4). pap. 8.99 (978-0-316-16498-6(4)) Little, Brown Bks. for Young Readers.

—Soccer 'Cats: Switch Play! Vasconcellos, Daniel, illus. 9th ed. 2003. (ENG.). 64p. (J). (gr. 1-4). pap. 8.99 (978-0-316-73807-1(7)) Little, Brown Bks. for Young Readers.

—Soccer 'Cats: You Lucky Dog. Vasconcellos, Daniel, illus. 8th ed. 2003. (ENG.). 64p. (J). (gr. 1-4). pap. 8.99 (978-0-316-73805-7(0)) Little, Brown Bks. for Young Readers.

—Soccer Halfback. l.t. ed. 2007. (New Matt Christopher Sports Library). 160p. (J). (gr. 4-6). lib. bdg. 26.60 (978-1-59953-110-6(0)) Norwood Hse. Pr.

—Soccer Scoop. 2007. (New Matt Christopher Sports Library). 133p. (J). (gr. 4-6). lib. bdg. 26.60 (978-1-59953-117-5(8)) Norwood Hse. Pr.

—You Lucky Dog. Vasconcellos, Daniel, illus. 2003. (Soccer Cats Ser.: Bk. 8). 49p. (J). (gr. 2-4). 12.65 (978-0-7569-3907-6(0)) Perfection Learning Corp.

Clark, Sherryl & Perry, Ellyse. Ellyse Perry: Double Time. 2017. (Ellyse Perry Ser.: 4). 160p. (J). (gr. 4-7). 13.99 (978-0-14-378130-1(8)) Random Hse. Australia AUS. Dist: Independent Pubs. Group.

—Ellyse Perry: Winning Touch. 2017. (Ellyse Perry Ser.: 3). 160p. (J). (gr. 4-7). 13.99 (978-0-14-378128-8(6)) Random Hse. Australia AUS. Dist: Independent Pubs. Group.

Clinch, Kelly. The Soccer Princess. 2008. (Illus.). (J). 10.95 (978-0-9800835-1-4(6)) Clinch Media.

Coleman, K. R. The Freshman. 2018. (Kick! Ser.). (ENG.). 112p. (YA). (gr. 6-12). 25.32 (978-1-5415-0020-4(2), a463568b-d9ed-4186-a3bf-7295efd14ec1, Darby Creek) Lerner Publishing Group.

—The Recruit. 2018. (Kick! Ser.). (ENG.). 104p. (YA). (gr. 6-12). pap. 7.99 (978-1-5415-0033-4(4), 8714fcaf-1a32-43d7-a256-c6d64123d3d0); lib. bdg. 25.32 (978-1-5415-0023-5(7), 12d0d5b1-c032-4689-a2b7-81d88d28de4b) Lerner Publishing Group. (Darby Creek).

Cooper, Ilene. Absolutely Lucy #4: Lucy on the Ball. Merrell, David, illus. 2011. (Lucy Ser.: 4). 112p. (J). (gr. 1-4). 5.99 (978-0-375-85559-7(9), Random Hse. Bks. for Young Readers) Random Hse. Children's Bks.

—Lucy on the Ball, 4. Merrell, David, illus. 2011. (Absolutely Lucy Ser.). (ENG.). 112p. (J). (gr. 2-4). lib. bdg. 17.44 (978-0-375-95559-4(3)) Random House Publishing Group.

Courtney, Richard, illus. Reds Against Blues! 2016. 22p. (J). (978-1-4806-9772-0(9)) Random Hse., Inc.

Cousins, Lucy. Maisy Plays Soccer. 2014. (Maisy First Experiences Ser.). lib. bdg. 17.20 (978-0-606-35155-3(8)) Turtleback.

—Maisy Plays Soccer: A Maisy First Experiences Book. Cousins, Lucy, illus. 2014. (Maisy Ser.). (ENG., Illus.). 32p. (J). (gr. -1-2). pap. 7.99 (978-0-7636-7238-6(6)) Candlewick Pr.

Coy, John. Eyes on the Goal, Bk. 2. 2012. (4 For 4 Ser.: 2). (ENG.). 192p. (J). (gr. 3-7). pap. 16.99 (978-0-312-65922-6(9), 900070508) Square Fish.

Crespo, Ana. The Sock Thief. 2016. (Av2 Fiction Readalong 2017 Ser.). (ENG.). (J). (gr. -1-2). 34.28 (978-1-4896-5329-1(5), AV2 by Weigl) Weigl Pubs., Inc.

Crowley, Kieran. The Mighty Dynamo. 2018. (ENG.). 384p. (J). pap. 9.99 (978-1-250-12952-9(4), 900176093) Square Fish.

Cunningham, Elaine. Ethan, a Soccer Player for Jesus. Valliant, Kristi, illus. 2010. 32p. (J). (978-0-8341-2486-8(6)) Beacon Hill Pr. of Kansas City.

Dakota, Heather. Emma's Very Busy Week. Panaccione, Nancy, illus. 2009. 31p. (J). (978-0-545-17227-1(6)) Scholastic, Inc.

Davies, Elgan Philip. Cic O'r Smotyn. 2005. (WEL., Illus.). 56p. pap. (978-1-902416-18-2(X)) Cymdeithas Lyfrau Ceredigion.

DiDomenico, Allison. You Can Do It, Fiona! 2010. 28p. pap. 12.95 (978-1-4490-9913-8(0)) AuthorHouse.

Diersch, Sandra. Play On, 1 vol. 2004. (Lorimer Sports Stories Ser.). (ENG.). 118p. (J). (gr. 4-8). 16.95 (978-1-55028-857-5(1), 857) James Lorimer & Co. Ltd., Pubs. CAN. Dist: Formac Lorimer Bks. Ltd.

Douglass Thom, Kara. Soccer Girl Cassie's Story: Teamwork Is the Goal. Seatter, Pamela, illus. 2014. (Go! Go! Sports Girls Ser.). (ENG.). 32p. (J). (gr. k-2). pap. 4.99 (978-1-940731-00-1(3)) Dream Big Toy Co.

Doyle, Malachy & Parsons, Garry. Spooky Soccer (Reading Ladder Level 3) Parsons, Garry, illus. 2nd ed. 2016. (Reading Ladder Level 3 Ser.). (ENG., Illus.). 48p. (gr. k-2). 4.99 (978-1-4052-8245-1(2), Reading Ladder) Farshore GBR. Dist: HarperCollins Pubs.

Dungy, Tony & Dungy, Lauren. Justin & the Bully: Ready-To-Read Level 2. Brantley-Newton, Vanessa, illus. 2012. (Team Dungy Ser.). (ENG.). 32p. (J). (gr. k-2). pap. 4.99 (978-1-4424-5718-8(X), Simon Spotlight) Simon Spotlight.

—Maria Finds Courage: A Team Dungy Story about Soccer. 2018. (Team Dungy Ser.). (ENG., Illus.). 32p. (J). (gr. 1-4). 16.99 (978-0-7369-7323-6(0), 6973236) Harvest Hse. Pubs.

Esckilsen, Erik E. Offsides. 2004. (ENG.). 176p. (J). (gr. 5-7). tchr. ed. 15.00 (978-0-618-46284-1(8), 543211, Clarion Bks.) HarperCollins Pubs.

Feinstein, John. Benchwarmers. 2019. (Benchwarmers Ser.: 1). (ENG.). 320p. (J). 16.99 (978-0-374-31203-9(6), 900198272, Farrar, Straus & Giroux (BYR)) Farrar, Straus & Giroux.

Fergus, Maureen. The Day Dad Joined My Soccer Team. Lowery, Mike, illus. 2018. (ENG.). 32p. (J). (gr. -1-2). 16.99 (978-1-77138-654-8(1)) Kids Can Pr., Ltd. CAN. Dist: Hachette Bk. Group.

FitzGerald, Dawn. Soccer Chick Rules. 2007. (ENG.). 160p. (J). (gr. 5-9). per. 16.99 (978-0-312-37662-8(6), 900048593) Square Fish.

Flint, Shamini. Ten: A Soccer Story. 2019. (ENG.). 176p. (J). (gr. 5-7). pap. 7.99 (978-1-328-59632-1(X), 1731316, Clarion Bks.) HarperCollins Pubs.

Foreman, Michael. Wonder Goal! Foreman, Michael, illus. 2010. (ENG., Illus.). 32p. (J). (gr. k-2). pap. 12.99 (978-1-84270-934-4(8)) Andersen Pr. GBR. Dist: Independent Pubs. Group.

Fox, R. J. Stuart & His Incredibly Obnoxious Magical Book: Soccer, 1 vol. 2009. 86p. pap. 19.95 (978-1-4489-9833-3(6)) America Star Bks.

Furgang, Kathy. Shrimp Joins the Team & Chaparro se une al Equipo: 6 English, 6 Spanish Adaptations. 2011. (ENG & SPA.). (J). 75.00 net. (978-1-4108-5651-7(8)) Benchmark Education Co.

Gallo, Tina. Olivia Plays Soccer. 2013. (Olivia Ready-To-Read Level 1 Ser.). lib. bdg. 13.55 (978-0-606-32060-3(1)) Turtleback.

Giff, Patricia Reilly. Soccer Song. Sims, Blanche, illus. 2008. (ENG.). 24p. (J). (gr. k-2). pap. 4.99 (978-0-15-206565-2(2), 1199543, Clarion Bks.) HarperCollins Pubs.

Gomes, Alexandre de Castro. Folclore de Chuteiras. Visca, illus. 2014. (POR.). 67p. (J). (978-85-7596-341-8(4)) Editora Peiropolis Ltda.

Gorrell, Nancy. Corey's Story. 2007. (ENG., Illus.). 96p. (J). (gr. 2-5). per. 6.99 (978-1-84550-258-4(2), 16889563-d370-49af-98d4-d01b97170712) Christian Focus Pubns. GBR. Dist: Baker & Taylor Publisher Services (BTPS).

Green, Tim. Deep Zone. 2012. (Football Genius Ser.: 5). (ENG.). 304p. (J). (gr. 3-7). pap. 7.99 (978-0-06-201245-6(2), HarperCollins) HarperCollins Pubs.

Guest, Jacqueline. Soccer Star!, 1 vol. 2003. (Lorimer Sports Stories Ser.: 61). (ENG.). 104p. (J). (gr. 4-8). 16.95 (978-1-55028-789-9(3), 789) James Lorimer & Co. Ltd., Pubs. CAN. Dist: Formac Lorimer Bks. Ltd.

Guillain, Adam & Steiner, Elke. Bella's Brazilian Football, 1 vol. Steiner, Elke, illus. 2007. (Bella Balistica Ser.). (ENG., Illus.). 32p. (J). (gr. k-2). pap. 8.95 (978-1-84059-488-1(8)) Milet Publishing.

Hamley, Dennis. Beautiful Games. Fenoughty, Charles, illus. 2004. 104p. per. (978-1-904529-13-2(5), Back to Front) Solidus.

Hamm, Mia. Winners Never Quit! Thompson, Carol, illus. 2006. (ENG.). 32p. (J). (gr. -1-2). pap. 7.99 (978-0-06-074052-8(3), HarperCollins) HarperCollins Pubs.

Hardcastle, Michael. Hit It!, 1 vol. Moulder, Bob, illus. 2006. (Graphic Quest Ser.). (ENG.). 88p. (J). (gr. 3-8). per. 6.95 (978-1-59889-164-5(2), 86490, Stone Arch Bks.) Capstone.

Harrison, Paul. Billy on the Ball. Raga, Silvia, illus. 2010. 32p. pap. (978-1-84089-634-3(5)) Zero to Ten, Ltd.

Haselhurst, Maureen. The Emperor's New Uniform. Kennedy, Kelly, illus. 2015. (Tadpoles: Fairytale Twists Ser.). (ENG.). 32p. (J). (gr. 1-2). (978-0-7787-1933-5(2)) Crabtree Publishing Co.

Hazuka, Tom. Last Chance for First. 2008. 296p. (YA). (gr. 9-18). pap. 8.95 (978-0-9798824-0-1(0)) Brown Barn Bks.

Hegarty, Pat. If I Were a... Soccer Star. Pope, Liz & Pope, Kate, illus. 2008. (If I Were A Ser.). 10p. (J). (gr. -1-k). bds. 6.95 (978-1-58925-835-8(5)) Tiger Tales.

Heller, Alyson. Soccer Day: Ready-To-Read Level 1. Björkman, Steve, illus. 2009. (After-School Sports Club Ser.). (ENG.). 32p. (J). (gr. -1-1). pap. 4.99 (978-1-4169-9410-7(6), Simon Spotlight) Simon Spotlight.

Hellman, Charles. Adventures in SportsLand - the Soccer Bully (with accompanying CD) Tirilli, Robert, illus. 2008. (Adventures in SportsLand: the Bully Ser.). 32p. (gr. -1-3). pap. 19.95 (978-0-935938-26-5(5)) Stogo, Malcolm Assocs.

Herrera, Juan Felipe. Featherless: Desplumado (English & Spanish Edition), 1 vol. Cuevas, Ernesto, Jr., illus. 2013.Tr. of Desplumado. (ENG.). 32p. (J). (gr. k-3). pap. 11.95 (978-0-89239-303-9(3), leelowcbp) Lee & Low Bks., Inc.

Higgins, Chris. The Secrets Club: No Match for Dani. 3rd ed. 2016. (Secrets Club Ser.: 3). 176p. (J). (gr. 2-4). pap. 10.99 (978-0-14-133524-7(6)) Penguin Bks., Ltd. GBR. Dist: Independent Pubs. Group.

Higgins, M. G. Blow Out. 2013. (Counterattack Ser.). (ENG.). 112p. (YA). (gr. 6-12). pap. 7.95 (978-1-4677-0717-6(1), 2f5d4845-9305-4304-91c3-4e5048d72fe8); lib. bdg. 27.99 (978-1-4677-0302-4(8), 97be20cb-4713-4506-a1f6-2cda47e61ed3) Lerner Publishing Group. (Darby Creek).

—Offside. 2013. (Counterattack Ser.). (ENG.). 112p. (YA). (gr. 6-12). lib. bdg. 27.99 (978-1-4677-0305-5(2), eebd7605-2ab7-4e6c-8ed1-f31d88c43b74, Darby Creek) Lerner Publishing Group.

Hillert, Margaret. It's a Good Game, Dear Dragon. Schimmell, David, illus. 2009. (BeginningtoRead Ser.). 32p. (J). (gr. k-2). lib. bdg. 22.60 (978-1-59953-293-6(X)) Norwood Hse. Pr.

—It's a Good Game, Dear Dragon (Es un Buen Juego, Querido Dragon) Del Risco, Eida, tr. from ENG. Schimmell, David, illus. 2010. (BeginningtoRead Ser.). (SPA & ENG.). 32p. (J). (gr. k-2). lib. bdg. 22.60 (978-1-59953-362-9(6)) Norwood Hse. Pr.

Hinks, Roy H. Cybo Soccer & Heavens Above. 2011. 116p. pap. 13.32 (978-1-4567-7327-4(5)) AuthorHouse.

Hoena, Blake A. Spotlight Striker, 1 vol. Sandoval, Gerardo, illus. 2010. (Sports Illustrated Kids Graphic Novels Ser.). (ENG.). 56p. (J). (gr. 3-8). 26.65 (978-1-4342-2128-5(8), 102858); pap. 7.19 (978-1-4342-2787-4(1), 114054) Capstone. (Stone Arch Bks.).

Holm, Jennifer L. & Holm, Matthew. Captain Disaster. 2012. (Squish Ser.: 4). lib. bdg. 17.20 (978-0-606-26812-7(X)) Turtleback.

—Squish #4: Captain Disaster. Holm, Jennifer L. & Holm, Matthew, illus. 2012. (Squish Ser.: 4). (Illus.). 96p. (J). (gr. 2-5). pap. 6.99 (978-0-375-84392-1(2)) Penguin Random Hse. LLC.

Hueller, Patrick. Archenemy. 2013. (Counterattack Ser.). (ENG.). 112p. (YA). (gr. 6-12). lib. bdg. 27.99 (978-1-4677-0306-2(0), 216dd675-0b23-439f-a7a1-9e1be6e375cf, Darby Creek) Lerner Publishing Group.

—The Beast. 2013. (Counterattack Ser.). (ENG.). 112p. (YA). (gr. 6-12). pap. 7.95 (978-1-4677-0716-9(3), 3d0b5d44-6e68-4d43-9089-49da6cd0b86c); lib. bdg. 27.99 (978-1-4677-0301-7(X), f43b90d2-4382-4eb0-86e1-ed1610e913d8) Lerner Publishing Group. (Darby Creek).

Humann, Amanda. Out of Sync. 2013. (Counterattack Ser.). (ENG.). 104p. (YA). (gr. 6-12). lib. bdg. 27.99 (978-1-4677-0304-8(4), 326d0f2f-4de4-40d5-baf1-bfa40c87ed06, Darby Creek) Lerner Publishing Group.

Janovitz, Marilyn. Score One More. 2020. (I Like to Read Ser.). (Illus.). 32p. (J). (gr. -1-3). 15.99 (978-0-8234-4514-1(3)) Holiday Hse., Inc.

Javaherbin, Mina. Goal! Ford, A. G., illus. 2012. (ENG.). 40p. (J). (gr. 1-4). pap. 8.99 (978-0-7636-5822-9(7)) Candlewick Pr.

—Soccer Star. Alarcao, Renato, illus. 2019. (ENG.). 40p. (J). (gr. k-3). 7.99 (978-1-5362-0713-2(6)) Candlewick Pr.

Joven, C. C. Soccer Score. López, Alex, illus. 2017. (Sports Illustrated Kids Starting Line Readers Ser.). (ENG.). 32p. (J). (gr. -1-1). pap. 3.95 (978-1-4965-4258-8(4), 133942); lib. bdg. 22.65 (978-1-4965-4251-9(7), 133930) Capstone. (Stone Arch Bks.).

Kann, Victoria. Pinkalicious: Soccer Star. Kann, Victoria, illus. 2012. (I Can Read Level 1 Ser.). (ENG., Illus.). 32p. (J). (gr. -1-3). 17.99 (978-0-06-198965-0(7), HarperCollins) HarperCollins Pubs.

—Soccer Star. 2012. (Pinkalicious I Can Read Ser.). (J). lib. bdg. 13.55 (978-0-606-26280-4(6)) Turtleback.

Kaplan, Michael. Betty Bunny Wants a Goal. Jorisch, Stéphane, illus. 2014. (Betty Bunny Ser.). 32p. (J). (gr. -1-k). 17.99 (978-0-8037-3859-1(5), Dial Bks) Penguin Young Readers Group.

Keats, Israel. The Heir. 2018. (Kick! Ser.). (ENG.). 104p. (YA). (gr. 6-12). pap. 7.99 (978-1-5415-0031-0(8), 77235fd9-4dc6-471c-ae90-65c49b54210a); 25.32 (978-1-5415-0021-1(0), 4cf8e1b1-c047-4866-b372-67240732d868) Lerner Publishing Group. (Darby Creek).

Kelly, David A. MVP #2: the Soccer Surprise. Brundage, Scott, illus. 2016. (Most Valuable Players Ser.: 2). 128p. (J). (gr. 1-4). 5.99 (978-0-553-51322-6(2), Random Hse. Bks. for Young Readers) Random Hse. Children's Bks.

Kenneally, Miranda. Defending Taylor. 2016. (Hundred Oaks Ser.: 7). 304p. (YA). (gr. 8-12). pap. 12.99 (978-1-4926-3008-1(X), 9781492630081) Sourcebooks, Inc.

Keplinger, Kody. Shut Out. 2012. (ENG.). 288p. (YA). (gr. 10-17). pap. 15.99 (978-0-316-17555-5(2), Poppy) Little, Brown Bks. for Young Readers.

Kew, Trevor. Trading Goals, 1 vol. 2009. (Lorimer Sports Stories Ser.). (ENG.). 144p. (J). (gr. 3-7). 26.19 (978-1-55277-425-0(2), 425) James Lorimer & Co. Ltd., Pubs. CAN. Dist: Children's Plus, Inc.

Kim, YoeongAh. The Shooting Stars Soccer Team. Lee, Hyeongjin, illus. rev. ed. 2014. (MySELF Bookshelf Ser.). (ENG.). 32p. (J). (gr. k-2). lib. bdg. 25.27 (978-1-59953-648-4(X)) Norwood Hse. Pr.

Kirby, Stan. Captain Awesome, Soccer Star. O'Connor, George, illus. 2012. (Captain Awesome Ser.: 5). (ENG.). 128p. (J). (gr. k-4). 17.99 (978-1-4424-4332-7(4)); pap. 6.99 (978-1-4424-4331-0(6)) Little Simon. (Little Simon).

—Captain Awesome, Soccer Star. 2012. (Captain Awesome Ser.: 5). lib. bdg. 16.00 (978-0-606-26545-4(7)) Turtleback.

Klass, David. Home of the Braves. 2004. 355p. (YA). (gr. 7-12). 17.65 (978-0-7569-2805-6(2)) Perfection Learning Corp.

Knowlton, Laurie. N 2 Deep. 2004. 128p. (J). pap. 5.99 (978-1-4003-0327-4(3)) Nelson, Thomas Inc.

Krech, Bob. Love Puppies & Corner Kicks. 2010. (ENG.). 192p. (J). (gr. 6-8). 22.44 (978-0-525-42197-9(1)) Penguin Young Readers Group.

Kreie, Chris. The Natural. 2018. (Kick! Ser.). (ENG.). 104p. (YA). (gr. 6-12). pap. 7.99 (978-1-5415-0025-9(3), 5c37029c-2df8-4087-a189-198db8ede35b); lib. bdg. 25.32 (978-1-5415-0019-8(9), 291afa5b-95d7-4b8b-ba09-32948c4c1298) Lerner Publishing Group. (Darby Creek).

—The Rookie Trap. 2019. (League of the Paranormal Ser.). (ENG.). 120p. (YA). (gr. 6-12). pap. 7.99 (978-1-5415-7297-3(1), d5045536-ee69-4a9a-a677-0a898fd75bc7); lib. bdg. 26.65 (978-1-5415-5684-3(4), 4ee2a27a-b9b1-42e0-808c-32cb611d5060) Lerner Publishing Group. (Darby Creek).

—The Superstar. 2018. (Kick! Ser.). (ENG.). 104p. (YA). (gr. 6-12). 25.32 (978-1-5415-0024-2(5), 1b86e765-43e2-4a01-aaa5-a2d1cf2da395, Darby Creek) Lerner Publishing Group.

—Who Wants to Play Just for Kicks?, 1 vol. Santillan, Jorge, illus. 2011. (Sports Illustrated Kids Victory School Superstars Ser.). (ENG.). 56p. (J). (gr. 1-3). pap. 5.95 (978-1-4342-3079-9(1), 114713); lib. bdg. 26.65 (978-1-4342-2229-9(2), 103092) Capstone. (Stone Arch Bks.).

Krivitzky, Nathan & Nathan, Krivitzky. Always Late Nate. O'Connell, Dave, illus. 2009. (ENG.). 32p. (J). pap. 10.95 (978-1-933916-41-5(9)) Nelson Publishing & Marketing.

Krulik, Nancy & Burwasser, Amanda. Soccer Shocker! Project Droid #2. Moran, Mike, illus. 2016. (Project Droid Ser.). (ENG.). 104p. (J). (gr. 1-4). 13.99 (978-1-5107-1019-1(1)); pap. 5.99 (978-1-5107-1029-0(9)) Skyhorse Publishing Co., Inc. (Sky Pony Pr.).

Lampard, Frank. Frankie vs. the Mummy's Menace. 2014. (Illus.). 97p. (J). (978-1-4242-6085-0(X)) Scholastic, Inc.

Latumau, Joseph. A Goal for Cindy. 2003. (ENG., Illus.). 24p. pap. 11.00 (978-1-4120-1465-6(4)) Trafford Publishing.

Lewman, David. SpongeBob, Soccer Star! Reed, Stephen, illus. 2010. (SpongeBob SquarePants Ser.). (ENG.). 24p. (J). (gr. -1-3). pap. 3.99 (978-1-4169-9445-9(9), Simon Spotlight/Nickelodeon) Simon Spotlight/Nickelodeon.

Lineker, Gary. More of Gary Lineker's Favourite Football Stories. 2003. (ENG.). 224p. (J). 19.99 (978-0-333-73782-8(2)) Macmillan Pubs., Ltd. GBR. Dist: Trafalgar Square Publishing.

Lupica, Mike. Shoot-Out. 2018. (ENG.). 208p. (J). (gr. 3-7). pap. 8.99 (978-0-451-47934-1(3), Puffin Books) Penguin Young Readers Group.

Maddox, Jake. Jake Maddox: Definición Por Penales. Heck, Claudia, tr. Tiffany, Sean, illus. 2012. (Jake Maddox en Español Ser.). (SPA.). 72p. (J). (gr. 3-6). 25.32 (978-1-4342-3814-6(8), 117503, Stone Arch Bks.) Capstone.

—Second-Chance Soccer, 1 vol. Ray, Michael, illus. 2014. (Jake Maddox JV Ser.). (ENG.). 96p. (J). (gr. 4-6). 26.65 (978-1-4342-9154-7(5), 125604, Stone Arch Bks.) Capstone.

—Soccer Sabotage. 2018. (Jake Maddox JV Ser.). (ENG., Illus.). 96p. (J). (gr. 4-6). lib. bdg. 26.65 (978-1-4965-5932-6(0), 137134, Stone Arch Bks.) Capstone.

—Soccer Shake-Up. Aburto, Jesus, illus. 2015. (Jake Maddox Sports Stories Ser.). (ENG.). 72p. (J). (gr. 3-6). lib. bdg. 25.99 (978-1-4965-0495-1(X), 128567, Stone Arch Bks.) Capstone.

—Soccer Shootout, 1 vol. Tiffany, Sean, illus. 2007. (Jake Maddox Sports Stories Ser.). (ENG.). 72p. (J). (gr. 3-6). 25.99 (978-1-59889-844-6(2), 94241); per. 5.95 (978-1-59889-896-5(5), 94320) Capstone. (Stone Arch Bks.).

—Soccer Show-Off, 1 vol. Wood, Katie, illus. 2014. (Jake Maddox Girl Sports Stories Ser.). (ENG.). 72p. (J). (gr. 3-6). 25.32 (978-1-4342-4144-3(0), 119879, Stone Arch Bks.) Capstone.

—Soccer Spirit. Mourning, Tuesday, illus. 2008. (Jake Maddox Girl Sports Stories Ser.). (ENG.). 72p. (J). (gr. 3-6). 25.32 (978-1-4342-0780-7(3), 95185, Stone Arch Bks.) Capstone.

—Soccer Stand-Off. 2016. (Jake Maddox JV Ser.). (ENG., Illus.). 96p. (J). (gr. 4-6). lib. bdg. 26.65 (978-1-4965-3983-0(4), 133206, Stone Arch Bks.) Capstone.

—Soccer Step-Up. 2016. (Jake Maddox JV Girls Ser.). (ENG., Illus.). 96p. (J). (gr. 4-8). lib. bdg. 26.65 (978-1-4965-3675-4(4), 132926, Stone Arch Bks.) Capstone.

—Soccer Surprise, 1 vol. Wood, Katie, illus. 2012. (Jake Maddox Girl Sports Stories Ser.). (ENG.). 72p. (J). (gr. 3-6). pap. 5.95 (978-1-4342-3906-8(3), 118091); lib. bdg. 25.32 (978-1-4342-3291-5(3), 116255) Capstone. (Stone Arch Bks.).

—Soccer Switch. Aburto, Jesus, illus. 2017. (Jake Maddox Graphic Novels Ser.). (ENG.). 72p. (J). (gr. 3-8). lib. bdg. 26.65 (978-1-4965-3699-0(1), 132938, Stone Arch Bks.) Capstone.

—Striker's Sister. Wood, Katie, illus. 2018. (Jake Maddox Girl Sports Stories Ser.). (ENG.). 72p. (J). (gr. 3-6). lib. bdg. 25.32 (978-1-4965-6355-2(7), 138071, Stone Arch Bks.) Capstone.

Manushkin, Fran. El Golazo de Pedro. Trusted Translations, Trusted, tr. Lyon, Tammie, illus. 2018. (Pedro en Español Ser.). (SPA.). 32p. (J). (gr. k-2). lib. bdg. 21.32 (978-1-5158-2511-1(6), 137570, Picture Window Bks.) Capstone.

—Pedro's Big Goal. Lyon, Tammie, illus. 2016. (Pedro Ser.). (ENG.). 32p. (J). (gr. k-2). lib. bdg. 21.32 (978-1-5158-0086-6(5), 132125, Picture Window Bks.) Capstone.

Marsh, Carole. The Secret Soccer Ball. 2006. 64p. (gr. 2-4). 14.95 (978-0-635-06219-2(4)); pap. 3.99 (978-0-635-06213-0(5)) Gallopade International.

Masannek, Joachim. The Wild Soccer Bunch, Book 2, Diego the Tornado: Diego the Tornado. Part, Michael, ed. Schier, Helga, tr. Birck, Jan, illus. 2011. (ENG.). 148p. (J). (gr. 4-7). 12.95 (978-0-9844257-1-6(3)) Sole Bks.

Maurer, Shari. Change of Heart. 2010. 290p. (YA). 16.95 (978-1-934813-36-2(2)) Westside Bks.

May, Eleanor. The Great Shape-up. 2008. pap. 34.95 (978-1-58013-763-8(6)) Astra Publishing Hse.

McAnulty, Stacy. Max Explains Everything: Soccer Expert. Hocking, Deborah, illus. 2019. 32p. (J). (gr. -1-2). 17.99 (978-1-101-99640-9(4), G.P. Putnam's Sons Books for Young Readers) Penguin Young Readers Group.

McKnight, Marty. Jim Nasium Is a Soccer Goofball. Jones, Chris B., illus. 2015. (Jim Nasium Ser.). (ENG.). 88p. (J). (gr. 2-3). pap. 5.95 (978-1-4965-0525-5(5), 128597, Stone Arch Bks.) Capstone.

McNamara, Margaret. Playground Problem: Ready-To-Read Level 1. Gordon, Mike, illus. 2004. (Robin Hill School Ser.). (ENG.). 32p. (J). (gr. -1-1). pap. 4.99 (978-0-689-85876-5(0), Simon Spotlight) Simon Spotlight.

Meister, Cari. Goalkeeper Goof, 1 vol. Doerrfeld, Cori, illus. 2009. (My First Graphic Novel Ser.). (ENG.). 32p. (J). (gr. k-2). pap. 6.25 (978-1-4342-1409-6(5), 95687, Stone Arch Bks.) Capstone.

Milway, Katie Smith. The Banana-Leaf Ball: How Play Can Change the World. Milway, Katie Smith, illus. 2017. (CitizenKid Ser.). (ENG., Illus.). 32p. (J). (gr. 3-7). 18.99 (978-1-77138-331-8(3)) Kids Can Pr., Ltd. CAN. Dist: Hachette Bk. Group.

Montalbano, Andrea. Caught Offside. 2017. (Soccer Sisters Ser.: 2). 176p. (J). (gr. 3-7). pap. 7.99 (978-1-4926-4484-2(6)) Sourcebooks, Inc.

—Lily Out of Bounds. 2012. (ENG.). 132p. (J). pap. 8.99 (978-0-9858956-1-7(6)) In This Together Media.

—One on One. 2018. (Soccer Sisters Ser.: 3). (Illus.). 192p. (J). (gr. 3-7). pap. 7.99 (978-1-4926-4487-3(0)) Sourcebooks, Inc.

—Out of Bounds. 2017. (ENG., Illus.). (J). (gr. 3-6). 18.99 (978-1-4926-6233-4(X)) Sourcebooks, Inc.

—Out of Bounds. 2017. (Soccer Sisters Ser.: 1). lib. bdg. 18.40 (978-0-606-40353-5(1)) Turtleback.

—Out of Bounds: Soccer Sisters. 2017. (Soccer Sisters Ser.: 1). 176p. (J). (gr. 3-7). pap. 7.99 (978-1-4926-4481-1(1), 9781492644811) Sourcebooks, Inc.

Montelia, Leonora Linda. Nora & Her Magic Cleats. 2010. (ENG.). 32p. pap. 18.65 (978-1-4415-9093-0(5)) Xlibris Corp.

S

Morgan, Alex. Choosing Sides. 2018. (Kicks Ser.). (ENG., Illus.). 112p. (J). (gr. 3-7). 17.99 *(978-1-4814-8156-4(8)*, Simon & Schuster Bks. For Young Readers) Simon & Schuster Bks. For Young Readers.

—Hat Trick. 2015. (Kicks Ser.). (ENG., Illus.). 128p. (J). (gr. 3-7). 17.99 *(978-1-4814-5096-6(4)*, Simon & Schuster Bks. For Young Readers) Simon & Schuster Bks. For Young Readers.

—In the Zone. 2018. (Kicks Ser.). (ENG., Illus.). 128p. (J). (gr. 3-7). 17.99 *(978-1-4814-8153-3(3)*, Simon & Schuster Bks. For Young Readers) Simon & Schuster Bks. For Young Readers.

—Sabotage Season. (Kicks Ser.). (ENG., Illus.). (J). (gr. 3-7). 2014. 192p. pap. 7.99 *(978-1-4424-8576-1(0))* 2013. 176p. 17.99 *(978-1-4424-8574-7(4))* Simon & Schuster Bks. For Young Readers. (Simon & Schuster Bks. For Young Readers).

—Saving the Team. (Kicks Ser.). (ENG., Illus.). (J). (gr. 3-7). 2014. 192p. pap. 7.99 *(978-1-4424-8571-6(X))* 2013. 176p. 17.99 *(978-1-4424-8570-9(1))* Simon & Schuster Bks. For Young Readers. (Simon & Schuster Bks. For Young Readers).

—Saving the Team. 2021. (Kicks Ser.). (ENG.). 176p. (J). (gr. 3-7). lib. bdg. 31.36 *(978-1-5321-4994-8(8)*, 36990, Chapter Bks.) Spotlight.

—Settle the Score. 2016. (Kicks Ser.). (ENG., Illus.). 128p. (J). (gr. 3-7). 16.99 *(978-1-4814-5104-8(9)*, Simon & Schuster Bks. For Young Readers) Simon & Schuster Bks. For Young Readers.

—Shaken Up. 2015. (Kicks Ser.). (ENG., Illus.). 128p. (J). (gr. 3-7). 16.99 *(978-1-4814-5100-0(6)*, Simon & Schuster Bks. For Young Readers) Simon & Schuster Bks. For Young Readers.

—Switching Goals. (Kicks Ser.). (ENG.). (J). (gr. 3-7). 2020. 144p. pap. 7.99 *(978-1-5344-2796-9(1))* 2019. 128p. 17.99 *(978-1-5344-2795-2(3))* Simon & Schuster Bks. For Young Readers. (Simon & Schuster Bks. For Young Readers).

—Under Pressure. 2018. (Kicks Ser.). (ENG.). 144p. (J). (gr. 3-7). pap. 7.99 *(978-1-4814-8151-9(7)*, Simon & Schuster Bks. For Young Readers) Simon & Schuster Bks. For Young Readers.

—Win or Lose. 2014. (Kicks Ser.). (ENG., Illus.). 160p. (J). (gr. 3-7). 15.99 *(978-1-4424-8580-8(9)*, Simon & Schuster Bks. For Young Readers) Simon & Schuster Bks. For Young Readers.

Morningstar, Jeremy. Penalty Kick. 2005. 56p. pap. 9.00 *(978-1-4116-6572-9(4))* Lulu Pr., Inc.

Murray, Stuart A. P. Matty in the Goal, 1 vol. 2012. (Champion Sports Story Ser.). (ENG.). 104p. (J). (gr. 3-5). 30.60 *(978-0-7660-3877-6(7)*, 7cd5aacf-9446-4ecc-a170-384455d3c3f5); pap. 13.88 *(978-1-4644-0003-2(2)*, cf8888ef-6c05-46e8-828c-b0584784f0c5) Enslow Publishing, LLC.

—Todd Goes for the Goal, 1 vol. 2012. (Champion Sports Story Ser.). (ENG.). 104p. (J). (gr. 3-5). pap. 13.88 *(978-1-4644-0000-1(8)*, 87b16cab-bcf9-4436-b487-a5de5c41931f); lib. bdg. 30.60 *(978-0-7660-3887-5(4)*, 08a03198-79a7-4c86-82be-341a28864a30) Enslow Publishing, LLC.

Myers, Bill. My Life as a Stupendously Stomped Soccer Star, 1 vol., 26. 2006. (Incredible Worlds of Wally Mcdoogle Ser.: 26). (ENG.). 128p. (J). (gr. 3-7). per. 6.99 *(978-1-4003-0635-0(3)*, Tommy Nelson) Nelson, Thomas Inc.

Myers, Bob. Trinity Goes to Soccer Camp. Bunker, Tom, illus. 2012. 36p. 24.95 *(978-1-4560-2906-7(1))* America Star Bks.

Myers, Walter Dean & Workman, Ross. Kick. 2012. (ENG.). 224p. (YA). (gr. 9). pap. 10.99 *(978-0-06-200491-8(3)*, HarperTeen) HarperCollins Pubs.

Nesbo, Jo. The Magical Fruit. Chace, Tara F., tr. Lowery, Mike, illus. (Doctor Proctor's Fart Powder Ser.). (ENG.). 320p. (J). (gr. 3-7). 2014. pap. 8.99 *(978-1-4424-9343-8(7))* 2013. 17.99 *(978-1-4424-9342-1(9))* Simon & Schuster Children's Publishing. (Aladdin).

Nunes, Ernest. Oh! How I Wish I Could Play Soccer with Ernie & the Dreamers. 2013. 70p. pap. 12.99 *(978-1-62509-705-7(0))* Salem Author Services.

O'Brien, Joe. Legends' Lair. 2016. (ENG., Illus.). 192p. (J). pap. 14.00 *(978-1-84717-826-8(X))* O'Brien Pr., Ltd., The IRL. Dist: Casemate Pubs. & Bk. Distributors, LLC.

O'Connor, Heather M. Betting Game, 1 vol. 2015. (Orca Sports Ser.). (ENG.). 216p. (J). (gr. 4-7). pap. 10.95 *(978-1-4598-0930-7(0))* Orca Bk. Pubs. USA.

O'Connor, Jane. Fancy Nancy: Nancy Clancy, Soccer Mania. Glasser, Robin Preiss, illus. 2016. (Nancy Clancy Ser.: 6). (ENG.). 144p. (J). (gr. 1-5). pap. 4.99 *(978-0-06-226966-9(6)*, HarperCollins) HarperCollins Pubs.

—Fancy Nancy: Nancy Clancy, Soccer Mania. Glasser, Robin Preiss, illus. 2015. (Nancy Clancy Ser.: 6). (ENG.). 128p. (J). (gr. 1-5). 9.99 *(978-0-06-226967-6(4)*, HarperCollins) HarperCollins Pubs.

—Nancy Clancy, Soccer Mania. Glasser, Robin Preiss, illus. 2016. (Nancy Clancy Ser.: 6). (ENG.). 144p. (J). (gr. 1-5). 14.75 *(978-0-606-39270-9(X))* Turtleback.

O'Donnell, Liam. Soccer Sabotage: A Graphic Guide Adventure, 1 vol. Deas, Mike, illus. 2009. (Graphic Guides: 3). (ENG.). 64p. (J). (gr. 4-7). pap. 9.95 *(978-1-55143-884-9(4))* Orca Bk. Pubs. USA.

O'Hara, Susan. Tim's First Soccer Game. Barrett, Rebecca, illus. 2012. 38p. pap. 14.97 *(978-1-61897-199-9(9)*, Strategic Bk. Publishing) Strategic Book Publishing & Rights Agency (SBPRA).

Oldfield, Matt. Aguero: From the Playground to the Pitch. 2018. (Ultimate Football Heroes Ser.). (ENG., Illus.). 176p. (J). (gr. 2-7). pap. 9.99 *(978-1-78606-807-1(9))* Blake, John Publishing, Ltd. GBR. Dist: Independent Pubs. Group.

—Bale: From the Playground to the Pitch. 2018. (Ultimate Football Heroes Ser.). (ENG., Illus.). 176p. (J). (gr. 2-7). pap. 11.99 *(978-1-78606-801-9(X))* Blake, John Publishing, Ltd. GBR. Dist: Independent Pubs. Group.

—Gerrard: From the Playground to the Pitch. 2018. (Classic Football Heroes Ser.). (ENG., Illus.). 176p. (J). (gr. 2-7). pap. 11.99 *(978-1-78606-812-5(5))* Blake, John Publishing, Ltd. GBR. Dist: Independent Pubs. Group.

—Hazard: From the Playground to the Pitch. 2018. (Ultimate Football Heroes Ser.). (ENG., Illus.). 176p. (J). (gr. 2-7). pap. 9.99 *(978-1-78606-808-8(7))* Blake, John Publishing, Ltd. GBR. Dist: Independent Pubs. Group.

—Iniesta: From the Playground to the Pitch. 2018. (Ultimate Football Heroes Ser.). (ENG., Illus.). 176p. (J). (gr. 2-7). pap. 11.99 *(978-1-78606-804-0(4))* Blake, John Publishing, Ltd. GBR. Dist: Independent Pubs. Group.

—Lukaku: From the Playground to the Pitch. 2018. (Ultimate Football Heroes Ser.). (ENG.). 176p. (J). (gr. 2-7). pap. 9.99 *(978-1-78606-885-9(0))* Blake, John Publishing, Ltd. GBR. Dist: Independent Pubs. Group.

—Neuer: From the Playground to the Pitch. 2018. (Ultimate Football Heroes Ser.). (ENG.). 176p. (J). (gr. 4-7). pap. 9.99 *(978-1-78606-915-3(6))* Blake, John Publishing, Ltd. GBR. Dist: Independent Pubs. Group.

—Neymar: From the Playground to the Pitch. 2018. (Heroes Ser.). (ENG., Illus.). 176p. (J). (gr. 4-8). pap. 10.99 *(978-1-78606-404-2(9))* Blake, John Publishing, Ltd. GBR. Dist: Independent Pubs. Group.

—Sanchez: From the Playground to the Pitch. 2018. (Ultimate Football Heroes Ser.). (ENG., Illus.). 176p. (J). (gr. 2-7). pap. 9.99 *(978-1-78606-809-5(5))* Blake, John Publishing, Ltd. GBR. Dist: Independent Pubs. Group.

—Suarez: From the Playground to the Pitch. 2018. (Ultimate Football Heroes Ser.). (ENG., Illus.). 176p. (J). (gr. 2-7). pap. 9.99 *(978-1-78606-806-4(0))* Blake, John Publishing, Ltd. GBR. Dist: Independent Pubs. Group.

—Zlatan: From the Playground to the Pitch. 2018. (Ultimate Football Heroes Ser.). (ENG., Illus.). 176p. (J). (gr. 2-7). pap. 11.99 *(978-1-78606-810-1(9))* Blake, John Publishing, Ltd. GBR. Dist: Independent Pubs. Group.

Oldfield, Matt & Oldfield, Tom. Beckham. 2018. (Football Heroes - International Editions Ser.). (ENG., Illus.). 176p. (J). (gr. 4-7). pap. 9.99 *(978-1-78606-921-4(0))* Blake, John Publishing, Ltd. GBR. Dist: Independent Pubs. Group.

—Figo. 2018. (Football Heroes - International Editions Ser.). (ENG., Illus.). 176p. (J). (gr. 4-7). pap. 9.99 *(978-1-78606-923-8(7))* Blake, John Publishing, Ltd. GBR. Dist: Independent Pubs. Group.

—Klinsmann. 2018. (Football Heroes - International Editions Ser.). (ENG.). 176p. (gr. 4-7). pap. 9.99 *(978-1-78606-922-1(9))* Blake, John Publishing, Ltd. GBR. Dist: Independent Pubs. Group.

—Maradona. 2018. (Football Heroes - International Editions Ser.). (ENG., Illus.). 176p. (J). (gr. 4-7). pap. 9.99 *(978-1-78606-924-5(5))* Blake, John Publishing, Ltd. GBR. Dist: Independent Pubs. Group.

—Messi. 2018. (ENG., Illus.). 176p. (J). (gr. 4-7). pap. 9.99 *(978-1-78606-931-3(8))* Blake, John Publishing, Ltd. GBR. Dist: Independent Pubs. Group.

—Neymar. 2018. (ENG., Illus.). 176p. (J). (gr. 4-7). pap. 9.99 *(978-1-78606-939-9(3))* Blake, John Publishing, Ltd. GBR. Dist: Independent Pubs. Group.

—Pogba. 2018. (Ultimate Football Heroes Ser.). (ENG., Illus.). 176p. (J). (gr. 4-7). pap. 9.99 *(978-1-78606-929-0(6))* Blake, John Publishing, Ltd. GBR. Dist: Independent Pubs. Group.

—Road to the World Cup. 2018. (Ultimate Football Heroes Ser.). (ENG., Illus.). 192p. (J). (gr. 4-7). pap. 9.99 *(978-1-78606-920-7(2))* Blake, John Publishing, Ltd. GBR. Dist: Independent Pubs. Group.

—Ronaldo. 2018. (Football Heroes - International Editions Ser.). (ENG., Illus.). 176p. (J). (gr. 4-7). pap. 9.99 *(978-1-78606-937-5(7))* Blake, John Publishing, Ltd. GBR. Dist: Independent Pubs. Group.

—Rooney: Manchester United. 2018. (Classic Football Heroes Ser.). (ENG., Illus.). 176p. (J). (gr. 2-7). pap. 9.99 *(978-1-78606-802-6(8))* Blake, John Publishing, Ltd. GBR. Dist: Independent Pubs. Group.

—Sterling. 2018. (Ultimate Football Heroes Ser.). (ENG.). 176p. (J). (gr. 2-7). pap. 9.99 *(978-1-78606-811-8(7))* Blake, John Publishing, Ltd. GBR. Dist: Independent Pubs. Group.

—Zidane. 2018. (Football Heroes - International Editions Ser.). (ENG., Illus.). 176p. (J). (gr. 4-7). pap. 9.99 *(978-1-78606-933-7(4))* Blake, John Publishing, Ltd. GBR. Dist: Independent Pubs. Group.

Olin, Rita & Olin, Spencer. Trouble in Soccertown: A Lazer Mcnulty Adventure. 2009. 108p. 20.95 *(978-1-4401-5374-7(4))*; pap. 10.95 *(978-1-4401-5376-1(0))* iUniverse, Inc.

O'Nan, Gerald D. The Adventures of Andy Ant: Lawn Mower on the Loose. McGary, Norman, illus. 2014. (ENG.). 28p. (gr. -1-4). pap. 9.95 *(978-1-61448-673-2(5))* Morgan James Publishing.

Orr, Tamra. No Hands Allowed, Plus Robbie & Ryan Play Indoor Soccer, 11 vols., Set. 2006. (Robbie Reader, Weekend Soccer Ser.). (J). (gr. 1-4). lib. bdg. *(978-1-58415-490-7(X))* Mitchell Lane Pubs.

Osborne, Mary Pope. Soccer on Sunday. Murdocca, Sal, illus. 2016. (Magic Tree House (R) Merlin Mission Ser.: 24). 144p. (J). (gr. 2-5). 6.99 *(978-0-307-98056-4(1)*, Random Hse. Bks. for Young Readers) Random Hse. Children's Bks.

Padian, Maria. Out of Nowhere. 2015. (ENG.). 352p. (YA). (gr. 7). pap. 10.99 *(978-0-375-86562-6(4)*, Ember) Random Hse. Children's Bks.

Palmer, Tom. Boys United. 2009. (Football Academy Ser.). (Illus.). 176p. (J). (gr. 2-4). pap. 10.99 *(978-0-14-132467-8(8))* Penguin Bks., Ltd. GBR. Dist: Independent Pubs. Group.

—Football Academy: Reading the Game, Bk. 4. 4th ed. 2009. (Football Academy Ser.). (Illus.). 160p. (J). (gr. 2-4). pap. 10.99 *(978-0-14-132470-8(8))* Penguin Bks., Ltd. GBR. Dist: Independent Pubs. Group.

—The Real Thing, Bk. 3. 3rd ed. 2009. (Football Academy Ser.). (Illus.). 176p. (J). (gr. 2-4). pap. 10.99 *(978-0-14-132469-2(4))* Penguin Bks., Ltd. GBR. Dist: Independent Pubs. Group.

—Striking Out. 2nd ed. 2009. (Football Academy Ser.). (Illus.). 160p. (J). (gr. 2-4). pap. 10.99 *(978-0-14-132468-5(6))* Penguin Bks., Ltd. GBR. Dist: Independent Pubs. Group.

Paul, Baptiste. The Field. Alcántara, Jacqueline, illus. 2018. (ENG.). 32p. (J). (gr. -1-3). 17.95 *(978-0-7358-4312-7(0))* North-South Bks., Inc.

Pedraza, M. Eugenia Rueda. Nico's Voyage. 2013. 32p. pap. *(978-1-4602-2360-4(8))* FriesenPress.

Pedro, Coach & Rita, Susan Adam. The Magic Soccer Ball: Trapping & My 1st Game. 2008. 44p. pap. 18.49 *(978-1-4343-6593-4(X))* AuthorHouse.

Pee-Wee Soccer. 2003. (J). per. *(978-1-57657-941-1(7))* Paradise Pr., Inc.

Peet, Mal. Alf Saves the Day. Hammond, Andy, illus. 2004. (ENG.). 24p. (J). lib. bdg. 23.65 *(978-1-59646-692-0(8))* Dingles & Co.

—Keeper. (ENG.). 240p. (YA). (gr. 5). 2016. pap. 9.99 *(978-0-7636-8746-5(4))* 2005. 15.99 *(978-0-7636-2749-2(6))* Candlewick Pr.

Peirce, Lincoln. Big Nate — Here Goes Nothing. 2012. (Big Nate Graphic Novels Ser.: 6). (J). lib. bdg. 20.85 *(978-0-606-26526-3(0))* Turtleback.

Peschke, Marci. Soccer Queen. Mourning, Tuesday, illus. 2015. (Kylie Jean Ser.). (ENG.). 112p. (J). (gr. 1-3). 22.65 *(978-1-4795-5882-7(6)*, 126953, Picture Window Bks.) Capstone.

Phillips, Dee. Goal, 1 vol. unabr. ed. 2010. (Right Now! Ser.). (ENG., Illus.). 45p. (YA). (gr. 9-12). pap. 10.75 *(978-1-61651-249-1(0))* Saddleback Educational Publishing, Inc.

Pierce, Terry. Soccer Time! McMahon, Bob, illus. 2019. (Step into Reading Ser.). 32p. (J). (gr. -1-1). pap. 5.99 *(978-0-525-58203-8(7)*, Random Hse. Bks. for Young Readers) Random Hse. Children's Bks.

Popescu, Petru. Weregirls: Birth of the Pack: Birth of the Pack. rev. ed. 2007. (ENG.). 352p. (YA). (gr. 8-12). pap. 18.99 *(978-0-7653-1641-7(2)*, 900039012, Tor Teen) Doherty, Tom Assocs., LLC.

Price, Mathew. Me Encanta el Futbol. (SPA.). pap. 11.95 *(978-950-07-2081-6(7))* Editorial Sudamericana S.A. ARG. Dist: Distribooks, Inc.

Priebe, Val. It's Hard to Dribble with Your Feet. Santillan, Jorge, illus. 2010. (Sports Illustrated Kids Victory School Superstars Ser.). (ENG.). 56p. (J). (gr. 1-3). pap. 5.95 *(978-1-4342-2782-9(0)*, 114049, Stone Arch Bks.) Capstone.

Quinn, Jason. The Beautiful Game: Survival. Sharma, Lalit Kumar, illus. 2017. (Campfire Graphic Novels Ser.: 9). 160p. (J). (gr. 5). pap. 12.99 *(978-93-81182-11-6(6)*, Campfire) Steerforth Pr.

Random House. You Can Be a Soccer Player. 2018. (Barbie Step into Reading Level 2 Ser.). lib. bdg. 14.75 *(978-0-606-40927-8(0))* Turtleback.

Random House Editors. Reds Against Blues! 2016. (Thomas & Friends Step into Reading Ser.). lib. bdg. 14.75 *(978-0-606-38474-2(X))* Turtleback.

Rayner, Robert. Falling Star, 1 vol. 2007. (Lorimer Sports Stories Ser.). (ENG.). 136p. (J). (gr. 4-8). 16.95 *(978-1-55028-971-8(3)*, 971) James Lorimer & Co. Ltd., Pubs. CAN. Dist: Formac Lorimer Bks. Ltd.

—Out of Sight, 1 vol. 2006. (Lorimer Sports Stories Ser.). (ENG.). 138p. (J). (gr. 3-7). 17.44 *(978-1-55028-919-0(5))* James Lorimer & Co. Ltd., Pubs. CAN. Dist: Children's Plus, Inc.

—Suspended, 1 vol. 2004. (Lorimer Sports Stories Ser.). (ENG.). 112p. (J). (gr. 4-8). 16.95 *(978-1-55028-861-2(X)*, 861) James Lorimer & Co. Ltd., Pubs. CAN. Dist: Formac Lorimer Bks. Ltd.

Rayner, Shoo. Ginger Ninja 5: World Cup Winners. (ENG., Illus.). 63p. (J). (gr. k-6). pap. 8.99 *(978-0-340-69379-7(7))* Hodder & Stoughton GBR. Dist: Trafalgar Square Publishing.

Regan, Peter. Riverside: Spring Fever. 2007. (ENG.). 112p. (J). pap. *(978-1-901737-56-1(X)*, Anvil Bks.) Mercier Pr., Ltd., The.

—Riverside: The Curse. Myler, Terry, illus. 2004. (Riverside Ser.). (ENG.). 127p. (J). pap. *(978-1-901737-46-2(2)*, Anvil Bks.) Mercier Pr., Ltd., The.

—Riverside: The Spy. 2007. (ENG.). 112p. (J). pap. *(978-1-901737-53-0(5)*, Anvil Bks.) Mercier Pr., Ltd., The.

Renner, C. J. Soccer Longshot, 1 vol. Aburto, Jesus, illus. 2011. (Sports Illustrated Kids Graphic Novels Ser.). (ENG.). 56p. (J). (gr. 3-8). pap. 7.19 *(978-1-4342-3402-5(9)*, 116415); lib. bdg. 26.65 *(978-1-4342-2241-1(1)*, 103105) Capstone. (Stone Arch Bks.).

Rey, H. A. Curious George Plays Soccer. 2017. (Curious George Ser.). (ENG., Illus.). 24p. (J). (gr. -1-3). 14.99 *(978-0-544-91246-5(2)*, 1655200, Clarion Bks.) HarperCollins Pubs.

Rigby, Robert. Goal! The Dream Begins. 2006. (ENG., Illus.). 240p. (YA). (gr. 7-9). pap. 7.99 *(978-0-15-205798-5(6)*, 1197425, Clarion Bks.) HarperCollins Pubs.

—Goal: Glory Days. 2010. (ENG., Illus.). 252p. (YA). (gr. 7-18). pap. 7.99 *(978-0-15-205921-7(0)*, 1197776, Clarion Bks.) HarperCollins Pubs.

—Goal Ii: Living the Dream. 2007. (ENG., Illus.). 224p. (YA). (gr. 7-7). pap. 14.95 *(978-0-15-205881-4(8)*, 1197657, Clarion Bks.) HarperCollins Pubs.

Riley, Zach. Surprise Kick. Ricci, Andrés, illus. 2012. (Zach Riley Ser.). (ENG.). 80p. (J). (gr. 2-5). lib. bdg. 35.64 *(978-1-61783-536-0(6)*, 15863, Calico Chapter Bks.) ABDO Publishing Co.

Rippin, Sally. The Soccer Star. Fukuoka, Aki, illus. (ENG.). (J). 2013. 48p. pap. 4.99 *(978-1-61067-096-8(5))* 2012. 44p. *(978-1-61067-133-0(3))* Kane Miller.

—The Winning Goal. Spartels, Stephanie, illus. (ENG.). (J). 2013. 48p. pap. 4.99 *(978-1-61067-123-1(6))* 2012. 43p. *(978-1-61067-137-8(6))* Kane Miller.

Ross, Jeff. Above All Else, 1 vol. 2014. (Orca Sports Ser.). (ENG.). 176p. (J). (gr. 4-7). pap. 10.95 *(978-1-4598-0388-6(4))* Orca Bk. Pubs. USA.

Rue, Nancy N. Lucy Out of Bounds, 1 vol. 2016. (Faithgirlz / a Lucy Novel Ser.: 2). (ENG.). 224p. (J). pap. 7.99 *(978-0-310-75505-0(0))* Zonderkidz.

Sanchez, Ricardo. Spotlight Soccer, 1 vol. Waryanto, Ian, illus. 2014. (Sports Illustrated Kids Graphic Novels Ser.). (ENG.). 72p. (J). (gr. 3-8). 26.65 *(978-1-4342-4165-8(3)*, 119967, Stone Arch Bks.) Capstone.

Scholastic. Peppa Plays Soccer (Peppa Pig), 1 vol. EOne, illus. 2016. (ENG.). 24p. (J). (gr. -1-k). pap. 4.99 *(978-1-338-03279-6(8))* Scholastic, Inc.

Scholastic Editors. Peppa Plays Soccer. 2016. (Peppa Pig 8X8 Ser.). lib. bdg. 14.75 *(978-0-606-38825-2(7))* Turtleback.

Scudamore, Beverly. Foul Play, 1 vol. 2005. (Lorimer Sports Stories Ser.). (ENG.). 112p. (J). (gr. 4-8). 16.95 *(978-1-55028-875-9(X)*, 875) James Lorimer & Co. Ltd., Pubs. CAN. Dist: Formac Lorimer Bks. Ltd.

Shaw, Natalie. A Special Day with Dad. 2014. (Olivia 8x8 Ser.). lib. bdg. 14.75 *(978-0-606-35460-8(3))* Turtleback.

Simmons, Cari. Picture Perfect #2: You First. 2015. (Picture Perfect Ser.: 2). (ENG.). 256p. (J). (gr. 3-7). pap. 6.99 *(978-0-06-231058-3(5)*, HarperCollins) HarperCollins Pubs.

Simon, Francesca. Horrid Henry & the Soccer Fiend. Ross, Tony, illus. 2009. (Horrid Henry Ser.: 0). (ENG.). 112p. (J). (gr. 2-5). pap. 7.99 *(978-1-4022-1778-4(1)*, Sourcebooks Jabberwocky) Sourcebooks, Inc.

—Horrid Henry & the Soccer Fiend. 2009. (Horrid Henry Ser.). lib. bdg. 17.20 *(978-0-606-06798-0(1))* Turtleback.

Sis, Peter. Madlenka. Sis, Peter, illus. 2010. (Madlenka Ser.). (ENG., Illus.). 48p. (J). (gr. k-2). pap. 12.99 *(978-0-312-65912-7(1)*, 900070485) Square Fish.

Skead, Robert. Elves Can't Kick. 2005. 84p. per. 7.99 *(978-1-929478-66-8(6))* Cross Training Publishing.

Sloan, Holly Goldberg. Keeper. 2003. (Touchdown Editions Ser.). (ENG.). 146p. (J). (gr. 7-12). 26.19 *(978-0-9708992-3-1(8))* Scobre Pr. Corp.

Smith, Annette. Saturday Morning Soccer. Hoit, Richard, illus. 2009. 16p. pap. 10.67 *(978-1-4190-5503-4(8))* Rigby Education.

Spring, Debbie. Breathing Soccer, 1 vol. 2008. (ENG.). 208p. (J). (gr. 4-8). pap. 10.95 *(978-1-897235-42-3(9))* Thistledown Pr., Ltd. CAN. Dist: Univ. of Toronto Pr.

Springstubb, Tricia. Cody & the Heart of a Champion. Wheeler, Eliza, illus. (Cody Ser.). (ENG.). 160p. (J). (gr. 2-5). 2019. pap. 7.99 *(978-1-5362-0633-3(4))* 2018. 14.99 *(978-0-7636-7921-7(6))* Candlewick Pr.

Stamper, Judith Bauer & Stamper, Judith. Go, Fractions! Demarest, Chris, illus. 2003. (All Aboard Math Readers Ser.). 48p. (J). (gr. k-3). 16.19 *(978-0-448-43113-0(0))* Penguin Young Readers Group.

Staunton, Ted. Great Play, Morgan. Slavin, Bill, illus. 2008. (First Novel Ser.). (ENG.). 64p. (J). (gr. 2-6). *(978-0-88780-772-5(0))* Formac Publishing Co., Ltd. CAN. Dist: Casemate Pubs. & Bk. Distributors, LLC.

Stein, Joshua. Chasing the King. 2005. (Dream Ser.). 150p. (gr. 3-8). pap. 9.95 *(978-0-9708992-4-8(6))* Scobre Pr. Corp.

Stiles, Amanda. The Runaway Soccer Ball. Torrey, Rich, illus. 2010. 16p. (J). pap. *(978-0-545-24819-8(1))* Scholastic, Inc.

Stultz, Janice. Harry Turnaround. 2012. 24p. pap. 15.99 *(978-1-4691-7141-8(4))* Xlibris Corp.

Stuve-Bodeen, Stephanie. Babu's Song. Boyd, Aaron, illus. 2003. (ENG.). 32p. (J). 16.95 *(978-1-58430-058-8(2))* Lee & Low Bks., Inc.

Styles, Walker. The Soccer Ball Monster Mystery. Whitehouse, Ben, illus. 2016. (Rider Woofson Ser.: 6). (ENG.). 128p. (J). (gr. k-4). pap. 5.99 *(978-1-4814-7110-7(4)*, Little Simon) Little Simon.

Swanson, Julie A. Going for the Record. 2004. 223p. (YA). pap. 8.00 *(978-0-8028-5273-1(4))* Eerdmans, William B. Publishing Co.

Swanson Sateren, Shelley. Max & Zoe at Soccer Practice, 1 vol. Sullivan, Mary & Sullivan, Mary, illus. 2012. (Max & Zoe Ser.). (ENG.). 32p. (J). (gr. k-2). lib. bdg. 21.32 *(978-1-4048-6213-5(7)*, 113590, Picture Window Bks.) Capstone.

Tamar, Erika. Venus & the Comets. 2004. (Junior Library Guild Selection Ser.). 96p. (J). (gr. 2-18). 14.95 *(978-1-58196-007-5(7))*; pap. 4.99 *(978-1-58196-018-1(2))* Lerner Publishing Group. (Darby Creek).

Taylor, Dereen. Paulo & the Football Thieves: Peek Inside the Pop-Up Windows! Hutchinson, Tim, illus. 2014. 12p. (J). (gr. -1-12). 16.99 *(978-1-86147-409-4(1)*, Armadillo) Anness Publishing GBR. Dist: National Bk. Network.

Teamwork Works. 2005. 39p. (J). 3.99 *(978-0-9763213-3-0(5))* OHC Group LLC.

Terrell, Brandon. Break to the Goal. 2015. (Game On! Ser.). (ENG.). 80p. (J). (gr. 3-6). *(978-1-63235-045-9(9)*, 11656, 12-Story Library) Bookstaves, LLC.

Thielbar, Melinda. The Hundred-Dollar Robber. 2nd rev. ed. 2010. pap. 39.62 *(978-0-7613-6943-1(0))* Lerner Publishing Group.

—The Hundred-Dollar Robber: A Mystery with Money. Pantoja, Maria Kristina Sb., illus. 2010. (Manga Math Mysteries Ser.: 2). (ENG.). 48p. (J). (gr. 3-5). pap. 6.99 *(978-0-7613-5243-3(0)*, eb5149e7-387a-4f32-8264-1a6ba34243fa, Graphic Universe™) Lerner Publishing Group.

—The Hundred-Dollar Robber: A Mystery with Money. Pantoja, Maria Kristina, illus. 2009. (Manga Math Mysteries Ser.: 2). (ENG.). 48p. (gr. 3-5). 29.27 *(978-0-7613-3854-3(3))* Lerner Publishing Group.

Thorpe, Kiki. In the Game. 2016. (Never Girls Ser.: 12). lib. bdg. 16.00 *(978-0-606-38468-1(5))* Turtleback.

Torrey, Richard. Beans Baker's Best Shot. 2006. (Step into Reading Ser.: Vol. 3). (Illus.). 48p. (J). (gr. k-3). per. 5.99 *(978-0-375-82839-3(7)*, Random Hse. Bks. for Young Readers) Random Hse. Children's Bks.

Toye, Clive. Toby & the Greatest Game. 2012. 136p. (gr. 4-6). pap. 11.95 *(978-1-4697-9516-4(7))* iUniverse, Inc.

Voigt, David & Voigt, Grady. Socky, the Soft-Hearted Soccer Ball. Wagner, Steve, illus. 2011. pap. 12.00 *(978-0-9833310-6-3(5))* Aperture Pr., LLC.

Wallace, Rich. Between the Sticks, 1 vol. Heitz, Tim, illus. 2015. (Game Face Ser.). (ENG.). 112p. (J). (gr. 2-5). 38.50 *(978-1-62402-132-9(8)*, 19192, Calico Chapter Bks.) ABDO Publishing Co.

—Fake Out, 2. Holder, Jimmy, illus. 2011. (Kickers Ser.: Bk. 2). (ENG.). 128p. (J). (gr. 2-5). lib. bdg. 18.69 *(978-0-375-95755-0(3)*, Knopf Bks. for Young Readers) Random Hse. Children's Bks.

—Kickers #1: the Ball Hogs, Bk. 1. Holder, Jimmy, illus. 2011. (Kickers Ser.: 1). 128p. (J). (gr. 1-4). 6.99 *(978-0-375-85092-9(9)*, Yearling) Random Hse. Children's Bks.

—Kickers #2: Fake Out. Holder, Jimmy, illus. 2011. (Kickers Ser.: 2). 128p. (J). (gr. 1-4). 6.99 *(978-0-375-85093-6(7)*, Yearling) Random Hse. Children's Bks.

—Kickers #3: Benched. Holder, Jimmy, illus. 2011. (Kickers Ser.: 3). 128p. (J). (gr. 1-4). 5.99 *(978-0-375-85094-3(5)*, Yearling) Random Hse. Children's Bks.

—Kickers #4: Game-Day Jitters. Holder, Jimmy, illus. 2012. (Kickers Ser.: 4). 128p. (J). (gr. 2-5). 5.99

(978-0-375-85095-0(3), Yearling) Random Hse. Children's Bks.

—Shots on Goal. 2005. 160p. (YA). (gr. 7-11). per. 5.99 *(978-0-679-88671-6(0),* Laurel Leaf) Random Hse. Children's Bks.

Warner, Gertrude Chandler, creator. The Mystery of the Soccer Snitch. 2014. (Boxcar Children Mysteries Ser.: 136). (ENG., Illus.). 128p. (J). (gr. 2-5). pap. 6.99 *(978-0-8075-0896-1(9),* 807508969, Random Hse. Bks. for Young Readers) Random Hse. Children's Bks.

Westcott, Jim. The Gift. 2014. (Red Rhino Ser.). (J). lib. bdg. 18.40 *(978-0-606-36201-6(0))* Turtleback.

Wheeler, Lisa. Dino-Soccer. Gott, Barry, illus. 2009. (Dino-Sports Ser.). (ENG.). 32p. (J). (gr. k-3). 18.99 *(978-0-8225-9028-6(X),* 3a7e422c-294d-4475-b765-8a7f45376638, Carolrhoda Bks.) Lerner Publishing Group.

Williams, Michael. Now Is the Time for Running. 2013. (ENG.). 240p. (YA). (gr. 7-17). pap. 10.99 *(978-0-316-07788-0(7))* Little, Brown Bks. for Young Readers.

Wilson, Bob. Stanley Bagshaw & the Short-Sighted Football Trainer. 2006. (Stanley Bagshaw Ser.). (Illus.). 32p. (J). (gr. k-2). pap. 6.95 *(978-1-903015-26-1(X))* Barn Owl Bks, London GBR. Dist: Independent Pubs. Group.

Young, Julian. The Daniel Model: Understanding the Pathway to Promotion & Power in the Kingdom of God. 2017. (ENG.). pap. 13.99 *(978-0-9990279-9-8(9))* Crown Media Publishing.

—The Peter Model: Understanding the Key That Unlock Maximum Kingdom Impact. 2017. (ENG.). pap. 14.99 *(978-0-9990279-8-1(0))* Crown Media Publishing.

Yu, Bill. Star Striker. Siragusa, Renato, illus. 2018. (Get in the Game Ser.). (ENG.). 32p. (J). (gr. 3-8). lib. bdg. 32.79 *(978-1-5321-3297-1(2),* 28499, Graphic Planet - Fiction) Magic Wagon.

Zepeda, Gwendolyn. I Kick the Ball: Pateo el Balón. Ventura, Gabriela Baeza, tr. Torrecilla, Pablo, illus. 2011. (SPA & ENG.). 32p. (J). (gr. -1-3). 16.95 *(978-1-55885-688-2(9),* Piñata Books) Arte Publico Pr.

SOCIAL ADJUSTMENT

Amos, Janine. Don't Do That! How Not to Act, 1 vol. 2009. (Best Behavior Ser.). (ENG., Illus.). 32p. (J). (gr. -1-2). pap. 11.55 *(978-1-60754-052-6(5),* b763b5fa-043f-4306-a4e8-5d824e2de8c4, Windmill Bks.) Rosen Publishing Group, Inc., The.

Paisley, Erinne. Can Your Conversations Change the World?, 1 vol. 2018. (PopActivism Ser.: 3). (ENG., Illus.). 160p. (YA). (gr. 8-12). pap. 14.95 *(978-1-4598-1309-0(X))* Orca Bk. Pubs. USA.

Rocha, Toni L. Coping When Someone in Your Family Has Cancer. 2009. (Coping Ser.). 192p. (gr. 7-12). 63.90 *(978-1-61511-988-2(4))* Rosen Publishing Group, Inc., The.

SOCIAL CHANGE

Amidon Lusted, Marcia. Civic Unrest: Investigate the Struggle for Social Change. Chandhok, Lena, illus. 2015. (Inquire & Investigate Ser.). (ENG.). 128p. (J). (gr. 6-10). 22.95 *(978-1-61930-241-9(1),* 3a620118-4228-4934-9619-91c246a64440) Nomad Pr.

Arégui, Matthias, et al. Before After. Arégui, Matthias et al, illus. 2014. (ENG.). 176p. (J). (gr. -1-3). 19.99 *(978-0-7636-7621-6(7))* Candlewick Pr.

Braun, Sandra. Women Inventors Who Changed the World, 1 vol. 2011. (Great Women of Achievement Ser.). (ENG., Illus.). 120p. (YA). (gr. 5-6). lib. bdg. 39.80 *(978-1-4488-5996-2(4),* 74a1163a-b33f-4640-aacc-883a75afabae, Rosen Reference) Rosen Publishing Group, Inc., The.

Bryan, Bethany. Social Change in the Twenty-First Century. 2019. (Defining Events of the Twenty-First Century Ser.). (ENG.). 80p. (J). (gr. 6-12). 41.27 *(978-1-68282-607-2(4))* ReferencePoint Pr., Inc.

Chambers, Veronica. Resist: 35 Profiles of Ordinary People Who Rose up Against Tyranny & Injustice. Turnbull, Tracy, illus. 2018. (ENG.). 224p. (J). (gr. 3-7). 16.99 *(978-0-06-279625-7(9),* HarperCollins) HarperCollins Pubs.

Clinton, Chelsea. It's Your World: Get Informed, Get Inspired & Get Going! (ENG., Illus.). (J). (gr. 5). 2017. 432p. pap. 9.99 *(978-0-399-54532-0(8),* Puffin Books) 2015. 416p. 18.99 *(978-0-399-17612-8(8),* Philomel Bks.) Penguin Young Readers Group.

Cohen, Marina. Changing Cultural Landscapes: How Are People & Their Communities Affected by Migration & Settlement?, 1 vol. 2010. (Investigating Human Migration & Settlement Ser.). (ENG., Illus.). 48p. (J). (gr. 5-8). *(978-0-7787-5178-6(3));* pap. *(978-0-7787-5193-9(7))* Crabtree Publishing Co.

Craats, Rennay. Trends. 2008. (USA Past Present Future Ser.). (Illus.). 48p. (J). (gr. 4-6). pap. 10.95 *(978-1-59036-977-7(7));* lib. bdg. 29.05 *(978-1-59036-976-0(9))* Weigl Pubs., Inc.

Davies, Monika. You Can Too! Change the World (Level 4) 2017. (TIME for KIDS(r): Informational Text Ser.). (ENG., Illus.). 32p. (J). (gr. 3-5). pap. 12.99 *(978-1-4258-4978-8(4))* Teacher Created Materials, Inc.

Dodge Cummings, Judy. Rebels & Revolutions: Real Tales of Radical Change in America. 2017. (Mystery & Mayhem Ser.). (ENG., Illus.). 128p. (J). (gr. 4-6). 19.95 *(978-1-61930-547-2(X),* 0a649428-fd58-42af-8dba-5550571227e2); pap. 9.95 *(978-1-61930-551-9(8),* 7ed208fc-70b4-4e66-ad8d-04e7a7442e25) Nomad Pr.

Drake, Jane & Love, Ann. Yes You Can! Your Guide to Becoming an Activist. 2010. 144p. (J). (gr. 5-18). pap. 12.95 *(978-0-88776-942-9(X),* Tundra Bks.) Tundra Bks. CAN. Dist: Penguin Random Hse. LLC.

Drayton, Bill, frwd. Be a Changemaker: How to Start Something That Matters. 2014. (ENG., Illus.). 240p. (YA). (gr. 7). 19.99 *(978-1-58270-465-4(1));* pap. 15.99 *(978-1-58270-464-7(3))* Simon Pulse/Beyond Words.

Duhig, Holly. Change & Resilience. 2018. (Our Values - Level 3 Ser.). (Illus.). 32p. (J). (gr. 5-6). *(978-0-7787-5433-6(2))* Crabtree Publishing Co.

Etheredge, Laura. Saudi Arabia & Yemen, 1 vol. 2011. (Middle East: Region in Transition Ser.). (ENG., Illus.). 176p. (YA). (gr. 10-10). lib. bdg. 43.59 *(978-1-61530-335-9(9),* 86e57c40-80e3-4846-a697-0c5a3ea2c306) Rosen Publishing Group, Inc., The.

—Syria, Lebanon, & Jordan, 1 vol. 2011. (Middle East: Region in Transition Ser.). (ENG., Illus.). 248p. (YA). (gr. 10-10). lib. bdg. 43.59 *(978-1-61530-329-8(4),* b19482da-7bc4-4f09-9f95-b00cd6590743) Rosen Publishing Group, Inc., The.

Etheredge, Laura S., ed. Egypt, 1 vol. 2011. (Middle East: Region in Transition Ser.). (ENG., Illus.). 208p. (YA). (gr. 10-10). 43.59 *(978-1-61530-325-0(1),* 20064351-277f-469b-8386-f0d2d5f8ebc6) Rosen Publishing Group, Inc., The.

Faulkner, Nicholas, ed. Top 101 Reformers, Revolutionaries, Activists, & Change Agents, 1 vol. 2016. (People You Should Know Ser.). (ENG.). 184p. (J). (gr. 8-8). lib. bdg. 38.84 *(978-1-68048-509-7(1),* 749d7355-96be-4e83-8f64-e594d02e586a) Rosen Publishing Group, Inc., The.

Ganeri, Anita. The Top Ten Leaders That Changed the World. 2009. (J). 60.00 *(978-1-4358-9166-1(X),* PowerKids Pr.); (ENG., Illus.). 32p. (J). (gr. 4-5). pap. 11.00 *(978-1-4358-9165-4(1),* 3b811668-8509-412a-9644-35bfef082751, PowerKids Pr.); (ENG., Illus.). 32p. (YA). (gr. 4-5). 30.27 *(978-1-4358-9164-7(3),* 2ce1f0bb-e00f-44c3-8ff3-31056aced95f) Rosen Publishing Group, Inc., The.

Heinz, Brian J. Nathan of Yesteryear & Michael of Today. Friar, Joanne, illus. 2006. (Exceptional Social Studies Titles for Intermediate Grades). (ENG.). 32p. (J). (gr. 3-6). lib. bdg. 22.60 *(978-0-7613-2893-3(9),* Millbrook Pr.) Lerner Publishing Group.

La Bella, Laura. World Financial Meltdown. 2010. (Doomsday Scenarios: Separating Fact from Fiction Ser.). 64p. (YA). (gr. 5-8). E-Book 58.50 *(978-1-4488-1209-7(7))* Rosen Publishing Group, Inc., The.

Lindeen, Mary. Then & Now, 1 vol. (Wonder Readers: Social Studies). (ENG.). (gr. -1-2). 2012. 20p. (J). lib. bdg. 25.32 *(978-1-4296-9616-6(8),* 120532) 2011. 16p. (J). pap. 6.25 *(978-1-4296-7972-5(7),* 118304) 2011. 16p. pap. 35.94 *(978-1-4296-8177-3(2))* Capstone. (Capstone Pr.).

Paul, Caroline. You Are Mighty: A Guide to Changing the World. Tamaki, Lauren, illus. 2018. (ENG.). 128p. (J). 17.99 *(978-1-68119-822-4(3),* 900188032, Bloomsbury Children's Bks.) Bloomsbury Publishing USA.

Pegis, Jessica. I Can Make a Difference! 2016. (Citizenship in Action Ser.). (ENG., Illus.). 24p. (J). (gr. 1-3). *(978-0-7787-2599-2(5));* pap. *(978-0-7787-2605-0(3))* Crabtree Publishing Co.

Penguin Young Readers. The Little Book of Little Activists. 2017. (Illus.). 48p. (J). (gr. k-4). 10.99 *(978-0-451-47854-2(1),* Viking Books for Young Readers) Penguin Young Readers Group.

Petrikowski, Nicki Peter. Working for Tolerance & Social Change Through Service Learning, 1 vol. 2014. (Service Learning for Teens Ser.). (ENG.). 80p. (J). (gr. 7-7). 37.80 *(978-1-4777-7967-5(1),* 627a9b71-1638-4068-81f9-ae1220cb52fa, Rosen Young Adult) Rosen Publishing Group, Inc., The.

Pinkney, Andrea. Hand in Hand: Ten Black Men Who Changed America (Coretta Scott King Author Award Winner) Pinkney, Brian, illus. 2012. (ENG.). 256p. (J). (gr. 3-7). 19.99 *(978-1-4231-4257-7(8))* Little, Brown Bks. for Young Readers.

Progressivism. 2010. (ENG., Illus.). 128p. (gr. 6-12). 45.00 *(978-1-60413-223-6(X),* P179250, Facts On File) Infobase Holdings, Inc.

Rosen, Michael J. & Kaboom! Staff. Let's Build a Playground. Kelson, Ellen & Cecil, Jennifer, illus. 2013. (ENG.). 32p. (J). (gr. 1-4). 15.99 *(978-0-7636-5532-7(5))* Candlewick Pr.

Russell, Bernadette. Be the Change, Make It Happen. Russell, Bernadette, illus. 2017. (ENG., Illus.). 96p. (J). pap. 14.99 *(978-1-61067-404-1(9))* Kane Miller.

Scirri, Kaitlin. How Facebook Changed the World, 1 vol. 2018. (Inventions That Changed the World Ser.). (ENG.). 64p. (gr. 5-5). pap. 16.28 *(978-1-5026-4107-6(0),* 970668d9-173e-4893-bba4-f0b04d94c456) Cavendish Square Publishing LLC.

Stanley, Diane. Resist! Peaceful Acts That Changed Our World. 2020. (ENG., Illus.). 48p. (J). (gr. 2-5). 18.99 *(978-0-8234-4487-8(2),* Neal Porter Bks) Holiday Hse., Inc.

Thompson, Laurie Ann. Be a Changemaker: How to Start Something That Matters. 2014. (ENG., Illus.). (YA). (gr. 7). lib. bdg. 24.60 *(978-1-68065-004-4(1))* Perfection Learning Corp.

Zabinski, Tanya. Peace, Love, Action! Everyday Acts of Goodness from a to Z. 2019. (Illus.). 120p. (J). (gr. 3-7). 19.95 *(978-1-946764-47-8(7),* Plum Blossom Bks.) Parallax Pr.

SOCIAL CLASSES

see also Aristocracy (Social Class); Middle Class; Working Class

Geragotelis, Brittany. What the Spell. 2014. (Life's a Witch Ser.). (ENG., Illus.). 352p. (YA). (gr. 9). pap. 9.99 *(978-1-4424-6707-1(X),* Simon & Schuster Bks. For Young Readers) Simon & Schuster Bks. For Young Readers.

Hartley Steiner. This Is Gabriel Making Sense of School: A Book about Sensory Processing Disorder. 2010. 28p. pap. 13.95 *(978-1-4269-2777-5(0))* Trafford Publishing.

Haugen, David M. & Musser, Susan, eds. The Middle Class, 1 vol. 2010. (Opposing Viewpoints Ser.). (ENG., Illus.). 256p. (gr. 10-12). 50.43 *(978-0-7377-4777-5(3),* e5771fce-f05d-4f77-9c39-9c9c7ca9732f); pap. 34.80 *(978-0-7377-4778-2(1),* 213d3475-c0eb-4951-9b2b-e910633f6773) Greenhaven Publishing LLC. (Greenhaven Publishing).

Henneberg, Susan, ed. The Wealth Gap, 1 vol. 2016. (Opposing Viewpoints Ser.). (ENG.). 216p. (J). (gr. 10-12). pap. 34.80 *(978-1-5345-0034-1(0),* ca12ace0-d5cf-47ca-8dcf-6e7ab8e82d3d); lib. bdg. 50.43 *(978-1-5345-0024-2(3),* 38666cb8-1af4-4cf7-83ce-98c98ed6d726) Greenhaven Publishing LLC. (Greenhaven Publishing).

Hinds, Kathryn. Everyday Life in the Roman Empire, 1 vol. 2010. (Everyday Life Ser.). (ENG.). 320p. (gr. 6-7). 45.50 *(978-0-7614-4484-8(X),* 9653d0c2-588b-46fb-a9dd-9bb0146b4e0d) Cavendish Square Publishing LLC.

—The Patricians, 1 vol. 2006. (Life in the Roman Empire (2006) Ser.). (ENG., Illus.). 80p. (gr. 6-6). 36.93 *(978-0-7614-1654-8(4),* 528ef3e1-3bb3-4a98-ac95-a0cb893ca44e) Cavendish Square Publishing LLC.

Jacobs, Denise. Patricians in the Roman Empire, 1 vol. 2016. (Life in the Roman Empire Ser.). (ENG., Illus.). 80p. (J). (gr. 6-6). 37.36 *(978-1-5026-2257-0(2),* e9332088-2e9b-482b-8de5-d326c39245dc) Cavendish Square Publishing LLC.

Nardo, Don. Lords, Ladies, Peasants, & Knights: Class in the Middle Ages, 1 vol. 2006. (Lucent Library of Historical Eras Ser.). (ENG., Illus.). 104p. (gr. 7-10). lib. bdg. 35.73 *(978-1-59018-928-3(0),* e7dfb5e6-cf73-4532-b183-7169bf59cb46, Lucent Pr.) Greenhaven Publishing LLC.

Robertson, J. Jean. My Community. 2010. (Little World Social Studies). (ENG., Illus.). 24p. (gr. k-2). pap. 9.95 *(978-1-61590-565-2(0),* 9781615905652) Rourke Educational Media.

SOCIAL CONDITIONS

see Social History

SOCIAL CONFLICT

Gallagher, Jim & Kavanaugh, Dorothy. A Guys' Guide to Conflict; a Girls' Guide to Conflict, 1 vol. 2008. (Flip-It-Over Guides to Teen Emotions Ser.). (ENG., Illus.). 128p. (gr. 5-6). lib. bdg. 35.93 *(978-0-7660-2852-4(6),* d7d166a8-ca84-4be5-976e-e54345be766e) Enslow Publishing, LLC.

Gibson, Brylee. Scams. 2007. (Connectors Ser.). (gr. 2-5). pap. *(978-1-877453-01-4(3))* Global Education Systems Ltd.

Hiber, Amanda, ed. Should Governments Negotiate with Terrorists?, 1 vol. 2008. (At Issue Ser.). (ENG., Illus.). 128p. (J). (gr. 10-12). lib. bdg. 41.03 *(978-0-7377-3932-9(0),* ada12ba7-2d6a-400a-b051-712fd7c04f5b); pap. 28.80 *(978-0-7377-3933-6(9),* ca4a01f1-b2dc-4d34-95e1-229833261930) Greenhaven Publishing LLC. (Greenhaven Publishing).

Holt, Rinehart and Winston Staff. Decisions for Health Blue, Chptr. 12: Conflict Management. 4th ed. 2004. pap. 11.20 *(978-0-03-068046-5(8))* Holt McDougal.

Judson, Karen Faye. Resolving Conflicts: How to Get along When You Don't Get Along, 1 vol. 2005. (Issues in Focus Today Ser.). (ENG., Illus.). 112p. (gr. 6-7). lib. bdg. 35.93 *(978-0-7660-2359-8(1),* becf4f5e-9e4a-4d0e-b76b-abe9b0a58a02) Enslow Publishing, LLC.

Naidoo, Beverley. Making It Home: Real-Life Stories from Children Forced to Flee. 2005. (Illus.). 117p. (gr. 3-7). 17.00 *(978-0-7569-5823-7(7))* Perfection Learning Corp.

Obadina, Elizabeth. Ethnic Groups in Africa. Ojakorotu, Victor & Rotberg, Robert I., eds. 2013. (Africa: Progress & Problems Ser.: 13). (Illus.). 112p. (J). (gr. 7-18). 24.95 *(978-1-4222-2939-2(4))* Mason Crest.

Rue, Nancy N. Everything You Need to Know about Peer Mediation. 2009. (Need to Know Library). 64p. (gr. 5-5). 58.50 *(978-1-60854-080-8(4))* Rosen Publishing Group, Inc., The.

Slavens, Elaine. Arguing: Deal with It Word by Word, 1 vol. Murray, Steven, illus. 2010. (Lorimer Deal with It Ser.). (ENG.). 32p. (J). (gr. 4-9). 24.95 *(978-1-55277-498-4(8),* 44deeac5-6965-45a8-848b-df78ba98c048) James Lorimer & Co. Ltd., Pubs. CAN. Dist: Lerner Publishing Group.

—Fighting: Deal with It Without Coming to Blows, 1 vol. Murray, Steven, illus. 2nd ed. 2010. (Lorimer Deal with It Ser.). (ENG.). 32p. (J). (gr. 4-9). 24.95 *(978-1-55277-501-1(1),* 22515bca-f1a4-44a7-a633-0635b9123f86) James Lorimer & Co. Ltd., Pubs. CAN. Dist: Lerner Publishing Group.

—Fighting Deal with It: Deal with It Without Coming to Blows, 1 vol. Murray, Steven, illus. 2nd ed. 2010. (Lorimer Deal with It Ser.). (ENG.). 32p. (J). (gr. 4-8). pap. 12.95 *(978-1-55277-517-2(8),* 9781552775172) James Lorimer & Co. Ltd., Pubs. CAN. Dist: Orca Bk. Pubs. USA.

SOCIAL CUSTOMS

see Manners and Customs

SOCIAL DEMOCRACY

see Socialism

SOCIAL DISTINCTIONS

see Social Classes

SOCIAL EQUALITY

see Equality

SOCIAL HISTORY

see also Economic History; Social Problems; Social Surveys

Amery, Heather. Then & Now. Firmin, Peter, illus. 2008. (Then & Now Ser.). 24p. (J). (gr. -1-3). pap. 4.99 *(978-0-7945-2211-7(4),* Usborne) EDC Publishing.

Barraclough, Sue & Hachette Children's Books Staff. Be an Eco Hero at Home. 2013. (Be an Eco Hero Ser.). (ENG., Illus.). 24p. (J). (gr. 2-4). lib. bdg. 25.65 *(978-1-59771-379-5(1))* Sea-To-Sea Pubns.

Barraclough, Sue & Hachette Children's Group. Be an Eco Hero Outdoors. 2013. (Be an Eco Hero Ser.). (ENG., Illus.). 24p. (J). (gr. 2-4). lib. bdg. 25.65 *(978-1-59771-382-5(1))* Sea-To-Sea Pubns.

Barraclough, Sue, et al. Be an Eco Hero on the Move. 2013. (Be an Eco Hero Ser.). (ENG., Illus.). 24p. (J). (gr. 2-4). lib. bdg. 25.65 *(978-1-59771-380-1(5))* Sea-To-Sea Pubns.

Bryan, Bethany. Social Change in the Twenty-First Century. 2019. (Defining Events of the Twenty-First Century Ser.). (ENG.). 80p. (J). (gr. 6-12). 41.27 *(978-1-68282-607-2(4))* ReferencePoint Pr., Inc.

Butterfield, Moira. Lady of the Manor. 2009. (Medieval Lives Ser.). 32.80 *(978-1-59920-169-6(0))* Black Rabbit Bks.

Davies, Gill. The One Wind. 2008. 32p. (J). pap. 7.99 *(978-1-905470-22-8(3))* SeaSquirt Pubns. GBR. Dist: Basic Distribution, Inc.

Deal, Heidi. Male Privilege. 2017. (Being Female in America Ser.). (ENG., Illus.). 112p. (J). (gr. 6-12). lib. bdg. 41.36 *(978-1-5321-1307-9(2),* 27515, Essential Library) ABDO Publishing Co.

Down, Susan. Theodore Weld: Architect of Abolitionism. 2013. (ENG., Illus.). 64p. (J). *(978-0-7787-1062-2(9));* pap. *(978-0-7787-1065-3(3))* Crabtree Publishing Co.

Global Hotspots, 12 vols., Set. Incl. Afghanistan. Downing, David. (Illus.). (J). lib. bdg. 21.27 *(978-0-7614-3177-0(2),* 133e9d9a-f4ce-420f-8b81-20c4cb3bb67d); Indian Subcontinent. Mason, Paul. lib. bdg. 21.27 *(978-0-7614-3178-7(0),* b4d0ca0a-284c-4fd3-a4ae-4ef69259727c); Iran. Downing, David. lib. bdg. 21.27 *(978-0-7614-3179-4(9),* 4ec1ec8f-235f-4acd-843f-aa915d799997); Iraq. Mason, Paul. lib. bdg. 21.27 *(978-0-7614-3180-0(2),* 7668a935-7646-46b8-895c-c028c2b5791b); Israel & Palestine. Mason, Paul. lib. bdg. 21.27 *(978-0-7614-3181-7(0),* 934277a6-9922-4bda-bb3e-f52728915c35); Sudan. Barker, Geoff. lib. bdg. 21.27 *(978-0-7614-3182-4(9),* 6baf70c8-b2e8-49d2-9ea1-2457e7b53943); 32p. (gr. 5-5). (Global Hotspots Ser.). (ENG.). 2009. Set lib. bdg. 127.62 *(978-0-7614-3175-6(6),* a3611918-f376-42b9-a807-d8ea62a374d6, Cavendish Square) Cavendish Square Publishing LLC.

Grayson, Robert. Ed Begley, Jr. Living Green. 2009. (Voices for Green Choices Ser.). (ENG., Illus.). 48p. (J). (gr. 5-9). lib. bdg. *(978-0-7787-4667-6(4))* Crabtree Publishing Co.

McCarthy, Pat. Friends of the Earth: A History of American Environmentalism with 21 Activities. 2013. (For Kids Ser.: 42). (ENG., Illus.). 144p. (J). (gr. 4). pap. 16.95 *(978-1-56976-718-4(1))* Chicago Review Pr., Inc.

McFall, Sally, ed. Pro/Con 2, 6 vols. 2003. (Illus.). 1392p. (YA). 339.00 *(978-0-7172-5753-9(3))* Scholastic Library Publishing.

—Pro/Con 3, 12 vols. 2004. (Illus.). (YA). 339.00 *(978-0-7172-5927-4(7),* Grolier) Scholastic Library Publishing.

Parker, Victoria. Helping the Environment, 1 vol. 2012. (I Can Make a Difference Ser.). (ENG., Illus.). 32p. (gr. 1-3). pap. 8.29 *(978-1-4329-5951-7(4),* 117714, Heinemann) Capstone.

Perritano, John. Education, Poverty, & Inequality. 2017. (Illus.). 64p. (J). *(978-1-4222-3634-5(X))* Mason Crest.

Wormwood: Solution to Terrorism, Poverty, & Despair. 2004. *(978-0-9755927-0-0(X))* Masha, Segun Inc.

Young, Mary. Nos Gusta Vivir Verde: We Like to Live Green. Parker, Zachary, illus. 2010. (SPA.). 32p. pap. 10.95 *(978-1-935387-01-5(4))* Kalindi Pr.

SOCIAL HYGIENE

see Health; Public Health

SOCIAL LIFE AND CUSTOMS

see Manners and Customs

SOCIAL POLICY

see also Multiculturalism

Drake, Jane & Love, Ann. Yes You Can! Your Guide to Becoming an Activist. 2010. 144p. (J). (gr. 5-18). pap. 12.95 *(978-0-88776-942-9(X),* Tundra Bks.) Tundra Bks. CAN. Dist: Penguin Random Hse. LLC.

Marzilli, Alan. Affirmative Action. 2004. (Point/Counterpoint: Issues in Contemporary American Society Ser.). (ENG., Illus.). 110p. (gr. 9-13). 35.00 *(978-0-7910-7918-8(X),* P114071, Facts On File) Infobase Holdings, Inc.

Open for Debate, 12 vols., Group 2. Incl. Animal Testing. Judson, Karen Faye. lib. bdg. 45.50 *(978-0-7614-1882-5(2),* 4eedcdeb-c370-4d38-b72b-6255bbbe8165); Censorship. Gottfried, Ted. lib. bdg. 45.50 *(978-0-7614-1883-2(0),* ac942367-a37a-44ad-a73b-1a3242157757); Civil Liberties. Spangenburg, Ray & Moser, Kit. lib. bdg. 45.50 *(978-0-7614-1886-3(5),* 415e3099-0f0f-4c1e-b712-c12da5691d1b); Environmental Issues. Fridell, Ron. lib. bdg. 45.50 *(978-0-7614-1885-6(7),* 7edccc67-4f0c-4d8f-a76c-81f6d7453dc9); Taxes. Kowalski, Kathiann M. lib. bdg. 45.50 *(978-0-7614-1887-0(3),* 895cfd0a-fdd4-42af-94f1-3f712dad7f51); (Illus.). 144p. (YA). (gr. 8-8). (Open for Debate Ser.). (ENG.). 2007. 273.00 *(978-0-7614-1881-8(4),* 81b0ec17-e6e6-41d9-9714-19bbc9387136, Cavendish Square) Cavendish Square Publishing LLC.

SOCIAL PROBLEMS

see also Child Labor; Crime; Discrimination; Divorce; Emigration and Immigration; Ethnic Relations; Housing; Juvenile Delinquency; Migrant Labor; Public Health; Race Relations; Social Surveys

Barghoorn, Linda. Zuriel Oduwole: Filmmaker & Campaigner for Girls' Education. 2018. (Remarkable Lives Revealed Ser.). (ENG., Illus.). 32p. (J). (gr. 3-3). *(978-0-7787-4703-1(4));* pap. *(978-0-7787-4714-7(X))* Crabtree Publishing Co.

Brooks, Ben. Stories for Kids Who Dare to Be Different: True Tales of Amazing People Who Stood up & Stood Out. Winter, Quinton, illus. 2019. (Dare to Be Different Ser.). (ENG.). 160p. (J). (gr. 3-7). 17.99 *(978-0-7624-6855-3(6),* Running Pr. Kids) Running Pr.

Bryfonski, Dedria, ed. Class Conflict in Charles Dickens' a Tale of Two Cities, 1 vol. 2013. (Social Issues in Literature Ser.). (ENG., Illus.). 208p. (gr. 10-12). pap. 33.00 *(978-0-7377-6975-3(0),* 852ba0e3-cb97-4a04-b147-fa1da614363f); lib. bdg. 48.03 *(978-0-7377-6974-6(2),* d47d082e-6661-4472-91db-789265ab6786) Greenhaven Publishing LLC. (Greenhaven Publishing).

—Death in Ernest Hemingway's the Old Man & the Sea, 1 vol. 2014. (Social Issues in Literature Ser.). (ENG., Illus.). 176p. (gr. 10-12). pap. 33.00 *(978-0-7377-6979-1(3),* 51eeebcc-2bd4-46e1-a28f-43b824b3dae7); lib. bdg. 48.03 *(978-0-7377-6978-4(5),* 5a7230d2-4467-4c7a-954a-1b3ce68eaa1d) Greenhaven Publishing LLC. (Greenhaven Publishing).

Chambers, Veronica. Resist: 35 Profiles of Ordinary People Who Rose up Against Tyranny & Injustice. Turnbull, Tracy, illus. 2018. (ENG.). 224p. (J). (gr. 3-7). 16.99 *(978-0-06-279625-7(9),* HarperCollins) HarperCollins Pubs.

Edwards, Nicola. Bullying. (Illus.). 32p. 18.95 *(978-1-932333-07-7(X))* Chrysalis Education.

Espejo, Roman, ed. Urban America, 1 vol. 2011. (Opposing Viewpoints Ser.). (ENG.). 208p. (gr. 10-12). lib. bdg. 50.43 *(978-0-7377-5249-6(1),* be2ebae3-b2cb-45b1-b33e-226e516606ce, Greenhaven Publishing) Greenhaven Publishing LLC.

—What Is Humanity's Greatest Challenge?, 1 vol. 2010. (At Issue Ser.). (ENG., Illus.). 112p. (gr. 10-12). 41.03

S

(978-0-7377-4314-2(X), 237aa490-2284-4c57-b39d-9a0d9c0a2c31); pap. 28.80 *(978-0-7377-4313-5(1),* 6f367c06-4f23-4281-978c-88e9e78df705) Greenhaven Publishing LLC. (Greenhaven Publishing).

Furgang, Kathy. Ending Hunger & Homelessness Through Service Learning, 1 vol. 2014. (Service Learning for Teens Ser.). (ENG.). 80p. (YA). (gr. 7-7). 37.80 *(978-1-4777-7959-0(0),* 6792312c-dc05-4a31-aa26-6623c80fe6b5, Rosen Young Adult) Rosen Publishing Group, Inc., The.

Gallagher, Aileen. The Muckrakers: American Journalism During the Age of Reform. 2009. (Progressive Movement 1900-1920: Efforts to Reform America's New Industrial Society Ser.). 32p. (gr. 3-4). 47.90 *(978-1-60854-173-7(8))* Rosen Publishing Group, Inc., The.

Global Issues, 9 bks., Set. Incl. Closing the Borders. Davies, Wendy. 1995. lib. bdg. 19.98 *(978-1-56847-335-2(4),* AS335-4); Exploitation of Children. Ennew, Judith. 1996. lib. bdg. 19.98 *(978-0-8172-4546-7(4));* Gender Issues. Stearman, Kaye & Vander Gaag, Nikki. 1996. lib. bdg. 19.98 *(978-0-8172-4545-0(6));* Genetic Engineering. Bryan, Jenny. 1997. lib. bdg. 19.98 *(978-0-8172-4860-4(9));* Racism. Garg, Samidha & Hardy, Jan. 1997. lib. bdg. 19.98 *(978-0-8172-4548-1(0));* Refugees. Warner, Rachel. 1997. lib. bdg. 19.98 *(978-0-8172-4547-4(2));* Rich-Poor Divide. Garlake, Teresa. 1995. lib. bdg. 19.98 *(978-1-56847-336-9(2),* AS336-2); United Nations - Peacekeeper? Johnson, Edward. 1995. lib. bdg. 19.98 *(978-1-56847-267-6(6),* AS267-6); (Illus.). 64p. (YA). (gr. 5-10). Set lib. bdg. 179.82 *(978-0-7398-1534-2(2))* Heinemann-Raintree.

Hamilton, Jill, ed. Activism, 1 vol. 2009. (Issues That Concern You Ser.). (ENG., Illus.). 120p. (gr. 7-10). 43.63 *(978-0-7377-4493-4(6),* e7775855-2254-456c-9806-1d5bc59f717f, Greenhaven Publishing) Greenhaven Publishing LLC.

Harmony Island: ATropical Adventure in Conflict Resolutuion. 2005. (YA). cd-rom *(978-0-9754754-4-7(4))* Academic Edge, Inc.

Hazen, Walter A. Everyday Life: Reform in America. 2004. (Illus.). iv, 100p. pap. 12.95 *(978-0-673-58898-2(X))* Good Year Bks.

Herman, Gail. Who Was Coretta Scott King? 2019. (Who HQ Ser.). (ENG.). 108p. (J). (gr. 2-3). 16.36 *(978-1-64310-859-9(X))* Penworthy Co., LLC, The.

Herman, Gail & Who HQ. Who Was Coretta Scott King? Copeland, Gregory, illus. 2017. (Who Was? Ser.). 112p. (J). (gr. 3-7). 5.99 *(978-0-451-53261-9(9),* Penguin Workshop) Penguin Young Readers Group.

Kallen, Stuart A., ed. Does Equality Exist in America?, 1 vol. 2006. (At Issue Ser.). (ENG., Illus.). 112p. (gr. 10-12). pap. 28.80 *(978-0-7377-3434-8(5),* 3bb18673-7efb-4926-a1eb-3da071dedc26); lib. bdg. 41.03 *(978-0-7377-3433-1(7),* 66bb5b16-77b8-48fe-83f4-9c404136a65c) Greenhaven Publishing LLC. (Greenhaven Publishing).

Kent, Deborah. Dorothy Day: Friend to the Forgotten. 2004. (ENG., Illus.). 179p. (J). pap. 12.00 *(978-0-8028-5265-6(3))* Eerdmans, William B. Publishing Co.

Krull, Kathleen. The Only Woman in the Photo: Frances Perkins & Her New Deal for America. Bye, Alexandra, illus. 2020. (ENG.). 48p. (J). (gr. -1-3). 19.99 *(978-1-4814-9151-8(2),* Simon & Schuster Bks. For Young Readers) Simon & Schuster Bks. For Young Readers.

Let's work together to build a cultured family 5: Kindle eBook, 8 vols., Set. Incl. How to Deal with Bullies. Kravetz, Jonathan. (J). lib. bdg. 26.27 *(978-1-4042-3670-7(8),* 4357e347-2e94-48ae-8613-094b4ea22c45); How to Deal with Fighting. Kravetz, Jonathan. (J). lib. bdg. 26.27 *(978-1-4042-3672-1(4),* 535d463a-ce52-4df0-af06-fc41da62cbf4); How to Deal with Insults. Fiedler, Julie. (J). lib. bdg. 26.27 *(978-1-4042-3673-8(2),* eefea0ff-423c-47ff-95c8-cce3045af684); How to Deal with Jealousy. Kravetz, Jonathan. (YA). lib. bdg. 26.27 *(978-1-4042-3674-5(0),* 927c1478-91b5-4e19-a2ad-2b2c31a5aa15); How to Deal with Teasing. Fiedler, Julie. (J). lib. bdg. 26.27 *(978-1-4042-3675-2(9),* e44bd11e-0634-45f0-845a-93b496a60ed5, PowerKids Pr.); (Illus.). 24p. (gr. 2-3). (Let's Work It Out Ser.). (ENG.). 2006. Set lib. bdg. 105.08 *(978-1-4042-3607-3(4),* 978682f4-1cf1-4555-a814-93b08f005314, PowerKids Pr.) Rosen Publishing Group, Inc., The.

McFall, Sally, ed. Pro/Con 2, 6 vols. 2003. (Illus.). 1392p. (YA). 339.00 *(978-0-7172-5753-9(3))* Scholastic Library Publishing.

—Pro/Con 3, 12 vols. 2004. (Illus.). (YA). 339.00 *(978-0-7172-5927-4(7),* Grolier) Scholastic Library Publishing.

Mortmain, Beatrice. Social Activism: Working Together to Create Change in Our Society, 1 vol. 2017. (Spotlight on Civic Action Ser.). (ENG.). 32p. (J). (gr. 4-5). 27.93 *(978-1-5081-6398-5(7),* 11e2ab07-5478-43f8-9354-fae2dd98020e, PowerKids Pr.) Rosen Publishing Group, Inc., The.

Open for Debate - Group 5, 8 vols., Set. Incl. National Health Care. Kowalski, Kathiann M. lib. bdg. 45.50 *(978-0-7614-2943-2(3),* edaa0977-a53f-47fe-aa23-2e0389c5e727); Political Campaigns. Naden, Corinne. lib. bdg. 45.50 *(978-0-7614-2944-9(1),* 9d2e64a5-2c0c-4a63-9836-204d64ed8840); Religious Fundamentalism. Fridell, Ron. lib. bdg. 45.50 *(978-0-7614-2945-6(X),* d9d1f5c0-2b35-4938-9b69-3cde347cd370); Right to Die. Stefoff, Rebecca. lib. bdg. 45.50 *(978-0-7614-2948-7(4),* bcbd0407-c7ba-4a50-9da6-fe926a35d042); 144p. (YA). (gr. 8-8). (Open for Debate Ser.). (ENG.). 2009. Set lib. bdg. 182.00 *(978-0-7614-2940-1(9),* dee07674-67e9-492f-9ba3-039659ed2638, Cavendish Square) Cavendish Square Publishing LLC.

Paul, Caroline. You Are Mighty: A Guide to Changing the World. Tamaki, Lauren, illus. 2018. (ENG.). 128p. (J). 17.99 *(978-1-68119-822-4(3),* 900188032, Bloomsbury Children's Bks.) Bloomsbury Publishing USA.

Peters, Elisa. Malala Yousafzai: Pakistani Activist for Female Education, 1 vol. 2017. (Spotlight on Civic Courage: Heroes of Conscience Ser.). (ENG., Illus.). 48p. (J). (gr. 6-6). 33.47 *(978-1-5081-7749-4(X),* 92731d4f-26f7-4da6-ae6b-19013b03ff01) Rosen Publishing Group, Inc., The.

Progressivism. 2010. (ENG., Illus.). 128p. (gr. 6-12). 45.00 *(978-1-60413-223-6(X),* P179250, Facts On File) Infobase Holdings, Inc.

Rodger, Ellen & Field, Jon Eben. Social Justice Activist. 2009. (Get Involved! Ser.). (ENG., Illus.). 32p. (J). (gr. 3-6). *(978-0-7787-4696-6(8));* pap. *(978-0-7787-4708-6(5))* Crabtree Publishing Co.

Runstedler, Nancy. Pay It Forward Kids: Small Acts, Big Change, 1 vol. 2013. (Ripple Effects Ser.). (ENG., Illus.). 64p. (YA). (gr. 6-10). 19.95 *(978-1-55455-301-3(6),* 5c6c46af-048a-40df-8bac-ae0eaef09ed4) Fitzhenry & Whiteside, Ltd. CAN. Dist: Firefly Bks., Ltd.

Sakany, Lois. Progressive Leaders: The Platforms & Policies of America's Reform Politicians. (Progressive Movement 1900-1920: Efforts to Reform America's New Industrial Society Ser.). 32p. (gr. 3-4). 2009. 47.90 *(978-1-60854-168-3(1))* 2006. (ENG., Illus.). (YA). lib. bdg. 30.47 *(978-1-4042-0193-4(9),* 440d7278-674c-4b79-8c8c-36efba421ac9) Rosen Publishing Group, Inc., The.

Scherer, Lauri S., ed. Death & Dying, 1 vol. 2014. (Issues That Concern You Ser.). (ENG., Illus.). 104p. (gr. 7-10). lib. bdg. 43.63 *(978-0-7377-6937-1(8),* 73ba075b-729e-468a-851a-53df43ebf82a, Greenhaven Publishing) Greenhaven Publishing LLC.

Smith, Paula. Be the Change in the World. 2014. (Be the Change! Ser.). (ENG., Illus.). 24p. (J). (gr. 2-3). *(978-0-7787-0622-9(2));* pap. *(978-0-7787-0634-2(6))* Crabtree Publishing Co.

Spence, Kelly. Yusra Mardini: Refugee Hero & Olympic Swimmer. 2018. (Remarkable Lives Revealed Ser.). (ENG., Illus.). 32p. (J). (gr. 3-3). *(978-0-7787-4711-6(5));* pap. *(978-0-7787-4726-0(3))* Crabtree Publishing Co.

Steele, Philip. Activists, 1 vol. 2011. (20th Century Lives Ser.). (ENG., Illus.). 32p. (YA). (gr. 5-5). 30.27 *(978-1-4488-3292-7(6),* dd57bb80-0f38-4720-92a2-71a168739e3c) Rosen Publishing Group, Inc., The.

Swarts, Katherine, ed. Welfare, 1 vol. 2008. (Social Issues Firsthand Ser.). (ENG., Illus.). 128p. (gr. 10-12). lib. bdg. 39.93 *(978-0-7377-4079-0(5),* 86740813-f723-4d97-87ef-9925ce9be46c, Greenhaven Publishing) Greenhaven Publishing LLC.

The March for Our Lives Founders. Glimmer of Hope: How Tragedy Sparked a Movement. 2018. (ENG., Illus.). 208p. (YA). 18.00 *(978-1-9848-3609-0(9),* Razorbill) Penguin Young Readers Group.

Vogel, Elizabeth. The Conflict Resolution Library: Set 4: Facing Changes, 6 bks. Incl. Dealing with Choices. lib. bdg. 26.27 *(978-0-8239-5410-0(2),* 3a5a910b-b77b-42f9-b7cf-628fdf06446e); Dealing with Rules at Home. lib. bdg. 26.27 *(978-0-8239-5411-7(0),* b906c612-b724-4226-99ae-c98d79e50970, PowerKids Pr.); Dealing with Showoffs. lib. bdg. 26.27 *(978-0-8239-5412-4(9),* b027c89b-1b93-4071-b3c5-c94619eaa576, PowerKids Pr.); 24p. (J). (gr. 2-3). 1999. (Illus.). Set lib. bdg. 73.80 o.p. *(978-0-8239-7007-0(8),* PowerKids Pr.) Rosen Publishing Group, Inc., The.

SOCIAL PROBLEMS—FICTION

Alexander, Adam. The Flurple Woozle. 2013. 26p. 16.99 *(978-0-9910324-7-1(0))* Mindstir Media.

Alexiou, Michelle. A Bully for Berl: Playground Escapades. 2012. (ENG.). 45p. (J). pap. 26.95 *(978-1-4327-8370-9(X));* pap. 22.95 *(978-1-4327-8364-8(5))* Outskirts Pr., Inc.

Andrews, Jesse. Munmun. 2018. (ENG.). 416p. (YA). (gr. 9-17). 18.99 *(978-1-4197-2871-6(7),* 1140101, Amulet Bks.) Abrams, Inc.

The Ask & the Answer (with Bonus Short Story) Chaos Walking: Book Two. 2014. (Chaos Walking Ser.: 2). (ENG., Illus.). 560p. (YA). (gr. 9). pap. 12.00 *(978-0-7636-7617-9(9))* Candlewick Pr.

Berenstain, Jan, et al. The Berenstain Bears & the Bad Influence. Berenstain, Stan & Jan & Berenstain, Mike, illus. 2008. (Berenstain Bears Ser.). (ENG.). 32p. (J). (gr. -1-3). pap. 4.99 *(978-0-06-057388-1(0),* HarperFestival) HarperCollins Pubs.

Berenstain, Stan, et al. The Berenstain Bears & the Bad Influence. Berenstain, Stan et al, illus. 2008. (Berenstain Bears Ser.). 32p. (J). (gr. -1-2). 8.99 *(978-0-06-057404-8(6),* HarperFestival) HarperCollins Pubs.

Blume, Judy. Then Again, Maybe I Won't. (J). 125p. pap. 3.99 *(978-0-8072-1445-9(0));* 2004. 164p. (gr. 5-9). pap. 29.00 incl. audio *(978-0-8072-0796-3(9),* LYA 354 SP) Random Hse. Audio Publishing Group. (Listening Library).

Christopher, Matt. Power Pitcher. 2008. (ENG.). 112p. (J). (gr. 3-7). pap. 9.99 *(978-0-316-05207-8(8))* Little, Brown Bks. for Young Readers.

Coleman, Sadie. The Biggest Heart Ever. Coleman, Sadie, illus. 2013. (Illus.). 24p. 14.99 *(978-0-9881969-0-2(5))* Vorpal Words, LLC.

Dana, Kimberly. Lucy & Cecee's How to Survive (and Thrive) in Middle School. 2012. 278p. (gr. 4-6). 27.95 *(978-1-4620-3967-8(7));* pap. 17.95 *(978-1-4620-3966-1(9))* iUniverse, Inc.

Davies, Stephen. Outlaw. 2011. (ENG.). 304p. (YA). (gr. 7). 16.99 *(978-0-547-39017-8(3))* Houghton Mifflin Harcourt Publishing Co.

Defrange, Tom. A Tinker Tale: Celebrating Differences. 2011. 36p. pap. 24.95 *(978-1-4560-5081-8(8))* America Star Bks.

Dickens, Charles. Hard Times. 2020. (ENG.). (J). 242p. 19.95 *(978-1-61895-950-8(6));* 240p. pap. 12.95 *(978-1-61895-949-2(2))* Bibliotech Pr.

—Hard Times. 2019. (ENG.). (J). 312p. pap. 8.99 *(978-0-368-97109-9(0));* 146p. pap. 12.96 *(978-0-368-26154-1(9))* Blurb, Inc.

—Hard Times. 2019. (ENG.). 274p. (J). pap. 12.89 *(978-1-7278-8597-2(X))* CreateSpace Independent Publishing Platform.

—Hard Times. (ENG.). (J). 2019. 234p. pap. 9.99 *(978-1-7105-9345-7(8))* 2019. 662p. pap. 24.99 *(978-1-6984-8207-1(8))* 2019. (Illus.). 280p. pap. 12.99 *(978-1-7024-2791-3(9))* 2019. (Illus.). 406p. pap. 21.45 *(978-1-7031-0980-1(5))* 2019. 294p. pap. 18.99 *(978-1-0891-3857-0(1))* 2019. 426p. pap. 20.00 *(978-1-6895-7107-4(1))* 2019. 582p. pap. 33.99 *(978-1-6895-4630-0(1))* 2019. 328p. pap. 17.99 *(978-1-6867-1385-9(1))* 2019. 660p. pap. 36.99 *(978-1-0861-5141-1(0))* 2019. 624p. pap. 37.99 *(978-1-0799-3468-7(5))* 2019. 662p. pap. 32.99 *(978-1-0784-4326-5(2))* 2019. 662p. pap. 40.99 *(978-1-0777-7594-7(6))* 2019. 660p. pap. 40.99 *(978-1-0753-8733-3(7))* 2019. 662p. pap. 39.99 *(978-1-0711-8399-1(0))* 2019. 328p. pap. 17.99 *(978-1-0972-9877-8(9))* 2019. 662p. pap. 36.99 *(978-1-0708-9682-3(9))* 2019. 582p. pap. 33.99 *(978-1-0932-0880-1(5))* 2019. 660p. pap. 38.99 *(978-1-0959-2916-2(X))* 2019. 660p. pap. 40.99 *(978-1-0913-6966-5(6))* 2019. 660p. pap. 38.99 *(978-1-0913-7346-4(9))* 2019. 582p. pap. 37.99 *(978-1-7992-5524-6(7))* 2019. 662p. pap. 41.99 *(978-1-7969-8839-0(1))* 2019. (Illus.). 426p. pap. 20.00 *(978-1-7946-9134-6(0))* 2018. (Illus.). 206p. pap. 9.60 *(978-1-7906-4063-8(6))* 2018. (Illus.). 582p. pap. 33.99 *(978-1-7915-8534-1(5))* 2018. (Illus.). 206p. pap. 9.70 *(978-1-7903-1345-7(7))* 2018. (Illus.). 320p. pap. 16.82 *(978-1-7267-6668-5(3))* 2018. (Illus.). 320p. pap. 16.82 *(978-1-7267-6666-1(7))* Independently Published.

—Hard Times. 2020. (ENG.). 228p. (J). pap. *(978-1-716-13517-0(6))* Lulu Pr., Inc.

—Hard Times, 1 vol. 2009. (Real Reads Ser.). (ENG., Illus.). 64p. (J). (gr. 5-5). pap. 14.55 *(978-1-60754-386-2(9),* 32765c58-45b5-41ee-9eb9-e9f42462683f); lib. bdg. 33.93 *(978-1-60754-385-5(0),* f89548eb-e14d-4e6d-a8f5-55ffbcdd0b83) Rosen Publishing Group, Inc., The. (Windmill Bks.).

Dickens, Charles, creator. Hard Times. 2020. (ENG.). 498p. (J). pap. *(978-0-371-24651-1(2))* HardPr.

Ellis, Ann Dee. This Is What I Did: 2009. (ENG.). 176p. (J). (gr. 7-17). pap. 11.99 *(978-0-316-01362-8(5))* Little, Brown Bks. for Young Readers.

Feder, Aliza & Sofer, Rochel. We Need to Talk. 2008. 250p. 18.95 *(978-1-934440-30-8(2),* Devora Publishing) Simcha Media Group.

Fisk, Katie. Flying with the Angels. 2008. 62p. pap. 19.95 *(978-1-60563-608-5(8))* America Star Bks.

Fleming, Candace. Lowji Discovers America. 2008. (ENG.). 160p. (J). (gr. 2-6). pap. 7.99 *(978-1-4169-5832-1(0),* Aladdin) Simon & Schuster Children's Publishing.

Forler, Nan. Bird Child. Thisdale, François, illus. 2009. 32p. (J). (gr. k-3). 19.95 *(978-0-88776-894-1(6),* Tundra Bks.) Tundra Bks. CAN. Dist: Penguin Random Hse. LLC.

Galante, Cecilia. Hershey Herself. 2008. (Mix Ser.). (ENG.). 336p. (J). (gr. 4-8). pap. 15.99 *(978-1-4169-5463-7(5))* Simon & Schuster, Inc.

Garrett, Troy. Kramer's World. 204p. 2010. pap. 12.50 *(978-1-60693-155-4(5))* 2008. 23.50 *(978-1-60693-518-7(6))* Strategic Book Publishing & Rights Agency (SBPRA). (Eloquent Bks.).

Godbersen, Anna. Envy. (Luxe Ser.: 3). (ENG.). (YA). (gr. 9). 2018. 448p. pap. 9.99 *(978-0-06-285218-2(3),* HarperTeen) 2009. 432p. pap. 9.99 *(978-0-06-134574-6(1))* HarperCollins Pubs.

Gómez Cerda, Alfredo. Barro de Medellin/ Mud of Medellin. Lopez, Xan, illus. 2010. (SPA.). 146p. (YA). (gr. 5-8). *(978-84-263-6849-2(2))* Vives, Luis Editorial (Edelvives).

Gorman, Amanda. Change Sings: A Children's Anthem. Long, Loren, illus. 2021. (ENG.). 32p. (J). (gr. -1-3). 18.99 *(978-0-593-20322-4(4),* Viking Books for Young Readers) Penguin Young Readers Group.

Handy Manny Pop-up Tool Book. 2009. 6p. 12.99 *(978-1-4231-2114-5(7))* Disney Pr.

Hichens, Joanne. Stained. 2008. (Cutting Edge Ser.). (ENG.). 200p. pap. *(978-1-84167-715-6(9))* Ransom Publishing Ltd.

Hinton, S. E. Esto Ya Es Otra Historia. (SPA.). (J). 6.95 *(978-84-204-4121-4(X))* Santillana USA Publishing Co., Inc.

—Rumble Fish. 2006. 21.50 *(978-0-8446-7283-0(1))* Smith, Peter Pub., Inc.

—Rumble Fish. 2013. lib. bdg. 18.40 *(978-0-606-35120-1(5))* Turtleback.

Hoban, Russell. Best Friends for Frances. Hoban, Lillian, illus. 2009. (I Can Read Book 2 Ser.). 48p. (J). (gr. -1-3). 16.99 *(978-0-06-083801-0(9))* HarperCollins Pubs.

Holcomb, T. Toot-Toot & Her Troubles: Name Calling. 2008. 12p. pap. 24.95 *(978-1-60563-472-2(7))* America Star Bks.

Horvath, Polly. My One Hundred Adventures. 2008. (My One Hundred Adventures Ser.). (ENG., Illus.). 272p. (J). (gr. 4-6). lib. bdg. 22.44 *(978-0-375-95582-2(8))* Random House Publishing Group.

Immenschuh, Marilyn Y. Samantha & the Kids of Room 220. 2007. 148p. per. 11.95 *(978-0-595-46842-3(X))* iUniverse, Inc.

Ireland, Justina. Dread Nation. (ENG.). (YA). (gr. 9). 2019. 480p. pap. 11.99 *(978-0-06-257061-1(7))* 2018. 464p. 17.99 *(978-0-06-257060-4(9))* HarperCollins Pubs. (Balzer & Bray).

Irwin, Judy. What's It to You? 2013. 106p. pap. *(978-0-9877088-7-8(2))* Irwin, Judy.

Island of Legends. 2014. (Unwanteds Ser.: 4). (ENG., Illus.). 496p. (J). (gr. 3-7). 19.99 *(978-1-4424-9328-5(3),* Aladdin) Simon & Schuster Children's Publishing.

James, Debra & James, Jessica. The Social Pyramid. 2010. 57p. pap. 7.50 *(978-0-557-40789-7(3))* Lulu Pr., Inc.

Jens, Charlene. Ookie Gets a New Best Friend. 2008. 39p. pap. 24.95 *(978-1-60474-475-0(8))* America Star Bks.

Jones Med, Marquita J. Marvette Made Fun of Me. 2012. (ENG.). 34p. (J). pap. 23.95 *(978-1-4327-8551-2(6))* Outskirts Pr., Inc.

Martinez, Rafael. El Deseo de Aurelio. Martinez, Enrique, illus. 2006. (la Orilla del Viento Ser.). (SPA.). 48p. (J). (gr. 8-10). pap. *(978-968-16-7988-0(1))* Fondo de Cultura Economica.

McKee, David. The Conquerors. 2005. (ENG., Illus.). 32p. (J). (gr. k-2). pap. 12.99 *(978-1-84270-468-4(0))* Andersen Pr. GBR. Dist: Independent Pubs. Group.

McMann, Lisa. Island of Shipwrecks. 2015. (Unwanteds Ser.: 5). (ENG., Illus.). 480p. (J). (gr. 3-7). pap. 9.99 *(978-1-4424-9332-2(1),* Aladdin) Simon & Schuster Children's Publishing.

—Island of Silence. 2013. (Unwanteds Ser.: 2). (ENG., Illus.). 432p. (J). (gr. 3-7). pap. 8.99 *(978-1-4424-0772-5(7),* Aladdin) Simon & Schuster Children's Publishing.

—Island of Silence. 2013. (Unwanteds Ser.: 2). lib. bdg. 18.40 *(978-0-606-32044-3(X))* Turtleback.

Milan, D. S. A Year of Starless Nights. 2013. 154p. pap. 14.95 *(978-1-62432-012-5(0))* Loose Leaves Publishing.

Miller, Jonathan. Kim's Introductions. 2009. 48p. pap. 21.99 *(978-1-4389-0856-4(3))* AuthorHouse.

Monsters of Men (with Bonus Short Story) Chaos Walking: Book Three. 2014. (Chaos Walking Ser.: 3). (ENG., Illus.). 656p. (YA). (gr. 9). pap. 14.00 *(978-0-7636-7619-3(5))* Candlewick Pr.

Ness, Patrick. Chaos Walking Movie Tie-In Edition: the Knife of Never Letting Go. 2020. (Chaos Walking Ser.: 1). (ENG.). 496p. (YA). (gr. 9). pap. 12.00 *(978-1-5362-0052-2(2))* Candlewick Pr.

—The Knife of Never Letting Go. 2018. (Chaos Walking Ser.: 1). (ENG.). 496p. (YA). (gr. 9). 24.99 *(978-1-5362-0053-9(0))* Candlewick Pr.

—The Knife of Never Letting Go. 2010. 20.00 *(978-1-60686-704-4(0))* Perfection Learning Corp.

—The Knife of Never Letting Go. 2014. (Chaos Walking Ser.: 1). 479p. lib. bdg. 22.10 *(978-0-606-35873-6(0))* Turtleback.

Novel Units. Animal Farm Novel Units Student Packet. 2019. (ENG.). (YA). pap. 13.99 *(978-1-56137-306-2(0),* Novel Units, Inc.) Classroom Library Co.

Olaogbebikan, Michael Olumide. Playmate. 2013. (Illus.). 20p. pap. 19.82 *(978-1-4772-4659-7(2))* AuthorHouse.

Pérez, Celia C. Strange Birds: A Field Guide to Ruffling Feathers. 2019. (Illus.). 384p. (J). (gr. 4-7). 17.99 *(978-0-425-29043-9(3),* Kokila) Penguin Young Readers Group.

Root, Phyllis. Toot Toot Zoom! Cordell, Matthew, illus. 2009. (ENG.). 40p. (J). (gr. -1-2). 15.99 *(978-0-7636-3452-0(2))* Candlewick Pr.

Sposito, Pipi, illus. Charles Dickens: Hard Times. 2021. (Sweet Cherry Easy Classics Ser.: 2). (ENG.). 96p. (J). 6.95 *(978-1-78226-746-1(8),* c45e9dcf-9689-4e0e-862b-f00e43b98e2a) Sweet Cherry Publishing GBR. Dist: Baker & Taylor Publisher Services (BTPS).

Students of John Marshall High School, Students of John Marshall High. The Elotes Man Will Soon Be Gone. 2008. (ENG.). 176p. (J). pap. 15.00 *(978-0-9790073-3-0(X))* 826 Valencia.

Sullivan, Therese M. & Bitner, Pamela. A Gift from Valentine. 2007. 24p. (J). per. 12.95 *(978-1-58939-981-5(1))* Virtualbookworm.com Publishing, Inc.

Sydor, Colleen. Timmerman Was Here. Debon, Nicolas, illus. 2009. 32p. (J). (gr. -1-1). 19.95 *(978-0-88776-890-3(3),* Tundra Bks.) Tundra Bks. CAN. Dist: Penguin Random Hse. LLC.

Thomas, Joyce Carol. Linda Brown, You Are Not Alone: The Brown v. Board of Education Decision. 2003. (ENG., Illus.). 128p. (J). 16.49 *(978-0-7868-2640-7(1))* Hyperion Pr.

Topakian, Patricia E. The Mystery of the Old Brown Suitcase. 2007. (ENG.). 26p. pap. 15.99 *(978-1-4196-2819-1(4))* CreateSpace Independent Publishing Platform.

Valentine, Billy. Trust Love: A Tale of Angels. 2008. 176p. (J). pap. 13.95 *(978-0-595-44989-7(1))* iUniverse, Inc.

Wagner, Jane. J. T. 125p. (J). (gr. 3-5). pap. 3.00 *(978-0-8072-1403-9(5),* Listening Library) Random Hse. Audio Publishing Group.

SOCIAL PSYCHOLOGY

see also Attitude (Psychology); Interpersonal Relations; Psychology, Applied; Social Adjustment; Violence

Amos, Janine & Spenceley, Annabel. Let's Make Friends, 1 vol. 2009. (Best Behavior Ser.). (ENG., Illus.). 32p. (J). (gr. -1-2). 27.27 *(978-1-60754-500-2(4),* 5ef76246-1f11-4b51-ac0e-43d1d162d3e5); pap. 11.55 *(978-1-60754-499-9(7),* 68eecf9b-33f3-4e9f-a397-a4b05ebc8154) Rosen Publishing Group, Inc., The. (Windmill Bks.).

Antill, Sara. Social Intelligence, 1 vol. 2013. (Character Strength Ser.). 24p. (J). (ENG.). (gr. 2-3). pap. 9.25 *(978-1-4488-9818-3(8),* e6502f80-d565-4e92-82b0-4e4965c761b2); (ENG.). (gr. 2-3). lib. bdg. 26.27 *(978-1-4488-9680-6(0),* 76f11b70-54e4-4d9a-b269-dc424ec0918d); (gr. 3-6). pap. 49.50 *(978-1-4488-9819-0(6))* Rosen Publishing Group, Inc., The. (PowerKids Pr.).

Brown Bear Books. The Individual & Society. 2011. (Psychology Ser.). (ENG., Illus.). 112p. (J). (gr. 9-12). lib. bdg. 42.80 *(978-1-936333-19-6(8),* 16779) Brown Bear Bks.

Cómo Organizar una Manifestación, 1 vol. 2014. (Sé un líder de la Comunidad (Be a Community Leader) Ser.). (SPA.). 32p. (J). (gr. 5-5). lib. bdg. 27.93 *(978-1-4777-6913-3(7),* 84ad41f3-f84f-48e9-b32c-d2e8d1bfb514, PowerKids Pr.) Rosen Publishing Group, Inc., The.

Evans, Christine. Objectification of Women in the Media. 2019. (Women & Society Ser.). (ENG.). 80p. (J). (gr. 6-12). *(978-1-68282-543-3(4))* ReferencePoint Pr., Inc.

Ford, Jeanne Marie. Challenging Stereotypes & Prejudices, 1 vol. 2017. (Active Citizenship Today Ser.). (ENG.). 32p. (gr. 3-3). pap. 11.58 *(978-1-5026-2916-6(X),* fbb62af8-e662-4ac3-87ed-4874cfbcf064) Cavendish Square Publishing LLC.

Harris, Duchess & Mooney, Carla. Fighting Stereotypes in Sports. 2018. (Race & Sports Ser.). (ENG., Illus.). 112p. (J). (gr. 6-12). lib. bdg. 41.36 *(978-1-5321-1669-8(1),* 30590, Essential Library) ABDO Publishing Co.

HolmesKaren. Slow Motion: Taking Your Time High Beginning Book with Online Access, 1 vol. 2014. (ENG., Illus.). 24p. (J). pap., E-Book, E-Book 7.50 *(978-1-107-69129-2(X))* Cambridge Univ. Pr.

How to Organize a Rally, 1 vol. 2014. (Be a Community Leader Ser.). (ENG., Illus.). 32p. (J). (gr. 5-5). lib. bdg. 27.93 *(978-1-4777-6693-4(6),* 50218642-211c-4c20-8cb1-42459f90bc6e, PowerKids Pr.) Rosen Publishing Group, Inc., The.

January, Brendan. Information Insecurity: Privacy under Siege. 2015. (ENG., Illus.). 96p. (YA). (gr. 6-12). lib. bdg. 34.65 *(978-1-4677-2517-0(X),* bd8a68e6-cc49-473a-8510-e0f202122f9e, Twenty-First Century Bks.) Lerner Publishing Group.

Lowery, Zoe & Mills, J. Elizabeth. Social Roles & Stereotypes, 1 vol. 2017. (Women in the World Ser.). (ENG., Illus.). 112p. (J). (gr. 6-6). 38.80 *(978-1-5081-7441-7(5),* 461dd125-e5a7-4467-9223-6b78b507b25a, Rosen Young Adult) Rosen Publishing Group, Inc., The.

Lynette, Rachel. How to Deal with Feeling Left Out. (Let's Work It Out Ser.). 24p. (gr. 2-3). 2009. 42.50 *(978-1-61514-260-6(6),* PowerKids Pr.) 2008. (ENG., Illus.). (J). lib. bdg. 26.27 *(978-1-4042-4520-4(0),* 3b59ab31-1365-4df7-adf1-29af2c26794e) Rosen Publishing Group, Inc., The.

Meiners, Cheri J. I Belong: A Book about Being Part of a Family & a Group. Weber, Penny, illus. 2018. (Learning about Me & You Ser.). (ENG.). 26p. (J). (— 1). bds. 9.99 *(978-1-63198-214-9(1),* 82149) Free Spirit Publishing Inc.

Mills, J. Elizabeth. Expectations for Women: Confronting Stereotypes. 2010. (Young Woman's Guide to Contemporary Issues Ser.). 112p. (YA). (gr. 9-12). lib. bdg., E-Book 63.90 *(978-1-61532-907-6(2))* Rosen Publishing Group, Inc., The.

Ricciuti, Edward R. Somos un Equipo / We Are a Team, 1 vol. 2008. (Listos para Ir a la Escuela / Ready for School Ser.). (ENG & SPA., Illus.). 24p. (gr. k-1). lib. bdg. 25.50 *(978-0-7614-2436-9(9),* 3cf0f01b-8774-40f9-8154-3301d5082d2a) Cavendish Square Publishing LLC.

—Somos un Equipo (We Are a Team), 1 vol. 2008. (Listos para Ir a la Escuela (Ready for School) Ser.). (SPA., Illus.). 24p. (gr. k-1). lib. bdg. 25.50 *(978-0-7614-2357-7(5),* 26424f33-a340-4359-91d0-86218711856e) Cavendish Square Publishing LLC.

Rodriguez, Gaby. The Pregnancy Project: A Memoir. 2013. (ENG., Illus.). 240p. (YA). (gr. 9). pap. 12.99 *(978-1-4424-4623-6(4),* Simon & Schuster Bks. For Young Readers) Simon & Schuster Bks. For Young Readers.

Souder, Patti. On the Edge of Disaster: Youth in the Juvenile Court System, 15 vols. 2004. (Youth with Special Needs Ser.). (Illus.). 128p. (J). lib. bdg. *(978-1-59084-727-5(X))* Mason Crest.

Wenzel, Anna, ed. Male Privilege, 1 vol. 2019. (At Issue Ser.). (ENG.). 128p. (gr. 10-12). 41.03 *(978-1-5345-0521-6(0),* c9b2d82d-1b5c-46df-879a-8b8bccec859b) Greenhaven Publishing LLC.

SOCIAL REFORM

see Social Problems

SOCIAL SCIENCES

see also Economics; Political Science; Social Change; Sociology

Accelerated Curriculum for Social Studies Grade 11 Exit TAKS Student Edition. 2005. (Region IV ESC Resources for Social Studies Ser.). spiral bd. *(978-1-932797-29-9(7))* Region 4 Education Service Ctr.

Ahearn, Janet Reed. A Bird's-Eye View. 2003. (Shutterbug Books: Social Studies). (Illus.). 16p. (J). (gr. -1-3). pap. 4.10 *(978-0-7398-7649-7(X))* Steck-Vaughn.

—Lady Liberty. 2003. (Shutterbug Books: Social Studies). (Illus.). 16p. pap. 4.10 *(978-0-7398-7646-6(5))* Steck-Vaughn.

Al rescate de Ballenas: Libros Aventuras (Adventure Books) 2003. (MacMillan/McGraw-Hill. Estudios Sociales Ser.). (ENG & SPA.). (gr. 4-18). *(978-0-02-150115-1(7))* Macmillan/McGraw-Hill Schl. Div.

The Allyn & Bacon Atlas for Elementary Social Studies. 2005. (J). *(978-1-930194-19-9(6))* Maps.com.

Analyzing the Issues: Set 1, 12 vols. 2016. (Analyzing the Issues Ser.). (ENG.). 208p. (gr. 8-8). lib. bdg. 305.58 *(978-0-7660-7503-0(6),* 718470a7-f237-4e28-989d-814c3ce35d6f) Enslow Publishing, LLC.

Analyzing the Issues: Set 2, 12 vols. 2016. (Analyzing the Issues Ser.). (ENG.). 208p. (YA). (gr. 8-8). lib. bdg. 305.58 *(978-0-7660-8374-5(8),* 7034259f-42c2-45a5-880f-a48ab48f1227) Enslow Publishing, LLC.

Andersen, Jill. The Great Debate, 1 vol. 2016. (Rosen REAL Readers: Social Studies Nonfiction / Fiction: Myself, My Community, My World Ser.). (ENG.). 12p. (gr. k-1). pap. 6.33 *(978-1-5081-2553-2(8),* c415fce0-c0e8-4552-bfbb-ca7760262fc6, Rosen Classroom) Rosen Publishing Group, Inc., The.

Andersen, W. H. Hooray for the Red, White, & Blue: A Content Area Reader-Social Studies. 2005. (Emergent/Early (Prek-2) Social Studies Package Ser.). 16p. (gr. k-2). 25.20 *(978-0-8215-7819-3(7))* Sadlier, William H. Inc.

Antarctica (Early Intervention Levels Ser.). 31.86 *(978-0-7362-0664-8(7))* CENGAGE Learning.

Aprenda Preparacion y Practica: Assessment. 2003. (MacMillan/McGraw-Hill. Estudios Sociales Ser.). (ENG & SPA.). (gr. 1-18). *(978-0-02-149775-1(3));* (gr. 4-18). *(978-0-02-149778-2(8))* Macmillan/McGraw-Hill Schl. Div.

Aprenda preparacion y practica, Guia del Maestro: Assessment. 2003. (MacMillan/McGraw-Hill. Estudios Sociales Ser.). (ENG & SPA.). (gr. 2-18). *(978-0-02-150016-1(9))* Macmillan/McGraw-Hill Schl. Div.

Aprenda preparacion y practica, Libro del Estudiante: Assessment. 2003. (MacMillan/McGraw-Hill. Estudios Sociales Ser.). (ENG & SPA.). (gr. 2-18). *(978-0-02-149776-8(1))* Macmillan/McGraw-Hill Schl. Div.

Aprenda preparacion y practica, Pupil Edition: Assessment. 2003. (MacMillan/McGraw-Hill. Estudios Sociales Ser.). (ENG & SPA.). (gr. 3-18). *(978-0-02-149777-5(X));* (gr. 5-18). *(978-0-02-149779-9(6))* Macmillan/McGraw-Hill Schl. Div.

Archer, Anita, et al. REWARDS Plus: Application to Social Studies: Reading Excellence: Word Attack & Rate Development Strategies: Student Book. 2003. (Illus.). 154p. (gr. 6-8). pap. 11.49 *(978-1-57035-803-6(6),* 136SOCSE) Cambium Education, Inc.

Archibald, Donna, et al. NETS*S Curriculum Series: Social Studies Units for Grades 9-12. McKenzie, Walter, ed. 2004. (Nets-S Curriculum Ser.). (Illus.). 195p. pap. 38.95 *(978-1-56484-212-1(6))* International Society for Technology in Education.

Ashbe, Jeanne. Es hora de Recoger: Traduccion Anna Coll-Vinent. 2004. (SPA.). 16p. *(978-84-8470-163-7(8))* Corimbo, Editorial S.L.

—La hora del Bano. 2004. (SPA.). 16p. *(978-84-8470-165-1(4))* Corimbo, Editorial S.L.

—Oh!, esta Oscuro. 2004. (SPA.). 16p. *(978-84-8470-164-4(6))* Corimbo, Editorial S.L.

At Play in the USA, 6 vols. (Book2WebTM Ser.). (gr. 4-8). 36.50 *(978-0-322-02983-5(X))* Wright Group/McGraw-Hill.

Auch, Allison. Electrifying Personalities: Set Of 6. 2011. (Navigators Ser.). (J). pap. 48.00 net. *(978-1-4108-0440-2(2))* Benchmark Education Co.

Auld, Mary. Conoce la Familia, 12 vols. Incl. Mi Hermana (My Sister) lib. bdg. 24.67 *(978-0-8368-3930-2(7),* 77757a0b-a436-4666-82a3-f01e51b0dd7e); Mi Hermano (My Brother) lib. bdg. 24.67 *(978-0-8368-3931-9(5),* dcbaf077-2d15-4eeb-b7f6-06f1dc106053); Mi Mamá (My Mom) lib. bdg. 24.67 *(978-0-8368-3932-6(3),* 09a7108c-fe6c-4f22-aac9-75bde0928475); Mi Papá (My Dad) lib. bdg. 24.67 *(978-0-8368-3933-3(1),* 97064b3c-6d64-4d42-9c2e-d7470efb2de0); Mis Abuelos (My Grandparents) lib. bdg. 24.67 *(978-0-8368-3934-0(X),* e7277374-85de-4cde-a9bb-5813322efacb); Mis Tíos (My Aunt & Uncle) lib. bdg. 24.67 *(978-0-8368-3935-7(8),* f07ffe92-cf8f-42a5-aa8b-db7e9ce6497a); (gr. k-2). (Conoce la Familia (Meet the Family) Ser.). (SPA., Illus.). 24p. 2004. Set lib. bdg. 148.02 *(978-0-8368-3929-6(3),* 4614e660-23ff-4719-b85c-44b87fad6862, Gareth Stevens Learning Library) Stevens, Gareth Publishing LLLP.

Axiom Press, ed. CultureGrams Kids Edition. 2003. spiral bd. 69.99 *(978-1-931694-63-6(X));* ring bd. 69.99 incl. cd-rom *(978-1-931694-64-3(8))* ProQuest LLC.

—CultureGrams States Edition. 2003. spiral bd. 59.99 incl. cd-rom *(978-1-931694-65-0(6));* ring bd. 59.99 incl. cd-rom *(978-1-931694-66-7(4))* ProQuest LLC.

Bauer, David. People Change the Land, 6 vols., Set. 2003. (Yellow Umbrella Early Level Ser.). (ENG.). 16p. (gr. k-1). pap. 35.70 *(978-0-7368-3006-5(5),* Capstone Pr.) Capstone.

Bednarz, Robert, et al. About My Community. 3rd ed. 2003. (Harcourt School Publishers Horizons Ser.). (ENG.). 376p. (gr. 2-2). pupil's gde. ed. 60.75 *(978-0-15-320179-0(7))* Harcourt Schl. Pubs.

Benchmark Education Company, LLC Staff, compiled by. Being a Good Citizen: Theme Set. 2006. (J). 136.00 *(978-1-4108-7065-0(0))* Benchmark Education Co.

—Civic Ideals & Practices. 2005. spiral bd. 60.00 *(978-1-4108-5428-5(0));* spiral bd. 90.00 *(978-1-4108-3937-4(0));* spiral bd. 65.00 *(978-1-4108-4504-7(4));* spiral bd. 110.00 *(978-1-4108-5427-8(2))* Benchmark Education Co.

—Community Counts & Community Change. 2005. spiral bd. 225.00 *(978-1-4108-5803-0(0))* Benchmark Education Co.

—Community Counts & Local GOVT. 2005. spiral bd. 225.00 *(978-1-4108-5802-3(2))* Benchmark Education Co.

—Individual Development & Identity. 2005. spiral bd. 685.00 *(978-1-4108-4505-4(2));* spiral bd. 1050.00 *(978-1-4108-5424-7(8));* spiral bd. 715.00 *(978-1-4108-5840-5(5));* spiral bd. 400.00 *(978-1-4108-3938-1(9));* spiral bd. 35.00 *(978-1-4108-3981-7(8));* spiral bd. 75.00 *(978-1-4108-3973-2(7));* spiral bd. 1100.00 *(978-1-4108-3746-2(7));* spiral bd. 360.00 *(978-1-4108-3964-0(8));* spiral bd. 585.00 *(978-1-4108-3963-3(X));* spiral bd. 245.00 *(978-1-4108-3939-8(7))* Benchmark Education Co.

—Individuals, Groups & Institutions. 2005. spiral bd. 25.00 *(978-1-4108-4500-9(1))* Benchmark Education Co.

—Individuals, Groups, & Institutions. 2005. spiral bd. 55.00 *(978-1-4108-3969-5(9));* spiral bd. 80.00 *(978-1-4108-5431-5(0))* Benchmark Education Co.

—Neighborhoods & Communities. 2006. (J). 235.00 *(978-1-4108-7040-7(5))* Benchmark Education Co.

—Neighborhoods & Communities: Theme Set. 2006. (J). 258.00 *(978-1-4108-7085-8(5))* Benchmark Education Co.

—People, Places & Environments. 2005. spiral bd. 235.00 *(978-1-4108-5836-8(7));* spiral bd. 55.00 *(978-1-4108-3968-8(0));* spiral bd. 575.00 *(978-1-4108-3748-6(3));* spiral bd. 150.00 *(978-1-4108-5837-5(5))* Benchmark Education Co.

—People, Places, & Environments. 2005. spiral bd. 50.00 *(978-1-4108-3975-6(3));* spiral bd. 450.00 *(978-1-4108-5420-9(5));* spiral bd. 245.00 *(978-1-4108-3944-2(3));* spiral bd. 185.00 *(978-1-4108-3945-9(1));* spiral bd. 315.00 *(978-1-4108-5421-6(3));* spiral bd. 145.00 *(978-1-4108-3955-8(9));* spiral bd. 75.00 *(978-1-4108-3956-5(7));* spiral bd. 110.00 *(978-1-4108-3967-1(2));* spiral bd. 315.00 *(978-1-4108-4503-0(6))* Benchmark Education Co.

—Regions of the U. S. 2006. spiral bd. 330.00 *(978-1-4108-7006-3(5))* 2005. (J). spiral bd. 265.00 *(978-1-4108-5769-9(7))* Benchmark Education Co.

—Regions of the U. S. Theme Set. 2006. (J). 259.00 *(978-1-4108-7111-4(8))* Benchmark Education Co.

—Social Studies Theme: People, Places & Environments. 2005. spiral bd. 220.00 *(978-1-4108-5328-8(4))* Benchmark Education Co.

—Social Studies Theme: Time, Continuity & Change. 2005. spiral bd. 560.00 *(978-1-4108-5322-6(5))* Benchmark Education Co.

—Spanish Social Studies Standard Set. 2005. spiral bd. 3225.00 *(978-1-4108-5845-0(6))* Benchmark Education Co.

—Time, Continuity, & Change. 2005. spiral bd. 365.00 *(978-1-4108-4502-3(8));* spiral bd. 110.00 *(978-1-4108-3978-7(8));* spiral bd. 190.00 *(978-1-4108-3977-0(X));* spiral bd. 55.00 *(978-1-4108-3970-1(2));* spiral bd. 75.00 *(978-1-4108-3953-4(2));* spiral bd. 640.00 *(978-1-4108-3952-7(4));* spiral bd. 1250.00 *(978-1-4108-3745-5(9));* spiral bd. 715.00 *(978-1-4108-5835-1(9));* spiral bd. 265.00 *(978-1-4108-5834-4(0));* spiral bd. 120.00 *(978-1-4108-3943-5(5));* spiral bd. 340.00 *(978-1-4108-3942-8(7));* spiral bd. 55.00 *(978-1-4108-3971-8(0))* Benchmark Education Co.

—Time, Continuity & Change. 2005. spiral bd. 1050.00 *(978-1-4108-5418-6(3));* spiral bd. 550.00 *(978-1-4108-5417-9(5))* Benchmark Education Co.

—World Communities: Theme Set. 2006. (J). 121.00 *(978-1-4108-7098-8(7))* Benchmark Education Co.

Billings. How: People, Places, & Ideas. 2003. (Steck-Vaughn History of Our World Ser.). (ENG., Illus.). 296p. (gr. 6-12). pap. 48.80 *(978-0-7398-7948-1(0))* Houghton Mifflin Harcourt Publishing Co.

—The Modern World, Vol. 2. 2003. (Steck-Vaughn History of Our World Ser.). (ENG., Illus.). 296p. (gr. 6-12). pap. 48.80 *(978-0-7398-7949-8(9))* Houghton Mifflin Harcourt Publishing Co.

BJU Staff. Geography Activity Student Gr9. 2004. 14.50 *(978-1-57924-300-5(2))* BJU Pr.

—World Studies Activity St Grd7. 2004. pap. 14.50 *(978-1-57924-302-9(9))* BJU Pr.

Blane, Francisco. What Will You Be? Lap Book. 2009. (My First Reader's Theater Set B Ser.). (J). 28.00 *(978-1-60634-993-9(7))* Benchmark Education Co.

Boehm, Richard G., et al. Activity Books: Communities. 2003. (Harcourt Brace Social Studies). (gr. k-7). act. bk. ed. 7.70 *(978-0-15-310306-3(X))* Harcourt Schl. Pubs.

—Activity Books: Making a Difference. 2003. (Harcourt Brace Social Studies). (gr. k-7). act. bk. ed. 5.80 *(978-0-15-310305-6(1))* Harcourt Schl. Pubs.

—Assessment Programs: A Child's Place. 2003. (Harcourt Brace Social Studies). (gr. k-7). 44.60 *(978-0-15-310297-4(7))* Harcourt Schl. Pubs.

—Assessment Programs: Making a Difference. 2003. (Harcourt Brace Social Studies). (gr. k-7). 44.60 *(978-0-15-310298-1(5))* Harcourt Schl. Pubs.

—Big Book Libraries. 2003. (Harcourt Brace Social Studies). (gr. 1-18). 317.70 *(978-0-15-310448-0(1));* (gr. 2-18). 317.70 *(978-0-15-310455-8(4))* Harcourt Schl. Pubs.

—Game Time! A Child's Place. 2003. (Harcourt Brace Social Studies). (gr. k-7). 7.30 *(978-0-15-312349-8(4))* Harcourt Schl. Pubs.

—Game Time! Making a Difference. 2003. (Harcourt Brace Social Studies). (gr. k-7). 7.30 *(978-0-15-312351-1(6))* Harcourt Schl. Pubs.

—Great Beginnings. 2003. (Harcourt Brace Estudios Sociales Ser.). (SPA.). (gr. k-7). pap. 107.90 *(978-0-15-306559-0(1));* (gr. k-7). pap., act. bk. ed. 12.90 *(978-0-15-306554-5(0));* 97th ed. (gr. k-7). pap., tchr. ed. 184.50 *(978-0-15-309127-8(4));* 97th ed. (gr. k-7). pap., suppl. ed. 233.60 *(978-0-15-309148-3(7));* 97th ed. (gr. k-7). pap., act. bk. ed. 11.40 *(978-0-15-309128-5(2));* 97th ed. (gr. k-7). pap., act. bk. ed. 12.90 *(978-0-15-309143-8(6));* 97th ed. (gr. 3-7). pap., tchr. ed., act. bk. ed. 21.30 *(978-0-15-307926-9(6));* 97th ed. (gr. 3-7). pap., tchr. ed., act. bk. ed. 21.30 *(978-0-15-309144-5(4));* 97th ed. (gr. 3-7). pap., tchr. ed., act. bk. ed. 18.70 *(978-0-15-309129-2(0));* Vol. 1. (gr. k-7). tchr. ed. 141.30 *(978-0-15-306548-4(6));* Vol. 1. 97th ed. (gr. k-7). pap., tchr. ed. 143.90 *(978-0-15-309141-4(X));* Vol. 2. (gr. k-7). tchr. ed. 141.30 *(978-0-15-306549-1(4));* Vol. 2. 97th ed. (gr. k-7). pap., tchr. ed. 143.90 *(978-0-15-309142-1(8))* Harcourt Schl. Pubs.

—El Mundo y Sus Gentes: Hemisferio Occidental, Europa y Rusia. 2005. (Illus.). 570p. (J). (gr. 4-7). 60.00 *(978-0-07-868380-0(7))* Glencoe/McGraw-Hill.

—My World & Me: A Kindergarten Program. 2003. (Harcourt Brace Social Studies). (gr. k-7). act. bk. ed. 5.30 *(978-0-15-310303-2(5))* Harcourt Schl. Pubs.

—Reading Support & Test Preparation: Communities. 2003. (Harcourt Brace Social Studies). (gr. k-7). 27.00 *(978-0-15-312379-5(6))* Harcourt Schl. Pubs.

—Reading Support & Test Preparation: Making a Difference. 2003. (Harcourt Brace Social Studies). (gr. k-7). 27.00 *(978-0-15-312376-4(1))* Harcourt Schl. Pubs.

—Relatos de la Historia: La Historia de Estados Unidos. 2003. (Harcourt Brace Estudios Sociales Ser.). (SPA.). (gr. k-7). pupil's gde. ed. 88.40 *(978-0-15-306543-9(5))* Harcourt Schl. Pubs.

—Social Studies Libraries: Making a Difference. 2003. (Harcourt Brace Social Studies). (gr. k-7). 95.70 *(978-0-15-310443-5(0))* Harcourt Schl. Pubs.

—Vocabulary Picture Cards. 2003. (Harcourt Brace Social Studies). (SPA.). (gr. 1-18). 61.90 *(978-0-15-310295-0(0));* (gr. 2-18). 69.30 *(978-0-15-310296-7(9))* Harcourt Schl. Pubs.

—Write-on Charts. 2003. (Harcourt Brace Social Studies). (SPA.). (gr. 3-18). 216.40 *(978-0-15-310292-9(6))* Harcourt Schl. Pubs.

Bolivar, Simon. Champion of Freedom. 2007. (Read on! Special Edition: Level BA Ser.). (Illus.). 23p. pap. 18.51 *(978-1-4190-3527-2(4))* Steck-Vaughn.

Bozek, Rachel, ed. The Political Elite & Special Interests, 1 vol. 2017. (Current Controversies Ser.). (ENG.). 136p. (gr. 10-12). pap. 33.00 *(978-1-5345-0105-8(3),* 322e9023-4d0e-4cb9-8243-1ddfa7001125); lib. bdg. 48.03 *(978-1-5345-0106-5(1),* 21fc5139-b0b1-47cd-8511-a1fd8d40ca35) Greenhaven Publishing LLC.

Brocker, Susan. Voices from the Civil War: Set Of 6. 2011. (Navigators Ser.). (J). pap. 48.00 net. *(978-1-4108-0434-1(8))* Benchmark Education Co.

Burke, Juliet. Let's Play!, 1 vol. 2012. (InfoMax Readers Ser.). (ENG., Illus.). 16p. (J). (gr. k-k). pap. 7.00 *(978-1-4488-8899-3(9),* d6f976d3-194d-473a-852a-b43eac237abb, Rosen Classroom) Rosen Publishing Group, Inc., The.

El campamento de Lewis y Clark: Libros Aventuras (Adventure Books) 2003. (MacMillan/McGraw-Hill. Estudios Sociales Ser.). (ENG & SPA.). (gr. 4-18). *(978-0-02-150121-2(1))* Macmillan/McGraw-Hill Schl. Div.

Cane, Ella. My World. 2013. (My World Ser.). (ENG.). 24p. (J). (gr. -1-2). pap., pap., pap. 41.70 *(978-1-4765-3683-5(X),* 20175, Pebble) Capstone.

—Neighborhoods in My World, 1 vol. 2013. (My World Ser.). (ENG.). 24p. (J). (gr. -1-2). 24.65 *(978-1-4765-3119-9(6),* 123101); pap. 6.95 *(978-1-4765-3461-9(6),* 123560) Capstone.

Cannon, Shannon. The Letter Qq Set: Past & Present, 6. 2004. (Letter Bks.). (ENG.). 8p. (gr. k-1). pap. 29.70 *(978-0-7368-4116-0(4))* Capstone.

Catala, Ellen. What Does a Firefighter Do?, 6 vols., Set. 2003. (Yellow Umbrella Early Level Ser.). (ENG.). 16p. (gr. k-1). pap. 35.70 *(978-0-7368-2988-5(1),* Capstone Pr.) Capstone.

La ceramica de los indigenas Pueblo: Libros Aventuras (Adventure Books) 2003. (MacMillan/McGraw-Hill. Estudios Sociales Ser.). (ENG & SPA.). (gr. 5-18). *(978-0-02-150124-3(6))* Macmillan/McGraw-Hill Schl. Div.

Cheyney, Arnold. History Challenge Level 1: 190 Brainteasers about the United States. 2005. (Challenge Ser.). (Illus.). 192p. (J). (gr. 3-5). per. 9.95 *(978-1-59647-065-1(8),* EAS002) Good Year Bks.

—History Challenge Level 2: 190 Brainteasers about the World. 2005. (Challenge Ser.). 192p. (J). (gr. 4-7). per. 9.95 *(978-1-59647-066-8(6),* EAS002) Good Year Bks.

A Child's Day (Group 2), 10 vols., Set. 2003. (Child's Day Ser.). (ENG.). (gr. 2-2). 163.20 *(978-0-7614-1406-3(1),* 16fb8054-95be-4f8c-9ca4-11c4752ca854, Cavendish Square) Cavendish Square Publishing LLC.

Cipriano, Jeri S. At the Park, 6 vols., Set. 2003. (Yellow Umbrella Early Level Ser.). (ENG.). 16p. (gr. k-1). pap. 35.70 *(978-0-7368-2984-7(9),* Capstone Pr.) Capstone.

—Celebrations, 6, Set. 2003. (Yellow Umbrella Early Level Ser.). (ENG.). 16p. (gr. k-1). pap. 35.70 *(978-0-7368-3002-7(2),* Capstone Pr.) Capstone.

—Harvest Time, 6 vols., Set. 2003. (Yellow Umbrella Early Level Ser.). (ENG.). 16p. (gr. k-1). pap. 35.70 *(978-0-7368-3003-4(0),* Capstone Pr.) Capstone.

Coetzee, Eirka, et al. Social Science Matters Grade 8 Learner's Book Afrikaans Translation. 2nd ed. 2006. (AFR., Illus.). 192p. pap., stu. ed. 14.00 *(978-0-521-67890-2(0))* Cambridge Univ. Pr.

Coletti, Sharon. The Power of One: A Guide to Service-Learning & Social Science Research. 2005. (YA). ring bd. 99.95 *(978-1-933558-07-3(5))* InspirEd Educators.

Coll-Seck, Jayden. Our School Motto, 1 vol., 1. 2015. (Rosen REAL Readers: Social Studies Nonfiction / Fiction: Myself, My Community, My World Ser.). (ENG.). 12p. (J). (gr. k-1). pap. 6.33 *(978-1-5081-1749-0(7),* eb4ba0d8-b358-4f80-8f71-90b7fc115e97, Rosen Classroom) Rosen Publishing Group, Inc., The.

—Sally Does Not Like Broccoli, 1 vol., 1. 2015. (Rosen REAL Readers: Social Studies Nonfiction / Fiction: Myself, My Community, My World Ser.). (ENG.). 8p. (J). (gr. k-1). pap. 5.46 *(978-1-5081-1656-1(3),* db3da43a-dcd8-467f-9a73-bdfb384c441a, Rosen Classroom) Rosen Publishing Group, Inc., The.

—This Is My Class, 1 vol., 1. 2015. (Rosen REAL Readers: Social Studies Nonfiction / Fiction: Myself, My Community, My World Ser.). (ENG.). 8p. (J). (gr. k-1). pap. 5.46 *(978-1-5081-1674-5(1),* 2fb304bf-8f55-460c-8b94-b58887ddbfc9, Rosen Classroom) Rosen Publishing Group, Inc., The.

—We Are All Different, 1 vol., 1. 2015. (Rosen REAL Readers: Social Studies Nonfiction / Fiction: Myself, My Community, My World Ser.). (ENG.). 8p. (J). (gr. k-1). pap. 5.46 *(978-1-5081-1707-0(1),* d1082981-df41-4fbb-891c-d8a36dce102f, Rosen Classroom) Rosen Publishing Group, Inc., The.

—We Buy Food at the Store, 1 vol., 1. 2015. (Rosen REAL Readers: Social Studies Nonfiction / Fiction: Myself, My Community, My World Ser.). (ENG.). 12p. (J). (gr. k-1). pap. 6.33 *(978-1-5081-1725-4(X),* a5569043-c9a2-42dc-9cbc-a7735d66eef4, Rosen Classroom) Rosen Publishing Group, Inc., The.

—We Celebrate Kwanzaa, 1 vol., 1. 2015. (Rosen REAL Readers: Social Studies Nonfiction / Fiction: Myself, My Community, My World Ser.). (ENG.). 12p. (J). (gr. k-1). pap. 6.33 *(978-1-5081-1797-1(7),* d9872aae-a006-4f0e-ab50-2dca5fb95e56, Rosen Classroom) Rosen Publishing Group, Inc., The.

Colonial America Classroom Library. (gr. 2-5). lib. bdg. 49.95 *(978-0-7368-4488-8(0),* Red Brick Learning) Capstone.

Community Helpers Classroom Library. (gr. 2-5). lib. bdg. 116.95 *(978-0-7368-7074-0(1),* Red Brick Learning) Capstone.

Community Helpers Complete Unit. (gr. 2-5). 664.95 *(978-0-7368-7075-7(X),* Red Brick Learning) Capstone.

The Continents Collection. 2005. (J). pap. *(978-1-60015-012-8(8))* Steps To Literacy, LLC.

The Cotton Tale. abr. ed. 2004. (Thrilling Tales in Time Ser.: Vol. 41). (J). 19.95 *(978-1-58123-372-8(8))* Larson Learning, Inc.

Cuaderno de Evaluacion: Student & Teacher Support Resources. 2003. (MacMillan/McGraw-Hill. Estudios Sociales Ser.). (ENG & SPA.). (gr. 1-18). *(978-0-02-149458-3(4));* (gr. 2-18). *(978-0-02-149459-0(2));* (gr. 3-18). *(978-0-02-149461-3(4));* (gr. 4-18). *(978-0-02-149971-7(3));* (gr. 5-18). *(978-0-02-149463-7(0))* Macmillan/McGraw-Hill Schl. Div.

Cuaderno de practica y Actividades: Student & Teacher Support Resources. 2003. (MacMillan/McGraw-Hill. Estudios Sociales Ser.). (ENG & SPA.). (gr. 1-18). *(978-0-02-149453-8(3));* (gr. 1-18). *(978-0-02-150009-3(6));* (gr. 2-18). *(978-0-02-150010-9(X));* (gr. 2-18). *(978-0-02-149454-5(1));* (gr. 3-18). *(978-0-02-149455-2(X));* (gr. 3-18). *(978-0-02-150011-6(8));* (gr. 4-18). *(978-0-02-149970-0(5));* (gr. 5-18). *(978-0-02-149457-6(6));* (gr. 5-18). *(978-0-02-150014-7(2))* Macmillan/McGraw-Hill Schl. Div.

CultureGrams 2005 World Edition. 2004. (YA). per. 129.99 *(978-1-931694-87-2(7));* ring bd. 139.99 *(978-1-931694-88-9(5))* ProQuest LLC.

Currie-McGhee, Leanne K. & Miller, Debra A. Civil Liberties, 1 vol. 2009. (Hot Topics Ser.). (ENG., Illus.). 112p. (J). (gr. 7-7). 41.03 *(978-1-4205-0080-6(5),* 7c6707fa-4721-4ea5-9a4c-1f33f213a71d, Lucent Pr.) Greenhaven Publishing LLC.

Cushing, Christopher. Let's Celebrate!, 1 vol. 2012. (InfoMax Readers Ser.). (ENG., Illus.). 16p. (J). (gr. k-k). pap. 7.00 *(978-1-4488-8962-4(6),* 3f166bb0-9a73-4b8e-bf9a-d0e13a576f6c, Rosen Classroom) Rosen Publishing Group, Inc., The.

Daily Activity Bank: Scott Foresman Social Studies: All Together. 2003. (gr. 1-18). *(978-0-328-03919-7(5),* Scott Foresman) Addison-Wesley Educational Pubs., Inc.

Daily Activity Bank: Scott Foresman Social Studies: Communities. 2003. (gr. 3-18). *(978-0-328-03921-0(7),* Scott Foresman) Addison-Wesley Educational Pubs., Inc.

Daily Activity Bank: Scott Foresman Social Studies: People & Places. 2003. (gr. 2-18). *(978-0-328-03920-3(9),* Scott Foresman) Addison-Wesley Educational Pubs., Inc.

Daily Activity Bank: Scott Foresman Social Studies: Regions. 2003. (gr. 4-18). *(978-0-328-03922-7(5),* Scott Foresman) Addison-Wesley Educational Pubs., Inc.

S

Daily Activity Bank: Scott Foresman Social Studies: The United States. 2003. (gr. 5-18). *(978-0-328-03926-5(8),* Scott Foresman) Addison-Wesley Educational Pubs., Inc.
Daily Activity Bank: Scott Foresman Social Studies: The World. 2003. (gr. 6-18). *(978-0-328-03927-2(6),* Scott Foresman) Addison-Wesley Educational Pubs., Inc.
Darity, William A. International Encyclopedia of Social Sciences, 9 vols., Set. 2nd rev. ed. 2007. (International Encyclopedia of the Social Sciences Ser.). (ENG., Illus.). 4000p. (C). 2009.00 *(978-0-02-865965-7(1))* Cengage Gale.
Daronco, Mickey & Ohanesian, Diane. Am I Sad? Set Of 6. 2nd rev. ed. 2011. (BuildUp Ser.). (J). pap. 27.00 net. *(978-1-4108-0740-3(1))* Benchmark Education Co.
Dell, Pamela. Honey for Sale. 2016. (Spring Forward Ser.). (J). (gr. 1). *(978-1-4900-2230-7(9))* Benchmark Education Co.
Diario de la Frontera: Libros Aventuras (Adventure Books) 2003. (MacMillan/McGraw-Hill. Estudios Sociales Ser.). (ENG & SPA.). (gr. 4-18). *(978-0-02-150118-2(1))* Macmillan/McGraw-Hill Schl. Div.
El diario de una nina Inmigrante: Libros Aventuras (Adventure Books) 2003. (MacMillan/McGraw-Hill. Estudios Sociales Ser.). (ENG & SPA.). (gr. 5-18). *(978-0-02-150126-7(2))* Macmillan/McGraw-Hill Schl. Div.
DiPiazza, Francesca Davis. Friend Me! 600 Years of Social Networking in America. 2015. (ENG., Illus.). 112p. (YA). (gr. 5-12). E-Book 53.32 *(978-1-4677-5931-1(7),* 9781467759311, Lerner Digital) Lerner Publishing Group.
Discos compactos: Libro del Estudiante: Technology. 2003. (MacMillan/McGraw-Hill. Estudios Sociales Ser.). (ENG & SPA.). (gr. 2-18). *(978-0-02-150052-9(5));* (gr. 3-18). *(978-0-02-150053-6(3));* (gr. 4-18). *(978-0-02-150055-0(X));* (gr. 5-18). *(978-0-02-150056-7(8))* Macmillan/McGraw-Hill Schl. Div.
Discovering Cultures Series - Group 1, 6 bks., Set. *(978-0-7614-1181-9(X),* Cavendish Square) Cavendish Square Publishing LLC.
Dunn, Justine. Hey! There's Social Studies in My Literature! Grades 1-2. Radtke, Becky, illus. 2007. (Rigby Best Teachers Press Ser.). 96p. per. 13.99 *(978-1-4190-3400-8(6))* Houghton Mifflin Harcourt Supplemental Pubs.
DynaNotes Grade 8 Social Studies Review Guide Transparency Set. 2006. (YA). trans. *(978-1-933854-35-9(9))* DynaStudy, Inc.
DynaNotes Grade 8 Social Studies TAKS Review Guide. 2006. pap. *(978-1-933854-31-1(6))* DynaStudy, Inc.
Endres, Hollie J. The Letter Gg Set: The World Around You, 6. 2004. (Letter Bks.). (ENG.). 8p. (gr. k-1). pap. 29.70 *(978-0-7368-4106-1(7))* Capstone.
—The Letter Vv Set: Sink or Float?, 6 vols. 2004. (Letter Bks.). (ENG.). 8p. (gr. k-1). pap. 29.70 *(978-0-7368-4121-4(0))* Capstone.
Engdahl, Sylvia, ed. Welfare, 1 vol. 2011. (Issues on Trial Ser.). (ENG.). 200p. (gr. 10-12). 49.93 *(978-0-7377-5110-9(X),* f7d8a679-2dce-45ad-9ac7-6f762eb3f92c, Greenhaven Publishing) Greenhaven Publishing LLC.
En busca de un Hogar: Libros Aventuras (Adventure Books) 2003. (MacMillan/McGraw-Hill. Estudios Sociales Ser.). (ENG & SPA.). (gr. 5-18). *(978-0-02-150123-6(8))* Macmillan/McGraw-Hill Schl. Div.
Estudios sociales Scott Foresman. 2003. (Scott Foresman Social Study Ser.). (SPA.). (gr. k-18). stu. ed. *(978-0-328-05613-2(8));* (gr. 1-18). stu. ed. *(978-0-328-05499-2(2));* (gr. 2-18). stu. ed. *(978-0-328-05500-5(X))* Addison-Wesley Educational Pubs., Inc. (Scott Foresman).
Estudios sociales Scott Foresman: Additional Resources. 2003. (Scott Foresman Social Study Ser.). (SPA.). (gr. k-2). *(978-0-328-03696-7(X));* (gr. k-2). tchr. ed. *(978-0-328-04213-5(7));* (gr. 1-18). *(978-0-328-05737-5(1));* (gr. 1-18). *(978-0-328-04202-9(1));* (gr. 1-18). *(978-0-328-05504-3(2));* (gr. 1-18). *(978-0-328-03867-1(9));* (gr. 1-18). *(978-0-328-03861-9(X));* (gr. 2-18). *(978-0-328-05738-2(X));* (gr. 2-18). *(978-0-328-04203-6(X));* (gr. 2-18). *(978-0-328-05505-0(0));* (gr. 2-18). *(978-0-328-03868-8(7));* (gr. 3-18). *(978-0-328-05506-7(9));* (gr. 3-18). *(978-0-328-03869-5(5));* (gr. 3-5). *(978-0-328-03698-1(6));* (gr. 3-5). tchr. ed. *(978-0-328-04214-2(5));* (gr. 4-18). *(978-0-328-05780-1(0));* (gr. 4-18). *(978-0-328-05777-1(0));* (gr. 4-18). *(978-0-328-05779-5(7));* (gr. 4-18). *(978-0-328-05776-4(2));* (gr. 4-18). *(978-0-328-05784-9(3));* (gr. 5-18). *(978-0-328-03865-7(2));* (gr. 5-18). *(978-0-328-05508-1(5));* (gr. 5-18). *(978-0-328-03871-8(7))* Addison-Wesley Educational Pubs., Inc. (Scott Foresman).
Estudios sociales Scott Foresman: Practice/Assessment. 2003. (Scott Foresman Social Study Ser.). (SPA.). (gr. 1-18). *(978-0-328-03463-5(0));* (gr. 1-18). *(978-0-328-03855-8(5));* (gr. 3-18). *(978-0-328-03465-9(7));* (gr. 4-18). *(978-0-328-05687-3(1));* (gr. 5-18). *(978-0-328-03467-3(3));* (gr. 5-18). *(978-0-328-03859-6(8))* Addison-Wesley Educational Pubs., Inc. (Scott Foresman).
Estudios Sociales Scott Foresman: Practice/Assessment. 2003. (SPA.). (gr. 2-18). *(978-0-328-03464-2(9),* Scott Foresman) Addison-Wesley Educational Pubs., Inc.
Estudios sociales Scott Foresman: Technology. 2003. (Scott Foresman Social Study Ser.). (SPA.). (gr. 1-18). *(978-0-328-09220-8(7));* (gr. 1-18). *(978-0-328-05726-9(6));* (gr. 1-18). cd-rom *(978-0-328-05744-3(4));* (gr. 1-18). cd-rom *(978-0-328-05932-4(3));* (gr. 2-18). *(978-0-328-09221-5(5));* (gr. 2-18). *(978-0-328-05727-6(4));* (gr. 2-18). cd-rom *(978-0-328-05933-1(1));* (gr. 2-18). cd-rom *(978-0-328-05745-0(2));* (gr. 3-18). *(978-0-328-05728-3(2));* (gr. 3-18). *(978-0-328-09222-2(3));* (gr. 3-18). cd-rom *(978-0-328-05746-7(0));* (gr. 3-18). cd-rom *(978-0-328-05934-8(X));* (gr. 4-18). *(978-0-328-05800-6(9));* (gr. 4-18). *(978-0-328-09223-9(1));* (gr. 4-18). cd-rom *(978-0-328-05786-3(X));* (gr. 4-18). cd-rom *(978-0-328-05936-2(6));* (gr. 5-18). *(978-0-328-05730-6(4));* (gr. 5-18). *(978-0-328-09224-6(X));* (gr. 5-18). cd-rom *(978-0-328-05748-1(7));* (gr. 5-18). cd-rom *(978-0-328-05937-9(4))* Addison-Wesley Educational Pubs., Inc. (Scott Foresman).
¡Estudios Sociales y más! Un enfoque practico: Estudios Sociales Scott Foresman. 2003. (SPA.). (gr. k-18). *(978-0-328-05503-6(4),* Scott Foresman) Addison-Wesley Educational Pubs., Inc.
The Events to Independence. 2004. (Thrilling Tales in Time Ser.: Vol. 3). (J). *(978-1-58123-369-8(8))* Larson Learning, Inc.
Every Student Learns: Scott Foresman Social Studies. 2003. (gr. k-18). tchr. ed. *(978-0-328-03608-0(0),* Scott Foresman) Addison-Wesley Educational Pubs., Inc.
Every Student Learns: Scott Foresman Social Studies: All Together. 2003. (SPA.). (gr. 1-18). tchr. ed. *(978-0-328-03609-7(9),* Scott Foresman) Addison-Wesley Educational Pubs., Inc.
Every Student Learns: Scott Foresman Social Studies: Communities. 2003. (SPA.). (gr. 3-18). tchr. ed. *(978-0-328-03611-0(0),* Scott Foresman) Addison-Wesley Educational Pubs., Inc.
Every Student Learns: Scott Foresman Social Studies: People & Places. 2003. (SPA.). (gr. 2-18). tchr. ed. *(978-0-328-03610-3(2),* Scott Foresman) Addison-Wesley Educational Pubs., Inc.
Every Student Learns: Scott Foresman Social Studies: Regions. 2003. (SPA.). (gr. 4-18). tchr. ed. *(978-0-328-03612-7(9),* Scott Foresman) Addison-Wesley Educational Pubs., Inc.
Every Student Learns: Scott Foresman Social Studies: The United States. 2003. (SPA.). (gr. 5-18). tchr. ed. *(978-0-328-03613-4(7),* Scott Foresman) Addison-Wesley Educational Pubs., Inc.
Every Student Learns: Scott Foresman Social Studies: The World. 2003. (gr. 6-18). tchr. ed. *(978-0-328-03614-1(5),* Scott Foresman) Addison-Wesley Educational Pubs., Inc.
Explora el Mundo. 288p. (J). (gr. 3-8). *(978-0-7166-7096-4(8))* World Bk., Inc.
Faherty, Sara. Welfare Reform. 2004. (Point/Counterpoint: Issues in Contemporary American Society Ser.). (ENG., Illus.). 112p. (gr. 9-14). 35.00 *(978-0-7910-8093-1(5),* P114112, Facts On File) Infobase Holdings, Inc.
Ferraro, Bonita. Be a Good Citizen: A Content Area Reader-Social Studies. 2005. (Sadlier-Oxford Content Area Readers Ser.). 12p. (gr. k-2). 25.20 *(978-0-8215-7820-9(0))* Sadlier, William H. Inc.
Firth, Rachel. Los Caballeros - Internet Linked. Gaudenzi, Giacinto, illus. 2004. (Titles in Spanish Ser.). (SPA.). 48p. (J). pap. 8.95 *(978-0-7460-5083-5(6),* Usborne) EDC Publishing.
For a Better Life. 2003. (Illus.). pap. 5.60 *(978-0-7398-7508-7(6))* Steck-Vaughn.
Foresman, Scott. Estudios sociales Scott Foresman. 2003. (SPA & ENG.). (gr. 4-4). stu. ed. 74.47 net. *(978-0-328-05001-7(6),* Scott Foresman) Savvas Learning Co.
—Estudios sociales Scott Foresman: Practice/Assessment. 2003. (SPA & ENG.). (gr. 4-4). pap. 16.47 net. *(978-0-328-05781-8(9),* Scott Foresman) Savvas Learning Co.
—Estudios sociales Scott Foresman: Technology. 2003. (SPA & ENG.). (gr. k-6). cd-rom 64.97 net. *(978-0-328-05749-8(5),* Scott Foresman) Savvas Learning Co.
—Scott Foresman Social Studies: Technology. 2003. (SPA & ENG.). (gr. 4-4). cd-rom 120.47 net. *(978-0-328-05667-5(7));* (ENG.). (gr. 1-1). cd-rom 72.97 net. *(978-0-328-05878-5(5));* (ENG.). (gr. 2-2). cd-rom 72.97 net. *(978-0-328-05879-2(3));* (ENG.). (gr. 3-3). cd-rom 70.47 net. *(978-0-328-05880-8(7));* (ENG.). (gr. 4-4). cd-rom 72.97 net. *(978-0-328-06259-1(6));* (SPA & ENG.). (gr. 4-4). cd-rom 120.47 net. *(978-0-328-05668-2(5));* (ENG.). (gr. 5-5). cd-rom 72.97 net. *(978-0-328-05882-2(3));* (ENG.). (gr. 6-6). cd-rom 120.47 net. *(978-0-328-05669-9(3))* Savvas Learning Co. (Scott Foresman).
Foster, Ruth. Nonfiction Reading Comprehension - Social Studies, Grades 1-2. 2006. (ENG.). 144p. pap. 16.99 *(978-1-4206-8027-0(7))* Teacher Created Resources, Inc.
—Nonfiction Reading Comprehension - Social Studies, Grades 2-3. 2006. (ENG.). 144p. pap. 16.99 *(978-1-4206-8023-2(4))* Teacher Created Resources, Inc.
—Social Studies, Grade 3. 2006. (Nonfiction Reading Comprehension Ser.). (ENG., Illus.). 144p. per. 16.99 *(978-1-4206-8024-9(2))* Teacher Created Resources, Inc.
Francis, Amy, ed. Road Rage, 1 vol. 2014. (At Issue Ser.). (ENG.). 104p. (gr. 10-12). lib. bdg. 41.03 *(978-0-7377-6197-9(0),* e41951cb-ecf6-4f8d-8c9b-a29cb720292e, Greenhaven Publishing) Greenhaven Publishing LLC.
Froman, Craig & Froman, Andrew. My Story 2: My Country, My World. 2018. 411p. (gr. 1-2). pap. 44.99 *(978-1-68344-118-2(4),* Master Books) New Leaf Publishing Group.
Frontline Coverage of Current Events, 12 vols., Set. 2004. (Frontline Coverage of Current Events Ser.). (ENG.). (J). (gr. 5-5). 206.82 *(978-1-4042-0378-5(8),* eddc6bbf-0133-4f10-9bf9-3992dc17f063) Rosen Publishing Group, Inc., The.
Gaertner, Meg. Miles's Birthday Week: A Book about the Days of the Week. 2018. (My Day Readers Ser.). (ENG.). 24p. (J). (gr. -1-2). lib. bdg. 32.79 *(978-1-5038-2758-5(5),* 212583) Child's World, Inc, The.
Garza, Carmen Lomas, illus. Cuadros de Familia. 15th anniv. ed. 2005.Tr. of Family Pictures. (ENG & SPA.). 32p. (J). (gr. -1-17). 16.95 *(978-0-89239-206-3(1))* Lee & Low Bks., Inc.
Gateway Biographies, 12 vols., Set. Incl. Al Gore: Fighting for a Greener Planet. Steloff, Rebecca. 2008. 26.60 *(978-1-57505-948-8(7));* Alberto Gonzales: Attorney General. McElroy, Lisa Tucker. (Illus.). (J). 2006. lib. bdg. 23.93 *(978-0-8225-3418-1(5));* Barack Obama: President for a New Era. Brill, Marlene Targ. 2009. 26.60 *(978-1-57505-950-1(9));* Condoleezza Rice. Wade, Mary Dodson. (Illus.). 2005. lib. bdg. 26.60 *(978-0-7613-9550-8(4));* Green Day: Keeping Their Edge. Doeden, Matt. (Illus.). 2006. lib. bdg. 26.60 *(978-0-8225-6390-7(8),* Lerner Pubns.); John G. Roberts, Jr.: Chief Justice. McElroy, Lisa Tucker. (Illus.). (J). 2006. lib. bdg. 26.60 *(978-0-8225-6389-1(4),* Lerner Pubns.); Michelle Obama: From Chicago's South Side to the White House. Brill, Marlene Targ. (Illus.). 2009. 26.60 *(978-0-7613-5033-0(0));* Nancy Pelosi: First Woman Speaker of the House. McElroy, Lisa Tucker. (Illus.). (J). 2007. lib. bdg. 26.60 *(978-0-8225-8685-2(1),* Lerner Pubns.); Ted Kennedy: A Remarkable Life in the Senate. McElroy, Lisa Tucker. (Illus.). (J). 2009. 26.60 *(978-0-7613-4457-5(8));* Tyra Banks: From Supermodel to Role Model. Hill, Anne E. 2009. 26.60 *(978-1-57505-949-5(5));* 48p. (gr. 4-8). 2010. Set lib. bdg. 319.20 *(978-0-8225-8069-0(1))* Lerner Publishing Group.
Gay, Kathlyn. Cultural Diversity: Conflicts & Challenges. 2003. (It Happened to Me Ser.: 6). (ENG., Illus.). 144p. pap. 55.00 *(978-0-8108-4805-4(8))* Scarecrow Pr., Inc.
Gensmer, Laura. Where We Live. 2011. (Wonder Readers Ser.). (ENG.). 16p. (J). (gr. -1-1). 25.95 *(978-1-4296-8668-6(5),* 195209, Capstone Pr.) Capstone.
Georgia Striving Readers Social Studies K-5. 2012. (CAP-Marketing Ser.). (ENG.). (gr. k-5). pap. 2161.30 *(978-1-62065-958-8(1))* Capstone.
Gerber, Paul. Is It Alive?, 1 vol. 2012. (InfoMax Readers Ser.). (ENG., Illus.). 16p. (J). (gr. k-k). pap. 7.00 *(978-1-4488-8965-5(0),* 3e520b30-20b8-45fb-9021-5f252d54ec0d, Rosen Classroom) Rosen Publishing Group, Inc., The.
Gerdes, Louise I., ed. Are Government Bailouts Effective?, 1 vol. 2012. (At Issue Ser.). (ENG.). 128p. (gr. 10-12). pap. 28.80 *(978-0-7377-6180-1(6),* 14c236be-ab97-4b24-9ab0-1930158f5ded); lib. bdg. 41.03 *(978-0-7377-6179-5(2),* b674386f-ba26-4e42-901a-871e232c61a8) Greenhaven Publishing LLC. (Greenhaven Publishing).
—Should the U. S. Close Its Borders?, 1 vol. 2014. (At Issue Ser.). (ENG.). 152p. (gr. 10-12). lib. bdg. 41.03 *(978-0-7377-6860-2(6),* 7f01c2b1-a5b6-4c7c-96b3-90408a1504db, Greenhaven Publishing) Greenhaven Publishing LLC.
Geschichte. (Duden-Schuelerduden Ser.). (GER., Illus.). 540p. (YA). *(978-3-411-05413-8(1))* Bibliographisches Institut & F. A. Brockhaus AG DEU. Dist: International Bk. Import Service, Inc.
Geschichte I. (Duden Abiturhilfen Ser.). (GER.). 86p. (YA). (gr. 12-13). *(978-3-411-02640-1(5))* Bibliographisches Institut & F. A. Brockhaus AG DEU. Dist: International Bk. Import Service, Inc.
Get a Clue: An Introduction to Primary Sources. 2005. (J). pap. *(978-1-932663-09-6(6))* History Compass, LLC.
Gifford, Clive. Racism. (Illus.). 64p. (YA). (gr. 5-18). lib. bdg. 29.95 *(978-1-931983-83-9(6))* Chrysalis Education.
—Racism, 1 vol. 2006. (Global Issues Ser.: 0). (ENG., Illus.). 64p. (YA). (gr. 6-10). pap. 12.95 *(978-1-55285-745-8(X),* bfa1b67a-af7f-4349-bd5e-4a5302a3ca65) Whitecap Bks., Ltd. CAN. Dist: Firefly Bks., Ltd.
Goodwin, Evelyn. Meet the Children from the Fifty States in Poetry. 2007. 106p. pap. 37.50 *(978-0-615-16145-7(6))* Goodwin, Evelyn.
Got Issues?: Set 2, 14 vols. 2015. (Got Issues? Ser.). (ENG.). 128p. (J). (gr. 7-7). lib. bdg. 272.51 *(978-0-7660-6697-7(5),* 8acb76f7-d08a-4bee-87bd-d55219cbe898) Enslow Publishing, LLC.
Gregoire, Maryellen. Storytime. 2011. (Wonder Readers Ser.). (ENG.). 16p. (J). (gr. -1-1). 25.95 *(978-1-4296-8670-9(7),* 195211) Capstone.
Gritzner, Charles F., contrib. by. Global Connections, 10 vols., Set. 2010. (Global Connections Ser.). (gr. 5-8). 350.00 *(978-1-60413-960-0(9),* Facts On File) Infobase Holdings, Inc.
Group/McGraw-Hill, Wright. Amazing Asia, 6 vols. (Book2WebTM Ser.). (gr. 4-8). 36.50 *(978-0-322-04437-1(5))* Wright Group/McGraw-Hill.
—Ancient Egypt: The Realm of Pharaohs, 6 vols. (Book2WebTM Ser.). (gr. 4-8). 36.50 *(978-0-322-04451-7(0))* Wright Group/McGraw-Hill.
—Las Aranas, 6 vols., Vol. 2. (First Explorers. Primeros Exploradores Nonfiction Sets Ser.). (SPA.). (gr. 1-2). 34.95 *(978-0-7699-1489-3(6))* Shortland Pubns. (U. S. A.) Inc.
—Cold Facts about Ice Ages, 6 vols. (Book2WebTM Ser.). (gr. 4-8). 36.50 *(978-0-322-04434-0(0))* Wright Group/McGraw-Hill.
—Como nos Transportamos, 6 vols. (First Explorers. Primeros Exploradores Nonfiction Sets Ser.). (SPA.). (gr. 1-2). 29.95 *(978-0-7699-1470-1(5))* Shortland Pubns. (U. S. A.) Inc.
—D-Man & Beans: Classroom Library Set. (D-Man Beans Ser.). (J). (gr. 4-6). 150.95 *(978-0-322-09210-5(8))* Wright Group/McGraw-Hill.
—D-Man & Beans: Complete Set. (D-Man Beans Ser.). (gr. 4-6). 479.95 *(978-0-322-09211-2(6))* Wright Group/McGraw-Hill.
—D-Man's Escape, 6 vols. (D-Man Beans Ser.). 47p. (gr. 4-6). 42.50 *(978-0-322-06267-2(5))* Wright Group/McGraw-Hill.
—Donde Vive la Gente, 6 vols., Vol. 2. (First Explorers. Primeros Exploradores Nonfiction Sets Ser.). (SPA.). (gr. 1-2). 29.95 *(978-0-7699-1486-2(1))* Shortland Pubns. (U. S. A.) Inc.
—Fuerzas de la Naturaleza, 6 vols., Vol. 2. (First Explorers. Primeros Exploradores Nonfiction Sets Ser.). (SPA.). (gr. 1-2). 34.95 *(978-0-7699-1482-4(9))* Shortland Pubns. (U. S. A.) Inc.
—Going Places: Level I, 6 vols. (First Explorers Ser.). 24p. (gr. 1-2). 29.95 *(978-0-7699-1446-6(2))* Shortland Pubns. (U. S. A.) Inc.
—Lagunas y Rios, 6 vols. (First Explorers. Primeros Exploradores Nonfiction Sets Ser.). (SPA.). (gr. 1-2). 29.95 *(978-0-7699-1475-6(6))* Shortland Pubns. (U. S. A.) Inc.
—Making Sense of Sound & Music, 6 vols. (Book2WebTM Ser.). (gr. 4-8). 36.50 *(978-0-322-04430-2(8))* Wright Group/McGraw-Hill.
—Mountain Majesty, 6 vols. (Book2WebTM Ser.). (gr. 4-8). 36.50 *(978-0-322-04440-1(5))* Wright Group/McGraw-Hill.
—Para Que Construye el Hombre, 6 vols., Vol. 2. (First Explorers. Primeros Exploradores Nonfiction Sets Ser.). (SPA.). (gr. 1-2). 34.95 *(978-0-7699-1480-0(2))* Shortland Pubns. (U. S. A.) Inc.
—People on the Path Toward Human Rights, 6 vols. (Book2WebTM Ser.). (gr. 4-8). 36.50 *(978-0-322-04466-1(9))* Wright Group/McGraw-Hill.
—Por Que se Mueven Las Cosas, 6 vols., Vol. 2. (First Explorers. Primeros Exploradores Nonfiction Sets Ser.). (SPA.). (gr. 1-2). 34.95 *(978-0-7699-1490-9(X))* Shortland Pubns. (U. S. A.) Inc.
—El Sonido, 6 vols., Vol. 2. (First Explorers. Primeros Exploradores Nonfiction Sets Ser.). (SPA.). (gr. 1-2). 34.95 *(978-0-7699-1488-6(8))* Shortland Pubns. (U. S. A.) Inc.
—Take-Twos Social Studies Vol. 2: Fluency - Complete Kit. (gr. 3-4). 483.50 *(978-0-322-09177-1(2))* Wright Group/McGraw-Hill.
—Take-Twos Social Studies Vol. 2: Fluency - Student Book Set - 1 Each of 12 Titles. (gr. 3-4). 81.95 *(978-0-322-09305-8(8))* Wright Group/McGraw-Hill.
—Why Things Move: Level K, 6 vols., Vol. 2. (First Explorers Ser.). 24p. (gr. 1-2). 34.95 *(978-0-7699-1466-4(7))* Shortland Pubns. (U. S. A.) Inc.
—Wonder World Complete Sets: Social Studies Set - 1 Each of 73 Titles. (Wonder Worldtm Ser.). (gr. k-6). 398.95 *(978-0-322-06713-4(8))* Wright Group/McGraw-Hill.
—Wonder World Early & Upper Emergent Sets: Social Studies Set - 1 Each of 43 Titles. (Wonder Worldtm Ser.). (gr. k-6). 204.95 *(978-0-322-06719-6(7))* Wright Group/McGraw-Hill.
—Wonder World Early Fluency & Fluency: Social Studies Set - 1 Each of 30 Titles. (Wonder Worldtm Ser.). (gr. k-6). 194.50 *(978-0-322-06716-5(2))* Wright Group/McGraw-Hill.
—World Leaders Through the Ages, 6 vols. (Book2WebTM Ser.). (gr. 4-8). 36.50 *(978-0-322-04471-5(5))* Wright Group/McGraw-Hill.
Gustando. (Coleccion Mil Preguntas). (SPA., Illus.). 24p. (J). pap. 5.50 *(978-950-11-0660-2(8),* SGM627) Sigmar ARG. Dist: Continental Bk. Co., Inc.
Haerens, Margaret, ed. Mexico's Drug War, 1 vol. 2013. (At Issue Ser.). (ENG.). 120p. (gr. 10-12). pap. 28.80 *(978-0-7377-6845-9(2),* 55998244-3df4-41c6-ad5a-ff80222ef546); lib. bdg. 41.03 *(978-0-7377-6844-2(4),* 42109a99-4713-4646-b8e7-627e48f26c44) Greenhaven Publishing LLC. (Greenhaven Publishing).
Hands: Level B, 6 vols. 8p. 24.95 *(978-0-7802-8915-4(3))* Wright Group/McGraw-Hill.
Hansen, Merrily P. Homes Around the World: A Content Area Reader-Social Studies. 2005. (Emergent/Early (Prek-2) Social Studies Package Ser.). 12p. (gr. k-2). 25.20 *(978-0-8215-7817-9(0))* Sadlier, William H. Inc.
Harcourt School Publishers Staff. All about People, Unit 4. 3rd ed. 2003. (Horizons Ser.). (Illus.). pap. 166.70 *(978-0-15-340223-4(7))* Harcourt Schl. Pubs.
—All the People, No. 4. 2nd ed. 2003. (Illus.). (gr. 1). pap. 139.70 *(978-0-15-337559-0(0))* Harcourt Schl. Pubs.
—At Home with the Family, Unit 2. 3rd ed. 2003. (Harcourt Brace Social Studies). pap. 76.00 *(978-0-15-341059-8(0))* Harcourt Schl. Pubs.
—Beginnings 2005. 3rd ed. 2003. (Harcourt Horizons Ser.). (ENG.). 744p. (gr. 4-5). stu. ed. 86.80 *(978-0-15-339620-5(2))* Harcourt Schl. Pubs.
—Being a Citizen, Unit 5. 3rd ed. 2003. (Harcourt Brace Social Studies). pap. 76.00 *(978-0-15-341070-3(1))* Harcourt Schl. Pubs.
—Catch a Dream Level 1-2. 3rd ed. 2003. (Harcourt School Publishers Trophies Ser.). (ENG., Illus.). 176p. (gr. 1-1). pupil's gde. ed. 38.10 *(978-0-15-322470-6(3))* Harcourt Schl. Pubs.
—Distant Voyages. 3rd ed. 2003. (Harcourt School Publishers Trophies Ser.). (ENG., Illus.). 768p. (gr. 5-5). pupil's gde. ed. 82.55 *(978-0-15-322479-9(7))* Harcourt Schl. Pubs.
—Going to School Big Book No. 1. 2nd ed. 2003. (Illus.). (gr. 1). pap. 139.70 *(978-0-15-337556-9(6))* Harcourt Schl. Pubs.
—Here & There 2003 Level 1-3. 3rd ed. 2003. (Harcourt School Publishers Trophies Ser.). (ENG., Illus.). 192p. (gr. 1-1). stu. ed. 42.10 *(978-0-15-322471-3(1))* Harcourt Schl. Pubs.
—Horizons. 3rd ed. 2003. (Harcourt School Publishers Horizons Ser.). (ENG., Illus.). 810p. (gr. 6-6). pupil's gde. ed. 93.40 *(978-0-15-320183-7(5))* Harcourt Schl. Pubs.
—Horizons: "All About Me" Unit. 3rd ed. 2003. (Harcourt Horizons Ser.). (Illus.). (gr. k-7). pap. 254.10 *(978-0-15-320943-7(7))* Harcourt Schl. Pubs.
—Horizons: Assessment Program. 3rd ed. 2003. (Harcourt Horizons Ser.). (ENG.). 48p. (gr. 1-1). pap. 72.15 *(978-0-15-340284-5(9));* pap. 72.15 *(978-0-15-340285-2(7))* Harcourt Schl. Pubs.
—Horizons Bk. 2: World Regions. 3rd ed. 2003. (Illus.). pap. 9.30 *(978-0-15-333944-8(6))* Harcourt Schl. Pubs.
—Horizons ESL Summary. 4th ed. 2004. (gr. 3). pap. 10.80 *(978-0-15-343720-5(0))* Harcourt Schl. Pubs.
—Horizons, Grade 2: Time for Kids Readers. 3rd ed. 2003. (Harcourt Horizons Ser.). pap., tchr. ed. 51.20 *(978-0-15-334647-7(7))* Harcourt Schl. Pubs.
—Horizons with Ancient Civilizations. 4th ed. 2004. (gr. 3). 53.20 *(978-0-15-344221-6(2))* Harcourt Schl. Pubs.
—Horizontes: Unit Big Book Collection. 3rd ed. 2003. (Harcourt Horizontes Ser.). (SPA., Illus.). (gr. k-6). 1112.80 *(978-0-15-325844-2(6));* 1112.80 *(978-0-15-325845-9(4))* Harcourt Schl. Pubs.
—Horizontes, Grade 1. 2nd ed. 2003. (Harcourt Horizontes Ser.). (SPA.). (gr. k-6). Vol. 1. tchr. ed. 114.40 *(978-0-15-328413-7(7))* Vol. 2. tchr. ed. 114.40 *(978-0-15-328414-4(5))* Harcourt Schl. Pubs.
—Horizontes, Grade 2, Vol. 1. 2nd ed. 2003. (Harcourt Horizontes Ser.). (SPA.). (gr. k-6). tchr. ed. 121.50 *(978-0-15-328415-1(3))* Harcourt Schl. Pubs.
—Horizontes, Grade 3. 2nd ed. 2003. (Harcourt Horizontes Ser.). (SPA.). (gr. k-6). Vol. 1. tchr. ed. 121.50 *(978-0-15-328509-7(5))* Vol. 2. tchr. ed. 121.50 *(978-0-15-328510-3(9))* Harcourt Schl. Pubs.
—In & Around the Land, Unit 4. 3rd ed. 2003. (Harcourt Brace Social Studies). pap. 76.00 *(978-0-15-341061-1(2))* Harcourt Schl. Pubs.
—Land Around, No. 3. 2nd ed. 2003. (Illus.). (gr. 1). pap. 139.70 *(978-0-15-337558-3(2))* Harcourt Schl. Pubs.
—Learn about People, Unit 4. 3rd ed. 2003. (Horizons Ser.). (Illus.). pap. 166.70 *(978-0-15-340230-2(X))* Harcourt Schl. Pubs.
—Learn about the People No. 4. 2nd ed. 2003. (Illus.). pap. 139.70 *(978-0-15-337569-9(8))* Harcourt Schl. Pubs.
—Lets Visit Museum, Above Level Reader Grade K: Harcourt School Publishers Social Studies. 2005. pap. 5.60 *(978-0-15-351872-0(3))* Harcourt Schl. Pubs.
—Living in a Community, Unit 1. 3rd ed. 2003. (Horizons Ser.). (Illus.). (gr. 2). pap. 166.70 *(978-0-15-340227-2(X))* Harcourt Schl. Pubs.
—Looking Back Big Book No. 5. 2nd ed. 2003. (Illus.). pap. 139.70 *(978-0-15-337560-6(4))* Harcourt Schl. Pubs.

—My Heros, Unit 5. 3rd ed. 2003. (Harcourt Brace Social Studies). pap. 76.00 *(978-0-15-341062-8(0))* Harcourt Schl. Pubs.

—Our Government, Unit 2. 3rd ed. 2003. (Horizons Ser.). (Illus.). pap. 166.70 *(978-0-15-340228-9(8))* Harcourt Schl. Pubs.

—Past & Present, Unit 5. 3rd ed. 2003. (Horizons Ser.). (Illus.). (gr. 2). pap. 166.70 *(978-0-15-340231-9(8))* Harcourt Schl. Pubs.

—Past & Present Big Book No. 5. 2nd ed. 2003. (Illus.). pap. 139.70 *(978-0-15-337570-5(1))* Harcourt Schl. Pubs.

—People at Work, Unit 6. 3rd ed. 2003. (Horizons Ser.). (Illus.). pap. 166.70 *(978-0-15-340232-6(6))* Harcourt Schl. Pubs.

—People in History, Unit 4. 3rd ed. 2003. (Harcourt Brace Social Studies). pap. 76.00 *(978-0-15-341069-7(8))* Harcourt Schl. Pubs.

—People in Time, Unit 6. 3rd ed. 2003. (Harcourt Brace Social Studies). pap. 76.00 *(978-0-15-341071-0(X))* Harcourt Schl. Pubs.

—School Days, Unit 1. 3rd ed. 2003. (Harcourt Brace Social Studies). (gr. 1). pap. 76.00 *(978-0-15-341058-1(2))* Harcourt Schl. Pubs.

—Social Studies: States & Regions: Library Book Collection. 2003. (Harcourt Brace Social Studies). (Illus.). (gr. k-7). 76.00 *(978-0-15-308392-1(1))* Harcourt Schl. Pubs.

—Social Studies Library. 2003. (Harcourt Brace Estudios Sociales Ser.). (SPA., Illus.). (gr. k-18). 37.60 *(978-0-15-310599-9(2))* Harcourt Schl. Pubs.

—TIME for Kids. 3rd ed. 2003. (Horizontes (Social Studies) Ser.). Bk. 1. (SPA.). (gr. 3). pap. 7.00 *(978-0-15-333782-6(6))*Bk. 2. (SPA.). pap. 7.00 *(978-0-15-333784-0(2))*Bk. 3. (SPA.). pap. 7.00 *(978-0-15-333786-4(9))*Bk. 4. (SPA.). pap. 7.00 *(978-0-15-333788-8(5))*Bk. 5. (SPA.). pap. 7.00 *(978-0-15-333790-1(7))*Bk. 6. (SPA.). pap. 7.00 *(978-0-15-333792-5(3))*Bk. 7. pap. 7.00 *(978-0-15-333794-9(X))*Bk. 8. (SPA.). pap. 7.00 *(978-0-15-333796-3(6))*Bk. 9. (SPA.). pap. 7.00 *(978-0-15-333798-7(2))*Bk. 13. (SPA.). pap. 7.00 *(978-0-15-333806-9(7))*Bk. 14. (SPA.). pap. 7.00 *(978-0-15-333808-3(3))*Bk. 15. (SPA.). pap. 7.00 *(978-0-15-333810-6(5))*Bk. 16. (SPA.). pap. 7.00 *(978-0-15-333812-0(1))*Bk. 17. (SPA.). pap. 7.00 *(978-0-15-333814-4(8))*Bk. 18. (SPA.). pap. 7.00 *(978-0-15-333816-8(4))* Harcourt Schl. Pubs.

—TIME for Kids: World Regions. 3rd ed. 2003. (Horizontes (Social Studies) Ser.). (SPA., Illus.). Bk. 1. pap. 9.30 *(978-0-15-333942-4(X))*Bk. 3. pap. 9.30 *(978-0-15-333946-2(2))*Bk. 4. pap. 9.30 *(978-0-15-333948-6(9))*Bk. 5. pap. 9.30 *(978-0-15-333950-9(0))*Bk. 6. pap. 9.30 *(978-0-15-333952-3(7))*Bk. 7. pap. 9.30 *(978-0-15-333954-7(3))*Bk. 8. pap. 9.30 *(978-0-15-333956-1(X))*Bk. 9. pap. 9.30 *(978-0-15-333958-5(6))*Bk. 10. pap. 9.30 *(978-0-15-333960-8(8))*Bk. 11. pap. 9.30 *(978-0-15-333962-2(4))*Bk. 12. pap. 9.30 *(978-0-15-333964-6(0))*Bk. 13. pap. 9.30 *(978-0-15-333966-0(7))*Bk. 14. pap. 9.30 *(978-0-15-333968-4(3))*Bk. 16. pap. 9.30 *(978-0-15-333972-1(1))*Bk. 17. pap. 9.30 *(978-0-15-333974-5(8))*Bk. 18. pap. 9.30 *(978-0-15-333976-9(4))*Bk. 19. pap. 9.30 *(978-0-15-333978-3(0))*Bk. 20. pap. 9.30 *(978-0-15-333980-6(2))*Bk. 21. pap. 9.30 *(978-0-15-333982-0(9))*Bk.15. pap. 9.30 *(978-0-15-333970-7(5))* Harcourt Schl. Pubs.

—TIME for Kids Bk. 11: World Region, 5 Packs. 3rd ed. 2003. (Horizontes (Social Studies) Ser.). (SPA.). (gr. 3-18). pap. 46.20 *(978-0-15-333963-9(2))* Harcourt Schl. Pubs.

—TIME for Kids 5 Pack. 3rd ed. 2003. (Horizontes (Social Studies) Ser.). (SPA.). (gr. 3-18). Bk. 2. pap. 34.90 *(978-0-15-333785-7(0))*Bk. 3. pap. 34.90 *(978-0-15-333787-1(7))* Harcourt Schl. Pubs.

—Timeless Treasure. 3rd ed. 2003. (Harcourt School Publishers Trophies Ser.). (ENG., Illus.). 752p. (gr. 6-6). pupil's gde. ed. 87.50 *(978-0-15-322480-5(0))* Harcourt Schl. Pubs.

—United States History Beginnings, Vol. 1. 3rd ed. 2003. (Harcourt Horizons Ser.). (ENG.). 756p. (gr. 4-5). tchr. ed., spiral bd. 191.95 *(978-0-15-339634-2(2))* Harcourt Schl. Pubs.

—United States History Civil War to Present. 3rd ed. 2003. (Harcourt Horizons Ser.). (ENG.). 576p. (gr. 5-6). tchr. ed., spiral bd. 192.00 *(978-0-15-339637-3(7))* Harcourt Schl. Pubs.

—US History: The Civil War to the Present, Vol. 1. 3rd ed. 2003. (Harcourt Horizons Ser.). (ENG.). 696p. (gr. 5-6). tchr. ed., spiral bd. 192.00 *(978-0-15-339636-6(9))* Harcourt Schl. Pubs.

—US History, Grade 5 Vol. 2: Beginnings. 3rd ed. 2003. (Harcourt Horizons Ser.). (ENG.). 648p. (gr. 4-5). tchr. ed., spiral bd. 191.95 *(978-0-15-339635-9(0))* Harcourt Schl. Pubs.

—We Belong in Groups, Unit 1. 3rd ed. 2003. (Harcourt Brace Social Studies). (gr. 2). pap. 76.00 *(978-0-15-341066-6(3))* Harcourt Schl. Pubs.

—We Work Together, Unit 3. 3rd ed. 2003. (Harcourt Brace Social Studies). pap. 76.00 *(978-0-15-341068-0(X))* Harcourt Schl. Pubs.

—World History: States & Regions. 3rd ed. 2003. (Harcourt Horizons Ser.). (ENG.). (gr. 3-4). 600p. tchr. ed., spiral bd. 153.45 *(978-0-15-339630-4(X))*; (Illus.). 584p. 79.75 *(978-0-15-339618-2(0))* Harcourt Schl. Pubs.

—World History, Grade 4 Vol. 2: States & Regions. 3rd ed. 2003. (Harcourt Horizons Ser.). (ENG.). 588p. (gr. 3-4). tchr. ed., spiral bd. 153.45 *(978-0-15-339631-1(8))* Harcourt Schl. Pubs.

Health Social Studies. Incl. The World Past to Present. pap., tchr. ed. 61.59: The World Past to Present. pap., tchr. ed. The World Past to Present. suppl. ed. *(978-0-669-11425-6(1))*; The World Past to Present. pap., wbk. ed. *(978-0-669-11405-8(7))*; The World Past to Present. tchr. ed., wbk. ed. *(978-0-669-11410-2(3))*; The World Past to Present. suppl. ed. *(978-0-669-11431-7(6))*; The World Past to Present. suppl. ed. *(978-0-669-11727-1(7))*; The World Past to Present. suppl. ed. 11.28 (J). (gr. 6-7). *(978-0-669-11391-4(3))* Houghton Mifflin Harcourt School Pubs.

Helgren. People, Places & Changes: Online Edition Plus. 3rd ed. 2003. 17.26 *(978-0-03-037418-0(9))* Holt McDougal.

Helgren, David M. People, Places & Change: Enhanced Online Edition. 3rd ed. 2003. 70.53 *(978-0-03-072533-3(X))* Holt McDougal.

Hellebuyck, Adam & Deimel, Laura. Tennis Grand Slam. 2019. (21st Century Skills Library: Global Citizens: Sports Ser.). (ENG., Illus.). 32p. (J). (gr. 4-7). pap. 14.21 *(978-1-5341-5036-2(6)*, 213451); lib. bdg. 32.07 *(978-1-5341-4750-8(0)*, 213450) Cherry Lake Publishing.

Hinds, Kathryn. The Palace, 1 vol. 2009. (Life in the Medieval Muslim World Ser.). (ENG.). 80p. (gr. 6-6). lib. bdg. 36.93 *(978-0-7614-3088-9(1)*, 14960366-c210-4045-bd8f-1ef36947278e) Cavendish Square Publishing LLC.

Hinton, Kerry. 10 Great Makerspace Projects Using Social Studies, 1 vol. 2017. (Using Makerspaces for School Projects Ser.). (ENG.). 64p. (gr. 6-6). 36.13 *(978-1-4994-3850-5(8)*, 6c070caa-b545-4d35-ac4a-b58b761e0fc2, Rosen Central) Rosen Publishing Group, Inc., The.

Hirsch, E. D., Jr., ed. History & Geography: Level 4. 2003. stu. ed. 44.50 *(978-0-7690-5025-6(5))* Pearson Learning.

—History & Geography: Level 5. 2003. stu. ed. 49.95 *(978-0-7690-5026-3(3))* Pearson Learning.

History Digs (Set), 10 vols., Set. Incl. America: Three Worlds Meet. Cosson, M. J. lib. bdg. 32.07 *(978-1-61080-193-5(8)*, 201162); America's Colonization & Settlement. Lusted, Marcia Amidon. lib. bdg. 32.07 *(978-1-61080-194-2(6)*, 201164); Birth of the United States. Brennan, Linda Crotta. lib. bdg. 32.07 *(978-1-61080-197-3(0)*, 201170); Contemporary United States. Cunningham, Kevin. lib. bdg. 32.07 *(978-1-61080-195-9(4)*, 201166); Development of U. S. Industry. Meinking, Mary. lib. bdg. 32.07 *(978-1-61080-198-0(9)*, 201172); Great Depression & World War II. Peterson, Sheryl. lib. bdg. 32.07 *(978-1-61080-199-7(7)*, 201174); Postwar United States. Combs, Maggie. lib. bdg. 32.07 *(978-1-61080-196-6(2)*, 201168); United States Enters the 20th Century. Herringshaw, DeAnn. lib. bdg. 32.07 *(978-1-61080-200-0(4)*, 201176); US Civil War & Reconstruction. Howell, Brian. lib. bdg. 32.07 *(978-1-61080-201-7(2)*, 201178); US Growth & Change in the 19th Century. Howell, Brian. lib. bdg. 32.07 *(978-1-61080-202-4(0)*, 201180); (gr. 4-8). (Explorer Library: Language Arts Explorer Ser.). (ENG., Illus.). 32p. 2011. 320.70 *(978-1-61080-243-7(8)*, 201030) Cherry Lake Publishing.

The History of the Humanities & Social Sciences, 6 vols. 2016. (History of the Humanities & Social Sciences Ser.). (ENG.). 208p. (gr. 8-8). 143.40 *(978-1-5081-7166-9(1)*, 5e6ea875-15de-4421-a107-3debb1f43868, Rosen Young Adult) Rosen Publishing Group, Inc., The.

Holba, Annette. Handbook for the Humanities Doctoral Student. 2005. 113p. pap. 19.95 *(978-1-4137-9929-3(9))* PublishAmerica, Inc.

Holidays & Celebrations Set. (gr. k-2). 346.95 *(978-0-7368-9406-7(3)*, Red Brick Learning) Capstone.

Holt, Rinehart and Winston Staff. People, Places & Change: Texas Online Edition. 2003. cd-rom 71.00 *(978-0-03-073348-2(0))* Holt McDougal.

Holzschuher, Cythnia. Our Country Thematic Unit. 2005. (Emergent/Early (Prek-2) Social Studies Package Ser.). 12p. (gr. -1-1). 25.20 *(978-0-8215-7832-2(4))* Sadlier, William H. Inc.

El Honesto Abe: Libros Aventuras (Adventure Books) 2003. (MacMillan/McGraw-Hill. Estudios Sociales Ser.). (ENG & SPA.). (gr. 1-18). *(978-0-02-150111-3(4))* Macmillan/McGraw-Hill Schl. Div.

Hord, Colleen. What's My Role? 2011. (Little World Social Studies Ser.). (ENG.). (J). (gr. k-2). lib. bdg. 19.55 *(978-1-68065-168-3(4))* Perfection Learning Corp.

Hotchkins, Dewayne. Our Man-Made Resources, 1 vol. 2016. (Rosen REAL Readers: Social Studies Nonfiction / Fiction: Myself, My Community, My World Ser.). (ENG.). 12p. (gr. k-1). pap. 6.33 *(978-1-5081-2347-7(0)*, ce4d882e-92c5-4891-9090-3fe997954863, Rosen Classroom) Rosen Publishing Group, Inc., The.

Hunter, Dru. Why Do We Behave Like That? (Think Like a Scientist Ser.). (ENG.). 48p. (J). (gr. 4-7). 2016. pap. 12.00 *(978-1-62832-202-6(0)*, 21076, Creative Paperbacks) 2015. *(978-1-60818-597-9(4)*, 21075, Creative Education) Creative Co., The.

Hutton, Stacie. Jr. Social Studies Investigator. 2005. (J). pap. 14.95 *(978-1-931334-64-8(1))* Pieces of Learning.

Ignite! Learning, compiled by. Social Studies COW Subscription. 2005. (J). *(978-0-9791935-1-4(6))* Ignite! Learning.

—Social Studies Texas COW Subscription. 2005. (J). *(978-0-9791935-2-1(4))* Ignite! Learning.

—SuperCOW - Science & Social Studies Subscription: Science & Social Studies US. 2005. (J). *(978-0-9791935-3-8(2))* Ignite! Learning.

—SuperCOW - Science & Social Studies TX Subscription: Science & Social Studies TX. 2005. (J). *(978-0-9791935-4-5(0))* Ignite! Learning.

La influencia espanola en Texas: Libros Aventuras (Adventure Books) 2003. (MacMillan/McGraw-Hill. Estudios Sociales Ser.). (ENG & SPA.). (gr. 4-18). *(978-0-02-150116-8(5))* Macmillan/McGraw-Hill Schl. Div.

International Day 6 Packs. Individual Title. (gr. -1-2). 23.00 *(978-0-7635-8801-4(6))* Rigby Education.

Iopeners: Big Book Collection, 20 vols. 2005. (J). (gr. k-18). 525.95 *(978-0-7652-4972-2(3))*; (gr. 1-18). 587.50 *(978-0-7652-4976-0(6))* Modern Curriculum Pr.

Iopeners: Classroom Library. 2005. (J). (gr. k-18). 440.50 *(978-0-7652-4969-2(3))*; (gr. 1-18). 518.50 *(978-0-7652-4973-9(1))*; (gr. 2-18). 518.50 *(978-0-7652-4977-7(4))*; (gr. 3-18). 616.50 *(978-0-7652-4980-7(4))*; (gr. 4-18). 616.50 *(978-0-7652-4983-8(9))*; (gr. 5-18). 694.50 *(978-0-7652-4986-9(3))*; (gr. 6-18). 694.50 *(978-0-7652-4989-0(8))* Modern Curriculum Pr.

It's Cool to Learn about Countries (Set), 4 vols., Set. Incl. It's Cool to Learn about Countries: Egypt. Marsico, Katie. lib. bdg. 34.93 *(978-1-61080-100-3(8)*, 201094); It's Cool to Learn about Countries: Ethiopia. Somervill, Barbara A. lib. bdg. 34.93 *(978-1-61080-099-0(0)*, 201092); It's Cool to Learn about Countries: Germany. Franchino, Vicky. lib. bdg. 34.93 *(978-1-61080-098-3(2)*, 201090); It's Cool to Learn about Countries: Vietnam. Rau, Dana Meachen. lib. bdg. 34.93 *(978-1-61080-097-6(4)*, 201088); 48p. (gr. 4-8). (Explorer Library: Social Studies Explorer Ser.). (ENG., Illus.). 2011. 125.44 *(978-1-61080-148-5(2)*, 201010) Cherry Lake Publishing.

Jackson, Abby. Homes, 6 vols., Set. 2003. (Yellow Umbrella Early Level Ser.). (ENG.). 16p. (gr. k-1). pap. 35.70 *(978-0-7368-3004-1(9)*, Capstone Pr.) Capstone.

—Making Money, 6 vols., Set. 2003. (Yellow Umbrella Early Level Ser.). (ENG.). 16p. (gr. k-1). pap. 35.70 *(978-0-7368-3005-8(7)*, Capstone Pr.) Capstone.

James, Eric. Up & Down, 1 vol. 2012. (InfoMax Readers Ser.). (ENG., Illus.). 16p. (J). (gr. k-k). pap. 7.00 *(978-1-4488-8878-8(6)*, 76321e24-b733-468c-bd29-cb3c7b9d04b8, Rosen Classroom) Rosen Publishing Group, Inc., The.

James, Wayan. Grandma Tells a Story, 1 vol. 2016. (Rosen REAL Readers: Social Studies Nonfiction / Fiction: Myself, My Community, My World Ser.). (ENG.). 8p. (gr. k-1). pap. 5.46 *(978-1-5081-2491-7(4)*, 2ef66939-a927-435e-8233-8155017b4f82, Rosen Classroom) Rosen Publishing Group, Inc., The.

Jarrett, Mark. Mastering New York's Elementary Social Studies Standards: Grade 5. 2007. (J). (gr. 5). pap. 11.95 *(978-0-9795493-3-5(7))* Jarrett Publishing Co.

The Journey West. 2004. (Thrilling Tales in Time Ser.: 5). (J). 19.95 *(978-1-58123-373-5(6))* Larson Learning, Inc.

Kachur, Matthew. Our Current World: Set Of 6. 2011. (Navigators Ser.). (J). pap. 44.00 net. *(978-1-4108-0415-0(1))* Benchmark Education Co.

Kohart, Georgia. A Heritage of the Heart Teaching Companion. 2003. (Illus.). ring bd. 24.95 *(978-0-9706348-1-8(1))* Heritage Heart Farm.

Kramer, Candice; Leon. Ben Franklin's Visit - a When Machine Play. Leon, Karen, illus. 2004. (Reader's Theater Content-Area Concepts Ser.). (ENG.). (J). (gr. 1-2). 5.00 net. *(978-1-4108-0799-1(1))* Benchmark Education Co.

—Cesar Chavez Comes to Visit. Leon, Karen, illus. 2004. (Reader's Theater Content-Area Concepts Ser.). (ENG.). (J). (gr. 1-2). 5.00 net. *(978-1-4108-0795-3(9))* Benchmark Education Co.

Language Arts Explorer (Set), 26 vols., Set. Incl. Save the Planet: Compost It. Barker, David M. 2010. lib. bdg. 32.07 *(978-1-60279-656-0(4)*, 200349); Save the Planet: Growing Your Own Garden. Hirsch, Rebecca. 2010. lib. bdg. 32.07 *(978-1-60279-657-7(2)*, 200350); Save the Planet: Helping Endangered Animals. Hirsch, Rebecca. 2010. lib. bdg. 32.07 *(978-1-60279-658-4(0)*, 200351); Save the Planet: Keeping Water Clean. Farrell, Courtney. 2010. lib. bdg. 32.07 *(978-1-60279-659-1(9)*, 200352); Save the Planet: Local Farms & Sustainable Foods. Vogel, Julia. 2010. lib. bdg. 32.07 *(978-1-60279-660-7(2)*, 200353); Save the Planet: Protecting Our Natural Resources. Hirsch, Rebecca. 2010. lib. bdg. 32.07 *(978-1-60279-661-4(0)*, 200354); Save the Planet: Reduce, Reuse, & Recycle. Minden, Cecilia. 2010. lib. bdg. 32.07 *(978-1-60279-662-1(9)*, 200355); Save the Planet: Using Alternative Energies. Farrell, Courtney. 2010. lib. bdg. 32.07 *(978-1-60279-663-8(7)*, 200356); Set. History Digs (Set) 2011. 320.70 *(978-1-61080-243-7(8)*, 201030); Set. Science Lab (Set) 2011. 256.56 *(978-1-61080-245-1(4)*, 201032); 32p. (gr. 4-8). (Explorer Library: Language Arts Explorer Ser.). (ENG., Illus.). 2011. 741.00 *(978-1-61080-239-0(X)*, 201026) Cherry Lake Publishing.

Lankford, Ronald D., Jr., ed. Green Cities, 1 vol. 2011. (At Issue Ser.). (ENG.). 112p. (gr. 10-12). pap. 28.80 *(978-0-7377-5152-9(5)*, e9fdc309-bf0d-4506-8dc4-447817702183); lib. bdg. 41.03 *(978-0-7377-5151-2(7)*, 9a2d91c5-c237-4a17-983c-50136722b9c7) Greenhaven Publishing LLC. (Greenhaven Publishing).

Lansford, Tom, ed. Dictatorships, 1 vol. 2013. (Opposing Viewpoints Ser.). (ENG., Illus.). 224p. (gr. 10-12). pap. 34.80 *(978-0-7377-6315-7(9)*, 986c6332-660a-44cc-86b4-a9742397e74a); lib. bdg. 50.43 *(978-0-7377-6314-0(0)*, ebc5897e-edfa-4a58-aa67-86bcf7f3fc66) Greenhaven Publishing LLC. (Greenhaven Publishing).

Lee, April. How We Get Around Town, 1 vol. 2012. (InfoMax Readers Ser.). (ENG., Illus.). 16p. (J). (gr. k-k). pap. 7.00 *(978-1-4488-8941-9(3)*, 5e9ca34d-70a0-419f-aa4d-32f009192669, Rosen Classroom) Rosen Publishing Group, Inc., The.

Let's See Library_Farms Complete Set. (Let's See Library-Farms Ser.). (gr. 1-3). 119.58 *(978-0-7565-0729-9(4)*, Compass Point Bks.) Capstone.

Lewis, Kelly. Making Choices. 2016. (Spring Forward Ser.). (J). (gr. 2). *(978-1-4900-9440-3(7))* Benchmark Education Co.

Libertad: Libros Aventuras (Adventure Books) 2003. (MacMillan/McGraw-Hill. Estudios Sociales Ser.). (ENG & SPA.). (gr. 4-18). *(978-0-02-150119-9(X))* Macmillan/McGraw-Hill Schl. Div.

Libro del Estudiante: Gente y Lugares. 2003. (MacMillan/McGraw-Hill. Estudios Sociales Ser.). (ENG & SPA.). (gr. 1-18). *(978-0-02-149960-1(8))* Macmillan/McGraw-Hill Schl. Div.

Libro del Estudiante: Nuestra Nacion. 2003. (MacMillan/McGraw-Hill. Estudios Sociales Ser.). (ENG & SPA.). (gr. 5-18). *(978-0-02-149964-9(0))* Macmillan/McGraw-Hill Schl. Div.

Libro del Estudiante: Nuestras Comunidades. 2003. (MacMillan/McGraw-Hill. Estudios Sociales Ser.). (ENG & SPA.). (gr. 3-18). *(978-0-02-149962-5(4))* Macmillan/McGraw-Hill Schl. Div.

Libro del Estudiante: Regiones de Nuestro Pais. 2003. (MacMillan/McGraw-Hill. Estudios Sociales Ser.). (ENG & SPA.). (gr. 4-18). *(978-0-02-149963-2(2))* Macmillan/McGraw-Hill Schl. Div.

Libro del Estudiante: Vivimos Juntos. 2003. (MacMillan/McGraw-Hill. Estudios Sociales Ser.). (ENG & SPA.). (gr. 2-18). *(978-0-02-149961-8(6))* Macmillan/McGraw-Hill Schl. Div.

Libros Aventuras Classroom Set: Libros Aventuras (Adventure Books) 2003. (MacMillan/McGraw-Hill. Estudios Sociales Ser.). (ENG & SPA.). (gr. 1-18). *(978-0-02-150096-3(7))*; (gr. 3-18). *(978-0-02-150098-7(3))*; (gr. 4-18). *(978-0-02-150059-8(2))*; (gr. 5-18). *(978-0-02-150100-7(9))* Macmillan/McGraw-Hill Schl. Div.

Libros Aventuras Deluxe Classroom Set: Libros Aventuras (Adventure Books) 2003. (MacMillan/McGraw-Hill. Estudios Sociales Ser.). (ENG & SPA.). (gr. 1-18). *(978-0-02-150101-4(7))*; (gr. 3-18). *(978-0-02-150103-8(3))*; (gr. 4-18). *(978-0-02-150060-4(6))*; (gr. 5-18). *(978-0-02-150105-2(X))* Macmillan/McGraw-Hill Schl. Div.

Lindeen, Mary. How Things Change, 6 vols., Set. 2004. (Letter Bks.). (ENG.). 8p. (gr. k-1). pap. 29.70 *(978-0-7368-4114-6(8))* Capstone.

Loria, Laura. How Do You Read Charts & Graphs?, 1 vol. 2018. (Let's Find Out! Social Studies Skills Ser.). (ENG., Illus.). 32p. (J). (gr. 2-3). lib. bdg. 26.06 *(978-1-5081-0700-2(9)*, cd96aa73-0c9d-4799-a706-73ffbd7b5801, Britannica Educational Publishing) Rosen Publishing Group, Inc., The.

Macmillan/Mcgraw. Alternative Learning Strategies: Staff Development Videotapes. (Staff Development Ser.). (gr. k-8). *(978-0-02-178701-2(8))* Macmillan/McGraw-Hill Schl. Div.

—Cooperative Learning: Staff Development Videotapes. (Staff Development Ser.). (gr. k-8). *(978-0-02-178702-9(6))* Macmillan/McGraw-Hill Schl. Div.

Making Headlines, 10 vols. 2016. (Making Headlines Ser.). (ENG.). 160p. (J). (gr. 7-7). lib. bdg. 208.00 *(978-0-7660-8399-8(3)*, 75ebdfad-765c-454a-a696-eb8b2e6ec70d) Enslow Publishing, LLC.

Making Patterns: Level C. 8p. 20.95 *(978-0-322-00361-3(X))* Wright Group/McGraw-Hill.

Martin, Elena. Working Together, 6 vols., Set. 2003. (Yellow Umbrella Early Level Ser.). (ENG.). 16p. (gr. k-1). pap. 35.70 *(978-0-7368-2987-8(3)*, Capstone Pr.) Capstone.

McCune, Susan. Our School Nurse, 1 vol., 1. 2015. (Rosen REAL Readers: Social Studies Nonfiction / Fiction: Myself, My Community, My World Ser.). (ENG.). 8p. (J). (gr. k-1). pap. 5.46 *(978-1-5081-1683-7(0)*, 66de05ce-2111-4709-959d-ea8d9affef9d, Rosen Classroom) Rosen Publishing Group, Inc., The.

—Tanika Walks Her Dog Every Day, 1 vol., 1. 2015. (Rosen REAL Readers: Social Studies Nonfiction / Fiction: Myself, My Community, My World Ser.). (ENG.). 8p. (J). (gr. k-1). pap. 5.46 *(978-1-5081-1668-4(7)*, 62afbf82-4a89-4d18-863d-676dab854ba5, Rosen Classroom) Rosen Publishing Group, Inc., The.

McDowell, Frank. Critical World Issues: Equal Opportunities, Vol. 16. 2016. (Critical World Issues Ser.: Vol. 16). (ENG., Illus.). 112p. (J). (gr. 7-12). 25.95 *(978-1-4222-3652-9(8))* Mason Crest.

McGraw Hill. Civics Today; Citizenship, Economics, & You, Student Edition. 2nd ed. 2004. (Civics Today: Citzshp Econ You Ser.). (ENG., Illus.). 710p. (gr. 7-10). lib. bdg., stu. ed. 63.24 *(978-0-07-860970-1(4)*, 0078609704) McGraw-Hill Higher Education.

—Journey Across Time, Early Ages, Activity Workbook, Student Edition. 2004. (MS World History Ser.). (ENG.). 48p. (gr. 6-9). stu. ed., spiral bd., wbk. ed. 8.36 *(978-0-07-868197-4(9)*, 0078681979) McGraw-Hill Education.

—The World & Its People, Active Reading Note-Taking Guide, Student Workbook. 2004. (GEOGRAPHY: WORLD & ITS PEOPLE Ser.). (ENG., Illus.). 416p. (gr. 6-9). stu. ed., per., wbk. ed. 14.04 *(978-0-07-868140-0(5)*, 0078681405) McGraw-Hill Education.

—The World & Its People: Eastern Hemisphere, Active Reading Note-Taking Guide, Student Workbook. 2004. (WORLD & ITS PEOPLE EASTERN Ser.). (ENG., Illus.). 336p. (gr. 6-9). stu. ed., per. 7.00 *(978-0-07-868058-8(1)*, 0078680581) McGraw-Hill Education.

—The World & Its People: Eastern Hemisphere, Activity Workbook, Student Edition. 2004. (WORLD & ITS PEOPLE EASTERN Ser.). (ENG., Illus.). 46p. (gr. 6-9). pap., wbk. ed. 4.08 *(978-0-07-868120-2(0)*, 0078681200) McGraw-Hill Education.

—The World & Its People, Reading Essentials & Study Guide, Student Workbook. 2004. (GEOGRAPHY: WORLD & ITS PEOPLE Ser.). (ENG., Illus.). 352p. (gr. 6-9). per., wbk. ed., pupil's gde. ed. 7.00 *(978-0-07-865513-5(7)*, 0078655137) McGraw-Hill Education.

—The World & Its People, Spanish Reading Essentials & Study Guide, Student Workbook. 2004. (GEOGRAPHY: WORLD & ITS PEOPLE Ser.). (SPA., Illus.). 346p. (gr. 6-9). stu. ed., per., wbk. ed. 7.00 *(978-0-07-865518-0(8)*, 0078655188) McGraw-Hill Education.

—The World & Its People, StudentWorks Plus CD-ROM. 2005. (GEOGRAPHY: WORLD & ITS PEOPLE Ser.). (ENG.). (gr. 6-9). 84.04 *(978-0-07-866345-1(8)*, 0078663458) McGraw-Hill Education.

—The World & Its People: Western Hemisphere, Europe, & Russia, Active Reading & Note-Taking Strategies, Student Edition. 2004. (WORLD & ITS PEOPLE WESTERN Ser.). (ENG., Illus.). 256p. (gr. 6-9). stu. ed., per. 14.04 *(978-0-07-868033-5(6)*, 0078680336) McGraw-Hill Education.

—The World & Its People: Western Hemisphere, Europe, & Russia, Activity Workbook, Student Edition. 2004. (WORLD & ITS PEOPLE WESTERN Ser.). (ENG., Illus.). 40p. (gr. 6-9). stu. ed., spiral bd., wbk. ed. 8.12 *(978-0-07-868026-7(3)*, 0078680263) McGraw-Hill Education.

—The World & Its People: Western Hemisphere, Europe, & Russia, Reading Essentials & Study Guide, Student Workbook. 2004. (WORLD & ITS PEOPLE WESTERN Ser.). (ENG., Illus.). 216p. (gr. 6-9). stu. ed., per., wbk. ed. 7.00 *(978-0-07-868030-4(1)*, 0078680301) McGraw-Hill Education.

—The World & Its People: Western Hemisphere, Europe, & Russia, StudentWorks Plus CD-ROM. 2005. (WORLD & ITS PEOPLE WESTERN Ser.). (ENG.). (gr. 6-9). 136.96 *(978-0-07-866322-2(9)*, 0078663229) McGraw-Hill Education.

McGraw Hill, creator. The World & Its People: Eastern Hemisphere, Reading Essentials & Study Guide, Student Workbook. 2004. (WORLD & ITS PEOPLE EASTERN Ser.). (ENG.). (gr. 6-9). stu. ed., wbk. ed. 7.60

(978-0-07-868055-7(7), 0078680557) McGraw-Hill Education.

McGraw-Hill Education Staff. The World & Its People: Western Hemisphere, Europe & Russia: Spanish Reading Essentials. 2004. (WORLD & ITS PEOPLE WESTERN Ser.). (SPA., Illus.). 216p. (gr. 6-9). stu. ed., per., wbk. ed. 6.80 (978-0-07-868050-2(6), 0078680506) McGraw-Hill Education.

Measure It: Big Book: Level D. 8p. 20.95 (978-0-322-00362-0(8)) Wright Group/McGraw-Hill.

El mejor Precio: Libros Aventuras (Adventure Books) 2003. (MacMillan/McGraw-Hill. Estudios Sociales Ser.). (ENG & SPA.). (gr. 3-18). (978-0-02-150113-7(0)) Macmillan/McGraw-Hill Schl. Div.

Meredith, Susan Markowitz. Connecting the World. 2016. (Spring Forward Ser.). (J). (gr. 2). (978-1-4900-9476-2(8)) Benchmark Education Co.

Merino, Noël, ed. The European Union, 1 vol. 2008. (Opposing Viewpoints Ser.). (ENG., Illus.). 200p. (gr. 10-12). lib. bdg. 50.43 (978-0-7377-3998-5(3), 7df05308-a9e7-4c01-9d3e-e42d9c9c0c7f, Greenhaven Publishing) Greenhaven Publishing LLC.

—The European Union, 1 vol. 2008. (Opposing Viewpoints Ser.). (ENG., Illus.). 200p. (gr. 10-12). pap. 34.80 (978-0-7377-3999-2(1), 3da7a178-9129-496a-b3e2-52508ddb84ba, Greenhaven Publishing) Greenhaven Publishing LLC.

—Privacy, 1 vol. 2014. (Global Viewpoints Ser.). (ENG., Illus.). 200p. (gr. 10-12). lib. bdg. 47.83 (978-0-7377-6912-8(2), 6d9df098-0b34-472e-a05b-5b0a360709f2, Greenhaven Publishing) Greenhaven Publishing LLC.

—Privacy, 1 vol. 2014. (Global Viewpoints Ser.). (ENG., Illus.). 200p. (gr. 10-12). pap. 32.70 (978-0-7377-6913-5(0), ce422721-6ead-4f23-b162-f0bd1c3d3fec, Greenhaven Publishing) Greenhaven Publishing LLC.

Meyers Schlaglichter des 20 Jahrhunderts. (978-3-411-07411-2(6)) Bibliographisches Institut & F. A. Brockhaus AG DEU. Dist: i. b. d., Ltd.

Meyers Taschenlexikon in einem Band. (978-3-411-10134-4(2)) Bibliographisches Institut & F. A. Brockhaus AG DEU. Dist: i. b. d., Ltd.

Milenio 1: Serie de Estudies Sociales para la Escuela Elemental. (SPA.). 25.00 (978-958-04-5593-6(7)) Norma S.A. COL. Dist: Distribuidora Norma, Inc.

Milenio 2: Serie de Estudies Sociales para la Escuela Elemental. (SPA.). 25.00 (978-958-04-5594-3(5)) Norma S.A. COL. Dist: Distribuidora Norma, Inc.

Milenio 3: Serie de Estudies Sociales para la Escuela Elemental. (SPA.). 30.00 (978-958-04-5595-0(3)) Norma S.A. COL. Dist: Distribuidora Norma, Inc.

Milenio 4: Serie de Estudies Sociales para la Escuela Elemental. (SPA.). 40.00 (978-958-04-5596-7(1)) Norma S.A. COL. Dist: Distribuidora Norma, Inc.

Milenio 5: Serie de Estudies Sociales para la Escuela Elemental. (SPA.). 45.00 (978-958-04-5597-4(X)) Norma S.A. COL. Dist: Distribuidora Norma, Inc.

Milenio 6: Serie de Estudies Sociales para la Escuela Elemental. (SPA.). 45.00 (978-958-04-5598-1(8)) Norma S.A. COL. Dist: Distribuidora Norma, Inc.

Milenio K: Serie de Estudies Sociales para la Escuela Elemental. (SPA.). 25.00 (978-958-04-5592-9(9)) Norma S.A. COL. Dist: Distribuidora Norma, Inc.

Miller, Debra A., ed. Social Security, 1 vol. 2013. (Current Controversies Ser.). (ENG., Illus.). 176p. (gr. 10-12). pap. 33.00 (978-0-7377-6246-4(2), a2d5a6d3-7e17-4daa-a990-2cc6fca555fd); lib. bdg. 48.03 (978-0-7377-6245-7(4), ecaff547-9e00-4c3a-89e5-ae36fa633b15) Greenhaven Publishing LLC. (Greenhaven Publishing).

Mills, Nathan. Living or Nonliving?, 1 vol. 2012. (Rosen Readers Ser.). (ENG., Illus.). 16p. (J). (gr. k-k). pap. 7.00 (978-1-4488-8746-0(1), c06efeba-0ac4-4493-9cc0-e906299a6a96, Rosen Classroom) Rosen Publishing Group, Inc., The.

Mills, Nathan & Allyn, Daisy. Around My Neighborhood, 1 vol. 2012. (Rosen Readers Ser.). (ENG., Illus.). 16p. (J). (gr. k-k). pap. 7.00 (978-1-4488-8646-3(5), 71ca028e-3189-4367-9dda-cda408983022, Rosen Classroom) Rosen Publishing Group, Inc., The.

Mills, Nathan & Baker, Rick. More or Less?, 1 vol. 2012. (Rosen Readers Ser.). (ENG., Illus.). 16p. (J). (gr. k-k). pap. 7.00 (978-1-4488-8649-4(X), cbebaaf9-bd06-4acd-9ace-a5f1d00b2736, Rosen Classroom) Rosen Publishing Group, Inc., The.

Mills, Nathan & Biehn, Mike. Things I Need, Things I Want, 1 vol. 2012. (Rosen Readers Ser.). (ENG., Illus.). 16p. (J). (gr. k-k). pap. 7.00 (978-1-4488-8728-6(3), 1f4e8243-f1bf-44d3-9bc7-16739ee96e2f, Rosen Classroom) Rosen Publishing Group, Inc., The.

Mills, Nathan & Christopher, Nick. Time for a Field Trip, 1 vol. 2012. (Rosen Readers Ser.). (ENG., Illus.). 16p. (J). (gr. k-k). pap. 7.00 (978-1-4488-8752-1(6), cb2bcd53-1835-4508-a77a-5874a907e1df, Rosen Classroom) Rosen Publishing Group, Inc., The.

Mills, Nathan & Davidson, Amy. My Busy Week, 1 vol. 2012. (Rosen Readers Ser.). (ENG., Illus.). 16p. (J). (gr. k-k). pap. 7.00 (978-1-4488-8689-0(9), 0dea7d70-1aa2-4c00-a9e0-15e9fd5b2833, Rosen Classroom) Rosen Publishing Group, Inc., The.

Mills, Nathan & Ericson, Emma. Up or Down?, 1 vol. 2012. (Rosen Readers Ser.). (ENG., Illus.). 16p. (J). (gr. k-k). pap. 7.00 (978-1-4488-8643-2(0), 7fb912cd-b423-40ed-8893-b9ce2ee39aa1, Rosen Classroom) Rosen Publishing Group, Inc., The.

Mills, Nathan & Fudoli, Melissa. I Have One More, 1 vol. 2012. (Rosen Readers Ser.). (ENG., Illus.). 16p. (J). (gr. k-k). pap. 7.00 (978-1-4488-8655-5(4), 1d7c2e3b-e0f0-4fb6-82fc-e2d298d2e2a2, Rosen Classroom) Rosen Publishing Group, Inc., The.

Mills, Nathan & Goodwin, Josh. How Do I Get There?, 1 vol. 2012. (Rosen Readers Ser.). (ENG., Illus.). 24p. (J). (gr. 1-1). pap. 8.25 (978-1-4488-8779-8(8), 018d7396-3ea7-48e5-9aa0-f4dd1aaa00b8, Rosen Classroom) Rosen Publishing Group, Inc., The.

Mills, Nathan & Miller, Andy. Is It Cloth, Clay, or Paper?, 1 vol. 2012. (Rosen Readers Ser.). (ENG., Illus.). 16p. (J). (gr. k-k). pap. 7.00 (978-1-4488-8707-1(0), 51e0c7ef-3a4b-4cff-96bb-a2bf17dfabc5, Rosen Classroom) Rosen Publishing Group, Inc., The.

Mills, Nathan & White, Ella. Months of the Year, 1 vol. 2012. (Rosen Readers Ser.). (ENG., Illus.). 24p. (J). (gr. 1-1). pap. 8.25 (978-1-4488-8785-9(2), a18f0f01-23dc-4ac1-b310-089445da9b55, Rosen Classroom) Rosen Publishing Group, Inc., The.

Mix It Up: Big Book: Level E. 8p. 20.95 (978-0-322-00363-7(6)) Wright Group/McGraw-Hill.

MoCasins: Level A, 6 vols. 8p. 24.95 (978-0-7802-9109-6(3)) Wright Group/McGraw-Hill.

Monsters in Myth, 8 vols., Set. Incl. Cerberus. Tracy, Kathleen. lib. bdg. 29.95 (978-1-58415-924-7(3)); Chimaera. LaRoche, Amy. lib. bdg. 29.95 (978-1-58415-925-4(1)); Cyclopes. Roberts, Russell. lib. bdg. 29.95 (978-1-58415-926-1(X)); Medusa. Tracy, Kathleen. lib. bdg. 29.95 (978-1-58415-928-5(6)); Minotaur. Roberts, Russell. lib. bdg. 29.95 (978-1-58415-929-2(4)); Monsters of Hercules. Orr, Tamra. lib. bdg. 29.95 (978-1-58415-927-8(8)); Sirens. Orr, Tamra. lib. bdg. 29.95 (978-1-58415-930-8(8)); Sphinx. DiPrimio, Pete. lib. bdg. 29.95 (978-1-58415-931-5(6)); (Illus.). 48p. (J). (gr. 4-7). 2010. 239.60 (978-1-58415-932-2(4)) Mitchell Lane Pubs.

Moore, Elizabeth & Gregory, Helen. Where Do People Work? 2011. (Wonder Readers Emergent Level Ser.). (ENG.). 16p. (gr. -1-1). pap. 35.94 (978-1-4296-8206-0(X), Capstone Pr.) Capstone.

Moran, Margaret. Cowhands & Cattle Trails: Set Of 6. 2011. (Navigators Ser.). (J). pap. 48.00 net. (978-1-4108-0426-6(7)) Benchmark Education Co.

Museums: Collections to Share, 6 vols. (Book2WebTM Ser.). (gr. 4-8). 36.50 (978-0-322-02986-6(4)) Wright Group/McGraw-Hill.

My Favorite Things. (Totally Girls Ser.). 16p. (J). (978-2-7643-0189-0(8)) Phidal Publishing, Inc./Editions Phidal, Inc.

My World: E-Journals. (Technology: Social Studies). (SPA.). (gr. k-1). (978-0-02-147228-4(9)) Macmillan/McGraw-Hill Schl. Div.

Mystery Hunters, 12 vols. 2016. (Mystery Hunters Ser.). (ENG.). 00048p. (J). (gr. 5-5). lib. bdg. 201.60 (978-1-4824-5857-2(8), fdeafb3a-9330-42e0-8623-94fb4f6c9e43) Stevens, Gareth Publishing LLLP.

Nations of the World Series, 4 vols., Set. 2003. pap. 137.12 (978-0-7398-7002-0(5)) Steck-Vaughn.

Nelid, Piper. Bill Is My Forever Dad, 1 vol., 1. 2015. (Rosen REAL Readers: Social Studies Nonfiction / Fiction: Myself, My Community, My World Ser.). (ENG.). 8p. (J). (gr. k-1). pap. 5.46 (978-1-5081-1629-5(6), 5fb81c9d-2452-45c1-b9d1-efa861667be7, Rosen Classroom) Rosen Publishing Group, Inc., The.

—Our School Is New, 1 vol., 1. 2015. (Rosen REAL Readers: Social Studies Nonfiction / Fiction: Myself, My Community, My World Ser.). (ENG.). 8p. (J). (gr. k-1). pap. 5.46 (978-1-5081-1680-6(6), 72a25155-8605-4a08-aadd-1593d8bd96a1, Rosen Classroom) Rosen Publishing Group, Inc., The.

—Our School Mission, 1 vol., 1. 2015. (Rosen REAL Readers: Social Studies Nonfiction / Fiction: Myself, My Community, My World Ser.). (ENG.). 12p. (J). (gr. k-1). pap. 6.33 (978-1-5081-1788-9(8), 32213670-2130-4a56-866c-0f49ecad979d, Rosen Classroom) Rosen Publishing Group, Inc., The.

—Saving for College, 1 vol., 1. 2015. (Rosen REAL Readers: Social Studies Nonfiction / Fiction: Myself, My Community, My World Ser.). (ENG.). 12p. (J). (gr. k-1). pap. 6.33 (978-1-5081-1770-4(5), 741bb19b-f3ad-47e8-a5a0-8ead6f823875, Rosen Classroom) Rosen Publishing Group, Inc., The.

—We Respect Our Classmates, 1 vol., 1. 2015. (Rosen REAL Readers: Social Studies Nonfiction / Fiction: Myself, My Community, My World Ser.). (ENG.). 12p. (J). (gr. k-1). pap. 6.33 (978-1-5081-1824-4(8), ba9e32cf-f9e1-47b6-bd24-873294c9b21a, Rosen Classroom) Rosen Publishing Group, Inc., The.

—Ximena Is from Colombia, 1 vol., 1. 2015. (Rosen REAL Readers: Social Studies Nonfiction / Fiction: Myself, My Community, My World Ser.). (ENG.). 12p. (J). (gr. k-1). pap. 6.33 (978-1-5081-1806-0(X), 5d231b3e-810b-4ad5-9ad5-d0fa9894c98b, Rosen Classroom) Rosen Publishing Group, Inc., The.

Nelson, Maria. I Am a Good Neighbor, 1 vol. 2013. (Kids of Character Ser.). 24p. (J). (gr. 1-2). (ENG.). 25.27 (978-1-4339-9021-2(0), d5783d81-9dc2-4af5-bb4a-139f68c0c343); pap. 48.90 (978-1-4339-9023-6(7)); (ENG., Illus.). pap. 9.15 (978-1-4339-9022-9(9), 9e30675f-025b-4fd4-b2d5-6cfad449d2e1) Stevens, Gareth Publishing LLLP.

The New World. 2004. (Thrilling Tales in Time Ser.: Vol. 2). (J). 19.95 (978-1-58123-371-1(X)) Larson Learning, Inc.

Nuestra primera Bandera: Libros Aventuras (Adventure Books) 2003. (MacMillan/McGraw-Hill. Estudios Sociales Ser.). (ENG & SPA.). (gr. 1-18). (978-0-02-150110-6(6)) Macmillan/McGraw-Hill Schl. Div.

Nunn, Tamara. My Global Address. 2017. (Learn-To-Read Ser.). (ENG., Illus.). (J). pap. 3.49 (978-1-68310-249-6(5)) Pacific Learning, Inc.

La Oficina de Libertos: Libros Aventuras (Adventure Books) 2003. (MacMillan/McGraw-Hill. Estudios Sociales Ser.). (ENG & SPA.). (gr. 4-18). (978-0-02-150117-5(3)) Macmillan/McGraw-Hill Schl. Div.

Ohio 8th Gr Social Studies. 2007. 52p. pap. 8.95 (978-0-9769459-6-3(7)) Hollandays Publishing Corp.

O'Keefe, Cynthia A. Exploring the Real World: Middle School Edition. Date not set. 200p. (Orig.). (J). pap. 85.00 (978-0-913956-89-2(9)) E B S C O Industries, Inc.

—Exploring the Real World: Primary School Edition. Date not set. 200p. (Orig.). (J). (gr. 4-6). pap. 65.00 (978-0-913956-88-5(0)) E B S C O Industries, Inc.

—Exploring the Real World: Secondary Edition. Date not set. 366p. (Orig.). (YA). (gr. 7-12). pap. 283.00 (978-0-913956-87-8(2)) E B S C O Industries, Inc.

O'Kelley, Jeff. Mapping the Way. 2006. (Early Explorers Ser.). (J). pap. (978-1-4108-6106-1(6)) Benchmark Education Co.

Open for Debate, 12 vols., Set. 2005. (Open for Debate Ser.). (ENG., Illus.). 128-144p. (gr. 8-8). lib. bdg. 273.00 (978-0-7614-1581-7(5), f8fc48ea-1c4c-4891-835f-81c1fbf8072d, Cavendish Square) Cavendish Square Publishing LLC.

Oxford Illustrated Social Studies Dictionary. 2013. (ENG., Illus.). 224p. pap. 29.70 (978-0-19-407132-1(4)) Oxford Univ. Pr., Inc.

Paderewski, Elliot. Global Citizens Protect the World Community, 1 vol. 2016. (Rosen REAL Readers: Social Studies Nonfiction / Fiction: Myself, My Community, My World Ser.). (ENG.). 12p. (gr. k-1). pap. 6.33 (978-1-5081-2353-8(5), 43b780cd-db75-42b2-b6ee-b313a907bef9, Rosen Classroom) Rosen Publishing Group, Inc., The.

Parnell, Declan. The Globe in Our Classroom, 1 vol., 1. 2015. (Rosen REAL Readers: Social Studies Nonfiction / Fiction: Myself, My Community, My World Ser.). (ENG.). 8p. (J). (gr. k-1). pap. 5.46 (978-1-5081-1635-6(0), 4a8ffaae-2eb8-449c-9b63-eeee2e15e682, Rosen Classroom) Rosen Publishing Group, Inc., The.

—My Aunt's Wedding, 1 vol., 1. 2015. (Rosen REAL Readers: Social Studies Nonfiction / Fiction: Myself, My Community, My World Ser.). (ENG.). 12p. (J). (gr. k-1). pap. 6.33 (978-1-5081-1758-2(6), 6ad257a9-824d-4c52-9dac-e954b18c41e5, Rosen Classroom) Rosen Publishing Group, Inc., The.

—Street Signs in My Neighborhood, 1 vol., 1. 2015. (Rosen REAL Readers: Social Studies Nonfiction / Fiction: Myself, My Community, My World Ser.). (ENG.). 12p. (J). (gr. k-1). pap. 6.33 (978-1-5081-1719-3(5), 4c4c1751-838b-4c85-a0bb-46be4b36deee, Rosen Classroom) Rosen Publishing Group, Inc., The.

—We Have Rules in School, 1 vol., 1. 2015. (Rosen REAL Readers: Social Studies Nonfiction / Fiction: Myself, My Community, My World Ser.). (ENG.). 8p. (J). (gr. k-1). pap. 5.46 (978-1-5081-1671-4(7), c06eb8da-ec12-4cc5-b6c9-7beb560e5758, Rosen Classroom) Rosen Publishing Group, Inc., The.

Pebble Books: One World, Many Cultures. 2005. (YA). (gr. k-3). 712.80 (978-0-7368-4217-4(9), Pebble) Capstone.

People to Know, 55 bks., Set. (Illus.). (YA). (gr. 6-12). lib. bdg. 1152.25 (978-0-89490-450-9(7)) Enslow Publishing, LLC.

El Pescador: Libros Aventuras (Adventure Books) 2003. (MacMillan/McGraw-Hill. Estudios Sociales Ser.). (ENG & SPA.). (gr. 3-18). (978-0-02-150112-0(2)) Macmillan/McGraw-Hill Schl. Div.

Peters, Jennifer, ed. Critical Perspectives on Social Justice, 1 vol. 2017. (Analyzing the Issues Ser.). (ENG.). 232p. (gr. 8-8). 50.93 (978-0-7660-9165-8(1), a6a97eb2-5e52-4929-b6a0-72f7763984ab) Enslow Publishing, LLC.

Pinkney, Andrea Davis. Peace Warriors (Profiles #6) 2013. (Profiles Ser.: 6). (ENG.). 144p. (J). (gr. 4-7). pap. 6.99 (978-0-545-51857-4(1), Scholastic Paperbacks) Scholastic, Inc.

Pohl, Kathleen. Descubramos Países del Mundo (Looking at Countries), 6 vols., Set. Incl. Descubramos Alemania (Looking at Germany) lib. bdg. 28.67 (978-0-8368-8781-5(6), a572e9f6-fc30-4480-8697-775b7c7c9ae7); Descubramos Argentina (Looking at Argentina) lib. bdg. 28.67 (978-0-8368-8779-2(4), f9d29693-28a3-4f52-be9c-44e1172f1d9c); Descubramos el Congo (Looking at the Congo) lib. bdg. 28.67 (978-0-8368-8780-8(8), 9a5867f5-6ba9-43db-b2bc-3fd7f070cd94); Descubramos Iran (Looking at Iran) (J). lib. bdg. 28.67 (978-0-8368-8782-2(4), 99c780a9-ce6e-4770-913e-82aeea1ea729); Descubramos Irlanda (Looking at Ireland) lib. bdg. 28.67 (978-0-8368-8783-9(2), bbf21f3e-51d9-4958-9af2-c5149120cc64); Descubramos Israel (Looking at Israel) lib. bdg. 28.67 (978-0-8368-8784-6(0), fb3a5782-3cbc-465a-a04f-ae313e267e57); (Illus.). (gr. 2-4). (Descubramos países del mundo (Looking at Countries) Ser.). (SPA.). 32p. 2008. 151.62 o.p. (978-0-8368-8778-5(6)) Stevens, Gareth Publishing LLLP.

—Looking at Countries, 6 vols., Set. Incl. Looking at Argentina. lib. bdg. 28.67 (978-0-8368-8765-5(4), 587f4477-8836-4b74-a699-cb3b3977d161); Looking at Germany. lib. bdg. 28.67 (978-0-8368-8767-9(0), d03cb753-784a-41d5-a69f-7693531085ad); Looking at Iran. lib. bdg. 28.67 (978-0-8368-8768-6(9), 92671d3e-82dd-4521-89b6-d9505cb8270c); Looking at Ireland. lib. bdg. 28.67 (978-0-8368-8769-3(7), b20375e3-c7b8-4702-87e1-f7e50070b329); Looking at Israel. lib. bdg. 28.67 (978-0-8368-8770-9(0), 265d70ed-8adf-412d-8ada-db56f9aa615c); Looking at the Congo. lib. bdg. 28.67 (978-0-8368-8766-2(2), dd5c1158-9a77-467b-ac9f-ea8328161fd5); (Illus.). (gr. 2-4)., Gareth Stevens Learning Library (Looking at Countries Ser.). 32p. 2008. 151.62 o.p. (978-0-8368-8764-8(6)) Stevens, Gareth Publishing LLLP.

Portalupi, Laura. Spies! Set: Real People, Real Stories, 6 vols. 2003. (High Five Reading - Green Ser.). (ENG.). 48p. (gr. 3-4). pap. 54.00 (978-0-7368-2840-6(0)) Capstone.

Prentiss, Timothy. What Is a Good Citizen? 2006. (Early Explorers Ser.). (J). pap. (978-1-4108-6110-8(4)) Benchmark Education Co.

PRESS, Celebration. Iopeners: Social Studies Library, 10 vols. 2004. (ENG.). (J). (gr. k-k). 220.95 (978-0-7652-4971-5(5), Celebration Pr.) Savvas Learning Co.

Price, Sean & Price, Sean Stewart. A Wicked History, 4 vols., Set. Incl. Wicked History: Attila the Hun. (Illus.). 128p. (J). (gr. 6-12). 2009. 31.00 (978-0-531-21801-3(5), Watts, Franklin); 2009. Set lib. bdg. 120.00 (978-0-531-26140-8(9), Watts, Franklin) Scholastic Library Publishing.

Proyecto Raices: un sueno hecho Realidad: Libros Aventuras (Adventure Books) 2003. (MacMillan/McGraw-Hill. Estudios Sociales Ser.). (ENG & SPA.). (gr. 5-18). (978-0-02-150127-4(0)) Macmillan/McGraw-Hill Schl. Div.

Que hay de Nuevo? Libros Aventuras (Adventure Books) 2003. (MacMillan/McGraw-Hill. Estudios Sociales Ser.). (ENG & SPA.). (gr. 1-18). (978-0-02-150109-0(2)) Macmillan/McGraw-Hill Schl. Div.

Raintree. Itip 2004 Grade 4 Soc Stud Sta. 2004. pap. (978-1-4109-1575-7(1)); pap. (978-1-4109-1577-1(8)) Harcourt Schl. Pubs.

—Itip 2004 Grades 2-4 Soc Stud. 2004. pap. (978-1-4109-1578-8(6)); pap. (978-1-4109-1573-3(5)) Harcourt Schl. Pubs.

—Itip 2004 Grades 3-4 Soc Stud. 2004. pap. (978-1-4109-1574-0(3)); pap. (978-1-4109-1576-4(X)) Harcourt Schl. Pubs.

—Itip 2004 Grades K-1 Soc Stud. 2004. pap. (978-1-4109-1572-6(7)) Harcourt Schl. Pubs.

—Itip 2004 Grades K-2 Science S. 2004. pap. (978-1-4109-1568-9(9)) Harcourt Schl. Pubs.

La rata Cambalachera: Libros Aventuras (Adventure Books) 2003. (MacMillan/McGraw-Hill. Estudios Sociales Ser.). (ENG & SPA.). (gr. 4-18). (978-0-02-150114-4(9)) Macmillan/McGraw-Hill Schl. Div.

Read Alouds & Primary Sources: Scott Foresman Social Studies. 2003. (gr. k-18). (978-0-328-03775-9(3), Scott Foresman) Addison-Wesley Educational Pubs., Inc.

Read Alouds & Primary Sources: Scott Foresman Social Studies: All Together. 2003. (gr. 1-18). (978-0-328-03776-6(1), Scott Foresman) Addison-Wesley Educational Pubs., Inc.

Read Alouds & Primary Sources: Scott Foresman Social Studies: Communities. 2003. (gr. 3-18). (978-0-328-03778-0(8), Scott Foresman) Addison-Wesley Educational Pubs., Inc.

Read Alouds & Primary Sources: Scott Foresman Social Studies: People & Places. 2003. (gr. 2-18). (978-0-328-03777-3(X), Scott Foresman) Addison-Wesley Educational Pubs., Inc.

Read Alouds & Primary Sources: Scott Foresman Social Studies:Regions. 2003. (gr. 4-18). (978-0-328-03779-7(6), Scott Foresman) Addison-Wesley Educational Pubs., Inc.

Read Alouds & Primary Sources: Scott Foresman Social Studies: The United States. 2003. (gr. 5-18). (978-0-328-03780-3(X), Scott Foresman) Addison-Wesley Educational Pubs., Inc.

Read Alouds & Primary Sources: Scott Foresman Social Studies: The World. 2003. (gr. 6-18). (978-0-328-03781-0(8), Scott Foresman) Addison-Wesley Educational Pubs., Inc.

Reed, Janet. Everyone Eats Bread!, 6 vols., Set. 2003. (Yellow Umbrella Early Level Ser.). (ENG.). 16p. (gr. k-1). pap. 35.70 (978-0-7368-2986-1(5), Capstone Pr.) Capstone.

—¡Todos Comen Pan!, 6 vols., Set. 2003. (Yellow Umbrella Spanish Emergent Level Ser.).Tr. of Everyone Eats Bread! Social Studies. (SPA.). 16p. (gr. k-1). pap. 35.70 (978-0-7368-3022-5(7)) Capstone.

Region 4 Education Service Center. Reading to Learn in Social Studies for Grades 6-8. 2006. spiral bd. (978-1-933049-56-4(1)) Region 4 Education Service Ctr.

—Reading to Learn in Social Studies for Grades 9-12. 2006. spiral bd. (978-1-933049-57-1(X)) Region 4 Education Service Ctr.

Regions Near & Far. (J). (gr. 4). suppl. ed. (978-0-669-11381-5(6)) Houghton Mifflin Harcourt School Pubs.

Regions Near & Far. Incl. suppl. ed. (978-0-669-11381-5(6)); Regions Near & Far. tchr. ed. (978-0-669-11397-6(2)); Regions Near & Far. suppl. ed. (978-0-669-11423-2(5)); Regions Near & Far. pap., wbk. ed. (978-0-669-11402-7(2)); Regions Near & Far. tchr. ed., wbk. ed. (978-0-669-11408-9(1)); Regions Near & Far. suppl. ed. (978-0-669-11428-7(6)); Regions Near & Far. suppl. ed. (978-0-669-11724-0(2)); Regions Near & Far. suppl. ed. (J). (gr. 4-6). pap. (978-0-669-11389-1(1)) Houghton Mifflin Harcourt School Pubs.

Resumenes de las Lecciones: Student & Teacher Support Resources. 2003. (MacMillan/McGraw-Hill. Estudios Sociales Ser.). (ENG & SPA.). (gr. 3-18). (978-0-02-149901-4(2)); (gr. 5-18). (978-0-02-149903-8(9)) Macmillan/McGraw-Hill Schl. Div.

Resumes de las Lecciones: Student & Teacher Support Resources. 2003. (MacMillan/McGraw-Hill. Estudios Sociales Ser.). (ENG & SPA.). (gr. 4-18). (978-0-02-150075-8(4)) Macmillan/McGraw-Hill Schl. Div.

Ring, Susan. From Here to There, 6 vols., Set. 2003. (Yellow Umbrella Early Level Ser.). (ENG.). 16p. (gr. k-1). pap. 35.70 (978-0-7368-2985-4(7), Capstone Pr.) Capstone.

Robertson, Charmaine. The Landmarks of My Town, 1 vol. 2016. (Rosen REAL Readers: Social Studies Nonfiction / Fiction: Myself, My Community, My World Ser.). (ENG.). 8p. (gr. k-1). pap. 5.46 (978-1-5081-2269-2(5), 58dd977e-d8b0-4559-8ff2-2e3367e52f21, Rosen Classroom) Rosen Publishing Group, Inc., The.

Ross, Stewart. Point of Impact Series, 12 bks., Set. (Illus.). (J). (gr. 5-7). lib. bdg. 290.64 (978-1-58810-187-7(8)) Heinemann-Raintree.

Rotsky, Leslie A. At Work in the Neighborhood: A Content Area Reader-Social Stuides. 2005. (Emergent/Early (Prek-2) Social Studies Package Ser.). 16p. (gr. k-2). 25.20 (978-0-8215-7818-6(9)) Sadlier, William H. Inc.

Schaefer, Lola M. Somos Iguales: Set Of 6. 2011. (Primeras Conexiones Ser.).Tr. of We Are All Alike. (SPA.). (J). pap. 40.00 net. (978-1-4108-0324-5(4)) Benchmark Education Co.

Schaub, Michelle. Where Are We? 2006. (Early Explorers Ser.). (J). pap. (978-1-4108-6108-5(2)) Benchmark Education Co.

School to Home Engagement: Grade 2 Social Studies. 2016. (ENG.). (gr. 2-2). pap., pap., pap. 20.00 (978-1-5157-5826-6(5), 176077) Capstone.

Schorr, Titus. Ben Is Good at Spelling, 1 vol., 1. 2015. (Rosen REAL Readers: Social Studies Nonfiction / Fiction: Myself, My Community, My World Ser.). (ENG.). 8p. (J). (gr. k-1). pap. 5.46 (978-1-5081-1662-2(8), 2c111711-25a2-40c3-8b38-cfb29cf64c76, Rosen Classroom) Rosen Publishing Group, Inc., The.

—Our Town Is 100 Years Old, 1 vol., 1. 2015. (Rosen REAL Readers: Social Studies Nonfiction / Fiction: Myself, My Community, My World Ser.). (ENG.). 8p. (J). (gr. k-1). pap. 5.46 (978-1-5081-1695-0(4), 2cc3733f-c7af-42d9-b7c4-4ea7c6232bc9, Rosen Classroom) Rosen Publishing Group, Inc., The.

—Places in Our Classroom, 1 vol., 1. 2015. (Rosen REAL Readers: Social Studies Nonfiction / Fiction: Myself, My

Community, My World Ser.). (ENG.). 8p. (J). (gr. k-1). pap. 5.46 *(978-1-5081-1644-8(X),* c764b64e-bf7c-48ad-aedf-fd8aa2cf8d9f, Rosen Classroom) Rosen Publishing Group, Inc., The.

—Symbols of America, 1 vol., 1. 2015. (Rosen REAL Readers: Social Studies Nonfiction / Fiction: Myself, My Community, My World Ser.). (ENG.). 12p. (J). (gr. k-1). pap. 6.33 *(978-1-5081-1767-4(5),* 51e42dbb-db31-4599-b9bd-cca0c785f3ca, Rosen Classroom) Rosen Publishing Group, Inc., The.

Schwartz, Linda. Social Studies & Science Quiz Whiz 3-5, Vol. 432. VanBlaricum, Pam, ed. Armstrong, Beverly, illus. 2004. 128p. (J). (gr. 3-5). pap. 10.99 *(978-0-88160-375-0(9),* LW-432) Creative Teaching Pr., Inc.

Scott Foresman Social Studies: Additional Resources. 2003. (gr. k-18). *(978-0-328-03918-0(7));* (gr. k-18). *(978-0-328-06262-1(6));* (gr. k-2). tchr. ed. *(978-0-328-04180-0(7));* (gr. 1-18). *(978-0-328-06263-8(4));* (gr. 2-18). *(978-0-328-06264-5(2));* (gr. 3-18). *(978-0-328-03601-1(3));* (gr. 3-18). *(978-0-328-06265-2(0));* (gr. 3-6). tchr. ed. *(978-0-328-04181-7(5));* (gr. 4-18). *(978-0-328-03602-8(1));* (gr. 4-18). *(978-0-328-06266-9(9));* (gr. 5-18). *(978-0-328-06267-6(7));* (gr. 6-18). *(978-0-328-03604-2(8));* (gr. 6-18). *(978-0-328-06268-3(5))* Addison-Wesley Educational Pubs., Inc. (Scott Foresman).

Scott Foresman Social Studies: Kindergarten Package. 2003. stu. ed. *(978-0-328-04348-4(6),* Scott Foresman) Addison-Wesley Educational Pubs., Inc.

Scott Foresman Social Studies: Practice/Assessment. 2003. (gr. k-18). *(978-0-328-03090-3(2));* (gr. 1-18). *(978-0-328-03091-0(0));* (gr. 2-18). *(978-0-328-03092-7(9));* (gr. 3-18). *(978-0-328-03093-4(7))* Addison-Wesley Educational Pubs., Inc. (Scott Foresman).

Scott Foresman Social Studies: Pupil Edition. 2003. (Scott Foresman Social Study Ser.). (gr. 5-18). *(978-0-328-01763-8(9),* Scott Foresman) Addison-Wesley Educational Pubs., Inc.

Scott Foresman Social Studies: Technology. 2003. (Multimedia Library). (gr. k-18). *(978-0-328-05696-5(0));* (SPA.). (gr. k-18). cd-rom *(978-0-328-05663-7(4));* (gr. k-18). cd-rom *(978-0-328-03875-6(X));* (gr. 1-18). *(978-0-328-05697-2(9));* (SPA.). (gr. 1-18). cd-rom *(978-0-328-05664-4(2));* (gr. 1-18). cd-rom *(978-0-328-03876-3(8));* (gr. 2-18). *(978-0-328-05698-9(7));* (SPA.). (gr. 2-18). cd-rom *(978-0-328-05665-1(0));* (gr. 2-18). cd-rom *(978-0-328-03877-0(6));* (gr. 3-18). *(978-0-328-05699-6(5));* (SPA.). (gr. 3-18). cd-rom *(978-0-328-05666-8(9));* (gr. 3-18). cd-rom *(978-0-328-03878-7(4));* (gr. 4-18). *(978-0-328-05700-9(2));* (gr. 4-18). cd-rom *(978-0-328-03879-4(2));* (gr. 5-18). *(978-0-328-05701-6(0));* (gr. 5-18). cd-rom *(978-0-328-03880-0(6));* (gr. 6-18). *(978-0-328-05702-3(9));* (gr. 6-18). cd-rom *(978-0-328-03881-7(4))* Addison-Wesley Educational Pubs., Inc. (Scott Foresman).

Scott Foresman Social Studies: Building A Nation: Practice/Assessment. 2003. (gr. 5-18). *(978-0-328-03100-9(3),* Scott Foresman) Addison-Wesley Educational Pubs., Inc.

Scott Foresman Social Studies: Regions: Practice/Assessment. 2003. (gr. 4-18). *(978-0-328-03094-1(5),* Scott Foresman) Addison-Wesley Educational Pubs., Inc.

Scott Foresman Social Studies: The United States: Practice/Assessment. 2003. (gr. 5-18). *(978-0-328-03095-8(3),* Scott Foresman) Addison-Wesley Educational Pubs., Inc.

Scott Foresman Social Studies: The World: Practice/Assessment. 2003. (gr. 6-18). *(978-0-328-03096-5(1),* Scott Foresman) Addison-Wesley Educational Pubs., Inc.

Shades of Gray. (J). pap., stu. ed. *(978-0-13-620188-5(1))* Prentice Hall (Schl. Div.).

Shafer, Jean. Learning from Charts & Graphs: Lessons in History, Civics, Geography, & Economics 2003. (Illus.). 48p. (J). 15.95 *(978-0-938682-76-9(8))* River Road Pubns., Inc.

Shava, Ryder. Baik Speaks Korean, 1 vol., 1. 2015. (Rosen REAL Readers: Social Studies Nonfiction / Fiction: Myself, My Community, My World Ser.). (ENG.). 12p. (J). (gr. k-1). pap. 6.33 *(978-1-5081-1818-3(3),* 91ed3e6a-e82c-4ab1-b1aa-18585a2205d1, Rosen Classroom) Rosen Publishing Group, Inc., The.

—Blonde Hair, Red Hair, 1 vol., 1. 2015. (Rosen REAL Readers: Social Studies Nonfiction / Fiction: Myself, My Community, My World Ser.). (ENG.). 8p. (J). (gr. k-1). pap. 5.46 *(978-1-5081-2021-6(8),* 2f44e4ac-210a-49a0-b913-959f1a41589a, Rosen Classroom) Rosen Publishing Group, Inc., The.

—Our School's Special Song, 1 vol., 1. 2015. (Rosen REAL Readers: Social Studies Nonfiction / Fiction: Myself, My Community, My World Ser.). (ENG.). 12p. (J). (gr. k-1). pap. 6.33 *(978-1-5081-1746-9(2),* 11f0fbf5-ec34-44c9-bd7c-94ffac035202, Rosen Classroom) Rosen Publishing Group, Inc., The.

—This Is My School, 1 vol., 1. 2015. (Rosen REAL Readers: Social Studies Nonfiction / Fiction: Myself, My Community, My World Ser.). (ENG.). 8p. (J). (gr. k-1). pap. 5.46 *(978-1-5081-1677-6(6),* 2b3a567b-8f28-4c68-a6fb-275f3c2e512a, Rosen Classroom) Rosen Publishing Group, Inc., The.

Shepard, Daniel. All Kinds of Farms, 6 vols., Set. 2003. (Yellow Umbrella Early Level Ser.). (ENG.). 16p. (gr. k-1). pap. 35.70 *(978-0-7368-2989-2(X),* Capstone Pr.) Capstone.

—What Did People Use Long Ago? 2003. (Shutterbug Books: Social Studies). (Illus.). 16p. (J). (gr. -1-3). pap. 4.10 *(978-0-7398-7643-5(0))* Steck-Vaughn.

Simpson, Louie. My Mom Votes!, 1 vol. 2012. (InfoMax Readers Ser.). (ENG., Illus.). 24p. (J). (gr. 1-1). pap. 8.25 *(978-1-4488-9055-2(1),* 0eaeb0e1-6144-4aae-9e82-3d16a911dd3e, Rosen Classroom) Rosen Publishing Group, Inc., The.

Sims, Kathy C., illus. & text. Louisiana Potpourri from A to Z. Sims, Kathy C., text. 2004.Tr. of Potpourri Louisianais d' A à Z. (FRE.). 64p. (YA). lib. bdg. 24.95 *(978-0-9753435-0-0(5))* Louisiana Ladybug Pr.

SIRS Enduring Issues 2006, 8 vols., Set. 2005. (Illus.). (YA). ring bd. 849.00 *(978-0-89777-554-0(6))* SIRS Publishing, Inc.

Snakes are Not Slimy, 6 vols. (Book2WebTM Ser.). (gr. 4-8). 36.50 *(978-0-322-02976-7(7))* Wright Group/McGraw-Hill.

Social Studies Explorer (Set), 21 vols., Set. Incl. It's Cool to Learn about Countries: Bangladesh. Orr, Tamra B. 2010. lib. bdg. 34.93 *(978-1-60279-829-8(X),* 200524); It's Cool to Learn about Countries: Brazil. Franchino, Vicky. 2010. lib. bdg. 34.93 *(978-1-60279-827-4(3),* 200520); It's Cool to Learn about Countries: China. Raatma, Lucia. 2010. lib. bdg. 34.93 *(978-1-60279-823-6(0),* 200512); It's Cool to Learn about Countries: India. Raatma, Lucia. 2010. lib. bdg. 34.93 *(978-1-60279-824-3(9),* 200514); It's Cool to Learn about Countries: Indonesia. Orr, Tamra B. 2010. lib. bdg. 34.93 *(978-1-60279-826-7(5),* 200518); It's Cool to Learn about Countries: Japan. Somervill, Barbara A. 2010. lib. bdg. 34.93 *(978-1-60279-832-8(X),* 200530); It's Cool to Learn about Countries: Mexico. Somervill, Barbara A. 2010. lib. bdg. 34.93 *(978-1-60279-833-5(8),* 200532); It's Cool to Learn about Countries: Nigeria. Rau, Dana Meachen. 2010. lib. bdg. 34.93 *(978-1-60279-830-4(3),* 200526); It's Cool to Learn about Countries: Pakistan. Labrecque, Ellen. 2010. lib. bdg. 34.93 *(978-1-60279-828-1(1),* 200522); It's Cool to Learn about Countries: Philippines. Franchino, Vicky. 2010. lib. bdg. 34.93 *(978-1-60279-834-2(6),* 200534); It's Cool to Learn about Countries: Russia. Marsico, Katie. 2010. lib. bdg. 34.93 *(978-1-60279-831-1(1),* 200528); It's Cool to Learn about Countries: United States. Marsico, Katie. 2010. lib. bdg. 34.93 *(978-1-60279-825-0(7),* 200516); Set. It's Cool to Learn about the United States (Set) 2011. 174.65 *(978-1-61080-191-1(1),* 201012); 48p. (gr. 4-8). (Explorer Library: Social Studies Explorer Ser.). (ENG., Illus.). 2011. 658.56 *(978-1-61080-253-6(5),* 201008) Cherry Lake Publishing.

Social Studies Program, Early Level. 2003. (Yellow Umbrella Early Level Ser.). (ENG.). 16p. (gr. k-1). pap. 428.40 *(978-0-7368-3060-7(X),* Capstone Pr.) Capstone.

Social Studies Set, 8 vols. (Content Collections). (gr. k-2). 265.66 *(978-0-7362-2270-9(7))* CENGAGE Learning.

Social Studies: The World: Scott Foresman Social Studies. 2003. (gr. 6-18). stu. ed. *(978-0-328-01766-9(3),* Scott Foresman) Addison-Wesley Educational Pubs., Inc.

Steck-Vaughn Staff. Arctic People. 2003. pap. 4.10 *(978-0-7398-7650-3(3))* Steck-Vaughn.

—Life on the Tallest Tree. 2003. pap. 4.10 *(978-0-7398-7636-7(8))* Steck-Vaughn.

—Matter All Around Us. 2003. pap. 4.10 *(978-0-7398-7639-8(2))* Steck-Vaughn.

—People & Places Nearby Level B. 2005. (Steck-Vaughn Social Studies). (ENG.). 112p. (gr. 2-2). pap. 29.50 *(978-0-7398-9219-0(3))* Houghton Mifflin Harcourt Publishing Co.

—Social Studies Level C: Living in Communities. 2005. (Steck-Vaughn Social Studies). (ENG.). 144p. (gr. 3-3). pap., stu. ed. 33.70 *(978-0-7398-9220-6(7))* Houghton Mifflin Harcourt Publishing Co.

—Social Studies Level C: Living in Communities. 2005. pap. 112.30 *(978-0-7398-9226-8(6));* pap., tchr. ed. 15.10 *(978-0-7398-9232-9(0))* Steck-Vaughn.

—Social Studies Level D: Regions of the Country. 2005. (Steck-Vaughn Social Studies). (ENG.). 160p. (gr. 4-4). pap. 33.70 *(978-0-7398-9221-3(5))* Houghton Mifflin Harcourt Publishing Co.

—Social Studies Level A: Homes & Families. 2005. (Steck-Vaughn Social Studies). (ENG.). 112p. (gr. 1-1). pap. 29.50 *(978-0-7398-9218-3(5))* Houghton Mifflin Harcourt Publishing Co.

—Social Studies Level A: Homes & Families. 2005. pap. 112.30 *(978-0-7398-9224-4(X));* pap., tchr. ed. 15.10 *(978-0-7398-9230-5(4))* Steck-Vaughn.

—Social Studies Level B: People & Places. 2005. (Steck-Vaughn Social Studies). (ENG.). 48p. (gr. 2-2). pap., tchr. ed. 26.60 *(978-0-7398-9231-2(2))* Houghton Mifflin Harcourt Publishing Co.

—Social Studies Level B: People & Places. 2005. pap. 112.30 *(978-0-7398-9225-1(8))* Steck-Vaughn.

—Social Studies Level E: History of the Country. 2005. pap. 137.30 *(978-0-7398-9228-2(2));* pap., tchr. ed. 15.10 *(978-0-7398-9234-3(7))* Steck-Vaughn.

—Social Studies Level F: World Cultures. 2005. (Steck-Vaughn Social Studies). (ENG.). 208p. (gr. 6-6). pap. 37.65 *(978-0-7398-9223-7(1))* Houghton Mifflin Harcourt Publishing Co.

—Social Studies Level F: World Cultures. 2005. pap. 96.70 *(978-0-7398-9229-9(0));* pap., tchr. ed. 15.10 *(978-0-7398-9235-0(5))* Steck-Vaughn.

—What's the Question? 2003. pap. 4.10 *(978-0-7398-7663-3(5))* Steck-Vaughn.

Stradling, Jan. People & Places: Level I, 6 vols., Vol. 2. (First Explorers Ser.). 24p. (gr. 1-2). 29.95 *(978-0-7699-1462-6(4))* Shortland Pubns. (U. S. A.) Inc.

—Under Attack: Level I, 6 vols. (First Explorers Ser.). 24p. (gr. 1-2). 29.95 *(978-0-7699-1453-4(5))* Shortland Pubns. (U. S. A.) Inc.

—You are Special: Level I, 6 vols. (First Explorers Ser.). 24p. (gr. 1-2). 29.95 *(978-0-7699-1454-1(3))* Shortland Pubns. (U. S. A.) Inc.

Sullivan, Erin Ash. Communities Helping Communities: Set Of 6. 2010. (Navigators Ser.). (J). pap. 44.00 net. *(978-1-4108-6246-4(1))* Benchmark Education Co.

Sundance/Newbridge LLC Staff. One World, Many Cultures. 2004. (Reading PowerWorks Ser.). (gr. 1-3). 37.50 *(978-0-7608-8952-7(X));* pap. 6.10 *(978-0-7608-8953-4(8))* Sundance/Newbridge Educational Publishing.

Superlibro Recursos: Superlibros. 2003. (MacMillan/McGraw-Hill. Estudios Sociales Ser.). (ENG & SPA.). (gr. 1-18). *(978-0-02-149977-9(2))* Macmillan/McGraw-Hill Schl. Div.

Superlibro Recursos: Vivimos Juntos: Superlibros. 2003. (MacMillan/McGraw-Hill. Estudios Sociales Ser.). (ENG & SPA.). (gr. 2-18). *(978-0-02-149978-6(0))* Macmillan/McGraw-Hill Schl. Div.

Syverson, Carolyn. Community Helpers. 2011. (Wonder Readers Ser.). (ENG.). 16p. (J). (gr. -1-1). 25.95 *(978-1-4296-8538-2(7),* 195206, Capstone Pr.) Capstone.

TAKS Social Studies Preparation Grade 11 Exit - Student Workbook. 2003. (Region IV ESC Resources for Social Studies Ser.). stu. ed., per. *(978-1-932524-67-3(3))* Region 4 Education Service Ctr.

TAKS Social Studies Preparation Grade 8. 2004. (Region IV ESC Resources for Social Studies Ser.). stu. ed., per., wbk. ed. *(978-1-932524-65-9(7))* Region 4 Education Service Ctr.

Talmadge Salle, Katherine. Daily Life Around the World: Set Of 6. 2011. (Navigators Ser.). (J). pap. 44.00 net. *(978-1-4108-6245-7(3))* Benchmark Education Co.

Test Generator: Technology. 2003. (MacMillan/McGraw-Hill. Estudios Sociales Ser.). (ENG & SPA.). (gr. 5-18). incl. audio compact disk *(978-0-02-150074-1(6))* Macmillan/McGraw-Hill Schl. Div.

Thompson, Tamara, ed. Extending the Human Lifespan, 1 vol. 2013. (At Issue Ser.). (ENG.). 128p. (gr. 10-12). pap. 28.80 *(978-0-7377-6837-4(1),* 1d4cc45e-7540-4012-b9b6-1cb8778a8378, Greenhaven Publishing) Greenhaven Publishing LLC.

Transgender Life, 10 vols. 2016. (Transgender Life Ser.). (ENG.). 00064p. (J). (gr. 6-6). 180.65 *(978-1-5081-7353-3(2),* 16b9d1bf-d4a1-41e4-9926-f61677f075ab, Rosen Young Adult) Rosen Publishing Group, Inc., The.

Trowell, Cynthia. Out of the Mist: A Survival Guide for Young Adults. 2004. (Illus.). 104p. (YA). per. 16.95 *(978-1-59094-045-7(6),* Top Shelf) Jawbone Publishing Corp.

True Book of the Continents Collection. 2005. (J). pap. *(978-1-60015-013-5(6))* Steps To Literacy, LLC.

Under Water: Big Book: Level C. 8p. 20.95 *(978-0-322-00625-6(2))* Wright Group/McGraw-Hill.

Underground: Big Book: Level D. 8p. 20.95 *(978-0-322-00345-3(8))* Wright Group/McGraw-Hill.

Unidad 1 Superlibro: Familias: Superlibros. 2003. (MacMillan/McGraw-Hill. Estudios Sociales Ser.). (ENG & SPA.). (gr. 1-18). *(978-0-02-149434-7(7))* Macmillan/McGraw-Hill Schl. Div.

Unidad 3 Superlibro: Civismo: Superlibros. 2003. (MacMillan/McGraw-Hill. Estudios Sociales Ser.). (ENG & SPA.). (gr. 1-18). *(978-0-02-149436-1(3))* Macmillan/McGraw-Hill Schl. Div.

Unidad 3 Superlibro: Historia: Vivimos Juntos: Superlibros (Big Books) 2003. (MacMillan/McGraw-Hill. Estudios Sociales Ser.). (ENG & SPA.). (gr. 2-18). *(978-0-02-149443-9(6))* Macmillan/McGraw-Hill Schl. Div.

Unidad 5 Superlibro: Gobierno: Vivimos Juntos: Superlibros (Big Books) 2003. (MacMillan/McGraw-Hill. Estudios Sociales Ser.). (ENG & SPA.). (gr. 2-18). *(978-0-02-149445-3(2))* Macmillan/McGraw-Hill Schl. Div.

Unidad 5 Superlibro: Historia: Superlibros. 2003. (MacMillan/McGraw-Hill. Estudios Sociales Ser.). (ENG & SPA.). (gr. 1-18). *(978-0-02-149438-5(X))* Macmillan/McGraw-Hill Schl. Div.

VanVoorst, Jennifer. The Letter Zz: How Things Move. 2004. (Letter Bks.). (ENG.). 8p. (gr. k-1). pap. 29.70 *(978-0-7368-4125-2(3))* Capstone.

—Things That Are Cold, 6 vols., Set. 2004. (Letter Bks.). (ENG.). 8p. (gr. k-1). pap. 29.70 *(978-0-7368-4108-5(3))* Capstone.

—Working, 6 vols., Set. 2003. (Yellow Umbrella Early Level Ser.). (ENG.). 16p. (gr. k-1). pap. 35.70 *(978-0-7368-3007-2(3),* Capstone Pr.) Capstone.

Verderosa, Laura. My Favorite Places. 2010. (Sight Word Readers Ser.). (J). 3.49 *(978-1-60719-611-2(5))* Newmark Learning LLC.

Viaje a la selva Tropical: Libros Aventuras (Adventure Books) 2003. (MacMillan/McGraw-Hill. Estudios Sociales Ser.). (ENG & SPA.). (gr. 5-18). *(978-0-02-150128-1(9))* Macmillan/McGraw-Hill Schl. Div.

Viaje por la Historia: Libros Aventuras (Adventure Books) 2003. (MacMillan/McGraw-Hill. Estudios Sociales Ser.). (ENG & SPA.). (gr. 4-18). *(978-0-02-150120-5(3))* Macmillan/McGraw-Hill Schl. Div.

The Viking Saga. 2004. (Thrilling Tales in Time Ser.: Vol. 1). (J). *(978-1-58123-370-4(1))* Larson Learning, Inc.

Warm up to Social Studies for Grade 11. 2005. spiral bd. *(978-1-933049-17-5(0))* Region 4 Education Service Ctr.

Waters, Carrie. A Look Back in Time: A Content Area Reader-Social Studies. 2005. (Emergent/Early (Prek-2) Social Studies Package Ser.). 20p. (gr. k-2). 25.20 *(978-0-8215-7816-2(2))* Sadlier, William H. Inc.

Weber, Rebecca. Lost Cities: Set Of 6. 2011. (Navigators Ser.). (J). pap. 48.00 net. *(978-1-4108-0419-8(4))* Benchmark Education Co.

What Kind of Dog Am I? Level C. 8p. 20.95 *(978-0-322-00371-2(7))* Wright Group/McGraw-Hill.

What's Black & White & Moos? Level F. 16p. 31.50 *(978-0-7802-9741-8(5))* Wright Group/McGraw-Hill.

Who Says? Big Book: Level F. 16p. 31.50 *(978-0-322-00377-4(6))* Wright Group/McGraw-Hill.

Why? Big Book: Level F. 16p. 31.50 *(978-0-322-00352-1(0))* Wright Group/McGraw-Hill.

Wiener, Gary, ed. War in Ernest Hemingway's for Whom the Bell Tolls, 1 vol. 2013. (Social Issues in Literature Ser.). (ENG., Illus.). 184p. (gr. 10-12). pap. 33.00 *(978-0-7377-6394-2(9),* 54ed712e-d443-487e-8d25-7d3e4f469ba1); lib. bdg. 48.03 *(978-0-7377-6393-5(0),* c3030e89-d0a3-435a-9f7a-935df8445be2) Greenhaven Publishing LLC. (Greenhaven Publishing).

William H. Sadlier Staff. Family Fun. 2005. (Social Studies). (gr. -1-2). 25.20 *(978-0-8215-7835-3(9))* Sadlier, William H. Inc.

—My Favorite Things. 2005. (Emergent/Early (Prek-2) Social Studies Package Ser.). 12p. (gr. -1-1). 25.20 *(978-0-8215-7831-5(6))* Sadlier, William H. Inc.

Williams, Brian. Way We Live: Biggest & Best. 2004. (Biggest & Best Ser.). (Illus.). 40p. (J). pap. 7.95 *(978-1-84236-064-4(7))* Miles Kelly Publishing, Ltd. GBR. Dist: Independent Pubs. Group.

Wilson, Mike. The Election Process. 2008. (Introducing Issues with Opposing Viewpoints Ser.). (ENG., Illus.). 112-144p. (YA). (gr. 7-10). 36.95 *(978-0-7377-3975-6(4),* Greenhaven Pr., Inc.) Cengage Gale.

Wood: Big Book: Level D. 8p. 20.95 *(978-0-7802-9743-2(1))* Wright Group/McGraw-Hill.

World Cultures Classroom Library. (gr. k-2). lib. bdg. 109.95 *(978-0-7368-9454-8(3),* Red Brick Learning) Capstone.

World Cultures Complete Unit. (gr. k-2). 624.95 *(978-0-7368-9455-5(1),* Red Brick Learning) Capstone.

World in Crisis, 12 vols. 2014. (World in Crisis Ser.). (ENG.). 48p. (YA). (gr. 5-5). 200.82 *(978-1-4777-7852-4(7),* 415ca6ac-bf9b-477e-8e87-7bd4319dc959, Rosen Reference) Rosen Publishing Group, Inc., The.

World Today: Heath Social Studies. Incl. The World Today. tchr. ed. *(978-0-669-11400-3(6));* The World Today. suppl. ed. *(978-0-669-11426-3(X));* The World Today. pap., wbk. ed. *(978-0-669-11406-5(5));* The World Today. pap., wbk. ed. *(978-0-669-11412-6(X));* The World Today. suppl. ed. *(978-0-669-11432-4(4));* The World Today. suppl. ed. *(978-0-669-11728-8(5));* The World Today. suppl. ed. (J). (gr. 6-7). *(978-0-669-11392-1(1))* Houghton Mifflin Harcourt School Pubs.

Yellowstone: Libros Aventuras (Adventure Books) 2003. (MacMillan/McGraw-Hill. Estudios Sociales Ser.). (ENG & SPA.). (gr. 4-18). *(978-0-02-150122-9(X))* Macmillan/McGraw-Hill Schl. Div.

Young, Ian. Amazing Journeys: Following in History's Footsteps, 6 vols. 2003. (High Five Reading - Green Ser.). (ENG.). 48p. (gr. 3-4). pap. 54.00 *(978-0-7368-2841-3(9))* Capstone.

Zoom in on Communities. 2016. (Zoom in on Communities Ser.). 24p. (gr. 2-2). pap. 56.10 *(978-0-7660-7976-2(7));* (ENG.). lib. bdg. 153.60 *(978-0-7660-7493-4(5),* 59b232a4-c758-4637-9c9f-ee97deb7ccb4) Enslow Publishing, LLC.

SOCIAL SCIENCES—STUDY AND TEACHING

Boehm, Richard G., et al. Carteles de la Unidad: La Historia de Nuestro Mundo: Relatos de la Historia. 97th ed. 2003. (Harcourt Brace Estudios Sociales Ser.). (SPA.). (gr. k-7). pap. 84.30 *(978-0-15-309146-9(0))* Harcourt Schl. Pubs.

—Desk Maps: Intermediate (3-7) Package Of 10. 2003. (Harcourt Brace Social Studies). (SPA.). (gr. 3-7). 27.00 *(978-0-15-310432-9(5))* Harcourt Schl. Pubs.

—Desk Maps: Primary (K-2) Package Of 10. 2003. (Harcourt Brace Social Studies). (SPA.). (gr. k-2). 27.00 *(978-0-15-310431-2(7))* Harcourt Schl. Pubs.

—Relatos de la Historia: Assessment Program. 97th ed. 2003. (Harcourt Brace Estudios Sociales Ser.). (SPA.). (gr. k-7). pap. 93.50 *(978-0-15-309130-8(4));* pap. 115.10 *(978-0-15-309145-2(2))* Harcourt Schl. Pubs.

—Relatos de la Historia: Estados y Regiones. 97th ed. 2003. (Harcourt Brace Estudios Sociales Ser.). (SPA.). (gr. k-7). pupil's gde. ed. 81.70 *(978-0-15-309126-1(6))* Harcourt Schl. Pubs.

—Relatos de la Historia: La Historia de Estados Mundo. 97th ed. 2003. (Harcourt Brace Estudios Sociales Ser.). (SPA.). (gr. k-7). pupil's gde. ed. 88.40 *(978-0-15-309140-7(1))* Harcourt Schl. Pubs.

—Transparencias: La Historia de Nuestro Mundo: Relatos de la Historia. 97th ed. 2003. (Harcourt Brace Estudios Sociales Ser.). (SPA.). (gr. k-7). pap. 138.70 *(978-0-15-309147-6(9))* Harcourt Schl. Pubs.

—Write-on Charts. 2003. (Harcourt Brace Estudios Sociales Ser.). (SPA.). (gr. 1-18). 248.40 *(978-0-15-313132-5(2));* (gr. 2-18). 248.40 *(978-0-15-313133-2(0))* Harcourt Schl. Pubs.

Hama, Larry. The Battle of First Bull Run: The War Begins!, 1 vol. 2006. (Graphic Battles of the Civil War Ser.). (ENG., Illus.). 48p. (gr. 4-5). pap. 14.05 *(978-1-4042-6476-2(0),* 5a9f1503-6cb6-4333-ba2e-51e98cec6b65, Rosen Classroom) Rosen Publishing Group, Inc., The.

—The Battle of Shiloh: Surprise Attack!, 1 vol. 2006. (Graphic Battles of the Civil War Ser.). (ENG., Illus.). 48p. (gr. 4-5). pap. 14.05 *(978-1-4042-6478-6(7),* 47c54eba-6131-4a1d-9181-d5c3a3bcc55e, Rosen Classroom) Rosen Publishing Group, Inc., The.

Harcourt School Publishers Staff. Horizontes. 3rd ed. 2003. (Harcourt Horizontes Ser.). (SPA., Illus.). (gr. k-6). 7.00 *(978-0-15-324549-7(2));* act. bk. ed. 8.40 *(978-0-15-324551-0(4));* act. bk. ed. 10.20 *(978-0-15-324552-7(2));* act. bk. ed. 8.40 *(978-0-15-324550-3(6));* pupil's gde. ed. 47.30 *(978-0-15-324531-2(X));* pupil's gde. ed. 54.10 *(978-0-15-324533-6(6))* Harcourt Schl. Pubs.

—Horizontes: Big Book. 3rd ed. 2003. (Harcourt Horizontes Ser.). (SPA., Illus.). (gr. k-6). tchr. ed. 268.00 *(978-0-15-324832-0(7))* Harcourt Schl. Pubs.

—Horizontes: States & Regions. 3rd ed. 2003. (Harcourt Horizontes Ser.). (SPA., Illus.). (gr. k-6). act. bk. ed. 10.50 *(978-0-15-324553-4(0));* pupil's gde. ed. 64.60 *(978-0-15-324534-3(4))* Harcourt Schl. Pubs.

—Horizontes: World Regions. 3rd ed. 2003. (Harcourt Horizontes Ser.). (SPA., Illus.). (gr. k-6). act. bk. ed. 11.80 *(978-0-15-324556-5(5))* Harcourt Schl. Pubs.

—Horizontes, Grade 2, Vol. 2. 2nd ed. 2003. (Harcourt Horizontes Ser.). (SPA.). (gr. k-6). tchr. ed. 121.50 *(978-0-15-328508-0(7))* Harcourt Schl. Pubs.

—Horizontes, Grade 4: States & Regions. 3rd ed. 2003. (Harcourt Horizontes Ser.). (SPA.). (gr. k-6). Vol. 1. tchr. ed. 133.80 *(978-0-15-321975-7(0))* Vol. 2. tchr. ed. 133.80 *(978-0-15-321976-4(9))* Harcourt Schl. Pubs.

—World Regions. 3rd ed. 2003. (Horizontes (Social Studies) Ser.). (SPA., Illus.). (gr. k-6). pupil's gde. ed. 75.50 *(978-0-15-324537-4(9))* Harcourt Schl. Pubs.

Kowalski, Kathiann M. It's Your World! A Crash Course in Social Studies, 1 vol. 2014. (Crash Course Ser.). (ENG.). 64p. (J). (gr. 4-8). pap. 8.95 *(978-1-4914-0783-7(2),* 126008) Capstone.

Provenzo, Eugene F., Jr., et al. 100 Experiential Learning Activities for Social Studies, Literature, & the Arts, Grades 5-12. 2008. (ENG., Illus.). 176p. 84.95 *(978-1-4129-3999-7(2),* B39992C) Corwin Pr.

Stevens, Stefan. Understanding Civilizations, 1 vol. 2013. (InfoMax Readers Ser.). (ENG.). 24p. (J). (gr. 3-3). pap. 8.25 *(978-1-4777-2619-8(5),* a402b0ea-e556-4943-9cdc-6ce5e89588d9); pap. 49.50 *(978-1-4777-2620-4(9))* Rosen Publishing Group, Inc., The. (Rosen Classroom).

Walch Publishing Staff. Humanities. 2007. (Daily Warm-Ups Ser.). 197p. (gr. 5-6). tchr. ed., spiral bd. 24.99 *(978-0-8251-6449-1(4))* Walch Education.

Wilkie, Sara. Social Studies Projects That Shine. 2011. (Explorer Library: Information Explorer Ser.). (ENG., Illus.). 32p. (gr. 4-8). lib. bdg. 32.07 *(978-1-61080-123-2(7),* 201132) Cherry Lake Publishing.

Yespolov, Johnson & Kalna-Dubinyuk, Arynova. Extension in Kazakhstan & the Experience of the Us: Lessons from a

S

Working National Model. 2012. 154p. 29.99 *(978-1-4771-4694-1(6))* Xlibris Corp.

SOCIAL SCIENTISTS

Hunter, Dru. Why Do We Behave Like That? 2016. (Think Like a Scientist Ser.). (ENG.). 48p. (J). (gr. 4-7). pap. 12.00 *(978-1-62832-202-6(0)*, 21076, Creative Paperbacks) Creative Co., The.

Levy, Janey. Careers in Criminal Profiling, 1 vol. 2008. (Careers in Forensics Ser.). (ENG., Illus.). 64p. (J). (gr. 5-5). lib. bdg. 37.13 *(978-1-4042-1342-5(2)*, a4305718-9b4a-4369-9661-b16d39c6bb95) Rosen Publishing Group, Inc., The.

SOCIAL SECURITY

Ruschmann, Paul. Social Security. 2011. (ENG., Illus.). 136p. (gr. 9). 35.00 *(978-1-60413-775-0(4)*, P189897, Facts On File) Infobase Holdings, Inc.

Worth, Richard. The Social Security Act, 1 vol. 2011. (Landmark Legislation Ser.). (ENG.). 128p. (YA). (gr. 8-8). 42.64 *(978-1-60870-043-1(7)*, c5a5ddf9-dce1-4405-94ef-cd43a78c2d77) Cavendish Square Publishing LLC.

SOCIAL SERVICE

see also Social Settlements

Bily, Cynthia A., ed. Welfare, 1 vol. 2009. (Introducing Issues with Opposing Viewpoints Ser.). (ENG., Illus.). 144p. (J). (gr. 7-10). 43.63 *(978-0-7377-4485-9(5)*, a2cc49a5-fa22-46fd-a879-d918d8108c5, Greenhaven Publishing) Greenhaven Publishing LLC.

Bryfonski, Dedria, ed. Street Teens, 1 vol. 2011. (Opposing Viewpoints Ser.). (ENG., Illus.). 224p. (gr. 10-12). 50.43 *(978-0-7377-5761-3(2)*, 586d14ae-665f-4f8c-8012-c378487e5821); pap. 34.80 *(978-0-7377-5762-0(0)*, 0c0a19cb-c896-4850-a471-75c786dce71c) Greenhaven Publishing LLC. (Greenhaven Publishing).

Byers, Ann. Working with Veterans & Military Families Through Service Learning, 1 vol. 2014. (Service Learning for Teens Ser.). (ENG.). 80p. (YA). (gr. 7-7). 37.80 *(978-1-4777-7963-7(9)*, 0d942f33-7109-4f8e-9786-33a992e65313, Rosen Young Adult) Rosen Publishing Group, Inc., The.

Catalano, Angela. Community Resources: The Land & the People in Communities. (Communities at Work Ser.). 24p. (gr. 2-2). 2009. 42.50 *(978-1-61511-891-5(8)*, PowerKids Pr.) 2004. (ENG., Illus.). (J). lib. bdg. 26.27 *(978-1-4042-2781-1(4)*, 07935c0f-0137-4cff-8ee3-d8856305043e) 2004. (ENG., Illus.). pap. 8.25 *(978-1-4042-5016-1(6)*, 8a337dc2-4913-41f0-ac19-4c867ba25828, PowerKids Pr.) Rosen Publishing Group, Inc., The.

Center for Learning Staff. Doing My Part: Curriculum Unit. 2003. (Cross-Curriculum Ser.). 42p. (YA). tchr. ed., spiral bd. 19.95 *(978-1-56077-740-3(0))* Center for Learning, The.

—Doing My Part Student Edition: Curriculum Unit. 2003. (Cross-Curriculum Ser.). 96p. (YA). stu. ed., per. 8.95 *(978-1-56077-741-0(9))* Center for Learning, The.

Cerone, Lulu. PhilanthroParties! A Party-Planning Guide for Kids Who Want to Give Back. 2017. (ENG., Illus.). 208p. (J). (gr. 5-9). 24.99 *(978-1-58270-587-3(9))* Aladdin/Beyond Words.

Christian, Mary Blount. Working with Immigrants & Migrant Populations Through Service Learning, 1 vol. 2014. (Service Learning for Teens Ser.). (ENG.). 80p. (YA). (gr. 7-7). 37.80 *(978-1-4777-7969-9(8)*, c6e5d08a-a33d-4db2-820b-946c124cf4ba, Rosen Young Adult) Rosen Publishing Group, Inc., The.

Chumin, Nancy. Manjhi Moves a Mountain. Popovici, Danny, illus. 2017. (ENG.). 36p. (J). (gr. k-5). 17.99 *(978-1-939547-34-7(2)*, 0a896958-b1ae-4265-a6a8-dcccf4c81698) Creston Bks.

Cohn, Jessica. Hand to Heart: Improving Communities, 1 vol. 2nd rev. ed. 2012. (TIME for KIDS(r): Informational Text Ser.). (ENG.). 48p. (gr. 4-5). pap. 11.99 *(978-1-4333-4866-2(7))* Teacher Created Materials, Inc.

Colby, Jennifer. Donating. Bane, Jeff, illus. 2018. (My Early Library: My Guide to Money Ser.). (ENG.). 24p. (J). (gr. k-1). lib. bdg. 30.64 *(978-1-5341-2899-6(9)*, 211640) Cherry Lake Publishing.

Community Workers, 12 vols. 2014. (Community Workers Ser.). (ENG.). 24p. (J). (gr. 1-1). 155.58 *(978-1-62713-140-7(X)*, 63d1943b-cb0f-46e8-802a-efb9e8ecee01, Cavendish Square) Cavendish Square Publishing LLC.

Davies, Elaine, et al. Dysgu Gofalu / Learning to Care. 2005. *(978-0-9543372-0-9(4))* Cofal Cymru.

Emmer, Rae. Community Service. 2009. (School Activities Ser.). 24p. (gr. 1-1). 42.50 *(978-1-60852-997-1(5)*, PowerKids Pr.) Rosen Publishing Group, Inc., The.

—Community Service: Servicio Comunitario, 1 vol. 2003. (School Activities / Actividades Escolares Ser.). (SPA & ENG., Illus.). 24p. (J). (gr. 1-2). lib. bdg. 26.27 *(978-0-8239-6900-5(2)*, 2d20d7c0-bc04-49b3-953d-7b3829a93b2c) Rosen Publishing Group, Inc., The.

—Community Service / Servicio Comunitario. 2009. (School Activities / Actividades escolares Ser.). (ENG & SPA.). 24p. (gr. 1-2). 42.50 *(978-1-60853-003-8(5)*, Editorial Buenas Letras) Rosen Publishing Group, Inc., The.

Flath, Camden. Social Workers: Finding Solutions for Tomorrow's Society. 2010. (New Careers for the 21st Century Ser.). (Illus.). 64p. (YA). (gr. 7-18). lib. bdg. 22.95 *(978-1-4222-1821-1(X))* Mason Crest.

Flikkema, Elizabeth. Make the World a Better Place! My Sharing Time, Talent & Treasure Activity Book. Olsen, Christian, illus. 2006. 47p. 19.95 *(978-0-9774155-0-2(3))* Learning to Give.

Gay, Kathlyn. Activism: The Ultimate Teen Guide. 2016. (It Happened to Me Ser.: 47). (Illus.). 234p. 55.00 *(978-1-4422-4293-7(0))* Rowman & Littlefield Publishers, Inc.

Gibbons, Susan. Love Grows: El Amor Crece. 2012. 32p. (-18). pap. 19.99 *(978-1-4772-6732-5(8))* AuthorHouse.

Graham, Amy. Choosing a Community Service Career: A How-To Guide, 1 vol. 2011. (Life: a How-To Guide Ser.). (ENG., Illus.). 128p. (gr. 6-7). pap. 13.88 *(978-1-59845-312-6(2)*, 16e90ecb-fc3a-4b69-9786-07df2732dd33); lib. bdg. 35.93 *(978-1-59845-147-4(2)*, b39c5830-b0a0-4c45-8b10-e49dc777c408) Enslow Publishing, LLC.

Haerens, Margaret, ed. Welfare, 1 vol. 2011. (Opposing Viewpoints Ser.). (ENG., Illus.). 224p. (gr. 10-12). 50.43 *(978-0-7377-5430-8(3)*, 59633cc1-68f2-48ea-8c6c-998b95598f69); pap. 34.80 *(978-0-7377-5431-5(1)*, c30d907a-fd30-4399-809d-080bc1b84a9e) Greenhaven Publishing LLC. (Greenhaven Publishing).

Hage, Sally M. & Romano, John L., eds. Best Practices in Prevention. 2012. (Prevention Practice Kit Ser.). (ENG.). 72p. pap. 30.00 *(978-1-4522-5797-6(3)*, B57976P) SAGE Pubns., Inc.

Honders, Jamie. Our Community Helpers, 1 vol. 2012. (InfoMax Readers Ser.). (ENG., Illus.). 16p. (J). (gr. k-k). pap. 7.00 *(978-1-4488-8917-4(0)*, e2890ab1-6ecc-4efc-8e10-b7486b015a07, Rosen Classroom) Rosen Publishing Group, Inc., The.

Houle, Michelle E. Lindsey Williams: Gardening for Impoverished Families, 1 vol. 2007. (Young Heroes Ser.). (ENG., Illus.). 48p. (gr. 4-8). lib. bdg. 30.38 *(978-0-7377-3867-4(7)*, fd01ea0c-813c-4ff0-b23b-0d81530eeeda, KidHaven Publishing) Greenhaven Publishing LLC.

Kreisman, Rachelle. Being a Good Citizen: A Kids' Guide to Community Involvement. Haggerty, Tim, illus. 2015. (Start Smart (tm) — Community Ser.). (ENG.). 32p. (J). (gr. 1-3). E-Book 39.99 *(978-1-937529-50-5(9))* Red Chair Pr.

—People Who Help: A Kids' Guide to Community Heroes. Haggerty, Tim, illus. 2015. (Start Smart (tm) — Community Ser.). (ENG.). 32p. (J). (gr. 1-3). E-Book 39.99 *(978-1-937529-35-2(5))* Red Chair Pr.

Leavitt, Amie Jane. Helping People with Disabilities & Special Needs Through Service Learning, 1 vol. 2014. (Service Learning for Teens Ser.). (ENG., Illus.). 80p. (J). (gr. 7-7). 37.80 *(978-1-4777-7965-1(5)*, 94b83274-be84-4c13-8f11-081438d7515b, Rosen Young Adult) Rosen Publishing Group, Inc., The.

Lewis, Barbara A. The Kid's Guide to Service Projects: Over 500 Service Ideas for Young People Who Want to Make a Difference. 2nd rev. ed. 2009. (ENG., Illus.). 160p. (J). (gr. 3-18). pap. 14.99 *(978-1-57542-338-8(3)*, 23388) Free Spirit Publishing Inc.

Lüsted, Marcia Amidon. Supporting the Elderly Through Service Learning, 1 vol. 2014. (Service Learning for Teens Ser.). (ENG.). 80p. (YA). (gr. 7-7). 37.80 *(978-1-4777-7957-6(4)*, 14cd395b-dc75-405d-9047-4c57c5993a79, Rosen Young Adult) Rosen Publishing Group, Inc., The.

Lynette, Rachel. What to Do When Your Family Is on Welfare, 1 vol. 2010. (Let's Work It Out Ser.). (ENG.). 24p. (J). (gr. 2-3). pap. 9.25 *(978-1-4358-9762-5(5)*, 587b9bf2-82fb-41bd-b615-69dd55acc367, PowerKids Pr.); (Illus.). lib. bdg. 26.27 *(978-1-4358-9337-5(9)*, 58dcac4d-a4c9-40d7-8646-f2af6047e426) Rosen Publishing Group, Inc., The.

Marsico, Katie. Doctors Without Borders. 2014. (Community Connections: How Do They Help? Ser.). (ENG., Illus.). 24p. (J). (gr. 2-5). 29.21 *(978-1-63188-027-8(6)*, 205515) Cherry Lake Publishing.

—The Red Cross. 2014. (Community Connections: How Do They Help? Ser.). (ENG., Illus.). 24p. (J). (gr. 2-5). 29.21 *(978-1-63188-028-5(4)*, 205519) Cherry Lake Publishing.

—Ymca. 2016. (Community Connections: How Do They Help? Ser.). (ENG., Illus.). 24p. (J). (gr. 2-5). 29.21 *(978-1-63471-056-5(8)*, 208304) Cherry Lake Publishing.

Mason, Helen. Dream Jobs in Human Services. 2018. (Cutting-Edge Careers in Technical Education Ser.). (ENG., Illus.). 32p. (J). (gr. 5-5). *(978-0-7787-4441-2(8))*; pap. *(978-0-7787-4452-8(3))* Crabtree Publishing Co.

O'Neal, Claire. Volunteering in School: A Guide to Giving Back. 2010. (How to Help Ser.). (Illus.). 48p. (J). (gr. 4-8). lib. bdg. 29.95 *(978-1-58415-920-9(0))* Mitchell Lane Pubs.

Pearl, Melissa Sherman. Alex's Lemonade Stand: Charities Started by Kids! 2018. (Community Connections: How Do They Help? Ser.). (ENG., Illus.). 24p. (J). (gr. 2-5). lib. bdg. 29.21 *(978-1-5341-0729-8(0)*, 210675) Cherry Lake Publishing.

—Alex's Lemonade Stand Foundation: Charities Started by Kids! 2018. (Community Connections: How Do They Help? Ser.). (ENG.). 24p. (J). (gr. 2-5). pap. 12.79 *(978-1-5341-0828-8(9)*, 210676) Cherry Lake Publishing.

—Katie's Krops: Charities Started by Kids! 2018. (Community Connections: How Do They Help? Ser.). (ENG.). 24p. (J). (gr. 2-5). pap. 12.79 *(978-1-5341-0831-8(9)*, 210688); (Illus.). lib. bdg. 29.21 *(978-1-5341-0732-8(0)*, 210687) Cherry Lake Publishing.

Pearl, Melissa Sherman & Sherman, David A. Coat-A-Kid: Charities Started by Kids! 2017. (Community Connections: How Do They Help? Ser.). (ENG., Illus.). 24p. (J). (gr. 2-5). lib. bdg. 29.21 *(978-1-63472-849-2(1)*, 209822) Cherry Lake Publishing.

—What's Mine Is Yours: Charities Started by Kids! 2017. (Community Connections: How Do They Help? Ser.). (ENG., Illus.). 24p. (J). (gr. 2-5). lib. bdg. 29.21 *(978-1-63472-847-8(5)*, 209814) Cherry Lake Publishing.

Pegis, Jessica. I Can Make a Difference! 2016. (Citizenship in Action Ser.). (ENG., Illus.). 24p. (J). (gr. 1-3). *(978-0-7787-2599-2(5))*; pap. *(978-0-7787-2605-0(3))* Crabtree Publishing Co.

Petrikowski, Nicki Peter. Working for Tolerance & Social Change Through Service Learning, 1 vol. 2014. (Service Learning for Teens Ser.). (ENG.). 80p. (J). (gr. 7-7). 37.80 *(978-1-4777-7967-5(1)*, 627a9b71-1638-4068-81f9-ae1220cb52fa, Rosen Young Adult) Rosen Publishing Group, Inc., The.

Poelman, Heidi. Courageous People Who Changed the World, Volume 1. Kershner, Kyle, illus. 2018. (People Who Changed the World Ser.: 1). (ENG.). 16p. (J). (gr. -1-k). bds. 9.99 *(978-1-945547-75-1(8)*, 554775) Familius LLC.

Prentiss, Timothy. A Volunteer Helps. 2006. (Early Explorers Ser.). (J). pap. *(978-1-4108-6112-2(0))* Benchmark Education Co.

Rauf, Don. Protecting the Environment Through Service Learning, 1 vol. 2014. (Service Learning for Teens Ser.). (ENG., Illus.). 80p. (J). (gr. 7-7). 37.80 *(978-1-4777-7961-3(2)*, 8b8e8fb3-467b-46e3-9588-22aeb85db7fa, Rosen Young Adult) Rosen Publishing Group, Inc., The.

Riddle, John & Simons, Rae. Veterinarian. 2013. 96p. (J). *(978-1-4222-2750-3(2))* Mason Crest.

Russell, Bernadette. Be the Change, Make It Happen. Russell, Bernadette, illus. 2017. (ENG., Illus.). 96p. (J). pap. 14.99 *(978-1-61067-404-1(9))* Kane Miller.

Sanna, Ellyn. Childcare Worker. Riggs, Ernestine G. & Gholar, Cheryl, eds. 2013. (Careers with Character Ser.: 18). 96p. (J). (gr. 7-18). 22.95 *(978-1-4222-2752-7(9))* Mason Crest.

Scraper, Katherine, et al. Around Town: Things You Can Do in Your Community. 2011. (J). pap. *(978-1-4509-5327-6(1))* Benchmark Education Co.

Shaw, Jessica. Working for Social Justice in Your Community, 1 vol. 2018. (Careers in Your Community Ser.). (ENG.). 80p. (gr. 7-7). 37.47 *(978-1-4994-6729-1(X)*, c2257481-14c9-4cef-9d7e-52020e4c406a) Rosen Publishing Group, Inc., The.

Staley, Erin. Improving Community Health & Safety Through Service Learning, 1 vol. 2014. (Service Learning for Teens Ser.). (ENG.). 80p. (YA). (gr. 7-7). 37.80 *(978-1-4777-7955-2(8)*, 5b33c48b-bab4-4dde-982f-726b6cb80c9f, Rosen Young Adult) Rosen Publishing Group, Inc., The.

Stanmyre, Jackie F. Supporting Groups That Fight for Fairness & Equality, 1 vol. 2017. (Active Citizenship Today Ser.). (ENG.). 32p. (gr. 3-3). pap. 11.58 *(978-1-5026-2932-6(1)*, 3d957acb-ed10-4e3b-9fb5-2a5a58e061f8) Cavendish Square Publishing LLC.

Swarts, Katherine, ed. Welfare, 1 vol. 2008. (Social Issues Firsthand Ser.). (ENG., Illus.). 128p. (gr. 10-12). lib. bdg. 39.93 *(978-0-7377-4079-0(5)*, 86740813-f723-4d97-87ef-9925ce9be46c, Greenhaven Publishing) Greenhaven Publishing LLC.

The Giving Tree. Expressions of Charity. 2012. 146p. pap. 26.95 *(978-0-7414-7754-5(8))* Infinity Publishing.

Warner, Emily B. Dottie Lamm: A Friend to Families. 2007. (Now You Know Bio Ser.: 8). (J). pap. 8.95 *(978-0-86541-085-5(2))* Filter Pr., LLC.

Wiener, Gary, ed. The Environment in Rachel Carson's Silent Spring, 1 vol. 2011. (Social Issues in Literature Ser.). (ENG., Illus.). 208p. (gr. 10-12). pap. 33.00 *(978-0-7377-5816-0(3)*, 89a202ee-7579-4f03-a7bc-5affbd32364b, Greenhaven Publishing) Greenhaven Publishing LLC.

SOCIAL SERVICE—FICTION

FableVision. Spf 40. Reynolds, Peter H., illus. 2013. (Zebrafish Ser.). (ENG.). 128p. (J). (gr. 5-9). pap. 9.99 *(978-1-4169-9709-2(1)*, Atheneum Bks. for Young Readers) Simon & Schuster Children's Publishing.

Lupica, Mike. Heat. 2007. (ENG.). 256p. (J). (gr. 5-18). 8.99 *(978-0-14-240757-8(7)*, Puffin Books) Penguin Young Readers Group.

—Heat. 2007. 220p. (gr. 5-9). 18.00 *(978-0-7569-8131-0(X))* Perfection Learning Corp.

—Heat. 2007. 18.40 *(978-1-4177-7264-3(6))* Turtleback.

Randall, Angel. Snow Angels. 2011. (Illus.). 32p. (J). 17.99 *(978-1-60641-046-2(6)*, Shadow Mountain) Shadow Mountain Publishing.

Schillow, Ned W. and Schillow. Titanic Hearts. 2007. 100p. per. 10.00 *(978-1-4257-3842-6(7))* Xlibris Corp.

SOCIAL SERVICE—VOCATIONAL GUIDANCE

Brinkerhoff, Shirley. Social Worker. Gholar, Cheryl & Riggs, Ernestine G., eds. 2013. (Careers with Character Ser.: 18). 96p. (J). (gr. 7-18). 22.95 *(978-1-4222-2766-4(9))* Mason Crest.

Flath, Camden. Social Workers: Finding Solutions for Tomorrow's Society. 2010. (New Careers for the 21st Century Ser.). (Illus.). 64p. (YA). (gr. 7-18). pap. 9.95 *(978-1-4222-2042-9(7))* Mason Crest.

Larocque, Katharine. Helping Seniors. 2019. (Careers Making a Difference Ser.). (Illus.). 80p. (J). (gr. 12). lib. bdg. 34.60 *(978-1-4222-4257-5(9))* Mason Crest.

Snyder, Gail. Careers If You Like Helping People. 2017. (ENG.). 80p. (YA). (gr. 5-12). 39.93 *(978-1-68282-136-7(6))* ReferencePoint Pr., Inc.

Turner, Amanda. Helping Children. 2019. (Careers Making a Difference Ser.). (Illus.). 80p. (J). (gr. 12). lib. bdg. 34.60 *(978-1-4222-4255-1(2))* Mason Crest.

—Helping Those in Poverty. 2019. (Careers Making a Difference Ser.). 80p. (J). (gr. 12). lib. bdg. 34.60 *(978-1-4222-4261-2(7))* Mason Crest.

—Helping Those with Addictions. 2019. (Careers Making a Difference Ser.). (Illus.). 80p. (J). (gr. 12). lib. bdg. 34.60 *(978-1-4222-4258-2(7))* Mason Crest.

—Helping Those with Disabilities. 2019. (Careers Making a Difference Ser.). (Illus.). 80p. (J). (gr. 12). lib. bdg. 34.60 *(978-1-4222-4259-9(5))* Mason Crest.

—Helping Victims. 2019. (Careers Making a Difference Ser.). (Illus.). 80p. (J). (gr. 12). lib. bdg. 34.60 *(978-1-4222-4262-9(5))* Mason Crest.

SOCIAL SETTLEMENTS

see also Playgrounds

also names of settlements, e.g. Hull House (Chicago, Ill.)

Friedman, Michael. Settlement Houses: Improving the Social Welfare of America's Immigrants. 2009. (Progressive Movement 1900-1920: Efforts to Reform America's New Industrial Society Ser.). 32p. (gr. 3-4). 47.90 *(978-1-60854-170-6(3))* Rosen Publishing Group, Inc., The.

Friedman, Michael & Friedman, Brett. Settlement Houses: Improving the Social Welfare of America's Immigrants, 1 vol. 2005. (Primary Sources of the Progressive Movement Ser.). (ENG., Illus.). 32p. (gr. 3-4). pap. 10.00 *(978-1-4042-0859-9(3)*, e609beb3-5f0e-4e71-9ae6-522240de7366) Rosen Publishing Group, Inc., The.

Owens, Tom. Immigrants & Neighbors. 2003. (Illus.). 40p. pap. 8.00 *(978-0-7891-5850-5(7))* Perfection Learning Corp.

Perez, Jessica. Hello Kitty Helps Out! 2003. (Illus.). 48p. (J). pap. *(978-0-439-44628-0(7))* Scholastic, Inc.

SOCIAL SETTLEMENTS—FICTION

Faigen, Anne G. New World Waiting. 2006. iii, 188p. (J). pap. *(978-0-9744715-5-6(0))* Local History Co., The.

SOCIAL STUDIES

see Geography; Social Sciences

SOCIAL SURVEYS

Davies, Monika. Life in Numbers: Polls & Surveys. 2018. (TIME(r): Informational Text Ser.). (ENG., Illus.). 48p. (J). (gr. 6-8). pap. 13.99 *(978-1-4258-5005-0(7))* Teacher Created Materials, Inc.

SOCIAL WELFARE

see Social Problems; Social Service

SOCIAL WORK

see Social Service

SOCIALISM

see also Capitalism; Communism; Labor Unions; National Socialism

Berne, Emma Carlson. Paris & Nicky Hilton. 2007. (Popular Culture: A View from the Paparazzi Ser.). (Illus.). 64p. (YA). (gr. 3-7). pap. 7.95 *(978-1-4222-0358-3(1))* Mason Crest.

Hunter, Nick. What Is Socialism?, 1 vol., Vol. 1. 2013. (Understanding Political Systems Ser.). (ENG.). 48p. (gr. 6-8). (J). pap. 15.05 *(978-1-4824-0322-0(6)*, 7e93d1ae-a704-455b-9709-aa227ffb3f82); (YA). lib. bdg. 34.61 *(978-1-4824-0321-3(8)*, c567679c-8d06-4ef2-ba13-71d59c11489c) Stevens, Gareth Publishing LLLP.

Jarrow, Jesse. Socialism: A Primary Source Analysis. (Primary Sources of Political Systems Ser.). 64p. (gr. 5-8). 2009. 58.50 *(978-1-60851-839-5(6))* 2004. (ENG., Illus.). (J). lib. bdg. 37.13 *(978-0-8239-4521-4(9)*, 91b9d6b8-2037-4b00-9aff-859b56dcb119) Rosen Publishing Group, Inc., The.

Murphy, John, ed. Socialism & Communism, 4 vols. 2014. (Political & Economic Systems Ser.). (ENG.). 288p. (YA). (gr. 10-10). 95.18 *(978-1-62275-336-9(4)*, fea3fa40-852a-4e0a-becc-8d93da2adb47); 47.59 *(978-1-62275-335-2(6)*, 88e95078-584a-4bc2-8565-6d96154dc2e5) Rosen Publishing Group, Inc., The.

Uhl, Xina M. & Jarrow, Jesse. Socialism, 1 vol. 2019. (Examining Political Systems Ser.). (ENG.). 64p. (gr. 6-6). pap. 13.95 *(978-1-5081-8528-4(X)*, 10cbf41e-5f8b-4b77-baa1-61cde32e13cf, Rosen Reference) Rosen Publishing Group, Inc., The.

SOCIALISM—UNITED STATES

Skahill, Carolyn M. The Socialist Party: Eugene V. Debs & the Radical Politics of the American Working Class. (Progressive Movement 1900-1920: Efforts to Reform America's New Industrial Society Ser.). 32p. (gr. 3-4). 2009. 47.90 *(978-1-60854-174-4(6))* 2006. (ENG., Illus.). (YA). lib. bdg. 30.47 *(978-1-4042-0198-9(X)*, 75f47ff0-c8ac-4b28-a3b6-e6a19f5d585b) Rosen Publishing Group, Inc., The.

SOCIETY OF FRIENDS

Haines, Marie. Lion-Hearted Quakers. Putman, Stanley, illus. 2011. 152p. 41.95 *(978-1-258-03120-6(5))* Literary Licensing, LLC.

Woog, Adam. What Makes Me a Quaker? 2004. (What Makes Me A — ? Ser.). (ENG., Illus.). 48p. (J). (gr. 3-7). lib. bdg. 27.50 *(978-0-7377-3082-1(X)*, Greenhaven Pr., Inc.) Cengage Gale.

SOCIETY OF FRIENDS—FICTION

Kerr, M. E., pseud. Slap Your Sides. 2003. 198p. (YA). 13.65 *(978-0-7569-4240-3(3))* Perfection Learning Corp.

Rinaldi, Ann. Finishing Becca: A Story about Peggy Shippen & Benedict Arnold. 2004. (Great Episodes Ser.). (ENG.). 384p. (YA). (gr. 7-8). pap. 17.95 *(978-0-15-205079-5(5)*, 1195340, Clarion Bks.) HarperCollins Pubs.

Roop, Connie & Roop, Peter. The Top-Secret Adventure of John Darragh, Revolutionary War Spy. Trover, Zachary, illus. 2010. (History's Kid Heroes Ser.). (ENG.). 32p. (J). (gr. 3-5). pap. 8.99 *(978-0-7613-6193-0(6)*, 7fa9c0ff-4a83-43e8-9a63-91b40b6156a7, Graphic Universe™) Lerner Publishing Group.

Vernon, Louise A. Key to the Prison. Eitzen, Allan, illus. 2nd ed. 2007. (Louise A. Vernon Ser.). (ENG.). 144p. (YA). (gr. 4-9). pap. 8.99 *(978-0-8361-1813-1(8))* Herald Pr.

SOCIOLOGY

see also Aristocracy (Social Class); Cities and Towns; Civilization; Communism; Emigration and Immigration; Equality; Ethnic Relations; Population; Psychology; Race Relations; Social Change; Social Classes; Social History; Social Problems; Social Surveys; Socialism

Alexander, Stephanie J. Sociology: The Study of Human Social Behavior, 1 vol., 1. 2015. (Britannica Guide to the Social Sciences Ser.). (ENG.). 160p. (J). (gr. 10-10). lib. bdg. 37.82 *(978-1-62275-555-4(3)*, 536cec6a-0a51-4112-a4be-98c2bcb04c6d, Britannica Educational Publishing) Rosen Publishing Group, Inc., The.

Analyzing the Issues: Set 3, 12 vols. 2017. (Analyzing the Issues Ser.). (ENG.). 208p. (gr. 8-8). lib. bdg. 305.58 *(978-0-7660-8569-5(4)*, fcacfdfa-bbf3-41d7-abb1-4bc5d8162ff3) Enslow Publishing, LLC.

Aucoin, Lee. Mi Comunidad. rev. ed. 2010. (Early Literacy Ser.).Tr. of My Community. (SPA., Illus.). 16p. (J). (gr. k-1). (J). 6.99 *(978-1-4333-1948-8(9))*; 19.99 *(978-1-4333-1949-5(7))* Teacher Created Materials, Inc.

Austen, Mary. I Learn from My Friends, 1 vol. 2016. (Things I Learn Ser.). (ENG., Illus.). 24p. (J). (gr. 1-1). pap. 9.25 *(978-1-4994-2345-7(4)*, 6c30e58b-75ef-4f24-a179-c098d3a47b18, PowerKids Pr.) Rosen Publishing Group, Inc., The.

Blundell, Jonathan. Cambridge Igcse(r) Sociology. Coursebook. Per le Scuole Superiori. 2014. (Cambridge International IGCSE Ser.). (ENG., Illus.). 288p. pap. 52.95 *(978-1-107-64513-4(1))* Cambridge Univ. Pr.

Blundell, Jonathan, et al. Sociology AS: The Complete Companion AQA. 2003. (ENG., Illus.). 168p. pap. 35.00 *(978-0-7487-7212-4(X))* Nelson Thornes Ltd. GBR. Dist: Trans-Atlantic Pubns., Inc.

Bond, Rebecca. My Bed: Enchanting Ways to Fall Asleep Around the World. Mavor, Salley, illus. 2020. (ENG.). 40p. (J). (gr. -1-3). 18.99 *(978-0-544-94906-5(4)*, 1660320, Clarion Bks.) HarperCollins Pubs.

Borgenicht, David & Epstein, Robin. Junior Edition. 2014. (Worst-Case Scenario Survival Handbook Ser.). (ENG.,

Illus.). 128p. (J). (gr. 4-7). 41.35 *(978-1-59920-976-0(4)*, 19405, Smart Apple Media) Black Rabbit Bks.

Borgenicht, David & Heimberg, Justin. Extreme Junior Edition. 2014. (Worst-Case Scenario Survival Handbook Ser.). (ENG.). 128p. (J). (gr. 4-7). 41.35 *(978-1-59920-973-9(X)*, 19403, Smart Apple Media) Black Rabbit Bks.

Coldwell, Lamar. A Folktale from the Dominican Republic, 1 vol. 2016. (Rosen REAL Readers: Social Studies Nonfiction / Fiction: Myself, My Community, My World Ser.). (ENG.). 12p. (gr. k-1). pap. 6.33 *(978-1-5081-2341-5(1)*, 77d4b96c-835c-4dff-8978-73f064fbb8d3, Rosen Classroom) Rosen Publishing Group, Inc., The.

Cook, Diane. Mohandas K. Gandi: Spiritual Leader. 2004. (Great Names Ser.). (Illus.). 32p. (J). (gr. 3-18). lib. bdg. 19.95 *(978-1-59084-143-3(3))* Mason Crest.

Cronin, Ali & Sayer, Melissa. Making a Difference: The Changing the World Handbook. 2009. (Really Useful Handbooks Ser.). (ENG., Illus.). 48p. (J). (gr. 5-11). lib. bdg. *(978-0-7787-4390-3(X))* Crabtree Publishing Co.

Cultures of the World (Third Edition, Group 6) (r), 12 vols. 2014. (Cultures of the World (Third Edition)(r) Ser.). (ENG.). 144p. (YA). (gr. 5-5). 292.74 *(978-0-7614-4990-4(6)*, ed09d2bb-8767-47d3-a815-0fe937dbeebc, Cavendish Square) Cavendish Square Publishing LLC.

Diamond, Susan. Social Rules for Kids-the Top 100 Social Rules Kids Need to Succeed. 2011. (ENG.). 132p. (J). pap. 19.95 *(978-1-934575-84-0(4))* Autism Asperger Publishing Co.

Diane O'Connell. People Person: The Story of Sociologist Marta Tienda. 2006. (ENG., Illus.). 128p. (gr. 7-9). per. 19.95 *(978-0-309-09557-0(3)*, Joseph Henry Pr.) National Academies Pr.

Dickmann, Nancy. What Are Eco-Cities? 2018. (Putting the Planet First Ser.). (Illus.). 32p. (J). (gr. 4-4). *(978-0-7787-5033-8(7))* Crabtree Publishing Co.

Dingles, Molly. Oval Opera. Brodie, Neale, illus. 2006. (Community of Shapes Ser.). 29p. (J). *(978-1-59646-047-8(4))* Dingles & Co.

—Star Ship. Brodie, Neale, illus. 2006. (Community of Shapes Ser.). 29p. (J). *(978-1-59646-039-3(3))* Dingles & Co.

—Sweet Hearts. Brodie, Neale, Illus. 2006. (Community of Shapes Ser.). (J). *(978-1-59646-037-9(7))* Dingles & Co.

Duffield, Katy. Neighborhood Helpers. 2018. (My World Ser.). (ENG., Illus.). 16p. (gr. -1-2). lib. bdg. 28.50 *(978-1-64156-199-0(8)*, 9781641561990) Rourke Educational Media.

Duffy, Beth. Sociology for Youth. 2006. 216p. spiral bd. *(978-0-9778602-0-3(5))* Newport Valley Pr.

Engdahl, Sylvia, ed. Driving, 1 vol. 2014. (Teen Rights & Freedoms Ser.). (ENG., Illus.). 120p. (gr. 10-12). lib. bdg. 43.63 *(978-0-7377-6997-5(1)*, d3bf3e1f-6f28-4edb-8b90-cacede71cb0e, Greenhaven Publishing) Greenhaven Publishing LLC.

Fields, Terri. Getting Along. 2018. (I Wonder Ser.). (ENG., Illus.). 16p. (gr. -1-2). lib. bdg. 28.50 *(978-1-64156-185-3(8)*, 9781641561853) Rourke Educational Media.

First Graphics: My Community. 2011. (First Graphics: My Community Ser.). (ENG.). 24p. (gr. 1-2). pap. 249.90 *(978-1-4296-6405-9(3))* Capstone.

Gardner, Alicia. We Are Different, We Are the Same, 1 vol. 2012. (InfoMax Readers Ser.). (ENG., Illus.). 16p. (J). (gr. k-k). pap. 7.00 *(978-1-4488-8950-1(2)*, d71f10ea-b0c6-46b1-be71-706820556778, Rosen Classroom) Rosen Publishing Group, Inc., The.

Gerdes, Louise I., ed. What Are the Causes of Prostitution?, 1 vol. 2007. (At Issue Ser.). (ENG.). 104p. (gr. 10-12). 41.03 *(978-0-7377-2737-1(3)*, a10e4c04-ad7e-4fcb-aa82-9ffc46300d62, Greenhaven Publishing) Greenhaven Publishing LLC.

Glencoe McGraw-Hill Staff. Sociology & You. 2007. (NTC: SOCIOLOGY & YOU Ser.). (ENG.). (gr. 9-12). cd-rom 148.96 *(978-0-07-878105-6(1)*, 0078781051) McGraw-Hill Higher Education.

Grant, John. Debunk It! Fake News Edition: How to Stay Sane in a World of Misinformation. 2019. (ENG., Illus.). 296p. (YA). (gr. 8-12). pap. 14.99 *(978-1-942186-59-5(2)*, ba11571f-df0d-43f6-9a4e-f10cddd2a26b, Zest Bks.) Lerner Publishing Group.

Greenan, Amy. Constructing Towns & Cities, 1 vol. 2018. (Impacting Earth: How People Change the Land Ser.). (ENG.). 24p. (gr. 2-2). pap. 9.25 *(978-1-5383-4185-8(9)*, d35ba34b-13a9-4090-9b8b-4845127646dd, PowerKids Pr.) Rosen Publishing Group, Inc., The.

Gunton, Sharon, ed. Cliques, 1 vol. 2009. (Social Issues Firsthand Ser.). (ENG.). 144p. (gr. 10-12). 39.93 *(978-0-7377-4029-5(9)*, 3d6ab7c5-fa4d-48af-b66b-92f4be6d93c2, Greenhaven Publishing) Greenhaven Publishing LLC.

Hawker, Louise, ed. Industrialism in John Steinbeck's the Grapes of Wrath, 1 vol. 2008. (Social Issues in Literature Ser.). (ENG., Illus.). 184p. (gr. 10-12). 48.03 *(978-0-7377-4034-9(5)*, 3b883ac2-f6b7-4c62-9bb0-026554b78235); pap. 33.00 *(978-0-7377-4035-6(3)*, 662198a8-ff58-4c54-9262-4d5e98b2088f) Greenhaven Publishing LLC. (Greenhaven Publishing).

Heing, Bridey, ed. America's Urban-Rural Divide, 1 vol. 2019. (Introducing Issues with Opposing Viewpoints Ser.). (ENG.). 120p. (J). (gr. 7-10). pap. 29.30 *(978-1-5345-0660-2(8)*, 3b9954bf-d1f9-4408-a474-b6e0c5d4dec0) Greenhaven Publishing LLC.

In the News: Set 4, 12 vols. Incl. Egg Donation: The Reasons & the Risks. Lew, Kristi. lib. bdg. 37.13 *(978-1-4358-5276-1(1)*, b694e186-33be-41c9-a132-6a4f05b42fdf); Hunger: Food Insecurity in America. Wilson, Michael R. lib. bdg. 37.13 *(978-1-4358-5278-5(8)*, 8f391cba-f485-4ca9-a070-6b6339df07ad); (Illus.). 64p. (YA). (gr. 6-6). 2009. (In the News Ser.). (ENG.). 2009. Set lib. bdg. 222.78 *(978-1-4358-3310-4(4)*, ef423cfc-7f62-4e05-9607-51f7b8dcd9a1) Rosen Publishing Group, Inc., The.

Kaplan, Arie. Social Intelligence. 2013. (7 Character Strengths of Highly Successful Students Ser.). 64p. (J). (gr. 5-8). pap. 77.70 *(978-1-4488-9566-3(9))*; (ENG.). (gr. 6-6). 37.12 *(978-1-4488-9552-6(9)*, 0835aa37-3591-4b7a-8bdc-75ad5ff641f1); (ENG.). (gr. 6-6). pap. 13.95 *(978-1-4488-9565-6(0)*, 96a0de8c-f8e7-410a-b232-f7c5c7504646) Rosen Publishing Group, Inc., The.

Krohn, Katherine E. Adele, 1 vol. 2013. (People in the News Ser.). (ENG., Illus.). 104p. (gr. 7-7). lib. bdg. 41.03 *(978-1-4205-0882-6(2)*, ac51c31a-6248-43d5-bd47-c41ddc491289, Lucent Pr.) Greenhaven Publishing LLC.

Laidlaw, Jill A. Cities. 2012. (What's in My Food Ser.). 32p. (gr. 1-4). lib. bdg. 27.10 *(978-1-59920-421-5(5))* Black Rabbit Bks.

Langston-George, Rebecca. For the Right to Learn: Malala Yousafzai's Story. Bock, Janna Rose, illus. 2015. (Encounter: Narrative Nonfiction Picture Bks.). (ENG.). 40p. (J). (gr. 3-6). 15.95 *(978-1-62370-426-1(X)*, 129042, Capstone Pr.) Capstone.

Lewis, Clare. History in Living Memory. 2015. (History in Living Memory Ser.). (ENG.). 24p. (J). (gr. k-2). 103.96 *(978-1-4846-0927-9(1)*, 22456, Heinemann) Capstone.

Lloyd Kyi, Tanya. 50 Body Questions: A Book That Spills Its Guts. Kinnaird, Ross, illus. 2014. (50 Questions Ser.). (ENG.). 108p. (J). (gr. 4-6). 22.95 *(978-1-55451-613-1(7)*, 9781554516131); 2nd ed. pap. 14.95 *(978-1-55451-612-4(9)*, 9781554516124) Annick Pr., Ltd. CAN. Dist: Publishers Group West (PGW).

McFall, Sally, ed. Pro/Con 2, 6 vols. 2003. (Illus.). 1392p. (YA). 339.00 *(978-0-7172-5753-9(3))* Scholastic Library Publishing.

—Pro/Con 3, 12 vols. 2004. (Illus.). (YA). 339.00 *(978-0-7172-5927-4(7)*, Grolier) Scholastic Library Publishing.

McGraw Hill. Sociology & You, Student Edition. 2006. (NTC: SOCIOLOGY & YOU Ser.). (ENG., Illus.). 601p. (gr. 9-12). pap., stu. ed. 134.28 *(978-0-07-874519-5(5)*, 0078745195) McGraw-Hill Education.

Miller, Jay. American Indian Families. 2006. (True Bks). (Illus.). 47p. (gr. 3-5). 16.95 *(978-0-7569-7130-4(6))* Perfection Learning Corp.

Moehn, Heather. Everything You Need to Know about Cliques. 2009. (Need to Know Library). 64p. (gr. 5-5). 58.50 *(978-1-60854-058-7(8))* Rosen Publishing Group, Inc., The.

Moran, Shelby. Why Do Towns Have Rules?, 1 vol. 2018. (Common Good Ser.). (ENG.). 24p. (gr. 2-2). 25.27 *(978-1-5383-3099-9(7)*, 48fc48d0-9644-4051-8ab5-c190494fef6e, PowerKids Pr.) Rosen Publishing Group, Inc., The.

Morrow, Carol. Forgiveness Is Smart for the Heart. Alley, R. W., illus. 2003. (Elf-Help Books for Kids). 32p. (J). per. 6.95 *(978-0-87029-370-2(2))* Abbey Pr.

Mototsune, Kat. Cliques: Deal with It Using What You Have Inside, 1 vol. Shannon, Ben, illus. 2010. (Lorimer Deal with It Ser.). (ENG.). 32p. (J). (gr. 4-9). lib. bdg. 24.95 *(978-1-55277-545-5(3)*, 13de2a69-3957-41d8-9a41-aae5b7bca6cb) James Lorimer & Co. Ltd., Pubs. CAN. Dist: Lerner Publishing Group.

—Cliques Deal with It: Deal with It Using What You Have Inside, 1 vol. Shannon, Ben, illus. 2011. (Lorimer Deal with It Ser.). (ENG.). 32p. (J). (gr. 4-12). pap. 12.95 *(978-1-55277-544-8(5)*, 9781552775448) James Lorimer & Co. Ltd., Pubs. CAN. Dist: Orca Bk. Pubs. USA.

Murphy Payne, Lauren. We Can Get Along: A Child's Book of Choices. Iwai, Melissa, illus. 2nd rev. ed. 2015. (ENG.). 40p. (Orig.). (J). (gr. -1-2). pap. 11.99 *(978-1-63198-027-5(0))* Free Spirit Publishing Inc.

O'Connell, Diane. People Person: The Story of Sociologist Marta Tienda. 2005. (Women's Adventures in Science Ser.). (ENG., Illus.). 120p. (YA). (gr. 5-9). lib. bdg. 31.50 *(978-0-531-16781-6(X))* Scholastic Library Publishing.

Oxfam. 2008. (Global Organizations Ser.). (ENG.). 48p. (J). 32.80 *(978-1-59920-305-8(7)*, 19275, Smart Apple Media) Black Rabbit Bks.

Parnell, Declan. Daniel Is Haitian American, 1 vol., 1. 2015. (Rosen REAL Readers: Social Studies Nonfiction / Fiction: Myself, My Community, My World Ser.). (ENG.). 12p. (J). (gr. k-1). pap. 6.33 *(978-1-5081-1794-0(2)*, 09a5b512-a46b-41b4-96df-d984e7035831, Rosen Classroom) Rosen Publishing Group, Inc., The.

Peters, Jennifer, ed. Critical Perspectives on Social Justice, 1 vol. 2017. (Analyzing the Issues Ser.). (ENG.). 232p. (gr. 8-8). pap. 26.23 *(978-0-7660-9563-2(0)*, 5a6920a1-818d-437f-b168-8dbde7dc59ad) Enslow Publishing, LLC.

Ratliff, Thomas. You Wouldn't Want to Be a Civil War Soldier! A War You'D Rather Not Fight. 2013. (You Wouldn't Want To Ser.). lib. bdg. 20.80 *(978-0-606-31627-9(2))* Turtleback.

Return of the Native. (ARA., Illus.). 48p. (J). 12.00 *(978-0-86685-625-6(0))* International Bk. Ctr., Inc.

Rice, Dona Herweck. Puedo Hacer Cualquier Cosa. rev. ed. 2010. (Early Literacy Ser.).Tr. of I Can Be Anything. (SPA., Illus.). 16p. (gr. k-1). (J). 6.99 *(978-1-4333-1950-1(0))*; 19.99 *(978-1-4333-1951-8(9))* Teacher Created Materials, Inc.

Ring, Susan. Helping Hands. 2005. (Yellow Umbrella Fluent Level Ser.). (ENG.). 16p. (gr. k-1). pap. 35.70 *(978-0-7368-5306-4(5)*, Capstone Pr.) Capstone.

Romain, Trevor & Verdick, Elizabeth. Cliques, Phonies & Other Baloney. Mark, Steve, illus. rev. ed. 2018. (Laugh & Learn(r) Ser.). (ENG.). 128p. (J). (gr. 3-8). pap. 10.99 *(978-1-63198-242-2(7)*, 82422) Free Spirit Publishing Inc.

Rothenberg, Annye. Why Do I Have To? Wenzel, David T., illus. 2009. 40p. (J). pap. 9.95 *(978-0-9790420-1-0(1))* Perfecting Parenting Pr.

Santos, Rita. Zoom in on Respect for Property, 1 vol. 2018. (Zoom in on Civic Virtues Ser.). (ENG.). 24p. (gr. 2-2). 25.60 *(978-0-7660-9783-4(8)*, 2bf3e175-12b4-45be-964a-110836f4acd3) Enslow Publishing, LLC.

Schuette, Sarah L. Communities: Revised Edition, 1 vol. rev. ed. 2009. (People Ser.). (ENG.). 24p. (J). (gr. -1-2). pap. 6.29 *(978-1-4296-3461-8(8)*, 96042) Capstone.

Suen, Anastasia. Medicos Sin Fronteras, 1 vol. 2003. (Organizaciones de Ayuda (Helping Organizations) Ser.). (SPA., Illus.). 24p. (J). (gr. 2-2). lib. bdg. 26.27 *(978-0-8239-6860-2(X)*, 9ddb44e4-6890-4970-9e1c-1c250066f29f) Rosen Publishing Group, Inc., The.

Thompson, Chad. Viera Madre Hubbard. rev. ed. 2010. (Early Literacy Ser.).Tr. of Old Mother Hubbard. (SPA., Illus.). 16p. (gr. k-1). 19.99 *(978-1-4333-1953-2(5))*; 6.99 *(978-1-4333-1952-5(7))* Teacher Created Materials, Inc.

Troupe, Thomas Kingsley. Extreme near-Death Stories. 2018. (That's Just Spooky! Ser.). (ENG.). 24p. (J). (gr. 4-6). pap. 8.99 *(978-1-64466-319-6(8)*, 12571, Hi Jinx) Black Rabbit Bks.

—Extreme Near-Death Stories. 2019. (Illus.). 24p. (J). pap. *(978-1-68072-766-1(4))* Black Rabbit Bks.

Turning Points in History, 8 vols., Set. Incl. Britannica Guide to Explorers & Explorations That Changed the Modern World. Pletcher, Kenneth. 352p. lib. bdg. 48.59 *(978-1-61530-028-0(7)*, 79cb531e-1d74-4c92-b4ad-ad724030f85f); Britannica Guide to Inventions That Changed the Modern World. Curley, Robert, ed. 392p. lib. bdg. 48.59 *(978-1-61530-020-4(1)*, bba4d0b9-7e2d-4177-831f-805bf7bf43f6); (YA). (gr. 10-10). (Turning Points in History Ser.). (ENG., Illus.). 392p. 2010. Set lib. bdg. 194.36 *(978-1-61530-034-1(1)*, 268cedcd-6aa1-4252-b38b-d7180145ee35) Rosen Publishing Group, Inc., The.

Warren, Rick H. Quinn at School: Relating, Connecting & Responding at School. 2011. (ENG., Illus.). 121p. (J). pap. 18.95 *(978-1-934575-87-1(9))* Autism Asperger Publishing Co.

Weitzman, Elizabeth. Let's Talk about Staying in a Shelter, 1 vol. 2003. (Let's Talk Library). (ENG., Illus.). 24p. (J). (gr. 2-3). lib. bdg. 26.27 *(978-0-8239-6812-1(X)*, 618cfedf-f853-4933-aeb0-a8b1b7f1490d, PowerKids Pr.) Rosen Publishing Group, Inc., The.

Willis, Laurie, ed. Extremism, 1 vol. 2011. (Opposing Viewpoints Ser.). (ENG., Illus.). 208p. (gr. 10-12). 50.43 *(978-0-7377-4964-9(4)*, 657ced25-a1e5-4bab-bfc4-60a3db8609b7); pap. 34.80 *(978-0-7377-4965-6(2)*, d4eddfe5-f708-4658-8556-c2b5429744d9) Greenhaven Publishing LLC. (Greenhaven Publishing).

SOCIOLOGY, RURAL

see also Country Life; Peasants

Miller, Jake. Who's Who in a Rural Community. 2009. (Communities at Work Ser.). 24p. (gr. 2-2). 42.50 *(978-1-61511-899-1(3)*, PowerKids Pr.) Rosen Publishing Group, Inc., The.

Sterling, Kristin. Living in Rural Communities. 2008. pap. 34.95 *(978-0-8225-9478-9(1))*; (ENG., Illus.). 24p. lib. bdg. 23.93 *(978-0-8225-8599-2(5)*, Lerner Pubns.) Lerner Publishing Group.

SOCIOLOGY, URBAN

see also Cities and Towns; Urban Renewal

Braun, Eric. The Guys' Guide to Making City Life More Awesome, 1 vol. 2014. (Guys' Guides). (ENG., Illus.). 32p. (J). (gr. 3-9). lib. bdg. 28.65 *(978-1-4765-3923-2(5)*, 123922, Capstone Pr.) Capstone.

Cane, Ella. Communities in My World, 1 vol. 2013. (My World Ser.). (ENG.). 24p. (J). (gr. -1-2). pap. 6.95 *(978-1-4765-3462-6(4)*, 123561) Capstone.

Colligan, L. H. The City. 2014. (J). pap. *(978-1-62712-883-4(2))* Cavendish Square Publishing LLC.

Gordon, Sharon. At Home in the City, 1 vol. 2007. (At Home Ser.). (ENG.). 32p. (gr. k-2). pap. 9.23 *(978-0-7614-3306-4(6)*, 7b58ea65-4129-4e6e-bb81-e1f8353abe5f) Cavendish Square Publishing LLC.

Harasymiw, Therese. Life in a Colonial City, 1 vol. 2008. (Real Life Readers Ser.). (ENG.). 32p. (gr. 4-5). pap. 10.00 *(978-1-4358-0165-3(2)*, 1da3a2af-a0fd-458c-aa42-482fadd545a7, Rosen Classroom) Rosen Publishing Group, Inc., The.

Held, George. Neighbors: The Yard Critters Too. Kim, Joung Un, illus. 2013. (ENG.). 32p. 20.00 *(978-0-916754-26-6(X))* Filsinger & Co., Ltd.

Hopkinson, Deborah. Shutting Out the Sky: Life in the Tenements of New York, 1880-1924 (Scholastic Focus) 2003. (ENG., Illus.). 144p. (J). (gr. 4-7). 19.99 *(978-0-439-37590-0(8))* Scholastic, Inc.

Laidlaw, Jill. Cities. 2010. (Sustaining Our Environment Ser.). 48p. (J). lib. bdg. 35.65 *(978-1-60753-135-7(6))* Amicus Learning.

Leardi, Jeanette. Making Cities Green. 2009. (Going Green Ser.). (Illus.). 32p. (YA). (gr. 3-6). lib. bdg. 28.50 *(978-1-59716-961-5(7))* Bearport Publishing Co., Inc.

McAllan, Kate. Urban Habitats, 1 vol. 2013. (Discovery Education: Habitats Ser.). (ENG.). 32p. (J). (gr. 4-5). 28.93 *(978-1-4777-1327-3(1)*, eb4d415a-bf9b-4c3e-aa63-2cf29d3bcaa8); pap. 11.00 *(978-1-4777-1489-8(8)*, 37257041-e976-47be-87b6-34f8a264d147) Rosen Publishing Group, Inc., The. (PowerKids Pr.).

McDonald, Caryl. Rural Life, Urban Life, 1 vol. 2013. (InfoMax Readers Ser.). (ENG.). 24p. (J). (gr. 2-2). pap. 8.25 *(978-1-4777-2346-3(3)*, f9cba6f6-85af-4690-9f52-227e3eb49552); pap. 49.50 *(978-1-4777-2347-0(1))* Rosen Publishing Group, Inc., The. (Rosen Classroom).

Meissner, David. My Neighborhood. 2011. (Early Connections Ser.). (J). *(978-1-61672-666-9(0))* Benchmark Education Co.

Urban Habitats. 2013. (Discovery Education: Habitats Ser.). 32p. (J). (gr. 3-6). pap. 60.00 *(978-1-4777-1490-4(1)*, PowerKids Pr.) Rosen Publishing Group, Inc., The.

Wirkner, Linda. Learning about Urban Growth in America with Graphic Organizers. 2009. (Graphic Organizers in Social Studies). 24p. (gr. 3-4). 42.50 *(978-1-61513-087-0(X)*, PowerKids Pr.) Rosen Publishing Group, Inc., The.

SOCRATES

Bowen, Richard. Socrates: Greek Philosopher. (Illus.). 32p. (J). 2013. (People of Importance Ser.: 21). (gr. 4-18). 19.95 *(978-1-4222-2857-9(6))* 2004. (Great Names Ser.). (gr. 3-18). lib. bdg. 19.95 *(978-1-59084-150-1(6))* Mason Crest.

Dhillon, Natasha C. & Lim, Jun. Socrates: The Father of Ethics & Inquiry, 1 vol. 2015. (Greatest Greek Philosophers Ser.). (ENG.). 112p. (J). (gr. 7-8). 38.80 *(978-1-4994-6134-3(8)*, 4581f937-e9a9-4dbb-95d1-36a58e935818, Rosen Young Adult) Rosen Publishing Group, Inc., The.

Zamosky, Lisa. Socrates: Greek Philosopher, 1 vol. rev. ed. 2007. (Social Studies: Informational Text Ser.). (ENG.). 32p. (J). (gr. 4-8). pap. 11.99 *(978-0-7439-0435-3(4))* Teacher Created Materials, Inc.

Zannos, Susan. The Life & Times of Socrates. 2004. (Biography from Ancient Civilizations Ser.). (Illus.). 48p. (J). (gr. 4-8). lib. bdg. 29.95 *(978-1-58415-282-8(6))* Mitchell Lane Pubs.

SOFTBALL

Baker, Jayne & Hofstetter, Adam. An Insider's Guide to Softball, 1 vol. 2014. (Sports Tips, Techniques, & Strategies Ser.). (ENG., Illus.). 48p. (J). (gr. 6-6). pap. 12.75 *(978-1-4777-8588-1(4)*, 36ae73d6-ea17-4487-b376-a42df5791a1d, Rosen Reference) Rosen Publishing Group, Inc., The.

Bonnet, Robert L. & Keen, Dan. Home Run! Science Projects with Baseball & Softball, 1 vol. 2009. (Score! Sports Science Projects Ser.). (ENG., Illus.). 104p. (gr. 5-6). lib. bdg. 35.93 *(978-0-7660-3365-8(1)*, dba14f41-8d17-48fa-a413-92e4bc29a7a0) Enslow Publishing, LLC.

Bratton, Deboral B. & Bratton, Ashley D. Record-a-Sport Baseball & Softball Organizer. Bratton, Deboral B. & Bratton, Ashley D., eds. Bratton, Deboral B. & Bratton, Ashley D., illus. 2003. (Illus.). (gr. 1-18). 18.95 *(978-1-931746-03-8(6))* Sport Your Stuff Corp.

Buckey, A. W. Women in Softball. 2020. (She's Got Game Ser.). (ENG., Illus.). 32p. (J). (gr. 3-5). pap. 9.95 *(978-1-64493-142-4(7)*, 1644931427); lib. bdg. 31.35 *(978-1-64493-063-2(3)*, 1644930633) North Star Editions. (Focus Readers).

Cooper, Brigitte Henry. Softball Surprise. Heitz, Tim, illus. 2017. (Game Face Ser.). (ENG.). 112p. (J). (gr. 2-5). lib. bdg. 38.50 *(978-1-5321-3044-1(9)*, 27046, Calico Chapter Bks.) ABDO Publishing Co.

Douglas, Peter. Baseball & Softball: Success on the Diamond. 2017. (Preparing for Game Day Ser.: Vol. 10). (ENG., Illus.). 79p. (J). (gr. 7-12). 24.95 *(978-1-4222-3913-1(6))* Mason Crest.

Fauchald, Nick. Batter Up! You Can Play Softball, 1 vol. Rooney, Ronnie, illus. 2005. (Game Day Ser.). (ENG.). 24p. (J). (gr. k-3). lib. bdg. 27.32 *(978-1-4048-1152-2(4)*, 87377, Picture Window Bks.) Capstone.

Gitlin, Marty. Girls Play to Win Softball. 2011. (Girls Play to Win Ser.). 64p. (J). (gr. 3-6). lib. bdg. 27.93 *(978-1-59953-465-7(7))* Norwood Hse. Pr.

Gola, Mark. Winning Softball for Girls, Second Edition. 2nd rev. ed. 2009. (Winning Sports for Girls Ser.). 224p. (gr. 6-12). pap. 14.95 *(978-0-8160-7717-5(7)*, Checkmark Bks.) Infobase Holdings, Inc.

Hofstetter, Adam B. Softball: Rules, Tips, Strategy, & Safety. (Sports from Coast to Coast Ser.). 48p. (gr. 6-6). 2009. 53.00 *(978-1-60853-130-1(9)*, Rosen Reference) 2007. (ENG., Illus.). (J). lib. bdg. 34.47 *(978-1-4042-0996-1(4)*, 21adf7f1-e005-4453-a8a4-0471a6f9be6e) Rosen Publishing Group, Inc., The.

Howell, Brian. Girls' Softball, 1 vol. 2013. (Girls' SportsZone Ser.). (ENG., Illus.). 48p. (J). (gr. 3-6). lib. bdg. 34.21 *(978-1-61783-990-0(6)*, 8878, SportsZone) ABDO Publishing Co.

McIntyre, Abigael & Wesley, Ann. Fastpitch Softball: Girls Rocking It, 1 vol., 1. 2015. (Title IX Rocks! Ser.). (ENG.). 64p. (J). (gr. 6-6). 36.13 *(978-1-4994-6241-8(7)*, 550f6e26-ede4-490c-b198-6a4eeea358eb, Rosen Young Adult) Rosen Publishing Group, Inc., The.

Nitz, Kristin Wolden. Softball. King, Andy, photos by. 2005. (Play-by-Play Ser.). (Illus.). 80p. (gr. 4-8). pap., lib. bdg. 23.93 *(978-0-8225-9875-6(2))* Lerner Publishing Group.

Rissman, Rebecca. Top Softball Tips. 2017. (Top Sports Tips Ser.). (ENG., Illus.). 32p. (J). (gr. 3-9). lib. bdg. 28.65 *(978-1-5157-4721-5(2)*, 134356, Capstone Pr.) Capstone.

Rogers, Amy B. Girls Play Softball, 1 vol. 2016. (Girls Join the Team Ser.). (ENG.). 24p. (J). (gr. 3-3). pap. 9.25 *(978-1-5081-4964-4(X)*, cbfb7473-d014-4783-8b3e-7c1e762c9e0e, PowerKids Pr.) Rosen Publishing Group, Inc., The.

Sanna, Gabriel. Baseball & Softball. 2010. (Getting the Edge Ser.). 96p. (YA). lib. bdg. 24.95 *(978-1-4222-1730-6(2))* Mason Crest.

Smith-Richard, Dean. Softball & Baseball for Fun & Fitness, 1 vol. 2019. (Sports for Fun & Fitness Ser.). (ENG.). 32p. (gr. 3-3). pap. 11.53 *(978-1-9785-1349-5(6)*, 46282a83-25eb-4637-be2d-1051c4321ad7) Enslow Publishing, LLC.

Woodyard, Janelle Valido. A Girl's Guide to Softball, 1 vol. 2012. (Get in the Game Ser.). (ENG.). 32p. (J). (gr. 3-9). lib. bdg. 28.65 *(978-1-4296-7672-4(8)*, 117269) Capstone.

SOFTBALL—FICTION

Alpine, Rachele. You Throw Like a Girl. 2017. (Mix Ser.). (ENG., Illus.). 272p. (J). (gr. 4-8). pap. 8.99 *(978-1-4814-5984-6(8)*, Simon & Schuster/Paula Wiseman Bks.) Simon & Schuster/Paula Wiseman Bks.

Barkley, Callie. Ellie Steps up to the Plate. Bishop, Tracy, illus. 2018. (Critter Club Ser.: 18). (ENG.). 128p. (J). (gr. k-4). 17.99 *(978-1-5344-1179-1(8))*; pap. 6.99 *(978-1-5344-1178-4(X))* Little Simon. (Little Simon).

Bowe, Julie. Curveball. 2017. (Victoria Torres, Unfortunately Average Ser.). (ENG., Illus.). 160p. (J). (gr. 4-8). pap. 5.95 *(978-1-4965-3820-8(X)*, 133120); lib. bdg. 27.99 *(978-1-4965-3818-5(8)*, 133117) Capstone. (Stone Arch Bks.).

Cook, Jacqueline. On to Nationals. 2008. 296p. per. 12.95 *(978-1-4327-1681-3(6))* Outskirts Pr., Inc.

Funk, Constance J. Holy as Thou. 2009. (Illus.). 400p. pap. 22.00 *(978-1-933002-66-8(2))* PublishingWorks.

The Grumpy Millionaire: Individual Title Six-Packs. (Bookweb Ser.). 32p. (gr. 5-18). 34.00 *(978-0-7635-3777-7(2))* Rigby Education.

Johnson, Maureen. The Key to the Golden Firebird. 2004. (ENG.). 304p. (J). (gr. 7-18). 15.99 *(978-0-06-054138-5(5))* HarperCollins Pubs.

Key, Anne. Stealing Bases. 2016. (ENG., Illus.). (YA). 24.99 *(978-1-63533-075-5(0)*, Harmony Ink Pr.) Dreamspinner Pr.

Lupica, Mike. Team Players. (Home Team Ser.). (ENG.). (J). (gr. 3-7). 2019. 320p. pap. 8.99 *(978-1-4814-1008-3(3))* 2018. (Illus.). 304p. 16.99 *(978-1-4814-1007-6(5))* Simon & Schuster Bks. For Young Readers. (Simon & Schuster Bks. For Young Readers).

Mackel, Kathy. MadCat. 2005. (Illus.). 192p. (J). 15.99 *(978-0-06-054869-8(X))* HarperCollins Pubs.

S

Mackey, Weezie Kerr. Throwing Like a Girl, 0 vols. 2013. (ENG.). 272p. (YA). (gr. 7-12). pap. 9.99 (978-0-7614-5606-3(6), 9780761456063, Skyscape) Amazon Publishing.

Maddox, Jake. Catching Confidence. 2018. (Jake Maddox JV Girls Ser.). (ENG., Illus.). 96p. (J). (gr. 4-8). lib. bdg. 26.65 (978-1-4965-5915-9(0), 137122, Stone Arch Bks.) Capstone.

—Softball Switch-Up. Wood, Katie, illus. 2019. (Jake Maddox Girl Sports Stories Ser.). (ENG.). 72p. (J). (gr. 3-6). pap. 5.95 (978-1-4965-8450-2(3), 140975, Stone Arch Bks.) Capstone.

—Stolen Bases. Mourning, Tuesday, illus. 2008. (Jake Maddox Girl Sports Stories Ser.). (ENG.). 72p. (J). (gr. 3-6). 25.32 (978-1-4342-0779-1(X), 95184, Stone Arch Bks.) Capstone.

McCorkle, Denise. On Angels Wings - Softball. 2008. 32p. pap. 17.95 (978-1-4327-3102-1(5)) Outskirts Pr., Inc.

Mendoza, Jessica & Mendoza, Alana. There's No Base Like Home, 1 vol. McNally Barshaw, Ruth, illus. 2018. (ENG.). 240p. (J). (gr. 3-7). 18.95 (978-1-62014-588-3(X), leelowtu, Tu Bks.) Lee & Low Bks., Inc.

RealBuzz Studios Staff. Hits & Misses. 2007. 128p. (YA). No. 1. pap. 4.97 (978-1-59789-569-9(5))No. 2. pap. 4.97 (978-1-59789-570-5(9))No. 3. pap. 4.97 (978-1-59789-571-2(7))No. 4. pap. 4.97 (978-1-59789-572-9(5)) Barbour Publishing, Inc. (Barbour Bks.).

Ritter, John H. Under the Baseball Moon. 2008. (Illus.). 283p. (gr. 8-12). 17.00 (978-0-7569-8934-7(5)) Perfection Learning Corp.

Robyn Washburn. Singled Out in Center Field: Diamonds Are A Girl's Best Friend - Book One. Lisa Byers, illus. 2009. 80p. pap. 12.00 (978-1-4389-6245-0(2)) AuthorHouse.

Van Draanen, Wendelin. Sammy Keyes & the Search for Snake Eyes. 2008. (Sammy Keyes Ser.: Bk. 7). (J). 64.99 (978-1-60640-645-8(0)) Findaway World, LLC.

—Sammy Keyes & the Search for Snake Eyes. Van Draanen, Wendelin, illus. 2003. (Sammy Keyes Ser.: Bk. 7). (Illus.). pap. 54.95 incl. audio compact disk (978-1-59112-281-4(3)); pap. 36.95 incl. audio (978-1-59112-273-9(2)) Live Oak Media.

—Sammy Keyes & the Search for Snake Eyes. 2003. (Sammy Keyes Ser.: Bk. 7). (Illus.). 277p. (gr. 5-9). 17.00 (978-0-7569-1445-5(0)) Perfection Learning Corp.

—Sammy Keyes & the Search for Snake Eyes. 2003. (Sammy Keyes Ser.: 7). 320p. (J). (gr. 5-7). 8.99 (978-0-440-41900-6(X), Yearling) Random Hse. Children's Bks.

—Sammy Keyes & the Sisters of Mercy. 2008. (Sammy Keyes Ser.: Bk. 3). (J). 59.99 (978-1-60640-646-5(9)) Findaway World, LLC.

Wilson, Wendy. Just Desserts. 2007. 53p. pap. 16.95 (978-1-4241-9285-4(4)) America Star Bks.

Winkler, Henry & Oliver, Lin. A Tale of Two Tails #15. 2008. (Hank Zipzer Ser.: 15). (ENG., Illus.). 160p. (J). (gr. 3-7). pap. 6.99 (978-0-448-44378-2(3), Grosset & Dunlap) Penguin Young Readers Group.

—The Zippity Zinger. 2004. (Hank Zipzer Ser.: No. 4). 160p. (J). (gr. 2-6). pap. 29.00 incl. audio (978-1-4000-9009-9(1), Listening Library) Random Hse. Audio Publishing Group.

—The Zippity Zinger. 2006. (Hank Zipzer Ser.: No. 4). 154p. (J). (gr. 3-9). lib. bdg. 24.21 (978-1-59961-103-7(1)) Spotlight.

Wolff, Virginia Euwer. Bat 6. 256p. (J). (gr. 4-6). pap. 4.99 (978-0-8072-8223-6(5)); 2004. (gr. 5-9). pap. 36.00 incl. audio (978-0-8072-8222-9(7), YYA144SP) Random Hse. Audio Publishing Group. (Listening Library).

SOIL CONSERVATION

see also Erosion

Cunningham, Kevin. Soil. 2009. (Diminishing Resources Ser.). 111p. (J). 28.95 (978-1-59935-114-8(5)) Reynolds, Morgan Inc.

Stefoff, Rebecca. Soil for Agriculture, 1 vol. 2016. (Science of Soil Ser.). (ENG., Illus.). 48p. (J). (gr. 4-4). 33.07 (978-1-5026-2225-9(4), 6196ec28-83c9-4e25-8a34-0bb96cdbca46) Cavendish Square Publishing LLC.

SOIL EROSION

see Erosion

SOIL FERTILITY

see Soils

SOILS

see also Clay; Irrigation; Reclamation of Land
also headings beginning with the word Soil

Aloian, Molly. Different Kinds of Soil, 1 vol. 2010. (Everybody Digs Soil Ser.). (ENG., Illus.). 32p. (J). (gr. 3-4). pap. (978-0-7787-5413-8(8)); lib. bdg. (978-0-7787-5400-8(6)) Crabtree Publishing Co.

Barker, David M. Science Lab: Soil. 2011. (Explorer Library: Language Arts Explorer Ser.). (ENG.). 32p. (gr. 4-8). pap. 14.21 (978-1-61080-296-3(9), 201218) Cherry Lake Publishing.

—Science Lab: Soil. 2011. (Explorer Library: Language Arts Explorer Ser.). (ENG., Illus.). 32p. (gr. 4-8). lib. bdg. 32.07 (978-1-61080-207-9(1), 201190) Cherry Lake Publishing.

Bowman, Chris. Soil. 2014. (Earth Science Rocks! Ser.). (ENG., Illus.). 24p. (J). (gr. k-3). lib. bdg. 26.95 (978-1-60014-982-5(0), Blastoff! Readers) Bellwether Media.

Cardenas, Ernesto A. Soils. 2009. pap. 4.95 (978-1-60698-088-0(2)) Milo Educational Bks. & Resources.

Coldwell, Lamar. All about Soil, 1 vol. 2016. (Rosen REAL Readers: STEM & STEAM Collection). (ENG.). 8p. (gr. k-1). pap. 5.46 (978-1-5081-2413-9(2), 9f5555b7-a7ed-4ea9-b8d7-9a10a4502032, Rosen Classroom) Rosen Publishing Group, Inc., The.

Conners, Cathy. Let's Look at Soil, 1 vol. 2013. (Rosen Readers Ser.). (ENG.). 24p. (J). (gr. 2-2). pap. 8.25 (978-1-4777-2342-5(0), 56fa0b95-bc85-4503-a196-74dfa9a27bf5, Rosen Classroom) Rosen Publishing Group, Inc., The.

Connors, Cathy. Let's Look at Soil. 2013. (Rosen Readers Ser.). (ENG.). 24p. (J). (gr. 2-3). pap. 49.50 (978-1-4777-2768-3(X), Rosen Classroom) Rosen Publishing Group, Inc., The.

Cunningham, Kevin. Soil. 2009. (Diminishing Resources Ser.). 111p. (J). 28.95 (978-1-59935-114-8(5)) Reynolds, Morgan Inc.

Ditchfield, Christin. Soil (a True Book: Natural Resources) 2003. (True Book Ser.). (ENG., Illus.). 48p. (J). (gr. 3-5). pap. 6.95 (978-0-516-29368-4(0), Children's Pr.) Scholastic Library Publishing.

Franchino, Vicky. Junior Scientists: Experiment with Soil. 2010. (Explorer Junior Library: Science Explorer Junior Ser.). (ENG., Illus.). 32p. (gr. 3-6). lib. bdg. 32.07 (978-1-60279-837-3(0), 200540) Cherry Lake Publishing.

—Soil. 2009. (Explorer Library: Science Explorer Ser.). (ENG., Illus.). 32p. (gr. 4-8). lib. bdg. 32.07 (978-1-60279-526-6(6), 200297) Cherry Lake Publishing.

Freed, Kira. The Secrets of Soil. 2017. (Text Connections Guided Close Reading Ser.). (J). (gr. 2). (978-1-4900-1835-5(2)) Benchmark Education Co.

Gardner, Robert. Science Fair Projects about Water & Soil, 1 vol. 2016. (Hands-On Science Ser.). (ENG.). 48p. (gr. 4-4). pap. 12.70 (978-0-7660-8211-3(3), a401950b-3da0-424a-a345-84a667eafd0f) Enslow Publishing, LLC.

—Soil: Green Science Projects for a Sustainable Planet, 1 vol. 2011. (Team Green Science Projects Ser.). (ENG., Illus.). 128p. (gr. 5-6). lib. bdg. 35.93 (978-0-7660-3647-5(2), 4e4025f5-d910-4e34-aeef-00c93859fee4) Enslow Publishing, LLC.

Greek, Joe. What Is Soil?, 1 vol., 1. 2015. (Junior Geologist Ser.). (ENG., Illus.). 32p. (J). (gr. 2-3). pap. 13.90 (978-1-5081-0051-5(9), 3b48a0c9-9677-4762-8c4d-ebd28500373c, Britannica Educational Publishing) Rosen Publishing Group, Inc., The.

Green, Jen. Rocks & Soil, 1 vol. 2007. (Our Earth Ser.). (ENG., Illus.). 24p. (YA). (gr. 2-3). lib. bdg. 26.27 (978-1-4042-4271-5(6), 3052c8a7-4172-41d2-b5c1-bc6dfcf217e8) Rosen Publishing Group, Inc., The.

Grover, Samantha. Exploring Soils: A Hidden World Underground. Heisler, Camille, illus. 2017. (ENG.). 32p. (J). (gr. 9-13). 18.95 (978-1-4863-0500-1(8)) CSIRO Publishing AUS. Dist: Stylus Publishing, LLC.

Gurney, Beth. Sand & Soil. 2004. (Rocks, Minerals, & Resources Ser.). (ENG., Illus.). 32p. (J). pap. (978-0-7787-1449-1(7)) Crabtree Publishing Co.

Hagler, Gina. Soils. 2016. (J). (978-1-4896-5289-8(2)) Weigl Pubs., Inc.

Hansen, Grace. Soils, 1 vol. 2015. (Geology Rocks! (Abdo Kids Jumbo) Ser.). (ENG., Illus.). 24p. (J). (gr. -1-2). 32.79 (978-1-62970-910-9(7), 18278, Abdo Kids) ABDO Publishing Co.

Hayes, Amy. We Need Worms, 1 vol. 2015. (Creatures We Can't Live Without Ser.). (ENG., Illus.). 24p. (J). (gr. 3-4). pap. 9.25 (978-1-4994-0986-4(9), 77fe12f8-34e0-405b-8586-f675591432f2, PowerKids Pr.) Rosen Publishing Group, Inc., The.

Hodge, Judith. Riches from Earth & Las riquezas de la Tierra: 6 English, 6 Spanish Adaptations. 2011. (ENG & SPA.). (J). 97.00 net. (978-1-4108-5716-3(6)) Benchmark Education Co.

Hoffman, Steven M. Rocks & Soil, 1 vol. 2011. (Rock It! Ser.). (ENG., Illus.). 24p. (J). (gr. 3-4). pap. 9.25 (978-1-4488-2706-0(X), bea46204-ff6f-4bbf-b3c5-2afb3edd4845); lib. bdg. 26.27 (978-1-4488-2560-8(1), 9ef2c467-0b44-4941-8b33-ed55e5f3d48f) Rosen Publishing Group, Inc., The. (PowerKids Pr.).

Holt, Rinehart and Winston Staff. Holt Science & Technology Chapter 10: Earth Science: Weathering of Soil. 5th ed. 2004. (Illus.). pap. 12.86 (978-0-03-030311-1(7)) Holt McDougal.

Hyde, Natalie. Micro Life in Soil. 2010. (Everybody Digs Soil Ser.). (ENG., Illus.). 32p. (J). (gr. 3-4). pap. (978-0-7787-5415-2(4)); lib. bdg. (978-0-7787-5402-2(2)) Crabtree Publishing Co.

Ivancic, Linda. Soil for Tools & Art, 1 vol. 2016. (Science of Soil Ser.). (ENG., Illus.). 48p. (J). (gr. 4-4). 33.07 (978-1-5026-2166-5(5), 0c13b27c-cab6-49f7-a6d7-0ed59dab694d) Cavendish Square Publishing LLC.

James, Emily. The Simple Science of Dirt. 2017. (Simply Science Ser.). (ENG., Illus.). 32p. (J). (gr. -1-2). lib. bdg. 27.99 (978-1-5157-7085-5(0), 135509, Capstone Pr.) Capstone.

Jennings, Terry. Rocas y Suelos (Rocks & Soils) (SPA.). 32p. (J). 6.95 (978-84-348-1912-2(0)) SM Ediciones ESP. Dist: AIMS International Bks., Inc.

Jones Waring, Kerry. Soil for Minerals & Medicine, 1 vol. 2016. (Science of Soil Ser.). (ENG., Illus.). 48p. (J). (gr. 4-4). 33.07 (978-1-5026-2162-7(2), 27401459-26b9-4344-9390-2ed4bd1a72a3) Cavendish Square Publishing LLC.

Kwarta, James. The Science of Soil, 1 vol. 2008. (Real Life Readers Ser.). (ENG.). 16p. (gr. 2-3). pap. 7.05 (978-1-4358-0033-5(8), acd3e713-9b45-45d8-9aa3-8830fa9fd1f0, Rosen Classroom) Rosen Publishing Group, Inc., The.

Latham, Donna. Tundra. 2010. (Endangered Biomes Ser.). (ENG., Illus.). 32p. (J). (gr. 3-6). 18.69 (978-1-934670-56-9(1)) Nomad Pr.

Lawrence, Ellen. Dirt. 2013. (Science Slam: FUN-Damental Experiments Ser.). 24p. (J). (gr. -1-3). lib. bdg. 26.99 (978-1-61772-737-5(7)) Bearport Publishing Co., Inc.

—Dirt or Soil: What's the Difference? 2015. (Down & Dirty Ser.). (ENG., Illus.). 24p. (J). (gr. -1-3). lib. bdg. 26.99 (978-1-62724-833-4(1)) Bearport Publishing Co., Inc.

—How Do Animals Help Make Soil? 2015. (Down & Dirty Ser.). (ENG., Illus.). 24p. (J). (gr. -1-3). lib. bdg. 26.99 (978-1-62724-835-8(8)) Bearport Publishing Co., Inc.

—Is Soil All the Same? 2015. (Down & Dirty Ser.). (ENG., Illus.). 24p. (J). (gr. -1-3). lib. bdg. 26.99 (978-1-62724-836-5(6)) Bearport Publishing Co., Inc.

—What Is Soil Made Of? 2015. (Down & Dirty Ser.). (ENG., Illus.). 24p. (J). (gr. -1-3). lib. bdg. 26.99 (978-1-62724-834-1(X)) Bearport Publishing Co., Inc.

—Why Do Most Plants Need Soil? 2015. (Down & Dirty Ser.). (ENG., Illus.). 24p. (J). (gr. -1-3). lib. bdg. 26.99 (978-1-62724-837-2(4)) Bearport Publishing Co., Inc.

Lindbo, David L., et al, texts. Soil! Get the Inside Scoop. 2008. (J). 20.00 (978-0-89118-848-3(7)) ASA-CSSA-SSSA.

MacAulay, Kelley. Why Do We Need Soil? 2014. (Natural Resources Close-Up Ser.). (ENG., Illus.). 24p. (J). (gr. 1-1). lib. bdg. (978-0-7787-0493-5(9)) Crabtree Publishing Co.

Mack, Dave L. In the Soil, 1 vol. 2015. (Garden Squad! Ser.). (ENG., Illus.). 24p. (J). (gr. 3-4). pap. 9.25 (978-1-4994-0975-8(3), b4994f9e-1d91-493c-b8b4-d9a8c70e8121, PowerKids Pr.) Rosen Publishing Group, Inc., The.

Meredith, Susan. Las Rocas, los Minerales y el Suelo. 2012. (Let's Explore Science Ser.). (SPA.). 48p. (gr. 4-8). pap. 10.95 (978-1-61810-470-0(5), 9781618104700) Rourke Educational Media.

—Rocks, Minerals, & Soil. 2009. (Let's Explore Science Ser.). (Illus.). 48p. (J). (gr. 4-8). lib. bdg. 32.79 (978-1-60694-411-0(8)) Rourke Educational Media.

Messner, Kate. Up in the Garden & down in the Dirt: (Nature Book for Kids, Gardening & Vegetable Planting, Outdoor Nature Book) Neal, Christopher Silas, illus. 2017. (Over & Under Ser.). (ENG.). 56p. (J). (gr. k-3). pap. 7.99 (978-1-4521-6136-5(4)) Chronicle Bks. LLC.

—Up in the Garden & down in the Dirt: (Spring Books for Kids, Gardening for Kids, Preschool Science Books, Children's Nature Books) Neal, Christopher Silas, illus. 2015. (Over & Under Ser.). (ENG.). 52p. (J). (gr. k-3). 17.99 (978-1-4521-1936-6(8)) Chronicle Bks. LLC.

Montgomery, Heather L. How Is Soil Made? 2010. (Everybody Digs Soil Ser.). (ENG., Illus.). 32p. (J). (gr. 3-4). pap. (978-0-7787-5414-5(6)) Crabtree Publishing Co.

Nelson, Robin. Soil. 2005. (First Step Nonfiction Ser.). (J). (Illus.). 23p. (gr. 3-7). lib. bdg. 18.60 (978-0-8225-2612-4(3), Lerner Pubns.); pap. 5.95 (978-0-8225-5376-2(7)) Lerner Publishing Group.

Newson, Lesley & Wadsworth, Pamela. Rhagor Am Greigiau, Pridd a Thywydd. 2005. (WEL., Illus.). 24p. pap. (978-1-85596-238-5(1)) Dref Wen.

Owen, Ruth. Science & Craft Projects with Rocks & Soil, 1 vol. 2013. (Get Crafty Outdoors Ser.). (ENG., Illus.). 32p. (J). (gr. 2-3). 30.27 (978-1-4777-0246-8(6), f2a967f2-9843-4ea9-bb1c-19b48ee2cca2); pap. 12.75 (978-1-4777-0255-0(5), d0be45d2-a926-4418-bc9e-b297f565040d) Rosen Publishing Group, Inc., The. (PowerKids Pr.).

Parker, Steve. Microlife That Lives in Soil, 1 vol. 2005. (Amazing World of Microlife Ser.). (ENG., Illus.). 32p. (gr. 3-3). pap. 7.99 (978-1-4109-1851-2(3), Raintree) Capstone.

Peterson, Cris. Seed, Soil, Sun: Earth's Recipe for Food. Lundquist, David R., photos by. (ENG., Illus.). 32p. (J). (gr. k-3). 2012. pap. 8.99 (978-1-59078-947-6(4)) 2010. 17.95 (978-1-59078-713-7(7)) Astra Publishing Hse. (Astra Young Readers).

Rake, Jody S. Roots, Bulbs, & Bacteria: Growths of the Underground. 2015. (Underground Safari Ser.). (ENG., Illus.). 24p. (J). (gr. 1-3). lib. bdg. 27.99 (978-1-4914-5062-8(2), 128773, Capstone Pr.) Capstone.

—Soil, Silt, & Sand: Layers of the Underground. 2015. (Underground Safari Ser.). (ENG., Illus.). 24p. (J). (gr. 1-3). lib. bdg. 27.99 (978-1-4914-5063-5(0), 128772, Capstone Pr.) Capstone.

Redlin, Janice L., ed. Land Abuse & Soil Erosion. 2006. (Understanding Global Issues Ser.). (Illus.). 56p. (J). (gr. 3-7). lib. bdg. 28.50 (978-1-59036-237-2(3)) Weigl Pubs., Inc.

Reilly, Kathleen M. Explore Soil! With 25 Great Projects. 2015. (Explore Your World Ser.). (ENG., Illus.). 96p. (J). (gr. 1-5). pap. 14.95 (978-1-61930-295-2(0), a0e206b2-c729-40b1-b792-5c07eb2befa9) Nomad Pr.

Reynolds, Shaye. Volcanoes, 1 vol. 2016. (Spotlight on Earth Science Ser.). (ENG.). 24p. (J). (gr. 4-6). pap. 11.00 (978-1-4994-2537-6(6), f8ca81ff-e7e7-439b-ae9a-0d270f3d1cf8, PowerKids Pr.) Rosen Publishing Group, Inc., The.

Riley, Peter. Rocks & Soil, 1 vol. 2016. (Moving up with Science Ser.). (ENG.). 32p. (J). (gr. 3-4). pap. 11.00 (978-1-4994-3153-7(8), 4ba9fcd8-eea1-4dbe-b21a-897f487f00be, PowerKids Pr.) Rosen Publishing Group, Inc., The.

Rissman, Rebecca. Rocks & Soil: Real Size Science. 2013. (Real Size Science Ser.). (ENG., Illus.). 24p. (J). (gr. -1-1). 25.32 (978-1-4329-7882-2(9), 122823); pap. 6.95 (978-1-4329-7889-1(6), 122829) Capstone. (Heinemann).

Rivera, Andrea. Soils. 2017. (Rocks & Minerals (Launch!) Ser.). (ENG., Illus.). 24p. (J). (gr. -1-2). lib. bdg. 31.36 (978-1-5321-2048-0(6), 25346, Abdo Zoom-Launch) ABDO Publishing Co.

Rosinsky, Natalie M. El Suelo: Tierra y Arena, 1 vol. Robledo, Sol, tr. Boyd, Sheree, illus. 2007. (Ciencia Asombrosa Ser.). (SPA.). 24p. (J). (gr. k-4). lib. bdg. 27.32 (978-1-4048-3211-4(4), 93769, Picture Window Bks.) Capstone.

Royston, Angela. Soil: Let's Look at a Garden. 2005. (J). (978-1-4109-1821-5(1)); (ENG.). 24p. pap. (978-1-4109-1830-7(0)) Steck-Vaughn.

Schuh, Mari. Soil Basics, 1 vol. 2011. (Science Builders Ser.). (ENG.). 24p. (J). (gr. -1-2). lib. bdg. 27.32 (978-1-4296-6071-6(6), 115004); (gr. -1-2). pap. 7.29 (978-1-4296-7110-1(6), 116770); (gr. k-1). pap. 44.74 (978-1-4296-7116-3(5), 16697, Capstone Pr.) Capstone.

The Science of Soil, 12 vols. 2016. (Science of Soil Ser.). (ENG.). 48p. (J). (gr. 4-4). lib. bdg. 198.42 (978-1-5026-2437-6(0), ca171cf3-9e05-422d-8cd9-b70c549d027a, Cavendish Square) Cavendish Square Publishing LLC.

Sharpe, Katie. Soil. 2009. (21st Century Skills Library: Real World Science Ser.). (ENG., Illus.). 32p. (gr. 4-8). lib. bdg. 32.07 (978-1-60279-464-1(2), 200234) Cherry Lake Publishing.

Sherman, Jill. Fertile Land & Soil, 1 vol. 2017. (Let's Learn about Natural Resources Ser.). (ENG.). 24p. (gr. 1-2). pap. 10.35 (978-0-7660-9139-9(2), aef7571c-6a71-43f4-90d4-bd497d3a853c) Enslow Publishing, LLC.

Sian Revision Soil Studies. 2004. (J). (978-1-59242-071-1(0)) Delta Education, LLC.

Sohn, Emily. Pebbles, Sand, & Silt. 2019. (IScience Ser.). (ENG., Illus.). 24p. (J). (gr. k-2). pap. 13.26 (978-1-68404-363-7(8)) Norwood Hse. Pr.

Soil. 2007. 48p. (gr. 3-8). 26.20 (978-0-7377-3638-0(0), Kidhaven) Cengage Gale.

Spilsbury, Louise. El Suelo. 2011. (Las Rocas Ser.). (SPA.). 32p. (gr. 3-6). pap. 8.29 (978-1-4329-5663-9(9), 117359, Heinemann) Capstone.

Spilsbury, Richard & Spilsbury, Louise. Soil, 1 vol. 2011. (Let's Rock Ser.). (ENG.). 32p. (J). (gr. 3-6). pap. 8.29 (978-1-4329-4693-7(5), 114425, Heinemann) Capstone.

Stefoff, Rebecca. Soil for Building Materials, 1 vol. 2016. (Science of Soil Ser.). (ENG., Illus.). 48p. (gr. 4-4). 33.07 (978-1-5026-2164-1(9), 7f0daaad-e3f1-4a84-a476-809fab58ad13) Cavendish Square Publishing LLC.

Sullivan, Laura. Soil for Fossils & History, 1 vol. 2016. (Science of Soil Ser.). (ENG.). 48p. (gr. 4-4). 33.07 (978-1-5026-2203-7(3), a2dd51be-725a-49e2-aed8-da79fd27f8af) Cavendish Square Publishing LLC.

Sundance/Newbridge LLC Staff. Rocks & Soil. 2007. (Early Science Ser.). (gr. k-3). 18.95 (978-1-4007-6441-9(6)); pap. 6.10 (978-1-4007-6437-2(8)) Sundance/Newbridge Educational Publishing.

Tillen, James. A Close Look at Soil, 1 vol. 2013. (InfoMax Readers Ser.). (ENG.). 24p. (J). (gr. 2-2). pap. 8.25 (978-1-4777-2767-6(1), 4685fd36-6d52-4fb8-84d8-98f21c248e3e); pap. 49.50 (978-1-4777-2327-2(7)) Rosen Publishing Group, Inc., The. (Rosen Classroom).

Tomecek, Steve. Dirt. 2014. 16.95 (978-1-63419-657-4(0)) Perfection Learning Corp.

—Jump into Science!: Dirt. 2016. (Jump into Science Ser.). (Illus.). 32p. (J). (gr. -1-k). pap. 7.99 (978-1-4263-2362-1(X), National Geographic Kids) Disney Publishing Worldwide.

Wade, Mary Dodson. Tiny Life on the Ground. 2005. (Rookie Read-About Science Ser.). (ENG., Illus.). 32p. (J). (gr. 1-2). 20.50 (978-0-516-25298-8(4), Children's Pr.) Scholastic Library Publishing.

Wadsworth, Pamela. Creigiau, Pridd a Thywydd. 2005. (WEL., Illus.). 24p. pap. (978-1-85596-237-8(3)) Dref Wen.

Wadsworth, Pamela & Tate, Sylvia. Golwg Gyntaf Ar Greigiau, Pridd a Thywydd. 2005. (WEL., Illus.). 24p. pap. (978-1-85596-253-8(5)) Dref Wen.

Walker, Kate. Soil, 1 vol. 2012. (Investigating Earth Ser.). (ENG.). 32p. (gr. 2-2). 31.21 (978-1-60870-561-0(7), 78c01612-cbb5-4a42-b2dd-74e9f85356b9) Cavendish Square Publishing LLC.

Walker, Sally M. Soil. (Illus.). 48p. (J). 2007. pap. 8.95 (978-0-8225-6622-9(2)) 2006. (gr. 3-7). lib. bdg. 25.26 (978-0-8225-5948-1(X), Lerner Pubns.) Lerner Publishing Group.

—Studying Soil. 2013. (Searchlight Books (tm) — Do You Dig Earth Science? Ser.). (ENG., Illus.). 40p. (J). (gr. 3-5). pap. 9.99 (978-1-4677-0794-7(5), aa59a434-d865-4b7b-9642-4859737c5baf); lib. bdg. 30.65 (978-1-4677-0023-8(1), 5dc6cd86-e7cc-45b4-8984-a5b1962f46ab, Lerner Pubns.) Lerner Publishing Group.

Watts, Pam. Soil. 2016. (Geology Rocks! Ser.). (ENG.). 24p. (J). (gr. 3-6). 32.79 (978-1-5038-0806-5(8), 210641) Child's World, Inc, The.

Wermund, Jerry. Soil: More Than Just Dirt. 2009. (Illus.). 48p. 18.95 (978-0-9726255-3-1(4)) Rockon Publishing.

SOLAR ENERGY

Alkire, Jessie. Solar Energy: Putting the Sun to Work. 2018. (Earth's Energy Innovations Ser.). (ENG., Illus.). 24p. (J). (gr. k-4). lib. bdg. 32.79 (978-1-5321-1574-5(1), 29002, Super SandCastle) ABDO Publishing Co.

—Solar Energy Projects: Easy Energy Activities for Future Engineers! 2018. (Earth's Energy Experiments Ser.). (ENG., Illus.). 32p. (J). (gr. k-4). lib. bdg. 34.21 (978-1-5321-1565-3(2), 28984, Super SandCastle) ABDO Publishing Co.

Bailey, Diane. Solar Power. 2014. (Harnessing Energy Ser.). (ENG.). 48p. (J). (gr. 5-8). pap. 12.00 (978-0-89812-998-4(2), 21362, Creative Paperbacks); lib. bdg. 35.65 (978-1-60818-412-5(9), 21361, Creative Education) Creative Co., The.

Bearce, Stephanie. How to Harness Solar Power for Your Home. 2009. (Tell Your Parents Ser.). (Illus.). 48p. (J). (gr. 4-7). lib. bdg. 29.95 (978-1-58415-761-8(5)) Mitchell Lane Pubs.

Benduhn, Tea. Energía Solar (Solar Power), 1 vol. 2008. (Energía para el Presente (Energy for Today) Ser.). (SPA.). 24p. (gr. 3-3). (J). lib. bdg. 24.67 (978-0-8368-9269-7(0), 311f6ee4-5d03-4bee-9e86-66b55aa45de4); pap. 9.15 (978-0-8368-9368-7(9), 617077fd-326a-487f-ba92-4c0a91974cb6) Stevens, Gareth Publishing LLLP. (Weekly Reader Leveled Readers).

—Solar Power, 1 vol. 2008. (Energy for Today Ser.). (ENG.). 24p. (gr. 3-3). (J). lib. bdg. 24.67 (978-0-8368-9263-5(1), 00ea634b-05b8-49a6-a454-a6097b38e363); pap. 9.15 (978-0-8368-9362-5(X), 52b8eae1-7221-4d42-8de3-13e122439133) Stevens, Gareth Publishing LLLP. (Weekly Reader Leveled Readers).

Benson, Jodyanne. The Sun & Earth's Surface, 1 vol. 2019. (Power of the Sun Ser.). (ENG.). 32p. (gr. 3-3). pap. 11.58 (978-1-5026-4666-8(8), 0724a52e-3b08-4485-b63e-31ff0e5b074d) Cavendish Square Publishing LLC.

Bow, James. Energy from the Sun: Solar Power. 2015. (Next Generation Energy Ser.). (ENG., Illus.). 32p. (J). (gr. 5-5). (978-0-7787-1982-3(0)) Crabtree Publishing Co.

—Understanding Our Sun. 2019. (Mission: Space Science Ser.). (Illus.). 48p. (J). (gr. 5-5). (978-0-7787-5395-7(6)); pap. (978-0-7787-5406-0(5)) Crabtree Publishing Co.

Brearley, Laurie. Solar Power: Capturing the Sun's Energy (a True Book: Alternative Energy) 2018. (True Book (Relaunch) Ser.). (ENG., Illus.). 48p. (J). (gr. 3-5). pap. 7.95 (978-0-531-23943-8(8), Children's Pr.) Scholastic Library Publishing.

—Solar Power: Capturing the Sun's Energy (a True Book: Alternative Energy) (Library Edition) 2018. (True Book (Relaunch) Ser.). (ENG., Illus.). 48p. (J). (gr. 3-5). lib. bdg. 31.00 (978-0-531-23686-4(2), Children's Pr.) Scholastic Library Publishing.

Bright, Michael. From Sunshine to Light Bulb. 2016. (Source to Resource Ser.). (Illus.). 32p. (J). (gr. 3-6). *(978-0-7787-2707-1(6))* Crabtree Publishing Co.

Coldwell, Lamar. My Uncle's Factory Produces Solar Panels, 1 vol. 2016. (Rosen REAL Readers: Social Studies Nonfiction / Fiction: Myself, My Community, My World Ser.). (ENG.). 12p. (gr. k-1). pap. 6.33 *(978-1-5081-2359-0(4),* efa3dba2-e7da-4047-bb59-e0cf8455c2eb, Rosen Classroom) Rosen Publishing Group, Inc., The.

Conley, Kate. Solar Energy. 2016. (Alternative Energy Ser.). (ENG., Illus.). 48p. (J). (gr. 4-8). lib. bdg. 35.64 *(978-1-68078-459-6(5),* 23855) ABDO Publishing Co.

DeCristofano, Carolyn Cinami. Running on Sunshine: How Does Solar Energy Work? Medeiros, Giovana, illus. 2018. (Let's-Read-And-Find-Out Science 2 Ser.). (ENG.). 40p. (J). (gr. -1-3). 17.99 *(978-0-06-247311-0(5))*; pap. 8.99 *(978-0-06-247310-3(7))* HarperCollins Pubs. (HarperCollins).

Dickmann, Nancy. Harnessing Solar Energy, 1 vol. 2016. (Future of Power Ser.). (ENG., Illus.). 32p. (J). (gr. 4-5). pap. 11.00 *(978-1-4994-3214-5(3),* e600a406-7aba-4fbb-beab-0fe97a437a87, PowerKids Pr.) Rosen Publishing Group, Inc., The.

Drummond, Allan. Solar Story: How One Community Lives Alongside the World's Biggest Solar Plant. 2020. (Green Power Ser.). (ENG., Illus.). 40p. (J). 18.99 *(978-0-374-30899-5(3),* 900188024, Farrar, Straus & Giroux (BYR)) Farrar, Straus & Giroux.

Duling, Kaitlyn. The Sun & Renewable Energy, 1 vol. 2019. (Power of the Sun Ser.). (ENG.). 32p. (J). (gr. 3-3). lib. bdg. 30.21 *(978-1-5026-4680-4(3),* 872e0106-0a92-42dc-ad2a-c3589d713072) Cavendish Square Publishing LLC.

Farris Naff, Clay, ed. Solar Power, 1 vol. 2006. (Fueling the Future Ser.). (ENG., Illus.). 128p. (gr. 10-12). lib. bdg. 46.23 *(978-0-7377-3565-9(1),* d95085a3-612d-46cd-a099-ba56a06322b7, Greenhaven Publishing) Greenhaven Publishing LLC.

Felix, Rebecca. Solar Energy. 2018. (Earth's Energy Resources Ser.). (ENG., Illus.). 24p. (J). (gr. -1-3). lib. bdg. 29.93 *(978-1-5321-1556-1(3),* 28966, SandCastle) ABDO Publishing Co.

friend, robyn C. & cohen, Judith Love. A Clean Planet: The Solar Power Story. katz, david A., illus. 2009. 48p. (J). pap. 7.00 *(978-1-880599-86-0(4))* Cascade Pass, Inc.

friend, robyn C. & Cohen, Judith Love. A Clean Planet: The Solar Power Story. Katz, David A., illus. 2009. 48p. (J). 13.95 *(978-1-880599-87-7(2))* Cascade Pass, Inc.

Garbe, Suzanne. The Science Behind Wonders of the Sun: Sun Dogs, Lunar Eclipses, & Green Flash. 2016. (Science Behind Natural Phenomena Ser.). (ENG., Illus.). 32p. (J). (gr. 3-9). lib. bdg. 28.65 *(978-1-5157-0778-3(4),* 132118, Capstone Pr.) Capstone.

Gould, Alan. Hot Water & Warm Homes from Sunlight. Gould, Alan et al, illus. Sneider, Cary I., photos by. rev. ed. 2005. (Great Explorations in Math & Science Ser.). 80p. 13.50 *(978-1-931542-04-3(X),* GEMS) Univ. of California, Berkeley, Lawrence Hall of Science.

Grady, Colin. Solar Energy, 1 vol. 2016. (Saving the Planet Through Green Energy Ser.). (ENG.). 24p. (gr. 3-3). pap. 10.35 *(978-0-7660-8292-2(X),* 63428589-9614-420f-bd74-f18d6f17d432) Enslow Publishing, LLC.

Hansen, Amy. Solar Energy: Running on Sunshine, 1 vol. 2010. (Powering Our World Ser.). (ENG.). 24p. (J). (gr. 3-3). pap. 9.25 *(978-1-4358-9740-3(4),* 9033a36e-6bcd-47e2-8c2e-44637f8a42f4) Rosen Publishing Group, Inc., The.

Hansen, Amy S. Solar Energy: Running on Sunshine. 2010. (Powering Our World Ser.). 24p. (J). (gr. 2-5). E-Book 42.50 *(978-1-4488-0197-8(4))*; (ENG., Illus.). (gr. 3-3). lib. bdg. 26.27 *(978-1-4358-9326-9(3),* ca2a6f22-b7c0-45b3-8c03-dda61f3c5fef) Rosen Publishing Group, Inc., The.

Hantula, Richard & Voege, Debra. How Do Solar Panels Work? 2009. (Science in the Real World Ser.). (ENG., Illus.). 32p. (gr. 4-6). 28.00 *(978-1-60413-472-8(0),* P173438, Chelsea Clubhse.) Infobase Holdings, Inc.

—Solar Power. 2010. (ENG.). 48p. (gr. 3-6). 30.00 *(978-1-60413-779-8(7),* P197784, Facts On File) Infobase Holdings, Inc.

Hardyman, Robyn. How a Solar-Powered Home Works, 1 vol. 2013. (EcoWorks Ser.). 32p. (J). (gr. 3-4). (ENG.). pap. 11.50 *(978-1-4339-9549-1(2),* 2cb33b20-341d-4863-a78c-680bf76c3326, Gareth Stevens Learning Library); pap. 63.00 *(978-1-4339-9550-7(6))*; (ENG., Illus.). lib. bdg. 29.27 *(978-1-4339-9548-4(4),* 6d9fcfcd-910a-467e-b0f3-981d79c3a70a) Stevens, Gareth Publishing LLLP.

Harper, Reggie. Using the Sun's Energy: If... Then, 1 vol. 2017. (Computer Science for the Real World Ser.). (ENG.). 16p. (gr. 2-3). pap. *(978-1-5383-5249-6(4),* 49f1b2f5-dac8-4512-9c6a-4a88a9da80c4, Rosen Classroom) Rosen Publishing Group, Inc., The.

Huggett, Audrey. Solar Energy Projects. 2016. (21st Century Skills Innovation Library: Makers As Innovators Ser.). (ENG., Illus.). 32p. (J). (gr. 4-8). lib. bdg. 32.07 *(978-1-63471-417-4(2),* 208447) Cherry Lake Publishing.

Jones, Susan. Solar Power of the Future: New Ways of Turning Sunlight into Energy. 2009. (Library of Future Energy Ser.). 64p. (gr. 5-5). 58.50 *(978-1-60853-629-0(7))* Rosen Publishing Group, Inc., The.

Kallen, Stuart A. Real-World STEM: Develop Economical Solar Power. 2017. (Real-World Stem Ser.). (ENG.). 80p. (YA). (gr. 5-12). *(978-1-68282-239-5(7))* ReferencePoint Pr., Inc.

Kenney, Karen Latchana. Energy Investigations. 2017. (Key Questions in Physical Science (Alternator Books (r)) Ser.). (ENG., Illus.). 32p. (J). (gr. 3-6). 29.32 *(978-1-5124-4003-4(5),* 3474451b-a346-4366-9111-ff41cef7335f, Lerner Pubns.) Lerner Publishing Group.

—Solar Energy. 2019. (Energy Revolution Ser.). (ENG., Illus.). 32p. (J). (gr. 3-6). lib. bdg. 27.99 *(978-1-5435-5540-0(3),* 139390, Capstone Pr.) Capstone.

Lachner, Elizabeth. Solar Power, 1 vol. 2018. (Exploring Energy Technology Ser.). (ENG.). 48p. (gr. 6-6). pap. 15.05 *(978-1-5081-0621-0(5),* a43d5910-00bd-466f-97af-fec0661c283c, Britannica Educational Publishing) Rosen Publishing Group, Inc., The.

Mahaney, Ian. Solar Energy. 2007. 28p. pap. 21.25 *(978-1-4358-3825-3(4),* PowerKids Pr.) Rosen Publishing Group, Inc., The.

Mahaney, Ian F. Solar Energy, 1 vol. (Energy in Action Ser.). (ENG., Illus.). 24p. (gr. 3-3). 2007. (J). lib. bdg. 26.27 *(978-1-4042-3479-6(9),* caa8fd1d-7f50-4d7e-9267-b4708a556374) 2006. pap. 7.05 *(978-1-4042-2188-8(3),* 8feb3df8-21d8-458b-80e7-4176675fb6fc) Rosen Publishing Group, Inc., The. (PowerKids Pr.).

Marquardt, Meg. Solar Energy. 2019. (Tech Bytes Ser.). (ENG., Illus.). 48p. (J). (gr. 4-6). 26.60 *(978-1-68450-916-4(5))* Norwood Hse. Pr.

Morey, Allan. Solar Storm. 2019. (It's the End of the World! Ser.). (ENG., Illus.). 24p. (J). (gr. 3-7). lib. bdg. 26.95 *(978-1-64487-084-6(3),* Torque Bks.) Bellwether Media.

Morris, Neil. Solar Power. 2007. (Energy Sources Ser.). (Illus.). 32p. (YA). (gr. 4-7). lib. bdg. 28.50 *(978-1-58340-908-4(4))* Black Rabbit Bks.

—Solar Power: Now & in the Future. 2010. (J). 34.25 *(978-1-59920-342-3(1))* Black Rabbit Bks.

Muschal, Frank. Energy from Wind, Sun, & Tides. 2007. (21st Century Skills Library: Power Up! Ser.). (ENG.). 32p. (gr. 4-8). pap. 14.21 *(978-1-60279-096-4(5),* 200657); (Illus.). lib. bdg. 32.07 *(978-1-60279-046-9(9),* 200052) Cherry Lake Publishing.

Owen, Ruth. Energy from the Sun: Solar Power, 1 vol. 2013. (Power: Yesterday, Today, Tomorrow Ser.). (ENG., Illus.). 32p. (J). (gr. 4-5). 28.93 *(978-1-4777-0270-3(9),* 42e33e94-879c-450d-9591-82f80e9a9e33); pap. 12.75 *(978-1-4777-0279-6(2),* ac7f1742-39b3-4f75-b5fa-91a6bfa78e0b) Rosen Publishing Group, Inc., The. (PowerKids Pr.).

Parker, Steve. Solar Power, 1 vol. 2004. (Science Files: Energy Ser.). (ENG., Illus.). 32p. (gr. 3-5). lib. bdg. 28.67 *(978-0-8368-4032-2(1),* 237e90cc-6ebc-469e-8ace-1ef2b6d23f4b, Gareth Stevens Learning Library) Stevens, Gareth Publishing LLLP.

Pipe, Jim. Solar Power. 2011. (J). 28.50 *(978-1-59604-215-5(X))* Black Rabbit Bks.

Porter, Esther. Sun Power: A Book about Renewable Energy, 1 vol. 2013. (Earth Matters Ser.). (ENG.). 32p. (J). (gr. -1-2). pap. 8.10 *(978-1-62065-739-3(2),* 121725); (gr. 1-2). pap. 49.60 *(978-1-62065-740-9(6),* 19322, Capstone Pr.) Capstone.

Reynoldson, Fiona. Understanding Solar Power, 1 vol. 2010. (World of Energy Ser.). (ENG.). 48p. (J). (gr. 5-6). lib. bdg. 34.60 *(978-1-4339-4127-6(9),* 700d4340-9128-40b4-98b3-1647ad66de24, Gareth Stevens Learning Library) Stevens, Gareth Publishing LLLP.

Rice, Dona & Otterman, Joseph. Powered by the Sun. rev. ed. 2019. (Smithsonian: Informational Text Ser.). (ENG., Illus.). 24p. (J). (gr. 1-2). pap. 8.99 *(978-1-4938-6658-8(3))* Teacher Created Materials, Inc.

Richards, Julie. Solar Energy, 1 vol. 2010. (Energy Choices Ser.). (ENG.). 32p. (gr. 3-3). 31.21 *(978-0-7614-4427-5(0),* 6fee630d-d4b6-4d39-a1f2-198046d56176) Cavendish Square Publishing LLC.

Ringstad, Arnold. The Science of Solar Energy. 2018. (ENG.). 80p. (YA). (gr. 5-12). *(978-1-68282-307-1(5))* ReferencePoint Pr., Inc.

Rivera, Andrea. Solar Power. 2016. (Our Renewable Earth Ser.). (ENG., Illus.). 24p. (J). (gr. -1-2). lib. bdg. 31.36 *(978-1-68079-941-5(X),* 24186, Abdo Zoom-Launch) ABDO Publishing Co.

Rooney, Anne. Solar Power, 1 vol. 2007. (Energy for the Future & Global Warming Ser.). (ENG.). 32p. (gr. 3-3). pap. 12.70 *(978-0-8368-8412-8(4),* e25ca2b0-0b76-4adb-a977-336aab6ee4d9); (Illus.). lib. bdg. 29.67 *(978-0-8368-8403-6(5),* 8c21aafb-3dec-46a2-b196-6c1a2e4b99c7) Stevens, Gareth Publishing LLLP.

Rowe, Brooke. Playing with Solar Heat. Bane, Jeff, illus. 2016. (My Early Library: My Science Fun Ser.). (ENG.). 24p. (J). (gr. k-1). 30.64 *(978-1-63471-031-2(2),* 208204) Cherry Lake Publishing.

Scibilia, Jade Zora. Solar Panels: Harnessing the Power of the Sun, 1 vol. 2017. (Powered up! a STEM Approach to Energy Sources Ser.). (ENG.). 24p. (J). (gr. 3-3). 25.27 *(978-1-5081-6425-8(8),* bb5e8f5c-3a01-4250-a916-9b3f7493533f, PowerKids Pr.) Rosen Publishing Group, Inc., The.

Science stories foss spanish solar energy ea Cr05. 2005. (J). *(978-1-59242-595-2(X))* Delta Education, LLC.

Sohn, Emily. Solar Energy. 2019. (IScience Ser.). (ENG., Illus.). 48p. (J). (gr. 5-6). pap. 13.26 *(978-1-68404-407-8(3))* Norwood Hse. Pr.

Solar-Wind-Riding Electric Sail: Meet NASA Inventor Bruce Wiegmann & His Team's. 2017. (J). *(978-0-7166-6162-7(4))* World Bk., Inc.

Solway, Andrew. From Sunlight to Blockbuster Movies: An Energy Journey Through the World of Light. 2015. (Energy Journeys Ser.). (ENG., Illus.). 48p. (J). (gr. 3-6). 35.99 *(978-1-4846-0882-1(8),* 127966, Heinemann) Capstone.

Spilsbury, Richard & Spilsbury, Louise. Solar Power, 1 vol. 2011. (Let's Discuss Energy Resources Ser.). (ENG., Illus.). 32p. (YA). (gr. 4-5). lib. bdg. 30.27 *(978-1-4488-5262-8(5),* 05bb6b22-2515-45f5-a3a1-afccbd83275b) Rosen Publishing Group, Inc., The.

Spiro, Ruth. Baby Loves Thermodynamics! Chan, Irene, illus. 2017. (Baby Loves Science Ser.: 3). 22p. (J). (— 1). bds. 8.99 *(978-1-58089-768-6(1))* Charlesbridge Publishing, Inc.

Sullivan, Laura. The Pros & Cons of Solar Power, 1 vol. 2014. (Economics of Energy Ser.). (ENG., Illus.). 80p. (YA). (gr. 7-7). lib. bdg. 37.36 *(978-1-62712-924-4(3),* df0d3f6d-92ea-4da6-ad55-6cd7ae5b6791) Cavendish Square Publishing LLC.

Sundance/Newbridge LLC Staff. Energy from the Sun. 2004. (Reading PowerWorks Ser.). (gr. 1-3). 37.50 *(978-0-7608-9711-9(5))*; pap. 6.10 *(978-0-7608-9712-6(3))* Sundance/Newbridge Educational Publishing.

Taylor-Butler, Christine. Junior Scientists: Experiment with Solar Energy. 2010. (Explorer Junior Library: Science Explorer Junior Ser.). (ENG., Illus.). 32p. (gr. 3-6). lib. bdg. 32.07 *(978-1-60279-840-3(0),* 200546) Cherry Lake Publishing.

—Solar Energy. 2009. (Explorer Library: Science Explorer Ser.). (ENG., Illus.). 32p. (gr. 4-8). lib. bdg. 32.07 *(978-1-60279-527-3(4),* 200295) Cherry Lake Publishing.

Thomas, Isabel. The Pros & Cons of Solar Power, 1 vol. 2007. (Energy Debate Ser.). (ENG., Illus.). 48p. (YA). (gr. 6-6). lib. bdg. 34.47 *(978-1-4042-3741-4(0),* f7c74371-4a23-487c-9f0f-84ab2443ed6a) Rosen Publishing Group, Inc., The.

Vogel, Julia. Solar Power. 2013. (Explorer Library: Language Arts Explorer Ser.). (ENG.). 32p. (gr. 4-8). pap. 14.21 *(978-1-61080-923-8(8),* 202573); (Illus.). 32.07 *(978-1-61080-898-9(3),* 202571); (Illus.). E-Book 49.21 *(978-1-61080-973-3(4),* 202574) Cherry Lake Publishing.

Walker, Niki. Harnessing Power from the Sun. 2006. (Energy Revolution Ser.). (ENG., Illus.). 32p. (J). (gr. 3-7). pap. *(978-0-7787-2926-6(5))* Crabtree Publishing Co.

SOLAR HEATING

see Solar Energy; Sun

SOLAR PHYSICS

see Sun

SOLAR POWER

see Solar Energy

SOLAR SYSTEM

Adamson, Thomas K. Sun, Moon, & Stars Pack [Scholastic]. 2011. (Exploring the Galaxy Ser.). 24p. pap. 1.50 *(978-1-4296-6292-5(1),* Capstone Pr.) Capstone.

Aguilar, David A. Seven Wonders of the Solar System. 2017. (Smithsonian Ser.). (Illus.). 80p. (J). (gr. 5). 18.99 *(978-0-451-47685-2(9),* Viking Books for Young Readers) Penguin Young Readers Group.

—13 Planets: The Latest View of the Solar System. 2011. (Illus.). 64p. (J). (gr. 3-7). 16.95 *(978-1-4263-0770-6(5),* National Geographic Kids) Disney Publishing Worldwide.

Anderson, Michael. The Nature of Planets, Dwarf Planets, & Space Objects, 1 vol. 2011. (Solar System Ser.). (ENG., Illus.). 96p. (J). (gr. 8-8). lib. bdg. 35.29 *(978-1-61530-517-9(3),* 58422bec-8a3c-42ac-8ffa-a5a83dda5ab4) Rosen Publishing Group, Inc., The.

Arlon, Penelope & Gordon-Harris, Tory. Planets. 2012. (J). lib. bdg. *(978-0-531-22957-6(2))* Scholastic, Inc.

Ashby, Ruth. How the Solar System Was Formed. 2003. (New Solar System Ser.). (J). lib. bdg. 28.50 *(978-1-58340-285-6(3))* Black Rabbit Bks.

Asselin, Kristine Carlson. Our Sun. 2010. (Solar System & Beyond Ser.). (ENG.). 32p. (J). (gr. 3-4). pap. 48.60 *(978-1-4296-6409-7(6),* 16155, Capstone Pr.) Capstone.

Asteroids. 2015. (Across the Universe Ser.). (ENG.). 24p. (J). (gr. 1-4). *(978-1-60818-480-4(3),* 21108, Creative Education) Creative Co., The.

Astronomy Now!, 4 vols., Set. Incl. Look at Pluto & Other Dwarf Planets. Kaspar, Anna. (YA). lib. bdg. 26.27 *(978-1-4042-3824-4(7),* 1cf8028f-d4c3-4751-9b44-778c3cd11f24); Look at Uranus. Slade, Suzanne. (J). lib. bdg. 26.27 *(978-1-4042-3831-2(X),* 1e40ce88-fc15-4ea2-8cb8-7770358167c5); (Illus.). 24p. (gr. 2-3). (Astronomy Now! Ser.). (ENG.). 2007. Set lib. bdg. 52.54 *(978-1-4042-3863-3(8),* c5609b92-a82e-44b5-aa90-6c5e73d73a96) Rosen Publishing Group, Inc., The.

Autumn Publishing Staff, illus. Solar System. 2004. (Wall Charts Ser.). (J). pap. 4.99 *(978-1-85997-257-1(8))* Byeway Bks.

Baines, Becky. Explore My World Planets. 2016. (Explore My World Ser.). (Illus.). 32p. (J). (gr. -1-k). pap. 4.99 *(978-1-4263-2322-5(0),* National Geographic Kids) Disney Publishing Worldwide.

Ball, Nate. Let's Investigate with Nate #2: The Solar System. Hargis, Wes, illus. 2017. (Let's Investigate with Nate Ser.: 2). (ENG.). 40p. (J). (gr. -1-3). pap. 6.99 *(978-0-06-235742-7(5),* HarperCollins) HarperCollins Pubs.

Basher, Simon & Green, Dan. Basher Science: Astronomy: Out of This World! Basher, Simon, illus. 2009. (Basher Science Ser.). (ENG., Illus.). 128p. (J). (gr. 5-9). pap. 9.99 *(978-0-7534-6290-4(7),* 900056024, Kingfisher) Roaring Brook Pr.

Believe It Or Not!, Ripleys, compiled by. Ripley Twists PB: Space. 2018. (Twist Ser.: 3). (ENG.). 48p. (J). pap. 7.99 *(978-1-60991-236-9(5))* Ripley Entertainment, Inc.

Bell, Samantha. Solar System. Bane, Jeff, illus. 2018. (Mi Mini Biografía (My Itty-Bitty Bio): My Early Library). (ENG.). 24p. (J). (gr. k-1). pap. 12.79 *(978-1-5341-0821-9(1),* 210648); lib. bdg. 30.64 *(978-1-5341-0722-9(3),* 210647) Cherry Lake Publishing.

Bell, Trudy E. Comets, Meteors, Asteroids, & the Outer Reaches. 2003. (New Solar System Ser.). (J). lib. bdg. 28.50 *(978-1-58340-289-4(6))* Black Rabbit Bks.

Benchmark Education Company, LLC Staff, compiled by. Earth & Space. 2005. spiral bd. 110.00 *(978-1-4108-3873-5(0))* Benchmark Education Co.

—Earth & Space: Theme Set. 2006. (J). 239.00 *(978-1-4108-7120-6(7))*; 237.00 *(978-1-4108-7106-0(1))* Benchmark Education Co.

—Our Solar System: Theme Set. 2006. (J). 105.00 *(978-1-4108-7062-9(6))* Benchmark Education Co.

Berger, Melvin & Berger, Gilda. El Sistema Solar: The Solar System. 2006. (ENG & SPA., Illus.). (J). *(978-0-439-82865-9(1))* Scholastic, Inc.

—Think Factory: Solar System. 2005. (Illus.). 47p. (J). *(978-0-439-51155-1(0))* Scholastic, Inc.

Berkes, Marianne. Going Around the Sun: Some Planetary Fun, 1 vol. Mason, Janeen, illus. 2012. (ENG.). 32p. (J). (gr. k-4). 16.95 *(978-1-58469-099-3(2))*; pap. 8.95 *(978-1-58469-100-6(X))* Sourcebooks, Inc. (Dawn Pubns.).

Beullens-Maoui, Nathalie, ed. Our Solar System: Armenian, 01 vols., 1. 2016. (Our Wonderful World Ser.). (ENG & SPA.). 8p. (J). pap. 9.35 *(978-1-5081-1211-2(8),* Rosen Classroom) Rosen Publishing Group, Inc., The.

—Our Solar System: Filipino, 01 vols., 1. 2016. (Our Wonderful World Ser.). (ENG & SPA.). 8p. (J). pap. 9.35 *(978-1-5081-1217-4(7),* Rosen Classroom) Rosen Publishing Group, Inc., The.

—Our Solar System: Hmong Green, 01 vols., 1. 2016. (Our Wonderful World Ser.). (ENG & SPA.). 8p. (J). pap. 9.35 *(978-1-5081-1229-7(0),* Rosen Classroom) Rosen Publishing Group, Inc., The.

Block, Dakota. Exploring the Solar System, 1 vol. 2012. (Exploring Earth & Space Ser.). (ENG., Illus.). 24p. (J). (gr. 1-2). 26.27 *(978-1-4488-8572-5(8),* 0fa49534-491c-44f5-b5df-f9eca902d269, PowerKids Pr.) Rosen Publishing Group, Inc., The.

Bloom, J. P. Jupiter (Jupiter), 1 vol. 2016. (Planetas (Planets) Ser.). (SPA., Illus.). 24p. (J). (gr. -1-2). lib. bdg. 32.79 *(978-1-68080-753-0(6),* 22668, Abdo Kids) ABDO Publishing Co.

—Mars, 1 vol. 2015. (Planets Ser.). (ENG., Illus.). 24p. (J). (gr. -1-2). lib. bdg. 32.79 *(978-1-62970-717-4(1),* 17233, Abdo Kids) ABDO Publishing Co.

—Mars. 2017. (Planets Ser.). (ENG.). 24p. (J). (gr. -1-2). pap. 7.95 *(978-1-4966-1282-3(5),* 135014, Capstone Classroom) Capstone.

—Marte (Mars), 1 vol. 2016. (Planetas (Planets) Ser.). (SPA., Illus.). 24p. (J). (gr. -1-2). lib. bdg. 32.79 *(978-1-68080-754-7(4),* 22670, Abdo Kids) ABDO Publishing Co.

—Mercurio (Mercury), 1 vol. 2016. (Planetas (Planets) Ser.). (SPA., Illus.). 24p. (J). (gr. -1-2). lib. bdg. 32.79 *(978-1-68080-755-4(2),* 22672, Abdo Kids) ABDO Publishing Co.

—Neptuno (Neptune), 1 vol. 2016. (Planetas (Planets) Ser.). (SPA., Illus.). 24p. (J). (gr. -1-2). lib. bdg. 32.79 *(978-1-68080-756-1(0),* 22674, Abdo Kids) ABDO Publishing Co.

—Saturno (Saturn), 1 vol. 2016. (Planetas (Planets) Ser.). (SPA., Illus.). 24p. (J). (gr. -1-2). lib. bdg. 32.79 *(978-1-68080-757-8(9),* 22676, Abdo Kids) ABDO Publishing Co.

—La Tierra (Earth), 1 vol. 2016. (Planetas (Planets) Ser.). (SPA., Illus.). 24p. (J). (gr. -1-2). lib. bdg. 32.79 *(978-1-68080-752-3(8),* 22666, Abdo Kids) ABDO Publishing Co.

—Urano (Uranus), 1 vol. 2016. (Planetas (Planets) Ser.). (SPA., Illus.). 24p. (J). (gr. -1-2). lib. bdg. 32.79 *(978-1-68080-758-5(7),* 22678, Abdo Kids) ABDO Publishing Co.

—Venus (Venus), 1 vol. 2016. (Planetas (Planets) Ser.). (SPA., Illus.). 24p. (J). (gr. -1-2). lib. bdg. 32.79 *(978-1-68080-759-2(5),* 22680, Abdo Kids) ABDO Publishing Co.

Bone, Emily. The Solar System Internet Referenced. Pastor, Terry & Haggerty, Tim, illus. 2010. (Beginner's Science Ser.). 32p. (J). (gr. 1). 4.99 *(978-0-7945-2812-6(0),* Usborne) EDC Publishing.

Bow, James. Space Mysteries Revealed. 2010. (ENG., Illus.). 32p. (J). pap. *(978-0-7787-7431-0(7))*; (gr. 4-7). lib. bdg. *(978-0-7787-7416-7(3))* Crabtree Publishing Co.

Bowman, Donna H. What Is the Moon Made Of? And Other Questions Kids Have about Space, 1 vol. Lubach, Peter, illus. 2010. (Kids' Questions Ser.). (ENG.). 24p. (J). (gr. k-2). pap. 7.49 *(978-1-4048-6726-0(0),* 115554, Picture Window Bks.) Capstone.

Brake, Mark. Lonely Planet Kids How to Be a Space Explorer 1: Your Out-Of-this-World Adventure. 2014. (Lonely Planet Kids Ser.). (ENG., Illus.). 160p. (J). (gr. 4-7). 17.99 *(978-1-74360-434-2(3),* 4798) Lonely Planet Global Ltd. IRL. Dist: Hachette Bk. Group.

Bredeson, Carmen & Dyson, Marianne. Exploring the Solar System, 1 vol. 2015. (Launch into Space! Ser.). (ENG.). 32p. (gr. 3-4). pap. 11.52 *(978-0-7660-6825-4(0),* 4b64b9fb-0a7e-440c-b8c2-341749f50b25); (Illus.). 26.93 *(978-0-7660-6827-8(7),* ed937177-22ca-436f-8a1b-517879459bec) Enslow Publishing, LLC.

Briggs, Andrew, et al. Rocky Road to Galileo: What Is Our Place in the Solar System. Hudson, Brett, illus. 2018. (Curious Science Quest Ser.). (ENG.). 112p. (J). (gr. 4-7). pap. 9.99 *(978-0-7459-7752-2(9),* ebfe0159-0667-4a65-b662-1a99c486f5c3, Lion Children's) Lion Hudson PLC GBR. Dist: Baker & Taylor Publisher Services (BTPS).

Britannica, Learning Library. Exploring Space. 2003. (Illus.). 64p. 14.95 *(978-1-59339-031-0(9))* Encyclopaedia Britannica, Inc.

Cain, Marie Mowery. What's Out There. 2013. (Big Books, Red Ser.). (ENG & SPA., Illus.). 16p. pap. 33.00 *(978-1-59246-220-9(0))* Big Books, by George!

Carroll, Jillian. Zoom Around a Moon. 2003. (J). pap. *(978-1-58417-241-3(X))*; lib. bdg. *(978-1-58417-240-6(1))* Lake Street Pubs.

Carson-Dellosa Publishing Staff. Solar System. 2006. (Just the Facts: Information at Your Fingertips Ser.). (ENG., Illus.). 64p. (J). (gr. 5-8). 28.69 *(978-0-7696-4259-8(4))* School Specialty, Incorporated.

Carson, Mary Kay. Far-Out Guide to Asteroids & Comets, 1 vol. 2010. (Far-Out Guide to the Solar System Ser.). (ENG.). 48p. (gr. 4-6). 27.93 *(978-0-7660-3188-3(8),* ef621ce9-a9c4-4391-af35-ff224f2f3616); (Illus.). pap. 11.53 *(978-1-59845-191-7(X),* af49b015-2798-4dc0-b943-dd4255ef1c75, Enslow Elementary) Enslow Publishing, LLC.

—Far-Out Guide to Earth, 1 vol. 2010. (Far-Out Guide to the Solar System Ser.). (ENG., Illus.). 48p. (gr. 4-6). 27.93 *(978-0-7660-3182-1(9),* a97e976e-f3e1-46c8-adf9-ec6caf395793); pap. 11.53 *(978-1-59845-183-2(9),* 490ff62c-f68d-4ca0-80d1-47ea4a62001d, Enslow Elementary) Enslow Publishing, LLC.

—Far-Out Guide to Jupiter, 1 vol. 2010. (Far-Out Guide to the Solar System Ser.). (ENG., Illus.). 48p. (gr. 4-6). 27.93 *(978-0-7660-3184-5(5),* 6a16612d-06e6-4802-ac66-df8c9269eafe); pap. 11.53 *(978-1-59845-186-3(3),* 4b5484a6-d5b3-4d70-8e96-e53c1da4f205, Enslow Elementary) Enslow Publishing, LLC.

—Far-Out Guide to Mars, 1 vol. 2010. (Far-Out Guide to the Solar System Ser.). (ENG.). 48p. (gr. 4-6). 27.93 *(978-0-7660-3183-8(7),* 7d349ac4-2183-49c2-8f16-66babd497cf1); (Illus.). pap. 11.53 *(978-1-59845-185-6(5),* 66d79d97-21a4-4979-a50c-96e67ab5898c, Enslow Elementary) Enslow Publishing, LLC.

—Far-Out Guide to Mercury, 1 vol. 2010. (Far-Out Guide to the Solar System Ser.). (ENG.). 48p. (gr. 4-6). 27.93 *(978-0-7660-3180-7(2),* 75115966-2db2-45ef-b2d9-5b206ba9ef2f); (Illus.). pap. 11.53 *(978-1-59845-181-8(2),* 8ef5e73a-5a47-461e-a11c-1ee8f2535537, Enslow Elementary) Enslow Publishing, LLC.

—Far-Out Guide to Neptune, 1 vol. 2010. (Far-Out Guide to the Solar System Ser.). (ENG., Illus.). 48p. (gr. 4-6). 27.93 *(978-0-7660-3186-9(1),* 425d9053-44bb-4ac5-93c6-9be12d72702f); pap. 11.53 *(978-1-59845-189-4(8),* 441e756c-3661-4b0f-8ee9-89f36210b720, Enslow Elementary) Enslow Publishing, LLC.

—Far-Out Guide to Saturn, 1 vol. 2010. (Far-Out Guide to the Solar System Ser.). (ENG., Illus.). 48p. (gr. 4-6). 27.93 *(978-0-7660-3178-4(0),* f610accb-d855-4c03-8b9b-b0e463631f97); pap. 11.53 *(978-1-59845-187-0(1),* 4f3a3150-9627-4cc0-be5f-ba66b622b612, Enslow Elementary) Enslow Publishing, LLC.

—Far-Out Guide to the Icy Dwarf Planets, 1 vol. 2010. (Far-Out Guide to the Solar System Ser.). (ENG.). 48p. (gr. 4-6). 27.93 *(978-0-7660-3187-6(X),* 376518fd-e04e-4c0a-b22c-0c29b8ac92f6); (Illus.). pap. 11.53 *(978-1-59845-190-0(1),* 08d57ebd-172e-463a-adb1-2d5f7cc42352, Enslow Elementary) Enslow Publishing, LLC.

—Far-Out Guide to the Moon, 1 vol. 2010. (Far-Out Guide to the Solar System Ser.). (ENG., Illus.). 48p. (J). (gr. 4-6). 27.93 *(978-0-7660-3189-0(6),* 826e8346-b03a-4610-8f7d-5061c75e655c); pap. 11.53 *(978-1-59845-184-9(7),* f8c0fc43-18f4-42c5-822b-3c4cfab1bf73, Enslow Elementary) Enslow Publishing, LLC.

—Far-Out Guide to the Sun, 1 vol. 2010. (Far-Out Guide to the Solar System Ser.). (ENG., Illus.). 48p. (gr. 4-6). 27.93 *(978-0-7660-3179-1(9),* d196138e-e746-4a4e-ad8b-fe4084661cfa); pap. 11.53 *(978-1-59845-180-1(4),* 4782d60f-ea5c-4554-b13e-75df8985cb22, Enslow Elementary) Enslow Publishing, LLC.

—Far-Out Guide to Uranus, 1 vol. 2010. (Far-Out Guide to the Solar System Ser.). (ENG., Illus.). 48p. (gr. 4-6). 27.93 *(978-0-7660-3185-2(3),* c4f8ee8d-959a-4c90-9bb3-c86e9dfa2bf1); pap. 11.53 *(978-1-59845-188-7(X),* 29076029-53d5-438d-8fe2-7ae24254afca, Enslow Elementary) Enslow Publishing, LLC.

—Far-Out Guide to Venus, 1 vol. 2010. (Far-Out Guide to the Solar System Ser.). (ENG.). 48p. (gr. 4-6). 27.93 *(978-0-7660-3181-4(0),* f16b2313-fd0a-426e-804d-3d39f93c40cd); (Illus.). pap. 11.53 *(978-1-59845-182-5(0),* 70aacc1f-a42e-41a4-9620-10a972218964, Enslow Elementary) Enslow Publishing, LLC.

Carson, Mary Kay & Carson, Mary K. Extreme Planets Q & A. 2008. (Illus.). 48p. (J). (gr. k-4). 17.99 *(978-0-06-089975-2(1))* HarperCollins Pubs.

Chiger, Arielle & Houk Maley, Adrienne. 20 Fun Facts about Asteroids & Comets, 1 vol. 2014. (Fun Fact File: Space! Ser.). (ENG.). 32p. (J). (gr. 2-3). pap. 11.50 *(978-1-4824-0792-1(2),* a01b2aa5-6c85-45c4-9e30-65c53120aec0) Stevens, Gareth Publishing LLLP.

Close, Edward. Earth's Place in Space, 1 vol., 1. 2014. (Discovery Education: Earth & Space Science Ser.). (ENG.). 32p. (gr. 4-5). 28.93 *(978-1-4777-6174-8(8),* c6899b64-60a4-4306-97ce-ecbfa9a24883, PowerKids Pr.) Rosen Publishing Group, Inc., The.

Cole, Joanna. Lost in the Solar System. Degen, Bruce, illus. 2010. (Magic School Bus Ser.). (ENG.). (J). (gr. 2-5). audio compact disk 18.99 *(978-0-545-22337-9(7))* Scholastic, Inc.

—Our Solar System. 2014. (Magic School Bus Presents Ser.). lib. bdg. 17.20 *(978-0-606-35816-3(1))* Turtleback.

Crabtree Publishing, compiled by. Exploring Our Solar System Set. 2008. (J). (gr. 4-7). pap. *(978-0-7787-3744-5(6))* Crabtree Publishing Co.

Dalmatian Press Staff. My Race into Space! 2008. (ENG.). 9p. bds. 4.95 *(978-1-58117-717-6(8),* Intervisual/Piggy Toes) Bendon, Inc.

Davis, Kenneth C. Don't Know Much about the Solar System. Martin, Pedro, illus. 2004. (ENG.). 48p. (J). (gr. 1-4). pap. 7.99 *(978-0-06-446230-3(7),* HarperCollins) HarperCollins Pubs.

Delta Education. Sci Res Bk Foss Grade 5 Next Gen Ea. 2015. (Illus.). 336p. (J). lib. bdg. *(978-1-62571-448-0(3))* Delta Education, LLC.

Demuth, Patricia Brennan. The Sun: Our Amazing Star. 2016. (Illus.). 32p. (J). (gr. -1-1). pap. 4.99 *(978-0-448-48828-8(0),* Grosset & Dunlap) Penguin Young Readers Group.

Dickmann, Nancy. Exploring Beyond the Solar System, 1 vol. 2015. (Spectacular Space Science Ser.). (ENG., Illus.). 48p. (J). (gr. 5-6). 33.47 *(978-1-4994-3641-9(6),* c661c4b7-cd32-45d1-9413-c0fe5359a666, Rosen Central) Rosen Publishing Group, Inc., The.

—The Sun & the Solar System, 1 vol. 2018. (Space Facts & Figures Ser.). (ENG.). 32p. (gr. 2-3). 28.93 *(978-1-5081-9522-1(6),* 2e87bdaa-6b4b-4f46-ab7b-8c23b3685cf3, Windmill Bks.) Rosen Publishing Group, Inc., The.

Dillard, Mark. Journey Through the Asteroid Belt, 1 vol. 2014. (Spotlight on Space Science Ser.). (ENG., Illus.). 32p. (J). (gr. 5-5). pap. 12.75 *(978-1-4994-3641-9(6),* 65b9e245-219d-4e23-994d-5e081d483242, PowerKids Pr.) Rosen Publishing Group, Inc., The.

Dils, Tracey E. Around the Moon 1,2,3: A Space Counting Book. 2015. (1, 2, 3... Count with Me Ser.). (ENG., Illus.). 24p. (J). (gr. k-2). 19.95 *(978-1-60753-714-4(1))* Amicus Learning.

DiSiena, Laura Lyn & Eliot, Hannah. Saturn Could Sail: And Other Fun Facts. Oswald, Pete & Spurgeon, Aaron, illus. 2014. (Did You Know? Ser.). (ENG.). 32p. (J). (gr. -1-3). 17.99 *(978-1-4814-1429-6(1));* pap. 7.99 *(978-1-4814-1428-9(3))* Little Simon. (Little Simon).

DK. DKfindout! Solar System. 2016. (DK Findout! Ser.). (ENG., Illus.). 64p. (J). (gr. 1-4). pap. 10.99 *(978-1-4654-5428-7(4),* DK Children) Dorling Kindersley Publishing, Inc.

—Eyewitness Explorer: Night Sky Detective: Explore Nature with Loads of Fun Activities. 2015. (DK Eyewitness Explorers Ser.). (ENG., Illus.). 72p. (J). (gr. 3-7). pap. 9.99 *(978-1-4654-3501-9(8),* DK Children) Dorling Kindersley Publishing, Inc.

—First Space Encyclopedia: A Reference Guide to Our Galaxy & Beyond. 2016. (DK First Reference Ser.). (ENG., Illus.). 136p. (J). (gr. 1-4). 16.99 *(978-1-4654-4343-4(6),* DK Children) Dorling Kindersley Publishing, Inc.

—My Best Pop-Up Space Book. 2015. (Noisy Pop-Up Bks.). (ENG., Illus.). 18p. (J). (-k). bds. 15.99 *(978-1-4654-3914-7(5),* DK Children) Dorling Kindersley Publishing, Inc.

—Super Space Encyclopedia: The Furthest, Largest, Most Spectacular Features of Our Universe. 2019. (DK Super Nature Encyclopedias Ser.). (ENG., Illus.). 208p. (J). (gr. 4-7). 24.99 *(978-1-4654-8171-9(0),* DK Children) Dorling Kindersley Publishing, Inc.

Dobeck, Maryann. Circling the Sun. 2004. (Reading PowerWorks Ser.). (Illus.). 16p. (gr. 1-3). pap. 6.10 *(978-0-7608-8917-6(1))* Sundance/Newbridge Educational Publishing.

Dompierre, Judith E. No More Than Four of a Kind. 2012. 36p. pap. 24.95 *(978-1-4626-9329-0(6))* America Star Bks.

Dyer, Alan. Space. 2007. (Insiders Ser.). (ENG., Illus.). 64p. (J). (gr. 3-7). 19.99 *(978-1-4169-3860-6(5),* Simon & Schuster Bks. For Young Readers) Simon & Schuster Bks. For Young Readers.

Early Bird Astronomy, 15 vols., Set. Incl. Dwarf Planet Pluto. Vogt, Gregory. 2009. lib. bdg. 26.60 *(978-0-7613-4157-4(9));* Earth. Zuehlke, Jeffrey. 2009. lib. bdg. 26.60 *(978-0-7613-4149-9(8));* Jupiter. Hansen, Rosanna. 2009. lib. bdg. 26.60 *(978-0-7613-4153-6(6));* Mars. Storad, Conrad J. 2009. lib. bdg. 26.60 *(978-0-7613-4152-9(8));* Mercury. Vogt, Gregory. 2009. lib. bdg. 26.60 *(978-0-7613-4150-5(1));* Meteors & Comets. Vogt, Gregory. 2010. lib. bdg. 26.60 *(978-0-7613-3876-5(4));* Milky Way. Vogt, Gregory. 2010. lib. bdg. 26.60 *(978-0-7613-3875-8(6));* Moon. Waxman, Laura Hamilton. 2010. lib. bdg. 26.60 *(978-0-7613-3872-7(1));* Neptune. Fleisher, Paul. 2009. lib. bdg. 26.60 *(978-0-7613-4155-0(2));* Saturn. Waxman, Laura Hamilton. 2009. lib. bdg. 26.60 *(978-0-7613-4154-3(4));* Solar System. Waxman, Laura Hamilton. 2010. lib. bdg. 26.60 *(978-0-7613-3874-1(8));* Stars. Vogt, Gregory. 2010. lib. bdg. 26.60 *(978-0-7613-3873-4(X));* Sun. Waxman, Laura Hamilton. 2010. lib. bdg. 26.60 *(978-0-7613-3871-0(3));* Uranus. Vogt, Gregory. 2009. lib. bdg. 26.60 *(978-0-7613-4156-7(0));* Venus. Fleisher, Paul. 2009. lib. bdg. 26.60 *(978-0-7613-4151-2(X));* 48p. (gr. 2-5). 2009. Set lib. bdg. 399.00 *(978-0-7613-3870-3(5),* Lerner Pubns.) Lerner Publishing Group.

Ehlmann, Bethany. Dr. e's Super Stellar Solar System: Massive Mountains! Supersize Storms! Alien Atmospheres! 2018. (Science Superheroes Ser.). (Illus.). 128p. (J). (gr. 3-7). pap. 12.99 *(978-1-4263-2798-8(6),* National Geographic Kids) Disney Publishing Worldwide.

Exploring the Galaxy Pack [Scholastic]. 2010. (Exploring the Galaxy Ser.). 24p. pap. 4.41 *(978-1-4296-5818-8(5),* Capstone Pr.) Capstone.

Faulkner, Nicholas & Gregersen, Erik. The Inner Planets, 1 vol. 2018. (Universe & Our Place in It Ser.). (ENG., Illus.). 128p. (YA). (gr. 10-10). pap. 20.95 *(978-1-5081-0607-4(X),* e1e432dd-73fe-439a-b801-5ca0617acbb5, Britannica Educational Publishing) Rosen Publishing Group, Inc., The.

—The Milky Way & Other Galaxies, 1 vol. 2018. (Universe & Our Place in It Ser.). (ENG., Illus.). 128p. (J). (gr. 10-10). pap. 20.95 *(978-1-5081-0610-4(X),* 3f8f62f2-5360-48df-9a84-ca92018e98c3, Britannica Educational Publishing) Rosen Publishing Group, Inc., The.

—The Outer Planets, 1 vol. 2018. (Universe & Our Place in It Ser.). (ENG.). 128p. (gr. 10-10). pap. 20.95 *(978-1-5081-0598-5(7),* aaf04b41-74a7-4a2b-8097-1bf55150abde, Britannica Educational Publishing) Rosen Publishing Group, Inc., The.

—The Sun & the Origins of the Solar System, 1 vol. 2018. (Universe & Our Place in It Ser.). (ENG.). 128p. (gr. 10-10). pap. 20.95 *(978-1-5081-0604-3(5),* f7416183-e1f7-4006-a8d8-5502f3dd64e5, Britannica Educational Publishing) Rosen Publishing Group, Inc., The.

Ferrie, Chris. 8 Little Planets. Doyle, Lizzy, illus. 2018. 18p. (J). (gr. -1-k). bds. 10.99 *(978-1-4926-7124-4(X))* Sourcebooks, Inc.

Finton, Nancy. Explore the Solar System! 2010. (Illus.). 29p. (J). *(978-0-545-28884-2(3))* Scholastic, Inc.

Fleisher, Paul. Venus. 2009. (Early Bird Astronomy Ser.). (ENG.). 48p. (gr. 2-5). lib. bdg. 26.60 *(978-0-7613-4151-2(X))* Lerner Publishing Group.

Ford, Adam. Stars: A Family Guide to the Night Sky. 2016. (Discover Together Guides). (ENG., Illus.). 48p. 16.95 *(978-1-61180-283-2(0),* Roost Books) Shambhala Pubns., Inc.

Fraknoi, Andrew & Schatz, Dennis. When the Sun Goes Dark. 2017. (ENG., Illus.). 36p. (J). (gr. 4-7). pap. 14.95 *(978-1-68140-011-2(1),* P541847) National Science Teachers Assn.

Fun Fact File: Space! 2014. (Fun Fact File: Space! Ser.). 32p. (J). (gr. 2-5). pap. 63.00 *(978-1-4824-1603-9(4))* Stevens, Gareth Publishing LLLP.

Gendell, Megan & Sweitzer, James. Spinning 'round the Sun: Everything You Wanted to Know about the Solar System & Everything in It. 2008. (Illus.). 32p. (J). pap. *(978-0-545-04459-2(6))* Scholastic, Inc.

Gifford, Clive. Out of This World: All the Cool Stuff about Space You Want to Knkow. 2012. (ENG., Illus.). 144p. (J). (gr. 4-6). 9.99 *(978-1-60652-519-7(0))* Reader's Digest Assn., Inc., The.

—Out of This World: All the Cool Stuff about Space You Want to Know. Pinder, Andrew, illus. 2012. 143p. (J). *(978-1-60652-571-5(9))* Reader's Digest Assn., Inc., The.

—The Solar System, Meteors, & Comets. 2015. (Watch This Space! Ser.). (ENG., Illus.). 32p. (J). (gr. 4-5). lib. bdg. *(978-0-7787-2023-2(3))* Crabtree Publishing Co.

Goldsmith, Mike. The Kingfisher Space Encyclopedia. 2017. (Kingfisher Encyclopedias Ser.). (ENG.). 160p. (J). pap. 13.99 *(978-0-7534-7353-5(4),* 900174958, Kingfisher) Roaring Brook Pr.

—Listopia: Space. 2016. (ENG., Illus.). 208p. (J). (gr. 2-5). pap. 9.99 *(978-1-4998-0280-1(3))* Little Bee Books Inc.

—Space. 2010. (Ripley Twists Ser.). 48p. (J). (gr. 3-18). lib. bdg. 19.95 *(978-1-4222-1833-4(3))* Mason Crest.

—Space Adventure. Abbott, Simon, illus. 2011. (Flip Flap Science Ser.). (ENG.). 10p. (J). (gr. -1-k). 9.95 *(978-1-84898-364-9(6),* TickTock Books) Octopus Publishing Group GBR. Dist: Independent Pubs. Group.

Goldstein, Margaret. The Sun. 2009. pap. 6.95 *(978-0-8225-4760-0(0))* Lerner Publishing Group.

Goldstein, Margaret J. The Solar System. 2003. (Our Universe Ser.). (ENG., Illus.). 32p. (gr. 2-4). lib. bdg. 22.60 *(978-0-8225-4657-3(4))* Lerner Publishing Group.

—The Sun. 2003. (Our Universe Ser.). (ENG., Illus.). 32p. (gr. 2-4). lib. bdg. 22.60 *(978-0-8225-4647-4(7))* Lerner Publishing Group.

Graham, Ian. Solar System. Kelly, Richard, ed. 2017. 48p. (J). pap. 9.95 *(978-1-78209-646-7(9))* Miles Kelly Publishing, Ltd. GBR. Dist: Parkwest Pubns., Inc.

Group/McGraw-Hill, Wright. Earth & Physical Science: Our Solar System, 6 vols. (Book2WebTM Ser.). (gr. 4-8). 36.50 *(978-0-322-04427-2(8))* Wright Group/McGraw-Hill.

Hansen, Grace. Asteroids & Meteoroids. 2017. (Our Galaxy Ser.). (ENG., Illus.). 24p. (J). (gr. -1-2). lib. bdg. 32.79 *(978-1-5321-0049-9(3),* 25172, Abdo Kids) ABDO Publishing Co.

Hantula, Richard & Asimov, Isaac. Our Planetary System, 1 vol. 2004. (Isaac Asimov's 21st Century Library of the Universe: near & Far Ser.). (ENG., Illus.). 32p. (gr. 3-5). lib. bdg. 28.67 *(978-0-8368-3969-2(2),* 23b2763f-e3ec-42a1-8d08-e916b0b7e303) Stevens, Gareth Publishing LLLP.

Harman, Alice. Planets, 1 vol., 1. 2015. (Fact Finders: Space Ser.). (ENG., Illus.). 24p. (J). (gr. 2-2). pap. 9.25 *(978-1-5081-9133-9(6),* 1b6bc0e0-f267-457f-8e9e-da57821281fb, Windmill Bks.) Rosen Publishing Group, Inc., The.

Hartson, Tamara. Planets, 1 vol. 2018. (Mega Machines Ser.). (ENG., Illus.). 64p. (J). pap. 6.99 *(978-1-926700-88-5(0),* 9d23404f-6062-4abf-bf4b-368c290af7e8) Blue Bike Bks. CAN. Dist: Lone Pine Publishing USA.

Hawksett, David. Interstellar! Can You Explore Beyond the Solar System?, 1 vol. 2017. (Be a Space Scientist! Ser.). (ENG.). 48p. (J). (gr. 5-5). 31.93 *(978-1-5383-2203-1(X),* 03d76bc6-e3c8-4724-a1a4-02a910e3d059); pap. 12.75 *(978-1-5383-2296-3(X),* fadc571d-a9dc-4eb2-8669-4dfa14612597) Rosen Publishing Group, Inc., The. (PowerKids Pr.).

Heather Zschock. Solar System Scratch & Sketch. 2006. (Activity Book Ser.). 64p. (J). spiral bd. 12.99 *(978-1-59359-917-1(X))* Peter Pauper Pr. Inc.

Higgins, Nadia. The Solar System Through Infographics. Waananen, Lisa, illus. 2013. (Super Science Infographics Ser.). (ENG.). 32p. (J). (gr. 3-5). pap. 8.99 *(978-1-4677-1594-2(8),* 3acd4aaa-7a00-416d-a3d2-3842cb643a8a); lib. bdg. 26.65 *(978-1-4677-1289-7(2),* 5f6dcd81-0f00-413a-9ae7-a11ba64858a9, Lerner Pubns.) Lerner Publishing Group.

Hill, Carolyn L. Journey Through Eclipses, 1 vol. 2014. (Spotlight on Space Science Ser.). (ENG.). 32p. (J). (gr. 5-5). pap. 12.75 *(978-1-4994-0377-0(1),* 9d1318e2-a635-45e2-bfd3-34b7fadc1a52, PowerKids Pr.) Rosen Publishing Group, Inc., The.

Hirsch, Rebecca E. Planets in Action (an Augmented Reality Experience) 2020. (Space in Action: Augmented Reality (Alternator Books (r)) Ser.). (ENG., Illus.). 32p. (J). (gr. 3-6). 31.99 *(978-1-5415-7878-4(3),* ef4d75cc-e332-4a14-8ef4-1e3fb085f32c, Lerner Pubns.) Lerner Publishing Group.

—Stars & Galaxies in Action (an Augmented Reality Experience) 2020. (Space in Action: Augmented Reality (Alternator Books (r)) Ser.). (ENG., Illus.). 32p. (J). (gr. 3-6). 31.99 *(978-1-5415-7879-1(1),* 686a08b9-0661-4a79-8f0e-c7872e988b9d, Lerner Pubns.) Lerner Publishing Group.

Hoffmann, Sara. The Little Book of Space. 2005. (Little Bks.). (ENG., Illus.). 24p. (J). (gr. -1-2). 9.95 *(978-1-58728-485-4(5))* Cooper Square Publishing Llc.

Holt, Rinehart and Winston Staff. Holt Science & Technology Chapter 20: Earth Science: Formation of the Solar System. 5th ed. 2004. (Illus.). pap. 12.86 *(978-0-03-030341-8(9))* Holt McDougal.

—Holt Science Spectrum Chptr. 19: The Solar System. 4th ed. Date not set. pap. 11.20 *(978-0-03-068058-8(1))* Holt McDougal.

Jackson, Ellen. Worlds Around Us: A Space Voyage. Miller, Ron, illus. 2006. (Exceptional Science Title for Intermediate Grades). 37p. (J). (gr. 3-7). lib. bdg. 23.93 *(978-0-7613-3405-7(X),* Millbrook Pr.) Lerner Publishing Group.

Jackson, Tom. The Magic School Bus Presents: Our Solar System: a Nonfiction Companion to the Original Magic School Bus Series. Bracken, Carolyn, illus. 2014. (Magic School Bus Presents Ser.). (ENG.). 32p. (J). (gr. 1-3). pap. 7.99 *(978-0-545-68365-4(3),* Scholastic Paperbacks) Scholastic, Inc.

Jacobson, Bray. Cycles in Space, 1 vol. 2019. (Look at Nature's Cycles Ser.). (ENG.). 32p. (gr. 2-2). pap. 11.50 *(978-1-5382-4102-8(1),* 7760a719-9624-474b-a10c-07e61e7af6b8) Stevens, Gareth Publishing LLLP.

Jacobson, Linda. Our Super Solar System, 1 vol. 2012. (InfoMax Readers Ser.). (ENG., Illus.). 24p. (J). (gr. 1-1). pap. 8.25 *(978-1-4488-9070-5(5),* d28250de-aa8f-4668-836b-86a8a652178b, Rosen Classroom) Rosen Publishing Group, Inc., The.

Jankéliowitch, Anne. Barefoot Books Solar System. Buxton, Annabelle, illus. 2019. (ENG.). 52p. (J). (gr. 3-7). 19.99 *(978-1-78285-823-2(7))* Barefoot Bks., Inc.

Jemison, Mae & Rau, Dana Meachen. Journey Through Our Solar System. 2013. (True Book™—Dr. Mae Jemison & 100 Year Starship™ Ser.). (ENG., Illus.). 48p. (J). lib. bdg. 29.00 *(978-0-531-25501-8(8))* Scholastic Library Publishing.

Jenkins, Martin. Exploring Space: from Galileo to the Mars Rover & Beyond. Biesty, Stephen, illus. 2017. (ENG.). 64p. (J). (gr. 3-7). 17.99 *(978-0-7636-8931-5(9))* Candlewick Pr.

Kazlow, Samuel, ed. Astronomy: Understanding Celestial Bodies, 1 vol. 2014. (Study of Science Ser.). (ENG.). 136p. (YA). (gr. 8-8). 37.82 *(978-1-62275-406-9(9),* b2697070-f990-4c14-bff5-4257f194b114) Rosen Publishing Group, Inc., The.

Kessler, Colleen. A Project Guide to the Solar System. 2010. (Earth Science Projects for Kids Ser.). (Illus.). 48p. (J). (gr. 4-7). lib. bdg. 29.95 *(978-1-58415-867-7(0))* Mitchell Lane Pubs.

Kizer Whitt, Kelly. Solar System Forecast, 1 vol. Allen Klein, Laurie, illus. 2012. 32p. (J). (SPA.). (gr. -1-4). 17.95 *(978-1-60718-678-6(0));* (ENG.). (gr. -1-4). 17.95 *(978-1-60718-523-9(7));* (ENG.). (gr. -1-4). pap. 9.95 *(978-1-60718-532-1(6));* (SPA.). (gr. 4-5). pap. 11.95 *(978-1-62855-425-0(8),* 37d710b2-fba7-4415-9f35-5e65258eecc7) Arbordale Publishing.

Kopp, Megan. Unlocking the Secrets of the Solar System. 2019. (Mission: Space Science Ser.). (Illus.). 48p. (J). (gr. 5-5). *(978-0-7787-5396-4(4));* pap. *(978-0-7787-5407-7(3))* Crabtree Publishing Co.

Kortenkamp, Steve. Asteroids, Comets, & Meteoroids. 2011. (Solar System & Beyond Ser.). (ENG.). 32p. (J). (gr. 3-4). pap. 48.60 *(978-1-4296-7224-5(2),* 16779); pap. 8.10 *(978-1-4296-7223-8(4),* 116833) Capstone. (Capstone Pr.).

—The Dwarf Planets. 2010. (Solar System & Beyond Ser.). (ENG.). 32p. (J). (gr. 3-4). pap. 48.60 *(978-1-4296-6406-6(1),* 16152, Capstone Pr.) Capstone.

—The Planets of Our Solar System. 2010. (Solar System & Beyond Ser.). (ENG.). 32p. (J). (gr. 3-4). pap. 48.60 *(978-1-4296-6410-3(X),* 16156, Capstone Pr.); lib. bdg. 27.99 *(978-1-4296-5396-1(5),* 113819) Capstone.

Koupelis, Theo. In Quest of the Solar System. rev. ed. 2010. (ENG.). 399p. (J). pap. 194.95 *(978-0-7637-6629-0(1))* Jones & Bartlett Learning, LLC.

Kruesi, Liz. Discover Space Exploration. 2016. (Searchlight Books (tm) — What's Cool about Science? Ser.). (ENG., Illus.). 40p. (J). (gr. 3-5). 30.65 *(978-1-5124-0811-9(5),* 1fb5a99a-38ad-49de-bf70-ed8d315026f8, Lerner Pubns.) Lerner Publishing Group.

Kruszelnicki, Karl. Dr Karl's Little Book of Space. 2017. (ENG.). 160p. (J). (gr. 2-4). pap. 9.99 *(978-1-925481-23-5(9),* Pan) Pan Macmillan Australia Pty, Ltd. AUS. Dist: Independent Pubs. Group.

Kukla, Lauren. The Amazing Universe. 2016. (Exploring Our Universe Ser.). (ENG., Illus.). 32p. (J). (gr. 3-6). lib. bdg. 32.79 *(978-1-68078-402-2(1),* 23663, Checkerboard Library) ABDO Publishing Co.

Labrecque, Ellen. Earth & Other Planets. 2019. (Our Place in the Universe Ser.). (ENG., Illus.). 24p. (J). (gr. 1-3). 25.99 *(978-1-9771-0848-7(2),* 140466, Pebble) Capstone.

Ladybird. Our Solar System - Read It Yourself with Ladybird Level 4. 2016. (Read It Yourself with Ladybird Ser.). 48p. (J). (gr. 2-4). (ENG.). 5.99 *(978-0-241-23743-4(2));* pap. 9.99 *(978-0-241-23741-0(6))* Penguin Bks., Ltd. GBR. Dist: Independent Pubs. Group.

Law, Felicia & Bailey, Gerry. Trouble in Space. Noyes, Leighton, illus. 2015. (Science to the Rescue Ser.). (ENG.). 32p. (J). (gr. 4-4). *(978-0-7787-1676-1(7))* Crabtree Publishing Co.

Lawrence, Richard. Our Universe. 2004. (Illus.). vi, 134p. (gr. 1-6). pap. 18.00 *(978-0-9725365-4-7(X))* Boarding House Publishing.

Leigh, Autumn. A Trip Through Our Solar System. (Reading Room Collection 1 Ser.). 16p. (gr. 2-3). 2009. 37.50 *(978-1-60851-940-8(6),* PowerKids Pr.) 2006. (ENG.). 37.95 *(978-1-4042-6219-5(9))* 2005. (ENG., Illus.). (J). lib. bdg. 22.27 *(978-1-4042-3345-4(8),* 2f245f59-80a4-4f91-bc4b-eb088fbe60b6, PowerKids Pr.) Rosen Publishing Group, Inc., The.

L'Hommedieu, Arthur John. Children of the Sun. L'Hommedieu, Arthur John, illus. (Illus.). 24p. (J). (gr. k-11). spiral bd. 10.99 *(978-0-85953-939-5(3))* Child's Play International Ltd. GBR. Dist: Child's Play-International.

—Our Solar System. 2018. (Information Bks.). (Illus.). 36p. (J). *(978-1-84643-594-2(3))* Child's Play International Ltd.

Linde, Barbara. Math in Our Solar System: Applying Problem-Solving Strategies. 2009. (PowerMath: Proficiency Plus Ser.). 32p. (gr. 4-5). 47.90 *(978-1-60851-413-7(7),* PowerKids Pr.) Rosen Publishing Group, Inc., The.

Linde, Barbara M. Math in Our Solar System: Applying Problem-Solving Strategies, 1 vol. (Math for the REAL World Ser.). (ENG.). 32p. (gr. 5-6). 2009. pap. 10.00 *(978-1-4042-5135-9(9),* 47c1cfe1-7782-47b5-8a24-378e22c6764a) 2004. (Illus.). (J). lib. bdg. 28.93 *(978-1-4042-2936-5(1),* 381f9a73-425d-4ac2-aeb8-53eda63581f4, PowerKids Pr.) Rosen Publishing Group, Inc., The.

Loomis, Ilima. Eclipse Chaser: Science in the Moon's Shadow. 2019. (Scientists in the Field Ser.). (ENG., Illus.). 80p. (J). (gr. 5-7). 18.99 *(978-1-328-77096-7(6),* 1681112, Clarion Bks.) HarperCollins Pubs.

Lopez, Delano. The Solar System: Out of This World with Science Activities for Kids. Slater, Jason, illus. 2019. (Build It Yourself Ser.). (ENG.). 128p. (J). (gr. 4-6). 22.95 *(978-1-61930-794-0(4),* 329dacbf-73b3-4968-82a1-3ee65b64455a); pap. 17.95 *(978-1-61930-797-1(9),* dda7d1f8-af61-46a6-a5fa-223afd67b1a8) Nomad Pr.

Loria, Laura. What Is a Constellation?, 1 vol. 2014. (Let's Find Out! Space Science Ser.). (ENG.). 32p. (J). (gr. 2-3). 26.06 *(978-1-62275-476-2(X),* 7eed2aac-c84c-4391-b199-d071a2a9dca2) Rosen Publishing Group, Inc., The.

The Magic School Bus: Lost in the Solar System. 2011. (J). audio compact disk 9.99 *(978-0-545-22880-0(8))* Scholastic, Inc.

Margles, Samantha. Earth's Solar System. 2014. (Illus.). 32p. (J). pap. *(978-0-545-58517-0(X))* Scholastic, Inc.

Martin, Justin McCory. Planets. 2010. (Illus.). 16p. (J). pap. *(978-0-545-13738-6(1))* Scholastic, Inc.

Mason Crest. Far Planets & Beyond, Vol. 7. 2016. (Solar System Ser.: Vol. 7). (ENG., Illus.). 48p. (J). (gr. 5-8). 20.95 *(978-1-4222-3550-8(5))* Mason Crest.

—Our Home Planet, Vol. 7. 2016. (Solar System Ser.: Vol. 7). (ENG., Illus.). 48p. (J). (gr. 5-8). 20.95 *(978-1-4222-3549-2(1))* Mason Crest.

Mattern, Joanne. Our Moon. 2010. (Solar System & Beyond Ser.). (ENG.). 32p. (J). (gr. 3-4). pap. 48.60 *(978-1-4296-6408-0(8)*, 16153, Capstone Pr.) Capstone.

Maunsell, Simonne. Fluffy Clouds. 2013. 20p. pap. 10.95 *(978-1-4525-7180-5(5)*, Balboa Pr.) Author Solutions, LLC.

McAnulty, Stacy. Moon! Earth's Best Friend. Lewis, Stevie, illus. 2019. (Our Universe Ser.: 3). (ENG.). 40p. (J). 19.99 *(978-1-250-19934-8(4)*, 900194811, Holt, Henry & Co. Bks. For Young Readers) Holt, Henry & Co.

McDonald, Jill. Hello, World! Solar System. 2016. (Hello, World! Ser.). (Illus.). 26p. (J). (— 1). bds. 8.99 *(978-0-553-52103-0(9)*, Doubleday Bks. for Young Readers) Random Hse. Children's Bks.

McGranaghan, John. Meet the Planets, 1 vol. Allen Klein, Laurie, illus. 2011. (ENG.). 32p. (J). (gr. k-5). 16.95 *(978-1-60718-123-1(1))* Arbordale Publishing.

—Meet the Planets, 1 vol. Klein, Laurie Allen, illus. 2011. (ENG.). 32p. (J). (gr. 2-3). pap. 10.95 *(978-1-60718-869-8(4)*, 5e404ef3-2e85-459a-8a0e-313c78697a63) Arbordale Publishing.

—Meet the Planets, 1 vol. Allen Klein, Laurie, illus. 2011. (SPA.). 32p. (J). (gr. 2-3). pap. 11.95 *(978-1-62855-411-3(8)*, 9eb8a5f1-e6ae-4452-a965-6f7128491aa7) Arbordale Publishing.

McMahon, Michael. Why Do Stars Twinkle?, 1 vol. 2010. (Solving Science Mysteries Ser.). (ENG., Illus.). 24p. (gr. 4-5). (J). pap. 9.25 *(978-1-61531-921-3(2)*, ee0bbc47-47cf-4000-9754-0d04979b329a, PowerKids Pr.); (YA). lib. bdg. 26.27 *(978-1-61531-895-7(X)*, 5cb41215-5515-48d4-961e-8de23820e0e3) Rosen Publishing Group, Inc., The.

Meachen Rau, Dana & Picture Window Books Staff. Giran en el Espacio: Un Libro Sobre Los Planetas. Robledo, Sol, tr. Shea, Denise, illus. 2007. (Ciencia Asombrosa: Exploremos el Espacio Ser.). (SPA.). 24p. (J). (gr. k-4). 27.32 *(978-1-4048-3231-2(9)*, 93780, Picture Window Bks.) Capstone.

Miller, Ron. Stars & Galaxies. 2006. (Worlds Beyond Ser.). (Illus.). 96p. (J). (gr. 5-9). 27.93 *(978-0-7613-3466-8(1)*, Twenty-First Century Bks.) Lerner Publishing Group.

Mills, Nathan & Block, Dakota. Exploring the Solar System, 1 vol. 2012. (Rosen Readers Ser.). (ENG., Illus.). 24p. (J). (gr. 1-2). pap. 8.25 *(978-1-4488-8857-3(3)*, 299c01d7-d01b-4f63-af8e-f4cbbba42b72, Rosen Classroom) Rosen Publishing Group, Inc., The.

Monier, Eric M., ed. How Life on Earth Is Affected by Earth's Unique Placement & Orientation in Our Solar System: An Anthology of Current Thought. 2009. (Contemporary Discourse in the Field of Astronomy Ser.). 240p. (gr. 10-10). 63.90 *(978-1-61511-903-5(5))* Rosen Publishing Group, Inc., The.

Moore, Patrick & Lawrence, Pete. Exploring the Mysteries of Astronomy, 1 vol. 2016. (STEM Guide to the Universe Ser.). (ENG.). 192p. (YA). (gr. 9-9). lib. bdg. 47.80 *(978-1-4994-6411-5(8)*, 475029ed-8b83-4680-9afe-1a89e0ca780b) Rosen Publishing Group, Inc., The.

Mosco, Rosemary. Science Comics: Solar System: Our Place in Space. Chad, Jon, illus. 2018. (Science Comics Ser.). (ENG.). 128p. (J). 21.99 *(978-1-62672-142-5(4)*, 900140352); pap. 12.99 *(978-1-62672-141-8(6)*, 900140351) Roaring Brook Pr. (First Second Bks.).

Nagelhout, Ryan. What Is a Moon?, 1 vol. 2014. (Let's Find Out! Space Science Ser.). (ENG.). 32p. (J). (gr. 2-3). 26.06 *(978-1-62275-466-3(2)*, 69130890-627f-4f2a-9f1e-0f1236a5c654) Rosen Publishing Group, Inc., The.

Nardo, Don. Asteroids & Comets. 2009. (Extreme Threats Ser.). 112p. (YA). lib. bdg. 28.95 *(978-1-59935-121-6(8))* Reynolds, Morgan Inc.

National Geographic Learning. Language, Literacy & Vocabulary - Reading Expeditions (Earth Science): Earth in Space. 2007. (ENG., Illus.). 36p. (J). pap. 20.95 *(978-0-7922-5428-7(7))* CENGAGE Learning.

Nelson, John. Collision Course: Asteroids & Earth. 2008. (Jr. Graphic Environmental Dangers Ser.). (ENG.). 24p. (J). 47.90 *(978-1-61532-098-1(9)*, PowerKids Pr.) Rosen Publishing Group, Inc., The.

—Trayectoría de Choque: Los Asteroides y la Tierra, 1 vol. 2009. (Historietas Juveniles: Peligros Del Medicambiente (Jr. Graphic Environmental Dangers) Ser.). (SPA., Illus.). 24p. (gr. 4-4). pap. 10.60 *(978-1-4358-8478-6(7)*, 45ea6c5c-bd39-4c77-a92c-2a1929fbc226); (YA). lib. bdg. 28.93 *(978-1-4358-8477-9(9)*, d51818e0-5943-445b-93ac-06f1a95ae46f) Rosen Publishing Group, Inc., The.

The New Solar System, 12 Vol Set. 2009. (New Solar System Ser.). (ENG.). (gr. 4-6). 276.00 *(978-1-60413-244-1(2)*, P166427, Chelsea Clubhse.) Infobase Holdings, Inc.

Nicolson, Cynthia Pratt & Bourgeois, Paulette. The Jumbo Book of Space. Nicolson, Cynthia Pratt & Slavin, Bill, illus. 2007. (Jumbo Bks.). 208p. (J). 17.95 *(978-1-55453-020-5(2))* Kids Can Pr., Ltd. CAN. Dist: Hachette Bk. Group.

O'Donnell, Kerri. Moons of Our Solar System. (Science Scope Ser.). 32p. (gr. 5-5). 2009. 47.90 *(978-1-60853-055-7(8))* 2009. (ENG.). (J). lib. bdg. 28.93 *(978-1-4358-2996-1(4)*, e812ee38-93b8-4e22-9080-80f8167da808) 2008. (ENG., Illus.). (J). pap. 10.00 *(978-1-4358-0181-3(4)*, d32936cf-3d23-405d-9e01-1e5543f22dcb) Rosen Publishing Group, Inc., The. (PowerKids Pr.).

—Space Circles: Learning about Radius & Diameter, 1 vol. (Math for the REAL World Ser.). (ENG., 32p. (gr. 4-5). 2010. Illus.). pap. 10.00 *(978-0-8239-8878-5(3)*, 03e2b502-0b41-4e57-b524-707195876408, PowerKids Pr.) 2004. 47.50 *(978-0-8239-7651-5(3))* Rosen Publishing Group, Inc., The.

Olien, Rebecca. Exploring the Planets in Our Solar System. (Objects in the Sky Ser.). 24p. (gr. 3-3). 2009. 42.50 *(978-1-60851-141-9(3))* 2007. (ENG., Illus.). (J). lib. bdg. 26.27 *(978-1-4042-3467-3(5)*, a3e1acfe-1a80-4987-9269-aac56a1fa428) Rosen Publishing Group, Inc., The. (PowerKids Pr.).

Orme, David. Comets. 2009. (Fact to Fiction Ser.). (Illus.). 36p. (J). pap. 6.95 *(978-0-7891-7899-2(0))* Perfection Learning Corp.

Orme, Helen. Solar System. 2010. (Science Everywhere! Ser.). 24p. 24.25 *(978-1-84898-292-5(5))* Black Rabbit Bks.

Our Solar System. (Jump Ser.). 36p. (J). (gr. 2-7). pap. *(978-1-882210-23-7(9))* Action Publishing, Inc.

Our Solar System, 1 vol., 1. 2015. (Our Wonderful World Ser.). 8p. (J). (gr. 2-4). pap. 9.35 *(978-1-5081-1235-8(5)*, b7a4ec17-74e6-4bbd-9c8f-a9abe3190bbb); pap. 9.35 *(978-1-5081-1259-4(2)*, e41f6251-a545-4962-b747-60846d6f2ed5); (ENG & SPA.). pap. 9.35 *(978-1-5081-1253-2(3)*, 80d04961-1e2a-4c82-a3c0-db41d46761f7); pap. 9.35 *(978-1-5081-1241-9(X)*, 314c2b09-51f4-43e4-b4be-05a66307a62f); pap. 9.35 *(978-1-5081-1247-1(9)*, a0b7095a-abd2-44a1-b2ef-47424e438965); pap. 9.35 *(978-1-5081-1223-5(1)*, b41c2c2f-f3a9-4e76-b9f8-016fa5dbf5fc) Rosen Publishing Group, Inc., The. (Rosen Classroom).

Our Solar System: An easy, practical book to understand the planets in our Solar System. Written especially for kids to learn about science & Nature. 2006. 108p. per. *(978-956-291-336-2(8))* Editorial Benei Noaj.

Our Solar System: Level Q, 6 vols. (Wonder Worldtm Ser.). 48p. 39.95 *(978-0-7802-2952-5(5))* Wright Group/McGraw-Hill.

Outer Space. 2014. (Ken Jennings' Junior Genius Guides). (ENG., Illus.). 160p. (J). (gr. 3-5). pap. 9.99 *(978-1-4814-0170-8(X)*, Little Simon) Little Simon.

Owen, Ruth. Asteroids & the Asteroid Belt, 1 vol. 2012. (Explore Outer Space Ser.). (ENG., Illus.). 32p. (J). (gr. 2-3). 29.93 *(978-1-4488-8073-7(4)*, 639f4d8a-5ae7-4cdd-af50-22283b99c762); pap. 11.00 *(978-1-4488-8115-4(3)*, c9b14d62-64aa-49a9-a252-1ade427d9544) Rosen Publishing Group, Inc., The. (Windmill Bks.).

Oxlade, Chris. Space Watch: The Sun. 2010. (Eye on Space Ser.). 24p. (J). pap. 8.25 *(978-1-61532-550-4(6)*, PowerKids Pr.); (ENG.). (gr. 1-1). lib. bdg. 26.27 *(978-1-61532-543-6(3)*, 8c49acef-9257-4f16-b0ad-883f41c43021) Rosen Publishing Group, Inc., The.

Pamplona, Alberto Hernández. A Visual Guide to the Universe, 1 vol. 2017. (Visual Exploration of Science Ser.). (ENG.). 104p. (J). (gr. 8-8). 38.80 *(978-1-5081-7585-8(3)*, 84f6d373-825b-4bd3-8716-7be994ea572d, Rosen Young Adult) Rosen Publishing Group, Inc., The.

Parker, Steve. Beyond the Solar System: From Red Giants to Black Holes, 1 vol. 2007. (Earth & Space Ser.). (ENG., Illus.). 48p. (YA). (gr. 6-6). lib. bdg. 34.47 *(978-1-4042-3739-1(9)*, d6e8bf1b-23e2-473d-a945-c78caa20dd00) Rosen Publishing Group, Inc., The.

Peddicord, Jane Anne. Night Wonders. Peddicord, Jane Anne, illus. 2005. (Illus.). 32p. (J). (gr. 1-4). pap. 7.95 *(978-1-57091-878-0(3))* Charlesbridge Publishing, Inc.

Peters, Elisa. The Planets, 1 vol. 2012. (PowerKids Readers: the Universe Ser.). (ENG., Illus.). 24p. (J). (gr. k-k). pap. 9.25 *(978-1-4488-7468-2(8)*, 61ef777b-7c63-4423-b844-ff3e09940789); lib. bdg. 26.27 *(978-1-4488-7389-0(4)*, 6a069236-6acb-4c72-87f4-a82cd76b7241) Rosen Publishing Group, Inc., The. (PowerKids Pr.).

—The Planets: Los Planetas, 1 vol. 2012. (PowerKids Readers: el Universo / the Universe Ser.). (SPA & ENG., Illus.). 24p. (J). (gr. k-k). lib. bdg. 26.27 *(978-1-4488-7825-3(X)*, 4be1d7d2-c7de-47a4-a856-e6dda99b01a8, PowerKids Pr.) Rosen Publishing Group, Inc., The.

Pop-Out Play Pak: Solar System. Orig. Title: Child's Play. (Illus.). 24p. (J). (gr. -1-4). reprint ed. *(978-1-881469-77-3(8))* Safari, Ltd.

Portman, Michael. Are There Other Earths?, 1 vol. 2013. (Space Mysteries Ser.). (ENG., Illus.). 32p. (gr. 2-3). 29.27 *(978-1-4339-8257-6(9)*, cd7a7a65-6058-4c35-89f2-8301d2fb0c05); pap. 11.50 *(978-1-4339-8258-3(7)*, fdbb7dc5-bb23-44e2-8dc9-b78d54e13c49) Stevens, Gareth Publishing LLLP. (Gareth Stevens Learning Library).

—Could an Asteroid Harm Earth?, 1 vol. 2013. (Space Mysteries Ser.). (ENG., Illus.). 32p. (J). (gr. 2-3). pap. 11.50 *(978-1-4339-8268-2(4)*, 25afa75b-2c45-4999-96b3-165f097edc08); lib. bdg. 29.27 *(978-1-4339-8267-5(6)*, ca005ed8-1850-494b-9248-93422aba580a) Stevens, Gareth Publishing LLLP.

Poynter, Margaret. Doomsday Rocks from Space, 1 vol. 2011. (Bizarre Science Ser.). (ENG., Illus.). 48p. (gr. 5-7). pap. 11.53 *(978-1-59845-221-1(5)*, dae07014-6bdf-4323-9137-9a1957131214); lib. bdg. 27.93 *(978-0-7660-3673-4(1)*, f079c330-9fef-49e3-b70a-91766494ca8f) Enslow Publishing, LLC.

Prendergast, Gabrielle. If Pluto Was a Pea. Gerlings, Rebecca, illus. 2019. (ENG.). 40p. (J). (gr. -1-3). 17.99 *(978-1-5344-0435-9(X)*, McElderry, Margaret K. Bks.) McElderry, Margaret K. Bks.

Prokos, Anna. Star Light, Star Bright: Exploring Our Solar System. Clegg, Dave, illus. 2017. (Imagine That! Ser.). (ENG.). 32p. (J). (gr. 2-4). E-Book 39.99 *(978-1-63440-164-7(6))* Red Chair Pr.

Publications International Ltd. Staff, ed. Solar System Puzzle. 2010. (J). 13.98 *(978-1-60553-351-3(3))* Publications International, Ltd.

Pulliam, Christine & Daniels, Patricia. Space Encyclopedia: A Tour of Our Solar System & Beyond. Aguilar, David A., illus. 2013. 191p. (J). *(978-1-4263-1629-6(1))* National Geographic Society.

Rabe, Tish. Planet Name Game. 2015. (Step into Reading Level 2 Ser.). lib. bdg. 13.55 *(978-0-606-37271-8(7))* Turtleback.

Rathburn, Betsy. Asteroids. 2018. (Space Science Ser.). (ENG., Illus.). 24p. (J). (gr. 3-7). lib. bdg. 26.95 *(978-1-62617-857-1(7)*, Torque Bks.) Bellwether Media.

Reid, Stephanie. Space. 2012. (Early Literacy Ser.). (ENG.). 16p. (gr. k-1). 19.99 *(978-1-4333-3468-9(2))*; 6.99 *(978-1-4333-3467-2(4))* Teacher Created Materials, Inc.

Reyes, Sonja. How Do Planets Move? What Will Happen?, 1 vol. 2017. (Computer Science for the Real World Ser.). (ENG.). 16p. (gr. 2-3). pap. *(978-1-5383-5234-2(6)*, 7d3dd3b8-f52c-45cf-858a-da71edb69505, Rosen Classroom) Rosen Publishing Group, Inc., The.

Rhatigan, Joe. Space: Planets, Moons, Stars, & More! 2019. (Step into Reading Ser.). (ENG.). 48p. (J). (gr. 2-3). 14.96 *(978-1-64310-863-6(8))* Penworthy Co., LLC, The.

—Space: Planets, Moons, Stars, & More! Girard, Thomas, illus. 2016. (Step into Reading Ser.). 48p. (J). (gr. k-3). 4.99 *(978-0-553-52316-4(3)*, Random Hse. Bks. for Young Readers) Random Hse. Children's Bks.

Ride, Sally & O'Shaughnessy, Tam E. Voyager: An Adventure to the Edge of the Solar System. 2nd rev. ed. 2005. (J). per. 20.00 *(978-0-9753920-5-8(0))* Sally Ride Science.

Riggs, Kate. Asteroids. 2015. (Across the Universe Ser.). (ENG.). 24p. (J). (gr. 1-4). pap. 9.99 *(978-1-62832-080-0(X)*, 21109, Creative Paperbacks) Creative Co., The.

—Moons. 2015. (Across the Universe Ser.). (ENG.). 24p. (J). (gr. 1-4). *(978-1-60818-483-5(8)*, 21120, Creative Education) Creative Co., The.

—Planets. 2015. (Across the Universe Ser.). (ENG.). 24p. (J). (gr. 1-4). pap. 9.99 *(978-1-62832-084-8(2)*, 21125, Creative Paperbacks); *(978-1-60818-484-2(6)*, 21124, Creative Education) Creative Co., The.

Riley, Peter. Earth, Moon & Sun. 2007. (Essential Science/Watts Ser.). (Illus.). 32p. (YA). (gr. 3-6). lib. bdg. 28.50 *(978-1-59920-025-5(2))* Black Rabbit Bks.

Ring, Susan & Roumanis, Alexis. Dwarf Planets. 2016. (Illus.). 24p. (J). *(978-1-5105-0968-9(2))* SmartBook Media, Inc.

—Earth. 2016. (Illus.). 24p. (J). *(978-1-5105-0971-9(2))* SmartBook Media, Inc.

—Jupiter. 2016. (Illus.). 24p. (J). *(978-1-5105-0974-0(7))* SmartBook Media, Inc.

—Neptune. 2016. (Illus.). 24p. (J). *(978-1-5105-0986-3(0))* SmartBook Media, Inc.

—Saturn. 2016. (Illus.). 24p. (J). *(978-1-5105-0989-4(5))* SmartBook Media, Inc.

—Venus. 2016. (Illus.). 24p. (J). *(978-1-5105-0995-5(X))* SmartBook Media, Inc.

Roop, Connie & Roop, Peter. Our Solar System. 2016. (Science for Toddlers Ser.: 1). (Illus.). 26p. (J). (gr. -1 — 1). bds. 8.99 *(978-1-4549-1418-1(1)*, 1404673) Sterling Publishing Co., Inc.

Rosen Publishing Group, creator. Mysteries of the Milky Way, 1 vol. 2008. (Scientific American Cutting-Edge Science Ser.). (ENG., Illus.). 136p. (YA). (gr. 9-9). lib. bdg. 39.80 *(978-1-4042-1404-0(6)*, 15ec5c20-d195-4f35-b800-04b76d5dd655) Rosen Publishing Group, Inc., The.

Roumanis, Alexis. Dwarf Planets. 2016. (J). *(978-1-5105-2043-1(0))* SmartBook Media, Inc.

—The Sun. 2016. (Illus.). 24p. (J). *(978-1-5105-0983-2(6))* SmartBook Media, Inc.

Rowe, Dana. Pavo Explores the Solar System. 2013. 40p. pap. 14.95 *(978-1-937829-67-4(7)*, Total Publishing & Media) Yorkshire Publishing Group.

Rowland, Andrew, illus. Space. 2015. 17p. (J). *(978-1-4351-5936-5(5))* Barnes & Noble, Inc.

Roza, Greg. Comets & Asteroids, 1 vol. 2010. (Our Solar System Ser.). (ENG.). 24p. (J). (gr. k-2). pap. 9.15 *(978-1-4339-3816-0(2)*, b05d5184-fb30-41ff-aaf6-79554c021ab0); (Illus.). lib. bdg. 25.27 *(978-1-4339-3815-3(4)*, 845a1937-59cb-46ea-85d1-8ab2643635dc) Stevens, Gareth Publishing LLLP.

—Neptune, 1 vol. 2010. (Our Solar System Ser.). (ENG.). 24p. (J). (gr. k-2). pap. 9.15 *(978-1-4339-3834-4(0)*, 5836b9b0-5c4a-49a3-b669-110776997034); (Illus.). lib. bdg. 25.27 *(978-1-4339-3833-7(2)*, c9acc356-3fea-4d9c-a656-3e8153d626db) Stevens, Gareth Publishing LLLP.

Rustad, Martha E. H. Space, 1 vol. 2013. (Little Scientist Ser.). (ENG., Illus.). 32p. (J). (gr. -1-2). pap. 6.95 *(978-1-4765-3551-7(5)*, 123597, Capstone Pr.) Capstone.

Sabol, Stephanie. Where Is Our Solar System? 2019. (Who HQ Ser.). (ENG.). 112p. (J). (gr. 2-4). 16.36 *(978-1-64310-813-1(1))* Penworthy Co., LLC, The.

Sabol, Stephanie & Who HQ. Where Is Our Solar System? Hammond, Ted, illus. 2018. (Where Is? Ser.). 112p. (J). (gr. 3-7). 5.99 *(978-0-515-15818-2(6)*, Penguin Workshop) Penguin Young Readers Group.

Sandy Creek (Firm) Staff, contrib. by. Our Solar System & Beyond: Planets, Stars, Space Travel & Fun Facts! 2014. (Illus.). (J). *(978-1-4351-5603-6(X))* Barnes & Noble, Inc.

Seluk, Nick. The Sun Is Kind of a Big Deal. Seluk, Nick, illus. 2018. (ENG., Illus.). 40p. (J). (gr. -1-3). 17.99 *(978-1-338-16697-2(2)*, Orchard Bks.) Scholastic, Inc.

Semadini, Tomassino. Lukie the Astro-Dog. 2008. 52p. pap. 10.49 *(978-1-4389-0359-0(6))* AuthorHouse.

Sexton, Colleen. Pluto. 2010. (Exploring Space Ser.). (ENG., Illus.). 24p. (J). (gr. k-3). lib. bdg. 26.95 *(978-1-60014-410-3(1)*, Blastoff! Readers) Bellwether Media.

—The Solar System. 2010. (Exploring Space Ser.). (ENG., Illus.). 24p. (J). (gr. k-3). lib. bdg. 26.95 *(978-1-60014-411-0(X)*, Blastoff! Readers) Bellwether Media.

Shealy, Dennis R. My Little Golden Book about the Solar System. Johnson, Richard, illus. 2018. (Little Golden Book Ser.). 24p. (J). (-k). 5.99 *(978-1-5247-6684-9(4)*, Golden Bks.) Random Hse. Children's Bks.

Sherman, Josepha. Asteroids, Meteors, & Comets, 1 vol. 2010. (Space! Ser.). (ENG.). 64p. (gr. 5-5). lib. bdg. 35.50 *(978-0-7614-4252-3(9)*, cc1d488f-8aac-4101-980d-527efb6bf637) Cavendish Square Publishing LLC.

Sian revision Earth-sun. 2004. (J). *(978-1-59242-020-9(6))* Delta Education, LLC.

Silverstein, Alvin, et al. The Universe. rev. ed. 2009. (Science Concepts, Second Ser.). (ENG.). 112p. (gr. 6-8). 31.93 *(978-0-7613-3937-3(X))* Lerner Publishing Group.

Simon, Seymour. Our Solar System. (ENG.). (J). (gr. 1-5). 2014. 48p. 17.99 *(978-0-06-233379-7(8))* 2007. (Illus.). 72p. 19.99 *(978-0-06-114008-2(2))* HarperCollins Pubs. (HarperCollins).

—Our Solar System: Revised Edition. rev. ed. 2014. (ENG.). 48p. (J). (gr. 1-5). pap. 7.99 *(978-0-06-114010-5(4)*, HarperCollins) HarperCollins Pubs.

El Sistema Solar. (Coleccion Ventana Transparente). (SPA.). *(978-950-11-1135-4(0)*, SG5232) Sigmar ARG. Dist: Lectorum Pubns., Inc.

Smith, Alexander Gordon. The Solar System. 2010. (Illus.). 128p. (J). (gr. -1-12). pap. 17.99 *(978-1-84476-893-6(7))* Anness Publishing GBR. Dist: National Bk. Network.

—The Solar System: A Breathtaking Tour of the Universe & How It Works with More Than 300 Incredible Photographs & Illustrations. 2014. (Illus.). 128p. (J). (gr. -1-12). 14.99 *(978-1-86147-327-1(3)*, Armadillo) Anness Publishing GBR. Dist: National Bk. Network.

Smyer, Lori. Journey Through Galaxies, 1 vol. 2014. (Spotlight on Space Science Ser.). (ENG.). 32p. (J). (gr. 5-5). pap. 12.75 *(978-1-4994-0369-5(0)*, a14b1df0-8929-472c-afa4-a003bed10c77, PowerKids Pr.) Rosen Publishing Group, Inc., The.

Sohn, Emily. Sun, Moon, & Stars. 2019. (IScience Ser.). (ENG., Illus.). 32p. (J). (gr. 3-4). pap. 13.26 *(978-1-68404-386-6(7))* Norwood Hse. Pr.

The Solar System. (First Facts about Ser.). 24p. (J). (gr. 3-7). pap. *(978-1-882210-16-9(6))* Action Publishing, Inc.

The Solar System. 2004. (Illus.). 32p. (J). (gr. 2-4). pap. 6.95 *(978-0-8225-4769-3(4))* Lerner Publishing Group.

The Solar System & Beyond. (Solar System & Beyond Ser.). (ENG.). 32p. (gr. 3-4). 2011. pap. 286.20 *(978-1-4296-6412-7(6))* 2010. pap. 47.70 *(978-1-4296-6244-4(1))* 2010. lib. bdg. 167.94 *(978-1-4296-5399-2(X))* Capstone. (Capstone Pr.).

Solar System (Collins Fascinating Facts) rev. ed. 2016. (Collins Fascinating Facts Ser.). (ENG., Illus.). 72p. (J). (gr. 1-3). pap. 10.99 *(978-0-00-816922-0(5))* HarperCollins Pubs. Ltd. GBR. Dist: Independent Pubs. Group.

Solar System (Set), 8 vols., Set. Incl. Earth. Simon, Charnan. lib. bdg. 29.21 *(978-1-61080-081-5(8)*, 201072); Jupiter. Kazunas, Ariel. lib. bdg. 29.21 *(978-1-61080-086-0(9)*, 201082); Mars. Simon, Charnan. lib. bdg. 29.21 *(978-1-61080-082-2(6)*, 201074); Mercury. Kazunas, Ariel. lib. bdg. 29.21 *(978-1-61080-088-4(5)*, 201086); Neptune. Kazunas, Ariel. lib. bdg. 29.21 *(978-1-61080-083-9(4)*, 201076); Saturn. Kazunas, Ariel. lib. bdg. 29.21 *(978-1-61080-087-7(7)*, 201084); Uranus. Kazunas, Ariel. lib. bdg. 29.21 *(978-1-61080-084-6(2)*, 201078); Venus. Kazunas, Ariel. lib. bdg. 29.21 *(978-1-61080-085-3(0)*, 201080); (gr. 2-5). (21st Century Junior Library: Solar System Ser.). (ENG., Illus.). 24p. 2011. 233.68 *(978-1-61080-147-8(4)*, 201006) Cherry Lake Publishing.

Solner Heimer, Patricia. Li'l Earth. Solner Heimer, Patricia, illus. 2010. (Illus.). 32p. (J). (gr. k-4). 15.99 *(978-0-9844453-0-1(7))* Maple Road Publishing, Inc.

Space Quest: Exploring Our Solar System: Individual Title Six-Packs. (Discovery World Ser.). 24p. (gr. 1-2). 33.00 *(978-0-7635-8481-8(9))* Rigby Education.

Sparrow, Giles. Destination Asteroids, Comets, & Meteors, 1 vol. 2009. (Destination Solar System Ser.). (ENG., Illus.). 32p. (J). (gr. 3-4). 28.93 *(978-1-4358-3449-1(6)*, 2c8c0ba9-b825-4430-875a-9e5821e56f6d); pap. 11.00 *(978-1-4358-3469-9(0)*, 76f52369-b13b-4db2-bc41-04a122032829) Rosen Publishing Group, Inc., The. (PowerKids Pr.).

—Our Solar System, 1 vol. 2017. (Space Explorers Ser.). (ENG.). 32p. (gr. 2-2). 26.93 *(978-0-7660-9267-9(4)*, 0d1a1111-b60b-44a8-af17-f7baf9b54c7b) Enslow Publishing, LLC.

Sparrow, Giles, et al. The Solar System, 1 vol. 2015. (Discoveries in Space Science Ser.). (ENG., Illus.). 80p. (YA). (gr. 9-9). lib. bdg. 37.36 *(978-1-5026-1018-8(3)*, 350aed88-fd94-4f8d-a845-010c20be72e9) Cavendish Square Publishing LLC.

Stefoff, Rebecca. Earth or Sun: Which One Is in the Center? 2013. (J). *(978-0-7614-8147-8(8))* Marshall Cavendish.

Storad, Conrad J. Mars. 2009. (Early Bird Astronomy Ser.). (ENG., Illus.). 48p. (gr. 2-5). pap. 8.95 *(978-0-7613-4980-8(4)*, Lerner Pubns.) Lerner Publishing Group.

Stott, Carole. Mission: Space: Explore the Galaxy. 2016. (Illus.). 128p. (J). *(978-1-4654-5376-1(8))* Dorling Kindersley Publishing, Inc.

Sundance/Newbridge LLC Staff. Circling the Sun. 2004. (Reading PowerWorks Ser.). (gr. 1-3). 37.50 *(978-0-7608-8916-9(3))* Sundance/Newbridge Educational Publishing.

Teacher Created Resources Staff. Space Guides: Discovering the Solar System. 2008. (ENG., Illus.). 32p. pap. 7.99 *(978-1-4206-8267-0(9))* Teacher Created Resources, Inc.

Terp, Gail. Earth & Other Inner Planets. 2018. (Deep Space Discovery Ser.). (ENG.). 32p. (gr. 2-7). 9.95 *(978-1-68072-713-5(3))*; (J). (gr. 4-6). pap. 9.99 *(978-1-64466-266-3(3)*, 12317); (Illus.). (J). (gr. 4-6). lib. bdg. *(978-1-68072-419-6(3)*, 12316) Black Rabbit Bks. (Bolt).

—Saturn & Other Outer Planets. 2018. (Deep Space Discovery Ser.). (ENG.). 32p. (gr. 2-7). 9.95 *(978-1-68072-716-6(8))*; (J). (gr. 4-6). pap. 9.99 *(978-1-64466-269-4(8)*, 12329); (Illus.). (J). (gr. 4-6). lib. bdg. *(978-1-68072-422-6(3)*, 12328) Black Rabbit Bks. (Bolt).

—Saturno y Otros Planetas Exteriores. 2018. (Descubrimiento Del Espacio Profundo Ser.). (SPA., Illus.). 32p. (J). (gr. 4-6). lib. bdg. *(978-1-68072-972-6(1)*, 12453, Bolt) Black Rabbit Bks.

—La Tierra y Otros Planetas Interiores. 2018. (Descubrimiento Del Espacio Profundo Ser.). (SPA.). 32p. (J). (gr. 4-6). lib. bdg. *(978-1-68072-969-6(1)*, 12444, Bolt) Black Rabbit Bks.

Time for Kids Editors. Time for Kids - Planets! 2005. (Time for Kids Ser.). (ENG., Illus.). 32p. (J). 14.99 *(978-0-06-078203-0(X))* HarperCollins Pubs.

Trammel, Howard K. The Solar System. 2009. (True Book Ser.). (ENG.). 48p. (J). (gr. 2-5). 29.00 *(978-0-531-16898-1(0))* Scholastic Library Publishing.

A True Book & Trade - Dr. Mae Jemison & 100 Year Starship & Trade. 2013. (True Book™—Dr. Mae Jemison & 100 Year Starship™ Ser.). (J). 116.00 *(978-0-531-25339-7(2)*, Children's Pr.) Scholastic Library Publishing.

Turiel, Isaac. How Do We Know the Size of the Solar System? 2009. (Great Scientific Questions & the Scientists Who Answered Them Ser.). 112p. (gr. 7-12). 63.90 *(978-1-61513-206-5(6))* Rosen Publishing Group, Inc., The.

Vogt, Gregory. The Dwarf Planet Pluto. 2009. (Early Bird Astronomy Ser.). (ENG.). 48p. (gr. 2-5). lib. bdg. 26.60 (978-0-7613-4157-4(9)) Lerner Publishing Group.

—Pluto: A Dwarf Planet. 2009. (Early Bird Astronomy Ser.). (ENG., Illus.). 48p. (gr. 2-5). pap. 8.95 (978-0-7613-4988-4(X), Lerner Pubns.) Lerner Publishing Group.

—Solar System. 2012. (Scholastic Reader Level 2 Ser.). (ENG.). 32p. (J). (gr. -1-3). pap. 3.99 (978-0-545-38267-0(X), Scholastic Paperbacks) Scholastic, Inc.

Waldeck, Aaron. Space Rocks: A Look at Asteriods & Comets. 2003. (Rosen Real Readers Big Bookstm Ser.). (ENG.). 24p. (gr. 3-4). 43.95 (978-0-8239-8729-0(9)) Rosen Publishing Group, Inc., The.

—Space Rocks: A Look at Asteroids & Comets. 2009. (Reading Room Collection 2 Ser.). 24p. (gr. 3-4). 42.50 (978-1-60851-990-3(2), PowerKids Pr.) Rosen Publishing Group, Inc., The.

Walsh, Kenneth. The Solar System, 1 vol. 2nd rev. ed. 2011. (TIME for KIDS(r): Informational Text Ser.). (ENG.). 28p. (gr. 2-3). pap. 10.99 (978-1-4333-3633-1(2)) Teacher Created Materials, Inc.

Waxman, Laura Hamilton. The Solar System. 2010. (Early Bird Astronomy Ser.). 48p. (ENG.). (gr. 2-5). lib. bdg. 26.60 (978-0-7613-3874-1(8)); (Illus.). (J). 8.95 (978-0-7613-4990-7(1), 1306464, Lerner Pubns.) Lerner Publishing Group.

Wells, Robert E. What's So Special about Planet Earth? 2012. (J). (978-1-61913-154-5(4)) Weigl Pubs., Inc.

Wilkins, Mary-Jane. Asteroids, Comets, & Meteors. 2017. (Fast Track: Our Solar System Ser.). 24p. (J). (gr. k-3). 28.50 (978-1-78121-368-1(2)) Brown Bear Bks.

—Earth. 2017. (Our Solar System Ser.). (ENG.). 24p. (J). (gr. 2-4). 28.50 (978-1-78121-364-3(X), 16653) Brown Bear Bks.

—The Inner Planets. 2017. (Our Solar System Ser.). (ENG., Illus.). 24p. (J). (gr. 2-4). 28.50 (978-1-78121-366-7(6), 16654) Brown Bear Bks.

—The Moon. 2017. (Our Solar System Ser.). (ENG.). 24p. (J). (gr. 2-4). 28.50 (978-1-78121-365-0(8), 16655) Brown Bear Bks.

—The Outer Planets. 2017. (Our Solar System Ser.). (ENG., Illus.). 24p. (J). (gr. 2-4). 28.50 (978-1-78121-367-4(4), 16656) Brown Bear Bks.

—The Sun. 2017. (Our Solar System Ser.). (ENG., Illus.). 24p. (J). (gr. 2-4). 28.50 (978-1-78121-363-6(1), 16657) Brown Bear Bks.

Willett, Edward. Space Q&a. 2014. (Science Discovery Ser.). (ENG., Illus.). 48p. (J). (gr. 4-7). lib. bdg. 28.55 (978-1-4896-0692-1(0), AV2 by Weigl) Weigl Pubs., Inc.

Williams, Brian & Egan, Vicky. The Solar System. Dogi, Flammetta, illus. 2007. (Back to Basics Ser.). 32p. (J). lib. bdg. (978-88-6098-049-6(6)) McRae Bks. Srl.

Wood, Matthew Brenden. Planetary Science: Explore New Frontiers. Carbaugh, Samuel, illus. 2017. (Inquire & Investigate Ser.). (ENG.). 128p. (J). (gr. 7-9). 22.95 (978-1-61930-567-0(4), 3f0c280f-7c1a-45b1-9ed3-d288037cb3b9); pap. 17.95 (978-1-61930-571-7(2), 42affcf1-61b1-43f4-955e-d02fa7b29d04) Nomad Pr.

World Book, Inc. Staff, contrib. by. Earth & Earth's Moon. 2010. (J). (978-0-7166-9540-0(5)) World Bk., Inc.

—Galaxies & the Universe. (J). 2010. (978-0-7166-9542-4(1)) 2nd ed. 2006. (Illus.). 64p. (978-0-7166-9513-4(8)) World Bk., Inc.

—Mars. 2010. (J). (978-0-7166-9536-3(7)) World Bk., Inc.

—Mercury & Venus. 2010. (J). (978-0-7166-9534-9(0)) World Bk., Inc.

—Neptune, Comets, & Dwarf Planets. 2010. (J). (978-0-7166-9538-7(3)) World Bk., Inc.

—A Place in Space. 2017. (J). (978-0-7166-7950-9(7)) World Bk., Inc.

—Saturn & Uranus. 2010. (J). (978-0-7166-9535-6(9)) World Bk., Inc.

—The Solar System. 2019. (Illus.). 96p. (J). (978-0-7166-3733-2(2)) World Bk., Inc.

—The Sun & Other Stars. 2010. (Illus.). 64p. (J). (978-0-7166-9539-4(1)) World Bk., Inc.

—Telescopes & Space Probes. 2010. (J). (978-0-7166-9541-7(3)) World Bk., Inc.

—Zac Newton Investigates Spectacular Space. 2018. (J). (978-0-7166-4061-5(9)) World Bk., Inc.

Yomtov, Nel. Sailing the Solar System: The Next 100 Years of Space Exploration. Pota, Giovanni & Brown, Alan, illus. 2016. (Our World: the Next 100 Years Ser.). (ENG.). 32p. (J). (gr. 3-9). lib. bdg. 31.32 (978-1-4914-8265-0(6), 130754, Capstone Pr.) Capstone.

Young-Brown, Fiona. The Universe to Scale: Similarities & Differences in Objects in Our Solar System, 1 vol. 2016. (Space Systems Ser.). (ENG., Illus.). 112p. (YA). (gr. 8-8). 44.50 (978-1-5026-2289-1(0), ece1adab-8861-44af-99d0-697a79ce0e77) Cavendish Square Publishing LLC.

Zobel, Derek. Asteroids. 2010. (Exploring Space Ser.). (ENG., Illus.). 24p. (J). (gr. k-3). lib. bdg. 26.95 (978-1-60014-196-6(X), Blastoff! Readers) Bellwether Media.

SOLDIERS

Here are entered works dealing with members of the armed forces in general, including the Navy, Marine Corps, etc. as well as the Army.

see also Armies; Generals; Military Art and Science; Scouts and Scouting

also names of countries with the subdivision Army—Military Life, e.g. United States—Army—Military life; etc.

Acton, Vanessa. Momcilo Gavric's World War I Story. Kronheimer, Ann, illus. 2018. (Narrative Nonfiction: Kids in War Ser.). (ENG.). 32p. (J). (gr. 2-4). 27.99 (978-1-5124-5679-0(9), 5300603e-3906-4416-9734-1ea47dd1a084, Lerner Pubns.); pap. 9.99 (978-1-5415-1193-4(X), 95ef1b3c-5db0-4edb-8ae0-fb702f810dc6) Lerner Publishing Group.

Adams, Simon. DK Eyewitness Books: Soldier: Discover the World of Soldiers — Their Training, Tactics, Vehicles, & Weapons. 2009. (DK Eyewitness Ser.). (ENG., Illus.). 72p. (J). (gr. 3-7). 16.99 (978-0-7566-4539-7(5), DK Children) Dorling Kindersley Publishing, Inc.

Anderson, Dale. Soldiers & Sailors in the American Revolution, 1 vol. 2005. (World Almanac(r) Library of the American Revolution Ser.). (ENG.). 48p. (gr. 5-8). pap. 15.05 (978-0-8368-5938-6(3), fefcb9af-19a9-4101-b561-c76c583fb122); lib. bdg. 33.67 (978-0-8368-5929-4(4), 29863a8e-4cf7-476a-957d-381f6117ed23) Stevens, Gareth Publishing LLLP. (Gareth Stevens Secondary Library).

AZ Books Staff. Great Warriors. Aksinovich, Natalia & Yaroshevich, Angelica, eds. 2012. (Sounds Around Us Ser.). (ENG.). 16p. (J). (gr. 1-3). bds. 17.95 (978-1-61889-033-7(6)) AZ Bks. LLC.

Barile, Mary. Alphonso Wetmore: Soldier, Adventurer, & Writer. 2015. (ENG., Illus.). 48p. (J). 24.00 (978-1-61248-147-0(7)) Truman State Univ. Pr.

Beller, Susan Provost. Yankee Doodle & the Redcoats: Soldiering in the Revolutionary War. Day, Larry, illus. 2003. (Single Titles Ser.). (ENG.). 96p. (gr. 5-8). lib. bdg. 26.60 (978-0-7613-2612-0(X), Twenty-First Century Bks.) Lerner Publishing Group.

Bodden, Valerie. X-Books: Gladiators. 2017. (X-Bks.). (Illus.). 32p. (J). (gr. 3-7). pap. 9.99 (978-1-62832-416-7(3), 20373, Creative Paperbacks) Creative Co., The.

Braun, Eric Mark. The Real Aaron Burr: The Truth Behind the Legend. 2019. (Real Revolutionaries Ser.). (ENG., Illus.). 64p. (J). (gr. 5-9). lib. bdg. 34.65 (978-0-7565-6250-2(3), 141182, Compass Point Bks.) Capstone.

Brooker, Marion Fargey. Hold the Oxo! A Teenage Soldier Writes Home. 2011. (Canadians at War Ser.: 6). (ENG., Illus.). 144p. (YA). pap. 14.99 (978-1-55488-870-2(0)) Dundurn Pr. CAN. Dist: Publishers Group West (PGW).

Burns, Kylie. Sparta!, 1 vol. 2013. (ENG., Illus.). 48p. (J). pap. (978-0-7787-1105-6(6)) Crabtree Publishing Co.

Byers, Ann. Working with Veterans & Military Families Through Service Learning, 1 vol. 2014. (Service Learning for Teens Ser.). (ENG.). 80p. (YA). (gr. 7-7). 37.80 (978-1-4777-7963-7(9), 0d942f33-7109-4f8e-9786-33a992e65313, Rosen Young Adult) Rosen Publishing Group, Inc., The.

Calvert, Patricia. Kit Carson: He Led the Way, 1 vol. 2007. (Great Explorations Ser.). (ENG., Illus.). 80p. (gr. 6-6). lib. bdg. 36.93 (978-0-7614-2223-5(4), 963e1330-9bef-4967-b147-72bb2846fbe9) Cavendish Square Publishing LLC.

Capstone Press. You Choose: Warriors. 2010. (You Choose: Warriors Ser.). (ENG.). 32p. 153.25 (978-1-4296-5897-3(5), Capstone Pr.) Capstone.

Cheatham, Mark. The Life of a Colonial Soldier, 1 vol. 2013. (Jr. Graphic Colonial America Ser.). (ENG., Illus.). 24p. (J). (gr. 2-3). pap. 11.60 (978-1-4777-1439-3(1), 856a9e2a-d842-4008-9543-7caf6bd62692); lib. bdg. 28.93 (978-1-4777-1310-5(7), f24ac1b8-8ed4-4c67-bb3c-083387a6d554) Rosen Publishing Group, Inc., The. (PowerKids Pr.).

Chikwanine, Michel & Humphreys, Jessica Dee. Child Soldier: When Boys & Girls Are Used in War. Dávila, Claudia, illus. 2015. (CitizenKid Ser.). (ENG.). 48p. (J). (gr. 5-9). 17.99 (978-1-77138-126-0(4)) Kids Can Pr., Ltd. CAN. Dist: Hachette Bk. Group.

Coleman, Miriam. Women in the Military, 1 vol. 2015. (Women Groundbreakers Ser.). (ENG.). 32p. (J). (gr. 4-5). pap. 11.00 (978-1-4994-1052-5(2), 03b6bd8a-34e7-4b3b-9ec4-f6f3fb5cfe5f, PowerKids Pr.) Rosen Publishing Group, Inc., The.

Collins, Kathleen. Marques de Lafayette: Heroe Frances de la Revolucion Estadounidense, 1 vol. 2003. (Grandes Personajes en la Historia de Los Estados Unidos (Famous People in American History) Ser.). (SPA., Illus.). 32p. (gr. 3-4). lib. bdg. 29.13 (978-0-8239-4139-1(6), a74adad7-370c-4ffc-9b68-cf8170ec0101, Editorial Buenas Letras) Rosen Publishing Group, Inc., The.

Crew, Hilary S. Women Engaged in War in Literature for Youth: A Guide to Resources for Children & Young Adults. 2007. (Literature for Youth Ser.: 11). (ENG.). 324p. per. 93.00 (978-0-8108-4929-7(1)) Scarecrow Pr., Inc.

Dinzeo, Paul. Spartans. 2012. (History's Greatest Warriors Ser.). (ENG., Illus.). 24p. (J). (gr. 3-7). lib. bdg. 26.95 (978-1-60014-749-4(6), Torque Bks.) Bellwether Media.

Doyle, Bill H. Behind Enemy Lines. 2009. 135p. (J). pap. (978-0-545-14705-7(0)) Scholastic, Inc.

Ehman, Ashley M. True Teen Stories from Iraq: Surviving ISIS, 1 vol. 2018. (Surviving Terror: True Teen Stories from Around the World Ser.). (ENG.). 112p. (YA). (gr. 8-8). 45.93 (978-1-5026-3544-0(5), 7db7ccff-816e-4490-b269-d3c4f175bc1b) Cavendish Square Publishing LLC.

Elliott, David. Voices: The Final Hours of Joan of Arc. 2019. (ENG., Illus.). 208p. (YA). (gr. 9). 17.99 (978-1-328-98759-4(0), 1709990, Clarion Bks.) HarperCollins Pubs.

Ellis, Deborah. Off to War: Voices of Soldiers' Children. 2008. (ENG., Illus.). 144p. (J). (gr. 2-18). 15.95 (978-0-88899-894-1(5)) Groundwood Bks. CAN. Dist: Publishers Group West (PGW).

Frontline Families. 2015. (Frontline Families Ser.). (ENG.). 48p. (J). (gr. 5-6). pap., pap., pap. 505.80 (978-1-4824-3471-2(7)) Stevens, Gareth Publishing LLLP.

Greenwood, Mark. The Donkey of Gallipoli: A True Story of Courage in World War I. Lessac, Frane, illus. 2008. (ENG.). 32p. (J). (gr. 1-4). 17.99 (978-0-7636-3913-6(3)) Candlewick Pr.

Gunderson, Jessica. Conquistadors. 2012. (Fearsome Fighters Ser.). (ENG.). 48p. (J). (gr. 5-9). 23.95 (978-1-60818-183-4(9), 21885, Creative Education) Creative Co., The.

Hawes, Alison. A Roman Soldier's Handbook. 2010. (Crabtree Connections Ser.). (ENG.). 24p. (J). (gr. 3-6). (978-0-7787-9952-8(2)); pap. (978-0-7787-9974-0(3)) Crabtree Publishing Co.

Heing, Bridey. The Children Soldiers of ISIS, 1 vol. 2017. (Crimes of ISIS Ser.). (ENG.). 104p. (gr. 8-8). pap. 20.95 (978-0-7660-9580-9(0), a0925f5f-024d-4e7d-90ec-860cd03151a9) Enslow Publishing, LLC.

Hepplewhite, Peter. Roman Soldiers. 2013. (Greatest Warriors Ser.). 32p. (gr. 3-7). 28.50 (978-1-78212-402-3(0)) Arcturus Publishing GBR. Dist: Black Rabbit Bks.

Himler, Ronald, illus. Why Did Daddy Have to Leave? 2018. (J). 17.95 (978-0-9885295-9-5(9)) Blue Marlin Pubns.

History's Greatest Warriors. 2011. (History's Greatest Warriors Ser.). (ENG.). 48p. (gr. 3-4). lib. bdg. 65.30 (978-1-4296-6604-6(8)) Capstone.

Innes, Stephanie & Endrulat, Harry. A Bear in War. Deines, Brian, illus. 2019. (ENG.). 40p. (J). (gr. k-4). pap. 14.95 (978-1-77278-086-4(3)) Pajama Pr. CAN. Dist: Publishers Group West (PGW).

Jones, Emma. Who Are Veterans?, 1 vol. 2019. (What's the Issue? Ser.). (ENG.). 24p. (gr. 3-3). pap. 9.25 (978-1-5345-2998-4(5), 01823712-8d56-45c8-870d-e7c3aa5d2033, KidHaven Publishing) Greenhaven Publishing LLC.

Kerley, Barbara. Brave Like Me. 2016. (Illus.). 48p. (J). (gr. -1-k). 17.99 (978-1-4263-2360-7(3), National Geographic Kids) Disney Publishing Worldwide.

Klepeis, Alicia Z. Nathan Hale: Revolutionary War Hero, 1 vol. William, Lorna, illus. 2018. (American Legends & Folktales Ser.). (ENG.). 32p. (gr. 3-3). 30.21 (978-1-5026-3689-8(1), dda8da1d-d3e0-4133-a44f-cbe0b3153926) Cavendish Square Publishing LLC.

Kohl, Peter. My Dad Is in the Army, 1 vol., 1. 2015. (Military Families Ser.). (ENG., Illus.). 24p. (J). (gr. 3-4). pap. 9.25 (978-1-5081-4434-2(6), 12d64cc3-617d-4733-ab90-7d2386fba3aa, PowerKids Pr.) Rosen Publishing Group, Inc., The.

Krasner, Barbara, ed. Returning Soldiers & PTSD, 1 vol. 2017. (Current Controversies Ser.). (ENG.). 296p. (gr. 10-12). pap. 33.00 (978-1-5345-0087-7(1), fda6ba1c-fabb-4687-ad55-1c334b886e98) Greenhaven Publishing LLC.

Lassieur, Allison. At Battle in the Civil War: An Interactive Battlefield Adventure. 2015. (You Choose: Battlefields Ser.). (ENG., Illus.). 112p. (J). (gr. 3-7). lib. bdg. 32.65 (978-1-4914-2149-9(5), 127630, Capstone Pr.) Capstone.

Levete, Sarah. Special Forces, 1 vol. 2015. (Defend & Protect Ser.). (ENG.). 48p. (J). (gr. 4-5). pap. 15.05 (978-1-4824-4115-4(2), d3d19342-08db-462e-a5dc-b9d6549bbaf3) Stevens, Gareth Publishing LLLP.

—Undercover Operations, 1 vol. 2015. (Defend & Protect Ser.). (ENG.). 48p. (J). (gr. 4-5). pap. 15.05 (978-1-4824-4127-7(6), 112bfda6-842e-450f-b640-a313f0faa90d) Stevens, Gareth Publishing LLLP.

Lewis, Mark L. Combat Rescues. 2019. (Rescues in Focus Ser.). (ENG., Illus.). 32p. (J). (gr. 2-3). pap. 9.95 (978-1-64185-840-3(0), 1641858400, Focus Readers) North Star Editions.

Liebman, Dan. I Want to Be a Soldier. 2012. (I Want to Be Ser.). (ENG., Illus.). 24p. (J). (gr. -1-2). pap. 3.99 (978-1-77085-036-1(8), ff303b13-c578-47cd-8943-2b9162efeb0b) Firefly Bks., Ltd.

Liebman, Dan & Liebman, Dan. I Want to Be a Soldier. 2012. (I Want to Be Ser.). (ENG., Illus.). 24p. (J). (gr. -1-2). 14.95 (978-1-77085-035-4(X), 5a998b59-8f4d-48a8-b4f8-65b44d2ab966) Firefly Bks., Ltd.

The Life of a Colonial Soldier. 2013. (Jr. Graphic Colonial America Ser.). 24p. (J). (gr. 3-6). pap. 63.60 (978-1-4777-1440-9(5), PowerKids Pr.) Rosen Publishing Group, Inc., The.

Linde, Barbara M. Heroes of the U. S. Army, 1 vol. 2012. (Heroes of the U. S. Military Ser.). (ENG., Illus.). 32p. (J). (gr. 3-4). pap. 11.50 (978-1-4339-7237-9(9), 6dfcf812-3593-438f-8ea8-dfe303031833); lib. bdg. 29.27 (978-1-4339-7236-2(0), 76711755-28cb-4350-81c2-f249f5c3fa80) Stevens, Gareth Publishing LLLP.

Loh-Hagan, Virginia. Aztecs vs. Spartans. 2019. (Battle Royale: Lethal Warriors Ser.). (ENG., Illus.). 32p. (J). (gr. 4-8). pap. 14.21 (978-1-5341-5054-6(4), 213523); lib. bdg. 32.07 (978-1-5341-4768-3(3), 213522) Cherry Lake Publishing. (45th Parallel Press).

—Immortals vs. Navy SEALs. 2019. (Battle Royale: Lethal Warriors Ser.). (ENG., Illus.). 32p. (J). (gr. 4-8). pap. 14.21 (978-1-5341-5053-9(6), 213519); lib. bdg. 32.07 (978-1-5341-4767-6(5), 213518) Cherry Lake Publishing. (45th Parallel Press).

Loveless, Antony & Nixon, James. Infantry Soldiers. 2012. (ENG., Illus.). 32p. (J). (978-0-7787-5100-7(7)); (The World's Most Dangerous Jobs Ser.: No. 7). pap. (978-0-7787-5114-4(7)) Crabtree Publishing Co.

MacCarald, Clara. Living Through the Revolutionary War. 2018. (American Culture & Conflict Ser.). (ENG., Illus.). 48p. (gr. 4-8). lib. bdg. 35.64 (978-1-64156-414-4(8), 9781641564144) Rourke Educational Media.

Macdonald, Fiona. Do You Want to Be a Roman Soldier? 2015. (Do You Want to Be... Ser.). (Illus.). 32p. (gr. 3-6). 28.50 (978-1-909645-38-7(9)) Book Hse. GBR. Dist: Black Rabbit Bks.

—Top 10 Worst Ruthless Warriors, 1 vol. Antram, David, illus. 2012. (Top 10 Worst Ser.). (ENG.). 32p. (J). (gr. 3-5). pap. 11.50 (978-1-4339-6686-6(7), 61436c43-ce49-4ece-b5e8-9a1d479bf1b6); lib. bdg. 29.27 (978-1-4339-6685-9(9), b8b7cc54-3972-4678-8765-14c346f65f35) Stevens, Gareth Publishing LLLP. (Gareth Stevens Learning Library).

Malam, John. Warriors. 2013. (Illus.). 48p. (J). (978-1-4351-5100-0(3)) Barnes & Noble, Inc.

—Warriors. 2010. (Remarkable Man & Beast Ser.). (Illus.). 48p. (J). (gr. 3-18). lib. bdg. 19.95 (978-1-4222-1979-9(8)) Mason Crest.

Mancini, Candice L., ed. Child Soldiers, 1 vol. 2010. (Global Viewpoints Ser.). (ENG., Illus.). 216p. (J). (gr. 10-12). 47.83 (978-0-7377-4839-0(7), 7fe0972a-8343-4055-bf46-6d9202084041); pap. 32.70 (978-0-7377-4840-6(0), 227c63c5-f321-469d-b6e8-c594b2d2eb55) Greenhaven Publishing LLC. (Greenhaven Publishing).

Margulies, Phillip. A Timeline of the Continental Army. 2009. (Timelines of American History Ser.). 32p. (gr. 4-4). 47.90 (978-1-60854-383-0(8), Rosen Reference) Rosen Publishing Group, Inc., The.

Marston, Elsa. The Compassionate Warrior: Abd el-Kader of Algeria. 2013. (Illus.). 184p. (J). (gr. 8-12). pap. 16.95 (978-1-937786-10-6(2), Wisdom Tales) World Wisdom, Inc.

Matthews, Rupert. Assyrian Soldier! An Ancient Army You'd Rather Not Join. Antram, David, illus. 2007. (You Wouldn't Want to... Ser.). (ENG.). 32p. (J). (gr. 2-5). 29.00 (978-0-531-18727-2(6)) Scholastic Library Publishing.

—Spartans, 1 vol. 2015. (History's Fearless Fighters Ser.). (ENG., Illus.). 48p. (J). (gr. 5-6). pap. 15.05 (978-1-4824-3181-0(5), b03d711c-4af3-4195-ade1-faa1c9d9b154) Stevens, Gareth Publishing LLLP.

McDonnell, Peter. A Soldier in Disguise. Tormey, Carlotta, illus. 2005. 16p. (J). pap. (978-0-7367-2909-3(7)) Zaner-Bloser, Inc.

McLeese, Don. Spartans. 2009. 32p. pap. 7.99 (978-0-8249-1446-2(5), Ideals Pubns.) Worthy Publishing.

Micklos, John & Micklos, John, Jr. Why We Won the American Revolution: Through Primary Sources, 1 vol. 2013. (American Revolution Through Primary Sources Ser.). (ENG.). 48p. (gr. 4-6). pap. 11.53 (978-1-4644-0192-3(6), 5895a7f8-08c5-4a37-9a5e-45c01416fbb5) Enslow Publishing, LLC.

Miller, Mara. The Iraq War: A Controversial War in Perspective, 1 vol. 2011. (Issues in Focus Today Ser.). (ENG., Illus.). 128p. (gr. 6-7). 35.93 (978-0-7660-3488-4(7), 2c09db48-4b7f-429d-b942-d6ba138bb2b4) Enslow Publishing, LLC.

Murrell, Deborah Jane & Dennis, Peter. Greek Warrior. 2012. (ENG., Illus.). 32p. (gr. 3-5). pap. 8.95 (978-1-926853-53-6(9)) Saunders Bk. Co. CAN. Dist: RiverStream Publishing.

Nelson, Sheila & Zoldak, Joyce. In Defense of Our Country: Survivors of Military Conflict. 2009. (J). pap. 24.95 (978-1-4222-1465-7(6)) Mason Crest.

Nelson, Sheila, et al. In Defense of Our Country: Survivors of Military Conflict. 2010. (Survivors Ser.). 128p. (YA). (gr. 7-12). 24.95 (978-1-4222-0452-8(9)) Mason Crest.

Osborne, Mary Pope & Boyce, Natalie Pope. Warriors: A Nonfiction Companion to Magic Tree House #31: Warriors in Winter. Mones, Isidre, illus. 2019. (Magic Tree House (R) Fact Tracker Ser.: 40). 128p. (J). (gr. 2-5). 6.99 (978-1-101-93651-1(7), Random Hse. Bks. for Young Readers) Random Hse. Children's Bks.

Otfinoski, Steven. Spartans. 2013. (Great Warriors Ser.:). (ENG., Illus.). 48p. (J). (gr. 4-8). pap. 18.50 (978-1-61783-778-4(4), 10810) ABDO Publishing Co.

Park, Louise & Love, Timothy. Spartan Hoplites, 1 vol. 2010. (Ancient & Medieval People Ser.). (ENG.). 32p. (gr. 5-5). 31.21 (978-0-7614-4449-7(1), cf1ff527-d52f-4dce-b8bf-9551f4fa4543) Cavendish Square Publishing LLC.

Pearl, Melissa Sherman & Sherman, David A. Cell Phones for Soldiers: Charities Started by Kids! 2017. (Community Connections: How Do They Help? Ser.). (ENG., Illus.). 24p. (J). (gr. 2-5). lib. bdg. 29.21 (978-1-63472-842-3(4), 209794) Cherry Lake Publishing.

Perritano, John. Saving Private Lynch! a Rescue Story from Operation Iraqi Freedom, Vol. 8. 2018. (Special Forces Stories Ser.). 64p. (J). (gr. 7). lib. bdg. 31.93 (978-1-4222-4081-6(9)) Mason Crest.

Poole, H. W. Military Families, Vol. 12. 2016. (Families Today Ser.). (Illus.). 48p. (J). (gr. 5). 20.95 (978-1-4222-3620-8(X)) Mason Crest.

Pullen, John J. Something Abides: The Story of Joshua Chamberlain. 2003. (Illus.). 67p. (J). per. 7.95 (978-0-9704408-1-5(2)) 20th Maine, Inc.

Quasha, Jennifer. Robert Rogers: Rogers' Rangers, & the French & Indian War. 2009. (Library of American Lives & Times Ser.). 112p. (gr. 5-5). 69.20 (978-1-60853-503-3(7)) Rosen Publishing Group, Inc., The.

Ratliff, Thamas. Do You Want to Be a Revolutionary War Soldier? 2015. (Do You Want to Be... Ser.). (Illus.). 32p. (gr. 3-6). 28.50 (978-1-909645-37-0(0)) Book Hse. GBR. Dist: Black Rabbit Bks.

Rhimer, Linda. Is He Really Coming Home! 2010. 20p. 13.77 (978-1-4269-3109-3(3)) Trafford Publishing.

Richards, Tracy. My Navy Dad. 2010. 20p. pap. 14.95 (978-1-4490-3217-3(6)) AuthorHouse.

Robertson, David A. The Scout: Tommy Prince. Henderson, Scott B., illus. 2014. (Tales from Big Spirit Ser.: 3). (ENG.). 30p. (J). (gr. 4-6). pap. (978-1-55379-478-3(8), 78912685-2d85-4153-9f88-b7d8feb31ffe, HighWater Pr.) Portage & Main Pr.

Russell, Marcia. A Visit to a Marine Base, 1 vol. 2nd rev. ed. 2011. (TIME for KIDS(r): Informational Text Ser.). (ENG.). 24p. (gr. 2-3). pap. 9.99 (978-1-4333-3609-6(X)) Teacher Created Materials, Inc.

Russo, Kristen J. Surprising Facts about Being an Army Soldier. 2017. (What You Didn't Know about the U. S. Military Life Ser.). (ENG., Illus.). 32p. (J). (gr. 3-9). lib. bdg. 28.65 (978-1-5157-7429-7(5), 135788, Capstone Pr.) Capstone.

Samuels, Charles. Soldiers. 2012. (World War II: Sourcebook Ser.). (ENG., Illus.). 48p. (J). (gr. 5-8). lib. bdg. 37.10 (978-1-936333-24-0(4), 16835) Brown Bear Bks.

Sawyer, Kem Knapp. Grace Akallo & the Pursuit of Justice for Child Soldiers. 2015. (J). (978-1-59935-456-9(X)) Reynolds, Morgan Inc.

Schomp, Virginia. World War II, 1 vol. 2005. (Letters from the Battlefront Ser.). (ENG., Illus.). 96p. (gr. 6-6). lib. bdg. 36.93 (978-0-7614-1662-3(5), 2ef22db5-a487-414b-9d38-8a7ab9b6be67) Cavendish Square Publishing LLC.

Schorr, Titus. My Dad Is in the Army Overseas, 1 vol., 1. 2015. (Rosen REAL Readers: Social Studies Nonfiction / Fiction: Myself, My Community, My World Ser.). (ENG.). 12p. (J). (gr. k-1). pap. 6.33 (978-1-5081-1821-3(3), d544f29c-3196-4a24-96af-21efc45fdb5b, Rosen Classroom) Rosen Publishing Group, Inc., The.

Schumacher, Cassandra. True Teen Stories from Afghanistan & Pakistan: Surviving the Taliban, 1 vol. 2018. (Surviving Terror: True Teen Stories from Around the World Ser.). (ENG.). 112p. (J). (gr. 8-8). 45.93 (978-1-5026-3550-1(X), dbc4abf8-86f7-438c-ab95-d6449c760225) Cavendish Square Publishing LLC.

Shames, Stephen. Transforming Lives: Turning Uganda's Forgotten Children into Leaders. Shames, Stephen, photos by. 2009. (Illus.). 40p. (YA). pap. 12.95 *(978-1-59572-213-3(0))* Star Bright Bks., Inc.
Shepard, Ray Anthony. Now or Never! Fifty-Fourth Massachusetts Infantry's War to End Slavery. 2017. (ENG., Illus.). 144p. (J). (gr. 5-12). 17.95 *(978-1-62979-340-5(X)*, Calkins Creek) Highlights Pr., c/o Highlights for Children, Inc.
Sims, Lesley. The Roman Soldier's Handbook: Everything a Beginner Soldier Needs to Know. McNee, Ian, illus. 2006. (English Heritage Ser.). 80p. (J). (gr. 4-7). 12.99 *(978-0-7945-0837-1(5)*, Usborne) EDC Publishing.
A Soldier Comes Home. 2011. (ENG., Illus.). 32p. (J). pap. 9.99 *(978-0-578-06838-1(9))* Yari Publishing.
Soriano, Joan & Malizia, Diana, eds. A Visual History of Soldiers & Armies Around the World, 1 vol. 2016. (Visual History of the World Ser.). (ENG., Illus.). 96p. (J). (gr. 8-8). 38.80 *(978-1-4994-6592-1(0)*, ece7bd18-1bd9-4d15-86d0-1b3ea7277c4f, Rosen Young Adult) Rosen Publishing Group, Inc., The.
Spradlin, Michael P. Ryan Pitts: Afghanistan: a Firefight in the Mountains of Wanat. 2019. (Medal of Honor Ser.: 2). (ENG., Illus.). 112p. (J). pap. 8.99 *(978-1-250-15710-2(2)*, 900185142, Farrar, Straus & Giroux (BYR)) Farrar, Straus & Giroux.
Stark, William N. Mighty Military Robots. 2016. (Military Machines on Duty Ser.). (ENG., Illus.). 24p. (J). (gr. 1-3). lib. bdg. 27.99 *(978-1-4914-8847-8(6)*, 131474, Capstone Pr.) Capstone.
Stewart, Alex. Gladiators. 2013. (Greatest Warriors Ser.). 32p. (gr. 3-7). 28.50 *(978-1-78212-398-9(9))* Arcturus Publishing GBR. Dist: Black Rabbit Bks.
—Greek Soldiers. 2013. (Greatest Warriors Ser.). 32p. (gr. 3-7). 28.50 *(978-1-78212-399-6(7))* Arcturus Publishing GBR. Dist: Black Rabbit Bks.
Stotts, Stuart. Lucius Fairchild: Civil War Hero. 2011. (Badger Biographies Ser.). (ENG., Illus.). 112p. (J). pap. 12.95 *(978-0-87020-460-9(2))* Wisconsin Historical Society.
Thiel, Kristin. Joan of Arc, 1 vol. 2017. (Great Military Leaders Ser.). (ENG.). 128p. (YA). (gr. 9-9). 47.36 *(978-1-5026-2791-9(4)*, 61492b8d-dfdd-49d4-9b3c-8b9f9c6129f2) Cavendish Square Publishing LLC.
—True Stories of Teen Soldiers, 1 vol. 2017. (True Teen Stories Ser.). (ENG.). 112p. (YA). (gr. 9-9). 44.50 *(978-1-5026-3164-0(4)*, b47c7b3a-ccce-4ba4-a7ae-e212f0331e28); pap. 20.99 *(978-1-5026-3401-6(5)*, cb95eec0-6fc6-42bd-8453-6ee3f6caf87b) Cavendish Square Publishing LLC.
—True Teen Stories from Syria: Surviving Civil War, 1 vol. 2018. (Surviving Terror: True Teen Stories from Around the World Ser.). (ENG.). 112p. (YA). (gr. 8-8). 45.93 *(978-1-5026-3541-9(0)*, 2eeee78a-55f8-4749-8b4f-bf490be5c502) Cavendish Square Publishing LLC.
Tripp, Natalie. We Care! Making Care Packages: Understand the Relationship Between Multiplication & Division, 1 vol. 2014. (Rosen Math Readers Ser.). (ENG., Illus.). 24p. (J). (gr. 3-3). pap. 8.25 *(978-1-4777-4955-5(1)*, 360c9e5d-b6b5-439c-a088-ffdeb984b3c3, PowerKids Pr.) Rosen Publishing Group, Inc., The.
A True Book: the U. S Army in World War II (Library Edition) 2014. (ENG.). 48p. (J). lib. bdg. 29.00 *(978-0-531-20496-2(0))* Scholastic Library Publishing.
Turner, Tracey. Hard as Nails Warriors. Lenman, Jamie, illus. 2015. (Hard As Nails in History Ser.). (ENG.). 64p. (J). (gr. 4-5). pap. *(978-0-7787-1517-7(5))* Crabtree Publishing Co.
Weaver, Susan B. Heroes! Activities for Kids Dealing with Deployment. 2011. (ENG., Illus.). 80p. (J). pap. 13.95 *(978-0-9829490-2-3(2))* Rainbow Reach.
Williams, Brian. Heroes of the Battlefield. 2015. (Heroes of World War II Ser.). (ENG., Illus.). 48p. (J). (gr. 4-6). 35.32 *(978-1-4109-8048-9(0)*, 130127, Raintree) Capstone.
Williams, Jack S. & Davis, Thomas L. Soldiers & Their Families of the California Mission Frontier, 1 vol. 2003. (People of the California Missions Ser.). (ENG., Illus.). 64p. (J). (gr. 4-4). lib. bdg. 32.93 *(978-0-8239-6285-3(7)*, 086e78d2-099a-4db3-abd3-9f67a8f32e61) Rosen Publishing Group, Inc., The.
Yomtov, Nel. True Stories of World War I, 1 vol. Proctor, Jon & Proctor, Jon, illus. 2012. (Stories of War Ser.). (ENG.). 32p. (J). (gr. 3-9). pap. 8.10 *(978-1-4296-9344-8(4)*, 120379); lib. bdg. 31.32 *(978-1-4296-8625-9(1)*, 118646) Capstone. (Capstone Pr.).
You Choose: Warriors. 2010. (You Choose: Warriors Ser.). (ENG.). 112p. (gr. 3-4). pap. 13.90 *(978-1-4296-5731-0(6))*; pap. 83.40 *(978-1-4296-5732-7(4))*; pap. 13.90 *(978-1-4296-5730-3(8))*; pap. 13.90 *(978-1-4296-5729-7(4))* Capstone. (Capstone Pr.).
Zullo, Allan. Vietnam War Heroes (10 True Tales) 2015. (10 True Tales Ser.). (ENG.). 192p. (J). (gr. 3-7). pap. 5.99 *(978-0-545-83750-7(2))* Scholastic, Inc.
—World War I Heroes. (Ten True Tales Ser.). (J). 2015. (ENG.). 176p. (gr. 3-7). pap. 5.99 *(978-0-545-83751-4(0))* 2014. 162p. pap. *(978-0-545-67533-8(2))* Scholastic, Inc.

SOLDIERS—FICTION

Addison, George R. III. When Mom Came Home. 2012. 32p. pap. 21.99 *(978-1-4691-6406-9(X))* Xlibris Corp.
Almond, David. Raven Summer. 2011. (ENG.). 208p. (YA). (gr. 7). pap. 7.99 *(978-0-385-73807-1(2)*, Ember) Random Hse. Children's Bks.
Altsheler, Joseph A. The Forest of Swords: A Story of Paris & the Marne. 2006. (World War I Ser.: Vol. 3). 284p. (J). reprint ed. 28.95 *(978-1-4218-1772-9(1))*; pap. 13.95 *(978-1-4218-1872-6(8))* 1st World Publishing, Inc. (1st World Library - Literary Society).
—The Forest of Swords: A Story of Paris & the Marne. 2004. (World War I Ser.: Vol. 3). (J). reprint ed. 32.95 *(978-0-8488-3005-2(9))* Amereon Ltd.
—The Forest of Swords: A Story of Paris & the Marne. 2006. (World War I Ser.: Vol. 3). (J). reprint ed. pap. *(978-1-4065-0809-3(8))* Dodo Pr.
—The Forest of Swords: A Story of Paris & the Marne. 2006. (World War I Ser.: Vol. 3). (J). reprint ed. pap. *(978-1-4068-0742-4(7))* Echo Library.
—The Forest of Swords: A Story of Paris & the Marne. 2010. (World War I Ser.: Vol. 3). 216p. (J). reprint ed. pap. *(978-1-4076-1521-9(1))* HardPr.
—The Forest of Swords: A Story of Paris & the Marne. 2011. (World War I Ser.: Vol. 3). 252p. (J). (gr. 4-7). reprint ed. pap. *(978-3-8424-7930-2(1))* tredition Verlag.
Amodeo, Darlene. Samantha & the Soldier: A Letter of Love. 2012. 40p. pap. 20.99 *(978-1-4772-9263-1(2))* AuthorHouse.
Andersen, Hans Christian. The Tinderbox. Yerko, Vladyslav, illus. 2016.Tr. of ??????? (ENG.). 24p. (J). 17.95 *(978-0-9965606-4-1(5)*, 9780996560641) A-BA-BA HAUS.
Anderson, Laurie Halse. Forge. (Seeds of America Trilogy Ser.). (ENG., Illus.). (J). (gr. 5-9). 2012. 320p. pap. 8.99 *(978-1-4169-6145-1(3))* 2010. 304p. 19.99 *(978-1-4169-6144-4(5))* Simon & Schuster Children's Publishing. (Atheneum Bks. for Young Readers).
Ayers, Michelle. Michael. 2011. 134p. pap. 9.99 *(978-0-557-78630-5(4))* Lulu Pr., Inc.
Ayozie, Ben-EL. Ants Everywhere. 2011. 20p. 11.49 *(978-1-4520-3431-7(1))* AuthorHouse.
Bacigalupi, Paolo. The Drowned Cities. 2013. (ENG.). 464p. (J). (gr. 10-17). pap. 12.99 *(978-0-316-05622-9(7))* 2012. 448p. (YA). 17.99 *(978-0-316-20037-0(9))* Little, Brown Bks. for Young Readers.
—The Drowned Cities. 2012. 352p. *(978-1-59606-506-2(0))* Subterranean Pr.
—The Drowned Cities. 2013. (J). lib. bdg. 22.10 *(978-0-606-31749-8(X))* Turtleback.
—Tool of War. (Ship Breaker Ser.). (ENG.). 384p. (YA). 2018. (gr. 9-17). pap. 19.99 *(978-0-316-22081-1(7))* 2017. (gr. 10-17). 17.99 *(978-0-316-22083-5(3))* Little, Brown Bks. for Young Readers.
Barry, Rick. Gunner's Run: A World War II Novel. 2007. 215p. (YA). (gr. 8-12). per. 8.99 *(978-1-59166-761-2(5))* BJU Pr.
Bates, Gordon. The Khaki Boys over the Top: Doing & Daring for Uncle Sam. 2017. (ENG., Illus.). (J). 23.95 *(978-1-374-94649-1(4))*; pap. 13.95 *(978-1-374-94648-4(6))* Capital Communications, Inc.
Beaty, Erin. The Traitor's Kiss. 2018. (Traitor's Trilogy Ser.: 1). (ENG.). 368p. (YA). pap. 12.99 *(978-1-250-15884-0(2)*, 900172348) Square Fish.
Blevins, Wiley. Ten Missing Princesses. Cox, Steve, illus. 2017. (Scary Tales Retold Ser.). (ENG.). 24p. (J). (gr. k-3). lib. bdg. 27.99 *(978-1-63440-168-5(9)*, 1aaeb31e-b7b1-4f1d-805e-10da6b4e6aaf) Red Chair Pr.
Boat, Patty. A Disappointing Homecoming: (A Soldier's Story), 1 vol. 2009. 158p. pap. 24.95 *(978-1-61546-997-0(4))* PublishAmerica, Inc.
Bond, Douglas. Guns of Providence. 2010. (J). pap. *(978-1-59638-156-8(6))* P & R Publishing.
Borden, Louise. Across the Blue Pacific: A World War II Story. Parker, Robert Andrew, illus. 2015. (ENG.). 48p. (J). (gr. -1-3). 7.99 *(978-0-544-55552-5(X)*, 1610459, Clarion Bks.) HarperCollins Pubs.
Bowen, Carl. Shadow Squadron: Rogue Agent. Tortosa, Wilson, illus. 2015. (Shadow Squadron Ser.). (ENG.). 224p. (J). (gr. 4-8). pap., pap., pap. 8.95 *(978-1-62370-296-0(8)*, 128369, Capstone Young Readers) Capstone.
Brandes, Nadine. Romanov. 2019. 341p. (YA). *(978-1-4041-1165-3(4))* Nelson, Thomas Inc.
Brenes, Carlos A. Private Billy. 2011. 32p. pap. 16.95 *(978-1-4560-9096-8(8))* America Star Bks.
Brown, Bruce, et al. Awol, 3 vols., Vol. 2. Kirkman, Robert, ed. 2008. (ENG., Illus.). 160p. (YA). pap. 14.99 *(978-1-58240-864-4(5)*, 0deb1600-a376-4769-8966-2a76a6a23c94) Image Comics.
Campbell, Suzy. My Daddy Is a Soldier, 1 vol. 2009. 19p. pap. 24.95 *(978-1-61546-724-2(6))* America Star Bks.
—My Daddy is a Soldier, 1 vol. 2010. 20p. 24.95 *(978-1-4512-1163-4(5))* PublishAmerica, Inc.
Carradice, Phil. The Black Chair. 2009. (ENG.). 128p. (J). pap. 10.50 *(978-1-84323-978-9(7))* Gomer Pr. GBR. Dist: Casemate Pubs. & Bk. Distributors, LLC.
Carroll, James Christopher. Papa's Backpack. Carroll, James Christopher, illus. 2015. (ENG., Illus.). 32p. (J). (gr. 1-3). 15.99 *(978-1-58536-613-2(7)*, 203942) Sleeping Bear Pr.
Cauvin, Raoul. Bluecoats - Greenhorn, Vol. 4. Lambil, Willy, illus. 4th ed. 2011. (Bluecoats Ser.: 4). 48p. (J). (gr. -1-12). pap. 11.95 *(978-1-84918-066-5(0))* CineBook GBR. Dist: National Bk. Network.
—The Blues in the Mud. Lambil, Willy, illus. 2014. (Bluecoats Ser.: 7). 48p. (J). (gr. -1-12). pap. 11.95 *(978-1-84918-183-9(7))* CineBook GBR. Dist: National Bk. Network.
—Bronco Benny. Lambil, Willy, illus. 2013. (Bluecoats Ser.: 6). 48p. (J). (gr. -1-12). pap. 11.95 *(978-1-84918-146-4(2))* CineBook GBR. Dist: National Bk. Network.
—The Navy Blues. Lambil, Willy, illus. 2009. (Bluecoats Ser.: 2). 46p. (J). (gr. 4-7). pap. 11.95 *(978-1-905460-82-3(1))* CineBook GBR. Dist: National Bk. Network.
—Robertsonville Prison, Volume 1. Lambil, Willy, illus. 2009. (Bluecoats Ser.: 1). 46p. (J). (gr. -1-17). pap. 11.95 *(978-1-905460-71-7(6))* CineBook GBR. Dist: National Bk. Network.
—Rumberley. Lambil, Willy, illus. 2012. (Bluecoats Ser.: 5). 48p. (J). (gr. 3-8). pap. 11.95 *(978-1-84918-108-2(X))* CineBook GBR. Dist: National Bk. Network.
Cohen, Miriam. My Big Brother, 1 vol. Himler, Ronald, illus. (ENG.). 32p. (J). 2008. (gr. -1-3). pap. 5.95 *(978-1-59572-037-5(5))* 2005. 15.95 *(978-1-59572-007-8(3))* 2005. pap. 6.95 *(978-1-59572-158-7(4))* Star Bright Bks., Inc.
Coleman, Jennifer. The Texas Nutcracker, 1 vol. 2018. (ENG., Illus.). 32p. (gr. k-3). 16.99 *(978-1-4556-2331-0(8)*, Pelican Publishing) Arcadia Publishing.
Collins, Suzanne. Year of the Jungle: Memories from the Home Front. Proimos, James, illus. 2013. (ENG.). 40p. (J). (gr. k-7). 18.99 *(978-0-545-42516-2(6)*, Scholastic Pr.) Scholastic, Inc.
Connell, Kate. Yankee Blue or Rebel Gray? The Civil War Adventures of Sam Shaw. 2003. (I Am American Ser.). (Illus.). 40p. (J). (gr. 3-7). pap. 6.99 *(978-0-7922-5179-8(2)*, National Geographic Children's Bks.) Disney Publishing Worldwide.
Coy, John. Eyes on the Goal, Bk. 2. 2012. (4 For 4 Ser.: 2). (ENG.). 192p. (J). (gr. 3-7). pap. 16.99 *(978-0-312-65922-6(9)*, 900070508) Square Fish.
Crump, Fred, Jr. The Brave Toy Soldier. 2007. (Illus.). 32p. (J). 12.95 *(978-1-934056-20-2(0))* UMI (Urban Ministries, Inc.).
Crump Jr., Fred. The Brave Toy Soldier. 2007. (Illus.). 32p. (J). (gr. -1). pap. 9.95 *(978-1-932715-82-8(7))* UMI (Urban Ministries, Inc.).
de Graaf, Anne. Son of a Gun. 2013. (ENG., Illus.). 125p. (J). (gr. 6-8). pap. 22.44 *(978-0-8028-5406-3(0))* Eerdmans, William B. Publishing Co.
DePalma, Johnny & Crabapple, Molly. Once upon a Christmas Tree: A Holiday Fairy Tale. 2007. (ENG.). 88p. pap. 10.50 *(978-0-615-15448-0(4))* Umbrelly Bks.
Dixon, Franklin W. The Secret of the Soldier's Gold. 2003. (Hardy Boys Ser.: 182). (ENG., Illus.). 160p. (J). (gr. 3-7). pap. 7.99 *(978-0-689-85885-7(X)*, Aladdin) Simon & Schuster Children's Publishing.
Doreen Norberg. The Soldier's Dog. 2010. 24p. pap. 15.99 *(978-1-4535-0898-5(8))* Xlibris Corp.
Duey, Kathleen. Pony Express: Time Soldiers Book #7. 2009. (Time Soldiers Ser.). (ENG., Illus.). (J). (gr. k-2). 48p. 15.95 *(978-1-929945-68-9(X))*; 96p. pap. 5.95 *(978-1-929945-69-6(8))* Big Guy Bks., Inc.
Dumbleton, Mike. Digger. Cowcher, Robin, illus. 2018. (ENG.). 32p. (J). (gr. k-3). 19.99 *(978-1-76029-673-5(2))* Allen & Unwin AUS. Dist: Independent Pubs. Group.
Ehrmantraut, Brenda. Hope Weavers. Magnuson, Diana, illus. 2009. (J). *(978-0-9729833-8-9(4))* Bubble Gum Pr.
Ellis, Deborah. The Cat at the Wall, 1 vol. 2014. (ENG., Illus.). 144p. (J). (gr. 4-7). 16.95 *(978-1-55498-491-6(2))*; pap. 9.95 *(978-1-55498-707-8(5))* Groundwood Bks. CAN. Dist: Publishers Group West (PGW).
Etheridge, Judy. Olivia's Wish. 2009. 32p. pap. 21.99 *(978-1-4415-3915-1(8))* Xlibris Corp.
Everett-Green, Evelyn. A Heroine of France. 2006. (ENG.). 188p. pap. 19.99 *(978-1-4264-7060-8(6))* Creative Media Partners, LLC.
Flanagan, John. The Battle of Hackham Heath. 2017. (Ranger's Apprentice: the Early Years Ser.: 2). (ENG.). 368p. (J). (gr. 5). 8.99 *(978-0-14-242733-0(0)*, Puffin Books) Penguin Young Readers Group.
Forde, Winston. Airborne Soldiers. 2010. (Illus.). 120p. 29.99 *(978-1-4535-6451-6(9))* Xlibris Corp.
Fortner, Tama. God Is Always Good: Comfort for Kids Facing Grief, Fear, or Change, 1 vol. Vasylenko, Veronica, illus. 2014. (ENG.). 32p. (J). 12.99 *(978-0-7180-1145-1(7)*, Tommy Nelson) Nelson, Thomas Inc.
Frost, Helen. Crossing Stones. 2009. (ENG., Illus.). 192p. (YA). (gr. 7-18). 19.99 *(978-0-374-31653-2(8)*, 900050356, Farrar, Straus & Giroux (BYR)) Farrar, Straus & Giroux.
Furtney, Charles S. Tryconnel: An Antebellum Adventure along the C & O Canal. 2004. (Illus.). iii, 156p. (J). pap. *(978-0-9711835-3-7(8))* Local History Co., The.
Garland, Sherry. The Buffalo Soldier, 1 vol. Himler, Ronald, illus. 2006. (ENG.). 32p. (J). (gr. k-3). 16.99 *(978-1-58980-391-6(4)*, Pelican Publishing) Arcadia Publishing.
George, Jessica Day. Princess of the Midnight Ball. 2010. (Twelve Dancing Princesses Ser.). (ENG.). 304p. (YA). (gr. 7-9). pap. 10.99 *(978-1-59990-455-9(1)*, 900064161, Bloomsbury USA Childrens) Bloomsbury Publishing USA.
Gilberstadt, Debra Pack. Unmarked Grave: Remembering an American Patriot. 2005. (YA). lib. bdg. 29.95 *(978-0-9763033-0-5(2))* Eslinger Hse. Publishing.
Grant, Michael. Front Lines. 2016. (Front Lines Ser.: 1). (ENG.). 576p. (YA). (gr. 9). 18.99 *(978-0-06-234215-7(0)*, Tegen, Katherine Bks) HarperCollins Pubs.
—Purple Hearts. (Front Lines Ser.: 3). (ENG.). 576p. (YA). (gr. 9). 2019. pap. 9.99 *(978-0-06-234222-5(3))* 2018. 18.99 *(978-0-06-234221-8(5))* HarperCollins Pubs. (Tegen, Katherine Bks).
—Silver Stars. (Front Lines Ser.: 2). (ENG.). (YA). (gr. 9). 2018. 592p. pap. 9.99 *(978-0-06-234219-5(3))* 2017. (Illus.). 576p. 18.99 *(978-0-06-234218-8(5))* HarperCollins Pubs. (Tegen, Katherine Bks).
—Silver Stars: A Front Lines Novel, Volume 2. 2017. (ENG., Illus.). 496p. (YA). pap. *(978-1-4052-8786-9(1))* HarperCollins Pubs.
Gray, Anthony. The Confederate Adventure of Jed Bodine & Ruefus: The Old Tulip Train Raid. 2012. (ENG.). (J). pap. 4.99 *(978-1-4675-2270-0(8))* Independent Pub.
Gray, Claudia. Defy the Fates. 2019. (Defy the Stars Ser.: 3). (ENG.). 480p. (YA). (gr. 9-17). 18.99 *(978-0-316-44075-2(2))* Little, Brown Bks. for Young Readers.
—Defy the Stars. 2018. (Defy the Stars Ser.: 1). (ENG.). 528p. (YA). (gr. 9-17). pap. 23.99 *(978-0-316-39404-8(1))* Little, Brown Bks. for Young Readers.
—Defy the Worlds. 2019. (Defy the Stars Ser.: 2). (ENG.). 496p. (YA). (gr. 9-17). pap. 12.99 *(978-0-316-39407-9(6))* Little, Brown Bks. for Young Readers.
Gray, Mila. Come Back to Me. 2015. (ENG., Illus.). 352p. (YA). (gr. 11). 17.99 *(978-1-4814-3965-7(0)*, Simon Pulse) Simon Pulse.
Haar, Jaap Ter & Meams, Martha. Boris. Poortvliet, Rien, illus. 2009. (J). pap. *(978-0-921100-72-0(8))* Inheritance Pubns.
Halse Anderson, Laurie. Forge. 2012. 18.00 *(978-1-61383-316-2(4))* Perfection Learning Corp.
—Forge. 2012. (Seeds of America Trilogy Ser.: 2). lib. bdg. 18.40 *(978-0-606-23680-5(5))* Turtleback.
Hardin, Melinda. Hero Dad, 0 vols. Langdo, Bryan, illus. 2012. (ENG.). 24p. (J). (gr. -1-2). 12.99 *(978-0-7614-5713-8(5)*, 9780761457138, Two Lions) Amazon Publishing.
Hart, Alison. Darling, Mercy Dog of World War I, 1 vol. Montgomery, Michael G., illus. 2013. (Dog Chronicles Ser.). 160p. (J). (gr. 2-5). 12.95 *(978-1-56145-705-2(1))* Peachtree Publishing Co. Inc.
—Gabriel's Journey, 1 vol. 2011. (Racing to Freedom Ser.: 2). 160p. (J). (gr. 3-7). pap. 4.99 *(978-1-56145-530-0(X))* Peachtree Publishing Co. Inc.
Hartnett, Sonya. The Silver Donkey. Spudvilas, Anne, illus. 2004. viii, 193p. (J). *(978-0-670-04240-1(4)*, Viking Adult) Penguin Publishing Group.
Hemphill, Stephanie. The Language of Fire: Joan of Arc Reimagined. 2019. (ENG.). 512p. (YA). (gr. 8). 17.99 *(978-0-06-249011-7(7)*, Balzer & Bray) HarperCollins Pubs.
Hendrix, John, illus. Shooting at the Stars. 2014. (ENG.). 40p. (J). (gr. 3-7). 19.99 *(978-1-4197-1175-6(X)*, 697001, Abrams Bks. for Young Readers) Abrams, Inc.
Henty, George. Wulf the Saxon: A Story of the Norman Conquest. Peacock, Ralph, illus. 2010. (Dover Children's Classics Ser.). (ENG.). 352p. (YA). (gr. 3-8). pap. 14.95 *(978-0-486-47595-0(6)*, 475956) Dover Pubns., Inc.
Higgins, M. G. The Soldier. 2014. (Red Rhino Ser.). (J). lib. bdg. 18.40 *(978-0-606-36204-7(5))* Turtleback.
Hoffman, Mary. The Twelve Dancing Princesses. Clara, Miss, illus. 2013. 40p. (J). (gr. 1-5). 17.99 *(978-1-84686-966-2(8))* Barefoot Bks., Inc.
Holmes, Sara. Operation Yes. 2009. 234p. (J). pap. *(978-0-545-20418-7(6))* Scholastic, Inc.
Holsey, Chanda Nicole. Precious Pete, Will You Remember Me, When I Am Out to Sea? A Salute to All Navy Dads. 2011. 20p. 11.99 *(978-1-4520-9651-3(1))* AuthorHouse.
Holsey, Dr Chanda Nicole & Holsey, Chanda Nicole. Savvie Sunshine, Will You Remember Daddy When I Am Out to Sea? A Salute to All Navy Dads. 2010. 24p. pap. 13.50 *(978-1-4490-7729-7(3))* AuthorHouse.
Hopkinson, Deborah. Billy & the Rebel: Based on a True Civil War Story. Floca, Brian, illus. 2005. 44p. (J). lib. bdg. 15.00 *(978-1-4242-1148-7(4))* Fitzgerald Bks.
—Billy & the Rebel: Based on a True Civil War Story. Floca, Brian, illus. 2006. (Ready-to-Read Ser.). 44p. (gr. 1-3). 14.00 *(978-0-7569-6390-3(7))* Perfection Learning Corp.
—Billy & the Rebel: Based on a True Civil War Story (Ready-To-Read Level 3) Floca, Brian, illus. (Ready-To-Read Ser.). (ENG.). 48p. (J). (gr. 1-3). 2006. pap. 4.99 *(978-0-689-83396-0(2))* 2005. 17.99 *(978-0-689-83964-1(2))* Simon Spotlight. (Simon Spotlight).
—From Slave to Soldier: Based on a True Civil War Story (Ready-To-Read Level 3) Floca, Brian, illus. (Ready-To-Read Ser.). (ENG.). 48p. (J). (gr. 1-3). 2007. pap. 4.99 *(978-0-689-83966-5(9))* 2005. 16.99 *(978-0-689-83965-8(0))* Simon Spotlight. (Simon Spotlight).
Hughes, Dean. Four-Four-Two. 2016. (ENG., Illus.). 272p. (YA). (gr. 7). 18.99 *(978-1-4814-6252-5(0)*, Atheneum Bks. for Young Readers) Simon & Schuster Children's Publishing.
—Soldier Boys. 2004. 230p. (gr. 7-12). 17.00 *(978-0-7569-4566-4(6))* Perfection Learning Corp.
—Soldier Boys. 2015. (ENG., Illus.). 240p. (YA). (gr. 7). pap. 11.99 *(978-1-4814-2704-3(0)*, Atheneum Bks. for Young Readers) Simon & Schuster Children's Publishing.
Hulme-Cross, Benjamin. The Spartan's March. 2016. (Warrior Heroes Ser.). (ENG., Illus.). 160p. (J). (gr. 5-9). *(978-0-7787-2865-8(X))* Crabtree Publishing Co.
Hutton, Keely. Secret Soldiers: A Novel of World War I. 2019. (ENG.). 320p. (J). 17.99 *(978-0-374-30903-9(5)*, 900188381, Farrar, Straus & Giroux (BYR)) Farrar, Straus & Giroux.
—Soldier Boy. 2018. (ENG.). 336p. (YA). pap. 16.99 *(978-1-250-15844-4(3)*, 900164407) Square Fish.
—Soldier Boy. 2018. (YA). lib. bdg. 20.85 *(978-0-606-41114-1(3))* Turtleback.
Ibbott, Penny. Scarcode. 2013. 358p. pap. *(978-1-78299-864-8(0))* FeedARead.com.
Jackson, Corrine. If I Lie. 2013. (ENG.). 288p. (YA). (gr. 9). pap. 12.99 *(978-1-4424-4000-5(7)*, Simon Pulse) Simon Pulse.
Johnson, Nancy. A Sweet-Sounding Place: A Civil War Story. 2008. (ENG.). 128p. (J). (gr. 3-7). pap. 10.95 *(978-0-89272-770-4(5))* Down East Bks.
Johnston, Annie Fellows. The Little Colonel: Maid of Honor. 2018. (ENG., Illus.). 172p. (YA). (gr. 7-12). pap. *(978-93-5297-427-6(1))* Alpha Editions.
Johnston, K. E. M. The Witness Tree & the Shadow of the Noose: Mystery, Lies, & Spies in Manassas. 2009. 111p. (J). (gr. 5-7). pap. 8.95 *(978-1-57249-397-1(6)*, White Mane Kids) White Mane Publishing Co., Inc.
Jones, Patrick. Combat Zone. 2015. (Support & Defend Ser.). (ENG.). 96p. (YA). (gr. 6-12). pap. 7.99 *(978-1-4677-8094-0(4)*, 7fcd07df-4780-48e5-8547-63a22f685b50, Darby Creek) Lerner Publishing Group.
Jones Yang, Dori. Daughter of Xanadu. 2012. (ENG.). 352p. (YA). (gr. 7). pap. 9.99 *(978-0-385-73924-5(9)*, Ember) Random Hse. Children's Bks.
Jorgensen, Norman. In Flanders Fields. Harrison-Lever, Brian, illus. 2003. (ENG.). 32p. (J). (gr. -1-3). 16.95 *(978-1-894965-01-9(9))* Simply Read Bks. CAN. Dist: Ingram Publisher Services.
Jorgensen, Norman & Harrison-Lever, Brian. In Flanders Fields. 2004. (Illus.). 32p. pap. 13.50 *(978-1-920731-03-8(2))* Fremantle Pr. AUS. Dist: Independent Pubs. Group.
Kagawa, Julie. Rogue. 2015. (Talon Saga Ser.: 2). (ENG.). 464p. (YA). (gr. 9-12). 17.99 *(978-0-373-21146-3(5)*, Harlequin Teen) Harlequin Enterprises ULC CAN. Dist: HarperCollins Pubs.
Kantorek, Keith A. A Soldier's Choice. 2009. (ENG.). 108p. 24.50 *(978-0-557-10928-9(0))*; pap. 9.50 *(978-0-557-10764-3(4))* Lulu Pr., Inc.
Karesh, Tracy Ann. Brave Little Soldier. 2005. (J). pap. 15.00 *(978-0-8059-6742-5(7))* Dorrance Publishing Co., Inc.
Kidd, Virginia Bates. The Children's Escape. 2011. 90p. pap. 19.95 *(978-1-4560-5406-9(6))* America Star Bks.
Krensky, Stephen. Davy Crockett A Life on the Frontier. Dacey, Bob & Bandelin, Debra, illus. 2005. (Ready-to-Read Ser.). 48p. (J). lib. bdg. 15.00 *(978-1-59054-959-9(7))* Fitzgerald Bks.
Landis, Matthew. The Not So Boring Letters of Private Nobody. 2019. (ENG.). 320p. (J). (gr. 5-9). 8.99 *(978-0-7352-2799-6(3)*, Puffin Books) Penguin Young Readers Group.
Le Feuvre, Amy. Teddy's Button. 2007. 92p. per. *(978-1-4065-2383-6(6))* Dodo Pr.
—Teddy's Button. 2004. reprint ed. pap. 1.99 *(978-1-4192-5094-1(9))*; pap. 15.95 *(978-1-4191-5094-4(4))* Kessinger Publishing, LLC.
Lee, Fonda. Cross Fire: an Exo Novel. (ENG.). 384p. (YA). (gr. 7-7). 2019. pap. 9.99 *(978-1-338-13911-2(8)*, Scholastic Paperbacks) 2018. 17.99 *(978-1-338-13909-9(6)*, Scholastic Pr.) Scholastic, Inc.
Lemke, Donald. Basic Training: Call of Doodie. Lentz, Bob, illus. 2018. (Basic Training Ser.). (ENG.). 30p. (J). (gr. -1 —

S

1). bds. 7.99 *(978-1-68446-008-3(5)*, 138937, Picture Window Bks.) Capstone.

LeSourd, Nancy. Secrets of Civil War Spies, 1 vol. 2008. (Liberty Letters Ser.). (ENG.). 224p. (J). pap. 7.99 *(978-0-310-71390-6(0))* Zonderkidz.

Lewis, Ellen Parry. An Unremarkable Girl. 2011. 434p. (YA). pap. 19.99 *(978-0-9843437-8-2(4))* Metal Lunchbox Publishing.

Lewis, Floyd. The Foundered Mule. 2006. (YA). 9.95 *(978-0-9788283-2-5(1))* Acacia Publishing, Inc.

Lieberman Hackelberg, Lori. Shep & the Wounded Soldier. 2012. pap. 11.95 *(978-0-7414-7353-0(4))* Infinity Publishing.

Lu, Marie. Legend. aut. ltd. collector's ed. 2013. (Legend Trilogy: Bk. 1). (Illus.). 306p. (YA). mass mkt. 100.00 net. *(978-1-934267-38-7(4))* Gauntlet, Inc.

—Legend. 2011. (Legend Trilogy: Bk. 1). (ENG.). (YA). (gr. 8-12). 54.99 *(978-1-61657-044-6(X)*, Penguin AudioBooks) Penguin Publishing Group.

—Legend. (Legend Ser.: 1). (ENG.). (YA). (gr. 7). 2013. 352p. pap. 12.99 *(978-0-14-242207-6(X)*, Speak) 2011. 320p. 19.99 *(978-0-399-25675-2(X)*, G.P. Putnam's Sons Books for Young Readers) Penguin Young Readers Group.

—Legend. l.t. ed. 2012. (Legend Trilogy: Bk. 1). (ENG.). 394p. (J). (gr. 7-12). 23.99 *(978-1-4104-4606-0(9))* Thorndike Pr.

—Legend. (Legend Graphic Novels Ser.: 1). 2015. lib. bdg. 26.95 *(978-0-606-38424-7(3))* 2013. lib. bdg. 20.85 *(978-0-606-31701-6(5))* Turtleback.

—Prodigy. l.t. ed. 2013. (Legend Trilogy: Bk. 2). (ENG.). 486p. 23.99 *(978-1-4104-5512-3(2))* Thorndike Pr.

—Prodigy. 2014. (Legend Ser.: 2). lib. bdg. 20.85 *(978-0-606-35716-6(5))* Turtleback.

—Prodigy: A Legend Novel. (Legend Ser.: 2). (ENG.). (YA). (gr. 7). 2014. Illus.). 416p. pap. 12.99 *(978-0-14-242755-2(1)*, Speak) 2013. 384p. 19.99 *(978-0-399-25676-9(8)*, G.P. Putnam's Sons Books for Young Readers) Penguin Young Readers Group.

—Prodigy: the Graphic Novel. 2016. (Legend Ser.: 2). (ENG., Illus.). 160p. (YA). (gr. 7). pap. 14.99 *(978-0-399-17190-1(8)*, G.P. Putnam's Sons Books for Young Readers) Penguin Young Readers Group.

Lynch, Chris. Free-Fire Zone. 2012. 183p. (J). *(978-0-545-49427-4(3)*, Scholastic Pr.) Scholastic, Inc.

—Free-Fire Zone. 2013. (Vietnam Ser.: 3). lib. bdg. 18.40 *(978-0-606-31963-8(8))* Turtleback.

—I Pledge Allegiance. 2011. 183p. (YA). *(978-0-545-38415-5(X))* Scholastic, Inc.

—I Pledge Allegiance. 2013. (Vietnam Ser.: 1). lib. bdg. 17.20 *(978-0-606-31961-4(1))* Turtleback.

—The Right Fight. 2014. 189p. (YA). *(978-0-545-63728-2(7)*, Scholastic Pr.) Scholastic, Inc.

—Sharpshooter. 2012. (J). *(978-0-545-43650-2(8)*, Scholastic Pr.);2. (Vietnam Ser.: 2). (ENG.). 192p. (gr. 6-8). 22.44 *(978-0-545-27026-7(X))* Scholastic, Inc.

—Sharpshooter. 2013. (Vietnam Ser.: 2). lib. bdg. 18.40 *(978-0-606-31962-1(X))* Turtleback.

Lynch, Keven R. What's a Buffalo Soldier? The Historical Adventures of Amber & Trevor. 2005. (J). pap. 12.00 *(978-0-8059-6750-0(8))* Dorrance Publishing Co., Inc.

Lyra, Luciana. De Como Meninas Guerreiras Contaram Heroínas. Medeiros, Vânia, illus. 2011. (POR.). 173p. (J). *(978-85-60676-35-4(X))* Confraria Do Vento.

MacKenzie, Ross. My Sailor Dad. 2008. (J). pap. 12.95 *(978-1-934666-34-0(3))* High-Pitched Hum Inc.

Maddox, Joseph & Maddox, Diana. See You in Hell. 2004. 215p. (YA). pap. 14.95 *(978-0-7414-1872-2(X))* Infinity Publishing.

Mafi, Tahereh. Defy Me. (Shatter Me Ser.: 5). (ENG.). (YA). (gr. 9). 2020. 384p. pap. 15.99 *(978-0-06-267640-5(7))* 2019. 368p. 19.99 *(978-0-06-267639-9(3))* HarperCollins Pubs. (HarperCollins).

—Ignite Me. 2014. (Shatter Me Ser.: 3). (ENG.). 416p. (YA). (gr. 9). 19.99 *(978-0-06-208557-3(3)*, HarperCollins) HarperCollins Pubs.

—Restore Me. 2018. 435p. (YA). *(978-0-06-284176-6(9))* Harper & Row Ltd.

—Restore Me. 2019. (Shatter Me Ser.: 4). (ENG.). 464p. (YA). (gr. 9). pap. 15.99 *(978-0-06-267637-5(7)*, HarperCollins) HarperCollins Pubs.

—Shatter Me. 2018. (Shatter Me Ser.: 1). (ENG.). (YA). (gr. 9). 448p. 21.99 *(978-0-06-274173-8(X))*; 368p. pap. 15.99 *(978-0-06-208550-4(6))* HarperCollins Pubs. (HarperCollins).

—Shatter Me. 2012. (Shatter Me Ser.: 1). (YA). lib. bdg. 20.85 *(978-0-606-26868-4(5))* Turtleback.

—Unravel Me. 2013. (Shatter Me Ser.: 2). (ENG.). (YA). (gr. 9). 496p. pap. 15.99 *(978-0-06-208554-2(9))*; 480p. 19.99 *(978-0-06-208553-5(0))* HarperCollins Pubs. (HarperCollins).

—Unravel Me. 2013. (Shatter Me Ser.: 2). (YA). lib. bdg. 20.85 *(978-0-606-35049-5(7))* Turtleback.

Manning, C. V. Cyon: Veritas. 2004. (ENG.). 289p. pap. 16.00 *(978-1-4116-1939-5(0))* Lulu Pr., Inc.

Manning, Matthew K. EOD Soldiers, 4 vols. Lima, Rico & Lima, Dijjo, illus. 2016. (EOD Soldiers Ser.). (ENG.). 40p. (J). (gr. 4-8). 109.28 *(978-1-4965-3415-6(8)*, 24961, Stone Arch Bks.) Capstone.

—Go Slow. Lima, Dijjo & Furuzono, Carlos, illus. 2016. (EOD Soldiers Ser.). (ENG.). 40p. (J). (gr. 4-8). lib. bdg. 26.65 *(978-1-4965-3109-4(4)*, 132175, Stone Arch Bks.) Capstone.

—The List. Lima, Rico et al, illus. 2016. (EOD Soldiers Ser.). (ENG.). 40p. (J). (gr. 4-8). lib. bdg. 26.65 *(978-1-4965-3110-0(8)*, 132176, Stone Arch Bks.) Capstone.

Massey, David. Taken. 2014. (ENG.). 320p. (YA). E-Book *(978-0-545-66129-4(3))*; (gr. 9). 18.99 *(978-0-545-66128-7(5)*, Chicken Hse., The) Scholastic, Inc.

Mattick, Lindsay. Finding Winnie: The True Story of the World's Most Famous Bear (Caldecott Medal Winner) Blackall, Sophie, illus. 2015. (ENG.). 56p. (J). (gr. -1-3). 18.99 *(978-0-316-32490-8(6))* Little, Brown Bks. for Young Readers.

McCormick, Patricia. Never Fall Down: A Novel. (ENG.). 224p. (YA). (gr. 9). 2013. pap. 11.99 *(978-0-06-173095-5(5))* 2012. 17.99 *(978-0-06-173093-1(9))* HarperCollins Pubs. (Balzer & Bray).

—Purple Heart. (ENG.). (YA). (gr. 8-12). 2011. 224p. pap. 10.99 *(978-0-06-173092-4(0))* 2009. 208p. 16.99 *(978-0-06-173090-0(4))* HarperCollins Pubs. (Balzer & Bray).

McElroy, Lisa Tucker. Love, Lizzie: Letters to a Military Mom. Paterson, Diane, illus. 2009. (ENG.). 32p. (J). (gr. -1-3). pap. 7.99 *(978-0-8075-4778-6(6)*, 807547786) Whitman, Albert & Co.

McKay, Sharon E. War Brothers: The Graphic Novel. Bell, Jennifer A., illus. 3rd ed. 2013. (ENG.). 208p. (YA). (gr. 9-12). pap. 18.95 *(978-1-55451-488-5(6)*, 9781554514885) Annick Pr., Ltd. CAN. Dist: Publishers Group West (PGW).

Meehan, William. Fife. 2006. (ENG.). 180p. (YA). (gr. 4-6). per. 12.95 *(978-0-595-39223-0(7))* iUniverse, Inc.

Millhouse, Jackie. The Tiger & the General. Girouard, Patrick, illus. 2007. 21p. (J). *(978-1-932911-32-9(4))* World Tribune Pr.

Monte, Diane E. Coming Home: Welcome Home at Last. 2012. 24p. pap. 17.99 *(978-1-4772-5713-5(6))* AuthorHouse.

Morpurgo, Michael. Private Peaceful. 2006. 18.00 *(978-0-7569-6630-0(2))* Perfection Learning Corp.

—Private Peaceful. 2006. (YA). 1.25 *(978-1-4193-2976-0(6))* Recorded Bks., Inc.

—Private Peaceful. 2006. (ENG., Illus.). 224p. (J). (gr. 7-12). per. 8.99 *(978-0-439-63653-7(1)*, Scholastic Paperbacks) Scholastic, Inc.

Moverley, Richard. The Reluctant Rajput. Dean, David, illus. 2005. (Yellow Go Bananas Ser.). (ENG.). 48p. (J). (gr. 3-4). lib. bdg. *(978-0-7787-2723-1(8))* Crabtree Publishing Co.

Murdock, Catherine Gilbert. Wisdom's Kiss. 2013. (ENG.). 320p. (YA). (gr. 7). pap. 8.99 *(978-0-547-85540-0(0)*, 1501132, Clarion Bks.) HarperCollins Pubs.

Myers, Walter Dean. Invasion. (ENG.). 224p. (YA). 2015. (gr. 7). pap. 12.99 *(978-0-545-38429-2(X))* 2013. E-Book *(978-0-545-57659-8(8))* Scholastic, Inc. (Scholastic Pr.).

—Patrol: An American Soldier in Vietnam. 2005. 17.00 *(978-0-7569-5428-4(2))* Perfection Learning Corp.

Nelson, Birgitta. The Sacking of Visby. 2011. 150p. 30.00 *(978-1-257-05686-6(7))*; pap. 14.99 *(978-1-257-05680-4(8))* Lulu Pr., Inc.

Nix, Garth. Sir Thursday. 2007. (Keys to the Kingdom Ser.: No. 4). 344p. (gr. 4-7). 18.00 *(978-0-7569-8121-1(2))* Perfection Learning Corp.

Novel Units. Sopa de Piedras (Stone Soup) Novel Units Teacher Guide. 2019.Tr. of Stone Soup. (ENG.). (J). (gr. k-3). pap. 12.99 *(978-1-56137-559-2(4)*, NU5657, Novel Units, Inc.) Classroom Library Co.

—Summer of My German Soldier Novel Units Teacher Guide. 2019. (ENG.). (YA). pap. 12.99 *(978-1-56137-113-6(0)*, Novel Units, Inc.) Classroom Library Co.

Ober, Pierre-Jacques. The Good Son: a Story from the First World War, Told in Miniature. Ober, Jules & Coonan, Felicity, illus. 2019. (ENG.). 104p. (J). (gr. 9). 22.00 *(978-1-5362-0482-7(X))* Candlewick Pr.

Oh, Ellen. Warrior. 2015. (Prophecy Ser.: 2). (ENG.). 352p. (YA). (gr. 8). pap. 9.99 *(978-0-06-209113-0(1)*, HarperTeen) HarperCollins Pubs.

Orzechowski, Shawneen. Sarah's Secret: Civil War Deserter at Fredericksburg. 2011. 104p. (J). pap. 8.95 *(978-1-57249-400-8(X)*, White Mane Kids) White Mane Publishing Co., Inc.

Otter, Isabel. My Daddy Is a Hero. 2018. *(978-1-61067-720-2(X))* Kane Miller.

Parry, Rosanne. Second Fiddle. 2012. 240p. (J). (gr. 3-7). 6.99 *(978-0-375-86166-6(1)*, Yearling) Random Hse. Children's Bks.

Patterson, Valerie O. Operation Oleander. 2015. (ENG.). 192p. (J). (gr. 5-7). pap. 7.99 *(978-0-544-43935-1(X)*, 1596834, Clarion Bks.) HarperCollins Pubs.

Paulsen, Gary. A Soldier's Heart. 2004. 128p. (J). (gr. 7-18). pap. 29.00 incl. audio *(978-0-8072-8301-1(0)*, Listening Library) Random Hse. Audio Publishing Group.

—Woods Runner. 2011. (ENG.). 176p. (YA). (gr. 7). pap. 9.99 *(978-0-375-85908-3(X)*, Lamb, Wendy Bks.) Random Hse. Children's Bks.

Phillips, Dee. Blast, 1 vol. unabr. ed. 2010. (Right Now! Ser.). (ENG.). 45p. (YA). (gr. 9-12). pap. 10.75 *(978-1-61651-245-3(8))* Saddleback Educational Publishing, Inc.

—Over the Top. 2014. (Yesterday's Voices Ser.). (YA). lib. bdg. 19.60 *(978-0-606-35582-7(0))* Turtleback.

Polacco, Patricia. Tucky Jo & Little Heart. Polacco, Patricia, illus. 2015. (ENG., Illus.). 48p. (J). (gr. -1-3). 19.99 *(978-1-4814-1584-2(0)*, Simon & Schuster Bks. For Young Readers) Simon & Schuster Bks. For Young Readers.

Raughley, Sarah. Siege of Shadows. (Effigies Ser.: 2). (ENG.). (YA). (gr. 9). 2018. 464p. pap. 12.99 *(978-1-4814-6681-3(X))* 2017. (Illus.). 448p. 18.99 *(978-1-4814-6680-6(1))* Simon Pulse. (Simon Pulse).

Remarque, Erich-Maria. All Quiet on the Western Front: With Related Readings. Wheen, A. W., tr. from GER. 2003. (EMC Masterpiece Series Access Editions). (Illus.). xxv, 249p. (YA). 13.99 *(978-0-8219-2420-4(6))* EMC/Paradigm Publishing.

Robbins, Dennis L. A Soldier's Christmas. 2011. 44p. pap. 21.99 *(978-1-4653-4097-9(1))* Xlibris Corp.

Rosenblatt, Darcey. Lost Boys. 2018. (ENG.). 288p. (J). pap. 12.99 *(978-1-250-15882-6(6)*, 900159430) Square Fish.

Sarah Taylor. The Teddy That Went to Iraq. Baker, David, illus. 2011. 28p. pap. 24.95 *(978-1-4560-8382-3(1))* America Star Bks.

Schmidt, Gary D. Anson's Way. 2009. (ENG.). 224p. (J). (gr. 3-7). pap. 15.95 *(978-0-547-23761-9(8)*, 1083874, Clarion Bks.) HarperCollins Pubs.

Schwabach, Karen. The Storm Before Atlanta. 2011. 320p. (J). (gr. 3-7). pap. 7.99 *(978-0-375-85867-3(9)*, Yearling) Random Hse. Children's Bks.

Sherman, M. Zachary. Blood Brotherhood, 1 vol. Casas, Fritz, illus. 2011. (Bloodlines Ser.). (ENG.). 88p. (J). (gr. 4-8). pap. 6.95 *(978-1-4342-3098-0(8)*, 114738, Stone Arch Bks.) Capstone.

—Control under Fire, 1 vol. Casas, Fritz, illus. 2011. (Bloodlines Ser.). (ENG.). 88p. (J). (gr. 4-8). pap. 6.95 *(978-1-4342-3100-0(3)*, 114739); lib. bdg. 27.32 *(978-1-4342-2561-0(5)*, 113620) Capstone. (Stone Arch Bks.).

—Fighting Phantoms, 1 vol. Casas, Fritz, illus. 2011. (Bloodlines Ser.). (ENG.). 88p. (J). (gr. 4-8). lib. bdg. 27.32 *(978-1-4342-2560-3(7)*, 113619, Stone Arch Bks.) Capstone.

—Heart of War. Casas, Fritz et al, illus. 2013. (Bloodlines Ser.). (ENG.). 240p. (J). (gr. 4-8). pap., pap., pap. 7.95 *(978-1-62370-002-7(7)*, 122308, Capstone Young Readers) Capstone.

—A Time for War, 1 vol. Casas, Fritz, illus. 2011. (Bloodlines Ser.). (ENG.). 88p. (J). (gr. 4-8). 27.32 *(978-1-4342-2558-0(5)*, 113616, Stone Arch Bks.) Capstone.

Shoulders, Michael. Crossing the Deadline: Stephen's Journey Through the Civil War. 2016. (ENG.). 384p. (YA). (gr. 4-7). 16.99 *(978-1-58536-951-5(9)*, 204098) Sleeping Bear Pr.

Skrutskie, Emily. Hullmetal Girls. 2018. 320p. (YA). (gr. 9). 17.99 *(978-1-5247-7019-8(1)*, Delacorte Pr.) Random Hse. Children's Bks.

Skye, Evelyn. Circle of Shadows. 2019. (YA). (Circle of Shadows Ser.: 1). (ENG.). 480p. (gr. 8). pap. 10.99 *(978-0-06-264373-5(8))*; (Illus.). 464p. *(978-0-06-291540-5(1))*; (Circle of Shadows Ser.: 1). (ENG., Illus.). 464p. (gr. 8). 17.99 *(978-0-06-264372-8(X))* HarperCollins Pubs. (Balzer & Bray).

Smith, Annie Laura. Saving da Vinci. 2005. (YA). mass mkt. 6.99 *(978-0-9753367-6-2(2))* Onstage Publishing, LLC.

Smith, W. J. Gorte 2: The Awakening. 2010. 174p. pap. *(978-1-84748-452-9(2))* Athena Pr.

Stewart-Goodair, Madonna. Key to the Golden Gates: The Mystic Soldier, Book 1, 1 vol. 2009. 48p. pap. 16.95 *(978-1-61582-625-4(4))* PublishAmerica, Inc.

—The Mystic Soldier: Warlock of Fire, 1 vol. 2009. 57p. pap. 16.95 *(978-1-61546-840-9(4))* PublishAmerica, Inc.

Strasser, Todd. Price of Duty. 2018. (ENG., Illus.). 192p. (YA). (gr. 9). 17.99 *(978-1-4814-9709-1(X)*, Simon & Schuster Bks. For Young Readers) Simon & Schuster Bks. For Young Readers.

—Price of Duty. 2019. (ENG.). 192p. (YA). (gr. 9). pap. 11.99 *(978-1-4814-9710-7(3))* Simon & Schuster, Inc.

Stratemeyer, Edward. Marching on Niagara: The Soldier Boys of the Old Frontier. 2011. 191p. (YA). pap. *(978-0-9843717-2-3(9))* Gask Castle Pr.

—With Washington in the West: A Soldier Boy's Battles in the Wilderness. 2011. 198p. (J). pap. *(978-0-9843717-1-6(0))* Gask Castle Pr.

Stratford, Anne Margaret. My Daddy Is A Soldier. 2008. (Illus.). 40p. (J). 17.99 *(978-0-9817938-0-1(0))* Diamond Fly Publishing, Inc.

Styles, Showell. The Flying Ensign: Greencoats Against Napoleon. 2003. (Budget Bks). Orig. Title: Greencoat Against Napoleon. (ENG.). 340p. (J). (gr. 7-9). pap. 14.95 *(978-1-883937-70-6(1))* Ignatius Pr.

Sullivan, Jacqueline Levering. Annie's War. 2007. (Illus.). 183p. (J). (gr. 3-7). 15.00 *(978-0-8028-5325-7(0)*, Eerdmans Bks For Young Readers) Eerdmans, William B. Publishing Co.

Sutcliff, Rosemary. The Eagle. movie tie-in ed. 2011. (Roman Britain Trilogy Ser.: 1). (ENG.). 240p. (YA). (gr. 5). pap. 10.99 *(978-0-312-56434-6(1)*, 900074782) Square Fish.

—The Eagle of the Ninth. 2010. (Roman Britain Trilogy Ser.: 1). (ENG.). 240p. (YA). (gr. 7). pap. 11.99 *(978-0-312-64429-1(9)*, 900068423) Square Fish.

Sutter, Marcus. Soldier Dogs #1: Air Raid Search & Rescue. Kinsella, Pat, illus. 2018. (Soldier Dogs Ser.: 1). (ENG.). 224p. (J). (gr. 3-7). pap. 7.99 *(978-0-06-284403-3(2)*, HarperFestival) HarperCollins Pubs.

Sykes, Shelley & Szymanski, Lois. The Soldier in the Cellar. 2011. (Gettysburg Ghost Gang Ser.: Vol. 5). 96p. (J). pap. 7.95 *(978-1-57249-299-8(6)*, White Mane Kids) White Mane Publishing Co., Inc.

Tak, Bibi Dumon. Soldier Bear. Philip Hopman, illus. 2011. (ENG.). 158p. (J). 13.00 *(978-0-8028-5375-2(7)*, Eerdmans Bks For Young Readers) Eerdmans, William B. Publishing Co.

Tallec, Olivier. Waterloo & Trafalgar. 2012. (Illus.). 64p. (J). (gr. k). 17.95 *(978-1-59270-127-8(2))* Enchanted Lion Bks., LLC.

Teacher Created Resources Staff & Collins, Susan. A Guide for Using Time Soldiers in the Classroom. 2009. (ENG.). 48p. pap. 9.99 *(978-1-4206-2003-0(7))* Teacher Created Resources, Inc.

Tintera, Amy. Rebel. (Reboot Ser.: 2). 352p. (YA). (gr. 8). 2015. (ENG.). pap. 10.99 *(978-0-06-221711-0(9))* 2014. pap. 12.00 *(978-0-06-233790-0(4))* HarperCollins Pubs. (HarperTeen).

—Reboot. 2013. (Reboot Ser.: 1). (ENG.). 384p. (YA). (gr. 8). 17.99 *(978-0-06-221707-3(0)*, HarperTeen) HarperCollins Pubs.

Tischler, Tracey. Heroes in the Sandbox. 2009. 28p. pap. 13.95 *(978-1-4490-5502-8(8))* AuthorHouse.

To Keep Me SAFE! A Story for Children Affected by Military Deployments. 2003. (J). 12.00 *(978-0-9740289-0-3(8))* State of Growth Publishing Co.

Turner, Megan Whalen. The King of Attolia. (Queen's Thief Ser.: 3). (ENG.). (YA). (gr. 8). 2017. 432p. pap. 10.99 *(978-0-06-264298-1(7))* 2007. 432p. pap. 7.99 *(978-0-06-083579-8(6))* 2006. 400p. 17.99 *(978-0-06-083577-4(X))* HarperCollins Pubs. (Greenwillow Bks.).

—The King of Attolia. 2007. (Queen's Thief Ser.: BK.3). 387p. (YA). 18.00 *(978-0-7569-8106-8(9))* Perfection Learning Corp.

—The King of Attolia. (YA). 2008. (Queen's Thief Ser.: BK.3). (ENG.). 84.49 *(978-1-4281-8027-7(3))* 2007. (Attolia Ser.: 3). 119.75 *(978-1-4281-1722-8(9))* 2007. (Queen's Thief Ser.: BK.3). (ENG.). 92.75 *(978-1-4281-1716-7(4))* 2006. (Queen's Thief Ser.: BK.3). (ENG.). 90.75 *(978-1-4281-1718-1(0))* 2006. (Queen's Thief Ser.: BK.3). (ENG.). 122.75 *(978-1-4281-1720-4(2))* 2006. (Queen's Thief Ser.: BK.3). 281.75 *(978-1-4281-1721-1(0))* 2006. (Queen's Thief Ser.: BK.3). (ENG.). 1.25 *(978-1-4281-1713-6(X))* 2006. (Queen's Thief Ser.: BK.3). (ENG.). 251.75 *(978-1-4281-1717-4(2))* Recorded Bks., Inc.

Verne, Jules. The Secret of the Island. Kingston, W. H. G., tr. 2008. 160p. 24.95 *(978-1-60664-753-0(9))* Rodgers, Alan Bks.

Warner, Susan. Daisy in the Field. 2017. (ENG., Illus.). (J). 26.95 *(978-1-374-97071-7(9))* Capital Communications, Inc.

Warner, Susan & Wetherell, Elizabeth. Daisy in the Field. 2011. 272p. 29.95 *(978-1-4638-9964-6(5))*; pap. 16.95 *(978-1-4638-0163-2(7))* Rodgers, Alan Bks.

Weston Woods Staff, creator. Stone Soup. 2011. 38.75 *(978-0-439-84572-4(6))*; 29.95 *(978-0-439-74595-6(0))* Weston Woods Studios, Inc.

Wiechman, Kathy Cannon. Like a River: A Civil War Novel. (ENG.). 336p. (J). (gr. 4-7). 2015. 18.99 *(978-1-62979-209-5(8))* 2012. (Illus.). E-Book *(978-1-62979-061-9(3))* Highlights Pr., c/o Highlights for Children, Inc. (Calkins Creek).

Wills, Cheryl. The Emancipation of Grandpa Sandy Wills. Pearson, Randell, illus. 2016. (ENG.). 48p. (J). pap. 18.63 *(978-1-61717-886-3(1))* Sussman Sales Co.

Wilson, John. Flames of the Tiger. 2003. (Illus.). 176p. (J). (gr. 13-18). 6.95 *(978-1-55337-619-4(6))* Kids Can Pr., Ltd. CAN. Dist: Hachette Bk. Group.

Winders, Gertrude Hecker. Jeb Stuart: Boy in the Saddle. Doremus, Robert, illus. 2011. 202p. 44.95 *(978-1-258-08155-3(5))* Literary Licensing, LLC.

Wolfer, Dianne & Harrison-Lever, Brian. Photographs in the Mud. 2007. (Illus.). 32p. pap. 15.50 *(978-1-921361-04-3(2))* Fremantle Pr. AUS. Dist: Independent Pubs. Group.

Wooten, Laura. With My Little Box of Crayons. Pennington, Kelly, illus. 2008. 50p. pap. 18.95 *(978-1-4251-7103-2(6))* Trafford Publishing.

Wright, Caleb E. Marcus Blair A Story of Provincial Times. 2006. pap. 22.95 *(978-1-4286-6303-9(7))* Kessinger Publishing, LLC.

Wulffson, Don L. Soldier X. 2003. 240p. (YA). (gr. 7-18). 6.99 *(978-0-14-250073-6(9)*, Puffin Books) Penguin Young Readers Group.

Wynne-Jones, Tim. The Emperor of Any Place. 2015. 336p. (YA). (gr. 9). 17.99 *(978-0-7636-6973-7(3))* Candlewick Pr.

Young, Miriam. Miss Suzy. Lobel, Arnold, illus. (J). 40th anniv. ed. 2004. 44p. 18.95 *(978-1-930900-28-8(7))* 50th ed. 2014. (ENG.). 40p. (gr. -1-3). 18.95 *(978-1-930900-75-2(9))* Purple Hse. Pr.

SOLDIERS—UNITED STATES

see also African American Soldiers

Ades, Audrey. Ethan Allen & the Green Mountain Boys. 2017. (Illus.). 32p. (J). 25.70 *(978-1-61228-952-6(5))* Mitchell Lane Pubs.

Anderson, Dale. A Soldier's Life in the Civil War, 1 vol. 2004. (World Almanac(r) Library of the Civil War Ser.). (ENG., Illus.). 48p. (gr. 5-8). pap. 15.05 *(978-0-8368-5595-1(7)*, 644f6601-6cb3-4513-a5bb-f0753119da8b, Gareth Stevens Secondary Library) Stevens, Gareth Publishing LLLP.

Beller, Susan Provost. Billy Yank & Johnny Reb: Soldiering in the Civil War. rev. ed. 2007. (Soldiers on the Battlefront Ser.). (ENG., Illus.). 112p. (gr. 6-8). lib. bdg. 33.26 *(978-0-8225-6803-2(9))* Lerner Publishing Group.

—The Doughboys over There: Soldiering in World War I. 2007. (Soldiers on the Battlefront Ser.). (ENG., Illus.). 112p. (J). (gr. 6-8). lib. bdg. 33.26 *(978-0-8225-6295-5(2))* Lerner Publishing Group.

—Yankee Doodle & the Redcoats: Soldiering in the Revolutionary War. rev. ed. 2007. (Soldiers on the Battlefront Ser.). (ENG., Illus.). 112p. (gr. 6-8). lib. bdg. 33.26 *(978-0-8225-6655-7(9))* Lerner Publishing Group.

Bryfonski, Dedria, ed. Veterans, 1 vol. 2015. (Opposing Viewpoints Ser.). (ENG., Illus.). 240p. (gr. 10-12). pap. 34.80 *(978-0-7377-7299-9(9)*, dd36cab3-31ac-4e6e-b7c5-4b42c8a706e6, Greenhaven Publishing) Greenhaven Publishing LLC.

Burns, Heidi A., contrib. by. U. S. Army True Stories: Tales of Bravery. 2014. (Courage under Fire Ser.). (ENG.). 32p. (J). (gr. 3-9). lib. bdg. 28.65 *(978-1-4765-9938-0(6)*, 125756, Capstone Pr.) Capstone.

Castrovilla, Selene. By the Sword. Farnsworth, Bill, illus. 2007. (ENG.). 40p. (J). (gr. 1-4). 17.95 *(978-1-59078-427-3(8)*, Calkins Creek) Highlights Pr., c/o Highlights for Children, Inc.

Cefrey, Holly. One Life to Lose for My Country: The Arrest & Execution of Nathan Hale. (Great Moments in American History Ser.). 32p. (gr. 3-3). 2009. 47.90 *(978-1-61513-135-8(3))* 2003. (ENG., Illus.). lib. bdg. 29.13 *(978-0-8239-4371-5(2)*, ffc71398-7cd2-4bd6-9226-931d0ff47e52, Rosen Reference) Rosen Publishing Group, Inc., The.

Collier, Peter. Choosing Courage: Inspiring True Stories of What It Means to Be a Hero. 2016. (ENG., Illus.). 272p. (J). (gr. 4-7). pap. 8.95 *(978-1-57965-705-5(2)*, 85705) Artisan.

Conkling, Winifred. Heroism Begins with Her: Inspiring Stories of Bold, Brave, & Gutsy Women in the U. S. Military. Kuo, Julia, illus. 2019. (ENG.). 240p. (J). (gr. 3-7). 18.99 *(978-0-06-284741-6(4)*, HarperCollins) HarperCollins Pubs.

Curtis, Suzanne. John Wesley Powell: American Hero. 2013. (ENG & SPA., Illus.). 78p. (J). pap. 8.95 *(978-0-86541-178-4(6))* Filter Pr., LLC.

Dell, Pamela & Raatma, Lucia. The Science of Soldiers, 1 vol. 2012. (Science of War Ser.). (ENG.). 48p. (J). (gr. 6-9). lib. bdg. 34.65 *(978-0-7565-4460-7(2)*, 115723, Compass Point Bks.) Capstone.

Dixon Jr., John T. Mommy, What Is a POW/MIA? 2008. 48p. pap. 24.95 *(978-1-60474-029-5(9))* PublishAmerica, Inc.

Doeden, Matt. Can You Survive in the Special Forces? An Interactive Survival Adventure. 2012. (You Choose: Survival Ser.). (ENG.). 112p. (J). (gr. 3-4). pap. 41.70 *(978-1-4296-9481-0(5)*, 18654, Capstone Pr.) Capstone.

Doyle, Bill H. Behind Enemy Lines: Under Fire in the Middle East. 2011. 136p. (J). pap. *(978-0-545-33463-1(2))* Scholastic, Inc.

Ellis, Edward S. The Life of Kit Carson: Hunter, Trapper, Guide, Indian Agent & Colonel U. S. A. 2007. 176p. per. *(978-1-4065-2477-2(8))* Dodo Pr.

Farrell, Mary Cronk. Standing up Against Hate: How Black Women in the Army Helped Change the Course of WWII. 2019. (ENG., Illus.). 208p. (J). (gr. 5-9). 17.99 *(978-1-4197-3160-0(2)*, 1151301, Abrams Bks. for Young Readers) Abrams, Inc.

Gauch, Patricia Lee. The Impossible Major Rogers. Parker, Robert Andrew, illus. 2008. (J). *(978-1-59078-334-4(4))* Highlights Pr., c/o Highlights for Children, Inc.

Goldish, Meish. Army: Civilian to Soldier. 2010. (Becoming a Soldier Ser.). 24p. (YA). (gr. 3-6). lib. bdg. 26.99 *(978-1-936088-11-9(8))* Bearport Publishing Co., Inc.

Goldsmith, Connie. Women in the Military: From Drill Sergeants to Fighter Pilots. 2019. (ENG., Illus.). 120p. (YA). (gr. 6-12). 37.32 *(978-1-5415-2812-3(3)*, 926b05ea-eead-4685-b89f-468374efd7d4, Twenty-First Century Bks.) Lerner Publishing Group.

Gonzalez, Lissette. The U. S. Military: Defending the Nation. (Dangerous Jobs Ser.). 24p. (gr. 2-3). 2009. 42.50 *(978-1-61512-137-3(4)*, PowerKids Pr.) 2007. (ENG., Illus.). (J). lib. bdg. 26.27 *(978-1-4042-3777-3(1)*,

1824257e-f710-4fc7-b56c-43f1b2c32996) Rosen Publishing Group, Inc., The.

Grossi, Craig. Craig & Fred Young Readers' Edition: A Marine, a Stray Dog, & How They Rescued Each Other. (ENG.). 256p. (J). (gr. 3). 2018. pap. 7.99 (978-0-06-269336-5(0)) 2017. (Illus.). 16.99 (978-0-06-269335-8(2)) HarperCollins Pubs. (HarperCollins).

Gunderson, Jessica. U. S. Navy True Stories: Tales of Bravery. 2014. (Courage under Fire Ser.). (ENG.). 32p. (J). (gr. 3-9). lib. bdg. 28.65 (978-1-4765-9937-3(8), 125758, Capstone Pr.) Capstone.

Hart, Joyce. Frequently Asked Questions about Being Part of a Military Family, 1 vol. 2009. (FAQ: Teen Life Ser.). (ENG., Illus.). 64p. (J). (gr. 5-6). lib. bdg. 37.13 (978-1-4358-5328-7(8), 55819231-6297-4ce2-aa7b-669164ab6757) Rosen Publishing Group, Inc., The.

Henrickson, Beth. The Marquis de Lafayette & Other International Champions of the American Revolution, 1 vol. 2015. (Spotlight on American History Ser.). (ENG., Illus.). 24p. (J). (gr. 4-6). pap. 11.00 (978-1-4994-1745-6(4), 6fd49d9d-45b0-422a-832d-c0f0b5b867d7, PowerKids Pr.) Rosen Publishing Group, Inc., The.

Hollmann, Robert E. William Barret Travis. 2012. (ENG.). 130p. pap. 9.95 (978-0-9779863-9-2(X)) Fireside Pr., Inc.

Kann, Bob. Cordelia Harvey: Civil War Angel. 2011. (Badger Biographies Ser.). (ENG., Illus.). 128p. (J). pap. 12.95 (978-0-87020-458-6(0)) Wisconsin Historical Society.

Levy, Janey. The Battle of the Alamo. (American History Flashpoints! Ser.). 32p. (gr. 4-4). 2009. 47.90 (978-1-61511-369-9(X), PowerKids Pr.) 2009. (ENG.). (J). lib. bdg. 28.93 (978-1-4358-2991-6(3), 8be7db00-99bc-423d-9fff-680274e8149e, PowerKids Pr.) 2008. (ENG.). pap. 10.00 (978-1-4358-0167-7(9), 92794efd-7ddf-4f34-9dcb-d7c99ab32b7c, Rosen Classroom) Rosen Publishing Group, Inc., The.

Lewis, Noah & Graham, Loretta. Edward Ned Hector. 2005. (ENG., Illus.). 36p. per. 19.99 (978-1-4208-6817-3(9)) AuthorHouse.

Libertson, Jody. Nathan Hale: Hero of the American Revolution. (Primary Sources of Famous People in American History Ser.). 32p. (gr. 2-3). 2009. 47.90 (978-1-60851-709-1(8)) 2003. (ENG & SPA., Illus.). lib. bdg. 29.13 (978-0-8239-4165-0(5), 6ba7c6c5-6c5b-48d6-8893-ff86061206ad, Editorial Buenas Letras) Rosen Publishing Group, Inc., The.

—Nathan Hale: Heroe de la guerra de Independencia, 1 vol. 2003. (Grandes Personajes en la Historia de Los Estados Unidos (Famous People in American History) Ser.). (SPA.). 32p. (gr. 3-4). pap. 10.00 (978-0-8239-4235-0(X), 6a95018e-f493-428b-81c2-a4423aaa0918, Rosen Classroom) Rosen Publishing Group, Inc., The.

—Nathan Hale: Heroe Revolucionario, 1 vol. 2003. (Grandes Personajes en la Historia de Los Estados Unidos (Famous People in American History) Ser.). (SPA., Illus.). 32p. (gr. 3-4). lib. bdg. 29.13 (978-0-8239-4141-4(8), bbc97f46-967b-45e2-a513-8a16ffafddad, Editorial Buenas Letras) Rosen Publishing Group, Inc., The.

—Nathan Hale: Héroe revolucionario / Hero of the American Revolution. 2009. (Famous People in American History/Grandes personajes en la historia de los Estados Unidos Ser.). (ENG & SPA.). 32p. (gr. 2-3). 47.90 (978-1-61512-552-4(3), Editorial Buenas Letras) Rosen Publishing Group, Inc., The.

—Nathan Hale: Héroe revolucionario (Nathan Hale: Hero of the American Revolution) 2009. (Grandes personajes en la historia de los Estados Unidos (Famous People in American History) Ser.). (SPA.). 32p. (gr. 2-3). 47.90 (978-1-61512-805-1(0), Editorial Buenas Letras) Rosen Publishing Group, Inc., The.

Link, Theodore. George Armstrong Custer: General de la Caballeria Estadounidense, 1 vol. 2003. (Grandes Personajes en la Historia de Los Estados Unidos (Famous People in American History) Ser.). (SPA., Illus.). 32p. (gr. 3-4). lib. bdg. 29.13 (978-0-8239-4134-6(5), de5d73c4-f45c-4127-8d2c-c8fca0a6b9c1, Editorial Buenas Letras) Rosen Publishing Group, Inc., The.

Markovics, Joyce L. & Pushies, Fred J. Today's Army Heroes. 2012. (Acts of Courage: Inside America's Military Ser.). 32p. (J). (gr. 2-7). lib. bdg. 28.50 (978-1-61772-445-9(9)) Bearport Publishing Co., Inc.

Marsico, Katie. John Cook's Civil War Story. Belmonte, David, illus. 2018. (Narrative Nonfiction: Kids in War Ser.). (ENG.). 32p. (J). (gr. 2-4). 27.99 (978-1-5124-5680-6(2), 5f6f9e26-2fd6-4442-9c13-4ea16f171ba8, Lerner Pubns.); pap. 9.99 (978-1-5415-1191-0(3), 22ac3d17-499b-4ec8-b3fc-10cf1dced47f) Lerner Publishing Group.

Marx, Mandy R. Amazing U. S. Marine Facts. 2016. (Amazing Military Facts Ser.). (ENG., Illus.). 24p. (J). (gr. -1-2). lib. bdg. 27.32 (978-1-5157-0954-1(X), 132278, Capstone Pr.) Capstone.

Maynard, Charles W. John Wesley Powell: Soldier, Scientist, & Explorer. 2009. (Famous Explorers of the American West Ser.). 24p. (gr. 3-4). 42.50 (978-1-61512-505-0(1), PowerKids Pr.) Rosen Publishing Group, Inc., The.

McNab, Chris. Learning Mental Endurance for Survival. Carney, John, ed. 2014. (Extreme Survival in the Military Ser.: 12). 64p. (J). (gr. 7-18). lib. bdg. 23.95 (978-1-4222-3082-4(1)) Mason Crest.

Micklos, John & Micklos, John, Jr. Why We Won the American Revolution: Through Primary Sources, 1 vol. 2013. (American Revolution Through Primary Sources Ser.). (ENG., Illus.). 48p. (J). (gr. 4-6). 27.93 (978-0-7660-4134-9(4), 1427223b-d0b5-47ed-ad69-7c1c441a1350) Enslow Publishing, LLC.

Miller, Adam, et al. Courage under Fire: True Stories of Bravery from the U. S. Army, Navy, Air Force, & Marines, 1 vol. 2014. (Courage under Fire Ser.). (ENG., Illus.). 112p. (J). (gr. 3-9). pap., pap., pap. 9.95 (978-1-4914-1065-3(5), 126702, Capstone Pr.) Capstone.

Miller, Reagan & Claus, J. Matteson. Life on a Civil War Battlefield. 2011. (ENG.). 48p. (J). pap. (978-0-7787-5357-5(3)); lib. bdg. (978-0-7787-5340-7(9)) Crabtree Publishing Co.

Moss, Marissa. Nurse, Soldier, Spy: The Story of Sarah Edmonds, a Civil War Hero. Hendrix, John, illus. 2011. (ENG.). 48p. (J). (gr. 3-7). 19.95 (978-0-8109-9735-6(5), 658701, Abrams Bks. for Young Readers) Abrams, Inc.

Norfolk, Sherry & Norfolk, Bobby. The Virginia Giant: The True Story of Peter Francisco. Brennan, Cait, illus. 2014. (ENG.). 160p. (J). (gr. 4-7). 16.99 (978-1-62619-117-4(4), History Pr., The) Arcadia Publishing.

Olson, Nathan & Glaser, Jason. Nathan Hale: Revolutionary Spy, 1 vol. Martin, Cynthia & Schoonover, Brent, illus. 2006. (Graphic Biographies Ser.). (ENG.). 32p. (J). (gr. 3-9). per. 8.10 (978-0-7368-6199-1(8), 87898, Capstone Pr.) Capstone.

Peppas, Lynn. Why Sam Houston Matters to Texas, 1 vol. 2013. (Texas Perspectives Ser.). (ENG., Illus.). 32p. (J). (gr. 4-4). lib. bdg. 28.93 (978-1-4777-0912-2(6), 60e60101-a7ab-4741-8c21-e08fda6394f0) Rosen Publishing Group, Inc., The.

Porterfield, Jason. The Third Amendment: The Right to Privacy in the Home, 1 vol. 2011. (Amendments to the United States Constitution: the Bill of Rights Ser.). (ENG., Illus.). 64p. (YA). (gr. 6-6). lib. bdg. 37.13 (978-1-4488-1256-1(9), c65b7d1b-4a76-4763-a116-93973e0541c2) Rosen Publishing Group, Inc., The.

—Third Amendment: Upholding the Right to Privacy, 1 vol. 2011. (Amendments to the United States Constitution: the Bill of Rights Ser.). (ENG.). 64p. (YA). (gr. 6-6). pap. 13.95 (978-1-4488-2304-8(8), f030c4a2-1fe0-422e-9906-b883ae76e358, Rosen Reference) Rosen Publishing Group, Inc., The.

Ratliff, Thomas. You Wouldn't Want to Be a Civil War Soldier! A War You'd Rather Not Fight. Antram, David, illus. 2013. (You Wouldn't Want to... Ser.). (ENG.). 32p. (J). 29.00 (978-0-531-25947-4(1), Watts, Franklin) Scholastic Library Publishing.

—You Wouldn't Want to Be a Civil War Soldier! A War You'D Rather Not Fight. 2013. (You Wouldn't Want To Ser.). lib. bdg. 20.80 (978-0-606-31627-9(2)) Turtleback.

Raum, Elizabeth. At Battle in the Revolutionary War: An Interactive Battlefield Adventure. 2015. (You Choose: Battlefields Ser.). (ENG., Illus.). 112p. (J). (gr. 3-7). pap. 6.95 (978-1-4914-2392-9(7), 127800, Capstone Pr.) Capstone.

Rice, Earle. The Life & Times of the Brothers Custer: Galloping to Glory. 2008. (Profiles in American History Ser.). (Illus.). 48p. (J). (gr. 4-8). lib. bdg. 29.95 (978-1-58415-665-9(1)) Mitchell Lane Pubs.

Sanford, William R. & Green, Carl R. Kit Carson: Courageous Mountain Man, 1 vol. 2013. (Courageous Heroes of the American West Ser.). (ENG., Illus.). 48p. (J). (gr. 5-7). pap. 11.53 (978-1-4644-0094-0(6), c76bd838-258d-431a-a120-4cfb04bb164f) Enslow Publishing, LLC.

Shoup, Kate. Life As a Soldier in the Civil War, 1 vol. 2015. (Life As... Ser.). (ENG., Illus.). 32p. (gr. 3-3). pap. 11.58 (978-1-5026-1083-6(3), 5dc3d5b6-a27f-4e0c-9e90-74c7d6dd040a) Cavendish Square Publishing LLC.

Siddons, Brian. Crispus Attucks & African American Patriots of the American Revolution, 1 vol. 2015. (Spotlight on American History Ser.). (ENG., Illus.). 24p. (J). (gr. 4-6). pap. 11.00 (978-1-4994-1739-5(X), 36a9b1bb-9134-4ab4-8115-56689f89d55d, PowerKids Pr.) Rosen Publishing Group, Inc., The.

Smithson, Ryan. Ghosts of War. 2010. (ENG.). 360p. (YA). (gr. 9). pap. 10.99 (978-0-06-166471-7(5), HarperTeen) HarperCollins Pubs.

Souza, D. M. John Wesley Powell. 2004. (Watts Library). (ENG., Illus.). 64p. (J). (gr. 5-7). pap. 8.95 (978-0-531-16653-6(8), Watts, Franklin) Scholastic Library Publishing.

Spradlin, Michael P. Jack Montgomery: World War II: Gallantry at Anzio. 2019. (Medal of Honor Ser.: 1). (ENG., Illus.). 112p. (J). pap. 8.99 (978-1-250-15707-2(2), 900185139, Farrar, Straus & Giroux (BYR)) Farrar, Straus & Giroux.

Stewart, Gail B. Life of a Soldier in Washington's Army. 2003. (American War Library). (ENG., Illus.). 112p. (J). 30.85 (978-1-59018-215-4(4), Lucent Bks.) Cengage Gale.

Stout, Glenn. Soldier Athletes. 2011. (Good Sports Ser.). (ENG.). 112p. (J). (gr. 5-7). pap. 6.99 (978-0-547-41729-5(2), 1430259, Clarion Bks.) HarperCollins Pubs.

Thornton, Jeremy. Foreign-Born Champions of the American Revolution. 2009. (Building America's Democracy Ser.). 24p. (gr. 3-3). 42.50 (978-1-61511-764-2(4), PowerKids Pr.) Rosen Publishing Group, Inc., The.

Vonne, Mira. Gross Facts about the American Civil War. 2017. (Gross History Ser.). (ENG., Illus.). 32p. (J). (gr. 3-9). lib. bdg. 27.32 (978-1-5157-4155-8(9), 133955, Capstone Pr.) Capstone.

Walsh, Steve. Zebulon Montgomery Pike: Explorer & Military Officer. 2011. (ENG & SPA., Illus.). 54p. (J). pap. 8.95 (978-0-86541-123-4(9)) Filter Pr., LLC.

Williams, Jack S. Soldiers & Their Families of the California Mission Frontier. 2009. (People of the California Missions Ser.). 64p. (gr. 4-4). 58.50 (978-1-60851-160-0(X), PowerKids Pr.) Rosen Publishing Group, Inc., The.

Yomtov, Nelson. Courage on the Battlefield: True Tales of Survival in the Military. 2015. (True Stories of Survival Ser.). (ENG., Illus.). 32p. (J). (gr. 3-9). lib. bdg. 31.32 (978-1-4914-6571-4(9), 129051, Capstone Pr.) Capstone.

Zullo, Allan. War Heroes: Voices from Iraq. 2009. 48p. (J). pap. (978-0-545-09026-1(1)) Scholastic, Inc.

SOLDIERS, AFRICAN AMERICAN

see African American Soldiers

SOLDIERS IN ART

Bergin, Mark. Soldiers, 1 vol. 2012. (How to Draw Ser.). (ENG.). 32p. (J). (gr. 4-5). pap. 12.75 (978-1-4488-6473-7(9), 5e4496cf-2c02-4105-a25a-6d1fe40afc82); lib. bdg. 30.27 (978-1-4488-6463-8(1), 7bb87737-0861-4bde-91f1-797136f1665b) Rosen Publishing Group, Inc., The. (PowerKids Pr.).

O'Connor, Jane. Hidden Army: Clay Soldiers of Ancient China. 2011. (All Aboard Reading Ser.). 48p. (J). (gr. 1-3). mass mkt. 4.99 (978-0-448-45580-8(3), Grosset & Dunlap) Penguin Young Readers Group.

SOLDIERS' LIFE

see Soldiers

SOLID GEOMETRY

see Geometry

SOLO, HAN (FICTITIOUS CHARACTER)—FICTION

Aaron, Jason. Skywalker Strikes. Cassaday, John & Martin, Laura, illus. 2016. (Star Wars: Skywalker Strikes Ser.). (ENG.). (J). (gr. 6-12). 24p. lib. bdg. 31.36 (978-1-61479-532-2(0), 21432); 24p. lib. bdg. 31.36 (978-1-61479-530-8(4), 21430); Vol. 1. 32p. lib. bdg. 31.36 (978-1-61479-527-8(4), 21427); Vol. 2. 24p. lib. bdg. 31.36 (978-1-61479-528-5(2), 21428); Vol. 3. 24p. lib. bdg. 31.36 (978-1-61479-529-2(0), 21429); Vol. 5. 24p. lib. bdg. 31.36 (978-1-61479-531-5(2), 21431) Spotlight. (Graphic Novels).

Barlow, Jeremy & Soriano, Carlo. Star Wars Adventures: Princess Leia & the Royal Ransom. 2011. (Star Wars Digests Ser.). (ENG., Illus.). 80p. (J). (gr. 3-8). 34.21 (978-1-59961-902-6(4), 13750, Graphic Novels) Spotlight.

Disney Book Group. Trapped in the Death Star! 2016. (Star Wars: World of Reading Ser.). (Illus.). 30p. (J). lib. bdg. 14.75 (978-0-606-39174-0(6)) Turtleback.

Kent, Lindsay. DK Readers L2: Star Wars: the Adventures of Han Solo. 2011. (DK Readers Level 2 Ser.). (ENG.). 32p. (J). (gr. -1-1). 3.99 (978-0-7566-8252-1(5), DK Children) Dorling Kindersley Publishing, Inc.

King, Trey. Death Star Battle. 2016. (Illus.). 30p. (J). (978-1-4806-9628-0(5), Disney Lucasfilm Press) Disney Publishing Worldwide.

Schreiber, Joe. Solo: A Star Wars Story. 2018. (Illus.). 201p. (J). (978-1-5444-2608-2(9)) Disney Publishing Worldwide.

Scott, Cavan. A Han & Chewie Adventure, 1. 2019. (Star Wars Choose Your Destiny Ser.). (ENG.). 144p. (J). (gr. 2-4). 15.59 (978-1-64310-797-4(6)) Penworthy Co., LLC, The.

Wang, Jack & Wang, Holman. Star Wars Epic Yarns: Return of the Jedi. 2015. (ENG., Illus.). 24p. (J). (gr. -1 — 1). 9.95 (978-1-4521-3500-7(2)) Chronicle Bks. LLC.

SOLOMON, KING OF ISRAEL

Myers, Glenn, illus. Solomon Builds the Temple: 1 Kings 5:1-8:66. 2005. (Little Learner Bible Story Books). 16p. (J). pap. 2.29 (978-0-7586-0944-1(2)) Concordia Publishing Hse.

Steinberg, Sari. King Solomon Figures It Out. Taulo, Tuija, illus. 2005. 32p. (J). (gr. k-3). 9.95 (978-965-465-004-5(5), Devora Publishing) Simcha Media Group.

Woodman, Ros. The Wise King: A Puzzle Book about Solomon. rev. ed. 2008. (Puzzle Ser.). (ENG.). 24p. (J). 4.99 (978-1-84550-404-5(6), d6891568-f6e9-441c-b87d-6cfe6c786595) Christian Focus Pubns. GBR. Dist: Baker & Taylor Publisher Services (BTPS).

SOLOMON, KING OF ISRAEL—FICTION

Haggard, H. Rider. Las Minas del Rey Salomon.Tr. of King Solomon's Mines. (SPA., Illus.). 184p. (YA). 11.95 (978-84-7281-094-5(1), AF1094) Auriga, Ediciones S.A. ESP. Dist: Continental Bk. Co., Inc.

—Las Minas del Rey Salomon. Eric, F. Rowe, illus. 5th ed. (Coleccion Clasicos en Accion).Tr. of King Solomon's Mines. (SPA.). 80p. (YA). (gr. 5-8). 12.76 (978-84-241-5779-1(6)) Everest Editora ESP. Dist: Lectorum Pubns., Inc.

Jules, Jacqueline. The Princess & the Ziz. Kahn, Katherine Janus, illus. 2008. 32p. (J). (gr. -1-3). lib. bdg. 17.95 (978-0-8225-7377-7(6), Kar-Ben Publishing) Lerner Publishing Group.

Kimmel, Eric A. Search for the Shamir. Stevanovic, Ivica, illus. 2018. (Scarlett & Sam Ser.). (ENG.). 152p. (J). (gr. 1-3). pap. 6.99 (978-1-5124-2938-1(4), fa05c70d-97fc-4c41-af59-93be9cd9769f, Kar-Ben Publishing) Lerner Publishing Group.

SONG BOOKS

see Songbooks

SONGBOOKS

see also School Songbooks

Barretta, Gene, illus. On Top of Spaghetti: A Silly Song Book. 2005. 12p. (J). 12.95 (978-1-58117-331-4(8), Intervisual/Piggy Toes) Bendon, Inc.

Big's Big Baby. (Looney Tunes Song & Sound Bks.). (Illus.). 16p. (J). (gr. -1-k). 7.98 (978-0-7853-1608-4(6), PI10) Publications International, Ltd.

Boytim, Joan Frey. Daffodils, Violets & Snowflakes - Low Voice: 24 Classical Songs for Young Women Ages Ten to Mid-Teens. 2003. (ENG.). 88p. pap. 16.99 (978-0-634-06212-4(3), 00740245) Leonard, Hal Corp.

Boytim, Joan Frey, ed. Daffodils, Violets & Snowflakes - High Voice: Classical Songs for Young Women High Voice Edition. 2003. (ENG.). 88p. (gr. 5-18). pap. 17.99 (978-0-634-06181-3(X), 00740244) Leonard, Hal Corp.

Diaper Days Songs. (Baby Looney Tunes Song Bks.). (Illus.). 16p. (J). (gr. -1). 7.98 (978-0-7853-1612-1(4), PI112) Publications International, Ltd.

Dockery, L. D. The Multiplication Song Book. 2012. 24p. pap. 17.99 (978-1-4772-6900-8(2)) AuthorHouse.

Frosty the Snowman: Songs of the Season: 5-Button Song Book. (Illus.). 10p. (J). (gr. -1-2). 7.98 (978-0-7853-2067-8(9), PI27) Publications International, Ltd.

Glazer, Tom. Tom Glazer's Treasury of Songs for Children. Seiden, Art, illus. 2nd ed. 2003. 256p. (J). (gr. 3-6). pap. 20.00 (978-1-58690-003-8(X)) Empire Publishing Service.

Goldstein, Rose B. Songs to Share. Schloss, E., illus. (ENG & HEB.). 64p. (J). (gr. -1-5). 2.95 (978-0-8381-0720-1(6), 10-720) United Synagogue of America Bk. Service.

Grant, Carrie and David. Elephant's Birthday Bells: Jump up & Join In. Busby, Ailie, illus. 2013. 32p. (J). pap. 7.99 (978-1-61067-181-1(3)) Kane Miller.

—Lion's Speedy Sauce: Jump up & Join In. Busby, Ailie, illus. 2013. 32p. (J). pap. 7.99 (978-1-61067-180-4(5)) Kane Miller.

Hal Leonard Corp. Staff. Still More Disney Solos for Kids Voice & Piano with Online Recorded Performances & Accompaniments. 2010. (ENG.). 44p. pap. 21.99 (978-1-4234-8333-5(2), 00230032) Leonard, Hal Corp.

Hop! Hop! Hop! (J). 15.95 (978-0-8126-0086-5(X)) Open Court Publishing Co.

Mickey's Favorites. (Sing-Along Ser.). (J). 11.99 incl. audio (978-1-55723-962-4(2)) Walt Disney Records.

Miller, Carolyn. Teaching Little Fingers to Play More Broadway Songs: Mid to Later Elementary Level. 2012. (ENG.). 32p. pap. 6.99 (978-1-4584-1767-1(0), 00416928) Willis Music Co.

Okun, Milton, ed. Cliff Eberhardt Songbook. Date not set. 56p. (YA). pap. 15.95 (978-0-89524-957-9(X)) Cherry Lane Music Co.

—Just for Kids. 32p. (YA). pap. 7.95 (978-0-89524-950-0(2), 02505506) Cherry Lane Music Co.

PI Kids. Disney Sofia the First: Princess in Training Sound Book. 2013. (ENG.). 12p. (J). (gr. k-3). bds. 15.99 (978-1-4508-6278-3(0), 1530, PI Kids) Phoenix International Publications, Inc.

Pingry, Patricia A. O Little Town of Bethlehem. 2008. (ENG., Illus.). 16p. (J). bds. 12.99 (978-0-8249-6566-2(3), Ideals Pubns.) Worthy Publishing.

Publications International Ltd. Staff, ed. Disney Princess: Canciones the Princesas. 2011. 24p. (J). 17.98 (978-1-4508-1615-1(0)) Publications International, Ltd.

—Disney Princess: Magical Princess Songs. 2011. 14p. (J). bds. 17.98 (978-1-4508-1132-3(9)) Publications International, Ltd.

—Disney Princess: Royal Recital. 2011. 14p. (J). bds. 17.98 (978-1-4508-1006-7(3)) Phoenix International Publications, Inc.

—Disney Princess: Songs to Treasure: Little Pop-Up Song Book. 2013. 10p. (J). (gr. k-4). bds. 10.99 (978-1-4508-6225-7(X), d48145fd-2550-4549-b020-98778a694300) Phoenix International Publications, Inc.

—Hello Kitty: Hello Songs: Play-A-Sound Digital Music Player Book. 2013. 14p. (J). (gr. k-4). bds. 22.98 (978-1-4508-6605-7(0), 4d3710ac-97b9-4b41-a7cd-23b43c501ffa) Phoenix International Publications, Inc.

—Minnie Mouse: Pretty Piano Play-Along: Piano Book. 2013. (Illus.). 14p. (J). (gr. k-3). bds. 18.98 (978-1-4508-6770-2(7), a4f2852b-3a90-4b10-ac4c-e802ee4cfa50) Phoenix International Publications, Inc.

—Minnie Mouse: Surprise, Surprise! Play-A-Sound Book. 2012. 10p. (J). (gr. k-3). bds. 7.99 (978-1-4508-6848-8(7), 0897e306-d7d1-4df0-a08f-afd88e1cfa82) Phoenix International Publications, Inc.

—Nickelodeon Dora the Explorer: Follow the Music. 2011. 14p. (J). 18.98 (978-1-4508-0712-8(7)) Phoenix International Publications, Inc.

—Rudolph the Red-Nosed Reindeer: Little Pop-Up Song Book. 2013. 10p. (J). (gr. k-4). bds. 18.98 (978-1-4508-5363-7(3), e80b43a2-a0ce-4d2a-8c6e-90c92a828ab9) Phoenix International Publications, Inc.

—Thomas & Friends: Play-a-Tune Puzzle Book. 2010. 10p. (J). bds. 13.98 (978-1-60553-756-6(X)) Publications International, Ltd.

Seuss. The Cat in the Hat Songbook: 50th Anniversary Edition. 2017. (Classic Seuss Ser.). (ENG., Illus.). 72p. (J). (gr. 2-12). 16.99 (978-0-394-81695-1(1), Random Hse. Bks. for Young Readers) Random Hse. Children's Bks.

Shake It up! Songbook. 120p. (J). 16.99 (978-0-8307-2769-8(8), Gospel Light) Gospel Light Pubns.

Shrubshall & Free. Around the Pind in 80 Days: A Musical for Children. 2011. (ENG.). 47p. 9.95 (978-0-573-08130-9(1), French, Samuel , Ltd.) Concord Theatricals.

Sweet Dreams Lullabies. (Baby Looney Tunes Song Bks.). (Illus.). 16p. (J). (gr. -1). 7.98 (978-0-7853-1613-8(2), PI13) Publications International, Ltd.

Taz TV. (Looney Tunes Song & Sound Bks.). (Illus.). 16p. (J). (gr. -1-k). 7.98 (978-0-7853-1609-1(4), PI9) Publications International, Ltd.

Trapani, Iza. How Much Is That Doggie in the Window? 2004. (Iza Trapani's Extended Nursery Rhymes Ser.). (ENG., Illus.). 32p. (J). (gr. k-k). pap. 7.95 (978-1-58089-030-4(X)) Charlesbridge Publishing, Inc.

SONGS

see also Ballads; Carols; Folk Songs; Hymns; Lullabies; National Songs; Popular Music; School Songbooks; Songbooks

A&C Black, A&C. Apusskidu: Songs for Children. 2017. (ENG.). 98p. (J). pap. 29.95 (978-1-4729-2991-4(8)) HarperCollins Pubs. Ltd. GBR. Dist: Independent Pubs. Group.

Ableman, Aaron & Room, Dave. Pacha's Pajamas: A Story Written by Nature. 2016. (ENG.). 200p. (J). pap. 12.95 (978-1-63047-704-2(4)) Morgan James Publishing.

Adlerman, Danny, et al. Rub a Dub Dub with CD. 2013. (Illus.). 32p. (J). (gr. -1-3). pap. 8.95 (978-1-58089-575-0(1)) Charlesbridge Publishing, Inc.

Albee, Sarah. Elmo's 12 Days of Christmas (Sesame Street) Swanson, Maggie, illus. 2003. (Big Bird's Favorites Board Bks.). (ENG.). 24p. (J). (gr. k — 1). bds. 4.99 (978-0-375-82506-4(1), Random Hse. Bks. for Young Readers) Random Hse. Children's Bks.

Albrecht, Sally K., et al. I Sing, You Sing, Too! 30 Echo Songs for Young Singers. 2008. (I Sing, You Sing Ser.). (ENG.). 68p. pap. 19.95 (978-0-7390-5259-4(4)) Alfred Publishing Co., Inc.

—I Sing, You Sing, Too! 30 Echo Songs for Young Singers, Book & CD. 2008. (I Sing, You Sing Ser.). (ENG.). 68p. pap. 44.95 (978-0-7390-5257-0(8)) Alfred Publishing Co., Inc.

—Rhythm All Around: 10 Rhythmic Songs for Singing & Learning (Teacher's Handbook) 2007. (ENG.). 72p. pap. 29.95 (978-0-7390-4643-2(8)) Alfred Publishing Co., Inc.

Alexander, Martha. A You're Adorable. Alexander, Martha, illus. 2nd ed. 2011. (ENG., Illus.). 20p. (J). (gr. -1 — 1). bds. 7.99 (978-0-7636-5332-3(2)) Candlewick Pr.

Allingham, William. Rhymes for the Young Folk. unabr. ed. 2012. (Illus.). 81p. 39.99 (978-1-4622-9303-2(4)) Repressed Publishing LLC.

Almeida, Artie. Recorder Express (Soprano Recorder Method for Classroom or Individual Use) Soprano Recorder Method for Classroom or Individual Use, Book & CD. 2007. (ENG.). 48p. pap. 14.95 (978-0-7390-4726-2(4)) Alfred Publishing Co., Inc.

Amador Family Staff & Barefoot Books Staff. The Wheels on the Bus. Williamson, Melanie, illus. 2014. 24p. (J). 16.99 (978-1-84686-787-3(8)) Barefoot Bks., Inc.

AMSCO Publications Staff & Hal Leonard Corp. Staff, creators. The Super Songbook for Kids. 2007. (ENG., Illus.). 80p. pap.

14.95 *(978-0-8256-3464-2(4)*, 14032042, Amsco Music) Music Sales Corp.

Antonini, Gabriele. Wheels on the Bus: Sing-Along Storybook. 2013. (ENG., Illus.). 20p. (J). 7.99 *(978-1-4508-3332-5(2)*, 1462, PI Kids) Phoenix International Publications, Inc.

The Ants Go Marching. 2009. (Rookie Preschool-NEW Ser.). (ENG.). 24p. (J). pap. 6.95 *(978-0-531-24581-1(0)*, Children's Pr.) Scholastic Library Publishing.

Archambault, John & Plummer, David. Two Birds SAT upon a Stone. Hollander, Sarah, illus. 2006. (J). pap. *(978-1-58669-187-5(2))* Childcraft Education Corp.

Arrullos. (SPA & ENG.). (J). (gr. -1-3). 10.00 net. *(978-1-57417-032-0(5)*, AC30087) Arcoiris Records, Inc.

Audio & Kidzup Productions Staff. Best Toddler Songbook. 2003. (Toddler Ser.). (J). pap. 12.99 incl. audio *(978-1-894281-76-8(4))* Kidzup Productions.

Axford, Elizabeth C. & compiled by. Kidtunes Songbook & Activity Guide Axford, Elizabeth C., compiled by. 2003. (ENG., Illus.). 52p. (J). 14.95 *(978-1-931844-01-7(1)*, PP1013) Piano Pr.

Ayotte-Irwin, Tracy & Jordan, Sara. Bilingual Songs - English-French, 2 vols., Vol. 2. 2003. (Bilingual Song English-French Ser.: 2). (ENG., Illus.). 48p. (J). 17.95 *(978-1-894262-80-4(8)*, 1894262808) Jordan, Sara Publishing.

The B-I-B-L-E Online Children Song. 2.00 *(978-0-687-07975-9(6))* Abingdon Pr.

Baby Signing Time. 2005. (J). Bk. 1. bds. *(978-1-933543-06-2(X))*Bk. 2. bds. *(978-1-933543-07-9(8))* Two Little Hands Productions LLC.

Baker, Clara Belle & Kohlsaat, Caroline. Songs for the Little Child. 2005. reprint ed. pap. 19.95 *(978-1-4179-3304-4(6))* Kessinger Publishing, LLC.

Barker, Dan. Mary Had a Little Lamb Songbook. 2003. 44p. (J). 5.00 *(978-1-58302-239-9(2))* Creative Ministry Solutions.

Baron, Andrew, illus. The Adventures of Octopus Rex. 2003. (J). per. 17.95 *(978-0-9760348-0-3(8))* Bh Pubns.

Basaluzzo, Constanza, illus. Old MacDonald Had a Farm. 2019. (Nursery Rhyme Board Bks.). (ENG.). 10p. bds. 5.99 *(978-1-68446-114-1(6)*, 141956, Capstone Editions) Capstone.

—Wheels on the Bus. 2019. (Nursery Rhyme Board Bks.). (ENG.). 10p. (J). bds. 5.99 *(978-1-68446-115-8(4)*, 141958, Capstone Editions) Capstone.

Bauer, Marion Dane. Love Song for a Baby. Andreasen, Dan, illus. 2011. (Classic Board Bks.). (ENG.). 40p. (J). (gr. -1 — 1). bds. 7.99 *(978-1-4169-6395-0(2)*, Little Simon) Little Simon.

Baxter, Nicola. Sing-Along Songs for Children: Join in with Your Free CD. Finn, Rebecca, illus. 2014. (ENG.). 12p. (J). (gr. -1-k). bds. 14.99 *(978-1-84322-892-9(0)*, Armadillo) Anness Publishing GBR. Dist: National Bk. Network.

Beall, Pamela Conn & Nipp, Susan Hagen. The Best of Wee Sing, 1 vol. 13th ed. 2007. (Wee Sing Ser.). (Illus.). 64p. (J). (gr. -1-2). 11.99 *(978-0-8431-2184-1(X)*, Price Stern Sloan) Penguin Young Readers Group.

—Wee Sing Around the World, 1 vol. 2006. (Wee Sing Ser.). (Illus.). 64p. (J). (gr. -1-2). 10.99 *(978-0-8431-2005-9(3)*, Price Stern Sloan) Penguin Young Readers Group.

—Wee Sing Bible Songs, 1 vol. 2005. (Wee Sing Ser.). 64p. (J). (gr. -1-2). 10.99 *(978-0-8431-1300-6(6)*, Price Stern Sloan) Penguin Young Readers Group.

—Wee Sing Children's Songs & Fingerplays, 1 vol. 2005. (Wee Sing Ser.). (ENG.). 64p. (J). (gr. -1-2). 10.99 *(978-0-8431-1362-4(6)*, Price Stern Sloan) Penguin Young Readers Group.

—Wee Sing for Baby, 1 vol. 2005. (Wee Sing Ser.). 64p. (J). (gr. -1-2). 10.99 *(978-0-8431-1338-9(3)*, Price Stern Sloan) Penguin Young Readers Group.

—Wee Sing in the Car, 1 vol. 2005. (Wee Sing Ser.). 64p. (J). (gr. -1-2). 10.99 *(978-0-8431-1339-6(1)*, Price Stern Sloan) Penguin Young Readers Group.

Beaton, Clare & Kletter, Dana. Mrs. Moon: Lullabies for Bedtime. 2007. (ENG., Illus.). 48p. (J). 19.99 *(978-1-84686-067-6(9))* Barefoot Bks., Inc.

Beaumont. Miss Polly Wolly Doodle from T. (J). 15.95 *(978-0-8118-4825-1(6))* Chronicle Bks. LLC.

Bee, Kati. Mrs. Flutterbee & the Funny Farm. 2007. (Illus.). 32p. (J). 15.99 *(978-0-9793760-0-9(9))* Kati Bee & Friends Publishing.

Berkner, Laurie. The Laurie Berkner Songbook Piano, Vocal & Guitar Chords Book/Online Audio. 2006. (ENG., Illus.). 56p. pap. 17.99 *(978-0-8256-3544-1(6)*, 14018683, Amsco Music) Music Sales Corp.

—Monster Boogie. Clanton, Ben, illus. 2018. (ENG.). 40p. (J). (gr. -1-3). 17.99 *(978-1-4814-6465-9(5)*, Simon & Schuster Bks. For Young Readers) Simon & Schuster Bks. For Young Readers.

—Pillowland. Garoche, Camille, illus. 2017. (ENG.). 32p. (J). (gr. -1-3). 17.99 *(978-1-4814-6467-3(1)*, Simon & Schuster Bks. For Young Readers) Simon & Schuster Bks. For Young Readers.

—We Are the Dinosaurs. Clanton, Ben, illus. 2017. (ENG.). 40p. (J). (gr. -1-3). 18.99 *(978-1-4814-6463-5(9)*, Simon & Schuster Bks. For Young Readers) Simon & Schuster Bks. For Young Readers.

Berlin, Irving. Easter Parade. McCue, Lisa, illus. 2003. 32p. (J). 16.89 *(978-0-06-029126-6(5))* HarperCollins Pubs.

—White Christmas: A Christmas Holiday Book for Kids. Hague, Michael, illus. 2010. (ENG.). 32p. (J). 16.99 *(978-0-06-029123-5(0)*, HarperCollins) HarperCollins Pubs.

Bernay, Emma & Berne, Emma Carlson. The Crow & the Pitcher. Palin, Tim, illus. 2019. (Classic Fables in Rhythm & Rhyme Ser.). (ENG.). 24p. (J). (gr. -1-2). lib. bdg. 33.99 *(978-1-68410-330-0(4)*, 140250) Cantata Learning.

—The Goose & the Golden Eggs. Gray, Howard, illus. 2019. (Classic Fables in Rhythm & Rhyme Ser.). (ENG.). 24p. (J). (gr. -1-2). lib. bdg. 33.99 *(978-1-68410-333-1(9)*, 140253) Cantata Learning.

—The Honest Woodcutter. Whitehouse, Ben, illus. 2019. (Classic Fables in Rhythm & Rhyme Ser.). (ENG.). 24p. (J). (gr. -1-2). lib. bdg. 33.99 *(978-1-68410-334-8(7)*, 140254) Cantata Learning.

—The Town Mouse & the Country Mouse. Poh, Jennie, illus. 2019. (Classic Fables in Rhythm & Rhyme Ser.). (ENG.). 24p. (J). (gr. -1-2). lib. bdg. 33.99 *(978-1-68410-335-5(5)*, 140255) Cantata Learning.

Big Animal Songbook. 2009. pap. 12.95 *(978-1-84772-546-2(5)*, AM993553) Wise Pubns. GBR. Dist: Music Sales Corp.

Bingo. 2017. (Illus.). (J). *(978-1-62885-390-2(5))* Kidsbooks, LLC.

Birchard, C. C. Boy Scout Song Book. 2004. reprint ed. pap. 20.95 *(978-1-4179-5741-5(7))* Kessinger Publishing, LLC.

Bixley, Donovan. Nga Wira o Te Pahi (the Wheels on the Bus Maori Edition) 2022. (ENG., Illus.). 24p. (J). (gr. -1-k). pap. 17.99 *(978-1-86971-359-1(1))* Hachette Australia AUS. Dist: Hachette Bk. Group.

Black, Joe. Boker Tov! Good Morning! Brown, Rick, illus. 2009. (Kar-Ben Favorites Ser.). (ENG.). 24p. (J). (gr. -1 — 1). pap. 8.95 *(978-0-7613-3951-9(5)*, Kar-Ben Publishing) Lerner Publishing Group.

Blecker, Lisa. Sweet Neighbors Come in All Colors. 2018. (ENG.). 32p. (J). (gr. -1-k). 11.95 *(978-1-61851-128-7(9))* Baha'i Publishing.

Blomgren, Jennifer. Why Do I Sing? Animal Songs of the Pacific Northwest. Gabriel, Andrea, illus. 2015. 20p. (J). (— 1). bds. 9.99 *(978-1-63217-020-0(5)*, Little Bigfoot) Sasquatch Bks.

Bouchard, David. An Aboriginal Carol: French Edition, 1 vol. Beaver, Moses, illus. 2007. (FRE.). 32p. (J). (gr. 3-18). 24.95 *(978-0-88995-413-7(5)*, 02e2f111-4d71-484c-92fa-1a7cb7a7a160) Fitzhenry & Whiteside, Ltd. CAN. Dist: Firefly Bks., Ltd.

Bower, Gary. Jingle in My Pocket. Bower, Jan, illus. 2009. 32p. 11.99 *(978-0-9704621-9-0(0))* Storybook Meadow Publishing.

Bowers, Tim, illus. Dinosaur Pet. 2012. (ENG.). 28p. (J). (gr. -1-3). 17.95 *(978-1-936140-36-7(5))* Charlesbridge Publishing, Inc.

Brady, Janeen. I Have a Song for You Vol. 1: About People & Nature. rev. ed. (Illus.). (J). (gr. -1-4). pap., stu. ed. 9.95 incl. audio *(978-0-944803-01-1(6))* Brite Music, Inc.

Brannon, Tom, illus. I Love You Valentine Songs. 2012. (J). *(978-1-4508-3303-5(9))* Phoenix International Publications, Inc.

Brighter Minds, creator. My Little Pony Sing & Play: Follow-Th-Lights Paino Songbook. gif. ed. 2005. (Illus.). 24p. (J). (gr. -1-4). bds. 13.99 *(978-1-57791-192-0(X))* Brighter Minds Children's Publishing.

Brimhall, John. My Favorite Classics: Level One. 120p. (J). (gr. 3-6). 13.95 *(978-0-8494-2180-8(2)*, 0114) Hansen, Charles Educational Music & Bks., Inc.

Brooks, Amy. Home Songs for Little Darlings: Children. 2005. pap. 24.95 *(978-1-4179-9169-3(0))* Kessinger Publishing, LLC.

Brown, Greg. Down at the Sea Hotel: A Greg Brown Song. Levert, Mireille, illus. 2007. (ENG.). 36p. (J). (gr. -1-2). 16.95 *(978-2-923163-34-5(6))* La Montagne Secrete CAN. Dist: Independent Pubs. Group.

Brown, Linda Kayse. Jerboth Weaves a Song. Noble, Penny, illus. 2007. (ENG.). 20p. (J). pap. 9.95 *(978-0-9769742-0-8(7))* Bay Villager, The.

Brown, Lisa Marie. The New Orleans Twelve Days of Christmas, 1 vol. Cotton, Sarah, illus. 2020. (Twelve Days of Christmas Ser.). (ENG.). 32p. (J). (gr. -1-3). 17.99 *(978-1-4556-2453-9(5)*, Pelican Publishing) Arcadia Publishing.

Brown, Tameka Fryer. Brown Baby Lullaby. Ford, A. G., illus. 2020. (ENG.). 32p. (J). 17.99 *(978-0-374-30752-3(0)*, 900180735, Farrar, Straus & Giroux (BYR)) Farrar, Straus & Giroux.

Brumfield, Susan. Over the Garden Wall: Children's Songs & Games from England. 2010. (ENG.). 160p. pap. 36.99 incl. audio compact disk *(978-1-4234-7337-4(X)*, 09971301) Leonard, Hal Corp.

Bryan, Ashley, illus. & selected by. All Night, All Day: A Child's First Book of African-American Spirituals. Bryan, Ashley, selected by. 2004. (ENG.). 48p. (J). (gr. -1-3). 7.99 *(978-0-689-86786-6(7)*, Atheneum Bks. for Young Readers) Simon & Schuster Children's Publishing.

Bucchino, John. Grateful: A Song of Giving Thanks. Hakkarainen, Anna-Liisa, illus. (Julie Andrews Collection). 40p. (J). (gr. -1-3). 2006. pap. 6.99 *(978-0-06-051635-2(6)*, Julie Andrews Collection) 2003. (ENG.). 17.99 *(978-0-06-051633-8(X)*, HarperCollins) HarperCollins Pubs.

Buchanan, Colin. Remember the Lord. rev. ed. 2007. (ENG., Illus.). 32p. (J). 14.99 *(978-1-84550-293-5(0)*, b4827e48-4220-4dd8-84ac-37cff67e2666) Christian Focus Pubns. GBR. Dist: Baker & Taylor Publisher Services (BTPS).

Busy Bees: Cassette. (Song Box Ser.). (gr. 1-2). 8.50 incl. audio *(978-0-7802-2269-4(5))* Wright Group/McGraw-Hill.

Cabrera, Jane. Here We Go Round the Mulberry Bush. 2019. (Jane Cabrera's Story Time Ser.). 32p. (J). (Illus.). (-k). 18.99 *(978-0-8234-4463-2(5))*; (gr. -1 — 1). bds. 7.99 *(978-0-8234-4462-5(7))* Holiday Hse., Inc.

—If You're Happy & You Know It. 2019. (Jane Cabrera's Story Time Ser.). (Illus.). 24p. (J). (-k). 18.99 *(978-0-8234-4465-6(1))*; (gr. -1 — 1). bds. 7.99 *(978-0-8234-4464-9(3))* Holiday Hse., Inc.

—Rock-A-bye Baby. 2017. (Jane Cabrera's Story Time Ser.). (ENG., Illus.). 32p. (J). (-k). 16.95 *(978-0-8234-3753-5(1))* Holiday Hse., Inc.

—Row, Row, Row Your Boat. 2015. (Jane Cabrera's Story Time Ser.). (ENG., Illus.). 32p. (J). (gr. -1-k). 7.99 *(978-0-8234-3302-5(1))* Holiday Hse., Inc.

Cabrera, Mirna Y., et al, eds. A La Rueda, Rueda: Traditional Latin American Folk Songs for Children. Jones, Juan Luis, illus. 2010. (ENG.). 64p. pap. 29.99 incl. audio compact disk *(978-1-4234-7797-6(9)*, 09971338) Leonard, Hal Corp.

Cameron, Andrea. The 10 Most Revolutionary Songs. 2008. 14.99 *(978-1-55448-493-5(6))* Scholastic Library Publishing.

La Cancion del Rey. (SPA.). (J). 3.99 *(978-0-7899-0482-9(9)*, 495652) Editorial Unilit.

Canciones de Mi Tierra Española: Songs of My Spanish Land: Canary Islands. 2005. 32p. *(978-0-9766568-0-7(9))* ERPublishing, LLC.

Cantos al maiz: un poeta hopi habla del Maiz: 6 Softcover Books. (Saludos Ser.: Vol. 2). (SPA.). (gr. 3-5). 31.00 *(978-0-7635-1813-4(1))* Rigby Education.

Carpenter-Pezoldt, Wendy. Grandma's Unique Birthday Songs. 2012. 40p. pap. 24.95 *(978-1-4626-8945-3(0))* America Star Bks.

Cartwright, Stephen, illus. Children's Songbook - Internet Referenced. 2004. (Songbooks Ser.). 32p. (J). pap. 6.95 *(978-0-7945-0710-7(7)*, Usborne) EDC Publishing.

Carus, Marianne. Higglety Pigglety Pop! Or There Must Be More to Life. (J). 19.95 incl. audio *(978-0-8126-0057-5(6))* Open Court Publishing Co.

—Sing, Clap, & Dance with Ladybug. (J). 19.95 incl. audio *(978-0-8126-0053-7(3))* Open Court Publishing Co.

—Sing Together with Ladybug. (J). 19.95 incl. audio *(978-0-8126-0081-0(9))* Open Court Publishing Co.

Caswell, Kelly. Hickory Dickory Dock. 2015. (Classic Books with Holes Ser.). (Illus.). 16p. (J). *(978-1-84643-677-2(X))* Child's Play International Ltd.

Chadwick, Stephen & MacGregor, Helen. Singing Languages - Singing Spanish (Book + CD): 22 Photocopiable Songs & Chants for Learning Spanish, 1 vol. Harding, Emma & Gosney, Joy, illus. 2008. (Singing Languages Ser.). (ENG.). 64p. (J). (gr. 2-6). pap. 32.95 incl. audio compact disk *(978-0-7136-8880-1(7))* HarperCollins Pubs. Ltd. GBR. Dist: Independent Pubs. Group.

Champagne, Melanie, illus. My Aunt Came Back. 2008. (First Steps in Music Ser.). (ENG.). 32p. (J). (gr. -1-k). 17.95 *(978-1-57999-680-2(9))* G I A Pubns., Inc.

Chapin, Harry. Mr. Tanner. Langdo, Bryan, illus. 2017. (ENG.). 40p. (J). (gr. k-2). 17.99 *(978-0-9913866-8-0(X))* Ripple Grove Pr.

Chapin, Tom & Forster, John. The Backwards Birthday Party. Groenink, Chuck, illus. 2015. (ENG.). 40p. (J). (gr. -1-3). 17.99 *(978-1-4424-6798-9(3)*, Atheneum Bks. for Young Readers) Simon & Schuster Children's Publishing.

Chapin, Tom & Mark, Michael. The Library Book. Groenink, Chuck, illus. 2017. (ENG.). 40p. (J). (gr. -1-3). 19.99 *(978-1-4814-6092-7(7))* Simon & Schuster Children's Publishing.

Clement, Debbie, et al. You're Wonderful. 2004. (Illus.). (J). *(978-0-9705987-4-5(2))* Rainbows Within Reach.

Clement, Gary. Swimming, Swimming, 1 vol. 2015. (ENG., Illus.). 48p. (J). (gr. -1-2). 18.95 *(978-1-55498-449-7(1))* Groundwood Bks. CAN. Dist: Publishers Group West (PGW).

Clydesdale, David T., contrib. by. King of the Jungle: The God of Creation Is Lord of My Heart. 2007. (Illus.). 116p. pap. 6.95 *(978-5-557-71505-8(3)*, Word Music) Word Entertainment.

Cohan, George M. & Schwaeber, Barbie. Give My Regards to Broadway. Newsom, Carol, illus. 2008. (American Favorites Ser.). (ENG.). 32p. (J). (gr. -1-3). 8.95 *(978-1-59249-727-0(6))*; 14.95 *(978-1-59249-726-3(8))* Soundprints.

Coleccion A, Level A. (De Canciones A Cuentos Ser.). (SPA.). (gr. k-18). 444.07 *(978-1-56334-873-0(X))* CENGAGE Learning.

Coleccion B, Level B. (De Canciones A Cuentos Ser.). (SPA.). (gr. 1-18). 434.56 *(978-1-56334-991-1(4))* CENGAGE Learning.

Coleccion C, Level C. (De Canciones A Cuentos Ser.). (SPA.). (gr. 2-18). 406.81 *(978-0-7362-0440-8(7))* CENGAGE Learning.

Collins Music. Apusskidu: Songs for Children (2016 Edition) 3rd ed. 2017. (ENG.). 96p. (J). pap. 39.95 *(978-1-4729-3269-3(2))* HarperCollins Pubs. Ltd. GBR. Dist: Independent Pubs. Group.

Connors, Stompin' Tom. Hockey Night Tonight (Board Book), 1 vol. Jones, Brenda, illus. 2009. (ENG.). 24p. (J). (gr. -1 — 1). bds. 12.95 *(978-1-55109-733-6(8)*, b34d41fd-74ed-4a33-b038-7b69c690d70e) Nimbus Publishing, Ltd. CAN. Dist: Baker & Taylor Publisher Services (BTPS).

Coots, J. Fred. Santa Claus Is Comin' to Town. Kellogg, Steven, illus. 2004. 40p. (J). (gr. -1-3). 16.89 *(978-0-06-623849-4(8))* HarperCollins Pubs.

Court, Shirley, et al. Singing Sherlock Vol. 2: The Complete Singing Resorce for Primary Schools. 2004. (ENG.). 88p. pap. 79.00 incl. audio compact disk *(978-0-85162-353-5(0)*, 48012149) Leonard, Hal Corp.

Crabtree, Sally. Magic Train Ride. Esplugas, Sonia, illus. 2012. (ENG.). 32p. (J). (gr. -1-2). pap. 9.99 *(978-1-84686-657-9(X))* Barefoot Bks., Inc.

Crews, Nina. Neighborhood Sing-Along. 2011. (ENG., Illus.). 64p. (J). (gr. -1-3). 17.99 *(978-0-06-185063-9(2)*, Greenwillow Bks.) HarperCollins Pubs.

Crisp, Dan, illus. Five Little Men in a Flying Saucer. 2005. (Classic Books with Holes Soft Cover Ser.). 16p. (J). pap. *(978-1-904550-30-3(4))* Child's Play International Ltd.

Dalmatian Press Staff. On Top of Spaghetti. 2008. (ENG.). 6p. (J). bds. 4.95 *(978-1-58117-720-6(8)*, Intervisual/Piggy Toes) Bendon, Inc.

Dalton, Pamela, illus. Under the Silver Moon: Lullabies, Night Songs & Poems. 2017. (ENG.). 48p. (J). 17.99 *(978-1-4521-1673-0(3))* Chronicle Bks. LLC.

Dann, Penny. Eensy Weensy Spider. 2003. (ENG., Illus.). 16p. (J). bds. 4.99 *(978-0-7641-5662-5(4))* Sourcebooks, Inc.

Dansicker, Michael, ed. Kid's Theatre Audition Songs - Boys Edition. 2007. (ENG.). 40p. pap. 19.95 incl. audio compact disk *(978-1-4234-2880-0(3)*, 00001125) Leonard, Hal Corp.

—Kids' Musical Theatre Audition - Girls Edition. 2007. (ENG.). 36p. pap. 19.99 *(978-1-4234-2877-0(3)*, 00001124) Leonard, Hal Corp.

Dathini, Desiré. Memez: Songs to Make You Shout & Dance. 2012. 24p. pap. 15.99 *(978-1-4691-8597-2(0))* Xlibris Corp.

de La Cour, Gary, et al, illus. Wheels on the Bus. rev. ed. 2007. (ENG.). 24p. (J). (gr. -1-3). 4.99 *(978-1-59069-562-3(3))* Studio Mouse LLC.

Dean, James & Dean, Kimberly. Pete the Cat: the Petes Go Marching. Dean, James, illus. 2018. (Pete the Cat Ser.). (ENG., Illus.). 40p. (J). (gr. -1-3). 9.99 *(978-0-06-230412-4(7)*, HarperCollins) HarperCollins Pubs.

—Pete the Cat: the Wheels on the Bus. Dean, James, illus. 2013. (Pete the Cat Ser.). (ENG., Illus.). 32p. (J). (gr. -1-3). 10.99 *(978-0-06-219871-6(8)*, HarperCollins) HarperCollins Pubs.

Decker, William. Songs That Honor America, 1 vol. 2012. (InfoMax Readers Ser.). (ENG., Illus.). 24p. (J). (gr. 1-1). pap. 8.25 *(978-1-4488-9037-8(3)*, 1bfc5d2e-43d6-496f-9585-0c4a967cb2f3, Rosen Classroom) Rosen Publishing Group, Inc., The.

Denver, John. Ancient Rhymes: A Dolphin Lullaby, 1 vol. Canyon, Christopher, illus. 2004. 36p. (J). (gr. -1-6). pap. 8.95 *(978-1-58469-065-8(8)*, Dawn Pubns.) Sourcebooks, Inc.

—For Baby (For Bobbie) Mason, Janeen, illus. 2009. 32p. (J). (gr. -1-6). pap. 8.95 *(978-1-58469-121-1(2)*, Dawn Pubns.) Sourcebooks, Inc.

—Grandma's Feather Bed, 1 vol. Canyon, Christopher, illus. 2007. 36p. (J). (gr. -1-6). pap. 8.95 *(978-1-58469-096-2(8)*, Dawn Pubns.) Sourcebooks, Inc.

—John Denver's Take Me Home, Country Roads, 1 vol. Canyon, Christopher, illus. 2005. 34p. (J). (gr. -1-6). 8.99 *(978-1-58469-073-3(9))*; (ENG.). 19.99 *(978-1-58469-072-6(0))* Sourcebooks, Inc. (Dawn Pubns.).

Deters, Kevin, illus. Care Bears Sing & Play: Follow-the-Lights Piano Songbook. 2006. (Care Bears Ser.). 24p. (J). (gr. -1-3). bds. 13.99 *(978-1-57791-300-9(0))* Brighter Minds Children's Publishing.

Diamond, Eileen. Everyday Songbook: 29 Bright & Happy Songs & Activities for Children, Book & 2 CDs. 2008. (Faber Edition Ser.). (ENG., Illus.). 999p. pap. 30.25 *(978-0-571-52887-5(2))* Faber & Faber, Ltd. GBR. Dist: Alfred Publishing Co., Inc.

Dickens, Charles & Sims, Lesley. A Christmas Carol. gif. ed. 2004. 64p. (Orig.). (J). (gr. 2-18). 8.95 *(978-0-7945-0584-4(8)*, Usborne) EDC Publishing.

Disney Storybook Artists Staff, contrib. by. Princess Songs. 2011. (Illus.). 12p. (J). bds. *(978-1-4508-2074-5(3)*, 1450820743) Publications International, Ltd.

Dobbins, Jan. A Farmer's Life for Me. Huliska-Beith, Laura, illus. 2013. 24p. (J). (gr. k-3). 16.99 *(978-1-84686-790-3(8))* Barefoot Bks., Inc.

Doni, Mama. Sing along Alef Bet. Gilboa, Rinat, illus. 2016. (ENG.). 32p. (J). 17.95 *(978-1-68115-509-8(5)*, a4087939-120e-443e-9851-b52106dddbb9) Behrman Hse., Inc.

Dorn, Susy. Cantemos en Español Song-Book: Spanish Learning Song-Book for Children. Carbajal, Diego, illus. 2006. (SPA.). (J). *(978-0-9764010-6-3(1))* Susy Dorn Productions, LLC.

—Sal y Pimienta Song-Book: Spanish Learning Song-Book for Children. Carbajal, Diego, illus. 2006. (SPA.). (J). *(978-0-9764010-7-0(X))* Susy Dorn Productions, LLC.

Duder, Tessa, ed. A Book of Pacific Lullabies. Hagin, Sally, illus. 2003. 32p. (J). pap. *(978-1-86950-393-2(7))* HarperCollins Pubs. New Zealand.

Duebber, Carol. Praise Power for Kids. 2005. pap. 40.99 *(978-1-4208-7465-5(9))* AuthorHouse.

Dylan, Bob. If Dogs Run Free. Campbell, Scott, illus. 2013. (ENG.). 40p. (J). (gr. -1-3). 19.99 *(978-1-4516-4879-9(0))* Simon & Schuster Children's Publishing.

Egielski, Richard. Itsy Bitsy Spider. Egielski, Richard, illus. 2012. (ENG., Illus.). 12p. (J). (gr. -1-1). 19.99 *(978-1-4169-9895-2(0)*, Atheneum Bks. for Young Readers) Simon & Schuster Children's Publishing.

Elementary Piggyback Song Book. 2003. (J). *(978-0-9745630-4-6(8))* F & S Music KS Publishing Co.

Elkins, Stephen. Little Dongs for Little Souls: Sharing God's Love. Davis, Lynne, illus. 2005. 32p. (J). 9.99 incl. audio compact disk *(978-0-8054-2673-1(6))* B&H Publishing Group.

—Little Songs for Little Souls: God Cares for Me. Davis, Lynne, illus. 2005. 32p. (J). 9.99 incl. audio compact disk *(978-0-8054-2675-5(2))* B&H Publishing Group.

—Little Songs for Little Souls: I Can Be Happy in Jesus. Davis, Lynne, illus. 2005. 32p. (J). 9.99 incl. audio compact disk *(978-0-8054-2676-2(0))* B&H Publishing Group.

—Little Songs for Little Souls: I Can Praise the Lord. Davis, Lynne, illus. 2005. 32p. (J). 9.99 incl. audio compact disk *(978-0-8054-2677-9(9))* B&H Publishing Group.

—LullaBible: A Musical Treasury for Mother & Baby. 2004. (Illus.). 224p. (J). 21.99 incl. audio compact disk *(978-0-8054-2390-7(7))* B&H Publishing Group.

—The LullaBible: A Musical Treasury for Mother & Baby. 2004. (Illus.). (J). 9.99 *(978-0-8054-2391-4(5))* B&H Publishing Group.

—The LullaBible: A Musical Treasury for Mother & Baby. Colton, Ellie, illus. 2004. (J). (gr. -1). 223p. 14.99 *(978-0-8054-2388-4(5))*; 224p. 19.99 incl. audio *(978-0-8054-2389-1(3))* B&H Publishing Group.

—My Sing-Along Bible: 50 Easy-Read Stories + 50 Fun Bible Songs. Reagan, Susan, illus. 2015. (ENG.). 96p. (J). 12.99 *(978-1-4964-0543-2(9)*, 4612218) Tyndale Hse. Pubs.

Elliott, Rebecca, et al, illus. Five Little Monkeys: And Other Counting Rhymes. 2004. (Mother Goose Ser.). (ENG.). 36p. (J). 15.95 *(978-1-59249-523-8(0)*, 1D026) Soundprints.

Elwell, Ellen Banks & Turk, Caron, illus. The Toddler's Songbook. 2009. (J). *(978-1-4335-0597-3(5))* Crossway.

Emerson, Roger. Cover Your Sneeze, Please! A Short Musical Play about Kids' Healthy Habits. 2013. (ENG.). 32p. pap. 39.99 *(978-1-4803-3393-2(X)*, 00117746) Leonard, Hal Corp.

Engvick, William. Lullabies & Night Songs. Sendak, Maurice, illus. 2004. (Sendak Reissues Ser.). 80p. (J). 40.00 *(978-0-06-029733-6(6))* HarperCollins Pubs.

Essential Audition Songs for Kids. (J). 21.95 incl. audio compact disk *(978-1-85909-867-7(3)*, Warner Bros. Pubns.) Alfred Publishing Co., Inc.

Faber, Nancy, et al. BigTime Piano Kids' Songs - Level 4. 2012. (ENG.). 40p. pap. 8.99 *(978-1-61677-629-9(3)*, 00420325) Faber Piano Adventures(r).

Fallon, Kathy Reilly & Pellegrino, Frank. Heavenly Skies & Lullabies: Illustrated Songbook & CD. Kelly, Becky, illus. 2006. (J). (gr. -1-3). 29.95 incl. audio compact disk *(978-1-933626-06-2(2)*, Lumina Pr.) Aeon Publishing Inc.

Fatus, Sophie. Here We Go Round the Mulberry Bush. 2007. (J). *(978-1-84686-036-2(9))* Barefoot Bks., Inc.

Fatus, Sophie & Penner, Fred. Here We Go Round the Mulberry Bush. Fatus, Sophie, illus. 2007. (ENG., Illus.). 24p. (J). (gr. -1-2). 16.99 *(978-1-84686-035-5(0))* Barefoot Bks., Inc.

Feierabend, John M. The Book of Finger Plays & Action Songs: Let's Pretend. 2003. (First Steps in Music Ser.). (ENG., Illus.). 88p. (J). (gr. -1-2). pap. 14.95 *(978-1-57999-212-5(9))* G I A Pubns., Inc.

—The Book of Song Dances. 2015. (First Steps in Music Ser.). (ENG., Illus.). 122p. (J). (gr. 2-4). pap. 17.95 *(978-1-62277-086-1(2))* G I A Pubns., Inc.
—The Book of Song Tales for Upper Grades. 2015. (First Steps in Music Ser.). (ENG., Illus.). 144p. (J). (gr. 4-7). pap. 18.95 *(978-1-62277-087-8(0))* G I A Pubns., Inc.
—The Book of Songs & Rhymes with Beat Motions: Let's Clap Our Hands Together. 2004. (First Steps in Music Ser.). (ENG., Illus.). 142p. (J). (gr. -1-2). pap. 19.95 *(978-1-57999-267-5(6),* G-5879) G I A Pubns., Inc.
—The Other Day I Met a Bear. Miller, Julia Love, illus. 2014. (First Steps in Music Ser.). (ENG.). 32p. (J). (gr. -1-k). 16.95 *(978-1-62277-076-2(5))* G I A Pubns., Inc.
—Over in the Meadow. Napoletano, Marissa, illus. 2016. (First Steps in Music Ser.). (ENG.). 32p. (J). (gr. k-2). 16.95 *(978-1-62277-178-3(8))* G I A Pubns., Inc.
Feldman, Jean. Birdies Lap Book. 2009. pap. 8.99 *(978-1-60689-099-8(9))* Creative Teaching Pr., Inc.
—Color Train Lap Book. 2009. pap. 8.99 *(978-1-60689-094-3(8))* Creative Teaching Pr., Inc.
—Dinosaur Boogie Lap Book. 2009. (J). pap. 8.99 *(978-1-60689-097-4(2))* Creative Teaching Pr., Inc.
—Five Little Monkeys Lap Book. 2009. pap. 8.99 *(978-1-60689-095-0(6))* Creative Teaching Pr., Inc.
—I Know an Old Lady Who Swallowed A One Lap Book. 2009. pap. 8.99 *(978-1-60689-102-5(2))* Creative Teaching Pr., Inc.
—May There Always Be Sunshine Lap Book. 2009. pap. 8.99 *(978-1-60689-101-8(4))* Creative Teaching Pr., Inc.
—My Hands on My Head Lap Book. 2009. pap. 8.99 *(978-1-60689-105-6(7))* Creative Teaching Pr., Inc.
—My Mother Is A Baker Lap Book. 2009. pap. 8.99 *(978-1-60689-104-9(9))* Creative Teaching Pr., Inc.
—Nursey Rhyme Rally Lap Book. 2009. pap. 8.99 *(978-1-60689-100-1(6))* Creative Teaching Pr., Inc.
—Rules Rap Lap Book. 2009. pap. 8.99 *(978-1-60689-098-1(0))* Creative Teaching Pr., Inc.
—Twinkle Friends Lap Book. 2009. pap. 8.99 *(978-1-60689-103-2(0))* Creative Teaching Pr., Inc.
Feldman, Jean & Karapetkova, Holly. Math Songs. unabr. ed. 2010. (ENG.). 16p. (gr. -1-k). 12.99 *(978-1-61741-588-3(X))* Rourke Educational Media.
Fletcher, Terri. Scrumpy's Educational Kid Songs. 2003. (Illus.). 16p. (J). (gr. -1-1). pap. 12.95 incl. audio compact disk *(978-0-9672279-1-7(7))* Scrumps Entertainment, Inc.
Flor Ada, Alma & Zubizarreta, Rosalma, trs. Uncle Nacho's Hat Reisberg, Mira, illus. 2013.Tr. of El Sombrero Del Tio Nacho. (ENG & SPA.). 32p. (J). (gr. 1-18). pap. 8.95 *(978-0-89239-043-4(3),* CBP0433S) Lee & Low Bks., Inc.
Flores, Carolyn Dee. Canta, Rana, Canta. Rosales-Yeomans, Natalia, tr. from SPA. Flores, Carolyn Dee, illus. 2013.Tr. of Sing, Froggie, Sing. (ENG & SPA., Illus.). 32p. (J). 16.95 *(978-1-55885-764-3(8),* Piñata Books) Arte Publico Pr.
Friedman, Debbie. Lullaby. Bubar, Lorraine, illus. 2014. (ENG.). 32p. (J). 18.99 *(978-1-58023-807-6(6),* d9c32597-badd-475b-8a24-b8382e4bea2d, Jewish Lights Publishing) LongHill Partners, Inc.
Friedman, Randee & Lander, Donna, eds. The New Rabbi Joe Black Songbook: Selected Songs from Aleph Bet Boogie, Everybody's Got A Little Music, Leave A Little Bit Undone, Sabbatical. 2004. (ENG & HEB.). 111p. (YA). per. 25.95 *(978-1-890161-52-1(7))* Sounds Write Productions, Inc.
Fyke, Laurie & Sindair, Kerrie. Songs, 1 vol. Stephen, Lib, illus. 2005. (ENG.). (J). pap. 17.50 incl. audio compact disk *(978-1-84414-079-4(2),* Jolly Learning) Jolly Learning, Ltd. GBR. Dist: American International Distribution Corp.
G-Mo. Shmu Songs. 2008. 81p. pap. 19.95 *(978-1-60672-098-1(8))* America Star Bks.
Gallina, Michael, et al. Sing & Play about the USA! 2007. (ENG.). 48p. (gr. k-4). pap. 29.95 *(978-1-59235-184-8(0),* 35020093) Shawnee Pr., Inc.
Galvin, Laura Gates. Oh Where, Oh Where Has My Little Dog Gone? Villnave, Erica Pelton, illus. 2008. (ENG.). 32p. (J). (gr. -1-2). 17.95 *(978-1-59249-859-8(0))* Soundprints.
García Lorca, Federico. Canciones (1921-1924) (SPA.). 96p. (J). 13.25 *(978-84-206-6106-3(6),* AZ6106) Alianza Editorial, S. A. ESP. Dist: Continental Bk. Co., Inc.
—Canciones y Poemas para Ninos. (Coleccion Poemas Juvenil). (SPA., Illus.). 96p. (J). 9.50 *(978-84-335-8401-4(4),* DD4014) Labor, Editorial S. A. ESP. Dist: Continental Bk. Co., Inc.
—Canciones y Poemas para Ninos. (SPA., Illus.). 64p. (J). (gr. 4-6). pap. 6.95 net. *(978-1-887578-59-2(5),* SQ0128) SpanPress, Inc.
Gardner, Louise, et al, illus. Old MacDonald & Other Sing-along Rhymes. 2006. (Mother Goose Ser.). (ENG.). 36p. (J). 12.95 *(978-1-59249-525-2(7),* 1D028) Soundprints.
The Ghosts Go Haunting. 2014. (ENG., Illus.). 32p. (J). (gr. -1-3). 16.99 *(978-0-8075-2852-5(8),* 807528528) Whitman, Albert & Co.
Gillespie, Haven & Coots, J. Fred. Santa Claus Is Comin' to Town. Kellogg, Steven, tr. Kellogg, Steven, illus. 2004. (ENG.). 40p. (J). (gr. -1-3). 15.99 *(978-0-688-14938-3(3))* HarperCollins Pubs.
Gitarren Songs. 2004. (YA). cd-rom *(978-1-891155-20-8(2))* EMedia Corp.
Gobo Books Staff. Sleepytime Songs. 2007. (Baby Sing & Play Ser.). 8p. (J). (gr. -1). bds. 12.95 incl. audio compact disk *(978-1-932915-42-6(7))* Sandvik Innovations, LLC.
God Is with You in Sleep. Date not set. 44p. (J). (gr. -1-5). 16.99 incl. audio compact disk *(978-0-9702219-0-2(8))* Bowden Music Co.
Golio, Gary. Strange Fruit: Billie Holiday & the Power of a Protest Song. Riley-Webb, Charlotte, illus. 2017. (ENG.). 40p. (J). (gr. 3-6). 19.99 *(978-1-4677-5123-0(5),* c6877f85-9906-4704-b83f-564414dd4300, Millbrook Pr.) Lerner Publishing Group.
Goodman, Steve. The Train They Call the City of New Orleans. McCurdy, Michael, illus. pap. 16.95 incl. audio *(978-1-59112-899-1(4));* pap. incl. audio compact disk *(978-1-59112-905-9(2));* pap. incl. audio *(978-1-59112-901-1(X));* pap. 18.95 incl. audio compact disk *(978-1-59112-903-5(6))* Live Oak Media.
Gott, Barry, illus. Head, Shoulders, Knees, & Toes. 2006. (J). *(978-1-58987-056-7(5))* Kindermusik International.
Graham, Pat, et al. A Children's Songbook Companion. Grover, Nina, illus. 2005. per. *(978-0-88290-795-6(6),* Horizon Pubs.) Cedar Fort, Inc./CFI Distribution.
Graper, Helen, illus. Bingo. 2016. (J). *(978-1-62885-144-1(9))* Kidsbooks, LLC.
Graves, Harmon. I'm Only Three¿ & Look at All the Things That I Can Do! Ritchie, Scot, illus. 2013. 30p. pap. 13.95 *(978-1-4349-3729-2(1))* Dorrance Publishing Co., Inc.
Group/McGraw-Hill, Wright. The Song Box Social Studies Songs: 1 Each of 4 Big Books. (Song Box Ser.). (gr. 1-2). 124.95 *(978-0-322-03797-7(2))* Wright Group/McGraw-Hill.
—The Song Box Social Studies Songs: 1 Each of 4 Cassettes. (Song Box Ser.). (gr. 1-2). 33.95 *(978-0-322-03795-3(6))* Wright Group/McGraw-Hill.
—The Song Box Social Studies Songs: 1 Each of 4 Student Books. (Song Box Ser.). (gr. 1-2). 18.95 *(978-0-322-03961-2(4))* Wright Group/McGraw-Hill.
—The Song Box Social Studies Songs: 6 Each of 4 Student Books. (Song Box Ser.). (gr. 1-2). 116.50 *(978-0-322-03796-0(4))* Wright Group/McGraw-Hill.
Guilmartin, Kenneth K. One Little Owl. 2012. (Illus.). 32p. (J). 12.95 *(978-0-9855719-4-8(2))* Music Together, LLC.
Gullible, Ru. The Phantom. 2008. 24p. pap. 14.50 *(978-1-4389-0229-6(8))* AuthorHouse.
Guthrie, Arlo. Me & My Goose. Garren, Kathy, illus. 2014. (ENG.). (J). 15.00 *(978-0-9915370-6-8(8))* Rising Son International, Ltd.
Guthrie, Woody. Enviarme a Ti, Level 2. Flor Ada, Alma, tr. Rosenberry, Vera, illus. 2003. (Dejame Leer Ser.). (SPA.). 8p. (J). (gr. -1-1). 6.50 *(978-0-673-36301-5(5),* Good Year Bks.) Celebration Pr.
Haas, Peter Michael. Geschichten Für Akkordeon - 25 Lustige und Wehmütige Kinderstücke. 2009.Tr. of Squeeze Box Fairy Tales - 25 Amusing & Wistful Children's Songs. (ENG.). 48p. 16.99 *(978-3-89922-124-4(9))* AMA Verlag GmbH DEU. Dist: Mel Bay Pubns., Inc.
Hal Leonard Corp. Staff. Children's Songs: Budget Books, 1 vol. 2009. (ENG.). 304p. pap. 12.99 *(978-1-4234-8033-4(3),* 1423480333) Leonard, Hal Corp.
Hal Leonard Corp. Staff, creator. Disney's My First Songbook - Volume 2: A Treasury of Favorite Songs to Sing & Play. 2003. (Easy Piano Songbook Ser.). (ENG., Illus.). 88p. pap. 19.99 *(978-0-634-04792-3(2),* 00316085) Leonard, Hal Corp.
—Disney's My First Songbook - Volume 4. 2011. (ENG.). 96p. pap. 17.99 *(978-1-4584-0698-9(9),* 00316160) Leonard, Hal Corp.
—Kids' Fun Songs: Learn & Play Recorder Pack. 2012. (ENG.). (J). pap. 19.99 *(978-1-4768-1507-7(0),* 00102843) Leonard, Hal Corp.
—Songs Children Can Sing! Pro Vocal Boys' & Girls' Edition Volume 1. 2012. (ENG.). 40p. pap. 14.99 incl. audio compact disk *(978-1-4584-2367-2(0),* 00740451) Leonard, Hal Corp.
—Songs for Kids - Audition Songs: Piano/Vocal/Guitar Arrangements with CD Backing Tracks. 2016. (ENG.). 48p. pap. 14.99 incl. audio compact disk *(978-1-4234-8955-9(1),* 1423489551) Music Sales Corp.
—Teaching Little Fingers to Play Broadway Songs. 2012. (ENG.). 32p. pap. 12.99 incl. audio compact disk *(978-1-4584-1766-4(2),* 00416927); pap. 7.99 *(978-1-4584-1765-7(4),* 00416926) Willis Music Co.
—Worship Together Favorites for Kids. 2007. (ENG.). 72p. pap. 12.95 *(978-1-4234-2541-0(3),* 00316109) Leonard, Hal Corp.
—15 Recital Songs in English: Low Voice. 2008. (ENG.). 48p. pap. 19.99 *(978-1-4234-4113-7(3),* 48019745) Boosey & Hawkes, Inc.
Harburg, E. Y. Over the Rainbow. Noonan, Julia, illus. Date not set. 32p. (J). 5.99 *(978-0-06-443677-9(2))* HarperCollins Pubs.
Harburg, E. Y. & Arlen, Harold. Over the Rainbow. Noonan, Julia, illus. 2004. 24p. (J). (gr. 4-8). reprint ed. 16.00 *(978-0-7567-7340-3(7))* DIANE Publishing Co.
Harnick, Sheldon. Sunrise, Sunset. Schoenherr, Ian, illus. 2005. 32p. (J). (gr. -1-1). lib. bdg. 16.89 *(978-0-06-051527-0(9))* HarperCollins Pubs.
Harris, Charisse N. Mama Please. 2009. (J). 6.95 *(978-1-61584-843-0(6))* Independent Pub.
Harter, Debbie. The Animal Boogie. Harter, Debbie, illus. (Illus.). 32p. pap. 6.99 *(978-1-84148-996-4(4))* Barefoot Bks., Inc.
—The Animal Boogie. 2005. (ENG., Illus.). 32p. (J). (gr. -1-2). 9.99 *(978-1-905236-22-0(0))* Barefoot Bks., Inc.
—The Animal Boogie. Harter, Debbie, illus. 2005. (ENG., Illus.). 32p. (J). (gr. -1-2). 6.99 *(978-1-905236-60-2(3))* Barefoot Bks., Inc.
Hayes, Larry E. My Name Starts with A (Library Version) 2004. (My Name Starts With Ser.). (Illus.). 32p. (J). lib. bdg. 12.95 *(978-0-9725292-7-3(6))* Inspire Pubns.
Henneberg, Susan. What Is a Song?, 1 vol. 2014. (Britannica Common Core Library). (ENG., Illus.). 32p. (J). (gr. 2-3). 27.04 *(978-1-62275-664-3(9),* 39b68636-a5dd-4104-88c2-f22c1ff69702, Britannica Educational Publishing) Rosen Publishing Group, Inc., The.
Heras, Theo. What Will We Do with the Baby-O? Herbert, Jennifer, illus. 2004. 32p. (J). (gr. k-k). 12.95 *(978-0-88776-689-3(7),* Tundra Bks.) Tundra Bks. CAN. Dist: Penguin Random House. LLC.
Heyge, Lorna Lutz. Music Garden for Babies from Birth to 18 Months: Songbook 1. 2003. (ENG.). 40p. pap. 22.99 incl. audio compact disk *(978-3-937315-00-3(4),* 49011105) Schott Music Corp.
Hilderbrand, Karen Mitzo & Thompson, Kim Mitzo. Essential Preschool Skills. 2008. (J). 44.99 *(978-1-59922-321-6(X))* Findaway World, LLC.
Hills, Tad. Duck & Goose, Let's Dance! (with an Original Song) Hills, Tad, illus. 2016. (Duck & Goose Ser.). (ENG., Illus.). 26p. (J). (gr. -1-2). bds. 8.99 *(978-0-385-37245-9(0),* Schwartz & Wade Bks.) Random Hse. Children's Bks.
Hinkler Studios Staff., ed. Jack & the Beanstalk. 2011. (Fairytale Pop-Ups Ser.). 12p. (J). 12.99 *(978-1-74185-087-1(8))* Hinkler Bks. Pty, Ltd. AUS. Dist: Ideals Pubns.
Hirao, Amiko, illus. Take Me Out to the Ball Game. 2011. 26p. (J). (gr. k-4). 17.95 *(978-1-936140-26-8(8))* Charlesbridge Publishing, Inc.
His Fleece Was White As Snow: Songbook. 2003. 66p. (YA). 5.00 *(978-1-58302-243-6(0))* Creative Ministry Solutions.
Hoberman, Mary Ann. The Eensy-Weensy Spider. Westcott, Nadine Bernard, illus. 2004. (ENG.). 32p. (J). (gr. -1-1). pap. 7.99 *(978-0-316-73412-7(8))* Little, Brown Bks. for Young Readers.
Hodges, Lynn & Buchanan, Sue. I Love You This Much, 1 vol. Bendall-Brunello, John, illus. (ENG.). (J). 2010. 36p. pap. 6.99 *(978-0-310-72265-6(9))* 2005. 16p. (gr. -1). bds. 8.99 *(978-0-310-70961-9(X))* Zonderkidz.
Holiday, Billie. God Bless the Child. Pinkney, Jerry, illus. 2004. 32p. (J). lib. bdg. 17.89 *(978-0-06-029487-8(6),* Amistad) HarperCollins Pubs.
Holiday, Billie & Herzog, Arthur, Jr. God Bless the Child. Pinkney, Jerry, illus. 2008. (ENG.). 40p. (J). (gr. -1-3). per. 7.99 *(978-0-06-443646-5(2))* HarperCollins Pubs.
Hollingworth, Denise, et al. Jammin' in the Jungle! 2013. (ENG.). 64p. pap. 39.99 incl. audio compact disk *(978-1-4584-1749-7(2),* 35028123) Shawnee Pr., Inc.
Hook, Dianne J., creator. All about Me: Creative Scrapbooking Templates & Clip Art for Classroom & Home. 2005. (Illus.). 64p. pap. 22.99 incl. cd-rom *(978-1-59441-191-5(3),* DJ-604010, DJ Inkers) Carson-Dellosa Publishing, LLC.
Hop! Hop! Hop! (J). 19.95 incl. audio *(978-0-8126-0088-9(6))* Open Court Publishing Co.
Hort, Lenny. The Seals on the Bus. Karas, G. Brian, illus. 2008. (ENG.). 32p. (J). (gr. -1-k). pap. 27.99 *(978-0-8050-8678-2(1),* 900045720, Holt, Henry & Co. Bks. For Young Readers) Holt, Henry & Co.
—The Seals on the Bus. Karas, G. Brian, illus. rev. ed. 2003. (ENG.). 32p. (J). (gr. -1-k). pap. 7.99 *(978-0-8050-7263-1(2),* 900018971) Square Fish.
Houston, Scott. Play Piano in a Flash Fake Book for Kids! A song book for kids in lead sheet Format, 1. l.t. ed. 2006. 88p. (J). spiral bd. 24.95 *(978-0-9712861-2-2(4),* 75) Houston Enterprises.
Houston, Scott & Sowash, Bradley. Play Piano in a Flash! the Next Step: The Next Step. l.t. ed. 2006. 100p. spiral bd. 24.95 *(978-0-9712861-3-9(2))* Houston Enterprises.
How Much Wood Could a Woodchuck Chuck? unabr. ed. 2007. (J). (gr. -1-k). 17.00 incl. audio compact disk *(978-0-9705773-4-4(6))* Kids At Our House, Inc., The.
Hull, Bunny. Happy, Happy Kwanzaa: Kwanzaa for the World. Saint-James, Synthia, illus. 2003. 24p. (J). (gr. k-5). pap. 16.95 incl. audio compact disk *(978-0-9721478-1-1(0),* KCC/HHKCD810, Kid's Creative Classics) BrassHeart Music.
If You're Happy: Individual Title Six-Packs. (Literatura 2000 Ser.). (gr. 1-2). 28.00 *(978-0-7635-0137-2(9))* Rigby Education.
In My Daughter's Eyes. 2006. (Illus.). 20p. (J). 9.99 incl. audio compact disk *(978-1-57791-218-7(7))* Brighter Minds Children's Publishing.
Ingram, Scott. The Writing of the Star-Spangled Banner, 1 vol. 2004. (Landmark Events in American History Ser.). (ENG., Illus.). 48p. (gr. 5-8). pap. 15.05 *(978-0-8368-5418-3(7),* e93295b0-1af5-42c3-842e-4db0ec8fced3); lib. bdg. 33.67 *(978-0-8368-5390-2(3),* 5058ce85-66a6-4f57-9bab-0adc8a80c538) Stevens, Gareth Publishing LLLP. (Gareth Stevens Secondary Library).
Itsy Bitsy Spider. 2004. (J). per. *(978-1-57657-427-0(X))* Paradise Pr., Inc.
Ivanov, Olga & Ivanov, Aleksey. Hanukkah, Oh Hanukkah!, 0 vols. Ivanov, Olga & Ivanov, Aleksey, illus. 2012. (ENG., Illus.). 24p. (J). (gr. -1-2). 12.99 *(978-0-7614-5845-6(X),* 9780761458456, Two Lions) Amazon Publishing.
I've Been Working on the Railroad. (Song Box Ser.). (gr. 1-2). 31.50 *(978-0-7802-0936-7(2));* 8.50 incl. audio *(978-0-7802-0938-1(9))* Wright Group/McGraw-Hill.
I've Been Working on the Railroad: 1 Big Book, 6 Each of 1 Student Book, & 1 Cassette. (Song Box Ser.). (gr. 1-2). 68.95 *(978-0-7802-0939-8(7))* Wright Group/McGraw-Hill.
I've Been Working on the Railroad: 6 Each of 1 Student Book, 6 vols. (Song Box Ser.). (gr. 1-2). 29.50 *(978-0-7802-0937-4(0))* Wright Group/McGraw-Hill.
J, Harris. Salam Alaikum: A Message of Peace. Jenkins, Ward, illus. 2017. (ENG.). 40p. (J). (gr. -1-3). 17.99 *(978-1-4814-8938-6(0),* Salaam Reads) Simon & Schuster Bks. For Young Readers.
Jacobs, Paul DuBois & Swender, Jennifer. Children's Songbag. 2005. (ENG., Illus.). 112p. (J). (gr. 3-4). spiral bd. 12.99 *(978-1-58685-356-3(2))* Gibbs Smith, Publisher.
Jacobson, John. ImagiBOP: Creative Movement & Songs for Grades K-2. 2011. (ENG.). 48p. pap. 29.99 *(978-1-61774-284-2(8),* 09971496) Leonard, Hal Corp.
Jacobson, John, et al. Say Hello Wherever You Go: Music Strategies, Songs & Activities for Grades K-2. 2010. (ENG.). 40p. pap. 19.99 incl. audio compact disk *(978-1-4234-8824-8(5),* 09971397) Leonard, Hal Corp.
Jensema, Marissa, illus. ASL Songs for Kids - 1: With Songs in American Sign Language. 2003. (J). cd-rom 29.95 *(978-0-9752933-1-7(1))* Institute for Disabilities Research & Training, Inc.
Jesus Loves Me. (Illus.). 16p. (J). pap. 1.50 *(978-0-87162-970-8(4),* E4983) Warner Pr., Inc.
Jewel. Sweet Dreams. Bates, Amy June, illus. 2013. (ENG.). 32p. (J). (gr. -1-k). 17.99 *(978-1-4424-8931-8(6),* Simon & Schuster/Paula Wiseman Bks.) Simon & Schuster/Paula Wiseman Bks.
Joachimowski, Paula L. Swamp Band Lullaby. McGrath, Ryan, illus. 2008. 32p. 17.99 *(978-1-59879-433-5(7))* Lifevest Publishing, Inc.
Johnson, James Weldon. Lift Every Voice & Sing. 2019. (ENG., Illus.). 32p. (J). 17.99 *(978-1-68119-955-9(6),* 900194335, Bloomsbury Children's Bks.) Bloomsbury Publishing USA.
Jordan, Sara. Fonetica Funky y Algo Mas, 2 vols., Kit. 2007. (ENG.). 48p. (J). (gr. k-4). 17.95 *(978-1-55386-080-8(2),* 1553860802) Jordan, Sara Publishing.
Joshua, Aaron, illus. There Was a Man & He Was Mad. 2008. (First Steps in Music Ser.). (ENG.). 24p. (J). (gr. -1-k). 18.95 *(978-1-57999-681-9(7))* G I A Pubns., Inc.
Kaiser, Cecily. On the First Night of Chanukah. Schatell, Brian, illus. 2007. (ENG.). 24p. (J). (gr. -1-3). pap. 3.99 *(978-0-439-75802-4(5))* Scholastic, Inc.
Kanzler, John. Rock-a -Bye Baby. Tiger Tales Staff, ed. Kanzler, John, illus. 2011. (ENG., Illus.). 24p. (J). (gr. -1-k). bds. 8.95 *(978-1-58925-853-2(3))* Tiger Tales.
Kanzler, John, tr. & illus. The Big Rock Candy Mountain. Kanzler, John, illus. 2004. 24p. (J). 15.95 *(978-1-59336-062-7(2));* pap. *(978-1-59336-063-4(0))* Mondo Publishing.
Katz, Alan. Are You Quite Polite? Are You Quite Polite? 2006. (ENG., Illus.). 32p. (J). (gr. -1-3). 19.99 *(978-0-689-86970-9(3),* McElderry, Margaret K. Bks.) McElderry, Margaret K. Bks.
—Going, Going, Gone! And Other Silly Dilly Sports Songs. Catrow, David, illus. 2009. (ENG.). 32p. (J). (gr. -1-3). 16.99 *(978-1-4169-0696-4(7),* McElderry, Margaret K. Bks.) McElderry, Margaret K. Bks.
—I'm Still Here in the Bathtub: I'm Still Here in the Bathtub. 2003. (ENG., Illus.). 32p. (J). (gr. -1-3). 19.99 *(978-0-689-84551-2(0),* McElderry, Margaret K. Bks.) McElderry, Margaret K. Bks.
—Mosquitoes Are Ruining My Summer! And Other Silly Dilly Camp Songs. Catrow, David, illus. 2011. (ENG.). 32p. (J). (gr. -1-3). 16.99 *(978-1-4169-5568-9(2),* McElderry, Margaret K. Bks.) McElderry, Margaret K. Bks.
—On Top of the Potty: On Top of the Potty. Catrow, David, illus. 2008. (ENG.). 32p. (J). (gr. -1-3). 19.99 *(978-0-689-86215-1(6),* McElderry, Margaret K. Bks.) McElderry, Margaret K. Bks.
—Smelly Locker: Silly Dilly School Songs. Catrow, David, illus. 2010. (ENG.). 32p. (J). (gr. -1-3). 9.99 *(978-1-4424-0251-5(2),* McElderry, Margaret K. Bks.) McElderry, Margaret K. Bks.
—Smelly Locker: Silly Dilly School Songs. Catrow, David, illus. 2008. (ENG.). 32p. (J). (gr. -1-3). 16.99 *(978-1-4169-0695-7(9))* Simon & Schuster, Inc.
—Too Much Kissing! And Other Silly Dilly Songs about Parents. Catrow, David, illus. 2009. (ENG.). 32p. (J). (gr. -1-2). 16.99 *(978-1-4169-4199-6(1),* McElderry, Margaret K. Bks.) McElderry, Margaret K. Bks.
Katz, Karen. The Babies on the Bus. Katz, Karen, illus. 2013. (ENG., Illus.). 28p. (J). (gr. -1-k). bds. 8.99 *(978-0-8050-9779-5(1),* 900119432, Holt, Henry & Co. Bks. For Young Readers) Holt, Henry & Co.
Kempf, Joe & Pescarino, Cathy. Faith-Filled Lullabies with Big Al & Annie. Sharp, Chris, illus. 2012. 32p. (J). *(978-1-61278-689-6(8))* Our Sunday Visitor, Publishing Div.
Kim, Daeshin. A Horse with Wings: And Other Songs for Children Sung by Characters from Shakespeare with CD. 2012. 25.95 *(978-0-7414-8050-7(6))* Infinity Publishing.
Kinkade, Thomas. Away in a Manger. 2009. (ENG., Illus.). 32p. (J). (gr. -1-3). pap. 7.99 *(978-0-06-078734-9(1),* HarperCollins) HarperCollins Pubs.
Kraft, Tamera & Colkmire, Lance. Kid Konnection: Kids Entering the Presence of God, Vol. 5. 2003. (Illus.). 112p. ring bd. 69.99 *(978-0-87148-383-6(1))* Pathway Pr.
Krauss, Gene & adapted by. Awesome Performance Music & Tracks. Krauss, Gene, adapted by. 2nd ed. 2005. (YA). spiral bd. 20.00 *(978-0-9785992-0-1(9))* GuitarVoyager Inc.
Kulling, Monica. Francis Scott Key's Star-Spangled Banner. Walz, Richard, illus. 2012. (Step into Reading Ser.). (ENG.). 48p. (J). (gr. k-3). pap. 3.99 *(978-0-375-86725-5(2),* Random Hse. Bks. for Young Readers) Random Hse. Children's Bks.
Kurtz, John. What Belongs? Baby Looney Tunes. Shively, Julie, illus. 2004. 12p. bds. 6.95 *(978-0-8249-6560-0(4),* Ideals Pubns.) Worthy Publishing.
Kwasi: a Storysong: Six-Pack. (Greetings Ser.: Vol. 2). 24p. (gr. 2-3). 31.00 *(978-0-7635-9415-2(6))* Rigby Education.
Lait, Alain le. It's So Good, 1 bk & 1 CD. 2003. (Illus.). 28p. (J). audio compact disk 15.95 *(978-0-9747122-0-8(5),* ENG100) Yadeeda.com.
Lakeshore Learning Materials Staff, contrib. by. Big Book of Learning Songs. 2007. (J). 19.95 *(978-1-59746-016-3(8))* Lakeshore Learning Materials.
Lamb, Amy And Chris. The Our World Series: Friends around our Home. 2010. (Illus.). 32p. pap. 14.49 *(978-1-4490-8098-3(7))* AuthorHouse.
Langham, Tony. Creepy Crawly Calypso. Harter, Debbie, illus. (Barefoot Singalongs Ser.). (ENG.). 32p. (J). 2012. (gr. -1-2). pap. 10.99 *(978-1-84686-828-3(9))* 2007. pap. 6.99 *(978-1-84686-133-8(0))* Barefoot Bks., Inc.
Langham, Tony & Harter, Debbie. Mira Quien Toca Calipso! Harter, Debbie, illus. 2009. (Illus.). 32p. (J). (gr. -1-2). pap. 7.99 *(978-1-84686-281-6(7))* Barefoot Bks., Inc.
Lansky, Bruce, ed. I've Been Burping in the Classroom: And Other Silly Sing-along Songs. Carpenter, Stephen, illus. 2007. 32p. (J). *(978-0-88166-521-5(5))* Meadowbrook Pr.
Larsen, Donna R. In My Own Backyard. Reilly, Michelle, illus. 2011. 30p. (J). *(978-0-615-52915-8(1))* DeuxRay Productions.
Law, Jessica. A Hole in the Bottom of the Sea. McDonald, Jill, illus. 2013. (Barefoot Singalongs Ser.). 24p. (J). (ENG.). (gr. -1-2). pap. 10.99 *(978-1-84686-862-7(9));* (gr. k-3). 16.99 *(978-1-84686-861-0(0))* Barefoot Bks., Inc.
Le Lait, Alain. Parapluie: Fabulous French Songs for Children. Le Lait, Alain, . 2006. (FRE.). (J). pap. 15.95 incl. audio compact disk *(978-0-9747122-5-3(6))* Yadeeda.com.
LeBuis, Peter. Character Building Songs, 2 vols., Kit. 2009. (ENG.). 48p. (J). 17.95 *(978-1-55386-104-1(3),* 1553861043) Jordan, Sara Publishing.
Lennon, John. Imagine. Jullien, Jean, illus. 2017. (ENG.). 32p. (J). (gr. -1-3). 18.99 *(978-1-328-80865-3(3),* 1688259, Clarion Bks.) HarperCollins Pubs.
Lennon, John & McCartney, Paul. Good Night. Paganelli, Elisa, illus. 2018. (J). *(978-1-4926-4979-3(1))* Sourcebooks, Inc.
Lettice, Jenna. The 12 Days of Kindergarten: A Book for Kindergarteners. Madden, Colleen, illus. 2017. (12 Days Of Ser.). 24p. (J). (gr. -1-2). pap. 5.99 *(978-0-399-55733-0(4),* Random Hse. Bks. for Young Readers) Random Hse. Children's Bks.
—The 12 Days of Preschool. Madden, Colleen, illus. 2018. (12 Days Of Ser.). 24p. (J). (gr. -1-2). pap. 5.99 *(978-1-5247-6660-3(7),* Random Hse. Bks. for Young Readers) Random Hse. Children's Bks.
Lichfield, Wilma B. Pocketful of Melodies. 2007. (J). per. 17.95 *(978-1-60002-236-4(7))* Mountain Valley Publishing, LLC.

S

Light, John. Are These Rhymes Nonsense? 2005. (Illus.). 60p. 12.00 (978-0-907759-71-3(8)) KT Pubns. GBR. Dist: Photon Pr.

Linn, Jennifer. The Hungry Spider: Hal Leonard Student Piano Library Showcase Solos Early Level 1 (Pre-Staff) 2003. (ENG.). 4p. pap. 4.99 (978-0-634-05819-6(3), 00296368) Leonard, Hal Corp.

Lithgow, John. I Got Two Dogs: (Book & CD) Neubecker, Robert, illus. 2008. (ENG.). 32p. (J). (gr. -1-1). 19.99 (978-1-4169-5881-9(9), Simon & Schuster Bks. For Young Readers) Simon & Schuster Bks. For Young Readers.

—Never Play Music Right Next to the Zoo. Hernandez, Leeza, illus. 2013. (ENG.). 40p. (J). (gr. -1-1). 19.99 (978-1-4424-6743-9(6), Simon & Schuster Bks. For Young Readers) Simon & Schuster Bks. For Young Readers.

Little Song Book. (De Canciones A Cuentos Ser.). (SPA.). (gr. 1-18). 8.91 (978-1-56334-892-1(6)) CENGAGE Learning.

Litton, Jonathan. Big Fish Little Fish. Galloway, Fiona, illus. 2016. (My Little World Ser.). (ENG.). 16p. (J). (gr. -1-k). bds. 8.99 (978-1-58925-215-8(2)) Tiger Tales.

Lowitz, Sadyebeth & Lowitz, Anson. Mr Key's Song: The Star Spangled Banner. 2011. 58p. 36.95 (978-1-258-10511-2(X)) Literary Licensing, LLC.

Lowry, Mark & Greene, Buddy. Mary, Did You Know? Bond, Denny, illus. 2005. 24p. (J). (gr. -1-k). bds. 9.99 incl. audio compact disk (978-1-57791-176-0(8)) Brighter Minds Children's Publishing.

MacDonald, Margaret Read & Jaeger, Winifred. The Round Book: Rounds Kids Love to Sing. Davis, Yvonne LeBrun, illus. 2006. (ENG.). 136p. (J). (gr. -1-3). per. 18.95 (978-0-87483-786-5(3)) August Hse. Pubs., Inc.

MacGregor, Helen & Birt, Catherine. Singing Subjects - Singing Phonics, 1 vol. 2008. (Singing Phonics Ser.). (ENG., Illus.). 80p. (J). pap. 32.95 incl. audio compact disk (978-1-4081-0472-9(5)) HarperCollins Pubs. Ltd. GBR. Dist: Independent Pubs. Group.

Madonna, Marissa, illus. There's a Hole in the Bucket! 2013. (First Steps in Music Ser.). (ENG.). 32p. (J). (gr. k-2). 16.95 (978-1-57999-970-4(0)) G I A Pubns., Inc.

Mahoney, Judy & Mahoney, Anne. Teach Me... French Spiritual Songs. 2005. (ENG., Illus.). 24p. (J). 15.95 (978-0-934633-50-5(9)) Teach Me Tapes, Inc.

Mantle, Ben & Mills, J. Elizabeth. The Spooky Wheels on the Bus: (a Holiday Wheels on the Bus Book) Mantle, Ben, illus. 2010. (ENG., Illus.). 24p. (J). (gr. -1-k). pap. 5.99 (978-0-545-17480-0(5)) Scholastic, Inc.

Marks, Anthony. The Usborne Farmyard Tales Songbook. Tyler, Jenny, ed. Cartwright, Stephen, illus. 2005. 31p. (J). (gr. -1-7). per. 6.95 (978-0-7945-0918-7(5), Usborne) EDC Publishing.

Marley, Cedella. One Love: (Multicultural Childrens Book, Mixed Race Childrens Book, Bob Marley Book for Kids, Music Books for Kids) Newton, Vanessa, illus. 2011. (Marley Ser.). (ENG.). 32p. (J). (gr. -1 — 1). 16.99 (978-1-4521-0224-5(4)) Chronicle Bks. LLC.

Marley, Cedella & Marley, Bob. One Love. Brantley-Newton, Vanessa, illus. 2014. (Marley Ser.). (ENG.). 24p. (J). (gr. -1 — 1). bds. 7.99 (978-1-4521-3855-8(9)) Chronicle Bks. LLC.

Martin, Joseph M., et al. Sing & Celebrate! Sacred Songs for Young Voices: Book/Enhanced CD (with Teaching Resources & Reproducible Pages) 2012. (ENG.). 56p. pap. 39.99 incl. audio compact disk (978-1-4584-2103-6(1), 35028238) Shawnee Pr., Inc.

McCabe, Larry. Easiest Mandolin Tunes for Children, 1 vol. 2007. (ENG.). 32p. 14.99 (978-0-7866-7535-7(7)) Mel Bay Pubns., Inc.

McCarthy, John. The Only Chord Book You Will Ever Need! Guitar Edition. 2007. (ENG.). 160p. pap. 19.99 (978-0-9764347-8-8(4), 14027259, Rock Hse. Method, The) Russell, Fred Publishing.

McKay-Lawton, Toni. Family Favourites. Manning, Eddie, illus. 2007. (Just in Rhyme Ser.). (ENG.). 12p. (J). (gr. -1-3). pap. (978-1-84167-028-7(6)) Ransom Publishing Ltd.

—Under the Sea. Manning, Eddie, illus. 2007. (Just in Rhyme Ser.). (ENG.). 12p. (J). (gr. -1-3). pap. (978-1-84167-027-0(8)) Ransom Publishing Ltd.

McQuinn, Anna. If You're Happy & You Know It. Fatus, Sophie, illus. 2011. (ENG.). 80p. (J). pap. 6.99 (978-1-84686-434-6(8)) Barefoot Bks., Inc.

—If You're Happy & You Know It! Fatus, Sophie, illus. 2011. (Barefoot Singalongs Ser.). (ENG.). 24p. (J). (gr. -1-2). pap. 10.99 (978-1-84686-619-7(7)) Barefoot Bks., Inc.

McQuinn, Anna & Fatus, Sophie. If You're Happy & You Know It. 2009. (ENG., Illus.). (J). (gr. k-2). 16.99 (978-1-84686-288-5(4)) Barefoot Bks., Inc.

Mendoza, Javier, et al. El Mundo. 2008. (Illus.). 32p. (J). pap. 7.99 (978-1-84686-209-0(4)) Barefoot Bks., Inc.

Mercer, Johnny & Mancini, Henry. Moon River. Hopgood, Tim, illus. 2018. (ENG.). 32p. (J). 24.99 (978-1-250-15900-7(8), 900185546, Holt, Henry & Co. Bks. For Young Readers) Holt, Henry & Co.

Metzger, Steve. The Leaves Are Falling One by One. Sagasti, Miriam, illus. 2007. (J). (978-0-439-02444-0(7)) Scholastic, Inc.

Michels-Boyce, Steven, illus. When Jesus Was A Kid Like Me: A Counting Song about Jesus When He Was a Kid Like You & Me. 2005. (J). 15.95 (978-0-9761477-0-1(X)) SoJam Pr.

Miles, Sandy. Birthday: Words by John Lennon & Paul Mccartney. 2009. 20p. pap. 11.25 (978-1-4389-4951-2(0)) AuthorHouse.

Miller, Philip J. We All Sing with the Same Voice. 2005. (ENG., Illus.). 40p. (J). (gr. -1-2). reprint ed. pap. 8.99 (978-0-06-073900-3(2), HarperCollins) HarperCollins Pubs.

Mitchell, Loretta. One, Two, Three... Echo Me! Ready-to-Use Songs, Games & Activities to Help Children Sing in Tune. 2003. (Illus.). 203p. pap. 29.95 (978-0-89328-157-1(3), 30/1800H) Heritage Music Pr.

Miyares, Daniel, illus. Waking up Is Hard to Do. 2010. (ENG.). 26p. (J). (gr. k-4). 19.99 (978-1-936140-13-8(6)) Charlesbridge Publishing, Inc.

Moore, Felicia. Children, Sing along & Learn with Me in Support of Antibullying Awareness! 2012. 16p. pap. 12.68 (978-1-4669-4831-0(0)) Trafford Publishing.

Moore Niver, Heather. Songs, 1 vol. 2018. (Let's Learn about Literature Ser.). (ENG.). 24p. (gr. 1-2). 24.27 (978-0-7660-9759-9(5), 7b81f67e-bcd6-4614-b91b-5e6a89833ff3) Enslow Publishing, LLC.

Naji, Jamilla. Musical Storyland: A Sing-A-Long Book with Musical Disc. Lt. ed. 2004. (Illus.). 32p. (J). per. 19.99 (978-0-9745568-0-2(7)) Words In Ink Publishing, Inc.

Nelson, Kadir. He's Got the Whole World in His Hands. 2010. (ENG.). 32p. (J). pap. 6.99 (978-0-14-241635-8(5), Puffin) Penguin Publishing Group.

Nelson, Steve & Rollins, Jack. Here Comes Peter Cottontail! 2021. (ENG.). 26p. (J). (gr. -1-1). pap. 5.99 (978-1-5460-1500-0(0)) Worthy Publishing.

—Here Comes Peter Cottontail! Walkley, Lizzie, illus. 2020. (ENG.). (J). (gr. -1 — 1). 20p. bds. 7.99 (978-1-5460-1430-0(6)); 16p. bds. 13.99 (978-1-5460-1431-7(4)) Worthy Publishing. (Worthy Kids/Ideals).

—Here Comes Peter Cottontail! Levy, Pamela R., illus. 2007. (ENG.). 26p. (J). bds. 12.99 (978-0-8249-6701-7(1), Ideals Pubns.) Worthy Publishing.

Norworth, Jack. Take Me Out to the Ball Game. Hirao, Amiko, illus. 2016. 24p. (J). (— 1). bds. 7.95 (978-1-62354-071-5(2)) Charlesbridge Publishing, Inc.

Numeroff, Laura Joffe. Mouse Stroller Songs. Date not set. (J). 9.99 (978-0-694-01420-0(6)) HarperCollins Pubs.

Okun, Milton, ed. All My Life - Karla Bonoff (Piano - Vocal) (Illus.). 64p. (Orig.). (YA). pap. 14.95 (978-0-89524-707-0(0)) Cherry Lane Music Co.

—From the Heart - 30 Love Songs. 117p. (Orig.). (YA). pap. 14.95 (978-0-89524-864-0(6), 02502146) Cherry Lane Music Co.

Omoto, Garrett, illus. Na Waihooluu. 2006.Tr. of Colors. (HAW & ENG.). 16p. (J). 8.95 (978-1-933835-00-6(1)) Partners in Development Foundation.

Orozco, Jose-Luis. Diez Deditos. 2014. 18.00 (978-1-63419-695-6(3)) Perfection Learning Corp.

Pair, Karma A. On My Way to the Market. Pressey, Deborah, illus. 2009. 24p. pap. 15.00 (978-1-4389-6299-3(1)) AuthorHouse.

Pancho Claus con Jose-Luis Orozco - Christmas with Jose-Luis Orozco. (SPA & ENG.). (J). (gr. k-3). 10.00 (978-1-57417-031-3(7)) Arcoiris Records, Inc.

Parisi, Bettie. Lullabies of Love. 2009. 28p. pap. 13.00 (978-1-4269-1016-6(9)) Trafford Publishing.

Partin, Judith E. Songs in the Night: (A Collection of Hymns, Choruses, & Songs...) 2004. 211p. (YA). 25.00 (978-0-9748494-1-6(3)) Omega Publishing.

Pax Lodge Songbook. 2005. (J). (978-0-88441-690-6(9)) Girl Scouts of the USA.

Paxton, Tom. The Jungle Baseball Game. Schmidt, Karenlee, illus. 2005. 30p. (J). (gr. -1-2). reprint ed. 16.00 (978-0-7567-8932-9(X)) DIANE Publishing Co.

Penner, Fred. Here We Go Round the Mulberry Bush. Fatus, Sophie, illus. 2008. (ENG.). 24p. (J). 9.99 (978-1-84686-079-9(2)) Barefoot Bks., Inc.

Perkins, Jill E. Cherubs Chatter: A Collection of Original Songs & Poems. 2004. (Illus.). 88p. (J). per. 7.95 (978-0-9749862-2-7(4)) Theragogy.com.

Perry, Rex, illus. Over the River & Through the Woods. 2004. 24p. (J). lib. bdg. 8.00 (978-1-4242-0640-7(5)) Fitzgerald Bks.

Petersen, George & Jenkins, J. J. Crazy Campsongs. Davis, Jack, illus. 2003. 64p. (J). bds. 9.99 (978-0-9726794-9-7(9)) Jenpet Publishing.

PI Kids. Disney Junior Mickey Mouse Clubhouse: I Can Play Christmas Songs! Sound Book. 2014. (ENG.). 12p. (J). bds. 14.99 (978-1-4508-8515-7(2), 1654, PI Kids) Phoenix International Publications, Inc.

—Disney Junior Mickey Mouse Clubhouse: Sing-Along Songs Sound Book. 2010. (ENG.). 12p. (J). bds. 23.99 (978-1-4127-4553-6(5), 1360, PI Kids) Phoenix International Publications, Inc.

PI Kids. Nickelodeon Blaze & the Monster Machines Monster Machine Music Sound Book. 2017. (ENG., Illus.). 12p. bds. 15.99 (978-1-5037-0997-3(3), 2145, PI Kids) Phoenix International Publications, Inc.

Pingry, Patricia A. The Story of Saint Patrick's Day. 2013. (ENG.). 22p. (J). (gr. -1-1). bds. 7.99 (978-0-8249-1893-4(2), Ideals Pubns.) Worthy Publishing.

Pingry, Patricia A. & Urbano, Aide. One Baby Jesus/Un Nino Dios. Edelson, Wendy, illus. 2003. (ENG & SPA.). 30p. (J). pap. 3.95 (978-0-8249-5472-7(6), Ideals Pubns.) Worthy Publishing.

Playaway, creator. Praise Songs for Kids. 2008. (Playaway Children Ser.). (J). 59.99 (978-1-59922-326-1(0)) Findaway World, LLC.

—Scripture Memory Songs. 2008. (Playaway Adult Nonfiction Ser.). (J). (gr. -1-3). 59.99 (978-1-59922-325-4(2)) Findaway World, LLC.

Pooh Songs. (Play-A-Song Ser.). (Illus.). 20p. (J). pap. 15.98 (978-0-7853-1326-7(5)) Publications International, Ltd.

The Predator. (Song Box Ser.). (gr. 1-2). 8.50 incl. audio (978-0-7802-2261-8(X)) Wright Group/McGraw-Hill.

The Predator: 1 Big Book, 6 Each of 1 Student Book, & 1 Cassette. (Song Box Ser.). (gr. 1-2). 68.95 (978-0-7802-3205-1(4)) Wright Group/McGraw-Hill.

The Predator: Big Book. (Song Box Ser.). (gr. 1-2). 31.50 (978-0-7802-2260-1(1)) Wright Group/McGraw-Hill.

Presley, Elvis. Elvis Presley's Love Me Tender. Graegin, Stephanie, illus. 2017. 40p. (J). (-k). 18.99 (978-0-7352-3122-1(2), Dial Bks) Penguin Young Readers Group.

Prévert, Jacques. Chanson des Escargotsqui Vont l'Enterrement. 2004. (Illus.). (J). (gr. 1-6). spiral bd. (978-0-616-07265-3(1)) Canadian National Institute for the Blind/Institut National Canadien pour les Aveugles.

Priddy, Roger. Sing-Along Songs with CD: With a Sing-Along Music CD. 2009. (Sing-Along Ser.). 28p. (J). (gr. -1 — 1). bds. 12.99 (978-0-312-50648-3(1), 900062944) St. Martin's Pr.

Publications International Ltd. Staff. Dora Ballerina Little Music Note Sound. 2010. 12p. bds. 9.98 (978-1-4508-1018-0(7)) Phoenix International Publications, Inc.

—Enchanted Songs. (Disney Princess Ser.). (Illus.). 10p. (J). bds. 9.98 (978-0-7853-8279-9(8), 7182300) Publications International, Ltd.

—Lenticular 1 Button Sesame Street. 2010. (SPA.). 12p. (J). bds. 10.98 (978-1-4127-4468-3(7), PIL Kids) Publications International, Ltd.

—Lenticular 1 Button Thomas. 2010. 12p. (J). bds. 10.98 (978-1-4127-4543-7(8), PIL Kids) Publications International, Ltd.

—My Little Pony Magic Friendship Songs. 2013. 10p. (J). (gr. k-4). bds. 10.99 (978-1-4508-6352-0(3), e11c6844-0b70-40b4-a490-b56ef2e7ed9f) Phoenix International Publications, Inc.

Publications International Ltd. Staff, creator. Dora the Explorer Laugh-along Sing-along. 2007. (Play-A-Song Ser.). (Illus.). bds. 15.98 (978-1-4127-7417-8(9)) Publications International, Ltd.

—Help along Sing a Song. 2007. (Play-A-Song Ser.). (Illus.). bds. 15.98 (978-1-4127-7419-2(5)) Publications International, Ltd.

—Learning Songs. 2007. (Take-along Songs Ser.). (Illus.). 16p. (J). (gr. -1). bds. 9.98 incl. audio compact disk (978-1-4127-7437-6(3)) Publications International, Ltd.

—Magic Songs. 2007. (Play-A-Song Ser.). (Illus.). (gr. -1-k). bds. 15.98 (978-1-4127-8813-7(7)) Publications International, Ltd.

—Scooby Doo!: Spooky Scooby Songs. 2007. (Play-A-Song Ser.). (Illus.). (J). (gr. -1-3). 16.98 (978-1-4127-7408-6(X)) Publications International, Ltd.

—Songs That Go. 2007. (Take-along Songs Ser.). (Illus.). 14p. (J). (gr. -1-3). bds. 9.98 incl. audio compact disk (978-1-4127-7440-6(3)) Publications International, Ltd.

Publications International Ltd. Staff, ed. All the World's Asleep. 2010. 14p. (J). bds. 7.98 net. (978-1-4127-4496-6(2), 1412744962, PIL Kids) Publications International, Ltd.

—Barney: I Love You Songs. 2011. 14p. (J). bds. 22.98 (978-1-4508-1249-8(X)) Publications International, Ltd.

—Car Tunes. 2010. 12p. (J). bds. 14.98 (978-1-60553-400-8(5), PIL Kids) Publications International, Ltd.

—Disney Mickey Mouse Clubhouse Let's Sing! Play-A-Sound Book & Cuddly Mickey. 2014. 6p. (J). bds. 19.98 (978-1-4508-7451-9(7), cbf92671-51dc-428b-801c-1493d85def5e) Publications International, Ltd.

—Disney Pixar Cars: Radiator Springs Sings. 2011. 14p. (J). bds. 17.98 (978-1-60553-389-6(0)) Publications International, Ltd.

—Disney Princess. 2010. 14p. (J). bds. 19.98 (978-1-60553-621-7(0)) Phoenix International Publications, Inc.

—Dora Digital Music Player. 2010. 14p. (J). bds. 9.39 net. (978-1-4508-1437-9(9), 1450814379) Phoenix International Publications, Inc.

—Elmos Garden Little Sound Book. 2005. (Play-a-Sound Ser.). (Illus.). 10p. (J). bds. 10.50 (978-1-4127-3291-8(3), 7244300) Publications International, Ltd.

—Friendship Songs. 2010. 24p. (J). 17.98 (978-1-60553-399-5(8), PIL Kids) Publications International, Ltd.

—Hello Kitty Sweet Songs: Play-A-Sound. 2013. 12p. (J). bds. 9.98 (978-1-4508-6167-0(9), 1450861679) Phoenix International Publications, Inc.

—Holiday Easter Play a Song Disney Bunnies. 2010. 10p. (J). bds. 12.98 (978-1-4127-9887-7(6)) Phoenix International Publications, Inc.

—Mickey Mouse 10 Song Sound. 2011. 24p. (J). 17.98 (978-1-4508-1472-0(7)) Publications International, Ltd.

—Mickey Mouse Clubhouse: Play Day Songs. 2011. (Illus.). 12p. (J). bds. 15.98 (978-1-4508-0925-2(1)) Publications International, Ltd.

—Mickey's Clubhouse Drum Song Sound. 2011. 14p. (J). bds. 20.98 (978-1-4508-1240-5(6)) Phoenix International Publications, Inc.

—Move to the Music. 2011. 14p. (J). bds. 20.98 (978-1-4508-1242-9(2)) Phoenix International Publications, Inc.

—Play & Learn Piano Elmo. 2011. 24p. (J). 17.98 (978-1-4508-0871-2(9)) Phoenix International Publications, Inc.

—Record a Song Old Mac Donald. 2011. 18p. 17.98 (978-1-4508-2179-7(0)) Phoenix International Publications, Inc.

—Sesame Street: Potty Time Songs. 2011. 12p. (J). bds. (978-1-4508-0401-1(2)) Phoenix International Publications, Inc.

—Starry Sky Songs. 2010. 14p. (J). bds. 17.98 (978-1-4127-4497-3(0)) Phoenix International Publications, Inc.

—Sunny Sing-Along Songs. 2010. 10p. (J). bds. 12.98 (978-1-4127-4493-5(8), PIL Kids) Publications International, Ltd.

—Thomas & Friends: Sing-Along Songs. 2011. 14p. (J). bds. 17.98 (978-1-4508-1130-9(2)) Phoenix International Publications, Inc.

—Winnie the Pooh: Sing along with Pooh (Little Pop-up Songbook) 2011. 10p. (J). bds. (978-1-60553-145-8(6)) Publications International, Ltd.

—The World of Eric Carle: Merry Christmas: Play-A-Sound Book. 2012. 14p. (J). (gr. k-3). bds. 16.99 (978-1-4508-6623-1(9), df3db359-6e89-4107-9d94-fec814a161da) Phoenix International Publications, Inc.

—9 Button Record Song Mickey'S Christmas. 2011. 18p. 19.98 (978-1-4508-1985-5(0)) Publications International, Ltd.

—9 Button Record Song Thomas Sing Along. 2011. 12p. (J). bds. 17.98 (978-1-4508-1995-4(8), 1450819958) Phoenix International Publications, Inc.

—9 Button Record Story Elmo Silly Stories. 2011. 18p. 19.98 (978-1-4508-1986-2(9)) Publications International, Ltd.

Puybaret, Eric, illus. Over the Rainbow. 2010. (ENG.). 26p. (J). (gr. k-4). 19.99 (978-1-936140-00-8(4)) Charlesbridge Publishing, Inc.

Racknor & Morrow. Wordszart. 2011. 92p. pap. 29.99 (978-0-557-55589-5(2)) Lulu Pr., Inc.

Raposo, Joe. Sing. Lichtenheld, Tom, illus. 2013. (ENG.). 40p. (J). (gr. -1-3). 16.99 (978-0-8050-9071-0(1), 900061330, Holt, Henry & Co. Bks. For Young Readers) Holt, Henry & Co.

Rappin' Heart Rhyme. (Song Box Ser.). (gr. 1-2). 8.50 incl. audio (978-0-322-00248-7(6)) Wright Group/McGraw-Hill.

Rappin' Heart Rhyme: 1 Big Book, 6 Each of 1 Student Book, & 1 Cassette. (Song Box Ser.). (gr. 1-2). 68.95 (978-0-322-00274-6(5)) Wright Group/McGraw-Hill.

Rappin' Heart Rhyme: 6 Each of 1 Student Book, 6 vols. (Song Box Ser.). (gr. 1-2). 29.50 (978-0-322-00270-8(2)) Wright Group/McGraw-Hill.

Rappin' Heart Rhyme: Big Book. (Song Box Ser.). (gr. 1-2). 31.50 (978-0-322-00265-4(6)) Wright Group/McGraw-Hill.

Rauenhorst, Linda. Frohliche Weihnachten: Learning Songs & Traditions in German. Collier, Roberta, illus. 2007. (Teach Me Ser.). (GER.). 32p. (J). (gr. -1-3). 19.95 (978-1-59972-063-0(9)) Teach Me Tapes, Inc.

Reasoner, Charles. Inside Old MacDonald's Barn. 2014. (Illus.). (J). (978-1-4351-5467-4(3)) Barnes & Noble, Inc.

Reed, Jennifer. Yankee Doodle, 1 vol. 2019. (America's Songs Ser.). (ENG.). 32p. (gr. 3-3). pap. 11.58 (978-1-5026-4877-8(6), ee0eadd7-381e-4755-9ba0-c1a24ae4458b) Cavendish Square Publishing LLC.

Rescek, Sanja, et al, illus. Itsy Bitsy Spider & Other Clap-along Rhymes. 2004. (Clap-Alongs Ser.). (ENG.). 36p. (J). (gr. -1-k). 12.95 (978-1-59249-522-1(2), 1D025) Soundprints.

Rice, Ruth Mason & Villar, Rose. Cycle, Children's Games & Other Songs. Browne, Anita, illus. 2012. 56p. 36.95 (978-1-258-23019-7(4)); pap. 21.95 (978-1-258-24214-5(1)) Literary Licensing, LLC.

Roberts, Sheena. Birds & Beasts: Animal songs, games & Activities. Price, David & Ursell, Martin, illus. 2006. (Classroom Music Ser.). (ENG.). 80p. (J). (gr. 1-6). (978-0-7136-5653-4(0), A&C Black) Bloomsbury Publishing Plc.

Rojo, Andrea Szekasy & Bardsley, Maggie. I Love Spanish Songs: Songbook & CD. 2003. (SPA., Illus.). 30p. (J). (gr. -1-2). pap. 15.99 (978-0-9671053-7-6(4)) Language Adventure Pubns.

Romendik, Irena, illus. The Musical Muffin Man. 2003. (Rub a Dub Books Ser.). 8p. (J). (gr. -1-k). vinyl bd. 7.00 (978-1-883043-45-2(X)) Straight Edge Pr., The.

Romendik, Irene, illus. I've Been Working on the Railroad: Musical Book. 2003. (J). 6.49 (978-1-883043-48-3(4)) Straight Edge Pr., The.

Rookie Preschool: Rookie Learn about Nauture: the Ants Go Marching. 2009. (Rookie Preschool Ser.). (ENG.). 24p. (J). (gr. -1). 23.00 (978-0-531-24406-7(7), Children's Pr.) Scholastic Library Publishing.

Rothero, Chris, illus. Strawberry Fair. 2004. 96p. (gr. 1-6). 14.95 (978-0-7136-2676-6(3), A&C Black) Bloomsbury Publishing Plc GBR. Dist: Consortium Bk. Sales & Distribution.

Ruesga, Rita Rosa & Scholastic, Inc. Staff. Cantaba la Rana. Sebastián, Soledad, illus. 2011. (SPA & ENG.). 32p. (J). (gr. -1-3). pap. 6.99 (978-0-545-27357-2(9), Scholastic en Espanol) Scholastic, Inc.

Rupprecht, Karen & Minor, Pamela. Months of Music & More. 2005. (Illus.). 28p. (J). per. 18.95 (978-0-9704184-3-2(4)) Pennypack Productions, Inc.

Sabol, Elizabeth, illus. Day Is Done: A Lullaby l.t. ed. 2004. 26p. (J). pap. incl. audio compact disk (978-0-9747382-0-8(4)) LeDor Publishing.

Sadlier We Believe Program Songbook. 2003. (J). per. (978-0-8215-5448-7(4), Sadlier) Sadlier, William H. Inc.

Salgado. Nuevas Canciones Infantiles. 2018.Tr. of New Children's Songs. (SPA.). 152p. (YA). pap. 6.95 (978-968-403-664-2(7)) Selector, S.A. de C.V. MEX. Dist: Spanish Pubs., LLC.

Salmon, Shirley. Hello Children: A Collection of Songs & Related Activities for Children Aged 4-9. 2007. (ENG.). 48p. pap. 21.95 (978-1-84761-052-2(8), 49016748) Schott Music Corp.

Sangam Songbook (Revised) 2005. (J). (978-0-88441-689-0(5)) Girl Scouts of the USA.

Save a Tree for Me: 1 Big Book, 6 Each of 1 Student Book, & 1 Cassette. (Song Box Ser.). (gr. 1-2). 68.95 (978-0-7802-3206-8(2)) Wright Group/McGraw-Hill.

Sawyer, Louise. The Phantom. 2003. (YA). 12.95 (978-0-9719842-1-9(2)) Martin & Brothers.

Schnetzler, Pattie. Earth Day Birthday. Wallace, Chad, illus. 2004. (Sharing Nature with Children Book Ser.). 32p. (J). 8.95 (978-1-58469-054-2(2)); 16.95 (978-1-58469-053-5(4)) Take Heart Pubns.

Schoenburg, Jane & Schoenburg, Steven. My Bodyworks: Songs about Your Bones, Muscles, Heart & More! Fisher, Cynthia, illus. 2014. (ENG.). 32p. (J). (gr. k-3). 16.95 (978-1-56656-583-7(9), Crocodile Bks.) Interlink Publishing Group, Inc.

Scholastic. The Wheels on the Truck Go 'Round & 'Round (Rookie Toddler) 2012. (Rookie Toddler Ser.). (ENG.). 14p. (J). (gr. -1 — 1). bds. 6.95 (978-0-531-20855-7(9), Children's Pr.) Scholastic Library Publishing.

Schwaeber, Barbie. Make New Friends. Brooks, Nan, illus. (American Favorites Ser.). (ENG.). 32p. (J). (gr. -1-3). 2008. 14.95 (978-1-59249-728-7(4)) 2007. 8.95 (978-1-59249-729-4(2)) Soundprints.

Schwaeber, Barbie H. She'll Be Comin Round the Mountain. Beaky, Suzanne, illus. 2007. (American Favorites Ser.). (ENG.). 32p. (J). (gr. -1-3). 9.85 (978-1-59249-688-4(1)) Soundprints.

Schwaeber, Barbie H., ed. She'll Be Comin' Round the Mountain. Beaky, Suzanne, illus. 2007. (American Favorites Ser.). (ENG.). 32p. (J). (gr. -1-3). 14.95 (978-1-59249-687-7(3)) Soundprints.

Schwortz, Anna M. A B C Rhymetime. Schwortz, Anna M., ed. Schwortz, Anna M., illus. 2005. (Illus.). 48p. (J). (gr. k-3). pap. (978-0-9769719-0-0(9)) AnnArt Pr.

Scribens, Sunny & Barefoot Books Staff. Space Song Rocket Ride. 2014. (Illus.). 24p. (J). 16.99 (978-1-78285-097-7(X)) Barefoot Bks., Inc.

Scruggs, Kathy. Espanol Con Senora Scruggs! 2003. (Illus.). 46p. (J). spiral bd. (978-0-9747272-0-2(2)) Permiso Por Favor Publishing Co.

Seasons & Celebrations. 2003. (Toddler Ser.). (Illus.). 36p. (J). pap. 12.99 (978-1-894677-48-6(X)) Kidzup Productions.

Sehgal, Kabir & Sehgal, Surishtha. Thread of Love. Hoang, Zara Gonzalez, illus. 2018. (ENG.). 40p. (J). (gr. -1-3). 18.99 (978-1-5344-0473-1(2), Beach Lane Bks.) Beach Lane Bks.

—The Wheels on the Tuk Tuk. Golden, Jess, illus. 2016. (ENG.). 40p. (J). (gr. -1-k). 18.99 *(978-1-4814-4831-4(5),* Beach Lane Bks.) Beach Lane Bks.
Selbert, Kathryn, illus. Ye Cannae Shove Yer Granny off a Bus: A Favourite Scottish Rhyme with Moving Parts, 20 vols. 2018. (Scottish Rhymes Ser.). 12p. (J). 9.95 *(978-1-78250-478-8(8),* Kelpies) Floris Bks. GBR. Dist: Consortium Bk. Sales & Distribution.
Sharp, Cecil James. English Folk-Chanteys: With Pianoforte Accompaniment, Introduction & Notes. unabr. ed. 2012. (Illus.). 91p. 39.99 *(978-1-4622-9398-8(0))* Repressed Publishing LLC.
Shyu, Theresa. Bilingual Songs - English-Mandarin-Chinese, 2 vols., Vol. 1. 2009. (Bilingual Songs English Mandarin Ser.: 1). (ENG., Illus.). 48p. (J). 17.95 *(978-1-55386-107-2(8),* 1553861078) Jordan, Sara Publishing.
Sickler, Jonas, illus. Indestructibles: Frere Jacques: Chew Proof · Rip Proof · Nontoxic · 100% Washable (Book for Babies, Newborn Books, Safe to Chew) 2011. (Indestructibles Ser.). (ENG.). 12p. (J). (gr. -1 — 1). pap. 5.95 *(978-0-7611-5923-0(1),* 15923) Workman Publishing Co., Inc.
Sign2Me, creator. Pick Me up! (Music & ASL) Fun Songs for Learning Signs. 2003. (ENG., Illus.). 64p. act. bk. ed. 36.95 incl. audio compact disk *(978-0-9668367-8-3(2),* Sign2Me) Sign2Me Early Learning / Northlight Communications, Inc.
Silver, Skye. Dump Truck Disco. Engel, Christiane, illus. 2018. (ENG.). 32p. (J). (gr. -1-2). 16.99 *(978-1-78285-407-4(X))* Barefoot Bks., Inc.
—Dump Truck Disco. 2019. (ENG.). (J). (gr. k-1). 18.96 *(978-1-64310-890-2(5))* Penworthy Co., LLC, The.
Smart Kidz, creator. Jesus Loves the Little Children. 2013. (Bible Sing along Bks.). (ENG., Illus.). 12p. (gr. -1). bds. 12.99 *(978-1-891100-34-5(3),* Smart Kids) Penton Overseas, Inc.
Smith, Craig. The Wonky Donkey. 2019. (ENG.). 22p. (J). (gr. k-1). 18.59 *(978-0-87617-275-9(3))* Penworthy Co., LLC, The.
—The Wonky Donkey. Cowley, Katz, illus. 2010. (ENG.). 24p. (J). (gr. -1-k). pap. 7.99 *(978-0-545-26124-1(4),* Scholastic Paperbacks) Scholastic, Inc.
Smith, Janet Kay. Sing A Song of Science: Lyrics for Kids From 1-99. 2005. (Illus.). 27p. (J). spiral bd. *(978-0-9768786-0-5(7))* Kay, Janet Consulting.
Smith, Richard B. & Bernard, Felix. Walking in a Winter Wonderland: Based on the Song by Felix Bernard & Richard B. Smith. Hopgood, Tim, illus. 2016. (J). *(978-0-19-275988-7(4))* Holt, Henry & Co.
Smithsonian Institution Staff. Home on the Range. Schwaeber, Barbie H., ed. Magnuson, Diana, illus. 2007. (ENG.). 32p. (J). (gr. -1-3). 9.85 *(978-1-59249-686-0(5))* Soundprints.
The Song Box Science Songs: 1 Each of 12 Big Books. (Song Box Ser.). (gr. 1-2). 375.50 *(978-0-322-02962-0(7))* Wright Group/McGraw-Hill.
The Song Box Science Songs: 1 Each of 12 Cassettes. (Song Box Ser.). (gr. 1-2). 101.95 *(978-0-322-02963-7(5))* Wright Group/McGraw-Hill.
The Song Box Science Songs: 1 Each of 12 Student Books. (Song Box Ser.). (gr. 1-2). 57.95 *(978-0-322-02959-0(7))* Wright Group/McGraw-Hill.
The Song Box Science Songs: 6 Each of 12 Student Books. (Song Box Ser.). (gr. 1-2). 349.95 *(978-0-322-02960-6(0))* Wright Group/McGraw-Hill.
Songs to the Corn: A Hopi Poet Writes about Corn, 6 packs. (Greetings Ser.: Vol. 2). (gr. 3-5). 31.00 *(978-0-7635-1808-0(5))* Rigby Education.
Soundprints Staff. Make New Friends. Schwaeber, Barbie Heit & Williams, Tracee, eds. Brooks, Nan, illus. 2008. (ENG.). 24p. (J). (gr. -1). 4.99 *(978-1-59069-651-4(4))* Studio Mouse LLC.
Soussana, Nathalie. Songs from the Garden of Eden: Jewish Lullabies & Nursery Rhymes. Alemagna, Beatrice, illus. 2009. (ENG & ARA.). 52p. (J). (gr. -1-2). 16.95 *(978-2-923163-46-8(X))* La Montagne Secrete CAN. Dist: Independent Pubs. Group.
Stannard, Kevin. Junior Voiceworks 1: 33 Songs for Children. 2003. (Voiceworks Ser.). (ENG., Illus.). 136p. 65.99 *(978-0-19-343551-3(9))* Oxford Univ. Pr., Inc.
Stein, Kristen. Oh Sweet Child of Mine. 2009. 32p. pap. 16.50 *(978-0-557-09407-3(0))* Lulu Pr., Inc.
SteveSongs Staff. The Shape Song Singalong. Sim, David, illus. 2011. 36p. (J). 16.99 *(978-1-84686-671-5(5))* Barefoot Bks., Inc.
Stotts, Stuart. We Shall Overcome: A Song That Changed the World. Cummings, Terrance, illus. 2010. (ENG.). 80p. (J). (gr. 5-7). 18.00 *(978-0-547-18210-0(4),* 1055966, Clarion Bks.) HarperCollins Pubs.
Strauss, Kurt & Strauss, Kim. Little Boy's Lullaby: A Songbook. 2005. (J). 35.00 *(978-0-9760929-0-2(5));* DVD, audio compact disk 35.00 *(978-0-9760929-3-3(X))* Blanket Street Publishing.
Street, Alison & Bance, Linda. Voiceplay: 22 Songs for Young Children, Pack. ldr.'s ed. 2006. (Voiceworks Ser.). (ENG., Illus.). 64p. 45.50 *(978-0-19-321060-8(6))* Oxford Univ. Pr., Inc.
Stroniarz, Christina V., illus. Let's Sing & Celebrate! 105 Original Songs for Seasons & Festivals. 2003. 224p. pap. 24.95 *(978-0-9720913-9-8(4))* Songbird Pr.
Studio Mouse, creator. Let's Play: Nursery Rhymes for Playing & Learning. 2005. (Read-Aloud Book Ser.). (ENG., Illus.). 36p. (J). 7.95 *(978-1-59249-535-1(4),* 1D205) Soundprints.
Sullivan, Carolyn Rose, illus. The Music Box: Songs, Rhymes, & Games for Young Children, 1 box. 2006. 200p. (J). 49.95 *(978-0-9772717-1-9(4))* ELZ Publishing.
Sullivan, James Kevin, illus. What Went Right Today? Journal: WWRT Journal. 2007. 72p. (J). spiral bd. 12.95 *(978-0-9766990-1-9(X))* Buz-Land Presentations, Inc.
Tagore, Rabindranath. Gitanjali - Song Offerings. 2007. 52p. per. 11.99 *(978-1-59547-773-6(X))* NuVision Pubns., LLC.
Tarsky, Sue. The Wheels on The... Uh-Oh! Willmore, Alex, illus. 2018. (ENG.). 32p. (J). (gr. -1-3). 16.99 *(978-0-8075-8869-7(5),* 807588695) Whitman, Albert & Co.
Taylor, Michaelle. Singing Across the Old North State: Story-Songs of North Carolina. 2004. 44p. (J). pap. *(978-1-880970-89-8(9))* Aerial Photography Services, Inc.
Temporin, Elena, illus. The Usborne Book of Christmas Lullabies. 2006. (Christmas Lullabies Ser.). 8p. (J). bds. 14.99 incl. audio compact disk *(978-0-7945-1469-3(3),* Usborne) EDC Publishing.
Thiele, Bob & Weiss, George David. What a Wonderful World. Hopgood, Tim, illus. 2014. (ENG.). 32p. (J). (gr. -1-k). 19.99 *(978-1-62779-254-7(6),* 900144000, Holt, Henry & Co. Bks. For Young Readers) Holt, Henry & Co.
Thomas: It's Great to Be an Engine. 2004. (Little Music Note Ser.). (Illus.). 10p. (J). bds. *(978-0-7853-9950-6(X),* 7209400) Phoenix International Publications, Inc.
Thomas, Joyce Carol. Singing Mama's Songs. Date not set. 32p. (J). 16.00 *(978-0-06-025379-0(7));* lib. bdg. 15.89 *(978-0-06-025382-0(7))* HarperCollins Pubs.
Thompson, Kim Mitzo. Bible Songs. 2011. (J). (gr. k-1). audio compact disk 4.99 *(978-1-59922-874-7(2))* Twin Sisters IP, LLC.
—The Easter Story. 2010. (J). (gr. k-2). pap. 4.99 *(978-1-59922-494-7(1))* Twin Sisters IP, LLC.
Thompson, Kim Mitzo & Hilderbrand, Karen Mitzo. Alphabet. 2010. 12p. (J). (gr. k-2). bds. 8.99 *(978-1-59922-569-2(7))* Twin Sisters IP, LLC.
—Counting. 2010. 12p. (J). (gr. k-2). bds. 8.99 *(978-1-59922-570-8(0))* Twin Sisters IP, LLC.
—Multiplication Rap. 2008. (Playaway Children Ser.). (J). 44.99 *(978-1-59922-324-7(4))* Findaway World, LLC.
Ticktock Media, Ltd. Staff. Itsy Bitsy Spider. 2011. (Sing-Along Songs Ser.). (ENG.). 10p. (J). (gr. k — 1). bds. 6.95 *(978-1-84898-170-6(8),* TickTock Books) Octopus Publishing Group GBR. Dist: Independent Pubs. Group.
—Old McDonald Had a Farm. 2011. (Sing-Along Songs Ser.). (ENG.). 10p. (J). (gr. k — 1). bds. 6.95 *(978-1-84898-169-0(4),* TickTock Books) Octopus Publishing Group GBR. Dist: Independent Pubs. Group.
—The Wheels on the Bus. 2011. (Sing-Along Songs Ser.). (ENG.). 10p. (J). (gr. k — 1). bds. 6.95 *(978-1-84898-172-0(4),* TickTock Books) Octopus Publishing Group GBR. Dist: Independent Pubs. Group.
Tiger Tales Staff, ed. Jingle Bells: A Collection of Songs & Carols. Kolvanovic, Dubravka, illus. 2014. (ENG.). 22p. (J). (gr. -1-k). bds. 8.99 *(978-1-58925-568-5(2))* Tiger Tales.
Time to Sign. Time to Sign with Children Infant/Toddler: Time to Sign with Music Infant/Toddler. 2003. Orig. Title: Time to Sign with Music Infant/Toddler. (Illus.). 42p. per. 19.95 *(978-0-9713666-0-2(8))* Time to Sign, Incorporated.
Todd, Traci N. Wiggle Waggle Bee. Barner, Bob, illus. 2013. (J). *(978-1-58987-327-8(0))* Kindermusik International.
Traditional. Dayenu! a Favorite Passover Song. Latimer, Miriam, illus. 2012. (ENG.). 14p. (J). (gr. -1 — 1). bds. 7.99 *(978-0-545-31236-3(1),* Cartwheel Bks.) Scholastic, Inc.
Traditional. Jesus Loves Me. 2009. (ENG., Illus.). 20p. (J). (gr. -1 — 1). bds. 7.99 *(978-0-8249-1839-2(8),* Worthy Kids/Ideals) Worthy Publishing.
Trapani, Iza. The Bear Went over the Mountain. 2012. (ENG., Illus.). 32p. (J). (gr. k-3). 16.95 *(978-1-61608-510-0(X),* 608510, Sky Pony Pr.) Skyhorse Publishing Co., Inc.
—Mary Had a Little Lamb. Trapani, Iza, illus. 2003. (Iza Trapani's Extended Nursery Rhymes Ser.). (Illus.). 32p. (J). (gr. -1-k). 7.95 *(978-1-58089-090-8(3))* Charlesbridge Publishing, Inc.
—Shoo Fly! Trapani, Iza, illus. 2007. (Iza Trapani's Extended Nursery Rhymes Ser.). (Illus.). 32p. (J). (gr. k-3). per. 7.95 *(978-1-58089-076-2(8))* Charlesbridge Publishing, Inc.
—Sing along with Iza & Friends: Row Row Row Your Boat. Trapani, Iza, illus. 2004. (Illus.). 32p. (J). pap. 11.95 incl. audio compact disk *(978-1-58089-102-8(0))* Charlesbridge Publishing, Inc.
—Sing along with Iza & Friends: The Itsy Bitsy Spider. Trapani, Iza, illus. 2004. (Illus.). 32p. (J). pap. 11.95 incl. audio compact disk *(978-1-58089-100-4(4))* Charlesbridge Publishing, Inc.
Tricia Lowenfield design. S Is for Shepherd. 2004. (Illus.). 32p. (J). per. 19.99 incl. audio compact disk *(978-0-9747367-0-9(8))* Pumpkins Pansies Bunnies & Bears.
Twin Sisters(r) Staff. B-I-N-G-O. 2009. 16p. 4.99 *(978-1-59922-368-1(6))* Twin Sisters IP, LLC.
—Bible Songs Workbook/CD Set. 2008. 96p. 10.99 *(978-1-57583-897-7(4))* Twin Sisters IP, LLC.
—Down Through the Chimney. 2009. 16p. 4.99 *(978-1-59922-413-8(5))* Twin Sisters IP, LLC.
—The Farmer in the Dell. 2009. 16p. 4.99 *(978-1-59922-370-4(8))* Twin Sisters IP, LLC.
—Five Little Monkeys Jumping on the Bed. 2009. 16p. 4.99 *(978-1-59922-372-8(4))* Twin Sisters IP, LLC.
—Jesus Loves the Little Children. 2010. (J). (gr. k-2). pap. 4.99 *(978-1-59922-495-4(X))* Twin Sisters IP, LLC.
—Jolly Old St.Nicholas. 2009. 16p. 4.99 *(978-1-59922-412-1(7))* Twin Sisters IP, LLC.
—The Lord Is My Shepherd. 2010. (J). (gr. k-1). 14.99 *(978-1-59922-632-3(4))* Twin Sisters IP, LLC.
—Multiplication Workbook & Music CD. 2009. pap. 12.99 incl. audio compact disk *(978-1-57583-894-6(X))* Twin Sisters IP, LLC.
—Old MacDonald Had a Farm. 2009. 16p. 4.99 *(978-1-59922-369-8(4))* Twin Sisters IP, LLC.
—Old Testament Handlebox-4 books. 2009. 12.99 *(978-1-59922-112-0(8))* Twin Sisters IP, LLC.
—Rise & Shine. 2010. (J). (gr. k-2). pap. 4.99 *(978-1-59922-496-1(8))* Twin Sisters IP, LLC.
—Six Little Ducks. 2010. (J). (gr. k-1). 14.99 *(978-1-59922-631-6(6));* pap. 4.99 *(978-1-59922-504-3(2))* Twin Sisters IP, LLC.
—The Story of Jesus Handlebox-4books. 2009. 12.99 *(978-1-59922-111-3(X))* Twin Sisters IP, LLC.
—Ten in the Bed. 2010. (J). (gr. k-2). pap. 4.99 *(978-1-59922-503-6(4))* Twin Sisters IP, LLC.
—The Wheels on the Bus. 2009. 16p. 4.99 *(978-1-59922-371-1(6))* Twin Sisters IP, LLC.
—When I Go Trick or Treating. 2009. 16p. 4.99 *(978-1-59922-416-9(X))* Twin Sisters IP, LLC.
—120 Kids' Songs 4CD Digipack. 2008. (Illus.). 14.99 *(978-1-59922-106-9(3))* Twin Sisters IP, LLC.
Twin Sisters(r) Staff, et al, adapted by. Six Little Ducks. 2010. (J). (gr. k-1). 14.99 *(978-1-59922-423-7(2))* Twin Sisters IP, LLC.
Twin Sisters(r) Staff & Hilderbrand, Karen Mitzo, adapted by. Ten in the Bed. 2010. (J). (gr. k-1). 14.99 *(978-1-59922-420-6(8))* Twin Sisters IP, LLC.
Twin Sisters(r) Staff, et al. I Thank God for You. 2010. (J). (gr. k-2). pap. 4.99 *(978-1-59922-497-8(6))* Twin Sisters IP, LLC.
—It's Silly Time. 2010. (J). (gr. k-2). pap. 4.99 *(978-1-59922-508-1(5))* Twin Sisters IP, LLC.
Vasilovich, Guy. The 13 Nights of Halloween. Vasilovich, Guy, illus. 2011. (ENG., Illus.). 40p. (J). (gr. -1-3). 16.99 *(978-0-06-180445-8(2),* HarperCollins) HarperCollins Pubs.
Vasylenko, Veronica, illus. Jingle Bells. 2007. (Padded Board Bks.). 18p. (J). (gr. -1-k). bds. 7.95 *(978-1-58925-821-1(5))* Tiger Tales.
VBS Ready, Set, Gold! Music Guide. 2003. (J). pap. *(978-0-8100-1528-9(5))* Northwestern Publishing Hse.
Vilsaint, Fequiere. Children Songs from Haiti: Chante Timoun Ayiti. Date not set. 28p. (J). (gr. 1-5). wbk. ed. 25.00 *(978-1-881839-55-2(9))* Educa Vision Inc.
Wade, Connie Morgan. Bible Songs & Action Rhymes (Ages 3-6) 2016. (ENG., Illus.). 224p. (J). (gr. -1-3). per. 16.99 *(978-0-7847-1781-3(8),* 140202) Standard Publishing.
Wagner, Veronica. DreamWorks Trolls: Get Back up Again Sound Book. 2016. (ENG., Illus.). 12p. (J). bds. 15.99 *(978-1-5037-1242-3(7),* 2222, PI Kids) Phoenix International Publications, Inc.
Walty, Margaret T., illus. Rock-a-Bye Baby: Lullabies for Bedtime. 2005. 40p. (J). (gr. k-4). reprint ed. 15.00 *(978-0-7567-8555-0(3))* DIANE Publishing Co.
Wang, Margaret. Eency Weency Spider. Rueda, Claudia, illus. 2006. (ENG.). 22p. (J). (gr. -1-3). bds. 10.95 *(978-1-58117-418-2(7),* Intervisual/Piggy Toes) Bendon, Inc.
Warhola, James. If You're Happy & You Know It. Geist, Ken, ed. Warhola, James, illus. 2007. (ENG., Illus.). 32p. (J). (gr. -1-k). 16.99 *(978-0-439-72766-2(9),* Orchard Bks.) Scholastic, Inc.
—If You're Happy & You Know It. 2007. (Illus.). (J). pap. *(978-0-545-01981-1(8))* Scholastic, Inc.
Weeks, Sarah. Don't Discover Me. Date not set. (J). (gr. -1-3). 15.99 *(978-0-06-028139-7(1))* HarperCollins Pubs.
Welfing, Melanie Rook. Sing for Joy. 2005. (J). pap. 1.69 *(978-1-59317-119-3(6))* Warner Pr., Inc.
Westerman, Robert. Santa We've Been Good: Sheet Music & Lyrics. 2006. (Illus.). 10p. (J). 6.95 *(978-0-9761992-2-9(X))* Gold Boy Music & Pubn.
Weston Woods Staff, creator. Over in the Meadow. 2004. 38.75 *(978-1-55592-759-2(9));* 18.95 *(978-1-55592-809-4(9));* 29.95 *(978-1-55592-852-0(8))* Weston Woods Studios, Inc.
White, Jack. We're Going to Be Friends. Blake, Elinor, illus. 2017. 32p. (J). (gr. 1-5). 21.00 *(978-0-9964016-9-2(5))* Third Man Books.
Wilcox, Ella Wheeler. Historical Mother Goose: A Jingle Book O. 2006. pap. 15.95 *(978-1-4179-7078-0(2))* Kessinger Publishing, LLC.
Williams, Pharrell. Happy! (ENG., Illus.). (J). (gr. -1 — 1). 2016. 30p. bds. 7.99 *(978-0-399-54812-3(2))* 2015. 32p. 19.99 *(978-0-399-17643-2(8))* Penguin Young Readers Group. (G.P. Putnam's Sons Books for Young Readers).
Winter's Gift. (Song Box Ser.). (gr. 1-2). 31.50 *(978-0-322-00267-8(2))* Wright Group/McGraw-Hill.
Winter's Gift: 6 Each of 1 Student Book. (Song Box Ser.). (gr. 1-2). 68.95 *(978-0-322-00277-7(X));* 29.50 *(978-0-322-00272-2(9))* Wright Group/McGraw-Hill.
Winter's Gift: Cassette. (Song Box Ser.). (gr. 1-2). 8.50 incl. audio *(978-0-322-00251-7(6))* Wright Group/McGraw-Hill.
Yarrow, Peter & Lipton, Lenny. Puff, the Magic Dragon. Puybaret, Eric, illus. (J). 2012. 24p. (gr. k — 1). bds. 8.99 *(978-1-4549-0114-3(4))* 2010. 32p. (gr. k-2). 9.95 *(978-1-4027-7216-0(5))* 2007. 24p. (gr. -1-2). 19.99 *(978-1-4027-4782-3(9))* Sterling Publishing Co., Inc.
Zahares, Wade, illus. Frosty the Snowman. 2013. (ENG.). 28p. (J). (gr. -1-3). 17.95 *(978-1-62354-012-8(7))* Charlesbridge Publishing, Inc.
Zondervan Staff. He's Got the Whole World in His Hands, 1 vol. Idle, Molly, illus. 2008. (I Can Read! / Song Ser.). (ENG.). 32p. (J). (gr. -1-3). pap. 4.99 *(978-0-310-71622-8(5))* Zonderkidz.
—If You're Happy & You Know It, 1 vol. Haley, Amanda, illus. 2008. (I Can Read! / Song Ser.). (ENG.). 32p. (J). (gr. -1-3). pap. 4.99 *(978-0-310-71621-1(7))* Zonderkidz.
—Jesus Loves Me, 1 vol. Borlasca, Hector, illus. 2008. (I Can Read! / Song Ser.). (ENG.). 32p. (J). (gr. -1-3). pap. 4.99 *(978-0-310-71619-8(5))* Zonderkidz.
—Jesus Loves the Little Children, 1 vol. Trasler, Janee, illus. 2008. (I Can Read! / Song Ser.). (ENG.). 32p. (J). (gr. -1-3). pap. 4.99 *(978-0-310-71620-4(9))* Zonderkidz.
2005 VBS SongBook. 2005. (J). *(978-1-58942-262-9(7))* R.H. Boyd Publishing Corp.

SONGS, AFRICAN AMERICAN
see African Americans—Music

SONGS, NATIONAL
see National Songs

SONGS, POPULAR
see Popular Music

SOOTHSAYING
see Divination

SOPORIFICS
see Narcotics

SORCERY
see Occultism; Witchcraft

SOSA, SAMMY, 1968-

Castle, George. Sammy Sosa: Slammin' Sammy. Rains, Rob, ed. 2003. (Superstar Ser.). (Illus.). 96p. (J). (gr. 4-7). pap. 4.95 *(978-1-58261-029-0(0))* Sports Publishing, LLC.
Kirkpatrick, Rob. Sammy Sosa: Bateador de Home Runs (Home-Run Hitter) 2009. (Deportistas de Poder (Power Players) Ser.). (SPA.). 24p. (gr. 1-1). 42.50 *(978-1-61512-160-1(9),* Editorial Buenas Letras) Rosen Publishing Group, Inc., The.
—Sammy Sosa: Home Run Hitter/Bateador de home Runs. 2009. (Power Players / Deportistas de Poder Ser.). (ENG & SPA.). 24p. (gr. 1-2). 42.50 *(978-1-60851-333-8(5),* Editorial Buenas Letras) Rosen Publishing Group, Inc., The.
Malone, Julio. Sammy Sosa en 9 Innings. 2nd exp. ed. 2004. (SPA.). (YA). pap. 12.95 net. *(978-0-9671705-0-3(8))* Editorial Miglo Inc.
—Sammy Sosa in 9 Innings. 2004. (YA). pap. 12.95 *(978-0-9671705-1-0(6))* Editorial Miglo Inc.
Morrison, John. Sammy Sosa. 2006. (Great Hispanic Heritage Ser.). (ENG., Illus.). 112p. (gr. 6-12). lib. bdg. 35.00 *(978-0-7910-8845-6(6),* P114457, Facts On File) Infobase Holdings, Inc.
Sammy Sosa - Sports Action Flipp Book. 2003. (J). mass mkt. 4.99 *(978-0-9744443-3-8(2))* Flipp Sports.
Savage, Jeff. Sammy Sosa. 2005. (Amazing Athletes Ser.). (Illus.). 32p. (J). (gr. 2-5). per. 5.95 *(978-0-8225-2041-2(9))* Lerner Publishing Group.
—Sammy Sosa: Home Run Hero. (Sports Achievers Biographies Ser.). (Illus.). 2005. (SPA.). 80p. (gr. 7-12). lib. bdg. 22.60 *(978-0-8225-3681-9(1))* 2003. 64p. (J). (gr. 4-9). 5.95 *(978-0-8225-9858-9(2),* Carolrhoda Bks.) Lerner Publishing Group.
Stewart, Mark. Sammy Sosa: Touching All the Bases. 2004. (American Literary Greats Ser.). (Illus.). 64p. (J). (gr. 5-18). lib. bdg. 25.26 *(978-0-7613-2778-3(9),* Millbrook Pr.) Lerner Publishing Group.

SOTO, HERNANDO DE, APPROXIMATELY 1500-1542

Donohue, Moira Rose. Hernando de Soto. 2015. (Illus.). 24p. (J). *(978-1-938813-20-7(0))* State Standards Publishing, LLC.
Goldberg, Jan. Hernando de Soto: Trailblazer of the American Southeast. 2009. (Library of Explorers & Exploration Ser.). 112p. (gr. 5-8). 66.50 *(978-1-60853-607-8(6),* Rosen Reference) Rosen Publishing Group, Inc., The.
Hubbard-Brown, Janet. Hernando de Soto & His Expeditions Across the Americas. 2005. (Explorers of New Lands Ser.). (ENG., Illus.). 100p. (gr. 5-8). lib. bdg. 30.00 *(978-0-7910-8610-0(0),* P114326, Facts On File) Infobase Holdings, Inc.
Marsh, Carole. Hernando de Soto: First Discovered the Mississippi River: First Discovered the Mississippi River. 2003. 12p. (gr. k-4). 2.95 *(978-0-635-02134-2(X))* Gallopade International.
Stuckey, Rachel. Explore with Hernando de Soto. 2016. (Travel with the Great Explorers Ser.). (ENG., Illus.). 32p. (J). (gr. 3-6). *(978-0-7787-2849-8(8))* Crabtree Publishing Co.
Young, Jeff C. Hernando de Soto: Spanish Conquistador in the Americas, 1 vol. 2009. (Great Explorers of the World Ser.). (ENG., Illus.). 112p. (gr. 6-7). lib. bdg. 35.93 *(978-1-59845-104-7(9),* 7fbdf9e0-91cc-47ae-9b32-2d3838629a61) Enslow Publishing, LLC.

SOUND
see also High-Fidelity Sound Systems

Albertson, Margaret & Emick, Paula. Music: the Sound of Science. 2018. (Project: STEAM Ser.). (ENG., Illus.). 48p. (gr. 4-8). pap. 10.95 *(978-1-64156-589-9(6),* 9781641565899) Rourke Educational Media.
Amson-Bradshaw, Georgia. Sound, 1 vol. 2017. (Science in a Flash Ser.). (ENG.). 32p. (J). (gr. 5-5). pap. 11.50 *(978-1-5382-1480-0(6),* c4054f92-c4c7-4757-8f52-7f2d726480ce); lib. bdg. 28.27 *(978-1-5382-1400-8(8),* de6e487a-7e8b-41bf-bf93-1e84be8307d7) Stevens, Gareth Publishing LLLP.
At My Grandfather's, 6 Pcks. (gr. -1-2). 27.00 *(978-0-7635-9435-0(0))* Rigby Education.
AZ Books Staff. Buzzing Meadow. Tulup, Natalia, ed. 2012. (How We Speak Ser.). (ENG.). 12p. (J). (gr. -1-k). bds. 10.95 *(978-1-61889-095-5(6))* AZ Bks. LLC.
—Feathered Singers. Tulup, Natalia, ed. 2012. (How We Speak Ser.). (ENG.). 12p. (J). (gr. -1-k). bds. 10.95 *(978-1-61889-096-2(4))* AZ Bks. LLC.
—Loud Farm. Tulup, Natalia, ed. 2012. (How We Speak Ser.). (ENG.). 12p. (J). (-k). bds. 10.95 *(978-1-61889-093-1(X))* AZ Bks. LLC.
Baker, Wendy, et al. Sound. (Make It Work! (Eureka!) Ser.). (FRE., Illus.). (J). pap. 9.99 *(978-0-590-24631-6(3))* Scholastic, Inc.
Ballard, Carol. Exploring Sound, 1 vol. 2007. (How Does Science Work? Ser.). (ENG., Illus.). 32p. (J). (gr. 2-3). lib. bdg. 30.27 *(978-1-4042-4279-1(1),* d1dccbdd-c144-428e-b84d-8f15529f0c4a) Rosen Publishing Group, Inc., The.
Barchers, Suzanne I. I've Discovered Sound!, 1 vol. 2009. (Eureka! Ser.). (ENG.). 32p. (gr. 4-4). lib. bdg. 31.21 *(978-0-7614-3207-4(8),* 384b9b1e-19cb-494e-ab9c-6bd64e3a429f) Cavendish Square Publishing LLC.
Bari, Ellen. Does Your Dog Speak Hebrew? A Book of Animal Sounds. Clifton-Brown, Holly, illus. 2020. (ENG.). 14p. (J). (gr. -1 — 1). bds. 7.99 *(978-1-5415-6089-5(2),* 36d82c5a-b2dd-43bf-af99-463931d0c2cb, Kar-Ben Publishing) Lerner Publishing Group.
Barlex, David & Wadsworth, Pamela. Rhagor Am Sain a Cherddoriaeth. 2005. (WEL., Illus.). 24p. pap. *(978-1-85596-240-8(3))* Dref Wen.
—Sain a Cherddoriaeth. 2005. (WEL., Illus.). 24p. pap. *(978-1-85596-239-2(X))* Dref Wen.
Beech, Linda Ward. The Magic School Bus in the Haunted Museum: A Book about Sound. Duchesne, Lucie, tr. Schick, Joel, illus. (Magic School Bus Ser.). (FRE.). 32p. (J). (gr. 1-4). pap. 5.99 *(978-0-590-24657-6(7))* Scholastic, Inc.
Benchmark Education Co., LLC. What Is That Sound? Big Book. 2014. (Shared Reading Foundations Ser.). (J). (gr. -1). *(978-1-4509-9437-8(7))* Benchmark Education Co.
Benchmark Education Company, LLC Staff, compiled by. Light & Sound: Theme Set. 2006. (J). 215.00 *(978-1-4108-7121-3(5))* Benchmark Education Co.
Bernhardt, Carolyn. Sound. 2018. (Science Starters Ser.). (ENG., Illus.). 24p. (J). (gr. k-3). lib. bdg. 26.95 *(978-1-62617-811-3(9),* Blastoff! Readers) Bellwether Media.
Boothroyd, Jennifer. Loud or Soft? High or Low? A Look at Sound. 2011. (Lightning Bolt Books Exploring Physical Science Ser.). 32p. pap. 45.32 *(978-0-7613-7650-7(X))* Lerner Publishing Group.
—Sending Messages with Light & Sound. 2014. (First Step Nonfiction — Light & Sound Ser.). (ENG., Illus.). 24p. (J). (gr. k-2). pap. 6.99 *(978-1-4677-4504-8(9),* 7d501c9a-3689-405d-b5b6-437bbb351e1a) Lerner Publishing Group.
Brasch, Nicolas. Tricks of Sound & Light. 2010. (Science Behind Ser.). 32p. lib. bdg. 28.50 *(978-1-59920-564-9(5))* Black Rabbit Bks.

S

—Why Does Sound Travel? All about Sound. 2010. (Illus.). 24p. (J). 49.50 *(978-1-61531-909-1(3)*, 1307169, PowerKids Pr.) Rosen Publishing Group, Inc., The.

—Why Is It So Loud?, 1 vol. 2010. (Solving Science Mysteries Ser.). (ENG., Illus.). 24p. (gr. 4-5). (J). pap. 9.25 *(978-1-61531-908-4(5)*, 04161079-3e60-46ab-b5fb-88e85aacaf0e, PowerKids Pr.); (YA). lib. bdg. 26.27 *(978-1-61531-888-9(7)*, be0e23e3-0ff9-4975-91cf-320daa17e939) Rosen Publishing Group, Inc., The.

Brooke, Susan Rich. World of Eric Carle: Sing Sound Book. 2018. (ENG., Illus.). 12p. (J). bds. 15.99 *(978-1-5037-2205-7(8)*, 2509, PI Kids) Phoenix International Publications, Inc.

Brown Bear Books. Light & Sound. 2011. (Introducing Physics Ser.). (ENG.). 64p. (J). (gr. 8-11). lib. bdg. 39.95 *(978-1-936333-06-6(6)*, 16503) Brown Bear Bks.

Burton, Margie, et al. I Hear! 2011. (Early Connections Ser.). (J). *(978-1-61672-294-4(0))* Benchmark Education Co.

Carlson Berne, Emma. Loud! Sound Energy, 1 vol. 2013. (Energy Everywhere Ser.). (ENG., Illus.). 24p. (J). (gr. 2-3). 26.27 *(978-1-4488-9648-6(7)*, 37e5063b-3eb1-4bd8-b433-9a0d8fbbb08f); pap. 9.25 *(978-1-4488-9754-4(8)*, e35fe831-6c0a-4464-b8e3-c7b5b8f9e6d1) Rosen Publishing Group, Inc., The. (PowerKids Pr.).

Casado, Dami & Casado, Alicia. El Sueño. 2005. (Sentidos y Algo Más). (SPA & ESP.). 16p. 8.99 *(978-84-272-6417-5(8))* Molino, Editorial ESP. Dist: Santillana USA Publishing Co., Inc.

Catasús Jennings, Terry. Sonidos en la Sabana, 1 vol. Saroff, Phyllis, illus. 2015.Tr. of Sounds of the Savanna. (SPA.). 32p. (J). (gr. k-3). pap. 11.95 *(978-1-62855-642-1(0))* Arbordale Publishing.

—Sounds of the Savanna, 1 vol. Saroff, Phyllis, illus. 2015.Tr. of Sounds of the Savanna. (ENG.). 32p. (J). (gr. k-3). pap. 9.95 *(978-1-62855-637-7(4))* Arbordale Publishing.

Claybourne, Anna. Ear-Splitting Sounds & Other Vile Noises. 2013. (ENG., Illus.). 32p. (J). *(978-0-7787-0925-1(6))*; pap. *(978-0-7787-0951-0(5))* Crabtree Publishing Co.

—Sound, 1 vol. 2013. (Physical Science Ser.). 48p. (J). (gr. 4-5). (ENG.). pap. 15.05 *(978-1-4339-9521-7(2)*, d51f368c-3dec-46c2-82d2-57ca94d70c44); pap. 84.30 *(978-1-4339-9522-4(0))*; (ENG., Illus.). lib. bdg. 34.61 *(978-1-4339-9520-0(4)*, 05b59618-f570-4059-98da-63449da71d14) Stevens, Gareth Publishing LLLP.

Coan, Sharon. How Sound Moves, 1 vol. rev. ed. 2014. (Science: Informational Text Ser.). (ENG., Illus.). 24p. (gr. 1-2). pap. 9.99 *(978-1-4807-4564-3(2))* Teacher Created Materials, Inc.

Connors, Kathleen. Sound, 1 vol. 2018. (Look at Physical Science Ser.). (ENG.). 32p. (gr. 2-2). 28.27 *(978-1-5382-2159-4(4)*, d6c22321-a0ff-4344-8d42-66f6e8fcd5f8) Stevens, Gareth Publishing LLLP.

Cooper, Christopher. The Basics of Sound, 1 vol. 2014. (Core Concepts Ser.). (ENG., Illus.). 96p. (YA). (gr. 7-7). 39.77 *(978-1-4777-7766-4(0)*, d64668b1-295f-4ae1-94c0-089e37c08238) Rosen Publishing Group, Inc., The.

Delta Education. Sci Res Bk Foss Grade 1 Next Gen Ea. 2015. (Illus.). 244p. (J). lib. bdg. *(978-1-62571-445-9(9))* Delta Education, LLC.

DK. Baby Faces Peekaboo! With Mirror, Touch-And-Feel, & Flaps. 2009. (Peekaboo! Ser.). (ENG.). 12p. (J). (gr. -1 — 1). bds. 10.99 *(978-0-7566-5506-8(4)*, DK Children) Dorling Kindersley Publishing, Inc.

Dunne, Abbie. Sound. 2016. (Physical Science Ser.). (ENG., Illus.). 24p. (J). (gr. -1-2). lib. bdg. 27.32 *(978-1-5157-0940-4(X)*, 132239, Capstone Pr.) Capstone.

Flesch Connors, Abigail. Exploring the Science of Sounds: 100 Musical Activities for Young Children. 2017. (ENG., Illus.). 216p. (gr. 13). pap. 16.95 *(978-0-87659-731-6(2)*, Gryphon House Inc) Gryphon Hse., Inc.

Fonder, Toni. The Science of Sound, 1 vol. 2008. (Real Life Readers Ser.). (ENG.). 16p. (gr. 2-3). pap. 7.05 *(978-1-4358-0093-9(1)*, 867bda98-7279-4867-a0b1-456307aa2554, Rosen Classroom) Rosen Publishing Group, Inc., The.

Frenkel, Karen A. Light & Sound Technology: Text Pairs. 2008. (Bridges/Navigators Ser.). (J). (gr. 4). 94.00 *(978-1-4108-8386-5(8))* Benchmark Education Co.

—Listening to Sound: Set Of 6. 2011. (Navigators Ser.). (J). pap. 48.00 net. *(978-1-4108-6227-3(5))* Benchmark Education Co.

—Listening to Sound: Text Pairs. 2008. (Bridges/Navigators Ser.). (J). (gr. 4). 94.00 *(978-1-4108-8387-2(6))* Benchmark Education Co.

Gardner, Jane P. Music Science, Vol. 11. Lewin, Russ, ed. 2015. (Science 24/7 Ser.). (Illus.). 48p. (J). (gr. 5). 20.95 *(978-1-4222-3412-9(6))* Mason Crest.

Gardner, Robert & Conklin, Joshua. A Kid's Book of Experiments with Sound, 1 vol. 2015. (Surprising Science Experiments Ser.). (ENG., Illus.). 48p. (gr. 4-4). 29.60 *(978-0-7660-7209-1(6)*, 7844d024-d3f5-421c-a5f1-7b20dd35cc1d) Enslow Publishing, LLC.

Gish, Melissa. Sound. 2005. (My First Look at Science Ser.). (Illus.). 24p. (J). (gr. k-3). lib. bdg. 15.95 *(978-1-58341-374-6(X)*, Creative Education) Creative Co., The.

Gregoire, Maryellen. All Kinds of Sounds, 1 vol. 2011. (Wonder Readers Emergent Level Ser.). (ENG.). 8p. (gr. -1-1). (J). pap. 6.25 *(978-1-4296-7838-4(0)*, 118151); pap. 35.94 *(978-1-4296-8217-6(5))* Capstone. (Capstone Pr.).

Gregory, Josh. Sound (a True Book: Physical Science) (Library Edition) 2019. (True Book (Relaunch) Ser.). (ENG., Illus.). 48p. (J). (gr. 3-5). lib. bdg. 31.00 *(978-0-531-13142-8(4)*, Children's Pr.) Scholastic Library Publishing.

Hansen, Grace. El Sonido. 2018. (Ciencia Básica (Beginning Science) Ser.).Tr. of Sound. (SPA.). 24p. (J). (gr. -1-2). lib. bdg. 32.79 *(978-1-5321-8392-8(5)*, 29977, Abdo Kids) ABDO Publishing Co.

—Sound. 2018. (Beginning Science Ser.). (ENG., Illus.). 24p. (J). (gr. -1-2). lib. bdg. 32.79 *(978-1-5321-0812-9(5)*, 28185, Abdo Kids) ABDO Publishing Co.

Harkrader, Lisa. The Science of Sound. 2016. (Spring Forward Ser.). (J). (gr. 1). *(978-1-4900-9401-4(6))* Benchmark Education Co.

Hartman, Eve & Meshbesher, Wendy. Light & Sound. rev. ed. 2016. (Sci-Hi: Physical Science Ser.). (ENG.). 48p. (J). (gr. 6-10). pap. 8.99 *(978-1-4109-8536-1(9)*, 134122, Raintree) Capstone.

Haslam, Andrew, et al. Sound. (Make It Work! Ser.). (Illus.). 48p. (J). pap. 7.99 *(978-0-590-24615-6(1))* Scholastic, Inc.

Herold, Vickey. Breaking the Sound Barrier. 2006. (J). pap. *(978-1-4108-6487-1(1))* Benchmark Education Co.

—Discover Sound. 2006. (J). pap. *(978-1-4108-6489-5(8))* Benchmark Education Co.

—Sound Is Energy. 2006. (J). pap. *(978-1-4108-6486-4(3))* Benchmark Education Co.

Hewitt, Sally. Amazing Sound. 2007. (Amazing Science Ser.). (ENG., Illus.). 32p. (J). (gr. 3-7). pap. *(978-0-7787-3629-5(6))* Crabtree Publishing Co.

Higgins, Nadia. Stupendous Sound Site CD+Book. Martinez Ricci, Andres, illus. 2010. (Science Rocks! Set 2 Site CD+Book Ser.). 32p. lib. bdg. 84.14 incl. cd-rom *(978-1-61641-012-4(4))* ABDO Publishing Co.

Hollar, Sherman. Sound, 1 vol. 2012. (Introduction to Physics Ser.). (ENG., Illus.). 80p. (J). (gr. 8-8). 35.29 *(978-1-61530-841-5(5)*, 4003ef28-e458-4c72-af90-79f8bbf28e2a) Rosen Publishing Group, Inc., The.

Hollar, Sherman, ed. Sound, 4 vols. 2012. (Introduction to Physics Ser.). (ENG., Illus.). 80p. (YA). (gr. 8-8). 70.58 *(978-1-61530-849-1(0)*, 8e89d4ed-e394-4cd0-b61d-c8c1c0e5d4cb) Rosen Publishing Group, Inc., The.

Holt, Rinehart and Winston Staff. Holt Science & Technology Chapter 21: Physical Science: The Nature of Sound. 5th ed. 2004. (Illus.). pap. 12.86 *(978-0-03-030436-1(9))* Holt McDougal.

Horne, Jane. Busy Baby Noisy Book. 2007. (Busy Baby Ser.). (Illus.). 12p. (gr. -1). per., bds. *(978-1-84610-434-3(3))* Make Believe Ideas.

Issa, Joanna. What Can I Hear?, 1 vol. 2014. (These Are My Senses Ser.). (ENG., Illus.). 24p. (J). (gr. -1-1). pap. 5.99 *(978-1-4846-0433-5(4)*, 126589, Heinemann) Capstone.

James, Emily. The Simple Science of Sound. 2018. (Simply Science Ser.). (ENG., Illus.). 32p. (J). (gr. -1-2). lib. bdg. 27.99 *(978-1-5435-1226-7(7)*, 137734, Capstone Pr.) Capstone.

Jankowski, Connie. All about Light & Sound, 1 vol. rev. ed. 2007. (Science: Informational Text Ser.). (ENG.). 32p. (J). (gr. 3-6). pap. 12.99 *(978-0-7439-0579-4(2))* Teacher Created Materials, Inc.

—Pioneers of Light & Sound, 1 vol. rev. ed. 2007. (Science: Informational Text Ser.). (ENG.). 32p. (gr. 3-6). pap. 12.99 *(978-0-7439-0580-0(6))* Teacher Created Materials, Inc.

Johnson, Robin. How Does Sound Change? 2014. (Light & Sound Waves Close-Up Ser.). (ENG., Illus.). 24p. (J). (gr. 1-2). *(978-0-7787-0520-8(X))* Crabtree Publishing Co.

Jordan, Apple. Noisy / Quiet, 1 vol. 2nd rev. ed. 2012. (Opposites Ser.). (ENG.). 16p. (gr. k-1). 24.07 *(978-1-60870-421-7(1)*, 4b235804-e819-4282-8b39-840ebcb00bda) Cavendish Square Publishing LLC.

Kelly, Lynne. Simple Concepts in Physics: Sound & Light. (Illus.). 88p. (J). (gr. 5-6). pap. *(978-1-875739-69-1(6))* Wizard Bks.

Kenney, Karen Latchana. The Science of Music: Discovering Sound. 2015. (Science in Action Ser.). (ENG., Illus.). 32p. (J). (gr. 3-6). 32.79 *(978-1-62403-962-1(6)*, 19421, Checkerboard Library) ABDO Publishing Co.

Kids, National Geographic. National Geographic Kids Little Kids First Board Book: Wild Animal Sounds. 2019. (First Board Bks.). (Illus.). 26p. (J). (gr. -1 — 1). bds. 7.99 *(978-1-4263-3466-5(4)*, National Geographic Kids) Disney Publishing Worldwide.

Lawrence, Ellen. Sound. 2014. (Science Slam: FUN-Damentals Ser.). 24p. (J). (gr. -1-3). lib. bdg. 26.99 *(978-1-62724-094-9(2))* Bearport Publishing Co., Inc.

LIGHT & SOUND. 2010. (ENG., Illus.). 128p. (gr. 6-12). 35.00 *(978-1-60413-344-8(9)*, P179270, Facts On File) Infobase Holdings, Inc.

Lindeen, Mary. Sound. 2018. (BeginningtoRead Ser.). (ENG.). 32p. (J). (gr. -1-2). lib. bdg. 22.60 *(978-1-59953-903-4(9))*; (gr. k-2). pap. 13.26 *(978-1-68404-150-3(3))* Norwood Hse. Pr.

Llewellyn, Claire. Sound. 2005. (I Know That! Ser.). (Illus.). 24p. (J). (gr. 1-3). lib. bdg. 22.80 *(978-1-932889-37-6(X))* Sea-To-Sea Pubns.

Lockyer, John. Sound, 1 vol. 2018. (ENG., Illus.). 21p. (J). pap. *(978-1-77654-256-7(8)*, Red Rocket Readers) Flying Start Bks.

Loria, Laura. What Is Sound Energy?, 1 vol. 2017. (Let's Find Out! Forms of Energy Ser.). (ENG., Illus.). 32p. (J). (gr. 2-3). pap. 13.90 *(978-1-68048-713-8(2)*, d7a98c03-b702-4563-a026-d2f5d03f0663, Britannica Educational Publishing) Rosen Publishing Group, Inc., The.

Lowery, Lawrence F. Quiet As a Butterfly. 2017. (I Wonder Why Ser.). (ENG., Illus.). 36p. (J). (gr. k-2). pap. 13.99 *(978-1-68140-354-0(4)*, P531929) National Science Teachers Assn.

Manolis, Kay. Sound. 2007. (First Science Ser.). (ENG., Illus.). 24p. (J). (gr. 2-5). lib. bdg. 26.95 *(978-1-60014-099-0(8))* Bellwether Media.

—Sound. 2007. (Blastoff! Readers Ser.). (ENG.). 24p. (J). (gr. k-2). 20.00 *(978-0-531-14728-3(2)*, Children's Pr.) Scholastic Library Publishing.

Marsico, Katie. Sound Waves. Bane, Jeff, illus. 2018. (My Early Library: My World of Science Ser.). (ENG.). 24p. (J). (gr. k-1). lib. bdg. 30.64 *(978-1-5341-2894-1(8)*, 211620) Cherry Lake Publishing.

Mason, Adrienne. Lost & Found. Cupples, Pat, illus. 2008. (Kids Can Read Ser.). 32p. (J). (gr. 1-2). 14.95 *(978-1-55453-251-3(5))*; pap. 3.95 *(978-1-55453-252-0(3))* Kids Can Pr., Ltd. CAN. Dist: Hachette Bk. Group.

Maurer, Daniel D. Do You Really Want to Yell in a Cave? A Book about Sound. Alberini, Teresa, illus. 2016. (Adventures in Science Ser.). (ENG.). 24p. (J). (gr. 1-4). lib. bdg. 20.95 *(978-1-60753-956-8(X)*, 15633) Amicus.

McGregor, Harriet. Sound, 1 vol. 2010. (Sherlock Bones Looks at Physical Science Ser.). (ENG.). 32p. (YA). (gr. 5-5). lib. bdg. 29.93 *(978-1-61533-215-1(4)*, 45e8bc0f-5ad6-4f42-bfaa-3b50892b4b0a, Windmill Bks.) Rosen Publishing Group, Inc., The.

Mendez, Horatio. Understanding Sound. 2013. (InfoMax Readers Ser.). (ENG.). 24p. (J). (gr. 2-3). pap. 49.50 *(978-1-4777-2394-4(3))*; (Illus.). pap. 8.25 *(978-1-4777-2393-7(5)*, 6441fe45-257f-4f84-9ce6-28b3e2cdcb34) Rosen Publishing Group, Inc., The. (Rosen Classroom).

Midthun, Joseph & Hiti, Samuel. Gravity. 2012. (Illus.). 32p. (J). *(978-0-7166-1420-3(0))* World Bk., Inc.

Milios, Rita. Sound in the Real World. 2013. (Science in the Real World Ser.). (ENG.). 48p. (J). (gr. 4-8). pap. 18.50 *(978-1-61783-794-4(6)*, 14618) ABDO Publishing Co.

Mortensen, Lori. What's That Sound? 2016. (Spring Forward Ser.). (J). (gr. 1). *(978-1-4900-9387-1(7))* Benchmark Education Co.

National Geographic Learning. Reading Expeditions (Science: Physical Science): the Magic of Light & Sound. 2006. (Nonfiction Reading & Writing Workshops Ser.). (ENG., Illus.). 32p. (J). pap. 18.95 *(978-0-7922-8886-2(6))* CENGAGE Learning.

Nsrc, prod. Science & Technology for Children BOOKS: Sound. 2008. 64p. (J). *(978-1-933008-42-4(3)*, Science and Technology Concepts (STC)) Smithsonian Science Education Ctr. (SSEC).

O'Hara, Nicholas. Sonidos / Sort It by Sound, 1 vol. de la Vega, Eida, tr. 2015. (Vamos a Agrupar Por... / Sort It Out! Ser.). (ENG & SPA.). 24p. (J). (gr. k-1). lib. bdg. 24.27 *(978-1-4824-3221-3(8)*, eb6f992a-e70e-4f70-8077-e4941c1f6bdf) Stevens, Gareth Publishing LLLP.

—Sort It by Sound, 1 vol. 2015. (Sort It Out! Ser.). (ENG., Illus.). 24p. (J). (gr. k-1). 24.27 *(978-1-4824-2579-6(3)*, f60f6376-fdc4-42a2-893c-8c1862e545a5) Stevens, Gareth Publishing LLLP.

Orr, Tamra. Understanding Sound. 2018. *(978-1-5105-3720-0(1))* SmartBook Media, Inc.

Orr, Tamra B. Understanding Sound. 2015. (Explorer Library: Science Explorer Ser.). (ENG., Illus.). 32p. (J). (gr. 4-8). pap. 14.21 *(978-1-63362-421-4(8)*, 206993) Cherry Lake Publishing.

Peterson, Megan Cooley. Scooby-Doo! a Science of Sound Mystery: A Song for Zombies. Cornia, Christian, illus. 2016. (Scooby-Doo Solves It with S. T. E. M. Ser.). (ENG.). 32p. (J). (gr. 3-6). 28.65 *(978-1-5157-2593-0(6)*, 132937, Capstone Pr.) Capstone.

—Sound. 2019. (Little Physicist Ser.). (ENG., Illus.). 32p. (J). (gr. 1-3). pap. 6.95 *(978-1-9771-1067-1(3)*, 141141); lib. bdg. 28.65 *(978-1-9771-0991-0(8)*, 140711) Capstone. (Pebble).

Prentice Hall Direct Education Staff. Science Explorer - Sound & Light. 2004. (ENG.). (gr. 6-8). stu. ed. 14.97 *(978-0-13-115101-7(0)*, Prentice Hall) Savvas Learning Co.

Prentice-Hall Staff. Sound & Light. 2nd ed. (J). stu. ed. 7.97 *(978-0-13-400565-2(1))*; pap., act. bk. ed. *(978-0-13-400581-2(3))* Prentice Hall (Schl. Div.).

Publications International Ltd. Staff, creator. Baby Einstein Animal Melodies. 2005. (Baby Einstein Ser.). (Illus.). 10p. (J). (gr. -1-k). 10.50 *(978-1-4127-3495-0(9)*, 7262600) Publications International, Ltd.

Randolph, Joanne. Sounds in My World. (My World of Science Ser.). 24p. (gr. 2-2). 2009. 37.50 *(978-1-61514-729-8(2))* 2005. (ENG., Illus.). (J). lib. bdg. 22.27 *(978-1-4042-3287-7(7)*, e0864a4e-66b4-4e04-b424-d34f9583509f) Rosen Publishing Group, Inc., The. (PowerKids Pr.).

—Sounds in My World: Los Sonidos en Mi Mundo, 1 vol. 2005. (My World of Science / la Ciencia en Mi Mundo Ser.). (ENG & SPA.). 24p. (J). (gr. 2-2). 22.27 *(978-1-4042-3318-8(0)*, 53185a91-403a-417d-85bc-e74ab0daaf97) Rosen Publishing Group, Inc., The.

—Sounds in My World/Los sonidos en mi Mundo. 2009. (My World of Science/la ciencia en mi mundo Ser.). (ENG & SPA.). 48p. (gr. 2-2). 37.50 *(978-1-61514-741-0(1)*, Editorial Buenas Letras) Rosen Publishing Group, Inc., The.

Riley, Peter. Changing Sounds. 2007. (Essential Science/Watts Ser.). (Illus.). 32p. (YA). (gr. 3-6). lib. bdg. 28.50 *(978-1-59920-023-1(6))* Black Rabbit Bks.

—Sound, 1 vol. 2016. (Moving up with Science Ser.). (ENG.). 32p. (J). (gr. 3-4). pap. 11.00 *(978-1-4994-3157-5(0)*, b9df8c20-0102-4b5b-82d6-24ede53ede8e, PowerKids Pr.) Rosen Publishing Group, Inc., The.

Riley, Peter D. Sound. 2011. (Real Scientist Investigates Ser.). (Illus.). 32p. (J). (gr. 3-5). lib. bdg. 28.50 *(978-1-59771-283-5(3))* Sea-To-Sea Pubns.

Rivera, Andrea. Sound. 2017. (Science Concepts Ser.). (ENG., Illus.). 24p. (J). (gr. -1-2). lib. bdg. 31.36 *(978-1-5321-2055-8(9)*, 25360, Abdo Zoom-Launch) ABDO Publishing Co.

Rogers, K. Light, Sound & Electricity. 2004. (Library of Science Ser.). 64p. (J). lib. bdg. 17.95 *(978-1-58086-376-6(0))* EDC Publishing.

Rooney, Anne. Audio Engineering & the Science of Soundwaves. 2013. (ENG., Illus.). 32p. (J). *(978-0-7787-1196-4(X))*; pap. *(978-0-7787-1229-9(X))* Crabtree Publishing Co.

Rosinsky, Natalie M. El Sonido: Fuerte, Suave, Alto y Bajo, 1 vol. Robledo, Sol, tr. John, Matthew, illus. 2007. (Ciencia Asombrosa Ser.). (SPA.). 24p. (J). (gr. k-4). per. 8.19 *(978-1-4048-2493-5(6)*, 93825, Picture Window Bks.) Capstone.

Rosinsky, Natalie M. & Picture Window Books Staff. El Sonido: Fuerte, Suave, Alto y Bajo, 1 vol. Robledo, Sol, tr. John, Matthew, illus. 2007. (Ciencia Asombrosa Ser.). (SPA.). 24p. (J). (gr. k-4). 27.32 *(978-1-4048-3229-9(7)*, 93766, Picture Window Bks.) Capstone.

Royston, Angela. All about Sound. 2016. (All about Science Ser.). (ENG., Illus.). 32p. (J). (gr. 1-3). lib. bdg. 29.99 *(978-1-4846-2691-7(5)*, 131134, Heinemann) Capstone.

—Sound & Hearing, 1 vol. 2011. (Science Corner Ser.). (ENG., Illus.). 24p. (J). (gr. 2-2). lib. bdg. 26.27 *(978-1-4488-5259-8(5)*, f51f97c2-3870-452c-9dd3-8e944bcbee85) Rosen Publishing Group, Inc., The.

Science Stories Foss Spanish Physics of Sound EA CR05. 2005. (J). *(978-1-59242-587-7(9))* Delta Education, LLC.

Sian Revision Sound Vibrations. 2004. (J). *(978-1-59242-075-9(3))* Delta Education, LLC.

Silverman, Buffy. The Amazing Facts about Sound. 2012. (My Science Library). (ENG.). 24p. (gr. 4-5). pap. 8.95 *(978-1-61810-242-3(7)*, 9781618102423) Rourke Educational Media.

Sohn, Emily. Adventures in Sound with Max Axiom, Super Scientist, 1 vol. Martin, Cynthia, illus. 2007. (Graphic Science Ser.). (ENG.). 32p. (J). (gr. 3-9). per. 8.10 *(978-0-7368-7889-0(0)*, 93886) Capstone.

—Adventures in Sound with Max Axiom Super Scientist: 4D an Augmented Reading Science Experience. Martin, Cynthia, illus. 2018. (Graphic Science 4D Ser.). (ENG.). 32p. (J). (gr. 3-9). pap. 7.95 *(978-1-5435-2955-5(0)*, 138555, Capstone Pr.) Capstone.

Solway, Andrew. From Crashing Waves to Music Download: An Energy Journey Through the World of Sound. 2015. (Energy Journeys Ser.). (ENG., Illus.). 48p. (J). (gr. 3-6). 35.99 *(978-1-4846-0883-8(6)*, 127967, Heinemann) Capstone.

Somervill, Barbara A. Ticks: Digging for Blood, 1 vol. 2007. (Bloodsuckers Ser.). (ENG., Illus.). 24p. (J). (gr. 2-3). lib. bdg. 26.27 *(978-1-4042-3800-8(X)*, 1f25b829-562f-4aed-aa9b-d75761182a91) Rosen Publishing Group, Inc., The.

Sound. (Make It Work Ser.). 42p. (J). (gr. 4-8). pap. *(978-1-882210-46-6(8))* Action Publishing, Inc.

Spilsbury, Louise. The Science of Sound, 1 vol. 2015. (Flowchart Smart Ser.). (ENG.). 48p. (J). (gr. 4-5). pap. 15.05 *(978-1-4824-4150-5(0)*, 995f7d30-d653-43d0-baa9-e293e5f169c1) Stevens, Gareth Publishing LLLP.

Stiegemeyer, Julie. Things I Hear in Church. Mitter, Kathy, illus. 2003. 20p. (J). bds. 5.49 *(978-0-7586-0125-4(5))* Concordia Publishing Hse.

Stradling, Jan. Sounds all Around: Level K, 6 vols., Vol. 2. (First Explorers Ser.). 24p. (gr. 1-2). 34.95 *(978-0-7699-1464-0(0))* Shortland Pubns. (U. S. A.) Inc.

Sullivan, Laura L. How Does Sound Move?, 1 vol. 2018. (How Does It Move? Forces & Motion Ser.). (ENG.). 32p. (gr. 3-3). 30.21 *(978-1-5026-3783-3(9)*, 8cf4f809-2594-41d6-b539-e1866eb7f71b) Cavendish Square Publishing LLC.

Sundance/Newbridge LLC Staff. Sound. 2007. (Early Science Ser.). (gr. k-3). 18.95 *(978-1-4007-6395-5(9))*; pap. 6.10 *(978-1-4007-6391-7(6))* Sundance/Newbridge Educational Publishing.

—What's That Sound? 2004. (Reading PowerWorks Ser.). (gr. 1-3). 37.50 *(978-0-7608-9807-9(3))*; pap. 6.10 *(978-0-7608-9808-6(1))* Sundance/Newbridge Educational Publishing.

Taplin, Sam. Night Sounds. 2018. (Press-A-Sound Bks.). (ENG.). 10p. (J). 19.99 *(978-0-7945-4142-2(9)*, Usborne) EDC Publishing.

Troupe, Thomas Kingsley. What's That Sound, Cinderella? The Fairy-Tale Physics of Sound. Tejido, Jomike, illus. 2018. (STEM-Twisted Fairy Tales Ser.). (ENG.). 32p. (J). (gr. k-3). pap. 7.95 *(978-1-5158-2901-0(4)*, 138423); lib. bdg. 27.99 *(978-1-5158-2897-6(2)*, 138419) Capstone. (Picture Window Bks.).

Trumbauer, Lisa. All about Sound (Rookie Read-About Science: Physical Science: Previous Editions) 2004. (Rookie Read-About Science Ser.). (ENG.). 32p. (J). (gr. 1-2). pap. 4.95 *(978-0-516-25847-8(8)*, Children's Pr.) Scholastic Library Publishing.

Twist, Clint. Light & Sound: The Best Start in Science. 2013. (Little Science Stars Ser.). (ENG.). 24p. (J). (gr. k-3). 18.69 *(978-1-84696-191-5(2)*, TickTock Books) Octopus Publishing Group GBR. Dist: Children's Plus, Inc.

Wacholtz, Anthony. Mummies & Sound, 6 vols. Mallea, Cristian, illus. 2013. (Monster Science Ser.). (ENG.). 32p. (J). (gr. 3-4). pap. 48.60 *(978-1-62065-819-2(4)*, 19401, Capstone Pr.) Capstone.

Wadsworth, Pamela. Golwg Gyntaf Ar Sain a Cherddoriaeth. 2005. (WEL., Illus.). 24p. pap. *(978-1-85596-247-7(0))* Dref Wen.

Walker, Sally M. Investigating Sound. 2011. (Searchlight Books (tm) — How Does Energy Work? Ser.). (ENG., Illus.). (gr. 3-5). 40p. (J). pap. 9.99 *(978-0-7613-7876-1(6)*, 9ba77bdb-0df9-4a4c-97c7-144ede9f6b41); pap. 51.01 *(978-0-7613-8410-6(3))* Lerner Publishing Group.

—El Sonido. Translations.com Staff, tr. from ENG. King, Andy, photos by. 2007. (Libros de Energía para madrugadores (Early Bird Energy) Ser.). (SPA., Illus.). 48p. (J). (gr. 2-5). lib. bdg. 26.60 *(978-0-8225-7722-5(4))* Lerner Publishing Group.

—El Sonido; Sound. 2008. pap. 52.95 *(978-0-8225-9867-1(1))* Lerner Publishing Group.

Ward, David J. I Heard a Sound. Comstock, Eric, illus. 2020. 40p. (J). (gr. 1-4). 18.99 *(978-0-8234-3704-7(3))* Holiday Hse., Inc.

What Is Noisy?, 6 Packs. (gr. 1-2). 22.00 *(978-0-7635-9095-6(9))* Rigby Education.

Winnick, Neil. Hearing. 2009. (World of Wonder Ser.). (Illus.). 24p. (J). (gr. 2-4). pap. 8.95 *(978-1-60596-055-5(1))* Weigl Pubs., Inc.

Winnick, Nick. Hearing. 2009. (World of Wonder Ser.). (Illus.). 24p. (J). (gr. 2-4). lib. bdg. 24.45 *(978-1-60596-054-8(3))* Weigl Pubs., Inc.

Winterberg, Jenna. Sound Waves & Communication. 2015. (Science: Informational Text Ser.). (ENG., Illus.). 32p. (J). (gr. 3-5). pap. 11.99 *(978-1-4807-4684-8(3))* Teacher Created Materials, Inc.

World Book, Inc. Staff, contrib. by. Sound. 2011. (J). *(978-0-7166-1430-2(8))* World Bk., Inc.

SOUND—EXPERIMENTS

Baker, Wendy, et al. Sound. (Make It Work! Ser.). (Illus.). 48p. (J). pap. 15.95 *(978-0-590-74522-2(0))* Scholastic, Inc.

Canavan, Thomas. Super Experiments with Light & Sound. Linley, Adam, illus. 2017. (Mind-Blowing Science Experiments Ser.). 32p. (gr. 4-5). pap. 63.00 *(978-1-5382-0733-8(8))* Stevens, Gareth Publishing LLLP.

Clark, Michael. Shattering Sounds, 1 vol. 2017. (Strange Science & Explosive Experiments Ser.). (ENG.). 32p. (J). (gr. 4-5). 29.27 *(978-1-5383-2272-7(2)*, f5928782-15e4-4e34-a4d7-5b9ca4364559); pap. 12.75

(978-1-5383-2368-7(0), 8e911f69-b383-41fe-b9d9-e6d75c7cab6b) Rosen Publishing Group, Inc., The. (PowerKids Pr.).

Claybourne, Anna. Noisy Experiments, 1 vol. 2018. (Ultimate Science Lab Ser.). (ENG.). 32p. (gr. 4-5). pap. 11.50 *(978-1-5382-3530-0(7),* dcdccc86-76f0-4d85-ba5c-1b0be066f4c7) Stevens, Gareth Publishing LLLP.

—Recreate Discoveries about Sound. 2018. (Recreate Scientific Discoveries Ser.). (Illus.). 32p. (J). (gr. 4-5). *(978-0-7787-5054-3(X))* Crabtree Publishing Co.

Cobb, Vicki. Bangs & Twangs: Science Fun with Sound. Haefele, Steve, illus. 2007. (Science Fun with Vicki Cobb Ser.). 48p. (J). (gr. 4-7). per. 7.95 *(978-0-8225-7022-6(X),* First Avenue Editions) Lerner Publishing Group.

Cook, Trevor. Experiments with Light & Sound, 1 vol. 2009. (Science Lab Ser.). (ENG.). 32p. (J). (gr. 4-4). lib. bdg. 30.27 *(978-1-4358-2808-7(9),* b61bea01-717d-45c1-b683-2575f99682f9); (Illus.). pap. 11.00 *(978-1-4358-3221-3(3),* cad2d49f-cf1b-4498-a90d-b9ac44faa841) Rosen Publishing Group, Inc., The. (PowerKids Pr.).

Gardner, Robert. Experimenting with Sound Science Projects, 1 vol. 2013. (Exploring Hands-On Science Projects Ser.). (ENG.). 128p. (gr. 5-6). lib. bdg. 30.60 *(978-0-7660-4148-6(4),* 89e468de-c44a-4b66-b7bb-1eaeb4864a65) Enslow Publishing, LLC.

—Jazzy Science Projects with Sound & Music, 1 vol. 2006. (Fantastic Physical Science Experiments Ser.). (ENG., Illus.). 48p. (gr. 3-3). lib. bdg. 27.93 *(978-0-7660-2588-2(8),* 053de9b3-8076-4eb7-9f97-894fbfb28c9a, Enslow Elementary) Enslow Publishing, LLC.

—Light, Sound, & Waves Science Fair Projects, Using the Scientific Method, 1 vol. 2010. (Physics Science Projects Using the Scientific Method Ser.). (ENG., Illus.). 160p. (gr. 5-6). 38.60 *(978-0-7660-3416-7(X),* a9e26572-5a3f-47d1-bd08-f3116b6e00ac) Enslow Publishing, LLC.

—Sound Experiments in Your Own Music Lab, 1 vol. 2015. (Design, Build, Experiment Ser.). (ENG.). 128p. (gr. 7-7). lib. bdg. 38.93 *(978-0-7660-6960-2(5),* 3dc44853-f2e5-4fd4-924d-cd00fe7cc268) Enslow Publishing, LLC.

Gardner, Robert & Conklin, Joshua. A Kid's Book of Experiments with Sound, 1 vol. 2015. (Surprising Science Experiments Ser.). (ENG.). 48p. (gr. 4-4). pap. 12.70 *(978-0-7660-7207-7(X),* 372e6173-77c1-47ec-8b22-be71f943e572) Enslow Publishing, LLC.

Hagler, Gina. Sound. 2016. (J). *(978-1-4896-5292-8(2))* Weigl Pubs., Inc.

Hawkins, Jay. Super Sonic: The Science of Sound, 1 vol. 2013. (Big Bang Science Experiments Ser.). (ENG., Illus.). 32p. (gr. 4-5). pap. 12.75 *(978-1-4777-0370-0(5),* f4d05e41-fc6a-44d2-b6e9-2d37dd4b72bc, Windmill Bks.) Rosen Publishing Group, Inc., The.

Merrill, Amy French. Everyday Physical Science Experiments with Light, 1 vol. 2005. (Content-Area Literacy Collections). (ENG.). 24p. (gr. 3-4). pap. 8.85 *(978-1-4042-5679-8(2),* 0470f6a5-c2b4-451a-90f6-00627ebbb844) Rosen Publishing Group, Inc., The.

—Everyday Physical Science Experiments with Light & Sound. 2009. (Science Surprises Ser.). 24p. (gr. 3-3). 42.50 *(978-1-60853-061-8(2),* PowerKids Pr.) Rosen Publishing Group, Inc., The.

Oxlade, Chris. Experiments with Sound & Light, 1 vol. 2014. (Excellent Science Experiments Ser.). (ENG., Illus.). 32p. (J). (gr. 4-5). lib. bdg. 29.27 *(978-1-4777-5965-3(4),* 8ceee608-5c78-425e-82f9-1b8d9e130ea2, PowerKids Pr.) Rosen Publishing Group, Inc., The.

—Super Science Light & Sound Experiments: 10 Amazing Experiments with Step-By-Step Photographs. 2016. (ENG., Illus.). (J). pap. *(978-1-78209-421-0(0))* Miles Kelly Publishing, Ltd.

Rake, Jody S. What Is Sound? 2019. (Science Basics Ser.). (ENG., Illus.). 24p. (J). (gr. 1-3). lib. bdg. 25.99 *(978-1-9771-0269-0(7),* 139269, Capstone Pr.) Capstone.

Rowe, Brooke. Making a Telephone. Bane, Jeff, illus. 2016. (My Early Library: My Science Fun Ser.). (ENG.). 24p. (J). (gr. k-1). 30.64 *(978-1-63471-029-9(0),* 208196) Cherry Lake Publishing.

—Playing Musical Bottles. Bane, Jeff, illus. 2016. (My Early Library: My Science Fun Ser.). (ENG.). 24p. (J). (gr. k-1). 30.64 *(978-1-63471-028-2(2),* 208192) Cherry Lake Publishing.

Spilsbury, Richard. Investigating Sound. 2018. (Investigating Science Challenges Ser.). (ENG., Illus.). 32p. (J). (gr. 4-4). *(978-0-7787-4209-8(1));* pap. *(978-0-7787-4380-4(2))* Crabtree Publishing Co.

Taylor-Butler, Christine. Sound. 2009. (Explorer Library: Science Explorer Ser.). (ENG., Illus.). 32p. (gr. 4-8). lib. bdg. 32.07 *(978-1-60279-532-7(0),* 200301) Cherry Lake Publishing.

Walker, Richard. Light & Sound, 1 vol. 2005. (Real World Science Ser.). (ENG., Illus.). 32p. (gr. 3-5). lib. bdg. 28.67 *(978-0-8368-6306-2(2),* 9809b3f3-dd5e-495a-8481-dce1ae4538e1, Gareth Stevens Learning Library) Stevens, Gareth Publishing LLLP.

Woodford, Chris. Experiments with Sound & Hearing, 1 vol. 2010. (Cool Science Ser.). (ENG., Illus.). 32p. (J). (gr. 4-5). pap. 11.50 *(978-1-4339-3457-5(4),* 81101c3b-a5f6-43be-9a7a-b37728255e67); lib. bdg. 30.67 *(978-1-4339-3456-8(6),* 5fafcb8d-3542-4533-8501-4e9c2fc0b430) Stevens, Gareth Publishing LLLP. (Gareth Stevens Learning Library).

SOUND—FICTION

Ann, Sharrie. Granddaughter & King Green Warts. 2008. 24p. pap. 12.99 *(978-1-4343-9470-5(0))* AuthorHouse.

Arthur, Clint. Bleep Blop Bloop, 1. Schedeen, Minnie, illus. 2006. 24p. (J). per. 8.99 net. *(978-1-4276-0218-3(2))* Aardvark Global Publishing.

AZ Books Staff. Babbling Pond. Tulup, Natalia, ed. 2012. (How We Speak Ser.). (ENG.). 12p. (J). (gr. -1-k). bds. 10.95 *(978-1-61889-097-9(2))* AZ Bks. LLC.

—My Farm. Yaroshevich, Angelica, ed. 2012. (Open the Book-I Am Alive Ser.). (ENG.). 8p. (J). (— 1). bds. 5.95 *(978-1-61889-043-6(3))* AZ Bks. LLC.

—My Forest. Yaroshevich, Angelica, ed. 2012. (Open the Book-I Am Alive Ser.). (ENG.). 8p. (J). (— 1). bds. 5.95 *(978-1-61889-042-9(5))* AZ Bks. LLC.

—My Pets. Yaroshevich, Angelica, ed. 2012. (Open the Book-I Am Alive Ser.). (ENG.). 8p. (J). (— 1). bds. 5.95 *(978-1-61889-045-0(X))* AZ Bks. LLC.

—My Zoo. Yaroshevich, Angelica, ed. 2012. (Open the Book-I Am Alive Ser.). (ENG.). 8p. (J). (— 1). bds. 5.95 *(978-1-61889-044-3(1))* AZ Bks. LLC.

Bentley, Dawn. Disney Pixar Cars Rhymes on the Go. Schwaeber, Barbie Heit, ed. 2011. (Carry a Tune Ser.). (ENG., Illus.). 24p. (J). (gr. -1-1). 4.99 *(978-1-60727-306-6(3))* Studio Mouse LLC.

Berg, Jean Horton. The Noisy Clock Shop. Seiden, Art, illus. 2015. (G&d Vintage Ser.). 32p. (J). (gr. -1-k). bds. 7.99 *(978-0-448-48216-3(9),* Grosset & Dunlap) Penguin Young Readers Group.

Berry, Ron. Can You Roar Like a Lion? Sharp, Chris, illus. 2009. (ENG.). 14p. bds. 10.99 *(978-0-8249-1433-2(3),* Ideals Pubns.) Worthy Publishing.

Berry, Ron & Mead, David. All Aboard! Charlie the Can-Do Choo Choo. Sharp, Chris, illus. 2009. (ENG.). 8p. 12.99 *(978-0-8249-1420-2(1),* Ideals Pubns.) Worthy Publishing.

Bickell, Elaine. The Little Ghost Who Lost Her Boo! McGrath, Raymond, illus. 2020. (ENG.). 32p. (J). (gr. -1-3). 17.99 *(978-0-593-20215-9(5))* Flamingo Bks.

Blevins, Wiley. The Big Crunch (Book 4), Bk. 4. Paillot, Jim, illus. 2017. (Funny Bone Books (tm) First Chapters — Ick & Crud Ser.). (ENG.). 32p. (J). (gr. k-2). pap. 6.99 *(978-1-63440-207-1(3),* 0e36fee4-1d0f-44d6-a030-21d9a04e2969) Red Chair Pr.

Boynton, Sandra. Sandra Boynton's Moo, Baa, la la La! Boynton, Sandra, illus. 2009. (ENG., Illus.). 16p. (J). bds. 16.99 *(978-1-4169-5035-6(4),* Little Simon) Little Simon.

Braun, Sebastien, illus. Can You Say It, Too? Stomp! Stomp! 2018. (Can You Say It, Too? Ser.). (ENG.). 10p. (J). (— 1). bds. 8.99 *(978-0-7636-9934-5(9))* Candlewick Pr.

Brown, Margaret Wise. The Noisy Book Board Book. Weisgard, Leonard, illus. 2017. (ENG.). 36p. (J). (gr. -1 — 1). bds. 7.99 *(978-0-06-248465-9(6),* HarperFestival) HarperCollins Pubs.

Burleigh, Robert. Clang! Clang! Beep! Beep! Listen to the City. Giacobbe, Beppe, illus. 2009. (ENG.). 32p. (J). (gr. -1-2). 19.99 *(978-1-4169-4052-4(9),* Simon & Schuster/Paula Wiseman Bks.) Simon & Schuster/Paula Wiseman Bks.

—Zoom! Zoom! Sounds of Things That Go in the City. Carpenter, Tad, illus. 2014. (ENG.). 32p. (J). (gr. -1-3). 18.99 *(978-1-4424-8315-6(6),* Simon & Schuster Bks. For Young Readers) Simon & Schuster Bks. For Young Readers.

Carle, Eric. My First Busy Book. Carle, Eric, illus. 2015. (World of Eric Carle Ser.). (ENG., Illus.). 12p. (J). (gr. -1). bds. 16.99 *(978-1-4814-5791-0(8),* Little Simon) Little Simon.

Carlson, Lavelle. Eek! I Hear a Squeak & the Scurrying of Little Feet. Loehr, Jenny, illus. 2006. (ENG.). 28p. (J). (gr. -1-3). 19.95 incl. audio compact disk *(978-0-9725803-8-0(7))* Children's Publishing.

Carluccio, Maria. The Sounds Around Town. Carluccio, Maria, illus. 2010. (ENG., Illus.). 13p. (J). 14.99 *(978-1-84686-362-2(7))* Barefoot Bks., Inc.

—The Sounds Around Town. 2008. (Illus.). 24p. (J). (gr. -1-k). 16.99 *(978-1-905236-28-2(X))* Barefoot Bks., Inc.

Carluccio, Maria, illus. The Sounds Around Town. 2011. 24p. (J). (gr. -1-3). pap. 7.99 *(978-1-84686-430-8(5))* Barefoot Bks., Inc.

Choo Choo. 2011. (Dora the Explorer Ser.). (Illus.). 10p. (J). bds. 10.98 *(978-0-7853-8278-2(X),* 7182700) Publications International, Ltd.

Clayton, Darcy M. Making Mouth Sounds All Day Long. Freeswick, Jill, illus. 2013. 36p. pap. 9.95 *(978-1-889131-90-0(3),* Castlebridge Bks.) Big Tent Bks.

Colato Lainez, Rene. Vamonos! / Let's Go! 2016. (ENG & SPA.). lib. bdg. 17.20 *(978-0-606-39166-5(5))* Turtleback.

Cook, Sherry & Johnson, Terri. Susie Sound, 26. Kuhn, Jesse, illus. l.t. ed. 2006. 32p. (J). 7.99 *(978-1-933815-18-3(3),* Quirkles, The) Creative 3, LLC.

Cornwell, Charles Scott. The Bell. 2009. 24p. pap. 12.95 *(978-1-60844-255-3(1))* Dog Ear Publishing, LLC.

Czekaj, Jef. Oink-A-Doodle-Moo. Czekaj, Jef, illus. 2012. (ENG., Illus.). 32p. (J). (gr. -1-1). 16.99 *(978-0-06-206011-2(2),* Balzer & Bray) HarperCollins Pubs.

Dicamillo, Kate. La La La: A Story of Hope. Kim, Jaime, illus. 2017. (ENG.). 72p. (J). (gr. -1-3). 17.99 *(978-0-7636-5833-5(2))* Candlewick Pr.

DiPucchio, Kelly. Dinosnores. Goembel, Ponder, illus. 2005. 32p. (J). (gr. -1 — 1). 17.99 *(978-0-06-051577-5(5));* lib. bdg. 16.89 *(978-0-06-051578-2(3))* HarperCollins Pubs.

Disney Publishing Staff. What's That Sound?, 15 vols. 2003. (It's Fun to Learn Ser.). (Illus.). 32p. (J). (gr. -1-3). 3.99 *(978-1-57973-132-8(5))* Advance Pubs. LLC.

Doyle, Malachy. Rory's Lost His Voice. Semple, David, illus. 2005. (ENG.). 24p. (J). lib. bdg. 23.65 *(978-1-59646-714-9(2))* Dingles & Co.

Duskey Rinker, Sherri. It's So Quiet: A Not-Quite-Going-To-Bed Book. Fucile, Tony, illus. 2021. (ENG.). 56p. (J). (gr. -1-k). 17.99 *(978-1-4521-4544-0(X))* Chronicle Bks. LLC.

Eastman, Brock & Eastman, Kinley. Daddy's Favorite Sound: What's Better Than a Woosh or a Giggle? 2019. (ENG., Illus.). 32p. (J). (gr. -1-3). 16.99 *(978-0-7369-7474-5(1),* 6974745) Harvest Hse. Pubs.

Eggleton, Jill. Where Are You, Mouse? McGrath, Raymond, illus. 2003. (Rigby Sails Early Ser.). (ENG.). 16p. (gr. 1-2). pap. 6.95 *(978-0-7578-8741-3(4))* Houghton Mifflin Harcourt Publishing Co.

Field, Elaine. Sounds (Cuddly Cuffs with Hang Tag) (Cuddly Cuffs Ser.). (Illus.). 12p. (J). tchr. ed. 5.95 *(978-1-58925-708-5(1))* Tiger Tales.

Fleming, Denise. The Cow Who Clucked. 2007. (J). (gr. -1-1). 27.95 incl. audio *(978-0-8045-6951-4(7))* Spoken Arts, Inc.

Forhan, Mary C. & Forhan, Mary C. Introduction to Letter Sounds: Fun, Active, Multisensory. 2003. (Illus.). 88p. spiral bd. 59.95 *(978-0-9744575-0-5(7))* Butterfly Park Educational Materials, Inc.

Freedman, Claire. The Monster of the Woods!/By Claire Freedman & Russell Julian. Julian, Russell, illus. 2013. (J). *(978-0-545-56837-1(4),* Cartwheel Bks.) Scholastic, Inc.

Galvin, Laura Gates. Quack's Masterpiece. 2006. (ENG., Illus.). 28p. (J). (gr. -1-3). pap. 2.99 *(978-1-59249-550-4(8))* Soundprints.

—What's That Sound? 2006. (ENG., Illus.). 28p. (J). (gr. -1-3). pap. 2.99 *(978-1-59249-553-5(2))* Soundprints.

Garcia, Emma. Tip Tip Dig Dig. 2013. (All about Sounds Ser.). (ENG., Illus.). 26p. (J). (— 1). bds. 7.99 *(978-1-906250-82-9(0))* Boxer Bks., Ltd. GBR. Dist: Sterling Publishing Co., Inc.

—Toot Toot Beep Beep. 2013. (All about Sounds Ser.). (ENG., Illus.). 26p. (J). (— 1). bds. 7.99 *(978-1-906250-84-3(7))* Boxer Bks., Ltd. GBR. Dist: Sterling Publishing Co., Inc.

Gershator, Phillis. Listen, Listen. Jay, Alison, illus. (ENG.). 32p. (J). (gr. -1-2). 2008. bds. 14.99 *(978-1-84686-201-4(9))* 2007. 16.99 *(978-1-84686-084-3(9))* Barefoot Bks., Inc.

Going, K. L. Bumpety, Dunkety, Thumpety-Thump! Shin, Simone, illus. 2017. (ENG.). 48p. (J). (gr. -1-k). 17.99 *(978-1-4424-3414-1(7),* Beach Lane Bks.) Beach Lane Bks.

Goldsaito, Katrina. The Sound of Silence. 2016. (ENG., Illus.). 40p. (J). (gr. -1-3). 18.99 *(978-0-316-20337-1(8))* Little, Brown Bks. for Young Readers.

Good Morning, Who's Snoring? Individual Title Six-Packs. (Story Steps Ser.). (gr. k-2). 32.00 *(978-0-7635-9619-4(1))* Rigby Education.

Gott, Barry. Honk! Splat! Vroom! Gott, Barry, illus. 2018. (ENG., Illus.). 32p. (J). (gr. -1-k). lib. bdg. 17.99 *(978-1-5124-4140-6(6),* ebdc41f3-e48d-40e3-8fac-8e165507d02d, Carolrhoda Bks.) Lerner Publishing Group.

Greenwell, Jessica. Noisy Body Book. 2012. (Noisy Bks). 10p. (J). ring bd. 18.99 *(978-0-7945-3133-1(4),* Usborne) EDC Publishing.

Harshman, Marc. All the Way to Morning. Dávalos, Felipe, illus. 2006. (J). per. 7.95 *(978-1-891852-49-7(3))* Quarrier Pr.

Hays, Anna Jane. The Pup Speaks Up. Petrone, Valeria, illus. 2003. (Step into Reading Ser.). 32p. (gr. -1-1). 14.00 *(978-0-7569-1696-1(8))* Perfection Learning Corp.

—The Pup Speaks Up. Petrone, Valeria, illus. 2003. (Step into Reading Ser.). 32p. (J). (gr. -1-1). pap. 4.99 *(978-0-375-81232-3(6),* Random Hse. Bks. for Young Readers) Random Hse. Children's Bks.

Horacek, Petr. Beep Beep. Horacek, Petr, illus. 2008. (ENG., Illus.). 16p. (J). (gr. k-k). bds. 6.99 *(978-0-7636-3482-7(4))* Candlewick Pr.

Hudson, Cheryl Willis. Sounds I Love to Hear. 2009. 24p. 3.99 *(978-1-60349-010-8(8),* Marimba Bks.) Just Us Bks., Inc.

Johnson, Errol. What's That Sound?, 1 vol. 2006. (Neighborhood Readers Ser.). (ENG., Illus.). 12p. (gr. k-1). pap. 5.90 *(978-1-4042-6738-1(7),* dee34506-d1ee-4047-a2c2-8897615c4ab4, Rosen Classroom) Rosen Publishing Group, Inc., The.

Ka Hulu Kohukohu. 2003. (J). 11.95 *(978-0-89610-463-1(X))* Island Heritage Publishing.

Kidd, Ron. Bookee Presents Colors, Shapes & Sounds. Nord, Mary, illus. (Talking Book Adventures Ser.). 12p. (J). (gr. -1-18). 16.95 *(978-0-9627001-1-8(8))* Futech Educational Products, Inc.

Lawrence, Mary. ¿Qué es Ese Sonido? (What's That Sound?) Adams, Lynn, illus. 2009. (Science Solves It! (r) en Espanol Ser.). (SPA.). (gr. k-2). pap. 33.92 *(978-0-7613-4801-6(8))* Lerner Publishing Group.

Long, Kathy. Christopher SAT Straight up in Bed. Cantor, Patricia, illus. 2013. (ENG.). 40p. (J). 16.00 *(978-0-8028-5359-2(5),* Eerdmans Bks For Young Readers) Eerdmans, William B. Publishing Co.

Lynn, Michelle. Fall Leaves. 2008. 17p. pap. 24.95 *(978-1-60672-027-1(9))* America Star Bks.

Mack, Karen. Who Makes the Sound? 2008. 11p. pap. 24.95 *(978-1-60610-852-9(2))* America Star Bks.

Mazza, Barbara. How the Short Vowels Got Their Sound. 2007. 28p. per. 17.32 *(978-1-4257-2721-5(2))* Xlibris Corp.

McCanna, Tim. So Many Sounds. Miller, Andy, illus. 2018. (ENG.). 24p. (J). (gr. -1-k). 12.99 *(978-1-4197-3156-3(4),* 1197101, Abrams Appleseed) Abrams, Inc.

McTaggart, Stephen & McTaggart, Debra. Bookee's Sounds Around. Nord, Mary, illus. (Talking Book Adventures Ser.). 12p. (J). (gr. -1-18). 16.95 *(978-0-9627001-0-1(X))* Futech Educational Products, Inc.

Munsch, Robert. Roar! Martchenko, Michael, illus. 2019. (ENG.). 32p. (J). pap. 7.99 *(978-0-545-98020-3(8))* Scholastic Canada, Ltd. CAN. Dist: Publishers Group West (PGW).

Mysak, Mary. Little Train! Stickley, Kelly, illus. 2004. 16p. (J). 7.50 *(978-0-9762274-0-3(1))* Helping Hands Children's Bks.

O'Connell, Rebecca. The Baby Goes Beep. Wilson-Max, Ken, illus. 2010. (ENG.). 16p. (J). (gr. -1 — 1). bds. 7.99 *(978-0-8075-0508-3(0),* 807505080) Whitman, Albert & Co.

Palatini, Margie. Boo-Hoo Moo. Graves, Keith, illus. 2009. 32p. (J). (gr. -1-3). lib. bdg. 18.89 *(978-0-06-114376-2(6))* HarperCollins Pubs.

—Moo Who? Graves, Keith, illus. 2007. (ENG.). 40p. (J). (gr. -1-2). pap. 7.99 *(978-0-06-000107-0(0),* Tegen, Katherine Bks) HarperCollins Pubs.

Perkins, Al. The Ear Book. Payne, Henry, illus. 2007. (Bright & Early Books(R) Ser.). 36p. (J). (gr. k-k). 9.99 *(978-0-375-84251-1(9),* Random Hse. Bks. for Young Readers) Random Hse. Children's Bks.

Perkins, Lynne Rae. Snow Music. Perkins, Lynne Rae, illus. 2003. (Illus.). 40p. (J). lib. bdg. 16.89 *(978-0-06-623958-3(3))* HarperCollins Pubs.

—Snow Music. 2003. (ENG., Illus.). 40p. (J). (gr. -1-3). 17.99 *(978-0-06-623956-9(7),* Greenwillow Bks.) HarperCollins Pubs.

Pfeffer, Wendy. Sounds All Around. Chernyshova, Anna, illus. 2016. (Let's-Read-And-Find-Out Science 1 Ser.). (ENG.). 40p. (J). (gr. -1-3). pap. 8.99 *(978-0-06-238669-4(7),* HarperCollins) HarperCollins Pubs.

Philips, L. Sometime after Midnight. 2018. 400p. (YA). (gr. 9). 18.99 *(978-0-425-29163-4(4),* Viking Books for Young Readers) Penguin Young Readers Group.

Pilney, Dovie. Charlie the Cocky Rooster: Another Adventure. 2008. 52p. pap. 20.95 *(978-1-4389-3517-1(X))* AuthorHouse.

Play a Sound Sesame Street 3 Pack. 2010. (J). 12.98 *(978-1-4127-8258-6(9))* Phoenix International Publications, Inc.

Pocahontas: Who's Making that Sound? (My First Read Along Ser.). (Illus.). (J). 7.99 incl. audio *(978-1-55723-961-7(4))* Walt Disney Records.

Potter, Beatrix. The Tale of Peter Rabbit: A Sound Story Book. 2013. (Peter Rabbit Ser.). (ENG., Illus.). 10p. (J). (gr. -1-2). 16.99 *(978-0-7232-6856-7(8),* Warne) Penguin Young Readers Group.

Publications International Ltd. Staff, ed. Race Day. 2010. 10p. (J). bds. 11.98 *(978-1-4127-4931-2(X),* PIL Kids) Publications International, Ltd.

—Ring-a-Ling! A Friend Is Here. 2010. 12p. (J). 9.98 *(978-1-4127-7939-5(1))* Phoenix International Publications, Inc.

Rubin, Susan Goldman. Jacob Lawrence in the City. 2009. (Mini Masters Modern Ser.). (ENG., Illus.). 24p. (J). (gr. -1 — 1). bds. 7.99 *(978-0-8118-6582-1(7))* Chronicle Bks. LLC.

Scarry, Richard. Splish-Splash.Tr. of Splish-Splash. (SPA., Illus.). (J). pap. 6.95 *(978-950-04-0676-5(4))* Emecé Editores S.A. ARG. Dist: Planeta Publishing Corp.

Seltzer, Eric. Arf! Buzz! Cluck! A Rather Noisy Alphabet. Creighton-Pester, David, illus. 2018. (ENG.). 24p. (J). (gr. -1 — 1). bds. 7.99 *(978-1-5344-1297-2(2),* Little Simon) Little Simon.

Seuss. Gerald Mcboing Boing. Crawford, Mel, illus. 2017. (Classic Seuss Ser.). (ENG.). 40p. (J). (gr. k-4). 16.99 *(978-1-5247-1635-6(9),* Random Hse. Bks. for Young Readers) Random Hse. Children's Bks.

—Gerald Mcboing Boing. Seuss, illus. 2004. (Little Golden Book Ser.). (ENG., Illus.). 24p. (J). (gr. -1-2). 5.99 *(978-0-375-82721-1(8),* Golden Bks.) Random Hse. Children's Bks.

—Mr. Brown Can Moo! Can You? 2014. (Big Bright & Early Board Book Ser.). (ENG., Illus.). 24p. (J). (-k). bds. 6.99 *(978-0-385-38712-5(1),* Random Hse. Bks. for Young Readers) Random Hse. Children's Bks.

Snider, Grant. What Sound Is Morning? 2020. (ENG., Illus.). 48p. (J). (gr. -1 — 1). 15.99 *(978-1-4521-7993-3(X))* Chronicle Bks. LLC.

Snow, Peggy. My Favorite Sounds from a to Z. 2007. (ENG.). 32p. (J). lib. bdg. 15.99 *(978-1-934277-02-7(9))* Mam Green Publishing, Inc.

Stute, Lela LaBree. The Big Bad Blonde, 1 vol. 2010. 18p. pap. 24.95 *(978-1-4489-9621-6(X))* PublishAmerica, Inc.

Sullivan, John. Kitten & the Night Watchman. Yoo, Taeeun, illus. 2018. (ENG.). 40p. (J). (gr. -1-3). 17.99 *(978-1-4814-6191-7(5),* Simon & Schuster/Paula Wiseman Bks.) Simon & Schuster/Paula Wiseman Bks.

Thompson, Lauren. Mouse Loves Spring. 2018. (Simon & Schuster Ready-To-Read Level 1 Ser.). lib. bdg. 13.55 *(978-0-606-40862-2(2))* Turtleback.

—Mouse Loves Spring: Ready-To-Read Pre-Level 1. Erdogan, Buket, illus. 2018. (Mouse Ser.). (ENG.). 32p. (J). (gr. -1-k). 17.99 *(978-1-5344-0185-3(7));* pap. 4.99 *(978-1-5344-0184-6(9))* Simon Spotlight. (Simon Spotlight).

Viau, Nancy. City Street Beat. 2015. (Illus.). 32p. (J). *(978-1-4896-3855-7(5))* Weigl Pubs., Inc.

Waring, Geoff. Oscar & the Bat: A Book about Sound. Waring, Geoff, illus. 2009. (Start with Science Ser.). (ENG., Illus.). 32p. (J). (gr. -1-3). pap. 6.99 *(978-0-7636-4513-7(3))* Candlewick Pr.

Watts, Kevin Bradley. Ben & the Mysterious Sound: Series: the Adventures of Tug Boat Ben. 2007. (Illus.). 32p. (J). *(978-0-9782625-2-5(2));* pap. *(978-0-9782625-1-8(4))* Alderney Publishing, Inc.

Weiner, Marcella Bakur & Neimark, Jill. I Want Your Moo: A Story for Children about Self-Esteem. Adinolfi, JoAnn, illus. 2nd ed. 2009. 32p. (J). (gr. -1-3). 14.95 *(978-1-4338-0542-4(1));* pap. 9.95 *(978-1-4338-0552-3(9))* American Psychological Assn. (Magination Pr.).

Williams, Rozanne. Mr. Noisy. 2017. (Learn-To-Read Ser.). (ENG., Illus.). (J). pap. 3.49 *(978-1-68310-208-3(8))* Pacific Learning, Inc.

Ylvis & Løchstøer, Christian. What Does the Fox Say? Nyhus, Svein, illus. 2013. (ENG.). 32p. (J). (gr. -1-3). 17.99 *(978-1-4814-2223-9(5),* Simon & Schuster Bks. For Young Readers) Simon & Schuster Bks. For Young Readers.

Young, Jessica. Pet This Book. Wiseman, Daniel, illus. 2018. (ENG.). 32p. (J). 15.99 *(978-1-68119-507-0(0),* 900175607, Bloomsbury Children's Bks.) Bloomsbury Publishing USA.

SOUND—POETRY

Cleary, Brian P. Bow-Tie Pasta: Acrostic Poems. Rowland, Andy, illus. 2015. (Poetry Adventures Ser.). (ENG.). 32p. (J). (gr. 2-5). 26.65 *(978-1-4677-2046-5(1),* 0adbb7ff-4e32-4fca-a185-e1662ffef733, Millbrook Pr.) Lerner Publishing Group.

SOUND—RECORDING AND REPRODUCING

Ambrosek, Renee. Shawn Fanning: The Founder of Napster. (Internet Career Biographies Ser.). 112p. (gr. 8-8). 2009. 63.90 *(978-1-61513-600-1(2))* 2006. (ENG., Illus.). (YA). lib. bdg. 39.80 *(978-1-4042-0720-2(1),* ebe36c69-b4cf-482a-bd7c-c7f3324ae510) Rosen Publishing Group, Inc., The.

Anniss, Matt. The Music Industry. 2015. (Music Scene Ser.). (J). lib. bdg. 37.10 *(978-1-59920-911-1(X))* Black Rabbit Bks.

Badach Doyle, Abby. Podcasters, 1 vol. 2019. (Digital Insiders Ser.). (ENG.). 32p. (gr. 3-4). pap. 11.50 *(978-1-5382-4759-4(3),* 79661fb6-3a91-43bc-8256-fe36cfdc6e53) Stevens, Gareth Publishing LLLP.

Bailey, Diane. The Story of Interscope Records. 2012. (J). pap. *(978-1-4222-2128-0(8));* 64p. (gr. 4). 22.95 *(978-1-4222-2115-0(6))* Mason Crest.

Baughan, Brian. The Story of Def Jam Records. 2012. (J). pap. *(978-1-4222-2127-3(X));* 64p. (gr. 4). 22.95 *(978-1-4222-2114-3(8))* Mason Crest.

Bell, Samantha S. Before Streaming Music. 2020. (What Did We Do? Ser.). (ENG., Illus.). 32p. (J). (gr. 2-3). pap. 9.95 *(978-1-64493-124-0(9),* 1644931249); lib. bdg. 31.35 *(978-1-64493-045-8(5),* 1644930455) North Star Editions. (Focus Readers).

Burgan, Michael. Spotify, Pandora, & Streaming Music, Vol. 6. 2018. (Tech 2. 0: World-Changing Entertainment Companies Ser.). (Illus.). 64p. (J). (gr. 7). lib. bdg. 31.93 *(978-1-4222-4058-8(4))* Mason Crest.

Colby, Jennifer. Phonograph to Streaming Music. 2019. (21st Century Junior Library: Then to Now Tech Ser.). (ENG., Illus.). 24p. (J). (gr. 2-5). pap. 12.79 *(978-1-5341-5013-3(7),* 213359); lib. bdg. 30.64 *(978-1-5341-4727-0(6),* 213358) Cherry Lake Publishing.

Cole, Joanna. The Magic School Bus Inside the Human Body, 1 vol. Degen, Bruce, illus. 2011. (Magic School Bus Ser.). (ENG.). (J). (gr. 2-5). audio compact disk 10.99 *(978-0-545-24083-3(2))* Scholastic, Inc.

Culp, Jennifer. Using Computer Science in Digital Music Careers, 1 vol. 2017. (Coding Your Passion Ser.). (ENG., Illus.). 80p. (J). (gr. 7-7). 37.47 *(978-1-5081-7517-9(9),* 2be9d75c-d4d1-4fdd-9711-827a91b2c331, Rosen Young Adult) Rosen Publishing Group, Inc., The.

Daniels, Leonard & Orr, Tamra. Web-Based Digital Presentations, 1 vol., 1. 2015. (Digital & Information Literacy Ser.). (ENG.). 48p. (J). (gr. 6-6). pap. 12.75 *(978-1-4994-3773-7(0),* 78e543c6-282e-4d3b-be5e-e84fe820adcf, Rosen Central) Rosen Publishing Group, Inc., The.

Finley, Toiya Kristen. Russell Simmons. 2009. (Sharing the American Dream Ser.). (Illus.). 64p. (YA). (gr. 7-12). 22.95 *(978-1-4222-0584-6(3))* Mason Crest.

Foy, Debbie. Simon Cowell: Global Music Mogul, 1 vol. 2011. (Famous Lives Ser.). (ENG., Illus.). 32p. (YA). (gr. 3-4). lib. bdg. 30.27 *(978-1-4488-3290-3(X),* 3eb63517-e24c-4a07-9554-7b46af24f2ae) Rosen Publishing Group, Inc., The.

Golus, Carrie. Biography Russell Simmons. 2007. (Biography Ser.). (Illus.). 112p. (J). (gr. -1). lib. bdg. *(978-0-8225-7158-2(7))* Twenty First Century Bks.

Heidelberger, David. Sound Mixing in TV & Film, 1 vol. 2018. (Exploring Careers in TV & Film Ser.). (ENG.). 96p. (gr. 7-7). pap. 20.99 *(978-1-5026-4155-7(0),* 31966f32-10ff-4661-9120-1131c205e3dd) Cavendish Square Publishing LLC.

Higgins, Nadia. Making a Podcast. 2018. (Sequence Entertainment Ser.). (ENG.). 32p. (J). (gr. 2-5). pap. 9.99 *(978-1-68152-362-0(0),* 15202) Amicus.

Hill, Z. B. Sean "Diddy" Combs. 2012. (J). pap. *(978-1-4222-2540-0(2));* (Illus.). 48p. (gr. 3-4). 19.95 *(978-1-4222-2514-1(3))* Mason Crest.

Indovino, Shaina C. Russell Simmons: From Drug Dealer to Music Mogul. 2012. (Extraordinary Success with a High School Diploma or Less Ser.). 64p. (J). (gr. 7-8). 22.95 *(978-1-4222-2301-7(9))* Mason Crest.

—Simon Cowell: From the Mailroom to Idol Fame. 2012. (Extraordinary Success with a High School Diploma or Less Ser.). 64p. (J). (gr. 7-8). 22.95 *(978-1-4222-2296-6(9))* Mason Crest.

Indovino, Shaina Carmel. Russell Simmons: From Drug Dealer to Music Mogul. 2012. (J). pap. *(978-1-4222-2312-3(4))* Mason Crest.

—Simon Cowell: From the Mailroom to Idol Fame. 2012. pap. *(978-1-4222-2307-9(8))* Mason Crest.

Kallen, Stuart A. IPod & MP3 Players, 1 vol. 2010. (Technology 360 Ser.). (ENG., Illus.). 104p. (gr. 7-10). lib. bdg. 41.53 *(978-1-4205-0166-7(6),* f893e429-ee0d-46d4-881a-ac251549619d, Lucent Pr.) Greenhaven Publishing LLC.

Kowalski, Emma. The Story of Konvict Muzik. 2012. (J). pap. *(978-1-4222-2129-7(6));* 64p. (gr. 4). 22.95 *(978-1-4222-2116-7(4))* Mason Crest.

—The Story of Mosley Music Group. 2012. (J). pap. *(978-1-4222-2130-3(X));* 64p. (gr. 4). 22.95 *(978-1-4222-2117-4(2))* Mason Crest.

—The Story of Roc-A-Fella Records. 2012. (J). pap. *(978-1-4222-2132-7(6));* 64p. (gr. 4). 22.95 *(978-1-4222-2119-8(9))* Mason Crest.

Mara, Wil. Sound Engineer. 2015. (21st Century Skills Library: Cool STEAM Careers Ser.). (ENG., Illus.). 32p. (J). (gr. 4-7). 32.07 *(978-1-63362-563-1(X),* 206436) Cherry Lake Publishing.

Mintzer, Richard. The Story of So So Def Records. 2012. (J). pap. *(978-1-4222-2133-4(4));* 64p. (gr. 4). 22.95 *(978-1-4222-2120-4(2))* Mason Crest.

Nieuwland, Jackson. Careers for Tech Girls in Audio Engineering, 1 vol. 2018. (Tech Girls Ser.). (ENG.). 80p. (J). (gr. 7-7). 37.47 *(978-1-5081-8008-1(3),* 4876acd2-d82a-4fd2-8455-5c0fb211ea85) Rosen Publishing Group, Inc., The.

Sturm, Jeanne. MP3 Players. 2008. (Let's Explore Science Ser.). (Illus.). 48p. (J). (gr. 4-8). lib. bdg. 31.36 *(978-1-60472-332-8(7))* Rourke Educational Media.

Traugh, Susan M. Sean Combs, 1 vol. 2010. (People in the News Ser.). (ENG., Illus.). 104p. (gr. 7-7). 41.03 *(978-1-4205-0237-4(9),* 1598dc89-1611-4398-8f6c-d1702cd2b68e, Lucent Pr.) Greenhaven Publishing LLC.

Whiting, Jim. The Story of No Limit Records. 2012. (J). pap. *(978-1-4222-2131-0(8));* 64p. (gr. 4). 22.95 *(978-1-4222-2118-1(0))* Mason Crest.

Wood, Alix. Be a Sound Designer: Creating a Mood, 1 vol. 2017. (Moviemakers' Film Club Ser.). (ENG.). 32p. (J). (gr. 4-5). pap. 11.00 *(978-1-5383-2380-9(X),* 936a7438-ce98-4f28-b9f0-b22286acf547); lib. bdg. 27.93 *(978-1-5081-6257-5(3),* 75061fa9-e530-4949-b7dd-abbf826062a3) Rosen Publishing Group, Inc., The. (PowerKids Pr.).

Wooster, Patricia. Music Producer. 2011. (21st Century Skills Library: Cool Arts Careers Ser.). (ENG., Illus.). 32p. (gr. 4-8). lib. bdg. 32.07 *(978-1-61080-133-1(4),* 201144) Cherry Lake Publishing.

SOUND EFFECTS

see Sounds

SOUND WAVES

see also Ultrasonic Waves

Boothroyd, Jennifer. Loud or Soft? High or Low? A Look at Sound. 2011. (Lightning Bolt Books Exploring Physical Science Ser.). 32p. pap. 45.32 *(978-0-7613-7650-7(X))* Lerner Publishing Group.

Catasús Jennings, Terry. Sonidos en la Sabana, 1 vol. Saroff, Phyllis, illus. 2015.Tr. of Sounds of the Savanna. (SPA.). 32p. (J). (gr. k-3). pap. 11.95 *(978-1-62855-642-1(0))* Arbordale Publishing.

—Sounds of the Savanna, 1 vol. Saroff, Phyllis, illus. 2015.Tr. of Sounds of the Savanna. (ENG.). 32p. (J). (gr. k-3). pap. 9.95 *(978-1-62855-637-7(4))* Arbordale Publishing.

Coan, Sharon. How Sound Moves, 1 vol. rev. ed. 2014. (Science: Informational Text Ser.). (ENG., Illus.). 24p. (gr. 1-2). pap. 9.99 *(978-1-4807-4564-3(2))* Teacher Created Materials, Inc.

Connors, Kathleen. Sound, 1 vol. 2018. (Look at Physical Science Ser.). (ENG.). 32p. (gr. 2-2). 28.27 *(978-1-5382-2159-4(4),* d6c22321-a0ff-4344-8d42-66f6e8fcd5f8) Stevens, Gareth Publishing LLLP.

Corsaro, Nicola. What Are Sound Waves?, 1 vol. 2013. (Rosen Readers Ser.). (ENG.). 24p. (J). (gr. 2-2). pap. 8.25 *(978-1-4777-2397-5(8),* 08ddd7c1-d340-403a-9d34-9618efe50930); pap. 49.50 *(978-1-4777-2398-2(6))* Rosen Publishing Group, Inc., The. (Rosen Classroom).

Gardner, Jane P. Music Science, Vol. 11. Lewin, Russ, ed. 2015. (Science 24/7 Ser.). (Illus.). 48p. (J). (gr. 5). 20.95 *(978-1-4222-3412-9(6))* Mason Crest.

Hawkins, Jay. Super Sonic: The Science of Sound, 1 vol. 2013. (Big Bang Science Experiments Ser.). (ENG., Illus.). 32p. (gr. 4-5). pap. 12.75 *(978-1-4777-0370-0(5),* f4d05e41-fc6a-44d2-b6e9-2d37dd4b72bc, Windmill Bks.) Rosen Publishing Group, Inc., The.

Jennings, Terry J. Sound. 2009. (J). 28.50 *(978-1-59920-275-4(1))* Black Rabbit Bks.

Johnson, Robin. How Does Sound Change? 2014. (Light & Sound Waves Close-Up Ser.). (ENG., Illus.). 24p. (J). (gr. 1-2). *(978-0-7787-0520-8(X))* Crabtree Publishing Co.

—The Science of Sound Waves. 2017. (Catch a Wave Ser.). (Illus.). 32p. (J). (gr. 4-4). *(978-0-7787-2941-9(9))* Crabtree Publishing Co.

—What Are Sound Waves? 2014. (Light & Sound Waves Close-Up Ser.). (ENG., Illus.). 24p. (J). (gr. 1-2). *(978-0-7787-0522-2(6))* Crabtree Publishing Co.

Lilly, Melinda. Sound up & Down. Thompson, Scott M., illus. 2003. 24p. (J). 20.64 *(978-1-58952-644-0(9))* Rourke Educational Media.

Mahaney, Ian F. Sound Waves. (Energy in Action Ser.). 24p. (gr. 3-3). 2009. 42.50 *(978-1-61512-263-9(X))* 2006. (ENG., Illus.). pap. 7.05 *(978-1-4042-2189-5(1),* 3f1a2e7c-168d-4156-9373-c5bdae0bc4c3) Rosen Publishing Group, Inc., The. (PowerKids Pr.).

Riley, Peter. Changing Sounds. 2007. (Essential Science/Watts Ser.). (Illus.). 32p. (YA). (gr. 3-6). lib. bdg. 28.50 *(978-1-59920-023-1(6))* Black Rabbit Bks.

Rooney, Anne. Audio Engineering & the Science of Soundwaves. 2013. (ENG., Illus.). 32p. (J). *(978-0-7787-1196-4(X));* pap. *(978-0-7787-1229-9(X))* Crabtree Publishing Co.

Sohn, Emily. Adventures in Sound with Max Axiom Super Scientist: 4D an Augmented Reading Science Experience. Martin, Cynthia, illus. 2018. (Graphic Science 4D Ser.). (ENG.). 32p. (J). (gr. 3-9). lib. bdg. 36.65 *(978-1-5435-2944-9(5),* 138533, Capstone Pr.) Capstone.

Wacholtz, Anthony. Mummies & Sound, 1 vol. Mallea, Cristian, illus. 2013. (Monster Science Ser.). (ENG.). 32p. (J). (gr. 3-9). pap. 8.10 *(978-1-62065-818-5(6),* 121775, Capstone Pr.) Capstone.

Winterberg, Jenna. Sound Waves & Communication. 2015. (Science: Informational Text Ser.). (ENG., Illus.). 32p. (J). (gr. 3-5). pap. 11.99 *(978-1-4807-4684-8(3))* Teacher Created Materials, Inc.

SOUNDS

Adivina Lo Que Es: Individual 6-packs, Level 4. 2003. 23.95 *(978-0-673-57868-6(2))* Celebration Pr.

AZ Books. Our Planet. 2013. (Sounds Around Us Ser.). (ENG.). 16p. (J). (gr. 1-3). bds. 17.95 *(978-1-61889-282-9(7))* AZ Bks. LLC.

Baggott, Stella. Baby's Very First Noisy Book. Baggott, Stella, illus. 2010. (Illus.). 10p. (J). bds. 14.99 *(978-0-7945-2653-5(5),* Usborne) EDC Publishing.

Bullard, Lisa. Loud & Quiet [Scholastic]: An Animal Opposites Book. 2009. (Animal Opposites Ser.). 32p. (gr. 1-2). pap. 1.00 *(978-1-4296-4232-3(7),* Capstone Pr.) Capstone.

Burton, Margie, et al. Sounds. 2011. (Early Connections Ser.). (J). *(978-1-61672-506-8(0))* Benchmark Education Co.

Cardenas, Ernesto A. Sounds. 2009. pap. 4.95 *(978-1-60698-090-3(4))* Milo Educational Bks. & Resources.

Crick, Sharon. Sounds. 2014. 20p. pap. 16.00 *(978-1-4828-9215-4(4))* Partridge Pub.

—Sounds. 2012. 20p. pap. 16.00 *(978-1-4669-2832-9(8))* Trafford Publishing.

Dalmatian Press Staff. Say Moo! 2008. (ENG.). 5p. (J). bds. 4.95 *(978-1-58117-722-0(4),* Intervisual/Piggy Toes) Bendon, Inc.

Dobson, Jolie. Beep Beep Choo Choo. 2014. (Snappy Sounds Ser.). (ENG., Illus.). 22p. (J). (gr. -1 — 1). bds. 5.95 *(978-1-77085-436-9(3),* 590efcf2-f4f2-42ed-a1b0-422b99b19e14) Firefly Bks., Ltd.

—Ring Ring Pop Pop. 2014. (Snappy Sounds Ser.). (ENG., Illus.). 22p. (J). (gr. -1 — 1). bds. 5.95 *(978-1-77085-437-6(1),* c6d2441d-b8f8-4e49-8cdb-874c69f3fbd0) Firefly Bks., Ltd.

—Snap Snap Woof Woof. 2014. (Snappy Sounds Ser.). (ENG., Illus.). 22p. (J). (gr. -1 — 1). bds. 5.95 *(978-1-77085-435-2(5),* de566b53-e31b-4d43-abd7-a8a1151b1e61) Firefly Bks., Ltd.

Gardner, Robert. Experimenting with Sound Science Projects, 1 vol. 2013. (Exploring Hands-On Science Projects Ser.). (ENG.). 128p. (gr. 5-6). pap. 13.88 *(978-1-4644-0225-8(6),* 9f49216f-17da-4c41-af6b-61e7953ec594) Enslow Publishing, LLC.

Gold-Vukson, Marji. The Sounds of My Jewish Year. Urban, Suzanne, illus. 2003. (ENG.). 12p. (J). (gr. -1 — 1). bds. 4.95 *(978-1-58013-047-9(X),* 78d258a8-5876-40a7-8d1e-2f81ffc13bb2, Kar-Ben Publishing) Lerner Publishing Group.

Greenwell, Jessica. Noisy Monsters. Wildish, Lee, illus. 2010. (Busy Sounds Board Bks). 10p. (J). bds. 18.99 *(978-0-7945-2769-3(8),* Usborne) EDC Publishing.

Group, Cricket Magazine. Oink-Oink: And Other Animal Sounds. Conteh-Morgan, Jane, illus. 2007. (ENG.). 20p. (J). (gr. k-k). bds. 7.95 *(978-0-8126-7934-2(2))* Cricket Bks.

Hewitt, Sally. Hear This! 2008. (Let's Start Science Ser.). (ENG., Illus.). 24p. (J). (gr. 3-7). pap. *(978-0-7787-4058-2(7))* Crabtree Publishing Co.

Himmelman, John. Noisy Bug Sing-Along, 1 vol. 2013. (ENG., Illus.). 32p. (J). (gr. -1-4). pap. 8.99 *(978-1-58469-192-1(1),* Dawn Pubns.) Sourcebooks, Inc.

—Noisy Bug Sing-Along, 1 vol. Himmelman, John, illus. 2013. (ENG., Illus.). 32p. (J). (gr. -1-4). 16.95 *(978-1-58469-191-4(3))* Take Heart Pubns.

Jennings, Terry J. Sound. 2009. (J). 28.50 *(978-1-59920-275-4(1))* Black Rabbit Bks.

Marsalis, Wynton. Squeak, Rumble, Whomp! Whomp! Whomp! A Sonic Adventure. Rogers, Paul, illus. 2012. (ENG.). 40p. (J). (gr. -1-3). 19.99 *(978-0-7636-3991-4(5))* Candlewick Pr.

Martin, Dayna. Sounds. 2018. (Illus.). 31p. (J). *(978-1-4896-9657-1(1),* AV2 by Weigl) Weigl Pubs., Inc.

Matthews, Derek. Animales de la Granja. 2005. (Escucha y Aprende Ser.). (SPA., Illus.). 10p. (J). (gr. -1-1). *(978-970-718-300-1(4),* Silver Dolphin en Español) Advanced Marketing, S. de R. L. de C. V.

—Animales de la Selva. 2005. (Escucha y Aprende Ser.). (SPA., Illus.). 10p. (J). (gr. -1-1). *(978-970-718-298-1(9),* Silver Dolphin en Español) Advanced Marketing, S. de R. L. de C. V.

—Escucha y Aprende - Mascotas. 2005. (Escucha y Aprende Ser.). (SPA., Illus.). 10p. (J). (gr. -1-k). *(978-970-718-299-8(7),* Silver Dolphin en Español) Advanced Marketing, S. de R. L. de C. V.

—Tráfico: Con Graciosos Sonidos de vehículos. 2005. (Escucha y Aprende Ser.). (SPA., Illus.). 10p. (J). (gr. -1-1). *(978-970-718-297-4(0),* Silver Dolphin en Español) Advanced Marketing, S. de R. L. de C. V.

McFarlane, Sheryl. What's That Sound? at the Circus. LaFave, Kim, illus. 2006. (What's That Sound? Ser.). (ENG.). 20p. (J). (gr. -1-k). bds. 6.95 *(978-1-55041-959-7(5),* b5efee24-0eb3-457a-a4a2-77a756ac1cb1) Trifolium Bks., Inc. CAN. Dist: Firefly Bks., Ltd.

Perkins, Al. The Ear Book. Payne, Henry, illus. 2008. (Bright & Early Board Books(TM) Ser.). (ENG.). 24p. (J). (— 1). bds. 4.99 *(978-0-375-84279-5(9),* Random Hse. Bks. for Young Readers) Random Hse. Children's Bks.

Robertson, J. Jean. Listen! What Do You Hear? 2008. (Things That Go Board Bks.). (ENG., Illus.). 16p. (gr. -1-k). bds. 5.99 *(978-1-60472-451-6(X),* 9781604724516) Rourke Educational Media.

Smeldit, H. W. Farts in the Wild: A Spotter's Guide. 2012. (ENG., Illus.). 24p. (J). (gr. -1-17). 16.99 *(978-1-4521-0631-1(2))* Chronicle Bks. LLC.

Sounds Great! Complete Set. (gr. k-2). incl. cd-rom *(978-0-7327-2785-7(5))* McGraw-Hill Education (Australia) Pty Ltd.

Taplin, Sam. Noisy Spooky Book. 2012. (Noisy Bks). 10p. (J). bds. 19.99 *(978-0-7945-2913-0(5),* Usborne) EDC Publishing.

Twist, Clint. Light & Sound. 2010. (Science Everywhere! Ser.). 24p. 24.25 *(978-1-84898-297-0(6))* Black Rabbit Bks.

What's That Sound? (Peek A Boo Pockets Ser.). (Illus.). 12p. (J). bds. *(978-2-89393-877-6(9))* Phidal Publishing, Inc./Editions Phidal, Inc.

SOUPS

Goss, Gary. Blue Moon Soup: A Family Cookbook. Dyer, Jane, illus. 2013. (ENG.). 72p. (J). (gr. 1-1). 16.95 *(978-1-62087-990-0(5),* 620990, Sky Pony Pr.) Skyhorse Publishing Co., Inc.

Hunt, Santana. Making Soups with Math!, 1 vol. 2019. (Cooking with Math! Ser.). (ENG.). 24p. (gr. 1-2). pap. 9.15 *(978-1-5382-4566-8(3),* a6c99a70-f44c-498b-8e82-8234daf701be) Stevens, Gareth Publishing LLLP.

Kuskowski, Alex. Cool Soups & Stews: Easy & Fun Comfort Food. 2015. (Cool Home Cooking Ser.). (ENG.). 32p. (J). (gr. 3-6). 34.21 *(978-1-62403-504-3(3),* 16882, Checkerboard Library) ABDO Publishing Co.

SOUSA, JOHN PHILIP, 1854-1932

Venezia, Mike. John Philip Sousa (Revised Edition) (Getting to Know the World's Greatest Composers) (Library Edition) Venezia, Mike, illus. 2018. (Getting to Know the World's Greatest Composers Ser.). (ENG., Illus.). 40p. (J). (gr. 3-4). 29.00 *(978-0-531-22869-2(X),* Children's Pr.) Scholastic Library Publishing.

SOUTH, THE

see Southern States

SOUTH AFRICA

Here are entered works on the Republic of South Africa. Works on the area south of the countries of Zaire and Tanzania are entered under Africa, Southern.

Aloian, Molly. Cultural Traditions in South Africa. 2014. (Cultural Traditions in My World Ser.). (ENG., Illus.). 32p. (J). (gr. 2-3). *(978-0-7787-0304-4(5))* Crabtree Publishing Co.

Angelou, Maya. My Painted House, My Friendly Chicken, & Me. Courtney-Clarke, Margaret, illus. 2003. (ENG.). 48p. (J). (gr. -1-2). 8.99 *(978-0-375-82567-5(3),* Crown Books For Young Readers) Random Hse. Children's Bks.

—My Painted House, My Friendly Chicken, & Me. 2003. (gr. k-3). lib. bdg. 18.40 *(978-0-613-71911-7(5))* Turtleback.

Ayo's Awesome Adventures in Cape Town: Mother City. 2018. (J). *(978-0-7166-3639-7(5))* World Bk., Inc.

Barraclough, John. South Africa. (World Focus Ser.). (Illus.). 31p. (J). (gr. 3-7). pap. 3.99 *(978-0-431-07268-5(X))* Oxfam Publishing GBR. Dist: Stylus Publishing, LLC.

Blauer, Ettagale & Laure, Jason. South Africa. (Enchantment of the World™, Second Ser.). (ENG.). 144p. (J). 2013. 40.00 *(978-0-531-25603-9(0))* 2006. (Illus.). (gr. 5-9). 37.00 *(978-0-516-24853-0(7))* Scholastic Library Publishing. (Children's Pr.).

Bowden, Rob. Cape Town. 2006. (ENG., Illus.). 61p. (gr. 5-8). 30.00 *(978-0-7910-8856-2(1),* P114467, Facts On File) Infobase Holdings, Inc.

Clapper, Nikki Bruno. Let's Look at South Africa. 2018. (Let's Look at Countries Ser.). (ENG., Illus.). 24p. (J). (gr. -1-2). lib. bdg. 27.32 *(978-1-5157-9916-0(6),* 136922, Capstone Pr.) Capstone.

Clark, Domini. South Africa: The Culture. 3rd rev. ed. 2008. (Lands, Peoples, & Cultures Ser.). (ENG., Illus.). 32p. (J). (gr. 3-9). lib. bdg. *(978-0-7787-9292-5(7))* Crabtree Publishing Co.

—South Africa: The Land. 3rd rev. ed. 2008. (Lands, Peoples, & Cultures Ser.). (ENG., Illus.). 32p. (J). (gr. 3-9). lib. bdg. *(978-0-7787-9290-1(0))* Crabtree Publishing Co.

—South Africa: The People, 1 vol. 3rd rev. ed. 2008. (Lands, Peoples, & Cultures Ser.). (ENG., Illus.). 32p. (J). (gr. 3-9). pap. *(978-0-7787-9659-6(0))* Crabtree Publishing Co.

—South Africa - The Culture, 1 vol. 3rd rev. ed. 2008. (Lands, Peoples, & Cultures Ser.). (ENG., Illus.). 32p. (J). (gr. 3-9). pap. *(978-0-7787-9660-2(4))* Crabtree Publishing Co.

—South Africa - The Land, 1 vol. 3rd rev. ed. 2008. (Lands, Peoples, & Cultures Ser.). (ENG., Illus.). 32p. (J). (gr. 3-9). pap. *(978-0-7787-9658-9(2))* Crabtree Publishing Co.

—South Africa - The People. 3rd rev. ed. 2008. (Lands, Peoples, & Cultures Ser.). (ENG., Illus.). 32p. (J). (gr. 3-9). lib. bdg. *(978-0-7787-9291-8(9))* Crabtree Publishing Co.

Cottrell, Robert. South Africa: A State of Apartheid. 2005. (Arbitrary Borders Ser.). (ENG., Illus.). 112p. (gr. 9-13). 35.00 *(978-0-7910-8257-7(1),* P114241, Facts On File) Infobase Holdings, Inc.

Gagne, Tammy. We Visit South Africa. 2012. (J). lib. bdg. 33.95 *(978-1-61228-308-1(X))* Mitchell Lane Pubs.

Gallagher, Michael. South Africa. 2007. (Countries in the News/Watts Ser.). (Illus.). 32p. (YA). (gr. 4-7). lib. bdg. 27.10 *(978-1-59920-020-0(1))* Black Rabbit Bks.

Ganeri, Anita. South Africa: A Benjamin Blog & His Inquisitive Dog Guide, 1 vol. Isik, Semur, illus. 2014. (Country Guides, with Benjamin Blog & His Inquisitive Dog Ser.). (ENG.). 32p. (J). (gr. 3-5). pap. 7.99 *(978-1-4109-6677-3(1),* 126257, Raintree) Capstone.

Green, Jen. Focus on South Africa, 1 vol. 2007. (World in Focus Ser.). (ENG., Illus.). 64p. (gr. 5-8). pap. 15.05 *(978-0-8368-6745-9(9),* f66229d5-a13a-4154-8b78-ad53143ef226); lib. bdg. 36.67 *(978-0-8368-6738-1(6),* 8016ebe5-00d9-418c-9ca9-107185624e42) Stevens, Gareth Publishing LLLP. (Gareth Stevens Secondary Library).

Haskins, Jim & Benson, Kathleen. Count Your Way Through South Africa. Neibert, Alissa, illus. 2006. (Count Your Way Ser.). (ENG.). 24p. (gr. 2-5). lib. bdg. 19.93 *(978-1-57505-883-2(9),* Millbrook Pr.) Lerner Publishing Group.

Hollingsworth, Tamara. Nelson Mandela: Leading the Way, 1 vol. 2nd rev. ed. 2013. (TIME for KIDS(r): Informational Text Ser.). (ENG., Illus.). 48p. (J). (gr. 4-5). lib. bdg. 29.96 *(978-1-4807-1116-7(0))* Teacher Created Materials, Inc.

Kalman, Bobbie. Spotlight on South Africa. 2011. (Spotlight on My Country Ser.: No. 19). (ENG.). 32p. (J). (gr. k-3). pap. *(978-0-7787-3490-1(0))* Crabtree Publishing Co.

Koosman, Melissa. Meet Our New Student from South Africa. 2009. (Meet Our New Student Ser.). (Illus.). 47p. (J). (gr. 2-5). lib. bdg. 29.95 *(978-1-58415-781-6(X))* Mitchell Lane Pubs.

Langley, Andrew. Cape Town, 1 vol. 2004. (Great Cities of the World Ser.). (ENG., Illus.). 48p. (gr. 5-8). lib. bdg. 33.67 *(978-0-8368-5045-1(9),* 813c027d-2138-4f40-8b73-d376ce5d5940, Gareth Stevens Secondary Library) Stevens, Gareth Publishing LLLP.

Matthews, Sheelagh. South Africa. 2016. (Illus.). 32p. (J). *(978-1-5105-1907-7(6))* SmartBook Media, Inc.

—South Africa. 2014. (J). *(978-1-4896-1030-0(8))* Weigl Pubs., Inc.

Miller, Derek. Mahatma Gandhi: March to Independence, 1 vol. 2017. (Peaceful Protesters Ser.). (ENG.). 112p. (YA). (gr. 9-9). pap. 20.99 *(978-1-5026-3396-5(5),* 97541f3e-8abe-46ee-adf0-e21ca841f103) Cavendish Square Publishing LLC.

Mis, Melody S. How to Draw South Africa's Sights & Symbols. 2009. (Kid's Guide to Drawing the Countries of the World Ser.). 48p. (gr. 4-4). 53.00 *(978-1-61511-125-1(5),* PowerKids Pr.) Rosen Publishing Group, Inc., The.

Murphy, Patricia J. South Africa, 1 vol. 2005. (Discovering Cultures Ser.). (ENG., Illus.). 48p. (gr. 3-4). lib. bdg. 31.21 *(978-0-7614-1719-4(2),* db321af9-4138-4476-8058-db6912a04ca3) Cavendish Square Publishing LLC.

Noonan, Sheila Smith. South Africa. Rotberg, Robert I., ed. 2012. (Evolution of Africa's Major Nations Ser.). (Illus.). 88p. (J). (gr. 7). 22.95 *(978-1-4222-2184-6(9))* Mason Crest.

—South Africa. 2011. (J). pap. *(978-1-4222-2212-6(8))* Mason Crest.

Oluonye, Mary. South Africa. 2009. pap. 52.95 *(978-0-7613-4735-4(6))* Lerner Publishing Group.

Owings, Lisa. South Africa. 2011. (Exploring Countries Ser.). (ENG., Illus.). 32p. (J). (gr. 3-7). lib. bdg. 27.95 *(978-1-60014-623-7(6),* Blastoff! Readers) Bellwether Media.

Perkins, Chloe. Living in ... South Africa: Ready-To-Read Level 2. Woolley, Tom, illus. 2016. (Living In... Ser.). (ENG.). 32p. (J). (gr. k-2). pap. 4.99 *(978-1-4814-7092-6(2),* Simon Spotlight) Simon Spotlight.

Petersen, Christine. South Africa. 2009. (J). *(978-1-58415-786-1(0))* Mitchell Lane Pubs.

Pugliano-Martin, Carol. Cape Town, South Africa. 2006. (J). pap. *(978-1-4108-6422-2(7))* Benchmark Education Co.

—Discover Cape Town. 2006. (J). pap. *(978-1-4108-6425-3(1))* Benchmark Education Co.

Rankin, Joan & Hartmann, Wendy. The African Orchestra. 2019. (ENG., Illus.). 32p. (J). (gr. 1-2). pap. 8.95 *(978-1-56656-025-2(X),* Crocodile Bks.) Interlink Publishing Group, Inc.

Rosmarin, Ike & Rissik, Dee. South Africa, 1 vol. 2nd rev. ed. 2004. (Cultures of the World (Second Edition)(r) Ser.). (ENG., Illus.). 144p. (gr. 5-5). lib. bdg. 49.79 *(978-0-7614-1704-0(4),* 1589cd39-a9c0-4214-b4a3-440d56072b85) Cavendish Square Publishing LLC.

Savery, Annabel. South Africa. 2011. (ENG., Illus.). 32p. (J). pap. 10.95 *(978-1-77092-027-9(7))* Saunders Bk. Co. CAN. Dist: RiverStream Publishing.

Senker, Cath. South Africa. 2014. (My Country Ser.). 24p. (gr. k-3). lib. bdg. 28.50 *(978-1-59920-907-4(1))* Black Rabbit Bks.

Sheen, Barbara. Foods of South Africa, 1 vol. 2012. (Taste of Culture Ser.). (ENG., Illus.). 64p. (gr. 3-6). lib. bdg. 36.83 *(978-0-7377-5952-5(6),*

8726e8a8-1445-459d-950f-1e4d798d5d3a, KidHaven Publishing) Greenhaven Publishing LLC.
Shoup, Kate. South Africa, 1 vol. 2017. (Exploring World Cultures (First Edition) Ser.). (ENG., Illus.). 32p. (gr. 3-3). pap. 12.16 *(978-1-5026-2507-6(5),* 6503ba0f-6c25-4fb8-a3c0-e459f7509ae8) Cavendish Square Publishing LLC.
Stein, R. Conrad. In a South African City, 1 vol. 2003. (Child's Day Ser.). (ENG., Illus.). 32p. (gr. 2-2). 32.64 *(978-0-7614-1407-0(X),* 30c1eaec-f8a7-421c-804c-054d6f80099a) Cavendish Square Publishing LLC.
Taylor, Trace. South Africa. (ICP Our World Ser.). (gr. k-1). 2012. (ENG.). 16p. (J). pap. 8.00 *(978-1-61541-130-6(5))* 2010. pap. 39.62 *(978-1-61541-131-3(3))* American Reading Co.
Taylor, Trace & Sánchez, Lucía M. South Africa. 2015. (1Y Nuestro Mundo Ser.). (SPA.). 16p. (J). (gr. k-1). pap. 8.00 *(978-1-61541-153-5(4))* American Reading Co.
Taylor, Trace & SáNchez, LucíA M. South Africa. 2010. pap. 39.62 *(978-1-61541-154-2(2))* American Reading Co.
Ward, Chris. Discover South Africa. 2010. (Illus.). 32p. (J). 63.60 *(978-1-61532-300-5(7),* 1307266); (ENG., (gr. 4-4). pap. 11.60 *(978-1-61532-299-2(X),* ebfe267a-9008-47ca-980d-7c1867248081) Rosen Publishing Group, Inc., The. (PowerKids Pr.).
Wilson, Rosie & Ward, Chris. Discover South Africa, 1 vol. 2010. (Discover Countries Ser.). (ENG., Illus.). 32p. (J). (gr. 4-4). 30.27 *(978-1-61532-289-3(2),* 7b794029-391c-47cd-88c9-c2daca7616b5) Rosen Publishing Group, Inc., The.

SOUTH AFRICA—BIOGRAPHY

Baptiste, Tracey. Nelson Mandela: Nobel Peace Prize-Winning Champion for Hope & Harmony, 4 vols. 2015. (Britannica Beginner Bios Ser.). (ENG.). 32p. (J). (gr. 2-3). 52.12 *(978-1-62275-943-9(5),* a2f77d99-a713-4e04-9c46-41666fe29d1e, Britannica Educational Publishing) Rosen Publishing Group, Inc., The.
—Nelson Mandela: Nobel Peace Prize-Winning Warrior for Hope & Harmony, 1 vol. 2015. (Britannica Beginner Bios Ser.). (ENG., Illus.). 32p. (J). (gr. 2-3). 26.06 *(978-1-62275-941-5(9),* 9c880c74-7f67-442d-b141-497ece6499c4, Britannica Educational Publishing) Rosen Publishing Group, Inc., The.
Belviso, Meg & Pollack, Pam. Who Is Nelson Mandela? 2014. (Who Was... ? Ser.). lib. bdg. 16.00 *(978-0-606-34158-5(7))* Turtleback.
Boothroyd, Jennifer. Nelson Mandela: A Life of Persistence. (Pull Ahead Books — Biographies Ser.). (ENG., Illus.). 32p. (gr. k-3). 2007. (J). pap. 7.99 *(978-0-8225-6434-8(3),* 4ba9e03a-1644-4461-a60e-7c4961301a45) 2006. lib. bdg. 22.60 *(978-0-8225-6385-3(1),* Lerner Pubns.) Lerner Publishing Group.
Dakers, Diane. Nelson Mandela: South Africa's Anti-Apartheid Revolutionary. 2014. (Crabtree Groundbreaker Biographies Ser.). (ENG., Illus.). 112p. (J). (gr. 6-6). *(978-0-7787-1241-1(9))* Crabtree Publishing Co.
Denenberg, Barry. Nelson Mandela: No Easy Walk to Freedom. 2014. (ENG.). 240p. (J). (gr. 4-7). pap. 7.99 *(978-0-545-66911-5(1))* Scholastic, Inc.
Erskine, Kathryn. Mama Africa! How Miriam Makeba Spread Hope with Her Song. Palmer, Charly, illus. 2017. (ENG.). 48p. (J). 18.99 *(978-0-374-30301-3(0),* 900152887, Farrar, Straus & Giroux (BYR)) Farrar, Straus & Giroux.
Feldman, Lawrence Anthony and Graham Spence; adapted by Thea. The Elephant Whisperer (Young Readers Adaptation) My Life with the Herd in the African Wild. 2017. (Elephant Whisperer Ser.). (ENG., Illus.). 256p. (J). 19.99 *(978-1-62779-309-4(7),* 900146134, Holt, Henry & Co. Bks. For Young Readers) Holt, Henry & Co.
Furgang, Kathy. Elon Musk: Entrepreneur. 2019. (Junior Biographies Ser.). (ENG.). 24p. (gr. 3-4). 56.10 *(978-1-9785-0893-4(X))* Enslow Publishing, LLC.
Gormley, Beatrice. Nelson Mandela: South African Revolutionary. 2015. (Real-Life Story Ser.). (ENG., Illus.). 256p. (J). (gr. 3-7). 17.99 *(978-1-4814-2059-4(3),* Aladdin) Simon & Schuster Children's Publishing.
Graham Gaines Rodriguez, Ann. Nelson Mandela & the End of Apartheid, 1 vol. 2015. (People & Events That Changed the World Ser.). (ENG., Illus.). 128p. (J). (gr. 7-8). 38.93 *(978-0-7660-7300-5(9),* a27ea591-870c-45ea-8587-10e2d5002b79) Enslow Publishing, LLC.
Green, Sara. Elon Musk. 2014. (Tech Icons Ser.). (ENG., Illus.). 24p. (J). (gr. 3-8). lib. bdg. 27.95 *(978-1-60014-988-7(X),* Pilot Bks.) Bellwether Media.
Ingram, Doreen. My Sanctuary, a Place I Call Home. 2010. (Illus.). 54p. pap. 17.50 *(978-1-60911-480-0(9),* Eloquent Bks.) Strategic Book Publishing & Rights Agency (SBPRA).
Josephson, Judith P. Nelson Mandela. 2009. (History Maker Biographies Ser.). (ENG.). 48p. (gr. 3-6). 27.93 *(978-1-58013-703-4(2),* Lerner Pubns.) Lerner Publishing Group.
Kallen, Stuart A. Elon Musk & Tesla. 2015. (ENG., Illus.). 80p. (J). lib. bdg. *(978-1-60152-870-4(1))* ReferencePoint Pr., Inc.
Keller, Bill. Tree Shaker: The Life of Nelson Mandela. 2013. (New York Times Ser.). (ENG., Illus.). 128p. (J). (gr. 5-9). pap. 14.99 *(978-1-59643-533-9(X),* 900061088) Square Fish.
Kramer, Ann. World History Biographies: Mandela: The Hero Who Led His Nation to Freedom. 2008. (National Geographic World History Biographies Ser.). (Illus.). 64p. (J). (gr. 3-7). pap. 7.99 *(978-1-4263-0173-5(1),* National Geographic Kids) Disney Publishing Worldwide.
Magoon, Kekla. Nelson Mandela: A Leader for Freedom, 1 vol. 2008. (Essential Lives Set 2 Ser.). (ENG., Illus.). 112p. (YA). (gr. 6-12). lib. bdg. 41.36 *(978-1-60453-038-4(3),* 6657, Essential Library) ABDO Publishing Co.
Meyer, Susan. Nelson Mandela: South African President & Anti-Apartheid Activist. 2017. (Spotlight on Civic Courage: Heroes of Conscience Ser.). 48p. (J). (gr. 10-15). 70.50 *(978-1-5383-8089-5(7),* Rosen Young Adult) Rosen Publishing Group, Inc., The.
Morini, Manuel & Segesso, Ignacio. Nelson Mandela. 2017. (Graphic Lives Ser.). (ENG., Illus.). 80p. (J). (gr. 3-9). lib. bdg. 32.65 *(978-1-5157-9164-5(5),* 136606, Capstone Pr.) Capstone.
Nelson, Kadir. Nelson Mandela. Nelson, Kadir, illus. (ENG., Illus.). 40p. (J). (gr. -1-3). 2019. pap. 9.99 *(978-0-06-178377-7(3))* 2013. 17.99 *(978-0-06-178374-6(9))* 2013. lib. bdg. 18.89 *(978-0-06-178376-0(5))* HarperCollins Pubs. (Tegen, Katherine Bks).
—Nelson Mandela. 2014. (SPA.). (J). (gr. 2-4). 21.99 *(978-84-261-4069-2(6))* Juventud, Editorial ESP. Dist: Lectorum Pubns., Inc.
Noah, Trevor. It's Trevor Noah: Born a Crime: Stories from a South African Childhood (Adapted for Young Readers) 2019. (ENG.). 304p. (J). (gr. 5). 17.99 *(978-0-525-58216-8(9),* Delacorte Bks. for Young Readers) Random House Publishing Group.
—It's Trevor Noah: Born a Crime: Stories from a South African Childhood (Adapted for Young Readers) 2019. (ENG.). 304p. (J). (gr. 5). lib. bdg. 20.99 *(978-0-525-58217-5(7),* Delacorte Bks. for Young Readers) Random Hse. Children's Bks.
Rajczak Nelson, Kristen. Nelson Mandela, 1 vol. 2015. (Heroes of Black History Ser.). (ENG., Illus.). 32p. (J). (gr. 3-4). pap. 11.50 *(978-1-4824-2908-4(X),* b39b2d5c-3cb7-42ed-81f5-4043e85c1433) Stevens, Gareth Publishing LLLP.
Riggs, Kate. The Release of Nelson Mandela. 2009. (Days of Change Ser.). (ENG., Illus.). 48p. (J). (gr. 5-8). 22.95 *(978-1-58341-736-2(2),* 22145) Creative Co., The.
Rose, Simon. Nelson Mandela. 2010. (Remarkable People Ser.). (Illus.). 24p. (J). (gr. 3-5). lib. bdg. 25.70 *(978-1-61690-172-1(1));* (gr. 4-6). pap. 11.95 *(978-1-61690-173-8(X))* Weigl Pubs., Inc.
Senker, Cath. Nelson Mandela. 2015. (Against the Odds Biographies Ser.). (ENG., Illus.). 48p. (J). (gr. 3-6). 35.99 *(978-1-4846-2465-4(3),* 129623, Heinemann) Capstone.
Stamper, G. C. Nelson Mandela. 2005. (Illus.). 32p. (J). pap. *(978-0-7367-2922-2(4))* Zaner-Bloser, Inc.
Trussell-Cullen, Alan. Nelson Mandela. 2009. pap. 13.25 *(978-1-60559-067-7(3))* Hameray Publishing Group, Inc.
Turner, Myra Faye. People That Changed the Course of History: The Story of Nelson Mandela 100 Years after His Birth. 2017. (J). *(978-1-62023-450-1(5))* Atlantic Publishing Group, Inc.
—People Who Changed the Course of History: The Story of Nelson Mandela 100 Years after His Birth. 2018. (ENG.). 238p. (YA). pap. 19.95 *(978-1-62023-446-4(7),* 0df6c692-20ee-481c-b071-04ecc3e6f8e5) Atlantic Publishing Group, Inc.
Vandegrift, Tom. 24 New Moons. 2003. 429p. (YA). pap. 20.95 *(978-0-7414-1503-5(8))* Infinity Publishing.
Wilcox, Christine. Oscar Pistorius, 1 vol. 2014. (People in the News Ser.). (ENG., Illus.). 104p. (gr. 7-7). 41.03 *(978-1-4205-1041-6(X),* 247c588f-7096-4e4e-86d7-980895bd2530, Lucent Pr.) Greenhaven Publishing LLC.

SOUTH AFRICA—FICTION

Benjamin, Ruth. Yesterday's Child. Cohen, Deene, illus. (YA). 16.95 *(978-1-56062-176-8(1),* CFR122H); pap. 13.95 *(978-1-56062-177-5(X),* CFR122S) C I S Communications, Inc.
Benwell, Fox. Kaleidoscope Song. 2018. (ENG.). 416p. (YA). (gr. 9). pap. 12.99 *(978-1-4814-7768-0(4))* Simon & Schuster.
—Kaleidoscope Song. 2017. (ENG.). 416p. (YA). (gr. 9). 17.99 *(978-1-4814-7767-3(6),* Simon & Schuster Bks. For Young Readers) Simon & Schuster Bks. For Young Readers.
Beverley, Naidoo. Journey to Jo'Burg: A South African Story. 97th rev. ed. 2014. (ENG.). 96p. (J). (gr. k-4). 10.24 *(978-1-63245-264-1(2))* Lectorum Pubns., Inc.
Bildner, Phil. The Soccer Fence: A Story of Friendship, Hope, & Apartheid in South Africa. Watson, Jesse Joshua, illus. 2014. 40p. (J). (gr. 1-3). 18.99 *(978-0-399-24790-3(4),* G.P. Putnam's Sons Books for Young Readers) Penguin Young Readers Group.
Callen, Sharon. Anna Goes to Zambia, 1 vol. rev. ed. 2013. (Literary Text Ser.). (ENG., Illus.). 20p. (gr. 1-2). (J). lib. bdg. 15.96 *(978-1-4807-1151-8(9));* 7.99 *(978-1-4333-5495-3(0))* Teacher Created Materials, Inc.
Coman, Carolyn. Many Stones. 2011. 14.12 *(978-0-7848-3598-2(5),* Everbind) Marco Bk. Co.
Cumberland, Wendy. Inkwelo Mountain: A Child's Adventure in Kwa Zulu, South Africa. 2013. 46p. pap. 10.95 *(978-1-62857-135-6(7),* Strategic Bk. Publishing) Strategic Book Publishing & Rights Agency (SBPRA).
Daly, Niki. The Herd Boy. 2012. (ENG., Illus.). 32p. (J). 17.00 *(978-0-8028-5417-9(6),* Eerdmans Bks For Young Readers) Eerdmans, William B. Publishing Co.
Deeks, Graham. Ratrigues & the Invisible Intelligence. 2011. 264p. 27.08 *(978-1-4269-7019-1(6));* pap. 17.08 *(978-1-4269-7020-7(X))* Trafford Publishing.
Driftin' Aarong. Claude Henry, the Iditarod Mouse ~3: The Great Castaway Adventure. 2009. 92p. pap. 9.95 *(978-1-4401-1949-1(X))* iUniverse, Inc.
Fraser, Kayo. Listen to Your Spirit: A Novel. 2019. (ENG., Illus.). 180p. (J). pap. *(978-1-937849-53-5(8))* Raven Publishing Inc. of Montana.
Garisch, Dawn. Babyshoes. 2004. (ENG.). 288p. (J). pap. 9.99 *(978-0-689-83778-4(X))* Simon & Schuster, Ltd. GBR. Dist: Simon & Schuster, Inc.
Harris, Godfrey. Credit the Crocodile: A Tale of Survival in the African Wild. 2017. (ENG., Illus.). 260p. (YA). *(978-0-935047-89-9(1))* Americas Group, The.
Heale, Jay. African Animal Tales. 2004. (Illus.). 96p. *(978-1-86872-704-9(1))* Penguin Random House South Africa.
Henty, George. With Buller in Natal: Or a Born Leader. l.t. ed. 2007. (ENG.). 324p. pap. 24.99 *(978-1-4264-9739-1(3))* Creative Media Partners, LLC.
Hichens, Joanne. Stained. 2008. (Cutting Edge Ser.). (ENG.). 200p. pap. *(978-1-84167-715-6(9))* Ransom Publishing Ltd.
Hildahl, Violetta R. Peacock of Taj Mahal. 2011. 28p. (gr. -1). pap. 13.59 *(978-1-4520-0259-0(2))* AuthorHouse.
Irwin, Bindi & Black, Jess. Rescue! Bindi Wildlife Adventures. 2011. (Bindi's Wildlife Adventures Ser.: 2). (ENG.). 112p. (J). (gr. 3-6). pap. 8.99 *(978-1-4022-5517-5(9),* Sourcebooks Jabberwocky) Sourcebooks, Inc.
Jacobs, Jaco. A Good Day for Climbing Trees. Geldenhuys, Kobus, tr. 2018. (ENG., Illus.). 160p. (J). pap. 11.99 *(978-1-78607-317-4(X),* 178607317X, Rock the Boat) Oneworld Pubns. GBR. Dist: Grantham Bk. Services.
Javaherbin, Mina. Goal! Ford, A. G., illus. 2012. (ENG.). 40p. (J). (gr. 1-4). pap. 8.99 *(978-0-7636-5822-9(7))* Candlewick Pr.
Kent, Trilby. Stones for My Father. 176p. (YA). (gr. 7). 2018. pap. 9.99 *(978-0-7352-6270-6(5))* 2011. 19.95 *(978-1-77049-252-3(6))* Tundra Bks. CAN. (Tundra Bks.). Dist: Penguin Random Hse. LLC.
Kramer, Berri, photos by & text. Mbali: A story from South Africa. Kramer, Berri, text. 2nd ed. 2006. (Illus.). (J). per. *(978-0-9706901-1-1(8))* Rotaplast Pr.
Lea, Jenny & Lea, Henry, illus. Malela: A Childhood Long Ago. 2014. 42p. (J). *(978-1-4931-4231-6(3))* Xlibris Corp.
MacGregor, Joanne. Fault Lines. 2016. (ENG.). 272p. pap. 11.25 *(978-1-4853-0422-7(9))* Protea Boekhuis ZAF. Dist: Casemate Pubs. & Bk. Distributors, LLC.
Marsh, Carole. The Rip-Roaring Mystery on the African Safari. 2009. (Around the World in 80 Mysteries Ser.). (J). (gr. 2-9). lib. bdg. 18.99 *(978-0-635-06835-4(4));* 13. (ENG., Illus.). 123p. (gr. 4-6). 22.44 *(978-0-635-06829-3(X))* Gallopade International.
Mbuyazi, Phiwayinkosi G. The Wiby Kids - How It All Began. 2011. 204p. pap. 12.99 *(978-1-61667-337-6(0))* Raider Publishing International.
McMiller, Theresa R. Bessie Goes All over the World. 2012. 28p. pap. 24.95 *(978-1-4626-9464-8(0))* America Star Bks.
Methods, Bryan. Lessons from Underground. 2018. (Master Diplexito & Mr. Scant Ser.). (ENG., Illus.). 272p. (J). (gr. 5-8). 17.99 *(978-1-5124-0581-1(7),* 199f9813-c1d3-4053-bc16-93f1f1c16c72, Carolrhoda Bks.) Lerner Publishing Group.
Moodley, Ermila. Path to My African Eyes. 2007. 173p. (J). (gr. 6-13). per. 15.95 *(978-1-933491-09-7(4))* Just Us Bks., Inc.
Naidoo, Beverley. Journey to Jo'burg: A South African Story. Velasquez, Eric, illus. 2019. (ENG.). 112p. (J). (gr. 3-7). pap. 7.99 *(978-0-06-288179-3(5),* HarperCollins) HarperCollins Pubs.
—No Turning Back. 2017. 208p. (YA). (gr. 9). pap. 13.95 *(978-0-14-136890-0(X))* Penguin Bks., Ltd. GBR. Dist: Independent Pubs. Group.
—Out of Bounds: Seven Stories of Conflict & Hope. 2008. (ENG.). 208p. (J). (gr. 5). pap. 7.99 *(978-0-06-050801-2(9),* HarperCollins) HarperCollins Pubs.
The Other Side of the Invisible Fence. 2006. (YA). per. 9.95 *(978-0-9787783-8-5(3))* Romain, Trevor Co., The.
Patel, T. M. The Immigrant: Stargazer. 2013. 290p. (J). pap. *(978-1-78299-385-8(1))* FeedARead.com.
Pegler, Robin. Having Fun Together: A Collection of Children's Stories. 2010. 514p. pap. 23.95 *(978-1-60693-817-1(7),* Eloquent Bks.) Strategic Book Publishing & Rights Agency (SBPRA).
Pennels, Geraldine. The School Shenanigans of Amy & Nontand. 2009. 152p. pap. 33.50 *(978-1-60860-496-8(9),* Strategic Bk. Publishing) Strategic Book Publishing & Rights Agency (SBPRA).
Penning, L. & Nelson, Marietjie. The Hero of Spionkop. 2006. (Illus.). 166p. (YA). pap. *(978-1-894666-92-3(5))* Inheritance Pubns.
—The Lion of Modderspruit. 2004. (Illus.). 142p. (YA). pap. *(978-1-894666-91-6(7))* Inheritance Pubns.
Powers, J. L. This Thing Called the Future, 1 vol. 2011. (ENG.). 208p. (YA). (gr. 9-12). 16.95 *(978-1-933693-95-8(9),* 23353382, Cinco Puntos Press) Lee & Low Bks., Inc.
Raina, Arushi. When Morning Comes, 1 vol. 2017. (ENG.). 232p. (YA). (gr. 8-12). 16.95 *(978-1-896580-69-2(6));* (Illus.). pap. 10.95 *(978-1-926890-14-2(0))* Tradewind Bks. CAN. Dist: Orca Bk. Pubs. USA.
Reid, Mayne. Young Yagers or A Narrative of Hunting A. 2006. (Illus.). pap. 31.95 *(978-1-4286-2205-0(5))* Kessinger Publishing, LLC.
Remza, Freddie. Ride the Wave. 2011. 272p. pap. 16.95 *(978-1-4327-6642-9(2))* Outskirts Pr., Inc.
Shepherd, J. A., illus. Old Hendrik's Tales - 13 South African Folk Tales. 2013. 198p. pap. *(978-1-909302-15-0(5))* Abela Publishing.
Smith, E. The Adventures of Sir Ambrose Elephant: A Visit to the City. Apa, Ivy Marie, illus. 2012. 19p. pap. 9.95 *(978-1-4691-8378-7(1))* Xlibris Corp.
Smith, Pieter Ernst. A Donkey Is Not Stupid, a Donkey Can Think. Shirley-Smith, Sanette, illus. 2011. 24p. pap. 11.50 *(978-1-61204-039-4(X),* Eloquent Bks.) Strategic Book Publishing & Rights Agency (SBPRA).
St. John, Lauren. The Elephant's Tale. 2011. (Legend of the Animal Healer Ser.). (ENG.). (J). 208p. (gr. 4-6). 21.19 *(978-0-8037-3291-9(0));* 240p. (gr. 3-7). 6.99 *(978-0-14-241879-6(X),* Puffin Books) Penguin Young Readers Group.
—The White Giraffe. 2008. (ENG., Illus.). 208p. (J). (gr. 2-5). 8.99 *(978-0-14-241152-0(3),* Puffin Books) Penguin Young Readers Group.
Swedeen, Staci. Tombi-Ende & the Frog: A Fairy Tale from Southern Africa. 2006. (J). pap. *(978-1-4108-7151-0(7))* Benchmark Education Co.
Tlali, Miriam. Between Two Worlds. 2004. (ENG.). 222p. reprint ed. pap. 20.25 *(978-1-55111-605-1(7),* P173893) Broadview Pr. CAN. Dist: Eurospan Group, The.
True, J. J. Billy Brite: Africa & Beyond. 2011. (Illus.). 112p. pap. 14.03 *(978-1-4567-7281-9(3))* AuthorHouse.
Tutu, Desmond. Desmond & the Very Mean Word. Ford, A. G., illus. 2012. (ENG.). 32p. (J). (gr. 1-4). 17.99 *(978-0-7636-5229-6(6))* Candlewick Pr.
Uncle Markie. Piglettè & Bobo in Sud Africa. 2003. (YA). ring bd. 9.95 *(978-1-933129-15-0(8))* Studio 403.
—Piglettè & Bobo on Safari. 2003. (YA). ring bd. 9.95 *(978-1-933129-16-7(6))* Studio 403.
van de Ruit, John. Spud. 2005. 300p. pap. *(978-0-14-302484-2(1))* Penguin Publishing Group.
—Spud. 2008. (ENG.). 336p. (YA). (gr. 7-18). 9.99 *(978-1-59514-187-3(1),* Razorbill) Penguin Young Readers Group.
—Spud-The Madness Continues. 2009. (ENG.). 352p. (YA). (gr. 7-18). 9.99 *(978-1-59514-245-0(2),* Razorbill) Penguin Young Readers Group.
Waddilove, Guy. Dancing with the Dragleon. 2013. (Illus.). 222p. pap. *(978-1-78036-196-3(3))* Peach Publishing.
Williams, Geoffrey T. The Great White Red Alert. Artful Doodlers, illus. Campbell, Tom, photos by. 2008. (Save Our Seas Adventure Bks.). (ENG.). 64p. (J). (gr. 4-7). 8.95 *(978-0-9800444-0-9(5))* Save Our Seas, Ltd.
Wood, Amanda. Rainbow. 2009. 208p. pap. 13.50 *(978-1-60860-343-5(1),* Strategic Bk. Publishing) Strategic Book Publishing & Rights Agency (SBPRA).
Wulf, Linda Press. The Night of the Burning. 2007. 224p. pap. *(978-0-7475-9051-4(6))* Bloomsbury Publishing Plc.

SOUTH AFRICA—RACE RELATIONS

Cruden, Alexander & Bryfonski, Dedria, eds. The End of Apartheid, 1 vol. 2009. (Perspectives on Modern World History Ser.). (ENG., Illus.). 224p. (gr. 10-12). 49.43 *(978-0-7377-4557-3(6),* 87c45ee3-8c1a-4c39-8b27-7ceb29c6c8c7, Greenhaven Publishing) Greenhaven Publishing LLC.
Finlayson, Reggie. Nelson Mandela. 2005. (Just the Facts Biographies Ser.). (ENG., Illus.). 112p. (gr. 5-12). lib. bdg. 27.93 *(978-0-8225-2644-5(1),* Lerner Pubns.) Lerner Publishing Group.
Glaser, Jason. The End of Apartheid, 1 vol. 2018. (History Just Before You Were Born Ser.). (ENG.). 32p. (J). (gr. 4-5). 28.27 *(978-1-5382-3026-8(7),* ca0fbf99-9636-4934-8636-5dd3787b25a1) Stevens, Gareth Publishing LLLP.
Graham Gaines Rodriguez, Ann. Nelson Mandela & the End of Apartheid, 1 vol. 2015. (People & Events That Changed the World Ser.). (ENG., Illus.). 128p. (J). (gr. 7-8). 38.93 *(978-0-7660-7300-5(9),* a27ea591-870c-45ea-8587-10e2d5002b79) Enslow Publishing, LLC.
Koosman, Melissa. The Fall of Apartheid in South Africa. 2009. (Monumental Milestones Ser.). 48p. (YA). (gr. 4-7). lib. bdg. 29.95 *(978-1-58415-736-6(4))* Mitchell Lane Pubs.
Magoon, Kekla. Nelson Mandela: A Leader for Freedom, 1 vol. 2008. (Essential Lives Set 2 Ser.). (ENG., Illus.). 112p. (YA). (gr. 6-12). lib. bdg. 41.36 *(978-1-60453-038-4(3),* 6657, Essential Library) ABDO Publishing Co.
Malaspina, Ann. Nelson Mandela: Fighting to Dismantle Apartheid, 1 vol. 2017. (Rebels with a Cause Ser.). (ENG.). 128p. (YA). (gr. 8-8). lib. bdg. 38.93 *(978-0-7660-8517-6(1),* 0b4489f0-6cb5-4f8d-9265-b48760337c0e) Enslow Publishing, LLC.
Martin, Michael J. Apartheid in South Africa, 1 vol. 2006. (World History Ser.). (ENG., Illus.). 104p. (gr. 7-7). lib. bdg. 41.53 *(978-1-59018-696-1(6),* f95c59bf-e3a1-4a94-b590-8ba1c4839e56, Lucent Pr.) Greenhaven Publishing LLC.
World Book, Inc. Staff, contrib. by. South Africa's Anti-Apartheid Movement. 2010. (Illus.). 62p. (J). *(978-0-7166-1507-1(X))* World Bk., Inc.

SOUTH AMERICA

Aloian, Molly & Kalman, Bobbie. Explore South America, 1 vol. rev. ed. 2007. (Explore the Continents Ser.). (ENG., Illus.). 32p. (J). (gr. 2-3). pap. *(978-0-7787-3090-3(5))* Crabtree Publishing Co.
Banting, Erinn. South America. (Illus.). 32p. (J). 2016. *(978-1-4896-5728-2(2))* 2005. (gr. -1-7). pap. 9.95 *(978-1-59036-329-4(9))* 2005. (gr. 4-6). lib. bdg. 26.00 *(978-1-59036-322-5(1))* Weigl Pubs., Inc.
Benchmark Education Co., LLC. Ancient Cultures of South America. 2014. (PRIME Ser.). (J). (gr. 6-8). pap. *(978-1-4509-9485-9(7))* Benchmark Education Co.
—The Geography of North & South America. 2014. (PRIME Ser.). (J). (gr. 6-8). pap. *(978-1-4509-9505-4(5))* Benchmark Education Co.
Branden, Claire Vanden. South America. 2018. (Continents (Cody Koala) Ser.). (ENG., Illus.). 24p. (J). (gr. k-3). lib. bdg. 31.36 *(978-1-5321-6175-9(1),* 30133, Pop! Cody Koala) Pop!
Carr, Joaquin. Habitats of South America: Set Of 6. 2010. (Navigators Ser.). (J). pap. 44.00 net. *(978-1-4108-5073-7(0))* Benchmark Education Co.
Delacre, Lulu. Olinguito, from a to Z! �Olinguito, de la a a la Z!. 1 vol. 2016. (SPA., Illus.). 40p. (J). (gr. k-6). 20.95 *(978-0-89239-327-5(0),* leelowcbp) Lee & Low Bks., Inc.
Donaldson, Madeline. South America. 2005. (Pull Ahead Books — Continents Ser.). (Illus.). 32p. (J). (gr. k-3). (ENG.). pap. 7.99 *(978-0-8225-2495-3(3),* ccc653df-9c21-43ce-b3a8-d25e51cf219d); lib. bdg. 22.60 *(978-0-8225-4723-5(6))* Lerner Publishing Group.
Encyclopaedia Britannica, Inc. Staff, compiled by. My First Britannica: The Americas. 2008. (gr. 7-12). *(978-1-59339-409-7(8))* Encyclopaedia Britannica, Inc.
Encyclopaedia Britannica Publishers, Inc. Staff. Views of the Americas. 2003. (Britannica Learning Library). (Illus.). 14.95 *(978-1-59339-012-9(2))* Encyclopaedia Britannica, Inc.
Esquivel, Gloria Susana. South America (a True Book: the Seven Continents) (Library Edition) 2019. (True Book (Relaunch) Ser.). (ENG., Illus.). 48p. (J). (gr. 3-5). lib. bdg. 31.00 *(978-0-531-12810-7(5),* Children's Pr.) Scholastic Library Publishing.
Gibson, Karen Bush. South America. rev. ed. 2016. (Seven Continents Ser.). (ENG.). 24p. (J). (gr. 2-4). pap. 7.45 *(978-1-5157-4217-3(2),* 133980, Capstone Pr.) Capstone.
—Spotlight on South America. 2016. (Spotlight on the Continents Ser.). (ENG.). 24p. (J). (gr. 1-3). pap. 7.99 *(978-1-5157-6148-8(7),* 134872, Capstone Pr.) Capstone.
Henderson, James D., ed. Discovering South America, 13 vols., Set. (Illus.). 64p. (YA). (gr. 5-18). lib. bdg. *(978-1-59084-284-3(7))* Mason Crest.
Hernández, Roger E. South America: Facts & Figures. (South America Today Ser.). 64p. (gr. 4-7). 2009. (Illus.). (J). 21.95 *(978-1-4222-0640-9(8))* 2007. (YA). pap. 9.95 *(978-1-4222-0707-9(2))* Mason Crest.
Hirschmann, Kristine. Geography of South America: Set Of 6. 2011. (Navigators Ser.). (J). pap. 50.00 net. *(978-1-4108-6264-8(X))* Benchmark Education Co.
Hovanec, Erin M. An Online Visit to South America. 2009. (Internet Field Trips Ser.). 24p. (gr. 3-3). 45.00 *(978-1-61513-607-0(X),* PowerKids Pr.) Rosen Publishing Group, Inc., The.
Koponen, Libby. South America. (True Book (Relaunch) Ser.). (ENG., Illus.). 48p. (J). 2009. (gr. 3-5). pap. 6.95 *(978-0-531-21831-0(7),* Children's Pr.) 2008. (gr. 2-5). 29.00 *(978-0-531-16869-1(7))* Scholastic Library Publishing.

S

Marsh, Carole. South America: A Continent of Countries of Amazing Proportions! 2009. (It's Your World Ser.). 48p. (J). (gr. 2-9). pap. 7.99 *(978-0-635-06822-4(2))* Gallopade International.

McIntosh, Kenneth & McIntosh, Marsha. The Flight from Turmoil. 2007. (Hispanic Heritage Ser.). (Illus.). 112p. (YA). lib. bdg. 22.95 *(978-1-59084-930-9(2))* Mason Crest.

National Geographic Learning. Reading Expeditions (World Studies: World Regions): South America: Geography & Environments. 2007. (ENG., Illus.). 64p. (J). pap. 27.95 *(978-0-7922-4382-3(X))* CENGAGE Learning.

Proudfit, Benjamin. The Pan-American Highway, 1 vol. 2016. (Road Trip: Famous Routes Ser.). (ENG., Illus.). 24p. (J). (gr. 2-3). 25.27 *(978-1-4824-4669-2(3),* 4b03770c-476b-44ef-bca0-90ea4c6c5e26) Stevens, Gareth Publishing LLLP.

Sayre, April Pulley. South America, Surprise! 2003. 32p. (J). (gr. 2-5). pap. 7.95 *(978-0-7613-1989-4(1));* (Illus.). lib. bdg. 21.90 *(978-0-7613-2123-1(3))* Lerner Publishing Group. (Millbrook Pr.).

Scoones, Simon. South America, 1 vol. 2005. (Continents of the World Ser.). (ENG., Illus.). 64p. (gr. 5-8). pap. 15.05 *(978-0-8368-5922-5(7),* 9a0e6236-9651-4803-add0-c7df5af6d9ad, Gareth Stevens Secondary Library) Stevens, Gareth Publishing LLLP.

Tarbox, A. D. A Rainforest Food Chain: Nature's Bounty. 2nd ed. 2015. (Odysseys in Nature Ser.). (ENG., Illus.). 80p. (J). (gr. 7-10). *(978-1-60818-543-6(5),* 20977, Creative Education) Creative Co., The.

The Library of the Western Hemisphere: Set 2, 8 vols. 2004. (Library of the Western Hemisphere Ser.). (ENG.). (J). (gr. 4-4). 105.08 *(978-1-4042-2964-8(7),* fde7c6d7-7fa8-46df-ab9a-e8c45db0f4ec) Rosen Publishing Group, Inc., The.

The Libray of the Western Hemisphere: Set 1, 8 vols. 2004. (Library of the Western Hemisphere Ser.). (ENG.). (J). (gr. 4-4). 105.08 *(978-1-4042-2963-1(9),* 9e4d3bdc-ec44-4267-baa8-a92197cb5390) Rosen Publishing Group, Inc., The.

Vanden Branden, Claire. South America. 2019. (Continents Ser.). (ENG., Illus.). 24p. (J). (gr. 1-1). pap. 8.95 *(978-1-64185-546-4(0),* 1641855460) North Star Editions.

Vierow, Wendy. South America, 1 vol. 2003. (Atlas of the Seven Continents Ser.). (ENG., Illus.). 24p. (J). (gr. 3-3). lib. bdg. 26.27 *(978-0-8239-6693-6(3),* 17a0eddd-ccba-4463-a533-d28a1eb65503) Rosen Publishing Group, Inc., The.

Williams, Heather DiLorenzo & Rylands, Warren. South America. 2019. (Illus.). 24p. (J). *(978-1-4896-8327-4(5),* AV2 by Weigl) Weigl Pubs., Inc.

Woods, Michael & Woods, Mary B. Seven Natural Wonders of Central & South America. 2009. (Seven Wonders Ser.). (Illus.). 80p. (YA). (gr. 5-9). lib. bdg. 33.26 *(978-0-8225-9070-5(0))* Twenty First Century Bks.

SOUTH AMERICA—DESCRIPTION AND TRAVEL

Harasymiw, Mark. Mapping South America. 2013. (Mapping the World Ser.). 24p. (J). (gr. 2-5). pap. 48.90 *(978-1-4339-9121-9(7))* Stevens, Gareth Publishing LLLP.

Harasymiw, Mark J. Mapping South America, 1 vol. 2013. (Mapping the World Ser.). (ENG.). 24p. (J). (gr. 2-3). 25.27 *(978-1-4339-9119-6(5),* 0e05b24b-0fe3-49af-809b-641d35fa9c9c); (Illus.). pap. 9.15 *(978-1-4339-9120-2(9),* 08e69961-234e-4664-abf6-71bec3beaa74) Stevens, Gareth Publishing LLLP.

Lee, James, ed. South America in Charts & Graphs. 2004. (YA). cd-rom 25.00 *(978-0-9749905-0-7(7))* JLM CD-ROM Publishing Co.

Rockett, Paul. Mapping South America. 2016. (Mapping the Continents Ser.). (Illus.). 32p. (J). (gr. 3-6). *(978-0-7787-2617-3(7))* Crabtree Publishing Co.

Vierow, Wendy. South America. 2009. (Atlas of the Seven Continents Ser.). 24p. (gr. 3-3). 42.50 *(978-1-61511-484-9(X),* PowerKids Pr.) Rosen Publishing Group, Inc., The.

Zronik, John Paul & Zronik, John. Francisco Pizarro: Journeys Through Peru & South America, 1 vol. 2005. (In the Footsteps of Explorers Ser.). (ENG., Illus.). 32p. (J). (gr. -1-9). pap. *(978-0-7787-2447-6(6))* Crabtree Publishing Co.

SOUTH AMERICA—DISCOVERY AND EXPLORATION

see America—Discovery and Exploration

SOUTH AMERICA—FICTION

Appleton, Victor. Tom Swift in Captivity or A Daring Escap. 2006. pap. *(978-1-4065-0914-4(0))* Dodo Pr.

Baldini-Chavez, Cecilia. The Silver-Golden Feather Secreted at el Dorado, 1 vol. 2009. 92p. pap. 19.95 *(978-1-60813-664-3(7))* America Star Bks.

Ballantyne, R. M. The Lighthouse. 2006. pap. *(978-1-4065-0531-3(5))* Dodo Pr.

Breckenridge, Gerald. The Radio Boys Search for the Inca's Treasure. 2011. 282p. pap. *(978-1-907256-99-8(7))* Abela Publishing.

C.M.M. A Life of Many Forms. 2012. 52p. pap. 16.95 *(978-1-62709-318-7(4))* America Star Bks.

Day, Williamson. The Pretorius Stories. 2011. 96p. pap. 9.99 *(978-1-4634-7430-0(X))* AuthorHouse.

De Matos, Isabel Freire. Una Carta de Monica. Saez, Sofia, illus. 2004. (SPA.). 32p. (gr. k-3). pap. 8.95 *(978-1-57581-574-9(5))* Santillana USA Publishing Co., Inc.

Doyle, Arthur Conan. The Lost World, 1 vol. 2009. (Real Reads Ser.). (ENG., Illus.). 64p. (J). (gr. 5-5). pap. 14.55 *(978-1-60754-395-4(8),* 49a60ade-2b66-439a-88f7-600b078eef55); lib. bdg. 33.93 *(978-1-60754-394-7(X),* 222eeae2-6661-460a-8103-8cfc7225ef8f) Rosen Publishing Group, Inc., The. (Windmill Bks.).

Finger, Charles J. Tales from Silver Lands. Honore, Paul, illus. 2017. (ENG.). 256p. pap. 12.99 *(978-0-486-82093-4(9),* 820939) Dover Pubns., Inc.

Fraggalosch, Audrey. Land of the Wild Llama: A Story of the Patagonian Andes. Denman, Michael & Huiett, William J., illus. 2005. (Wild Habitats Ser.). (ENG.). (J). (gr. 1-4). 32p. 19.95 *(978-1-931465-83-0(5),* BC7022); 36p. 15.95 *(978-1-931465-81-6(9),* B7022) Soundprints.

—Land of the Wild Llama: A Story of the Patagonian Andes, Including 10" Toy. Denman, Michael & Huiett, William J., illus. 2005. (Wild Habitats Ser.). (ENG.). 36p. (J). (gr. 1-4). 17.95 *(978-1-931465-86-1(X),* PS7022) Soundprints.

Garis, Howard R. The Curlytops & Their Pets. 2009. 120p. 22.95 *(978-1-60664-609-0(5));* pap. 10.95 *(978-1-60664-341-9(X))* Rodgers, Alan Bks.

Graham-Morgan, Ivet. Peter the Parrot Misses Home: Misses Home. 2011. 16p. 9.98 *(978-1-4343-9791-1(2))* AuthorHouse.

Hayes, Celeste. Cacao & the Jaded Orb: A Sphinx & Trevi Adventure. 2011. (Illus.). 62p. (J). pap. 22.95 *(978-0-9785695-2-5(0))* Adam's Creations Publishing, LLC.

Hergé. The Broken Ear. (Illus.). 62p. (J). 24.95 *(978-0-8288-5086-5(0))* French & European Pubns., Inc.

—L' Oreille Cassee.Tr. of Broken Ear. (FRE., Illus.). 62p. (J). 19.95 *(978-0-8288-5054-4(2))* French & European Pubns., Inc.

Jones, Allan Frewin. Legend of the Anaconda King. 2006. 186p. (J). pap. *(978-0-439-85670-6(1))* Scholastic, Inc.

Kavanagh, Shannon & McKay, Jeffrey. Safari Jeff & Shannon Visit South America. 2005. (Great Green Adventure Ser.). (Illus.). 46p. 14.95 *(978-0-9734409-1-1(0))* Croctalk Publishing CAN. Dist: Hushion Hse. Publishing, Ltd.

King Sr., Billy. The Story. 2010. 73p. pap. 11.95 *(978-0-557-25606-8(2))* Lulu Pr., Inc.

Krebs, Laurie. We're Sailing to Galapagos. Restelli, Grazia, illus. 2007. (ENG.). 32p. (J). (gr. k-5). pap. 9.99 *(978-1-84686-102-4(0))* Barefoot Bks., Inc.

Marsh, Carole. The Mystery in the Amazon Rainforest: South America. 2009. (Around the World in 80 Mysteries Ser.). (Illus.). 131p. (J). lib. bdg. 18.99 *(978-0-635-07017-3(0),* Marsh, Carole Mysteries) Gallopade International.

Mattassi, Ezio. Pepito the Penguin, 1 vol. Mattassi, Ezio, illus. 2009. (Illus.). 15p. pap. 24.95 *(978-1-61582-731-2(5))* PublishAmerica, Inc.

Mitton, Tony. Rainforest Adventure. 2015. (Amazing Animals Ser.). (ENG., Illus.). 24p. (J). (gr. -1-1). pap. 6.99 *(978-0-7534-7227-9(9),* 900149031, Kingfisher) Roaring Brook Pr.

Myers, Bill. My Life As Crocodile Junk Food, 1 vol. 2020. (Incredible Worlds of Wally Mcdoogle Ser.: 4). (ENG., Illus.). 144p. (J). pap. 8.99 *(978-0-7852-3122-6(6),* Tommy Nelson) Nelson, Thomas Inc.

Oldfield, Matt. Suarez: From the Playground to the Pitch. 2018. (Ultimate Football Heroes Ser.). (ENG., Illus.). 176p. (J). (gr. 2-7). pap. 9.99 *(978-1-78606-806-4(0))* Blake, John Publishing, Ltd. GBR. Dist: Independent Pubs. Group.

O'Neill, Katrina. Key of the Mayan Kingdom. 2007. (Illus.). 52p. (J). pap. *(978-1-4207-0717-5(5))* Sundance/Newbridge Educational Publishing.

Paterson, John B., Jr. & Paterson, John B., Sr. Roberto's Trip to the Top. Alarcao, Renato, illus. 2009. (ENG.). 40p. (J). (gr. -1-3). 16.99 *(978-0-7636-2708-9(9))* Candlewick Pr.

Paulding, Steve. The Wonderful Adventures of Bradley the Bat. Schmidt, Caleb & Schmidt, Carter, illus. 2013. 70p. pap. 18.95 *(978-0-615-74591-6(1))* Slow on the Draw Productions.

Peet, Mal. The Penalty. 2016. (ENG.). 272p. (J). (gr. 7). pap. 8.99 *(978-0-7636-8747-2(2))* Candlewick Pr.

Pierson, Rich. Adventures of Fred the Donkey. 2012. 48p. pap. 21.99 *(978-1-4691-7343-6(3))* Xlibris Corp.

Rimes, Raleigh. Dinosaurology. 2013. (Ologies Ser.). (ENG.). 30p. (J). (gr. 3-7). 21.99 *(978-0-7636-6739-9(0))* Candlewick Pr.

Rockwood, Roy. Jack North's Treasure Hunt: Or, Daring Adventures in South America. 2007. (ENG.). 142p. pap. 18.99 *(978-1-4264-2654-4(2));* 146p. pap. 19.99 *(978-1-4264-2711-4(5))* Creative Media Partners, LLC.

Sherrow, Victoria. Galapagos Fur Seal. 2012. (ENG., Illus.). 24p. (J). pap. 3.95 *(978-1-60727-725-5(5))* Soundprints.

VanArsdale, Anthony, illus. The Khipu & the Final Key. 2017. (Boxcar Children Great Adventure Ser.: 5). (ENG.). 144p. (J). (gr. 2-5). 12.99 *(978-0-8075-0681-3(8),* 119189763, Random Hse. Bks. for Young Readers) Random Hse. Children's Bks.

Varon, Sara. New Shoes. 2018. (ENG., Illus.). 208p. (J). 19.99 *(978-1-59643-920-7(3),* 900121340, First Second Bks.) Roaring Brook Pr.

Wagner, Lori. Gateway of the Sun. 2007. 120p. pap. 9.95 *(978-0-9798627-2-4(8))* Affirming Faith.

Watson, Myrtle. Kite Flying in the Village: A Guyanese Girl's Story. 2011. 20p. 10.03 *(978-1-4520-8632-3(X))* AuthorHouse.

Winter, Barbara. The Golden Scarab. 2007. (Illus.). 48p. (J). lib. bdg. 15.00 *(978-1-4242-1617-8(6))* Dingles & Co.

SOUTH AMERICA—HISTORY

Adamson, Thomas K. Learning about South America. 2015. (Searchlight Books (tm) — Do You Know the Continents? Ser.). (ENG., Illus.). 40p. (J). (gr. 3-5). 30.65 *(978-1-4677-8021-6(9),* 4a335caf-f478-4912-a956-12bc9739ffc8, Lerner Pubns.) Lerner Publishing Group.

Aloian, Molly & Kalman, Bobbie. Explora America del Sur. 2007. (Explora Los Continentes Ser.). (SPA & ENG., Illus.). 32p. (J). (gr. 3-7). pap. *(978-0-7787-8301-5(4))* Crabtree Publishing Co.

Banting, Erinn. South America. 2012. (J). *(978-1-61913-453-9(5));* pap. *(978-1-61913-454-6(3))* Weigl Pubs., Inc.

Barnett, Tracy. Immigration from South America. 2005. (Changing Face of North America Ser.). (Illus.). 112p. (J). lib. bdg. 24.95 *(978-1-59084-687-2(7))* Mason Crest.

Boyd, Judy. South America, Vol. 10. 2016. (Social Progress & Sustainability Ser.). (Illus.). 80p. (J). (gr. 7). 24.95 *(978-1-4222-3499-0(1))* Mason Crest.

Brown, Risa. South America, 1 vol. 2013. (Continents Ser.). (ENG.). 48p. (J). (gr. 4-8). lib. bdg. 35.64 *(978-1-61783-934-4(5),* 4570) ABDO Publishing Co.

Colleen Madonna Flood Williams. Suriname, Vol. 13. Henderson, James D., ed. 2015. (Discovering South America: History, Politics, & Culture Ser.). (Illus.). 64p. (J). (gr. 7). lib. bdg. 22.95 *(978-1-4222-3304-7(9))* Mason Crest.

Cooke, Tim. The Exploration of South America, 1 vol. 2013. (Explorers Discovering the World Ser.). (ENG., Illus.). 48p. (gr. 4-5). 34.60 *(978-1-4339-8627-7(2),* 60b42b24-2a02-4dd9-82f3-d7f5fa41c730); pap. 15.05 *(978-1-4339-8628-4(0),* 80049545-939c-4041-993a-73ed06c844d4) Stevens, Gareth Publishing LLLP. (Gareth Stevens Learning Library).

Cruz, Bárbara C. Simón Bolívar: Fighting for Latin American Liberation, 1 vol. 2017. (Rebels with a Cause Ser.). (ENG.). 128p. (gr. 8-8). lib. bdg. 38.93 *(978-0-7660-8952-5(5),* 839e486e-f0eb-4d0b-b7d9-eee63be0ea5b) Enslow Publishing, LLC.

DePietro, Frank. South American Immigrants. 2013. (Illus.). 64p. (J). pap. *(978-1-4222-2346-8(9))* Mason Crest.

—South American Immigrants. Limón, José E., ed. 2012. (Hispanic Americans: Major Minority Ser.). (Illus.). 64p. (J). (gr. 4). 22.95 *(978-1-4222-2329-1(9))* Mason Crest.

Doane, Beth. From the Jungle: Stories & Original Art from Children Living in Rainforests. 2012. 40p. pap. 15.95 *(978-1-4525-6090-8(0))* Balboa Pr.

Ganeri, Anita. Introducing South America, 1 vol. 2013. (Introducing Continents Ser.). (ENG.). 32p. (J). (gr. 1-3). pap. 8.95 *(978-1-4329-8052-8(1),* 123215, Heinemann) Capstone.

Hernandez, Roger E. South America: Facts & Figures, Vol. 13. Henderson, James D., ed. 2015. (Discovering South America: History, Politics, & Culture Ser.). (Illus.). 64p. (J). (gr. 7). lib. bdg. 22.95 *(978-1-4222-3303-0(0))* Mason Crest.

Hirsch, Rebecca. South America (Rookie Read-About Geography: Continents) 2012. (Rookie Read-About Geography Ser.). (ENG., Illus.). 32p. (J). (gr. 1-2). pap. 5.95 *(978-0-531-29281-5(9),* Children's Pr.) Scholastic Library Publishing.

Hirschmann, Kristine. Geography of South America: Text Pairs. 2008. (Bridges/Navigators Ser.). (J). (gr. 6). 81.00 *(978-1-4108-8440-4(6))* Benchmark Education Co.

In North & South America. (J). (gr. 5). 3.80 *(978-0-8374-1454-6(7),* 405) Weekly Reader Corp.

Juarez, Christine. South America: A 4D Book. 2018. (Investigating Continents Ser.). (ENG., Illus.). 24p. (J). (gr. 1-3). lib. bdg. 27.99 *(978-1-5435-3182-4(2),* 138811, Capstone Pr.) Capstone.

Kalman, Bobbie. L'Amérique du Sud. 2012. (FRE.). 32p. (J). pap. 9.95 *(978-2-89579-461-5(8))* Bayard Canada CAN. Dist: Crabtree Publishing Co.

Kennedy, Mike & Stewart, Mark. Soccer in South America. 2011. (Smart about Soccer Ser.). 24p. (J). (gr. k-3). lib. bdg. 22.60 *(978-1-59953-446-6(0))* Norwood Hse. Pr.

Lindeen, Mary. South America. 2018. (Continents of the World Ser.). (ENG.). 24p. (J). (gr. -1-2). lib. bdg. 32.79 *(978-1-5038-2499-7(3),* 212323) Child's World, Inc, The.

Lynette, Rachel. South American Tapirs. 2013. (Jungle Babies of the Amazon Rain Forest Ser.). (Illus.). 24p. (J). (gr. -1-3). lib. bdg. 25.65 *(978-1-61772-759-7(8))* Bearport Publishing Co., Inc.

McClish, Bruce. New World Continents & Land Bridges: North & South America. rev. ed. 2016. (Continents Ser.). (ENG.). 32p. (J). (gr. 4-6). pap. 8.99 *(978-1-4846-3639-8(2),* 134035, Heinemann) Capstone.

National Geographic Learning. Reading Expeditions (World Studies: World Cultures): South America: People & Places. 2007. (ENG.). 64p. pap. 27.95 *(978-0-7922-4383-0(8))* National Geographic School Publishing, Inc.

Oachs, Emily Rose. South America. 2016. (Discover the Continents Ser.). (ENG., Illus.). 24p. (J). (gr. k-3). pap. 7.99 *(978-1-61891-260-2(7),* 12044); lib. bdg. 26.95 *(978-1-62617-329-3(X))* Bellwether Media. (Blastoff! Readers).

Roumanis, Alexis. Exploring Continents: South America. 2015. 24p. pap. 12.95 *(978-1-4896-3049-0(X))* Weigl Pubs., Inc.

—South America. 2014. (Illus.). 24p. (J). *(978-1-4896-3046-9(5))* Weigl Pubs., Inc.

Sirota, Lyn A. South America. 2014. (J). *(978-1-4896-0958-8(X))* Weigl Pubs., Inc.

South America: Regions of the World. 2003. spiral bd. 16.95 *(978-1-56004-158-0(7))* Social Studies Schl. Service.

Tylers, Michael. Predators of South America & Antarctica. 2015. (J). lib. bdg. *(978-1-62713-550-4(2))* Cavendish Square Publishing LLC.

Waxman, Malcolm & Porter, Malcolm. Atlas of South America & Antarctica, 1 vol. 2010. (Atlases of the World Ser.). (ENG., Illus.). 48p. (YA). (gr. 5-5). 34.47 *(978-1-4358-8459-5(0),* 507e3b28-3aa1-479a-b0ab-d765ce01bedb, Rosen Reference) Rosen Publishing Group, Inc., The.

World Book, Inc. Staff, contrib. by. Endangered Animals of the World. 2014. (J). *(978-0-7166-5620-3(5))* World Bk., Inc.

Zocchi, Judith Mazzeo. In South Africa. Brodie, Neale, illus. 2008. (J). *(978-1-59646-642-5(1));* pap. *(978-1-59646-643-2(X))* Dingles & Co.

SOUTH ATLANTIC STATES

see Atlantic States

SOUTH CAROLINA

Columbia in Pictures. 2004. (Illus.). lib. bdg. 27.93 *(978-0-8225-1996-6(8))* Lerner Publishing Group.

Crane, Carol. Net Numbers: A South Carolina Numbers Book. Palmer, Gary, illus. 2006. (America by the Numbers Ser.). (ENG.). 40p. (J). (gr. 1-3). 17.95 *(978-1-58536-202-8(6),* 202040) Sleeping Bear Pr.

Dykstra, Mary. South Carolina, 1 vol. 2005. (Portraits of the States Ser.). (ENG., Illus.). 32p. (gr. 3-5). pap. 11.50 *(978-0-8368-4694-2(X),* c67e2c67-4fc1-418f-888f-eeab9cb23eca); lib. bdg. 28.67 *(978-0-8368-4675-1(3),* 910ca9ee-81e3-4a3f-81bc-19d7f6107c6b) Stevens, Gareth Publishing LLLP. (Gareth Stevens Learning Library).

Fredeen, Charles. South Carolina. 2012. (J). lib. bdg. 25.26 *(978-0-7613-4556-5(6),* Lerner Pubns.) Lerner Publishing Group.

Hess, Debra. South Carolina, 1 vol. Santoro, Christopher, illus. 2004. (It's My State! (First Edition)(r) Ser.). (ENG.). 80p. (gr. 4-4). lib. bdg. 34.07 *(978-0-7614-1690-6(0),* 663cc77f-89b5-448f-94bc-c164584df453) Cavendish Square Publishing LLC.

Hoffman, Nancy & Hart, Joyce. South Carolina, 1 vol. 2nd rev. ed. 2010. (Celebrate the States (Second Edition) Ser.). (ENG.). 144p. (gr. 6-6). 39.79 *(978-0-7614-4034-5(8),* 4a376f40-a461-41dc-ac49-0c6e10a4b7c2) Cavendish Square Publishing LLC.

Kovacik, Charles F. & Steinke, Theodore R., eds. South Carolina: An Atlas. 2005. (Illus.). 40p. (YA). 9.95 *(978-0-9768247-0-1(1))* South Carolina Geographic Alliance.

Marsh, Carole. South Carolina Current Events Projects: 30 Cool, Activities, Crafts, Experiments & More for Kids to Do to Learn about Your State! 2003. (South Carolina Experience Ser.). 32p. (gr. k-8). pap. 5.95 *(978-0-635-02059-8(9),* Marsh, Carole Bks.) Gallopade International.

—South Carolina Geography Projects: 30 Cool, Activities, Crafts, Experiments & More for Kids to Do to Learn about Your State! 2003. (South Carolina Experience Ser.). 32p. (gr. k-5). pap. 5.95 *(978-0-635-01859-5(4),* Marsh, Carole Bks.) Gallopade International.

—South Carolina Government Projects: 30 Cool, Activities, Crafts, Experiments & More for Kids to Do to Learn about Your State! 2003. (South Carolina Experience Ser.). 32p. (gr. k-5). pap. 5.95 *(978-0-635-01959-2(0),* Marsh, Carole Bks.) Gallopade International.

—South Carolina People Projects: 30 Cool, Activities, Crafts, Experiments & More for Kids to Do to Learn about Your State! 2003. (South Carolina Experience Ser.). 32p. (gr. k-5). pap. 5.95 *(978-0-635-02009-3(2),* Marsh, Carole Bks.) Gallopade International.

—South Carolina Symbols & Facts Projects: 30 Cool, Activities, Crafts, Experiments & More for Kids to Do to Learn about Your State! 2003. (South Carolina Experience Ser.). 32p. (gr. k-5). pap. 5.95 *(978-0-635-01909-7(4),* Marsh, Carole Bks.) Gallopade International.

Murray, Julie. South Carolina, 1 vol. 2006. (United States Ser.). (ENG., Illus.). 32p. (gr. 2-4). 27.07 *(978-1-59197-699-8(5),* Buddy Bks.) ABDO Publishing Co.

O'Neill, Elizabeth. Alfred Visits South Carolina. 2007. (Illus.). 24p. (J). (gr. -1-3). pap. 12.00 *(978-0-9790240-5-4(6))* Funny Bone Bks.

Parker, Bridget. South Carolina. 2016. (States Ser.). (ENG., Illus.). 32p. (J). (gr. 3-6). lib. bdg. 27.99 *(978-1-5157-0428-7(9),* 132039, Capstone Pr.) Capstone.

Parker, Janice. South Carolina: The Palmetto State. 2016. (Illus.). 48p. (J). *(978-1-5105-2093-6(7))* SmartBook Media, Inc.

Schuetz, Kristin. South Carolina. 2013. (Exploring the States Ser.). (ENG., Illus.). 32p. (J). (gr. 3-7). lib. bdg. 27.95 *(978-1-62617-040-7(1),* Blastoff! Readers) Bellwether Media.

South Carolina. 2003. (Switched on Schoolhouse Ser.). cd-rom 24.95 *(978-0-7403-0664-8(2))* Alpha Omega Pubns., Inc.

Stroud, Cynthia. Carolina Children: The Sandhills. 2007. (Illus.). 30p. pap. 17.99 *(978-0-9794580-0-2(5))* Carolina Children.

Sullivan, E. J. S Is for South Carolina. Eldredge, Ernie, illus. 2007. (State Alphabet Bks.). 20p. *(978-1-58173-626-7(6))* Sweetwater Pr.

Way, Jennifer. South Carolina. 2009. (Bilingual Library of the United States of America Ser.). (ENG & SPA.). 32p. (gr. 2-2). 47.90 *(978-1-60853-385-5(9),* Editorial Buenas Letras) Rosen Publishing Group, Inc., The.

—South Carolina/Carolina del Sur, 1 vol. Brusca, Maria Cristina, tr. 2005. (Bilingual Library of the United States of America Ser.: Set 2). (ENG & SPA., Illus.). 32p. (J). (gr. 2-2). lib. bdg. 28.93 *(978-1-4042-3106-1(4),* 6061a60f-507d-47a6-b697-196d4b28434f) Rosen Publishing Group, Inc., The.

Weatherly, Myra S. From Sea to Shining Sea: South Carolina. 2008. (ENG.). 80p. (J). pap. 7.95 *(978-0-531-20813-7(3),* Children's Pr.) Scholastic Library Publishing.

Weintraub, A. How to Draw South Carolina's Sights & Symbols. 2009. (Kid's Guide to Drawing America Ser.). 32p. (gr. k-k). 50.50 *(978-1-61511-094-0(1),* PowerKids Pr.) Rosen Publishing Group, Inc., The.

SOUTH CAROLINA—FICTION

Alexander, Scott L. My Dog Named Whatever. 2007. 68p. per. 10.95 *(978-1-4327-1572-4(0))* Outskirts Pr., Inc.

Anderson, T. Neill. Horrors of History: Ocean of Fire: The Burning of Columbia 1865. 2014. (Horrors of History Ser.). (Illus.). 176p. (J). (gr. 5). 16.95 *(978-1-58089-516-3(6))* Charlesbridge Publishing, Inc.

Arrington, Linda. Ugly Trees. Arrington, Linda, photos by. 2012. (Illus.). 24p. pap. 24.95 *(978-1-4626-8925-5(6))* America Star Bks.

Asim, Jabari. The Road to Freedom: A Story of the Reconstruction. 2004. 131p. (J). lib. bdg. 16.92 *(978-1-4242-0765-7(7))* Fitzgerald Bks.

Baisley, Tilda & Wyrick, Monica. Crabbing: A Lowcountry Family Tradition. 2016. (Young Palmetto Bks.). (ENG., Illus.). 32p. 18.99 *(978-1-61117-640-7(9),* P496413) Univ. of South Carolina Pr.

Black, Chuck. Rise of the Fallen: Wars of the Realm, Book 2. 2015. (Wars of the Realm Ser.: 2). (ENG.). 320p. (YA). (gr. 7). pap. 13.00 *(978-1-60142-504-1(X),* Multnomah Bks.) Crown Publishing Group, The.

Blue, Rose & Naden, Corinne. Ron's Big Mission. Tate, Don, illus. 2009. 32p. (J). (gr. 1-3). 18.99 *(978-0-525-47849-2(3),* Dutton Books for Young Readers) Penguin Young Readers Group.

Boone, Martina. Illusion. 2016. (Heirs of Watson Island Ser.). (ENG., Illus.). 480p. (YA). (gr. 9). 17.99 *(978-1-4814-1128-8(4),* Simon Pulse) Simon Pulse.

Brown, Monica. Waiting for the Biblioburro. Parra, John, illus. 2011. (ENG.). 32p. (J). (gr. k-3). 18.99 *(978-1-58246-353-7(0),* Tricycle Pr.) Random Hse. Children's Bks.

Carmen & Thane Johnson. Dogs Don't Wear Underwear. Bianca & Annie West, illus. 2009. 20p. pap. 12.99 *(978-1-4389-4128-8(5))* AuthorHouse.

Charley's Columbia Backyard. 2006. (J). 14.95 *(978-0-9793808-0-8(4))* Backyard Ambassador Reader Publishing Co.

Clamp, Janet. The Adventures of Lilly the Bloodhound & Her Friends: Lilly Gets a New Home & Family. 2013. 20p. pap. 17.99 *(978-1-4817-0057-3(X))* AuthorHouse.

Crouse, Donna J. The Ruby Ring: The Whispering Cove Kids Club. 2005. 114p. pap. 12.99 *(978-0-9765339-0-0(1))* Crouse, Donna J.

Cullen, Lisa Anne. Three Wild Pigs: A Carolina Folktale. 2018. (Young Palmetto Bks.). (ENG., Illus.). 32p. 18.99 *(978-1-61117-944-6(0),* P599432) Univ. of South Carolina Pr.

Curtis, Christopher Paul. The Journey of Little Charlie. 2018. (ENG.). 256p. (J). (gr. 4-7). 19.99 *(978-0-545-15666-0(1),* Scholastic Pr.) Scholastic, Inc.

—The Journey of Little Charlie (Scholastic Gold) 2021. (ENG.). 272p. (J). (gr. 3-7). pap. 8.99 *(978-0-545-15667-7(X))* Scholastic, Inc.

Curtis, Christopher Paul & Vega, Eida de la. El Viaje de Charlie. 2019. (SPA.). (J). 12.99 *(978-1-63245-697-7(4))* Lectorum Pubns., Inc.

Davies, Anna. Wrecked. 2013. (ENG., Illus.). 336p. (YA). (gr. 9). pap. 9.99 *(978-1-4424-3279-6(9),* Simon & Schuster Bks. For Young Readers) Simon & Schuster Bks. For Young Readers.

Draper, Sharon M. Copper Sun. 2014. (ENG.). 336p. (YA). 14.24 *(978-1-63245-110-1(7))* Lectorum Pubns., Inc.

—Copper Sun. 2011. 11.04 *(978-0-7848-3373-5(7),* Everbind) Marco Bk. Co.

—Copper Sun. (ENG.). (YA). 2008. 336p. (gr. 9-12). pap. 12.99 *(978-1-4169-5348-7(5))* 2006. 320p. (gr. 8-18). 19.99 *(978-0-689-82181-3(6))* Simon & Schuster Children's Publishing. (Atheneum Bks. for Young Readers).

—Copper Sun. Lt. ed. 2006. 358p. (YA). (gr. 8-18). 22.95 *(978-0-7862-8948-6(1))* Thorndike Pr.

—Copper Sun. 2008. 316p. lib. bdg. 22.10 *(978-1-4177-9702-8(9))* Turtleback.

Echols, Jennifer. Such a Rush. 2012. (ENG.). 336p. (YA). (gr. 7). pap. 20.99 *(978-1-4516-5802-6(8),* Gallery Bks.) Gallery Bks.

Ellison, Joy D. Carol & Connie. 2008. 28p. per. 24.95 *(978-1-4241-9276-2(5))* America Star Bks.

Flood, Pansie Hart. Secret Holes. Marshall, Felicia, illus. 2004. 128p. (J). (gr. 3-6). 15.95 *(978-0-87614-923-2(9),* Carolrhoda Bks.) Lerner Publishing Group.

—Sometimey Friend. Marshall, Felicia, illus. 2005. 124p. (J). (gr. 3-7). 15.95 *(978-1-57505-866-5(9))* Lerner Publishing Group.

—Sylvia & Miz Lula Maye. Marshall, Felicia, illus. 2003. (Middle Grade Fiction Ser.). 120p. (J). (gr. 3-6). 15.95 *(978-0-87614-204-2(8),* Carolrhoda Bks.) Lerner Publishing Group.

Garcia, Kami & Stohl, Margaret. Beautiful Chaos. 2012. (Beautiful Creatures Ser.: 3). (ENG.). 528p. (YA). (gr. 7-17). pap. 16.99 *(978-0-316-12351-8(X))* Little, Brown Bks. for Young Readers.

—Beautiful Creatures. 2010. (Beautiful Creatures Ser.: 1). (ENG.). 592p. (YA). (gr. 7-17). pap. 16.99 *(978-0-316-07703-3(8))* Little, Brown Bks. for Young Readers.

Garcia, Kami & Stohl, Margaret. Beautiful Creatures. 2010. (Beautiful Creatures Ser.: 1). (YA). lib. bdg. 23.30 *(978-0-606-26699-4(2))* Turtleback.

—Beautiful Darkness. 2010. (Beautiful Creatures Ser.: Bk. 2). (YA). 59.99 *(978-1-60941-036-0(X))* Findaway World, LLC.

—Beautiful Darkness. 2010. (Beautiful Creatures Ser.: Bk. 2). 512p. pap. 17.99 *(978-0-316-09861-8(2))* Little, Brown Bks. for Young Readers.

Garcia, Kami & Stohl, Margaret. Beautiful Darkness. 2011. (Beautiful Creatures Ser.: 2). (ENG.). 528p. (YA). (gr. 7-17). pap. 15.99 *(978-0-316-07704-0(6))* Little, Brown Bks. for Young Readers.

Garcia, Kami & Stohl, Margaret. Beautiful Darkness. 2011. (Beautiful Creatures Ser.: 2). (YA). lib. bdg. 24.50 *(978-0-606-26700-7(X))* Turtleback.

—Beautiful Redemption. 2012. (Beautiful Creatures Ser.: Bk. 4). (ENG.). 576p. (YA). (gr. 7-17). pap. 9.99 *(978-0-316-22519-9(3))* Little, Brown Bks. for Young Readers.

Garcia, Kami & Stohl, Margaret. Beautiful Redemption. 2013. (Beautiful Creatures Ser.: 4). (ENG.). 496p. (YA). (gr. 7-17). pap. 15.99 *(978-0-316-12356-3(0))* Little, Brown Bks. for Young Readers.

Garcia, Kami & Stohl, Margaret. Beautiful Redemption. 2013. (Beautiful Creatures Ser.: 4). (YA). lib. bdg. 24.50 *(978-0-606-32282-9(5))* Turtleback.

Hampton, Patrick. Down by the Mulberry Tree, 1 vol. 2009. 15p. pap. 24.95 *(978-1-60703-672-2(X))* America Star Bks.

Haskins, James. The March on Washington. 2004. (Illus.). 192p. (J). (gr. 5-18). pap. 10.95 *(978-0-940975-93-4(9),* Sankofa Bks.) Just Us Bks., Inc.

Hay, Angela. Grace S Incredible! Unforgettable! Summer! 2012. 38p. pap. 19.99 *(978-1-62419-562-4(8))* Salem Author Services.

Himes, Rachel. Princess & the Peas. Himes, Rachel, illus. 2017. (Illus.). 32p. (J). (gr. k-3). 16.99 *(978-1-58089-718-1(5))* Charlesbridge Publishing, Inc.

Howard, Greg. Social Intercourse. 2018. (ENG., Illus.). 320p. (YA). (gr. 9). 18.99 *(978-1-4814-9781-7(2),* Simon & Schuster Bks. For Young Readers) Simon & Schuster Bks. For Young Readers.

Ingle, Sheila. Courageous Kate: A Daughter of the American Revolution. 2006. (ENG.). 130p. pap. 11.95 *(978-1-891885-52-5(9))* Hub City Pr.

Jacobs, Lily. The Littlest Bunny in South Carolina: An Easter Adventure. Dunn, Robert, illus. 2015. (Littlest Bunny Ser.). (ENG.). 32p. (J). (gr. -1-3). 9.99 *(978-1-4926-1195-0(6),* Hometown World) Sourcebooks, Inc.

James, Eric. Santa's Sleigh Is on Its Way to South Carolina: A Christmas Adventure. Dunn, Robert, illus. 2015. (Santa's Sleigh Is on Its Way Ser.). (ENG.). 32p. (J). (gr. k-2). 12.99 *(978-1-4926-2757-9(7),* Hometown World) Sourcebooks, Inc.

—The Spooky Express South Carolina. Piwowarski, Marcin, illus. 2017. (Spooky Express Ser.). (ENG.). 32p. (J). (gr. k-6). 9.99 *(978-1-4926-5398-1(5),* Hometown World) Sourcebooks, Inc.

—Tiny the South Carolina Easter Bunny. 2018. (Tiny the Easter Bunny Ser.). (ENG.). 40p. (J). (gr. k-3). 9.99 *(978-1-4926-5963-1(0),* Hometown World) Sourcebooks, Inc.

Johnson, Varian. The Parker Inheritance (Scholastic Gold) (ENG.). (J). (gr. 3-7). 2019. 368p. pap. 8.99 *(978-0-545-95278-1(6))* 2018. 352p. 18.99 *(978-0-545-94617-9(4))* Scholastic, Inc. (Levine, Arthur A. Bks.).

Jones, Joyce Elaine. For Such a Journey. 2005. (J). 5.99 *(978-0-9766559-0-9(X))* Treorca Pr.

Joyce, S. E. Silas Saves the Friendly Crab: A Low Country Tale. 2011. (Illus.). 28p. (J). (gr. 1-2). pap. 14.99 *(978-1-4634-0285-3(6))* AuthorHouse.

Karr, Kathleen. Worlds Apart, 0 vols. unabr. ed. 2013. (ENG.). 208p. (J). (gr. 4-6). pap. 9.99 *(978-1-4778-1710-0(7),* 9781477817100, Two Lions) Amazon Publishing.

Long, Melinda & Wyrick, Monica. Art Smart, Science Detective: The Case of the Sliding Spaceship. 2018. (Young Palmetto Bks.). (ENG., Illus.). 64p. pap. 12.99 *(978-1-61117-935-4(1),* P599510) Univ. of South Carolina Pr.

Luddy, Karon. Spelldown: The Big-Time Dreams of a Small-Town Word Whiz. 2008. (Mix Ser.). (ENG.). 224p. (J). (gr. 4-8). pap. 10.99 *(978-1-4169-5452-1(X),* Simon & Schuster/Paula Wiseman Bks.) Simon & Schuster/Paula Wiseman Bks.

McKinney-Whitaker, Courtney. The Last Sister: A Novel. 2014. (Young Palmetto Bks.). (ENG.). 232p. 41.99 *(978-1-61117-429-8(5),* P235023) Univ. of South Carolina Pr.

Monroe, Mary Alice. The Islanders. (Islanders Ser.: 1). (ENG.). (J). (gr. 3-7). 2022. 320p. pap. 8.99 *(978-1-5344-2728-0(7))* 2021. (Illus.). 304p. 17.99 *(978-1-5344-2727-3(9))* Simon & Schuster Children's Publishing. (Aladdin).

Monroe, Mary Alice. Search for Treasure. (Islanders Ser.: 2). (ENG.). (J). (gr. 3-7). 2023. 288p. pap. 8.99 *(978-1-5344-2731-0(7))* 2022. (Illus.). 272p. 17.99 *(978-1-5344-2730-3(9))* Simon & Schuster Children's Publishing. (Aladdin).

Mosier, Pamela. Elizabeth, the Eastern Gray Squirrel. 2008. 44p. pap. 18.95 *(978-1-4357-5407-2(7))* Lulu Pr., Inc.

Moulder, Holly. Eyes of the Calusa. 2007. 111p. (J). pap. 8.95 *(978-0-9790405-0-4(7))* White Pelican Pr.

Mullinax, Jerry. Encoree. 2009. (YA). pap. *(978-0-88092-646-1(5))* Royal Fireworks Publishing Co.

Muschla, Gary Robert. The Sword & the Cross. 2009. (YA). pap. *(978-0-88092-472-6(1))* Royal Fireworks Publishing Co.

Myers, Walter Dean. The Glory Field. 2008. (ENG.). 400p. (J). (gr. 7). pap. 9.99 *(978-0-545-05575-8(X),* Scholastic Paperbacks) Scholastic, Inc.

Myracle, Lauren. Thirteen Plus One. 2011. (Winnie Years Ser.: 5). (ENG.). 304p. (J). (gr. 5-18). 8.99 *(978-0-14-241901-4(X),* Puffin Books) Penguin Young Readers Group.

O'Connor, Barbara. On the Road to Mr. Mineo's. 2014. (ENG., Illus.). 208p. (J). (gr. 3-7). pap. 10.99 *(978-1-250-03993-4(2),* 900123696) Square Fish.

—The Small Adventure of Popeye & Elvis. 2011. (ENG.). 176p. (J). (gr. 3-7). pap. 8.99 *(978-0-312-65932-5(6),* 900070518) Square Fish.

Parsons, Karyn. How High the Moon. 2019. (ENG.). 320p. (J). (gr. 3-7). 16.99 *(978-0-316-48400-8(8))* Little, Brown Bks. for Young Readers.

Reichs, Kathy. Code: A Virals Novel. 2013. (Virals Ser.: 3). (ENG.). 432p. (J). (gr. 5). pap. 11.99 *(978-1-59514-572-7(9),* Puffin Books) Penguin Young Readers Group.

—Virals. 2014. lthr. 79.00 *(978-1-62715-582-3(1))* Leatherbound Bestsellers.

—Virals. 2011. (Virals Ser.: 1). (ENG.). 480p. (J). (gr. 5-18). 11.99 *(978-1-59514-426-3(9),* Puffin Books) Penguin Young Readers Group.

—Virals. 2011. 20.00 *(978-1-61383-226-4(5))* Perfection Learning Corp.

Reichs, Kathy & Reichs, Brendan. Code. 2013. (Virals Ser.: 3). lib. bdg. 19.65 *(978-0-606-32140-2(3))* Turtleback.

—Virals. 2011. (Virals Ser.: 1). lib. bdg. 20.85 *(978-0-606-23069-8(6))* Turtleback.

Rinaldi, Ann. Cast Two Shadows: The American Revolution in the South. 2004. (Great Episodes Ser.). (ENG., Illus.). 304p. (YA). (gr. 7-8). pap. 7.99 *(978-0-15-205077-1(9),* 1195334, Clarion Bks.) HarperCollins Pubs.

Rubin, Sarah. Someday Dancer. 2012. (J). *(978-0-545-39379-9(5))* Scholastic, Inc.

Seabrooke, Brenda. The Bridges of Summer. 2007. (ENG.). 160p. per. 12.95 *(978-0-595-43720-7(6),* Backinprint.com) iUniverse, Inc.

Skelton, Vonda Skinner. Bitsy & the Mystery at Hilton Head Island. 2008. 192p. (J). (gr. 4-7). pap. 8.95 *(978-1-57072-325-4(7))* Overmountain Pr.

Sully, Katherine. Night-Night South Carolina. Poole, Helen, illus. 2017. (Night-Night Ser.). (ENG.). 20p. (J). (gr. -1-1). bds. 9.99 *(978-1-4926-4779-9(9),* 9781492647799, Hometown World) Sourcebooks, Inc.

Teaster, Gerald Fred. Spirit up the People: Four Days to the Cowpens. 2006. (Illus.). 236p. per. 12.95 *(978-0-9744556-2-4(8))* Junior History Pr.

Todd, Anne. Teddy Powers: The Stone Keepers. 2012. 394p. pap. 13.99 *(978-1-938993-00-8(4))* Keogh, Anne.

Victoria & the Baby Tree. 2005. pap. 14.95 *(978-1-59526-525-8(2))* Aeon Publishing Inc.

Vrabel, Beth. A Blind Guide to Stinkville. (ENG.). (J). (gr. 2-7). 2016. 280p. pap. 7.99 *(978-1-5107-0382-7(9))* 2015. 264p. 16.99 *(978-1-63450-157-6(8))* Skyhorse Publishing Co., Inc. (Sky Pony Pr.).

Woods, Brenda. The Unsung Hero of Birdsong, USA. 2019. 208p. (J). (gr. 5). 16.99 *(978-1-5247-3709-2(7),* Nancy Paulsen Books) Penguin Young Readers Group.

SOUTH CAROLINA—HISTORY

Antle, Bhagavan "Doc". Bubbles: An Elephant's Story. 2018. (ENG., Illus.). 32p. (J). 14.99 *(978-1-68383-196-9(9),* Earth Aware Editions) Insight Editions.

Bodie, Idella. The Wizard Owl. 2003. (Illus.). 86p. (J). pap. 6.95 *(978-0-87844-167-9(0))* Sandlapper Publishing Co., Inc.

Boehm Jerome, Kate. Columbia & the State of South Carolina: Cool Stuff Every Kid Should Know. 2011. (Arcadia Kids Ser.). (ENG., Illus.). 48p. (J). (gr. 3-6). pap. 11.99 *(978-1-4396-0090-0(2))* Arcadia Publishing.

Born, Mark Alan. TIDELOG 2003 Graphic Almanac for Southeastern States: Covering the Entire South Carolina Coast, North to Wilmington NC, & South to Brunswick, Ga. Escher, M. C., illus. 2004. 144p. spiral bd. 14.95 *(978-1-933120-05-8(3))* Pacific Pubs.

Brett, Jeannie & Crane, Carol. Little South Carolina. 2011. (Little State Ser.). (ENG., Illus.). 20p. (J). (gr. -1-1). bds. 9.95 *(978-1-58536-486-2(X),* 202249) Sleeping Bear Pr.

Cunningham, Kevin. The South Carolina Colony. 2011. (True Book-the Thirteen Colonies Ser.). (ENG., Illus.). 48p. (J). lib. bdg. 29.00 *(978-0-531-25398-4(8));* (gr. 3-5). pap. 6.95 *(978-0-531-26611-3(7))* Scholastic Library Publishing. (Children's Pr.).

Gamble, Adam, et al. Good Night South Carolina. 2014. (Good Night Our World Ser.). (ENG.). 20p. (J). (— 1). bds. 9.95 *(978-1-60219-190-7(5))* Good Night Bks.

Gilbert, Sara. South Carolina. 2009. (This Land Called America Ser.). 32p. (YA). (gr. 3-6). 19.95 *(978-1-58341-793-5(1))* Creative Co., The.

Hamilton, John. South Carolina, 1 vol. 2016. (United States of America Ser.). (ENG., Illus.). 48p. (J). (gr. 5-9). 34.21 *(978-1-68078-343-8(2),* 21671, Abdo & Daughters) ABDO Publishing Co.

Harmon, Daniel E. Lower Atlantic: Florida, Georgia, South Carolina, Vol. 19. 2015. (Let's Explore the States Ser.). (Illus.). 64p. (J). (gr. 5). 23.95 *(978-1-4222-3325-2(1))* Mason Crest.

—South Carolina: Past & Present, 1 vol. 2010. (United States: Past & Present Ser.). (ENG.). 48p. (YA). (gr. 5-5). pap. 12.75 *(978-1-4358-9522-5(3),* 49695bc8-fcfc-4bc2-817e-fb4e9cc991fb); lib. bdg. 34.47 *(978-1-4358-9495-2(2),* 0c4a2347-7ded-4560-8e58-c819deece380) Rosen Publishing Group, Inc., The. (Rosen Reference).

Hasan, Heather. A Primary Source History of the Colony of South Carolina. (Primary Sources of the Thirteen Colonies & the Lost Colony Ser.). 64p. 2009. (gr. 5-8). 58.50 *(978-1-60851-889-0(2))* 2005. (ENG., Illus.). (gr. 4-6). per. 12.95 *(978-1-4042-0667-0(1),* 241c6f63-021e-435c-a04f-2865c60a6dfb) 2005. (ENG., Illus.). (YA). (gr. 4-6). lib. bdg. 37.13 *(978-1-4042-0436-2(9),* c8e07ee5-8d84-463c-abca-d9721f2dae98) Rosen Publishing Group, Inc., The.

Hawk, Fran. The Story of the H. L. Hunley & Queenie's Coin. Nance, Dan, illus. 2004. (ENG.). 40p. (J). (gr. 1-4). 16.95 *(978-1-58536-218-9(2),* 202048) Sleeping Bear Pr.

Hess, Debra & McGeveran, William. South Carolina, 1 vol. 2nd rev. ed. 2012. (It's My State! (Second Edition)(r) Ser.). (ENG.). 80p. (gr. 4-4). 34.07 *(978-1-60870-526-9(9),* ca7038f3-66c0-4c9f-8d3e-ae4fd3934439) Cavendish Square Publishing LLC.

Hess, Debra, et al. South Carolina, 1 vol. 3rd rev. ed. 2015. (It's My State! (Third Edition)(r) Ser.). (ENG., Illus.). 80p. (gr. 4-4). 35.93 *(978-1-62713-175-9(2),* ed210098-26d2-44ee-b368-1c9d3f353b4f) Cavendish Square Publishing LLC.

Jerome, Kate B. Lucky to Live in South Carolina. 2017. (Arcadia Kids Ser.). (ENG., Illus.). 32p. (J). 16.99 *(978-0-7385-2794-9(7))* Arcadia Publishing.

—The Wise Animal Handbook South Carolina. 2017. (Arcadia Kids Ser.). (ENG., Illus.). 32p. (J). 16.99 *(978-0-7385-2841-0(2))* Arcadia Publishing.

Kauffman, Scott. Francis Marion: Swamp Fox of South Carolina. 2006. (Forgotten Heroes of the American Revolution Ser.). (Illus.). 88p. (YA). (gr. 5-11). lib. bdg. 23.95 *(978-1-59556-014-8(9))* OTTN Publishing.

Kelly Edwards Elementary School (Williston, S.C.) Staff, contrib. by. The ABCs of Williston History. 2007. (J). pap. *(978-0-87844-185-3(9))* Sandlapper Publishing Co., Inc.

Krebs, Laurie. A Day in the Life of a Colonial Indigo Planter. (Library of Living & Working in Colonial Times Ser.). 24p. (gr. 3-3). 2009. 42.50 *(978-1-60853-732-7(3),* PowerKids Pr.) 2003. (ENG., Illus.). (J). lib. bdg. 26.27 *(978-0-8239-6229-7(6),* 4fbf7f8a-1b2e-4518-ba28-11908a0c5cf6) Rosen Publishing Group, Inc., The.

Marsh, Carole. Exploring South Carolina Through Project-Based Learning: Geography, History, Government, Economics & More. 2016. (South Carolina Experience Ser.). (ENG.). (J). pap. 9.99 *(978-0-635-12364-0(9))* Gallopade International.

—South Carolina History Projects: 30 Cool, Activities, Crafts, Experiments & More for Kids to Do to Learn about Your State! 2003. (South Carolina Experience Ser.). 32p. (gr. k-5). pap. 5.95 *(978-0-635-01809-0(8),* Marsh, Carole Bks.) Gallopade International.

Maynard, Charles W. Fort Sumter. 2009. (Famous Forts Throughout American History Ser.). 24p. (gr. 3-4). 42.50 *(978-1-61512-520-3(5),* PowerKids Pr.) Rosen Publishing Group, Inc., The.

Mis, Melody S. The Colony of South Carolina: A Primary Source History, 1 vol. 2006. (Primary Source Library of the Thirteen Colonies & the Lost Colony Ser.). (ENG., Illus.). 24p. (J). (gr. 3-4). lib. bdg. 26.27 *(978-1-4042-3438-3(1),* cb43e2a8-0e50-4781-8b73-ca7c9bfc885d, PowerKids Pr.) Rosen Publishing Group, Inc., The.

Parker, Janice. South Carolina. 2011. (Guide to American States Ser.). (Illus.). 48p. (YA). (gr. 3-6). 29.99 *(978-1-61690-813-3(0));* (J). *(978-1-61690-489-0(5))* Weigl Pubs., Inc.

—South Carolina: The Palmetto State. 2016. (J). *(978-1-4896-4938-6(7))* Weigl Pubs., Inc.

Pohl, Amelia J. Savannah River. 2009. (J). *(978-1-935077-58-9(9));* pap. *(978-1-935077-65-7(1))* State Standards Publishing, LLC.

Somervill, Barbara A. America the Beautiful: South Carolina (Revised Edition) 2014. (America the Beautiful, Third Ser. (Revised Edition) Ser.). (ENG.). 144p. (J). lib. bdg. 40.00 *(978-0-531-28292-2(9))* Scholastic Library Publishing.

—South Carolina (a True Book: My United States) (Library Edition) 2018. (True Book (Relaunch) Ser.). (ENG., Illus.). 48p. (J). (gr. 3-5). 31.00 *(978-0-531-23579-9(3),* Children's Pr.) Scholastic Library Publishing.

Vierow, Wendy. The Assault on Fort Wagner: Black Union Soldiers Make a Stand in South Carolina Battle. 2009. (Headlines from History Ser.). 24p. (gr. 3-3). 42.50 *(978-1-61513-240-9(6),* PowerKids Pr.) Rosen Publishing Group, Inc., The.

Walker, Sally M. Shipwreck Search: Discovery of the H. L. Hunley. Verstraete, Elaine, illus. (On My Own Science Ser.). (ENG.). 48p. (gr. 2-4). 2007. (J). per. 7.99 *(978-0-8225-6449-2(1),* c091eaf0-8595-4cc4-81dd-f04fe879a8c7, First Avenue Editions) 2006. lib. bdg. 25.26 *(978-1-57505-878-8(2),* Millbrook Pr.) Lerner Publishing Group.

Winter, Jeanette. Biblioburro: A True Story from Colombia. Winter, Jeanette, illus. 2010. (ENG., Illus.). 32p. (J). (gr. 1-4). 18.99 *(978-1-4169-9778-8(4),* Beach Lane Bks.) Beach Lane Bks.

Yasuda, Anita. South Carolina: The Palmetto State. 2012. (J). *(978-1-61913-401-0(2));* pap. *(978-1-61913-402-7(0))* Weigl Pubs., Inc.

Zepke, Terrance. Pirates of the Carolinas for Kids. 2009. (Carolinas for Kids Ser.). (ENG.). 72p. (J). (gr. -1-12). pap. 12.95 *(978-1-56164-459-9(5))* Pineapple Pr., Inc.

SOUTH DAKOTA

Bjorklund, Ruth. South Dakota, 1 vol. Santoro, Christopher, illus. 2005. (It's My State! (First Edition)(r) Ser.). (ENG.). 80p. (gr. 4-4). lib. bdg. 34.07 *(978-0-7614-1531-2(9),* c6e5b1d0-577e-44df-9c95-48ee1df5971c) Cavendish Square Publishing LLC.

—South Dakota, 1 vol. 2nd rev. ed. 2013. (It's My State! (Second Edition)(r) Ser.). (ENG.). 80p. (gr. 4-4). pap. 18.64 *(978-1-62712-097-5(1),* 7589cc71-d6a1-41bf-ac34-670215508637) Cavendish Square Publishing LLC.

Brown, Jonatha A. South Dakota, 1 vol. 2006. (Portraits of the States Ser.). (ENG.). 32p. (gr. 3-5). pap. 11.50 *(978-0-8368-4725-3(3),* e6a107a0-4031-48f8-83e5-a07ab62a9906); (Illus.). lib. bdg. 28.67 *(978-0-8368-4708-6(3),* ea481aed-6429-472a-b406-4406c7a00641) Stevens, Gareth Publishing LLLP. (Gareth Stevens Learning Library).

Brown, Vanessa. South Dakota/Dakota del Sur, 1 vol. Brusca, Maria Cristina, tr. 2005. (Bilingual Library of the United States of America Ser.: Set 2). (ENG & SPA., Illus.). 32p. (J). (gr. 2-2). lib. bdg. 28.93 *(978-1-4042-3107-8(2),* 1886b16e-9d2d-46cf-8123-4b645d64af80) Rosen Publishing Group, Inc., The.

Bryan, Dale-Marie. South Dakota. 2006. (Rookie Read-About Geography Ser.). (ENG., Illus.). 32p. (J). (gr. 1-2). lib. bdg. 20.50 *(978-0-516-25444-9(8))* Scholastic Library Publishing.

Glaser, Jason. South Dakota: The Mount Rushmore State, 1 vol. 2010. (Our Amazing States Ser.). (ENG.). 24p. (J). (gr. 3-3). pap. 9.25 *(978-1-4358-9774-8(9),* 94cd3f16-2fb9-480f-9540-cb6fce9b7430); lib. bdg. 26.27 *(978-1-4358-9343-6(3),* 3b0bb895-8c73-47ca-9712-e91f6d42b691) Rosen Publishing Group, Inc., The. (PowerKids Pr.).

Hamilton, John. South Dakota, 1 vol. 2016. (United States of America Ser.). (ENG., Illus.). 48p. (J). (gr. 5-9). 34.21 *(978-1-68078-344-5(0),* 21673, Abdo & Daughters) ABDO Publishing Co.

Heinrichs, Ann. South Dakota. Kania, Matt, illus. 2017. (U. S. A. Travel Guides). (ENG.). 40p. (J). (gr. 2-5). lib. bdg. 38.50 *(978-1-5038-1981-8(7),* 211618) Child's World, Inc, The.

Hirschmann, Kris. South Dakota, 1 vol. 2003. (World Almanac(r) Library of the States Ser.). (ENG., Illus.). 48p. (gr. 4-6). pap. 15.05 *(978-0-8368-5331-5(8),* d0bd9141-6a33-47a5-bd40-0823d09d1aa4); lib. bdg. 33.67 *(978-0-8368-5160-1(9),* 8d1b954c-6921-45c5-8711-701fbcc1bdf9) Stevens, Gareth Publishing LLLP. (Gareth Stevens Learning Library).

Marsh, Carole. South Dakota Current Events Projects: 30 Cool, Activities, Crafts, Experiments & More for Kids to Do to Learn about Your State! 2003. (South Dakota Experience Ser.). 32p. (gr. k-8). pap. 5.95 *(978-0-635-02060-4(2),* Marsh, Carole Bks.) Gallopade International.

—South Dakota Geography Projects: 30 Cool, Activities, Crafts, Experiments & More for Kids to Do to Learn about Your State! 2003. (South Dakota Experience Ser.). 32p. (gr. k-5). pap. 5.95 *(978-0-635-01875-5(6),* Marsh, Carole Bks.) Gallopade International.

—South Dakota Government Projects: 30 Cool, Activities, Crafts, Experiments & More for Kids to Do to Learn about Your State! 2003. (South Dakota Experience Ser.). 32p. (gr. k-5). pap. 5.95 *(978-0-635-01960-8(4),* Marsh, Carole Bks.) Gallopade International.

—South Dakota People Projects: 30 Cool, Activities, Crafts, Experiments & More for Kids to Do to Learn about Your State! 2003. (South Dakota Experience Ser.). 32p. (gr. k-5). pap. 5.95 *(978-0-635-02010-9(6),* Marsh, Carole Bks.) Gallopade International.

—South Dakota Symbols & Facts Projects: 30 Cool, Activities, Crafts, Experiments & More for Kids to Do to Learn about Your State! 2003. (South Dakota Experience Ser.). 32p. (gr. k-5). pap. 5.95 *(978-0-635-01910-3(8),* Marsh, Carole Bks.) Gallopade International.

Mcdaniel, Melissa. South Dakota, 1 vol. 2nd rev. ed. 2007. (Celebrate the States (Second Edition) Ser.). (ENG., Illus.). 144p. (gr. 6-6). lib. bdg. 39.79 *(978-0-7614-2156-6(4),* 18d64417-4340-4aa6-9df5-d3765b159ba4) Cavendish Square Publishing LLC.

Murray, Julie. South Dakota, 1 vol. 2006. (United States Ser.). (ENG., Illus.). 32p. (gr. 2-4). 27.07 *(978-1-59197-700-1(2),* Buddy Bks.) ABDO Publishing Co.

Parker, Bridget. South Dakota. 2016. (States Ser.). (ENG., Illus.). 32p. (J). (gr. 3-6). lib. bdg. 27.99 *(978-1-5157-0429-4(7),* 132040, Capstone Pr.) Capstone.

Peters, S. True. How to Draw South Dakota's Sights & Symbols. 2009. (Kid's Guide to Drawing America Ser.). 32p. (gr. k-4). 50.50 *(978-1-61511-095-7(X),* PowerKids Pr.) Rosen Publishing Group, Inc., The.

Peterson, Sheryl. North Dakota. 2009. (This Land Called America Ser.). 32p. (YA). (gr. 3-6). 19.95 *(978-1-58341-794-2(X))* Creative Co., The.

Schuler, Harold H. Fort Sisseton. 2012. (Prairie Plains Ser.: No. 5). (Illus.). 283p. (Orig.). reprint ed. pap. 22.95 *(978-0-931170-62-1(1))* Ctr. for Western Studies.

Sirvaitis, Karen. South Dakota. 2nd exp. rev. ed. 2003. (Hello U. S. A. Ser.). (Illus.). 84p. (J). (gr. 3-6). pap. 6.95 *(978-0-8225-4139-4(4))* Lerner Publishing Group.

Townsley, Janet Howe. Dakota Dreams: Fannie Sabra Howe's Own Story, 1881-1884. 2003. (Illus.). 77p. (J). 19.95 *(978-0-9715171-4-1(2))* South Dakota Historical Society Pr.

Turnipseed, Susan. South Dakota: A Journey Through Time Student Workbook. Heers, Matt & Heers, Nate, illus. 2003. 28p. (J). pap. *(978-1-57579-268-2(0))* Pine Hill Pr.

—South Dakota: A Journey Through Time Student Workbook Answer Key. Heers, Matt & Heers, Nate, illus. 2003. 28p. (J). pap. *(978-1-57579-269-9(9))* Pine Hill Pr.

Waldman, Nomi J. Deadwood, South Dakota: A Frontier Community: Text Pairs. 2008. (Bridges/Navigators Ser.). (J). (gr. 3). 81.00 *(978-1-4108-8358-2(2))* Benchmark Education Co.

SOUTH DAKOTA—FICTION

Anderson, William. M Is for Mount Rushmore: A South Dakota Alphabet. Harness, Cheryl, illus. 2005. (Discover America

S

State by State Ser.). (ENG.). 40p. (J). (gr. 1-3). 18.99 *(978-1-58536-141-0(0),* 202001) Sleeping Bear Pr.

Baum, L. Frank & Conahan, Carolyn Digby. The Discontented Gopher. 2006. (Prairie Tales Ser.). (ENG., Illus.). 40p. (gr. 3-7). 14.95 *(978-0-9749195-9-1(4),* P240877, South Dakota State Historical Society Pr.) South Dakota Historical Society Pr.

Black Hills Summer. 2003. (YA). per. *(978-0-9740718-0-0(3))* Strathmoor Pr.

Brezenoff, Steve. Field Trip Mysteries: the Mount Rushmore Face That Couldn't See. Canga, Chris & Calo, Marcos, illus. 2012. (Field Trip Mysteries Ser.). (ENG.). 88p. (J). (gr. 3-6). pap. 5.95 *(978-1-4342-4199-3(8),* 120257, Stone Arch Bks.) Capstone.

Brown, Jeff. Flat Stanley's Worldwide Adventures #1: the Mount Rushmore Calamity. Pamintuan, Macky, illus. 2009. (Flat Stanley's Worldwide Adventures Ser.: 1). (ENG.). 96p. (J). (gr. 2-5). 15.99 *(978-0-06-142991-0(0));* pap. 4.99 *(978-0-06-142990-3(2),* 91be4692-a157-4cdf-bf09-64fa0741a507) HarperCollins Pubs. (HarperCollins).

Browne, Chris. The Monster Who Ate the State. 2014. (ENG., Illus.). 29p. 19.95 *(978-0-9860355-9-3(9),* P233290) South Dakota Historical Society Pr.

Cartwright, Nancy & Jones, Joanna. Henry's Adventure at the Franklin Hotel. Feterl, Bill, illus. 2011. (YA). lib. bdg. *(978-0-913062-44-9(8))* Fenwyn Pr.

Chace, Rebecca. June Sparrow & the Million-Dollar Penny. Schwartz, Kacey, illus. 2017. (ENG.). 352p. (J). (gr. 3-7). 16.99 *(978-0-06-246498-9(1),* Balzer & Bray) HarperCollins Pubs.

Eastman, Charles A. & Eastman, Elaine Goodale. The Raccoon & the Bee Tree. Susan, Turnbull, illus. 2013. 32p. (J). *(978-0-9860355-4-8(8))* South Dakota Historical Society Pr.

Erickson, Mary Ellen. What Happened to the Deer? Peanut Butter Club Mysteries. 2007. 182p. (J). 23.95 *(978-0-595-68396-3(7));* per. 13.95 *(978-0-595-42799-4(5))* iUniverse, Inc.

Glaser, Linda. Hannah's Way. Gustavson, Adam, illus. 2012. (Shabbat Ser.). 32p. (J). (gr. k-3). lib. bdg. 17.95 *(978-0-7613-5137-5(X),* Kar-Ben Publishing) Lerner Publishing Group.

Hardesty, Ann A. Lucy's Trials in the Black Hills. 2009. 104p. pap. 10.99 *(978-1-4490-5368-0(8))* AuthorHouse.

Hobbs, Will. Go Big or Go Home. 2009. (ENG.). 208p. (J). (gr. 5). pap. 6.99 *(978-0-06-074143-3(0),* HarperCollins) HarperCollins Pubs.

House, Peggy. Prairie Anna. 2012. (J). *(978-1-60682-395-8(7))* BJU Pr.

Jacobs, Lily. The Littlest Bunny in South Dakota: An Easter Adventure. Dunn, Robert, illus. 2015. (Littlest Bunny Ser.). (ENG.). 32p. (J). (gr. -1-3). 9.99 *(978-1-4926-1198-1(0),* Hometown World) Sourcebooks, Inc.

James, Eric. Santa's Sleigh Is on Its Way to South Dakota: A Christmas Adventure. Dunn, Robert, illus. 2016. (Santa's Sleigh Is on Its Way Ser.). (ENG.). 32p. (J). (gr. k-2). 12.99 *(978-1-4926-4355-5(6),* 9781492643555, Hometown World) Sourcebooks, Inc.

—The Spooky Express South Dakota. Piwowarski, Marcin, illus. 2017. (Spooky Express Ser.). (ENG.). 32p. (J). (gr. k-6). 9.99 *(978-1-4926-5399-8(3),* Hometown World) Sourcebooks, Inc.

—Tiny the South Dakota Easter Bunny. 2018. (Tiny the Easter Bunny Ser.). (ENG.). 40p. (J). (gr. k-3). 9.99 *(978-1-4926-5964-8(9),* Hometown World) Sourcebooks, Inc.

Kropp, Joseph P. Hickok's Gold. 2006. (J). 11.95 *(978-1-890905-25-5(9))* Day to Day Enterprises.

McNeely, Marian Hurd. The Jumping-Off Place. Siegel, William, illus. 2017. (ENG.). 320p. (J). pap. 9.95 *(978-0-486-81568-8(4),* 815684) Dover Pubns., Inc.

McNeely, Marian Hurd & L., Jean. The Jumping-Off Place. 2008. (ENG., Illus.). 320p. (J). pap. 15.95 *(978-0-9798940-4-6(2),* P240879, South Dakota State Historical Society Pr.) South Dakota Historical Society Pr.

Mehnert, Robert. Spelunkers. 2012. 108p. pap. 19.95 *(978-1-62709-036-0(3))* America Star Bks.

Meierhenry, Mark, et al. The Mystery of the Maize. 2010. (Mystery Ser.). (ENG., Illus.). 44p. (J). 13.95 *(978-0-9822749-1-0(2),* P240880, South Dakota State Historical Society Pr.) South Dakota Historical Society Pr.

—The Mystery of the Pheasants. 2012. (Mystery Ser.). (ENG., Illus.). 44p. (J). 14.95 *(978-0-9845041-9-0(2),* P240881) South Dakota Historical Society Pr.

Meyer, Deanna. Buffalo on the Ridge. 2010. pap. 12.95 *(978-0-7414-6103-2(X))* Infinity Publishing.

Moore, Ted. Eagle Eye & the Fall of Creek Canyon. 2007. 112p. per. 10.95 *(978-0-595-43133-5(X))* iUniverse, Inc.

Neal, Michael. Bonnie's Rescue: A Courageous Critters« Series Book. 2009. 56p. pap. 8.95 *(978-1-4401-1237-9(1))* iUniverse, Inc.

Patrick, Jean. Four Famous Faces. Graef, Renee, illus. 2014. 32p. (J). lib. bdg. 16.99 *(978-0-9798823-8-8(9))* Mount Rushmore Bookstores.

Peterson, Esther Allen. Will Spring Come? 2009. (Illus.). 157p. (J). *(978-0-88092-768-0(2))* Royal Fireworks Publishing Co.

Schurch, Maylan Henry. The Meatless Mayhem Mystery. 2003. (Justin Case Adventures Ser.: 5). 121p. (J). pap. 7.99 *(978-0-8280-1615-5(1),* 133-650) Review & Herald Publishing Assn.

Sully, Katherine. Night-Night South Dakota. Poole, Helen, illus. 2017. (Night-Night Ser.). (ENG.). 20p. (J). (gr. -1-1). bds. 9.99 *(978-1-4926-4775-1(6),* 9781492647751, Hometown World) Sourcebooks, Inc.

Wilder, Laura Ingalls. The First Four Years. Williams, Garth, illus. 2008. (Little House Ser.: 9). (ENG.). 160p. (J). (gr. 3-7). pap. 9.99 *(978-0-06-440031-2(X),* HarperCollins) HarperCollins Pubs.

—The First Four Years: Full Color Edition. Williams, Garth, illus. 2004. (Little House Ser.: 9). (ENG.). 160p. (J). (gr. 3-7). pap. 9.99 *(978-0-06-058188-6(3),* HarperCollins) HarperCollins Pubs.

—Little Town on the Prairie. Williams, Garth, illus. 2003. (Little House Ser.). 320p. (J). pap. 5.99 *(978-0-06-052242-1(9))* HarperCollins Pubs.

—Little Town on the Prairie: A Newbery Honor Award Winner. Williams, Garth, illus. 2008. (Little House Ser.: 7). (ENG.). 320p. (J). (gr. 3-7). pap. 8.99 *(978-0-06-440007-7(7),* HarperCollins) HarperCollins Pubs.

—Little Town on the Prairie: Full Color Edition: A Newbery Honor Award Winner. Williams, Garth, illus. 2004. (Little House Ser.: 7). (ENG.). 320p. (J). (gr. 3-7). pap. 9.99 *(978-0-06-058186-2(7),* HarperCollins) HarperCollins Pubs.

—The Long Winter: A Newbery Honor Award Winner. Williams, Garth, illus. 2008. (Little House Ser.: 6). (ENG.). 352p. (J). (gr. 3-7). pap. 9.99 *(978-0-06-440006-0(9),* HarperCollins) HarperCollins Pubs.

—The Long Winter: Full Color Edition: A Newbery Honor Award Winner. Williams, Garth, illus. 2004. (Little House Ser.: 6). (ENG.). 352p. (J). (gr. 3-7). pap. 10.99 *(978-0-06-058185-5(9),* HarperCollins) HarperCollins Pubs.

—These Happy Golden Years. 2007. (Little House Ser.). (ENG.). 304p. (J). (gr. 3-7). pap., pap. 6.99 *(978-0-06-088544-1(0),* Harper Trophy) HarperCollins Pubs.

—These Happy Golden Years. l.t. ed. (J). (gr. 3-6). 35.95 *(978-1-58118-102-9(7))* LRS.

—These Happy Golden Years: A Newbery Honor Award Winner. Williams, Garth, illus. rev. ed. 2008. (Little House Ser.: 8). (ENG.). 304p. (J). (gr. 3-7). pap. 8.99 *(978-0-06-440008-4(5),* HarperCollins) HarperCollins Pubs.

—These Happy Golden Years: Full Color Edition: A Newbery Honor Award Winner. Williams, Garth, illus. 2004. (Little House Ser.: 8). (ENG.). 304p. (J). (gr. 3-7). pap. 9.99 *(978-0-06-058187-9(5),* HarperCollins) HarperCollins Pubs.

SOUTH DAKOTA—HISTORY

Bjorklund, Ruth. South Dakota, 1 vol. 2nd rev. ed. 2013. (It's My State! (Second Edition)(r) Ser.). (ENG.). 80p. (gr. 4-4). 35.93 *(978-1-60870-884-0(5),* 9b1b0014-dd8e-42ac-893e-b80263660560) Cavendish Square Publishing LLC.

Bjorklund, Ruth, et al. South Dakota: The Mount Rushmore State, 1 vol. 3rd rev. ed. 2016. (It's My State! (Third Edition)(r) Ser.). (ENG., Illus.). 80p. (gr. 4-4). 35.93 *(978-1-62713-222-0(8),* e73b5828-b686-453a-addb-2753e0b02408) Cavendish Square Publishing LLC.

Burgan, Michael. America the Beautiful: South Dakota (Revised Edition) 2014. (America the Beautiful, Third Ser. (Revised Edition) Ser.). (ENG., Illus.). 144p. (J). lib. bdg. 40.00 *(978-0-531-28293-9(7))* Scholastic Library Publishing.

Dell, Pamela. Last Battle: Causes & Effects of the Massacre at Wounded Knee. 2015. (Cause & Effect: American Indian History Ser.). (ENG., Illus.). 32p. (J). (gr. 3-6). lib. bdg. 27.99 *(978-1-4914-4835-9(0),* 128721) Capstone.

Gitlin, Martin. Wounded Knee Massacre, 1 vol. 2010. (ENG.). 216p. (gr. 7-18). 43.00 *(978-1-59884-409-2(1),* 900301679, Bloomsbury Academic) Bloomsbury Publishing Plc GBR. Dist: Macmillan.

Goldsworthy, Kaite. El Monte Rushmore. 2013. (Iconos Americanos Ser.). (SPA., Illus.). 24p. (J). (gr. k-2). lib. bdg. 27.13 *(978-1-62127-621-0(X),* AV2 by Weigl) Weigl Pubs., Inc.

—Mount Rushmore. 2014. (Illus.). 24p. (J). *(978-1-62127-465-0(9))* Weigl Pubs., Inc.

Jerome, Kate B. Lucky to Live in South Dakota. 2017. (Arcadia Kids Ser.). (ENG., Illus.). 32p. (J). 16.99 *(978-0-7385-2808-3(0))* Arcadia Publishing.

—The Wise Animal Handbook South Dakota. 2017. (Arcadia Kids Ser.). (ENG., Illus.). 32p. (J). 16.99 *(978-0-7385-2842-7(0))* Arcadia Publishing.

Kittinger, Jo S. South Dakota (a True Book: My United States) (Library Edition) 2018. (True Book (Relaunch) Ser.). (ENG., Illus.). 48p. (J). (gr. 3-5). lib. bdg. 31.00 *(978-0-531-23580-5(7),* Children's Pr.) Scholastic Library Publishing.

Kopp, Megan. South Dakota: Mount Rushmore State. 2012. (J). *(978-1-61913-403-4(9));* pap. *(978-1-61913-404-1(7))* Weigl Pubs., Inc.

Marsh, Carole. Exploring South Dakota Through Project-Based Learning: Geography, History, Government, Economics & More. 2016. (South Dakota Experience Ser.). (ENG.). (J). pap. 9.99 *(978-0-635-12365-7(7))* Gallopade International.

—I'm Reading about Mount Rushmore. 2016. (I'm Reading about Mount Rushmore Ser.). (ENG., Illus.). (J). lib. bdg. 24.99 *(978-0-635-12215-5(4))* Gallopade International.

—I'm Reading about South Dakota. 2014. (South Dakota Experience Ser.). (ENG., Illus.). (J). pap., pap. 8.99 *(978-0-635-11316-0(3))* Gallopade International.

—South Dakota History Projects: 30 Cool, Activities, Crafts, Experiments & More for Kids to Do to Learn about Your State! 2003. (South Dakota Experience Ser.). 32p. (gr. k-5). pap. 5.95 *(978-0-635-01810-6(1),* Marsh, Carole Bks.) Gallopade International.

Pearson, Jaci Conrad. Adams A to Z. Nelson, Darrel, illus. 2011. 51p. (J). *(978-0-9793584-3-2(4))* TDG Communications, Inc.

Petersen, Christine. South Dakota: Past & Present, 1 vol. 2010. (United States: Past & Present Ser.). (ENG., Illus.). 48p. (J). (gr. 5-5). pap. 12.75 *(978-1-4358-9523-2(1),* f1c8a7bb-e974-4fcd-b2d5-7f6ae00b7fce); lib. bdg. 34.47 *(978-1-4358-9496-9(0),* 1e1fd9a4-bba7-4593-ad51-ccff73796fb6) Rosen Publishing Group, Inc., The. (Rosen Reference).

Strudwick, Leslie. South Dakota. 2011. (Guide to American States Ser.). (Illus.). 48p. (YA). (gr. 3-6). 29.99 *(978-1-61690-814-0(9));* (J). 29.99 *(978-1-61690-490-6(9))* Weigl Pubs., Inc.

—South Dakota: The Mount Rushmore State. 2016. (J). *(978-1-4896-4941-6(7))* Weigl Pubs., Inc.

Waldman, Nomi J. Deadwood, South Dakota A Frontier Community: Set Of 6. 2011. (Navigators Ser.). (J). pap. 44.00 net. *(978-1-4108-6247-1(X))* Benchmark Education Co.

Westcott, Jim. Upper Plains: Montana, North Dakota, South Dakota, Vol. 19. 2015. (Let's Explore the States Ser.). (Illus.). 64p. (J). (gr. 5). 23.95 *(978-1-4222-3336-8(7))* Mason Crest.

Yacowitz, Caryn. South Dakota. 2009. (From Sea to Shining Sea, Second Ser.). (ENG.). 80p. (J). pap. 7.95 *(978-0-531-21143-4(6),* Children's Pr.) Scholastic Library Publishing.

SOUTH POLE

Bluthenthal, Todd. The South Pole, 1 vol. 2017. (Where on Earth? Mapping Parts of the World Ser.). 24p. (J). (gr. 1-2). (ENG.). pap. 9.15 *(978-1-4824-6433-7(0),* daeb26a0-f52b-479a-a0b0-9b2a9c109056); pap. 48.90 *(978-1-4824-6434-4(9))* Stevens, Gareth Publishing LLLP.

Bodden, Valerie. To the South Pole. 2011. (Great Expeditions Ser.). (ENG.). 48p. (J). (gr. 5-8). pap. 12.00 *(978-0-89812-667-9(3),* 22161, Creative Paperbacks); (Illus.). 35.65 *(978-1-60818-069-1(7),* 22155, Creative Education) Creative Co., The.

Cooke, Tim. The Exploration of the North & South Poles, 1 vol. 2013. (Explorers Discovering the World Ser.). (ENG., Illus.). 48p. (J). (gr. 4-5). 34.60 *(978-1-4339-8631-4(0),* 2313c10c-11d4-4c82-bda1-79ec3d5d0908); pap. 15.05 *(978-1-4339-8632-1(9),* 2c8796b4-bddb-4528-b8fe-758db89089b2) Stevens, Gareth Publishing LLLP. (Gareth Stevens Learning Library).

Grochowicz, Joanna. Amundsen's Way: The Race to the South Pole. 2019. (ENG., Illus.). 320p. (J). (gr. 5-9). pap. 14.99 *(978-1-76063-766-8(1),* A&U Children's) Allen & Unwin AUS. Dist: Independent Pubs. Group.

Llanas, Sheila Griffin. Who Reached the South Pole First? (Race for History Ser.). (ENG.). 32p. (gr. 3-4). 2011. pap. 47.70 *(978-1-4296-6413-4(4))* 2010. (J). lib. bdg. 27.99 *(978-1-4296-3344-4(1),* 95851) Capstone. (Capstone Pr.).

Mason, Theodore. The South Pole Ponies. 2007. 232p. (gr. 7). per. 18.00 *(978-1-59048-251-3(4))* Long Riders' Guild Pr., The.

Morlock, Rachael. Roald Amundsen Reaches the South Pole, 1 vol. 2018. (Real-Life Scientific Adventures Ser.). (ENG.). 32p. (gr. 4-5). 29.27 *(978-1-5081-6858-4(X),* d5803a1a-65b1-4f9e-a5e0-64c465907cac, PowerKids Pr.) Rosen Publishing Group, Inc., The.

Pipe, Jim. The Race to the South Pole. 2006. (Stories from History Ser.). (ENG., Illus.). 48p. (J). (gr. 3-6). 21.19 *(978-0-7696-4722-7(7))* School Specialty, Incorporated.

Worth, Bonnie. Ice Is Nice! All about the North & South Poles. Ruiz, Aristides & Mathieu, Joe, illus. 2010. (Cat in the Hat's Learning Library). (ENG.). 48p. (J). (gr. -1-3). 9.99 *(978-0-375-82885-0(0),* Random Hse. Bks. for Young Readers) Random Hse. Children's Bks.

Yomtov, Nel. Roald Amundsen Explores the South Pole. 2015. (Extraordinary Explorers Ser.). (ENG., Illus.). 24p. (J). (gr. 3-8). lib. bdg. 29.95 *(978-1-62617-295-1(1),* Black Sheep) Bellwether Media.

SOUTH POLE—FICTION

Berenstain, Stan & Berenstain, Jan. Nothing Ever Happens at the South Pole. Berenstain, Jan & Berenstain, Mike, illus. 2012. (ENG.). 40p. (J). (gr. -1-3). 10.99 *(978-0-06-207532-1(2),* HarperCollins) HarperCollins Pubs.

Burks, James. Bird & Squirrel on Ice. 2014. (Illus.). 125p. (J). *(978-0-605-86251-7(6),* Graphix) Scholastic, Inc.

—Bird & Squirrel on Ice: a Graphic Novel (Bird & Squirrel #2) Burks, James, illus. 2014. (Bird & Squirrel Ser.). (ENG., Illus.). 128p. (J). (gr. 2-5). pap. 10.99 *(978-0-545-56318-5(6),* Graphix) Scholastic, Inc.

Coyle, Carmela LaVigna. Thank You, Aunt Tallulah! MacPherson, Bruce, illus. 2006. (ENG.). 32p. (J). (gr. -1-3). 15.95 *(978-0-87358-891-1(6))* Cooper Square Publishing Llc.

Heidenreich, Elke. Some Folk Think the South Pole's Hot: The Three Tenors Play the Antarctic. Buchholz, Quint, illus. 2004. (ENG.). 64p. (J). 17.95 *(978-1-56792-170-0(1))* Godine, David R. Pub.

Kimmel, Elizabeth Cody. My Penguin Osbert in Love: Midi Edition. Lewis, H. B., illus. 2010. (ENG.). 48p. (J). (gr. -1-3). 7.99 *(978-0-7636-5001-8(3))* Candlewick Pr.

Lawrence, Iain. The Winter Pony. 2012. (ENG., Illus.). 256p. (J). (gr. 4-6). lib. bdg. 21.19 *(978-0-385-90394-3(4))* Random Hse. Bks. for Young Readers.

—The Winter Pony. 2012. (Illus.). 256p. (J). (gr. 4-7). 7.99 *(978-0-440-23972-7(9),* Yearling) Random Hse. Children's Bks.

Rockwood, Roy. Under the Ocean to the South Pole. 2007. 120p. per. *(978-1-4068-3972-2(8))* Echo Library.

—Under the Ocean to the South Pole. 2009. 152p. 24.95 *(978-1-60664-626-7(5));* pap. 12.95 *(978-1-60664-365-5(7))* Rodgers, Alan Bks.

—Under the Ocean to the South Pole: Or, the Strange Cruise of the Submarine Wonder. 2017. (ENG., Illus.). (J). 23.95 *(978-1-374-84548-0(5))* Capital Communications, Inc.

—Under the Ocean to the South Pole or the Strange Cruise of the Submarine Wonder. 2007. 180p. 95.99 *(978-1-4280-7589-4(5));* per. 89.99 *(978-1-4280-7588-7(7))* IndyPublish.com.

Spinelli, Eileen. Something to Tell the Grandcows. Slavin, Bill, illus. 2004. 32p. (J). 16.00 *(978-0-8028-5236-6(X));* (gr. -1-3). 8.00 *(978-0-8028-5304-2(8),* Eerdmans Bks For Young Readers) Eerdmans, William B. Publishing Co.

SOUTH SEA ISLANDS

see Islands of the Pacific

SOUTHEAST ASIA

Here are entered works dealing collectively with the mainland and insular regions of Asia lying south of China and east of India, including Burma, Thailand, Laos, Cambodia, Vietnam, Malaysia, Singapore, Brunei, Indonesia, East Timor, and the Philippines.

Boomgaard, Peter. Southeast Asia: An Environmental History, 1 vol. Stoll, Mark R., ed. 2006. (Nature & Human Societies Ser.). (ENG., Illus.). 392p. (C). 103.00 *(978-1-85109-419-6(9),* 900299378) ABC-CLIO, LLC.

Chandler, Julia. The Colonial & Postcolonial Experience in East & Southeast Asia, 1 vol. 2016. (Colonial & Postcolonial Experience Ser.). (ENG., Illus.). 304p. (J). (gr. 10-10). 55.59 *(978-1-5081-0438-4(7),* 9c5db86f-5f8e-4f42-8ebc-95fd3c5a8235) Rosen Publishing Group, Inc., The.

Orr, Tamra B. Brunei, 1 vol. 2009. (Cultures of the World (First Edition)(r) Ser.). (ENG.). 144p. (gr. 5-5). lib. bdg. 49.79 *(978-0-7614-3121-3(7),* 920daf83-c0e8-4e71-bb4c-d46e1fd52096) Cavendish Square Publishing LLC.

Philips, Douglas. Southeast Asia. 2005. (Modern World Cultures Ser.). (ENG., Illus.). 136p. (gr. 6-12). lib. bdg. 30.00 *(978-0-7910-8149-5(4),* P114156, Facts On File) Infobase Holdings, Inc.

Robbins, Gerald. Azerbaijan. 2006. (Growth & Influence of Islam in the Nations of Asia & Central Asia Ser.). (Illus.). 128p. (J). lib. bdg. 25.95 *(978-1-59084-878-4(0))* Mason Crest.

Southeast Asia: Regions of the World. 2003. spiral bd. 16.95 *(978-1-56004-159-7(5))* Social Studies Schl. Service.

Yomtov, Nel. Immigrants from India & Southeast Asia. 2018. (Immigration Today Ser.). (ENG., Illus.). 32p. (J). (gr. 3-6). lib. bdg. 27.99 *(978-1-5435-1382-0(4),* 137787, Capstone Pr.) Capstone.

SOUTHEAST ASIA—FICTION

Coburn, Jewell Reinhard & Lee, Tzexa Cherta. Jouanah: A Hmong Cinderella, 1 vol. O'Brien, Anne Sibley, illus. 2014. (Cinderella Ser.). (ENG.). 32p. (J). (gr. 2-5). pap. 11.95 *(978-1-885008-41-1(4),* leelowshens, Shen's Bks.) Lee & Low Bks., Inc.

Cornwell, Autumn. Carpe Diem. 2009. (ENG.). 368p. (YA). (gr. 7-12). pap. 18.99 *(978-0-312-56129-1(6),* 900058864) Square Fish.

Kingston, William H. In the Eastern Seas. 2013. 396p. pap. *(978-3-943850-66-6(8))* weitsüchtig. in Europäischer Hochschulverlag GmbH & Co. KG.

Kingston, William Henry Giles. In the Eastern Seas. 2017. (ENG., Illus.). (J). 28.95 *(978-1-374-86270-8(3));* pap. 18.95 *(978-1-374-86269-2(X))* Capital Communications, Inc.

SOUTHERN STATES

Andrews, Barbara. Discover the Southeast Region. 2006. (J). pap. *(978-1-4108-6435-2(9))* Benchmark Education Co.

Bethea, Nikole. G Is for Grits: A Southern Alphabet, 1 vol. Lyne, Alison, illus. 2012. (ABC Ser.). (ENG.). 32p. (J). (gr. k-3). 19.99 *(978-1-4556-1698-5(2),* Pelican Publishing) Arcadia Publishing.

Currie, Stephen. A Peculiar Institution: Slavery in the Plantation South. 2005. (Lucent Library of Black History). (ENG., Illus.). 112p. (J). (gr. 7-10). lib. bdg. 33.45 *(978-1-59018-704-3(0),* Lucent Bks.) Cengage Gale.

Davidson, Tish. East South-Central States: Kentucky & Tennessee, Vol. 19. 2015. (Let's Explore the States Ser.). (Illus.). 64p. (J). (gr. 5). 23.95 *(978-1-4222-3322-1(7))* Mason Crest.

Dunn, Mary. My Adventure in the Southeast: Advanced My Adventure. 2007. 44p. (J). pap. 8.99 *(978-1-59092-436-5(3))* Blue Forge Pr.

Erickson, Paul. Daily Life on a Southern Plantation. Gabbey, Terry, illus. Slingsby, Miki, photos by. 2006. 48p. (J). (gr. 2-5). reprint ed. pap. 8.00 *(978-1-4223-5727-9(9))* DIANE Publishing Co.

Gullo, Jim. A Travel Guide to the Plantation South. 2005. (Travel Guide To Ser.). (ENG., Illus.). 112p. (J). (gr. 5-8). lib. bdg. 30.85 *(978-1-59018-360-1(6),* Lucent Bks.) Cengage Gale.

Johnson, Marlys & Clarke, Duncan. Native Tribes of the Southeast, 1 vol. 2004. (Native Tribes of North America Ser.). (ENG., Illus.). 64p. (J). (gr. 5-8). lib. bdg. 36.67 *(978-0-8368-5614-9(7),* c2a7cbe4-4300-474a-a6d8-4ec06cacf3bd, Gareth Stevens Secondary Library) Stevens, Gareth Publishing LLLP.

Micklos, John, Jr. People & Places of the Southeast. 2016. (United States by Region Ser.). (ENG., Illus.). 32p. (J). (gr. 3-6). lib. bdg. 27.99 *(978-1-5157-2443-8(3),* 132823, Capstone Pr.) Capstone.

National Geographic Learning. Reading Expeditions (Social Studies: Readings about America): the Southeast Today. 2007. (ENG., Illus.). 32p. (J). pap. 18.95 *(978-0-7922-4533-9(4))* CENGAGE Learning.

Rikson, Paule. Daily Life on a Southern Plantation 1853. 2004. (Illus.). 48p. (J). (gr. 4-8). reprint ed. 17.00 *(978-0-7567-7709-8(7))* DIANE Publishing Co.

Smith-Llera, Danielle. TV Exposes Brutality on the Selma March: 4D an Augmented Reading Experience. 2019. (Captured Television History 4D Ser.). (ENG., Illus.). 64p. (J). (gr. 5-9). pap. 8.99 *(978-0-7565-6005-8(5),* 139136); 39.99 *(978-0-7565-6001-0(2),* 139132) Capstone. (Compass Point Bks.).

The South, 1 vol. 2014. (Land That I Love: Regions of the United States Ser.). (ENG., Illus.). 32p. (J). (gr. 3-3). lib. bdg. 27.93 *(978-1-4777-6857-0(2),* 2949dc7c-888b-4618-a057-bda0b2ff345a, PowerKids Pr.) Rosen Publishing Group, Inc., The.

Yannuzzi, Della A. The Life of Zora Neale Hurston: Author & Folklorist, 1 vol. 2014. (Legendary African Americans Ser.). (ENG.). 96p. (gr. 6-6). 31.61 *(978-0-7660-6275-7(9),* f0dd1f0e-d807-4ece-bd31-b58971173adf) Enslow Publishing, LLC.

SOUTHERN STATES—FICTION

Carter, Noni. Good Fortune. 2011. (ENG.). 496p. (YA). (gr. 7). pap. 12.99 *(978-1-4169-8481-8(X),* Simon & Schuster Bks. For Young Readers) Simon & Schuster Bks. For Young Readers.

—Good Fortune. 2010. (ENG.). 496p. (YA). (gr. 7-6). 16.99 *(978-1-4169-8480-1(1))* Simon & Schuster, Inc.

Cline-Ransome, Lesa. Light in the Darkness: A Story about How Slaves Learned in Secret. Ransome, James E., illus. 2013. (ENG.). 40p. (J). (gr. -1-3). 18.99 *(978-1-4231-3495-4(8))* Little, Brown Bks. for Young Readers.

DAVIS**DECEASED**, David. Ten Redneck Babies: A Southern Counting Book, 1 vol. 2004. (ENG., Illus.). 32p. (J). (gr. k-k). 16.99 *(978-1-58980-232-2(2),* Pelican Publishing) Arcadia Publishing.

DeLong, Lucianne. A Tall Southern Tale. Ungureanu, Dan Paul, illus. l.t. ed. 2013. (Possum Squat Ser.). (ENG.). 40p. (J). 15.95 *(978-0-9833237-1-6(2))* Krullstone Publishing, LLC.

—Whiskers Takes a Walk: A Possum Squat Tale. Ungureanu, Dan Paul, illus. 2013. (Possum Squat Ser.). (ENG.). 40p. (J). 15.95 *(978-0-9833237-3-0(9))* Krullstone Publishing, LLC.

Dicamillo, Kate. Because of Winn-Dixie. 2015. (ENG.). 208p. (J). (gr. 4-7). lib. bdg. 18.80 *(978-1-68065-673-2(2))* Perfection Learning Corp.

—Because of Winn-Dixie. l.t. ed. 2019. (ENG.). 148p. (J). (gr. 4-7). pap. 12.99 *(978-1-4328-6406-4(8),* Large Print Pr.) Thorndike Pr.

DiCamillo, Kate. Gracias a Winn-Dixie. 2010. (SPA.). 152p. (gr. 4-6). pap. 12.99 *(978-84-279-3265-4(0))* Noguer y Caralt Editores, S. A. ESP. Dist: Lectorum Pubns., Inc.

Evans, Freddi Williams. Hush Harbor: Praying in Secret. Banks, Erin, illus. 2008. (ENG.). 32p. (J). (gr. k-3). 16.95 *(978-0-8225-7965-6(0)*, Carolrhoda Bks.) Lerner Publishing Group.

Finley, Martha. Elsie's Kith & Kin. 2006. 28.95 *(978-1-4218-2994-4(0))*; pap. 13.95 *(978-1-4218-3094-0(9))* 1st World Publishing, Inc.

—Elsie's Kith & Kin. 2018. (ENG., Illus.). 232p. (YA). (gr. 7-12). pap. *(978-93-5297-357-6(7))* Alpha Editions.

—Elsie's Motherhood. 2006. 29.95 *(978-1-4218-2995-1(9))*; pap. 14.95 *(978-1-4218-3095-7(7))* 1st World Publishing, Inc.

—Elsie's Motherhood. 2018. (ENG., Illus.). 252p. (YA). (gr. 7-12). pap. *(978-93-5297-358-3(5))* Alpha Editions.

—Elsie's Motherhood. 2017. (ENG., Illus.). (J). 25.95 *(978-1-374-95817-3(4))* Capital Communications, Inc.

—Elsie's Womanhood. 2018. (ENG., Illus.). 268p. (YA). (gr. 7-12). pap. *(978-93-5297-361-3(5))* Alpha Editions.

Friedman, Aimee. Sea Change. 2009. (ENG.). 320p. (J). (gr. 7-12). 16.99 *(978-0-439-92228-9(3))* Scholastic, Inc.

Gutman, Dan. The Genius Files #3: You Only Die Twice. 2013. (Genius Files Ser.: 3). (ENG.). (J). (gr. 3-7). 320p. pap. 7.99 *(978-0-06-182772-3(X))*; (Illus.). 304p. 16.99 *(978-0-06-182770-9(3))* HarperCollins Pubs. (HarperCollins).

—You Only Die Twice. 2013. (Genius Files Ser.: 3). (J). lib. bdg. 17.20 *(978-0-606-35043-3(8))* Turtleback.

Hamilton, Martha & Weiss, Mitch. The Hidden Feast: A Folktale from the American South. Tate, Don, illus. 2006. (ENG.). 32p. (J). (gr. k-3). 16.95 *(978-0-87483-758-2(8))* August Hse. Pubs., Inc.

Johnson, Allen, Jr. My Brother's Story. McMorris, Kelley, illus. 2014. (Blackwater Novels Ser.: Vol. 1). (ENG.). 191p. (J). (gr. 4-7). 14.99 *(978-1-933725-37-6(0))* Premium Pr. America.

Kendall, Jane. Horse Diaries #9: Tennessee Rose. Sheckels, Astrid, illus. 2012. (Horse Diaries: 9). (ENG.). 160p. (J). (gr. 3-7). pap. 7.99 *(978-0-375-87006-4(7)*, Random Hse. Bks. for Young Readers) Random Hse. Children's Bks.

LaFaye, A. Stella Stands Alone. 2010. (ENG.). 256p. (YA). (gr. 7). pap. 7.99 *(978-1-4169-8647-8(2)*, Simon & Schuster Bks. For Young Readers) Simon & Schuster Bks. For Young Readers.

Lawson, Jessica. Waiting for Augusta. 2016. (ENG., Illus.). 336p. (J). (gr. 3-7). 17.99 *(978-1-4814-4839-0(0)*, Simon & Schuster Bks. For Young Readers) Simon & Schuster Bks. For Young Readers.

Mitchell, Margaree King. When Grandmama Sings. Ransome, James, illus. 2012. (ENG.). 40p. (J). (gr. k-4). 16.99 *(978-0-688-17563-4(5)*, HarperCollins) HarperCollins Pubs.

Optic, Oliver, pseud. Watch & Wait; or, the Young Fugitives a Story for Young People by Oliver Optic [Pseud.]. 2006. 284p. per. 23.99 *(978-1-4255-2683-2(7))* Michigan Publishing.

Patrick, Denise Lewis. A Matter of Souls. 2018. (ENG.). 192p. (YA). (gr. 6-12). pap. 9.99 *(978-1-5415-1482-9(3)*, 4161e4af-dc7d-4119-a82e-dde17ece88ec, Carolrhoda Lab™) Lerner Publishing Group.

Payne, C. C. The Thing about Leftovers. 2017. 288p. (J). (gr. 5). 8.99 *(978-0-14-751422-6(3)*, Puffin Books) Penguin Young Readers Group.

Phillips, Lyda. Mr Touchdown. 2008. 184p. 23.95 *(978-1-4401-0976-8(1))*; pap. 13.95 *(978-1-60528-029-5(1))* iUniverse, Inc. (iUniverse Star).

Pineda, Jon. Let's No One Get Hurt: A Novel. 2018. *(978-0-374-90306-0(9))* Farrar, Straus & Giroux.

Ramsnips, Tunder. The Hardly Boys. 2010. 196p. pap. 15.95 *(978-0-557-38767-0(1))* Lulu Pr., Inc.

Sam's Last Summer. 2006. (J). per. 5.95 *(978-0-9790796-3-4(2))* PJR Assocs., Ltd.

San Souci, Robert D. & San Souci, Daniel, illus. Sister Tricksters: Rollicking Tales of Clever Females. 2006. (ENG.). 70p. (J). (gr. 3-7). 19.95 *(978-0-87483-791-9(X))* August Hse. Pubs., Inc.

Schronk, Julie. The Grass Grows Green. 2007. 208p. per. 24.95 *(978-1-60441-057-0(4))* America Star Bks.

Sorensen. Curious Missie C. 2003. (J). *(978-0-15-204717-7(4))* Harcourt Trade Pubs.

—Curious Missie P. 2003. (J). pap. *(978-0-15-204716-0(6))* Harcourt Trade Pubs.

Standish, Burt L. Frank Merriwell down South. 2017. (ENG., Illus.). (J). 25.95 *(978-1-374-86900-4(7))*; pap. 15.95 *(978-1-374-86899-1(X))* Capital Communications, Inc.

—Frank Merriwell down South. Rudman, Jack, ed. (Frank Merriwell Ser.). (YA). (gr. 9-18). 29.95 *(978-0-8373-9305-6(1))*; 2003. pap. 9.95 *(978-0-8373-9005-5(2)*, FM-005) Merriwell, Frank Inc.

Taylor, Mildred D. The Friendship. 2014. (ENG.). 56p. (J). (gr. 3-7). 11.24 *(978-1-63245-342-6(8))* Lectorum Pubns., Inc.

Whelan, Gloria. The Listeners. Benny, Mike, illus. 2009. (Tales of Young Americans Ser.). (ENG.). 40p. (J). (gr. 1-4). 18.99 *(978-1-58536-419-0(3)*, 202154) Sleeping Bear Pr.

Wiles, Deborah. Each Little Bird That Sings. 2006. (ENG., Illus.). 288p. (J). (gr. 3-7). reprint ed. pap. 8.99 *(978-0-15-205657-5(2)*, 1197010, Clarion Bks.) HarperCollins Pubs.

—Freedom Summer. Lagarrigue, Jerome, illus. 2005. (ENG.). 32p. (J). (gr. -1-3). reprint ed. 8.99 *(978-0-689-87829-9(X)*, Aladdin) Simon & Schuster Children's Publishing.

Williams, Rozanne, adapted by. Way down South. 2017. (Learn-To-Read Ser.). (ENG., Illus.). (J). pap. 3.49 *(978-1-68310-203-8(7))* Pacific Learning, Inc.

SOUTHERN STATES—HISTORY

Anderson, Dale. The Aftermath of the Civil War, 1 vol. 2004. (World Almanac(r) Library of the Civil War Ser.). (ENG., Illus.). 48p. (gr. 5-8). pap. 15.05 *(978-0-8368-5597-5(3)*, ad27f227-78f5-47db-a4a4-11d6eaec8003); lib. bdg. 33.67 *(978-0-8368-5588-3(4)*, c777ffc3-916f-4e09-bf81-5fbda0f6625d) Stevens, Gareth Publishing LLLP. (Gareth Stevens Secondary Library).

—World Almanac Library of the Civil War, 10 vols. Incl. Aftermath of the Civil War. lib. bdg. 33.67 *(978-0-8368-5588-3(4)*, c777ffc3-916f-4e09-bf81-5fbda0f6625d); Causes of the Civil War. lib. bdg. 33.67 *(978-0-8368-5581-4(7)*, 88052b64-ee89-4168-9b03-c8645b27670f); Civil War at Sea. lib. bdg. 33.67 *(978-0-8368-5585-2(X)*, abaa704c-54ab-437b-a508-a47da1d3dc87); Civil War in the East (1861-July 1863) lib. bdg. 33.67 *(978-0-8368-5582-1(5)*, ea65b134-2894-4b4a-b659-255a776186b0); Civil War in the West (1861-July 1863) lib. bdg. 33.67 *(978-0-8368-5583-8(3)*, a497de3e-669b-4027-92d0-df03b0280971); Home Fronts in the Civil War. lib. bdg. 33.67 *(978-0-8368-5587-6(6)*, f82d4d42-0c19-4e83-844b-321427333a72); Union Victory (July 1863 - 1865) lib. bdg. 33.67 *(978-0-8368-5584-5(1)*, e28734b4-0c65-4c17-9779-244cfe64b88f); (gr. 5-8). (World Almanac(r) Library of the Civil War Ser.). (ENG., Illus.). 48p. 2004. Set lib. bdg. 168.35 *(978-0-8368-5580-7(9)*, 6d23f6f8-b267-4c3a-8417-931f1aeca97a, Gareth Stevens Secondary Library) Stevens, Gareth Publishing LLLP.

Aretha, David. Sit-Ins & Freedom Rides. 2009. (Civil Rights Movement Ser.). 128p. (J). (gr. 4-7). 28.95 *(978-1-59935-098-1(X))* Reynolds, Morgan Inc.

—The Story of the Civil Rights Freedom Rides in Photographs, 1 vol. 2014. (Story of the Civil Rights Movement in Photographs Ser.). (ENG.). 48p. (gr. 5-6). lib. bdg. 27.93 *(978-0-7660-4236-0(7)*, 83f796b1-a975-446e-a063-7e23e397c7af) Enslow Publishing, LLC.

Bartley, Niccole. The South. 2014. (Land That I Love: Regions of the United States Ser.). 32p. (J). (gr. 3-6). pap. 60.00 *(978-1-4777-6636-1(7)*, PowerKids Pr.) Rosen Publishing Group, Inc., The.

Chandler, Matt. Fantasmas de el Álamo y Otros Lugares Embrujados Del Sur. Aparicio Publishing LLC, Aparicio Publishing, tr. 2020. (América Embrujada Ser.).Tr. of Ghosts of the Alamo & Other Hauntings of the South. (SPA., Illus.). 32p. (J). (gr. 3-9). lib. bdg. 30.65 *(978-1-4966-8511-7(3)*, 200617, Capstone Pr.) Capstone.

Connors, Kathleen. Let's Explore the Southeast, 1 vol. 2013. (Road Trip: Exploring America's Regions Ser.). (ENG.). 24p. (J). (gr. 2-3). pap. 9.15 *(978-1-4339-9145-5(4)*, f54fb6ce-c116-4f46-a608-2853ca40ea24); (Illus.). lib. bdg. 25.27 *(978-1-4339-9144-8(6)*, 369316bf-1f1e-4ccb-8ed4-de15b49c192f) Stevens, Gareth Publishing LLLP.

Hazelton, Amie. Hernando de Soto: An Explorer of the Southeast. 2017. (World Explorers Ser.). (ENG., Illus.). 32p. (J). (gr. 3-6). lib. bdg. 27.99 *(978-1-5157-4204-3(0)*, 133971, Capstone Pr.) Capstone.

Hernández, Roger E. & Hernández, Roger E. Early Explorations, The 1500s, 1 vol. 2009. (Hispanic America Ser.). (ENG.). 80p. (gr. 5-5). lib. bdg. 36.93 *(978-0-7614-2937-1(9)*, b16d1ad5-064e-49b4-aaa7-c60082b1692b) Cavendish Square Publishing LLC.

Hinton, Kerry. Sit-Ins & Nonviolent Protest for Racial Equality, 1 vol. 2017. (Spotlight on the Civil Rights Movement Ser.). (ENG., Illus.). 48p. (J). (gr. 6-6). pap. 12.75 *(978-1-5383-8064-2(1)*, 6766c7e7-1637-4622-98c3-92162a48c4ee, Rosen Young Adult) Rosen Publishing Group, Inc., The.

Jameson, W. C. Buried Treasures of the South: Legends of Lost, Buried, & Forgotten Treasures, from Tidewater Virginia to Coastal Carolina to Cajun Louisiana. 2006. (Buried Treasure Ser.). (ENG., Illus.). 192p. (J). (gr. 4-17). pap. 14.95 *(978-0-87483-286-0(1))* August Hse. Pubs., Inc.

LaClair, Teresa. The Southern Colonies: The Search for Wealth (1600-1770) 2012. (J). pap. *(978-1-4222-2412-0(0))* Mason Crest.

—The Southern Colonies: The Search for Wealth (1600-1770) Rakove, Jack N., ed. 2012. (How America Became America Ser.). 48p. (J). (gr. 3-4). 19.95 *(978-1-4222-2398-7(1))* Mason Crest.

—The Southern Colonies: The Search for Wealth (1600-1770) 2018. (J). *(978-1-5105-3590-9(X))* SmartBook Media, Inc.

Let's Explore the Southeast. 2013. (Road Trip: Exploring America's Regions Ser.). 24p. (J). (gr. 2-5). pap. 48.90 *(978-1-4339-9146-2(2))* Stevens, Gareth Publishing LLLP.

Lombardo, Jennifer. The Trail of Tears, 1 vol. 2020. (Turning Points Ser.). (ENG.). 104p. (gr. 7-7). pap. 20.99 *(978-1-5026-5774-9(0)*, 39987c52-b678-4336-8274-8d7d38864c3d) Cavendish Square Publishing LLC.

Maloof, Torrey. Reconstruction: Freedom Delayed. rev. ed. 2017. (Social Studies: Informational Text Ser.). (ENG., Illus.). 32p. (gr. 4-8). pap. 11.99 *(978-1-4938-3806-6(7))* Teacher Created Materials, Inc.

Marsico, Katie. It's Cool to Learn about the United States Southeast. 2011. (Explorer Library: Social Studies Explorer Ser.). (ENG.). 48p. (gr. 4-8). pap. 15.64 *(978-1-61080-303-8(5)*, 201199) Cherry Lake Publishing.

—It's Cool to Learn about the United States: Southeast. 2011. (Explorer Library: Social Studies Explorer Ser.). (ENG., Illus.). 48p. (gr. 4-8). lib. bdg. 34.93 *(978-1-61080-181-2(4)*, 201156) Cherry Lake Publishing.

National Geographic Learning. Reading Expeditions (Social Studies: Travels Across America's Past): the Southeast: Its History & People. 2007. (ENG., Illus.). 32p. (J). pap. 18.95 *(978-0-7922-8613-4(8))* CENGAGE Learning.

Nelson, Sheila. The Southern Colonies: The Quest for Prosperity. 2006. (How America Became America Ser.). (Illus.). 96p. (YA). lib. bdg. 22.95 *(978-1-59084-902-6(7))* Mason Crest.

Rau, Dana Meachen. A True Book: the Southeast. 2012. (True Book Ser.). (ENG., Illus.). 48p. (J). 29.00 *(978-0-531-24852-2(6)*, Children's Pr.) Scholastic Library Publishing.

Roberts, Russell. The Formation of the Confederacy. 2020. (Civil War Ser.). (ENG., Illus.). 48p. (J). (gr. 5-6). pap. 11.95 *(978-1-64493-160-8(5)*, 1644931605); lib. bdg. 34.21 *(978-1-64493-081-6(1)*, 1644930811) North Star Editions. (Focus Readers).

Santella, Andrew. Mountain Men. 2003. (Cornerstones of Freedom Ser.). (ENG., Illus.). 48p. (YA). (gr. 4-7). 26.00 *(978-0-516-24216-3(4))* Scholastic Library Publishing.

Stanborough, Rebecca. Exploring the South. 2017. (Exploring America's Regions Ser.). (ENG., Illus.). 48p. (J). (gr. 4-8). lib. bdg. 35.64 *(978-1-5321-1383-3(8)*, 27681) ABDO Publishing Co.

Streissguth, Tom. Perspectives on Reconstruction. 2018. (Perspectives on US History Ser.). (ENG., Illus.). 32p. (J). (gr. 3-6). 32.80 *(978-1-63235-403-7(9)*, 13725, 12-Story Library) Bookstaves, LLC.

Uhl, Xina M. & Flanagan, Timothy. A Primary Source Investigation of Reconstruction, 1 vol. 2018. (Uncovering American History Ser.). (ENG.). 64p. (gr. 6-6). pap. 13.95 *(978-1-5081-8405-8(4)*, b6716a0c-44ee-418b-b9fc-be349d9fb5e8, Rosen Reference) Rosen Publishing Group, Inc., The.

Uschan, Michael V. Murder & Lynching in the Deep South, 1 vol. 2006. (Lucent Library of Black History Ser.). (ENG., Illus.). 104p. (gr. 7-7). lib. bdg. 37.73 *(978-1-59018-845-3(4)*, ce6b490c-7d1f-4065-a5f5-cc0abcd95d67, Lucent Pr.) Greenhaven Publishing LLC.

Wiseman, Blaine. The Southeast. 2016. (Illus.). 48p. (J). *(978-1-5105-1140-8(7))* SmartBook Media, Inc.

SOUTHERN STATES—RACE RELATIONS

Brimner, Larry Dane. Twelve Days in May: Freedom Ride 1961. 2017. (ENG., Illus.). 112p. (YA). (gr. 5-12). 18.95 *(978-1-62979-586-7(0)*, Calkins Creek) Highlights Pr., c/o Highlights for Children, Inc.

Coles, Robert. The Story of Ruby Bridges. 2009. 8.44 *(978-0-7848-3016-1(9)*, Everbind) Marco Bk. Co.

—The Story of Ruby Bridges. 2011. 17.00 *(978-1-61383-173-1(0))* Perfection Learning Corp.

—The Story of Ruby Bridges. Ford, George, illus. 50th anniv. ed. 2010. (ENG.). 32p. (J). (gr. -1-3). pap. 7.99 *(978-0-439-47226-5(1)*, Scholastic Paperbacks) Scholastic, Inc.

—The Story of Ruby Bridges. 2010. lib. bdg. 17.20 *(978-0-606-23189-3(7))* Turtleback.

Crayton, Lisa A. Freedom Riders, 1 vol. 2017. (Spotlight on the Civil Rights Movement Ser.). (ENG., Illus.). 48p. (J). (gr. 6-6). pap. 12.75 *(978-1-5383-8026-0(9)*, 25b8f5e8-d5c9-43d2-bb6e-bb032e8b0356) Rosen Publishing Group, Inc., The.

Doeden, Matt. John Lewis: Courage in Action. 2018. (Gateway Biographies Ser.). (ENG., Illus.). 48p. (J). (gr. 4-8). 31.99 *(978-1-5415-1238-2(3)*, c3bd6e6c-7a71-4a92-a1fb-b9894d102410, Lerner Pubns.) Lerner Publishing Group.

Fremon, David K. The Jim Crow Laws & Racism in United States History, 1 vol. 2014. (In United States History Ser.). (ENG., Illus.). 96p. (J). (gr. 5-6). pap. 13.88 *(978-0-7660-6093-7(4)*, 1fa3834b-0b6a-42f9-9e05-83d934804825) Enslow Publishing, LLC.

Hinton, Kerry. Sit-Ins & Nonviolent Protest for Racial Equality, 1 vol. 2017. (Spotlight on the Civil Rights Movement Ser.). (ENG., Illus.). 48p. (J). (gr. 6-6). pap. 12.75 *(978-1-5383-8064-2(1)*, 6766c7e7-1637-4622-98c3-92162a48c4ee, Rosen Young Adult) Rosen Publishing Group, Inc., The.

Hunter-Gault, Charlayne. To the Mountaintop: My Journey Through the Civil Rights Movement. 2014. (New York Times Ser.). (ENG., Illus.). 224p. (YA). (gr. 7). pap. 16.00 *(978-1-250-04062-6(0)*, 900124083) Square Fish.

Hussey, Maria. The Rise of the Jim Crow ERA, 1 vol. 2015. (African American Experience: from Slavery to the Presidency Ser.). (ENG., Illus.). 80p. (J). (gr. 7-8). 35.47 *(978-1-68048-042-9(1)*, a8ce4d36-15e5-4b4b-be24-79033d0d3e75, Britannica Educational Publishing) Rosen Publishing Group, Inc., The.

Hussey, Maria, ed. The Rise of the Jim Crow Era, 4 vols. 2015. (African American Experience: from Slavery to the Presidency Ser.). (ENG.). 80p. (YA). (gr. 7-8). 70.94 *(978-1-68048-043-6(X)*, 62dddc2c-3921-4b30-b75b-4189b361ea36, Britannica Educational Publishing) Rosen Publishing Group, Inc., The.

Latta, Susan M. Reconstruction Era, 1 vol. 2014. (African-American History Ser.). (ENG.). 48p. (J). (gr. 4-8). lib. bdg. 35.64 *(978-1-62403-147-2(1)*, 1175) ABDO Publishing Co.

Levy, Debbie. Slaves on a Southern Plantation. 2004. (Daily Life Ser.). (ENG., Illus.). 48p. (J). 27.50 *(978-0-7377-1827-0(7)*, Greenhaven Pr., Inc.) Cengage Gale.

Machajewski, Sarah. The Freedom Rides: The Rise of the Civil Rights Movement, 1 vol. 2017. (Lucent Library of Black History Ser.). (ENG.). 104p. (YA). (gr. 7-7). pap. 20.99 *(978-1-5345-6298-1(2)*, b930c3e5-bb00-4a19-bad6-f4564c9f28ad); lib. bdg. 41.03 *(978-1-5345-6239-4(7)*, 5d382c93-59ab-40ea-97c0-a7aec6f9e606) Greenhaven Publishing LLC. (Lucent Pr.).

Maloof, Torrey. Reconstruction: Freedom Delayed. rev. ed. 2017. (Social Studies: Informational Text Ser.). (ENG., Illus.). 32p. (gr. 4-8). pap. 11.99 *(978-1-4938-3806-6(7))* Teacher Created Materials, Inc.

Maraniss, Andrew. Strong Inside (Young Readers Edition) The True Story of How Perry Wallace Broke College Basketball's Color Line. 2017. (Illus.). 272p. (J). (gr. 5). 10.99 *(978-1-5247-3727-6(5)*, Puffin Books) Penguin Young Readers Group.

Miller, Jake. Sit-Ins & Freedom Rides: The Power of Nonviolent Resistance. (Library of the Civil Rights Movement Ser.). 24p. (gr. 3-3). 2009. 42.50 *(978-1-60853-892-8(3))* 2003. (ENG., Illus.). (J). lib. bdg. 26.27 *(978-0-8239-6253-2(9)*, 820657be-4c2f-44d5-96a6-c913fba1c55d) Rosen Publishing Group, Inc., The. (PowerKids Pr.).

Mortensen, Lori. Voices of the Civil Rights Movement. 2015. (We Shall Overcome Ser.). (ENG., Illus.). 32p. (J). (gr. 3-6). lib. bdg. 27.99 *(978-1-4914-2044-7(8)*, 127522) Capstone.

Muldoon, Kathleen M. Jim Crow Era, 1 vol. 2014. (African-American History Ser.). (ENG., Illus.). 48p. (J). (gr. 4-8). lib. bdg. 35.64 *(978-1-62403-146-5(3)*, 1173) ABDO Publishing Co.

Pinkney, Andrea Davis. Sit-In: How Four Friends Stood up by Sitting Down. 2010. (ENG., Illus.). 40p. (J). (gr. 1-17). 18.99 *(978-0-316-07016-4(5))* Little, Brown Bks. for Young Readers.

Rappaport, Doreen. Free at Last! Stories & Songs of Emancipation. Evans, Shane W., illus. 2006. (ENG.). 64p. (J). (gr. 4-7). pap. 9.99 *(978-0-7636-3147-5(7))* Candlewick Pr.

Sapet, Kerrily. John Lewis. 2009. (Political Profiles Ser.). 100p. (YA). (gr. 5-9). 28.95 *(978-1-59935-130-8(7))* Reynolds, Morgan Inc.

Tisdale, Rachel. The Freedom Riders, 1 vol., 1. 2013. (We Shall Overcome Ser.). (ENG.). 32p. (J). (gr. 4-6). 28.93 *(978-1-4777-6061-1(X)*, f142af66-6ae7-44b2-9331-8ef88702bdbb, PowerKids Pr.) Rosen Publishing Group, Inc., The.

Uschan, Michael V. Murder & Lynching in the Deep South, 1 vol. 2006. (Lucent Library of Black History Ser.). (ENG., Illus.). 104p. (gr. 7-7). lib. bdg. 37.73 *(978-1-59018-845-3(4)*, ce6b490c-7d1f-4065-a5f5-cc0abcd95d67, Lucent Pr.) Greenhaven Publishing LLC.

Welch, Catherine A. Children of the Civil Rights Era. 2005. (Picture the American Past Ser.). (Illus.). 48p. (J). (gr. 2-5). lib. bdg. 22.60 *(978-1-57505-481-0(7))* Lerner Publishing Group.

SOUTHWEST, NEW

Here are entered works on that part of the United States which roughly corresponds to the old Spanish province of New Mexico, including the present Arizona, New Mexico, southern Colorado, Utah, Nevada and California.

Alagna, Magdalena. Wyatt Earp: Lawman of the American West. 2009. (Primary Sources of Famous People in American History Ser.). 32p. (gr. 2-3). 47.90 *(978-1-60851-747-3(0))* Rosen Publishing Group, Inc., The.

—Wyatt Earp: Lawman of the American West / Sheriff del oeste Americano. 2009. (Famous People in American History/Grandes personajes en la historia de los Estados Unidos Ser.). (ENG & SPA.). 32p. (gr. 2-3). 47.90 *(978-1-61512-558-6(2)*, Editorial Buenas Letras) Rosen Publishing Group, Inc., The.

—Wyatt Earp: Sheriff del oeste americano (Wyatt Earp: Lawman of the American West) 2009. (Grandes personajes en la historia de los Estados Unidos (Famous People in American History) Ser.). (SPA.). 32p. (gr. 2-3). 47.90 *(978-1-61512-811-2(5)*, Editorial Buenas Letras) Rosen Publishing Group, Inc., The.

Aldridge, Rebecca. The Hoover Dam. 2009. (Building America: Then & Now Ser.). (ENG., Illus.). 120p. (gr. 5-8). 35.00 *(978-1-60413-069-0(5)*, P161625, Facts On File) Infobase Holdings, Inc.

Alpers, Jody. T Is for Tortilla: A Southwestern Alphabet Book. Johnson, Celeste, illus. 2006. (J). (gr. -1-3). *(978-1-929115-14-3(8))* Azro Pr., Inc.

Anderson, Dale. The Anasazi Culture at Mesa Verde, 1 vol. 2003. (Landmark Events in American History Ser.). (ENG., Illus.). 48p. (gr. 5-8). lib. bdg. 33.67 *(978-0-8368-5371-1(7)*, d8a2b8ef-2688-4037-9941-f19b059b0349, Gareth Stevens Secondary Library) Stevens, Gareth Publishing LLLP.

Andrews, Barbara. The Southwest Region. 2006. (J). pap. *(978-1-4108-6433-8(2))* Benchmark Education Co.

Connors, Kathleen. Let's Explore the Great Basin, 1 vol. 2013. (Road Trip: Exploring America's Regions Ser.). 24p. (J). (gr. 2-3). (ENG.). pap. 9.15 *(978-1-4339-9125-7(X)*, c666168a-eced-4cbd-8c3f-8d29da4d1b8f); pap. 48.90 *(978-1-4339-9126-4(8))*; (ENG., Illus.). lib. bdg. 25.27 *(978-1-4339-9124-0(1)*, a1f4c056-8766-48fc-9f32-0911608a9712) Stevens, Gareth Publishing LLLP.

—Let's Explore the Southwest, 1 vol. 2013. (Road Trip: Exploring America's Regions Ser.). (ENG.). 24p. (J). (gr. 2-3). pap. 9.15 *(978-1-4339-9150-9(0)*, 4ee82a8d-5ce9-4343-8469-83c76dfb91f2); (Illus.). lib. bdg. 25.27 *(978-1-4339-9149-3(7)*, c4111111-1d5e-4dd0-8a2f-834a0f08659a) Stevens, Gareth Publishing LLLP.

Cooke, Tim. Billy the Kid: A Notorious Gunfighter of the Wild West, 1 vol. 2015. (Wanted! Famous Outlaws Ser.). (ENG., Illus.). 48p. (J). (gr. 6-8). pap. 15.05 *(978-1-4824-4243-4(4)*, db263247-1a67-4b89-9656-f6d897eddd3b) Stevens, Gareth Publishing LLLP.

—Explore with Francisco Vazquez de Coronado. 2016. (Travel with the Great Explorers Ser.). (ENG., Illus.). 32p. (J). (gr. 3-6). *(978-0-7787-2847-4(1))* Crabtree Publishing Co.

Cunningham, Kevin & Benoit, Peter. The Ute. 2011. (True Bk Ser.). 48p. (J). pap. 6.95 *(978-0-531-29307-2(6))*; (gr. 3-5). 29.00 *(978-0-531-20765-9(X))* Scholastic Library Publishing. (Children's Pr.).

Dean, Arlan. The Old Spanish Trail: From Santa Fe, New Mexico to Los Angeles, California. 2009. (Famous American Trails Ser.). 24p. (gr. 3-3). 42.50 *(978-1-61512-489-3(6)*, PowerKids Pr.) Rosen Publishing Group, Inc., The.

—The Santa Fe Trail: From Independence, Missouri to Santa Fe, New Mexico. 2009. (Famous American Trails Ser.). 24p. (gr. 3-3). 42.50 *(978-1-61512-492-3(6)*, PowerKids Pr.) Rosen Publishing Group, Inc., The.

Dewey, Jennifer Owings. The Shaman & the Water Serpent. Yazzie, Benton, illus. 2007. (ENG.). 40p. (J). 19.95 *(978-0-8263-4211-9(6)*, P123732) Univ. of New Mexico Pr.

Freedman, Russell. In the Days of the Vaqueros. 2008. (ENG., Illus.). 80p. (YA). (gr. 7). pap. 9.99 *(978-0-547-13365-2(0)*, 1048765, Clarion Bks.) HarperCollins Pubs.

Gagne, Tammy. Exploring the Southwest. 2017. (Exploring America's Regions Ser.). (ENG., Illus.). 48p. (J). (gr. 4-8). lib. bdg. 35.64 *(978-1-5321-1384-0(6)*, 27682) ABDO Publishing Co.

Glasscock, Sarah. The Southwest: Set Of 6. 2011. (Navigators Ser.). (J). pap. 48.00 net. *(978-1-4108-5104-8(4))* Benchmark Education Co.

—The Southwest: Text Pairs. 2008. (Bridges/Navigators Ser.). (J). (gr. 4). 89.00 *(978-1-4108-8397-1(3))* Benchmark Education Co.

Goodman, Michael E. Wyatt Earp. 2005. (Legends of the West Ser.). (Illus.). 48p. (J). (gr. 5-9). lib. bdg. 21.95 *(978-1-58341-339-5(1)*, Creative Education) Creative Co., The.

Hall, Margaret. Venom & Visions: Art of the Southwest. 2007. (Shockwave: Arts & Culture Ser.). (ENG., Illus.). 36p. (J). (gr. 4-8). 25.00 *(978-0-531-17788-4(2)*, Children's Pr.) Scholastic Library Publishing.

Hazelton, Amie. Francisco Vasquez de Coronado: An Explorer of the Southwest. 2017. (World Explorers Ser.). (ENG., Illus.). 32p. (J). (gr. 3-6). lib. bdg. 27.99 *(978-1-5157-4203-6(2)*, 133970, Capstone Pr.) Capstone.

S

Healy, Nick. Billy the Kid. 2005. (Legends of the West (Creative Education) Ser.). (Illus.). 48p. (J). (gr. 5-9). lib. bdg. 21.95 *(978-1-58341-335-7(9)*, Creative Education) Creative Co., The.

HELMAN, Wolfe Jecan. C Is for Coyote: A Southwest Alphabet Book. 2017. (Illus.). 32p. (J). (gr. k-3). bds. 7.95 *(978-1-63076-300-8(4))* Muddy Boots Pr.

Hernández, Roger E. & Hernández, Roger E. Early Explorations, The 1500s, 1 vol. 2009. (Hispanic America Ser.). (ENG.). 80p. (gr. 5-5). lib. bdg. 36.93 *(978-0-7614-2937-1(9)*, b16d1ad5-064e-49b4-aaa7-c60082b1692b) Cavendish Square Publishing LLC.

King, David C. Projects about the Spanish West, 1 vol. 2007. (Hands-On History Ser.). (ENG., Illus.). 48p. (gr. 3-3). lib. bdg. 34.07 *(978-0-7614-1982-2(9)*, a52eb496-efaf-4d41-8b47-36b641d7e99d) Cavendish Square Publishing LLC.

Let's Explore the Southwest. 2013. (Road Trip: Exploring America's Regions Ser.). 24p. (J). (gr. 2-5). pap. 48.90 *(978-1-4339-9151-6(9))* Stevens, Gareth Publishing LLLP.

Maynard, Charles W. Zebulon Pike: Soldier-Explorer of the American Southwest. 2009. (Famous Explorers of the American West Ser.). 24p. (gr. 3-4). 42.50 *(978-1-61512-506-7(X)*, PowerKids Pr.) Rosen Publishing Group, Inc., The.

Miller, Reagan & Peppas, Lynn. What's in the Southwest? Crabtree Publishing Staff, ed. 2011. (All Around the U.S. Ser.: No. 4). (ENG.). 32p. (J). (gr. 3-6). pap. *(978-0-7787-1832-1(8))* Crabtree Publishing Co.

Mountjoy, Shane. Francisco Coronado & the Seven Cities of Gold. 2005. (Explorers of New Lands Ser.). (ENG., Illus.). 160p. (gr. 5-8). lib. bdg. 30.00 *(978-0-7910-8631-5(3)*, P114347, Facts On File) Infobase Holdings, Inc.

National Geographic Learning. Reading Expeditions (Social Studies: Readings about America): the Southwest Today. 2007. (Nonfiction Reading & Writing Workshops Ser.). (ENG., Illus.). 32p. (J). pap. 18.95 *(978-0-7922-4535-3(0))* CENGAGE Learning.

Peppas, Lynn. Why Francisco Coronado Matters to Texas, 1 vol. 2013. (Texas Perspectives Ser.). (ENG., Illus.). 32p. (J). (gr. 4-4). lib. bdg. 28.93 *(978-1-4777-0909-2(6)*, ea11e18a-2750-4bf4-ad7a-d5d0300c739e) Rosen Publishing Group, Inc., The.

Perritano, John. Spanish Missions. 2010. (True Book Ser.). (Illus.). 48p. (J). pap. 6.95 *(978-0-531-21238-7(6))*; (ENG., (gr. 3-5). 21.19 *(978-0-531-20575-4(4)*, Children's Pr.) Scholastic Library Publishing.

Smith-Llera, Danielle. People & Places of the Southwest. 2016. (United States by Region Ser.). (ENG., Illus.). 32p. (J). (gr. 3-6). lib. bdg. 27.99 *(978-1-5157-2442-1(5)*, 132821, Capstone Pr.) Capstone.

Steele, Christy. California & the Southwest Join the United States, 1 vol. 2004. (America's Westward Expansion Ser.). (ENG., Illus.). 48p. (gr. 5-8). lib. bdg. 33.67 *(978-0-8368-5786-3(0)*, 12bac90f-b38b-4e68-9457-aecac44c0b39, Gareth Stevens Secondary Library) Stevens, Gareth Publishing LLLP.

Steloff, Rebecca. Texas & the Far West, 1 vol. 2003. (North American Historical Atlases Ser.). (ENG., Illus.). 48p. (gr. 5-5). 32.64 *(978-0-7614-1345-5(6)*, 0ac39afa-f94c-43f2-bb35-12911614d67a) Cavendish Square Publishing LLC.

Tarbox, A. D. A Desert Food Chain: Nature's Bounty. 2nd ed. 2015. (Odysseys in Nature Ser.). (ENG., Illus.). 80p. (J). (gr. 7-10). *(978-1-60818-539-9(7)*, 20965, Creative Education) Creative Co., The.

Thompson, Paul B. Billy the Kid: It Was a Game of Two & I Got There First, 1 vol. 2008. (Americans: the Spirit of a Nation Ser.). (ENG., Illus.). 128p. (gr. 5-6). lib. bdg. 35.93 *(978-0-7660-3480-8(1)*, efb3071a-90e0-4603-bfb4-ea376dda4901) Enslow Publishing, LLC.

Urban, William. Wyatt Earp: The O. K. Corral & the Law of the American West. 2009. (Library of American Lives & Times Ser.). 112p. (gr. 5-5). 69.20 *(978-1-60853-512-5(6))* Rosen Publishing Group, Inc., The.

Walsh, Steve. Zebulon Montgomery Pike: Explorer & Military Officer. 2011. (ENG & SPA., Illus.). 54p. (J). pap. 8.95 *(978-0-86541-123-4(9))* Filter Pr., LLC.

Weisberg, Barbara & Haley, Alex. Coronado's Golden Quest. Eagle, Mike, illus. 2009. (Steck-Vaughn Stories of America Ser.). (ENG.). 88p. (gr. 3-8). pap. 14.20 *(978-0-8114-8072-7(0))* Houghton Mifflin Harcourt Publishing Co.

Wiewandt, Thomas A. Hidden Life of the Desert. 2nd ed. 2010. (J). *(978-0-87842-555-6(1))* Mountain Pr. Publishing Co., Inc.

Wiseman, Blaine. The Southwest. 2016. (Illus.). 48p. (J). *(978-1-5105-1142-2(3))* SmartBook Media, Inc.

World Book, Inc. Staff, contrib. by. Indians of the Southwest. 2009. (J). *(978-0-7166-2142-3(8))* World Bk., Inc.

Worth, Richard. The Texas War of Independence: The 1800s, 1 vol. 2009. (Hispanic America Ser.). (ENG.). 80p. (gr. 5-5). lib. bdg. 36.93 *(978-0-7614-2934-0(4)*, 15e26fa2-4c55-418b-9cdd-d43ad23078b) Cavendish Square Publishing LLC.

Wyatt Earp. 2010. (ENG., Illus.). 112p. (gr. 6-12). 35.00 *(978-1-60413-597-8(2)*, P179311, Facts On File) Infobase Holdings, Inc.

SOUTHWEST, NEW—FICTION

Allred, Sylvester. Jabber the Steller's Jay. Iverson, Diane, illus. 2017. (ENG.). 32p. (J). (gr. k-3). 16.99 *(978-1-943328-89-5(7)*, West Winds Pr.) West Margin Pr.

Browne, Vee. The Stone Cutter & the Navajo Maiden. Manavi, Lorraine Begay, tr. from ENG. Brycelea, Clifford & Yazzie, Johnson, illus. 2008. (NAV & ENG.). 32p. (J). (gr. -1-3). 17.95 *(978-1-893354-92-0(X))* Salina Bookshelf Inc.

Bruchac, Joseph. Killer of Enemies, 1 vol. 2013. (Killer of Enemies Ser.). (ENG.). 400p. (YA). 19.95 *(978-1-62014-143-4(4)*, 1620141434, Tu Bks.) Lee & Low Bks., Inc.

—Trail of the Dead, 1 vol. 2015. (Killer of Enemies Ser.: 2). (ENG.). 400p. (YA). (gr. 7-12). 19.95 *(978-1-62014-261-5(9)*, leelowtu) Lee & Low Bks., Inc.

Carrillo, P. S. Desert Passage. 2008. (ENG.). 192p. (YA). (gr. 6-18). pap. 10.95 *(978-1-55885-517-5(3)*, Piñata Books) Arte Publico Pr.

Crum, Sally. Race to the River: The Ancient Journey Continues. 2009. (YA). pap. 12.95 *(978-1-932738-72-8(X))* Western Reflections Publishing Co.

Gutman, Dan. From Texas with Love. 2014. (Genius Files Ser.: 4). (J). lib. bdg. 17.20 *(978-0-606-36462-1(5))* Turtleback.

—The Genius Files #4: from Texas with Love. 2014. (Genius Files Ser.: 4). (ENG.). (J). (gr. 3-7). 304p. pap. 9.99 *(978-0-06-182775-4(4))*; (Illus.). 288p. 16.99 *(978-0-06-182773-0(8))* HarperCollins Pubs. (HarperCollins).

Hobbs, Will. The Big Wander. 2004. (Illus.). 181p. (J). (gr. 5-9). 13.65 *(978-0-7569-4970-9(X))* Perfection Learning Corp.

Jennings, Terry Catasús. Vivian & the Legend of the Hoodoos. Saroff, Phyllis, illus. 2017. (ENG.). 32p. (J). (gr. k-3). 17.95 *(978-1-62855-957-6(8))* Arbordale Publishing.

—Viviana y la Leyenda de Los Hoodoos. Saroff, Phyllis, illus. 2017. (SPA.). 32p. (J). (gr. 2-3). pap. 11.95 *(978-1-62855-959-0(4)*, bcd3114a-be6e-4f61-816b-c75146a5cb44) Arbordale Publishing.

La Farge, Oliver. Cochise of Arizona. 2014. 222p. pap. 24.95 *(978-0-86534-675-8(5))* Sunstone Pr.

Lamadrid, Enrique R. Amadito & the Hero Children: Amadito y Los Niños Héroes. Córdova, Amy, illus. 2011. (SPA & ENG.). (J). *(978-0-8263-4978-1(1))* Univ. of New Mexico Pr.

—Amadito & the Hero Children: Amadito y Los niños Héroes. Córdova, Amy & Córdova, Amy, illus. 2011. (ENG.). 60p. (J). E-Book *(978-0-8263-4980-4(3))* Univ. of New Mexico Pr.

Lowell, Susan. A Very Hairy Christmas. Harris, Jim, illus. 2012. (J). *(978-1-933855-80-6(0))* Rio Nuevo Pubs.

McCormack, Caren McNelly. The Fiesta Dress: A Quinceanera Tale, 0 vols. Aviles, Martha, illus. 2012. (ENG.). 42p. (J). (gr. -1-3). pap. 9.99 *(978-0-7614-6236-1(8)*, 9780761462361, Two Lions) Amazon Publishing.

Muldoon, Kathleen M. The Runaway Skeleton. Hilliker, Phillip, illus. 2008. (Vortex Bks.). (ENG.). 112p. (J). (gr. 5-9). 26.65 *(978-1-4342-0800-2(1)*, 95205, Stone Arch Bks.) Capstone.

Muller, Seth. The Day of Storms, 3 vols. Dubay, Tayloe, ed. Whitethorne, Bahe, Jr., illus. 2010. (Keepers of the WindClaw Chronicles: Bk. 3). 224p. (J). pap. 12.95 *(978-1-893354-10-4(5))* Salina Bookshelf Inc.

—The Mockingbird's Manual. Tayloe, McConnell Dubay, ed. Whitethorne, Bahe, Jr., illus. 2009. (Keepers of the WindClaw Chronicles: Bk. 1). (ENG.). 128p. (J). (gr. 4-7). pap. 12.95 *(978-1-893354-04-3(0))* Salina Bookshelf Inc.

O'Dell, Scott. Sing down the Moon. 2011. 9.00 *(978-0-7848-3596-8(9)*, Everbind) Marco Bk. Co.

—Sing down the Moon: A Newbery Honor Award Winner. 2010. (ENG.). 144p. (J). (gr. 3-7). pap. 7.99 *(978-0-547-40632-9(0)*, 1428509, Clarion Bks.) HarperCollins Pubs.

Parpan, Justin, illus. Gwango's Lonesome Trail. 2006. 32p. (J). (gr. -1-3). 15.95 *(978-0-60106-004-2(2))* Red Cygnet Pr.

Randles, Slim. Ol' Jimmy Dollar. Montoya, Jerry, illus. 2018. (ENG.). 52p. (J). (gr. 1-3). pap. 17.95 *(978-1-943681-24-2(4))* Nuevo Bks.

Randles, Slim & Montoya, Jerry, illus. Ol' Jimmy Dollar. 2015. 42p. (J). *(978-1-936744-40-4(6))* LPD Pr.

Rivera-Ashford, Roni Capin & Johnson, Richard. Hip Hip Hooray, It's Monsoon Day! 2007. (ENG & SPA.). (YA). pap. 15.95 *(978-1-886679-36-8(3))* Arizona Sonora Desert Museum Pr.

Spady, Angela. Channing o'Banning & the Turquoise Trail, 1 vol. 2015. (ENG., Illus.). 128p. (J). pap. 6.99 *(978-0-7180-3236-4(5)*, Tommy Nelson) Nelson, Thomas Inc.

Wells, Rosemary. Ivy Takes Care. LaMarche, Jim, illus. 2015. (ENG.). 208p. (J). (gr. 3-7). pap. 6.99 *(978-0-7636-7660-5(8))* Candlewick Pr.

SOUTHWEST, OLD

Here are entered works on the section which comprised the southwestern part of the United States before the cessions of land from Mexico following the Mexican War. It includes Louisiana, Texas, Arkansas, Tennessee, Kentucky and Missouri.

Gallagher, Derek, text. Ancient Dwellings of the Southwest. 2004. (Illus.). 10p. (J). 16.95 *(978-1-58369-048-2(4))* Western National Parks Assn.

SOUTHWEST, OLD—FICTION

Ts'o, Pauline. Whispers of the Wolf. 2015. (Illus.). 40p. (J). (gr. k-3). 16.95 *(978-1-937786-45-8(5)*, Wisdom Tales) World Wisdom, Inc.

SOVEREIGNS

see Kings, Queens, Rulers, etc.

SOVIET UNION

Baker, Lawrence W. Cold War Reference Library Cumulative Index. 2003. (Cold War Reference Library). (ENG.). 85p. (J). 5.00 *(978-0-7876-7667-4(5)*, UXL) Cengage Gale.

—Immigration & Migration Reference. 2004. (US Immigration & Migration Reference Library). (ENG.). (J). 5.00 *(978-0-7876-7734-3(5)*, UXL) Cengage Gale.

Hanes, Sharon M., et al. Cold War: Almanac, 2 vols. 2003. (U-X-L Cold War Reference Library). (Illus.). (J). *(978-0-7876-9087-8(2))*; (ENG., 376p. lib. bdg. 233.00 *(978-0-7876-9089-2(9))* Cengage Gale. (UXL).

Kallen, Stuart A. Primary Sources. 2003. (American War Library). (ENG., Illus.). 112p. (J). 30.85 *(978-1-59018-243-7(X)*, Lucent Bks.) Cengage Gale.

Márquez, Herón. Russia in Pictures. 2nd ed. 2003. (Visual Geography Series, Second Ser.). (ENG., Illus.). 80p. (gr. 5-12). 31.93 *(978-0-8225-0937-0(7))* Lerner Publishing Group.

SOVIET UNION—BIOGRAPHY

Feldman, Heather. Valentina Tereshkova: The First Woman in Space. 2009. (Space Firsts Ser.). 24p. (gr. 3-4). 42.50 *(978-1-60853-114-1(7)*, PowerKids Pr.) Rosen Publishing Group, Inc., The.

Glaser, Jason. Maria Sharapova, 1 vol. 2007. (Sports Idols Ser.). (ENG., Illus.). 24p. (J). (gr. 2-3). lib. bdg. 26.27 *(978-1-4042-4181-7(7)*, 156bb605-656e-463c-9237-31009e5b6526) Rosen Publishing Group, Inc., The.

Goldstein, Margaret J. V. I. Lenin. 2007. (Biography Ser.). (Illus.). 112p. (J). (gr. 3-7). lib. bdg. 29.27 *(978-0-8225-5977-1(3)*, Twenty-First Century Bks.) Lerner Publishing Group.

Hubbard, Ben. Yuri Gagarin & the Race to Space. 2015. (Adventures in Space Ser.). (ENG., Illus.). 48p. (J). (gr. 4-6). 35.99 *(978-1-4846-2514-9(5)*, 130011, Heinemann) Capstone.

McCollum, Sean. Joseph Stalin. 2010. (Wicked History Ser.). (ENG., Illus.). 128p. (J). 31.00 *(978-0-531-20755-0(2)*, Watts, Franklin) Scholastic Library Publishing.

—Joseph Stalin (a Wicked History) 2010. (Wicked History Ser.). (ENG.). 128p. (J). (gr. 6-12). pap. 5.95 *(978-0-531-22355-0(8)*, Watts, Franklin) Scholastic Library Publishing.

Resnick, Abraham. Lenin: Founder of the Soviet Union. 2004. 132p. (YA). pap. 13.95 *(978-0-595-30701-2(9)*, Authors Choice Pr.) iUniverse, Inc.

Stewart, Mark. Maria Sharapova, 1 vol. 2009. (Today's Superstars Ser.). (ENG.). 48p. (J). (gr. 3-3). pap. 15.05 *(978-1-4339-2160-5(X)*, 24baefdc-301b-4986-bba8-d9089f3150cb); lib. bdg. 34.60 *(978-1-4339-1967-1(2)*, 51b4d2c6-8be2-4fd4-961d-13284c76cb8e) Stevens, Gareth Publishing LLLP.

SOVIET UNION—FICTION

Abadzis, Nick. Laika. 2014. (YA). lib. bdg. 22.10 *(978-0-606-36130-9(8))* Turtleback.

Anthony, Horowitz. Russian Roulette. 2014. (Alex Rider Ser.: 10). lib. bdg. 19.65 *(978-0-606-36189-7(8))* Turtleback.

Appleton, Victor. Tom Swift & his Air Glider. 2005. 26.95 *(978-1-4218-1500-8(1)*, 1st World Library - Literary Society) 1st World Publishing, Inc.

Blaine, John. The Boy Scouts in Russia. 2018. (ENG., Illus.). 118p. (YA). (gr. 7-12). pap. *(978-93-5297-261-6(9))* Alpha Editions.

—Boy Scouts in Russia. 2006. 25.95 *(978-1-4218-2968-5(1))*; pap. 10.95 *(978-1-4218-3068-1(X))* 1st World Publishing, Inc.

Blue, Sebastien. Liquid Diamond. 2013. 176p. *(978-1-4602-3345-0(X))* FriesenPress.

Brooks, Kaarina. Boy from Karelia. 2017. (ENG., Illus.). 248p. pap. 14.95 *(978-1-988763-09-5(6))* Villa Wisteria Pubns.

Carson, John E. & Carson, Marlene R. Ramblin' Rose: The Porcelain Mines in Russia. 2007. (Ramblin' Rose Ser.). 191p. (J). (gr. 8-12). per. 8.99 *(978-0-9776043-7-1(3))* Aspirations Media, Inc.

Celenza, Anna Harwell. Pictures at an Exhibition. Kitchel, JoAnn E., illus. 2016. (Once upon a Masterpiece Ser.: 2). 32p. (J). (gr. 1-4). lib. bdg. 16.95 *(978-1-58089-528-6(X))* Charlesbridge Publishing, Inc.

Durbin, William. The Darkest Evening. 3rd ed. 2011. (Fesler-Lampert Minnesota Heritage Ser.). (ENG.). 248p. pap. 9.95 *(978-0-8166-7568-5(6))* Univ. of Minnesota Pr.

Flannigan, Liz. Starlight Grey. Docampo, Valeria, illus. 2013. (Magic Stories Ser.). 48p. (J). (gr. 1-4). pap. 8.99 *(978-1-84686-778-1(9))* Barefoot Bks., Inc.

Grant, Myrna. Ivan & the American Journey. 2006. (Flamingo Fiction 9-13s Ser.). (ENG., Illus.). 144p. (J). (gr. 4-7). per. 6.99 *(978-1-84550-131-0(4)*, b03f49c8-dc2a-4123-856a-b53453a4d806) Christian Focus Pubns. GBR. Dist: Baker & Taylor Publisher Services (BTPS).

—Ivan & the Hidden Bible. rev. ed. 2006. (Flamingo Fiction 9-13s Ser.). (ENG., Illus.). 144p. (J). (gr. 4-7). per. 6.99 *(978-1-84550-133-4(0)*, a73bcfb0-1d15-46e7-ad2b-7adb1c86a432) Christian Focus Pubns. GBR. Dist: Baker & Taylor Publisher Services (BTPS).

—Ivan & the Informer. 2013. (Flamingo Fiction 9-13s Ser.). (ENG., Illus.). 128p. (J). (gr. 1-8). per. 6.99 *(978-1-84550-134-1(9)*, 71281e29-3b04-49d6-b46d-9ed4f2583007) Christian Focus Pubns. GBR. Dist: Baker & Taylor Publisher Services (BTPS).

—Ivan & the Secret in the Suitcase. 2006. (Flamingo Fiction 9-13s Ser.). (ENG., Illus.). 144p. (J). (gr. 4-7). per. 6.99 *(978-1-84550-136-5(5)*, 90cf7cab-dea4-49c0-a1e1-347bc14e92d3) Christian Focus Pubns. GBR. Dist: Baker & Taylor Publisher Services (BTPS).

Hergé. The Calculus Affair. (Illus.). 62p. (J). 19.95 *(978-0-8288-5014-8(3))* French & European Pubns., Inc.

Hergé & Hergé. Tintin in the Land of the Soviets. 2007. (Adventures of Tintin: Original Classic Ser.). (ENG., Illus.). 144p. (J). (gr. 3-17). pap. 14.99 *(978-0-316-00374-2(3))* Little, Brown Bks. for Young Readers.

Horowitz, Anthony. Russian Roulette: The Story of an Assassin. 2014. (Alex Rider Ser.: 10). (ENG.). 432p. (J). (gr. 5). pap. 9.99 *(978-0-14-751231-4(X)*, Puffin Books) Penguin Young Readers Group.

Howell, Gill. Snow King. Cann, Helen, illus. 2005. (ENG.). 24p. (J). lib. bdg. 23.65 *(978-1-59646-742-2(8))* Dingles & Co.

Johnson, Vargie. Catherine the Great the Victorious: What Made Them Famous? 2006. 156p. (J). per. 15.00 *(978-1-931195-96-6(X))* KiwE Publishing, Ltd.

Katz, Gwen C. Among the Red Stars. (ENG.). 384p. (YA). (gr. 8). 2018. pap. 9.99 *(978-0-06-264275-2(8))* 2017. 17.99 *(978-0-06-264274-5(X))* HarperCollins Pubs. (HarperTeen).

Kiem, Elizabeth. Dancer, Daughter, Traitor, Spy. 2014. (Bolshoi Saga Ser.: 1). (Illus.). 304p. (YA). (gr. 9). pap. 10.99 *(978-1-61695-422-2(1)*, Soho Teen) Soho Pr., Inc.

King, Dedie. I See the Sun in Russia. Ossapova, Irina, tr. Inglese, Judith, illus. 2012. (I See the Sun Ser.: 4). (RUS.). 40p. (J). (gr. 1-7). 12.95 *(978-1-935874-08-9(X))* Satya Hse. Pubns.

Lasky, Kathryn. Night Witches: A Novel of World War II. 2017. 211p. (J). *(978-1-338-15866-3(X)*, Scholastic Pr.) Scholastic, Inc.

Litvina, Alexandra. The Apartment: a Century of Russian History. Bouis, Antonina W., tr. Desnitskaya, Anna, illus. 2019. (ENG.). 64p. (J). (gr. 3-7). 25.99 *(978-1-4197-3403-8(2)*, 1249901, Abrams Bks. for Young Readers) Abrams, Inc.

Ludmila's Way - Teaching Guide. 2003. (J). 17.95 *(978-1-55942-192-8(4))* Witcher Productions.

Maguire, Gregory. Egg & Spoon. (ENG.). 496p. (YA). (gr. 7). 2015. pap. 12.99 *(978-0-7636-8016-9(8))* 2014. (Illus.). 17.99 *(978-0-7636-7220-1(3))* Candlewick Pr.

Mayhew, Julie. Mother Tongue. 2019. (ENG.). 304p. (J). (gr. 9). 16.99 *(978-1-5362-0263-2(0))* Candlewick Pr.

Optic, Oliver, pseud. Northern Lands: Or, Young America in Russia & Prussia; A Story of Travel & Adventure / by William T. Adams (Oliver Optic). 2006. 384p. per. 26.99 *(978-1-4255-4074-6(0))* Michigan Publishing.

Pushkin, Alexksandr Sergeevich. The Daughter of the Commandant. 2017. (ENG., Illus.). (J). (gr. -1-7). 22.95 *(978-1-374-95089-4(0))*; pap. 12.95 *(978-1-374-95088-7(2))* Capital Communications, Inc.

Ransome, Arthur. Old Peter's Russian Tales. 2007. 180p. per. 12.95 *(978-1-60312-321-1(0))*; 24.95 *(978-1-60312-739-4(9))* Aegypan.

—Old Peter's Russian Tales. 2007. (ENG.). 200p. pap. 19.99 *(978-1-4346-0606-8(6))* Creative Media Partners, LLC.

—Old Peter's Russian Tales. 2005. 35.00 *(978-1-55742-465-5(9))*; pap. 15.95 *(978-1-55742-456-3(X))* Wildside Pr., LLC.

Stilton, Thea. Thea Stilton & the Lost Letters. 2015. (Thea Stilton Ser.: 21). (Illus.). 159p. (J). lib. bdg. 18.40 *(978-0-606-37061-5(7))* Turtleback.

Yehoshua, A. B. The Story of Crime & Punishment. Schoffman, Stuart, tr. Bougaeva, Sonja, illus. 2016. (Save the Story Ser.: 4). (ENG.). 104p. (J). (gr. 3-7). 19.95 *(978-1-78269-014-6(X)*, Pushkin Children's Bks.) Steerforth Pr.

Yelchin, Eugene. Breaking Stalin's Nose. 2013. (J). lib. bdg. 18.40 *(978-0-606-32308-6(2))* Turtleback.

SOVIET UNION—HISTORY

Allen, John. Debates on the Soviet Union's Collapse. 2018. (Debating History Ser.). (ENG.). 80p. (YA). (gr. 6-12). 39.93 *(978-1-68282-375-0(X))* ReferencePoint Pr., Inc.

Anderson, Matthew. Symphony for the City of the Dead: Dmitri Shostakovich & the Siege of Leningrad. 2017. (ENG.). 464p. (YA). (gr. 9). 26.95 *(978-0-606-39102-3(9))* Turtleback.

Bailey, Budd. The Formation & Dissolution of the Soviet Union, 1 vol. 2018. (Redrawing the Map Ser.). (ENG.). 112p. (YA). (gr. 9-9). lib. bdg. 45.93 *(978-1-5026-3565-5(8)*, 8a7ad011-9e58-4bda-adc7-58cdf87d98be) Cavendish Square Publishing LLC.

Blomquist, Christopher. A Primary Source Guide to Russia, 1 vol. 2004. (Countries of the World: a Primary Source Journey Ser.). (ENG., Illus.). 24p. (J). (gr. 2-3). lib. bdg. 26.27 *(978-1-4042-2756-9(3)*, 1abede21-a15b-446c-b4b0-dd1baa5f43df, PowerKids Pr.) Rosen Publishing Group, Inc., The.

Burgan, Michael. Miracle on Ice: How a Stunning Upset United a Country. 2016. (Captured History Sports Ser.). (ENG., Illus.). 64p. (J). (gr. 5-9). pap. 8.95 *(978-0-7565-5294-7(X)*, 131254, Compass Point Bks.) Capstone.

Favreau, Marc. Spies: The Secret Showdown Between America & Russia. 2019. (ENG., Illus.). 320p. (YA). (gr. 7-17). 19.99 *(978-0-316-54592-1(9))* Little, Brown Bks. for Young Readers.

Gay, Kathlyn. The Aftermath of the Russian Revolution. 2009. (Aftermath of History Ser.). (ENG.). 160p. (gr. 9-12). 38.60 *(978-0-8225-9092-7(1))* Lerner Publishing Group.

Goodman, Michael E. The KGB & Other Russian Spies. 2013. (Spies Around the World Ser.). (ENG., Illus.). 48p. (J). (gr. 5-9). pap. 12.00 *(978-0-89812-970-0(2)*, 21965, Creative Paperbacks) Creative Co., The.

Harkins, Susan Sales & Harkins, William H. The Fall of the Soviet Union 1991. 2007. (Monumental Milestones Ser.). (Illus.). 48p. (J). (gr. 4-7). lib. bdg. 29.95 *(978-1-58415-539-3(6))* Mitchell Lane Pubs.

Hudak, Heather C. The Space Race. 2018. (Uncovering the Past: Analyzing Primary Sources Ser.). (Illus.). 48p. (J). (gr. 5-6). *(978-0-7787-4749-9(2))* Crabtree Publishing Co.

Murray, Laura K. Spies in the KGB. 2016. (I Spy Ser.). (ENG., Illus.). 24p. (J). (gr. 1-4). *(978-1-60818-617-4(2)*, 20471, Creative Education) Creative Co., The.

The Russian Federation: Then & Now. 2014. (The Former Soviet Union: Then & Now). (ENG., Illus.). 80p. (J). lib. bdg. *(978-1-60152-692-2(X))* ReferencePoint Pr., Inc.

Suib, Stella. Inside Russia's SVR: The Foreign Intelligence Service. 2005. (Illus.). 63p. (YA). reprint ed. 26.00 *(978-0-7567-8668-7(1))* DIANE Publishing Co.

Wittrock, Jeni. Laika the Space Dog: First Hero in Outer Space, 1 vol. Toth, Shannon, illus. 2014. (Animal Heroes Ser.). (ENG.). 32p. (J). (gr. k-2). 29.32 *(978-1-4795-5463-8(4)*, 126113, Picture Window Bks.) Capstone.

Wittrock, Jeni, et al. Animal Heroes, 1 vol. 2014. (Animal Heroes Ser.). (ENG.). 32p. (J). (gr. k-2). 125.28 *(978-1-4795-5555-0(X)*, 21764, Picture Window Bks.) Capstone.

SOVIET UNION—HISTORY—FICTION

Brandes, Nadine. Romanov. 2019. 341p. (YA). *(978-1-4041-1165-3(4))* Nelson, Thomas Inc.

Durbin, William. The Darkest Evening. 3rd ed. 2011. (Fesler-Lampert Minnesota Heritage Ser.). (ENG.). 248p. pap. 9.95 *(978-0-8166-7568-5(6))* Univ. of Minnesota Pr.

Haar, Jaap Ter & Mearns, Martha. Boris. Poortvliet, Rien, illus. 2009. (J). pap. *(978-0-921100-72-0(8))* Inheritance Pubns.

Haddix, Margaret Peterson. Risked. 2013. (Missing Ser.: 6). (ENG., Illus.). 320p. (J). (gr. 3-7). 18.99 *(978-1-4169-8984-4(6)*, Simon & Schuster Bks. For Young Readers) Simon & Schuster Bks. For Young Readers.

—Risked. 2014. (Missing Ser.: 6). lib. bdg. 19.65 *(978-0-606-36096-8(4))* Turtleback.

Kiem, Elizabeth. Orphan, Agent, Prima, Pawn. 2018. (Bolshoi Saga Ser.: 3). 336p. (YA). (gr. 9). pap. 10.99 *(978-1-61695-908-1(8)*, Soho Teen) Soho Pr., Inc.

Lasky, Kathryn. The Night Journey. 2005. 151p. (gr. 3-7). 16.00 *(978-0-7569-5062-0(7))* Perfection Learning Corp.

Lough, Amber. Open Fire. 2020. (ENG.). 264p. (YA). (gr. 6-12). 18.99 *(978-1-5415-7289-8(0)*, 26390117-2d45-4720-a977-2ce45d9ddfb3, Carolrhoda Lab™) Lerner Publishing Group.

Miller, Sarah. The Lost Crown. 2012. (ENG., Illus.). 448p. (YA). (gr. 7). pap. 12.99 *(978-1-4169-8341-5(4)*, Atheneum Bks. for Young Readers) Simon & Schuster Children's Publishing.

Sedgwick, Marcus. Blood Red Snow White. 2017. (YA). lib. bdg. 22.10 *(978-0-606-40589-8(5))* Turtleback.

—Blood Red Snow White: A Novel. 2017. (ENG.). 336p. (YA). pap. 23.99 *(978-1-250-12963-5(X)*, 900160941) Square Fish.

Sepetys, Ruta. Ashes in the Snow (Movie Tie-In) 2018. (ENG.). 384p. (YA). (gr. 7). pap. 11.99

(978-1-9848-3674-8(9), Penguin Books) Penguin Young Readers Group.
—Between Shades of Gray. 2012. (ENG & JPN.). 398p. (YA). (gr. 7). pap. (978-4-00-115651-5(2)) Iwanami Shoten.
—Between Shades of Gray. 2009. 10.36 (978-0-7848-3779-5(1), Everbind) Marco Bk. Co.
—Between Shades of Gray. (ENG., (YA). (gr. 7-18). 2012. Illus.). 384p. pap. 12.99 (978-0-14-242059-1(X), Penguin Books) 2011. 352p. 19.99 (978-0-399-25412-3(9), Philomel Bks.) Penguin Young Readers Group.
—Between Shades of Gray. lt. ed. (ENG.). 2020. lib. bdg. 22.99 (978-1-4328-7360-8(1)) 2011. 432p. (YA). 23.99 (978-1-4104-4083-9(4)) Thorndike Pr.
—Between Shades of Gray. 2012. lib. bdg. 20.85 (978-0-606-26089-3(7)) Turtleback.
Vern, Jules. Michael Strogoff. 2006. 408p. pap. 26.45 (978-1-59462-432-2(1), Bk. Jungle) Standard Publications, Inc.
—Miguel Strogoff. (SPA., Illus.). 176p. (YA). 11.95 (978-84-7281-109-6(3), AF1109) Auriga, Ediciones S.A. ESP. Dist: Continental Bk. Co., Inc.
Vern, Jules & Verne, Julio. Miguel Strogoff. (Coleccion Clasicos de la Juventud). (SPA., Illus.). 236p. (J). 12.95 (978-84-7189-106-8(9), ORT305) Ortells, Alfredo Editorial S.L. ESP. Dist: Continental Bk. Co., Inc.
Whelan, Gloria. Angel on the Square. 2004. 288p. (gr. 5-9). 20.00 (978-0-7569-4062-1(1)) Perfection Learning Corp.
—Burying the Sun. 2004. 224p. (J). (gr. 5-18). (ENG.). 15.99 (978-0-06-054112-5(1)); lib. bdg. 16.89 (978-0-06-054113-2(X)) HarperCollins Pubs.
Wulffson, Don L. Soldier X. 2003. 240p. (YA). (gr. 7-18). 6.99 (978-0-14-250073-6(9), Puffin Books) Penguin Young Readers Group.
Yelchin, Eugene. Breaking Stalin's Nose. Yelchin, Eugene, illus. 2013. (ENG., Illus.). 176p. (J). (gr. 4-7). pap. 8.99 (978-1-250-03410-6(8), 900120580) Square Fish.

SOVIET UNION—HISTORY—1689-1800

Catherine the Great & the Enlightenment in Russia. 2005. (World Leaders Ser.). (Illus.). 160p. (gr. 6-12). lib. bdg. 28.95 (978-1-931798-27-3(3)) Reynolds, Morgan Inc.
Gibson, Karen Bush. The Life & Times of Catherine the Great. 2005. (Biography from Ancient Civilizations Ser.). (Illus.). 48p. (J). (gr. 4-7). lib. bdg. 29.95 (978-1-58415-347-4(4)) Mitchell Lane Pubs.

SOVIET UNION—HISTORY—REVOLUTION, 1905-1907

Engdahl, Sylvia, ed. The Bolshevik Revolution, 1 vol. 2013. (Perspectives on Modern World History Ser.). (ENG., Illus.). 232p. (gr. 10-12). lib. bdg. 49.43 (978-0-7377-6363-8(9), df75a956-0aa5-423b-9224-806e329e7449, Greenhaven Publishing) Greenhaven Publishing LLC.

SOVIET UNION—HISTORY—1917-1991

Choices Program - Brown University. The Russian Revolution, 2 vols. 2005. (ENG., Illus.). 124p. pap., lab manual ed. 34.00 (978-1-891306-79-2(0)) Choices Program, Brown Univ.
Johnson, Robert, compiled by. Lenin, Stalin & Communist Russia: The Myth & Reality of Communism. 2003. (Studymates Ser.). (Illus.). 132p. (C). pap. 27.50 (978-1-84285-039-8(3)) GLMP Ltd. GBR. Dist: Chicago Distribution Ctr.
Sherman, Josepha. The Cold War. 2004. (Chronicle of America's Wars Ser.). (Illus.). 96p. (J). (gr. 5-12). 27.93 (978-0-8225-0150-3(3)) Lerner Publishing Group.

SOVIET UNION—HISTORY—REVOLUTION, 1917-1921

Adcock, Michael. Cambridge Checkpoints VCE History - Russian Revolution 2014-16 & Quiz Me More, 1 vol. 2013. (Cambridge Checkpoints Ser.). (ENG.). pap., stu. ed., E-Book (978-1-107-66979-6(0)) Cambridge Univ. Pr.
Bjornlund, Lydia. Eyewitness to the Russian Revolution. 2018. (Eyewitness to World War I Ser.). (ENG.). 32p. (J). (gr. 4-7). lib. bdg. 35.64 (978-1-5038-1606-0(0), 211164) Child's World, Inc, The.
The BOLSHEVIK REVOLUTION. 2010. (ENG., Illus.). 120p. (gr. 9-18). 35.00 (978-1-60413-279-3(5), P179261, Facts On File) Infobase Holdings, Inc.
Fleming, Candace. The Family Romanov: Murder, Rebellion, & the Fall of Imperial Russia. 2014. (ENG., Illus.). 304p. (YA). (gr. 7). 19.99 (978-0-375-86782-8(1), Schwartz & Wade Bks.) Random Hse. Children's Bks.
Schmermund, Elizabeth & Edwards, Judith. Vladimir Lenin & the Russian Revolution, 1 vol. 2015. (People & Events That Changed the World Ser.). (ENG., Illus.). 128p. (gr. 7-8). 38.93 (978-0-7660-7414-9(5), d258c502-f6ad-49b2-a0ec-49c69ee3ba93) Enslow Publishing, LLC.
Trenton, Russell. The Russian Revolution: The Fall of the Tsars & the Rise of Communism, 1 vol. 2015. (Age of Revolution Ser.). (ENG., Illus.). 168p. (J). (gr. 9-10). 37.82 (978-1-68048-032-0(4), da4ab504-7d74-4c9c-ad97-3443afda5dd9, Britannica Educational Publishing) Rosen Publishing Group, Inc., The.
Whiting, Jim. The Russian Revolution 1917. 2007. (Monumental Milestones Ser.). (Illus.). 48p. (YA). (gr. 4-7). lib. bdg. 29.95 (978-1-58415-537-9(X)) Mitchell Lane Pubs.

SOVIET UNION—HISTORY—1925-1953

Abdo Publishing. Joseph Stalin, 1 vol. 2015. (Essential Lives Set 9 Ser.). (ENG., Illus.). 112p. (YA). (gr. 6-12). 41.36 (978-1-62403-896-9(4), 17824, Essential Library) ABDO Publishing Co.
Johnson, Robert, compiled by. Lenin, Stalin & Communist Russia: The Myth & Reality of Communism. 2003. (Studymates Ser.). (Illus.). 132p. (C). pap. 27.50 (978-1-84285-039-8(3)) GLMP Ltd. GBR. Dist: Chicago Distribution Ctr.
Jukes, Geoffrey & O'Neill, Robert John. World War II: The Eastern Front 1941-1945, 1 vol. 2010. (World War II: Essential Histories Ser.). (ENG., Illus.). 96p. (YA). (gr. 10-10). lib. bdg. 38.47 (978-1-4358-9134-0(1), 364c546d-4d20-4553-90dc-f1789407d04f) Rosen Publishing Group, Inc., The.
McCollum, Sean. Joseph Stalin. 2010. (Wicked History Ser.). (ENG., Illus.). 128p. (J). 31.00 (978-0-531-20755-0(2), Watts, Franklin) Scholastic Library Publishing.
—Joseph Stalin (a Wicked History) 2010. (Wicked History Ser.). (ENG.). 128p. (J). (gr. 6-12). pap. 5.95 (978-0-531-22355-0(8), Watts, Franklin) Scholastic Library Publishing.
Wein, Elizabeth. A Thousand Sisters: The Heroic Airwomen of the Soviet Union in World War II. 2019. (ENG., Illus.). 400p. (YA). (gr. 8). 19.99 (978-0-06-245301-3(7), Balzer & Bray) HarperCollins Pubs.
Zuehlke, Jeffrey. Joseph Stalin. 2006. (Biography Ser.). (Illus.). 112p. (J). (gr. 3-7). lib. bdg. 27.93 (978-0-8225-3421-1(5), Twenty-First Century Bks.) Lerner Publishing Group.

SOVIET UNION—POLITICS AND GOVERNMENT

Baier, Bret & Whitney, Catherine. Three Days in Moscow Young Readers' Edition: Ronald Reagan & the Fall of the Soviet Empire. 2018. (ENG., Illus.). 240p. (J). (gr. 3-7). 17.99 (978-0-06-286445-1(9), HarperCollins) HarperCollins Pubs.
Hurt, Avery Elizabeth. Superpower Rivalries & Proxy Warfare, 1 vol. 2017. (Cold War Chronicles Ser.). (ENG.). 112p. (YA). (gr. 9-9). lib. bdg. 44.50 (978-1-5026-2729-2(9), ea03d290-a7a9-4ca9-ae78-5843b274a9c7) Cavendish Square Publishing LLC.
Immell, Myra, ed. The Dissolution of the Soviet Union, 1 vol. 2010. (Perspectives on Modern World History Ser.). (ENG., Illus.). 216p. (gr. 10-12). 49.43 (978-0-7377-4794-2(3), 2ba433b8-6bcc-4cec-9404-a088cf5d4f21, Greenhaven Publishing) Greenhaven Publishing LLC.
Marcovitz, Hal. Cause & Effect the Fall of the Soviet Union: The Fall of the Soviet Union. 2015. (ENG., Illus.). 80p. (J). lib. bdg. (978-1-60152-792-9(6)) ReferencePoint Pr., Inc.
Roxburgh, Ellis. John F. Kennedy vs. Nikita Khrushchev: Cold War Adversaries, 1 vol. 2014. (History's Greatest Rivals Ser.). (ENG., Illus.). 48p. (J). (gr. 6-8). lib. bdg. 33.60 (978-1-4824-2221-4(2), bfc1cb51-8eeb-416d-af93-4cb9dbc51ac4) Stevens, Gareth Publishing LLLP.
Sasley, Brent. The Cold War in the Middle East, 1950-1991. 2009. (Making of the Middle East Ser.). (Illus.). 80p. (YA). (gr. 7-18). lib. bdg. 22.95 (978-1-4222-0173-2(2)) Mason Crest.
Small, Cathleen. The Collapse of Communism & the Breakup of the Soviet Union, 1 vol. 2017. (Cold War Chronicles Ser.). (ENG., Illus.). 112p. (YA). (gr. 9-9). 44.50 (978-1-5026-2728-5(0), 413d6192-bfc7-4333-ad83-081404abe46f) Cavendish Square Publishing LLC.

SPACE, OUTER

see Outer Space

SPACE AND TIME

see also Cyberspace; Relativity (Physics); Time Travel

Brezina, Corona. Time Travel, 1 vol. 2018. (Sci-Fi or STEM? Ser.). (ENG.). 64p. (gr. 7-7). 36.13 (978-1-5081-8046-3(6), 7d15399e-6b4e-4497-aa8e-89dbebbdcae3) Rosen Publishing Group, Inc., The.
Butterfield, Moira. Space. Biggin, Gary & Lipscombe, Nick, illus. 32p. (J). mass mkt. 8.99 (978-0-590-24424-4(8)) Scholastic, Inc.
Gaughan, Richard. Wormholes Explained, 1 vol. 2018. (Mysteries of Space Ser.). (ENG.). 80p. (gr. 7-7). 38.93 (978-0-7660-9965-4(2), 50898e31-3da7-4939-83fc-32809f8340db) Enslow Publishing, LLC.
Hantula, Richard & Asimov, Isaac. Space Junk, 1 vol. 2005. (Isaac Asimov's 21st Century Library of the Universe: Past & Present Ser.). (ENG., Illus.). 32p. (gr. 3-5). lib. bdg. 28.67 (978-0-8368-3983-8(8), 5a159410-ffad-46f9-94f5-3b38f21ab56a) Stevens, Gareth Publishing LLLP.
Jacklin, Karl. A Space in Time. (Illus.). (J). (gr. 3-6). pap. (978-1-876367-04-6(0)) Wizard Bks.
Kagayame, Johnny & Sherman, Josepha. Discovering the Construct of Time, 1 vol. 2011. (Scientist's Guide to Physics Ser.). (ENG.). 112p. (YA). (gr. 7-7). lib. bdg. 39.80 (978-1-4488-4703-7(6), 8308ad51-f29e-4641-aaef-4fb44890c71d) Rosen Publishing Group, Inc., The.
O'Byrne, John, ed. Space. 2007. (Little Guides). (Illus.). 320p. pap. 7.98 (978-1-74089-348-0(4)) Fog City Pr.
Perrin, Clotilde. At the Same Moment, Around the World. 2014. (ENG., Illus.). 36p. (J). (gr. k-3). 17.99 (978-1-4521-2208-3(3)) Chronicle Bks. LLC.
Rebman, Nick. What Is on Top? A Book about Positions. 2016. (Concept Fun Ser.). (ENG.). 16p. (J). (gr. -1-2). 29.93 (978-1-5038-0769-3(X), 210617) Child's World, Inc, The.
Robinson, Peg. The Science of Time Travel, 1 vol. 2018. (Science of Superpowers Ser.). (ENG.). 48p. (gr. 4-4). pap. 13.93 (978-1-5026-3802-1(9), 8bdff7fc-b48e-441d-88a3-cd70d80445d7) Cavendish Square Publishing LLC.
The Science of Space. 2016. (Illus.). 48p. (J). (978-1-4222-3515-7(7)) Mason Crest.
The Science of Time. 2016. (Illus.). 48p. (J). (978-1-4222-3516-4(5)) Mason Crest.
Tyson, Neil deGrasse & Mone, Gregory. Astrophysics for Young People in a Hurry. 2019. (ENG., Illus.). (J). (gr. 3-7). 192p. 17.95 (978-1-324-00328-1(6), 340328); 176p. pap. 11.95 (978-0-393-35650-2(7), 35650) Norton, W. W. & Co., Inc. (Norton Young Readers).
Wadsworth, Pamela. Amser a Gofod. 2005. (WEL., Illus.). 24p. pap. (978-1-85596-241-5(1)) Dref Wen.
—Golwg Gyntaf Ar Amser a Gofod. 2005. (WEL., Illus.). 24p. pap. (978-1-85596-248-4(9)) Dref Wen.
—Rhagor Am Amser a Gofod. 2005. (WEL., Illus.). 24p. pap. (978-1-85596-242-2(X)) Dref Wen.
Whiting, Jim. Space & Time. (Mysteries of the Universe Ser.). (ENG., Illus.). 48p. (J). (gr. 5-9). 2013. pap. 12.00 (978-0-89812-917-5(6), 21931, Creative Paperbacks) 2012. 23.95 (978-1-60818-192-6(8), 21924, Creative Education) Creative Co., The.
Windsor, Susan, illus. Space: God's Majestic Handiwork. 2017. 111p. (J). pap. (978-1-946246-03-5(4)) Institute for Creation Research.

SPACE AND TIME—FICTION

Abela, Deborah. Mission: Hollywood. O'Connor, George, illus. 2007. (Spy Force Ser.: 4). (ENG.). 240p. (J). (gr. 3-7). pap. 10.99 (978-1-4169-3969-6(5), Aladdin) Simon & Schuster Children's Publishing.
Accardo, Jus. Omega. 2017. (Infinity Division Novel Ser.: 2). (ENG.). 320p. (YA). pap. 9.99 (978-1-63375-825-4(7), 900180795) Entangled Publishing, LLC.
Ali, Khayyam Esab. The Wormhole Kids Visit President Kennedy. 2004. (ENG., Illus.). 56p. (J). per. 7.95 (978-1-59526-231-8(8)) Aeon Publishing Inc.
Alton, Steve. The Firehills. 2005. (ENG.). 192p. (YA). (gr. 5-12). 15.95 (978-1-57505-798-9(0), Carolrhoda Bks.) Lerner Publishing Group.
—The Malifex. 2003. (Middle Readers Ser.). (Illus.). 182p. (J). (gr. 3-7). 14.95 (978-0-8225-0959-2(8)) Lerner Publishing Group.
Baggott, Julianna. The Ever Breath. 2011. (ENG.). 240p. (J). (gr. 4-6). lib. bdg. 21.19 (978-0-385-90676-0(5), Delacorte Pr.) Random Hse. Children's Bks.
Banks, Lynne Reid. The Indian in the Cupboard. 181p. (J). (Indian in the Cupboard Ser.: No. 1). (gr. 4-7). pap. 4.99 (978-0-8072-1433-6(7)); 2004. (Indian in the Cupboard Ser.). (gr. 3-7). pap. 36.00 incl. audio (978-0-8072-7308-1(2), YA809SP) Random Hse. Audio Publishing Group. (Listening Library).
—The Key to the Indian. 2004. (Indian in the Cupboard Ser.: 5). (J). (gr. 3-6). lib. bdg. 17.20 (978-0-613-23006-3(X)) Turtleback.
—The Secret of the Indian. 2010. (Indian in the Cupboard Ser.). (ENG.). 192p. (J). (gr. 3-7). 7.99 (978-0-375-85524-5(6), Yearling) Random Hse. Children's Bks.
—Secret of the Indian. 2003. (ENG., Illus.). 160p. pap. (978-0-00-714900-1(X), Collins) HarperCollins Pubs. Ltd.
Barker, Clive. Abarat. 119.90 (978-0-06-056894-8(1)) HarperCollins Pubs.
—Abarat. Barker, Clive, illus. 2005. (Abarat Ser.: 1). (ENG., Illus.). (YA). (gr. 8). 2011. 528p. pap. 10.99 (978-0-06-209410-0(6)) 2004. 496p. reprint ed. pap. 9.99 (978-0-06-059637-8(6)) HarperCollins Pubs. (HarperCollins).
—Abarat: Days of Magic, Nights of War, 4 vols., Vol. 2. Barker, Clive, illus. ltd. num. aut. ed. 2004. (Illus.). 493p. 175.00 (978-1-890885-17-5(7)) Trice, B.E. Publishing.
—Abarat: Absolute Midnight. Barker, Clive, illus. 2013. (Abarat Ser.: 3). (ENG., Illus.). 640p. (YA). (gr. 8). pap. 10.99 (978-0-06-440933-9(3), HarperCollins) HarperCollins Pubs.
—Abarat: Days of Magic, Nights of War. Barker, Clive, illus. (Abarat Ser.: 2). (ENG., Illus.). (YA). (gr. 8). 2011. 624p. pap. 9.99 (978-0-06-209411-7(4)) 2006. 576p. reprint ed. pap. 9.99 (978-0-06-059638-5(4)) HarperCollins Pubs. (HarperCollins).
Bernstein, Nina. Magic by the Book, 4 vols. unabr. ed. 2005. (J). 65.75 (978-1-4193-3607-2(X), 42048) Recorded Bks., Inc.
Birney, Betty G. The Princess & the Peabodys. 2007. (ENG.). 256p. (J). (gr. 5-9). 15.99 (978-0-06-084720-3(4)) HarperCollins Pubs.
Boné, Thomas H., illus. The Teacher Who Would Not Retire Discovers a New Planet. 2009. (J). 17.95 (978-0-9792918-3-8(6)) Blue Marlin Pubns.
Boston, Lucy M. The Children of Green Knowe Collection. 2013. (ENG., Illus.). 368p. (J). 12.95 (978-0-571-30347-2(1)) Faber & Faber, Inc.
British Broadcasting Corporation Children's Books Staff & Richards, Justin. The American Adventures. 2016. (ENG.). 192p. (J). 14.99 (978-1-4059-2872-4(7), 693ad97d-0494-487c-b36a-3f38d2afcbed) Penguin Bks., Ltd. GBR. Dist: Diamond Comic Distributors, Inc.
Carlson, Caroline. The Door at the End of the World. 2019. (ENG.). 304p. (J). (gr. 3-7). 16.99 (978-0-06-236830-0(3), HarperCollins) HarperCollins Pubs.
Carter, Mike. Access to the Universe. 2005. (Illus.). 160p. (Orig.). pap. (978-0-7344-0696-5(7), Lothian Children's Bks.) Hachette Australia.
Caterer, Claire M. The Key & the Flame. (ENG.). (J). (gr. 3-7). 2015. 496p. pap. 7.99 (978-1-4424-5742-3(2)) 2013. 480p. 17.99 (978-1-4424-5741-6(4)) McElderry, Margaret K. Bks. (McElderry, Margaret K. Bks.).
Christopher, John. Dragon Dance. 2015. (Fireball Trilogy Ser.: 3). (ENG., Illus.). 224p. (J). (gr. 4-8). pap. 8.99 (978-1-4814-2015-0(1), Aladdin) Simon & Schuster Children's Publishing.
—Fireball. 2015. (Fireball Trilogy Ser.: 1). (ENG., Illus.). 256p. (J). (gr. 4-8). pap. 7.99 (978-1-4814-2009-9(7), Aladdin) Simon & Schuster Children's Publishing.
—New Found Land. 2015. (Fireball Trilogy Ser.: 2). (ENG., Illus.). 224p. (J). (gr. 4-8). pap. 7.99 (978-1-4814-2012-9(7), Aladdin) Simon & Schuster Children's Publishing.
Cockcroft, Jason. Counter Clockwise. 2009. 208p. (J). lib. bdg. 16.89 (978-0-06-125555-7(6), Tegen, Katherine Bks) HarperCollins Pubs.
Cody, Matthew. The Dead Gentleman. 2012. 288p. (J). (gr. 5). 7.99 (978-0-375-84490-4(2), Yearling) Random Hse. Children's Bks.
Cole, Frank L. Hashbrown Winters & Whiz-Tastrophe. 2013. pap. 14.99 (978-1-4621-1056-8(8), Bonneville Bks.) Cedar Fort, Inc./CFI Distribution.
Colfer, Eoin. The Atlantis Complex. 2012. (Artemis Fowl Ser.: 7). (J). lib. bdg. 19.65 (978-0-606-23614-0(7)) Turtleback.
—The Last Guardian. 2014. (Artemis Fowl Ser.: 8). (J). lib. bdg. 19.65 (978-0-606-32288-1(4)) Turtleback.
—The Time Paradox. 2009. (Artemis Fowl Ser.: 6). (J). lib. bdg. 19.65 (978-0-606-10579-8(4)) Turtleback.
Cooper, Susan. The Dark Is Rising. 2007. (YA). 1.25 (978-1-4193-7923-9(2)) Recorded Bks., Inc.
Corlett, William. The Door in the Tree. 2010. (Magician's House Quartet Ser.: 2). (ENG.). 304p. (YA). (gr. 5-8). pap. 13.99 (978-1-4424-1414-3(6), Simon Pulse) Simon Pulse.
—The Steps up the Chimney. 2011. (Magician's House Quartet Ser.: 1). (ENG.). 288p. (YA). (gr. 7). pap. 13.99 (978-1-4424-2935-2(6), Simon Pulse) Simon Pulse.
Corp, Carey & Langdon, Lorie. Doon, 1 vol. 2014. (Doon Novel Ser.: 1). (ENG.). 416p. (YA). pap. 12.99 (978-0-310-74239-5(0)) Blink.
Cotterill, Colin. Average Alan. 2013. 150p. pap. (978-616-7503-18-9(4)) Asia Document Bureau, Ltd.
Curry, Jane Louise. The Birdstones. 2017. (ENG., Illus.). 176p. (J). pap. 19.99 (978-1-62524-318-8(9), Candlewood Pr.) Harding Hse. Publishing Sebice Inc.
Dalton, Annie. Feeling the Vibes: Babysit a Buddha! 2008. (Mel Beeby Agent Angel Ser.). (ENG.). 208p. (J). (gr. 4-7). pap. 6.95 (978-0-00-716140-9(9)) HarperCollins Pubs. Ltd. GBR. Dist: Independent Pubs. Group.
Dashner, James. The Blade of Shattered Hope. 2010. (13th Reality Ser.: Bk. 3). 432p. (J). 18.99 (978-1-60641-239-8(6), Shadow Mountain) Shadow Mountain Publishing.
—The Blade of Shattered Hope. Dorman, Brandon, illus. 2011. (13th Reality Ser.: 3). (ENG.). 528p. (J). (gr. 3-7). pap. 9.99 (978-1-4424-0871-5(5), Aladdin) Simon & Schuster Children's Publishing.
—The Hunt for Dark Infinity. Beus, Bryan, illus. 2009. (13th Reality Ser.: Bk. 2). 446p. (J). 18.95 (978-1-60641-034-9(2), Shadow Mountain) Shadow Mountain Publishing.
—The Hunt for Dark Infinity. Beus, Bryan, illus. 2010. (13th Reality Ser.: 2). (ENG.). 544p. (J). (gr. 3-7). pap. 9.99 (978-1-4169-9153-3(0), Aladdin) Simon & Schuster Children's Publishing.
—The Journal of Curious Letters. Beus, Bryan, illus. 2008. (13th Reality Ser.: Bk. 1). 434p. (J). (gr. 4-7). 17.95 (978-1-59038-831-0(3), Shadow Mountain) Shadow Mountain Publishing.
—The Journal of Curious Letters. Beus, Bryan, illus. 2009. (13th Reality Ser.: 1). (ENG.). 528p. (J). (gr. 3-7). pap. 9.99 (978-1-4169-9152-6(2), Aladdin) Simon & Schuster Children's Publishing.
—The Void of Mist & Thunder. Dorman, Brandon, illus. 2013. (13th Reality Ser.: 4). (ENG.). 496p. (J). (gr. 3-7). pap. 9.99 (978-1-4424-0873-9(1), Aladdin) Simon & Schuster Children's Publishing.
Dateno, Maria Grace. Braving the Storm, 6 vols., Vol. 2. Cunningham, Paul, illus. 2013. 70p. (J). pap. 5.95 (978-0-8198-1204-9(8)) Pauline Bks. & Media.
—Shepherds to the Rescue, 6 vols., Vol. 1. Cunningham, Paul, illus. 2013. 71p. (J). pap. 5.95 (978-0-8198-7251-7(2)) Pauline Bks. & Media.
Davis, Heather. The Clearing. 2010. (ENG., Illus.). 224p. (YA). (gr. 9). pap. 13.99 (978-0-547-26367-0(8), 1406284, Clarion Bks.) HarperCollins Pubs.
Doty, Jean Slaughter. Can I Get There by Candlelight? 2012. (ENG.). 128p. (YA). (gr. 7). pap. 7.99 (978-1-4424-8608-9(2), Simon & Schuster Bks. For Young Readers) Simon & Schuster Bks. For Young Readers.
Edge, Christopher. The Many Worlds of Albie Bright. 2019. (ENG.). 192p. (J). (gr. 4-7). 6.99 (978-1-5247-1360-7(0), Yearling) Random Hse. Children's Bks.
Elaine Vanier. Crystal Lights: Awaken the Power. 2009. 116p. pap. 10.95 (978-1-4401-8357-7(0)) iUniverse, Inc.
Engdahl, Sylvia. Enchantress from the Stars. 2018. (ENG.). 368p. (J). pap. 10.99 (978-1-68119-613-8(1), 900179035, Bloomsbury USA Childrens) Bloomsbury Publishing USA.
—Enchantress from the Stars. 2003. (ENG.). 304p. (YA). (gr. 7-18). pap. 9.99 (978-0-14-250037-8(2), Firebird) Penguin Young Readers Group.
Ephron, Delia. Frannie in Pieces. Beckerman, Chad, illus. 2007. 374p. (YA). (gr. 7-12). lib. bdg. 17.89 (978-0-06-074717-6(X), HarperTeen) HarperCollins Pubs.
Evans, Alison. Ida. 2017. (ENG.). 176p. (YA). (gr. 7). pap. 15.95 (978-1-76040-438-3(1)) Bonnier Publishing GBR. Dist: Independent Pubs. Group.
Fisher, Catherine. Darkhenge. 2006. 340p. (YA). (gr. 7-12). 15.99 (978-0-06-078582-6(9)) HarperCollins Pubs.
Flavin, Teresa. The Crimson Shard. (ENG.). (J). (gr. 4-7). 2015. 288p. pap. 6.99 (978-0-7636-7172-3(X)) 2012. (Illus.). 256p. 15.99 (978-0-7636-6093-2(0)) Candlewick Pr. (Templar).
Fox Mazer, Norma. Saturday, the Twelfth of October. 2015. (ENG.). 274p. (J). (gr. 3). pap. 13.95 (978-1-939601-31-5(2)) Ig Publishing, Inc.
Gaiman, Neil. Fortunately, the Milk. Young, Skottie, illus. (ENG.). 128p. (J). (gr. 3-7). 2014. pap. 7.99 (978-0-06-222408-8(5)) 2013. 18.99 (978-0-06-222407-1(7)) HarperCollins Pubs. (HarperCollins).
—Fortunately, the Milk. 2014. (J). lib. bdg. 16.00 (978-0-606-35965-8(6)) Turtleback.
Gaiman, Neil & Reaves, Michael. Interworld. 2008. (Illus.). 181p. (J). (gr. 5-9). 60.00 (978-1-59606-173-6(1)) Subterranean Pr.
—InterWorld. (InterWorld Trilogy Ser.: 1). (ENG.). (YA). (gr. 8). 2013. 304p. pap. 9.99 (978-0-06-212530-9(3), HarperTeen) 2008. 256p. pap. 10.99 (978-0-06-123898-7(8), HarperCollins) HarperCollins Pubs.
Gaiman, Neil, et al. Eternity's Wheel. (InterWorld Trilogy Ser.: 3). (ENG.). 288p. (YA). (gr. 8). 2016. pap. 9.99 (978-0-06-206800-2(8)) 2015. 17.99 (978-0-06-206799-9(0)) HarperCollins Pubs. (HarperTeen).
—The Silver Dream. (InterWorld Trilogy Ser.: 2). (ENG.). (YA). (gr. 8). 2015. 272p. pap. 9.99 (978-0-06-206797-5(4)) 2013. 256p. 18.99 (978-0-06-206796-8(6)) HarperCollins Pubs. (HarperTeen).
Garner, Alan. The Owl Service. 2006. (Odyssey Classics Ser.). (ENG., Illus.). 240p. (J). (gr. 7-12). pap. 14.95 (978-0-15-205618-6(1)) Houghton Mifflin Harcourt Publishing Co.
Germano, Yveta. Bring Me Back. 2013. 298p. 27.99 (978-1-938516-75-7(3)); 318p. pap. 13.99 (978-1-938516-17-7(6)) Midnight Hologram, LLC.
Graham, Judith A. The Didley-Doo's Go on an Adventure, 1 vol. 2009. 33p. pap. 24.95 (978-1-60749-897-1(9)) America Star Bks.
Gray, Claudia. A Million Worlds with You. 2016. 419p. (YA). (978-0-06-257364-3(0), HarperTeen) HarperCollins Pubs.
—Ten Thousand Skies above You. (Firebird Ser.: 2). (ENG.). (YA). (gr. 9). 2016. 448p. pap. 11.99 (978-0-06-227900-2(9)) 2015. 432p. 17.99 (978-0-06-227899-9(1)) HarperCollins Pubs. (HarperTeen).
Haddix, Margaret Peterson. Caught. (Missing Ser.: 5). (ENG.). (J). (gr. 3-7). 2013. Illus.). 368p. pap. 8.99 (978-1-4169-8983-7(8)) 2012. 352p. 16.99 (978-1-4169-8982-0(X)) Simon & Schuster Bks. For Young Readers. (Simon & Schuster Bks. For Young Readers).
—Redeemed. 2015. (Missing Ser.: 8). (ENG.). 416p. (J). (gr. 3-7). 19.99 (978-1-4424-9756-6(4), Simon & Schuster Bks. For Young Readers) Simon & Schuster Bks. For Young Readers.
—Redeemed. 2016. (Missing Ser.: 8). lib. bdg. 18.40 (978-0-606-39234-1(3)) Turtleback.
—Sabotaged. (Missing Ser.: 3). (ENG.). (J). (gr. 3-7). 2011. 400p. pap. 8.99 (978-1-4169-5425-5(2)) 2010. 384p. 17.99 (978-1-4169-5424-8(4)) Simon & Schuster Bks. For Young Readers. (Simon & Schuster Bks. For Young Readers).

S

—Sent. (Missing Ser.: 2). (YA). 2011. 82.75 (978-1-4407-2678-1(7)) 2009. 1.25 (978-1-4407-2679-8(5)) 2009. 98.75 (978-1-4407-2675-0(2)) 2009. 218.75 (978-1-4407-2670-5(1)) Recorded Bks., Inc.

—Sent. (Missing Ser.: 2). (ENG.). (J). (gr. 3-7). 2010. 336p. pap. 8.99 (978-1-4169-5423-1(6)) 2009. 320p. 16.99 (978-1-4169-5422-4(8)) Simon & Schuster Bks. For Young Readers. (Simon & Schuster Bks. For Young Readers).

—Sent. abr. ed. 2009. (978-1-4424-0767-1(0)) Simon & Schuster Children's Publishing.

—Sent. l.t. ed. 2010. (Missing Ser.: Bk. 2). (ENG.). 345p. 23.99 (978-1-4104-3245-2(9)) Thorndike Pr.

—Sent. 2010. (Missing Ser.: 2). lib. bdg. 18.40 (978-0-606-14699-9(7)) Turtleback.

Hautman, Pete. The Cydonian Pyramid. (Klaatu Diskos Ser.: 2). (ENG.). 368p. (YA). (gr. 7). 2014. pap. 8.99 (978-0-7636-6933-1(4)) 2013. 16.99 (978-0-7636-5404-7(3)) Candlewick Pr.

—The Klaatu Terminus. (Klaatu Diskos Ser.: 3). 368p. (YA). (gr. 7). 2015. (ENG.). pap. 8.99 (978-0-7636-7675-9(6)) 2014. 16.99 (978-0-7636-5405-4(1)) Candlewick Pr.

Hering, Marianne & Sanders, Nancy I. Captured on the High Seas. 2014. (AIO Imagination Station Bks.: 14). (ENG.). 144p. (J). pap. 5.99 (978-1-58997-775-4(0), 4609675) Focus on the Family Publishing.

Hering, Marianne, et al. Doomsday in Pompeii. 2015. (AIO Imagination Station Bks.: 16). (ENG., Illus.). 144p. (J). pap. 5.99 (978-1-58997-803-4(X), 4622295) Focus on the Family Publishing.

House, David James. The Key to Space. 2006. (ENM.). 364p. (YA). 24.95 (978-0-9777086-0-4(8)) House, David.

Hubbard, L. Ron, contrib. by. The Crossroads: Literature Guide for Teachers & Librarians, Based on Common Core ELA Standards for Classrooms 6-9. 2013. (Stories from the Golden Age Ser.). (ENG.). 35p. (gr. 6-9). pap., tchr. ed. 14.95 (978-1-59212-810-5(6)) Galaxy Pr., LLC.

Hubert, Jerry. They Were Not Gods: A Space-Age Fairytale. 2003. 170p. (YA). 23.95 (978-0-595-66091-9(6)); pap. 13.95 (978-0-595-29970-6(9)) iUniverse, Inc.

Jacques, Brian. The Angel's Command. 2005. (Castaways of the Flying Dutchman Ser.). (ENG., Illus.). 384p. (J). (gr. 3-7). 9.99 (978-0-14-240285-6(0), Firebird) Penguin Young Readers Group.

—The Angel's Command. 2003. (Castaways of the Flying Dutchman Ser.: No. 2). 1.00 (978-1-4175-5393-8(6)) Recorded Bks., Inc.

—Voyage of Slaves. 2007. (Castaways of the Flying Dutchman Ser.: 3). (ENG.). 320p. (gr. 12-18). 7.99 (978-0-441-01528-3(X), Ace) Penguin Publishing Group.

Jaffe, Charlotte & Doherty, Barbara. The Space Race. 2003. (Illus.). (J). (gr. 2-3). 60.00 (978-1-57336-395-2(2), I5077) Interaction Pubs., Inc.

James, Nick. Strikeforce. 2013. (Skyship Academy Ser.: 3). (ENG., Illus.). 360p. (YA). (gr. 9-12). pap. 9.99 (978-0-7387-3637-2(6), 0738736376, Flux) North Star Editions.

Jansen, Patty. The Far Horizon. 2012. 176p. pap. (978-0-9872009-4-5(1)) Capricornica Pubns.

Johnson, Cara. Looking Forward Back: The Dream Travelers Book Three. 2008. 162p. (J). per. 9.99 (978-0-9768870-3-4(7)) Whirling Dirvish Publishing.

Johnson, Jane. Legends of the Shadow World: The Secret Country; the Shadow World; Dragon's Fire. Stower, Adam, illus. 2010. (ENG.). 1120p. (J). (gr. 3-7). pap. 14.99 (978-1-4169-9082-6(8), Simon & Schuster Bks. For Young Readers) Simon & Schuster Bks. For Young Readers.

—The Secret Country. Stower, Adam, illus. 2007. (Eidolon Chronicles Ser.: 1). (ENG.). 336p. (J). (gr. 3-7). per. 15.99 (978-1-4169-3815-6(X), Simon & Schuster Bks. For Young Readers) Simon & Schuster Bks. For Young Readers.

Kagan, Dale A. Trip into Space. 2004. (ENG.). 30p. per. 13.99 (978-1-4134-5159-7(4)) Xlibris Corp.

Kirsch, R. A. The Big One: (A Bicycle Tale), 1 vol. 2009. 191p. pap. 24.95 (978-1-60703-341-7(0)) PublishAmerica, Inc.

Klass, David. Firestorm. rev. l.t. ed. 2007. (Caretaker Trilogy: Bk. 1). 435p. (YA). (gr. 9). 23.95 (978-0-7862-9364-3(0)) Thorndike Pr.

—Firestorm: The Caretaker Trilogy: Book 1, 1. 2008. (Caretaker Trilogy Ser.: 1). (ENG.). 320p. (YA). (gr. 7-12). pap. 17.99 (978-0-312-38018-2(6), 900050543) Square Fish.

—Whirlwind: The Caretaker Trilogy: Book 2. 2009. (Caretaker Trilogy Ser.: 2). (ENG.). 320p. (YA). (gr. 9-12). pap. 18.99 (978-0-312-38429-6(7), 900053364) Square Fish.

Klingele, Lindsey. The Broken World. (ENG.). (YA). (gr. 8). 2018. 448p. pap. 9.99 (978-0-06-238037-1(0)) 2017. 432p. 17.99 (978-0-06-238036-4(2)) HarperCollins Pubs. (HarperTeen).

Kogge, Michael. Star Wars: The Force Awakens. 2016. (Illus.). 186p. (J). (978-1-338-13324-0(1)) Disney Publishing Worldwide.

Krpata, Mitch. The End of Time (Poptropica Book 4) Merritt, Kory, illus. 2017. (Poptropica Ser.). (ENG.). 112p. (J). (gr. 1-4). 9.99 (978-1-4197-2557-9(2), 1140501, Amulet Bks.) Abrams, Inc.

Kuykendall, Roger. All Day September. 2011. 28p. 12.95 (978-1-4638-9782-6(0)); pap. 6.95 (978-1-4638-0109-0(2)) Rodgers, Alan Bks.

Langton, Jane. The Diamond in the Window. Blegvad, Erik, illus. 2018. (Hall Family Chronicles) xi, 245p. (J). pap. (978-1-930900-93-6(7)) Purple Hse. Pr.

Larbalestier, Justine. Magic's Child. 2007. (Magic or Madness Trilogy). 291p. (YA). (978-1-4287-3603-0(4), Razorbill) Penguin Publishing Group.

Laurie, Victoria. The Curse of Deadman's Forest. (ENG.). 432p. (J). 2011. (gr. 3-7). 8.99 (978-0-440-42259-4(0), Yearling)2. 2010. (Oracles of Delphi Keep Ser.: No. 2). (gr. 6-8). lib. bdg. 22.44 (978-0-385-90562-6(9), Delacorte Pr.) Random Hse. Children's Bks.

—Oracles of Delphi Keep. (Oracles of Delphi Keep Ser.: 1). (J). 2010. 576p. (gr. 3-7). 8.99 (978-0-440-42258-7(2), Yearling)1. 2009. (ENG.). 560p. (gr. 6-8). lib. bdg. 22.44 (978-0-385-90561-9(0), Delacorte Pr.) Random Hse. Children's Bks.

Lawrence, Michael. A Crack in the Line. 2004. (Withern Rise Ser.). (ENG.). 336p. (J). 15.99 (978-0-06-072477-1(3)) HarperCollins Pubs.

—A Crack in the Line. 2005. (Withern Rise Trilogy). 323p. (YA). (gr. 9). 16.65 (978-0-7569-5739-1(7)) Perfection Learning Corp.

—Small Eternities. (Withern Rise Ser.). 336p. 2006. (Illus.). (J). (gr. 7). pap. 7.99 (978-0-06-072482-5(X), HarperTeen) 2005. (YA). 16.89 (978-0-06-072481-8(1)) 2005. (ENG.). (J). (gr. 8). 15.99 (978-0-06-072480-1(3), Greenwillow Bks.) HarperCollins Pubs.

—The Underwood See. 2007. (Withern Rise Ser.). (gr. 9). (ENG.). 384p. (J). pap. 7.99 (978-0-06-072485-6(4), Greenwillow Bks.); 372p. (YA). 16.99 (978-0-06-072483-2(8)) HarperCollins Pubs.

L'Engle, Madeleine. An Acceptable Time. 2007. (Wrinkle in Time Quintet Ser.: 5). (ENG.). 384p. (J). (gr. 5-9). per. 7.99 (978-0-312-36858-6(5), 900042675) Square Fish.

Lipsyte, Robert. The Twinning Project. 2014. (ENG.). 288p. (J). (gr. 5-7). pap. 16.99 (978-0-544-22522-0(8), 1563389, Clarion Bks.) HarperCollins Pubs.

MacHale, D. J. The Pilgrims of Rayne. 2008. (Pendragon Ser.: 8). (ENG.). 576p. (J). (gr. 5-9). pap. 10.99 (978-1-4169-1417-4(X), Aladdin) Simon & Schuster Children's Publishing.

—The Soldiers of Halla. (Pendragon Ser.: 10). (ENG.). 608p. (J). (gr. 5-9). 2010. pap. 10.99 (978-1-4169-1421-1(8)) 2009. 19.99 (978-1-4169-1420-4(X)) Simon & Schuster Children's Publishing. (Aladdin).

Mason, Timothy. The Last Synapsid. Cronan, Paul, illus. 2011. (ENG.). 320p. (J). (gr. 4-6). lib. bdg. 22.44 (978-0-385-90567-1(X), Yearling) Random Hse. Children's Bks.

McCool, Ben. Souljacker. Rousseau, Craig, illus. 2012. (Captain America: the Korvac Saga Ser.). (ENG.). 24p. (J). (gr. 3-5). lib. bdg. 31.36 (978-1-61479-020-4(5), 4111, Marvel Age) Spotlight.

—The Star Lord. Rousseau, Craig, illus. 2012. (Captain America: the Korvac Saga Ser.). (ENG.). 24p. (J). (gr. 3-5). lib. bdg. 31.36 (978-1-61479-022-8(1), 4113, Marvel Age) Spotlight.

—Strange Days. Rousseau, Craig, illus. 2012. (Captain America: the Korvac Saga Ser.). (ENG.). 24p. (J). (gr. 3-5). lib. bdg. 31.36 (978-1-61479-019-8(1), 4110, Marvel Age) Spotlight.

—The Traveler. Rousseau, Craig, illus. 2012. (Captain America: the Korvac Saga Ser.). (ENG.). 24p. (J). (gr. 3-5). lib. bdg. 31.36 (978-1-61479-021-1(3), 4112, Marvel Age) Spotlight.

McDonald, Joyce. Shades of Simon Gray. 2003. (Readers Circle Ser.). 245p. (YA). 14.15 (978-0-7569-1880-4(4)) Perfection Learning Corp.

Mcentire, Myra. Hourglass, 1. 2012. (Hourglass Ser.). (ENG.). 400p. (YA). (gr. 9-12). 26.19 (978-1-60684-144-0(0)) Farshore GBR. Dist: Children's Plus, Inc.

McOmber, Rachel B., ed. McOmber Phonics Storybooks: The Time Box. rev. ed. (Illus.). (J). (978-0-944991-52-7(1)) Swift Learning Resources.

McQuerry, Maureen Doyle. Time Out of Time: Book One: Beyond the Door. (Time Out of Time Ser.). (ENG., Illus.). (J). 2015. 400p. (gr. 5-9). pap. 7.95 (978-1-4197-1493-1(7), 683303) 2014. 384p. (gr. 3-7). 16.95 (978-1-4197-1016-2(8), 683301) Abrams, Inc. (Amulet Bks.).

Mebus, Scott. Gods of Manhattan, 1 vol. 2009. (ENG.). 368p. (J). (gr. 3-7). 9.99 (978-0-14-241307-4(0), Puffin Books) Penguin Young Readers Group.

—Gods of Manhattan 2: Spirits in the Park, Vol. 2. 2010. (ENG.). 400p. (J). (gr. 3-7). 8.99 (978-0-14-241645-7(2), Puffin Books) Penguin Young Readers Group.

—Gods of Manhattan 3: Sorcerer's Secret, Bk. 3. 2011. 384p. (J). (gr. 5-18). 8.99 (978-0-14-241878-9(1), Puffin Books) Penguin Young Readers Group.

—Spirits in the Park. 2009. (Gods of Manhattan Ser.: No. 2). (J). (978-0-525-47963-5(5), Dutton Juvenile) Penguin Publishing Group.

Miller, Chris & Miller, Allan. Hunter Brown & the Consuming Fire, 3 bks., Bk.2. 2009. (ENG., Illus.). 352p. (J). pap. 13.99 (978-1-59317-357-9(1)) Warner Pr., Inc.

Miller, Christopher & Miller, Allan. Hunter Brown & the Eye of Ends, 3 bks., Bk.3. 2011. (J). pap. 13.99 (978-1-59317-400-2(4)) Warner Pr., Inc.

—Hunter Brown & the Secret of the Shadow, 3 bks., Bk.1. 2008. (ENG., Illus.). 384p. (J). (gr. 9-18). pap. 13.99 (978-1-59317-328-9(8)) Warner Pr., Inc.

Millici, Nate, et al. Star Wars. Roux, Stéphane, illus. 2017. (J). (978-1-368-01493-9(3)) Disney Publishing Worldwide.

Monson, Marianne. The Enchanted Tunnel Vol. 3: Journey to Jerusalem. Burr, Dan, illus. 2011. 85p. (YA). (gr. 3-6). pap. 7.99 (978-1-60908-068-6(8)) Deseret Bk. Co.

—The Enchanted Tunnel Vol. 4: Wandering in the Wilderness. Burr, Dan, illus. 2011. 85p. (YA). (gr. 3-6). pap. 7.99 (978-1-60908-069-3(6)) Deseret Bk. Co.

—Escape from Egypt. 2010. (Illus.). 85p. (J). (978-1-60641-670-9(7)) Deseret Bk. Co.

Moreau, Chris. The Professor's Telescope. Marek, Jane, illus. 2006. (YA). 10.95 (978-0-9785399-0-0(7)); cd-rom 7.95 (978-0-9785399-2-4(3)) Windows of Discovery.

Morris, Chad. Cragbridge Hall, Book 2: The Avatar Battle. 2014. (Cragbridge Hall Ser.: 2). (ENG., Illus.). 360p. (J). (gr. 3-9). 17.99 (978-1-60907-809-6(8), Shadow Mountain) Shadow Mountain Publishing.

—Cragbridge Hall, Book 3: The Impossible Race. 2015. (Cragbridge Hall Ser.: 3). (ENG., Illus.). 432p. (J). (gr. 3-9). 18.99 (978-1-60907-979-6(5), 5127575, Shadow Mountain) Shadow Mountain Publishing.

Mull, Brandon. Beyonders the Complete Set (Boxed Set) A World Without Heroes; Seeds of Rebellion; Chasing the Prophecy, Set. 2013. (Beyonders Ser.). (ENG., Illus.). 1456p. (J). (gr. 3-7). 59.99 (978-1-4424-8593-8(0), Aladdin) Simon & Schuster Children's Publishing.

—Chasing the Prophecy. (Beyonders Ser.: 3). (ENG.). (J). (gr. 3-7). 2014. 528p. pap. 9.99 (978-1-4169-9797-9(0)) 2013. 512p. 21.99 (978-1-4169-9796-2(2)) Simon & Schuster Children's Publishing. (Aladdin).

—Seeds of Rebellion. (Beyonders Ser.: 2). (ENG., Illus.). 512p. (J). (gr. 3-7). 2013. pap. 9.99 (978-1-4169-9795-5(4)) 2012. 21.99 (978-1-4169-9794-8(6)) Simon & Schuster Children's Publishing. (Aladdin).

—Seeds of Rebellion. 2012. (Beyonders Ser.: Bk. 2). (ENG., Illus.). 512p. (J). pap. 10.99 (978-1-4424-4965-7(9), Simon & Schuster/Paula Wiseman Bks.) Simon & Schuster/Paula Wiseman Bks.

—Seeds of Rebellion. 2013. (Beyonders Ser.: 2). lib. bdg. 19.65 (978-0-606-27030-4(2)) Turtleback.

—A World Without Heroes. (J). 2011. (Beyonders Ser.: 1). 1.25 (978-1-4640-0920-4(1)) (Beyonders Ser.: 1). 92.75 (978-1-4618-0338-6(1)) 2011. (Beyonders Ser.: 1). 124.75 (978-1-4618-0353-9(5)) 2011. 122.75 (978-1-4618-0363-8(2)) Recorded Bks., Inc.

—A World Without Heroes. (Beyonders Ser.: 1). (ENG.). (J). (gr. 3-7). 2012. 512p. pap. 9.99 (978-1-4169-9793-1(8)) 2011. 464p. 21.99 (978-1-4169-9792-4(X)) Simon & Schuster Children's Publishing. (Aladdin).

—A World Without Heroes. 2011. (Beyonders Ser.: Bk. 1). (ENG.). 464p. (J). pap. 10.99 (978-1-4424-3530-8(5), Simon & Schuster/Paula Wiseman Bks.) Simon & Schuster/Paula Wiseman Bks.

—A World Without Heroes. 2012. (Beyonders Ser.: 1). lib. bdg. 19.65 (978-0-606-23675-1(9)) Turtleback.

National Children's Book and Literacy Alliance Staff, contrib. by. The Exquisite Corpse Adventure. 2011. (ENG., Illus.). 288p. (J). (gr. 4-6). 22.44 (978-0-7636-5149-7(4)) Candlewick Pr.

Natl Children's Book & Literacy Alliance. The Exquisite Corpse Adventure. 2011. (ENG., Illus.). 288p. (J). (gr. 4-7). pap. 9.99 (978-0-7636-5773-4(5)) Candlewick Pr.

Naujokaitis, Pranas T. Dinosaurs in Space. 2019. (Balloon Toons Ser.). (ENG.). 36p. (J). (gr. k-1). 22.96 (978-1-64310-899-5(9)) Penworthy Co., LLC, The.

Neimark, Gillian. The Golden Rectangle. (ENG., 160p. (J). (gr. 3-7). 2014. Illus.). pap. 6.99 (978-1-4169-8043-8(1)) 2013. 15.99 (978-1-4169-8042-1(3)) Simon & Schuster Children's Publishing. (Aladdin).

—The Secret Spiral. 2013. (ENG.). (J). 208p. (gr. 4-6). 18.69 (978-1-4169-8040-7(7)); 224p. (gr. 3-7). pap. 5.99 (978-1-4169-8041-4(5)) Simon & Schuster Children's Publishing. (Aladdin).

New York Hall of Science, The. Charlie & Kiwi: An Evolutionary Adventure. FableVision & Reynolds, Peter H., illus. 2011. (ENG.). 48p. (J). (gr. -1-3). 19.99 (978-1-4424-2112-7(6), Atheneum Bks. for Young Readers) Simon & Schuster Children's Publishing.

Nix, Garth. Sir Thursday. 2007. (Keys to the Kingdom Ser.: No. 4). 344p. (gr. 4-7). 18.00 (978-0-7569-8121-1(2)) Perfection Learning Corp.

Norris, Christine. The Sword of Danu. 2012. (Library of Athena Ser.: bk.4). (J). 268p. (gr. 3-7). pap. 14.99 (978-1-61271-095-2(6)); (978-1-61271-096-9(4)); (978-1-61271-097-6(2)) Zumaya Pubns. LLC.

Osborne, Mary Pope. El Invierno Del Hechicero Del Hielo. 2015. (Casa De árbol Ser.: 32). (SPA., Illus.). 144p. (J). (gr. 2-4). pap. 6.99 (978-1-63245-535-2(8)) Lectorum Pubns., Inc.

—A Perfect Time for Pandas, Bk. 20. Murdocca, Sal, illus. 2014. (Magic Tree House (R) Merlin Mission Ser.: 20). (ENG.). 144p. (J). (gr. 2-5). pap. 6.99 (978-0-375-86798-9(8), Random Hse. Bks. for Young Readers) Random Hse. Children's Bks.

—A Perfect Time for Pandas. 2014. (Magic Tree House Merlin Missions Ser.: 20). lib. bdg. 16.00 (978-0-606-35564-3(2)) Turtleback.

—Tigers at Twilight. unabr. ed. 2004. (Magic Tree House Ser.: No. 19). 72p. (J). (gr. k-3). pap. 17.00 incl. audio (978-0-8072-0928-8(7), S FTR 251 SP, Listening Library) Random Hse. Audio Publishing Group.

—To the Future, Ben Franklin! Ford, A. G., illus. 2019. (Magic Tree House (R) Ser.: 32). (J). (gr. 1-4). 96p. 13.99 (978-0-525-64832-1(1)); (ENG.). 112p. lib. bdg. 16.99 (978-0-525-64833-8(X)) Random Hse. Children's Bks. (Random Hse. Bks. for Young Readers).

—Vacation under the Volcano. unabr. ed. 2004. (Magic Tree House Ser.: No. 13). 74p. (J). (gr. k-3). pap. 17.00 incl. audio (978-0-8072-0782-6(9), LFTR 241 SP, Listening Library) Random Hse. Audio Publishing Group.

Osborne, Mary Pope, et al. Perros Salvajes a la Hora de la Cena. Murdocca, Sal, illus. 2008. (Casa del Arbol Ser.: 20).Tr. of Dingoes at Dinnertime. (SPA.). (J). (gr. 2-4). pap. 6.99 (978-1-933032-50-4(2)) Lectorum Pubns., Inc.

—Tigres Al Anochecer. Murdocca, Sal, illus. 2008. (Casa del Arbol Ser.: 19).Tr. of Tigers at Twilight. (SPA.). (J). (gr. 2-4). pap. 8.99 (978-1-933032-49-8(9)) Lectorum Pubns., Inc.

Paul, Donita K. Two Renegade Realms, 1 vol. 2014. (Realm Walkers Ser.). (ENG.). 416p. (YA). pap. 13.99 (978-0-310-73581-6(5)) Zondervan.

Paulsen, Gary. The Time Hackers. 2006. (ENG.). 96p. (J). (gr. 3-7). 5.99 (978-0-553-48788-6(4), Yearling) Random Hse. Children's Bks.

Pilkington, Linda Rash. Arthur Collins & the Three Wishes: Arthur the Brave! 322p. (gr. 4-18). 2009. (YA). pap. 13.95 (978-0-615-26743-2(2)) 2008. (J). 20.95 (978-0-615-22213-4(7)) City Castles Publishing.

Pinkwater, Daniel M. The Yggyssey: How Iggy Wondered What Happened to All the Ghosts, Found Out Where They Went, & Went There. Brown, Calef, illus. 2009. (ENG.). 256p. (J). (gr. 4-6). 18.69 (978-0-618-59445-0(0)) Houghton Mifflin Harcourt Publishing Co.

Prince, Maggie. The House on Hound Hill. 2003. (ENG.). 256p. (J). (gr. 5-7). pap. 15.95 (978-0-618-33124-6(7), 493932, Clarion Bks.) HarperCollins Pubs.

Rebecca, Stead. When You Reach Me. 2014. (ENG.). 208p. (J). (gr. 12-12). 11.24 (978-1-63245-235-1(9)) Lectorum Pubns., Inc.

Revealed. 2014. (Missing Ser.: 7). (ENG., Illus.). 448p. (J). (gr. 3-7). 19.99 (978-1-4169-8986-8(2), Simon & Schuster Bks. For Young Readers) Simon & Schuster Bks. For Young Readers.

Rockwood, Roy. Through Space to Mars. 2008. 128p. (gr. 4-7). pap. 11.95 (978-1-60664-173-6(5)) Aegypan.

Rollins, James. Jake Ransom & the Howling Sphinx. 2012. (Jake Ransom Ser.: 2). (ENG.). 160p. (J). (gr. 5). pap. 7.99 (978-0-06-147384-5(7), HarperCollins) HarperCollins Pubs.

Rust, Ned. Patrick Griffin's First Birthday on Ith. 2018. (Patrick Griffin & the Three Worlds Ser.: 2). (ENG., Illus.). 304p. (J). pap. 15.99 (978-1-250-15892-5(3), 900185538) Square Fish.

Salerni, Dianne K. The Inquisitor's Mark. 2015. (Eighth Day Ser.: 2). (ENG.). 352p. (J). (gr. 3-7). 16.99 (978-0-06-227218-8(7), HarperCollins) HarperCollins Pubs.

Sanders, Ted. The Box & the Dragonfly. Bruno, Iacopo, illus. 2015. (Keepers Ser.: No. 1). 534p. (J). (978-0-06-239019-6(8)) Harper & Row Ltd.

—The Keepers: the Box & the Dragonfly. Bruno, Iacopo, illus. 2015. (Keepers Ser.: 1). (ENG.). 544p. (J). (gr. 3-7). 16.99 (978-0-06-227582-0(8), HarperCollins) HarperCollins Pubs.

Santat, Dan. Are We There Yet? 2016. (ENG., Illus.). 40p. (J). (gr. -1-3). 17.99 (978-0-316-19999-5(0)) Little, Brown Bks. for Young Readers.

Scarrow, Alex & Bale, Tim. TimeRiders, 1. 2011. (TimeRiders Ser.). (ENG.). 416p. (YA). (gr. 7-12). 26.19 (978-0-8027-2172-3(9), 9780802721723) Walker & Co.

Schmatz, Pat. Circle the Truth. 2007. (Exceptional Reading & Language Arts Titles for Intermediate Grades Ser.). (ENG.). 192p. (YA). (gr. 7-12). 16.95 (978-0-8225-7268-8(0)) Lerner Publishing Group.

Sedgwick, Marcus. The Ghosts of Heaven. 2016. (ENG.). 384p. (YA). pap. 10.99 (978-1-250-07367-9(7), 900150798) Square Fish.

Shire, Poppy. Magic Pony Carousel #1: Sparkle the Circus Pony. Berg, Ron, illus. 2007. (Magic Pony Carousel Ser.: 1). (ENG.). 96p. (J). (gr. 2-5). pap. 3.99 (978-0-06-083779-2(9), HarperCollins) HarperCollins Pubs.

—Magic Pony Carousel #3: Star the Western Pony. Berg, Ron, illus. 2007. (Magic Pony Carousel Ser.: 3). (ENG.). 96p. (J). (gr. 2-5). pap. 3.99 (978-0-06-083785-3(3), HarperCollins) HarperCollins Pubs.

—Magic Pony Carousel #4: Jewel the Midnight Pony. Berg, Ron, illus. 2008. (Magic Pony Carousel Ser.: 4). (ENG.). 96p. (J). (gr. 2-5). pap. 4.99 (978-0-06-083788-4(8), HarperCollins) HarperCollins Pubs.

Signorino, John. Billy & the Aliens of Alpha-C, 1 vol. 2008. (ENG.). 36p. pap. 24.95 (978-1-60474-882-6(6)) America Star Bks.

Sividious Stark & the Stadium Between Worlds. 2013. (ENG.). 236p. (YA). pap. 12.99 (978-1-62108-273-6(3)) Covenant Communications, Inc.

Snyder, Laurel. Any Which Wall. Pham, LeUyen, illus. 256p. (J). 2010. (gr. 3-7). pap. 7.99 (978-0-375-85561-0(0)) 2009. (ENG.). (gr. 6-8). lib. bdg. 21.19 (978-0-375-95560-0(7)) Random Hse. Children's Bks. (Yearling).

—Seven Stories Up. 2015. 240p. (J). (gr. 3-7). 7.99 (978-0-375-87326-3(0), Yearling) Random Hse. Children's Bks.

Sorrells, Aaron. A Trip through the Solar System. 2010. 34p. pap. 16.00 (978-0-557-49151-3(7)) Lulu Pr., Inc.

Starmer, Aaron. The Riverman. 2015. (Riverman Trilogy Ser.: 1). (ENG.). 336p. (YA). (gr. 5-9). pap. 12.99 (978-1-250-05685-6(3), 900139058) Square Fish.

Stead, Rebecca. Cuando Me Alcances. 2011.Tr. of When You Reach Me. (SPA.). 294p. pap. (978-958-45-3215-2(4)) Norma S.A.

—When You Reach Me. 2010. lib. bdg. 18.40 (978-0-606-15179-5(6)) Turtleback.

—When You Reach Me: (Newbery Medal Winner) (ENG.). (J). (gr. 3-7). 2010. 240p. 8.99 (978-0-375-85086-8(4), Yearling) 2009. 208p. 16.99 (978-0-385-73742-5(4), Lamb, Wendy Bks.) Random Hse. Children's Bks.

Stephens, Berin L. Time Gangsters. 2012. pap. 14.99 (978-1-59955-966-7(8)) Cedar Fort, Inc./CFI Distribution.

Stephens, John. The Emerald Atlas. 2012. (Books of Beginning Ser.: 1). (ENG.). 464p. (J). (gr. 3-7). 10.99 (978-0-375-87271-6(X), Yearling) Random Hse. Children's Bks.

—The Emerald Atlas. l.t. ed. 2012. (Books of Beginning Ser.). (ENG.). 547p. (J). (gr. 4-7). 23.99 (978-1-4104-4234-5(9)) Thorndike Pr.

—The Fire Chronicle. 2012. (Illus.). 437p. (J). (978-0-449-81015-6(1)) Knopf, Alfred A. Inc.

—The Fire Chronicle. 2013. (Books of Beginning Ser.: 2). (ENG., Illus.). 464p. (J). (gr. 3-7). 9.99 (978-0-375-87272-3(8), Yearling) Random Hse. Children's Bks.

Stevenson, Patricia. The Z Family Coloring Book. 2012. 60p. (gr. -1). pap. 8.99 (978-1-4582-0242-0(9), Abbott Pr.) Author Solutions, LLC.

Stone, Tamara Ireland. Time after Time. 2014. (ENG.). 368p. (J). (gr. 7-12). pap. 18.99 (978-1-4231-5981-0(0)) Hyperion Bks. for Children.

—Time Between Us. 2013. (ENG.). 384p. (J). (gr. 7-12). pap. 19.99 (978-1-4231-5977-3(2)) Hyperion Pr.

Stories Beyond Time & Space. (J). pap. 15.50 (978-0-8359-0158-1(0)) Globe Fearon Educational Publishing.

Studio Mouse Staff. Space Adventure. rev. ed. 2008. (ENG., Illus.). (J). 12.99 (978-1-59069-609-5(3)) Studio Mouse LLC.

Tebbetts, Chris. Me Myself & Him. 2019. (ENG.). 304p. (YA). (gr. 9). 17.99 (978-1-5247-1522-9(0), Delacorte Pr.) Random Hse. Children's Bks.

Thompson, Kate. The New Policeman. 2008. (New Policeman Trilogy Ser.: 1). (ENG., Illus.). 464p. (YA). (gr. 8-12). pap. 9.99 (978-0-06-117429-2(7), Greenwillow Bks.) HarperCollins Pubs.

—The New Policeman. pap. 1.00 (978-1-4074-4550-2(2)) Recorded Bks., Inc.

A Thousand Pieces of You. 2014. (Firebird Ser.: 1). (ENG.). 368p. (YA). (gr. 9). 18.99 (978-0-06-227896-8(7), HarperTeen) HarperCollins Pubs.

Turetsky, Bianca. The Time-Traveling Fashionista at the Palace of Marie Antoinette. 2013. (Time-Traveling Fashionista Ser.: 2). (ENG., Illus.). 272p. (J). (gr. 3-7). pap. 9.00 (978-0-316-10535-4(X), Poppy) Little, Brown Bks. for Young Readers.

Valentine, James. The Past Is Gone. 2007. (TimeJumpers Ser.: 1). (ENG.). 288p. (J). (gr. 3-7). pap. 13.99 (978-1-4169-3955-9(5), Simon & Schuster/Paula Wiseman Bks.) Simon & Schuster/Paula Wiseman Bks.

Waid, Mark. Man Out of Time. Molina, Jorge, illus. 2011. (Captain America Ser.). (ENG.). 24p. (J). (gr. 4-8). Pt. 1. lib. bdg. 31.36 (978-1-59961-936-1(9), 4104)Pt. 2. lib. bdg. 31.36 (978-1-59961-937-8(7), 4105)Pt. 3. lib. bdg. 31.36 (978-1-59961-938-5(5), 4106)Pt. 4. lib. bdg. 31.36 (978-1-59961-939-2(3), 4107)Pt. 5. lib. bdg. 31.36 (978-1-59961-940-8(7), 4108) Spotlight. (Marvel Age).

Warner, Michael N. The Titanic Game. Ordaz, Frank, illus. 2018. (ENG.). 208p. (J). pap. 11.95 *(978-0-9744446-2-8(6))* All About Kids Publishing.
Wells, Rosemary. On the Blue Comet. Ibatoulline, Bagram, illus. (ENG.). 336p. (J). (gr. 5). 2012. pap. 9.99 *(978-0-7636-5815-1(4))* 2010. 16.99 *(978-0-7636-3722-4(X))* Candlewick Pr.
West, Jacqueline. The Second Spy. 2013. (Books of Elsewhere Ser.: 3). lib. bdg. 18.40 *(978-0-606-31698-9(1))* Turtleback.
—The Second Spy: The Books of Elsewhere: Volume 3. 2013. (Books of Elsewhere Ser.: 3). (ENG., Illus.). 320p. (J). (gr. 5). pap. 9.99 *(978-0-14-242608-1(3)*, Puffin Books) Penguin Young Readers Group.
—The Shadows. l.t. ed. 2010. (Books of Elsewhere Ser.: Vol. 1). (ENG.). 268p. 23.99 *(978-1-4104-3139-4(8))* Thorndike Pr.
—The Shadows. 2011. (Books of Elsewhere Ser.: 1). lib. bdg. 17.20 *(978-0-606-23070-4(X))* Turtleback.
—The Shadows: The Books of Elsewhere: Volume 1. 2011. (Books of Elsewhere Ser.: 1). (ENG.). 272p. (J). (gr. 5-7). 8.99 *(978-0-14-241872-7(2)*, Puffin Books) Penguin Young Readers Group.
—Spellbound, 2. 2012. (Books of Elsewhere Ser.: 2). (ENG., Illus.). 304p. (J). (gr. 6-8). 21.19 *(978-0-8037-3441-8(7))* Penguin Young Readers Group.
—Spellbound: The Books of Elsewhere: Volume 2, 2 vols. 2012. (Books of Elsewhere Ser.: 2). (ENG.). 320p. (J). (gr. 5-18). pap. 8.99 *(978-0-14-242102-4(2)*, Puffin Books) Penguin Young Readers Group.
—Still Life: The Books of Elsewhere: Volume 5. Bernatene, Poly, illus. 2015. (Books of Elsewhere Ser.: 5). (ENG.). 352p. (J). (gr. 5). 8.99 *(978-0-14-242297-7(5)*, Puffin Books) Penguin Young Readers Group.
—The Strangers. 2014. (Books of Elsewhere Ser.: 4). lib. bdg. 18.40 *(978-0-606-35680-0(0))* Turtleback.
—The Strangers: The Books of Elsewhere: Volume 4. Bernatene, Poly, illus. 2014. (Books of Elsewhere Ser.: 4). (ENG.). 336p. (J). (gr. 5). pap. 8.99 *(978-0-14-242575-6(3)*, Puffin Books) Penguin Young Readers Group.
Weyn, Suzanne. The Renaissance Kids. Graves, Linda Dockey, illus. 2003. (ENG.). 56p. (J). (gr. 6-8). pap. 7.97 net. *(978-0-7652-3277-9(4)*, Celebration Pr.) Savvas Learning Co.
White, Dorine. The Emerald Ring (Cleopatra's Legacy) 2013. 183p. (YA). pap. 13.99 *(978-1-4621-1133-6(5)*, Horizon Pubs.) Cedar Fort, Inc./CFI Distribution.
Williams, Sean. Twinmaker. 2013. (Twinmaker Ser.: 1). (ENG.). 496p. (YA). (gr. 8). 17.99 *(978-0-06-220321-2(5)*, Balzer & Bray) HarperCollins Pubs.
Willis, Jeanne. Shamanka. 2009. (J). pap. *(978-0-7636-3767-5(X))* Candlewick Pr.
Wilson, N. D. The Chestnut King (100 Cupboards Book 3) 2011. (100 Cupboards Ser.: 3). (ENG., Illus.). 512p. (J). (gr. 3-7). 9.99 *(978-0-375-83886-6(4)*, Yearling) Random Hse. Children's Bks.
—Dandelion Fire (100 Cupboards Book 2) 2009. (100 Cupboards Ser.: 2). (ENG., Illus.). 480p. (J). (gr. 3-7). 9.99 *(978-0-375-83884-2(8)*, Yearling) Random Hse. Children's Bks.
—The Door Before (100 Cupboards Prequel) 2018. (100 Cupboards Ser.). 256p. (J). (gr. 3-7). 8.99 *(978-0-449-81680-6(X)*, Yearling) Random Hse. Children's Bks.
—Outlaws of Time #3: the Last of the Lost Boys. 2018. (Outlaws of Time Ser.: 3). (ENG., Illus.). 256p. (J). (gr. 3-7). 16.99 *(978-0-06-232732-1(1)*, Tegen, Katherine Bks) HarperCollins Pubs.
—100 Cupboards, 1. 2007. (100 Cupboards Ser.: Bk. 1). (ENG., Illus.). 289p. (J). (gr. 4-6). lib. bdg. 22.44 *(978-0-375-93881-8(8))* Random House Publishing Group.
—100 Cupboards (100 Cupboards Book 1) 2008. (100 Cupboards Ser.: 1). (ENG.). 320p. (J). (gr. 3-7). 8.99 *(978-0-375-83882-8(1)*, Yearling) Random Hse. Children's Bks.
Winters, Jeffrey. Mystic Uncle & the Magical Bridge. 2005. 116p. (J). (gr. 3-7). pap. 10.95 *(978-1-59526-167-0(2)*, Llumina Pr.) Aeon Publishing Inc.
Wood, Maryrose. How I Found the Perfect Dress. 2008. (Morgan Rawlinson Novel Ser.). (ENG.). 240p. (YA). (gr. 9-18). 11.00 *(978-0-425-21939-3(9)*, Berkley) Penguin Publishing Group.
Woodruff, Elvira. George Washington's Spy. 2012. (ENG.). 240p. (J). (gr. 4-7). pap. 7.99 *(978-0-545-10488-3(2)*, Scholastic Paperbacks) Scholastic, Inc.
—George Washington's Spy. 2012. lib. bdg. 17.20 *(978-0-606-26216-3(4))* Turtleback.

SPACE EXPLORATION (ASTRONAUTICS)
see Outer Space—Exploration

SPACE FLIGHT
see also Interplanetary Voyages; Outer Space—Exploration; Space Stations

Aldrin, Buzz. Look to the Stars. Minor, Wendell, illus. 2009. (ENG.). 40p. (J). (gr. 1-3). 18.99 *(978-0-399-24721-7(1)*, G.P. Putnam's Sons Books for Young Readers) Penguin Young Readers Group.
Baker, David. Living in Space. 2008. (Exploring Space Ser.). (Illus.). 32p. (J). (gr. 4-6). lib. bdg. 26.00 *(978-1-59036-769-8(3))* Weigl Pubs., Inc.
Baker, David & Kissock, Heather. Living in Space. 2008. (Exploring Space Ser.). (Illus.). 32p. (J). (gr. 4-6). pap. 9.95 *(978-1-59036-770-4(7))* Weigl Pubs., Inc.
Blast off with Ellen Ochoa! (Greetings Ser.: Vol. 3). 24p. (gr. 2-3). 31.00 *(978-0-7635-5861-1(3))* Rigby Education.
Blast off with Ellen Ochoa! 6 Small Books. (Greetings Ser.: Vol. 3). 24p. (gr. 2-3). 31.00 *(978-0-7635-9432-9(6))* Rigby Education.
Bortz, Fred. Envisioning Outer Space: Where Science & Fiction Meet. 2015. (J). *(978-1-4677-6305-9(5))*; lib. bdg. *(978-1-4677-3740-1(2))* Twenty First Century Bks.
Carroll, Jillian. Where to Stay. 2003. (J). pap. *(978-1-58417-233-8(9))* Lake Street Pubs.
Carson, Mary Kay. Mission to Pluto: The First Visit to an Ice Dwarf & the Kuiper Belt. 2017. (Scientists in the Field Ser.). (ENG., Illus.). 80p. (J). (gr. 5-7). 18.99 *(978-0-544-41671-0(6)*, 1594758, Clarion Bks.) HarperCollins Pubs.
Clark, Julie. The 10 Greatest Breakthroughs in Space Exploration. 2008. (J). 14.99 *(978-1-55448-520-8(7))* Scholastic Library Publishing.
Dalmatian Press Staff. My Race into Space! 2008. (ENG.). 9p. bds. 4.95 *(978-1-58117-717-6(8)*, Intervisual/Piggy Toes) Bendon, Inc.
Davis, Barbara J. & Voege, Debra. How Does a Spacecraft Reach the Moon? 2009. (Science in the Real World Ser.). (ENG., Illus.). 32p. (gr. 4-6). 28.00 *(978-1-60413-470-4(4)*, P173437, Chelsea Clubhse.) Infobase Holdings, Inc.
DK. DKfindout! Space Travel. 2019. (DK Findout! Ser.). (ENG., Illus.). 64p. (J). (gr. 1-4). 16.99 *(978-1-4654-7932-7(5))*; pap. 10.99 *(978-1-4654-7931-0(7))* Dorling Kindersley Publishing, Inc. (DK Children).
Dorling Kindersley Publishing Staff. Space Travel. 2019. (ENG., Illus.). 64p. (J). pap. *(978-0-241-35839-9(6))* Dorling Kindersley Publishing, Inc.
Dubbs, Chris. Space Dogs: Pioneers of Space Travel. 2003. 102p. (YA). pap. 11.95 *(978-0-595-26735-4(1)*, Writer's Showcase Pr.) iUniverse, Inc.
Duhig, Holly. Faster-Than-Light Space Travel, 1 vol. 2017. (Science Fiction to Science Fact Ser.). (ENG.). 32p. (J). (gr. 4-5). pap. 11.50 *(978-1-5382-1497-8(0)*, cb42f800-5d99-448a-ac4b-9ae0ec825fdf); lib. bdg. 28.27 *(978-1-5382-1382-7(6)*, 8d96a194-2462-4e42-a91f-a151a8a69c69) Stevens, Gareth Publishing LLLP.
Fabiny, Sarah & Who HQ. What Is NASA? Hammond, Ted, illus. 2019. (What Was? Ser.). 112p. (J). (gr. 3-7). 5.99 *(978-1-5247-8603-8(9))*; 15.99 *(978-1-5247-8605-2(5))* Penguin Young Readers Group. (Penguin Workshop).
Feldman, Heather. Dennis Tito: The First Space Tourist. 2009. (Space Firsts Ser.). 24p. (gr. 3-4). 42.50 *(978-1-60853-112-7(0)*, PowerKids Pr.) Rosen Publishing Group, Inc., The.
From Earth to the Stars. 2017. (From Earth to the Stars Ser.). 48p. (gr. 10-12). pap. 56.20 *(978-1-5081-0529-9(4))*; (ENG.). (gr. 6-7). 113.64 *(978-1-5081-0527-5(8)*, 85bb2ff4-2339-451d-b368-04a3447c1c16) Rosen Publishing Group, Inc., The. (Britannica Educational Publishing).
Gardner, Jane P. Travel Science, Vol. 11. Lewin, Russ, ed. 2015. (Science 24/7 Ser.). (Illus.). 48p. (J). (gr. 5). 20.95 *(978-1-4222-3415-0(0))* Mason Crest.
Goldstein, Margaret J. Astronauts: A Space Discovery Guide. 2017. (Space Discovery Guides). (ENG., Illus.). 48p. (J). (gr. 4-6). 31.99 *(978-1-5124-2588-8(5)*, f66640b4-d476-4f07-bf0d-2992b97f5148); E-Book 47.99 *(978-1-5124-3801-7(4)*, 9781512438017); E-Book 4.99 *(978-1-5124-3800-0(6)*, 9781512438000) Lerner Publishing Group. (Lerner Pubns.).
The Great Space Race. (Color & Learn Ser.). 36p. (J). (gr. 1-5). pap. *(978-1-882210-15-2(8))* Action Publishing, Inc.
Gross, Miriam J. All about Space Missions, 1 vol. 2009. (Blast Off! Ser.). (ENG.). 24p. (J). (gr. 2-3). pap. 9.25 *(978-1-4358-3138-4(1)*, 2c9aa5cb-9bae-4a8e-b34e-87d3674163db); lib. bdg. 26.27 *(978-1-4358-2740-0(6)*, 255befb5-8e9f-4767-9624-23cb3c6fd2c9) Rosen Publishing Group, Inc., The. (PowerKids Pr.).
Hansen, Ole Steen. Space Flight. 2003. (Story of Flight Ser.). (ENG., Illus.). 32p. (J). (gr. 2-9). lib. bdg. *(978-0-7787-1207-7(9))* Crabtree Publishing Co.
Holcroft, John & Candlewick Press Staff. Space Exploration: Panorama Pops. Holcroft, John, illus. 2015. (Panorama Pops Ser.). (ENG., Illus.). 30p. (J). (gr. k-4). 8.99 *(978-0-7636-7699-5(3))* Candlewick Pr.
Houran, Lori Haskins. A Trip into Space: An Adventure to the International Space Station. 2014. (Av2 Fiction Readalong 2015 Ser.). (ENG.). (J). (gr. -1-2). lib. bdg. 32.71 *(978-1-4896-2837-4(1)*, AV2 by Weigl) Weigl Pubs., Inc.
—A Trip into Space: An Adventure to the International Space Station. Marquez, Francisca, illus. 2019. (ENG.). 24p. (J). (gr. -1-3). pap. 7.99 *(978-0-8075-8093-6(7)*, 807580937) Whitman, Albert & Co.
Jefferis, David. The Astronauts: Space Survival. 2019. (Moon Flight Atlas Ser.). (Illus.). 32p. (J). (gr. 5-5). *(978-0-7787-5411-4(1))*; pap. *(978-0-7787-5420-6(0))* Crabtree Publishing Co.
—Space Explorers. 2017. (Our Future in Space Ser.). (Illus.). 32p. (J). (gr. 5-5). *(978-0-7787-3535-9(4))*; pap. *(978-0-7787-3540-3(0))* Crabtree Publishing Co.
Jones, Tom. Ask the Astronaut: A Galaxy of Astonishing Answers to Your Questions on Spaceflight. 2016. (Illus.). 224p. (gr. 5-12). pap. 12.95 *(978-1-58834-537-0(8)*, Smithsonian Bks.) Smithsonian Institution Scholarly Pr.
Kelley, K. C. Blast off to Space. 2018. (Amazing Adventures Ser.). (ENG.). 16p. (J). (gr. k-2). lib. bdg. *(978-1-68151-315-7(3)*, 14881); (Illus.). pap. 7.99 *(978-1-68152-271-5(3)*, 14887) Amicus.
Kemoun, Hubert Ben & Grenier, Christian. Half & Half-Voyage into Space. Moutarde & Blanchin, Matthieu, illus. 2008. (J). 48p. pap. 4.99 *(978-1-60115-210-7(8))*; (ENG.). 45p. 17.44 *(978-1-60115-209-1(4))* Treasure Bay, Inc.
Klepeis, Alicia Z. Space Survival: Keeping People Alive in Space. 2019. (Future Space Ser.). (ENG., Illus.). 32p. (J). (gr. 3-9). pap. 7.95 *(978-1-5435-7521-7(8)*, 141052); lib. bdg. 28.65 *(978-1-5435-7265-0(0)*, 140596) Capstone.
Kruesi, Liz. Voyage to Pluto. 2018. (Illus.). 48p. (J). pap. *(978-1-4896-9801-8(9)*, AV2 by Weigl) Weigl Pubs., Inc.
Ladybird. Space Activity Book - Ladybird Readers Level 4. 2016. (Ladybird Readers Ser.). (ENG.). 16p. (J). (gr. 2-4). pap., act. bk. ed. 5.99 *(978-0-241-25377-9(2))* Penguin Bks., Ltd. GBR. Dist: Independent Pubs. Group.
Lakin, Patricia. The Stellar Story of Space Travel: Ready-To-Read Level 3. Burroughs, Scott, illus. 2016. (History of Fun Stuff Ser.). (ENG.). 48p. (J). (gr. 1-3). pap. 4.99 *(978-1-4814-5623-4(7)*, Simon Spotlight) Simon Spotlight.
Lassieur, Allison. International Space Station: An Interactive Space Exploration Adventure. 2016. (You Choose: Space Ser.). (ENG., Illus.). 112p. (J). (gr. 3-7). lib. bdg. 32.65 *(978-1-4914-8104-2(8)*, 130588, Capstone Pr.) Capstone.
Launch into Space! 2015. (Launch into Space! Ser.). (ENG.). 32p. (J). (gr. 3-4). pap., pap., pap. 63.12 *(978-0-7660-7056-1(5))* Enslow Publishing, LLC.
Llimós, Anna & Llimós, Anna. Space Adventure Crafts, 1 vol. 2010. (Fun Adventure Crafts Ser.). (ENG., Illus.). 32p. (gr. k-2). 26.60 *(978-0-7660-3732-8(0)*, 774d4439-51b5-4f80-bd8c-51adade1ce2f, Enslow Elementary) Enslow Publishing, LLC.
—Space Adventure Crafts, 1 vol. 2010. (Fun Adventure Crafts Ser.). (ENG., Illus.). 32p. (gr. k-2). pap. 10.35 *(978-0-7660-3733-5(9)*, b19ca19c-8762-40d6-be0e-32d4c79ec7bb, Enslow Elementary) Enslow Publishing, LLC.
Loh-Hagan, Virginia. Lost in Space Hacks. 2019. (Could You Survive? Ser.). (ENG.). 32p. (J). (gr. 4-8). pap. 14.21 *(978-1-5341-5069-0(2)*, 213583); (Illus.). lib. bdg. 32.07 *(978-1-5341-4783-6(7)*, 213582) Cherry Lake Publishing. (45th Parallel Press).
Lombardo, Jennifer. Space Exploration Throughout History: From Telescopes to Tourism, 1 vol. 2019. (World History Ser.). (ENG.). 104p. (gr. 7-7). 41.53 *(978-1-5345-6712-2(7)*, 47fb66b6-eab7-446c-ae36-dc30db49b477, Lucent Pr.) Greenhaven Publishing LLC.
Lubka, S. Ruth. Pupniks: The Story of Two Space Dogs, 1 vol. 2003. (ENG., Illus.). 32p. (J). (gr. k-3). 16.95 *(978-0-7614-5137-2(4))* Marshall Cavendish Corp.
MacCarald, Clara. Colonizing Mars. 2019. (Science for the Future Ser.). (ENG., Illus.). 48p. (J). (gr. 5-6). pap. 11.95 *(978-1-64185-847-2(8)*, 1641858478); lib. bdg. 34.21 *(978-1-64185-778-9(1)*, 1641857781) North Star Editions. (Focus Readers).
Meet NASA Inventor Masahiro Ono & His Team's Asteroid-Harpooning Hitcher. 2017. (J). *(978-0-7166-6161-0(6))* World Bk., Inc.
Miles, Lisa & Smith, Alastair. Astronomy & Space. 2003. (Complete Bks.). (ENG., Illus.). 1p. (YA). (gr. 3-18). pap. 14.95 *(978-0-7460-3104-9(1))* EDC Publishing.
Miller, Gary. The Outer Limits: The Future of Space Exploration. 2009. (Current Science Ser.). (ENG.). 48p. (J). (gr. 4-6). pap. 8.95 *(978-1-4339-2246-6(0)*, Gareth Stevens Learning Library) Stevens, Gareth Publishing LLLP.
—The Outer Limits: the Future of Space Exploration, 1 vol. 2009. (Current Science Ser.). (ENG.). 48p. (YA). (gr. 4-6). lib. bdg. 33.67 *(978-1-4339-2242-8(8)*, 0a3856e3-925d-4df0-a4d0-35b9136b6483) Stevens, Gareth Publishing LLLP.
Milligan, Aiyanna. Cutting-Edge SpaceX News. 2019. (Searchlight Books (tm) — New Frontiers of Space Ser.). (ENG., Illus.). 32p. (J). (gr. 3-5). pap. 9.99 *(978-1-5415-7487-8(7)*, 40d4d969-d2ea-49a0-be32-6ac4f37dd983); lib. bdg. 30.65 *(978-1-5415-5583-9(X)*, de6fb458-ff9c-4ac1-971f-c5ec46d02b30) Lerner Publishing Group. (Lerner Pubns.).
Newland, Sonya. Space Exploration: Triumphs & Tragedies, 1 vol. 2016. (Crabtree Chrome Ser.). (ENG., Illus.). 48p. (J). (gr. 6-9). pap. *(978-0-7787-2231-1(7))* Crabtree Publishing Co.
Parker, Steve & Snedding, Robert. A Brief Illustrated History of Space Exploration. 2017. (Brief Illustrated History Ser.). (ENG., Illus.). 32p. (J). (gr. 3-6). lib. bdg. 27.99 *(978-1-5157-2519-0(7)*, Capstone Pr.) Capstone.
Porterfield, Jason. The Benefits of Spaceflight & Space Exploration, 1 vol. 2017. (From Earth to the Stars Ser.). (ENG., Illus.). 48p. (J). (gr. 6-7). pap. 15.05 *(978-1-68048-661-2(6)*, 07a1fc2e-e593-4f4c-8cc2-4edd2b8b4411, Britannica Educational Publishing) Rosen Publishing Group, Inc., The.
Randolph, Joanne. Dennis Tito: First Space Tourist. 2009. (Reading Room Collection 2 Ser.). 24p. (gr. 3-4). 42.50 *(978-1-60851-962-0(7)*, PowerKids Pr.) Rosen Publishing Group, Inc., The.
Rice, William B. & Wolfe, Hillary. Blast off to Space Camp, 1 vol. 2nd rev. ed. 2012. (TIME for KIDS(r): Informational Text Ser.). (ENG.). 32p. (gr. 3-5). pap. 12.99 *(978-1-4333-3673-7(1))* Teacher Created Materials, Inc.
Richards, Patti. The Space Shuttle Missions. 2018. (Destination Space Ser.). (ENG., Illus.). 48p. (J). (gr. 5-6). pap. 11.95 *(978-1-63517-570-7(4)*, 1635175704); lib. bdg. 34.21 *(978-1-63517-498-4(8)*, 1635174988) North Star Editions. (Focus Readers).
Roby, Cynthia A. Building Aircraft & Spacecraft: Aerospace Engineers, 1 vol., 1. 2015. (Engineers Rule! Ser.). (ENG., Illus.). 32p. (J). (gr. 4-5). pap. 12.75 *(978-1-5081-4528-8(8)*, 68cf95a4-db79-43bb-8ce9-d7a6b7f5c885, PowerKids Pr.) Rosen Publishing Group, Inc., The.
Rooney, Anne. A Math Journey Through Space. 2014. (Go Figure! Ser.). (ENG., Illus.). 32p. (J). (gr. 4-4). *(978-0-7787-0730-1(X))* Crabtree Publishing Co.
Royston, Angela. Space Blog. 2010. (ENG., Illus.). 32p. (J). *(978-0-7787-9910-8(7))*; pap. *(978-0-7787-9931-3(X))* Crabtree Publishing Co.
Rustad, Martha E. H. Space Travel. 2018. (Astronaut's Life Ser.). (ENG., Illus.). 24p. (J). (gr. -1-2). lib. bdg. 27.32 *(978-1-5157-9818-7(6)*, 136886, Capstone Pr.) Capstone.
Shaughnessy, Mara. LEGO Man in Space: A True Story. 2013. (ENG., Illus.). 32p. (J). (gr. -1-3). 14.95 *(978-1-62087-544-5(6)*, 620544, Sky Pony Pr.) Skyhorse Publishing Co., Inc.
Sibila, Tom. SpaceShipOne: Making Dreams Come True. 2005. (High Five Reading - Blue Ser.). (ENG., Illus.). 48p. (gr. 3-4). per. 9.00 *(978-0-7368-5744-4(3))* Capstone.
Space Exploration: Science, Technology, Engineering (Calling All Innovators: a Career for You) (Library Edition) 2014. (Calling All Innovators: a Career for You Ser.). (ENG.). 64p. (J). (gr. 5-8). lib. bdg. 32.00 *(978-0-531-20615-7(7)*, Children's Pr.) Scholastic Library Publishing.
Sparrow, Giles. Space Travel, 1 vol. 2017. (Space Explorers Ser.). (ENG.). 32p. (gr. 2-2). 26.93 *(978-0-7660-9268-6(2)*, 971af130-d004-4de1-aa0a-aea03a7e081a) Enslow Publishing, LLC.
Thompson, Ben & Slader, Erik. The Race to Space: Countdown to Liftoff (Epic Fails #2) Foley, Tim, illus. 2018. (Epic Fails Ser.: 2). (ENG.). 160p. (J). pap. 8.99 *(978-1-250-15062-2(0)*, 900182551) Roaring Brook Pr.
Top That Publishing Staff, ed. Lets Explore Space. 2004. (Fun Kits Ser.). (Illus.). 48p. (J). *(978-1-84510-244-9(4))* Top That! Publishing PLC.
A Trip into Space: Individual Title Six-Pack. (Story Steps Ser.). (gr. k-2). 23.00 *(978-0-7635-9614-9(0))* Rigby Education.
West, David. Spacecraft. 2017. (What's Inside? Ser.). (ENG., Illus.). 24p. (J). (gr. k-3). 28.50 *(978-1-62588-404-6(4)*, 19389, Smart Apple Media) Black Rabbit Bks.
—Ten of the Best Adventures in Space. 2015. (Ten of the Best: Stories of Exploration & Adventure Ser.). (ENG., Illus.). 24p. (J). (gr. 3-4). *(978-0-7787-1836-9(0))* Crabtree Publishing Co.
Williams, Dave & Cunti, Loredana. To Burp or Not to Burp: A Guide to Your Body in Space. Krynauw, Theo, illus. 2016. (Dr. Dave — Astronaut Ser.). (ENG.). 56p. (J). (gr. 1-5). pap. 12.95 *(978-1-55451-853-1(9))* Annick Pr., Ltd. CAN. Dist: Publishers Group West (PGW).
Woods, David & Harland, David M. Inside Gemini, 1 vol. 2017. (Geek's Guide to Space Ser.). (ENG., Illus.). 192p. (J). (gr. 9-9). 46.27 *(978-1-4994-6697-3(8)*, 2b1d5611-5887-42ac-bc60-cb6ed128bacb, Rosen Young Adult) Rosen Publishing Group, Inc., The.
Woolf, Alex. The Science of Spacecraft: the Cosmic Truth about Rockets, Satellites, & Probes (the Science of Engineering) (Library Edition) Myer, Ed & Beach, Bryan, illus. 2019. (Science Of... Ser.). (ENG.). 32p. (J). (gr. 3-3). lib. bdg. 29.00 *(978-0-531-13197-8(1)*, Watts, Franklin) Scholastic Library Publishing.
World Book, Inc. Staff, contrib. by. Human Space Exploration. 2010. (J). *(978-0-7166-9543-1(X))* World Bk., Inc.
Zelon, Helen. The Endeavor Mission STS-61: Fixing the Hubble Space Telescope. 2009. (Space Missions Ser.). 24p. (gr. 3-4). 42.50 *(978-1-60853-117-2(1)*, PowerKids Pr.) Rosen Publishing Group, Inc., The.

SPACE FLIGHT—FICTION

Alafaci, Marie. Zelda's Big Adventure. McG, Shane, illus. 2017. (ENG.). 32p. (J). (gr. -1-3). 16.99 *(978-1-328-66081-7(8)*, 1667182, Clarion Bks.) HarperCollins Pubs.
Applegate, K. A., pseud. Survival. 2003. (Remnants Ser.: No. 13). 165p. (J). (gr. 4-8). 12.65 *(978-0-7569-5301-0(4))* Perfection Learning Corp.
Appleton, Victor. The Alien Probe. (Tom Swift Ser.). (J). (gr. 3-7). 20.95 *(978-0-88411-464-2(3))* Amereon Ltd.
—The Rescue Mission. (Tom Swift Ser.). (J). (gr. 3-7). 20.95 *(978-0-88411-458-1(9))* Amereon Ltd.
—Terror on the Moons of Jupiter. (Tom Swift Ser.). (J). (gr. 3-7). 20.95 *(978-0-88411-460-4(0))* Amereon Ltd.
Ashley, Jonathan. Lily & Kosmo in Outer Outer Space. Ashley, Jonathan, illus. 2018. (ENG., Illus.). 208p. (J). (gr. 2-5). 16.99 *(978-1-5344-1364-1(2)*, Simon & Schuster Bks. For Young Readers) Simon & Schuster Bks. For Young Readers.
Aston, Dianna Hutts. The Moon over Star. Pinkney, Jerry, illus. 2008. (ENG.). 32p. (J). (gr. 1-3). 17.99 *(978-0-8037-3107-3(8)*, Dial Bks) Penguin Young Readers Group.
Barbini, F. T. Tijaran Tales: White Child. 2011. 214p. pap. *(978-0-7552-1349-8(1))* Authors OnLine, Ltd.
Bell, David. Pyjamas in Space. 2007. (Dawn Gray Ser.). (ENG.). 260p. pap. *(978-1-84167-580-0(6))* Ransom Publishing Ltd.
Bennett, Jeffrey. Max Goes to the Moon: A Science Adventure with Max the Dog. Okamoto, Alan, illus. 2nd ed. 2012. (Science Adventures with Max the Dog Ser.). (ENG.). 32p. (J). (gr. 2-4). 15.00 *(978-1-937548-20-9(1))* Big Kid Science.
Bergman, Mara. Oliver Who Would Not Sleep! Maland, Nick, illus. 2007. (J). *(978-0-439-92827-4(3)*, Levine, Arthur A. Bks.) Scholastic, Inc.
Brallier, Max. Galactic Hot Dogs 2: The Wiener Strikes Back. Maguire, Rachel & Kelley, Nichole, illus. 2016. (Galactic Hot Dogs Ser.: 2). (ENG.). 288p. (J). (gr. 3-7). 13.99 *(978-1-4814-2496-7(3)*, Aladdin) Simon & Schuster Children's Publishing.
Bransford, Nathan. Jacob Wonderbar for President of the Universe, 2 vols., 2. 2013. (Jacob Wonderbar Ser.: 2). (ENG.). 224p. (J). (gr. 4-6). 22.44 *(978-0-8037-3538-5(3)*, Dial) Penguin Publishing Group.
Brown, Jeff. Stanley in Space. Pamintuan, Macky, illus. 2009. (Flat Stanley Ser.). (ENG.). 128p. (J). (gr. 2-5). pap. 4.99 *(978-0-06-442174-4(0)*, HarperCollins) HarperCollins Pubs.
—Stanley in Space. Nash, Scott, illus. 2009. (Flat Stanley Ser.: 3). (J). (gr. k-3). lib. bdg. 14.75 *(978-0-613-66735-7(2))* Turtleback.
Burns, Dal. The Adventures of Phoo. 2006. 148p. pap. 24.95 *(978-1-4241-1773-4(9))* PublishAmerica, Inc.
Cameron, Eleanor. Stowaway to the Mushroom Planet. 2003. (J). (gr. 4-8). 21.50 *(978-0-8446-7237-3(8))* Smith, Peter Pub., Inc.
Card, Orson Scott. Pathfinder. (Pathfinder Trilogy Ser.). (ENG.). 672p. (YA). (gr. 7). 2011. pap. 13.99 *(978-1-4169-9179-3(4))* 2010. 21.99 *(978-1-4169-9176-2(X))* Simon Pulse. (Simon Pulse).
—Pathfinder. l.t. ed. 2011. (Pathfinder Ser.). (ENG.). 802p. 23.99 *(978-1-4104-3681-8(0))* Thorndike Pr.
Cerberus Jones. The Ancient Starship. 2017. (ENG.). 160p. (J). pap. 5.99 *(978-1-61067-501-7(0))* Kane Miller.
—The Midnight Mercenary: The Gateway. 2017. (ENG., Illus.). 160p. (J). pap. 5.99 *(978-1-61067-500-0(2))* Kane Miller.
Dare, Danni. Jake Jett: Adventures in Space. 2010. 32p. pap. 12.99 *(978-1-4520-4981-6(5))* AuthorHouse.
Davies, Benji, illus. Bizzy Bear: Space Rocket. 2015. (Bizzy Bear Ser.). (ENG.). 8p. (J). (— 1). bds. 7.99 *(978-0-7636-8003-9(6))* Candlewick Pr.
Deluca, Alison. Christmas O'Clock: A Collection. Daly, Lisa, illus. 2013. 198p. pap. 9.99 *(978-1-939296-98-6(6))* Myrddin Publishing Group.
Dixon, Andy. Star Quest. Brooks, Felicity, ed. Harris, Nick, illus. 2006. (Usborne Fantasy Puzzle Bks.). 32p. (YA). (gr. 7). lib. bdg. 15.99 *(978-1-58086-906-5(8)*, Usborne) EDC Publishing.
Draper, Sharon M. The Space Mission Adventure. Watson, Jesse Joshua, illus. 2012. (Clubhouse Mysteries Ser.: 4). (ENG.). 112p. (J). (gr. 3-7). 17.99 *(978-1-4424-4225-2(5))*; pap. 6.99 *(978-1-4424-4226-9(3))* Simon & Schuster Children's Publishing. (Aladdin).
Eastman, Brock. Hope. 2019. 509p. (J). pap. *(978-1-59638-249-7(X))* P & R Publishing.
Espluga, Maria. I, Astronaut: Yo, Astronauta. 2009. (SPA & ENG.). 28p. (J). 13.95 *(978-1-931398-56-5(9))* Me+Mi Publishing.
Fruchter, Jason, illus. Space Race. 2017. (J). *(978-1-5182-2283-2(8)*, Golden Bks.) Random Hse. Children's Bks.

Fyfe, H. b. & Fyfe, H. B. The Outbreak of Peace. 2011. 18p. 13.95 *(978-1-4638-9705-5(7))* Rodgers, Alan Bks.

Ganz-Schmitt, Sue. Planet Kindergarten. Prigmore, Shane, illus. 2016. (ENG.). 36p. (J). (gr. -1-k). 7.99 *(978-1-4521-5644-6(1))* Chronicle Bks. LLC.

Gehl, Laura. Baby Astronaut. Wiseman, Daniel, illus. 2019. (Baby Scientist Ser.: 2). (ENG.). 22p. (J). (gr. -1 — 1). bds. 8.99 *(978-0-06-284134-6(3)*, HarperFestival) HarperCollins Pubs.

Gehrt, Linda. My Trip, My Spaceship. 2004. 26p. pap. 24.95 *(978-1-4137-3392-1(1))* PublishAmerica, Inc.

Gibbs, Stuart. Space Case. 2015. (Moon Base Alpha Ser.). (ENG., Illus.). 368p. (J). (gr. 3-7). pap. 8.99 *(978-1-4424-9487-9(5)*, Simon & Schuster Bks. For Young Readers) Simon & Schuster Bks. For Young Readers.

—Space Case. 2015. (Moon Base Alpha Ser.: 1). lib. bdg. 18.40 *(978-0-606-37883-3(9))* Turtleback.

Goulbourne, Nathaniel. The Aliens Zoo. 2013. (Illus.). 28p. pap. 21.35 *(978-1-4817-8198-5(7))* AuthorHouse.

Handford, Martin. Where's Waldo? Spaer Adventure: The Great Space Adventure. (Illus.). 24p. (J). (gr. k-18). 19.95 *(978-0-9627001-4-9(2))* Futech Educational Products, Inc.

Harstad, Johan. 172 Hours on the Moon. 2012. (ENG.). 368p. (YA). (gr. 7-17). 36.99 *(978-0-316-18288-1(5))* Little, Brown Bks. for Young Readers.

Hawking, Lucy & Hawking, Stephen. George's Cosmic Treasure Hunt. Parsons, Garry, illus. 2009. (George's Secret Key Ser.). (ENG.). 320p. (J). (gr. 3-7). 19.99 *(978-1-4169-8671-3(5)*, Simon & Schuster Bks. For Young Readers) Simon & Schuster Bks. For Young Readers.

—George's Cosmic Treasure Hunt. Parsons, Garry, illus. 2011. (George's Secret Key Ser.). (ENG.). 352p. (J). (gr. 3-7). pap. 12.99 *(978-1-4424-2175-2(4)*, Simon & Schuster Bks. For Young Readers) Simon & Schuster Bks. For Young Readers.

Hawking, Stephen & Hawking, Lucy. George & the Unbreakable Code. Parsons, Garry, illus. (George's Secret Key Ser.). (ENG.). (J). (gr. 3-7). 2017. 368p. pap. 12.99 *(978-1-4814-6628-8(3))* 2016. 352p. 19.99 *(978-1-4814-6627-1(5))* Simon & Schuster Bks. For Young Readers. (Simon & Schuster Bks. For Young Readers).

Hergé. Destination Moon.Tr. of Objectif Lune. (J). (gr. 3-8). ring bd. 19.95 *(978-0-8288-5026-1(7))*; (Illus.). 62p. 19.95 *(978-0-8288-5027-8(5))* French & European Pubns., Inc.

—Objectif Lune.Tr. of Destination Moon. (FRE., Illus.). (J). (gr. 7-9). ring bd. 19.95 *(978-0-8288-5051-3(8))* French & European Pubns., Inc.

—On a Marche sur la Lune. (Tintin Ser.).Tr. of Explorers on the Moon. (FRE., Illus.). 62p. (J). pap. 21.95 *(978-2-203-00116-9(X))* Casterman, Editions FRA. Dist: Distribooks, Inc.

—On a Marche sur la Lune.Tr. of Explorers on the Moon. (FRE., Illus.). (J). (gr. 7-9). ring bd. 19.95 *(978-0-8288-5053-7(4))* French & European Pubns., Inc.

Hillert, Margaret. Up, up & Away. 2016. (BeginningtoRead Ser.). (ENG., Illus.). 32p. (J). (gr. 1-2). 22.60 *(978-1-59953-806-8(7))* Norwood Hse. Pr.

Jeapes, Ben. His Majesty's Starship. 2013. 348p. pap. *(978-1-909016-18-7(7))* Monico.

Jeffers, Oliver. The Way Back Home. Jeffers, Oliver, illus. 2008. (ENG., Illus.). 32p. (J). (gr. -1-3). 18.99 *(978-0-399-25074-3(3)*, Philomel Bks.) Penguin Young Readers Group.

Jones, Allan Frewin. Starship. (Hunter & Moon Mystery Ser.: Vol. 5). (ENG.). 169p. (J). pap. 8.99 *(978-0-340-70964-1(2))* Hodder & Stoughton GBR. Dist: Trafalgar Square Publishing.

Jones, Cerberus. The Midnight Mercenary. 2016. (Illus.). 146p. (J). *(978-1-61067-573-4(8))* Kane Miller.

Kaczynski, Heather. Dare Mighty Things. 2017. (ENG.). 384p. (YA). (gr. 8). 17.99 *(978-0-06-247986-0(5)*, HarperTeen) HarperCollins Pubs.

Kaufman, Amie. Illuminae. 2017. lib. bdg. 24.50 *(978-0-606-39847-3(3))* Turtleback.

Kaufman, Amie & Kristoff, Jay. Aurora Rising. (Aurora Cycle Ser.: 1). (ENG., Illus.). (YA). (gr. 7). 2020. 496p. pap. 12.99 *(978-1-5247-2099-5(2)*, Ember) 2019. 480p. 19.99 *(978-1-5247-2096-4(8)*, Knopf Bks. for Young Readers) 2019. 480p. lib. bdg. 21.99 *(978-1-5247-2097-1(6)*, Knopf Bks. for Young Readers) Random Hse. Children's Bks.

—Gemina. (Illuminae Files Ser.: 2). (ENG.). 672p. (YA). (gr. 9). 2018. pap. 12.99 *(978-0-553-49918-6(1)*, Ember) 2016. (Illus.). 21.99 *(978-0-553-49915-5(7)*, Knopf Bks. for Young Readers) Random Hse. Children's Bks.

—Obsidio. (Illuminae Files Ser.: 3). (ENG., Illus.). (YA). (gr. 9). 2019. 640p. pap. 12.99 *(978-0-553-49922-3(X)*, Ember) 2018. 624p. 21.99 *(978-0-553-49919-3(X)*, Knopf Bks. for Young Readers) Random Hse. Children's Bks.

Kelly, Mark. Astrotwins — Project Rescue. 2016. (Astrotwins Ser.). (ENG., Illus.). 256p. (J). (gr. 3-7). 16.99 *(978-1-4814-2458-5(0)*, Simon & Schuster/Paula Wiseman Bks.) Simon & Schuster/Paula Wiseman Bks.

—Mousetronaut Goes to Mars. Payne, C. F., illus. 2013. (Mousetronaut Ser.). (ENG.). 40p. (J). (gr. -1-3). 19.99 *(978-1-4424-8426-9(8)*, Simon & Schuster/Paula Wiseman Bks.) Simon & Schuster/Paula Wiseman Bks.

Kerr, P. B., pseud. One Small Step. 2009. (ENG.). 320p. (J). (gr. 3-9). pap. 8.99 *(978-1-4169-4214-6(9)*, McElderry, Margaret K. Bks.) McElderry, Margaret K. Bks.

Lavoie, Rejean. Des Legumes Pour Frank Einstein. Begin, Jean-Guy, illus. 2004. (Des 9 Ans. Ser.: Vol. 44). (FRE.). 120p. (J). 8.95 *(978-2-89599-006-2(9))* Editions de la Paix CAN. Dist: World of Reading, Ltd.

Layton, Neal. Tony Spears: the Invincible Tony Spears & the Brilliant Blob: Book 2, Bk. 2. 2018. (Tony Spears Ser.). (ENG., Illus.). 224p. (J). (gr. k-2). pap. 9.99 *(978-1-4449-1963-9(6))* Hachette Children's Group GBR. Dist: Hachette Bk. Group.

Lee, Yoon. Dragon Pearl. 2019. (ENG.). 320p. lib. bdg. 18.80 *(978-1-6636-2730-8(4))* Perfection Learning Corp.

—Rick Riordan Presents Dragon Pearl (a Thousand Worlds Novel, Book 1) 2019. (ENG., Illus.). 320p. (J). (gr. 3-7). 16.99 *(978-1-368-01335-2(X)*, Riordan, Rick) Disney Publishing Worldwide.

—Rick Riordan Presents Dragon Pearl (a Thousand Worlds Novel Book 1) 2020. 320p. (J). (gr. 3-7). pap. 8.99 *(978-1-368-01474-8(7)*, Riordan, Rick) Disney Publishing Worldwide.

Lee, Yoon Ha. Dragon Pearl. 2020. (Thousand Worlds (Trade) Ser.). (ENG.). 320p. (gr. 4-7). 24.94 *(978-1-5364-6113-8(X)*, Riordan, Rick) Disney Pr.

—Dragon Pearl. 2019. 320p. 16.99 *(978-1-368-01519-6(0))* Disney Publishing Worldwide.

Litton, Jonathan. Planet Pop-Up: Monkey on the Moon. Anderson, Nicola, illus. 2015. (Planet Pop-Up Ser.). (ENG.). 12p. (J). (gr. -1). 12.95 *(978-1-62686-372-9(5)*, Silver Dolphin Bks.) Readerlink Distribution Services, LLC.

Mak, D P. Invisible Pill. 2005. 44p. pap. *(978-1-84401-210-7(7))* Athena Pr.

Marazano, Richard. The Sons of Ares, 2 vols. Ponzio, Jean-Michel, illus. 2009. (Chimpanzee Complex Ser.: 1). 56p. pap. 13.95 *(978-1-84918-002-3(4))* CineBook GBR. Dist: National Bk. Network.

Marbury, Stephanie. Off to the Moon! Leigh, Tom, illus. 2006. 20p. (J). *(978-1-59939-100-7(7)*, Reader's Digest Young Families, Inc.) Studio Fun International.

Marshall, Sandra K. Tom's Space Adventure. 2007. 60p. per. 16.95 *(978-1-4241-7840-7(1))* America Star Bks.

Martin, Carrie Waddington. Ham the Astrochimp: Anything Is Possible. 2012. 52p. (-18). pap. 24.99 *(978-1-4797-1059-1(8))* Xlibris Corp.

Mass, Wendy. Voyagers: the Seventh Element (Book 6) 2016. (Voyager Ser.: 6). 208p. (J). (gr. 3-7). 12.99 *(978-0-385-38673-9(7)*, Random Hse. Bks. for Young Readers) Random Hse. Children's Bks.

Moesta, Rebecca, et al. Star Challengers Trilogy. 2013. (J). pap. 18.99 *(978-1-61475-124-3(2)*, WordFire Pr.) WordFire Pr.

Montgomery, R. A. War with the Evil Power Master. 2005. (Illus.). 123p. (J). pap. *(978-0-7608-9700-3(X))* Sundance/Newbridge Educational Publishing.

—War with the Evil Power Master. Millet, Jason, illus. 2006. (ENG.). 144p. (J). (gr. 4-8). per. 7.99 *(978-1-933390-12-3(3)*, CHCL12) Chooseco LLC.

Munzel, Alexander. Where the Holy Thistle Blooms. 2003. (Illus.). 98p. (J). per. *(978-0-9672566-1-0(5))* Technical Software, Inc.

North, Phoebe. Starglass. 2013. (Starglass Sequence Ser.). (ENG., Illus.). 448p. (YA). (gr. 7). 17.99 *(978-1-4424-5953-3(0)*, Simon & Schuster Bks. For Young Readers) Simon & Schuster Bks. For Young Readers.

Olivas, John D. Endeavour's Long Journey/la Larga Travesía de Endeavour. Roski, Gayle G., illus. 2016. (SPA.). 40p. (J). 19.95 *(978-0-9973947-2-6(2))* East West Discovery Pr.

Parker, Emma. The Space Rocket. 2010. (Illus.). pap. *(978-1-877547-87-4(5))* First Edition Ltd.

Patchett, Mary E. Flight to the Misty Planet. 2011. 236p. 46.95 *(978-1-258-07100-4(2))* Literary Licensing, LLC.

Pati, Geeta. Finny's Voyage Through the Universe: Nebula, Supernova, Open Star Cluster. 2007. 100p. per. 11.95 *(978-1-59526-422-0(1)*, Llumina Pr.) Aeon Publishing Inc.

Puttock, Simon. Earth to Stella! Hopman, Philip, illus. 2006. (ENG.). 32p. (J). (gr. -1-3). 16.00 *(978-0-618-58535-9(4)*, 100428, Clarion Bks.) HarperCollins Pubs.

Rau, Dana. Moon Walk. Buchs, Thomas, illus. 3rd ed. 2003. (Soundprints' Read-and-Discover Ser.). (ENG.). 48p. (J). (gr. -1-3). pap. 4.35 *(978-1-59249-015-8(8)*, S2006) Soundprints.

Rau, Dana Meachen. Moon Walk. Buchs, Thomas, illus. 2004. (Soundprints' Read-and-Discover Ser.). 48p. (gr. -1-3). 13.95 *(978-0-7569-3370-8(6))* Perfection Learning Corp.

Revis, Beth. Across the Universe. 2012. (Across the Universe Trilogy: Bk. 1). (ENG.). (YA). (gr. 7-12). 54.99 *(978-1-61587-857-4(2)*, Penguin AudioBooks) Penguin Publishing Group.

—Across the Universe, 1. 2011. (Across the Universe Ser.: 1). (ENG.). 448p. (YA). (gr. 9-12). pap. 11.99 *(978-1-59514-467-6(6)*, Razorbill) Penguin Young Readers Group.

—Across the Universe. 2011. (Across the Universe Trilogy Ser.: 1). lib. bdg. 20.85 *(978-0-606-23139-8(0))* Turtleback.

Riggs, Kate & Sheban, Chris. Beyond the Stars. 2019. (Illus.). 12p. (J). (gr. -1-k). bds. 8.99 *(978-1-56846-336-0(7)*, 18678, Creative Editions) Creative Co., The.

Robinson, Alise. Shining Stars: A Colors Book. Reich, Carin, illus. 2005. (Space Craze Ser.). 16p. (J). (gr. -1-k). per., bds. 6.95 *(978-1-58117-392-5(X)*, Intervisual/Piggy Toes) Bendon, Inc.

Rockwell, Carey. The Revolt on Venus. 2007. 120p. per. *(978-1-4068-3961-6(2))* Echo Library.

—Sabotage in Space. 2007. 108p. per. *(978-1-4068-3959-3(0))* Echo Library.

—The Space Pioneers. 2007. 120p. per. *(978-1-4068-3962-3(0))* Echo Library.

Rockwood, Roy. Lost on the Moon. 2008. 132p. pap. 10.95 *(978-1-60664-236-8(7))* Rodgers, Alan Bks.

—Through Space to Mars. 2008. 128p. (gr. 4-7). 23.95 *(978-1-60664-801-8(2))* Aegypan.

Ryan, Candace. Zoo Zoom! Pamintuan, Macky, illus. 2015. (ENG.). 32p. (J). (gr. -1-1). 16.99 *(978-1-61963-357-5(4)*, 900134207, Bloomsbury USA Childrens) Bloomsbury Publishing USA.

Sander, Sonia. 3, 2, 1, Liftoff! (LEGO City: Level 1 Reader) 2011. (LEGO City Ser.). (ENG.). 32p. (J). (gr. -1-k). pap. 3.99 *(978-0-545-33167-8(6))* Scholastic, Inc.

Schaefer, Elizabeth & Hopps, Kevin. Hera's Phantom Flight. 2017. (World of Reading Level 2 (Leveled Readers) Ser.). (ENG., Illus.). 32p. (J). (gr. k-3). 31.36 *(978-1-5321-4067-9(3)*, 25438) Spotlight.

Schindler, Roslyn. Zeon. Schindler, Roslyn, illus. 2013. (Illus.). 28p. pap. 13.95 *(978-1-61493-192-8(5))* Peppertree Pr., The.

The Secret Life of Jack O' Lanterns. 2004. 32p. 15.00 *(978-1-883211-35-6(2))* Laughing Elephant.

Shaw, Nancy E. Sheep Blast Off! Apple, Margot, illus. 2011. (Sheep in a Jeep Ser.). (ENG.). 32p. (J). (gr. -1-3). pap. 6.99 *(978-0-547-52025-4(5)*, 1445464, Clarion Bks.) HarperCollins Pubs.

Sloane, William, ed. Space, Space, Space: Stories about the Time When Men Will Be Adventuring to the Stars. 2011. 288p. 48.95 *(978-1-258-10156-5(4))* Literary Licensing, LLC.

Snyder, Lavinia Branca. Mission in Space: Softi's Adventures. 2003. (Illus.). (J). mass mkt. *(978-1-932233-35-3(0))* Aurora Libris Corp.

Space Case. 2014. (Moon Base Alpha Ser.). (ENG., Illus.). 352p. (J). (gr. 3-7). 18.99 *(978-1-4424-9486-2(7)*, Simon & Schuster Bks. For Young Readers) Simon & Schuster Bks. For Young Readers.

Stanek, Robert, pseud. Bugville Critters Explore the Solar System. 2011. (Illus.). 42p. pap. 5.99 *(978-1-57545-262-3(6)*, Reagent Pr. Bks. for Young Readers) RP Media.

Stilton, Gerónimo & Mckeon, Kathryn. Mouse in Space! 2013. (Geronimo Stilton Ser.: 52). lib. bdg. 18.40 *(978-0-606-31525-8(X))* Turtleback.

Tesler, Monica. Bounders. 2016. (Bounders Ser.: 1). (ENG., Illus.). 384p. (J). (gr. 5-9). 16.99 *(978-1-4814-4593-1(6)*, Aladdin) Simon & Schuster Children's Publishing.

Todd, Ruthven. Space Cat & the Kittens. Galdone, Paul, illus. 2018. (ENG.). 96p. (gr. 1-5). 16.95 *(978-0-486-82275-4(3)*, 822753) Dover Pubns., Inc.

Troupe, Thomas Kingsley. The Squadron. 2015. (Tartan House Ser.). (ENG.). 96p. (J). (gr. 3-6). *(978-1-63235-057-2(2)*, 11684, 12-Story Library) Bookstaves, LLC.

Verba, Joan Marie. Action Alert. 2008. 176p. (YA). pap. 15.95 *(978-0-9653575-8-6(9))* FTL Pubns.

Walker, Peter Lancaster. Space Travelers Land at Buckingham Palace. Dixit, Rama, illus. 2007. 275p. (J). 19.95 *(978-1-934138-12-0(6))* Bouncing Ball Bks., Inc.

Westerfeld, Scott. The Manual of Aeronautics: An Illustrated Guide to the Leviathan Series. Thompson, Keith, illus. 2012. (ENG.). 64p. (YA). (gr. 7). 19.99 *(978-1-4169-7179-5(3)*, Simon Pulse) Simon Pulse.

Wheeler, Kim. Jonny Plumb's New Adventures... 2013. 172p. pap. *(978-0-7552-1569-0(9)*, Bright Pen) Authors OnLine, Ltd.

Zakour, John. Baxter Moon Galactic Scout. 2008. 198p. (J). (gr. 5-10). per. 8.95 *(978-0-9768126-9-2(X))* Brown Barn Bks.

SPACE FLIGHT, MANNED

see Manned Space Flight

SPACE FLIGHT—POETRY

Carthew, Mark. Footprints on the Moon: Poems about Space, 1 vol. rev. ed. 2013. (Literary Text Ser.). (ENG., Illus.). 28p. (gr. 2-3). pap. 9.99 *(978-1-4333-5564-6(7))* Teacher Created Materials, Inc.

SPACE FLIGHT TO MARS

Anderson, Rane. Stem: Mission to Mars: Problem Solving (Grade 3) 2017. (Mathematics in the Real World Ser.). (ENG., Illus.). 32p. (J). (gr. 3-4). pap. 11.99 *(978-1-4807-5801-8(9))* Teacher Created Materials, Inc.

Bellisario, Gina. To Mars! Moran, Mike, illus. 2017. (Cloverleaf Books (tm) — Space Adventures Ser.). (ENG.). 24p. (J). (gr. k-2). 25.32 *(978-1-5124-2539-0(7)*, df57e8ce-22db-41b2-9a4c-913f1808335c); E-Book 4.99 *(978-1-5124-3888-8(X)*, 9781512438888); E-Book 38.65 *(978-1-5124-3887-1(1)*, 9781512438871); E-Book 38.65 *(978-1-5124-2832-2(9))* Lerner Publishing Group. (Millbrook Pr.).

Carson, Mary Kay. Mission to Mars. 2018. (Beyond Planet Earth Ser.). (Illus.). 32p. (J). (gr. 1). 16.95 *(978-1-4549-2351-0(2))* Sterling Publishing Co., Inc.

Collins, Ailynn. Mars or Bust! Orion & the Mission to Deep Space. 2019. (Future Space Ser.). (ENG., Illus.). 32p. (J). (gr. 3-9). pap. 7.95 *(978-1-5435-7514-9(5)*, 141045); lib. bdg. 28.65 *(978-1-5435-7268-1(5)*, 140599) Capstone.

Hawksett, David. Living on Mars: Can You Colonize a Planet?, 1 vol. 2017. (Be a Space Scientist! Ser.). (ENG.). 48p. (J). (gr. 5-5). 31.93 *(978-1-5383-2205-5(6)*, 364ab89d-04a4-4a62-92d7-407629468fc4); pap. 12.75 *(978-1-5383-2298-7(6)*, cba58767-1d72-4f5d-9fe0-28747d343e18) Rosen Publishing Group, Inc., The. (PowerKids Pr.).

Kenney, Karen Latchana. Cutting-Edge Journey to Mars. 2019. (Searchlight Books (tm) — New Frontiers of Space Ser.). (ENG., Illus.). 32p. (J). (gr. 3-5). pap. 9.99 *(978-1-5415-7485-4(0)*, b8ec822a-c817-4ca7-91e2-00d114dfacf1); lib. bdg. 30.65 *(978-1-5415-5745-1(X)*, 307656cb-9ae5-40cd-b8fa-e8d4b19b269e) Lerner Publishing Group. (Lerner Pubns.).

MacCarald, Clara. How Did Robots Land on Mars? 2018. (How'd They Do That? Ser.). (ENG., Illus.). 32p. (J). (gr. 4-6). lib. bdg. 28.65 *(978-1-5435-4136-6(4)*, 139090, Capstone Pr.) Capstone.

Silverman, Buffy. Mars Missions: A Space Discovery Guide. 2017. (Space Discovery Guides). (ENG., Illus.). 48p. (J). (gr. 4-6). 31.99 *(978-1-5124-2585-7(0)*, 72b2d712-8724-4432-84d7-5be2d3aacef4); E-Book 47.99 *(978-1-5124-2795-0(0))*; E-Book 47.99 *(978-1-5124-3810-9(3)*, 9781512438109); E-Book 4.99 *(978-1-5124-3809-3(X)*, 9781512438093) Lerner Publishing Group. (Lerner Pubns.).

Vogt, Gregory. Missions to Mars. 2018. (Illus.). 48p. (J). pap. *(978-1-4896-9818-6(3)*, AV2 by Weigl) Weigl Pubs., Inc.

Vogt, Gregory L. Missions to Mars. 2018. (Destination Space Ser.). (ENG., Illus.). 48p. (J). (gr. 5-6). pap. 11.95 *(978-1-63517-568-4(2)*, 1635175682); lib. bdg. 34.21 *(978-1-63517-496-0(1)*, 1635174961) North Star Editions. (Focus Readers).

SPACE FLIGHT TO THE MOON

see also Moon—Exploration; Project Apollo (U.S.)

Adamson, Thomas K. Apollo 11 Moon Landing: An Interactive Space Exploration Adventure. 2016. (You Choose: Space Ser.). (ENG., Illus.). 112p. (J). (gr. 3-7). lib. bdg. 32.65 *(978-1-4914-8103-5(X)*, 130587, Capstone Pr.) Capstone.

—The First Moon Landing, 1 vol. Purcell, Gordon & Beatty, Terry, illus. 2006. (Graphic History Ser.). (ENG.). 32p. (J). (gr. 3-9). per. 8.10 *(978-0-7368-9654-2(6)*, 93409) Capstone.

Aldrin, Buzz. Reaching for the Moon. Minor, Wendell, illus. (ENG.). 40p. (J). (gr. 1-4). 2008. 8.99 *(978-0-06-055447-7(9))* 2005. 17.99 *(978-0-06-055445-3(2))* HarperCollins Pubs. (HarperCollins).

—Reaching for the Moon. Minor, Wendell, illus. unabr. ed. 2005. (Picture Book Readalong Ser.). (gr. k-4). 28.95 incl. audio compact disk *(978-1-59519-582-1(3))* Live Oak Media.

—To the Moon & Back: My Apollo 11 Adventure. 2018. (Illus.). 16p. (J). (gr. 3-7). 32.00 *(978-1-4263-3249-4(1)*, National Geographic Kids) Disney Publishing Worldwide.

Anderson, Dale. The First Moon Landing, 1 vol. 2003. (Landmark Events in American History Ser.). (ENG., Illus.). 48p. (gr. 5-8). pap. 15.05 *(978-0-8368-5406-0(3)*, 8331f41a-909d-4aac-b3ea-e6dc480dd8f7, Gareth Stevens Secondary Library) Stevens, Gareth Publishing LLLP.

Anderson, Dale & Hudson Goff, Elizabeth. The First Moon Landing, 1 vol. 2005. (Graphic Histories Ser.). (ENG., Illus.). 32p. (gr. 3-3). pap. 11.50 *(978-0-8368-6255-3(4)*, 491167e5-ee10-48f6-ace4-7d028e5f1452) Stevens, Gareth Publishing LLLP.

—El Primer Alunizaje (the First Moon Landing), 1 vol. 2007. (Historias Gráficas (Graphic Histories) Ser.). (SPA., Illus.). 32p. (gr. 3-3). pap. 11.50 *(978-0-8368-7904-9(X)*, 302c3f42-3b16-49b2-9303-b4d8f8170ff9); lib. bdg. 29.67 *(978-0-8368-7897-4(3)*, 8703cb2d-af44-4bc5-a497-3658ee3652f6) Stevens, Gareth Publishing LLLP.

Bailey, Gerry & Foster, Karen. Armstrong's Moon Rock. Radford, Karen & Noyes, Leighton, illus. 2008. (Stories of Great People Ser.). (ENG.). 40p. (J). (gr. 3-8). lib. bdg. *(978-0-7787-3684-4(9))*; (gr. 5-8). pap. *(978-0-7787-3706-3(3))* Crabtree Publishing Co.

Bodden, Valerie. Man Walks on the Moon. 2009. (Days of Change Ser.). 48p. (YA). (gr. 4-7). 22.95 *(978-1-58341-735-5(4))* Creative Co., The.

—Man Walks on the Moon: Days of Change. 2015. (Odysseys in History Ser.). (ENG., Illus.). 80p. (J). (gr. 7-10). *(978-1-60818-528-3(1)*, 20956, Creative Education) Creative Co., The.

—Man Walks on the Moon: Odysseys in History. 2016. (Odysseys in History Ser.). (ENG.). 80p. (J). (gr. 7-10). pap. 14.99 *(978-1-62832-129-6(6)*, 20957, Creative Paperbacks) Creative Co., The.

—To the Moon. 2011. (Great Expeditions Ser.). (ENG., Illus.). 48p. (J). (gr. 5-8). 35.65 *(978-1-60818-068-4(9)*, 22153, Creative Education); pap. 12.00 *(978-0-89812-666-2(5)*, 22159, Creative Paperbacks) Creative Co., The.

Brinkley, Douglas. American Moonshot Young Readers' Edition: John F. Kennedy & the Great Space Race. 2019. (ENG., Illus.). 272p. (J). (gr. 3-7). 16.99 *(978-0-06-266028-2(4)*, HarperCollins) HarperCollins Pubs.

Brouwer, Sigmund. Moon Mission: The Epic 400-Year Journey to Apollo 11. 2019. (ENG., Illus.). 128p. (J). (gr. 7-11). 17.99 *(978-1-5253-0036-3(9))* Kids Can Pr., Ltd. CAN. Dist: Hachette Bk. Group.

Brown, Don. Rocket to the Moon! Big Ideas That Changed the World #1. 2019. (Big Ideas That Changed the World Ser.). (ENG., Illus.). 136p. (J). (gr. 3-7). 14.99 *(978-1-4197-3404-5(0)*, 1254701) Abrams, Inc.

Buckley, James, Jr. Michael Collins: Discovering History's Heroes. 2019. (Jeter Publishing Ser.). (ENG.). 160p. (J). (gr. 2-5). 18.99 *(978-1-5344-2480-7(6))*; (Illus.). pap. 7.99 *(978-1-5344-2479-1(2))* Simon & Schuster Children's Publishing. (Aladdin).

Burleigh, Robert. One Giant Leap. Wimmer, Mike, illus. 2014. 40p. (J). (gr. 1-3). 8.99 *(978-0-14-751165-2(8)*, Puffin Books) Penguin Young Readers Group.

Calkhoven, Laurie. You Can't Bring a Sandwich to the Moon ... & Other Stories about Space! Space Age (Ready-To-Read Level 3) Fabbretti, Valerio, illus. 2018. (Secrets of American History Ser.). (ENG.). 48p. (J). (gr. 1-3). 17.99 *(978-1-5344-1781-6(8))*; pap. 4.99 *(978-1-5344-1780-9(X))* Simon Spotlight. (Simon Spotlight).

Choi, John & McGowen, Tom. Reaching for the Moon: The Cold War Space Race. 2019. (J). *(978-1-9785-1530-7(8))* Enslow Publishing, LLC.

Close, Edward. Moon Missions, 1 vol., 1. 2014. (Discovery Education: Earth & Space Science Ser.). (ENG.). 32p. (gr. 4-5). 28.93 *(978-1-4777-6178-6(0)*, 3a958377-1ebb-4f7a-814b-0b9ad8ffa8bf, PowerKids Pr.) Rosen Publishing Group, Inc., The.

Collins, Michael. Flying to the Moon: An Astronaut's Story. 3rd ed. 2019. (ENG., Illus.). 224p. (J). 19.99 *(978-0-374-31202-2(8)*, 900197771, Farrar, Straus & Giroux (BYR)) Farrar, Straus & Giroux.

Dell, Pamela. Man on the Moon: How a Photograph Made Anything Seem Possible, 1 vol. 2010. (Captured History Ser.). (ENG.). 64p. (J). (gr. 5-7). pap. 8.95 *(978-0-7565-4447-8(5)*, 115528, Compass Point Bks.) Capstone.

Dorling Kindersley Publishing Staff. Moon Landings: Level 3. 2019. (ENG., Illus.). 64p. (J). *(978-0-241-35853-5(1))* Dorling Kindersley Publishing, Inc.

Dunn, Joe. Moon Landing, 1 vol. Espinosa, Rod et al, illus. 2007. (Graphic History Ser.). (ENG.). 32p. (J). (gr. 3-8). 32.79 *(978-1-60270-078-9(8)*, 9042, Graphic Planet - Fiction) Magic Wagon.

Dyer, Alan. Mission to the Moon: (Book & DVD) 2009. (ENG., Illus.). 80p. (J). (gr. 3-7). 19.99 *(978-1-4169-7935-7(2)*, Simon & Schuster Bks. For Young Readers) Simon & Schuster Bks. For Young Readers.

Engdahl, Sylvia, ed. The Apollo 11 Moon Landing, 1 vol. 2011. (Perspectives on Modern World History Ser.). (ENG., Illus.). 224p. (gr. 10-12). 49.43 *(978-0-7377-5785-9(X)*, ddcbb0d3-d8df-4659-bfb5-3001aa465dee, Greenhaven Publishing) Greenhaven Publishing LLC.

Floca, Brian. Moonshot: The Flight of Apollo 11. Floca, Brian, illus. 2019. (ENG., Illus.). 56p. (J). (gr. -1-5). 19.99 *(978-1-5344-4030-2(5)*, Atheneum/Richard Jackson Bks.) Simon & Schuster Children's Publishing.

Gall, Chris. Go for the Moon: A Rocket, a Boy, & the First Moon Landing. Gall, Chris, illus. 2019. (ENG., Illus.). 48p. (J). 19.99 *(978-1-250-15579-5(7)*, 900184774) Roaring Brook Pr.

Graham, Ian. You Wouldn't Want to Be on Apollo 13! A Mission You'd Rather Not Go On. Antram, David, illus. 2003. (You Wouldn't Want to Ser.). (ENG.). 32p. (J). (gr. 2-5). pap. 9.95 *(978-0-531-16650-5(3)*, Watts, Franklin) Scholastic Library Publishing.

Green, Carl R. Walking on the Moon: The Amazing APOLLO 11 Mission, 1 vol. 2012. (American Space Missions: Astronauts, Exploration, & Discovery Ser.). (ENG., Illus.). 48p. (gr. 5-7). 27.93 *(978-0-7660-4076-2(3)*, 74153f82-5742-4637-87b7-a4d7636392e5) Enslow Publishing, LLC.

Hubbard, Ben. Neil Armstrong & Traveling to the Moon. 2015. (Adventures in Space Ser.). (ENG., Illus.). 48p. (J). (gr. 4-6).

35.99 (978-1-4846-2515-6(3), 130012, Heinemann) Capstone.

Irwin, James. Destination Moon. 15th anniv. ed. 2004. 52p. 16.00 (978-1-929241-98-9(4)) Send The Light Distribution LLC.

Jazynka, Kitson. National Geographic Readers: Buzz Aldrin (L3) 2018. (Readers Ser.). (ENG., Illus.). 48p. (J). (gr. 3-7). lib. bdg. 14.90 (978-1-4263-3207-4(6), National Geographic Kids) Disney Publishing Worldwide.

Jefferis, David. The Astronauts: Space Survival. 2019. (Moon Flight Atlas Ser.). (Illus.). 32p. (J). (gr. 5-5). (978-0-7787-5411-4(1)); pap. (978-0-7787-5420-6(0)) Crabtree Publishing Co.

—Exploring the Moon: 1969-1972. 2019. (Moon Flight Atlas Ser.). (Illus.). 32p. (J). (gr. 5-5). (978-0-7787-5409-1(X)); pap. (978-0-7787-5418-3(9)) Crabtree Publishing Co.

—Project Apollo: the Race to Land on the Moon. 2019. (Moon Flight Atlas Ser.). (Illus.). 32p. (J). (gr. 5-5). (978-0-7787-5410-7(3)); pap. (978-0-7787-5419-0(7)) Crabtree Publishing Co.

Kelly, Nigel & Tames, Richard. Point of Impact Series, 7 bks., Set 1. (Illus.). (J). (gr. 5-7). lib. bdg. 169.54 (978-1-57572-419-5(7)) Heinemann-Raintree.

Keppeler, Eric. Apollo 11 & the First Men on the Moon, 1 vol. 2018. (Real-Life Scientific Adventures Ser.). (ENG.). 32p. (gr. 4-5). 29.27 (978-1-5081-6842-3(3), 75daa6bc-a2bd-4928-83f4-5a1c877e70f4, PowerKids Pr.) Rosen Publishing Group, Inc., The.

Klepeis, Alicia Z. Moon Base & Beyond: The Lunar Gateway to Deep Space. 2019. (Future Space Ser.). (ENG., Illus.). 32p. (J). (gr. 3-9). pap. 7.95 (978-1-5435-7515-6(3), 141046); lib. bdg. 28.65 (978-1-5435-7267-4(7), 140598) Capstone.

Kluger, Jeffrey & Shamir, Ruby. To the Moon! The True Story of the American Heroes on the Apollo 8 Spaceship. 2019. (Illus.). 304p. (J). (gr. 5). 9.99 (978-1-5247-4103-7(5), Puffin Books) Penguin Young Readers Group.

Koestler-Grack, Rachel. Neil Armstrong, 1 vol. 2009. (People We Should Know (Second Series) Ser.). (ENG.). 48p. (J). (gr. 3-5). pap. 11.50 (978-1-4339-2147-6(2), e4006eee-7361-4818-886b-857c8686683d); lib. bdg. 33.67 (978-1-4339-1948-0(6), c5c0766e-8dda-41a3-b758-f5c155112e75) Stevens, Gareth Publishing LLLP. (Gareth Stevens Learning Library).

Loh-Hagan, Virginia. Apollo 13: Mission to the Moon. 2018. (True Survival Ser.). (ENG.). 32p. (J). (gr. 4-8). pap. 14.21 (978-1-5341-0871-4(8), 210848); (Illus.). lib. bdg. 32.07 (978-1-5341-0772-4(X), 210847) Cherry Lake Publishing. (45th Parallel Press).

Lovitt, Charles. My Little Golden Book about the First Moon Landing. Sims, Bryan, illus. 2019. (Little Golden Book Ser.). (ENG.). 24p. (J). (-k). 5.99 (978-0-525-58007-2(7), Golden Bks.) Random Hse. Children's Bks.

Malam, John. Man Walks on the Moon. 2003. (Dates with History Ser.). 45p. (J). lib. bdg. 28.50 (978-1-58340-407-2(4)) Black Rabbit Bks.

McNulty, Faith. If You Decide to Go to the Moon. Kellogg, Steven, illus. 2005. (ENG.). 48p. (J). (gr. -1-k). 18.99 (978-0-590-48359-9(5), Scholastic Pr.) Scholastic, Inc.

McReynolds, Linda. Eight Days Gone. O'Rourke, Ryan, illus. 2019. 28p. (J). (— 1). bds. 8.99 (978-1-57091-024-1(3)) Charlesbridge Publishing, Inc.

Nagelhout, Ryan. The First Moon Walk, 1 vol. 2014. (Incredible True Adventures Ser.). (ENG.). 32p. (J). (gr. 3-4). pap. 11.50 (978-1-4824-2038-8(4), 3c771659-10cf-426c-baae-192665f12123) Stevens, Gareth Publishing LLLP.

—Neil Armstrong in His Own Words, 1 vol. 2015. (Eyewitness to History Ser.). (ENG., Illus.). 32p. (J). (gr. 4-5). pap. 11.50 (978-1-4824-4078-2(4), e99a42bf-4083-426c-a3dd-dfa2fc1e89f5) Stevens, Gareth Publishing LLLP.

Olson, Elsie. Breakthroughs in Moon Exploration. 2019. (Cosmos Chronicles (Alternator Books (r)) Ser.). (ENG., Illus.). 32p. (J). (gr. 3-6). pap. 10.99 (978-1-5415-7369-7(2), 5ff50d8f-8878-4f7d-ab5d-e8341f177e7e); lib. bdg. 29.32 (978-1-5415-5596-9(1), 49e56b8f-bdaa-4a09-9ea0-63920cff5d63) Lerner Publishing Group. (Lerner Pubns.).

Oxlade, Chris. The Moon. 2010. (Eye on Space Ser.). 24p. (J). pap. 8.25 (978-1-61532-546-7(8), PowerKids Pr.); (ENG.). (gr. 1-1). lib. bdg. 26.27 (978-1-61532-541-2(7), 46e50f19-85f1-40a9-83de-9e71bf1de938) Rosen Publishing Group, Inc., The.

Pohlen, Jerome. The Apollo Missions for Kids: The People & Engineering Behind the Race to the Moon, with 21 Activities. 2019. (For Kids Ser.: 71). (Illus.). 160p. (J). (gr. 4). pap. 18.99 (978-0-912777-17-7(6)) Chicago Review Pr., Inc.

Richards, Patti. The Apollo Missions. 2018. (Destination Space Ser.). (ENG., Illus.). 48p. (J). (gr. 5-6). pap. 11.95 (978-1-63517-565-3(8), 1635175658); lib. bdg. 34.21 (978-1-63517-493-9(7), 1635174937) North Star Editions. (Focus Readers).

—The Apollo Missions. 2018. (Illus.). 48p. (J). pap. (978-1-4896-9831-5(0), AV2 by Weigl) Weigl Pubs., Inc.

Riley, Christopher & Dolling, Phil. Inside Apollo 11, 1 vol. 2017. (Geek's Guide to Space Ser.). (ENG.). 192p. (J). (gr. 9-9). 46.27 (978-1-4994-6696-6(X), 079cca55-62a2-4f68-89b2-60cd0402a04b, Rosen Young Adult) Rosen Publishing Group, Inc., The.

Rissman, Rebecca. Houston, We've Had a Problem: The Story of the Apollo 13 Disaster. 2018. (Tangled History Ser.). (ENG.). 112p. (J). (gr. 3-9). pap. 6.95 (978-1-5157-7964-3(5), 136044); lib. bdg. 32.65 (978-1-5157-7940-7(8), 136036) Capstone. (Capstone Pr.).

Robbins, Dean. The Astronaut Who Painted the Moon: the True Story of Alan Bean. Rubin, Sean, illus. 2019. (ENG.). 40p. (J). (gr. -1-3). 17.99 (978-1-338-25953-7(9), Orchard Bks.) Scholastic, Inc.

Rocco, John. How We Got to the Moon: The People, Technology, & Daring Feats of Science Behind Humanity's Greatest Adventure. 2020. (Illus.). 264p. (J). (gr. 5). 29.99 (978-0-525-64741-6(4), Crown Books For Young Readers) Random Hse. Children's Bks.

Sandler, Martin W. Apollo 8: The Mission That Changed Everything. 2018. (ENG., Illus.). 176p. (J). (gr. 5). 24.99 (978-0-7636-9489-0(4)) Candlewick Pr.

Schyffert, Bea Uusma. The Man Who Went to the Far Side of the Moon: The Story of Apollo 11 Astronaut Michael Collins (NASA Books, Apollo 11 Book for Kids, Children's Astronaut Books) 2019. (ENG.). 80p. (J). (gr. 3-7). pap. 12.99 (978-1-4521-8023-6(7)) Chronicle Bks. LLC.

Scott, Elaine. Our Moon: New Discoveries about Earth's Closest Companion. 2016. (ENG., Illus.). 72p. (J). (gr. 5-7). 18.99 (978-0-547-48394-8(5), 1439925, Clarion Bks.) HarperCollins Pubs.

Sipe, Nicole. The History of the First Moon Landing. 2018. (Mathematics in the Real World Ser.). (ENG., Illus.). 32p. (J). (gr. 4-8). pap. 11.99 (978-1-4258-5822-3(8)) Teacher Created Materials, Inc.

Slade, Suzanne. Countdown: 2979 Days to the Moon. Gonzalez, Thomas, illus. 2018. 144p. (J). (gr. 5-9). 22.95 (978-1-68263-013-6(7)) Peachtree Publishing Co. Inc.

Smibert, Angie. 12 Incredible Facts about the First Moon Landing. 2016. (Turning Points in US History Ser.). (ENG., Illus.). 32p. (J). (gr. 3-5). 32.80 (978-1-63235-130-2(7), 12-Story Library) Bookstaves, LLC.

Tan, Sheri. Handshake in Space: The Apollo-Soyuz Test Project. Bond, Higgins, illus. 2009. 32p. (J). (gr. 1-5). pap. 9.95 incl. audio (978-1-60727-104-8(4)); (ENG.). 9.95 (978-1-60727-115-4(X)); (ENG.). 17.95 (978-1-60727-114-7(1)); pap. 9.95 incl. reel tape (978-1-59249-203-9(7)) Soundprints.

Thimmesh, Catherine. Team Moon: How 400,000 People Landed Apollo 11 on the Moon. 2006. (ENG., Illus.). 80p. (J). (gr. 5-7). 19.95 (978-0-618-50757-3(4), 510514, Clarion Bks.) HarperCollins Pubs.

Troupe, Thomas Kingsley. Apollo's First Moon Landing: A Fly on the Wall History. Tejido, Jomike, illus. 2018. (Fly on the Wall History Ser.). (ENG.). 32p. (J). (gr. 1-3). lib. bdg. 27.99 (978-1-5158-1598-3(6), 136251, Picture Window Bks.) Capstone.

Tunby, Benjamin. Surviving a Space Disaster: Apollo 13. 2019. (They Survived (Alternator Books (r)) Ser.). (ENG., Illus.). 32p. (J). (gr. 3-6). 29.32 (978-1-5415-2350-0(4), ab165ec4-a23d-4f4c-889b-fa9cfccea128, Lerner Pubns.) Lerner Publishing Group.

Turner, Myra Faye. Events That Changed the Course of History: The Story of Apollo 11 & the Men on the Moon 50 Years Later. Lieneman, Danielle, ed. 2018. (ENG.). 208p. (YA). pap. 19.95 (978-1-62023-527-0(7), 5be831af-1e65-4060-9f68-0aceed51edae) Atlantic Publishing Group, Inc.

—The Story of Apollo 11 & the Men on the Moon 50 Years Later. 2018. (J). lib. bdg. (978-1-62023-528-7(5)) Atlantic Publishing Group, Inc.

Weakland, Mark. When Neil Armstrong Built a Wind Tunnel. Lozano, Luciano, illus. 2017. (Leaders Doing Headstands Ser.). (ENG.). 32p. (J). (gr. 1-4). lib. bdg. 28.65 (978-1-5158-1575-4(7), 136245, Picture Window Bks.) Capstone.

Wilkinson, Philip. Spacebusters: The Race to the Moon. 2012. (DK Readers Level 3 Ser.). (ENG.). 48p. (J). (gr. 1-3). 16.19 (978-0-7566-9085-4(4)) Dorling Kindersley Publishing, Inc.

Wishinsky, Frieda. Could We Live on the Moon? 2004. (ENG., Illus.). 24p. (J). (gr. 2-2). pap. 10.92 (978-0-7652-5178-7(7), Celebration Pr.) Savvas Learning Co.

Woolf, Alex. Trailblazers: Neil Armstrong: First Man on the Moon. 2019. (Trailblazers Ser.). (ENG., Illus.). 192p. (J). (gr. 3-7). 7.99 (978-0-593-12401-7(4), Random Hse. Bks. for Young Readers) Random Hse. Children's Bks.

Yomtov, Nel. The Apollo 11 Moon Landing: July 20 1969, 1 vol. Chiu, Andrew, illus. 2014. (24-Hour History Ser.). (ENG.). 48p. (J). (gr. 3-9). pap. 8.95 (978-1-4329-9298-9(8), 124614); lib. bdg. 33.99 (978-1-4329-9292-7(9), 124609) Capstone. (Heinemann).

Zemlicka, Shannon. Neil Armstrong. 2003. (History Maker Bios Ser.). (Illus.). 48p. (J). (gr. 2-4). 26.60 (978-0-8225-0395-8(6), Lerner Pubns.) Lerner Publishing Group.

SPACE MEDICINE

see also Life Support Systems (Space Environment); Manned Space Flight

Linde, Barbara M. Rocket Scientists, 1 vol., 1. 2015. (Out of the Lab: Extreme Jobs in Science Ser.). (ENG., Illus.). 32p. (J). (gr. 4-5). pap. 11.00 (978-1-4994-1855-2(8), 5cbe70a5-4786-443f-87c6-fea5ae820431, PowerKids Pr.) Rosen Publishing Group, Inc., The.

SPACE PROBES

see also Lunar Probes

also names of space vehicles and space projects, e.g. Mariner project; etc.

Baker, David & Kissock, Heather. Probing Space. 2009. (Exploring Space Ser.). (Illus.). 32p. (J). (gr. 2-4). pap. 9.95 (978-1-60596-026-5(8)); lib. bdg. 26.00 (978-1-60596-025-8(X)) Weigl Pubs., Inc.

Collins, Ailynn. Probe Power: How Space Probes Do What Humans Can't. 2019. (Future Space Ser.). (ENG., Illus.). 32p. (J). (gr. 3-9). pap. 7.95 (978-1-5435-7518-7(8), 141049); lib. bdg. 28.65 (978-1-5435-7269-8(3), 140600) Capstone.

Furstinger, Nancy. Robots in Space. 2014. (Lightning Bolt Books (r) — Robots Everywhere! Ser.). (ENG., Illus.). 32p. (J). (gr. 1-3). pap. 9.99 (978-1-4677-4510-9(3), 865977fb-31b3-4865-a160-1ef1d1c30c35); lib. bdg. 29.32 (978-1-4677-4055-5(1), ea912cc8-ca06-4b2d-a579-a1c46f9dc90f, Lerner Pubns.) Lerner Publishing Group.

Gross, Miriam. All about Space Missions. 2009. (Blast Off! Ser.). 24p. (gr. 2-3). 42.50 (978-1-61511-623-2(0), PowerKids Pr.) Rosen Publishing Group, Inc., The.

Gross, Miriam J. All about Space Missions, 1 vol. 2009. (Blast Off! Ser.). (ENG.). 24p. (J). (gr. 2-3). pap. 9.25 (978-1-4358-3138-4(1), 2c9aa5cb-9bae-4a8e-b34e-87d3674163db); lib. bdg. 26.27 (978-1-4358-2740-0(6), 255befb5-8e9f-4767-9624-23cb3c6fd2c9) Rosen Publishing Group, Inc., The. (PowerKids Pr.).

Hantula, Richard & Asimov, Isaac. Exploring Outer Space, 1 vol. 2005. (Isaac Asimov's 21st Century Library of the Universe: Past & Present Ser.). (ENG., Illus.). 32p. (gr. 3-5). lib. bdg. 28.67 (978-0-8368-3981-4(1), 178ac6e2-ad74-41c4-8f5b-ea4798022921) Stevens, Gareth Publishing LLLP.

Jefferis, David. Space Probes: Exploring Beyond Earth. 2008. (Exploring our Solar System Ser.). (ENG., Illus.). 32p. (J). (gr. 3-8). pap. (978-0-7787-3741-4(1)) Crabtree Publishing Co.

Jemison, Mae & Rau, Dana Meachen. Journey Through Our Solar System. 2013. (True Book™—Dr. Mae Jemison & 100 Year Starship™ Ser.). (ENG., Illus.). 48p. (J). lib. bdg. 29.00 (978-0-531-25501-8(8)) Scholastic Library Publishing.

Kain, Kathleen. Telescopes & Space Probes. 2006. (World Book's Solar System & Space Exploration Library). (Illus.). 63p. (J). (978-0-7166-9510-3(3)) World Bk., Inc.

Kenney, Karen Latchana. Breakthroughs in Planet & Comet Research. 2019. (Space Exploration (Alternator Books (r)) Ser.). (ENG., Illus.). 32p. (J). (gr. 3-6). 29.32 (978-1-5415-3870-2(6), fee970a7-9c67-48b0-a7b4-dc837a3ff879, Lerner Pubns.) Lerner Publishing Group.

Larson, Kirsten W. Space Robots. 2018. (Robotics in Our World Ser.). (ENG., Illus.). 32p. (J). (gr. 2-5). pap. 9.99 (978-1-68152-178-7(4), 14809) Amicus.

Meet NASA Inventor Kendra Short & Her Printable Probes & Cosmic Confetti. 2017. (J). (978-0-7166-6158-0(6)) World Bk., Inc.

Miller, Ron. Robot Explorers. 2007. (Space Innovations Ser.). (ENG., Illus.). 112p. (gr. 6-8). lib. bdg. 31.93 (978-0-8225-7152-0(8)) Lerner Publishing Group.

Mills, Nathan & Stiegler, Lorraine. Space Probes, 1 vol. 2012. (Rosen Readers Ser.). (ENG., Illus.). 24p. (J). (gr. 1-2). pap. 8.25 (978-1-4488-8869-6(7), 01e87361-02cb-470b-82d9-7854c8f69298, Rosen Classroom) Rosen Publishing Group, Inc., The.

O'Hearn, Michael. Awesome Space Robots. 2013. (Robots Ser.). (ENG.). 32p. (J). (gr. 3-4). pap. 50.74 (978-1-62065-779-9(1), 19361, Capstone Pr.) Capstone.

O'Hearn, Michael. Awesome Space Robots, 1 vol. 2013. (Robots Ser.). (ENG.). 32p. (J). (gr. 3-9). lib. bdg. 28.65 (978-1-4296-9918-1(3), 120630); (Illus.). pap. 8.29 (978-1-62065-778-2(3), 121743) Capstone.

Riggs, Kate. New Horizons. 2018. (Now That's Fast! Ser.). (ENG.). 24p. (J). (gr. 1-4). pap. 8.99 (978-1-62832-588-1(7), 19857, Creative Paperbacks) Creative Co., The.

Saunders-Smith, Gail. Robots in Space, 1 vol. 2014. (Cool Robots Ser.). (ENG., Illus.). 24p. (J). (gr. -1-2). 27.32 (978-1-4914-0585-7(6), 125923, Capstone Pr.) Capstone.

Shea, Therese. Gareth's Guide to Building a Space Probe. 2017. (Gareth Guides to an Extraordinary Life Ser.). 32p. (gr. 4-5). pap. 63.00 (978-1-5382-0337-8(5)) Stevens, Gareth Publishing LLLP.

Sparrow, Giles. Destination Mars, 1 vol. 2009. (Destination Solar System Ser.). (ENG., Illus.). 32p. (J). (gr. 3-4). pap. 11.00 (978-1-4358-3459-0(3), fbad798e-9438-4b98-8603-3bfdce8eb4c9); lib. bdg. 28.93 (978-1-4358-3443-9(7), d68da343-bd95-4d14-b8cb-7ebaddfd7ed1) Rosen Publishing Group, Inc., The. (PowerKids Pr.).

—Destination Mercury, 1 vol. 2009. (Destination Solar System Ser.). (ENG.). 32p. (J). (gr. 3-4). lib. bdg. 28.93 (978-1-4358-3441-5(0), d02370b7-5a8c-46b0-acb1-669ebad14c24); (Illus.). pap. 11.00 (978-1-4358-3455-2(0), 9dbf2a09-30ef-4a3e-a76c-e17e114079c4) Rosen Publishing Group, Inc., The. (PowerKids Pr.).

Stiegler, Lorraine. Space Probes, 1 vol. 2012. (Exploring Earth & Space Ser.). (ENG., Illus.). 24p. (J). (gr. 1-2). 26.27 (978-1-4488-8580-0(9), eca19de1-0ae6-4e72-9bee-c32de37e94dd, PowerKids Pr.) Rosen Publishing Group, Inc., The.

Swatling, Todd. What Happens to Space Probes?, 1 vol. 2018. (Space Mysteries Ser.). (ENG.). 32p. (gr. 2-3). 29.27 (978-1-5382-1959-1(X), 41b9eae3-a043-4dcc-95fc-2b04d56f53fc) Stevens, Gareth Publishing LLLP.

World Book, Inc. Staff, contrib. by. Telescopes & Space Probes. (J). 2010. (978-0-7166-9541-7(3)) 2nd ed. 2006. (Illus.). 64p. (978-0-7166-9520-2(0)) World Bk., Inc.

SPACE RESEARCH

see Outer Space—Exploration; Space Sciences

SPACE SCIENCES

see also Astronautics; Astronomy; Geophysics; Outer Space; Space Medicine

Be a Space Scientist!, 12 vols. 2017. (Be a Space Scientist! Ser.). (ENG.). (J). (gr. 5-5). lib. bdg. 191.58 (978-1-5081-6263-6(8), 57e8e602-518d-4f5c-8189-a0948105350a, PowerKids Pr.) Rosen Publishing Group, Inc., The.

Becklake, Sue & Parker, Steve. Astronomy. 2013. (Illus.). 48p. (J). (978-1-4351-5086-7(4)) Barnes & Noble, Inc.

Benchmark Education Company, LLC Staff, compiled by. Earth & Space Science. 2006. spiral bd. 695.00 (978-1-4108-6942-5(3)) 2006. spiral bd. 365.00 (978-1-4108-6939-5(3)) 2006. spiral bd. 235.00 (978-1-4108-6934-0(2)) 2006. spiral bd. 80.00 (978-1-4108-6927-2(X)) 2006. spiral bd. 365.00 (978-1-4108-6925-8(3)) 2006. spiral bd. 365.00 (978-1-4108-6946-3(6)) 2005. spiral bd. 405.00 (978-1-4108-5852-8(9)) 2005. spiral bd. 675.00 (978-1-4108-5851-1(0)) 2005. spiral bd. 950.00 (978-1-4108-5441-4(8)) 2005. spiral bd. 1025.00 (978-1-4108-5440-7(X)) 2005. spiral bd. 870.00 (978-1-4108-4518-4(4)) 2005. spiral bd. 75.00 (978-1-4108-3870-4(6)) 2005. spiral bd. 220.00 (978-1-4108-3859-9(5)) 2005. spiral bd. 370.00 (978-1-4108-3858-2(7)) 2005. spiral bd. 220.00 (978-1-4108-3851-3(X)) 2005. spiral bd. 305.00 (978-1-4108-3850-6(1)) 2005. spiral bd. 335.00 (978-1-4108-3829-2(3)) 2005. spiral bd. 580.00 (978-1-4108-3826-1(9)) 2005. spiral bd. 55.00 (978-1-4108-3874-2(9)) Benchmark Education Co.

—Science Theme: Earth & Space Science. 2005. spiral bd. 340.00 (978-1-4108-5314-1(4)) Benchmark Education Co.

Bortz, Fred. Astrobiology. 2008. pap. 52.95 (978-0-8225-9326-3(2)) 2007. (ENG., Illus.). 48p. (gr. 4-8). lib. bdg. 27.93 (978-0-8225-6771-4(7), Lerner Pubns.) Lerner Publishing Group.

Chapman, Cindy. What Is in the Sky?, 6 vols., Set. 2003. (Phonics Readers 1-36 Ser.). (ENG.). 8p. (gr. k-1). pap. 29.70 (978-0-7368-3202-1(5)) Capstone.

Cientificos! 9: Ciencias Terrestres y del Espacio. (SPA.). (J). 60.00 (978-958-04-6348-1(4)) Norma S.A. COL. Dist: Distribuidora Norma, Inc.

Daynes, Katie. Living in Space. Wray, Zoe & Fox, Christyan, illus. 2006. (Beginners Nature: Level 2 Ser.). 32p. (J). (gr. 1-3). 4.99 (978-0-7945-1339-9(5), Usborne) EDC Publishing.

Dickmann, Nancy. Exploring Comets, Asteroids, & Other Objects in Space, 1 vol. 2015. (Spectacular Space Science Ser.). (ENG., Illus.). 48p. (J). (gr. 5-6). 33.47 (978-1-4994-3637-2(8), 670562d8-c46b-4c18-a44e-6c803f2766d7, Rosen Central) Rosen Publishing Group, Inc., The.

—Math in Space. 2018. (Amazing World of Math Ser.). (ENG., Illus.). 32p. (J). (gr. 3-6). 27.99 (978-1-5415-0100-3(4), 5717b2a1-3b14-4d24-ae55-e5a375d9cf44, Hungry Tomato (r)) Lerner Publishing Group.

Dowswell, Paul. First Encyclopedia of Space. 2004. (First Encyclopedia Ser.). (SPA & ENG., Illus.). (J). (gr. 3-18). 1p. pap. 9.99 (978-0-7945-0035-1(8), Usborne); 1p. pap. 9.99 (978-0-7945-0035-1(8), Usborne); 64p. lib. bdg. 17.95 (978-1-58086-357-5(4)) EDC Publishing.

Earth & Space Science. 2011. (Earth & Space Science Ser.). (ENG.). 24p. (gr. k-1). lib. bdg. 54.64 (978-1-4296-6836-1(9), Capstone Pr.) Capstone.

Elish, Dan. Kaleidoscope Space Gorup 2, 4 bks., Set. Incl. Galaxies. 32.64 (978-0-7614-2047-7(9), 132cdea3-d223-4344-86ea-7ce04501ced6); NASA. lib. bdg. 32.64 (978-0-7614-2046-0(0), 7d2c4392-852c-4109-8304-40daa8b73ba5); Satellites. lib. bdg. 32.64 (978-0-7614-2098-9(3), 622d009d-5c37-410e-8c56-c4e7dfa0043b); Sun. lib. bdg. 32.64 (978-0-7614-2048-4(7), 667aed39-e166-4330-9f9f-e25201fd813e); (Illus.). 48p. (gr. 4-4). 2007. lib. bdg. (978-0-7614-2045-3(2), Cavendish Square) Cavendish Square Publishing LLC.

Encyclopaedia Britannica, Inc. Staff, compiled by. Science & Nature. 2003. (Britannica Learning Library). (Illus.). (gr. 2-5). 14.95 (978-1-59339-002-0(5), 049903-EN-REF) Encyclopaedia Britannica, Inc.

—Technology & Inventions. 2003. (Britannica Learning Library). (Illus.). (gr. 2-5). 14.95 (978-1-59339-003-7(3), 049904-EN-REF) Encyclopaedia Britannica, Inc.

Erickson, John, et al. AfterSchool KidzScience: Earth & Space Science: Sunlight Science Kit. 2013. (J). 225.00 (978-1-61003-142-4(3)) Center for the Collaborative Classroom.

Exploracion del Espacio, 6 vols., Vol. 3. (Explorers. Exploradores Nonfiction Sets Ser.). (SPA.). (gr. 3-6). (978-0-7699-0653-9(2)) Shortland Pubns. (U. S. A.) Inc.

Explore Space! Classroom Library. (gr. 2-5). lib. bdg. 22.95 (978-0-7368-9250-6(8), Red Brick Learning) Capstone.

Explore Space! II Classroom Library. (gr. 2-5). lib. bdg. 22.95 (978-0-7368-4536-6(4), Red Brick Learning) Capstone.

Exploring Space: Level Q, 6 vols., Vol. 3. (Explorers Ser.). 32p. (gr. 3-6). 44.95 (978-0-7699-0617-1(6)) Shortland Pubns. (U. S. A.) Inc.

Gardner, Robert & Goodstein, Madeline. Ace Your Space Science Project: Great Science Fair Ideas, 1 vol. 2009. (Ace Your Science Project Ser.). (ENG., Illus.). 128p. (gr. 5-6). lib. bdg. 35.93 (978-0-7660-3230-9(2), 4b435834-8e1d-493e-94dc-af7e8e16e91a) Enslow Publishing, LLC.

Gibson, Brylee. The World Beyond Earth. 2007. (Connectors Ser.). (gr. 2-5). pap. (978-1-877453-11-3(0)) Global Education Systems Ltd.

Goldsmith, Mike. The Kingfisher Space Encyclopedia. 2017. (Kingfisher Encyclopedias Ser.). (ENG.). 160p. (J). pap. 13.99 (978-0-7534-7353-5(4), 900174958, Kingfisher) Roaring Brook Pr.

Goldstein, Margaret J. Discover Jupiter. 2018. (Searchlight Books (tm) — Discover Planets Ser.). (ENG., Illus.). 32p. (J). (gr. 3-5). 30.65 (978-1-5415-2335-7(0), 33b5311d-1f09-4c8b-b340-e673428817c4, Lerner Pubns.) Lerner Publishing Group.

Goodman, Susan E. Ultimate Field Trip #5: Blasting off to Space Academy. Doolittle, Michael J., illus. 2011. (ENG.). 48p. (J). (gr. 3-7). pap. 19.99 (978-1-4424-4345-7(6), Atheneum Bks. for Young Readers) Simon & Schuster Children's Publishing.

Graham, Ian & Jones, Geriant. H. Exploring Science: Space an Amazing Fact File & Hands-On Project Book. 2015. (ENG., Illus.). 64p. (J). (gr. -1-6). 12.99 (978-1-86147-386-8(9), Armadillo) Anness Publishing GBR. Dist: National Bk. Network.

Grant, Donald. Atlas of Space. Grant, Donald, illus. 2012. (ENG., Illus.). 36p. (J). (gr. -1-k). 19.99 (978-1-85103-407-9(2)) Moonlight Publishing, Ltd. GBR. Dist: Independent Pubs. Group.

Grolier Educational Staff, contrib. by. Space Science, 8 vols. 2004. (Illus.). (J). 309.00 (978-0-7172-5825-3(4), Grolier) Scholastic Library Publishing.

Hantula, Richard & Asimov, Isaac. Global Space Programs, 1 vol. 2005. (Isaac Asimov's 21st Century Library of the Universe: Past & Present Ser.). (ENG., Illus.). 32p. (gr. 3-5). lib. bdg. 28.67 (978-0-8368-3982-1(X), c7836922-1a80-4909-93cd-08c7133b3aa2) Stevens, Gareth Publishing LLLP.

Harris, Tim. Space Science, 1 vol. 2015. (Science Q & A Ser.). (ENG., Illus.). 32p. (gr. 3-3). pap. 11.58 (978-1-5026-0612-9(7), 0539d64f-57ce-4f6b-9cc7-9047e3b6df77) Cavendish Square Publishing LLC.

Hewitt, Sally. Earth & Space. (Illus.). 32p. (YA). (gr. 2-18). lib. bdg. 27.10 (978-1-932333-31-2(2)) Chrysalis Education.

Holden, Henry M. The Coolest Job in the Universe: Working Aboard the International Space Station, 1 vol. 2012. (American Space Missions: Astronauts, Exploration, & Discovery Ser.). (ENG., Illus.). 48p. (gr. 5-7). lib. bdg. 27.93 (978-0-7660-4074-8(7), 2a655c2e-ef54-4c2c-9324-2b92f1c91bec) Enslow Publishing, LLC.

Holt, Rinehart and Winston Staff. Holt Science & Technology Chapter 19: Earth Science: Stars, the Galaxy, & the Universe. 5th ed. 2004. (Illus.). pap. 12.86 (978-0-03-030336-4(2)) Holt McDougal.

—Holt Science & Technology Chapter 22: Earth Science: Exploring Space. 5th ed. 2004. (Illus.). pap. 12.86 *(978-0-03-030351-7(6))* Holt McDougal.

Hunter, Dru. What Is Out There? 2016. (Think Like a Scientist Ser.). (ENG.). 48p. (J). (gr. 4-7). pap. 12.00 *(978-1-62832-199-9(7)*, 21067, Creative Paperbacks) Creative Co., The.

Hutmacher, Kimberly M. The Universe Began with a Bang & Other Cool Space Facts. 2019. (Mind-Blowing Science Facts Ser.). (ENG., Illus.). 32p. (J). (gr. 4-6). lib. bdg. 28.65 *(978-1-5435-5769-5(4)*, 139725) Capstone.

Hutson, Matt. What Do You Want to Be? Explore Aerospace. 2005. (J). 6.00 *(978-0-9753920-7-2(7))* Sally Ride Science.

Ivey, Catherine. Totally Amazing Careers in Space Sciences. 2006. (J). 7.80 *(978-1-933798-00-4(9))* Sally Ride Science.

Johnson, Rose. Discoveries in Earth & Space Science That Changed the World, 1 vol. 2014. (Scientific Breakthroughs Ser.). (ENG.). 48p. (YA). (gr. 6-6). 33.47 *(978-1-4777-8609-3(0)*, 05dc91f9-73c7-4339-a809-eef3c8153518, Rosen Reference) Rosen Publishing Group, Inc., The.

Kawa, Katie. Freaky Space Stories, 1 vol. 2015. (Freaky True Science Ser.). (ENG., Illus.). 32p. (J). (gr. 4-5). 28.27 *(978-1-4824-2958-9(6)*, d51a66dc-47f0-4ab2-a788-3bb723be4cab) Stevens, Gareth Publishing LLLP.

Kenney, Karen Latchana. Breakthroughs in Planet & Comet Research. 2019. (Space Exploration (Alternator Books (r)) Ser.). (ENG., Illus.). 32p. (J). (gr. 3-6). 29.32 *(978-1-5415-3870-2(6)*, fee970a7-9c67-48b0-a7b4-dc837a3ff879, Lerner Pubns.) Lerner Publishing Group.

—Cutting-Edge Astronaut Training. 2019. (Searchlight Books (tm) — New Frontiers of Space Ser.). (ENG., Illus.). 32p. (J). (gr. 3-5). pap. 9.99 *(978-1-5415-7482-3(6)*, f932a244-3985-4799-95dd-166b23a7bf42); lib. bdg. 30.65 *(978-1-5415-5580-8(5)*, 1d34cccc-e8ab-4c86-b3f2-adf735803d35) Lerner Publishing Group. (Lerner Pubns.).

Keppeler, Eric. More Freaky Space Stories, 1 vol. 2019. (Freaky True Science Ser.). (ENG.). 32p. (gr. 4-5). pap. 11.50 *(978-1-5382-4062-5(9)*, 242e9922-9f68-4957-a807-c0a26d7fdb35) Stevens, Gareth Publishing LLLP.

Khan, Hena & Dyson, Marianne J. The Space Explorer's Guide to Out-Of-This-World Science. 2004. (Space University Ser.). (Illus.). 48p. (J). *(978-0-439-55747-4(X))* Scholastic, Inc.

Koellhoffer, Tara, ed. Space & Astronomy. 2006. (Science News for Kids Ser.). (Illus.). 136p. (gr. 4-6). lib. bdg. 30.00 *(978-0-7910-9125-8(2)*, Chelsea Clubhse.) Infobase Holdings, Inc.

Kruesi, Liz. Discover Space Exploration. 2016. (Searchlight Books (tm) — What's Cool about Science? Ser.). (ENG., Illus.). 40p. (J). (gr. 3-5). 30.65 *(978-1-5124-0811-9(5)*, 1fb5a99a-38ad-49de-bf70-ed8d315026f8, Lerner Pubns.) Lerner Publishing Group.

Let's Find Out! Space Science, 12 vols. 2014. (Let's Find Out! Space Science Ser.). (ENG.). 32p. (J). (gr. 2-3). 156.36 *(978-1-62275-486-1(7)*, 60ba4beb-fe9b-499a-a0d4-a3dd2ff2d78f) Rosen Publishing Group, Inc., The.

Lombardo, Jennifer. Space Exploration Throughout History: From Telescopes to Tourism, 1 vol. 2019. (World History Ser.). (ENG.). 104p. (gr. 7-7). 41.53 *(978-1-5345-6712-2(7)*, 47fb66b6-eab7-446c-ae36-dc30db49b477, Lucent Pr.) Greenhaven Publishing LLC.

Macmillan Reference USA, ed. Space Sciences: 4 Volume Set, 4 vols. 2nd ed. 2012. (Macmillan Science Library). (ENG., Illus.). 1850p. 925.00 *(978-0-02-866214-5(8)*, Macmillan Reference USA) Cengage Gale.

McDougal-Littell Publishing Staff. Modules: Physical Science - Space Science. 2004. (McDougal Littell Science Ser.). (ENG.). 64p. (gr. 6-8). pap., lab manual ed. 15.30 *(978-0-618-43734-4(7)*, 2-01227) Great Source Education Group, Inc.

Michael, Allaby. El Planeta Tierra.Tr. of Planet Earth. (SPA.). 96p. (YA). (gr. 5-8). 18.36 *(978-84-241-1994-2(0))* Everest Editora ESP. Dist: Lectorum Pubns., Inc.

Milbourne, Anna. On the Moon. 2004. (On the Moon Ser.). 24p. (J). 9.95 *(978-0-7945-0617-9(8)*, Usborne) EDC Publishing.

Minter, Laura & Williams, Tia. The Space Craft Book: 15 Things a Space Fan Can't Do Without! 2018. (ENG., Illus.). 64p. pap. 9.95 *(978-1-78494-365-3(7)*, GM0309) GMC Distribution GBR. Dist: Ingram Publisher Services.

Modules: Earth Science; Space Science TE. 2005. (gr. 6-12). *(978-0-618-33422-3(X)*, 2-01012) Holt McDougal.

Out in Space. 2005. (Earth & Outer Space Ser.). (YA). (gr. k-3). 118.80 *(978-0-7368-4211-2(X)*, Pebble) Capstone.

Owen, Ruth. Space Survival Guide. 2010. (ENG., Illus.). 32p. (J). pap. *(978-0-7787-7553-9(4))*; lib. bdg. *(978-0-7787-7531-7(3))* Crabtree Publishing Co.

Parker. Space Mysteries - Space Busters. 2004. (YA). pap. 48.30 *(978-1-4109-0293-1(5))* Harcourt Schl. Pubs.

Parker, Steve. Probes to the Planets. West, David, illus. 2015. (Story of Space Ser.). (ENG.). 32p. (J). (gr. 3-6). 31.35 *(978-1-62588-077-2(4))* Black Rabbit Bks.

Parks, Peggy J. Space Research. 2010. (Inside Science Ser.). (Illus.). 96p. (J). (gr. 7-12). 41.27 *(978-1-60152-111-8(1)*, 1316146) ReferencePoint Pr., Inc.

Pebble Books: Earth & Outer Space. 2005. (YA). (gr. k-3). 594.00 *(978-0-7368-4222-8(5)*, Pebble) Capstone.

Perritano, John. Space Science, Vol. 10. 2016. (Stem in Current Events Ser.). (Illus.). 64p. (J). (gr. 7). 23.95 *(978-1-4222-3595-9(5))* Mason Crest.

Pinna, Lorenzo. La Conquista del Espacio. (SPA.). 88p. (YA). (gr. 5-8). *(978-84-7131-926-5(8))* Editex, Editorial S.A. ESP. Dist: Lectorum Pubns., Inc.

Rathburn, Betsy. Galaxies. 2018. (Space Science Ser.). (ENG., Illus.). 24p. (J). (gr. 3-7). lib. bdg. 26.95 *(978-1-62617-859-5(3)*, Torque Bks.) Bellwether Media.

Rauf, Don. Choose a Career Adventure at NASA. 2016. (Bright Futures Press: Choose a Career Adventure Ser.). (ENG., Illus.). 32p. (J). (gr. 4-6). 32.07 *(978-1-63471-913-1(1)*, 208973) Cherry Lake Publishing.

Rice, Dona Herweck, et al. Let's Explore Earth & Space Science, Grades 4-5. 2015. (Book Collection). (ENG., Illus.). 32p. (gr. 4-5). 89.90 *(978-1-4938-1423-7(0))* Teacher Created Materials, Inc.

Rich, Mari. Space, Vol. 10. Gilmore, Malinda & Pouson, Mel, eds. 2016. (Black Achievement in Science Ser.). (Illus.). 64p. (J). (gr. 7). 23.95 *(978-1-4222-3563-8(7))* Mason Crest.

Romaine, Garret. Solar System, Space Rocks, & Beyond: Exploring the Wonders of Space Particles & Meteorites. 2018. (Geology Lab for Kids Ser.). (ENG., Illus.). 32p. (J). (gr. 3-6). lib. bdg. 27.99 *(978-1-63159-457-1(5)*, 56468e7a-d008-44da-aa7c-7ad266addf08, Quarry Bks.) Quarto Publishing Group USA.

Rudy, Lisa Jo. Eyes in the Sky (24/7: Science Behind the Scenes: Spy Files) (Library Edition) 2007. (24/7: Science Behind the Scenes Ser.). (ENG., Illus.). 64p. (J). (gr. 8-12). 29.00 *(978-0-531-12082-8(1)*, Watts, Franklin) Scholastic Library Publishing.

Rustad, Martha E. H. Working in Space. 2018. (Astronaut's Life Ser.). (ENG., Illus.). 24p. (J). (gr. -1-2). lib. bdg. 27.32 *(978-1-5157-9820-0(8)*, 136888, Capstone Pr.) Capstone.

Scholastic News Nonficiton Readers - Space Science, 12 vols., Set. Incl. Jupiter. Taylor-Butler, Christine. 22.00 *(978-0-531-14696-5(0))*; Mars. Chrismer, Melanie. 22.00 *(978-0-531-14697-2(9))*; Mercury. Taylor-Butler, Christine. 22.00 *(978-0-531-14698-9(7))*; Neptune. Chrismer, Melanie. 22.00 *(978-0-531-14750-4(9))*; Pluto: Dwarf Planet. Taylor-Butler, Christine. 22.00 *(978-0-531-14751-1(7))*; Saturn. Taylor-Butler, Christine. 22.00 *(978-0-531-14752-8(5))*; Uranus. Taylor-Butler, Christine. 22.00 *(978-0-531-14754-2(1))*; Venus. Chrismer, Melanie. 22.00 *(978-0-531-14755-9(X))*; (Illus.). 24p. (J). (gr. 1-2). 2007. 2007. Set lib. bdg. 240.00 o.p. *(978-0-531-18674-9(1)*, Children's Pr.) Scholastic Library Publishing.

The Science of Space. 2016. (Illus.). 48p. (J). *(978-1-4222-3515-7(7))* Mason Crest.

Spectacular Space Science. 2015. (Spectacular Space Science Ser.). (ENG.). 48p. (J). (gr. 5-6). pap., pap., pap. 423.00 *(978-1-4777-8623-9(6)*, Rosen Central) Rosen Publishing Group, Inc., The.

Spotlight on Space Science, 28 vols. 2014. (Spotlight on Space Science Ser.). (ENG.). 32p. (J). (gr. 5-5). lib. bdg. 391.02 *(978-1-4994-0438-8(7)*, 4dd1fb48-3e07-4192-bbe1-611455b6887d, PowerKids Pr.) Rosen Publishing Group, Inc., The.

Steinkraus, Kyla. Planetas Rocosos - Mercurio, Venus, la Tierra y Marte. 2017. (Inside Outer Space Ser.).Tr. of Rocky Planets - Mercury, Venus, Earth, & Mars. (SPA.). 24p. (gr. k-3). pap. 9.95 *(978-1-68342-262-4(7)*, 9781683422624) Rourke Educational Media.

Steps To Literacy Staff, compiled by. Explore Space Collection: Capv220. 2005. (ENG., Illus.). (J). pap. *(978-1-60015-016-6(0))* Steps To Literacy, LLC.

Stott, Carole. I Wonder Why Stars Twinkle. Tremblay, Marie-Ave, illus. 2011. (I Wonder Why Ser.). (ENG.). 32p. (J). (gr. k-3). pap. 6.99 *(978-0-7534-6520-2(5)*, 900070300, Kingfisher) Roaring Brook Pr.

Teacher Created Materials Staff, ed. Earth & Space Science: Add-on Pack. 2007. (Science Readers Ser.). 89.99 *(978-1-4333-0067-7(2))* Teacher Created Materials, Inc.

Top That Publishing Staff, ed. Space. 2004. (Know How Know Why Ser.). (Illus.). (J). 48p. pap. *(978-1-84510-026-1(3))*; 24p. pap. *(978-1-84510-114-5(6))*; 48p. per. *(978-1-84510-012-4(3))* Top That! Publishing PLC.

Wadsworth, Pamela. Golwg Gyntaf Ar Amser a Gofod. 2005. (WEL., Illus.). 24p. pap. *(978-1-85596-248-4(9))* Dref Wen.

What Is in Space?, 6 vols. (Sunshinetm Science Ser.). 24p. (gr. 1-2). 31.50 *(978-0-7802-0292-4(9))* Wright Group/McGraw-Hill.

Willett, Edward. Space. 2009. (Science Q & A Ser.). (Illus.). 48p. (YA). (gr. 5-8). pap. 10.95 *(978-1-60596-073-9(X))*; lib. bdg. 29.05 *(978-1-60596-072-2(1))* Weigl Pubs., Inc.

World Book, Inc. Staff, contrib. by. Encyclopedia of Space. 2013. (J). *(978-0-7166-7523-5(4))* World Bk., Inc.

SPACE SCIENCES—HISTORY

Brown Bear Books. Chemistry, Earth, & Space Sciences. 2009. (Great Scientists Ser.). (ENG.). 64p. (J). (gr. 8-11). 35.65 *(978-1-933834-47-4(1)*, 16492) Brown Bear Bks.

SPACE SHIPS—PILOTS

see Astronauts

SPACE SHUTTLES

Amato, William. The Space Shuttle. 2009. (High-Tech Vehicles Ser.). 24p. (gr. 2-3). 42.50 *(978-1-61513-308-6(9)*, PowerKids Pr.) Rosen Publishing Group, Inc., The.

—Transbordadores Espaciales, 1 vol. 2003. (Vehículos de Alta Tecnología (High-Tech Vehicles) Ser.). (SPA., Illus.). 24p. (J). (gr. 2-2). lib. bdg. 26.27 *(978-0-8239-6885-5(5)*, 240d13e8-ed14-4403-9737-a92b27f97ea3) Rosen Publishing Group, Inc., The.

—Transbordadores espaciales (the Space Shuttle) 2009. (Vehículos de alta tecnología (High-Tech Vehicles) Ser.). (SPA.). 24p. (gr. 2-3). 42.50 *(978-1-60854-721-0(3)*, Editorial Buenas Letras) Rosen Publishing Group, Inc., The.

Baker, David. Living in Space. 2008. (Exploring Space Ser.). (Illus.). 32p. (J). (gr. 4-6). lib. bdg. 26.00 *(978-1-59036-769-8(3))* Weigl Pubs., Inc.

—The Shuttle. 2008. (Exploring Space Ser.). (Illus.). 32p. (J). (gr. 4-6). lib. bdg. 26.00 *(978-1-59036-767-4(7))* Weigl Pubs., Inc.

Baker, David & Kissock, Heather. Living in Space. 2008. (Exploring Space Ser.). (Illus.). 32p. (J). (gr. 4-6). pap. 9.95 *(978-1-59036-770-4(7))* Weigl Pubs., Inc.

—The Shuttle. 2008. (Exploring Space Ser.). (Illus.). 32p. (J). (gr. 4-6). pap. 9.95 *(978-1-59036-768-1(5))* Weigl Pubs., Inc.

Channing, Margot. Space & Other Flying Machines. 2015. (Inside Eye Ser.). (Illus.). 32p. (gr. 3-6). 31.35 *(978-1-906370-79-4(6))* Book Hse. GBR. Dist: Black Rabbit Bks.

Dahl, Michael. On the Launch Pad: A Counting Book about Rockets, 1 vol. Shea, Denise & Alderman, Derrick, illus. 2004. (Know Your Numbers Ser.). (ENG.). 24p. (J). (gr. -1-2). per. 8.95 *(978-1-4048-1119-5(2)*, 92614, Picture Window Bks.) Capstone.

Fahey, Kathleen. Challenger & Columbia, 1 vol. 2004. (Disasters Ser.). (ENG., Illus.). 32p. (gr. 3-5). lib. bdg. 28.67 *(978-0-8368-4496-2(0)*, 4d9eeb51-0067-4e39-a081-7c046ef62ae1, Gareth Stevens Learning Library) Stevens, Gareth Publishing LLLP.

Gross, Miriam. All about Space Shuttles. 2009. (Blast Off! Ser.). 24p. (gr. 2-3). 42.50 *(978-1-61511-626-3(5))*; (ENG., Illus.). (J). pap. 9.25 *(978-1-4358-3136-0(5)*, 93e89b8f-6b1d-40bf-b00e-a43e39c89bd8) Rosen Publishing Group, Inc., The. (PowerKids Pr.).

Gross, Miriam J. All about Space Shuttles, 1 vol. 2009. (Blast Off! Ser.). (ENG.). 24p. (J). (gr. 2-3). lib. bdg. 26.27 *(978-1-4358-2738-7(4)*, 30669b7f-4d2e-413a-9667-9abee59d4c53, PowerKids Pr.) Rosen Publishing Group, Inc., The.

Holden, Henry M. Space Shuttle Disaster: The Tragic Mission of the Challenger, 1 vol. 2012. (American Space Missions: Astronauts, Exploration, & Discovery Ser.). (ENG., Illus.). 48p. (gr. 5-7). 27.93 *(978-0-7660-4073-1(9)*, f2db5b2f-3726-437e-8cc8-7ad611aa8195) Enslow Publishing, LLC.

Kerrod, Robin. Space Shuttles, 1 vol. 2004. (History of Space Exploration Ser.). (ENG., Illus.). 48p. (gr. 5-8). lib. bdg. 33.67 *(978-0-8368-5709-2(7)*, 37876d2b-02ab-4ee4-a49c-067f08aac24f) Stevens, Gareth Publishing LLLP.

Langley, Andrew. Sally Ride & the Shuttle Missions. 2015. (Adventures in Space Ser.). (ENG., Illus.). 48p. (J). (gr. 4-6). 35.99 *(978-1-4846-2516-3(1)*, 130013, Heinemann) Capstone.

Littlejohn, Randy. Life in Outer Space. (Life in Extreme Environments Ser.). 64p. (gr. 5-8). 2009. 53.00 *(978-1-61514-269-9(X))* 2003. (ENG., Illus.). lib. bdg. 37.13 *(978-0-8239-3989-3(8)*, e1a48f16-b307-4fad-a22f-dde0324840fa) Rosen Publishing Group, Inc., The. (Rosen Reference).

Morey, Allan. Space Shuttles. 2017. (Space Tech Ser.). (ENG., Illus.). 24p. (J). (gr. 3-7). lib. bdg. 26.95 *(978-1-62617-706-2(6)*, Epic Bks.) Bellwether Media.

Murray, Julie. Spaceships, 1 vol. 2014. (Transportation Ser.). (ENG.). 24p. (J). (gr. -1-2). lib. bdg. 32.79 *(978-1-62970-081-6(9)*, 1705, Abdo Kids) ABDO Publishing Co.

Orr, Tamra B. Columbia Space Shuttle Explosion & Space Exploration. 2017. (Perspectives Library: Modern Perspectives Ser.). (ENG., Illus.). 32p. (J). (gr. 4-7). lib. bdg. 32.07 *(978-1-63472-861-4(0)*, 209870) Cherry Lake Publishing.

Rees, Peter. Shockwave: Secrets of the Space Shuttle. 2007. (Shockwave: Technology & Manufacturing Ser.). (ENG., Illus.). 36p. (J). (gr. 4-6). lib. bdg. 25.00 *(978-0-531-17590-3(1)*, Children's Pr.) Scholastic Library Publishing.

Richards, Patti. The Space Shuttle Missions. 2018. (Illus.). 48p. (J). *(978-1-4896-9809-4(4)*, AV2 by Weigl) Weigl Pubs., Inc.

Roza, Greg. The Hubble Space Telescope: Understanding & Representing Numbers in the Billions, 1 vol. 2004. (PowerMath: Proficiency Plus Ser.). (ENG., Illus.). 32p. (J). (gr. 5-6). lib. bdg. 28.93 *(978-1-4042-2931-0(0)*, 7af2f6d7-2234-4b48-ae6e-bc071138672d, PowerKids Pr.) Rosen Publishing Group, Inc., The.

—The Hubble Space Telescope: Understanding & Representing Numbers up to 1 Billion, 1 vol. 2010. (Math for the REAL World Ser.). (ENG., Illus.). 32p. (gr. 5-6). pap. 10.00 *(978-1-4042-5129-8(4)*, 881be7c6-f2f5-4e5e-bf41-3aab27d0b7a2) Rosen Publishing Group, Inc., The.

Sexton, Colleen. Space Shuttles. 2010. (Exploring Space Ser.). (ENG., Illus.). 24p. (J). (gr. k-3). lib. bdg. 26.95 *(978-1-60014-294-9(X)*, Blastoff! Readers) Bellwether Media.

Sofer, Barbara. Ilan Ramon: Israel's Space Hero. 2003. (Illus.). 64p. (J). (gr. 3-6). 16.95 *(978-1-58013-115-5(8))*; (ENG., pap. 6.95 *(978-1-58013-116-2(6))* Lerner Publishing Group. (Kar-Ben Publishing).

Spray, Sally. Awesome Engineering Spacecraft. 2018. (Awesome Engineering Ser.). (ENG., Illus.). 32p. (J). (gr. 3-6). lib. bdg. 27.99 *(978-1-5435-1337-0(9)*, 137768, Capstone Pr.) Capstone.

Stone, Adam. The Challenger Explosion. 2014. (Disaster Stories Ser.). (ENG., Illus.). 24p. (J). (gr. 3-8). 29.95 *(978-1-62617-151-0(3)*, Black Sheep) Bellwether Media.

A Trip into Space: Individual Title Six-Pack. (Story Steps Ser.). (gr. k-2). 23.00 *(978-0-7635-9614-9(0))* Rigby Education.

Zelon, Helen. The Endeavor SRTM: Mapping the Earth. 2009. (Space Missions Ser.). 24p. (gr. 3-4). 42.50 *(978-1-60853-118-9(X)*, PowerKids Pr.) Rosen Publishing Group, Inc., The.

Zuehlke, Jeffrey. The Space Shuttle. 2006. (Pull Ahead Bks.). (Illus.). 32p. (J). (gr. 3-7). lib. bdg. 22.60 *(978-0-8225-6420-1(3)*, Lerner Pubns.) Lerner Publishing Group.

SPACE SHUTTLES—FICTION

Arnett, Mindee. Avalon. 2014. (Avalon Ser.: 1). (ENG.). 432p. (YA). (gr. 8). 17.99 *(978-0-06-223559-6(1)*, Balzer & Bray) HarperCollins Pubs.

Bannister, Bram. Rupert, the Alien & the Bank Robbery. 2007. 56p. per. 8.95 *(978-0-595-44839-5(9))* iUniverse, Inc.

Barth, Kathleen E. The Amazing Adventures of Quigley D Pigley & His Friends. 2009. 16p. pap. 8.49 *(978-1-4389-8322-6(0))* AuthorHouse.

Brezenoff, Steve. The Final Mission. Calle Velez, Juan, illus. 2019. (Michael Dahl Presents: Screams in Space 4D Ser.). (ENG.). 112p. (J). (gr. 3-5). lib. bdg. 27.32 *(978-1-4965-7902-7(X)*, 139612, Stone Arch Bks.) Capstone.

Colvin, Denise Marie. Suzy's Big Dream Comes True. 2007. 61p. pap. 19.95 *(978-1-4241-8157-5(7))* America Star Bks.

Douglas, Atom. Mathew's Space Ship. Douglas, Atom, . 2007. (Illus.). 32p. (J). 6.50 *(978-0-9798316-0-7(1))* JaxPublishing.net.

Edick, Grant. Space Station. 2004. (Two Boys Adventure Story Ser.). 98p. (J). (gr. 3-6). 15.95 *(978-0-9677839-9-4(2))* Wysteria Publishing.

Flintham, Thomas. Super Rabbit Boy Blasts Off!, 5. 2019. (Branches Early Ch Bks). (ENG.). 72p. (J). (gr. 2-3). 15.96 *(978-1-64310-895-7(6))* Penworthy Co., LLC, The.

—Super Rabbit Boy Blasts off!: a Branches Book (Press Start! #5) Flintham, Thomas, illus. 2018. (Press Start! Ser.: 5). (ENG., Illus.). 80p. (J). (gr. k-2). pap. 6.99 *(978-1-338-23962-1(7))* Scholastic, Inc.

—Super Rabbit Boy Blasts off!: a Branches Book (Press Start! #5) (Library Edition) Flintham, Thomas, illus. 5th ed. 2018. (Press Start! Ser.: 5). (ENG., Illus.). 80p. (J). (gr. k-2). lib. bdg. 24.99 *(978-1-338-23970-6(8))* Scholastic, Inc.

Gentry, Stephen. Journey to the Stars & Back. 2005. 52p. (J). pap. 16.49 *(978-1-4116-5985-8(6))* Lulu Pr., Inc.

Greenburg, Dan. Weird Planet #1: Dude, Where's My Spaceship. Pamintuan, Macky, illus. 2006. (Weird Planet Ser.: 1). (ENG.). 96p. (J). (gr. 1-4). 6.99 *(978-0-375-83344-1(7)*, Random Hse. Bks. for Young Readers) Random Hse. Children's Bks.

Kelly, Erin Entrada. We Dream of Space: A Newbery Honor Award Winner. 2020. (ENG., Illus.). 400p. (J). (gr. 3-7). 16.99 *(978-0-06-274730-3(4)*, Greenwillow Bks.) HarperCollins Pubs.

Kelly, Mark. Mousetronaut: Based on a (Partially) True Story. Payne, C. F., illus. 2012. (Mousetronaut Ser.). (ENG.). 40p. (J). (gr. -1-3). 19.99 *(978-1-4424-5824-6(0)*, Simon & Schuster/Paula Wiseman Bks.) Simon & Schuster/Paula Wiseman Bks.

Manship, Paul. The Cube. 2006. (ENG.). 128p. (J). pap. 7.50 *(978-1-84323-739-6(3))* Gomer Pr. GBR. Dist: Casemate Pubs. & Bk. Distributors, LLC.

Olivas, John D. Endeavour's Long Journey: Celebrating 19 Years of Space Exploration. Roski, Gayle Garner, illus. 2013. (J). pap. *(978-0-9856237-3-9(X))* East West Discovery Pr.

—Endeavour's Long Journey/la Larga Travesía de Endeavour. Roski, Gayle G., illus. 2016. (SPA.). 40p. (J). 19.95 *(978-0-9973947-2-6(2))* East West Discovery Pr.

Rigby Education Staff. The Space Cat. (Sails Literacy Ser.). (Illus.). 16p. (gr. 2-3). 27.00 *(978-0-7635-9949-2(2)*, 699492C99) Rigby Education.

Rockwell, Carey. On the Trail of Space Pirates. Ley, Willy, ed. 2007. 140p. per. 11.95 *(978-1-60312-283-2(4))* Aegypan.

Steele, Andrew. The Galaxy Boys & the Sphere. 2008. (ENG.). 285p. (J). (gr. 4-7). pap. *(978-1-85756-687-1(4))* Janus Publishing Co.

Turner, Paul. ULYSSES: the Pegasi Incident. 2007. 216p. pap. 15.95 *(978-1-84753-642-6(5))* Lulu Pr., Inc.

West, Robert. There's a Spaceship in My Tree!, 1 vol., 1. 2008. (Star-Fighters of Murphy Street Ser.: 1). (ENG., Illus.). 144p. (J). (gr. 4-6). pap. 6.99 *(978-0-310-71425-5(7))* Zonderkidz.

Woodsonrick. Poodles in Space. 2012. 24p. 24.95 *(978-1-4626-5333-1(2))* America Star Bks.

Wyre, Yvonne. The Further Adventures of Cuthbert the Coal Lorry & all His Friends. 2007. (Illus.). 204p. pap. *(978-1-84401-801-7(6))* Athena Pr.

Zakour, John. Baxter Moon Galactic Scout. 2008. 198p. (J). (gr. 5-10). per. 8.95 *(978-0-9768126-9-2(X))* Brown Barn Bks.

SPACE STATIONS

Here are entered works dealing with manned installations existing for specific functions, such as servicing space ships, etc., in orbit around the earth or other natural extraterrestrial bodies.

Baker, David. Inside the International Space Station, 1 vol. 2017. (Geek's Guide to Space Ser.). (ENG., Illus.). 192p. (J). (gr. 9-9). 46.27 *(978-1-4994-6698-0(6)*, cb95ac67-9c24-4e3c-a89a-80006984f2cf, Rosen Young Adult) Rosen Publishing Group, Inc., The.

—The International Space Station. 2009. 32p. 26.00 *(978-1-59036-775-9(8))* Weigl Pubs., Inc.

Baker, David & Kissock, Heather. The International Space Station. (Illus.). 32p. (J). 2016. *(978-1-4896-5824-1(6)*, AV2 by Weigl) 2009. (gr. 2-4). pap. 9.95 *(978-1-60596-024-1(1))* 2009. (gr. 2-4). lib. bdg. 26.00 *(978-1-60596-023-4(3))* Weigl Pubs., Inc.

Brown, Carron. En la Estación Espacial: Shine-A-light. Johnson, Bee, illus. 2019.Tr. of On the Space Station. (SPA.). (J). 12.99 *(978-1-61067-913-8(X))* Kane Miller.

—Space Station. Johnson, Bee, illus. 2016. (ENG.). 36p. (J). 12.99 *(978-1-61067-411-9(1))* Kane Miller.

Buckley, James. Home Address: ISS: International Space Station. 2015. (Illus.). 48p. (J). *(978-1-4806-9866-6(0)*, Warne, Frederick Pubs.) Penguin Bks., Ltd.

—Home Address: ISS: International Space Station. 2015. (Smithsonian Ser.). (ENG., Illus.). 48p. (J). (gr. 3-4). pap. 4.99 *(978-0-448-48709-0(8)*, Penguin Young Readers) Penguin Young Readers Group.

Carroll, Jillian. Where to Stay. 2003. (J). lib. bdg. *(978-1-58417-232-1(0))* Lake Street Pubs.

Clay, Kathryn. Living in Space. 2017. (Little Astronauts Ser.). (ENG., Illus.). 32p. (J). (gr. -1-2). lib. bdg. 28.65 *(978-1-5157-3657-8(1)*, 133642, Capstone Pr.) Capstone.

Claybourne, Anna. The International Space Station: Band 11/Lime, Bd. 11. 2018. (Collins Big Cat Ser.). (ENG., Illus.). 32p. (J). pap. 8.99 *(978-0-00-823041-8(2))* HarperCollins Pubs. Ltd. GBR. Dist: Independent Pubs. Group.

Dickins, Rosie. See Inside a Space Station & Other Spacecraft. 2017. (See Inside Board Bks.). (ENG.). 16p. 14.99 *(978-0-7945-4020-3(1)*, Usborne) EDC Publishing.

Dyson, Marianne J. Space Station Science. Klug, Dave, illus. 2nd ed. 2004. (ENG.). 128p. (J). pap. 11.95 *(978-0-89317-059-2(3)*, WW-0593, Windward Publishing) Finney Co., Inc.

Editors of YES Mag, Editors of. The Amazing International Space Station. 2003. (ENG., Illus.). 48p. (J). (gr. 3-7). 11.99 *(978-1-55337-523-4(8))* Kids Can Pr., Ltd. CAN. Dist: Hachette Bk. Group.

Einspruch, Andrew. Life on a Space Station, 1 vol. 2012. (Discovery Education: Technology Ser.). (ENG., Illus.). 32p. (J). (gr. 4-5). pap. 11.00 *(978-1-4488-7966-3(3)*, 8f083993-e463-4902-92a5-51d76a604e72); lib. bdg. 28.93 *(978-1-4488-7884-0(5)*, 0068c8b2-d8a9-4e0f-8c46-c7ab599a9dc4) Rosen Publishing Group, Inc., The. (PowerKids Pr.).

Faust, Daniel R. Más Allá de la Tierra: Vivir en Otro Planeta, 1 vol. 2009. (Historietas Juveniles: Peligros Del Medioambiente (Jr. Graphic Environmental Dangers) Ser.). (SPA., Illus.). 24p. (gr. 4-4). pap. 10.60 *(978-1-4358-8472-4(8)*, 7b74d532-cf15-43b9-bf13-828cca7b1dea); (YA). lib. bdg. 28.93 *(978-1-4358-8471-7(X)*, 564ad328-dade-409e-b98f-5396878a160c) Rosen Publishing Group, Inc., The.

Feldman, Heather. Skylab: The First American Space Station. 2009. (Space Firsts Ser.). 24p. (gr. 3-4). 42.50 *(978-1-60853-113-4(9)*, PowerKids Pr.) Rosen Publishing Group, Inc., The.

Gifford, Clive. The International Space Station. Schlitzkus, Dan, illus. 2019. (ENG.). 32p. (J). (gr. 4-6). pap. 11.99 *(978-1-5263-0217-5(9)*, Wayland) Hachette Children's Group GBR. Dist: Hachette Bk. Group.

Gross, Miriam. All about Space Stations. 2009. (Blast Off! Ser.). 24p. (gr. 2-3). 42.50 *(978-1-61511-629-4(X))*; (ENG.). (J). lib. bdg. 26.27 *(978-1-4358-2737-0(6)*, 5fd8b406-e835-4c01-86b0-27f50529fdd1) Rosen Publishing Group, Inc., The. (PowerKids Pr.).

Gross, Miriam J. All about Space Stations, 1 vol. 2009. (Blast Off! Ser.). (ENG., Illus.). 24p. (J). (gr. 2-3). pap. 9.25 *(978-1-4358-3135-3(7)*, 6a006a33-e623-4e20-962b-5a441c8326bf, PowerKids Pr.) Rosen Publishing Group, Inc., The.

Hamilton, John. International Space Station: The Science Lab in Space. 2017. (Xtreme Spacecraft Ser.). (ENG., Illus.). 32p. (J). (gr. 3-9). lib. bdg. 32.79 *(978-1-5321-1008-5(1)*, 25592, Abdo & Daughters) ABDO Publishing Co.

—Space Stations & Beyond. 2018. (Space Race Ser.). (ENG., Illus.). 48p. (J). (gr. 5-9). lib. bdg. 34.21 *(978-1-5321-1834-0(1)*, 30544, Abdo & Daughters) ABDO Publishing Co.

Hogan, Christa C. Space Stations. 2018. (Destination Space Ser.). (ENG., Illus.). 48p. (J). (gr. 5-6). pap. 11.95 *(978-1-63517-571-4(2)*, 1635175712); lib. bdg. 34.21 *(978-1-63517-499-1(6)*, 1635174996) North Star Editions. (Focus Readers).

—Space Stations. 2018. (Illus.). xi, 423p. (J). pap. *(978-1-4896-9806-3(X)*, AV2 by Weigl) Weigl Pubs., Inc.

Holden, Henry M. The Coolest Job in the Universe: Working Aboard the International Space Station, 1 vol. 2012. (American Space Missions: Astronauts, Exploration, & Discovery Ser.). (ENG., Illus.). 48p. (gr. 5-7). lib. bdg. 27.93 *(978-0-7660-4074-8(7)*, 2a655c2e-ef54-4c2c-9324-2b92f1c91bec) Enslow Publishing, LLC.

Jefferis, David. Space Colonists. 2017. (Our Future in Space Ser.). (Illus.). 32p. (J). (gr. 5-5). *(978-0-7787-3534-2(6))*; pap. *(978-0-7787-3538-0(9))* Crabtree Publishing Co.

Jenkins, Martin. Exploring Space: from Galileo to the Mars Rover & Beyond. Biesty, Stephen, illus. 2017. (ENG.). 64p. (J). (gr. 3-7). 17.99 *(978-0-7636-8931-5(9))* Candlewick Pr.

Kelly, Scott. My Journey to the Stars. Ceolin, André, illus. 2020. (ENG.). 48p. (J). (gr. k-3). pap. 8.99 *(978-0-593-12465-9(0)*, Dragonfly Bks.) Random Hse. Children's Bks.

—My Journey to the Stars (Step into Reading) Ceolin, André, illus. 2019. (Step into Reading Ser.). (ENG.). 48p. (J). (gr. k-3). pap. 5.99 *(978-1-5247-6380-0(2)*, Random Hse. Bks. for Young Readers) Random Hse. Children's Bks.

Kerrod, Robin. Space Stations, 1 vol. 2004. (History of Space Exploration Ser.). (ENG., Illus.). 48p. (gr. 5-8). lib. bdg. 33.67 *(978-0-8368-5710-8(0)*, 150e4c50-8e65-4630-9756-ecec9e7d35ce) Stevens, Gareth Publishing LLLP.

Klepeis, Alicia Z. Moon Base & Beyond: The Lunar Gateway to Deep Space. 2019. (Future Space Ser.). (ENG., Illus.). 32p. (J). (gr. 3-9). pap. 7.95 *(978-1-5435-7515-6(3)*, 141046); lib. bdg. 28.65 *(978-1-5435-7267-4(7)*, 140598) Capstone.

Larson, Kirsten. International Space Station. 2017. (Engineering Wonders Ser.). (ENG.). 48p. (gr. 3-5). pap. 10.95 *(978-1-68342-459-8(X)*, 9781683424598) Rourke Educational Media.

Lassieur, Allison. International Space Station: An Interactive Space Exploration Adventure. 2016. (You Choose: Space Ser.). (ENG., Illus.). 112p. (J). (gr. 3-7). lib. bdg. 32.65 *(978-1-4914-8104-2(8)*, 130588, Capstone Pr.) Capstone.

Littlejohn, Randy. Life in Outer Space. (Life in Extreme Environments Ser.). 64p. (gr. 5-8). 2009. 53.00 *(978-1-61514-269-9(X))* 2003. (ENG., Illus.). lib. bdg. 37.13 *(978-0-8239-3989-3(8)*, e1a48f16-b307-4fad-a22f-dde0324840fa) Rosen Publishing Group, Inc., The. (Rosen Reference).

McCarthy, Cecilia Pinto. Engineering the International Space Station. 2017. (Building by Design Set 2 Ser.). (ENG., Illus.). 48p. (J). (gr. 4-8). lib. bdg. 35.64 *(978-1-5321-1372-7(2)*, 27670) ABDO Publishing Co.

Morey, Alla. The International Space Station. 2017. (Space Tech Ser.). (ENG., Illus.). 24p. (J). (gr. 3-7). lib. bdg. 26.95 *(978-1-62617-701-7(5)*, Epic Bks.) Bellwether Media.

Murray, Julie. International Space Station. 2018. (Super Structures Ser.). (ENG., Illus.). 24p. (J). (gr. k-4). lib. bdg. 31.36 *(978-1-5321-2311-5(6)*, 28389, Abdo Zoom-Dash) ABDO Publishing Co.

Nipaul, Devi. The International Space Station: An Orbiting Laboratory. 2004. (High Interest Books: Architectural Wonders Ser.). (ENG., Illus.). 48p. (J). (gr. 7-9). 18.69 *(978-0-516-24076-3(5))* Scholastic Library Publishing.

Olson, Elsie. Spectacular Space Stations. 2019. (Cosmos Chronicles (Alternator Books (r)) Ser.). (ENG., Illus.). 32p. (J). (gr. 3-6). pap. 10.99 *(978-1-5415-7371-0(4)*, 228285eb-bf56-4aa3-80e0-637d0ff0c258); lib. bdg. 29.32 *(978-1-5415-5597-6(X)*, 01ded9db-0e47-4f52-9992-23844aacf036) Lerner Publishing Group. (Lerner Pubns.).

Owen, Ruth. Space Stations, 1 vol. 2014. (Objects in Space Ser.). (ENG., Illus.). 32p. (J). (gr. 4-4). 27.93 *(978-1-4777-5869-4(0)*, 03a7e351-84ae-407a-9b4d-35d0b6b60956, PowerKids Pr.) Rosen Publishing Group, Inc., The.

Parker, Steve. Space Stations. West, David, illus. 2015. (Story of Space Ser.). (ENG.). 32p. (J). (gr. 3-6). 31.35 *(978-1-62588-081-9(2))* Black Rabbit Bks.

Rustad, Martha E. H. Space Stations. 2012. (Exploring Space Ser.). (ENG.). 24p. (gr. k-1). pap. 41.70 *(978-1-4296-8330-2(9)*, Capstone Pr.) Capstone.

Sexton, Colleen. Space Stations. 2010. (Exploring Space Ser.). (ENG., Illus.). 24p. (J). (gr. k-3). lib. bdg. 26.95 *(978-1-60014-295-6(8)*, Blastoff! Readers) Bellwether Media.

Sipe, Nicole. Living & Working in Space. rev. ed. 2018. (Smithsonian: Informational Text Ser.). (ENG., Illus.). 32p. (J). (gr. 4-8). pap. 11.99 *(978-1-4938-6712-7(1))* Teacher Created Materials, Inc.

Throp, Claire. A Visit to a Space Station: Fantasy Science Field Trips, 1 vol. 2014. (Fantasy Science Field Trips Ser.). (ENG.). 32p. (J). (gr. 3-5). pap. 8.95 *(978-1-4109-6202-7(4)*, 124812, Raintree) Capstone.

Waxman, Laura Hamilton. Exploring the International Space Station. 2011. (Searchlight Books (tm) — What's Amazing about Space? Ser.). (ENG., Illus.). (gr. 3-5). 40p. (J). pap. 9.99 *(978-0-7613-7879-2(0)*, e1d5558f-abe3-4f30-89bb-8718aae45cf8); pap. 51.01 *(978-0-7613-8416-8(2))* Lerner Publishing Group.

SPACE STATIONS—FICTION

Appleton, Victor. The Space Hotel. 2007. (Tom Swift, Young Inventor Ser.). (ENG.). 160p. (gr. 4-7). 27.07 *(978-1-59961-353-6(0))* Spotlight.

Bean, Raymond. The Curse of Mars. Vimislik, Matthew, illus. 2016. (Out of This World Ser.). (ENG.). 112p. (J). (gr. 2-5). lib. bdg. 32.65 *(978-1-4965-3615-0(0)*, 132831, Stone Arch Bks.) Capstone.

—First Family in Space. Vimislik, Matthew, illus. 2016. (Out of This World Ser.). (ENG.). 112p. (J). (gr. 2-5). lib. bdg. 32.65 *(978-1-4965-3617-4(7)*, 132833, Stone Arch Bks.) Capstone.

—Trouble on Venus. Vimislik, Matthew, illus. 2016. (Out of This World Ser.). (ENG.). 112p. (J). (gr. 2-5). lib. bdg. 32.65 *(978-1-4965-3614-3(2)*, 132830, Stone Arch Bks.) Capstone.

Brooks, Molly. Sanity & Tallulah. Brooks, Molly, illus. 2018. (Sanity & Tallulah Ser.: 1). (ENG., Illus.). 240p. (J). (gr. 3-7). 21.99 *(978-1-368-00844-0(5))*; pap. 12.99 *(978-1-368-02280-4(4))* Little, Brown Bks. for Young Readers.

Brouwer, Sigmund. Death Trap. 2009. (Robot Wars Ser.: 1). (ENG.). 288p. (J). pap. 7.99 *(978-1-4143-2309-1(3)*, 4601299, Tyndale Kids) Tyndale Hse. Pubs.

Cahill, Byron. Space Pox. 2005. (J). pap. *(978-1-4108-4220-6(7))* Benchmark Education Co.

Childress, Jamie. Lost Universe. Braun, Chris, illus. 2007. (ENG.). 162p. (gr. 4-7). per. 4.99 *(978-1-931882-74-3(6))* Adventures Unlimited Pr.

Collins, Ailynn. Alien Lockdown. Calle Velez, Juan, illus. 2019. (Michael Dahl Presents: Screams in Space 4D Ser.). (ENG.). 112p. (J). (gr. 3-5). lib. bdg. 27.32 *(978-1-4965-7905-8(4)*, 139615, Stone Arch Bks.) Capstone.

Curious George Discovers Space. 2015. (Curious George Ser.). (ENG., Illus.). 32p. (J). (gr. -1-3). 6.99 *(978-0-544-50028-0(8)*, 1604444, Clarion Bks.) HarperCollins Pubs.

Daley, Michael J. Rat Trap. 2008. (ENG.). 272p. (J). (gr. 3-7). 16.95 *(978-0-8234-2093-3(0))* Holiday Hse., Inc.

Dean, James. Out of This World. 2017. (Pete the Cat (HarperCollins) Ser.). (J). lib. bdg. 14.75 *(978-0-606-40077-0(X))* Turtleback.

Edick, Grant. Space Station. 2004. (Two Boys Adventure Story Ser.). 98p. (J). (gr. 3-6). 15.95 *(978-0-9677839-9-4(2))* Wysteria Publishing.

Flounders, Anne, ed. Return to Earth. Wolk-Stanley, Jessica; Flounders, illus. 2004. (Reader's Theater Content-Area Concepts Ser.). (ENG.). (J). (gr. 3-5). 5.00 net. *(978-1-4108-2306-9(7)*, A23067) Benchmark Education Co.

Kaufman, Amie & Kristoff, Jay. Gemina. (Illuminae Files Ser.: 2). (ENG.). 672p. (YA). (gr. 9). 2018. pap. 12.99 *(978-0-553-49918-6(1)*, Ember) 2016. (Illus.). 21.99 *(978-0-553-49915-5(7)*, Knopf Bks. for Young Readers) Random Hse. Children's Bks.

Lake, Nick. Satellite. (ENG.). 464p. (YA). (gr. 7). 2019. pap. 10.99 *(978-1-5247-1356-0(2)*, Ember) 2017. 17.99 *(978-1-5247-1353-9(8)*, Knopf Bks. for Young Readers) Random Hse. Children's Bks.

Leo. The Group, 3 vols., Vol. 2. 2009. (Aldebaran Ser.: 2). (Illus.). 96p. pap. 19.95 *(978-1-905460-70-0(8))* CineBook GBR. Dist: National Bk. Network.

Levigne, Michelle. Commonwealth Universe: Modern Era. 2013. 110p. pap. *(978-1-922066-35-0(4))*; 146p. pap. *(978-1-922066-33-6(8))*; 134p. pap. *(978-1-922066-32-9(X))*; 110p. pap. *(978-1-922066-31-2(1))* Writers Exchange E-Publishing.

Marsh, Carole. The Mission Possible Mystery at Space Center Houston. 2009. 160p. (J). 18.99 *(978-0-635-06833-0(8)*, Marsh, Carole Bks.) Gallopade International.

Monroe, Chris. Monkey with a Tool Belt Blasts Off! Monroe, Chris, illus. 2020. (Monkey with a Tool Belt Ser.). (ENG., Illus.). 32p. (J). (gr. -1-2). 17.99 *(978-1-5415-7757-2(4)*, eed07eba-23fa-4179-a41f-6af4139dabb2, Carolrhoda Bks.) Lerner Publishing Group.

Morgan, Kass. Light Years. 2018. (ENG.). 384p. (YA). E-Book *(978-0-316-51046-2(7))* Little Brown & Co.

—Light Years. (Light Years Ser.: 1). (ENG.). (YA). (gr. 9-17). 2019. 416p. pap. 10.99 *(978-0-316-51043-1(2))* 2018. 384p. 17.99 *(978-0-316-51044-8(0))* Little, Brown Bks. for Young Readers.

—Supernova. 2019. (ENG.). 368p. (YA). (gr. 9-17). 18.99 *(978-0-316-51051-6(3))* Little, Brown Bks. for Young Readers.

Rockwell, Carey. The Revolt on Venus: The TOM CORBETT Space Cadet Adventure. 2007. (ENG.). 180p. pap. 19.99 *(978-1-4264-9548-9(X))* Creative Media Partners, LLC.

Seegert, Scott & Martin, John. Sci-Fi Junior High: Crash Landing. 2018. (Sci-Fi Junior High Ser.: 2). (ENG., Illus.). 336p. (J). (gr. 3-7). 13.99 *(978-0-316-31521-0(4)*, Jimmy Patterson) Little Brown & Co.

Seigel, Jonathan & Rother, Beverly S. Myrtle the Turtle & Popeye the Mouse: Learning about Our Solar System. 2012. 40p. pap. 24.95 *(978-1-4626-6587-7(X))* America Star Bks.

Williams, Allen. Claude the Backward-Jumping Bullfrog: Space Shuttle Commander. 2009. 32p. pap. 17.99 *(978-1-4490-0479-8(2))* AuthorHouse.

SPACE SUITS

see Astronauts—Clothing

SPACE TELECOMMUNICATION

see Interstellar Communication

SPACE TRAVEL

see Interplanetary Voyages; Manned Space Flight; Space Flight

SPACE VEHICLES

see also Artificial Satellites; Space Probes; Space Stations

Adams, Gloria G. 21st-Century Spaceships, 1 vol. 2018. (Feats of 21st-Century Engineering Ser.). (ENG.). 48p. (gr. 4-4). 29.60 *(978-0-7660-9706-3(4)*, c4b32885-38b3-47d0-b8bd-345f7d5bb8e7) Enslow Publishing, LLC.

Avera, Randy. The Truth about Challenger. 2003. (Illus.). 344p. 34.00 *(978-1-932258-00-4(0)*, SAN # 254-9522) Randolph Publishing.

Baxter, Roberta. Challenger Explosion. 2013. (History's Greatest Disasters Ser.). (ENG., Illus.). 48p. (J). (gr. 4-8). pap. 18.50 *(978-1-62403-019-2(X)*, 10768); lib. bdg. 35.64 *(978-1-61783-954-2(X)*, 9479) ABDO Publishing Co.

Bodden, Valerie. The Challenger Explosion. 2018. (Disasters for All Time Ser.). (ENG.). 48p. (J). (gr. 4-7). pap. 12.00 *(978-1-62832-547-8(X)*, 19724, Creative Paperbacks) Creative Co., The.

Bow, James. Space Vehicles. 2018. (Vehicles on the Job Ser.). (ENG., Illus.). 24p. (J). (gr. 1-3). 25.27 *(978-1-59953-941-6(1))* Norwood Hse. Pr.

Brasch, Nicolas. Machines of Speed & Flight. 2011. (Technology Behind Ser.). 32p. (YA). (gr. 3-6). 28.50 *(978-1-59920-568-7(8))* Black Rabbit Bks.

Braun, Eric Mark & Raum, Elizabeth. Fighting to Survive Space Disasters: Terrifying True Stories. 2019. (Fighting to Survive Ser.). (ENG., Illus.). 64p. (J). (gr. 4-9). pap. 8.95 *(978-0-7565-6233-5(3)*, 140935); lib. bdg. 35.32 *(978-0-7565-6186-4(8)*, 140665) Capstone. (Compass Point Bks.).

Bricker, Sandra D. Challenger. Miller, Zachary N., ed. Taylor, Marjorie, illus. rev. ed. 2003. (Take Ten Ser.). 47p. (J). (gr. 4-18). pap. 4.95 *(978-1-58659-021-5(9))* Artesian Pr.

Caper, William. The Challenger Space Shuttle Explosion. 2007. (Code Red Ser.). (Illus.). 32p. (YA). (gr. 2-5). lib. bdg. 28.50 *(978-1-59716-367-5(8))* Bearport Publishing Co., Inc.

Claybourne, Anna. Make a Space Center. 2020. (J). *(978-0-7787-7355-9(8))* Crabtree Publishing Co.

Collins, Ailynn. Mars or Bust! Orion & the Mission to Deep Space. 2019. (Future Space Ser.). (ENG., Illus.). 32p. (J). (gr. 3-9). pap. 7.95 *(978-1-5435-7514-9(5)*, 141045); lib. bdg. 28.65 *(978-1-5435-7268-1(5)*, 140599) Capstone.

Dickins, Rosie. See Inside a Space Station & Other Spacecraft. 2017. (See Inside Board Bks.). (ENG.). 16p. 14.99 *(978-0-7945-4020-3(1)*, Usborne) EDC Publishing.

Duhig, Holly. Solar Sails, 1 vol. 2017. (Science Fiction to Science Fact Ser.). (ENG.). 32p. (J). (gr. 4-5). pap. 11.50 *(978-1-5382-1491-6(1)*, da8eeada-01a9-4839-90d7-52b67ed8875a); lib. bdg. 28.27 *(978-1-5382-1388-9(5)*, eae241b9-4e7d-4ae2-ad7b-f982d2160151) Stevens, Gareth Publishing LLLP.

Edge, Laura B. Apollo 13: A Successful Failure. 2020. (ENG., Illus.). 136p. (YA). (gr. 6-12). lib. bdg. 37.32 *(978-1-5415-5900-4(2)*, ac06a4cc-af4f-479a-91d1-7c354675f7e7, Twenty-First Century Bks.) Lerner Publishing Group.

Fahey, Kathleen. Challenger & Columbia, 1 vol. 2004. (Disasters Ser.). (ENG., Illus.). 32p. (gr. 3-5). lib. bdg. 28.67 *(978-0-8368-4496-2(3)*, 4d9eeb51-0067-4e39-a081-7c046ef62ae1, Gareth Stevens Learning Library) Stevens, Gareth Publishing LLLP.

Felix, Rebecca. Ellen Ochoa: Dynamic Space Director. 2018. (Space Crusaders Ser.). (ENG., Illus.). 32p. (J). (gr. 3-6). lib. bdg. 32.79 *(978-1-5321-1703-9(5)*, 30694, Checkerboard Library) ABDO Publishing Co.

Floca, Brian. Moonshot: The Flight of Apollo 11. Floca, Brian, illus. 2019. (ENG., Illus.). 56p. (J). (gr. -1-5). 19.99 *(978-1-5344-4030-2(5)*, Atheneum/Richard Jackson Bks.) Simon & Schuster Children's Publishing.

Furniss. Spacecraft 6-Pack. 2004. (Illus.). (J). pap. 48.30 *(978-1-4109-1203-9(5))* Harcourt Schl. Pubs.

The Geek's Guide to Space, 10 vols. 2017. (Geek's Guide to Space Ser.). (ENG.). 192p. (gr. 9-9). 231.35 *(978-1-4994-6664-5(1)*, f2d85375-6e2c-4fc4-ba4c-1ac30436e3af, Rosen Young Adult) Rosen Publishing Group, Inc., The.

Gilpin, Daniel. Spacecraft, 1 vol. Pang, Alex, illus. 2011. (Machines Close-Up Ser.). (ENG.). 32p. (gr. 4-4). 31.21 *(978-1-60870-112-4(3)*, 3d924006-0a5a-4d82-a29b-abe9a8227f78) Cavendish Square Publishing LLC.

Goldberg, Jan. James Lovell: The Rescue of Apollo 13. (Library of Astronaut Biographies Ser.). 112p. (gr. 5-8). 2009. 63.90 *(978-1-60853-522-4(3))* 2003. (ENG., Illus.). lib. bdg. 39.80 *(978-0-8239-4459-0(X)*, cf5be92f-7a3b-418d-a041-bfde2da85369) Rosen Publishing Group, Inc., The. (Rosen Reference).

Graham, Ian. In Space. 2008. (QEB Machines at Work Ser.). (Illus.). 36p. (YA). (gr. 4-7). 19.95 *(978-1-59566-318-4(5))* QEB Publishing Inc.

Hamilton, John. Mars Landers. 2018. (Mission to Mars Ser.). (ENG.). 48p. (J). (gr. 5-9). lib. bdg. 34.21 *(978-1-5321-1593-6(8)*, 28762, Abdo & Daughters) ABDO Publishing Co.

—Mars Orbiters. 2018. (Mission to Mars Ser.). (ENG., Illus.). 48p. (J). (gr. 5-9). lib. bdg. 34.21 *(978-1-5321-1595-0(4)*, 28766, Abdo & Daughters) ABDO Publishing Co.

—Mars Rovers. 2018. (Mission to Mars Ser.). (ENG., Illus.). 48p. (J). (gr. 5-9). lib. bdg. 34.21 *(978-1-5321-1596-7(2)*, 28768, Abdo & Daughters) ABDO Publishing Co.

Hamilton, Tracy Brown. All about Spacecraft, 1 vol. 2016. (Let's Find Out! Transportation Ser.). (ENG., Illus.). 32p. (J). (gr. 2-3). lib. bdg. 26.06 *(978-1-68048-445-8(1)*, 5bc59e5b-21fc-43ba-9dd5-62c742978fcd) Rosen Publishing Group, Inc., The.

Hawcock, David. Make Your Own Press-Out Spaceships. 2018. (ENG.). 22p. (gr. 1-5). pap. 12.99 *(978-0-486-82503-8(5)*, 825035) Dover Pubns., Inc.

Hirsch, Rebecca E. Space Vehicles in Action (an Augmented Reality Experience) 2020. (Space in Action: Augmented Reality (Alternator Books (r)) Ser.). (ENG., Illus.). 32p. (J). (gr. 3-6). lib. bdg. 31.99 *(978-1-5415-7882-1(1)*, 7771913d-8045-4c13-8e35-f0c00ee7aa90, Lerner Pubns.) Lerner Publishing Group.

Hofer, Charles. Spacecraft. (World's Fastest Machines Ser.). 24p. (gr. 2-3). 2009. 42.50 *(978-1-60854-855-2(4))* 2007. (ENG., Illus.). lib. bdg. 26.27 *(978-1-4042-4178-7(7)*, dd6386e5-aacf-44eb-9c62-fef0e351ba99) Rosen Publishing Group, Inc., The. (PowerKids Pr.).

Jackson, Tom. Spacecraft. 2015. (Technology Timelines Ser.). (ENG., Illus.). 32p. (J). (gr. 2-4). 31.35 *(978-1-78121-237-0(6)*, 16812) Brown Bear Bks.

Kelly, Tracey. Communication Technology: From Smoke Signals to Smartphones. 2019. (History of Inventions Ser.). (ENG.). 24p. (J). (gr. 2-4). lib. bdg. *(978-1-78121-456-5(5)*, 16733) Brown Bear Bks.

Kortenkamp, Steve. Mars Exploration Rovers: An Interactive Space Exploration Adventure. 2016. (You Choose: Space Ser.). (ENG., Illus.). 112p. (J). (gr. 3-7). lib. bdg. 32.65 *(978-1-4914-8106-6(4)*, 130589, Capstone Pr.) Capstone.

Land-Sailing Venus Rover: Meet NASA Inventor Geoffrey Landis & His Team's. 2017. (J). *(978-0-7166-6160-3(8))* World Bk., Inc.

Laser-Sailing Starships: Meet NASA Inventor Philip Lubin & His Team's. 2017. (J). *(978-0-7166-6159-7(4))* World Bk., Inc.

Lemke, Donald B. The Apollo 13 Mission, 1 vol. Tucker, Keith, illus. 2006. (Disasters in History Ser.). (ENG.). 32p. (J). (gr. 3-9). 31.32 *(978-0-7368-5476-4(2)*, 90156, Capstone Pr.) Capstone.

Loh-Hagan, Virginia. Apollo 13: Mission to the Moon. 2018. (True Survival Ser.). (ENG.). 32p. (J). (gr. 4-8). pap. 14.21 *(978-1-5341-0871-4(8)*, 210848); (Illus.). lib. bdg. 32.07 *(978-1-5341-0772-4(X)*, 210847) Cherry Lake Publishing. (45th Parallel Press).

MacCarald, Clara. How Did Robots Land on Mars? 2018. (How'd They Do That? Ser.). (ENG., Illus.). 32p. (J). (gr. 4-6). lib. bdg. 28.65 *(978-1-5435-4136-6(4)*, 139090, Capstone Pr.) Capstone.

Meet NASA Inventor Robert Hoyt & His Team's Web-Spinning Space Spiders. 2017. (J). *(978-0-7166-6157-3(8))* World Bk., Inc.

Morey, Allan. The Hubble Space Telescope. 2017. (Space Tech Ser.). (ENG., Illus.). 24p. (J). (gr. 3-7). lib. bdg. 26.95 *(978-1-62617-700-0(7)*, Epic Bks.) Bellwether Media.

Motum, Markus. Curiosity: the Story of a Mars Rover. Motum, Markus, illus. 2018. (ENG., Illus.). 56p. (J). (gr. 3-7). 22.99 *(978-0-7636-9504-0(1))* Candlewick Pr.

Owen, Ruth. Saturn, 1 vol. 2013. (Explore Outer Space Ser.). (ENG.). 32p. (J). (gr. 2-3). 29.93 *(978-1-61533-727-9(X)*, 75a81bac-edb4-4435-a8c9-0744ad268c18); pap. 11.00 *(978-1-61533-771-2(7)*, cf637717-e3a9-42ab-956c-336652c3548e) Rosen Publishing Group, Inc., The. (Windmill Bks.).

—Saturn. 2013. (Explore Outer Space Ser.). 32p. (J). (gr. 3-6). pap. 60.00 *(978-1-61533-772-9(5))* Windmill Bks.

—Spacecraft, 1 vol. 2014. (Objects in Space Ser.). (ENG., Illus.). 32p. (J). (gr. 4-4). pap. 11.00 *(978-1-4777-5875-5(5)*, ea4aa1bd-668c-4272-ad14-0efe28408761, PowerKids Pr.) Rosen Publishing Group, Inc., The.

Oxlade, Chris & West, David. The Apollo Missions & Other Adventures in Space, 1 vol. 2011. (Incredible True Adventures Ser.). (ENG., Illus.). 48p. (YA). (gr. 5-5). pap. 12.75 *(978-1-4488-6664-9(2)*, ae16a48b-3a24-4c61-977a-04d14674e3ce); lib. bdg. 34.47 *(978-1-4488-6660-1(X)*, 607a5fbc-cf3d-4888-9f7a-20ba7795eddf) Rosen Publishing Group, Inc., The. (Rosen Reference).

Parker, Steve. Space Exploration. 2010. (How It Works Ser.). 40p. (J). (gr. 3-18). lib. bdg. 19.95 *(978-1-4222-1799-3(X))* Mason Crest.

Perritano, John. Space Machines, 1 vol. 2013. (Machines in Motion Ser.). 48p. (J). (gr. 3-3). (ENG.). pap. 15.05 *(978-1-4339-9613-9(8)*, 548bed3f-a380-48af-a936-4b864a78df08); pap. 84.30 *(978-1-4339-9614-6(6))*; (ENG., Illus.). lib. bdg. 34.61 *(978-1-4339-9612-2(X)*, 19d4c740-b09d-4d6b-848b-1d2ea2bb359a) Stevens, Gareth Publishing LLLP.

Peterson, Christy. Cutting-Edge Hubble Telescope Data. 2019. (Searchlight Books (tm) — New Frontiers of Space Ser.). (ENG., Illus.). 32p. (J). (gr. 3-5). pap. 9.99 *(978-1-5415-7484-7(2)*, 693e0d9b-052e-4873-9c6a-b5ed1addd6f4); lib. bdg. 30.65 *(978-1-5415-5581-5(3)*, a753add7-1035-45de-a9bf-367b895f49d6) Lerner Publishing Group. (Lerner Pubns.).

Radomski, Kassandra. The Apollo 13 Mission: Core Events of a Crisis in Space, 1 vol. 2014. (What Went Wrong? Ser.). (ENG., Illus.). 32p. (J). (gr. 3-6). pap. 7.95 *(978-1-4765-5130-2(8)*, 124448, Capstone Pr.) Capstone.

Rice Jr., Earle. The Orion Spacecraft. 2018. lib. bdg. 29.95 *(978-1-68020-168-0(9))* Mitchell Lane Pubs.

Rissman, Rebecca. Houston, We've Had a Problem: The Story of the Apollo 13 Disaster. 2018. (Tangled History Ser.). (ENG.). 112p. (J). (gr. 3-9). pap. 6.95 *(978-1-5157-7964-3(5)*, 136044, Capstone Pr.) Capstone.

—TV Displays Disaster As the Challenger Explodes: 4D an Augmented Reading Experience. 2019. (Captured Television History 4D Ser.). (ENG., Illus.). 64p. (J). (gr. 5-9). pap. 8.99 *(978-0-7565-6002-7(0)*, 139133, Compass Point Bks.) Capstone.

Roza, Greg. The Hubble Space Telescope: Understanding & Representing Numbers in the Billions. 2009. (PowerMath: Proficiency Plus Ser.). 32p. (gr. 4-5). 47.90 *(978-1-60851-422-9(6)*, PowerKids Pr.) Rosen Publishing Group, Inc., The.

Rustad, Martha E. H. Space Vehicles. 2012. (Exploring Space Ser.). (ENG.). 24p. (gr. k-1). pap. 41.70 *(978-1-4296-8331-9(7))*; (Illus.). (J). (gr. -1-2). lib. bdg. 27.32 *(978-1-4296-7580-2(2)*, 117177) Capstone. (Capstone Pr.).

Scott, Elaine. Space, Stars, & the Beginning of Time: What the Hubble Telescope Saw. (ENG., Illus.). 72p. (J). (gr. 5-7). 2018. pap. 9.99 *(978-1-328-89577-6(7)*, 1699657) 2011. 17.99 *(978-0-547-24189-0(5)*, 1099036) HarperCollins Pubs. (Clarion Bks.).

Silverman, Buffy. How Do Space Vehicles Work? 2013. (Lightning Bolt Books (r) — How Flight Works). (ENG., Illus.). 32p. (J). (gr. 1-3). pap. 9.99 *(978-1-4677-0788-6(0)*, 75da9b00-a162-477e-ba03-d0795510bc57); lib. bdg. 29.32 *(978-0-7613-8971-2(7)*, 4416f7c1-a0b9-46df-a132-30082ac14895, Lerner Pubns.) Lerner Publishing Group.

Simon, Seymour. Destination Space. 2006. (Illus.). 32p. (gr. k-4). 17.00 *(978-0-7569-6746-8(5))* Perfection Learning Corp.

—Destination: Space. 2006. (ENG., Illus.). 32p. (J). (gr. k-4). pap. 7.99 *(978-0-06-087723-1(5),* HarperCollins) HarperCollins Pubs.

Slade, Suzanne. Daring Dozen: The Twelve Who Walked on the Moon. Marks, Alan, illus. 2019. 48p. (J). (gr. k-4). lib. bdg. 17.99 *(978-1-58089-773-0(8))* Charlesbridge Publishing, Inc.

Solar-Wind-Riding Electric Sail: Meet NASA Inventor Bruce Wiegmann & His Team's. 2017. (J). *(978-0-7166-6162-7(4))* World Bk., Inc.

Space Systems, 12 vols. 2016. (Space Systems Ser.). (ENG.). 112p. (YA). (gr. 8-8). lib. bdg. 267.00 *(978-1-5026-2404-8(4),* ab1c61b1-c625-4204-975c-fa71dc64a8d3, Cavendish Square) Cavendish Square Publishing LLC.

Sparrow, Giles. Exploring the Universe, 1 vol. 2006. (Secrets of the Universe Ser.). (ENG., Illus.). 48p. (gr. 6-8). lib. bdg. 33.67 *(978-0-8368-7276-7(2),* b9c1e309-ac1e-4409-923b-d6b8b6a1a3cd, Gareth Stevens Secondary Library) Stevens, Gareth Publishing LLLP.

Spizzirri, Linda, ed. Space Craft. Spizzirri, Peter M., illus. 32p. (J). (gr. 1-8). pap. 4.98 incl. audio *(978-0-86545-036-3(6))* Spizzirri Pr., Inc.

Thimmesh, Catherine. Team Moon: How 400,000 People Landed Apollo 11 on the Moon. 2006. (ENG., Illus.). 80p. (J). (gr. 5-7). 19.95 *(978-0-618-50757-3(4),* 510514, Clarion Bks.) HarperCollins Pubs.

Thomas, Rachael L. Make a Spaceship Your Way! 2018. (Super Simple DIY Ser.). (ENG., Illus.). 32p. (J). (gr. k-4). lib. bdg. 34.21 *(978-1-5321-1720-6(5),* 30728, Super SandCastle) ABDO Publishing Co.

Time, Nicholas O. Houston, We Have a Klutz! 2016. (In Due Time Ser.: 4). (ENG., Illus.). 160p. (J). (gr. 3-7). 17.99 *(978-1-4814-7237-1(2),* Simon Spotlight) Simon Spotlight.

Tunby, Benjamin. Surviving a Space Disaster: Apollo 13. 2019. (They Survived (Alternator Books (r)) Ser.). (ENG., Illus.). 32p. (J). (gr. 3-6). 29.32 *(978-1-5415-2350-0(4),* ab165ec4-a23d-4f4c-889b-fa9cfccea128, Lerner Pubns.) Lerner Publishing Group.

Vallejo, Harry. Dropping Clues from the Sky. 2011. 48p. (gr. 10-12). 19.89 *(978-1-4269-9297-1(1));* pap. 9.89 *(978-1-4269-9296-4(3))* Trafford Publishing.

Visca, Curt. How to Draw Cartoon Spacecraft & Astronauts in Action. 2009. (Kid's Guide to Drawing Ser.). 24p. (gr. 3-3). 47.90 *(978-1-61511-019-3(4),* PowerKids Pr.) Rosen Publishing Group, Inc., The.

Visca, Curt & Visca, Kelley. How to Draw Cartoon Spacecraft & Astronauts in Action, 1 vol. 2003. (Kid's Guide to Drawing Ser.). (ENG., Illus.). 24p. (J). (gr. 3-3). lib. bdg. 28.93 *(978-0-8239-6729-2(8),* 0ef6c7d9-a3c8-409c-882e-a8008f4babec, PowerKids Pr.) Rosen Publishing Group, Inc., The.

Vogt, Gregory L. Disasters in Space Exploration. rev. ed. 2003. (Worlds Beyond Ser.). (Illus.). 80p. (gr. 5-8). lib. bdg. 25.90 *(978-0-7613-2895-7(5),* Twenty-First Century Bks.) Lerner Publishing Group.

Walker, Landry Q. Star Wars Encyclopedia of Starfighters & Other Vehicles. 2018. (ENG., Illus.). 208p. (J). (gr. 3-7). 19.99 *(978-1-4654-6665-5(7),* DK Children) Dorling Kindersley Publishing, Inc.

Walliman, Dominic. Professor Astro Cat's Space Rockets. Newman, Ben, illus. 2018. (ENG.). 32p. (J). (gr. k-2). 13.99 *(978-1-911171-94-2(1))* Flying Eye Bks. GBR. Dist: Penguin Random Hse. LLC.

West, David. Spacecraft. (What's Inside? Ser.). (ENG., Illus.). 24p. (J). (gr. k-3). 2017. 28.50 *(978-1-62588-404-6(4),* 19389) 2015. 27.10 *(978-1-62588-067-3(7),* 19318) Black Rabbit Bks. (Smart Apple Media).

Williams, Dave & Cunti, Loredana. Mighty Mission Machines: From Rockets to Rovers. 2018. (ENG., Illus.). 52p. (J). (gr. 3-7). 22.95 *(978-1-77321-013-1(0));* pap. 12.95 *(978-1-77321-012-4(2))* Annick Pr., Ltd. CAN. Dist: Publishers Group West (PGW).

Woolf, Alex. The Science of Spacecraft: the Cosmic Truth about Rockets, Satellites, & Probes (the Science of Engineering) (Library Edition) Myer, Ed & Beach, Bryan, illus. 2019. (Science Of... Ser.). (ENG.). 32p. (J). (gr. 3-3). lib. bdg. 29.00 *(978-0-531-13197-8(1),* Watts, Franklin) Scholastic Library Publishing.

World Book, Inc. Staff, contrib. by. Robots in Action. 2019. (Illus.). 48p. (J). *(978-0-7166-4135-3(6))* World Bk., Inc.

Zelon, Helen. The Apollo 13 Mission: Surviving an Explosion in Space. 2009. (Space Missions Ser.). 24p. (gr. 3-4). 42.50 *(978-1-60853-116-5(3),* PowerKids Pr.) Rosen Publishing Group, Inc., The.

Zobel, Derek. The Hubble Telescope. 2010. (Exploring Space Ser.). (ENG., Illus.). 24p. (J). (gr. k-3). lib. bdg. 26.95 *(978-1-60014-296-3(6),* Blastoff! Readers) Bellwether Media.

Zoehfeld, Kathleen Weidner. Apollo 13 (Totally True Adventures) How Three Brave Astronauts Survived a Space Disaster. Lowe, Wesley, illus. 2015. (Totally True Adventures Ser.). 112p. (J). (gr. 2-5). pap. 6.99 *(978-0-385-39125-2(0),* Random Hse. Bks. for Young Readers) Random Hse. Children's Bks.

SPAIN

Ainsley, Dominic J. Spain, Vol. 16. 2018. (European Countries Today Ser.). (Illus.). 96p. (J). (gr. 7). 34.60 *(978-1-4222-3991-9(8))* Mason Crest.

Bader, Bonnie & Who HQ. Who Was Christopher Columbus? Harrison, Nancy, illus. 2013. (Who Was? Ser.). 112p. (J). (gr. 3-7). pap. 5.99 *(978-0-448-46333-9(4),* Penguin Workshop) Penguin Young Readers Group.

Blomquist, Christopher. A Primary Source Guide to Spain. (Countries of the World). 24p. (gr. 2-3). 2009. 42.50 *(978-1-61512-045-1(9))* 2004. (ENG., Illus.). (J). lib. bdg. 26.27 *(978-1-4042-2757-6(1),* dafbbab2-95c3-4b07-8c7c-e9d6b978eca8) Rosen Publishing Group, Inc., The. (PowerKids Pr.).

Bowden, Rob, et al. Focus on Spain, 1 vol. 2006. (World in Focus Ser.). (ENG., Illus.). 64p. (gr. 5-8). pap. 15.05 *(978-0-8368-6730-5(0),* 0b3ac136-3bfb-466e-b81f-2d953237a573); lib. bdg. 36.67 *(978-0-8368-6723-7(8),* 8a8c41e3-61d9-40ad-b260-49463da24bc9) Stevens, Gareth Publishing LLLP. (Gareth Stevens Secondary Library).

Brooks, Susie. Let's Visit Spain, 1 vol. 2009. (Around the World Ser.). (ENG., Illus.). 32p. (J). (gr. 2-3). pap. 11.00 *(978-1-4358-8608-7(9),* 2b1a96f3-e65d-488f-9d0c-cf8ddc843281); lib. bdg. 28.93 *(978-1-4358-3027-1(X),* dfce59fb-0139-497d-8f2c-b1da00f7223a) Rosen Publishing Group, Inc., The. (PowerKids Pr.).

Burlingame, Jeff. Soccer Star Andrés Iniesta, 1 vol. 2014. (Goal! Latin Stars of Soccer Ser.). (ENG.). 48p. (gr. 4-6). pap. 11.53 *(978-1-62285-226-0(5),* 282a18fb-01d9-4055-b47a-3b5abe7264f2) Enslow Publishing, LLC.

Cefrey, Holly. The Pinckney Treaty: America Wins the Right to Travel the Mississippi River. 2009. (Life in the New American Nation Ser.). 32p. (gr. 4-4). 47.90 *(978-1-61514-286-6(X))* Rosen Publishing Group, Inc., The.

Dyan, Penelope. The Rain in Spain — -A Kid's Guide to Barcelona, Spain. Weigand, John D., photos by. 2011. (Illus.). 38p. pap. 12.95 *(978-1-935630-56-2(3))* Bellissima Publishing, LLC.

Elgin, Kathy. Costume Around the World: Spain. 2008. (Costume Around the World Ser.). (ENG., Illus.). 32p. (gr. 4-6). 28.00 *(978-0-7910-9772-4(2),* P459460, Chelsea Clubhse.) Infobase Holdings, Inc.

Faiella, Graham. Spain: A Primary Source Cultural Guide. (Primary Sources of World Cultures Ser.). 128p. (gr. 4-5). 2009. 79.90 *(978-1-60851-930-9(9))* 2003. (ENG., Illus.). lib. bdg. 43.60 *(978-0-8239-4002-8(0),* c351b9a1-4f5f-43ec-936a-6624cd067f72) Rosen Publishing Group, Inc., The.

Feinstein, Stephen. Columbus: Opening up the New World, 1 vol. 2009. (Great Explorers of the World Ser.). (ENG., Illus.). 112p. (gr. 6-7). lib. bdg. 35.93 *(978-1-59845-101-6(4),* c7df4c23-961d-4fde-8204-2c16a7e9a732) Enslow Publishing, LLC.

Flynn, Claire E. Running with the Bulls, 1 vol. 2013. (Thrill Seekers Ser.). (ENG., Illus.). 32p. (J). (gr. 3-4). pap. 11.50 *(978-1-4824-3294-7(3),* 11be7de3-8e16-4ae6-8805-62e5d3a09286) Rosen Publishing Group, Inc., The.

Goldberg, Jan. Hernando de Soto: Trailblazer of the American Southeast. 2009. (Library of Explorers & Exploration Ser.). 112p. (gr. 5-8). 66.50 *(978-1-60853-607-8(6),* Rosen Reference) Rosen Publishing Group, Inc., The.

Graham, Ian. Spain. 2003. (Country Files Ser.). 32p. (J). lib. bdg. 24.25 *(978-1-58340-240-5(3))* Black Rabbit Bks.

Hoogenboom, Lynn. Amerigo Vespucci. 2009. (Primary Source Library of Famous Explorers Ser.). 24p. (gr. 4-4). 42.50 *(978-1-60854-118-8(5),* PowerKids Pr.) Rosen Publishing Group, Inc., The.

Horn, Geoffrey M. & Stewart, Mark. Rafael Nadal, 1 vol. 2009. (Today's Superstars Ser.). (ENG.). 32p. (J). (gr. 3-3). lib. bdg. 34.60 *(978-1-4339-1965-7(6),* 485a588f-296a-4bd2-aa45-69a314348e2d) Stevens, Gareth Publishing LLLP.

James, Yolanda. In Spain. Brodie, Neale, illus. 2008. (J). *(978-1-59646-772-9(X))* Dingles & Co.

Kent, Su. Living in Spain. Hampton, David, photos by. 2006. (Living In- Ser.). (Illus.). 32p. (J). (gr. 4-7). lib. bdg. 27.10 *(978-1-59771-048-0(2))* Sea-To-Sea Pubns.

Kenyon, John. Spain. 2004. (QEB Travel Through Ser.). (Illus.). 32p. (J). lib. bdg. 18.95 *(978-1-59566-061-9(5))* QEB Publishing Inc.

Kohen, Elizabeth, et al. Spain, 1 vol. 3rd rev. ed. 2013. (Cultures of the World (Third Edition)(r) Ser.). (ENG.). 144p. (gr. 5-5). pap. 24.51 *(978-1-62712-162-0(5),* 34e0b7d9-3b37-48ce-a0b3-6c07f9e18387) Cavendish Square Publishing LLC.

Lusted, Marcia Amidon. Spain, 1 vol. 2013. (Countries of the World Set 2 Ser.). (ENG.). 144p. (YA). (gr. 6-12). lib. bdg. 42.79 *(978-1-61783-637-4(0),* 4898, Essential Library) ABDO Publishing Co.

Markovics, Joyce. Spain. 2017. (Countries We Come From Ser.). (ENG., Illus.). 32p. (J). (gr. k-3). 19.95 *(978-1-68402-251-9(7))* Bearport Publishing Co., Inc.

Mattern, Joanne. Spain, 1 vol. 2016. (Exploring World Cultures (First Edition) Ser.). (ENG., Illus.). 32p. (gr. 3-3). pap. 12.16 *(978-1-5026-2146-7(0),* de540adc-2eb7-4fbe-a5c7-0d88234af46c) Cavendish Square Publishing LLC.

Parker, Lewis K. Spain, 1 vol. Murdocca, Sal, illus. 2003. (Discovering Cultures Ser.). (ENG.). 48p. (gr. 3-4). 31.21 *(978-0-7614-1520-6(3),* 5dcf3b74-04bf-4e29-b3e3-231c3f57e111) Cavendish Square Publishing LLC.

Peppas, Lynn. Why Francisco Coronado Matters to Texas, 1 vol. 2013. (Texas Perspectives Ser.). (ENG., Illus.). 32p. (J). (gr. 4-4). lib. bdg. 28.93 *(978-1-4777-0909-2(6),* ea11e18a-2750-4bf4-ad7a-d5d0300c739e) Rosen Publishing Group, Inc., The.

Powell, Jillian. Descubramos España (Looking at Spain), 1 vol. 2007. (Descubramos Países Del Mundo (Looking at Countries) Ser.). (SPA., Illus.). 32p. (gr. 2-4). lib. bdg. 28.67 *(978-0-8368-7952-0(X),* 0c2d73b1-59b4-4701-8cf4-4f2d7d22eb9c, Gareth Stevens Learning Library) Stevens, Gareth Publishing LLLP.

—Looking at Spain, 1 vol. 2007. (Looking at Countries Ser.). (ENG., Illus.). 32p. (gr. 2-4). pap. 11.50 *(978-0-8368-7679-6(2),* 0f87fafc-b86e-4114-aa3f-0092f323c8a7); lib. bdg. 28.67 *(978-0-8368-7672-7(5),* 6187d90c-6421-4170-bd7a-c4db8e30f619) Stevens, Gareth Publishing LLLP. (Gareth Stevens Learning Library).

Rechner, Amy. Spain. 2018. (Country Profiles Ser.). (ENG., Illus.). 32p. (J). (gr. 3-8). lib. bdg. 27.95 *(978-1-62617-844-1(5),* Blastoff! Discovery) Bellwether Media.

Reis, Ronald A. Christopher Columbus & the Age of Exploration for Kids: With 21 Activities. 2013. (For Kids Ser.: 52). (ENG., Illus.). 160p. (J). (gr. 4). pap. 16.95 *(978-1-61374-674-5(1))* Chicago Review Pr., Inc.

Rice, Simon & Campbell, Polly. Discover Spain, 1 vol. 2010. (Discover Countries Ser.). (ENG., Illus.). 32p. (J). (gr. 4-4). lib. bdg. 30.27 *(978-1-61532-301-2(5),* 943902f5-a457-438b-82b2-e4cc192112c8) Rosen Publishing Group, Inc., The.

Savery, Annabel. Spain. 2011. (ENG., Illus.). 32p. (J). pap. 10.95 *(978-1-77092-028-6(5))* Saunders Bk. Co. CAN. Dist: RiverStream Publishing.

Schon, Isabel. The Best of Latino Heritage, 1996-2002: A Guide to the Best Juvenile Books about Latino People. 2003. (ENG., Illus.). 272p. 87.00 *(978-0-8108-4669-2(1))* Scarecrow Pr., Inc.

Taus-Bolstad, Stacy. Spain in Pictures. 2nd rev. expurg. ed. 2004. (Visual Geography Series, Second Ser.). (ENG., Illus.). 80p. (gr. 5-12). 31.93 *(978-0-8225-1993-5(3))* Lerner Publishing Group.

Teacher Created Resources Staff. Travel Through - Spain: Come on a Journey of Discovery. 2008. (Qeb Travel Through Ser.). (ENG., Illus.). 32p. (gr. 4-7). pap. 7.99 *(978-1-4206-8286-1(5))* Teacher Created Resources, Inc.

Thompson, Linda. The Spanish in America. 2005. (Expansion of America II Ser.). (Illus.). 48p. (J). (gr. 4-8). lib. bdg. 31.36 *(978-1-59515-514-6(7))* Rourke Educational Media.

SPAIN—FICTION

Alonso, Manuel L. Tiempo de Nubes Negras. 4th ed. 2004.Tr. of Time for Black Clouds. (SPA., Illus.). 88p. (J). (gr. 6-8). pap. 12.99 *(978-84-207-7770-2(6))* Grupo Anaya, S.A. ESP. Dist: Lectorum Pubns., Inc.

Angel, Ido. Vipo in Madrid: Billy Must Win! 2015. (AV2 Animated Storytime Ser.). (ENG.). (J). lib. bdg. 29.99 *(978-1-4896-3893-9(8),* AV2 by Weigl) Weigl Pubs., Inc.

Bentley, Sue. Sunshine Shimmers. 2014. (Magic Puppy Ser.: 12). lib. bdg. 14.75 *(978-0-606-34141-7(2))* Turtleback.

Bostick, B. k. Huber Hill & the Brotherhood of Coronado. 2012. 282p. (J). 14.99 *(978-1-59955-981-0(1))* Cedar Fort, Inc./CFI Distribution.

Butcher, Nicholas. The Hand above the Gate. 2008. 204p. pap. *(978-1-84923-348-4(9))* YouWriteOn.

El Cid. (SPA., Illus.). 128p. (J). 11.95 *(978-84-7281-098-3(4),* AF1098) Auriga, Ediciones S.A. ESP. Dist: Continental Bk. Co., Inc.

de Trevino, Elizabeth Borton. I, Juan de Pareja. 3rd ed. pap. 3.95 *(978-0-13-800129-2(4))* Prentice Hall (Schl. Div.).

—I, Juan de Pareja. l.t. ed. 2005. 244p. 20.95 *(978-0-7862-7666-0(5))* Thorndike Pr.

De Trevino, Elizabeth Borton. I, Juan de Pareja: The Story of a Great Painter & the Slave He Helped Become a Great Artist. 2008. (ENG.). 192p. (YA). (gr. 7-12). pap. 9.99 *(978-0-312-38005-2(4),* 900050528) Square Fish.

Elmokadem, Shirley. Serena & The Moor's Last Sigh. 2007. 80p. per. *(978-1-84549-229-8(3))* arima publishing.

Following Isabella - Evaluation Guide: Evaluation Guide. 2006. (J). *(978-1-55942-406-6(0))* Witcher Productions.

Gabán, Jesús. El libro de Don Quijote para niños: Nueva edición) 2016. (SPA., Illus.). 112p. (J). (gr. 4-7). 20.95 *(978-84-16075-98-0(0),* B De Blook) Penguin Random House Grupo Editorial ESP. Dist: Penguin Random Hse. LLC.

Galdos, Benito Perez. Tristana. Costa, Margaret Jull, tr. 2014. (NYRB Classics Ser.). 192p. pap. 14.95 *(978-1-59017-765-5(7),* NYRB Classics) New York Review of Bks., Inc., The.

Gibbs, Stuart. The Last Musketeer #2: Traitor's Chase. 2019. (ENG.). 272p. (J). (gr. 3-7). pap. 7.99 *(978-0-06-204842-4(2),* HarperCollins) HarperCollins Pubs.

Gray, Kes. Daisy & the Trouble with Kittens. Sharratt, Nick & Parsons, Garry, illus. 2010. (Daisy Ser.). (ENG.). 256p. (J). (gr. 2-4). pap. 11.99 *(978-1-86230-834-3(9),* Red Fox) Random House Children's Books GBR. Dist: Independent Pubs. Group.

Green, Elaine. The Adventures of Abigale Green in Spain. Alston, Brad, illus. 2012. 38p. (J). 14.95 *(978-1-937406-10-3(5))* Amplify Publishing Group.

Haddix, Margaret Peterson. The Summer of Broken Things. 2018. (ENG., Illus.). 400p. (YA). (gr. 7). 17.99 *(978-1-4814-1764-8(9))* Simon & Schuster Children's Publishing.

Harrison, Lisi, creator. Alicia. 2008. (Clique Summer Collection: 3). (ENG., Illus.). 144p. (YA). (gr. 7-17). pap. 10.99 *(978-0-316-02753-3(7),* Poppy) Little, Brown Bks. for Young Readers.

I, Juan de Pareja. 3rd ed. (J). pap., stu. ed. *(978-0-13-667452-8(6))* Prentice Hall (Schl. Div.).

Jiménez, Juan Ramón. Platero y Yo. (SPA.). 192p. (J). 13.95 *(978-84-206-1851-7(9),* AZ1851); (Illus.). 159p. 15.95 *(978-84-206-3408-1(5))* Alianza Editorial, S. A. ESP. Dist: Continental Bk. Co., Inc., Distribooks, Inc.

—Platero y Yo. (SPA.). (J). pap. 9.95 *(978-968-432-357-5(3),* PM223) Editorial Porrua MEX. Dist: Continental Bk. Co., Inc.

—Platero y Yo. annot. ed. (SPA., Illus.). 232p. (J). 15.95 *(978-84-207-2636-6(2),* ANY010) Grupo Anaya, S.A. ESP. Dist: Continental Bk. Co., Inc.

—Platero y Yo (Platero & I) (SPA.). (J). pap. 9.95 *(978-968-416-022-4(4),* AOR01) Fernandez USA Publishing.

Johnson, Jane. La Princesa y el Pintor. Johnson, Jane, illus. 2003.Tr. of Princess & the Painter. (SPA., Illus.). 32p. (J). (gr. -1-3). pap. 14.95 *(978-1-56014-618-6(4),* SAN6184) Santillana USA Publishing Co., Inc.

Kephart, Beth. Small Damages. 2013. (Illus.). 304p. (YA). (gr. 9). pap. 8.99 *(978-0-14-242641-8(5),* Speak) Penguin Young Readers Group.

Krantz, Hazel. In the Garden of the Caliph. 2012. 132p. (gr. 4-6). 23.14 *(978-1-4669-2888-6(3));* (J). pap. 13.14 *(978-1-4669-2886-2(7))* Trafford Publishing.

Kurlansky, Mark. The Girl Who Swam to Euskadi: Euskadiraino Igerian Joan Zen Neska. Kurlansky, Mark, illus. 2005. (ENG & BAQ., Illus.). 32p. (J). (gr. -1-3). 18.95 *(978-1-877802-54-6(9))* Ctr. for Basque Studies.

Kyle, Tracey. Food Fight Fiesta: A Tale about la Tomatina. Gomez, Ana, illus. 2018. 32p. (J). (gr. k-3). 16.99 *(978-1-5107-3215-5(2),* Sky Pony Pr.) Skyhorse Publishing Co., Inc.

Lindo, Elvira. Manolito Four-Eyes: The 1st Volume of the Great Encyclopedia of My Life, 0 vols. Moriarty, Joanne, tr. Urberuaga, Emilio, illus. 2010. (Manolito Four-Eyes Ser.: 1). (ENG.). 155p. (J). (gr. 4-6). pap. 9.99 *(978-0-7614-5729-9(1),* 9780761457299, Two Lions) Amazon Publishing.

—Manolito Four-Eyes: the 2nd Volume of the Great Encyclopedia of My Life, 0 vols. Travalia, Caroline, tr. Urberuaga, Emilio, illus. unabr. ed. 2013. (Manolito Four-Eyes Ser.: 2). (ENG.). 162p. (J). (gr. 4-6). pap. 9.99 *(978-1-4778-1700-1(X),* 9781477817001, Two Lions) Amazon Publishing.

—Manolito Gafotas, 0 vols. Urberuaga, Emilio, illus. 2012. (SPA.). 192p. (J). (gr. 4-6). pap. 9.99 *(978-0-7614-5730-5(5),* 9780761457305, Two Lions) Amazon Publishing.

Martinez, Rueben. Once upon a Time/Habia una Vez: Traditional Latin American Tales/Cuentos Tradicionales Latinoamericanos (Bilingual English-Spanish) ón, Raúl, illus. 2010. (ENG.). 96p. (J). (gr. -1-3). 19.99 *(978-0-06-146895-7(9))* HarperCollins Español.

McDougal-Littell Publishing Staff. Literature Connections Spanish: Yo, Juan de Pareja (I, Juan de Pareja) 2004. (McDougal Littell Literature Connections Ser.). (SPA.). 256p. (gr. 7-7). 16.90 *(978-0-395-84375-8(8),* 2-70788) Great Source Education Group, Inc.

Morningstar, Jeremy. Penalty Kick. 2005. 56p. pap. 9.00 *(978-1-4116-6572-9(4))* Lulu Pr., Inc.

Muñiz-Huberman, Angelina & Menton, Seymour. Dreaming of Safed. 2014. 126p. (YA). pap. *(978-1-935604-61-7(9))* Gaon Bks.

Narváez, Concha López. El Fuego de los Pastores.Tr. of Shepherds' Fire. (SPA.). (YA). (gr. 5). pap. *(978-84-395-0902-8(2))* Espasa Calpe, S.A. ESP. Dist: Lectorum Pubns., Inc.

Oldfield, Matt. Iniesta: From the Playground to the Pitch. 2018. (Ultimate Football Heroes Ser.). (ENG., Illus.). 176p. (J). (gr. 2-7). pap. 11.99 *(978-1-78606-804-0(4))* Blake, John Publishing, Ltd. GBR. Dist: Independent Pubs. Group.

—Suarez: From the Playground to the Pitch. 2018. (Ultimate Football Heroes Ser.). (ENG., Illus.). 176p. (J). (gr. 2-7). pap. 9.99 *(978-1-78606-806-4(0))* Blake, John Publishing, Ltd. GBR. Dist: Independent Pubs. Group.

Oldfield, Matt & Oldfield, Tom. Figo. 2018. (Football Heroes - International Editions Ser.). (ENG., Illus.). 176p. (J). (gr. 4-7). pap. 9.99 *(978-1-78606-923-8(7))* Blake, John Publishing, Ltd. GBR. Dist: Independent Pubs. Group.

Pérez Anton, Pablo. THE GLUTTON. 2007. (ENG., Illus.). 48p. (J). 18.95 *(978-84-96788-91-6(1))* OQO, Editora ESP. Dist: Baker & Taylor Bks.

Pérez Galdós, Benito. Marianela. 2003. (SPA.). 159p. (YA). 12.95 *(978-968-6966-08-4(0))* EDITER'S Publishing Hse. MEX. Dist: EDITER'S Publishing Hse.

—Marianela. 9th ed. (SPA., Illus.). 240p. 18.50 *(978-84-376-0380-3(3),* CT1174) Ediciones Cátedra ESP. Dist: Continental Bk. Co., Inc.

—Marianela. 10th ed. 2003. (SPA., Illus.). 208p. *(978-84-207-3415-6(2),* GS1219) Grupo Anaya, S.A. ESP. Dist: Lectorum Pubns., Inc.

Sedgwick, Julian. The Palace of Memory, No. 2. Moffett, Patricia, illus. 2017. (Mysterium Ser.: 2). (ENG.). 352p. (J). (gr. 4-8). 18.99 *(978-1-4677-7568-7(1),* a33df367-d91f-4e23-aeec-f2976f2a8368, Carolrhoda Bks.) Lerner Publishing Group.

Servi Machlin, Edda. My Puppy Marrano. 2007. (YA). 19.95 *(978-1-878857-13-2(4))* Giro Pr.

Sierra, Judy. The Beautiful Butterfly: A Folktale from Spain. Chess, Victoria, illus. 2005. 32p. (J). (gr. k-4). reprint ed. 19.00 *(978-0-7567-9593-1(1))* DIANE Publishing Co.

Song-i, Yoon. Saint Teresa of Avila, God's Troublemaker. 2014. (ENG., Illus.). 208p. (J). pap. 14.95 *(978-0-8198-9038-2(3))* Pauline Bks. & Media.

Staley, Samuel. The Pirate of Panther Bay Classroom Guide. 2007. 75p. spiral bd. 15.00 *(978-0-9764684-2-4(5))* IZS, Inc.

Stilton, Thea. Thea Stilton & the Spanish Dance Mission (Thea Stilton #16) A Geronimo Stilton Adventure. 2018. (True Book (Relaunch) Ser.: 16). (ENG.). 176p. (J). (gr. 3-5). E-Book 7.95 *(978-0-545-55685-9(6),* Scholastic Paperbacks) Scholastic, Inc.

Strange, Derek. Level 1: Girl Meets Boy. 2nd ed. 2008. (Pearson English Graded Readers Ser.). (ENG., Illus.). 32p. pap. 11.99 *(978-1-4058-6971-3(2),* Pearson ELT) Pearson Education.

Suguitan, Jazel A. We're Moving?! Shari Tucker's Wacky World #1. 2010. 124p. 20.95 *(978-1-4502-6874-5(9));* pap. 10.95 *(978-1-4502-6871-4(4))* iUniverse, Inc.

Terrell, Brandon. Harmony & Hoops. Garcia, Eduardo, illus. 2016. (Time Machine Magazine Ser.). (ENG.). 128p. (J). (gr. 3-6). lib. bdg. 23.99 *(978-1-4965-2596-3(5),* 130725) Capstone.

Terry, Alana. What Hurricane? My Solar-Powered History on a Supply Ship to the Jamestown Colony. Steffen, Jeremy, illus. 2013. 136p. pap. 12.99 *(978-1-937848-05-7(1))* Do Life Right, Inc.

Tulien, Sean. The Pit & the Pendulum, 1 vol. Fabul, J. C., illus. 2013. (Edgar Allan Poe Graphic Novels Ser.). (ENG.). 72p. (J). (gr. 5-9). pap. 6.10 *(978-1-4342-4260-0(9),* 120322); lib. bdg. 27.99 *(978-1-4342-4024-8(X),* 118405) Capstone. (Stone Arch Bks.).

Waller, Stephen. Level 1: Run for Your Life. 2nd ed. 2008. (Pearson English Graded Readers Ser.). (ENG., Illus.). 32p. pap. 11.99 *(978-1-4058-6970-6(4),* Pearson ELT) Pearson Education.

Wojciechowska, Maia. Shadow of a Bull. 2011. 8.32 *(978-0-7848-3457-2(1),* Everbind) Marco Bk. Co.

SPAIN—HISTORY

Anderson, Wayne. The ETA: Spain's Basque Terrorists. 2009. (Inside the World's Most Infamous Terrorist Organizations Ser.). 64p. (gr. 5-5). 58.50 *(978-1-61513-578-3(2))* Rosen Publishing Group, Inc., The.

Bader, Bonnie. Who Was Christopher Columbus? 2013. (Who Was... ? Ser.). lib. bdg. 16.00 *(978-0-606-31684-2(1))* Turtleback.

Baicker, Karen. Conquistador: Francisco Pizarro Ravages the Inca Empire. 2011. (J). pap. *(978-0-545-32940-8(X))* Scholastic, Inc.

Behar, Yvonne. Out of Spain Vol. 3: Celebrating Sephardi Culture. Brooks, Andree Aelion, illus. 58p. (J). (gr. 5-7). pap. 4.95 *(978-0-9702700-3-0(8))* Brooks, Andree Aelion.

Bodden, Valerie. Conquistadors. 2013. 24p. pap. *(978-1-60818-467-5(6))* Creative Co., The.

Cohen, Robert Z. Hernando de Soto, 1 vol. 2016. (Spotlight on Explorers & Colonization Ser.). (ENG.). 48p. (J). (gr. 6-6). pap. 12.75 *(978-1-5081-7210-9(2),* 5b649c52-63fc-4d8c-a0be-960b8f0072ca) Rosen Publishing Group, Inc., The.

Cultures of the Past - Group 6, 4 bks. *(978-0-7614-1491-9(6),* Cavendish Square) Cavendish Square Publishing LLC.

DiConsiglio, John. Francisco Pizarro: Destroyer of the Inca Empire. 2008. (Wicked History Ser.). (ENG., Illus.). 128p. (J). 31.00 *(978-0-531-18551-3(6),* Watts, Franklin) Scholastic Library Publishing.

Donohue, Moira Rose. Christopher Columbus. 2013. (Illus.). 24p. (J). *(978-1-938813-04-7(9));* pap. *(978-1-938813-08-5(1))* State Standards Publishing, LLC.

—Hernando de Soto. 2015. (Illus.). 24p. (J). *(978-1-938813-20-7(0))* State Standards Publishing, LLC.

—Juan Ponce de León. 2013. (Illus.). 24p. (J). *(978-1-938813-06-1(5))* State Standards Publishing, LLC.

Dyan, Penelope. Around Corners — -A Kid's Guide to Malaga, Spain. Weigand, John D., photos by. 2012. (Illus.). 34p. pap. 11.95 *(978-1-61477-032-9(8))* Bellissima Publishing, LLC.

—¡Hola Córdoba! a Kid's Guide to Córdoba, Spain. Weigand, John D., photos by. 2012. (Illus.). 34p. pap. 11.95 *(978-1-61477-035-0(2))* Bellissima Publishing, LLC.

—¡Hola Madrid! a Kid's Guide to Madrid, Spain. Weigand, John D., photos by. 2012. (Illus.). 34p. pap. 11.95 *(978-1-61477-031-2(X))* Bellissima Publishing, LLC.

—I Remember Still, a Kid's Guide to Seville, Spain. Weigand, John D., photos by. 2012. (Illus.). 34p. pap. 11.95 *(978-1-61477-034-3(4))* Bellissima Publishing, LLC.

—A Lot o' Granada, a Kid's Guide to Granada, Spain. Weigand, John D., photos by. 2012. (Illus.). 34p. pap. 11.95 *(978-1-61477-033-6(6))* Bellissima Publishing, LLC.

Greene, Meg. The Transcontinental Treaty 1819: A Primary Source Examination of the Treaty Between the United States & Spain over the American West. (Primary Sources of American Treaties Ser.). 64p. (gr. 5-8). 2009. 58.50 *(978-1-60851-514-1(1))* 2005. (ENG., Illus.). (J). lib. bdg. 37.13 *(978-1-4042-0439-3(3),* b6d892eb-9f77-4d3a-9466-87b58369515b) Rosen Publishing Group, Inc., The.

Gunderson, Jessica. Christopher Columbus: New World Explorer or Fortune Hunter?, 1 vol. 2013. (Perspectives on History Ser.). (ENG.). 32p. (J). (gr. 3-6). pap. 7.95 *(978-1-4765-3406-0(3),* 123537) Capstone.

Hernández, Roger E. & Hernández, Roger E. Early Explorations, The 1500s, 1 vol. 2009. (Hispanic America Ser.). (ENG.). 80p. (gr. 5-5). lib. bdg. 36.93 *(978-0-7614-2937-1(9),* b16d1ad5-064e-49b4-aaa7-c60082b1692b) Cavendish Square Publishing LLC.

Herrero, Teresa. Me llamo… Gaudí. 2010. (Me Llamo... Ser.). (SPA., Illus.). 63p. (J). pap. *(978-84-342-3337-9(1))* Parramon Ediciones S.A.

Hilliam, David. Philip II: King of Spain & Leader of the Counter-Reformation. 2009. (Rulers, Scholars, & Artists of the Renaissance Ser.). 112p. (gr. 5-8). 66.50 *(978-1-60852-944-5(4),* Rosen Reference) Rosen Publishing Group, Inc., The.

Howse, Jennifer. Spain. 2018. (Illus.). 32p. (J). *(978-1-4896-7506-4(X),* AV2 by Weigl) Weigl Pubs., Inc.

Kallen, Stuart A. A Journey with Christopher Columbus. 2017. (Primary Source Explorers Ser.). (ENG., Illus.). 40p. (J). (gr. 3-5). lib. bdg. 30.65 *(978-1-5124-0772-3(0),* a4e6d874-7e43-4bd3-91fb-6f8d4860869f, Lerner Pubns.) Lerner Publishing Group.

Lee, Michelle. Guggenheim Museum. 2015. (How Did They Build That? Ser.). (ENG., Illus.). 32p. (gr. 3-8). 27.99 *(978-1-62920-563-2(X))* Scobre Pr. Corp.

Malam, John. You Wouldn't Want to Sail in the Spanish Armada! An Invasion You'd Rather Not Launch. Antram, David, illus. 2006. (You Wouldn't Want to Ser.). (ENG.). 32p. (J). (gr. 2-5). 29.00 *(978-0-531-14974-4(9))* Scholastic Library Publishing.

Matthews, Rupert. Conquistadors, 1 vol. 2015. (History's Fearless Fighters Ser.). (ENG., Illus.). 48p. (J). (gr. 5-6). pap. 15.05 *(978-1-4824-3161-2(0),* df78be3f-e654-441e-a876-58fd4d3854ba) Stevens, Gareth Publishing LLLP.

Nagelhout, Ryan. Vasco Núñez de Balboa, 1 vol. 2016. (Spotlight on Explorers & Colonization Ser.). (ENG., Illus.). 48p. (J). (gr. 6-6). pap. 12.75 *(978-1-4777-8828-8(X),* 4cf61e68-f789-41e8-9338-29be4c5b7bdc) Rosen Publishing Group, Inc., The.

Nardo, Don. The Spanish Conquistadors, 1 vol. 2009. (World History Ser.). (ENG.). 104p. (gr. 7-7). 41.53 *(978-1-4205-0133-9(X),* f892900d-9097-425b-a89d-f0ed83da84b9, Lucent Pr.) Greenhaven Publishing LLC.

O'Brien, Cynthia. Explore with Francisco Pizarro. 2015. (Travel with the Great Explorers Ser.). (ENG., Illus.). 32p. (J). (gr. 4-5). *(978-0-7787-1700-3(3))* Crabtree Publishing Co.

—Explore with Ponce de León. 2014. (Travel with the Great Explorers Ser.). (ENG., Illus.). 32p. (J). (gr. 4-5). *(978-0-7787-1429-3(2))* Crabtree Publishing Co.

Owens, Lisa L. A Journey with Hernán Cortés. 2017. (Primary Source Explorers Ser.). (ENG., Illus.). 40p. (J). (gr. 3-5). 30.65 *(978-1-5124-0777-8(1),* 1a7f988c-a4ce-4b11-a824-160a4148d5c3, Lerner Pubns.) Lerner Publishing Group.

Parker, Lewis K. Spanish Colonies in the Americas. 2009. (European Colonies in the Americas Ser.). 24p. (gr. 2-2). 42.50 *(978-1-61512-320-9(2),* PowerKids Pr.) Rosen Publishing Group, Inc., The.

Pavlovic, Zoran, et al. Spain, Updated Edition. 2nd rev. ed. 2011. (ENG.). (gr. 6-12). 35.00 *(978-1-61753-047-0(6),* P210468, Facts On File) Infobase Holdings, Inc.

Pelleschi, Andrea. Juan Ponce de Leon, 1 vol. 2013. (Jr. Graphic Famous Explorers Ser.). (ENG., Illus.). 24p. (J). (gr. 2-3). pap. 11.60 *(978-1-4777-0131-7(1),* f6946dde-86cf-4540-899d-5cf107a78138); lib. bdg. 28.93 *(978-1-4777-0073-0(0),* 43e92445-d896-4a81-9b3f-e4a887366395) Rosen Publishing Group, Inc., The. (PowerKids Pr.).

Peppas, Lynn. Why Cabeza de Vaca Matters to Texas, 1 vol. 2013. (Texas Perspectives Ser.). (ENG., Illus.). 32p. (J). (gr. 4-4). lib. bdg. 28.93 *(978-1-4777-0913-9(4),* 99187d06-5c9b-4171-8e2d-abd99916f04f) Rosen Publishing Group, Inc., The.

Ramen, Fred. Albucasis (Abu al-Qasim Al-Zahrawi) Renowned Muslim Surgeon of the Tenth Century. 2009. (Great Muslim Philosophers & Scientists of the Middle Ages Ser.). 112p. (gr. 6-6). 66.50 *(978-1-61513-178-5(7),* Rosen Reference) Rosen Publishing Group, Inc., The.

—Hernán Cortés: The Conquest of Mexico & the Aztec Empire. 2009. (Library of Explorers & Exploration Ser.). 112p. (gr. 5-8). 66.50 *(978-1-60853-606-1(8),* Rosen Reference) Rosen Publishing Group, Inc., The.

Ray, Michael, ed. Portugal & Spain, 4 vols. 2013. (Britannica Guide to Countries of the European Union Ser.). (ENG.). 344p. (YA). (gr. 10-10). 113.18 *(978-1-61530-994-8(2),* bae25e48-a1c3-4d1d-b9c1-1c01ab935d54); 56.59 *(978-1-61530-967-2(5),* 974873cf-0eec-4910-a3e1-d4fc24fec110) Rosen Publishing Group, Inc., The.

Rice, Simon. Discover Spain. 2010. (Illus.). 32p. (J). 63.60 *(978-1-61532-303-6(1));* (ENG., (gr. 4-4). pap. 11.60 *(978-1-61532-302-9(3),* 047c25c3-193a-47f8-8eba-52ddfeaae37d) Rosen Publishing Group, Inc., The. (PowerKids Pr.).

Roberts, Steven. Francisco Vasquez de Coronado, 1 vol. 2013. (Jr. Graphic Famous Explorers Ser.). (ENG., Illus.). 24p. (J). (gr. 2-3). pap. 11.60 *(978-1-4777-0125-6(7),* 77a4e6c9-2632-45f0-958b-8dc67e5aab63); lib. bdg. 28.93 *(978-1-4777-0070-9(6),* 423b48d7-28a6-4797-8302-25088c166fa5) Rosen Publishing Group, Inc., The. (PowerKids Pr.).

Ryan, Sean. Spain in Our World. 2010. (Countries in Our World Ser.). 32p. (gr. 4-7). lib. bdg. 31.35 *(978-1-59920-438-3(X))* Black Rabbit Bks.

Sebastian, Emily. The Colonial & Postcolonial Experience in Latin America & the Caribbean, 1 vol. 2016. (Colonial & Postcolonial Experience Ser.). (ENG., Illus.). 256p. (J). (gr. 10-10). 55.59 *(978-1-5081-0439-1(5),* 6083d7af-3889-4012-9b3a-9c8057fca86a) Rosen Publishing Group, Inc., The.

Sexton, Colleen & Grack, Rachel. Spain. 2010. (Exploring Countries Ser.). (ENG., Illus.). 32p. (J). (gr. 3-7). lib. bdg. 27.95 *(978-1-60014-489-9(6),* Blastoff! Readers) Bellwether Media.

Sheen, Barbara. Foods of Spain, 1 vol. 2007. (Taste of Culture Ser.). (ENG., Illus.). 64p. (gr. 3-6). lib. bdg. 33.58 *(978-0-7377-3539-0(2),* 4faab20b-3652-4460-9652-6372216579c3, KidHaven Publishing) Greenhaven Publishing LLC.

Simons, Rae & Indovino, Shaina C. Spain. Bruton, John, ed. 2012. (Major European Union Nations Ser.). 64p. (J). (gr. 7). 22.95 *(978-1-4222-2259-1(4))* Mason Crest.

Simons, Rae & Indovino, Shaina Carmel. Spain. 2012. (J). pap. *(978-1-4222-2290-4(X))* Mason Crest.

Somervill, Barbara A. Enchantment of the World: Spain. 2012. (ENG., Illus.). 144p. (J). 40.00 *(978-0-531-27546-7(9),* Children's Pr.) Scholastic Library Publishing.

Sonneborn, Liz. The Acquisition of Florida: America's Twenty-Seventh State. 2009. (ENG., Illus.). 120p. (gr. 6-12). 35.00 *(978-1-60413-054-6(7),* P161432, Facts On File) Infobase Holdings, Inc.

Sutherland, Katrice. Spanish Explorers. 2016. (Illus.). 32p. (J). *(978-1-5105-1872-8(X))* SmartBook Media, Inc.

Thomson, Ruth. Spain, 1 vol. 2011. (Countries Ser.). (ENG., Illus.). 24p. (J). (gr. 2-2). lib. bdg. 26.27 *(978-1-4488-3278-1(0),* a4af7158-1d17-452e-ade1-e84c95f00e39) Rosen Publishing Group, Inc., The.

Tieck, Sarah. Spain, 1 vol. 2013. (Explore the Countries Ser.). (ENG.). 40p. (J). (gr. 2-5). lib. bdg. 35.64 *(978-1-61783-818-7(7),* 6941, Big Buddy Bks.) ABDO Publishing Co.

Urrutia, Maria Christina & Libura, Krystyna. Ecos de la Conquista. 2005. (SPA.). (J). pap. 14.25 *(978-968-7381-21-3(3))* Tecolote, Ediciones, S.A. de C.V. MEX. Dist: Iaconi, Mariuccia Bk. Imports.

Usborne Books Staff & Doherty, Gillian. 1001 Cosas Que Buscar en el Pasado. 2004. (SPA., Illus.). 32p. (J). (gr. -1-18). lib. bdg. 14.95 *(978-1-58086-286-8(1),* EU1375) EDC Publishing.

Wade, Mary Dodson. Christopher Columbus (Rookie Biographies) 2014. (Rookie Biographies Ser.). (ENG., Illus.). 32p. (J). (gr. 1-2). pap. 5.95 *(978-0-531-21202-8(5),* Children's Pr.) Scholastic Library Publishing.

Wallus Sammons, Sandra. Ponce de Leon & the Discovery of Florida. 2013. (ENG., Illus.). 72p. (J). (gr. -1-12). pap. 9.95 *(978-1-56164-593-0(1))* Pineapple Pr., Inc.

Williams, Jack S. Soldiers & Their Families of the California Mission Frontier. 2009. (People of the California Missions Ser.). 64p. (gr. 4-4). 58.50 *(978-1-60851-160-0(X),* PowerKids Pr.) Rosen Publishing Group, Inc., The.

Woog, Adam. Life During the Spanish Inquisition. 2014. (Living History Ser.). (ENG., Illus.). 96p. (J). lib. bdg. 22.95 *(978-1-60152-722-6(5))* ReferencePoint Pr., Inc.

Yim Bridges, Shirin. Isabella of Castile. Nguyen, Albert, illus. 2010. (Thinking Girl's Treasury of Real Princesses Ser.). (ENG.). 24p. (J). (gr. 3-8). 18.95 *(978-0-9845098-4-3(4))* Goosebottom Bks. LLC.

SPAIN—HISTORY—FICTION

Aiken, Joan. Go Saddle the Sea. 2007. (ENG., Illus.). 384p. (YA). (gr. 7). pap. 6.95 *(978-0-15-206064-0(2),* 1198214, Clarion Bks.) HarperCollins Pubs.

—The Teeth of the Gale. 2007. (ENG., Illus.). 352p. (YA). (gr. 7). pap. 18.99 *(978-0-15-206070-1(7),* 1198233, Clarion Bks.) HarperCollins Pubs.

Collingwood, Harry. Across the Spanish Main. 2009. 204p. pap. 14.95 *(978-1-60664-390-7(8))* Rodgers, Alan Bks.

Eiseman, Joan. Ricardo & the Fisherman. Eiseman, Joan, illus. 2007. (Illus.). 32p. (J). per. 12.95 *(978-0-9786745-4-0(5))* Marble Hse. Editions.

Freire, Espido. El Chico de la Flecha. 2017. (SPA., Illus.). 239p. (J). (gr. 7-9). pap. 19.99 *(978-84-698-0907-5(5))* Grupo Anaya, S.A. ESP. Dist: Lectorum Pubns., Inc.

Gibbs, Stuart. The Last Musketeer #2: The Traitor's Chase. 2nd ed. 2012. (Last Musketeer Ser.: 2). (ENG.). 256p. (J). (gr. 3-7). 16.99 *(978-0-06-204841-7(4),* HarperCollins) HarperCollins Pubs.

Gonzalez, Christina Diaz. A Thunderous Whisper. 2013. (Illus.). 320p. (J). (gr. 5). pap. 8.99 *(978-0-375-87371-3(6),* Yearling) Random Hse. Children's Bks.

Greene, Jacqueline Dembar. The Secret Shofar of Barcelona. Chayka, Doug, illus. 2009. (High Holidays Ser.). (ENG.). 32p. (J). (gr. k-3). 17.95 *(978-0-8225-9915-9(5),* Kar-Ben Publishing) Lerner Publishing Group.

Henty, George. With Moore at Corunna: A Tale of the Peninsular War. 2004. reprint ed. pap. 1.99 *(978-1-4192-9445-7(8));* pap. 30.95 *(978-1-4191-9445-0(3))* Kessinger Publishing, LLC.

Hoffman, Alice. Incantation. rev. ed. 2007. (ENG., Illus.). 192p. (YA). (gr. 7-17). per. 12.99 *(978-0-316-15428-4(8))* Little, Brown Bks. for Young Readers.

Holub, Joan. Isabel Saves the Prince: Based on a True Story of Isabel I of Spain (Ready-To-Read Level 3) Aleshina, Nonna, illus. 2007. (Young Princesses Around the World Ser.). (ENG.). 48p. (J). (gr. 1-3). pap. 13.99 *(978-0-689-87197-9(X),* Simon Spotlight) Simon Spotlight.

Jules, Jacqueline. Never Say a Mean Word Again: A Tale from Medieval Spain. Bernhard, Durga Yael, illus. 2014. 32p. (J). (gr. -1-3). 16.95 *(978-1-937786-20-5(X),* Wisdom Tales) World Wisdom, Inc.

Miklowitz, Gloria D. Secrets in the House of Delgado. 2004. (ENG.). 192p. (J). (gr. 4-18). pap. 8.00 *(978-0-8028-5210-6(6))* Eerdmans, William B. Publishing Co.

Muschla, Gary Robert. The Sword & the Cross. 2009. (YA). lib. bdg. *(978-0-88092-471-9(3))* Royal Fireworks Publishing Co.

Narvaez, Concha Lopez. La Colina de Edeta. (SPA.). 124p. (YA). (gr. 5-8). *(978-84-239-9050-4(8),* EC3401) Espasa Calpe, S.A. ESP. Dist: Lectorum Pubns., Inc.

Narváez, Concha López. El Tiempo y la Promesa.Tr. of Time & the Promise. (SPA.). (YA). (gr. 5-8). 164p. *(978-84-216-2558-3(6),* BU7323); 9th ed. (Illus.). 208p. *(978-84-216-1538-6(6),* BU6188) Bruño, Editorial ESP. Dist: Lectorum Pubns., Inc.

Orgad, Dorit. The Boy from Seville. Silverston, Sondra, tr. Katz, Avi, illus. 2007. (Kar-Ben for Older Readers Ser.). (ENG.). 200p. (J). (gr. 5-7). lib. bdg. 16.95 *(978-1-58013-253-4(7),* Kar-Ben Publishing) Lerner Publishing Group.

Ricci, Dorothy. Through Goya's Eyes: The World of the Spanish Painter & His Friend & Mentor, Gaspar Jovellanos. 2008. (YA). pap. *(978-0-88092-763-5(1));* lib. bdg. *(978-0-88092-762-8(3))* Royal Fireworks Publishing Co.

RollasonJane. Freddie's War Level 6 Advanced. 2010. (Cambridge Experience Readers Ser.). (ENG.). 128p. pap. 14.75 *(978-84-8323-909-4(4))* Cambridge Univ. Pr.

Sanderson, Whitney. Horse Diaries #14: Calvino. Sanderson, Ruth, illus. 2017. (Horse Diaries: 12). 160p. (J). (gr. 3-7). pap. 7.99 *(978-1-101-93779-2(3),* Random Hse. Bks. for Young Readers) Random Hse. Children's Bks.

Styles, Showell. The Flying Ensign: Greencoats Against Napoleon. 2003. (Budget Bks). Orig. Title: Greencoat Against Napoleon. (ENG.). 340p. (J). (gr. 7-9). pap. 14.95 *(978-1-883937-70-6(1))* Ignatius Pr.

Wilson, John. Lost in Spain. 2009. (ENG., Illus.). 216p. (YA). (gr. 7-18). pap. *(978-1-55470-177-3(5))* Me to We.

Wiseman, Eva. The Last Song. 2012. (Illus.). 232p. (YA). (gr. 7). 17.95 *(978-0-88776-979-5(9),* Tundra Bks.) Tundra Bks. CAN. Dist: Penguin Random Hse. LLC.

Zafon, Carlos. Marina. 2011. (FRE.). (YA). (gr. 8-12). pap. *(978-2-266-21302-8(4))* Le Robert.

Zafon, Carlos Ruiz. Marina. 2014. (ENG.). 336p. (YA). (gr. 7-17). 34.99 *(978-0-316-04471-4(7))* Little, Brown Bks. for Young Readers.

SPAIN—HISTORY—CIVIL WAR, 1936-1939

Byers, Ann. Strategic Inventions of the Spanish Civil War, 1 vol. 2016. (Tech in the Trenches Ser.). (ENG., Illus.). 112p. (YA). (gr. 9-9). lib. bdg. 44.50 *(978-1-5026-2355-3(2),* a112fc74-eceb-4205-bbb7-86fa4ddc415e) Cavendish Square Publishing LLC.

Griffiths, Katie. The Spanish Civil War, 1 vol. 2017. (Interwar Years Ser.). (ENG., Illus.). 128p. (YA). (gr. 9-9). 47.36 *(978-1-5026-2719-3(1),* 8bc56fdc-750d-46ad-8a07-a702f075c344) Cavendish Square Publishing LLC.

Katz, William Loren & Crawford, Marc. The Lincoln Brigade: A Picture History. 2013. (ENG.). 96p. pap. 15.00 *(978-1-62032-901-6(8),* Wipf and Stock) Wipf & Stock Pubs.

Robeson, Susan. Grandpa Stops a War: A Paul Robeson Story. Brown, Rod, illus. 2019. 32p. (J). (gr. k-4). 17.95 *(978-1-60980-882-2(7),* Triangle Square) Seven Stories Pr.

SPANISH AMERICA

see Latin America

SPANISH-AMERICAN WAR, 1898

Baker, Brynn. Roosevelt's Rough Riders: Fearless Cavalry of the Spanish-American War. 2015. (Military Heroes Ser.). (ENG., Illus.). 32p. (J). (gr. 3-6). lib. bdg. 27.99 *(978-1-4914-4840-3(7),* 128725, Capstone Pr.) Capstone.

Brannen Jr., Daniel E., et al. Spanish American War. 2003. (Spanish-American War Ser.). (ENG., Illus.). 264p. (J). 129.00 *(978-0-7876-6561-6(4),* UXL) Cengage Gale.

Clinton, Greg. Puerto Rico & the Spanish-American War, 1 vol. 2015. (Expanding America Ser.). (ENG., Illus.). 96p. (YA). (gr. 8-8). 44.50 *(978-1-5026-0972-4(X),* a88a02e6-28c6-4cee-955a-e503c5193061) Cavendish Square Publishing LLC.

Golay, Michael. Spanish-American War. Bowman, John S., ed. 3rd rev. ed. 2010. (America at War Ser.). (ENG., Illus.). 192p. (gr. 6-12). 45.00 *(978-0-8160-8189-9(1),* P495244, Facts On File) Infobase Holdings, Inc.

Griffin, Brett. Yellow Journalism, Sensationalism, & Circulation Wars, 1 vol. 2018. (Fourth Estate: Journalism in North America Ser.). (ENG.). 112p. (gr. 8-8). lib. bdg. 44.50 *(978-1-5026-3471-9(6),* d8f78bff-ca76-4d27-bbed-512e5d87bc81) Cavendish Square Publishing LLC.

Hernández, Roger E. & Hernández, Roger E. The Spanish-American War, 1 vol. 2010. (Hispanic America Ser.). (ENG.). 80p. (gr. 5-5). 36.93 *(978-0-7614-4174-8(3),* 1499d798-45f4-46ae-b565-4231da694cd1) Cavendish Square Publishing LLC.

Johanson, Paula. The Spanish-American War, 1 vol. 2016. (United States at War Ser.). (ENG., Illus.). 128p. (gr. 6-6). 38.93 *(978-0-7660-7665-5(2),* 5aa081a5-110c-408f-adf6-a8e11be99557) Enslow Publishing, LLC.

McNeese, Tim. Remember the Maine! The Spanish-American War Begins. 2004. (First Battles Ser.). (Illus.). 112p. (YA). (gr. 6-12). 23.95 *(978-1-883846-79-4(X),* First Biographies) Reynolds, Morgan Inc.

Poulakidas, Georgene. The Spanish-American War. 2009. (Primary Sources of American Wars Ser.). 24p. (gr. 3-4). 42.50 *(978-1-60851-528-8(1),* PowerKids Pr.) Rosen Publishing Group, Inc., The.

Rice, Katelyn. The Spanish-American War. rev. ed. 2016. (Social Studies: Informational Text Ser.). (ENG.). 32p. (J). (gr. 4-8). pap. 11.99 *(978-1-4938-3541-6(6))* Teacher Created Materials, Inc.

Roesser, Marie. The Spanish-American War, 1 vol. 2019. (Look at U. S. History Ser.). (ENG.). 32p. (gr. 2-2). pap. 11.50 *(978-1-5382-4883-6(2),* 6846e425-b842-430b-88d3-dc69f6153a38) Stevens, Gareth Publishing LLLP.

SPANISH-AMERICAN WAR, 1898—FICTION

Finley, Martha. Elsie's Young Folks. 2008. 296p. 34.99 *(978-1-58960-287-8(0))* Sovereign Grace Pubs., Inc.

Morrison, Harry Steele. The Adventures of A Boy Reporter. 2004. reprint ed. pap. 20.95 *(978-1-4191-5137-8(1));* pap. 1.99 *(978-1-4192-5137-5(6))* Kessinger Publishing, LLC.

Munroe, Kirk. 'Forward, March' 2007. 148p. per. 11.95 *(978-1-60312-029-6(7))* Aegypan.

SPANISH LANGUAGE

La Abeja Trabajadora. 2003. (J). 23.95 *(978-0-673-77796-6(0))* Celebration Pr.

Ace Academics, ed. Spanish: A Whole Course in a Box! 2007. (Exambusters Ser.). 384p. (gr. 7-18). 12.95 *(978-1-881374-97-8(1),* Exambusters) Ace Academics, Inc.

Aigner-Clark, Julie. La Guardería de Idiomas (The Guarderia Language) 2004. (Baby Einstein Ser.). (SPA., Illus.). 16p. (J). bds. *(978-970-718-153-3(2),* Silver Dolphin en Español) Advanced Marketing, S. de R. L. de C. V.

Amery, H. First Thousand Words. 2004. (SPA.). 70p. (J). pap. 9.99 *(978-0-7945-0463-2(9))* EDC Publishing.

—First Thousand Words in Spanish IL. rev. ed. 2004. (First Thousand Words Ser.). (SPA & ENG.). 64p. (J). 12.99 *(978-0-7945-0284-3(9));* lib. bdg. 20.99 *(978-1-58086-564-7(X))* EDC Publishing.

Amery, H. & Cartwright, S. First Spanish Word Book. 2004. (Treasury of Farmyard Tales Ser.). (SPA & ENG.). 48p. (J). 10.95 *(978-0-7945-0476-2(0))* EDC Publishing.

Anaya, Rudolfo A. How Chile Came to New Mexico. Nasario, Garcia, tr. from ENG. Nicolas, Otero, illus. 2014. (SPA & ENG.). 48p. (J). (gr. -1-3). 24.95 *(978-1-936744-20-6(1),* Rio Grande Bks.) LPD Pr.

Anderson, Jill, ed. Let's Go on Safari!/Vamos de Safari! Utton, Peter, illus. 2005. (Word Play/Juegos con Pala Ser.). (ENG.). 20p. (J). (gr. -1-17). bds. 6.95 *(978-1-58728-522-6(3))* Cooper Square Publishing Llc.

Animals Habitats, 1 vol., 1. 2015. (Our Wonderful World Ser.). (ENG & SPA.). 8p. (J). (gr. 2-4). pap. 9.35 *(978-1-5081-1251-8(7),* 8381f755-80e3-4e2c-a12f-372821758bec, Rosen Classroom) Rosen Publishing Group, Inc., The.

Appleby, Alex. Lo Que Oigo / What I Hear, 1 vol. 2014. (Mis Cinco Sentidos / My Five Senses Ser.). (SPA & ENG.). 24p. (J). (gr. k-k). 24.27 *(978-1-4824-0869-0(4),* 5af715a4-fe82-4a1d-9bb7-f08d22b7bbf8) Stevens, Gareth Publishing LLLP.

La Arana. 2003. 23.95 *(978-0-673-77156-8(3))* Celebration Pr.

Baker, Mary. English - Spanish Counting Book. Mason, Alfonso & Mason, Ruth, illus. 2008. 24p. pap. 24.95 *(978-1-60672-035-6(X))* America Star Bks.

Barfell, Judith A. Learn & Sign Funtime-Beginnings-Spanish. 2005. (Beginnings Ser.: Bk. 1). (SPA.). (J). per. 14.95 *(978-0-9753717-2-5(X))* Learn & Sign Funtime Bks.

Barron's Educational Series & Rabley, Stephen. A New World/Un Nuevo Mundo: Spanish/English Edition. Lopez, David, illus. 2010. (Let's Read! Spanish-English Ser.). (ENG.). 32p. (J). (gr. k-3). 17.44 *(978-0-7641-4471-4(5),* B.E.S. Publishing) Peterson's.

Bauman, Carey. God Controls the Storm. Bauman, Carey, tr. 2007. (Little Jewel Book Ser.). (Illus.). 24p. (J). (gr. 2). pap. 2.70 *(978-0-7399-2396-2(X))* Rod & Staff Pubs., Inc.

Beaton, Clare, illus. English-Spanish Bilingual First Books, 6 bks. (J). lib. bdg. 86.70 *(978-1-56674-944-2(1))* Forest Hse. Publishing Co., Inc.

Beck, Jeanine. First Spanish: Mi Casa: An Introduction to Commonly Used Spanish Words & Phrases Around the Home, with 500 Lively Photographs. 2016. (Illus.). 64p. (J). (gr. -1-12). 12.99 *(978-1-86147-697-5(3),* Armadillo) Anness Publishing GBR. Dist: National Bk. Network.

—Mi Casa: An Introduction to Commonly Used Spanish Words & Phrases Around the Home, with 500 Lively Photographs. 2008. (Illus.). 64p. pap. 7.99 *(978-1-84476-525-6(3))* Anness Publishing GBR. Dist: National Bk. Network.

Berkes, Marianne. The Tortoise & Hare's Amazing Race, 1 vol. Morrison, Cathy, illus. 2015. (ENG & SPA.). 32p. (J). (gr. k-3). 17.95 *(978-1-62855-635-3(8))* Arbordale Publishing.

Berry, Shilo. E-Mails Home. 2008. (Illus.). 24p. (J). pap. 10.95 *(978-1-59646-565-7(4))* Dingles & Co.

Brandenberg, Aliki & Aliki. La Fiesta Medieval. (SPA.). 32p. 15.95 *(978-84-261-2696-2(0))* Juventud, Editorial ESP. Dist: Distribooks, Inc.

Brooks, Felicity. Easy Spanish Words Sticker Book. 2012. (First Sticker Language Bks). 24p. (J). pap. 6.99 *(978-0-7945-3323-6(X),* Usborne) EDC Publishing.

—Everyday Words in Spanish. Litchfield, Jo, illus. rev. ed. 2004. (Everyday Words Ser.). 48p. (J). pap. 9.95 *(978-0-7945-0881-4(2),* Usborne) EDC Publishing.

—My First Spanish Word Book. 2015. (My First Word Bks.). (ENG.). 20p. (J). 9.99 *(978-0-7945-3493-6(7),* Usborne) EDC Publishing.

Budds, Sam. 1000 First Words in Spanish. Lacome, Susie, illus. 2013. 96p. (J). (gr. k-4). 12.99 *(978-1-84322-959-9(5))* Anness Publishing GBR. Dist: National Bk. Network.

Burke, David. GOLDILOCKS (Spanish to English - Level 2) Learn ENGLISH Through Fairy Tales. 2007. (SPA & ENG.). (J). per. 14.95 incl. audio compact disk *(978-1-891888-96-0(X))* Slangman Publishing.

Cacciapuoti, Aurora. Let's Learn Spanish: First Words for Everyone (Learning Spanish for Children; Spanish for Preschooler; Spanish Learning Book) 2020. (ENG., Illus.). 48p. (J). 12.99 *(978-1-4521-6626-1(9))* Chronicle Bks. LLC.

Camarena, Cathy & Ruff, Gloria B. Valeria y Victor. 2006. (Primeros Sonidos Ser.). (J). pap. 48.42 *(978-1-59679-908-0(0))* ABDO Publishing Co.

S

Canetti, Yanitzia. Colores escolares/School Colors: A World of Color. 2010. (ENG & SPA.). 24p. (J). pap. 6.99 (978-1-59835-272-6(5), BrickHouse Education) Cambridge BrickHouse, Inc.

—Colorful Shapes/Figuras de Colores: A World of Color. 2010. (SPA & ENG.). 24p. (J). pap. 6.99 (978-1-59835-278-8(4), BrickHouse Education) Cambridge BrickHouse, Inc.

—Colorful Sights Paisajes de Colores: A World of Color. 2010. (SPA & ENG.). 24p. (J). pap. 6.99 (978-1-59835-280-1(6), BrickHouse Education) Cambridge BrickHouse, Inc.

—Colors on Colors/Colores Sobre Colores: A World of Color. 2010. (SPA & ENG.). 24p. (J). pap. 6.99 (978-1-59835-276-4(8), BrickHouse Education) Cambridge BrickHouse, Inc.

—Tasty Colors/Colores de Sabores: A World of Color. 2010. (SPA & ENG.). 24p. (J). pap. 6.99 (978-1-59835-270-2(9), BrickHouse Education) Cambridge BrickHouse, Inc.

Carole Marsh. Uh,Oh,Amigo! Spanish for Kids. 2004. (Little Linguist Ser.). 32p. (gr. 2-6). pap. 5.95 (978-0-635-02428-2(4)) Gallopade International.

Carson, Jana. We Both Read Bilingual Edition-About Space/Acerca Del Espacio. 2011. (SPA., Illus.). 44p. (J). pap. 5.99 (978-1-60115-052-3(0)) Treasure Bay, Inc.

Chano: Individual Title Six-Packs. (Literatura 2000 Ser.). (gr. 2-3). 33.00 (978-0-7635-0194-5(8)) Rigby Education.

Chappell, Jackie. Our School Is Like A Family. 2007. (ENG., Illus.). 16p. (gr. k-2). 28.50 (978-1-60472-110-2(3)) Rourke Educational Media.

Charlie: Individual Title Six-Packs. (Literatura 2000 Ser.). (gr. 2-3). 33.00 (978-0-7635-0221-8(9)) Rigby Education.

La Charreada. 2003. 23.95 (978-0-673-77782-9(0)) Celebration Pr.

Chiquilibros: Activity Masters. (SPA.). (gr. -1-1). 26.00 (978-0-7635-2366-4(6)); 21.00 (978-0-7635-2557-6(X)) Rigby Education.

Chiquilibros: Add-to Packs. (SPA.). (gr. k-1). 61.00 (978-0-7635-8587-7(4)); 30.00 (978-0-7635-8585-3(8)); 30.00 (978-0-7635-8586-0(6)); 30.00 (978-0-7635-8584-6(X)) Rigby Education.

Chiquilibros: Chiquicuentos Complete Package. (SPA.). (gr. -1-1). 250.00 (978-0-7635-8571-6(8)) Rigby Education.

Chiquilibros: Chiquicuentos Grupo A Add-to Pack. (SPA.). (gr. -1-1). 125.00 (978-0-7635-8568-6(8)) Rigby Education.

Chiquilibros: Chiquicuentos Grupo B Add-to Pack. (SPA.). (gr. -1-1). 125.00 (978-0-7635-8569-3(6)) Rigby Education.

Chiquilibros: Cuentos listos Complete Packages. (SPA.). (gr. k-1). 114.00 (978-0-7635-8582-2(3)); 114.00 (978-0-7635-8581-5(5)); 114.00 (978-0-7635-8580-8(7)); 203.00 (978-0-7635-8583-9(1)) Rigby Education.

Chiquilibros: Grupo A Activity Guide. (SPA.). (gr. k-1). 18.00 (978-0-7635-2400-5(X)) Rigby Education.

Chiquilibros: Grupo B Activity Guide. (SPA.). (gr. k-1). 18.00 (978-0-7635-2401-2(8)) Rigby Education.

Chiquilibros: Grupo C Activity Guide. (SPA.). (gr. k-1). 18.00 (978-0-7635-2402-9(6)) Rigby Education.

Chiquilibros: Grupo D Activity Guide. (SPA.). (gr. k-1). 18.00 (978-0-7635-2403-6(4)) Rigby Education.

Chiquilibros: Grupos consonanticos Add-to Pack. (SPA.). (gr. -1-1). 38.00 (978-0-7635-8579-2(3)) Rigby Education.

Chiquilibros: Grupos consonanticos Complete Package. (SPA.). (gr. -1-1). 166.00 (978-0-7635-8578-5(5)) Rigby Education.

Chiquilibros: Silabas Add-to Pack. (SPA.). (gr. -1-1). 78.00 (978-0-7635-8576-1(9)) Rigby Education.

Chiquilibros: Silabas Complete Package. (SPA.). (gr. -1-1). 307.00 (978-0-7635-8577-8(7)) Rigby Education.

Ciencia Física (Physical Science) 2011. (Ciencia Física/Physical Science Ser.). (MUL.). 24p. (gr. k-1). lib. bdg. 109.28 (978-1-4296-6908-5(X)) Capstone.

Clothes-Ropa Bilingual Board Book. 2008. (ENG & SPA.). (J). pap. 5.99 (978-0-9727886-9-4(7)) Osmosis, LLC.

Collins UK. A Volar Pupil Book Level 4: Primary Spanish for the Caribbean. 2015. (ENG.). 72p. (J). (gr. 3-4). pap. 13.99 (978-0-00-813637-6(8)) HarperCollins Pubs. Ltd. GBR. Dist: Independent Pubs. Group.

El Coqui. 2003. 23.95 (978-0-673-77382-1(5)) Celebration Pr.

El Coqui: Poems, Rhymes, & Songs Listening Packs. 2003. 34.50 (978-0-673-58630-8(8)) Celebration Pr.

Coupe, Robert. Antiguo Egipto/Acient Egypt. 2011. 16p. pap. (978-607-404-320-4(5), Silver Dolphin en Español) Advanced Marketing, S. de R. L. de C. V.

Cuaderno Suenos y Palabras. (SPA.). (J). (gr. k-6). wbk. ed. 18.00 (978-958-04-7094-6(4)); Vol. 2. (gr. k-6). wbk. ed. 18.00 (978-958-04-7095-3(2)); Vol. 3. (gr. k-6). wbk. ed. 18.00 (978-958-04-7096-0(0)); Vol. 4. (gr. k-6). wbk. ed. 18.00 (978-958-04-7737-2(X)); Vol. 5. (gr. k-6). wbk. ed. 18.00 (978-958-04-7738-9(8)); Vol. 6. (gr. k-6). wbk. ed. 18.00 (978-958-04-7739-6(6)); Vol. 7. (gr. 7-12). wbk. ed. 18.00 (978-958-04-5653-7(4)); Vol. 8. (gr. 7-12). wbk. ed. 18.00 (978-958-04-5654-4(2)); Vol. 9. (gr. 7-12). wbk. ed. 18.00 (978-958-04-5655-1(0)); Vol. 10. (gr. 7-12). wbk. ed. 18.00 (978-958-04-5956-9(8)); Vol. 11. (gr. 7-12). wbk. ed. 18.00 (978-958-04-5958-3(4)); Vol. 12. (gr. 7-12). wbk. ed. 18.00 (978-958-04-5960-6(6)) Norma S.A. COL. Dist: Distribuidora Norma, Inc.

Cuando el senor Rey ronco: When Mr Quinn Snored. 2005. (Take-Home Bks.). (SPA.). (YA). (gr. -1-3). 15.75 (978-0-8215-1207-4(2)) Sadlier, William H. Inc.

Cuidando a los animales/Keeping Baby Animals Safe. 2005. (Libros en Espanol Para Ninos Ser.). (SPA.). (YA). (gr. -1-1). 11.97 (978-0-8215-0996-8(9)) Sadlier, William H. Inc.

Dayton, Connor. Tricks with Bikes/Trucos con la Moto, 1 vol. Alaman, Eduardo, tr. 2007. (Motorcycles: Made for Speed / Motocicletas: a Toda Velocidad Ser.). (SPA & ENG., Illus.). 24p. (J). (gr. 1-1). lib. bdg. 26.27 (978-1-4042-7615-4(7), 114c80ad-5625-4254-916c-744d9b09eb48) Rosen Publishing Group, Inc., The.

Deacon, Carol. Manualidades Divertidas. 2003. (SPA.). 64p. 12.98 (978-1-4054-1483-8(9)) Parragon, Inc.

Dee, Nora. Spanish Words at the Zoo, 1 vol., Vol. 1. 2013. (Learn My Language! Spanish Ser.). (ENG.). 24p. (J). (gr. 1-2). 25.27 (978-1-4824-0355-8(2), d63433d1-6aec-4924-af1b-ee016c0578fc); pap. 9.15 (978-1-4824-0358-9(7), 2d22ae17-b141-49ba-ac74-7b9351482ec2) Stevens, Gareth Publishing LLLP.

Denmark-Allen, Eva. I Was, I Am, i Will Be! - Yo Fui! Yo soy! Yo Sere! 2007. (ENG & SPA., Illus.). 56p. (J). per. 12.00 (978-0-9792016-8-4(3)) Professional Publishing Hse. LLC.

Dingles, Molly. Blue as a Blueberry/Azul como un Arandano. Velez, Walter, illus. 2003. (SPA.). 32p. (J). lib. bdg. 21.65 (978-1-891997-28-0(9)) Dingles & Co.

—Brown as an Acorn. Velez, Walter, illus. 2004. (Community of Color Ser.). 32p. (J). pap. 10.95 (978-1-59646-346-2(5)) Dingles & Co.

—Brown as an Acorn/Marrón como una Bellota. Velez, Walter, illus. 2004. (Community of Color Ser.).Tr. of Marrón como una Bellota. (ENG & SPA.). 32p. (J). lib. bdg. 21.65 (978-1-891997-37-2(8)) Dingles & Co.

—Gray as a Dolphin. Velez, Walter, illus. 2004. (Community of Color Ser.). 32p. (J). pap. 10.95 (978-1-59646-342-4(2)) Dingles & Co.

—Gray as a Dolphin/Gris como un Delfín. Velez, Walter, illus. 2004. (Community of Color Ser.).Tr. of Gris como un Delfín. (ENG & SPA.). 32p. (J). pap. 10.95 (978-1-59646-092-8(X)); lib. bdg. 21.65 (978-1-891997-58-7(0)) Dingles & Co.

—Green as a Frog/Verde como una Rana. Velez, Walter, illus. 2003. (Community of Color Ser.). (SPA & ENG.). 32p. (J). lib. bdg. 21.65 (978-1-891997-29-7(7), 1228150) Dingles & Co.

—Green as a Frog/Vert comme une Grenouille. Velez, Walter, illus. 2004. (Community of Color Ser.).Tr. of Vert comme une Grenouille. (ENG & FRE.). 32p. (J). lib. bdg. 21.65 (978-1-891997-71-6(8)) Dingles & Co.

—Red as a Fire Truck/Rojo como un camion de Bomberos. Velez, Walter, illus. 2003. (Community of Color Ser.).Tr. of Rojo Como un Camion de Bomberos. (SPA.). 32p. (J). lib. bdg. 21.65 (978-1-891997-27-3(0)) Dingles & Co.

—Yellow as a Lemon/Amarillo como un Limon. Velez, Walter, illus. 2003. (Community of Color Ser.). (SPA.). 32p. (J). lib. bdg. 21.65 (978-1-891997-30-3(0)) Dingles & Co.

Dorling Kindersley Smart Steps: DK Smart Steps Complete Package. 2003. cd-rom 123.95 (978-0-673-61614-2(2)) Celebration Pr.

Dorn, Susy. Cantemos en Español Song-Book: Spanish Learning Song-Book for Children. Carbajal, Diego, illus. 2006. (SPA.). (J). (978-0-9764010-6-3(1)) Susy Dorn Productions, LLC.

—Sal y Pimienta Song-Book: Spanish Learning Song-Book for Children. Carbajal, Diego, illus. 2006. (SPA.). (J). (978-0-9764010-7-0(X)) Susy Dorn Productions, LLC.

Downing, Julie, illus. All the Ways I Love You (bilingual Edition) 2005. (SPA & ENG.). 10p. (J). 8.95 (978-1-58117-335-2(0), Intervisual/Piggy Toes) Bendon, Inc.

Drawing Conclusions & Inferences Spanish Version, Gr. 1-3. 2005. (J). per. (978-1-58232-148-6(5)) ECS Learning Systems, Inc.

Drawing Conclusions & Inferences Spanish Version, Gr. 4-5. 2005. (J). per. (978-1-58232-143-1(4)) ECS Learning Systems, Inc.

Early Macken, JoAnn. Penguins / Los Pinguinos, 1 vol. 2004. (Animals I See at the Zoo / Animales Que Veo en el Zoológico Ser.). (ENG & SPA., Illus.). 24p. (J). (gr. k-2). pap. 9.15 (978-0-8368-4006-3(2), 74d6e910-2d98-4e43-adf6-203bc5265399, Weekly Reader Leveled Readers) Stevens, Gareth Publishing LLLP.

Egan, Tracie. Cynthia Ann Parker: Cautiva de los Comanches, 1 vol. Gonzalez, Tomas, tr. 2003. (Grandes Personajes en la Historia de Los Estados Unidos (Famous People in American History) Ser.). (SPA.). 32p. (gr. 3-4). pap. 10.00 (978-0-8239-4225-1(2), 5843e5b5-d80d-4f57-9417-a17007949bba); (Illus.). lib. bdg. 29.13 (978-0-8239-4131-5(0), 507592c3-ab4c-44d1-b4e0-abe5e02fb61a, Editorial Buenas Letras) Rosen Publishing Group, Inc., The.

Ellis, Martyn & Martín, Rosa Maria. Aventura Nueva, Bk. 1. 2003. (ENG., Illus.). 224p. pap., stu. ed. 42.50 (978-0-340-86880-5(5)) Hodder Education Group GBR. Dist: Trans-Atlantic Pubns., Inc.

Elya, Susan Middleton. La Princesa & the Pea. Martinez-Neal, Juana, illus. 2017. 32p. (J). (gr. -1-3). 18.99 (978-0-399-25156-6(1), G.P. Putnam's Sons Books for Young Readers) Penguin Young Readers Group.

—Say Hola to Spanish at the Circus, 1 vol. Lopez, Loretta, illus. 2013. (ENG.). 32p. (J). (gr. k-5). pap. 10.95 (978-1-58430-042-7(6), leelowbooks) Lee & Low Bks., Inc.

—Say Hola to Spanish, Otra Vez (Say Hola to Spanish (Paperback)) (English & Spanish Edition), 1 vol. 2013. (ENG., Illus.). 32p. (J). (gr. k-5). pap. 9.95 (978-1-880000-83-0(0), leelowbooks) Lee & Low Bks., Inc.

—Say Hola to Spanish (Say Hola to Spanish (Paperback)) (English & Spanish Edition), 1 vol. 2013. (ENG., Illus.). 32p. (J). (gr. k-5). pap. 10.95 (978-1-880000-64-9(4), leelowbooks) Lee & Low Bks., Inc.

En el Bosque. 2003. 23.95 (978-0-673-77175-9(X)) Celebration Pr.

En el Mercado. 2003. 23.95 (978-0-673-77790-4(1)) Celebration Pr.

En Mi Jardin. 2003. 23.95 (978-0-673-77131-5(8)) Celebration Pr.

El Enanito Maloigoloso. 2003. (J). (gr. -1-2). 28.95 (978-0-673-77377-7(9)) Celebration Pr.

Estoy Enojado. 2003. (J). (gr. -1-2). 23.95 (978-0-673-77391-3(4)) Celebration Pr.

Estrada, Altamira Perea. Un Abecedario Muy Sabroso. (SPA.). (J). pap. 4.76 net. (978-0-590-93319-3(1)) Scholastic, Inc.

Fact & Opinion Spanish Version, Gr. 1-3. 2005. (J). per. (978-1-58232-149-3(3)) ECS Learning Systems, Inc.

Fact & Opinion Spanish Version, Gr. 4-5. 2005. (Spanish Version Ser.). (J). per. (978-1-58232-144-8(2)) ECS Learning Systems, Inc.

Fatus, Sophie & París, Merbxe. My Big Barefoot Book of Spanish & English Words. 2016. (SPA & ENG.). (J). pap. (978-1-78285-275-9(1)) Barefoot Bks., Inc.

Fedoruk, Dennis, prod. Bilingual Baby - Flashcard Set - Spanish. 2013. (SPA.). (J). 7.99 (978-1-892703-75-0(0)) Small Fry Beginnings.

First Explorers Primeros Exploradores Set 1: Spanish - 1 Each of 12 Student Books. (First Explorers. Primeros Exploradores Nonfiction Sets Ser.). (gr. 1-2). 59.95 (978-0-7699-1370-4(9)) Shortland Pubns. (U. S. A.) Inc.

First Explorers Primeros Exploradores Set 1: Spanish - 1 Each of 12 Student Books, 1 Each of 12 Lesson Plans. (First Explorers. Primeros Exploradores Nonfiction Sets Ser.). (gr. 1-2). 107.95 (978-0-7699-1368-1(7)) Shortland Pubns. (U. S. A.) Inc.

First Explorers Primeros Exploradores Set 1: Spanish - 6 Each of 12 Student Books, 1 Each of 12 Lesson Plans. (First Explorers. Primeros Exploradores Nonfiction Sets Ser.). (SPA.). (gr. 1-2). 407.50 (978-0-7699-1372-8(5)) Shortland Pubns. (U. S. A.) Inc.

First Explorers Primeros Exploradores Set 2: Spanish - 1 Each of 12 Student Books. (First Explorers. Primeros Exploradores Nonfiction Sets Ser.). (gr. 1-2). 67.50 (978-0-7699-1371-1(7)) Shortland Pubns. (U. S. A.) Inc.

First Explorers Primeros Exploradores Set 2: Spanish - 1 Each of 12 Student Books, 1 Each of 12 Lesson Plans. (First Explorers. Primeros Exploradores Nonfiction Sets Ser.). (gr. 1-2). 115.50 (978-0-7699-1369-8(5)) Shortland Pubns. (U. S. A.) Inc.

First Explorers Primeros Exploradores Set 2: Spanish - 6 Each of 12 Student Books, 1 Each of 12 Lesson Plans. (First Explorers. Primeros Exploradores Nonfiction Sets Ser.). (SPA.). (gr. 1-2). 452.50 (978-0-7699-1373-5(3)) Shortland Pubns. (U. S. A.) Inc.

First Explorers Primeros Exploradores Sets 1-2: Spanish - 1 Each of 24 Student Books, 1 Each of 24 Lesson Plans. (First Explorers. Primeros Exploradores Nonfiction Sets Ser.). (gr. 1-2). 223.50 (978-0-7699-1358-2(X)) Shortland Pubns. (U. S. A.) Inc.

First Explorers Primeros Exploradores Sets 1-2: Spanish - 6 Each of 24 Student Books, 1 Each of 24 Lesson Plans. (First Explorers. Primeros Exploradores Nonfiction Sets Ser.). (SPA.). (gr. 1-2). 816.95 (978-0-7699-1367-4(9)) Shortland Pubns. (U. S. A.) Inc.

Flor Ada, Alma & Campoy, F. Isabel, contrib. by. Steps. (Literature Collection of Gateways to the Sun Ser.). 32p. (J). (gr. k-6). pap. 13.95 (978-1-59437-716-7(2)) Santillana USA Publishing Co., Inc.

Friends Are Forever: Individual Title Six-Packs. (Literatura 2000 Ser.). (gr. 2-3). 33.00 (978-0-7635-0169-3(7)) Rigby Education.

Fui Al Mar. 2003. 23.95 (978-0-673-77162-9(8)) Celebration Pr.

Fulcher, Roz. Color & Learn Easy Spanish Phrases for Kids. 2015. (Dover Little Activity Bks.). (ENG.). 64p. (J). (gr. k-3). pap. 2.99 (978-0-486-79759-5(7), 797597) Dover Pubns., Inc.

—My First Spanish Lesson: Color & Learn! 2019. (Dover Bilingual Books for Kids Ser.). (ENG., Illus.). 64p. (J). (gr. k-3). pap. 4.99 (978-0-486-83309-5(7), 833097) Dover Pubns., Inc.

Ganeri, Anita. Volcanes y terremotos/Earthquakes & Volcanoes. 2011. 16p. pap. (978-607-404-319-8(1), Silver Dolphin en Español) Advanced Marketing, S. de R. L. de C. V.

Getting the Sequence Spanish Version, Gr. 1-3. 2005. (J). per. (978-1-58232-146-2(9)) ECS Learning Systems, Inc.

Getting the Sequence Spanish Version, Gr. 4-5. 2005. (J). per. (978-1-58232-141-7(8)) ECS Learning Systems, Inc.

Gibbons, Gail. De Sol a Sol.Tr. of Sun Up, Sun Down. (SPA., Illus.). (J). (gr. 1-3). pap. 3.96 net. (978-0-590-46903-6(7), SO30343, Scholastic en Espanol) Scholastic, Inc.

Glencoe McGraw-Hill Staff. Glencoe Middle School Spanish: ¿Cómo Te Va? B Nivel Azul. 2005. (Glencoe Spanish Ser.). (ENG.). (gr. 6-8). stu. ed. 128.36 incl. cd-rom (978-0-07-874279-8(X), 007874279X) McGraw-Hill Higher Education.

Glencoe McGraw-Hill Staff, creator. Repaso: A Review Workbook for Grammar, Communication, & Culture. 2nd ed. 2004. (SPA., Illus.). 719p. (gr. 6-12). per., wbk. ed. 26.64 (978-0-07-846050-0(6), 9780078460500) Glencoe/McGraw-Hill.

Gómez, Carlos Humberto. Workbook 1. (Coleccion Nos Comunicamos). (SPA & ENG.). (J). (gr. 1). pap., wbk. ed. 11.50 (978-958-04-2074-3(2), 01021255) Norma S.A. COL. Dist: Continental Bk. Co., Inc.

—Workbook 2. (Coleccion Nos Comunicamos). (SPA & ENG.). (J). (gr. 2). pap., wbk. ed. 11.50 (978-958-04-2075-0(0), 01021256) Norma S.A. COL. Dist: Continental Bk. Co., Inc.

—Workbook 3. (Coleccion Nos Comunicamos). (SPA & ENG.). (J). (gr. 3). pap., wbk. ed. 11.50 (978-958-04-2076-7(9), 01021257) Norma S.A. COL. Dist: Continental Bk. Co., Inc.

—Workbook 4. (Coleccion Nos Comunicamos). (SPA & ENG.). (J). (gr. 4). pap., wbk. ed. 11.50 (978-958-04-1784-2(9), 01021258) Norma S.A. COL. Dist: Continental Bk. Co., Inc.

—Workbook 6. (Coleccion Nos Comunicamos). (SPA & ENG.). (J). (gr. 6). pap., wbk. ed. 11.50 (978-958-04-1791-0(1), 01021260) Norma S.A. COL. Dist: Continental Bk. Co., Inc.

—Workbook Kindergarten. (Coleccion Nos Comunicamos). (SPA & ENG.). (J). pap., wbk. ed. 11.50 (978-958-04-2035-4(1), 01021254) Norma S.A. COL. Dist: Continental Bk. Co., Inc.

Gose, Senora. Flip Flop Spanish: Ages 3-5: Level 2. 2008. (Illus.). 108p. (J). spiral bd. 29.95 (978-0-9801772-0-6(0)) Flip n Flop Learning, LLC.

Grades 1-2 Complete Pinata/Mas Pinata Package. 2003. 1943.95 (978-0-673-58717-6(7)) Celebration Pr.

Grainger, Lesley, illus. My First Spanish Words Sticker Activity Book/Mi Primer Libro de Palabras en Espanol. 2018. (ENG.). 32p. (J). pap. 6.99 (978-1-68119-614-5(X), 900179036, Bloomsbury Activity Bks.) Bloomsbury Publishing USA.

Guy, Ginger Foglesong. Perros! Perros!/Dogs! Dogs! Bilingual English-Spanish. Glick, Sharon, illus. 2006. (ENG.). 32p. (J). (gr. -1-3). 17.99 (978-0-06-083574-3(5), Greenwillow Bks.) HarperCollins Pubs.

Harte, May. Halloween, 1 vol. Gonzalez, Tomas, tr. 2003. (My Library of Holidays / Mi Biblioteca de Celebraciones Ser.). (SPA & ENG., Illus.). 24p. (J). (gr. 1-1). lib. bdg. 22.27 (978-1-4042-7529-4(0), e0e6a4a7-e699-4132-9889-197f8cd76824, PowerKids Pr.) Rosen Publishing Group, Inc., The.

Hayhurst, Chris. Sitting Bull: Sioux Chief = Toro Sentado: Jefe Sioux, 1 vol. de la Vega, Eida, tr. 2003. (Famous People in American History / Grandes Personajes en la Historia de Los Estados Unidos Ser.). (ENG & SPA., Illus.). 32p. (gr. 2-3). lib. bdg. 29.13 (978-0-8239-4168-1(X), 7c2b3e50-df9d-4b60-95e9-904698643800, Editorial Buenas Letras) Rosen Publishing Group, Inc., The.

—Toro Sentado: Jefe Sioux, 1 vol. 2003. (Grandes Personajes en la Historia de Los Estados Unidos (Famous People in American History) Ser.). (SPA.). 32p. (gr. 3-4). pap. 10.00 (978-0-8239-4238-1(4), 3bb38c5c-d5ef-4f35-9217-a163596589ee); (Illus.). lib. bdg. 29.13 (978-0-8239-4144-5(2), 76f2b3f4-2601-49c2-9de3-680b1ae6835e, Editorial Buenas Letras) Rosen Publishing Group, Inc., The.

Hazan, Maurice, creator. El Camino: Practicing Everyday Vocabulary. (SPA.). (J). 124.95 (978-1-932770-44-5(5), SG5) Symtalk, Inc.

—The Conversation Game for Spanish. (SPA.). (YA). 124.95 (978-1-932770-47-6(X), SG8) Symtalk, Inc.

—Dime quien Es: Spanish Dialogues Level 1. (SPA.). (J). 134.95 (978-1-932770-43-8(7), SG4) Symtalk, Inc.

—Dime quien Es: Spanish Dialogues Level 2. (SPA.). (J). 134.95 (978-1-932770-45-2(3), SG6) Symtalk, Inc.

—Dime quien Es: Spanish Dialogues Level 3. (SPA.). (YA). 199.95 (978-1-932770-55-1(0), SG16) Symtalk, Inc.

—Frases y Fotos: Long Sentence Bingo. (SPA.). (YA). 124.95 (978-1-932770-46-9(1), SG7) Symtalk, Inc.

—Object, Color & Number Bingo. (SPA.). (J). 124.95 (978-1-932770-41-4(0), SG2) Symtalk, Inc.

—Los Perdidos: Directions in the City. (SPA.). (YA). 199.95 (978-1-932770-54-4(2), SG15) Symtalk, Inc.

—The Prom Game for Spanish. (YA). 44.95 (978-1-932770-51-3(8), SG12) Symtalk, Inc.

—Resto Presto. (SPA.). (J). 169.95 (978-1-932770-42-1(9), SG3) Symtalk, Inc.

Heller, Daryl. Hanukkah/Januca, 1 vol. 2003. (My Library of Holidays / Mi Biblioteca de Celebraciones Ser.). (SPA & ENG., Illus.). 24p. (J). (gr. 1-1). lib. bdg. 22.27 (978-1-4042-7525-6(8), 2187698e-4640-4433-a7f6-222405da8ffb, PowerKids Pr.) Rosen Publishing Group, Inc., The.

Holland, Gini. Alive & Not Alive / Vivo y No Vivo, 1 vol. 2007. (I Know Opposites / Conceptos Contrarios Ser.). (SPA & ENG., Illus.). 16p. (gr. k-2). pap. 6.30 (978-0-8368-8308-4(X), c2e80e72-8498-4d2e-a788-c8d25a7094cd); lib. bdg. 21.67 (978-0-8368-8303-9(9), 1def279f-722c-4e9a-bc9a-0e458e5edf24) Stevens, Gareth Publishing LLLP. (Weekly Reader Leveled Readers).

—Hot & Cold / Caliente y Frío, 1 vol. 2007. (I Know Opposites / Conceptos Contrarios Ser.). (SPA & ENG.). 16p. (gr. k-2). lib. bdg. 21.67 (978-0-8368-8304-6(7), d0357d1d-e518-4359-a91c-aa0ee1f5ed73, Weekly Reader Leveled Readers) Stevens, Gareth Publishing LLLP.

Holt, Rinehart and Winston Staff. Expresate: Premier Online Edition. 6th ed. Date not set. (SPA.). 76.80 (978-0-03-074564-5(0));Level 1. 75.13 (978-0-03-074563-8(2)) Holt McDougal.

HOP, LLC. Hooked on Spanish. 2006. 64.99 (978-1-931020-92-3(2)); 99.99 (978-1-931020-75-6(2)) HOP, LLC.

—Hooked on Spanish Beginning Spanish. 2006. 24.99 (978-1-933863-14-6(5)) HOP, LLC.

Howard, Linda & Dockray, Tracy Arah, illus. Mi Gran Libro de Palabras Play-Doh. 2006. (SPA.). 10p. (J). (gr. -1-4). reprint ed. 10.00 (978-1-4223-5586-2(1)) DIANE Publishing Co.

Hudson, Amanda. This Is My Ball / Ésta Es Mi Pelota, 1 vol. 2008. (Our Toys / Nuestros Juguetes Ser.). (SPA & ENG., Illus.). 16p. (J). (gr. k-k). lib. bdg. 21.67 (978-0-8368-9256-7(9), 7a578453-083d-411a-aee4-e2afbde908e1, Weekly Reader Leveled Readers) Stevens, Gareth Publishing LLLP.

—This Is My Bear / Éste Es Mi Oso, 1 vol. 2008. (Our Toys / Nuestros Juguetes Ser.). (SPA & ENG.). 16p. (gr. k-k). pap. 6.30 (978-0-8368-9356-4(5), c0f08e9a-97e6-4d05-a8ab-c3e7ee4c5936); (Illus.). (J). lib. bdg. 21.67 (978-0-8368-9257-4(7), f77425f0-d46b-4c49-bca2-e13c85e883ff) Stevens, Gareth Publishing LLLP. (Weekly Reader Leveled Readers).

Humbach. Expresate: Premier Online Edition. 6th ed. Date not set. (SPA.). Level 1. stu. ed. 19.93 (978-0-03-040457-3(6))Level 1a. stu. ed. 14.60 (978-0-03-040449-8(5))Level 1b. 14.60 (978-0-03-040453-5(3))Level 2. stu. ed. 19.93 (978-0-03-040459-7(2))Level 3. stu. ed. 19.93 (978-0-03-040463-4(0)) Holt McDougal.

—Ven Conmigo: Online Edition, Level 3. 3rd ed. 2003. (SPA.). 71.40 (978-0-03-036149-4(4)) Holt McDougal.

Hutchins, J. Spanish First Words / Primeras Palabras en Español (Bilingual) (Bilingual Edition) 2013. (SPA., Illus.). 32p. (J). (gr. -1-3). pap. 4.99 (978-0-545-56328-4(3), Scholastic en Espanol) Scholastic, Inc.

—Spanish First Words (Primeras Palabras en Espanol) 2013. (SPA & ENG.). lib. bdg. 14.75 (978-0-606-32400-7(3)) Turtleback.

I'm Learning Spanish, Vol. 3. 2005. (J). 12.99 (978-1-894677-77-6(3)) Kidzup Productions.

Johnson, J. Bradley. Surround Yourself with Essential Vacation Spanish. 2005. per. 49.99 (978-0-9765236-2-8(0)) Innovative Language, LLC.

—Surround Yourself with Spanish: Beginner Level. 2005. (ENG & SPA.). 156p. (C). per. 99.99 (978-0-9765236-0-4(4)) Innovative Language, LLC.

—Surround Yourself with Spanish Conversations, Vol. 1. 2005. (ENG & SPA.). 92p. (C). per. 39.99 (978-0-9765236-1-1(2)) Innovative Language, LLC.

Jordan, Sara. Fonetica Funky y Algo Mas, 2 vols., Kit. 2007. (ENG.). 48p. (J). (gr. k-4). 17.95 (978-1-55386-080-8(2), 1553860802) Jordan, Sara Publishing.

Jordan, Sara & Gomez, Patricia. Bilingual Beginners: English-Spanish, 2 vols. abr. ed. 2010. (SPA.). 64p. (J). 17.95 (978-1-55386-114-0(0), 1553861140) Jordan, Sara Publishing.

Kelley, Michelle. Rules, Rules, Rules. 2007. (ENG., Illus.). 16p. (gr. k-2). 28.50 (978-1-60472-111-9(1)) Rourke Educational Media.

Kennedy, Robert. Spanish Words in the House, 1 vol., Vol. 1. 2013. (Learn My Language! Spanish Ser.). (ENG.). 24p. (J). (gr. 1-2). 25.27 (978-1-4824-0360-2(9), 2bd02798-6614-4f99-b91e-61d6e016087d); pap. 9.15 (978-1-4824-0363-3(3), 6b4f8d99-6847-4313-8792-71c3060349b0) Stevens, Gareth Publishing LLLP.

Kids, Lonely Planet. Lonely Planet Kids First Words - Spanish 1. Iwohn, Sebastien & Mansfield, Andy, illus. 2017. (Lonely Planet Kids Ser.). (ENG.). 208p. (J). (gr. 1-3). pap. 12.99 *(978-1-78657-317-9(2)*, 5403) Lonely Planet Global Ltd. IRL. Dist: Hachette Bk. Group.

Kidzup Productions Staff. I'm Learning Spanish. 2005. (J). Vol. 1. 12.99 *(978-1-894677-75-2(7))* Vol. 2. 12.99 *(978-1-894677-76-9(5))* Kidzup Productions.

Kim, illus. Colors All Around. 2008. (SPA & ENG.). 28p. (J). pap. 8.95 *(978-1-60448-009-2(2))* Lectura Bks.

Leigh, Johanna. Spanish Words at the Park, 1 vol., Vol. 1. 2013. (Learn My Language! Spanish Ser.). (ENG.). 24p. (J). (gr. 1-2). 25.27 *(978-1-4824-0346-6(3)*, 576ce367-3d68-4c54-8a91-801c317592b8); pap. 9.15 *(978-1-4824-0345-9(5)*, 365f1974-969b-4503-bad9-f33df113f046) Stevens, Gareth Publishing LLLP.

Leonard, Marcia. Mi Dia de Campamento: My Camp Out. 2008. pap. 34.95 *(978-0-8225-9496-3(X))* Lerner Publishing Group.

Link, Theodore. Annie Oakley: Wild West Sharpshooter = Pistolera Del Lejano Oeste, 1 vol. 2003. (Famous People in American History / Grandes Personajes en la Historia de Los Estados Unidos Ser.). (SPA & ENG., Illus.). 32p. (J). (gr. 2-3). lib. bdg. 29.13 *(978-0-8239-4150-6(7)*, c9bf44a4-8733-4b7d-9fe7-c08803ad5713) Rosen Publishing Group, Inc., The.

Listen & Learn First Spanish Words. 2017. (Listen & Learn First Words Ser.). (ENG.). (J). bds. 19.99 *(978-0-7945-3886-6(X)*, Usborne) EDC Publishing.

Litchfield, Jo, illus. Very First Words in Spanish. 2009. (Very First Words in Spanish Ser.). (SPA & ENG.). 18p. (J). (gr. -1). bds. 7.99 *(978-0-7945-2446-3(X)*, Usborne) EDC Publishing.

LiveABC (Firm) Staff & McGraw-Hill Companies Staff, contrib. by. McGraw-Hill's Spanish Illustrated Dictionary. 2011. (ENG & SPA., Illus.). iv, 140p. (J). cd-rom *(978-0-07-174916-9(0))* McGraw-Hill Cos., The.

Lome, Emilio Angel. Lottery of Riddles. Martinez, Enrique, illus. 2011. 46p. (gr. 2-5). pap. 6.95 *(978-968-19-0663-4(2))* Aguilar, Altea, Taurus, Alfaguara, S.A. de C.V MEX. Dist: Santillana USA Publishing Co., Inc.

Lomp, Stephan. Indestructibles: Bebé, Vamos a Comer! / Baby, Let's Eat! Chew Proof · Rip Proof · Nontoxic · 100% Washable (Book for Babies, Newborn Books, Safe to Chew) 2018. (Indestructibles Ser.). (SPA., Illus.). 12p. (J). (gr. -1 — 1). pap. 5.99 *(978-1-5235-0318-6(1)*, 100318) Workman Publishing Co., Inc.

Long, Sara. nexos Multimedia: Used with ... Long-Nexos: Introductory Spanish. 2004. cd-rom 2.76 *(978-0-618-06865-4(1)*, 334239) CENGAGE Learning.

The Lost Feet. 2003. 28.95 *(978-0-673-78113-0(5))* Celebration Pr.

Main Idea & Details Spanish Version, Gr. 4-5. 2005. (J). per. *(978-1-58232-142-4(6))* ECS Learning Systems, Inc.

El Maiz De Quetzalcoatl. 2003. 28.95 *(978-0-673-78095-9(3))* Celebration Pr.

Maldonado, Premier. Animales. 2006. (SPA.). 14.99 *(978-0-9727886-5-6(4))* Osmosis, LLC.

—Cuerpo. 2006. (SPA., Illus.). 14.99 *(978-0-9727886-4-9(6))* Osmosis, LLC.

El Mariachi. 2003. 23.95 *(978-0-673-77788-1(X))* Celebration Pr.

Mariachi Tradition Videotape: Videotape Packages. 2003. (Share the Music Ser.). (gr. 1-8). *(978-0-02-295488-8(0))* Macmillan/McGraw-Hill Schl. Div.

Marsh, Carole. Uh, Oh, Amigo! Spanish for Kids. Beard, Chad, ed. 2004. (Little Linguist Ser.). (Illus.). 32p. 29.95 *(978-0-635-02436-7(5))* Gallopade International.

Martin, Dayna. The Toddler's Handbook: Bilingual (English / Spanish) (Ingles / Espanol) Numbers, Colors, Shapes, Sizes, ABC Animals, Opposites, & Sounds, with over 100 Words That Every Kid Should Know (Engage Early Readers: Children's Learning Books) Roumanis, A. r., ed. I.t. ed. 2015. (SPA & ENG., Illus.). 48p. (J). pap. *(978-1-77226-225-4(0))* AD Classic.

Martin, Rosa Maria & Ellis, Martyn. Nueva. 2004. (ENG., Illus.). 208p. pap. 42.50 *(978-0-340-86887-4(2))* Hodder Education Group GBR. Dist: Trans-Atlantic Pubns., Inc.

Maurice, creator. The Spanish Question Game. (SPA.). (YA). 134.95 *(978-1-932770-48-3(8)*, SG9) Symtalk, Inc.

Mazzeo, J. L. Xavia's X Book (BL) el libro X de Xavia (PB), 24 vols. 2007. (My Letter Library Ser.: 24). (SPA., Illus.). (J). pap. 10.95 *(978-1-59646-558-9(1))* Dingles & Co.

Mazzeo, J. L. Bebe's B Book/ el libro B de Bebé, 2 vols. 2007. (My Letter Library Ser.: 2). (SPA & ENG., Illus.). (J). pap. 10.95 *(978-1-59646-426-1(7))*; lib. bdg. 23.60 *(978-1-59646-425-4(9))* Dingles & Co.

—Delia's D Book /el libro D de Delia, 4 vols. 2007. (My Letter Library Ser.: 4). (SPA., Illus.). (J). pap. 10.95 *(978-1-59646-438-4(0))*; lib. bdg. 23.60 *(978-1-59646-437-7(2))* Dingles & Co.

—Emma's E-Book / El Libro E de Emma, 5 vols. 2007. (My Letter Library Ser.: 5). (SPA & ENG.). (J). pap. 10.95 *(978-1-59646-444-5(5))*; lib. bdg. 23.60 *(978-1-59646-443-8(7))* Dingles & Co.

—Faye's F Book (BL) el libro F de Faye (PB), 6 vols. 2007. (My Letter Library Ser.: 6). (SPA.). (J). pap. 10.95 *(978-1-59646-450-6(X))* Dingles & Co.

—George's G Book (BL) el libro G de George, 7 vols. 2007. (My Letter Library Ser.: 7). (J). lib. bdg. 23.60 *(978-1-59646-455-1(0))* Dingles & Co.

—George's G Book (BL) el libro G de George (PB), 7 vols. 2007. (My Letter Library Ser.: 7). (SPA.). (J). pap. 10.95 *(978-1-59646-456-8(9))* Dingles & Co.

—Henry's H Book (BL) el libro H de Henry, 8 vols. 2007. (My Letter Library Ser.: 8). (J). lib. bdg. 23.60 *(978-1-59646-461-2(5))* Dingles & Co.

—Henry's H Book (BL) el libro H de Henry (PB), 8 vols. 2007. (My Letter Library Ser.: 8). (SPA.). (J). pap. 10.95 *(978-1-59646-462-9(3))* Dingles & Co.

—Izzy's I Book (BL) el libro I de Izzy, 9 vols. 2007. (My Letter Library Ser.: 9). (SPA.). (J). lib. bdg. 23.60 *(978-1-59646-467-4(4))* Dingles & Co.

—Izzy's I Book (BL) el libro I de Izzy (PB), 9 vols. 2007. (My Letter Library Ser.: 9). (SPA.). (J). pap. 10.95 *(978-1-59646-468-1(2))* Dingles & Co.

—Jade's J Book (BL) el libro J de Jade, 10 vols. 2007. (My Letter Library Ser.: 10). (SPA.). (J). lib. bdg. 23.60 *(978-1-59646-473-5(9))* Dingles & Co.

—Jade's J Book (BL) el libro J de Jade (PB), 10 vols. 2007. (My Letter Library Ser.: 10). (SPA.). (J). pap. 10.95 *(978-1-59646-474-2(7))* Dingles & Co.

—Jade's J Book (PB), 10 vols. 2007. (My Letter Library Ser.: 10). (J). pap. 10.95 *(978-1-59646-471-1(2))* Dingles & Co.

—Kelsey's K Book (BL) el libro K de Kelsey, 11 vols. 2007. (My Letter Library Ser.: 11). (SPA.). (J). lib. bdg. 23.60 *(978-1-59646-479-7(8))* Dingles & Co.

—Kelsey's K Book (BL) el libro K de Kelsey (PB), 11 vols. 2007. (My Letter Library Ser.: 11). (SPA.). (J). pap. 10.95 *(978-1-59646-480-3(1))* Dingles & Co.

—El Libro F de Faye, 5 vols. 2007. (My Letter Library Ser.: 6).Tr. of Faye's F Book. (SPA.). (J). lib. bdg. 23.60 *(978-1-59646-449-0(6))* Dingles & Co.

—Logan's L Book (BL) el libro L de Logan, 12 vols. 2007. (My Letter Library Ser.: 12). (SPA.). (J). lib. bdg. 23.60 *(978-1-59646-485-8(2))* Dingles & Co.

—Logan's L Book (BL) el libro L de Logan (PB), 12 vols. 2007. (My Letter Library Ser.: 12). (SPA.). (J). pap. 10.95 *(978-1-59646-486-5(0))* Dingles & Co.

—Mia's M Book (BL) el libro M de Mia, 13 vols. 2007. (My Letter Library Ser.: 13). (SPA.). (J). lib. bdg. 23.60 *(978-1-59646-491-9(7))* Dingles & Co.

—Mia's M Book (BL) el libro M de Mia (PB), 13 vols. 2007. (My Letter Library Ser.: 13). (SPA.). (J). pap. 10.95 *(978-1-59646-492-6(5))* Dingles & Co.

—Nate's N Book (BL) el libro N de Nate, 14 vols. 2007. (My Letter Library Ser.: 14). (SPA.). (J). lib. bdg. 23.60 *(978-1-59646-497-1(6))* Dingles & Co.

—Nate's N Book (BL) el libro N de Nate (PB), 14 vols. 2007. (My Letter Library Ser.: 14). (SPA.). (J). pap. 10.95 *(978-1-59646-498-8(4))* Dingles & Co.

—Owen's O Book (BL) el libro O de Owen, 15 vols. 2007. (My Letter Library Ser.: 15). (SPA.). (J). lib. bdg. 23.60 *(978-1-59646-503-9(4))* Dingles & Co.

—Owen's O Book (BL) el libro O de Owen (PB), 15 vols. 2007. (My Letter Library Ser.: 15). (SPA.). (J). pap. 10.95 *(978-1-59646-504-6(2))* Dingles & Co.

—Owen's O Book (PB), 15 vols. 2007. (My Letter Library Ser.: 15). (J). pap. 10.95 *(978-1-59646-501-5(8))* Dingles & Co.

—Peter's P Book (BL) el libro P de Peter, 16 vols. 2007. (My Letter Library Ser.: 16). (SPA.). (J). lib. bdg. 23.60 *(978-1-59646-509-1(3))* Dingles & Co.

—Peter's P Book (BL) el libro P de Peter (PB), 16 vols. 2007. (My Letter Library Ser.: 16). (SPA.). (J). pap. 10.95 *(978-1-59646-510-7(7))* Dingles & Co.

—Quinn's Q Book (BL) el libro Q de Quinn, 17 vols. 2007. (My Letter Library Ser.: 17). (SPA.). (J). lib. bdg. 23.60 *(978-1-59646-515-2(8))* Dingles & Co.

—Quinn's Q Book (BL) el libro Q de Quinn (PB), 17 vols. 2007. (My Letter Library Ser.: 17). (SPA.). (J). pap. 10.95 *(978-1-59646-516-9(6))* Dingles & Co.

—Rosie's R Book (BL) el libro R de Rosie, 18 vols. 2007. (My Letter Library Ser.: 18). (SPA.). (J). lib. bdg. 23.60 *(978-1-59646-521-3(2))* Dingles & Co.

—Rosie's R Book (BL) el libro R de Rosie (PB), 18 vols. 2007. (My Letter Library Ser.: 18). (SPA.). (J). pap. 10.95 *(978-1-59646-522-0(0))* Dingles & Co.

—Sofie's S Book (BL) el libro S de Sofie, 19 vols. 2007. (My Letter Library Ser.: 19). (SPA.). (J). lib. bdg. 23.60 *(978-1-59646-527-5(1))* Dingles & Co.

—Sofie's S Book (BL) el libro S de Sofie (PB), 19 vols. 2007. (My Letter Library Ser.: 19). (SPA.). (J). pap. 10.95 *(978-1-59646-528-2(X))* Dingles & Co.

—Tad's T Book (BL) el libro T de Tad, 20 vols. 2007. (My Letter Library Ser.: 20). (SPA.). (J). lib. bdg. 23.60 *(978-1-59646-533-6(6))* Dingles & Co.

—Tad's T Book (BL) el libro T de Tad (PB), 20 vols. 2007. (My Letter Library Ser.: 20). (SPA.). (J). pap. 10.95 *(978-1-59646-534-3(4))* Dingles & Co.

—Uri's U Book (BL) el libro U de Uri, 21 vols. 2007. (My Letter Library Ser.: 21). (SPA.). (J). lib. bdg. 23.60 *(978-1-59646-539-8(5))* Dingles & Co.

—Uri's U Book (BL) el libro U de Uri (PB), 21 vols. 2007. (My Letter Library Ser.: 21). (SPA.). (J). pap. 10.95 *(978-1-59646-540-4(9))* Dingles & Co.

—Vera's V Book (BL) el libro V de Vera, 22 vols. 2007. (My Letter Library Ser.: 22). (SPA & ENG., Illus.). (J). lib. bdg. 23.60 *(978-1-59646-545-9(X))* Dingles & Co.

—Vera's V Book (BL) el libro V de Vera (PB), 22 vols. 2007. (My Letter Library Ser.: 22). (SPA & ENG., Illus.). (J). pap. 10.95 *(978-1-59646-546-6(8))* Dingles & Co.

—Will's W Book (BL) el libro W de Will, 23 vols. 2007. (My Letter Library Ser.: 23). (SPA.). (J). lib. bdg. 23.60 *(978-1-59646-551-0(4))* Dingles & Co.

—Will's W Book (BL) el libro W de Will (PB), 23 vols. 2007. (My Letter Library Ser.: 23). (SPA.). (J). pap. 10.95 *(978-1-59646-552-7(2))* Dingles & Co.

—Xavia's X Book (BL) el libro X de Xavia, 24 vols. 2007. (My Letter Library Ser.: 24). (SPA., Illus.). (J). lib. bdg. 23.60 *(978-1-59646-557-2(3))* Dingles & Co.

—Yola's Y Book (BL) el libro Y de Yola, 25 vols. 2007. (My Letter Library Ser.: 25). (SPA.). (J). lib. bdg. 23.60 *(978-1-59646-563-3(8))* Dingles & Co.

—Yola's Y Book (BL) el libro Y de Yola (PB), 25 vols. 2007. (My Letter Library Ser.: 25). (SPA.). (J). pap. 10.95 *(978-1-59646-564-0(6))* Dingles & Co.

McGraw Hill. ¿Cómo Te Va? Intro Nivel Rojo, Interactive Student Edition. 2003. (Middle School Spanish Intro Ser.). (SPA.). (gr. 6-8). stu. ed. 67.76 *(978-0-07-861026-4(5)*, 0078610265) Glencoe/McGraw-Hill.

—¿Cómo Te Va? Intro Nivel Rojo, Student Edition. 2003. (Middle School Spanish Intro Ser.). (SPA., Illus.). 144p. (gr. 6-8). stu. ed. 67.76 *(978-0-07-860350-1(1)*, 0078603501) McGraw-Hill Higher Education.

McGraw Hill, et al. ¿Cómo Te Va? Level a Nivel Verde, Interactive Student Edition CD-ROM. 2003. (Glencoe Spanish Ser.). (ENG.). (gr. 6-8). stu. ed. 96.64 *(978-0-07-861024-0(9)*, 0078610249) Glencoe/McGraw-Hill.

McKay, Sindy. We Both Read Bilingual Edition-About Dinosaurs/Acerca de Los Dinosaurios: Updated Cover, Information & Illustrations For 2020. Walters, Robert, illus. 2011. (SPA & ENG.). 44p. (J). pap. 5.99 *(978-1-60115-050-9(4))* Treasure Bay, Inc.

Mi Amigo. 2003. stu. ed. 35.50 *(978-0-8136-8135-1(9))* Modern Curriculum Pr.

Milet Publishing. My First Bilingual Book-Jobs (English-Spanish), 1 vol. 2012. (My First Bilingual Book Ser.). (ENG & SPA., Illus.). 24p. (J). (gr. k — 1). bds. 7.99 *(978-1-84059-712-7(7))* Milet Publishing.

Milet Publishing Staff. Animals - My First Bilingual Book, 1 vol. 2011. (My First Bilingual Book Ser.). (ENG & SPA., Illus.). 24p. (J). (gr. k — 1). bds. 8.99 *(978-1-84059-620-5(1))* Milet Publishing.

—Bilingual Visual Dictionary. 2011. (Milet Multimedia Ser.). (SPA & ENG., Illus.). 1p. (J). (gr. k-2). cd-rom 19.95 *(978-1-84059-592-5(2))* Milet Publishing.

—Home - My First Bilingual Book, 60 vols. 2011. (My First Bilingual Book Ser.). (ENG & SPA., Illus.). 24p. (J). (gr. k — 1). bds. 8.99 *(978-1-84059-652-6(X))* Milet Publishing.

—Milet Interactive for Kids - Spanish for English Speakers. 2012. (Milet Interactive for Kids Ser.). (SPA & ENG., Illus.). 1p. (J). (gr. k-2). cd-rom 24.95 *(978-1-84059-678-6(3))* Milet Publishing.

—My Bilingual Book-Sight (English-Spanish), 1 vol. 2014. (My Bilingual Book Ser.). (ENG & SPA., Illus.). 24p. (J). (gr. -1-k). 9.95 *(978-1-84059-800-1(X))* Milet Publishing.

—My First Bilingual Book-Fruit (English-Spanish), 60 vols. 2011. (My First Bilingual Book Ser.). (ENG & SPA., Illus.). 24p. (J). (gr. k — 1). bds. 8.99 *(978-1-84059-636-6(8))* Milet Publishing.

—My First Bilingual Book-Vegetables (English-Spanish), 1 vol. 2011. (My First Bilingual Book Ser.). (ENG & SPA., Illus.). 24p. (J). (gr. k — 1). bds. 8.99 *(978-1-84059-668-7(6))* Milet Publishing.

Mis Primeras Palabras (My First Words) (SPA.). (J). 6.95 *(978-970-05-0284-7(8))* Grijalbo, Editorial MEX. Dist: AIMS International Bks., Inc.

Mlawer, Teresa, tr. What Do I Feel? / ¿Qué Siento? Kubler, Annie, illus. 2015. (Small Senses Bilingual Ser.: 5). (ENG.). 12p. (J). bds. *(978-1-84643-721-2(0))* Child's Play International Ltd.

Monckeberg, Paulina. Artilugia Spanish 2008. 2007. (Pascualina Family of Products Ser.). 114p. (J). spiral bd. 14.95 *(978-956-8222-58-1(8))* Pascualina Producciones S.A.

Mora, Pat, et al. Water Rolls, Water Rises, 1 vol. So, Meilo, illus. 2014. (SPA & ENG.). 32p. (J). 18.95 *(978-1-60060-899-5(X))* Lee & Low Bks., Inc.

My Español Book Level I. 2005. pap. *(978-0-9767837-0-1(3))* Linguatechnics Publishing.

My Español Book, Level II. 2005. pap. *(978-0-9767837-1-8(1))*; pap., tchr. ed. *(978-0-9767837-3-2(8))* Linguatechnics Publishing.

My First Coloring Book of Spansih Words. 1000th ed. 2003. (ENG & SPA., Illus.). 34p. (J). 5.95 *(978-0-9722999-0-9(4))* Three Sisters Pr.

Nance, Kimberly A. & Rivera, Isidro J. Aprendizaje: Tecnicas de Composicion. 2nd ed. 2003. (SPA., Illus.). 196p. tchr. ed. *(978-0-618-23127-0(7))* CENGAGE Learning.

Nelson, Robin. Empujar Y Jalar; Push & Pull. 2008. pap. 34.95 *(978-0-8225-9895-4(7))* Lerner Publishing Group.

Nextext, creator. Ana Maria Matute. 2006. (Spanish Readers Ser.). (SPA., Illus.). 223p. (YA). (gr. 8-12). *(978-0-618-04826-7(X))* Holt McDougal.

Nickelodeon Staff, ed. Words - Dora the Explorer. 2010. (Write, Slide & Learn Ser.). 14p. (J). (gr. -1-1). 9.99 *(978-1-74184-519-8(X)*, Ideals Pubns.) Worthy Publishing.

Ninos Aprenden Ingles Corp. Children Learning Spanish. 2005. (Illus.). 119p. (J). pap. 19.95 *(978-1-934665-04-6(5))* Ninos Aprenden Ingles Corp.

No Diga Si Cuando Quiera Decir No (Don't Say Yes When You Mean No) (SPA.). pap. *(978-968-419-347-5(5))* Grijalbo, Editorial.

Nunn, Daniel. Families in Spanish: Las Familias, 1 vol. 2013. (World Languages - Families Ser.). (SPA., Illus.). 24p. (J). (gr. 1-3). lib. bdg. 25.32 *(978-1-4329-7173-1(5)*, 121187, Heinemann) Capstone.

Oliver, Stephen, photos by. Tamanos. 2005. (Coleccion Primeras Imagenes).Tr. of My First Look at Sizes. (SPA., Illus.). (J). (gr. -1-18). pap. 7.95 *(978-950-11-0907-8(0)*, SGM9070) Sigmar ARG. Dist: Continental Bk. Co., Inc.

Oquendo, Lisa, illus. Abecedario. 2006. (SPA.). bds. 5.99 *(978-1-934113-04-2(2))* Little Cubans, LLC.

Orero, Maria Jesus. Nico y Sus Trajes. 2006. (Nico Collection). (SPA & ESP., Illus.). 12p. (gr. -1-2). per., bds. 6.99 *(978-84-272-6152-5(7))* Molino, Editorial ESP. Dist: Santillana USA Publishing Co., Inc.

Ortells, Estela. En el Bosque. (Coleccion Pequeno Simon). (SPA., Illus.). 32p. (J). 7.95 *(978-84-7189-166-2(2)*, ORT347) Ortells, Alfredo Editorial S.L. ESP. Dist: Continental Bk. Co., Inc.

Un Pajarito. 2003. 23.95 *(978-0-673-77778-2(2))* Celebration Pr.

Parish, Ellen. Spanish: Level 2. 2003. (Skill Builders Ser.). 80p. 2.95 *(978-1-932210-15-6(0))* Rainbow Bridge Publishing.

Parker, Helen. Trace, Stick Learn Borrar Primeras Palabras/Wipe Clean First Words. 2007. (Trace, Stick & Learn Ser.). (Illus.). 12p. (gr. -1-k). pap. *(978-1-84610-645-3(1))* Make Believe Ideas.

Parnell, Declan. Luis Speaks Spanish, 1 vol., 1. 2015. (Rosen REAL Readers: Social Studies Nonfiction / Fiction: Myself, My Community, My World Ser.). (ENG.). 12p. (J). (gr. k-1). pap. 6.33 *(978-1-5081-1776-6(4)*, d976394d-ffed-4216-b302-05342b820001, Rosen Classroom) Rosen Publishing Group, Inc., The.

El parque de Juegos, 2 Packs. (Chiquilibros Ser.). (SPA.). (gr. -1-1). 12.00 *(978-0-7635-8548-8(3))* Rigby Education.

El paseo en Trineo: Individual Title Two-Packs. (Chiquilibros Ser.). (SPA.). (gr. -1-1). 12.00 *(978-0-7635-8546-4(7))* Rigby Education.

Patrick, Roman. Spanish Words at the Post Office, 1 vol., Vol. 1. 2013. (Learn My Language! Spanish Ser.). (ENG., Illus.). 24p. (J). (gr. 1-2). 25.27 *(978-1-4824-0350-3(1)*, 9b8b1ff8-487b-4887-8194-78f13114b7ae) Stevens, Gareth Publishing LLLP.

PatrickGeorge. Contrarios. 2012. (SPA.). 26p. (J). (gr. -1-1). pap. 19.99 *(978-84-261-3885-9(3))* Juventud, Editorial ESP. Dist: Lectorum Pubns., Inc.

Patterson, Irania & McElvane, Catherine. Wings & Dreams (Alas y Suenos) The Legend of Angel Falls (La Leyenda del Salto Angel) 2010. (ENG & SPA.). 40p. (J). (gr. 1-3). 19.95 *(978-0-9815192-4-1(5))* Novello Festival Pr.

El Payaso, 6 Packs. (Chiquilibros Ser.). (SPA.). (gr. k-1). 23.00 *(978-0-7635-8785-7(0))* Rigby Education.

Pebble Soup Exploraciones: Pebble Soup Exploraciones Extra Ingredients. 239.00 *(978-0-7578-3342-7(X))* Rigby Education.

El Pequenito Tonito. 2003. 23.95 *(978-0-673-77368-5(X))* Celebration Pr.

Phillips, Larissa. Cochise: Jefe Apache, 1 vol. de la Vega, Eida, tr. 2003. (Grandes Personajes en la Historia de Los Estados Unidos (Famous People in American History) Ser.). (SPA., Illus.). 32p. (gr. 3-4). pap. 10.00 *(978-0-8239-4223-7(6)*, 78727065-ac30-44c5-8197-d0ca1e0721c8); (J). lib. bdg. 29.13 *(978-0-8239-4129-2(9)*, 792cb486-94fb-48f0-bcc7-1ac55441242a, Editorial Buenas Letras) Rosen Publishing Group, Inc., The.

Pisonero, Isidoro, et al. Pasacalle 2: Curso de Espanol para Ninos. (SPA & ENG.). (J). (gr. 3-7). 96p. tchr. ed. *(978-84-7143-715-0(5))*; 96p. stu. ed. *(978-84-7143-708-2(2))*; 64p. wbk. ed. *(978-84-7143-709-9(0))* Sociedad General Espanola de Libreria.

Portavoz. Libro Abc-dario. 2004. (Sabio Y Prudente Ser.).Tr. of ABC Book. (SPA.). 32p. (J). pap. 2.50 *(978-0-8254-0925-7(X))* Kregel Pubns.

Potey Mollina, José Luis. El pergamino de Zenit y el descubrimiento de los sellos Divinos. 2010. (SPA.). 224p. (YA). pap. 18.99 *(978-1-59835-099-9(4)*, CBH Bks.) Cambridge BrickHouse, Inc.

Prosser, Charonne. Cambridge IGCSE(tm) Spanish Workbook. 2019. (Cambridge Assessment International Educa Ser.). (SPA.). 96p. (YA). (gr. 7-9). pap. 16.95 *(978-0-00-830039-5(9))* HarperCollins Pubs. Ltd. GBR. Dist: Independent Pubs. Group.

Publications International Ltd. Staff. Little English Spanish Sound Diego. 2007. 12p. (J). 10.98 *(978-1-4127-6738-5(5))* Publications International, Ltd.

Publications International Ltd. Staff, ed. Baby Einstein. 2007. (J). 10.98 *(978-1-4127-7467-3(5))* Publications International, Ltd.

Que Sigue? 2003. 23.95 *(978-0-673-77129-2(6))* Celebration Pr.

Que Soy? 2003.Tr. of What Am I? (J). (gr. -1-2). 23.95 *(978-0-673-77408-8(2))* Celebration Pr.

Que Soy? Big Book Packages. 2003. 64.95 *(978-0-673-58600-1(6))* Celebration Pr.

Que Susto Me Dio! 2003. (J). (gr. -1-2). 23.95 *(978-0-673-77397-5(3))* Celebration Pr.

Quetzalcoatl's Corn. 2003. 28.95 *(978-0-673-78116-1(X))* Celebration Pr.

Quien Vive Aqui? 2003. (J). (gr. -1-2). 23.95 *(978-0-673-77396-8(5))* Celebration Pr.

Quien Vive Aqui? Big Book Packages. 2003. 64.95 *(978-0-673-58601-8(4))* Celebration Pr.

Randolph, Joanne. All about A Months/Los Meses, 1 vol. Brusca, Maria Cristina, tr. 2007. (It's about Time / Los Libros Del Tiempo Ser.). (SPA & ENG., Illus.). 24p. (J). (gr. 1-1). lib. bdg. 26.27 *(978-1-4042-7628-4(9)*, 7a299ee6-755c-4d3a-aee7-b3087c44e510) Rosen Publishing Group, Inc., The.

Random House. 500 Palabras Nuevas para Ti (500 Words to Grow on Spanish Edition) Kest, Kristin, illus. 2005. (Pictureback(R) Ser.). (SPA.). 32p. (J). (gr. -1-2). pap. 5.99 *(978-0-375-83308-3(0)*, Random House Para Ninos) Random Hse. Children's Bks.

—500 Words to Grow On. Kest, Kristin, illus. 2005. (Pictureback(R) Ser.). 32p. (J). (gr. -1-k). pap. 3.99 *(978-0-375-83307-6(2)*, Random Hse. Bks. for Young Readers) Random Hse. Children's Bks.

El Rebozo: Big Book Packages. 2003. 64.95 *(978-0-673-58595-0(6))* Celebration Pr.

El Recreo. 2003. 23.95 *(978-0-673-77180-3(6))* Celebration Pr.

El Renacuajo. 2003. 23.95 *(978-0-673-77169-8(5))* Celebration Pr.

Robleda, Margarita. Jugando con Las Vocales. Suarez, Maribel, illus. 2006. (Rana, Rema, Rimas Ser.).Tr. of Playing with Vowels. (SPA.). 12p. (J). (gr. -1-k). 7.95 *(978-1-59820-210-6(3)*, Alfaguara) Santillana USA Publishing Co., Inc.

Rodriguez, Patty & Stein, Ariana. Cuauhtemoc: Shapes/Formas, 1 vol. Reyes, Citlali, illus. 2018.Tr. of Spanish. (SPA.). 22p. (J). (gr. -1-k). bds. 9.99 *(978-0-9861099-3-5(2))* Little Libros, LLC.

—Guadalupe: First Words/Primeras Palabras, 1 vol. Reyes, Citlali, illus. 2018. 22p. (J). bds. 9.99 *(978-0-9861099-0-4(8))* Little Libros, LLC.

Rojo, Andrea Szekasy. Arcoiris, Level 1 Activity Book: Spanish for Children. 2003. (SPA., Illus.). 48p. (Orig.). (J). (gr. 1-6). pap., act. bk. ed. 10.99 *(978-0-9671053-5-2(6)*, 0510) Language Adventure Pubns.

Rosa-Mendoza, Gladys. English-Spanish Foundations Series: The Alphabet; Numbers; Colors & Shapes. Cifuentes, Carolina, ed. Noiset, Michele, illus. 2004. (Spanish Foundations Ser.). (ENG & SPA.). (J). bds. 19.95 *(978-0-9679748-1-1(X))* Me+Mi Publishing.

—Let's Go to the Zoo!/Vamos Al Zoologico! Elkerton, Andy, illus. 2007. (English Spanish Foundations Ser.). (ENG & SPA.). 20p. (J). (gr. -1-k). bds. 6.95 *(978-1-931398-20-6(8))* Me+Mi Publishing.

—Lupe Lupita, Where Are You?/Lupe Lupita Donde Estas? Ochoa, Ana, illus. 2007. (English Spanish Foundations Ser.). 20p. (gr. -1-k). pap. 19.95 *(978-1-931398-82-4(8))* Me+Mi Publishing.

—My House/Mi Casa. Borlasca, Hector, illus. (English Spanish Foundations Ser.). (gr. -1-1). 2007. per. 19.95 *(978-1-931398-84-8(4))* 2006. (ENG & SPA.). 20p. (J). bds. 6.95 *(978-1-931398-18-3(6))* Me+Mi Publishing.

—My School/Mi Escuela. Murphy, Terri, illus. 2007. (English Spanish Foundations Ser.). (ENG & SPA.). (J). (gr. -1-k). bds. 6.95 *(978-1-931398-23-7(2))* Me+Mi Publishing.

—My Senses/Mis Sentidos. Merer, Laura, illus. 2007. (English Spanish Foundations Ser.). (ENG & SPA.). 20p. (J). (gr. -1-k). bds. 6.95 *(978-1-931398-21-3(6))* Me+Mi Publishing.

—My Week/Mi Semana. Wesley, Milliana, ed. Grosshauser, Peter, illus. 2007. (English Spanish Foundations Ser.). (gr. -1-k). bds. 6.95 *(978-1-931398-25-1(9))* Me+Mi Publishing.

S

—Opposites/Opuestos. Cifuentes, Carolina, ed. McGeehan, Dan, illus. 2008. (English-Spanish Foundations Ser.). (gr. -1-k). bds. 6.95 *(978-1-931398-04-6(6))* Me+Mi Publishing.

—When I Am/Cuando Estoy. Regan, Dana, illus. 2007. (English Spanish Foundations Ser.). 20p. (gr. -1-k). pap. 19.95 *(978-1-931398-83-1(6))* Me+Mi Publishing.

—Who Lives in the Sea?/Qui'n Vive en el Mar? O'Neil, Sharron, illus. 2007. (English Spanish Foundations Ser.). (ENG & SPA.). 20p. (J). (gr. -1-k). bds. 6.95 *(978-1-931398-24-4(0))* Me+Mi Publishing.

Rosa y Sus Amigos. 2003. 23.95 *(978-0-673-77793-5(6))* Celebration Pr.

Rosier, Michelle. Elementary Spanish - Worktext Step 1. 2006. 72p. per. 15.00 *(978-1-59166-276-1(1))* BJU Pr.

—Elementary Spanish — Worktext Step 2. 2006. 72p. per. 15.00 *(978-1-59166-277-8(X))* BJU Pr.

—Elementary Spanish — Worktext Step 3. 2006. 72p. per. 15.00 *(978-1-59166-278-5(8))* BJU Pr.

Ryan, Pam Muñoz. Nuestra California / Our California. López, Rafael, illus. 2008.Tr. of Our California. 48p. (J). (gr. 1-4). 17.95 *(978-1-58089-226-1(4))* Charlesbridge Publishing, Inc.

Salazar, Julia. Spanish Words on the Road, 1 vol., Vol. 1. 2013. (Learn My Language! Spanish Ser.). (ENG., Illus.). 24p. (J). (gr. 1-2). 25.27 *(978-1-4824-0365-7(X),* 19b4adc3-af80-4fc0-bd13-e7f4a671247f) Stevens, Gareth Publishing LLLP.

Saludos! Complete Blue Level Packages. 697.00 *(978-0-7635-9510-4(1))* Rigby Education.

Santiago, Carmen. Fun & Easy Spanish for You, Vol. 2. 2003. 48p. (J). per. 29.95 *(978-1-56167-794-3(9))* American Literary Pr.

Santiago, Carmen Angelica. Fun & Easy Spanish for You. 2003. (SPA.). 50p. (J). Vol. 1. per. 29.95 *(978-1-56167-793-1(0))* Vol. 3. (Illus.). per. 29.95 *(978-1-56167-795-5(7))* American Literary Pr.

Sara, Sarita. 2003. (SPA.). 23.95 *(978-0-673-77366-1(3))* Celebration Pr.

Scarry, Richard & Luna Rising Editors. Richard Scarry's Best Word Book Ever. 2004. (ENG., Illus.). 64p. (J). (gr. -1-2). 16.95 *(978-0-87358-873-7(8))* Cooper Square Publishing Llc.

—Richard Scarry's Best Word Book Ever. Scarry, Richard, illus. 2004. (ENG., Illus.). 64p. (J). (gr. -1-2). pap. 10.95 *(978-0-87358-874-4(6))* Cooper Square Publishing Llc.

Schmitt, Conrad J. ¿Cómo Te Va? Intro Nivel Rojo, Workbook. 2003. (Middle School Spanish Intro Ser.). (ENG., Illus.). 72p. (gr. 6-8). pap., wbk. ed. 11.44 *(978-0-07-860542-0(3),* 0078605423) McGraw-Hill Higher Education.

—¿Cómo Te Va? Level B Nivel Azul, Interactive Student Edition CD-ROM. 2003. (Glencoe Spanish Ser.). (ENG.). (gr. 6-8). stu. ed. 99.60 *(978-0-07-861025-7(7),* 0078610257) Glencoe/McGraw-Hill.

—¿Cómo Te Va? Level B Nivel Azul, Workbook. 2003. (Glencoe Spanish Ser.). (ENG., Illus.). 128p. (gr. 6-8). pap., wbk. ed. 18.68 *(978-0-07-860556-7(3),* 0078605563) McGraw-Hill Education.

School Zone Publishing Company Staff. Bilingual Preschool Big Get Ready! 2005. (ENG.). 320p. (J). (gr. k). pap. 9.99 *(978-1-58947-493-2(7))* School Zone Publishing Co.

Schumacher, Bev. Where Will You Find Me? / Donde Me Encontraras. 2008. (SPA.). 20p. (J). lib. bdg. 9.95 *(978-1-935292-07-4(2))* Learning Props.

Segal, Robin. ABC in Albuquerque. 2009. (All 'Bout Cities Ser.). (ENG.). 32p. (J). (gr. -1-k). *(978-1-935139-01-0(0))* Murray Hill Bks., LLC.

—ABC in San Antonio. 2009. (All 'Bout Cities Ser.). (ENG.). 32p. (J). (gr. -1-k). *(978-1-935139-04-1(5))* Murray Hill Bks., LLC.

Segal, Robin & Adler, Tasha. ABC in Los Angeles: And la County. 2009. (All 'Bout Cities Ser.). (ENG.). 32p. (J). (gr. -1-k). *(978-1-935139-02-7(9))* Murray Hill Bks., LLC.

Senor Cascaron. 2003. (SPA.). 23.95 *(978-0-673-77170-4(9))* Celebration Pr.

Senor Cascaron: Poems, Rhymes, & Songs Listening Packs. 2003. (SPA.). 34.50 *(978-0-673-58623-0(5))* Celebration Pr.

Seuss. The Cat in the Hat/el Gato Ensombrerado (the Cat in the Hat Spanish Edition) Bilingual Edition. 2015. (Classic Seuss Ser.).Tr. of Cat in the Hat/el Gato Ensombrerado. (Illus.). 72p. (J). (gr. -1-2). 16.99 *(978-0-553-52443-7(7),* Random Hse. Bks. for Young Readers) Random Hse. Children's Bks.

Sierra i Fabra, Jordi. Aydin. 97th ed. 2003. (SPA., Illus.). 144p. pap. 23.40 *(978-84-236-3708-9(5),* ED6264) Harcourt Schl. Pubs.

Sombreros. 2003. (SPA.). 23.95 *(978-0-673-77798-0(7))* Celebration Pr.

Sosa, Carlos. Celebrations. 2007. (Familia Banderas Ser.). (Illus.). 48p. (J). (gr. 3-7). per. 9.95 *(978-1-933669-11-3(X))* Literary Architects, LLC.

—Cultures. 2007. (Familia Banderas Ser.). (Illus.). 48p. (J). (gr. 3-7). per. 9.95 *(978-1-933669-12-0(8))* Literary Architects, LLC.

Soy la Cafetera. 2003. 23.95 *(978-0-673-77386-9(8))* Celebration Pr.

Soy La Cafetera: Poems, Rhymes, & Songs Listening Packs. 2003. 34.50 *(978-0-673-58634-6(0))* Celebration Pr.

Spanish II, Set. 2004. (YA). (gr. 9-12). 99.95 *(978-0-7403-0241-1(8),* ES9915, Lifepac) Alpha Omega Pubns., Inc.

Spanish Intro Kit. 2004. (ENG & SPA.). (J). 44.99 *(978-0-943343-76-1(3))* Learning Wrap-Ups, Inc.

Spanish School Thesaurus: Sinonimos, Antonimos, Paronimos. 2004th ed. 2004. 380p. pap. 9.95 *(978-950-11-1158-3(X))* Los Andes Publishing Co.

Spanish/English Desk Cards. 2004. (J). 8.95 *(978-1-56911-177-2(4))* Learning Resources, Inc.

Sterling Publishing Co., Inc. First Words/Primeras Palabras. 2013. (Say & Play Ser.). (ENG & SPA., Illus.). 28p. (J). (— 1). bds. 6.95 *(978-1-4549-1039-8(9))* Sterling Publishing Co., Inc.

Stillman, David. Repaso: Answer Key. 2004. (SPA & ENG.). 416p. (gr. 6-12). pap. 8.95 *(978-0-8442-7422-5(4),* NTC4224) Glencoe/McGraw-Hill.

Stokes, Jeffery D. ¡Qué Bien Suena! Text. 2004. 224p. (YA). pap. 104.76 incl. cd-rom *(978-0-618-23502-5(7),* 354274) CENGAGE Learning.

Suenos y Palabras. (SPA.). (J). (gr. k-6). 30.00 *(978-958-04-7091-5(X));* 30.00 *(978-958-04-7090-8(1));* Vol. 2. 30.00 *(978-958-04-7092-2(8));* Vol. 3. 30.00 *(978-958-04-7093-9(6));* Vol. 4. *(978-958-04-7734-1(5));* Vol. 5. *(978-958-04-7735-8(3));* Vol. 6. *(978-958-04-7736-5(1))* Norma S.A. COL. Dist: Distribuidora Norma, Inc.

Suenos y Palabras 1. (J). 26.50 *(978-958-04-4036-9(0))* Norma S.A. COL. Dist: Distribuidora Norma, Inc.

Suenos y Palabras 10. (SPA.). (J). (gr. 7-12). 40.00 *(978-958-04-5955-2(X))* Norma S.A. COL. Dist: Distribuidora Norma, Inc.

Suenos y Palabras 11. (SPA.). (J). (gr. 7-12). 45.00 *(978-958-04-5957-6(6))* Norma S.A. COL. Dist: Distribuidora Norma, Inc.

Suenos y Palabras 12. (SPA.). (J). (gr. 7-12). 50.00 *(978-958-04-5959-0(2))* Norma S.A. COL. Dist: Distribuidora Norma, Inc.

Suenos y Palabras 2. (SPA.). (J). 26.50 *(978-958-04-4037-6(9))* Norma S.A. COL. Dist: Distribuidora Norma, Inc.

Suenos y Palabras 3. (SPA.). (J). 26.50 *(978-958-04-4038-3(7))* Norma S.A. COL. Dist: Distribuidora Norma, Inc.

Suenos y Palabras 4. (SPA.). (J). 26.50 *(978-958-04-4039-0(5))* Norma S.A. COL. Dist: Distribuidora Norma, Inc.

Suenos y Palabras 5. (SPA.). (J). 26.50 *(978-958-04-4040-6(9))* Norma S.A. COL. Dist: Distribuidora Norma, Inc.

Suenos y Palabras 6. (SPA.). (J). 26.50 *(978-958-04-4041-3(7))* Norma S.A. COL. Dist: Distribuidora Norma, Inc.

Suenos y Palabras 7, Vol. 7. (SPA.). (J). (gr. 7-12). 35.00 *(978-958-04-5650-6(X))* Norma S.A. COL. Dist: Distribuidora Norma, Inc.

Suenos y Palabras 8. (SPA.). (J). (gr. 7-12). 35.00 *(978-958-04-5651-3(8))* Norma S.A. COL. Dist: Distribuidora Norma, Inc.

Suenos y Palabras 9. (SPA.). (J). (gr. 7-12). 40.00 *(978-958-04-5652-0(6))* Norma S.A. COL. Dist: Distribuidora Norma, Inc.

Suenos y Palabras K. (SPA.). (J). 26.50 *(978-958-04-4355-1(6))* Norma S.A. COL. Dist: Distribuidora Norma, Inc.

Taylor, Trace & Sánchez, Lucía M. Delfines: Dolphins. 2014. (2G Animales Marinos Ser.). (SPA.). 12p. (J). (gr. k-2). pap. 8.00 *(978-1-61541-282-2(4))* American Reading Co.

Teckentrup, Britta, illus. Fast & Slow Spanish. 2013. 14p. (J). (gr. -1-k). bds. 6.99 *(978-1-78285-035-9(X))* Barefoot Bks., Inc.

TestWorks. 2004. (Scott Foresman Reading Ser.). (gr. k-18). cd-rom 99.00 *(978-0-328-02541-1(0));* (gr. 1-18). tchr. ed. 99.00 incl. cd-rom *(978-0-673-62281-5(9));* (gr. 2-18). cd-rom 99.00 *(978-0-673-62282-2(7));* (gr. 3-18). cd-rom 99.00 *(978-0-673-62283-9(5));* (gr. 4-18). tchr. ed. 99.00 incl. cd-rom *(978-0-673-62284-6(3));* (gr. 5-18). tchr. ed. 99.00 incl. cd-rom *(978-0-673-62285-3(1));* (gr. 6-18). tchr. ed. 99.00 incl. cd-rom *(978-0-673-62286-0(X))* Addison-Wesley Educational Pubs., Inc.

Tipton, Stacey. The Complete Musical Spanish: With New Bonus Verbs Learning CD, 1. 2nd ed. 2005. (SPA., Illus.). 112p. 49.99 *(978-0-9706829-7-0(2))* Musical Linguist, The.

Todos Somos Amigos. 2003. 23.50 *(978-0-673-77190-2(3))* Celebration Pr.

Travis, Joelle & Figueras, Ligaya, eds. Los Animales y los Verbos. Hazan, Maurice, illus. 2003. (SPA.). 89p. (J). per. 20.00 *(978-1-932770-16-2(X),* SWLB1) Symtalk, Inc.

Traynor, Tracy & Pérez, María. Spanish with Abby & Zak, 1 vol. Hambleton, Laura, illus. 2008. (Abby & Zak Ser.). (ENG & SPA.). 48p. (J). (gr. k-2). pap. 16.95 *(978-1-84059-515-4(9))* Milet Publishing.

Tu Amigo, Jorge. 2003. 28.95 *(978-0-673-78106-2(2))* Celebration Pr.

Uriz, Francisco J. & Harling, Birgit. En el Mundo Hispanico. stu. ed. 19.95 *(978-0-8219-2324-5(2),* 70376); pap., tchr.'s training gde. ed. 15.95 *(978-0-8219-2325-2(0),* 70865) EMC/Paradigm Publishing.

Vargo, Sharon Hawkins. Senor Felipes Alphabet Adventure: El Alfabeto Espanol. 2003. (Single Titles Ser.: Vol. 3). 32p. (J). (gr. -1). 7.95 *(978-0-7613-1897-2(6))* Lerner Publishing Group.

Velázquez Press, creator. Diario de Escritura Académica para Matemáticas. 2018. (SPA.) (YA). pap. 4.95 *(978-1-59495-717-8(7))* Velázquez Pr.

—Velázquez Biliteracy Program PreK Hora de la Comida Set. 2017. (SPA.). (J). *(978-1-59495-709-3(6))* Velázquez Pr.

El Viaje de Carlos y Ceci. 2003. (Illus.). (J). 28.95 *(978-0-673-78103-1(8))* Celebration Pr.

Villafane-Leon, Ines. A Story for All Seasons: Un Cuento Para Cada Estacion: Immigration of One. 2004. (ENG & SPA.). xiii, 367p. (YA). pap. 22.95 *(978-1-882897-78-0(1))* Lost Coast Pr.

A Volar Pupil Book Level 3: Primary Spanish for the Caribbean. 2015. (ENG., Illus.). 72p. (J). (gr. 2-3). pap. 13.99 *(978-0-00-813634-5(3))* HarperCollins Pubs. Ltd. GBR. Dist: Independent Pubs. Group.

A Volar Workbook Level 1: Primary Spanish for the Caribbean. 2015. (ENG.). 48p. (J). (gr. k-1). pap. 8.99 *(978-0-00-813629-1(7))* HarperCollins Pubs. Ltd. GBR. Dist: Independent Pubs. Group.

Way, Jennifer. The Running Book: Correr, 1 vol. 2003. (Let's Get Moving / Diviértete en Movimiento Ser.). (ENG & SPA., Illus.). 24p. (J). (gr. k-1). lib. bdg. 26.27 *(978-1-4042-7512-6(6),* 5ac87a7c-aec7-42c8-a1bc-9b65d2f78a46) Rosen Publishing Group, Inc., The.

Who is Michael Ramirez? 2003. (J). 28.95 *(978-0-673-78107-9(0))* Celebration Pr.

Williams-Ashe, Marcella Norton. Granny Says. Williams Jr., Anthony, illus. 2012. 46p. pap. 12.00 *(978-0-9764198-4-6(X))* Allecram Publishing.

Ya Llego el Mariachi! 2003. (J). 28.95 *(978-0-673-78104-8(6))* Celebration Pr.

Ya Mero Llegamos, Mami? 2003. 23.95 *(978-0-673-78081-2(3))* Celebration Pr.

Yellow Umbrella Spanish Big Books [Kaplan]. 2011. (Big Book - Spanish Edition Ser.). (SPA.). 16p. 149.70 *(978-1-4296-6642-8(0),* Capstone Pr.) Capstone.

Yo Bailo! 2003. (J). 23.95 *(978-0-673-77781-2(2))* Celebration Pr.

Yo Tengo una Tia. 2003. (J). 23.95 *(978-0-673-78059-1(7))* Celebration Pr.

Yo Vivo Aqui. 2003. (J). 23.95 *(978-0-673-77792-8(8))* Celebration Pr.

Zaz! 2003. 23.95 *(978-0-673-77367-8(1))* Celebration Pr.

Zoo-Zológico Bilingual Board Book. 2008. (ENG & SPA., Illus.). (J). pap. 5.99 *(978-0-9727886-8-7(9))* Osmosis, LLC.

Zorzi, Gina & Sánchez, Lucía M. Bosques: This is a Forest. 2010. (2G Ecosistemas Ser.). (SPA.). 28p. (J). (gr. k-2). pap. 9.60 *(978-1-61541-426-0(6))* American Reading Co.

The 5 W's & H Spanish Version, Gr. 4-5. 2005. (Spanish Version Ser.). (J). per. *(978-1-58232-140-0(X))* ECS Learning Systems, Inc.

The 5 W's Spanish Version, Gr. 1-3. 2005. (J). per. *(978-1-58232-145-5(0))* ECS Learning Systems, Inc.

SPANISH LANGUAGE—CONVERSATION AND PHRASE BOOKS

Brooks, Felicity & Mackinnon, Mairi. Spanish Words & Phrases - Internet Referenced. 2008. (First Picture Spanish Ser.). (Illus.). 50p. (J). 9.99 *(978-0-7945-2229-2(7),* Usborne) EDC Publishing.

Bruzzone, Catherine & Martineau, Susan. Hide & Speak Spanish. Comfort, Louise, illus. 2003. (Hide & Speak Ser.). (ENG.). 32p. (J). (gr. 2-6). pap. 9.99 *(978-0-7641-2589-8(3))* Sourcebooks, Inc.

Candel, Arianna. Los Contrarios. Rovira, Francesc, illus. 2004. (Osito Estudiante / Little Bear's Firsts Ser.).Tr. of Opposites. (SPA.). 36p. (J). (gr. k-3). 21.19 *(978-0-7641-2993-3(7),* B.E.S. Publishing) Peterson's.

—Las Formas. Rovira, Francesc, illus. 2004. (Osito Estudiante / Little Bear's Firsts Ser.).Tr. of Shapes. (SPA.). 36p. (J). (gr. k-3). 21.19 *(978-0-7641-2995-7(3),* B.E.S. Publishing) Peterson's.

—Los Numeros. Rovira, Francesc, illus. 2004. (Osito Estudiante / Little Bear's Firsts Ser.).Tr. of Numbers. (SPA.). 36p. (J). (gr. k-3). 21.19 *(978-0-7641-2996-4(1),* B.E.S. Publishing) Peterson's.

Gose, Senora. Flip Flop Spanish: Ages 3-5: Level 1. 2008. (Illus.). 84p. (J). spiral bd. 29.95 *(978-0-9801772-1-3(9))* Flip n Flop Learning, LLC.

Mahoney, Judy. Teach Me Everyday Spanish: Celebrating the Seasons, 22 vols., Vol. 2. Girouard, Patrick, illus. adapted ed. 2009. (SPA & ENG.). 32p. (J). (gr. -1-2). lib. bdg. 19.95 incl. audio compact disk *(978-1-59972-202-3(X))* Teach Me Tapes, Inc.

—Teach Me Everyday Spanish Vol 1, Volume 1. Girouard, Patrick, illus. 2008. (ENG.). 32p. (J). (gr. -1). 19.95 *(978-1-59972-102-6(3))* Teach Me Tapes, Inc.

McGraw Hill. ¿Cómo Te Va? Level B Nivel Azul, Audio Activities. 2003. (Glencoe Spanish Ser.). (SPA., Illus.). 48p. (gr. 6-8). spiral bd. 9.80 *(978-0-07-860557-4(1),* 0078605571) McGraw-Hill Higher Education.

Pirz, Therese Slevin. Language Helper Spanish: Helping You Speak More Spanish. 2006. (Language Helper Ser.). (Illus.). 218p. (J). pap. 20.00 *(978-0-9716605-8-8(1))* Chou Chou Pr.

Press, J. P. Welcome to Spanish with Sesame Street (r). 2019. (Sesame Street (r) Welcoming Words Ser.). (ENG.). 32p. (J). (gr. -1-2). pap. 7.99 *(978-1-5415-7497-7(4),* 26de0094-726f-4d76-9284-0c9f47f1e979); lib. bdg. 27.99 *(978-1-5415-5500-6(7),* 1b4f0418-4568-47d3-a115-50bf3b8d1d5f) Lerner Publishing Group. (Lerner Pubns.).

Reyes, Raquel, et al. I May Bien! Level E. 2005. (I May Bien! Ser.).Tr. of Very Good. (SPA.). 130p. (J). 22.95 *(978-0-9718696-9-1(3))* Double R Publishing, LLC.

Roca, Nuria. La Primavera (Spring) 2004. (Estaciones / Seasons Ser.).Tr. of Spring. (SPA., Illus.). 36p. (J). (gr. k-3). 22.44 *(978-0-7641-2734-2(9),* B.E.S. Publishing) Peterson's.

Schmitt, Conrad J. ¿Cómo Te Va? Level a Nivel Verde, Audio Activities. 2003. (Glencoe Spanish Ser.). (ENG., Illus.). 48p. (gr. 6-8). spiral bd. 9.92 *(978-0-07-860550-5(4),* 0078605504) McGraw-Hill Education.

Sojo, Cecilia I. The Everything Kids' Learning Spanish Book: Exercises & Puzzles to Help You Learn Espanol. 2nd rev. ed. 2010. (Everything(r) Kids Ser.). (ENG., Illus.). 144p. pap. 9.99 *(978-1-4405-0676-5(0))* Adams Media Corp.

Spanish for Business: Beginning Level. (J). (gr. k-6). suppl. ed. 59.00 *(978-0-8219-0144-1(3),* 70036) EMC/Paradigm Publishing.

Spanish for Business Interm: Intermediate Level. (J). (gr. k-6). suppl. ed. 59.00 *(978-0-8219-0145-8(1),* 70037) EMC/Paradigm Publishing.

Tulip, Jenny. My First Spanish Word Book. 2004. (ENG & SPA., Illus.). 48p. (J). 5.99 *(978-1-85854-394-9(0))* Brimax Books Ltd. GBR. Dist: Byeway Bks.

Vaamonde, Conchita, tr. My First Spanish Words. Tulip, Jenny, illus. 2004. (SPA.). 12p. (J). bds. 7.99 *(978-1-85854-512-7(9))* Brimax Books Ltd. GBR. Dist: Byeway Bks.

Watson, Carol, et al. Let's Learn Spanish. 2003. (Let's Learn Ser.). (ENG., Illus.). 32p. pap. 9.95 *(978-0-7818-1013-5(2))* Hippocrene Bks., Inc.

SPANISH LANGUAGE—DICTIONARIES

Brooks, Felicity & MacKinnon, Mairi. The Usborne Picture Dictionary in Spanish. rev. ed. 2007. (Picture Dictionaries Ser.). (Illus.). 111p. (J). 16.99 *(978-0-7945-1608-6(4),* Usborne) EDC Publishing.

Bruzzone, Catherine, et al. Spanish-English Picture Dictionary. 2011. (First Bilingual Picture Dictionaries Ser.). (ENG., Illus.). 48p. (J). (gr. 2-4). pap. 7.99 *(978-0-7641-4661-9(0))* Sourcebooks, Inc.

Continental Press Staff. English-Spanish Picture Dictionary. 2017. (SPA & ENG., Illus.). 92p. (J). (gr. k-8). pap., stu. ed. 18.95 *(978-1-5240-0263-3(1))* Continental Pr., Inc.

Davies, H. Spanish Dictionary for Beginners. 2004. (Beginner's Dictionaries Ser.). (SPA & ENG.). 128p. (J). pap. 12.99 *(978-0-7945-0288-1(1))* EDC Publishing.

Davies, Helen. Spanish Dictionary for Beginners. Irving, Nicole, ed. Shackell, John, illus. 2003. (Beginner's Dictionaries Ser.). (SPA.). 128p. lib. bdg. 20.99 *(978-1-58086-488-6(0))* EDC Publishing.

Diaz-Cubero, Jose H. Practicas de Ortografia: 3 Grado. (SPA & ENG.). (J). (gr. 3). 9.95 *(978-84-357-0127-3(1),* CPR88) Ediciones y Distribuciones Codice, S.A. ESP. Dist: Continental Bk. Co., Inc.

Diccionario de la Lengua Espanola Basico. (SPA., Illus.). (J). 5.95 *(978-958-04-4116-8(2))* Norma S.A. COL. Dist: Distribuidora Norma, Inc.

Diccionario de la Lengua Espanola Mini. (SPA.). (J). 2.50 *(978-958-04-4584-5(2))* Norma S.A. COL. Dist: Distribuidora Norma, Inc.

Diccionario de Primaria de la Lengua Española. 2nd ed. 2003. (SPA., Illus.). 1006p. (J). (gr. 3-7). *(978-84-8332-061-7(4))* Bibliograf, S.A.

Diccionario Didactico de Espanol Elemental (Didactic Dictionary of Elementary Spanish) Edicion Mexicana (Mexican Edition) (SPA., Illus.). 880p. *(978-84-348-4715-6(9),* SM1932) SM Ediciones.

Diccionario Esencial. (SPA.). 1376p. 19.95 *(978-84-294-3415-6(1))* Santillana USA Publishing Co., Inc.

Diccionario Inicial de la Lengua Espanola. (SPA., Illus.). 336p. (J). 8.95 *(978-84-7153-199-5(2),* VX992) Bibliograf, S.A. ESP. Dist: Continental Bk. Co., Inc.

Diccionario Usual Larousse.Tr. of Handy Larousse Spanish Dictionary. (SPA.). 782p. pap. *(978-970-22-0126-7(8))* Larousse, Ediciones, S. A. de C. V.

DK. DK First Picture Dictionary: Spanish: 2,000 Words to Get You Started in Spanish. 2005. (ENG., Illus.). 128p. (J). (gr. 5-12). 16.99 *(978-0-7566-1370-9(1),* DK Children) Dorling Kindersley Publishing, Inc.

—First Spanish Dictionary. 2018. (DK First Reference Ser.). (ENG., Illus.). 128p. (J). (gr. 1-4). 16.99 *(978-1-4654-6949-6(4),* DK Children) Dorling Kindersley Publishing, Inc.

Enciclopedia Juvenil, 4 vols., Set. (J). 59.00 *(978-84-272-5995-9(6),* MO501) Molino, Editorial ESP. Dist: Continental Bk. Co., Inc.

Equipo Staff. Diccionario Inicial Everest. Jorge, Gutiérrez Sahagún, illus. (SPA.). 336p. *(978-84-241-1013-0(7))* Everest Editora ESP. Dist: Lectorum Pubns., Inc.

—Everest Diccionario Cima de la Lengua Espanola.Tr. of Everest Cima Dictionary of the Spanish Language. (SPA.). 868p. 22.95 *(978-84-241-1036-9(6),* EV7041); 566p. 19.95 *(978-84-241-1027-7(7),* EV6705) Everest Editora ESP. Dist: Lectorum Pubns., Inc.

Equipo Staff & Equipo Lexicográfico Everest. Everest Diccionario Practico de Sinonimos y Antonimos.Tr. of Everest Practical Thesaurus. (SPA.). 576p. 12.99 *(978-84-241-1508-1(2),* EV7151) Everest Editora ESP. Dist: Lectorum Pubns., Inc.

Goodman, Marlene. Let's Learn Spanish Picture Dictionary. 2004. 80p. 9.95 *(978-0-07-140828-8(2))* McGraw-Hill/Contemporary.

Liccioni, Tina. The Clownfish/el Pez Payaso: An English/Spanish Bilingual Book. Vesazquez, Gloria, tr. 2013. (ENG.). 36p. (J). pap. 21.95 *(978-1-4327-9060-8(9))* Outskirts Pr., Inc.

Magic Spanish Picture Dictionary. 2009. (ENG.). 144p. pap. 9.99 *(978-1-4231-2265-4(8))* Disney Pr.

McGraw Hill. El Español para Nosotros: Curso para Hispanohablantes Level 2, Workbook & Audio Activities Student Edition. 2005. (Spanish Heritage Speaker Ser.). (SPA.). 224p. (gr. 9-12). stu. ed., per., wbk. ed. 31.00 *(978-0-07-867656-7(8),* 0078676568) McGraw-Hill Education.

—McGraw-Hill's Spanish Picture Dictionary. 2004. (ENG., Illus.). 96p. 24.00 *(978-0-07-142812-5(7),* 0071428127) McGraw-Hill Education.

Merriam-Webster, ed. Merriam-Webster's Illustrated Spanish-English Student Dictionary. 2012. (ENG., Illus.). 496p. (J). (gr. 4-8). pap. 21.95 *(978-0-87779-177-5(5),* d16b9935-0de2-4e4c-9d65-7b84061e6992) Merriam-Webster, Inc.

Norma Staff. Mi Primer Vocabulario (My First Vocabulary Dict.), 2 vols., Set. (SPA.). (J). 50.00 *(978-958-04-3093-3(4))* Norma S.A. COL. Dist: AIMS International Bks., Inc.

Oxford, ed. Oxford Learner's Spanish Dictionary. 2017. (ENG., Illus.). 704p. 13.99 *(978-0-19-840796-6(3))* Oxford Univ. Pr., Inc.

Rey, Alain. Robert junior Poche. pap. 29.95 *(978-2-85036-687-1(0))* Le Robert FRA. Dist: Distribooks, Inc.

Richmond Concise Dictionary. (SPA.). 716p. (J). (gr. 3-8). pap. 30.95 *(978-970-29-0661-2(X))* Santillana USA Publishing Co., Inc.

Santillana. Pictodiccionario: Diccionario en Im Genes. Sangregorio, Fernando et al, illus. 2003.Tr. of Child's First Spanish Dictionary. (SPA.). 144p. (gr. k-3). 29.95 *(978-1-58105-973-1(6),* Santillana) Santillana USA Publishing Co., Inc.

SPANISH LANGUAGE—DICTIONARIES—ENGLISH

Amery, Heather. First Hundred Words in Spanish II. 2015. (First Hundred Words Ser.). (ENG.). 32p. (J). pap. 6.99 *(978-0-7945-3513-1(5),* Usborne) EDC Publishing.

Brooks, Felicity. Very First Dictionary in Spanish - Internet Referenced. 2008. (Very First Dictionaries Ser.). 80p. (J). 11.99 *(978-0-7945-2104-2(5),* Usborne) EDC Publishing.

Collins Dictionaries. Collins Primary Illustrated Spanish Dictionary: Get Started, for Ages 7-11. 2015. (ENG., Illus.). 640p. (gr. 3-6). 14.95 *(978-0-00-811196-0(0))* HarperCollins Pubs. Ltd. GBR. Dist: Independent Pubs. Group.

—Spanish School Gem Dictionary: Trusted Support for Learning, in a Mini-Format (Collins School Dictionaries) 3rd rev. ed. 2015. (ENG.). 640p. (YA). (gr. 6-11). pap. 7.99 *(978-0-00-756930-4(0))* HarperCollins Pubs. Ltd. GBR. Dist: Independent Pubs. Group.

Collins Dictionary Staff. Collins Spanish School Dictionary. 2nd ed. 2011. (SPA & ENG.). 640p. (J). pap. 9.95 *(978-0-00-736784-9(8))* HarperCollins Pubs. Ltd. GBR. Dist: Independent Pubs. Group.

Diccionario Basico Ingles/Espanol (1540) 2003. (SPA & ENG.). 528p. pap. 5.98 *(978-970-22-0480-0(1))* Larousse, Ediciones, S. A. de C. V. MEX. Dist: Giron Bks.

Diccionario Bilingue Basico. (SPA & ENG.). (J). 5.95 *(978-958-04-4118-2(9))* Norma S.A. COL. Dist: Distribuidora Norma, Inc.

Hanson, Tracie, des. New World Baby - Spanish. 2007. (ENG, SPA, FRE, GER & ITA., Illus.). 28p. (J). 14.00 (978-0-9799185-0-6(2)) Hanson, Tracie.
Hippocrene Books Staff, creator. Children's Picture Dictionary. 2006. (Hippocrene Children's Illustrated Dictionaries Ser.). (ENG & SPA., Illus.). 108p. (J). (gr. 3-7). pap. 14.95 (978-0-7818-1130-9(9)) Hippocrene Bks., Inc.
Hochstatter, Daniel J. Just Look 'n Learn Spanish Picture Dictionary. 2004. 96p. 11.95 (978-0-07-140829-5(0)) McGraw-Hill/Contemporary.
Kudela, Katy R. My First Book of Spanish Words, 1 vol. 2009. (Bilingual Picture Dictionaries Ser.). (MUL.). 32p. (J). (gr. -1-2). lib. bdg. 27.99 (978-1-4296-3298-0(4), 95707, Capstone Pr.) Capstone.
Laud, Valerie. The Picture Book Dictionary: The Essential Source for Bilingual Families, English-Spanish Edition. Latushkin, Valentin, illus. l.t. ed. 2005. (ENG & SPA.). 96p. (J). (978-0-9747387-0-3(0)) EKADOO Publishing Group.
Longman Diccionario Pocket Mexico Paper. 2004. (Illus.). 832p. (C). pap. 27.27 (978-0-582-51157-6(7)) Pearson Education.
Merriam-Webster, ed. Merriam-Webster's Notebook Spanish-English Dictionary. 2004. (MUL.). 112p. (J). (gr. 5). pap. 5.95 (978-0-87779-672-5(6), 9970c54f-2fd5-4585-a058-5073682b4aab) Merriam-Webster, Inc.
Merriam-Webster Editors. Merriam-Webster's Spanish-English Dictionary. 2014. (SPA.). (gr. 7-12). lib. bdg. 17.20 (978-0-613-09430-6(1)) Turtleback.
Richmond Advanced Dictionary: Spanish/English, English/Spanish. (ENG & SPA.). 720p. (J). (gr. 9-12). 30.95 (978-84-294-9861-5(3), Richmond) Santillana USA Publishing Co., Inc.
Richmond Pocket Dictionary: Spanish-English, English-Spanish. (SPA & ENG.). 806p. (J). (gr. 6-12). pap. 10.95 (978-84-294-9860-8(5)) Santillana USA Publishing Co., Inc.
Sauri, Trudy. Gift of Yucatan Nouns A-Z. 2008. (ENG & SPA., Illus.). 64p. (J). per. 18.00 (978-0-9797637-3-1(8)) Your Culture Gifts.
Spanish-English Picture Dictionary. 2003. (SPA & ENG.). (J). per. (978-1-884907-30-2(X)) Paradise Pr., Inc.
Stanley, Mandy. My First English-Spanish Library. 2018. (ENG., Illus.). 60p. (J). 29.99 (978-0-7534-7467-9(0), 900197795, Kingfisher) Roaring Brook Pr.
Thomas, Mar Andres. Mi Primer Libro Bilingue: la Comida/My First Bilingual Book: Food. 2013. (ENG & SPA., Illus.). 69p. (J). (gr. -1-3). pap. 14.95 (978-1-938690-43-3(5)) Salem Author Services.
York, M. J. Learn Spanish Words. Petelinsek, Kathleen, illus. 2014. (Foreign Language Basics Ser.). (ENG & SPA.). 24p. (J). (gr. 2-5). 32.79 (978-1-62687-379-7(8), 207126) Child's World, Inc, The.

SPANISH LANGUAGE—GRAMMAR

ABC. 2003. (J). per. (978-1-884907-44-9(X)); per. (978-1-884907-40-1(7)) Paradise Pr., Inc.
ABC. 2003. (First Concepts Book Ser.). 32p. (J). 3.98 (978-0-7525-8892-6(3)) Parragon, Inc.
ABC. (Coleccion Picaros Peluchines). (SPA.). (J). 5.50 (978-950-11-0398-4(6), SGM398) Sigmar ARG. Dist: Continental Bk. Co., Inc.
La Abeja Trabajadora. 2003. (J). 23.95 (978-0-673-77796-6(0)) Celebration Pr.
Acento 8: Cuaderno de Ortografia. (SPA.). (J). (gr. 1-9). 16.00 (978-958-04-3831-1(5)) Norma S.A. COL. Dist: Distribuidora Norma, Inc.
Acento 9: Cuaderno de Ortografia. (SPA., Illus.). (J). (gr. 1-9). 16.00 (978-958-04-3832-8(3)) Norma S.A. COL. Dist: Distribuidora Norma, Inc.
Advina Quien Soy? 2003. 23.95 (978-0-673-77182-7(2)) Celebration Pr.
Al Juego! 2003. 23.95 (978-0-673-77777-5(4)) Celebration Pr.
Ana Y Tito. 2003. 23.95 (978-0-673-77783-6(9)) Celebration Pr.
Los Animales Nos Ayudan. 2003. 23.95 (978-0-673-77393-7(0)) Celebration Pr.
Antonio Y Su Poncho. 2003. 28.95 (978-0-673-78086-7(4)) Celebration Pr.
El Apartamento. 2003. 23.95 (978-0-673-77183-4(0)) Celebration Pr.
La Arana. 2003. 23.95 (978-0-673-77156-8(3)) Celebration Pr.
El Arco Iris. 2003. 23.95 (978-0-673-77128-5(8)) Celebration Pr.
Ashley, Moana. Wonders of the Worlds. 2008. (Illus.). 24p. (J). pap. 10.95 (978-1-59646-541-1(7)) Dingles & Co.
Ay, Caramba! 2003. 28.95 (978-0-673-78097-3(X)) Celebration Pr.
Los Ayudantes. 2003. 23.95 (978-0-673-77164-3(4)) Celebration Pr.
Borreguita Negra: Poems, Rhymes, & Songs Listening Packs. 2003. 34.50 (978-0-673-58629-2(4)) Celebration Pr.
Brilla, Brilla, Estrellita. 2003. 23.95 (978-0-673-77365-4(5)) Celebration Pr.
Brinca La Tablita: Big Book Packages. 2003. 64.95 (978-0-673-58603-2(0)) Celebration Pr.
Las Buenas Noches. 2003. 23.95 (978-0-673-77392-0(2)) Celebration Pr.
El Caldo. 2003. 23.95 (978-0-673-77773-7(1)) Celebration Pr.
Camarena, Cathy & Ruff, Gloria B. Carmen y Carlos. 2006. (Primeros Sonidos Ser.). (SPA., Illus.). 23p. (J). pap. 48.42 (978-1-59679-848-9(3)) ABDO Publishing Co.
—Cindi y César. 2006. (Primeros Sonidos Ser.). (SPA., Illus.). 23p. (J). pap. 48.42 (978-1-59679-852-6(1)) ABDO Publishing Co.
—Crisma y Cristián. 2006. (Primeros Sonidos Ser.). (SPA., Illus.). 23p. (J). pap. 48.42 (978-1-59679-850-2(5)) ABDO Publishing Co.
—Ema y Eduardo. 2006. (Primeros Sonidos Ser.). (J). pap. 48.42 (978-1-59679-858-8(0)) ABDO Publishing Co.
—Fey y Félix. 2006. (Primeros Sonidos Ser.). (SPA., Illus.). 23p. (J). pap. 48.42 (978-1-59679-860-1(2)) ABDO Publishing Co.
—Florinda y Flavio. 2006. (Primeros Sonidos Ser.). (SPA., Illus.). 23p. (J). pap. 48.42 (978-1-59679-862-5(9)) ABDO Publishing Co.
—Gilda y Gilberto. 2006. (Primeros Sonidos Ser.). (SPA., Illus.). 23p. (J). pap. 48.42 (978-1-59679-870-0(X)) ABDO Publishing Co.
—Isabel e Iván. 2006. (Primeros Sonidos Ser.). (SPA., Illus.). 23p. (J). pap. 48.42 (978-1-59679-876-2(9)) ABDO Publishing Co.
—Kelli y Avellino. 2006. (Primeros Sonidos Ser.). (SPA., Illus.). 23p. (J). pap. 48.42 (978-1-59679-882-3(3)) ABDO Publishing Co.
—Olivia y Oscar. 2006. (Primeros Sonidos Ser.). (J). pap. 48.42 (978-1-59679-890-8(4)) ABDO Publishing Co.
—Toñis y Toño. 2006. (Primeros Sonidos Ser.). (SPA., Illus.). 23p. (J). pap. 48.42 (978-1-59679-888-5(2)) ABDO Publishing Co.
Celebramos las Fiestas. 2003. 23.95 (978-0-673-77389-0(2)) Celebration Pr.
La Charreada. 2003. 23.95 (978-0-673-77782-9(0)) Celebration Pr.
Los Cinco Hermanos. 2003. 23.95 (978-0-673-77192-6(X)) Celebration Pr.
Los Cinco Sentidos. 2003. 23.95 (978-0-673-77126-1(1)) Celebration Pr.
El Conejo Magico. 2003. 23.95 (978-0-673-77191-9(1)) Celebration Pr.
Conozco una Viejita. 2003. 23.95 (978-0-673-77364-7(7)) Celebration Pr.
Los Contrarios (Opposites) (SPA.). (J). 6.95 (978-968-419-087-0(5)) Grijalbo, Editorial MEX. Dist: AIMS International Bks., Inc.
El Coqui: Big Book Packages. 2003. 64.95 (978-0-673-58596-7(4)) Celebration Pr.
El Correo: Individual Title Two-Packs. (Chiquilibros Ser.). (SPA.). (gr. -1-1). 12.00 (978-0-7635-8561-7(0)) Rigby Education.
Cual Contiene Mas? 2003. 23.95 (978-0-673-77400-2(7)) Celebration Pr.
Cuando Me Bano. 2003. 23.95 (978-0-673-77160-5(1)) Celebration Pr.
Cuando Sea Grande. 2003. 23.95 (978-0-673-77388-3(4)) Celebration Pr.
Cuantos Hay? 2003. 23.95 (978-0-673-77159-9(8)) Celebration Pr.
La Cucaracha: Big Book Packages. 2003. 64.95 (978-0-673-58594-3(8)) Celebration Pr.
De Colores: Big Book Packages. 2003. 64.95 (978-0-673-58602-5(2)) Celebration Pr.
Denne, B. & Irving, N. Easy Spanish. 2004. (Easy Languages Ser.). (SPA., Illus.). 128p. (J). (gr. 6-18). lib. bdg. 20.95 (978-1-58086-431-2(7)) EDC Publishing.
Diaz-Cubero, Jose H. Practicas de Ortografia: 2 Grado. (SPA & ENG.). (J). (gr. 2). 9.95 (978-84-357-0128-0(X), CPR86) Ediciones y Distribuciones Codice, S.A. ESP. Dist: Continental Bk. Co., Inc.
Diez Ositos. 2003. 23.95 (978-0-673-77362-3(0)) Celebration Pr.
Los Dinosaurios. 2003.Tr. of Great Dinosaur Search. 28.95 (978-0-673-77403-3(1)) Celebration Pr.
Donde Aprendo Yo. 2003. (J). (gr. -1-2). 23.95 (978-0-673-77390-6(6)) Celebration Pr.
Donde Juego Yo. 2003. 23.95 (978-0-673-77185-8(7)) Celebration Pr.
Emberley, Rebecca. My Room/Mi Cuarto. 2005. (SPA., Illus.). 10p. (J). (gr. -1 — 1). bds. 7.99 (978-0-316-00052-9(3)) Little, Brown Bks. for Young Readers.
En el Mercado. 2003. 23.95 (978-0-673-77790-4(1)) Celebration Pr.
En Mi Jardin. 2003. 23.95 (978-0-673-77131-5(8)) Celebration Pr.
Las Estaciones. 2003. 23.95 (978-0-673-77127-8(X)) Celebration Pr.
Estoy Enojado. 2003. (J). (gr. -1-2). 23.95 (978-0-673-77391-3(4)) Celebration Pr.
Fabulas Fabulosas. 2006. (SPA.). (J). (978-1-933485-24-9(8)) Publicaciones Puertorriquenas, Inc.
Figueras, Ligaya, ed. En Plena Vista Level 1. Hazan, Maurice, illus. 5th ed. 2003. (SPA.). 140p. per. 22.00 (978-1-932770-98-8(4), SHB-SM) Symtalk, Inc.
Las Figuras Geometricas. 2003. 23.95 (978-0-673-77123-0(7)) Celebration Pr.
Fui Al Mar. 2003. 23.95 (978-0-673-77162-9(8)) Celebration Pr.
Gordon, Ronni L. & Stillman, David M. Cuaderno 2: An Intermediate Workbook for Grammar & Communication: Answer Key & Progress Checks, Vol. 2. 2004. (ENG & SPA.). (J). (gr. 6-12). pap., suppl. ed. (978-0-8442-7927-5(7), EC79277) Glencoe/McGraw-Hill.
Grades 1-2 Complete Pinata/Mas Pinata Package. 2003. 1943.95 (978-0-673-58717-6(7)) Celebration Pr.
Hazan, Maurice. Saber, Deber, Querer, Poder: Symtalk Verb + Verb Infinitive Game for Spanish. (SPA.). (YA). 134.95 (978-1-932770-49-0(6), SG10) Symtalk, Inc.
Hazan, Maurice, creator. Spanish Conjugating Cards. (SPA.). 149.95 (978-1-932770-86-5(0), SCC) Symtalk, Inc.
—Los Verbos: Symtalk Verb Bingo. (SPA.). (J). 124.95 (978-1-932770-40-7(2), SG1) Symtalk, Inc.
Holt, Rinehart and Winston Staff. ¡Ven Conmigo! 3rd ed. 2003. (¡Ven Conmigo! Ser.). (SPA & ENG.). 112p. (gr. 6-6). pap. 17.45 (978-0-03-064982-0(X)) Houghton Mifflin Harcourt Publishing Co.
—Ven Conmigo! Level 1: Cuaderno/Act. 3rd ed. 2003. (SPA.). pap., tchr. ed. 22.93 (978-0-03-064981-3(1)) Holt McDougal.
—Ven Conmigo! Level 1: Cuadero/Hispanic. 3rd ed. 2003. (Holt ?Ven Conmigo! Ser.). (SPA & ENG.). 64p. (gr. 6-6). pap. 16.20 (978-0-03-065538-8(2)) Houghton Mifflin Harcourt Publishing Co.
—Ven Conmigo! Level 2: Cuadero/Hispanic. 3rd ed. 2003. (SPA.). pap. 14.60 (978-0-03-065546-3(3)) Holt McDougal.
—¡Ven Conmigo!, Level 2. 3rd ed. 2003. (¡Ven Conmigo! Ser.). (SPA & ENG.). 112p. (gr. 8-8). pap. 17.95 (978-0-03-064983-7(8)) Houghton Mifflin Harcourt Publishing Co.
—Ven Conmigo!, Level 2: Cuaderno de Act. 3rd ed. 2003. (¡Ven Conmigo! Ser.). (SPA & ENG.). 160p. (gr. 8-8). pap. 21.85 (978-0-03-064986-8(2)) Houghton Mifflin Harcourt Publishing Co.
A La Cama! 2003. 23.95 (978-0-673-77399-9(X)) Celebration Pr.
Lakeshore Learning Materials Staff, contrib. by. Spanish Alphabet Big Book. 2006. (SPA.). (J). pap. 19.95 (978-1-59746-000-2(1)) Lakeshore Learning Materials.
Lasetras. 2003. 23.95 (978-0-673-77167-4(9)) Celebration Pr.
Leeme un Cuento. 2003. 23.95 (978-0-673-77189-6(X)) Celebration Pr.
Lengua Espanola: Cuarto Grado. (SPA & ENG.). (J). (gr. 4). 21.95 (978-84-357-0027-6(5), CPR76) Ediciones y Distribuciones Codice, S.A. ESP. Dist: Continental Bk. Co., Inc.
Lengua Espanola: Quinto Grado. (SPA & ENG.). (J). (gr. 5). 22.00 (978-84-357-0171-6(9), CPR78) Ediciones y Distribuciones Codice, S.A. ESP. Dist: Continental Bk. Co., Inc.
Lengua Espanola: Segundo Grado. (SPA & ENG.). (J). (gr. 2). 17.95 (978-84-357-0137-2(9), CPR72) Ediciones y Distribuciones Codice, S.A. ESP. Dist: Continental Bk. Co., Inc.
Lengua Espanola: Sexto Grado. (SPA & ENG.). (J). (gr. 6). 22.00 (978-84-357-0170-9(0), CPR80) Ediciones y Distribuciones Codice, S.A. ESP. Dist: Continental Bk. Co., Inc.
Lengua Espanola: Tercer Grado. (SPA & ENG.). (J). (gr. 3). 17.95 (978-84-357-0028-3(3), CPR74) Ediciones y Distribuciones Codice, S.A. ESP. Dist: Continental Bk. Co., Inc.
Lo Que Sale De un Huevo. 2003. 23.95 (978-0-673-77161-2(X)) Celebration Pr.
Looking for Insects. 2003. (J). 28.95 (978-0-673-78112-3(7)) Celebration Pr.
Los Tres Deseos. 2003. 23.95 (978-0-673-77193-3(8)) Celebration Pr.
Lupita Y David. 2003. (J). (gr. -1-2). 28.95 (978-0-673-77380-7(9)) Celebration Pr.
Las Maquinas. 2003. (J). (gr. -1-2). 28.95 (978-0-673-77401-9(5)) Celebration Pr.
La Mariposa. 2003.Tr. of Butterfly. 23.95 (978-0-673-77125-4(3)) Celebration Pr.
Las Mariposas de Alicia. 2003. 28.95 (978-0-673-78105-5(4)) Celebration Pr.
La Mariquita Triste. 2003. 23.95 (978-0-673-77795-9(2)) Celebration Pr.
Mazzeo, J. L. Aimee's A Book (BL) el libro A de Aimée, 1. 2007. (My Letter Library Ser.: 1). (SPA., Illus.). (J). pap. 10.95 (978-1-59646-420-9(8)); lib. bdg. 23.60 (978-1-59646-419-3(4)) Dingles & Co.
—Cassie's C Book (BL) el libro C de Cassie: S, 3 vols. 2007. (My Letter Library Ser.: 3). (SPA & ENG., Illus.). (J). lib. bdg. 23.60 (978-1-59646-431-5(3)) Dingles & Co.
—Cassie's C Book (BL) el libro C de Cassie (PB), 3 vols. 2007. (My Letter Library Ser.: 3). (SPA & ENG., Illus.). (J). pap. 10.95 (978-1-59646-432-2(1)) Dingles & Co.
—Zach's Z Book (BL) el libro Z de Zach, 26 vols. 2007. (My Letter Library Ser.: 26). (SPA & ENG., Illus.). (J). lib. bdg. 23.60 (978-1-59646-569-5(7)) Dingles & Co.
—Zach's Z Book (BL) el libro Z de Zach (PB), 26 vols. 2007. (My Letter Library Ser.: 26). (SPA & ENG., Illus.). (J). pap. 10.95 (978-1-59646-570-1(0)) Dingles & Co.
Me Encontre una Piedra. 2003. 23.95 (978-0-673-77158-2(X)) Celebration Pr.
Me Siento Feliz. 2003. (J). (gr. -1-2). 23.95 (978-0-673-77394-4(9)) Celebration Pr.
Mi Bicicleta. 2003. 23.95 (978-0-673-77775-1(8)) Celebration Pr.
Mi Camion. 2003. 23.95 (978-0-673-77780-5(4)) Celebration Pr.
Mi Casa Nueva. 2003. 23.95 (978-0-673-77172-8(5)) Celebration Pr.
Mi Cuerpo. 2003. 23.95 (978-0-673-77124-7(5)) Celebration Pr.
Mi Dia. 2003. 23.95 (978-0-673-77165-0(2)) Celebration Pr.
Mi Gatito Fachoso. 2003. 23.95 (978-0-673-77176-6(8)) Celebration Pr.
Mi Libro de Cocina. 2003. (Illus.). 28.95 (978-0-673-78085-0(6)) Celebration Pr.
Mi Mama Trabaja. 2003. 23.95 (978-0-673-77184-1(9)) Celebration Pr.
A Mi Me Gusta. 2003. 23.95 (978-0-673-77387-6(6)) Celebration Pr.
Mi Mejor Amigo. 2003. 23.95 (978-0-673-77181-0(4)) Celebration Pr.
Mi Mundo. 2003. (J). (gr. -1-2). 23.95 (978-0-673-77406-4(6)) Celebration Pr.
Mi Muneco De Nieve. 2003. 23.95 (978-0-673-77779-9(0)) Celebration Pr.
Mi Nana Chalita. 2003. 23.95 (978-0-673-77171-1(7)) Celebration Pr.
Milet Publishing Staff. Music - English-Spanish, 1 vol. 2012. (My First Bilingual Book Ser.). (ENG & SPA., Illus.). 24p. (J). (gr. k — 1). bds. 8.99 (978-1-84059-728-8(3)) Milet Publishing.
—My First Bilingual Book-Sports (English-Spanish), 1 vol. 2012. (My First Bilingual Book Ser.). (ENG & SPA., Illus.). 24p. (J). (gr. k — 1). bds. 7.99 (978-1-84059-760-8(7)) Milet Publishing.
Mis Cinco Perritos. 2003. 23.95 (978-0-673-77363-0(9)) Celebration Pr.
Mis Comidas Favoritas. 2003. (SPA.). 23.95 (978-0-673-77799-7(5)) Celebration Pr.
Mis Mascotas. 2003. 23.95 (978-0-673-77177-3(6)) Celebration Pr.
Mis Zapatos Ruevos. 2003. 23.95 (978-0-673-77188-9(1)) Celebration Pr.
More Pizza. 2003. 28.95 (978-0-673-78111-6(9)) Celebration Pr.
Muchos Frijoles. 2003. 23.95 (978-0-673-77774-4(X)) Celebration Pr.
La Muneca Azul. 2003. (J). (gr. -1-2). 23.95 (978-0-673-77383-8(3)) Celebration Pr.
La Muneca Azul: Poems, Rhymes, & Songs Listening Packs. 2003. 34.50 (978-0-673-58631-5(6)) Celebration Pr.
My Grandma's Memory Trunk. 2003. 28.95 (978-0-673-78110-9(0)) Celebration Pr.
Necesito Mi Desayuno. 2003. 23.95 (978-0-673-77178-0(4)) Celebration Pr.
No Les Tengo Miedo. 2003. 23.95 (978-0-673-77130-8(X)) Celebration Pr.
No Me Quiero Banar. 2003. (J). (gr. -1-2). 23.95 (978-0-673-77395-1(7)) Celebration Pr.
No Quiero Ir Al Dentista. 2003. 23.95 (978-0-673-77174-2(1)) Celebration Pr.
Oscar. 2003. 23.95 (978-0-673-77369-2(8)) Celebration Pr.
A Paco. 2003. 23.95 (978-0-673-77797-3(9)) Celebration Pr.
Palencia del Burgo, Ramón. Uso de la gramática junior - nivel avanzado. (SPA.). 128p. 24.95 (978-84-7711-555-7(9)) Edelsa Grupo Didascalia, S.A. ESP. Dist: Distribooks, Inc.
Las Partes De una Planta. 2003. (J). (gr. -1-2). 23.95 (978-0-673-77402-6(3)) Celebration Pr.
Pattis, Anne-Francoise. Let's Learn Spanish Coloring Book. 2003. (ENG., Illus.). 64p. pap. 9.00 (978-0-07-142142-3(4), 0071421424) McGraw-Hill Education.
Pedro, Pedrito. 2003. (J). (gr. -1-2). 23.95 (978-0-673-77384-5(1)) Celebration Pr.
Pedro, Pedrito: Big Book Packages. 2003. 64.95 (978-0-673-58598-1(0)) Celebration Pr.
Pedro, Pedrito: Poems, Rhymes, & Songs Listening Packs. 2003. 34.50 (978-0-673-58632-2(4)) Celebration Pr.
La Primavera. 2003. (J). (gr. -1-2). 23.95 (978-0-673-77385-2(X)) Celebration Pr.
La Primavera: Poems, Rhymes, & Songs Listening Packs. 2003. 34.50 (978-0-673-58633-9(2)) Celebration Pr.
Primer Dia de Clases. 2003. 23.95 (978-0-673-77187-2(3)) Celebration Pr.
Que Alegria! 2003. 23.95 (978-0-673-77173-5(3)) Celebration Pr.
Que Comes Tu? 2003. 23.95 (978-0-673-77186-5(5)) Celebration Pr.
Que Dia Es Hoy? 2003. 23.95 (978-0-673-77157-5(1)) Celebration Pr.
Que Mala Suerte! 2003. (J). (gr. -1-2). 23.95 (978-0-673-77398-2(1)) Celebration Pr.
Que Me Pongo? 2003. (J). (gr. -1-2). 23.95 (978-0-673-77407-1(4)) Celebration Pr.
Que Me Pongo? Big Book Packages. 2003. 64.95 (978-0-673-58599-8(9)) Celebration Pr.
Que Miedo! 2003. 23.95 (978-0-673-77794-2(4)) Celebration Pr.
Ranchetti, Sebastiano. Animal Opposites / Opuestos Animales, 1 vol. 2008. (Learn with Animals / Aprende con Los Animales Ser.). (SPA & ENG., Illus.). 24p. (gr. k-1). pap. 9.15 (978-0-8368-9043-3(4), 631077de-3557-4a93-a323-ad969f2ad9b4); lib. bdg. 24.67 (978-0-8368-9038-9(8), c90b0b17-e3be-4eee-8f10-e0a029403ea9) Stevens, Gareth Publishing LLLP. (Weekly Reader Leveled Readers).
Saber Es Poder: A Basic Grammar Book, Easy, Fun & Practical. (ENG & SPA.). 45.00 (978-0-944356-08-1(7)) Alegria Hispana Pubns.
Sigmar Staff. Sinonimos - Ant - Paraonimos (Synonyms - Ant - Homonyms) (SPA.). (J). 9.95 (978-950-11-0639-8(X)) Sigmar ARG. Dist: AIMS International Bks., Inc.
La Sirenita. 2003. (SPA.). 28.95 (978-0-673-77379-1(5)) Celebration Pr.
Thayer, Tanya. La Primavera. Translations.com Staff, tr. 2005. (Mi Primer Paso Al Mundo Real Las Estaciones Del Ano (First Step Nonfiction - Seasons) Ser.).Tr. of Spring. (SPA., Illus.). 24p. (gr. k-2). lib. bdg. 23.93 (978-0-8225-3165-4(8)); per. 6.95 (978-0-8225-3158-6(5)) Lerner Publishing Group.
Thomas, Keith A. The Idioms. Thomas, Keith A., illus. (ENG & SPA., Illus.). 44p. (J). (gr. 3-18). pap. (978-0-9617451-4-1(2)) KALEXT Productions, LLC.
La Tostada. 2003. 23.95 (978-0-673-77800-0(2)) Celebration Pr.
Travis, Joelle & Figueras, Ligaya, eds. Numeros, Colores, Verbos y Frases. Hazan, Maurice, illus. 2003. (SPA.). 112p. (J). per. 20.00 (978-1-932770-17-9(8), SWLB2) Symtalk, Inc.
Tulip, Jenny. My First Spanish Word Book. 2004. (ENG & SPA., Illus.). 48p. (J). 5.99 (978-1-85854-394-9(0)) Brimax Books Ltd. GBR. Dist: Byeway Bks.
Vaamonde, Conchita, tr. My First Spanish Words. Tulip, Jenny, illus. 2004. (SPA.). 12p. (J). bds. 7.99 (978-1-85854-512-7(9)) Brimax Books Ltd. GBR. Dist: Byeway Bks.
Watts, Catherine & Phillips, Hilary. Bringing Spanish to Life: Creative Activities For 5-11. 2015. (ENG., Illus.). 120p. (C). pap. 47.95 (978-1-138-79768-0(5), Y169544) Routledge.
Wise, Sue. How Do I Say That? / ¿Cómo Se Dice?, 1 vol. 2005. (Reference Ser.). (ENG & SPA., Illus.). 32p. (gr. 2-4). pap. 11.50 (978-0-8368-6583-7(9), 14d262c5-a77c-4846-8610-5f4700215d4d); lib. bdg. 28.67 (978-0-8368-6259-1(7), d7f78b4d-090d-42e7-ae3b-d39e993c0815) Stevens, Gareth Publishing LLLP. (Gareth Stevens Learning Library).
With addition of Elefonetica Phonics Storybooks Green & Orange Collections. (De Canciones A Cuentos Ser.). (SPA.). (gr. 1-18). 987.10 (978-0-7362-0703-4(1)) CENGAGE Learning.
Zocchi, Judith Mazzeo. Will's W Book: El Libro "W" de Will. 2005. (ENG & SPA., Illus.). (978-1-59646-553-4(0)) Dingles & Co.
Zocchi, Judith Mazzeo, et al. Aimee's A Book: El Libro a de Aimee. Revutsky, Helen Ross, illus. 2005. (J). (978-1-59646-421-6(6)) Dingles & Co.
—Bebe's "B" Book: El Libro "B" de Bibi. Revutsky, Helen Ross, illus. 2005. (SPA & ENG.). (J). (978-1-59646-427-8(5)) Dingles & Co.
—Delia's D Book: El Libro D de Delia. Revutsky, Helen Ross, illus. 2005. (SPA.). (J). (978-1-59646-439-1(9)) Dingles & Co.
—Tad's "T" Book: El Libro "T" de Tad. 2005. (ENG & SPA., Illus.). (J). (978-1-59646-535-0(2)) Dingles & Co.
—Vera's "V" Book: El Libro "V" de Vera. 2005. (ENG & SPA., Illus.). (J). (978-1-59646-547-3(6)) Dingles & Co.
—Xavia's "X" Book: El Libro "X" de Xavia. Revutsky, Helen Ross, illus. 2005. (SPA.). (978-1-59646-559-6(X)) Dingles & Co.
Zocchi, Judy. Cassie's "C" Book: El Libro "C" de Cassie. 2005. (SPA & ENG., Illus.). (J). (978-1-59646-433-9(X)) Dingles & Co.

SPANISH LANGUAGE—READERS

Abrapalabra! (SPA.). (gr. -1-1). 161.67 (978-0-7362-2592-2(7)) CENGAGE Learning.
Abuelita y Yo. (Spanish Early Intervention Levels Ser.). (SPA.). 23.10 (978-1-56334-777-1(6)) CENGAGE Learning.

S

Acento 1: Cuaderno de Ortografia. (SPA.). (J). (gr. 1-9). 16.00 *(978-958-04-3823-6(4))* Norma S.A. COL. Dist: Distribuidora Norma, Inc.

Acento 2: Cuaderno de Ortografia. (SPA.). (J). 16.00 *(978-958-04-3822-9(6))* Norma S.A. COL. Dist: Distribuidora Norma, Inc.

Acento 3: Cuaderno de Ortografia. (SPA.). (J). (gr. 1-9). 16.00 *(978-958-04-3821-2(8))* Norma S.A. COL. Dist: Distribuidora Norma, Inc.

Acento 4: Cuaderno de Ortografia. (SPA.). (J). (gr. 1-9). 16.00 *(978-958-04-3820-5(X))* Norma S.A. COL. Dist: Distribuidora Norma, Inc.

Acento 5: Cuaderno de Ortografia. (SPA.). (J). (gr. 1-9). 16.00 *(978-958-04-3819-9(6))* Norma S.A. COL. Dist: Distribuidora Norma, Inc.

Acento 6: Cuaderno de Ortografia. (SPA.). (J). (gr. 1-9). 16.00 *(978-958-04-3829-8(3))* Norma S.A. COL. Dist: Distribuidora Norma, Inc.

Acento 7: Cuaderno de Ortografia. (SPA.). (J). (gr. 1-9). 16.00 *(978-958-04-3830-4(7))* Norma S.A. COL. Dist: Distribuidora Norma, Inc.

Ada, Alma Flor & Campoy, F. Isabel. Muu, Moo! Rimas de Animales/Animal Nursery Rhymes: Bilingual English-Spanish. Escriva, Vivi, illus. 2010. (ENG.). 48p. (J). (gr. -1-3). 16.99 *(978-0-06-134613-2(6))*; lib. bdg. 17.89 *(978-0-06-134614-9(4))* HarperCollins Español.

Ada, Alma Flor & Wensell, Ulises. Ten Little Puppies/Diez Perritos. 2011. (ENG., Illus.). 32p. (J). (gr. -1-3). 16.99 *(978-0-06-147043-1(0))* HarperCollins Español.

Ada, Alma Flor & Zubizarreta, Gabriel M. Con Cariño, Amalia (Love, Amalia) (SPA., Illus.). (J). (gr. 3-7). 2013. 160p. pap. 7.99 *(978-1-4424-2406-7(0))* 2012. 144p. 18.99 *(978-1-4424-2405-0(2)*, Atheneum Bks. for Young Readers) Simon & Schuster Children's Publishing.

Adivinalo!, 6, Pack. (Literatura 2000 Ser.). (SPA.). (gr. k-1). 28.00 *(978-0-7635-1009-1(2))* Rigby Education.

El Aeropuerto, 2, Pack. (Chiquilibros Ser.). (SPA.). (gr. -1-1). 12.00 *(978-0-7635-8557-0(2))* Rigby Education.

Aguilar, Jose. Jovenes piratas/Youngs Pirates. 2008. 36p. *(978-84-934160-7-2(X))* Atalante.

Ahumada. Juguemos a Leer-Texto.Tr. of Lets Play to Read. (SPA.). (J). 7.98 *(978-968-24-5631-2(2))* Trillas Editorial, S. A. MEX. Dist: Continental Bk. Co., Inc.

Al Circo, Al Circo! 2003. 63.50 *(978-0-8136-8085-9(9))*; suppl. ed. 8.95 *(978-0-8136-8082-8(4))* Modern Curriculum Pr.

Alagna, Magdalena. Wyatt Earp: Lawman of the American West / Sheriff del oeste Americano. 2009. (Famous People in American History/Grandes personajes en la historia de los Estados Unidos Ser.). (ENG & SPA.). 32p. (gr. 2-3). 47.90 *(978-1-61512-558-6(2)*, Editorial Buenas Letras) Rosen Publishing Group, Inc., The.

—Wyatt Earp: Sheriff del oeste americano (Wyatt Earp: Lawman of the American West) 2009. (Grandes personajes en la historia de los Estados Unidos (Famous People in American History) Ser.). (SPA.). 32p. (gr. 2-3). 47.90 *(978-1-61512-811-2(5)*, Editorial Buenas Letras) Rosen Publishing Group, Inc., The.

Alcántara, Ricardo. Cuenta Estrellas.Tr. of Counting Stars. (SPA.). 64p. (J). (gr. 3-5). 6.36 *(978-84-261-2146-2(2))* Juventud, Editorial ESP. Dist: Lectorum Pubns., Inc.

Alfaro Sifontes, Manuel Guillermo. Alboroto en un Lugar Remoto. 2005. (Illus.). 32p. (J). *(978-1-58018-052-8(3))* Cambridge BrickHouse, Inc.

Allsop, Marcus. Nos Gustan Nuestros Dientes We Like Our Teeth. 2nd ed. 2012. (We Like Toi Ser.). (ENG.). 32p. (J). pap. 10.95 *(978-1-935826-09-5(3))* Kalindi Pr.

Aloian, Molly. Columbus Day. 2010. (ENG., Illus.). 32p. (J). *(978-0-7787-4760-4(3))*; pap. *(978-0-7787-4778-9(6))* Crabtree Publishing Co.

Alphabet Sorting Box. (gr. -1-12). 22.40 *(978-0-7362-1095-9(4))* CENGAGE Learning.

Alvarez, Julia. Devolver Al Remitente (Return to Sender Spanish Edition) 2010. (SPA.). 368p. (J). (gr. 3-7). 8.99 *(978-0-375-85124-7(0)*, Yearling) Random Hse. Children's Bks.

Alvarez, Mrinali, illus. Pon, Pon: ¡A Jugar con el Bebé! 2005. (SPA.). 28p. (J). 8.95 *(978-0-8477-1550-3(7))* Univ. of Puerto Rico Pr.

Amanecer Grade K: Student Anthology. (Nuevos Horizontes Ser.). (SPA.). (J). 9.95 *(978-1-56014-499-1(8))* Santillana USA Publishing Co., Inc.

Ambrus, Victor G. Busca a Dracula (Search for Dracula) (J). 5.95 *(978-950-08-1288-7(6))* Atlantida ARG. Dist: AIMS International Bks., Inc.

—Cuenta con Dracula (Count with Dracula) (J). 5.95 *(978-950-08-1286-3(X))* Atlantida ARG. Dist: AIMS International Bks., Inc.

—Lee Con Dracula (Read with Dracula) (J). 5.95 *(978-950-08-1287-0(8))* Atlantida ARG. Dist: AIMS International Bks., Inc.

—Que Hora Es, Dracula? (What Time Is It, Dracula?) (J). 5.95 *(978-950-08-1285-6(1))* Atlantida ARG. Dist: AIMS International Bks., Inc.

Amigos, 6 vols., Pack. (Literatura 2000 Ser.). (SPA.). (gr. k-1). 28.00 *(978-0-7635-1010-7(6))* Rigby Education.

Los amigos del Mono, 6 Pack. (Literatura 2000 Ser.). (SPA.). (gr. 1-2). 28.00 *(978-0-7635-1033-6(5))* Rigby Education.

Amigos para Siempre: Individual Title Six-Packs. (Literatura 2000 Ser.). (SPA.). (gr. 2-3). 33.00 *(978-0-7635-1081-7(5))* Rigby Education.

El Amor de Beatriz. (SPA.). pap. 5.95 *(978-88-8148-806-3(X))* EMC/Paradigm Publishing.

Anastasio, Dina. How Raven Became Black & Owl Got Its Spots & Por qué el cuervo es negro y el búho tiene Manchitas: 6 English, 6 Spanish Adaptations. 2011. (ENG & SPA.). (J). 75.00 net. *(978-1-4108-5626-5(7))* Benchmark Education Co.

Anaya Publishers Staff. Aprender a Vivir 1. (SPA.). 56p. (J). *(978-84-207-7136-6(8))* Grupo Anaya, S.A.

—Aprender a Vivir 2. (SPA.). (J). *(978-84-207-7190-8(2))* Grupo Anaya, S.A.

—Aprender a Vivir 3. (SPA.). 88p. (J). *(978-84-207-6555-6(4))* Grupo Anaya, S.A.

—Aprender a Vivir 3: Propuesta Didactica. (SPA.). 128p. (J). *(978-84-207-6556-3(2))* Grupo Anaya, S.A.

—Aprender a Vivir 4. (SPA.). 88p. (J). *(978-84-207-6557-0(0))* Grupo Anaya, S.A.

—Aprender a Vivir 4: Propuesta Didactica. (SPA.). 128p. (J). *(978-84-207-6558-7(9))* Grupo Anaya, S.A.

—Aprender a Vivir 5. (SPA.). 88p. (J). *(978-84-207-6559-4(7))* Grupo Anaya, S.A.

—Aprender a Vivir 5: Propuesta Didactica. (SPA.). 128p. (J). *(978-84-207-6560-0(0))* Grupo Anaya, S.A.

—Aprender a Vivir 6. (SPA.). 88p. (J). *(978-84-207-6561-7(9))* Grupo Anaya, S.A.

—Aprender a Vivir 6: Propuesta Didactica. (SPA.). 128p. (J). *(978-84-207-6562-4(7))* Grupo Anaya, S.A.

Anaya, Rudolfo. The First Tortilla: A Bilingual Story. Lamadrid, Enrique R., tr. Córdova, Amy, illus. 2012. (ENG & SPA.). 32p. (J). pap. 16.95 *(978-0-8263-4215-7(9)*, P208966) Univ. of New Mexico Pr.

—La Llorona: The Crying Woman. Lamadrid, Enrique R., tr. Córdova, Amy, illus. 2011. (ENG.). 40p. (J). 19.95 *(978-0-8263-4460-1(7)*, P196646) Univ. of New Mexico Pr.

El Apicultor, 6 vols., Pack. (Literatura 2000 Ser.). (SPA.). (gr. 2-3). 33.00 *(978-0-7635-1083-1(1))* Rigby Education.

Appleby, Alex. It's Sunny! / ¡Está Soleado!, 1 vol. 2013. (What's the Weather? / ¿Qué Tiempo Hace? Ser.). (SPA & ENG., Illus.). 24p. (J). (gr. k-k). 25.27 *(978-1-4339-9454-8(2)*, 8520c099-825c-40d9-9a9e-704fd347d662) Stevens, Gareth Publishing LLLP.

—It's Windy! / ¡Está Ventoso!, 1 vol. 2013. (What's the Weather? / ¿Qué Tiempo Hace? Ser.). (SPA & ENG., Illus.). 24p. (J). (gr. k-k). 25.27 *(978-1-4339-9452-4(6)*, ae6c9bf0-db7a-4c8c-945a-3b8e69bee130) Stevens, Gareth Publishing LLLP.

—Lo Que Toco / What I Touch, 1 vol. 2014. (Mis Cinco Sentidos / My Five Senses Ser.). (SPA & ENG.). 24p. (J). (gr. k-k). 24.27 *(978-1-4824-0877-5(5)*, eaa24db5-9dd7-476d-9819-f4ffbe35e3c5) Stevens, Gareth Publishing LLLP.

April, Elyse. We Like to Move - Spanish / English Edition: Exercise Is Fun. 2012. (We Like To Ser.). (ENG., Illus.). 32p. (J). pap. 10.95 *(978-1-935826-08-8(5))* Kalindi Pr.

Aquel que Escucha: Individual Title Six-Packs. (Literatura 2000 Ser.). (SPA.). (gr. 2-3). 33.00 *(978-0-7635-1084-8(X))* Rigby Education.

Aquellos Dias de Dinosaurios: Little Book, Level 14, Vol. 14. 2003. (Fonolibros Ser.). 35.50 *(978-0-7652-0124-9(0))* Modern Curriculum Pr.

El arbol de Diego: Individual Title Six-Packs. (Literatura 2000 Ser.). (SPA.). (gr. 1-2). 28.00 *(978-0-7635-1034-3(3))* Rigby Education.

El arbol de la Miel: Individual Title Six-Packs. (Literatura 2000 Ser.). (SPA.). (gr. 2-3). 33.00 *(978-0-7635-1254-5(0))* Rigby Education.

Are We There Yet, Mama? 2003. 23.95 *(978-0-673-78136-9(4))* Celebration Pr.

Arnold, George. Los Gatos of the CIA. 2005. (SPA & ENG., Illus.). 225p. pap. 22.95 *(978-1-57168-861-3(7)*, Nortex Pr.) Eakin Pr.

Arrugas: Individual Title Six-Packs. (Literatura 2000 Ser.). (SPA.). (gr. 1-2). 28.00 *(978-0-7635-1035-0(1))* Rigby Education.

Aventuras Infantiles/Adventures for Kids. (ENG & SPA.). 80p. (J). 17.00 *(978-0-944356-04-3(4))* Alegria Hispana Pubns.

Ayer Vino Santa Clos: Individuel, 6-packs. 2003. 23.95 *(978-0-673-77137-7(7))* Celebration Pr.

AZ Books Staff. Animales - Farm Animals: Farm Animals. Gorbachenok, Ekaterina, ed. 2012. (Spanish for Kids Ser.). (ENG & SPA.). 10p. (J). (gr. -1-k). 11.95 *(978-1-61889-135-8(9))* AZ Bks. LLC.

—Colores - Colorful Animals: Colorful Animals. Gorbachenok, Ekaterina, ed. 2012. (Spanish for Kids Ser.). (ENG & SPA.). 10p. (J). (gr. -1-k). bds. 11.95 *(978-1-61889-136-5(7))* AZ Bks. LLC.

—Numeros - Count the Toys: Count the Toys. Gorbachenok, Ekaterina, ed. 2012. (Spanish for Kids Ser.). (ENG & SPA.). 10p. (J). (-k). bds. 11.95 *(978-1-61889-137-2(5))* AZ Bks. LLC.

Baca, Ana. Tía's Tamales. Chilton, Noël, illus. 2012. (ENG & SPA.). 32p. (J). pap. 16.95 *(978-0-8263-5027-5(5)*, P225697) Univ. of New Mexico Pr.

Bain, Michelle. The Adventures of Thumbs up Johnnie Rules of Thumb for Going Green: Rules of Thumb for Going Green. Lizana, Lorenzo, illus. 2008. 18p. (J). pap. 5.95 *(978-0-9795832-4-7(1))* Pixie Stuff LLC.

—Las aventuras de Juanito el Pulgarcito Zipp, Pequeño Dígito, las señales y las Señas: Zipp, Pequeño Dígito, las señales y las Señas. Lizana, Lorenzo, illus. 2007.Tr. of Zipp, Digit & the Happy Signs! (SPA.). 28p. (J). *(978-0-9795832-3-0(3))* Pixie Stuff LLC.

El bano de Benito. (Spanish Early Intervention Levels Ser.). (SPA.). 21.30 *(978-0-7362-0824-6(0))* CENGAGE Learning.

El Bano de Papa, 6, Pack. (Literatura 2000 Ser.). (SPA.). (gr. 1-2). 28.00 *(978-0-7635-1058-9(0))* Rigby Education.

Bansch, Helga. Petra. 2010. (SPA., Illus.). 48p. (J). 15.95 *(978-84-9871-003-8(0))* OQO, Editora ESP. Dist: Baker & Taylor Bks.

Barker, Henry. Vino Del Espacio (It Came from Outer Space) Gott, Barry, illus. 2009. (Science Solves It! (r) en Espanol Ser.). (SPA.). 32p. (J). (gr. 1-3). pap. 33.92 *(978-1-58013-771-3(7))* Lerner Publishing Group.

Barner, Bob. The Day of the Dead / el día de Los Muertos: A Bilingual Celebration. 2011.Tr. of Day of the Dead / el día de Los Muertos. (Illus.). 32p. (J). (gr. -1-3). pap. 7.99 *(978-0-8234-2381-1(6))* Holiday Hse., Inc.

Barredo, Jose Eduardo. Mundo Azul. (Torre de Papel Ser.). (SPA.). 284p. (YA). (gr. 7-18). 7.95 *(978-958-04-4522-7(2))* Norma S.A. COL. Dist: Distribuidora Norma, Inc.

Un Barrio Muy Especial. (Coleccion Leo Con Figuras). (SPA., Illus.). 14p. (J). pap. 4.50 *(978-950-11-0928-3(3)*, SGM293) Sigmar ARG. Dist: Continental Bk. Co., Inc.

Barry, Frances. Salvemos a Los Animales. 2012. (SPA.). 26p. (J). (gr. k-1). pap. 23.99 *(978-84-261-3856-9(X))* Juventud, Editorial ESP. Dist: Lectorum Pubns., Inc.

Beaton, Clare & Blackstone, Stella. Un Alce, Veinte Ratones. Beaton, Clare, illus. 2006.Tr. of One Moose, Twenty Mice. (Illus.). 32p. (J). (gr. -1-k). bds. 6.99 *(978-1-84686-019-5(9))* Barefoot Bks., Inc.

Beaude, Pierre Marie. Flora, la Desconocida del Espacio. (Torre de Papel Ser.). (SPA.). (YA). (gr. 6-18). 7.95 *(978-958-04-1033-1(X))* Norma S.A. COL. Dist: Distribuidora Norma, Inc.

Beck, Paul. El Cuerpo Humano. Fairman, Jennifer, illus. 2007. (SPA.). 48p. (J). (gr. k-5). *(978-970-718-436-7(1)*, Silver Dolphin en Español) Advanced Marketing, S. de R. L. de C. V.

Beckstrand, Karl. Crumbs on the Stairs - Migas en Las Escaleras: A Mystery. Beckstrand, Karl, illus. 2011. (Mini-Mysteries for Minors Ser.: 2).Tr. of Migas en Las Escaleras. (ENG & SPA., Illus.). 24p. (J). pap. 14.95 *(978-0-9776065-9-7(7)*, Gozo Bks.) Premio Publishing & Gozo Bks., LLC.

Beltran, Andrea. Juliet's Day. 2009. 34p. pap. 24.20 *(978-0-557-18983-0(7))* Lulu Pr., Inc.

Benchmark Education Company, LLC Staff. Spanish Emergent Supplement. 2005. (BookRoom Collection Ser.). (J). spiral bd. 880.00 *(978-1-4108-5613-5(5))* Benchmark Education Co.

Benchmark Education Company, LLC Staff, compiled by. Spanish Early/Fluent Supplement. 2005. spiral bd. 1350.00 *(978-1-4108-5661-6(5))* Benchmark Education Co.

—Spanish Grade 3 Small Group Set. 2005. spiral bd. 4000.00 *(978-1-4108-5667-8(4))*; spiral bd. 1000.00 *(978-1-4108-5668-5(2))* Benchmark Education Co.

—Spanish Grade 4 Small Group Set. 2005. spiral bd. 4000.00 *(978-1-4108-5669-2(0))*; spiral bd. 1000.00 *(978-1-4108-5670-8(4))* Benchmark Education Co.

—Spanish Grade 5 Small Group Set. 2005. spiral bd. 1000.00 *(978-1-4108-4960-1(0))* Benchmark Education Co.

Benegas, Candela. Una Rayuela: Level 1. (SPA & ENG.). 128p. (J). (gr. 3-7). stu. ed. 21.95 *(978-84-7143-804-1(6)*, SGS8046) Sociedad General Espanola de Libreria ESP. Dist: Continental Bk. Co., Inc.

Benoist, Cathy & Gilmore, Cathy. El Conejito de Pascua: El Cuento de un Dia Extraordinario. Sundy, Jonathan, illus. 2014. (SPA.). 40p. (J). (gr. 4-7). 16.99 *(978-0-7648-2456-2(2)*, Libros Liguori) Liguori Pubns.

Bernier-Grand, Carmen T. Shake It, Morena! And Other Folklore from Puerto Rico. Delacre, Lulu, illus. 2007. 48p. (J). (gr. -1-3). per. 6.95 *(978-0-8225-7026-4(2)*, First Avenue Editions) Lerner Publishing Group.

Bertrand, Diane Gonzales. El Momento de Trino. Sanmiguel, Rosario, tr. from ENG. 2006. (SPA.). 181p. (J). (gr. 3-7). per. 9.95 *(978-1-55885-473-4(8)*, Piñata Books) Arte Publico Pr.

Bertrand, Diane Gonzales & Ventura, Gabriela Baeza. The Party for Papá Luis/La Fiesta para Papá Luis. Galindo, Alejandro, illus. 2010. (ENG.). 32p. (J). (gr. -1-3). 16.95 *(978-1-55885-532-8(7))* Arte Publico Pr.

Biblioteca Saltamontes Spanish Chapter Books Coleccion Viva Chivito! Classroom Set & Manipulatives. (SPA.). (gr. 1-2). 521.25 incl. reel tape *(978-0-7362-1589-3(1))*; 517.82 incl. audio compact disk *(978-0-7362-1591-6(3))* CENGAGE Learning.

La Bicicross de Alex: Individual Title Six-Packs. (Literatura 2000 Ser.). (SPA.). (gr. 1-2). 28.00 *(978-0-7635-1036-7(X))* Rigby Education.

Biello, David. Portaaviones: Por dentro y por fuera (Aircraft Carriers: Inside & Out) 2009. (Tecnología: Mapas para el Futuro Ser.). (SPA.). 48p. (gr. 4-4). 53.00 *(978-1-60853-287-2(9)*, Editorial Buenas Letras) Rosen Publishing Group, Inc., The.

Bienvenidos! (Illus.). 96p. (J). (gr. k-5). Level 1. (ENG & SPA.). pap., wbk. ed. 18.95 *(978-88-8148-038-8(7))*Level 2. (SPA & ENG., pap., wbk. ed. 18.95 *(978-88-8148-045-6(X))*Level 3. (SPA & ENG., pap., wbk. ed. 18.95 *(978-88-8148-046-3(8))* European Language Institute ITA. Dist: Distribooks, Inc.

Blackaby, Susan. El Lugar de Luis, 1 vol. Ruíz, Carlos & Ruíz, Carlos, trs. Gallagher-Cole, Mernie, illus. 2006. (Read-It! Readers en Español: Story Collection).Tr. of Place for Mike. (SPA.). 24p. (J). (gr. -1-3). 22.65 *(978-1-4048-1688-6(7)*, 90854, Picture Window Bks.) Capstone.

Blackstone, Stella. Bear at Work. Harter, Debbie, illus. 2011. (ENG & SPA.). 24p. (J). (gr. -1-k). pap. 6.99 *(978-1-84686-554-1(9))* Barefoot Bks., Inc.

—Bear at Work (Oso en el Trabajo) 2012. (ENG & SPA., Illus.). 24p. (J). pap. 7.99 *(978-1-84686-769-9(X))* Barefoot Bks., Inc.

—Bear on a Bike / Oso en Bicicleta. Harter, Debbie, illus. 2014. (Bear Ser.). (ENG.). 32p. (J). (gr. -1-1). pap. 8.99 *(978-1-78285-079-3(1))* Barefoot Bks., Inc.

—Bear's Busy Family / la Familia Ocupada de Oso. Harter, Debbie, illus. 2014. (Bear Ser.). (ENG.). 32p. (J). (gr. -1-1). pap. 8.99 *(978-1-84686-771-2(1))* Barefoot Bks., Inc.

Blackstone, Stella & Scribens, Sunny. Mis Primeras Palabras. 2017. (SPA.). 30p. (J). (gr. -1-k). bds. 14.99 *(978-1-78285-325-1(1))* Barefoot Bks., Inc.

Blair, Eric. El Lobo y Los Siete Cabritos: Versión Del Cuento de Los Hermanos Grimm. Abello, Patricia, tr. Petrusek, Brett, illus. 2006. (Read-It! Readers en Español: Cuentos de Hadas Ser.). (SPA.). 32p. (J). (gr. k-3). 22.65 *(978-1-4048-1645-9(3)*, 86680, Picture Window Bks.) Capstone.

—El Ninito de Jengibre, 1 vol. Abello, Patricia, tr. Peterson, Ben, illus. 2006. (Read-It! Readers en Español: Cuentos Folclóricos Ser.).Tr. of Gingerbread Man. (SPA.). 32p. (J). (gr. k-3). 22.65 *(978-1-4048-1647-3(X)*, 91757, Picture Window Bks.) Capstone.

—El Pastorcito Mentiroso: Versión de la Fábula de Esopo. Abello, Patricia, tr. Silverman, Dianne, illus. 2006. (Read-It! Readers en Español: Fábulas Ser.).Tr. of Boy Who Cried Wolf - A Retelling of Aesop's Fable. (SPA.). 24p. (J). (gr. k-3). 22.65 *(978-1-4048-1616-9(X)*, 91876, Picture Window Bks.) Capstone.

Blake, Stéphanie. No Quiero Ir a la Escuela. 2007. (SPA., Illus.). 40p. (gr. k-2). 17.99 *(978-84-8470-268-9(5))* Corimbo, Editorial S.L. ESP. Dist: Lectorum Pubns., Inc.

Blue Collection. (Elefonetica Ser.). (SPA.). (gr. 1-2). 373.22 *(978-0-7362-0795-9(3))* CENGAGE Learning.

Boada, Francesc. Princess & the Pea / la Princesesa y el Guisante. Estrada, Pau, illus. 2013. (Bilingual Fairy Tales Ser.). (SPA & ENG.). 32p. (J). (gr. 1-4). lib. bdg. 28.50 *(978-1-60753-357-3(X)*, 16284) Amicus.

Boada, Francesc, adapted by. Cinderella/Cenicienta: Bilingual Edition. 2005. (Bilingual Fairy Tales Ser.: BILI). (ENG., Illus.). 32p. (J). (gr. -1-7). pap. 8.99 *(978-0-8118-3090-4(X))* Chronicle Bks. LLC.

La Boda, 6, Pack. 2003. 23.95 *(978-0-673-77138-4(5))* Celebration Pr.

La Boda, 6 pack. (Literatura 2000 Ser.). (SPA.). (gr. k-1). 28.00 *(978-0-7635-1011-4(4))* Rigby Education.

La Boda de Trazo y Rayita. (SPA.). (J). 12.00 *(978-958-02-1364-2(X))* Editorial Voluntad S.A. COL. Dist: Distribuidora Norma, Inc.

Bofil, Francesc. Rapunzel. Joma, illus. 2013. (Bilingual Fairy Tales Ser.). (SPA & ENG.). 32p. (J). (gr. 1-4). lib. bdg. 28.50 *(978-1-60753-360-3(X)*, 16286) Amicus.

Boie, Kirsten. King-Kong, el Conejillo de Indias Viajeros. (Torre de Papel Ser.). (SPA.). (J). (gr. 2). 7.95 *(978-958-04-1311-0(8))* Norma S.A. COL. Dist: Distribuidora Norma, Inc.

Bojunga, Lygia. La Casa de la Madrina. (Torre de Papel Ser.). (SPA.). (J). (gr. 4-18). 8.95 *(978-958-04-3396-5(8)*, NR30562) Norma S.A. COL. Dist: Lectorum Pubns., Inc., Distribuidora Norma, Inc.

—La Cuerda Floja. (Torre de Papel Ser.).Tr. of Tightrope. (SPA.). (J). (gr. 4-18). 8.95 *(978-958-04-4527-2(3))* Norma S.A. COL. Dist: Distribuidora Norma, Inc.

Boo! Matching English, 6 Pack. 2003. 23.95 *(978-0-673-76188-0(6))* Celebration Pr.

Bornemann, Elsa. El Libro de los Chicos Enamorados. (SPA.). (J). (gr. 5-8). 8.95 *(978-958-04-3454-2(9)*, NR7681) Norma S.A. COL. Dist: Lectorum Pubns., Inc., Distribuidora Norma, Inc.

—El Ultimo Mago de Bilembambudin. (Torre de Papel Ser.). (SPA.). (J). (gr. 4-18). 8.95 *(978-958-04-3455-9(7))* Norma S.A. COL. Dist: Distribuidora Norma, Inc.

Borreguita Negra. 2003. 23.95 *(978-0-673-77381-4(7))* Celebration Pr.

Borth, Teddy. Animales Azules (Blue Animals), 1 vol. 2016. (Animales de Colores (Animal Colors) Ser.). (SPA., Illus.). 24p. (J). (gr. -1-2). lib. bdg. 32.79 *(978-1-68080-724-0(2)*, 22610, Abdo Kids) ABDO Publishing Co.

—Animales Rojos (Red Animals), 1 vol. 2016. (Animales de Colores (Animal Colors) Ser.). (SPA., Illus.). 24p. (J). (gr. -1-2). lib. bdg. 32.79 *(978-1-68080-727-1(7)*, 22616, Abdo Kids) ABDO Publishing Co.

—Futbol Americano: Grandes Momentos, Récords y Datos (Spanish Version) 2016. (Grandes Deportes (Great Sports) Ser.). (SPA., Illus.). 24p. (J). (gr. -1-2). lib. bdg. 32.79 *(978-1-68080-736-3(6)*, 22634, Abdo Kids) ABDO Publishing Co.

—Gimnasia: Grandes Momentos, Récords y Datos (Spanish Version) 2016. (Grandes Deportes (Great Sports) Ser.). (SPA., Illus.). 24p. (J). (gr. -1-2). lib. bdg. 32.79 *(978-1-68080-734-9(X)*, 22630, Abdo Kids) ABDO Publishing Co.

El bosque de Miel. (Saludos Ser.: Vol. 1). (SPA.). (gr. 2-3). 31.00 *(978-0-7635-5731-7(5))* Rigby Education.

El bosque de Miel: 6 Small Books. (Saludos Ser.: Vol. 1). (SPA.). (gr. 2-3). 31.00 *(978-0-7635-9538-8(1))* Rigby Education.

Bravo, Queta!, 6 pack. 2003. 23.95 *(978-0-673-78072-0(4))* Celebration Pr.

Brinca la Tablita. 2003. 28.95 *(978-0-673-78091-1(0))* Celebration Pr.

Brooks, Felicity & MacKinnon, Mairi. First Picture Spanish. Litchfield, Jo, illus. 2006. (First Picture Flap Bks.). 18p. (J). (gr. 1-4). bds. 14.99 *(978-0-7945-1384-9(0)*, Usborne) EDC Publishing.

Brown, Jonatha A. La Piel y el Pelo de Los Animales (Animal Skin & Fur), 1 vol. 2006. (En Qué Se Diferencian Los Animales (Why Animals Look Different) Ser.). (SPA., Illus.). 24p. (J). (gr. 2-4). lib. bdg. 24.67 *(978-0-8368-7415-0(3)*, 69d9c034-0cb3-4f43-83f3-a959826224be, Weekly Reader Leveled Readers) Stevens, Gareth Publishing LLLP.

Brown, Monica. Marisol Mcdonald Doesn't Match: Marisol Mcdonald No Combina, 1 vol. Palacios, Sara, illus. 2013. (Marisol Mcdonald Ser.). (ENG.). 32p. (J). (gr. k-3). 19.95 *(978-0-89239-235-3(5)*, leelowcbp) Lee & Low Bks., Inc.

—Maya's Blanket / la Manta de Maya, 1 vol. Diaz, David, illus. 2015. (ENG.). 32p. (J). (gr. k-4). 19.95 *(978-0-89239-292-6(4)*, leelowcbp) Lee & Low Bks., Inc.

Brown, Monica & Ventura, Gabriela Baeza. Clara & the Curandera / Clara y la Curandera. Muraida, Thelma, illus. 2011. (J). 16.95 *(978-1-55885-700-1(1)*, Piñata Books) Arte Publico Pr.

Broyles, Anne. Arturo & the Bienvenido Feast, 1 vol. Cortes, Maru, tr. from SPA. Lewis, K. E., illus. 2017. (ENG & SPA.). 32p. (J). (gr. -1-3). 16.99 *(978-1-4556-2283-2(4)*, Pelican Publishing) Arcadia Publishing.

Buceando en el Misterio. (SPA., Illus.). 70p. (YA). (gr. 8-10). pap. 14.95 *(978-88-8148-333-4(5))* EMC/Paradigm Publishing.

Un buen Lugar. (Spanish Early Intervention Levels Ser.). (SPA.). 31.14 *(978-0-7362-0326-5(5))* CENGAGE Learning.

Buen Viaje Pinguinos! (Coleccion Leo Con Figuras). (SPA., Illus.). 14p. (J). pap. 4.50 *(978-950-11-0929-0(1)*, SGM291) Sigmar ARG. Dist: Continental Bk. Co., Inc.

Buenas noches, Hermanito: Individual Title Six-Packs. (Literatura 2000 Ser.). (SPA.). (gr. 1-2). 28.00 *(978-0-7635-1037-4(8))* Rigby Education.

A Bully Named Laura Sue: Social/Emotional Lap Book. (Pebble Soup Explorations Ser.). (SPA.). (gr. -1-18). 16.00 *(978-0-7635-7568-7(2))* Rigby Education.

Burke, David. Beauty & the Beast: Level 3: Learn Spanish Through Fairy Tales. Sandoval, Migs, illus. 2006. (Learn Spanish Through Fairy Tales Ser.). (ENG & SPA.). 29p. (J). (gr. -1-3). pap. 14.95 incl. audio compact disk *(978-1-891888-86-1(2))* Slangman Publishing.

—Goldilocks & the 3 Bears: Level 2: Learn Spanish Through Fairy Tales. Sandoval, Migs, illus. 2006. (Learn Spanish Through Fairy Tales Ser.). (ENG & SPA.). 29p. (J). (gr. -1-3). pap. 14.95 incl. audio compact disk *(978-1-891888-80-9(3))* Slangman Publishing.

Burton, Margie, et al. Clean Beaches & Playas Limpias: 6 English, 6 Spanish Adaptations. 2011. (J). spiral bd. 75.00 net. *(978-1-4108-5625-8(9))* Benchmark Education Co.

Cabal, Graciela Beatriz. Toby. (Torre de Papel Ser.). (SPA., Illus.). (J). (gr. 4-18). 8.95 *(978-958-04-4222-6(3))* Norma S.A. COL. Dist: Distribuidora Norma, Inc.

Caballero, D., tr. Que? Como? Por Que?: Autos y Camiones. Weller, Ursula, illus. 2007. (Junior (Silver Dolphin) Ser.). 16p. (J). (gr. -1). *(978-970-718-490-9(6)*, Silver Dolphin en Español) Advanced Marketing, S. de R. L. de C. V.

El Caballo Blanco, 6 Pack. (Literatura 2000 Ser.). (SPA.). (gr. 2-3). 33.00 *(978-0-7635-1255-2(9))* Rigby Education.

El Caballo Comilon, 6 Pack. (Literatura 2000 Ser.). (SPA.). (gr. 1-2). 28.00 *(978-0-7635-1038-1(6))* Rigby Education.
El caballo Mecanico, 6 Pack. (Chiquilibros Ser.). (SPA.). (gr. k-1). 23.00 *(978-0-7635-8613-3(7))* Rigby Education.
Cae una Nuez. (Spanish Early Intervention Levels Ser.). 28.38 *(978-0-7362-0838-3(0))* CENGAGE Learning.
Caicedo, Maria Victoria. En la Casa con la Abuelita. (SPA.). (J). 8.95 *(978-958-04-7445-6(1))* Norma S.A. COL. Dist: Distribuidora Norma, Inc.
Cajas: Individual Title Six-Packs. (Literatura 2000 Ser.). (SPA.). (gr. 1-2). 28.00 *(978-0-7635-1059-6(9))* Rigby Education.
El Calcetin. (Spanish Early Intervention Levels Ser.). (SPA.). 23.10 *(978-0-7362-0324-1(9))* CENGAGE Learning.
Camila y la Anciana-del-Barro: 6 Softcover Books. (Saludos Ser.: Vol. 1). (SPA.). (gr. 3-5). 31.00 *(978-0-7635-1752-6(6))* Rigby Education.
Caminando: Individual Title Six-Packs. (Literatura 2000 Ser.). (SPA.). (gr. 2-3). 33.00 *(978-0-7635-1085-5(8))* Rigby Education.
Caminata en la Ciudad, 6 Packs. (Chiquilibros Ser.). (SPA.). (gr. -1-1). 12.00 *(978-0-7635-8553-2(X))* Rigby Education.
Una Caminata Por el Bosque, 2 pack. (Chiquilibros Ser.). (SPA.). (gr. -1-1). 12.00 *(978-0-7635-8547-1(5))* Rigby Education.
La Camisa de Guerrero, 6 Pack. (Saludos Ser.: Vol. 2). (SPA.). (gr. 2-3). 31.00 *(978-0-7635-9523-4(3))* Rigby Education.
Campbell, Eric. El Lugar de los Leones. (Torre de Papel Ser.).Tr. of Where Lions Live Wild. (SPA.). (YA). (gr. 6-18). 8.95 *(978-958-04-3150-3(7))* Norma S.A. COL. Dist: Distribuidora Norma, Inc.
Campbell, Kathy. Let's Draw a Bear with Squares / Vamos a dibujar un oso usando Cuadrados. 2009. (Let's Draw with Shapes / Vamos a dibujar con figuras Ser.). (ENG & SPA.). 24p. (gr. k-1). 42.50 *(978-1-61514-220-0(7))*, Editorial Buenas Letras) Rosen Publishing Group, Inc., The.
—Let's Draw a Fish with Triangles / Vamos a dibujar un pez usando Triángulos. 2009. (Let's Draw with Shapes / Vamos a dibujar con figuras Ser.). (ENG & SPA.). 24p. (gr. k-1). 42.50 *(978-1-61514-222-4(3))*, Editorial Buenas Letras) Rosen Publishing Group, Inc., The.
—Let's Draw a Frog with Ovals / Vamos a dibujar una rana Usando óvalos. 2009. (Let's Draw with Shapes / Vamos a dibujar con figuras Ser.). (ENG & SPA.). 24p. (gr. k-1). 42.50 *(978-1-61514-223-1(1))*, Editorial Buenas Letras) Rosen Publishing Group, Inc., The.
Candela, Pilar. Una Rayuela Bk. A: Level 1. (SPA & ENG.). 96p. (J). (gr. 3-7). wbk. ed. 12.95 *(978-84-7143-810-2(0))*, SGS8100) Sociedad General Espanola de Libreria ESP. Dist: Continental Bk. Co., Inc.
—Una Rayuela Bk. B: Level 1. (SPA & ENG.). 98p. (J). (gr. 3-7). wbk. ed. 12.95 *(978-84-7143-811-9(9))*, SGS8119) Sociedad General Espanola de Libreria ESP. Dist: Continental Bk. Co., Inc.
Canetti, Yanitzia. Abecedario Nutritivo. 2009. (SPA.). 40p. (J). pap. 8.99 *(978-1-59835-115-6(X))*, BrickHouse Education) Cambridge BrickHouse, Inc.
El cangrejo al fondo del Mar: Individual Title Six-Packs. (Literatura 2000 Ser.). (SPA.). (gr. 1-2). 28.00 *(978-0-7635-1060-2(2))* Rigby Education.
Canizares, Susan & Chessen, Betsey. Storms: Tormentas. 2004. (Science Emergent Readers Ser.). (ENG & SPA., Illus.). (J). *(978-0-439-66392-2(X))* Scholastic, Inc.
Cann, Kate. Viviendo Juntos. (SPA.). (YA). 9.95 *(978-958-04-6873-8(7))* Norma S.A. COL. Dist: Distribuidora Norma, Inc.
Cano, Carles & Cano Peiró, Carles. El Arbol de las Hojas Din A-4. (SPA., Illus.). 28p. (J). (gr. k-2). *(978-84-8464-027-1(2))*, KA30310) Kalandraka Editora, S.L. ESP. Dist: Lectorum Pubns., Inc.
Caraballo, Samuel. My Big Sister / Mi Hermana Mayor. Muraida, Thelma, illus. 2012. (ENG & SPA.). (J). (gr. 3-8). 16.95 *(978-1-55885-750-6(8))*, Piñata Books) Arte Publico Pr.
Caritas. (Spanish Early Intervention Levels Ser.). 23.10 *(978-1-56334-785-6(7))* CENGAGE Learning.
Carle, Eric. Amigos. Carle, Eric, illus. 2016. (SPA., Illus.). 22p. (J). (— 1). bds. 7.99 *(978-0-399-54506-1(9))* Penguin Young Readers Group.
—My Very First Book of Numbers / Mi Primer Libro de Números: Bilingual Edition. Carle, Eric, illus. 2013. (Illus.). 20p. (J). (gr. -1 — 1). bds. 7.99 *(978-0-399-16141-4(4))* Penguin Young Readers Group.
—My Very First Book of Shapes / Mi Primer Libro de Formas: Bilingual Edition. Carle, Eric, illus. 2013. (Illus.). 20p. (J). (gr. -1 — 1). bds. 6.99 *(978-0-399-16142-1(2))* Penguin Young Readers Group.
Carlitos: Individual Title Six-Packs. (Literatura 2000 Ser.). (SPA.). (gr. 2-3). 33.00 *(978-0-7635-1256-9(7))* Rigby Education.
Carr, Elias. Jo y la Sopa Lenta. Garton, Michael, illus. 2016. (SPA.). (J). *(978-1-5064-2097-4(4))*, Sparkhouse Pr.) Spark Hse.
Carrasco, Xavier. Rumpelstiltskin. Infante, Francesc, illus. 2013. (Bilingual Fairy Tales Ser.). (SPA & ENG.). 32p. (J). (gr. 1-4). lib. bdg. 28.50 *(978-1-60753-359-7(6))*, 16287) Amicus.
Carson Dellosa Education, compiled by. Everyday Words in Spanish: Photographic. 2004. (ENG.). 104p. (gr. -1-8). 7.99 *(978-1-936022-83-0(4))*, 3924) Carson-Dellosa Publishing, LLC.
La casa de Calabaza: Individual Title Six-Packs. (Literatura 2000 Ser.). (SPA.). (gr. 2-3). 33.00 *(978-0-7635-1086-2(6))* Rigby Education.
La casa de Tita: Individual Title Six-Packs. (Literatura 2000 Ser.). (SPA.). (gr. 2-3). 33.00 *(978-0-7635-1257-6(5))* Rigby Education.
La casa nueva de los Ortega: Individual Title Six-Packs. (Literatura 2000 Ser.). (SPA.). (gr. 1-2). 28.00 *(978-0-7635-1061-9(0))* Rigby Education.
Una casa para Sergin: Six-Pack. (Saludos Ser.: Vol. 2). (SPA.). (gr. 2-3). 31.00 *(978-0-7635-9542-5(X))* Rigby Education.
Casado, Dami & Casado, Alicia. La Nieve. 2005. (Yo Te Hablare De... Ser.). (SPA., Illus.). 14p. (J). per., bds. 8.99 *(978-84-272-7297-2(9))* Molino, Editorial ESP. Dist: Santillana USA Publishing Co., Inc.
Casanueva, Idilian. I Like to Flap My Hands. 2009. 32p. pap. 12.95 *(978-1-60844-001-6(X))* Dog Ear Publishing, LLC.
Casas. (Spanish Early Intervention Levels Ser.). (SPA.). 23.10 *(978-1-56334-774-0(1))* CENGAGE Learning.
Chano: Individual Title Six-Packs. (Literatura 2000 Ser.). (SPA.). (gr. 2-3). 33.00 *(978-0-7635-1087-9(4))* Rigby Education.
Chiles. (Spanish Early Intervention Levels Ser.). (SPA.). 23.10 *(978-1-56334-778-8(4))* CENGAGE Learning.
Chiquilibros: Letras Add-to Pack. (SPA.). (gr. -1-1). 103.00 *(978-0-7635-8575-4(0))* Rigby Education.
Chiquilibros: Letras Complete Package. (SPA.). (gr. -1-1). 374.00 *(978-0-7635-8574-7(2))* Rigby Education.
Chirridos!, 6, Pack. (Literatura 2000 Ser.). (SPA.). (gr. 1-2). 28.00 *(978-0-7635-1039-8(4))* Rigby Education.
El chivo Comilon. (Spanish Early Intervention Levels Ser.). (SPA.). 23.10 *(978-1-56334-767-2(9))* CENGAGE Learning.
Christelow, Eileen. Cinco Monitos Brincando en la Cama/Five Little Monkeys Jumping on the Bed: Bilingual Spanish-English. Christelow, Eileen, illus. 2014. (Five Little Monkeys Story Ser.). (ENG., Illus.). 30p. (J). (— 1). bds. 9.99 *(978-0-544-08900-6(6))*, 1537638, Clarion Bks.) HarperCollins Pubs.
—5 Little Monkeys Bake Birthday Cake/Cinco Monitos Hacen un Pastel de Cumpleanos: Bilingual English-Spanish. Christelow, Eileen, illus. 2014. (Five Little Monkeys Story Ser.).Tr. of Five Little Monkeys Bake a Birthday Cake. (ENG., Illus.). 30p. (J). (— 1). bds. 7.99 *(978-0-544-08899-3(9))*, 1537637, Clarion Bks.) HarperCollins Pubs.
El Circo: Individual Title Six-Packs. (Literatura 2000 Ser.). (SPA.). (gr. -1-1). 28.00 *(978-0-7635-1188-3(9))* Rigby Education.
Cirilo, el gallo Desafinado. (Spanish Early Intervention Levels Ser.). (SPA.). 28.38 *(978-0-7362-0840-6(2))* CENGAGE Learning.
The City Walk: Individual Title Two-Packs. (Chiquilibros Ser.). (gr. -1-1). 12.00 *(978-0-7635-8533-4(5))* Rigby Education.
Una ciudad, una escuela, muchas Comidas: 6 Small Books. (Saludos Ser.: Vol. 1). (SPA.). (gr. 3-5). 31.00 *(978-0-7635-1805-9(0))* Rigby Education.
Clark, Sarah Kartchner. ¡En Equipo Con el Sr. Supercoyote! rev. ed. 2007. (Reader's Theater Ser.).Tr. of Teaming with Mr. Cool! (SPA., Illus.). 24p. (gr. 3-4). pap. 8.99 *(978-1-4333-0025-7(7))* Teacher Created Materials, Inc.
Claro Que Si. (Spanish Early Intervention Levels Ser.). 28.38 *(978-0-7362-0844-4(5))* CENGAGE Learning.
Clavel, Bernard. Leyendas de Montanas. (Torre de Papel Ser.). (SPA.). (YA). (gr. 6-18). 7.95 *(978-958-04-1529-9(3))* Norma S.A. COL. Dist: Distribuidora Norma, Inc.
—Leyendas del Mar. (Torre de Papel Ser.). (SPA.). (YA). (gr. 6-18). 8.95 *(978-958-04-1387-5(8))* Norma S.A. COL. Dist: Distribuidora Norma, Inc.
Cochinita bien Vestida. (Spanish Early Intervention Levels Ser.). 21.30 *(978-0-7362-0830-7(5))* CENGAGE Learning.
La Cocina: Individual Title Two-Packs. (Chiquilibros Ser.). (SPA.). (gr. -1-1). 12.00 *(978-0-7635-8560-0(2))* Rigby Education.
El cocinero Feroz: Individual Title Six-Packs. (Literatura 2000 Ser.). (SPA.). (gr. 2-3). 33.00 *(978-0-7635-1258-3(3))* Rigby Education.
Cofer, Judith Ortiz. Animal Jamboree / La Fiesta de los Animales: Latino Folktales / Leyendas Latinas. Rosales-Yeomans, Natalia, tr. 2012. (SPA & ENG.). (J). pap. 9.95 *(978-1-55885-743-8(5))*, Piñata Books) Arte Publico Pr.
Colasanti, Marina. Lejos Como Mi Querer y Otros Cuentos. (SPA.). (YA). 8.95 *(978-958-04-3651-5(7))* Norma S.A. COL. Dist: Distribuidora Norma, Inc.
Cole, Babette. El Principe Ceniciento.Tr. of Prince Cinders. (SPA.). 32p. (J). 12.95 *(978-84-233-1687-8(4))* Ediciones Destino ESP. Dist: Planeta Publishing Corp.
Cole, Carol A. La Dama de Los Pingüinos, 1 vol. Rogers, Sherry, illus. 2012. (SPA.). 32p. (J). (gr. -1-3). 17.95 *(978-1-60718-697-7(7))* Arbordale Publishing.
Los Collaros. 2003. 23.95 *(978-0-673-77776-8(6))* Celebration Pr.
Collins, Kathleen. Sojourner Truth: Defensora de los derechos civiles (Sojourner Truth: Equal Rights Advocate) 2009. (Grandes personajes en la historia de los Estados Unidos (Famous People in American History) Ser.). (SPA.). 32p. (gr. 2-3). 47.90 *(978-1-61512-808-2(5))*, Editorial Buenas Letras) Rosen Publishing Group, Inc., The.
—Sojourner Truth: Equal Rights Advocate. 2009. (Primary Sources of Famous People in American History Ser.). 32p. (gr. 2-3). 47.90 *(978-1-60851-727-5(6))* Rosen Publishing Group, Inc., The.
—Sojourner Truth: Equal Rights Advocate / Defensora de los derechos Civiles. 2009. (Famous People in American History/Grandes personajes en la historia de los Estados Unidos Ser.). (ENG & SPA.). 32p. (gr. 2-3). 47.90 *(978-1-61512-556-2(6))*, Editorial Buenas Letras) Rosen Publishing Group, Inc., The.
Come See My Farm. 2003. 23.95 *(978-0-673-78129-1(1))* Celebration Pr.
Comida Magica: Individual Title-Six Packs. (Chiquilibros Ser.). (SPA.). (gr. k-1). 23.00 *(978-0-7635-8615-7(3))* Rigby Education.
Una Comida Tradicional. 2003. 28.95 *(978-0-673-78092-8(9))* Celebration Pr.
Como funciona? Interactive Packages: A rodar, a Rodar. (Pebble Soup Exploraciones Ser.). (SPA.). (gr. -1-18). 52.00 *(978-0-7578-5268-8(8))* Rigby Education.
Como funciona? Interactive Packages: Mirandolo Bien. (Pebble Soup Exploraciones Ser.). (SPA.). (gr. -1-18). 52.00 *(978-0-7578-5270-1(X))* Rigby Education.
Compartiendo: Individual Title Six-Packs. (Literatura 2000 Ser.). (SPA.). (gr. k-1). 28.00 *(978-0-7635-1013-8(0))* Rigby Education.
Complete Spanish, Set. 2004. 13.99 incl. audio compact disk *(978-1-57583-299-9(2))* Twin Sisters IP, LLC.
Complete Spanish DRA Pack, 96 vols. (Spanish Dra Levels Ser.). (SPA.). 353.75 *(978-0-7362-0993-9(X))* CENGAGE Learning.
Complete Spanish Guided Reading Pack, 96 vols. (Spanish Guided Reading Levels Ser.). (SPA.). 353.75 *(978-0-7362-0991-5(3))* CENGAGE Learning.
Complete Spanish Lexile Pack, 92 vols. (Spanish Lexile Levels Ser.). (SPA.). 339.89 *(978-0-7362-1512-1(3))* CENGAGE Learning.
Conklin, Wendy. Dos Amigos Planos Viajan por el Mundo. rev. ed. 2007. (Reader's Theater Ser.).Tr. of Two Flat Friends Travel the World. (SPA.). 24p. (gr. 3-4). pap. 8.99 *(978-1-4333-0022-6(2))* Teacher Created Materials, Inc.
Conoce las Nubes. 2006. (Real Readers en español Ser.). (J). pap. 24.95 *(978-1-4042-2486-5(6))*, Rosen Classroom) Rosen Publishing Group, Inc., The.
Contro, Arturo. Rafael Marquez. 2009. (World Soccer Stars / Estrellas del fútbol mundial Ser.). (ENG & SPA.). 24p. (gr. 2-2). 42.50 *(978-1-60854-849-1(X))*, Editorial Buenas Letras) Rosen Publishing Group, Inc., The.
El corderito mas Chiquito: Lap Book. (Pebble Soup Exploraciones Ser.). (SPA.). 16p. (gr. -1-18). 21.00 *(978-0-7578-1678-9(9))* Rigby Education.
El corderito mas Chiquito: Small Book. (Pebble Soup Exploraciones Ser.). (SPA.). 16p. (gr. -1-18). 5.00 *(978-0-7578-1718-2(1))* Rigby Education.
El coro de Gatos: Individual Title Six-Packs. (Literatura 2000 Ser.). (SPA.). (gr. 2-3). 33.00 *(978-0-7635-1088-6(2))* Rigby Education.
El Correo: Individual Title Two-Packs. (Chiquilibros Ser.). (SPA.). (gr. -1-1). 12.00 *(978-0-7635-8561-7(0))* Rigby Education.
Costales, Amy. Abuelo Vivia Solo/Grandpa Used to Live Alone. Gama, Esperanza, illus. 2010. (ENG.). 32p. (J). (gr. -1-3). 16.95 *(978-1-55885-531-1(9))* Arte Publico Pr.
Cowan, Catherine & Buehner, Mark. Mi Vida con la Ola. Rubio, Esther, tr. Buehner, Mark, illus. 2004. (SPA., Illus.). 29p. (J). 19.99 *(978-84-88342-45-4(4))* S.A. Kokinos ESP. Dist: Lectorum Pubns., Inc.
Cowen-Fletcher, Jane. Se Necesita Todo un Pueblo. 2003. (SPA., Illus.). (J). pap. 4.76 net. *(978-0-590-29394-5(X))*, SO30915) Scholastic, Inc.
Creo que Si! (Spanish Early Intervention Levels Ser.). (SPA.). 31.14 *(978-0-7362-0332-6(X))* CENGAGE Learning.
Crisp, Dan. Trabajo/ Work. 2007. 14p. 10.95 *(978-84-263-6452-4(7))* Vives, Luis Editorial (Edelvives) ESP. Dist: Baker & Taylor Bks.
Cronin, Doreen. Dubi Dubi Muu. Jimenez Rioja, Alberto, tr. from ENG. 2007.Tr. of Dooby Dooby Moo. (SPA., Illus.). 35p. (J). (gr. -1-1). 15.95 *(978-1-933032-33-7(2))* Lectorum Pubns., Inc.
Cual es el Mio? (Spanish Early Intervention Levels Ser.). (SPA.). 23.10 *(978-1-56334-791-7(1))* CENGAGE Learning.
Cuando estaba Enferma: Individual Title Six-Packs. (Literatura 2000 Ser.). (SPA.). (gr. 1-2). 28.00 *(978-0-7635-1040-4(8))* Rigby Education.
Cuando sea mas Grande: Individual Title Six-Packs. (Literatura 2000 Ser.). (SPA.). (gr. 1-2). 28.00 *(978-0-7635-1063-3(7))* Rigby Education.
Cuando tienes Susto: Social/Emotional Lap Book. (Pebble Soup Exploraciones Ser.). (SPA.). (gr. -1-18). 16.00 *(978-0-7578-1792-2(0))* Rigby Education.
Cuatro Ardillitas. (Spanish Early Intervention Levels Ser.). (SPA.). 31.14 *(978-0-7362-0336-4(2))* CENGAGE Learning.
La Cucaracha: Individual 6-packs. 2003. 23.95 *(978-0-673-78071-3(6))* Celebration Pr.
Cuenta con la Familia. (Spanish Early Intervention Levels Ser.). (SPA.). 23.10 *(978-1-56334-758-0(X))* CENGAGE Learning.
Cuentitos mios Classroom Set: Green Series. (Rimas Y Risas Ser.). (SPA.). (gr. -1-2). 352.70 *(978-0-7362-0057-8(6))* CENGAGE Learning.
Cuentitos Mios Classroom Set: Green Series with addition of Manipulatives. (Rimas Y Risas Ser.). (SPA.). (gr. -1-2). 477.31 *(978-0-917837-96-8(7))* CENGAGE Learning.
El cuento de Dona Chila: 6 Softcover Books. (Saludos Ser.: Vol. 3). (SPA.). (gr. 3-5). 31.00 *(978-0-7635-1780-9(1))* Rigby Education.
Cuentos de Muchos Mundos/Stories of Many Worlds. (ENG & SPA.). 160p. 20.00 *(978-0-944356-19-7(2))* Alegria Hispana Pubns.
Cuentos Favoritos/Favorite Tales. (ENG & SPA.). 80p. 15.00 *(978-0-944356-01-2(X))* Alegria Hispana Pubns.
Cuentos Matematicos/Math Tales. (ENG & SPA.). 80p. 17.00 *(978-0-944356-05-0(2))* Alegria Hispana Pubns.
Cuidado! Individual Title Six-Packs. (Literatura 2000 Ser.). (SPA.). (gr. -1-1). 28.00 *(978-0-7635-1189-0(7))* Rigby Education.
El cumpleanos de Alisa: Individual Title Six-Packs. (Literatura 2000 Ser.). (SPA.). (gr. k-1). 28.00 *(978-0-7635-1014-5(9))* Rigby Education.
El cumpleanos de Bruno: Individual Title Six-Packs. (Literatura 2000 Ser.). (SPA.). (gr. 1-2). 28.00 *(978-0-7635-1041-1(6))* Rigby Education.
El cumpleanos de mi Abuelito: Individual Title Six-Packs. (Literatura 2000 Ser.). (SPA.). (gr. 2-3). 33.00 *(978-0-7635-1089-3(0))* Rigby Education.
Cuno, Sabine. Abre, Cierra y Aprende! Caballero, D., tr. Senner, Katja, illus. 2007. 14p. (J). (gr. -1). *(978-970-718-489-3(2))*, Silver Dolphin en Español) Advanced Marketing, S. de R. L. de C. V.
Curry, Don L. Rookie Ready to Learn en Español: en Mi Patio. O'Leary Brown, Erin, illus. 2011. (Rookie Ready to Learn Español Ser.). Orig. Title: Rookie Ready to Learn: In My Backyard. (SPA.). 32p. (J). pap. 5.95 *(978-0-531-26784-4(9))*, Children's Pr.) Scholastic Library Publishing.
Curry, Don L. & O'Leary Brown, Erin. En Mi Patio. O'Leary Brown, Erin, illus. 2011. (Rookie Ready to Learn Español Ser.). (SPA., Illus.). 32p. (J). lib. bdg. 23.00 *(978-0-531-26116-3(6))*, Children's Pr.) Scholastic Library Publishing.
Curtis, Christopher Paul & Jiménez Rioja, Alberto. Me Llamo Bud, No Buddy. 2016. (SPA.). 240p. (J). (gr. 5-12). pap. 12.99 *(978-1-63245-639-7(7))* Lectorum Pubns., Inc.
Cusimano Love, Maryann. You Are My I Love You. Ichikawa, Satomi, illus. 2012. 30p. (J). (gr. -1 — 1). bds. 7.99 *(978-0-399-24396-7(8))*, Philomel Bks.) Penguin Young Readers Group.
Da Vacaciones. (Mi Primer Diccionario Illustrado Espanol Ser.). (SPA.). pap. 4.95 *(978-88-8148-844-5(2))* EMC/Paradigm Publishing.
Daniel: Individual Title Six-Packs. (Literatura 2000 Ser.). (SPA.). (gr. 1-2). 28.00 *(978-0-7635-1064-0(5))* Rigby Education.
Danziger, Paula. Es Dia de Feria, Ambar Dorado. Ross, Tony, illus. 2007. (de Ámbar / a Is for Amber Easy-To-Read Ser.).Tr. of It's a Fair Day, Amber Brown. (SPA.). 48p. (gr. k-3). pap. 8.95 *(978-1-59820-596-1(X))* Santillana USA Publishing Co., Inc.
—Segundo Grado Es Increible, Ambar Dorado. Ross, Tony, illus. 2007. (de Ámbar / a Is for Amber Easy-To-Read Ser.).Tr. of Second Grade Rules, Amber Brown. (SPA.). 48p. (gr. k-3). pap. 8.95 *(978-1-59820-594-7(3))* Santillana USA Publishing Co., Inc.
de Alba, Laura, tr. Caritas Felices. 2007. (Disney Winnie the Pooh (SilverDolphin) Ser.). (Illus.). 8p. (J). (gr. -1). bds. *(978-970-718-391-9(8))*, Silver Dolphin en Español) Advanced Marketing, S. de R. L. de C. V.
De Anda, Diane. The Patchwork Garden. Ventura, Gabriela Baeza, tr. Kemarskaya, Oksana, illus. 2013.Tr. of Pedacitos de Huerto. (ENG & SPA.). 32p. (J). 16.95 *(978-1-55885-763-6(X))*, Piñata Books) Arte Publico Pr.
De Compras. (Spanish Early Intervention Levels Ser.). 23.10 *(978-1-56334-784-9(9))* CENGAGE Learning.
de Lambana, Martha Lucia Martinez. Grafias 4 4: Escritura Asociativa Script: Ejercitacion. (SPA.). (J). (gr. k-6). 12.00 *(978-958-04-5329-1(2))* Norma S.A. COL. Dist: Distribuidora Norma, Inc.
—Grafias 5 5: Escritura Asociativa Script: Intermedio. (SPA.). (J). (gr. k-6). 12.00 *(978-958-04-5330-7(6))* Norma S.A. COL. Dist: Distribuidora Norma, Inc.
—Grafias 6 6: Escritura Asociativa Script: Avanzada. (SPA.). (J). (gr. k-6). 12.00 *(978-958-04-5331-4(4))* Norma S.A. COL. Dist: Distribuidora Norma, Inc.
—Grafias K: Escritura Asociativa Script: Aprestamiento. (SPA.). (J). (gr. k-6). 12.00 *(978-958-04-5316-1(0))* Norma S.A. COL. Dist: Distribuidora Norma, Inc.
De lo Que Contaron - Fraile (What They Told the Friar (XV!)) 2005. (SPA.). (J). pap. *(978-968-7381-04-6(3))* Tecolote, Ediciones, S.A. de C.V.
De padre a Hijo: 6 Small Books. (Saludos Ser.: Vol. 1). (SPA.). (gr. 3-5). 31.00 *(978-0-7635-1755-7(0))* Rigby Education.
De Safari: Individual Title-Six Packs. (Chiquilibros Ser.). (SPA.). (gr. k-1). 23.00 *(978-0-7635-8605-8(6))* Rigby Education.
De Valdenebro, Eladio. Tono y el Bosque. (Torre de Papel Ser.). (SPA.). (J). (gr. 4-18). 8.95 *(978-958-04-3397-2(6))* Norma S.A. COL. Dist: Distribuidora Norma, Inc.
Debajo de la Cama, 6 Packs. (Chiquilibros Ser.). (SPA.). (gr. k-1). 23.00 *(978-0-7635-8619-5(6))* Rigby Education.
Del Moral, S., tr. Animales. 2006. (Disney Learning (Silver Dolphin en Espanol) Ser.). (Illus.). 22p. (J). (gr. -1). *(978-970-718-431-2(0))*, Silver Dolphin en Español) Advanced Marketing, S. de R. L. de C. V.
—Colores. 2006. (Disney Learning (Silver Dolphin en Espanol) Ser.). (Illus.). 22p. (J). (gr. -1). *(978-970-718-430-5(2))*, Silver Dolphin en Español) Advanced Marketing, S. de R. L. de C. V.
—Contrarios. 2006. (Disney Learning (Silver Dolphin en Espanol) Ser.). (Illus.). 22p. (J). (gr. -1). *(978-970-718-428-2(0))*, Silver Dolphin en Español) Advanced Marketing, S. de R. L. de C. V.
—Formas. 2006. (Disney Learning (Silver Dolphin en Espanol) Ser.). (Illus.). 22p. (J). (gr. -1). *(978-970-718-429-9(9))*, Silver Dolphin en Español) Advanced Marketing, S. de R. L. de C. V.
Del Moral, Susana. Baby Da Vinci, Mi Cuerpo. Zaidi, Nadeem, illus. 2006. (Baby Einstein Ser.). (SPA.). 6p. (J). (gr. -1-k). bds. *(978-970-718-455-8(8))*, Silver Dolphin en Español) Advanced Marketing, S. de R. L. de C. V.
del Moral Zavariz, Susana & Zaidi, Nadeem. El Concurso: Un Libro con Espejos. 2006. (SPA., Illus.). 5p. (J). (gr. -1-k). bds. *(978-970-718-458-9(2))*, Silver Dolphin en Español) Advanced Marketing, S. de R. L. de C. V.
Delacre, Lulu. Rafi y Rosi, 1 vol. Delacre, Lulu, illus. 2016. (Rafi & Rosi Ser.).Tr. of Rafi & Rosi. (SPA., Illus.). 64p. (J). (gr. k-3). pap. 10.95 *(978-0-89239-378-7(5))*, leelowcbp) Lee & Low Bks., Inc.
—Rafi y Rosi Carnival, 1 vol. 2016. (Rafi & Rosi Ser.).Tr. of Rafi & Rosi Carnival. (SPA., Illus.). 64p. (J). (gr. k-3). pap. 11.95 *(978-0-89239-380-0(7))*, leelowcbp) Lee & Low Bks., Inc.
Demado. En Avant: Enhanced Online Edition. 4th ed. 2003. (SPA.). cd-rom 54.80 *(978-0-03-031974-7(9))* Holt McDougal.
Demasiada Ropa, 6 Pack. (Literatura 2000 Ser.). (SPA.). (gr. k-1). 28.00 *(978-0-7635-1015-2(7))* Rigby Education.
DeMolay, Jack. El Triángulo de las Bermudas: La desaparición del vuelo 19 (the Bermuda Triangle:the Disappearance of Flight 19) 2009. (Historietas Juveniles: Misterios (Jr. Graphic Mysteries) Ser.). (SPA.). 24p. (gr. 2-3). 47.90 *(978-1-61513-348-2(8))*, Editorial Buenas Letras) Rosen Publishing Group, Inc., The.
Den Vueltas, 6 Packs. (Literatura 2000 Ser.). (SPA.). (gr. 1-2). 28.00 *(978-0-7635-1065-7(3))* Rigby Education.
El Dentista, 2 Packs. (Chiquilibros Ser.). (SPA.). (gr. -1-1). 12.00 *(978-0-7635-8565-5(3))* Rigby Education.
Despegue con Ellen Ochoa! 6 Small Books. (Saludos Ser.: Vol. 3). (SPA.). (gr. 2-3). 31.00 *(978-0-7635-9548-7(9))* Rigby Education.
Despegue con Ellen Ochoa! Big Book. (Saludos Ser.: Vol. 3). (SPA.). (gr. 2-3). 31.00 *(978-0-7635-5863-5(X))* Rigby Education.
El dia de Escuela, 2 packs. (Chiquilibros Ser.). (SPA.). (gr. -1-1). 12.00 *(978-0-7635-8562-4(9))* Rigby Education.
El Dia de los Muertos: 6 Small Books. (Saludos Ser.: Vol. 1). (SPA.). 24p. (gr. 2-3). 31.00 *(978-0-7635-9520-3(9))* Rigby Education.
El Dia lluvioso, 2 packs. (Chiquilibros Ser.). (SPA.). (gr. -1-1). 12.00 *(978-0-7635-8552-5(1))* Rigby Education.
Diario de una Marquesa (Diary of a Marchioness) 2005. (SPA.). (J). pap. *(978-968-7381-05-3(1))* Tecolote, Ediciones, S.A. de C.V.
El Diario de Val. (SPA., Illus.). 70p. (YA). (gr. 7-9). pap. *(978-88-8148-328-0(9))* EMC/Paradigm Publishing.
Dias de Alegria. (Spanish Early Intervention Levels Ser.). (SPA.). 23.10 *(978-1-56334-781-8(4))* CENGAGE Learning.
Diaz, Nelbaliz. Laura y Su Caja de Sorpresas. 2007. (SPA.). 48p. 14.95 *(978-0-8477-0452-1(1))* Univ. of Puerto Rico Pr.
Dickens, Charles. Las Campanas.Tr. of Chimes. (SPA.). 7.75 *(978-958-04-2124-5(2))* Norma S.A. COL. Dist: Distribuidora Norma, Inc.
Diez Ositos: Big Book Packages. 2003. 64.95 *(978-0-673-58578-3(6))* Celebration Pr.

S

Dime como te Sientes: Big Book. (Pebble Soup Exploraciones Ser.). (SPA.). 16p. (gr. -1-18). 31.00 *(978-0-7578-1685-7(1))* Rigby Education.

Dime como te Sientes: Small Book. (Pebble Soup Exploraciones Ser.). (SPA.). 16p. (gr. -1-18). 5.00 *(978-0-7578-1725-0(4))* Rigby Education.

Los Dinosaurios: Big Book Packages. 2003. 64.95 *(978-0-673-58597-4(2))* Celebration Pr.

La diosa del Volcan: 6 Small Books. (Saludos Ser.: Vol. 1). (SPA.). (gr. 3-5). 31.00 *(978-0-7635-2055-7(1))* Rigby Education.

Disfraces, 6 Pack. (Chiquilibros Ser.). (SPA.). (gr. k-1). 23.00 *(978-0-7635-8601-0(3))* Rigby Education.

Disher, Garry. Flaminio, el Piano. (Torre de Papel Ser.). (SPA.). (J). (gr. 4-18). 8.95 *(978-958-04-4139-7(1))* Norma S.A. COL. Dist: Distribuidora Norma, Inc.

Disney Enterprises Inc. Staff, creator. Caritas Felices. 2007. (Disney Princesa (Silver Dolphin) Ser.). (Illus.). 8p. (J). (gr. -1). bds. *(978-970-718-389-6(6)*, Silver Dolphin en Español) Advanced Marketing, S. de R. L. de C. V.

—Disney Caritas Felices: Simba. 2007. (Illus.). 8p. (J). (gr. -1). *(978-970-718-392-6(6)*, Silver Dolphin en Español) Advanced Marketing, S. de R. L. de C. V.

El doctor Buscapistas: Social/Emotional Lap Book. (Pebble Soup Exploraciones Ser.). (SPA.). (gr. -1-18). 16.00 *(978-0-7578-1790-8(4))* Rigby Education.

Dominguez, Angela. Maria Had a Little Llama / María Tenía una Llamita: Bilingual. Dominguez, Angela, illus. 2013.Tr. of Maria Had a Little Llama. (SPA., Illus.). 32p. (J). (gr. -1-2). 19.99 *(978-0-8050-9333-9(8)*, 900070912, Holt, Henry & Co. Bks. For Young Readers) Holt, Henry & Co.

Dominguez, Ramon Garcia. El Grillo del Tercer Milenium. (SPA.). (J). 8.95 *(978-958-04-6266-8(6))* Norma S.A. COL. Dist: Distribuidora Norma, Inc.

Dona Coneja. (Spanish Early Intervention Levels Ser.). (SPA.). 21.30 *(978-0-7362-0826-0(7))* CENGAGE Learning.

Dona Flora's Flowers. 2003. 23.95 *(978-0-673-78133-8(X))* Celebration Pr.

Donde esta Claudia? Individual Title Six-Packs. (Literatura 2000 Ser.). (SPA.). (gr. k-1). 28.00 *(978-0-7635-1017-6(3))* Rigby Education.

Donde esta mi Mascota? Individual Title-Six Packs. (Chiquilibros Ser.). (SPA.). (gr. k-1). 23.00 *(978-0-7635-8624-9(2))* Rigby Education.

Donde vivimos Interactive Packages: En mi Vecindario. (Pebble Soup Exploraciones Ser.). (SPA.). (gr. -1-18). 52.00 *(978-0-7578-5258-9(0))* Rigby Education.

Donde vivimos Interactive Packages: Los Trabajos. (Pebble Soup Exploraciones Ser.). (SPA.). (gr. -1-18). 52.00 *(978-0-7578-5256-5(4))* Rigby Education.

Donde Vivo Yo: Individual 6-packs. 2003. 23.95 *(978-0-673-77136-0(9))* Celebration Pr.

Doro, el Potrillo. (Coleccion Leo Con Figuras). (SPA., Illus.). 14p. (J). pap. 5.50 *(978-950-11-0841-5(4)*, SGM414) Sigmar ARG. Dist: Continental Bk. Co., Inc.

Dos gatos Tontos, 6 Packs. (Literatura 2000 Ser.). (SPA.). (gr. 2-3). 33.00 *(978-0-7635-1090-9(4))* Rigby Education.

Los Dos Volcanes. 2003. 28.95 *(978-0-673-78100-0(3))* Celebration Pr.

El dragon Grunon. (Spanish Early Intervention Levels Ser.). (SPA.). 31.14 *(978-0-7362-0338-8(9))* CENGAGE Learning.

Droop, Constanza. Que? Como? Por Que?: Las Estaciones del Ano. Caballero, D., tr. Droop, Constanza, illus. 2007. (Junior (Silver Dolphin) Ser.). (Illus.). 16p. (J). (gr. -1). *(978-970-718-492-3(2)*, Silver Dolphin en Español) Advanced Marketing, S. de R. L. de C. V.

Dugan, Christine. Marcha Hacia Delante. rev. ed. 2007. (Reader's Theater Ser.). (SPA., Illus.). 20p. (J). (gr. 1-2). 7.99 *(978-1-4333-0019-6(2))* Teacher Created Materials, Inc.

—Muchas Manos Ayudan. rev. ed. 2007. (Reader's Theater Ser.). (SPA.). 20p. (gr. 1-2). 7.99 *(978-1-4333-0017-2(6))* Teacher Created Materials, Inc.

Los Dulces. 2003. 23.95 *(978-0-673-77163-6(6))* Celebration Pr.

Dulces Recuerdos. 2003. 28.95 *(978-0-673-78102-4(X))* Celebration Pr.

Duncan, E. E. Ralph Carr: Defender of Japanese Americans. 2011. (ENG & SPA., Illus.). 66p. (J). pap. 8.95 *(978-0-86541-116-6(6))* Filter Pr., LLC.

Durmiendo: Individual Title Six-Packs. (Literatura 2000 Ser.). (SPA.). (gr. 1-2). 28.00 *(978-0-7635-1043-5(2))* Rigby Education.

Each Big Book Set: Green Series. (Rimas Y Risas Ser.). (SPA.). (gr. -1-2). 212.23 *(978-1-56334-004-8(6))* CENGAGE Learning.

Each Big Book Set: Green Series with addition of Manipulatives. (Rimas Y Risas Ser.). (SPA.). (gr. -1-2). 344.62 *(978-0-7362-0054-7(1))* CENGAGE Learning.

East, Jacqueline. No Quiero comer Eso! (SPA.). (J). 8.95 *(978-958-04-7345-9(5))* Norma S.A. COL. Dist: Distribuidora Norma, Inc.

Eastman, P. D. El Mejor Nido. Mlawer, Teresa, tr. from ENG. 2005.Tr. of Best Nest. (SPA., Illus.). 64p. (J). (gr. k-2). 12.99 *(978-1-930332-84-3(X)*, LC33270) Lectorum Pubns., Inc.

El/Dibujo de Maria: Individual Title, 6 packs. (Literatura 2000 Ser.). (SPA.). (gr. 1-2). 28.00 *(978-0-7635-1042-8(4))* Rigby Education.

Elena y el Monito. (Spanish Early Intervention Levels Ser.). (SPA.). 21.30 *(978-0-7362-0807-9(0))* CENGAGE Learning.

Ellis, Catherine. Cars & Trucks/Autos y Camiones. 2009. (Mega Military Machines/Megamaquinas militares Ser.). (ENG & SPA.). 24p. (gr. 1-1). 42.50 *(978-1-61514-639-0(3)*, Editorial Buenas Letras) Rosen Publishing Group, Inc., The.

—Helicopters/Helicópteros. 2009. (Mega Military Machines/Megamaquinas militares Ser.). (ENG & SPA.). 24p. (gr. 1-1). 42.50 *(978-1-61514-640-6(7)*, Editorial Buenas Letras) Rosen Publishing Group, Inc., The.

Elovitz Marshall, Linda. Rainbow Weavery, 1 vol. Chavarri, Elisa, illus. 2016. (ENG.). 40p. (J). (gr. k-4). 20.95 *(978-0-89239-374-9(2)*, leelowcbp) Lee & Low Bks., Inc.

Elsa's Shawl. 2003. 23.95 *(978-0-673-78130-7(5))* Celebration Pr.

En Busca De Insectos. 2003. 28.95 *(978-0-673-78096-6(1))* Celebration Pr.

En Busca del Amigo Desaparecido. (SPA., Illus.). 70p. (YA). (gr. 6-8). *(978-88-8148-323-5(8))* EMC/Paradigm Publishing.

En casa de mis Padrinos. (Spanish Early Intervention Levels Ser.). (SPA.). 28.38 *(978-0-7362-0847-5(X))* CENGAGE Learning.

En Donde Marchan los Elefantes? (Pebble Soup Exploraciones Ser.). (SPA.). 16p. (gr. -1-18). 31.00 *(978-0-7578-1679-6(7))* Rigby Education.

En donde marchan los Elefantes? Small Book. (Pebble Soup Exploraciones Ser.). (SPA.). 16p. (gr. -1-18). 5.00 *(978-0-7578-1719-9(X))* Rigby Education.

En el cielo de Medianoche: Big Book. (Pebble Soup Exploraciones Ser.). (SPA.). 16p. (gr. -1-18). 31.00 *(978-0-7578-1693-2(2))* Rigby Education.

En el cielo de Medianoche: Small Book. (Pebble Soup Exploraciones Ser.). (SPA.). 16p. (gr. -1-18). 5.00 *(978-0-7578-1733-5(5))* Rigby Education.

En el Jardin: Individual Title Six-Packs. (Literatura 2000 Ser.). (SPA.). (gr. 1-2). 28.00 *(978-0-7635-1067-1(X))* Rigby Education.

En el Mundo. (Spanish Early Intervention Levels Ser.). (SPA.). 23.10 *(978-1-56334-794-8(6))* CENGAGE Learning.

En el Rancho, 6, Pack. (Literatura 2000 Ser.). (SPA.). (gr. k-1). 28.00 *(978-0-7635-1018-3(1))* Rigby Education.

En el restaurante de mis Tios. (Spanish Early Intervention Levels Ser.). (SPA.). 23.10 *(978-1-56334-780-1(6))* CENGAGE Learning.

En el Supermercado, 6, Pack. (Chiquilibros Ser.). (SPA.). (gr. k-1). 23.00 *(978-0-7635-8617-1(X))* Rigby Education.

En el Zoologico, 6, Pack. 2003. 23.95 *(978-0-673-77146-9(6))* Celebration Pr.

En la Ciudad. (Spanish Early Intervention Levels Ser.). (SPA.). 23.10 *(978-1-56334-776-4(8))* CENGAGE Learning.

En la ciudad de Roma: Individual Title Six-Packs. (Literatura 2000 Ser.). (SPA.). (gr. 2-3). 33.00 *(978-0-7635-1091-6(2))* Rigby Education.

En la ciudad de San Antonio: Lap Book. (Pebble Soup Exploraciones Ser.). (SPA.). 16p. (gr. -1-18). 21.00 *(978-0-7578-1680-2(0))* Rigby Education.

En la ciudad de San Antonio: Small Book. (Pebble Soup Exploraciones Ser.). (SPA.). 16p. (gr. -1-18). 5.00 *(978-0-7578-1720-5(3))* Rigby Education.

En la Mananita. (Spanish Early Intervention Levels Ser.). (SPA.). 23.10 *(978-1-56334-796-2(2))* CENGAGE Learning.

En la oscuridad Interactive Packages: Duermete, mi Amor. (Pebble Soup Exploraciones Ser.). (SPA.). (gr. -1-18). 52.00 *(978-0-7578-5271-8(8))* Rigby Education.

En La Playa, 6 Pks. 2003. 23.95 *(978-0-673-77135-3(0))* Celebration Pr.

En la Playa, 6, Pack. (Chiquilibros Ser.). (SPA.). (gr. k-1). 23.00 *(978-0-7635-8618-8(8))* Rigby Education.

En mi Cama, 6 Pks. (Literatura 2000 Ser.). (SPA.). (gr. k-1). 28.00 *(978-0-7635-1019-0(X))* Rigby Education.

En mi Cuarto: Individual Title Six-Packs. (Literatura 2000 Ser.). (SPA.). (gr. k-1). 28.00 *(978-0-7635-1020-6(3))* Rigby Education.

En mi Escuela. (Spanish Early Intervention Levels Ser.). (SPA.). 23.10 *(978-1-56334-757-3(1))* CENGAGE Learning.

En Mi Jardin: Big Book Packages. 2003. 64.95 *(978-0-673-58579-0(4))* Celebration Pr.

Encuentros. (Nuevos Horizontes Ser.). (SPA.). (J). (gr. 5). wbk. ed. 9.95 *(978-1-56014-523-3(4))* Santillana USA Publishing Co., Inc.

Encuentros: Evaluations, Grade 5. (Nuevos Horizontes Ser.). (SPA.). (J). 22.50 *(978-1-56014-524-0(2))* Santillana USA Publishing Co., Inc.

Encuentros: Student Anthology. (Nuevos Horizontes Ser.). (SPA.). (J). (gr. 5). 19.95 *(978-1-56014-522-6(6))* Santillana USA Publishing Co., Inc.

English-Spanish Book Set 800937, 4 vols. 2005. (J). bds. *(978-1-59794-096-2(8))* Environments, Inc.

La Ensalada, 6 Packs. 2003. 23.95 *(978-0-673-77147-6(4))* Celebration Pr.

Es Mejor Dar Que Recibir. 2003. 28.95 *(978-0-673-78099-7(6))* Celebration Pr.

Es Mia! Social/Emotional Lap Book. (Pebble Soup Exploraciones Ser.). (SPA.). (gr. -1-18). 16.00 *(978-0-7578-1786-1(6))* Rigby Education.

Es un Elefante? (Spanish Early Intervention Levels Ser.). (SPA.). 21.30 *(978-0-7362-0800-0(3))* CENGAGE Learning.

Escalando: Individual Title Six-Packs. (Literatura 2000 Ser.). (SPA.). (gr. k-1). 28.00 *(978-0-7635-1021-3(1))* Rigby Education.

El Escondite: Individual Title, 6 pack. (Chiquilibros Ser.). (SPA.). (gr. k-1). 23.00 *(978-0-7635-8625-6(0))* Rigby Education.

Escudos Rotos (Broken Shields (XVI Century)) 2005. (SPA.). (J). pap. *(978-968-7381-00-8(0))* Tecolote, Ediciones, S.A. de C.V.

Espanol Correcto. (SPA.). (J). 29.00 *(978-958-04-5925-5(8))* Norma S.A. COL. Dist: Distribuidora Norma, Inc.

Espluga, Maria. I, Astronaut: Yo, Astronauta. 2009. (SPA & ENG.). 28p. (J). 13.95 *(978-1-931398-56-5(9))* Me+Mi Publishing.

—I, Ballerina: Yo, Bailarina. 2009. (ENG & SPA.). 28p. (J). 13.95 *(978-1-931398-55-8(0))* Me+Mi Publishing.

—I, Sailor: Yo, Marinero. 2009. (SPA & ENG.). 28p. (J). 13.95 *(978-1-931398-53-4(4))* Me+Mi Publishing.

Estados Unidos: Formacion, Desarrollo y Transformacion. (SPA.). (J). *(978-958-04-7743-3(4))* Norma S.A. COL. Dist: Distribuidora Norma, Inc.

Estice, Rose Mary & Fried, Mary. Big Keep Books- Spanish Emergent Reader 1: Mira como Juego; ¡Curitas!; Los Animales del Zoológico: Construyendo una Casa; la Alberca; ¡Agua y Jabón!; Me Visto; Mi Gato, 8 bks., Set. Elías, Annette, tr. Simon, Sue A. et al, illus. 2005.Tr. of Emergent Reader 1. (SPA.). 8p. (J). 20.00 *(978-1-893986-42-8(X))* Keep Bks.

Evan-Moor. Spanish / English Read & nderstand Science Grades 4-6. 2007. (Spanish/English Read & Understand Ser.). (ENG., Illus.). 304p. (J). (gr. 4-6). pap. 29.99 *(978-1-59673-077-9(3)*, EMC 5312) Evan-Moor Educational Pubs.

—Spanish/English Read & Understand Nonfiction: Grades 4-6. 2007. (Spanish/English Read & Understand Ser.). (ENG.). 304p. (J). (gr. 4-6). pap. 29.99 *(978-1-59673-076-2(5)*, EMC 5311) Evan-Moor Educational Pubs.

Expertas en Terremotos. (Saludos Ser.: Vol. 2). (SPA.). (gr. 3-5). 31.00 *(978-0-7635-3235-2(5))* Rigby Education.

Expertas en Terremotos: 6 Small Books. (Saludos Ser.: Vol. 2). (SPA.). (gr. 3-5). 31.00 *(978-0-7635-2066-3(7))* Rigby Education.

Falconer, Ian. Olivia y Las Princesas. 2012. (SPA., Illus.). 32p. (J). (gr. -1-1). 17.99 *(978-1-933032-82-5(0))* Lectorum Pubns., Inc.

Fallon, Jimmy & Lopez, Jennifer. Con Pollo: A Bilingual Playtime Adventure. Campos, Andrea, illus. 2022. (ENG.). 48p. (J). 18.99 *(978-1-250-83041-8(9)*, 900252853) Feiwel & Friends.

La Familia Ruidosa: Lap Book. (Pebble Soup Exploraciones Ser.). 16p. (gr. -1-18). 21.00 *(978-0-7578-1671-0(1))* Rigby Education.

La Familia Ruidosa: Small Book. (Pebble Soup Exploraciones Ser.). 16p. (gr. -1-18). 5.00 *(978-0-7578-1711-3(4))* Rigby Education.

Familias de animales salvajes (Wild Animal Families), 8 vols. 2007. (Familias de Animales Salvajes (Wild Animal Families) Ser.). (SPA.). 24p. (gr. 2-4). lib. bdg. 106.68 *(978-0-8368-7965-0(1)*, 9d98c97a-926e-4db8-b31f-b79e65ba75bb, Gareth Stevens Learning Library) Stevens, Gareth Publishing LLLP.

Fantasia Bilingue/Bilingual Fantasy. (ENG & SPA.). 80p. 15.00 *(978-0-944356-02-9(8))* Alegria Hispana Pubns.

Feeling Scared: Social/Emotional Lap Book. (Pebble Soup Explorations Ser.). (SPA.). (gr. -1-18). 16.00 *(978-0-7635-7573-1(9))* Rigby Education.

Felipa y el Dragon: Individual Title Six-Packs. (Literatura 2000 Ser.). (SPA.). (gr. 1-2). 28.00 *(978-0-7635-1069-5(6))* Rigby Education.

Feliz Ano Nuevo. 2003. 23.95 *(978-0-673-78079-9(1))* Celebration Pr.

Fente, et al. Curso Intensivo de Espanol: Ejercicios Practicos: Nivel de Iniciacion y Elemental. (SPA.). 288p. stu. ed. 26.95 *(978-84-85786-43-5(2)*, SGS694) Edelsa Grupo Didascalia, S.A. ESP. Dist: Continental Bk. Co., Inc.

La Feria. (Spanish Early Intervention Levels Ser.). (SPA.). 23.10 *(978-1-56334-770-2(9))* CENGAGE Learning.

Fernández de Lizardi, José Joaquín. El Periquillo Sarniento. 2003. (SPA.). 351p. (YA). 12.95 *(978-968-6966-10-7(2))* EDITER'S Publishing Hse. MEX. Dist: EDITER'S Publishing Hse.

Fernández, Jesús, et al. Curso Intensivo de Espanol: Niveles Elemental e Intermedio: Clave. (SPA.). 32p. *(978-84-7143-416-6(4))* Sociedad General Espanola de Libreria.

—Curso Intensivo de Espanol: Niveles Intermedio y Superior: Clave. (SPA.). 64p. *(978-84-7143-418-0(0))* Sociedad General Espanola de Libreria.

Fernandez, Joyce. Little Bird - Pajarito. 2010. 31p. 15.95 *(978-0-615-23709-1(6))* My Second Language Publishing, USA.

Fernández, Mayra. Los Colores de Mi Mundo (Rainbow Kids) (SPA & ENG., Illus.). 20p. (J). pap. 6.95 *(978-1-887578-01-1(3)*, STK1SP) SpanPress, Inc.

Fiction & Nonfiction Packs: Combo Packs. (SPA.). (gr. k-2). 85.92 *(978-1-56334-403-9(3))* CENGAGE Learning.

Fiction & Nonfiction Packs: Jumbo Packs. (SPA.). (gr. k-2). 438.19 *(978-1-56334-400-8(9))* CENGAGE Learning.

La fiesta de Cumpleanos. (Spanish Early Intervention Levels Ser.). (SPA.). 23.10 *(978-1-56334-759-7(8))* CENGAGE Learning.

Fiesta de Dinosaurios, 6 Pks. (Chiquilibros Ser.). (SPA.). (gr. k-1). 23.00 *(978-0-7635-8786-4(9))* Rigby Education.

La Fiesta Monstruosa, 6 Pks. (Chiquilibros Ser.). (SPA.). (gr. k-1). 23.00 *(978-0-7635-8600-3(5))* Rigby Education.

Fisher, Doris & Sneed, Dani. My Even Day: Spanish, 1 vol. Lee, Karen, illus. 2007. (SPA.). 32p. (J). (gr. -1-3). 17.95 *(978-1-60718-692-2(6))* Arbordale Publishing.

—One Odd Day, 1 vol. Lee, Karen, illus. 2006. (SPA.). 32p. (J). (gr. -1-3). 17.95 *(978-1-60718-694-6(2))* Arbordale Publishing.

"Fisher" Suedmeyer, Paul A. The 12 Eternals on the Great Voyage. 2013. 40p. pap. *(978-1-4602-1731-3(4))* FriesenPress.

Fito, el Perro. (Coleccion Leo Con Figuras). (SPA., Illus.). 14p. (J). pap. 5.50 *(978-950-11-0840-8(6)*, SGM410) Sigmar ARG. Dist: Continental Bk. Co., Inc.

Fleming, Candace. Nam! Nam! Nam! Schmidt, Alejandra, tr. from ENG. Karas, G. Brian, illus. 2007. (SPA.). 32p. (J). (gr. -1-2). 15.95 *(978-1-933032-35-1(9))* Lectorum Pubns., Inc.

Fleming, Candace, et al. ¡Ñam! ¡Ñam! ¡Ñam! 2018. 32p. (J). pap. 9.99 *(978-1-63245-672-4(9))* Lectorum Pubns., Inc.

Flip Chart. 2003. (Scott Foresman Science Ser.). (gr. k-18). suppl. ed. 294.00 *(978-0-673-59350-4(9))*; (gr. 1-18). suppl. ed. 435.75 *(978-0-673-59351-1(7))*; (gr. 2-18). suppl. ed. 435.75 *(978-0-673-59352-8(5))* Addison-Wesley Educational Pubs., Inc.

Flor Ada, Alma. Celebra el Ano Nuevo Chino con la Familia Fong. 2006. (Cuentos para Celebrar / Stories to Celebrate Ser.). (Illus.). 30p. (gr. k-6). per. 11.95 *(978-1-59820-114-7(X)*, Alfaguara) Santillana USA Publishing Co., Inc.

—Celebra el Cinco de Mayo con un Jarabe Tapatio. Gomez, Marcela & Silva, David, illus. 2006. (Cuentos para Celebrar / Stories to Celebrate Ser.). 30p. (gr. k-6). per. 11.95 *(978-1-59820-118-5(2))* Ediciones Alfaguara ESP. Dist: Santillana USA Publishing Co., Inc.

Las Flores De Dona Flora: Individual 6-packs. 2003. 23.95 *(978-0-673-78073-7(2))* Celebration Pr.

Focas. (Spanish Early Intervention Levels Ser.). (SPA.). 21.30 *(978-0-7362-0827-7(5))* CENGAGE Learning.

Fonolibros Series: Complete Stage One. 2003. (SPA.). 1230.95 *(978-0-7652-1052-4(5))* Modern Curriculum Pr.

Fonolibros Series: Complete Stage Two. 2003. (SPA.). 895.50 *(978-0-7652-1053-1(3))* Modern Curriculum Pr.

Fontes, Justine. Daniel el Descortes: Rude Ralph. Jordan, Charles, illus. 2005. (Rookie Reader Español Ser.). 32p. (gr. k-2). 19.50 *(978-0-516-24444-0(2)*, Children's Pr.) Scholastic Library Publishing.

—Rookie Ready to Learn en Español: Daniel el Descortés. Jordan, Charles, illus. 2011. (Rookie Ready to Learn Español Ser.). Orig. Title: Rookie Ready to Learn: Rude Ralph. (SPA.). 40p. (J). pap. 5.95 *(978-0-531-26790-5(3)*, Children's Pr.) Scholastic Library Publishing.

Franks, Katie. Dirt Bikes. 2009. (Motorcycles Made for Speed/Motocicletas a toda velocidad Ser.). (ENG & SPA.). 24p. (gr. 1-1). 42.50 *(978-1-61514-672-7(5)*, Editorial Buenas Letras) Rosen Publishing Group, Inc., The.

Fraser, Janine M. La Mariposa de Abdullah. (Torre de Papel Ser.). (SPA., Illus.). (J). (gr. 2). 7.95 *(978-958-04-4917-1(1))* Norma S.A. COL. Dist: Distribuidora Norma, Inc.

Freddy the Fish. 2003. 23.95 *(978-0-673-78128-4(3))* Celebration Pr.

Freed, Herb. Sing & Learn Spanish. 2004. 271p. (J). pap. 14.95 *(978-0-9760472-0-9(9))* Global Village Kids, LLC.

French, Cathy. Make an Animal Mobile & Haz un móvil de Animales: 6 English, 6 Spanish Adaptations. 2011. (SPA & ENG.). (J). 75.00 net. *(978-1-4108-5619-7(4))* Benchmark Education Co.

—Make an Island & Haz una Isla: 6 English, 6 Spanish Adaptations. 2011. (ENG & SPA.). (J). 75.00 net. *(978-1-4108-5632-6(1))* Benchmark Education Co.

Fruits & Vegetables I Like to Eat - Spanish Take Home Book. 2007. (Journeys Ser.). (J). pap. 49.95 *(978-1-4042-5513-5(3)*, Rosen Classroom) Rosen Publishing Group, Inc., The.

La Fruta. (Spanish Early Intervention Levels Ser.). (SPA.). 23.10 *(978-1-56334-762-7(8))* CENGAGE Learning.

Galindo-Leal, Carlos. De dos mundos = of Two Worlds: Las ranas, sapos y salamandras de la Península de Yucatán, México = the Frogs, Toads & Salamanders of the Yucatan Peninsula, Mexico. Arreola Alemón, Roberto, illus. 2003. (SPA & ENG.). 152p. pap. 19.95 *(978-1-929165-52-0(8))* PANGAEA.

La Gallinita Roja: Lap Book. (Pebble Soup Exploraciones Ser.). (SPA.). 16p. (gr. -1-18). 21.00 *(978-0-7578-1684-0(3))* Rigby Education.

La Gallinita Roja: Small Book. (Pebble Soup Exploraciones Ser.). (SPA.). 16p. (gr. -1-18). 5.00 *(978-0-7578-1724-3(6))* Rigby Education.

La Gallinita Roja: Video Tape. (ENG & SPA.). (gr. k-1). 26.00 *(978-0-7635-6276-2(9))* Rigby Education.

Gamblin, Rose Tooley & Hernández, Oscar. Bill's Lunch: El Almuerzo de Bill. 2010. (ENG & SPA., Illus.). 32p. (J). *(978-0-8127-0472-3(X))* Review & Herald Publishing Assn.

Game Time: Matching English 6-packs. 2003. 23.95 *(978-0-673-57558-6(6))* Celebration Pr.

García Márquez, Gabriel. La Siesta del Martes.Tr. of Tuesday's Siesta. (SPA.). 28p. 10.50 *(978-958-04-5574-5(0))* Norma S.A. COL. Dist: Distribuidora Norma, Inc.

García, Nasario. Grandpa Lolo & Trampa: A Story of Surprise & Mystery = Abuelito Lolo y Trampa: Un Cuento de Sorpresa y Misterio. Montoya, Jeremy, illus. 2014. (SPA & ENG.). 41p. (J). 9.99 *(978-1-936744-30-5(9))* LPD Pr.

—Grandpa Lolo's Navajo Saddle Blanket: La Tilma de Abuelito Lolo. Moeller, Richard, illus. Moeller, Richard, photos by. 2012. (J). *(978-0-8263-5078-7(X))* Univ. of New Mexico Pr.

—Grandpa Lolo's Navajo Saddle Blanket: La Tilma de Abuelito Lolo. 2012. (ENG., Illus.). 72p. (J). E-Book *(978-0-8263-5080-0(1))* Univ. of New Mexico Pr.

La gatita Presumida. (Spanish Early Intervention Levels Ser.). (SPA.). 28.38 *(978-0-7362-0846-8(1))* CENGAGE Learning.

Gatitos: Individual Title Six-Packs. (Literatura 2000 Ser.). (SPA.). (gr. -1-1). 28.00 *(978-0-7635-1195-1(1))* Rigby Education.

Gedovius, Juan. Purple Cubed. Gedovius, Juan, illus. (Illus.). 32p. (J). (gr. k-6). 13.95 *(978-968-19-0751-8(5))* Santillana USA Publishing Co., Inc.

El gigante Solitario: Individual Title Six-Packs. (Literatura 2000 Ser.). (SPA.). (gr. 2-3). 33.00 *(978-0-7635-1092-3(0))* Rigby Education.

Gol! (Spanish Early Intervention Levels Ser.). (SPA.). 23.10 *(978-0-7362-0323-4(0))* CENGAGE Learning.

Gol!, 6, Pack. 2003. 23.95 *(978-0-673-78064-5(3))* Celebration Pr.

Gómez, Carlos Humberto. Nos Comunicamos 1. (Coleccion Nos Comunicamos). (SPA & ENG.). (J). (gr. 1). pap. 23.50 *(978-958-04-1580-0(3)*, 15017309) Norma S.A. COL. Dist: Continental Bk. Co., Inc.

—Nos Comunicamos 2. (Coleccion Nos Comunicamos). (SPA & ENG.). (J). (gr. 2). pap. 23.50 *(978-958-04-1581-7(1)*, 15017310) Norma S.A. COL. Dist: Continental Bk. Co., Inc.

—Nos Comunicamos 4. (Coleccion Nos Comunicamos). (SPA & ENG.). (J). (gr. 4). pap. 23.50 *(978-958-04-1583-1(8)*, 1021251) Norma S.A. COL. Dist: Continental Bk. Co., Inc.

—Nos Comunicamos 6. (Coleccion Nos Comunicamos). (SPA & ENG.). (J). (gr. 6). pap. 23.50 *(978-958-04-1585-5(4)*, 1021253) Norma S.A. COL. Dist: Continental Bk. Co., Inc.

—Nos Comunicamos Kindergarten. (Coleccion Nos Comunicamos). (SPA & ENG.). (J). 23.50 *(978-958-04-1579-4(X)*, NOR5794) Norma S.A. COL. Dist: Continental Bk. Co., Inc.

Gonzalez, Maya Christina. Call Me Tree: Ll�mame �rbol, 1 vol. 2014.Tr. of Call Me Tree. (ENG.). 24p. (J). (gr. k-4). 19.95 *(978-0-89239-294-0(0)*, leelowcbp) Lee & Low Bks., Inc.

—My Colors, My World/Mis Colores, Mi Mundo (English & Spanish Edition), 1 vol. 2013.Tr. of Mis Colores, Mi Mundo. (ENG., Illus.). 32p. (J). (gr. k-2). pap. 11.95 *(978-0-89239-278-0(9)*, leelowcbp, Children's Book Press) Lee & Low Bks., Inc.

La Granja De Don Manuel: Individual 6-packs. 2003. 23.95 *(978-0-673-77151-3(2))* Celebration Pr.

Granny Says. 2005. (Illus.). (J). pap. 11.00 *(978-0-9764198-0-8(7))* Allecram Publishing.

Green Collection. (Elefonetica Ser.). (SPA.). (gr. 1-2). 324.85 *(978-0-7362-0784-3(8))* CENGAGE Learning.

Greene, Inez. Adonde Esta Me Topito?, Level 1. Flor Ada, Alma, tr. 2003. (Dejame Leer Ser.). (SPA., Illus.). (J). (gr. -1-3). 6.50 *(978-0-673-36328-2(7)*, Good Year Bks.) Celebration Pr.

Gregorio El Gallo, 6 Pack. 2003. 23.95 *(978-0-673-78078-2(3))* Celebration Pr.

The Grocery Store: Individual Title Two-Packs. (Chiquilibros Ser.). (gr. -1-1). 12.00 *(978-0-7635-8539-6(4))* Rigby Education.

El grupo musical Lac Hong: 6 Small Books. (Saludos Ser.: Vol. 1). (SPA.). (gr. 3-5). 31.00 *(978-0-7635-1757-1(7))* Rigby Education.

El Guerito Travieso, 6 Packs. 2003. 23.95 (978-0-673-77154-4(7)) Celebration Pr.

Guy, Ginger Foglesong. Fiesta! Bilingual English-Spanish. Moreno, Rene King, illus. 2007. (ENG.). 32p. (J). (gr. -1-3). 6.99 (978-0-06-088226-6(3), Greenwillow Bks.) HarperCollins Pubs.

Hansen, Grace. Animales Extraordinarios! (Weird Animals to Shock You!) 2016. (Ver para Creer (Seeing Is Believing) Ser.). (SPA., Illus.). 24p. (J). (gr. -1-2). lib. bdg. 32.79 (978-1-68080-772-1(2), 22706, Abdo Kids) ABDO Publishing Co.

—Caballitos de Mar (Seahorses), 1 vol. 2016. (Vida en el Océano (Ocean Life) Ser.). (SPA., Illus.). 24p. (J). (gr. -1-2). lib. bdg. 32.79 (978-1-68080-748-6(X), 22658, Abdo Kids) ABDO Publishing Co.

—Curiosidades Cientificas Increibles! (Science Facts to Surprise You!) 2016. (Ver para Creer (Seeing Is Believing) Ser.). (SPA., Illus.). 24p. (J). (gr. -1-2). lib. bdg. 32.79 (978-1-68080-771-4(4), 22704, Abdo Kids) ABDO Publishing Co.

—Delfines (Dolphins), 1 vol. 2016. (Vida en el Océano (Ocean Life) Ser.). (SPA., Illus.). 24p. (J). (gr. -1-2). lib. bdg. 32.79 (978-1-68080-745-5(5), 22652, Abdo Kids) ABDO Publishing Co.

—Jane Goodall: Activista y Experta en Chimpancés (Spanish Version) 2016. (Biografías: Personas Que Han Hecho Historia (History Maker Biographies) Ser.). (SPA., Illus.). 24p. (J). (gr. -1-2). lib. bdg. 32.79 (978-1-68080-739-4(0), 22640, Abdo Kids) ABDO Publishing Co.

—Maquinas Asombrosas! (Machines to Thrill You!) 2016. (Ver para Creer (Seeing Is Believing) Ser.). (SPA., Illus.). 24p. (J). (gr. -1-2). lib. bdg. 32.79 (978-1-68080-769-1(2), 22700, Abdo Kids) ABDO Publishing Co.

—Pulpos (Octopuses), 1 vol. 2016. (Vida en el Océano (Ocean Life) Ser.). (SPA., Illus.). 24p. (J). (gr. -1-2). lib. bdg. 32.79 (978-1-68080-747-9(1), 22656, Abdo Kids) ABDO Publishing Co.

—Records Mundiales Insolitos! (World Records to Wow You!) 2016. (Ver para Creer (Seeing Is Believing) Ser.). (SPA., Illus.). 24p. (J). (gr. -1-2). lib. bdg. 32.79 (978-1-68080-773-8(0), 22708, Abdo Kids) ABDO Publishing Co.

Harris, Dorothy Joan. Un Perro Muy Diferente. Rioja, Alberto Jimenez, tr. from ENG. LaFave, Kim, illus. 2006. (SPA.). 28p. (J). (gr. 5-6). pap. 9.99 (978-1-933032-04-7(9)) Lectorum Pubns., Inc.

Harvey, Sarah N. El Blanco, 1 vol. 2010. (Spanish Soundings Ser.). (SPA.). 128p. (YA). (gr. 8-12). pap. 9.95 (978-1-55469-317-7(9)) Orca Bk. Pubs. USA.

Has visto al jabali que anda por Aqui? Individual Title Six-Packs. (Literatura 2000 Ser.). (SPA.). (gr. 2-3). 33.00 (978-0-7635-1093-0(9)) Rigby Education.

Hay un esqueleto en el Autobus: Individual Title Six-Packs. (Literatura 2000 Ser.). (SPA.). (gr. 2-3). 33.00 (978-0-7635-1094-7(7)) Rigby Education.

Hayes, Joe. The Coyote under the Table: El Coyote Debajo de la Mesa, 1 vol. Castro L., Antonio, illus. 2022.Tr. of Folk Tales Told in Spanish & English. (ENG.). 136p. (J). (gr. 1-7). pap. 15.95 (978-1-935955-06-1(3), 23353382, Cinco Puntos Press) Lee & Low Bks., Inc.

—The Day It Snowed Tortillas - El DÃ a que Nevaron Tortillas: Folktales Told in Spanish & English, 1 vol. Castro L., Antonio, illus. 2003. (SPA & ENG.). 144p. (J). (gr. 3-6). pap. 14.95 (978-0-938317-76-0(8), 3488840c-6617-4886-98d7-0a90d3b6bce5, Cinco Puntos Press) Lee & Low Bks., Inc.

—Don't Say a Word, MamÃ¡ - No Digas Nada, MamÃ¡, 1 vol. Valencia, Esau Andrade, illus. 2013. (ENG.). 40p. (J). (gr. -1-3). pap. 12.95 (978-1-935955-45-0(4), 23353382, Cinco Puntos Press) Lee & Low Bks., Inc.

Hayhurst, Chris. John Sutter: California Pioneer / Pionero de California. 2009. (Famous People in American History/Grandes personajes en la historia de los Estados Unidos Ser.). (ENG & SPA.). 32p. (gr. 2-3). 47.90 (978-1-61512-549-4(3), Editorial Buenas Letras) Rosen Publishing Group, Inc., The.

—John Sutter: Pionero de California (John Sutter: California Pioneer) 2009. (Grandes personajes en la historia de los Estados Unidos (Famous People in American History) Ser.). (SPA.). 32p. (gr. 2-3). 47.90 (978-1-61512-803-7(4), Editorial Buenas Letras) Rosen Publishing Group, Inc., The.

—Sitting Bull / Toro Sentado: Sioux War Chief / Jefe Sioux. 2009. (Famous People in American History/Grandes personajes en la historia de los Estados Unidos Ser.). (SPA.). 32p. (gr. 2-3). 47.90 (978-1-61512-555-5(8), Editorial Buenas Letras) Rosen Publishing Group, Inc., The.

Hecho en Corea: 6 Small Books. (Saludos Ser.: Vol. 3). (SPA.). (gr. 3-5). 31.00 (978-0-7635-1830-1(1)) Rigby Education.

Hector tiene Hipo. (Spanish Early Intervention Levels Ser.). 21.30 (978-0-7362-0833-8(X)) CENGAGE Learning.

Hermoso, A. S., et al. Curso Practico de la Gramatica de Espanol Lengua Extranjera: Curso Practico I. 2nd ed. (SPA.). 116p. wbk. ed. 18.95 (978-84-7711-073-6(5), EDI0735) Edelsa Grupo Didascalia, S.A. ESP. Dist: Continental Bk. Co., Inc.

—Curso Practico de la Gramatica de Espanol Lengua Extranjera: Curso Practico II. (SPA.). 116p. wbk. ed. 18.95 (978-84-7711-074-3(3), EDI0743) Edelsa Grupo Didascalia, S.A. ESP. Dist: Continental Bk. Co., Inc.

—Curso Practico de la Gramatica de Espanol Lengua Extranjera: Curso Practico III. (SPA., Illus.). 128p. wbk. ed. 24.95 (978-84-7711-075-0(1), EDI0751) Edelsa Grupo Didascalia, S.A. ESP. Dist: Continental Bk. Co., Inc.

Herrera, Juan Felipe. Upside down Boy/el Nino de Cabeza, 1 vol. 2013.Tr. of Nino de Cabeza. (ENG., Illus.). 32p. (J). (gr. 1-5). per. 11.95 (978-0-89239-217-9(7), leelowcbp, Children's Book Press) Lee & Low Bks., Inc.

Hill, Eric. Donde Esta Spot? (SPA.). pap. 10.95 (978-950-07-1960-5(6)) Editorial Sudamericana S.A. ARG. Dist: Distribooks, Inc.

Hillert, Margaret. Dear Dragon Goes to the Library (Querido Dragon Va a la Biblioteca) Del Risco, Eida, tr. from ENG. Schimmell, David, illus. 2010. (BeginningtoRead Ser.). (SPA & ENG.). 32p. (J). (gr. k-2). lib. bdg. 22.60 (978-1-59953-361-2(8)) Norwood Hse. Pr.

—Dear Dragon's Day with Father (Querido Dragon Pasa el Dia con Papa) Del Risco, Eida, tr. from ENG. Schimmell, David, illus. 2010. (BeginningtoRead Ser.). (SPA & ENG.). 32p. (J). (gr. k-2). lib. bdg. 22.60 (978-1-59953-360-5(X)) Norwood Hse. Pr.

—Es Primavera, Querido Dragón/It's Spring, Dear Dragon. Schimmell, David, illus. 2011. (BeginningtoRead Ser.). 32p. (J). (-2). pap. 11.94 (978-1-60357-555-3(3)) Norwood Hse. Pr.

—Es Primavera, Querido Dragón/It's Spring, Dear Dragon. del Risco, Eida, tr. from ENG. Schimmell, David, illus. 2011. (BeginningtoRead Ser.). 32p. (J). (gr. k-2). lib. bdg. 22.60 (978-1-59953-471-8(1)) Norwood Hse. Pr.

—Es un Buen Juego, Querido Dragón/It's a Good Game, Dear Dragon. Schimmell, David, illus. 2010. (BeginningtoRead Ser.). 32p. (J). (-2). pap. 11.94 (978-1-60357-550-8(2)) Norwood Hse. Pr.

—It's a Good Game, Dear Dragon (Es un Buen Juego, Querido Dragon) Del Risco, Eida, tr. from ENG. Schimmell, David, illus. 2010. (BeginningtoRead Ser.). (SPA & ENG.). 32p. (J). (gr. k-2). lib. bdg. 22.60 (978-1-59953-362-9(6)) Norwood Hse. Pr.

—Juega, Juega, Juega, Querido Dragón/Play, Play, Play, Dear Dragon. del Risco, Eida, tr. Schimmell, David, illus. 2010. (BeginningtoRead Ser.). 32p. (J). (-2). pap. 11.94 (978-1-60357-551-5(0)) Norwood Hse. Pr.

—Play, Play, Play, Dear Dragon (Juega, Juega, Juega, Querido Dragon) Del Risco, Eida, tr. Schimmell, David, illus. 2010. (BeginningtoRead Ser.). (SPA & ENG.). 32p. (J). (gr. k-2). lib. bdg. 22.60 (978-1-59953-363-6(4)) Norwood Hse. Pr.

Hipp, Andrew. El Girasol: Por dentro y por fuera (Sunflower:Inside & Out) 2009. (Explora la Naturaleza (Getting into Nature) Ser.). (SPA.). 32p. (gr. 3-4). 47.90 (978-1-61512-336-0(9), Editorial Buenas Letras) Rosen Publishing Group, Inc., The.

—El Maiz: Por dentro y por fuera (Corn: Inside & Out) 2009. (Explora la Naturaleza (Getting into Nature) Ser.). (SPA.). 32p. (gr. 3-4). 47.90 (978-1-61512-337-7(7), Editorial Buenas Letras) Rosen Publishing Group, Inc., The.

—El Roble: Por dentro y por fuera (Oak Tree: Inside & Out) 2009. (Explora la Naturaleza (Getting into Nature) Ser.). (SPA.). 32p. (gr. 3-4). 47.90 (978-1-61512-338-4(5), Editorial Buenas Letras) Rosen Publishing Group, Inc., The.

Hoffman, Mary Ann. LeBron James: Basketball Star. 2009. (Sports Superstars Ser.). 24p. (gr. 1-1). 42.50 (978-1-60853-178-3(3), PowerKids Pr.) Rosen Publishing Group, Inc., The.

Hola! (Spanish Early Intervention Levels Ser.). (SPA.). 23.10 (978-1-56334-761-0(X)) CENGAGE Learning.

Hola y Adios, 6 Packs. (Literatura 2000 Ser.). (SPA.). (gr. k-1). 28.00 (978-0-7635-1023-7(8)) Rigby Education.

Holt, Rinehart and Winston Staff. En Avant: Online Edition. 4th ed. 2003. 43.86 (978-0-03-031718-7(5)) Holt McDougal.

—Ven Conmigo! Level 1: Storytelling Book. 3rd ed. 2003. (Holt Spanish Ser.). (SPA.). pap. 14.60 (978-0-03-065474-9(2)) Holt McDougal.

El Hombrecito de pan de Jengibre. (ENG & SPA.). (gr. k-1). 26.00 incl. VHS (978-0-7635-6277-9(7)) Rigby Education.

Las Horas. (Coleccion Libritos Acordeon). (SPA., Illus.). 10p. (J). pap. 5.50 (978-950-11-0827-9(9), SGM279) Sigmar ARG. Dist: Continental Bk. Co., Inc.

La Hormiga y el Saltamontes: Lap Book. (Pebble Soup Exploraciones Ser.). (SPA.). 16p. (gr. -1-18). 21.00 (978-0-7578-1682-6(7)) Rigby Education.

La hormiga y el Saltamontes: Small Book. (Pebble Soup Exploraciones Ser.). (SPA.). 16p. (gr. -1-18). 5.00 (978-0-7578-1722-9(X)) Rigby Education.

Houghton, Gillian. Abejas: Por dentro y por fuera (Bees: Inside & Out) 2009. (Explora la Naturaleza (Getting into Nature) Ser.). (SPA.). 32p. (gr. 3-4). 47.90 (978-1-61512-333-9(4), Editorial Buenas Letras) Rosen Publishing Group, Inc., The.

Hudson, Amanda. This Is My Ball / Ésta Es Mi Pelota, 1 vol. 2008. (Our Toys / Nuestros Juguetes Ser.). (SPA & ENG.). 16p. (gr. k-k). pap. 6.30 (978-0-8368-9355-7(7), 90b25969-7e82-4470-9892-d7cdfb7bb3a0, Weekly Reader Leveled Readers) Stevens, Gareth Publishing LLLP.

Huevo rojo y Jengibre: Six-Pack. (Saludos Ser.: Vol. 1). (SPA.). (gr. 2-3). 31.00 (978-0-7635-9518-0(7)) Rigby Education.

Huracan a la Vista! 6 Small Books. (Saludos Ser.: Vol. 2). (SPA.). (gr. 3-5). 31.00 (978-0-7635-2069-4(1)) Rigby Education.

Hurt-Newton, Tania. Vamos de Paseo. (SPA.). pap. 7.95 (978-950-07-2027-4(2)) Editorial Sudamericana S.A. ARG. Dist: Distribooks, Inc.

I Dance 6 Packs: Matching English. 2003. 23.95 (978-0-673-57559-3(4)) Celebration Pr.

I Live Here: Matching English, 6 Packs. 2003. 23.95 (978-0-673-57560-9(8)) Celebration Pr.

The Ice Cream Shop: Individual Title, 2 Packs. (Chiquilibros Ser.). (gr. -1-1). 12.00 (978-0-7635-8534-1(3)) Rigby Education.

Igual a mi Abuelo: Individual Title, 6 Packs. (Literatura 2000 Ser.). (SPA.). (gr. 1-2). 28.00 (978-0-7635-1045-9(9)) Rigby Education.

In the Dark Interactive Packages: Bedtime. (Pebble Soup Explorations Ser.). (SPA.). (gr. -1-18). 52.00 (978-0-7578-5247-3(5)) Rigby Education.

In the Dark Interactive Packages: Nighttime Jobs. (Pebble Soup Explorations Ser.). (SPA.). (gr. -1-18). 52.00 (978-0-7578-5250-3(5)) Rigby Education.

In the Midnight Sky. (Pebble Soup Explorations Ser.). (SPA.). 16p. (gr. -1-18). 31.00 (978-0-7578-1669-7(X)) Rigby Education.

In the Midnight Sky: Small Book. (Pebble Soup Explorations Ser.). (SPA.). 16p. (gr. -1-18). 5.00 (978-0-7578-1709-0(2)) Rigby Education.

Infante, Begona. Fatima Yo Soy de El Salvador.Tr. of I'm from El Salvador. (SPA.). 48p. (J). 12.95 (978-84-246-9403-6(1)) La Galera, S.A. Editorial ESP. Dist: AIMS International Bks., Inc.

El Ingles Animado por Walt Disney.Tr. of Animated English by Walt Disney. (SPA.). (978-970-22-0098-7(9)) Larousse, Ediciones, S. A. de C. V.

Inkiow, Dimiter. Yo, Clara y el Papagayo Pipo. (Torre de Papel Ser.). (SPA.). (J). (gr. 2). 7.95 (978-958-04-2072-9(6)) Norma S.A. COL. Dist: Distribuidora Norma, Inc.

—Yo, Clara y el Poni Miguelin. (SPA., Illus.). 7.95 (978-958-04-2389-8(X)) Norma S.A. COL. Dist: Distribuidora Norma, Inc.

Insectos, Insectos, 6 Packs. 2003. 23.95 (978-0-673-78070-6(8)) Celebration Pr.

Insects, Insects. 2003. 23.95 (978-0-673-78132-1(1)) Celebration Pr.

The Iron Horse, 6 Packs. (Chiquilibros Ser.). (gr. k-1). 23.00 (978-0-7635-0443-4(2)) Rigby Education.

Iturralde, Edna. Conoce a Miguel de Cervantes: Get to Know Miguel de Cervantes. 2014. (Personajes Del Mundo Hispnico Ser.). (ENG & SPA., Illus.). 32p. (J). (gr. -1-3). 15.95 (978-1-61435-352-2(2), Alfaguara) Santillana USA Publishing Co., Inc.

Izquierdo, Ana, tr. Caritas Felices: Winnie-the-Pooh. 2007. (Disney Winnie the Pooh (SilverDolphin) Ser.). (SPA., Illus.). 10p. (J). (gr. -1). bds. (978-970-718-393-3(4), Silver Dolphin en Español) Advanced Marketing, S. de R. L. de C. V.

Jackson, Nikki. Georgia & Reed's: My Potty & Me. 2012. 16p. pap. 15.99 (978-1-4772-4516-3(2)) AuthorHouse.

—Georgia & Reeds: The AL-PHA-BET Book. 2012. 20p. pap. 17.99 (978-1-4772-2939-2(6)) AuthorHouse.

Jarkins, Sheila. The Adventures of Marco Flamingo in the Jungle. Jarkins, Sheila, illus. 2012. (Illus.). 32p. (J). 1.99 (978-1-936299-31-7(3), Raven Tree Pr.) Delta Systems Company, Inc.

Jeffries, Joyce. Meet the Mayor / Conoce a Los Alcaldes, 1 vol. 2013. (People Around Town / Gente de Mi Ciudad Ser.). (SPA & ENG., Illus.). 24p. (J). (gr. k-k). 25.27 (978-1-4339-9470-8(4), b2aa7e90-b2d6-4cc0-aadb-29ceb8786c8f) Stevens, Gareth Publishing LLLP.

—Meet the Pilot / Conoce a Los Pilotos, 1 vol. 2013. (People Around Town / Gente de Mi Ciudad Ser.). (SPA & ENG.). 24p. (J). (gr. k-k). 25.27 (978-1-4339-9472-2(0), 95bd2d81-8eb3-45c9-a2f8-848d4aec7c6d) Stevens, Gareth Publishing LLLP.

Johansen, Heidi. What I Look Like When I am Angry / Cómo me veo cuando estoy Enojado. 2009. (Let's Look at Feelings / un vistazo a los sentimientos Ser.). (ENG & SPA.). 24p. (gr. k-1). 42.50 (978-1-61514-245-3(2), Editorial Buenas Letras) Rosen Publishing Group, Inc., The.

—What I Look Like When I am Happy / Cómo me veo cuando estoy Contento. 2009. (Let's Look at Feelings / un vistazo a los sentimientos Ser.). (ENG & SPA.). 24p. (gr. k-1). 42.50 (978-1-61514-244-6(4), Editorial Buenas Letras) Rosen Publishing Group, Inc., The.

Johnson, Bruce & McKay, Sindy. We Both Read Bilingual Edition-About Dogs/Acerca de Los Perros. 2011.Tr. of Acerca de Los Perros. (ENG & SPA., Illus.). 44p. (J). pap. 5.99 (978-1-60115-048-6(2)) Treasure Bay, Inc.

Johnson, Gee & Sánchez, Lucía M. El Pulpo. 2013. (2G Vida Marina Ser.). (SPA., Illus.). 20p. (J). (gr. k-2). pap. 9.60 (978-1-61541-452-9(5)) American Reading Co.

Jones, Christianne C. Pruebalo, 1 vol. Ruíz, Carlos, tr. Won Yi, Hye, illus. 2006. (Read-It! Readers en Español: Story Collection). (SPA.). 24p. (J). (gr. -1-3). 22.65 (978-1-4048-1692-3(5), 91277, Picture Window Bks.) Capstone.

Juan y Paula en la Granja. (Coleccion Leo Con Figuras). (SPA.). 14p. (J). pap. 4.50 (978-950-11-0837-8(6), SGM376) Sigmar ARG. Dist: Continental Bk. Co., Inc.

Juego de Dedos. (Spanish Early Intervention Levels Ser.). (SPA.). 21.30 (978-0-7362-0805-5(4)) CENGAGE Learning.

Juez por un Dia: 6 Small Books. (Saludos Ser.: Vol. 1). (SPA.). (gr. 3-5). 31.00 (978-0-7635-1802-8(6)) Rigby Education.

Juez por un Dia: Big Book. (Saludos Ser.: Vol. 1). (SPA.). (gr. 3-5). 31.00 (978-0-7635-3172-0(3)) Rigby Education.

Juguemos con la Musica.Tr. of Let's Play with Music. (SPA.). (J). (gr. k-2). pap., stu. ed. 11.16 (978-968-24-3081-7(X)) Trillas Editorial, S. A. MEX. Dist: Lectorum Pubns., Inc.

Jules, Jacqueline. Cantante Súper Estrella. Smith, Kim, illus. 2018. (Sofia Martinez en Español Ser.). (SPA.). 32p. (J). (gr. k-2). lib. bdg. 21.32 (978-1-5158-2452-7(7), 137555, Picture Window Bks.) Capstone.

—El Cumpleaños de la Abuela. Smith, Kim, illus. 2018. (Sofia Martinez en Español Ser.). (SPA.). 32p. (J). (gr. k-2). lib. bdg. 21.32 (978-1-5158-2443-5(8), 137546, Picture Window Bks.) Capstone.

—Las Cartas Especiales de la Abuela. Smith, Kim, illus. 2018. (Sofia Martinez en Español Ser.). (SPA.). 32p. (J). (gr. k-2). lib. bdg. 21.32 (978-1-5158-2444-2(6), 137547, Picture Window Bks.) Capstone.

—Lío de Caléndulas. Smith, Kim, illus. 2018. (Sofia Martinez en Español Ser.). (SPA.). 32p. (J). (gr. k-2). lib. bdg. 21.32 (978-1-5158-2447-3(0), 137550, Picture Window Bks.) Capstone.

—Lista para la Foto. Smith, Kim, illus. 2018. (Sofia Martinez en Español Ser.). (SPA.). 32p. (J). (gr. k-2). lib. bdg. 21.32 (978-1-5158-2449-7(7), 137552, Picture Window Bks.) Capstone.

—A Oscuras. Smith, Kim, illus. 2018. (Sofia Martinez en Español Ser.). (SPA.). 32p. (J). (gr. k-2). lib. bdg. 21.32 (978-1-5158-2446-6(2), 137549, Picture Window Bks.) Capstone.

—Un Paseo de Compras Problemático. Smith, Kim, illus. 2018. (Sofia Martinez en Español Ser.). (SPA.). 32p. (J). (gr. k-2). lib. bdg. 21.32 (978-1-5158-2451-0(9), 137554, Picture Window Bks.) Capstone.

—La Receta Secreta. Trusted Translations, Trusted, tr. Smith, Kim, illus. 2018. (Sofia Martinez en Español Ser.). (SPA.). 32p. (J). (gr. k-2). lib. bdg. 22.65 (978-1-5158-2450-3(0), 137553, Picture Window Bks.) Capstone.

Jung, Scott. Verdades bíblicas eternas (Timeless Bible Truths) 2011. 32p. pap. 6.99 (978-0-7586-2680-6(0)) Concordia Publishing Hse.

—Verdades bíblicas eternas (Timeless Bible Truths) - Bilingual. 2011. 64p. pap. 7.99 (978-0-7586-2681-3(9)) Concordia Publishing Hse.

Just Bunny & Me: Big Book. (Pebble Soup Explorations Ser.). (SPA.). 16p. (gr. -1-18). 31.00 (978-0-7578-1666-6(5)) Rigby Education.

Just Bunny & Me: Small Book. (Pebble Soup Explorations Ser.). (SPA.). 16p. (gr. -1-18). 5.00 (978-0-7578-1706-9(8)) Rigby Education.

Kalman, Bobbie & Johnson, Robin. El Ciclo de Vida Del Pinguino Emperador. 2007. (Libro de Bobbie Kalman Ser.). (SPA., Illus.). 32p. (J). (978-1-4287-3238-4(1)) Crabtree Publishing Co.

Kanellos, Nicolás. El Torneo de Trabalenguas / the Tongue Twister Tournament. Vega, Anne, illus. 2016. (SPA & ENG.). 32p. (J). (gr. k-4). 17.95 (978-1-55885-832-9(6), Piñata Books) Arte Publico Pr.

Kasza, Keiko. El Mas Poderoso. (SPA.). (J). 8.95 (978-958-04-6490-7(1)) Norma S.A. COL. Dist: Distribuidora Norma, Inc.

Katz, Karen. ¡Cu-Cú, Bebé! (Peek-A-Baby) Katz, Karen, illus. 2009. (SPA., Illus.). 14p. (J). (gr. -1 — 1). bds. 7.99 (978-1-4169-7938-8(7), Libros Para Ninos) Libros Para Ninos.

Kaut, Ellis. El Duende del Carpintero. (Torre de Papel Ser.). (SPA.). (J). (gr. 4-18). 7.95 (978-958-04-2889-3(1)) Norma S.A. COL. Dist: Distribuidora Norma, Inc.

Kelly, Harold G. El Sol por dentro (Inside the Sun) 2009. (Reading Room Collection: Spanish Ser.). (SPA.). 24p. (gr. 3-4). 42.50 (978-1-60854-177-5(0), Editorial Buenas Letras) Rosen Publishing Group, Inc., The.

Khu, Jannel. Let's Draw a School Bus with Shapes/Vamos a dibujar un autobus escolar usando Figuras. 2009. (Let's Draw with Shapes / Vamos a dibujar con figuras Ser.). (ENG & SPA.). 24p. (gr. k-1). 42.50 (978-1-61514-218-7(5), Editorial Buenas Letras) Rosen Publishing Group, Inc., The.

Kique el Taxista. (Spanish Early Intervention Levels Ser.). (SPA.). 21.30 (978-0-7362-0835-2(6)) CENGAGE Learning.

The Kitchen: Individual Title Two-Packs. (Chiquilibros Ser.). (gr. -1-1). 12.00 (978-0-7635-8540-2(8)) Rigby Education.

Kittinger, Jo S. Cuando sea Grande: When I Grow Up. Lucas, Margeaux, illus. 2005. (Rookie Reader Español Ser.). 24p. (gr. k-2). 19.50 (978-0-516-24443-3(4), Children's Pr.) Scholastic Library Publishing.

Kline, Trish & Donev, Mary. Celebration of Letters A & B: Busy Preschoolers. 2007. (Illus.). 16p. (J). per. 20.00 (978-1-934307-04-5(1)) Ghost Hunter Productions.

—Celebration of Letters C & D: Busy Preschoolers. 2007. (Illus.). 16p. (J). per. 20.00 (978-1-934307-05-2(X)) Ghost Hunter Productions.

—Celebration of Letters E & F: Busy Preschoolers. 2007. (Illus.). 16p. (J). per. 20.00 (978-1-934307-06-9(8)) Ghost Hunter Productions.

—Celebration of Letters G & H: Busy Preschoolers. 2007. (Illus.). 16p. (J). per. 20.00 (978-1-934307-07-6(6)) Ghost Hunter Productions.

—Celebration of Letters I & J: Busy Preschoolers. 2007. (Illus.). 16p. (J). per. 20.00 (978-1-934307-08-3(4)) Ghost Hunter Productions.

—Celebration of Letters K & L: Busy Preschoolers. 2007. (Illus.). 16p. (J). per. 20.00 (978-1-934307-09-0(2)) Ghost Hunter Productions.

—Celebration of Letters M & N: Busy Preschoolers. 2007. (Illus.). 16p. (J). per. 20.00 (978-1-934307-10-6(6)) Ghost Hunter Productions.

—Celebration of Letters O & Q: Busy Preschoolers. 2007. (Illus.). 16p. (J). per. 20.00 (978-1-934307-11-3(4)) Ghost Hunter Productions.

—Celebration of Letters P & R: Busy Preschoolers. 2007. (Illus.). 16p. (J). per. 20.00 (978-1-934307-12-0(2)) Ghost Hunter Productions.

—Celebration of Letters S & T: Busy Preschoolers. 2007. (Illus.). 16p. (J). per. 20.00 (978-1-934307-13-7(0)) Ghost Hunter Productions.

—Celebration of Letters U & V: Busy Preschoolers. 2007. (Illus.). 16p. (J). per. 20.00 (978-1-934307-14-4(9)) Ghost Hunter Productions.

—Celebration of Letters W & X: Busy Preschoolers. 2007. (Illus.). 16p. (J). per. 20.00 (978-1-934307-15-1(7)) Ghost Hunter Productions.

—Celebration of Letters Y & Z: Busy Preschoolers. 2007. (Illus.). 16p. (J). per. 20.00 (978-1-934307-16-8(5)) Ghost Hunter Productions.

Klingel, Cynthia & Noyed, Robert B. Hair, 1 vol. 2010. (Let's Read about Our Bodies (Second Edition) Ser.). (ENG., Illus.). 24p. (gr. k-2). pap. 9.15 (978-1-4339-3363-9(2), 447f226d-1139-4a0e-8603-ef654f2714d5) Stevens, Gareth Publishing LLLP.

—Hair / el Cabello, 1 vol. 2010. (Let's Read about Our Bodies / Hablemos Del Cuerpo Humano Ser.). (SPA & ENG., Illus.). 24p. (gr. k-2). pap. 9.15 (978-1-4339-3739-2(5), 9660fe2f-a969-4b58-b901-52b57ffc5367); (J). lib. bdg. 24.67 (978-1-4339-3738-5(7), 46c30145-1386-46f7-addb-721c12096d2d) Stevens, Gareth Publishing LLLP.

—Hands, 1 vol. 2010. (Let's Read about Our Bodies (Second Edition) Ser.). (ENG., Illus.). 24p. (gr. k-2). pap. 9.15 (978-1-4339-3366-0(7), 5844324f-ed31-46b3-a161-2b9f77b53327); (J). lib. bdg. 24.67 (978-1-4339-3365-3(9), 623f3927-68ad-4335-8c10-a8e724d933ea) Stevens, Gareth Publishing LLLP.

—Hands / Las Manos, 1 vol. 2010. (Let's Read about Our Bodies / Hablemos Del Cuerpo Humano Ser.). (SPA & ENG., Illus.). 24p. (gr. k-2). pap. 9.15 (978-1-4339-3742-2(5), c2781f53-5f66-4dc5-90f5-4a289ddf7e05); (J). lib. bdg. 24.67 (978-1-4339-3741-5(7), 488aa1c8-bcb8-4f7e-953d-c81a76e89f00) Stevens, Gareth Publishing LLLP.

—Nose, 1 vol. 2010. (Let's Read about Our Bodies (Second Edition) Ser.). (ENG., Illus.). 24p. (gr. k-2). pap. 9.15 (978-1-4339-3372-1(1), 0fba4b99-b136-4f40-afde-bd52b6e6ec8e); (J). lib. bdg. 24.67 (978-1-4339-3371-4(3), ba20bc52-5f23-4e5c-9ec3-f0515eb949ed) Stevens, Gareth Publishing LLLP.

—Nose / la Nariz, 1 vol. 2010. (Let's Read about Our Bodies / Hablemos Del Cuerpo Humano Ser.). (SPA & ENG., Illus.). 24p. (gr. k-2). pap. 9.15 (978-1-4339-3748-4(4), 78273cbd-e597-47e1-b311-29989cac650c); (J). lib. bdg. 24.67 (978-1-4339-3747-7(6), 86aed606-2438-4275-9026-266bcfe8a324) Stevens, Gareth Publishing LLLP.

—Skin, 1 vol. 2010. (Let's Read about Our Bodies (Second Edition) Ser.). (ENG., Illus.). 24p. (gr. k-2). pap. 9.15 (978-1-4339-3375-2(6), 1d406892-af7e-4222-b782-8ac08fc49cae); (J). lib. bdg. 24.67 (978-1-4339-3374-5(8), d0d25068-b7a9-47ea-80a9-0d88a5dc66e2) Stevens, Gareth Publishing LLLP.

—Skin / la Piel, 1 vol. 2010. (Let's Read about Our Bodies / Hablemos Del Cuerpo Humano Ser.). (SPA & ENG., Illus.). 24p. (gr. k-2). pap. 9.15 *(978-1-4339-3751-4(4),* 43c38744-5a3e-4bc3-b245-9b7602f2ee99); (J). lib. bdg. 24.67 *(978-1-4339-3750-7(6),* a79cc109-3cba-41c1-a978-597de8cb9d6c) Stevens, Gareth Publishing LLLP.

Kondrchek, Jamie. A Day in the Life (Un Dia en la Vida), 4 vols., Set. Vega, Eida de la, tr. Rasemas, Joe, illus. Incl. My Favorite Time of Day (Mi Hora Preferida del Dia) lib. bdg. 25.70 *(978-1-58415-837-0(9))*; On My Way to School (De Camino a la Escuela) Rasemas, Joe. 25.70 *(978-1-58415-840-0(9))*; What Day Is It? (Que Dia Es Hoy?) Rasemas, Joe. 25.70 *(978-1-58415-838-7(7))*; What Should I Wear Today? (Que Ropa Me Pondre Hoy?) Rasemas, Joe. 25.70 *(978-1-58415-839-4(5))*; (Illus.). 32p. (J). (gr. -1-1). 2009. (ENG & SPA.). 2009. Set lib. bdg. 102.80 *(978-1-58415-844-8(1))* Mitchell Lane Pubs.

Kranz, Linda. Only One You / Nadie Como Tu. Mlawer, Teresa, tr. 2014. (Illus.). 32p. (J). (gr. -1-1). 12.95 *(978-1-63076-023-6(4))* Taylor Trade Publishing.

—You Be You/Sé Siempre Tú. Mlawer, Teresa, tr. 2014. (Illus.). 32p. (J). (gr. -1-1). 12.95 *(978-1-63076-021-2(8))* Taylor Trade Publishing.

Kwasi: un cuento Cancion: 6 Small Books. (Saludos Ser.: Vol. 2). (SPA.). 24p. (gr. 2-3). 31.00 *(978-0-7635-9525-8(X))* Rigby Education.

Lab Manual. 2003. (Scott Foresman Science Ser.). (gr. 1-18). tchr. ed., lab manual ed. 13.25 *(978-0-673-59344-3(4))*; (gr. 2-18). tchr. ed., lab manual ed. 13.25 *(978-0-673-59345-0(2))*; (gr. 3-18). tchr. ed., lab manual ed. 13.25 *(978-0-673-59346-7(0))*; (gr. 4-18). tchr. ed., lab manual ed. 13.25 *(978-0-673-59347-4(9))*; (gr. 5-18). tchr. ed., lab manual ed. 13.25 *(978-0-673-59348-1(7))* Addison-Wesley Educational Pubs., Inc.

Lachtman, Ofelia Dumas. Pepita Packs Up: Pepita Empaca. Ventura, Gabriela Baeza, tr. from ENG. Delange, Alex Pardo, illus. 2005. 48p. (J). (gr. -1-k). lib. bdg. 16.95 *(978-1-55885-431-4(2),* Piñata Books) Arte Publico Pr.

El Ladron: Individual Title-Six Packs. (Chiquilibros Ser.). (SPA.). (gr. k-1). 23.00 *(978-0-7635-8606-5(4))* Rigby Education.

Lakeshore Learning Materials Staff, contrib. by. Spanish Emergent Readers: Set of 8 Books. 2007. (SPA.). (J). 44.95 *(978-1-59746-020-0(6))* Lakeshore Learning Materials.

Lamadrid, Enrique R. Amadito & the Hero Children: Amadito y Los Niños Héroes. Córdova, Amy, illus. 2011. (SPA & ENG.). (J). *(978-0-8263-4978-1(1))* Univ. of New Mexico Pr.

—Amadito & the Hero Children: Amadito y Los niños Héroes. Córdova, Amy & Córdova, Amy, illus. 2011. (ENG.). 60p. (J). E-Book *(978-0-8263-4980-4(3))* Univ. of New Mexico Pr.

Landrón, Rafael & Landrón, José Rafael. Beba y la Isla Nena: Beba & the Little Island. Ordóñez, María Antonia, illus. 2010. (SPA & ENG.). 32p. (J). *(978-1-934370-05-6(3),* Campanita Bks.) Editorial Campana.

Las dos Hermanas: Lap Book. (Pebble Soup Exploraciones Ser.). (SPA.). 16p. (gr. -1-18). 21.00 *(978-0-7578-1692-5(4))* Rigby Education.

Las dos Hermanas: Small Book. (Pebble Soup Exploraciones Ser.). (SPA.). 16p. (gr. -1-18). 5.00 *(978-0-7578-1732-8(7))* Rigby Education.

Las Escondidas. (Spanish Early Intervention Levels Ser.). (SPA.). 31.14 *(978-0-7362-0337-1(0))* CENGAGE Learning.

Las huellas Verdes: Individual Title Six-Packs. (Literatura 2000 Ser.). (SPA.). (gr. 1-2). 28.00 *(978-0-7635-1044-2(0))* Rigby Education.

Las Ovejitas. (Spanish Early Intervention Levels Ser.). (SPA.). 21.30 *(978-0-7362-0825-3(9))* CENGAGE Learning.

Las Pinatas. (Spanish Early Intervention Levels Ser.). (SPA.). 21.30 *(978-0-7362-0808-6(9))* CENGAGE Learning.

Las Visitas: Individual Title Six-Packs. (Literatura 2000 Ser.). (SPA.). (gr. k-1). 28.00 *(978-0-7635-1032-9(7))* Rigby Education.

Lavaca BLANCA de botas NEGRAS. (SPA.). (J). 12.00 *(978-958-02-1235-5(X))* Editorial Voluntad S.A. COL. Dist: Distribuidora Norma, Inc.

Lawton, Wendy. A La Sombra de Su Mano, 1 vol. 2009. Orig. Title: Shadow of His Hand. (SPA.). 160p. pap. 4.99 *(978-0-8254-1379-7(6),* Editorial Portavoz) Kregel Pubns.

Lebscky, Ibi. Albert. Cardoni, Paolo, illus. (Coleccion Seran Famosos).Tr. of Little Albert Einstein. (SPA.). 28p. (J). (gr. 2-4). 10.36 *(978-84-233-1400-3(6))* Ediciones Destino ESP. Dist: Lectorum Pubns., Inc.

Lechermeier, Philippe. Princesas/ Princesses: Mini Album. 2008. (SPA.). 108p. 15.95 *(978-84-263-6701-3(1))* Vives, Luis Editorial (Edelvives) ESP. Dist: Lectorum Pubns., Inc.

Lectura en Familia: Spanish Easy Reading Combo. (SPA.). (gr. -1-2). 122.04 *(978-1-56334-402-2(5))* CENGAGE Learning.

Lectura en Familia: Spanish Phonics Grade 1 Combo. (SPA.). (gr. 1-18). 200.04 *(978-0-7362-1490-2(9))* CENGAGE Learning.

Lectura en Familia: Spanish Phonics Grade 2 Combo. (SPA.). (gr. 2-18). 114.18 *(978-0-7362-1491-9(7))* CENGAGE Learning.

Leo 1. (SPA.). (J). 16.00 *(978-958-04-5657-5(7))* Norma S.A. COL. Dist: Distribuidora Norma, Inc.

Leo 2. (SPA.). (J). 16.00 *(978-958-04-5658-2(5))* Norma S.A. COL. Dist: Distribuidora Norma, Inc.

Leo 3. (SPA.). (J). 16.00 *(978-958-04-5659-9(3))* Norma S.A. COL. Dist: Distribuidora Norma, Inc.

Leo 4. (SPA.). (J). 16.00 *(978-958-04-5660-5(7))* Norma S.A. COL. Dist: Distribuidora Norma, Inc.

Leo 5. (SPA.). (J). 16.00 *(978-958-04-5661-2(5))* Norma S.A. COL. Dist: Distribuidora Norma, Inc.

Leo 6. (SPA.). (J). 16.00 *(978-958-04-5662-9(3))* Norma S.A. COL. Dist: Distribuidora Norma, Inc.

Leonard, Marcia. El Hombre de Hojalata. Handelman, Dorothy, photos by. 2005. (ENG & SPA., Illus.). 32p. (J). (gr. -1-1). pap. 4.99 *(978-0-8225-3310-8(3))* Lerner Publishing Group.

Leonard, Marcia & Handelman, Dorothy. The Pet Vet. Handelman, Dorothy, illus. Leonard, Marcia, photos by. 2005. (ENG & SPA., Illus.). 32p. (J). (gr. -1-1). pap. 4.99 *(978-0-8225-3299-6(9))* Lerner Publishing Group.

Levy, Janice & Arisa, Miguel. I Remember Abuelito: A Day of the Dead Story. Lopez, Loretta, illus. 2012.Tr. of Yo Recuerdo a Abuelito - Un Cuento del Dia de los Muertos. (SPA & ENG.). (J). *(978-1-61913-114-9(5))* Weigl Pubs., Inc.

Levy, Robert. Not Just Mustard & Ketchup/ No Solo Mostaza y Salsa de Tomate. 2007. 58p. pap. 9.95 *(978-0-7414-4304-5(X))* Infinity Publishing.

La Leyenda del Dorado. (SPA.). (J). 12.00 *(978-958-02-1355-0(0))* Editorial Voluntad S.A. COL. Dist: Distribuidora Norma, Inc.

Libertson, Jody. Nathan Hale: Hero of the American Revolution. 2009. (Primary Sources of Famous People in American History Ser.). 32p. (gr. 2-3). 47.90 *(978-1-60851-709-1(8))* Rosen Publishing Group, Inc., The.

—Nathan Hale: Héroe revolucionario / Hero of the American Revolution. 2009. (Famous People in American History/Grandes personajes en la historia de los Estados Unidos Ser.). (ENG & SPA.). 32p. (gr. 2-3). 47.90 *(978-1-61512-552-4(3),* Editorial Buenas Letras) Rosen Publishing Group, Inc., The.

—Nathan Hale: Héroe revolucionario (Nathan Hale: Hero of the American Revolution) 2009. (Grandes personajes en la historia de los Estados Unidos (Famous People in American History) Ser.). (SPA.). 32p. (gr. 2-3). 47.90 *(978-1-61512-805-1(0),* Editorial Buenas Letras) Rosen Publishing Group, Inc., The.

Libritos Mios staff, et al. Spanish Emergent Reader 1: Mira como Juego; ¡Curitas!; Los Animales del Zoológico; Construyendo una Casa; la Alberca; ¡Agua y Jabón!; Me Visto; Mi Gato, 8 bks. Elías, Annette, tr. Clayman, Fillys et al, illus. 2003.Tr. of Emergent Reader 1. (SPA.). 8p. (J). 120.00 *(978-1-893986-24-4(1))* Keep Bks.

Libritos para Mi: Blue Set. (SPA.). (gr. k-2). 129.00 *(978-0-7362-0711-9(2))* CENGAGE Learning.

Libritos para Mi: Green Set. (SPA.). (gr. k-2). 129.00 *(978-0-7362-0709-6(0))* CENGAGE Learning.

Libritos para Mi: Orange Set. (SPA.). (gr. k-2). 129.00 *(978-0-7362-0710-2(4))* CENGAGE Learning.

Libritos para Mi: Purple Set. (SPA.). (gr. k-2). 129.00 *(978-0-7362-0708-9(2))* CENGAGE Learning.

Libritos para Mi: Red Set. (SPA.). (gr. k-2). 129.00 *(978-0-7362-0707-2(4))* CENGAGE Learning.

Lillegard, Dee. Papas el Martes, Level 1. 2003. (Dejame Leer Ser.). (SPA., Illus.). (J). (gr. -1-3). 6.50 *(978-0-673-36327-5(9),* Good Year Bks.) Celebration Pr.

Linari, Adrian. Los Cuentos de Aguara. (SPA.). (J). 8.95 *(978-958-04-5031-3(5))* Norma S.A. COL. Dist: Distribuidora Norma, Inc.

Lionni, Leo. Su Propio Color (a Color of His Own, Spanish-English Bilingual Edition) Lionni, Leo, illus. 2016. (Illus.). 30p. (J). (gr. -1-k). bds. 8.99 *(978-0-553-53873-1(X),* Knopf Bks. for Young Readers) Random Hse. Children's Bks.

Lisansky, Sue, illus. Cinderella. 2011. (First Fairy Tales Ser.). (ENG.). 20p. (J). (gr. -1-3). pap. 4.99 *(978-1-934004-19-7(7))* Byeway Bks.

El Liston. (Spanish Early Intervention Levels Ser.). (SPA.). 23.10 *(978-1-56334-773-3(3))* CENGAGE Learning.

Little Books Collection: Includes 18 Little Books. 2003. 83.50 *(978-0-7652-0130-0(5))* Modern Curriculum Pr.

Llega la Abuelita: 6 Small Books. (Saludos Ser.: Vol. 2). (SPA.). (gr. 2-3). 31.00 *(978-0-7635-9544-9(6))* Rigby Education.

La Llegada del Virrey (Arrival of the Viceroy) 2005. (SPA.). (J). pap. *(978-968-7381-01-5(9))* Tecolote, Ediciones, S.A. de C.V.

Llego la Banda (E) (Spanish Early Intervention Levels Ser.). (SPA.). 21.30 *(978-0-7362-0831-4(3))* CENGAGE Learning.

Llorente, Maria Isabel Molina. El Misterio del Hombre Que Desaparecio. (Torre de Papel Ser.). (SPA.). (J). (gr. 4-18). 7.95 *(978-958-04-0729-4(0))* Norma S.A. COL. Dist: Distribuidora Norma, Inc.

Lo mas Importante. (Spanish Early Intervention Levels Ser.). (SPA.). 31.14 *(978-0-7362-0340-1(0))* CENGAGE Learning.

Lo mas quieto que Puedo: 6 Small Books. (Saludos Ser.: Vol. 3). (SPA.). (gr. 2-3). 31.00 *(978-0-7635-9549-4(7))* Rigby Education.

Lo Que Sale De Un Huevo: Big Book Packages. 2003. 64.95 *(978-0-673-58590-5(5))* Celebration Pr.

Lodge, Jo. La Casa del Senor Coc/ The House of Mr Coc. 2007. 8p. bds. 36.95 *(978-84-263-6454-8(3))* Vives, Luis Editorial (Edelvives) ESP. Dist: Baker & Taylor Bks.

—Imita Al Senor Coc/ Imitate Mr Coc. 2007. 22p. bds. 18.95 *(978-84-263-6221-6(4))* Vives, Luis Editorial (Edelvives) ESP. Dist: Baker & Taylor Bks.

Lolita Y Su Familia: Individual 6-packs. 2003. 23.95 *(978-0-673-78062-1(7))* Celebration Pr.

Lolita's Family, 6 Packs. 2003. 23.95 *(978-0-673-78126-0(7))* Celebration Pr.

Los animales Astutos: Individual Title Six-Packs. (Literatura 2000 Ser.). (SPA.). (gr. 2-3). 33.00 *(978-0-7635-1082-4(3))* Rigby Education.

Los animalitos de Oaxaca: Lap Book. (Pebble Soup Exploraciones Ser.). (SPA.). 16p. (gr. -1-18). 21.00 *(978-0-7578-1688-8(6))* Rigby Education.

Los animalitos de Oaxaca: Small Book. (Pebble Soup Exploraciones Ser.). (SPA.). 16p. (gr. -1-18). 5.00 *(978-0-7578-1728-1(9))* Rigby Education.

Los cinco Pollitos: Individual Title Six-Packs. (Literatura 2000 Ser.). (SPA.). (gr. 1-2). 28.00 *(978-0-7635-1062-6(9))* Rigby Education.

Los Comilones: Individual Title Six-Packs. (Literatura 2000 Ser.). (SPA.). (gr. k-1). 28.00 *(978-0-7635-1012-1(2))* Rigby Education.

A los dos Anos: 6 Small Books. (SPA.). (gr. k-1). 20.00 *(978-0-7635-6254-0(8))* Rigby Education.

Los fideos de Papa: Individual Title Six-Packs. (Literatura 2000 Ser.). (SPA.). (gr. 1-2). 28.00 *(978-0-7635-1070-1(X))* Rigby Education.

Los recuerdos de mi Abuelita: Individual Title Six-Packs. (Literatura 2000 Ser.). (SPA.). (gr. 1-2). 28.00 *(978-0-7635-1077-0(7))* Rigby Education.

Los regalos de mi Abuelito. (Spanish Early Intervention Levels Ser.). (SPA.). 23.10 *(978-1-56334-790-0(3))* CENGAGE Learning.

Los Sentidos. (Spanish Early Intervention Levels Ser.). (SPA.). 23.10 *(978-1-56334-787-0(3))* CENGAGE Learning.

Los tres chivos Vivos: Video Tape. (ENG & SPA.). (gr. k-1). 26.00 *(978-0-7635-6280-9(7))* Rigby Education.

Los tres Cochinitos: Video Tape. (ENG & SPA.). (gr. k-1). 26.00 *(978-0-7635-6228-1(9))* Rigby Education.

Los trucos de Paco: Individual Title Six-Packs. (Literatura 2000 Ser.). (SPA.). (gr. 1-2). 28.00 *(978-0-7635-1056-5(4))* Rigby Education.

Losantos, Cristina, illus. Beauty & the Beast (La Bella y la Bestia) 2013. (Bilingual Fairy Tales Ser.). (SPA & ENG.). 32p. (J). (gr. 1-4). lib. bdg. 28.50 *(978-1-60753-355-9(3))* Amicus Learning.

Louise, Cristina & McIlroy, Michelle. Where Is Paco Now? Louise, Cristina & McIlroy, Michelle, illus. 2012. (SPA & ENG., Illus.). (J). *(978-1-934370-26-1(6),* Campanita Bks.) Editorial Campana.

Lucia encuentra un Dragon: Individual Title, 6 packs. (Literatura 2000 Ser.). (SPA.). (gr. 2-3). 33.00 *(978-0-7635-1095-4(5))* Rigby Education.

Luis y la Mariposa: Individual Title Six-Packs. (Literatura 2000 Ser.). (SPA.). (gr. 2-3). 33.00 *(978-0-7635-1263-7(X))* Rigby Education.

MacHado, Ana Maria. Eso No Me lo Quita Nadie.Tr. of No One Can Take That Away from Me. (SPA.). (YA). (gr. 7-8). 8.95 *(978-958-04-4530-2(3),* NR4358) Norma S.A. COL. Dist: Lectorum Pubns., Inc., Distribuidora Norma, Inc.

Maddox, Jake. Jake Maddox: Definición Por Penales. Heck, Claudia, tr. Tiffany, Sean, illus. 2012. (Jake Maddox en Español Ser.). (SPA.). 72p. (J). (gr. 3-6). 25.32 *(978-1-4342-3814-6(8),* 117503, Stone Arch Bks.) Capstone.

—El Lanzador Bajo Presión. Heck, Claudia, tr. from ENG. Tiffany, Sean, illus. 2012. (Jake Maddox en Español Ser.). (SPA.). 72p. (J). (gr. 3-6). 25.32 *(978-1-4342-3815-3(6),* 117504, Stone Arch Bks.) Capstone.

—El Rebelde de la Patineta, 1 vol. Heck, Claudia, tr. Tiffany, Sean, illus. 2012. (Jake Maddox en Español Ser.). (SPA.). 72p. (J). (gr. 3-6). 25.32 *(978-1-4342-3816-0(4),* 117505, Stone Arch Bks.) Capstone.

—El Tramposo de BMX, 1 vol. Heck, Claudia, tr. Tiffany, Sean & Tiffany, Sean, illus. 2012. (Jake Maddox en Español Ser.). (SPA.). 72p. (J). (gr. 3-6). 25.32 *(978-1-4342-3817-7(2),* 117507, Stone Arch Bks.) Capstone.

Mahoney, Judy. Teach Me Even More Spanish Book Box: Twenty-One Songs to Sing & a Story about Pen Pals. (Foreign Language Ser.). (SPA.). (J). incl. audio NewSound, LLC.

Mami, Mami! (Spanish Early Intervention Levels Ser.). (SPA.). 21.30 *(978-0-7362-0801-7(1))* CENGAGE Learning.

La Manana: Individual Title Two-Packs. (Chiquilibros Ser.). (SPA.). (gr. -1-1). 12.00 *(978-0-7635-8551-8(3))* Rigby Education.

Manushkin, Fran. Adiós a Goldie. Lyon, Tammie & Lyon, Tammie, illus. 2012. (Katie Woo en Español Ser.). (SPA.). 32p. (J). (gr. k-2). pap. 6.95 *(978-1-4048-7676-7(6),* 120350, Picture Window Bks.) Capstone.

—El Golazo de Pedro. Trusted Translations, Trusted, tr. Lyon, Tammie, illus. 2018. (Pedro en Español Ser.). (SPA.). 32p. (J). (gr. k-2). lib. bdg. 21.32 *(978-1-5158-2511-1(6),* 137570, Picture Window Bks.) Capstone.

—La Gran Mentira, 1 vol. Lyon, Tammie & Lyon, Tammie, illus. 2012. (Katie Woo en Español Ser.). (SPA.). 32p. (J). (gr. k-2). pap. 6.95 *(978-1-4048-7678-1(2),* 120354); lib. bdg. 21.32 *(978-1-4048-7522-7(0),* 119824) Capstone. (Picture Window Bks.).

—La Jefa Del Mundo, 1 vol. Lyon, Tammie & Lyon, Tammie, illus. 2012. (Katie Woo en Español Ser.). (SPA.). 32p. (J). (gr. k-2). pap. 6.95 *(978-1-4048-7679-8(0),* 120353); lib. bdg. 21.32 *(978-1-4048-7523-4(9),* 119825) Capstone. (Picture Window Bks.).

—Pedro, Candidato a Presidente. Trusted Translations, Trusted, tr. Lyon, Tammie, illus. 2018. (Pedro en Español Ser.). (SPA.). 32p. (J). (gr. k-2). lib. bdg. 21.32 *(978-1-5158-2508-1(6),* 137567, Picture Window Bks.) Capstone.

—Pedro el Ninja. Trusted Translations, Trusted, tr. Lyon, Tammie, illus. 2018. (Pedro en Español Ser.). (SPA.). 32p. (J). (gr. k-2). lib. bdg. 21.32 *(978-1-5158-2510-4(8),* 137568, Picture Window Bks.) Capstone.

—Pedro el Pirata. Trusted Translations, Trusted, tr. Lyon, Tammie, illus. 2018. (Pedro en Español Ser.). (SPA.). 32p. (J). (gr. k-2). lib. bdg. 21.32 *(978-1-5158-2514-2(0),* 137573, Picture Window Bks.) Capstone.

—Pedro y el Tiburón. Trusted Translations, Trusted, tr. Lyon, Tammie, illus. 2018. (Pedro en Español Ser.). (SPA.). 32p. (J). (gr. k-2). lib. bdg. 21.32 *(978-1-5158-2507-4(8),* 137566, Picture Window Bks.) Capstone.

—La Torre Embromada de Pedro. Trusted Translations, Trusted, tr. Lyon, Tammie, illus. 2018. (Pedro en Español Ser.). (SPA.). 32p. (J). (gr. k-2). lib. bdg. 21.32 *(978-1-5158-2513-5(2),* 137572, Picture Window Bks.) Capstone.

Manushkin, Fran & Lyon, Tammie. Basta de Burlas, 1 vol. Lyon, Tammie, illus. 2012. (Katie Woo en Español Ser.). (SPA., Illus.). 32p. (J). (gr. k-2). pap. 6.95 *(978-1-4048-7677-4(4),* 120351, Picture Window Bks.) Capstone.

Many Hats: Matching English, 6-packs. 2003. 23.95 *(978-0-673-57561-6(6))* Celebration Pr.

La maquina de Imprimir: Individual Title Six-Packs. (Literatura 2000 Ser.). (SPA.). (gr. 1-2). 28.00 *(978-0-7635-1046-6(7))* Rigby Education.

La Marca en la Roca. (SPA., Illus.). 70p. (YA). (gr. 8-10). pap. *(978-88-8148-466-9(8))* EMC/Paradigm Publishing.

El Mariachi: Big Book Packages. 2003. 64.95 *(978-0-673-58585-1(9))* Celebration Pr.

Mariachi 6 Packs: Matching English. 2003. 23.95 *(978-0-673-57562-3(4))* Celebration Pr.

Marianela. (Coleccion Centro Literario). (SPA.). (J). pap., stu. ed. 7.95 *(978-958-02-0483-1(7),* CAR017) Editorial Voluntad S.A. COL. Dist: Continental Bk. Co., Inc.

Mariconda, Barbara. Sort It Out! Spanish. Rogers, Sherry, illus. 2008.Tr. of Sort It Out! (SPA.). 32p. (J). (gr. k-4). 17.95 *(978-1-60718-695-3(0))* Arbordale Publishing.

Marina la Ballena. 2003. 28.95 *(978-0-673-78090-4(2))* Celebration Pr.

Mariño, Ricardo. Lo Unico del Mundo. (Torre de Papel Ser.). (SPA.). (YA). (gr. 6-18). 8.95 *(978-958-04-3812-0(9))* Norma S.A. COL. Dist: Distribuidora Norma, Inc.

Martin, Ann M. Claudia y la Nueva Alumna. Peraire del Molino, C., tr. (Club de Las Canguro Ser.: Vol. 12).Tr. of Claudia & the New Girl. (SPA.). 156p. (J). 11.95 *(978-84-272-3662-2(X))* Molino, Editorial ESP. Dist: AIMS International Bks., Inc.

—Claudia y la Triste Despedida. Peraire del Molino, Conchita, tr. (El Club de las Canguro Ser.: Vol. 26).Tr. of Claudia & the Sad Good-Bye. (SPA.). 150p. (J). 11.95 *(978-84-272-3676-9(X))* Molino, Editorial ESP. Dist: AIMS International Bks., Inc.

—Kristy y el Secreto de Susan. (El Club de las Canguro Ser.: Vol. 32).Tr. of Kristy & the Susan's Secret. (SPA.). 150p. (J). 11.95 *(978-84-272-3682-0(4))* Molino, Editorial ESP. Dist: AIMS International Bks., Inc.

—Kristy y los Esnobs. (Club de Las Canguro Ser.: Vol. 11).Tr. of Kristy & the Snobs. (SPA.). 158p. (J). 11.95 *(978-84-272-3661-5(1))* Molino, Editorial ESP. Dist: AIMS International Bks., Inc.

—Mala Suerte de Mary Anne. Peraire del Molino, Conchita, tr. (Club de Las Canguro Ser.: Vol. 17).Tr. of Mary Anne's Bad-Luck Mystery. (SPA.). 142p. (J). 11.95 *(978-84-272-3667-7(0))* Molino, Editorial ESP. Dist: AIMS International Bks., Inc.

Martin, Bill, Jr. Oso Panda, Oso Panda, Que Ves Ahi? / Panda Bear, Panda Bear, What Do You Hear? (Spanish Edition) Mlawer, Teresa, tr. Carle, Eric, illus. 2009. (Brown Bear & Friends Ser.).Tr. of Brown Bear, Brown Bear, What Do You See? (SPA.). 26p. (J). (gr. -1-k). bds. 10.99 *(978-0-8050-8756-7(7),* 900049804, Holt, Henry & Co. Bks. For Young Readers) Holt, Henry & Co.

Mary and Rich Chamberlin. Las Crepes de Mama Panya: Un Relato de Kenia. Cairns, Julia, illus. 2016. (SPA.). 40p. (J). (gr. k-5). pap. 9.99 *(978-1-78285-072-4(4))* Barefoot Bks., Inc.

Mas Pizza! 2003. 28.95 *(978-0-673-78089-8(9))* Celebration Pr.

Masters, Susan Rowan. La Vida Secreta de Hubie Hatzel. (Torre de Papel Ser.). (SPA.). (J). (gr. 4-18). 7.95 *(978-958-04-1900-6(0))* Norma S.A. COL. Dist: Distribuidora Norma, Inc.

Mattern, Joanne. Sojourner Truth: Early Abolitionist. 2009. (Women Who Shaped History Ser.). 24p. (gr. 2-3). 42.50 *(978-1-60854-821-7(X),* PowerKids Pr.) Rosen Publishing Group, Inc., The.

Matthias, Catherine. Rookie Ready to Learn en Español: Demasiados Globos. Sharp, Gene, illus. 2011. (Rookie Ready to Learn Español Ser.). Orig. Title: Rookie Ready to Learn: Too Many Balloons. (SPA.). 40p. (J). pap. 5.95 *(978-0-531-26792-9(X),* Children's Pr.) Scholastic Library Publishing.

Mayra y el baile de Disfraces: Individual Title Six-Packs. (Literatura 2000 Ser.). (SPA.). (gr. 2-3). 33.00 *(978-0-7635-1096-1(3))* Rigby Education.

McDonald, Megan. Judy Moody & Stink: la Loca, Loca Búsqueda Del Tesoro / JM & Stink: the Mad, Mad, Mad, Mad Treasure Hunt. 2011. (Judy Moody & Stink Ser.). (SPA., Illus.). 144p. (J). (gr. 2-5). pap. 14.95 *(978-1-61605-137-2(X),* Alfaguara) Penguin Random House Grupo Editorial ESP. Dist: Penguin Random Hse. LLC.

McGraw Hill. ¡Buen Viaje! Level 1, StudentWorks Plus CD-ROM. 2005. (Glencoe Spanish Ser.). (SPA.). (gr. 7-12). stu. ed. 177.96 incl. cd-rom *(978-0-07-868622-1(9),* 0078686229) McGraw-Hill Education.

—¡Buen Viaje!, Level 2, StudentWorks Plus CD-ROM. 2005. (Glencoe Spanish Ser.). (SPA.). (gr. 8-12). cd-rom 180.08 *(978-0-07-868623-8(7),* 0078686237) McGraw-Hill Education.

—¡Buen Viaje! Level 3, StudentWorks Plus CD-ROM. 2004. (Glencoe Spanish Ser.). (SPA.). (gr. 9-12). stu. ed. 171.48 incl. cd-rom *(978-0-07-868624-5(5),* 0078686245) McGraw-Hill Education.

McQuinn, Anna. Lola Planta un Jardín / Lola Plants a Garden. Beardshaw, Rosalind, illus. 2017. (Lola Reads Ser.: 4).Tr. of Lola Plants a Garden. 28p. (J). (-k). pap. 7.99 *(978-1-58089-786-0(X))* Charlesbridge Publishing, Inc.

Me Encontre Una Piedra: Big Book Packages. 2003. 64.95 *(978-0-673-58591-2(3))* Celebration Pr.

Me gusta Leer. (Spanish Early Intervention Levels Ser.). (SPA.). 21.30 *(978-0-7362-0806-2(2))* CENGAGE Learning.

Meachen Rau, Dana. ¡a Rodar! (Rolling), 1 vol. 2008. (En Movimiento (on the Move) Ser.). (SPA., Illus.). 32p. (gr. k-1). lib. bdg. 25.50 *(978-0-7614-2419-2(9),* 9332c010-8b6a-4b38-970a-84a3088edc44) Cavendish Square Publishing LLC.

—En el Parque (at the Park), 1 vol. 2009. (Tiempo de la Diversión (Fun Time) Ser.). (SPA., Illus.). 24p. (gr. k-1). lib. bdg. 25.50 *(978-0-7614-2775-9(9),* 0189c902-e46f-48d6-856a-7c204806d681) Cavendish Square Publishing LLC.

—En el Parque de Atracciones (at the Fair), 1 vol. 2009. (Tiempo de la Diversión (Fun Time) Ser.). (SPA., Illus.). 24p. (gr. k-1). lib. bdg. 25.50 *(978-0-7614-2749-0(X),* 9cb26d57-373c-487f-a28e-ad3f6ed1b049) Cavendish Square Publishing LLC.

—En el Zoológico (at the Zoo), 1 vol. 2009. (Tiempo de la Diversión (Fun Time) Ser.). (SPA., Illus.). 24p. (gr. k-1). lib. bdg. 25.50 *(978-0-7614-2777-3(5),* b63f8050-3988-480a-9027-3d00fc989b66) Cavendish Square Publishing LLC.

Meachen Rau, Dana & Vargus, Nanci Reginelli. En la Granja (on a Farm), 1 vol. 2009. (Tiempo de la Diversión (Fun Time) Ser.). (SPA., Illus.). 24p. (gr. k-1). lib. bdg. 25.50 *(978-0-7614-2778-0(3),* 4a9c0a4a-81c3-4673-b2ec-ec8187ea265c) Cavendish Square Publishing LLC.

Meddaugh, Susan. Fireworks for All. 2011. (Martha Speaks Ser.). (ENG., Illus.). 24p. (J). (gr. -1-3). pap. 3.99 *(978-0-547-55620-8(9))* Houghton Mifflin Harcourt Publishing Co.

—Martha Habla: Conoce a Martha/Martha Speaks: Meet Martha Bilingual Reader. 2015. (Martha Speaks Ser.). (ENG., Illus.). 24p. (J). (gr. -1-3). 12.99 *(978-0-544-43508-7(7),* HMH Books For Young Readers) Houghton Mifflin Harcourt Publishing Co.

Medina, Conni. Haz Papel Picado. 2nd rev. ed. 2012. (TIME for KIDS(r): Informational Text Ser.).Tr. of Make Papel Picado. (SPA.). 20p. (gr. 1-2). 8.99 *(978-1-4333-4425-1(4))* Teacher Created Materials, Inc.

—Haz un Dragón del Año Nuevo Chino. 2nd rev. ed. 2012. (TIME for KIDS(r): Informational Text Ser.). (SPA.). 20p. (gr. 1-2). 6.99 (978-1-4333-4426-8(2)) Teacher Created Materials, Inc.
—Haz un Muñequito de Jengibre. 2nd rev. ed. 2012. (TIME for KIDS(r): Informational Text Ser.). (SPA.). 20p. (gr. 1-2). 8.99 (978-1-4333-4427-5(0)) Teacher Created Materials, Inc.
Medina, Meg. Tia Isa Quiere un Carro. Munoz, Claudio, illus. 2012.Tr. of Tia Isa Wants a Car. (SPA.). 32p. (J). (gr. -1-2). pap. 7.99 (978-0-7636-5751-2(4)) Candlewick Pr.
—Tía Isa Quiere un Carro. 2012.Tr. of Tia Isa Wants a Car. (SPA.). lib. bdg. 17.20 (978-0-606-23801-4(8)) Turtleback.
Mejías, Mónica. Aprendiendo a Leer con Mili y Molo: Learn How to Read in Spanish. Mejías, Mónica, illus. 2004.Tr. of Lernen Sie Spanish Lesen, Impara a leggere in Spagnolo, Aprenda a ler Espanhol, Apprenez à lire L'espagnol. (Illus.). 40p. (J). audio compact disk 12.00 (978-0-9753799-0-5(9)) Ediciones Alas, Inc.
El mejor regalo de Cumpleanos: Individual Title Six-Packs. (Literatura 2000 Ser.). (SPA.). (gr. 2-3). 33.00 (978-0-7635-1264-4(8)) Rigby Education.
El mensaje de las Estrellas: Lap Book. (Pebble Soup Exploraciones Ser.). (SPA.). 16p. (gr. -1-18). 21.00 (978-0-7578-1677-2(0)) Rigby Education.
Los Meses Del Ano. 2003. 23.95 (978-0-673-77168-1(7)) Celebration Pr.
Mi amiga Laura. (Spanish Early Intervention Levels Ser.). (SPA.). 31.14 (978-0-7362-0329-6(X)) CENGAGE Learning.
Mi Amigo. 2003. 35.50 (978-0-8136-8137-5(5)); 63.50 (978-0-8136-8139-9(1)) Modern Curriculum Pr.
Mi Caballito. (Spanish Early Intervention Levels Ser.). (SPA.). 23.10 (978-1-56334-775-7(X)) CENGAGE Learning.
Mi Caja: Individual Title-Six Packs. (Chiquilibros Ser.). (SPA.). (gr. k-1). 23.00 (978-0-7635-8604-1(8)) Rigby Education.
Mi conejito y Yo: Big Book. (Pebble Soup Exploraciones Ser.). (SPA.). 16p. (gr. -1-18). 31.00 (978-0-7578-1690-1(8)) Rigby Education.
Mi Dia. (Spanish Early Intervention Levels Ser.). (SPA.). 23.10 (978-1-56334-771-9(7)) CENGAGE Learning.
Mi Escuelita: Individual 6-packs. 2003. 23.95 (978-0-673-77142-1(3)) Celebration Pr.
Mi Familia. (Spanish Early Intervention Levels Ser.). (SPA.). 31.14 (978-0-7362-0327-2(3)) CENGAGE Learning.
Mi Familia: Individual 6-packs. 2003. 23.95 (978-0-673-77133-9(4)) Celebration Pr.
Mi Hermanita: Individual Title Six-Packs. (Literatura 2000 Ser.). (SPA.). (gr. -1-1). 28.00 (978-0-7635-1196-8(X)) Rigby Education.
Mi Hermanito. (Spanish Early Intervention Levels Ser.). (SPA.). 23.10 (978-1-56334-772-6(5)) CENGAGE Learning.
Mi Hogar: Individual Title-Six Packs. (Chiquilibros Ser.). (SPA.). (gr. k-1). 23.00 (978-0-7635-8621-8(8)) Rigby Education.
Mi Maestra, 6 Packs. 2003. 23.95 (978-0-673-77148-3(2)) Celebration Pr.
Mi Mami: Individual 6-packs. 2003. 23.95 (978-0-673-77143-8(1)) Celebration Pr.
Mi Perrita Chata, 6 Packs. 2003. 23.95 (978-0-673-77149-0(0)) Celebration Pr.
Mi Tata Chuy, 6 Packs. 2003. 23.95 (978-0-673-77139-1(3)) Celebration Pr.
Milet Publishing. My First Bilingual Book-Numbers (English-Spanish), 1 vol. 2010. (My First Bilingual Book Ser.). (ENG & SPA., Illus.). 24p. (J). (gr. k — 1). bds. 8.99 (978-1-84059-545-1(0)) Milet Publishing.
Milet Publishing Staff. Colors, 1 vol. 2010. (My First Bilingual Book Ser.). (ENG & SPA., Illus.). 24p. (J). (gr. k — 1). bds. 8.99 (978-1-84059-539-0(6)) Milet Publishing.
Mira el Dinosaurio! (Spanish Early Intervention Levels Ser.). (SPA.). 31.14 (978-0-7362-0334-0(6)) CENGAGE Learning.
Mira lo que hizo Tomas, 6 vols., Pack. (Literatura 2000 Ser.). (SPA.). (gr. 1-2). 28.00 (978-0-7635-1072-5(6)) Rigby Education.
Mis Animalitos: Individual Title Six-Packs. (Literatura 2000 Ser.). (SPA.). (gr. k-1). 28.00 (978-0-7635-1024-4(6)) Rigby Education.
Mis Cinco Perritos: Big Book Packages. 2003. 64.95 (978-0-673-58580-6(8)) Celebration Pr.
Mis Cumpleanos: Individual 6-packs. 2003. 23.95 (978-0-673-77150-6(4)) Celebration Pr.
Mis Juguetes, 6 Packs. 2003. 23.95 (978-0-673-77141-4(5)) Celebration Pr.
Mis Quehaceres, 6 Packs. 2003. 23.95 (978-0-673-77145-2(8)) Celebration Pr.
Mlawer, Teresa, tr. What Do I Hear? / ¿Qué Oigo? Kubler, Annie, illus. 2015. (Small Senses Bilingual Ser.: 5). (ENG.). 12p. (J). bds. (978-1-84643-724-3(5)) Child's Play International Ltd.
—What Do I See? / ¿Qué Veo? Kubler, Annie, illus. 2015. (Small Senses Bilingual Ser.: 5). (ENG.). 12p. (J). bds. (978-1-84643-725-0(3)) Child's Play International Ltd.
—What Do I Smell? / ¿Qué Huelo? Kubler, Annie, illus. 2015. (Small Senses Bilingual Ser.: 5). (ENG.). 12p. (J). bds. (978-1-84643-723-6(7)) Child's Play International Ltd.
—What Do I Taste? / ¿Qué Saboreo? Kubler, Annie, illus. 2015. (Small Senses Bilingual Ser.: 5). (ENG.). 12p. (J). bds. (978-1-84643-722-9(9)) Child's Play International Ltd.
El Modelo: Individual Title Six-Packs. (Chiquilibros Ser.). (SPA.). (gr. k-1). 23.00 (978-0-7635-8596-9(3)) Rigby Education.
Molina, Angeles. El Principe Que No Queria Ser Principe. 2007. (SPA.). 64p. 14.95 (978-0-8477-0455-2(6)) Univ. of Puerto Rico Pr.
Monica Brown. Marisol Mcdonald & the Monster: Marisol Mcdonald y el Monstruo (English & Spanish Edition), 1 vol. 2016. (Marisol Mcdonald Ser.). (ENG., Illus.). 32p. (J). (gr. k-3). 19.95 (978-0-89239-326-8(2), leelowcbp) Lee & Low Bks., Inc.
Los Monstruos, 6 packs. 2003. 23.95 (978-0-673-77144-5(X)) Celebration Pr.
La Montana que Llora. (Saludos Ser.: Vol. 1). (SPA.). (gr. 3-5). 31.00 (978-0-7635-3221-5(5)) Rigby Education.
La Montana que Llora: 6 Small Books. (Saludos Ser.: Vol. 1). (SPA.). (gr. 3-5). 31.00 (978-0-7635-1848-6(4)) Rigby Education.
Montes, Marisa. A Crazy Mixed-Up Spanglish Day. Cepeda, Joe, illus. 2004. (Get Ready for Gabi Ser.). 120p. (gr. 2-5). 14.00 (978-0-7569-3403-3(6)) Perfection Learning Corp.
Montoya, Martha, creator. Cenando con el Monstruo: Take-Home. 2005. (Los Kitos Ser.). (SPA.). (YA). (gr. 1-3). 15.00 (978-0-8215-8813-0(3)) Sadlier, William H. Inc.
—Mi heroe Favorito: Take-Home. 2005. (Los Kitos Ser.). (SPA.). (YA). (gr. 1-3). 15.00 (978-0-8215-8811-6(7)) Sadlier, William H. Inc.
—No, no a la Biblioteca! Take-Home. 2005. (Los Kitos Ser.). (SPA.). (YA). (gr. 1-3). 15.00 (978-0-8215-8812-3(5)) Sadlier, William H. Inc.
La Mosquita Lista. 2003. 23.95 (978-0-673-77122-3(9)) Celebration Pr.
Multicultural Activities Blackline Masters: Fuerzas de la Naturaleza. (Saludos Ser.). (SPA.). (gr. 3-5). 21.00 (978-0-7635-2228-5(7)) Rigby Education.
Multicultural Activities Blackline Masters: Regalos de la Tierra. (Saludos Ser.). (SPA.). (gr. 3-5). 21.00 (978-0-7635-2227-8(9)) Rigby Education.
Multicultural Activities Blackline Masters: Vivan las Tradiciones. (Saludos Ser.). (SPA.). (gr. 3-5). 21.00 (978-0-7635-2226-1(0)) Rigby Education.
El mundo de los Pajaros. (Spanish Early Intervention Levels Ser.). (SPA.). 23.10 (978-0-7362-0325-8(7)) CENGAGE Learning.
La Muneca De Galleta: Individual 6-packs. 2003. 23.95 (978-0-673-77152-0(0)) Celebration Pr.
El muneco de Nieve, 6 vols., Pack. (Chiquilibros Ser.).Tr. of Little Snowman. (SPA.). (gr. k-1). 23.00 (978-0-7635-8592-1(0)) Rigby Education.
Murphy, Stuart J. ¡Bien Hecho, Ajay! 2011. (I See I Learn Ser.: 20).Tr. of Good Job, Ajay! (SPA., Illus.). 32p. (J). (-k). 14.95 (978-1-58089-486-9(0)) Charlesbridge Publishing, Inc.
—Camila y Su Equipo. 2012. (I See I Learn Ser.: 21). (Illus.). 32p. (J). (-k). 14.95 (978-1-58089-490-6(9)) Charlesbridge Publishing, Inc.
—Carlos Escribe Su Nombre. 2014. (I See I Learn Ser.: 24). (Illus.). 32p. (J). (-k). 14.95 (978-1-58089-496-8(8)) Charlesbridge Publishing, Inc.
—Emma Hace Amigos. 2011. (I See I Learn Ser.: 17). (Illus.). 32p. (J). (-k). 14.95 (978-1-58089-482-1(8)); pap. 6.95 (978-1-58089-483-8(6)) Charlesbridge Publishing, Inc.
—En Busca de Freda. 2012. (I See I Learn Ser.: 23). (Illus.). 32p. (J). (-k). 14.95 (978-1-58089-494-4(1)) Charlesbridge Publishing, Inc.
—Freda Organiza una Merienda. 2011. (I See I Learn Ser.: 18). (Illus.). 32p. (J). (-k). 14.95 (978-1-58089-488-3(7)) Charlesbridge Publishing, Inc.
Muy bien, Mayra! (Spanish Early Intervention Levels Ser.). (SPA.). 28.38 (978-0-7362-0836-9(4)) CENGAGE Learning.
My Cook Book. 2003. 28.95 (978-0-673-78108-6(9)) Celebration Pr.
My Family Set - Spanish 800799, 6. 2005. (J). bds. (978-1-59794-043-6(7)) Environments, Inc.
My Snowman: Matching English 6-packs. 2003. 23.95 (978-0-673-57563-0(2)) Celebration Pr.
Nada Extra: Individual Title Six-Packs. (Literatura 2000 Ser.). (SPA.). (gr. 1-2). 28.00 (978-0-7635-1048-0(3)) Rigby Education.
Nelson, Mary Beth & Linn, Laurent, illus. Elmo's Big Word Book: El Libro Grande de Palabras de Elmo. Barrett, John E., photos by. 2006. (Elmo's Big Word Book/el Libro Grande de Palabras de Elmo Ser.). (ENG.). 12p. (J). (gr. -1 — 1). bds. 8.95 (978-0-87358-906-2(8)) Cooper Square Publishing Llc.
Nelson, Robin. El Ciclo Del Agua. 2003. (SPA.). 23p. (J). pap. 5.95 (978-0-8225-4824-9(0), Lerner Pubns.) Lerner Publishing Group.
—Usamos el Agua. 2003. (Primeros Pasos Ser.). (SPA., Illus.). 23p. (J). pap. 6.95 (978-0-8225-4825-6(9), Lerner Pubns.) Lerner Publishing Group.
Niebisch, Jackie. La Escuela de los Vampiritos. (SPA.). (J). (gr. 4-18). 8.95 (978-958-04-5042-9(0)) Norma S.A. COL. Dist: Distribuidora Norma, Inc.
—La Escuela de los Vampiritos - Examen. (SPA.). (J). 8.95 (978-958-04-5641-4(0)) Norma S.A. COL. Dist: Distribuidora Norma, Inc.
La Nina Del Poncho. 2003. (J). (gr. -1-2). 28.95 (978-0-673-77378-4(7)) Celebration Pr.
El Nino que fue al Viento Norte: Individual Title, 6 packs. (Literatura 2000 Ser.). (SPA.). (gr. 2-3). 33.00 (978-0-7635-1266-8(4)) Rigby Education.
Niven, David. Los 100 Secretos de la Gente Feliz: Lo que los Cientificos han Descubierto y como Puede Aplicarlo a su Vida. (SPA.). (J). 12.00 (978-958-04-7180-6(0)) Norma S.A. COL. Dist: Distribuidora Norma, Inc.
No, Chayito, No: Individual 6-packs. 2003. 23.95 (978-0-673-78074-4(0)) Celebration Pr.
No Les Tengo Miedo: Big Book Packages. 2003. 64.95 (978-0-673-58581-3(6)) Celebration Pr.
No te dejes de Laura Sue: Social/Emotional Lap Book. (Pebble Soup Exploraciones Ser.). (SPA.). (gr. -1-18). 16.00 (978-0-7578-1793-9(9)) Rigby Education.
No te Preocupes: Individual Title, 6 packs. (Literatura 2000 Ser.). (SPA.). (gr. 2-3). 33.00 (978-0-7635-1098-5(X)) Rigby Education.
Nonfiction Packs. (SPA.). 288.75 (978-0-7362-2578-6(1)) CENGAGE Learning.
Nonfiction Packs: Spanish Nonfiction Pack, 33 vols. 117.53 (978-0-7362-1511-4(5)) CENGAGE Learning.
North, Sherry. Champ's Story: Dogs Get Cancer Too! (Spanish Edition) Rietz, Kathleen, illus. 2010. (SPA.). 32p. (J). (gr. -1-4). 17.95 (978-1-60718-681-6(0)) Arbordale Publishing.
—Champ's Story: Dogs Get Cancer Too!, 1 vol. Rietz, Kathleen, illus. 2010. (ENG.). 32p. (J). (gr. -1-4). 16.95 (978-1-60718-077-7(4)); pap. 8.95 (978-1-60718-088-3(X)) Arbordale Publishing.
Nos traen Agua. (Saludos Ser.: Vol. 3). (SPA.). (gr. 3-5). 31.00 (978-0-7635-3268-0(1)) Rigby Education.
Nos traen Agua: 6 Small Books. (Saludos Ser.: Vol. 3). (SPA.). (gr. 3-5). 31.00 (978-0-7635-1827-1(1)) Rigby Education.
Nosotros Interactive Packages: Aqui me Tienen. (Pebble Soup Exploraciones Ser.). (gr. -1-18). 52.00 (978-0-7578-5251-0(3)) Rigby Education.
Nöstlinger, Christine. Las Enfermedades de Franz. (Torre de Papel Ser.). (SPA.). (J). 7.95 (978-958-04-1930-3(2)) Norma S.A. COL. Dist: Distribuidora Norma, Inc.
—Franz Se Mete en Problemas de Amor. (Torre de Papel Ser.). (SPA.). (J). 7.95 (978-958-04-2697-4(X)) Norma S.A. COL. Dist: Distribuidora Norma, Inc.
—El Lobo y los Siete Cabritos. (Torre de Papel Ser.). (SPA., Illus.). (J). (gr. 2). 7.95 (978-958-04-4532-6(X)) Norma S.A. COL. Dist: Distribuidora Norma, Inc.
—Un Marido para Mamá. 2011. (Torre de Papel Ser.). (SPA.). 184p. (gr. 6-8). pap. 12.99 (978-958-04-2382-9(2)) Norma S.A. COL. Dist: Lectorum Pubns., Inc.
—Las Vacaciones de Franz. (Torre de Papel Ser.). (SPA.). (J). (gr. 2). 7.95 (978-958-04-1931-0(0)) Norma S.A. COL. Dist: Distribuidora Norma, Inc.
Nuestra casa de Adobe: 6 Small Books. (Saludos Ser.: Vol. 2). (SPA.). (gr. 2-3). 31.00 (978-0-7635-9543-2(8)) Rigby Education.
Nuestras geniales Orejas. (Spanish Early Intervention Levels Ser.). (SPA.). 28.38 (978-0-7362-0841-3(0)) CENGAGE Learning.
Nuestro Mundo. (Nuevos Horizontes Ser.). (SPA.). (J). (gr. 1). No. 1. wbk. ed. 7.95 (978-1-56014-504-2(8))No. 2. wbk. ed. 7.95 (978-1-56014-505-9(6)) Santillana USA Publishing Co., Inc.
Nuestro Mundo: Evaluations, Grade 1. (Nuevos Horizontes Ser.). (SPA.). (J). 22.50 (978-1-56014-506-6(4)) Santillana USA Publishing Co., Inc.
Nuestro Mundo No. 1: Student Anthology. (Nuevos Horizontes Ser.). (SPA.). (J). (gr. 1). 14.95 (978-1-56014-502-8(1)) Santillana USA Publishing Co., Inc.
Nuestro Mundo No. 2: Student Anthology. (Nuevos Horizontes Ser.). (SPA.). (J). (gr. 1). 14.95 (978-1-56014-503-5(X)) Santillana USA Publishing Co., Inc.
Nuestro perro Sam 6 Packs. Individual Title. (Literatura 2000 Ser.). (SPA.). (gr. k-1). 28.00 (978-0-7635-1025-1(4)) Rigby Education.
Nuestro viaje hacia la Libertad: 6 Small Books. (Saludos Ser.: Vol. 3). (SPA.). (gr. 3-5). 31.00 (978-0-7635-1782-3(8)) Rigby Education.
Nuevas Aventuras. (Nuevos Horizontes Ser.). (SPA.). (J). (gr. 3). wbk. ed. 8.95 (978-1-56014-515-8(3)) Santillana USA Publishing Co., Inc.
Nuevas Aventuras: Evaluations, Grade 3. (Nuevos Horizontes Ser.). (SPA.). (J). 22.50 (978-1-56014-516-5(1)) Santillana USA Publishing Co., Inc.
Nuevas Aventuras: Student Anthology. (Nuevos Horizontes Ser.). (SPA.). (J). (gr. 3). 18.95 (978-1-56014-514-1(5)) Santillana USA Publishing Co., Inc.
Nuevas Fronteras. (Nuevos Horizontes Ser.). (SPA.). (J). (gr. 4). wbk. ed. 8.95 (978-1-56014-519-6(6)) Santillana USA Publishing Co., Inc.
Nuevas Fronteras: Evaluations, Grade 4. (Nuevos Horizontes Ser.). (SPA.). (J). 22.50 (978-1-56014-520-2(X)) Santillana USA Publishing Co., Inc.
Nuevas Fronteras: Student Anthology. (Nuevos Horizontes Ser.). (SPA.). (J). (gr. 4). 18.95 (978-1-56014-518-9(8)) Santillana USA Publishing Co., Inc.
Obregón, José María. Nevada. 2009. (Bilingual Library of the United States of America Ser.). (ENG & SPA.). 32p. (gr. 2-2). 47.90 (978-1-60853-372-5(7), Editorial Buenas Letras) Rosen Publishing Group, Inc., The.
—New York / Nueva York. 2009. (Bilingual Library of the United States of America Ser.). (ENG & SPA.). 32p. (gr. 2-2). 47.90 (978-1-60853-376-3(X), Editorial Buenas Letras) Rosen Publishing Group, Inc., The.
Ohara, Maricarmen. Amiguitos. (SPA., Illus.). 144p. (J). (gr. k-3). 23.00 (978-0-944356-22-7(2)) Alegria Hispana Pubns.
—Capullitos. (SPA., Illus.). 70p. (J). (gr. k-3). 15.00 (978-0-944356-03-6(6)) Alegria Hispana Pubns.
—Tesoro de Poesia Juvenil. (SPA.). 144p. 20.00 (978-0-944356-09-8(5)) Alegria Hispana Pubns.
Ojos, Orejas y Pecas. (SPA.). (J). 12.00 (978-958-02-1236-2(8)) Editorial Voluntad S.A. COL. Dist: Distribuidora Norma, Inc.
Olivas, Daniel. Benjamin & the Word: Benjamín y la Palabra. Baeza Ventura, Gabriela, tr. Dyen, Don, illus. 2011. 32p. (J). pap. 7.95 (978-1-55885-687-5(0), Piñata Books) Arte Publico Pr.
On Safari: Individual Title-Six Packs. (Chiquilibros Ser.). (gr. k-1). 23.00 (978-0-7635-0434-2(3)) Rigby Education.
Once upon a Time Spanish Version-Little Red Riding Hood. 2005. (J). (978-1-57022-562-8(1)) ECS Learning Systems, Inc.
Once upon a Time Spanish Version-the Boy Who Cried Wolf. 2005. (J). (978-1-57022-557-4(5)) ECS Learning Systems, Inc.
Once upon a Time Spanish Version-the Elves & the Shoemaker. 2005. (J). (978-1-57022-559-8(1)) ECS Learning Systems, Inc.
Once upon a Time Spanish Version-the Gingerbread Man. 2005. (J). (978-1-57022-556-7(7)) ECS Learning Systems, Inc.
Once upon a Time Spanish Version-the Little Red Hen. 2005. (J). (978-1-57022-561-1(3)) ECS Learning Systems, Inc.
Once upon a Time Spanish Version-the Three Bears. 2005. (J). (978-1-57022-563-5(X)) ECS Learning Systems, Inc.
Once upon a Time Spanish Version-the Three Billy Goats Gruff. 2005. (J). (978-1-57022-564-2(8)) ECS Learning Systems, Inc.
Once upon a Time Spanish Version-the Three Little Pigs. 2005. (J). (978-1-57022-565-9(6)) ECS Learning Systems, Inc.
Onetti, Juan Carlos. Los Adioses. (SPA.). (J). 9.00 (978-958-04-7258-2(0)) Norma S.A. COL. Dist: Distribuidora Norma, Inc.
Onieva Morales, Juan Luis. Como Dominar la Ortografia: Ortografia Moderna. (SPA.). 176p. 18.95 (978-84-359-0467-4(9), ARG502) Playor, Editorial, S.A. ESP. Dist: Continental Bk. Co., Inc.
Oppenheim, Joanne. El Principe No Duerme. Latimer, Miriam, illus. 2014. (SPA.). 32p. (J). (gr. -1-2). pap. 9.99 (978-1-78285-077-9(5)) Barefoot Bks., Inc.
Orange Collection. (Elefonetica Ser.). (SPA.). (gr. 1-2). 296.76 (978-0-7362-0790-4(2)) CENGAGE Learning.
Orejas. (Spanish Early Intervention Levels Ser.). (SPA.). 23.10 (978-1-56334-783-2(0)) CENGAGE Learning.
Orlev, Uri. La Pequena Nina Grande. Gleich, Jacky, illus. (Buenas Noches Ser.). (SPA.). (J). 8.95 (978-958-04-4902-7(3)) Norma S.A. COL. Dist: Distribuidora Norma, Inc.
Osborne, Mary Pope, et al. Carnaval a Media Luz. Murdocca, Sal, illus. 2016. (SPA.). 113p. (J). (gr. 2-4). pap. 6.99 (978-1-63245-643-4(5)) Lectorum Pubns., Inc.
—La Estación de Las Tormentas de Arena. Murdocca, Sal, illus. 2016. (SPA.). 107p. (J). (gr. 2-4). pap. 5.99 (978-1-63245-644-1(3)) Lectorum Pubns., Inc.
—La Noche de Los Nuevos Magos. Murdocca, Sal, illus. 2016. (SPA.). 111p. (J). (gr. 2-4). pap. 6.99 (978-1-63245-645-8(1)) Lectorum Pubns., Inc.
—Tormenta de Nieve en Luna Azul. Murdocca, Sal, illus. 2016. (SPA.). (J). (gr. 2-4). pap. 6.99 (978-1-63245-646-5(X)) Lectorum Pubns., Inc.
El Oso Meno, 6 Packs. 2003. 23.95 (978-0-673-78067-6(8)) Celebration Pr.
Los Osos. 2003. (J). (gr. -1-2). 28.95 (978-0-673-77404-0(X)) Celebration Pr.
Palabras. (Coleccion Libritos Acordeon). (SPA., Illus.). 10p. (J). pap. 5.50 (978-950-11-0824-8(4), SGM244) Sigmar ARG. Dist: Continental Bk. Co., Inc.
Palermo, Miguel Angel. Lo Que Cuentan los Tehuelches. (Cuentamerica Ser.). (SPA.). (YA). (gr. 4-18). pap. (978-950-07-1405-1(1), SA30067) Editorial Sudamericana S.A. ARG. Dist: Lectorum Pubns., Inc.
—Lo Que Cuentan los Wichis. (Cuentamerica Ser.). (SPA.). (YA). (gr. 4-18). (978-950-07-1616-1(X), SA30068) Editorial Sudamericana S.A. ARG. Dist: Lectorum Pubns., Inc.
Pan y Canela. (SPA.). (gr. k-2). 426.37 (978-1-56334-543-2(9), CO8206); (gr. k-2). 519.49 (978-1-56334-643-9(5), SE8103); (gr. k-2). 500.86 (978-1-56334-642-2(7), SE8102); (gr. k-2). 1533.42 (978-0-7362-0446-0(6), PA8220); (gr. k-2). 426.37 (978-1-56334-542-5(0), CO8205);Level C. (gr. 2-18). 738.56 (978-0-7362-0705-8(8), SU8100) CENGAGE Learning.
Pan y Canela: Collection C. (SPA.). (gr. k-2). 615.30 (978-0-7362-0343-2(5)); 522.85 (978-0-7362-0342-5(7)) CENGAGE Learning.
A Papa no le Molesto: Individual Title Six-Packs. (Literatura 2000 Ser.). (SPA.). (gr. 1-2). 28.00 (978-0-7635-1057-2(2)) Rigby Education.
Papa salvo la Fiesta: Six-Pack. (Saludos Ser.: Vol. 3). (SPA.). (gr. 2-3). 31.00 (978-0-7635-9528-9(4)) Rigby Education.
Papas. (Spanish Early Intervention Levels Ser.). (SPA.). 21.30 (978-0-7362-0802-4(X)) CENGAGE Learning.
Papi y Yo. (Spanish Early Intervention Levels Ser.). (SPA.). 23.10 (978-1-56334-786-3(5)) CENGAGE Learning.
Paquito y los frijoles Magicos: Video Tape. (ENG & SPA.). (gr. k-1). 26.00 (978-0-7635-6278-6(5)) Rigby Education.
Parker, David & Lyon, Tammie. ¡Soy Optimista! Lyon, Tammie, illus. 2011. (SPA., Illus.). (J). (978-0-545-27356-5(0)) Scholastic, Inc.
Parramón, José María. Mi Calle. Borday, Irene, illus. (Coleccion Estoy En...).Tr. of My Street. (SPA.). 32p. (J). (gr. k-3). 6.36 (978-84-342-1003-5(7)) Parramon Ediciones S.A. ESP. Dist: Lectorum Pubns., Inc.
—Mi Casa. Borday, Irene, illus. (Coleccion Estoy En...).Tr. of My House. (SPA.). 32p. (J). (gr. k-3). 6.36 (978-84-342-1002-8(9)) Parramon Ediciones S.A. ESP. Dist: Lectorum Pubns., Inc.
—Mi Jardin. Borday, Irene, illus. (Coleccion Estoy En...).Tr. of My Garden. (SPA.). 32p. (J). (gr. k-3). 6.36 (978-84-342-1005-9(3)) Parramon Ediciones S.A. ESP. Dist: Lectorum Pubns., Inc.
Parramón, José María & Bordoy, Irene. Mi Calle.Tr. of My Street. (SPA., Illus.). (J). (gr. -1-1). 6.95 (978-958-04-1277-9(4)) Norma S.A. COL. Dist: Distribuidora Norma, Inc.
Pastel de Lodo: Individual Title Six-Packs. (Literatura 2000 Ser.). (SPA.). (gr. -1-1). 28.00 (978-0-7635-1000-8(9)) Rigby Education.
Patas, 6 Packs. (Literatura 2000 Ser.). (SPA.). (gr. 1-2). 28.00 (978-0-7635-1049-7(1)) Rigby Education.
El patito y los Gusanos. (Spanish Early Intervention Levels Ser.). (SPA.). 21.30 (978-0-7362-0811-6(9)) CENGAGE Learning.
Patricelli, Leslie. Faster! Faster!/Mas Rapido! Mas Rapido! Patricelli, Leslie, illus. 2013. (Leslie Patricelli Board Bks.). (Illus.). 30p. (J). (-k). bds. 8.99 (978-0-7636-6611-8(4)) Candlewick Pr.
Paty la Pequenita, 6 Packs. (Literatura 2000 Ser.). (SPA.). (gr. 1-2). 28.00 (978-0-7635-1050-3(5)) Rigby Education.
Pebble Soup Exploraciones: Complete Pebble Soup Exploraciones Package. 1650.00 (978-0-7578-3315-1(2)) Rigby Education.
El Pececito Andres: Individual 6-packs. 2003. 23.95 (978-0-673-78065-2(1)) Celebration Pr.
Penn, Sarah. Nat Love: African American Cowboy / Vaquero Afroamericano. 2009. (Famous People in American History/Grandes personajes en la historia de los Estados Unidos Ser.). (ENG & SPA.). 32p. (gr. 2-3). 47.90 (978-1-61512-551-7(5), Editorial Buenas Letras) Rosen Publishing Group, Inc., The.
Pennac, Daniel. La Mirada del Lobo. (Torre de Papel Ser.). (SPA.). (J). (gr. 4-18). 8.95 (978-958-04-4145-8(6)) Norma S.A. COL. Dist: Distribuidora Norma, Inc.
Penovi, Celina. Alboroto a la Hora Del Desayuno / Scrambled Breakfast. 2009. 20p. pap. 14.99 (978-1-4490-2743-8(1)) AuthorHouse.
Pensando. (Coleccion Mil Preguntas). (SPA., Illus.). 24p. (J). pap. 5.50 (978-950-11-0661-9(6), SGM629) Sigmar ARG. Dist: Continental Bk. Co., Inc.
Pepe El Panadero, 6 Packs. 2003. 23.95 (978-0-673-78061-4(9)) Celebration Pr.
Pérez-Mercado, Mary Margaret & Pérez-Mercado, Mary Margaret. Rookie Ready to Learn en Español: ¡Zas! Torrey, Richard L., illus. 2011. (Rookie Ready to Learn Español Ser.). Orig. Title: Rookie Ready to Learn: Splat! (SPA.). 32p. (J). pap. 5.95 (978-0-531-26788-2(1), Children's Pr.) Scholastic Library Publishing.
Perrault, Charles. Cinderella (Cenicienta) Fransoy, Monse, illus. 2013. (Bilingual Fairy Tales Ser.). (ENG & SPA.). 32p. (gr. 1-4). lib. bdg. 28.50 (978-1-60753-356-6(1)) Amicus Learning.
Perrin. (Spanish Early Intervention Levels Ser.). (SPA.). 21.30 (978-0-7362-0834-5(8)) CENGAGE Learning.
Perritos, 6 Packs. 2003. 23.95 (978-0-673-78063-8(5)) Celebration Pr.

Pesce, Elena. La Cola de los Ingleses. (SPA.). (J). (gr. 4-18). 7.95 *(978-958-04-5033-7(1))* Norma S.A. COL. Dist: Distribuidora Norma, Inc.

Peters, Elisa. It's a Bird! / ¡Es un Ave! 2009. (Everyday Wonders / Maravillas de todos los días Ser.). (ENG & SPA.). 24p. (gr. 1-1). 42.50 *(978-1-61512-327-6(X)*, Editorial Buenas Letras) Rosen Publishing Group, Inc., The.

—It's a Caterpillar! / ¡Es una Oruga! 2009. (Everyday Wonders / Maravillas de todos los días Ser.). (ENG & SPA.). 24p. (gr. 1-1). 42.50 *(978-1-61512-328-5(8)*, Editorial Buenas Letras) Rosen Publishing Group, Inc., The.

—It's a Dragonfly! / ¡Es una Libélula! 2009. (Everyday Wonders / Maravillas de todos los días Ser.). (ENG & SPA.). 24p. (gr. 1-1). 42.50 *(978-1-61512-329-2(6)*, Editorial Buenas Letras) Rosen Publishing Group, Inc., The.

—It's a Sunflower! / ¡Es un Girasol! 2009. (Everyday Wonders / Maravillas de todos los días Ser.). (ENG & SPA.). 24p. (gr. 1-1). 42.50 *(978-1-61512-330-8(X)*, Editorial Buenas Letras) Rosen Publishing Group, Inc., The.

—It's an Apple Tree! / ¡Es un Manzano! 2009. (Everyday Wonders / Maravillas de todos los días Ser.). (ENG & SPA.). 24p. (gr. 1-1). 42.50 *(978-1-61512-331-5(8)*, Editorial Buenas Letras) Rosen Publishing Group, Inc., The.

—It's Snow! / ¡la Nieve! 2009. (Everyday Wonders / Maravillas de todos los días Ser.). (ENG & SPA.). 24p. (gr. 1-1). 42.50 *(978-1-61512-332-2(6)*, Editorial Buenas Letras) Rosen Publishing Group, Inc., The.

Petersen, Kathleen C. Null. ¿Poesía? ¡Qué Horror! rev. ed. 2007. (Reader's Theater Ser.). (SPA.). 20p. (J). (gr. 1-2). 7.99 *(978-1-4333-0020-2(6))* Teacher Created Materials, Inc.

Phillips, Larissa. Cochise: Apache Chief. 2009. (Primary Sources of Famous People in American History Ser.). 32p. (gr. 2-3). 47.90 *(978-1-60851-660-5(1))* Rosen Publishing Group, Inc., The.

—Cochise: Apache Chief / Cochise: Jefe Apache. 2009. (Famous People in American History/Grandes personajes en la historia de los Estados Unidos Ser.). (ENG & SPA.). 32p. (gr. 2-3). 47.90 *(978-1-61512-540-1(X)*, Editorial Buenas Letras) Rosen Publishing Group, Inc., The.

—Cochise: Jefe apache (Cochise: Apache Chief) 2009. (Grandes personajes en la historia de los Estados Unidos (Famous People in American History) Ser.). (SPA.). 32p. (gr. 2-3). 47.90 *(978-1-61512-792-4(5)*, Editorial Buenas Letras) Rosen Publishing Group, Inc., The.

Phonics Songs & Rhymes Flip Chart. 2004. (gr. k-18). suppl. ed. 109.15 *(978-0-328-02213-7(6))*; (gr. 3-18). suppl. ed. 109.50 *(978-0-673-59718-2(0))* Addison-Wesley Educational Pubs., Inc.

Pin uno, pin dos, pin Tres: Individual Title Six-Packs. (Literatura 2000 Ser.). (SPA.). (gr. 2-3). 33.00 *(978-0-7635-1269-9(9))* Rigby Education.

Pinata, 6 Packs. 2003. 23.95 *(978-0-673-77134-6(2))* Celebration Pr.

Pinata: Mas Pinata Package. 2003. 1744.95 *(978-0-673-58718-3(5))* Celebration Pr.

Pinguete y Miguela. (Spanish Early Intervention Levels Ser.). (SPA.). 28.38 *(978-0-7362-0842-0(9))* CENGAGE Learning.

Pinto, Pinto. (Spanish Early Intervention Levels Ser.). (SPA.). 23.10 *(978-1-56334-769-6(5))* CENGAGE Learning.

Pisa Y Ve! Little Books, Level 6, Vol. 10. 2003. (Fonolibros Ser.). 25.50 *(978-0-7652-0087-7(2))* Modern Curriculum Pr.

Pitt, Marilyn, et al. Perro en Apuros: Let Me In. Bianchi, John & Taylor, Trace, illus. 2010. (1G Our World Ser.). (ENG.). 24p. (J). pap. 9.60 *(978-1-61541-170-2(4))* American Reading Co.

La Playa: Individual Title Six-Packs. (Literatura 2000 Ser.). (SPA.). (gr. -1-1). 28.00 *(978-0-7635-1001-5(7))* Rigby Education.

Polacco, Patricia. Gracias, Senor Falker. 2006. (SPA., Illus.). 34p. (J). (gr. 2-3). per. 9.99 *(978-1-933032-02-3(2)*, LC34004) Lectorum Pubns., Inc.

Pollack, Pam & Belviso, Meg. I Can't Sit Still! Living with ADHD. Fabrega, Marta, illus. 2009. (Live & Learn Ser.). (ENG.). 36p. (J). (gr. k-3). 21.19 *(978-0-7641-4419-6(7)*, B.E.S. Publishing) Peterson's.

—No Puedo Estar Quieto! Mi Vida con ADHD. Fabrega, Marta, illus. 2009. (Vive y Aprende Libros Ser.). (ENG.). 36p. (J). (gr. k-2). pap. 6.99 *(978-0-7641-4420-2(0))* Sourcebooks, Inc.

La pollita Vivita: Video Tape. (ENG & SPA.). (gr. k-1). 26.00 *(978-0-7635-6279-3(3))* Rigby Education.

El Pollito Huerfanito: Individual 6-packs. 2003. 23.95 *(978-0-673-77153-7(9))* Celebration Pr.

Los Pollitos. 2003. (J). (gr. -1-2). 28.95 *(978-0-673-77405-7(8))* Celebration Pr.

Por amor a las Tortugas: Six-Pack. (Saludos Ser.: Vol. 1). (SPA.). (gr. 2-3). 31.00 *(978-0-7635-9537-1(3))* Rigby Education.

Por Que? (Coleccion Mil Preguntas). (SPA., Illus.). 24p. (J). pap. 5.50 *(978-950-11-0611-4(X)*, SGM11X) Sigmar ARG. Dist: Continental Bk. Co., Inc.

Por que el conejo tiene las orejas tan Largas? Lap Book. (Pebble Soup Exploraciones Ser.). (SPA.). 16p. (gr. -1-18). 21.00 *(978-0-7578-1691-8(6))* Rigby Education.

Por que el conejo tiene las orejas tan Largas? Small Book. (Pebble Soup Exploraciones Ser.). (SPA.). 16p. (gr. -1-18). 5.00 *(978-0-7578-1731-1(9))* Rigby Education.

Por que el mar es Salado: Individual Title Six-Packs. (Literatura 2000 Ser.). (SPA.). (gr. 2-3). 33.00 *(978-0-7635-1270-5(2))* Rigby Education.

Por que los conejos tienen las orejas Largas: Individual Title Six-Packs. (Literatura 2000 Ser.). (SPA.). (gr. 2-3). 33.00 *(978-0-7635-1271-2(0))* Rigby Education.

Por que soplan los vientos Salvajes: 6 Softcover Books. (Saludos Ser.: Vol. 1). (SPA.). (gr. 3-5). 31.00 *(978-0-7635-1845-5(X))* Rigby Education.

Porque los elefantes tienen narices Largas: Individual Title Six-Packs. (Literatura 2000 Ser.). (SPA.). (gr. 1-2). 28.00 *(978-0-7635-1073-2(4))* Rigby Education.

Preparandose para la Fiesta, 6 Packs. (Literatura 2000 Ser.). (SPA.). (gr. -1-1). 28.00 *(978-0-7635-1002-2(5))* Rigby Education.

Price, Mara & Ventura, Gabriela Baeza. Grandma's Chocolate/El Chocolate de Abuelita. Fields, Lisa, illus. 2010. (SPA.). 32p. (J). (gr. -1-3). 16.95 *(978-1-55885-587-8(4)*, Piñata Books) Arte Publico Pr.

Price, Mathew. Vueltas y Vueltas en Patin. (SPA.). pap. 3.95 *(978-950-07-2062-5(0))* Editorial Sudamericana S.A. ARG. Dist: Distribooks, Inc.

Prieto, Iliana. La Princesa del Retrato y el Dragon Rey. (Torre de Papel Ser.). (SPA.). (J). (gr. 4-18). 8.95 *(978-958-04-4219-6(3))* Norma S.A. COL. Dist: Distribuidora Norma, Inc.

La Princesa De Verdad. 2003. 28.95 *(978-0-673-78087-4(2))* Celebration Pr.

El problema de Ema, 6 Packs. (Literatura 2000 Ser.). (SPA.). (gr. 1-2). 28.00 *(978-0-7635-1074-9(2))* Rigby Education.

Publications International Ltd. Staff, ed. PNO BK Spa Disney Princess. 2009. 12p. 15.98 *(978-1-4127-9243-1(6))* Phoenix International Publications, Inc.

Puedo Salir? 2003. (Coleccion Parvulitos). 63.50 *(978-0-8136-8103-0(0))* Modern Curriculum Pr.

Puedo Salir? Big Book. 2003. 35.50 *(978-0-8136-8101-6(4))* Modern Curriculum Pr.

Puertas al sol / Gold Set. (SPA.). (J). (gr. 3-5). 65.00 *(978-1-59437-849-2(5))* Santillana USA Publishing Co., Inc.

Puertas al sol / Silver Set. (SPA.). (J). (gr. k-2). 65.00 *(978-1-59437-848-5(7))* Santillana USA Publishing Co., Inc.

Pullman, Philip. Luces del Norte. (SPA.). (YA). 2007. 672p. pap. 8.95 *(978-84-666-1635-5(7))* 8th ed. 2005. (Illus.). 379p. (gr. 7-11). 13.95 *(978-84-406-3296-8(7))* Ediciones B ESP. Dist: Spanish Pubs., LLC, Independent Pubs. Group.

—Luces del Norte. (SPA.). 672p. 18.95 *(978-84-663-0673-7(0))* Suma de Letras, S.L. ESP. Dist: Distribooks, Inc.

Puppies. 2003. 23.95 *(978-0-673-78127-7(5))* Celebration Pr.

Puppies. 10.95 *(978-3-8238-4703-8(1))* teNeues Publishing Co.

Puzo, Mario. Las Extranas Vacaciones de Davie Shaw. (SPA.). 124p. (YA). (gr. 5-18). *(978-84-279-3318-7(5)*, NG2827) Noguer y Caralt Editores, S. A. ESP. Dist: Lectorum Pubns., Inc.

Que agarro Rigo? Individual Title Six-Packs. (Literatura 2000 Ser.). (SPA.). (gr. k-1). 28.00 *(978-0-7635-1027-5(0))* Rigby Education.

Que debes decir? Que debes Hacer? Social/Emotional Lap Book. (Pebble Soup Exploraciones Ser.). (SPA.). (gr. -1-18). 16.00 *(978-0-7578-1791-5(2))* Rigby Education.

Que es Chiquito? (Spanish Early Intervention Levels Ser.). (SPA.). 23.10 *(978-1-56334-760-3(1))* CENGAGE Learning.

Que es Rojo? (Spanish Early Intervention Levels Ser.). (SPA.). 31.14 *(978-0-7362-0339-5(7))* CENGAGE Learning.

Que Es un Murcielago? Individual Title Six-Packs. (Literatura 2000 Ser.). (SPA.). (gr. 1-2). 28.00 *(978-0-7635-1051-0(3))* Rigby Education.

Que hay a la vuelta de la Esquina? Individual Title Six-Packs. (Literatura 2000 Ser.). (SPA.). (gr. 1-2). 28.00 *(978-0-7635-1075-6(0))* Rigby Education.

Que hizo Zoe Zapata? (Spanish Early Intervention Levels Ser.). (SPA.). 21.30 *(978-0-7362-0828-4(3))* CENGAGE Learning.

Que puede Volar? Individual Title Six-Packs. (Literatura 2000 Ser.). (SPA.). (gr. k-1). 28.00 *(978-0-7635-1028-2(9))* Rigby Education.

Que puedo yo Hacer? 6 Small Books. (Saludos Ser.: Vol. 1). (SPA.). (gr. 2-3). 31.00 *(978-0-7635-9539-5(X))* Rigby Education.

Que quiere Beto? Individual Title-Six Packs. (Chiquilibros Ser.). (SPA.). (gr. k-1). 23.00 *(978-0-7635-8610-2(2))* Rigby Education.

Que quieren Ellos? Individual Title-Six Packs. (Chiquilibros Ser.). (SPA.). (gr. k-1). 23.00 *(978-0-7635-8611-9(0))* Rigby Education.

Que Revoltijo! Individual Title Six-Packs. (Chiquilibros Ser.). (SPA.). (gr. k-1). 23.00 *(978-0-7635-8593-8(9))* Rigby Education.

Que sale de las Semillas? (Spanish Early Intervention Levels Ser.). (SPA.). 23.10 *(978-1-56334-768-9(7))* CENGAGE Learning.

Que Sera? 2003. 28.95 *(978-0-673-78093-5(7))* Celebration Pr.

Que Sera? Big Book. (Pebble Soup Exploraciones Ser.). (SPA.). 16p. (gr. -1-18). 31.00 *(978-0-7578-1689-5(4))* Rigby Education.

Que Sera? Small Book. (Pebble Soup Exploraciones Ser.). (SPA.). 16p. (gr. -1-18). 5.00 *(978-0-7578-1729-8(7))* Rigby Education.

Que Sigue? Big Book Packages. 2003. 64.95 *(978-0-673-58584-4(0))* Celebration Pr.

Que suerte Tengo! Individual Title Six-Packs. (Literatura 2000 Ser.). (SPA.). (gr. 1-2). 28.00 *(978-0-7635-1076-3(9))* Rigby Education.

Que va en la Tina? Individual Title Six-Packs. (Literatura 2000 Ser.). (SPA.). (gr. k-1). 28.00 *(978-0-7635-1029-9(7))* Rigby Education.

Querida Abuelita: 6 Small Books. (Saludos Ser.: Vol. 2). (SPA.). (gr. 3-5). 31.00 *(978-0-7635-1770-0(4))* Rigby Education.

Querida Gilda. (Spanish Early Intervention Levels Ser.). (SPA.). 23.10 *(978-0-7362-0322-7(2))* CENGAGE Learning.

Querido Santa, 6 Packs. (Literatura 2000 Ser.). (SPA.). (gr. k-1). 28.00 *(978-0-7635-1030-5(0))* Rigby Education.

Quien? (Coleccion Mil Preguntas). (SPA., Illus.). 24p. (J). pap. 5.50 *(978-950-11-0607-7(1)*, SGM110) Sigmar ARG. Dist: Continental Bk. Co., Inc.

Quien es Michael Ramirez? 2003. 28.95 *(978-0-673-78084-3(8))* Celebration Pr.

A quien le gusta la Noche? (Spanish Early Intervention Levels Ser.). (SPA.). 31.14 *(978-0-7362-0330-2(3))* CENGAGE Learning.

Quien paso por Aqui? (Spanish Early Intervention Levels Ser.). (SPA.). 23.10 *(978-1-56334-788-7(1))* CENGAGE Learning.

Quien soy Yo? (Spanish Early Intervention Levels Ser.). (SPA.). 23.10 *(978-1-56334-793-1(8))* CENGAGE Learning.

Quienes Son Tus Amigos? 2003. 35.50 *(978-0-8136-8047-7(6))* Modern Curriculum Pr.

Quieres Jugar? Big Book. (Pebble Soup Exploraciones Ser.). 16p. (gr. -1-18). 31.00 *(978-0-7578-1672-7(X))* Rigby Education.

Quieres Jugar? Small Book. (Pebble Soup Exploraciones Ser.). 16p. (gr. -1-18). 5.00 *(978-0-7578-1712-0(2))* Rigby Education.

Rabbits: Individual Title Six-Packs. (Literatura 2000 Ser.). (gr. 2-3). 33.00 *(978-0-7635-0235-5(9))* Rigby Education.

Rabe, Tish. ¡Te Amo, Te Abrazo, Leo Contigo!/Love You, Hug You, Read to You! Endersby, Frank, illus. 2015. 32p. (J). (gr. -1 — 1). bds. 7.99 *(978-1-101-93657-3(6)*, Random Hse. Bks. for Young Readers) Random Hse. Children's Bks.

Ramos, Maria Cristina. De Barrio Somos. (Torre de Papel Ser.). (SPA.). (J). (gr. 4). 7.95 *(978-958-04-4221-9(5))* Norma S.A. COL. Dist: Distribuidora Norma, Inc.

Ramos, Pilar. La NUEVA CASA. (SPA.). 32p. (J). 10.00 *(978-84-342-2517-6(4))* Parramon Ediciones S.A. ESP. Dist: Distribuidora Norma, Inc.

La rana que se creia Caballo: Individual Title Six-Packs. (Literatura 2000 Ser.). (SPA.). (gr. 2-3). 33.00 *(978-0-7635-1272-9(9))* Rigby Education.

El Ranchito. (Spanish Early Intervention Levels Ser.). (SPA.). 23.10 *(978-1-56334-764-1(4))* CENGAGE Learning.

El Rancho: Individual Title Six-Packs. (Literatura 2000 Ser.). (SPA.). (gr. -1-1). 28.00 *(978-0-7635-1006-0(8))* Rigby Education.

Randolph, Joanne. Fire Trucks. 2009. (To the Rescue! Ser.). 24p. (gr. 1-1). 42.50 *(978-1-60854-397-7(8)*, PowerKids Pr.) Rosen Publishing Group, Inc., The.

—Fire Trucks/Camiones de Bomberos. 2009. (To the Rescue! / ¡Al rescate! Ser.). (ENG & SPA.). 24p. (gr. 1-1). 42.50 *(978-1-60854-403-5(6)*, Editorial Buenas Letras) Rosen Publishing Group, Inc., The.

—Gases in My World, 1 vol. 2006. (Journeys Ser.). (ENG.). 24p. (gr. k-2). pap. 7.05 *(978-1-4042-8419-7(2)*, d5f9afc6-d1af-4d12-a54d-446d2221cf87, Rosen Classroom) Rosen Publishing Group, Inc., The.

—Gears in My World, 1 vol. 2006. (Journeys Ser.). (ENG.). 24p. (gr. k-2). pap. 7.05 *(978-1-4042-8423-4(0)*, fd623d93-fcd6-45a7-a99b-7319d5211970, Rosen Classroom) Rosen Publishing Group, Inc., The.

—Let's Draw a Butterfly with Circles / Vamos a dibujar una mariposa usando Círculos. 2009. (Let's Draw with Shapes / Vamos a dibujar con figuras Ser.). (ENG & SPA.). 24p. (gr. k-1). 42.50 *(978-1-61514-221-7(5)*, Editorial Buenas Letras) Rosen Publishing Group, Inc., The.

—Let's Draw a Horse with Rectangles / Vamos a dibujar un caballo usando Rectángulos. 2009. (Let's Draw with Shapes / Vamos a dibujar con figuras Ser.). (ENG & SPA.). 24p. (gr. k-1). 42.50 *(978-1-61514-224-8(X)*, Editorial Buenas Letras) Rosen Publishing Group, Inc., The.

—Police Cars. 2009. (To the Rescue! Ser.). 24p. (gr. 1-1). 42.50 *(978-1-60854-398-4(6)*, PowerKids Pr.) Rosen Publishing Group, Inc., The.

—Police Cars/Patrullas. 2009. (To the Rescue! / ¡Al rescate! Ser.). (ENG & SPA.). 24p. (gr. 1-1). 42.50 *(978-1-60854-404-2(4)*, Editorial Buenas Letras) Rosen Publishing Group, Inc., The.

—Wedges in My World, 1 vol. 2006. (Journeys Ser.). (ENG.). 24p. (gr. k-2). pap. 7.05 *(978-1-4042-8426-5(5)*, e5722743-6b08-4bcf-a8f8-bbf72ee84dae, Rosen Classroom) Rosen Publishing Group, Inc., The.

—What I Look Like When I am Confused / Cómo me veo cuando estoy Confundido. 2009. (Let's Look at Feelings / un vistazo a los sentimientos Ser.). (ENG & SPA.). 24p. (gr. k-1). 42.50 *(978-1-61514-246-0(0)*, Editorial Buenas Letras) Rosen Publishing Group, Inc., The.

—Wheels & Axels in My World/Ejes y ruedas en mi Mundo. 2009. (My World of Science/la ciencia en mi mundo Ser.). (ENG & SPA.). 48p. (gr. 2-2). 37.50 *(978-1-61514-743-4(8)*, Editorial Buenas Letras) Rosen Publishing Group, Inc., The.

—Whose Back Is This? / ¿de quién es esta Espalda? 2009. (Animal Clues / ¿Adivina de Quién Es? Ser.). (ENG & SPA.). 24p. (gr. 1-1). 42.50 *(978-1-61511-437-5(8)*, Editorial Buenas Letras) Rosen Publishing Group, Inc., The.

—Whose Eyes Are These? / ¿de quién son estos Ojos? 2009. (Animal Clues / ¿Adivina de Quién Es? Ser.). (ENG & SPA.). 24p. (gr. 1-1). 42.50 *(978-1-61511-438-2(6)*, Editorial Buenas Letras) Rosen Publishing Group, Inc., The.

—Whose Nose Is This? / ¿de quién es esta Nariz? 2009. (Animal Clues / ¿Adivina de Quién Es? Ser.). (ENG & SPA.). 24p. (gr. 1-1). 42.50 *(978-1-61511-439-9(4)*, Editorial Buenas Letras) Rosen Publishing Group, Inc., The.

—Whose Teeth Are These? / ¿de quién son estos Dientes? 2009. (Animal Clues / ¿Adivina de Quién Es? Ser.). (ENG & SPA.). 24p. (gr. 1-1). 42.50 *(978-1-61511-440-5(8)*, Editorial Buenas Letras) Rosen Publishing Group, Inc., The.

—Whose Toes Are Those? / ¿de quién son estas Patas? 2009. (Animal Clues / ¿Adivina de Quién Es? Ser.). (ENG & SPA.). 24p. (gr. 1-1). 42.50 *(978-1-61511-441-2(6)*, Editorial Buenas Letras) Rosen Publishing Group, Inc., The.

—Whose Tongue Is This? / ¿de quién es esta Lengua? 2009. (Animal Clues / ¿Adivina de Quién Es? Ser.). (ENG & SPA.). 24p. (gr. 1-1). 42.50 *(978-1-61511-442-9(4)*, Editorial Buenas Letras) Rosen Publishing Group, Inc., The.

Los Raspados. 2003. 23.95 *(978-0-673-77786-7(3))* Celebration Pr.

Ratita y Raton. (Spanish Early Intervention Levels Ser.). (SPA.). 21.30 *(978-0-7362-0810-9(0))* CENGAGE Learning.

El raton Audaz. (Spanish Early Intervention Levels Ser.). (SPA.). 28.38 *(978-0-7362-0839-0(9))* CENGAGE Learning.

Rau, Dana Meachen. Cansada de Esperar, 1 vol. Ruiz, Carlos, tr. Fitzpatrick, Brad, illus. 2006. (Read-It! Readers en Español: Story Collection). (SPA.). 32p. (J). (gr. -1-3). 22.65 *(978-1-4048-1695-4(X)*, 86647, Picture Window Bks.) Capstone.

Reach for Reading: Reaching up en espanol Self-Training Package. (SPA.). (gr. 1-3). 675.00 *(978-0-7578-5933-5(X))* Rigby Education.

Reaching up en espanol Additional Resources: Additional Tutor's Manual. (Reach for Reading Ser.). (SPA.). (gr. 1-3). 31.00 *(978-0-7635-7622-6(0))* Rigby Education.

Reaching up en espanol Additional Resources: Spanish Books (75 Titles) (Reach for Reading Ser.). (SPA.). (gr. 1-3). 205.00 *(978-0-7578-4878-0(8))* Rigby Education.

Reaching up en espanol Additional Workstations: With Books. (Reach for Reading Ser.). (SPA.). (gr. 1-3). 390.00 *(978-0-7635-3711-1(X))* Rigby Education.

Reaching up en espanol Additional Workstations: Without Books. (Reach for Reading Ser.). (SPA.). (gr. 1-3). 285.00 *(978-0-7578-3544-5(9))* Rigby Education.

Read & Understand Spanish / English, Fiction. 2005. (J). 29.99 *(978-1-59673-075-5(7)*, EMC 5310) Evan-Moor Educational Pubs.

Reading 2000 Phonics Songs & Rhymes Flip Chart. 2004. (gr. 2-18). suppl. ed. 109.15 *(978-0-673-59717-5(2))* Addison-Wesley Educational Pubs., Inc.

El Rebozo De Elsa, 6 packs. 2003. 23.95 *(978-0-673-78068-3(6))* Celebration Pr.

Recortes. (Spanish Early Intervention Levels Ser.). (SPA.). 23.10 *(978-1-56334-779-5(2))* CENGAGE Learning.

Recuerdos: Individual Title Six-Packs. (Literatura 2000 Ser.). (SPA.). (gr. 2-3). 33.00 *(978-0-7635-1099-2(8))* Rigby Education.

Un Regalo del Mar, 6 Packs. (Literatura 2000 Ser.). (SPA.). (gr. 2-3). 33.00 *(978-0-7635-1273-6(7))* Rigby Education.

Regalos de Navidad, 6 Packs. (Literatura 2000 Ser.). (SPA.). (gr. 1-2). 28.00 *(978-0-7635-1052-7(1))* Rigby Education.

Reiser, Lynn. My Way/a Mi Manera: Bilingual English-Spanish. Reiser, Lynn, illus. 2007. (ENG., Illus.). 32p. (J). (gr. -1-k). 16.99 *(978-0-06-084101-0(X))* HarperCollins Español.

El Renacuajo: Big Book Packages. 2003. 64.95 *(978-0-673-58587-5(5))* Celebration Pr.

Rene Colato Lainez. Mama the Alien/Mama la Extraterrestre (Bilingual Edition) (Spanish & English Edition), 1 vol. 2016. (ENG., Illus.). 32p. (J). (gr. 1-4). 18.95 *(978-0-89239-298-8(3)*, leelowcbp) Lee & Low Bks., Inc.

Reno ensucia: Messy Moose. 2005. (Take-Home Bks.). (SPA.). (YA). (gr. -1-3). 15.75 *(978-0-8215-1201-2(3))* Sadlier, William H. Inc.

Reno ensucia/Messy Moose. 2005. (Libros en Espanol Para Ninos Ser.). (SPA.). (YA). (gr. -1-1). 11.97 *(978-0-8215-0991-3(8))* Sadlier, William H. Inc.

El rey de la Laguna. (Spanish Early Intervention Levels Ser.). (SPA.). 31.14 *(978-0-7362-0328-9(1))* CENGAGE Learning.

Rey, H. A. Curious George Curious You: on Your Way!/¡Eres Curioso Todo el Tiempo! Bilingual English-Spanish. 2012. (Curious George Ser.). (ENG.). 32p. (J). (gr. -1-3). 9.99 *(978-0-547-79368-9(5)*, 1493387, Clarion Bks.) HarperCollins Pubs.

—Curious George Dance Party/Jorge el Curioso el Baile: Bilingual English-Spanish. 2013. (Curious George TV Ser.). (ENG., Illus.). 24p. (J). (gr. -1-3). pap. 4.99 *(978-0-547-96822-3(1)*, 1521358, Clarion Bks.) HarperCollins Pubs.

Rice, Dona Herweck. Agua. 2nd rev. ed. 2011. (TIME for KIDS(r): Informational Text Ser.). (SPA.). 12p. (gr. k-1). 7.99 *(978-1-4333-4415-2(7))* Teacher Created Materials, Inc.

—Casas Alrededor Del Mundo. 2nd rev. ed. 2012. (TIME for KIDS(r): Informational Text Ser.).Tr. of Homes Around the World. (SPA., Illus.). 20p. (gr. 1-2). 8.99 *(978-1-4333-4431-2(9))* Teacher Created Materials, Inc.

—Colores. 2nd rev. ed. 2011. (TIME for KIDS(r): Informational Text Ser.). (SPA.). 12p. (gr. k-1). 7.99 *(978-1-4333-4405-3(X))* Teacher Created Materials, Inc.

—Comer Bien. 2nd rev. ed. 2012. (TIME for KIDS(r): Informational Text Ser.). (SPA.). 20p. (gr. 1-2). 8.99 *(978-1-4333-4430-5(0))* Teacher Created Materials, Inc.

—Cómo Crecen las Plantas. 2nd rev. ed. 2011. (TIME for KIDS(r): Informational Text Ser.). (SPA.). 12p. (gr. k-1). 7.99 *(978-1-4333-4416-9(5))* Teacher Created Materials, Inc.

—Cosas con Alas. 2nd rev. ed. 2012. (TIME for KIDS(r): Informational Text Ser.). (SPA.). 20p. (gr. 1-2). 6.99 *(978-1-4333-4422-0(X))* Teacher Created Materials, Inc.

—A Dónde Ir. 2nd rev. ed. 2011. (TIME for KIDS(r): Informational Text Ser.). (SPA.). 12p. (gr. k-1). 7.99 *(978-1-4333-4412-1(2))* Teacher Created Materials, Inc.

—En Movimiento. 2nd rev. ed. 2011. (TIME for KIDS(r): Informational Text Ser.). (SPA.). 12p. (gr. k-1). 7.99 *(978-1-4333-4410-7(6))* Teacher Created Materials, Inc.

—Esta Soy Yo. 2nd rev. ed. 2011. (TIME for KIDS(r): Informational Text Ser.). (SPA.). 12p. (gr. k-1). 7.99 *(978-1-4333-4407-7(6))* Teacher Created Materials, Inc.

—Figuras. 2nd rev. ed. 2011. (TIME for KIDS(r): Informational Text Ser.). (SPA.). 12p. (gr. k-1). 7.99 *(978-1-4333-4406-0(8))* Teacher Created Materials, Inc.

—Grande y Pequeño. 2nd rev. ed. 2011. (TIME for KIDS(r): Informational Text Ser.). (SPA.). 12p. (gr. k-1). 7.99 *(978-1-4333-4404-6(1))* Teacher Created Materials, Inc.

—¡Locos por Insectos y Arañas! 2nd rev. ed. 2012. (TIME for KIDS(r): Informational Text Ser.).Tr. of Going Buggy. (SPA.). 20p. (gr. 1-2). 8.99 *(978-1-4333-4424-4(6))* Teacher Created Materials, Inc.

—Lugares del Mundo. 2nd rev. ed. 2012. (TIME for KIDS(r): Informational Text Ser.).Tr. of Places Around the World. (SPA.). 20p. (gr. 1-2). 8.99 *(978-1-4333-4433-6(5))* Teacher Created Materials, Inc.

—Madres Animales y Sus Crías. 2nd rev. ed. 2011. (TIME for KIDS(r): Informational Text Ser.). (SPA., Illus.). 12p. (gr. k-1). 7.99 *(978-1-4333-4418-3(1))* Teacher Created Materials, Inc.

—Mantenerse en Forma con Deportes. 2nd rev. ed. 2012. (TIME for KIDS(r): Informational Text Ser.). (SPA.). 20p. (gr. 1-2). 6.99 *(978-1-4333-4429-9(7))* Teacher Created Materials, Inc.

—Mantenerse Sano. 2nd rev. ed. 2012. (TIME for KIDS(r): Informational Text Ser.).Tr. of Staying Healthy. (SPA., Illus.). 20p. (gr. 1-2). 8.99 *(978-1-4333-4428-2(9))* Teacher Created Materials, Inc.

—Mi Gran Familia. 2nd rev. ed. 2011. (TIME for KIDS(r): Informational Text Ser.). (SPA.). 12p. (gr. k-1). 7.99 *(978-1-4333-4409-1(2))* Teacher Created Materials, Inc.

—Niños Alrededor del Mundo. 2nd rev. ed. 2012. (TIME for KIDS(r): Informational Text Ser.). (SPA.). 20p. (gr. 1-2). 6.99 *(978-1-4333-4432-9(7))* Teacher Created Materials, Inc.

—Ojos de Animales. 2nd rev. ed. 2011. (TIME for KIDS(r): Informational Text Ser.). (SPA.). 12p. (gr. k-1). 6.99 *(978-1-4333-4417-6(3))* Teacher Created Materials, Inc.

—Terreno. 2nd rev. ed. 2011. (TIME for KIDS(r): Informational Text Ser.). (SPA.). 12p. (gr. k-1). 7.99 *(978-1-4333-4413-8(0))* Teacher Created Materials, Inc.

—El Tiempo. 2nd rev. ed. 2011. (TIME for KIDS(r): Informational Text Ser.). (SPA.). 12p. (gr. k-1). 7.99 *(978-1-4333-4414-5(9))* Teacher Created Materials, Inc.

—Trabajadores. 2nd rev. ed. 2011. (TIME for KIDS(r): Informational Text Ser.). (SPA.). 12p. (gr. k-1). 7.99 *(978-1-4333-4411-4(4))* Teacher Created Materials, Inc.

—La Vida de una Abeja. 2nd rev. ed. 2012. (TIME for KIDS(r): Informational Text Ser.). (SPA.). 20p. (gr. 1-2). 8.99 (978-1-4333-4421-3(1)) Teacher Created Materials, Inc.
—La Vida de una Mariposa. 2nd rev. ed. 2012. (TIME for KIDS(r): Informational Text Ser.). (SPA.). 20p. (gr. 1-2). 8.99 (978-1-4333-4420-6(3)) Teacher Created Materials, Inc.
—La Vida de Una Rana. 2nd rev. ed. 2012. (TIME for KIDS(r): Informational Text Ser.).Tr. of Frog's Life. (SPA.). 20p. (gr. 1-2). 8.99 (978-1-4333-4419-0(X)) Teacher Created Materials, Inc.
—La Vida Marina. 2nd rev. ed. 2012. (TIME for KIDS(r): Informational Text Ser.). (SPA.). 20p. (gr. 1-2). 6.99 (978-1-4333-4423-7(8)) Teacher Created Materials, Inc.
—Yo Sé. 2nd rev. ed. 2011. (TIME for KIDS(r): Informational Text Ser.). (SPA.). 12p. (gr. k-1). 7.99 (978-1-4333-4408-4(4)) Teacher Created Materials, Inc.
Riddell, Chris. Ottoline va al Colegio. 2008. (SPA.). 172p. (J). 13.95 (978-84-263-6833-1(6)) Vives, Luis Editorial (Edelvives) ESP. Dist: Baker & Taylor Bks.
—Ottoline y la Gata Amarilla. 2008. (SPA.). 172p. (J). 13.95 (978-84-263-6832-4(8)) Vives, Luis Editorial (Edelvives) ESP. Dist: Baker & Taylor Bks.
El Rio: Big Book. (Pebble Soup Exploraciones Ser.). (SPA.). 16p. (gr. -1-18). 31.00 (978-0-7578-1683-3(5)) Rigby Education.
El Rio: Small Book. (Pebble Soup Exploraciones Ser.). (SPA.). 16p. (gr. -1-18). 5.00 (978-0-7578-1723-6(8)) Rigby Education.
El rio es mi Vida: 6 Small Books. (Saludos Ser.: Vol. 3). (SPA.). (gr. 3-5). 31.00 (978-0-7635-1829-5(8)) Rigby Education.
Riqui y el Carnaval. (Spanish Early Intervention Levels Ser.). (SPA.). 21.30 (978-0-7362-0832-1(1)) CENGAGE Learning.
Risley, Jacqueline & Tim. Alpha's ABC's Games: Spanish & English Ages 2-6. Risley, Jacqueline & Tim, illus. 2007.Tr. of Alfa y sus Juegos de la A a la Z. (SPA & ENG., Illus.). 32p. (J). 6.99 (978-0-9791680-0-0(7)) Alpha Learning World, Inc.
Rivas, Spelile. The Cucuy Stole My Cascarones / el Coco Me Robó Los Cascarones. Baeza Ventura, Gabriela, tr. Cervantes, Valeria, illus. 2013. (SPA & ENG.). 32p. (J). 17.95 (978-1-55885-771-0(0), Piñata Books) Arte Publico Pr.
Rivas, Spelile & Plascencia, Amira. No Time for Monsters/No Hay Tiempo para Monstruos. Cervantes, Valeria, illus. 2010. (SPA & ENG.). 32p. (J). (gr. -1-3). 16.95 (978-1-55885-445-0(2)) Arte Publico Pr.
Rivera, Jose E. La Voragine (The Vortex) (Coleccion Centro Literario). (SPA.). (J). pap., stu. ed. 7.95 (978-958-02-0502-9(7), CAR027) Editorial Voluntad S.A. COL. Dist: Continental Bk. Co., Inc.
Rivera, Lassen. Mi Silla de Ruedas. Alvarez, Mrinali, illus. 2006. (SPA.). 28p. 8.95 (978-0-8477-1568-8(X)) Univ. of Puerto Rico Pr.
—Soy Gordito. Alvarez, Mrinali, illus. 2006. (SPA.). 28p. 8.95 (978-0-8477-1565-7(5)) Univ. of Puerto Rico Pr.
El Robot, 6, Pack. (Chiquilibros Ser.). (SPA.). (gr. k-1). 23.00 (978-0-7635-8612-6(9)) Rigby Education.
Rodriguez, Angelica. Mia y Primos/Mia & Cousins: Yo grito,corro y grito / I scream, run & Scream. 2009. 24p. pap. 12.49 (978-1-4389-7095-0(1)) AuthorHouse.
Rodriguez, Orlando A. Valores Morales y Buenos Hábitos — Rangel, Mario Hugo, illus. (SPA.). 32p. (J). 2004. (978-0-311-38596-6(6)) 2004. (978-0-311-38597-3(4)) 2003. (978-0-311-38595-9(8)) Baptist Spanish Publishing Hse./Casa Bavtista de Publicaciones: Mundo Hispano.
Rojas, Emilio. Ortografía Real de la Lengua Española: Libro con Ejercicios. 2003. 328p. (YA). (gr. 5-18). 17.95 (978-968-6966-15-2(3)) EDITER'S Publishing Hse. MEX. Dist: EDITER'S Publishing Hse.
El Rompecabezas: Individual Title-Six Packs. (Chiquilibros Ser.). (SPA.). (gr. k-1). 23.00 (978-0-7635-8614-0(5)) Rigby Education.
Rosa-Mendoza, Gladys. Animals at the Farm/Animales de la Granja Big Book. 2009. (ENG & SPA.). 20p. (J). pap. 19.95 (978-1-931398-89-3(5)) Me+Mi Publishing.
—Jobs Around My Neighborhood/Oficios en Mi Vecindario. Iosa, Ann, illus. 2007. (English Spanish Foundations Ser.). 20p. (gr. -1-k). pap. 19.95 (978-1-931398-81-7(X)) Me+Mi Publishing.
Rosa-Mendoza, Gladys, creator. I Can! 2004. (English-Spanish Foundations Ser.: Vol. 11).Tr. of Yo Puedo! (SPA & ENG., Illus.). 20p. (J). bds. 6.95 (978-1-931398-11-4(9)) Me+Mi Publishing.
Rossetti-Shustak, Bernadette. I Love You Through & Through / Te Quiero, Yo Te Quiero (Bilingual) (Bilingual Edition) Church, Caroline Jayne, illus. 2013. (SPA.). 24p. (J). (gr. -1 — 1). bds. 8.95 (978-0-545-58416-6(7)) Scholastic, Inc.
Ruedas. (Spanish Early Intervention Levels Ser.). (SPA.). 23.10 (978-1-56334-789-4(X)) CENGAGE Learning.
Ruedas, 6 Packs. (Literatura 2000 Ser.). (SPA.). (gr. k-1). 28.00 (978-0-7635-1031-2(9)) Rigby Education.
Ruffin, Fran. Whales / Ballenas. 2009. (My World of Animals / Yo y los animales Ser.). (ENG & SPA.). 24p. (gr. 1-1). 37.50 (978-1-61514-719-9(5), Editorial Buenas Letras) Rosen Publishing Group, Inc., The.
Ruiz-Flores, Lupe. Lupita's First Dance / el Primer Baile de Lupita. Baeza Ventura, Gabriela, tr. Utomo, Gabhor, illus. 2013. (SPA.). 32p. (J). 17.95 (978-1-55885-772-8(9), Piñata Books) Arte Publico Pr.
Ruiz-Flores, Lupe & Rosales-Yeomans, Natalia. Let's Salsa. Rosales-Yeomans, Natalia, tr. Casilla, Robert, illus. 2013.Tr. of Bailemos Salsa. (SPA & ENG.). 32p. (J). 17.95 (978-1-55885-762-9(1), Piñata Books) Arte Publico Pr.
Ruiz, Olivia, et al. La Amiga Nueva De Roberto: Guias De Observacion, Level 12. 2003. 3.95 (978-0-673-61538-1(3)) Celebration Pr.
—Las Cajas De Zapatos: Guias De Observacion, Level 10. 2003. 3.95 (978-0-673-61537-4(5)) Celebration Pr.
—Debes Ser Atento Con Josefina: Resumen Del Cuento, Level 34. 2003. 3.95 (978-0-673-61562-6(6)) Celebration Pr.
—Debes Ser Atento Con Josefina: Guias De Observacion, Level 34. 2003. (SPA.). 3.95 (978-0-673-61546-6(4)) Celebration Pr.
—El Dia Mas Maravilloso: Guias De Observacion, Level 24. 2003. 3.95 (978-0-673-61543-5(X)) Celebration Pr.
—Donde Esta Mi Gorra? Guias De Observacion, Level 4. 2003. 3.95 (978-0-673-61534-3(0)) Celebration Pr.
—Duque: Guias De Observacion, Level 8. 2003. 3.95 (978-0-673-61536-7(7)) Celebration Pr.
—Evaluacion Del Desarrollo De la Lectura Package. 2003. 123.50 (978-0-673-61724-8(6)) Celebration Pr.
—Un Gigante En El Bosque: Guias De Observacion, Level 18. 2003. 3.95 (978-0-673-61541-1(3)) Celebration Pr.
—Mas Astuto Que El Viejo Camilo Canoso: Guias De Observacion, Level 40. 2003. 3.95 (978-0-673-61548-0(0)) Celebration Pr.
—La Olla De Oro: Guias De Observacion, Level 16. 2003. 3.95 (978-0-673-61540-4(5)) Celebration Pr.
—Peligro En las Profundidades: Guias De Observacion, Level 44. 2003. 3.95 (978-0-673-61549-7(9)) Celebration Pr.
—Por Que Paramos? Guias De Observacion, Level 6. 2003. 3.95 (978-0-673-61535-0(9)) Celebration Pr.
—Que Te Gusta? Guias De Observacion, Level 3. 2003. 3.95 (978-0-673-61533-6(2)) Celebration Pr.
—Reni la Rana: Guias De Observacion, Level 20. 2003. 3.95 (978-0-673-61542-8(1)) Celebration Pr.
—Sabes Cantar? Mira Lo Que Se Va: Registro De la Lectura Oral. 2003. (SPA.). 3.95 (978-0-673-61566-4(9)) Celebration Pr.
—Sabes Cantar? Mira Lo Que Se Va Yo Veo: Guias De Observacion, Level 2. 2003. (SPA.). 3.95 (978-0-673-61532-9(4)) Celebration Pr.
—El Vagon: Guias De Observacion, Level 14. 2003. (SPA.). 3.95 (978-0-673-61539-8(1)) Celebration Pr.
—Yo No Te Veo Hermosa: Guias De Observacion, Level 28. 2003. (SPA.). 3.95 (978-0-673-61544-2(8)) Celebration Pr.
—Yo Veo Que Te Gusta? Registro De la Lectura Oral, Level 3. 2003. (SPA.). 3.95 (978-0-673-61567-1(7)) Celebration Pr.
Rusty the Rooster. 2003. 23.95 (978-0-673-78134-5(8)) Celebration Pr.
Rylant, Cynthia. El Caso de la Perezosa Dormilona. (SPA.). (J). 7.95 (978-958-04-7539-2(3)) Norma S.A. COL. Dist: Distribuidora Norma, Inc.
El sacudon de San Francisco: 6 Small Books. (Saludos Ser.: Vol. 3). (SPA.). (gr. 3-5). 31.00 (978-0-7635-2081-6(0)) Rigby Education.
Sad Ladybug: Matching English 6-packs. 2003. 23.95 (978-0-673-57564-7(0)) Celebration Pr.
Sal, Solecito. (Spanish Early Intervention Levels Ser.). (SPA.). 23.10 (978-0-7362-0321-0(4)) CENGAGE Learning.
Saldaña, René. Dancing with the Devil & Other Tales from Beyond / Bailando con el Diablo y Otros Cuentos del Más Allá. Baeza Ventura, Gabriela, tr. from ENG. 2012. (SPA & ENG.). (YA). pap. 9.95 (978-1-55885-744-5(3), Piñata Books) Arte Publico Pr.
Sale un Patito. (Spanish Early Intervention Levels Ser.). (SPA.). 21.30 (978-0-7362-0804-8(6)) CENGAGE Learning.
Saludos! Add-to Pack. (SPA.). 47.00 (978-0-7635-9515-9(2)) Rigby Education.
Saludos! Complete Blue Level Packages. (ENG & SPA.). 1279.00 (978-0-7635-9511-1(X)); (SPA.). 697.00 (978-0-7635-9509-8(8)) Rigby Education.
Saludos! Complete Pasado valioso, futuro Brillante. (SPA.). 385.00 (978-0-7635-9512-8(8)) Rigby Education.
Saludos! Complete Pasado valioso, futuro brillante Rich Past, Bright Future Theme Packages. (ENG & SPA.). 693.00 (978-0-7635-9514-2(4)) Rigby Education.
Saludos! Rich Past, Bright Future Theme Packages. 385.00 (978-0-7635-9513-5(6)) Rigby Education.
Sánchez, Isidro. Mi Gato. Ruis, Maria, illus. (Coleccion Mis Animales Preferidos).Tr. of My Cat. (SPA.). 32p. (J). (gr. k-3). 6.36 (978-84-342-1127-8(0), PR0482) Parramon Ediciones S.A. ESP. Dist: Lectorum Pubns., Inc.
—Mi Hamster. Ruis, Maria, illus. (Coleccion Mis Animales Preferidos).Tr. of My Hamster. (SPA.). 32p. (J). (gr. k-3). 6.36 (978-84-342-1129-2(7), PR0485) Parramon Ediciones S.A. ESP. Dist: Lectorum Pubns., Inc.
—Mi Pajaro. Ruis, Maria, illus. (Coleccion Mis Animales Preferidos).Tr. of My Bird. (SPA.). 32p. (J). (gr. k-3). 6.36 (978-84-342-1128-5(9), PR0483) Parramon Ediciones S.A. ESP. Dist: Lectorum Pubns., Inc.
—Mi Perro. Ruis, Maria, illus. (Coleccion Mis Animales Preferidos).Tr. of My Dog. (SPA.). 32p. (J). (gr. k-3). (978-84-342-1126-1(2), PR0481) Parramon Ediciones S.A. ESP. Dist: Lectorum Pubns., Inc.
Sánchez, Lucía M. & Dibble, Traci. Delfines. 2013. (1-3A Vida Marina Ser.). (SPA., Illus.). 20p. (J). pap. 9.60 (978-1-61406-058-1(4)) American Reading Co.
La Sandia. (Spanish Early Intervention Levels Ser.). (SPA.). 23.10 (978-1-56334-795-5(4)) CENGAGE Learning.
Sandviks HOP, Inc. Staff. Learn to Read: Localized Spanish for U. S. 2007. (J). (gr. k). 64.99 (978-1-60143-890-4(7)); (gr. k-1). 139.99 (978-1-60143-889-8(3)); (gr. 1). 64.99 (978-1-60143-891-1(5)) HOP, LLC.
Sastrias, Martha. Como Motivar a los Ninos a Leer: Lecto-Juegos y Algo Mas. 2005. (ENG., Illus.). 180p. (gr. 2-4). per. 11.95 (978-968-860-449-6(6)) Editorial Pax MEX. Dist: Independent Pubs. Group.
Schreiber-Wicke, Edith. Cuando Decir No. (SPA.). (J). 8.95 (978-958-04-6534-8(7)) Norma S.A. COL. Dist: Distribuidora Norma, Inc.
Schuette, Sarah L. Rectángulos: Rectángulos a Nuestro Alrededor. 2012. (Figuras Geométricas/Shapes Ser.).Tr. of Rectangles - Seeing Rectangles All Around Us. (MUL.). 32p. (gr. 1-2). pap. 47.70 (978-1-4296-8532-0(8), Capstone Pr.) Capstone.
Schwartz, David M. Cuanto Es un Millon? Kellogg, Steven, illus. 2003. (SPA.). (J). (gr. k-3). pap. 3.96 net. (978-0-590-47393-4(X), SO30942) Scholastic, Inc.
Scott, Ann Herbert. On Mother's Lap/en Las Piernas de Mamá: Bilingual English-Spanish. Coalson, Glo, illus. 2007.Tr. of On Mother's Lap. (ENG.). 14p. (J). (gr. k — 1). bds. 5.95 (978-0-618-75247-8(1), 100529, Clarion Bks.) HarperCollins Pubs.
Scott Foresman Family Reading Guide. 2004. (gr. k-18). 13.25 (978-0-673-63394-1(2)); (gr. 1-18). 13.25 (978-0-673-63395-8(0)); (gr. 2-18). 13.25 (978-0-673-63396-5(9)); (gr. 3-18). 13.50 (978-0-673-63397-2(7)); (gr. 4-18). 13.50 (978-0-673-63398-9(5)); (gr. 5-18). 13.50 (978-0-673-63399-6(3)) Addison-Wesley Educational Pubs., Inc.
Scott, Alberto Douglas. Cocina y Ciencia. 2012. 44p. (J). (gr. 3-5). pap. 23.99 (978-958-30-3715-3(X)) Juventud, Editorial ESP. Dist: Lectorum Pubns., Inc.
Se venden Pasteles. (Spanish Early Intervention Levels Ser.). (SPA.). 31.14 (978-0-7362-0333-3(8)) CENGAGE Learning.
Segal, John. Sopa de Zanahoria. Mlawer, Teresa, tr. from ENG. 2006. (Illus.). (gr. -1-k). 12.99 (978-1-933032-13-9(8)) Lectorum Pubns., Inc.
Un Segundo Cumpleanos: 6 Small Books. (Saludos Ser.: Vol. 2). (SPA.). 24p. (gr. 2-3). 31.00 (978-0-7635-9524-1(1)) Rigby Education.
Seki, Sunny. The Tale of the Lucky Cat. Seki, Sunny, illus. 2008. (ENG & SPA., Illus.). 32p. (J). 18.95 (978-0-9669437-9-5(1)) East West Discovery Pr.
Senor Cascaron: Big Book Packages. 2003. (SPA.). 64.95 (978-0-673-58592-9(1)) Celebration Pr.
La Senora Audaz, 6 Pack. (Literatura 2000 Ser.). (SPA.). (gr. 1-2). 28.00 (978-0-7635-1053-4(X)) Rigby Education.
Set of 10 Titles, Vol. 4. (Spanish Early Intervention Levels Ser.). (SPA.). 37.00 (978-0-7362-1180-2(2)) CENGAGE Learning.
Set of 10 Titles: Levels 14-18. (Spanish Early Intervention Levels Ser.). (SPA.). 51.44 (978-0-7362-1184-0(5)) CENGAGE Learning.
Set of 11 Titles, Vol. 3. (Spanish Early Intervention Levels Ser.). (SPA.). 41.15 (978-0-7362-1179-6(9)) CENGAGE Learning.
Set of 11 Titles: Levels 19-20. (Spanish Early Intervention Levels Ser.). (SPA.). 52.03 (978-0-7362-1185-7(3)) CENGAGE Learning.
Set of 14 Titles: Levels 5-7. (Spanish Early Intervention Levels Ser.). (SPA.). 52.10 (978-0-7362-1181-9(0)) CENGAGE Learning.
Set of 20 Titles: Level B. (Spanish Guided Reading Levels Ser.). (SPA.). 75.80 (978-0-7362-1195-6(0)) CENGAGE Learning.
Set of 8 Titles. (Spanish Early Intervention Levels Ser.). (SPA.). 30.80 (978-0-7362-1010-2(5)) CENGAGE Learning.
Set of 9 Titles: Levels 10-13. (Spanish Early Intervention Levels Ser.). (SPA.). 42.09 (978-0-7362-1183-3(7)) CENGAGE Learning.
Set of 9 Titles: Levels 8-9. (Spanish Early Intervention Levels Ser.). (SPA.). 33.75 (978-0-7362-1182-6(9)) CENGAGE Learning.
Seuss, Dr. Un Pez, Dos Peces, Pez Rojo. Canetti, Yanitzia, tr. from ENG. 2005. 64p. (J). 8.99 (978-1-930332-83-6(1)) Lectorum Pubns., Inc.
Sh! Sh! 2003. 23.95 (978-0-673-78060-7(0)) Celebration Pr.
Shaw, Diana. Dias de Terror. (Torre de Papel Ser.). (SPA.). (YA). (gr. 6-18). 8.95 (978-958-04-1504-6(8)) Norma S.A. COL. Dist: Distribuidora Norma, Inc.
Shepherd, Joanne. What I Look Like When I am Scared / Cómo me veo cuando estoy Asustado. 2009. (Let's Look at Feelings / un vistazo a los sentimientos Ser.). (ENG & SPA.). 24p. (gr. k-1). 42.50 (978-1-61514-248-4(7), Editorial Buenas Letras) Rosen Publishing Group, Inc., The.
—What I Look Like When I am Surprised / Cómo me veo cuando estoy Sorprendido. 2009. (Let's Look at Feelings / un vistazo a los sentimientos Ser.). (ENG & SPA.). 24p. (gr. k-1). 42.50 (978-1-61514-249-1(5), Editorial Buenas Letras) Rosen Publishing Group, Inc., The.
Si Camino Por Laz Ciudad... 2003. (SPA.). 35.50 (978-0-8136-8089-7(1)) Modern Curriculum Pr.
Sierra I Fabra, Jordi. El Disco Magico. (SPA.). (YA). 8.95 (978-958-04-6264-4(X)) Norma S.A. COL. Dist: Distribuidora Norma, Inc.
—Martes XXIII. (SPA.). (YA). 9.95 (978-958-04-6025-1(6)) Norma S.A. COL. Dist: Distribuidora Norma, Inc.
Silate, Jennifer. Betsy Ross: Creator of the American Flag. 2009. (Primary Sources of Famous People in American History Ser.). 32p. (gr. 2-3). 47.90 (978-1-60851-657-5(1)) Rosen Publishing Group, Inc., The.
Silver Dolphin en Español Editors. Disney Tesoro de libros de Calcomanias: Disney Sticker Book Treasury, Spanish-Language Edition. 2007. (Illus.). 48p. (J). (978-970-718-447-3(7), Silver Dolphin en Español) Advanced Marketing, S. de R. L. de C. V.
Silver Dolphin en Español Editors, creator. El Gusto. 2007. (Baby Senses (Silver Dolphin en Espanol) Ser.). (Illus.). 10p. (J). (gr. -1). bds. (978-970-718-473-2(6), Silver Dolphin en Español) Advanced Marketing, S. de R. L. de C. V.
—El Olfato. 2007. (Baby Senses (Silver Dolphin en Espanol) Ser.). (Illus.). 10p. (J). (gr. 5). bds. (978-970-718-471-8(X), Silver Dolphin en Español) Advanced Marketing, S. de R. L. de C. V.
—La Vista. 2007. (Baby Senses (Silver Dolphin en Espanol) Ser.). (Illus.). 8p. (J). (gr. -1). bds. (978-970-718-472-5(8), Silver Dolphin en Español) Advanced Marketing, S. de R. L. de C. V.
Silver Dolphin Staff, creator. Disney Caritas Felices: Dumbo. 2007. (Illus.). 8p. (J). (gr. -1). bds. (978-970-718-394-0(2), Silver Dolphin en Español) Advanced Marketing, S. de R. L. de C. V.
Sinon Sinonimo y Horacio Contrario. (SPA.). (J). 12.00 (978-958-02-1238-6(4)) Editorial Voluntad S.A. COL. Dist: Distribuidora Norma, Inc.
La Sirenita. (SPA & ENG., Illus.). (J). (gr. -1-5). pap. 5.95 incl. audio compact disk (978-88-8148-363-1(7)) EMC/Paradigm Publishing.
Skinner, Daphne. Tod el Apretado: Math Matters en Espanol. Nez, John, illus. 2005. (SPA.). 32p. (J). pap. 5.95 (978-1-57565-155-2(6)) Astra Publishing Hse.
Small Book Classroom Set: Green Series. (Rimas Y Risas Ser.). (SPA.). (gr. -1-2). 337.22 (978-1-56334-129-8(8)) CENGAGE Learning.
Small Book Classroom Set: Green Series with addition of Manipulatives. (Rimas Y Risas Ser.). (SPA.). (gr. -1-2). 461.82 (978-0-7362-0882-6(8)) CENGAGE Learning.
Smith, Michael. Thomas the T. Rex: The Journey of a Young Dinosaur to Los Angeles. Roski, Gayle Garner, illus. 2011. (J). (978-0-9832278-4-7(5)) East West Discovery Pr.
Smith, Michael & Roski, Gayle Garner. Thomas the T. Rex: The Journey of a Young Dinosaur to Los Angeles. Roski, Gayle Garner, illus. 2011. (SPA & ENG., Illus.). (J). (978-0-9832278-2-3(9)) East West Discovery Pr.
El Soldadito de Plomo.Tr. of Staunch Tin Soldier. (SPA & ENG., Illus.). (J). (gr. -1-5). pap. 5.95 incl. audio compact disk (978-88-8148-293-1(2)) EMC/Paradigm Publishing.
El Sombrero de Juan: Harry's Hat. 2005. (Take-Home Bks.). (SPA.). (YA). (gr. -1-3). 15.75 (978-0-8215-1203-6(X)) Sadlier, William H. Inc.
El Sombrero de Juan/Harry's Hat. 2005. (Libros en Espanol Para Ninos Ser.). (SPA.). (YA). (gr. -1-1). 11.97 (978-0-8215-0993-7(4)) Sadlier, William H. Inc.
Sommer, Carl. Can You Help Me Find My Smile? Me Puedes Ayudar a Encontrar Mi Sonrisa? Budwine, Greg, illus. 2009. (Another Sommer-Time Story Bilingual Ser.). (SPA & ENG.). 48p. (J). lib. bdg. 16.95 (978-1-57537-150-4(2)) Advance Publishing, Inc.
—Dare to Dream! ¡Atrévete a Soñar! Martinez, Jorge et al, illus. 2009. 48p. (J). 26.95 incl. audio compact disk (978-1-57537-176-4(6)) Advance Publishing, Inc.
—Dream (Sueña) Martinez, Jorge et al, illus. 2009. (Quest for Success Bilingual Ser.). (SPA & ENG.). 104p. (YA). (gr. 6-18). lib. bdg. 14.95 (978-1-57537-226-6(6)) Advance Publishing, Inc.
—Fast Forward(Avance Acelarado) Budwine, Greg, illus. 2009. (Quest for Success Bilingual Ser.). (SPA & ENG.). 104p. (YA). lib. bdg. 14.95 (978-1-57537-227-3(4)) Advance Publishing, Inc.
—The Great Deception(El Gran Engaño) Noé, illus. 2009. (Quest for Success Bilingual Ser.). (ENG & SPA.). 72p. (YA). lib. bdg. 14.95 (978-1-57537-228-0(2)) Advance Publishing, Inc.
—The Great Royal Race(La Gran Carrera Real) Westbrook, Dick, illus. 2009. (Another Sommer-Time Story Bilingual Ser.). (SPA & ENG.). 48p. (J). lib. bdg. 16.95 (978-1-57537-152-8(9)) Advance Publishing, Inc.
—I Am a Lion!(Yo Soy un León!) Budwine, Greg, illus. 2009. (Another Sommer-Time Story Bilingual Ser.). (SPA & ENG.). 48p. (J). lib. bdg. 16.95 (978-1-57537-153-5(7)) Advance Publishing, Inc.
—If Only I Were...(Si Yo Fuese...) James, Kennon, illus. 2009. (Another Sommer-Time Story Bilingual Ser.). (SPA & ENG.). 48p. (J). lib. bdg. 16.95 (978-1-57537-154-2(5)) Advance Publishing, Inc.
—It's Not Fair!(No Es Justo) ! Budwine, Greg, illus. 2009. (Another Sommer-Time Story Bilingual Ser.). (SPA & ENG.). 48p. (J). lib. bdg. 16.95 (978-1-57537-155-9(3)) Advance Publishing, Inc.
—King of the Pond(El Rey Del Estanque) Budwine, Greg, illus. 2009. (Another Sommer-Time Story Bilingual Ser.). (SPA & ENG.). 48p. (J). lib. bdg. 16.95 (978-1-57537-156-6(1)) Advance Publishing, Inc.
—Light Your Candle(Enciende Tu Vela) James, Kennon, illus. 2009. (Another Sommer-Time Story Bilingual Ser.). (SPA & ENG.). 48p. (J). lib. bdg. 16.95 (978-1-57537-157-3(X)) Advance Publishing, Inc.
—The Little Red Train(El Trenecito Rojo) James, Kennon, illus. 2009. (Another Sommer-Time Story Bilingual Ser.). (SPA & ENG.). 48p. (J). lib. bdg. 16.95 (978-1-57537-158-0(8)) Advance Publishing, Inc.
—Lost & Found(Perdida y Encontrada) Budwine, Greg, illus. 2009. (Quest for Success Bilingual Ser.). (ENG & SPA.). 96p. (YA). lib. bdg. 14.95 (978-1-57537-229-7(0)) Advance Publishing, Inc.
—Mayor for a Day: Alcalde Por un Dia. Westbrook, Dick, illus. 2009. (Another Sommer-Time Story Bilingual Ser.). (SPA & ENG.). 48p. (J). lib. bdg. 16.95 (978-1-57537-159-7(6)) Advance Publishing, Inc.
—Miserable Millie(La Pobrecita Mili) Vignolo, Enrique, illus. 2009. (Another Sommer-Time Story Bilingual Ser.). (SPA & ENG.). 48p. (J). lib. bdg. 16.95 (978-1-57537-160-3(X)) Advance Publishing, Inc.
—No Longer a Dilly Dally(Nunca Mas a Troche y Moche) James, Kennon, illus. 2009. (Another Sommer-Time Story Bilingual Ser.). (SPA & ENG.). 48p. (J). lib. bdg. 16.95 (978-1-57537-162-7(6)) Advance Publishing, Inc.
—No One Will Ever Know(Nadie Se Va a Enterar) Westbrook, Dick, illus. 2009. (Another Sommer-Time Story Bilingual Ser.). (SPA & ENG.). 48p. (J). lib. bdg. 16.95 (978-1-57537-163-4(4)) Advance Publishing, Inc.
—Noise! Noise! Noise!(Ruido! Ruido! Ruido!) James, Kennon, illus. 2009. (Another Sommer-Time Story Bilingual Ser.). (SPA & ENG.). 48p. (J). lib. bdg. 16.95 (978-1-57537-161-0(8)) Advance Publishing, Inc.
—Proud Rooster & Little Hen(Gallito Orgulloso y Gallinita) Budwine, Greg, illus. 2009. (Another Sommer-Time Story Bilingual Ser.). (SPA & ENG.). 48p. (J). 16.95 (978-1-57537-164-1(2)) Advance Publishing, Inc.
—The Race(La Carrera) Budwine, Greg, illus. 2009. (Quest for Success Bilingual Ser.). (SPA & ENG.). 104p. (YA). lib. bdg. 14.95 (978-1-57537-230-3(4)) Advance Publishing, Inc.
—The Rebel(El Rebelde) Vignolo, Enrique, illus. 2009. (Quest for Success Bilingual Ser.). (ENG & SPA.). 104p. (J). lib. bdg. 14.95 (978-1-57537-231-0(2)) Advance Publishing, Inc.
—The Revolt(La Revuelta) Budwine, Greg, illus. 2009. (Quest for Success Bilingual Ser.). (SPA & ENG.). 104p. (YA). lib. bdg. 14.95 (978-1-57537-232-7(0)) Advance Publishing, Inc.
—The Roar(El Rugido) Budwine, Greg, illus. 2009. (Quest for Success Bilingual Ser.). (SPA & ENG.). 96p. (YA). lib. bdg. 14.95 (978-1-57537-233-4(9)) Advance Publishing, Inc.
—The Runaway(La Escapeda) Vignolo, Enrique, illus. 2009. (Quest for Success Bilingual Ser.). (SPA & ENG.). 104p. (YA). lib. bdg. 14.95 (978-1-57537-234-1(7)) Advance Publishing, Inc.
—The Sly Fox & the Chicks(El Zorro Astuto y los Pollitos) James, Kennon, illus. 2009. (Another Sommer-Time Story Bilingual Ser.). (SPA & ENG.). 48p. (J). lib. bdg. 16.95 (978-1-57537-166-5(9)) Advance Publishing, Inc.
—Spike the Rebel!(pua, el Rebelde!) Vignolo, Enrique, illus. 2009. (Another Sommer-Time Story Bilingual Ser.). (SPA & ENG.). 48p. (J). lib. bdg. 16.95 (978-1-57537-167-2(7)) Advance Publishing, Inc.
—Three Little Pigs(Los Tres Cerditos) Budwine, Greg & Vignolo, Enrique, illus. 2009. (Another Sommer-Time Story Bilingual Ser.). (SPA & ENG.). 48p. (J). lib. bdg. 16.95 (978-1-57537-168-9(5)) Advance Publishing, Inc.
—Tied up In Knots(Enredados) Budwine, Greg, illus. 2009. (Another Sommer-Time Story Bilingual Ser.). (SPA & ENG.). 48p. (J). lib. bdg. 16.95 (978-1-57537-169-6(3)) Advance Publishing, Inc.
—Time Remote!(El Control Del Tiempo!) Budwine, Greg, illus. 2009. (Another Sommer-Time Story Bilingual Ser.). (SPA & ENG.). 48p. (J). lib. bdg. 16.95 (978-1-57537-170-2(7)) Advance Publishing, Inc.
—The Ugly Caterpillar(La Oruga Fea) Budwine, Greg, illus. 2009. (Another Sommer-Time Story Bilingual Ser.). (SPA &

S

ENG.). 48p. (J). (gr. k-3). lib. bdg. 16.95 *(978-1-57537-171-9(5))* Advance Publishing, Inc.
—You Move You Lose(El Que Se Mueva, Pierde) James, Kennon, illus. 2009. (Another Sommer-Time Story Bilingual Ser.). (SPA & ENG.). 48p. (J). lib. bdg. 16.95 *(978-1-57537-172-6(3))* Advance Publishing, Inc.
—Your Job Is Easy(Tu Trabajo Es Facil) James, Kennon, illus. 2009. (Another Sommer-Time Story Bilingual Ser.). (SPA & ENG.). 48p. (J). lib. bdg. 16.95 *(978-1-57537-173-3(1))* Advance Publishing, Inc.
Sommer, Carl & Aesop, Aesop. Divide to Conquer(Divide y Venceras) Mercado, Jorge, illus. 2009. (Quest for Success Bilingual Ser.). (ENG & SPA.). 72p. (YA). lib. bdg. 14.95 *(978-1-57537-225-9(8))* Advance Publishing, Inc.
—The Silent Scream(El Grito Silencioso) Bogdan, Enache, illus. 2009. (Quest for Success Bilingual Ser.). (SPA & ENG.). 72p. (YA). lib. bdg. 14.95 *(978-1-57537-235-8(5))* Advance Publishing, Inc.
—Tiny Giant(La Gigante Pequeña) Mercado, Jorge, illus. 2009. (Quest for Success Bilingual Ser.). (ENG & SPA.). 72p. (YA). lib. bdg. 14.95 *(978-1-57537-236-5(3))* Advance Publishing, Inc.
Somos Amigos. (Spanish Early Intervention Levels Ser.). (SPA.). 23.10 *(978-1-56334-763-4(6))* CENGAGE Learning.
La sopa Especial: Individual Title, 6 packs. (Literatura 2000 Ser.). (SPA.). (gr. 1-2). 28.00 *(978-0-7635-1054-1(8))* Rigby Education.
Una sorpresa para Monica: 6 Small Books. (Saludos Ser.: Vol. 2). (SPA.). (gr. 3-5). 31.00 *(978-0-7635-1816-5(6))* Rigby Education.
Spanish Board Book Set 800782, 7. 2005. (J). bds. *(978-1-59794-017-7(8))* Environments, Inc.
Spanish Book Set #2 800875, 8 vols. 2005. (J). pap. *(978-1-59794-053-5(4))* Environments, Inc.
Spanish DRA Levels, 7 bks., Set. (Spanish Dra Levels Ser.). (SPA.). Level 1. 26.65 *(978-0-7362-1213-7(2))*Level 10-14. 49.19 *(978-0-7362-1219-9(1))*Level 16-18. 35.41 *(978-0-7362-1220-5(5))*Level 20-28. 68.06 *(978-0-7362-1221-2(3))*Level A. 18.65 *(978-0-7362-1212-0(4))* Vol. 2. 61.00 *(978-0-7362-1214-4(0))* Vol. 3. 49.15 *(978-0-7362-1215-1(9))* Vol. 4. 33.15 *(978-0-7362-1216-8(7))* Vol. 6. 22.20 *(978-0-7362-1217-5(5))* Vol. 8. 29.60 *(978-0-7362-1218-2(3))* CENGAGE Learning.
Spanish-English Books 800878, 4 vols. 2005. (J). bds. *(978-1-59794-056-6(9))* Environments, Inc.
Spanish Guided Reading Levels, 28 bks., Set. (Spanish Guided Reading Levels Ser.). (SPA.). Level C. 105.10 *(978-0-7362-1196-3(9))*Level D. 14.80 *(978-0-7362-1197-0(7))*Level A. 15.40 *(978-0-7362-1194-9(2))*Levels E-F. 46.78 *(978-0-7362-1198-7(5))*Levels G-J. 77.96 *(978-0-7362-1199-4(3))*Levels K-M. 57.22 *(978-0-7362-1200-7(0))* Vol. 2. 52.70 *(978-0-7362-1178-9(0))* CENGAGE Learning.
Spanish Guided Reading Levels Series, 96 vols. (Spanish Early Intervention Levels Ser.). (SPA.). 393.06 *(978-0-7362-1177-2(2))* CENGAGE Learning.
Spanish Paperbacks 800718, 10. 2005. (J). *(978-1-59794-016-0(X))* Environments, Inc.
Spanish TAKS MASTER Reading Grade 3. 2004. *(978-1-57022-464-5(1))* ECS Learning Systems, Inc.
Spanish TAKS MASTER Reading Grade 4. 2004. *(978-1-57022-465-2(X))* ECS Learning Systems, Inc.
Spencer, Mignon. I'm Living My Dream: An Inspirational Rhyme for all Ages in English & Spanish. Mack, Travis, illus. 2008.Tr. of Hago mi sueno Realidad. (ENG & SPA.). 32p. (J). 12.99 *(978-0-9763871-2-1(3))* Solomon's Bks.
Stalcup, La Loncheria. Arroyo, illus. 2008. (SPA & ENG.). 28p. (J). pap. 8.95 *(978-1-60448-006-1(8))* Lectura Bks.
—La Loncheria. Arroyo, illus. 2008. (SPA & ENG.). 28p. (J). 15.95 *(978-1-60448-005-4(X))* Lectura Bks.
Stanley, Diane. El Caballero y la Doncella.Tr. of Gentleman & the Kitchen Maid. (SPA.). 30p. (J). (gr. 3-5). 11.96 *(978-84-261-2876-8(9))* Juventud, Editorial ESP. Dist: Lectorum Pubns., Inc.
Star Bright Books. Eating the Rainbow: Spanish, 1 vol. 2010. (Libro de Comidas de Colores Ser.).Tr. of Eating the Rainbow. (SPA., Illus.). 32p. (J). bds. 6.95 *(978-1-59572-225-6(4))* Star Bright Bks., Inc.
—Eating the Rainbow: Spanish/English, 1 vol. 2010. (Libro de Comidas de Colores/Colorful Food Bks.). (ENG., Illus.). 16p. (J). bds. 6.95 *(978-1-59572-203-4(3))* Star Bright Bks., Inc.
Steinsiek, Sabra Brown. The Tale of the Pronghorned Cantaloupe. Chilton, Noel Dora, illus. 2013. 48p. 24.95 *(978-1-936744-11-4(2)*, Rio Grande Bks.) LPD Pr.
Sterling Publishing Co., Inc. Things That Go/Cosas Que Se Mueven. 2013. (Say & Play Ser.). (ENG & SPA., Illus.). 28p. (J). (— 1). bds. 6.95 *(978-1-4549-1042-8(9))* Sterling Publishing Co., Inc.
Street, Sesame. Elmo's Guessing Game about Colors/Elmo y Su Juego de Adivinar Los Colores. 2006. (Elmo's Guessing Game about Colors / Elmo y Su Juego de Adivinar Los Colores Ser.). (SPA, ENG & MUL., Illus.). 10p. (J). (gr. -1 — 1). bds. 5.95 *(978-0-87358-905-5(X))* Cooper Square Publishing Llc.
Student Pack. (Cuentacuentos Ser.). (SPA.). (gr. k-18). 83.31 *(978-1-56334-798-6(9))* CENGAGE Learning.
Suen, Anastasia. Hábitat para la Humanidad (Habitat for Humanity) 2009. (Organizaciones de ayuda (Helping Organizations) Ser.). (SPA.). 24p. (gr. 2-2). 42.50 *(978-1-60851-145-7(6)*, Editorial Buenas Letras) Rosen Publishing Group, Inc., The.
Suenos y Fantasias. (Nuevos Horizontes Ser.). (SPA.). (J). (gr. 2). No. 1. wbk. ed. 8.95 *(978-1-56014-510-3(2))*No. 2. wbk. ed. 8.95 *(978-1-56014-511-0(0))* Santillana USA Publishing Co., Inc.
Suenos y Fantasias: Evaluations, Grade 2. (Nuevos Horizontes Ser.). (SPA.). (J). 22.50 *(978-1-56014-512-7(9))* Santillana USA Publishing Co., Inc.
Suenos y Fantasias No. 1: Student Anthology. (Nuevos Horizontes Ser.). (SPA.). (J). (gr. 2). 14.95 *(978-1-56014-508-0(0))* Santillana USA Publishing Co., Inc.
Suenos y Fantasias No. 2: Student Anthology. (Nuevos Horizontes Ser.). (SPA.). (J). (gr. 2). 16.95 *(978-1-56014-509-7(9))* Santillana USA Publishing Co., Inc.
Super Classroom Set. (Elefonetica Ser.). (SPA.). (gr. 1-2). 939.56 *(978-0-7362-0782-9(1))* CENGAGE Learning.
Superflaco! (Spanish Early Intervention Levels Ser.). (SPA.). 28.38 *(978-0-7362-0843-7(7))* CENGAGE Learning.
Susaeta, Equipo. La bella durmiente - Sleeping beauty. 2011. (Cuentos Bilingües Ser.). (SPA & ENG.). 34p. (J). (gr. k-2). 8.99 *(978-84-305-2453-2(3))* Susaeta Ediciones, S.A. ESP. Dist: Independent Pubs. Group.
—Blancanieves - Snow White. 2011. (Cuentos Bilingües Ser.). (SPA & ENG.). 34p. (J). (gr. k-2). 8.99 *(978-84-305-2454-9(1))* Susaeta Ediciones, S.A. ESP. Dist: Independent Pubs. Group.
—LAS BRUJAS. (SPA.). (J). 3.48 *(978-84-305-9406-1(X))* Susaeta Ediciones, S.A. ESP. Dist: AIMS International Bks., Inc.
—Leo y Veo, las Hadas.Tr. of I Read & See, the Fairies. (SPA.). 24p. (J). 3.48 *(978-84-305-9408-5(6))* Susaeta Ediciones, S.A. ESP. Dist: AIMS International Bks., Inc.
—Leo y Veo, los Gnomos.Tr. of I Read & See, the Elves. (SPA.). 24p. (J). 3.48 *(978-84-305-9407-8(8))* Susaeta Ediciones, S.A. ESP. Dist: AIMS International Bks., Inc.
—LOS GIGANTES. (SPA.). 24p. (J). 3.48 *(978-84-305-9409-2(4))* Susaeta Ediciones, S.A. ESP. Dist: AIMS International Bks., Inc.
TAKS Reading Preparation Grade 3 - Spanish. 2004. (SPA.). per., wbk. ed. *(978-1-932524-91-8(6))* Region 4 Education Service Ctr.
TAKS Reading Preparation Grade 4 - Spanish. 2004. (SPA.). stu. ed., per., wbk. ed. *(978-1-932524-92-5(4))* Region 4 Education Service Ctr.
TAKS Reading Preparation Grade 5 - Spanish. 2004. (SPA.). stu. ed., per., wbk. ed. *(978-1-932524-93-2(2))* Region 4 Education Service Ctr.
El Taller de Pinatas. 2003. (SPA.). 23.95 *(978-0-673-78082-9(1))* Celebration Pr.
Los Tamales. 2003. 23.95 *(978-0-673-77132-2(6))* Celebration Pr.
Tan Set. (Dias y Dias de Poesia Ser.). (SPA.). (gr. -1-6). 207.23 *(978-1-56334-271-4(5)*, DI8631); 293.52 *(978-1-56334-272-1(3)*, DI8632) CENGAGE Learning.
Taylor, Mildred D. Lloro por la Tierra. (SPA.). (YA). 10.95 *(978-958-04-1838-2(1))* Norma S.A. COL. Dist: AIMS International Bks., Inc.
Taylor, Trace. Afghanistan. 2010. pap. 39.62 *(978-1-61541-135-1(6))* American Reading Co.
Taylor, Trace & SáNchez, LucíA M. Afghanistan. 2010. pap. 39.62 *(978-1-61541-158-0(5))* American Reading Co.
Taylor, Trace & Sánchez, Lucía M. Ballenas: Whales. 2015. (2G Animales Marinos Ser.). (SPA.). 12p. (J). (gr. k-2). pap. 8.00 *(978-1-61541-280-8(8))* American Reading Co.
—Pingüinos de la AntáRtida: Antarctic Penguins. 2015. (2G Animales Marinos Ser.). (ENG & SPA.). 12p. (J). (gr. k-2). pap. 8.00 *(978-1-61541-274-7(3))* American Reading Co.
Taylor, Trace & Sanchez, Lucia M. Vamos de acampada (Let's Go Camping) 2011. (Lugares adonde voy Ser.). (SPA.). 16p. pap. 39.62 *(978-1-61541-418-5(5))* American Reading Co.
Taylor, Trace, et al. Vamos de Acampada: Let's Go Camping. 2010. (2Y Lugares Adonde Voy Ser.). (SPA.). 16p. (J). (gr. k-2). pap. 9.60 *(978-1-61541-417-8(7))* American Reading Co.
El tesoro de Tono: Individual Title Six-Packs. (Literatura 2000 Ser.). (SPA.). (gr. 2-3). 33.00 *(978-0-7635-1252-1(4))* Rigby Education.
Tesoro Escondido, 6, Pack. (Chiquilibros Ser.). (SPA.). (gr. k-1). 23.00 *(978-0-7635-8589-1(0))* Rigby Education.
Theme Library, 10 vols. (High Point Ser.). (gr. 6-12). Level C. 74.53 *(978-0-7362-0983-0(2))*Level B. (Illus.). 91.19 *(978-0-7362-0951-9(4))* CENGAGE Learning.
Thompson, Lauren. Cuaquito (Little Quack) Anderson, Derek, illus. 2010. (SPA.). 34p. (J). (gr. -1-1). bds. 8.99 *(978-1-4169-9894-5(2)*, Libros Para Ninos) Libros Para Ninos.
Thompson, Michael. Los Otros Osos/ the Other Bears (Spanish Edition) (Spanish & English Edition) 2013. (ENG., Illus.). 40p. (J). 16.99 *(978-1-59572-644-5(6))* Star Bright Bks., Inc.
La tia Rosalia: Individual Title Six-Packs. (Literatura 2000 Ser.). (SPA.). (gr. 1-2). 28.00 *(978-0-7635-1079-4(3))* Rigby Education.
Tibo, Gilles. Corre, Nicolas, Corre! Rioja, Alberto Jimenez, tr. from FRE. St. Aubin, Bruno, illus. 2009. (SPA & ENG.). 32p. (J). (gr. 2-4). pap. 6.99 *(978-1-933032-57-3(X))* Lectorum Pubns., Inc.
Tiburones. 2003.Tr. of Sharks. (SPA.). 23.95 *(978-0-673-78080-5(5))* Celebration Pr.
El Tiempo: Individual Title Six-Packs. (Chiquilibros Ser.). (SPA.). (gr. k-1). 23.00 *(978-0-7635-8588-4(2))* Rigby Education.
El tigre Comilon, 6, Pack. (Literatura 2000 Ser.). (SPA.). (gr. -1-1). 28.00 *(978-0-7635-1007-7(6))* Rigby Education.
Time for Bed: Individual Title Six-Packs. (Chiquilibros Ser.). (gr. k-1). 23.00 *(978-0-7635-0425-0(4))* Rigby Education.
A Tina le gustan las Herramientas: Lap Book. (Pebble Soup Exploraciones Ser.). (SPA.). 16p. (gr. -1-18). 21.00 *(978-0-7578-1686-4(X))* Rigby Education.
A Tina le gustan las Herramientas: Small Book. (Pebble Soup Exploraciones Ser.). (SPA.). 16p. (gr. -1-18). 5.00 *(978-0-7578-1726-7(2))* Rigby Education.
Titanes de la Literatura Infantil.Tr. of Infant Literature. (SPA.). (J). *(978-968-15-0412-0(7))* Editores Mexicanos Unidos.
A Tocar! Individual 6-packs. 2003. 23.95 *(978-0-673-78075-1(9))* Celebration Pr.
Toconayo. 2003. 28.95 *(978-0-673-78101-7(1))* Celebration Pr.
Todas las Mananas: Lap Book. (Pebble Soup Exploraciones Ser.). 16p. (gr. -1-18). 21.00 *(978-0-7578-1673-4(8))* Rigby Education.
Todas las Mananas: Small Book. (Pebble Soup Exploraciones Ser.). 16p. (gr. -1-18). 5.00 *(978-0-7578-1713-7(0))* Rigby Education.
Todo cambia Interactive Packages: El agua Cambia. (Pebble Soup Exploraciones Ser.). (SPA.). (gr. -1-18). 52.00 *(978-0-7578-5263-3(7))* Rigby Education.
Todo cambia Interactive Packages: Los Sentimientos. (Pebble Soup Exploraciones Ser.). (SPA.). (gr. -1-18). 52.00 *(978-0-7578-5266-4(1))* Rigby Education.
Todo Rojo. (Spanish Early Intervention Levels Ser.). (SPA.). 21.30 *(978-0-7362-0803-1(8))* CENGAGE Learning.
Todos Enojados: Social/Emotional Lap Book. (Pebble Soup Exploraciones Ser.). (SPA.). (gr. -1-18). 16.00 *(978-0-7578-1788-5(2))* Rigby Education.
Todos Somos Amigos: Big Book Packages. 2003. 64.95 *(978-0-673-58593-6(X))* Celebration Pr.
Tolstoi, Leo. La Muerte de Ivan Ilich. (SPA.). 6.25 *(978-958-04-2126-9(9))* Norma S.A. COL. Dist: Distribuidora Norma, Inc.
Tomas: Individual Title Six-Packs. (Literatura 2000 Ser.). (SPA.). (gr. 1-2). 28.00 *(978-0-7635-1055-8(6))* Rigby Education.
Tomas's Tops. 2003. 23.95 *(978-0-673-78131-4(3))* Celebration Pr.
Torres, Jennifer. Finding the Music: En Pos de la Música, 1 vol. Alarcão, Renato, illus. 2015.Tr. of En Pos de la Música. (ENG.). 40p. (J). 18.95 *(978-0-89239-291-9(6))* Lee & Low Bks., Inc.
Tostada: Matching English 6-packs. 2003. 23.95 *(978-0-673-57565-4(9))* Celebration Pr.
El Traje Perdido. (Spanish Early Intervention Levels Ser.). (SPA.). 31.14 *(978-0-7362-0335-7(4))* CENGAGE Learning.
Trapp, Kyrima. Que? Como? Por Que?: Los Colores. 2007. (Illus.). 16p. (J). (gr. -1). *(978-970-718-491-6(4)*, Silver Dolphin en Español) Advanced Marketing, S. de R. L. de C. V.
Los tres Bobos: Individual Title, 6 Packs. (Literatura 2000 Ser.). (SPA.). (gr. 2-3). 33.00 *(978-0-7635-1274-3(5))* Rigby Education.
Los tres Cerditos: Lap Book. (Pebble Soup Exploraciones Ser.). (SPA.). 16p. (gr. -1-18). 21.00 *(978-0-7578-1674-1(6))* Rigby Education.
Los Tres Cerditos Desobedientes: Individual 6-packs. 2003. 23.95 *(978-0-673-77155-1(5))* Celebration Pr.
Los tres Magos: Individual Title, 6 Packs. (Literatura 2000 Ser.). (SPA.). (gr. 2-3). 33.00 *(978-0-7635-1275-0(3))* Rigby Education.
Los Trillizos: Individual Title, 6 Packs. (Literatura 2000 Ser.). (SPA.). (gr. 2-3). 33.00 *(978-0-7635-1253-8(2))* Rigby Education.
Los Trompos De Tomas, 6 packs. 2003. 23.95 *(978-0-673-78069-0(4))* Celebration Pr.
Tu, Alice. A Fair Is Fun, 6 vols., Set. 2003. (Phonics Readers 1-36 Ser.). (ENG.). 8p. (gr. k-1). pap. 29.70 *(978-0-7368-3203-8(3))* Capstone.
Tullet, Hervé. Presiona Aquí (Press Here Spanish Language Edition) Press Here Spanish Language Edition. 2012. (ENG., Illus.). 56p. (J). (gr. -1-3). 15.99 *(978-1-4521-1287-9(8))* Chronicle Bks. LLC.
Twin Sisters(r) Staff. Kids Learn Spanish Handlebox- 4 books. 2009. 12.99 *(978-1-59922-110-6(1))* Twin Sisters IP, LLC.
Twine, Alice. Puppies/Cachorros. 2009. (Baby Animals/Animales bebé Ser.). (ENG & SPA.). 24p. (gr. 1-1). 42.50 *(978-1-61511-507-5(2)*, Editorial Buenas Letras) Rosen Publishing Group, Inc., The.
Two Volcanoes. 2003. 28.95 *(978-0-673-78117-8(8))* Celebration Pr.
Los uniformes Amarillos: Individual Title, 6 Packs. (Literatura 2000 Ser.). (SPA.). (gr. 2-3). 33.00 *(978-0-7635-1276-7(1))* Rigby Education.
Uno, dos, tres y Cuatro. (Spanish Early Intervention Levels Ser.). (SPA.). 23.10 *(978-1-56334-792-4(X))* CENGAGE Learning.
Urraca, Maraca, Urraca: Little Books, Level 1, Vol. 13. 2003. (Fonolibros Ser.). 25.50 *(978-0-7652-0090-7(2))* Modern Curriculum Pr.
Usen la Cabeza: Social/Emotional Lap Book. (Pebble Soup Exploraciones Ser.). (SPA.). (gr. -1-18). 16.00 *(978-0-7578-1784-7(X))* Rigby Education.
Valentin, Karen. Allie's World: Abuela & Abuelo Move: Abuela & Abuelo Move. 2009. 32p. 6.95 *(978-1-60349-021-4(3)*, Marimba Bks.) Just Us Bks., Inc.
Vamos! (Spanish Early Intervention Levels Ser.). (SPA.). 21.30 *(978-0-7362-0809-3(7))* CENGAGE Learning.
Vamos De Viaje. 2003. (SPA.). 23.95 *(978-0-673-77179-7(2))* Celebration Pr.
Vamos, Samantha R. The Cazuela That the Farm Maiden Stirred. López, Rafael & López, Rafael, illus. 2013. (ENG.). 32p. (J). (gr. k-3). pap. 8.95 *(978-1-58089-243-8(4))* Charlesbridge Publishing, Inc.
Vaughan, Richard. Levantemos el Cielo, Level 3. 2003. (Dejame Leer Ser.). (SPA., Illus.). (J). (gr. -1-3). 4.50 *(978-0-673-36332-9(5)*, Good Year Bks.) Celebration Pr.
—El Universo, Level 2. 2003. (Dejame Leer Ser.). (SPA., Illus.). (J). (gr. -1-3). 6.50 *(978-0-673-36329-9(5)*, Good Year Bks.) Celebration Pr.
Vaughn, Inés. Potatoes/Papas. 2009. (Native Foods of Latin America / Alimentos indígenas de Latino América Ser.). (ENG & SPA.). 24p. (gr. 2-3). 42.50 *(978-1-61514-798-4(5)*, Editorial Buenas Letras) Rosen Publishing Group, Inc., The.
Vázquez-Figueroa, Alberto. Anaconda. (SPA.). 400p. 12.95 *(978-84-01-46951-0(1))* Plaza & Janes Editories, S.A. ESP. Dist: Distribooks, Inc.
El Veliz De los Recuerdos. 2003. 28.95 *(978-0-673-78088-1(0))* Celebration Pr.
El venado de Mario. (Spanish Early Intervention Levels Ser.). (SPA.). 28.38 *(978-0-7362-0837-6(2))* CENGAGE Learning.
El venado y el Cocodrilo: Individual Title Six-Packs. (Literatura 2000 Ser.). (SPA.). (gr. 1-2). 28.00 *(978-0-7635-1080-0(7))* Rigby Education.
Veo, veo Colas. (Spanish Early Intervention Levels Ser.). (SPA.). 23.10 *(978-1-56334-766-5(0))* CENGAGE Learning.
Vestimos con Orgullo: 6 Small Books. (Saludos Ser.: Vol. 2). (SPA.). (gr. 3-5). 31.00 *(978-0-7635-1769-4(0))* Rigby Education.
El viaje de la abuelita Jenny: 6 Small Books. (Saludos Ser.: Vol. 3). (SPA.). (gr. 3-5). 31.00 *(978-0-7635-1783-0(6))* Rigby Education.
Viento Bravo. (Spanish Early Intervention Levels Ser.). (SPA.). 28.38 *(978-0-7362-0845-1(3))* CENGAGE Learning.
Vingan A Ver Mi Rancho! Individual 6-packs. 2003. 23.95 *(978-0-673-78066-9(X))* Celebration Pr.
Viva la Musica! (Spanish Early Intervention Levels Ser.). (SPA.). 31.14 *(978-0-7362-0331-9(1))* CENGAGE Learning.
Vjva el Midsommar! (Saludos Ser.: Vol. 1). (SPA.). 24p. (gr. 2-3). 31.00 *(978-0-7635-5719-5(6))* Rigby Education.
Vjva el Midsommar! 6 Small Books. (Saludos Ser.: Vol. 1). (SPA.). 24p. (gr. 2-3). 31.00 *(978-0-7635-9519-7(5))* Rigby Education.
Las Vocales: Big Book Packages. 2003. 64.95 *(978-0-673-58588-2(3))* Celebration Pr.
Vogel, Elizabeth. ¡A hacer ejercicio! (Let's Exercise) 2009. (Limpieza y salud todo el día (Clean & Healthy All Day Long) Ser.). (SPA.). 24p. (gr. 1-1). 37.50 *(978-1-61514-291-0(6)*, Editorial Buenas Letras) Rosen Publishing Group, Inc., The.
—¡A lavarse las manos! (Washing My Hands) 2009. (Limpieza y salud todo el día (Clean & Healthy All Day Long) Ser.). (SPA.). 24p. (gr. 1-1). 37.50 *(978-1-61514-292-7(4)*, Editorial Buenas Letras) Rosen Publishing Group, Inc., The.
—¡Al agua patos! (Taking My Bath) 2009. (Limpieza y salud todo el día (Clean & Healthy All Day Long) Ser.). (SPA.). 24p. (gr. 1-1). 37.50 *(978-1-61514-294-1(0)*, Editorial Buenas Letras) Rosen Publishing Group, Inc., The.
—¡el cuidado de tu cabello! (Taking Care of My Hair) 2009. (Limpieza y salud todo el día (Clean & Healthy All Day Long) Ser.). (SPA.). 24p. (gr. 1-1). 37.50 *(978-1-61514-295-8(9)*, Editorial Buenas Letras) Rosen Publishing Group, Inc., The.
Volver a Empezar: 6 Softcover Books. (Saludos Ser.: Vol. 3). (SPA.). (gr. 3-5). 31.00 *(978-0-7635-2079-3(9))* Rigby Education.
Wall Chart. 2003. (gr. 1-18). suppl. ed. 81.90 *(978-0-673-59355-9(X))* Addison-Wesley Educational Pubs., Inc.
Washington, Joi. Wasps. 2011. (Predator Bugs Ser.). 16p. pap. 39.62 *(978-1-61541-352-2(9))* American Reading Co.
Wax, Wendy A. Musica en Casa: Libro de Cuentos. de Alba, Ariette, tr. 2005. (Disney Princess Ser.). (SPA., Illus.). 38p. (J). (gr. -1-7). incl. audio compact disk *(978-970-718-289-9(X)*, Silver Dolphin en Español) Advanced Marketing, S. de R. L. de C. V.
The Wedding: Individual Title Six-Packs. (Literatura 2000 Ser.). (gr. k-1). 28.00 *(978-0-7635-0071-9(2))* Rigby Education.
Weinhold, Angela. El Bosque. 2007. (Junior (Silver Dolphin) Ser.). (Illus.). 16p. (J). (gr. -1). *(978-970-718-493-0(0)*, Silver Dolphin en Español) Advanced Marketing, S. de R. L. de C. V.
Werther, Scott P. Powerboats / Lanchas Motorizadas. 2009. (Extreme Machines / Máquinas extremas Ser.). (ENG & SPA.). 24p. (gr. 1-2). 42.50 *(978-1-61512-448-0(9)*, Editorial Buenas Letras) Rosen Publishing Group, Inc., The.
What's in the Box? 2003. 28.95 *(978-0-673-78114-7(3))* Celebration Pr.
The White Horse: Individual Title Six-Packs. (Literatura 2000 Ser.). (gr. 2-3). 33.00 *(978-0-7635-0244-7(8))* Rigby Education.
Wilde, Oscar. El Fantasma de Canterville: Y otros Cuentos. (SPA.). (YA). 8.75 *(978-958-04-6746-5(3))* Norma S.A. COL. Dist: Distribuidora Norma, Inc.
Willems, Mo. El Conejito Knuffle: Un Cuento Aleccionador. rev. ed. 2007. (Knuffle Bunny Ser.). (SPA., Illus.). 40p. (J). (gr. -1-k). pap. 7.99 *(978-1-4231-0567-1(2)*, Hyperion Books for Children) Disney Publishing Worldwide.
Williams, Rozanne. Who Lives Here? 2017. (Learn-To-Read Ser.). (ENG., Illus.). (J). pap. 3.49 *(978-1-68310-178-9(2))* Pacific Learning, Inc.
Williamson, Melanie. El magnifico plan de Lobo/ Wolf's Magnificent Plan. Williamson, Melanie, illus. 2008. (SPA., Illus.). 29p. 20.95 *(978-84-263-6837-9(9))* Vives, Luis Editorial (Edelvives) ESP. Dist: Baker & Taylor Bks.
With addition of Elefonetica & Pan y Canela. (De Canciones A Cuentos Ser.). (SPA.). (gr. 1-18). 1413.46 *(978-0-7362-0704-1(X))*; (gr. 2-18). 1261.41 *(978-0-7362-0706-5(6))* CENGAGE Learning.
A With Addition of Pan y Canela Collection. (Cuentacuentos Ser.). (SPA.). (gr. k-18). 1238.34 *(978-1-56334-801-3(2))* CENGAGE Learning.
A With Addition of Pan y Canela Little Reader Collection. (De Canciones A Cuentos Ser.). (SPA.). (gr. k-18). 870.44 *(978-1-56334-571-5(4))* CENGAGE Learning.
With Addition of Pan y Canela Little Reader Collection B. (De Canciones A Cuentos Ser.). (SPA.). (gr. 1-18). 860.93 *(978-1-56334-993-5(0))* CENGAGE Learning.
With addition of Pan y Canela Little Reader Collection C. (De Canciones A Cuentos Ser.). (SPA.). (gr. 2-18). 929.66 *(978-0-7362-0442-2(3))* CENGAGE Learning.
Witte, Anna. El Fandango de Lola. Archer, Micha, illus. 2011. 32p. (J). (gr. k-5). 9.99 *(978-1-84686-359-2(7))* Barefoot Bks., Inc.
Word Pocket with Letras Moviles. (SPA.). (gr. 2-18). 7.40 *(978-0-7362-0853-6(4))* CENGAGE Learning.
Y Ahora, Que Leo? 2003. (J). 28.95 *(978-0-673-78098-0(8))* Celebration Pr.
Yo Me Visto Solo, 6-packs. 2003. (J). 23.95 *(978-0-673-77140-7(7))* Celebration Pr.
Yo quiero Ser. (Spanish Early Intervention Levels Ser.). (SPA.). 23.10 *(978-1-56334-782-5(2))* CENGAGE Learning.
Yo Vivo Aqui: Big Book Packages. 2003. (J). 64.95 *(978-0-673-58586-8(7))* Celebration Pr.
Your Friend, Jorge. 2003. 28.95 *(978-0-673-78118-5(6))* Celebration Pr.
El yoyo de Mayito. (Spanish Early Intervention Levels Ser.). (SPA.). 21.30 *(978-0-7362-0829-1(1))* CENGAGE Learning.
Zepeda, Gwendolyn. Level up / Paso de Nivel. Baeza Ventura, Gabriela, tr. from ENG. Torrecilla, Pablo, illus. 2012. (SPA & ENG.). (J). (gr. 5-9). 16.95 *(978-1-55885-747-6(8)*, Piñata Books) Arte Publico Pr.
Zepeda, Gwendolyn & Ventura, Gabriela Baeza. Growing up with Tamales: Los Tamales de Ana. Ward, April, illus. 2008. (SPA & ENG.). 32p. (J). (gr. -1-2). 16.95 *(978-1-55885-493-2(2)*, Piñata Books) Arte Publico Pr.
Ziegler, Argentina Palacios, tr. Dora y la Princesa de la Nieve (Dora Saves the Snow Princess) Aikins, Dave, illus. 2008. (Dora la Exploradora Ser.). (SPA.). 24p. (J). (gr. -1-2). pap. 3.99 *(978-1-4169-5870-3(3)*, Libros Para Ninos) Libros Para Ninos.
Zimmermann, Natalie. Un Principe para Lila. (Torre de Papel Ser.). (SPA., Illus.). (J). 7.95 *(978-958-04-5051-1(X))* Norma S.A. COL. Dist: Distribuidora Norma, Inc.
Un Zoologico, 6 Packs. (Literatura 2000 Ser.). (SPA.). (gr. -1-1). 28.00 *(978-0-7635-1008-4(4))* Rigby Education.
6-Pack Collection: Includes 180 books (30 6-Packs) 2003. (J). 769.95 *(978-0-7652-0558-2(0))* Modern Curriculum Pr.

SPANISH LITERATURE

Pascal, Francine. Rebelde con Causa. Orig. Title: Taking Charge. (SPA.). 136p. (J). 6.95 *(978-84-272-3796-4(0))* Molino, Editorial ESP. Dist: AIMS International Bks., Inc.

SPANISH MAIN

Malam, John. Do You Want to Be a Pirate? 2015. (Do You Want to Be... Ser.). (Illus.). 32p. (gr. 3-6). 28.50 *(978-1-909645-36-3(2))* Book Hse. GBR. Dist: Black Rabbit Bks.

—You Wouldn't Want to... Be a Pirate's Prisoner! Antram, David, illus. rev. ed. 2012. (ENG.). 32p. (J). lib. bdg. 29.00 *(978-0-531-27502-3(7))* Scholastic Library Publishing.

SPANISH MAIN—FICTION

Batson, Wayne Thomas. Isle of Fire, 1 vol. 2009. (ENG.). 352p. (J). pap. 9.99 *(978-1-4003-1512-3(3),* Tommy Nelson) Nelson, Thomas Inc.

—Isle of Swords, 1 vol. 2008. (ENG.). 352p. (J). pap. 9.99 *(978-1-4003-1363-1(5),* Tommy Nelson) Nelson, Thomas Inc.

Henty, George. Under Drake's Flag: A Tale of the Spanish Main. 2011. 316p. pap. 19.95 *(978-1-61179-182-2(0))* Fireship Pr.

SPANISH POETRY—COLLECTIONS

Polo, Eduardo. Chamario. 2005. (SPA., Illus.). 48p. (J). 8.99 *(978-980-257-278-6(0))* Ekare, Ediciones VEN. Dist: Iaconi, Mariuccia Bk. Imports.

SPARRING

see Boxing

SPARROWS

Amstutz, Lisa J. House Sparrows. 2015. (Backyard Birds Ser.). (ENG., Illus.). 24p. (J). (gr. -1-2). lib. bdg. 27.32 *(978-1-4914-6109-9(8),* 129002, Capstone Pr.) Capstone.

Klukow, Mary Ellen. A Sparrow's Disappearing Home. Pinilla, Albert, illus. 2019. (Animal Habitats at Risk Ser.). (ENG.). 24p. (J). (gr. 1-3). pap. 9.99 *(978-1-68152-490-0(2),* 11076) Amicus.

Thornhill, Jan. The Triumphant Tale of the House Sparrow, 1 vol. 2018. (ENG., Illus.). 44p. (J). (gr. 4-7). 18.95 *(978-1-77306-006-4(6))* Groundwood Bks. CAN. Dist: Publishers Group West (PGW).

Vail, Grace. A Bird Watcher's Guide to Sparrows, 1 vol. 2015. (Backyard Bird Watchers Ser.). (ENG., Illus.). 32p. (J). (gr. 2-3). pap. 11.50 *(978-1-4824-3911-3(5),* d7d4ec44-73e6-40eb-9d67-e2cb8bdcd137) Stevens, Gareth Publishing LLLP.

Webster, Christine. Sparrows. 2007. (Backyard Animals Ser.). (Illus.). 24p. (J). (gr. -1-3). lib. bdg. 24.45 *(978-1-59036-681-3(6))* Weigl Pubs., Inc.

—Sparrows. Hudak, Heather C., ed. 2007. (Backyard Animals Ser.). (Illus.). 24p. (J). (gr. -1-3). pap. 8.95 *(978-1-59036-682-0(4))* Weigl Pubs., Inc.

SPARROWS—FICTION

Albright, Ann. Samuel Sparrow & the Tree of Light. Albright, Ann, illus. 2nd ed. 2003. (ENG., Illus.). 28p. (J). pap. *(978-0-9715472-5-4(4))* Ascension Lutheran Church.

Bischoff, Marlene A. Charming Chirp. 2013. 26p. pap. 13.95 *(978-1-4796-0132-5(2))* TEACH Services, Inc.

Dalton, Sherry A. Do Indians Eat Soup? 2011. 32p. pap. 24.95 *(978-1-4560-7463-0(6))* America Star Bks.

Doney, Meryl. The Very Worried Sparrow. Hansen, Gaby, illus. 2008. (J). (gr. -1-3). 12.95 *(978-0-8198-8038-3(8))* Pauline Bks. & Media.

Ebers, Georg. A Question. 2005. 96p. pap. 10.95 *(978-1-4218-0443-9(3),* 1st World Library - Literary Society) 1st World Publishing, Inc.

English, Frank. Honey. 2019. (ENG., Illus.). 80p. (J). (gr. 2-3). pap. *(978-1-913071-00-4(6))* Andrews UK Ltd.

Ferry, Beth. Sealed with a Kiss. Taliec, Olivier, illus. 2019. (ENG.). 32p. (J). (gr. -1-3). 19.99 *(978-0-06-247577-0(0),* HarperCollins) HarperCollins Pubs.

Flounders, Anne; DuFalla, ed. Sumac & the Magic Lake. DuFalla, Anita, illus. 2004. (Reader's Theater Content-Area Concepts Ser.). (ENG.). (J). (gr. 1-2). 5.00 net. *(978-1-4108-2291-8(5),* A22915) Benchmark Education Co.

Glass, Stephen. Sara Sparrow. 2006. (J). per. 14.95 *(978-1-59858-065-5(5))* Dog Ear Publishing, LLC.

Grandmother Sparrow: Copyright TXu1-280-697. 2007. (J). *(978-0-9792641-0-8(3))* Shelle, Carole Creative Arts.

Griffin, Molly Beth. Silhouette of a Sparrow. 2013. (Milkweed Prize for Children's Literature Ser.). (Illus.). 208p. pap. 12.00 *(978-1-57131-704-9(X))* Milkweed Editions.

Hicks, Constance. Florabelle Bunny & the Sparrow. 2011. 24p. pap. 12.99 *(978-1-4490-9969-5(6))* AuthorHouse.

Himes, John. Beauty. 2012. 24p. pap. 17.99 *(978-1-4772-9440-6(6))* AuthorHouse.

Howell, Julie Ann. The Tooth Be Told. Cotton, Sue Lynn, illus. 2011. 24p. 18.95 *(978-1-61493-061-7(9))* Peppertree Pr., The.

Kasbarian, Lucine. The Greedy Sparrow: An Armenian Tale, 0 vols. Zaikina, Maria, illus. 2012. (ENG.). 32p. (J). (gr. -1-3). 17.99 *(978-0-7614-5821-0(2),* 9780761458210, Two Lions) Amazon Publishing.

Kassel, Roger de. Mr P & the Bully Birds. 2013. (ENG., Illus.). 12p. pap. 8.75 *(978-1-78035-677-8(3),* Fastprint Publishing) Upfront Publishing Ltd. GBR. Dist: Printondemand-worldwide.com.

—Mr P & the Red Poppy. 2013. (ENG., Illus.). 22p. pap. 8.75 *(978-1-78035-707-2(9),* Fastprint Publishing) Upfront Publishing Ltd. GBR. Dist: Printondemand-worldwide.com.

Kerven, Rosalind. Sparrow, the Crow & the Pearl. Williamson, Melanie, illus. 2005. (ENG.). 24p. (J). lib. bdg. 23.65 *(978-1-59646-754-5(1))* Dingles & Co.

Kircher, Jean. Bertie Can't Fly. 2007. 24p. pap. 24.95 *(978-1-4241-8477-4(0))* America Star Bks.

Lampley, David Gerald. Shorty's Dilemm. 2011. 74p. pap. 19.95 *(978-1-4560-4189-2(4))* America Star Bks.

Larson, Michael J. The Easter Sparrows. Schmidt, Janine Ringdahl, illus. 2010. (ENG.). 28p. pap. 10.95 *(978-1-4497-0012-6(8),* WestBow Pr.) Author Solutions, LLC.

Lewis, C. A. Harold the Sparrow & His Bellybutton. 2013. 48p. pap. *(978-1-4602-1117-5(0))* FriesenPress.

Maguire, Thomas Aquinas. A Growling Place. 2007. (Illus.). 32p. (J). (gr. -1-3). 16.95 *(978-1-894965-74-3(4))* Simply Read Bks. CAN. Dist: Ingram Publisher Services.

Mitchell, Ronnie & May, Leslie. Catching the Wind: Beanie's First Flight. 2011. 24p. pap. 12.79 *(978-1-4567-5613-0(3))* AuthorHouse.

Moore, Sherry. The Crab Is Back in Town. 2007. (ENG.). 100p. (J). per. *(978-1-894936-78-1(7))* Saga Bks.

Narváez, Concha López & Concha, López Narváez. El Cernicalo Porque. Salmeron, Rafael, illus. (Pajaros de Cuento Coleccion). (SPA.). 84p. (YA). (gr. 5-8). *(978-84-241-7927-4(7))* Everest Editora ESP. Dist: Lectorum Pubns., Inc.

Otenbaker, Audrey Lee. God's Jewel. 2009. 48p. (J). pap. 17.95 *(978-1-4327-3340-7(0))* Outskirts Pr., Inc.

Paiva, Teresa & Pinto, Helena Rebelo. My Friend, Sleep. 2011. (Illus.). 68p. pap. 35.25 *(978-1-4567-8990-9(2))*; 60p. (gr. 1-2). pap. 14.95 *(978-1-4567-8952-7(X))* AuthorHouse.

Pennypacker, Sara. Sparrow Girl. Tanaka, Yoko, illus. 2009. (ENG.). 40p. (J). (gr. -1-3). 17.99 *(978-1-4231-1187-0(7))* Little, Brown Bks. for Young Readers.

Pugliano-Martin, Carol. The Very Mean King & el rey Malo: 6 English, 6 Spanish Adaptations. 2011. (ENG & SPA.). (J). 75.00 net. *(978-1-4108-5648-7(8))* Benchmark Education Co.

Santilli, Shirley. Trouble in Treeville. Santilli Wolfinger, Lorrie, illus. 2013. 42p. 19.99 *(978-0-9910962-0-6(7))* Aperture Pr., LLC.

Sargent, Dave & Sargent, David M. Cindy Sparrow: Respect the Property of Others, 19 vols., Vol. 6. Lenoir, Jane, illus. 2003. (Feather Tales Ser.: 6). 42p. (J). pap. 10.95 *(978-1-56763-730-4(2))*; 2nd ed. lib. bdg. 20.95 *(978-1-56763-729-8(9))* Ozark Publishing.

Sharp, Euan. Diggedy Dozer in Treetop Troubles. 2008. 34p. 15.95 *(978-1-4357-0982-9(9))* Lulu Pr., Inc.

Thompson, Anne. Arrow Sparrow. 2009. (Illus.). 32p. pap. *(978-1-84549-369-1(9),* Swirl) arima publishing.

Urbain, Christophe, photos by. Emma in Paris. 2013. (ENG., Illus.). 56p. (J). (gr. k). 17.95 *(978-1-59270-139-1(6))* Enchanted Lion Bks., LLC.

Von Michaelis, Carol. Magpie Grows Up. 2012. 16p. pap. 15.99 *(978-1-4772-6115-6(X))* AuthorHouse.

Wittenbach, Jennie. Little Stories for Little Folks. 2011. 36p. pap. 21.99 *(978-1-4628-8818-4(6))* Xlibris Corp.

SPASTIC PARALYSIS

see Cerebral Palsy

SPEAKING

see Debates and Debating; Public Speaking; Rhetoric; Voice

SPECIAL EFFECTS (CINEMATOGRAPHY)

see Cinematography—Special Effects

SPECIE

see Money

SPECIMENS, PRESERVATION OF

see Taxidermy

SPECTACLES

see Eyeglasses

SPECTERS

see Apparitions; Ghosts

SPEECH

see also Language and Languages; Phonetics; Voice

Beaumont, Susanna. Baby Senses Speech: Look! I'm Talking! 2005. (Baby Senses Ser.). (Illus.). 16p. (gr. -1-k). bds. *(978-1-905051-52-6(2))* Make Believe Ideas.

Carillo, Christina Martin. Come Smile with Me. 2011. 40p. pap. 24.95 *(978-1-4560-8297-0(3))* America Star Bks.

Dow, Kathy & Dow, Danica, illus. Low-Down Dirty Words. 2004. 28p. (J). *(978-0-9749886-0-3(X))* KayStar Publishing.

First Experiences - Going to the Doctor. 2005. (J). per. 8.95 *(978-1-59566-130-2(1))* QEB Publishing Inc.

Galvin, Kathleen M., et al. The Basics of Speech: Learning to Be a Competent Communicator. 4th ed. 2004. (Ntc: Basics of Speech Ser.). (ENG., Illus.). 606p. (gr. 6-12). stu. ed. 99.00 *(978-0-07-861620-4(4),* 0078616204) McGraw-Hill Higher Education.

Hodson, Sarah E. Wh- Questions. 2012. (Illus.). 7p. (J). *(978-0-7606-1382-5(6))* LinguiSystems, Inc.

Holzer, Angela. Fat Freddy. Tucker, Barclay, illus. 2009. 36p. (J). lib. bdg. 8.99 *(978-0-9821563-4-6(0))* Good Sound Publishing.

—Gooey Gummy Geese. Smith, Ashley, illus. 2008. (ENG.). (J). lib. bdg. 8.99 *(978-0-9821563-1-5(6))* Good Sound Publishing.

—My Dog, Eddie. Funk, Debbie, illus. 2009. 36p. (J). lib. bdg. 8.99 *(978-0-9821563-5-3(9))* Good Sound Publishing.

Kawa, Katie. The Most Powerful Presidential Words, 1 vol. 2019. (Words That Shaped America Ser.). (ENG.). 32p. (gr. 4-5). pap. 11.50 *(978-1-5382-4795-2(X),* a7a51070-e634-4726-b426-d350f2e5ccce) Stevens, Gareth Publishing LLLP.

Lenny's Lost Spots. 2005. (J). per. 8.95 *(978-1-59566-131-9(X))* QEB Publishing Inc.

Libal, Joyce. Finding My Voice: Youth with Speech Impairment. 2003. (Youth with Special Needs Ser.). (Illus.). 127p. (YA). pap. 14.95 *(978-1-4222-0422-1(7))* Mason Crest.

—Speech Impairment. Albers, Lisa et al, eds. 2014. (Living with a Special Need Ser.: 16). 128p. (J). (gr. 7-18). 25.95 *(978-1-4222-3043-5(0))* Mason Crest.

Life Cycles - from Seed to Sunflower. 2005. (J). per. 8.95 *(978-1-59566-145-6(X))* QEB Publishing Inc.

Life Cycles: From Caterpillar to Butterfly. 2005. (J). per. 8.95 *(978-1-59566-129-6(8))* QEB Publishing Inc.

LoGiudice, Carolyn & McConnell, Nancy. Room 28 a Social Language Program. 2004. (YA). per. 25.95 *(978-0-7606-0530-1(0))* LinguiSystems, Inc.

MagneTalk Match-Up Adventure Kit (with Barrier) Gb181. 2006. (J). 59.99 *(978-1-58650-616-2(1))* Super Duper Pubns.

MagneTalk Match-Up Adventure Kit (without Barrier) Gb182. 2006. (J). 59.99 *(978-1-58650-653-7(6))* Super Duper Pubns.

Matheson, Hughena. The 10 Most Historic Speeches. 2007. 14.99 *(978-1-55448-478-2(2))* Scholastic Library Publishing.

McCutcheon, Randall, et al. Glencoe Speech, Student Edition. 3rd ed. 2004. (Ntc: Speech Comm Matters Ser.). (ENG., Illus.). 605p. (gr. 9-12). stu. ed. 123.68 *(978-0-07-861618-1(2),* 0078616182) McGraw-Hill Education.

O'Connor, Frances. Frequently Asked Questions about Stuttering, 1 vol. 2007. (FAQ: Teen Life Ser.). (ENG., Illus.). 64p. (YA). (gr. 5-6). lib. bdg. 37.13 *(978-1-4042-1931-1(5),* 790d4745-9848-45a5-9e7f-a3298be78962) Rosen Publishing Group, Inc., The.

Rembisz, Linda. Count with Balloons. Liebeck, Lisa, illus. 2009. 28p. pap. 12.49 *(978-1-4490-1989-1(7))* AuthorHouse.

Sleeper, Amanda A. Speech & Language. Chudler, Eric H., ed. 2006. (Gray Matter Ser.). (ENG., Illus.). 123p. (gr. 9-12). lib. bdg. 35.00 *(978-0-7910-8952-1(5),* P114491, Facts On File) Infobase Holdings, Inc.

Sparks, Sarah Constance. Omfg: Owning My Future Greatness. 2010. 56p. pap. 21.99 *(978-1-4520-2684-8(X))* AuthorHouse.

SPEECH, LIBERTY OF

see Freedom of Speech

SPEECH THERAPY

Buesser, Jeanne. He Talks Funny: A Heartwarming Story of Everyday Life. 2010. 28p. 12.49 *(978-1-4520-2595-7(9))* AuthorHouse.

Cottrell, Sue. Can I Tell You about Stammering? A Guide for Friends, Family & Professionals. Khan, Sophie, illus. 2013. (Can I Tell You About... ? Ser.). 48p. (C). pap. 15.95 *(978-1-84905-415-7(0),* 694233) Kingsley, Jessica Pubs. GBR. Dist: Hachette UK Distribution.

—Can I Tell You about Stuttering? A Guide for Friends, Family & Professionals. Khan, Sophie, illus. 2013. (Can I Tell You About... ? Ser.). 48p. (C). pap. 15.95 *(978-1-84905-435-5(5),* 694276) Kingsley, Jessica Pubs. GBR. Dist: Hachette UK Distribution.

Flath, Camden. Therapy Jobs in Educational Settings: Speech, Physical, Occupational & Audiology. 2010. (New Careers for the 21st Century Ser.). (Illus.). 64p. (YA). (gr. 7-18). pap. 9.95 *(978-1-4222-2047-4(8))*; lib. bdg. 22.95 *(978-1-4222-1826-6(0))* Mason Crest.

Gustafson, Monica. Quick Make Artic Activities. 2006. (J). per. 27.95 *(978-0-7606-0656-8(0))* LinguiSystems, Inc.

Kaufman, Nancy R. Kaufman Speech Praxis Workout Book. 2005. (Illus.). 127p. (J). pap. *(978-0-9765497-1-0(9))* Northern Speech Services.

Libal, Joyce. Finding My Voice: Youth with Speech Impairment. 2004. (Youth with Special Needs Ser.). (Illus.). 128p. (YA). 24.95 *(978-1-59084-738-1(5))* Mason Crest.

—Finding My Voice: Youth with Speech Impairment. 2003. (Youth with Special Needs Ser.). (Illus.). 127p. (YA). pap. 14.95 *(978-1-4222-0422-1(7))* Mason Crest.

Sargisson, Lisa. Quick Connect Articulation 1. 2006. (J). 15.95 *(978-0-7606-0661-2(7))* LinguiSystems, Inc.

Sarrgisson, Lisa. Quick Connect Articulaton 2. 2006. (J). 15.95 *(978-0-7606-0662-9(5))* LinguiSystems, Inc.

Simon, Samantha. Speech Pathologists & Audiologists. 2017. (Careers in Healthcare Ser.: Vol. 13). (ENG., Illus.). 64p. (YA). (gr. 7-12). 23.95 *(978-1-4222-3806-6(7))* Mason Crest.

Wojcicki, Ronda M. Speech Class Rules: An Introduction to Speech Therapy for Children. 2007. (Illus.). 32p. (J). 19.95 *(978-0-9794102-0-8(7))* Speech Place Publishing, The.

SPEECH THERAPY—FICTION

Carillo, Christina. Life Can Be A Smile. 2010. 30p. pap. 21.99 *(978-1-4500-2848-6(9))* Xlibris Corp.

Feiffer, Jules. Bark, George. 2004. 29.95 *(978-1-55592-700-4(9))* Weston Woods Studios, Inc.

Gutman, Dan. Miss Laney Is Zany! 2010. (My Weird School Daze Ser.: 8). (J). lib. bdg. 14.75 *(978-0-606-10112-7(8))* Turtleback.

—My Weird School Daze #8: Miss Laney Is Zany! Paillot, Jim, illus. 2010. (My Weird School Daze Ser.: 8). (ENG.). 112p. (J). (gr. 1-5). pap. 4.99 *(978-0-06-155415-5(4),* HarperCollins) HarperCollins Pubs.

Patterson, Nancy Ruth. The Shiniest Rock of All. 2009. 84p. pap. 8.95 *(978-1-4401-1620-9(2))* iUniverse, Inc.

SPEED

Adamson, Heather. Animals with Speed. 2010. (Amicus Readers. Our Animal World (Level 1) Ser.). (ENG.). 24p. (J). (gr. k-2). lib. bdg. 25.65 *(978-1-60753-007-7(4),* 17162) Amicus.

Armentrout, David & Armentrout, Patricia. Speed Demons. 2008. (Illus.). 32p. (J). 28.50 *(978-1-60472-305-2(X))* Rourke Educational Media.

Baer, T. H. Measuring Speed, 1 vol. 2015. (Measure It! Ser.). (ENG.). 24p. (J). (gr. 1-2). pap. 9.15 *(978-1-4824-3864-2(X),* b2ce9707-3ff2-42eb-9dac-58b68f1e19df) Stevens, Gareth Publishing LLLP.

Barkan, Joanne. What Is Velocity? (Rookie Read-About Science: Physical Science: Previous Editions) 2005. (Rookie Read-About Science Ser.). (ENG., Illus.). 32p. (J). (gr. 1-2). pap. 4.95 *(978-0-516-24664-2(X),* Children's Pr.) Scholastic Library Publishing.

Brunner- Jass, Renata. Field of Play: Measuring Distance, Rate, & Time. 2013. (IMath Ser.). (ENG., Illus.). 48p. (J). (gr. 5-6). pap. 13.26 *(978-1-60357-510-2(3))* Norwood Hse. Pr.

Butterfield, Moira, et al. Record Breakers & Other Speed Machines. (ENG., Illus.). 32p. (J). mass mkt. 8.99 *(978-0-590-24653-8(4))* Scholastic, Inc.

Caes, Charles J. Discovering the Speed of Light, 1 vol. 2011. (Scientist's Guide to Physics Ser.). (ENG., Illus.). 112p. (YA). (gr. 7-7). lib. bdg. 39.80 *(978-1-4488-4699-3(4),* 1b8657cc-8041-42be-8f09-06206583a90f) Rosen Publishing Group, Inc., The.

—How Do We Know the Speed of Light? 2009. (Great Scientific Questions & the Scientists Who Answered Them Ser.). 112p. (gr. 7-12). 63.90 *(978-1-61513-207-2(4))* Rosen Publishing Group, Inc., The.

Dintiman, George Blough. Speed Improvement for Young Athletes: How to Sprint Faster in Your Sport in 30 Workouts. rev. ed. 2006. (Illus.). 153p. pap. 17.95 *(978-0-938074-26-7(1))* National Assn. of Speed & Explosion.

Enz, Tammy. Outrunning Bullets: Superman & the Science of Speed. 2016. (Superman Science Ser.). (ENG., Illus.). 32p. (J). (gr. 3-9). lib. bdg. 27.99 *(978-1-5157-0915-2(9),* 132213, Stone Arch Bks.) Capstone.

Frederick, Shane. Speed Training for Teen Athletes: Exercises to Take Your Game to the Next Level. 2012. (Sports Training Zone Ser.). (ENG.). 48p. (gr. 4-5). pap. 47.70 *(978-1-4296-8487-3(9))* Capstone.

Gardner, Robert. Bicycle Science Fair Projects, 1 vol. 2015. (Prize-Winning Science Fair Projects Ser.). (ENG.). 128p. (gr. 7-7). lib. bdg. 38.93 *(978-0-7660-7016-5(6),* 94c3e29f-cf18-4fcb-ac51-f24b10357a7c) Enslow Publishing, LLC.

—How Fast Is Fast? Science Projects with Speed, 1 vol. 2014. (Hot Science Experiments Ser.). (ENG.). 48p. (gr. 3-4). 26.93 *(978-0-7660-6615-1(0),* 29456ae8-f1b0-4655-be51-d3e2a910adb8); pap. 11.53 *(978-0-7660-6616-8(9),* 07c9a8fc-9197-4b00-bcf4-8b7e6f45bbef, Enslow Elementary) Enslow Publishing, LLC.

Gordon, Sharon. Fast, Slow, 1 vol. (Just the Opposite Ser.). (ENG.). 24p. (gr. k-1). 2008. pap. 9.23 *(978-0-7614-3281-4(7),* f218e495-952f-454b-bcd1-27ce65deb44a) 2003. (Illus.). lib. bdg. 25.50 *(978-0-7614-1570-1(X),* 26f23ffd-f5e2-4020-8fcb-f4b5419afa79, Cavendish Square) Cavendish Square Publishing LLC.

—Rapido, Lento / Fast, Slow, 1 vol. 2008. (Exactamente lo Opuesto / Just the Opposite Ser.). (ENG & SPA., Illus.). 24p. (gr. k-1). lib. bdg. 25.50 *(978-0-7614-2447-5(4),* c9a1db90-b7b1-4bb7-8403-86a7dd0b0861) Cavendish Square Publishing LLC.

—Rapido, Lento (Fast, Slow), 1 vol. 2008. (Exactamente lo Opuesto (Just the Opposite) Ser.). (SPA., Illus.). 24p. (gr. k-1). lib. bdg. 25.50 *(978-0-7614-2367-6(2),* 8e3a2a49-9830-474b-97b7-88c66e82fba2) Cavendish Square Publishing LLC.

Greathouse, Lisa. Farm Animals: Classifying & Sorting. rev. ed. 2011. (Mathematics in the Real World Ser.). (ENG.). 32p. (gr. k-1). pap. 9.99 *(978-1-4333-3442-9(9))* Teacher Created Materials, Inc.

—Wild Animals, Level K. rev. ed. 2011. (Mathematics in the Real World Ser.). (ENG.). 32p. (gr. k-1). pap. 9.99 *(978-1-4333-3443-6(7))* Teacher Created Materials, Inc.

Gregoire, Maryellen. Moving Fast, 1 vol. 2011. (Wonder Readers Emergent Level Ser.). (ENG.). 16p. (gr. -1-1). (J). pap. 6.25 *(978-1-4296-8060-8(1),* 118378); pap. 35.94 *(978-1-4296-8130-8(6))* Capstone. (Capstone Pr.).

Group/McGraw-Hill, Wright. Speed: Magazine Anthology: Level 6, 6 vols. (Comprehension Strand Ser.). (gr. 4-8). 54.00 *(978-0-322-06040-1(0))* Wright Group/McGraw-Hill.

Harrison, Paul. Speed Machines. (Up Close Ser.). 24p. (gr. 3-3). 2009. 47.90 *(978-1-60854-705-0(1))* 2007. (ENG., Illus.). (J). lib. bdg. 28.93 *(978-1-4042-4222-7(8),* 0cc7297d-c4a0-451f-b09e-2535c2a0696c) Rosen Publishing Group, Inc., The. (PowerKids Pr.).

Herrington, Lisa M. Built for Speed: Kangaroos! Cheetahs! Lizards! (Rookie Star: Extraordinary Animals) (Library Edition) 2018. (Rookie Star Ser.). (ENG., Illus.). 32p. (J). (gr. 2-3). lib. bdg. 25.00 *(978-0-531-23089-3(9),* Children's Pr.) Scholastic Library Publishing.

Holden, Pam. So Fast, 1 vol. Webb, Philip, illus. 2009. (Red Rocket Readers Ser.). (ENG.). 16p. (gr. -1-1). pap. *(978-1-877363-20-7(0),* Red Rocket Readers) Flying Start Bks.

Hyde, Natalie. Speeding up, Slowing Down. 2014. (Motion Close-Up Ser.). (ENG., Illus.). 24p. (J). (-1). *(978-0-7787-0530-7(7))* Crabtree Publishing Co.

Ipcizade, Catherine. The Fastest Animals. 2011. (Extreme Animals Ser.). (ENG.). 24p. (gr. k-1). pap. 41.70 *(978-1-4296-6377-9(4),* Capstone Pr.) Capstone.

KociendaGenevieve. FAST: THE NEED FOR SPEED HIGH BEGINNING BOOK WITH ONLINE ACCESS, 1 vol. 2014. (ENG., Illus.). 24p. pap., E-Book, E-Book 9.50 *(978-1-107-68068-5(9))* Cambridge Univ. Pr.

Kramer, Nash. What Goes Fastest? 2012. (Level B Ser.). (ENG., Illus.). 16p. (J). (gr. k-2). pap. 7.95 *(978-1-927136-19-5(9),* 19421) RiverStream Publishing.

Lanier, Wendy Hinote. The Science of Speed, 1 vol. 2016. (Super-Awesome Science Ser.). (ENG., Illus.). 48p. (J). (gr. 4-8). lib. bdg. 35.64 *(978-1-68078-249-3(5),* 22099) ABDO Publishing Co.

Lindeen, Mary. Speed. 2017. (Beginning-To-Read Ser.). (ENG.). 32p. (J). (gr. k-2). pap. 13.26 *(978-1-68404-099-5(X))*; (Illus.). 22.60 *(978-1-59953-880-8(6))* Norwood Hse. Pr.

Loughran, Donna & Brunner-Jass, Renata. Field of Play: Measuring Distance, Rate, & Time. 2013. (IMath Ser.). (Illus.). 48p. (J). (gr. 5-6). lib. bdg. 23.94 *(978-1-59953-571-5(8))* Norwood Hse. Pr.

Mapua, Jeff. Extreme Motorsports, 1 vol. 2015. (Sports to the Extreme Ser.). (ENG., Illus.). 48p. (J). (gr. 5-6). 33.47 *(978-1-4994-3549-8(5),* d6a61ed0-27e4-4924-8c97-758d1e50445b, Rosen Central) Rosen Publishing Group, Inc., The.

Meyer, Eileen R. Who's Faster? Animals on the Move. Bergum, Constance Rummel, illus. 2012. (J). *(978-0-87842-592-1(6))* Mountain Pr. Publishing Co., Inc.

Minden, Cecilia. Fast & Slow. 2016. (21st Century Basic Skills Library: Animal Opposites Ser.). (ENG., Illus.). 24p. (J). (gr. k-3). 26.35 *(978-1-63470-472-4(X),* 207619) Cherry Lake Publishing.

Orme, David. Speed. 2008. (Trailblazers Ser.). (ENG., Illus.). 36p. pap. *(978-1-84167-647-0(0))* Ransom Publishing Ltd.

—Speed. 2009. (Fact to Fiction Ser.). (Illus.). 36p. (J). 16.95 *(978-0-7569-9283-5(4))*; pap. 6.95 *(978-0-7891-7906-7(7))* Perfection Learning Corp.

Owen, Ruth. Speed Machines, 1 vol., 1. 2014. (DIY for Boys Ser.). (ENG.). 32p. (J). (gr. 4-4). 30.17 *(978-1-4777-6274-5(4),* 7bc6d818-5cbe-4785-b5c6-17b21ce228ea, PowerKids Pr.) Rosen Publishing Group, Inc., The.

—Top 10 Fastest. 2010. (Crabtree Contact Ser.). (ENG., Illus.). 32p. (J). (gr. 3-6). pap. *(978-0-7787-7509-6(7),* 1308102); lib. bdg. *(978-0-7787-7488-4(0),* 1308102) Crabtree Publishing Co.

—Top 10 Slowest. 2010. (ENG., Illus.). 32p. (J). pap. *(978-0-7787-7511-9(9))*; lib. bdg. *(978-0-7787-7490-7(2))* Crabtree Publishing Co.

Parham, Jerrill. Shockwave: Thrills & Spills. 2007. (Shockwave: the Human Experience Ser.). (ENG., Illus.). 36p. (J). (gr. 3-5). 25.00 *(978-0-531-17762-4(9),* Children's Pr.) Scholastic Library Publishing.

Paris, Stephanie. Vroom! Speed & Acceleration, 1 vol. 2nd rev. ed. 2013. (TIME for KIDS(r): Informational Text Ser.). (ENG.).

S

64p. (gr. 4-8). pap. 14.99 *(978-1-4333-4938-6(8))*; (Illus.). (J). lib. bdg. 31.96 *(978-1-4333-7437-1(4))* Teacher Created Materials, Inc.

Parker, Steve & Kelly, Miles. Speed. Kelly, Richard, ed. 2017. (Illus.). 48p. (J). pap. 9.95 *(978-1-84810-532-4(0))* Miles Kelly Publishing, Ltd. GBR. Dist: Parkwest Pubns., Inc.

Rossiter, Brienna. Fast & Slow. 2019. (Opposites Ser.). (ENG., Illus.). 16p. (J). (gr. k-1). 25.64 *(978-1-64185-345-3(X)*, 164185345X, Focus Readers) North Star Editions.

Roza, Greg. Severe Storms: Measuring Velocity, 1 vol. (Math for the REAL World Ser.). 32p. (gr. 5-5). 2009. (ENG., Illus.). pap. 10.00 *(978-1-4042-6085-6(4)*, 0b31cbfb-c655-4696-96cc-52fbb0356a3b) 2009. 47.90 *(978-1-60851-365-9(3)*, PowerKids Pr.) 2006. (ENG., Illus.). (YA). lib. bdg. 28.93 *(978-1-4042-3366-9(0)*, 8be3ba0f-3d3f-44cf-a60b-868b2ada3ce4) Rosen Publishing Group, Inc., The.

Schuh, Mari C. Shockwave: Full Speed Anead. 2007. (Shockwave: Earth & Physical Science Ser.). (ENG., Illus.). 36p. (J). (gr. 4-8). 25.00 *(978-0-531-17792-1(0)*, Children's Pr.) Scholastic Library Publishing.

Schwartz, Heather E. The Science of a Race Car: Reactions in Action. 2010. (Action Science Ser.). (ENG.). 32p. (gr. 3-4). pap. 47.70 *(978-1-4296-5074-8(5)*, Capstone Pr.) Capstone.

Starke, John. Speed Machines: Mission Xtreme 3D. 2004. (Mission Xtreme 3D Ser.). (Illus.). 18p. (J). pap. 5.95 *(978-1-902626-50-5(8))* Red Bird Publishing GBR. Dist: Weatherhill, Inc.

Sullivan, Navin. Speed, 1 vol. 2007. (Measure Up! Ser.). (ENG., Illus.). 48p. (gr. 4-4). lib. bdg. 34.07 *(978-0-7614-2325-6(7)*, 4134ce9b-6ecf-4306-8497-746ff7ef782a) Cavendish Square Publishing LLC.

Tan, Richard. Fast & Slow, 1 vol. 2015. (Rosen REAL Readers: STEM & STEAM Collection). (ENG.). 8p. (gr. k-1). pap. 5.46 *(978-1-4994-9652-9(4)*, 16ce65ec-e0e8-4f23-9a30-1a6fdbd0ee7c, Rosen Classroom) Rosen Publishing Group, Inc., The.

Vilardi, Debbie & Vilardi, Deborah. Amazing Human Feats of Speed. 2018. (Superhuman Feats Ser.). (ENG., Illus.). 32p. (J). (gr. 4-6). lib. bdg. 28.65 *(978-1-5435-4121-2(6)*, 139075, Capstone Pr.) Capstone.

Weakland, Mark. Zoom! Wile E. Coyote Experiments with Speed & Velocity. Sordo, Paco, illus. 2017. (Wile E. Coyote, Physical Science Genius Ser.). (ENG.). 32p. (J). (gr. 3-5). lib. bdg. 31.32 *(978-1-5157-3734-6(9)*, 133678, Capstone Pr.) Capstone.

Wells, Robert E. What's Faster Than a Speeding Cheetah? 2012. (J). *(978-1-61913-153-8(6))* Weigl Pubs., Inc.

What Is Fast?, 6 Packs. (gr. 1-2). 22.00 *(978-0-7635-9104-5(1))* Rigby Education.

Woodford, Chris. Speed, 1 vol. 2012. (Measure up Math Ser.). (ENG., Illus.). 32p. (J). (gr. 4-4). 29.27 *(978-1-4339-7445-8(2)*, b6390704-0b5b-4ad8-9847-f3a29d1a8b62); pap. 11.50 *(978-1-4339-7446-5(0)*, e29cd7cf-e33b-4b49-b255-ab701f7d0c49) Stevens, Gareth Publishing LLLP. (Gareth Stevens Learning Library).

Woods, Bob. Wild Racers, 1 vol. 2010. (Racing Mania Ser.). (ENG.). 48p. (gr. 4-4). lib. bdg. 34.07 *(978-0-7614-4389-6(4)*, 84e59eb8-835a-4c9c-b9c8-4a92797537e2) Cavendish Square Publishing LLC.

World Book, Inc. Staff, contrib. by. Biggest, Fastest, Smallest, Slowest! 2017. (J). *(978-0-7166-7946-2(9))* World Bk., Inc.

Zubek, Adeline. Fast or Slow?, 1 vol. 2019. (All about Opposites Ser.). (ENG.). 24p. (gr. k-k). 24.27 *(978-1-5382-3716-8(4)*, 60fb01b2-8fb8-4e67-96a0-20fcc3052a0f) Stevens, Gareth Publishing LLLP.

SPEED, SUPERSONIC

see Aerodynamics, Supersonic

SPELEOLOGY

see Caves

SPELLERS

Cundy, David. Animals Spell Love. Cundy, David, illus. 2016. (ENG., Illus.). 40p. 15.95 *(978-1-56792-586-9(3))* Godine, David R. Pub.

Siede Preis Photography (Firm) Staff & Brian Warling Photography (Firm) Staff, contrib. by. First Words. 2003. (Lift-A-Flap Ser.). (Illus.). 12p. (J). bds. 12.98 *(978-0-7853-8624-7(6)*, 7188400) Publications International, Ltd.

SPELLING

see names of languages with the subdivision Spelling, e.g. English Language—Spelling

The Battle of Bowling Street: Level 4, 6 vols. (Fluency Strand Ser.). (gr. 4-8). 45.00 *(978-1-4045-1224-5(1))* Wright Group/McGraw-Hill.

Diaz-Cubero, Jose H. Practicas de Ortografia: 6 Grado. (SPA & ENG.). (J). (gr. 6). 9.95 *(978-84-357-0124-2(7)*, CPR94) Ediciones y Distribuciones Codice, S.A. ESP. Dist: Continental Bk. Co., Inc.

Disney Staff, contrib. by. Write, Slide & Learn Disney Princess: Spelling. 2011. (Disney Write, Slide & Learn Ser.). 12p. (J). 9.99 *(978-1-74183-852-7(5))* Hinkler Bks. Pty. Ltd. AUS. Dist: Ideals Pubns.

Dr Awkward: Level 6, 6 vols. (Fluency Strand Ser.). (gr. 4-8). 45.00 *(978-1-4045-1239-9(X))* Wright Group/McGraw-Hill.

Heinrichs, Ann. Spelling Rules. 2019. (English Grammar Ser.). (ENG.). 32p. (J). (gr. 2-5). lib. bdg. 35.64 *(978-1-5038-3248-0(1)*, 213007) Child's World, Inc, The.

Herbold, Marvin. Marvin Teaches Fingerspelling. 2003. (YA). cd-rom 19.95 *(978-0-9752933-1-0(8))* Institute for Disabilities Research & Training, Inc.

Hinkler Studios Staff., ed. Disney Princess: Counting & Spelling. 2011. 12p. 9.99 *(978-1-74183-871-8(1))* Hinkler Bks. Pty. Ltd. AUS. Dist: Ideals Pubns.

Holt, Rinehart and Winston Staff. Elements of Language: Spelling - Grade 6. 2003. (Elements of Language Ser.). 13.86 *(978-0-03-056326-3(7))* Holt McDougal.

HOP, LLC. Hooked on Spelling. 2006. 99.99 *(978-1-933863-98-6(6))*; 64.99 *(978-1-60143-000-7(0))*; 24.99 *(978-1-60143-001-4(9))* HOP, LLC.

Howard, Cheryl Lee. Daisy Dustbunny Seven Days a Week: Learning to spell the days of the week is fun with Daisy Dustbunny. 2011. 24p. pap. 24.95 *(978-1-4560-6777-9(X))* America Star Bks.

Just Around the Block. (J). (gr. k-2). 75.00 *(978-0-669-13448-3(1))*; pap. 9.90 *(978-0-669-15288-3(9))* Houghton Mifflin Harcourt School Pubs.

Learning Company Books Staff, ed. Reader Rabbit Spelling Challenge. 2004. (Illus.). 64p. (J). (gr. 1-18). pap. *(978-0-7630-7740-2(2))*; (gr. 2-18). pap. *(978-0-7630-7741-9(0))* Magma

Marcel Meringue: Level 2, 6 vols. (Fluency Strand Ser.). (gr. 4-8). 45.00 *(978-1-4045-1212-2(8))* Wright Group/McGraw-Hill.

More Spelling. 2004. (Help with Homework Ser.). 32p. (J). (gr. 1-4). wbk. ed. 3.99 *(978-1-904596-27-2(9))* Byeway Bks.

Night Mare Trip: Level 5, 6 vols. (Fluency Strand Ser.). (gr. 4-8). 45.00 *(978-1-4045-1230-6(6))* Wright Group/McGraw-Hill.

Olo: Level 6, 6 vols. (Fluency Strand Ser.). (gr. 4-8). 45.00 *(978-1-4045-1237-5(3))* Wright Group/McGraw-Hill.

Once, Twice, Boom: Level 7, 6 vols. (Fluency Strand Ser.). (gr. 4-8). 45.00 *(978-1-4045-1240-5(3))* Wright Group/McGraw-Hill.

Pulse- Fun with Vocabulary & Spelling. 2006. cd-rom 4.99 *(978-1-60245-041-7(2))* GDL Multimedia, LLC.

Rechtschreibung und Wortkunde. (Duden-Schuelerduden Ser.). (GER.). 384p. (YA). (gr. 4-18). pap. *(978-3-411-05175-5(2))* Bibliographisches Institut & F. A. Brockhaus AG DEU. Dist: International Bk. Import Service, Inc.

Rieder, E. & Toth, M. Das ABC-Haus: Arbeitsheft 1. (Illus.). 64p. pap. *(978-3-12-675645-7(X))* Klett Lerntraining bei PONS DEU. Dist: International Bk. Import Service, Inc.

—Das ABC-Haus: Schuelerbuch. (Illus.). 96p. (J). pap. *(978-3-12-675644-0(1))* Klett Lerntraining bei PONS DEU. Dist: International Bk. Import Service, Inc.

—Das ABC-Haus. Arbeitsheft 2: Deutsch als Fremd- oder Zweitsprache mit wenigen oder keinen Vorkenntnissen. (Illus.). 64p. pap. *(978-3-12-675648-8(4))* Klett Lerntraining bei PONS DEU. Dist: International Bk. Import Service, Inc.

School Zone Publishing. Spelling Puzzles. 2003. (Language Arts Ser.). (ENG.). cd-rom 19.99 *(978-1-58947-914-2(9))* School Zone Publishing Co.

Schwartz, Linda. Conquer Spelling: Word Lists, Roles, & Activities to Help Kids Become Spelling Heros. Scott, Kelly, ed. Armstrong, Beverly & Grayson, Rick, illus. 2003. 112p. (J). pap. 13.99 *(978-0-88160-362-0(7)*, LW-420, Learning Works, The) Creative Teaching Pr., Inc.

Spelling & Vocabulary, Set. 2004. (gr. 2). 38.95 *(978-0-7403-0219-0(1)*, Horizons) Alpha Omega Pubns., Inc.

Spelling Words & Sentences. 2011. (Spelling by Sound & Structure Ser.). 87p. (J). (gr. 2-8). pap. 4.35 *(978-0-7399-0708-5(5))* Rod & Staff Pubs., Inc.

Spelling Workout. (J). Bk. A. 3rd ed. (gr. 1). 11.95 net. *(978-0-8136-2815-8(6))*Bk. F. 3rd ed. (gr. 6). 11.95 net. *(978-0-8136-2820-2(2))*Bk. G. 3rd ed. (gr. 7). 11.95 net. *(978-0-8136-2821-9(0))*Bk. H. 3rd ed. (gr. 8). 12.50 net. *(978-0-8136-2847-9(4))*Bk. H. 3rd ed. (gr. 8). 11.95 net. *(978-0-8136-2822-6(9))*Rev. B. (gr. 2). *(978-0-8136-2808-0(3))* Modern Curriculum Pr.

Studio Mouse Staff. Spelling Fun. 2011. (Cars Ser.). (ENG., Illus.). 28p. (J). 15.99 *(978-1-59069-938-6(6))* Studio Mouse LLC.

Terror Bear Canyon: Level 5, 6 vols. (Fluency Strand Ser.). (gr. 4-8). 45.00 *(978-1-4045-1225-2(X))* Wright Group/McGraw-Hill.

To Catch a Thief: Level 3, 6 vols. (Fluency Strand Ser.). (gr. 4-8). 45.00 *(978-1-4045-1219-1(5))* Wright Group/McGraw-Hill.

Trocki, Phillip. Spelling Workout. rev. ed. 2003. (Illus.). (J). Level C. (gr. 3). tchr. ed. 10.50 *(978-0-7652-2490-3(9))*Level A. (gr. 1). tchr. ed. 10.50 *(978-0-7652-2488-0(7))*Level B. (gr. 2). tchr. ed. 10.50 *(978-0-7652-2489-7(5))* Modern Curriculum Pr.

Unccor: Level 5, 6 vols. (Fluency Strand Ser.). (gr. 4-8). 45.00 *(978-1-4045-1231-3(4))* Wright Group/McGraw-Hill.

Vinopol, Corinne. Spell Well: CD-ROM American Sign Language Spelling Game. 2003. (YA). cd-rom 19.95 *(978-0-9752933-0-3(3))* Institute for Disabilities Research & Training, Inc.

Zone Zoomers: Level 2, 6 vols. (Fluency Strand Ser.). (gr. 4-8). 45.00 *(978-1-4045-1213-9(6))* Wright Group/McGraw-Hill.

SPELLS

see Charms

SPHERICAL TRIGONOMETRY

see Trigonometry

SPICES

Rodger, Ellen. The Biography of Spices, 1 vol. 2005. (How did That Get There? Ser.). (ENG., Illus.). 32p. (J). (gr. 4-5). pap. *(978-0-7787-2520-6(0))*; lib. bdg. *(978-0-7787-2484-1(0))* Crabtree Publishing Co.

Wells, Donald. The Spice Trade. 2005. (Great Journeys Ser.). (Illus.). 32p. (J). (gr. 6-7). lib. bdg. 26.00 *(978-1-59036-208-2(X))* Weigl Pubs., Inc.

World Book, Inc. Staff, contrib. by. Salt & Pepper. 2019. (Illus.). 48p. (J). *(978-0-7166-2864-4(3))* World Bk., Inc.

SPIDER-MAN (FICTITIOUS CHARACTER)—FICTION

Andrews, Kaare. Spider-Man Legend of the Spider-Clan, 3 vols. Young, Skott, illus. 2003. (Mangaverse Ser.: Vol. 3). 128p. (YA). pap. 11.99 *(978-0-7851-1114-6(X))* Marvel Worldwide, Inc.

Bendis, Brian Michael. Spider-Man - Miles Morales, Vol. 3. Brown, Patrick & Kudranski, Szymon, illus. 2017. (Spider-Man Ser.: 3). 160p. (gr. 4-17). pap. 19.99 *(978-1-302-90597-2(X)*, Marvel Universe) Marvel Worldwide, Inc.

Berrios, Frank. The Amazing Spider-Man (Marvel: Spider-Man) Legramandi, Francesco & Cagol, Andrea, illus. 2012. (Little Golden Book Ser.). (ENG.). 24p. (J). (gr. k-k). 5.99 *(978-0-307-93107-8(2)*, Golden Bks.) Random Hse. Children's Bks.

—High Voltage! (Marvel: Spider-Man) Cagol, Andrea & Legramandi, Francesco, illus. 2014. (Little Golden Book Ser.). (ENG.). 24p. (J). (-k). 5.99 *(978-0-385-37427-9(5)*, Golden Bks.) Random Hse. Children's Bks.

—Night of the Vulture! (Marvel: Spider-Man) Legramandi, Francesco & Scolari, Silvano, illus. 2017. (Little Golden Book Ser.). (ENG.). 24p. (J). (-k). 5.99 *(978-1-5247-1728-5(2)*, Golden Bks.) Random Hse. Children's Bks.

—Trapped by the Green Goblin! (Marvel: Spider-Man) Cagol, Andrea & Legramandi, Francesco, illus. 2013. (Little Golden Book Ser.). (ENG.). 24p. (J). (-k). 5.99 *(978-0-307-97655-0(6)*, Golden Bks.) Random Hse. Children's Bks.

Cadenhead, MacKenzie. Marvel Super Hero Adventures: Buggin' Out! An Early Chapter Book. 2018. (Super Hero Adventures Chapter Bks.: 3). (ENG., Illus.). 80p. (J). (gr. 1-3). pap. 4.99 *(978-1-368-00857-0(7))* Marvel Worldwide, Inc.

David, Erica. Prison Break. Scherberger, Patrick, illus. 2007. (Spider-Man Ser.: No. 2). (ENG.). 24p. (J). (gr. 2-6). lib. bdg. 31.36 *(978-1-59961-214-0(3)*, 13626, Marvel Age) Spotlight.

—The Sinister Six. Hamscher, Cory, illus. 2007. (Spider-Man Ser.: No. 2). (ENG.). 24p. (J). (gr. 2-6). lib. bdg. 31.36 *(978-1-59961-216-4(X)*, 13628, Marvel Age) Spotlight.

David, Peter, et al. Wizard Spiderman, Vol. 11. 2006. (Illus.). 272p. (YA). 50.00 *(978-0-9743253-6-1(8))* Diamond Comic Distributors, Inc.

Davis, Alan. Killraven. Davis, Alan, illus. 2003. (Spider-Man Ser.). (Illus.). 144p. (YA). pap. 16.99 *(978-0-7851-1083-5(6))* Marvel Worldwide, Inc.

DBG. The Story of SpiderMan (Level 2) 2012. (World of Reading Ser.). (ENG.). 32p. (J). (gr. 1-3). pap. 5.99 *(978-1-4231-5409-9(6))* Marvel Worldwide, Inc.

DeMatteis, J. M., et al. Son of the Goblin. 2004. (Spider-Man Ser.). (Illus.). 144p. (YA). pap. 15.99 *(978-0-7851-1563-2(3))* Marvel Worldwide, Inc.

Dezago, Todd. Captain America: Stars, Stripes, & Spiders! 2006. (Spider-Man Team Up Ser.). (ENG., Illus.). 24p. (J). (gr. 2-6). lib. bdg. 31.36 *(978-1-59961-001-6(9)*, 13641, Marvel Age) Spotlight.

—Fantastic Four: The Chameleon Strikes! Fridolfs, Derek, illus. 2006. (Spider-Man Team Up Ser.). (ENG.). 24p. (J). (gr. 2-6). lib. bdg. 31.36 *(978-1-59961-005-4(1)*, 13645, Marvel Age) Spotlight.

—Fantastic Four: The Menace of Monster Isle! Davis, Shane, illus. 2006. (Spider-Man Team Up Ser.). (ENG.). 24p. (J). (gr. 2-6). lib. bdg. 31.36 *(978-1-59961-006-1(X)*, 13646, Marvel Age) Spotlight.

—Spider-Man: Change the Weather. 2006. (Spider-Man Team Up Ser.). (ENG., Illus.). 24p. (J). (gr. 2-6). lib. bdg. 31.36 *(978-1-59961-003-0(5)*, 13643, Marvel Age) Spotlight.

—Thor: Out of Time! 2006. (Spider-Man Team Up Ser.). (ENG., Illus.). 24p. (J). (gr. 2-6). lib. bdg. 31.36 *(978-1-59961-004-7(3)*, 13644, Marvel Age) Spotlight.

Dezago, Todd, et al. Duel with Daredevil! 2006. (Spider-Man Ser.: No. 1). (ENG., Illus.). 24p. (J). (gr. 2-6). 31.36 *(978-1-59961-013-9(2)*, 13608, Marvel Age) Spotlight.

—The Enforcers! 2006. (Spider-Man Ser.: No. 1). (ENG., Illus.). 24p. (J). (gr. 2-6). 31.36 *(978-1-59961-019-1(1)*, 13614, Marvel Age) Spotlight.

—Spidey Strikes Back! 2006. (Spider-Man Ser.: No. 1). (ENG., Illus.). 24p. (J). (gr. 2-6). 31.36 *(978-1-59961-017-7(5)*, 13612, Marvel Age) Spotlight.

Disney Book Group & Marvel Book Group. Spider-Man: Love Bug. 2015. (Marvel 8x8s Ser.). (J). lib. bdg. 16.00 *(978-0-606-37542-9(2))* Turtleback.

Egan, Kate. Evil Comes in Pairs. Merkel, Joe F., illus. 2009. (Spider-Man Ser.). 64p. (J). (gr. 2-5). pap. 4.99 *(978-0-06-162625-8(2)*, HarperFestival) HarperCollins Pubs.

Figueroa, Acton. Spider-Man 2: Everyday Hero. Vasquez, Ivan & Redondo, Jesus, illus. movie tie-in ed. 2004. (Festival Reader Ser.). 32p. (J). (gr. -1-2). pap. 3.99 *(978-0-06-057363-8(5)*, HarperFestival) HarperCollins Pubs.

Golden Books, illus. Spider-Man Little Golden Book Library (Marvel) Spider-Man!; Trapped by the Green Goblin; the Big Freeze!; High Voltage!; Night of the Vulture!, 5 vols. 2017. (Little Golden Book Ser.). (ENG.). 120p. (J). (-k). 29.95 *(978-1-5247-6409-8(4)*, Golden Bks.) Random Hse. Children's Bks.

Gunter, Jacob Ben, et al. The Daily Bugle Stories. 2004. (Spider-Man 2 Ser.). (Illus.). 144p. pap. *(978-0-00-717815-5(8)*, HarperCollins Entertainment) HarperCollins Pubs. Ltd.

Jenkins, Paul. Here There Be the Monsters, Vol. 3. Scott, Damion, illus. 2004. (Spider-Man Ser.). 144p. (YA). 9.99 *(978-0-7851-1333-1(9))* Marvel Worldwide, Inc.

Lee, Stan. Here Comes Spider-Man. 2007. (Spider-Man Ser.: No. 2). (ENG., Illus.). 24p. (J). (gr. 2-6). lib. bdg. 31.36 *(978-1-59961-210-2(0)*, 13622, Marvel Age) Spotlight.

—Make Mine Mysterio! Norton, Mike, illus. 2007. (Spider-Man Ser.: No. 2). (ENG.). 24p. (J). (gr. 2-6). lib. bdg. 31.36 *(978-1-59961-211-9(9)*, 13623, Marvel Age) Spotlight.

—The Man Called Electro! O' Hare, Michael, illus. 2006. (Spider-Man Ser.: No. 1). (ENG.). 24p. (J). (gr. 2-6). 31.36 *(978-1-59961-021-4(3)*, 13616, Marvel Age) Spotlight.

—Picture-Perfect Peril! Scherberger, Patrick, illus. 2007. (Spider-Man Ser.: No. 2). (ENG.). 24p. (J). (gr. 2-6). lib. bdg. 31.36 *(978-1-59961-212-6(7)*, 13624, Marvel Age) Spotlight.

—The Terrible Threat of the Living Brain! Meyers, Jonboy, illus. 2006. (Spider-Man Ser.: No. 1). (ENG.). 24p. (J). (gr. 2-6). 31.36 *(978-1-59961-008-5(6)*, 13603, Marvel Age) Spotlight.

Lee, Stan, et al. Unmasked by Doctor Octopus! 2006. (Spider-Man Ser.: No. 1). (ENG., Illus.). 24p. (J). (gr. 2-6). 31.36 *(978-1-59961-010-8(8)*, 13605, Marvel Age) Spotlight.

Lime, Harry. Spider-Man 3: Meet the Heroes & Villains. Gordon, Steven E., illus. 2007. (I Can Read Bks.). 32p. (J). pap. 3.99 *(978-0-06-083721-1(7)*, Harper Trophy) HarperCollins Pubs.

Loeb, Jeph. Blue. Sale, Tim, illus. 2003. (Spider-Man Ser.). 160p. (YA). 21.99 *(978-0-7851-1062-0(3))* Marvel Worldwide, Inc.

Marvel Book Group & Macri, Thomas. This Is Spider-Man. 2012. (Marvel World of Reading Level 1 Ser.). (J). lib. bdg. 13.55 *(978-0-606-23787-1(9))* Turtleback.

Marvel Book Group Staff. Ultimate Spider-Man Halloween. 2014. (Marvel 8x8s Ser.). (J). lib. bdg. 16.00 *(978-0-606-35286-4(4))* Turtleback.

Marvel Press Book Group, Marvel Press. World of Reading Marvel: Meet the Super Heroes!-Pre-Level 1 Boxed Set. Set. 2017. (World of Reading Ser.). (ENG., Illus.). 144p. (J). (gr. -1-k). 12.99 *(978-1-368-00852-5(6))* Marvel Worldwide, Inc.

—World of Reading: This Is Miles Morales. 2018. (World of Reading Ser.). (ENG., Illus.). 32p. (J). (gr. 1-3). pap. 4.99 *(978-1-368-02863-9(2))* Marvel Worldwide, Inc.

—5-Minute SpiderMan Stories. 2017. (5-Minute Stories Ser.). (ENG.). 192p. (J). (gr. 1-3). 12.99 *(978-1-4847-8142-5(2))* Marvel Worldwide, Inc.

McDonnell, David, ed. Spiderman & Other Amazing Heroes. 2004. (Starlog Movie Magic Ser.). (YA). pap. *(978-0-88013-065-3(2))* Profile Entertainment, Inc.

McKeever, Sean. Rush Hour! Scherberger, Patrick, illus. 2007. (Spider-Man Ser.: No. 2). (ENG.). 24p. (J). (gr. 2-6). lib. bdg. 31.36 *(978-1-59961-215-7(1)*, 13627, Marvel Age) Spotlight.

—Vulture Hunt! Hamscher, Cory, illus. 2007. (Spider-Man Ser.: No. 2). (ENG.). 24p. (J). (gr. 2-6). lib. bdg. 31.36 *(978-1-59961-217-1(8)*, 13629, Marvel Age) Spotlight.

McKeever, Sean & Lee, Stan. Doom with a View! Norton, Mike, illus. 2007. (Spider-Man Ser.: No. 2). (ENG.). 24p. (J). (gr. 2-6). lib. bdg. 31.36 *(978-1-59961-208-9(9)*, 13620, Marvel Age) Spotlight.

McVeigh, Mark W. The Lizard's Legacy. Sazaklis, John, illus. 2009. (Spider-Man Ser.). 64p. (J). (gr. 2-5). pap. 4.99 *(978-0-06-162627-2(9)*, HarperFestival) HarperCollins Pubs.

Parker, Jeff & Lee, Stan. Goom Got Game! Scherberger, Patrick, illus. 2007. (Spider-Man Ser.: No. 2). (ENG.). 24p. (J). (gr. 2-6). lib. bdg. 31.36 *(978-1-59961-209-6(7)*, 13621, Marvel Age) Spotlight.

Publications International Ltd. Staff, ed. Spider Sense Spider-Man: Super Villain Showdown. 2010. 12p. (J). bds. 12.98 *(978-1-4127-9911-9(2))* Phoenix International Publications, Inc.

Quantz, Daniel, et al. Face-to-Face with the Lizard! 2006. (Spider-Man Ser.: No. 1). (ENG., Illus.). 24p. (J). (gr. 2-6). 31.36 *(978-1-59961-014-6(0)*, 13609, Marvel Age) Spotlight.

—Marked for Destruction by Dr. Doom! 2006. (Spider-Man Ser.: No. 1). (ENG., Illus.). 24p. (J). (gr. 2-6). 31.36 *(978-1-59961-015-3(9)*, 13610, Marvel Age) Spotlight.

—Nothing Can Stop the Sandman! 2006. (Spider-Man Ser.: No. 1). (ENG., Illus.). 24p. (J). (gr. 2-6). 31.36 *(978-1-59961-016-0(7)*, 13611, Marvel Age) Spotlight.

—Spider-Man Versus Doctor Octopus. 2006. (Spider-Man Ser.: No. 1). (ENG., Illus.). 24p. (J). (gr. 2-6). 31.36 *(978-1-59961-011-5(6)*, 13606, Marvel Age) Spotlight.

Raicht, Mike, et al. The Grotesque Adventure of the Green Goblin! 2006. (Spider-Man Ser.: No. 1). (ENG., Illus.). 24p. (J). (gr. 2-6). 31.36 *(978-1-59961-020-7(5)*, 13615, Marvel Age) Spotlight.

—Kraven the Hunter. 2006. (Spider-Man Ser.: No. 1). (ENG., Illus.). 24p. (J). (gr. 2-6). 31.36 *(978-1-59961-009-2(4)*, 13604, Marvel Age) Spotlight.

—The Menace of Mysterio. 2006. (Spider-Man Ser.: No. 1). (ENG., Illus.). 24p. (J). (gr. 2-6). 31.36 *(978-1-59961-022-1(1)*, 13617, Marvel Age) Spotlight.

—Where Flies the Beetle! Guest-Starring the Human Torch. 2006. (Spider-Man Ser.: No. 1). (ENG., Illus.). 24p. (J). (gr. 2-6). 31.36 *(978-1-59961-023-8(X)*, 13618, Marvel Age) Spotlight.

Reynolds, Jason. Miles Morales. 2018. (YA). lib. bdg. 20.85 *(978-0-606-40966-7(1))* Turtleback.

—Miles Morales: Spider-Man. 2018. (Marvel YA Novel Ser.). (ENG., Illus.). 272p. (YA). (gr. 7-12). pap. 10.99 *(978-1-4847-8850-9(8))* Marvel Worldwide, Inc.

—Miles Morales: SpiderMan. 2017. (Marvel YA Novel Ser.). (ENG., Illus.). 272p. (YA). (gr. 7-12). 17.99 *(978-1-4847-8748-9(X))* Marvel Worldwide, Inc.

Spider-Man & Friends. 2003. (J). per. *(978-1-57657-858-2(5))* Paradise Pr., Inc.

Straczynski, J. Michael. Best of Spider-Man, Vol. 3. Youngquist, Jeff, ed. 2004. (Spider-Man Ser.). (Illus.). 368p. (YA). 29.99 *(978-0-7851-1339-3(8))* Marvel Worldwide, Inc.

—The Book of Ezekiel, Vol. 7. Romita, John, Jr., illus. 2004. (Spider-Man Ser.). 144p. (YA). pap. 12.99 *(978-0-7851-1525-0(0))* Marvel Worldwide, Inc.

Teitelbaum, Michael. The Secret Life of Black Cat. Sazaklis, John, illus. 2009. (Spider-Man Ser.). 64p. (J). (gr. 2-5). pap. 4.99 *(978-0-06-162626-5(0)*, HarperFestival) HarperCollins Pubs.

Thomas, Rich. The Amazing Spider-Man. Clark, Jeff, illus. 2012. (Marvel Origins Ser.). (ENG.). 48p. (J). (gr. k-5). lib. bdg. 31.36 *(978-1-61479-007-5(8)*, 11335, Marvel Age) Spotlight.

—Spider-Man: Attack of the Heroes. 2014. (Mighty Marvel Chapter Bks.). (J). lib. bdg. 16.00 *(978-0-606-35271-0(6))* Turtleback.

Thompson, Robbie. Spidey #1. Bradshaw, Nick & Campbell, Jim, illus. 2016. (Spidey Ser.). (ENG.). 24p. (J). (gr. 2-8). lib. bdg. 31.36 *(978-1-61479-593-3(2)*, 24374, Marvel Age) Spotlight.

—Spidey #2. Bradshaw, Nick & Campbell, Jim, illus. 2016. (Spidey Ser.). (ENG.). 24p. (J). (gr. 2-8). lib. bdg. 31.36 *(978-1-61479-594-0(0)*, 24375, Marvel Age) Spotlight.

—Spidey #3. Bradshaw, Nick & Campbell, Jim, illus. 2016. (Spidey Ser.). (ENG.). 24p. (J). (gr. 2-8). lib. bdg. 31.36 *(978-1-61479-595-7(9)*, 24376, Marvel Age) Spotlight.

—Spidey #4. Araujo, Andre Lima & Rosenberg, Rachelle, illus. 2016. (Spidey Ser.). (ENG.). 24p. (J). (gr. 2-8). lib. bdg. 31.36 *(978-1-61479-596-4(7)*, 24377, Marvel Age) Spotlight.

—Spidey #5. Araujo, Andre Lima & Campbell, Jim, illus. 2016. (Spidey Ser.). (ENG.). 24p. (J). (gr. 2-8). lib. bdg. 31.36 *(978-1-61479-597-1(5)*, 24378, Marvel Age) Spotlight.

—Spidey #6. Araujo, Andre Lima & Campbell, Jim, illus. 2016. (Spidey Ser.). (ENG.). 24p. (J). (gr. 2-8). lib. bdg. 31.36 *(978-1-61479-598-8(3)*, 24379, Marvel Age) Spotlight.

Tobin, Paul. Spider-Man & the Secret Wars GN. Scherberger, Patrick, illus. 2010. (ENG.). 128p. pap. 14.99 *(978-0-7851-4443-4(9))* Marvel Worldwide, Inc.

Van Lente, Fred. Breaking up Is Venomous to Do! Paniccia, Mark, ed. Hamscher, Cory, illus. 2007. (Spider-Man Ser.: No. 3). (ENG.). 24p. (J). (gr. 2-6). lib. bdg. 31.36 *(978-1-59961-393-2(X)*, 13631, Marvel Age) Spotlight.

—World War G. Paniccia, Mark, ed. Hamscher, Cory, illus. 2007. (Spider-Man Ser.: No. 3). (ENG.). 24p. (J). (gr. 2-6). lib. bdg. 31.36 *(978-1-59961-396-3(4)*, 13634, Marvel Age) Spotlight.

West, Alexandra. Thwip! You Are It! Brizuela, Dario, illus. 2017. (J). *(978-1-5182-2667-0(1))* Disney Pr.

—Thwip! You Are It! 2018. (World of Reading Ser.). (ENG.). 32p. (J). (gr. -1-1). 13.89 (978-1-64310-770-7(4)) Penworthy Co., LLC, The.

Wrecks, Billy & Berrios, Frank. Marvel Spider-Man Little Golden Book Favorites (Marvel: Spider-Man), Vol. 2. Golden Books, illus. 2021. (Little Golden Book Ser.). (ENG.). 80p. (J). (-k). 8.99 (978-0-307-97659-8(9), Golden Bks.) Random Hse. Children's Bks.

SPIDERS

Abbott, Simon, illus. 100 Questions about Bugs: And All the Answers, Too! 2018. (100 Questions Ser.). (ENG.). 48p. (J). 7.99 (978-1-4413-2618-8(9), ff72d12a-2883-49e2-9efd-5a780a2d627c) Peter Pauper Pr. Inc.

Allen, Judy. Are You a Spider? Humphries, Tudor, illus. 2003. (Backyard Bks.). (ENG.). 31p. (J). (gr. k-3). pap. 7.99 (978-0-7534-5609-5(5), 900052554, Kingfisher) Roaring Brook Pr.

—Are You a Spider? 2003. (Backyard Bks.). (J). (gr. -1-2). lib. bdg. 17.20 (978-0-613-90776-7(0)) Turtleback.

Allman, Toney. From Spider Webs to Man-Made Silk. 2005. (Imitating Nature Ser.). (ENG., Illus.). 32p. (J). (gr. 4-8). lib. bdg. 26.20 (978-0-7377-3124-8(9), Greenhaven Pr., Inc.) Cengage Gale.

Amstutz, Lisa J. Spiders. 2017. (Little Critters Ser.). (ENG., Illus.). 24p. (J). (gr. -1-2). lib. bdg. 22.65 (978-1-5157-7826-4(6), 135977, Pebble) Capstone.

Anderson, Catherine. Daddy Longlegs. 2003. (Bug Bks.). (Illus.). (J). 32p. lib. bdg. 22.79 (978-1-4034-0763-4(0)); (ENG., 24p. pap. 6.50 (978-1-4034-0994-2(3)) Heinemann-Raintree.

Archer, Claire. Araña Lobo, 1 vol. 2014. (Arañas (Spiders) Ser.). (SPA.). 24p. (J). (gr. k-2). lib. bdg. 32.79 (978-1-62970-370-1(2), 2809, Abdo Kids) ABDO Publishing Co.

—Bird-Eating Spiders, 1 vol. 2014. (Spiders (Abdo Kids) Ser.). (ENG.). 24p. (J). (gr. -1-2). lib. bdg. 32.79 (978-1-62970-071-7(1), 1650, Abdo Kids) ABDO Publishing Co.

—Black Widow Spiders, 1 vol. 2014. (Spiders (Abdo Kids) Ser.). (ENG.). 24p. (J). (gr. -1-2). lib. bdg. 32.79 (978-1-62970-072-4(X), 1651, Abdo Kids) ABDO Publishing Co.

—Jumping Spiders, 1 vol. 2014. (Spiders (Abdo Kids) Ser.). (ENG.). 24p. (J). (gr. -1-2). lib. bdg. 32.79 (978-1-62970-073-1(8), 1652, Abdo Kids) ABDO Publishing Co.

—Tarantula Spiders, 1 vol. 2014. (Spiders (Abdo Kids) Ser.). (ENG.). 24p. (J). (gr. -1-2). lib. bdg. 32.79 (978-1-62970-074-8(6), 1653, Abdo Kids) ABDO Publishing Co.

—Trapdoor Spiders, 1 vol. 2014. (Spiders (Abdo Kids) Ser.). (ENG.). 24p. (J). (gr. -1-2). lib. bdg. 32.79 (978-1-62970-075-5(4), 1654, Abdo Kids) ABDO Publishing Co.

—Wolf Spiders, 1 vol. 2014. (Spiders (Abdo Kids) Ser.). (ENG.). 24p. (J). (gr. k-2). lib. bdg. 32.79 (978-1-62970-076-2(2), 1655, Abdo Kids) ABDO Publishing Co.

Archer, Claire, et al. Arañas Tramperas. 2015. (Arañas Ser.). (SPA., Illus.). 24p. (J). (gr. -1-2). pap. 7.95 (978-1-4966-0391-3(5), 130246, Capstone Classroom) Capstone.

—Tarántulas Goliat. 2015. (Arañas Ser.). (SPA., Illus.). 24p. (J). (gr. -1-2). pap. 7.95 (978-1-4966-0397-5(4), 130249, Capstone Classroom) Capstone.

Barton, Bethany. I'm Trying to Love Spiders. Barton, Bethany, illus. (Illus.). (J). (gr. -1-3). 2019. 40p. pap. 8.99 (978-0-593-11371-4(3), Puffin Books) 2015. 34p. 18.99 (978-0-670-01693-8(4), Viking Books for Young Readers) Penguin Young Readers Group.

Believe It Or Not!, Ripleys, compiled by. Ripley Twists PB: Spiders & Scary Creepy Crawlies. 2018. (Twist Ser.: 12). (ENG.). 48p. (J). pap. 7.99 (978-1-60991-234-5(9)) Ripley Entertainment, Inc.

Berger, Melvin. Spinning Spiders. Schindler, S. D., illus. 2015. 40p. pap. 6.00 (978-1-61003-617-7(4)) Center for the Collaborative Classroom.

—Spinning Spiders. Schindler, S. D., illus. 2003. (Let's-Read-and-Find-Out-Science Ser.: Vol. 2). 40p. (J). (gr. k-4). lib. bdg. 16.89 (978-0-06-028697-2(0)) HarperCollins Pubs.

—Spinning Spiders. Schindler, S. D., illus. 2003. (Let's-Read-and-Find-Out Science Ser.). 33p. (gr. k-4). 16.00 (978-0-7569-1449-3(3)) Perfection Learning Corp.

Bergeron, Alain M. & Quintin, Michel. Do You Know Spiders?, 1 vol. Sampar, illus. 2013. (Do You Know? Ser.). (ENG.). 64p. (J). (gr. 2-4). 9.95 (978-1-55455-302-0(4), eee083c2-9508-468f-9166-37b5e072450e) Trifolium Bks., Inc. CAN. Dist: Firefly Bks., Ltd.

Biel, Timothy Levi. Aranas. Rountree, Monica, tr. 2003. (Zoobooks Ser.). Orig. Title: Spiders. (SPA., Illus.). 24p. (J). (gr. 1-7). lib. bdg. 15.95 (978-1-888153-82-8(2)) National Wildlife Federation.

Bishop, Celeste. Scrambling Spiders, 1 vol. 2015. (Icky Animals! Small & Gross Ser.). (ENG.). 24p. (J). (gr. 1-1). pap. 9.25 (978-1-4994-0717-4(3), a3de59cf-78ee-484e-9a86-c91b1c944061, PowerKids Pr.) Rosen Publishing Group, Inc., The.

Bishop, Nic. Nic Bishop: Spiders, 1 vol. Bishop, Nic, photos by. 2007. (ENG., Illus.). 48p. (J). (gr. -1-3). 19.99 (978-0-439-87756-5(3), Scholastic Nonfiction) Scholastic, Inc.

—Spiders. 2012. (Scholastic Reader Level 2 Ser.). lib. bdg. 13.55 (978-0-606-26742-7(5)) Turtleback.

—Spiders (Nic Bishop: Scholastic Reader, Level 2) Bishop, Nic, photos by. 2012. (Scholastic Reader, Level 2 Ser.). (ENG., Illus.). 32p. (J). (gr. k-2). pap. 3.99 (978-0-545-23757-4(2), Scholastic Paperbacks) Scholastic, Inc.

Black, Nessa. Spiders. (Spot Creepy Crawlies Ser.). (ENG., Illus.). 16p. (J). (gr. -1-2). 2018. pap. 7.99 (978-1-68152-229-6(2), 14760) 2017. 17.95 (978-1-68151-110-8(X), 14641) Amicus.

Blake, Kevin. Deadly Spider Bite! 2018. (Envenomators Ser.). (ENG.). 24p. (J). (gr. 2-7). 19.45 (978-1-68402-656-2(3)) Bearport Publishing Co., Inc.

Bodden, Valerie. Spider. 2014. 32p. (J). (Illus.). (978-1-60818-407-1(2), Creative Education); (ENG.). (gr. 3-6). pap. 9.99 (978-0-89812-993-9(1), 21346, Creative Paperbacks) Creative Co., The.

—Spiders. 2011. (Creepy Creatures Ser.). 24p. (J). (gr. 1-3). 24.25 (978-1-58341-996-0(9), Creative Education); (ENG.). pap. 7.99 (978-0-89812-569-6(3), 22677, Creative Paperbacks) Creative Co., The.

—Spiders. 2010. (ENG., Illus.). 24p. (J). pap. 8.95 (978-1-926853-76-5(8)) Saunders Bk. Co. CAN. Dist: Creative Co., The.

Books Are Fun 8 Title Animal Lives Set: Spiders. 2006. (J). (978-1-59566-313-9(4)) QEB Publishing Inc.

Borgert-Spaniol, Megan. Black Widow Spiders. 2016. (Creepy Crawlies Ser.). (ENG., Illus.). 24p. (J). (gr. k-3). lib. bdg. 26.95 (978-1-62617-299-9(4), Blastoff! Readers) Bellwether Media.

—Spiders. 2013. (Backyard Wildlife Ser.). (ENG., Illus.). 24p. (J). (gr. k-3). lib. bdg. 26.95 (978-1-60014-921-4(9), Blastoff! Readers) Bellwether Media.

Boutland, Craig. Anansi the Talking Spider & Other Legendary Creatures of Africa, 1 vol. 2018. (Cryptozoologist's Guide to Curious Creatures Ser.). (ENG.). 32p. (gr. 4-5). lib. bdg. 28.27 (978-1-5382-2706-0(1), fd8e5bf2-3ab2-4403-9467-e47242605031) Stevens, Gareth Publishing LLLP.

Bredeson, Carmen. Hair-Shooting Tarantulas & Other Weird Spiders, 1 vol. 2009. (I Like Weird Animals! Ser.). (ENG., Illus.). 24p. (gr. k-2). lib. bdg. 25.27 (978-0-7660-3127-2(6), 72923f9d-5be1-4814-9eaa-56e9aafb3626, Enslow Elementary) Enslow Publishing, LLC.

—Tarantulas up Close, 1 vol. 2008. (Zoom in on Animals! Ser.). (ENG., Illus.). 24p. (gr. k-2). pap. 10.95 (978-1-59845-421-5(8), 2a31ed64-4162-4abf-8654-a0ae3f43de30); lib. bdg. 25.60 (978-0-7660-3076-3(8), 4e50b369-a087-4d54-9df1-67a4e68b2e9f) Enslow Publishing, LLC. (Enslow Elementary).

Breene, Robert G., III. A Widow Spider in Its Web. 2003. (Where Do Animals Live? Ser.). (J). (978-1-58417-186-7(3)); pap. (978-1-58417-187-4(1)) Lake Street Pubs.

Buckley, James, et al. Discovery Bugopedia. 2015. (J). lib. bdg. 33.00 (978-0-606-36892-6(2)) Turtleback.

Camisa, Kathryn. Hairy Tarantulas. 2008. (No Backbone! Ser.). (Illus.). 24p. (J). (gr. k-3). lib. bdg. 26.99 (978-1-59716-704-8(5), 1284308) Bearport Publishing Co., Inc.

Camisa, Kathryn & Brown, Brian Victor. Hairy Tarantulas. 2019. (J). pap. (978-1-64280-749-3(4)) Bearport Publishing Co., Inc.

Canetti, Yanitzia. Canta y Cuenta Las Arañas. 2010. (J). (978-1-59835-226-9(1)) Cambridge BrickHouse, Inc.

—1-2-3 Do, Re, Mi Spiders. 2010. (J). (978-1-59835-225-2(3)) Cambridge BrickHouse, Inc.

Caputo, Christine A. Insects & Spiders. 2012. (Illus.). 32p. (J). (978-0-545-46703-2(9)) Scholastic, Inc.

Carle, Eric. My Own Very Busy Spider Coloring Book. Carle, Eric, illus. 2004. (Illus.). 32p. (J). (gr. -1-k). 5.99 (978-0-399-24309-7(7), Philomel Bks.) Penguin Young Readers Group.

Charner, Kathy, ed. Learn Every Day about Bugs & Spiders: 100 Best Ideas from Teachers. 2010. (Learn Every Day Ser.). (ENG.). 128p. pap. 12.95 (978-0-87659-128-4(4), Gryphon House Inc) Gryphon Hse., Inc.

Christiansen, Per. Poisonous Spiders, 1 vol. 2008. (Nature's Monsters: Insects & Spiders Ser.). (ENG., Illus.). 32p. (J). (gr. 3-5). lib. bdg. 28.67 (978-0-8368-9219-2(4), 06a71a16-6bd0-4f58-bd48-87e5b708f4d3) Stevens, Gareth Publishing LLLP.

Clark, Willow. Black Widow Spider!, 1 vol. 2010. (Animal Danger Zone Ser.). (ENG.). 24p. (J). (gr. 2-3). lib. bdg. 27.27 (978-1-60754-959-8(X), 5b255290-1aff-447f-83d5-1cd94c1b77e4); (Illus.). pap. 9.15 (978-1-60754-968-0(9), fb7274f9-c0cf-44ca-926c-d7c107309741) Rosen Publishing Group, Inc., The. (Windmill Bks.).

Cooper, Jason. Black Widow Spiders. 2005. (Rourke Discovery Library). (Illus.). 24p. (J). (gr. 2-5). lib. bdg. 22.79 (978-1-59515-445-3(0)) Rourke Educational Media.

—Black Widows. Rourke Publishing Staff, ed. 2009. 24p. (J). pap. 3.99 (978-0-8249-5141-2(7), Ideals Pubns.) Worthy Publishing.

—Fishing Spiders. 2005. (Rourke Discovery Library). (Illus.). 24p. (J). (gr. 2-5). lib. bdg. 22.79 (978-1-59515-446-0(9)) Rourke Educational Media.

—Garden Spiders. 2005. (Rourke Discovery Library). (Illus.). 24p. (J). (gr. 2-5). lib. bdg. 14.95 (978-1-59515-447-7(7)) Rourke Educational Media.

—Jumping Spiders. 2005. (Rourke Discovery Library). (Illus.). 24p. (J). (gr. 2-5). lib. bdg. 22.79 (978-1-59515-448-4(5)) Rourke Educational Media.

—Jumping Spiders. Rourke Publishing Staff, ed. 2009. 24p. (J). pap. 3.99 (978-0-8249-5142-9(5), Ideals Pubns.) Worthy Publishing.

—Tarantulas. 2005. (Spiders Discovery Ser.). (Illus.). 24p. (J). (gr. 2-5). lib. bdg. 14.95 (978-1-59515-449-1(3)) Rourke Educational Media.

—Tarantulas. Rourke Publishing Staff, ed. 2009. 24p. (J). pap. 3.99 (978-0-8249-5143-6(3), Ideals Pubns.) Worthy Publishing.

Creepy Crawly Creatures. 2007. (ENG., Illus.). 14p. (J). (gr. -1-3). 16.95 (978-1-58117-623-0(6), Intervisual/Piggy Toes) Bendon, Inc.

de Nijs, Erika. A Spider's Web, 1 vol. 2016. (Animal Builders Ser.). (ENG., Illus.). 24p. (gr. 1-1). pap. 9.22 (978-1-5026-2071-2(5), 36023350-ab94-44d0-9529-9ad8758507ff) Cavendish Square Publishing LLC.

Dean, James & Dean, Kimberly. Pete the Cat & the Itsy Bitsy Spider. Dean, James, illus. 2019. (Pete the Cat Ser.). (ENG., Illus.). 32p. (J). (gr. -1-3). 9.99 (978-0-06-267544-6(3), HarperCollins) HarperCollins Pubs.

Dellaccio, Tanya. Spiders Lived with the Dinosaurs!, 1 vol. 2016. (Living with the Dinosaurs Ser.). (ENG., Illus.). 24p. (J). (gr. 2-3). pap. 9.15 (978-1-4824-5681-3(8), 65ff175f-705e-4da7-a58f-1f0b2cd4b4b3) Stevens, Gareth Publishing LLLP.

DK. Insects & Spiders. 2019. (Nature Explorers Ser.). (ENG., Illus.). 64p. (J). (gr. 1-3). 9.99 (978-1-4654-7909-9(0), DK Children) Dorling Kindersley Publishing, Inc.

Editors of Kingfisher. It's All about... Scary Spiders. 2016. (It's All About... Ser.). (ENG., Illus.). 32p. (J). pap. 5.99 (978-0-7534-7265-1(1), 900156433, Kingfisher) Roaring Brook Pr.

Ethan, Eric. Black Widow Spiders, 1 vol. 2003. (Dangerous Spiders Ser.). (ENG., Illus.). 24p. (gr. 2-4). lib. bdg. 25.67 (978-0-8368-3765-0(7), 444a0ecb-ddc2-4b90-b7ca-e5455bdd9521, Gareth Stevens Learning Library) Stevens, Gareth Publishing LLLP.

—Brown Recluse Spiders, 1 vol. 2003. (Dangerous Spiders Ser.). (ENG., Illus.). 24p. (gr. 2-4). lib. bdg. 25.67 (978-0-8368-3766-7(5), b096f02e-e321-4802-be15-adc9c58f81da, Gareth Stevens Learning Library) Stevens, Gareth Publishing LLLP.

—Dangerous Spiders, 12 vols. Incl. Black Widow Spiders. lib. bdg. 25.67 (978-0-8368-3765-0(7), 444a0ecb-ddc2-4b90-b7ca-e5455bdd9521); Brown Recluse Spiders. lib. bdg. 25.67 (978-0-8368-3766-7(5), b096f02e-e321-4802-be15-adc9c58f81da); Funnel-Web Spiders. lib. bdg. 25.67 (978-0-8368-3767-4(3), c10fa522-3e1c-4c3b-acf4-78f42b7d094c); Hobo Spiders. lib. bdg. 25.67 (978-0-8368-3768-1(1), 45b78075-5552-41ca-9f80-f74d063bdad0); Tarantulas. lib. bdg. 25.67 (978-0-8368-3769-8(X), 9eb2102c-9ccc-4539-905a-84545163c4de); Yellow Sac Spiders. lib. bdg. 25.67 (978-0-8368-3770-4(3), 34993946-90e1-4ddf-9ead-893c338db9ae); (gr. 2-4). (Dangerous Spiders Ser.). (ENG., Illus.). 24p. 2003. Set lib. bdg. 154.02 (978-0-8368-3764-3(9), 49a94941-a112-4f8f-874d-f44b894455cd, Gareth Stevens Learning Library) Stevens, Gareth Publishing LLLP.

—Funnel-Web Spiders, 1 vol. 2003. (Dangerous Spiders Ser.). (ENG., Illus.). 24p. (gr. 2-4). lib. bdg. 25.67 (978-0-8368-3767-4(3), c10fa522-3e1c-4c3b-acf4-78f42b7d094c, Gareth Stevens Learning Library) Stevens, Gareth Publishing LLLP.

—Hobo Spiders, 1 vol. 2003. (Dangerous Spiders Ser.). (ENG., Illus.). 24p. (gr. 2-4). lib. bdg. 25.67 (978-0-8368-3768-1(1), 45b78075-5552-41ca-9f80-f74d063bdad0, Gareth Stevens Learning Library) Stevens, Gareth Publishing LLLP.

—Tarantulas, 1 vol. 2003. (Dangerous Spiders Ser.). (ENG., Illus.). 24p. (gr. 2-4). lib. bdg. 25.67 (978-0-8368-3769-8(X), 9eb2102c-9ccc-4539-905a-84545163c4de, Gareth Stevens Learning Library) Stevens, Gareth Publishing LLLP.

—Yellow Sac Spiders, 1 vol. 2003. (Dangerous Spiders Ser.). (ENG., Illus.). 24p. (gr. 2-4). lib. bdg. 25.67 (978-0-8368-3770-4(3), 34993946-90e1-4ddf-9ead-893c338db9ae, Gareth Stevens Learning Library) Stevens, Gareth Publishing LLLP.

Evans, Arthur V., et al. Grzimek's Student Animal Life Resource, 2 vols. 2005. (Illus.). l, 442p. (J). (978-0-7876-9244-5(1)); (978-0-7876-9245-2(X)) Cengage Gale. (UXL).

Evans, Barbara Greene. Oscar, the Inquisitive Spider. Greene, Kelly Evelyn, illus. 2013. (ENG.). 45p. (J). pap. 24.95 (978-1-4787-1779-9(3)) Outskirts Pr., Inc.

Farndon, John. Incredible Bugs. Portolano, Cristina, illus. 2016. (Animal Bests Ser.). (ENG.). 32p. (J). (gr. 3-6). lib. bdg. 27.99 (978-1-5124-0640-5(6), d5a42811-cac0-4ca5-b000-d4b9cf060eac, Hungry Tomato (r)) Lerner Publishing Group.

Franchino, Vicky. Tarantulas. 2012. (Nature's Children Ser.). (ENG., Illus.). 48p. (J). pap. 6.95 (978-0-531-21083-3(9)); (gr. 3-5). lib. bdg. 28.00 (978-0-531-20908-0(3)) Scholastic Library Publishing. (Children's Pr.).

Franks, Katie. Spiders up Close. (Nature up Close Ser.). 24p. 2009. (gr. k-1). 42.50 (978-1-61514-828-8(0)) 2007. (ENG., Illus.). (J). (gr. 1-1). lib. bdg. 26.27 (978-1-4042-4138-1(8), ff6ef8fc-c9c4-4561-957a-8ef3ef4ceb86) Rosen Publishing Group, Inc., The. (PowerKids Pr.).

—Spiders up Close / Las Aranas. 2009. (Nature up Close / la naturaleza de cerca Ser.). (ENG & SPA.). 24p. (gr. k-1). 42.50 (978-1-61514-834-9(5), Editorial Buenas Letras) Rosen Publishing Group, Inc., The.

—Spiders up Close/Las Aranas, 1 vol. Sanz, Pilar, tr. 2007. (Nature up Close / la Naturaleza de Cerca Ser.). (ENG & SPA., Illus.). 24p. (J). (gr. 1-1). lib. bdg. 26.27 (978-1-4042-7679-6(3), de825364-84af-4943-827c-80007b3b9b79, Editorial Buenas Letras) Rosen Publishing Group, Inc., The.

Furstinger, Nancy. How Do Spiders Hear? 2018. (Crazy Animal Facts Ser.). (ENG., Illus.). 32p. (J). (gr. 4-6). lib. bdg. 28.65 (978-1-5435-4116-8(X), 139070, Capstone Pr.) Capstone.

—Spiders Are Awesome. 2018. (Animals Are Awesome Ser.). (ENG., Illus.). 32p. (J). (gr. 3-6). 32.80 (978-1-63235-441-9(1), 13819, 12-Story Library) Bookstaves, LLC.

—Spiderwebs. 2018. (Animal Engineers Ser.). (ENG., Illus.). 32p. (J). (gr. 2-3). pap. 9.95 (978-1-63517-964-4(5), 1635179645); lib. bdg. 31.35 (978-1-63517-863-0(0), 1635178630) North Star Editions. (Focus Readers).

Gaertner, Meg. Diving Bell Spiders. 2019. (Unique Animal Adaptations Ser.). (ENG., Illus.). 32p. (J). (gr. 4-6). pap. 7.95 (978-1-5435-7506-4(4), 141036) Capstone.

Gallagher, Debbie & Gallagher, Brendan. Spiders, 1 vol. 2012. (Mighty Minibeasts Ser.). (ENG.). 32p. (gr. 3-3). 31.21 (978-1-60870-547-4(1), 4293622e-55bc-4dd2-90bf-20d76cee2036) Cavendish Square Publishing LLC.

Gilpin, R. Spiders. 2003. (Usborne Beginners Ser.). (ENG., Illus.). 32p. (J). (gr. 1-3). 17.44 (978-0-7945-0167-9(2), Usborne) EDC Publishing.

Gilpin, Rebecca. Spiders. Kushii, Tetsuo & Wright, David, illus. 2006. (Usborne Beginners Ser.). 32p. (J). (gr. 1). lib. bdg. 12.99 (978-1-58086-946-1(7), Usborne) EDC Publishing.

—Spiders. Kushii, Tetsuo et al, illus. 2006. (Beginners Nature: Level 1 Ser.). 32p. (J). (gr. k-2). 4.99 (978-0-7945-1398-6(0), Usborne) EDC Publishing.

Gitlin, Marty. Las Tarántulas. 2019. (Criaturas Rastreras Ser.). (SPA., Illus.). 32p. (J). (gr. 4-6). lib. bdg. (978-1-62310-202-9(2), 12852, Bolt) Black Rabbit Bks.

—Tarantulas. 2019. (Crawly Creatures Ser.). (ENG.). 32p. (J). (gr. 4-6). pap. 9.99 (978-1-64466-024-9(5), 12685); (Illus.). lib. bdg. (978-1-68072-813-2(X), 12684) Black Rabbit Bks. (Bolt).

Giulieri, Anne. The Banana Spider. 2012. (Engage Literacy Blue Ser.). (ENG.). 16p. (J). (gr. k-2). pap. 36.94 (978-1-4296-8983-0(8), 18388); pap. 6.99 (978-1-4296-8982-3(X), 119996) Capstone. (Capstone Pr.).

Goldish, Meish. Jumping Spiders. 2008. (No Backbone! Ser.). (Illus.). 24p. (J). (gr. k-3). lib. bdg. 26.99 (978-1-59716-705-5(3), 1284307) Bearport Publishing Co., Inc.

—Spider-Tizers & Other Creepy Treats. (Extreme Cuisine Ser.). 24p. (J). (gr. 1-6). 2018. (ENG.). 7.99 (978-1-64280-073-9(2)) 2009. (Illus.). lib. bdg. 26.99 (978-1-59716-759-8(2)) Bearport Publishing Co., Inc.

—Spooky Wolf Spiders. 2008. (No Backbone! Ser.). (Illus.). 24p. (J). (gr. k-3). lib. bdg. 26.99 (978-1-59716-706-2(1), 1284306) Bearport Publishing Co., Inc.

—Tricky Trapdoor Spiders. 2008. (No Backbone! Ser.). (Illus.). 24p. (J). (gr. k-3). lib. bdg. 26.99 (978-1-59716-707-9(X), 1284305) Bearport Publishing Co., Inc.

Gravel, Elise. The Spider: The Disgusting Critters Series. (Disgusting Critters Ser.). (ENG., Illus.). 32p. (J). (gr. 1-4). 2016. pap. 6.99 (978-1-101-91854-8(3)) 2015. 10.99 (978-1-77049-664-4(5)) Tundra Bks. CAN. (Tundra Bks.). Dist: Penguin Random Hse. LLC.

Gregory, Josh. Nature's Children: Wolf Spiders. 2013. (ENG.). 48p. (J). 28.00 (978-0-531-23363-4(4)); pap. 6.95 (978-0-531-25161-4(6)) Scholastic Library Publishing.

Group/McGraw-Hill, Wright. Spider & Buffalo: Level N, 6 vols. (Summer Skies Ser.). 128p. (gr. 3-6). 36.95 (978-0-322-05887-3(2)) Wright Group/McGraw-Hill.

Guillain, Charlotte. Super Spiders, 1 vol. 2013. (Walk on the Wild Side Ser.). (ENG.). 32p. (J). (gr. 3-5). pap. 8.95 (978-1-4109-5226-4(6), 122558, Raintree) Capstone.

Hamilton, Robert M. Ticks, 1 vol. 2015. (Freaky Freeloaders: Bugs That Feed on People Ser.). (ENG., Illus.). 24p. (J). (gr. 2-3). 25.27 (978-1-4994-0770-9(X), 2ea58752-f886-4e95-8992-aeaf267cee69, PowerKids Pr.) Rosen Publishing Group, Inc., The.

Harris, Monica. Black Widow Spider. 2003. (Bug Bks.). (Illus.). 32p. (J). lib. bdg. 22.79 (978-1-4034-0762-7(2)) Heinemann-Raintree.

—Tarantula. 2003. (Bug Bks.). (Illus.). 32p. (J). lib. bdg. 22.79 (978-1-4034-0764-1(9)) Heinemann-Raintree.

Hartson, Tamara. Spiders, 1 vol. 2018. (KidsWorld Ser.). (ENG., Illus.). 64p. (J). pap. 6.99 (978-1-988183-40-4(5), 96f0f4b1-653e-4155-9ff0-161f9b7ca48b) KidsWorld Bks. CAN. Dist: Lone Pine Publishing USA.

Hayes, Amy. Funnel-Web Spiders, 1 vol. 2017. (Spiders: Eight-Legged Terrors Ser.). (ENG.). 24p. (J). (gr. 2-3). pap. 9.15 (978-1-5382-0205-0(0), f735fbc1-37ed-490a-9b26-6a62eff2dc3b) Stevens, Gareth Publishing LLLP.

Heos, Bridget. Stronger Than Steel: Spider Silk DNA & the Quest for Better Bulletproof Vests, Sutures, & Parachute Rope. Comins, Andy, illus. 2013. (Scientists in the Field Ser.). (ENG.). 80p. (J). (gr. 5-7). 18.99 (978-0-547-68126-9(7), 1475667, Clarion Bks.) HarperCollins Pubs.

Herrington, Lisa M. It's a Good Thing There Are Spiders. 2014. (Rookie Read-About(r) Science — It's a Good Thing... Ser.). (ENG.). 32p. (J). pap. 5.95 (978-0-531-22832-6(0)) Scholastic Library Publishing.

Hesper, Sam. Black Widow Spiders, 1 vol. 2014. (Animal Cannibals Ser.). (ENG., Illus.). 24p. (J). (gr. 2-3). lib. bdg. 25.27 (978-1-4777-5745-1(7), 567a7201-a299-488f-acee-e3d09024f603, PowerKids Pr.) Rosen Publishing Group, Inc., The.

Hilb, Nora, illus. Itsy Bitsy Spider. 2017. (Classic Books with Holes 8x8 Ser.). (ENG.). 16p. (J). pap. (978-1-84643-974-2(4)) Child's Play International Ltd.

Hileman, Jane. Spiders Are Hunters. 2015. (2B Wild Animals Ser.). (ENG., Illus.). 32p. (J). pap. 8.00 (978-1-63437-124-7(0)) American Reading Co.

Hirschmann, Kris. Deadliest Spiders. 2016. (ENG.). 80p. (J). (gr. 5-12). lib. bdg. (978-1-68282-058-2(0)) ReferencePoint Pr., Inc.

Houghton, Gillian. Abejas: Por Dentro y Por Fuera, 1 vol. Velazquez De Leon, Mauricio, tr. Studio Stalio, illus. 2003. (Explora la Naturaleza (Getting into Nature) Ser.). (SPA.). 32p. (YA). (gr. 3-4). lib. bdg. 28.93 (978-1-4042-2862-7(4), d3be9d93-f3fc-4338-8427-b52d9a10ff29) Rosen Publishing Group, Inc., The.

—Aranas: Por Dentro y Por Fuera, 1 vol. Gonzalez, Tomas, tr. Studio Stalio, illus. 2003. (Explora la Naturaleza (Getting into Nature) Ser.). (SPA.). 32p. (YA). (gr. 3-4). lib. bdg. 28.93 (978-1-4042-2867-2(5), 30e45ecd-aac2-41bc-b5af-b40482c21396) Rosen Publishing Group, Inc., The.

—Aranas: Por dentro y por fuera (Spiders: Inside & Out) 2009. (Explora la Naturaleza (Getting into Nature) Ser.). 32p. (gr. 3-4). 47.90 (978-1-61512-334-6(2), Editorial Buenas Letras) Rosen Publishing Group, Inc., The.

—Spider, 1 vol. 2004. (Getting into Nature Ser.). (ENG., Illus.). 32p. (J). (gr. 3-4). lib. bdg. 28.93 (978-0-8239-4209-1(0), 6feaaa3f-b922-451d-8d9f-581c2636066d) Rosen Publishing Group, Inc., The.

—Spiders: Inside & Out. 2009. (Getting into Nature Ser.). 32p. (gr. 3-4). 47.90 (978-1-61512-725-2(9), PowerKids Pr.) Rosen Publishing Group, Inc., The.

How Spiders Live, 6 vols. (Sunshinetm Science Ser.). 24p. (gr. 1-2). 31.50 (978-0-7802-0283-2(X)); 36.95 (978-0-7802-0534-5(0)) Wright Group/McGraw-Hill.

Huggins-Cooper, Lynn. Minibeasts. 2003. (Starters Ser.). 24p. (J). lib. bdg. 21.35 (978-1-58340-263-4(2)) Black Rabbit Bks.

—Scary Spiders. 2006. (Killer Nature! Ser.). (Illus.). 32p. (J). (gr. 3-5). lib. bdg. 28.50 (978-1-58340-935-0(1)) Black Rabbit Bks.

Ingram, Kevin. Spider. 2017. (Up Close & Scary Ser.). (Illus.). 32p. (gr. 2-5). 31.35 (978-1-911242-06-2(7)) Book Hse. GBR. Dist: Black Rabbit Bks.

Insects & Spiders. (Action Bks.). 64p. (J). (gr. 3-7). pap. (978-1-882210-67-1(0)) Action Publishing, Inc.

Iorio, Nicole & Time for Kids Editors. Spiders! 2005. (Time for Kids Science Scoops Ser.). (ENG., Illus.). 48p. (J). 14.99

(978-0-06-057635-6(9)); (gr. 1-3). pap. 3.99 *(978-0-06-057634-9(0))* HarperCollins Pubs.

Jackson, Tom. Spiders. 2008. (Nature's Children. Set 3 Ser.). (Illus.). 52p. (J). *(978-0-7172-6287-8(1))* Grolier, Ltd.

—Spooky Spiders, 1 vol. 2010. (Dangerous Animals Ser.). (ENG.). 32p. (gr. 2-4). (J). pap. 11.50 *(978-1-4339-4050-7(7)*, 62986c34-830f-4286-8b15-f6b666e0f445, Gareth Stevens Learning Library); (YA). lib. bdg. 29.27 *(978-1-4339-4049-1(3)*, 465681b2-3bd0-4d84-a9b8-b4ae3d9c929c) Stevens, Gareth Publishing LLLP.

Jordan, Apple. Guess Who Spins, 1 vol. 2009. (Guess Who? Ser.). (ENG.). 32p. (gr. k-1). pap. 9.23 *(978-0-7614-3558-7(1)*, 2ce8411c-0aae-4c71-b4f3-904caa827179) Cavendish Square Publishing LLC.

Kalman, Bobbie & Smithyman, Kathryn. El Ciclo de Vida de la Araña. 2006. (Ciclos de Vida Ser.). (SPA., Illus.). 32p. (J). (gr. 3-7). pap. *(978-0-7787-8714-3(1))* Crabtree Publishing Co.

—El Ciclo de Vida de la Arana. 2006. (Ciclos de Vida Ser.). (SPA., Illus.). 32p. (J). (gr. 3-7). lib. bdg. *(978-0-7787-8668-9(4))* Crabtree Publishing Co.

Keppeler, Jill. Black Widows, 1 vol. 2017. (Spiders: Eight-Legged Terrors Ser.). (ENG.). 24p. (J). (gr. 2-3). pap. 9.15 *(978-1-4824-6495-5(0)*, e9bbd82e-9b8d-4e81-a67f-02f83d9d8e56) Stevens, Gareth Publishing LLLP.

Khu, Jannell. Spiders. (My World of Animals Ser.). 24p. (gr. 1-1). 2009. 37.50 *(978-1-61514-713-7(6))* 2003. (ENG., Illus.). (J). lib. bdg. 22.27 *(978-1-4042-2523-7(4)*, 4765f555-a32d-40ff-900e-0a7ec3215e86) Rosen Publishing Group, Inc., The. (PowerKids Pr.).

—Spiders / Arañas. 2009. (My World of Animals / Yo y los animales Ser.). (ENG & SPA.). 24p. (gr. 1-1). 37.50 *(978-1-61514-718-2(7)*, Editorial Buenas Letras) Rosen Publishing Group, Inc., The.

—Spiders/Aranas, 1 vol. Beuliens, Nathalie, tr. 2003. (My World of Animals / Yo y Los Animales Ser.). (ENG & SPA., Illus.). 24p. (J). (gr. 1-1). lib. bdg. 22.27 *(978-1-4042-7523-2(1)*, 39264ffa-8ff3-46bc-b803-e41615e43f69, PowerKids Pr.) Rosen Publishing Group, Inc., The.

Klepeis, Alicia Z. Assassin Bug vs. Ogre-Faced Spider: When Cunning Hunters Collide. 2016. (Bug Wars Ser.). (ENG., Illus.). 32p. (J). (gr. 3-9). lib. bdg. 28.65 *(978-1-4914-8065-6(3)*, 130569, Capstone Pr.) Capstone.

Kolpin, Molly. Black Widow Spiders, 1 vol. 2010. (Spiders Ser.). (ENG.). 24p. (J). (gr. 1-3). lib. bdg. 25.99 *(978-1-4296-4519-5(9)*, 103011, Capstone Pr.) Capstone.

Kopp, Megan. Black Widow Spiders. 2011. (gr. 2-4). (J). pap. 12.95 *(978-1-61690-628-3(6)*, AV2 by Weigl); (Illus.). 24p. (YA). 27.13 *(978-1-61690-622-1(7))* Weigl Pubs., Inc.

Kubler, Annie. Incey Wincey Spider. 2005. (Illus.). 12p. (J). spiral bd. *(978-1-904550-03-7(7))* Child's Play International Ltd.

Ladybird. Minibeasts - Read It Yourself with Ladybird Level 3. 2016. (Read It Yourself with Ladybird Ser.). (ENG., Illus.). 48p. (J). 5.99 *(978-0-241-23737-3(8))* Penguin Bks., Ltd. GBR. Dist: Independent Pubs. Group.

Lawrence, Ellen. A Spider's Life. 2012. (Animal Diaries: Life Cycles Ser.). 24p. (J). (gr. -1-3). lib. bdg. 26.99 *(978-1-61772-414-5(9))* Bearport Publishing Co., Inc.

Leavitt, Amie Jane. Care for a Pet Tarantula. 2007. (How to Convince Your Parents You Can ... Ser.). (Illus.). 32p. (J). (gr. 1-4). lib. bdg. 25.70 *(978-1-58415-603-1(1))* Mitchell Lane Pubs.

Levy, Janey. Bird-Eating Spiders. 2017. (Spiders: Eight-Legged Terrors Ser.). 24p. (J). (gr. 2-3). pap. 48.90 *(978-1-4824-6485-6(3))* Stevens, Gareth Publishing LLLP.

Lewis, Clare. Bug Body Parts. 2015. (J). *(978-1-4846-2555-2(2))* Heinemann-Raintree.

Lomberg, Michelle. Caring for Your Spider. 2004. (Caring for Your Pet Ser.). (Illus.). 32p. (J). (gr. 4-7). per. 9.95 *(978-1-59036-155-9(5))*; lib. bdg. 26.00 *(978-1-59036-120-7(2))* Weigl Pubs., Inc.

—Spider. 2009. (My Pet Ser.). (Illus.). 32p. (J). (gr. 3-5). pap. 9.95 *(978-1-60596-095-1(0))*; lib. bdg. 26.00 *(978-1-60596-094-4(2))* Weigl Pubs., Inc.

Lomberg, Michelle & Gillespie, Katie. Spider. 2015. (J). *(978-1-4896-2970-8(X))* Weigl Pubs., Inc.

Lunis, Natalie. Deadly Black Widows. (No Backbone! Spiders Ser.). (Illus.). 24p. (J). (gr. k-3). 2016. (ENG.). pap. 7.99 *(978-1-944998-44-8(6))* 2008. lib. bdg. 26.99 *(978-1-59716-667-6(7)*, 1284310) Bearport Publishing Co., Inc.

—Inside the Spider's Web. 2013. (Science Slam: Snug As a Bug-Where Bugs Live Ser.). 24p. (J). (gr. -1-3). lib. bdg. 26.99 *(978-1-61772-903-4(5))* Bearport Publishing Co., Inc.

—Inside the Tarantula's Burrow. 2013. (Science Slam: Snug As a Bug-Where Bugs Live Ser.). 24p. (J). (gr. -1-3). lib. bdg. 26.99 *(978-1-61772-907-2(8))* Bearport Publishing Co., Inc.

Lynette, Rachel. Tarantulas, 1 vol. 2013. (Monsters of the Animal Kingdom Ser.). (ENG., Illus.). 24p. (J). (gr. 2-3). pap. 9.25 *(978-1-4488-9720-9(3)*, 72df513c-38bb-4c47-81a6-7cdfe83f872c); lib. bdg. 26.27 *(978-1-4488-9632-5(0)*, e4015e93-0155-4b5f-92b2-bcd084952ad6) Rosen Publishing Group, Inc., The. (PowerKids Pr.).

Machajewski, Sarah. Brown Recluse Spiders, 1 vol. 2017. (Spiders: Eight-Legged Terrors Ser.). (ENG.). 24p. (J). (gr. 2-3). pap. 9.15 *(978-1-5382-0202-9(6)*, 39ebf302-a7d1-4233-9b6a-6737920f0200) Stevens, Gareth Publishing LLLP.

Macheske, Felicia. Hairy Hunter: Tarantula. 2016. (Guess What Ser.). (ENG., Illus.). 24p. (J). (gr. k-2). 30.64 *(978-1-63470-722-0(2)*, 207599) Cherry Lake Publishing.

Markle, Sandra. Spiders: Biggest! Littlest! Pollard, Simon, photos by. 2011. (Biggest! Littlest! Ser.). (ENG., Illus.). 32p. (J). (gr. k-2). pap. 10.95 *(978-1-59078-875-2(3)*, Astra Young Readers) Astra Publishing Hse.

—Wolf Spiders: Mothers on Guard. 2011. (Arachnid World Ser.). (ENG., Illus.). 48p. (J). (gr. 4-8). lib. bdg. 29.32 *(978-0-7613-5040-8(3)*, 472e4549-7d45-4153-9ea7-1567490c64b2, Lerner Pubns.) Lerner Publishing Group.

Marsh, Laura. National Geographic Readers: Spiders. 2011. (Readers Ser.). (Illus.). 32p. (J). (gr. -1-k). pap. 4.99 *(978-1-4263-0851-2(5))*; (ENG., lib. bdg. 15.99 *(978-1-4263-0852-9(3))* Disney Publishing Worldwide. (National Geographic Kids).

Marshall Cavendish Corporation Staff, contrib. by. Insects & Spiders of the World, 11 vols., Set. 2003. (Illus.). 704p. lib. bdg. *(978-0-7614-7334-3(3)*, Cavendish Square) Cavendish Square Publishing LLC.

Marsico, Katie. Spiders Weave Webs. 2015. (Tell Me Why Library). (ENG., Illus.). 24p. (J). (gr. 2-5). 29.21 *(978-1-63362-617-1(2)*, 206652) Cherry Lake Publishing.

Martin, Claudia. Spiders & Bugs Around the World. 2014. (Animals Around the World Ser.). (ENG., Illus.). 32p. (J). (gr. 2-5). 31.35 *(978-1-62588-198-4(3)*, 19264, Smart Apple Media) Black Rabbit Bks.

Mattern, Joanne. Water Spiders, 1 vol. 2010. (Spiders Ser.). (ENG.). 24p. (J). (gr. 1-3). lib. bdg. 25.99 *(978-1-4296-4522-5(9)*, 103014, Capstone Pr.) Capstone.

McAneney, Caitie. Scorpion vs. Black Widow, 1 vol. 2015. (Bizarre Beast Battles Ser.). (ENG., Illus.). 24p. (J). (gr. 2-3). pap. 9.15 *(978-1-4824-2792-9(3)*, 8c506fca-aaf9-4e8e-8d82-6f3f4c477db2) Stevens, Gareth Publishing LLLP.

McFee, Shane. Deadly Spiders. 2009. (Poison! Ser.). 24p. (gr. 2-3). 42.50 *(978-1-60851-323-9(8)*, PowerKids Pr.) Rosen Publishing Group, Inc., The.

Mcginty, Alice B. The Jumping Spider. 2009. (Library of Spiders Ser.). 24p. (gr. 3-3). 42.50 *(978-1-60853-872-0(9)*, PowerKids Pr.) Rosen Publishing Group, Inc., The.

—The Tarantula. 2009. (Library of Spiders Ser.). 24p. (gr. 3-3). 42.50 *(978-1-60853-873-7(7)*, PowerKids Pr.) Rosen Publishing Group, Inc., The.

—The Wolf Spider. 2009. (Library of Spiders Ser.). 24p. (gr. 3-3). 42.50 *(978-1-60853-874-4(5)*, PowerKids Pr.) Rosen Publishing Group, Inc., The.

McNab, Chris & Sutherland, Johnathan. Dangerous Insects & Spiders, 1 vol. 2006. (Nature's Monsters: Insects & Spiders Ser.). (ENG., Illus.). 32p. (gr. 3-5). lib. bdg. 28.67 *(978-0-8368-6848-7(X)*, 47f7d10f-ce2f-4121-a097-e5f8e9d0afe7, Gareth Stevens Learning Library) Stevens, Gareth Publishing LLLP.

—Giant Spiders & Insects, 1 vol. 2006. (Nature's Monsters: Insects & Spiders Ser.). (ENG., Illus.). 32p. (gr. 3-5). lib. bdg. 28.67 *(978-0-8368-6850-0(1)*, c4294f01-08d4-4247-b973-f45bc445e80d, Gareth Stevens Learning Library) Stevens, Gareth Publishing LLLP.

Meachen Rau, Dana. Spin, Spider, Spin!, 1 vol. 2008. (Go, Critter, Go! Ser.). (ENG., Illus.). 24p. (gr. k-1). lib. bdg. 25.50 *(978-0-7614-2653-0(1)*, 4b6901ac-0f25-4f1e-a824-235317b78614) Cavendish Square Publishing LLC.

—¡Teje Araña, Teje! / Spin, Spider, Spin!, 1 vol. 2009. (¡Vamos, Insecto, Vamos! / Go, Critter, Go! Ser.). (ENG & SPA., Illus.). 24p. (gr. k-1). lib. bdg. 25.50 *(978-0-7614-2818-3(6)*, 09882752-5462-4dcd-853e-477ca4c16146) Cavendish Square Publishing LLC.

—¡Teje Araña, Teje! (Spin, Spider, Spin!), 1 vol. 2009. (¡Vamos, Insecto, Vamos! (Go, Critter, Go!) Ser.). (SPA., Illus.). 24p. (gr. k-1). lib. bdg. 25.50 *(978-0-7614-2794-0(5)*, d76ae637-295f-464c-8889-737ac6d3e1b9) Cavendish Square Publishing LLC.

Mehta, Baldev. I Like Spiders. 2009. (Illus.). 24p. pap. 11.49 *(978-1-4490-2879-4(9))* AuthorHouse.

Merlino, Kim. Insects & Spiders: Grades 2 & 3. (Illus.). (J). pap., wbk. ed. 4.99 *(978-0-88743-960-5(8))* School Zone Publishing Co.

Miller, Jake. Brown Recluse Spiders, 1 vol. 2003. (Library of Spiders Ser.). (ENG., Illus.). 24p. (J). (gr. 3-3). lib. bdg. 26.27 *(978-0-8239-6707-0(7)*, d15d6650-0544-4207-a14c-1e6c2438272f, PowerKids Pr.) Rosen Publishing Group, Inc., The.

—Cobweb Weavers. (Library of Spiders Ser.). 24p. (gr. 3-3). 2009. 42.50 *(978-1-60853-866-9(4)*, PowerKids Pr.) 2003. (ENG., Illus.). (YA). lib. bdg. 26.27 *(978-0-8239-6708-7(5)*, 9b101ff0-9647-43f2-9327-4a051fcb756c) Rosen Publishing Group, Inc., The.

—Fishing Spiders. (Library of Spiders Ser.). 24p. (gr. 3-3). 2009. 42.50 *(978-1-60853-868-3(0))* 2003. (ENG., Illus.). (J). lib. bdg. 26.27 *(978-0-8239-6711-7(5)*, c79afbcd-8613-4679-b458-7dbc1141f03b) Rosen Publishing Group, Inc., The. (PowerKids Pr.).

—Funnel Weavers. (Library of Spiders Ser.). 24p. (gr. 3-3). 2009. 42.50 *(978-1-60853-869-0(9))* 2003. (ENG., Illus.). (J). lib. bdg. 26.27 *(978-0-8239-6709-4(3)*, 93496402-ab50-4e96-b730-06b84a1ffde7) Rosen Publishing Group, Inc., The. (PowerKids Pr.).

—Trap-Door Spiders. 2009. (Library of Spiders Ser.). 24p. (gr. 3-3). 42.50 *(978-1-60853-875-1(3)*, PowerKids Pr.) Rosen Publishing Group, Inc., The.

—Trap Door Spiders, 1 vol. 2003. (Library of Spiders Ser.). (ENG., Illus.). 24p. (J). (gr. 3-3). lib. bdg. 26.27 *(978-0-8239-6710-0(7)*, 7893ffd4-e696-4007-b450-5825875bcaa1, PowerKids Pr.) Rosen Publishing Group, Inc., The.

Mitchell, Susan K. Biggest vs. Smallest Creepy, Crawly Creatures, 1 vol. 2010. (Biggest vs. Smallest Animals Ser.). (ENG., Illus.). 24p. (gr. k-2). 25.27 *(978-0-7660-3581-2(6)*, 4e77b2a2-6e9d-4810-a5ff-98770a3c0885, Enslow Elementary) Enslow Publishing, LLC.

Montgomery, Sy. The Tarantula Scientist. Bishop, Nic, photos by. 2007. (Scientists in the Field Ser.). (ENG., Illus.). 80p. (J). (gr. 5-7). pap. 9.99 *(978-0-618-91577-4(X)*, 1014892, Clarion Bks.) HarperCollins Pubs.

Morgan, Emily. Next Time You See a Spiderweb. 2016. (Next Time You See Ser.). (ENG., Illus.). 32p. (J). (gr. k-2). pap. 13.99 *(978-1-938946-34-9(0)*, 9781938946349) National Science Teachers Assn.

Morgan, Sally. Spiders. 2010. (Amazing Animal Hunters Ser.). (ENG.). 32p. (J). (gr. 3-5). lib. bdg. 28.50 *(978-1-60753-048-0(1)*, 17203) Amicus.

—Spiders. 2004. (QEB Animal Lives Ser.). (Illus.). 32p. (J). lib. bdg. 18.95 *(978-1-59566-036-7(4))* QEB Publishing Inc.

—Spiders. 2012. (ENG., Illus.). 32p. (gr. 3-5). pap. 8.95 *(978-1-926722-52-8(3))* Saunders Bk. Co. CAN. Dist: RiverStream Publishing.

Morley, Christine. Freaky Facts about Spiders. 2007. (Freaky Facts Ser.). (ENG., Illus.). 32p. (J). (gr. 2-5). 13.95 *(978-1-58728-596-7(7))*; pap. 8.95 *(978-1-58728-597-4(5))* Cooper Square Publishing Llc.

Murawski, Darlyne A. Spiders & Their Webs. Murawski, Darlyne A., photos by. 2007. (Illus.). 31p. (J). reprint ed. 17.00 *(978-1-4223-6813-8(0))* DIANE Publishing Co.

—Spiders & Their Webs. 2004. (Illus.). 32p. (J). (gr. 1-3). 16.95 *(978-0-7922-6979-3(9)*, National Geographic Kids) Disney Publishing Worldwide.

Murray, Julie. Black Widow Spiders. 2019. (Animal Kingdom Ser.). (ENG.). 32p. (J). (gr. 2-5). lib. bdg. 34.21 *(978-1-5321-1618-6(7)*, 32347, Big Buddy Bks.) ABDO Publishing Co.

—Tarantula Spiders. 2019. (Animal Kingdom Ser.). (ENG., Illus.). 32p. (J). (gr. 2-5). lib. bdg. 34.21 *(978-1-5321-1653-7(5)*, 32417, Big Buddy Bks.) ABDO Publishing Co.

Murray, Laura K. Spiders. (Seedlings Ser.). (ENG.). 24p. (J). 2016. (gr. k-2). pap. 10.99 *(978-1-62832-189-0(X)*, 21035, Creative Paperbacks) 2015. (Illus.). (gr. -1-k). *(978-1-60818-584-9(2)*, 21034, Creative Education) Creative Co., The.

O'Brien, Lindsy. Tarantula vs. Tarantula Hawk: Clash of the Giants. 2016. (Bug Wars Ser.). (ENG., Illus.). 32p. (J). (gr. 3-9). lib. bdg. 28.65 *(978-1-4914-8064-9(5)*, 130568, Capstone Pr.) Capstone.

Orme, David. Bugs & Spiders. 2010. (Fact to Fiction Grafx Ser.). (Illus.). 36p. (J). lib. bdg. 16.95 *(978-1-60686-465-4(3))* Perfection Learning Corp.

Owen, Ruth. Science & Craft Projects with Insects, Spiders, & Other Minibeasts, 1 vol. 2013. (Get Crafty Outdoors Ser.). (ENG., Illus.). 32p. (J). (gr. 2-3). 30.27 *(978-1-4777-0245-1(8)*, b38403ee-8fe0-4313-aa33-cf81a4f5796a); pap. 12.75 *(978-1-4777-0253-6(9)*, 322fcfd3-8985-46ba-ba68-fb515ce013f5) Rosen Publishing Group, Inc., The. (PowerKids Pr.).

Pallotta, Jerry. Tarantula vs. Scorpion (Who Would Win?) Bolster, Rob, illus. 2016. (Who Would Win? Ser.). (ENG.). 32p. (J). (gr. 1-3). pap. 3.99 *(978-0-545-30172-5(6))* Scholastic, Inc.

Parker, Steve. Insects & Spiders, 1 vol. 2015. (100 Facts You Should Know Ser.). (ENG., Illus.). 48p. (J). (gr. 4-5). pap. 15.05 *(978-1-4824-3203-9(X)*, a4b38a74-387e-4ba2-89c4-a0a96f3f610f) Stevens, Gareth Publishing LLLP.

—Spiders, 1 vol. Draper, Richard, illus. 2010. (I Love Animals Ser.). (ENG.). 24p. (J). (gr. 2-2). pap. 9.15 *(978-1-61533-256-4(1)*, 6b4b0877-a645-4682-b11f-dc002e19d31c); lib. bdg. 27.27 *(978-1-61533-250-2(2)*, 19e0fa5c-9d4e-44b4-9178-65411794c3da) Rosen Publishing Group, Inc., The. (Windmill Bks.).

—10 Things You Should Know about Spiders. Gallagher, Belinda & Borton, Paula, eds. Draper, Richard, illus. 2004. (10 Things You Should Know Ser.). 24p. (J). 6.99 *(978-1-84236-122-1(8))* Miles Kelly Publishing, Ltd. GBR. Dist: Independent Pubs. Group.

Patterson, Jack K. Spiders, 1 vol. 2018. (Creepy Crawlers Ser.). (ENG.). 24p. (gr. 1-1). 25.93 *(978-1-5026-4269-1(7)*, 582964bf-3f11-4a38-a97d-7aa2d048469e) Cavendish Square Publishing LLC.

Perkins, Wendy. Spider. 2011. (Amicus Readers. Animal Life Cycles (Level 2) Ser.). (ENG.). 24p. (J). (gr. 1-4). lib. bdg. 25.65 *(978-1-60753-160-9(7)*, 17067) Amicus.

Powell, Patricia Hruby. Zinnia: How the Corn Was Saved. Ruffenach, Jessie, ed. Thomas, Peter, tr. from NAV. Benally, Kendrick, illus. 2004. (ENG & NAV.). 32p. (J). (gr. -1-3). 17.95 *(978-1-893354-38-8(5))* Salina Bookshelf Inc.

Pringle, Laurence. Spiders! Strange & Wonderful. Henderson, Meryl Learnihan, illus. 2017. (Strange & Wonderful Ser.). (ENG.). 32p. (J). (gr. 2-5). 17.95 *(978-1-62979-321-4(3)*, Astra Young Readers) Astra Publishing Hse.

Randolph, Joanne. Black Widow Spiders, 1 vol., 1. 2014. (Nightmare Creatures: Spiders! Ser.). (ENG.). 24p. (J). (gr. 2-3). 26.27 *(978-1-4777-2888-8(0)*, 6ccad4dc-c579-4fcd-b022-7374483d7db7, PowerKids Pr.) Rosen Publishing Group, Inc., The.

—Crab Spiders, 1 vol., 1. 2014. (Nightmare Creatures: Spiders! Ser.). (ENG.). 24p. (J). (gr. 2-3). 26.27 *(978-1-4777-2892-5(9)*, 5a6eec19-3d88-4c96-a927-f3f96ecde3f9, PowerKids Pr.) Rosen Publishing Group, Inc., The.

—Jumping Spiders, 1 vol., 1. 2014. (Nightmare Creatures: Spiders! Ser.). (ENG.). 24p. (J). (gr. 2-3). 26.27 *(978-1-4777-2889-5(9)*, c733d551-b6fe-41b5-9266-a41aa3654e11, PowerKids Pr.) Rosen Publishing Group, Inc., The.

—Orb-Weaver Spiders, 1 vol., 1. 2014. (Nightmare Creatures: Spiders! Ser.). (ENG., Illus.). 24p. (J). (gr. 2-3). 26.27 *(978-1-4777-2893-2(7)*, b0217ebf-bf73-4895-a3c8-0909ea2d4ae5, PowerKids Pr.) Rosen Publishing Group, Inc., The.

—Tarantulas. (Classroom Pets Ser.). 2009. 24p. (gr. 2-3). 42.50 *(978-1-61511-860-1(8))* 2007. 28p. (gr. 3-7). pap. 21.25 *(978-1-4358-3835-2(1))* 2006. (ENG., Illus.). 24p. (J). (gr. 2-3). lib. bdg. 26.27 *(978-1-4042-3678-3(3)*, d606a576-9005-425a-a0a2-968259d1afd7)1. 2014. (ENG.). 24p. (J). (gr. 2-3). 26.27 *(978-1-4777-2891-8(0)*, 5b05fac7-a423-45c8-ba6a-ddf48e6131c3) Rosen Publishing Group, Inc., The. (PowerKids Pr.).

—Wolf Spiders, 1 vol., 1. 2014. (Nightmare Creatures: Spiders! Ser.). (ENG.). 24p. (J). (gr. 2-3). 26.27 *(978-1-4777-2890-1(2)*, 2e016ead-12a9-45c6-8fb2-cfb7c24b3c6e, PowerKids Pr.) Rosen Publishing Group, Inc., The.

Raum, Elizabeth. Black Widow Spiders. 2015. (Poisonous Animals Ser.). (ENG., Illus.). 32p. (J). (gr. 2-5). lib. bdg. 19.95 *(978-1-60753-784-7(2)*, 15300) Amicus.

Reher, Matt. All about Spiders. 2016. (2G Bugs Ser.). (ENG., Illus.). 24p. (J). pap. 8.00 *(978-1-63437-096-7(1))* American Reading Co.

—Spiders Don't Suck Blood. 2010. (2B Wild Animals Ser.). (ENG., Illus.). 24p. (J). pap. 8.00 *(978-1-63437-143-8(7))* American Reading Co.

René, Ellen. Investigating Spiders & Their Webs. (Science Detectives Ser.). 24p. (gr. 2-3). 2009. 42.50 *(978-1-60853-013-7(2)*, PowerKids Pr.) 2008. (ENG., Illus.). (J). lib. bdg. 26.27 *(978-1-4042-4482-5(4)*, 41d5818d-155e-4f0b-8f87-2af68fb5e468) Rosen Publishing Group, Inc., The.

Ricciuti, Edward R. Adivina Quién Teje / Guess Who Spins, 1 vol. 2009. (Adivina Quién / Guess Who? Ser.). (ENG & SPA.). 32p. (gr. k-2). 25.50 *(978-0-7614-2887-9(9)*, 1d62cea7-c519-4667-87ed-7a2a0edfe8cb) Cavendish Square Publishing LLC.

—Adivina Quién Teje (Guess Who Spins), 1 vol. 2009. (Adivina Quién (Guess Who?) Ser.). (SPA.). 32p. (gr. k-2). 25.50 *(978-0-7614-2871-8(2)*, 965148be-fa9d-4957-a019-6b9780497ebb) Cavendish Square Publishing LLC.

—Guess Who Spins, 1 vol. 2006. (Guess Who? Ser.). (ENG., Illus.). 32p. (gr. k-1). lib. bdg. 25.50 *(978-0-7614-1768-2(0)*, 76871426-f95c-40c5-86d6-dbba4db6cec6) Cavendish Square Publishing LLC.

Riley, Joelle. Hairy Tarantulas. 2009. pap. 40.95 *(978-0-8225-9318-8(1))* 2007. (ENG., Illus.). 32p. (J). lib. bdg. 22.60 *(978-0-8225-6702-8(4)*, Lerner Pubns.) Lerner Publishing Group.

Rin, Bo. Insects & Spiders: Insects & Spiders. Do, Gam, illus. 2015. (Science Storybooks Ser.). (ENG.). 32p. (J). (gr. k-4). 27.99 *(978-1-925233-61-2(8)*, 08951cb0-8239-4e9e-ae56-3faa02434702, Big and SMALL) ChoiceMaker Pty. Ltd., The AUS. Dist: Lerner Publishing Group.

Ripley's Believe It Or Not! Ripley Twists: Spiders & Scary Creepy Crawlies. 2014. (Twist Ser.: 12). (ENG.). 48p. (J). 12.95 *(978-1-60991-115-7(6))* Ripley Entertainment, Inc.

Robb, Jackie & Stringle, Berny. The Story of Spider. Duncan, Karen & Stringle, Sam, illus. 2004. (Bang on the Door Ser.). 32p. (YA). pap. *(978-1-85602-318-4(4)*, Pavilion Children's Books) Pavilion Bks.

Robbins, Lynette. Jumping Spiders. (J). 2012. 49.50 *(978-1-4488-5166-9(1)*, PowerKids Pr.) 2011. (ENG.). 24p. (gr. 2-3). pap. 9.25 *(978-1-4488-5165-2(3)*, 2b45b24f-1dc6-4a02-a912-89c42a22e334, PowerKids Pr.) 2011. (ENG.). 24p. (gr. 2-3). lib. bdg. 26.27 *(978-1-4488-5016-7(9)*, 0bb0a367-0e77-4635-b878-28aea853edca) Rosen Publishing Group, Inc., The.

Rodríguez, Ana María. The Secret of the Scuba Diving Spider... & More!, 1 vol. 2017. (Animal Secrets Revealed! Ser.). (ENG.). 48p. (gr. 4-4). lib. bdg. 29.60 *(978-0-7660-8629-6(1)*, 63bce324-8009-413a-b10f-a33a1d754f7f) Enslow Publishing, LLC.

Ross, Michael Elsohn. Spiderology. Erickson, Darren, illus. Grogan, Brian, photos by. (Backyard Buddies Ser.). 48p. (gr. 3-6). 2005. lib. bdg. 19.93 *(978-1-57505-387-5(X))* 2003. (YA). 6.95 *(978-1-57505-438-4(8)*, Carolrhoda Bks.) Lerner Publishing Group.

Roza, Greg. Deadly Black Widows, 1 vol. 2011. (Small but Deadly Ser.). (ENG.). 24p. (J). (gr. 2-3). pap. 9.15 *(978-1-4339-5732-1(9)*, 1b58a13f-0d0a-4916-8a77-63d08d356967); lib. bdg. 25.27 *(978-1-4339-5730-7(2)*, 463f3775-be07-4198-a411-9b1f5f7436d7) Stevens, Gareth Publishing LLLP. (Gareth Stevens Learning Library).

—Strange Spiders. 2011. (World of Bugs Ser.). (Illus.). 24p. (gr. k-2). 69.20 *(978-1-4339-6145-8(8))*; (ENG., (J). pap. 9.15 *(978-1-4339-4612-7(2)*, f888c636-7874-402e-87e2-0ce2ff13aee3); (ENG., (J). lib. bdg. 25.27 *(978-1-4339-4611-0(4)*, 468a637b-ff68-43bd-8558-4e5226a99240) Stevens, Gareth Publishing LLLP.

Rupert, Matthews. Visual Factfinder Bugs. 2008. 512p. pap. *(978-1-84810-079-4(5))* Miles Kelly Publishing, Ltd.

Rustad, Martha E. H. Stunning Spiders. 2017. (Bugs Are Beautiful! Ser.). (ENG., Illus.). 32p. (J). (gr. -1-2). lib. bdg. 27.99 *(978-1-5157-4500-6(7)*, 134199, Capstone Pr.) Capstone.

School Zone Publishing Company Staff. Insects & Spiders. (Illus.). (J). 19.99 incl. audio compact disk *(978-0-88743-977-3(2))*; 19.99 incl. audio compact disk *(978-0-88743-944-5(6))* School Zone Publishing Co.

Schuetz, Kari. Tarantulas. 2015. (Creepy Crawlies Ser.). (ENG., Illus.). 24p. (J). (gr. k-3). lib. bdg. 26.95 *(978-1-62617-227-2(7)*, Blastoff! Readers) Bellwether Media.

Seeley, M. H. Trap-Door Spiders, 1 vol. 2017. (Spiders: Eight-Legged Terrors Ser.). (ENG.). 24p. (J). (gr. 2-3). pap. 9.15 *(978-1-5382-0213-5(1)*, 381d3e2b-d7f0-4cdf-94e5-e8b5bec2ae8c) Stevens, Gareth Publishing LLLP.

Sharif, Meghan. Why Do Wolf Spiders Make Burrows? And Other Odd Arachnid Adaptations, 1 vol. 2018. (Odd Adaptations Ser.). (ENG.). 32p. (gr. 3-4). 28.27 *(978-1-5382-2035-1(0)*, 3472a88f-1675-48bc-8cf6-8da7a6692965) Stevens, Gareth Publishing LLLP.

Shea, Therese. Spider Biters. (Big Bad Biters Ser.). 24p. (gr. 2-3). 2009. 42.50 *(978-1-61511-565-5(X))* 2006. (ENG., Illus.). (J). lib. bdg. 26.27 *(978-1-4042-3521-2(3)*, e945f69c-845b-4c59-85f9-4021a220acf0) Rosen Publishing Group, Inc., The. (PowerKids Pr.).

—We Need Spiders, 1 vol. 2015. (Creatures We Can't Live Without Ser.). (ENG.). 24p. (J). (gr. 3-4). 25.27 *(978-1-4994-1044-0(1)*, ab56d140-1095-4b5b-945a-b43ff51972e7, PowerKids Pr.) Rosen Publishing Group, Inc., The.

Shea, Therese M. 20 Fun Facts about Spiders, 1 vol. 2013. (Fun Fact File: Bugs! Ser.). (ENG., Illus.). 32p. (gr. 2-3). 27.93 *(978-1-4339-8245-3(5)*, 17002003-0a37-495b-8d56-8def7504f849); pap. 11.50 *(978-1-4339-8246-0(3)*, 80d3f012-e764-43d6-9cfb-0d82f1b0d119) Stevens, Gareth Publishing LLLP. (Gareth Stevens Learning Library).

Shofner, Melissa Raé. Giant Huntsman Spiders, 1 vol. 2017. (Spiders: Eight-Legged Terrors Ser.). (ENG.). 24p. (J). (gr. 2-3). pap. 9.15 *(978-1-5382-0209-8(3)*, 8a9ed137-552d-4da1-a1c8-d8786c06ea75) Stevens, Gareth Publishing LLLP.

Sill, Cathryn. About Arachnids: A Guide for Children, 1 vol. Sill, John, illus. 2003. (About... Ser.: 7). 40p. (J). (gr. -1-2). 16.95 *(978-1-56145-038-1(3))* Peachtree Publishing Co. Inc.

Silverstein, Alvin, et al. Tarantulas: Cool Pets!, 1 vol. 2012. (Far-Out & Unusual Pets Ser.). (ENG., Illus.). 48p. (gr. 3-3). pap. 11.53 *(978-1-4644-0128-2(4),* 5e073838-cca2-4500-b75b-9e5dba74d480, Enslow Elementary) Enslow Publishing, LLC.
Simon, Seymour. Smithsonian: Spiders. 2007. (ENG., Illus.). 32p. (J). (gr. k-4). pap. 7.99 *(978-0-06-089103-9(3),* HarperCollins) HarperCollins Pubs.
—Spiders. 2003. (Illus.). 32p. (J). (gr. k-4). lib. bdg. 17.89 *(978-0-06-028392-6(0))* HarperCollins Pubs.
Simons, Lisa M. B. From Egg to Spider. 2003. (Grow up! Ser.). (J). pap. *(978-1-58417-178-2(2));* lib. bdg. *(978-1-58417-172-0(3))* Lake Street Pubs.
Siy, Alexandra. Up Close with Spiders. Kunkel, Dennis, photos by. 2018. (Illus.). 48p. (J). (gr. 2-5). pap. 8.99 *(978-0-8234-4044-3(3))* Holiday Hse., Inc.
Smith, Sian. Spiders, 1 vol. 2012. (Creepy Critters Ser.). (ENG., Illus.). 24p. (J). (gr. -1-k). pap. 9.95 *(978-1-4109-4823-6(4),* 119460, Raintree) Capstone.
The Spider Bank: Individual Title Six-Packs. (Story Steps Ser.). (gr. k-2). 32.00 *(978-0-7635-9845-7(3))* Rigby Education.
Spiders (Eyes on Nature Ser.). 32p. (J). (gr. 1). pap. *(978-1-882210-59-6(X))* Action Publishing, Inc.
Spiders (Eyes on Nature Ser.). (Illus.). 32p. (J). (gr. 1-18). 7.95 *(978-1-56156-462-0(1))* Kidsbooks, LLC.
Spiders: Eight-Legged Terrors. 2017. (Spiders: Eight-Legged Terrors Ser.). 24p. (gr. 2-3). pap. 48.90 *(978-1-5382-0489-4(4));* (ENG.). lib. bdg. 145.62 *(978-1-5382-0475-7(4),* 021eec83-6c7f-4865-ad7f-da6995f410e7) Stevens, Gareth Publishing LLLP.
Spiders: Level I, 6 vols. (Wonder Worldtm Ser.). 16p. 29.95 *(978-0-7802-1237-4(1))* Wright Group/McGraw-Hill.
Spiders & their Webs, 6 vols. (Sunshinetm Science Ser.). 24p. (gr. 1-2). 36.95 *(978-0-7802-0535-2(9));* 31.50 *(978-0-7802-0284-9(8))* Wright Group/McGraw-Hill.
Spiders are Special Animals, 6 vols. (Sunshinetm Science Ser.). 24p. (gr. 1-2). 36.95 *(978-0-7802-0536-9(7));* 31.50 *(978-0-7802-0285-6(6))* Wright Group/McGraw-Hill.
Staff, Gareth Editorial Staff. Spiders, 1 vol. 2004. (All about Wild Animals Ser.). (ENG., Illus.). 32p. (gr. 2-4). lib. bdg. 28.67 *(978-0-8368-4172-5(7),* 1d2493e0-0c2f-4846-b183-af7b966597cb, Gareth Stevens Learning Library) Stevens, Gareth Publishing LLLP.
Stark, Kristy. Terrarium Pets: Volume (Grade 6) 2019. (Mathematics in the Real World Ser.). (ENG., Illus.). 32p. (gr. 5-8). pap. 11.99 *(978-1-4258-5891-9(0))* Teacher Created Materials, Inc.
Statts, Leo. Tarantulas. 2016. (Rain Forest Animals Ser.). (ENG.). 24p. (J). (gr. -1-2). 49.94 *(978-1-68079-364-2(0),* 22985, Abdo Zoom-Launch) ABDO Publishing Co.
Stewart, Melissa. How Do Spiders Make Webs?, 1 vol. 2009. (Tell Me Why, Tell Me How Ser.). (ENG., Illus.). 32p. (gr. 3-3). lib. bdg. 32.64 *(978-0-7614-2920-3(4),* 2af2b0a9-d741-4150-848f-3fc7a1399c01) Cavendish Square Publishing LLC.
—Insect or Spider? How Do You Know?, 1 vol. 2011. (Which Animal Is Which? Ser.). (ENG., Illus.). 24p. (gr. k-2). pap. 10.35 *(978-1-59845-237-2(1),* 9f811824-f9c6-48c8-9233-22ed11d4fe38, Enslow Elementary); lib. bdg. 25.27 *(978-0-7660-3681-9(2),* c4de5651-36e9-4e71-89b8-f68482a7f4c7) Enslow Publishing, LLC.
Stradling, Jan. Spy on Spiders: Level K, 6 vols., Vol. 2. (First Explorers Ser.). 24p. (gr. 1-2). 34.95 *(978-0-7699-1465-7(9))* Shortland Pubns. (U. S. A.) Inc.
Strain Trueit, Trudi. Spiders, 1 vol. (Backyard Safari Ser.). (ENG.). 2012. 32p. (gr. 3-3). 31.21 *(978-1-60870-249-7(9),* 9796599a-2be1-4176-a423-47ece010bf4d) 2010. 24p. (gr. k-1). 25.50 *(978-0-7614-3965-3(X),* a2bc4ced-d21d-4065-aeb8-e4801ca8cceb) Cavendish Square Publishing LLC.
Strother, Ruth. Tarantula Paperback. 2013. (Great Predators Ser.). (ENG., Illus.). 48p. (J). (gr. 4-8). pap. 18.50 *(978-1-62403-017-8(3),* 10793) ABDO Publishing Co.
Sullivan, Laura. Insects & Arachnids Explained, 1 vol. 2016. (Distinctions in Nature Ser.). (ENG., Illus.). 32p. (gr. 3-3). pap. 11.58 *(978-1-5026-2189-4(4),* 27a4e3b2-8015-4a40-9397-a7dba43d8ceb) Cavendish Square Publishing LLC.
Sundance/Newbridge LLC Staff. Spinning a Web. 2007. (Early Science Ser.). (gr. k-3). 18.95 *(978-1-4007-6233-0(2));* pap. 6.10 *(978-1-4007-6229-3(4))* Sundance/Newbridge Educational Publishing.
Tait, Noel. Insects & Spiders. 2008. (Insiders Ser.). (ENG.). 64p. (J). (gr. 3-7). 19.99 *(978-1-4169-3868-2(0),* Simon & Schuster Bks. For Young Readers) Simon & Schuster Bks. For Young Readers.
Taylor, Barbara. Exploring Nature - Sensational Spiders: A Comprehensive Guide to Some of the Most Intriguing Creatures in the Animal Kingdom, with over 220 Pictures. 2013. (ENG., Illus.). 64p. (J). (gr. k-8). 12.99 *(978-1-84322-854-7(8),* Armadillo) Anness Publishing GBR. Dist: National Bk. Network.
Taylor-Butler, Christine. Insects & Spiders. 2013. (ENG.). 48p. (J). 29.00 *(978-0-531-21753-5(1))* Scholastic Library Publishing.
Taylor, Trace. Jumping Spiders. Taylor, Trace, illus. 2012. (1-3Y Bugs Ser.). (ENG., Illus.). 20p. (J). pap. 8.00 *(978-1-61406-687-3(6))* American Reading Co.
—Tarantulas. 2009. (Bugs Ser.). (ENG.). 12p. (J). (gr. k-2). pap. 9.60 *(978-1-59301-852-8(5))* American Reading Co.
Taylor, Trace & Rupp, Kristina. Tarantulas (English) 2016. (2G Bugs Ser.). (ENG., Illus.). 20p. (J). pap. 8.00 *(978-1-61406-692-7(2))* American Reading Co.
Taylor, Trace & Sanchez, Lucia M. Tarántulas (Tarantulas) 2011. (poder de 100 - Bichos Ser.). (SPA.). 12p. pap. 33.92 *(978-1-61541-291-4(3))* American Reading Co.
Titmus, Dawn. Insects & Spiders, 1 vol. 2018. (Cool Pets for Kids Ser.). (ENG.). 32p. (J). (gr. 3-3). 27.93 *(978-1-5383-3801-8(7),* 21a175d6-3feb-47b8-8e26-0fd93223c935, PowerKids Pr.) Rosen Publishing Group, Inc., The.
Turner, Matt. Deadly Spiders. Calle, Santiago, illus. 2017. (Crazy Creepy Crawlers Ser.). (ENG.). 32p. (J). (gr. 3-6). 27.99 *(978-1-5124-1553-7(7),* bfecdfb1-9a44-46c7-b330-07cea47d687e); E-Book 42.65 *(978-1-5124-3596-2(1),* 9781512435962); E-Book 4.99 *(978-1-5124-3597-9(X),* 9781512435979); E-Book 42.65 *(978-1-5124-2713-4(6))* Lerner Publishing Group. (Hungry Tomato (r)).
Underwater Spiders: Early Level Satellite Individual Title Six-Packs. (Sails Literacy Ser.). 16p. (gr. 1-2). 27.00 *(978-0-7578-3162-1(1))* Rigby Education.
Vilardi, Debbie. Why Do Spiders Make Webs? 2019. (Science Questions Ser.). (ENG., Illus.). 24p. (J). (gr. 1-1). pap. 8.95 *(978-1-64185-589-1(4),* 1641855894) North Star Editions.
—Why Do Spiders Make Webs? 2018. (Science Questions Ser.). (ENG., Illus.). 24p. (J). (gr. k-3). lib. bdg. 31.36 *(978-1-5321-6218-3(9),* 30219, Pop! Cody Koala) Pop!
Washington, Joi. Jumping Spiders. 2011. (Predator Bugs Ser.). 16p. pap. 39.62 *(978-1-61541-356-0(1))* American Reading Co.
—The Wolf Spider. 2011. (Power 50 - Predator Bugs Ser.). 32p. (J). (gr. k-2). pap. 7.95 *(978-1-61541-379-9(0))* American Reading Co.
Washington, Joi & Sanchez, Lucia M. ArañAs Saltadoras: Jumping Spiders. 2011. (Bichos depredadores (Predator Bugs) Ser.). 16p. (J). pap. 6.95 *(978-1-61541-357-7(X))* American Reading Co.
Waxman, Laura Hamilton. Web-Spinning Spiders. 2016. (First Step Nonfiction — Backyard Critters Ser.). (ENG., Illus.). 24p. (J). (gr. k-2). 23.99 *(978-1-5124-0884-3(0),* faab2501-d11d-4c92-9eef-509bbcd2b42f, Lerner Pubns.) Lerner Publishing Group.
Weber, Valerie J. Por Qué Algunos Animales Tejen Telarañas (Why Animals Live in Webs), 1 vol. 2008. (Donde Viven Los Animales (Where Animals Live) Ser.). (SPA.). 24p. (gr. 2-4). pap. 9.15 *(978-0-8368-8819-5(7),* abd6c368-0e61-4723-90fb-b63b5941ab9a, Weekly Reader Leveled Readers) Stevens, Gareth Publishing LLLP.
—Por Qué Algunos Animales Tejen Telarañas (Why Animals Live in Webs), 1 vol. 2008. (Donde Viven Los Animales (Where Animals Live) Ser.). (SPA., Illus.). 24p. (gr. 2-4). lib. bdg. 24.67 *(978-0-8368-8812-6(X),* dc43b668-8a47-41f9-941b-beaef87653ae, Weekly Reader Leveled Readers) Stevens, Gareth Publishing LLLP.
—Why Animals Live in Webs, 1 vol. 2008. (Where Animals Live Ser.). (ENG.). 24p. (gr. 2-4). pap. 9.15 *(978-0-8368-8805-8(7),* c72824dd-873a-45a1-a537-da12d9c903b6, Weekly Reader Leveled Readers) Stevens, Gareth Publishing LLLP.
—Why Animals Live in Webs, 1 vol. 2008. (Where Animals Live Ser.). (ENG., Illus.). 24p. (gr. 2-4). lib. bdg. 24.67 *(978-0-8368-8798-3(0),* 1f3ae027-03ab-4382-bfb0-8d561e2fe00f, Weekly Reader Leveled Readers) Stevens, Gareth Publishing LLLP.
West, David. Spiders & Other Creepy-Crawlies, 1 vol. 2017. (Inside Animals Ser.). (ENG., Illus.). 24p. (J). (gr. 3-3). 26.27 *(978-1-5081-9389-0(4),* 41b662d8-0d4f-48e0-b101-3f5ada865790); pap. 9.25 *(978-1-5081-9430-9(0),* f5358fb4-3e99-43e9-a712-abdd979a1b52) Rosen Publishing Group, Inc., The. (Windmill Bks.).
What's This Spider Doing? Individual Title Six-Packs. (Story Steps Ser.). (gr. k-2). 32.00 *(978-0-7635-9617-0(5))* Rigby Education.
White, Nancy. Crafty Garden Spiders. 2008. (No Backbone! Ser.). (Illus.). 24p. (YA). (gr. k-3). lib. bdg. 26.99 *(978-1-59716-703-1(7))* Bearport Publishing Co., Inc.
Wilson, Emily. Trap-Door Spiders, 1 vol. 2016. (Dig Deep! Bugs That Live Underground Ser.). (ENG., Illus.). 24p. (J). (gr. 3-3). pap. 9.25 *(978-1-4994-2066-1(8),* 78a60825-b6e4-4e95-942d-c73d104cb932, PowerKids Pr.) Rosen Publishing Group, Inc., The.
Wimmer, Teresa. Spiders. 2006. (My First Look at Insects Ser.). (Illus.). 24p. (J). (gr. k-2). 15.95 *(978-1-58341-456-9(8),* Creative Education) Creative Co., The.
Wood, Selina. Spiders. 2009. (Extreme Pets Ser.). (YA). (gr. 4-7). 28.50 *(978-1-59920-234-1(4))* Black Rabbit Bks.
Woodward, John. Spider. 2010. (Garden Minibeasts up Close Ser.). 32p. (gr. 2-4). 30.00 *(978-1-60413-895-5(5),* Chelsea Clubhse.) Infobase Holdings, Inc.
World Book, Inc. Staff, contrib. by. Animal Lives, 7 vols. 2009. (Illus.). 336p. (J). (gr. 3-5). 139.00 *(978-0-7166-0401-3(9))* World Bk., Inc.
—Insects & Spiders. (J). 2011. *(978-0-7166-1789-1(7))* 2009. *(978-0-7166-0405-1(1))* World Bk., Inc.
—Insects, Spiders, & Creepy Crawlers: A Supplement to Childcraft, the How & Why Library. 2007. (J). *(978-0-7166-0618-5(6))* World Bk., Inc.
—Pinktoes & Other Tarantulas. 2007. (World Book's Animals of the World Ser.). (Illus.). 64p. (J). *(978-0-7166-1332-9(8))* World Bk., Inc.
Zabludoff, Marc. Spiders, 1 vol. 2007. (Animal Ways Ser.). (ENG., Illus.). 112p. (gr. 6-6). lib. bdg. 38.36 *(978-0-7614-1747-7(8),* 072784af-4277-484e-b331-e89d7806a4c2) Cavendish Square Publishing LLC.
Zondervan Staff. Spiders, Snakes, Bees, & Bats, 1 vol. 2010. (I Can Read! / Made by God Ser.). (ENG., Illus.). 32p. (J). (gr. -1-2). pap. 4.99 *(978-0-310-72007-2(9))* Zonderkidz.

SPIDERS—FICTION

Abbott Orloff, Chrissy. Lady Humming Fly's Lesson on Staying Safe. 2009. 80p. pap. 28.99 *(978-1-4389-9938-8(0))* AuthorHouse.
Alexander, R. W. Spider Fight. 2010. (J). pap. 9.95 *(978-0-7414-5924-4(8))* Infinity Publishing.
Allen, Jean M. A Tangled Web. 2012. 26p. 24.95 *(978-1-4512-9475-0(1))* America Star Bks.
Anderson, Jane. Anansi the Spider & the Sky King: A Tale from Africa. 2006. (J). pap. *(978-1-4108-6175-7(9))* Benchmark Education Co.
Anderson, Michael. Woolly Bargains: A Scary Story for Young People. 2013. (ENG.). 27p. (J). pap. 22.95 *(978-1-4787-0654-0(6))* Outskirts Pr., Inc.
Archer, Dosh. Itsy Bitsy Spider. Archer, Dosh, illus. (Urgency Emergency! Ser.). (ENG., Illus.). 48p. (J). (gr. k-2). 2015. pap. 9.99 *(978-0-8075-8360-9(X),* 080758360X) 2013. 12.99 *(978-0-8075-8358-6(8),* 807583588) Whitman, Albert & Co.
Arrington, H. Anansi's Narrow Waist: A Tale from Ghana, 1 vol. Allin, Nicole, illus. 2017. (ENG.). 32p. (J). (gr. k-3). 16.99 *(978-1-4556-2216-0(8),* Pelican Publishing) Arcadia Publishing.
Austrian, J. J. Worm Loves Worm. Curato, Mike, illus. 2016. (ENG.). 32p. (J). (gr. -1-3). 17.99 *(978-0-06-238633-5(6),* Balzer & Bray) HarperCollins Pubs.
Baldwin, C. R. Henry the Spider. 2011. (Illus.). 44p. pap. 16.76 *(978-1-4567-8649-6(0))* AuthorHouse.
Baldwin, Kevin. Beetle Dan & the Big Purple Slide: A Beetle Dan Story. 2006. (ENG., Illus.). 32p. (J). (gr. -1-2). 14.99 *(978-1-59185-921-5(2),* 9212, Creation Hse.) Charisma Media.
Beeson, Jan. Mysterious World of the Puffins the Treasure Hunt Book 1. 2013. 74p. pap. 19.99 *(978-0-9890482-0-0(9))* Beeson, Jan.
Bennett, Angela K. Herbert the Helpful Spider. 2018. (ENG., Illus.). 18p. (J). (gr. -1-3). pap. *(978-1-5289-2479-5(7))* Austin Macauley Pubs. Ltd.
—Herbert the Helpful Spider. 2018. (ENG., Illus.). 15p. (J). pap. 13.95 *(978-1-78710-547-8(4),* 40730a8e-b79f-49bc-99dd-3b5acbb78f1d) Austin Macauley Pubs. Ltd. GBR. Dist: Baker & Taylor Publisher Services (BTPS).
Bentley, Dawn. Three Hungry Spiders & One Fat Fly! Twinem, Neecy, illus. 2010. (Stretchies Book Ser.). 16p. (J). (gr. -1-k). 8.99 *(978-0-8249-1460-8(0),* Ideals Pubns.) Worthy Publishing.
Berger, Melvin. Spinning Spiders. 2003. (Let's-Read-And-Find-Out Science 2 Ser.). (ENG., Illus.). 40p. (J). (gr. k-4). pap. 6.99 *(978-0-06-445207-6(7),* HarperCollins) HarperCollins Pubs.
—Spinning Spiders. Schindler, S. D., illus. 2003. (Let's-Read-and-Find-Out Science Ser.). (ENG.). 40p. (J). (gr. k-4). 15.99 *(978-0-06-028696-5(2))* HarperCollins Pubs.
Berlin, Ethan T. The Hugely-Wugely Spider. Edwards, Karl Newsom, illus. 2018. (ENG.). 40p. (J). 18.99 *(978-0-374-30616-8(8),* 900174319, Farrar, Straus & Giroux (BYR)) Farrar, Straus & Giroux.
Beus, Bryan. Westly: A Spider's Tale. Beus, Bryan, illus. 2015. (ENG., Illus.). 176p. (J). (gr. 4-6). 15.99 *(978-1-62972-068-5(2),* 5136479, Shadow Mountain) Shadow Mountain Publishing.
Blocker, Adam P. Joshua & the Spider. Taylor, Josh, illus. 2013. (ENG.). 72p. 17.99 *(978-1-939418-08-1(9))* Writer of the Round Table Pr.
Bolander, Sharon Miller. At the Stroke of Midnight. 2012. 40p. pap. 24.95 *(978-1-4626-8905-7(1))* America Star Bks.
Boniface, William. Lights Out, Night's Out. Kirkova, Milena, illus. 2011. (ENG.). 24p. (J). pap. 6.99 *(978-1-4494-0236-5(4))* Andrews McMeel Publishing.
Bonnell, Kris. Spiders. 2009. (J). pap. 7.95 *(978-1-60892-000-6(3))* Reading Reading Bks., LLC.
Bowman, Chaliece. Sarah's Camping Trip. 2012. 20p. pap. 17.99 *(978-1-4772-5531-5(1))* AuthorHouse.
Brewis, Alan. Boris Returns A Hero! 2008. 72p. pap. 12.50 *(978-1-4357-4377-9(6))* Lulu Pr., Inc.
Brightwood, Laura, illus. Anansi & the Turtle. Brightwood, Laura, . 2006. (J). *(978-0-9779290-0-9(0))* 3-C Institute for Social Development.
Brooks, Donna. The Golden Spindle. 2010. 112p. pap. 30.00 *(978-1-60860-852-2(2),* Eloquent Bks.) Strategic Book Publishing & Rights Agency (SBPRA).
Cairo, Anna. The Spider in My Shower. 2012. 28p. pap. 16.99 *(978-1-4634-8768-3(1))* AuthorHouse.
Callen, Sharon. Happy Faces Leave Home, 1 vol. rev. ed. 2013. (Literary Text Ser.). (ENG., Illus.). 28p. (gr. 2-3). pap. 9.99 *(978-1-4333-5560-8(4))* Teacher Created Materials, Inc.
Carle, Eric. La Araña Muy Ocupada. Carle, Eric, illus. 2004. Tr. of Very Busy Spider. (SPA., Illus.). 32p. (J). (gr. -1-k). 21.99 *(978-0-399-24241-0(4))* Penguin Young Readers Group.
—The Very Busy Spider. Carle, Eric, illus. 2011. (ENG., Illus.). 24p. (J). (gr. -1 — 1). bds. 16.99 *(978-0-399-25601-1(6),* Philomel Bks.) Penguin Young Readers Group.
—The Very Busy Spider: A Lift-The-Flap Book. 2006. (World of Eric Carle Ser.). (Illus.). 24p. (J). (gr. -1-k). 9.99 *(978-0-448-44421-5(6))* Penguin Young Readers Group.
Carlson, Melody. Bitsy's Harvest Party. Reagan, Susan Joy, illus. 2005. 32p. (J). (gr. -1-4). 12.99 *(978-0-8054-2684-7(1))* B&H Publishing Group.
Chapman, Keith. Itsy Bitsy Spider. Tickle, Jack, illus. (Tiger Tales Ser.). (J). 2008. 24p. (gr. -1-2). pap. 6.95 *(978-1-58925-407-7(4))* 2006. 32p. 15.95 *(978-1-58925-055-0(9))* Tiger Tales.
Chronicle Books, Chronicle & ImageBooks. Little Spider: Finger Puppet Book: (Finger Puppet Book for Toddlers & Babies, Baby Books for Halloween, Animal Finger Puppets) 2007. (Little Finger Puppet Board Bks.: FING). (ENG., Illus.). 12p. (J). (gr. -1 — 1). bds. 7.99 *(978-0-8118-6104-5(X))* Chronicle Bks. LLC.
Clark, Janice Stump. Miss Golden-Silk Unties a Tangle. 2011. (ENG., Illus.). 34p. (J). (gr. -1-3). pap. 19.99 *(978-0-9996323-0-7(2))* Garden Gallery.
Coffman, Dan. Titu Miata's Spider. 2012. (ENG.). pap. *(978-1-4675-2424-7(7))* Independent Pub.
Cook, Beatrice. A Journey with the Spider & Snake to Arizona. Campis, Adrian, Jr., illus. 2007. (J). 14.95 *(978-0-9795867-0-5(4))* Travel America Bks.
Cook, Sherry & Johnson, Terri. Susie Sound, 26. Kuhn, Jesse, illus. Lt. ed. 2006. 32p. (J). 7.99 *(978-1-933815-18-3(3),* Quirkles, The) Creative 3, LLC.
Cox, Tracey M. Arachnabet- an Alphabet of Spiders. 2013. 20p. pap. 9.95 *(978-1-61633-362-1(6))* Guardian Angel Publishing, Inc.
Cronin, Doreen. Diary of a Spider. Bliss, Harry, illus. (ENG.). 40p. (J). (gr. -1-3). 2013. 12.99 *(978-0-06-223300-4(9))* 2005. 18.99 *(978-0-06-000153-7(4))* HarperCollins Pubs. (HarperCollins).
—Diary of a Spider. Bliss, Harry, illus. unabr. ed. 2006. (Picture Book Readalong Ser.). (J). (gr. -1-2). 28.95 incl. audio compact disk *(978-1-59519-486-2(X))* Live Oak Media.
—Diary of a Spider. Bliss, Harry, illus. unabr. ed. 2006. (J). (gr. -1-3). 29.95 *(978-0-439-90579-4(6))* Weston Woods Studios, Inc.
Czajak, Paul. Seaver the Weaver. The Brothers Hilts, The Brothers, illus. 2015. (ENG.). 32p. (J). (-k). 15.95 *(978-1-938063-57-2(0),* Mighty Media Kids) Mighty Media Pr.
Danley, Jerry J. Billy Black Ant's Exciting Adventures. Hilley, Thomas, illus. 2012. 56p. pap. 12.99 *(978-0-9885180-5-6(8))* Mindstir Media.
Delessert, Etienne. Spartacus the Spider. 2010. (ENG., Illus.). 32p. (J). (gr. 1-3). 17.95 *(978-1-56846-213-4(1),* 22062, Creative Editions) Creative Co., The.
Diaz, S. Jemmy & the Little Spider of Hope. 2012. 40p. pap. 20.99 *(978-1-4772-7032-5(9))* AuthorHouse.
Dj Caz. Spiders & Cupcakes. 2009. 28p. pap. 12.49 *(978-1-4389-7243-5(1))* AuthorHouse.
Dodson, Emma. Speckle the Spider. Dodson, Emma, illus. 2010. (ENG., Illus.). 32p. (J). (gr. -1-2). 14.99 *(978-0-7636-4778-0(0))* Candlewick Pr.
Donaldson, Julia. Spinderella. Pichon, Liz, illus. 2005. (Blue Go Bananas Ser.). (ENG.). 48p. (J). (gr. 1-2). lib. bdg. *(978-0-7787-2628-9(2))* Crabtree Publishing Co.
Donbavand, Tommy. Scream Street: Heart of the Mummy, Bk. 3. Cartoon Saloon, Ltd., illus. 2010. (Scream Street Ser.: 3). (ENG.). 128p. (J). (gr. 3-7). pap. 5.99 *(978-0-7636-4636-3(9))* Candlewick Pr.
Dyan, Penelope. Mikey & Me & the Spider — -the Continuing Story of a Girl & Her Dog. Dyan, Penelope, illus. 2010. (Illus.). 50p. pap. 14.95 *(978-1-935118-95-4(1))* Bellissima Publishing, LLC.
Eddy, Olivia. The Hatchling. 2008. 112p. pap. 9.99 *(978-1-60693-546-0(1),* Strategic Bk. Publishing) Strategic Book Publishing & Rights Agency (SBPRA).
El-Magazy, Rowzaa. Ali & the Spider. 2016. (ENG., Illus.). 18p. (J). (gr. -1-2). 8.95 *(978-0-86037-325-4(8))* Kube Publishing Ltd. GBR. Dist: Consortium Bk. Sales & Distribution.
Ewers, Hans Heinz. The Spider. 2004. reprint ed. pap. 1.99 *(978-1-4192-8326-0(X))* Kessinger Publishing, LLC.
Farahay, Michael L. The Butterfly, The Bee & The Spider. Farahay, Naomi E., ed. 2007. (ENG.). 80p. pap. 36.95 *(978-1-4303-2623-6(9))* Lulu Pr., Inc.
Finn, Isobel. La Mariquita Perezosa. 2003. (SPA., Illus.). 26p. (J). *(978-84-8418-029-6(8),* ZZ4475) Zendrera Zariquiey, Editorial ESP. Dist: Lectorum Pubns., Inc.
Fletcher, Ralph. Spider Boy. 2009. (ENG.). 192p. (J). (gr. 5-7). pap. 7.99 *(978-0-547-24820-2(2),* 1100710, Clarion Bks.) HarperCollins Pubs.
Flores, Travis. The Spider Who Never Gave Up. Michelle, Ciappa, illus. 2004. (J). *(978-0-9759077-0-2(0))* Inclusive Global Inc.
Flores, Vanessa. Tasha Tries to Fly: If... Then, 1 vol. 2017. (Computer Science for the Real World Ser.). (ENG.). 12p. (gr. 1-2). pap. *(978-1-5383-5178-9(1),* be14957c-1f2d-4363-beda-30df3d293c5d, Rosen Classroom) Rosen Publishing Group, Inc., The.
Fogwill, Joyce Graham. Bubs the Bumblebee & the Spider's Web. 2012. (ENG.). 24p. (J). pap. 12.95 *(978-1-4327-9586-3(4))* Outskirts Pr., Inc.
Friar, Christine. Anansi & the Scarecrow. 2011. 32p. pap. 15.99 *(978-1-4568-7143-7(9))* Xlibris Corp.
Fuerst, Jeffrey B. The Itsy Bitsy Spider. Collins, Daryll, illus. 2010. (Rising Readers Ser.). (J). 3.49 *(978-1-60719-689-1(1))* Newmark Learning LLC.
Georgiana, Vanessa. Lulu: And the Garden of Life. 2013. 104p. (gr. 4-6). pap. 8.99 *(978-1-4582-0936-8(9),* Abbott Pr.) Author Solutions, LLC.
Gilson, Jamie. Gotcha! Wummer, Amy, illus. 2006. (ENG.). 80p. (J). (gr. -1-3). 15.00 *(978-0-618-54356-4(2),* 100819, Clarion Bks.) HarperCollins Pubs.
Grant, Jacob. Bear Out There. 2019. (ENG., Illus.). 40p. (J). 17.99 *(978-1-68119-745-6(6),* 900184203, Bloomsbury Children's Bks.) Bloomsbury Publishing USA.
—Bear's Scare. (ENG., Illus.). 40p. (J). 2019. bds. 7.99 *(978-1-68119-994-8(7),* 900194726) 2018. 17.99 *(978-1-68119-720-3(0),* 900182263) Bloomsbury Publishing USA. (Bloomsbury Children's Bks.).
Greens, Olivia. My Dream. 2012. 28p. pap. 21.99 *(978-1-4797-1305-9(8))* Xlibris Corp.
Guillain, Charlotte. Why the Spider Has Long Legs: An African Folk Tale, 1 vol. Dorado, Steve, illus. 2014. (Folk Tales from Around the World Ser.). (ENG.). 24p. (J). (gr. -1-3). pap. 6.95 *(978-1-4109-6701-5(8),* 126279, Raintree) Capstone.
Harjo, Benjamin, et al, illus. Spider Spins a Story: Fourteen Legends from Native America. 2007. (ENG.). 72p. (J). (gr. 3-7). pap. 8.95 *(978-0-87358-936-9(X))* Cooper Square Publishing Llc.
Harney Jr., Robert. The Clumsiest Spider. Scott, Jennifer, illus. 2011. 44p. pap. 24.95 *(978-1-4626-2166-8(X))* America Star Bks.
Hart, Teresa. The Ant & the Lost Spider, 1 vol. 2009. 76p. pap. 19.95 *(978-1-60749-296-2(2))* America Star Bks.
Harwell, Andrew. The Spider Ring. 2015. (ENG.). 224p. (J). (gr. 3-7). 16.99 *(978-0-545-68290-9(8),* Scholastic Pr.) Scholastic, Inc.
Hilb, Nora. Itsy Bitsy Spider. 2015. (Classic Books with Holes Ser.). (Illus.). 16p. (J). *(978-1-84643-676-5(1))* Child's Play International Ltd.
Hilb, Nora, illus. Itsy Bitsy Spider. (Classic Books with Holes 8x8 with CD Ser.). (J). 2017. (ENG.). 16p. *(978-1-78628-079-4(5))* 2012. 14p. spiral bd. *(978-1-84643-509-6(9))* 2012. 16p. pap. *(978-1-84643-498-3(X))* Child's Play International Ltd.
Hilton, Marcel. The Magical Web. 2007. 38p. 19.50 *(978-1-4303-2678-6(6))* Lulu Pr., Inc.
Hilton, Nette. The Web. Millard, Kerry, illus. 2013. (ENG.). 80p. (J). (gr. 2-4). 18.69 *(978-1-61067-087-6(6))* Kane Miller.
Holden, Pam. Sneaky Spider, 1 vol. Storey, Jim, illus. 2009. (Red Rocket Readers Ser.). (ENG.). 17p. (gr. 2-2). pap. *(978-1-877363-83-2(9))* Flying Start Bks.
Holub, Joan. More Snacks! A Thanksgiving Play. Terry, Will, illus. 2006. (Ant Hill Ser.: 1). (ENG.). 24p. (J). (gr. -1-k). lib. bdg. 11.89 *(978-1-4169-2559-0(7),* Simon Spotlight) Simon Spotlight.
—More Snacks! A Thanksgiving Play (Ready-To-Read Pre-Level 1) Terry, Will, illus. 2006. (Ant Hill Ser.: 1). (ENG.). 24p. (J). (gr. -1-k). pap. 4.99 *(978-1-4169-0954-5(0),* Simon Spotlight) Simon Spotlight.
—Picnic! A Day in the Park (Ready-To-Read Pre-Level 1) Terry, Will, illus. 2008. (Ant Hill Ser.). (ENG.). 24p. (J). (gr. -1-k). pap. 4.99 *(978-1-4169-5133-9(4),* Simon Spotlight) Simon Spotlight.
Hopgood, Tim. Walter's Wonderful Web: A First Book about Shapes. 2016. (ENG., Illus.). 32p. (J). 18.99

S

(978-0-374-30352-5(5), 900156325, Farrar, Straus & Giroux (BYR)) Farrar, Straus & Giroux.
Housel, Debra. Charlotte's Web: An Instructional Guide for Literature. rev. ed. 2015. (Great Works). (ENG., Illus.). 72p. (gr. 3-5). pap. 9.99 *(978-1-4807-6995-3(9))* Shell Educational Publishing.
Hulme-Cross, Benjamin. The House of Memories. Evergreen, Nelson, illus. 2015. (Dark Hunter Ser.). (ENG.). 64p. (J). (gr. 4-8). pap. 4.99 *(978-1-4677-8085-8(5)*, dc2a87ce-8f71-42e9-b061-e920ab07c356, Darby Creek) Lerner Publishing Group.
Jarman, Julia. Harry the Clever Spider at School: Band 07/Turquoise (Collins Big Cat) Fowkes, Charlie, illus. 2007. (Collins Big Cat Ser.). (ENG.). 24p. (J). (gr. 1-2). pap. 6.99 *(978-0-00-718670-9(3))* HarperCollins Pubs. Ltd. GBR. Dist: Independent Pubs. Group.
Jenkins, Steven. The Spider House: Battle for the Wall. 2007. 264p. 26.95 *(978-0-595-69910-0(3))*; per. 16.95 *(978-0-595-44488-5(1))* iUniverse, Inc.
Johnson, Gerald J. Miss Spinny, the Spider. Miltenberger, Jeri & Miltenberger, Dave, illus. 2012. 24p. 24.95 *(978-1-4626-6488-7(1))* America Star Bks.
Johnson, Myrna. Let's Take a Hike. 2013. (ENG., Illus.). 32p. (gr. -1-1). pap. 13.95 *(978-1-936205-79-0(3)*, P223206) Austin, Stephen F. State Univ. Pr.
Kelly, Martin & Legris, Phil. Itsy Bitsy Spider. (Illus.). 6p. (J). 4.95 *(978-1-929766-25-3(4))* Handprint Bks.
Kemp, Dane. Imaginary Tales. 2011. 186p. pap. 24.95 *(978-1-4560-4686-6(1))* America Star Bks.
Khan, Aliyah. The Adventures of Solomon Spider: Solomon Sees the City. 2011. 28p. (gr. -1 — 1). pap. 14.09 *(978-1-4490-1546-6(8))* AuthorHouse.
Kimmel, Eric A. Anansi Series. Stevens, Janet, illus. 2003. pap. 68.95 incl. audio compact disk *(978-1-59112-840-3(4))*;Set. (J). pap. 61.95 incl. audio *(978-0-87499-469-8(1))* Live Oak Media.
Kirk, Bill. There's a Spider in My Sink! Brown, Suzy, illus. 2008. 16p. pap. 9.95 *(978-1-935137-25-2(5))* Guardian Angel Publishing, Inc.
Kirk, David. Bedtime Story. 2006. (Illus.). 32p. (J). *(978-0-448-44514-4(X))* Penguin Publishing Group.
—Captain Sunny Patch. 2006. (Illus.). 32p. (J). *(978-0-448-44515-1(8))* Callaway Editions, Inc.
—Little Miss Spider. 2018. (ENG., Illus.). 32p. (J). (gr. -1-k). 14.95 *(978-0-935112-14-6(6))* Callaway Editions, Inc.
—Miss Spider's Sunny Patch Surprise. 2005. (Play-a-Sound Ser.). (Illus.). 24p. (J). 16.98 *(978-1-4127-3558-2(0)*, 7262900) Publications International, Ltd.
Kroupa, Robert J. Just Like You. 2011. (J). *(978-0-9825503-4-2(0))* IGI Pr.
Krumwiede, Lana. Just Itzy. Pizzoli, Greg, illus. 2015. (ENG.). 40p. (J). (-k). 15.99 *(978-0-7636-5811-3(1))* Candlewick Pr.
Lancaster, Melinda. Tyler & the Spider. Gillen, Rosemarie, illus. 2010. 32p. (J). pap. 9.95 *(978-1-935706-08-3(X))* Wiggles Pr.
Lane, Jeanette, et al. The Magic School Bus Gets Caught in a Web. Enik, Ted, illus. 2007. (Scholastic Reader Ser.). (J). *(978-0-545-03587-3(2))* Scholastic, Inc.
Lasky, Kathryn. The Deadlies: Felix Takes the Stage. Gilpin, Stephen, illus. 2011. (Deadlies Ser.). (ENG.). 144p. (J). (gr. 2-5). pap. 5.99 *(978-0-545-11730-2(5)*, Scholastic Paperbacks) Scholastic, Inc.
—Felix Takes the Stage. Gilpin, Stephen, illus. 2010. (ENG.). 144p. (J). (gr. 2-5). 15.99 *(978-0-545-11681-7(3)*, Scholastic Pr.) Scholastic, Inc.
—Spiders on the Case, Bk. 2. Gilpin, Stephen, illus. 2011. (ENG.). 176p. (J). (gr. 2-5). 15.99 *(978-0-545-11682-4(1)*, Scholastic Pr.) Scholastic, Inc.
Lindsay, Sierra. Spindly the Spider. Lindsay, Sierra, illus. 2012. (Illus.). 20p. pap. 10.99 *(978-0-9836641-9-2(6))* Kids At Heart Publishing, LLC.
Lobo, Julia. Eek! That's Creepy! Look & Find. Cavallini, Linda, illus. 2010. 24p. (J). 7.98 *(978-1-60553-898-3(1))* Publications International, Ltd.
Lucado, Max & Schmidt, Troy. Webster, the Scaredy Spider. 2005. 32p. (J). pap. 3.99 *(978-1-4003-0665-7(5))* Nelson, Thomas Inc.
Lyssenko, Taras. Wendy's Fear of Heights. 2003. 14p. (J). *(978-0-9740542-0-9(8))* Prairie Shore Creative, Inc.
Magsamen, Sandra. Itsy-Bitsy I Love You! (heart-Felt Books) Heartfelt Stories. Magsamen, Sandra, illus. 2016. (Heart-Felt Bks.). (ENG., Illus.). 10p. (J). (— 1). 7.99 *(978-0-545-46841-1(8)*, Cartwheel Bks.) Scholastic, Inc.
Marchi, Mary V. The Web in the Halo: A Tale of a Spider Who Learns about Christmas. 2012. 32p. pap. 19.99 *(978-1-4685-6624-6(5))* AuthorHouse.
Marshall, Geraldine Ann. Spider's Gift: A Christmas Story. Sorge, Rebecca, illus. 2016. 40p. (J). pap. 14.95 *(978-0-8198-9058-0(8))* Pauline Bks. & Media.
Matt and Dave, Matt and. Yuck's Amazing Underpants. Baines, Nigel, illus. 2012. (Yuck Ser.). (ENG.). 112p. (J). (gr. 2-5). pap. 4.99 *(978-1-4424-5122-3(X)*, Simon & Schuster/Paula Wiseman Bks.) Simon & Schuster/Paula Wiseman Bks.
—Yuck's Slime Monster. Baines, Nigel, illus. 2012. (Yuck Ser.). (ENG.). 112p. (J). (gr. 2-5). 14.99 *(978-1-4424-5124-7(6))*; pap. 5.99 *(978-1-4424-5126-1(2))* Simon & Schuster/Paula Wiseman Bks. (Simon & Schuster/Paula Wiseman Bks.).
Miceli, Mary Anne. Boston North Shore's. 2011. 44p. pap. 21.99 *(978-1-4568-1135-8(5))* Xlibris Corp.
Miller, John. Red Spider Hero. Cucco, Giuliano, illus. 2015. 40p. (J). (gr. -1-3). 16.95 *(978-1-59270-176-6(0))* Enchanted Lion Bks., LLC.
Miss Spider Activity Kit. 2005. (Illus.). (J). *(978-0-448-44063-7(6)*, Grosset & Dunlap) Penguin Publishing Group.
Monks, Lydia. Aaaarrgghh! Spider! 2004. (ENG., Illus.). 32p. (J). *(978-1-4052-0688-4(8))* Farshore.
—Aaaarrgghh Spider! Monks, Lydia, illus. 2004. (ENG., Illus.). 32p. (J). pap. *(978-1-4052-1044-7(3))* Farshore.
Moore, James W. & Moore, Eileen. Dark at the Foot of the Stairs. (ENG., Illus.). 92p. (J). pap. *(978-0-340-64873-5(2))* Hodder & Stoughton.
Morgan, C. M. Silver Doorway #2: Dwarves in the Dark. 2003. 104p. (J). pap. *(978-0-9702189-3-3(1))* Sabledrake Enterprises.
Morley, Farah, illus. The Spider & the Doves: The Story of the Hijra. 2012. (ENG.). 30p. (J). (gr. -1-2). 8.95 *(978-0-86037-449-7(1))* Kube Publishing Ltd. GBR. Dist: Consortium Bk. Sales & Distribution.
Moulton, Mark K. A Royal Wedding. Good, Karen H., illus. 2007. (ENG.). 32p. (J). (gr. k-3). 14.99 *(978-0-8249-8677-3(6)*, Ideals Pubns.) Worthy Publishing.
Moulton, Mark Kimball. One Enchanted Evening. Crouch, Karen Hillard, illus. 2003. 32p. (J). 14.95 *(978-0-8249-5480-2(7)*, Ideals Pubns.) Worthy Publishing.
Nagbe, Bakeh N. Wleh, Sr. Greedy Spider. 2005. (ENG.). 44p. per. 16.99 *(978-1-4134-9097-8(2))* Xlibris Corp.
Nanny, B. The Spider who Lived in our Grandads Car. 2011. (Illus.). 12p. 10.17 *(978-1-4567-7645-9(2))* AuthorHouse.
Niddrie, June. Sweetpea & His Friends. 2010. 36p. pap. 17.30 *(978-0-557-31853-7(X))* Lulu Pr., Inc.
Norfolk, Bobby & Norfolk, Sherry. Anansi & the Pot of Beans. Hoffmire, Baird, illus. 2006. (Story Cove Ser.). (ENG.). 32p. (J). (gr. -1-3). 4.95 *(978-0-87483-811-4(8))* August Hse. Pubs., Inc.
Novel Units. Anansi the Spider Novel Units Teacher Guide. 2019. (ENG.). (J). pap. 12.99 *(978-1-56137-278-2(1)*, Novel Units, Inc.) Classroom Library Co.
—Charlotte's Web Novel Units Student Packet. 2019. (ENG.). (J). pap. 13.99 *(978-1-56137-630-8(2)*, NU6302SP, Novel Units, Inc.) Classroom Library Co.
—Scorpions Novel Units Teacher Guide. 2019. (ENG.). (YA). pap. 12.99 *(978-1-56137-293-5(5)*, Novel Units, Inc.) Classroom Library Co.
Oaklee, Mammy. My Keyboard Was Hi~Jacked! 2013. 40p. pap. *(978-1-4602-2616-2(X))* FriesenPress.
Oguneye, Kunle. Sikulu & Harambe by the Zambezi River: An African Vversion of the Good Samaritan Story. McCorkindale, Bruce & Youtsey, Scott, illus. 2008. 32p. (J). (gr. -1-5). 14.99 *(978-0-9777362-4-3(8))* Blue Brush Media.
Olson, Kevin Noel. Eerey Tocsin in the Cryptoid Zoo. Hammack, Debi, illus. 2006. (ENG.). 176p. (YA). per. 15.95 *(978-1-887560-17-7(3)*, Cornerstone Bk. Publishers) Cornerstone Bk. Pubs.
Orme, David. Bugs & Spiders. Mongiovi, Jorge, illus. 2010. (Fact to Fiction Ser.). 36p. pap. 7.45 *(978-0-7891-7990-6(3))* Perfection Learning Corp.
Osborne, Mary Pope. The Mysteries of Spider Kane. 2006. (ENG.). 240p. (J). (gr. 3-7). 6.99 *(978-0-440-42097-2(0)*, Yearling) Random Hse. Children's Bks.
Osei, Leah. Why Anansi Has Eight Thin Legs: A Tale from West Africa, 1 vol. rev. ed. 2013. (Literary Text Ser.). (ENG., Illus.). 24p. (gr. 1-3). pap. 8.99 *(978-1-4333-5524-0(8))* Teacher Created Materials, Inc.
Pandya, Ashish. Ping the Spider: The journey Begins... 2008. 16p. pap. 12.99 *(978-1-4343-9261-9(9))* AuthorHouse.
Pantelides, Sherry. Make A Choice to Rejoice! A Story about Being Cheerful. Perez, Debi, illus. 2007. 32p. (J). 12.99 *(978-0-9771076-2-9(0))* Lacey Productions.
Perry, Taily. Saving Sunny Stream, a Wormie Wormald Adventure. 2009. 60p. pap. 22.00 *(978-1-60860-296-4(6)*, Eloquent Bks.) Strategic Book Publishing & Rights Agency (SBPRA).
Phillips, Gina & Martin, Stuart. Ants & Caterpillars. 2003. (Busy Bugs Ser.). 12p. (J). bds. 14.95 *(978-1-74047-240-1(3))* Book Co. Publishing Pty, Ltd., The AUS. Dist: Penton Overseas, Inc.
Pollock, Terry. A Spider Like Me. 2011. 28p. pap. 21.99 *(978-1-4628-6791-2(X))* Xlibris Corp.
Publications International Ltd. Staff, ed. Sesame Street: The Itsy Bitsy Spider. 2011. 10p. (J). bds. 7.98 *(978-1-4508-0858-3(1)*, 6461bf3e-ab03-4ebc-81c6-091daf4fbc8e) Phoenix International Publications, Inc.
Ray, Michelle. A Huntsman Spider in My House: Little Aussie Critters. Ashford, Sylvie, illus. 2014. (ENG.). 34p. pap. 8.95 *(978-1-61448-842-2(8)*, 9781614488422) Morgan James Publishing.
Raye, Donna. Edison the Firefly & Sierra the Special Spider. 2013. 28p. pap. 9.99 *(978-0-9910324-9-5(7))* Mindstir Media.
Razi, Michaele. Frank the Seven-Legged Spider. 2017. (Illus.). 32p. (J). (gr. -1-3). 16.99 *(978-1-63217-128-3(7)*, Little Bigfoot) Sasquatch Bks.
Read, Laurie. Blacky Longlegs Meets Freddy the Fly. 2008. 20p. pap. 14.00 *(978-1-4389-1231-8(5))* AuthorHouse.
Redepenning, George. The Adventures of Webster. 2008. pap. 9.00 *(978-0-8059-8629-7(4))* Dorrance Publishing Co., Inc.
Reed, Len. Monsters at My Bed. 2011. 16p. (gr. 1-2). pap. 8.49 *(978-1-4567-6786-0(0))* AuthorHouse.
ReWalt, Nancy E. Aerial: A Spider's Tale. Cranford, Darren, illus. 2009. 32p. (J). 16.95 *(978-0-9821110-0-0(2))* Ronan Enterprises, Inc.
—Aerial: A Trip to Remember. Cranford, Darren, illus. 2010. 32p. (J). 16.95 *(978-0-9821110-1-7(0))* Ronan Enterprises, Inc.
Rewalt, Nancy E. Aerial Meets Farmer Fedamore. Cranford, Darren, illus. 2012. 64p. (J). 17.95 *(978-0-9821110-3-1(7))* Ronan Enterprises, Inc.
Rivera, Monica O. Lola the Spider & the Purple Crayon. 2009. 20p. pap. 15.00 *(978-1-4389-7487-3(6))* AuthorHouse.
Roberts, Pauline. Miss Spider Misses Supper. 2012. 28p. pap. 16.09 *(978-1-4669-5264-5(4))* Trafford Publishing.
Rouss, Sylvia A. Sammy Spider Series, 11 vols., Set. Kahn, Katherine Janus, illus. 2003. (J). (gr. -1-3). 70.61 *(978-1-58013-046-2(1)*, Kar-Ben Publishing) Lerner Publishing Group.
—Sammy Spider's First Bar Mitzvah. Kahn, Katherine Janus, illus. 2016. (ENG.). 32p. (J). (gr. -1-3). 17.99 *(978-1-4677-8931-8(3)*, 609c49a2-6f53-4b33-820b-3bbf958d88b8, Kar-Ben Publishing) Lerner Publishing Group.
—Sammy Spider's First Day of School. Kahn, Katherine Janus, illus. 2009. (Kar-Ben Favorites Ser.). (ENG.). 32p. (J). (gr. -1-2). 16.95 *(978-0-8225-8583-1(9)*, Kar-Ben Publishing) Lerner Publishing Group.
—Sammy Spider's First Haggadah. Kahn, Katherine Janus, illus. 2007. (ENG.). 32p. (J). (gr. -1-3). per. 7.99 *(978-1-58013-230-5(8)*, a576058b-9534-4121-80bf-9ba351c5c0af, Kar-Ben Publishing) Lerner Publishing Group.
—Sammy Spider's First Mitzvah. Kahn, Katherine Janus, illus. 2014. (ENG.). 24p. (J). (gr. -1-3). 17.95 *(978-1-4677-1947-6(1)*, a8861aa7-d249-435f-ac41-dc242b6e1326, Kar-Ben Publishing) Lerner Publishing Group.
—Sammy Spider's First Shavuot. Kahn, Katherine Janus, illus. 2008. (ENG.). 32p. (J). (gr. -1-3). lib. bdg. 9.99 *(978-0-8225-7224-4(9)*, c79a4b2f-eed5-4ab2-9ff9-40e1c8e3bbca); per. 8.99 *(978-0-8225-7225-1(7)*, 4ac00b78-7450-41c1-8879-8889127582ea) Lerner Publishing Group. (Kar-Ben Publishing).
—Sammy Spider's First Simchat Torah. Kahn, Katherine Janus, illus. 2010. (ENG.). 32p. (J). (gr. -1-2). pap. 7.99 *(978-0-7613-3966-3(3)*, 76cc09d4-c84c-4eda-8cb1-822a72ea2811, Kar-Ben Publishing) Lerner Publishing Group.
—Sammy Spider's First Sukkot. Kahn, Katherine Janus, illus. 2004. (ENG.). 32p. (J). (gr. -1-3). 17.95 *(978-1-58013-142-1(5)*, Kar-Ben Publishing) Lerner Publishing Group.
—Sammy Spider's First Sukkot. Kahn, Katherine Janus, illus. 2004. (ENG.). 32p. (J). (gr. -1-3). pap. 8.99 *(978-1-58013-083-7(6)*, 30089e0a-abc2-4e86-8e0f-4cc8ea2d1fd6, Kar-Ben Publishing) Lerner Publishing Group.
—Sammy Spider's First Wedding. Kahn, Katherine Janus, illus. 2019. (ENG.). 32p. (J). (gr. -1-3). 12.99 *(978-1-5124-8366-6(4)*, a2b8388f-a654-45a7-b287-15c8d6352996, Kar-Ben Publishing) Lerner Publishing Group.
—Sammy Spider's First Yom Kippur. Kahn, Katherine Janus, illus. 2013. (ENG.). 32p. (J). (gr. -1-3). 7.99 *(978-0-7613-9196-8(7)*, 583af9d7-d61d-4ca1-ae6b-8befc99b7c80); E-Book 27.99 *(978-1-4677-1639-0(1))* Lerner Publishing Group. (Kar-Ben Publishing).
—Sammy Spider's Hanukkah Colors. Kahn, Katherine Janus, illus. 2017. (ENG.). 12p. (J). (gr. -1 — 1). bds. 5.99 *(978-1-4677-5238-1(X)*, 2f9f5071-1e9b-4c00-abb8-936a4314e444, Kar-Ben Publishing) Lerner Publishing Group.
—Sammy Spider's New Friend. Kahn, Katherine, illus. 2012. (Kar-Ben Favorites Ser.). (ENG.). 32p. (J). (gr. -1-2). lib. bdg. 17.95 *(978-0-7613-6663-8(6)*, Kar-Ben Publishing) Lerner Publishing Group.
—Sammy Spider's Passover Shapes. Kahn, Katherine Janus, illus. 2017. (ENG.). 12p. (J). (gr. -1 — 1). bds. 5.99 *(978-1-4677-7970-8(9)*, ff930d1d-18ff-4e40-ae02-3260511dc5f1); E-Book 23.99 *(978-1-5124-2727-1(6)*, 9781512427271) Lerner Publishing Group. (Kar-Ben Publishing).
Sanders, Terri L. Rainbow Spider. 2003. E-Book 4.95 incl. cd-rom *(978-1-59201-011-0(3))* Bks. Unbound E-Publishing Co.
Satterfield, April. Leah Bug & Her Flying Friends. Guthrie, Lewis, illus. 2011. 20p. pap. 24.95 *(978-1-4560-8422-6(4))* America Star Bks.
Schandle, Julie. Little Wishes Big Dreams: Around the World. 2005. (Illus.). 22p. (J). 11.95 *(978-0-9771868-0-8(6)*, 303-503-3289) Big Dreams Publishing.
Schmickl, Angela. The Matador Who Ran Away from the Spider. 2013. 24p. pap. 10.96 *(978-1-4251-9190-0(8))* Trafford Publishing.
Schweizer, Chris. Tricky Spider Tales. Huddleston, Courtney, illus. 2011. (Tricky Journeys Ser.: 5). (ENG.). (J). (gr. 2-4). pap. 39.62 *(978-0-7613-8629-2(7))* Lerner Publishing Group.
Scorpions. 2003. 50p. (YA). tchr. ed., ring bd. *(978-1-58049-470-0(6)*, TU226) Prestwick Hse., Inc.
Seuling, Barbara. Robert & the Attack of the Giant Tarantula. Brewer, Paul, illus. 2003. (Oh No, It's Robert Ser.). (ENG.). 64p. (J). pap. 3.99 *(978-0-439-23545-7(6)*, Scholastic Paperbacks) Scholastic, Inc.
Shan, Darren, pseud. Cirque du Freak: Trials of Death. 2004. (Cirque du Freak Ser.: 5). (Illus.). 224p. (J). (gr. 7-17). pap. 13.99 *(978-0-316-60395-9(3))* Little, Brown Bks. for Young Readers.
Sherlock, Philip. Anansi & the Alligator Eggs y Los Huevos Del Caimán. Rickham, Elethia, tr. Judah, Susan, illus. 2nd ed. 2013. 42p. pap. 15.00 *(978-976-95510-6-0(6))* Minna Pr.
Simler, Isabelle, illus. A Web. 2018. (ENG.). 48p. (J). 16.99 *(978-1-4413-2843-4(2)*, a81ee573-86b8-4cb0-9ebc-1e5d399ac580) Peter Pauper Pr. Inc.
Simpson, Tj. Tiny Paul the Tarantula Takes a Walk, 1 vol. Register, J. R., illus. 2010. 70p. pap. 19.95 *(978-1-60703-117-8(5))* America Star Bks.
Smart Kidz, creator. The Itsy Bitsy Spider. 2013. (Sing N Play Songs Ser.). (ENG., Illus.). 12p. (J). (gr. -1). bds. 12.99 *(978-1-891100-56-7(4)*, Smart Kids) Penton Overseas, Inc.
Smith, Alex T. Mr. Penguin & the Fortress of Secrets, 1 vol. 2019. (Mr. Penguin Ser.: 2). (ENG., Illus.). 288p. (J). (gr. 3-7). 16.95 *(978-1-68263-130-0(3))* Peachtree Publishing Co. Inc.
—Mr. Penguin & the Lost Treasure. 2019. (Mr. Penguin Ser.: 1). (ENG., Illus.). 208p. (J). (gr. 3-7). 16.95 *(978-1-68263-120-1(6))* Peachtree Publishing Co. Inc.
Smith, Craig & Thomson, Maureen. Willbee the Bumblebee. Cowley, Katz, illus. 2019. (ENG.). 32p. (J). (gr. -1-k). pap. 7.99 *(978-1-338-57521-7(X))* Scholastic, Inc.
Smith, Kim. Leroy's Long Journey: Leroy Baxter, the near-Sighted Spider Volume I, 4 vols., Vol. 1. 2009. (Leroy Baxter, the Near-Sighted Spider Ser.: Vol. 1). (Illus.). 28p. (J). (gr. k-3). pap. 8.99 *(978-0-9818190-0-6(1)*, Candy Cane Bks.) Sunlight Publishing.
Smith, Pamela Colman. Annancy Stories. 2006. (YA). reprint ed. pap. 19.99 *(978-0-9769612-2-2(9))* Darker Intentions Pr.
Soileau, Hodges, illus. The Black Widow Spider Mystery. 2004. (Boxcar Children Special Ser.). 130p. (gr. 2-7). 15.50 *(978-0-7569-3266-4(1))* Perfection Learning Corp.
Sorenson, Jack R. Eibhlin & Her Dragon, 1 vol. 2009. 131p. pap. 24.95 *(978-1-60749-634-2(8))* America Star Bks.
Soundprints Staff. Itsy Bitsy Spider: And Other Favorites. 2005. (Meet Mother Goose Ser.). (ENG., Illus.). 36p. (J). 10.95 *(978-1-931465-31-2(2)*, MD1100); 14.95 *(978-1-931465-51-9(7)*, MPD1100) Soundprints.
Spider Night! (Early Intervention Levels Ser.). 28.38 *(978-0-7362-0411-8(3))* CENGAGE Learning.
Spinelli, Eileen. Sophie's Masterpiece: A Spider's Tale. Dyer, Jane, illus. 2004. (ENG.). 32p. (J). (gr. -1-2). reprint ed. 7.99 *(978-0-689-86680-7(1)*, Simon & Schuster Bks. For Young Readers) Simon & Schuster Bks. For Young Readers.
Stoh, Emily. Roger Meets Sam. Stoh, Judy, illus. 2009. 24p. pap. 9.95 *(978-1-935105-41-1(8))* Avid Readers Publishing Group.
Stoner, Eileen M. Inky & Dinky: Mindy ... . A Tale of Change. 2009. 48p. pap. 17.49 *(978-1-4490-0488-0(1))* AuthorHouse.
Stringer, Beverly. Joe the Dancing Spider. 2004. (ENG., Illus.). 26p. pap. 13.50 *(978-1-4120-2020-6(4))* Trafford Publishing.
Sydor, Colleen. Raising a Little Stink. Constantin, Pascale, illus. 2006. 32p. (J). (gr. -1-2). 16.95 *(978-1-55337-896-9(2))* Kids Can Pr., Ltd. CAN. Dist: Hachette Bk. Group.
.T. Ozzie the Spider. 2013. 24p. pap. 11.95 *(978-1-4575-2025-9(7))* Dog Ear Publishing, LLC.
Tandy, Clive. Quarry Grove. 2008. 60p. per. 11.59 *(978-1-4251-4974-1(X))* Trafford Publishing.
Thomas, Susan. Beyond the Mist: Sequel to Mist on the Window. 2012. 352p. pap. 24.34 *(978-1-4772-4627-6(4))* AuthorHouse.
Thompson, Chad. The Itsy Bitsy Spider. 2009. (Early Literacy Ser.). (ENG., Illus.). 16p. (gr. k-1). 19.99 *(978-1-4333-1455-1(X))*; 6.99 *(978-1-4333-1454-4(1))* Teacher Created Materials, Inc.
Trapani, Iza. Sing along with Iza & Friends: The Itsy Bitsy Spider. Trapani, Iza, illus. 2004. (Illus.). 32p. (J). pap. 11.95 incl. audio compact disk *(978-1-58089-100-4(4))* Charlesbridge Publishing, Inc.
Treviño, Hilda L. Ladybugs on a Mission. 2013. 70p. (gr. 4-6). pap. 8.95 *(978-1-4759-7762-2(X))* iUniverse, Inc.
Vermeulen, Thomas. Gabangani Guinea Fowl & Huzu the Bird Eating Spider. 2009. 50p. pap. 19.50 *(978-1-60693-741-9(3)*, Eloquent Bks.) Strategic Book Publishing & Rights Agency (SBPRA).
Wakefield, Beth. The Cleaner. 2010. 151p. pap. 14.50 *(978-1-4457-6809-0(7))* Lulu Pr., Inc.
Walsh, Melanie. Trick or Treat? Walsh, Melanie, illus. 2009. (ENG., Illus.). 16p. (J). (gr. -1-2). bds. 7.99 *(978-0-7636-4295-2(9))* Candlewick Pr.
Wang, Margaret. Eency Weency Spider. Rueda, Claudia, illus. 2006. (ENG.). (J). 12p. bds. 5.95 *(978-1-58117-505-9(1))*; 22p. (gr. -1-3). bds. 10.95 *(978-1-58117-418-2(7))* Bendon, Inc. (Intervisual/Piggy Toes).
West, Robert. Escape from the Drooling Octopod!, 1 vol., 3. 2008. (Star-Fighters of Murphy Street Ser.: 3). (ENG., Illus.). 144p. (J). (gr. 4-6). pap. 6.99 *(978-0-310-71427-9(3))* Zonderkidz.
West, Tracey. Waking the Rainbow Dragon, 10. 2019. (Branches Early Ch Bks). (ENG.). 89p. (J). (gr. 2-3). 15.36 *(978-0-87617-978-9(2))* Penworthy Co., LLC, The.
—Waking the Rainbow Dragon: a Branches Book (Dragon Masters #10), 1 vol. Jones, Damien, illus. 2018. (Dragon Masters Ser.: 10). (ENG.). 96p. (J). (gr. 1-3). pap. 5.99 *(978-1-338-16989-8(0))* Scholastic, Inc.
—Waking the Rainbow Dragon: a Branches Book (Dragon Masters #10) (Library Edition) Jones, Damien, illus. 2018. (Dragon Masters Ser.: 10). (ENG.). 96p. (J). (gr. 1-3). lib. bdg. 24.99 *(978-1-338-16990-4(4))* Scholastic, Inc.
Weston Woods Staff, creator. Anansi the Spider. 2011. 18.95 *(978-0-439-88174-6(9))*; 38.75 *(978-0-439-84573-1(4))* Weston Woods Studios, Inc.
Whincup, Sara. The St John's Cross Spider. Yapsangco, Kenn, illus. 2015. (ENG.). 28p. (J). pap. 28.22 *(978-1-5035-0985-6(0))* Xlibris Corp.
White. Tela di Carlotta. pap. 13.95 *(978-88-04-46241-5(8))* Mondadori ITA. Dist: Distribooks, Inc.
White, E. B. Charlotte's Web. Williams, Garth, illus. 2005. (Charming Classics). 192p. (J). pap. 7.99 *(978-0-06-084594-0(5)*, HarperFestival) HarperCollins Pubs.
—Charlotte's Web. movie tie-in ed. 2006. (Charlotte's Web Ser.). (ENG., Illus.). 192p. (J). (gr. 4-7). per. 7.99 *(978-0-06-112026-8(X))* HarperCollins Pubs.
—Charlotte's Web. Williams, Garth, illus. movie tie-in ed. 2006. (Charlotte's Web Ser.). (J). 192p. mass mkt. 7.99 *(978-0-06-122874-2(5)*, Harper Trophy);Set. pap. 19.99 *(978-0-06-121502-5(3))* HarperCollins Pubs.
—Charlotte's Web. Williams, Garth, illus. 2004. (CHI.). 158p. (YA). pap. *(978-957-08-2568-8(5))* Linking Publishing Co., Ltd.
—Charlotte's Web. Williams, Garth, illus. 184p. (J). pap. 5.95 *(978-0-8072-8305-9(3)*, Listening Library) Random Hse. Audio Publishing Group.
—Charlotte's Web. unabr. ed. 2004. 184p. (J). (gr. 3-7). pap. 36.00 incl. audio *(978-0-8072-8304-2(5)*, YYA156SP, Listening Library) Random Hse. Audio Publishing Group.
—Charlotte's Web. 2012. (J). (gr. 3-6). 18.40 *(978-0-8085-3772-4(5))* Turtleback.
—Wilbur's Adventure: A Charlotte's Web Picture Book. Kneen, Maggie, illus. 2008. (Charlotte's Web Ser.). 32p. (J). (gr. k-2). lib. bdg. 17.89 *(978-0-06-078165-1(3))* HarperCollins Pubs.
White, E. B. & DiCamillo, Kate. Charlotte's Web: A Newbery Honor Award Winner. Williams, Garth, illus. 2012. (ENG.). (J). (gr. 3-7). 192p. 9.99 *(978-0-06-112495-2(8))*; 192p. 17.99 *(978-0-06-026385-0(7))*; 384p. pap. 8.99 *(978-0-06-440055-8(7))* HarperCollins Pubs. (HarperCollins).
—Charlotte's Web Read-Aloud Edition: A Newbery Honor Award Winner. Williams, Garth, illus. 2006. (ENG.). 192p. (J). (gr. 3-7). 17.99 *(978-0-06-088261-7(1)*, HarperCollins) HarperCollins Pubs.
Williams, Rozanne. Spiders, Spiders Everywhere. 2017. (Learn-To-Read Ser.). (ENG., Illus.). (J). pap. 3.49 *(978-1-68310-230-4(4))* Pacific Learning, Inc.
Wilson, George H. The Message of the Writing Spider. 2010. (Illus.). 50p. (J). 15.00 *(978-0-9778477-1-6(3))* A Story Plus Children Bks.
Winter, Barbara. Spider Saga. 2004. (Amazing Dictionary Ser.). (Illus.). 64p. pap. *(978-0-921156-96-3(0))* Plumleaf Press.
Zimmerman, Carol. Charlie the Spider. 2011. 32p. pap. 13.95 *(978-1-4567-9523-8(6))* AuthorHouse.

SPIES

see also Secret Service; World War, 1939-1945—Underground Movements see also subdivisions Secret Service and Underground Movements under individual wars, e.g. World War, 1939-1945—Secret Service; World War, 1939-1945—Underground Movements.

Allen, Thomas B. George Washington, Spymaster: How the Americans Outspied the British & Won the Revolutionary War. 2007. (Illus.). 192p. (J). (gr. 5-9). per. 7.95 (978-1-4263-0041-7(7), National Geographic Kids) Disney Publishing Worldwide.

Anniss, Matt. Espionage, 1 vol. 2013. (Crime Science Ser.). 48p. (J). (gr. 4-5). (ENG.). pap. 15.05 (978-1-4339-9489-0(5), 28151101-65ea-492e-91b4-375394024309); pap. 84.30 (978-1-4339-9490-6(9)); (ENG., Illus.). lib. bdg. 34.61 (978-1-4339-9488-3(7), 3fed191e-9def-4a89-ac90-10b35f4dd340) Stevens, Gareth Publishing LLLP.

Baden-Powell, Robert. My Adventures as a Spy. 2014. (Eyewitness Accounts Ser.). (ENG., Illus.). 128p. pap. 13.95 (978-1-4456-3610-8(7)) Amberley Publishing GBR. Dist: Independent Pubs. Group.

—My Adventures As a Spy. 2017. (ENG., Illus.). (J). 22.95 (978-1-374-81844-6(5)); pap. 12.95 (978-1-374-81843-9(7)) Capital Communications, Inc.

—My Adventures As a Spy. (ENG., Illus.). (J). 2017. pap. 12.87 (978-1-375-40147-0(5)) 2015. 22.95 (978-1-297-49249-5(8)) Creative Media Partners, LLC.

Botones para el General Washington (Buttons for General Washington) 2006. (J). pap. 6.95 (978-0-8225-6617-5(6), Ediciones Lerner) Lerner Publishing Group.

Boyer, Crispin & Zimbler, Suzanne. Top Secret: Spies, Codes, Capers, Gadgets, & Classified Cases Revealed. 2021. (ENG., Illus.). 192p. (J). (gr. 3-7). 19.99 (978-1-4263-3912-7(7), National Geographic Kids) Disney Publishing Worldwide.

Brian, Sarah Jane. Brainiac's Secret Agent: Fun Activities for Spies of All Ages. 2004. (ENG., Illus.). 128p. (J). spiral bd., act. bk. ed. 12.99 (978-0-88088-446-4(0), fcd2348a-df74-4c82-b862-cd446ccbc491) Peter Pauper Pr. Inc.

Brook, Henry. Spying. Frith, Alex, ed. Johnson, Staz & Roots, Adrian, illus. 2014. (ENG.). 80p. (J). (gr. 4-7). pap. 8.99 (978-0-7945-2809-6(0), Usborne) EDC Publishing.

Brown, Alex. Secret Missions. 2009. (Difficult & Dangerous Ser.). (ENG., Illus.). 32p. (J). pap. (978-1-897563-26-7(4)) Saunders Bk. Co.

Brown Bear Books. Spies: Behind Enemy Lines. 2012. (Mission Impossible Ser.). (ENG.). 32p. (J). (gr. 4-6). lib. bdg. 31.35 (978-1-936333-29-5(5), 16753) Brown Bear Bks.

Burgan, Michael. Spies of the Civil War: An Interactive History Adventure. 2015. (You Choose: Spies Ser.). (ENG., Illus.). 112p. (J). (gr. 3-7). pap. 6.95 (978-1-4914-5932-4(8), 128852, Capstone Pr.) Capstone.

—World War II Spies, 1 vol. 2013. (You Choose: World War II Ser.). (ENG., Illus.). 112p. (J). (gr. 3-7). pap. 6.95 (978-1-62065-722-5(8), 121706, Capstone Pr.) Capstone.

—World War II Spies: An Interactive History Adventure. 2013. (You Choose: World War II Ser.). (ENG.). 112p. (J). (gr. 3-4). pap. 41.70 (978-1-62065-723-2(6), 19313, Capstone Pr.) Capstone.

—World War II Spies: An Interactive History Adventure, 1 vol. 2013. (You Choose: World War II Ser.). (ENG., Illus.). 112p. (J). (gr. 3-7). lib. bdg. 32.65 (978-1-4296-9898-6(5), 120614, Capstone Pr.) Capstone.

Caravantes, Peggy. The Many Faces of Josephine Baker: Dancer, Singer, Activist, Spy. (Women of Action Ser.). (ENG.). 208p. (YA). (gr. 7). 2018. pap. 14.99 (978-1-61373-832-0(3)) 2015. (Illus.). 19.95 (978-1-61373-034-8(9)) Chicago Review Pr., Inc.

—Petticoat Spies: Six Women Spies of the US Civil War. 2004. (Notable Americans Ser.). (Illus.). 112p. (YA). (gr. 6-12). 23.95 (978-1-883846-88-6(9), First Biographies) Reynolds, Morgan Inc.

Caswell, Deanna. Famous Spies. 24p. (J). 2019. (Illus.). pap. (978-1-68072-739-5(7)) 2018. (ENG.). (gr. 4-6). pap. 8.99 (978-1-64466-292-2(2), 12463, Hi Jinx) 2018. (ENG., Illus.). (gr. 4-6). lib. bdg. 28.50 (978-1-68072-585-8(8), 12462, Hi Jinx) Black Rabbit Bks.

—Famous Spy Missions. 24p. (J). 2019. (Illus.). pap. (978-1-68072-740-1(0)) 2018. (ENG.). (gr. 4-6). pap. 8.99 (978-1-64466-293-9(0), 12467, Hi Jinx) 2018. (ENG., Illus.). (gr. 4-6). lib. bdg. 28.50 (978-1-68072-586-5(6), 12466, Hi Jinx) Black Rabbit Bks.

—Making Spy Disguises. 24p. (J). 2019. (Illus.). pap. (978-1-68072-741-8(9)) 2018. (ENG.). (gr. 4-6). pap. 8.99 (978-1-64466-294-6(9), 12471, Hi Jinx) 2018. (ENG., Illus.). (gr. 4-6). lib. bdg. 28.50 (978-1-68072-587-2(4), 12470, Hi Jinx) Black Rabbit Bks.

—Mastering Spy Techniques. 24p. (J). 2019. (Illus.). pap. (978-1-68072-743-2(5)) 2018. (ENG.). (gr. 1-3). pap. 10.99 (978-1-64466-296-0(5), 12479, Hi Jinx) 2018. (ENG., Illus.). (gr. 4-6). lib. bdg. 28.50 (978-1-68072-589-6(0), 12478, Hi Jinx) Black Rabbit Bks.

—Real Spy Gadgets. 24p. (J). 2019. (Illus.). pap. (978-1-68072-744-9(3)) 2018. (ENG.). (gr. 4-6). pap. 8.99 (978-1-64466-297-7(3), 12483, Hi Jinx) 2018. (ENG., Illus.). (gr. 4-6). lib. bdg. 28.50 (978-1-68072-590-2(4), 12482, Hi Jinx) Black Rabbit Bks.

Cefrey, Holly. One Life to Lose for My Country: The Arrest & Execution of Nathan Hale. (Great Moments in American History Ser.). 32p. (gr. 3-3). 2009. 47.90 (978-1-61513-135-8(3)) 2003. (ENG., Illus.). lib. bdg. 29.13 (978-0-8239-4371-5(2), ffc71398-7cd2-4bd6-9226-931d0ff47e52, Rosen Reference) Rosen Publishing Group, Inc., The.

Cerasini, Marc, et al. Keep It Hidden! The Best Places to Stash Your Stuff. 2007. (Illus.). 32p. (J). pap. (978-0-439-90850-4(7)) Scholastic, Inc.

—Spy to Spy: Sharing Your Secrets Safely. 2007. (Illus.). 32p. (J). (978-0-545-01560-8(X)) Scholastic, Inc.

Chaline, Eric. Secret Heroes of World War II: Tales of Courage from the Worlds of Espionage & Resistance. 2016. (Illus.). 224p. (YA). (978-1-4351-6251-8(X)) Metro Bks.

Cipriano, Jeri. Moe Berg: Spy Catcher. Brooks, Scott R., illus. 2018. (Hidden History — Spies Ser.). (ENG.). 32p. (J). (gr. 2-5). pap. 8.99 (978-1-63440-294-1(4), ef609875-eac4-4c2b-890c-414d134f3af7) Red Chair Pr.

Clapper, Kathryn N., et al. CIA Agents. 2018. (U. S. Federal Agents Ser.). (ENG., Illus.). 32p. (J). (gr. 3-9). lib. bdg. 27.32 (978-1-5435-0142-1(7), 137079, Capstone Pr.) Capstone.

Coddington, Andrew. Code Breakers & Spies of the Civil War, 1 vol. 2018. (Code Breakers & Spies Ser.). (ENG.). 80p. (YA). (gr. 8-8). 38.79 (978-1-5026-3847-2(9), c7cda8cb-7fe6-498b-95b0-4c1d964379a7) Cavendish Square Publishing LLC.

—Code Breakers & Spies of the Vietnam War, 1 vol. 2018. (Code Breakers & Spies Ser.). (ENG.). 80p. (J). (gr. 8-8). 38.79 (978-1-5026-3859-5(2), 3e16192e-bf41-42c1-893c-961a10c6934c) Cavendish Square Publishing LLC.

Cordello, Red, et al. The Stakeout: Spying & Secret Surveillance. 2007. 32p. (J). (978-0-439-90851-1(5)) Scholastic, Inc.

Costain, Meredith. Spies Revealed, 1 vol. 2013. (Discovery Education: Sensational True Stories Ser.). (ENG., Illus.). 32p. (J). (gr. 4-5). pap. 11.00 (978-1-4777-0103-4(6), 11898d18-742b-418f-a4b6-6bfb0c8a0c6b); lib. bdg. 28.93 (978-1-4777-0059-4(5), 3bf85882-32bd-485b-be1e-1a7ad9c1868a) Rosen Publishing Group, Inc., The. (PowerKids Pr.).

Curley, Robert. Spy Agencies, Intelligence Operations, & the People Behind Them, 1 vol. Curley, Robert, ed. 2013. (Intelligence & Counterintelligence Ser.). (ENG.). 120p. (YA). (gr. 9-9). 36.49 (978-1-62275-035-1(7), 285a9b74-bdbd-4ecf-b4c0-436196f5042b) Rosen Publishing Group, Inc., The.

Curley, Robert, ed. Spy Agencies, Intelligence Operations, & the People Behind Them, 4 vols. 2013. (Intelligence & Counterintelligence Ser.). (ENG.). 120p. (YA). (gr. 9-9). 72.98 (978-1-62275-039-9(X), 1bc7b88e-37cf-4d52-b746-686ce88dec4b) Rosen Publishing Group, Inc., The.

Daigneau, Jean. Code Cracking for Kids: Secret Communications Throughout History, with 21 Codes & Ciphers. 2019. (For Kids Ser.: 75). (Illus.). 144p. (J). (gr. 4-7). pap. 18.99 (978-1-64160-138-2(8)) Chicago Review Pr., Inc.

De Winter, James. Amazing Tricks of Real Spies. 2010. (Extreme! Ser.). (ENG.). 32p. (gr. 3-4). pap. 47.70 (978-1-4296-5118-9(0), Capstone Pr.) Capstone.

Derr, Aaron. Benedict Arnold: Hero or Enemy Spy? Brooks, Scott R., illus. 2018. (Hidden History — Spies Ser.). (ENG.). 32p. (J). (gr. 2-5). pap. 8.99 (978-1-63440-293-4(6), 2a403f3a-520f-4990-b238-6df35a52cbfe); lib. bdg. 26.65 (978-1-63440-279-8(0), 6a2568e9-210c-4247-a276-ddbee47fd7b9) Red Chair Pr.

—Nathan Hale: America's First Spy. Wicinas, Tami, illus. 2018. (Hidden History — Spies Ser.). (ENG.). 32p. (J). (gr. 2-5). pap. 8.99 (978-1-63440-296-5(0), 8a2a9e91-5332-4f0e-8e8a-8e1d098cc8a6) Red Chair Pr.

Dowswell, P. Secret Agent Spy. 2009. (Kid Kits Ser.). 144p. (J). 16.99 (978-1-60130-152-9(9)); 16.99 (978-1-60130-153-6(7)) EDC Publishing. (Usborne).

Dowswell, Paul & Fleming, Fergus. Spies. 2008. (Usborne True Stories Ser.). (Illus.). 139p. (J). pap. 4.99 (978-0-7945-1842-4(7), Usborne) EDC Publishing.

—True Spy Stories. 2004. (True Adventure Stories Ser.). (J). 144p. pap. 4.95 (978-0-7945-0088-7(9)); (Illus.). 139p. (gr. 5). lib. bdg. 12.95 (978-1-58086-682-8(4)) EDC Publishing. (Usborne).

Doyle, Bill H. Behind Enemy Lines. 2009. 135p. (J). pap. (978-0-545-14705-7(0)) Scholastic, Inc.

Favreau, Marc. Spies: The Secret Showdown Between America & Russia. 2019. (ENG., Illus.). 320p. (YA). (gr. 7-17). 19.99 (978-0-316-54592-1(9)) Little, Brown Bks. for Young Readers.

Ford, Jeanne Marie. Code Breakers & Spies of World War I, 1 vol. 2018. (Code Breakers & Spies Ser.). (ENG.). 80p. (YA). (gr. 8-8). 38.79 (978-1-5026-3850-2(9), f8938ee1-8a7c-4260-b9b9-74c7d69b6c0a) Cavendish Square Publishing LLC.

Francis, Suzanne, et al. Spy by Night: Stealth & Secrets after Dark. 2007. (Illus.). 32p. (J). pap. (978-0-545-01557-8(X)) Scholastic, Inc.

Friddell, Claudia. George Washington's Spies (Totally True Adventures) 2016. (Totally True Adventures Ser.). (Illus.). 112p. (J). (gr. 2-5). pap. 5.99 (978-0-399-55077-5(1), Random Hse. Bks. for Young Readers) Random Hse. Children's Bks.

Gifford, Clive. Spies & Spying. 2013. (Illus.). 128p. (J). (978-1-4351-5016-4(3)) Barnes & Noble, Inc.

Gilbert, Adrian. Secret Agents. 2009. (Spy Files Ser.). (ENG., Illus.). 32p. (J). (gr. 3-12). pap. 6.95 (978-1-55407-574-4(2), fadfa7ce-8dd3-46c1-964f-72b65edf0586) Firefly Bks., Ltd.

—Top Technology. 2009. (Spy Files Ser.). (ENG., Illus.). 32p. (J). (gr. 3-12). pap. 6.95 (978-1-55407-576-8(9), 6a7b9166-1fad-4c47-bd5d-eafc56e978a6) Firefly Bks., Ltd.

Goodman, Michael. World War I Spies. 2015. (Wartime Spies Ser.). (ENG., Illus.). 48p. (J). (gr. 4-7). (978-1-60818-602-0(4), 21090, Creative Education) Creative Co., The.

Goodman, Michael E. The CIA & Other American Spies. (Spies Around the World Ser.). (ENG., Illus.). 48p. (J). (gr. 5-9). 2013. pap. 12.00 (978-0-89812-969-4(9), 21964, Creative Paperbacks) 2012. 23.95 (978-1-60818-226-8(6), 21960) Creative Co., The.

—Civil War Spies. (Wartime Spies Ser.). (ENG.). 48p. (J). (gr. 4-7). 2016. pap. 12.00 (978-1-62832-203-3(9), 21079, Creative Paperbacks) 2015. (Illus.). (978-1-60818-598-6(2), 21078, Creative Education) Creative Co., The.

—Cold War Spies. (Wartime Spies Ser.). (ENG., Illus.). 48p. (J). (gr. 4-7). 2016. pap. 12.00 (978-1-62832-204-0(7), 21082, Creative Paperbacks) 2015. (978-1-60818-599-3(0), 21081, Creative Education) Creative Co., The.

—The KGB & Other Russian Spies. (Spies Around the World Ser.). (ENG., Illus.). 48p. (J). (gr. 5-9). 2013. pap. 12.00 (978-0-89812-970-0(2), 21965, Creative Paperbacks) 2012. 23.95 (978-1-60818-227-5(4), 21961, Creative Education) Creative Co., The.

—Modern Spies. (Wartime Spies Ser.). (ENG., Illus.). 48p. (J). (gr. 4-7). 2016. pap. 12.00 (978-1-62832-205-7(5), 21085, Creative Paperbacks) 2015. (978-1-60818-600-6(8), 21084, Creative Education) Creative Co., The.

—The Mossad & Other Israeli Spies. 2013. (Spies Around the World Ser.). (ENG., Illus.). 48p. (J). (gr. 5-9). pap. 12.00 (978-0-89812-971-7(0), 21966, Creative Paperbacks) Creative Co., The.

—Revolutionary War Spies. (Wartime Spies Ser.). (ENG.). 48p. (J). (gr. 4-7). 2016. pap. 12.00 (978-1-62832-206-4(3), 21088, Creative Paperbacks) 2015. (Illus.). (978-1-60818-601-3(6), 21087, Creative Education) Creative Co., The.

—The SIS & Other British Spies. (Spies Around the World Ser.). (ENG., Illus.). 48p. (J). (gr. 5-9). 2013. pap. 12.00 (978-0-89812-972-4(9), 21967, Creative Paperbacks) 2012. 23.95 (978-1-60818-229-9(0), 21963, Creative Education) Creative Co., The.

—World War I Spies. 2016. (Wartime Spies Ser.). (Illus.). 48p. (J). (gr. 4-7). pap. 12.00 (978-1-62832-207-1(1), 21091, Creative Paperbacks) Creative Co., The.

—World War II Spies. (Wartime Spies Ser.). (Illus.). 48p. (J). (gr. 4-7). 2016. pap. 12.00 (978-1-62832-208-8(X), 21094, Creative Paperbacks) 2015. (ENG., (978-1-60818-603-7(2), 21093, Creative Education) Creative Co., The.

Grayson, Robert. Civil War Spies, 1 vol. 2016. (Essential Library of the Civil War Ser.). (ENG., Illus.). 112p. (J). (gr. 8-12). lib. bdg. 41.36 (978-1-68078-277-6(0), 21709, Essential Library) ABDO Publishing Co.

Hale, Nathan. Nathan Hale's Hazardous Tales: One Dead Spy. 2012. (Nathan Hale's Hazardous Tales Ser.). (ENG., Illus.). 128p. (J). (gr. 3-7). 14.99 (978-1-4197-0396-6(X), 1000101) Abrams, Inc.

Harmon, Daniel E. Special Ops: Military Intelligence, 1 vol. 2014. (Inside Special Forces Ser.). (ENG.). 64p. (J). (gr. 6-6). 36.13 (978-1-4777-7587-5(0), 6b234487-65cf-4578-9bf4-22b687b0c7db, Rosen Reference) Rosen Publishing Group, Inc., The.

Harvey, Gill. True Stories of Crime & Detection. 2004. (True Adventure Stories Ser.). 144p. (J). lib. bdg. 12.95 (978-1-58086-644-6(1), Usborne) EDC Publishing.

—True Stories of Crime & Detection. Chisholm, Jane, ed. 2004. (True Adventure Stories Ser.). 144p. (J). pap. 4.95 (978-0-7945-0613-1(5), Usborne) EDC Publishing.

Hastedt, Glenn Peter. Espionage: A Reference Handbook, 1 vol. 2003. (Contemporary World Issues Ser.). (ENG., Illus.). 240p. (C). 65.00 (978-1-57607-950-8(3), 900301573) ABC-CLIO, LLC.

Head, Honor. Famous Spies. 2010. (Spies & Spying Ser.). (J). (gr. 4-7). 28.50 (978-1-59920-358-4(8)) Black Rabbit Bks.

Hunter, Ryan Ann. In Disguise! Stories of Real Women Spies. 2004. (Illus.). 133p. (J). (gr. 4-7). per. 9.95 (978-1-58270-095-3(8)) Beyond Words Publishing, Inc.

—In Disguise! Undercover with Real Women Spies. Little, Jeanette, illus. 2013. (ENG.). 176p. (J). (gr. 3-7). pap. 9.99 (978-1-58270-382-4(5)) Aladdin/Beyond Words.

Hurt, Avery Elizabeth. Code Breakers & Spies of the Cold War, 1 vol. 2018. (Code Breakers & Spies Ser.). (ENG.). 80p. (J). (gr. 8-8). lib. bdg. 38.79 (978-1-5026-3856-4(8), 60d051b5-8abb-4ccc-a8e8-a1f49ed21693) Cavendish Square Publishing LLC.

Hyde, Natalie. Classified: Spies at Work. 2014. (Crabtree Chrome Ser.). (ENG., Illus.). 48p. (J). (gr. 2-2). (978-0-7787-1335-7(0)) Crabtree Publishing Co.

Janeczko, Paul B. The Dark Game: True Spy Stories from Invisible Ink to CIA Moles. 2012. (ENG.). 256p. (YA). (gr. 5-9). pap. 11.99 (978-0-7636-6066-6(3)) Candlewick Pr.

Jeffrey, Gary. Secret Agents. 2009. (Graphic Careers Ser.). (ENG.). 48p. (YA). (gr. 5-5). 58.50 (978-1-61512-891-4(3), Rosen Reference) Rosen Publishing Group, Inc., The.

—Secret Agents, 1 vol. Riley, Terry, illus. 2008. (Graphic Careers Ser.). (ENG.). 48p. (gr. 5-5). per. 14.05 (978-1-4042-1465-1(8), ec60b871-fb2d-43bd-8fdf-2763a0385ae8); (YA). lib. bdg. 37.13 (978-1-4042-1464-4(X), 600bda56-1c6c-4364-94ee-8b17ceb3fea4) Rosen Publishing Group, Inc., The.

Kallen, Stuart A. Primary Sources. 2003. (American War Library). (ENG., Illus.). 112p. (J). 30.85 (978-1-59018-243-7(X), Lucent Bks.) Cengage Gale.

Kelley, K. C. How Spies Work. 2010. (Spies & Spying Ser.). (J). (gr. 4-7). 28.50 (978-1-59920-359-1(6)) Black Rabbit Bks.

Kids, Lonely Planet. Lonely Planet Kids How to Be an International Spy 1: Your Training Manual, Should You Choose to Accept It. 2015. (Lonely Planet Kids Ser.). (ENG., Illus.). 160p. (J). (gr. 4-7). 17.99 (978-1-74360-773-2(3), 4979) Lonely Planet Global Ltd. IRL. Dist: Hachette Bk. Group.

Kilmeade, Brian & Yaeger, Don. George Washington's Secret Six (Young Readers Adaptation) The Spies Who Saved America. 2020. (Illus.). 176p. (J). (gr. 5). pap. 9.99 (978-0-425-28901-3(X), Puffin Books) Penguin Young Readers Group.

Kim, F. S. Undercover Women: History's Greatest Spies. 2015. (Illus.). 32p. (J). pap. (978-0-545-59146-1(5)) Scholastic, Inc.

King, Bart. The Pocket Guide to Spy Stuff, 1 vol. Miller, Russ, illus. 2018. (Pocket Guide Ser.). 216p. (J). (gr. 3-8). pap. 9.99 (978-1-4236-4982-3(6)) Gibbs Smith, Publisher.

Klepeis, Alicia Z. Nathan Hale: Revolutionary War Hero, 1 vol. William, Lorna, illus. 2018. (American Legends & Folktales Ser.). (ENG.). 32p. (gr. 3-3). 30.21 (978-1-5026-3689-8(1), dda8da1d-d3e0-4133-a44f-cbe0b3153926) Cavendish Square Publishing LLC.

Kudlinski, Kathleen V. Rebel with a Cause: The Daring Adventure of Dicey Langston, Girl Spy of the American Revolution. Faber, Rudy, illus. 2015. (Encounter: Narrative Nonfiction Picture Bks.). (ENG.). 40p. (J). (gr. 3-6). lib. bdg. 29.32 (978-1-4914-6073-3(3), 128973, Capstone Young Readers) Capstone.

Langley, Andrew. Wartime Spies. 2010. (Spies & Spying Ser.). (J). (gr. 4-7). 28.50 (978-1-59920-362-1(6)) Black Rabbit Bks.

Langston-George, Rebecca. Deep-Cover Spies & Double-Crossers of the Cold War. 2017. (Spies! Ser.). (ENG., Illus.). 64p. (J). (gr. 4-8). lib. bdg. 34.65 (978-0-7565-5497-2(7), 134226, Compass Point Bks.) Capstone.

—Fearless Spies & Daring Deeds of World War II. 2017. (Spies! Ser.). (ENG., Illus.). 64p. (J). (gr. 4-8). lib. bdg. 34.65 (978-0-7565-5500-9(0), 134229, Compass Point Bks.) Capstone.

Lassieur, Allison. Courageous Spies & International Intrigue of World War I. 2017. (Spies! Ser.). (ENG., Illus.). 64p. (J). (gr. 4-8). lib. bdg. 34.65 (978-0-7565-5499-6(3), 134228, Compass Point Bks.) Capstone.

—Cyber Spies & Secret Agents of Modern Times. 2017. (Spies! Ser.). (ENG., Illus.). 64p. (J). (gr. 4-8). lib. bdg. 34.65 (978-0-7565-5498-9(5), 134227, Compass Point Bks.) Capstone.

Lassieur, Allison & Langston-George, Rebecca. Spies! 2017. (Spies! Ser.). (ENG., Illus.). 64p. (J). (gr. 4-8). 146.60 (978-0-7565-5518-4(3), 25806, Compass Point Bks.) Capstone.

—Spies! The History of Secret Agents & Double-Crossers. 2017. (ENG., Illus.). 240p. (J). (gr. 4-8). pap., pap., pap. 14.95 (978-1-62370-911-2(3), 136389, Capstone Young Readers) Capstone.

Libertson, Jody. Nathan Hale: Hero of the American Revolution. (Primary Sources of Famous People in American History Ser.). 32p. 2009. (gr. 2-3). 47.90 (978-1-60851-709-1(8)) 2003. (ENG., Illus.). (gr. 3-4). pap. 10.00 (978-0-8239-4189-6(2), 22d23725-2467-4f07-94a5-866661b41ee6) 2003. (ENG & SPA., Illus.). (gr. 2-3). lib. bdg. 29.13 (978-0-8239-4165-0(5), 6ba7c6c5-6c5b-48d6-8893-ff86061206ad, Editorial Buenas Letras) 2003. (ENG., Illus.). (gr. 3-4). lib. bdg. 29.13 (978-0-8239-4117-9(5), 63522eaa-0eb2-4695-ba53-02a3b3819817, Rosen Reference) Rosen Publishing Group, Inc., The.

—Nathan Hale: Heroe de la guerra de Independencia, 1 vol. 2003. (Grandes Personajes en la Historia de Los Estados Unidos (Famous People in American History) Ser.). (SPA.). 32p. (gr. 3-4). pap. 10.00 (978-0-8239-4235-0(X), 6a95018e-f493-428b-81c2-a4423aaa0918, Rosen Classroom) Rosen Publishing Group, Inc., The.

—Nathan Hale: Heroe Revolucionario, 1 vol. 2003. (Grandes Personajes en la Historia de Los Estados Unidos (Famous People in American History) Ser.). (SPA., Illus.). 32p. (gr. 3-4). lib. bdg. 29.13 (978-0-8239-4141-4(8), bbc97f46-967b-45e2-a513-8a16ffafddad, Editorial Buenas Letras) Rosen Publishing Group, Inc., The.

—Nathan Hale: Héroe revolucionario / Hero of the American Revolution. 2009. (Famous People in American History/Grandes personajes en la historia de los Estados Unidos Ser.). (ENG & SPA.). 32p. (gr. 2-3). 47.90 (978-1-61512-552-4(3), Editorial Buenas Letras) Rosen Publishing Group, Inc., The.

—Nathan Hale: Héroe revolucionario (Nathan Hale: Hero of the American Revolution) 2009. (Grandes personajes en la historia de los Estados Unidos (Famous People in American History) Ser.). (SPA.). 32p. (gr. 2-3). 47.90 (978-1-61512-805-1(0), Editorial Buenas Letras) Rosen Publishing Group, Inc., The.

Lockwood, Brad. Domestic Spying & Wiretapping. 2009. (In the News Ser.). 64p. (gr. 6-6). 58.50 (978-1-61513-465-6(4)) Rosen Publishing Group, Inc., The.

Loh-Hagan, Virginia. Girl Spies. 2019. (History's Yearbook Ser.). (ENG.). 32p. (J). (gr. 4-8). pap. 14.21 (978-1-5341-5080-5(3), 213627); (Illus.). lib. bdg. 32.07 (978-1-5341-4794-2(2), 213626) Cherry Lake Publishing. (45th Parallel Press).

McCollum, Sean. Secrets of World War I. 2017. (Top Secret Files Ser.). (ENG., Illus.). 32p. (J). (gr. 3-9). lib. bdg. 28.65 (978-1-5157-4139-8(7), 133947, Capstone Pr.) Capstone.

—Secrets of World War II. 2017. (Top Secret Files Ser.). (ENG., Illus.). 32p. (J). (gr. 3-9). lib. bdg. 28.65 (978-1-5157-4140-4(0), 133948, Capstone Pr.) Capstone.

McCormick, Patricia. The Plot to Kill Hitler: Dietrich Bonhoeffer: Pastor, Spy, Unlikely Hero. (ENG.). 192p. (J). (gr. 3). 2018. pap. 9.99 (978-0-06-241109-9(8)) 2016. (Illus.). 18.99 (978-0-06-241108-2(X)) HarperCollins Pubs. (Balzer & Bray).

Mendez, Antonio J. & Mendez, Jonna. Gathering Info: Getting the Scoop by Using Your Wits. 2007. (Illus.). 32p. (J). (978-0-439-90849-8(3)) Scholastic, Inc.

Micklos, John & Micklos, John, Jr. Courageous Children & Women of the American Revolution: Through Primary Sources, 1 vol. 2013. (American Revolution Through Primary Sources Ser.). (ENG., Illus.). 48p. (J). (gr. 4-6). 27.93 (978-0-7660-4131-8(X), 40dceef4-2d11-43ca-8481-3586da810fef) Enslow Publishing, LLC.

—Why We Won the American Revolution: Through Primary Sources, 1 vol. 2013. (American Revolution Through Primary Sources Ser.). (ENG.). 48p. (gr. 4-6). pap. 11.53 (978-1-4644-0192-3(6), 5895a7f8-08c5-4a37-9a5e-45c01416fbb5); (Illus.). (J). 27.93 (978-0-7660-4134-9(4), 1427223b-d0b5-47ed-ad69-7c1c441a1350) Enslow Publishing, LLC.

MILES, Kelly. Spies. Kelly, Richard, ed. 2017. 48p. (J). pap. 9.95 (978-1-78617-302-7(6)) Miles Kelly Publishing, Ltd. GBR. Dist: Parkwest Pubns., Inc.

Mitchell, Don. The Lady Is a Spy: Virginia Hall, World War II Hero of the French Resistance (Scholastic Focus) 2019. (ENG., Illus.). 288p. (YA). (gr. 7-7). 18.99 (978-0-545-93612-5(8), Scholastic Nonfiction) Scholastic, Inc.

Mitchell, Susan K. The Secret World of Spy Agencies, 1 vol. 2012. (Secret World of Spies Ser.). (ENG., Illus.). 48p. (gr. 4-6). pap. 11.53 (978-1-59845-352-2(1), 43ad0874-8726-49ec-ac2f-54ee2bde66f6); lib. bdg. 27.93 (978-0-7660-3714-4(2), fe1c45ab-9bfb-4038-bacc-48d2066d9675) Enslow Publishing, LLC.

—Spies & Lies: Famous & Infamous Spies, 1 vol. 2012. (Secret World of Spies Ser.). (ENG., Illus.). 48p. (gr. 4-6). pap. 11.53 (978-1-59845-349-2(1), 78389286-5ac3-476a-9d35-4acabfa240e0) Enslow Publishing, LLC.

—Spies, Double Agents, & Traitors, 1 vol. 2012. (Secret World of Spies Ser.). (ENG., Illus.). 48p. (gr. 4-6). pap. 11.53 (978-1-59845-351-5(3), 6dcaf12e-1ed8-4408-ba31-efe28d452e75); lib. bdg. 27.93 (978-0-7660-3711-3(8), cf4b35b4-d678-4589-83dc-dd14ba760f2a) Enslow Publishing, LLC.

—Spy Codes & Ciphers, 1 vol. 2012. (Secret World of Spies Ser.). (ENG., Illus.). 48p. (gr. 4-6). pap. 11.53 (978-1-59845-353-9(X), 1cc3ae90-03ac-46e6-824d-5ab583572b3c); lib. bdg. 27.93

(978-0-7660-3709-0(6), 2aee1d6f-77b9-4d41-b2a5-6c21f7090fe7) Enslow Publishing, LLC.

—Spy Gizmos & Gadgets, 1 vol. 2012. (Secret World of Spies Ser.). (ENG., Illus.). 48p. (gr. 4-6). pap. 11.53 (978-1-59845-354-6(8), b59662e3-dd2c-4a35-9af1-22194edbb22f); lib. bdg. 27.93 (978-0-7660-3710-6(X), 75f0b8c3-1745-48aa-83e5-4a7ac1ae7cf2) Enslow Publishing, LLC.

—Spy Tech: Digital Dangers, 1 vol. 2012. (Secret World of Spies Ser.). (ENG., Illus.). 48p. (gr. 4-6). pap. 11.53 (978-1-59845-350-8(5), 98d81f2c-ad98-41b5-aae1-4c95d7f948a4); lib. bdg. 27.93 (978-0-7660-3712-0(6), 16b5eac6-437e-4e75-9f63-dd134efd20b0) Enslow Publishing, LLC.

Moss, Marissa. Nurse, Soldier, Spy: The Story of Sarah Edmonds, a Civil War Hero. Hendrix, John, illus. 2011. (ENG.). 48p. (J). (gr. 3-7). 19.95 (978-0-8109-9735-6(5), 658701, Abrams Bks. for Young Readers) Abrams, Inc.

Murray, Hallie. The Role of Female Confederate Spies in the Civil War, 1 vol. 2019. (Warrior Women in American History Ser.). (ENG.). 104p. (gr. 7-7). pap. 21.00 (978-1-5026-5540-0(3), eaa72ffe-9b57-4ea3-8b26-a98d4ac093e2); lib. bdg. 44.50 (978-1-5026-5541-7(1), 813ee375-f83d-4738-8a94-3357dd568210) Cavendish Square Publishing LLC.

—The Role of Female Confederate Spies in the Civil War. 2019. (J). pap. (978-1-9785-1404-1(2)) Enslow Publishing, LLC.

—The Role of Female Union Spies in the Civil War, 1 vol. 2019. (Warrior Women in American History Ser.). (ENG.). 104p. (gr. 7-7). pap. 21.00 (978-1-5026-5552-3(7), 40c157e3-a9ba-4c9a-b76e-20fdbcf1acbe); lib. bdg. 44.50 (978-1-5026-5553-0(5), 5447ba82-d148-40f6-aebd-ab6b1462b113) Cavendish Square Publishing LLC.

—The Role of Female Union Spies in the Civil War. 2020. (J). pap. (978-1-9785-1416-4(6)) Enslow Publishing, LLC.

Murray, Laura K. Spies in the CIA. 2016. (I Spy Ser.). (ENG.). 24p. (J). (gr. 1-4). (978-1-60818-616-7(4), 20468, Creative Education) Creative Co., The.

—Spies in the KGB. 2016. (I Spy Ser.). (ENG., Illus.). 24p. (J). (gr. 1-4). (978-1-60818-617-4(2), 20471, Creative Education) Creative Co., The.

—Spies in the Mossad. 2016. (I Spy Ser.). (ENG., Illus.). 24p. (J). (gr. 1-4). (978-1-60818-618-1(0), 20474, Creative Education) Creative Co., The.

—Spies in the SIS. 2016. (I Spy Ser.). (ENG., Illus.). 24p. (J). (gr. 1-4). (978-1-60818-619-8(9), 20477, Creative Education) Creative Co., The.

Narayan, Natasha. Spies, Secret Agents & Spooks of London. 2004. (Of London Ser.). (ENG., Illus.). 96p. (J). pap. 8.99 (978-1-904153-14-6(3)) Tempus ESP. Dist: Independent Pubs. Group.

Oliver, Martin. Spycraft: How to Be the Best Secret Agent Ever. 2019. (Buster Know-How Ser.). (ENG., Illus.). 128p. (J). (gr. 4-6). pap. 16.99 (978-1-78055-510-2(5)) O'Mara, Michael Bks., Ltd. GBR. Dist: Independent Pubs. Group.

Olson, Elsie. Spies! Smart & Secretive Schemers. 2017. (History's Hotshots Ser.). (ENG., Illus.). 32p. (J). (gr. 3-6). lib. bdg. 32.79 (978-1-5321-1275-1(0), 27599, Checkerboard Library) ABDO Publishing Co.

Olson, Nathan & Glaser, Jason. Nathan Hale: Revolutionary Spy, 1 vol. Martin, Cynthia & Schoonover, Brent, illus. 2006. (Graphic Biographies Ser.). (ENG.). 32p. (J). (gr. 3-9). per. 8.10 (978-0-7368-6199-1(8), 87898, Capstone Pr.) Capstone.

Omoth, Tyler. Secrets of the American Revolution. 2017. (Top Secret Files Ser.). (ENG., Illus.). 32p. (J). (gr. 3-9). lib. bdg. 28.65 (978-1-5157-4137-4(0), 133945, Capstone Pr.) Capstone.

Orme, David. Spies. 2008. (Trailblazers Ser.). (ENG., Illus.). 36p. pap. (978-1-84167-695-1(0)) Ransom Publishing Ltd.

—Spies. 2010. (Fact to Fiction Grafx Ser.). (Illus.). 36p. (J). lib. bdg. 16.95 (978-1-60686-473-9(4)) Perfection Learning Corp.

Owen, David. Spies: The Undercover World of Secrets, Gadgets & Lies. 2004. (ENG., Illus.). 128p. (J). (gr. 5-9). pap. 9.95 (978-1-55297-794-1(3), 1666b851-6d76-4fa0-89c5-123b72f14072) Firefly Bks., Ltd.

Owen, Ruth. The Superspy Handbook, 1 vol., 1. 2014. (DIY for Boys Ser.). (ENG.). 32p. (J). (gr. 4-4). 30.17 (978-1-4777-6282-0(5), de9b02ad-d301-43d7-9b0a-94251e3041ef, PowerKids Pr.) Rosen Publishing Group, Inc., The.

Payne, Matt. Secret Agent Gear: Spy Tools & Tech: Past, Present, & Future. 2013. (Illus.). 32p. (J). pap. (978-0-545-59143-0(0)) Scholastic, Inc.

Pender, Lionel. Spy vs. Spy: Intelligence Organizations, 1 vol. 2016. (Law Enforcement & Intelligence Gathering Ser.). (ENG.). 104p. (YA). (gr. 8-8). lib. bdg. 37.82 (978-1-5081-0370-7(4), ef87a714-1d87-4a0f-8d69-2f89983a5f05, Britannica Educational Publishing) Rosen Publishing Group, Inc., The.

Perrin, Pat & Coleman, Wim. The Mystery of the Murdered Playwright. 2004. (Cover-To-Cover Books). (Illus.). 56p. pap. 9.00 (978-0-7891-6001-0(3)); (gr. 4-7). lib. bdg. 17.95 (978-0-7569-1353-3(5)) Perfection Learning Corp.

Phillips, Larissa. Women Civil War Spies of the Confederacy. (American Women at War Ser.). 112p. (gr. 8-8). 2009. 63.90 (978-1-61511-402-3(5)) 2004. (ENG., Illus.). lib. bdg. 39.80 (978-0-8239-4451-4(4), 0e231b97-a361-4988-a631-9ba03b3bf6f3) Rosen Publishing Group, Inc., The.

Portalupi, Laura. Spies! Real People, Real Stories. 2003. (High Five Reading - Green Ser.). (ENG., Illus.). 48p. (gr. 3-4). per. 9.00 (978-0-7368-2830-7(3)) Capstone.

Price, Sean. Modern Spies. 2014. pap. (978-1-4765-3593-7(0)) Capstone.

Purcell, Martha Sias. Spies of the American Revolution. 2003. (Reading Essentials in Social Studies). (Illus.). 48p. pap. 9.00 (978-0-7891-5854-3(X)) Perfection Learning Corp.

Rauf, Don. Killer Lipstick: And Other Spy Gadgets. (24/7 Science Behind the Scenes: Spy Files Ser.). (ENG., Illus.). 64p. (J). 2008. (gr. 7-12). 22.44 (978-0-531-12084-2(8)) 2007. (gr. 8-12). pap. 7.95 (978-0-531-17536-1(7)) Scholastic Library Publishing. (Watts, Franklin).

Raum, Elizabeth. Spies of the American Revolution: An Interactive Espionage Adventure. 2015. (You Choose: Spies Ser.). (ENG., Illus.). 112p. (J). (gr. 3-7). lib. bdg. 32.65 (978-1-4914-5858-7(5), 128821, Capstone Pr.) Capstone.

—Stealing Nazi Secrets in World War II: An Interactive Espionage Adventure. 2015. (You Choose: Spies Ser.). (ENG., Illus.). 112p. (J). (gr. 3-7). pap. 6.95 (978-1-4914-5934-8(4), 128854, Capstone Pr.) Capstone.

Rigby Education Staff. Spy Manual. (Sails Literacy Ser.). (Illus.). 16p. (gr. 2-3). 27.00 (978-0-7635-9938-6(7), 699387C99) Rigby Education.

Rockwell, Anne. A Spy Called James: The True Story of James Lafayette, Revolutionary War Double Agent. Cooper, Floyd, illus. 2016. (ENG.). 32p. (J). (gr. 2-5). lib. bdg. 19.99 (978-1-4677-4933-6(8), 2dc8d93e-186e-4737-9f52-c724b0f2aff9); E-Book 29.32 (978-1-4677-6178-9(8)) Lerner Publishing Group. (Carolrhoda Bks.).

Rodger, Ellen. Top Secret Science in Cybercrime & Espionage. 2019. (Top Secret Science Ser.). (Illus.). 48p. (J). (gr. 5-5). (978-0-7787-5992-8(X)); pap. (978-0-7787-5998-0(9)) Crabtree Publishing Co.

Rooney, Anne. Spies. 2003. (Wicked Wallets Ser.). (ENG., Illus.). 24p. (YA). (978-1-84347-036-6(5), Pavilion Children's Books) Pavilion Bks.

Roop, Peter & Roop, Connie. Botones Para el General Washington. Hanson, Peter E., illus. 2006. (Yo Solo - Historia (on My Own - History) Ser.).Tr. of Buttons for General Washington. (SPA.). 48p. (gr. 2-4). lib. bdg. 25.26 (978-0-8225-6261-0(8)) Lerner Publishing Group.

Rose, Alexa. Spy Games. 2014. (PACKtivities Ser.: 3). (ENG.). 48p. (J). 11.99 (978-1-935703-38-9(2)) Downtown Bookworks.

Ruelle, Karen Gray. Surprising Spies: Unexpected Heroes of World War II. 2020. (Illus.). 160p. (J). (gr. 3-7). 19.99 (978-0-8234-3757-3(4)) Holiday Hse., Inc.

Sakany, Lois. Women Civil War Spies of the Union. (American Women at War Ser.). 112p. (gr. 8-8). 2009. 63.90 (978-1-61511-403-0(3)) 2004. (ENG., Illus.). lib. bdg. 39.80 (978-0-8239-4450-7(6), badfd22d-70f2-4115-bb75-98ffbe423da6) Rosen Publishing Group, Inc., The.

Samuels, Charles. Spying & Security. 2012. (World War II: Sourcebook Ser.). (ENG.). 48p. (J). (gr. 5-8). lib. bdg. 37.10 (978-1-936333-25-7(2), 16836) Brown Bear Bks.

Schumacher, Cassandra. Code Breakers & Spies of the American Revolution, 1 vol. 2018. (Code Breakers & Spies Ser.). (ENG.). 80p. (J). (gr. 8-8). 38.79 (978-1-5026-3844-1(4), 015f9852-f119-411b-beea-21221643f68d) Cavendish Square Publishing LLC.

Seiple, Samantha. Nazi Saboteurs: Hitler's Secret Attack on America. 2019. (Illus.). 206p. (J). pap. (978-1-338-25919-3(9)) Scholastic, Inc.

—Nazi Saboteurs: Hitler's Secret Attack on America (Scholastic Focus) 2019. (ENG., Illus.). 224p. (YA). (gr. 7-7). 17.99 (978-1-338-25914-8(8), Scholastic Nonfiction) Scholastic, Inc.

Small, Cathleen. Code Breakers & Spies of World War II, 1 vol. 2018. (Code Breakers & Spies Ser.). (ENG.). 80p. (J). (gr. 8-8). lib. bdg. 38.79 (978-1-5026-3853-3(3), 8e8ea6af-5a7a-4270-a993-896000b0f30a) Cavendish Square Publishing LLC.

Sodaro, Craig. Civil War Spies. 2013. 48p. pap. 9.95 (978-1-4765-3590-6(6)) Capstone.

The Spy, 6 vols., Pack. (Sails Literacy Ser.). 16p. (gr. k-18). 27.00 (978-0-7635-4437-9(X)) Rigby Education.

Spy Files Set, 6 vols., Set. Incl. Bioterror: Deadly Invisible Weapons. Rudy, Lisa Jo. (gr. 7-12). 2008. 22.44 (978-0-531-12080-4(5)); Eyes in the Sky (24/7: Science Behind the Scenes: Spy Files) (Library Edition) Rudy, Lisa Jo. (gr. 8-12). 2007. 29.00 (978-0-531-12082-8(1)); Killer Lipstick: And Other Spy Gadgets. Rauf, Don. (gr. 7-12). 2008. 22.44 (978-0-531-12084-2(8)); 64p. (J)., Watts, Franklin (24/7: Science Behind the Scenes Ser.). (Illus.). 2007. 174.00 (978-0-531-12477-2(0)) Scholastic Library Publishing.

Stemple, Heidi E. Y. Ready for Anything! Training Your Brain for Expert Espionage. 2006. (Illus.). 32p. (J). (978-0-439-90504-6(4)) Scholastic, Inc.

Stewart, James. Spies & Traitors. 2008. (Amazing History Ser.). (Illus.). 32p. (J). (gr. 2-6). pap. 28.50 (978-1-59920-109-2(7)) Black Rabbit Bks.

—Spies & Traitors. 2009. (Amazing History Ser.). (Illus.). 32p. (J). pap. 7.95 (978-1-59920-210-5(7)) Black Rabbit Bks.

Sullivan, Laura. Life As a Spy in the American Revolution, 1 vol. 2015. (Life As... Ser.). (ENG., Illus.). 32p. (gr. 3-3). 30.21 (978-1-5026-1081-2(7), 5d4dacd8-8e62-4603-84c8-63bd892ca5df) Cavendish Square Publishing LLC.

Swanson, Jennifer. Top Secret Science: Projects You Aren't Supposed to Know About, 1 vol. 2014. (Scary Science Ser.). (ENG., Illus.). 32p. (J). (gr. 3-6). lib. bdg. 27.99 (978-1-4765-3926-3(X), 123924, Capstone Pr.) Capstone.

Terp, Gail. Ninja. 2019. (History's Warriors Ser.). (ENG., Illus.). 32p. (J). (gr. 4-6). pap. 9.99 (978-1-64466-042-3(3), 12757); lib. bdg. (978-1-68072-851-4(2), 12756) Black Rabbit Bks. (Bolt).

Tracy, Kathleen. Nathan Hale. 2006. (Profiles in American History Ser.). (Illus.). 48p. (J). (gr. 3-7). lib. bdg. 29.95 (978-1-58415-447-1(0)) Mitchell Lane Pubs.

Troupe, Thomas Kingsley. Sneaky Spies: The Inspiring Truth Behind Popular Stealth Video Games. 2018. (Video Games vs. Reality Ser.). (ENG., Illus.). 32p. (J). (gr. 3-9). pap. 7.95 (978-1-5435-2576-2(8), 138060); lib. bdg. 28.65 (978-1-5435-2572-4(5), 138054) Capstone. (Capstone Pr.).

Wiese, Jim & Melton, H. Keith. The Spy's Guide to Counterintelligence. 2003. (Illus.). 48p. (J). (978-0-439-33646-8(5)) Scholastic, Inc.

Wilson, Camilla. Civil War Spies: Behind Enemy Lines. 2010. vii, 104p. (J). pap. (978-0-545-13002-8(6)) Scholastic, Inc.

Zullo, Allan. The Secret Agent & Other Spy Kids. 2006. 147p. (J). pap. (978-0-439-84835-0(0)) Scholastic, Inc.

SPIES—FICTION

Aaron, Chester. Alex, Who Won His War. 2014. 225p. (YA). (978-1-936144-26-6(3)) Zumaya Pubns. LLC.

Abela, Deborah. In Search of the Time & Space Machine: Max Remy Superspy 1. Murphy, Jobi, illus. 2005. (Spy Force Ser.). 256p. (Orig.). (J). 14.95 (978-1-74051-765-2(2), Simon & Schuster Bks. For Young Readers) Simon & Schuster Bks. For Young Readers.

—Mission: Hollywood. O'Connor, George, illus. 2007. (Spy Force Ser.: 4). (ENG.). 240p. (J). (gr. 3-7). pap. 10.99 (978-1-4169-3969-6(5), Aladdin) Simon & Schuster Children's Publishing.

Allen, Elise & Daryle Connors. Gabby Duran & the Unsittables. 2016. (Gabby Duran Ser.: 1). (J). lib. bdg. 18.40 (978-0-606-39443-7(5)) Turtleback.

Anderson, Danny. Santa's Spy. 2012. 28p. pap. 15.99 (978-1-4771-1007-2(0)) Xlibris Corp.

Anderson, Laurie Halse. Chains. (Seeds of America Trilogy Ser.). (ENG., Illus.). (J). (gr. 5-9). 2010. 336p. pap. 8.99 (978-1-4169-0586-8(3)) 2008. 320p. 19.99 (978-1-4169-0585-1(5)) Simon & Schuster Children's Publishing. (Atheneum Bks. for Young Readers).

Anderson, M. T. Agent Q, or the Smell of Danger! Cyrus, Kurt, illus. 2011. (Pals in Peril Tale Ser.). (ENG.). 320p. (J). (gr. 5-9). pap. 8.99 (978-1-4424-2640-5(3), Beach Lane Bks.) Beach Lane Bks.

Anderson, Matthew. Agent Q, or the Smell of Danger! Cyrus, Kurt, illus. 2010. (Pals in Peril Tale Ser.). (ENG.). 304p. (J). (gr. 5-9). 16.99 (978-1-4169-8640-9(5), Beach Lane Bks.) Beach Lane Bks.

Angleberger, Tom. Didi Dodo, Future Spy: Double-O Dodo (Didi Dodo, Future Spy #3) Chapman, Jared, illus. 2020. (Flytrap Files Ser.). (ENG.). 112p. (J). (gr. 1-4). 12.99 (978-1-4197-4097-8(0), 1259601, Amulet Bks.) Abrams, Inc.

—Didi Dodo, Future Spy: Recipe for Disaster (Didi Dodo, Future Spy #1) Chapman, Jared, illus. 2019. (Flytrap Files Ser.). (ENG.). (J). (gr. 1-4). 128p. pap. 5.99 (978-1-4197-3706-0(6), 1259503); 112p. 12.99 (978-1-4197-3370-3(2), 1259501) Abrams, Inc. (Amulet Bks.).

—Didi Dodo, Future Spy: Robo-Dodo Rumble (Didi Dodo, Future Spy #2) Chapman, Jared, illus. 2019. (Flytrap Files Ser.). (ENG.). 112p. (J). (gr. 1-4). 12.99 (978-1-4197-3688-9(4), 1259401) Abrams, Inc.

Anthony, Horowitz. Ark Angel. 2007. (Alex Rider Ser.: Bk. 6). 326p. (gr. 5-9). 19.00 (978-0-7569-8134-1(4)) Perfection Learning Corp.

—Ark Angel. 2007. (Alex Rider Ser.: 6). 326p. lib. bdg. 19.65 (978-1-4177-7664-1(1)) Turtleback.

—Crocodile Tears, 9 vols. 2010. (Alex Rider Adventure Ser.: 8). (J). 81.75 (978-1-4407-5451-7(9)); 79.75 (978-1-4407-5453-1(5)); 102.75 (978-1-4407-5456-2(X)); 100.75 (978-1-4407-5458-6(6)); 1.25 (978-1-4407-5459-3(4)) Recorded Bks., Inc.

—Crocodile Tears. 2010. (Alex Rider Ser.: 8). lib. bdg. 19.65 (978-0-606-23639-3(2)) Turtleback.

—Point Blanc. 2004. (Alex Rider Ser.: Bk. 2). (SPA.). 264p. 7.95 (978-84-414-1410-5(6)) Editorial Edaf, S.L. ESP. Dist: Spanish Pubs., LLC.

—Scorpia Rising, 9 vols. (J). 2012. 90.75 (978-1-4561-3363-4(2)) 2012. 1.25 (978-1-4640-0577-0(X)) 2012. 256.75 (978-1-4561-3362-7(4)) 2011. 122.75 (978-1-4561-3365-8(9)) 2011. 120.75 (978-1-4561-3367-2(5)) Recorded Bks., Inc.

—Scorpia Rising. 2012. (Alex Rider Ser.: 9). lib. bdg. 19.65 (978-0-606-23638-6(4)) Turtleback.

—Stormbreaker. 2004. (Alex Rider Ser.: Bk. 1). 208p. (J). (gr. 4-7). pap. 38.00 incl. audio (978-0-8072-2277-5(1), Listening Library) Random Hse. Audio Publishing Group.

Arena, Felice & Kettle, Phil. Secret Agent Heroes. Vane, Mitch, illus. 2004. (J). pap. (978-1-59336-355-0(9)) Mondo Publishing.

Author TBD. I Lie for a Living. 2006. (Illus.). 192p. per. 14.95 (978-0-7922-5316-7(7), National Geographic) Disney Publishing Worldwide.

Avi. Sophia's War: A Tale of the Revolution. 2012. (ENG., Illus.). 320p. (J). (gr. 3-7). 19.99 (978-1-4424-1441-9(3), Beach Lane Bks.) Beach Lane Bks.

—Sophia's War: A Tale of the Revolution. 2013. (ENG., Illus.). 336p. (J). (gr. 3-7). pap. 8.99 (978-1-4424-1442-6(1)) Simon & Schuster Children's Publishing.

Backues, E. Sharol. Stories of a Dragonfly Spy, a Dog Named Droop & a Little Calf That Wondered Why? 2011. 28p. pap. 21.99 (978-1-4653-6343-5(2)) Xlibris Corp.

The Balloon Ride, 6, Pack. (Sails Literacy Ser.). 16p. (gr. k-18). 27.00 (978-0-7635-4427-0(2)) Rigby Education.

The Balloon Ride: KinderConcepts Individual Title Six-Packs. (Kinderstarters Ser.). 8p. (gr. -1-1). 21.00 (978-0-7635-8736-9(2)) Rigby Education.

Barba, Rick. The Secret of Stoneship Woods. 2006. (Spy Gear Adventures Ser.: 1). (ENG., Illus.). 160p. (J). (gr. 3-7). pap. 8.99 (978-1-4169-0887-6(0), Simon & Schuster/Paula Wiseman Bks.) Simon & Schuster/Paula Wiseman Bks.

Barchers, Suzanne I. Spy It!, 1 vol. rev. ed. 2011. (Phonics Ser.). (ENG., Illus.). 16p. (gr. k-2). 6.99 (978-1-4333-2910-4(7)) Teacher Created Materials, Inc.

Barnes, Jennifer Lynn. The Squad: Perfect Cover. 2008. (Squad Ser.). (ENG.). 288p. (YA). (gr. 7). mass mkt. 7.99 (978-0-385-73454-7(9), Laurel Leaf) Random Hse. Children's Bks.

Barnett, Mac. The Impossible Crime (Mac B. , Kid Spy #2) Lowery, Mike, illus. 2018. (Mac B. , Kid Spy Ser.: 2). (ENG.). 160p. (J). (gr. 2-5). 12.99 (978-1-338-14368-3(9), Orchard Bks.) Scholastic, Inc.

—Mac Undercover (Mac B. , Kid Spy #1) Lowery, Mike, illus. 2018. (Mac B. , Kid Spy Ser.: 1). (ENG.). 160p. (J). (gr. 2-5). 12.99 (978-1-338-14359-1(X), Orchard Bks.) Scholastic, Inc.

Becker, Helaine. Dirk Daring, Secret Agent, 1 vol. 2014. (Dirk Daring, Secret Agent Ser.: 1). (ENG., Illus.). 208p. (J). (gr. 4-7). pap. 9.95 (978-1-4598-0683-2(2)) Orca Bk. Pubs. USA.

Bell, Michele Ashman. Dragon's Jaw: A Heart-Pounding Adventure. 2005. 241p. (J). (978-1-59156-880-3(3)) Covenant Communications.

—Spyhunt: A Heart-Pounding Adventure: A Novel. 2004. 187p. (J). (978-1-59156-457-7(3)) Covenant Communications.

Bernstein, Jonathan. Bridget Wilder: Spy-In-Training. 2016. (Bridget Wilder Ser.: 1). (J). lib. bdg. 17.20 (978-0-606-38746-0(3)) Turtleback.

—Bridget Wilder: Spy-In-Training. 2016. (Bridget Wilder Ser.: 1). (ENG.). 320p. (J). (gr. 3-7). pap. 6.99 (978-0-06-238267-2(5), Tegen, Katherine Bks) HarperCollins Pubs.

Blakemore, Megan Frazer. The Spy Catchers of Maple Hill. 2014. (ENG.). 320p. (J). (gr. 3-6). 16.99 (978-1-61963-348-3(5), 900134200, Bloomsbury USA Childrens) Bloomsbury Publishing USA.

Boyd, David. Hidden Message. Alward, Jeff, illus. 2007. 48p. (J). lib. bdg. 23.08 (978-1-4242-1637-6(0)) Fitzgerald Bks.

Bradbury, Jennifer. Wrapped. 2011. (ENG., Illus.). 320p. (YA). (gr. 7-18). 16.99 (978-1-4169-9007-9(0), Atheneum Bks. for Young Readers) Simon & Schuster Children's Publishing.

Bradley, F. T. Double Vision. 2013. (Double Vision Ser.: 1). (ENG.). 272p. (J). (gr. 3-7). pap. 6.99 (978-0-06-210438-0(1), HarperCollins) HarperCollins Pubs.

—Double Vision: the Alias Men. 2015. (Double Vision Ser.: 3). (ENG.). 256p. (J). (gr. 3-7). pap. 7.99 (978-0-06-210444-1(6), HarperCollins) HarperCollins Pubs.

Bradley, Kimberly Brubaker. For Freedom: The Story of a French Spy. 2005. 181p. 16.00 (978-0-7569-5091-0(0)) Perfection Learning Corp.

—For Freedom: The Story of a French Spy. 2005. (ENG.). 192p. (YA). (gr. 7-9). mass mkt. 8.99 (978-0-440-41831-3(3), Laurel Leaf) Random Hse. Children's Bks.

Broad, Michael. Ghost Diamond!, No. 1. Broad, Michael, illus. 2011. (Agent Amelia Ser.: 1). (ENG., Illus.). 144p. (J). (gr. 2-5). lib. bdg. 22.60 (978-0-7613-8056-6(6)) Lerner Publishing Group.

—Zombie Cows!, 2 vols., No. 2. Broad, Michael, illus. 2011. (Agent Amelia Ser.: 2). (ENG., Illus.). 144p. (J). (gr. 2-5). lib. bdg. 22.65 (978-0-7613-8057-3(4), 6ab86559-2b7d-4b2e-bf35-1cbee740a7c1, Darby Creek) Lerner Publishing Group.

—#1 Ghost Diamond! 2011. (Agent Amelia Ser.). pap. 33.92 (978-0-7613-8341-3(7), Darby Creek) Lerner Publishing Group.

—#2 Zombie Cows! 2011. (Agent Amelia Ser.). pap. 33.92 (978-0-7613-8342-0(5), Darby Creek) Lerner Publishing Group.

—#3 Hypno Hounds! 2011. (Agent Amelia Ser.). pap. 33.92 (978-0-7613-8343-7(3), Darby Creek) Lerner Publishing Group.

—#4 Spooky Ballet! 2011. (Agent Amelia Ser.). pap. 33.92 (978-0-7613-8344-4(1), Darby Creek) Lerner Publishing Group.

Brown, Teri. Velvet Undercover. 2015. (ENG.). 336p. (YA). (gr. 8). 17.99 (978-0-06-232127-5(7), Balzer & Bray) HarperCollins Pubs.

Bruchac, Joseph. Code Talker: A Novel about the Navajo Marines of World War Two. 2005. 240p. (YA). (gr. 7-18). 17.99 (978-0-8037-2921-6(9), Dial Bks) Penguin Young Readers Group.

—Wolf Mark, 1 vol. 2011. (ENG.). 392p. (YA). (gr. 7-12). 20.95 (978-1-60060-661-8(X), leelowtu, Tu Bks.) Lee & Low Bks., Inc.

Buckley, Michael. The Cheerleaders of Doom. 2012. (Nerds Ser.: 3). (YA). lib. bdg. 18.40 (978-0-606-26927-8(4)) Turtleback.

—Nerds: Book Five: Attack of the BULLIES, Bk. 5. 2014. (ENG., Illus.). 352p. (J). (gr. 3-7). pap. 9.99 (978-1-4197-1222-7(5), 695503) Abrams, Inc.

—Nerds: Book Four: the Villain Virus, Bk. 4. 2013. (Nerds Ser.). (ENG.). 304p. (J). (gr. 3-7). pap. 8.99 (978-1-4197-0975-3(5), 695403, Amulet Bks.) Abrams, Inc.

—Nerds: Book Two: M Is for Mama's Boy, Bk. 2. 2011. (ENG., Illus.). 288p. (J). (gr. 3-7). pap. 9.99 (978-1-4197-0023-1(5), Amulet Bks.) Abrams, Inc.

—NERDS: National Espionage, Rescue, & Defense Society, 5 vols. 2009. (N. E. R. D. S. Ser.: 1). (J). 190.75 (978-1-4407-4234-7(0)); 1.25 (978-1-4407-4243-9(X)); 71.75 (978-1-4407-4235-4(9)); 86.75 (978-1-4407-4239-2(1)); 73.75 (978-1-4407-4233-0(2)); 88.75 (978-1-4407-4237-8(5)) Recorded Bks., Inc.

—Nerds: National Espionage, Rescue, & Defense Society (Book One), Bk. 1. 2010. (ENG., Illus.). 352p. (J). (gr. 3-7). pap. 9.99 (978-0-8109-8985-6(9), 660103, Amulet Bks.) Abrams, Inc.

—NERDS - National Espionage, Rescue, & Defense Society. 2010. (Nerds Ser.: 1). (J). lib. bdg. 18.40 (978-0-606-15084-2(6)) Turtleback.

—NERDS 2: M für Muttersöhnchen. 2011. (SPA.). 260p. (J). (gr. 6-8). pap. 10.99 (978-987-612-335-8(1)) V&R Editoras.

—Nerds 3: Cheerleaders of Doom. 2011. (Nerds Ser.). (ENG., Illus.). 288p. (J). (gr. 3-7). pap. 7.95 (978-1-4197-0124-5(X)) Abrams, Inc.

—Nerds 5: Attack of the Bullies. 2013. (Nerds Ser.). (ENG.). 336p. (YA). (gr. 3-7). pap. 7.95 (978-1-4197-1046-9(X)) Abrams, Inc.

—NERDS: Book Three: The Cheerleaders of Doom, Bk. 3. 2012. (Nerds Ser.). (ENG.). 304p. (YA). (gr. 3-7). pap. 8.99 (978-1-4197-0414-7(1), 661503, Amulet Bks.) Abrams, Inc.

Burgis, Stephanie. The Girl with the Dragon Heart. 2019. (Dragon Heart Ser.). (ENG.). 304p. (J). pap. 8.99 (978-1-5476-0244-5(9), 900207565, Bloomsbury Children's Bks.) Bloomsbury Publishing USA.

Butcher, A. J. Spy High Mission One. 2004. (ENG.). 224p. (YA). (gr. 5-8). pap. 13.99 (978-0-316-73760-9(7)) Little, Brown Bks. for Young Readers.

—Spy High Mission Three: the Serpent Scenario. 2004. (ENG.). 224p. (YA). (gr. 5-8). pap. 13.99 (978-0-316-73766-1(6)) Little, Brown Bks. for Young Readers.

—Spy High Mission Two: Chaos Rising. 2004. (ENG., Illus.). 240p. (YA). (gr. 5-8). pap. 14.99 (978-0-316-73765-4(8)) Little, Brown Bks. for Young Readers.

Cage, Elizabeth. Covert Affairs 2: Spy Girls Are Forever; Dial "V" for Vengeance; If Looks Could Kill. 2014. (ENG., Illus.). 640p. (YA). (gr. 7). pap. 12.99 (978-1-4424-8229-6(X), Simon Pulse) Simon Pulse.

—Dial "V" for Vengeance. 2013. (Spy Girls Ser.: 5). (ENG., Illus.). 192p. (YA). (gr. 7). pap. 13.99 (978-1-4814-2084-6(4), Simon Pulse) Simon Pulse.

—If Looks Could Kill. 2013. (Spy Girls Ser.: 6). (ENG., Illus.). 192p. (YA). (gr. 7). pap. 13.99 *(978-1-4814-2085-3(2),* Simon Pulse) Simon Pulse.

—License to Thrill. 2013. (Spy Girls Ser.: 1). (ENG., Illus.). 192p. (YA). (gr. 7). pap. 13.99 *(978-1-4814-2078-5(X),* Simon Pulse) Simon Pulse.

—Live & Let Spy. 2013. (Spy Girls Ser.: 2). (ENG., Illus.). 192p. (YA). (gr. 7). pap. 13.99 *(978-1-4814-2079-2(8),* Simon Pulse) Simon Pulse.

—Nobody Does It Better. 2013. (Spy Girls Ser.: 3). (ENG., Illus.). 192p. (YA). (gr. 7). pap. 13.99 *(978-1-4814-2080-8(1),* Simon Pulse) Simon Pulse.

—Spy Girls Are Forever. 2013. (Spy Girls Ser.: 4). (ENG., Illus.). 192p. (YA). (gr. 7). pap. 13.99 *(978-1-4814-2082-2(8),* Simon Pulse) Simon Pulse.

Caletti, Deb. The Last Forever. 2016. (ENG., Illus.). 352p. (YA). (gr. 7-7). pap. 11.99 *(978-1-4424-5002-8(9),* Simon & Schuster Bks. For Young Readers) Simon & Schuster Bks. For Young Readers.

Calkhoven, Laurie. Boys of Wartime: Daniel at the Siege of Boston 1776, 1. 2011. (Boys of Wartime Ser.: 1). 224p. (J). (gr. 4-7). 8.99 *(978-0-14-241750-8(5),* Puffin) Penguin Young Readers Group.

Carey, John. Cook Spies. 2005. 34p. (J). per. *(978-0-9773723-2-4(4))* Trent's Prints.

Carriger, Gail. Curtsies & Conspiracies. 2014. (Finishing School Ser.: 2). (ENG.). 336p. (YA). (gr. 7-17). pap. 10.99 *(978-0-316-19020-6(9))* Little, Brown Bks. for Young Readers.

—Etiquette & Espionage. 2013. (Finishing School Ser.: 1). (ENG.). 336p. (YA). (gr. 7-17). pap. 11.99 *(978-0-316-19010-7(1))* Little, Brown Bks. for Young Readers.

—Waistcoats & Weaponry. 2015. (Finishing School Ser.: 3). (ENG.). 320p. (YA). (gr. 7-17). pap. 18.99 *(978-0-316-19025-1(X))* Little, Brown Bks. for Young Readers.

Carter, Ally. Cross My Heart & Hope to Spy. 2016. (Gallagher Girls Ser.: 2). (ENG.). 256p. (YA). (gr. 7-17). pap. 10.99 *(978-1-4847-8503-4(7))* Little, Brown Bks. for Young Readers.

—Cross My Heart & Hope to Spy. 2016. (Gallagher Girls Ser.: 2). (J). lib. bdg. 20.85 *(978-0-606-38296-0(8))* Turtleback.

—I'd Tell You I Love You, but Then I'd Have to Kill You. 2016. (Gallagher Girls Ser.: 1). (ENG.). 304p. (YA). (gr. 7-17). pap. 11.99 *(978-1-4847-8505-8(3))* Hyperion Bks. for Children.

—Only the Good Spy Young. 10th anniv. ed. 2016. (Gallagher Girls Ser.: 4). (ENG.). 288p. (YA). (gr. 7-17). pap. 9.99 *(978-1-4847-8506-5(1))* Little, Brown Bks. for Young Readers.

—Out of Sight, Out of Time. 10th anniv. ed. 2016. (Gallagher Girls Ser.: 5). (ENG.). 320p. (YA). (gr. 7-17). pap. 9.99 *(978-1-4847-8507-2(X))* Hyperion Bks. for Children.

—Out of Sight, Out of Time. 2016. (Gallagher Girls Ser.: 5). (YA). lib. bdg. 20.85 *(978-0-606-38299-1(2))* Turtleback.

—United We Spy. 2016. (Gallagher Girls Ser.: 6). (ENG.). 320p. (YA). (gr. 7-17). pap. 10.99 *(978-1-4847-8508-9(8))* Hyperion Bks. for Children.

—United We Spy. 2016. (Gallagher Girls Ser.: 6). (YA). lib. bdg. 20.85 *(978-0-606-38300-4(X))* Turtleback.

Chalk, Gary, et al. The Spy Master. 2005. (F. E. A. R. Adventures S. Ser.). (ENG., Illus.). 128p. (J). 8.00 *(978-1-84046-692-8(8),* Wizard Books) Icon Bks., Ltd. GBR. Dist: Publishers Group Canada.

Cherub: The Recruit; the Dealer; Maximum Security. 2013. (Cherub Ser.). (ENG.). 1008p. (YA). (gr. 7). pap. 29.99 *(978-1-4424-8376-7(8),* Simon Pulse) Simon Pulse.

CHERUB: Black Friday: Book 15, Bk. 15. 2014. (Cherub Ser.). (ENG.). 400p. (gr. 7). 11.99 *(978-0-340-99924-0(1))* Hachette Children's Group GBR. Dist: Hachette Bk. Group.

CHERUB: Dark Sun & Other Stories. 2013. (ENG.). 208p. (YA). pap. 11.99 *(978-1-4449-1644-7(0))* Hachette Children's Group GBR. Dist: Hachette Bk. Group.

Child, Lauren. Ruby Redfort Feel the Fear. Child, Lauren, illus. (Ruby Redfort Ser.: 4). (ENG., Illus.). 528p. (J). (gr. 5-9). 2018. pap. 7.99 *(978-0-7636-9452-4(5))* 2016. 16.99 *(978-0-7636-5470-2(1))* Candlewick Pr.

Clements, Andrew. The Whites of Their Eyes. Stower, Adam, illus. 2013. (Benjamin Pratt & the Keepers of the School Ser.: 3). (ENG.). 240p. (J). (gr. 2-5). pap. 7.99 *(978-1-4169-3909-2(1),* Atheneum Bks. for Young Readers) Simon & Schuster Children's Publishing.

Cook, Lyn. Flight from the Fortress. 1 vol. 2006. (ENG.). 156p. (J). (gr. 5-8). per. 7.95 *(978-1-55041-792-0(4),* 92ef756c-8e41-4829-b659-cf8fe5b05d66) Trifolium Bks., Inc. CAN. Dist: Firefly Bks., Ltd.

Cope, Andrew. Captured! 2nd ed. 2006. (Spy Dog Ser.: 2). (Illus.). 176p. (J). (gr. 2-7). pap. 10.99 *(978-0-14-131885-1(6))* Penguin Bks., Ltd. GBR. Dist: Independent Pubs. Group.

—Spy Cat: Safari. 3rd ed. 2016. (Illus.). 160p. (J). (gr. 2-7). pap. 10.99 *(978-0-14-135718-8(5))* Penguin Bks., Ltd. GBR. Dist: Independent Pubs. Group.

—Spy Dog. Wallace, Tig, ed. 2005. (Spy Dog Ser.: 1). (Illus.). 176p. (J). (gr. 2-7). pap. 10.99 *(978-0-14-131884-4(8))* Penguin Bks., Ltd. GBR. Dist: Independent Pubs. Group.

—Spy Dog. 7th ed. 2011. (Spy Dog Ser.: 6). (Illus.). 160p. (J). (gr. 2-7). pap. 10.99 *(978-0-14-133620-6(X))* Penguin Bks., Ltd. GBR. Dist: Independent Pubs. Group.

—Spy Dog: Roller Coaster. 7th ed. 2015. (Spy Dog Ser.). (Illus.). 160p. (J). (gr. 2-7). pap. 10.99 *(978-0-14-133882-8(2))* Penguin Bks., Ltd. GBR. Dist: Independent Pubs. Group.

—Spy Dog 12. 2017. (Spy Dog Ser.: 12). (Illus.). 176p. (J). (gr. 2-7). pap. 10.99 *(978-0-14-136999-0(X))* Penguin Bks., Ltd. GBR. Dist: Independent Pubs. Group.

—Spy Dog Storm Chaser. 10th ed. 2015. (Spy Dog Ser.: 11). (Illus.). 160p. (J). (gr. 2-7). pap. 10.99 *(978-0-14-135715-7(0))* Penguin Bks., Ltd. GBR. Dist: Independent Pubs. Group.

—Spy Dog Unleashed. 3rd ed. 2007. (Spy Dog Ser.: 3). (Illus.). 160p. (J). (gr. 2-7). pap. 10.99 *(978-0-14-132123-3(7))* Penguin Bks., Ltd. GBR. Dist: Independent Pubs. Group.

—Spy Pups: Survival Camp. 5th ed. 2015. (Spy Pups Ser.: 5). (Illus.). 160p. (J). (gr. 2-7). pap. 10.99 *(978-0-14-133880-4(6))* Penguin Bks., Ltd. GBR. Dist: Independent Pubs. Group.

—Superbrain. 4th ed. 2008. (Spy Dog Ser.: 4). (Illus.). 160p. (J). (gr. 2-7). pap. 10.99 *(978-0-14-132244-5(6))* Penguin Bks., Ltd. GBR. Dist: Independent Pubs. Group.

—Training School. 6th ed. 2015. (Spy Pups Ser.: 6). (Illus.). 144p. (J). (gr. 2-7). pap. 10.99 *(978-0-14-133881-1(4))* Penguin Bks., Ltd. GBR. Dist: Independent Pubs. Group.

Coven, Wanda. Heidi Heckelbeck & the Snoopy Spy. Burris, Priscilla, illus. 2018. (Heidi Heckelbeck Ser.: 23). (ENG.). 128p. (J). (gr. k-4). 17.99 *(978-1-5344-1111-1(9));* pap. 6.99 *(978-1-5344-1110-4(0))* Little Simon. (Little Simon).

Crane, Laura Dent. The Automobile Girls at Washington. rev. ed. 2006. (ENG.). 196p. 26.95 *(978-1-4218-2096-5(X),* 1st World Library - Literary Society) 1st World Publishing, Inc.

Cross, Julie. Tempest: A Novel. 2012. (Tempest Trilogy Ser.: 1). (ENG.). 368p. (YA). (gr. 9-12). pap. 14.99 *(978-1-250-01120-6(5),* 900084879, St. Martin's Griffin) St. Martin's Pr.

—Vortex: A Tempest Novel. 2013. (Tempest Trilogy Ser.: 2). (ENG.). 384p. (YA). (gr. 9-12). pap. 14.99 *(978-1-250-04478-5(2),* 900127471, St. Martin's Griffin) St. Martin's Pr.

Daneshvari, Gitty. The League of Unexceptional Children. (League of Unexceptional Children Ser.: 1). (ENG., Illus.). (J). (gr. 3-7). 2016. 256p. pap. 7.99 *(978-0-316-40568-3(X))* 2015. 240p. 17.00 *(978-0-316-40570-6(1))* Little, Brown Bks. for Young Readers.

—The League of Unexceptional Children: the Kids Who Knew Too Little. 2017. (League of Unexceptional Children Ser.: 3). (ENG., Illus.). 208p. (J). (gr. 3-7). 16.99 *(978-0-316-40576-8(0))* Little, Brown Bks. for Young Readers.

Davis, Tim, illus. The Case of the Purple Diamonds. 2011. 88p. pap. 9.95 *(978-1-934606-07-0(3))* TAG Publishing, LLC.

Del Toro, Gladys. The Mutation of Black Cat, 1 vol. 2009. 76p. pap. 16.95 *(978-1-61546-487-6(5))* PublishAmerica, Inc.

Dietrich, Cale. The Love Interest. 2018. (ENG.). 384p. (YA). pap. 11.99 *(978-1-250-15864-2(8),* 900164748) Square Fish.

Diver, Lucienne. Fangtabulous. 2017. (Vamped Ser.: Vol. 4). (ENG., Illus.). (YA). pap. 14.95 *(978-1-62268-121-1(5))* Bella Rosa Bks.

—Fangtastic. 2017. (Vamped Ser.: Vol. 3). (ENG., Illus.). (YA). pap. 14.95 *(978-1-62268-119-8(3))* Bella Rosa Bks.

Divine Madness. (Cherub Ser.: 5). (ENG.). (YA). (gr. 7). 2013. 400p. pap. 12.99 *(978-1-4424-1364-1(6))* 2012. 384p. 19.99 *(978-1-4169-9944-7(2))* Simon Pulse. (Simon Pulse).

Dixon, Franklin W. The Secret of the Caves #7, Bk. 7. 2017. (Hardy Boys Ser.: 7). 192p. (J). (gr. 3-7). 8.99 *(978-0-515-15909-7(3),* Grosset & Dunlap) Penguin Young Readers Group.

Duble, Kathleen Benner. Quest. 2008. (ENG.). 256p. (J). (gr. 5-9). 19.99 *(978-1-4169-3386-1(7),* McElderry, Margaret K. Bks.) McElderry, Margaret K. Bks.

Duggan, Olive. Spy Kitties Create a Better World. 2013. 158p. pap. 7.95 *(978-1-62137-257-8(X))* Virtualbookworm.com Publishing, Inc.

Durham, Victor G. Submarine Boys & the Spies. 2006. 27.95 *(978-1-4218-3008-7(6));* pap. 12.95 *(978-1-4218-3108-4(2))* 1st World Publishing, Inc.

Edmondson, Nathan. Where Is Jake Ellis? 2016. (ENG., Illus.). 124p. (YA). pap. 14.99 *(978-1-60706-744-3(7),* a55fdff3-d47e-43f1-99a8-79a9defb1d4f) Image Comics.

—Who Is Jake Ellis?, Vol. 1. 2011. (ENG., Illus.). 136p. (YA). pap. 16.99 *(978-1-60706-459-6(6),* 1d740148-ea58-4001-bd58-b97d0d3749d0) Image Comics.

Eisenstein, Ann. Fallen Prey, a Sean Gray Junior Special Agent Mystery. Waugh, Leslie, ed. 2013. 190p. pap. 9.99 *(978-1-935711-31-5(8))* Peak City Publishing, LLC.

Enna, Bruno. Double Duck. Soffritti, Donald, illus. 2010. (ENG.). 112p. (J). pap. 9.99 *(978-1-60886-545-1(2))* BOOM! Studios.

Ericson, Helen. Harriet Spies Again. 2004. 240p. (J). (gr. 3-7). pap. 36.00 incl. audio *(978-0-8072-2091-7(4),* Listening Library) Random Hse. Audio Publishing Group.

The Fall. 2014. (Cherub Ser.: 7). (ENG., Illus.). 368p. (YA). (gr. 7). pap. 12.99 *(978-1-4424-9947-8(8),* Simon Pulse) Simon Pulse.

Farrant, Natasha. What We Did for Love: Resistance, Heartbreak, Betrayal, 1 vol. 2014. (Scarlet Voyage Ser.). (ENG.). 208p. (gr. 6-7). 39.93 *(978-1-62324-028-8(X),* d31625c5-9ff5-4d47-8330-f4de9d508ec8) Enslow Publishing, LLC.

Fisher, Cyrus. The Avion My Uncle Flew. Floethe, Richard, illus. 2018. xi, 262p. (J). pap. *(978-1-948959-00-1(3))* Purple Hse. Pr.

Fisher, Linda C. A Will of Her Own. 2006. (YA). pap. *(978-0-88092-641-6(4));* lib. bdg. *(978-0-88092-640-9(6))* Royal Fireworks Publishing Co.

Fitzhugh, Louise. Harriet l'Espionne. (FRE.). pap. 19.95 *(978-2-07-058141-2(1))* Gallimard, Editions FRA. Dist: Distribooks, Inc.

—Harriet the Spy. 298p. (J). (gr. 3-5). pap. 5.95 *(978-0-8072-1535-7(X),* Listening Library) Random Hse. Audio Publishing Group.

—Harriet the Spy: 50th Anniversary Edition. 50th anniv. ed. 2014. (Harriet the Spy Ser.). (ENG., Illus.). 336p. (J). (gr. 3-7). 18.99 *(978-0-385-37610-5(3),* Delacorte Bks. for Young Readers) Random Hse. Children's Bks.

Fitzhugh, Louise & Ericson, Helen. Harriet Spies Again. 2003. (ENG.). 256p. (J). (gr. 3-7). mass mkt. 7.99 *(978-0-440-41688-3(4),* Yearling) Random Hse. Children's Bks.

Fitzhugh, Louise & Gold, Maya. Harriet the Spy, Double Agent. 2007. (ENG.). 160p. (J). (gr. 3-7). 6.99 *(978-0-440-41691-3(4),* Yearling) Random Hse. Children's Bks.

Francia, Giada, ed. Ballooning over Italy: An Extraordinary Voyage Packed with Games & Fantastic Adventures; Special Agents. Ezrin, Amy, tr. Colombo, Angelo, illus. 2007. (Alex & Penny Ser.). (ENG.). 80p. (J). (gr. 2-5). 14.95 *(978-88-544-0160-0(9),* White Star) Rizzoli International Pubns., Inc.

Frederick, Heather Vogel. The Black Paw, 1. 2013. (Spy Mice Ser.: 1). (ENG., Illus.). 224p. (J). (gr. 3-6). pap. 7.99 *(978-1-4424-6701-9(0))* Simon & Schuster, Inc.

—For Your Paws Only. 2013. (Spy Mice Ser.: 2). (ENG., Illus.). 240p. (J). (gr. 3-6). pap. 6.99 *(978-1-4424-6703-3(7),* Simon & Schuster Bks. For Young Readers) Simon & Schuster Bks. For Young Readers.

—For Your Paws Only. Comport, Sally Wern, illus. 2006. (Spy Mice Ser.: 2). (ENG.). 272p. (J). (gr. 3-6). pap. 5.99 *(978-1-4169-4025-8(1),* Simon & Schuster Bks. For Young Readers) Simon & Schuster Bks. For Young Readers.

Gale, Emily. My Explosive Diary. Dreidemy, Joëlle & Dreidemy, Joëlle, illus. 2014. (Eliza Boom Ser.: 1). (ENG.). 128p. (J). (gr. 1-4). 16.99 *(978-1-4814-0650-5(7),* Simon & Schuster/Paula Wiseman Bks.) Simon & Schuster/Paula Wiseman Bks.

—My Super-Spy Diary. Dreidemy, Joëlle & Dreidemy, Joëlle, illus. 2014. (Eliza Boom Ser.: 2). (ENG.). 128p. (J). (gr. 1-4). pap. 5.99 *(978-1-4814-0652-9(3),* Aladdin) Simon & Schuster Children's Publishing.

Gibbs, Stuart. Charlie Thorne & the Last Equation. (Charlie Thorne Ser.). (ENG., Illus.). (J). (gr. 5). 2020. 416p. pap. 8.99 *(978-1-5344-2477-7(6))* 2019. 400p. 17.99 *(978-1-5344-2476-0(8))* 2019. 400p. E-Book *(978-1-5344-2478-4(4))* Simon & Schuster Bks. For Young Readers. (Simon & Schuster Bks. For Young Readers).

—Charlie Thorne & the Last Equation, 1. 2020. (Charlie Thorne Ser.). (ENG.). 416p. (gr. 5-8). 24.94 *(978-1-5364-6985-1(8))* Simon & Schuster, Inc.

—Charlie Thorne & the Lost City. (Charlie Thorne Ser.). (ENG.). (J). (gr. 5). 2022. 416p. pap. 8.99 *(978-1-5344-4382-2(7))* 2021. (Illus.). 384p. 17.99 *(978-1-5344-4381-5(9))* Simon & Schuster Bks. For Young Readers. (Simon & Schuster Bks. For Young Readers).

—Charlie Thorne & the Lost City, 2. 2022. (Charlie Thorne Ser.). (ENG.). 416p. (gr. 5-8). 24.94 *(978-1-5364-7253-0(0))* Simon & Schuster, Inc.

—Evil Spy School. 2015. (Spy School Ser.). (ENG., Illus.). 336p. (J). (gr. 3-7). 18.99 *(978-1-4424-9489-3(1),* Simon & Schuster Bks. For Young Readers) Simon & Schuster Bks. For Young Readers.

—Spy Camp. (Spy School Ser.). (ENG., Illus.). (J). (gr. 3-7). 2014. 352p. pap. 8.99 *(978-1-4424-5754-6(6))* 2013. 336p. 18.99 *(978-1-4424-5753-9(8))* Simon & Schuster Bks. For Young Readers. (Simon & Schuster Bks. For Young Readers).

—Spy School. (Spy School Ser.). (ENG., (J). (gr. 3-7). 2013. Illus.). 320p. pap. 8.99 *(978-1-4424-2183-7(5))* 2012. 304p. 18.99 *(978-1-4424-2182-0(7))* Simon & Schuster Bks. For Young Readers. (Simon & Schuster Bks. For Young Readers).

—Spy School British Invasion. 2019. (Spy School Ser.). (ENG., Illus.). 320p. (J). (gr. 3-7). 17.99 *(978-1-5344-2470-8(9),* Simon & Schuster Bks. For Young Readers) Simon & Schuster Bks. For Young Readers.

—Spy School Goes South. 2018. (Spy School Ser.). (ENG., Illus.). 352p. (J). (gr. 3-7). 17.99 *(978-1-4814-7785-7(4),* Simon & Schuster Bks. For Young Readers) Simon & Schuster Bks. For Young Readers.

—Spy School Secret Service. (Spy School Ser.). (ENG.). (J). (gr. 3-7). 2018. 368p. pap. 8.99 *(978-1-4814-7783-3(8))* 2017. (Illus.). 352p. 18.99 *(978-1-4814-7782-6(X))* Simon & Schuster Bks. For Young Readers. (Simon & Schuster Bks. For Young Readers).

—Spy Ski School. (Spy School Ser.). (ENG.). (J). (gr. 3-7). 2017. 384p. pap. 8.99 *(978-1-4814-4563-4(4))* 2016. (Illus.). 368p. 18.99 *(978-1-4814-4562-7(6))* Simon & Schuster Bks. For Young Readers. (Simon & Schuster Bks. For Young Readers).

Gifford, Clive. Spies Revealed. 2008. (ENG., Illus.). 32p. (J). (gr. 1-7). 21.99 *(978-1-4169-7113-9(0),* Atheneum Bks. for Young Readers) Simon & Schuster Children's Publishing.

Glass, George. Black-Tie Spy. 2013. 94p. (J). pap. *(978-0-545-47271-5(7))* Scholastic, Inc.

Gonzalez, Christina Diaz. A Thunderous Whisper. 2013. (Illus.). 320p. (J). (gr. 5). pap. 8.99 *(978-0-375-87371-3(6),* Yearling) Random Hse. Children's Bks.

Gratz, Alan. Projekt 1065: a Novel of World War II. 2016. (ENG.). 320p. (J). (gr. 4-7). 17.99 *(978-0-545-88016-9(5),* Scholastic Pr.) Scholastic, Inc.

Greene, Stephanie. Owen Foote, Super Spy. Weston, Martha, illus. 2005. (ENG.). 96p. (J). (gr. 1-4). pap. 8.95 *(978-0-618-55159-0(X),* 100825, Clarion Bks.) HarperCollins Pubs.

Griffis, Molly Levite. The Rachel Resistance. 224p. 8.95 *(978-1-57168-553-7(7))* Eakin Pr.

Griffith, A. J. America's Child. 2008. (J). pap. 9.99 *(978-0-88092-493-1(4))* Royal Fireworks Publishing Co.

Gutman, Dan. My Weird School #7: Mrs. Cooney Is Loony! Paillot, Jim, illus. 2005. (My Weird School Ser.: 7). (ENG.). 112p. (J). (gr. 1-5). pap. 5.99 *(978-0-06-074522-6(3),* HarperCollins) HarperCollins Pubs.

Guzman, Lila & Guzman, Rick. Lorenzo's Revolutionary Quest. 2003. 176p. (J). pap. 9.95 *(978-1-55885-392-8(8),* Piñata Books) Arte Publico Pr.

Halse Anderson, Laurie. Chains. l.t. ed. 2017. (Seeds of America Ser.). (ENG.). 442p. 22.99 *(978-1-4104-9917-2(0))* Cengage Gale.

—Chains. 2014. (Seeds of America Trilogy). (ENG.). 336p. (J). 12.24 *(978-1-63245-094-4(1))* Lectorum Pubns., Inc.

—Chains. 2009. 9.00 *(978-0-7848-3678-1(7),* Everbind) Marco Bk. Co.

—Chains. l.t. ed. 2009. (ENG.). 390p. (YA). 23.95 *(978-1-4104-1425-0(6))* Thorndike Pr.

—Chains. 2010. (Seeds of America Trilogy Ser.: 1). lib. bdg. 19.65 *(978-0-606-14520-6(6))* Turtleback.

Harlow, Joan Hiatt. Midnight Rider. 2006. (ENG.). 384p. (J). (gr. 4-9). pap. 8.99 *(978-0-689-87010-1(8),* McElderry, Margaret K. Bks.) McElderry, Margaret K. Bks.

Hayner, Linda K. Ellanor's Exchange. 2005. 195p. (YA). 8.99 *(978-1-59166-462-8(4))* BJU Pr.

Henderson's Boys: Scorched Earth: Book 7, Bk. 7. 2013. (Henderson's Boys Ser.). (ENG., Illus.). 368p. (YA). (gr. 7-17). pap. 10.99 *(978-1-4449-0233-4(4))* Hachette Children's Group GBR. Dist: Hachette Bk. Group.

Higgins, Jack & Richards, Justin. Death Run. 2009. (ENG.). 288p. (YA). (gr. 7-18). 8.99 *(978-0-14-241475-0(1),* Speak) Penguin Young Readers Group.

—First Strike. 2011. (Chance Twins Ser.: Bk. 4). (ENG.). 240p. (YA). (gr. 7-12). 24.94 *(978-0-399-25240-2(1))* Penguin Young Readers Group.

—Sharp Shot. 2010. (ENG.). 240p. (YA). (gr. 7-18). 8.99 *(978-0-14-241730-0(0),* Speak) Penguin Young Readers Group.

—Sure Fire. 2008. (ENG.). 272p. (YA). (gr. 7-18). 8.99 *(978-0-14-241213-8(9),* Speak) Penguin Young Readers Group.

Higgins, Simon. Moonshadow: Rise of the Ninja. 2011. (Moonshadow Ser.: 1). (ENG.). 352p. (J). (gr. 3-7). pap. 18.99 *(978-0-316-05532-1(8))* Little, Brown Bks. for Young Readers.

Higson, Charlie. Hurricane Gold, 4. 2011. (Young Bond Ser.). (ENG.). 384p. (J). (gr. 6-8). 22.44 *(978-1-4231-1415-4(9))* Hyperion Bks. for Children.

—The Young Bond Series, Book Three: Double or Die, 3. 2011. (Young Bond Ser.: Bk. 3). (ENG.). 400p. (YA). (gr. 6-8). 22.44 *(978-1-4231-1099-6(4))* Hyperion Bks. for Children.

Hildebrand, Jens. Team 002: The Abduction of the Queen. Garcia, Juan F., illus. 2013. 224p. pap. *(978-3-929892-46-8(4))* Hildebrand, Jutta Warped Tomato Publishing.

—Team 002 und das Utopia-Element. Garcia, Juan F., illus. 2013. 270p. pap. *(978-3-929892-39-0(1))* Hildebrand, Jutta Warped Tomato Publishing.

—Team 002 und Die Entführung der Queen. Garcia, Juan F., illus. 2013. 240p. pap. *(978-3-929892-37-6(5))* Hildebrand, Jutta Warped Tomato Publishing.

S

Holm, Jennifer L. & Hamel, Jonathan. The Postman Always Brings Mice. Weinman, Brad, illus. 2005. (Stink Files Ser.: No. 1). 129p. (J). 12.65 *(978-0-7569-6529-7(2))* Perfection Learning Corp.

—To Scratch a Thief. Weinman, Brad, illus. (Stink Files Ser.: No. 2). 144p. 2005. pap. 4.99 *(978-0-06-052984-0(9),* Harper Trophy) 2004. (J). 14.99 *(978-0-06-052982-6(2))* 2004. (J). lib. bdg. 15.89 *(978-0-06-052983-3(0))* HarperCollins Pubs.

Horowitz, Anthony. Alex Rider: Secret Weapon: Seven Untold Adventures from the Life of a Teenaged Spy. 2019. (Alex Rider Ser.: 12). (ENG., Illus.). 336p. (J). (gr. 5). 17.99 *(978-1-5247-3933-1(2),* Philomel Bks.) Penguin Young Readers Group.

—Ark Angel. 2007. (Alex Rider Ser.: 6). (ENG.). 352p. (J). (gr. 5-18). 8.99 *(978-0-14-240738-7(0),* Puffin Books) Penguin Young Readers Group.

—Crocodile Tears. 2010. (Alex Rider Ser.: 8). (ENG.). 416p. (J). (gr. 5-18). 8.99 *(978-0-14-241719-5(X),* Puffin Books) Penguin Young Readers Group.

—Eagle Strike. 2006. (Alex Rider Ser.: 4). (ENG.). 368p. (J). (gr. 5-18). 8.99 *(978-0-14-240613-7(9),* Puffin Books) Penguin Young Readers Group.

—The Falcon's Malteser. 2004. (Diamond Brothers Ser.: No. 1). (ENG.). 208p. (J). (gr. 3-7). 7.99 *(978-0-14-240219-1(2),* Puffin Books) Penguin Young Readers Group.

—Never Say Die. (Alex Rider Ser.: 11). (ENG.). 368p. (J). (gr. 5). 2018. 9.99 *(978-1-5247-3932-4(4),* Puffin Books) 2017. 17.99 *(978-1-5247-3930-0(8),* Philomel Bks.) Penguin Young Readers Group.

—Point Blank. 2006. (Alex Rider Ser.: 2). (ENG.). 320p. (J). (gr. 5-18). 9.99 *(978-0-14-240612-0(0),* Puffin Books) Penguin Young Readers Group.

—Scorpia. 2006. (Alex Rider Ser.: 5). (ENG.). 416p. (J). (gr. 5-18). pap. 8.99 *(978-0-14-240578-9(7),* Puffin Books) Penguin Young Readers Group.

—Scorpia Rising. 2012. (Alex Rider Ser.: 9). (ENG.). 432p. (J). (gr. 5-18). 9.99 *(978-0-14-241985-4(0),* Puffin Books) Penguin Young Readers Group.

—Skeleton Key. 2006. (Alex Rider Ser.: 3). (ENG.). 368p. (J). (gr. 5-18). 8.99 *(978-0-14-240614-4(7),* Puffin Books) Penguin Young Readers Group.

—Skeleton Key: the Graphic Novel. Kanako & Yuzuru, illus. 2009. (Alex Rider Ser.: Bk. 3). (ENG.). 176p. (J). (gr. 5-18). pap. 16.99 *(978-0-399-25418-5(8),* Philomel Bks.) Penguin Young Readers Group.

—Snakehead. 2008. (Alex Rider Ser.: 7). (ENG.). 432p. (J). (gr. 5-18). pap. 8.99 *(978-0-14-241212-1(0),* Puffin Books) Penguin Young Readers Group.

—Stormbreaker. 2006. (Alex Rider Ser.: 1). (ENG.). 304p. (J). (gr. 5-18). 9.99 *(978-0-14-240611-3(2),* Puffin Books) Penguin Young Readers Group.

—Stormbreaker: the Graphic Novel. Kanako & Yuzuru, illus. 2006. (Alex Rider Ser.). (ENG.). 144p. (J). (gr. 5-18). pap. 14.99 *(978-0-399-24633-3(9),* Philomel Bks.) Penguin Young Readers Group.

Horowitz, Anthony & Johnston, Antony. Scorpia: an Alex Rider Graphic Novel. Vieceli, Emma & Brown, Kate, illus. 2017. (Alex Rider Ser.). (ENG.). 176p. (J). (gr. 4-7). pap. 15.99 *(978-0-7636-9257-5(3))* Candlewick Pr.

Howard, Kate, adapted by. Spy vs. Spy. 2015. (Illus.). 32p. (J). *(978-1-4806-9048-6(1))* Scholastic, Inc.

Hulme-Cross, Benjamin. Grayfields. 2018. (Mission Alert Ser.). (ENG., Illus.). 72p. (J). (gr. 5-8). pap. 7.99 *(978-1-5415-2632-7(5),* a52730cf-d72c-4750-9477-584023c33d5b, Darby Creek) Lerner Publishing Group.

—Island X. 2018. (Mission Alert Ser.). (ENG., Illus.). 72p. (J). (gr. 5-8). pap. 7.99 *(978-1-5415-2633-4(3),* ac1afa40-f139-4730-918c-fb6bac75511b, Darby Creek) Lerner Publishing Group.

—Lab 101. 2018. (Mission Alert Ser.). (ENG., Illus.). 72p. (J). (gr. 5-8). pap. 7.99 *(978-1-5415-2634-1(1),* e0aa8cce-4b5c-4c27-ab6d-9182c2e44a05); lib. bdg. 26.65 *(978-1-5415-2581-8(7),* 8b70c8b2-a5c4-4888-8800-441922b9cd6b) Lerner Publishing Group. (Darby Creek).

—Viper Attack. 2018. (Mission Alert Ser.). (ENG., Illus.). 72p. (J). (gr. 5-8). pap. 7.99 *(978-1-5415-2635-8(X),* 37ed1a29-87bb-4c86-8008-c787d7fb4c3f); lib. bdg. 26.65 *(978-1-5415-2582-5(5),* 20dc948f-9702-402f-9a96-e489206343b6) Lerner Publishing Group. (Darby Creek).

Hunsaker, Joan. A Dagger in Time - the Web of Spies. 2010. 200p. 25.99 *(978-1-58930-247-1(8));* pap. 15.99 *(978-1-58930-248-8(6))* Selah Publishing Group, LLC.

Hunt, Elizabeth Singer. The Search for the Sunken Treasure Bk. 2: Australia. 2007. (Illus.). 110p. (J). *(978-1-4242-4190-3(1))* Hachette Bk. Group.

Hunter, John P. Red Thunder: Secrets, Spies, & Scoundrels at Yorktown. 2006. 234p. (J). (gr. 6-8). 7.95 *(978-0-87935-231-8(0))* Colonial Williamsburg Foundation.

I Spy: Individual Title Six-Packs. (Story Steps Ser.). (gr. k-2). 29.00 *(978-0-7635-9571-5(3))* Rigby Education.

Jacobs, Edgar P. The Mystery of the Great Pyramid. (Blake & Mortimer Ser.: 2). (Illus.). Pt. 1. 2007. 72p. pap. 15.95 *(978-1-905460-37-3(6))*Pt. 2. 2008. 56p. pap. 15.95 *(978-1-905460-38-0(4))* CineBook GBR. Dist: National Bk. Network.

—S. O. S. Meteors. 2009. (Blake & Mortimer Ser.: 6). (Illus.). 64p. pap. 15.95 *(978-1-905460-97-7(X))* CineBook GBR. Dist: National Bk. Network.

—The Yellow "M" 2007. (Blake & Mortimer Ser.: 1). (Illus.). 72p. per. 16.95 *(978-1-905460-21-2(X))* CineBook GBR. Dist: National Bk. Network.

James, Brian. Port of Spies #4. Zivoin, Jennifer, illus. 2007. (Pirate School Ser.: 4). 64p. (J). (gr. 1-3). pap. 4.99 *(978-0-448-44646-2(4)*, Grosset & Dunlap) Penguin Young Readers Group.

Johnston, K. E. M. The Witness Tree & the Shadow of the Noose: Mystery, Lies, & Spies in Manassas. 2009. 111p. (J). (gr. 5-7). pap. 8.95 *(978-1-57249-397-1(6)*, White Mane Kids) White Mane Publishing Co., Inc.

Jolley, Dan & Croall, Marie P. Agent Mongoose & the Attack of the Giant Insects. 15th rev. ed. 2010. (Twisted Journeys (r) Ser.: 15). (ENG.). (J). (gr. 4-7). pap. 45.32 *(978-0-7613-6998-1(8))* Lerner Publishing Group.

Jones, Allan. Codename Quicksilver 1: in the Zone. 2012. (Codename Quicksilver Ser.). (ENG.). 128p. (J). (gr. 4-6). pap. 6.99 *(978-1-4440-0545-5(6)*, Orion Children's Bks.) Hachette Children's Group GBR. Dist: Hachette Bk. Group.

Karash, Igor. Sir Drakon. Karash, Igor, illus. collector's ltd. num. ed. 2018. (ENG., Illus.). 72p. (J). pap. 19.95 *(978-1-62804-123-1(4))* Liberty Publishing Hse., Inc.

Kehoe, Tim. Furious Jones & the Assassin's Secret. 2014. (ENG., illus.). 336p. (J). (gr. 3-7). 16.99 *(978-1-4424-7337-9(1)*, Simon & Schuster Bks. For Young Readers) Simon & Schuster Bks. For Young Readers.

Kelly, Katy. Melonhead & the Undercover Operation. Johnson, Gillian, illus. 2012. (Melonhead Ser.: 3). 256p. (J). (gr. 3-7). 7.99 *(978-0-375-84528-4(3)*, Yearling) Random Hse. Children's Bks.

Kidd, Ronald. Undercover Kid: The Comic Book King. Sklar, Andy, illus. 2007. (All Aboard Mystery Reader Ser.). (ENG.). 48p. (J). pap. 3.99 *(978-0-448-44438-3(0)*, Grosset & Dunlap) Penguin Publishing Group.

Kiem, Elizabeth. Dancer, Daughter, Traitor, Spy. 2014. (Bolshoi Saga Ser.: 1). (Illus.). 304p. (YA). (gr. 9). pap. 10.99 *(978-1-61695-422-2(1)*, Soho Teen) Soho Pr., Inc.

Lagonegro, Melissa. Super Agents (Barbie Spy Squad) 2016. (Step into Reading Ser.). (ENG., Illus.). 24p. (J). (gr. -1-1). pap. 5.99 *(978-1-101-93140-0(X)*, Random Hse. Bks. for Young Readers) Random Hse. Children's Bks.

Lantigua, Lizette M. Mission Libertad. 2012. (ENG.). 192p. (YA). pap. 9.95 *(978-0-8198-4900-7(6))* Pauline Bks. & Media.

Larry, H. I. Zac Power #1: Poison Island: 24 Hours to Save the World ... & Walk the Dog. Oswald, Ash, illus. 2008. (Zac Power Ser.: 1). (ENG.). 96p. (J). (gr. 3-6). pap. 6.99 *(978-0-312-34659-1(X)*, 900042759) Square Fish.

—Zac Power #2: Deep Waters: 24 Hours to Save the World ... & Finish His Homework, 2. Oswald, Ash, illus. 2008. (Zac Power Ser.: 2). (ENG.). 96p. (J). (gr. 2-4). pap. 6.99 *(978-0-312-34655-3(7)*, 900042756) Square Fish.

—Zac Power #3: Mind Games: 24 Hours to Save the World ... & Put Out the Rubbish, 3. Oswald, Ash, illus. 2008. (Zac Power Ser.: 3). (ENG.). 96p. (J). (gr. 2-4). pap. 6.99 *(978-0-312-34657-7(3)*, 900042758) Square Fish.

—Zac Power #4: Frozen Fear: 24 Hours to Save the World ... & Get Home for Dinner. Oswald, Ash, illus. 2008. (Zac Power Ser.: 4). (ENG.). 96p. (J). (gr. 3-6). pap. 7.99 *(978-0-312-34656-0(5)*, 900042757) Square Fish.

Lee, M. C. Like I Know Jack. 2016. (ENG., Illus.). (YA). 27.99 *(978-1-63533-042-7(4))*; (Center Ser.: 3). 260p. pap. 16.99 *(978-1-63476-807-8(8))* Dreamspinner Pr. (Harmony Ink Pr.).

Leonard, Julia Platt. Cold Case. (ENG.). 288p. (J). (gr. 3-7). 2012. pap. 5.99 *(978-1-4424-2010-6(3))* 2011. (Illus.). 15.99 *(978-1-4424-2009-0(X))* Simon & Schuster/Paula Wiseman Bks. (Simon & Schuster/Paula Wiseman Bks.).

LeSourd, Nancy. Secrets of Civil War Spies, 1 vol. 2008. (Liberty Letters Ser.). (ENG.). 224p. (J). pap. 7.99 *(978-0-310-71390-6(0))* Zonderkidz.

Locke, Katherine. The Spy with the Red Balloon. 2019. (Balloonmakers Ser.: 2). (ENG.). 368p. (YA). (gr. 8-12). pap. 9.99 *(978-0-8075-2938-6(9)*, 807529389) Whitman, Albert & Co.

Long, Angela Pullam. Salvador the Spy in the Case of the Missing Cats. 2008. 32p. pap. 24.95 *(978-1-60672-724-9(9))* America Star Bks.

Long, Loren & Bildner, Phil. Blastin' the Blues. Long, Loren, illus. 2011. (Sluggers Ser.: 5). (ENG., Illus.). 448p. (J). (gr. 3-7). pap. 8.99 *(978-1-4169-1891-2(4)*, Simon & Schuster Bks. For Young Readers) Simon & Schuster Bks. For Young Readers.

Lord, Gabrielle. Black Ops Hunted: Conspiracy 365. 2014. 192p. (J). 10.99 *(978-1-61067-171-2(6))* Kane Miller.

—Black Ops Missing: Conspiracy 365. 2014. 192p. (J). 10.99 *(978-1-61067-168-2(6))* Kane Miller.

Lorimer, Janet. A Deadly Game (Spy), 1 vol. 2017. (Pageturners Ser.). (ENG.). 80p. (YA). (gr. 9-12). 10.75 *(978-1-68021-398-0(9))* Saddleback Educational Publishing, Inc.

—An Eye for an Eye (Spy), 1 vol. 2017. (Pageturners Ser.). (ENG.). 76p. (YA). (gr. 9-12). 10.75 *(978-1-68021-399-7(7))* Saddleback Educational Publishing, Inc.

—Scavenger Hunt (Spy), 1 vol. 2017. (Pageturners Ser.). (ENG.). 80p. (YA). (gr. 9-12). 10.75 *(978-1-68021-401-7(2))* Saddleback Educational Publishing, Inc.

—Tuesday Raven (Spy), 1 vol. 2017. (Pageturners Ser.). (ENG.). 80p. (YA). (gr. 9-12). 10.75 *(978-1-68021-402-4(0))* Saddleback Educational Publishing, Inc.

Lu, Marie. Warcross. l.t. ed. 2017. (ENG.). 514p. 24.95 *(978-1-4328-4371-7(0))* Cengage Gale.

—Warcross. (Warcross Ser.: 1). (ENG.). (YA). (gr. 7). 2019. 400p. 9.99 *(978-1-9848-1576-7(8)*, Penguin Books) 2018. 416p. pap. 11.99 *(978-0-399-54797-3(5)*, Speak) 2017. 368p. 18.99 *(978-0-399-54796-6(7)*, G.P. Putnam's Sons Books for Young Readers) Penguin Young Readers Group.

—Warcross. 2018. (SPA.). 520p. (YA). pap. 19.99 *(978-987-747-342-1(9))* V&R Editoras.

—Wildcard. (Warcross Ser.: 2). (ENG.). (YA). (gr. 7). 2019. 368p. pap. 12.99 *(978-0-399-54800-0(9)*, Penguin Books) 2018. 352p. 18.99 *(978-0-399-54799-7(1)*, G.P. Putnam's Sons Books for Young Readers) Penguin Young Readers Group.

Lubar, David. Enter the Zombie. 2011. (Nathan Abercrombie, Accidental Zombie Ser.: 5). (ENG.). 192p. (J). (gr. 4-8). 18.69 *(978-0-7653-2344-6(3)*, Starscape) Doherty, Tom Assocs., LLC.

Luper, Eric. The Spy's Secret (Key Hunters #2) 2016. (Key Hunters Ser.: 2). (ENG.). 128p. (J). (gr. 2-5). pap. 5.99 *(978-0-545-82206-0(8))* Scholastic, Inc.

Macauley, Jo. Inferno, 1 vol. 2014. (Secrets & Spies Ser.). (ENG.). 224p. (J). (gr. 4-7). 26.65 *(978-1-4342-9595-8(8)*, 126764, Stone Arch Bks.) Capstone.

—New World, 1 vol. 2014. (Secrets & Spies Ser.). (ENG.). 224p. (J). (gr. 4-7). 26.65 *(978-1-4342-9596-5(6)*, 126765, Stone Arch Bks.) Capstone.

—Plague, 1 vol. 2014. (Secrets & Spies Ser.). (ENG.). 224p. (J). (gr. 4-7). pap. 8.95 *(978-1-62370-053-9(1)*, 124410, Capstone Young Readers) Capstone.

—Treason. 2014. (J). pap. *(978-1-4342-7944-6(8)*, Stone Arch Bks.); (ENG.). 224p. (gr. 4-7). 26.65 *(978-1-4342-7946-0(4)*, 124693, Stone Arch Bks.); (ENG., Illus.). 224p. (gr. 4-7). pap. 8.95 *(978-1-62370-052-2(3)*, 124409, Capstone Young Readers) Capstone.

MacLean, Alistair. Circus. (J). 24.95 *(978-0-89190-672-8(X))* Amereon Ltd.

Mad Dogs. 2014. (Cherub Ser.: 8). (ENG., Illus.). 416p. (YA). (gr. 7). pap. 12.99 *(978-1-4424-9954-6(0))*; 17.99 *(978-1-4424-9953-9(2))* Simon Pulse. (Simon Pulse).

Mah, Adeline Yen. Chinese Cinderella & the Secret Dragon Society. 2006. (ENG., Illus.). 256p. (J). (gr. 5-9). pap. 7.99 *(978-0-06-056736-1(8)*, HarperCollins) HarperCollins Pubs.

Mahle, Melissa & Dennis, Kathryn. Camp Secret. Wong, Liz, illus. 2013. (Junior Spies Ser.: 1). (ENG.). 268p. (J). pap. 10.99 *(978-0-9852273-4-0(6))* SpyGirls Pr.

Maid of Deception. 2014. (Maids of Honor Ser.). (ENG., Illus.). 416p. (YA). (gr. 7). 17.99 *(978-1-4424-4141-5(0)*, Simon & Schuster Bks. For Young Readers) Simon & Schuster Bks. For Young Readers.

Man vs. Beast. 2013. (Cherub Ser.: 6). (ENG., (YA). (gr. 7). Illus.). 352p. pap. 13.99 *(978-1-4424-1365-8(4))*; 336p. 16.99 *(978-1-4169-9945-4(0))* Simon Pulse. (Simon Pulse).

Marathon. When You're Having Fun, Vol. 4. 2005. (Totally Spies! Ser.). (Illus.). 96p. pap. 14.99 *(978-1-59532-818-2(1)*, Tokyopop Kids) TOKYOPOP, Inc.

Marsh, Carole. The Counterfeit Constitution Mystery. 2008. (Real Kids, Real Places Ser.). (Illus.). 144p. (J). (gr. 3-5). 14.95 *(978-0-635-06517-9(7))*; per. 5.95 *(978-0-635-06512-4(6))* Gallopade International.

Martinek, Frank V. Don Winslow Breaks the Spy Net. Warren, F., illus. 2011. 226p. 44.95 *(978-1-258-07858-4(9))* Literary Licensing, LLC.

—Don Winslow Saves the Secret Formul. Warren, F., illus. 2011. 226p. 44.95 *(978-1-258-07446-3(X))* Literary Licensing, LLC.

Martinek, Frank Victor. Don Winslow: Face to Face with the Scorpion. Warren, F., illus. 2011. 224p. 44.95 *(978-1-258-07493-7(1))* Literary Licensing, LLC.

Marzollo, Jean. I Spy Lightning in the Sky (Scholastic Reader, Level 1) I Spy Lightning in the Sky. Wick, Walter, illus. 2005. (Scholastic Reader, Level 1 Ser.). (ENG.). 32p. (J). (gr. -1-3). pap. 3.99 *(978-0-439-68052-3(2)*, Cartwheel Bks.) Scholastic, Inc.

Marzollo, Jean & Scholastic / LeapFrog. I Spy Imagine That! Wick, Walter, illus. 2008. (J). 13.99 *(978-1-59319-933-3(3))* LeapFrog Enterprises, Inc.

Mason, Adrienne. Secret Spies. Cupples, Patricia & Cupples, Pat, illus. 2008. (Kids Can Read Ser.). 32p. (J). (gr. 1-2). 14.95 *(978-1-55453-276-6(0))* Kids Can Pr., Ltd. CAN. Dist: Hachette Bk. Group.

Mason, Jane B. & Hines-Stephens, Sarah. Disguised & Dangerous. Phillips, Craig, illus. 2011. 92p. (J). *(978-0-545-37469-9(3))* Scholastic, Inc.

Mason, Jane B. & Stephens, Sarah Hines. A Dog & His Girl Mysteries #2: Dead Man's Best Friend, 2. 2013. (Dog & His Girl Mysteries Ser.). (ENG.). 208p. (J). (gr. 4-6). 18.69 *(978-0-545-43625-0(7))* Scholastic, Inc.

Mass, Wendy & Brawer, Michael. Space Taxi: the Galactic B. U. R. P. 2016. (Space Taxi Ser.: 4). (ENG., Illus.). 128p. (J). (gr. 1-5). 14.99 *(978-0-316-24331-5(0))*; pap. 9.99 *(978-0-316-24330-8(2))* Little, Brown Bks. for Young Readers.

McCaffrey, Laura Williams. Marked. 2017. (ENG.). 368p. (YA). (gr. 7). pap. 9.99 *(978-0-544-93884-7(4)*, 1658461, Clarion Bks.) HarperCollins Pubs.

McCarthy, Meghan. Steal Back the Mona Lisa! McCarthy, Meghan, illus. 2006. (ENG., Illus.). 40p. (J). (gr. -1-3). 16.00 *(978-0-15-205368-0(9)*, 1196166, Clarion Bks.) HarperCollins Pubs.

McDivitt, Barry. The Youngest Spy. 2007. (ENG.). 176p. (YA). (gr. 3-9). per. 12.95 *(978-1-897235-17-1(8))* Thistledown Pr., Ltd. CAN. Dist: Univ. of Toronto Pr.

McFarlane, Susannah. Jump Start. 2015. 123p. (J). *(978-1-61067-444-7(8))* Kane Miller.

—Jump Start: EJ12 Girl Hero. 2016. 128p. (J). pap. 5.99 *(978-1-61067-382-2(4))* Kane Miller.

McGee, Ron. Ryan Quinn & the Rebel's Escape. 2016. (Ryan Quinn Ser.: 1). (ENG., Illus.). 368p. (J). (gr. 3-7). 16.99 *(978-0-06-242164-7(6)*, HarperCollins) HarperCollins Pubs.

McGowan, Jennifer. Maid of Secrets. (Maids of Honor Ser.). (ENG.). (YA). (gr. 7). 2014. 432p. pap. 9.99 *(978-1-4424-4139-2(9))* 2013. 416p. 17.99 *(978-1-4424-4138-5(0))* Simon & Schuster Bks. For Young Readers. (Simon & Schuster Bks. For Young Readers).

—Maid of Wonder. 2015. (Maids of Honor Ser.). (ENG., Illus.). 336p. (YA). (gr. 7). 17.99 *(978-1-4814-1826-3(2))* Simon & Schuster Children's Publishing.

McLean, Allan Campbell. The Hill of the Red Fox, 20 vols. 3rd rev. ed. 2015. 272p. (J). 9.95 *(978-1-78250-206-7(8)*, Kelpies) Floris Bks. GBR. Dist: Consortium Bk. Sales & Distribution.

McMullen, Beth. Double Cross. 2019. (Mrs. Smith's Spy School for Girls Ser.: 3). (ENG., Illus.). 272p. (J). (gr. 4-8). 18.99 *(978-1-4814-9026-9(5)*, Aladdin) Simon & Schuster Children's Publishing.

—Mrs. Smith's Spy School for Girls. 2017. (Mrs. Smith's Spy School for Girls Ser.: 1). (ENG., Illus.). 304p. (J). (gr. 4-8). 17.99 *(978-1-4814-9020-7(6)*, Aladdin) Simon & Schuster Children's Publishing.

—Mrs. Smith's Spy School for Girls. 2018. (Mrs. Smith's Spy School for Girls Ser.: 1). (ENG., Illus.). 320p. (J). (gr. 4-8). pap. 8.99 *(978-1-4814-9021-4(4)*, Simon & Schuster/Paula Wiseman Bks.) Simon & Schuster/Paula Wiseman Bks.

Menotti, Andrea. Operation Fowl Play. Kennedy, Kelly, illus. 2004. (Spy Five Ser.). 92p. (J). *(978-0-439-70349-9(2))* Scholastic, Inc.

—Operation Master Mole. Kennedy, Kelly, illus. 2004. (Spy Five Ser.). 93p. (J). *(978-0-439-70351-2(4))* Scholastic, Inc.

Meyer, L. A. Rapture of the Deep: Being an Account of the Further Adventures of Jacky Faber, Soldier, Sailor, Mermaid, Spy. 2011. (Bloody Jack Adventures Ser.: 7). (ENG.). 464p. (YA). (gr. 9). pap. 9.99 *(978-0-547-55120-3(7)*, 1450433, Clarion Bks.) HarperCollins Pubs.

Monroe, Ella. Secrets & Lies: A Capital Girls Novel. 2012. (Capital Girls Ser.: 2). (ENG.). 320p. (YA). (gr. 8). pap. 22.99 *(978-0-312-62305-0(4)*, 900076854, St. Martin's Griffin) St. Martin's Pr.

Morley, Elizabeth. Let Sleeping Hedgehogs Spy. 2013. (Illus.). 154p. pap. *(978-1-78299-107-6(7))* FeedARead.com.

Moss, Marissa. Bombs over London. 2014. (Mira's Diary Ser.). (ENG., Illus.). 190p. (J). (gr. 2-8). 12.99 *(978-1-939547-12-5(1)*, 5ad055a5-1363-4f46-accf-d31871e40e1f) Creston Bks.

—Emma's Journal. 2004. (Young American Voice Bks.). (Illus.). (gr. 3-7). 17.00 *(978-0-7569-4110-9(5))* Perfection Learning Corp.

Muchamore, Robert. Brigands M. C. 2016. (Cherub Ser.: 11). (ENG., Illus.). 416p. (YA). (gr. 9). 17.99 *(978-1-4814-5671-5(7)*, Simon Pulse) Simon Pulse.

—CHERUB: Brigands M. C. Book 11. 2010. (ENG.). 448p. (YA). (gr. 7-17). pap. 10.99 *(978-0-340-95646-5(1))* Hodder & Stoughton GBR. Dist: Hachette Bk. Group.

—CHERUB: Class a: the Graphic Novel: Book 2. Combet, David & Payen, Baptiste, illus. 2021. (Cherub Ser.). (ENG.). 128p. (J). (gr. 6-17). pap. 15.99 *(978-1-4449-3978-1(5))* Hachette Children's Group GBR. Dist: Hachette Bk. Group.

—CHERUB: Mad Dogs: Book 8, Bk. 8. 2007. (ENG.). 416p. (J). (gr. 7-17). pap. 10.99 *(978-0-340-91171-6(9))* Hodder & Stoughton GBR. Dist: Hachette Bk. Group.

—CHERUB: New Guard: Book 17, Bk. 17. 2017. (Cherub Ser.). (ENG.). 320p. (J). (gr. 7-17). 11.99 *(978-1-4449-1414-6(6))* Hachette Children's Group GBR. Dist: Hachette Bk. Group.

—CHERUB: Shadow Wave: Book 12, Bk. 12. 2011. (ENG.). 368p. (J). (gr. k-17). 10.99 *(978-0-340-99974-5(8))* Hodder & Stoughton GBR. Dist: Hachette Bk. Group.

—CHERUB: the General: Book 10. 2013. (ENG.). 352p. (J). (gr. 7-17). pap. 10.99 *(978-0-340-93184-4(1))* Hodder & Stoughton GBR. Dist: Hachette Bk. Group.

—CHERUB: the Sleepwalker: Book 9. 2008. (ENG.). 336p. (J). (gr. 7-17). pap. 10.99 *(978-0-340-93183-7(3))* Hodder & Stoughton GBR. Dist: Hachette Bk. Group.

—The Dealer. (Cherub Ser.: 2). (ENG.). (YA). (gr. 7). 2011. 336p. pap. 12.99 *(978-1-4424-1361-0(1))* 2010. 320p. 19.99 *(978-1-4169-9941-6(8))* Simon Pulse. (Simon Pulse).

—Henderson's Boys: Eagle Day: Book 2. 2009. (Henderson's Boys Ser.). (ENG., Illus.). 432p. (J). (gr. 7-17). 11.99 *(978-0-340-95649-6(6))* Hachette Children's Group GBR. Dist: Hachette Bk. Group.

—Henderson's Boys: Secret Army: Book 3. 2010. (Henderson's Boys Ser.). (ENG., Illus.). 384p. (YA). (gr. 7-17). pap. 11.99 *(978-0-340-95650-2(X))* Hachette Children's Group GBR. Dist: Hachette Bk. Group.

—The Killing. 2012. (Cherub Ser.: 4). (ENG.). 336p. (YA). (gr. 7). pap. 13.99 *(978-1-4424-1363-4(8))*; 21.99 *(978-1-4169-9943-0(4))* Simon Pulse. (Simon Pulse).

—Maximum Security. (Cherub Ser.: 3). (ENG.). 320p. (YA). (gr. 7). 2012. pap. 12.99 *(978-1-4424-1362-7(X))* 2011. lib. bdg. 19.99 *(978-1-4169-9942-3(6))* Simon Pulse. (Simon Pulse).

—The Recruit. 2010. (Cherub Ser.: 1). (ENG.). 352p. (YA). (gr. 7). pap. 12.99 *(978-1-4424-1360-3(3))*; 21.99 *(978-1-4169-9940-9(X))* Simon Pulse. (Simon Pulse).

—Shadow Wave. 2017. (Cherub Ser.: 12). (ENG., Illus.). 352p. (YA). (gr. 7). 19.99 *(978-1-4814-5674-6(1)*, Simon Pulse) Simon Pulse.

—The Sleepwalker. 2015. (Cherub Ser.: 9). (ENG., Illus.). 336p. (YA). (gr. 7). 17.99 *(978-1-4814-5663-0(6)*, Simon Pulse) Simon Pulse.

Muchamore, Robert & Edginton, Ian. CHERUB: the Recruit Graphic Novel: Book 1. Aggs, John, illus. 2012. (Cherub Ser.). (ENG.). 176p. (YA). (gr. 7-17). pap. 11.99 *(978-1-4449-0318-8(7))* Hachette Children's Group GBR. Dist: Hachette Bk. Group.

Mykiusch, Matt. Strangers in Atlantis. 2017. (Seaborne Ser.: 2). (ENG.). 280p. (J). (gr. 3-6). 18.99 *(978-1-5124-1375-5(5)*, e05ec5a2-2d78-405a-84fd-82f201d65d74); E-Book 29.32 *(978-1-5124-2691-5(1))* Lerner Publishing Group. (Carolrhoda Bks.).

Nick Barry. Revenge of Poseidon's Trident: An Ethan Sparks Adventure. 2010. 176p. 23.95 *(978-1-4502-1090-4(2))*; pap. 13.95 *(978-1-4502-1088-1(0))* iUniverse, Inc.

Nielsen, Jennifer A. Behind Enemy Lines. 2016. (Infinity Ring Ser.: 6). lib. bdg. 17.20 *(978-0-606-38623-4(8))* Turtleback.

—Behind Enemy Lines (Infinity Ring, Book 6) 6th ed. 2016. (Infinity Ring Ser.: 6). (ENG.). 192p. (J). (gr. 3-7). pap. 6.99 *(978-0-545-90121-5(9)*, Scholastic Pr.) Scholastic, Inc.

Noble, Trinka Hakes. The Scarlet Stockings Spy. Papp, Robert, illus. 2004. (Tales of Young Americans Ser.). (ENG.). 48p. (J). (gr. 1-4). 16.95 *(978-1-58536-230-1(1)*, 202055) Sleeping Bear Pr.

O'Brien, Jack. Silver Chief's Revenge. Wiese, Kurt, illus. 2011. 222p. 44.95 *(978-1-258-09709-7(5))* Literary Licensing, LLC.

O'Hely, Eileen. P. E. P. Squad. 2014. (ENG.). 320p. (J). 16.00 *(978-1-78117-195-0(5))* Mercier Pr., Ltd., The IRL. Dist: Dufour Editions, Inc.

O'Malley, Kevin. Herbert Fieldmouse, Secret Agent. 2003. (Illus.). 32p. (J). pap. *(978-1-59336-043-6(6))*; (gr. 1-6). 15.95 *(978-1-59336-042-9(8))* Mondo Publishing.

Orme, David. Spies. Martin, Jan, illus. 2010. (Fact to Fiction Grafx Ser.). 36p. pap. 7.45 *(978-0-7891-7998-2(9))* Perfection Learning Corp.

Parker, Jake. Rescue on Tankium3. 2011. (Missile Mouse Ser.: 2). (ENG., Illus.). 160p. (J). (gr. 3-7). 21.99 *(978-0-545-11716-6(X)*, Graphix) Scholastic, Inc.

Paulsen, Gary. Woods Runner. 2011. (ENG.). 176p. (YA). (gr. 7). pap. 9.99 *(978-0-375-85908-3(X)*, Lamb, Wendy Bks.) Random Hse. Children's Bks.

Pearce, Jackson. The Doublecross: (And Other Skills I Learned As a Superspy) 2015. (ENG.). 304p. (YA). (gr. 3-6). 16.99 *(978-1-61963-414-5(7)*, 9781619634145, Bloomsbury USA Childrens) Bloomsbury Publishing USA.

—The Doublecross: (and Other Skills I Learned As a Superspy) 2016. (ENG.). 304p. (J). pap. 8.99 *(978-1-61963-939-3(4)*, 900152561, Bloomsbury USA Childrens) Bloomsbury Publishing USA.

—The Doublecross: (And Other Skills I Learned As a Superspy) 2016. (J). lib. bdg. 18.40 *(978-0-606-38555-8(X))* Turtleback.

—The Inside Job: (and Other Skills I Learned As a Superspy) 2016. (ENG.). 272p. (J). 16.99 *(978-1-61963-420-6(1)*, 900135729, Bloomsbury USA Childrens) Bloomsbury Publishing USA.

Percival, Tom. The Secret Mountain. 2018. (Little Legends Ser.: 5). (ENG., Illus.). 192p. (J). (gr. 2-5). pap. 8.99 *(978-1-4926-6570-0(3)*, Sourcebooks Jabberwocky) Sourcebooks, Inc.

Perlman, Rhea. Canyon Catastrophe. Santat, Dan, illus. 2006. (Otto Undercover Ser.). 128p. (J). (gr. 4-7). 14.99 *(978-0-06-075498-3(2))* HarperCollins Pubs.

Peterfreund, Diana. Omega City: Infinity Base. 2018. (Omega City Ser.: 3). (ENG.). 304p. (J). (gr. 3-7). 16.99 *(978-0-06-231091-0(7)*, Balzer & Bray) HarperCollins Pubs.

Pierpoint, Eric. The Secret Mission of William Tuck. 2015. (ENG.). 320p. (J). (gr. 4-7). pap. 11.99 *(978-1-4022-8174-7(9)*, 9781402281747) Sourcebooks, Inc.

Plum-Ucci, Carol. Fire Will Fall. 2011. (ENG.). 492p. (YA). (gr. 9). pap. 25.99 *(978-0-547-55007-7(3)*, 1450217, Clarion Bks.) HarperCollins Pubs.

—Fire Will Fall. 2011. (ENG.). 496p. (YA). (gr. 9-12). 24.94 *(978-0-15-216562-8(2))* Houghton Mifflin Harcourt Publishing Co.

Ponnay, Brenda. Secret Agent Josephine in Paris. Ponnay, Brenda, illus. 2013. (ENG., Illus.). 32p. (J). (gr. -1-2). pap. 19.99 *(978-1-62395-524-3(6))* Xist Publishing.

Ponnay, Brenda & Ponnay, Brenda. Secret Agent Josephine in Paris. 2013. 32p. pap. 9.99 *(978-1-62395-552-6(1))* Xist Publishing.

Ponti, James. City Spies, 1. 2021. (City Spies Ser.). (ENG.). 400p. (gr. 4-7). 26.19 *(978-1-5364-6774-1(X)*, Aladdin) Simon & Schuster Children's Publishing.

—City Spies. (City Spies Ser.: 1). (ENG., Illus.). (J). (gr. 3-7). 2021. 400p. pap. 9.99 *(978-1-5344-1492-1(4))* 2020. 384p. 18.99 *(978-1-5344-1491-4(6))* Simon & Schuster/Paula Wiseman Bks. (Simon & Schuster/Paula Wiseman Bks.).

—Forbidden City. 2022. (City Spies Ser.: 3). (ENG., Illus.). 448p. (J). (gr. 3-7). 17.99 *(978-1-5344-7921-0(X)*, Aladdin) Simon & Schuster Children's Publishing.

—Golden Gate. (City Spies Ser.: 2). (ENG.). 2022. 448p. (J). (gr. 3-7). pap. 8.99 *(978-1-5344-1495-2(9))* 2021. (Illus.). 432p. (J). (gr. 3-7). 18.99 *(978-1-5344-1494-5(0))*2. 2022. 448p. (gr. 4-7). 24.94 *(978-1-5364-7207-3(7))* Simon & Schuster Children's Publishing. (Aladdin).

—Trapped! 2018. (Framed! Ser.: 3). (ENG., Illus.). 384p. (J). (gr. 3-7). 19.99 *(978-1-5344-0891-3(6))*, Aladdin) Simon & Schuster Children's Publishing.

Portes, Andrea. Liberty: The Spy Who (Kind of) Liked Me. 2017. (ENG.). 400p. (J). *(978-0-06-267332-9(7)*, HarperTeen) HarperCollins Pubs.

Preus, Margi. Shadow on the Mountain. 2014. (ENG., Illus.). 320p. (YA). (gr. 3-7). pap. 9.99 *(978-1-4197-1159-6(8)*, 1006603) Abrams, Inc.

Prins, Piet. The Grim Reaper. 2006. (Illus.). 130p. (J). pap. *(978-1-894666-74-9(7))* Inheritance Pubns.

Publications International Ltd. Staff, ed. Mater Saves the Day. 2011. 12p. (J). bds. 10.98 *(978-1-4508-0695-4(3))* Phoenix International Publications, Inc.

Rash, Andy. Agent A to Agent Z. 2004. (Illus.). (J). *(978-0-439-36883-4(9)*, Levine, Arthur A. Bks.) Scholastic, Inc.

Readler, Blaine C. Under the Radar: The Spy Drone Adventure. 2006. (ENG.). 248p. (J). (gr. 7-12). per. *(978-1-933255-18-7(8))* DNA Pr.

Regan, Peter. Riverside: The Spy. 2007. (ENG.). 112p. (J). pap. *(978-1-901737-53-0(5)*, Anvil Bks.) Mercier Pr., Ltd., The.

Reid, Kimberly. Prettyboy Must Die: A Novel. 2019. (ENG.). 288p. (YA). pap. 16.99 *(978-0-7653-9088-2(4)*, 900169701, Tor Teen) Doherty, Tom Assocs., LLC.

Reid, Roger. Space. 2008. (ENG.). 160p. (J). 19.95 *(978-1-58838-230-6(3)*, 9002, NewSouth Bks.) NewSouth, Inc.

Richards, Justin. Licence to Fish, Book 3. 2011. (Agent Alfie Ser.). (ENG., Illus.). 176p. (J). (gr. 2-4). 6.99 *(978-0-00-727359-1(2))* HarperCollins Pubs. Ltd. GBR. Dist: Independent Pubs. Group.

—Thunder Raker (Agent Alfie, Book 1) Book 1. 2008. (Agent Alfie Ser.: 1). (ENG., Illus.). 144p. (J). (gr. 2-4). pap. 6.99 *(978-0-00-727357-7(6)*, HarperCollins Children's Bks.) HarperCollins Pubs. Ltd. GBR. Dist: HarperCollins Pubs.

Richler, Mordecai. Jacob Two-Two's First Spy Case. Eyolfson, Norman, illus. 2003. (Jacob Two-Two Ser.). (ENG.). 144p. (J). (gr. 3-7). pap. 6.95 *(978-0-88776-694-7(3))* Tundra Bks. CAN. Dist: Random Hse., Inc.

—Jacob Two-Two's First Spy Case. Petricic, Dusan, illus. 2009. (Jacob Two-Two Ser.). (ENG.). 176p. (J). (gr. 4-7). 10.95 *(978-0-88776-927-6(6))* Tundra Bks. CAN. Dist: Random Hse., Inc.

Richmond, Caroline Tung. The Darkest Hour. 2016. (ENG.). 320p. (YA). (gr. 7). 17.99 *(978-0-545-80127-0(3)*, Scholastic Pr.) Scholastic, Inc.

Rinaldi, Ann. Finishing Becca: A Story about Peggy Shippen & Benedict Arnold. 2004. (Great Episodes Ser.). (ENG.). 384p. (YA). (gr. 7-8). pap. 17.95 *(978-0-15-205079-5(5)*, 1195340, Clarion Bks.) HarperCollins Pubs.

—The Secret of Sarah Revere. 2003. (Great Episodes Ser.). (ENG.). 336p. (J). (gr. 5-7). pap. 9.99 *(978-0-15-204684-2(4)*, 1194115, Clarion Bks.) HarperCollins Pubs.

Roberts, Daniel. Douglas Diggly Super Spy. 2011. (ENG.). 179p. pap. 12.50 *(978-1-105-49212-9(5))* Lulu Pr., Inc.

Roop, Connie & Roop, Peter. The Top-Secret Adventure of John Darragh, Revolutionary War Spy. Trover, Zachary, illus. 2010. (History's Kid Heroes Ser.). (ENG.). 32p. (J). (gr. 3-5). pap. 8.99 *(978-0-7613-6193-0(6)*, 7fa9c0ff-4a83-43e8-9a63-91b40b6156a7, Graphic Universe™) Lerner Publishing Group.

Roop, Peter & Roop, Connie. The Top-Secret Adventure of John Darragh, Revolutionary War Spy. Trover, Zachary, illus. 2010. pap. 51.02 *(978-0-7613-6923-3(6))* Lerner Publishing Group.

—The Top-Secret Adventure of John Darragh, Revolutionary War Spy. Trover, Zachary, illus. 2010. (History's Kid Heroes Ser.). (ENG.). 32p. (gr. 3-5). lib. bdg. 26.60 *(978-0-7613-6174-9(X))* Lerner Publishing Group.

Roy, Ron. Capital Mysteries #4: a Spy in the White House. Bush, Timothy, illus. 2004. (Capital Mysteries Ser.: 4). 96p. (J). (gr. 1-4). 6.99 *(978-0-375-82557-6(6)*, Random Hse. Bks. for Young Readers) Random Hse. Children's Bks.

—A Spy in the White House, 4. Bush, Timothy, tr. Bush, Timothy, illus. 2004. (Capital Mysteries Ser.: No. 4). (ENG.). 86p. (J). (gr. 2-4). lib. bdg. 17.44 *(978-0-375-92557-3(0))* Random House Publishing Group.

Rylander, Chris. Codename Zero. 2014. (Codename Conspiracy Ser.: 1). (ENG.). 368p. (J). (gr. 3-7). 16.99 *(978-0-06-212008-3(5)*, Waldon Pond Pr.) HarperCollins Pubs.

—Countdown Zero. 2015. (Codename Conspiracy Ser.: 2). (ENG.). 368p. (J). (gr. 3-7). 16.99 *(978-0-06-212011-3(5)*, Waldon Pond Pr.) HarperCollins Pubs.

Sadler, Heather. An Apatosaurus Would NOT Make a Good Spy. Calvert, Steph, illus. 2018. (Dinosaur Daydreams Ser.). (ENG.). 24p. (J). (gr. -1-2). lib. bdg. 27.99 *(978-1-5158-2128-1(5)*, 136732, Picture Window Bks.) Capstone.

Sager Weinstein, Jacob. Lyric Mckerrigan, Secret Librarian. Brosgol, Vera, illus. 2018. (ENG.). 48p. (J). (gr. -1-3). 17.99 *(978-0-544-80122-6(9)*, 1640248, Clarion Bks.) HarperCollins Pubs.

Sala, George Augustus. Captain Dangerous. 2011. 130p. 24.95 *(978-1-4638-9899-1(1))*; 124p. pap. 10.95 *(978-1-4638-0142-7(4))*; 126p. pap. 10.95 *(978-1-4638-0141-0(6))*; 130p. pap. 10.95 *(978-1-4638-0140-3(8))* Rodgers, Alan Bks.

Scieszka, Jon. The All-Purpose SPHDZ Boxed Set: SPHDZ Book #1!; SPHDZ Book #2!; SPHDZ Book #3!; SPHDZ 4 Life!, Set. Prigmore, Shane, illus. 2013. (Spaceheadz Ser.). (ENG.). 864p. (J). (gr. 2-5). pap. 23.99 *(978-1-4424-9858-7(7)*, Simon & Schuster Bks. For Young Readers) Simon & Schuster Bks. For Young Readers.

—SPHDZ 4 Life! Prigmore, Shane, illus. 2013. (Spaceheadz Ser.: 4). (ENG.). 192p. (J). (gr. 2-5). pap. 5.99 *(978-1-4169-7958-6(1))*;Bk. 4. 16.99 *(978-1-4169-7957-9(3))* Simon & Schuster Bks. For Young Readers. (Simon & Schuster Bks. For Young Readers).

—SPHDZ Book #1! Prigmore, Shane, illus. 2010. (Spaceheadz Ser.: 1). (ENG.). 176p. (J). (gr. 2-5). 14.99 *(978-1-4169-7951-7(4)*, Simon & Schuster Bks. For Young Readers) Simon & Schuster Bks. For Young Readers.

—SPHDZ Book #2! Prigmore, Shane, illus. 2011. (Spaceheadz Ser.: 2). (ENG.). 256p. (J). (gr. 2-5). pap. 7.99 *(978-1-4169-7954-8(9)*, Simon & Schuster Bks. For Young Readers) Simon & Schuster Bks. For Young Readers.

—SPHDZ Book #3! Prigmore, Shane, illus. (Spaceheadz Ser.: 3). (ENG.). 224p. (J). (gr. 2-5). 2012. pap. 8.99 *(978-1-4169-7956-2(5))* 2011. 15.99 *(978-1-4169-7955-5(7))* Simon & Schuster Bks. For Young Readers. (Simon & Schuster Bks. For Young Readers).

Scott, Kate. Spies in Disguise: Boy in Tights. 2016. (ENG., Illus.). 192p. (J). (gr. 1-5). pap. 7.99 *(978-1-63450-689-2(8)*, Sky Pony Pr.) Skyhorse Publishing Co., Inc.

Sealed with a Lie. 2014. (ENG., Illus.). 256p. (YA). (gr. 9). 17.99 *(978-1-4814-0052-7(5)*, Simon & Schuster Bks. For Young Readers) Simon & Schuster Bks. For Young Readers.

Sharmat, Marjorie Weinman & Sharmat, Mitchell. The Sly Spy. Brunkus, Denise, illus. 2005. (Olivia Sharp: Agent for Secrets Ser.). 80p. (J). (gr. 3-7). per. 6.99 *(978-0-440-42062-0(8)*, Yearling) Random Hse. Children's Bks.

Sharpe, Luke. Billy Sure, Kid Entrepreneur Is a Spy! Ross, Graham, illus. 2016. 141p. (J). *(978-1-4242-6367-7(0)*, Simon Spotlight) Simon Spotlight.

Singleton, Linda Joy. Kelsey the Spy. 2016. (Curious Cat Spy Club Ser.: 3). (ENG.). (J). (gr. 3-7). 304p. pap. 9.99 *(978-0-8075-1384-2(9)*, 807513849); 288p. 14.99 *(978-0-8075-1380-4(6)*, 807513806) Whitman, Albert & Co.

Skead, Robert A. Patriots Redcoats & Spies, 1 vol. 2015. (American Revolutionary War Adventures Ser.). (ENG.). 192p. (J). 14.99 *(978-0-310-74841-0(0))* Zonderkidz.

Skillchecks for Spy. 2005. (Double Fastback Ser.). (J). (gr. 6-12). 64p. pap. 5.95 *(978-0-13-024475-8(9))*; 32p. pap. 5.95 *(978-0-13-024458-1(9))* Globe Fearon Educational Publishing.

Slade, Arthur G. The Hunchback Assignments, 1. 2010. (Hunchback Assignments Ser.). (ENG.). 288p. (YA). (gr. 7-12). lib. bdg. 24.94 *(978-0-385-90694-4(3))* Random House Publishing Group.

Smith, Annie Laura. The Legacy of Bletchley Park. 2004. (YA). mass mkt. 6.99 *(978-0-9753367-1-7(1))* Onstage Publishing, LLC.

Smith, Icy. Three Years & Eight Months. Kindert, Jennifer C., illus. 2013. (J). *(978-0-9856237-8-4(0))* East West Discovery Pr.

Smith, Lindsay. Skandal. 2016. (Sekret Ser.: 2). (ENG.). 352p. (YA). pap. 20.99 *(978-1-250-07369-3(3)*, 900150800) Square Fish.

Smith, Nikki Shannon. Charlotte Spies for Justice: A Civil War Survival Story. Trunfio, Alessia, illus. 2019. (Girls Survive Ser.). (ENG.). 112p. (J). (gr. 3-7). pap. 7.95 *(978-1-4965-8446-5(5)*, 140971); E-Book 4.95 *(978-1-4965-8389-5(2)*, 186555) Capstone. (Stone Arch Bks.).

Smith, Roland. Independence Hall. (I, Q Ser.: Bk. 1). (ENG.). 312p. (YA). (gr. 6-8). 2009. Illus.). 15.95 *(978-1-58536-468-8(1)*, 202188) 2008. pap. 12.99 *(978-1-58536-325-4(1)*, 202289) Sleeping Bear Pr.

—The White House. 2010. (I, Q Ser.: Bk. 2). (ENG.). 256p. (YA). (gr. 6-8). pap. 9.99 *(978-1-58536-456-5(8)*, 202378);Bk. 2. 16.99 *(978-1-58536-478-7(9)*, 202191) Sleeping Bear Pr.

Smith, Roland & Spradlin, Michael P. The Alamo. 2013. (I, Q Ser.). (ENG.). 288p. (YA). (gr. 5-8). 16.99 *(978-1-58536-822-8(9)*, 202356); pap. 9.99 *(978-1-58536-821-1(0)*, 202369) Sleeping Bear Pr.

—Alcatraz. 2014. (I, Q Ser.). (ENG.). 272p. (J). (gr. 5-7). 16.99 *(978-1-58536-826-6(1)*, 203667);Bk. 6. pap. 9.99 *(978-1-58536-825-9(3)*, 203727) Sleeping Bear Pr.

—I, Q the Windy City, Bk.5. 2014. (I, Q Ser.). (ENG.). 240p. (YA). (gr. 5-7). 9.99 *(978-1-58536-823-5(7)*, 202902) Sleeping Bear Pr.

Sobol, Donald J. Secret Agents Four. Shortall, Leonard W., illus. 2003. (Adventure Library). (ENG.). 140p. (J). (gr. 4-6). pap. 10.95 *(978-1-883937-65-2(5))* Ignatius Pr.

Soup, Cuthbert. A Whole Nother Story. Timmins, Jeffrey Stewart, illus. 2010. (Whole Nother Story Ser.). (ENG.). 288p. (YA). (gr. 3-6). pap. 8.99 *(978-1-59990-518-1(3)*, 900068450, Bloomsbury USA Childrens) Bloomsbury Publishing USA.

Sparkes, Ali. Frozen in Time. 2011. (ENG.). 320p. (J). (gr. 4-6). 22.44 *(978-1-60684-077-1(0))* Farshore GBR. Dist: Children's Plus, Inc.

Speer, Cindy Lynn. Unbalanced. 2010. 241p. pap. *(978-1-934841-90-7(0))* Zumaya Pubns. LLC.

Spradlin, Michael P. Live & Let Shop. 2005. (Spy Goddess Ser.: Bk. 1). (ENG., Illus.). 224p. (gr. 7-18). 15.99 *(978-0-06-059407-7(1))* HarperCollins Pubs.

Spy, 10 vols. 2005. (Double Fastback Ser.). (J). (gr. 6-12). 64p. pap. 54.95 *(978-0-13-024468-0(6))*; 32p. pap. 44.95 *(978-0-13-024440-6(6))* Globe Fearon Educational Publishing.

The Spy down the Street, 6 vols., Vol. 2. (Woodland Mysteriestm Ser.). 133p. (gr. 3-7). 42.50 *(978-0-7802-7938-4(7))* Wright Group/McGraw-Hill.

Stead, Rebecca. Liar & Spy. 2013. (ENG.). 208p. (J). (gr. 3-7). 8.99 *(978-0-375-85087-5(2)*, Yearling) Random Hse. Children's Bks.

Stone, Sonja. Dark Divide: A Desert Dark Novel. 2018. (Desert Dark Novel Ser.: 2). (ENG.). 384p. (YA). (gr. 7). 18.99 *(978-0-8234-3836-5(8))* Holiday Hse., Inc.

—Desert Dark: A Desert Dark Novel. (Desert Dark Novel Ser.: 1). (ENG.). (YA). (gr. 7). 2017. 344p. pap. 7.99 *(978-0-8234-3766-5(3))* 2016. 336p. 17.95 *(978-0-8234-3562-3(8))* Holiday Hse., Inc.

Strange, Spencer. Operation Billion Gazillion. 2005. (Spy Five Ser.). 93p. *(978-0-439-70352-9(2))* Scholastic, Inc.

Taylor, Mary Ann. Spies: A Gander's Cove Mystery. Casteel, Kay, illus. 2006. (J). mass mkt. 5.99 *(978-0-9753367-7-9(0))* Onstage Publishing, LLC.

—Traitors: A Gander's Cove Mystery. Casteel, Kay, illus. 2006. (J). mass mkt. 5.99 *(978-0-9753367-9-3(7))* Onstage Publishing, LLC.

Thaler, Mike. Hubie Cool: Super Spy. Lee, Jared D., illus. 2016. 64p. (J). *(978-0-545-85076-6(2))* Scholastic, Inc.

Thomas, Jane Resh. The Counterfeit Princess. 2005. (J). (ENG.). 208p. (gr. 5-7). 15.00 *(978-0-395-93870-6(8)*, 112679); 197p. *(978-0-618-93780-6(3))* HarperCollins Pubs. (Clarion Bks.).

Thompson, Paul B. Liberty's Son: A Spy Story of the American Revolution, 1 vol. 2010. (Historical Fiction Adventures Ser.). (ENG.). 160p. (J). (gr. 3-5). pap. 13.88 *(978-0-7660-3654-3(5)*, e375b881-5db5-4312-8893-78b569ea53a8); (Illus.). lib. bdg. 31.93 *(978-0-7660-3309-2(0)*, d55f9c9c-b247-45b8-ab6e-3092d697d744) Enslow Publishing, LLC.

Toffler-Corrie, Laura. Noah Green Saves the World. Pamintuan, Macky, illus. 2020. (ENG.). 280p. (J). (gr. 4-7). 17.99 *(978-1-5415-6036-9(1)*, 4e539792-d4b9-48b5-a143-9e038eaf9c09, Kar-Ben Publishing) Lerner Publishing Group.

Tra, Frank. Spy School. O'Reilly, Sean Patrick, ed. 2011. (Illus.). 76p. (YA). pap. 14.95 *(978-1-926914-27-5(9))* Arcana Studio, Inc.

Two Lies & a Spy. 2014. (ENG., Illus.). 272p. (YA). (gr. 9). pap. 12.99 *(978-1-4424-8173-2(0)*, Simon & Schuster Bks. For Young Readers) Simon & Schuster Bks. For Young Readers.

Van Draanen, Wendelin. Shredderman: Enemy Spy. 2006. (Shredderman Ser.: 4). (ENG., Illus.). 192p. (J). (gr. 1-4). 7.99 *(978-0-440-41915-0(8)*, Yearling) Random Hse. Children's Bks.

Van Hamme, Jean. The Strange Encounter, Vol. 5. 2009. (Blake & Mortimer Ser.: 5). (Illus.). 66p. pap. 15.95 *(978-1-905460-75-5(9))* CineBook GBR. Dist: National Bk. Network.

Vaughan, M. M. Mindscape. Bruno, Iacopo, illus. 2015. (Ability Ser.). (ENG.). 336p. (YA). (gr. 3-7). pap. 7.99 *(978-1-4424-5205-3(6)*, McElderry, Margaret K. Bks.) McElderry, Margaret K. Bks.

Viorst, Judith. Lulu's Mysterious Mission. 2015. (Lulu Ser.). (ENG., Illus.). 192p. (J). (gr. 1-5). pap. 8.99 *(978-1-4424-9747-4(5))* Simon & Schuster Children's Publishing.

Walden, Mark. Rogue. (H. I. V. E. Ser.: 5). (ENG.). (J). (gr. 3-7). 2012. 320p. pap. 8.99 *(978-1-4424-1369-6(7))* 2011. 304p. 18.99 *(978-1-4424-2187-5(8))* Simon & Schuster Bks. For Young Readers. (Simon & Schuster Bks. For Young Readers).

Walters, Eric. Sleeper, 1 vol. 2014. (Seven Sequels Ser.: 1). (ENG., Illus.). 240p. (J). (gr. 4-7). pap. 10.95 *(978-1-4598-0543-9(7))* Orca Bk. Pubs. USA.

Warner, Penny. The Hunt for the Missing Spy. 2016. (Code Busters Club Ser.: 5). (ENG.). 168p. (J). (gr. 3-6). E-Book 26.65 *(978-1-5124-0305-3(9)*, Darby Creek) Lerner Publishing Group.

Watson, Mary. The Wren Hunt. 2018. (ENG.). 416p. (YA). 17.99 *(978-1-68119-859-0(2)*, 900189933, Bloomsbury Young Adult) Bloomsbury Publishing USA.

Webb, Robert N. We Were There at the Boston Tea Party. Ward, E. F., illus. 2013. (ENG.). 192p. (J). (gr. 3-8). pap. 9.99 *(978-0-486-49260-5(5)*, 492605) Dover Pubns., Inc.

Wein, Elizabeth. Code Name Verity. l.t. ed. 2018. (ENG.). (J). pap. 12.99 *(978-1-4328-5038-8(5))* Cengage Gale.

—Code Name Verity. 2012. (ENG.). 352p. (YA). (gr. 9-12). 16.99 *(978-1-4231-5219-4(0))* Little, Brown Bks. for Young Readers.

—Code Name Verity. 2013. (YA). lib. bdg. 20.85 *(978-0-606-31760-3(0))* Turtleback.

Westerfeld, Scott, et al. Nexus. 2018. (Zeroes Ser.: 3). (ENG.). 496p. (YA). (gr. 9). 19.99 *(978-1-4814-4342-5(9)*, Simon Pulse) Simon Pulse.

Whelan, Gloria. Parade of Shadows. 2007. 304p. (J). (gr. 5-18). lib. bdg. 16.89 *(978-0-06-089029-2(0))* HarperCollins Pubs.

Wickstrom, Lois June & Darling, Lucrecia. The Orange Forest Rabbit Mysteries: Book One. 2003. (J). per. 13.95 *(978-0-916176-23-5(1))* Gripper Products.

Wild, Ailsa. Squishy Taylor, 6 vols. Wood, Ben, illus. 2018. (Squishy Taylor Ser.). (ENG.). 128p. (J). (gr. 2-4). pap., pap., pap. 41.70 *(978-1-5158-1996-7(5)*, 27348, Picture Window Bks.) Capstone.

Winston, Sherri. Jada Sly, Artist & Spy. 2019. (ENG., Illus.). 272p. (J). (gr. 3-7). 32.99 *(978-0-316-50536-9(6))* Little, Brown Bks. for Young Readers.

Wolfe, Jack & Wolfe, Jennifer. The Tales of Spy Dogs Archie & Hazel. 2011. 44p. pap. 16.59 *(978-1-4567-6244-5(3))* AuthorHouse.

Woodruff, Elvira. George Washington's Spy. 2012. (ENG.). 240p. (J). (gr. 4-7). pap. 7.99 *(978-0-545-10488-3(2)*, Scholastic Paperbacks) Scholastic, Inc.

—George Washington's Spy. 2012. lib. bdg. 17.20 *(978-0-606-26216-3(4))* Turtleback.

Yelchin, Eugene. Spy Runner. Yelchin, Eugene, illus. 2019. (ENG., Illus.). 352p. (J). 21.99 *(978-1-250-12081-6(0)*, 900173090, Holt, Henry & Co. Bks. For Young Readers) Holt, Henry & Co.

Young, Jessica. Spy Guy: The Not-So-Secret Agent. Santoso, Charles, illus. 2015. (ENG.). 40p. (J). (gr. -1-3). 16.99 *(978-0-544-20859-9(5)*, 1560872, Clarion Bks.) HarperCollins Pubs.

Zindel, Paul. The Gadget. 2003. (ENG., Illus.). 192p. (YA). (gr. 7). mass mkt. 7.99 *(978-0-440-22951-3(0)*, Laurel Leaf) Random Hse. Children's Bks.

SPINAL PARALYSIS, ANTERIOR

see Poliomyelitis

SPIRITS

see also Angels; Apparitions; Ghosts; Witchcraft

Cox, Barbara & Forbes, Scott. Spooky Spirits & Creepy Creatures, 1 vol., Vol. 1. 2014. (Creepy Chronicles Ser.). (ENG., Illus.). 32p. (J). (gr. 5-6). 29.27 *(978-1-4824-0243-8(2)*, 6cc5b9f5-3189-4879-974b-4339c8ee5299) Stevens, Gareth Publishing LLLP.

Howard, Ian T. One Love, Two Worlds. Bishop, Tracey, illus. 2010. 36p. pap. 14.75 *(978-1-60911-771-9(9)*, Eloquent Bks.) Strategic Book Publishing & Rights Agency (SBPRA).

Juettner, Bonnie. Genies, 1 vol. 2010. (Monsters Ser.). (ENG., Illus.). 48p. (gr. 4-8). 36.83 *(978-0-7377-5051-5(0)*, e5f1048d-6625-44b3-a013-b987d13e8f49, KidHaven Publishing) Greenhaven Publishing LLC.

Krensky, Stephen. Zombies. 2007. (Monster Chronicles Ser.). (ENG., Illus.). 48p. (gr. 4-7). lib. bdg. 26.60 *(978-0-8225-6759-2(8)*, Lerner Pubns.) Lerner Publishing Group.

Loh-Hagan, Virginia. Genies. 2017. (Magic, Myth, & Mystery Ser.). (ENG., Illus.). 32p. (J). (gr. 4-8). lib. bdg. 32.07 *(978-1-63472-885-0(8)*, 209966, 45th Parallel Press) Cherry Lake Publishing.

netzley, patricia. Paranormal Activity. 2011. (Mysterious & Unknown Ser.). 96p. (YA). (gr. 7-12). lib. bdg. 43.93 *(978-1-60152-240-5(1))* ReferencePoint Pr., Inc.

SPIRITUAL HEALING

Ferguson, Isabel & Frederick, Heather Vogel. A World More Bright: The Life of Mary Baker Eddy. 2013. (Illus.). vi, 279p. *(978-0-87510-494-2(0)*, Christian Science Publishing Society, The) Christian Science Publishing Society.

Galloway, Tammy. I Am Healed: Praying God's Word for Children. 2010. 28p. 13.95 *(978-1-4497-0428-5(X)*, WestBow Pr.) Author Solutions, LLC.

Ives, Pastor Carla. Healed from the Inside Out! 2010. 32p. pap. 12.99 *(978-1-4490-3000-1(9))* AuthorHouse.

Taylor, Mary J. God's Miracle Process: Trauma Transformed into Treasures 2005. (Illus.). 144p. per. 12.95 *(978-0-9768530-0-8(0))* Choices International.

Walker, Kathryn. Mysterious Healing. 2009. (Unsolved! Ser.). (ENG., Illus.). 32p. (J). (gr. 3-5). pap. *(978-0-7787-4163-3(X))*; (gr. 4-6). lib. bdg. *(978-0-7787-4150-3(8))* Crabtree Publishing Co.

SPIRITUAL HEALING—FICTION

Bruce, Ann Elizabeth. Inspire Your Spirit. 2007. 48p. per. *(978-1-897312-54-4(7))* Adlibbed Ltd.

Conley, Autumn. Colby's Peace. 2005. 197p. pap. 24.95 *(978-1-4137-8937-9(4))* America Star Bks.

Harris, Janice. The Journey: Subtle Lessons in Spiritual Awakening. 2007. 180p. per. 19.95 *(978-1-4327-0795-8(7))* Outskirts Pr., Inc.

Harwell, Wiley D. Knowing Truth by Name: The Stories of White Bear. 2006. 144p. per. *(978-1-59298-130-4(5))* Beaver's Pond Pr., Inc.

An Inner Child Speaks. 2006. (J). 17.99 *(978-0-9779130-0-8(7))* Zy Iman Pubng.

Kolb, Joseph J. Reservation Dreams. 2004. 185p. pap. 24.95 *(978-1-4137-3054-8(X))* America Star Bks.

Lansdowne, Marcella. The Adventures of Patty & Annabel: The Monsoon & the Auric Field. 2009. 28p. pap. 15.95 *(978-1-4389-4786-0(0))* AuthorHouse.

Richardson, Faith. Tree Root & River Rat. 2003. (Illus.). 248p. (J). pap. 12.95 *(978-0-9744989-5-9(5))* Fox Song Bks.

Sanderson, Whitney. Horse Diaries #5: Golden Sun. Sanderson, Ruth, illus. 2010. (Horse Diaries: 5). 160p. (J). (gr. 3-7). pap. 7.99 *(978-0-375-86194-9(7)*, Random Hse. Bks. for Young Readers) Random Hse. Children's Bks.

Thompson, John & Thompson, Susan. The Lilychild. 2011. 256p. 35.95 *(978-1-4497-1331-7(9))*; pap. 19.95 *(978-1-4497-1330-0(0))* Author Solutions, LLC. (WestBow Pr.).

SPIRITUAL LIFE

see also Christian Life; Faith

Allah in Person, Royall. The Center Page, Volume 1. 2003. (Illus.). 241p. 51.00 *(978-0-9768502-0-5(6))* United Nation of Islam, The.

Anderson, Carolyn B. Exchanging God's Glory for the Pleasures of the Flesh. 2004. 120p. (YA). per. 8.95 *(978-0-9718249-8-0(3))* Anderson Publishing.

Armbrecht, Doug, compiled by. Quiet Time Prepack for Families (Quiet Time Devotionals). 21. 2006. (Illus.). (YA). per. 347.79 *(978-1-931235-53-2(8)*, gbookpack) Word of Life Fellowship, Inc.

Arons, Marsha. Teen Miracles: Extraordinary Life-Changing Stories by America's Teenagers. 2004. (Illus.). 256p. pap. 9.95 *(978-1-58062-758-0(7))* Adams Media Corp.

Artworks. Faith, Hope & Love. 2004. (YA). 16.95 *(978-1-57938-856-0(6))* Artworks International.

Bewes, Richard & Thompson, Ian. Top 100 Questions Remix: Spiritual Answers to Real Questions. 2010. (ENG.). 224p. (gr. 7-12). pap. 14.99 *(978-1-84550-191-4(8)*, 1ed4fed1-cdb7-43e5-94aa-96d3cbf0dea9) Christian Focus Pubns. GBR. Dist: Baker & Taylor Publisher Services (BTPS).

Blosser, Connie S. Destiny's Trouble: A True Story. 2013. 20p. pap. 24.95 *(978-1-4626-9341-2(5))* America Star Bks.

Bowman, Crystal. Is God Always with Me? Kucharik, Elena, illus. 2006. (Little Blessings Ser.). (ENG.). 64p. (J). 9.99 *(978-1-4143-0287-4(8)*, 6002878) Tyndale Hse. Pubs.

Box, Su. You Are Very Special. Poole, Susie, illus. 2003. 32p. (J). pap. 6.95 *(978-0-8198-8807-5(9)*, 332-417) Pauline Bks. & Media.

S

Butler, David. Redeemer: Who He Is & Who He Will Always Be. 2019. (Illus.). 169p. (J). pap. 15.99 *(978-1-62972-574-1(9))* Deseret Bk. Co.

Cardero, Patrick & JFA Productions Staff. Hello It's Me: An Ineterview with God. 2003. 225p. pap. 19.95 *(978-0-9723024-0-1(9))* JFA Productions.

Carr, Dan. God, I Need to Talk to You about Lying. Clark, Bartholomew & Clark, Bill, illus. 16p. (J). 1.19 *(978-0-7586-0512-2(9))* Concordia Publishing Hse.

—God, I Need to Talk to You about Sharing. Clark, Bartholomew & Clark, Bill, illus. 16p. (J). 1.19 *(978-0-7586-0511-5(0))* Concordia Publishing Hse.

—God, I Need to Talk to You about Stealing. Clark, Bartholomew & Clark, Bill, illus. 16p. (J). 1.19 *(978-0-7586-0509-2(9))* Concordia Publishing Hse.

—God, I Need to Talk to You about Vandalism. Clark, Bartholomew & Clark, Bill, illus. 16p. (J). 1.19 *(978-0-7586-0510-8(2))* Concordia Publishing Hse.

Chopra, Deepak. Fire in the Heart: A Spiritual Guide for Teens. 2006. (ENG., Illus.). 208p. (YA). (gr. 7-12). pap. 15.99 *(978-0-689-86217-5(2)*, Simon & Schuster Bks. For Young Readers) Simon & Schuster Bks. For Young Readers.

—Teens Ask Deepak: All the Right Questions. Barchowsky, Damien, illus. 2006. (ENG.). 208p. (YA). (gr. 7). pap. 17.99 *(978-0-689-86218-2(0)*, Simon Pulse) Simon Pulse.

Christensen, Catherine. The Holy Ghost Is My Friend. 2017. (ENG., Illus.). (J). (gr. -1-2). 14.99 *(978-1-4621-2083-3(0))* Cedar Fort, Inc./CFI Distribution.

Cummings Moore, Thelma Wyatt. Living with a Passion. 2003. 103p. (YA). (gr. 8-18). pap. 5.95 *(978-0-942683-40-0(4))* Publishing Assocs., Inc.

Dent, Jenny. The Giant Jigsaw Puzzle: Democratic Committee Assignments in the Modern House. (Spiritual Teachings for Children Ser.). (Illus.). 32p. (J). (gr. k-9). 17.95 *(978-0-85487-053-0(9))* White Eagle Publishing Trust GBR. Dist: DeVorss & Co.

Dobson, Shirley. God Helps Me Share: Coloring Book about Abigail & David. 2004. (Illus.). 12p. pap. 1.49 *(978-0-8307-2894-7(5)*, Gospel Light) Gospel Light Pubns.

—God Made the World Coloring Book. 2004. (Illus.). 16p. 1.49 *(978-0-8307-2487-1(7)*, Gospel Light) Gospel Light Pubns.

—God Made the World Coloring Book: 100-Unit Counter Merchandiser. 2004. 16p. 99.00 *(978-0-8307-2488-8(5)*, Gospel Light) Gospel Light Pubns.

—God's Little Helper Coloring Book. 2004. (Illus.). 16p. pap. 1.49 *(978-0-8307-2188-7(6)*, Gospel Light) Gospel Light Pubns.

Dobson, Shirley, contrib. by. God Gives Me Joy Coloring Book. 2004. 16p. 1.49 *(978-0-8307-3054-4(0)*, Gospel Light) Gospel Light Pubns.

Dunagan, Cindy. Journaling Toward Moral Excellence Volume Four for Young Adults: A Character Building Workbook of 100 Thought-Provoking Questions to Help the Young Discover the Value of Moral Strength. 2004. (Journaling Toward Moral Excellence Ser.: Vol. 4). 107p. (YA). (gr. 11-18). 11.95 *(978-0-9759871-3-1(5))* Straight Paths Pr.

—Journaling Toward Moral Excellence Volume Three for Teenagers: A Character Building Workbook of 100 Thought-Provoking Questions to Help the Young Discover the Value of Moral Strength. 2004. (Journaling Toward Moral Excellence Ser.: Vol. 3). 107p. (YA). (gr. 8-10). 11.95 *(978-0-9759871-2-4(7))* Straight Paths Pr.

—Journaling Toward Moral Excellence Volume Two for Pre-Teens Vol. 2: A Character Building Workbook of 100 Thought-Provoking Questions to Help the Young Discover the Value of Moral Strength. 2004. (Journaling Toward Moral Excellence Ser.: Vol. 2). 107p. (J). (gr. 5-7). 11.95 *(978-0-9759871-1-7(9))* Straight Paths Pr.

Eagle, Golden. It's Good to Laugh at Yourself (Coyote Medicine. l.t. ed. 2004. (Illus.). 22p. (J). per. 12.99 *(978-1-932338-36-2(5))* Lifevest Publishing, Inc.

Enloe, Rochelle & Enloe, Tim. Kid-Power! How Kids Can Get the Holy Spirit's Power! 2007. (Illus.). (J). per. 5.99 *(978-0-9794331-0-8(X))* E M Pubns.

Fear Not My Child, I Am Here: Emerging from the Spiral of Fear the Practical Mystic's Guide for Embracing Your Heart's Desire. 2003rd ed. 2003. 240p. per. 15.95 *(978-0-9742213-0-4(9))* Community Works!

Feinberg, Margaret & Gillespie, Natalie. Text Messages from God for Kids. 2005. (Instant Messages Ser.). 160p. mass mkt. 9.99 *(978-1-59379-040-0(6))* White Stone Bks.

Fernandez, Mayte. Secrets of Your Guardian Angels. 2013. 68p. pap. 24.45 *(978-1-4525-6765-5(4))* Balboa Pr.

Fitzhugh, Steve. Who Will Survive: The Teenager's Ultimate Struggle for Survival. 2003. (YA). per. 10.00 (978-0-9748298-0-7(3)) PowerMoves.

Foster, Kathryn Joy. Always Room for One More. l.t. ed. 2004. (Illus.). 12p. (J). spiral bd. 13.00 (978-0-9728779-6-1(7), TBK-21007) Read All Over Publishing.

Francis I, pseud. Anointed: Gifts of the Holy Spirit. 2017. (ENG.). (J). 18.95 (978-0-8198-0653-6(6)) Pauline Bks. & Media.

Fryberger, Phil. Dad's Magic Oatmeal Breakfast. 2007. (ENG.). 28p. 14.95 (978-1-4303-2072-2(9)) Lulu Pr., Inc.

Gilven, Edwin. Blubaugh, Spiritually Speaking. 2005. 27p. spiral bd. 13.58 (978-1-4116-4623-0(1)) Lulu Pr., Inc.

Hallinan, P. K. Love Letter from God. 2014. (ENG., Illus.). 24p. (J). (gr. -1-2). 12.99 (978-0-8249-5662-2(1), Ideals Pubns.) Worthy Publishing.

Havergal, Frances Ridley. Little Pillows & Morning Bells: Good-Night Thoughts & Waking Thoughts for the Little Ones. 2004. 200p. (J). per. 14.95 (978-1-932474-25-1(0)) Solid Ground Christian Bks.

Hemry, Melanie & Lynnes, Gina. Anointing for Children w/ anointing oil Vial. 2007. (Illus.). 192p. 14.99 (978-0-88368-686-7(4), 776867) Whitaker Hse.

Hill, Harriet, et al. Healing Heart's Club Story & Activity Book. 2018. (ENG., Illus.). 74p. (J). (gr. 3-6). pap. 2.99 (978-1-937628-90-1(6)) American Bible Society.

Hodgson, Joan. Hullo Sun. Ripper, Peter, illus. 2003. 32p. (gr. -1-3). 8.95 (978-0-85487-072-1(5)) White Eagle Publishing Trust GBR. Dist: DeVorss & Co.

How to Hear the Voice of God Today! 2003. 52p. per. (978-1-932833-09-6(9)) Dickow, Gregory Ministries.

Jackson, Vanessa Wyse. Recipes for Life: Fifty Ready-To-Use Spiritual Talks for Children. 2012. (ENG., Illus.). 134p. pap. 15.95 (978-1-84730-360-8(9)) Veritas Pubns. IRL. Dist: Casemate Pubs. & Bk. Distributors, LLC.

Jones, Kidada. School of Awake: A Girl's Guide to the Universe. Jones, Koa, illus. 2017. (ENG.). 168p. (YA). (gr. 9-13). pap. 18.95 (978-1-60868-458-8(X)) New World Library.

Jones, Nona C. When the Soul Won't Let Go: No-Nonsense Answers to a Broken Woman's Questions. 2004. 90p. (YA). pap. 10.00 (978-0-9762770-0-2(X)) TNJ Ministries.

Klemp, Joan & Moore, Anthony N. Sounds of HU. Brouhard, Crary & Carrol, Patrick, illus. 2013. (J). pap. (978-1-57043-363-4(1)) Eckankar.

Liebenow, Todd & VonSeggen, Liz. Join the Hall of Faith. 2004. 20p. (J). 18.00 (978-1-58302-256-6(2)) Creative Ministry Solutions.

Lucado, Max & Lucado, Jenna. Redefining Beautiful: What God Sees When God Sees You, 1 vol. 2009. (ENG.). 240p. (YA). (gr. 7-12). pap. 14.99 (978-1-4003-1428-7(3), Tommy Nelson) Nelson, Thomas Inc.

The Man of Destiny. 2005. (YA). per. 8.95 (978-1-59872-161-4(5)) Instant Pub.

Mattern, Joanne. Mystics & Psychics. 2011. (World Religions & Beliefs Ser.). 128p. (gr. 7-12). 28.95 (978-1-59935-148-3(X)) Reynolds, Morgan Inc.

Meyer, Richard. This Faith Is Mine. 2005. 176p. 10.49 (978-0-7586-0727-0(X)) Concordia Publishing Hse.

Monge, Marlyn. Mary & the Little Shepherds of Fatima. Lopez, Maria Joao, illus. 2017. (ENG.). 34p. (J). 14.95 (978-0-8198-4959-5(6)) Pauline Bks. & Media.

Montgomery, Sharon, text. Your Invisible Bodies: A Reference Book for Children & Adults about Human Energy Fields. 2011. (Illus.). (978-0-9811089-2-6(X)) Words By Montgomery.

Nagaraja, Dharmachari. The Buddha's Apprentice at Bedtime: Tales of Compassion & Kindness for You to Read with Your Child - to Delight & Inspire. 2013. (Illus.). 128p. (J). (gr. -1-3). pap. 18.95 (978-1-78028-514-6(0), Watkins Publishing) Watkins Media Limited GBR. Dist: Penguin Random Hse. LLC.

Oaks, Kristen M. & Phillips, JoAnn. The Testimony Glove. Burr, Dan, illus. 2010. 31p. (J). (gr. -1-4). 17.99 (978-1-60641-151-3(9)) Deseret Bk. Co.

Overstreet, Betty. The Lord Still Speaks - Are You Listening?, 1 book. 2004. 113p. (YA). per. 14.95 (978-0-9746253-0-0(2)) Overstreet Pub. & Mktg.

Parr, Susan Sherwood. 30 Days Out of Depression. 2004. (ENG., Illus.). 58p. 3.95 (978-0-9728590-5-9(5)) Word Productions.

Power Twins Handbook Volume One. 2006. (J). spiral bd. (978-0-9742355-1-6(2)) Brda, Tracy.

Promiseland. 2008. (J). per. 8.00 (978-0-9664736-0-5(4)) Grace Walk Resources, LLC.

Rees, Rebecca. It Is Good to Be a Part of All This: Stories of a Small Part in the Great Work. 2011. 122p. pap. 19.99 (978-1-4568-8875-6(7)) Xlibris Corp.

Simmons, Judy. Where Is Heaven? 2009. 32p. pap. 12.99 (978-1-4389-5900-9(1)) AuthorHouse.

Sisters of Notre Dame, Chardon, Ohio. God Cares for Us: Grade 2. 2008. (Christ Our Life 2009 Ser.). (ENG.). 222p. (gr. 1-8). pap., stu. ed. 15.20 (978-0-8294-2407-2(5)) Loyola Pr.

—We Believe: Grade 3. 2008. (Christ Our Life 2009 Ser.). (ENG.). 252p. (gr. 1-8). pap., stu. ed. 15.20 (978-0-8294-2410-2(5)) Loyola Pr.

SL Resources Staff, prod. Inhabit Student Book. 2010. 47p. (YA). 3.99 (978-1-935040-77-4(4)) SL Resources.

—SEQUENCE Student Work Book. 2009. 47p. (YA). 3.99 (978-1-935040-74-3(X)) SL Resources.

Spiritual Leaders & Thinkers. 2005. (Spiritual Leaders & Thinkers Ser.). 120p. (C). (gr. 9). 270.00 (978-0-7910-8734-3(4), Facts On File) Infobase Holdings, Inc.

Stillman, Sarah. Soul Searching: A Girl's Guide to Finding Herself. Gross, Susan, illus. 2012. (ENG.). 176p. (YA). (gr. 7). pap. 9.99 (978-1-58270-303-9(5)) Simon Pulse/Beyond Words.

Terpstra, Marcia J. Splinters from My Rocking Chair: A Journey Through Incest Survival. 2011. 128p. pap. 14.99 (978-1-4634-3928-6(8)) AuthorHouse.

Ume, Anne. A Spiritual Trilogy. Hudson, David W., photos by. 2003. (ENG., Illus.). 352p. (YA). pap. 21.00 (978-0-9727967-0-5(3), 77707) Bois Pubns.

Valeri, Jennifer. God from A-Z: A Child's Guide to Learning about God. 2009. 32p. pap. 15.00 (978-1-60860-761-7(5), Eloquent Bks.) Strategic Book Publishing & Rights Agency (SBPRA).

Vukelic, Deneen. Soaring - a Teen's Guide to Spirit & Spirituality. 2015. (ENG., Illus.). 209p. (J). (gr. -1-12). pap. 19.95 (978-1-78279-874-3(9), Soul Rocks Bks.) Hunt, John Publishing Ltd. GBR. Dist: National Bk. Network.

Walker, Peggy, illus. My First Book of Buddhist Treasures. 2003. 38p. (J). 8.95 (978-0-915678-81-5(0)) World Tribune Pr.

Walsch, Neale Donald. The Little Soul & the Earth: I'm Somebody! Riccio, Frank, illus. 2005. 32p. (J). 20.00 (978-1-57174-451-7(7)) Hampton Roads Publishing Co., Inc.

Watson, W. Hamp, Jr. Frederick Wilson Still Speaks - Big Words for Our Time. Watson, W. Hamp, Jr., ed. l.t. ed. 2004. (J). per. 12.95 (978-0-9746976-0-4(5)) Cambridge Way Publishing.

SPIRITUALS (SONGS)

Bryan, Ashley. Let It Shine. 2007. (ENG., Illus.). 40p. (J). (gr. -1-3). 19.99 (978-0-689-84732-5(7), Atheneum Bks. for Young Readers) Simon & Schuster Children's Publishing.

Corr, Christopher, illus. Whole World: PB with CD. 2010. (ENG.). 32p. (J). (gr. -1-2). 9.99 (978-1-84686-085-0(7)) Barefoot Bks., Inc.

Corr, Christopher & Penner, Fred. Whole World. Corr, Christopher, illus. 2007. (ENG., Illus.). 32p. (J). (gr. -1-4). 16.99 (978-1-84686-043-0(1)) Barefoot Bks., Inc.

—Whole World. 2007. (ENG., Illus.). 32p. (J). (gr. -1-3). 9.99 (978-1-84686-092-8(X)) Barefoot Bks., Inc.

Edmunds, Kate, illus. Dry Bones. 2007. (Classic Books with Holes Board Book Ser.). (J). 14p. (gr. -1-1). spiral bd. (978-1-84643-112-8(3)); 16p. (gr. 1-1). pap. (978-1-84643-108-1(5)) Child's Play International Ltd.

Giovanni, Nikki. On My Journey Now: Looking at African-American History Through the Spirituals. 2009. (ENG., Illus.). 128p. (J). (gr. 7-9). pap. 9.99 (978-0-7636-4380-5(7)) Candlewick Pr.

Holiday, Billie. God Bless the Child. Pinkney, Jerry, illus. 2004. 32p. (J). lib. bdg. 17.89 (978-0-06-029487-8(6), Amistad) HarperCollins Pubs.

Holiday, Billie & Herzog, Arthur, Jr. God Bless the Child. Pinkney, Jerry, illus. 2008. (ENG.). 40p. (J). (gr. -1-3). per. 7.99 (978-0-06-443646-5(2)) HarperCollins Pubs.

Penner, Fred & Corr, Christopher. Whole World. 2012. (Illus.). 32p. (J). (gr. -1-2). 9.99 (978-1-84686-832-0(7)) Barefoot Bks., Inc.

Pinkney, Gloria Jean. Music from Our Lord's Holy Heaven. Pinkney, Jerry et al, illus. 2005. 48p. (J). (gr. -1-18). lib. bdg. 18.89 incl. audio compact disk (978-0-06-000769-0(9)) HarperCollins Pubs.

SPLICING

see Knots and Splices

SPONGEBOB SQUAREPANTS (FICTITIOUS CHARACTER)—FICTION

Aikins, Dave. Haunted Houseboat. 2013. (SpongeBob Squarepants 8X8 Ser.). lib. bdg. 13.55 (978-0-606-32220-1(5)) Turtleback.

Artifact Group Staff & Artifact Group, The. Atlantis SquarePantis. 2007. (SpongeBob SquarePants Ser.). (ENG., Illus.). 24p. (J). (gr. k-3). pap. 3.99 (978-1-4169-3799-9(4), Simon Spotlight/Nickelodeon) Simon Spotlight/Nickelodeon.

Banks, Steven. The Art Contest: No Cheating Allowed! Dress, Robert, illus. 2006. (SpongeBob SquarePants Ser.: 12). (ENG.). 24p. (J). (gr. -1-3). pap. 3.99 (978-1-4169-0667-4(3), Simon Spotlight/Nickelodeon) Simon Spotlight/Nickelodeon.

—Lost in Time. The Artifact Group, illus. 2006. 22p. (J). lib. bdg. 15.00 (978-1-4242-0977-4(3)) Fitzgerald Bks.

—The Song That Never Ends. DePorter, Vince, illus. 2005. 32p. (J). lib. bdg. 15.00 (978-1-59054-984-1(8)) Fitzgerald Bks.

—SpongeBob Goes to the Doctor. Saunders, Zina, illus. 2005. (SpongeBob SquarePants Ser.: 9). (ENG.). 24p. (J). pap. 3.99 (978-1-4169-0359-8(3), Simon Spotlight/Nickelodeon) Simon Spotlight/Nickelodeon.

—Spongebob Goes to the Doctor. Saunders, Zina, illus. 2005. 22p. (J). lib. bdg. 15.00 (978-1-4242-0976-7(5)) Fitzgerald Bks.

—Stop the Presses! DePorter, Vince, illus. 2005. 22p. (J). lib. bdg. 15.00 (978-1-4242-0973-6(0)) Fitzgerald Bks.

Bond, Clint & Clark, Andy, illus. The Great Snail Race. 2005. (SpongeBob SquarePants Ser.). (ENG.). 24p. (J). pap. 3.99 (978-0-689-87313-3(1), Simon Spotlight/Nickelodeon) Simon Spotlight/Nickelodeon.

Carbone, Courtney. Food Fight! 2015. (Spongebob Squarepants Step into Reading Ser.). lib. bdg. 14.75 (978-0-606-36398-3(X)) Turtleback.

Chipponeri, Kelli. The Big Win. Aikins, Dave, illus. 2008. (SpongeBob SquarePants Ser.: 13). (ENG.). 32p. (J). (gr. k-2). pap. 3.99 (978-1-4169-4938-1(0), Simon Spotlight/Nickelodeon) Simon Spotlight/Nickelodeon.

Dart, Allan, ed. SpongeBob SquarePants & Other TV Tunes, No. 2. 2003. (Illus.). 16p. (J). pap. 3.99 (978-0-88013-060-8(1)) Profile Entertainment, Inc.

David, Erica. Christmas with Krabby Klaws. Martinez, Heather, illus. 2010. (SpongeBob SquarePants Ser.). (ENG.). 16p. (J). pap. 5.99 (978-1-4424-0805-0(7), Simon Spotlight/Nickelodeon) Simon Spotlight/Nickelodeon.

David, Erica & Artifact Group Staff. Good Times! 10th anniv. ed. 2009. (SpongeBob SquarePants Ser.). (ENG.). 32p. (J). (gr. k-2). pap. 3.99 (978-1-4169-8500-6(X), Simon Spotlight/Nickelodeon) Simon Spotlight/Nickelodeon.

Eliot, Chip & Lewman, David. Funny-Side Up! A SpongeBob Joke Book. 2014. lib. bdg. 16.00 (978-0-606-36279-5(7)) Turtleback.

Giddy Up Staff. SpongeBob Abraca Dazzle. 2006. 24p. 4.99 (978-1-59524-079-8(9)) Giddy Up, LLC.

Goldberg, Barry, illus. Bubble Blowers, Beware! 2004. (SpongeBob SquarePants Ser.). (ENG.). 24p. (J). pap. 3.99 (978-0-689-86862-7(6), Simon Spotlight/Nickelodeon) Simon Spotlight/Nickelodeon.

Harvey, Alex. Dancing with the Star. 2013. (Spongebob Squarepants Step into Reading Ser.). lib. bdg. 13.55 (978-0-606-23687-4(2)) Turtleback.

Hillenburg, Stephen. SpongeBob Comics: Book 1: Silly Sea Stories. 2017. (SpongeBob Comics Ser.). (ENG., Illus.). 112p. (J). (gr. 3-7). pap. 12.99 (978-1-4197-2319-3(7), 1151801) Abrams, Inc.

—SpongeBob Comics: Book 2: Aquatic Adventurers, Unite! 2017. (SpongeBob Comics Ser.). (ENG., Illus.). 112p. (J). (gr. 3-7). pap. 12.99 (978-1-4197-2320-9(0), 1151901) Abrams, Inc.

—SpongeBob Comics: Book 3: Tales from the Haunted Pineapple. 2017. (SpongeBob Comics Ser.). (ENG., Illus.). 112p. (J). (gr. 3-7). pap. 12.99 (978-1-4197-2560-9(2), 1152001, Amulet Bks.) Abrams, Inc.

—SpongeBob Comics: Treasure Chest. 2017. (SpongeBob Comics Ser.). (ENG., Illus.). 208p. (gr. k-2). 32.99 (978-1-4197-2561-6(0), 1152101, Abrams ComicArts) Abrams, Inc.

Hillenburg, Steven. SpongeBob SquarePants, Vol. 7. 2005. (SpongeBob SquarePants Ser.). (Illus.). 89p. pap. 14.99 (978-1-59532-678-2(2), Tokyopop Kids) TOKYOPOP, Inc.

—SpongeBob SquarePants: Another Day Another Dollar, Vol. 5. 2004. (Nickelodeon Ser.). (Illus.). 96p. pap. 14.99 (978-1-59532-209-8(4), Tokyopop Kids) TOKYOPOP, Inc.

Hillenburg, Steven, creator. Crime & Funishment Vol. 4, 7 vols. 2004. (Illus.). 96p. (gr. 2-5). pap. 14.99 (978-1-59182-576-0(8), Tokyopop Kids) TOKYOPOP, Inc.

—SpongeBob SquarePants Vol. 1: Krusty Krab Adventures, 2 vols. 2003. (Illus.). 96p. (J). pap. 14.99 (978-1-59182-398-8(6), Tokyopop Kids) TOKYOPOP, Inc.

—SpongeBob SquarePantsTM: Friends Forever. 2003. (Illus.). 96p. pap. 14.99 (978-1-59182-399-5(4), Tokyopop Kids) TOKYOPOP, Inc.

Krulik, Nancy. Ice-Cream Dreams. Martinez, Heather, illus. 2004. 22p. (J). lib. bdg. 15.00 (978-1-4242-0975-0(7)) Fitzgerald Bks.

Lewman, David. The Case of the Vanished Squirrel. Moore, Harry, illus. 2008. (SpongeBob SquarePants Ser.). (ENG.). 16p. (J). (gr. -1-3). pap. 5.99 (978-1-4169-4939-8(9), Simon Spotlight/Nickelodeon) Simon Spotlight/Nickelodeon.

—Double Trouble: The Case of the Missing Spatula - The Case of the Vanished Squirrel. Moore, Harry, Jr., illus. 2010. (SpongeBob SquarePants Ser.). (ENG.). 36p. (J). bds. 10.99 (978-1-4424-1337-5(9), Simon Spotlight/Nickelodeon) Simon Spotlight/Nickelodeon.

—Oh, Barnacles! SpongeBob's Handbook for Bad Days. Style Guide Staff, illus. 2005. (SpongeBob SquarePants Ser.). (ENG.). 48p. (J). pap. 3.99 (978-1-4169-0641-4(X), Simon Spotlight/Nickelodeon) Simon Spotlight/Nickelodeon.

—SpongeBob, Soccer Star! Reed, Stephen, illus. 2010. (SpongeBob SquarePants Ser.). (ENG.). 24p. (J). (gr. -1-3). pap. 3.99 (978-1-4169-9445-9(9), Simon Spotlight/Nickelodeon) Simon Spotlight/Nickelodeon.

—SpongeBob's Slap Shot. Moore, Harry, illus. 2008. (SpongeBob SquarePants Ser.). (ENG.). 24p. (J). (gr. -1-3). pap. 3.99 (978-1-4169-6153-6(4), Simon Spotlight/Nickelodeon) Simon Spotlight/Nickelodeon.

—Spongebob's Slap Shot. 2014. (SpongeBob Squarepants 8X8 Ser.). lib. bdg. 13.55 (978-0-606-36280-1(0)) Turtleback.

Miglis, Jenny. And the Winner Is... Meurer, Caleb, illus. 2005. (SpongeBob SquarePants Ser.: 4). 22p. (J). lib. bdg. 15.00 (978-1-59054-824-0(8)) Fitzgerald Bks.

—New Student Starfish. Martinez, Heather, illus. 2003. (SpongeBob SquarePants Ser.). (ENG.). 64p. (J). pap. 3.99 (978-0-689-86164-2(8), Simon Spotlight/Nickelodeon) Simon Spotlight/Nickelodeon.

Nickelodeon Staff. Party Time! 2013. (Spongebob Squarepants Step into Reading Ser.). lib. bdg. 13.55 (978-0-606-32221-8(3)) Turtleback.

Nickelodeon Staff & Nickelodeon / LeapFrog. SpongeBob SquarePants: The Tour de Bikini Bottom. 2008. (J). 13.99 (978-1-59319-926-5(0)) LeapFrog Enterprises, Inc.

Ostrow, Kim. The Great Snail Race. Bond, Clint & Clark, Andy, illus. 2005. (SpongeBob SquarePants Ser.: No. 6). 22p. (J). lib. bdg. 15.00 (978-1-59054-830-1(2)) Fitzgerald Bks.

Pass, Erica. Hooray for Dads! 2014. (SpongeBob Squarepants 8X8 Ser.). lib. bdg. 14.75 (978-0-606-35560-5(X)) Turtleback.

—SpongeBob LovePants. Schigiel, Gregg, illus. 2006. (Ready-to-Read Ser.). (ENG.). 32p. (J). (gr. k-2). pap. 3.99 (978-1-4169-1758-8(6), Simon Spotlight/Nickelodeon) Simon Spotlight/Nickelodeon.

Publications International Ltd. Staff, ed. Nickelodeon(tm) Spongebob Squarepants: Look & Find(r). 2014. 24p. (J). (978-1-4508-9354-1(6), 1450893546) Publications International, Ltd.

—Spongebob Clock It's Time Sound Book. 2004. 10p. (J). bds. 16.98 (978-1-4127-3030-3(9), 7226500) Publications International, Ltd.

—SpongeBob Squarepants (Little Look & Find) 2010. 24p. (J). 2.98 (978-1-4508-0205-5(2)) Phoenix International Publications, Inc.

Random House. Five Undersea Stories (SpongeBob SquarePants) Random House, illus. 2015. (Step into Reading Ser.). (ENG., Illus.). 160p. (J). (gr. -1-1). 8.99 (978-0-553-50860-4(1), Random Hse. Bks. for Young Readers) Random Hse. Children's Bks.

—Party Time! (SpongeBob SquarePants) Moore, Harry, illus. 2013. (Step into Reading Ser.). (ENG.). 32p. (J). (gr. -1-1). 5.99 (978-0-449-81875-6(6), Random Hse. Bks. for Young Readers) Random Hse. Children's Bks.

Random House Staff. You're Fired! 2014. (SpongeBob Squarepants 8X8 Ser.). lib. bdg. 13.55 (978-0-606-35204-8(X)) Turtleback.

Richards, Kitty. SpongeBob Airpants: The Lost Episode. Martinez, Heather, illus. 2003. (SpongeBob SquarePants Ser.). (ENG.). 64p. (J). pap. 3.99 (978-0-689-86163-5(X), Simon Spotlight/Nickelodeon) Simon Spotlight/Nickelodeon.

Silverhardt, Lauryn. SpongeBob SpookyPants. Style Guide Staff, illus. 2004. (SpongeBob SquarePants Ser.). (ENG.). 16p. (J). bds. 5.99 (978-0-689-87320-1(4), Simon Spotlight/Nickelodeon) Simon Spotlight/Nickelodeon.

SpongeBob Squarepants WOW! Scratchers. 2005. 4p. (J). 6.99 (978-1-59524-031-6(4)) Giddy Up, LLC.

SpongeBob WOW Paper Scribble & Giggle Pad. 2004. 36p. (J). 7.99 (978-1-59524-006-4(3)) Giddy Up, LLC.

SpongeBob WOW! Surprise & Shine. 2005. 4p. (J). 6.99 (978-1-59524-049-1(7)) Giddy Up, LLC.

SpongeBob's Box of Books. 2005. (SpongeBob SquarePants Ser.). (ENG.). 144p. (J). pap. 10.99 (978-1-4169-1186-9(3), Simon Spotlight/Nickelodeon) Simon Spotlight/Nickelodeon.

Taylor, Nicole & Watts, Michael. SpongeBob Squarepants: Wormy. 2014. (ENG.). 32p. (J). pap. incl. audio compact disk (978-1-909221-71-0(6)) Glasgow, Mary Pubns.

Willson, Sarah. Behold, No Cavities! A Visit to the Dentist. Moore, Harry, illus. 2007. (SpongeBob SquarePants Ser.: 15). (ENG.). 24p. (J). (gr. -1-3). pap. 3.99 (978-1-4169-3566-7(5), Simon Spotlight/Nickelodeon) Simon Spotlight/Nickelodeon.

—Just Say Please! Moore, Harry, illus. 2007. (SpongeBob SquarePants Ser.). (ENG.). 32p. (J). (gr. k-2). pap. 3.99 (978-1-4169-4129-3(0), Simon Spotlight/Nickelodeon) Simon Spotlight/Nickelodeon.

—Mother Knows Best. Dress, Robert, illus. 2006. (SpongeBob SquarePants Chapter Bks.: Vol. 11). (ENG.). 64p. (J). (gr. 3-7). pap. 4.99 (978-1-4169-0793-0(9), Simon Spotlight/Nickelodeon) Simon Spotlight/Nickelodeon.

SPORTS

see also Aeronautical Sports; Amusements; Aquatic Sports; Athletics; Coaching (Athletics); Games; Gymnastics; Olympics; Outdoor Life; Physical Education and Training; Rodeos; School Sports; Winter Sports

also names of sports, e.g. baseball; etc.

Abramovitz, Melissa. The Science & Technology of Football. 2019. (Science & Technology of Sports Ser.). (ENG.). 80p. (J). (gr. 6-12). 41.27 (978-1-68282-651-5(1)) ReferencePoint Pr., Inc.

Action Sports, 6 vols. 2017. (Action Sports (Fly!) Ser.). (ENG., Illus.). 24p. (J). (gr. 2-8). lib. bdg. 188.16 (978-1-5321-2091-6(5), 26774, Abdo Zoom-Fly) ABDO Publishing Co.

Adamson, Thomas K. The Kids' Guide to Sports Design & Engineering, 1 vol. 2014. (SI Kids Guide Bks.). (ENG.). 48p. (J). (gr. 4-5). lib. bdg. 32.65 (978-1-4765-4155-6(8), 124261) Capstone.

Adamson, Thomas K. & Frederick, Shane. Sports Math. 2011. (Sports Math Ser.). (ENG.). 48p. (J). (gr. 5-9). pap., pap., pap. 31.80 (978-1-4296-7323-5(0), 16829) Capstone.

—Sports Math Classroom Collection. 2011. (Sports Math Ser.). (ENG.). 48p. (J). (gr. 5-6). pap., pap. 197.56 (978-1-4296-7324-2(9), 16830) Capstone.

Adamson, Thomas K., et al. High-Tech Sports Classroom Collection. 2013. (High-Tech Sports Ser.). (ENG.). 48p. (J). (gr. 3-9). pap., pap. 215.80 (978-1-62065-915-1(8), 19463) Capstone.

—SI Kids Guide Books, 1 vol. 2014. (SI Kids Guide Bks.). (ENG.). 48p. (J). (gr. 4-5). 138.60 (978-1-4765-6214-8(8), 20611) Capstone.

Aksomitis, Linda. Sports Champions. 2008. (Science Solves It Ser.). (ENG., Illus.). 32p. (J). (gr. 3-7). pap. (978-0-7787-4179-4(6)); lib. bdg. (978-0-7787-4172-5(9)) Crabtree Publishing Co.

Alcraft, Rob. Four-Desert Challenge: Band 14/Ruby (Collins Big Cat) 2015. (Collins Big Cat Ser.). (ENG., Illus.). 48p. (J). (gr. 3-4). pap. 10.99 (978-0-00-812781-7(6)) HarperCollins Pubs. Ltd. GBR. Dist: Independent Pubs. Group.

Alexander, Kwame. The Playbook: 52 Rules to Aim, Shoot, & Score in This Game Called Life. 2023. (ENG., Illus.). 176p. (J). (gr. 3-7). pap. 9.99 (978-0-06-328877-5(X), Clarion Bks.) HarperCollins Pubs.

—The Playbook: 52 Rules to Aim, Shoot, & Score in This Game Called Life. Neave, Thai, illus. 2017. (ENG.). 176p. (J). (gr. 3-7). 16.99 (978-0-544-57097-9(9), 1612556, Clarion Bks.) HarperCollins Pubs.

—The Playbook: 52 Rules to Aim, Shoot, & Score in This Game Called Life. Neave, Thai, photos by. 2017. (ENG., Illus.). (J). (gr. 5-7). lib. bdg. 26.95 (978-0-606-39814-5(7)) Turtleback.

Alexander, Lori. A Sporting Chance: How Ludwig Guttmann Created the Paralympic Games. Drummond, Allan, illus. 2020. (ENG.). 128p. (J). (gr. 3-7). 17.99 (978-1-328-58079-5(2), 1728624, Clarion Bks.) HarperCollins Pubs.

The All-Time Best of Sports. 2011. (All-Time Best of Sports Ser.). (ENG.). 64p. (gr. 3-4). pap. 214.80 (978-1-4296-6456-1(8)) Capstone.

Ana, Reverend & Binkow, Howard. Howard B. Wigglebottom Learns about Sportsmanship: Winning Isn't Everything. Cornelison, Susan F., illus. 2012. (Howard B. Wigglebottom Ser.). (ENG.). 32p. (J). (gr. -1-3). 18.00 (978-0-9826165-6-7(2), 0331f3ab-7cc1-4753-8cf0-73d1c1d21578, We Do Listen) We Do Listen Foundation.

Anniss, Matthew. The Impact of Technology in Sports. 2015. (Impact of Technology Ser.). (ENG., Illus.). 56p. (J). (gr. 6-9). pap. 9.49 (978-1-4846-2641-2(9), 130099, Heinemann) Capstone.

Aretha, David. Top 10 Worst Injuries in Football, 1 vol. 2016. (Sports Greats Ser.). (ENG., Illus.). 48p. (gr. 5-6). pap. 12.70 (978-0-7660-8300-4(4), 1605d358-136e-423d-9821-82c4c3e8105d) Enslow Publishing, LLC.

At the Top of Their Game, 16 vols. 2017. (At the Top of Their Game Ser.). (ENG.). 112p. (gr. 9-9). lib. bdg. 356.00 (978-1-5026-2682-0(9), fabdb4c9-cb6d-49d9-99e6-11666db5e6f0, Cavendish Square) Cavendish Square Publishing LLC.

Atlantic, Leonard. We Play Sports!, 1 vol. 2017. (Ways to Play Ser.). (ENG.). 24p. (gr. k-k). pap. 9.15 (978-1-4824-6353-8(9), 8aa22be6-c1c3-4c24-bd48-962445d3b39b) Stevens, Gareth Publishing LLLP.

Baltzell, Amy, et al. Whose Game Is It, Anyway? A Guide to Helping Your Child Get the Most from Sports, Organized by Age & Stage. 2006. (ENG.). 336p. pap. 21.99 (978-0-618-47460-8(9), 689439, Mariner Bks.) HarperCollins Pubs.

Barber, Nicola. Ancient Roman Sports & Pastimes, 1 vol. 2010. (Ancient Communities: Roman Life Ser.). (ENG.). 32p. (J). (gr. 4-4). pap. 11.60 (978-1-61532-315-9(5), c9e3a8a9-cf7b-45c5-b1eb-27f5b7275fe5); (Illus.). lib. bdg. 30.27 (978-1-61532-306-7(6), d2bcfc1a-44df-494f-ab3b-ec082266c837) Rosen Publishing Group, Inc., The. (PowerKids Pr.).

Barceló, Josefina. Vamos a Jugar. Álvarez, Mrinalí, illus. 2006. (SPA.). (J). 8.95 (978-0-8477-1560-2(4)) Univ. of Puerto Rico Pr.

Barker, Geoff. Sports & Leisure Careers. 2010. (In the Workplace Ser.). 48p. (J). 35.65 (978-1-60753-094-7(5)) Amicus Learning.

Barker, Geoff & Savery, Annabel. Sports & Leisure Careers. 2011. (Been There! Ser.). 32p. (gr. 3-6). lib. bdg. 31.35 (978-1-59920-474-1(6)) Black Rabbit Bks.

Be a Plant Scientist: Level L, 6 vols. (Take-Twostm Ser.). 16p. 36.95 (978-0-322-03403-7(5)) Wright Group/McGraw-Hill.

Beard, Daniel Carter. The American Boy's Handy Book: What to Do & How to Do It. 2018. (Illus.). 416p. (J). (gr. 4-12). 19.95 (978-1-4930-3680-6(7), Lyons Pr.) Globe Pequot Pr., The.

BeaverSimon. SPORT, GAME OR HOBBY? LOW INTERMEDIATE BOOK WITH ONLINE ACCESS, 1 vol. 2014. (ENG., Illus.). 48p. (J). pap., E-Book, E-Book 9.50 (978-1-107-68658-8(X)) Cambridge Univ. Pr.

Believe It Or Not!, Ripleys. Ripley Twists PB: Sports. 2018. (Twist Ser.: 6). (ENG.). 48p. (J). pap. 7.99 (978-1-60991-235-2(7)) Ripley Entertainment, Inc.

Benched: Dealing with Sports Injuries, 12 vols. 2016. (Benched: Dealing with Sports Injuries Ser.). 24p. (ENG.). (gr. 2-3). lib. bdg. 145.62 (978-1-4824-4593-0(X), c3a89f5c-7b9d-451c-9d45-2aed87cd9b96); (gr. 3-2). pap. 48.90 (978-1-4824-5311-9(8)) Stevens, Gareth Publishing LLLP.

Berman, Len. And Nobody Got Hurt! The World's Weirdest, Wackiest True Sports Stories. Gamble, Kent, illus. 2005. (ENG.). 128p. (J). (gr. 3-7). per. 9.99 (978-0-316-01029-0(4)) Little, Brown Bks. for Young Readers.

—And Nobody Got Hurt 2! The World's Weirdest, Wackiest, Most Amazing True Sports Stories. rev. ed. 2007. (ENG., Illus.). 144p. (J). (gr. 3-7). per. 10.99 (978-0-316-06705-8(9)) Little, Brown Bks. for Young Readers.

Berman, Ron. Sports. 2012. (Urban Entrepreneurs Ser.). (ENG., Illus.). 40p. (gr. 3-8). pap. 9.95 (978-1-61570-519-1(8)) Scobre Pr. Corp.

Berry, Joy. Help Me Be Good about Being a Bad Sport. 2009. (Help Me Be Good Ser.). 40p. pap. 7.95 (978-1-60577-108-3(2)) Berry, Joy Enterprises.

—Help Me Be Good Being a Bad Sport. Bartholomew, illus. 2010. (Help Me Be Good Ser.). (ENG.). 32p. (J). (gr. -1-2). pap. 4.99 (978-1-60577-139-7(2)) Berry, Joy Enterprises.

Beth, Georgia. Stem: The Science of Fitness: Multiplying Fractions (Grade 5) 2018. (Mathematics in the Real World Ser.). (ENG., Illus.). 32p. (J). (gr. 4-8). pap. 11.99 (978-1-4258-5815-5(5)) Teacher Created Materials, Inc.

Bethea, Nikole Brooks. The Science of Basketball with Max Axiom, Super Scientist. Campidelli, Maurizio, illus. 2015. (Science of Sports with Max Axiom Ser.). (ENG.). 32p. (J). (gr. 3-9). lib. bdg. 31.32 (978-1-4914-6084-9(9), 128983, Capstone Pr.) Capstone.

—The Science of Football with Max Axiom, Super Scientist. 2015. (Science of Sports with Max Axiom Ser.). (ENG., Illus.). 32p. (J). (gr. 3-9). lib. bdg. 31.32 (978-1-4914-6085-6(7), 128984, Capstone Pr.) Capstone.

Big Time 64p. (YA). (gr. 6-12). pap. (978-0-8224-2390-4(1)) Globe Fearon Educational Publishing.

Bildner, Phil. Martina & Chrissie: The Greatest Rivalry in the History of Sports. Helquist, Brett, illus. (ENG.). 40p. (J). (gr. 2-5). 2019. 8.99 (978-1-5362-0564-0(8)) 2017. 16.99 (978-0-7636-7308-6(0)) Candlewick Pr.

Borth, Teddy. Great Sports, 6 vols. 2015. (Great Sports Ser.: 6). (ENG.). 24p. (J). (gr. -1-2). lib. bdg. 196.74 (978-1-62970-686-3(8), 16698, Abdo Kids) ABDO Publishing Co.

Bourassa, Barbara. Sports Club. 2012. (Illus.). 120p. (J). (978-1-4351-4414-9(7)) Barnes & Noble, Inc.

Bow, James. Evaluating Arguments about Sports & Entertainment. 2018. (State Your Case Ser.). (Illus.). 48p. (J). (gr. 5-6). (978-0-7787-5078-9(7)) Crabtree Publishing Co.

Bowers, Matt. Team Sports at the Paralympics. 2020. (Paralympic Sports Ser.). (ENG.). 32p. (J). (gr. 2-4). pap. 9.99 (978-1-68152-558-7(5), 10757) Amicus.

—Wheelchair Sports at the Paralympics. 2020. (Paralympic Sports Ser.). (ENG.). 32p. (J). (gr. 2-4). pap. 9.99 (978-1-68152-555-6(0), 10754) Amicus.

Bowker, Paul. Playing Pro Football. 2014. (Playing Pro Sports Ser.). (ENG., Illus.). 64p. (J). (gr. 4-8). lib. bdg. 26.65 (978-1-4677-3844-6(1), 32e6f0b9-3294-4454-b4a7-30498135a8b7, Lerner Pubns.) Lerner Publishing Group.

Bowker, Paul D. Total Lacrosse. 2016. (Total Sports Ser.). (ENG., Illus.). 64p. (J). (gr. 3-6). lib. bdg. 35.64 (978-1-68078-506-7(0), 23835, SportsZone) ABDO Publishing Co.

Bowman, Chris. Stadiums. 2018. (Everyday Engineering Ser.). (ENG., Illus.). 24p. (J). (gr. k-3). lib. bdg. 26.95 (978-1-62617-826-7(7), Blastoff! Readers) Bellwether Media.

Bradley, Michael & Braun, Eric. Sports Shockers! 2017. (Sports Shockers! Ser.). (ENG., Illus.). 32p. (J). (gr. 3-9). 122.60 (978-1-5157-8061-8(9), 26979, Capstone Pr.) Capstone.

Branon, Dave. Heads Up! Sports Devotions for All-Star Kids, 1 vol. rev. ed. 2012. (ENG.). 346p. (J). pap. 9.99 (978-0-310-72544-2(5)) Zondervan.

Braun, Eric. Awesome, Disgusting, Unusual Facts about Sports. 2018. (Our Gross, Awesome World Ser.). (ENG.). 24p. (J). (gr. 4-6). pap. 8.99 (978-1-64466-309-7(0), 12531); (Illus.). lib. bdg. 28.50 (978-1-68072-614-5(5), 12530) Black Rabbit Bks. (Hi Jinx).

—Beurk! le Livre Différent et Fascinant Sur le Sport. 2018. (Notre Monde: dégoûtant Mais Génial! Ser.). (FRE.). 24p. (J). (gr. 4-6). (978-1-77092-452-9(3), 12587, Hi Jinx) Black Rabbit Bks.

—Incredible Sports Trivia: Fun Facts & Quizzes. 2018. (Trivia Time! (Alternator Books (r)) Ser.). (ENG., Illus.). 32p. (J). (gr. 3-6). 29.32 (978-1-5124-8333-8(8), 77ce9daf-dd21-4869-8140-e707abe3570f, Lerner Pubns.) Lerner Publishing Group.

Braun, Eric, et al. Stathead Sports: How Data Changed the Sport. 2018. (Stathead Sports Ser.). (ENG.). 48p. (J). (gr. 3-9). 122.60 (978-1-5435-1458-2(8), 27984, Compass Point Bks.) Capstone.

Brocker, Susan. Sports Legends: Set Of 6. 2011. (Navigators Ser.). (J). pap. 44.00 net. (978-1-4108-0406-8(2)) Benchmark Education Co.

Brush, Jim. Extreme Summer Sports. 2013. (ENG., Illus.). 46p. (J). 35.65 (978-1-59771-407-5(0)) Sea-To-Sea Pubns.

Buckley, James, Jr. Scholastic Year in Sports 2016. 2015. lib. bdg. 20.85 (978-0-606-37763-8(8)) Turtleback.

—Scholastic Year in Sports 2017. 2016. (ENG.). 192p. (J). (gr. 3-7). 20.85 (978-0-606-39153-5(3)) Turtleback.

Buckley, James. Scholastic Year in Sports 2018. 2017. (Illus.). 192p. (J). lib. bdg. 20.85 (978-0-606-40654-3(9)) Turtleback.

—Sports Media Relations, Vol. 10. Ferrer, Al, ed. 2015. (Careers off the Field Ser.). (Illus.). 64p. (J). (gr. 7). lib. bdg. 23.95 (978-1-4222-3269-9(7)) Mason Crest.

—STEM in Sports. 2015. (STEM in Sports Ser.). (Illus.). 64p. (J). (gr. 7). 23.95 (978-1-4222-3232-3(8)) Mason Crest.

Burdick, Jeff. Super Sports Trivia, 1 vol. 2013. (Ultimate Trivia Challenge Ser.). 32p. (J). (gr. 2-3). (ENG.). pap. 11.50 (978-1-4339-8301-6(X), e1791604-79e8-423b-9830-6fbf5936fa8d); pap. 63.00 (978-1-4339-8302-3(8)); (ENG., Illus.). lib. bdg. 27.92 (978-1-4339-8300-9(1), 8a070ec0-f4fe-403b-a4c7-d33a3b84f6b1) Stevens, Gareth Publishing LLLP.

Burgan, Michael. Working in College Sports, Vol. 10. Ferrer, Al, ed. 2015. (Careers off the Field Ser.). (Illus.). 64p. (J). (gr. 7). lib. bdg. 23.95 (978-1-4222-3274-3(3)) Mason Crest.

Bussell, Linda. Vamos a Usar la DIVISIÓN en el Campamento de Deportes (Using DIVISION at Sports Camp), 1 vol. 2008. (Las Matemáticas en Nuestro Mundo - Nivel 3 (Math in Our World - Level 3) Ser.). (SPA.). 24p. (gr. 3-3). (J). lib. bdg. 24.67 (978-0-8368-9296-3(8), ea493467-e6c7-445d-aa7f-4c08e14e11a4); pap. 9.15 (978-0-8368-9395-3(6), c6a01d97-4738-49ff-8be0-f9038f414673) Stevens, Gareth Publishing LLLP. (Weekly Reader Leveled Readers).

Butler, Erin K. Sports to the Extreme. 2017. (Sports to the Extreme Ser.). (ENG., Illus.). 32p. (J). (gr. 3-9). 122.60 (978-1-5157-7875-2(4), 26918, Capstone Pr.) Capstone.

Butterfield, Moira & Hachette Children's Group. The Olympics Scandals. 2011. (Olympics Ser.). (ENG.). 32p. (YA). (gr. 4-7). 28.50 (978-1-59771-320-7(1)) Sea-To-Sea Pubns.

Canetti, Yanitzia. Sporty Colors/Colores Deportivos: A World of Color. 2010. (ENG & SPA.). 24p. (J). pap. 6.99 (978-1-59835-268-9(7), BrickHouse Education) Cambridge BrickHouse, Inc.

Capstone Press. Passport to World Sports. 2010. (Passport to World Sports Ser.). (ENG.). 32p. lib. bdg. 159.90 (978-1-4296-5917-8(3), Capstone Pr.) Capstone.

—Play Like the Pros, 1 vol. 2010. (Play Like the Pros (Sports Illustrated for Kids) Ser.). (ENG.). 32p. lib. bdg. 101.28 (978-1-4296-5916-1(5)) Capstone.

—Ultimate Pro Team Guides, 1 vol. 2010. (Ultimate Pro Team Guides (Sports Illustrated for Kids) Ser.). (ENG.). 32p. lib. bdg. 133.28 (978-1-4296-5900-0(9)) Capstone.

—Wild Outdoors. 2010. (Wild Outdoors Ser.). (ENG.). 32p. lib. bdg. 101.28 (978-1-4296-5904-8(1), Capstone Pr.) Capstone.

Carothers, Thomas. Sports' One-Hit Wonders. 2017. (Wild World of Sports Ser.). (ENG., Illus.). 48p. (J). (gr. 3-6). lib. bdg. 34.21 (978-1-5321-1369-7(2), 27667, SportsZone) ABDO Publishing Co.

Carr, Aaron. BMX. 2013. (978-1-62127-627-2(9)) Weigl Pubs., Inc.

—Esqui. 2013. (Deportes de Moda Ser.). (SPA., Illus.). 24p. (J). (gr. k-2). lib. bdg. 27.13 (978-1-62127-633-3(3), AV2 by Weigl) Weigl Pubs., Inc.

—Moto X. 2012. (Cool Sports (Av2) Ser.). (ENG., Illus.). 24p. (J). lib. bdg. 27.13 (978-1-61913-511-6(6), AV2 by Weigl) Weigl Pubs., Inc.

—Moto X with Code. 2012. (Cool Sports (Av2) Ser.). (ENG., Illus.). 24p. (J). (gr. k-2). pap. 12.95 (978-1-61913-517-8(5), AV2 by Weigl) Weigl Pubs., Inc.

Carter, Andre & Nicholls, Shawn. You Call That a Sport? Strange Sports from Around the Globe. 2003. (J). 3.99 (978-1-930623-32-3(1)) Sports Illustrated For Kids.

Champion, Neil. Orienteering, 1 vol. 2009. (Get Outdoors Ser.). (ENG., Illus.). 32p. (gr. 4-4). (J). pap. 11.00 (978-1-4358-3052-3(0), da1e10ed-7078-4bfb-bdac-0a6d3bfd8e37, PowerKids Pr.); (YA). lib. bdg. 28.93 (978-1-4358-3044-8(X), ea7e2e27-062f-4bd6-b3f0-35dab72c488f) Rosen Publishing Group, Inc., The.

Chandler, Matt, et al. All-Star Goofball Trivia: Weird & Wild Sports Trivia. 2017. (Sports Illustrated Kids Ser.). (ENG., Illus.). 144p. (J). (gr. 3-9). pap., pap., pap. 9.95 (978-1-62370-778-1(1), 132653, Capstone Young Readers) Capstone.

Chastain, Zachary. Rooting for the Home Team: Sports in The 1800s. 2009. (Daily Life in America in the 1800s Ser.). 64p. (YA). (gr. 7-18). pap. 9.95 (978-1-4222-1859-4(7)); lib. bdg. 22.95 (978-1-4222-1786-3(8)) Mason Crest.

Ching, Jacqueline. Adventure Racing. 2009. (Ultra Sports Ser.). 64p. (gr. 5-8). 58.50 (978-1-60854-606-0(3), Rosen Reference) Rosen Publishing Group, Inc., The.

Clark, Jeff. Dad's Masterpiece: The Patricia Masotto Story. 2009. 112p. 22.50 (978-1-60693-873-7(8), Strategic Bk. Publishing) Strategic Book Publishing & Rights Agency (SBPRA).

Clausen, Nicki & Grace, Jeff. Basketball Science. 2017. (Got Game Ser.). (ENG., Illus.). 32p. (J). (gr. 2-7). 9.95 (978-1-68072-493-6(2), Bolt) Black Rabbit Bks.

Clay, Kathryn, et al. Cool Sports Facts. 2011. (Cool Sports Facts Ser.). (ENG.). 24p. (gr. k-1). pap. 166.80 (978-1-4296-6375-5(8), Capstone Pr.) Capstone.

Cohn, Jessica. On the Job in the Game. Scheuer, Lauren, illus. 2016. (Core Content Social Studies — on the Job Ser.). (ENG.). 32p. (J). (gr. 2-5). lib. bdg. 26.65 (978-1-63440-111-1(5), 0d4c6a11-e3a4-43f6-bc45-697dfe49f39f) Red Chair Pr.

Connolly, Sean. The Book of Wildly Spectacular Sports Science: 54 All-Star Experiments. 2016. (Irresponsible Science Ser.). (ENG., Illus.). 256p. (J). (gr. 4-7). 14.95 (978-0-7611-8928-2(9), 18928) Workman Publishing Co., Inc.

Cool Sports Facts. 2011. (Cool Sports Facts Ser.). (ENG.). 24p. (gr. k-1). pap. 375.30 (978-1-4296-7401-0(6), Capstone Pr.) Capstone.

Cooper, Brigitte Henry. Sports Report. Heitz, Tim, illus. 2017. (Game Face Ser.). (ENG.). 112p. (J). (gr. 2-5). lib. bdg. 38.50 (978-1-5321-3045-8(7), 27047, Calico Chapter Bks.) ABDO Publishing Co.

Corrigan, Delia Stubbs & Tighe, Elizabeth. Go Team! Mascots of the SEC. 2008. (Illus.). 64p. (J). pap. 10.99 (978-0-9797040-0-0(6)) Go Team, LLC.

Crabtree Publishing, creator. Sports Starters. 2008. pap. (978-0-7787-3166-5(9)) Crabtree Publishing Co.

Creighton, Jayne. Sports. 2009. (Science Q & A Ser.). (Illus.). 48p. (YA). (gr. 5-8). pap. 10.95 (978-1-60596-071-5(3)); lib. bdg. 29.05 (978-1-60596-070-8(5)) Weigl Pubs., Inc.

Crossingham, John. Lacrosse in Action. 2003. (Sports in Action Ser.). (ENG., Illus.). 32p. (J). (gr. 4). pap. (978-0-7787-0349-5(5)) Crabtree Publishing Co.

Currie, Stephen. Cheating. 2007. (Ripped from the Headlines Ser.). (YA). (gr. 7-12). 23.95 (978-1-60217-011-7(8)) Erickson Pr.

Daredevil Sports. 2015. (Daredevil Sports Ser.). (ENG.). 32p. (J). (gr. 1-1). pap., pap., pap. 63.00 (978-1-4824-3451-4(2)) Stevens, Gareth Publishing LLLP.

Davies, Monika. No Way! Spectacular Sports Stories (Grade 7) 2nd rev. ed. 2017. (TIME(r): Informational Text Ser.). (ENG., Illus.). 48p. (J). (gr. 5-8). pap. 13.99 (978-1-4938-3609-3(9)) Teacher Created Materials, Inc.

—Spectacular Sports: Playing Like a Girl: Problem Solving (Grade 4) 2017. (Mathematics in the Real World Ser.). (ENG., Illus.). 32p. (J). (gr. 4-5). pap. 11.99 (978-1-4258-5552-9(0)) Teacher Created Materials, Inc.

Davis, Bela. Diseños en Los Deportes. 2018. (¡Diseños Divertidos! (Patterns Are Fun!) Ser.).Tr. of Patterns in Sports. (SPA.). 24p. (J). (gr. -1-2). lib. bdg. 31.36 (978-1-5321-8377-5(1), 29947, Abdo Kids) ABDO Publishing Co.

—Patterns in Sports. 2018. (Patterns Are Fun! Ser.). (ENG., Illus.). 24p. (J). (gr. -1-2). lib. bdg. 31.36 (978-1-5321-0797-9(8), 28155, Abdo Kids) ABDO Publishing Co.

Deportes Atleticos, 6 vols., Vol. 2. (Explorers. Exploradores Nonfiction Sets Ser.). (SPA.). 32p. (gr. 3-6). 44.95 (978-0-7699-0648-5(6)) Shortland Pubns. (U. S. A.) Inc.

Deportes Con Pelota, 6 vols., Vol. 3. (Explorers. Exploradores Nonfiction Sets Ser.). (SPA.). (gr. 3-6). (978-0-7699-0660-7(5)) Shortland Pubns. (U. S. A.) Inc.

Doeden, Matt. More Than a Game: Race, Gender, & Politics in Sports. 2019. (ENG., Illus.). 64p. (J). (gr. 5-12). lib. bdg. 34.65 (978-1-5415-4094-1(8), 82a60aff-b280-455c-94bf-9444fd815bac, Millbrook Pr.) Lerner Publishing Group.

Domnauer, Teresa. Ultimate Sports, Level 3. 2007. (Extreme Readers Level 3 - Confident Reader Ser.). (ENG., Illus.). 32p. (gr. k-3). 16.19 (978-0-7696-4338-0(8)) School Specialty, Incorporated.

Doudna, Kelly. Play Fair!, 1 vol. 2007. (Character Concepts Ser.). (Illus.). 24p. (J). (gr. k-3). lib. bdg. 24.21 (978-1-59928-739-3(0), SandCastle) ABDO Publishing Co.

Downey, Glen R. The 10 Greatest Sports Showdowns. 2008. 14.99 (978-1-55448-535-2(5)) Scholastic Library Publishing.

—The 10 Most Shocking Sports Scandals. 2007. 14.99 (978-1-55448-505-5(3)) Scholastic Library Publishing.

Downs, Alison. Dream Jobs in Sports Retail, 1 vol. 2017. (Great Careers in the Sports Industry Ser.). (ENG., Illus.). 128p. (J). (gr. 7-7). pap. 21.00 (978-1-5081-7865-1(8), b539e715-441a-49bb-b5b7-22bbeecc7e08) Rosen Publishing Group, Inc., The.

Duncan, David A. Dude, Where's Your Helmet?, 1 vol. 2009. (ENG., Illus.). 48p. (J). pap. (978-1-897522-59-2(2)) RMB Rocky Mountain Bks.

Dyan, Penelope. The Rain in Spain — -A Kid's Guide to Barcelona, Spain. Weigand, John D., photos by. 2011. (Illus.). 38p. pap. 12.95 (978-1-935630-56-2(3)) Bellissima Publishing, LLC.

Egendorf, Laura K. Performance Enhancing Drugs. 2007. (Compact Research Ser.). (Illus.). 96p. (YA). (gr. 7-12). lib. bdg. 43.93 (978-1-60152-003-6(4)) ReferencePoint Pr., Inc.

Egendorf, Laura K., ed. Girls & Sports, 1 vol. 2012. (Issues That Concern You Ser.). (ENG., Illus.). 120p. (gr. 7-10). lib. bdg. 43.63 (978-0-7377-5693-7(4), 21ed1593-1e88-48e9-a471-dc74e016eb20, Greenhaven Publishing) Greenhaven Publishing LLC.

El-Hewie, Mohamed F. Essentials of Weightlifting & Strength Training. 2nd rev. exp. ed. 2005. (Illus.). 700p. lib. bdg. 85.00 (978-0-9719581-9-7(X)) Shaymaa Publishing Corp.

Eliot, Hannah. Turkeys Strike Out: And Other Fun Facts. Spurgeon, Aaron, illus. 2016. (Did You Know? Ser.). (ENG.). 32p. (J). (gr. -1-3). 17.99 (978-1-4814-5169-7(3)); pap. 6.99 (978-1-4814-5168-0(5)) Little Simon. (Little Simon).

Encarnacion, Elizabeth. Sports Stadiums. 2007. (Qeb Buildings at Work Ser.). (Illus.). 36p. (J). (gr. 4-7). lib. bdg. 19.95 (978-1-59566-372-6(X)) QEB Publishing Inc.

Entrenamiento Deportivo Series, 10 vols., Set. 2003. (Entrenamiento Deportivo (Sports Training) Ser.). (SPA., Illus.). (J). (gr. 1-2). 131.35 (978-0-8239-6913-5(4), 154d9ebf-6dad-4f9f-9bdb-fe9c2363efd5, Editorial Buenas Letras) Rosen Publishing Group, Inc., The.

ESPN Staff. The ESPN Book, No. 9. 2005. (ENG.). 96p. (J). pap. 3.99 (978-0-7868-1261-5(3)) Hyperion Pr.

Evans, Gwydion, et al. Ar Dîm Duw: Cyfres o Sesiynau Sydd Yn Defnyddio Byd Chwaraeon I Son Am y Ffydd Gristnogol. 2005. (WEL., Illus.). 24p. pap. (978-1-85994-036-5(6)) Cyhoeddiadau'r Gair.

Extreme! 2010. (Extreme! Ser.). (ENG.). 32p. (gr. 3-4). pap. 1526.40 (978-1-4296-5204-9(7), Capstone Pr.) Capstone.

Extreme Sports, 6 bks. Incl. In-Line Skating. Woods, Bob. lib. bdg. 25.67 (978-0-8368-3722-3(3), 6845160e-f898-4a40-a67e-297369c18320); Mountain Biking. Kelley, K. C. lib. bdg. 25.67 (978-0-8368-3723-0(1), 0676d3d5-9a31-4fc9-a9f7-5eea6719d82c); Snowboarding. Woods, Bob. lib. bdg. 25.67 (978-0-8368-3725-4(8), 6bb21f20-f8ad-4c2c-b740-e4b6f75ae3fa); Stunt Bicycle Riding. Kelley, K. C. (J). lib. bdg. 25.67 (978-0-8368-3726-1(6), 893c67ff-0780-417e-8b01-d5943661cbc5); Water Sports. Woods, Bob. lib. bdg. 25.67 (978-0-8368-3727-8(4), 01e8d627-d049-4468-a538-e53dd25ef0b2); 24p. (gr. 2-4). 2003., Gareth Stevens Learning Library (Illus.). 2003. Set lib. bdg. 127.60 o.p. (978-0-8368-3721-6(5)) Stevens, Gareth Publishing LLLP.

Feldman, Heidi C. Great Jobs in Sports. 2019. (Great Jobs Ser.). (ENG.). 80p. (YA). (gr. 6-12). (978-1-68282-527-3(2)) ReferencePoint Pr., Inc.

Felix, Rebecca. Patterns in Sports. 2015. (21st Century Basic Skills Library: Patterns All Around Ser.). (ENG., Illus.). 24p. (gr. k-3). 26.35 (978-1-63188-921-9(4), 206008) Cherry Lake Publishing.

—They Won One! 2014. (Hear Homophones Here Ser.). (ENG.). 16p. (J). (gr. k-2). lib. bdg. 25.65 (978-1-60753-573-7(4), 15829) Amicus.

Ferguson, creator. Coaches & Fitness Professionals. 2nd rev. ed. 2008. (Ferguson's Careers in Focus Ser.). (ENG.). 188p. (gr. 6-12). 32.95 (978-0-8160-7284-2(1), P179088, Ferguson Publishing Company) Infobase Holdings, Inc.

—Sports. 4th rev. ed. 2008. (Ferguson's Careers in Focus Ser.). (ENG.). 204p. (gr. 6-12). 32.95 (978-0-8160-7287-3(6), P179091, Ferguson Publishing Company) Infobase Holdings, Inc.

Fisher, Doris & Gibbs, D. L. Bowling Alley Adjectives, 1 vol. 2008. (Grammar All-Stars: the Parts of Speech Ser.). (ENG., Illus.). 32p. (gr. 2-4). (J). lib. bdg. 28.67 (978-0-8368-8901-7(0), a7aaa854-c1e7-40b0-a7e1-9ed6e3ce91bd); pap. 11.50 (978-0-8368-8908-6(8), 0f0747e3-e3b1-4137-ad29-d69efa69fbc2) Stevens, Gareth Publishing LLLP. (Gareth Stevens Learning Library).

—Hole-In-One Adverbs, 1 vol. 2008. (Grammar All-Stars: the Parts of Speech Ser.). (ENG., Illus.). 32p. (gr. 2-4). (J). lib. bdg. 28.67 (978-0-8368-8902-4(9), 0d4c48df-eeb2-46e5-9653-e570750250c8); pap. 11.50 (978-0-8368-8909-3(6), 076d0f0f-9d59-4be8-a370-f1638e90f268) Stevens, Gareth Publishing LLLP. (Gareth Stevens Learning Library).

—Home Run Verbs, 1 vol. 2008. (Grammar All-Stars: the Parts of Speech Ser.). (ENG., Illus.). 32p. (gr. 2-4). (J). lib. bdg. 28.67 (978-0-8368-8903-1(7), 485ccf4c-01a8-4058-bf69-cd30bb96bb9f); pap. 11.50 (978-0-8368-8910-9(X), ae8f5ce9-59dc-4504-96bb-ed8f1d8311e2) Stevens, Gareth Publishing LLLP. (Gareth Stevens Learning Library).

—Slam Dunk Pronouns, 1 vol. 2008. (Grammar All-Stars: the Parts of Speech Ser.). (ENG., Illus.). 32p. (gr. 2-4). (J). lib. bdg. 28.67 (978-0-8368-8904-8(5), 9230da51-dfd1-4565-bf2d-14e8766b4581); pap. 11.50 (978-0-8368-8911-6(8), 09a0ba83-3db0-49cb-b7ce-80fbef6cfd11) Stevens, Gareth Publishing LLLP. (Gareth Stevens Learning Library).

—Tennis Court Conjunctions, 1 vol. 2008. (Grammar All-Stars: the Parts of Speech Ser.). (ENG., Illus.). 32p. (gr. 2-4). (J). lib. bdg. 28.67 (978-0-8368-8905-5(3), 3a183b48-e0f8-499c-99ff-c0350484ac63); pap. 11.50 (978-0-8368-8912-3(6), f4f1f366-51f3-4c8c-b855-dd6a60139152) Stevens, Gareth Publishing LLLP. (Gareth Stevens Learning Library).

—Touchdown Nouns, 1 vol. 2008. (Grammar All-Stars: the Parts of Speech Ser.). (ENG., Illus.). 32p. (gr. 2-4). (J). lib. bdg. 28.67 (978-0-8368-8906-2(1), 16d86d7d-4647-4d8b-bb8c-f9ef0a9cceeb); pap. 11.50 (978-0-8368-8913-0(4), cc6b7941-1946-47aa-a0e3-6aa9e45fc202) Stevens, Gareth Publishing LLLP. (Gareth Stevens Learning Library).

Fishman, Jon M. Crayola (r) Team Colors: The Wonderful, Colorful World of Sports. 2019. (ENG., Illus.). 32p. (J). (gr. k-3). lib. bdg. 27.99 (978-1-5415-5471-9(X), 6fb79650-5b33-4f4d-bac7-b50d4b3d8f1e, Lerner Pubns.) Lerner Publishing Group.

Fitzpatrick, Tom & Grogan, Jerry. All about Gaelic Football. 2004. (ENG., Illus.). 32p. pap. 15.95 (978-0-86278-892-6(7)) O'Brien Pr., Ltd., The IRL. Dist: Casemate Pubs. & Bk. Distributors, LLC.

Forest, Christopher. The Kids' Guide to Sports Ethics, 1 vol. 2014. (SI Kids Guide Bks.). (ENG.). 48p. (J). (gr. 4-5). lib. bdg. 32.65 (978-1-4765-4153-2(1), 124258) Capstone.

Frederick, Shane. The Kids' Guide to Sports Media, 1 vol. 2014. (SI Kids Guide Bks.). (ENG.). 48p. (J). (gr. 4-5). lib. bdg. 32.65 (978-1-4765-4152-5(3), 124257) Capstone.

—Stamina Training for Teen Athletes: Exercises to Take Your Game to the Next Level, 1 vol. 2012. (Sports Training Zone Ser.). (ENG.). 48p. (J). (gr. 5-9). pap. 8.19 (978-1-4296-8001-1(6), 118333) Capstone.

Frederick, Shane & Hetrick, Hans. Record Breakers. 2017. (Record Breakers Ser.). (ENG., Illus.). 32p. (J). (gr. 3-9). 119.96 (978-1-5157-3801-5(9), 25487, Capstone Pr.) Capstone.

Freedman, Jeri. Dream Jobs in Sports Management & Administration, 1 vol. 2012. (Great Careers in the Sports Industry Ser.). (ENG., Illus.). 136p. (J). (gr. 7-7). lib. bdg. 44.13 (978-1-4488-6901-5(3), 49d7a34b-b3f2-4b16-89c0-1b35b55f8012) Rosen Publishing Group, Inc., The.

Fridell, Ron. Sports Technology. 2009. pap. 52.95 (978-0-7613-4785-9(2)) Lerner Publishing Group.

Furgang, Kathy. Dream Jobs in Sports Law, 1 vol. 2014. (Great Careers in the Sports Industry Ser.). (ENG., Illus.). 136p. (J). (gr. 7-7). 44.13 (978-1-4777-7527-1(7), 82b892c3-fbd4-4697-9cc9-0a423f717b2f) Rosen Publishing Group, Inc., The.

Furgang, Kathy & Furgang, Adam. Dream Jobs in Stadium & Sports Facility Operations, 1 vol. 2014. (Great Careers in the Sports Industry Ser.). (ENG., Illus.). 128p. (J). (gr. 7-7). 44.13 (978-1-4777-7529-5(3), 16a07468-b909-4c75-86e1-41ba99986853) Rosen Publishing Group, Inc., The.

Gaarder-Juntti, Oona. Shapes in Sports, 1 vol. 2013. (Shapes Everywhere Ser.). (ENG.). 24p. (J). (gr. k-4). lib. bdg. 32.79 (978-1-61783-415-8(7), 13334, Super SandCastle) ABDO Publishing Co.

Galvin, Laura. Oh Where, Oh Where Has My Little Dog Gone? Villnave, Erica Pelton, illus. 2008. (ENG.). 32p. (J). (gr. -1-2). 9.95 (978-1-59249-860-4(4)) Soundprints.

Game Day: From the Locker Room to the Press Box (and Everything in Between) 2011. (Game Day (Sports Illustrated for Kids) Ser.). (ENG.). 32p. (gr. 3-4). pap. 190.80 (978-1-4296-6451-6(7)) Capstone.

Ganeri, Anita. Get Active! Orange Band. 2017. (Cambridge Reading Adventures Ser.). (ENG., Illus.). 16p. pap. 7.35 (978-1-108-43973-2(X)) Cambridge Univ. Pr.

—Who Is the Greatest? 2 Wayfarers. 2017. (Cambridge Reading Adventures Ser.). (ENG., Illus.). 32p. pap. 8.60 *(978-1-108-43617-5(X))* Cambridge Univ. Pr.

Gardner, Jane P. Sports Science, Vol. 11. Lewin, Russ, ed. 2015. (Science 24/7 Ser.). (Illus.). 48p. (J). (gr. 5). lib. bdg. 20.95 *(978-1-4222-3414-3(2))* Mason Crest.

Gardner, Robert. The Physics of Sports Science Projects, 1 vol. 2013. (Exploring Hands-On Science Projects Ser.). (ENG.). 128p. (gr. 5-6). pap. 13.88 *(978-1-4644-0222-7(1),* 0257ffe0-eddf-4a37-8257-690a9f6c4745); lib. bdg. 30.60 *(978-0-7660-4146-2(8),* 1cfcb805-a91a-4b9a-91f7-951871acdc1a) Enslow Publishing, LLC.

Gerber, Larry. Dream Jobs in Sports Refereeing, 1 vol. 2014. (Great Careers in the Sports Industry Ser.). (ENG., Illus.). 128p. (J). (gr. 7-7). 44.13 *(978-1-4777-7525-7(0),* ebf2e9c6-9265-461e-b7f6-3711172c0eaf) Rosen Publishing Group, Inc., The.

Gifford, Clive. Sports. 2010. (Healthy Lifestyles Ser.). 48p. (J). 35.65 *(978-1-60753-088-6(0))* Amicus Learning.

—Teamwork in Soccer, 1 vol. 2010. (Spotlight on Soccer Ser.). (ENG., Illus.). 32p. (J). (gr. 4-4). lib. bdg. 28.93 *(978-1-61532-609-9(X),* 0067f2e5-de79-4757-9c00-0c368a18f13d, PowerKids Pr.) Rosen Publishing Group, Inc., The.

—Tell Me about Sports, 8 vols., Set. Incl. Baseball. 31.21 *(978-0-7614-4453-4(X),* b85b3e71-bfbc-48fa-bc6a-aba61b9ac99a); Basketball. 31.21 *(978-0-7614-4455-8(6),* 07f8f32b-2ee5-4da9-841f-6f1611a45f6d); Football. 31.21 *(978-0-7614-4456-5(4),* e8b76e79-2fb6-4dee-8521-b0186722106f); Martial Arts. 31.21 *(978-0-7614-4457-2(2),* 860d3c39-ca9a-4240-b9c7-f0b79739ab29); Running. 31.21 *(978-0-7614-4459-6(9),* b08933e2-6b99-4e1b-8466-19a6a2e8b2ea); Soccer. 31.21 *(978-0-7614-4460-2(2),* 26d87a40-55f5-48a2-b4dd-69753ed9635c); Swimming. (Illus.). 31.21 *(978-0-7614-4462-6(9),* 69c73e57-5015-492c-88fe-6e5fa7ffac2e); Tennis. 31.21 *(978-0-7614-4463-3(7),* 4daa638d-adec-4d4f-a9ac-41559367ee8c); 32p. (gr. 4-4). 2010. (Tell Me about Sports Ser.). 2009. Set lib. bdg. 228.00 o.p. *(978-0-7614-4452-7(1),* Cavendish Square) Cavendish Square Publishing LLC.

Gigliotti, Jim. Animal Sports, 1 vol. 2011. (Extreme Sports Ser.). (ENG., Illus.). 32p. (J). (gr. 2-4). 32.65 *(978-1-4109-4216-6(3),* 115656); pap. 8.29 *(978-1-4109-4223-4(6),* 115662) Capstone. (Raintree).

—Sports Arena & Event Management, Vol. 10. Ferrer, Al, ed. 2015. (Careers off the Field Ser.). (Illus.). 64p. (J). (gr. 7). lib. bdg. 23.95 *(978-1-4222-3266-8(2))* Mason Crest.

—STEM in Sports. 2015. (STEM in Sports Ser.). (Illus.). 64p. (J). (gr. 7). 23.95 *(978-1-4222-3233-0(6))* Mason Crest.

Girls Join the Team, 12 vols. 2016. (Girls Join the Team Ser.). 24p. (gr. 3-3). (ENG.). 151.62 *(978-1-5081-4900-2(3),* f592b709-0b88-420c-8471-887231e2be0d); pap. 49.50 *(978-1-4994-2472-0(8))* Rosen Publishing Group, Inc., The. (PowerKids Pr.).

Girls' SportsZone: Set Of 8, 6 vols. 2013. (Girls' SportsZone Ser.: 8). (ENG.). 48p. (J). (gr. 3-6). lib. bdg. 205.32 *(978-1-61783-983-2(3),* 8864, SportsZone) ABDO Publishing Co.

Gitlin, Martin. Dream Jobs in Sports Finance & Administration, 1 vol. 2014. (Great Careers in the Sports Industry Ser.). (ENG., Illus.). 144p. (YA). (gr. 7-7). 44.13 *(978-1-4777-7520-2(X),* ceded921-9f4a-4aa0-b0e7-196fda742fab) Rosen Publishing Group, Inc., The.

—Dream Jobs in Sports Scouting, 1 vol. 2014. (Great Careers in the Sports Industry Ser.). (ENG., Illus.). 128p. (YA). (gr. 7-7). 44.13 *(978-1-4777-7518-9(8),* 4b58cda5-90ec-437a-b37c-d2ec000feef5) Rosen Publishing Group, Inc., The.

—Referee. 2013. (Earning $50,000 - $100,000 with a High School Diploma or Less Ser.: 14). 64p. (J). (gr. 7-18). 22.95 *(978-1-4222-2899-9(1))* Mason Crest.

Gitlin, Martin, ed. Athletes, Ethics, & Morality, 1 vol. 2018. (Opposing Viewpoints Ser.). (ENG.). 200p. (gr. 10-12). lib. bdg. 50.43 *(978-1-5345-0410-3(9),* 7bf1750b-46ca-4ad1-8582-0fce3b60918c, Greenhaven Publishing) Greenhaven Publishing LLC.

Gitlin, Marty. A Dream Job As a Sports Statistician, 1 vol. 2017. (Great Careers in the Sports Industry Ser.). (ENG., Illus.). 128p. (J). (gr. 7-7). 44.13 *(978-1-5383-8138-0(9),* 80f657fb-a281-4368-97b4-1fb9474bb74b); pap. 21.00 *(978-1-5081-7861-3(5),* 636db28e-6189-4bec-98f3-c9c860619426) Rosen Publishing Group, Inc., The.

—Sports' Most Memorable Characters. 2017. (Wild World of Sports Ser.). (ENG., Illus.). 48p. (J). (gr. 3-6). lib. bdg. 34.21 *(978-1-5321-1368-0(4),* 27666, SportsZone) ABDO Publishing Co.

Gleisner, Jenna Lee. Sports in Winter. 2018. (Welcoming the Seasons Ser.). (ENG.). 24p. (J). (gr. -1-2). lib. bdg. 32.79 *(978-1-5038-2389-1(X),* 212232) Child's World, Inc, The.

Goh, Michelle. The 10 Best Cinderella Stories in Sports. 2008. 14.99 *(978-1-55448-495-9(2))* Scholastic Library Publishing.

Going Pro, 12 vols. 2014. (Going Pro Ser.). (ENG.). 32p. (J). (gr. 3-4). lib. bdg. 169.62 *(978-1-4824-1647-3(6),* eef1f078-beac-4323-8ae4-2d22c503e792) Stevens, Gareth Publishing LLLP.

Gonzales, Debbie. Girls with Guts! The Road to Breaking Barriers & Bashing Records. Gibbon, Rebecca, illus. 2019. 32p. (J). (gr. 1-4). lib. bdg. 16.99 *(978-1-58089-747-1(9))* Charlesbridge Publishing, Inc.

Gonzalez, Tony & Brown, Greg. Tony Gonzalez: Catch & Connect. 2004. (Football Ser.). (Illus.). 48p. (J). 15.95 *(978-0-9634650-8-5(2))* Positively for Kids, Inc.

Goodstein, Madeline. Sports Science Fair Projects, 1 vol. 2015. (Prize-Winning Science Fair Projects Ser.). (ENG.). 128p. (gr. 7-7). lib. bdg. 38.93 *(978-0-7660-7026-4(3),* 3e3997a0-ca8c-4617-b8a2-0586ef09d1e4) Enslow Publishing, LLC.

Goranson, Christopher D. Danny Harf: Wakeboarding Superstar, 1 vol. 2004. (Extreme Sports Biographies Ser.). (ENG., Illus.). 64p. (YA). (gr. 5-8). lib. bdg. 37.13 *(978-1-4042-0066-1(5),* 71e33346-ad16-40bf-857d-3461d0d5dbf4) Rosen Publishing Group, Inc., The.

Gosman, Gillian. Simple Machines in Sports, 1 vol. 2014. (Simple Machines Everywhere Ser.). (ENG., Illus.). 24p. (J). (gr. 2-3). 25.27 *(978-1-4777-6829-7(7),* 34603074-eae7-45c7-b80f-b288e150f932, PowerKids Pr.) Rosen Publishing Group, Inc., The.

Grace, Nicki Clausen & Grace, Jeff. Basketball Science. 2017. (Got Game Ser.). (ENG.). 32p. (J). (gr. 4-6). pap. 9.99 *(978-1-64466-184-0(5),* 11416); (Illus.). lib. bdg. *(978-1-68072-144-7(5),* 10472) Black Rabbit Bks. (Bolt).

Graubart, Norman D. The Science of Basketball, 1 vol. 2015. (Sports Science Ser.). (ENG., Illus.). 32p. (J). (gr. 4-5). pap. 11.00 *(978-1-4994-1064-8(6),* daa596d0-bf1e-4dd0-9d31-7b13fee32576, PowerKids Pr.) Rosen Publishing Group, Inc., The.

Graves, Will. Greatest Teams That Didn't Win It All. 2017. (Wild World of Sports Ser.). (ENG., Illus.). 48p. (J). (gr. 3-6). lib. bdg. 34.21 *(978-1-5321-1364-2(1),* 27662, SportsZone) ABDO Publishing Co.

Great Careers in the Sports Industry: Set 2, 12 vols. 2014. (Great Careers in the Sports Industry Ser.). (ENG.). 160p. (YA). (gr. 7-7). 264.78 *(978-1-4777-7522-6(6),* ff8daf26-bee7-431d-aa0e-5c4750baa08a) Rosen Publishing Group, Inc., The.

Great Careers in the Sports Industry: Sets 1-2. 2014. (Great Careers in the Sports Industry Ser.). 160p. (YA). (gr. 7-12). 409.50 *(978-1-4777-8098-5(X))* Rosen Publishing Group, Inc., The.

Greathead, Helen. Supersports, 1 vol. 2016. (What Would You Choose? Ser.). (ENG.). 32p. (J). (gr. 4-5). pap. 11.50 *(978-1-4824-6118-3(8),* 39317cc1-a625-4c08-bbfe-e2064f185604) Stevens, Gareth Publishing LLLP.

Green, Sara. Nike. 2015. (Brands We Know Ser.). (ENG., Illus.). 24p. (J). (gr. 3-8). 27.95 *(978-1-62617-210-4(2))*; pap. 8.99 *(978-1-61891-250-3(X),* 12002) Bellwether Media. (Pilot Bks.).

Group/McGraw-Hill, Wright. Take-Twos Sports Vol. 2: Early Fluency - Complete Kit. (gr. 2-18). 420.50 *(978-0-322-09173-3(X))* Wright Group/McGraw-Hill.

—Take-Twos Sports Vol. 2: Early Fluency - Student Book Set - 1 Each of 12 Titles. (gr. 2-18). 69.95 *(978-0-322-09301-0(5))* Wright Group/McGraw-Hill.

Gutman, Dan. My Weird School Fast Facts: Sports. Paillot, Jim, illus. 2016. (My Weird School Fast Facts Ser.). (ENG.). 176p. (J). (gr. 1-5). pap. 5.99 *(978-0-06-230617-3(0),* HarperCollins) HarperCollins Pubs.

Haldy, Emma E. Florence Griffith Joyner. Bane, Jeff, illus. 2016. (My Early Library: My Itty-Bitty Bio Ser.). (ENG.). 24p. (J). (gr. k-1). 30.64 *(978-1-63471-019-0(3),* 208156) Cherry Lake Publishing.

Hamilton, Tracy Brown. Dream Jobs in Sports Equipment Design, 1 vol. 2017. (Great Careers in the Sports Industry Ser.). (ENG.). 128p. (J). (gr. 7-7). 44.13 *(978-1-5383-8140-3(0),* 94190847-71d9-4cfb-8415-258be7f6fa63); pap. 21.00 *(978-1-5081-7862-0(3),* 2fe611b9-109b-4c4d-a8af-531e598b11f9) Rosen Publishing Group, Inc., The.

Hammelef, Danielle S. Behind-The-Scenes Pro Sports Careers. 2017. (Behind the Glamour Ser.). (ENG., Illus.). 64p. (J). (gr. 4-8). lib. bdg. 31.99 *(978-1-5157-4896-0(0),* 134480, Capstone Pr.) Capstone.

Harris, Duchess & Conley, Kate. Gender & Race in Sports. 2018. (Race & Sports Ser.). (ENG., Illus.). 112p. (J). (gr. 6-12). lib. bdg. 41.36 *(978-1-5321-1670-4(5),* 30592, Essential Library) ABDO Publishing Co.

Harris, Duchess & Henzel, Cynthia Kennedy. Politics & Protest in Sports. 2018. (Race & Sports Ser.). (ENG., Illus.). 112p. (J). (gr. 6-12). lib. bdg. 41.36 *(978-1-5321-1671-1(3),* 30594, Essential Library) ABDO Publishing Co.

Harris, Duchess & Miller, Michael. Race & Sports Management. 2018. (Race & Sports Ser.). (ENG., Illus.). 112p. (J). (gr. 6-12). lib. bdg. 41.36 *(978-1-5321-1673-5(X),* 30598, Essential Library) ABDO Publishing Co.

Harris, Duchess & Mooney, Carla. Fighting Stereotypes in Sports. 2018. (Race & Sports Ser.). (ENG., Illus.). 112p. (J). (gr. 6-12). lib. bdg. 41.36 *(978-1-5321-1669-8(1),* 30590, Essential Library) ABDO Publishing Co.

Harris, Duchess & Streissguth, Tom. Race & College Sports. 2018. (Race & Sports Ser.). (ENG., Illus.). 112p. (J). (gr. 6-12). lib. bdg. 41.36 *(978-1-5321-1672-8(1),* 30596, Essential Library) ABDO Publishing Co.

Harris, Duchess & Wheeler, Jill C. Race in Sports Media Coverage. 2018. (Race & Sports Ser.). (ENG., Illus.). 112p. (J). (gr. 6-12). lib. bdg. 41.36 *(978-1-5321-1674-2(8),* 30600, Essential Library) ABDO Publishing Co.

Hay DeSimone, Corkey. Future Sports Legend Board Book: An Early Introduction to Sports in Maryland. Hay DeSimone, Corkey, illus. 2006. (Illus.). (J). bds. 4.99 *(978-0-9747921-5-6(2))* Gentle Giraffe Pr.

Healthy for Life (Set), 8 vols. 2007. (21st Century Skills Library: Healthy for Life Ser.). (ENG.). 32p. (gr. 4-8). 256.56 *(978-1-60279-105-3(8),* 200028) Cherry Lake Publishing.

Helget, N. & McCollum, Sean. Full STEAM Sports. 2018. (Full STEAM Sports Ser.). (ENG.). 32p. (J). (gr. 3-6). 119.96 *(978-1-5435-3049-0(4),* 28506, Capstone Pr.) Capstone.

Heling, Kathryn & Hembrook, Deborah. Clothesline Clues to Sports People Play. Davies, Andy Robert, illus. 2015. (ENG.). 40p. (J). (gr. -1-2). lib. bdg. 14.95 *(978-1-58089-602-3(2))* Charlesbridge Publishing, Inc.

Herman, Gail & Who HQ. What Are the Paralympic Games? Thomson, Andrew, illus. 2020. (What Was? Ser.). 112p. (J). (gr. 3-7). 5.99 *(978-1-5247-9262-6(4))*; lib. bdg. 15.99 *(978-1-5247-9263-3(2))* Penguin Young Readers Group. (Penguin Workshop).

Herweck, Diana. In the Game: An Athlete's Life, 1 vol. 2nd rev. ed. 2013. (TIME for KIDS(r): Informational Text Ser.). (ENG., Illus.). 48p. (J). (gr. 4-5). lib. bdg. 29.96 *(978-1-4807-1100-6(4))* Teacher Created Materials, Inc.

Herzog, Brad. A Is for Amazing Moments: A Sports Alphabet. Rose, Melanie, illus. 2015. (Av2 Fiction Readalong 2016 Ser.). (ENG.). (J). (gr. 1-4). lib. bdg. 34.28 *(978-1-4896-3729-1(X),* AV2 by Weigl) Weigl Pubs., Inc.

—A Is for Amazing Moments: A Sports Alphabet. Rose, Melanie, illus. 2008. (Sports Alphabet Ser.). (ENG.). 40p. (J). (gr. 1-4). 17.95 *(978-1-58536-360-5(X),* 202145) Sleeping Bear Pr.

Hetrick, Hans. Breaking Barriers. 2017. (Real Heroes of Sports Ser.). (ENG., Illus.). 32p. (J). (gr. 3-9). lib. bdg. 26.65 *(978-1-5157-4434-4(5),* 134125, Capstone Pr.) Capstone.

High Five Reading: Sports / Adventure [Really Good Stuff]. 2010. (High Five Reading Ser.). pap. 90.00 *(978-1-4296-5360-2(4),* Red Brick Learning) Capstone.

Hoena, B. A. The Science of Hockey with Max Axiom, Super Scientist. 2015. (Science of Sports with Max Axiom Ser.). (ENG., Illus.). 32p. (J). (gr. 3-9). lib. bdg. 31.32 *(978-1-4914-6086-3(5),* 128985, Capstone Pr.) Capstone.

Hoena, Blake. Sports Illustrated Kids All-Star Jokes! 2017. (Sports Illustrated Kids All-Star Jokes! Ser.). (ENG., Illus.). 64p. (J). (gr. 2-6). 98.60 *(978-1-4965-5106-1(0),* 26970, Stone Arch Bks.) Capstone.

Hoena, Blake & Dreier, David L. The Science of Sports with Max Axiom. Cacau, Caio, illus. 2015. (Science of Sports with Max Axiom Ser.). (ENG.). 32p. (J). (gr. 3-9). 133.28 *(978-1-4914-6914-9(5),* 22968, Capstone Pr.) Capstone.

Hofer, Charles. Motorcycles, 1 vol. 2007. (World's Fastest Machines Ser.). (ENG., Illus.). 24p. (J). (gr. 2-3). lib. bdg. 26.27 *(978-1-4042-4177-0(9),* ce9d5c96-1723-438b-81c4-cf50583583cd, PowerKids Pr.) Rosen Publishing Group, Inc., The.

Hogenkamp, S. All Sorts of Sports: Learning the or Sound. 2009. (PowerPhonics Ser.). 24p. (gr. 1-1). 39.90 *(978-1-60851-431-1(5),* PowerKids Pr.) Rosen Publishing Group, Inc., The.

Holden, Pam. We Like Sports, 1 vol. 2015. (ENG., Illus.). 16p. (-1). pap. *(978-1-77654-120-1(0),* Red Rocket Readers) Flying Start Bks.

Holder, Sherie. More Amazing Sports Photos: More Funny, Famous, & Fantastic Photographs from the World of Sports. rev. ed. Date not set. 32p. (J). pap. 3.95 *(978-1-886749-13-9(2))* Sports Illustrated For Kids.

Hollow, Michele C. Nifty Thrifty Sports Crafts, 1 vol. 2007. (Nifty Thrifty Crafts for Kids Ser.). (ENG., Illus.). 32p. (gr. 3-3). lib. bdg. 26.60 *(978-0-7660-2782-4(1),* 6721e36d-47e3-4ee5-a591-df5a0d3f7f08, Enslow Elementary) Enslow Publishing, LLC.

Horn, Geoffrey M. Sports Therapist, 1 vol. 2008. (Cool Careers: Helping Careers Ser.). (ENG.). 32p. (gr. 3-3). pap. 11.50 *(978-0-8368-9329-8(8),* 15eca04e-76c2-45d7-8de3-7ce4de80e92a); lib. bdg. 28.67 *(978-0-8368-9196-6(1),* 6b71aba5-04fc-450e-8801-b68fe7757499) Stevens, Gareth Publishing LLLP.

Howse, Jennifer. Sports: African American History. 2011. (J). (gr. 5-8). pap. 14.95 *(978-1-61690-664-1(2),* AV2 by Weigl); (Illus.). 48p. (YA). (gr. 1-4). 29.99 *(978-1-61690-660-3(X))* Weigl Pubs., Inc.

Hudson, Amanda. This Is My Ball / Ésta Es Mi Pelota, 1 vol. 2008. (Our Toys / Nuestros Juguetes Ser.). (SPA & ENG., Illus.). 16p. (J). (gr. k-k). lib. bdg. 21.67 *(978-0-8368-9256-7(9),* 7a578453-083d-411a-aee4-e2afbde908e1, Weekly Reader Leveled Readers) Stevens, Gareth Publishing LLLP.

Hughes, Morgan. Cheerleading. 2005. (Junior Sports Ser.). (Illus.). 32p. (gr. 2-4). 19.95 *(978-1-59515-194-0(X))* Rourke Educational Media.

Hustad, Douglas. Gaming & Professional Sports Teams. 2018. (ESports: Game On! Ser.). (ENG.). 48p. (J). (gr. 5-8). 29.27 *(978-1-59953-965-2(9))* Norwood Hse. Pr.

Ingham, Anne. The Ball Book. 2012. 28p. pap. 21.99 *(978-1-4691-8747-1(7))* Xlibris Corp.

Inside Sports: Set 2, 12 vols. 2014. (Inside Sports Ser.). (ENG.). 96p. (YA). (gr. 6-6). lib. bdg. 211.74 *(978-1-62275-598-1(7),* e5424c9f-b4af-4941-8b65-a6d07243a196, Britannica Educational Publishing) Rosen Publishing Group, Inc., The.

Ivy, Darlene Sigda. Working in Sports. 2018. (Career Files Ser.). (ENG., Illus.). 32p. (J). (gr. 3-6). 32.80 *(978-1-63235-449-5(7),* 13842, 12-Story Library) Bookstaves, LLC.

Jobs to Do. 2017. (J). *(978-0-7166-7945-5(0))* World Bk., Inc.

Johanson, Paula. Supercharged Sports. 2017. (Techno Planet Ser.). (Illus.). 32p. (J). (gr. 5-5). *(978-0-7787-3603-5(2))* Crabtree Publishing Co.

Johnson, Haley S. Amazing Human Feats of Endurance. 2018. (Superhuman Feats Ser.). (ENG., Illus.). 32p. (J). (gr. 4-6). lib. bdg. 28.65 *(978-1-5435-4123-6(2),* 139077, Capstone Pr.) Capstone.

Johnson, Jeremy. Unusual & Awesome Jobs in Sports: Pro Team Mascot, Pit Crew Member, & More. 2015. (You Get Paid for THAT? Ser.). (ENG., Illus.). 32p. (J). (gr. 3-9). lib. bdg. 28.65 *(978-1-4914-2032-4(4),* 127510, Capstone Pr.) Capstone.

Johnson, Robin. Sports in Different Places. 2017. (Learning about Our Global Community Ser.). 24p. (J). (gr. 2-2). *(978-0-7787-3656-1(3))*; pap. *(978-0-7787-3665-3(2))* Crabtree Publishing Co.

Jones, Rob Lloyd. Look Inside Sports. 2012. (Look Inside Board Bks). 16p. (J). bds. 15.99 *(978-0-7945-3250-5(0),* Usborne) EDC Publishing.

Jones, Tammy. I Like to Play Sports. 2009. (Sight Word Readers Set A Ser.). (J). 3.49 net. *(978-1-60719-135-3(0))* Newmark Learning LLC.

Kallen, Stuart A. Careers If You Like Sports. 2017. (Career Discovery Ser.). (ENG.). 80p. (YA). (gr. 5-12). *(978-1-68282-142-8(0))* ReferencePoint Pr., Inc.

Kamberg, Mary-Lane. A Dream Job As a Sports Agent, 1 vol. 2017. (Great Careers in the Sports Industry Ser.). (ENG.). 128p. (J). (gr. 7-7). 44.13 *(978-1-5383-8136-6(2),* e1dfcbf1-3274-407e-84c3-18aca92b1f77); pap. 21.00 *(978-1-5081-7860-6(7),* 6fba67f5-48b9-4b8e-bdc2-ffdf0e426502) Rosen Publishing Group, Inc., The.

Katz, Ben & Nyman, Debbie. The 10 Greatest Sports Dynasties. 2008. 14.99 *(978-1-55448-525-3(8))* Scholastic Library Publishing.

Kaufman, Gabriel. Sporting Events: From Baseball to Skateboarding. 2006. (Which Came First? Ser.). (Illus.). 32p. (YA). (gr. 3-6). lib. bdg. 28.50 *(978-1-59716-132-9(2))* Bearport Publishing Co., Inc.

Kawa, Katie. Mujeres en Los Deportes (Women in Sports), 1 vol. 2015. (Ellas Abrieron Camino (Women Groundbreakers) Ser.). (SPA.). 32p. (J). (gr. 4-5). 27.93 *(978-1-4994-0518-7(9),* 7fcffca2-3a20-4f13-bf5f-b932e00c4f01, PowerKids Pr.) Rosen Publishing Group, Inc., The.

—Staying Fit with Sports!, 1 vol. 2013. (Rosen Readers Ser.). (ENG.). 24p. (J). (gr. 3-3). pap. 8.25 *(978-1-4777-2590-0(3),* ffcab87a-9029-4d6e-9ccd-e440bb9234e8); pap. 49.50 *(978-1-4777-2592-4(X))* Rosen Publishing Group, Inc., The. (Rosen Classroom).

—Women in Sports, 1 vol. 2015. (Women Groundbreakers Ser.). (ENG., Illus.). 32p. (J). (gr. 4-5). 27.93 *(978-1-4994-1095-2(6),* 5aa4029d-0fbd-4fa2-a071-7370fb3048bd, PowerKids Pr.) Rosen Publishing Group, Inc., The.

Kelley, K. C. Choose a Career Adventure at the Olympics. 2016. (Bright Futures Press: Choose a Career Adventure Ser.). (ENG., Illus.). 32p. (J). (gr. 4-6). 32.07 *(978-1-63471-914-8(X),* 208977) Cherry Lake Publishing.

—Choose a Career Adventure at the Super Bowl. 2016. (Bright Futures Press: Choose a Career Adventure Ser.). (ENG., Illus.). 32p. (J). (gr. 4-6). 32.07 *(978-1-63471-915-5(8),* 208981) Cherry Lake Publishing.

—Stadium. 2018. (Field Trips, Let's Go! Ser.). (ENG.). 16p. (J). (gr. k-2). 25.65 *(978-1-68151-309-6(9),* 14863) Amicus.

Kerr, Jim. Sports. 2010. (Media Power Ser.). 48p. (YA). (gr. 5-9). 35.65 *(978-1-60753-115-9(1))* Amicus Learning.

Kerstetter, Greg. Work in the Professional Sports Industry. 2019. (Career Finder Ser.). (ENG.). 80p. (YA). (gr. 6-12). 41.27 *(978-1-68282-733-8(X),* BrightPoint Pr.) ReferencePoint Pr., Inc.

Kids, National Geographic. Sports Sticker Activity Book. 2019. 56p. (J). (gr. -1-k). pap. 6.99 *(978-1-4263-3365-1(X),* National Geographic Kids) Disney Publishing Worldwide.

Kleist, Nick. Super Sports Numbers: Understand Place Value, 1 vol. 2014. (Math Masters: Number & Operations in Base Ten Ser.). (ENG.). 24p. (J). (gr. 2-2). 25.27 *(978-1-4777-6401-5(1),* 2ccfad17-15d1-436e-814a-4d96a3abb0fd); pap. 8.25 *(978-1-4777-4666-0(8),* 87bbad0d-8297-443f-9552-a8111c462add) Rosen Publishing Group, Inc., The. (Rosen Classroom).

Kortemeier, Todd. Courage in Sports. 2018. (Sports Build Character Ser.). (ENG., Illus.). 32p. (J). (gr. 2-3). lib. bdg. 31.35 *(978-1-63517-531-8(3),* 1635175313, Focus Readers) North Star Editions.

—It's Great to Be a Fan in California. 2018. (Sports Nation Ser.). (ENG., Illus.). 48p. (J). (gr. 5-6). pap. 11.95 *(978-1-64185-028-5(0),* 1641850280); lib. bdg. 34.21 *(978-1-63517-926-2(2),* 1635179262) North Star Editions. (Focus Readers).

—It's Great to Be a Fan in Colorado. 2018. (Sports Nation Ser.). (ENG., Illus.). 48p. (J). (gr. 5-6). pap. 11.95 *(978-1-64185-029-2(9),* 1641850299); lib. bdg. 34.21 *(978-1-63517-927-9(0),* 1635179270) North Star Editions. (Focus Readers).

—It's Great to Be a Fan in Illinois. 2018. (Sports Nation Ser.). (ENG., Illus.). 48p. (J). (gr. 5-6). pap. 11.95 *(978-1-64185-031-5(0),* 1641850310); lib. bdg. 34.21 *(978-1-63517-929-3(7),* 1635179297) North Star Editions. (Focus Readers).

—It's Great to Be a Fan in Ohio. 2018. (Sports Nation Ser.). (ENG., Illus.). 48p. (J). (gr. 5-6). pap. 11.95 *(978-1-64185-037-7(X),* 164185037X); lib. bdg. 34.21 *(978-1-63517-935-4(1),* 1635179351) North Star Editions. (Focus Readers).

—12 Reasons to Love Lacrosse. 2018. (ENG.). 32p. (gr. 3-6). pap. 9.95 *(978-1-62143-550-1(4))* Pr. Room Editions LLC.

Kortemeier, Tom. Pro Sports by the Numbers. 2016. (Pro Sports by the Numbers Ser.). (ENG., Illus.). 32p. (J). (gr. 3-9). 122.60 *(978-1-4914-9073-0(X),* 24530, Capstone Pr.) Capstone.

Koya, Lena & La Bella, Laura. Female Athletes, 1 vol. 2017. (Women in the World Ser.). (ENG., Illus.). 112p. (J). (gr. 6-6). 38.80 *(978-1-5081-7718-0(X),* c6f6606e-e453-42a4-a7e5-41d59a4abc07); pap. 18.65 *(978-1-5081-7855-2(0),* d61265e0-9446-4d57-8cb9-e90843e4ee8f) Rosen Publishing Group, Inc., The.

Kreisman, Rachelle. Things We Do: A Kids' Guide to Community Activity. Haggerty, Tim, illus. 2015. (Start Smart (tm) — Community Ser.). (ENG.). 32p. (J). (gr. 1-3). E-Book 39.99 *(978-1-937529-51-2(7))* Red Chair Pr.

Kurtz, Kevin. What Makes Sports Gear Safer? 2015. (Engineering Keeps Us Safe Ser.). (ENG., Illus.). 32p. (J). (gr. 4-6). E-Book 39.99 *(978-1-4677-8650-8(0),* Lerner Pubns.) Lerner Publishing Group.

Kuskowski, Alex. Know Your Numbers: Sports. 2014. (Numbers 1-20 Ser.). (ENG.). 24p. (J). (gr. -1-3). lib. bdg. 29.93 *(978-1-62403-268-4(0),* 1598, SandCastle) ABDO Publishing Co.

La Bella, Laura. Women & Sports, 1 vol. 2012. (Young Woman's Guide to Contemporary Issues Ser.). (ENG., Illus.). 112p. (YA). (gr. 8-9). lib. bdg. 39.80 *(978-1-4488-8398-1(9),* 3ada87d5-7266-4e3c-90d6-2aefb94a6e61) Rosen Publishing Group, Inc., The.

Laks Gorman, Jacqueline. The Playground / el Parque, 1 vol. 2004. (I Like to Visit / Me Gusta Visitar Ser.). (Illus.). 24p. (gr. k-2). (ENG & SPA.). pap. 9.15 *(978-0-8368-4605-8(2),* e88b3f05-bf56-4c66-82ef-683c241275c9); (SPA & ENG., lib. bdg. 24.67 *(978-0-8368-4598-3(6),* 73c99212-fc4d-4e63-837f-4217008e847f) Stevens, Gareth Publishing LLLP. (Weekly Reader Leveled Readers).

Lancaster, Scott B. Fair Play: Making Organized Sports a Great Experience for Your Kids. 2004. 194p. reprint ed. pap. 15.00 *(978-0-7567-8419-5(0))* DIANE Publishing Co.

Lanier, Wendy Hinote. The Science of Sports, 1 vol. 2016. (Super-Awesome Science Ser.). (ENG., Illus.). 48p. (J). (gr. 4-8). lib. bdg. 35.64 *(978-1-68078-250-9(9),* 22101) ABDO Publishing Co.

LeBoutillier, Nate. Ultimate Pro Team Guides, 1 vol., Set. Incl. Ultimate Guide to Pro Basketball Teams. (ENG.). 72p. (J). (gr. 3-9). 2010. lib. bdg. 35.32 *(978-1-4296-4821-9(X),* 103348, Capstone Pr.); (Ultimate Pro Team Guides (Sports Illustrated for Kids) Ser.). (ENG.). 72p. 2010. Set lib. bdg. 138.60 o.p. *(978-1-4296-4823-3(6))* Capstone.

Lee, Michelle. Spectacular Sports. 2019. (Mathematics in the Real World Ser.). (ENG., Illus.). 32p. (gr. 5-8). pap. 11.99 *(978-1-4258-5882-7(1))* Teacher Created Materials, Inc.
Let's Talk Sports! 2016. (Let's Talk Sports! Ser.). 00032p. (J). pap. 63.00 *(978-1-4824-5836-7(5))* Stevens, Gareth Publishing LLLP.
Levete, Sarah. Maker Projects for Kids Who Love Sports. 2017. (Be a Maker! Ser.). (ENG., Illus.). 32p. (J). (gr. 5-5). *(978-0-7787-2877-1(3))*; pap. *(978-0-7787-2891-7(9))* Crabtree Publishing Co.
Libal, Joyce & Simons, Rae. Professional Athlete & Sports Official. Riggs, Ernestine G. & Gholar, Cheryl, eds. 2013. (Careers with Character Ser.: 18). 96p. (J). (gr. 7-18). 22.95 *(978-1-4222-2763-3(4))* Mason Crest.
Linde, Barbara M. Ice Hockey: Science on Ice, 1 vol. 2017. (Science Behind Sports Ser.). (ENG.). 112p. (gr. 7-7). lib. bdg. 41.03 *(978-1-5345-6113-7(7),* 7d175cbe-e878-4cf0-8ed9-0878ff74b811, Lucent Pr.) Greenhaven Publishing LLC.
Living Legends of Sports: Set 1, 32 vols. 2015. (Living Legends of Sports Ser.). (ENG.). 48p. (J). (gr. 5-6). 454.56 *(978-1-68048-196-9(7),* a5d1ae75-93a3-4adc-ac67-3bbf1569cdf0, Britannica Educational Publishing) Rosen Publishing Group, Inc., The.
LoaderMandy. Amazing Young Sports People Level 1 Beginner/Elementary. 2010. (Cambridge Experience Readers Ser.). (ENG.). 48p. pap. 14.75 *(978-84-8323-572-0(2))* Cambridge Univ. Pr.
Loh-Hagan, Virginia. Extreme Cliff Diving. 2016. (Nailed It! Ser.). (ENG., Illus.). 32p. (J). (gr. 4-8). 32.07 *(978-1-63471-089-3(4),* 208467, 45th Parallel Press) Cherry Lake Publishing.
—Extreme Downhill Ski Racing. 2016. (Nailed It! Ser.). (ENG., Illus.). 32p. (J). (gr. 4-8). 32.07 *(978-1-63471-092-3(4),* 208479, 45th Parallel Press) Cherry Lake Publishing.
—Extreme MotoGP. 2016. (Nailed It! Ser.). (ENG., Illus.). 32p. (J). (gr. 4-8). 32.07 *(978-1-63471-091-6(6),* 208475, 45th Parallel Press) Cherry Lake Publishing.
—Stadiums. 2017. (21st Century Junior Library: Extraordinary Engineering Ser.). (ENG., Illus.). 24p. (J). (gr. 2-5). lib. bdg. 29.21 *(978-1-63472-166-0(7),* 209236) Cherry Lake Publishing.
—Wacky Sports. 2017. (Stranger Than Fiction Ser.). (ENG., Illus.). 32p. (J). (gr. 4-8). lib. bdg. 32.07 *(978-1-63472-889-8(0),* 209982, 45th Parallel Press) Cherry Lake Publishing.
Louck, Cheryl. The ABC's of Motocross. Zielinski, Dave, photos by. 2003. (Illus.). 24p. (J). per. 14.95 *(978-0-9744230-0-5(9))* Louck, Cheryl.
Loya, Allyssa. Sporty Algorithms. 2020. (Sports Coding Concepts Ser.). (ENG., Illus.). 32p. (J). (gr. 1-3). 27.99 *(978-1-5415-7691-9(8),* 06928cdf-6bde-4660-b0fe-80cf5bc61aa6, Lerner Pubns.) Lerner Publishing Group.
—Sporty Bugs & Errors. 2020. (Sports Coding Concepts Ser.). (ENG., Illus.). 32p. (J). (gr. 1-3). lib. bdg. 27.99 *(978-1-5415-7693-3(4),* 1652dcbc-12ea-452e-8e60-3dbb030fcb03, Lerner Pubns.) Lerner Publishing Group.
—Sporty Conditionals. 2020. (Sports Coding Concepts Ser.). (ENG., Illus.). 32p. (J). (gr. 1-3). lib. bdg. 27.99 *(978-1-5415-7692-6(6),* 8de3d337-ae57-4fde-892d-5517f84a2a02, Lerner Pubns.) Lerner Publishing Group.
Luke, Andrew. Lacrosse, Vol. 13. 2016. (Inside the World of Sports Ser.: Vol. 13). (ENG., Illus.). 80p. (J). (gr. 7-12). 24.95 *(978-1-4222-3464-8(9))* Mason Crest.
Lyon, Drew & McCollum, Sean. The Best & Worst of Sports: A Guide to the Game's Good, Bad, & Ugly. 2018. (Best & Worst of Sports Ser.). (ENG.). 32p. (J). (gr. 3-9). 122.60 *(978-1-5435-0631-0(3),* 27682, Capstone Pr.) Capstone.
Lyon, Drew & Omoth, Tyler. Pro Sports Team Guides. 2017. (Pro Sports Team Guides). (ENG.). 72p. (J). (gr. 3-9). 149.28 *(978-1-5157-8870-6(9),* 27152, Capstone Pr.) Capstone.
MacDonald, Margaret. What Does the Referee Do? 2011. (Learn-Abouts Ser.). (Illus.). 16p. (J). pap. 7.95 *(978-1-59920-632-5(3))* Black Rabbit Bks.
MacDonald, Steele Lisa. The Science of Waves & Surfboards. rev. ed. 2018. (Smithsonian: Informational Text Ser.). (ENG., Illus.). 32p. (J). (gr. 3-5). pap. 11.99 *(978-1-4938-6705-9(9))* Teacher Created Materials, Inc.
Mack, Gail. Kickboxing, 1 vol. 2012. (Martial Arts in Action Ser.). (ENG.). 48p. (gr. 5-5). lib. bdg. 32.64 *(978-0-7614-4936-2(1),* d8f32aa3-567f-49f4-bb7b-1e8056990c3f) Cavendish Square Publishing LLC.
MacKinnon, Christopher. Canadian Sports Sites for Kids: Places Named for Speedsters, Scorers, & Other Sportsworld Citizens. 2012. (ENG., Illus.). 144p. (J). pap. 14.99 *(978-1-4597-0705-4(2))* Dundurn Pr. CAN. Dist: Publishers Group West (PGW).
—Canadian Sports Sites for Kids: Places Named for Speedsters, Scorers, & Other Sportsworld Citizens (Large Print 16pt) 2013. 208p. pap. *(978-1-4596-6305-3(5))* ReadHowYouWant.com, Ltd.
MacNab, Chris. Weight Training. 2005. (Sports Injuries Ser.). (Illus.). 64p. (YA). lib. bdg. 19.95 *(978-1-59084-641-4(9))* Mason Crest.
marcovitz, hal. How Serious a Problem Is Drug Use in Sports? 2012. (Illus.). 80p. (J). lib. bdg. *(978-1-60152-448-5(X))* ReferencePoint Pr., Inc.
Marini, Matt. Analytics: Sports Stats & More, Vol. 10. Ferrer, Al, ed. 2015. (Careers off the Field Ser.). (Illus.). 64p. (J). (gr. 7). lib. bdg. 23.95 *(978-1-4222-3265-1(4))* Mason Crest.
Markegard, Blake. Rey Mysterio. 2014. (Wrestling Superstars Ser.). (ENG., Illus.). 24p. (J). (gr. 3-7). pap. 8.99 *(978-1-61891-239-8(9),* 11990, Epic Bks.) Bellwether Media.
Marquardt, Meg. Great e-Sports Debates. 2018. (Great Sports Debates Ser.). (ENG.). 48p. (J). (gr. 3-6). lib. bdg. 34.21 *(978-1-5321-1443-4(5),* 29028, SportsZone) ABDO Publishing Co.
Marthaler, Jon. Offbeat Sports. 2017. (Wild World of Sports Ser.). (ENG., Illus.). 48p. (J). (gr. 3-6). lib. bdg. 34.21 *(978-1-5321-1366-6(8),* 27664, SportsZone) ABDO Publishing Co.
Martin, Dayna. Sports. 2018. (Illus.). 31p. (J). *(978-1-4896-9661-8(X),* AV2 by Weigl) Weigl Pubs., Inc.
Martin, Oscar, Jr., creator. Sports Legends l.t. ed. 2003. (Illus.). 25p. (J). E-Book 19.95 incl. cd-rom *(978-0-9748416-6-3(8))* Build Your Story.
Mason, Paul. How to Design the World's Best Sports Stadium: In 10 Simple Steps. 2019. (How to Design the World's Best Ser.). (ENG.). 32p. (J). (gr. 4-6). pap. 12.99 *(978-0-7502-9200-9(8),* Wayland) Hachette Children's Group GBR. Dist: Hachette Bk. Group.
—Sports Heroes of Ancient Greece. 2010. (ENG.). 32p. (J). (gr. 3-5). *(978-0-7787-9911-5(5))*; pap. *(978-0-7787-9932-0(8))* Crabtree Publishing Co.
—Training for Sports, 4 vols., Set. Incl. Improving Flexibility. (Illus.). 32p. (YA). (gr. 5-6). 2011. lib. bdg. 30.27 *(978-1-4488-3299-6(3),* 6946b587-9086-4e0b-90ba-9e1f729b7388); (Training for Sports Ser.). (Illus.). 32p. 2011. Set lib. bdg. 28.50 o.p. *(978-1-4488-3310-8(8),* PowerKids Pr.) Rosen Publishing Group, Inc., The.
Mattern, Joanne. Famous Mystics & Psychics. 2004. (gr. 7-10). 27.45 *(978-1-59018-558-2(7))* Cengage Gale.
—It's Great to Be a Fan in New York. 2018. (Sports Nation Ser.). (ENG., Illus.). 48p. (J). (gr. 5-6). pap. 11.95 *(978-1-64185-035-3(3),* 1641850353); lib. bdg. 34.21 *(978-1-63517-933-0(5),* 1635179335) North Star Editions. (Focus Readers).
—It's Great to Be a Fan in Pennsylvania. 2018. (Sports Nation Ser.). (ENG., Illus.). 48p. (J). (gr. 5-6). pap. 11.95 *(978-1-64185-038-4(8),* 1641850388); lib. bdg. 34.21 *(978-1-63517-936-1(X),* 163517936X) North Star Editions. (Focus Readers).
—So, You Want to Work in Sports? The Ultimate Guide to Exploring the Sports Industry. 2014. (Be What You Want Ser.). (ENG., Illus.). 224p. (J). (gr. 3-7). pap. 9.99 *(978-1-58270-448-7(1))* Aladdin/Beyond Words.
McAdon, Brad & Williams, Mary E., eds. Understanding & Engaging Humanity, 1 vol. 2009. (Opposing Viewpoints Ser.). (ENG.). 296p. (gr. 10-12). pap. 34.80 *(978-0-7377-4811-6(7),* d8646434-b680-496f-af2c-0ea3d51b741a, Greenhaven Publishing) Greenhaven Publishing LLC.
McCabe, Matthew. It's Great to Be a Fan in Florida. 2018. (Sports Nation Ser.). (ENG., Illus.). 48p. (J). (gr. 5-6). pap. 11.95 *(978-1-64185-030-8(2),* 1641850302); lib. bdg. 34.21 *(978-1-63517-928-6(9),* 1635179289) North Star Editions. (Focus Readers).
—It's Great to Be a Fan in Minnesota. 2018. (Sports Nation Ser.). (ENG., Illus.). 48p. (J). (gr. 5-6). pap. 11.95 *(978-1-64185-034-6(5),* 1641850345); lib. bdg. 34.21 *(978-1-63517-932-3(7),* 1635179327) North Star Editions. (Focus Readers).
Mccabe, Matthew. It's Great to Be a Fan in Florida. 2019. (Illus.). 48p. (J). *(978-1-64185-131-2(7),* Focus Readers) North Star Editions.
McDaniel, Melissa. Pushing the Limits: A Chapter Book. 2004. (True Tales Ser.). (ENG., Illus.). 48p. (J). 22.50 *(978-0-516-23734-3(9),* Children's Pr.) Scholastic Library Publishing.
McDonnell, Vincent. The Story of the GAA. 2009. (ENG.). 146p. (J). pap. 13.95 *(978-1-905172-96-2(6),* Collins Pr., The) M.H. Gill & Co. U. C. IRL. Dist: Dufour Editions, Inc.
McFee, Shane. Whitewater Rafting, 1 vol. 2008. (Living on the Edge Ser.). (ENG., Illus.). 24p. (J). (gr. 2-3). lib. bdg. 26.27 *(978-1-4042-4218-0(X),* 01f65719-002b-4442-90be-1244f518a052) Rosen Publishing Group, Inc., The.
McKinney, Donna B. It's Great to Be a Fan in North Carolina. 2018. (Sports Nation Ser.). (ENG., Illus.). 48p. (J). (gr. 5-6). pap. 11.95 *(978-1-64185-036-0(1),* 1641850361); lib. bdg. 34.21 *(978-1-63517-934-7(3),* 1635179343) North Star Editions. (Focus Readers).
—It's Great to Be a Fan in North Carolina. 2019. (Illus.). 48p. (J). *(978-1-64185-137-4(6),* Focus Readers) North Star Editions.
McLeish, Ewan. Sports Industry, 1 vol. 2010. (Closer Look: Global Industries Ser.). (ENG., Illus.). 48p. (J). (gr. 7-7). lib. bdg. 34.47 *(978-1-4358-9634-5(3),* e392c70d-abc8-43d3-a032-dacf4f0817dd, Rosen Reference) Rosen Publishing Group, Inc., The.
McMurchy-Barber, Gina. When Children Play: The Story of Right to Play, 1 vol. 2013. (Ripple Effects Ser.). (ENG.). 56p. (YA). (gr. 5-10). 19.95 *(978-1-55455-154-5(4),* 254c4623-4fbf-4088-9811-ad6bc7ec8564) Trifolium Bks., Inc. CAN. Dist: Firefly Bks., Ltd.
McNeil, Niki, et al. HOCPP 1128 the History of Sports. 2006. spiral bd. 12.50 *(978-1-60308-128-3(3))* In the Hands of a Child.
McPherson, Stephanie Sammartino. Doping in Sports: Winning at Any Cost? 2016. (ENG., Illus.). 104p. (YA). (gr. 6-12). E-Book 51.99 *(978-1-4677-9576-0(3),* Twenty-First Century Bks.) Lerner Publishing Group.
Meeks, Connor. Sports! Have Fun & Stay Healthy, 1 vol. 2013. (InfoMax Readers Ser.). (ENG.). 24p. (J). (gr. 3-3). pap. 8.25 *(978-1-4777-2646-4(2),* c5c4f6b4-5d45-48bc-b224-165181dd22e7); pap. 49.50 *(978-1-4777-2647-1(0))* Rosen Publishing Group, Inc., The. (Rosen Classroom).
Mental X 2003. (Illus.). 32p. (YA). pap. 5.50 *(978-0-9745066-8-5(0))* Sports In Mind.
Milet Publishing Staff. My First Bilingual Book-Sports, 1 vol. 2012. (My First Bilingual Book Ser.). (ENG., Illus.). 24p. (J). (gr. k — 1). bds. 7.99 *(978-1-84059-761-5(5))* Milet Publishing.
—My First Bilingual Book-Sports (English-Bengali), 1 vol. 2012. (My First Bilingual Book Ser.). (ENG., Illus.). 24p. (J). (gr. k — 1). bds. 7.99 *(978-1-84059-749-3(6))* Milet Publishing.
—My First Bilingual Book-Sports (English-Farsi), 1 vol. 2012. (My First Bilingual Book Ser.). (ENG., Illus.). 24p. (J). (gr. k — 1). bds. 7.99 *(978-1-84059-751-6(8))* Milet Publishing.
—My First Bilingual Book-Sports (English-German), 1 vol. 2012. (My First Bilingual Book Ser.). (ENG & GER., Illus.). 24p. (J). (gr. k — 1). bds. 7.99 *(978-1-84059-753-0(4))* Milet Publishing.
—My First Bilingual Book-Sports (English-Korean), 1 vol. 2012. (My First Bilingual Book Ser.). (ENG., Illus.). 24p. (J). (gr. k — 1). bds. 7.99 *(978-1-84059-755-4(0))* Milet Publishing.
—My First Bilingual Book-Sports (English-Polish), 1 vol. 2012. (My First Bilingual Book Ser.). (ENG & POL., Illus.). 24p. (J). (gr. k — 1). bds. 7.99 *(978-1-84059-756-1(9))* Milet Publishing.
—My First Bilingual Book-Sports (English-Russian), 1 vol. 2012. (My First Bilingual Book Ser.). (ENG., Illus.). 24p. (J). (gr. k — 1). bds. 7.99 *(978-1-84059-758-5(5))* Milet Publishing.
—My First Bilingual Book-Sports (English-Spanish), 1 vol. 2012. (My First Bilingual Book Ser.). (ENG & SPA., Illus.). 24p. (J). (gr. k — 1). bds. 7.99 *(978-1-84059-760-8(7))* Milet Publishing.
—My First Bilingual Book-Sports (English-Urdu), 1 vol. 2012. (My First Bilingual Book Ser.). (ENG., Illus.). 24p. (J). (gr. k — 1). bds. 7.99 *(978-1-84059-762-2(3))* Milet Publishing.
—My First Bilingual Book-Sports (English-Vietnamese), 1 vol. 2012. (My First Bilingual Book Ser.). (ENG., Illus.). 24p. (J). (gr. k — 1). bds. 7.99 *(978-1-84059-763-9(1))* Milet Publishing.
—Sports, 1 vol. 2012. (My First Bilingual Book Ser.). (ENG., Illus.). 24p. (J). (gr. k — 1). bds. 7.99 *(978-1-84059-757-8(7))*; bds. 7.99 *(978-1-84059-750-9(X))*; bds. 7.99 *(978-1-84059-748-6(8))* Milet Publishing.
—Sports - My First Bilingual Book, 1 vol. 2012. (My First Bilingual Book Ser.). (ENG & FRE., Illus.). 24p. (J). (gr. k — 1). bds. 7.99 *(978-1-84059-752-3(6))*; bds. 7.99 *(978-1-84059-759-2(3))* Milet Publishing.
—Sports (English-Italian), 1 vol. 2012. (My First Bilingual Book Ser.). (ENG & ITA., Illus.). 24p. (J). (gr. k — 1). bds. 7.99 *(978-1-84059-754-7(2))* Milet Publishing.
Miller, Connie Colwell. You Can Follow the Rules: Cheat or Play Fair? Assanelli, Victoria, illus. 2019. (Making Good Choices Ser.). (ENG.). 24p. (J). (gr. 1-3). pap. 9.99 *(978-1-68152-476-4(7),* 11062) Amicus.
Miller, Karen. Girls & Sports. 2009. (Opposing Viewpoints Ser.). (ENG., Illus.). 224p. (gr. 10-12). 48.80 *(978-0-7377-4516-0(9))* Cengage Gale.
Miller, Karen, ed. Girls & Sports, 1 vol. 2009. (Opposing Viewpoints Ser.). (ENG., Illus.). 224p. (gr. 10-12). pap. 34.80 *(978-0-7377-4517-7(7),* d81262e7-c5da-4600-ae67-6b29e15e10bd, Greenhaven Publishing) Greenhaven Publishing LLC.
Miller, Ray, et al. Beat the Clock Sports. Thorp, Cameron, illus. 2007. 48p. (J). *(978-0-439-02189-0(8))* Scholastic, Inc.
Mis Deportes Favoritos / My Favorite Sports, 12 vols. 2014. (Mis Deportes Favoritos / My Favorite Sports Ser.). (SPA & ENG.). 24p. (J). (gr. k-k). 145.62 *(978-1-4824-1186-7(5),* 2f7f5a92-4644-4f15-b3c7-82b431244016) Stevens, Gareth Publishing LLLP.
Mitchell-Hughes, Kimberley. The 10 Most Extreme Sports. 2008. 14.99 *(978-1-55448-555-0(X))* Scholastic Library Publishing.
Mooney, Carla. African Americans in Sports, 1 vol. 2012. (Lucent Library of Black History Ser.). (ENG., Illus.). 112p. (gr. 7-7). lib. bdg. 41.03 *(978-1-4205-0675-4(7),* 88a1cf1e-ae7d-4b91-8ebd-7bb05793b0a6, Lucent Pr.) Greenhaven Publishing LLC.
—Dream Jobs in Sports Personnel, 1 vol. 2017. (Great Careers in the Sports Industry Ser.). (ENG.). 128p. (J). (gr. 7-7). 44.13 *(978-1-5383-8142-7(7),* 5a1128ad-58ca-40e2-9b7a-6eab98faeabf) Rosen Publishing Group, Inc., The.
—For People Who Love Sports, 1 vol. 2016. (Cool Careers Without College Ser.). (ENG., Illus.). 104p. (J). (gr. 7-7). 41.12 *(978-1-5081-7266-4(2),* b8fe6922-c39f-43ed-aaed-156f2429d96c) Rosen Publishing Group, Inc., The.
—Using Math in Sports, 1 vol. 2017. (Math You Will Actually Use Ser.). (ENG.). 48p. (J). (gr. 5-5). pap. 12.75 *(978-1-4994-3872-7(9),* 62af4930-13cc-4070-83e1-5e7f0b40c0f6, Rosen Central) Rosen Publishing Group, Inc., The.
Mooney, Carla, contrib. by. Dream Jobs in Sports Personnel, 1 vol. 2017. (Great Careers in the Sports Industry Ser.). (ENG.). 128p. (J). (gr. 7-7). pap. 21.00 *(978-1-5081-7863-7(1),* bb628a19-693c-45cc-9f4e-a96bd935ab7d) Rosen Publishing Group, Inc., The.
Moore, Elizabeth. Sports Rules, 1 vol. (Wonder Readers Next Steps: Social Studies). (ENG.). (gr. -1-1). 2013. 20p. (J). 25.32 *(978-1-4765-2364-4(9),* 122881) 2011. 16p. (J). pap. 6.25 *(978-1-4296-7871-1(2),* 118203) 2011. 16p. pap. 35.94 *(978-1-4296-8158-2(6))* Capstone. (Capstone Pr.).
Moore, Tijon Adamson. Pigeon Toed. Baker, David, illus. 2011. 28p. pap. 24.95 *(978-1-4560-0607-5(X))* America Star Bks.
Mullins, Patty Rutland. All about Sports with Inspector McQ. Ebert, Len, illus. 2004. (Treasure Tree Ser.). 32p. (J). *(978-0-7166-1645-0(9))* World Bk., Inc.
Murphy, Bernadette & Surridge, Gerry. Sport Readiness. 2004. (Illus.). 160p. pap. 14.95 *(978-0-673-58914-9(5))* Good Year Bks.
Murphy, Frank. Stand up for Sportsmanship. 2019. (21st Century Junior Library: Growing Character Ser.). (ENG., Illus.). 24p. (J). (gr. 2-5). pap. 12.79 *(978-1-5341-5032-4(3),* 213435); lib. bdg. 30.64 *(978-1-5341-4746-1(2),* 213434) Cherry Lake Publishing.
Murray, Stuart A. P. Score with Track & Field Math, 1 vol. 2013. (Score with Sports Math Ser.). (ENG.). 48p. (gr. 3-3). pap. 11.53 *(978-1-4644-0291-3(4),* a26aa89f-1efd-435d-a556-8ae2ad74f4af); lib. bdg. 27.93 *(978-0-7660-4176-9(X),* a54f2385-784f-490a-b8da-a7ca623984be) Enslow Publishing, LLC. (Enslow Elementary).
My Favorite Sport, 6 vols. 2004. (My Favorite Sport Ser.). (ENG.). 24p. (gr. 2-4). lib. bdg. 74.01 *(978-0-8368-4336-1(3),* 5e10661e-bde4-465f-bb34-426ea4ca30fe, Weekly Reader Leveled Readers) Stevens, Gareth Publishing LLLP.
My Favorite Sports, 12 vols. 2014. (My Favorite Sports Ser.). 24p. (J). (gr. k-k). (ENG.). 145.62 *(978-1-4824-0773-0(6),* 2c3bda48-2c07-482b-a7cc-b7716eaebda1); pap. 48.90 *(978-1-4824-1575-9(5))* Stevens, Gareth Publishing LLLP.
Myers, Jess. Make Me the Best Lacrosse Player. 2016. (Make Me the Best Athlete Ser.). (ENG., Illus.). 48p. (J). (gr. 4-6). lib. bdg. 34.21 *(978-1-68078-490-9(0),* 23789, SportsZone) ABDO Publishing Co.
Nagelhout, Ryan. Lacrosse: Who Does What?, 1 vol. 2017. (Sports: What's Your Position? Ser.). (ENG.). 32p. (J). (gr. 3-4). lib. bdg. 28.27 *(978-1-5382-0411-5(8),* 7c43bfc7-5206-48f5-8214-daf90a9ba2db) Stevens, Gareth Publishing LLLP.
—The Science of Hockey, 1 vol. 2015. (Sports Science Ser.). (ENG., Illus.). 32p. (J). (gr. 4-5). pap. 11.00 *(978-1-4994-1070-9(0),* f1734121-a05a-49ed-8ff6-b679a29bd6e5, PowerKids Pr.) Rosen Publishing Group, Inc., The.
Nardo, Don. Arts, Leisure, & Sport in Ancient Egypt. 2005. (Lucent Library of Historical Eras Ser.). (ENG., Illus.). 112p. (YA). (gr. 7-12). lib. bdg. 33.45 *(978-1-59018-706-7(7))* Cengage Gale.
—A Roman Gladiator. 2004. (Working Life Ser.). (ENG., Illus.). 112p. (J). 30.85 *(978-1-59018-480-6(7),* Lucent Bks.) Cengage Gale.
Nasium, James. African Americans in Sports. 2012. (J). pap. *(978-1-4222-2394-9(9))* Mason Crest.
National Geographic Kids. Weird but True Sports: 300 Wacky Facts about Awesome Athletics. 2016. (Weird but True Ser.: 2). (Illus.). 208p. (J). (gr. 3-7). pap. 8.99 *(978-1-4263-2467-3(7),* National Geographic Kids) Disney Publishing Worldwide.
Newcomb, Tim. STEM in Sports: Engineering. 2015. (STEM in Sports Ser.). 64p. (J). (gr. 7). lib. bdg. 23.95 *(978-1-4222-3231-6(X))* Mason Crest.
Nitz, Kristin Wolden. Track. 2003. (Play-by-Play Ser.). (Illus.). 80p. (J). (gr. 5-18). pap. 7.95 *(978-0-8225-9873-2(6))* Lerner Publishing Group.
Nussbaum, Ben. Communicate! Sports Speeches. 2018. (TIME(r): Informational Text Ser.). (ENG., Illus.). 48p. (J). (gr. 6-8). pap. 13.99 *(978-1-4258-5006-7(5))* Teacher Created Materials, Inc.
Omoth, Tyler. Major Sports Championships. 2018. (Major Sports Championships Ser.). (ENG.). 32p. (J). (gr. 3-9). 117.28 *(978-1-5435-0526-9(0),* 27657, Capstone Pr.) Capstone.
Omoth, Tyler, et al. For the Record Classroom Collection. 2012. (For the Record Ser.). (ENG.). 32p. (J). (gr. 4-6). pap., pap. 107.40 *(978-1-4296-9437-7(8),* 18627) Capstone.
—Six Degrees of Sports. 2015. (Six Degrees of Sports Ser.). (ENG.). 48p. (J). (gr. 3-8). 138.60 *(978-1-4914-2624-1(1),* 22621) Capstone.
O'Neill, Dan. Stubborn Gal: The True Story of an Undefeated Sled Dog Racer. Maisch, Klara, illus. 2015. (ENG.). 48p. 17.95 *(978-1-60223-272-3(5))* Univ. of Alaska Pr.
O'Shei, Tim. The World's Zaniest Sports. 2015. (Library of Weird Ser.). (ENG., Illus.). 32p. (J). (gr. 3-9). lib. bdg. 28.65 *(978-1-4914-2020-1(0),* 127496, Capstone Pr.) Capstone.
Page, Jason. Cycling, Shooting, & Show Jumping: Archery, Weightlifting, & a Whole Lot More. 2008. (Olympic Sports Ser.). (ENG., Illus.). 32p. (J). (gr. 3-7). pap. *(978-0-7787-4030-8(7))*; (gr. 4-7). lib. bdg. *(978-0-7787-4013-1(7))* Crabtree Publishing Co.
Pawlett, Mark. The Tae Kwon Do Handbook. 2009. (Martial Arts Ser.). 256p. (gr. 8-8). 79.90 *(978-1-61514-370-2(X))* Rosen Publishing Group, Inc., The.
Pearl, Melissa Sherman & Sherman, David A. FUNDaFIELD: Charities Started by Kids! 2017. (Community Connections: How Do They Help? Ser.). (ENG., Illus.). 24p. (J). (gr. 2-5). lib. bdg. 29.21 *(978-1-63472-843-0(2),* 209798) Cherry Lake Publishing.
Pernu, Dennis. The Complete Guide to Sports. 2015. (Illus.). 144p. (J). *(978-1-4351-6166-5(1))* Barnes & Noble, Inc.
Perritano, John. Gnarly Sports Injuries, 1 vol. 2017. (Red Rhino Nonfiction Ser.). (ENG., Illus.). 60p. (J). (gr. 4-7). pap. 11.95 *(978-1-68021-071-2(8))* Saddleback Educational Publishing, Inc.
—Gnarly Sports Injuries. 2017. (Red Rhino Nonfiction Ser.). (J). lib. bdg. 19.60 *(978-0-606-39893-0(7))* Turtleback.
—Sports Science, 1 vol. 2011. (Cool Science Ser.). (ENG.). 48p. (gr. 4-4). 31.21 *(978-1-60870-081-3(X),* 590c3487-42c1-426c-a8d4-62b508e6b67b) Cavendish Square Publishing LLC.
Personal Best: Set, 8 vols. 2008. (Personal Best Ser.). (ENG.). (J). (gr. 4-4). lib. bdg. 121.08 *(978-1-4358-2566-6(7),* d1cce255-dfda-4866-b1f2-fe3e069bc71d, PowerKids Pr.) Rosen Publishing Group, Inc., The.
Peterson, Brian C. Sports Marketing: Careers off the Field, Vol. 10. Ferrer, Al, ed. 2015. (Careers off the Field Ser.). (Illus.). 64p. (J). (gr. 7). 23.95 *(978-1-4222-3272-9(7))* Mason Crest.
Pezzi, Bryan. Terry Fox. 2010. (Illus.). 24p. *(978-1-77071-598-1(3))*; pap. *(978-1-77071-604-9(1))* Weigl Educational Pubs. Ltd.
Phelan, Glen. Forces & Motion in Sports: Set Of 6. 2011. (Navigators Ser.). (J). pap. 50.00 net. *(978-1-4108-5088-1(9))* Benchmark Education Co.
—Forces & Motion in Sports: Text Pairs. 2008. (Bridges/Navigators Ser.). (J). (gr. 6). 81.00 *(978-1-4108-8435-0(X))* Benchmark Education Co.
Play Like the Pros. 2010. (Play Like the Pros (Sports Illustrated for Kids) Ser.). (ENG.). 32p. (J). (gr. 3-4). pap., pap., pap. 27.80 *(978-1-4296-5740-2(5),* 170779) Capstone.
Play Like the Pros, 1 vol., Set. Incl. Play Football Like a Pro: Key Skills & Tips. Doeden, Matt. lib. bdg. 27.32 *(978-1-4296-4825-7(2),* 103351); Play Soccer Like a Pro: Key Skills & Tips. Forest, Christopher. lib. bdg. 27.32 *(978-1-4296-4827-1(9),* 103353); (J). (gr. 3-9). (Play Like the Pros (Sports Illustrated for Kids) Ser.). (ENG.). 32p. 2010. 107.85 o.p. *(978-1-4296-4828-8(7),* 169364) Capstone.
Play Like the Pros Classroom Collection. 2010. (Play Like the Pros (Sports Illustrated for Kids) Ser.). (ENG.). 32p. (J). (gr. 3-4). pap., pap., pap. 166.80 *(978-1-4296-5743-3(X),* 170782) Capstone.
Play Sports! 2017. (J). *(978-0-7166-7952-3(3))* World Bk., Inc.
Polydoros, Lori. Motorcycle Racing, 1 vol. 2013. (Super Speed Ser.). (ENG.). 32p. (J). (gr. 3-9). 27.32 *(978-1-4765-0121-5(1),* 122186, Capstone Pr.) Capstone.
—Strange but True Sports, 1 vol. 2010. (Strange but True Ser.). (ENG.). 32p. (J). (gr. 3-9). lib. bdg. 27.32 *(978-1-4296-4550-8(4),* 103035, Capstone Pr.) Capstone.
Ponto, Joanna & Hollow, Michele C. Kids Love Sports Crafts, 1 vol. 2018. (Kids Love Crafts Ser.). (ENG.). 32p. (J). (gr. 3-3). 26.93 *(978-1-9785-0201-7(X),* fb193ce4-b0af-46b4-a8f3-03b7ec181bbd) Enslow Publishing, LLC.
Powless, Justin, Neal and Giles & Benchmark Education Co. Staff. Lasting Legacies - America's First Game. 2014. (Text

S

Connections Ser.). (J). (gr. 5). *(978-1-4900-1374-9(1))* Benchmark Education Co.

Publ, Griffin. Easy Olympic Sports Reader, 6 Bks, Set. 2004. (U. S. Olympic Committee Easy Olympic Sports Readers Ser.). (Illus.). 16p. (J). pap. 17.95 *(978-1-58000-116-8(5))* Griffin Publishing Group.

Publications International Ltd. Staff, ed. Pub Time Sports Trivia. 2013. 192p. *(978-1-4508-7827-2(X)*, 145087827X) Publications International, Ltd.

Publishing, Ferguson. Professional Sports Organizations. 2012. (Career Launcher Ser.). (ENG.). 130p. (gr. 9). 34.95 *(978-0-8160-7964-3(1)*, P179133, Ferguson Publishing Company) Infobase Holdings, Inc.

Publishing, Ferguson, et al. Preparing for a Career in Sports. 2006. (What Can I Do Now? Ser.). (ENG., Illus.). 172p. (gr. 6-12). 22.95 *(978-0-89434-254-7(1)*, P053083, Ferguson Publishing Company) Infobase Holdings, Inc.

Raatma, Lucia. Sportsmanship. 2013. (21st Century Junior Library: Character Education Ser.). (ENG., Illus.). 24p. (J). (gr. 1-4). 29.21 *(978-1-62431-158-1(X)*, 202952); pap. 12.79 *(978-1-62431-290-8(X)*, 202954) Cherry Lake Publishing.

Rappoport, Ken. Ladies First: Women Athletes Who Made a Difference, 1 vol. 2010. (Illus.). 192p. (J). (gr. 3-7). pap. 8.95 *(978-1-56145-534-8(2))* Peachtree Publishing Co. Inc.

Reeves, Diane Lindsey. Making Choices on My Team. 2018. (21st Century Junior Library: Smart Choices Ser.). (ENG., Illus.). 24p. (J). (gr. k-2). pap. 12.79 *(978-1-5341-0888-2(2)*, 210916); lib. bdg. 30.64 *(978-1-5341-0789-2(4)*, 210915) Cherry Lake Publishing.

Ricciuti, Edward R. Somos un Equipo / We Are a Team, 1 vol. 2008. (Listos para Ir a la Escuela / Ready for School Ser.). (ENG & SPA., Illus.). 24p. (gr. k-1). lib. bdg. 25.50 *(978-0-7614-2436-9(9)*, 3cf0f01b-8774-40f9-8154-3301d5082d2a) Cavendish Square Publishing LLC.

—Somos un Equipo (We Are a Team), 1 vol. 2008. (Listos para Ir a la Escuela (Ready for School) Ser.). (SPA., Illus.). 24p. (gr. k-1). lib. bdg. 25.50 *(978-0-7614-2357-7(5)*, 26424f33-a340-4359-91d0-86218711856e) Cavendish Square Publishing LLC.

—We Are a Team, 1 vol. (Ready for School Ser.). (ENG.). 24p. (gr. k-1). 2008. pap. 9.23 *(978-0-7614-3271-5(X)*, 68e73a3c-795e-42ae-82e3-ebf5a3f4cc0c) 2007. (Illus.). lib. bdg. 25.50 *(978-0-7614-1994-5(2)*, ed3f0415-c9d5-4e5b-a4b0-d3364c724224, Cavendish Square) Cavendish Square Publishing LLC.

Rice, Dona Herweck. Keeping Fit with Sports, 1 vol. 2nd rev. ed. 2011. (TIME for KIDS(r): Informational Text Ser.). (ENG.). 20p. (gr. 1-2). 6.99 *(978-1-4333-3596-9(4))* Teacher Created Materials, Inc.

—Mantenerse en Forma con Deportes. 2nd rev. ed. 2012. (TIME for KIDS(r): Informational Text Ser.). (SPA.). 20p. (gr. 1-2). 6.99 *(978-1-4333-4429-9(7))* Teacher Created Materials, Inc.

Richards, Jon & Simkins, Ed. Art, Culture, & Sports. 2016. (Mapographica Ser.). (ENG., Illus.). 32p. (J). (gr. 3-6). *(978-0-7787-2655-5(X))* Crabtree Publishing Co.

Riggs, Kate. The Great Recession. 2016. (Turning Points Ser.). (ENG.). 48p. (J). (gr. 4-7). pap. 12.00 *(978-1-62832-345-0(0)*, 20811, Creative Paperbacks) Creative Co., The.

Riggs, Thomas, ed. Are Players' Unions Good for Professional Sports Leagues?, 1 vol. 2012. (At Issue Ser.). (ENG.). 112p. (gr. 10-12). pap. 28.80 *(978-0-7377-6417-8(1)*, aa9eac10-046b-48b1-a5fe-c597a2ac4728); lib. bdg. 41.03 *(978-0-7377-6416-1(3)*, a4abd5d2-f826-45c2-a9db-131c3db2c880) Greenhaven Publishing LLC. (Greenhaven Publishing).

Ripley Publishing Staff & Mason Crest Publishers Staff, contrib. by. Extreme Endeavors. 2013. (Ripley's Believe It or Not! Enter If You Dare Ser.). (Illus.). 36p. (J). (gr. 4-18). pap. 9.95 *(978-1-4222-2797-8(9))* Mason Crest.

Ripley's Believe It Or Not! Staff. Extreme Endeavors. 2013. (Ripley's Believe It or Not! Enter If You Dare Ser.: 8). 36p. (J). (gr. 4-18). 19.95 *(978-1-4222-2780-0(4))* Mason Crest.

Rissman, Rebecca. Playing with Friends: Comparing Past & Present, 1 vol. 2014. (Comparing Past & Present Ser.). (ENG., Illus.). 24p. (J). (gr. -1-1). lib. bdg. 25.32 *(978-1-4329-8993-4(6)*, 124790, Heinemann) Capstone.

Rober, Harold. Starting a Sport. 2017. (Bumba Books (r) — Fun Firsts Ser.). (ENG., Illus.). 24p. (J). (gr. -1-1). 26.65 *(978-1-5124-2552-9(4)*, d5ed0281-130f-4f80-9284-52a5b473e24a); E-Book 39.99 *(978-1-5124-3689-1(5)*, 9781512436891); E-Book 4.99 *(978-1-5124-3690-7(9)*, 9781512436907); E-Book 39.99 *(978-1-5124-2748-6(9))* Lerner Publishing Group. (Lerner Pubns.).

Robinson, Garrick & Kjeldsen, Neil. Having A Ball: Youth Sports Done Right, 1 book. 2006. (ENG & SPA., Illus.). 44p. (J). per. 14.95 *(978-0-9777437-0-4(5))* Zeus Sports Florida LLC.

Rogers, Amy B. Should Girls Play Sports with Boys?, 1 vol. 2017. (Points of View Ser.). (ENG.). 24p. (J). (gr. 3-3). pap. 9.25 *(978-1-5345-2483-5(5)*, 701e7399-aa7d-4e1a-9a3e-a4b2c5206a0d); lib. bdg. 26.23 *(978-1-5345-2421-7(5)*, 9867a9c6-e41b-45ad-884e-ea7b6458bb26) Greenhaven Publishing LLC.

Roland, James. The Science & Technology of Soccer. 2019. (Science & Technology of Sports Ser.). (ENG.). 80p. (J). (gr. 6-12). 41.27 *(978-1-68282-655-3(4))* ReferencePoint Pr., Inc.

Rosen, Michael J. Balls! Margeson, John, illus. 2006. 72p. (J). (gr. 4-8). 18.95 *(978-1-58196-030-3(1)*, Darby Creek) Lerner Publishing Group.

Ross, Michael & Ross, Christopher. A Kid's Game Plan for Great Choices: An All-Sports Devotional. 2019. (ENG., Illus.). 208p. (J). (gr. 2-7). pap. 12.99 *(978-0-7369-7524-7(1)*, 6975247) Harvest Hse. Pubs.

Ross, Stewart. Sport Technology. 2010. (New Technology Ser.). (ENG., Illus.). 48p. (J). 26.99 *(978-0-237-54077-7(0))* Evans Brothers, Ltd. GBR. Dist: Independent Pubs. Group.

Rowe, Brooke. What Kind of Sports Pro Are You? 2015. (Best Quiz Ever Ser.). (ENG., Illus.). 32p. (J). (gr. 4-8). 32.07 *(978-1-63470-036-8(8)*, 206804) Cherry Lake Publishing.

Royston, Angela. Win That Sprint! Forces in Sport. 2015. (Feel the Force Ser.). (ENG., Illus.). 48p. (J). (gr. 3-6). 35.99 *(978-1-4846-2597-2(8)*, 130075, Heinemann) Capstone.

Rumsch, BreAnn. Good Sports Don't Give Up. Petrik, Mike, illus. 2019. (Good Sports Ser.). (ENG.). 24p. (J). (gr. -1-2). pap. 7.95 *(978-1-68410-427-7(0)*, 141221); lib. bdg. 33.99 *(978-1-68410-400-0(9)*, 141210) Cantata Learning.

—Good Sports Use Teamwork. Petrik, Mike, illus. 2019. (Good Sports Ser.). (ENG.). 24p. (J). (gr. -1-2). 33.99 *(978-1-68410-402-4(5)*, 141212) Cantata Learning.

—Good Sports, Win or Lose. Petrik, Mike, illus. 2019. (Good Sports Ser.). (ENG.). 24p. (J). (gr. -1-2). pap. 7.95 *(978-1-68410-430-7(0)*, 141225) Cantata Learning.

Ruscoe, Michael. Kick Ball Capitalization, 1 vol. 2009. (Grammar All-Stars: Writing Tools Ser.). (ENG.). 32p. (J). (gr. 2-4). lib. bdg. 28.67 *(978-1-4339-1942-8(7)*, 94dfc141-fcef-4a68-9ba6-b0742a37f417, Gareth Stevens Learning Library) Stevens, Gareth Publishing LLLP.

Salas, Laura Purdie. Colors of Sports, 1 vol. 2010. (Colors All Around Ser.). (ENG.). 32p. (J). (gr. -1-2). pap. 8.10 *(978-1-4296-6149-2(6)*, 115298); (gr. 1-2). pap. 48.60 *(978-1-4296-6150-8(X)*, 16039) Capstone. (Capstone Pr.).

—S Is for Score! A Sports Alphabet. 2010. (Alphabet Fun Ser.). (ENG.). 32p. (gr. 1-2). pap. 47.70 *(978-1-4296-5087-8(7)*, Capstone Pr.) Capstone.

Samuel, Adele. Wild World of Sports. 2007. (Steck-Vaughn BOLDPRINT Anthologies Ser.). (ENG., Illus.). 48p. (gr. 4-7). pap. 16.90 *(978-1-4190-4020-7(0))* Houghton Mifflin Harcourt Publishing Co.

Sandler, Michael. Stupendous Sports Stadiums. 2018. (So Big Compared to What? Ser.). (ENG.). 24p. (J). (gr. 1-6). 7.99 *(978-1-64280-084-5(8))* Bearport Publishing Co., Inc.

Santillan, Jorge, illus. Sports Illustrated Kids Victory School Superstars, 6 vols., Set. Incl. Five Fouls & You're Out! Priebe, Val. lib. bdg. 26.65 *(978-1-4342-2228-2(4)*, 103091); There's No Crying in Baseball. Yasuda, Anita. lib. bdg. 26.65 *(978-1-4342-2226-8(8)*, 103089); Who Wants to Play Just for Kicks? Kreie, Chris. lib. bdg. 26.65 *(978-1-4342-2229-9(2)*, 103092); You Can't Spike Your Serves. Gassman, Julie. lib. bdg. 26.65 *(978-1-4342-2231-2(4)*, 103094); (Illus.). (J). (gr. 1-3). (Sports Illustrated Kids Victory School Superstars Ser.). (ENG.). 56p. 2011. Set lib. bdg. 159.90 *(978-1-4342-3126-0(7)*, Stone Arch Bks.) Capstone.

Schaefer, Adam. Steroids. 2008. (21st Century Skills Library: Health at Risk Ser.). (ENG., Illus.). 32p. (gr. 4-8). lib. bdg. 32.07 *(978-1-60279-287-6(9)*, 200136) Cherry Lake Publishing.

Scheff, Matt. Amazing Human Feats of Distance. 2018. (Superhuman Feats Ser.). (ENG., Illus.). 32p. (J). (gr. 4-6). lib. bdg. 28.65 *(978-1-5435-4125-0(9)*, 139079, Capstone Pr.) Capstone.

Schmidt, Debra. Careers in Sports & Fitness. 2016. (Exploring Careers Ser.). (ENG., Illus.). 80p. (J). (gr. 5-12). 38.60 *(978-1-60152-814-8(0))* ReferencePoint Pr., Inc.

Scholastic Library Publishing. Rookie Read-about(r) Sports. 2012. (Rookie Read-about Ser.). (J). (gr. -1-1). 92.00 *(978-0-531-26524-6(2)*, Children's Pr.) Scholastic Library Publishing.

Schuette, Sarah L. Sports Zone: A Spot-It Challenge, 1 vol. 2012. (Spot It Ser.). (ENG.). 32p. (J). (gr. -1-2). lib. bdg. 27.99 *(978-1-4296-8712-6(6)*, 119505, Capstone Pr.) Capstone.

Schwaeber, Barbie Heit. Alphabet of Sports. Lowe, David, illus. (Alphabet Bks.). (ENG.). 40p. 2011. (J). (gr. -1-3). 9.95 *(978-1-60727-446-9(9))* 2009. 9.95 *(978-1-59249-994-6(5))* 2008. (J). (gr. k-2). 15.95 *(978-1-59249-769-0(1))* Soundprints.

Schwartz, Heather E. Cheerleading, 1 vol. 2012. (Science Behind Sports Ser.). (ENG., Illus.). 104p. (gr. 7-7). lib. bdg. 41.03 *(978-1-4205-0818-5(0)*, b76379ec-d4d0-4c30-8910-760de79ec070, Lucent Pr.) Greenhaven Publishing LLC.

The Science of Sports [Capstone Sole Source]. 2010. (Science of Sports (Sports Illustrated for Kids) Ser.). 48p. lib. bdg. 179.94 *(978-1-4296-5880-5(0))* Capstone.

The Science of Sports [Kurtz]. 2010. (Science of Sports (Sports Illustrated for Kids) Ser.). 32p. pap. 59.70 *(978-1-4296-5961-1(0))* Capstone.

Scott, Celicia. Sports & Fitness. Hart, Diane H., ed. 2014. (Integrated Life of Fitness Ser.). 64p. (J). (gr. 7-18). pap. 11.95 *(978-1-4222-3201-9(8))*; 23.95 *(978-1-4222-3163-0(1))* Mason Crest.

Scott, John, text. Athletic Quest Total Sports System. 2004. (YA). 30.00 *(978-1-879498-82-2(0))* SportAmerica.

—Seniors: How to Get Recruited. 2004. (YA). 30.00 *(978-1-879498-77-8(4))* SportAmerica.

—Sophomore: How to Make the Team. 2004. (YA). 30.00 *(978-1-879498-79-2(0))* SportAmerica.

Seidel, Jeff. Ultimate College Basketball Road Trip. 2018. (Ultimate Sports Road Trips Ser.). (ENG., Illus.). 48p. (J). (gr. 3-9). lib. bdg. 34.21 *(978-1-5321-1750-3(7)*, 30788, SportsZone) ABDO Publishing Co.

Shannon, Terry Miller. Good Sports. 2016. (Spring Forward Ser.). (J). (gr. 1). *(978-1-4900-2236-9(8))* Benchmark Education Co.

Shapiro, Simon. Faster, Higher, Smarter: Bright Ideas That Transformed Sports. 2016. (ENG., Illus.). 120p. (J). (gr. 5). pap. 12.95 *(978-1-55451-813-5(X))* Annick Pr., Ltd. CAN. Dist: Publishers Group West (PGW).

Shaw, Jessica. Dream Jobs in Sports Psychology, 1 vol. 2017. (Great Careers in the Sports Industry Ser.). (ENG., Illus.). 128p. (J). (gr. 7-7). 44.13 *(978-1-5383-8144-1(3)*, ac94670e-c36e-44e0-afec-60f4c492e1b5); pap. 21.00 *(978-1-5081-7864-4(X)*, 9251ba13-4dc3-4ff6-b900-ca522bfb2278) Rosen Publishing Group, Inc., The.

Sichol, Lowey Bundy. From an Idea to Nike: How Marketing Made Nike a Global Success. Jennings, C. S., illus. 2019. (From an Idea To Ser.). (ENG.). 128p. (J). (gr. 1-5). pap. 7.99 *(978-1-328-45363-1(4)*, 1711807, Clarion Bks.) HarperCollins Pubs.

Side-By-Side Sports, 1 vol. 2014. (Side-By-Side Sports Ser.). (ENG.). 48p. (J). (gr. 4-6). pap., pap., pap. 31.80 *(978-1-4765-6173-8(7)*, 173191) Capstone.

Simonds, Lucy. Indoor Sports. 2007. (Trackers-Math Ser.). (gr. 2-5). pap. 5.00 *(978-1-59055-921-5(5))* Pacific Learning, Inc.

Simons, Rae. Sports Math. 2013. (Math 24/7 Ser.: 10). 48p. (J). (gr. 5-18). 19.95 *(978-1-4222-2909-5(2))* Mason Crest.

Sipe, Nicole. Safe Cycling. rev. ed. 2019. (Smithsonian: Informational Text Ser.). (ENG., Illus.). 32p. (J). (gr. 2-3). pap. 10.99 *(978-1-4938-6669-4(9))* Teacher Created Materials, Inc.

Slade, Suzanne. The Kids' Guide to Money in Sports, 1 vol. 2014. (SI Kids Guide Bks.). (ENG.). 48p. (J). (gr. 4-5). lib. bdg. 32.65 *(978-1-4765-4154-9(X)*, 124259) Capstone.

—Who Invented Basketball? And Other Questions Kids Have about Sports, 1 vol. Pillo, Cary, illus. 2010. (Kids' Questions Ser.). (ENG.). 24p. (J). (gr. k-2). pap. 7.49 *(978-1-4048-6730-7(9)*, 115555, Picture Window Bks.) Capstone.

Slingerland, Janet. Sports Science & Technology in the Real World. 2016. (STEM in the Real World Set 2 Ser.). (ENG., Illus.). 48p. (J). (gr. 4-8). lib. bdg. 35.64 *(978-1-68078-483-1(8)*, 23903) ABDO Publishing Co.

Small, Cathleen. Lacrosse, 1 vol. 2018. (Mind vs Muscle: the Psychology of Sports Ser.). (ENG.). 48p. (gr. 5-6). pap. 15.05 *(978-1-5382-2531-8(X)*, 83ab677a-2f14-4b3b-928f-19c0de9bc1a1) Stevens, Gareth Publishing LLLP.

Smibert, Angie. Building a Stadium. 2018. (Sequence Amazing Structures Ser.). (ENG.). 32p. (J). (gr. 2-5). pap. 9.99 *(978-1-68152-352-1(3)*, 15167) Amicus.

So Many Sports! (Girls' World Ser.). 16p. (J). *(978-2-7643-0143-2(X))* Phidal Publishing, Inc./Editions Phidal, Inc.

Sosieski, Shanti. Who's Next: The Hottest Young Stars in Action Sports. 2004. (J). 3.99 *(978-1-930623-34-7(8))* Sports Illustrated For Kids.

Sports, 10 vols. 2005. (Double Fastback Ser.). (J). (gr. 6-12). 64p. pap. 54.95 *(978-0-13-024465-9(1))*; 32p. pap. 44.95 *(978-0-13-024446-8(5))* Globe Fearon Educational Publishing.

Sports: What's Your Position? 2017. (Sports: What's Your Position? Ser.). 32p. (gr. 3-4). pap. 63.00 *(978-1-5382-0490-0(8))*; (ENG.). lib. bdg. 169.62 *(978-1-5382-0476-4(2)*, d505dc97-92b2-4e2d-9785-35e9421666fa) Stevens, Gareth Publishing LLLP.

Sports & Fitness (Gr. PreK-5) 2003. (J). *(978-1-58232-026-7(8))* ECS Learning Systems, Inc.

Sports Around the World, 6 vols. (Book2WebTM Ser.). (gr. 4-8). 36.50 *(978-0-322-02989-7(9))* Wright Group/McGraw-Hill.

Sports' Best Ever, 6 vols. 2015. (Sports' Best Ever Ser.: 6). (ENG.). 64p. (J). (gr. 3-6). lib. bdg. 213.84 *(978-1-62403-616-3(3)*, 17309, SportsZone) ABDO Publishing Co.

Sports Families, 12 vols., Set. Incl. Archie, Peyton, & Eli Manning: Football's Royal Family. Nagle, Jeanne. lib. bdg. 34.47 *(978-1-4358-3550-4(6)*, a61f0764-f8eb-4007-a652-c8bec2d0c9ea); Calvin Hill & Grant Hill: One Family's Legacy in Football & Basketball. Porterfield, Jason. lib. bdg. 34.47 *(978-1-4358-3549-8(2)*, c9c2cd7f-1463-42c4-b9f7-34ea7df22919); Earnhardt NASCAR Dynasty: The Legacy of Dale Sr. & Dale Jr. Watson, Stephanie. lib. bdg. 34.47 *(978-1-4358-3551-1(4)*, 9513eac1-03a4-4f5f-a59c-736ea7e466e0); Ken Griffey Sr. & Ken Griffey Jr. Baseball Heroes. Mills, J. Elizabeth. lib. bdg. 34.47 *(978-1-4358-3554-2(9)*, b57b0b5e-b5df-412c-926a-b58a2182958d); Ronde & Tiki Barber: Football Stars. Heos, Bridget. lib. bdg. 34.47 *(978-1-4358-3553-5(0)*, b9ec456e-ca02-425a-b1b6-55110faea611); Venus & Serena Williams: Tennis Champions. Bailey, Diane. lib. bdg. 34.47 *(978-1-4358-3552-8(2)*, 241aae56-ad15-4a0f-97ba-c0b7fd676cf3); (YA). (gr. 5-5). 2010. (Sports Families Ser.). (ENG., Illus.). 48p. 2009. Set lib. bdg. 206.82 *(978-1-4358-3601-3(4)*, 26368be7-4dda-41e6-825c-4df516844e08, Rosen Reference) Rosen Publishing Group, Inc., The.

Sports for All: Level P, 6 vols., Vol. 2. (Explorers Ser.). 32p. (gr. 3-6). 44.95 *(978-0-7699-0612-6(5))* Shortland Pubns. (U. S. A.) Inc.

Sports from Coast to Coast. 2005. (Illus.). 48p. (gr. 5-8). lib. bdg. 159.00 *(978-1-4042-0347-1(8))* Rosen Publishing Group, Inc., The.

Sports from Coast to Coast, 6 bks., Set 2. Incl. Baseball: Rules, Tips, Strategy, & Safety. Porterfield, Jason. (J). lib. bdg. 34.47 *(978-1-4042-0991-6(3)*, 708b2c49-c38f-41ba-90c4-bd9983180bc0); Basketball: Rules, Tips, Strategy, & Safety. Ramen, Fred. (J). lib. bdg. 34.47 *(978-1-4042-0992-3(1)*, d512f253-2e5f-4384-9cbf-0f4d7e429e5a); Football: Rules, Tips, Strategy, & Safety. Wingate, Brian. (J). lib. bdg. 34.47 *(978-1-4042-0993-0(X)*, bb367b45-d480-4dd1-8beb-91800177a2d4); Paintball: Rules, Tips, Strategy, & Safety. Roza, Greg. (YA). lib. bdg. 34.47 *(978-1-4042-0994-7(8)*, 14ed9362-26e7-4ad6-bb87-e6439acbe62b); Soccer: Rules, Tips, Strategy, & Safety. Wingate, Brian. (J). lib. bdg. 34.47 *(978-1-4042-0995-4(6)*, 1f7842d4-8c2f-4ff3-b8d4-c01a7f337b6c); Softball: Rules, Tips, Strategy, & Safety. Hofstetter, Adam B. (J). lib. bdg. 34.47 *(978-1-4042-0996-1(4)*, 21adf7f1-e005-4453-a8a4-0471a6f9be6e); (Illus.). 48p. (gr. 6-6). 2007. 2007. Set lib. bdg. 196.50 o.p. *(978-1-4042-1044-8(X))* Rosen Publishing Group, Inc., The.

Sports Illustrated for Kids: Year in Sports 2006. 2005. (J). 99.90 *(978-0-439-82763-8(9))* Scholastic, Inc.

Sports Reports, 50 bks., Set. (Illus.). (YA). (gr. 4-10). lib. bdg. 1047.50 *(978-0-89490-568-1(6))* Enslow Publishing, LLC.

Sports Science. 2015. (Sports Science Ser.). (ENG.). 32p. (J). (gr. 4-5). pap., pap., pap. 360.00 *(978-1-4994-1311-3(4)*, PowerKids Pr.) Rosen Publishing Group, Inc., The.

Sports (Set), 8 vols. Incl. Baseball. Minden, Cecilia. (Illus.). lib. bdg. 32.07 *(978-1-60279-243-2(7)*, 200194); Basketball. Minden, Cecilia. (Illus.). lib. bdg. 32.07 *(978-1-60279-245-6(3)*, 200196); Football. Marsico, Katie. (Illus.). lib. bdg. 32.07 *(978-1-60279-247-0(X)*, 200198); Running. Marsico, Katie & Minden, Cecilia. (Illus.). lib. bdg. 32.07 *(978-1-60279-249-4(6)*, 200032); Soccer. Minden, Cecilia. (Illus.). lib. bdg. 32.07 *(978-1-60279-244-9(5)*, 200195); Speed Skating. Marsico, Katie. lib. bdg. 32.07 *(978-1-60279-250-0(X)*, 200128); Swimming. Minden, Cecilia. (Illus.). lib. bdg. 32.07 *(978-1-60279-246-3(1)*, 200197); Tennis. Marsico, Katie. (Illus.). lib. bdg. 32.07 *(978-1-60279-248-7(8)*, 200127); (gr. 4-8). (21st Century Skills Library: Real World Math Ser.). (ENG.). 32p. 2008. 256.56 *(978-1-60279-289-0(5)*, 200185) Cherry Lake Publishing.

Sports Tips, Techniques, & Strategies: Set 1. 2014. (Sports Tips, Techniques, & Strategies Ser.). 48p. (YA). (gr. 5-8). pap. 423.00 *(978-1-4777-8125-8(0))*; pap. 70.50 *(978-1-4777-8124-1(2))* Rosen Publishing Group, Inc., The. (Rosen Reference).

Sports Tips, Techniques, & Strategies: Set 2, 12 vols. 2014. (Sports Tips, Techniques, & Strategies Ser.). (ENG.). 48p. (YA). (gr. 6-6). lib. bdg. 200.82 *(978-1-4777-8097-8(1)*, a2111e2d-de1e-4ce6-8729-fcd87a8d59a0, Rosen Central) Rosen Publishing Group, Inc., The.

Sports Trivia, 6 vols. 2015. (Sports Trivia Ser.: 6). (ENG.). 48p. (J). (gr. 3-9). lib. bdg. 205.32 *(978-1-68078-000-0(X)*, 19494, SportsZone) ABDO Publishing Co.

SportsGirl, 8 bks. Incl. Competitive Gymnastics for Girls. Wesley, Ann. lib. bdg. 37.13 *(978-0-8239-3406-5(3)*, 91cb8203-5100-4788-96cb-d8387ed4fee3); Competitive Track & Field for Girls. Manley, Claudia B. lib. bdg. 37.13 *(978-0-8239-3408-9(X)*, 1ecc7fed-04e2-40e9-bd49-2dec7bbd55df); (YA). (gr. 5-8). 2000. (Illus.). 64p. 2005. Set lib. bdg. 35.45 o.p. *(978-0-8239-9426-7(0))* Rosen Publishing Group, Inc., The.

Staeger, Rob. Native American Sports & Games. Johnson, Troy, ed. 2013. (Native American Life Ser.: 15). 64p. (J). (gr. 5-18). 19.95 *(978-1-4222-2976-7(9))* Mason Crest.

Stark, Kristy. Diversión y Juegos: Campos, Pistas y Canchas - Partición de Figuras. rev. ed. 2018. (Mathematics in the Real World Ser.). (SPA., Illus.). 32p. (J). (gr. 2-3). pap. 10.99 *(978-1-4258-2877-6(9))* Teacher Created Materials, Inc.

—Fun & Games: Fields, Rinks, & Courts: Partitioning Shapes (Grade 2) 2018. (Mathematics in the Real World Ser.). (ENG., Illus.). 32p. (J). (gr. 2-3). pap. 10.99 *(978-1-4258-5760-8(4))* Teacher Created Materials, Inc.

—¡No te limites! Los equipos (Outside the Box: Teams) (Spanish Version) (Level K) rev. ed. 2019. (TIME for KIDS(r): Informational Text Ser.). (SPA., Illus.). 12p. (J). (gr. k-1). 7.99 *(978-1-4258-2683-3(0))* Teacher Created Materials, Inc.

—Outside the Box: Teams (Level K) 2018. (TIME for KIDS(r): Informational Text Ser.). (ENG., Illus.). 12p. (J). (gr. k-1). 7.99 *(978-1-4258-4946-7(6))* Teacher Created Materials, Inc.

Stephens, Ronald, ed. Sports. 2014. (Safety First Ser.: 11). 48p. (J). (gr. 5-18). 20.95 *(978-1-4222-3053-4(8))* Mason Crest.

Stewart, Mark. Classic Rivalries, 1 vol. 2009. (Ultimate 10: Sports Ser.). (ENG.). 48p. (gr. 3-3). (J). pap. 11.50 *(978-1-4339-2205-3(3)*, 324a36ab-ed45-488f-8a23-4654cfe0668d); (YA). lib. bdg. 33.67 *(978-0-8368-9161-4(9)*, 19a55f59-e60d-4fa6-9ce4-800eeaea13b0) Stevens, Gareth Publishing LLLP.

—The Ultimate 10: Sports, 12 vols., Set. Incl. Baseball. (J). lib. bdg. 33.67 *(978-0-8368-9156-0(2)*, 80cc05fe-7c02-4fb1-baaa-0623b3ac87e6); Basketball. (YA). lib. bdg. 33.67 *(978-0-8368-9157-7(0)*, f462b359-7f53-40e6-b438-d6ecd7ec96a9); Classic Rivalries. (YA). lib. bdg. 33.67 *(978-0-8368-9161-4(9)*, 19a55f59-e60d-4fa6-9ce4-800eeaea13b0); Clutch Performers. (YA). lib. bdg. 33.67 *(978-0-8368-9158-4(9)*, 6ea0ec6a-62f5-4f7e-989d-eadaca3ef89c); Football. (YA). lib. bdg. 33.67 *(978-0-8368-9159-1(7)*, 404c21ea-962d-44e4-8f83-f1ae36afd57e); Olympics. (YA). lib. bdg. 33.67 *(978-0-8368-9160-7(0)*, 09b366d3-4a5d-4694-87e8-ea2b518b17b9); (gr. 3-3). (Ultimate 10: Sports Ser.). (ENG.). 48p. 2009. Set lib. bdg. 202.02 *(978-0-8368-9187-4(2)*, 1d5fecf8-24f0-423d-a1dd-66f4ed0e4a9f) Stevens, Gareth Publishing LLLP.

—The Ultimate 10: Sports - Fall 2009 Release Set, 6 vols. 2009. (Ultimate 10: Sports Ser.). (ENG.). 48p. (J). (gr. 3-8). pap. 53.70 *(978-1-4339-2209-1(6)*, Gareth Stevens Hi-Lo Must Reads) Stevens, Gareth Publishing LLLP.

Stock Car Racers. (Cool Cars Ser.). 16p. (J). *(978-2-7643-0131-9(6))* Phidal Publishing, Inc./Editions Phidal, Inc.

Streissguth, Tom. It's Great to Be a Fan in Michigan. 2018. (Sports Nation Ser.). (ENG., Illus.). 48p. (J). (gr. 5-6). pap. 11.95 *(978-1-64185-033-9(7)*, 1641850337); lib. bdg. 34.21 *(978-1-63517-931-6(9)*, 1635179319) North Star Editions. (Focus Readers).

Sullivan, Erin. Sports Math & Matemáticas en los Deportes: 6 English, 6 Spanish Adaptations, 122 vols., Vol. 2. 2011. (Navigators Ser.). (J). instr.'s gde. ed. 97.00 net. *(978-1-4108-1774-7(1)*, 17741) Benchmark Education Co.

Super Racing. (Cool Cars Ser.). 16p. (J). *(978-2-7643-0002-2(6))* Phidal Publishing, Inc./Editions Phidal, Inc.

Super Speeders. (Cool Cars Ser.). 16p. (J). *(978-2-7643-0004-6(2))* Phidal Publishing, Inc./Editions Phidal, Inc.

Sutherland, Steve. Courage to Win. 2010. 94p. pap. 9.99 *(978-1-60860-804-1(2)*, Eloquent Bks.) Strategic Book Publishing & Rights Agency (SBPRA).

Tallarico, Tony J., Jr. SPARK Favorite Sports Spot-The-Differences. 2017. (Dover Kids Activity Bks.). (ENG.). 64p. (J). (gr. 1-4). pap. 5.99 *(978-0-486-81925-9(6)*, 819256) Dover Pubns., Inc.

Tammen, Christina. C h u m P. 2010. 42p. pap. 13.95 *(978-1-935268-21-5(X))* Halo Publishing International.

Technosports: Individual Title, 6 packs. (Bookweb Ser.). 32p. (gr. 4-18). 34.00 *(978-0-7635-3746-3(2))* Rigby Education.

Teitelbaum, Michael. Sports Broadcasting. 2008. (21st Century Skills Innovation Library: Innovation in Entertainment Ser.). (ENG., Illus.). 32p. (gr. 4-8). lib. bdg. 32.07 *(978-1-60279-216-6(X)*, 200147) Cherry Lake Publishing.

Tellier, Derek, et al. What's Your Dream? 2016. (What's Your Dream? Ser.). (ENG.). 96p. (J). (gr. 4-6). 103.96 *(978-1-4965-3469-9(7)*, 24988) Capstone.

Terp, Gail. The Debate about Paying College Athletes. 2018. (Pros & Cons Ser.). (ENG., Illus.). 48p. (J). (gr. 5-6). pap. 11.95 *(978-1-63517-595-0(X)*, 163517595X); lib. bdg. 34.21 *(978-1-63517-523-3(2)*, 1635175232) North Star Editions. (Focus Readers).

The Editors of Sports Illustrated Kids. Sports Illustrated Kids Stats! The Greatest Numbers in Sports. 2013. (ENG.). 128p. (J). (gr. k-17). pap. 14.95 *(978-1-61893-039-2(7))* Sports Illustrated For Kids.

—The Top 10 of Everything in Sports. 2013. (Sports Illustrated Kids Top 10 Lists Ser.). (ENG.). 96p. (J). (gr. 3-17). 19.95 *(978-1-61893-079-8(6))* Sports Illustrated For Kids.

Thomas, Ron & Herran, Joe. Getting into Sports. 2005. (Getting into Sports Ser.). (Illus.). 32p. (gr. 4-6). 140.00 *(978-0-7910-9067-1(1)*, Chelsea Clubhse.) Infobase Holdings, Inc.

Thrasher, Travis & DudePerfect. Dude Perfect 101 Tricks, Tips, & Cool Stuff, 1 vol. 2021. (ENG., Illus.). 256p. (J). 28.99 *(978-1-4002-1707-6(5)*, Tommy Nelson) Nelson, Thomas Inc.

Tibballs, Geoff. Sports. 2010. (Ripley Twists Ser.). (Illus.). 48p. (J). (gr. 3-18). lib. bdg. 19.95 *(978-1-4222-1834-1(1))* Mason Crest.

Time Out: Star Athletes Who Shine off the Field. (Illus.). 32p. (J). (gr. 3-9). pap. 3.99 *(978-1-930623-19-4(4))* Sports Illustrated For Kids.

To the Extreme [Really Good Stuff]. 2010. (To the Extreme Ser.). 32p. pap. 79.50 *(978-1-4296-5362-6(0)*, Capstone Pr.) Capstone.

Tocci, Salvatore. True Books: Experiments with Sports. 2003. (True Book: Science Experiments Ser.). (ENG., Illus.). 48p. (J). (gr. 3-5). 18.69 *(978-0-516-22789-4(0))* Scholastic Library Publishing.

Torres, John A. Critical Perspectives on Minors Playing High-Contact Sports, 1 vol. 2016. (Analyzing the Issues Ser.). (ENG.). 208p. (gr. 8-8). lib. bdg. 50.93 *(978-0-7660-8137-6(0)*, d6e5e675-9599-4151-9a01-ffdbe52b3fd4) Enslow Publishing, LLC.

Torrisi, Cathy. Take a Stand. 2011. pap. 39.95 *(978-0-7664-3753-1(1))* Abrams & Co. Pubs., Inc.

Turnbull, Stephanie. Sports Horses. 2015. (ENG., Illus.). 24p. (J). pap. 8.95 *(978-1-77092-230-3(X))* RiverStream Publishing.

Ultimate Pro Team Guides Classroom Collection. 2010. (Ultimate Pro Team Guides (Sports Illustrated for Kids) Ser.). (ENG.). 72p. (gr. 3-4). pap. 214.80 *(978-1-4296-5739-6(1))* Capstone.

Ultimate Sports Force Staff. Super Squad: Basketball's Superstars. 2003. (Illus.). 56p. (J). pap. 7.95 *(978-1-57243-601-5(8))* Triumph Bks.

Ultimate Trivia Challenge, 10 vols. 2013. (Ultimate Trivia Challenge Ser.). 32p. (J). (gr. 2-3). (ENG.). 139.60 *(978-1-4339-8308-5(7)*, a450ffc2-e311-41ac-a24a-b0fe80800aea); pap. 315.00 *(978-1-4339-9740-2(1))*; pap. 52.50 *(978-1-4339-9739-6(8))* Stevens, Gareth Publishing LLLP.

Valat, Pierre-Marie. El Deporte. (Coleccion Mundo Maravilloso). (SPA., Illus.). 168p. (J). (gr. 2-4). 13.56 *(978-84-348-4486-5(9)*, SM1438) SM Ediciones ESP. Dist: Lectorum Pubns., Inc.

Wacky World of Sports, 12 vols. 2014. (Wacky World of Sports Ser.). (ENG.). 32p. (J). (gr. 3-4). 169.62 *(978-1-4824-1176-8(8)*, 62b7ef9a-4547-4673-9136-217aa6f46fa9) Stevens, Gareth Publishing LLLP.

Walsh, Kieran. Sports Math. 2005. (Math & My World Ser.). (Illus.). 48p. (J). (gr. 4-6). lib. bdg. 20.95 *(978-1-59515-495-8(7))* Rourke Educational Media.

Ward, Lesley. Showdown: Players Around the World (Level 2) 2017. (TIME for KIDS(r): Informational Text Ser.). (ENG., Illus.). 28p. (J). (gr. 2-3). pap. 10.99 *(978-1-4258-4967-2(9))* Teacher Created Materials, Inc.

Watkins, Christine, ed. Sports & Athletes, 1 vol., No. 9. 2009. (Opposing Viewpoints Ser.). (ENG., Illus.). 232p. (gr. 10-12). 50.43 *(978-0-7377-4542-9(8)*, 981c6051-89f2-49a8-89e2-563b0284748d); pap. 34.80 *(978-0-7377-4543-6(6)*, 96aa0f82-d37d-4d8f-99e2-fae46cc17bc7) Greenhaven Publishing LLC. (Greenhaven Publishing).

Watson, Stephanie. The Science Behind Soccer, Volleyball, Cycling, & Other Popular Sports. 2016. (Science of the Summer Olympics Ser.). (ENG., Illus.). 32p. (J). (gr. 3-9). lib. bdg. 28.65 *(978-1-4914-8160-8(9)*, 130639, Capstone Pr.) Capstone.

Watt, Fiona. Sports Sticker Book. 2011. (Sticker Activity Bks). 24p. (J). pap. 8.99 *(978-0-7945-3121-8(0)*, Usborne) EDC Publishing.

Wells, Don. Lacrosse. 2005. (For the Love of Sports Ser.). (Illus.). 24p. (J). (gr. 4-6). lib. bdg. 24.45 *(978-1-59036-297-6(7))* Weigl Pubs., Inc.

What's Your Dream? 2016. (What's Your Dream? Ser.). (ENG.). 96p. (J). (gr. 3-4). pap., pap., pap. 23.80 *(978-1-4965-3470-5(0)*, 175346) Capstone.

Whelon, Chuck. What to Doodle? All Sorts of Sports! 2009. (Dover Doodle Bks.). (ENG., Illus.). 64p. (J). (gr. 2-5). pap. 5.99 *(978-0-486-47267-6(1)*, 472671) Dover Pubns., Inc.

Wiener, Gary, ed. Athlete Activism, 1 vol. 2019. (At Issue Ser.). (ENG.). 128p. (gr. 10-12). pap. 28.80 *(978-1-5345-0634-3(9)*, fe688cc2-136b-4596-8ffb-22851c2fba48) Greenhaven Publishing LLC.

Wild Outdoors, 1 vol. 2010. (Wild Outdoors Ser.). (ENG.). 32p. (gr. 1-2). lib. bdg. 54.64 *(978-1-4296-4813-4(9)*, Capstone Pr.) Capstone.

Wilder, K. C. Tour de You: Swirling Circles of Freedom. 2010. 24p. 11.49 *(978-1-4520-1099-1(4))* AuthorHouse.

Williams, Brian. Sport & Entertainment: Biggest & Best. 2003. (Biggest & Best Ser.). (Illus.). 40p. (J). pap. 7.95 *(978-1-84236-063-7(9))* Miles Kelly Publishing, Ltd. GBR. Dist: Independent Pubs. Group.

Williams, Heather. Girls' Lacrosse: A Guide for Players & Fans. 2019. (Sports Zone Ser.). (ENG., Illus.). 32p. (J). (gr. 3-6). pap. 7.95 *(978-1-5435-7460-9(2)*, 140900); lib. bdg. 27.99 *(978-1-5435-7427-2(0)*, 140713) Capstone.

Wilner, Barry. Hard-To-Beat Sports Records. 2017. (Wild World of Sports Ser.). (ENG., Illus.). 48p. (J). (gr. 3-6). lib. bdg. 34.21 *(978-1-5321-1365-9(X)*, 27663, SportsZone) ABDO Publishing Co.

Wingate, Brian. Violence at Sports Events. (Violence & Society Ser.). 64p. (gr. 6-6). 2009. 58.50 *(978-1-60854-727-2(2))* 2008. (ENG., Illus.). (YA). lib. bdg. 37.13 *(978-1-4042-1796-6(7)*, f99384c3-3864-4210-ab14-1885f7044649) Rosen Publishing Group, Inc., The.

Wood, Alix. Sports on the Map, 1 vol. 2014. (Fun with Map Skills Ser.). (ENG., Illus.). 32p. (J). (gr. 4-4). lib. bdg. 27.93 *(978-1-4777-6972-0(2)*, 00276323-63ed-4b71-9d5d-285a2dddebc8, PowerKids Pr.) Rosen Publishing Group, Inc., The.

—Wacky Moments in Sports, 1 vol. 2014. (Wacky World of Sports Ser.). (ENG., Illus.). 32p. (J). (gr. 3-4). pap. 11.50 *(978-1-4824-1221-5(7)*, 0ceb8342-036e-49d2-8553-b8a0995aef51) Stevens, Gareth Publishing LLLP.

—Wacky Races, 1 vol. 2014. (Wacky World of Sports Ser.). (ENG.). 32p. (J). (gr. 3-4). pap. 11.50 *(978-1-4824-1222-2(5)*, fd798b01-734a-46d3-87b3-9719ee5eead3) Stevens, Gareth Publishing LLLP.

—Wacky Team Sports, 1 vol. 2014. (Wacky World of Sports Ser.). (ENG., Illus.). 32p. (J). (gr. 3-4). pap. 11.50 *(978-1-4824-1224-6(1)*, c3f3413a-6f65-4ae4-a751-4d08c4102b90) Stevens, Gareth Publishing LLLP.

—Wacky Throwing Sports. 2014. (Wacky World of Sports Ser.). 32p. (J). (gr. 3-6). pap. 63.00 *(978-1-4824-0876-8(7))* Stevens, Gareth Publishing LLLP.

World Book, Inc. Staff, contrib. by. Sports. 2019. (J). *(978-0-7166-3769-1(3))* World Bk., Inc.

Wunderlich, Rick. Math on the Job: Working in Sports. 2016. (ENG., Illus.). 32p. (J). *(978-0-7787-2362-2(3))* Crabtree Publishing Co.

Yomtov, Nel. The Science of a Carve Turn. 2015. (21st Century Skills Library: Full-Speed Sports Ser.). (ENG., Illus.). 32p. (J). (gr. 4-7). 32.07 *(978-1-63362-580-8(X)*, 206504) Cherry Lake Publishing.

—The Science of a Cutback. 2015. (21st Century Skills Library: Full-Speed Sports Ser.). (ENG., Illus.). 32p. (J). (gr. 4-7). 32.07 *(978-1-63362-581-5(8)*, 206508) Cherry Lake Publishing.

You Can Canoe! Individual Title Six-Packs. (Action Packs Ser.). 120p. (gr. 3-5). 44.00 *(978-0-7635-8393-4(6))* Rigby Education.

Zuckerman, Gregory, et al. Rising Above: How 11 Athletes Overcame Challenges in Their Youth to Become Stars. 2016. 256p. (J). (gr. 5-9). 17.99 *(978-0-399-17382-0(X)*, Philomel Bks.) Penguin Young Readers Group.

SPORTS—BIOGRAPHY

Adams, Sean. Tim Duncan. 2004. (Sports Heroes & Legends Ser.). (ENG., Illus.). 112p. (J). (gr. 5-12). lib. bdg. 30.60 *(978-0-8225-1793-1(0))* Lerner Publishing Group.

All-Star Players, 12 vols., Sets 1-2. Incl. All-Star Players: Set 1. 2006. lib. bdg. 115.72 *(978-1-4042-3601-1(5)*, ee6f4b42-d882-4d9d-89a6-a982e7b38577); All-Star Players: Set 2. 2008. lib. bdg. 86.79 *(978-1-4358-2564-2(0)*, f8cacf69-255e-445a-9789-a59ccc4a8526, PowerKids Pr.); (J). (gr. 4-5). 2008. Set lib. bdg. 287.40 *(978-1-4358-2669-4(8))* Rosen Publishing Group, Inc., The.

Allyson, Jackie. Chris Jesus Ferguson. 2009. (Superstars of Poker Ser.). (Illus.). 64p. (YA). (gr. 4-7). lib. bdg. 22.95 *(978-1-4222-0218-0(6))* Mason Crest.

—Doyle Texas Dolly Brunson. 2009. (Superstars of Poker Ser.). (Illus.). 64p. (YA). (gr. 4-7). lib. bdg. 22.95 *(978-1-4222-0216-6(X))* Mason Crest.

—Gus the Great Dane Hansen. 2009. (Superstars of Poker Ser.). (Illus.). 64p. (YA). (gr. 4-7). lib. bdg. 22.95 *(978-1-4222-0219-7(4))* Mason Crest.

Anthony, Carmelo & Brown, Greg. Carmelo Anthony: It's Just the Beginning. 2004. (Basketball Ser.). (Illus.). 48p. (J). 15.95 *(978-0-9634650-7-8(4))* Positively for Kids, Inc.

Armentrout, David & Armentrout, Patricia. Tony Hawk. 2005. (Discover the Life of a Sports Star Ser.). (Illus.). 24p. (gr. 1-4). 14.95 *(978-1-59515-129-2(X))* Rourke Educational Media.

Armstrong, Jesse. Big Show. 2015. (Wrestling Superstars Ser.). (ENG., Illus.). 24p. (J). (gr. 3-7). pap. 8.99 *(978-1-61891-246-6(1)*, 11998, Epic Bks.) Bellwether Media.

Benchmark All-Stars: Group 2, 12 vols., Set. 2006. (All-Stars Ser.). (ENG.). (J). (gr. 4-4). 204.42 *(978-0-7614-1755-2(9)*, ed546666-960a-4fa4-ba24-f37bfa5d4988, Cavendish Square) Cavendish Square Publishing LLC.

Bradley, Michael. Serena Williams, 1 vol. 2006. (All-Stars Ser.). (ENG., Illus.). 48p. (gr. 4-4). 34.07 *(978-0-7614-1760-6(5)*, eaaed1f9-01fa-49a4-88ab-92b4e111e18f) Cavendish Square Publishing LLC.

Carter, Vince & Brown, Greg. Vince Carter: Choose Your Course. 2004. (Basketball Ser.). (Illus.). 48p. (J). 15.95 *(978-0-9634650-2-3(3))* Positively for Kids, Inc.

Christopher, Matt. Babe Ruth. 2015. (Great Americans in Sports Ser.). (J). lib. bdg. 16.00 *(978-0-606-37519-1(8))* Turtleback.

—Mia Hamm. 2015. (Great Americans in Sports Ser.). (J). lib. bdg. 16.00 *(978-0-606-37520-7(1))* Turtleback.

—On the Court with... Yao Ming. 2004. (ENG., Illus.). 112p. (J). (gr. 5-8). pap. 9.99 *(978-0-316-73574-2(4))* Little, Brown Bks. for Young Readers.

Contro, Arturo. Gianluigi Buffon, 1 vol. Benson, Megan, tr. 2008. (World Soccer Stars / Estrellas Del Fútbol Mundial Ser.). (SPA & ENG., Illus.). 24p. (J). (gr. 2-2). lib. bdg. 26.27 *(978-1-4042-7668-0(8)*, f6bc9999-9c62-4d5f-b759-0b9a080256f3) Rosen Publishing Group, Inc., The.

—Landon Donovan, 1 vol. Benson, Megan, tr. 2008. (World Soccer Stars / Estrellas Del Fútbol Mundial Ser.). (SPA & ENG., Illus.). 24p. (J). (gr. 2-2). lib. bdg. 26.27 *(978-1-4042-7666-6(1)*, afb00a3b-138e-462c-bc34-f2d6500b3bbd) Rosen Publishing Group, Inc., The.

Dodson Wade, Mary. Amazing Olympic Athlete Wilma Rudolph, 1 vol. 2009. (Amazing Americans Ser.). (ENG., Illus.). 24p. (gr. k-2). lib. bdg. 25.27 *(978-0-7660-3282-8(5)*, 34b5dfbd-0b67-4e34-97fe-24c1037bcaa6) Enslow Publishing, LLC.

Doeden, Matt. Shaun White, 2nd Edition. 2nd rev. ed. 2012. (Amazing Athletes Ser.). (ENG., Illus.). 32p. (J). (gr. 2-5). pap. 7.95 *(978-0-7613-9067-1(7)*, 7d1285d1-659d-4f04-8025-b2ba4549ca7e) Lerner Publishing Group.

—Shaun White (Revised Edition) 2012. (Amazing Athletes Ser.). 32p. (J). (gr. 2-5). pap. 45.32 *(978-0-7613-9139-5(8))* Lerner Publishing Group.

Edwards, Ethan. All-Star Players: Set 2, 6 vols. Incl. Meet Derek Jeter: Captain of the New York Yankees. lib. bdg. 28.93 *(978-1-4042-4488-7(3)*, 24d1ceed-b96f-4658-9d25-85ded96adc7f); Meet Kevin Garnett: Basketball's Big Ticket. lib. bdg. 28.93 *(978-1-4042-4490-0(5)*, 84b490fb-50de-4512-b8dd-aef5080f8b2a); Meet LaDainian Tomlinson: Football's Fastest Running Back. lib. bdg. 28.93 *(978-1-4042-4491-7(3)*, ebe26808-364d-40ec-8670-44cc1f5490a6); (Illus.). 32p. (YA). (gr. 4-5). 2008. (All-Star Players Ser.). (ENG.). 2008. Set lib. bdg. 86.79 *(978-1-4358-2564-2(0)*, f8cacf69-255e-445a-9789-a59ccc4a8526, PowerKids Pr.) Rosen Publishing Group, Inc., The.

Extreme Sports Biographies, 8 vols. 2004. (Extreme Sports Biographies Ser.). (ENG., Illus.). (J). (gr. 3-4). 105.08 *(978-1-4042-2954-9(X)*, 72c61c63-b250-42f4-b883-d341bc946582); 64p. (gr. 5-8). lib. bdg. 111.39 *(978-1-4042-0344-0(3)*, 5d57971f-6fae-4199-9942-47d3556a0695) Rosen Publishing Group, Inc., The.

Galán, Johnn. Luis Tejada -Vida Breve, Crítica Crónica. 2006. (SPA.). 192p. (YA). *(978-958-30-1692-9(6))* Panamericana Editorial.

Gitlin, Marty. Lindsey Vonn, 1 vol. 2012. (People in the News Ser.). (ENG., Illus.). 104p. (gr. 7-7). lib. bdg. 41.03 *(978-1-4205-0614-3(5)*, fd9f887e-9664-499d-b56b-ada11c8b8d71, Lucent Pr.) Greenhaven Publishing LLC.

Golus, Carrie. Muhammad Ali. 2006. (Sports Heroes & Legends Ser.). (ENG., Illus.). 120p. (J). (gr. 5-12). lib. bdg. 30.60 *(978-0-8225-5960-3(9))* Lerner Publishing Group.

Goranson, Christopher D. Danny Harf: Wakeboarding Superstar, 1 vol. 2004. (Extreme Sports Biographies Ser.). (ENG., Illus.). 64p. (YA). (gr. 5-8). lib. bdg. 37.13 *(978-1-4042-0066-1(5)*, 71e33346-ad16-40bf-857d-3461d0d5dbf4) Rosen Publishing Group, Inc., The.

The Greatest Records in Sports, 12 vols. 2014. (Greatest Records in Sports Ser.). (ENG.). 32p. (J). (gr. 4-5). lib. bdg. 167.58 *(978-1-4777-5743-7(0)*, 66a86b57-684b-494a-9b40-7ebf3451c9be, PowerKids Pr.) Rosen Publishing Group, Inc., The.

Greenberg, Michael. Sword of a Champion: The Sharon Monplaisir Story. 2003. (Anything You Can Do. . .Ser.: Vol. 2). (Illus.). 96p. (J). (gr. 2-5). pap. 9.95 *(978-1-930546-39-4(4))* Wish Publishing.

Hall, Kirsten. Kids in Sports. 2005. (True Tales Ser.). (ENG., Illus.). 48p. (J). (gr. 2-4). pap. 4.95 *(978-0-516-24685-7(2)*, Children's Pr.) Scholastic Library Publishing.

Johnson, Brad & Brown, Greg. Brad Johnson: Play with Passion. 2004. (Football Ser.). (Illus.). 48p. (J). 15.95 *(978-0-9634650-4-7(X))* Positively for Kids, Inc.

Jones, Jeremy V. Toward the Goal, Revised Edition: The Kaka Story, 1 vol. rev. ed. 2014. (ZonderKidz Biography Ser.). (ENG.). 160p. (J). pap. 7.99 *(978-0-310-73840-4(7))* Zonderkidz.

Kennedy, Mike. Tony Hawk, 1 vol. 2009. (People We Should Know (Second Series) Ser.). (ENG.). 48p. (J). (gr. 3-5). pap. 11.50 *(978-1-4339-2191-9(X)*, 50efe211-bfe9-4ae6-a322-b0117570e90b); lib. bdg. 33.67 *(978-1-4339-1952-7(4)*, 449999e6-f670-459d-8244-b2820381bce2) Stevens, Gareth Publishing LLLP. (Gareth Stevens Learning Library).

Kirkpatrick, Rob. Hot Shots, 6 bks. Incl. Dale Earnhardt, Jr. NASCAR Road Racer. (Illus.). 24p. (J). (gr. 1). 2000. lib. bdg. 17.25 *(978-0-8239-5545-9(1)*, PKDAEA, PowerKids Pr.); (Illus.). Set lib. bdg. 96.00 *(978-0-8239-7001-8(9)*, PKPOHS, PowerKids Pr.) Rosen Publishing Group, Inc., The.

—Power Players, 6 bks. Incl. Doug Flutie: International Football Star. lib. bdg. 17.25 *(978-0-8239-5537-4(0))*; Grant Hill: Basketball All-Star. lib. bdg. 17.25 *(978-0-8239-5538-1(9))*; 24p. (J). (gr. 1). 2003. (Illus.). Set lib. bdg. 24.60 o.p. *(978-0-8239-7000-1(0)*, PowerKids Pr.) Rosen Publishing Group, Inc., The.

Kjelle, Marylou Morano. Dwayne the Rock Johnson. 2008. (Robbie Reader Ser.). (Illus.). 32p. (J). (gr. 2-5). lib. bdg. 25.70 *(978-1-58415-722-9(4))* Mitchell Lane Pubs.

Lewis, Wendy A. Fire on the Water: The Red-Hot Career of Superstar Rower Ned Hanlan, 1 vol. 2007. (Lorimer Recordbooks Ser.). (ENG., Illus.). 112p. (J). (gr. 4-6). 9.95 *(978-1-55028-972-5(1)*, 972); 16.95 *(978-1-55028-973-2(X)*, 973) James Lorimer & Co. Ltd., Pubs. CAN. Dist: Formac Lorimer Bks. Ltd.

—Lacrosse Warrior: The Life of Mohawk Lacrosse Champion Gaylord Powless, 1 vol. 3rd ed. 2008. (Lorimer Recordbooks Ser.). (ENG., Illus.). 120p. (YA). (gr. 7-12). 8.99 *(978-1-55277-001-6(X)*, 4176b0b7-f16a-4bfe-99e7-6d1312032c98) James Lorimer & Co. Ltd., Pubs. CAN. Dist: Lerner Publishing Group.

Living Legends of Sports: Set 2, 10 vols. 2018. (Living Legends of Sports Ser.). (ENG.). 48p. (gr. 5-6). lib. bdg. 142.05 *(978-1-5383-0318-4(3)*, e8f728cf-1bfc-463e-bbd2-526a37cff940) Rosen Publishing Group, Inc., The.

Lyon, Drew, et al. Real Heroes of Sports. 2017. (Real Heroes of Sports Ser.). (ENG.). 32p. (J). (gr. 3-9). pap., pap., pap. 28.76 *(978-1-5157-4464-1(7)*, 25769) Capstone.

Macrae, Sloan. The Greatest Records in Sports, 1 vol. 2015. (Greatest Records in Sports Ser.). (ENG.). 32p. (J). 60.00 *(978-1-4994-0310-7(0)*, PowerKids Pr.) Rosen Publishing Group, Inc., The.

Mahaney, Ian. Tony Hawk: Skateboarding Champ, 1 vol. 2004. (Extreme Sports Biographies Ser.). (ENG., Illus.). 24p. (J). (gr. 3-4). 26.27 *(978-1-4042-2747-7(4)*, 927bcbbf-3613-42cd-a44c-4a1b742f9194, PowerKids Pr.) Rosen Publishing Group, Inc., The.

Mahaney, Ian F. Kevin Jones: Snowboarding Champion, 1 vol. 2004. (Extreme Sports Biographies Ser.). (ENG., Illus.). 24p. (J). (gr. 3-4). 26.27 *(978-1-4042-2745-3(8)*, c839ecb5-b812-4541-b24f-83b1287cfb95, PowerKids Pr.) Rosen Publishing Group, Inc., The.

—Taig Khris: In-Line Skate Champion, 1 vol. 2004. (Extreme Sports Biographies Ser.). (ENG., Illus.). 24p. (J). (gr. 3-4). 26.27 *(978-1-4042-2746-0(6)*, 5c3b9f77-7b3b-4c24-8800-6d895c0b7302, PowerKids Pr.) Rosen Publishing Group, Inc., The.

McClellan, Ray. Undertaker. 2014. (Wrestling Superstars Ser.). (ENG., Illus.). 24p. (J). (gr. 3-7). pap. 8.99 *(978-1-61891-245-9(3)*, 11991, Epic Bks.) Bellwether Media.

Micklos, John & Micklos, John, Jr. Muhammad Ali: I Am the Greatest, 1 vol. 2010. (American Rebels Ser.). (ENG.). 160p. (J). (gr. 9-10). 38.60 *(978-0-7660-3381-8(3)*, d42fe273-d034-4514-abe8-94559090d86a) Enslow Publishing, LLC.

Miller, Raymond H. Tony Hawk. 2004. (Stars of Sport Ser.). (ENG., Illus.). 48p. (J). 27.50 *(978-0-7377-1568-2(5)*, Greenhaven Pr., Inc.) Cengage Gale.

Moussavi, Sam. It's Great to Be a Fan in Massachusetts. 2018. (Sports Nation Ser.). (ENG., Illus.). 48p. (J). (gr. 5-6). pap. 11.95 *(978-1-64185-032-2(9)*, 1641850329); lib. bdg. 34.21 *(978-1-63517-930-9(0)*, 1635179300) North Star Editions. (Focus Readers).

Nagle, Jeanne. Top 101 Athletes, 1 vol., 1. 2013. (People You Should Know Ser.). (ENG.). 168p. (YA). (gr. 8-8). 38.84 *(978-1-62275-136-5(1)*, 6edd56c7-ae60-46fd-9ab7-73a37ecb8fd1) Rosen Publishing Group, Inc., The.

Obregón, José María. Freddy Adu, 1 vol. 2009. (World Soccer Stars / Estrellas Del Fútbol Mundial Ser.). (SPA & ENG., Illus.). 24p. (J). (gr. 2-2). lib. bdg. 26.27 *(978-1-4358-2730-1(9)*, 4771c84f-07fd-41b8-92de-b40238df6d29) Rosen Publishing Group, Inc., The.

Parham, Jerrill. Shockwave: Thrills & Spills. 2007. (Shockwave: the Human Experience Ser.). (ENG., Illus.). 36p. (J). (gr. 3-5). 25.00 *(978-0-531-17762-4(9)*, Children's Pr.) Scholastic Library Publishing.

Real Heroes of Sports. 2017. (Real Heroes of Sports Ser.). (ENG.). 32p. (J). (gr. 3-4). 114.60 *(978-1-5157-4463-4(9)*, 175672) Capstone.

Roberts, Jeremy. Tiger Woods. 2007. (Biography Ser.). (Illus.). 112p. (J). (gr. 4-7). per. 7.95 *(978-0-8225-8563-3(4)*, First Avenue Editions) Lerner Publishing Group.

Rosenberg, Aaron. Dave Mirra, 1 vol. 2004. (Extreme Sports Biographies Ser.). (ENG., Illus.). 64p. (J). (gr. 5-8). lib. bdg. 37.13 *(978-1-4042-0067-8(3)*, 089087d0-d280-40ed-91a7-13ffe0033a46) Rosen Publishing Group, Inc., The.

Savage, Jeff. Marion Jones. 2005. (J). pap. 5.95 *(978-0-8225-2040-5(0)*, First Avenue Editions); (Illus.). (gr. 3-4). lib. bdg. 22.60 *(978-0-8225-3657-4(9))* Lerner Publishing Group.

—Usain Bolt. 2012. (Amazing Athletes Ser.). (ENG., Illus.). 32p. (J). (gr. 2-5). pap. 7.95 *(978-1-4677-1097-8(0)*, f5a26ce6-46a0-43ce-9cf2-d7cc5d8a13de) Lerner Publishing Group.

Sherrow, Victoria. Wilma Rudolph. Johnson, Larry, illus. 2006. (Yo Solo Biografías Ser.). (ENG & SPA.). 48p. (J). (gr. 2-3). lib. bdg. 23.93 *(978-0-8225-6260-3(X)*, Ediciones Lerner) Lerner Publishing Group.

Smithwick, John. All-Star Players: Set 1, 8 vols. Incl. Meet Alex Rodriguez: Baseball's Lightning Rod. lib. bdg. 28.93 *(978-1-4042-3636-3(8)*, c3cfdddc-5d8d-4f27-a525-61ca0eb84d3d); Meet David Ortiz: Baseball's Top Slugger. lib. bdg. 28.93 *(978-1-4042-3637-0(6)*, 0c12cf4c-8808-4e11-8c1d-a5b76656ce59); Meet Dwyane Wade: Basketball's Rising Star. lib. bdg. 28.93 *(978-1-4042-3639-4(2)*, 6d5c92d5-781a-4753-8656-f549a7e35f1d); Meet Lebron James: Basketball's King James. lib. bdg. 28.93 *(978-1-4042-3638-7(4)*, 5cc93377-b064-4475-aeab-47e633317325); Meet Shaun Alexander: Football's Top Running Back. lib. bdg. 28.93 *(978-1-4042-3635-6(X)*, 9a73e01b-b60c-48af-bf08-fde51a839c2a); (Illus.). 32p. (YA). (gr. 4-5). 2007. (All-Star Players Ser.). (ENG.). 2006. Set lib. bdg. 115.72 *(978-1-4042-3601-1(5)*, ee6f4b42-d882-4d9d-89a6-a982e7b38577) Rosen Publishing Group, Inc., The.

Snow, D. C. Champ Bailey. 2009. (Superstars of Pro Football Ser.). (Illus.). 64p. (YA). (gr. 7-12). lib. bdg. 22.95 *(978-1-4222-0544-0(4))* Mason Crest.

Sporting Heroes. Date not set. 32p. (J). 3.98 *(978-0-7525-9875-8(9))* Parragon, Inc.

Sports Idols, 8 vols., Set. 2007. (Sports Idols Ser.). (ENG.). (J). (gr. 2-3). lib. bdg. 105.08 *(978-1-4042-4239-5(2)*, f8e74ecc-54cb-4bf4-9946-447c9ae192ac) Rosen Publishing Group, Inc., The.

Sports Star Champions: Set 2. 2017. (Sports Star Champions Ser.). 48p. (gr. 5-6). pap. 70.20 *(978-0-7660-8805-4(7))*; (ENG.). lib. bdg. 177.60 *(978-0-7660-8598-5(8)*, 5ce12e50-c032-4e7c-b78c-b6e7565058a1) Enslow Publishing, LLC.

Stewart, Mark. New Wave, 27 vols. Incl. Allen Iverson: Motion & Emotion. 2001. lib. bdg. 22.90 *(978-0-7613-1958-0(1))*; Andruw Jones: Love That Glove. 2001. lib. bdg. 22.90 *(978-0-7613-1967-2(0))*; Daunte Culpepper: Command & Control. 2002. lib. bdg. 22.90 *(978-0-7613-2613-7(8))*; Ichiro Suzuki: The Best in the West. 2002. lib. bdg. 22.90 *(978-0-7613-2616-8(2))*; Jackie Stiles: Gym Dandy. 2002. lib. bdg. 22.90 *(978-0-7613-2614-4(6))*; Jevon Kearse: Force of One. 2001. lib. bdg. 22.90 *(978-0-7613-2269-6(8))*; Kevin Garnett/Shake up the Game. 2002. lib. bdg. 22.90 *(978-0-7613-2615-1(4))*; Kurt Warner: Can't Keep Him Down. 2001. lib. bdg. 22.90 *(978-0-7613-1953-5(0))*; Scott Gomez: Open up the Ice. 2001. lib. bdg. 22.90 *(978-0-7613-2268-9(X))*; Todd Helton: The Hits Keep Coming. 2001. lib. bdg. 22.90 *(978-0-7613-2271-9(X))*; Vince Carter: The Fire Burns Bright. 2001. lib. bdg. 22.90 *(978-0-7613-2270-2(1))*; 48p. (gr. 4-18)., Millbrook Pr. (Illus.). 2004. 595.40 o.p. *(978-0-7613-3080-6(1)*, Twenty-First Century Bks.) Lerner Publishing Group.

Streissguth, Tom. Wilma Rudolph. 2007. (Illus.). 110p. (YA). pap. 9.95 *(978-0-8225-6693-9(1))* Lerner Publishing Group.

Timblin, Stephen. MX Champions: The Stars of the Show - Past & Present. 2008. (MXplosion! Ser.). (ENG., Illus.). 32p. (J). (gr. 3-7). pap. *(978-0-7787-4002-5(1))*; lib. bdg. *(978-0-7787-3989-0(9))* Crabtree Publishing Co.

S

Valay, Ana Patricia. Giovani Dos Santos. 2012. (Superstars of Soccer ENGLISH Ser.). (ENG., Illus.). 32p. (J). (gr. 4-7). lib. bdg. 19.95 (978-1-4222-2650-6(6)) Mason Crest.

Velázquez de León, Mauricio. 20 Soccer Legends, 1 vol. 2010. (World Soccer Bks.). (ENG., Illus.). 64p. (YA). (gr. 5-5). lib. bdg. 37.13 (978-1-4358-9136-4(8), 64593dbc-9d22-4ae5-88ff-4e950d308951, Rosen Reference) Rosen Publishing Group, Inc., The.

Who's Who in Sports 2003-2004: High School Edition. 26th ed. 2004. (YA). 39.95 (978-0-9724667-2-1(X), Who's Who In Sports) Guidry Assocs., Inc.

Woods, Mark. Top Score Math, 8 vols., Set. Incl. Ace! Tennis Facts & Stats. Owen, Ruth. lib. bdg. 29.27 (978-1-4339-4986-9(5), 50bda16d-ab8c-4787-b50f-1e0fc32ca3ab); Goal! Soccer Facts & Stats. Owen, Ruth. lib. bdg. 29.27 (978-1-4339-5015-5(4), 8b988238-466a-4044-9a40-5d1ad3ae6974); Xtreme! Extreme Sports Facts & Stats. lib. bdg. 29.27 (978-1-4339-5020-9(0), 50cb46ae-451f-470d-bfd2-e164982d9752); (J). (gr. 4-5). (Top Score Math Ser.). (ENG., Illus.). 32p. 2011. Set lib. bdg. 117.08 (978-1-4339-5035-3(9), 94a2eb92-ae6b-49eb-9a90-0f72c69db8a3, Gareth Stevens Learning Library) Stevens, Gareth Publishing LLLP.

The World's Greatest Sports Stars [Kurtz]. 2010. (World's Greatest Sports Stars (Sports Illustrated for Kids) Ser.). 32p. pap. 35.80 (978-1-4296-5960-4(2)) Capstone.

Wrestling Greats. 2005. (Illus.). 112p. (gr. 7-12). lib. bdg. 265.30 (978-0-8239-3911-4(1)) Rosen Publishing Group, Inc., The.

Zuehlke, Jeffrey. Ben Roethlisberger. 2007. (Amazing Athletes Ser.). (ENG., Illus.). 32p. (gr. 2-5). lib. bdg. 25.26 (978-0-8225-7660-0(0)) Lerner Publishing Group.

—Dirk Nowitzki. 2007. (Amazing Athletes Ser.). (ENG., Illus.). 32p. (gr. 2-5). lib. bdg. 25.26 (978-0-8225-7661-7(9)) Lerner Publishing Group.

SPORTS—FICTION

Adler, David A. Cam Jansen & the Sports Day Mysteries. Allen, Joy, illus. 2009. (Cam Jansen: A Super Special Ser.). 118p. 16.00 (978-1-60686-431-9(9)) Perfection Learning Corp.

—Cam Jansen & the Sports Day Mysteries: A Super Special. 2009. (Cam Jansen Ser.). lib. bdg. 16.00 (978-0-606-00110-6(7)) Turtleback.

—Cam Jansen: Cam Jansen & the Sports Day Mysteries: A Super Special. Allen, Joy, illus. 2009. (Cam Jansen Ser.). 128p. (J). (gr. 2-5). 5.99 (978-0-14-241225-1(2), Puffin Books) Penguin Young Readers Group.

—Get a Hit, Mo! 2017. (Penguin Young Readers Level 2 Ser.). lib. bdg. 13.55 (978-0-606-39770-4(1)) Turtleback.

—Pass the Ball, Mo! 2019. (Penguin Young Readers Ser.). (ENG.). 29p. (J). (gr. k-1). 14.89 (978-0-87617-760-0(7)) Penworthy Co., LLC, The.

Alexander, Samantha. Team Spirit, Bk. 2. 2nd ed. (ENG.). 128p. (J). mass mkt. 6.99 (978-0-330-34534-7(6), Pan) Pan Macmillan GBR. Dist: Trafalgar Square Publishing.

Alonge, L. J. Frank #3. Allen, Raul, illus. 2017. (Blacktop Ser.: 3). 128p. (YA). (gr. 7). mass mkt. 7.99 (978-1-101-99566-2(1), Grosset & Dunlap) Penguin Young Readers Group.

—Janae #2. Allen, Raul, illus. 2016. (Blacktop Ser.: 2). 144p. (YA). (gr. 7). mass mkt. 7.99 (978-1-101-99564-8(5), Grosset & Dunlap) Penguin Young Readers Group.

Arena, Felice. Handball. Jarrett, Tom, illus. 6th ed. 2017. (Sporty Kids Ser.). 80p. (J). (gr. 1-3). 8.99 (978-0-14-330890-4(4)) Random Hse. Australia AUS. Dist: Independent Pubs. Group.

—Netball. Jellett, Tom, illus. 2017. (Sporty Kids Ser.). 80p. (J). (gr. 1-3). 12.99 (978-0-14-330908-6(0)) Random Hse. Australia AUS. Dist: Independent Pubs. Group.

Aretha, David. Rounding Third, Heading Home!, 1 vol. 2012. (Champion Sports Story Ser.). (ENG.). 112p. (J). (gr. 3-5). 30.60 (978-0-7660-3876-9(9), a1388efb-6562-4268-8850-9e304174a703) Enslow Publishing, LLC.

Aronson, Jeff & Aronson, Miriam. Little Mike & Maddie's First Motorcycle Ride. Aronson, Jeff & Zephyr, Jay, illus. 2007. 32p. (J). 16.00 (978-0-9795302-0-3(2), CrumbGobbler Pr.) Downtown Wetmore Pr.

Aryal, Aimee. Hello, Brutus! De Angel, Miguel & Moore, D., illus. 2006. 24p. (J). lib. bdg. 14.95 (978-1-932888-51-5(9)) Amplify Publishing Group.

—Hello, Paws! 2007. (YA). 14.95 (978-1-932888-74-4(8)) Amplify Publishing Group.

—Let's Go, Giants! De Angel, Miguel, illus. 2007. 24p. (J). lib. bdg. 14.95 (978-1-932888-92-8(6)) Amplify Publishing Group.

Aryal, Aimee & Halligan, Chris. Meet Cort the Sport. 2006. (Cort the Sport Adventures Ser.). (Illus.). 24p. (J). (gr. -1-3). per. 5.95 (978-1-932888-61-4(6), 91-100-01) Amplify Publishing Group.

The Autumn Marathon. 2005. (J). 16.95 (978-0-9771495-0-6(1)) Artistic Ventures LLC.

Avivi, Karen. Shredded. 2013. 316p. pap. (978-0-9918079-3-2(6)) Avivi, Karen.

Baker, Theo. Do Robots Get Space Sick? López, Àlex, illus. 2017. (Galaxy Games Ser.). (ENG.). 48p. (gr. 3-5). pap. 8.95 (978-1-68342-434-5(4), 9781683424345) Rourke Educational Media.

—Gas Giant Jump. López, Àlex, illus. 2017. (Galaxy Games Ser.). (ENG.). 48p. (gr. 3-5). 25.64 (978-1-68342-336-2(4), 9781683423362) Rourke Educational Media.

Barber, Tiki & Barber, Ronde. Jump Shot. 2013. (Barber Game Time Bks.). (ENG., Illus.). 160p. (J). (gr. 3-7). 16.99 (978-1-4424-5729-4(5), Simon & Schuster/Paula Wiseman Bks.) Simon & Schuster/Paula Wiseman Bks.

Barbo, Maria S. & Preller, James. The Case of the Four-Leaf Clover. Smith, Jamie, illus. 2008. 104p. (J). pap. (978-0-545-03837-9(5)) Scholastic, Inc.

Barnes, Derrick D. Ruby Flips for Attention (Ruby & the Booker Boys #4) Newton, Vanessa Brantley, illus. 2009. (Ruby & the Booker Boys Ser.: 4). (ENG.). 144p. (J). (gr. 2-5). pap. 5.99 (978-0-545-01763-3(7), Scholastic Paperbacks) Scholastic, Inc.

Barwin, Steven. Making Select, 1 vol. 2011. (Lorimer Sports Stories Ser.). (ENG.). 104p. (J). (gr. 4-8). 16.95 (978-1-55277-875-3(4), 875); pap. 9.95 (978-1-55277-874-6(6), 874) James Lorimer & Co. Ltd., Pubs. CAN. Dist: Formac Lorimer Bks. Ltd.

—Sk8er, 1 vol. 2007. (Lorimer Sports Stories Ser.). (ENG.). 128p. (J). (gr. 4-8). Illus.). 16.95 (978-1-55028-985-5(3), 985); 8.95 (978-1-55028-983-1(7), 983) James Lorimer & Co. Ltd., Pubs. CAN. Dist: Formac Lorimer Bks. Ltd.

—Spiked, 1 vol. 2013. (Lorimer Sports Stories Ser.). (ENG.). 120p. (J). (gr. 4-8). pap. 9.95 (978-1-4594-0528-8(5), c41d73bb-b0f5-47a2-ad55-8f547ccb58c8) James Lorimer & Co. Ltd., Pubs. CAN. Dist: Lerner Publishing Group.

Beka. Why Are We Here Again? Poupard et al, illus. 2007. (Rugger Boys Ser.: 1). (ENG.). 48p. (J). (gr. 4-7). per. 9.99 (978-1-905460-33-5(3)) CineBook GBR. Dist: National Bk. Network.

Bently, Peter. The Yoga Ogre. Rickerty, Simon, illus. 2012. (ENG.). 32p. (J). 15.99 (978-1-84738-902-2(3)) Simon & Schuster, Ltd. GBR. Dist: Simon & Schuster, Inc.

Berenstain, Jan, et al. The Berenstain Bears Play a Good Game, 1 vol. 2009. (Berenstain Bears/Living Lights: a Faith Story Ser.). (ENG., Illus.). 32p. (J). (gr. -1-2). pap. 4.99 (978-0-310-71252-7(1)) Zonderkidz.

Berenstain, Stan & Berenstain, Jan. The Berenstain Bears' Report Card Trouble. 2004. (Berenstain Bears First Time Bks.). (J). (gr. k-3). spiral bd. (978-0-616-11096-6(0)); spiral bd. (978-0-616-11095-9(2)) Canadian National Institute for the Blind/Institut National Canadien pour les Aveugles.

Berk, Josh. Say It Ain't So. 2015. (Lenny & the Mikes Ser.: 2). (ENG.). 288p. (J). (gr. 3-7). pap. 9.99 (978-0-307-93007-1(6), Yearling) Random Hse. Children's Bks.

Bittmann, Suzy. Life with Molly Mcgee - Sports Chick: Caught in a Pickle. 2010. 211p. pap. 15.99 (978-0-557-46339-8(4)) Lulu Pr., Inc.

Bonehill, Ralph. Guns & Snowshoes or the Winter Outing of the Young Hunters. 2004. reprint ed. pap. 19.95 (978-1-4191-2252-1(5)); pap. 1.99 (978-1-4192-2252-8(X)) Kessinger Publishing, LLC.

BookSource Staff, compiled by. Sports Sabotage. 2012. (Hardy Boys: Secret Files Ser.: 8). lib. bdg. 16.00 (978-0-606-23673-7(2)) Turtleback.

Bossley, Michele Martin. Goon Squad, 1 vol. 2003. (Lorimer Sports Stories Ser.). (ENG.). 104p. (J). (gr. 4-8). 8.95 (978-1-55028-808-7(3), 808); 16.95 (978-1-55028-809-4(1), 809) James Lorimer & Co. Ltd., Pubs. CAN. Dist: Formac Lorimer Bks. Ltd.

Bowe, Julie. Curveball. 2017. (Victoria Torres, Unfortunately Average Ser.). (ENG., Illus.). 160p. (J). (gr. 4-8). lib. bdg. 27.99 (978-1-4965-3818-5(8), 133117, Stone Arch Bks.) Capstone.

Bowen, Fred. Go for the Goal!, 1 vol. 2012. (Fred Bowen Sports Story Ser.: 17). 128p. (J). (gr. 2-6). pap. 6.99 (978-1-56145-632-1(2)) Peachtree Publishing Co. Inc.

—Real Hoops, 1 vol. 2011. (Fred Bowen Sports Story Ser.: 16). 128p. (J). (gr. 2-6). pap. 6.99 (978-1-56145-566-9(0)) Peachtree Publishing Co. Inc.

Breisacher, Cathy. Chip & Curly: The Great Potato Race. Heinsz, Joshua, illus. 2019. (ENG.). 32p. (J). (gr. k-3). 16.99 (978-1-58536-408-4(8), 204660) Sleeping Bear Pr.

Bridwell, Norman. Clifford's Sports Day. (Clifford, the Big Red Dog Ser.). (Illus.). 32p. (J). (gr. k-2). pap. 5.99 (978-0-590-16002-5(8)) Scholastic, Inc.

Brouwer, Sigmund. La Course-Poursuite des Loups Gris, 1 vol. Gingras, Gaston, tr. from ENG. Griffiths, Dean, illus. 2011. (Loups Gris Ser.: 1). (FRE.). 72p. (J). (gr. 1-3). pap. 6.95 (978-1-4598-0009-0(5)) Orca Bk. Pubs. USA.

Brown, Dustin. The Sports Pages. Scieszka, Jon, ed. 2012. (Guys Read Ser.). (J). lib. bdg. 17.20 (978-0-606-26877-6(4)) Turtleback.

Bruchac, Joseph, et al. Sports Shorts. 2007. (Illus.). 127p. (J). per. 4.99 (978-1-58196-058-7(1), Darby Creek) Lerner Publishing Group.

—Sports Shorts: An Anthology of Short Stories. 2005. (Illus.). 127p. (J). (gr. 4-7). 15.95 (978-1-58196-040-2(9), Darby Creek) Lerner Publishing Group.

Buffington, Cecil. High School Super-Star: The Junior Year. 2008. 244p. pap. 16.95 (978-0-595-51914-9(8)) iUniverse, Inc.

Burton, Jennifer. Christopher's Dilemma. 2003. (Topeka Heights Ser.). (YA). (gr. 9-12). pap. 10.99 (978-0-9724733-1-6(9)) ALEXZUS Bks.

Campbell, Tonie. The Highest Stand. 2005. (Dream Ser.). 150p. (gr. 3-8). pap. 9.95 (978-0-9708992-5-5(4)) Scobre Pr. Corp.

Casciano, Christie & Moziak, Rose Mary Casciano, illus. Haunted Hockey in Lake Placid. 2012. (ENG.). 72p. (J). pap. (978-1-59531-040-8(1)) North Country Bks., Inc.

—The Puck Hog. 2011. (ENG.). 44p. (J). pap. 9.95 (978-1-59531-037-8(1)) North Country Bks., Inc.

Cayen, Alise. Patty Pom-Poms. 2009. 36p. pap. 16.50 (978-1-60693-685-6(9), Strategic Bk. Publishing) Strategic Book Publishing & Rights Agency (SBPRA).

Chambers, Sam T. & Rotella, Bob. Head Case Lacrosse Goalie: Sports Fiction with a Winning Edge. 2009. (ENG., Illus.). 95p. (gr. 4-7). pap. 9.95 (978-1-933979-40-3(2), ce9ea0d0-6568-4f71-9693-7cc89d338e18) Night Heron Media.

Chapman, Megan Joy. Lion Heart & Alessio Book 2: Mission, Peace, Patience, Kindness. 2014. (Lion Heart & Alessio Ser.: 2). (ENG.). 192p. (J). (gr. 3-7). pap. 11.99 (978-1-62136-755-0(X), Creation Hse.) Charisma Media.

Christopher, Matt. Comeback of the Home Run Kid. 2006. (ENG.). 128p. (J). (gr. 2-5). per. 9.99 (978-0-316-05987-9(0)) Little, Brown Bks. for Young Readers.

—Lacrosse Face-Off. 2006. (ENG.). 128p. (J). (gr. 3-7). per. 9.99 (978-0-316-79641-5(7)) Little, Brown Bks. for Young Readers.

—Soccer 'Cats: Making the Save. Vasconcellos, Daniel, illus. 11th ed. 2004. (ENG.). 64p. (J). (gr. 1-4). pap. 8.99 (978-0-316-73745-6(3)) Little, Brown Bks. for Young Readers.

Ciencin, Scott. End Zone Thunder, 1 vol. Sandoval, Gerardo, illus. 2010. (Sports Illustrated Kids Graphic Novels Ser.). (ENG.). 56p. (J). (gr. 3-8). 26.65 (978-1-4342-2010-3(9), 102774); pap. 7.19 (978-1-4342-2784-3(7), 114051) Capstone. (Stone Arch Bks.).

—Full Court Flash, 1 vol. Sandoval, Gerardo, illus. 2011. (Sports Illustrated Kids Graphic Novels Ser.). (ENG.). 56p. (J). (gr. 3-8). pap. 7.19 (978-1-4342-3074-4(0), 114690); lib. bdg. 26.65 (978-1-4342-2225-1(X), 103088) Capstone. (Stone Arch Bks.).

Collins, Terry. High-Flying Sam. Date not set. (Rocket Power Ready-to-Read Ser.: Vol. 5). (J). pap. 3.50 (978-0-689-86582-4(1), Simon Spotlight/Nickelodeon) Simon Spotlight/Nickelodeon.

Connelly, Neil. Brawler. 2019. (ENG.). 320p. (YA). (gr. 7-7). 17.99 (978-1-338-15775-8(2), Levine, Arthur A. Bks.) Scholastic, Inc.

Cook, Julia. My Mom Thinks She's My Volleyball Coach... but She's Not! Valentine, Allison, illus. 2007. (ENG.). 32p. (J). (gr. 3-8). 8.00 (978-1-934073-10-0(5), A252); pap. 5.00 (978-1-934073-09-4(1), A144) National Ctr. For Youth Issues.

—Teamwork Isn't My Thing, & I Don't Like to Share!, Volume 4. De Weerd, Kelsey, illus. 2012. (Best Me I Can Be Ser.). (ENG.). 31p. (J). (gr. k-6). pap. 10.95 (978-1-934490-35-8(0)) Boys Town Pr.

Coombs, Charles Ira. Indoor Sports Stories. Geer, Charles H., illus. 2011. 190p. 42.95 (978-1-258-09130-9(5)) Literary Licensing, LLC.

Cortright, Celeste. Ready, Set, Go! Sports of All Sorts. Engel, Christiane, illus. 2020. (ENG.). 24p. (J). (gr. -1-2). 16.99 (978-1-78285-985-7(3)); pap. 9.99 (978-1-78285-991-8(8)) Barefoot Bks., Inc.

Coven, Wanda. Heidi Heckelbeck Tries Out for the Team. Burris, Priscilla, illus. 2017. (Heidi Heckelbeck Ser.: 19). (ENG.). 128p. (J). (gr. k-4). pap. 6.99 (978-1-4814-7172-5(4), Little Simon) Little Simon.

—Heidi Heckelbeck Tries Out for the Team. 2017. (Heidi Heckelbeck Ser.: 19). lib. bdg. 16.00 (978-0-606-39741-4(8)) Turtleback.

Cross, Julie. Off the Ice. 2017. (Juniper Falls Ser.). (ENG.). 370p. (YA). pap. 9.99 (978-1-63375-655-7(6), 9781633756557) Entangled Publishing, LLC.

Crutcher, Chris. Whale Talk. (ENG.). (YA). 2018. 352p. (gr. 9). pap. 11.99 (978-0-06-268775-3(1)) 2009. 304p. (gr. 8). pap. 9.99 (978-0-06-177131-6(7)) HarperCollins Pubs. (Greenwillow Bks.).

—Whale Talk. 2004. 224p. (J). (gr. 7-18). pap. 38.00 incl. audio (978-0-8072-2289-8(5), Listening Library) Random Hse. Audio Publishing Group.

Damman, Matthew. The Small Sports Take the Field! Eisenbraun, Patty, illus. 2nd ed. 2013. (ENG.). 32p. (J). 15.99 (978-0-9856967-0-2(2)) MAP Creative LLC.

Darlison, Aleesah. Willow's Victory. Brailsford, Jill, illus. 2017. (Unicorn Riders Ser.). (ENG.). 112p. (J). (gr. 3-5). pap. 5.95 (978-1-4795-6557-3(1), 128547, Picture Window Bks.) Capstone.

Delashmutt, Amy. Hello, Cy! Torgeson, Sarah, illus. 2007. 24p. (J). lib. bdg. 14.95 (978-1-932888-53-9(5)) Amplify Publishing Group.

deRubertis, Barbara. Rosie Raccoon's Rock & Roll Raft. Alley, R. W., illus. 2011. (Animal Antics A to Z Ser.). 32p. (J). pap. 45.32 (978-0-7613-7664-4(X)) Astra Publishing Hse.

Derubertis, Barbara. Tessa Tiger's Temper Tantrums. Alley, R. W., illus. 2011. (Animal Antics A to Z Set III Ser.). pap. 45.32 (978-0-7613-8429-8(4)) Astra Publishing Hse.

deRubertis, Barbara & DeRubertis, Barbara. Rosie Raccoon's Rock & Roll Raft. Alley, R. W., illus. 2012. (Animal Antics A to Z Ser.). 32p. (J). (gr. 2 — 1). cd-rom 7.95 (978-1-57565-411-9(3)) Astra Publishing Hse.

Diersch, Sandra. Ceiling Stars, 1 vol. 2004. (Lorimer SideStreets Ser.). (ENG.). 144p. (YA). (gr. 9-12). 8.99 (978-1-55028-834-6(2), fb77ad92-8952-405d-9d3b-cbaed8c05244); 16.95 (978-1-55028-835-3(0), 835) James Lorimer & Co. Ltd., Pubs. CAN. Dist: Lerner Publishing Group, Formac Lorimer Bks. Ltd.

Dillard, Mary Gregory. The Days of My Youth. 2011. 184p. pap. 24.95 (978-1-4560-7513-2(6)) America Star Bks.

Dixon, Amy. Marathon Mouse. Denlinger, Sam, illus. 2012. (ENG.). 32p. (J). (gr. -1-k). 16.95 (978-1-61608-966-5(0), 608966, Sky Pony Pr.) Skyhorse Publishing Co., Inc.

Dixon, Franklin W. Sports Sabotage. 8. Burroughs, Scott, illus. 2012. (Hardy Boys: the Secret Files Ser.: 8). (ENG.). 112p. (J). (gr. 1-4). pap. 5.99 (978-1-4424-2316-9(1), Aladdin) Simon & Schuster Children's Publishing.

Drummond, Ree. Charlie Plays Ball. deGroat, Diane, illus. 2015. (Charlie the Ranch Dog Ser.). (ENG.). 40p. (J). (gr. -1-3). 18.99 (978-0-06-229752-5(X), HarperCollins) HarperCollins Pubs.

Duane, Diane, et al. Tom Clancy's Net Force: Death Match. 2003. (Net Force YA Ser.: 18). (ENG.). 192p. (YA). (gr. 7-18). 7.99 (978-0-425-18448-6(X), Berkley) Penguin Publishing Group.

Dungy, Tony & Dungy, Lauren. Carson Chooses Forgiveness: A Team Dungy Story about Basketball. 2019. (Team Dungy Ser.). (ENG., Illus.). 32p. (J). (gr. 1-4). 16.99 (978-0-7369-7322-9(2), 6973229) Harvest Hse. Pubs.

Earhart, Kristin. Arctic Freeze. Kaban, Eda, illus. 2015. 121p. (J). (978-1-5182-0297-1(7)) Scholastic, Inc.

—Arctic Freeze. 2015. (Race the Wild Ser.: 3). lib. bdg. 14.75 (978-0-606-37773-7(5)) Turtleback.

Evans, Zoe. Bevan vs. Evan: (and Other School Rivalries). 4. Barrager, Brigette, illus. 2012. (Cheer! Ser.: 4). (ENG.). 224p. (J). (gr. 3-7). pap. 6.99 (978-1-4424-3364-9(7), Simon Spotlight) Simon & Schuster Children's Publishing.

—Confessions of a Wannabe Cheerleader. Barrager, Brigette, illus. 2011. (Cheer! Ser.: 1). (ENG.). 240p. (J). (gr. 3-7). pap. 6.99 (978-1-4424-2241-4(6), Simon Spotlight) Simon Spotlight.

Ferguson, Donald. Chums of Scranton High on the Cinder Pat. 2006. 25.95 (978-1-4218-2937-1(1)); pap. 10.95 (978-1-4218-3037-7(X)) 1st World Publishing, Inc.

—The Chums of Scranton High on the Cinder Path. 2007. 124p. per. (978-1-4065-2363-8(1)) Dodo Pr.

—Chums of Scranton High Out for the Penna. 2006. 25.95 (978-1-4218-2938-8(X)); pap. 10.95 (978-1-4218-3038-4(8)) 1st World Publishing, Inc.

—The Chums of Scranton High Out for the Pennant, or, in the Three Town League. 2007. 124p. per. (978-1-4065-2364-5(X)) Dodo Pr.

Ferreira, Ninha. The Breakthrough: All Star Cheer Articles - Book 1. 2008. (ENG.). 194p. (YA). per. 13.95 (978-0-9815202-0-9(0)) Higgins Publishing.

Froggatt, Sarah H. E. Leopard Spots: How the Clouded Leopard Got Her Spots. 2012. 32p. pap. 32.70 (978-1-4771-3891-5(9)) Xlibris Corp.

Galloway, Priscilla. Atalante: La Coureuse la Plus Rapide au Monde. Cousineau, Normand, illus. 2006. (FRE.). 75p. (J). (gr. k-4). reprint ed. pap. 15.00 (978-1-4223-5394-3(X)) DIANE Publishing Co.

Game Face, 4 vols. 2015. (Game Face Ser.: 4). (ENG.). 112p. (J). (gr. 2-5). lib. bdg. 154.00 (978-1-62402-131-2(X), 19190, Calico Chapter Bks.) ABDO Publishing Co.

Gassman, Julie. Cheerleading Really Is a Sport, 1 vol. Santillan, Jorge, illus. 2010. (Sports Illustrated Kids Victory School Superstars Ser.). (ENG.). 56p. (J). (gr. 1-3). 26.65 (978-1-4342-2130-8(X), 102860); pap. 5.95 (978-1-4342-2809-3(6), 114079) Capstone. (Stone Arch Bks.).

—Nobody Wants to Play with a Ball Hog. Santillan, Jorge, illus. 2010. (Sports Illustrated Kids Victory School Superstars Ser.). (ENG.). 56p. (J). (gr. 1-3). pap. 5.95 (978-1-4342-2806-2(1), 114076, Stone Arch Bks.) Capstone.

—You Can't Spike Your Serves, 1 vol. Santillan, Jorge, illus. 2011. (Sports Illustrated Kids Victory School Superstars Ser.). (ENG.). 56p. (J). (gr. 1-3). pap. 5.95 (978-1-4342-3080-5(5), 114714); lib. bdg. 26.65 (978-1-4342-2231-2(4), 103094) Capstone. (Stone Arch Bks.).

Graham, Georgia. A Team Like No Other, 1 vol. Graham, Georgia, illus. 2004. (ENG., Illus.). 32p. (J). (gr. 1-2). 9.95 (978-0-88995-290-4(6), d3dbce51-2cd4-43dd-83f0-8311a06bd57a) Trifolium Bks., Inc. CAN. Dist: Firefly Bks., Ltd.

Gray, Kes. Daisy & the Trouble with Sports Day. 2014. (Daisy Ser.). (ENG., Illus.). 320p. (J). (gr. 2-4). pap. 11.99 (978-1-78295-285-5(3), Red Fox) Random House Children's Books GBR. Dist: Independent Pubs. Group.

Green, Tim. Kid Owner. 2016. (ENG.). 352p. (J). (gr. 3-7). 17.20 (978-0-606-39256-3(4)) Turtleback.

Groth, Darren & Groth, Simon. Infinite Blue, 1 vol. 2018. (ENG.). 192p. (YA). (gr. 8-12). pap. 14.95 (978-1-4598-1513-1(0)) Orca Bk. Pubs. USA.

Hallinan, P. K. Let's Play As a Team. 2003. (ENG., Illus.). 28p. (J). 8.75 (978-0-8249-5452-9(1), Ideals Pubns.) Worthy Publishing.

Hancock, H. Irving. The High School Freshmen. rev. ed. 2006. 212p. 27.95 (978-1-4218-1741-5(1)); pap. 12.95 (978-1-4218-1841-2(8)) 1st World Publishing, Inc. (1st World Library - Literary Society).

—The High School Freshmen. 2007. 180p. per. (978-1-4065-1988-4(X)) Dodo Pr.

—The High School Freshmen: Or, Dick & Co. 's First Year Pranks & Sports. 2017. (ENG., Illus.). (J). 23.95 (978-1-374-93030-8(X)); pap. 13.95 (978-1-374-93029-2(6)) Capital Communications, Inc.

—The High School Freshmen: Or, Dick & Co. 's First Year Pranks & Sports. 2017. (ENG., Illus.). (J). pap. (978-0-649-60244-5(7)) Trieste Publishing Pty Ltd.

—The High School Freshmen; or, Dick & Co. 's First Year Pranks & Sports. 2017. (ENG., Illus.). (J). pap. (978-0-649-14431-0(7)) Trieste Publishing Pty Ltd.

—The High School Pitcher. rev. ed. 2006. 212p. 27.95 (978-1-4218-1743-9(8)); pap. 12.95 (978-1-4218-1843-6(4)) 1st World Publishing, Inc. (1st World Library - Literary Society).

Harding, David. Chance of a Lifetime: Izzy Folau 1. Fosdike, James, illus. 2015. (Izzy Folau Ser.: 1). 176p. (J). (gr. 4-7). pap. 9.99 (978-0-85798-661-0(9)) Random Hse. Australia AUS. Dist: Independent Pubs. Group.

Harris, Devon D. Yes I Can. 2006. (Illus.). 48p. (J). (978-0-9764082-4-6(4)) Waterhouse Publishing.

Hartman, Mike. Take Your Dreams to the ICE. 2003. (Illus.). 60p. (YA). per. 9.99 (978-0-9760419-1-7(X)) ThatsMyLife Co.

He, Xu. Happy Taichichuan. 2007. (ENG.). 60p. pap. 9.50 (978-1-4303-2610-6(7)) Lulu Pr., Inc.

Health New England, creator. Sammie Sportz My Summer of Sports Safety. 2007. (Illus.). 16p. (J). 9.95 (978-0-9777159-3-0(0)) Health New England.

Hegerhorst, Bethany. The Soccer Princess: Josephina & the Gown Fashion Runway Show, 13 bks., bk. 1. Abbott, Kristin, illus. 2011. 32p. (J). 17.99 (978-0-615-35488-0(2)) Leo Publishing Works, Inc.

—The Soccer Princess: Josephina & the Gown Fashion Runway Show, 12. Abbott, Kristin, illus. 2011. 32p. (J). (978-0-9803829-6-9(3)) Murray Bks.

Heidbreder, Robert. Crocodiles Play! Mate, Rae, illus. 2009. (ENG.). 32p. (J). (gr. -1-3). 16.95 (978-1-894965-86-6(8)) Simply Read Bks. CAN. Dist: Ingram Publisher Services.

—Crocodiles Play!, 1 vol. Maté, Rae, illus. 2008. (ENG.). 32p. (J). (gr. -1-k). 16.95 (978-1-896580-89-0(0)) Tradewind Bks. CAN. Dist: Orca Bk. Pubs. USA.

Hellard, B. & Gibbs, L. Chase Your Goal. 2016. (Netball Gems Ser.: 2). 160p. (J). (gr. 4-7). pap. 10.99 (978-0-85798-766-2(6)) Random Hse. Australia AUS. Dist: Independent Pubs. Group.

—Defend to the End. 2016. (Netball Gems Ser.: 4). (Illus.). 160p. (J). (gr. 4-7). pap. 8.99 (978-0-85798-770-9(4)) Random Hse. Australia AUS. Dist: Independent Pubs. Group.

—Hooked on Netball. 2016. (Netball Gems Ser.: 1). (Illus.). 144p. (J). (gr. 4-7). 10.99 (978-0-85798-763-1(1)) Random Hse. Australia AUS. Dist: Independent Pubs. Group.

—Pivot & Win. 2016. (Netball Gems Ser.: 3). (Illus.). 160p. (J). (gr. 4-7). pap. 10.99 (978-0-85798-768-6(2)) Random Hse. Australia AUS. Dist: Independent Pubs. Group.

Hellard, B. & Gibbs, Lisa. Netball Gems Bindup 1. 2017. (Netball Gems Ser.). 304p. (J). (gr. 2-4). 19.99 (978-0-14-378088-5(3)) Random Hse. Australia AUS. Dist: Independent Pubs. Group.

Hellman, Charles. Fun Is... 2005. 124p. (gr. 4-7). per. 9.95 (978-0-935938-16-6(8)) LuckySports.

Hellman, Charles S. Discovering Sportsland. Tiritilli, Robert A., illus. 2013. 44p. pap. 9.49 (978-0-935938-51-7(6)) LuckySports.

—The Volleyball Bully. Tiritilli, Robert A., illus. 2013. 34p. pap. 9.25 (978-0-935938-53-1(2)) LuckySports.

Hicks, Betty. Basketball Bats / Goof-Off Goalie. McCauley, Adam, illus. 2009. (Gym Shorts Ser.). (ENG.). 128p. (J). (gr. 2-4). pap. 14.99 (978-0-312-58247-0(1), 900062060) Square Fish.

Higgins, Kitty. Mushing in Alaska. 2005. (J). pap. (978-1-4108-4228-2(2)) Benchmark Education Co.

Hitchhiking Flat Kid. 2004. (J). ring bd. 4.50 (978-0-9763328-0-0(9), Flat Kids) Smart Smiles Co., The.

Hoban, Russell. How Tom Beat Captain Najork & His Hired Sportsmen. Blake, Quentin, illus. 2006. (ENG.). 32p. (J). (gr. k-4). pap. 7.95 (978-1-56792-322-3(4)) Godine, David R. Pub.

Hoese, Ray. My Dad Is an Ironman. Steinbach, Coreen, illus. 2004. (ENG.). 32p. (J). 15.00 (978-1-891369-51-3(2)) Breakaway Bks.

Holm, Jennifer L. & Holm, Matthew. Captain Disaster. 2012. (Squish Ser.: 4). lib. bdg. 17.20 (978-0-606-26812-7(X)) Turtleback.

—Squish #4: Captain Disaster. Holm, Jennifer L. & Holm, Matthew, illus. 2012. (Squish Ser.: 4). (Illus.). 96p. (J). (gr. 2-5). pap. 6.99 (978-0-375-84392-1(2)) Penguin Random Hse. LLC.

Houran, Lori Haskins. Alien in the Outfield (Book 6) Warrick, Jessica, illus. 2017. (How to Be an Earthling Ser.: 6). 64p. (J). (gr. 1-4). 6.99 (978-1-57565-848-3(8), 6b5c279a-7e30-4bcd-be2d-055ec8834290, Kane Press) Astra Publishing Hse.

Howling, Eric. Hoop Magic, 1 vol. 2013. (Lorimer Sports Stories Ser.). (ENG.). 136p. (J). (gr. 4-8). pap. 9.95 (978-1-4594-0525-7(0), 6a2cdd0e-1968-44a0-a9d8-1ef2e3c07bfd) James Lorimer & Co. Ltd., Pubs. CAN. Dist: Lerner Publishing Group.

Hutchins, Hazel. TJ & the Sports Fanatic, 1 vol. 2006. (Orca Young Readers Ser.). (ENG., Illus.). 144p. (J). (gr. 4-7). per. 5.95 (978-1-55143-461-2(X)) Orca Bk. Pubs. USA.

I Play for Notre Dame. 2004. (J). bds. (978-0-9749156-0-9(2)) Mandell, Ted.

Jeter, Derek. Change Up. 2016. (Jeter Publishing Ser.). (ENG., Illus.). 176p. (J). (gr. 3-7). 17.99 (978-1-4814-6445-1(0), Simon & Schuster/Paula Wiseman Bks.) Simon & Schuster/Paula Wiseman Bks.

Jones Beehler, Jayne J. Drop the Puck, It's Hockey Season. Dohm, Katrina G., illus. 2015. (Official Adventures Ser.). (ENG.). (J). (gr. 2-5). 17.95 (978-1-59298-881-5(4)) Beaver's Pond Pr., Inc.

Jones, Jasmine. Coach Carter. 2004. (Amistad Ser.). (ENG., Illus.). 144p. (J). (gr. 8-18). pap. 6.99 (978-0-06-077252-9(2), Amistad) HarperCollins Pubs.

Kellerhals-Stewart, Heather. SAR: Powderhounds, 1 vol. 2013. (ENG.). 176p. (YA). (gr. 8-12). 19.95 (978-1-4594-0518-9(8), 0518); pap. 12.95 (978-1-4594-0519-6(6), 0519) James Lorimer & Co. Ltd., Pubs. CAN. Dist: Formac Lorimer Bks. Ltd.

Kelli Hunter Beamon. Mommy, I Want to Be a Cheerleader! 2009. 16p. pap. 8.49 (978-1-4389-7037-0(4)) AuthorHouse.

Kelly, David A. MVP #1: the Gold Medal Mess. Brundage, Scott, illus. 2016. (Most Valuable Players Ser.: 1). 128p. (J). (gr. 1-4). 5.99 (978-0-553-51319-6(2), Random Hse. Bks. for Young Readers) Random Hse. Children's Bks.

Kelsey, Stacy. Sproket the Moto Dog, 1 vol. 2009. 40p. pap. 24.95 (978-1-60749-899-5(5)) America Star Bks.

Kew, Trevor. Breakaway, 1 vol. 2011. (Lorimer Sports Stories Ser.). (ENG.). 144p. (J). (gr. 4-8). pap. 9.95 (978-1-55277-862-3(2), 3e9b4547-1644-4539-a964-b339abedd96e) James Lorimer & Co. Ltd., Pubs. CAN. Dist: Lerner Publishing Group.

Kilby, Tracie. Gymnastics Gina. 2010. 32p. pap. 16.00 (978-1-4520-6277-8(3)) AuthorHouse.

Kishimoto, Masashi. Naruto: Chapter Book, Vol. 2: The Tests of a Ninja. 2008. (Naruto: Chapter Bks.: 2). (ENG., Illus.). 80p. (J). (gr. 1-5). pap. 4.99 (978-1-4215-2213-5(6)) Viz Media.

Klass, David. Losers Take All. 2016. (YA). lib. bdg. 20.85 (978-0-606-39480-2(X)) Turtleback.

Koertge, Ron. Shakespeare Makes the Playoffs. 2012. (ENG., Illus.). 176p. (YA). (gr. 7). pap. 7.99 (978-0-7636-5852-6(9)) Candlewick Pr.

Könnecke, Ole. Sports Are Fantastic Fun! Könnecke, Ole, illus. 2018. (ENG., Illus.). 56p. (J). (gr. -1-k). 19.99 (978-1-77657-201-4(7), 4bb59a55-4dc5-4cec-a2a1-54ead8ff0079) Gecko Pr. NZL. Dist: Lerner Publishing Group.

Kosgei, William. The Talented & Gifted: African Writers Series. 2013. 106p. pap. 10.95 (978-1-62516-165-9(4), Strategic Bk. Publishing) Strategic Book Publishing & Rights Agency (SBPRA).

Krakow, Amy. The Matt & the Morster 60 Sking & Snowboarding. Williams, Steve, illus. 2005. 32p. (J). (gr. k-6). 15.00 (978-0-9715224-2-8(1)) Wagging Tales Publishing.

Kreie, Chris. Shot Clock Slam. Aburto, Jesus & Esparza, Andres, illus. 2010. (Sports Illustrated Kids Graphic Novels Ser.). (ENG.). 56p. (J). (gr. 3-8). pap. 7.19 (978-1-4342-2786-7(3), 114053, Stone Arch Bks.) Capstone.

Krinsky, Lee. The Longest Fall. 2009. 228p. 25.95 (978-0-595-71908-2(2)); pap. 15.95 (978-0-595-42719-2(7)) iUniverse, Inc.

Ladybird. Topsy & Tim: the Big Race Ladybird Readers Level 2. 2016. (Ladybird Readers Ser.). (Illus.). 48p. (J). (gr. 2-4). pap. 9.99 (978-0-241-25448-6(5)) Penguin Bks., Ltd. GBR. Dist: Independent Pubs. Group.

Landers, Ace. Race for Treasure. White, Dave, illus. 2011. 32p. (J). pap. (978-0-545-33454-9(3)) Scholastic, Inc.

Lewis, Axel. Canyon Chaos, 1 vol. 2014. (Robot Racers Ser.). (ENG., Illus.). 160p. (J). (gr. 2-4). pap. 6.95 (978-1-4342-7936-1(7), 124681, Stone Arch Bks.) Capstone.

—Rain Forest Rampage, 1 vol. 2014. (Robot Racers Ser.). (ENG.). 160p. (J). (gr. 2-4). 26.65 (978-1-4342-6571-5(4), 124406); (Illus.). pap. 6.95 (978-1-4342-7937-8(5), 124682) Capstone. (Stone Arch Bks.).

Ley, Mary. Tri-Son: The Little Triathlete. Ley, Mary, illus. 2003. (Illus.). per. (978-0-9707547-1-4(X)) Woodburn Graphics, Inc.

Lin, Chris. Mandy & Pandy Play Sports. Villalta, Ingrid, illus. 2008. 20p. (J). (gr. -1-3). bds. 9.99 (978-0-9800156-7-6(7)) Mandy & Pandy Bks., LLC.

London, Jonathan. Desolation Canyon. London, Sean, illus. 2015. (Aaron's Wilderness Ser.: 1). (ENG.). 168p. (J). (gr. 3-5). pap. 12.99 (978-1-941821-29-9(4), West Winds Pr.) West Margin Pr.

—Froggy Plays T-Ball. Remkiewicz, Frank, illus. 2009. (Froggy Ser.). (ENG.). 32p. (J). (gr. -1-k). pap. 7.99 (978-0-14-241304-3(6), Puffin Books) Penguin Young Readers Group.

Long, Loren & Bildner, Phil. Blastin' the Blues. Long, Loren, illus. 2011. (Sluggers Ser.: 5). (ENG., Illus.). 448p. (J). (gr. 3-7). pap. 8.99 (978-1-4169-1891-2(4), Simon & Schuster Bks. For Young Readers) Simon & Schuster Bks. For Young Readers.

Loughlin, Patrick. Super Sports Stories for Children. 2016. (Illus.). 208p. (J). (gr. 1-3). pap. 13.99 (978-0-85798-966-6(9)) Random Hse. Australia AUS. Dist: Independent Pubs. Group.

Lubar, David. Lay Ups & Long Shots: Eight Short Stories. 2008. 128p. (YA). (gr. 5-8). 14.95 (978-1-58196-078-5(6), Darby Creek) Lerner Publishing Group.

Luciani, Brigitte. What a Team! Gauvin, Edward, tr. from FRE. Tharlet, Eve, illus. 2011. (Mr. Badger & Mrs. Fox Ser.: 3). (ENG.). 32p. (J). (gr. k-3). 25.26 (978-0-7613-5627-1(4)) Lerner Publishing Group.

Lupica, Mike. Game Changers (Game Changers, Book 1), Bk. 1. 2013. (Game Changers Ser.: 1). (ENG.). 224p. (J). (gr. 3-7). pap. 7.99 (978-0-545-38179-6(7), Scholastic Pr.) Scholastic, Inc.

Lynch, Chris. Slot Machine. 2003. 23.00 (978-0-8446-7249-6(1)) Smith, Peter Pub., Inc.

Maccarone, Grace. Bunny Race! Long, Ethan, illus. 2009. (J). (978-0-545-11290-1(7)) Scholastic, Inc.

Macdonald, Kelly. They Shoot! They Score! Life's Lessons on Ice. Luca, Bogdan, illus. 2005. 32p. 9.99 (978-0-9736893-0-3(7)) MacDonald, Kelly CAN. Dist: Hushion Hse. Publishing, Ltd.

MacGregor, Roy. The Highest Number in the World. Després, Geneviève, illus. 2014. 32p. (J). (gr. 1-4). 17.99 (978-1-77049-575-3(4), Tundra Bks.) Tundra Bks. CAN. Dist: Penguin Random Hse. LLC.

—The Night They Stole the Stanley Cup, 2. 2013. (Screech Owls Ser.: 2). (ENG.). 176p. (J). (gr. 4-7). pap. 8.99 (978-1-77049-414-5(6), Tundra Bks.) Tundra Bks. CAN. Dist: Penguin Random Hse. LLC.

Maddox, Jake. Caught Stealing. Aburto, Jesus, illus. 2015. (Jake Maddox Sports Stories Ser.). (ENG.). 72p. (J). (gr. 3-6). lib. bdg. 25.99 (978-1-4965-0493-7(3), 128565, Stone Arch Bks.) Capstone.

—Digging Deep. Wood, Katie, illus. 2018. (Jake Maddox Girl Sports Stories Ser.). (ENG.). 72p. (J). (gr. 3-6). lib. bdg. 25.32 (978-1-4965-6356-9(5), 138075, Stone Arch Bks.) Capstone.

—Free Climb, 1 vol. Tiffany, Sean, illus. 2008. (Jake Maddox Sports Stories Ser.). (ENG.). 72p. (J). (gr. 3-6). pap. 5.95 (978-1-4342-0880-4(X), 95237, Stone Arch Bks.) Capstone.

—Gridiron Showdown, 1 vol. Ray, Michael, illus. 2014. (Jake Maddox JV Ser.). (ENG.). 96p. (J). (gr. 4-6). 26.65 (978-1-4342-9155-4(3), 125605, Stone Arch Bks.) Capstone.

—Jake Maddox: Definición Por Penales. Heck, Claudia, tr. Tiffany, Sean, illus. 2012. (Jake Maddox en Español Ser.). (SPA.). 72p. (J). (gr. 3-6). 25.32 (978-1-4342-3814-6(8), 117503, Stone Arch Bks.) Capstone.

—Jake Maddox: Tiro Libre, 1 vol. Heck, Claudia, tr. from ENG. Tiffany, Sean, illus. 2012. (Jake Maddox en Español Ser.). (SPA.). 72p. (J). (gr. 3-6). 25.32 (978-1-4342-3812-2(1), 117500, Stone Arch Bks.) Capstone.

—Jump Serve, 1 vol. Mourning, Tuesday, illus. 2008. (Jake Maddox Girl Sports Stories Ser.). (ENG.). 72p. (J). (gr. 3-6). per. 5.95 (978-1-4342-0520-9(7), 94460, Stone Arch Bks.) Capstone.

—Lacrosse Attack. Tiffany, Sean, illus. 2008. (Jake Maddox Sports Stories Ser.). (ENG.). 72p. (J). (gr. 3-6). 25.99 (978-1-4342-0776-0(5), 95181); pap. 5.95 (978-1-4342-0872-9(9), 95233) Capstone. (Stone Arch Bks.).

—Lacrosse Laser. Aburto, Jesus, illus. 2016. (Jake Maddox Sports Stories Ser.). (ENG.). 72p. (J). (gr. 3-6). lib. bdg. 25.99 (978-1-4965-3051-6(9), 131933, Stone Arch Bks.) Capstone.

—On the Line, 1 vol. Tiffany, Sean, illus. 2006. (Jake Maddox Sports Stories Ser.). (ENG.). 72p. (J). (gr. 3-6). 25.99 (978-1-59889-062-4(X), 86533, Stone Arch Bks.) Capstone.

—Paintball Boss. 2016. (Jake Maddox JV Ser.). (ENG., Illus.). 96p. (J). (gr. 4-6). lib. bdg. 26.65 (978-1-4965-3982-3(6), 133205, Stone Arch Bks.) Capstone.

—Pick & Roll. Tiffany, Sean, illus. 2018. (Jake Maddox Sports Stories Ser.). (ENG.). 72p. (J). (gr. 3-6). pap. 5.95 (978-1-4965-6320-0(4), 138059, Stone Arch Bks.) Capstone.

—Pool Panic. Wood, Katie, illus. 2016. (Jake Maddox Girl Sports Stories Ser.). (ENG.). 72p. (J). (gr. 3-6). lib. bdg. 25.32 (978-1-4965-2618-2(X), 131174, Stone Arch Bks.) Capstone.

—Soccer Sabotage. 2018. (Jake Maddox JV Ser.). (ENG., Illus.). 96p. (J). (gr. 4-6). lib. bdg. 26.65 (978-1-4965-5932-6(0), 137134, Stone Arch Bks.) Capstone.

—Soccer Shootout, 1 vol. Tiffany, Sean, illus. 2007. (Jake Maddox Sports Stories Ser.). (ENG.). 72p. (J). (gr. 3-6). 25.99 (978-1-59889-844-6(2), 94241, Stone Arch Bks.) Capstone.

—Soccer Surprise, 1 vol. Wood, Katie, illus. 2012. (Jake Maddox Girl Sports Stories Ser.). (ENG.). 72p. (J). (gr. 3-6). pap. 5.95 (978-1-4342-3906-8(3), 118091); lib. bdg. 25.32 (978-1-4342-3291-5(3), 116255) Capstone. (Stone Arch Bks.).

—Touchdown Turmoil. 2018. (Jake Maddox JV Ser.). (ENG., Illus.). 96p. (J). (gr. 4-6). lib. bdg. 25.99 (978-1-4965-6331-6(X), 138062, Stone Arch Bks.) Capstone.

—El Tramposo de BMX, 1 vol. Heck, Claudia, tr. Tiffany, Sean & Tiffany, Sean, illus. 2012. (Jake Maddox en Español Ser.). (SPA.). 72p. (J). (gr. 3-6). 25.32 (978-1-4342-3817-7(2), 117507, Stone Arch Bks.) Capstone.

—Volleyball Dreams, 1 vol. Wood, Katie, illus. 2012. (Jake Maddox Girl Sports Stories Ser.). (ENG.). 72p. (J). (gr. 3-6). pap. 5.95 (978-1-4342-3907-5(1), 118092); lib. bdg. 25.32 (978-1-4342-3292-2(1), 116256) Capstone. (Stone Arch Bks.).

—Volleyball Victory. Wood, Katie, illus. 2016. (Jake Maddox Girl Sports Stories Ser.). (ENG.). 72p. (J). (gr. 3-6). lib. bdg. 25.32 (978-1-4965-2619-9(8), 131175, Stone Arch Bks.) Capstone.

Maddox, Jake & Maddox, Jake. Gold Medal Swim, 1 vol. Garcia, Eduardo, illus. 2012. (Jake Maddox Sports Stories Ser.). (ENG.). 72p. (J). (gr. 3-6). lib. bdg. 25.99 (978-1-4342-3288-5(3), 116252, Stone Arch Bks.) Capstone.

Magness, Vicki. Stephen: A Strong Man to Run a Race. 2012. 40p. pap. 21.99 (978-1-4771-2562-5(0)) Xlibris Corp.

Maiocco, Chris & Maiocco, Kimberly. Things My Father Taught Me Through Sports... Playing the Game of Baseball: Playing the Game of Baseball. Cox, Tom, illus. 2003. 20p. (J). 12.99 (978-0-9720417-0-6(2), 0-9720417-0-2) His Kids Publishing, Inc.

Mantell, Paul & Christopher, Matt. Snowboard Champ. 2005. (Matt Christopher Sports Ser.). 146p. (gr. 3-7). 16.00 (978-0-7569-5198-6(4)) Perfection Learning Corp.

Mantlo, Mickey A. & Cook, Darren A. Tennis Shoes & Toe Clips, 1 vol. 2010. 204p. pap. 24.95 (978-1-4512-9683-9(5)) America Star Bks.

Manushkin, Fran. El Golazo de Pedro. Trusted Translations, Trusted, tr. Lyon, Tammie, illus. 2018. (Pedro en Español Ser.). (SPA.). 32p. (J). (gr. k-2). lib. bdg. 21.32 (978-1-5158-2511-1(6), 137570, Picture Window Bks.) Capstone.

Marsh, Carole. The Castaway Cheerleaders. 2006. 64p. (gr. 2-4). 14.95 (978-0-635-06224-6(0)); pap. 3.99 (978-0-635-06218-5(6)) Gallopade International.

—The Mystery on Alaska's Iditarod Trail. 2009. (Real Kids, Real Places Ser.). 145p. (J). 18.99 (978-0-635-06997-9(0), Marsh, Carole Mysteries) Gallopade International.

Martin, R. T. Pod Racer. 2017. (Level Up Ser.). (ENG.). 112p. (YA). (gr. 6-12). pap. 7.99 (978-1-5124-5358-4(7), ca2a9320-8539-4cd2-b818-bbab252d30a7); lib. bdg. 26.65 (978-1-5124-3988-5(6), c051e999-497c-4d60-b57b-c3aac1520b93) Lerner Publishing Group. (Darby Creek).

Mayer, Mercer. Fair Play. 2012. (Big Little Critter Ser.: 1). (ENG., Illus.). 98p. (J). 12.95 (978-1-60746-763-2(1), Premiere) FastPrncl, Inc.

McCann, James. Flying Feet, 1 vol. 2010. (Orca Sports Ser.). (ENG., Illus.). 152p. (J). (gr. 4-7). pap. 9.95 (978-1-55469-290-3(3)) Orca Bk. Pubs. USA.

McCoy, Mary. Camp So-And-So. 2017. (ENG.). 424p. (YA). (gr. 8-12). E-Book 27.99 (978-1-5124-3429-3(9), 9781512434293); E-Book 9.99 (978-1-5124-3428-6(0), 9781512434286) Lerner Publishing Group. (Carolrhoda Lab™).

McCully, Emily Arnold. Late Nate in a Race. 2013. (I Like to Read Ser.). (ENG., Illus.). 24p. (J). (gr. -1-3). pap. 7.99 (978-0-8234-2755-0(2)) Holiday Hse., Inc.

Mcdonald, Megan. Stink & the Ultimate Thumb-Wrestling Smackdown, 1 vol. Reynolds, Peter H., illus. 2012. (Stink Ser.: No. 2). (ENG.). 144p. (J). (gr. 1-5). 31.36 (978-1-59961-194-5(5), 13835, Chapter Bks.) Spotlight.

McDonald, Megan. Stink: the Ultimate Thumb-Wrestling Smackdown, Bk. 6. Reynolds, Peter H., illus. 2013. (Stink Ser.: 6). (ENG.). 144p. (J). (gr. 1-4). 15.99 (978-0-7636-6393-3(X)) Candlewick Pr.

McDonnell, Vincent. Race Against Time. 2005. (SPA & ENG.). 96p. (J). pap. 11.95 (978-1-903464-62-5(5), Collins Pr., The) M.H. Gill & Co. U. C. IRL. Dist: Dufour Editions, Inc.

McEwan, Jamie. Willy the Scrub. Kennedy, Victor, illus. 2004. (Junior Library Guild Selection Ser.). (ENG.). 64p. (J). (gr. 2-5). 11.95 (978-1-58196-010-5(7), Darby Creek) Lerner Publishing Group.

McKee, David. Elmer & the Whales. McKee, David, illus. 2014. (Elmer Ser.). (ENG., Illus.). 32p. (J). (gr. -1-3). 16.95 (978-1-4677-3453-0(5), 38181d9e-acb0-45e5-8042-73782a258a4d) Lerner Publishing Group.

McKissack, Robert. Try Your Best. Cepeda, Joe, illus. 2004. (ENG.). 24p. (J). (gr. -1-3). pap. 4.99 (978-0-15-205090-0(6), 1195368, Clarion Bks.) HarperCollins Pubs.

McKissack, Robert L. Try Your Best. Cepeda, Joe, illus. 2005. (Green Light Readers Level 2 Ser.). (gr. k-2). 13.95 (978-0-7569-5630-1(7)) Perfection Learning Corp.

McMahon, Kate. That Touch of Magic. 2009. (ENG.). 112p. (J). pap. (978-1-901737-60-8(8), Anvil Bks.) Mercier Pr., Ltd., The.

McMullan, Kate. Go for the Gold, Atalanta!, 1 vol. Zilber, Denis, illus. 2011. (Myth-O-Mania Ser.: Bk. 8). (ENG.). 192p. (J). (gr. 4-8). pap. 5.95 (978-1-4342-3441-4(X), 116462, Stone Arch Bks.) Capstone.

—Go for the Gold, Atalanta! 2003. (Myth-o-Mania Ser.: No. 8). (Illus.). 160p. (J). 9.99 (978-0-7868-0864-9(0)) Hyperion Bks. for Children.

McOmber, Rachel B., ed. McOmber Phonics Storybooks: A Game for Champions. rev. ed. (Illus.). (J). (978-0-944991-68-8(8)) Swift Learning Resources.

Meister, Cari. The Kickball Kids, 1 vol. Olson, Julie, illus. 2009. (My First Graphic Novel Ser.). (ENG.). 32p. (J). (gr. k-2). pap. 6.25 (978-1-4342-1410-2(9), 95688, Stone Arch Bks.) Capstone.

Mills, Tricia. Heartbreak River. 2009. (YA). (978-1-59514-220-7(7), Razorbill) Penguin Publishing Group.

Montalbano, Andrea. Lily Out of Bounds. 2012. (ENG.). 132p. (J). pap. 8.99 (978-0-9858956-1-7(6)) In This Together Media.

Montgomery, R. A. Always Picked Last. Newton, Keith, illus. 2009. 64p. (J). (gr. 2). pap. 7.99 (978-1-933390-38-3(7)) Chooseco LLC.

Moore, Stephanie Perry. Keep Jumping/No Hating. 2012. (Lockwood Lions Ser.). (YA). lib. bdg. 26.90 (978-0-606-26494-5(9)) Turtleback.

—Settle down/Be Real. 2012. (Lockwood Lions Ser.). (YA). lib. bdg. 26.90 (978-0-606-26495-2(7)) Turtleback.

Moore, Stephanie Perry & Moore, Derrick. Real Diva/Man Up. 2014. (Grovehill Giants Ser.). (YA). lib. bdg. 26.90 (978-0-606-31879-2(8)) Turtleback.

—Scream Loud/Quiet Strength. 2014. (Grovehill Giants Ser.). (YA). lib. bdg. 26.90 (978-0-606-31880-8(1)) Turtleback.

Moore, Steve. King of the Bench: No Fear! Moore, Steve, illus. 2017. (King of the Bench Ser.: 1). (ENG., Illus.). 224p. (J). (gr. 3-7). 13.99 (978-0-06-220330-4(4), HarperCollins) HarperCollins Pubs.

Morgan, Alex. Under Pressure. 2017. (Kicks Ser.). (ENG., Illus.). 128p. (J). (gr. 3-7). 18.99 (978-1-4814-8150-2(9), Simon & Schuster Bks. For Young Readers) Simon & Schuster Bks. For Young Readers.

—Win or Lose. 2014. (Kicks Ser.). (ENG., Illus.). 160p. (J). (gr. 3-7). 15.99 (978-1-4424-8580-8(9), Simon & Schuster Bks. For Young Readers) Simon & Schuster Bks. For Young Readers.

Morningstar, Jeremy. My Own Special Angel. 2005. 24p. 7.00 (978-1-4116-6574-3(0)) Lulu Pr., Inc.

Murphy, Harriet. Diego in Action! Follow the Reader Level 2. 2007. (Go, Diego, Go! Ser.). (ENG., Illus.). 24p. (J). (gr. -1-2). 24.99 (978-1-4169-4993-0(3), Simon Scribbles) Simon Scribbles.

Murray, Stuart A. P. Matty in the Goal, 1 vol. 2012. (Champion Sports Story Ser.). (ENG.). 104p. (J). (gr. 3-5). 30.60 (978-0-7660-3877-6(7), 7cd5aacf-9446-4ecc-a170-384455d3c3f5); pap. 13.88 (978-1-4644-0003-2(2), cf8888ef-6c05-46e8-828c-b0584784f0c5) Enslow Publishing, LLC.

Myers, Walter Dean. Game. (ENG.). (YA). (gr. 8). 2009. 240p. pap. 15.99 (978-0-06-058296-8(0)) 2008. 224p. 17.99 (978-0-06-058294-4(4)) HarperCollins Pubs. (HarperTeen).

Neighbors, Jared. Rivals, 1 vol. 2009. 73p. pap. 19.95 (978-1-61582-021-4(3)) America Star Bks.

New Coach Blues. 2003. (Illus.). pap. 5.60 (978-0-7398-7509-4(4)) Steck-Vaughn.

Nickel, Scott. I Could Be a One-Man Relay, 1 vol. Santillan, Jorge H., illus. 2012. (Sports Illustrated Kids Victory School Superstars Ser.). (ENG.). 56p. (J). (gr. 1-3). pap. 5.95 (978-1-4342-3867-2(9), 118049); lib. bdg. 26.65 (978-1-4342-2246-6(2), 103109) Capstone. (Stone Arch Bks.).

Olivas, Daniel. Benjamin & Word Benjamin Y la Palabra. (SPA & ENG., Illus.). 32p. 15.95 (978-1-55885-413-0(4), Piñata Books) Arte Publico Pr.

O'Neal, Shaquille. Little Shaq. Taylor, Theodore, III, illus. 2015. (ENG.). 80p. (J). (gr. k-2). 9.99 (978-1-61963-721-4(9), 900146374, Bloomsbury USA Childrens) Bloomsbury Publishing USA.

Owen, Frank, ed. Teenage Winter Sports Stories. Ricketts, William, illus. 2011. 254p. 46.95 (978-1-258-10167-1(X)) Literary Licensing, LLC.

Parish, Herman. Amelia Bedelia Chapter Book #5. Avril, Lynne, illus. 2014. (Amelia Bedelia Ser.). (ENG.). 160p. (J). (gr. 1-5). 9.99 (978-0-06-233399-5(2), Greenwillow Bks.) HarperCollins Pubs.

—Amelia Bedelia Chapter Book #5: Amelia Bedelia Shapes Up. 2014. (Amelia Bedelia Ser.). (ENG., Illus.). 160p. (J). (gr. 1-5). pap. 5.99 (978-0-06-233396-4(8), Greenwillow Bks.) HarperCollins Pubs.

Pee-Wee T-Ball. 2003. (J). per. (978-1-57657-942-8(5)) Paradise Pr., Inc.

Peirce, Lincoln. Big Nate: Thunka, Thunka, Thunka. 2016. (Big Nate Ser.: Vol. 14). (ENG., Illus.). (J). (gr. 3-6). 29.99 (978-1-4494-7581-9(7)) Andrews McMeel Publishing.

—Big Nate: Thunka, Thunka, Thunka, Volume 14. 2016. (Big Nate Ser.: 14). (ENG., Illus.). 176p. (J). (gr. 3-6). pap. 12.99 (978-1-4494-6227-7(8)) Andrews McMeel Publishing.

Petrillo, Genevieve. Keep Your Ear on the Ball, 1 vol. Lyon, Lea, illus. 2009. (ENG.). 32p. (J). (gr. 2-6). pap. 9.95 (978-0-88448-324-3(X), 884324) Tilbury Hse. Pubs.

Phillips, Lyda. Mr Touchdown. 2008. 184p. 23.95 (978-1-4401-0976-8(1)); pap. 13.95 (978-1-60528-029-5(1)) iUniverse, Inc. (iUniverse Star).

Posada, Jorge. Sí, Puedes (Play Ball!) ón, Raúl, illus. 2010. (SPA.). 32p. (J). (gr. 1-5). 8.99 (978-1-4169-9826-6(8), Simon & Schuster/Paula Wiseman Bks.) Simon & Schuster/Paula Wiseman Bks.

Poulsen, David A. Blind Date. 2nd rev. ed. 2008. (Lawrence High Yearbook Ser.). (ENG.). 96p. (J). (gr. 2-7). pap. (978-1-55263-933-7(9)) Me to We.

—Wild Thing. 2008. (Lawrence High Yearbook Ser.). (ENG.). 96p. (gr. 2-7). pap. (978-1-55263-931-3(2)) Me to We.

Random House. You Can Be a Soccer Player (Barbie) 2018. (Step into Reading Ser.). (ENG., Illus.). 24p. (J). (gr. -1-1). pap. 5.99 (978-1-5247-6911-6(8), Random Hse. Bks. for Young Readers) Random Hse. Children's Bks.

Rayburn, Tricia. Maggie Bean Stays Afloat. 2008. (ENG.). 320p. (J). (gr. 4-8). pap. 6.99 (978-1-4169-3347-2(6), Aladdin) Simon & Schuster Children's Publishing.

Rayner, Robert. Just for Kicks, 1 vol. 2004. (Lorimer Sports Stories Ser.). (ENG.). 152p. (J). (gr. 4-8). 16.95 (978-1-55028-825-4(3), 825) James Lorimer & Co. Ltd., Pubs. CAN. Dist: Formac Lorimer Bks. Ltd.

Ricci, Christine. The Super Soccer Game. Hall, Susan & Roper, Robert, illus. 2007. (J). pap. (978-1-4127-8926-4(5)) Publications International, Ltd.

Richardson, Charisse. The Real Slam Dunk. 2005. (Illus.). 96p. (J). (gr. k-3). 6.99 (978-0-14-240212-2(5), Puffin Books) Penguin Young Readers Group.

Riley, Zach. Quarterback Crisis. Ricci, Andrés, illus. 2012. (Zach Riley Ser.). (ENG.). 80p. (J). (gr. 2-5). lib. bdg. 35.64 (978-1-61783-534-6(X), 15859, Calico Chapter Bks.) ABDO Publishing Co.

Rippin, Sally. The Soccer Star. Fukuoka, Aki, illus. 2012. (Billie B. Brown Ser.). (ENG.). 44p. (J). (978-1-61067-133-0(3)) Kane Miller.

Robins, Eleanor. Back-Up Quarterback, 1 vol. unabr. ed. 2010. (Carter High Chronicles Ser.). (ENG.). 52p. (YA). (gr. 9-12). pap. 9.75 (978-1-61651-303-0(9)) Saddleback Educational Publishing, Inc.

—Don't Blame Me 2011, 1 vol. unabr. ed. 2010. (Carter High Chronicles Ser.). (ENG.). 52p. (YA). (gr. 9-12). pap. 9.75 (978-1-61651-306-1(3)) Saddleback Educational Publishing, Inc.

—One More Chance, 1 vol. unabr. ed. 2010. (Carter High Senior Year Ser.). (ENG.). 52p. (YA). (gr. 9-12). pap. 9.75 *(978-1-61651-327-6(6))* Saddleback Educational Publishing, Inc.

Rocking & Rolling Along, 6 vols., Set B. 32p. (gr. 1-3). 26.50 *(978-0-7802-8053-3(9))* Wright Group/McGraw-Hill.

Roddy, Lee. Escape down the Raging Rapids. 2008. (D. J. Dillon Adventure Ser.: No. 10). (Illus.). 117p. (J). 7.99 *(978-0-88062-274-5(1))* Mott Media.

Rosen, Robert. My Favorite Sport. De Polonia, Nina, illus. 2017. (Play Time Ser.). (ENG.). 24p. (gr. -1-2). 28.50 *(978-1-68342-716-2(5)*, 9781683427162) Rourke Educational Media.

—My Favorite Sport. de Polonia, Nina, illus. 2017. (Play Time Ser.). (ENG.). 24p. (gr. -1-2). pap. 9.95 *(978-1-68342-768-1(8)*, 9781683427681) Rourke Educational Media.

Rosselson, Leon. Gordon & the Giantkillers. (ENG., Illus.). 127p. (J). pap. 7.99 *(978-0-340-64072-2(3))* Hodder & Stoughton GBR. Dist: Trafalgar Square Publishing.

Roza, Greg. Goal!, 1 vol. 2006. (Neighborhood Readers Ser.). (ENG.). 16p. (gr. 1-2). pap. 6.50 *(978-1-4042-7046-6(9)*, 08747fa9-73fa-4f31-b945-f1530a3ff6fb, Rosen Classroom) Rosen Publishing Group, Inc., The.

Rud, Jeff. High & Inside, 1 vol. 2006. (ENG.). 180p. (J). (gr. 4-7). per. 7.95 *(978-1-55143-532-9(2))* Orca Bk. Pubs. USA.

Sander, Sonia. Play Ball, Pikachu! (Pokémon Alola Reader), 1 vol. 2018. (ENG.). 32p. (J). (gr. -1-3). pap. 5.99 *(978-1-338-23752-8(7))* Scholastic, Inc.

Schultz Nicholson, Lorna. Big Air, 1 vol. 2013. (Lorimer Podium Sports Academy Ser.). (ENG.). 144p. (YA). (gr. 9-12). pap. 9.95 *(978-1-4594-0531-8(5)*, 5bb98421-debc-4bf6-9c80-b84b59d54841) James Lorimer & Co. Ltd., Pubs. CAN. Dist: Lerner Publishing Group.

Scieszka, Jon, et al. Guys Read: the Sports Pages. Santat, Dan, illus. 2012. (Guys Read Ser.: 3). (ENG.). 272p. (J). (gr. 3-7). pap. 7.99 *(978-0-06-196377-3(1)*, Waldon Pond Pr.) HarperCollins Pubs.

Scott, Danny. Calum's Big Break, 44 vols. Morentorn, Alice A., illus. 2016. (Scotland Stars FC Ser.). 144p. (J). pap. 6.95 *(978-1-78250-265-4(3)*, Kelpies) Floris Bks. GBR. Dist: Consortium Bk. Sales & Distribution.

—Calum's Cup Final, 34 vols. Morentorn, Alice A., illus. 2016. (Scotland Stars FC Ser.). 144p. (J). pap. 6.95 *(978-1-78250-282-1(3)*, Kelpies) Floris Bks. GBR. Dist: Consortium Bk. Sales & Distribution.

—Calum's Hard Knock, 36 vols. Morentorn, Alice A., illus. 2016. (Scotland Stars FC Ser.). 144p. (J). pap. 6.95 *(978-1-78250-280-7(7)*, Kelpies) Floris Bks. GBR. Dist: Consortium Bk. Sales & Distribution.

—Calum's New Boots, 44 vols. Morentorn, Alice A., illus. 2016. (Scotland Stars FC Ser.). 144p. (J). pap. 6.95 *(978-1-78250-264-7(5)*, Kelpies) Floris Bks. GBR. Dist: Consortium Bk. Sales & Distribution.

—Calum's Tough Match, 36 vols. Morentorn, Alice A., illus. 2016. (Scotland Stars FC Ser.). 144p. (J). pap. 6.95 *(978-1-78250-281-4(5)*, Kelpies) Floris Bks. GBR. Dist: Consortium Bk. Sales & Distribution.

Sedgwick, Chantele. Switching Gears. (Love, Lucas Novel Ser.: 2). (ENG.). (J). (gr. 6-6). 2018. 300p. pap. 8.99 *(978-1-5107-2492-1(3))* 2017. 288p. 16.99 *(978-1-5107-0506-7(6))* Skyhorse Publishing Co., Inc. (Sky Pony Pr.).

Sharifi, David & Sharifi, Jason. Moonlight Valley: The Great Race. 2008. 28p. pap. 13.99 *(978-1-4389-1865-5(8))* AuthorHouse.

Shaw, Mary. Brady Brady & the Big Mistake, 11vols. Temple, Chuck, illus. l.t. ed. 2004. 32p. (J). per. *(978-0-9735557-4-5(2))* Brady Brady, Inc.

—Brady Brady & the Great Exchange, 11 vols. Temple, Chuck, illus. l.t. ed. 2003. 32p. (J). per. *(978-0-9735557-5-2(0))* Brady Brady, Inc.

Shaw, Michael. Slider: The Leo Butterburger Story. 2004. per. 14.95 *(978-0-9747666-4-5(X))* American Retrospects, LLC.

Siggins, Gerard. Rugby Runner: Ancient Roots, Modern Boots. 2017. (Rugby Spirit Ser.: 5). (ENG.). 208p. (J). 14.00 *(978-1-84717-913-5(4))* O'Brien Pr., Ltd., The IRL. Dist: Casemate Pubs. & Bk. Distributors, LLC.

Sikes, Richard. Laughing with Uncle Adolph. 2008. pap. 14.95 *(978-0-9745854-2-0(4))* Old Bay Publishing.

Skillchecks for Sports. 2005. (Double Fastback Ser.). (J). (gr. 6-12). 64p. pap. 5.95 *(978-0-13-024471-0(6))*; 32p. pap. 5.95 *(978-0-13-024454-3(6))* Globe Fearon Educational Publishing.

Skuy, David. Striker, 1 vol. 2013. (ENG.). 216p. (J). (gr. 4-7). 19.95 *(978-1-4594-0512-7(9)*, 9781459405127); pap. 12.95 *(978-1-4594-0513-4(7)*, 9781459405134) James Lorimer & Co. Ltd., Pubs. CAN. Dist: Casemate Pubs. & Bk. Distributors, LLC.

Slam Dunk. Date not set. 9.95 *(978-0-89868-289-2(4))*; pap. 3.95 *(978-0-89868-288-5(6))* ARO Publishing Co.

Smith, Bryan. If Winning Isn't Everything, Why Do I Hate to Lose? Martin, Brian, illus. 2015. (ENG.). 31p. (J). (gr. k-6). pap. 10.95 *(978-1-934490-85-3(7))* Boys Town Pr.

Snyder, Betsy, illus. I Can Play. 2015. (I Can Interactive Board Bks.). (ENG.). 14p. (J). (gr. -1 — 1). bds. 8.99 *(978-1-4521-2905-1(3))* Chronicle Bks. LLC.

Sporteller Staff. Race to Win (Auto Racing) 64p. (YA). (gr. 6-12). pap. 10.95 *(978-0-8224-6479-2(9))* Globe Fearon Educational Publishing.

Sports Day: Individual Title Six-Packs. (gr. -1-2). 23.00 *(978-0-7635-8804-5(0))* Rigby Education.

Sports Double Fastbacks, 10 bks. (YA). (gr. 6-12). pap. 59.95 *(978-0-8224-2389-8(8))* Globe Fearon Educational Publishing.

Sports Illustrated Kids Graphic Novels Fall 2010 Set, 1 vol., Set. 2010. (Sports Illustrated Kids Graphic Novels Ser.). (ENG.). 56p. (gr. 2-3). 133.25 *(978-1-4342-2692-1(1)*, Stone Arch Bks.) Capstone.

Standish, Burt L. Dick Merriwell at Fardale. Rudman, Jack, ed. 2003. (Frank Merriwell Ser.). 29.95 *(978-0-8373-9376-6(0))* Merriwell, Frank Inc.

—Dick Merriwell, Freshman. Rudman, Jack, ed. 2003. (Frank Merriwell Ser.). pap. 9.95 *(978-0-8373-9142-7(3))* Merriwell, Frank Inc.

—Dick Merriwell in the Wilds. Rudman, Jack, ed. 2003. (Frank Merriwell Ser.). pap. 9.95 *(978-0-8373-9167-0(9))* Merriwell, Frank Inc.

—Dick Merriwell on the Gridiron. Rudman, Jack, ed. 2003. (Frank Merriwell Ser.). pap. 9.95 *(978-0-8373-9102-1(4))* Merriwell, Frank Inc.

—Dick Merriwell, the Wizard. Rudman, Jack, ed. 2003. (Frank Merriwell Ser.). pap. 9.95 *(978-0-8373-9126-7(1))* Merriwell, Frank Inc.

—Dick Merriwell's Ability. Rudman, Jack, ed. 2003. (Frank Merriwell Ser.). 29.95 *(978-0-8373-9390-2(6))*; pap. 9.95 *(978-0-8373-9090-1(7))* Merriwell, Frank Inc.

—Dick Merriwell's Assurance. Rudman, Jack, ed. 2003. (Frank Merriwell Ser.). pap. 9.95 *(978-0-8373-9109-0(1))* Merriwell, Frank Inc.

—Dick Merriwell's Backers. Rudman, Jack, ed. 2003. (Frank Merriwell Ser.). pap. 9.95 *(978-0-8373-9149-6(0))* Merriwell, Frank Inc.

—Dick Merriwell's Backstop. Rudman, Jack, ed. 2003. (Frank Merriwell Ser.). 29.95 *(978-0-8373-9396-4(5))*; pap. 9.95 *(978-0-8373-9096-3(6))* Merriwell, Frank Inc.

—Dick Merriwell's Best Work. Rudman, Jack, ed. 2003. (Frank Merriwell Ser.). pap. 9.95 *(978-0-8373-9150-2(4))* Merriwell, Frank Inc.

—Dick Merriwell's Black Star. Rudman, Jack, ed. 2003. (Frank Merriwell Ser.). pap. 9.95 *(978-0-8373-9158-8(X))* Merriwell, Frank Inc.

—Dick Merriwell's Cleverness. Rudman, Jack, ed. 2003. (Frank Merriwell Ser.). pap. 9.95 *(978-0-8373-9124-3(5))* Merriwell, Frank Inc.

—Dick Merriwell's Close Call. Rudman, Jack, ed. 2003. (Frank Merriwell Ser.). pap. 9.95 *(978-0-8373-9156-4(3))* Merriwell, Frank Inc.

—Dick Merriwell's Dare. Rudman, Jack, ed. 2003. (Frank Merriwell Ser.). pap. 9.95 *(978-0-8373-9136-6(9))* Merriwell, Frank Inc.

—Dick Merriwell's Dash. Rudman, Jack, ed. 2003. (Frank Merriwell Ser.). 29.95 *(978-0-8373-9389-6(2))*; pap. 9.95 *(978-0-8373-9089-5(3))* Merriwell, Frank Inc.

—Dick Merriwell's Day. Rudman, Jack, ed. 2003. (Frank Merriwell Ser.). pap. 9.95 *(978-0-8373-9114-4(8))* Merriwell, Frank Inc.

—Dick Merriwell's Debt. Rudman, Jack, ed. 2003. (Frank Merriwell Ser.). pap. 9.95 *(978-0-8373-9152-6(0))* Merriwell, Frank Inc.

—Dick Merriwell's Defense. Rudman, Jack, ed. 2003. (Frank Merriwell Ser.). 29.95 *(978-0-8373-9392-6(2))*; pap. 9.95 *(978-0-8373-9092-5(3))* Merriwell, Frank Inc.

—Dick Merriwell's Delivery. Rudman, Jack, ed. 2003. (Frank Merriwell Ser.). 29.95 *(978-0-8373-9384-1(1))*; pap. 9.95 *(978-0-8373-9084-0(2))* Merriwell, Frank Inc.

—Dick Merriwell's Diamond. Rudman, Jack, ed. 2003. (Frank Merriwell Ser.). 29.95 *(978-0-8373-9387-2(6))*; pap. 9.95 *(978-0-8373-9087-1(7))* Merriwell, Frank Inc.

—Dick Merriwell's Disguise. Rudman, Jack, ed. 2003. (Frank Merriwell Ser.). pap. 9.95 *(978-0-8373-9103-8(2))* Merriwell, Frank Inc.

—Dick Merriwell's Distrust. Rudman, Jack, ed. 2003. (Frank Merriwell Ser.). pap. 9.95 *(978-0-8373-9151-9(2))* Merriwell, Frank Inc.

—Dick Merriwell's Downfall. Rudman, Jack, ed. 2003. (Frank Merriwell Ser.). pap. 9.95 *(978-0-8373-9116-8(4))* Merriwell, Frank Inc.

—Dick Merriwell's Example. Rudman, Jack, ed. 2003. (Frank Merriwell Ser.). pap. 9.95 *(978-0-8373-9166-3(0))* Merriwell, Frank Inc.

—Dick Merriwell's Five. Rudman, Jack, ed. 2003. (Frank Merriwell Ser.). pap. 9.95 *(978-0-8373-9130-4(X))* Merriwell, Frank Inc.

—Dick Merriwell's Glory. Rudman, Jack, ed. 2003. (Frank Merriwell Ser.). 29.95 *(978-0-8373-9377-3(9))*; pap. 9.95 *(978-0-8373-9077-2(X))* Merriwell, Frank Inc.

—Dick Merriwell's Grit. Rudman, Jack, ed. 2003. (Frank Merriwell Ser.). pap. 9.95 *(978-0-8373-9108-3(3))* Merriwell, Frank Inc.

—Dick Merriwell's Home Run. Rudman, Jack, ed. 2003. (Frank Merriwell Ser.). pap. 9.95 *(978-0-8373-9135-9(0))* Merriwell, Frank Inc.

—Dick Merriwell's Honors. Rudman, Jack, ed. 2003. (Frank Merriwell Ser.). pap. 9.95 *(978-0-8373-9173-1(3))* Merriwell, Frank Inc.

—Dick Merriwell's Influence. Rudman, Jack, ed. 2003. (Frank Merriwell Ser.). pap. 9.95 *(978-0-8373-9141-0(5))* Merriwell, Frank Inc.

—Dick Merriwell's Joke. Rudman, Jack, ed. 2003. (Frank Merriwell Ser.). pap. 9.95 *(978-0-8373-9144-1(X))* Merriwell, Frank Inc.

—Dick Merriwell's Long Slide. Rudman, Jack, ed. 2003. (Frank Merriwell Ser.). pap. 9.95 *(978-0-8373-9110-6(5))* Merriwell, Frank Inc.

—Dick Merriwell's Magnetism. Rudman, Jack, ed. 2003. (Frank Merriwell Ser.). pap. 9.95 *(978-0-8373-9148-9(2))* Merriwell, Frank Inc.

—Dick Merriwell's Marked Money. Rudman, Jack, ed. 2003. (Frank Merriwell Ser.). pap. 9.95 *(978-0-8373-9100-7(8))* Merriwell, Frank Inc.

—Dick Merriwell's Mastery. Rudman, Jack, ed. 2003. (Frank Merriwell Ser.). pap. 9.95 *(978-0-8373-9153-3(9))* Merriwell, Frank Inc.

—Dick Merriwell's Model. Rudman, Jack, ed. 2003. (Frank Merriwell Ser.). 29.95 *(978-0-8373-9393-3(0))*; pap. 9.95 *(978-0-8373-9093-2(1))* Merriwell, Frank Inc.

—Dick Merriwell's Mystery. Rudman, Jack, ed. 2003. (Frank Merriwell Ser.). 29.95 *(978-0-8373-9394-0(9))*; pap. 9.95 *(978-0-8373-9094-9(X))* Merriwell, Frank Inc.

—Dick Merriwell's Narrow Escape. Rudman, Jack, ed. 2003. (Frank Merriwell Ser.). 29.95 *(978-0-8373-9380-3(9))*; pap. 9.95 *(978-0-8373-9080-2(X))* Merriwell, Frank Inc.

—Dick Merriwell's Persistence. Rudman, Jack, ed. 2003. (Frank Merriwell Ser.). pap. 9.95 *(978-0-8373-9113-7(X))* Merriwell, Frank Inc.

—Dick Merriwell's Polo Team. Rudman, Jack, ed. 2003. (Frank Merriwell Ser.). pap. 9.95 *(978-0-8373-9132-8(6))* Merriwell, Frank Inc.

—Dick Merriwell's Pranks. Rudman, Jack, ed. 2003. (Frank Merriwell Ser.). pap. 9.95 *(978-0-8373-9120-5(2))* Merriwell, Frank Inc.

—Dick Merriwell's Promise. Rudman, Jack, ed. 2003. (Frank Merriwell Ser.). 29.95 *(978-0-8373-9378-0(7))*; pap. 9.95 *(978-0-8373-9078-9(8))* Merriwell, Frank Inc.

—Dick Merriwell's Racket. Rudman, Jack, ed. 2003. (Frank Merriwell Ser.). 29.95 *(978-0-8373-9381-0(7))*; pap. 9.95 *(978-0-8373-9081-9(8))* Merriwell, Frank Inc.

—Dick Merriwell's Regret. Rudman, Jack, ed. 2003. (Frank Merriwell Ser.). pap. 9.95 *(978-0-8373-9147-2(4))* Merriwell, Frank Inc.

—Dick Merriwell's Reputation. Rudman, Jack, ed. 2003. (Frank Merriwell Ser.). pap. 9.95 *(978-0-8373-9171-7(7))* Merriwell, Frank Inc.

—Dick Merriwell's Rescue. Rudman, Jack, ed. 2003. (Frank Merriwell Ser.). 29.95 *(978-0-8373-9379-7(5))*; pap. 9.95 *(978-0-8373-9079-6(6))* Merriwell, Frank Inc.

—Dick Merriwell's Resource. Rudman, Jack, ed. 2003. (Frank Merriwell Ser.). pap. 9.95 *(978-0-8373-9129-8(6))* Merriwell, Frank Inc.

—Dick Merriwell's Return. Rudman, Jack, ed. 2003. (Frank Merriwell Ser.). pap. 9.95 *(978-0-8373-9128-1(8))* Merriwell, Frank Inc.

—Dick Merriwell's Revenge. Rudman, Jack, ed. 2003. (Frank Merriwell Ser.). 29.95 *(978-0-8373-9382-7(5))*; pap. 9.95 *(978-0-8373-9082-6(6))* Merriwell, Frank Inc.

—Dick Merriwell's Ruse. Rudman, Jack, ed. 2003. (Frank Merriwell Ser.). 29.95 *(978-0-8373-9383-4(3))*; pap. 9.95 *(978-0-8373-9083-3(4))* Merriwell, Frank Inc.

—Dick Merriwell's Stanchness. Rudman, Jack, ed. 2003. (Frank Merriwell Ser.). pap. 9.95 *(978-0-8373-9161-8(X))* Merriwell, Frank Inc.

—Dick Merriwell's Stand. Rudman, Jack, ed. 2003. (Frank Merriwell Ser.). pap. 9.95 *(978-0-8373-9163-2(6))* Merriwell, Frank Inc.

—Dick Merriwell's Staying Power. Rudman, Jack, ed. 2003. (Frank Merriwell Ser.). pap. 9.95 *(978-0-8373-9143-4(1))* Merriwell, Frank Inc.

—Dick Merriwell's Stroke. Rudman, Jack, ed. 2003. (Frank Merriwell Ser.). pap. 9.95 *(978-0-8373-9127-4(X))* Merriwell, Frank Inc.

—Dick Merriwell's Team Mate. Rudman, Jack, ed. 2003. (Frank Merriwell Ser.). pap. 9.95 *(978-0-8373-9138-0(5))* Merriwell, Frank Inc.

—Dick Merriwell's Test. Rudman, Jack, ed. 2003. (Frank Merriwell Ser.). pap. 9.95 *(978-0-8373-9104-5(0))* Merriwell, Frank Inc.

—Frank Merriwell as Coach. Rudman, Jack, ed. 2003. (Frank Merriwell Ser.). 29.95 *(978-0-8373-9372-8(8))*; pap. 9.95 *(978-0-8373-9072-7(9))* Merriwell, Frank Inc.

—Frank Merriwell Facing His Foes. Rudman, Jack, ed. 2003. (Frank Merriwell Ser.). pap. 9.95 *(978-0-8373-9160-1(1))* Merriwell, Frank Inc.

—Frank Merriwell in Camp. Rudman, Jack, ed. 2003. (Frank Merriwell Ser.). (YA). (gr. 9-18). 29.95 *(978-0-8373-9324-7(8))*; pap. 9.95 *(978-0-8373-9024-6(9)*, FM-024) Merriwell, Frank Inc.

—Frank Merriwell in Maine. Rudman, Jack, ed. 2003. (Frank Merriwell Ser.). (YA). (gr. 9-18). 29.95 *(978-0-8373-9328-5(0))*; pap. 9.95 *(978-0-8373-9028-4(1)*, FM-028) Merriwell, Frank Inc.

—Frank Merriwell's Alarm. Rudman, Jack, ed. 2003. (Frank Merriwell Ser.). (YA). (gr. 9-18). 29.95 *(978-0-8373-9316-2(7))*; pap. 9.95 *(978-0-8373-9016-1(8)*, FM-016) Merriwell, Frank Inc.

—Frank Merriwell's Athletes. Rudman, Jack, ed. 2003. (Frank Merriwell Ser.). (YA). (gr. 9-18). 29.95 *(978-0-8373-9317-9(5))*; pap. 9.95 *(978-0-8373-9017-8(6)*, FM-017) Merriwell, Frank Inc.

—Frank Merriwell's Champions. Rudman, Jack, ed. 2003. (Frank Merriwell Ser.). (YA). (gr. 9-18). 29.95 *(978-0-8373-9319-3(1))*; pap. 9.95 *(978-0-8373-9019-2(2)*, FM-019) Merriwell, Frank Inc.

—Frank Merriwell's Chase. Rudman, Jack, ed. 2003. (Frank Merriwell Ser.). (YA). (gr. 9-18). 29.95 *(978-0-8373-9327-8(2))*; pap. 9.95 *(978-0-8373-9027-7(3)*, FM-027) Merriwell, Frank Inc.

—Frank Merriwell's Courage. Rudman, Jack, ed. 2003. (Frank Merriwell Ser.). (YA). (gr. 9-18). 29.95 *(978-0-8373-9314-8(0))*; pap. 9.95 *(978-0-8373-9014-7(1)*, FM-014) Merriwell, Frank Inc.

—Frank Merriwell's Double Shot. Rudman, Jack, ed. 2003. (Frank Merriwell Ser.). 29.95 *(978-0-8373-9347-6(7))*; pap. 9.95 *(978-0-8373-9047-5(8))* Merriwell, Frank Inc.

—Frank Merriwell's Hard Luck. Rudman, Jack, ed. 2003. (Frank Merriwell Ser.). 29.95 *(978-0-8373-9332-2(9))*; pap. 9.95 *(978-0-8373-9032-1(X))* Merriwell, Frank Inc.

—Frank Merriwell's Honor. Rudman, Jack, ed. 2003. (Frank Merriwell Ser.). 29.95 *(978-0-8373-9386-5(8))*; pap. 9.95 *(978-0-8373-9086-4(9))* Merriwell, Frank Inc.

—Frank Merriwell's Leaguers. Rudman, Jack, ed. 2003. (Frank Merriwell Ser.). pap. 9.95 *(978-0-8373-9139-7(3))* Merriwell, Frank Inc.

—Frank Merriwell's Lesson. Rudman, Jack, ed. 2003. (Frank Merriwell Ser.). pap. 9.95 *(978-0-8373-9170-0(9))* Merriwell, Frank Inc.

—Frank Merriwell's Luck. Rudman, Jack, ed. 2003. (Frank Merriwell Ser.). 29.95 *(978-0-8373-9356-8(6))*; pap. 9.95 *(978-0-8373-9056-7(7))* Merriwell, Frank Inc.

—Frank Merriwell's Marvel. Rudman, Jack, ed. 2003. (Frank Merriwell Ser.). 29.95 *(978-0-8373-9374-2(4))*; pap. 9.95 *(978-0-8373-9074-1(5))* Merriwell, Frank Inc.

—Frank Merriwell's Mascot. Rudman, Jack, ed. 2003. (Frank Merriwell Ser.). 29.95 *(978-0-8373-9357-5(4))*; pap. 9.95 *(978-0-8373-9057-4(5))* Merriwell, Frank Inc.

—Frank Merriwell's New Comedian. Rudman, Jack, ed. 2003. (Frank Merriwell Ser.). 29.95 *(978-0-8373-9340-7(X))*; pap. 29.95 *(978-0-8373-9040-6(0))* Merriwell, Frank Inc.

—Frank Merriwell's Nomads. Rudman, Jack, ed. 2003. (Frank Merriwell Ser.). pap. 9.95 *(978-0-8373-9101-4(6))* Merriwell, Frank Inc.

—Frank Merriwell's Opportunity. Rudman, Jack, ed. 2003. (Frank Merriwell Ser.). 29.95 *(978-0-8373-9331-5(0))*; pap. 9.95 *(978-0-8373-9031-4(1))* Merriwell, Frank Inc.

—Frank Merriwell's Own Company. Rudman, Jack, ed. 2003. (Frank Merriwell Ser.). 29.95 *(978-0-8373-9335-3(3))*; pap. 9.95 *(978-0-8373-9035-2(4))* Merriwell, Frank Inc.

—Frank Merriwell's Peril. Rudman, Jack, ed. 2003. (Frank Merriwell Ser.). pap. 9.95 *(978-0-8373-9115-1(6))* Merriwell, Frank Inc.

—Frank Merriwell's Phantom. Rudman, Jack, ed. 2003. (Frank Merriwell Ser.). 29.95 *(978-0-8373-9359-9(0))*; pap. 9.95 *(978-0-8373-9059-8(1))* Merriwell, Frank Inc.

—Frank Merriwell's Power. Rudman, Jack, ed. 2003. (Frank Merriwell Ser.). 29.95 *(978-0-8373-9364-3(7))*; pap. 9.95 *(978-0-8373-9064-2(8))* Merriwell, Frank Inc.

—Frank Merriwell's Pride. Rudman, Jack, ed. 2003. (Frank Merriwell Ser.). pap. 9.95 *(978-0-8373-9121-2(0))* Merriwell, Frank Inc.

—Frank Merriwell's Problem. Rudman, Jack, ed. 2003. (Frank Merriwell Ser.). 29.95 *(978-0-8373-9338-4(8))*; pap. 9.95 *(978-0-8373-9038-3(9))* Merriwell, Frank Inc.

—Frank Merriwell's Prosperity. Rudman, Jack, ed. 2003. (Frank Merriwell Ser.). 29.95 *(978-0-8373-9341-4(8))*; pap. 9.95 *(978-0-8373-9041-3(9))* Merriwell, Frank Inc.

—Frank Merriwell's Protege. Rudman, Jack, ed. 2003. (Frank Merriwell Ser.). 29.95 *(978-0-8373-9333-9(7))*; pap. 9.95 *(978-0-8373-9033-8(8))* Merriwell, Frank Inc.

—Frank Merriwell's Pursuit. Rudman, Jack, ed. 2003. (Frank Merriwell Ser.). pap. 9.95 *(978-0-8373-9117-5(2))* Merriwell, Frank Inc.

—Frank Merriwell's Rescue. Rudman, Jack, ed. 2003. (Frank Merriwell Ser.). 29.95 *(978-0-8373-9398-8(1))*; pap. 9.95 *(978-0-8373-9098-7(2))* Merriwell, Frank Inc.

—Frank Merriwell's Reward. Rudman, Jack, ed. 2003. (Frank Merriwell Ser.). 29.95 *(978-0-8373-9358-2(2))*; pap. 9.95 *(978-0-8373-9058-1(3))* Merriwell, Frank Inc.

—Frank Merriwell's Rough Deal. Rudman, Jack, ed. 2003. (Frank Merriwell Ser.). pap. 9.95 *(978-0-8373-9111-3(3))* Merriwell, Frank Inc.

—Frank Merriwell's Search. Rudman, Jack, ed. 2003. (Frank Merriwell Ser.). 29.95 *(978-0-8373-9367-4(1))*; pap. 9.95 *(978-0-8373-9067-3(2))* Merriwell, Frank Inc.

—Frank Merriwell's Setback. Rudman, Jack, ed. 2003. (Frank Merriwell Ser.). 29.95 *(978-0-8373-9366-7(3))*; pap. 9.95 *(978-0-8373-9066-6(4))* Merriwell, Frank Inc.

—Frank Merriwell's Shrewdness. Rudman, Jack, ed. 2003. (Frank Merriwell Ser.). 29.95 *(978-0-8373-9365-0(5))*; pap. 9.95 *(978-0-8373-9065-9(6))* Merriwell, Frank Inc.

—Frank Merriwell's Sports Afield. Rudman, Jack, ed. (Frank Merriwell Ser.). (YA). (gr. 9-18). 29.95 *(978-0-8373-9310-0(8))*; pap. 9.95 *(978-0-8373-9010-9(9)*, FM-010) Merriwell, Frank Inc.

—Frank Merriwell's Stage Hit. Rudman, Jack, ed. 2003. (Frank Merriwell Ser.). 29.95 *(978-0-8373-9342-1(6))*; pap. 9.95 *(978-0-8373-9042-0(7))* Merriwell, Frank Inc.

—Frank Merriwell's Steadying Hand. Rudman, Jack, ed. 2003. (Frank Merriwell Ser.). pap. 9.95 *(978-0-8373-9165-6(2))* Merriwell, Frank Inc.

—Frank Merriwell's Strategy. Rudman, Jack, ed. 2003. (Frank Merriwell Ser.). pap. 9.95 *(978-0-8373-9106-9(7))* Merriwell, Frank Inc.

—Frank Merriwell's Strong Arm. Rudman, Jack, ed. 2003. (Frank Merriwell Ser.). 29.95 *(978-0-8373-9371-1(X))*; pap. 9.95 *(978-0-8373-9071-0(0))* Merriwell, Frank Inc.

—Frank Merriwell's Support. Rudman, Jack, ed. 2003. (Frank Merriwell Ser.). 29.95 *(978-0-8373-9375-9(2))*; pap. 9.95 *(978-0-8373-9075-8(3))* Merriwell, Frank Inc.

—Frank Merriwell's Talisman. Rudman, Jack, ed. 2003. (Frank Merriwell Ser.). pap. 9.95 *(978-0-8373-9145-8(8))* Merriwell, Frank Inc.

—Frank Merriwell's Temptation. Rudman, Jack, ed. 2003. (Frank Merriwell Ser.). 29.95 *(978-0-8373-9354-4(X))*; pap. 9.95 *(978-0-8373-9054-3(0))* Merriwell, Frank Inc.

—Frank Merriwell's Tigers. Rudman, Jack, ed. 2003. (Frank Merriwell Ser.). pap. 9.95 *(978-0-8373-9131-1(8))* Merriwell, Frank Inc.

—Frank Merriwell's Tricks. Rudman, Jack, ed. 2003. (Frank Merriwell Ser.). 29.95 *(978-0-8373-9353-7(1))*; pap. 9.95 *(978-0-8373-9053-6(2))* Merriwell, Frank Inc.

—Frank Merriwell's Triumph. Rudman, Jack, ed. 2003. (Frank Merriwell Ser.). pap. 9.95 *(978-0-8373-9107-6(5))* Merriwell, Frank Inc.

—Frank Merriwell's Trump Card. Rudman, Jack, ed. 2003. (Frank Merriwell Ser.). pap. 9.95 *(978-0-8373-9105-2(9))* Merriwell, Frank Inc.

—Frank Merriwell's Trust. Rudman, Jack, ed. 2003. (Frank Merriwell Ser.). 29.95 *(978-0-8373-9369-8(8))*; pap. 9.95 *(978-0-8373-9069-7(9))* Merriwell, Frank Inc.

—Frank Merriwell's Victories. Rudman, Jack, ed. 2003. (Frank Merriwell Ser.). 29.95 *(978-0-8373-9361-2(2))*; pap. 9.95 *(978-0-8373-9061-1(3))* Merriwell, Frank Inc.

—Frank Merriwell's Winners. Rudman, Jack, ed. 2003. (Frank Merriwell Ser.). 29.95 *(978-0-8373-9388-9(4))*; pap. 9.95 *(978-0-8373-9088-8(5))* Merriwell, Frank Inc.

—Frank Merriwell's Wizard. Rudman, Jack, ed. 2003. (Frank Merriwell Ser.). pap. 9.95 *(978-0-8373-9174-8(1))* Merriwell, Frank Inc.

—Frank Merriwell's Worst Boy. Rudman, Jack, ed. 2003. (Frank Merriwell Ser.). pap. 9.95 *(978-0-8373-9155-7(5))* Merriwell, Frank Inc.

Stanwood Pier, Arthu. The Jester of St. Timothy's. 2006. pap. 14.95 *(978-1-55742-546-1(9))* Wildside Pr., LLC.

Stevens, Eric & Maddox, Jake. Playing Forward. Tiffany, Sean, illus. 2010. (Jake Maddox Sports Story Ser.). 72p. pap. 0.60 *(978-1-4342-3206-9(9)*, Stone Arch Bks.) Capstone.

Sticker Dolly Dressing Sports (Revised) 2017. (Sticker Dolly Dressing Ser.). (ENG.). (J). pap. 9.99 *(978-0-7945-3782-1(0)*, Usborne) EDC Publishing.

Strasser, Todd. Close Out. 2004. (ENG.). 304p. (YA). (gr. 9). mass mkt. 5.99 *(978-0-689-87031-6(0)*, Simon Pulse) Simon Pulse.

Stroke of Luck (Swimming) 64p. (YA). (gr. 6-12). pap. 10.95 *(978-0-8224-6482-2(9))* Globe Fearon Educational Publishing.

Swan, Bill. Corner Kick, 1 vol. 2004. (Lorimer Sports Stories Ser.: 66). (ENG.). 144p. (J). (gr. 4-8). 16.95 *(978-1-55028-817-9(2)*, 817) James Lorimer & Co. Ltd., Pubs. CAN. Dist: Formac Lorimer Bks. Ltd.

—Mud Happens, 1 vol. 2005. (Lorimer Sports Stories Ser.: 82). (ENG.). 112p. (J). (gr. 4-8). 16.95 *(978-1-55028-899-5(7)*, 899); 8.95 *(978-1-55028-898-8(9)*, 898) James Lorimer & Co. Ltd., Pubs. CAN. Dist: Formac Lorimer Bks. Ltd.

—Road Rage, 1 vol. 2006. (Lorimer Sports Stories Ser.). (ENG.). 120p. (J). (gr. 4-8). 8.95 (978-1-55028-916-9(0), 916) James Lorimer & Co. Ltd., Pubs. CAN. Dist: Formac Lorimer Bks. Ltd.

Swann, Stephen. The Blooter Boys. 2009. (ENG.). 42p. pap. 21.50 (978-1-4452-2665-1(0)) Lulu Pr., Inc.

Tammen, Christina. Chump Ii Every Team Has an Undiscovered Secret Weapon! 2013. 30p. pap. 14.95 (978-1-61244-081-1(9)) Halo Publishing International.

Tate, Nikki. Deadpoint. 2017. (Orca Sports Ser.). lib. bdg. 20.80 (978-0-606-40454-9(6)) Turtleback.

Terrell, Brandon. Grit & Gold. Garcia, Eduardo, illus. 2016. (Time Machine Magazine Ser.). (ENG.). 128p. (J). (gr. 3-6). lib. bdg. 23.99 (978-1-4965-2597-0(3), 130726) Capstone.

Thaler, Mike. The Field Day from the Black Lagoon. Lee, Jared, illus. 2008. (From the Black Lagoon Ser.). 64p. (gr. 2-5). 14.00 (978-0-7569-8801-2(2)) Perfection Learning Corp.

—The Field Day from the Black Lagoon. Lee, Jared, illus. 2011. (Black Lagoon Adventures Ser.: No. 1). (ENG.). 64p. (J). (gr. 2-6). 31.36 (978-1-59961-812-8(5), 3598, Chapter Bks.) Spotlight.

—The Field Day from the Black Lagoon (Black Lagoon Adventures #6) Lee, Jared, illus. 2008. (Black Lagoon Adventures Ser.: 6). (ENG.). 64p. (J). (gr. 2-5). pap. 4.99 (978-0-439-68076-9(X), Scholastic Paperbacks) Scholastic, Inc.

Thomas, Michelle. Bubble World & the Olympics. 2010. 28p. 12.49 (978-1-4520-1682-5(8)) AuthorHouse.

Tomlinson, Everett T. Winning His W. 2006. pap. (978-1-4068-1194-0(7)) Echo Library.

Truckey, Don. The Adventures of Caraway Kim... Southpaw. 2006. (ENG.). 192p. pap. 10.95 (978-1-894345-90-3(8)) Thistledown Pr., Ltd. CAN. Dist: Univ. of Toronto Pr.

Tulien, Sean. Paintball Punk, 1 vol. Aburto, Jesus & Esparza, Andres, illus. 2010. (Sports Illustrated Kids Graphic Novels Ser.). (ENG.). 56p. (J). (gr. 3-8). 26.65 (978-1-4342-2219-0(5), 103082); pap. 7.19 (978-1-4342-2788-1(X), 114055) Capstone. (Stone Arch Bks.).

Twigg, Aeres. The Green Hawk. 2003. (ENG., Illus.). 88p. (J). pap. 12.95 (978-1-85902-787-5(3)) Beekman Bks., Inc.

Wallace, Rich. Kickers #1: the Ball Hogs, Bk. 1. Holder, Jimmy, illus. 2011. (Kickers Ser.: 1). 128p. (J). (gr. 1-4). 6.99 (978-0-375-85092-9(9), Yearling) Random Hse. Children's Bks.

—Sports Camp. 2012. 160p. (J). (gr. 4-6). (ENG.). lib. bdg. 21.19 (978-0-375-94059-0(6), Knopf Bks. for Young Readers); 6.99 (978-0-440-23993-2(1), Yearling) Random Hse. Children's Bks.

—Technical Foul. 2004. (Winning Season Ser.: Bk. 2). (ENG.). 112p. (J). (gr. 3-6). 17.44 (978-0-670-05941-6(2)) Penguin Young Readers Group.

Walters, Eric. Underdog, 1 vol. 2004. (Orca Young Readers Ser.). (ENG., Illus.). 176p. (J). (gr. 4-7). pap., tchr. ed. 6.95 (978-1-55143-302-8(8), 1234544) Orca Bk. Pubs. USA.

Ward, Stephen J. The GREATEST Togger Story Ever Told - Part 1: Thrifty's Stand. 2010. 66p. pap. 14.95 (978-1-4461-3060-5(6)) Lulu Pr., Inc.

—The GREATEST Togger Story Ever Told - Part 2: the Boot of All Evil. 2010. 84p. pap. 16.95 (978-1-4461-3069-8(X)) Lulu Pr., Inc.

—The GREATEST Togger Story Ever Told - Part 3: Far from the Screaming Crowd. 2010. 86p. pap. 16.95 (978-1-4461-3075-9(4)) Lulu Pr., Inc.

—The GREATEST Togger Story Ever Told - Part 4: the Raiders of Leaf. 2010. 170p. pap. 21.50 (978-1-4461-3076-6(2)) Lulu Pr., Inc.

Weston Woods Staff, creator. Clown of God. 2011. 38.75 (978-0-545-14915-0(0)) Weston Woods Studios, Inc.

Wheeler, Lee Alden. Bucking the Odds 2004. (YA). pap. 13.00 (978-0-9760824-0-8(3)) United Writers Pr.

Whyte, Janet M. Rescue Rider, 1 vol. 2011. (Lorimer Sports Stories Ser.). (ENG.). 136p. (J). (gr. 4-8). 16.95 (978-1-55277-869-2(X), 869); pap. 9.95 (978-1-55277-868-5(1), 7cb515cf-1302-4faa-8cc9-3bb4033662d8) James Lorimer & Co. Ltd., Pubs. CAN. Dist: Formac Lorimer Bks. Ltd., Lerner Publishing Group.

Wight, Eric. Frankie Pickle & the Pine Run 3000. Wight, Eric, illus. 2010. (Frankie Pickle Ser.). (ENG., Illus.). 96p. (J). (gr. 2-5). 10.99 (978-1-4169-6485-8(1), Simon & Schuster Bks. For Young Readers) Simon & Schuster Bks. For Young Readers.

Wilson, George. Arron the Royal Archer. 2010. (Illus.). 50p. (J). 15.00 (978-0-9778477-3-0(X)) A Story Plus Children Bks.

Winfield, Arthur M. Putnam Hall Champions or Bound to Win Ou. 2006. pap. 28.95 (978-1-4286-2346-0(9)) Kessinger Publishing, LLC.

Wisler, Joelle. Ariana Gold. 2016. (What's Your Dream? Ser.). (ENG., Illus.). 96p. (J). (gr. 4-6). lib. bdg. 25.99 (978-1-4965-3442-2(5), 132564, Stone Arch Bks.) Capstone.

Wyler, Melissa. The Adventures of Henry the Sports Bug: Book 1. 2012. 36p. pap. 19.99 (978-1-105-64532-7(0)) Lulu Pr., Inc.

Yasuda, Anita. Beach Volleyball Is No Joke, 1 vol. Santillan, Jorge, illus. 2011. (Sports Illustrated Kids Victory School Superstars Ser.). (ENG.). 56p. (J). (gr. 1-3). pap. 5.95 (978-1-4342-3393-6(6), 116406, Stone Arch Bks.) Capstone.

Zullo, Allan. The Haunted Shortstop: True Ghostly Sports Stories. 2007. 128p. (J). pap. (978-0-439-88618-5(X)) Scholastic, Inc.

SPORTS—HISTORY

Brignall, Richard. Forever Champions: The Enduring Legacy of the Record-Setting Edmonton Grads, 1 vol. 2007. (Lorimer Recordbooks Ser.). (ENG., Illus.). 112p. (gr. 4-8). (J). 9.95 (978-1-55028-976-3(4), 976); (978-1-55028-977-0(2)) James Lorimer & Co. Ltd., Pubs. CAN. Dist: Formac Lorimer Bks. Ltd., Casemate Pubs. & Bk. Distributors, LLC.

Campbell, Grace. Great Sports Fails. 2020. (Searchlight Books (tm) — Celebrating Failure Ser.). (ENG., Illus.). 32p. (J). (gr. 3-5). lib. bdg. 30.65 (978-1-5415-7736-7(1), 62a46f9b-8642-4e53-bb42-b3f6bc117d75, Lerner Pubns.) Lerner Publishing Group.

Christopher, Matt. The Greatest Sports Team Rivalries. 2012. (ENG., Illus.). 144p. (J). (gr. 3-7). pap. 10.99 (978-0-316-17687-3(7)) Little, Brown Bks. for Young Readers.

Craats, Rennay. Sports. 2008. (USA Past Present Future Ser.). (Illus.). 48p. (J). (gr. 4-6). pap. 10.95 (978-1-59036-975-3(0)); lib. bdg. 29.05 (978-1-59036-974-6(2)) Weigl Pubs., Inc.

Davies, Monika. No Way! Spectacular Sports Stories. 2017. (Time for Kids Nonfiction Readers Ser.). lib. bdg. 20.85 (978-0-606-40272-9(1)) Turtleback.

Doeden, Matt. All about Sports. 2015. (All about Sports Ser.). (ENG.). 32p. (J). (gr. -1-2). 119.96 (978-1-4914-2433-9(8), 22366, Capstone Pr.) Capstone.

—Coming up Clutch: The Greatest Upsets, Comebacks, & Finishes in Sports History. 2018. (Spectacular Sports Ser.). (ENG., Illus.). 64p. (J). (gr. 5-8). lib. bdg. 34.65 (978-1-5124-2756-1(X), 883e11ed-3346-4be3-bd97-f972c3a8fed0, Millbrook Pr.) Lerner Publishing Group.

Ford, Jeanne Marie. The 12 Most Influential Athletes of All Time. 2018. (Most Influential Ser.). (ENG., Illus.). 32p. (J). (gr. 3-6). 32.80 (978-1-63235-407-5(1), 13744, 12-Story Library) Bookstaves, LLC.

Ford, Michael. You Wouldn't Want to Be A Greek Athlete! 2014. (You Wouldn't Want to... Ser.). (ENG.). 32p. (J). lib. bdg. 29.00 (978-0-531-21175-5(4), Watts, Franklin) Scholastic Library Publishing.

Gatto, Steve. Da Curse of the Billy Goat: The Chicago Cubs, Pennant Races, & Curses. 2004. 144p. per. 19.95 (978-0-9720910-4-6(1)) Protar Hse., LLC.

Gilpin, Daniel. Record-Breaking People, 1 vol. 2011. (Record Breakers Ser.). (ENG., Illus.). 32p. (J). (gr. 2-3). lib. bdg. 30.27 (978-1-4488-5293-2(5), cbc4a9d5-bc4a-495f-8aeb-cb5d06ab8e26, PowerKids Pr.) Rosen Publishing Group, Inc., The.

Historia de los Deportes Series: Set, 12 vols. 2003. (Historia de Los Deportes (Sports History) Ser.). (SPA., Illus.). (J). (gr. 2-2). 157.62 (978-0-8239-6917-3(7), b9d866ba-5ad9-4f3b-9899-55a9b4319faa, Editorial Buenas Letras) Rosen Publishing Group, Inc., The.

Krull, Kathleen. Lives of the Athletes: Thrills, Spills (and What the Neighbors Thought) Hewitt, Kathryn, illus. 2013. (Lives Of ... Ser.). (ENG.). 96p. (J). (gr. 5-7). pap. 8.99 (978-0-544-24760-4(4), 1566172, Clarion Bks.) HarperCollins Pubs.

Marthaler, Jon. Bad Days in Sports. 2017. (Whoops! a History of Bad Days Ser.). (ENG., Illus.). 48p. (J). (gr. 5-8). lib. bdg. 35.99 (978-1-4109-8564-4(4), 134314, Raintree) Capstone.

Mason, Tyler. Biggest Scandals in Sports. 2017. (Wild World of Sports Ser.). (ENG., Illus.). 48p. (J). (gr. 3-6). lib. bdg. 34.21 (978-1-5321-1362-8(5), 27660, SportsZone) ABDO Publishing Co.

Mattern, Joanne. Legendary Athletic Achievements. 2018. (Unbelievable Ser.). (ENG., Illus.). 32p. (J). (gr. 3-6). 32.80 (978-1-63235-423-5(3), 13771, 12-Story Library) Bookstaves, LLC.

Monteverde, Matthew. Giants vs. Cowboys. 2014. (J). 49.50 (978-1-4777-2783-6(3), PowerKids Pr.) Rosen Publishing Group, Inc., The.

Morley, Jacqueline. How to Be an Ancient Greek Athlete. 2008. (How to Be Ser.). (ENG., Illus.). 32p. (J). (gr. 3-7). pap. 5.95 (978-1-4263-0278-7(9), National Geographic Children's Bks.) National Geographic Society.

Murray, Laura K. The Story of Lululemon Athletica. 2016. (Built for Success Ser.). (ENG., Illus.). 48p. (J). (gr. 4-7). pap. 12.00 (978-1-62832-159-3(8), 20859, Creative Paperbacks) Creative Co., The.

Nasium, James. African Americans in Sports. Hill, Marc Lamont, ed. 2012. (Major Black Contributions from Emancipation to Civil Rights Ser.). 64p. (J). (gr. 5). 22.95 (978-1-4222-2381-9(7)) Mason Crest.

Platt, Richard. They Played What?! The Weird History of Sports & Recreation. 2007. (Weird History Ser.). (ENG.). 48p. (J). (gr. 3-6). 16.95 (978-1-58728-585-1(1)); (Illus.). pap. 9.95 (978-1-58728-586-8(X)) Cooper Square Publishing Llc.

Rule, Heather. Sports' Greatest Turnarounds. 2017. (Wild World of Sports Ser.). (ENG., Illus.). 48p. (J). (gr. 3-6). lib. bdg. 34.21 (978-1-5321-1367-3(6), 27665, SportsZone) ABDO Publishing Co.

Scheppler, Bill. The Iron Man Triathlon. 2009. (Ultra Sports Ser.). 64p. (gr. 5-8). 58.50 (978-1-60854-608-4(X), Rosen Reference) Rosen Publishing Group, Inc., The.

Sports Greats: Set 2, 12 vols. 2016. (Sports Greats Ser.). 48p. (ENG.). (gr. 5-6). lib. bdg. 177.60 (978-0-7660-7500-9(1), 0be6d809-e035-4830-bf41-481e7e469e75); (gr. 6-5). pap. 70.20 (978-0-7660-7972-4(4)) Enslow Publishing, LLC.

SPORTS in AMERICA: 1990 to 1999, 2ND EDITION. 2nd rev. ed. 2010. (Sports in America: Decade by Decade Ser.). (ENG., Illus.). 96p. (gr. 7-12). 39.95 (978-1-60413-456-8(9), P179283, Facts On File) Infobase Holdings, Inc.

Stokes, Erica M. Sports of Mexico. (Mexico: Beautiful Land, Diverse People Ser.). 64p. (YA). (gr. 7-12). 2009. (Illus.). 21.95 (978-1-4222-0654-6(8)) 2007. pap. 9.95 (978-1-4222-0721-5(8)) Mason Crest.

Zweig, Eric. National Geographic Kids Everything Sports: All the Photos, Facts, & Fun to Make You Jump! 2016. (National Geographic Kids Everything Ser.). (Illus.). 64p. (J). (gr. 3-7). pap. 12.99 (978-1-4263-2333-1(6), National Geographic Kids) Disney Publishing Worldwide.

SPORTS—POETRY

Akister, Finola, et al, selected by. Sports Poems & Mouse Poems. 2008. (Illus.). 32p. (J). pap. 10.95 (978-1-59646-619-7(7)) Dingles & Co.

Akister, Finola, et al. Sports Poems & Mouse Poems. 2008. (Illus.). 32p. (J). lib. bdg. 23.65 (978-1-59646-618-0(9)) Dingles & Co.

Alvarez, Mrinali, illus. Pon, Pon: ¡A Jugar con el Bebé! 2005. (SPA.). 28p. (J). 8.95 (978-0-8477-1550-3(7)) Univ. of Puerto Rico Pr.

Gutman, Dan. Casey Back at Bat. Johnson, Steve & Fancher, Lou, illus. 2009. (ENG.). 32p. (J). (gr. -1-3). pap. 7.99 (978-0-06-056027-0(4), HarperCollins) HarperCollins Pubs.

Hoyte, Carol-Ann. And the Crowd Goes Wild! A Global Gathering of Sports Poems. Roemer, Heidi Bee, ed. Sylvester, Kevin, illus. 2012. 80p. pap. (978-1-77097-953-6(0)) FriesenPress.

Ipcizade, Catherine, et al. Pucks, Clubs, & Baseball Gloves: Reading & Writing Sports Poems, 1 vol. Loveridge, Matthew et al, illus. 2014. (Poet in You Ser.). (ENG.). 32p. (J). (gr. 2-4). pap. 9.95 (978-1-4795-2947-6(8), 124545, Picture Window Bks.) Capstone.

Lansky, Bruce. I Hope I Don't Strike Out! & Other Funny Sports Poems. Carpenter, Stephen, illus. 2008. 30p. (978-0-88166-535-2(5)) Meadowbrook Pr.

Smith Jr., Charles R. Hoop Kings. 2007. (Sports Royalty Ser.). (ENG., Illus.). 40p. (J). (gr. 3-7). pap. 7.99 (978-0-7636-3560-2(X)) Candlewick Pr.

—Hoop Queens. 2007. (Sports Royalty Ser.). (ENG., Illus.). 40p. (J). (gr. 3-7). pap. 7.99 (978-0-7636-3561-9(8)) Candlewick Pr.

SPORTS IN ART

Antram, David. Extreme Sports, 1 vol. 2012. (How to Draw Ser.). (ENG.). 32p. (J). (gr. 4-5). pap. 12.75 (978-1-4488-6465-2(8), e4813516-948e-42f4-b1af-b832a082c870); lib. bdg. 30.27 (978-1-4488-6459-1(3), f6f59ce3-a555-4533-8fb2-4271581a8b55) Rosen Publishing Group, Inc., The. (PowerKids Pr.).

Cook, Trevor & Miles, Lisa. Drawing Sports Figures, 1 vol. 2011. (Drawing Is Fun Ser.). (ENG., Illus.). 32p. (J). (gr. 1-2). pap. 11.50 (978-1-4339-5074-2(X), 22db3a9b-81c6-4bd9-a6fc-d9f7eb2da5c8, Gareth Stevens Learning Library); lib. bdg. 29.27 (978-1-4339-5028-5(6), 80245e2a-e3ed-48a5-b6b5-16b94117cc8d) Stevens, Gareth Publishing LLLP.

Kissock, Heather. Extreme Sports. 2012. (J). (978-1-61913-239-9(7)); pap. (978-1-61913-244-3(3)) Weigl Pubs., Inc.

Reid, Emily. Sports Claymation, 1 vol. 2016. (Claymation Sensation Ser.). (ENG.). 32p. (gr. 3-3). pap. 12.75 (978-1-4994-8104-4(7), 39ca1238-4448-4e52-987f-c6f370df48e3, Windmill Bks.) Rosen Publishing Group, Inc., The.

Wacholtz, Anthony. Drawing with Sports Illustrated Kids, 1 vol. Ray, Michael & Haya, Erwin, illus. 2013. (Drawing with Sports Illustrated Kids Ser.). (ENG.). 144p. (J). (gr. 5-9). pap., pap., pap. 14.95 (978-1-4765-3581-4(7), 123606, Capstone Pr.) Capstone.

—Picture a Home Run: A Baseball Drawing Book, 1 vol. Haya, Erwin, illus. 2013. (Drawing with Sports Illustrated Kids Ser.). (ENG.). 64p. (J). (gr. 5-9). 34.65 (978-1-4765-3106-9(4), 123087) Capstone.

—Picture a Slam Dunk: A Basketball Drawing Book, 1 vol. Haya, Erwin, illus. 2013. (Drawing with Sports Illustrated Kids Ser.). (ENG.). 64p. (J). (gr. 5-9). 34.65 (978-1-4765-3107-6(2), 123088) Capstone.

—Picture a Touchdown: A Football Drawing Book, 1 vol. Ray, Michael, illus. 2013. (Drawing with Sports Illustrated Kids Ser.). (ENG.). 64p. (J). (gr. 5-9). 34.65 (978-1-4765-3104-5(8), 123085) Capstone.

SPORTS JOURNALISM

Christopher, Dale. Behind the Desk with... Matt Christopher: The #1 Sportswriter for Kids. 2004. (ENG., Illus.). 128p. (J). (gr. 2-5). pap. 9.99 (978-0-316-10952-9(5)) Little, Brown Bks. for Young Readers.

Dakers, Diane. Sports Journalism. 2018. (Investigative Journalism That Inspired Change Ser.). (Illus.). 48p. (J). (gr. 6-6). (978-0-7787-5352-0(2)) Crabtree Publishing Co.

Marlowe, Christie. Announcer. 2013. (Earning $50,000 - $100,000 with a High School Diploma or Less Ser.: 14). 64p. (J). (gr. 7-18). 22.95 (978-1-4222-2887-6(8)) Mason Crest.

Peterson, Brian C. Sports Marketing: Careers off the Field, Vol. 10. Ferrer, Al, ed. 2015. (Careers off the Field Ser.). (Illus.). 64p. (J). (gr. 7). 23.95 (978-1-4222-3272-9(7)) Mason Crest.

Schwartzenberger, Tina. Don Cherry. 2010. (Illus.). 24p. (978-1-77071-625-4(4)); pap. (978-1-77071-626-1(2)) Weigl Educational Pubs. Ltd.

Suen, Anastasia. Read & Write Sports: Readers Theatre & Writing Activities for Grades 3-8, 1 vol. 2011. (ENG.). 232p. pap. 45.00 (978-1-59884-631-7(0), 836852, Libraries Unlimited) Bloomsbury Publishing USA.

Thomas, Stephen, ed. Hot Summer Fun, Cool Summer Stars. Staake, Bob et al, illus. Date not set. 28p. (Orig.). (J). (gr. 3-7). pap. (978-1-886749-26-9(4)) Sports Illustrated For Kids.

Tracy, Kathleen. Matt Christopher. 2008. (Classic Storytellers Ser.). (Illus.). 48p. (J). (gr. 4-7). lib. bdg. 29.95 (978-1-58415-535-5(3)) Mitchell Lane Pubs.

Walters, John. Sports Broadcasting, Vol. 10. Ferrer, Al, ed. 2015. (Careers off the Field Ser.). (Illus.). 64p. (J). (gr. 7). 23.95 (978-1-4222-3271-2(9)) Mason Crest.

—Sportswriting & Sports Photography, Vol. 10. Ferrer, Al, ed. 2015. (Careers off the Field Ser.). (Illus.). 64p. (J). (gr. 7). lib. bdg. 23.95 (978-1-4222-3273-6(5)) Mason Crest.

SPRING

Aloian, Molly. How Do We Know It Is Spring? 2013. (ENG., Illus.). 24p. (J). (978-0-7787-0959-6(0)); (gr. 2-2). pap. (978-0-7787-0963-3(9)) Crabtree Publishing Co.

Anderson, Maxine & Berkenkamp, Lauri. Explore Spring! 25 Great Ways to Learn about Spring. Frederick-Frost, Alexis, illus. 2007. (Explore Your World Ser.). (ENG.). 96p. (J). (gr. k-4). per. 12.95 (978-0-9785037-4-1(0), 78cc76a9-c8fc-43ca-9a84-475c2da9df6b) Nomad Pr.

Appleby, Alex. ¿Qué Sucede en Primavera? / What Happens in Spring?, 1 vol., Vol. 1. 2013. (Cuatro Estaciones Estupendas / Four Super Seasons Ser.). (SPA & ENG.). 24p. (J). (gr. k-k). 25.27 (978-1-4824-0119-6(3), 3ce3c190-4f18-4c1f-b30b-50c350bb6fe4) Stevens, Gareth Publishing LLLP.

—What Happens in Spring?, 1 vol., Vol. 1. 2013. (Four Super Seasons Ser.). (ENG.). 24p. (J). (gr. k-k). 25.27 (978-1-4824-0105-9(3), c9800c58-68c9-46f4-b9ab-236ca009bc4f) Stevens, Gareth Publishing LLLP.

Barnham, Kay. Spring, 1 vol. 2010. (Seasons Ser.). (ENG.). 24p. (J). (gr. 1-1). lib. bdg. 26.27 (978-1-61532-569-6(7), edbd3919-fbd7-4180-9c8a-cee38eeac2ef, PowerKids Pr.) Rosen Publishing Group, Inc., The.

Bekkering, Annalise. Spring. 2010. (J). pap. 9.95 (978-1-61690-050-2(4)); 24p. (gr. 2-4). lib. bdg. 25.70 (978-1-61690-046-5(6)) Weigl Pubs., Inc.

—Spring: World of Wonder Seasons. 2010. (J). (978-1-60596-766-0(1)) Weigl Pubs., Inc.

Best, Arthur. Springs, 1 vol. 2017. (Our World of Water Ser.). (ENG.). 24p. (gr. 1-1). pap. 9.22 (978-1-5026-3102-2(4), 5bd73274-303b-4248-94a2-dae02fac71dc) Cavendish Square Publishing LLC.

Bridge, Chris Helene. Spring Is Coming! 2018. (ENG., Illus.). 32p. (J). 19.95 (978-1-942945-48-2(5), f8784901-b803-4cb9-94e3-3a165a836043) Night Heron Media.

Brode, Robyn. April, 1 vol. 2nd rev. ed. 2009. (Months of the Year (Second Edition) Ser.). (ENG.). 24p. (J). (gr. 1-1). pap. 9.15 (978-1-4339-2097-4(2), a0799db3-8e0b-4f65-9c4a-c30a4d92b0e3); lib. bdg. 24.67 (978-1-4339-1920-6(6), 80c9e860-0476-4789-9641-24fbb0f10c7f) Stevens, Gareth Publishing LLLP. (Weekly Reader Leveled Readers).

—April / Abril, 1 vol. 2009. (Months of the Year / Meses Del Ano Ser.). (ENG & SPA.). 24p. (J). (gr. 1-1). pap. 9.15 (978-1-4339-2109-4(X), 00b7e47e-eeb2-47d0-bced-74a8ef9fc932); lib. bdg. 24.67 (978-1-4339-1932-9(X), 901f9bc7-a39e-4b04-bd6f-cd31a2143530) Stevens, Gareth Publishing LLLP. (Weekly Reader Leveled Readers).

—March, 1 vol. 2nd rev. ed. 2009. (Months of the Year (Second Edition) Ser.). (ENG.). 24p. (J). (gr. 1-1). pap. 9.15 (978-1-4339-2096-7(4), 62e73f46-8aaf-4d7d-b091-291322a7e869); lib. bdg. 24.67 (978-1-4339-1919-0(2), fac8673a-5f8d-4e68-ba95-ff92f245184c) Stevens, Gareth Publishing LLLP. (Weekly Reader Leveled Readers).

—March / Marzo, 1 vol. 2009. (Months of the Year / Meses Del Ano Ser.). (ENG & SPA.). 24p. (J). (gr. 1-1). pap. 9.15 (978-1-4339-2108-7(1), 839d1464-433a-405f-8f81-b9f61b190a66); lib. bdg. 24.67 (978-1-4339-1931-2(1), 2f0d421e-b6a6-43f7-9bcd-639b5b03d6b6) Stevens, Gareth Publishing LLLP. (Weekly Reader Leveled Readers).

—May, 1 vol. 2nd rev. ed. 2009. (Months of the Year (Second Edition) Ser.). (ENG.). 24p. (J). (gr. 1-1). pap. 9.15 (978-1-4339-2098-1(0), a6c97378-63c3-4e60-9d3c-56328769676e); lib. bdg. 24.67 (978-1-4339-1921-3(4), eb7e4c47-8139-4d4b-92fe-3ee509d598af) Stevens, Gareth Publishing LLLP. (Weekly Reader Leveled Readers).

—May / Mayo, 1 vol. 2009. (Months of the Year / Meses Del Ano Ser.). (ENG & SPA.). 24p. (J). (gr. 1-1). pap. 9.15 (978-1-4339-2110-0(3), f9fb85d1-5065-43d9-9caf-09319f7e1944); lib. bdg. 24.67 (978-1-4339-1933-6(8), bcd818e9-b5e8-4ca5-97f8-76234f6d086c) Stevens, Gareth Publishing LLLP. (Weekly Reader Leveled Readers).

Bryant, Margaret A., et al. Learning about Spring with Children's Literature. 2006. (ENG., Illus.). 160p. (J). (gr. k-3). pap. 14.95 (978-1-56976-206-6(6), Zephyr Pr.) Chicago Review Pr., Inc.

Burke, Betty & Finer, Susie. Activités de Printemps. (FRE.). 32p. pap. (978-0-439-98520-8(X)) Scholastic Canada, Ltd.

Butterfield, Moira. Spring. James, Helen, illus. 2005. (Seasons (Smart Apple Media) Ser.). 32p. (YA). (gr. 2-4). lib. bdg. 27.10 (978-1-58340-614-4(X)) Black Rabbit Bks.

Carr, Aaron. Spring. 2013. 25.00 (978-1-62127-493-3(4)) Weigl Pubs., Inc.

Casado, Dami & Casado, Alicia. La Primavera. 2005. (Brujita Mo y las Cuatro Estaciones Ser.). (SPA & ESP., Illus.). 14p. (J). (gr. k-4). per., bds. 7.99 (978-84-272-6238-6(8)) Molino, Editorial ESP. Dist: Santillana USA Publishing Co., Inc.

Clay, Kathryn. Animals in Spring. 2016. (Celebrate Spring Ser.). (ENG., Illus.). 24p. (J). (gr. -1-2). lib. bdg. 22.65 (978-1-4914-8302-2(4), 130778, Pebble) Capstone.

—Celebrate Spring. 2016. (Celebrate Spring Ser.). (ENG., Illus.). 24p. (J). (gr. -1-2). 98.60 (978-1-4914-8318-3(0), 24037, Pebble) Capstone.

—Flowers. 2016. (Celebrate Spring Ser.). (ENG., Illus.). 24p. (J). (gr. -1-2). lib. bdg. 22.65 (978-1-4914-8304-6(0), 130780) Capstone.

—Planting Seeds. 2016. (Celebrate Spring Ser.). (ENG., Illus.). 24p. (J). (gr. -1-2). lib. bdg. 22.65 (978-1-4914-8305-3(9), 130781) Capstone.

Collinson, Clare. Spring. 2010. (Thinking about the Seasons Ser.). 32p. 28.50 (978-1-59771-260-6(4)) Sea-To-Sea Pubns.

Declus, Jennifer. What Might I Find in a Geyser. Kalasea, illus. 2004. (J). (978-0-9743690-0-6(4)) Britt Allcroft Productions.

DeGezelle, Terri. Exploring Spring, 1 vol. 2012. (Exploring the Seasons Ser.). (ENG.). 24p. (J). (gr. -1-2). pap. 7.29 (978-1-4296-7910-7(7), 118242); (gr. k-1). pap. 41.70 (978-1-4296-8351-7(1)) Capstone. (Capstone Pr.).

Early Macken, JoAnn. Spring, 1 vol. 2005. (Seasons of the Year Ser.). (ENG., Illus.). 16p. (gr. k-1). pap. 6.30 (978-0-8368-6359-8(3), d064738f-4b46-467c-8328-995b33e93e0a); lib. bdg. 21.67 (978-0-8368-6354-3(2), fac47fe0-4eb4-42b5-aa24-56560b16908c) Stevens, Gareth Publishing LLLP. (Weekly Reader Leveled Readers).

—Spring / Primavera, 1 vol. 2005. (Seasons of the Year / Las Estaciones Del Año Ser.). (Illus.). 16p. (gr. k-1). (SPA & ENG.). pap. 6.30 (978-0-8368-6538-7(3), 8f77a1f1-940b-4b7c-b14e-ca84d8fd1e61); (ENG & SPA., lib. bdg. 21.67 (978-0-8368-6533-2(2), ea650498-f034-488c-b765-2ba44dc26a51) Stevens, Gareth Publishing LLLP. (Weekly Reader Leveled Readers).

Endres, Hollie J. The Letter Ss Set: Spring & Summer, 6 vols. 2004. (Letter Bks.). (ENG.). 8p. (gr. k-1). pap. 29.70 (978-0-7368-4118-4(0)) Capstone.

Enslow, Brian. Spring Colors, 1 vol. 2011. (All about Colors of the Seasons Ser.). (ENG., Illus.). 24p. (gr. -1-1). pap. 10.35 (978-1-59845-265-5(7), 8d4c3810-64e1-43c7-a442-652bfd94e2b0, Enslow Publishing) Enslow Publishing, LLC.

Esbaum, Jill. Everything Spring. 2010. (Illus.). 16p. (J). (gr. -1-k). pap. 5.95 (978-1-4263-0607-5(5), National Geographic Kids) Disney Publishing Worldwide.

Fewer, Michael. Naturama: Open Your Eyes to the Wonders of Irish Nature. Doran, Melissa, illus. 2017. (ENG.). 96p. (J). 42.00 (978-0-7171-6980-1(4)) Gill Bks. IRL. Dist: Casemate Pubs. & Bk. Distributors, LLC.

Fretland VanVoorst, Jenny. Animals in Spring. 2015. (Illus.). 24p. (J). lib. bdg. (978-1-62031-234-6(4), Bullfrog Bks.) Jump! Inc.

—Birds in Spring. 2015. (Illus.). 24p. (J). lib. bdg. (978-1-62031-235-3(2)) Jump! Inc.
—El Clima en la Primavera. 2015.Tr. of Weather in Spring. (SPA., Illus.). 24p. (J). lib. bdg. (978-1-62031-252-0(2), Bullfrog Bks.) Jump! Inc.
—Gardens in Spring. 2015. (Illus.). 24p. (J). lib. bdg. (978-1-62031-236-0(0)) Jump! Inc.
—Las Aves en la Primavera. 2015.Tr. of Birds in Spring. (SPA., Illus.). 24p. (J). lib. bdg. (978-1-62031-250-6(6), Bullfrog Bks.) Jump! Inc.
—Los Animales en la Primavera. 2015.Tr. of Animals in Spring. (SPA., Illus.). 24p. (J). lib. bdg. (978-1-62031-241-4(7), Bullfrog Bks.) Jump! Inc.
—Los árboles en la Primavera. 2015.Tr. of Trees in Spring. (SPA., Illus.). 24p. (J). lib. bdg. (978-1-62031-251-3(4), Bullfrog Bks.) Jump! Inc.
—Los Jardines en la Primavera. 2015.Tr. of Gardens in Spring. (SPA., Illus.). 24p. (J). lib. bdg. (978-1-62031-242-1(5), Bullfrog Bks.) Jump! Inc.
—Trees in Spring. 2015. (Illus.). 24p. (J). lib. bdg. (978-1-62031-237-7(9), Bullfrog Bks.) Jump! Inc.
—Weather in Spring. 2015. (Illus.). 24p. (J). lib. bdg. (978-1-62031-238-4(7), Bullfrog Bks.) Jump! Inc.
Gaertner, Meg. People in Spring. 2020. (Spring Is Here Ser.). (ENG., Illus.). 16p. (J). (gr. k-1). pap. 7.95 (978-1-64493-100-4(1), 1644931001); lib. bdg. 25.64 (978-1-64493-021-2(8), 1644930218) North Star Editions. (Focus Readers).
—Spring Animals. 2020. (Spring Is Here Ser.). (ENG., Illus.). 16p. (J). (gr. k-1). 25.64 (978-1-64493-022-9(6), 1644930226, Focus Readers) North Star Editions.
—Spring Plants. 2020. (Spring Is Here Ser.). (ENG., Illus.). 16p. (J). (gr. k-1). 25.64 (978-1-64493-023-6(4), 1644930234, Focus Readers) North Star Editions.
—A Spring Pond. 2020. (Spring Is Here Ser.). (ENG., Illus.). 16p. (J). (gr. k-1). pap. 7.95 (978-1-64493-103-5(6), 1644931036); lib. bdg. 25.64 (978-1-64493-024-3(2), 1644930242) North Star Editions. (Focus Readers).
—Spring Weather. 2020. (Spring Is Here Ser.). (ENG., Illus.). 16p. (J). (gr. k-1). pap. 7.95 (978-1-64493-104-2(4), 1644931044); lib. bdg. 25.64 (978-1-64493-025-0(0), 1644930250) North Star Editions. (Focus Readers).
Gagliardi, Sue. Get Outside in Spring. 2019. (Get Outside Ser.). (ENG., Illus.). 32p. (J). (gr. 2-3). 31.35 (978-1-64185-332-3(8), 1641853328, Focus Readers) North Star Editions.
Ghigna, Charles. Raindrops Fall All Around. Watson, Laura, illus. 2015. (Springtime Weather Wonders Ser.). (ENG.). 24p. (J). (gr. -1-2). lib. bdg. 22.65 (978-1-4795-6030-1(8), 127289, Picture Window Bks.) Capstone.
Glaser, Rebecca. Spring. 2012. (ENG., Illus.). 24p. (J). lib. bdg. 25.65 (978-1-62031-014-4(7)) Jump! Inc.
Gleisner, Jenna Lee. How's the Weather in Spring? 2014. (21st Century Basic Skills Library: Let's Look at Spring Ser.). (ENG., Illus.). 24p. (J). (gr. k-3). pap. 12.79 (978-1-62431-681-4(6), 203129) Cherry Lake Publishing.
—What Blossoms in Spring? 2014. (21st Century Basic Skills Library: Let's Look at Spring Ser.). (ENG.). 24p. (J). (gr. k-3). pap. 12.79 (978-1-62431-686-9(7), 203149); (Illus.). 26.35 (978-1-62431-659-3(X), 203148) Cherry Lake Publishing.
—What Do Animals Do in Spring? 2014. (21st Century Basic Skills Library: Let's Look at Spring Ser.). (ENG., Illus.). 24p. (J). (gr. k-3). 26.35 (978-1-62431-660-9(3), 203152) Cherry Lake Publishing.
—What Do People Do in Spring? 2014. (21st Century Basic Skills Library: Let's Look at Spring Ser.). (ENG., Illus.). 24p. (J). (gr. k-3). 26.35 (978-1-62431-661-6(1), 203156) Cherry Lake Publishing.
Henkes, Kevin. When Spring Comes Board Book: An Easter & Springtime Book for Kids. Dronzek, Laura, illus. 2018. (ENG.). 36p. (J). (gr. -1-k). bds. 7.99 (978-0-06-274166-0(7), Greenwillow Bks.) HarperCollins Pubs.
Henshaw, Lorne. Birds in Spring, 1 vol. 2016. (We Love Spring! Ser.). (ENG., Illus.). 24p. (J). (gr. k-k). pap. 9.15 (978-1-4824-5477-2(7), 805828e4-43a0-46ec-aae7-91bd9dbb6975) Stevens, Gareth Publishing LLLP.
Here Comes Spring! 2003. (J). per. (978-1-57657-968-8(9)) Paradise Pr., Inc.
Herriges, Ann. Spring. 2006. (Seasons Ser.). (ENG., Illus.). 24p. (J). (gr. k-3). lib. bdg. 26.95 (978-1-60014-031-0(9)) Bellwether Media.
—Spring. 2011. (Blastoff! Readers Ser.). (ENG.). 24p. (J). pap. 5.95 (978-0-531-26247-4(2), Children's Pr.) Scholastic Library Publishing.
Herrington, Lisa M. How Do You Know It's Spring? 2013. (ENG.). 32p. (J). 23.00 (978-0-531-29947-0(3)) Scholastic Library Publishing.
Hollow, Stanley. First Spring Flowers, 1 vol. 2016. (We Love Spring! Ser.). (ENG., Illus.). 24p. (J). (gr. k-k). pap. 9.15 (978-1-4824-5489-5(0), fa427801-1d6a-4a3d-a47d-c7bef3d12a3f) Stevens, Gareth Publishing LLLP.
Jeffries, Joyce. Dinosaurs in the Spring, 1 vol. 2014. (Dinosaur School Ser.). (ENG.). 24p. (J). (gr. k-k). pap. 9.15 (978-1-4824-0622-1(5), 7a128365-f6a0-4ace-a246-e578f69f5c88c) Stevens, Gareth Publishing LLLP.
Jones, Tammy. I Like the Spring! 2009. (Sight Word Readers Set A Ser.). (J). 3.49 net. (978-1-60719-138-4(5)) Newmark Learning LLC.
Kalz, Jill. Spring. 2005. (My First Look at Seasons Ser.). (Illus.). 24p. (J). (gr. k-3). lib. bdg. 15.95 (978-1-58341-363-0(4), Creative Education) Creative Co., The.
Latta, Sara L. Why Is It Spring?, 1 vol. 2012. (Why Do We Have Seasons? Ser.). (ENG., Illus.). 24p. (gr. k-2). 25.27 (978-0-7660-3986-5(2), ee79cb96-5d69-4305-8286-91f597a2d7e0); pap. 10.35 (978-1-59845-389-8(0), 482a48cf-0736-49d7-81d6-82605ae602da, Enslow Elementary) Enslow Publishing, LLC.
Lim, Annalees. 10-Minute Seasonal Crafts for Spring, 1 vol. 2014. (10-Minute Seasonal Crafts Ser.). (ENG.). 24p. (J). (gr. 2-3). lib. bdg. 28.93 (978-1-4777-9206-3(6), a3ea3cf1-9b81-42e4-b031-7e8c3eafd443, Windmill Bks.) Rosen Publishing Group, Inc., The.
Lindeen, Mary. Spring! 2015. (BeginningtoRead Ser.). (ENG., Illus.). 32p. (J). (gr. k-2). lib. bdg. 22.60 (978-1-59953-679-8(X)) Norwood Hse. Pr.
—Spring. 2015. (Beginning-To-Read Ser.). (ENG., Illus.). 32p. (J). (gr. k-2). pap. 13.26 (978-1-60357-739-7(4)) Norwood Hse. Pr.
Macken, JoAnn Early. What We Do in Spring. 2018. (Seasons Can Be Fun (LOOK! Books (tm)) Ser.). (ENG., Illus.). 24p. (J). (gr. -1-3). lib. bdg. 25.32 (978-1-63440-306-1(1), 47f7adc1-6ba6-4902-85cd-0974d29892bd) Red Chair Pr.
McGee, Randel. Fun & Festive Spring Crafts: Flower Puppets, Bunny Masks, & Mother's Day Pop-Up Cards, 1 vol. 2014. (Fun & Festive Crafts for the Seasons Ser.). (ENG., Illus.). 48p. (gr. 3-3). lib. bdg. 26.93 (978-0-7660-4318-3(5), cf7f1cb2-0282-41d3-b570-debbcba0c810, Enslow Elementary) Enslow Publishing, LLC.
Meister, Cari. Spring Is Special. 2010. (First Graphics: Seasons Ser.). (ENG., Illus.). 24p. (J). (gr. 1-2). pap. 38.74 (978-1-4296-5693-1(X), 15485) Capstone.
Minden, Cecilia. What Can I See in the Spring? 2018. (Seasons Ser.). (ENG.). 16p. (J). (gr. -1-2). pap. 11.36 (978-1-5341-2874-3(3), 211543, Cherry Blossom Press) Cherry Lake Publishing.
Moon, Walt K. ¡la Primavera Es Divertida! (Spring Is Fun!) 2017. (Bumba Books (r) en Español — Diviértete con Las Estaciones (Season Fun) Ser.). (SPA., Illus.). 24p. (J). (gr. -1-1). 26.65 (978-1-5124-2861-2(2), 4b55454e-9e54-4ab8-a9d8-fc24b45cf0dd, Ediciones Lerner) Lerner Publishing Group.
—Spring Is Fun! 2016. (Bumba Books (r) — Season Fun Ser.). (ENG., Illus.). 24p. (J). (gr. -1-1). 26.65 (978-1-5124-1411-0(5), fbacb6ce-d925-4510-94e7-50bb06305071, Lerner Pubns.) Lerner Publishing Group.
Murray, Julie. La Primavera. 2016. (Las Estaciones Ser.). (SPA.). 24p. (J). (gr. -1-2). pap. 7.95 (978-1-4966-0709-6(0), 131744, Capstone Classroom) Capstone.
—Spring, 1 vol. 2015. (Seasons Ser.). (ENG., Illus.). 24p. (J). (gr. -1-2). 31.36 (978-1-62970-920-8(4), 18298, Abdo Kids) ABDO Publishing Co.
Owen, Ruth. How Do You Know It's Spring? (Signs of the Seasons Ser.). 24p. (J). 2016. (ENG., Illus.). (gr. k-3). pap. 7.99 (978-1-944998-49-3(7)) 2012. (gr. -1-3). lib. bdg. 26.99 (978-1-61772-398-8(3)) Bearport Publishing Co., Inc.
Peters, Katie. Spring Flowers. 2019. (Seasons All Around Me (Pull Ahead Readers — Nonfiction) Ser.). (ENG., Illus.). 16p. (J). (gr. -1-1). pap. 8.99 (978-1-5415-7345-1(5), 834c30d7-f293-4126-a5b3-0e6778cc0420); lib. bdg. 27.99 (978-1-5415-5870-0(7), 70896019-f6a9-4f9a-a44e-13efe19b7f4b) Lerner Publishing Group. (Lerner Pubns.).
Pettiford, Rebecca. Spring. 2018. (Seasons of the Year Ser.). (ENG., Illus.). 24p. (J). (gr. k-3). pap. 7.99 (978-1-61891-302-9(6), 12098, Blastoff! Readers) Bellwether Media.
Priddy, Roger. Bright Baby Touch & Feel Spring. 2011. (Bright Baby Touch & Feel Ser.). (ENG., Illus.). 10p. (J). (gr. -1 — 1). bds. 4.95 (978-0-312-51006-0(3), 900073555) St. Martin's Pr.
Roca, Nuria. La Primavera (Spring) 2004. (Estaciones / Seasons Ser.).Tr. of Spring. (SPA., Illus.). 36p. (J). (gr. k-3). 22.44 (978-0-7641-2734-2(9), B.E.S. Publishing) Peterson's.
Rotner, Shelley. Hello Spring! (Hello Seasons! Ser.). (Illus.). 32p. (J). (gr. -1-3). 2019. pap. 7.99 (978-0-8234-3995-9(X)) 2017. (ENG., 16.95 (978-0-8234-3752-8(3)) Holiday Hse., Inc.
—Hello Spring! 2019. (Hello Seasons! Ser.). (ENG.). 32p. (J). (gr. k-1). 18.79 (978-1-64310-987-9(1)) Penworthy Co., LLC, The.
Rustad, Martha E. H. All about Spring. 2012. (All about Spring Ser.). (ENG.). 24p. (J). (gr. -1-2). pap., pap., pap. 27.80 (978-1-4296-9366-0(5), 18578, Capstone Pr.) Capstone.
—All about Spring Classroom Collection. 2012. (All about Spring Ser.). (ENG.). 24p. (J). (gr. k-1). pap., pap., pap. 166.80 (978-1-4296-9367-7(3), 18579, Capstone Pr.) Capstone.
—Animals in Spring, 1 vol. 2012. (All about Spring Ser.). (ENG., Illus.). 24p. (J). (gr. -1-2). pap. 7.29 (978-1-4296-9358-5(4), 120384, Capstone Pr.) Capstone.
—Animals in Spring. 2012. (All about Spring Ser.). (ENG.). 24p. (J). (gr. k-1). pap. 43.74 (978-1-4296-9360-8(6), 18575, Capstone Pr.) Capstone.
—People in Spring, 1 vol. 2012. (All about Spring Ser.). (ENG.). 24p. (J). (gr. -1-2). pap. 7.29 (978-1-4296-9361-5(4), 120385); (Illus.). lib. bdg. 27.32 (978-1-4296-8657-0(X), 118994) Capstone. (Capstone Pr.).
—People in Spring. 2012. (All about Spring Ser.). (ENG.). 24p. (J). (gr. k-1). pap. 43.74 (978-1-4296-9359-2(2), 18574, Capstone Pr.) Capstone.
—Plants in Spring, 1 vol. 2012. (All about Spring Ser.). (ENG.). 24p. (J). (gr. -1-2). pap. 7.29 (978-1-4296-9362-2(2), 120386); (gr. -1-2). lib. bdg. 27.32 (978-1-4296-8656-3(1), 118993); (gr. k-1). pap. 43.74 (978-1-4296-9363-9(0), 18576) Capstone. (Capstone Pr.).
—Weather in Spring, 1 vol. 2012. (All about Spring Ser.). (ENG.). 24p. (J). (gr. -1-2). pap. 7.29 (978-1-4296-9364-6(9), 120387); (gr. k-1). pap. 43.74 (978-1-4296-9365-3(7), 18577) Capstone. (Capstone Pr.).
Salas, Laura Purdie. Snowman - Cold = Puddle: Spring Equations. Archer, Micha, illus. 2019. 32p. (J). (gr. -1-3). lib. bdg. 16.99 (978-1-58089-798-3(3)) Charlesbridge Publishing, Inc.
Schuette, Sarah L. Let's Look at Spring: A 4D Book. rev. ed. 2018. (Investigate the Seasons Ser.). (ENG., Illus.). 24p. (J). (gr. -1-2). lib. bdg. 29.32 (978-1-5435-0858-1(8), 137609, Capstone Pr.) Capstone.
Schuh, Mari. La Primavera. 2019. (Estaciones Ser.). (SPA.). 16p. (J). (gr. -1-2). (978-1-68151-626-4(8), 14527) Amicus.
—Le Printemps. 2019. (Spot les Saisons Ser.). (FRE.). 16p. (J). (gr. -1-2). (978-1-77092-439-0(6), 14528) Amicus.
—Spring. 2019. (Spot Seasons Ser.). (ENG.). 16p. (J). (gr. -1-2). lib. bdg. (978-1-68151-550-2(4), 14511) Amicus.
Shepherd, Jodie. Colores de la Primavera Crayola (r) (Crayola (r) Spring Colors) 2018. (Estaciones Crayola (r) (Crayola (r) Seasons) Ser.). (SPA., Illus.). 24p. (J). (gr. -1-3). 29.32 (978-1-5415-0954-2(4), 1bd4009c-60cb-49df-87ed-f8af08142635, Ediciones Lerner) Lerner Publishing Group.
Silverman, Buffy. On a Snow-Melting Day: Seeking Signs of Spring. 2020. (ENG., Illus.). 32p. (J). (gr. -1-3). 30.65 (978-1-5415-7813-5(9), 604d785a-5855-422f-8473-522051cd64bf, Millbrook Pr.) Lerner Publishing Group.
Smith, Sian. What Can You See in Spring?, 1 vol. 2014. (Seasons Ser.). (ENG.). 24p. (J). (gr. -1-1). pap. 5.99 (978-1-4846-0354-3(0), 126440, Heinemann) Capstone.
Storey, Rita. Art for Spring, 1 vol. 2017. (Outdoor Art Room Ser.). (ENG.). 32p. (J). (gr. 3-3). 30.27 (978-1-5081-9418-7(1), f962148f-c8b8-49ae-9649-2882f144e7c2); pap. 12.75 (978-1-5081-9467-5(X), b7100f3f-cf69-4017-b649-58cd4698db96) Rosen Publishing Group, Inc., The. (Windmill Bks.).
Thayer, Tanya. Spring. 2005. (First Step Nonfiction Ser.). (Illus.). 24p. (gr. k-2). lib. bdg. 17.27 (978-0-8225-1986-7(0)) Lerner Publishing Group.
Turnbull, Stephanie. Spring. 2013. (Seasons Ser.). (ENG., Illus.). 24p. (J). (gr. k-3). 25.65 (978-1-59920-847-3(4), 17377) Black Rabbit Bks.
Urban, Chieu Anh. Color Wonder Hooray for Spring! Urban, Chieu Anh, illus. 2016. (Color Wonder Ser.). (ENG., Illus.). 14p. (J). (gr. -1 — 1). bds. 7.99 (978-1-4814-8720-7(5), Little Simon) Little Simon.
Wargin, Kathy-jo. K Is for Kite: God's Springtime Alphabet, 1 vol. Gatto, Kim, illus. 2010. (ENG.). 40p. (J). (gr. -1-2). 15.99 (978-0-310-71662-4(4)) Zonderkidz.
We Love Spring! 2016. (We Love Spring! Ser.). 00024p. (J). pap. 48.90 (978-1-4824-5536-6(6)) Stevens, Gareth Publishing LLLP.
Welch, Martha Mckeen. Close Looks in a Spring Woods. 2011. (J). (978-0-396-07998-9(9)) Dodd, Mead & Co., U. S.
World Book, Inc. Staff, contrib. by. Spring Celebrations. 2009. (Illus.). 46p. (J). (978-0-7166-5042-3(8)) World Bk., Inc.
York, M. J. Plants in Spring. 2017. (Welcoming the Seasons Ser.). (ENG.). 24p. (J). (gr. -1-2). lib. bdg. 32.79 (978-1-5038-1654-1(0), 211507) Child's World, Inc, The.
—Spring on the Farm. 2017. (Welcoming the Seasons Ser.). (ENG.). 24p. (J). (gr. -1-2). lib. bdg. 32.79 (978-1-5038-1657-2(5), 211508) Child's World, Inc, The.
York, M. J. & Willis, John. Animals. 2018. (Illus.). 24p. (J). (978-1-4896-9665-6(2), AV2 by Weigl) Weigl Pubs., Inc.
—Plants. 2018. (Illus.). 24p. (J). pap. (978-1-4896-9670-0(9), AV2 by Weigl) Weigl Pubs., Inc.
—Weather. 2018. (Illus.). 24p. (J). pap. (978-1-4896-9674-8(1), AV2 by Weigl) Weigl Pubs., Inc.

SPRING—FICTION

Accord Publishing, Accord. Hop, Pop, & Play: A Mini Animotion Book. 2011. (ENG.). 12p. (J). 9.99 (978-1-4494-0177-1(5)) Andrews McMeel Publishing.
Alexander, Liza. Splish-Splash Spring! 2016. lib. bdg. 14.75 (978-0-606-38486-5(3)) Turtleback.
Allen, Elise & Stanford, Halle. Spring's Sparkle Sleepover. Poolier, Paige, illus. 2015. (Enchanted Sisters Ser.: 3). (J). lib. bdg. 16.00 (978-0-606-36218-4(5)) Turtleback.
Armstrong, Jeannette. Dancing with the Cranes, 1 vol. Hall, Ron, illus. 2nd rev. ed. 2017. (ENG.). 24p. (J). (gr. 1-3). pap. 10.95 (978-1-894778-70-1(7)) Theytus Bks., Ltd. CAN. Dist: Orca Bk. Pubs. USA.
Barklem, Jill. Cuento de Primavera.Tr. of Spring Story. (SPA.). (J). pap. 8.95 (978-84-233-2618-1(7)) Ediciones Destino ESP. Dist: Planeta Publishing Corp.
Bauer, Marion Dane. Crinkle, Crackle, CRACK: It's Spring! Shelley, John, illus. 2019. 32p. (J). (gr. -1-3). pap. 7.99 (978-0-8234-4177-8(6)) Holiday Hse., Inc.
—Crinkle, Crackle, CRACK: It's Spring! 2019. (ENG.). 32p. (J). (gr. k-1). 18.79 (978-1-64310-988-6(X)) Penworthy Co., LLC, The.
—In Like a Lion Out Like a Lamb. McCully, Emily Arnold, illus. 2012. (ENG.). 32p. (J). (gr. -1-3). pap. 7.99 (978-0-8234-2432-0(4)) Holiday Hse., Inc.
Bennett, Elizabeth. Hello Kitty: Garden Party. Hino, Sachiho, illus. 2015. 22p. (J). (978-0-545-73447-9(9)) Scholastic, Inc.
—It's Spring Time! Baccala, Gladys, illus. 2013. (ENG.). 16p. (J). (gr. -1). bds. 8.95 (978-1-58925-639-2(5)) Tiger Tales.
Berenstain, Jan & Mike. The Berenstain Bears Spring Storybook Favorites: Includes 7 Stories Plus Stickers!: a Springtime Book for Kids. Berenstain, Mike, illus. 2019. (Berenstain Bears Ser.). (ENG.). 192p. (J). (gr. -1-3). 13.99 (978-0-06-288310-0(0), HarperCollins) HarperCollins Pubs.
Berger, Carin. Finding Spring: A Springtime Book for Kids. Berger, Carin, illus. 2015. (ENG., Illus.). 40p. (J). (gr. -1-3). 17.99 (978-0-06-225019-3(1), Greenwillow Bks.) HarperCollins Pubs.
Berger, Samantha & Chanko, Pamela. It's Spring! (a StoryPlay Book) 2017. (StoryPlay Ser.). (ENG., Illus.). 40p. (J). (gr. -1-k). 5.99 (978-1-338-23218-9(5)) Scholastic, Inc.
Berner, Rotraut Susanne. All Around Bustletown: Spring. 2020. (All Around Bustletown Ser.). (ENG., Illus.). 14p. (J). (-k). bds. 14.95 (978-3-7913-7409-3(5)) Prestel Verlag GmbH & Co KG. DEU. Dist: Penguin Random Hse. LLC.
Bond, Rebecca. Pig & Goose & the First Day of Spring. Bond, Rebecca, illus. 2017. (Illus.). 48p. (J). (gr. k-3). lib. bdg. 12.99 (978-1-58089-594-1(8)) Charlesbridge Publishing, Inc.
Bonnell, Kris. Spring Is Coming! 2007. (J). pap. 6.95 (978-1-933727-64-6(0)) Reading Reading Bks., LLC.
Brooks, Donna. The Amazing Apple Tree. 2011. 40p. pap. 16.95 (978-1-61204-563-4(4), Strategic Bk. Publishing) Strategic Book Publishing & Rights Agency (SBPRA).
Carlstrom, Nancy White. Raven & River. Van Zyle, Jon, illus. 2011. (ENG.). 32p. pap. 13.95 (978-1-60223-150-4(8)) Univ. of Alaska Pr.
Carter, David A. Springtime in Bugland! Ready-To-Read Level 1. Carter, David A., illus. 2012. (David Carter's Bugs Ser.). (ENG., Illus.). 24p. (J). (gr. -1-1). 15.99 (978-1-4424-3892-7(4)); pap. 3.99 (978-1-4424-3890-3(8)) Simon Spotlight. (Simon Spotlight).
Chaconas, Dori. Looking for Easter, 1 vol. Moore, Margie, illus. 2011. (Holiday Books: Easter Ser.). (ENG.). 32p. (J). (gr. -1-3). 21.19 (978-0-8075-4749-6(2)) Whitman, Albert & Co.
—Looking for Easter. Moore, Margie, illus. 2012. 32p. (J). 34.28 (978-1-61913-120-0(X)) Weigl Pubs., Inc.
Cocca-Leffler, Maryann. Let It Rain. Cocca-Leffler, Maryann, illus. 2013. (ENG., Illus.). 24p. (J). (gr. k-3). pap. 16.19 (978-0-545-45343-1(7)) Scholastic, Inc.
Colandro, Lucille. There Was an Old Lady Who Swallowed a Frog! Lee, Jared D., illus. 2015. (J). (978-0-545-83213-7(6)) Scholastic, Inc.
—There Was an Old Lady Who Swallowed a Frog! Lee, Jared, illus. 2014. (ENG.). 32p. (J). (gr. -1-1). pap. 6.99 (978-0-545-69138-3(9), Cartwheel Bks.) Scholastic, Inc.
Curry, Don L. In My Backyard. O'Leary Brown, Erin, illus. 2011. (Rookie Ready to Learn — Animals Ser.). 32p. (J). (gr. -1-k). lib. bdg. 25.00 (978-0-531-26416-4(5)); pap. 5.95 (978-0-531-26697-7(4)) Scholastic Library Publishing. (Children's Pr.).
—Rookie Ready to Learn en Español: en Mi Patio. O'Leary Brown, Erin, illus. 2011. (Rookie Ready to Learn Español Ser.). Orig. Title: Rookie Ready to Learn: in My Backyard. (SPA.). 32p. (J). pap. 5.95 (978-0-531-26784-4(9), Children's Pr.) Scholastic Library Publishing.
Curry, Don L. & O'Leary Brown, Erin. En Mi Patio. O'Leary Brown, Erin, illus. 2011. (Rookie Ready to Learn Español Ser.). (SPA., Illus.). 32p. (J). lib. bdg. 23.00 (978-0-531-26116-3(6), Children's Pr.) Scholastic Library Publishing.
Cyrus, Kurt. Shake a Leg, Egg! Cyrus, Kurt, illus. 2017. (ENG., Illus.). 32p. (J). (gr. -1-3). 17.99 (978-1-4814-5848-1(5), Beach Lane Bks.) Beach Lane Bks.
Davis, Kathryn Lynn. Wake up! Wake Up! A Springtime Lift-The-Flap Book. Davis, Kathryn Lynn, illus. 2011. (ENG., Illus.). 14p. (J). (gr. -1 — 1). bds. 5.99 (978-1-4424-1217-0(8), Little Simon) Little Simon.
dePaola, Tomie. Four Friends in Summer. dePaola, Tomie, illus. 2003. (ENG., Illus.). 32p. (J). (gr. -1-3). reprint ed. 19.99 (978-0-689-85693-8(8), Simon & Schuster Bks. For Young Readers) Simon & Schuster Bks. For Young Readers.
Depken, Kristen L. A Royal Spring. 2016. (Disney Princess Step into Reading Ser.). lib. bdg. 14.75 (978-0-606-38466-7(9)) Turtleback.
Disney Books. Winnie the Pooh: Pooh's Secret Garden. 2012. (ENG., Illus.). 24p. (J). (gr. -1-k). pap. 4.99 (978-1-4231-4845-6(2), Disney Press Books) Disney Publishing Worldwide.
Dudás, Gergely. Bear's Springtime Book of Hidden Things: An Easter & Springtime Book for Kids. Dudás, Gergely, illus. 2019. (ENG., Illus.). 32p. (J). (gr. -1-3). pap. 8.99 (978-0-06-257080-2(3), HarperCollins) HarperCollins Pubs.
Dunham, Wendy. A Windy Spring Day: God Gives Us Friends When We're Afraid. 2018. (Tales of Buttercup Grove Ser.). (ENG., Illus.). 64p. (J). (gr. -1-2). 12.99 (978-0-7369-7200-0(5), 6972000) Harvest Hse. Pubs.
Earhart, Kristin. Roscoe & the Pony Parade. Gurney, John, illus. 2008. (Little Apple Ser.). 88p. (J). (978-0-545-08094-1(0)) Scholastic, Inc.
Ergün, Erol. The Hearer & the Seer of All. 2011. (ENG., Illus.). 160p. (J). (gr. -1-12). pap. 9.95 (978-1-59784-257-0(5), Tughra Bks.) Blue Dome, Inc.
Ernst, Lisa Campbell. Wake up, It's Spring! Ernst, Lisa Campbell, illus. 2004. (ENG., Illus.). 40p. (J). (gr. -1-3). 16.99 (978-0-06-008985-6(7)) HarperCollins Pubs.
Floyd, Jamie. The Spring Flower. 2008. 17p. pap. 24.95 (978-1-60610-810-9(7)) America Star Bks.
Fogliano, Julie. And Then It's Spring. Stead, Erin E., illus. 2012. (ENG.). 32p. (J). (gr. -1-2). 19.99 (978-1-59643-624-4(7), 900066722) Roaring Brook Pr.
—And Then It's Spring. 2013. (J). (gr. k-3). (978-0-545-57133-3(2)) Weston Woods Studios, Inc.
Francis-Harris, Annabel. The Other Side of the Forest. 2006. pap. 19.95 (978-1-59526-458-9(2)) Aeon Publishing Inc.
Galbraith, Kathryn O. Spring Babies. Pons, Adela, illus. 2019. (Babies in the Park Ser.). 20p. (J). (gr. -1 — 1). bds. 7.99 (978-1-68263-068-6(4)) Peachtree Publishing Co. Inc.
Galliez, Roxane Marie. Patience, Miyuki: (intergenerational Picture Book Ages 5-8 Teaches Life Lessons of Learning How to Wait, Japanese Art & Scenery) Ratanavanh, Seng Soun, illus. 2019. (ENG.). 32p. (J). (gr. k-3). 18.95 (978-1-61689-843-4(7)) Princeton Architectural Pr.
George, Kallie. Duck, Duck, Dinosaur: Spring Smiles. Vidal, Oriol, illus. 2019. (My First I Can Read Ser.). (ENG.). 32p. (J). (gr. -1-3). 16.99 (978-0-06-235322-1(5)); pap. 4.99 (978-0-06-235321-4(7)) HarperCollins Pubs. (HarperCollins).
Ghigna, Charles. I See Spring, 1 vol. Jatkowska, Agnieszka, illus. 2011. (I See Ser.). (ENG.). 24p. (J). (gr. -1 — 1). pap. 6.10 (978-1-4048-6849-6(6), 116430, Picture Window Bks.) Capstone.
Glaser, Linda. It's Spring! Swan, Susan, illus. 2003. (Celebrate the Seasons Ser.). (ENG.). 32p. (J). (gr. k-3). pap. 7.95 (978-0-7613-1345-8(1), 7b76d9d0-459e-4c2b-9c59-c0392071e43e, First Avenue Editions) Lerner Publishing Group.
Grandfather Pine & His Special Place: Book One - Spring. 2013. 48p. (978-1-4602-2520-2(1)) FriesenPress.
Hanson, Bonnie Compton. A Stormy Spring. 2004. (Ponytail Girls Ser.). (Illus.). 192p. (J). pap. 7.99 (978-1-58411-032-3(5), Legacy Pr.) Rainbow Pubs. & Legacy Pr.
Hays, Anna Jane. Spring Surprises. Swearingen, Hala Wittwer, illus. 2010. (Step into Reading: Step 2 Ser.). (ENG.). 24p. (J). (gr. -1-1). lib. bdg. 16.19 (978-0-375-95840-3(1)) Random House Publishing Group.
Heckt, Jackie. It's Spring, 1 vol. 2016. (Four Seasons Ser.). (ENG., Illus.). 24p. (gr. 1-1). pap. 9.25 (978-1-5081-5183-8(0), 882f4666-01a7-4420-aefc-22c6aa034c92, PowerKids Pr.) Rosen Publishing Group, Inc., The.
Henkes, Kevin. When Spring Comes. Dronzek, Laura, illus. 2016. (ENG.). 40p. (J). (gr. -1-3). 18.89 (978-0-06-233140-3(X), Greenwillow Bks.) HarperCollins Pubs.
—When Spring Comes: An Easter & Springtime Book for Kids. Dronzek, Laura, illus. 2019. (ENG.). 40p. (J). (gr. -1-3). pap. 8.99 (978-0-06-274167-7(5), Greenwillow Bks.) HarperCollins Pubs.
Hennessy, Mary L. Spring Breezes & Sneezes. 2012. 20p. pap. 17.99 (978-1-4772-6042-5(0)) AuthorHouse.
Hillenbrand, Will. Spring Is Here: A Bear & Mole Story. 2012. (Bear & Mole Ser.: 1). (ENG., Illus.). 32p. (J). (-k). pap. 7.99 (978-0-8234-2431-3(6)) Holiday Hse., Inc.

Hillert, Margaret. Es Primavera, Querido Dragón/It's Spring, Dear Dragon. Schimmell, David, illus. 2011. (BeginningtoRead Ser.). 32p. (J). (-2). pap. 11.94 *(978-1-60357-555-3(3))* Norwood Hse. Pr.
—Es Primavera, Querido Dragón/It's Spring, Dear Dragon. del Risco, Eida, tr. from ENG. Schimmell, David, illus. 2011. (BeginningtoRead Ser.). 32p. (J). (gr. k-2). lib. bdg. 22.60 *(978-1-59953-471-8(1))* Norwood Hse. Pr.
—It's Spring, Dear Dragon. Schimmell, David, illus. 2009. (BeginningtoRead Ser.). 32p. (J). (gr. k-2). lib. bdg. 22.60 *(978-1-59953-312-4(X))* Norwood Hse. Pr.
Hive Enterprise Staff, contrib. by. Spring Bee. 2016. (Hive Ser.). (ENG., Illus.). 24p. (J). (gr. -1-1). 16.19 *(978-1-4844-7010-7(9))* Penguin Publishing Group.
Iwamura, Kazuo. Good-Bye, Winter! Hello, Spring! 2019. (ENG., Illus.). 32p. (J). (gr. -1-2). 17.95 *(978-0-7358-4345-5(7))* North-South Bks., Inc.
Johnson, Crockett. Time for Spring. Johnson, Crockett, illus. 2016. (ENG., Illus.). 40p. (J). (gr. -1-3). 14.99 *(978-0-06-243033-5(5),* HarperCollins) HarperCollins Pubs.
—Will Spring Be Early? or Will Spring Be Late? Johnson, Crockett, illus. 2016. (ENG., Illus.). 48p. (J). (gr. -1-3). 14.99 *(978-0-06-243037-3(8),* HarperCollins) HarperCollins Pubs.
Kann, Victoria. Fairy House. 2013. (Pinkalicious I Can Read Ser.). (J). lib. bdg. 13.55 *(978-0-606-27134-9(1))* Turtleback.
—Pinkalicious: Fairy House. Kann, Victoria, illus. 2013. (I Can Read Level 1 Ser.). (ENG., Illus.). 32p. (J). (gr. -1-3). 16.99 *(978-0-06-218783-3(X),* HarperCollins) HarperCollins Pubs.
Katschke, Judy. Bring on Spring! Elsom, Clare, illus. 2015. 32p. (J). pap. *(978-0-545-82337-1(4))* Scholastic, Inc.
Katz, Karen. Baby Loves Spring! A Karen Katz Lift-The-Flap Book. Katz, Karen, illus. 2012. (ENG., Illus.). 14p. (J). (gr. -1 — 1). bds. 7.99 *(978-1-4424-2745-7(0),* Little Simon) Little Simon.
Kelley, Marty, illus. Spring Goes Squish: A Vibrant Volume of Vociferous Vernal Verse. 2008. (J). (gr. k-2). 14.95 *(978-1-55933-315-3(4))* Zino Pr. Children's Bks.
Kimura, Ken. 999 Frogs Wake Up. Murakami, Yasunari, illus. 2013. (ENG.). 48p. (J). (gr. -1-3). 19.95 *(978-0-7358-4108-6(X))* North-South Bks., Inc.
Koontz, Robin Michal & Elliott, Rebecca. Butterfly Spring. 2009. (Rhyme Time Readers Ser.). (Illus.). (J). *(978-0-545-08359-1(1))* Scholastic, Inc.
Lagerlöf, Selma. The Further Adventures of Nils. Howard, Velma Swanston, tr. 2003. 284p. pap. 14.95 *(978-1-59224-320-4(7));* 32.95 *(978-1-59224-541-3(2))* Wildside Pr., LLC.
Lewman, David. The Sound of Spring. 2018. (Step into Reading Level 2 Ser.). lib. bdg. 14.75 *(978-0-606-40956-8(4))* Turtleback.
Lloyd, Jennifer. Taffy Time. Lee, Jacqui, illus. 2015. (ENG.). 40p. (J). (gr. -1-3). 16.95 *(978-1-927018-62-0(5))* Simply Read Bks. CAN. Dist: Ingram Publisher Services.
Luker, Lynne M. Mr Mushroom's Busy Day: Little Forest People. 2009. 32p. pap. 21.95 *(978-1-4389-8971-6(7))* AuthorHouse.
Mackall, Dandi. The Super Gifts of Spring: Easter. 2015. (Seasons Ser.). (ENG., Illus.). 32p. (J). (gr. -1-3). 9.99 *(978-1-4336-8233-9(8),* B&H Kids) B&H Publishing Group.
Marmon, Carol. When Mommy Bird Comes to Visit. 2007. 32p. (J). pap. 8.00 *(978-0-8059-7079-1(7))* Dorrance Publishing Co., Inc.
Mazur, Kathy. It's Springtime in My Backyard. 2005. (J). bds. 16.95 *(978-0-9761076-0-6(0))* Spring Ducks Bks., LLC.
Mcdonnell, Patrick. The Mutts Spring Diaries. 2018. (Mutts Kids Ser.). (ENG., Illus.). 178p. (J). (gr. 3-6). 34.99 *(978-1-4494-9456-8(0))* Andrews McMeel Publishing.
McDonnell, Patrick. The Mutts Spring Diaries. 2018. (Mutts Kids Ser.: 4). (ENG., Illus.). 176p. (J). pap. 9.99 *(978-1-4494-8514-6(6))* Andrews McMeel Publishing.
—The Mutts Summer Diaries. 2019. (Mutts Kids Ser.: 5). (ENG.). (J). 176p. pap. 9.99 *(978-1-4494-9523-7(0));* (Illus.). 178p. (gr. 3-6). 35.99 *(978-1-5248-5131-6(0))* Andrews McMeel Publishing.
Mcintyre, Gary P. Jake Fall & Winter. 2011. 198p. pap. 24.95 *(978-1-4560-4085-7(5))* America Star Bks.
Menconi, James Pasqual. Queen Mariella & the Fable of the Peony. 2011. 24p. (gr. -1). pap. 13.50 *(978-1-4567-3934-8(4))* AuthorHouse.
Nakagawa, Masafumi. Dr. Mouse's Mission. Perry, Mia Lynn, tr. Yamawaki, Yuriko, illus. 2007. (R. I. C. Story Chest Ser.). 27p. (J). (gr. -1-1). 14.95 incl. audio compact disk *(978-1-74126-051-9(5))* R.I.C. Pubns. AUS. Dist: SCB Distributors.
Neusner, Dena Wallenstein. Colors of Spring. McKee, Darren, illus. 2003. (Barney Ser.). (ENG.). 32p. (J). pap., act. bk. ed. 3.99 *(978-1-58668-305-4(5))* Scholastic, Inc.
Nicholas, Nicki. Spring Has Sprung for Peter & Lil. 2012. 24p. pap. 15.50 *(978-1-4669-2211-2(7))* Trafford Publishing.
Nolen, Jerdine. Bradford Street Buddies: Springtime Blossoms. Henninger, Michelle, illus. 2017. (ENG.). 48p. (J). (gr. 1-4). pap. 4.99 *(978-0-544-87390-2(4),* 1649393, Clarion Bks.) HarperCollins Pubs.
O'Brien, Anne Sibley & Gal, Susan. Abracadabra, It's Spring! 2016. (Seasonal Magic Ser.). (ENG., Illus.). 24p. (J). (gr. -1-k). 15.99 *(978-1-4197-1891-5(6),* 1121301, Abrams Appleseed) Abrams, Inc.
O'Connor, Jane. Fancy Nancy: Spring Fashion Fling: A Springtime Book for Kids. Glasser, Robin Preiss, illus. 2015. (Fancy Nancy Ser.). (ENG.). 24p. (J). (gr. -1-3). pap. 4.99 *(978-0-06-226956-0(9),* HarperFestival) HarperCollins Pubs.
—Spring Fashion Fling. 2015. (Fancy Nancy Picture Bks.). (J). lib. bdg. 14.75 *(978-0-606-36476-8(5))* Turtleback.
Piper, Sophie. The Angel & the Dove: A Story for Easter, 1 vol. Stephenson, Kristina, illus. 2010. 32p. (J). 12.99 *(978-0-8254-7897-0(9),* Lion Children's) Lion Hudson PLC GBR. Dist: Kregel Pubns.
Pugliano-Martin, Carol. See You in Spring! 2006. (Early Explorers Ser.). (J). pap. *(978-1-4108-6105-4(8))* Benchmark Education Co.
Rabbit's Spring Adventure. 2012. (Illus.). (J). *(978-1-4351-4584-9(4))* Barnes & Noble, Inc.
Rawlinson, Julia. Fletcher & the Springtime Blossoms. 2011. (J). (gr. -1-2). 29.95 *(978-0-545-32738-1(5))* Weston Woods Studios, Inc.
—Fletcher & the Springtime Blossoms: A Springtime Book for Kids. Beeke, Tiphanie, illus. 2009. (ENG.). 32p. (J). (gr. -1-3). 17.99 *(978-0-06-168855-3(X),* Greenwillow Bks.) HarperCollins Pubs.
Reinlein, Ann. The Adventures of Mister Squirrel Acorn. 2008. 32p. pap. 15.00 *(978-1-4389-1879-2(8))* AuthorHouse.
Remenar, Kristen. Groundhog's Dilemma. Faulkner, Matt, illus. 2015. (ENG.). 32p. (J). (gr. -1-2). lib. bdg. 18.99 *(978-1-58089-600-9(6))* Charlesbridge Publishing, Inc.
RH Disney. Welcome, Spring! (Disney Frozen) RH Disney, illus. 2016. (Pictureback(R) Ser.). (ENG., Illus.). 16p. (J). (gr. -1-2). 4.99 *(978-0-7364-3385-3(6),* RH/Disney) Random Hse. Children's Bks.
Rife, Mary Lou "Dink" & Backman, Kathleen. Spring Is in the Air with Graeagle Bear. 2010. (ENG.). 38p. pap. 21.99 *(978-1-4500-4025-9(X))* Xlibris Corp.
Rockwell, Anne. My Spring Robin. Rockwell, Harlow, illus. 2015. (ENG.). 24p. (J). (gr. -1-3). 16.99 *(978-1-4814-1137-0(3),* Aladdin) Simon & Schuster Children's Publishing.
Russell, Rachel Renée. Dork Diaries 9, 3 vols. unabr. ed. 2015. (Dork Diaries: 8). (ENG.). 320p. (J). (gr. 4-8). audio compact disk 14.99 *(978-1-4423-7023-4(8))* Simon & Schuster Audio.
—Dork Diaries 9: Tales from a Not-So-Dorky Drama Queen. Russell, Rachel Renée, illus. 2015. (Dork Diaries: 9). (ENG., Illus.). 352p. (J). (gr. 4-8). 14.99 *(978-1-4424-8769-7(0),* Aladdin Paperbacks) Simon & Schuster Children's Publishing.
Saxon, Victoria. Olaf Waits for Spring. 2018. (Illus.). (J). *(978-1-5444-0196-6(5),* Golden Bks.) Random Hse. Children's Bks.
—Olaf Waits for Spring (Disney Frozen) RH Disney, illus. 2018. (Little Golden Book Ser.). (ENG.). 24p. (J). (-k). 4.99 *(978-0-7364-3765-3(7),* Golden/Disney) Random Hse. Children's Bks.
Schertle, Alice. Little Blue Truck's Springtime: An Easter & Springtime Book for Kids. McElmurry, Jill, illus. 2018. (ENG.). 16p. (J). (gr. -1 — 1). bds. 13.99 *(978-0-544-93809-0(7),* 1658575, Clarion Bks.) HarperCollins Pubs.
Senior, Patricia. Pip & the Magic Flute. 2008. (Illus.). 40p. pap. 18.49 *(978-1-4389-0023-0(6))* AuthorHouse.
Smith, Rosemary. Lizard Tales: Lizzie Walks on the Wild Side. 2010. 28p. pap. 12.50 *(978-1-60911-082-6(X),* Strategic Bk. Publishing) Strategic Book Publishing & Rights Agency (SBPRA).
Taylor, Michael. What Do You See? Fiorentino, Chiara, illus. 2017. (Seasons Around Me Ser.). (ENG.). 24p. (gr. -1-2). pap. 9.95 *(978-1-68342-763-6(7),* 9781683427636) Rourke Educational Media.
Thompson, Lauren. Mouse Loves Spring. 2018. (Simon & Schuster Ready-To-Read Level 1 Ser.). lib. bdg. 13.55 *(978-0-606-40862-2(2))* Turtleback.
—Mouse Loves Spring: Ready-To-Read Pre-Level 1. Erdogan, Buket, illus. 2018. (Mouse Ser.). (ENG.). 32p. (J). (gr. -1-k). 17.99 *(978-1-5344-0185-3(7));* pap. 4.99 *(978-1-5344-0184-6(9))* Simon Spotlight. (Simon Spotlight).
—Mouse's First Spring. Erdogan, Buket, illus. 2012. (Classic Board Bks.). (ENG.). 34p. (J). (gr. -1-3). bds. 8.99 *(978-1-4424-3431-8(7),* Little Simon) Little Simon.
—Mouse's First Spring. Erdogan, Buket, illus. 2005. (ENG.). 32p. (J). (gr. -1-3). 19.99 *(978-0-689-85838-3(8),* Simon & Schuster Bks. For Young Readers) Simon & Schuster Bks. For Young Readers.
Trover, Zachary. The Spring Chicken! 2013. (Step into Reading Level 2 Ser.). lib. bdg. 13.55 *(978-0-606-26979-7(7))* Turtleback.
Umphervile, Tina. The Spring Celebration, 1 vol. Rice, Christie, illus. 2015. (ENG.). 32p. (Orig.). (J). (gr. 1-2). mass mkt. 10.95 *(978-0-921827-46-7(6),* 1a2481c7-9a1b-4539-b7cd-5d00f3998955) Pemmican Pubns., Inc. CAN. Dist: Firefly Bks., Ltd.
Urbanovic, Jackie. Happy Go Ducky. Urbanovic, Jackie & Mathieu, Joe, illus. 2012. (I Can Read Level 1 Ser.). (ENG.). 32p. (J). (gr. k-3). 16.99 *(978-0-06-186440-7(4));* pap. 5.99 *(978-0-06-186439-1(0))* HarperCollins Pubs. (HarperCollins).
von Olfers, Sibylle. Mother Earth & Her Children: A Quilted Fairy Tale. Zipes, Jack, tr. Schoen-Smith, Sieglinde, illus. 2015. (ENG.). 32p. (J). (— 1). 12.95 *(978-1-933308-50-0(8))* Breckling Pr.
—Mother Earth & Her Children Coloring Book: Color the Wonderful World of Nature As You See It! 24 Magical, Mythical Coloring Scenes. Zipes, Jack, tr. Schoen-Smith, Sieglinde, illus. 2015. (ENG.). 24p. (J). (gr. 2-4). pap. 6.95 *(978-1-933308-54-8(0))* Breckling Pr.
Voorheis, Tracy. Nibbles... a strawberry Tale. Voorheis, Tracy, illus. 2007. (Illus.). 60p. (J). per. 19.00 *(978-0-9787113-0-6(0),* Ithaca Pr.) Authors & Artists Publishers of New York, Inc.
Walsh, Liza Gardner. Do Fairies Bring the Spring. Mitchell, Hazel, illus. 2019. 22p. (J). (gr. -1-12). 8.95 *(978-1-60893-660-1(0))* Down East Bks.
Walters, Jennifer Marino. Surprising Spring. Nez, John, illus. 2016. (Seasons Ser.). (ENG.). 24p. (J). (gr. -1 — 1). lib. bdg. 25.32 *(978-1-63440-047-3(X),* 3ce02d63-4297-4c10-b965-f130b6cfd455, Rocking Chair Kids) Red Chair Pr.
Walton, Mildred D. Spring Reborn. 2012. 28p. pap. 21.99 *(978-1-4691-2556-5(0))* Xlibris Corp.
Warfield, Laura Castillo. Daisy's Faith. 2011. 24p. pap. 15.99 *(978-1-4568-8348-5(8))* Xlibris Corp.
Washburn, Kim. Bunny Blessings, 1 vol. East, Jacqueline, illus. 2018. (ENG.). 18p. (J). bds. 8.99 *(978-0-310-76209-6(X))* Zonderkidz.
Werber, Yael. Spring for Sophie. Hill, Jen, illus. 2017. (ENG.). 32p. (J). (gr. -1-3). 19.99 *(978-1-4814-5134-5(0),* Simon & Schuster Bks. For Young Readers) Simon & Schuster Bks. For Young Readers.
Winnie the Pooh. Spring Cleaning. 2010. 32p. pap. 4.99 *(978-1-4231-3072-7(3))* Disney Pr.
Yang, Belle. A Nest in Springtime: A Mandarin Chinese-English Bilingual Book of Numbers. Yang, Belle, illus. 2012. (ENG., Illus.). 24p. (J). (gr. k — 1). bds. 6.99 *(978-0-7636-5279-1(2))* Candlewick Pr.
Yee, Wong Herbert. Mouse & Mole: Fine Feathered Friends. Yee, Wong Herbert, illus. 2011. (Mouse & Mole Story Ser.). (ENG., Illus.). 48p. (J). (gr. 1-4). pap. 4.99 *(978-0-547-51977-7(X),* 1445276, Clarion Bks.) HarperCollins Pubs.
Zimmerman, Amanda. The Spring Snowman. 2011. 48p. pap. 9.95 *(978-1-4502-9816-2(8))* iUniverse, Inc.
Zipf, Sean. What Color Is Spring? Antkowski, Marygrace, illus. 2008. 36p. pap. 24.95 *(978-1-60703-005-8(5))* America Star Bks.

SPRING—POETRY

Overton, Hollie. Baby Doll. 2018. (ENG., Illus.). 400p. mass mkt. 7.99 *(978-0-316-52710-1(6))* Orbit.

SPY FOX (FICTITIOUS CHARACTER)—FICTION

Kull, Cyndi. I Spy. 2011. 16p. pap. 8.50 *(978-1-4634-2279-0(2))* AuthorHouse.

SQUANTO

Byers, Ann. Squanto, 1 vol. 2020. (Inside Guide: Famous Native Americans Ser.). (ENG.). 32p. (gr. 4-5). pap. 11.58 *(978-1-5026-5060-3(6),* ce942a61-8809-40a3-9ae2-0e11b981a031) Cavendish Square Publishing LLC.
Isbell, Hannah. Squanto: Native American Translator & Guide, 1 vol. 2017. (Junior Biographies Ser.). (ENG.). 24p. (gr. 3-4). pap. 10.35 *(978-0-7660-9065-1(5),* bf71e6c5-83e5-46c8-af76-feebcd8d8af2) Enslow Publishing, LLC.
Kessel, Joyce K. Squanto & the First Thanksgiving. Donze, Lisa, illus. rev. ed. 2003. (On My Own Holidays Ser.). (ENG.). 48p. (gr. 2-4). lib. bdg. 25.26 *(978-0-87614-941-6(7))* Lerner Publishing Group.
—Squanto & the First Thanksgiving, 2nd Edition. Donze, Lisa, illus. 2nd rev. ed. 2003. (On My Own Holidays Ser.). (ENG.). 48p. (J). (gr. 2-4). pap. 8.99 *(978-1-57505-585-5(6),* 7a820627-e0ae-495a-9499-accc5d2a0944, First Avenue Editions) Lerner Publishing Group.
—Squanto y el Primer Dia de Accion de Gracias. Donze, Lisa, illus. 2007. (Yo Solo - Festividades (on My Own - Holidays) Ser.). 48p. (J). (gr. 4-7). per. 6.95 *(978-0-8225-7795-9(X))* Lerner Publishing Group.
—Squanto y el Primer Día de Acción de Gracias. Translations.com Staff, tr. from ENG. Donze, Lisa, illus. 2007. (Yo Solo - Festividades (on My Own - Holidays) Ser.). (SPA.). 48p. (gr. 2-4). lib. bdg. 25.26 *(978-0-8225-7792-8(5))* Lerner Publishing Group.
—Squanto Y el Primer Dia de Accion de Gracias; Squanto & the First Thanksgiving. 2008. pap. 40.95 *(978-0-8225-9678-3(4))* Lerner Publishing Group.
Metaxas, Eric. Squanto & the First Thanksgiving: The Legendary American Tale. Donato, Michael A., illus. 2004. 36p. (J). (gr. 3-8). reprint ed. 19.00 *(978-0-7567-7123-2(4))* DIANE Publishing Co.

SQUANTO—FICTION

Bruchac, Joseph. Squanto's Journey: The Story of the First Thanksgiving. 2014. 17.00 *(978-1-63419-743-4(7))* Perfection Learning Corp.

SQUASH (GAME)

Lord, Michelle. A Girl Called Genghis Khan: The Story of Maria Toorpakai Wazir. Malik, Shehzil, illus. 2019. (People Who Shaped Our World Ser.: 5). 48p. (J). (gr. k). 16.95 *(978-1-4549-3136-2(1))* Sterling Publishing Co., Inc.

SQUIDS

Andover, Max. Octopuses & Squid. 2011. (Illus.). 16p. (J). pap. *(978-0-545-24792-4(6))* Scholastic, Inc.
Dussling, Jennifer. Giant Squid: Mystery of the Deep. Johnson, Pamela, illus. 2004. (American Museum of Natural History Ser.). 48p. (gr. 1-3). 14.00 *(978-0-7569-1981-8(9))* Perfection Learning Corp.
Fleming, Candace. Giant Squid. Rohmann, Eric, illus. 2016. (ENG.). 40p. (J). (gr. 1-5). 19.99 *(978-1-59643-599-5(2),* 900065585) Roaring Brook Pr.
Kwan, Garfield & Song, Dana. Squidtoons: Exploring Ocean Science with Comics. 2018. (ENG., Illus.). 130p. (J). (gr. 3-6). 31.99 *(978-1-4494-9741-5(1))* Andrews McMeel Publishing.
Lunis, Natalie. Squirting Squids. 2007. (No Backbone! Ser.). (Illus.). 24p. (J). (gr. k-3). lib. bdg. 26.99 *(978-1-59716-513-6(1))* Bearport Publishing Co., Inc.
Lunis, Natalie & Murphy, Bill. Squirting Squids. 2016. (No Backbone! Marine Invertebrates Ser.). (ENG., Illus.). 24p. (J). (gr. k-3). pap. 7.99 *(978-1-944998-79-0(9))* Bearport Publishing Co., Inc.
Miller, Tori. Octopuses & Squid. 2009. (Freaky Fish Ser.). 24p. (gr. 2-3). 42.50 *(978-1-61512-640-8(6),* PowerKids Pr.); (ENG.). (J). lib. bdg. 26.27 *(978-1-4358-2757-8(0),* a2123354-0798-4fe4-961e-b248ded374cc); (ENG., Illus.). (J). pap. 9.25 *(978-1-4358-3174-2(8),* 875067de-e53e-4298-8a91-c0363376e20e, PowerKids Pr.) Rosen Publishing Group, Inc., The.
Nyikos, Stacy Ann. Squirt. Sisneros, Shawn, illus. l.t. ed. 2005. 32p. (J). lib. bdg. 15.95 *(978-0-9764199-0-7(4))* Stonehorse Publishing, LLC.
Owen, Ruth. Giant Squid & Octopuses, 1 vol., 1. 2014. (Real Life Sea Monsters Ser.). (ENG.). 32p. (J). (gr. 3-3). 28.93 *(978-1-4777-6261-5(2),* afeff637-d0e2-4d3d-bba5-adc88f143e64, PowerKids Pr.) Rosen Publishing Group, Inc., The.
Polinsky, Paige V. Giant Squid: Mysterious Monster of the Deep. 2016. (Real Monsters Ser.). (ENG., Illus.). 32p. (J). (gr. 3-6). lib. bdg. 32.79 *(978-1-68078-419-0(6),* 23697, Checkerboard Library) ABDO Publishing Co.
Redmond, Shirley Raye. Tentacles! Tales of the Giant Squid. Barnard, Bryn, illus. 2005. (Step into Reading Ser.). (gr. k-2). 14.00 *(978-0-7569-5576-2(9))* Perfection Learning Corp.
Schuh, Mari. Squids. 2015. (Illus.). 24p. (J). lib. bdg. *(978-1-62031-193-6(3),* Bullfrog Bks.) Jump! Inc.
Sexton, Colleen. Squids. 2008. (Oceans Alive Ser.). (ENG., Illus.). 24p. (J). (gr. k-3). lib. bdg. 26.95 *(978-1-60014-175-1(7))* Bellwether Media.
Sommer, Nathan. Squids. 2018. (Ocean Life up Close Ser.). (ENG., Illus.). 24p. (J). (gr. k-3). lib. bdg. 26.95 *(978-1-62617-767-3(8),* Blastoff! Readers) Bellwether Media.
Weber, Valerie J. Octopuses & Squids, 1 vol. 2008. (Animals That Live in the Ocean Ser.). (ENG., Illus.). 24p. (J). (gr. 1-1). lib. bdg. 25.27 *(978-0-8368-9242-0(9),* 4b2b859f-1912-446c-a41a-50ed9e5ab7f3, Weekly Reader Leveled Readers) Stevens, Gareth Publishing LLLP.
—Octopuses & Squids / Pulpos y Calamares, 1 vol. 2008. (Animals That Live in the Ocean / Animales Que Viven en el Océano Ser.). (SPA & ENG.). 24p. (gr. 1-1). (J). lib. bdg. 25.27 *(978-0-8368-9248-2(8),* f7699b10-e49f-41af-b08b-444ac4153781); pap. 9.15 *(978-0-8368-9347-2(6),* ccd18598-1f8a-43f0-866c-53589950c13d) Stevens, Gareth Publishing LLLP. (Weekly Reader Leveled Readers).
—Squids, 1 vol. 2004. (Weird Wonders of the Deep Ser.). (ENG., Illus.). 24p. (gr. 2-4). lib. bdg. 25.67 *(978-0-8368-4564-8(1),* 8042743c-1b81-495d-a18f-ba1102c97149, Gareth Stevens Learning Library) Stevens, Gareth Publishing LLLP.

SQUIRRELS

Appleby, Alex. I See a Squirrel, 1 vol. 2013. (In My Backyard Ser.). (ENG., Illus.). 24p. (J). (gr. k-k). pap. 9.15 *(978-1-4339-8560-7(8),* de87c582-5689-4221-a60b-b24c8826a569); lib. bdg. 25.27 *(978-1-4339-8559-1(4),* ea1f7df0-e9d5-4e49-94dc-c191b2752b77) Stevens, Gareth Publishing LLLP.
—I See a Squirrel / Puedo Ver una Ardilla, 1 vol. 2013. (In My Backyard / en Mi Jardin Ser.). (SPA & ENG., Illus.). 24p. (J). (gr. k-k). lib. bdg. 25.27 *(978-1-4339-8800-4(3),* 1eb3ab19-bb3b-4eab-87ee-7d2a49fdb69f) Stevens, Gareth Publishing LLLP.
Arnold, Quinn M. Squirrels. 2018. (Seedlings Ser.). (ENG.). 24p. (J). (gr. -1-k). *(978-1-60818-976-2(7),* 19923, Creative Education) Creative Co., The.
—Toads. 2018. (Seedlings Ser.). (ENG.). 24p. (J). (gr. -1-k). pap. 8.99 *(978-1-62832-603-1(4),* 19932, Creative Paperbacks) Creative Co., The.
Best, Arthur. A Squirrel's Hollow, 1 vol. 2018. (Animal Homes Ser.). (ENG.). 24p. (gr. 1-1). lib. bdg. 27.36 *(978-1-5026-3670-6(0),* 328ea296-62b3-4a42-a878-f6c9f84175f1) Cavendish Square Publishing LLC.
Booth, Anita K. Squirrels!!! An Informative & Entertaining Book about Our Favorite Mountain Mammal. Booth, Anita K., illus. 2nd ed. 2004. (Illus.). 76p. 12.95 *(978-0-9748702-1-2(8))* AKB Design.
Borgert-Spaniol, Megan. Baby Squirrels. 2015. (Super Cute! Ser.). (ENG., Illus.). 24p. (J). (gr. k-3). lib. bdg. 26.95 *(978-1-62617-220-3(X),* Blastoff! Readers) Bellwether Media.
Bowman, Chris. Red Squirrels. 2016. (North American Animals Ser.). (ENG., Illus.). 24p. (J). (gr. k-3). lib. bdg. 26.95 *(978-1-62617-336-1(2),* Blastoff! Readers) Bellwether Media.
Bradley, James. The Squirrel. 2006. (Nature Walk Ser.). (ENG., Illus.). 64p. (gr. 4-6). lib. bdg. 28.00 *(978-0-7910-9116-6(3),* P114529, Facts On File) Infobase Holdings, Inc.
Ciovacco, Justine. Squirrels, 1 vol. 2009. (Amazing Animals Ser.). (ENG.). 48p. (J). (gr. 3-5). pap. 11.50 *(978-1-4339-2029-5(8),* 630de16d-2885-4360-8272-fdb44c31aa44, Gareth Stevens Learning Library) Stevens, Gareth Publishing LLLP.
—Squirrels. 2007. (J). *(978-1-59939-133-5(3),* Reader's Digest Young Families, Inc.) Studio Fun International.
Clark Sawyer, J. Las Ardillas de Tierra de Trece Franjas. 2014. (¿a dónde Van en Invierno? Ser.). (SPA.). 24p. (J). (gr. -1-3). lib. bdg. 26.99 *(978-1-62724-459-6(X))* Bearport Publishing Co., Inc.
—Thirteen-Lined Ground Squirrels. 2015. (Illus.). 24p. (J). lib. bdg. 26.99 *(978-1-62724-317-9(8))* Bearport Publishing Co., Inc.
Dettman, Eileen. Determo: The true story of a very clever North Carolina red Squirrel. 2010. (J). 9.95 *(978-0-615-38527-3(3))* Dettman Design Services.
Dieker, Wendy Strobel. La Ardilla. 2017. (Spot Backyard Animals Ser.). (SPA & ENG., Illus.). 16p. (J). (gr. k-3). 17.95 *(978-1-68151-277-8(7))* Amicus Learning.
—Squirrels. (Spot Backyard Animals Ser.). (ENG., Illus.). 16p. (J). (gr. -1-2). 2018. pap. 7.99 *(978-1-68152-222-7(5),* 14753) 2017. 17.95 *(978-1-68151-097-2(9),* 14634) Amicus.
Diemer, Lauren. Squirrels. 2007. (Backyard Animals Ser.). (Illus.). 24p. (J). (gr. 2-4). lib. bdg. 24.45 *(978-1-59036-671-4(9))* Weigl Pubs., Inc.
—Squirrels. Hudak, Heather C., ed. 2007. (Backyard Animals Ser.). (Illus.). 24p. (J). (gr. -1-3). pap. 8.95 *(978-1-59036-672-1(7))* Weigl Pubs., Inc.
Ferry, Beth. Squirrel's Family Tree. Kang, A. N., illus. 2019. (ENG.). 40p. (J). (gr. -1-k). 17.99 *(978-1-338-18736-6(8),* Orchard Bks.) Scholastic, Inc.
Gagne, Tammy. Backyard Jungle Safari Gray Squirrels: Grey Squirrels. 2015. (ENG., Illus.). 32p. (J). 26.50 *(978-1-62469-104-1(8))* Purple Toad Publishing, Inc.
Gates, Margo. A Good Nut. Herring, Carol, illus. 2019. (Let's Look at Animal Habitats (Pull Ahead Readers — Fiction) Ser.). (ENG.). 16p. (J). (gr. -1-1). 27.99 *(978-1-5415-5865-6(0),* dcb05530-a226-4737-855b-0b26b518b851, Lerner Pubns.) Lerner Publishing Group.
Gilkerson, Patricia. My Adventure with Squirrels. 2009. (ENG.). 44p. (J). 8.99 *(978-1-59092-470-9(3))* Blue Forge Pr.
Hawksworth, Lorraine & Guzy, Adam. Fables from the Largetooth Animal Refuge. 2009. 52p. pap. 20.49 *(978-1-4389-6508-6(7))* AuthorHouse.
Jackson, Tom. Squirrels. 2008. (Nature's Children Ser.). (Illus.). 52p. (J). *(978-0-7172-6245-8(6))* Grolier, Ltd.
Lake, G. G. Gray Squirrels. 2016. (Woodland Wildlife Ser.). (ENG., Illus.). 24p. (J). (gr. -1-2). lib. bdg. 27.32 *(978-1-5157-0818-6(7),* 132154, Capstone Pr.) Capstone.
Leaf, Christina. Gray Squirrels. 2015. (North American Animals Ser.). (ENG., Illus.). 24p. (J). (gr. k-3). lib. bdg. 26.95 *(978-1-62617-187-9(4),* Blastoff! Readers) Bellwether Media.
McGill, Jordan. Ardillas. 2012. (SPA.). (J). *(978-1-61913-197-2(8))* Weigl Pubs., Inc.
—Squirrels. 2011. (J). *(978-1-61690-931-4(5));* *(978-1-61690-577-4(8))* Weigl Pubs., Inc.
O'Brien, Lindsy. Squirrels. 2016. (In My Backyard Ser.). (ENG., Illus.). 24p. (J). (gr. 1-3). *(978-1-60818-702-7(0),* 20602, Creative Education) Creative Co., The.
O'Brien, Lindsy J. Squirrels. 2016. (In My Backyard Ser.). (ENG., Illus.). 24p. (J). (gr. 1-3). pap. 8.99 *(978-1-62832-298-9(5),* 20600, Creative Paperbacks) Creative Co., The.
Otfinoski, Steven. Squirrels, 1 vol. 2011. (Animals, Animals Ser.). (ENG.). 48p. (gr. 5-5). 32.64 *(978-0-7614-4843-3(8),* 3f55d94e-8f96-4143-a5a4-8b7700b4e4ea) Cavendish Square Publishing LLC.

S

Owen, Ruth. Squirrel Kits. 2011. (Wild Baby Animals Ser.). 24p. (J). (gr. k-3). lib. bdg. 25.65 (978-1-61772-160-1(3)); lib. bdg., E-Book 39.93 (978-1-61772-244-8(8)) Bearport Publishing Co., Inc.

Petrie, Kristin. Squirrels, 1 vol. 2015. (Backyard Animals Ser.). (ENG.). 32p. (J). (gr. 3-6). 32.79 (978-1-62403-663-7(5), 16824, Checkerboard Library) ABDO Publishing Co.

Roza, Greg. Your Neighbor the Squirrel, 1 vol. 2011. (City Critters Ser.). (ENG., Illus.). 24p. (J). (gr. 2-3). pap. 9.25 (978-1-4488-5123-2(8), ae6f21ea-db04-47d3-babc-f48769005980); lib. bdg. 27.27 (978-1-61533-383-7(5), ae592d0d-e906-4d3c-8183-e4a904eca756) Rosen Publishing Group, Inc., The. (Windmill Bks.).

Russell, Justin Eric. Baby Squirrels. 2019. (Adorable Animals Ser.). (ENG., Illus.). 32p. (J). (gr. 4-6). pap. 9.99 (978-1-64466-006-5(7), 12613, Bolt) Black Rabbit Bks.

Sayre, April Pulley. Squirrels Leap, Squirrels Sleep. Jenkins, Steve, illus. 2016. (ENG.). 40p. (J). 18.99 (978-0-8050-9251-6(X), 900068146, Holt, Henry & Co. Bks. For Young Readers) Holt, Henry & Co.

Schuh, Mari C. Squirrels. 2015. (Backyard Animals Ser.). (ENG., Illus.). 24p. (J). (gr. -1-2). lib. bdg. 27.32 (978-1-4914-2088-1(X), 127568, Capstone Pr.) Capstone.

Somervill, Barbara A. Gray Squirrel. 2008. (21st Century Skills Library: Animal Invaders Ser.). (ENG., Illus.). 32p. (J). (gr. 4-8). lib. bdg. 32.07 (978-1-60279-116-9(3), 1280688) Cherry Lake Publishing.

Statts, Leo. Squirrels. 2017. (Backyard Animals (Launch!) Ser.). (ENG., Illus.). 24p. (J). (gr. -1-2). lib. bdg. 31.36 (978-1-5321-2006-0(0), 25276, Abdo Zoom-Launch) ABDO Publishing Co.

Strain Trueit, Trudi. Squirrels, 1 vol. 2012. (Backyard Safari Ser.). (ENG.). 32p. (gr. 3-3). 31.21 (978-1-60870-248-0(0), e61cac0d-2a02-4e5e-8cbb-5326ec07ee93) Cavendish Square Publishing LLC.

Sundance/Newbridge LLC Staff. Squirrels All Year Long. 2007. (Early Science Ser.). (gr. k-3). 18.95 (978-1-4007-6404-4(1)); pap. 6.10 (978-1-4007-6400-6(9)) Sundance/Newbridge Educational Publishing.

Watanabe, Lynne M. Squirrels. 2016. (Illus.). 32p. (J). (978-0-87659-709-5(6)) Gryphon Hse., Inc.

Zappa, Marcia. Flying Squirrels, 1 vol. 2015. (World's Weirdest Animals Ser.). (ENG., Illus.). 32p. (J). (gr. 2-5). 34.21 (978-1-62403-775-7(5), 17852, Big Buddy Bks.) ABDO Publishing Co.

Zobel, Derek. Squirrels. 2010. (Backyard Wildlife Ser.). (ENG., Illus.). 24p. (J). (gr. k-3). lib. bdg. 26.95 (978-1-60014-447-9(0), Blastoff! Readers) Bellwether Media.

SQUIRRELS—FICTION

Abbott, Jacob. Rollo at Play. 2008. 124p. (gr. 3-7). 23.95 (978-1-60664-760-8(1)); pap. 10.95 (978-1-60664-132-3(8)) Aegypan.

—Rollo at Play. 2009. 148p. pap. 8.95 (978-1-59915-343-8(2)) Yesterday's Classics.

Alaniz, Joshua. The Unfortunate yet Fortunate Squirrel. 2013. 20p. pap. 24.95 (978-1-63004-271-4(4)) America Star Bks.

Alexander, Ron. And God Created Squirrels. 2007. 28p. per. 19.95 (978-1-4327-1512-0(7)) Outskirts Pr., Inc.

Allard, Toni. Anything but Nuts. 2007. 20p. per. 24.95 (978-1-4241-8796-6(6)) America Star Bks.

Anderson, Steven. Leap & Twirl. DeAnguelo Hout, Sarah, illus. 2012. 34p. (J). pap. 10.99 (978-0-692-01667-1(8)) BalletMet Dance Centre.

Ardagh, Philip. High in the Clouds. Dunbar, Geoff, illus. 2007. 93p. (J). 20.00 (978-1-4223-6720-9(7)) DIANE Publishing Co.

Aryal, Aimee. Hello Buzz! Moore, Danny, illus. 2004. 24p. (J). 19.95 (978-1-932888-27-0(6)) Amplify Publishing Group.

Aschermann, Kurt. Bj & the Amazing Doctor Directions. 2008. 172p. pap. 11.99 (978-1-4343-7708-1(3)) AuthorHouse.

Atchison, David C. The Adventures of Black Bart: Dry Bones. 2008. (ENG.). 84p. pap. 7.94 (978-0-615-20238-9(1)) Black Bart Bks.

Avi. The Mayor of Central Park. Floca, Brian, illus. (ENG.). 208p. (J). (gr. 3-6). 2003. 15.99 (978-0-06-000682-2(X)) 2005. reprint ed. pap. 6.99 (978-0-06-051557-7(0), HarperCollins) HarperCollins Pubs.

—The Mayor of Central Park. Floca, Brian, illus. 2005. 193p. (J). (gr. 3-7). 13.65 (978-0-7569-5125-2(9)) Perfection Learning Corp.

AZ Books Staff. Squirrel Searches for a Home. 2012. (Plush Baby Ser.). (ENG., Illus.). 10p. (J). (gr. -1 — 1). bds. 11.95 (978-1-61889-220-1(7)) AZ Bks. LLC.

Bailey, Dawn Wentz. Joey & the Mighty Oak. 2008. 20p. pap. 24.95 (978-1-60813-377-2(X)) PublishAmerica, Inc.

Barba, Theresa. How Talia Met Tanner. 2012. 40p. pap. 20.99 (978-1-4772-1617-0(0)) AuthorHouse.

Barnard, Bobbie. The Fairies of the Big Forest. 2013. 16p. pap. 24.95 (978-1-63004-359-9(1)) America Star Bks.

Barnard, Lucy, illus. Squirrel's Busy Day. 2014. 24p. (J). (978-1-4351-5602-9(1)) Barnes & Noble, Inc.

Barone, Barbara. Leafy Trees & Bumbly Bees. 2012. 28p. pap. 16.09 (978-1-4669-6267-5(4)) Trafford Publishing.

Barrett, Hayley. Girl Versus Squirrel. Andriani, Renée, illus. 2020. 32p. (J). (gr. -1-3). 18.99 (978-0-8234-4251-5(9), Margaret Ferguson Books) Holiday Hse., Inc.

Bauman, Jill, illus. The Tale of Squirrel Nutkin. 2006. (J). 6.99 (978-1-59939-017-8(5)) Cornerstone Pr.

Bellew, Steve C. The Great Walnut War. 2012. 24p. pap. 24.95 (978-1-4626-7623-1(5)) America Star Bks.

Beranek, Malinda. Rocky, the Country Squirrel. 2008. 12p. pap. 24.95 (978-1-60563-018-2(7)) America Star Bks.

Berglund, Andrea Lloyd. A Good Little Horse: Thunder's Morning Stroll. 2009. 36p. (J). pap. 19.95 (978-1-4327-3822-8(4)) Outskirts Pr., Inc.

Biederman, Judy. Bushy Tail Squirrel's First Day Out. 2004. (J). lib. bdg. (978-0-9725485-2-6(1)) Waterfall Ridge.

Billows, Denis. Down in Bluebell Wood. 2010. 164p. pap. 11.99 (978-1-4490-8822-4(8)) AuthorHouse.

Blevins-Counts, Charlotte. Squirrel, Where Are You? 2009. 24p. pap. 12.95 (978-1-59858-963-4(6)) Dog Ear Publishing, LLC.

Bonnell, Kris. A House for Squirrel. 2007. (J). pap. 5.95 (978-1-933727-46-2(2)) Reading Reading Bks., LLC.

Bowers, Tim. A New Home. Bowers, Tim, illus. 2003. (Green Light Readers Level 1 Ser.). (ENG., Illus.). 24p. (J). (gr. -1-3). pap. 4.99 (978-0-15-204848-8(0), 1194639, Clarion Bks.) HarperCollins Pubs.

Bowlin, Serina. Wandering Sam. Thrasher, Brian, illus. 2011. 20p. pap. 9.97 (978-1-61204-280-0(5), Eloquent Bks.) Strategic Book Publishing & Rights Agency (SBPRA).

Bowman, Rachael Ann. Sammy the Karate Squirrel. 2013. 28p. pap. 13.95 (978-1-4624-0800-9(1), Inspiring Voices) Author Solutions, LLC.

Bright, Rachel. Snowflake in My Pocket. Rong, Yu, illus. 2017. 32p. (J). 12.99 (978-1-61067-551-2(7)) Kane Miller.

—The Squirrels Who Squabbled. Field, Jim, illus. 2019. (ENG.). 32p. (J). (gr. -1-k). 14.99 (978-1-338-53803-8(9), Scholastic Pr.) Scholastic, Inc.

Brown, Daniel. Chipper Learns a Lesson. 2013. 28p. pap. 5.99 (978-0-9897549-4-1(4)) Story and Logic Media Group.

Bruchac, Joseph. How Chipmunk Got His Stripes. 2003. (gr. k-3). lib. bdg. 17.20 (978-0-613-61631-7(6)) Turtleback.

Bryant, Phoebe. What Is That in the Air? A play date with Sayde. 2009. (Illus.). 28p. pap. 12.99 (978-1-4490-2209-9(X)) AuthorHouse.

Buckley, Michael. Nerds: Book Two: M Is for Mama's Boy, Bk. 2. 2011. (ENG., Illus.). 288p. (J). (gr. 3-7). pap. 9.99 (978-1-4197-0023-1(5), Amulet Bks.) Abrams, Inc.

—NERDS 2: M für Muttersöhnchen. 2011. (SPA.). 260p. (J). (gr. 6-8). pap. 10.99 (978-987-612-335-8(1)) V&R Editoras.

Buice, J. W. Silly Squirrel. 2011. 28p. pap. 15.99 (978-1-4568-3384-8(7)) Xlibris Corp.

Bunting, Sarah Clare. Why Are You So Lazy Owl? 2011. (ENG.). 16p. 12.50 (978-1-4709-4837-5(0)) Lulu Pr., Inc.

Burch, Minnie Kirby. The Adventures of Squir Squirrel: A Story of Love & Trust. 2012. 64p. pap. 31.99 (978-1-4771-2043-9(2)) Xlibris Corp.

Burgess, Thornton W. The Adventures of Chatterer the Red Squirrel. (J). 18.95 (978-0-8488-0376-6(0)) Amereon Ltd.

—The Adventures of Chatterer the Red Squirrel. 2006. pap. 10.95 (978-1-59605-783-8(1), Cosimo Classics) Cosimo, Inc.

—The Adventures of Happy Jack. 2004. (Dover Children's Thrift Classics Ser.). (ENG., Illus.). 128p. (J). (gr. 3-8). pap. 6.00 (978-0-486-43321-9(8), 433218) Dover Pubns., Inc.

—Happy Jack. 2011. 140p. 25.95 (978-1-4638-9558-7(5)) Rodgers, Alan Bks.

Burks, James. Bird & Squirrel on Fire: a Graphic Novel (Bird & Squirrel #4), Vol. 4. 2017. (Bird & Squirrel Ser.). (ENG., Illus.). 192p. (J). (gr. 2-5). 19.99 (978-0-545-80429-5(9), Graphix) Scholastic, Inc.

—Bird & Squirrel on Ice. 2014. (Illus.). 125p. (J). (978-0-605-86251-7(6), Graphix) Scholastic, Inc.

—Bird & Squirrel on Ice: a Graphic Novel (Bird & Squirrel #2) Burks, James, illus. 2014. (Bird & Squirrel Ser.). (ENG., Illus.). 128p. (J). (gr. 2-5). pap. 10.99 (978-0-545-56318-5(6), Graphix) Scholastic, Inc.

—Bird & Squirrel on the Run! 2012. (Bird Squirrel Ser.). (Illus.). 125p. (J). lib. bdg. 19.65 (978-0-606-26211-8(3)) Turtleback.

—Bird & Squirrel on the Run!: a Graphic Novel (Bird & Squirrel #1) 2012. (Bird & Squirrel Ser.). (ENG., Illus.). 128p. (J). (gr. 2-5). pap. 10.99 (978-0-545-31283-7(3), Graphix) Scholastic, Inc.

Byers, James. One Nutty Family. Collier, Kevin, illus. 2012. 16p. pap. 9.95 (978-1-61633-200-6(X)) Guardian Angel Publishing, Inc.

Cain, Karen L. Squirrel's Curl. 2011. 24p. 13.00 (978-1-4567-1466-6(X)) AuthorHouse.

Calvani, Mayra. Humberto, the Bookworm Hamster. Grady, Kit, illus. 2009. 20p. pap. 10.95 (978-1-935137-92-4(1)) Guardian Angel Publishing, Inc.

Carman, Patrick. The Walnut Cup. James, Steve, illus. 2009. (Elliot's Park Ser.: Bk. 3). 80p. (J). (gr. 1-5). 8.99 (978-0-545-01932-3(X), Orchard Bks.) Scholastic, Inc.

Case, Maggie. A Squirrel's Tale. 2011. 24p. (gr. -1). pap. 11.32 (978-1-4567-5118-0(2)) AuthorHouse.

Cavagnaro, Teresa Dunham. Sweet Sallie's Squirrel Scarf Factory. Cavagnaro, Larry, illus. 2012. 36p. 24.95 (978-1-4626-6126-8(2)) America Star Bks.

Chamberlain, Lyn. Quonby & the Tree Den. Weltner, Dave, illus. l.t. ed. 2004. 12p. (J). 7.95 (978-0-9706654-8-5(2)) Sprite Pr.

Charman, Katrina. The Cloud Kingdom: a Branches Book (the Last Firehawk #7) Tondora, Judit, illus. 2019. (Last Firehawk Ser.: 7). (ENG.). 96p. (J). (gr. 1-3). pap. 5.99 (978-1-338-30717-7(7)) Scholastic, Inc.

—The Cloud Kingdom: a Branches Book (the Last Firehawk #7) (Library Edition), Vol. 7. Tondora, Judit, illus. 2019. (Last Firehawk Ser.: 7). (ENG.). 96p. (J). (gr. 1-3). 24.99 (978-1-338-30718-4(5)) Scholastic, Inc.

—The Crystal Caverns: a Branches Book (the Last Firehawk #2) (Library Edition) Norton, Jeremy, illus. 2017. (Last Firehawk Ser.: 2). (ENG.). 96p. (J). (gr. 1-3). 15.99 (978-1-338-12252-7(5)) Scholastic, Inc.

—The Ember Stone: a Branches Book (the Last Firehawk #1) Norton, Jeremy, illus. 2017. (Last Firehawk Ser.: 1). (ENG.). 96p. (J). (gr. 1-3). pap. 5.99 (978-1-338-12213-8(4)) Scholastic, Inc.

—Lullaby Lake: a Branches Book (the Last Firehawk #4) Norton, Jeremy, illus. 2018. (Last Firehawk Ser.: 4). (ENG.). 96p. (J). (gr. 1-3). pap. 5.99 (978-1-338-12267-1(3)) Scholastic, Inc.

—Lullaby Lake: a Branches Book (the Last Firehawk #4) (Library Edition), Vol. 4. Norton, Jeremy, illus. 2018. (Last Firehawk Ser.: 4). (ENG.). 96p. (J). (gr. 1-3). lib. bdg. 24.99 (978-1-338-12271-8(1)) Scholastic, Inc.

—The Shadowlands: a Branches Book (the Last Firehawk #5) Norton, Jeremy, illus. 2019. (Last Firehawk Ser.: 5). (ENG.). 96p. (J). (gr. 1-3). pap. 5.99 (978-1-338-30711-5(8)) Scholastic, Inc.

—The Whispering Oak: a Branches Book (the Last Firehawk #3), 1 vol., Vol. 3. Norton, Jeremy, illus. 2018. (Last Firehawk Ser.: 3). (ENG.). 96p. (J). (gr. 1-3). pap. 5.99 (978-1-338-12255-8(X)) Scholastic, Inc.

Chichester Clark, Emma, tr. & illus. Will & Squill. Chichester Clark, Emma, illus. 2006. 32p. (J). (gr. -1-k). 15.95 (978-1-57505-936-5(3), Carolrhoda Bks.) Lerner Publishing Group.

Chicken Squad: The First Misadventure, 1 vol. 2015. (Your Reading Path Ser.: 1). (Illus.). 112p. (J). (gr. 3-3). pap. (978-1-4424-9677-4(0), 04928386-0b45-4e55-b035-177f94c93034, Rosen Classroom) Rosen Publishing Group, Inc., The.

Chinnery, Karen. Secret Agent Squirrel. 2006. (ENG.). 48p. per. 16.95 (978-1-4241-5459-3(6)) America Star Bks.

Chuang, Emily. Francis' Tail. 2010. (ENG.). 32p. pap. 23.95 (978-0-557-73632-4(3)) Lulu Pr., Inc.

Clayton, Emily. If my Parents Only Knew... 2011. (Illus.). 28p. (gr. -1). pap. 14.09 (978-1-4567-7405-9(0)) AuthorHouse.

Cocca-Leffler, Maryann. The Belonging Tree. Lombardi, Kristine A., illus. 2020. (ENG.). 40p. (J). 18.99 (978-1-250-30513-8(6), 900197497, Holt, Henry & Co. Bks. For Young Readers) Holt, Henry & Co.

Colleen, Marcie. Going Nuts: Super Happy Party Bears 4. James, Steve, illus. 2017. (Super Happy Party Bears Ser.: 4). (ENG.). 144p. (J). pap. 5.99 (978-1-250-10049-8(6), 900162461) Imprint IND. Dist: Macmillan.

Collins, Paul. A Tale of Two Squirrels. 2008. 104p. pap. 9.95 (978-1-60693-204-9(7), Eloquent Bks.) Strategic Book Publishing & Rights Agency (SBPRA).

Conroe, Lindy. Rockafella Jones & the Hidden Treasure. Riette, Susanne, illus. 2011. 108p. (J). pap. 10.95 (978-1-935199-00-7(5)) Blue Mustang Pr.

Cook, Kacy. Nuts, 0 vols. 2012. (ENG.). 160p. (J). (gr. 3-7). pap. 7.99 (978-0-7614-6311-5(9), 9780761463115, Two Lions) Amazon Publishing.

Cook, Sherry & Johnson, Terri. Vinnie Volcano, 26. Kuhn, Jesse, illus. l.t. ed. 2006. (Quirkles — Exploring Phonics through Science Ser.: 22). 32p. (J). 7.99 (978-1-933815-21-3(3), Quirkles, The) Creative 3, LLC.

Cooper, D. C. Rascal the Baby Squirrel. 2013. 32p. (978-1-4602-2658-2(5)) FriesenPress.

Cooper, Helen. Pumpkin Soup (Book & CD Set), Set. unabr. ed. 2009. (ENG., Illus.). 32p. (J). (gr. -1-3). 9.99 (978-1-4272-0740-1(2), 900061793) Macmillan Audio.

Cortina, Janice. Grandpa Kolbe & the Squirrels. 2009. 32p. pap. 12.99 (978-1-4389-6762-2(4)) AuthorHouse.

Councilman, Janet H. Rocky & His Responsible Band of Cowboys, 1 vol. 2009. pap. 24.95 (978-1-60749-384-6(5)) America Star Bks.

Covey, Sean. Sammy & the Pecan Pie: Habit 4. Curtis, Stacy, illus. (7 Habits of Happy Kids Ser.: 4). (ENG.). 32p. (J). (gr. -1-1). 2018. 6.99 (978-1-5344-1581-2(5)) 2013. 7.99 (978-1-4424-7647-9(8)) Simon & Schuster Bks. For Young Readers. (Simon & Schuster Bks. For Young Readers).

—Sammy & the Pecan Pie: Habit 4 (Ready-To-Read Level 2) Curtis, Stacy, illus. 2019. (7 Habits of Happy Kids Ser.: 4). (ENG.). 32p. (J). (gr. k-2). 17.99 (978-1-5344-4454-6(8)); pap. 4.99 (978-1-5344-4453-9(X)) Simon Spotlight. (Simon Spotlight).

—Sophie & the Perfect Poem: Habit 6. Curtis, Stacy, illus. (7 Habits of Happy Kids Ser.: 6). (ENG.). 32p. (J). (gr. -1-1). 2018. 6.99 (978-1-5344-1583-6(1)) 2013. 7.99 (978-1-4424-7651-6(6)) Simon & Schuster Bks. For Young Readers. (Simon & Schuster Bks. For Young Readers).

—Sophie & the Perfect Poem: Habit 6 (Ready-To-Read Level 2) Curtis, Stacy, illus. 2020. (7 Habits of Happy Kids Ser.: 6). (ENG.). 32p. (J). (gr. k-2). 17.99 (978-1-5344-4460-7(2)); pap. 4.99 (978-1-5344-4459-1(9)) Simon Spotlight. (Simon Spotlight).

Craig, Joni. A Shoulder for Oscar. Haddad-Hamwi, Louise, illus. 2013. 40p. pap. 11.95 (978-0-9887836-6-9(5)) Taylor and Seale Publishing.

Cronin, Doreen. The Chicken Squad. Cornell, Kevin, illus. 2014. 92p. (J). (978-0-605-90609-9(2)) Simon & Schuster Children's Publishing.

Crow, Marilee. A Short Tale about a Long Tail. Snider, K. C., illus. 2010. 16p. pap. 10.95 (978-1-61633-067-5(8)) Guardian Angel Publishing, Inc.

Cruea, Kim. Summer Falls Junior Rangers: The First Adventures. 2008. 73p. pap. 19.95 (978-1-60474-552-8(5)) America Star Bks.

Cummins, Judi, creator. It's Raining Acorns & Ladybugs. 2005. (Illus.). 28p. (J). per. (978-0-9760377-4-3(2)) Cummins, Judi.

Curtis, Jennifer Keats. Squirrel Rescue, 1 vol. 2012. (ENG., Illus.). 32p. (gr. 3-6). 16.99 (978-0-7643-4246-2(0), 4654) Schiffer Publishing, Ltd.

Cusack, Bob. The Squirming Squirrel. 2009. 16p. pap. 12.99 (978-1-4389-5551-3(0)) AuthorHouse.

Cusick, N. L. Tales from Grey Squirrel Manor #1 - a Tale of Two Squirrels. 2013. 24p. pap. (978-1-4602-0814-4(5)) FriesenPress.

Dalton, Kippy. Cat & Squirrel. 2016. (Spring Forward Ser.). (J). (gr. 1). (978-1-4900-3714-1(4)) Benchmark Education Co.

Daniels, Cheri & Nicewander, Carol. Shadow Tail Meets the Gang. 2008. 24p. pap. 11.49 (978-1-4389-3259-0(6)) AuthorHouse.

Davenport, Eddie. Bunnyburg: The Newcomers. 2013. (ENG.). 30p. (J). pap. 14.95 (978-1-4787-2062-1(X)) Outskirts Pr., Inc.

Davies, Caroline & Martin, Sharon. Chwarae Cuddio. 2005. (WEL., Illus.). 12p. pap. (978-1-86101-080-3(X)) Acen Limited.

—Cotiau Newydd. 2005. (WEL., Illus.). 12p. pap. (978-1-86101-081-0(8)) Acen Limited.

—Y Frech Goch. 2005. (WEL., Illus.). 12p. pap. (978-1-86101-079-7(6)) Acen Limited.

Davis, Holly. Thankful Together. Sokolova, Valerie, illus. 2006. 36p. (J). 5.99 (978-0-7847-1436-2(3), 04077) Standard Publishing.

Degen, Bruce. Snow Joke. 2014. 24p. pap. (978-0-8234-3223-3(8)) Holiday Hse., Inc.

DiCamillo, Kate. Flora & Ulysses: The Illuminated Adventures. Campbell, K. G., illus. (ENG.). (J). (gr. 3-7). 2016. 256p. pap. 8.99 (978-0-7636-8764-9(2)) 2013. 240p. 19.99 (978-0-7636-6040-6(X)) Candlewick Pr.

Dicamillo, Kate. Flora & Ulysses: The Illuminated Adventures. Campbell, K. G., illus. 2016. (ENG.). 256p. (J). (gr. 3-7). 17.20 (978-0-606-39100-9(2)) Turtleback.

—Flora & Ulysses: The Illuminated Adventures. 2015. lib. bdg. 19.65 (978-0-606-36861-2(2)) Turtleback.

Dillard, Mary Gregory. Jeepers Creepers! The Squirrels Are Coming. 2007. 85p. pap. 19.95 (978-1-4241-9951-8(4)) America Star Bks.

Dilley, Kristi. Squiggy the Squirrel Meets Wallis the Woodpecker. Dilley, Kristi, illus. 2013. (Illus.). 28p. pap. 9.99 (978-1-937165-47-5(7)) Orange Hat Publishing.

d'Lacey, Chris. The Fire Within (the Last Dragon Chronicles #1) 2007. (Last Dragon Chronicles Ser.: 1). (ENG.). 352p. (J). (gr. 3-7). pap. 9.99 (978-0-439-67244-3(9), Orchard Bks.) Scholastic, Inc.

—Icefire. d'Lacey, Chris, illus. 2007. (Last Dragon Chronicles Ser.: 2). (Illus.). lib. bdg. 19.65 (978-1-4177-9138-5(1)) Turtleback.

Dobson, Donna. Timmy's First Adventure. 2012. 28p. pap. 24.95 (978-1-4626-7945-4(5)) America Star Bks.

Dodd, Melissa. Santa Sheds, 1 vol. 2009. 17p. pap. 24.95 (978-1-60749-208-5(3)) America Star Bks.

Doodle, Nanny. Divorced at Six. 2006. 158p. pap. 24.95 (978-1-4241-3963-7(5)) PublishAmerica, Inc.

Doudna, Kelly. Squirrel Hollow. Chawla, Neena, illus. 2006. (Fact & Fiction Ser.). 24p. (J). pap. 48.42 (978-1-59679-968-4(4)) ABDO Publishing Co.

Douglass, E. The Squirrel Friends Adventures: The Monster & the Great Storm. 2013. 100p. 19.95 (978-1-4759-6640-4(7)); pap. 9.95 (978-1-4759-6638-1(5)) iUniverse, Inc.

Dowler, Pattie. Suzie Squirrel & the Disappearing Pies. 2012. 24p. pap. 24.95 (978-1-4626-7636-1(7)) America Star Bks.

Dubuc, Marianne. Otto & Pio (Read Aloud Book for Children about Friendship & Family) 2019. (ENG., Illus.). 66p. (J). (gr. k-3). 18.95 (978-1-61689-760-4(0)) Princeton Architectural Pr.

Duling, Astrid. The Guinea Pigs Twiggy & Molly. 2012. 134p. pap. (978-3-8423-1287-6(3)) Books on Demand GmbH.

Dunbar, Geoff & Ardagh, Philip. High in the Clouds. 2005. (Illus.). 91p. (J). (978-1-4156-2820-1(3), Dutton Juvenile) Penguin Publishing Group.

Duracell and the National Center for Missing & Exploited Children (NCMEC), creator. The Great Tomato Adventure: A Story about Smart Safety Choices. 2007. 0.00 (978-0-9795307-0-8(9)) Duracell & the National Ctr. for Missing & Exploited Children (NCMEC).

Earl the Squirrel & the Great Acorn Caper: None. 2003. (J). pap. 24.95 incl. cd-rom (978-0-9749041-0-8(4)) Big Lil' Bks.

Educational Insights. The Sneaky, Snacky Squirrel. Gaggiotti, Lucia, illus. 2017. (ENG.). 12p. (J). (— 1). bds. 11.99 (978-0-7636-9465-4(7), Candlewick Entertainment) Candlewick Pr.

Edwards, Jamee-Marie. But I Am a Cat! 2013. 44p. pap. 20.00 (978-1-4772-8231-1(9)) AuthorHouse.

Eller, Sylvia Klope. The Squirrel Who Hitchhiked to Atlanta. 2007. (Illus.). 32p. (J). pap. 8.00 (978-0-8059-7596-3(9)) Dorrance Publishing Co., Inc.

Elliott, Rebecca. Baxter Is Missing: a Branches Book (Owl Diaries #6) Elliott, Rebecca, illus. 2017. (Owl Diaries: 6). (ENG., Illus.). 80p. (J). (gr. k-2). pap. 6.99 (978-1-338-04284-9(X)) Scholastic, Inc.

Fenske, Jonathan. We Need More Nuts! Fenske, Jonathan, illus. (Illus.). 32p. (J). 2019. (gr. k-2). 4.99 (978-0-593-09599-7(5), Penguin Workshop) 2017. (gr. 1-2). pap. 5.99 (978-0-515-15913-4(1), Penguin Young Readers) Penguin Young Readers Group.

—We Need More Nuts! 2018. (Penguin Young Readers Ser.). (ENG.). 32p. (J). (gr. -1-1). 13.89 (978-1-64310-319-8(9)) Penworthy Co., LLC, The.

Fisher, Stacey & Paner, Amy, Illustrator. No Nuts for Nutty. 2008. 26p. 14.95 (978-0-615-19778-4(7)) Fisher-Paner Publishing.

Fitzgerald, J. Rupert, the Sturdy Oak Tree: Who thought he was a little better than the other Trees. 2010. 16p. (J). pap. 14.95 (978-1-4327-5734-2(2)) Outskirts Pr., Inc.

Flaxenwick, Dim. Dobbin, Our Favourite Pony: Dobbin & the Little Red Squirrel. 2012. 44p. pap. 20.72 (978-1-4669-2179-5(X)) Trafford Publishing.

Flynn, Caren. Exceptional Elvis. 2010. (Illus.). 24p. pap. 12.00 (978-1-60844-481-6(3)) Dog Ear Publishing, LLC.

Freeman, Don. Earl the Squirrel. Freeman, Don, illus. 2008. (Illus.). (J). (gr. -1-2). pap. 16.95 incl. audio (978-1-4301-0411-7(2)) Live Oak Media.

—Earl the Squirrel. 2007. (ENG., Illus.). 48p. (J). (gr. -1-2). pap. 8.99 (978-0-14-240893-3(X), Puffin Books) Penguin Young Readers Group.

Friend, Larry. Squirrelly the Squirrel & Starlett. 2012. (ENG.). 64p. pap. 10.95 (978-1-4327-8658-8(X)) Outskirts Pr., Inc.

Fyne, Olga. Squirrel Race. 2009. 28p. pap. 13.99 (978-1-4389-3676-5(1)) AuthorHouse.

Galjanic, Lisa. When Series 6 Volume Set, 6, 6. 2007. (Illus.). 100p. (J). 34.95 (978-1-933532-06-6(8)) LSG Pubns.

—When Squirrels Try. Hope, Michelle, illus. 2007. (J). 9.95 (978-1-933532-02-8(5)) LSG Pubns.

Gammage, Karen S. Nutty & Buddy. 2010. 32p. pap. 21.99 (978-1-4535-1182-4(2)) Xlibris Corp.

Gard, Don. The Adventures of Beezer. Giancanelli, Candace, illus. 2006. 100p. per. 12.95 (978-1-59858-157-7(0)) Dog Ear Publishing, LLC.

George, Lindsay Barrett. That Pup! George, Lindsay Barrett, illus. 2011. (ENG., Illus.). 32p. (J). (gr. -1-k). 16.99 (978-0-06-200413-0(1), Greenwillow Bks.) HarperCollins Pubs.

Giddens, Martha Anne. The Unluckiest Kid in the Universe. 2006. 56p. pap. 9.95 (978-1-4120-7935-8(7)) Trafford Publishing.

Gifford, Jerry. The Squirrel Highway. 2011. 32p. pap. 24.95 (978-1-4560-9397-6(5)) America Star Bks.

Godby, Michele. Mommy... Would You Still Love Me If I Was a Squirrel. 2012. 32p. pap. 21.99 (978-1-4797-6199-9(0)) Xlibris Corp.

Gordon, Pauline C. Animals in My Backyard! Joey, the Flying Squirrel. 2012. 28p. pap. 15.99 (978-1-4771-1961-7(2)) Xlibris Corp.

Graham, Janice C. The Little Country Girl & Frisky the Squirrel. Allen, S. Joan & Graham, Jerry L., illus. 2008. 32p. pap. 24.95 (978-1-60610-312-8(1)) America Star Bks.

Grambling, Lois G. Shoo! Scat!, 1 vol. Newman, Barbara Johansen, illus. 2004. (ENG.). 32p. (J). 16.95 (978-0-7614-5167-9(6)) Marshall Cavendish Corp.

Grandma. Harry's Adventure, 1 vol. 2009. 17p. pap. 24.95 (978-1-60836-943-0(9)) America Star Bks.

Gravett, Emily. Cyril & Pat. Gravett, Emily, illus. 2019. (ENG., Illus.). 32p. (J). (gr. -1-3). 17.99 (978-1-5344-3950-4(1), Simon & Schuster Bks. For Young Readers) Simon & Schuster Bks. For Young Readers.

Green, Poppy. The Clover Curse. Bell, Jennifer A., illus. 2016. (Adventures of Sophie Mouse Ser.: 7). (ENG.). 128p. (J). (gr.

k-4). 17.99 *(978-1-4814-5184-0(7)*, Little Simon) Little Simon.

—The Emerald Berries. Bell, Jennifer A., illus. 2015. (Adventures of Sophie Mouse Ser.: 2). (ENG.). 128p. (J). (gr. k-4). pap. 6.99 *(978-1-4814-2835-4(7)*, Little Simon) Little Simon.

Grossnickle, Mary. A Place in My Heart. Relyea, Alison, illus. 2014. 36p. (C). 17.95 *(978-1-84905-771-4(0)*, 694479) Kingsley, Jessica Pubs. GBR. Dist: Hachette UK Distribution.

Grove, Malachai. The Return of Malachai. 2011. 24p. pap. 14.99 *(978-1-4567-6257-5(5))* AuthorHouse.

Guillain, Charlotte. Rumplesnakeskin. 1 vol. Beacon, Dawn, illus. 2014. (Animal Fairy Tales Ser.). (ENG.). 24p. (J). (gr. -1-2). lib. bdg. 23.99 *(978-1-4109-6111-2(7)*, 124738, Raintree) Capstone.

Hagler, Chris E. Big Jim & the Squirrel. 2012. 28p. 24.95 *(978-1-4626-6085-8(1))* America Star Bks.

Hale, Shannon & Hale, Dean. The Unbeatable Squirrel Girl: Squirrel Meets World. 2018. (YA). lib. bdg. 19.65 *(978-0-606-40715-1(4))* Turtleback.

Harrington, Geri. Gray Squirrel at Pacific Avenue. Roosevelt, Michele Chopin, illus. 2011. (Smithsonian's Backyard Ser.). (ENG.). 32p. (J). (gr. -1-3). 19.95 *(978-1-60727-638-8(0))* Soundprints.

Harvey, Gwendolyn Fowlkes. The Backyard Plum Tree. 2009. (J). pap. *(978-1-61623-481-2(4))* Independent Pub.

Hasan, Jamal I. A Journey to Remember. 2007. 64p. per. 8.95 *(978-0-595-43375-9(8))* iUniverse, Inc.

Head, Murray, photos by. I Can Run. 2017. (I Like to Read Ser.). (ENG., Illus.). 32p. (J). (gr. -1-3). 7.99 *(978-0-8234-3846-4(5))* Holiday Hse., Inc.

Heigh, Stephen. Mr. George & the Red Hat. Burton, Kevin, ed. Heigh, Stephen, illus. 2004. (Illus.). 32p. (J). 18.95 *(978-0-9745715-2-2(0))* KRBY Creations, LLC.

Hein, Connie L. Toliver in Time; for a Journey West: History in a Nutshell. Theobald, Denise, illus. Lt. ed. 2005. 28p. (J). lib. bdg. 17.95 *(978-0-9740855-6-2(1))*; per. 9.95 *(978-0-9740855-7-9(X))* Still Water Publishing.

Hemming, Alice. The Leaf Thief. Slater, Nicola, illus. 2021. (Squirrel & Bird Book Ser.). (ENG.). 32p. (J). (gr. -1-3). 17.99 *(978-1-7282-3520-2(0)*, Sourcebooks Jabberwocky) Sourcebooks, Inc.

Hicks, Ron. Grumpy Stories. 2018. (ENG., Illus.). 46p. (J). *(978-1-5289-2509-9(2))*; pap. *(978-1-5289-2510-5(6))* Austin Macauley Pubs. Ltd.

Hills, Tad & Hills, Tad. Rocket's Very Fine Day. 2019. (Step into Reading Ser.). (Illus.). 32p. (J). (gr. -1-1). pap. 5.99 *(978-0-525-64494-1(6)*, Schwartz & Wade Bks.) Random Hse. Children's Bks.

Hoffer, Rod. The Strange Christmas Dream. 2012. 64p. pap. 24.99 *(978-1-4772-5949-8(X))* AuthorHouse.

Holland, Francis. KoKo's New Home. 2008. 32p. pap. 24.95 *(978-1-60474-706-5(4))* America Star Bks.

Holliday, Andrea. Squissy, the Little Grey Squirrel That Got a Second Chance. 2013. 28p. pap. 24.95 *(978-1-4626-9788-5(7))* America Star Bks.

Horn, Mildred D. Teeny the Squirrel Meets the Outside World. 2009. 15.95 *(978-1-61623-107-1(6))* Independent Pub.

Houser, Marlin. The Secret of Squirrel Meadow. 2006. (Adventures of Little Fox Ser.). (Illus.). 171p. (J). 16.95 *(978-0-9752703-4-9(6))*; per. 7.95 *(978-0-9752703-5-6(4))* Marhouse, Inc.

Howells, Angela. The Tails of Victoria Way. 2009. (Illus.). 32p. pap. 12.99 *(978-1-4490-4432-9(8))* AuthorHouse.

Hudson, Katy. The Golden Acorn. Hudson, Katy, illus. 2019. (ENG., Illus.). 32p. (J). (gr. -1-1). lib. bdg. 17.95 *(978-1-68446-036-6(0)*, 139807, Capstone Editions) Capstone.

Hughes, Diane Marie. Meet Wilbur the Squirrel. 2004. 21p. pap. 24.95 *(978-1-4137-2758-6(1))* PublishAmerica, Inc.

Humphreys, Dolores, illus. The Adventures of J. G. & Echo: The Land of All Creatures & the Swamp Creature, 1. 2003. 81p. (J). per. 16.00 *(978-0-9727415-2-1(6))* Cuccia, Louis.

Iverson, Diane. Rascal, the Tassel Eared Squirrel. 2007. 64p. pap. 9.95 *(978-0-932821-64-5(2))* Grand Canyon Conservancy.

Iwamura, Kazuo. Bedtime in the Forest. 2010. (ENG., Illus.). 32p. (J). (gr. -1-2). 19.95 *(978-0-7358-2310-5(3))* North-South Bks., Inc.

—Hooray for Snow! 2009. (ENG., Illus.). 24p. (J). (gr. -1-2). 17.95 *(978-0-7358-2219-1(0))* North-South Bks., Inc.

Jackson, Glenda K. Friends of the Hills. 2012. 20p. pap. 17.99 *(978-1-4685-4082-6(3))* AuthorHouse.

Jacques, Brian. Rakkety Tam. 17 vols. 2005. (Redwall Ser.: 17). (ENG.). 384p. (J). (gr. 5-18). mass mkt. 8.99 *(978-0-441-01318-0(X)*, Ace) Penguin Publishing Group.

—Rakkety Tam. 2004. (Redwall Ser.). 1.00 *(978-1-4175-5517-8(3))* Recorded Bks., Inc.

—Rakkety Tam: A Tale from Redwall. 2006. (Redwall Ser.: 17). (ENG., Illus.). 384p. (J). (gr. 5-18). 9.99 *(978-0-14-240683-0(X)*, Firebird) Penguin Young Readers Group.

Jasnoch, Dorothy. The Adventures of Oskar: Oskar's New School. Korzeniowski, Samson O., ed. Jasnoch, Dorothy, illus. 2013. (Illus.). 32p. 18.99 *(978-1-937752-27-9(5))* Owl About Bks. Pubs.

Jeanfield. Twinkle, a Christmas Story. 2009. 36p. pap. 13.95 *(978-1-60693-745-7(6)*, Eloquent Bks.) Strategic Book Publishing & Rights Agency (SBPRA).

Jenkins, Henry A. The Adventures of Monkey Squirrel & Frogman: Sand Trap. 2009. 16p. pap. 8.49 *(978-1-4343-7827-9(6))* AuthorHouse.

Jenkins, Martin. The Squirrels' Busy Year: A First Science Storybook. Jones, Richard, illus. 2018. (Science Storybooks Ser.). (ENG.). 32p. (J). (gr. -1-1). 17.99 *(978-0-7636-9600-9(5))* Candlewick Pr.

John, Clement. Best Friends: A Bedtime Story. 2011. (Illus.). 40p. pap. 21.93 *(978-1-4520-7922-6(6))* AuthorHouse.

Johnson, Dennis. The Tree That Went Sailing: (Based on a true story - Palm Beach, Florida) 2009. (ENG.). 40p. pap. 21.99 *(978-1-4415-0181-3(9))* Xlibris Corp.

Johnson, Donna. The Story of the Little Red Leaf. Johnson, Emily, illus. Lt. ed. 2006. (ENG.). 22p. (J). 25.00 *(978-0-9778774-0-9(X))* Choice Point Editions.

Jones, Janey Louise. Sonny the Daring Squirrel. Poh, Jennie, illus. 2016. (Superfairies Ser.). (ENG.). 56p. (J). (gr. k-3). lib. bdg. 23.99 *(978-1-5158-0433-8(X)*, 132554, Picture Window Bks.) Capstone.

Kabir, Shohag. Mice & Squirrel. 2009. 24p. pap. 13.99 *(978-1-4389-9164-1(9))* AuthorHouse.

Keller, George. Squirrelly Whirly & the Haunted House. 2005. 21p. 7.45 *(978-1-4116-4425-0(5))* Lulu Pr., Inc.

Kelly, Jacqueline. A Squirrelly Situation: Calpurnia Tate, Girl Vet. Meyer, Jennifer L., illus. 2021. (Calpurnia Tate, Girl Vet Ser.: 5). (ENG.). 112p. (J). pap. 6.99 *(978-1-250-21115-6(8)*, 900161298) Square Fish.

Klick, Lisa. Bailey & Friends. Stouch, Ryan, illus. 2008. 40p. pap. 14.95 *(978-1-59858-743-2(9))* Dog Ear Publishing, LLC.

Kirby, Lee. Super Turbo vs. the Flying Ninja Squirrels. O'Connor, George, illus. 2016. (Super Turbo Ser.: 2). (ENG.). 128p. (J). (gr. k-4). 17.99 *(978-1-4814-8888-4(0))*; pap. 5.99 *(978-1-4814-8887-7(2))* Little Simon. (Little Simon).

Kirkpatrick, Teresa. Roscoe's Forest Adventures. 2008. 177p. pap. 24.95 *(978-1-60672-328-9(6))* America Star Bks.

Kreidler, Shannon. The Adventures of Sally the Squirrel: Interactive... Educational & Earn Gold Stars. 2013. 28p. pap. 15.99 *(978-1-4797-7674-0(2))* Xlibris Corp.

Lang, Valerie E. Jet's Day: A Whisker Team Story. 2011. 32p. pap. 13.00 *(978-1-61204-178-0(7)*, Strategic Bk. Publishing) Strategic Book Publishing & Rights Agency (SBPRA).

Lawson, Tanya. Pawpaw Harry & the Baby Squirrel. 2011. 24p. pap. 12.00 *(978-1-4567-4616-2(2))* AuthorHouse.

Lease, Janice. Marigold Little Squirrel in a Cactus Patch. 2008. 48p. pap. 19.95 *(978-0-9800762-0-2(X))* Cinnamon Ridge Publishing.

Leatham, Marc Vincent. The Race. 2007. (Illus.). (J). (gr. -1-3). per. 15.99 *(978-1-59879-274-4(1))* Lifevest Publishing, Inc.

—The Story of the Five Squirrels. Leatham, Marc Vincent, illus. 2007. (Illus.). (J). (gr. -1-3). per. 15.99 *(978-1-59879-275-1(X))* Lifevest Publishing, Inc.

Leist, Christina. Jack the Bear. 2009. (ENG., Illus.). 40p. (J). (gr. -1-3). 16.95 *(978-1-894965-97-2(3))* Simply Read Bks. CAN. Dist: Ingram Publisher Services.

Levy, Elizabeth. The Mixed-Up Mask Mystery: A Fletcher Mystery. Gorstein, Mordicai, illus. unabr. ed. 2006. (First Chapter Bks.). (J). (gr. 2-4). pap. 17.95 incl. audio *(978-1-59519-710-8(9))*; pap. 20.95 incl. audio compact disk *(978-1-59519-711-5(7))* Live Oak Media.

Lewellyn, Natalie. Nutty to Meet You! Dr. Peanut Book #1. 2008. (Illus.). 32p. (J). 11.95 *(978-0-9777082-0-8(9))* One Monkey Bks.

Lipe, Riki. Hanging with Yum-Yum & Yuck. 2007. (Illus.). (J). 10.00 *(978-0-9659381-6-7(6))* Hoot N' Cackle Pr.

Lithgow, John. Micawber. Payne, C. F., illus. 2005. (ENG.). 40p. (J). (gr. -1-3). reprint ed. 9.99 *(978-0-689-83542-1(6)*, Simon & Schuster Bks. For Young Readers) Simon & Schuster Bks. For Young Readers.

Lloyd-Jones, Sally. Just Because You're Mine. Endersby, Frank, illus. 2011. (ENG.). 32p. (J). (gr. -1-2). 17.99 *(978-0-06-201476-4(5)*, HarperCollins) HarperCollins Pubs.

Loughead, Deb. A Pocketful of Fur. Birke, Lisa, tr. 2005. (Illus.). 60p. (J). (gr. 2-4). 6.95 *(978-0-9730831-6-3(6))* Hodgepog Bks. CAN. Dist: Fitzhenry & Whiteside, Ltd.

Lowery, Marie Hayes. Beau & Friends. 2012. 20p. pap. 17.99 *(978-1-4817-0106-8(1))* AuthorHouse.

Luberto, Bradley. Clide & Druce: A Repulsive Tale of Trolls & Tax Money. 2006. (ENG.). 48p. per. 16.95 *(978-1-4241-5012-0(4))* PublishAmerica, Inc.

Lush, Nelia. Gracie & Belle Never Again! 2007. 20p. per. 24.95 *(978-1-4241-8373-9(1))* America Star Bks.

Mabry, Virginia. Jolly Ollie from Olney. 2012. 16p. pap. 10.00 *(978-1-937260-25-5(9))* Sleepytown Pr.

MacVicar, Andrea. Tales of Zoffic. Morse, Patti, illus. 2007. 58p. (J). per. 16.95 *(978-0-9798395-0-4(5))* Inspiration Pr. Inc.

Mae, Darcie. Sammy & Robert. 2008. 24p. pap. 24.95 *(978-1-60474-811-6(7))* America Star Bks.

The Magical Adventures of Samuel the Squirrel & Oscar the Owl Journey to Mars. 2005. (J). per. 12.95 *(978-0-9762929-0-6(4))* Morning Glory Pubns.

Marinaro, Stacy. Carter the Acorn Collecting Cutie. 2008. 20p. pap. 10.50 *(978-0-615-20807-7(X))* Marinaro, Stacy.

Masini, Beatrice. The Right Place. Mulazzani, Simona, illus. 2020. (ENG.). 32p. (J). (gr. -1-2). 16.99 *(978-1-78285-981-9(0))*; pap. 9.99 *(978-1-78285-982-6(9))* Barefoot Bks., Inc.

Matthews, Ian. Albert the Big Eyed Squirrel. 2011. 25p. (J). pap. 15.95 *(978-1-4327-5904-9(3))* Outskirts Pr., Inc.

May, Kyla. Pug Blasts off: a Branches Book (Diary of a Pug #1) May, Kyla, illus. 2019. (Diary of a Pug Ser.: 1). (ENG., Illus.). 80p. (J). (gr. k-2). pap. 4.99 *(978-1-338-53003-2(8))* Scholastic, Inc.

—Pug's Snow Day: a Branches Book (Diary of a Pug #2) (Library Edition) May, Kyla, illus. 2019. (Diary of a Pug Ser.: 2). (ENG., Illus.). 80p. (J). (gr. k-2). 24.99 *(978-1-338-53007-0(0))* Scholastic, Inc.

May, Kyla, illus. Pug Blasts Off. 2019. 72p. (J). *(978-1-338-50034-9(1))* Scholastic, Inc.

Mayer, Marvin S. Sammy Squirrel & the Sunflower Seeds. Johns, Dick, illus. 2008. 73p. pap. 19.95 *(978-1-60672-193-3(3))* America Star Bks.

McAdams, Susan. Shubert. McAdams, Caleb, illus. 2008. 16p. per. 24.95 *(978-1-4241-9756-9(2))* America Star Bks.

McClurkan, Rob. Aw, Nuts! 2014. (ENG., Illus.). 32p. (J). (gr. -1-3). 17.99 *(978-0-06-231729-2(6)*, HarperCollins) HarperCollins Pubs.

McCorkle, Barbara. Bandit Raccoon. Taylor, David A., illus. Lt. ed. 2006. 39p. (J). 19.95 *(978-1-59879-170-9(2))*; per. 13.99 *(978-1-59879-123-5(0))* Lifevest Publishing, Inc.

—Brutis' New Friend. Taylor, David A., illus. 2007. 30p. (J). 13.99 *(978-1-59879-439-7(6))* Lifevest Publishing, Inc.

—Brutis' New Friend. 2005. (Illus.). 23p. (J). (gr. -1-3). per. 8.99 *(978-1-932338-60-7(8))* Lifevest Publishing, Inc.

McFarland, Myndie. Squigley the Squirrel. 2012. 46p. pap. 12.95 *(978-1-886057-11-1(7))* Warren Publishing, Inc.

McKelvey, Lonnie. Ralph & His New Friends. 2007. (J). *(978-0-9796519-1-5(3))* Mirror Publishing.

McLeod, Laura. George the Squirrel. 2015. (ENG., Illus.). (J). 15.99 *(978-1-58169-548-9(9)*, Evergreen Pr.) Genesis Communications, Inc.

McNease, Mitzy. Chester's Presents. Cox, Kim, illus. 2006. 28p. (J). 10.95 *(978-0-9779488-0-2(3))* Blancmange Publishing LLC.

McQueen, Todd, illus. Bob & Rob & Corn on the Cob. 2014. (ENG.). 40p. (J). (gr. -1-k). 16.95 *(978-1-62873-591-8(0)*, Sky Pony Pr.) Skyhorse Publishing Co., Inc.

Meaker, Mary. Quinton, Brewster & Chaley. 2011. 64p. (gr. -1). pap. 9.99 *(978-1-4634-3023-8(X))* AuthorHouse.

Meisel, Paul. Good Night, Bat! Good Morning, Squirrel! 2016. (ENG., Illus.). 40p. (J). (gr. -1-3). 17.95 *(978-1-62979-495-2(3)*, Astra Young Readers) Astra Publishing Hse.

Meschenmoser, Sebastian. It's Springtime, Mr. Squirrel. 2018. (ENG., Illus.). 64p. (J). (gr. -1-3). 18.95 *(978-0-7358-4310-3(4))* North-South Bks., Inc.

—Mr. Squirrel & the King of the Forest. 2019. (ENG., Illus.). 64p. (J). (gr. -1-2). 18.95 *(978-0-7358-4342-4(2))* North-South Bks., Inc.

—Mr. Squirrel & the Moon. 2015. (ENG., Illus.). 48p. (J). (gr. -1-1). 18.95 *(978-0-7358-4156-7(X))* North-South Bks., Inc.

—Waiting for Winter. 2015. (ENG., Illus.). 58p. (J). (gr. k-3). 10.99 *(978-1-61067-435-5(9))* Kane Miller.

Meyer, Linda. Jones & the Great Act. 2009. 118p. pap. 9.99 *(978-0-557-17339-6(6))* Lulu Pr., Inc.

Miller, Donna C. Me & Mister Squirrel. 2005. (J). pap. 8.00 *(978-0-8059-6523-0(8))* Dorrance Publishing Co., Inc.

Miller, Jennifer. Christmas Tails. Knight, Vanessa, illus. 2009. 56p. pap. 17.26 *(978-1-4251-8987-7(3))* Trafford Publishing.

Miller, Pat. Squirrel's New Year's Resolution. Ember, Kathi, illus. 2012. (J). 34.28 *(978-1-61913-135-4(8))* Weigl Pubs., Inc.

—Squirrel's New Year's Resolution. Ember, Kathi, illus. 2017. (ENG.). 32p. (J). (gr. -1-3). pap. 8.99 *(978-0-8075-7592-5(5)*, 807575925) Whitman, Albert & Co.

Mjolhus, Joy. Squirrel Babies & Friends. 2008. 16p. pap. 24.95 *(978-1-4241-8562-7(9))* America Star Bks.

Morgan, Allen. Matthew & the Midnight Hospital. 2004. (Illus.). (J). (gr. k-3). spiral bd. *(978-0-616-01529-2(1))* Canadian National Institute for the Blind/Institut National Canadien pour les Aveugles.

Moser, Lisa. Squirrel's World: Candlewick Sparks. Gorbachev, Valeri, illus. 2013. (Candlewick Sparks Ser.). (ENG.). 48p. (J). (gr. k-4). pap. 5.99 *(978-0-7636-6644-6(0))* Candlewick Pr.

Mosier, Pamela. Elizabeth, the Eastern Gray Squirrel. 2008. 44p. pap. 18.95 *(978-1-4357-5407-2(7))* Lulu Pr., Inc.

Muir, Leslie. C. R. Mudgeon. Hector, Julian, illus. 2012. (ENG.). 32p. (J). (gr. -1-3). 15.99 *(978-1-4169-7906-7(9)*, Atheneum Bks. for Young Readers) Simon & Schuster Children's Publishing.

Mullican, Norma Waldon & Zivney, Missy Mullican. A Collection of Squirrel Tales: Something to Crow About. 2009. 84p. pap. 10.99 *(978-1-60791-702-1(5))* Salem Author Services.

Munroe, C. K. Attack of the Mutant Squirrels. 2011. (Illus.). 118p. pap. *(978-1-908147-55-4(5))* YouWriteOn.

Music for Little People, contrib. by. Let's Go Chipper! Into the Great Outdoors. 2011. (ENG.). audio compact disk 9.98 *(978-1-56628-474-5(0))* Music for Little People, Inc.

Nair, Anita. Adventures of Nonu, the Skating Squirrel. 2006. (Illus.). 44p. (J). *(978-81-291-0892-0(5))* Rupa & Co.

Nawrocki, Mike. Boy Meets Squirrels. Séguin-Magee, Luke, illus. 2019. (Dead Sea Squirrels Ser.: 2). (ENG.). 128p. (J). pap. 6.99 *(978-1-4964-3502-6(8)*, 20_32041, Tyndale Kids) Tyndale Hse. Pubs.

—Nutty Study Buddies. Séguin-Magee, Luke, illus. 2019. (Dead Sea Squirrels Ser.: 3). (ENG.). 128p. (J). pap. 6.99 *(978-1-4964-3506-4(0)*, 20_32045, Tyndale Kids) Tyndale Hse. Pubs.

—Squirreled Away. Séguin-Magee, Luke, illus. 2019. (Dead Sea Squirrels Ser.: 1). (ENG.). 128p. (J). pap. 6.99 *(978-1-4964-3498-2(6)*, 20_31671, Tyndale Kids) Tyndale Hse. Pubs.

—Squirrelnapped! Séguin-Magee, Luke, illus. 2019. (Dead Sea Squirrels Ser.: 4). (ENG.). 128p. (J). pap. 6.99 *(978-1-4964-3510-1(9)*, 20_32049, Tyndale Kids) Tyndale Hse. Pubs.

—Tree-Mendous Trouble. Séguin-Magee, Luke, illus. 2020. (Dead Sea Squirrels Ser.: 5). (ENG.). 128p. (J). pap. 6.99 *(978-1-4964-3514-9(1)*, 20_32053, Tyndale Kids) Tyndale Hse. Pubs.

—Whirly Squirrelies. Séguin-Magee, Luke, illus. 2020. (Dead Sea Squirrels Ser.: 6). (ENG.). 128p. (J). pap. 6.99 *(978-1-4964-3518-7(4)*, 20_32057, Tyndale Kids) Tyndale Hse. Pubs.

Nicholas, Nicki. Peter & Lil on a Winter's Day. 2011. 24p. pap. *(978-1-4269-7316-1(0))* Trafford Publishing (UK) Ltd.

—Peter & Lil's Amazing Autumn Day. 2011. 24p. (gr. 1-2). pap. 15.50 *(978-1-4269-6047-5(6))* Trafford Publishing.

—Peter & Lil's Summer Day Adventure. 2011. 24p. pap. 15.50 *(978-1-4269-5358-3(5))* Trafford Publishing.

Nick, Papa. Never Ending Stories. 2011. 44p. pap. 24.95 *(978-1-4626-3792-8(2))* America Star Bks.

Nolan, Lucy A. Smarter Than Squirrels. 0 vols. Reed, Mike, illus. unabr. ed. 2012. (Down Girl & Sit Ser.: 1). (ENG.). 68p. (J). (gr. 1-3). pap. 9.99 *(978-0-7614-5571-4(X)*, 9780761455714, Two Lions) Amazon Publishing.

Nona Theresa Perez - Bayanin. Nadia Mei's First Spring: A Season of Growth. 2012. 32p. pap. 21.99 *(978-1-4771-1006-5(2))* Xlibris Corp.

O'Brien, Richard. Christopher & Joshua Go Fishing. 2012. (ENG., Illus.). 38p. pap. 11.00 *(978-1-78035-257-2(3)*, Fastprint Publishing) Upfront Publishing Ltd. GBR. Dist: Printondemand-worldwide.com.

Ohi, Debbie Ridpath. Where Are My Books? Ohi, Debbie Ridpath, illus. (ENG., Illus.). 40p. (J). (gr. -1-3). 2019. 7.99 *(978-1-5344-5320-3(2))* 2015. 19.99 *(978-1-4424-6741-5(X))* Simon & Schuster Bks. For Young Readers. (Simon & Schuster Bks. For Young Readers).

Ohi, Ruth. Fox & Squirrel. Ohi, Ruth, illus. 2013. (ENG., Illus.). 32p. (J). (gr. -1-2). *(978-1-4431-1914-6(8))* Scholastic Canada, Ltd.

Osuna, Rosa, illus. No es Facil, Pequena Ardilla. 2004.Tr. of It's Not Easy, Little Squirrel. (SPA.). (J). 15.99 *(978-84-8464-202-2(X))* Kalandraka Editora, S.L. ESP. Dist: Lectorum Pubns., Inc.

Otitoloju/Blazing Ideas ltd, Ololade/Adewunmi, retold by. Kunkuru, Jaba Da Kurege: The Tortoise, the Rat & the Squirrel. 2008. (YOR & ENG., Illus.). 36p. 16.00 *(978-0-9801243-7-8(9))* Blazing Ideas Ltd.

—Mbe, Nkapi na Osa. 2008. (YOR & ENG., Illus.). 36p. 16.00 *(978-0-9801243-3-0(6))* Blazing Ideas Ltd.

Page, Frank. Sometimes a Squirrel Is Just a Squirrel. 2005. (ENG.). 106p. pap. 9.99 *(978-1-4116-6062-5(5))* Lulu Pr., Inc.

Paner, Amy & Fisher, Stacey. Nutty Scurries to School. 2008. 25p. 14.95 *(978-0-615-23931-6(5))* Fisher-Paner Publishing.

Parker, Emma. Bill Hides Acorns. 2010. (Illus.). 24p. pap. *(978-1-877561-33-7(9))* First Edition Ltd.

Pearson, Iris & Merrill, Mike. The Adventures of Lady: The Big Storm. Pearson, Iris, ed. Project Firefly Animation Studios, illus. rev. ed. 2007. 34p. (J). 11.99 *(978-0-9789984-2-4(1))* Adventures of Lady LLC, The.

—The Adventures of Lady: The Big Storm Coloring Book. Pearson, Iris, ed. Project Firefly Animation Studios, illus. 2007. 34p. (J). pap. 5.49 *(978-0-9789984-3-1(X))* Adventures of Lady LLC, The.

Peck, Steven L. The Rifts of Rime (Quickened Chronicles) 2012. pap. 14.99 *(978-1-59955-967-4(6))* Cedar Fort, Inc./CFI Distribution.

Pedersen, Peggy A. Jasmine & the Magic Squirrel. 2008. 12p. pap. 24.95 *(978-1-60474-052-3(3))* America Star Bks.

Pellant, Terry. The Real Valentine's Story. 2004. 27p. (J). pap. 24.95 *(978-1-4137-2146-1(X))* PublishAmerica, Inc.

Perkins, Lynne Rae. Nuts to You. Perkins, Lynne Rae, illus. 2014. (ENG., Illus.). 272p. (J). (gr. 3-7). 16.99 *(978-0-06-009275-7(0)*, Greenwillow Bks.) HarperCollins Pubs.

Pernikoff, Doug. So What If Im a Bully. 2009. 40p. 11.99 *(978-0-9816923-3-3(8))* Cochran, Russ Co., The.

S

Pilutti, Deb. Bear & Squirrel Are Friends ... Yes, Really! Pilutti, Deb, illus. 2015. (ENG., Illus.). 40p. (J). (gr. -1-3). 19.99 *(978-1-4814-2913-9(2)*, Simon & Schuster Bks. For Young Readers) Simon & Schuster Bks. For Young Readers.

Pittman, Michael. Mackey's first Adventure. 2011. 24p. pap. 14.93 *(978-1-4269-5175-6(2))* Trafford Publishing.

Potter, Beatrix. The Tale of Squirrel Nutkin. (Beatrix Potter Bookmark Board Book Ser.). (Illus.). 6p. (J). bds. 3.95 *(978-1-58989-203-3(8))* Thurman Hse., LLC.

Powell, Jimmie. The Squirrel the Worm & the Nut Trees. 2007. 48p. per. 15.95 *(978-1-4327-1326-3(4))* Outskirts Pr., Inc.

Preus, Margi. The Littlest Voyageur. Pilgrim, Cheryl, illus. 2020. 176p. (J). (gr. 2-5). 16.99 *(978-0-8234-4247-8(0)*, Margaret Ferguson Books) Holiday Hse., Inc.

Ramoutar, Christine L. Tales from the Pine Forest. 2012. 108p. pap. 10.95 *(978-1-4620-7030-5(2))* iUniverse, Inc.

Randy. The Adventures of Rico. 2010. 28p. pap. 13.79 *(978-1-4490-8353-3(6))* AuthorHouse.

Ray, J. Hamilton. Squirrels on Skis. Lemaître, Pascal, illus. 2013. (Beginner Books(R) Ser.). 64p. (J). (gr. -1-2). 9.99 *(978-0-449-81081-1(X)*, Random Hse. Bks. for Young Readers) Random Hse. Children's Bks.

Reimiller, Diane L. Ike & Jamie. Jastrzebski, Brandy, illus. 2008. 32p. pap. 24.95 *(978-1-60610-227-5(3))* America Star Bks.

Reinlein, Ann. The Adventures of Mister Squirrel Acorn. 2008. 32p. pap. 15.00 *(978-1-4389-1879-2(8))* AuthorHouse.

Rey, H. A. Curious George Plants a Seed/Jorge el Curioso Siembra una Semilla: Bilingual English-Spanish. 2007. (Curious George TV Ser.). (ENG., Illus.). 24p. (J). (gr. -1-3). mass mkt. 5.99 *(978-0-618-89688-2(0)*, 498198, Clarion Bks.) HarperCollins Pubs.

Richardson, Lin Douglas. The Meaning of Me. 2011. 28p. pap. 24.95 *(978-1-4626-2891-9(5))* America Star Bks.

Rickards, Lynne. Rowan the Red Squirrel. 30 vols. Mitchell, Jon, illus. 2018. 32p. (J). 11.95 *(978-1-78250-477-1(X)*, Kelpies) Floris Bks. GBR. Dist: Consortium Bk. Sales & Distribution.

Ringler, Matt. It's Fall! Shearing, Leonie, illus. 2006. 28p. (J). pap. *(978-0-439-87146-4(8))* Scholastic, Inc.

Ringley, Patrick & Brown, Anne Corbett. The Adventures of the Nutters, the Tree Highway. Cotton, Sue Lynn, illus. 2013. 48p. pap. 19.95 *(978-1-61493-207-9(7))* Peppertree Pr., The.

Ritch, Catherine. Zipper Finds a Job. Trexler, Jennifer Suther, illus. 2014. (White Squirrel Parables Ser.: Vol. 2). (ENG.). 32p. (J). (gr. -1-3). 13.95 *(978-1-933341-40-8(8))* CRM.

Roberton, Fiona. A Tale of Two Beasts. 2015. (ENG., Illus.). 32p. (J). pap. 12.99 *(978-1-61067-361-7(1))* Kane Miller.

Rockas, Leo. Mice Make War. 2007. 53p. 16.95 *(978-1-4241-5708-2(0))* America Star Bks.

Rogers, Diana. Critters of Grassy Green Plains: Got to Get the Critters Counted. 2012. 20p. pap. 24.95 *(978-1-4626-7562-3(X))* America Star Bks.

Rose, Chloe Gayle & Rose, Tammy Marie. The Snake That Eats Cake. 2012. 28p. pap. 24.95 *(978-1-4626-9882-0(4))* America Star Bks.

Rose, Nancy. Merry Christmas, Squirrels! 2015. (ENG., Illus.). 32p. (J). (gr. -1-3). 17.00 *(978-0-316-30257-9(0))* Little, Brown Bks. for Young Readers.

—The Secret Life of Squirrels. 2014. (ENG., Illus.). 32p. (J). (gr. -1-3). 18.99 *(978-0-316-37027-1(4))* Little, Brown Bks. for Young Readers.

—The Secret Life of Squirrels: a Love Story. 2016. (ENG., Illus.). 32p. (J). (gr. -1-3). 16.99 *(978-0-316-27263-6(9))* Little, Brown Bks. for Young Readers.

—The Secret Life of Squirrels: Back to School! 2018. (ENG., Illus.). 32p. (J). (gr. -1-3). 17.99 *(978-0-316-50621-2(4))* Little, Brown Bks. for Young Readers.

Rubin, Adam. Those Darn Squirrels! Salmieri, Daniel, illus. (ENG.). 32p. (J). (gr. -1-3). 2011. pap. 7.99 *(978-0-547-57681-7(1)*, 1458442) 2008. 17.99 *(978-0-547-00703-8(5)*, 1029826) HarperCollins Pubs. (Clarion Bks.).

—Those Darn Squirrels & the Cat Next Door. Salmieri, Daniel, illus. 2011. (ENG.). 32p. (J). (gr. -1-3). 16.99 *(978-0-547-42922-9(3)*, 1432155, Clarion Bks.) HarperCollins Pubs.

—Those Darn Squirrels Fly South. Salmieri, Daniel, illus. 2012. (ENG.). 32p. (J). (gr. -1-3). 17.99 *(978-0-547-67823-8(1)*, 1475037, Clarion Bks.) HarperCollins Pubs.

Ruiz, John. The Squirrel, the Eagle & the Red Hawk. 2012. 32p. pap. 21.99 *(978-1-4691-7970-4(9))* Xlibris Corp.

Rylant, Cynthia. Gooseberry Park. Howard, Arthur, illus. 2007. (ENG.). 144p. (J). (gr. 3-7). pap. 7.99

(978-0-15-206159-3(2), 1198490, Clarion Bks.) HarperCollins Pubs.

Sackanay, Kathleen. Adventures in the Forest. Wood, Morgan, illus. 2007. 24p. (J). pap. 8.45 *(978-0-9791276-2-5(9))* Athanatos Publishing Group.

Saldivar, Jose A. The Adventures of Oskar: Oskar's New School. Nilsson, Janet Busbey, ed. Jasnoch, Dorothy, illus. 2013. 32p. pap. 13.99 *(978-1-937752-14-9(3))*; (ENG.). pap. 13.99 *(978-1-937752-07-1(0))* Owl About Bks. Pubs.

Salmon, Peg. Percy & His Family. 2007. 44p. per. 15.95 *(978-1-4327-0841-2(4))* Outskirts Pr., Inc.

Salten, Felix. Perri. Mussey, Barrows, tr. 2015. (Bambi's Classic Animal Tales Ser.). (ENG., Illus.). 256p. (J). (gr. 3-7). pap. 8.99 *(978-1-4424-8760-4(7)*, Aladdin) Simon & Schuster Children's Publishing.

Sargent, Dave & Sargent, David M. Cindy Sparrow: Respect the Property of Others, 19 vols., Vol. 6. Lenoir, Jane, illus. 2003. (Feather Tales Ser.: 6). 42p. (J). pap. 10.95 *(978-1-56763-730-4(2))*; 2nd ed. lib. bdg. 20.95 *(978-1-56763-729-8(9))* Ozark Publishing.

Satterly, Denise B. The Adventures of Icky & Weezy: Fall Has Arrived. 2011. 20p. (gr. -1 — 1). pap. 10.03 *(978-1-4520-2046-4(9))* AuthorHouse.

Scheber, George. Earl Joins the Circus. Spicer, Bridgett, illus. l.t. ed. 2005. (Adventures of Earl the Squirrel Ser.). 32p. (J). (gr. -1-3). 12.95 *(978-1-878847-01-0(5))* Make Me A Story Pr.

—Earl the Squirrel. Spicer, Bridgett, illus. l.t. ed. 2005. (Adventures of Earl the Squirrel Ser.). 32p. (J). (gr. -1-2). 12.95 *(978-1-878847-00-3(7))* Make Me A Story Pr.

Schwartz, Virginia Frances. Nutz!, 1 vol. Leist, Christina, illus. 2012. (ENG.). 152p. (J). (gr. 4-7). pap. 12.95 *(978-1-896580-87-6(4))* Tradewind Bks. CAN. Dist: Orca Bk. Pubs. USA.

Scott, Dee Mary. The Adventures of Charles & Camilla Chinchilla. 2012. (ENG., Illus.). 46p. pap. 6.99 *(978-1-78035-389-0(8)*, Fastprint Publishing) Upfront Publishing Ltd. GBR. Dist: Printondemand-worldwide.com.

Seidler, Tor. Oh, Rats! Evans, Gabriel, illus. 2020. (ENG.). 336p. (J). (gr. 3-7). pap. 8.99 *(978-1-5344-2685-6(X)*, Atheneum Bks. for Young Readers) Simon & Schuster Children's Publishing.

Seymour, Mary Sue. Friends in a Storm. Flynn, Samantha, illus. 2013. 20p. pap. 9.95 *(978-1-61633-376-8(6))* Guardian Angel Publishing, Inc.

Shelton, Ricky V. Quacker Meets His Dad the Squirrel: Tales from a Duck Named Quacker. Williams, Shan, illus. Date not set. (J). (gr. -1-1). pap. 7.00 *(978-0-9634257-3-7(0))* RVS Bks., Inc.

Shepherd, Melissa L. On Mother's Day. 2012. 24p. pap. 14.93 *(978-1-4669-1165-9(4))* Trafford Publishing.

Shields, Kathleen J. Hamilton Troll Meets Chatterton Squirrel. Klug, Leigh A. & Bryant, Carol W., illus. 4th ed. 2013. 42p. 14.00 *(978-0-9882745-3-2(1))* Erin Go Bragh Publishing.

Shongo Jr., Earl. Chippie the Squirrel. 2012. 20p. pap. 14.99 *(978-1-4772-8252-6(1))* AuthorHouse.

Sica, Diane. The Adventures of Sammy & Vinney. 2012. 48p. pap. 11.95 *(978-1-4685-6883-7(3))* AuthorHouse.

Simon, Mary Manz. Squirrel Says Thank You. Couri, Kathy & Clearwater, Linda, illus. 2006. (First Virtues for Toddlers Ser.). 20p. (J). 5.99 *(978-0-7847-1415-7(0)*, 04067) Standard Publishing.

Simpson, Richard. The Squirrel Who Was Afraid to Climb Trees. Hoch, Kevin, illus. 2003. 55p. (J). pap. 9.95 *(978-0-7414-1825-8(8))* Infinity Publishing.

Singhose, Rose. Granny's giggles book Four. 2010. 38p. pap. 16.95 *(978-0-557-59965-3(2))* Lulu Pr., Inc.

—Granny's GIGGLES BOOK SIX. 2010. 34p. pap. 16.95 *(978-0-557-61003-7(6))* Lulu Pr., Inc.

—Granny's giggles book Three. 2010. 33p. pap. 16.95 *(978-0-557-59768-0(4))* Lulu Pr., Inc.

Singhose, Rose & StGermain, Annette. Gramma's Sure Fire Cure for Insomnia in the Very Young. 2010. 67p. pap. 27.50 *(978-0-557-08697-9(3))* Lulu Pr., Inc.

Skidmore, Marlene. In Trouble Again! 2010. 24p. pap. 9.99 *(978-0-9845208-9-3(9))* Faithful Life Pubs.

—Wesley's Swoo-Foo. 2008. 28p. pap. 9.99 *(978-0-9821408-5-7(1))* Faithful Life Pubs.

Smith, Sharon. Speedy the Squirrel. 2012. 32p. pap. 17.25 *(978-1-4669-6438-9(3))* Trafford Publishing.

Smythe, Katie. Squirrel Gets Ready, 1 vol. 2015. (Rosen REAL Readers: STEM & STEAM Collection). (ENG.). 8p. (gr. k-1). pap. 5.46 *(978-1-4994-9611-6(7)*, 48f8e908-9b7e-458d-9784-cc0dca4cd65b, Rosen Classroom) Rosen Publishing Group, Inc., The.

Snider, Kc. Silence. Snider, Kc, illus. 2013. (Illus.). 28p. 19.95 *(978-1-61633-437-6(1))* Guardian Angel Publishing, Inc.

The Snowman, 6 vols., Pack. (Chiquilibros Ser.). (gr. k-1). 23.00 *(978-0-7635-0417-5(3))* Rigby Education.

The Snowman: Individual Title Six-Pack. (Story Steps Ser.). (gr. k-2). 20.00 *(978-0-7635-9578-4(0))* Rigby Education.

Sommer, Carl. No One Will Ever Know. Budwine, Greg, illus. 2014. (J). pap. *(978-1-57537-962-3(7))* Advance Publishing, Inc.

—No One Will Ever Know. 2003. (Another Sommer-Time Story Ser.). (Illus.). 48p. (J). (gr. 1-4). 16.95 incl. audio *(978-1-57537-555-7(9))* Advance Publishing, Inc.

—No One Will Ever Know. Westbrook, Dick, illus. 2003. (Another Sommer-Time Story Ser.). (ENG.). 48p. (J). (gr. 1-4). 16.95 incl. audio compact disk *(978-1-57537-506-9(0))* Advance Publishing, Inc.

—No One Will Ever Know(Nadie Se Va a Enterar) Westbrook, Dick, illus. 2009. (Another Sommer-Time Story Bilingual Ser.). (SPA & ENG.). 48p. (J). lib. bdg. 16.95 *(978-1-57537-163-4(4))* Advance Publishing, Inc.

Sparks, Joanne. Mr. Squirrel. Sparks, Jolene, illus. 2009. 29p. pap. 24.95 *(978-1-61546-375-6(5))* America Star Bks.

Spellman, Frankie. Pinky & Bubs' Stinky Night Out. Spellman, Susan, illus. 2005. (ENG.). 32p. (J). (gr. -1-3). per. 12.95 *(978-1-933002-16-3(6))* PublishingWorks.

Steiner, Dawn. The Silver Squirrel & Friends: The Original Book. 2009. 16p. pap. 8.99 *(978-1-4389-2944-6(7))* AuthorHouse.

—Silver Squirrel & Friends I Can Read Edition: For Beginner Readers. 2009. 16p. pap. 8.99 *(978-1-4389-2916-3(1))* AuthorHouse.

Stone, Chuck. Squizzy the Black Squirrel: A Fabulous Fable of Friendship. Jackson, Jeannie, tr. Jackson, Jeannie, illus. 2003. 30p. (J). 16.95 *(978-0-940880-71-9(7))* Open Hand Publishing, LLC.

Summerville, Justin. Forgetful Freddie. 2013. 44p. 17.99 *(978-0-9890288-1-3(X))* Mindstir Media.

Swallow, Pamela C. Groundhog Gets a Say. Bunkus, Denise, illus. 2007. (ENG.). 40p. (J). (gr. k-3). pap. 8.99 *(978-0-14-240896-4(4)*, Puffin Books) Penguin Young Readers Group.

Tafuri, Nancy. The Busy Little Squirrel. Tafuri, Nancy, illus. 2010. (Classic Board Bks.). (ENG., Illus.). 34p. (J). (gr. -1 — 1). bds. 7.99 *(978-1-4424-0721-3(2)*, Little Simon) Little Simon.

—Busy Little Squirrel. 2007. (ENG., Illus.). 32p. (J). (gr. -1-3). 18.99 *(978-0-689-87341-6(7)*, Simon & Schuster Bks. For Young Readers) Simon & Schuster Bks. For Young Readers.

Taher, Amr. Jimmy the Squirrel. Taher, Layal, ed. Graphics, Nataly, illus. 2011. (ENG.). 36p. (J). 14.99 *(978-1-4567-3526-5(8)*, aea46e17-dc7d-4818-9cb9-9fb2231098b2) AuthorHouse.

Tatsuyama, Sayuri. Happy Happy Clover, Vol. 4. Tatsuyama, Sayuri, illus. 2010. (Happy Happy Clover Ser.: 4). (ENG., Illus.). 192p. (J). pap. 7.99 *(978-1-4215-2735-2(9))* Viz Media.

Taylor, Anna. Sophia's Favorite Squirrel Browny. 2013. 24p. pap. 9.95 *(978-0-9891694-7-9(2))* Barringer Publishing.

Taylor, Pat Eytcheson. Scamper Tangles with Christmas. 2012. 56p. pap. 15.00 *(978-0-9845630-4-3(0))* Catch-A-Winner Publishing.

Tela, Carl M. Squnky's Big Awakening. Tela, Donna L., illus. 2009. 140p. pap. 14.99 *(978-1-4251-8145-1(7))* Trafford Publishing.

Terrell, Andrea M. The Adventures of Sammy the Squirrel: Buying Shoes. Mitchell, Anthony W., illus. 2008. (ENG.). 28p. pap. 13.99 *(978-1-4343-5608-6(6))* AuthorHouse.

Theodoridou, Despoina. Lola, the Lonely Doctor. 2012. (Illus.). 24p. pap. 15.99 *(978-1-4691-6637-7(2))* Xlibris Corp.

Thomson, Malcolm. Let's Go Nuts. 2012. (Illus.). 48p. pap. 24.40 *(978-1-4772-3913-1(8))* AuthorHouse.

Thorpe, Linda W. Teeny-Weeny's Two Front Teeth. 2007. (Illus.). 16p. (J). 6.95 *(978-0-9799671-0-8(4))* ThunderBolt Publishing.

Tollefson, Carol & Shelton, Kim. McTavich That Rascal Squirrel. 2015. (ENG., Illus.). 20p. pap. 12.00 *(978-1-62288-101-7(X)*, P476290) Austin, Stephen F. State Univ. Pr.

Tossell, David H. Charlie & Chippo Meet a Ghost. Pritchard, Louise, illus. 2012. 24p. pap. *(978-1-908773-25-8(1))* Iponymous Publishing, Ltd.

Utsler, Elaine. The Black Cherry Forest: Storybook 1. Wendle, Stan, ed. Jeannotte, Lawrence, illus. 2nd ed. 2003. 48p. (J). per. 6.95 *(978-0-9727787-1-8(3)*, BCF1B) EV Publishing Corp.

Van Genechten, Guido. Ricky & the Squirrel. 2010. (Ricky Ser.). (ENG., Illus.). 30p. (J). (gr. -1-k). 16.95 *(978-1-60537-078-1(9))* Clavis Publishing.

Vande Velde, Vivian. Squirrel in the House. Björkman, Steve, illus. 2017. (Twitch the Squirrel Ser.: 2). (ENG.). 80p. (J). (gr. 1-4). pap. 6.99 *(978-0-8234-3877-8(5))* Holiday Hse., Inc.

—Squirrel in the Museum. Björkman, Steve, illus. 2019. (Twitch the Squirrel Ser.: 3). (ENG.). 112p. (J). (gr. 1-4). 15.99 *(978-0-8234-4167-9(9))* Holiday Hse., Inc.

Vil, Steve. Arvid & Hornschwatz Go Skunk Scoffing. Witt, Eddie, illus. 2011. 32p. pap. 24.95 *(978-1-4560-6043-5(0))* America Star Bks.

Voake, Steve. Daisy Dawson & the Secret Pond. Meserve, Jessica, illus. 2010. (Daisy Dawson Ser.: 2). (ENG.). 96p. (J). (gr. 1-4). pap. 6.99 *(978-0-7636-4730-8(6))* Candlewick Pr.

—Daisy Dawson & the Secret Pond, 2. Meserve, Jessica, illus. 2009. (Daisy Dawson Ser.: 2). (ENG.). 96p. (J). (gr. 1-4). 18.69 *(978-0-7636-4009-5(3))* Candlewick Pr.

Voigt, Cynthia. Toaff's Way. 2018. (ENG., Illus.). 272p. (J). (gr. 3-7). 16.99 *(978-1-5247-6536-1(8)*, Knopf Bks. for Young Readers) Random Hse. Children's Bks.

Wall, Billy James. The Mystery of Marcy & the Stony Squirrel. 2009. 40.00 *(978-1-61584-580-4(1))* Independent Pub.

Walter-Goodspeed, Dee Dee. Friends Will Be There Forever. Jones, Ayanna, illus. 2012. 26p. (J). (-18). pap. 15.99 *(978-1-933846-36-1(4))* Fairwood Pr.

Watt, Mélanie. Scaredy Squirrel. 2011. (J). (gr. -1-3). 29.95 *(978-0-545-32740-4(7))*; 18.95 *(978-0-545-32752-7(0))*;Set. 38.75 *(978-0-545-32759-6(8))* Weston Woods Studios, Inc.

—Scaredy Squirrel at the Beach. Watt, Mélanie, illus. 2012. (ENG., Illus.). 32p. (J). (gr. -1-3). pap. 7.99 *(978-1-55453-462-3(3))* Kids Can Pr., Ltd. CAN. Dist: Hachette Bk. Group.

—Scaredy Squirrel at the Beach. Watt, Mélanie, illus. 2008. (Scaredy Squirrel Ser.). (ENG., Illus.). 32p. (J). (gr. -1-3). 16.99 *(978-1-55453-225-4(6))* Kids Can Pr., Ltd. CAN. Dist: Hachette Bk. Group.

Watt, Mélanie & Watt, Mélanie. Scaredy Squirrel. Watt, Mélanie & Watt, Mélanie, illus. (ENG., Illus.). 40p. (J). (gr. -1-3). 2008. pap. 8.99 *(978-1-55453-023-6(7))* 2006. 16.99 *(978-1-55337-959-1(4))* Kids Can Pr., Ltd. CAN. Dist: Hachette Bk. Group.

—Scaredy Squirrel at Night. Watt, Mélanie & Watt, Mélanie, illus. 2009. (Scaredy Squirrel Ser.). (ENG., Illus.). 32p. (J). (gr. -1-3). 16.99 *(978-1-55453-288-9(4))* Kids Can Pr., Ltd. CAN. Dist: Hachette Bk. Group.

—Scaredy Squirrel Has a Birthday Party, 0 vols. Watt, Mélanie & Watt, Mélanie, illus. (ENG., Illus.). 32p. (J). (gr. -1-3). 2014. pap. 7.99 *(978-1-55453-716-7(9))* 2011. 16.99 *(978-1-55453-468-5(2))* Kids Can Pr., Ltd. CAN. Dist: Hachette Bk. Group.

—Scaredy Squirrel Makes a Friend. Watt, Mélanie & Watt, Mélanie, illus. 2007. (ENG., Illus.). 32p. (J). (gr. -1-3). 16.99 *(978-1-55453-181-3(0))* Kids Can Pr., Ltd. CAN. Dist: Hachette Bk. Group.

West, Karen L. Tommy the Squirrel Wants to Be Human. 2009. 24p. pap. 12.99 *(978-1-4389-8096-6(5))* AuthorHouse.

Wheat, Tiffany. There's a Gopher in My Garden! 2013. (ENG., Illus.). (J). (gr. -1-3). pap. 9.95 *(978-1-62086-463-0(0))* Amplify Publishing Group.

Willems, Mo. I Lost My Tooth!-An Unlimited Squirrels Book. 2018. (Unlimited Squirrels Ser.: 1). (ENG.). 96p. (J). (gr. -1-3). 12.99 *(978-1-368-02457-0(2)*, Hyperion Books for Children) Disney Publishing Worldwide.

—I Want to Sleep under the Stars!-An Unlimited Squirrels Book. 2020. (Unlimited Squirrels Ser.). (ENG., Illus.). 96p. (J). (gr. 1-3). 12.99 *(978-1-368-05335-8(1)*, Hyperion Books for Children) Disney Publishing Worldwide.

—Who Is the Mystery Reader?-An Unlimited Squirrels Book. 2019. (Unlimited Squirrels Ser.). (ENG., Illus.). 96p. (J). (gr. -1-3). 12.99 *(978-1-368-04686-2(X)*, Hyperion Books for Children) Disney Publishing Worldwide.

Willett, Christie. Isabella. 2011. 52p. (gr. -1). pap. 19.39 *(978-1-4269-6387-2(4))* Trafford Publishing.

Williamgoldenpen. Quacker's Bedtime Stories. 2006. 49p. pap. 16.95 *(978-1-4241-2236-3(8))* PublishAmerica, Inc.

Williams, Antonio. A Day in the World of Todd the Squirrel. 2011. 28p. pap. 12.82 *(978-1-4634-4408-2(7))* AuthorHouse.

Williams, Greg. Airmont the Flying Squirrel. 2011. 30p. pap. 19.00 *(978-1-60746-219-4(2))* FastPrncil, Inc.

Williams, Levester. The Adventures od Crunchy & Munchy Squirrel: Field Nuts. 2005. pap. *(978-0-9774418-0-8(6))* L.Patrick Publishing.

Williams, M. Ed. Friends in the Meadow - Squirrels the Frolics of Scamp & Scooter. 2013. 72p. pap. *(978-1-77067-429-5(2))* FriesenPress.

Windhorst, Brenda. Do You Want a Henry Story? 2011. 24p. pap. 15.99 *(978-1-4628-8796-5(1))* Xlibris Corp.

Wright, Craig. Dolphin Read Start Silly Squirrel. 2010. (ENG., Illus.). 20p. 5.00 *(978-0-19-440076-3(X))* Oxford Univ. Pr., Inc.

Yalmeh, Jacklin. Scruffy & the Blue Hazelnut Tree. 2013. 38p. pap. 10.95 *(978-0-9885898-1-0(8))* i ZGOOL Media.

—Scruffy & the Walnuts. 2013. 38p. pap. 10.95 *(978-0-9885898-2-7(6))* i ZGOOL Media.

Yang, Stella, illus. The Snowman, 6 vols., Pack. (Sails Literacy Ser.). 16p. (gr. k-18). 27.00 *(978-0-7635-4439-3(6))* Rigby Education.

Yolen, Jane. Trash Mountain. Monroe, Chris, illus. 2015. (ENG.). 184p. (J). (gr. 3-6). E-Book 27.99 *(978-1-4677-7170-2(8)*, Carolrhoda Bks.) Lerner Publishing Group.

Young, Miriam. Miss Suzy. Lobel, Arnold, illus. (J). 40th anniv. ed. 2004. 44p. 18.95 *(978-1-930900-28-8(7))* 50th ed. 2014. (ENG.). 40p. (gr. -1-3). 18.95 *(978-1-930900-75-2(9))* Purple Hse. Pr.

Young, Sandra M. Daniel, the Little Red Squirrel: Learns His Lessons. 2008. 40p. pap. 18.49 *(978-1-4389-1844-0(5))* AuthorHouse.

Youngberg, Yvette M. The Tooting Squirrel. 2009. (Illus.). 20p. pap. 10.95 *(978-1-4389-1967-6(0))* AuthorHouse.

SRI LANKA

Berlatsky, Noah, ed. Sri Lanka, 1 vol. 2014. (Genocide & Persecution Ser.). (ENG., Illus.). 240p. (gr. 10-12). lib. bdg. 43.63 *(978-0-7377-6900-5(9)*, d22d0de0-5618-41c8-bde8-c7570326abf7, Greenhaven Publishing) Greenhaven Publishing LLC.

Hoffmann, Sara. Sri Lanka in Pictures. 2006. (Visual Geography Series, Second Ser.). (ENG., Illus.). 80p. (gr. 5-12). lib. bdg. 31.93 *(978-0-8225-3481-5(9))* Lerner Publishing Group.

O'Brien, Cynthia. Cultural Traditions in Sri Lanka. 2017. (Cultural Traditions in My World Ser.). (Illus.). 32p. (J). (gr. 3-2). *(978-0-7787-8099-1(6))* Crabtree Publishing Co.

Sullivan, Laura L. Sri Lanka. 2019. (Exploring World Cultures Ser.). (ENG.). 32p. (gr. 3-3). 66.96 *(978-1-5026-4719-1(2))* Cavendish Square Publishing LLC.

Wanasundera, Nanda P. Sri Lanka, 1 vol. 2003. (Cultures of the World (First Edition)(r) Ser.). (ENG., Illus.). 144p. (gr. 5-5). lib. bdg. 49.79 *(978-0-7614-1477-3(0)*, a850a9c2-198f-4c76-b4de-bf18ac975bb2) Cavendish Square Publishing LLC.

Wanasundera, Nanda P. & Spilling, Jo-Ann. Sri Lanka, 1 vol. 3rd rev. ed. 2012. (Cultures of the World (Third Edition)(r) Ser.). (ENG.). 144p. (gr. 5-5). lib. bdg. 48.79 *(978-1-60870-994-6(9)*, c3110edf-e8cc-4805-b0cc-4671c689b996) Cavendish Square Publishing LLC.

SRI LANKA—FICTION

Isbell, Tessa J. Animal Adventures: Goosey & Beauty Take a Mystery Magic Carpet Ride to Jamaica. 2013. 48p. pap. 21.99 *(978-1-4669-7217-9(3))* Trafford Publishing.

Lipp, Frederick J. Tea Leaves. Coloma, Lester, tr. Coloma, Lester, illus. 2003. (J). 32p. (gr. 1-6). 15.95 *(978-1-59034-998-4(9))*; 33p. pap. *(978-1-59034-999-1(7))* Mondo Publishing.

Wanasuriya, Chandrani. Favorite Folktales of Sri Lank. 2007. 108p. per. 19.95 *(978-1-4241-9965-5(4))* America Star Bks.

STABILIZATION IN INDUSTRY

see Economic History

STAGE

see Acting; Actors and Actresses; Theater

STAGE SCENERY

see Theaters—Stage Setting and Scenery

STAGE SETTING

see Theaters—Stage Setting and Scenery

STAINED GLASS

see Glass Painting and Staining

STALIN, JOSEPH, 1879-1953

Abdo Publishing. Joseph Stalin, 1 vol. 2015. (Essential Lives Set 9 Ser.). (ENG., Illus.). 112p. (YA). (gr. 6-12). 41.36 *(978-1-62403-896-9(4)*, 17824, Essential Library) ABDO Publishing Co.

Benchmark Education Company. Three Twentieth Century Dictators (Teacher Guide) 2004. *(978-1-4108-2593-3(0))* Benchmark Education Co.

Joihnson, Robert, compiled by. Lenin, Stalin & Communist Russia: The Myth & Reality of Communism. 2003. (Studymates Ser.). (Illus.). 132p. (C). pap. 27.50 *(978-1-84285-039-8(3))* GLMP Ltd. GBR. Dist: Chicago Distribution Ctr.

Jukes, Geoffrey & O'Neill, Robert John. World War II: The Eastern Front 1941-1945, 1 vol. 2010. (World War II: Essential Histories Ser.). (ENG., Illus.). 96p. (YA). (gr. 10-10). lib. bdg. 38.47 *(978-1-4358-9134-0(1)*, 364c546d-4d20-4553-90dc-f1789407d04f) Rosen Publishing Group, Inc., The.

McCollum, Sean. Joseph Stalin. 2010. (Wicked History Ser.). (ENG., Illus.). 128p. (J). 31.00 *(978-0-531-20755-0(2)*, Watts, Franklin) Scholastic Library Publishing.

—Joseph Stalin (a Wicked History) 2010. (Wicked History Ser.). (ENG.). 128p. (J). (gr. 6-12). pap. 5.95 *(978-0-531-22355-0(8)*, Watts, Franklin) Scholastic Library Publishing.

Ruby, India. Three Twentieth Century Dictators: Set Of 6. 2011. (Navigators Ser.). (J). pap. 50.00 net. *(978-1-4108-2578-0(7))* Benchmark Education Co.

Zuehlke, Jeffrey. Joseph Stalin. 2006. (Biography Ser.). (Illus.). 112p. (J). (gr. 3-7). lib. bdg. 27.93 *(978-0-8225-3421-1(5)*, Twenty-First Century Bks.) Lerner Publishing Group.

STALINGRAD, BATTLE OF, VOLGOGRAD, RUSSIA, 1942-1943

Wilson, John. Four Steps to Death. 2005. 208p. (YA). (gr. 7-9). 7.95 *(978-1-55337-705-4(2))* Kids Can Pr., Ltd. CAN. Dist: Hachette Bk. Group.

STAMINA, PHYSICAL

see Physical Fitness

STAMPS, POSTAGE

see Postage Stamps

STANDARD OF VALUE

see Money

STANDARD TIME

see Time

STANDISH, MYLES, 1584?-1656

Harness, Cheryl. The Adventurous Life of Myles Standish: And the Amazing-but-True Survival Story of Plymouth Colony. 2006. (Cheryl Harness Histories Ser.). (Illus.). 144p. (J). (gr. 5-9). 16.95 *(978-0-7922-5918-3(1)*, National Geographic Kids) Disney Publishing Worldwide.

STANLEY, HENRY M. (HENRY MORTON), 1841-1904

Henry Stanley & the Quest for the Source of the Nile. 2014. (ENG.). 176p. (J). (gr. 3-7). pap. 13.95 *(978-1-59077-348-2(9))* Evans, M. & Co., Inc.

O'Brien, Cynthia. Explore with Stanley & Livingstone. 2016. (Travel with the Great Explorers Ser.). (ENG., Illus.). 32p. (J). (gr. 3-6). *(978-0-7787-2848-1(X))* Crabtree Publishing Co.

STANTON, ELIZABETH CADY, 1815-1902

Adiletta, Dawn. Elizabeth Cady Stanton: Women's Suffrage & the First Vote. (Library of American Lives & Times Ser.). 112p. (gr. 5-5). 2009. 69.20 *(978-1-60853-479-1(0))* 2004. (ENG., Illus.). (J). lib. bdg. 38.27 *(978-1-4042-2647-0(8)*, c7dcb355-12ad-4a2b-9bd6-5e815734870e) Rosen Publishing Group, Inc., The.

Bohannon, Lisa Frederiksen. Women's Rights & Nothing Less: The Story of Elizabeth Cady Stanton. 2004. (Feminist Voices Ser.). (Illus.). 112p. (YA). (gr. 6-12). 23.95 *(978-1-883846-66-4(8)*, First Biographies) Reynolds, Morgan Inc.

Frey, Wendy. Citizen Heroes. 2007. (Illus.). 68p. (J). *(978-1-4105-0888-1(9))*; *(978-1-4105-0887-4(0))* Building Wings LLC.

Fry, Erin. The Power of Friendship. 2005. (Illus.). 16p. (J). pap. *(978-0-7367-2920-8(8))* Zaner-Bloser, Inc.

Isecke, Harriet. Susan B. Anthony & Elizabeth Cady Stanton: Early Suffragists. rev. ed. 2011. (Social Studies: Informational Text Ser.). (ENG., Illus.). 32p. (gr. 4-8). pap. 11.99 *(978-1-4333-1506-0(8))* Teacher Created Materials, Inc.

Kent, Deborah. Elizabeth Cady Stanton: Founder of the Women's Suffrage Movement, 1 vol. 2016. (Heroes of the Women's Suffrage Movement Ser.). (ENG.). 128p. (gr. 6-6). 38.93 *(978-0-7660-7889-5(2)*, 05025743-f964-4f6c-8e70-67989020d66a) Enslow Publishing, LLC.

—Elizabeth Cady Stanton: Woman Knows the Cost of Life, 1 vol. 2008. (Americans: the Spirit of a Nation Ser.). (ENG., Illus.). 128p. (gr. 5-6). lib. bdg. 35.93 *(978-0-7660-3357-3(0)*, a08165a5-32e5-45ad-8cb3-d3e3ffca7805) Enslow Publishing, LLC.

Marlgorz, Juliet. Elizabeth Cady Stanton & the Fight for Equal Rights, 1 vol. 2008. (Real Life Readers Ser.). (ENG.). 32p. (gr. 4-6). pap. 10.00 *(978-1-4358-0233-9(0)*, c6a2072f-8727-488c-b3bd-4dfd47097ed8, Rosen Classroom) Rosen Publishing Group, Inc., The.

Mattern, Joanne. Elizabeth Cady Stanton & Susan B. Anthony: Fighting Together for Women's Rights. 2009. (Women Who Shaped History Ser.). 24p. (gr. 2-3). 42.50 *(978-1-60854-818-7(X)*, PowerKids Pr.) Rosen Publishing Group, Inc., The.

Rappaport, Doreen. Elizabeth Started All the Trouble. Faulkner, Matt, illus. 2016. (ENG.). 40p. (J). (gr. -1-3). 18.99 *(978-0-7868-5142-3(2))* Disney Pr.

Shea, Nicole. Elizabeth Cady Stanton in Her Own Words. 2014. (Eyewitness to History Ser.). 32p. (J). (gr. 4-6). pap. 63.00 *(978-1-4824-1201-7(2))* Stevens, Gareth Publishing LLLP.

Stone, Tanya Lee. Elizabeth Leads the Way: Elizabeth Cady Stanton & the Right to Vote. Gibbon, Rebecca, illus. 2010. (ENG.). 32p. (J). (gr. 1-5). pap. 8.99 *(978-0-312-60236-9(7)*, 900064232) Square Fish.

STANTON, WILL (FICTITIOUS CHARACTER)—FICTION

Cooper, Susan. The Dark Is Rising. 2009. 7.64 *(978-0-7848-2212-8(3)*, Everbind) Marco Bk. Co.

—The Dark Is Rising. 15.85 *(978-0-7569-8464-9(5))* Perfection Learning Corp.

—The Dark Is Rising. (Dark Is Rising Sequence Ser.). 244p. (YA). (gr. 5-18). pap. 4.99 *(978-0-8072-1533-3(3)*, Listening Library) Random Hse. Audio Publishing Group.

STARFISHES

Anderson, Jo Marie. Sea Stars in the Tide Pool, 1 vol. 2017. (Critters by the Sea Ser.). (ENG.). 24p. (J). (gr. 3-3). 25.27 *(978-1-5383-2521-6(7)*, a893b0de-ce6d-4a5d-b13a-2b450b8dd29b, PowerKids Pr.) Rosen Publishing Group, Inc., The.

Fish, Lori Flying. One Shining Starfish. Fish, Lori Flying, illus. 2010. (Illus.). 16p. pap. 9.95 *(978-1-936343-12-6(6))* Peppertree Pr., The.

Gay, Marie-Louise. Stella, l'Etoile de Mer. braille ed. 2004. (FRE.). (J). (gr. -1-3). spiral bd. *(978-0-616-03072-1(X))* Canadian National Institute for the Blind/Institut National Canadien pour les Aveugles.

Gibbs, Maddie. Sea Stars, 1 vol. 2013. (PowerKids Readers: Fun Fish Ser.). 24p. (J). (gr. k-k). (ENG.). 26.27

(978-1-4777-0760-9(3), 8d7da585-63d5-4a6c-9640-44ea75da2a44); (ENG.). pap. 9.25 (978-1-4777-0853-8(7), 9f27f566-70ae-478b-a380-8118328fe51a); pap. 49.50 (978-1-4777-0854-5(5)) Rosen Publishing Group, Inc., The. (PowerKids Pr.).

—Sea Stars / Las Estrellas de Mar, 1 vol. De La Vega, Eida, ed. 2013. (PowerKids Readers: Peces Divertidos / Fun Fish Ser.). (ENG & SPA.). 24p. (J). (gr. k-k). 26.27 (978-1-4777-1218-4(6), b54e3a7b-8e7a-436a-88e7-48a732c0bf14, PowerKids Pr.) Rosen Publishing Group, Inc., The.

Gray, Susan H. Sea Star. 2014. (21st Century Skills Library: Exploring Our Oceans Ser.). (ENG., Illus.). 32p. (J). (gr. 3-6). 32.07 (978-1-63188-023-0(3), 205499) Cherry Lake Publishing.

Herriges, Ann. Sea Stars. 2006. (Oceans Alive Ser.). (ENG., Illus.). 24p. (J). (gr. k-3). lib. bdg. 26.95 (978-1-60014-021-1(1)) Bellwether Media.

James, Helen Foster. Discover Sea Stars. 2015. (21st Century Basic Skills Library: Splash! Ser.). (ENG., Illus.). 24p. (J). (gr. 2-4). pap. 12.79 (978-1-63362-696-6(2), 206609) Cherry Lake Publishing.

Jones, Tammy. At the Shore. 2009. (Sight Word Readers Set A Ser.). (J). 3.49 net. (978-1-60719-137-7(7)) Newmark Learning LLC.

Kenan, Tessa. ¡Mira, una Estrella de Mar! (Look, a Starfish!) 2017. (Bumba Books (r) en Español — Veo Animales Marinos (I See Ocean Animals) Ser.). (SPA., Illus.). 24p. (J). (gr. -1-1). 26.65 (978-1-5124-2869-8(8), 339c07a0-1b7c-46e4-b8e3-5de41deee81e, Ediciones Lerner) Lerner Publishing Group.

Laughlin, Kara L. Sea Stars. 2017. (In the Deep Blue Sea Ser.). (ENG.). 24p. (J). (gr. k-3). lib. bdg. 32.79 (978-1-5038-1693-0(1), 211527) Child's World, Inc, The.

Lunis, Natalie. Prickly Sea Stars. (No Backbone! Marine Invertebrates Ser.). (Illus.). 24p. (J). (gr. k-3). 2016. (ENG.). pap. 7.99 (978-1-944998-77-6(2)) 2007. lib. bdg. 26.99 (978-1-59716-508-2(5)) Bearport Publishing Co., Inc.

Meister, Cari. Sea Stars. 2012. (ENG., Illus.). 24p. (J). lib. bdg. 25.65 (978-1-62031-012-0(0)) Jump! Inc.

Metz, Lorijo. Discovering Starfish, 1 vol. 2011. (Along the Shore Ser.). (ENG., Illus.). 24p. (J). (gr. 2-3). lib. bdg. 26.27 (978-1-4488-4996-3(9), cfc178b3-7d91-4a8f-a589-edea6daeecaa) Rosen Publishing Group, Inc., The.

Mitchell, Susan K. Biggest vs. Smallest Sea Creatures, 1 vol. 2010. (Biggest vs. Smallest Animals Ser.). (ENG., Illus.). 24p. (gr. k-2). 25.27 (978-0-7660-3580-5(8), b870c237-3a34-4d45-82c2-5f3439953602, Enslow Elementary) Enslow Publishing, LLC.

Nagelhout, Ryan. Sea Stars, 1 vol. 2013. (Underwater World Ser.). (ENG., Illus.). 24p. (J). (gr. k-k). pap. 9.15 (978-1-4339-8572-0(1), c670b948-4ca1-4656-b3a1-ce99360e345a); lib. bdg. 25.27 (978-1-4339-8571-3(3), e013eb07-03fd-4e7a-b183-ab758a524d84) Stevens, Gareth Publishing LLLP.

—Sea Stars / Estrellas de Mar, 1 vol. 2013. (Underwater World / el Mundo Submarino Ser.). (SPA & ENG., Illus.). 24p. (J). (gr. k-k). lib. bdg. 25.27 (978-1-4339-8782-3(1), c620cc9e-8a3a-46e9-a385-99eb4606f343) Stevens, Gareth Publishing LLLP.

Pettiford, Rebecca. Sea Stars. 2016. (Ocean Life up Close Ser.). (ENG., Illus.). 24p. (J). (gr. k-3). 26.95 (978-1-62617-421-4(0)); pap. 7.99 (978-1-61891-268-8(2), 12058) Bellwether Media. (Blastoff! Readers).

Schaefer, Lola M. Sea Stars [Scholastic]. 2009. (Ocean Life Ser.). 24p. (gr. k-1). pap. 2.99 (978-1-4296-3678-0(5), Pebble) Capstone.

Schuh, Mari. Sea Stars. 2019. (Spot Ocean Animals Ser.). (ENG.). 16p. (J). (gr. -1-2). lib. bdg. (978-1-68151-632-5(2), 10764) Amicus.

Schuh, Mari C. Sea Stars. 2015. (Sea Life Ser.). (ENG., Illus.). 24p. (J). (gr. -1-2). lib. bdg. 27.32 (978-1-4914-6044-3(X), 128958, Capstone Pr.) Capstone.

Statts, Leo. Starfish. 2016. (Ocean Animals Ser.). (ENG., Illus.). 24p. (J). (gr. -1-2). lib. bdg. 31.36 (978-1-68079-915-6(0), 24134, Abdo Zoom-Launch) ABDO Publishing Co.

Stone, Lynn M. Sea Stars. 2005. (Rourke Discovery Library). (Illus.). 24p. (J). (gr. -1-3). lib. bdg. 21.36 (978-1-59515-442-2(6)) Rourke Educational Media.

Strain Trueit, Trudi. Starfish, 1 vol. 2011. (Ocean Life Ser.). (ENG.). 24p. (gr. k-1). 25.50 (978-0-7614-4894-5(2), e81b4e00-180e-48f8-9552-f0450432fdec) Cavendish Square Publishing LLC.

Sullivan, Jody. Sea Stars [Scholastic]. 2010. (Under the Sea Ser.). 24p. pap. 0.50 (978-1-4296-5066-3(4), Capstone Pr.) Capstone.

Zuchora-Walske, Christine. Spiny Sea Stars. 2003. (Pull Ahead Bks.). (Illus.). 32p. (J). (gr. k-2). pap. 6.95 (978-0-8225-3770-0(2)) Lerner Publishing Group.

STARLINGS

Bronson, Wilfrid S., illus. Starlings. 2008. 84p. (J). pap. 18.95 (978-0-86534-649-9(6)) Sunstone Pr.

Gray, Susan H. Starling. 2008. (21st Century Skills Library: Animal Invaders Ser.). (ENG., Illus.). 32p. (gr. 4-8). lib. bdg. 32.07 (978-1-60279-113-8(9), 200109) Cherry Lake Publishing.

STARR, BELLE, 1848-1899

Rau, Margaret. Belle of the West: The True Story of Belle Starr. 2004. (Women of the Frontier Ser.). (Illus.). 160p. (YA). (gr. 6-12). 23.95 (978-1-883846-68-8(4), First Biographies) Reynolds, Morgan Inc.

Sargent, Dave & Sargent, Pat. Lily: (Lilac Dun) A Second Chance, 30 vols., Vol. 38. Lenoir, Jane, illus. 2003. (Saddle up Ser.: Vol. 38). 42p. (J). pap. 10.95 (978-1-56763-698-7(5)); lib. bdg. 23.60 (978-1-56763-697-0(7)) Ozark Publishing.

STARR, EMILY (FICTITIOUS CHARACTER)—FICTION

see Starr, Emily Byrd (Fictitious Character)—Fiction

STARR, EMILY BYRD (FICTITIOUS CHARACTER)—FICTION

Montgomery, L. M. Emily Climbs: A Virago Modern Classic. 2014. (ENG.). 384p. (J). (gr. 4-9). pap. 10.99 (978-1-84408-989-5(4), Virago Press) Little, Brown Book Group Ltd. GBR. Dist: Hachette Bk. Group.

—Emily of New Moon. 2019. (ENG.). (J). (gr. 5-12). 704p. pap. 27.99 (978-1-6984-6657-6(9)); 700p. pap. 39.99 (978-1-6967-9800-6(0)); 700p. pap. 39.99 (978-1-6910-9002-0(6)); 700p. pap. 39.99 (978-1-6949-7463-1(4)); 562p. pap. 35.99 (978-1-0864-2303-7(8)); 342p. pap. 19.99 (978-1-6862-9811-0(0)); 562p. pap. 30.99 (978-1-0775-9085-4(7)); 704p. pap. 45.99 (978-1-0784-0299-6(X)); 704p. pap. 25.99 (978-1-0799-5146-2(6)); 704p. pap. 34.99 (978-1-0803-9453-1(2)); 704p. pap. 39.99 (978-1-0761-2343-5(0)); 702p. pap. 39.99 (978-1-0974-8467-6(X)); 468p. pap. 26.99 (978-1-0957-2882-6(2)); 704p. pap. 44.99 (978-1-0917-4644-2(3)); 704p. pap. 44.99 (978-1-7969-7316-7(5)); 702p. pap. 30.99 (978-1-7965-6239-2(4)) Independently Published.

—Emily of New Moon. 2019. (ENG.). (J). (gr. 5-12). 342p. pap. 14.99 (978-1-7018-6548-8(3)); 330p. pap. 33.99 (978-1-7077-8544-5(9)) Independently Published.

—Emily of New Moon: A Virago Modern Classic. 2014. (ENG.). 416p. (J). (gr. 4-9). pap. 10.99 (978-1-84408-988-8(6), Virago Press) Little, Brown Book Group Ltd. GBR. Dist: Hachette Bk. Group.

—Emily's Quest: A Virago Modern Classic. 2014. (ENG.). 272p. (J). (gr. 4-9). pap. 10.99 (978-1-84408-987-1(8), Virago Press) Little, Brown Book Group Ltd. GBR. Dist: Hachette Bk. Group.

Montgomery, Lucy Maud. Emily of New Moon. 2018. (ENG., Illus.). 184p. (J). (gr. 4-7). pap. 6.95 (978-0-464-89423-0(9)) Blurb, Inc.

—Emily of New Moon. (ENG.). (J). 2019. 626p. (gr. 4-7). pap. 35.99 (978-1-0865-5466-3(3)) 2019. 628p. (gr. k-6). pap. 34.99 (978-1-0934-3679-2(4)) 2018. (Illus.). 628p. (gr. 4-7). pap. 35.99 (978-1-7915-2706-8(X)) Independently Published.

Montgomery, Lucy Maud & Montgomery, L. M. Emily of New Moon. 2019. (ENG., Illus.). 316p. (J). (gr. k-6). 19.99 (978-1-5154-3983-7(6)); pap. 9.99 (978-1-5154-3982-0(8)) Wilder Pubns., Corp.

STARS

see also Astrology; Astronomy; Astrophysics; Meteors; Planets; Solar System

Adamson, Thomas K. Stars [Scholastic]. 2011. (Exploring the Galaxy Ser.). 24p. pap. 0.50 (978-1-4296-6291-8(3), Capstone Pr.) Capstone.

Anderson, Michael. The Sun, Stars, & Galaxies, 1 vol. 2011. (Solar System Ser.). (ENG., Illus.). 96p. (J). (gr. 8-8). lib. bdg. 35.29 (978-1-61530-519-3(X), 4da0729d-9c90-488b-b525-d7146a1edaa8) Rosen Publishing Group, Inc., The.

Aspen-Baxter, Linda & Kissock, Heather. Las Estrellas. 2012. (Mirando Al Cielo Ser.). (SPA., Illus.). 24p. (J). (gr. k-2). lib. bdg. 27.13 (978-1-61913-218-4(4), AV2 by Weigl) Weigl Pubs., Inc.

Asselin, Kristine Carlson. Stars. 2010. (Solar System & Beyond Ser.). (ENG.). 32p. (J). (gr. 3-4). pap. 48.60 (978-1-4296-6411-0(8), 16157); (Illus.). pap. 8.10 (978-1-4296-6243-7(3), 115395) Capstone. (Capstone Pr.).

Austen, Mary. Andromeda, 1 vol. 2015. (Constellation Collection). (ENG., Illus.). 24p. (J). (gr. 3-3). pap. 9.25 (978-1-4994-0931-4(1), 573aaf3a-68bc-44a2-8391-fa0aa72c6db5, PowerKids Pr.) Rosen Publishing Group, Inc., The.

Bayarri Dolz, Jordi. La Prehistòria. (SPA.). (J). 10.00 (978-84-342-1469-9(5)) Parramon Ediciones S.A. ESP. Dist: Distribuidora Norma, Inc.

Bellisario, Gina. To the Stars! Moran, Mike, illus. 2017. (Cloverleaf Books (tm) — Space Adventures Ser.). (ENG.). 24p. (J). (gr. k-2). 25.32 (978-1-5124-2537-6(0), 4b03fa2e-d854-4efa-8c3f-68749cf82c18); E-Book 38.65 (978-1-5124-3896-3(0), 9781512438963); E-Book 38.65 (978-1-5124-2834-6(5)) Lerner Publishing Group. (Millbrook Pr.).

Bennett, Elizabeth. Stars & Constellations. 2007. (Illus.). 16p. (J). (978-0-545-00734-4(8)) Scholastic, Inc.

Bredeson, Carmen & Dyson, Marianne. Exploring the Stars, 1 vol. 2015. (Launch into Space! Ser.). (ENG.). 32p. (gr. 3-4). pap. 11.52 (978-0-7660-6829-2(3), d6a63fd6-80a4-4189-8be1-3ca4ea45dd98); (Illus.). 26.93 (978-0-7660-6831-5(5), c4737d3b-d238-4f21-a56b-fe19c5fb328d) Enslow Publishing, LLC.

Buchanan, Shelly. Stars. 2015. (Science: Informational Text Ser.). (ENG., Illus.). 32p. (gr. 4-8). pap. 11.99 (978-1-4807-4728-9(9)) Teacher Created Materials, Inc.

Burton, Margie, et al. Counting Stars. 2011. (Early Connections Ser.). (J). (978-1-61672-519-8(2)) Benchmark Education Co.

Carlson-Berne, Emma. Totally Wacky Facts about Planets & Stars. 2015. (Mind Benders Ser.). (ENG., Illus.). 112p. (J). (gr. 3-6). lib. bdg. 23.99 (978-1-4914-6523-3(9), 129022, Capstone Pr.) Capstone.

Channing, Margot. Stars & Planets. 2014. (Closer Look At... Ser.). (Illus.). 32p. (gr. 3-6). 31.35 (978-1-905087-08-2(X), 1374553) Book Hse. GBR. Dist: Black Rabbit Bks.

Crabtree Editors & Wimbush, Jeff. The Stars. 2012. (Journey Through Space Ser.). (ENG.). 24p. (J). (gr. 3-6). lib. bdg. (978-0-7787-5308-7(5)) Crabtree Publishing Co.

Cram101 Textbook Reviews Staff. Outlines & Highlights for in Quest of the Stars & Galaxies by Theo Koupelis, Isbn: 9780763766306. 2014. (ENG.). 214p. (C). pap. 30.95 (978-1-61812-145-5(6)) Cram101 Inc.

Crane, Cody. The Stars (Rookie Read-About Science: the Universe) 2018. (Rookie Read-About Science Ser.). (ENG.). 32p. (J). (gr. 1-2). pap. 5.95 (978-0-531-22981-1(5), Children's Pr.) Scholastic Library Publishing.

—The Sun. 2018. (Getting to Know the World's Greatest Composers Ser.). (J). lib. bdg. 116.00 (978-0-531-22982-8(3), Children's Pr.) Scholastic Library Publishing.

Daynes, Katie. Lift-The-Flap Very First Questions & Answers What Are Stars. 2018. (Lift-The-Flap Very First Questions & Answers Ser.). (ENG.). 12p. (J). 12.99 (978-0-7945-4211-5(5), Usborne) EDC Publishing.

Demuth, Patricia Brennan. The Sun: Our Amazing Star. 2016. (Illus.). 32p. (J). (gr. -1-1). pap. 4.99 (978-0-448-48828-8(0), Grosset & Dunlap) Penguin Young Readers Group.

Deutsch, Stacia & Cohon, Rhody. Life of a Star: Set Of 6. 2010. (Navigators Ser.). (J). pap. 50.00 net. (978-1-4108-6241-9(0)) Benchmark Education Co.

—Life of a Star: Text Pairs. 2008. (Bridges/Navigators Ser.). (J). (gr. 6). 89.00 (978-1-4108-8444-2(9)) Benchmark Education Co.

Dickmann, Nancy. Exploring Beyond the Solar System, 1 vol. 2015. (Spectacular Space Science Ser.). (ENG., Illus.). 48p. (J). (gr. 5-6). 33.47 (978-1-4994-3641-9(6), c661c4b7-cd32-45d1-9413-c0fe5359a666, Rosen Central) Rosen Publishing Group, Inc., The.

—Galaxies & Stars, 1 vol. 2018. (Space Facts & Figures Ser.). (ENG., Illus.). 32p. (J). (gr. 2-3). 28.93 (978-1-5081-9514-6(5), d05058bb-c1c9-47ec-a14c-db25f4b66051, Windmill Bks.) Rosen Publishing Group, Inc., The.

Dilkes, D. H. I See Stars, 1 vol. 2010. (All about Shapes Ser.). (ENG., Illus.). 24p. (gr. -1-1). lib. bdg. 25.27 (978-0-7660-3803-5(3), 82b68912-a7d0-43ac-acbd-70969cf17239, Enslow Publishing) Enslow Publishing, LLC.

DK. DK Readers L2: Stars & Galaxies: Discover the Secrets of the Stars! 2017. (DK Readers Level 2 Ser.). (ENG., Illus.). 48p. (J). (gr. k-2). pap. 4.99 (978-1-4654-5863-6(8), DK Children) Dorling Kindersley Publishing, Inc.

Drimmer, Stephanie Warren. National Geographic Readers: Night Sky. 2017. (Readers Ser.). (Illus.). 32p. (J). (gr. 1-3). pap. 4.99 (978-1-4263-2815-2(X), National Geographic Kids) Disney Publishing Worldwide.

Duffey, Gary. Windows. 2012. 16p. pap. 7.95 (978-1-4582-0512-4(6), Abbott Pr.) Author Solutions, LLC.

Evert, Laura. Planets, Moons, & Stars. Garrow, Linda, illus. 2003. (Take along Guides). (ENG.). 48p. (J). (gr. 2-5). pap. 7.95 (978-1-55971-842-4(0)) Cooper Square Publishing Llc.

Faulkner, Nicholas & Gregersen, Erik. Stars & Nebulae, 1 vol. 2018. (Universe & Our Place in It Ser.). (ENG., Illus.). 128p. (YA). (gr. 10-10). pap. 20.95 (978-1-5081-0601-2(0), 5034aebf-f346-43d0-b46f-afbc9173fc6d, Britannica Educational Publishing) Rosen Publishing Group, Inc., The.

Finton, Nancy. Explore the Solar System! 2010. (Illus.). 29p. (J). (978-0-545-28884-2(3)) Scholastic, Inc.

Galat, Joan Marie. Black Holes & Supernovas. 2011. (Solar System & Beyond Ser.). (ENG.). 32p. (J). (gr. 3-4). pap. 48.60 (978-1-4296-7226-9(9), 16780); pap. 8.10 (978-1-4296-7225-2(0), 116834) Capstone. (Capstone Pr.).

Gardner, Robert & Conklin, Joshua. A Kid's Book of Experiments with Stars, 1 vol. 2015. (Surprising Science Experiments Ser.). (ENG.). 48p. (gr. 4-4). pap. 12.70 (978-0-7660-7268-8(1), 27bf4666-4815-4fc3-9024-fbc67c215637) Enslow Publishing, LLC.

Gendell, Megan & O'Dea, Tierney. Shoot for the Stars: Everything You Wanted to Know about Astronomy, Stars, & Constellations. 2008. (Illus.). 32p. (J). (978-0-545-04458-5(8)) Scholastic, Inc.

George, Michael. Stars: Beacons in the Sky. 2003. (LifeViews Ser.). (Illus.). 32p. (J). lib. bdg. (978-1-58341-250-3(6), Creative Education) Creative Co., The.

Gifford, Clive. Stars, Galaxies, & the Milky Way. 2015. (Watch This Space! Ser.). (ENG., Illus.). 32p. (J). (gr. 4-5). lib. bdg. (978-0-7787-2022-5(5)) Crabtree Publishing Co.

Gillingham, Sara. Seeing Stars: A Complete Guide to the 88 Constellations. 2018. (ENG., Illus.). 216p. 24.95 (978-0-7148-7722-8(0)) Phaidon Pr., Inc.

—Seeing Stars: A Complete Guide to the 88 Constellations. 2018. (ENG., Illus.). 216p. (gr. 2-5). 24.95 (978-0-7148-7772-3(7)) Phaidon Pr., Inc.

Goldsmith, Mike. Listopia: Space. 2016. (ENG., Illus.). 208p. (J). (gr. 2-5). pap. 9.99 (978-1-4998-0280-1(3)) Little Bee Books Inc.

Goldstein, Margaret. Stars. 2009. pap. 6.95 (978-0-8225-4759-4(7)) Lerner Publishing Group.

Goldstein, Margaret J. Mysteries of Stars. 2020. (Searchlight Books (tm) — Space Mysteries Ser.). (ENG., Illus.). 32p. (J). (gr. 3-5). 30.65 (978-1-5415-9738-9(9), b4ee4c2a-b714-451e-a622-cf98630f72b5, Lerner Pubns.) Lerner Publishing Group.

—Stars. 2003. (Our Universe Ser.). (ENG., Illus.). 32p. (gr. 2-4). lib. bdg. 22.60 (978-0-8225-4646-7(9)) Lerner Publishing Group.

Goldsworthy, Steve. Constellations. 2016. (Illus.). 32p. (J). (978-1-4896-5809-8(2), AV2 by Weigl) Weigl Pubs., Inc.

Graham, Ian. Galaxies & Stars. 2015. (Space Ser.). (ENG., Illus.). 24p. (J). (gr. 1-3). lib. bdg. 28.50 (978-1-62588-208-0(4), 17402) Black Rabbit Bks.

Graun, Ken. Our Constellations & Their Stars. 2004. (Twenty-First Century Astronomy Ser.: 3). (Illus.). 36p. (J). 15.95 (978-1-928771-09-8(2)) Ken Pr.

Griffin, Ingrid. The Story of the Great Bear, 1 vol. 2015. (Stories in the Stars Ser.). (ENG., Illus.). 24p. (J). (gr. 1-2). pap. 9.15 (978-1-4824-2665-6(X), 64f75325-a4ef-4a1b-8fad-7e066ca11e17) Stevens, Gareth Publishing LLLP.

Guillain, Charlotte. Stars, 1 vol. 2009. (Space Ser.). (ENG.). 24p. (gr. -1-1). 21.99 (978-1-4329-2748-6(5), Heinemann) Capstone.

Hansen, Grace. Stars. 2017. (Our Galaxy Ser.). (ENG., Illus.). 24p. (J). (gr. -1-2). lib. bdg. 32.79 (978-1-5321-0051-2(5), 25176, Abdo Kids) ABDO Publishing Co.

Hantula, Richard & Asimov, Isaac. The Life & Death of Stars, 1 vol. 2004. (Isaac Asimov's 21st Century Library of the Universe: near & Far Ser.). (ENG., Illus.). 32p. (gr. 3-5). lib. bdg. 28.67 (978-0-8368-3967-8(6), 84c0790f-daba-4370-9c94-546cea0547fa) Stevens, Gareth Publishing LLLP.

—A Stargazer's Guide, 1 vol. 2004. (Isaac Asimov's 21st Century Library of the Universe: Fact & Fantasy Ser.). (ENG., Illus.). 32p. (gr. 3-5). lib. bdg. 28.67 (978-0-8368-3953-1(6), f6d94989-05e6-4867-b024-1ac882f2e48c) Stevens, Gareth Publishing LLLP.

Harcourt School Publishers Staff. How the Sky Got Its Starr. 3rd ed. 2004. (Trophies Reading Program Ser.). (Illus.). (gr. k). pap. 11.50 (978-0-15-340895-3(2)) Harcourt Schl. Pubs.

Hirsch, Rebecca E. Stars & Galaxies in Action (an Augmented Reality Experience) 2020. (Space in Action: Augmented Reality (Alternator Books (r)) Ser.). (ENG., Illus.). 32p. (J). (gr. 3-6). 31.99 (978-1-5415-7879-1(1), 686a08b9-0661-4a79-8f0e-c7872e988b9d, Lerner Pubns.) Lerner Publishing Group.

How Are Stars Born? 2013. (Space Mysteries Ser.). 32p. (J). (gr. 2-5). pap. 63.00 (978-1-4339-9220-9(5)) Stevens, Gareth Publishing LLLP.

Hudd, Emily. How Long Do Stars Last? 2019. (How Long Does It Take? Ser.). (ENG., Illus.). 32p. (J). (gr. 3-6). pap. 7.95 (978-1-5435-7541-5(2), 141073); lib. bdg. 29.99 (978-1-5435-7296-4(0), 140613) Capstone.

Hutmacher, Kimberly. The Night Sky. 2012. (My Science Library). (ENG.). 24p. (gr. 3-4). pap. 8.95 (978-1-61810-225-6(7), 9781618102256) Rourke Educational Media.

Jacobson, Ryan. Constellations Activity Book, 1 vol. Nitzsche, Shane, illus. 2012. (ENG.). 64p. (J). (gr. k-5). pap. 6.95 (978-1-59193-325-0(0), Adventure Pubns.) AdventureKEEN.

Jefferis, David. Black Holes: And Other Bizarre Space Objects, 1 vol. 2006. (Science Frontiers Ser.). (ENG., Illus.). 32p. (J). (gr. 4-7). pap. (978-0-7787-2870-2(6), 1253434) Crabtree Publishing Co.

—The Stars: Glowing Spheres in the Sky. 2008. (Exploring our Solar System Ser.). (ENG., Illus.). 32p. (J). (gr. 3-8). pap. (978-0-7787-3743-8(8)) Crabtree Publishing Co.

Kelly, Miles. Stars & Galaxies. Kelly, Richard, ed. 2017. 48p. (J). pap. 9.95 (978-1-78209-648-1(5)) Miles Kelly Publishing, Ltd. GBR. Dist: Parkwest Pubns., Inc.

Kenney, Karen Latchana. The Science of Stars: Exploring Matter. 2015. (Science in Action Ser.). (ENG., Illus.). 32p. (J). (gr. 3-6). 32.79 (978-1-62403-965-2(0), 19427, Checkerboard Library) ABDO Publishing Co.

Keranen, Rachel. The Composition of the Universe: the Evolution of Stars & Galaxies, 1 vol. 2016. (Space Systems Ser.). (ENG., Illus.). 112p. (J). (gr. 8-8). 44.50 (978-1-5026-2285-3(8), 229b7660-80d5-4658-892a-6813bc61ff8f) Cavendish Square Publishing LLC.

Kim, Flora. Constellations. 2009. (True Book(tm), A — Space Ser.). (ENG.). 48p. (J). (gr. 2-5). 31.00 (978-0-531-16895-0(6)) Scholastic Library Publishing.

Kimmelman, Leslie. Star Pictures. 2004. (ENG., Illus.). 8p. (J). (gr. k-k). pap. 7.56 (978-0-7652-5134-3(5), Celebration Pr.) Savvas Learning Co.

Kissock, Heather. Stars. 2011. (J). (978-1-61690-601-6(4)); (ENG.). lib. bdg. 27.13 (978-1-61690-955-0(2)) Weigl Pubs., Inc.

Koupelis, Theo. In Quest of the Stars & Galaxies. rev. ed. 2010. (ENG.). 457p. (J). pap. 177.95 (978-0-7637-6630-6(5)) Jones & Bartlett Learning, LLC.

Kubuitsile, Lauri. Stars Yellow Band. 2016. (Cambridge Reading Adventures Ser.). (ENG., Illus.). 16p. pap. 7.95 (978-1-316-50315-7(1)) Cambridge Univ. Pr.

Kukla, Lauren. Stars. 2016. (Exploring Our Universe Ser.). (ENG., Illus.). 32p. (J). (gr. 3-6). lib. bdg. 32.79 (978-1-68078-408-4(0), 23675, Checkerboard Library) ABDO Publishing Co.

Labrecque, Ellen. The Sun & Stars. 2019. (Our Place in the Universe Ser.). (ENG., Illus.). 24p. (J). (gr. 1-3). 25.99 (978-1-9771-0847-0(4), 140465, Pebble) Capstone.

Lacey, Saskia. Art & Culture: The Stories of Constellations: Shapes (Grade 3) 2017. (Mathematics in the Real World Ser.). (ENG., Illus.). 32p. (J). (gr. 3-4). pap. 11.99 (978-1-4807-5812-4(4)) Teacher Created Materials, Inc.

Latta, Sara L. Exploring Constellations. 2017. (Discover the Night Sky Ser.). (ENG., Illus.). 32p. (J). (gr. 3-6). pap. 7.95 (978-1-5157-8739-6(7), 136315); lib. bdg. 27.99 (978-1-5157-8735-8(4), 136311) Capstone. (Capstone Pr.).

Layton, Neal. The Story of Stars: From the Stars, Solar Systems & Galaxies to Beyond. 2013. (Illus.). 19p. (J). (978-1-4351-5110-9(0)) Barnes & Noble, Inc.

Lois, Lowry. Number the Stars. 2004. 144p. (J). (gr. 5-9). pap. 29.00 incl. audio (978-1-4000-8637-5(X), Listening Library) Random Hse. Audio Publishing Group.

Low, Chen-Chen-Chen. Lizzie May the Immortal. 2008. (ENG.). 70p. pap. 29.99 (978-1-4092-4579-7(9)) Lulu Pr., Inc.

Lowry, Lois. Number the Stars. l.t. ed. 2019. (ENG.). 282p. (J). (gr. 5-7). pap. 12.99 (978-1-4328-6393-7(2), Large Print Pr.) Thorndike Pr.

Mack, Gail. The Stars, 1 vol. 2010. (Space! Ser.). (ENG.). 64p. (gr. 5-5). lib. bdg. 35.50 (978-0-7614-4250-9(2), ad10bcef-0904-4021-bccd-059791a73db8) Cavendish Square Publishing LLC.

Martin, Justin McCory. Stars. 2010. (Illus.). 16p. (J). (978-0-545-13736-2(5)) Scholastic, Inc.

Massey Steve. Space Stars & Planets. 2009. (Young Reed Ser.). 1p. (J). 14.95 (978-1-921073-06-9(3)) New Holland Pubs. Pty, Ltd. AUS. Dist: Tuttle Publishing.

Miller, Ron. Stars & Galaxies. 2006. (Worlds Beyond Ser.). (Illus.). 96p. (J). (gr. 5-9). 27.93 (978-0-7613-3466-8(1), Twenty-First Century Bks.) Lerner Publishing Group.

Mistral, Gabriela. Ronda de Astros. 3rd ed. (SPA., Illus.). 128p. (YA). (gr. 5). 9.95 (978-84-239-9019-1(2), EC5264) Espasa Calpe, S.A. ESP. Dist: Lectorum Pubns., Inc., Libros Sin Fronteras.

Mitchell, Melanie S. Stars. 2004. (First Step Nonfiction). (ENG., Illus.). 24p. (gr. k-2). lib. bdg. 23.93 (978-0-8225-5138-6(1)) Lerner Publishing Group.

—The Stars. 2003. (First Step Nonfiction Ser.). (Illus.). 22p. (J). pap. 5.95 (978-0-8225-3592-8(0), Lerner Pubns.) Lerner Publishing Group.

Mitton, Jacqueline. Once upon a Starry Night: A Book of Constellations. (ENG., Illus.). 32p. (J). (gr. 1-3). 2009. pap. 10.99 (978-1-4263-0391-3(2), National Geographic Kids) 2004. 16.95 (978-0-7922-6332-6(4), National Geographic Children's Bks.) Disney Publishing Worldwide.

—Zoo in the Sky: A Book of Animal Constellations. 2006. (ENG., Illus.). 32p. (J). (gr. 1-3). pap. 7.95 (978-0-7922-5935-0(1), National Geographic Kids) Disney Publishing Worldwide.

Mitton, Jacqueline & Balit, Christina. Zoo in the Sky: A Book of Animal Constellations. 2008. (ENG., Illus.). 32p. (gr. 1-4).

S

pap. 22.44 (978-0-7112-1319-7(4)) National Geographic Society.

Moon, Walt K. Let's Explore the Stars. 2017. (Bumba Books (r) — a First Look at Space Ser.). (ENG., Illus.). 24p. (J). (gr. -1-1). 26.65 (978-1-5124-3347-0(0), d129007a-efd0-49c7-8594-2c4195930935, Lerner Pubns.) Lerner Publishing Group.

Moore, David. National Geographic Science 1-2 (Earth Science: Sun, Moon, & Stars): Explore on Your Own: Stories in the Stars. 2009. 12p. (C). pap. 8.95 (978-0-7362-5593-6(1)) National Geographic School Publishing, Inc.

Moore, Patrick. First Book of Stars. 2010. (ENG., Illus.). 96p. pap. 22.95 (978-1-84868-291-7(3)) Amberley Publishing GBR. Dist: Independent Pubs. Group.

Nadeau, Isaac. Learning about the Movement of the Sun & Other Stars with Graphic Organizers, 1 vol. (Graphic Organizers in Science & Social Studies). (ENG., Illus.). 24p. (gr. 4-5). 2005. pap. 8.25 (978-1-4042-5040-6(9), 9fcb7273-1f54-4d12-b835-cf44a401dfc6) 2004. (J). 25.27 (978-1-4042-2805-4(5), 2f750e05-dfdc-4cf6-b853-f1c2f6caf1ff) Rosen Publishing Group, Inc., The. (PowerKids Pr.).

National Geographic Learning. Language, Literacy & Vocabulary - Reading Expeditions (Earth Science): Stars. 2007. (ENG., Illus.). 36p. (J). pap. 20.95 (978-0-7922-5433-1(3)) CENGAGE Learning.

—Reading Expeditions (Science: Earth Science): Stars & Galaxies. 2007. (ENG., Illus.). 32p. (J). pap. 18.95 (978-0-7922-4574-2(1)) CENGAGE Learning.

Negus, James. Supernovas Explained, 1 vol. 2018. (Mysteries of Space Ser.). (ENG.). 80p. (gr. 7-7). 38.93 (978-1-9785-0458-5(6), eb4ffc53-63c2-4889-9cbf-d8119157e5e4) Enslow Publishing, LLC.

Nicolson, Cynthia. Discover the Stars. Slavin, Bill, illus. 2006. 32p. (J). lib. bdg. 15.38 (978-1-4242-1196-8(4)) Fitzgerald Bks.

Orr, Tamra. I Spy in the Sky the Stars. 2011. (Randy's Corner Ser.). (Illus.). 32p. (J). (gr. k-3). lib. bdg. 25.70 (978-1-58415-975-9(8)) Mitchell Lane Pubs.

Owen, Ruth. Supernovas, 1 vol. 2012. (Explore Outer Space Ser.). (ENG., Illus.). 32p. (J). (gr. 2-3). pap. 11.00 (978-1-4488-8119-2(6), 2aaf97e2-0cb1-476c-864f-ce3c89da6907); lib. bdg. 29.93 (978-1-4488-8078-2(5), 0e9d9f94-1a84-450d-ba0f-8826a85a9bfc) Rosen Publishing Group, Inc., The. (Windmill Bks.).

Parker, Steve. Beyond the Solar System: From Red Giants to Black Holes, 1 vol. 2007. (Earth & Space Ser.). (ENG., Illus.). 48p. (YA). (gr. 6-6). lib. bdg. 34.47 (978-1-4042-3739-1(9), d6e8bf1b-23e2-473d-a945-c78caa20dd00) Rosen Publishing Group, Inc., The.

Pasachoff, Jay M. Peterson First Guide to Astronomy, Second Edition. 2nd ed. 2014. (Peterson First Guide Ser.). (ENG., Illus.). 128p. pap. 7.95 (978-0-544-16562-5(4), 1551341, Mariner Bks.) HarperCollins Pubs.

Peddicord, Jane Anne. Night Wonders. Peddicord, Jane Anne, illus. 2005. (Illus.). 32p. (J). (gr. 1-4). pap. 7.95 (978-1-57091-878-0(3)) Charlesbridge Publishing, Inc.

Peters, Elisa. Stars, 1 vol. 2012. (PowerKids Readers: the Universe Ser.). (ENG., Illus.). 24p. (J). (gr. k-k). pap. 9.25 (978-1-4488-7534-4(X), e4345bae-d851-4069-9331-dffcdd2f1a4e); lib. bdg. 26.27 (978-1-4488-7388-3(6), 3416e43b-5549-4950-8b44-072009a6e86c) Rosen Publishing Group, Inc., The. (PowerKids Pr.).

—Stars: Las Estrellas, 1 vol. 2012. (PowerKids Readers: el Universo / the Universe Ser.). (SPA & ENG., Illus.). 24p. (J). (gr. k-k). lib. bdg. 26.27 (978-1-4488-7824-6(1), a266f214-0384-457b-8773-439e10f7da5b, PowerKids Pr.) Rosen Publishing Group, Inc., The.

Peters, Stephanie True. Andromeda. 2009. (Library of Constellations Ser.). 24p. (gr. 3-4). 45.00 (978-1-60853-573-6(8), PowerKids Pr.) Rosen Publishing Group, Inc., The.

—Gemini. 2009. (Library of Constellations Ser.). 24p. (gr. 3-4). 45.00 (978-1-60853-574-3(6), PowerKids Pr.) Rosen Publishing Group, Inc., The.

—The Little Dipper. 2009. (Library of Constellations Ser.). 24p. (gr. 3-4). 45.00 (978-1-60853-577-4(0), PowerKids Pr.) Rosen Publishing Group, Inc., The.

Prokos, Anna. Star Light, Star Bright: Exploring Our Solar System. Clegg, Dave, illus. 2017. (Imagine That! Ser.). (ENG.). 32p. (J). (gr. 2-4). E-Book 39.99 (978-1-63440-164-7(6)) Red Chair Pr.

Rajczak Nelson, Kristen. 20 Fun Facts about Stars, 1 vol. 2014. (Fun Fact File: Space! Ser.). (ENG., Illus.). 32p. (J). (gr. 2-3). 27.93 (978-1-4824-1013-6(3), 388b9d8c-6b96-42ca-a24a-eaa0fe524c99); pap. 11.50 (978-1-4824-1014-3(1), 14110a1e-bb7c-43e3-8d90-36aaef92852e) Stevens, Gareth Publishing LLLP.

Rao, Joe. Looking Up! The Science of Stargazing (Ready-To-Read Level 3) Borgions, Mark, illus. 2017. (Science of Fun Stuff Ser.). (ENG.). 48p. (J). (gr. 1-3). pap. 4.99 (978-1-4814-7917-2(2), Simon Spotlight) Simon Spotlight.

Reilly, Carmel. The Stars, 1 vol. 2012. (Sky Watching Ser.). (ENG.). 32p. (gr. 5-5). 31.21 (978-1-60870-583-2(8), 465f8d09-78f1-455c-b275-2401af38eccd) Cavendish Square Publishing LLC.

Roesser, Blanche. The Story of Pegasus, 1 vol. 2015. (Stories in the Stars Ser.). (ENG., Illus.). 24p. (J). (gr. 1-2). pap. 9.15 (978-1-4824-2677-9(3), 36f45a46-54b1-40c7-b1ab-c9b093944a6e) Stevens, Gareth Publishing LLLP.

—The Story of Perseus, 1 vol. 2015. (Stories in the Stars Ser.). (ENG., Illus.). 24p. (J). (gr. 1-2). 24.27 (978-1-4824-2683-0(8), c474c835-92b6-4301-a844-88ac2424fce7) Stevens, Gareth Publishing LLLP.

Rogers, Amy B. Orion, 1 vol. 2015. (Constellation Collection). (ENG., Illus.). 24p. (J). (gr. 3-3). 25.27 (978-1-4994-0990-1(7), 8d7c40a3-1a96-436e-80d1-3138087894f9, PowerKids Pr.) Rosen Publishing Group, Inc., The.

Romero, Libby. Discover Stars. 2006. (J). pap. (978-1-4108-6509-0(6)) Benchmark Education Co.

—Stars. 2006. (J). pap. (978-1-4108-6506-9(1)) Benchmark Education Co.

Rose, Simon. Andromeda: The Myth & Science. 2015. (Illus.). 24p. (J). (978-1-5105-0265-9(3)) SmartBook Media, Inc.

—Andromeda: The Myth & Science. 2015. (J). (978-1-4896-3316-3(2)) Weigl Pubs., Inc.

—Cygnus the Swan: The Myth & Science. 2015. (Illus.). 24p. (J). pap. (978-1-5105-0266-6(1)) SmartBook Media, Inc.

—Cygnus the Swan: The Myth & Science. 2015. (J). (978-1-4896-3320-0(0)) Weigl Pubs., Inc.

—Hercules: The Myth & Science. 2015. (Illus.). 24p. (J). pap. (978-1-5105-0267-3(X)) SmartBook Media, Inc.

—Hercules: The Myth & Science. 2015. (J). (978-1-4896-3324-8(3)) Weigl Pubs., Inc.

—Orion: The Myth & Science. 2015. (Illus.). 24p. (J). pap. (978-1-5105-0268-0(8)) SmartBook Media, Inc.

—Orion: The Myth & Science. 2015. (J). (978-1-4896-3328-6(6)) Weigl Pubs., Inc.

—Pegasus: The Myth & Science. 2015. (J). (978-1-4896-3332-3(4)) Weigl Pubs., Inc.

Roza, Greg. How Are Stars Born?, 1 vol. 2013. (Space Mysteries Ser.). (ENG.). 32p. (J). (gr. 2-3). 29.27 (978-1-4339-9218-6(3), 7abe6a25-bd77-4d0f-99bd-67234eaf0ceb); pap. 11.50 (978-1-4339-9219-3(1), 26acb813-958f-4511-9ff0-2f6dba4fa1a4) Stevens, Gareth Publishing LLLP.

Rustad, Martha E. H. Constellations. 2012. (Exploring Space Ser.). (ENG.). 24p. (gr. k-1). pap. 41.70 (978-1-4296-8327-2(9), Capstone Pr.) Capstone.

—Las Estrellas. 2012. (En el Espacio/Out in Space Ser.).Tr. of The Stars. (MUL.). 24p. (gr. k-1). pap. 35.70 (978-1-4296-8551-1(4)) Capstone.

—Las Estrellas/the Stars. 2010. (En el Espacio/Out in Space Ser.). (MUL.). 24p. (J). (gr. -1-2). lib. bdg. 24.65 (978-1-4296-5342-8(6), 113768) Capstone.

—The Milky Way. 2012. (Exploring Space Ser.). (ENG.). 24p. (gr. k-1). pap. 41.70 (978-1-4296-8328-9(7), Capstone Pr.) Capstone.

—The Stars: Revised Edition. rev. ed. 2008. (Out in Space Ser.). (ENG., Illus.). 24p. (J). (gr. -1-2). pap. 6.29 (978-1-4296-2816-7(2), 95333) Capstone.

—The Stars [Scholastic]. 2009. (Out in Space Ser.). 24p. (gr. k-1). pap. 2.50 (978-1-4296-4051-0(0), Pebble) Capstone.

Ryback, Carol. The Stars, 1 vol. 2005. (In the Sky Ser.). (ENG., Illus.). 24p. (gr. 2-4). pap. 9.15 (978-0-8368-6350-5(X), 8c2f3164-cc1c-42f0-8c66-1712671fe51e); lib. bdg. 24.67 (978-0-8368-6345-1(3), f4b84a01-9413-4201-ba4e-9c02ccdd6dbd) Stevens, Gareth Publishing LLLP. (Weekly Reader Leveled Readers).

—The Sun, 1 vol. 2005. (In the Sky Ser.). (ENG., Illus.). 24p. (gr. 2-4). pap. 9.15 (978-0-8368-6351-2(8), a75fe222-451e-44e0-8b63-125fbe31525d); lib. bdg. 24.67 (978-0-8368-6346-8(1), 74f75f3b-e0cb-4e98-b88f-31d3323d973e) Stevens, Gareth Publishing LLLP. (Weekly Reader Leveled Readers).

Shadick, Stan. Skywatcher's Companion: Constellations & Their Mythology, 1 vol. 2007. (ENG., Illus.). 48p. (J). (gr. 4-7). pap. 9.95 (978-1-894974-36-3(0)) Heritage Hse. CAN. Dist: Orca Bk. Pubs. USA.

Sian revision Planets&stars. 2004. (J). (978-1-59242-057-5(5)) Delta Education, LLC.

Simon, Seymour. Stars. 2006. (ENG., Illus.). 32p. (J). (gr. k-4). pap. 7.99 (978-0-06-089001-8(0), HarperCollins) HarperCollins Pubs.

—Stars. 2006. (Illus.). 31p. (gr. k-4). 17.00 (978-0-7569-6747-5(3)) Perfection Learning Corp.

—Stars & Constellations. 2007. (Illus.). 24p. (J). (978-0-545-00403-9(9)) Scholastic, Inc.

Sipe, Nicole. Mapping the Milky Way (Grade 3) rev. ed. 2018. (Smithsonian: Informational Text Ser.). (ENG., Illus.). 32p. (J). (gr. 3-4). pap. 11.99 (978-1-4938-6689-2(3)) Teacher Created Materials, Inc.

Sipe, Roger. Guided by Stars (Grade 5) rev. ed. 2018. (Smithsonian: Informational Text Ser.). (ENG., Illus.). 32p. (gr. 4-8). pap. 11.99 (978-1-4938-6718-9(0)) Teacher Created Materials, Inc.

Sohn, Emily. Sun, Moon, & Stars. 2019. (IScience Ser.). (ENG., Illus.). 32p. (J). (gr. 3-4). pap. 13.26 (978-1-68404-386-6(7)) Norwood Hse. Pr.

Sparrow, Giles. The Stars, 1 vol. 2017. (Space Explorers Ser.). (ENG.). 32p. (gr. 2-2). 26.93 (978-0-7660-9265-5(8), c320606e-bb47-4599-9696-fc3c5b1e8e0c) Enslow Publishing, LLC.

—Stars & Galaxies, 1 vol. 2006. (Secrets of the Universe Ser.). (ENG., Illus.). 48p. (gr. 6-8). lib. bdg. 33.67 (978-0-8368-7280-4(0), cd6fe3e2-97af-4e68-9b6b-24b2c57d1773, Gareth Stevens Secondary Library) Stevens, Gareth Publishing LLLP.

—The Sun & Stars. 2011. (Exploring Space: Space Travel Guides). 32p. (gr. 3-6). lib. bdg. 31.35 (978-1-59920-666-0(8)) Black Rabbit Bks.

Sparrow, Giles, et al. Stars & Galaxies, 1 vol. 2015. (Discoveries in Space Science Ser.). (ENG., Illus.). 80p. (YA). (gr. 9-9). lib. bdg. 37.36 (978-1-5026-1020-1(5), 05422254-c5eb-460c-af4c-0c93f926f951) Cavendish Square Publishing LLC.

Stegenga, Wil. Spectacular Star Designs. 2009. (Dover Design Coloring Bks.). (ENG., Illus.). 32p. (gr. 3-5). pap. 3.99 (978-0-486-46993-5(X)) Dover Pubns., Inc.

Stoltman, Joan. What Are Stars Made Of?, 1 vol. 2018. (Space Mysteries Ser.). (ENG.). 32p. (gr. 2-3). 29.27 (978-1-5382-1955-3(7), 29d7a17e-b4aa-45ab-91e1-31c2398a0250) Stevens, Gareth Publishing LLLP.

Stories in the Stars. 2015. (Stories in the Stars Ser.). (ENG.). 24p. (J). (gr. 1-2). pap., pap., pap. 48.90 (978-1-4824-3504-7(7)); pap., pap., pap. 293.40 (978-1-4824-3495-8(4)); lib. bdg. 145.62 (978-1-4824-2542-0(4), 5b88190d-1260-419c-b642-350e6b30b7d6) Stevens, Gareth Publishing LLLP.

The Sun & Other Stars Instructional Guide. 2009. (Grade 8: Science Exit Project Kits Ser.). spiral bd. (978-1-4042-4026-1(8), Rosen Classroom) Rosen Publishing Group, Inc., The.

Terp, Gail. El Sol y Otras Estrellas. 2018. (Descubrimiento Del Espacio Profundo Ser.). (SPA.). 32p. (J). (gr. 4-6). lib. bdg. (978-1-68072-974-0(8), 12459, Bolt) Black Rabbit Bks.

—The Sun & Other Stars. 2018. (Deep Space Discovery Ser.). (ENG.). 32p. (gr. 2-7). 9.95 (978-1-68072-718-0(4)); (J). (gr. 4-6). pap. 9.99 (978-1-64466-271-7(X), 12337); (Illus.). (J). (gr. 4-6). lib. bdg. (978-1-68072-424-0(X), 12336) Black Rabbit Bks. (Bolt).

Than, Ker. Stars (a True Book: Space) 2010. (True Book (Relaunch) Ser.). (ENG., Illus.). 48p. (J). (gr. 3-5). pap. 6.95 (978-0-531-22806-7(1), Children's Pr.) Scholastic Library Publishing.

Thomson, Sarah L. Extreme Stars! Q&A. 2006. (ENG., Illus.). 48p. (J). (gr. k-4). pap. 6.99 (978-0-06-089933-2(6), Collins) HarperCollins Pubs.

Tomecek, Steve. Jump into Science: Stars. 2006. (Jump into Science Ser.). (Illus.). 32p. (J). (gr. -1-k). per. 6.95 (978-0-7922-5581-9(X), National Geographic Kids) Disney Publishing Worldwide.

—Stars. Guida, Liisa C., illus. 2003. (Jump into Science Ser.). (J). 16.95 (978-0-7922-8203-7(5)) CENGAGE Learning.

Turnbull, Stephanie. Sun, Moon & Stars. Chen, Kuo Kang & Mayer, Uwe, illus. 2006. (Beginners Nature: Level 2 Ser.). 32p. (J). (gr. 1-3). 4.99 (978-0-7945-1399-3(9), Usborne) EDC Publishing.

Vaughan, Jenny. Super Stars: Band 15/Emerald (Collins Big Cat) 2016. (Collins Big Cat Ser.). (ENG.). 48p. (J). (gr. 3-4). pap. 10.99 (978-0-00-816393-8(6)) HarperCollins Pubs. Ltd. GBR. Dist: Independent Pubs. Group.

Vigil, Angel. Papi, How Many Stars Are in the Sky? Ahmad, Aadil & James, Martin, illus. 2010. (J). (978-1-60617-151-6(8)) Teaching Strategies, LLC.

Vogt, Gregory. Stars. 2010. (Early Bird Astronomy Ser.). (ENG.). 48p. (gr. 2-5). lib. bdg. 26.60 (978-0-7613-3873-4(X)) Lerner Publishing Group.

What Is a Sun?, 1 vol. 2014. (Let's Find Out! Space Science Ser.). (ENG.). 32p. (J). (gr. 2-3). 26.06 (978-1-62275-461-8(1), a7b0de08-7633-4361-bce9-a70c6d108003) Rosen Publishing Group, Inc., The.

Whiting, Jim. Stars. 2012. (Mysteries of the Universe Ser.). (ENG., Illus.). 48p. (J). (gr. 5-9). 23.95 (978-1-60818-193-3(6), 21925, Creative Education) Creative Co., The.

Willis, John & Gillespie, Katie. Stars. 2018. (Illus.). 24p. (J). (978-1-4896-5698-8(7), AV2 by Weigl) Weigl Pubs., Inc.

Wimbush, Jeff. The Stars, 1 vol. 2012. (ENG.). 24p. (J). pap. (978-0-7787-5313-1(1)) Crabtree Publishing Co.

World Book, Inc. Staff, contrib. by. Stars — Birth & Death. 2010. (Illus.). 64p. (J). (978-0-7166-9548-6(0)) World Bk., Inc.

—Stars — the Inside Story. 2010. (Illus.). 64p. (J). (978-0-7166-9547-9(2)) World Bk., Inc.

—The Sun & Other Stars. (J). 2010. (Illus.). 64p. (978-0-7166-9539-4(1)) 2006. 63p. (978-0-7166-9501-1(4)) 2nd ed. 2006. (Illus.). 64p. (978-0-7166-9521-9(9)) World Bk., Inc.

Wright, Holly. Star. 2004. (J). pap. 3.75 (978-0-9743690-6-8(3)) Britt Allcroft Productions.

STARS, FALLING

see Meteors

STARS—FICTION

Addis, Tom. A Gift of Light. 2008. (ENG.). 42p. per. 21.99 (978-1-4257-7073-0(8)) Xlibris Corp.

Ayasta, Ayasta. Star. 2007. 117p. 34.95 (978-1-4303-1520-9(2)) Lulu Pr., Inc.

Batson, Susann. Sparkie: A Star Afraid of the Dark. Batson, Susann, illus. 2008. (Illus.). 16p. pap. 7.95 (978-1-935137-01-6(8)) Guardian Angel Publishing, Inc.

Bauer, Marion Dane. The Stuff of Stars. Holmes, Ekua, illus. 2018. (ENG.). 40p. (J). (gr. -1-3). 18.99 (978-0-7636-7883-8(X)) Candlewick Pr.

Bauman, Boomer. One Star at a Time. 2009. 68p. pap. 20.50 (978-1-60860-571-2(X), Eloquent Bks.) Strategic Book Publishing & Rights Agency (SBPRA).

Baumgart, Klaus. Laura's Secret. Waite, Judy, tr. from GER. 2003. (Illus.). 32p. (J). (gr. -1-2). tchr. ed. 16.95 (978-1-58925-031-4(1)) Tiger Tales.

Baxter, Nicola. Josie the Giraffe & the Starry Night. Fox, Lisa, illus. 2016. (ENG.). 16p. (J). (gr. -1-12). 7.99 (978-0-85723-526-8(5), Armadillo) Anness Publishing GBR. Dist: National Bk. Network.

—The Mermaid & the Star. Rigby, Deborah, illus. 2025. 14p. (J). bds. (978-1-84322-907-0(2), Armadillo) Anness Publishing.

Beavin, John. The Parable of the Stars. 2009. 24p. pap. 11.50 (978-1-60693-368-8(X), Strategic Bk. Publishing) Strategic Book Publishing & Rights Agency (SBPRA).

Benjamin, Sigalit. Garland of Stars. 2009. 26p. pap. 14.50 (978-1-60860-345-9(8), Eloquent Bks.) Strategic Book Publishing & Rights Agency (SBPRA).

Bennett, Deborah. The Christmas Star. 2013. 24p. pap. 24.95 (978-1-63000-934-2(2)) America Star Bks.

Bickford-Smith, Coralie. The Fox & the Star. 2015. (ENG., Illus.). 64p. 20.00 (978-0-14-310867-2(0), Penguin Bks.) Penguin Publishing Group.

Bishop, Charlie. The Lucky Purple Star. 2009. (ENG.). 26p. pap. 14.99 (978-1-4415-2482-9(7)) Xlibris Corp.

Bobbie, Gramma. The Bright Stars. 2009. 20p. pap. 11.49 (978-1-4490-3474-0(8)) AuthorHouse.

Bowman, Crystal. A Star for Jesus, 1 vol. Gevry, Claudine, illus. 2014. (ENG.). 14p. (J). bds. 6.99 (978-0-310-73826-8(1)) Zonderkidz.

Brown, Carl & Brown, Kay. The Little Star. 2006. 123p. (J). pap. 15.99 (978-1-4120-9079-7(2)) Trafford Publishing.

Brownlie, Marion. Star Is Happy. 2013. 36p. pap. (978-0-9875551-4-4(6)) Aurora House.

Burris, Shana Renee. Bailey the Bear: Sees Stars Everywhere! 2012. (ENG.). 31p. (J). pap. 12.95 (978-1-4327-9011-0(0)) Outskirts Pr., Inc.

Cannistra, Meg. The Trouble with Shooting Stars. 2019. (ENG., Illus.). 336p. (J). (gr. 3-7). 17.99 (978-1-5344-2896-6(8), Simon & Schuster Bks. For Young Readers) Simon & Schuster Bks. For Young Readers.

Cara al Cielo Vol.3: Six-Pack. (Saludos Ser.: Vol. 3). (SPA.). (gr. 2-3). 31.00 (978-0-7635-9547-0(0)) Rigby Education.

Carrie C Yakola. Lucy's Shooting Star. 2009. 32p. pap. 15.99 (978-1-4343-5276-7(5)) AuthorHouse.

Cherobin. Zoomy Boomy & the Moon: Zoomy & the Moon Learn the Strength of Love. 2009. 24p. pap. 14.99 (978-1-4490-2069-9(0)) AuthorHouse.

Cherobin & Cherobin. Zoomy Boomy Lights the Night: Zoomy Conquers Shyness. 2009. 24p. pap. 14.49 (978-1-4490-2068-2(2)) AuthorHouse.

Clark, Brenda. Spiro Goes West: More Adventures of Spiro the Shooting Star. 2008. 57p. pap. 16.95 (978-1-60474-770-6(6)) America Star Bks.

Clontz, Jay F. The Tiny Star. 2004. 39p. pap. 16.95 (978-1-4137-2339-7(X)) America Star Bks.

Coats, Vivian. His Star. 2009. (ENG.). 24p. pap. 11.49 (978-1-4490-3885-4(9)) AuthorHouse.

cordone-warner, debra. Starzzee & A Day of Play. 2010. 40p. pap. 18.99 (978-0-557-54780-7(6)) Lulu Pr., Inc.

Côté, Yvonne. Bago the Adventurer: A Star's Help Book 2. 2012. 28p. (-18). pap. 19.99 (978-1-4772-8822-1(8)) AuthorHouse.

Cumming, Hannah. The Lost Stars. Cumming, Hannah, illus. 2011. (Child's Play Library). (Illus.). 32p. (J). (978-1-84643-416-7(5)) Child's Play International Ltd.

Dale, Jenny. Little Star. Reid, Mick, illus. 2003. 109p. (J). (978-0-439-54363-7(0)) Scholastic, Inc.

Dalmatian Press Staff. Star Light, Star Bright. 2008. (ENG.). 6p. bds. 4.95 (978-1-58117-723-7(2), Intervisual/Piggy Toes) Bendon, Inc.

Das, Christina. Swinging under the Stars. l.t. ed. 2005. (Illus.). 32p. (J). 15.95 (978-0-9763082-1-8(5), A JuneOne Production) JuneOne Publishing Hub.

Davis, Darren. Atlas Gt Planets. 2006. (ENG.). 16p. (J). (gr. -1-12). bds. 5.99 (978-1-59559-103-6(6)) Left Field,Angel Gate.

Davis, Rachayl Eckstein & Schram, Peninnah. The Apple Tree's Discovery. Lee, Wendy W., illus. 2012. (ENG.). 24p. (J). (gr. -1-2). pap. 7.99 (978-0-7613-5132-0(9), 6adca0a0-d419-4ca4-82b0-6ee930438a2e, Kar-Ben Publishing) Lerner Publishing Group.

Dean, James & Dean, Kimberly. Pete the Cat: Twinkle, Twinkle, Little Star. Dean, James, illus. 2014. (Pete the Cat Ser.). (ENG., Illus.). 32p. (J). (gr. -1-3). 9.99 (978-0-06-230416-2(X), HarperCollins) HarperCollins Pubs.

DeStefano, Anthony. Little Star. 2013. (ENG., Illus.). 36p. (J). (gr. k-3). 15.99 (978-0-7369-5859-2(2), 6958592) Harvest Hse. Pubs.

Dixon, Franklin W. Galaxy X: Book One in the Galaxy X Trilogy, Bk. 1. 2009. (Hardy Boys (All New) Undercover Brothers Ser.: 28). (ENG.). 160p. (J). (gr. 3-7). pap. 6.99 (978-1-4169-7801-5(1), Aladdin) Simon & Schuster Children's Publishing.

Dukovich, Amanda J. A Star Named Little One (Boy) Pride, Matthew, illus. l.t. ed. 2006. 32p. (J). (gr. -1). 15.99 (978-1-59879-189-1(3)) Lifevest Publishing, Inc.

—A Star Named Little One (Girl) Pride, Matthew, illus. l.t. ed. 2006. 32p. (J). (gr. -1-k). 15.99 (978-1-59879-090-0(0)) Lifevest Publishing, Inc.

Dyan, Penelope. A Thousand Stars. Dyan, Penelope, illus. 2012. (Illus.). 34p. pap. 11.95 (978-1-61477-049-7(2)) Bellissima Publishing, LLC.

Edmonds, Lin. Patric the Pony & the Shining Star. 2010. 36p. pap. 17.49 (978-1-4520-7389-7(9)) AuthorHouse.

Elisabeth, Megan. A Star's Journey from Twinkle to Shine. 2012. 28p. pap. 24.95 (978-1-62709-789-5(9)) America Star Bks.

Face to the Sky, 6 pack. (Greetings Ser.: Vol. 3). 24p. (gr. 2-3). 31.00 (978-0-7635-9431-2(8)) Rigby Education.

Facklam, Margery. Only a Star. Carpenter, Nancy, illus. 2004. 32p. (J). (gr. -1-3). pap. 8.00 (978-0-8028-5174-1(6)) Eerdmans, William B. Publishing Co.

Faghih, Parisa. The Sign of Green Stars. 2008. (Illus.). 45p. (J). pap. 24.95 (978-1-4241-8967-0(5)) America Star Bks.

Fanny, Nanny. Touch the Stars: A Children's Book. Nanny Fanny, illus. 2013. 32p. pap. 12.99 (978-1-61204-275-6(9), Strategic Bk. Publishing) Strategic Book Publishing & Rights Agency (SBPRA).

Ferraro, Lynn. Joey Discovers Astronomy. Leslie, Melissa, illus. 2005. (ENG.). 23p. per. 12.99 (978-1-4134-9624-6(5)) Xlibris Corp.

Fischer, Kelly. The Moon Throws a Birthday Party. Duckworth, Michelle, illus. 2011. 32p. (J). 19.50 (978-1-58385-237-8(9)) ktf-writers-studio.

Foster, Patricia. Where Did You Come from, Tiny Drop? 2008. 24p. pap. 24.95 (978-1-60610-224-4(9)) America Star Bks.

Fox, Adrienne. Starstruck. 2012. 126p. 27.45 (978-1-4772-3558-4(2)); pap. 15.18 (978-1-4772-3556-0(6)) AuthorHouse.

Frank, Connie. Sadie & the Night Sky, 1 vol. 2009. 24p. pap. 24.95 (978-1-60703-911-2(7)) America Star Bks.

Galloway, Teresa A. The Tiny Star Birth of a Soul. 2009. 36p. pap. 15.95 (978-1-4389-3857-8(8)) AuthorHouse.

Garrett, Christine. Dream Bunny's Tales - Saving the Land of Dreams. 2009. (Illus.). 48p. pap. 13.95 (978-1-60860-451-7(9), Eloquent Bks.) Strategic Book Publishing & Rights Agency (SBPRA).

Gasior, Julie. Samy the Star. 2008. 46p. 27.95 (978-0-615-18884-3(2)) Gasior, Julie.

Gazzetta, Katherine Cutchin. Love from a Star. Gazzetta, Katherine Cutchin, illus. 2015. (ENG., Illus.). 32p. (J). (gr. -1-k). 14.99 (978-1-58536-950-8(0), 204017) Sleeping Bear Pr.

Geffert, Karen L. A Falling Star Is the Beginning of a Wish. 2012. 32p. pap. 19.99 (978-1-4772-5649-7(0)) AuthorHouse.

Ginolfi, Art. The Tiny Star. 2005. 32p. (J). pap. 3.99 (978-1-4003-0683-1(3)) Nelson, Thomas Inc.

Ginolfi, Arthur. The Tiny Star. 2019. (Faith-Based Picture Books for God's ChildrenTM Ser.). (ENG.). 32p. (J). (-1). 14.99 (978-1-68099-525-1(1), Good Bks.) Skyhorse Publishing Co., Inc.

Gooch, T. It Was My Star. 2003. (Illus.). 32p. 19.97 (978-0-9726119-0-9(8)) Dancing Force, The.

Grizzell, Larry. The Star: A Christmas Song. 2006. (Illus.). 25p. (J). 19.95 (978-0-9759542-2-5(9)) Adventures Galore.

Guillet, Jean-Pierre. La Puce Cosmique et le Rayon Bleuge. Guillet, Francois, illus. 2004. (Des 9 Ans. Ser.). (FRE.). 120p. (J). (978-2-922565-98-0(X)) Editions de la Paix CAN. Dist: World of Reading, Ltd.

Harmening, Gail. How Did Clancey Get His Color?, 1 vol. 2009. 45p. pap. 24.95 (978-1-60836-440-4(2)) America Star Bks.

Hay, Sam. The Star in the Jar. Massini, Sarah, illus. 2018. (ENG.). 32p. (J). (gr. -1-3). 17.99 (978-1-4926-6220-4(8), Sourcebooks Jabberwocky) Sourcebooks, Inc.

He Who Listens: Individual Title Six-Packs. (Literatura 2000 Ser.). (gr. 2-3). 33.00 (978-0-7635-0171-6(9)) Rigby Education.

Heine, Theresa & Tavares, Victor. Star Seeker: A Journey to Outer Space. Tavares, Victor, illus. 2006. (ENG., Illus.). 32p. (J). (gr. -1-3). 16.99 (978-1-905236-36-7(0)) Barefoot Bks., Inc.

Henkes, Kevin. Wemberly's Ice-Cream Star. Henkes, Kevin, illus. 2003. (ENG., Illus.). 24p. (J). (gr. -1-k). bds. 6.99 (978-0-06-050405-2(6), Greenwillow Bks.) HarperCollins Pubs.

Heos, Bridget. Twinkle, Twinkle, Little Lamb. Jennings, Sarah, illus. 2018. 32p. (J). (gr. k-3). 17.99 (978-1-68152-405-4(8), 15236) Amicus.

Hill, Harriet. The Star That Could Not Twinkle. 2010. 30p. 18.95 (978-1-4452-2689-7(8)) Lulu Pr., Inc.

Hoehn, Ron. The Windy Night: It happened one Night. 2011. 23p. (J). pap. 16.95 (978-1-4327-6408-1(X)) Outskirts Pr., Inc.

Holston-Holloway, Angela M. The Apple Pie Kids. 2006. (J). pap. 8.00 (978-0-8059-6899-6(7)) Dorrance Publishing Co., Inc.

Holub, Joan. Twinkle, Star of the Week. Nicholls, Paul, illus. 2012. (J). (978-1-61913-137-8(4)) Weigl Pubs., Inc.

Horacek, Petr. Suzy Goose & the Christmas Star: Midi Edition. Horacek, Petr, illus. 2010. (ENG., Illus.). 32p. (J). (gr. -1-2). 7.99 (978-0-7636-5000-1(5)) Candlewick Pr.

Hotz, Donna. The Christmas Star. 2009. 24p. pap. 12.99 (978-1-4490-2387-4(8)) AuthorHouse.

Ives, Suzanne Lintz. Bob, the Tree who Became a Star. 2010. 16p. (J). pap. 14.95 (978-1-4327-2748-2(6)) Outskirts Pr., Inc.

Jeffers, Oliver. The Boy: His Stories & How They Came to Be. 2019. (ENG., Illus.). 168p. (J). (gr. -1-3). 40.00 (978-0-593-11474-2(4), Philomel Bks.) Penguin Young Readers Group.

—How to Catch a Star. Jeffers, Oliver, illus. 2004. (ENG., Illus.). 32p. (J). (gr. -1-2). 18.99 (978-0-399-24286-1(4), Philomel Bks.) Penguin Young Readers Group.

Johnson-Carrigan, Ettarose. Old Rugged: How the Tree Became the Cross. 2008. 24p. pap. 11.99 (978-1-4389-2781-7(9)) AuthorHouse.

Kaye, Shannie. O, Little Star. 2012. 24p. 24.95 (978-1-62709-965-3(4)); pap. 24.95 (978-1-4626-9157-9(9)) America Star Bks.

Kazimierski, Diana. The Star. 2009. 24p. pap. 11.99 (978-1-4389-3799-1(7)) AuthorHouse.

Kiker, Jean. The Story of Misty: The star who became the most famous star of All. 2011. 20p. 11.59 (978-1-4269-5627-0(4)) Trafford Publishing.

Kowalik, Susie. Lumen: The Star That Shone for the Visit of the Composer-Conductor. 2013. (ENG.). 24p. pap. 10.99 (978-1-4624-0539-8(8), Inspiring Voices) Author Solutions, LLC.

Krishnaswami, Uma. Bright Sky, Starry City, 1 vol. Sicuro, Aimée, illus. 2015. (ENG.). 32p. (J). (gr. 1-4). 17.95 (978-1-55498-405-3(X)) Groundwood Bks. CAN. Dist: Publishers Group West (PGW).

The Land Beyond Forever. 2006. 25.00 (978-0-9785570-0-3(X)) Three Sisters Publishing Hse., Ltd.

Lemieux, Jean. Toby Shoots for Infinity. Cummins, Sarah, tr. Casson, Sophie, illus. 2005. (Formac First Novels Ser.: 55). (ENG.). 64p. (J). (gr. 2-5). 14.95 (978-0-88780-685-8(6), 685); 4.95 (978-0-88780-684-1(8), 684) Formac Publishing Co., Ltd. CAN. Dist: Formac Lorimer Bks. Ltd.

Leonard, Krystian. Shining Scars. Kelly, Lucas, illus. 2013. (ENG.). 31p. (J). 16.95 (978-0-938467-72-4(7)) Headline Bks., Inc.

Levasseur, Jody Rogers. The Forever Star. 2011. 28p. pap. 24.95 (978-1-4626-2729-5(3)) America Star Bks.

Lin, Grace. A Big Mooncake for Little Star (Caldecott Honor Book) 2018. (ENG., Illus.). 40p. (J). (gr. -1-3). 18.99 (978-0-316-40448-8(9)) Little, Brown Bks. for Young Readers.

Lobel, Gill. Little Bear's Special Wish. Hansen, Gaby, illus. 2004. 32p. (J). tchr. ed. 16.95 (978-1-58925-034-5(6)) Tiger Tales.

Lobo, Julia. Grandma Wishes. Cottage Door Press, ed. Rowe, Helen, illus. 2015. (ENG.). 18p. (J). (gr. -1-1). bds. 9.99 (978-1-68052-008-8(3), 1000090) Cottage Door Pr.

Lois, Lowry. Number the Stars. 2004. 144p. (J). (gr. 5-9). pap. 29.00 incl. audio (978-1-4000-8637-5(X), Listening Library) Random Hse. Audio Publishing Group.

Lowry, Lois. Number the Stars. l.t. ed. 2019. (ENG.). 282p. (J). (gr. 5-7). pap. 12.99 (978-1-4328-6393-7(2), Large Print Pr.) Thorndike Pr.

Lyon, George Ella. My Friend, the Starfinder. Gammell, Stephen, illus. 2008. (ENG.). 40p. (J). (gr. -1-2). 19.99 (978-1-4169-2738-9(7), Atheneum/Richard Jackson Bks.) Simon & Schuster Children's Publishing.

MacDonald, George. The Princess & the Goblin. 2010. 222p. pap. 13.95 (978-0-557-47296-3(2)) Lulu Pr., Inc.

Macgregor, Virginia. As Far As the Stars. 2019. (ENG.). 448p. (J). (gr. 7). 9.99 (978-0-00-827450-4(9), HQ) HarperCollins Pubs. Ltd. GBR. Dist: HarperCollins Pubs.

Maguire, Thomas Aquinas. Three Little Dreams, 3 vols. 2010. (ENG., Illus.). 36p. (J). (gr. -1). 16.95 (978-1-894965-79-8(5)) Simply Read Bks. CAN. Dist: Ingram Publisher Services.

March-Settle, Michelle. A Shining Star: A Journey for All Ages. 2004. (J). pap. 8.00 (978-0-8059-6368-7(5)) Dorrance Publishing Co., Inc.

McGhee, Alison. Star Bright: A Christmas Story. Reynolds, Peter H., illus. 2014. (ENG.). 40p. (J). (gr. -1-3). 17.99 (978-1-4169-5858-1(4), Atheneum Bks. for Young Readers) Simon & Schuster Children's Publishing.

McLellan, Dora. Stevie Star... the Star That Was Afraid to Shine. 2010. 21p. 14.99 (978-0-557-30108-9(4)) Lulu Pr., Inc.

Meehan, Kelly. A Star Named Symphony. 2009. 24p. pap. 12.99 (978-1-4389-6652-6(0)) AuthorHouse.

The Message in the Stars: Lap Book. (Pebble Soup Explorations Ser.). 16p. (gr. -1-18). 21.00 (978-0-7578-2113-4(8)) Rigby Education.

The Message in the Stars: Small Book. (Pebble Soup Explorations Ser.). 16p. (gr. -1-18). 5.00 (978-0-7578-2114-1(6)) Rigby Education.

Mincin, Sabrina. Catching a Shooting Star. 2012. 28p. pap. 12.95 (978-1-4575-0862-2(1)) Dog Ear Publishing, LLC.

Monroe, Jean Guard & Williamson, Ray A. They Dance in the Sky: Native American Star Myths. Stewart, Edgar, illus. 2007. (ENG.). 144p. (J). (gr. 5-7). pap. 9.99 (978-0-618-80912-7(0), 491700, Clarion Bks.) HarperCollins Pubs.

Morgan, Beverly. Gregory & the Stars: A Little Story about Independence. Joyful Noise, ed. 2005. (Illus.). 26p. (J). 4.95 (978-0-9772109-0-9(1)) Joyful Noise.

Nelson, S. D. The Star People: A Lakota Story. 2003. (ENG., Illus.). 40p. (J). (gr. -1-3). 19.99 (978-0-8109-4584-5(3)) Abrams, Inc.

Nyong'o, Lupita. Sulwe. Harrison, Vashti, illus. 2019. Orig. Title: Sulwe. (ENG.). 48p. (J). (gr. -1-3). 17.99 (978-1-5344-2536-1(5), Simon & Schuster Bks. For Young Readers) Simon & Schuster Bks. For Young Readers.

O'Connor, Jane. Fancy Nancy Sees Stars [60th Anniversary Edition]. 2017. (I Can Read Level 1 Ser.). (ENG., Illus.). 40p. (J). (gr. -1-3). 9.99 (978-0-06-257275-2(X), HarperCollins) HarperCollins Pubs.

O'Connor, Jane & Glasser, Robin Preiss. Fancy Nancy: Stellar Stargazer. 2011. (Fancy Nancy Ser.). (ENG., Illus.). 32p. (J). (gr. -1-2). 13.99 (978-0-06-191523-9(8), HarperCollins) HarperCollins Pubs.

Olsen, Bevan. Bethlehem's Star. 2008. 16p. pap. 2.99 (978-1-59955-181-4(0)) Cedar Fort, Inc./CFI Distribution.

Olsen, Leigh. The Stars in the Sky. 2009. (All Aboard Reading: Station Stop 2 Ser.). (ENG.). 48p. (J). (gr. 1-3). 16.19 (978-0-448-45240-1(5)) Penguin Young Readers Group.

Pangalos, Carol B. Gabriella & the Magic Stars. 2011. 36p. (gr. -1). pap. 15.14 (978-1-4634-1108-4(1)) AuthorHouse.

Peacock, Thomas. The Forever Sky. Lee, Annette S., illus. 2019. (ENG.). 32p. (J). 17.95 (978-1-68134-098-2(4)) Minnesota Historical Society Pr.

Penado, Martha. Star Stuff. 2009. 47p. pap. 24.95 (978-1-60813-991-0(3)) America Star Bks.

Penelope Panda's Shooting Star. 2008. (Illus.). 32p. (J). (gr. k-3). pap. 14.99 (978-0-9717290-3-2(4)) Adrema Pr.

Peredo, Roberto. Acoyani: El Nino y el Poeta. Sanchez, Andres & Arte Y Diseno, Tane, illus. 2nd rev. ed. 2006. (Castillo de la Lectura Naranja Ser.). (SPA & ENG.). 166p. (J). (gr. 4-7). pap. 7.95 (978-970-20-0146-1(3)) Castillo, Ediciones, S. A. de C. V. MEX. Dist: Macmillan.

Phifer, Larry. World on a String. 2013. (ENG.). 17.95 (978-0-9886984-0-6(4)) Storytime Works.

Phyllis Stella Jadosh. Well Then, You Must Be Lucky. 2011. 24p. pap. 11.95 (978-1-935268-70-3(8)) Halo Publishing International.

Pitman, Sandra. 10 Busy Bumble Bees, 1 vol. Sizemore, Carmen, illus. 2009. 20p. pap. 24.95 (978-1-60749-683-0(6)) America Star Bks.

Pohlemann, Terri. She Lives in the Stars. 2012. 24p. pap. 24.95 (978-1-4626-6190-9(4)) America Star Bks.

Randolph, Tammy. Cricket's Starry Night. 2011. 28p. pap. 15.99 (978-1-4568-4506-3(3)) Xlibris Corp.

Ranson, Erin. A Bright New Star: With Color-Changing Star Light. Crisp, Dan, illus. 2007. (Story Book Ser.). 16p. (J). (gr. -1-3). bds. (978-1-84666-161-7(7), Tide Mill Pr.) Top That! Publishing PLC.

Ray, Mary Lyn. Stars. Frazee, Marla, illus. 2011. (ENG.). 40p. (J). (gr. -1-3). 18.99 (978-1-4424-2249-0(1), Beach Lane Bks.) Beach Lane Bks.

—Stars. Frazee, Marla, illus. 2017. (Classic Board Bks.). (ENG.). 36p. (J). (gr. -1-k). bds. 7.99 (978-1-5344-0662-9(X), Little Simon) Little Simon.

Roberg, Robert & Whiting, Chuck. The Littlest Star: A Musical Story. 2003rd gif. l.t. ed. 2003. (Illus.). 40p. 10.95 incl. audio compact disk (978-0-9712398-0-7(0)) Shine Time Records & Bks.

Roberts, Phyllis. Teeny Tiny Star. 2007. (Illus.). 30p. (J). lib. bdg. 19.95 (978-1-933732-40-4(7)) Big Ransom Studio.

Rose, Robin. Reaching for the Stars. 2008. 24p. pap. 11.95 (978-1-4389-2299-7(X)) AuthorHouse.

Runnells, Treesha. Five Wishing Stars: Disappearing Die Cut. Dillard, Sarah, illus. 2005. (ENG.). 12p. (J). 14.95 (978-1-58117-265-2(6), Intervisual/Piggy Toes) Bendon, Inc.

Runton, Andy. Owly & Wormy, Bright Lights & Starry Nights. Runton, Andy, illus. 2012. (ENG., Illus.). 40p. (J). (gr. -1-3). 19.99 (978-1-4169-5775-1(8), Atheneum Bks. for Young Readers) Simon & Schuster Children's Publishing.

San Giacomo, Renee. Herbie's Star. 2012. 24p. pap. 24.95 (978-1-4626-7596-8(4)) America Star Bks.

Santillo, LuAnn. The Wish. Santillo, LuAnn, ed. 2003. (Half-Pint Kids Readers Ser.). (Illus.). 7p. (J). (gr. -1-1). pap. 1.00 (978-1-59256-048-6(2)) Half-Pint Kids, Inc.

Schram, Peninnah & Davis, Rachayl Eckstein. The Apple Tree's Discovery. Lee, Wendy W., illus. 2012. (Kar-Ben Favorites Ser.). (ENG.). 24p. (J). (gr. -1-2). lib. bdg. 16.95 (978-0-7613-5130-6(2), Kar-Ben Publishing) Lerner Publishing Group.

Sierra I Fabra, Jordi. El Nino Que Vivia en las Estrellas. (SPA.). 120p. (YA). (gr. 5-8). 8.95 (978-84-204-4429-1(4)) Ediciones Alfaguara ESP. Dist: Santillana USA Publishing Co., Inc.

Sills, Elizabeth & Patrice, Elena. Nana Star. Saker, Linda, illus. 32p. (J). (gr. -1-3). 2007. 15.95 (978-0-9753843-5-0(X)) 2004. 17.99 (978-0-9753843-0-5(9)) ee publishing & productions, inc.

—Nana Star & the Moonman. Saker, Linda, illus. 2008. 32p. (J). (gr. -1-3). 15.95 (978-0-9753843-6-7(8)) ee publishing & productions, inc.

Silver Dolphin en Español Editors, creator. Mis Figuras Geometricas, Srita Estrella. 2005. (Mis figuras Geometricas Ser.). (SPA., Illus.). 6p. (J). (gr. -1-k). (978-970-718-295-0(4), Silver Dolphin en Español) Advanced Marketing, S. de R. L. de C. V.

Sklyar, Igor. King & the Star. 2005. (Illus.). 50p. pap. (978-1-84401-048-6(1)) Athena Pr.

Slate, Joseph. The Secret Stars, 1 vol. Dávalos, Felipe, illus. 2005. (ENG.). 32p. (J). pap. 5.95 (978-0-7614-5152-5(8)) Marshall Cavendish Corp.

Solomon, Philippa. Settle down for Storytime. 2009. (Illus.). 64p. pap. 23.49 (978-1-4389-6032-6(8)) AuthorHouse.

Spires, Sharlene. The Grandsisters. 2010. 56p. pap. 15.99 (978-1-4535-3004-7(5)) Xlibris Corp.

Sprenkle, Connie L. My Shining Star. 2011. 24p. pap. 15.99 (978-1-4568-2168-5(7)) Xlibris Corp.

Stars of the Sky. 2004. (Illus.). 32p. (J). 12.95 (978-0-9759468-0-0(3)) Balanced Families.

Symington, Martha M. Global Heart Warming: Dream Believe Achieve Series. Sanderson, Jessica B., illus. 2009. 36p. pap. (978-1-897435-34-2(7)) Agio Publishing Hse.

Tiger Tales. The Gingerbread Man. Latimer, Miriam, illus. 2016. (My First Fairy Tales Ser.). (ENG.). 32p. (J). (gr. -1-2). pap. 8.99 (978-1-58925-477-0(5)) Tiger Tales.

—Ten Twinkly Stars. Julian, Russell, illus. 2016. (ENG.). 28p. (J). (gr. -1-k). mass mkt. 3.99 (978-1-58925-475-6(9)) Tiger Tales.

Titchenell, Elsa-Brita. Once Round the Sun. Gruelle, Justin C., illus. 2011. 62p. 36.95 (978-1-258-03323-1(2)) Literary Licensing, LLC.

Torres, Christopher S. Salma & the Christmas Star. Hildebrandt, Lowell, illus. 2010. 24p. 12.99 (978-1-4490-8981-8(X)) AuthorHouse.

Trapani, Iza. Sing along with Iza & Friends: Twinkle, Twinkle Little Star. Trapani, Iza, illus. 2004. (Illus.). 32p. (J). pap. 11.95 incl. audio compact disk (978-1-58089-101-1(2)) Charlesbridge Publishing, Inc.

—Twinkle, Twinkle, Little Star. Trapani, Iza, illus. 2008. (Iza Trapani's Extended Nursery Rhymes Ser.). (Illus.). 26p. (J). (gr. -1 — 1). bds. 7.95 (978-1-58089-015-1(6)) Charlesbridge Publishing, Inc.

Twinkle Twinkle Little Star. 2005. (J). bds. 6.99 (978-0-9753127-3-5(1)) Family Bks. at Home.

Valdez-Moore, Pura J. Tippy the Special Star. 2008. 24p. pap. 24.95 (978-1-4241-9943-3(3)) America Star Bks.

Vela, Eugenio H. Twinkle, Twinkle Little Harold. 2012. 28p. pap. 24.95 (978-1-4560-0901-4(X)) America Star Bks.

Venditti, Stacey Marie. Stashi the Rainbow Star: Her Journey Home. Provenzano, Jeannine, illus. 2008. 52p. pap. 24.95 (978-1-60474-786-7(2)) America Star Bks.

Wallace, Nancy Elizabeth. Stars! Stars! Stars!, 0 vols. Wallace, Nancy Elizabeth, illus. 2012. (ENG., Illus.). 40p. (J). (gr. 1-3). 17.99 (978-0-7614-5612-4(0), 9780761456124, Two Lions) Amazon Publishing.

Warden, Kristina. Sparkle: a Star's Story, 1 vol. 2009. (Nature Stories Ser.). (ENG., Illus.). 24p. (J). (gr. 1-2). pap. 9.15 (978-1-60754-087-8(8), 5544a69b-14ff-494d-b197-4f4ef54026a5); lib. bdg. 27.27 (978-1-60754-086-1(X), 1b87875b-dda3-4b7c-bc29-ca7ab697669f) Rosen Publishing Group, Inc., The. (Windmill Bks.).

Where Do the Stars Go? 2007. (J). 19.95 (978-0-9795877-1-9(9)) Pitcher, Jan.

Willson, Sarah & Thompson Bros. Estrellita. Thompson Brothers Studio Staff, illus. 2003. (Dora la Exploradora Ser.).Tr. of Little Star. (SPA.). 24p. (J). pap. 3.99 (978-0-689-86307-3(1), Libros Para Ninos) Libros Para Ninos.

Wilson, Jessica. Stary's Secret. Tintjer, Birgit, illus. 2007. 28p. pap. 24.95 (978-1-4241-9089-8(4)) America Star Bks.

Wisenrich, Athena. Sitar: Legend of the Morning Star. 2012. 32p. pap. 18.95 (978-1-4525-5351-1(3)) Balboa Pr.

Witschen, Kay. Clinker's Christmas Star. Witschen, Kay, illus. 2004. (Illus.). 24p. (J). 6.95 (978-0-9741352-1-2(6)) Dwitt Publishing.

Wolf, Mari. An Empty Bottle. 2011. 30p. 13.95 (978-1-4638-9995-0(5)) Rodgers, Alan Bks.

Wolfel, Ursula. Fliegender Stern. pap. 14.95 (978-3-570-26064-7(X)) Bertelsman, Verlagsgruppe C. GmbH DEU. Dist: Distribooks, Inc.

Woodall, Karen. Listen to the Stars. 2013. (ENG.). 34p. (J). 18.95 (978-1-4787-1446-0(8)) Outskirts Pr., Inc.

Woolf, Julia, illus. Special Star. 2008. (ENG.). 10p. (J). bds. 4.95 (978-1-58117-815-9(8), Intervisual/Piggy Toes) Bendon, Inc.

Zappa, Shana Muldoon, et al. Adora Finds a Friend, 10. 2016. (Star Darlings Ser.). (ENG.). 176p. (J). (gr. 3-6). 21.19 (978-1-4844-8574-3(2)) Disney Pr.

—Astra's Mixed-Up Mission, 8. 2016. (Star Darlings Ser.). (ENG.). 176p. (J). (gr. 3-6). 21.19 (978-1-4844-8084-7(8)) Disney Pr.

—Cassie Comes Through. 2016. 147p. (J). (978-1-4806-9840-6(7)) Disney Publishing Worldwide.

—Piper's Perfect Dream. 2016. 156p. (J). (978-1-4806-9807-9(5)) Disney Publishing Worldwide.

—Tessa's Lost & Found, 9. 2016. (Star Darlings Ser.). (ENG.). 176p. (J). (gr. 3-6). 21.19 (978-1-4844-8193-6(3)) Disney Pr.

—Vega & the Fashion Disaster, 4. 2016. (Star Darlings Ser.). (ENG., Illus.). 176p. (J). (gr. 3-6). lib. bdg. 21.19 (978-1-4844-7389-4(2)) Disney Pr.

STARS—POETRY

Taylor, Jane. Twinkle, Twinkle Little Star. Duffy, Katherine, illus. 2016. (ENG.). 32p. (J). (gr. -1-k). pap. 9.99 (978-1-5324-0073-5(X)) Xist Publishing.

Trapani, Iza. Twinkle, Twinkle, Little Star. Trapani, Iza, illus. 2008. (Iza Trapani's Extended Nursery Rhymes Ser.). (Illus.). 26p. (J). (gr. -1 — 1). bds. 7.95 (978-1-58089-015-1(6)) Charlesbridge Publishing, Inc.

STATE AND CHURCH

see Church and State

STATE AND EDUCATION

see Education and State

STATE BIRDS

Tait, Leia. Birds. 2008. (U. S. Sites & Symbols Ser.). (Illus.). 48p. (J). (gr. 3-5). pap. 10.95 (978-1-59036-891-6(6)); lib. bdg. 29.05 (978-1-59036-890-9(8)) Weigl Pubs., Inc.

Talbott, Hudson. United Tweets of America: 50 State Birds Their Stories, Their Glories. Talbott, Hudson, illus. 2015. (Illus.). 64p. (J). (gr. 1-3). 8.99 (978-0-14-751557-5(2), Puffin Books) Penguin Young Readers Group.

STATE CHURCH

see Church and State

STATE FLOWERS

Tait, Leia. Flowers. 2008. (U. S. Sites & Symbols Ser.). (Illus.). 48p. (J). (gr. 3-5). pap. 10.95 (978-1-59036-895-4(9)); lib. bdg. 29.05 (978-1-59036-894-7(0)) Weigl Pubs., Inc.

STATE GOVERNMENTS

see also Governors

also names of states with the subdivision Politics and Government, e.g. New York (State)—Politics and government; etc.

Benchmark Education Company. Local & State Government (Teacher Guide) 2005. (978-1-4108-4639-6(3)) Benchmark Education Co.

Benchmark Education Company, LLC Staff, compiled by. Social Studies Theme: GOVT & Citizenship. 2005. spiral bd. 115.00 (978-1-4108-5331-8(4)) Benchmark Education Co.

Brannon, Barbara. Discover Local & State Government. 2005. (J). pap. (978-1-4108-5145-1(1)) Benchmark Education Co.

Cefrey, Holly & Brexel, Bernadette. Your Governor: State Government in Action, 1 vol. 2003. (Primary Source Library of American Citizenship Ser.). (ENG., Illus.). 32p. (YA). (gr. 5-5). lib. bdg. 29.13 (978-0-8239-4480-4(8), de1303fb-e2e3-4478-bbb1-06f11d055284, Rosen Reference) Rosen Publishing Group, Inc., The.

Hurtig, Jennifer. Capitals. 2008. (U. S. Sites & Symbols Ser.). (Illus.). 48p. (J). (gr. 3-5). lib. bdg. 29.05 (978-1-59036-896-1(7)); (gr. 4-6). pap. 10.95 (978-1-59036-897-8(5)) Weigl Pubs., Inc.

Johnson, Etta. Local & State Government. 2005. (J). pap. (978-1-4108-4591-7(5)) Benchmark Education Co.

LeVert, Suzanne. How States Make Laws, 1 vol. 2005. (Kaleidoscope: Government Ser.). (ENG., Illus.). 48p. (gr. 4-4). lib. bdg. 32.64 (978-0-7614-1595-4(5), 0f73330b-051f-4516-95bc-6a5214d7f6ff) Cavendish Square Publishing LLC.

—State Government, 1 vol. 2005. (Kaleidoscope: Government Ser.). (ENG., Illus.). 48p. (gr. 4-4). lib. bdg. 32.64 (978-0-7614-1596-1(3), 0f003ae2-7593-4bfb-b67c-d9cdf5c8a0ef) Cavendish Square Publishing LLC.

Machajewski, Sarah. What Are State & Local Government?, 1 vol. 2015. (Let's Find Out! Government Ser.). (ENG., Illus.). 32p. (J). (gr. 2-3). 26.06 (978-1-62275-986-6(9), 52c5d263-c673-4f05-b5af-a24cb9564dbb, Britannica Educational Publishing) Rosen Publishing Group, Inc., The.

Mahoney, Emily. Becoming a State Governor, 1 vol. 2015. (Who's Your Candidate? Choosing Government Leaders Ser.). (ENG., Illus.). 32p. (J). (gr. 3-4). pap. 11.50 (978-1-4824-4047-8(4), 0e9803dd-c477-49f0-8306-d34bf9d96e31) Stevens, Gareth Publishing LLLP.

Mahoney, Emily Jankowski. Becoming a State Governor. 2016. (Who's Your Candidate? Choosing Government Leaders Ser.). (ENG.). 32p. (J). (gr. 3-6). 21.30 (978-1-5311-8608-1(4)) Perfection Learning Corp.

Manning, Jack. The State Governor, 1 vol. 2014. (Our Government Ser.). (ENG.). 24p. (J). (gr. 1-3). lib. bdg. 27.99 (978-1-4914-0335-8(7), 125848) Capstone.

Marsh, Carole. Alabama Government Projects: 30 Cool, Activities, Crafts, Experiments & More for Kids to Do to Learn about Your State! 2003. (Alabama Experience Ser.). 32p. (gr. k-5). pap. 5.95 (978-0-635-01920-2(5), Marsh, Carole Bks.) Gallopade International.

—Alaska Government Projects: 30 Cool, Activities, Crafts, Experiments & More for Kids to Do to Learn about Your State! 2003. (Alaska Experience Ser.). 32p. (gr. k-5). pap. 5.95 (978-0-635-01921-9(3), Marsh, Carole Bks.) Gallopade International.

—Arizona Government Projects: 30 Cool, Activities, Crafts, Experiments & More for Kids to Do to Learn about Your State! 2003. (Arizona Experience Ser.). 32p. (gr. k-5). pap. 5.95 (978-0-635-01922-6(1), Marsh, Carole Bks.) Gallopade International.

—Arkansas Government Projects: 30 Cool, Activities, Crafts, Experiments & More for Kids to Do to Learn about Your State! 2003. (Arkansas Experience Ser.). 32p. (gr. k-5). pap. 5.95 (978-0-635-01923-3(X), Marsh, Carole Bks.) Gallopade International.

—California Government Projects: 30 Cool, Activities, Crafts, Experiments & More for Kids to Do to Learn about Your State! 2003. (California Experience Ser.). 32p. (gr. k-5). pap. 5.95 (978-0-635-01924-0(8), Marsh, Carole Bks.) Gallopade International.

—Colorado Government Projects: 30 Cool, Activities, Crafts, Experiments & More for Kids to Do to Learn about Your State! 2003. (Colorado Experience Ser.). 32p. (gr. k-5). pap. 5.95 (978-0-635-01925-7(6), Marsh, Carole Bks.) Gallopade International.

—Connecticut Government Projects: 30 Cool, Activities, Crafts, Experiments & More for Kids to Do to Learn about Your State! 2003. (Connecticut Experience Ser.). 32p. (gr. k-5). pap. 5.95 (978-0-635-01926-4(4), Marsh, Carole Bks.) Gallopade International.

—Delaware Government Projects: 30 Cool, Activities, Crafts, Experiments & More for Kids to Do to Learn about Your State! 2003. (Delaware Experience Ser.). 32p. (gr. k-5). pap. 5.95 (978-0-635-01927-1(2), Marsh, Carole Bks.) Gallopade International.

—Florida Government Projects: 30 Cool, Activities, Crafts, Experiments & More for Kids to Do to Learn about Your State! 2003. (Florida Experience Ser.). 32p. (gr. k-5). pap. 5.95 (978-0-635-01928-8(0), Marsh, Carole Bks.) Gallopade International.

—Georgia Government Projects: 30 Cool, Activities, Crafts, Experiments & More for Kids to Do to Learn about Your State! 2003. (Georgia Experience Ser.). 32p. (gr. k-5). pap. 5.95 (978-0-635-01929-5(9), Marsh, Carole Bks.) Gallopade International.

—Hawaii Government Projects: 30 Cool, Activities, Crafts, Experiments & More for Kids to Do to Learn about Your State! 2003. (Hawaii Experience Ser.). 32p. (gr. k-5). pap. 5.95 (978-0-635-01930-1(2), Marsh, Carole Bks.) Gallopade International.

—Idaho Government Projects: 30 Cool, Activities, Crafts, Experiments & More for Kids to Do to Learn about Your State! 2003. (Idaho Experience Ser.). 32p. (gr. k-5). pap.

5.95 *(978-0-635-01931-8(0)*, Marsh, Carole Bks.) Gallopade International.

—Illinois Government Projects: 30 Cool, Activities, Crafts, Experiments & More for Kids to Do to Learn about Your State! 2003. (Illinois Experience Ser.). 32p. (gr. k-5). pap. 5.95 *(978-0-635-01932-5(9)*, Marsh, Carole Bks.) Gallopade International.

—Indiana Government Projects: 30 Cool, Activities, Crafts, Experiments & More for Kids to Do to Learn about Your State! 2003. (Indiana Experience Ser.). 32p. (gr. k-5). pap. 5.95 *(978-0-635-01933-2(7)*, Marsh, Carole Bks.) Gallopade International.

—Iowa Government Projects: 30 Cool, Activities, Crafts, Experiments & More for Kids to Do to Learn about Your State! 2003. (Iowa Experience Ser.). 32p. (gr. k-5). pap. 5.95 *(978-0-635-01934-9(5)*, Marsh, Carole Bks.) Gallopade International.

—Kansas Government Projects: 30 Cool, Activities, Crafts, Experiments & More for Kids to Do to Learn about Your State! 2003. (Kansas Experience Ser.). 32p. (gr. k-5). pap. 5.95 *(978-0-635-01935-6(3)*, Marsh, Carole Bks.) Gallopade International.

—Kentucky Government Projects #4: 30 Cool Activities, Crafts, Experiments & More for Kids to Do! 2003. (Kentucky Experience Ser.). (Illus.). 32p. (J). (gr. k-5). pap. 5.95 *(978-0-635-01936-3(1)*, Marsh, Carole Bks.) Gallopade International.

—Louisiana Government Projects: 30 Cool, Activities, Crafts, Experiments & More for Kids to Do to Learn about Your State! 2003. (Louisiana Experience Ser.). 32p. (gr. k-5). pap. 5.95 *(978-0-635-01937-0(X)*, Marsh, Carole Bks.) Gallopade International.

—Maine Government Projects: 30 Cool, Activities, Crafts, Experiments & More for Kids to Do to Learn about Your State! 2003. (Maine Experience Ser.). 32p. (gr. k-5). pap. 5.95 *(978-0-635-01938-7(8)*, Marsh, Carole Bks.) Gallopade International.

—Maryland Government Projects: 30 Cool, Activities, Crafts, Experiments & More for Kids to Do to Learn about Your State! 2003. (Maryland Experience Ser.). 32p. (gr. k-5). pap. 5.95 *(978-0-635-01939-4(6)*, Marsh, Carole Bks.) Gallopade International.

—Massachusetts Government Projects: 30 Cool, Activities, Crafts, Experiments & More for Kids to Do to Learn about Your State! 2003. (Massachusetts Experience Ser.). 32p. (gr. k-5). pap. 5.95 *(978-0-635-01940-0(X)*, Marsh, Carole Bks.) Gallopade International.

—Michigan Government Projects: 30 Cool, Activities, Crafts, Experiments & More for Kids to Do to Learn about Your State! 2003. (Michigan Experience Ser.). 32p. (gr. k-5). pap. 5.95 *(978-0-635-01941-7(8)*, Marsh, Carole Bks.) Gallopade International.

—Minnesota Government Projects: 30 Cool, Activities, Crafts, Experiments & More for Kids to Do to Learn about Your State! 2003. (Minnesota Experience Ser.). 32p. (gr. k-5). pap. 5.95 *(978-0-635-01942-4(6)*, Marsh, Carole Bks.) Gallopade International.

—Mississippi Government Projects: 30 Cool, Activities, Crafts, Experiments & More for Kids to Do to Learn about Your State! 2003. (Mississippi Experience Ser.). 32p. (gr. k-5). pap. 5.95 *(978-0-635-01943-1(4)*, Marsh, Carole Bks.) Gallopade International.

—Missouri Government Projects: 30 Cool, Activities, Crafts, Experiments & More for Kids to Do to Learn about Your State! 2003. (Missouri Experience Ser.). 32p. (gr. k-5). pap. 5.95 *(978-0-635-01944-8(2)*, Marsh, Carole Bks.) Gallopade International.

—Montana Government Projects: 30 Cool, Activities, Crafts, Experiments & More for Kids to Do to Learn about Your State! 2003. (Montana Experience Ser.). 32p. (gr. k-5). pap. 5.95 *(978-0-635-01945-5(0)*, Marsh, Carole Bks.) Gallopade International.

—Nebraska Government Projects: 30 Cool, Activities, Crafts, Experiments & More for Kids to Do to Learn about Your State! 2003. (Nebraska Experience Ser.). 32p. (gr. k-5). pap. 5.95 *(978-0-635-01946-2(9)*, Marsh, Carole Bks.) Gallopade International.

—Nevada Government Projects: 30 Cool, Activities, Crafts, Experiments & More for Kids to Do to Learn about Your State! 2003. (Nevada Experience Ser.). 32p. (gr. k-5). pap. 5.95 *(978-0-635-01947-9(7)*, Marsh, Carole Bks.) Gallopade International.

—New Hampshire Government Projects: 30 Cool, Activities, Crafts, Experiments & More for Kids to Do to Learn about Your State! 2003. (New Hampshire Experience Ser.). 32p. (gr. k-5). pap. 5.95 *(978-0-635-01948-6(5)*, Marsh, Carole Bks.) Gallopade International.

—New Jersey Government Projects: 30 Cool, Activities, Crafts, Experiments & More for Kids to Do to Learn about Your State! 2003. (New Jersey Experience Ser.). 32p. (gr. k-5). pap. 5.95 *(978-0-635-01949-3(3)*, Marsh, Carole Bks.) Gallopade International.

—New Mexico Government Projects: 30 Cool, Activities, Crafts, Experiments & More for Kids to Do to Learn about Your State! 2003. (New Mexico Experience Ser.). 32p. (gr. k-5). pap. 5.95 *(978-0-635-01950-9(7)*, Marsh, Carole Bks.) Gallopade International.

—North Carolina Government Projects: 30 Cool, Activities, Crafts, Experiments & More for Kids to Do to Learn about Your State! 2003. (North Carolina Experience Ser.). 32p. (gr. k-5). pap. 5.95 *(978-0-635-01952-3(3)*, Marsh, Carole Bks.) Gallopade International.

—North Dakota Government Projects: 30 Cool, Activities, Crafts, Experiments & More for Kids to Do to Learn about Your State! 2003. (North Dakota Experience Ser.). 32p. (gr. k-5). pap. 5.95 *(978-0-635-01953-0(1)*, Marsh, Carole Bks.) Gallopade International.

—Ohio Government Projects: 30 Cool, Activities, Crafts, Experiments & More for Kids to Do to Learn about Your State! 2003. (Ohio Experience Ser.). 32p. (gr. k-5). pap. 5.95 *(978-0-635-01954-7(X)*, Marsh, Carole Bks.) Gallopade International.

—Oklahoma Government Projects: 30 Cool, Activities, Crafts, Experiments & More for Kids to Do to Learn about Your State! 2003. (Oklahoma Experience Ser.). 32p. (gr. k-5). pap. 5.95 *(978-0-635-01955-4(8)*, Marsh, Carole Bks.) Gallopade International.

—Oregon Government Projects: 30 Cool, Activities, Crafts, Experiments & More for Kids to Do to Learn about Your State! 2003. (Oregon Experience Ser.). 32p. (gr. k-5). pap. 5.95 *(978-0-635-01956-1(6)*, Marsh, Carole Bks.) Gallopade International.

—Pennsylvania Government Projects: 30 Cool, Activities, Crafts, Experiments & More for Kids to Do to Learn about Your State! 2003. (Pennsylvania Experience Ser.). 32p. (gr. k-5). pap. 5.95 *(978-0-635-01957-8(4)*, Marsh, Carole Bks.) Gallopade International.

—Rhode Island Government Projects: 30 Cool, Activities, Crafts, Experiments & More for Kids to Do to Learn about Your State! 2003. (Rhode Island Experience Ser.). 32p. (gr. k-5). pap. 5.95 *(978-0-635-01958-5(2)*, Marsh, Carole Bks.) Gallopade International.

—South Carolina Government Projects: 30 Cool, Activities, Crafts, Experiments & More for Kids to Do to Learn about Your State! 2003. (South Carolina Experience Ser.). 32p. (gr. k-5). pap. 5.95 *(978-0-635-01959-2(0)*, Marsh, Carole Bks.) Gallopade International.

—South Dakota Government Projects: 30 Cool, Activities, Crafts, Experiments & More for Kids to Do to Learn about Your State! 2003. (South Dakota Experience Ser.). 32p. (gr. k-5). pap. 5.95 *(978-0-635-01960-8(4)*, Marsh, Carole Bks.) Gallopade International.

—Tennessee Government Projects: 30 Cool, Activities, Crafts, Experiments & More for Kids to Do to Learn about Your State! 2003. (Tennessee Experience Ser.). 32p. (gr. k-5). pap. 5.95 *(978-0-635-01961-5(2)*, Marsh, Carole Bks.) Gallopade International.

—Texas Government Projects: 30 Cool, Activities, Crafts, Experiments & More for Kids to Do to Learn about Your State! 2003. (Texas Experience Ser.). 32p. (gr. k-5). pap. 5.95 *(978-0-635-01962-2(0)*, Marsh, Carole Bks.) Gallopade International.

—Utah Government Projects: 30 Cool, Activities, Crafts, Experiments & More for Kids to Do to Learn about Your State! 2003. (Utah Experience Ser.). 32p. (gr. k-5). pap. 5.95 *(978-0-635-01963-9(9)*, Marsh, Carole Bks.) Gallopade International.

—Vermont Government Projects: 30 Cool, Activities, Crafts, Experiments & More for Kids to Do to Learn about Your State! 2003. (Vermont Experience Ser.). 32p. (gr. k-5). pap. 5.95 *(978-0-635-01964-6(7)*, Marsh, Carole Bks.) Gallopade International.

—Virginia Government Projects: 30 Cool, Activities, Crafts, Experiments & More for Kids to Do to Learn about Your State! 2003. (Virginia Experience Ser.). 32p. (gr. k-5). pap. 5.95 *(978-0-635-01965-3(5)*, Marsh, Carole Bks.) Gallopade International.

McAuliffe, Bill. State & Local Government. 2016. (By the People Ser.). (ENG., Illus.). 48p. (J). (gr. 4-7). 39.95 *(978-1-60818-674-7(1)*, 20569, Creative Education); pap. 12.00 *(978-1-62832-270-5(5)*, 20567, Creative Paperbacks) Creative Co., The.

Nagelhout, Ryan. Standing in a Governor's Shoes, 1 vol. 2015. (My Government Ser.). (ENG., Illus.). 32p. (gr. 4-4). pap. 11.58 *(978-1-5026-0475-0(2)*, d48671df-08fc-4e4b-968c-73e847e30acc) Cavendish Square Publishing LLC.

Othello: Activity Pack. 2003. 156p. (YA). pap. *(978-1-58049-631-5(8)*, PA6318) Prestwick Hse., Inc.

STATE PLANNING

see Social Policy

STATE TREES

Watson, Galadriel Findlay. Trees. 2008. (U. S. Sites & Symbols Ser.). (Illus.). 48p. (J). (gr. 3-5). pap. 10.95 *(978-1-59036-889-3(4))*; lib. bdg. 29.05 *(978-1-59036-888-6(6))* Weigl Pubs., Inc.

STATEN ISLAND (NEW YORK, N.Y.)—FICTION

Mercaldo, David. Little Boy Boo: The Adventures of A Yorkshire Terrier Who Thought He Was a Boy. 2009. 112p. pap. 11.99 *(978-1-61579-099-9(3))* Salem Author Services.

STATESMEN

see also Diplomats

Adams, Colleen. Benjamin Franklin: American Inventor. 2009. (Reading Room Collection 2 Ser.). 24p. (gr. 3-4). 42.50 *(978-1-60851-959-0(7)*, PowerKids Pr.) Rosen Publishing Group, Inc., The.

Adler, David A. A Picture Book of Alexander Hamilton. Collins, Matt, illus. 2019. (Picture Book Biography Ser.). 32p. (J). (gr. -1-3). 17.99 *(978-0-8234-3961-4(5))* Holiday Hse., Inc.

—A Picture Book of Benjamin Franklin. Wallner, John & Wallner, Alexandra, illus. 2018. (Picture Book Biography Ser.). 32p. (J). (gr. -1-3). pap. 7.99 *(978-0-8234-4057-3(5))* Holiday Hse., Inc.

—A Picture Book of Benjamin Franklin. Wallner, John & Wallner, Alexandra, illus. 2008. (Picture Book Biography Ser.). (J). (gr. k-3). 28.95 incl. audio compact disk *(978-1-4301-0340-0(X))* Live Oak Media.

—A Picture Book of Benjamin Franklin. 2008. (J). (gr. k-3). pap. 39.95 incl. audio compact disk *(978-1-4301-0341-7(8))* Live Oak Media.

—A Picture Book of Benjamin Franklin, 4 bks., Set. Wallner, John & Wallner, Alexandra, illus. 2008. (Picture Book Biography Ser.). (J). (gr. k-3). pap. 37.95 incl. audio *(978-1-4301-0338-7(8))* Live Oak Media.

Albee, Sarah. Alexander Hamilton: A Plan for America. Ko, Chin, illus. 2018. (I Can Read Level 2 Ser.). (ENG.). 32p. (J). (gr. -1-3). pap. 4.99 *(978-0-06-243290-2(7)*, HarperCollins) HarperCollins Pubs.

—Alexander Hamilton: a Plan for America. Ko, Chin, illus. 2018. (I Can Read Level 2 Ser.). (ENG.). 32p. (J). (gr. -1-3). 16.99 *(978-0-06-243291-9(5)*, HarperCollins) HarperCollins Pubs.

Aldridge, Rebecca. Ban Ki-Moon: United Nations Secretary-General. 2009. (Modern World Leaders Ser.). (ENG.). 128p. (gr. 7-12). 30.00 *(978-1-60413-070-6(9)*, P167308, Facts On File) Infobase Holdings, Inc.

Anderson, Dale. Leaders of the American Revolution, 1 vol. 2005. (World Almanac(r) Library of the American Revolution Ser.). (ENG.). 48p. (gr. 5-8). lib. bdg. 33.67 *(978-0-8368-5931-7(6)*, 5670f581-1e2e-4ddf-81e4-ea8e89f67c26, Gareth Stevens Secondary Library) Stevens, Gareth Publishing LLLP.

Aretha, David A. Jefferson Davis. 2009. (ENG., Illus.). 144p. (gr. 6-12). 35.00 *(978-1-60413-297-7(3)*, P163832, Facts On File) Infobase Holdings, Inc.

Ashby, Ruth. The Amazing Mr. Franklin: Or the Boy Who Read Everything, 1 vol. 2019. (Illus.). 112p. (J). (gr. 2-5). pap. 7.95 *(978-1-68263-102-7(8))* Peachtree Publishing Co. Inc.

Bailey, Diane. DK Life Stories: Gandhi. Ager, Charlotte, illus. 2019. (DK Life Stories Ser.). (ENG.). 128p. (J). (gr. 3-7). pap. 5.99 *(978-1-4654-7842-9(6)*, DK Children) Dorling Kindersley Publishing, Inc.

Baldwin, James. Four Great Americans. 2006. pap. *(978-1-4065-0509-2(9))* Dodo Pr.

—Four Great Americans: Washington Franklin Webster Lincoln: a Book for Young Americans. 2017. (ENG., Illus.). (J). (gr. 3-7). 23.95 *(978-1-374-89694-9(2))*; pap. 13.95 *(978-1-374-89693-2(4))* Capital Communications, Inc.

—Four Great Americans: Washington, Franklin, Webster, Lincoln. a Book for Young Americans. 2017. (ENG., Illus.). (J). (gr. 3-7). pap. *(978-0-649-58735-3(9))* Trieste Publishing Pty Ltd.

Bedell, J. M. & Greenhead, Bill. Superheroes of the Constitution: Action & Adventure Stories about Real-Life Heroes. 2017. (ENG., Illus.). 112p. (J). pap. 9.99 *(978-1-63158-233-2(X)*, Racehorse Publishing) Skyhorse Publishing Co., Inc.

Benge, Janet & Benge, Geoff. Heroes of History - Benjamin Franklin: Live Wire. 2005. (Heroes of History Ser.). (ENG., Illus.). 208p. (YA). (gr. 5). pap. 11.99 *(978-1-932096-14-9(0))* Emerald Bks.

Bennett, Doraine & Scott, Clark C. Benjamin Franklin. 2012. (Illus.). 24p. (J). *(978-1-935884-38-5(7))*; pap. *(978-1-935884-47-7(6))* State Standards Publishing, LLC.

Boekhoff, P. M. & Kallen, Stuart A. Benjamin Franklin. 2006. (Illus.). 48p. (J). (gr. 4-8). 17.00 *(978-1-4223-5322-6(2))* DIANE Publishing Co.

Brandt, Keith & Macken, JoAnn Early. Paul Revere, Son of Liberty. Livingston, Francis, illus. 2007. 50p. (J). *(978-0-439-02017-6(4))* Scholastic, Inc.

Brockenbrough, Martha. Alexander Hamilton, Revolutionary. 2019. (ENG.). 384p. (YA). pap. 12.99 *(978-1-250-21170-5(0)*, 900174028) Square Fish.

Burch, Joann J. Jefferson Davis: Soldier & President of the Confederacy, 1 vol. 2014. (Legendary American Biographies Ser.). (ENG.). 96p. (gr. 6-6). 29.60 *(978-0-7660-6465-2(4)*, 1fa4bcce-ff13-4db6-92b8-4245a0c2af0e); pap. 13.88 *(978-0-7660-6466-9(2)*, 6e28cb08-5155-4f1c-8bb7-3d1cb3483692) Enslow Publishing, LLC.

Byrd, Robert. Electric Ben: The Amazing Life & Times of Benjamin Franklin. 2012. 40p. (J). (gr. k-3). 17.99 *(978-0-8037-3749-5(1)*, Dial Bks) Penguin Young Readers Group.

Colbert, David. Benjamin Franklin. 2008. (10 Days Ser.). (ENG.). 160p. (J). (gr. 3-8). pap. 8.99 *(978-1-4169-6446-9(0)*, Simon & Schuster/Paula Wiseman Bks.) Simon & Schuster/Paula Wiseman Bks.

Collard, Sneed B., III. Benjamin Franklin: The Man Who Could Do Just about Anything, 1 vol. 2007. (American Heroes Ser.). (ENG., Illus.). 48p. (gr. 3-3). lib. bdg. 32.64 *(978-0-7614-2161-0(0)*, 92ba54e7-6855-43a1-b3f4-276d6a5eef30) Cavendish Square Publishing LLC.

Collins, Kathleen. El Marques de Lafayette: Heroe Frances de la Guerra de Independencia, 1 vol. 2003. (Grandes Personajes en la Historia de Los Estados Unidos (Famous People in American History) Ser.). (SPA.). 32p. (gr. 3-4). pap. 10.00 *(978-0-8239-4233-6(3)*, 611571c8-b964-4b87-9954-e1eb2363af67, Rosen Classroom) Rosen Publishing Group, Inc., The.

—Marquis de Lafayette: French Hero of the American Revolution, 1 vol. 2003. (Famous People in American History / Grandes Personajes en la Historia de Los Estados Unidos Ser.). (ENG & SPA., Illus.). 32p. (gr. 2-3). lib. bdg. 29.13 *(978-0-8239-4163-6(9)*, 22b96b9a-22f4-4124-a502-dda13c946bf7, Editorial Buenas Letras) Rosen Publishing Group, Inc., The.

Conklin, Wendy. Benjamin Franklin, 1 vol. rev. ed. 2004. (Social Studies: Informational Text Ser.). (ENG.). 24p. (gr. 4-8). pap. 10.99 *(978-0-7439-8755-4(1))* Teacher Created Materials, Inc.

Cook, Diane. Mohandas Gandhi: Spiritual Leader. 2013. (People of Importance Ser.: 21). (Illus.). 32p. (J). (gr. 4-18). 19.95 *(978-1-4222-2852-4(5))* Mason Crest.

Cooper, Meghan. Sun Tzu, 1 vol. 2017. (Great Military Leaders Ser.). (ENG., Illus.). 128p. (YA). (gr. 9-9). 47.36 *(978-1-5026-2867-1(8)*, 069f2f6c-dec4-48bb-a898-a978596e4fa6) Cavendish Square Publishing LLC.

Cox, Vicki. Fidel Castro. 2003. (Major World Leaders Ser.). (ENG., Illus.). 112p. (gr. 6-12). 30.00 *(978-0-7910-7651-4(2)*, P113944, Facts On File) Infobase Holdings, Inc.

Davies, Monika. True Life: Alexander Hamilton. 2nd rev. ed. 2016. (TIME(r): Informational Text Ser.). (ENG., Illus.). 48p. (gr. 6-8). pap. 13.99 *(978-1-4938-3633-8(1))* Teacher Created Materials, Inc.

DeCarolis, Lisa. Alexander Hamilton: Federalist & Founding Father. 2009. (Library of American Lives & Times Ser.). 112p. (gr. 5-5). 69.20 *(978-1-60853-470-8(7))* Rosen Publishing Group, Inc., The.

DeGraw, Aleine. Alexander Hamilton: American Statesman. 2009. (Primary Sources of Famous People in American History Ser.). 32p. (gr. 2-3). 47.90 *(978-1-60851-646-9(6))* Rosen Publishing Group, Inc., The.

—Alexander Hamilton: American Statesman / Estadista Estadounidense. 2009. (Famous People in American History/Grandes personajes en la historia de los Estados Unidos Ser.). (SPA.). 32p. (gr. 2-3). 47.90 *(978-1-61512-536-4(1)*, Editorial Buenas Letras) Rosen Publishing Group, Inc., The.

—Alexander Hamilton: Estadista Estadounidense, 1 vol. 2003. (Grandes Personajes en la Historia de Los Estados Unidos (Famous People in American History) Ser.). (SPA., Illus.). 32p. (gr. 3-4). pap. 10.00 *(978-0-8239-4219-0(8)*, fddf036c-d53d-4973-8e1e-b3966f9f7021) Rosen Publishing Group, Inc., The.

—Alexander Hamilton: Estadista estadounidense (Alexander Hamilton: American Statesman) 2009. (Grandes personajes en la historia de los Estados Unidos (Famous People in American History) Ser.). 32p. (gr. 2-3). 47.90 *(978-1-61512-788-7(7)*, Editorial Buenas Letras) Rosen Publishing Group, Inc., The.

Doeden, Matt. Darkness Everywhere: The Assassination of Mohandas Gandhi. 2013. (ENG., Illus.). 80p. (YA). (gr. 6-12). E-Book 47.99 *(978-1-4677-1659-8(6)*, Twenty-First Century Bks.) Lerner Publishing Group.

Duling, Kaitlyn. Benjamin Franklin: Inventor & Founding Father, 1 vol. 2019. (Great American Entrepreneurs Ser.). (ENG.). 128p. (gr. 9-9). pap. 22.16 *(978-1-5026-4536-4(X)*, 466b4ac5-f5a1-400d-bd8d-c6e4a33af683) Cavendish Square Publishing LLC.

—Benjamin Franklin: Inventor & Founding Father. 2018. (J). pap. *(978-1-5026-4023-9(6))* Musa Publishing.

Edwards, Roberta & Who HQ. Who Was Paul Revere? O'Brien, John, illus. 2011. (Who Was? Ser.). 112p. (J). (gr. 3-7). pap. 6.99 *(978-0-448-45715-4(6)*, Penguin Workshop) Penguin Young Readers Group.

Eric, Lily. Paul Revere. 2019. (Illus.). 24p. (J). *(978-1-4896-9550-5(8)*, AV2 by Weigl) Weigl Pubs., Inc.

EZ Comics, ed. James A. Baker, III: The Authorised Comic Book Biography. 2009. (ENG., Illus.). 44p. (YA). *(978-0-9795887-3-0(1))* EZ Comics.

Feinstein, Stephen. Colin Powell, 1 vol. 2008. (African-American Heroes Ser.). (ENG., Illus.). 24p. (gr. k-2). lib. bdg. 25.27 *(978-0-7660-2761-9(9)*, 0a493614-833f-471e-bd26-4f9998b1c6b1, Enslow Elementary) Enslow Publishing, LLC.

Fingeroth, Danny. Democracy's Signature: Benjamin Franklin & the Declaration of Independence. 2009. (Great Moments in American History Ser.). 32p. (gr. 3-3). 47.90 *(978-1-61513-141-9(8))* Rosen Publishing Group, Inc., The.

Finlayson, Reggie. Colin Powell. 2005. (Biography Ser.). (Illus.). 112p. (gr. 6-12). lib. bdg. 27.93 *(978-0-8225-4966-6(2))* Lerner Publishing Group.

Fleming, Candace. Ben Franklin's Almanac: Being a True Account of the Good Gentleman's Life. 2003. (ENG., Illus.). 128p. (J). (gr. 5-9). 22.99 *(978-0-689-83549-0(3)*, Atheneum Bks. for Young Readers) Simon & Schuster Children's Publishing.

Fleming, Thomas. Ben Franklin: Inventing America. 2017. (Great Leaders & Events Ser.). (ENG., Illus.). 208p. (J). (gr. 4-8). lib. bdg. 35.99 *(978-1-942875-23-9(1)*, ddb56499-e1ab-4552-9b39-62486bda3151, Voyageur Pr.) Quarto Publishing Group USA.

Ford, Barbara. Paul Revere: American Patriot, 1 vol. 2014. (Legendary American Biographies Ser.). (ENG.). 96p. (gr. 6-6). 29.60 *(978-0-7660-6485-0(9)*, 71b83a69-4129-48f5-bc63-b49d99ff4350); pap. 13.88 *(978-0-7660-6486-7(7)*, 16fec7fd-cdf8-4057-83a8-a000c6afe506) Enslow Publishing, LLC.

Ford, Nick. Niccolò Machiavelli: Florentine Statesman, Playwright, & Poet, 1 vol. 2004. (Rulers, Scholars, & Artists of the Renaissance Ser.). (ENG.). 112p. (J). (gr. 5-8). lib. bdg. 39.80 *(978-1-4042-0316-7(8)*, 2c8dd72f-ba94-426c-bbc4-49d82256ee92) Rosen Publishing Group, Inc., The.

—Niccolò Machiavelli: Florentine Statesman, Playwright, & Poet. 2009. (Rulers, Scholars, & Artists of the Renaissance Ser.). 112p. (gr. 5-8). 66.50 *(978-1-60852-943-8(6)*, Rosen Reference) Rosen Publishing Group, Inc., The.

Forsyth, Fiona. Cicero: Defender of the Republic. 2009. (Ancient Leaders Ser.). 112p. (gr. 5-8). 66.50 *(978-1-61511-420-7(3)*, Rosen Reference) Rosen Publishing Group, Inc., The.

Fradin, Dennis Brindell. The Signers: The 56 Stories Behind the Declaration of Independence. McCurdy, Michael, illus. 2003. (ENG.). 176p. (J). (gr. 5-18). 24.99 *(978-0-8027-8849-8(1)*, 900032845, Bloomsbury USA Childrens) Bloomsbury Publishing USA.

—Who Was Ben Franklin? O'brien, John, illus. 2003. (Who Was...? Ser.). 105p. (gr. 4-7). 15.00 *(978-0-7569-1589-6(9))* Perfection Learning Corp.

Franklin, Benjamin. Benjamin Franklin's Wise Words: How to Work Smart, Play Well, & Make Real Friends. 2017. (Illus.). 128p. (J). (gr. 3-7). 16.99 *(978-1-4263-2699-8(8)*, National Geographic Kids) Disney Publishing Worldwide.

Fritz, Jean. Alexander Hamilton: the Outsider. 2012. (ENG.). 144p. (J). (gr. 3-7). 8.99 *(978-0-14-241986-1(9)*, Puffin Books) Penguin Young Readers Group.

Furgang, Kathy. The Declaration of Independence & Benjamin Franklin of Pennsylvania. 2009. (Framers of the Declaration of Independence Ser.). 24p. (gr. 3-3). 42.50 *(978-1-61512-629-3(5)*, PowerKids Pr.) Rosen Publishing Group, Inc., The.

—The Declaration of Independence & Robert Livingston of New York. 2009. (Framers of the Declaration of Independence Ser.). 24p. (gr. 3-3). 42.50 *(978-1-61512-631-6(7)*, PowerKids Pr.) Rosen Publishing Group, Inc., The.

Gagne, Tammy. Who Were the Signers of the Declaration of Independence? 2017. (Young America Ser.). (Illus.). 47p. (J). (gr. 3-6). 29.95 *(978-1-61228-983-0(5))* Mitchell Lane Pubs.

Gandhi, Arun & Hegedus, Bethany. Be the Change: A Grandfather Gandhi Story. Turk, Evan, illus. 2016. (ENG.). 48p. (J). (gr. -1-3). 18.99 *(978-1-4814-4265-7(1))* Simon & Schuster Children's Publishing.

—Grandfather Gandhi. Turk, Evan, illus. 2014. (ENG.). 48p. (J). (gr. -1-3). 18.99 *(978-1-4424-2365-7(X))* Simon & Schuster Children's Publishing.

Gaustad, Edwin S. Benjamin Franklin: Inventing America. 2006. 143p. (J). (gr. 4-8). reprint ed. 22.00 *(978-1-4223-5227-4(7))* DIANE Publishing Co.

Giblin, James Cross. The Amazing Life of Benjamin Franklin. Dooling, Michael, illus. 2006. 48p. (gr. -1-3). 18.00 *(978-0-7569-6551-8(9))* Perfection Learning Corp.

Gilman, Sarah. Ben Franklin, 1 vol. 2016. (Explore Colonial America Ser.). (ENG., Illus.). 48p. (gr. 4-5). 29.60 *(978-0-7660-7873-4(6)*, 42aeadd0-ba2b-4e55-9437-cc525a643fff) Enslow Publishing, LLC.

Gimpel, Lee. Fighting Wars, Planning for Peace: The Story of George C. Marshall. 2005. (World Leaders Ser.). (Illus.). 176p. (J). (gr. 6-12). lib. bdg. 26.95 *(978-1-931798-66-2(4))* Reynolds, Morgan Inc.

Glass, Maya. Benjamin Franklin: Early American Genius. (Primary Sources of Famous People in American History Ser.). 32p. 2009. (gr. 2-3). 47.90 *(978-1-60851-654-4(7))* 2003. (ENG., Illus.). (gr. 3-4). pap. 10.00 *(978-0-8239-4175-9(2),* b45187dc-6b5e-4b22-9e71-9d53ecc04d6a) 2003. (ENG., Illus.). (J). (gr. 3-4). lib. bdg. 29.13 *(978-0-8239-4103-2(5),* 8b464c67-53c0-43ed-99f2-2206fe1f6d9d) Rosen Publishing Group, Inc., The.

—Benjamin Franklin: Early American Genius / Político e inventor Estadounidense. 2009. (Famous People in American History/Grandes personajes en la historia de los Estados Unidos Ser.). (ENG & SPA.). 32p. (gr. 2-3). 47.90 *(978-1-61512-538-8(8),* Editorial Buenas Letras) Rosen Publishing Group, Inc., The.

—Benjamin Franklin: Político e inventor Estadounidense, 1 vol. 2003. (Grandes Personajes en la Historia de Los Estados Unidos (Famous People in American History) Ser.). (SPA.). 32p. (gr. 3-4). pap. 10.00 *(978-0-8239-4221-3(X),* c2496fbf-eecd-4e55-90ef-221234038279, Rosen Classroom) Rosen Publishing Group, Inc., The.

—Benjamin Franklin: Político e inventor estadounidense (Benjamin Franklin: Early American Genius) 2009. (Grandes personajes en la historia de los Estados Unidos (Famous People in American History) Ser.). (SPA.). 32p. (gr. 2-3). 47.90 *(978-1-61512-790-0(9),* Editorial Buenas Letras) Rosen Publishing Group, Inc., The.

Golden, Nancy. The British Are Coming! The Midnight Ride of Paul Revere. 2009. (Great Moments in American History Ser.). 32p. (gr. 3-3). 47.90 *(978-1-61513-136-5(1))* Rosen Publishing Group, Inc., The.

Gosman, Gillian. Benjamin Franklin, 1 vol. 2011. (Life Stories Ser.). (ENG., Illus.). 24p. (J). (gr. 3-3). pap. 9.25 *(978-1-4488-2759-6(0),* d96f395d-ae34-43c9-9680-8de06d8c53e6); lib. bdg. 26.27 *(978-1-4488-2585-1(7),* 0ce2f8ab-182f-4f36-8495-052334f7703d) Rosen Publishing Group, Inc., The. (PowerKids Pr.).

Gould, Jane H. Alexander Hamilton, 1 vol. 2012. (Jr. Graphic Founding Fathers Ser.). (ENG., Illus.). 24p. (J). (gr. 2-3). pap. 11.60 *(978-1-4488-7989-2(2),* 1d6bf400-d883-42f3-9cf5-9ec5414ffb13); lib. bdg. 28.93 *(978-1-4488-7895-6(0),* 2bbd35e0-af34-4c29-b0ab-a3eb8774959f) Rosen Publishing Group, Inc., The. (PowerKids Pr.).

—Benjamin Franklin, 1 vol. 2012. (Jr. Graphic Founding Fathers Ser.). (ENG., Illus.). 24p. (J). (gr. 2-3). pap. 11.60 *(978-1-4488-7990-8(6),* c2607bf3-41ea-46f1-90c5-06cc7b530046); lib. bdg. 28.93 *(978-1-4488-7896-3(9),* 4e9506b1-7138-494a-9292-34a30a1d094c) Rosen Publishing Group, Inc., The. (PowerKids Pr.).

Greene, Victor. The Life of Benjamin Franklin, 1 vol. 2012. (InfoMax Readers Ser.). (ENG., Illus.). 24p. (J). (gr. 1-1). pap. 8.25 *(978-1-4488-8992-1(8),* 99f79325-30f1-4a45-b10b-27e9c99e0ad8, Rosen Classroom) Rosen Publishing Group, Inc., The.

Gunderson, Jessica. The Real Alexander Hamilton: The Truth Behind the Legend. 2019. (Real Revolutionaries Ser.). (ENG., Illus.). 64p. (J). (gr. 5-9). pap. 7.95 *(978-0-7565-6128-4(0),* 140075); lib. bdg. 34.65 *(978-0-7565-5892-5(1),* 138697) Capstone. (Compass Point Bks.).

—The Real Benjamin Franklin: The Truth Behind the Legend. 2019. (Real Revolutionaries Ser.). (ENG., Illus.). 64p. (J). (gr. 5-9). pap. 7.95 *(978-0-7565-6129-1(9),* 140076); lib. bdg. 34.65 *(978-0-7565-5893-2(X),* 138698) Capstone. (Compass Point Bks.).

Haldy, Emma E. Benjamin Franklin. Bane, Jeff, illus. 2016. (My Early Library: My Itty-Bitty Bio Ser.). (ENG.). 24p. (J). (gr. k-1). 30.64 *(978-1-63470-478-6(9),* 207643) Cherry Lake Publishing.

—Benjamin Franklin SP. Bane, Jeff, illus. 2018. (My Early Library: Mi Mini Biografía (My Itty-Bitty Bio) Ser.). (SPA.). 24p. (J). (gr. k-1). lib. bdg. 30.64 *(978-1-5341-2994-8(4),* 212024) Cherry Lake Publishing.

Hale, Sarah Elder, ed. Jefferson Davis & the Confederacy. 2005. (ENG., Illus.). 48p. (J). (gr. 3-9). 17.95 *(978-0-8126-7908-3(3))* Cobblestone Pr.

Hancock, Lee. Lorenzo de' Medici: Florence's Great Leader & Patron of the Arts. (Rulers, Scholars, & Artists of the Renaissance Ser.). 112p. (gr. 5-8). 2009. 66.50 *(978-1-60852-942-1(8),* Rosen Reference) 2004. (ENG., Illus.). (J). lib. bdg. 39.80 *(978-1-4042-0315-0(X),* ca8076a6-2614-4397-8ac0-414e3eda79d9) Rosen Publishing Group, Inc., The.

Hesleden, Michael. Benjamin Franklin: American Diplomat, 1 vol. 2015. (Spotlight on American History Ser.). (ENG., Illus.). 24p. (J). (gr. 4-6). pap. 11.00 *(978-1-4994-1782-1(9),* 9e07a93f-8acc-4758-91cb-ca59c6005d7f, PowerKids Pr.) Rosen Publishing Group, Inc., The.

Heuston, Kimberley. Mao Zedong. 2010. (Wicked History Ser.). (ENG.). 128p. (J). (gr. 6-12). pap. 5.95 *(978-0-531-22356-7(6),* Watts, Franklin) Scholastic Library Publishing.

—Otto von Bismarck: Iron Chancellor of Germany. (Wicked History Ser.). (ENG., Illus.). (YA). 2010. 128p. (gr. 6-12). pap. 5.95 *(978-0-531-22824-1(X),* Watts, Franklin) 2009. 224p. (gr. 5-9). 31.00 *(978-0-531-21278-3(5))* Scholastic Library Publishing.

Heuston, Kimberley Burton. Mao Zedong. 2010. (Wicked History Ser.). (ENG., Illus.). 128p. (J). (gr. 5-8). 31.00 *(978-0-531-20756-7(0))* Scholastic Library Publishing.

Hicks, Dwayne. Paul Revere: American Patriot, 1 vol. 2012. (Beginning Biographies Ser.). (ENG., Illus.). 24p. (J). (gr. 1-2). 26.27 *(978-1-4488-8599-2(X),* 2aa1337b-5524-4b90-af85-b6dbee02d41d, PowerKids Pr.) Rosen Publishing Group, Inc., The.

Hilliam, David. Thomas Becket: English Saint & Martyr. 2009. (Leaders of the Middle Ages Ser.). 112p. (gr. 5-8). 66.50 *(978-1-61513-902-6(8),* Rosen Reference) Rosen Publishing Group, Inc., The.

Hirschfeld, Leila & Hirschfeld, Tom. You Decide, Ben Franklin! Weber, Lisa K., illus. 2016. 269p. (J). pap. *(978-0-553-50952-6(7),* Salamander Bks.) Pavilion Bks.

Hollander, Barbara Gottfried. Harvey Milk: The First Openly Gay Elected Official in the United States. 2017. (Spotlight on Civic Courage: Heroes of Conscience Ser.). 48p. (J). (gr. 10-15). 70.50 *(978-1-5383-8093-2(5),* Rosen Young Adult) Rosen Publishing Group, Inc., The.

Hughes, Chris. The Constitutional Convention. 2005. (People at the Center of Ser.). (Illus.). 48p. (J). (gr. -1-7). lib. bdg. 24.95 *(978-1-56711-918-3(2),* Blackbirch Pr., Inc.) Cengage Gale.

Jeffrey, Gary. Paul Revere & His Midnight Ride, 1 vol. 2011. (Graphic Heroes of the American Revolution Ser.). (ENG.). 24p. (J). (gr. 3-3). pap. 9.15 *(978-1-4339-6020-8(6),* 0981fe11-ad56-49bb-ba3e-6601372ad8b3, Gareth Stevens Learning Library); lib. bdg. 26.60 *(978-1-4339-6019-2(2),* c3cd73f3-b213-499a-b80e-d68ebc2109bb) Stevens, Gareth Publishing LLLP.

—Thomas Jefferson & the Declaration of Independence, 1 vol. 2011. (Graphic Heroes of the American Revolution Ser.). (ENG., Illus.). 24p. (J). (gr. 3-3). 26.60 *(978-1-4339-6025-3(7),* b3ad44c5-2d19-400f-8ba3-6b2e6bef69a2); pap. 9.15 *(978-1-4339-6026-0(5),* 6bfbc259-f45e-48b1-85a7-4b2b3c1cce56, Gareth Stevens Learning Library) Stevens, Gareth Publishing LLLP.

Juarez, Christine. José Antonio Navarro. 2016. (Great Hispanic & Latino Americans Ser.). (ENG., Illus.). 24p. (J). (gr. -1-2). lib. bdg. 24.65 *(978-1-5157-1889-5(1),* 132588, Pebble) Capstone.

Katirgis, Jane & McCarthy, Rose. Meet Paul Revere: Revolutionary Hero, 1 vol. 2019. (Introducing Famous Americans Ser.). (ENG.). 32p. (gr. 3-4). pap. 11.53 *(978-1-9785-1130-9(2),* aabbf4d0-c3b3-4ca2-86a7-db6ef8ac5f6d) Enslow Publishing, LLC.

Keller, Susanna. Alexander Hamilton: America's First Treasury Secretary, 1 vol. 2017. (Britannica Beginner Bios Ser.). (ENG., Illus.). 32p. (J). (gr. 2-3). pap. 13.90 *(978-1-68048-808-1(2),* eab0f6a1-72cf-4eb2-a5eb-53313f8b7c28); lib. bdg. 26.06 *(978-1-68048-809-8(0),* 2896e138-b801-4476-9722-6e478e5423ba) Rosen Publishing Group, Inc., The. (Britannica Educational Publishing).

—The True Story of Paul Revere's Ride, 1 vol. 2013. (What Really Happened? Ser.). (ENG., Illus.). 24p. (J). (gr. 2-3). pap. 9.25 *(978-1-4488-9838-1(2),* efd634f7-c46f-44be-a810-8952a3a1d7af); lib. bdg. 26.27 *(978-1-4488-9690-5(8),* b9df1cc6-fbb3-44a4-8594-63505b0e3628) Rosen Publishing Group, Inc., The. (PowerKids Pr.).

Kelly, Jack. Benjamin Franklin. Tafalla, Ortiz, illus. 2005. (Heroes of America Ser.). 239p. (gr. 3-8). 27.07 *(978-1-59679-257-9(4),* Abdo & Daughters) ABDO Publishing Co.

Kuhn, Betsy. The Force Born of Truth: Mohandas Gandhi & the Salt March, India 1930. 2010. (Civil Rights Struggles Around the World Ser.). (ENG., Illus.). 160p. (YA). (gr. 6-12). lib. bdg. 38.65 *(978-0-8225-8968-6(0),* deaff85b-8573-436b-a823-e0da6015bbfa, Twenty-First Century Bks.) Lerner Publishing Group.

Kulling, Monica. Alexander Hamilton: from Orphan to Founding Father. Fabbretti, Valerio, illus. 2017. (Step into Reading Ser.). 48p. (J). (gr. k-3). pap. 4.99 *(978-1-5247-1698-1(7),* Random Hse. Bks. for Young Readers) Random Hse. Children's Bks.

Lace, William W. Benjamin Franklin. 2010. (ENG., Illus.). 120p. (gr. 5-8). 35.00 *(978-1-60413-737-8(1),* P210466, Facts On File) Infobase Holdings, Inc.

Let's Call It America! Meet Our Founding Fathers. 2013. (Illus.). 32p. (J). *(978-0-545-53539-7(5))* Scholastic, Inc.

Lowell, Barbara. Alexander Hamilton: American Hero. Ermos, George, illus. 2018. (Penguin Young Readers, Level 4 Ser.). 32p. (J). (gr. 1-3). pap. 4.99 *(978-1-5247-8773-8(6),* Penguin Young Readers) Penguin Young Readers Group.

Lowery, Zoe & Forsyth, Fiona. Cicero, 1 vol. 2016. (Leaders of the Ancient World Ser.). (ENG., Illus.). 112p. (J). (gr. 6-6). 38.80 *(978-1-5081-7258-1(7),* 381f80e6-0929-49e6-a725-c4b0d60d45ba) Rosen Publishing Group, Inc., The.

Lucas, Eileen. Mahatma Gandhi: Fighting for Indian Independence, 1 vol. 2017. (Rebels with a Cause Ser.). (ENG.). 128p. (gr. 8-8). lib. bdg. 38.93 *(978-0-7660-8513-8(9),* 7939188e-3ec5-4be9-bb21-fc0384bf8c3d) Enslow Publishing, LLC.

Mack, Molly. The Life of Paul Revere, 1 vol. 2012. (InfoMax Readers Ser.). (ENG., Illus.). 24p. (J). (gr. 1-1). pap. 8.25 *(978-1-4488-9049-1(7),* ed30d88c-450a-4152-abba-81a56a50f15f, Rosen Classroom) Rosen Publishing Group, Inc., The.

Major World Leaders. 2005. (Major World Leaders Ser.). 144p. (gr. 6-12). 270.00 *(978-0-7910-8410-6(8),* Facts On File) Infobase Holdings, Inc.

Malaspina, Ann. Mahatma Gandhi & India's Independence, 1 vol. 2015. (People & Events That Changed the World Ser.). (ENG., Illus.). 128p. (gr. 7-8). lib. bdg. 38.93 *(978-0-7660-7262-6(2),* 8f83c7cf-ac81-4ea0-81ba-a248f923ff26) Enslow Publishing, LLC.

Mara, Wil. Benjamin Franklin. (Rookie Biographies(tm) Ser.). (Illus.). (J). 2014. (ENG.). 32p. lib. bdg. 25.00 *(978-0-531-20558-7(4))* 2007. 31p. (gr. 1-2). pap. 4.95 *(978-0-531-12591-5(2),* Children's Pr.) Scholastic Library Publishing.

—Benjamin Franklin (Rookie Biographies) 2014. (Rookie Biographies Ser.). (ENG., Illus.). 32p. (J). (gr. 1-2). pap. 5.95 *(978-0-531-21201-1(7),* Children's Pr.) Scholastic Library Publishing.

—Rookie Biographies: Paul Revere. 2005. (Rookie Biographies Ser.). (ENG., Illus.). 32p. (J). (gr. 1-2). pap. 4.95 *(978-0-516-25820-1(6),* Children's Pr.) Scholastic Library Publishing.

Marsh, Carole. Jefferson Davis, Civil War Hero. 2004. 12p. (gr. k-4). 2.95 *(978-0-635-02366-7(0))* Gallopade International.

Marston, Elsa. The Compassionate Warrior: Abd el-Kader of Algeria. 2013. (Illus.). 184p. (J). (gr. 8-12). pap. 16.95 *(978-1-937786-10-6(2),* Wisdom Tales) World Wisdom, Inc.

Martí, Jose. Jose Martí: Cuatro cuentos Infantiles. Martinez, Enrique & Graullera, Fabiola, illus. (SPA.). 28p. (J). (gr. 3-5). 9.95 *(978-970-29-0522-6(2))* Santillana, Editorial, S.A. de C.V. MEX. Dist: Santillana USA Publishing Co., Inc.

Mattern, Joanne. Sam Houston: Un Estadista Audaz. 2013. (Primary Source Readers Ser.). (SPA.). lib. bdg. 19.65 *(978-0-606-31869-3(0))* Turtleback.

McCarthy, Rose. Dictatorship: A Primary Source Analysis. 2009. (Primary Sources of Political Systems Ser.). 64p. (gr. 5-8). 58.50 *(978-1-60851-837-1(X))* Rosen Publishing Group, Inc., The.

—Paul Revere: Freedom Rider. 2009. (Primary Sources of Famous People in American History Ser.). 32p. (gr. 2-3). 47.90 *(978-1-60851-714-5(4))* Rosen Publishing Group, Inc., The.

—Paul Revere: Freedom Rider / Jinete de la causa Revolucionaria. 2009. (Famous People in American History/Grandes personajes en la historia de los Estados Unidos Ser.). (ENG & SPA.). 32p. (gr. 2-3). 47.90 *(978-1-61512-553-1(1),* Editorial Buenas Letras) Rosen Publishing Group, Inc., The.

—Paul Revere: Jinete de la causa revolucionaria (Paul Revere: Freedom Rider) 2009. (Grandes personajes en la historia de los Estados Unidos (Famous People in American History) Ser.). (SPA.). 32p. (gr. 2-3). 47.90 *(978-1-61512-806-8(9),* Editorial Buenas Letras) Rosen Publishing Group, Inc., The.

—Paul Revere: Jinete de la guerra de Independencia, 1 vol. 2003. (Grandes Personajes en la Historia de Los Estados Unidos (Famous People in American History) Ser.). (SPA.). 32p. (gr. 3-4). pap. 10.00 *(978-0-8239-4236-7(8),* 7a9dae9c-1087-4ed3-af54-9ea70e742eec, Rosen Classroom) Rosen Publishing Group, Inc., The.

McCollum, Sean. The Chairman: Mao Unleashes Chaos in China. 2011. (J). pap. *(978-0-545-32935-4(3))* Scholastic, Inc.

—Joseph Stalin. 2010. (Wicked History Ser.). (ENG., Illus.). 128p. (J). 31.00 *(978-0-531-20755-0(2),* Watts, Franklin) Scholastic Library Publishing.

—Joseph Stalin (a Wicked History) 2010. (Wicked History Ser.). (ENG.). 128p. (J). (gr. 6-12). pap. 5.95 *(978-0-531-22355-0(8),* Watts, Franklin) Scholastic Library Publishing.

McCurdy, Michael, illus. So Said Ben. 2007. (ENG.). 32p. (J). (gr. 1-3). 17.95 *(978-1-56846-147-2(X),* 22702, Creative Editions) Creative Co., The.

McDonnell, Vincent. Michael Collins: Most Wanted Man. 2009. (ENG.). 136p. (J). pap. 15.95 *(978-1-905172-62-7(1),* Collins Pr., The) M.H. Gill & Co. U. C. IRL. Dist: Dufour Editions, Inc.

McDowell, Pamela. Benjamin Franklin. 2013. *(978-1-62127-307-3(5));* pap. *(978-1-62127-313-4(X))* Weigl Pubs., Inc.

McGrath, Brian. Aaron Burr: More Than a Villain (Alexander Hamilton) rev. ed. 2017. (Social Studies: Informational Text Ser.). (ENG., Illus.). 32p. (gr. 4-8). pap. 11.99 *(978-1-4258-6355-5(8))* Teacher Created Materials, Inc.

McLeese, Don. Alexander Hamilton. 2004. (Heroes of the American Revolution Ser.). (Illus.). 32p. (gr. 2-5). lib. bdg. *(978-1-59515-219-0(9))* Rourke Educational Media.

—Benjamin Franklin. 2005. (Heroes of the American Revolution Ser.). (Illus.). 32p. (gr. 2-5). 19.95 *(978-1-59515-216-9(4))* Rourke Educational Media.

Melton, Buckner F. Aaron Burr: The Rise & Fall of an American Politician. 2009. (Library of American Lives & Times Ser.). 112p. (gr. 5-5). 69.20 *(978-1-60853-468-5(5))* Rosen Publishing Group, Inc., The.

Meltzer, Brad. I Am Gandhi: A Graphic Biography of a Hero. Mack, David et al, illus. 2018. (Ordinary People Change the World Ser.). 64p. (J). (gr. 5-9). pap. 8.99 *(978-0-525-55269-7(3),* Dial Bks) Penguin Young Readers Group.

Meltzer, Brad & Eliopoulos, Christopher. I Am Gandhi. (Ordinary People Change the World Ser.). (Illus.). 40p. (J). (gr. k-4). 2023. pap. 9.99 ***(978-0-593-61921-6(8),*** Rocky Pond Bks.) 2017. 16.99 *(978-0-7352-2870-2(1),* Dial Bks) Penguin Young Readers Group.

Merrell Foster, Leila. Benjamin Franklin: Statesman & Inventor, 1 vol. 2014. (Legendary American Biographies Ser.). (ENG.). 96p. (gr. 6-6). 29.60 *(978-0-7660-6445-4(X),* 6f71ffbe-8abd-4301-95fb-7c002da289d3); pap. 13.88 *(978-0-7660-6446-1(8),* becd3130-d729-474f-a78f-4c9df4c93a65) Enslow Publishing, LLC.

Miller, Brandon Marie. Benjamin Franklin, American Genius: His Life & Ideas with 21 Activities. 2009. (For Kids Ser.: 28). (ENG., Illus.). 144p. (J). (gr. 4-7). pap. 18.99 *(978-1-55652-757-9(8))* Chicago Review Pr., Inc.

Miller, Derek. Mahatma Gandhi: March to Independence, 1 vol. 2017. (Peaceful Protesters Ser.). (ENG.). 112p. (YA). (gr. 9-9). pap. 20.99 *(978-1-5026-3396-5(5),* 97541f3e-8abe-46ee-adf0-e21ca841f103) Cavendish Square Publishing LLC.

Mills, Nathan & Coleridge, Margaret. Who Was Benjamin Franklin?, 1 vol. 2012. (Rosen Readers Ser.). (ENG., Illus.). 24p. (J). (gr. 1-1). pap. 8.25 *(978-1-4488-8773-6(9),* 65d597ea-9aaf-4279-9f06-cd6054727350, Rosen Classroom) Rosen Publishing Group, Inc., The.

Mills, Nathan & Hicks, Dwayne. Paul Revere: American Patriot, 1 vol. 2012. (Rosen Readers Ser.). (ENG., Illus.). 24p. (J). (gr. 1-2). pap. 8.25 *(978-1-4488-8836-8(0),* 134af41f-53e0-4456-a0f8-6e74a2a5ae8e, Rosen Classroom) Rosen Publishing Group, Inc., The.

Min, Ellen. The Midnight Ride of Paul Revere: One If by Land, Two If by Sea, 1 vol. 2015. (Spotlight on American History Ser.). (ENG., Illus.). 24p. (J). (gr. 4-6). pap. 11.00 *(978-1-4994-1734-0(9),* 6ebe0528-c359-4a33-b22f-cde39d20f9ee, PowerKids Pr.) Rosen Publishing Group, Inc., The.

Morlock, Theresa. 20 Fun Facts about Benjamin Franklin. 2017. (Fun Fact File: Founding Fathers Ser.). 32p. (gr. 2-3). pap. 63.00 *(978-1-5382-0271-5(9))* Stevens, Gareth Publishing LLLP.

Nagle, Jeanne, ed. Top 101 World Leaders, 1 vol., 1. 2013. (People You Should Know Ser.). (ENG.). 184p. (YA). (gr. 8-8). 38.84 *(978-1-62275-124-2(8),* 27187543-c140-40c6-9f53-a9c922e9fd92) Rosen Publishing Group, Inc., The.

National Geographic Learning. Reading Expeditions (Social Studies: Documents of Freedom): the Declaration of Independence. 2007. (ENG., Illus.). 32p. (J). pap. 18.95 *(978-0-7922-4554-4(7))* CENGAGE Learning.

Nelson, Maria. The Life of Ben Franklin, 1 vol. 2012. (Famous Lives Ser.). (ENG.). 24p. (J). (gr. 1-2). pap. 9.15 *(978-1-4339-6347-6(7),* 26557dd4-7694-49cb-9a64-92978e1c931d); lib. bdg. 25.27 *(978-1-4339-6345-2(0),* 46c95f44-0445-407d-a54d-e09def9de09c) Stevens, Gareth Publishing LLLP.

—The Life of Ben Franklin / la Vida de Benjamín Franklin, 1 vol. 2012. (Famous Lives / Vidas Extraordinarias Ser.). (ENG & SPA., Illus.). 24p. (J). (gr. 1-2). 25.27 *(978-1-4339-6653-8(0),* 9e202cf7-e254-4a33-8484-e8019e733ad8) Stevens, Gareth Publishing LLLP.

—The Life of Paul Revere, 1 vol. 2012. (Famous Lives Ser.). (ENG.). 24p. (J). (gr. 1-2). pap. 9.15 *(978-1-4339-6355-1(8),* 28f1d255-6234-4269-a325-eee483bc787f); lib. bdg. 25.27 *(978-1-4339-6353-7(1),* 94adfa60-b92a-4642-bf87-ccb0fbd3bbd7) Stevens, Gareth Publishing LLLP.

Newton, Michael E. Alexander Hamilton: The Formative Years. 2015. (ENG., Illus.). 774p. 40.00 *(978-0-9826040-3-8(3))* Eleftheria Publishing.

Osborne, Mary Pope & Boyce, Natalie Pope. Benjamin Franklin: A Nonfiction Companion to Magic Tree House #32: to the Future, Ben Franklin! 2019. (Magic Tree House (R) Fact Tracker Ser.: 41). (Illus.). 128p. (J). (gr. 2-5). pap. 6.99 *(978-1-9848-9317-8(3),* Random Hse. Bks. for Young Readers) Random Hse. Children's Bks.

Otfinoski, Steven. Patriots & Redcoats: Stories of American Revolutionary War Leaders. 2015. (Revolutionary War Ser.). (ENG., Illus.). 48p. (J). (gr. 3-6). pap. 8.95 *(978-1-4914-2158-1(4),* 127709, Capstone Pr.) Capstone.

Otheguy, Emma. Martí's Song for Freedom / Martí y Sus Versos Por la Libertad: Mart� y Sus Versos Por la Independencia, 1 vol. Vidal, Beatriz, illus. 2017. (ENG.). 32p. (J). (gr. 2-8). 19.95 *(978-0-89239-375-6(0),* leelowcbp, Children's Book Press) Lee & Low Bks., Inc.

Owens, L. L. Benjamin Franklin, 1 vol. 2007. (Essential Lives Set 1 Ser.). (ENG., Illus.). 112p. (YA). (gr. 6-12). lib. bdg. 41.36 *(978-1-59928-840-6(0),* 6633, Essential Library) ABDO Publishing Co.

Peppas, Lynn. Why José Antonio Navarro Matters to Texas, 1 vol. 2013. (Texas Perspectives Ser.). (ENG., Illus.). 32p. (J). (gr. 4-4). lib. bdg. 28.93 *(978-1-4777-0936-8(3),* 0143289d-1cb7-4f6e-8c3b-f4449a309e61) Rosen Publishing Group, Inc., The.

Phan, Sandy. Cecil Rhodes: The Man Who Expanded an Empire, 1 vol. rev. ed. 2012. (Social Studies: Informational Text Ser.). (ENG.). 32p. (gr. 4-8). pap. 11.99 *(978-1-4333-5016-0(5))* Teacher Created Materials, Inc.

Pollack, Pam, et al. Who Was Alexander Hamilton? Putra, Dede, illus. 2017. (Who Was? Ser.). 112p. (J). (gr. 3-7). 5.99 *(978-0-399-54427-9(5),* Penguin Workshop) Penguin Young Readers Group.

Price, Sean Stewart. Adolf Hitler. 2010. (Wicked History Ser.). (ENG., Illus.). 128p. (J). 31.00 *(978-0-531-20757-4(9),* Watts, Franklin) Scholastic Library Publishing.

Proudfit, Benjamin. Benjamin Franklin, 1 vol. 2014. (What You Didn't Know about History Ser.). (ENG., Illus.). 24p. (J). (gr. 2-3). pap. 9.15 *(978-1-4824-1926-9(2),* 66cc6acd-1c69-4e17-a047-f595f8d43b19) Stevens, Gareth Publishing LLLP.

Randolph, Joanne. The Call of Liberty: Marquis de Lafayette & the American Revolution. 2009. (Great Moments in American History Ser.). 32p. (gr. 3-3). 47.90 *(978-1-61513-152-5(3))* Rosen Publishing Group, Inc., The.

Randolph, Ryan P. Benjamin Franklin: Inventor, Writer, & Patriot. 2009. (Library of American Lives & Times Ser.). 112p. (gr. 5-5). 69.20 *(978-1-60853-472-2(3))* Rosen Publishing Group, Inc., The.

Ransom, Candice. John Hancock. 2005. (History Maker Bios Ser.). (Illus.). 48p. (J). (gr. 3-4). 26.60 *(978-0-8225-1547-0(4),* Lerner Pubns.) Lerner Publishing Group.

Rau, Dana Meachen & Who HQ. Who Was Gandhi? Hoare, Jerry, illus. 2014. (Who Was? Ser.). 112p. (J). (gr. 3-7). pap. 5.99 *(978-0-448-48235-4(5),* Penguin Workshop) Penguin Young Readers Group.

Rausch, Monica. Benjamin Franklin, 1 vol. 2007. (Great Americans Ser.). (ENG., Illus.). 24p. (gr. 2-4). pap. 9.15 *(978-0-8368-7689-5(X),* f9d7d902-1989-4c9f-a6ea-a5c5f1ef3960); lib. bdg. 24.67 *(978-0-8368-7682-6(2),* e5fe2671-81d7-496f-bd45-9a1d7ab28aad) Stevens, Gareth Publishing LLLP. (Weekly Reader Leveled Readers).

—Benjamín Franklin, 1 vol. 2007. (Grandes Personajes (Great Americans) Ser.). (SPA., Illus.). 24p. (gr. 2-4). lib. bdg. 24.67 *(978-0-8368-7981-0(3),* 1de6ba44-ef15-450a-bd7c-2aa5e00e911c) Stevens, Gareth Publishing LLLP.

Rice, William & Rice, Dona. Mohandas Gandhi. 2017. (TIME for Kids en Español - Level 3 Ser.). (SPA., Illus.). 32p. (J). (gr. 2-5). lib. bdg. 32.65 *(978-1-5157-5189-2(9),* 134708, Capstone Pr.) Capstone.

Riley, Gail Blasser. Cornerstones of Freedom: Benjamin Franklin & Electricity. 2004. (Cornerstones of Freedom Ser.). (ENG., Illus.). 48p. (J). (gr. 4-7). 26.00 *(978-0-516-24240-8(7))* Scholastic Library Publishing.

Riley, John B. Benjamin Franklin: A Photo Biography. l.t. ed. 2004. (First Biographies Ser.). (Illus.). 24p. (YA). (gr. 5-18). 16.95 *(978-1-883846-64-0(1),* First Biographies) Reynolds, Morgan Inc.

Rinaldo, Denise. Julius Caesar: Dictator for Life. 2010. (Wicked History Ser.). (ENG.). 128p. (J). (gr. 6-12). pap. 5.95 *(978-0-531-22822-7(3),* Watts, Franklin) Scholastic Library Publishing.

Rivera, Sheila. Mohandas Gandhi: A Life of Integrity. (Pull Ahead Books — Biographies Ser.). (Illus.). 32p. (J). 2007. (ENG.). (gr. k-3). pap. 7.99 *(978-0-8225-6432-4(7),* 80e01018-0109-487b-8579-e04d22a5e061) 2006. (gr. 3-7). lib. bdg. 22.60 *(978-0-8225-6383-9(5),* Lerner Pubns.) Lerner Publishing Group.

Romero, Libby. National Geographic Kids Readers: Alexander Hamilton (L3) 2018. (Readers Ser.). (Illus.). 48p. (J). (gr. 3-7). pap. 4.99 *(978-1-4263-3038-4(3));* (ENG., lib. bdg. 14.90

S

(978-1-4263-3039-1(1)) Disney Publishing Worldwide. (National Geographic Kids).

Ryckman, Tatiana. Alexander Hamilton: The First Secretary of the Treasury & an Author of the Federalist Papers, 1 vol. 2016. (Great American Thinkers Ser.). (ENG., Illus.). 128p. (J). (gr. 9-9). 47.36 *(978-1-5026-1934-1(2),* e61e020c-0a13-45b1-95be-cb5f62d6901b) Cavendish Square Publishing LLC.

Santillian, Beatriz & Aird, Hamish. Pericles: Athenian Statesman & Patron of the Arts, 1 vol. 2017. (Leaders of the Ancient World Ser.). (ENG., Illus.). 112p. (J). (gr. 6-6). 38.80 *(978-1-5081-7487-5(3),* 0bdf2823-7850-4d5e-a765-836c33750a1d, Rosen Young Adult) Rosen Publishing Group, Inc., The.

Santillian, Beatriz & Randall, Bernard. Solon: Athenian Statesman & Poet, 1 vol. 2017. (Leaders of the Ancient World Ser.). (ENG., Illus.). 112p. (J). (gr. 6-6). 38.80 *(978-1-5081-7493-6(8),* 9e229bc7-da52-47ff-8710-b22f9277c86a, Rosen Young Adult) Rosen Publishing Group, Inc., The.

Satterfield, Kathryn Hoffman. Benjamin Franklin A Man of Many Talents. 2005. 44p. (J). lib. bdg. 15.00 *(978-1-4242-0846-3(7))* Fitzgerald Bks.

Sawyer, Kem Knapp. Mohandas Gandhi. 2011. (Champion of Freedom Ser.). 144p. (gr. 7-12). 28.95 *(978-1-59935-166-7(8))* Reynolds, Morgan Inc.

Schwartz, Heather E. Alexander Hamilton: The Story of a Statesman. 2020. (Gateway Biographies Ser.). (ENG., Illus.). 48p. (J). (gr. 4-8). pap. 11.99 *(978-1-5415-8886-8(X),* 53c57c54-581f-4c89-9d64-f13c6a4b348c); lib. bdg. 31.99 *(978-1-5415-7748-0(5),* c9c12720-d8a7-4416-8f8b-af90f397aacf) Lerner Publishing Group. (Lerner Pubns.).

Seeley, M. H. 20 Fun Facts about Aaron Burr, 1 vol. 2017. (Fun Fact File: Founding Fathers Ser.). (ENG., Illus.). 32p. (J). (gr. 2-3). 27.93 *(978-1-5382-0281-4(6),* 19d6db15-b3b7-44f3-a5f4-0e7bc1f2b537) Stevens, Gareth Publishing LLLP.

—20 Fun Facts about Alexander Hamilton, 1 vol. 2017. (Fun Fact File: Founding Fathers Ser.). (ENG., Illus.). 32p. (J). (gr. 2-3). pap. 11.50 *(978-1-5382-0288-3(3),* 76d79366-9bf3-4b7d-a923-d9a526bd2a69) Stevens, Gareth Publishing LLLP.

Shaw, Maura D. Gandhi: India's Great Soul. Marchesi, Stephen, illus. 2003. (ENG.). 32p. (J). (gr. 1-3). 12.95 *(978-1-893361-91-1(8),* cae3cea7-a255-4b12-be7a-5ba52b13badc, Skylight Paths Publishing) LongHill Partners, Inc.

Shea, Therese M. Alexander Hamilton: Founding Father & Treasury Secretary, 1 vol. 2017. (Junior Biographies Ser.). (ENG.). 24p. (gr. 3-4). pap. 10.35 *(978-0-7660-9045-3(0),* c04e79f6-c80e-4ab8-974e-5cbba0de0d73) Enslow Publishing, LLC.

Smith, Andrea P. A Day in the Life of Colonial Silversmith Paul Revere. (Illus.). 24p. (J). 2012. 63.60 *(978-1-4488-5217-8(X))* 2011. (ENG., (gr. 2-3). pap. 11.60 *(978-1-4488-5216-1(1),* 222487a5-1e5c-4e48-abee-09b3e5f95238) 2011. (ENG., (gr. 2-3). lib. bdg. 28.93 *(978-1-4488-5189-8(0),* 2bb3a4f9-0113-4e50-be2f-9f17eb9f5dd4) Rosen Publishing Group, Inc., The. (PowerKids Pr.).

Stoltman, Joan. Mohandas Gandhi, 1 vol. 2018. (Little Biographies of Big People Ser.). (ENG.). 24p. (gr. 1-2). 24.27 *(978-1-5382-1851-8(8),* f4ac0609-56fb-461b-9558-e5943b4295cb) Stevens, Gareth Publishing LLLP.

Streissguth, Tom. Benjamin Franklin. 2005. (Bios for Challenged Readers Ser.). (Illus.). 112p. (J). (gr. 6-12). lib. bdg. 27.93 *(978-0-8225-2210-2(1))* Lerner Publishing Group.

Tarman, Mel. Judah: The Story of Judah P. Benjamin, Confederate Statesman. 2013. 46p. pap. 6.95 *(978-1-929919-50-5(6))* Camp Pope Publishing.

Thayer, William Makepeace. From Boyhood to Manhood: Life of Benjamin Franklin. 2006. pap. *(978-1-4068-0906-0(3))* Echo Library.

Time for Kids Editors. Benjamin Franklin - A Man of Many Talents. 2005. (Time for Kids Ser.). (ENG., Illus.). 48p. (J). (gr. 2-4). pap. 3.99 *(978-0-06-057609-7(X))* HarperCollins Pubs.

Time Magazine Editors. Alexander Hamilton: Life Stories of Extraordinary Americans. 2018. (Heroes of History Ser.: 1). (ENG., Illus.). 144p. (J). (gr. 6-17). pap. 9.99 *(978-1-68330-850-8(6),* Time Home Entertainment) Time Inc. Bks.

Todd, Anne M. Mohandas Gandhi. 2004. (Spiritual Leaders & Thinkers Ser.). (ENG., Illus.). 120p. (gr. 9-13). 30.00 *(978-0-7910-7864-8(7),* P114032, Facts On File) Infobase Holdings, Inc.

Tracy, Kathleen. The Life & Times of Cicero. 2006. (Biography from Ancient Civilizations Ser.). (Illus.). 48p. (J). (gr. 4-8). lib. bdg. 29.95 *(978-1-58415-510-2(3))* Mitchell Lane Pubs.

Troupe, Thomas Kingsley. Paul Revere's Ride: a Fly on the Wall History. Tejido, Jomike, illus. 2017. (Fly on the Wall History Ser.). (ENG.). 32p. (J). (gr. 1-3). lib. bdg. 27.99 *(978-1-4795-9785-7(6),* 133407, Picture Window Bks.) Capstone.

A True Book & Trade - Biographies. 2013. (True Book™—Biographies Ser.). (J). 116.00 *(978-0-531-28024-9(1),* Children's Pr.) Scholastic Library Publishing.

Trussell-Cullen, Alan. Mahatma Gandhi. 2009. pap. 13.25 *(978-1-60559-064-6(9))* Hameray Publishing Group, Inc.

Uschan, Michael V. Fidel Castro, 1 vol. 2008. (People in the News Ser.). (ENG., Illus.). 104p. (gr. 7-7). lib. bdg. 41.03 *(978-1-4205-0059-2(7),* 85489daf-72a5-4286-adcf-582eb9813e72, Lucent Pr.) Greenhaven Publishing LLC.

Vander Hook, Sue. Mahatma Gandhi: Proponent of Peace, 1 vol. 2010. (Essential Lives Set 5 Ser.). (ENG.). 112p. (YA). (gr. 6-12). lib. bdg. 41.36 *(978-1-61613-515-7(8),* 6713, Essential Library) ABDO Publishing Co.

Vescia, Monique & Nicholson, Michael. Mahatma Gandhi: Champion of the Indian Independence Movement. 2017. (Spotlight on Civic Courage: Heroes of Conscience Ser.). 48p. (J). (gr. 10-15). 70.50 *(978-1-5383-8084-0(6));* (ENG.). (gr. 6-6). pap. 12.75 *(978-1-5383-8083-3(8),* f3b85104-520d-4ce4-8ad0-bca42a298a39) Rosen Publishing Group, Inc., The. (Rosen Young Adult).

Wagner, Heather Lehr. Machiavelli: Renaissance Political Analyst & Author. 2005. (Makers of the Middle Ages & Renaissance Ser.). (ENG., Illus.). 136p. (gr. 5-8). lib. bdg. 32.95 *(978-0-7910-8629-2(1),* P114345, Facts On File) Infobase Holdings, Inc.

Wallace, Susan Helen & Jablonski, Patricia E. Saint Thomas More: Courage, Conscience, & the King. Lachuk, Dani, illus. 2014. (ENG.). 144p. (J). pap. 8.95 *(978-0-8198-9021-4(9))* Pauline Bks. & Media.

Waxman, Laura Hamilton. Colin Powell. 2005. (History Maker Bios Ser.). 48p. (J). pap. 8.95 *(978-0-8225-5463-9(1));* (ENG., Illus.). (gr. 3-6). lib. bdg. 27.93 *(978-0-8225-2433-5(3),* Lerner Pubns.) Lerner Publishing Group.

Weston Woods Staff, creator. Where Was Patrick Henry on the 29th of May? 2011. 38.75 *(978-1-55592-485-0(9))* 2004. 18.95 *(978-1-55592-483-6(2))* 2004. 29.95 *(978-1-55592-484-3(0))* Weston Woods Studios, Inc.

White, Casey. John Jay: Diplomat of the American Experiment, 1 vol. 2006. (Library of American Thinkers Ser.). (ENG., Illus.). 112p. (YA). (gr. 6-6). lib. bdg. 39.80 *(978-1-4042-0507-9(1),* d02aee73-ee35-409b-89c1-7c009ebf0d42) Rosen Publishing Group, Inc., The.

Whiting, Jim. Benjamin Franklin. 2006. (Profiles in American History Ser.). (Illus.). 48p. (J). (gr. 3-7). lib. bdg. 29.95 *(978-1-58415-435-8(7))* Mitchell Lane Pubs.

—The Life & Times of Pericles. 2005. (Biography from Ancient Civilizations Ser.). (Illus.). 48p. (J). (gr. -1-7). lib. bdg. 29.95 *(978-1-58415-339-9(3))* Mitchell Lane Pubs.

Willett, Edward. Ayatollah Khomeini. 2009. (Middle East Leaders Ser.). 112p. (gr. 5-8). 66.50 *(978-1-61514-645-1(8),* Rosen Reference) Rosen Publishing Group, Inc., The.

Winter, Jonah. Paul Revere & the Bell Ringers: Ready-To-Read Level 2. Dodson, Bert, illus. 2003. (Ready-To-Read Childhood of Famous Americans Ser.). (ENG.). 32p. (J). (gr. k-2). pap. 4.99 *(978-0-689-85635-8(0),* Simon Spotlight) Simon Spotlight.

World Leaders Set, vols. 8, vol. 8. Incl. Adolf Hitler & Nazi Germany. Rice, Earle. (Illus.). 176p. (J). (gr. 3-7). 2006. lib. bdg. 28.95 *(978-1-931798-78-5(8));* Alexander the Great: Conqueror of the Known World. Nardo, Don. (Illus.). 100p. (J). 2009. 28.95 *(978-1-59935-126-1(9));* Che Guevara: In Search of Revolution. Miller, Calvin Craig. (Illus.). 192p. (J). (gr. 6-12). 2006. lib. bdg. 26.95 *(978-1-931798-93-8(1));* Cleopatra: Ruler of Egypt. (Illus.). 176p. (gr. 6-12). 2007. lib. bdg. 27.95 *(978-1-59935-035-6(1));* Empire in the East: The Story of Genghis Khan. Rice, Earle, Jr. (Illus.). 160p. (J). (gr. 3-7). 2005. 28.95 *(978-1-931798-62-4(1));* Fidel Castro & the Cuban Revolution. Naden, Corinne J. & Blue, Rose. (Illus.). 144p. (J). (gr. 3-7). 2006. lib. bdg. 27.95 *(978-1-59935-029-5(7));* Fighting Wars, Planning for Peace: The Story of George C. Marshall. Gimpel, Lee. (Illus.). 176p. (J). (gr. 6-12). 2005. lib. bdg. 26.95 *(978-1-931798-66-2(4));* Hugo Chavez: Leader of Venezuela. (Illus.). 128p. 2007. lib. bdg. 27.95 *(978-1-59935-068-4(8));* Joseph Stalin & the Soviet Union. (Illus.). 208p. (J). (gr. 6-12). 2006. lib. bdg. 26.95 *(978-1-931798-94-5(X));* Mao Zedong & the Chinese Revolution. Naden, Corinne J. 144p. (YA). (gr. 6-9). 2008. lib. bdg. 28.95 *(978-1-59935-100-1(5));* Velvet Revolution: Vaclav Havel & the Fall of Communism. Duberstein, John. (Illus.). 160p. (gr. 6-12). 2006. lib. bdg. 28.95 *(978-1-931798-85-3(0));* Woodrow Wilson & the Progressive Era. Lukes, Bonnie L. (Illus.). 192p. (J). (gr. 6-10). 2006. lib. bdg. 26.95 *(978-1-931798-79-2(6));* 2009. Set lib. bdg. 247.60 *(978-1-59935-013-4(0))* Reynolds, Morgan Inc.

Wyborny, Sheila. Kim Jong Il, 1 vol. 2009. (People in the News Ser.). (ENG., Illus.). 104p. (gr. 7-7). lib. bdg. 41.03 *(978-1-4205-0091-2(0),* bce6fd4e-5a78-42b1-8c19-1ce498c0d927, Lucent Pr.) Greenhaven Publishing LLC.

Zamosky, Lisa. Government Leaders Then & Now, 1 vol. rev. ed. 2006. (Social Studies: Informational Text Ser.). (ENG.). 32p. (J). (gr. 2-3). pap. 11.99 *(978-0-7439-9386-9(1))* Teacher Created Materials, Inc.

STATISTICS

see also Probabilities

also general subjects and names of countries, cities, etc. with the subdivision Statistics, e.g. U. S.—Statistics; etc.

Adams, Colleen. The Everglades: Analyzing Graphs, Tables, & Charts, 1 vol. (Math for the REAL World Ser.). 32p. 2010. (ENG.). (gr. 5-6). pap. 10.00 *(978-1-4042-5127-4(8),* 3a7c14b2-85fc-471e-a450-89ce07c74867) 2009. (gr. 4-5). 47.90 *(978-1-60851-420-5(X))* 2004. (ENG., Illus.). (J). (gr. 5-6). lib. bdg. 28.93 *(978-1-4042-2933-4(7),* 646ef08d-58d4-4657-b51a-fe8b757246c4) Rosen Publishing Group, Inc., The. (PowerKids Pr.).

Arvoy, Marsha & Nardi, Dorianne. Percentage. 2010. (ENG., Illus.). 24p. (J). *(978-0-7787-5246-2(1));* pap. *(978-0-7787-5293-6(3))* Crabtree Publishing Co.

Brookie, Anna, et al. Mathematics & Statistics for the New Zealand Curriculum Year 9. 2nd ed. 2013. (Cambridge Mathematics & Statistics for the New Zealand Curriculum Ser.). (ENG.). pap., stu. ed. *(978-1-107-62840-3(7))* Cambridge Univ. Pr.

Burrill, Gail F., et al. Exploring Regression. (Data-Driven Mathematics Ser.). 96p. (YA). (gr. 7-12). pap., stu. ed. 18.95 *(978-1-57232-245-5(4))* Seymour, Dale Pubns.

Burton, Margie, et al. We All Scream for Ice Cream. 2011. (Early Connections Ser.). (J). *(978-1-61672-544-0(3))* Benchmark Education Co.

Bussell, Linda. Trabajemos con NÚMEROS en Las Noticias (Working with NUMBERS in the News), 1 vol. 2008. (Las Matemáticas en Nuestro Mundo - Nivel 3 (Math in Our World - Level 3) Ser.). (SPA.). 24p. (gr. 3-3). (J). lib. bdg. 24.67 *(978-0-8368-9292-5(5),* 9e717c71-dbc5-4ad3-993c-9ce031fb3c33); pap. 9.15 *(978-0-8368-9391-5(3),* 55f7ffd3-9a70-4e0b-b3a1-4518995133ca) Stevens, Gareth Publishing LLLP. (Weekly Reader Leveled Readers).

—Working with Numbers in the News, 1 vol. 2008. (Math in Our World - Level 3 Ser.). (ENG., Illus.). 24p. (J). (gr. 3-3). lib. bdg. 24.67 *(978-0-8368-9284-0(4),* e3359afe-c0e8-42cb-89b9-6fc62638b3c5, Weekly Reader Leveled Readers) Stevens, Gareth Publishing LLLP.

—Working with NUMBERS in the News, 1 vol. 2008. (Math in Our World - Level 3 Ser.). (ENG., Illus.). 24p. (J). (gr. 3-3). pap. 9.15 *(978-0-8368-9383-0(2),* df89f987-19bf-4190-93e7-a39da482c04c, Weekly Reader Leveled Readers) Stevens, Gareth Publishing LLLP.

D'Anna, Cindy. Field Day!, 1 vol. 2013. (Core Math Skills: Measurement & Geometry Ser.). (ENG.). 24p. (J). (gr. 1-1). 26.27 *(978-1-4777-2229-9(7),* 3ab7d6de-cac0-44ea-a8ba-3684a4950849); pap. 8.25 *(978-1-4777-2046-2(4),* 44154cad-16de-4e54-aea2-e4e029544d77) Rosen Publishing Group, Inc., The. (Rosen Classroom).

—Field Day! Represent & Interpret Data. 2013. (Rosen Math Readers Ser.). (ENG.). 24p. (J). (gr. 1-2). pap. 49.50 *(978-1-4777-2047-9(2),* Rosen Classroom) Rosen Publishing Group, Inc., The.

Dowdy, Penny. Estimation. 2008. (My Path to Math Ser.). (ENG., Illus.). 24p. (J). (gr. k-3). lib. bdg. *(978-0-7787-4337-8(3))* Crabtree Publishing Co.

Drawing Conclusions & Inferences (Gr. 4-5) 2004. (J). *(978-1-58232-134-9(5))* ECS Learning Systems, Inc.

Dugan, Christine. Tonight's Concert. rev. ed. 2012. (Mathematics in the Real World Ser.). (ENG.). 32p. (gr. 5-8). pap. 11.99 *(978-1-4333-3464-1(X))* Teacher Created Materials, Inc.

Edgar, Sherra G. Tally Charts. 2013. (21st Century Basic Skills Library: Let's Make Graphs Ser.). (ENG., Illus.). 24p. (J). (gr. k-3). 26.35 *(978-1-62431-395-0(7),* 202700); pap. 12.79 *(978-1-62431-471-1(6),* 202702) Cherry Lake Publishing.

Exploring Statistics. (J). (gr. k-2). 9.90 *(978-0-669-15890-8(9))* Houghton Mifflin Harcourt School Pubs.

Faulkner, Nicholas & Gregersen, Erik, eds. Statistics & Probability, 1 vol. 2017. (Foundations of Math Ser.). (ENG., Illus.). 400p. (J). (gr. 10-10). lib. bdg. 55.59 *(978-1-68048-779-4(5),* feec8536-3290-4507-8bf0-476670ee5ae8, Britannica Educational Publishing) Rosen Publishing Group, Inc., The.

Flatt, Lizann. Collecting Data. 2016. (Get Graphing! Building Data Literacy Skills Ser.). (ENG., Illus.). 24p. (J). (gr. 1-3). *(978-0-7787-2633-3(9))* Crabtree Publishing Co.

Frederick, Shane & Braun, Eric. Know the Stats: A Fan's Guide to Stats. 2018. (Know the Stats Ser.). (ENG.). 32p. (J). (gr. 3-9). 122.60 *(978-1-5435-0637-2(2),* 27683, Capstone Pr.) Capstone.

Freudenthal. Insights into Data. 3rd ed. 2003. (Math in Context Ser.). (Illus.). 7.86 *(978-0-03-071699-7(3))* Holt McDougal.

Gitlin, Marty. A Dream Job As a Sports Statistician, 1 vol. 2017. (Great Careers in the Sports Industry Ser.). (ENG., Illus.). 128p. (J). (gr. 7-7). 44.13 *(978-1-5383-8138-0(9),* 80f657fb-a281-4368-97b4-1fb9474bb74b) Rosen Publishing Group, Inc., The.

Gnanadesikan, Mrudulla. Art & Technique of Simulation. (YA). (gr. 7-12). pap., stu. ed. 12.95 *(978-0-86651-336-4(1),* DSO1704) Globe Fearon Educational Publishing.

Hernandez, Marissa. Baseball: Statistical Questions & Measures. 2019. (Mathematics in the Real World Ser.). (ENG., Illus.). 32p. (gr. 5-8). pap. 11.99 *(978-1-4258-5893-3(7))* Teacher Created Materials, Inc.

Higgins, Nadia. Sequences: Order Matters! Sanchez, Sr., illus. 2018. (Code It! Ser.). (ENG.). 24p. (J). (gr. 1-3). 33.99 *(978-1-68410-310-2(X),* 140702) Cantata Learning.

Kompelien, Tracy. You Can Estimate, Thats Really Great!, 1 vol. 2007. (Math Made Fun Ser.). (Illus.). 24p. (J). (gr. k-3). lib. bdg. 24.21 *(978-1-59928-551-1(7),* SandCastle) ABDO Publishing Co.

Loria, Laura. How Do You Read Charts & Graphs?, 1 vol. 2018. (Let's Find Out! Social Studies Skills Ser.). (ENG., Illus.). 32p. (J). (gr. 2-3). lib. bdg. 26.06 *(978-1-5081-0700-2(9),* cd96aa73-0c9d-4799-a706-73ffbd7b5801, Britannica Educational Publishing) Rosen Publishing Group, Inc., The.

MacGillivray, Helen & Petocz, Peter. Statistics & Probability in the Australian Curriculum Years 9 And 10. 2013. (ENG.). pap. *(978-1-107-65599-7(4))* Cambridge Univ. Pr.

Marsico, Katie. Mountains. 2009. (21st Century Skills Library: Real World Math Ser.). (ENG.). 32p. (gr. 4-8). lib. bdg. 32.07 *(978-1-60279-492-4(8),* 200316) Cherry Lake Publishing.

Mikoley, Kate. NASCAR: Stats, Facts, & Figures, 1 vol. 2017. (Do Math with Sports Stats! Ser.). (ENG.). 32p. (J). (gr. 3-4). pap. 11.50 *(978-1-5382-1141-0(6),* 721fdcf9-f35e-4dfe-97f8-3b951b9abd67) Stevens, Gareth Publishing LLLP.

Mineo, Kate. Compare with Bears, 1 vol. 2011. (Animal Math Ser.). (ENG., Illus.). 24p. (J). (gr. 1-2). pap. 9.15 *(978-1-4339-5660-7(8),* b95cafc9-5301-4171-b168-dce070d9c152); lib. bdg. 25.27 *(978-1-4339-5658-4(6),* 846b0876-4e3a-449b-8271-f0ac949558a6) Stevens, Gareth Publishing LLLP.

Oehrli, Jo Angela. Stats & Data Comprehension. 2017. (21st Century Skills Library: Data Geek Ser.). (ENG., Illus.). 32p. (J). (gr. 4-7). lib. bdg. 32.07 *(978-1-63472-710-5(X),* 210098) Cherry Lake Publishing.

Peters, Elisa. Statistics & Probability, 1 vol. 2014. (Story of Math Ser.). (ENG.). 64p. (YA). (gr. 8-8). 34.29 *(978-1-62275-533-2(2),* fd2ed37e-aa69-4c48-87ec-162e0bb68061, Britannica Educational Publishing) Rosen Publishing Group, Inc., The.

Puritz, Christian. Venture Mathematics Worksheets: Bk. S: Statistics & Extra Investigations: Blackline Masters for Higher Ability Classes Aged 11-16. 2006. (ENG.). 36p. pap. 14.99 *(978-1-899618-72-9(4))* Parkwest Pubns., Inc.

Robinson, C. L. MATH1on1 Statistics Foundation. 2006. (YA). per. 9.99 *(978-0-9786767-9-7(3))* Robinson, Consuelo.

Tallman, Teresa. Fun with Statistics. 2016. (ENG., Illus.). (J). pap. 9.95 *(978-1-55571-832-9(9),* Grid Pr.) L & R Publishing, LLC.

Understandable Statistics, Concepts & Methods. 7th ed. 2003. (gr. 11-12). instr.'s gde. ed. *(978-0-618-20560-8(8),* 3-07006); cd-rom *(978-0-618-20563-9(2),* 3-07010) CENGAGE Learning.

Visto, Joy. What Are the Chances? 2016. (Making Math Work Ser.). (ENG.). 48p. (J). (gr. 4-7). pap. 12.00 *(978-1-62832-174-6(1),* 20909, Creative Paperbacks) Creative Co., The.

Ward, Lesley. Life in Numbers: What Is Average? 2018. (TIME(r): Informational Text Ser.). (ENG., Illus.). 48p. (J). (gr. 5-8). pap. 13.99 *(978-1-4258-4997-9(0))* Teacher Created Materials, Inc.

STATISTICS—GRAPHIC METHODS

Cocca, Lisa Colozza. Bar Graphs. 2013. (Explorer Junior Library: Math Explorer Junior Ser.). (ENG.). 24p. (gr. 1-4). pap. 12.79 *(978-1-61080-936-8(X),* 202625); (Illus.). 32.07 *(978-1-61080-911-5(4),* 202623) Cherry Lake Publishing.

—Pictographs. 2013. (Explorer Junior Library: Math Explorer Junior Ser.). (ENG.). 24p. (gr. 1-4). pap. 12.79 *(978-1-61080-938-2(6),* 202633); (Illus.). 32.07 *(978-1-61080-913-9(0),* 202631) Cherry Lake Publishing.

—Tally Charts. 2013. (Explorer Junior Library: Math Explorer Junior Ser.). (ENG.). 24p. (gr. 1-4). pap. 12.79 *(978-1-61080-941-2(6),* 202645); (Illus.). 32.07 *(978-1-61080-916-0(5),* 202643) Cherry Lake Publishing.

Edgar, Sherra G. Pictographs. 2013. (21st Century Basic Skills Library: Let's Make Graphs Ser.). (ENG., Illus.). 24p. (J). (gr. k-3). 26.35 *(978-1-62431-393-6(0),* 202692); pap. 12.79 *(978-1-62431-469-8(4),* 202694) Cherry Lake Publishing.

Harris, Nancy. Mashed Potatoes: Collecting & Reporting Data. 2007. (Math Focal Points (Discovery Library) Ser.). (Illus.). 24p. (J). (gr. -1-3). lib. bdg. 22.79 *(978-1-60044-640-5(X))* Rourke Educational Media.

Rupert, Matthews. Visual Factfinder Bugs. 2008. 512p. pap. *(978-1-84810-079-4(5))* Miles Kelly Publishing, Ltd.

Wilson, Natashya. The Census & America's People: Analyzing Data Using Line Graphs & Tables, 1 vol. (Math for the REAL World Ser.). (ENG., 32p. (gr. 4-5). 2010. Illus.). pap. 10.00 *(978-0-8239-8903-4(8),* 5f6c0764-ecdb-44c5-b338-d62a8d91bff0, PowerKids Pr.) 2004. 47.50 *(978-0-8239-7647-8(5))* Rosen Publishing Group, Inc., The.

STATUE OF LIBERTY (NEW YORK, N.Y.)

Arena, Jen. My Little Golden Book about the Statue of Liberty. Garofoli, Viviana, illus. 2018. (Little Golden Book Ser.). 24p. (J). (-k). 5.99 *(978-1-5247-7033-4(7),* Golden Bks.) Random Hse. Children's Bks.

Bauer, Marion Dane. The Statue of Liberty. Wallace, John, illus. 2007. (Ready-To-Read Level 1 Ser.). (ENG.). 32p. (J). (gr. -1-1). lib. bdg. 16.19 *(978-1-4169-3480-6(4),* Aladdin) Simon & Schuster Children's Publishing.

—The Statue of Liberty: Ready-To-Read Level 1. Wallace, John, illus. (Wonders of America Ser.). (ENG.). 32p. (J). (gr. -1-1). 2018. 17.99 *(978-1-5344-3031-0(8))* 2007. pap. 4.99 *(978-1-4169-3479-0(0))* Simon Spotlight. (Simon Spotlight).

Behrens, Janice. What Is the Statue of Liberty? 2009. (Scholastic News Nonfiction Readers: American Symbols Ser.). (ENG., Illus.). 24p. (J). (gr. k-3). 21.19 *(978-0-531-21091-8(X),* Children's Pr.) Scholastic Library Publishing.

Blake, Kevin. Statue of Liberty. 2016. (American Places: from Vision to Reality Ser.). (ENG., Illus.). 32p. (J). (gr. 2-7). 28.50 *(978-1-944102-41-8(8))* Bearport Publishing Co., Inc.

Braithwaite, Jill. The Statue of Liberty. 2010. pap. 45.32 *(978-0-7613-6993-6(7))* 2004. (Illus.). 32p. (J). lib. bdg. 22.60 *(978-0-8225-3802-8(4))* 2003. (ENG., Illus.). 32p. (J). pap. 7.99 *(978-0-8225-3756-4(7),* 97632d5d-af02-421b-85d3-d964d5828a84, First Avenue Editions) Lerner Publishing Group.

Brannon, Cecelia H. Zoom in on the Statue of Liberty, 1 vol. 2016. (Zoom in on American Symbols Ser.). (ENG., Illus.). 24p. (gr. 2-2). pap. 10.95 *(978-0-7660-8450-6(7),* ad7e2b7a-b783-46c2-9869-b13484213848) Enslow Publishing, LLC.

Byrd, Robert. Liberty Arrives! How America's Grandest Statue Found Her Home. Byrd, Robert, illus. 2019. (Illus.). 40p. (J). (gr. 1-4). 17.99 *(978-0-7352-3082-8(X),* Dial Bks) Penguin Young Readers Group.

Curlee, Lynn. Liberty. Curlee, Lynn, illus. 2003. (ENG., Illus.). 48p. (J). (gr. 2-7). 9.99 *(978-0-689-85683-9(0),* Atheneum Bks. for Young Readers) Simon & Schuster Children's Publishing.

Douglas, Lloyd G. The Statue of Liberty. 2003. (Welcome Bks.). (ENG., Illus.). 24p. (J). (gr. -1-2). pap. 4.95 *(978-0-516-27877-3(0),* Children's Pr.) Scholastic Library Publishing.

Edison, Erin. The Statue of Liberty: A 4D Book. 2018. (National Landmarks Ser.). (ENG., Illus.). 24p. (J). (gr. 1-3). lib. bdg. 27.99 *(978-1-5435-3131-2(8),* 138736, Capstone Pr.) Capstone.

Eldridge, Alison & Eldridge, Stephen. The Statue of Liberty: An American Symbol, 1 vol. 2012. (All about American Symbols Ser.). (ENG., Illus.). 24p. (gr. -1-1). pap. 10.35 *(978-1-4644-0051-3(2),* ce6878a5-d808-48bc-9712-c3240405fd33, Enslow Publishing) Enslow Publishing, LLC.

Fandel, Jennifer. The Statue of Liberty. 2005. (What in the World? Ser.). (Illus.). 48p. (J). (gr. 5-9). lib. bdg. 21.95 *(978-1-58341-377-1(4),* Creative Education) Creative Co., The.

Firestone, Mary. The Statue of Liberty, 1 vol. Skeens, Matthew, illus. 2006. (American Symbols Ser.). (ENG.). 24p. (J). (gr. 1-3). 9.95 *(978-1-4048-2222-1(4),* 93436, Picture Window Bks.) Capstone.

Gamble, Adam & Jasper, Mark. Good Night Statue of Liberty. Stevenson, Harvey, illus. 2017. (Good Night Our World Ser.). 20p. (J). (gr. -1 — 1). bds. 9.95 *(978-1-60219-429-8(7))* Good Night Bks.

Gaspar, Joe. The Statue of Liberty, 1 vol. 2013. (PowerKids Readers: American Symbols Ser.). (Illus.). 24p. (J). (gr. k-k). (ENG.). pap. 9.25 *(978-1-4777-0811-8(1),* 6e252316-3561-4301-adbc-b6ff16338829); (ENG., lib. bdg. 26.27 *(978-1-4777-0735-7(2),* c7de9595-d0e3-475f-9951-748fdf3ea371); pap. 49.50 *(978-1-4777-0812-5(X))* Rosen Publishing Group, Inc., The. (PowerKids Pr.).

—The Statue of Liberty / la Estatua de la Libertad, 1 vol. Alamn, Eduardo, ed. 2013. (PowerKids Readers: Símbolos de América / American Symbols Ser.). (ENG & SPA.). 24p. (J). (gr. k-k). 26.27 *(978-1-4777-1203-0(8),* 081ab1a8-fb7a-412d-826d-cdaba8c2fab0, PowerKids Pr.) Rosen Publishing Group, Inc., The.

Glaser, Linda. Emma's Poem: The Voice of the Statue of Liberty. Nivola, Claire A., illus. (ENG.). 32p. (J). (gr. -1-3). 2013. pap. 9.99 *(978-0-544-10508-9(7),* 1540808) 2010.

17.99 (978-0-547-17184-5(6), 1054295) HarperCollins Pubs. (Clarion Bks.).

Goldsworthy, Steve. Estatua de la Libertad. 2013. (SPA.). (J). (978-1-62127-623-4(6)) Weigl Pubs., Inc.

—Statue of Liberty with Code. 2012. (AV2 American Icons Ser.). (ENG., Illus.). 24p. (J). (gr. -1-3). pap. 12.95 (978-1-61913-303-7(2), AV2 by Weigl) Weigl Pubs., Inc.

Healy, Nick. The Statue of Liberty. 2003. (J). pap. (978-1-58417-117-1(0)); lib. bdg. (978-1-58417-054-9(9)) Lake Street Pubs.

Hess, Debra. The Statue of Liberty, 1 vol. (Symbols of America Ser.). (ENG.). 40p. (gr. 3-3). 2008. pap. 9.23 (978-0-7614-3393-4(7), ac530130-fdb3-4d4d-bad4-b1325a1ddde6) 2005. (Illus.). lib. bdg. 32.64 (978-0-7614-1707-1(9), f62aff3b-b6a9-40fe-8fe8-1286532c4591, Cavendish Square) Cavendish Square Publishing LLC.

Hicks, Terry Allan. Symbols of America Group 2, 12 vols., Set. Incl. Bald Eagle. lib. bdg. 32.64 (978-0-7614-2133-7(5), 4cc77ac4-353f-4135-8229-fee1fad1bf3b); Capitol. lib. bdg. 32.64 (978-0-7614-2132-0(7), 983498dc-4064-4d9b-a5fd-9541490d6e2c); Declaration of Independence. lib. bdg. 32.64 (978-0-7614-2135-1(1), b672c79b-ebcf-460a-bf6f-c79934c3be91); Ellis Island. lib. bdg. 32.64 (978-0-7614-2134-4(3), eadd5cdd-45bd-4dab-99b1-a60a5a76c2ba); Pledge of Allegiance. lib. bdg. 32.64 (978-0-7614-2136-8(X), 4f80c1f0-d3ea-4dd5-b747-5d88842745e5); Uncle Sam. lib. bdg. 32.64 (978-0-7614-2137-5(8), e6f9da10-1cd5-4edb-8cd5-0e9e233d21ec); (Illus.). 40p. (gr. 3-3). (Symbols of America Ser.). (ENG.). 2007. Set lib. bdg. 195.84 (978-0-7614-2130-6(0), b2a0354a-8705-48f9-b041-df7983c1050e, Cavendish Square) Cavendish Square Publishing LLC.

Hochain, Serge. Building Liberty: A Statue Is Born. Hochain, Serge, illus. 2006. (Illus.). 46p. (J). (gr. 4-8). reprint ed. 25.00 (978-1-4223-5181-9(5)) DIANE Publishing Co.

Holub, Joan. What Is the Statue of Liberty? 2014. (What Is.... ? Ser.). lib. bdg. 16.00 (978-0-606-35687-9(8)) Turtleback.

Holub, Joan & Who HQ. What Is the Statue of Liberty? Hinderliter, John, illus. 2014. (What Was? Ser.). 112p. (J). (gr. 3-7). 5.99 (978-0-448-47917-0(6), Penguin Workshop) Penguin Young Readers Group.

Hurtig, Jennifer. The Statue of Liberty. 2008. (Structural Wonders Ser.). (Illus.). 32p. (J). (gr. 4-6). pap. 9.95 (978-1-59036-941-8(6)); lib. bdg. 26.00 (978-1-59036-940-1(8)) Weigl Pubs., Inc.

—Statue of Liberty. 2019. (Structural Wonders of the World Ser.). (ENG., Illus.). 24p. (J). (gr. 2-5). pap. 12.95 (978-1-4896-9944-2(9)); lib. bdg. 28.55 (978-1-4896-9943-5(0)) Weigl Pubs., Inc.

Hurtig, Jennifer & Kissock, Heather. The Statue of Liberty. 2014. (J). (978-1-4896-1966-2(6)) Weigl Pubs., Inc.

Lewison, Wendy Cheyette. L Is for Liberty. Hines, Laura Freeman, illus. 2003. 24p. (J). (gr. -1-3). mass mkt. 5.99 (978-0-448-43228-1(5), Grosset & Dunlap) Penguin Young Readers Group.

Malam, John. You Wouldn't Want to Be a Worker on the Statue of Liberty! Antram, David, illus. 2008. (You Wouldn't Want to...: American History Ser.). (ENG.). 32p. (J). 29.00 (978-0-531-20700-0(5), Watts, Franklin) Scholastic Library Publishing.

—You Wouldn't Want to Be a Worker on the Statue of Liberty! A Monument You'd Rather Not Build. Antram, David, illus. 2008. (You Wouldn't Want to...: American History Ser.). (ENG.). 32p. (J). (gr. 3-18). pap. 9.95 (978-0-531-21910-2(0), Watts, Franklin) Scholastic Library Publishing.

Malaspina, Ann. Nathan & Nicole Learn about Nouns. Hamblin, George, illus. 2014. (Language Builders Ser.). (ENG.). 32p. (J). (gr. 2-4). lib. bdg. 25.27 (978-1-59953-666-8(8)) Norwood Hse. Pr.

Mann, Elizabeth. Statue of Liberty: A Tale of Two Countries. Witschonke, Alan, illus. 2011. (Wonders of the World Book Ser.). (ENG.). 48p. (J). (gr. 3-18). 24.95 (978-1-931414-43-2(2), 030e5aed-098b-430a-9258-a5afcc7a9da4) Mikaya Pr.

Marcovitz, Hal. Statue of Liberty: A Beacon of Welcome & Hope. Moreno, Barry, ed. 2014. (Patriotic Symbols of America Ser.: 20). 48p. (J). (gr. 4-18). 20.95 (978-1-4222-3130-2(5)) Mason Crest.

Markovics, Joyce. Green & Spiky: What Am I? 2018. (American Place Puzzlers Ser.). (ENG.). 24p. (J). (gr. -1-3). E-Book 41.36 (978-1-68402-536-7(2)) Bearport Publishing Co., Inc.

Markovics, Joyce L. Green & Spiky: What Am I? 2018. (American Place Puzzlers Ser.). (ENG.). 24p. (J). (gr. -1-3). lib. bdg. 26.99 (978-1-68402-478-0(1)) Bearport Publishing Co., Inc.

Marsh, Carole. I'm Reading about the Statue of Liberty. 2016. (I'm Reading About Ser.). (ENG., Illus.). (J). lib. bdg. 24.99 (978-0-635-12207-0(3)); pap. 7.99 (978-0-635-12208-7(1)) Gallopade International.

Mattern, Joanne. The Statue of Liberty: A Welcome Gift. 2017. (Core Content Social Studies — Let's Celebrate America Ser.). (ENG., Illus.). 32p. (J). (gr. 2-5). lib. bdg. 26.65 (978-1-63440-224-8(3), 61c05d47-0186-438f-bf4e-84932585dea7) Red Chair Pr.

Monroe, Tyler. The Statue of Liberty. 2013. (U. S. Symbols Ser.). (ENG.). 24p. (J). (gr. -1-2). 27.32 (978-1-4765-3088-8(2), 123065); pap. 7.95 (978-1-4765-3537-1(X), 123583) Capstone.

Moriarty, Siobhan. Visit the Statue of Liberty, 1 vol. 2012. (Landmarks of Liberty Ser.). (ENG., Illus.). 24p. (J). (gr. 2-3). pap. 9.15 (978-1-4339-6402-2(3), 7d937197-1526-4045-8011-fa2ca79ec733, Gareth Stevens Learning Library); lib. bdg. 25.27 (978-1-4339-6400-8(7), 1f1d79cd-bcdd-49f0-afc6-fb3962804988) Stevens, Gareth Publishing LLLP.

Ohlin, Nancy. The Statue of Liberty. Simó, Roger, illus. 2017. (Blast Back! Ser.). (ENG.). 112p. (J). (gr. 2-5). pap. 5.99 (978-1-4998-0456-0(3)); 16.99 (978-1-4998-0457-7(1)) Little Bee Books Inc.

Orr, Tamra B. The Statue of Liberty: Introducing Primary Sources. 2016. (Introducing Primary Sources Ser.). (ENG., Illus.). 32p. (J). (gr. -1-2). lib. bdg. 28.65 (978-1-4914-8223-0(0), 130685, Capstone Pr.) Capstone.

Penner, Lucille Recht. The Statue of Liberty. 2003. (Step into Reading: Step 2 Ser.). (ENG., Illus.). 32p. (J). (gr. -1-1). 17.44 (978-0-679-96928-0(4)) Random House Publishing Group.

Qaiser, Annie. The Story of the Statue of Liberty: A History Perspectives Book. 2013. (Perspectives Library). (ENG., Illus.). 32p. (J). (gr. 4-8). 32.07 (978-1-62431-422-3(8), 202808); pap. 14.21 (978-1-62431-498-8(8), 202810) Cherry Lake Publishing.

Rappaport, Doreen. Lady Liberty: A Biography. Tavares, Matt, illus. 2011. (ENG.). 40p. (J). (gr. 3-7). pap. 8.99 (978-0-7636-5301-9(2)) Candlewick Pr.

—Lady Liberty: Candlewick Biographies: A Biography. Tavares, Matt, illus. 2014. (Candlewick Biographies Ser.). (ENG.). 48p. (J). (gr. 3-7). 14.99 (978-0-7636-7114-3(2)) Candlewick Pr.

RJF Publishing Staff & Staton, Hilarie. The Statue of Liberty. 2009. (Symbols of American Freedom Ser.). 48p. (gr. 4-6). 30.00 (978-1-60413-516-9(6), Chelsea Clubhse.) Infobase Holdings, Inc.

Rustad, Martha E. H. Why Is the Statue of Liberty Green? Conger, Holli, illus. 2014. (Cloverleaf Books (tm) — Our American Symbols Ser.). (ENG.). 24p. (J). (gr. k-2). pap. 8.99 (978-1-4677-4470-6(0), 66b27ff6-4eec-43de-880f-0fe0a52a0dc1, Millbrook Pr.) Lerner Publishing Group.

Schuh, Mari. The Statue of Liberty. 2018. (Symbols of American Freedom Ser.). (ENG., Illus.). 24p. (J). (gr. k-3). pap. 7.99 (978-1-61891-473-6(1), 12126); lib. bdg. 26.95 (978-1-62617-887-8(9)) Bellwether Media. (Blastoff! Readers).

Shea, Pegi Deitz. Liberty Rising: The Story of the Statue of Liberty. Zahares, Wade, illus. 2013. (ENG.). 44p. (J). (gr. k-4). 10.99 (978-1-250-02720-7(9), 900098291) Square Fish.

Shea, Therese. The Statue of Liberty Wasn't Made to Welcome Immigrants: Exposing Myths about U.S. Landmarks. 2019. (Exposed! More Myths about American History Ser.). (ENG.). 32p. (gr. 2-3). 63.00 (978-1-5382-3759-5(8)) Stevens, Gareth Publishing LLLP.

Shoup, Kate. Lady Liberty: Symbol of a Nation, 1 vol. Gennari, Joel, illus. 2018. (American Legends & Folktales Ser.). (ENG.). 32p. (J). (gr. 3-3). 30.21 (978-1-5026-3686-7(7), ffa5b6b2-bf0c-4b51-948a-9d56aa08b0b4) Cavendish Square Publishing LLC.

Silate, Jennifer. The Statue of Liberty. (Primary Sources of American Symbols Ser.). 24p. (gr. 3-3). 2009. 42.50 (978-1-60851-510-3(9), PowerKids Pr.) 2006. (ENG., Illus.). (J). lib. bdg. 26.27 (978-1-4042-2696-8(6), 021195ea-ca45-478d-8e1d-a934079862f0) Rosen Publishing Group, Inc., The.

Simms, Susan Rose. The Statue of Liberty. 2018. (US Symbols Ser.). (ENG., Illus.). 24p. (J). (gr. k-3). lib. bdg. 31.36 (978-1-5321-6048-6(8), 28728, Pop! Cody Koala) Pop!

Stevenson, Harvey. Looking at Liberty. Stevenson, Harvey, illus. 2003. (Illus.). 40p. (J). (gr. -1-2). 17.89 (978-0-06-000101-8(1)) HarperCollins Pubs.

Sullivan, Laura L. Building the Statue of Liberty, 1 vol. 2017. (Engineering North America's Landmarks Ser.). (ENG.). 32p. (gr. 3-3). pap. 11.58 (978-1-5026-2972-2(0), b8b169fb-bab1-4110-94d3-33a57802f29f) Cavendish Square Publishing LLC.

STEALING

see Theft

STEAM-ENGINES

Collier, James Lincoln. Steam Engines, 1 vol. 2007. (Great Inventions Ser.). (ENG., Illus.). 144p. (YA). (gr. 8-8). lib. bdg. 45.50 (978-0-7614-1880-1(6), 0d3dedd7-e3ba-4b33-86da-d2275ec61393) Cavendish Square Publishing LLC.

Johnson, Jordan. How the Steam Engine Changed the World, 1 vol. 2018. (Inventions That Changed the World Ser.). (ENG.). 64p. (gr. 5-5). pap. 16.28 (978-1-5026-4116-8(X), 64ac1cb2-1e20-4b61-af4f-8524e51135ed) Cavendish Square Publishing LLC.

Orr, Tamra B. The Steam Engine. 2006. (Inventions That Shaped the World Ser.). (Illus.). 80p. (J). (gr. 5-8). 17.60 (978-0-7569-6862-5(3)) Perfection Learning Corp.

Orr, Tamra B. & Orr, Tamra. The Steam Engine. 2005. (Inventions That Shaped the World Ser.). (ENG., Illus.). 80p. (J). (gr. 5-8). lib. bdg. 30.50 (978-0-531-12400-0(2), Watts, Franklin) Scholastic Library Publishing.

Stark, Kristy. Powered by Steam. rev. ed. 2018. (Smithsonian: Informational Text Ser.). (ENG., Illus.). 32p. (gr. 3-5). pap. 11.99 (978-1-4938-6694-6(X)) Teacher Created Materials, Inc.

STEAM SHOVELS—FICTION

Burton, Virginia Lee. Mike Mulligan & His Steam Shovel. 2006. (Illus.). 48p. pap. (978-1-84507-501-9(3), White Lion Publishing) Quarto Publishing Group UK.

—Mike Mulligan & His Steam Shovel 75th Anniversary. 75th anniv. ed. 2014. (ENG., Illus.). 56p. (J). (gr. -1-3). 17.99 (978-0-544-27992-6(1), 1570274, Clarion Bks.) HarperCollins Pubs.

—Mike Mulligan & His Steam Shovel Board Book. 2007. (ENG., Illus.). 40p. (J). (gr. -1 — 1). bds. 8.99 (978-0-618-84019-9(2), 589156, Clarion Bks.) HarperCollins Pubs.

—Mike Mulligan & His Steam Shovel Book & Cd, 1 vol. 2006. (ENG., Illus.). 48p. (J). (gr. -1-3). audio compact disk 10.99 (978-0-618-73756-7(1), 482681, Clarion Bks.) HarperCollins Pubs.

Weston Woods Staff, creator. Mike Mulligan & His Steam Shovel. 2011. 18.95 (978-0-439-72838-6(X)); 38.75 (978-0-439-72839-3(8)) Weston Woods Studios, Inc.

Zimmerman, Andrea & Clemesha, David. Digger Man. Zimmerman, Andrea, illus. 2007. (Digger Man Ser.: 1). (ENG., Illus.). 32p. (J). (gr. -1-k). pap. 8.99 (978-0-8050-8203-6(4), 900040876) Square Fish.

STEAMBOATS

Boothroyd, Jennifer. Robert Fulton: A Life of Innovation. 2007. (Pull Ahead Bks.). (Illus.). 32p. (J). (gr. 3-7). lib. bdg. 22.60 (978-0-8225-6458-4(0), Lerner Pubns.) Lerner Publishing Group.

Doeden, Matt. The Queen Mary: A Chilling Interactive Adventure. 2016. (You Choose: Haunted Places Ser.). (ENG., Illus.). 112p. (J). (gr. 3-7). lib. bdg. 32.65 (978-1-5157-2578-7(2), 132921, Capstone Pr.) Capstone.

Ferut, Michael. RMS Queen Mary. 2014. (Scariest Places on Earth Ser.). (ENG., Illus.). 24p. (J). (gr. 3-7). lib. bdg. 26.95 (978-1-60014-996-2(0), Torque Bks.) Bellwether Media.

Haunted! the Queen Mary. 2013. (History's Most Haunted Ser.). 32p. (J). (gr. 3-6). pap. 63.00 (978-1-4339-9260-5(4)) Stevens, Gareth Publishing LLLP.

Jordan, Shirley. Benjamin Brown & the Great Steamboat Race. Kemly, Kathleen, illus. 2011. (History Speaks: Picture Books Plus Reader's Theater Ser.). 48p. pap. 56.72 (978-0-7613-7630-9(5)); (ENG.). (gr. 2-4). pap. 9.95 (978-0-7613-6133-6(2)) Lerner Publishing Group.

Loh-Hagan, Virginia. Women & Children First: Sinking of the Titanic. 2019. (Behind the Curtain Ser.). (ENG., Illus.). 32p. (J). (gr. 4-8). pap. 14.21 (978-1-5341-3996-1(6), 212813); lib. bdg. 32.07 (978-1-5341-4340-1(8), 212812) Cherry Lake Publishing. (45th Parallel Press).

Macaulay, David. Crossing on Time: Steam Engines, Fast Ships, & a Journey to the New World. 2019. (ENG., Illus.). 128p. (J). 24.99 (978-1-59643-477-6(5), 900055833) Roaring Brook Pr.

Marsico, Katie. Robert Fulton. Bane, Jeff, illus. 2018. (My Early Library: My Itty-Bitty Bio Ser.). (ENG.). 24p. (J). (gr. k-1). lib. bdg. 30.64 (978-1-5341-2890-3(5), 211604) Cherry Lake Publishing.

McLeese, Don. Robert Fulton. 2005. (Rourke Discovery Library). (Illus.). 24p. (J). (gr. 2-5). lib. bdg. (978-1-59515-434-7(5), 1244323) Rourke Educational Media.

McVicker, Maryellen. Joseph Kinney: Steamboat Captain. Hare, John, illus. 2014. (ENG.). 48p. (J). lib. bdg. 24.00 (978-1-61248-116-6(7)) Truman State Univ. Pr.

Murdico, Suzanne J. Railroads & Steamships: Important Developments in American Transportation. (America's Industrial Society in the 19th Century Ser.). 32p. (gr. 4-4). 2009. 47.90 (978-1-61511-340-8(1)) 2003. (ENG., Illus.). (J). pap. 10.00 (978-0-8239-4278-7(3), 44a84b6b-b256-4ad5-a2e0-5367fe9c4a95) 2003. (ENG., Illus.). (J). lib. bdg. 29.13 (978-0-8239-4024-0(1), 9c5f4762-c197-4003-b7e8-465e5458522a, Rosen Reference) Rosen Publishing Group, Inc., The.

Parks, Peggy J. Robert Fulton: Innovator with Steam Power. 2003. (Giants of Science Ser.). (ENG., Illus.). 64p. (J). 28.35 (978-1-56711-492-8(X), Blackbirch Pr., Inc.) Cengage Gale.

Pierce, Morris A. Robert Fulton & the Development of the Steamboat. 2009. (Library of American Lives & Times Ser.). 112p. (gr. 5-5). 69.20 (978-1-60853-502-6(9)) Rosen Publishing Group, Inc., The.

Radford, James & Wooders, Dave. Adventures on the Queen Mary: ... tales of a Teenage Crew Member! 2015. (ENG., Illus.). 274p. pap. 25.00 (978-0-692-54554-6(9)) Perfect Page, The.

Roberts, Steven. Robert Fulton, 1 vol. 2013. (Jr. Graphic American Inventors Ser.). (ENG., Illus.). 24p. (J). (gr. 2-3). pap. 11.60 (978-1-4777-0139-3(7), c5dd61cb-9649-4ec8-9047-81ab9ae446ea); lib. bdg. 28.93 (978-1-4777-0077-8(3), 159a243a-5a03-4063-8f8a-03f2562d666b) Rosen Publishing Group, Inc., The. (PowerKids Pr.).

Rogers, Kate. Robert Fulton Invents the Steamboat, 1 vol. 2013. (Rosen Readers Ser.). (ENG.). 24p. (J). (gr. 3-3). pap. 8.25 (978-1-4777-2603-7(9), 93aaa7f4-609b-449e-ad53-f3d9b455482e); pap. 49.50 (978-1-4777-2604-4(7)) Rosen Publishing Group, Inc., The. (Rosen Classroom).

Shea, Therese M. Haunted! the Queen Mary, 1 vol. 2013. (History's Most Haunted Ser.). (ENG.). 32p. (J). (gr. 3-4). 29.27 (978-1-4339-9258-2(2), 907be61b-a374-49e5-8d48-885d36bb8f69); pap. 11.50 (978-1-4339-9259-9(0), f2133c99-b939-47ec-8187-2ae456796638) Stevens, Gareth Publishing LLLP.

Stone, Adam. The Titanic Disaster. 2014. (Disaster Stories Ser.). (ENG., Illus.). 24p. (J). (gr. 3-8). 29.95 (978-1-62617-154-1(8), Black Sheep) Bellwether Media.

Youngblood, Wayne. Mark Twain along the Mississippi, 1 vol. 2005. (In the Footsteps of American Heroes Ser.). (ENG., Illus.). 64p. (gr. 5-8). pap. 15.05 (978-0-8368-6435-9(2), fc650921-fafb-4dde-ae34-50f8069dd1ae); lib. bdg. 36.67 (978-0-8368-6430-4(1), 075f253e-b58f-4ce9-9e41-a0fcee83e823) Stevens, Gareth Publishing LLLP. (Gareth Stevens Secondary Library).

STEAMSHIPS

see Steamboats

STEEL

see also Iron

also headings beginning with the word Steel

Kassinger, Ruth. Iron & Steel: From Thor's Hammer to the Space Shuttle. 2003. (Material World Ser.). (ENG., Illus.). 80p. (gr. 5-9). lib. bdg. 26.60 (978-0-7613-2111-8(X), Twenty-First Century Bks.) Lerner Publishing Group.

Meister, Cari. From Metal to Bicycles. Pinilla, Albert, illus. 2019. (Who Made My Stuff? Ser.). (ENG.). 24p. (J). (gr. 1-4). lib. bdg. (978-1-68151-695-0(0), 10847) Amicus.

STEEL-ENGRAVING

see Engraving

STEEL INDUSTRY AND TRADE

see also Iron Industry and Trade

Jarnow, Jesse. Oil, Steel, & Railroads: America's Big Businesses in the Late 1800s. (America's Industrial Society in the 19th Century Ser.). 32p. (gr. 4-4). 2009. 47.90 (978-1-61511-337-8(1)) 2003. (ENG., Illus.). pap. 10.00 (978-0-8239-4276-3(7), a40b88e8-1561-410a-b257-646a9dc4260d) Rosen Publishing Group, Inc., The.

Kent, Zachary A. Andrew Carnegie: Industrialist & Philanthropist, 1 vol. 2014. (Legendary American Biographies Ser.). (ENG.). 96p. (gr. 6-6). 29.60 (978-0-7660-6435-5(2), 83cad165-d751-4ea5-9e03-e842c95bc454); pap. 13.88 (978-0-7660-6436-2(0), 699940b5-73e2-48a5-829d-05a6f6a0215d) Enslow Publishing, LLC.

Parker, Lewis K. Andrew Carnegie & the Steel Industry. 2009. (American Tycoons Ser.). 24p. (gr. 3-3). 42.50 (978-1-61511-388-0(6), PowerKids Pr.) Rosen Publishing Group, Inc., The.

Rajczak Nelson, Kristen. Andrew Carnegie & the Steel Industry, 1 vol. 2016. (Great Entrepreneurs in U. S. History Ser.). (ENG., Illus.). 32p. (J). (gr. 5-5). pap. 12.75 (978-1-4994-2115-6(X), 86a635c6-2e46-4123-87f9-cf147087a193, PowerKids Pr.) Rosen Publishing Group, Inc., The.

STEFANSSON, VILHJALMUR, 1879-1962

Montgomery, Richard. Pechuck. 2005. reprint ed. pap. 31.95 (978-1-4179-9755-8(9)) Kessinger Publishing, LLC.

STEIN, GERTRUDE, 1874-1946

Robillard, Evie. A Portrait in Poems: The Storied Life of Gertrude Stein & Alice B. Toklas. Katstaller, Rachel, illus. 2020. (ENG.). 48p. (J). (gr. 1-4). 17.99 (978-1-5253-0056-1(3)) Kids Can Pr., Ltd. CAN. Dist: Hachette Bk. Group.

Shaughnessy, Nicola. Gertrude Stein. 2007. (Writers & Their Work Ser.). (ENG.). 96p. pap. 32.95 (978-0-7463-0906-3(6), 9780746309063) Liverpool Univ. Pr. GBR. Dist: Oxford Univ. Pr., Inc.

Winter, Jonah. Gertrude Is Gertrude Is Gertrude Is Gertrude. Brown, Calef, illus. 2009. (ENG.). 40p. (J). (gr. -1-3). 19.99 (978-1-4169-4088-3(X), Atheneum Bks. for Young Readers) Simon & Schuster Children's Publishing.

STEINBECK, JOHN, 1902-1968

John Steinbeck: The Voice of the Land. 2014. (ENG.). 192p. (J). (gr. 3-7). pap. 13.95 (978-1-59077-358-1(6)) Evans, M. & Co., Inc.

Mcarthur, Debra. John Steinbeck: The Grapes of Wrath & of Mice & Men, 1 vol. 2009. (Writers & Their Works). (ENG., Illus.). 144p. (YA). (gr. 7-7). lib. bdg. 45.50 (978-0-7614-2964-7(6), eb334f1f-4b82-432b-9fcc-1aedfb40d310) Cavendish Square Publishing LLC.

Tracy, Kathleen. John Steinbeck. 2004. (Classic Storytellers Ser.). (Illus.). 48p. (J). (gr. 4-8). lib. bdg. 29.95 (978-1-58415-271-2(0)) Mitchell Lane Pubs.

STENCIL WORK

see also Screen Process Printing

Cartwright, Stephen, illus. Christmas Stencil Book. 2005. (Usborne Farmyard Tales Ser.). 10p. (J). (gr. -1-3). bds. 9.95 (978-0-7945-1142-5(2), Usborne) EDC Publishing.

Cleyet-Merle, Laurence, illus. Animal Stencil Book. 2006. (Stencil Bks.). 14p. (J). (gr. -1-3). bds. 12.99 (978-0-7945-1140-1(6), Usborne) EDC Publishing.

Doherty, Gillian. Stencil Book. 2005. (Stencil Book Ser.). 14p. (J). 9.95 (978-0-7945-0866-1(9), Usborne) EDC Publishing.

Editors of Klutz. Stencil Art. Editors of Klutz, ed. 2013. (ENG.). 48p. (J). (gr. 3). 19.99 (978-0-545-56166-2(3)) Klutz.

Green, John. Fun with Horseback Riding Stencils. 2004. (Dover Stencils Ser.). (ENG., Illus.). 6p. (J). (gr. 1-4). pap. 1.99 (978-0-486-43419-3(2), 434192) Dover Pubns., Inc.

Harper, Ellen. Fun with Egyptian Symbols Stencils. 2003. (Dover Stencils Ser.). (ENG., Illus.). 6p. (J). (gr. 1-4). pap. 2.50 (978-0-486-43109-3(6), 431096) Dover Pubns., Inc.

Kennedy, Paul E. Fun with Whales Stencils. 2008. (Dover Stencils Ser.). (ENG., Illus.). (J). (gr. -1-5). pap. 1.50 (978-0-486-46687-3(6)) Dover Pubns., Inc.

Leonard, Barry, ed. Drawing Trucks & Diggers: A Book of 10 Stencils. 2004. (Illus.). 34p. (J). (gr. k-4). reprint ed. ring bd. 10.00 (978-0-7567-8505-5(7)) DIANE Publishing Co.

Lovell, Katie, illus. Christmas Stencil Cards. 2007. (Christmas Stencil Cards Ser.). 16p. (J). 9.99 (978-0-7945-1896-7(6), Usborne) EDC Publishing.

Noble, Marty. Fun with Emergency Vehicles Stencils. 2003. (Dover Stencils Ser.). (ENG., Illus.). 6p. (J). (gr. -1-5). pap. 1.50 (978-0-486-42634-1(3)) Dover Pubns., Inc.

—Fun with Good Luck Symbols Stencils. 2004. (Dover Stencils Ser.). (ENG.). 6p. (J). (gr. -1-5). pap. 1.50 (978-0-486-43692-0(6)) Dover Pubns., Inc.

—Fun with Mother Goose Stencils. 2003. (Dover Stencils Ser.). (ENG.). 6p. (J). (gr. -1-5). pap. 1.50 (978-0-486-42351-7(4)) Dover Pubns., Inc.

—Fun with Noah's Ark Stencils. 2006. (Dover Stencils Ser.). (ENG., Illus.). 6p. (J). (gr. -1-5). pap. 1.50 (978-0-486-44881-7(9)) Dover Pubns., Inc.

—Fun with Wedding Stencils. 2004. (Dover Stencils Ser.). (ENG.). 6p. (gr. -1-5). pap. 1.50 (978-0-486-43683-8(7)) Dover Pubns., Inc.

Pearson, Maria, illus. Spooky Stencil Cards. 2008. (Stencil Cards Ser.). 16p. (J). 9.99 (978-0-7945-2415-9(X), Usborne) EDC Publishing.

QEB Learn Art National Book Stores Edition: Stencils & Prints. 2006. (J). per. (978-1-59566-283-5(9)) QEB Publishing Inc.

Robins, Deri. Stencils & Prints: Great Ideas for Art Prints, Cards, Wrapping Paper, & More. 2006. (Art Smart Ser.). (ENG., Illus.). 32p. (J). (gr. 2-5). pap. 9.95 (978-1-58728-544-8(4)) Cooper Square Publishing Llc.

School Zone Staff. Fun & Festive. 2004. (ENG.). 32p. (J). 12.99 (978-1-58947-471-0(6), 03602) School Zone Publishing Co.

—On the Farm. 2004. (ENG.). 32p. (J). 12.99 (978-1-58947-470-3(8), 03601) School Zone Publishing Co.

—Things That Go. 2004. (ENG.). 32p. (J). 12.99 (978-1-58947-472-7(4), 03603) School Zone Publishing Co.

Silver Dolphin en Español Editors. Libro de actividades con plantillas: Disney Animales: Animals Stencil. 2007. (Illus.). 10p. (J). bds. (978-970-718-435-0(3), Silver Dolphin en Español) Advanced Marketing, S. de R. L. de C. V.

Silver Dolphin en Español Editors, creator. Disney Favoritos 2: Libro de Actividades con Plantillas. 2007. (Illus.). 20p. (J). (gr. -1). bds. (978-970-718-433-6(7), Silver Dolphin en Español) Advanced Marketing, S. de R. L. de C. V.

—Disney Princesa Libro de Actividades con Plantillas. 2007. (Disney Princesa (Silver Dolphin) Ser.). (Illus.). 20p. (J). (gr. -1). bds. (978-970-718-434-3(5), Silver Dolphin en Español) Advanced Marketing, S. de R. L. de C. V.

Stanley, Mandy. Stencils. 2016. (Arty Mouse Creativity Kits Ser.). (ENG., Illus.). 12p. (J). (gr. -1-2). pap. 16.99 (978-1-78445-433-3(8)) Top That! Publishing PLC GBR. Dist: Independent Pubs. Group.

Stencils & Prints, 6 bks. 2005. (QEB Learn Art Ser.). (Illus.). 32p. (J). per. 8.95 *(978-1-59566-127-2(1))* QEB Publishing Inc.

Stowell, Louie & Pearcey, Alice. Diggers Stencil Book. Doherty, Gillian, ed. Tudor, Andy, illus. 2007. (Stencil Bks.). 14p. (J). bds. 12.99 *(978-0-7945-1576-8(2)*, Usborne) EDC Publishing.

Top That. Let's Stencil Things That Go. 2008. *(978-1-84666-584-4(1))* Top That! Publishing PLC.

STENGEL, CASEY, 1891-1975

Winter, Jonah. You Never Heard of Casey Stengel?! Blitt, Barry, illus. 2016. 40p. (J). (gr. -1-3). 17.99 *(978-0-375-87013-2(X)*, Schwartz & Wade Bks.) Random Hse. Children's Bks.

STEPFAMILIES

Beyl, Charles, illus. My Parents Are Divorced Too: A Book for Kids by Kids. 2nd ed. 2006. 64p. (J). (gr. 3-7). per. 9.95 *(978-1-59147-242-1(3)*, Magination Pr.) American Psychological Assn.

Delessert, Etienne. A Glass. Delessert, Etienne, illus. 2013. (ENG., Illus.). 32p. (J). (gr. 4-7). 18.99 *(978-1-56846-257-8(3)*, 21611, Creative Editions) Creative Co., The.

Ford, Melanie, et al. My Parents Are Divorced Too: A Book for Kids by Kids. Beyl, Charles, illus. 2nd ed. 2006. (ENG.). 72p. (J). (gr. 3-7). 14.95 *(978-1-59147-241-4(5)*, Magination Pr.) American Psychological Assn.

Gay, Kathlyn. Divorce: The Ultimate Teen Guide. 2014. (It Happened to Me Ser.: 41). (Illus.). 220p. 59.00 *(978-0-8108-9238-5(3))* Rowman & Littlefield Publishers, Inc.

Geisen, Cynthia. Growing into a Family: A Kids Guide to Living in a Blended Family. Alley, R. W., illus. 2015. 32p. (J). pap. 7.95 *(978-0-87029-684-0(1))* Abbey Pr.

Hagler, Gina. Everything You Need to Know about Living in a Blended Family, 1 vol. 2018. (Need to Know Library). (ENG.). 64p. (gr. 6-6). pap. 13.95 *(978-1-5081-8348-8(1)*, 48559724-adb7-4b5c-b22c-453e38e4fcfe) Rosen Publishing Group, Inc., The.

Hewitt, Sally. My Stepfamily. 2009. (J). 28.50 *(978-1-59920-229-7(8))* Black Rabbit Bks.

Houser, Grace. What's Life Like in a Blended Family?, 1 vol. 2018. (Help Me Understand Ser.). (ENG., Illus.). 24p. (J). (gr. 3-3). pap. 9.25 *(978-1-5383-4808-6(X)*, 8f5ea699-2c09-431c-b7a3-1a616f68887e, PowerKids Pr.) Rosen Publishing Group, Inc., The.

MacGregor, Cynthia. Jigsaw Puzzle Family: The Stepkids' Guide to Fitting It Together. 2005. (ENG.). 120p. (J). (gr. 4-8). per. 12.95 *(978-1-886230-63-7(3)*, I0637, Impact Pubs.) New Harbinger Pubns.

Myers, Nancy & Charles, Rodney. Where's My Brother Joshua? 2013. 20p. pap. 15.95 *(978-1-935323-14-3(8))* Westry Wingate Group, Inc.

Peterman, Rosie L., et al. Divorce & Stepfamilies, 1 vol. 2012. (Teen Mental Health Ser.). (ENG., Illus.). 48p. (J). (gr. 5-6). lib. bdg. 34.47 *(978-1-4488-6893-3(9)*, e921246d-921a-4248-848e-dd177071b0bc) Rosen Publishing Group, Inc., The.

Schuette, Sarah L. Blended Families, 1 vol. 2010. (My Family Ser.). (ENG.). 24p. (J). (gr. -1-2). pap. 6.29 *(978-1-4296-4835-6(X)*, 112814); (gr. k-1). pap. 38.74 *(978-1-4296-5158-5(X)*, 15190, Pebble) Capstone.

Simons, Rae. Blended Families. 2010. (Changing Face of Modern Families Ser.). (Illus.). 64p. (YA). (gr. 6-18). 22.95 *(978-1-4222-1492-3(3))* Mason Crest.

Stern, Zoe & Stern, Evan. Divorce Is Not the End of the World: Zoe's & Evan's Coping Guide for Kids. 2nd rev. ed. 2008. (Illus.). 112p. (J). (gr. 3-7). pap. 9.99 *(978-1-58246-241-7(0)*, Tricycle Pr.) Random Hse. Children's Bks.

Weitzman, Elizabeth. Let's Talk about Living in a Blended Family. 2009. (Let's Talk Library). 24p. (gr. 2-3). 42.50 *(978-1-60853-451-7(0)*, PowerKids Pr.) Rosen Publishing Group, Inc., The.

STEPFAMILIES—FICTION

Bach, Mette. Cinders. 2019. (Lorimer Real Love Ser.). (ENG.). 168p. (YA). (gr. 9-12). lib. bdg. 27.99 *(978-1-4594-1385-6(7)*, 95865eef-4a8c-4cbf-8a0c-2e9b8b685b46) James Lorimer & Co. Ltd., Pubs. CAN. Dist: Lerner Publishing Group.

Banks, Piper. Geek Abroad, 2 vols. 2008. (Geek High Ser.: 2). (ENG.). 256p. (YA). (gr. 9-18). 9.99 *(978-0-451-22393-7(4)*, Berkley) Penguin Publishing Group.

—Revenge of the Geek. 2010. (Geek High Ser.: 4). (ENG.). 256p. (gr. 12-18). 9.99 *(978-0-451-23134-5(1)*, Berkley) Penguin Publishing Group.

—Summer of the Geek. 2010. (Geek High Ser.: 3). (ENG.). 256p. (YA). (gr. 5-18). 9.99 *(978-0-451-22984-7(3)*, Berkley) Penguin Publishing Group.

Barwin, Steven. Icebreaker, 1 vol. 2006. (Lorimer Sports Stories Ser.). (ENG.). 128p. (J). (gr. 4-8). 16.95 *(978-1-55028-951-0(9)*, 951) James Lorimer & Co. Ltd., Pubs. CAN. Dist: Formac Lorimer Bks. Ltd.

Behrens, Rebecca. The Last Grand Adventure. (ENG.). (J). (gr. 3-7). 2019. 352p. pap. 8.99 *(978-1-4814-9693-3(X))* 2018. (Illus.). 336p. 17.99 *(978-1-4814-9692-6(1))* Simon & Schuster Children's Publishing. (Aladdin).

Bentley, Sue. Classroom Princess. 2013. (Magic Puppy Ser.: 9). lib. bdg. 16.00 *(978-0-606-32122-8(5))* Turtleback.

—Classroom Princess #9. Swan, Angela, illus. 2013. (Magic Puppy Ser.: 9). (ENG.). 128p. (J). (gr. 1-3). 6.99 *(978-0-448-46732-0(1)*, Grosset & Dunlap) Penguin Young Readers Group.

—Party Dreams #5, 5 vols., 5. Swan, Angela, illus. 2010. (Magic Puppy Ser.: 5). (ENG.). 128p. (J). (gr. 1-3). 5.99 *(978-0-448-45064-3(X)*, Grosset & Dunlap) Penguin Young Readers Group.

Boada, Francesc, adapted by. Cinderella/Cenicienta: Bilingual Edition. 2005. (Bilingual Fairy Tales Ser.: BIL). (ENG., Illus.). 32p. (J). (gr. -1-7). pap. 8.99 *(978-0-8118-3090-4(X))* Chronicle Bks. LLC.

Bobrick, Julie, ed. Cinderella: Level 1: Learn Mandarin Chinese Through Fairy Tales. Peters, Li Li & Tao, Ming, trs. Sandoval, Migs, illus. 2006. (Learn Chinese Through Fairy Tales Ser.). (ENG & CHI.). 29p. pap. 14.95 incl. audio compact disk *(978-1-891888-79-3(X))* Slangman Publishing.

Bodeen, S. A. Found: Book 4 of the Shipwreck Island Series. 2018. (Shipwreck Island Ser.: 4). (ENG.). 160p. (J). pap. 9.99 *(978-1-250-02784-9(5)*, 900104992) Square Fish.

Bowdish, Lynea. How to Be Nice -- & Other Lessons I Didn't Learn. Gray, Leslie, illus. 2006. 47p. (J). pap. *(978-1-59336-726-8(0))* Mondo Publishing.

Bowvayne. A Spell Behind Bars. Snow, Alan, illus. 2006. (Misadventures of Danny Cloke Ser.). 207p. (J). per. 4.99 *(978-0-7945-1293-4(3)*, Usborne) EDC Publishing.

—A Turn in the Grave. Snow, Alan, illus. 2006. (Misadventures of Danny Cloke Ser.). 143p. (J). per. 4.99 *(978-0-7945-1292-7(5)*, Usborne) EDC Publishing.

Bryant, Ann. Billie & the Parent Plan. 2007. (Billie & the Parent Plan Ser.). 191p. (J). (gr. 2-5). per. 4.99 *(978-0-7945-1721-2(8)*, Usborne) EDC Publishing.

Bullard, Lisa. Trick-or-Treat on Milton Street. Oeltjenbruns, Joni, illus. 2003. (Picture Bks.). 32p. (J). (gr. -1-3). 15.95 *(978-1-57505-158-1(3)*, Carolrhoda Bks.) Lerner Publishing Group.

Burke, David. Cinderella: Level 1: Learn German Through Fairy Tales. Bobrick, Julie, ed. Deese, Teut & Wirth, Petra, trs. Sandoval, Migs, illus. 2006. (Learn German Through Fairy Tales Ser.). (ENG & GER.). 29p. pap. 14.95 incl. audio compact disk *(978-1-891888-76-2(5))* Slangman Publishing.

Buxbaum, Julie. Tell Me Three Things. 2017. (ENG.). 352p. (YA). (gr. 7). pap. 11.99 *(978-0-553-53567-9(6)*, Ember) Random Hse. Children's Bks.

Cabot, Meg. The Mediator: Shadowland & Ninth Key. 2010. (Mediator Ser.). (ENG.). 544p. (YA). (gr. 8). pap. 9.99 *(978-0-06-204020-6(0)*, HarperTeen) HarperCollins Pubs.

Caletti, Deb. Love Is All You Need: Wild Roses; the Nature of Jade. 2013. (ENG.). 608p. (YA). (gr. 7-7). pap. 11.99 *(978-1-4424-6636-4(7)*, Simon Pulse) Simon Pulse.

Cartwright, Stephen, illus. Cinderella. 2006. (First Stories Sticker Bks.). 16p. (J). (gr. -1-3). pap. 6.99 *(978-0-7945-1311-5(5)*, Usborne) EDC Publishing.

Chambers, Pamela G. My Mommy's Getting Married. Stewart, Muriel, illus. 2009. 32p. (gr. -1-3). 17.95 *(978-0-9799487-0-1(3))* Infinity Publishing Co.

Cinderella. unabr. ed. (Read-Along Ser.). (J). 7.99 incl. audio *(978-1-55723-007-2(2))* Walt Disney Records.

Clawson, David. My Fairy Godmother Is a Drag Queen. 2017. (ENG.). 336p. (J). (gr. 8-8). 17.99 *(978-1-5107-1411-3(1)*, Sky Pony Pr.) Skyhorse Publishing Co., Inc.

Clifton, Lutricia. Freaky Fast Frankie Joe. 2013. (ENG.). 272p. (J). (gr. 3-7). pap. 7.99 *(978-0-8234-2867-0(2))* Holiday Hse., Inc.

Cohen, Tish. Inside Out Girl: A Novel. 2008. (ENG.). 352p. pap. 14.99 *(978-0-06-145295-6(5)*, Harper Perennial) HarperCollins Pubs.

Cohn, Rachel. Gingerbread. 2003. (ENG., Illus.). 224p. (YA). (gr. 9). pap. 9.99 *(978-0-689-86020-1(X)*, Simon & Schuster Bks. For Young Readers) Simon & Schuster Bks. For Young Readers.

—Shrimp, 7 vols. 2005. (YA). 171.75 *(978-1-4193-5253-9(9))* Recorded Bks., Inc.

—The Steps. 2004. (ENG.). 144p. (J). (gr. 3-7). reprint ed. pap. 7.99 *(978-0-689-87414-7(6)*, Simon & Schuster Bks. For Young Readers) Simon & Schuster Bks. For Young Readers.

—Two Steps Forward. (ENG., Illus.). 240p. (YA). 2013. (gr. 7). pap. 11.99 *(978-1-4424-9615-6(0))* 2006. 15.95 *(978-0-689-86614-2(3))* Simon & Schuster Bks. For Young Readers. (Simon & Schuster Bks. For Young Readers).

Cook, Eileen. Unraveling Isobel. 2012. (ENG.). 320p. (YA). (gr. 9). pap. 9.99 *(978-1-4424-1328-3(X)*, Simon Pulse) Simon Pulse.

Coolidge, Susan. What Katy Did. 2017. (Virago Modern Classics,What Katy Did Ser.). (ENG.). 208p. (J). (gr. 4-6). 11.99 *(978-0-349-00959-0(7)*, Virago Press) Little, Brown Book Group Ltd. GBR. Dist: Hachette Bk. Group.

Cooper, Floyd. The Ring Bearer. Cooper, Floyd, illus. 2017. (Illus.). 32p. (J). (gr. -1-2). 17.99 *(978-0-399-16740-9(4)*, Philomel Bks.) Penguin Young Readers Group.

Cooper, Ilene. The Worst Noel: A Novel. 2006. 143p. (J). (gr. 4-8). reprint ed. pap. 4.00 *(978-1-4223-5411-7(3))* DIANE Publishing Co.

Cray, Jordan. Dead Man's Hand. 2009. (Danger. com Ser.: 8). (ENG.). 224p. (YA). (gr. 7). pap. 10.99 *(978-1-4169-9852-5(7)*, Simon Pulse) Simon Pulse.

Cross, Frances. Marty's Diary. 2008. (Cutting Edge Ser.). (ENG.). 160p. pap. *(978-1-84167-697-5(7))* Ransom Publishing Ltd.

Cumbie, Patricia. Where People Like Us Live. 2008. 224p. (YA). (gr. 7-18). lib. bdg. 17.89 *(978-0-06-137598-9(5)*, Geringer, Laura Book) HarperCollins Pubs.

Daniels, Sara. Pieces of the Sky. 2005. 135p. pap. 15.99 *(978-1-4116-4291-1(0))* Lulu Pr., Inc.

de Gramont, Nina. Meet Me at the River. 2014. (ENG., Illus.). 384p. (YA). (gr. 9). pap. 11.99 *(978-1-4169-8016-2(4)*, Atheneum Bks. for Young Readers) Simon & Schuster Children's Publishing.

Deem, James M. 3 NBs of Julian Drew. 2004. (ENG.). 208p. (YA). (gr. 7-18). pap. 13.95 *(978-0-618-43907-2(2)*, 484394, Clarion Bks.) HarperCollins Pubs.

Deriso, Christine Hurley. The Right-Under Club: Second Stage. 2010. (J). *(978-0-385-73621-3(5))*; lib. bdg. *(978-0-385-90593-0(9))* Random House Publishing Group. (Delacorte Pr).

Dessen, Sarah. Along for the Ride. 2011. (ENG.). 432p. (YA). (gr. 7-18). pap. 12.99 *(978-0-14-241556-6(1)*, Speak) Penguin Young Readers Group.

—Along for the Ride. 2011. lib. bdg. 20.85 *(978-0-606-15360-7(8))* Turtleback.

—This Lullaby. 2004. (ENG.). 368p. (YA). (gr. 7-18). reprint ed. pap. 11.99 *(978-0-14-250155-9(7)*, Speak) Penguin Young Readers Group.

Dokey, Cameron. Before Midnight: A Retelling Of "Cinderella" 2007. (Once upon a Time Ser.). (ENG.). 208p. (YA). (gr. 7-12). mass mkt. 8.99 *(978-1-4169-3471-4(5)*, Simon Pulse) Simon Pulse.

Donnelly, Jennifer. Stepsister. (ENG.). (YA). 2020. 368p. (gr. 8-12). pap. 10.99 *(978-1-338-26847-8(3))* 2019. 352p. (gr. 7-7). 17.99 *(978-1-338-26846-1(5)*, Scholastic Pr.) Scholastic, Inc.

Draper, Sharon M. Forged by Fire. 2013. (Hazelwood High Trilogy Ser.: 2). (ENG., Illus.). 176p. (YA). (gr. 7). pap. 10.99 *(978-1-4424-8914-1(6)*, Atheneum Bks. for Young Readers) Simon & Schuster Children's Publishing.

—Forged by Fire. 2013. (Hazelwood High Trilogy Ser.: 2). lib. bdg. 20.85 *(978-0-606-32333-8(3))* Turtleback.

Dwyer, Mindy. The Salmon Princess: An Alaska Cinderella Story. 2004. (Paws IV Ser.). (ENG., Illus.). 32p. (J). (gr. -1-2). pap. 10.99 *(978-1-57061-355-5(9)*, Little Bigfoot) Sasquatch Bks.

Frederick, Heather Vogel. Once upon a Toad. 2013. (ENG., Illus.). 288p. (J). (gr. 5-9). pap. 7.99 *(978-1-4169-8479-5(8)*, Simon & Schuster Bks. For Young Readers) Simon & Schuster Bks. For Young Readers.

—Once upon a Toad. 2012. (ENG., Illus.). 272p. (J). (gr. 5-9). 16.99 *(978-1-4169-8478-8(X))* Simon & Schuster, Inc.

Friesen, Gayle. For Now. 2007. 248p. (J). (gr. 5-9). 7.95 *(978-1-55453-133-2(0))* Kids Can Pr., Ltd. CAN. Dist: Hachette Bk. Group.

Gaetz, Dayle Campbell. Spoiled Rotten. 2006. (Orca Currents Ser.). 103p. (gr. 5-9). 19.95 *(978-0-7569-6875-5(5))* Perfection Learning Corp.

Gervay, Susanne. Always Jack. Wilcox, Cathy, illus. 2013. 148p. (J). *(978-1-61067-226-9(7))* Kane Miller.

—Super Jack. Wilcox, Cathy, illus. 2003. (ENG.). 192p. *(978-0-207-19918-9(3))* HarperCollins Pubs. Australia.

—SuperJack. Wilcox, Cathy, illus. 2013. (ENG.). 192p. (J). pap. 5.99 *(978-1-61067-129-3(5))* Kane Miller.

Green, Shari. Macy Mcmillan & the Rainbow Goddess. 2017. (ENG.). 240p. (J). (gr. 3-7). pap. 12.95 *(978-1-77278-017-8(0))* Pajama Pr. CAN. Dist: Publishers Group West (PGW).

Greene, Stephanie. Falling into Place. 2006. (ENG.). 128p. (J). (gr. 5-7). pap. 8.95 *(978-0-618-68928-6(1)*, 100487, Clarion Bks.) HarperCollins Pubs.

Hahn, Mary Downing. Look for Me by Moonlight. 2008. (ENG.). 208p. (YA). (gr. 7). pap. 7.99 *(978-0-547-07616-4(9)*, 1042006, Clarion Bks.) HarperCollins Pubs.

—Wait till Helen Comes: A Ghost Story. 2008. (ENG., Illus.). 208p. (J). (gr. 5-7). pap. 9.99 *(978-0-547-02864-4(4)*, 1032983, Clarion Bks.) HarperCollins Pubs.

Hicks, Betty. Out of Order. 2007. (ENG.). 176p. (J). (gr. 3-7). pap. 15.99 *(978-0-312-37355-9(4)*, 900045404) Square Fish.

Hinton, S. E. Esto Ya Es Otra Historia. (SPA.). (J). 6.95 *(978-84-204-4121-4(X))* Santillana USA Publishing Co., Inc.

Johnson, Lois Walfrid. The Creeping Shadows. 2009. (Orig.). (J). 8.99 *(978-0-88062-277-6(6))* Mott Media.

—The Disappearing Stranger. 2009. (Orig.). (J). 8.99 *(978-0-88062-275-2(X))* Mott Media.

Jones, Jen. Maren's New Family. Franco, Paula, illus. 2015. (Sleepover Girls Ser.). (ENG.). 128p. (J). (gr. 3-5). lib. bdg. 22.65 *(978-1-4965-0540-8(9)*, 128612, Stone Arch Bks.) Capstone.

Kantor, Melissa. If I Have a Wicked Stepmother, Where's My Prince? 2005. 283p. (YA). *(978-1-4156-2763-1(0))* Hyperion Pr.

Kats, Jewel. Cinderella's Magical Wheelchair: An Empowering Fairy Tale. Kinra, Richa, illus. 2012. (J). 24p. 29.95 *(978-1-61599-113-6(1))*; 20p. pap. 16.95 *(978-1-61599-112-9(3))* Loving Healing Pr., Inc.

Kehoe, Tim. Vincent Shadow: Toy Inventor. Wohnoutka, Mike & Francis, Guy, illus. 2011. (Vincent Shadow Ser.: 1). (ENG.). 224p. (J). (gr. 3-7). pap. 13.99 *(978-0-316-05666-3(9))* Little, Brown Bks. for Young Readers.

Lane, Bryan. Stepbrothers the New Arrival. 2012. 16p. pap. 15.00 *(978-1-4685-7410-4(8))* AuthorHouse.

Langan, John. Search for Safety. 2006. (Bluford Ser.). 128p. (YA). (gr. 7-18). pap. 4.95 *(978-1-59194-070-8(2))* Townsend Pr.

Lee, Kathy. Space Invaders. 2011. 144p. pap. *(978-1-84427-507-6(8))* Scripture Union.

Levins, Sandra. Do You Sing Twinkle? A Story about Remarriage & New Family. Langdo, Bryan, illus. 2009. 32p. (J). (gr. -1-3). (ENG.). 14.95 *(978-1-4338-0539-4(1))*; pap. 9.95 *(978-1-4338-0551-6(0))* American Psychological Assn. (Magination Pr.).

Lockwood, Cara. Wuthering High: A Bard Academy Novel. 2006. (Bard Academy Ser.: 1). (ENG.). 272p. (YA). (gr. 8-12). pap. 17.99 *(978-1-4165-2475-5(4)*, MTV Bks.) MTV Books.

Luciani, Brigitte. A Hubbub: Book 2, No. 2. Tharlet, Eve, illus. 2010. (Mr. Badger & Mrs. Fox Ser.: 2). (ENG.). 32p. (J). (gr. k-3). pap. 7.99 *(978-0-7613-5632-5(0)*, 16271d6f-0029-4813-9c24-d51cd664aca3, Graphic Universe™) Lerner Publishing Group.

—Peace & Quiet: Book 4, No. 4. Tharlet, Eve, illus. 2012. (Mr. Badger & Mrs. Fox Ser.: 4). (ENG.). 32p. (J). (gr. k-3). pap. 7.99 *(978-0-8225-9163-4(4)*, c88a3e3a-49bd-4fd8-af9b-b8ad48fd6eb9, Graphic Universe™) Lerner Publishing Group.

—What a Team! Gauvin, Edward, tr. from FRE. Tharlet, Eve, illus. 2011. (Mr. Badger & Mrs. Fox Ser.: 3). (ENG.). 32p. (J). (gr. k-3). 25.26 *(978-0-7613-5627-1(4))* Lerner Publishing Group.

—What a Team! Book 3, No. 3. Tharlet, Eve, illus. 2011. (Mr. Badger & Mrs. Fox Ser.: 3). (ENG.). 32p. (J). (gr. k-3). pap. 7.99 *(978-0-7613-5633-2(9)*, 54e78c75-d598-4114-b1d2-9f724293d0ac, Graphic Universe™) Lerner Publishing Group.

—The Wild Cat: Book 6. Tharlet, Eve, illus. 2018. (Mr. Badger & Mrs. Fox Ser.). (ENG.). 32p. (J). (gr. k-3). 26.65 *(978-1-5415-0086-0(5)*, db60c918-cf2b-4049-8c66-c81a69da77ae, Graphic Universe™) Lerner Publishing Group.

Lundquist, Jenny. The Wondrous World of Violet Barnaby. 2017. (ENG.). 272p. (J). (gr. 3-7). 17.99 *(978-1-4814-6035-4(8))*; (Illus.). pap. 7.99 *(978-1-4814-6034-7(X))* Simon & Schuster Children's Publishing. (Aladdin).

Lynn, Tracy. Snow: A Retelling of "Snow White & the Seven Dwarfs" 2006. (Once upon a Time Ser.). (ENG.). 272p. (YA). (gr. 9-12). mass mkt. 7.99 *(978-1-4169-4015-9(4)*, Simon Pulse) Simon Pulse.

Mancusi, Mari. Princesses, Inc. 2017. (Mix Ser.). (ENG., Illus.). 320p. (J). (gr. 4-8). pap. 7.99 *(978-1-4814-7900-4(8)*, Aladdin) Simon & Schuster Children's Publishing.

Mangum, Kay Lynn. When the Bough Breaks. 2007. 352p. (YA). pap. 15.95 *(978-1-59038-748-1(1))* Deseret Bk. Co.

Manley, Candance. Skeeter's Dream. 2010. (ENG.). 192p. (J). (gr. 7-18). pap. 14.95 *(978-0-9785634-8-6(4))* La Frontera Publishing.

Marciniak, Christine. Lights, Camera, Ali! 2013. 232p. (J). pap. 13.99 *(978-1-61271-214-7(2))* Zumaya Pubns. LLC.

—Reality Ali. 2012. (J). *(978-1-61271-075-4(1))*; *(978-1-61271-076-1(X))*; pap. 13.99 *(978-1-61271-074-7(3))* Zumaya Pubns. LLC.

Maskame, Estelle. Did I Mention I Need You? 2016. (Did I Mention I Love You (DIMILY) Ser.: 2). (ENG.). 384p. (YA). (gr. 8-12). pap. 10.99 *(978-1-4926-3218-4(X)*, 9781492632184) Sourcebooks, Inc.

McCahan, Erin. I Now Pronounce You Someone Else. 2010. (ENG.). 272p. (J). (gr. 7-18). 16.99 *(978-0-545-08818-3(6)*, Levine, Arthur A. Bks.) Scholastic, Inc.

McCombie, Karen. My Big (Strange) Happy Family. Monks, Lydia, illus. 2009. (J). pap. *(978-0-385-73597-1(9)*, Yearling) Random Hse. Children's Bks.

McKay, Hilary. The Time of Green Magic. (ENG., Illus.). (J). (gr. 3-7). 2021. 272p. pap. 7.99 *(978-1-5344-6277-9(5))* 2020. 240p. 17.99 *(978-1-5344-6276-2(7))* McElderry, Margaret K. Bks. (McElderry, Margaret K. Bks.).

Meade, L. T. The Children's Pilgrimage. 2017. (ENG., Illus.). (J). 25.95 *(978-1-374-91664-7(1))*; pap. 15.95 *(978-1-374-91663-0(3))* Capital Communications, Inc.

Meyer, Marissa. Cinder. Lt. ed. 2012. (Lunar Chronicles: Bk. 1). (ENG.). 517p. (J). (gr. 7-12). 23.99 *(978-1-4104-4607-7(7))* Thorndike Pr.

—Cinder. 2013. (Lunar Chronicles Ser.: 1). (YA). lib. bdg. 20.85 *(978-0-606-28633-6(0))* Turtleback.

—Cinder. 2015. (Cinder Ser.: 1). (SPA.). 416p. (YA). (gr. 9-12). pap. 20.99 *(978-987-612-927-5(9))* V&R Editoras.

—Cinder: Book One of the Lunar Chronicles. 2012. (Lunar Chronicles Ser.: 1). (ENG.). 400p. (YA). (gr. 7-12). 24.99 *(978-0-312-64189-4(3)*, 900078307) Feiwel & Friends.

—Cinder: Book One of the Lunar Chronicles. 2020. (Lunar Chronicles Ser.: 1). (ENG.). 448p. (YA). pap. 11.99 *(978-1-250-76888-9(8)*, 900233163) Square Fish.

Miles, Brenda S. & Sweet, Susan D. Cinderstella: A Tale of Planets Not Princes. Docampo, Valeria, illus. 2016. 32p. (J). *(978-1-4338-2270-4(9)*, Magination Pr.) American Psychological Assn.

Miles, Cindy. Forevermore. 2013. (ENG.). 288p. (YA). (gr. 7). pap. 9.99 *(978-0-545-42622-0(7))* Scholastic, Inc.

Minh Quoc. Tam & Cam/Tam Cam: The Ancient Vietnamese Cinderella Story. Smith, William, tr. from VIE. Mai Long, illus. 2006. (ENG & VIE.). 32p. (J). (gr. 1-4). 16.95 *(978-0-9701654-4-2(7))* East West Discovery Pr.

Minke, Shari. The Airplane Story: A Blended Family's Journey. 2010. pap. 12.99 *(978-1-61579-944-2(3))* Salem Author Services.

Morgan, Melissa J. Extra Credit #22, 22. 2009. (Camp Confidential Ser.: 22). 160p. (J). (gr. 4-7). 4.99 *(978-0-448-45216-6(2)*, Grosset & Dunlap) Penguin Young Readers Group.

Musilli Whitesell, Marjorie. I Have Four Parents. 2009. (Illus.). 20p. pap. 10.95 *(978-1-60860-448-7(9)*, Eloquent Bks.) Strategic Book Publishing & Rights Agency (SBPRA).

Palmer, Robin. Girl vs. Superstar, 1. 2010. (Yours Truly, Lucy B. Parker Ser.: 1). 224p. (J). (gr. 6-8). 21.19 *(978-0-14-241500-9(6))* Penguin Young Readers Group.

—Love You Like a Sister. 2017. (Mix Ser.). (ENG., Illus.). 256p. (J). (gr. 4-8). pap. 7.99 *(978-1-4814-6642-4(9)*, Aladdin) Simon & Schuster Children's Publishing.

Payne, C. C. The Thing about Leftovers. 2017. 288p. (J). (gr. 5). 8.99 *(978-0-14-751422-6(3)*, Puffin Books) Penguin Young Readers Group.

Peters, Julie Anne. Keeping You a Secret. 2005. (ENG., Illus.). 272p. (J). (gr. 10-17). pap. 10.99 *(978-0-316-00985-0(7))* Little, Brown Bks. for Young Readers.

Peterson, Esther Allen. The House That Cared. 2010. (J). pap. *(978-0-88092-505-1(1))* Royal Fireworks Publishing Co.

Probst, Jeff & Tebbetts, Chris. Stranded. 2013. (Stranded Ser.: 1). lib. bdg. 17.20 *(978-0-606-36788-2(8))* Turtleback.

Probst, Jeff & Tebbetts, Christopher. Desperate Measures. 2016. (Stranded, Shadow Island Ser.: 3). 172p. (J). lib. bdg. 17.20 *(978-0-606-37562-7(7))* Turtleback.

—Shadow Island: Desperate Measures. 2016. (Stranded Ser.: 6). (ENG.). 192p. (J). (gr. 3-7). 6.99 *(978-0-14-751390-8(1)*, Puffin Books) Penguin Young Readers Group.

—Shadow Island: the Sabotage. 2015. (Stranded Ser.: 5). (ENG.). 224p. (J). (gr. 3-7). 6.99 *(978-0-14-751389-2(8)*, Puffin Books) Penguin Young Readers Group.

—Stranded. 2013. (Stranded Ser.: 1). (ENG.). 208p. (J). (gr. 3-7). pap. 8.99 *(978-0-14-242424-7(2)*, Puffin Books) Penguin Young Readers Group.

—Trial by Fire. 2013. 174p. (J). *(978-0-14-751195-9(X))* Penguin Publishing Group.

—Trial by Fire. 2013. (Stranded Ser.: 2). (ENG.). 208p. (J). (gr. 3-7). pap. 8.99 *(978-0-14-242425-4(0)*, Puffin Books) Penguin Young Readers Group.

Rallison, Janette. My Unfair Godmother. 2012. (ENG.). 352p. (YA). (gr. 7-12). 26.19 *(978-0-8027-2236-2(9)*, 9780802722362) Bloomsbury Publishing USA.

Readler, Blaine C. Under the Radar: The Spy Drone Adventure. 2006. (ENG.). 248p. (J). (gr. 7-12). per. *(978-1-933255-18-7(8))* DNA Pr.

Reinhardt, Dana. How to Build a House. 2009. (ENG.). 240p. (YA). (gr. 9-11). pap. 8.99 *(978-0-375-84454-6(6)*, Ember) Random Hse. Children's Bks.

Reinhart, Matthew. Cinderella: A Pop-Up Fairy Tale. Reinhart, Matthew, illus. 2005. (ENG., Illus.). 12p. (J). (gr. -1-3). 39.99 *(978-1-4169-0501-1(4)*, Little Simon) Little Simon.

Roehrig, Caleb. White Rabbit. 2019. (ENG.). 352p. (YA). pap. 13.99 *(978-1-250-29475-3(4)*, 900195091) Square Fish.

Ruby, Laura. Play Me. 2009. (ENG.). 336p. (YA). (gr. 9). pap. 9.99 *(978-0-06-124329-5(9)*, HarperTeen) HarperCollins Pubs.

Salenas, Bobbi. Cinderella Latina - Cinicienta Latina. La Madrid, Enriquee, tr. Salenas, Bobbi, illus. 2003. (SPA., Illus.). (YA). (gr. 3-12). 19.95 *(978-0-934925-05-8(X))* Pinata Pubns.

Salisbury, Graham. Lord of the Deep. braille ed. 2003. (J). (gr. 2). spiral bd. *(978-0-616-15872-2(6))* Canadian National Institute for the Blind/Institut National Canadien pour les Aveugles.

—Lord of the Deep. 2003. (ENG.). 192p. (YA). (gr. 7). mass mkt. 6.99 *(978-0-440-22911-7(1)*, Laurel Leaf) Random Hse. Children's Bks.

—Lord of the Deep: A Novel. 2006. 182p. (J). (gr. 6-10). reprint ed. 16.00 *(978-1-4223-5841-2(0))* DIANE Publishing Co.

Sandoval, Migs, illus. Cinderella: Level 1: Learn French Through Fairy Tales. 2006. (Learn French Through Fairy Tales Ser.). (ENG & FRE.). 29p. (J). (gr. -1-3). pap. 14.95 incl. audio compact disk *(978-1-891888-75-5(7))* Slangman Publishing.

Schroeder, Lisa. Far from You. (ENG.). (YA). 2010. 384p. (gr. 9). pap. 12.99 *(978-1-4169-7507-6(1))* 2008. 368p. (gr. 8-18). 15.99 *(978-1-4169-7506-9(3))* Simon Pulse. (Simon Pulse).

Scott, Mindi. Live Through This. 2012. (ENG.). 304p. (YA). (gr. 9). pap. 9.99 *(978-1-4424-4060-9(0))*; 17.99 *(978-1-4424-4059-3(7))* Simon Pulse. (Simon Pulse).

Seely, Debra. Grasslands. 2017. (ENG., Illus.). (J). (gr. 4-6). pap. 9.99 *(978-0-922820-18-4(X))* Watermark Pr., Inc.

Selfors, Suzanne. Wedgie & Gizmo. Fisinger, Barbara, illus. 2017. (Wedgie & Gizmo Ser.: 1). (ENG.). 176p. (J). (gr. 3-7). 13.99 *(978-0-06-244763-0(7)*, Tegen, Katherine Bks) HarperCollins Pubs.

—Wedgie & Gizmo vs. the Toof. 2018. (Wedgie & Gizmo Ser.: 2). (ENG., Illus.). 192p. (J). (gr. 3-7). 12.99 *(978-0-06-244765-4(3)*, Tegen, Katherine Bks) HarperCollins Pubs.

Shabazz, Ilyasah & Watson, RenAe. Betty Before X. 2018. (ENG.). 256p. (J). pap. 8.99 *(978-1-250-29418-0(5)*, 900173907) Square Fish.

Shabazz, Ilyasah & Watson, Renée. Betty Before X. 2018. (ENG.). 256p. (J). E-Book *(978-0-374-30611-3(7)*, 900173908, Farrar, Straus & Giroux (BYR)) Farrar, Straus & Giroux.

Shabazz, Ilyasah & Watson, Renee. Betty Before X. 2018. (ENG.). 256p. (J). 17.99 *(978-0-374-30610-6(9)*, 900173906, Farrar, Straus & Giroux (BYR)) Farrar, Straus & Giroux.

Sheinkin, Steve. Abraham Lincoln, Pro Wrestler. Swaab, Neil, illus. 2019. (Time Twisters Ser.). (ENG.). 176p. (J). pap. 8.99 *(978-1-250-20787-6(8)*, 900201775) Roaring Brook Pr.

Sheinmel, Courtney. All the Things You Are. 2011. (ENG.). 256p. (J). (gr. 4-8). 15.99 *(978-1-4169-9717-7(2)*, Simon & Schuster Bks. For Young Readers) Simon & Schuster Bks. For Young Readers.

—Positively. 2010. (ENG.). 240p. (J). (gr. 4-9). pap. 6.99 *(978-1-4424-0622-3(4)*, Simon & Schuster Bks. For Young Readers) Simon & Schuster Bks. For Young Readers.

—Positively. 2010. (ENG., Illus.). 224p. (J). (gr. 6-8). 21.19 *(978-1-4169-7169-6(6))* Simon & Schuster, Inc.

Shultz, Carrie. V. I. P. Stepkid. 2013. 24p. pap. 10.95 *(978-1-4908-0831-4(0)*, WestBow Pr.) Author Solutions, LLC.

Simon, Coco. Mia's Baker's Dozen. 2013. (Cupcake Diaries: 6). (ENG., Illus.). 160p. (J). (gr. 3-7). 17.99 *(978-1-4424-8566-2(3)*, Simon Spotlight) Simon Spotlight.

Smith, Roland & Spradlin, Michael P. The Alamo. 2013. (I, Q Ser.). (ENG.). 288p. (YA). (gr. 5-8). 16.99 *(978-1-58536-822-8(9)*, 202356); pap. 9.99 *(978-1-58536-821-1(0)*, 202369) Sleeping Bear Pr.

—Alcatraz. 2014. (I, Q Ser.). (ENG.). 272p. (J). (gr. 5-7). 16.99 *(978-1-58536-826-6(1)*, 203667);Bk. 6. pap. 9.99 *(978-1-58536-825-9(3)*, 203727) Sleeping Bear Pr.

—I, Q the Windy City, Bk.5. 2014. (I, Q Ser.). (ENG.). 240p. (YA). (gr. 5-7). 9.99 *(978-1-58536-823-5(7)*, 202902) Sleeping Bear Pr.

Snowe, Olivia. The Glass Voice, 1 vol. Lamoreaux, Michelle, illus. 2014. (Twicetold Tales Ser.). (ENG.). 128p. (J). (gr. 3-6). 25.32 *(978-1-4342-9148-6(0)*, 125596, Stone Arch Bks.) Capstone.

Snyder, Zilpha Keatley. The Headless Cupid. Raible, Alton, illus. 2009. (Stanley Family Ser.). (ENG.). 224p. (J). (gr. 3-7). 16.99 *(978-1-4169-9532-6(3)*, Atheneum Bks. for Young Readers) Simon & Schuster Children's Publishing.

Stockham, Jess, illus. Cinderella. 2007. (Flip-Up Fairy Tales Ser.). 24p. (J). (gr. -1-2). *(978-1-84643-091-6(7))* Child's Play International Ltd.

Tharp, Tim. The Spectacular Now. 2010. (ENG.). 304p. (YA). (gr. 9). pap. 9.99 *(978-0-375-86502-2(0)*, Knopf Bks. for Young Readers) Random Hse. Children's Bks.

Tooke, Wes. Lucky: Maris, Mantle, & My Best Summer Ever. (ENG.). 192p. (J). (gr. 3-7). 2011. pap. 6.99 *(978-1-4169-8664-5(2))* 2010. 15.99 *(978-1-4169-8663-8(4))* Simon & Schuster Bks. For Young Readers. (Simon & Schuster Bks. For Young Readers).

Tucker, Charlotte Maria. Driven into Exile: A Story of the Huguenots. 2003. (Huguenot Inheritance Ser.: Vol. 5). (Illus.). 141p. (J). *(978-0-921100-66-9(3))* Inheritance Pubns.

Ventresca, Yvonne. Black Flowers, White Lies. (ENG.). (J). 2018. 280p. (gr. 8-8). pap. 9.99 *(978-1-5107-2596-6(2))* 2016. 272p. (gr. 6-6). 16.99 *(978-1-5107-0988-1(6))* Skyhorse Publishing Co., Inc. (Sky Pony Pr.).

West, Carly Anne. The Bargaining. 2015. (ENG., Illus.). 416p. (YA). (gr. 9). 17.99 *(978-1-4424-4182-8(8)*, Simon Pulse) Simon Pulse.

Wild, Ailsa. Squishy Taylor & a Question of Trust. 2018. (Squishy Taylor Ser.). (ENG., Illus.). 128p. (J). (gr. 2-4). pap. 6.95 *(978-1-5158-1971-4(X)*, 136642, Picture Window Bks.) Capstone.

—Squishy Taylor & the Bonus Sisters. 2018. (Squishy Taylor Ser.). (ENG., Illus.). 128p. (J). (gr. 2-4). pap. 6.95 *(978-1-5158-1972-1(8)*, 136643, Picture Window Bks.) Capstone.

Wild, Alisa. Squishy Taylor & a Question of Trust. Wood, Ben, illus. 2017. (Squishy Taylor Ser.). (ENG.). 128p. (J). (gr. 2-4). lib. bdg. 25.32 *(978-1-5158-1955-4(8)*, 136638, Picture Window Bks.) Capstone.

—Squishy Taylor & the Bonus Sisters. Wood, Ben, illus. 2017. (Squishy Taylor Ser.). (ENG.). 128p. (J). (gr. 2-4). lib. bdg. 25.32 *(978-1-5158-1956-1(6)*, 136639, Picture Window Bks.) Capstone.

Wilhite, Becca. Bright Blue Miracle. 2009. 176p. (J). pap. 8.99 *(978-1-60641-031-8(8)*, Shadow Mountain) Shadow Mountain Publishing.

STEPPARENTS

Butcher, Tami. My Bonus Mom! Taking the Step Out of Stepmom. Nouf, Feras, illus. 2011. (ENG.). 54p. (J). (gr. -1-3). 16.95 *(978-1-58985-081-1(5)*, Story Monsters Pr.) Story Monsters LLC.

Hancock, Rusty. Dedicated Dads: Stepfathers of Famous People. Van Kampen, Megan, illus. 2004. 138p. *(978-0-934981-12-5(4))* Lawells Publishing.

MacGregor, Cynthia. Jigsaw Puzzle Family: The Stepkids' Guide to Fitting It Together. 2005. (ENG.). 120p. (J). (gr. 4-8). per. 12.95 *(978-1-886230-63-7(3)*, I0637, Impact Pubs.) New Harbinger Pubns.

Riggs, Kate. Wicked Stepmothers. 2013. (Happily Ever After Ser.). (ENG., Illus.). 24p. (J). (gr. 1-4). 25.65 *(978-1-60818-245-9(2)*, 21782, Creative Education) Creative Co., The.

Wells, Sherry A. Warm & Wonderful Stepmothers of Famous People. Van Kampen, Megan, illus. 2004. 131p. 20.00 *(978-0-934981-10-1(8))* Lawells Publishing.

STEPPARENTS—FICTION

Acton, Vanessa. Family Business. 2018. (Suddenly Royal Ser.). (ENG., Illus.). 112p. (YA). (gr. 6-12). pap. 7.99 *(978-1-5415-2637-2(6)*, ce440027-c29f-46af-a905-2758e76b3da7); lib. bdg. 26.65 *(978-1-5415-2568-9(X)*, be198e1c-5cc6-4753-98aa-6c163c230409) Lerner Publishing Group. (Darby Creek).

Alger, Horatio. Frank & Fearless or the Fortunes of Jasper Kent. 2007. 228p. 20.99 *(978-1-4280-7465-1(1))*; per. 14.99 *(978-1-4280-7470-5(8))* IndyPublish.com.

Appelt, Kathi. When Otis Courted Mama. McElmurry, Jill, illus. 2015. (ENG.). 40p. (J). (gr. -1-3). 17.99 *(978-0-15-216688-5(2)*, 1201655, Clarion Bks.) HarperCollins Pubs.

Ashworth, Sherry. Close-Up. 2006. (ENG.). 256p. (J). (gr. 7). pap. 11.95 *(978-1-4169-0474-8(3)*, Simon & Schuster Children's) Simon & Schuster, Ltd. GBR. Dist: Simon & Schuster, Inc.

Banting, Celia. I Only Said I Had No Choice. 2006. (I Only Said Ser.). (Illus.). 202p. (YA). pap. 14.99 *(978-0-9786648-0-0(9))* Wighita Pr.

Billingsley, Franny. Chime. 2012. (ENG.). 320p. (YA). (gr. 7-12). 26.19 *(978-0-8037-3552-1(9)*, Dial) Penguin Publishing Group.

—Chime. 2012. (ENG.). 384p. (YA). (gr. 7-18). 8.99 *(978-0-14-242092-8(1)*, Speak) Penguin Young Readers Group.

Bowvayne. A Spell Behind Bars. Snow, Alan, illus. 2006. (Misadventures of Danny Cloke Ser.). 208p. (J). (gr. 6). lib. bdg. 12.99 *(978-1-58086-926-3(2)*, Usborne) EDC Publishing.

Bradman, Tony. The Wicked Stepmother Helps Out, 1 vol. Warburton, Sarah, illus. 2014. (After Happily Ever After Ser.). (ENG.). 56p. (J). (gr. 3-6). lib. bdg. 25.99 *(978-1-4342-7951-4(0)*, 124699, Stone Arch Bks.) Capstone.

Brooks, Martha. Being with Henry, 1 vol. (ENG.). 174p. pap. 8.95 *(978-0-88899-502-5(4))* Groundwood Bks. CAN. Dist: Publishers Group West (PGW).

Caletti, Deb. Wild Roses. 2008. (ENG.). 320p. (YA). (gr. 7-12). pap. 8.99 *(978-1-4169-5782-9(0)*, Simon Pulse) Simon Pulse.

Connor, Leslie. Waiting for Normal. 2008. (ENG.). 304p. (J). (gr. 5-18). 16.99 *(978-0-06-089088-9(6)*, Tegen, Katherine Bks) HarperCollins Pubs.

Couloumbis, Audrey. Not Exactly a Love Story. 2014. (ENG.). 288p. (YA). (gr. 7). pap. 9.99 *(978-0-375-86606-7(X)*, Ember) Random Hse. Children's Bks.

Crystian, Carol Payne. Ebony Black & The 7. 2012. 28p. pap. 24.95 *(978-1-4626-9728-1(3))* America Star Bks.

Cullen, Lynn. Diary of Nelly Vandorn. Date not set. 128p. (gr. 3-18). mass mkt. 4.99 *(978-0-06-440926-1(0))* HarperCollins Pubs.

Cullen-Skowronski, Fiona. The Smugglers' Caves. 2009. 284p. pap. *(978-1-84923-435-1(3))* YouWriteOn.

Dickens, Charles. David Copperfield. 2008. (Bring the Classics to Life Ser.). (Illus.). 72p. (gr. 4-12). pap., act. bk. ed. 10.95 *(978-1-55576-322-0(7)*, EDCTR-408B) EDCON Publishing Group.

—David Copperfield. 2009. 186p. pap. 19.99 *(978-1-4590-4328-2(6))* General Bks. LLC.

—David Copperfield. 2006. (Oberon Modern Playwrights Ser.). (ENG.). 126p. per. 14.95 *(978-1-84002-570-5(0)*, 900242906) Oberon Bks., Ltd. GBR. Dist: Macmillan.

—David Copperfield, 1 vol. 2009. (Real Reads Ser.). (ENG., Illus.). 64p. (J). (gr. 5-5). pap. 14.55 *(978-1-60754-383-1(4)*, c5e07a78-19a4-4f2e-8cb9-6c68f7cc7a4c, Windmill Bks.) Rosen Publishing Group, Inc., The.

—David Copperfield, 1 vol. 2009. (Foundation Classics Ser.). (ENG.). 56p. (J). (gr. 5-5). lib. bdg. 32.60 *(978-1-60754-852-2(6)*, 2f99677f-33bf-48ec-ae78-c9d2ee798299, Windmill Bks.) Rosen Publishing Group, Inc., The.

—David Copperfield. 2006. (Oxford Progressive English Readers Ser.). (ENG., Illus.). 103p. (J). (gr. 4-7). per. *(978-0-19-597140-8(X))* Oxford Univ. Pr.

Dickerson, Melanie. The Fairest Beauty, 1 vol. 2013. (Fairy Tale Romance Ser.). (ENG.). 336p. (YA). pap. 12.99 *(978-0-310-72439-1(2))* Zondervan.

Dolenz, Ami. Harold & Agatha: The Mysterious Jewel. 2013. 176p. *(978-1-4602-0520-4(0))*; pap. *(978-1-4602-0420-7(4))* FriesenPress.

Ferguson, Tina. The Day i Disappeared. 2005. 83p. pap. 16.95 *(978-1-4137-9243-0(X))* PublishAmerica, Inc.

Frost, Helen. When My Sister Started Kissing. 2017. (ENG.). 208p. (J). 16.99 *(978-0-374-30303-7(7)*, 9780374303037, Farrar, Straus & Giroux (BYR)) Farrar, Straus & Giroux.

Galvin, Laura Gates & Studio Mouse Editorial. Cinderella: Dreams Do Come True. 2008. (ENG., Illus.). 36p. (J). (gr. -1). 7.99 *(978-1-59069-436-7(8))* Studio Mouse LLC.

Geras, Adèle & Geras, Adèle. Pictures of the Night: The Egerton Hall Novels, Volume Three. 2005. (ENG.). 192p. (YA). (gr. 7-12). pap. 11.95 *(978-0-15-205543-1(6)*, 1196670, Clarion Bks.) HarperCollins Pubs.

Gilani, Fawzia. Cinderella: an Islamic Tale: An Islamic Tale. 2011. (ENG., Illus.). 44p. (J). (gr. 5-8). 14.00 *(978-0-86037-473-2(4))* Kube Publishing Ltd. GBR. Dist: Consortium Bk. Sales & Distribution.

Grabenstein, Chris. The Crossroads. 2009. (Haunted Mystery Ser.: 1). (ENG.). 352p. (J). (gr. 3-7). 8.99 *(978-0-375-84698-4(0)*, Yearling) Random Hse. Children's Bks.

—The Demons' Door. 2017. (Haunted Mystery Ser.: 2). 352p. (J). (gr. 3-7). 8.99 *(978-1-5247-6520-0(1)*, Yearling) Random Hse. Children's Bks.

Grimm, Jacob & Grimm, Wilhelm. Hansel & Gretel, 20 vols. Archipova, Anastasiya, illus. 2008. (ENG.). 32p. (J). (gr. -1-3). *(978-0-86315-623-6(1))* Floris Bks.

Gunderson, Jessica. Snow White & the Seven Dwarfs: An Interactive Fairy Tale Adventure. Miramon, Sabrina, illus. 2017. (You Choose: Fractured Fairy Tales Ser.). (ENG.). 112p. (J). (gr. 3-7). lib. bdg. 32.65 *(978-1-5157-6943-9(7)*, 135417, Capstone Pr.) Capstone.

Hanson-Roberts, Mary, illus. Cinderella: A Tale of Kindness. 2006. (J). 6.99 *(978-1-59939-001-7(9))* Cornerstone Pr.

Hayes, Vicki C. The Garden Troll, 1 vol. 2015. (Red Rhino Ser.). (ENG.). 68p. (J). (gr. 4-7). pap. 9.95 *(978-1-62250-916-4(1))* Saddleback Educational Publishing, Inc.

Heathfield, Lisa. Paper Butterflies. 2019. (ENG.). 272p. (YA). (gr. 7-12). pap. 9.99 *(978-1-5415-6042-0(6)*, 07431f09-5118-4a8c-a304-97ae7ceefdcd, Carolrhoda Lab™) Lerner Publishing Group.

Helget, Nicole. The End of the Wild. 2018. (ENG., Illus.). 288p. (J). (gr. 3-7). pap. 7.99 *(978-0-316-24513-5(5))* Little, Brown Bks. for Young Readers.

—The End of the Wild. 2018. (J). lib. bdg. 18.40 *(978-0-606-40989-6(0))* Turtleback.

Hendry, Frances. Quest for a Queen: The Falcon. 2006. pap. *(978-1-905665-06-8(7))* Pollinger In Print.

Ius, Dawn. Lizzie. 2018. (ENG., Illus.). 336p. (YA). (gr. 7). 18.99 *(978-1-4814-9076-4(1)*, Simon Pulse) Simon Pulse.

Jackson, Ellen B. Cinnamon Brown & the Seven Dwarfs. Brown, Elbrite, illus. 2006. (J). *(978-0-670-06106-8(9)*, Viking Adult) Penguin Publishing Group.

Johnson, Angela. Bird. 2006. 133p. (gr. 3-7). 16.00 *(978-0-7569-6660-7(4))* Perfection Learning Corp.

Jukes, Mavis. Like Jake & Me. 2005. (ENG., Illus.). 64p. (J). (gr. 1-4). 6.99 *(978-0-440-42122-1(5)*, Yearling) Random Hse. Children's Bks.

Kelly, Erin Entrada. The Land of Forgotten Girls. 2016. (ENG.). 304p. (J). (gr. 3-7). 16.99 *(978-0-06-223864-1(7)*, Greenwillow Bks.) HarperCollins Pubs.

Konigsburg, E. L. Journey to an 800 Number. 2008. (ENG.). 160p. (J). (gr. 4-8). pap. 7.99 *(978-1-4169-5875-8(4)*, Atheneum Bks. for Young Readers) Simon & Schuster Children's Publishing.

LaFaye, A. Nissa's Place. 2010. (ENG.). 256p. (J). (gr. 2-8). pap. 8.00 *(978-1-57131-697-4(3))* Milkweed Editions.

Lake, Susan. Ebony & the Five Dwarfs. 2007. 56p. per. 10.00 *(978-1-4257-7841-5(0))* Xlibris Corp.

Little Reader Digital Storybook: Cinderella. 2005. (J). cd-rom 8.99 *(978-0-9767657-7-6(2))* Mullings Media.

MacLachlan, Patricia. Sarah, Plain & Tall: A Newbery Award Winner. 30th anniv. ed. 2015. (Sarah, Plain & Tall Ser.: 1). (ENG.). 112p. (J). (gr. 1-5). pap. 7.99 *(978-0-06-239952-6(7)*, HarperCollins) HarperCollins Pubs.

Maddox, Jake. Doubles Trouble. Tiffany, Sean, illus. 2017. (Jake Maddox Sports Stories Ser.). (ENG.). 72p. (J). (gr. 3-6). lib. bdg. 25.99 *(978-1-4965-4957-0(0)*, 135852, Stone Arch Bks.) Capstone.

McClintock, Norah. Tell. 2007. (Orca Soundings Ser.). 100p. (gr. 4-7). 19.95 *(978-0-7569-8069-6(0))* Perfection Learning Corp.

McGowan, Maureen. Cinderella: Ninja Warrior. 2010. 320p. pap. 8.95 *(978-1-60747-778-5(5)*, Pickwick Pr.) Phoenix Bks., Inc.

Meade, L. T. The Children's Pilgrimage. 2004. reprint ed. pap. 1.99 *(978-1-4192-5659-2(9))*; pap. 24.95 *(978-1-4191-5659-5(4))* Kessinger Publishing, LLC.

Messner, Kate. Spitfire. 2007. (ENG.). (J). pap. *(978-1-59531-018-7(5))* North Country Bks., Inc.

Meyer, Marissa. Winter. 2015. (Lunar Chronicles Ser.: 4). (ENG.). 832p. (YA). (gr. 7-12). 28.99 *(978-0-312-64298-3(9)*, 900078311) Feiwel & Friends.

—Winter. 2018. (Lunar Chronicles Ser.: 4). (YA). lib. bdg. 24.50 *(978-0-606-40586-7(0))* Turtleback.

Meyers, Susan A. Callie & the Stepmother. Gauss, Rose, illus. l.t. ed. 2005. (ENG.). 64p. (J). (gr. -1-3). pap. 6.95 *(978-0-9718348-0-4(6))* Blooming Tree Pr.

Milford, Kate. Bluecrowne: A Greenglass House Story. (Greenglass House Ser.). (ENG., Illus.). (J). (gr. 5-7). 2020. 288p. pap. 9.99 *(978-0-358-09754-9(1)*, 1747616) 2018. 272p. 17.99 *(978-1-328-46688-4(4)*, 1713526) HarperCollins Pubs. (Clarion Bks.).

Millner, Denene & Miller, Mitzi. If Only You Knew, Bk. 2. 2008. (Hotlanta Ser.: 2). (ENG.). 254p. (J). (gr. 7-18). 24.94 *(978-0-545-00309-4(1))* Scholastic, Inc.

Mullaly Hunt, Lynda. One for the Murphys. (J). (gr. 5). 2013. 256p. pap. 8.99 *(978-0-14-242652-4(0)*, Puffin Books) 2012. 240p. 17.99 *(978-0-399-25615-8(6)*, Nancy Paulsen Books) Penguin Young Readers Group.

Narsimhan, Mahtab. The Third Eye: Tara Trilogy. 2007. (Tara Trilogy Ser.: 1). (ENG.). 240p. (YA). (gr. 5-7). pap. 12.99 *(978-1-55002-750-1(6)*, Boardwalk Bks.) Dundurn Pr. CAN. Dist: Ingram Publisher Services.

Nixon, Joan Lowery. Nancy's Story, 1765. 2004. (J). *(978-0-87935-225-7(6))* Colonial Williamsburg Foundation.

Nussbaum, Ben & Studio Mouse Editorial. Snow White: A New Beginning. 2008. (ENG., Illus.). 36p. (J). (gr. -1). 7.99 *(978-1-59069-437-4(6))* Studio Mouse LLC.

Patricia, MacLachlan. Sarah, Plain & Tall. 2014. (Sarah, Plain & Tall Ser.). (ENG.). 96p. (J). 10.24 *(978-1-63245-125-5(5))* Lectorum Pubns., Inc.

Paulin, Chrita. Let's Bake a Family. Burns, Rosalyn, ed. Richards, Tanya, illus. 2009. (ENG.). 32p. (J). pap. 12.95 *(978-0-9763400-1-0(1))* Coal Under Pr.ure, LLC.

Peralta, Joaquin. Emma Snow: At the Edge of the World. 2009. 206p. (J). pap. 17.00 *(978-1-934376-19-5(1))* Balona Bks.

Polak, Monique. Home Invasion. 2006. (Orca Soundings Ser.). 105p. (gr. 7-11). 19.95 *(978-0-7569-6871-7(2))* Perfection Learning Corp.

Reynolds Naylor, Phyllis. Alice on Her Way. 2006. (Alice McKinley Ser.: No. 17). 322p. (gr. 9-12). 17.00 *(978-0-7569-6909-7(3))* Perfection Learning Corp.

—Alice on Her Way. 2006. (Alice Ser.: No. 17). (ENG.). 352p. (YA). (gr. 9-12). mass mkt. 6.99 *(978-0-689-87091-0(4)*, Simon Pulse) Simon Pulse.

Rinaldi, Ann. Keep Smiling Through. 2005. (ENG.). 208p. (J). (gr. 3-7). pap. 13.95 *(978-0-15-205399-4(9)*, 1196254, Clarion Bks.) HarperCollins Pubs.

Salisbury, Graham. Lord of the Deep. 2003. 182p. (J). (gr. 5-9). 13.65 *(978-0-7569-1455-4(8))* Perfection Learning Corp.

Sanchez, Alex. Bait. 2010. (ENG.). 256p. (YA). (gr. 7). pap. 12.99 *(978-1-4169-3774-6(9)*, Simon & Schuster Bks. For Young Readers) Simon & Schuster Bks. For Young Readers.

Schroeder, Lisa. Falling for You. 2013. (ENG.). 368p. (YA). (gr. 9). 16.99 *(978-1-4424-4399-0(5)*, Simon Pulse) Simon Pulse.

Sherrard, Valerie. Three Million Acres of Flame. 2007. (ENG.). 200p. (YA). pap. 12.99 *(978-1-55002-727-3(1))* Dundurn Pr. CAN. Dist: Publishers Group West (PGW).

Smith-Matheson, Shirlee. The Gambler's Daughter. 2nd ed. 2009. (ENG.). 144p. (YA). pap. 12.99 *(978-1-55002-718-1(2))* Dundurn Pr. CAN. Dist: Publishers Group West (PGW).

Sullivan, Derek E. Biggie. 2015. (ENG.). 272p. (YA). (gr. 8-12). 16.99 *(978-0-8075-0727-8(X)*, 080750727X) Whitman, Albert & Co.

Thomas, Kara. The Cheerleaders. 2019. (ENG.). 400p. (YA). (gr. 9). pap. 12.99 *(978-1-5247-1835-0(1)*, Ember) Random Hse. Children's Bks.

Timmins, Jeffrey Stewart, illus. Cinderella: The Graphic Novel, 1 vol. 2008. (Graphic Spin Ser.). (ENG.). 40p. (J). (gr. 3-6). pap. 5.95 *(978-1-4342-0860-6(5)*, 95220, Stone Arch Bks.) Capstone.

Weston Woods Staff, creator. James Marshall's Cinderella. 2011. 38.75 *(978-0-439-84886-2(5))* Weston Woods Studios, Inc.

Whitten, A. J. The Well. 2009. (ENG., Illus.). 336p. (YA). (gr. 7-18). pap. 18.95 *(978-0-547-23229-4(2)*, 1082742, Clarion Bks.) HarperCollins Pubs.

Wild, Ailsa. Squishy Taylor in Zero Gravity. 2018. (Squishy Taylor Ser.). (ENG., Illus.). 128p. (J). (gr. 2-4). lib. bdg. 25.32 *(978-1-5158-1980-6(9)*, 136647, Picture Window Bks.) Capstone.

Zimmer, Tracie Vaughn. Sketches from a Spy Tree. Glass, Andrew, illus. 2005. (ENG.). 64p. (J). (gr. 5-7). 16.00 *(978-0-618-23479-0(9)*, 111177, Clarion Bks.) HarperCollins Pubs.

STEROIDS

Benjamin, Daniel. Steroids, 1 vol. 2013. (Dangerous Drugs Ser.). (ENG.). 64p. (gr. 6-6). 36.93 *(978-1-60870-826-0(8)*, 5b6f13a5-bf9b-4b76-9c1b-782ae65663df); pap. 16.28 *(978-1-62712-062-3(9)*, ded6fdb1-24a0-4677-8a3b-9ca5b1835a00) Cavendish Square Publishing LLC.

Edwards, Sue Bradford. Steroids. 2018. (Drugs in Real Life Ser.). (ENG., Illus.). 112p. (J). (gr. 6-12). lib. bdg. 41.36 *(978-1-5321-1420-5(6)*, 28822, Essential Library) ABDO Publishing Co.

Friedman, Lauri S., ed. Steroids, 1 vol. 2008. (Writing the Critical Essay: an Opposing Viewpoints Guide Ser.). (ENG., Illus.). 120p. (gr. 7-12). lib. bdg. 39.93 *(978-0-7377-4267-1(4)*, c4d2be23-2134-4bc2-ae07-308e425e571f, Greenhaven Publishing) Greenhaven Publishing LLC.

Gerber, Larry. The Truth about Steroids, 1 vol. 2013. (Drugs & Consequences Ser.). (ENG., Illus.). 64p. (J). (gr. 5-5). 37.13 *(978-1-4777-1895-7(8)*, 6e44db4f-74aa-4094-a399-dec01b186422) Rosen Publishing Group, Inc., The.

Honders, Christine & Roleff, Tamara L. Steroids & Other Performance-Enhancing Drugs, 1 vol. 2016. (Drug Education Library). (ENG.). 112p. (YA). (gr. 7-7). lib. bdg. 39.08 *(978-1-5345-6003-1(3)*, 7c5d8b32-4b94-4620-b994-1d3e027bed87, Lucent Pr.) Greenhaven Publishing LLC.

Latta, Sara L. Investigate Steroids & Performance Drugs, 1 vol. 2014. (Investigate Drugs Ser.). (ENG., Illus.). 112p. (gr. 5-6). lib. bdg. 34.93 *(978-0-7660-4240-7(5)*, d1c7a737-a701-4cdf-8fa6-46b3e06c89f9) Enslow Publishing, LLC.

LeVert, Suzanne & Whiting, Jim. Steroids, 1 vol. 2010. (Drug Facts Ser.). (ENG.). 32p. (gr. 5-5). 31.21 *(978-0-7614-4352-0(5)*, 2007f6fa-fce1-4bab-b222-69fd6e646023) Cavendish Square Publishing LLC.

May, Suellen. Steroids & Other Performance-Enhancing Drugs. 2011. (ENG., Illus.). 112p. (gr. 9-12). 34.95 *(978-1-60413-552-7(2)*, P189864, Facts On File) Infobase Holdings, Inc.

Schaefer, Adam. Steroids. 2008. (21st Century Skills Library: Health at Risk Ser.). (ENG., Illus.). 32p. (gr. 4-8). lib. bdg. 32.07 *(978-1-60279-287-6(9)*, 200136) Cherry Lake Publishing.

Sterngass, Jon. Steroids, 1 vol. 2011. (Controversy! Ser.). (ENG.). 112p. (YA). (gr. 8-8). 39.79 *(978-0-7614-4903-4(5)*, 9b4c3adc-3be6-4d21-bb54-5110eb50ebbb) Cavendish Square Publishing LLC.

STEVENSON, ROBERT LOUIS, 1850-1894

Collins GCSE. Dr Jekyll & Mr Hyde: AQA GCSE 9-1 English Literature Text Guide: Ideal for Home Learning, 2022 & 2023 Exams. 2017. (ENG., Illus.). 80p. (YA). (gr. 9-11). pap. 8.99 *(978-0-00-824710-2(2))* HarperCollins Pubs. Ltd. GBR. Dist: Independent Pubs. Group.

Murphy, Jim. Across America on an Emigrant Train. 2003. (ENG., Illus.). 168p. (J). (gr. 5-7). pap. 10.95 *(978-0-395-76483-1(1)*, 111826, Clarion Bks.) HarperCollins Pubs.

STILTON, GERONIMO (FICTITIOUS CHARACTER)—FICTION

Geronimo Stilton 12: 12-Copy Solid Prepack. 2004. (J). *(978-0-439-64102-9(0)*, Scholastic Paperbacks) Scholastic, Inc.

Heim, Julia & Dami, Elisabetta. The Little Book of Happiness. Bluecheese, Wally, illus. 2013. 42p. (J). pap. *(978-0-545-48255-4(0))* Scholastic, Inc.

Scholastic, Inc. Staff, contrib. by. Geronimo Stilton 12: 12-copy Solid Self Shipper. 2004. (ENG.). (J). pap.

S

(978-0-439-64101-2(2), Scholastic Paperbacks) Scholastic, Inc.

Stilton, Geronimo. All Because of a Cup of Coffee (Geronimo Stilton #10), Volume 10. 2004. (Geronimo Stilton Ser.: 10). (ENG., Illus.). 128p. (J). (gr. 2-5). pap. 7.99 *(978-0-439-55972-0(3)*, Scholastic Paperbacks) Scholastic, Inc.

—Attack of the Bandit Cats (Geronimo Stilton #8) 2004. (Geronimo Stilton Ser.: 8). (ENG., Illus.). 128p. (J). (gr. 2-5). pap. 7.99 *(978-0-439-55970-6(7)*, Scholastic Paperbacks) Scholastic, Inc.

Stilton, Gerónimo. Cat & Mouse in a Haunted House. 2004. (Geronimo Stilton Ser.: 3). (gr. 3-6). lib. bdg. 18.40 *(978-0-613-72224-7(8))* Turtleback.

Stilton, Geronimo. Cat & Mouse in a Haunted House (Geronimo Stilton #3) Keys, Larry, illus. 2004. (Geronimo Stilton Ser.: 3). (ENG.). 128p. (J). (gr. 2-5). pap. 7.99 *(978-0-439-55965-2(0)*, Scholastic Paperbacks) Scholastic, Inc.

Stilton, Gerónimo. Christmas Catastrophe. 2007. (Geronimo Stilton Ser.). (Illus.). 93p. (J). (gr. 2-5). 14.65 *(978-0-7569-8804-3(7))* Perfection Learning Corp.

Stilton, Geronimo. The Curse of the Cheese Pyramid (Geronimo Stilton #2), Volume 2. Keys, Larry, illus. 2004. (Geronimo Stilton Ser.: No. 2). (ENG.). 128p. (J). (gr. 2-5). pap. 7.99 *(978-0-439-55964-5(2)*, Scholastic Paperbacks) Scholastic, Inc.

Stilton, Gerónimo. Down & Out down Under. 2007. (Geronimo Stilton Ser.: 29). lib. bdg. 18.40 *(978-1-4177-7837-9(7))* Turtleback.

Stilton, Geronimo. The Enchanted Charms (Geronimo Stilton & the Kingdom of Fantasy #7) 2015. (Geronimo Stilton & the Kingdom of Fantasy Ser.: 7). (ENG., Illus.). 320p. (J). (gr. 2-5). 16.99 *(978-0-545-74615-1(9)*, Scholastic Paperbacks) Scholastic, Inc.

Stilton, Gerónimo. The Enormouse Pearl Heist. 2012. (Geronimo Stilton Ser.: 51). lib. bdg. 18.40 *(978-0-606-26756-4(5))* Turtleback.

Stilton, Geronimo. A Fabumouse Vacation for Geronimo (Geronimo Stilton #9), Vol. 9. 2004. (Geronimo Stilton Ser.: 9). (ENG., Illus.). 128p. (J). (gr. 2-5). pap. 7.99 *(978-0-439-55971-3(5)*, Scholastic Paperbacks) Scholastic, Inc.

Stilton, Gerónimo. Field Trip to Niagara Falls. Keys, Larry et al, illus. 2005. (Geronimo Stilton Ser.: No. 24). 121p. (J). lib. bdg. 18.46 *(978-1-4242-0293-5(0))* Fitzgerald Bks.

—Flight of the Red Bandit. 2014. (Geronimo Stilton Ser.: 56). lib. bdg. 18.40 *(978-0-606-35195-9(7))* Turtleback.

Stilton, Geronimo. Flight of the Red Bandit (Geronimo Stilton #56), Volume 56. 2014. (Geronimo Stilton Ser.: 56). (ENG., Illus.). 128p. (J). (gr. 2-5). pap. 7.99 *(978-0-545-55630-9(9)*, Scholastic Paperbacks) Scholastic, Inc.

—Four Mice Deep in the Jungle (Geronimo Stilton #5), Volume 5. 2004. (Geronimo Stilton Ser.: No. 5). (ENG., Illus.). 128p. (J). (gr. 2-5). pap. 7.99 *(978-0-439-55967-6(7)*, Scholastic Paperbacks) Scholastic, Inc.

Stilton, Geronimo. Geronimo Stilton 12-Copy Prepack. 2004. (J). 71.88 *(978-0-439-70121-1(X)*, Scholastic Paperbacks) Scholastic, Inc.

Stilton, Geronimo. Geronimo Stilton Boxed Set Vol. #4-6, Set. 2011. (Geronimo Stilton Graphic Novels Ser.). (ENG., Illus.). 168p. (J). (gr. 2-6). 29.99 *(978-1-59707-271-7(0)*, 900078888, Papercutz) Mad Cave Studios.

—Geronimo Stilton Graphic Novels #10: Geronimo Stilton Saves the Olympics, Vol. 10. 10th ed. 2012. (Geronimo Stilton Graphic Novels Ser.: 10). (ENG., Illus.). 56p. (J). (gr. 2-6). 9.99 *(978-1-59707-319-6(9)*, 900085146, Papercutz) Mad Cave Studios.

—Geronimo Stilton Graphic Novels #12: The First Samurai, Vol. 12. 2013. (Geronimo Stilton Graphic Novels Ser.: 12). (ENG., Illus.). 56p. (J). (gr. 2-6). 9.99 *(978-1-59707-385-1(7)*, 900117449, Papercutz) Mad Cave Studios.

—Geronimo Stilton Graphic Novels #4: Following the Trail of Marco Polo, Vol. 4. 2010. (Geronimo Stilton Graphic Novels Ser.: 4). (ENG., Illus.). 56p. (J). (gr. 2-6). 9.99 *(978-1-59707-188-8(9)*, 900065778, Papercutz) Mad Cave Studios.

—Geronimo Stilton Graphic Novels #5: The Great Ice Age, Vol. 5. 2010. (Geronimo Stilton Graphic Novels Ser.: 5). (ENG., Illus.). 56p. (J). (gr. 2-6). 9.99 *(978-1-59707-202-1(8)*, 900068264, Papercutz) Mad Cave Studios.

—Geronimo Stilton Graphic Novels #6: Who Stole the Mona Lisa?, Vol. 6. 2010. (Geronimo Stilton Graphic Novels Ser.: 6). (ENG., Illus.). 56p. (J). (gr. 2-6). 9.99 *(978-1-59707-221-2(4)*, 900070133, Papercutz) Mad Cave Studios.

—Geronimo Stilton Graphic Novels #7: Dinosaurs in Action!, Vol. 7. 2011. (Geronimo Stilton Graphic Novels Ser.: 7). (ENG., Illus.). 56p. (J). (gr. 2-6). 9.99 *(978-1-59707-239-7(7)*, 900073808, Papercutz) Mad Cave Studios.

—Geronimo Stilton Graphic Novels #8: Play It Again, Mozart!, Vol. 8. 2011. (Geronimo Stilton Graphic Novels Ser.: 8). (ENG., Illus.). 56p. (J). (gr. 2-6). 9.99 *(978-1-59707-276-2(1)*, 900078848, Papercutz) Mad Cave Studios.

—Geronimo Stilton Graphic Novels #9: The Weird Book Machine, Vol. 9. 2012. (Geronimo Stilton Graphic Novels Ser.: 9). (ENG., Illus.). 56p. (J). (gr. 2-6). 9.99 *(978-1-59707-295-3(8)*, 900080966, Papercutz) Mad Cave Studios.

Stilton, Gerónimo. Geronimo's Valentine. 2009. (Geronimo Stilton Ser.: 36). (Illus.). 103p. (J). 18.40 *(978-1-4364-5051-5(9))* Turtleback.

—Ghost Pirate Treasure. 2012. (Geronimo Stilton — Creepella Von Cacklefur Ser.: 3). lib. bdg. 18.40 *(978-0-606-23931-8(6))* Turtleback.

—The Golden Statue Plot. 2013. (Geronimo Stilton Ser.: 55). (Illus.). 106p. lib. bdg. 18.40 *(978-0-606-32380-2(5))* Turtleback.

Stilton, Geronimo. I'm a Scaredy-Mouse! (Geronimo Stilton Cavemice #7) Bk. 7. 2015. (Geronimo Stilton Cavemice Ser.: 7). (ENG., Illus.). 128p. (J). (gr. 2-5). pap. 7.99 *(978-0-545-74616-8(7)*, Scholastic Paperbacks) Scholastic, Inc.

Stilton, Gerónimo. I'm Too Fond of My Fur! 2004. (Geronimo Stilton Ser.: 4). (Illus.). 116p. (gr. 3-6). lib. bdg. 18.40 *(978-0-613-72225-4(6))* Turtleback.

Stilton, Geronimo. I'm Too Fond of My Fur! (Geronimo Stilton #4) Keys, Larry, illus. 2004. (Geronimo Stilton Ser.: No. 4). (ENG.). 128p. (J). (gr. 2-5). pap. 7.99 *(978-0-439-55966-9(9)*, Scholastic Paperbacks) Scholastic, Inc.

—The Journey Through Time (Geronimo Stilton Special Edition) 2014. (Geronimo Stilton Journey Through Time Ser.). (ENG., Illus.). 320p. (J). (gr. 2-5). 16.99 *(978-0-545-55623-1(6)*, Scholastic Paperbacks) Scholastic, Inc.

Stilton, Gerónimo. The Karate Mouse. 2010. (Geronimo Stilton Ser.: 40). lib. bdg. 18.40 *(978-0-606-06847-5(3))* Turtleback.

—Kingdom of Fantasy. 2009. (Kingdom of Fantasy Ser.: No. 1). 320p. 14.99 *(978-0-439-69148-2(6)*, Scholastic Paperbacks) Scholastic, Inc.

Stilton, Geronimo. The Kingdom of Fantasy (Geronimo Stilton & the Kingdom of Fantasy #1), Volume 1. 2009. (Geronimo Stilton & the Kingdom of Fantasy Ser.: 1). (ENG., Illus.). 320p. (J). (gr. 2-5). 16.99 *(978-0-545-98025-8(9)*, Scholastic Paperbacks) Scholastic, Inc.

—Lost Treasure of the Emerald Eye. 2004. (Geronimo Stilton Ser.: 2). (gr. 3-6). lib. bdg. 18.40 *(978-0-613-72223-0(X))* Turtleback.

—Lost Treasure of the Emerald Eye (Geronimo Stilton #1), Volume 1. 2004. (Geronimo Stilton Ser.: 1). (ENG., Illus.). 128p. (J). (gr. 2-5). pap. 7.99 *(978-0-439-55963-8(4)*, Scholastic Paperbacks) Scholastic, Inc.

Stilton, Gerónimo. The Mona Mousa Code. Wolf, Matt, illus. 2005. (Geronimo Stilton Ser.: No. 15). 113p. (J). lib. bdg. 10.00 *(978-1-4242-0284-3(1))* Fitzgerald Bks.

—The Mouse Island Marathon. 2007. (Geronimo Stilton Ser.: 30). lib. bdg. 18.40 *(978-1-4177-7839-3(3))* Turtleback.

Stilton, Geronimo. My Name Is Stilton, Geronimo Stilton (Geronimo Stilton #19), Volume 19. 2005. (Geronimo Stilton Ser.: 19). (ENG., Illus.). 128p. (J). (gr. 2-5). pap. 7.99 *(978-0-439-69142-0(7)*, Scholastic Paperbacks) Scholastic, Inc.

Stilton, Gerónimo. The Mysterious Cheese Thief. 2007. (Geronimo Stilton Ser.). (Illus.). 111p. (J). (gr. 2-5). 14.65 *(978-0-7569-8303-1(7))* Perfection Learning Corp.

—The Mysterious Cheese Thief. 2007. (Geronimo Stilton Ser.: 31). (Illus.). 111p. (gr. 4-7). 18.40 *(978-1-4177-9646-5(4))* Turtleback.

—The Mystery in Venice. 2012. (Geronimo Stilton Ser.: 48). lib. bdg. 18.40 *(978-0-606-23729-1(1))* Turtleback.

—The Race Across America. 2009. (Geronimo Stilton Ser.: 37). lib. bdg. 18.40 *(978-0-606-00228-8(6))* Turtleback.

—Ride for Your Life! 2014. (Geronimo Stilton — Creepella Von Cacklefur Ser.: 6). lib. bdg. 18.40 *(978-0-606-35847-7(1))* Turtleback.

Stilton, Geronimo. Ride for Your Life! (Creepella Von Cacklefur #6) A Geronimo Stilton Adventure. 2014. (Creepella Von Cacklefur Ser.: 6). (ENG., Illus.). 128p. (J). (gr. 2-5). pap. 7.99 *(978-0-545-64659-8(6)*, Scholastic Paperbacks) Scholastic, Inc.

Stilton, Gerónimo. Rumble in the Jungle. 2013. (Geronimo Stilton Ser.: 53). lib. bdg. 18.40 *(978-0-606-31527-2(6))* Turtleback.

—The Search for Sunken Treasure. Wolf, Matt, illus. 2006. (Geronimo Stilton Ser.: No. 25). 111p. (J). lib. bdg. 10.00 *(978-1-4242-1519-5(6))* Fitzgerald Bks.

Stilton, Geronimo. The Search for Treasure (Geronimo Stilton & the Kingdom of Fantasy #6) (ENG.). 320p. (J). 2017. (gr. -1-k). E-Book 12.99 *(978-0-545-65895-9(0))*Volume 6. 2014. (Geronimo Stilton & the Kingdom of Fantasy Ser.: 6). (Illus.). (gr. 2-5). 16.99 *(978-0-545-55604-7(4))* Scholastic, Inc. (Scholastic Paperbacks).

Stilton, Gerónimo. Singing Sensation. 2009. (Geronimo Stilton Ser.: 39). lib. bdg. 18.40 *(978-0-606-00230-1(8))* Turtleback.

—The Stinky Cheese Vacation. 2014. (Geronimo Stilton Ser.: 57). lib. bdg. 18.40 *(978-0-606-35843-9(9))* Turtleback.

Stilton, Geronimo. A Suitcase Full of Ghosts (Creepella Von Cacklefur #7) A Geronimo Stilton Adventure. 2015. (Creepella Von Cacklefur Ser.: 7). (ENG.). 128p. (J). (gr. 2-5). pap. 7.99 *(978-0-545-74611-3(6)*, Scholastic Paperbacks) Scholastic, Inc.

Stilton, Gerónimo. The Super Chef Contest. 2014. (Geronimo Stilton Ser.: 58). lib. bdg. 18.40 *(978-0-606-36056-2(5))* Turtleback.

—This Hotel Is Haunted! 2012. (Geronimo Stilton Ser.: 50). lib. bdg. 18.40 *(978-0-606-26182-1(6))* Turtleback.

—Time Machine Trouble. 2016. (Illus.). 128p. (J). pap. *(978-1-338-05290-9(X))* Scholastic, Inc.

—Valley of the Giant Skeletons. 2008. (Illus.). 111p. (J). lib. bdg. 15.38 *(978-1-4242-4303-7(3))* Fitzgerald Bks.

—Valley of the Giant Skeletons. 2008. (Geronimo Stilton Ser.). (Illus.). 110p. (gr. 2-5). 17.00 *(978-0-7569-8805-0(5))* Perfection Learning Corp.

—Valley of the Giant Skeletons. 2008. (Geronimo Stilton Ser.: 32). lib. bdg. 18.40 *(978-1-4364-2713-5(4))* Turtleback.

Stilton, Geronimo. The Volcano of Fire (Geronimo Stilton & the Kingdom of Fantasy #5) 2013. (Geronimo Stilton & the Kingdom of Fantasy Ser.: 5). (ENG., Illus.). 320p. (J). (gr. 2-5). 16.99 *(978-0-545-55625-5(2)*, Scholastic Paperbacks) Scholastic, Inc.

Stilton, Gerónimo. Watch Your Tail! 2013. (Geronimo Stilton Cavemice Ser.: 2). lib. bdg. 18.40 *(978-0-606-31998-0(0))* Turtleback.

—The Way of the Samurai. 2012. (Geronimo Stilton Ser.: 49). lib. bdg. 18.40 *(978-0-606-26094-7(3))* Turtleback.

Stilton, Gerónimo & Mckeon, Kathryn. Mouse in Space! 2013. (Geronimo Stilton Ser.: 52). lib. bdg. 18.40 *(978-0-606-31525-8(X))* Turtleback.

Stilton, Gerónimo & Stilton, Thea. Thea Stilton & the Ghost of the Shipwreck. 2010. (Thea Stilton Ser.: 3). lib. bdg. 19.65 *(978-0-606-06843-7(0))* Turtleback.

Stilton, Gerónimo, et al. The Journey Through Time. 2014. (Illus.). 94p. (J). *(978-0-545-61129-9(6))* Scholastic, Inc.

Stilton, Thea. The Secret of the Snow (Thea Stilton: Special Edition #3) A Geronimo Stilton Adventure. (ENG.). 320p. (J). 2016. (gr. -1-k). E-Book 4.99 *(978-0-545-65902-4(7))* 2014. (gr. 2-5). 16.99 *(978-0-545-65605-4(2))* Scholastic, Inc. (Scholastic Paperbacks).

—Thea Stilton & the Missing Myth. 2014. (Thea Stilton Ser.: 20). lib. bdg. 19.65 *(978-0-606-36058-6(1))* Turtleback.

STOCK EXCHANGES

see also Bonds; Investments; Securities; Stocks

Connolly, Sean. The Stock Market. 2010. (World Economy Explained Ser.). (ENG.). 48p. (J). (gr. 6-10). lib. bdg. 35.65 *(978-1-60753-082-4(1)*, 17237) Amicus.

—The Stock Market. 2012. (ENG., Illus.). 48p. (gr. 6-10). pap. 9.95 *(978-1-926722-80-1(9))* Saunders Bk. Co. CAN. Dist: RiverStream Publishing.

Connolly, Sean & Pipe, Jim. The Stock Market. 2011. (On the Edge Ser.). 32p. (YA). (gr. 3-6). 28.50 *(978-1-59920-518-2(1))* Black Rabbit Bks.

Crayton, Lisa A. & Furgang, Kathy. The Stock Market: What It Is & How It Works, 1 vol. 2015. (Economics in the 21st Century Ser.). (ENG.). 96p. (gr. 8-8). 36.27 *(978-0-7660-7384-5(X)*, fb662e84-198d-414d-a8f9-ea4d0f161a2c) Enslow Publishing, LLC.

Crewe, Sabrina & Ingram, Scott. The Stock Market Crash Of 1929, 1 vol. 2004. (Events That Shaped America Ser.). (ENG., Illus.). 32p. (gr. 3-5). lib. bdg. 28.67 *(978-0-8368-3416-1(X)*, 0fb1953c-c7f7-4358-9de4-7c6b761ec8d7, Gareth Stevens Learning Library) Stevens, Gareth Publishing LLLP.

Fuller, Donna Jo. The Stock Market. 2005. (How Economics Works). (ENG., Illus.). 48p. (gr. 3-5). lib. bdg. 25.26 *(978-0-8225-2635-3(2)*, Lerner Pubns.) Lerner Publishing Group.

Furgang, Kathy. How the Stock Market Works, 1 vol. 2010. (Real World Economics Ser.). (ENG., Illus.). 80p. (YA). (gr. 6-6). lib. bdg. 38.47 *(978-1-4358-9466-2(9)*, 46ad7b2b-8ed9-4cc5-ad95-685a31acfaac) Rosen Publishing Group, Inc., The.

Grant, R. G. Why Did the Great Depression Happen?, 1 vol. 2010. (Moments in History Ser.). (ENG., Illus.). 48p. (YA). (gr. 6-8). pap. 15.05 *(978-1-4339-4170-2(8)*, ba126829-abf9-4869-a334-3e5a8993bc0a, Gareth Stevens Secondary Library); lib. bdg. 34.60 *(978-1-4339-4169-6(4)*, 2cef96c8-83ef-49c1-9b92-65399e65e0dc) Stevens, Gareth Publishing LLLP.

North, Charles & Caes, Charles J. The Stock Market. 2011. (J). 77.70 *(978-1-4488-4755-6(9))*; (ENG.). 64p. (J). (gr. 5-5). pap. 13.95 *(978-1-4488-4723-5(0)*, 1a5689c5-8098-4098-8e8c-95c59b30e717); (ENG.). 64p. (YA). (gr. 5-5). lib. bdg. 37.13 *(978-1-4488-4717-4(6)*, e5401597-aef2-4f08-b894-6f2983594809) Rosen Publishing Group, Inc., The.

Sebree, Chet'la. Understanding the Stock Market, 1 vol. 2019. (21st-Century Economics Ser.). (ENG.). 80p. (gr. 8-8). pap. 18.64 *(978-1-5026-4605-7(6)*, c352212a-a080-45d7-b8b9-e88ec289f531) Cavendish Square Publishing LLC.

Sepahban, Lois. 12 Things to Know about the Stock Market. 2015. (Today's News Ser.). (ENG., Illus.). 32p. (J). (gr. 3-6). 32.80 *(978-1-63235-034-3(3)*, 11612, 12-Story Library) Bookstaves, LLC.

Thompson, Helen. Understanding the Stock Market. 2010. (Junior Library of Money). 64p. (YA). (gr. 7-18). lib. bdg. 22.95 *(978-1-4222-1773-3(6))* Mason Crest.

Yasuda, Anita. The Stock Market Crash Bankrupts America. 2018. (Events That Changed America Ser.). (ENG.). 32p. (J). (gr. 3-6). lib. bdg. 35.64 *(978-1-5038-2523-9(X)*, 212330, MOMENTUM) Child's World, Inc, The.

Zuravicky, Orli. The Stock Market: Understanding & Applying Ratios, Decimals, Fractions, & Percentages, 1 vol. (Math for the REAL World Ser.). 32p. 2010. (ENG., Illus.). (gr. 5-6). pap. 10.00 *(978-1-4042-5121-2(9)*, ddd12023-3138-43e4-b1a9-6c64ae7727c1) 2009. (gr. 4-5). 47.90 *(978-1-60851-426-7(9)*, PowerKids Pr.) 2004. (ENG., Illus.). (J). (gr. 5-6). lib. bdg. 28.93 *(978-1-4042-2929-7(9)*, cb86b53e-920e-4daa-98e4-515caa73a877, PowerKids Pr.) Rosen Publishing Group, Inc., The.

STOCK MARKET

see Stock Exchanges

STOCK RAISING

see Livestock

STOCKS

see also Bonds; Investments; Securities; Stock Exchanges

Bateman, Katherine R. The Young Investor: Projects & Activities for Making Your Money Grow. 2nd ed. 2010. (ENG., Illus.). 144p. (J). (gr. 4). pap. 14.95 *(978-1-56976-546-3(4))* Chicago Review Pr., Inc.

Beach, Byron & Keck, Gayle. Stock Matters: An Introduction to Stock & Ownership for Kids. 2006. (Illus.). 72p. (J). pap. 6.99 *(978-0-9788438-0-9(0))* OneShare Educational Pr.

Connolly, Sean. The Stock Market. 2010. (World Economy Explained Ser.). (ENG.). 48p. (J). (gr. 6-10). lib. bdg. 35.65 *(978-1-60753-082-4(1)*, 17237) Amicus.

—The Stock Market. 2012. (ENG., Illus.). 48p. (gr. 6-10). pap. 9.95 *(978-1-926722-80-1(9))* Saunders Bk. Co. CAN. Dist: RiverStream Publishing.

Connolly, Sean & Pipe, Jim. The Stock Market. 2011. (On the Edge Ser.). 32p. (YA). (gr. 3-6). 28.50 *(978-1-59920-518-2(1))* Black Rabbit Bks.

Fuller, Donna Jo. The Stock Market. 2005. (How Economics Works). (ENG., Illus.). 48p. (gr. 3-5). lib. bdg. 25.26 *(978-0-8225-2635-3(2)*, Lerner Pubns.) Lerner Publishing Group.

Furgang, Kathy. How the Stock Market Works, 1 vol. 2010. (Real World Economics Ser.). (ENG., Illus.). 80p. (YA). (gr. 6-6). lib. bdg. 38.47 *(978-1-4358-9466-2(9)*, 46ad7b2b-8ed9-4cc5-ad95-685a31acfaac) Rosen Publishing Group, Inc., The.

Gagne, Tammy. A Dividend Stock Strategy for Teens. 2013. (Illus.). 48p. (gr. 4-8). lib. bdg. 29.95 *(978-1-61228-426-2(4))* Mitchell Lane Pubs.

Minden, Cecilia. Investing: Making Your Money Work for You. 2007. (21st Century Skills Library: Real World Math Ser.). (ENG., Illus.). 32p. (gr. 4-8). lib. bdg. 32.07 *(978-1-60279-003-2(5)*, 200069) Cherry Lake Publishing.

Orr, Tamra. A Kid's Guide to Stock Market Investing. 2008. (Money Matters Ser.). (Illus.). 48p. (YA). (gr. 3-6). lib. bdg. 29.95 *(978-1-58415-642-0(2))* Mitchell Lane Pubs.

Pellittiere II, Michael. GROW MONEY - A Kid's Guide to Saving & Investing. 2007. (ENG.). 60p. (YA). pap. 10.40 *(978-0-615-14589-1(2))* Dakota Assocs., Inc.

—GROW MONEY II - A Teenager's Guide to Saving & Investing. 2007. (ENG.). 118p. (YA). pap. 11.42 *(978-0-615-18343-5(3))* Dakota Assocs., Inc.

Thompson, Helen. Understanding the Stock Market. 2010. (Junior Library of Money). 64p. (YA). (gr. 7-18). lib. bdg. 22.95 *(978-1-4222-1773-3(6))* Mason Crest.

STOCKYARDS

see Meat Industry and Trade

STONE

see also Masonry; Rocks

Auster, Michael A. Stone Is Strong! 2005. (Yellow Umbrella Fluent Level Ser.). (ENG., Illus.). 16p. (gr. k-1). pap. 35.70 *(978-0-7368-5300-2(6)*, Capstone Pr.) Capstone.

Brenner, C. M. The Petoskey & Me: Look & Find. 2016. (Illus.). 24p. (J). 16.95 *(978-0-9980042-0-4(0))* SimplyCMB,LLC.

deMarin, Layne. Built from Stone, 1 vol. 2011. (Wonder Readers Fluent Level Ser.). (ENG.). 16p. (gr. -1-2). (J). pap. 6.25 *(978-1-4296-7911-4(5)*, 118243); pap. 35.94 *(978-1-4296-8074-5(1))* Capstone. (Capstone Pr.).

Royston, Angela. Rock: Let's Look at a Pebble. 2005. (J). *(978-1-4109-1826-0(2))*; (ENG.). 24p. pap. *(978-1-4109-1833-8(5))* Steck-Vaughn.

Storey, Rita. Rocks & Stones. 2007. (How We Use Materials/Watts Ser.). (Illus.). 30p. (J). (gr. 4-7). lib. bdg. 28.50 *(978-1-59920-006-4(6))* Black Rabbit Bks.

STONE AGE

see also Prehistoric Peoples

DK. DKfindout! Stone Age. 2017. (DK Findout! Ser.). (ENG., Illus.). 64p. (J). (gr. 1-4). pap. 10.99 *(978-1-4654-5750-9(X)*, DK Children) Dorling Kindersley Publishing, Inc.

Dyan, Penelope. High on a Hill! a Kid's Guide to Innsbruck, Austri. Weigand, John D., photos by. 2011. (Illus.). 40p. pap. 12.95 *(978-1-935630-76-0(8))* Bellissima Publishing, LLC.

Hibbert, Clare. The History Detective Investigates: Stone Age to Iron Age. 2017. (History Detective Investigates Ser.). (ENG., Illus.). 32p. (J). (gr. 4-6). pap. 12.99 *(978-0-7502-8197-3(9)*, Wayland) Hachette Children's Group GBR. Dist: Hachette Bk. Group.

Howell, Izzi. Fact Cat: History: Early Britons: Stone Age to Iron Age. 2017. (Fact Cat: History: Early Britons Ser.). (ENG., Illus.). 24p. (J). (gr. k-2). pap. 9.99 *(978-0-7502-9938-1(X)*, Wayland) Hachette Children's Group GBR. Dist: Hachette Bk. Group.

—The Genius of the Stone, Bronze, & Iron Ages. 2019. (Genius of the Ancients Ser.). (ENG.). 32p. (J). (gr. 4-5). pap. *(978-0-7787-6597-4(0)*, eacecb69-7a4f-49fb-9595-76c5efced2a9); lib. bdg. *(978-0-7787-6577-6(6)*, de4e945d-a2a1-4548-8257-d5cb3c914ce4) Crabtree Publishing Co.

Hurdman, Charlotte. Hands-on History! Stone Age. 2013. (ENG., Illus.). 64p. (J). (gr. k-3). 12.99 *(978-1-84322-974-2(9)*, Armadillo) Anness Publishing GBR. Dist: National Bk. Network.

Johanson, Paula. The Paleolithic Revolution, 1 vol. 2016. (First Humans & Early Civilizations Ser.). (ENG., Illus.). 64p. (J). (gr. 6-6). pap. 13.95 *(978-1-4994-6314-9(6)*, c074a745-4446-4ff8-bb67-5a7001211c4d) Rosen Publishing Group, Inc., The.

Kerrigan, Juliet. The Stone Age: Band 12/Copper (Collins Big Cat) 2016. (Collins Big Cat Ser.). (ENG., Illus.). 32p. (J). (gr. 2-3). pap. 9.99 *(978-0-00-816380-8(4))* HarperCollins Pubs. Ltd. GBR. Dist: Independent Pubs. Group.

Lisle, Rebecca. The First Underwear. Watson, Richard, illus. 2019. (Early Bird Readers — Purple (Early Bird Stories (tm)) Ser.). (ENG.). 32p. (J). (gr. k-3). 30.65 *(978-1-5415-4229-7(0)*, e5ae9783-29f7-4cbe-ad67-d127e9d9feb6); pap. 9.99 *(978-1-5415-7418-2(4)*, e22fbad4-dbb8-43c6-8790-dc08ac22e6ec) Lerner Publishing Group. (Lerner Pubns.).

Lock, Deborah. DK Readers L2: Life in the Stone Age. 2018. (DK Readers Level 2 Ser.). (ENG., Illus.). 48p. (J). (gr. k-2). pap. 4.99 *(978-1-4654-6845-1(5)*, DK Children) Dorling Kindersley Publishing, Inc.

Lock, Deborah & Dorling Kindersley Publishing Staff. Life in the Stone Age. 2018. (ENG., Illus.). 48p. (J). *(978-0-241-31593-4(X))* Dorling Kindersley Publishing, Inc.

Meyer, Susan. The Neolithic Revolution, 1 vol. 2016. (First Humans & Early Civilizations Ser.). (ENG., Illus.). 64p. (J). (gr. 6-6). pap. 13.95 *(978-1-4994-6322-4(7)*, 42f32161-ba61-4f24-9b96-7eee8eed313f) Rosen Publishing Group, Inc., The.

Newland, Sonya. Explore!: Stone, Bronze & Iron Ages. 2017. (Explore! Ser.). (ENG., Illus.). 32p. (J). (gr. 4-6). pap. 12.99 *(978-0-7502-9736-3(0)*, Wayland) Hachette Children's Group GBR. Dist: Hachette Bk. Group.

Oachs, Emily Rose. The Cave of Altamira. 2019. (Digging up the Past Ser.). (ENG., Illus.). 24p. (J). (gr. 3-7). lib. bdg. 26.95 *(978-1-64487-066-2(5)*, Torque Bks.) Bellwether Media.

Owings, Lisa. Skara Brae: The Lost Neolithic Village. 2020. (Abandoned Places Ser.). (ENG.). 24p. (J). (gr. 3-7). lib. bdg. 26.95 *(978-1-64487-164-5(5)*, Torque Bks.) Bellwether Media.

Spizzirri, Linda, ed. Prehistoric Birds. Spizzirri, Peter M., illus. 32p. (J). (gr. 1-8). pap. 4.98 incl. audio *(978-0-86545-023-3(4))* Spizzirri Pr., Inc.

—Prehistoric Sea Life. Kohn, Arnie, illus. 32p. (J). (gr. 1-8). pap. 4.98 incl. audio *(978-0-86545-020-2(X))* Spizzirri Pr., Inc.

Stevens, Noel. In the Never-Never-Converse with an Archangel. 2008. 132p. pap. 13.95 *(978-0-595-52727-4(2))* iUniverse, Inc.

STONE AGE—FICTION

Fidler, Kathleen. The Boy with the Bronze Axe, 56 vols. 3rd rev. ed. (ENG., Illus.). 176p. pap. 11.95 *(978-0-86315-488-1(3))* Floris Bks. GBR. Dist: SteinerBooks, Inc.

Hart, John. Mammoth Boy: A Lad's Epic Journey to Find Mammoths in the Ice Age. 2012. (ENG.). 240p. pap. *(978-1-78088-174-4(6))* Troubador Publishing Ltd.

McDonnell, Vincent. Children of Stone. 2006. (ENG.). 206p. (J). pap. 11.95 *(978-1-903464-88-5(9)*, Collins Pr., The) M.H. Gill & Co. U. C. IRL. Dist: Dufour Editions, Inc.

Paterson, Katherine & Paterson, John. The Flint Heart. Rocco, John, illus. 2018. (ENG.). 288p. (J). (gr. 2-5). pap. 7.99 *(978-1-5362-0371-4(8))* Candlewick Pr.

Scieszka, Jon. Your Mother Was a Neanderthal #4. Smith, Lane, illus. 2004. (Time Warp Trio Ser.: 4). 80p. (J). (gr. 2-4). pap. 5.99 *(978-0-14-240048-7(3),* Puffin Books) Penguin Young Readers Group.

Winterhager, Randerath -. Vuela, Yoa, vuela! 2012. (SPA.). 32p. (J). (gr. 2-3). pap. 19.99 *(978-84-261-3918-4(3))* Juventud, Editorial ESP. Dist: Lectorum Pubns., Inc.

STONEHENGE (ENGLAND)

Aronson, Marc. If Stones Could Speak: Unlocking the Secrets of Stonehenge. 2010. (Illus.). 64p. (J). (gr. 5-9). 17.95 *(978-1-4263-0599-3(0),* National Geographic Kids) Disney Publishing Worldwide.

Croy, Anita. What Was Stonehenge For?, 1 vol. 2017. (Mysteries in History: Solving the Mysteries of the Past Ser.). (ENG.). 48p. (gr. 5-5). lib. bdg. 33.07 *(978-1-5026-2794-0(9),* cda35e6d-3c08-434e-8fec-b9dcf62e1b04) Cavendish Square Publishing LLC.

Dalgleish, Sharon. It's a Mystery. 2003. (Real Deal Ser.). (Illus.). 32p. (J). pap. *(978-0-7608-6692-4(9))* Sundance/Newbridge Educational Publishing.

Dunn, Mary. My Adventure at Stonehenge. 2006. 44p. (J). 8.99 *(978-1-59092-412-9(6))* Blue Forge Pr.

Kelley, True & Who HQ. Where Is Stonehenge? Hinderliter, John, illus. 2016. (Where Is? Ser.). 112p. (J). (gr. 3-7). pap. 6.99 *(978-0-448-48693-2(8),* Penguin Workshop) Penguin Young Readers Group.

Kelly, Dave & Coddington, Andrew. The Bermuda Triangle, Stonehenge, & Unexplained Places, 1 vol. 2017. (Paranormal Investigations Ser.). (ENG.). 64p. (gr. 6-6). 35.93 *(978-1-5026-2843-5(0),* 6259e3f1-c705-4959-a995-7fe257b4b4f7) Cavendish Square Publishing LLC.

Loh-Hagan, Virginia. Stonehenge. 2018. (Urban Legends: Don't Read Alone! Ser.). (ENG., Illus.). 32p. (J). (gr. 4-8). pap. 14.21 *(978-1-5341-0865-3(3),* 210824); lib. bdg. 32.07 *(978-1-5341-0766-3(5),* 210823) Cherry Lake Publishing. (45th Parallel Press).

McDaniel, Sean. Stonehenge. 2011. (Unexplained Ser.). (ENG., Illus.). 24p. (J). (gr. 3-7). lib. bdg. 26.95 *(978-1-60014-645-9(7),* Torque Bks.) Bellwether Media.

Owings, Lisa. Stonehenge. 2015. (Unexplained Mysteries Ser.). (ENG., Illus.). 24p. (J). (gr. 3-7). lib. bdg. 26.95 *(978-1-62617-204-3(8),* Epic Bks.) Bellwether Media.

Peterson, Megan Cooley. Stonehenge: Who Built This Stone Formation? 2018. (History's Mysteries Ser.). (ENG.). 32p. (J). (gr. 4-6). pap. 9.99 *(978-1-64466-259-5(0),* 12289); (Illus.). lib. bdg. *(978-1-68072-412-7(6),* 12288) Black Rabbit Bks. (Bolt).

Raum, Elizabeth. Stonehenge. 2015. (Ancient Wonders Ser.). (Illus.). 32p. (J). 28.50 *(978-1-60753-469-3(X))* Amicus Learning.

Riggs, Kate. Stonehenge. 2009. (Places of Old Ser.). 24p. (J). (gr. 1-5). lib. bdg. 24.25 *(978-1-58341-711-9(7),* Creative Education) Creative Co., The.

Sabatino, Michael. 20 Fun Facts about Stonehenge, 1 vol., Vol. 1. 2013. (Fun Fact File: World Wonders! Ser.). (ENG.). 32p. (J). (gr. 2-3). 27.93 *(978-1-4824-0457-9(5),* 863bd00c-75ea-4bf2-a511-62327b4d1791) Stevens, Gareth Publishing LLLP.

Shofner, Shawndra. Stonehenge. 2005. (Ancient Wonders of the World Ser.). (Illus.). 32p. (J). (gr. 4-7). lib. bdg. 18.95 *(978-1-58341-360-9(X),* Creative Education) Creative Co., The.

World Book, Inc. Staff, contrib. by. The Mysteries of Stonehenge. 2014. (J). *(978-0-7166-2667-1(5))* World Bk., Inc.

STONES, PRECIOUS

see Precious Stones

STONEWARE

see Pottery

STORIES

see also Animals—Fiction; Ballet—Fiction; Bible Stories; Birds—Fiction; Christmas—Fiction; Fairy Tales; Horror Stories; Legends; Mystery and Detective Stories; Operas—Stories, Plots, Etc.; Sea Stories; Short Stories; Storytelling; Trees—Fiction

Alexander, Ian. Do You See a Dozen?, Vol. 2. l.t. ed. 2005. (Sadlier Phonics Reading Program). (Illus.). 8p. (gr. -1-1). 23.00 net. *(978-0-8215-7347-1(0))* Sadlier, William H. Inc.

Angela's Bookshelf Publishing Staff. Choice Stories for Children. Date not set. (Illus.). 144p. (J). pap. 6.95 *(978-1-878726-08-7(0))* A B Publishing.

Baldner, Jean V. Pebbles in the Wind. Webster, Carroll, illus. 52p. (Orig.). (YA). (gr. 7-18). pap. 5.95 *(978-0-9615317-0-6(3))* Baldner, Jean V.

Baum, L. Frank. Adventures of the Magical Monarch of Mo & His People. Date not set. (J). (gr. 5-6). lib. bdg. 20.95 *(978-0-88411-771-1(5))* Amereon Ltd.

Benchabbat, Edie C., et al. My Little Guardian Storybook. Date not set. (Illus.). 28p. (J). (gr. -1-5). pap. 5.99 *(978-0-9660879-0-1(9))* Little Guardians, Inc.

Berger, Melvin & Peck, Marshall H., III. A Whale Is Not a Fish & Other Animal Mix-Ups. (FRE., Illus.). 64p. (J). pap. 6.99 *(978-0-590-16026-1(5))* Scholastic, Inc.

Bertrand, Diane Gonzales. Upside down & Backwards. Hernandez, Karina, tr. 2004. (ENG & SPA., Illus.). 64p. (J). (gr. 2-5). pap. 9.95 *(978-1-55885-408-6(8),* Piñata Books) Arte Publico Pr.

Blyton, Enid. Mr Twiddle Stories. (ENG., Illus.). 224p. (J). pap. 5.95 *(978-0-09-965560-2(8))* Penguin Random Hse. GBR. Dist: Trafalgar Square Publishing.

—Well, Really, Mr Twiddle! 2nd ed. (Illus.). 111p. (J). pap. 6.95 *(978-0-7475-3852-3(2))* Bloomsbury Publishing Plc GBR. Dist: Trafalgar Square Publishing.

Brooks, Martha. Traveling on into the Light: And Other Stories. (J). 16.95 *(978-0-88899-220-8(3))* Groundwood Bks. CAN. Dist: Publishers Group West (PGW).

Castroviejo, Concha & Fedorchek, Robert M., trs. from SPA. The Garden with Seven Gates. 2003. (Illus.). 112p. (J). 32.50 *(978-0-8387-5559-4(3))* Bucknell Univ. Pr.

Cleary, Beverly. Jean & Johnny. 2007. (ENG.). 224p. (J). (gr. 5-18). pap. 10.99 *(978-0-380-72805-3(2),* HarperCollins) HarperCollins Pubs.

Cuentos para Soñar. 2010. (SPA.). (J). *(978-970-718-864-8(2),* Silver Dolphin en Español) Advanced Marketing, S. de R. L. de C. V.

Dale, Jenny. Boomerang Bob. Reid, Mick, illus. 2003. 105p. (J). *(978-0-439-45348-6(8))* Scholastic, Inc.

—Homeward Bound. Reid, Mick, illus. 2003. 110p. (J). *(978-0-439-45354-7(2))* Scholastic, Inc.

Disney Staff. La Belle et la Bete.Tr. of Beauty & the Beast. (FRE., Illus.). 96p. (J). (gr. -1-4). 11.95 *(978-2-89393-145-6(6))* Phidal Publishing, Inc./Editions Phidal, Inc. CAN. Dist: AIMS International Bks., Inc.

Elkins, Stephen. Special Times Bible Rhymes for Toddlers. 2005. (Special Times Ser.). (Illus.). 32p. (J). (gr. -1-18). 9.97 *(978-0-8054-2659-5(0))* B&H Publishing Group.

—Special Times Bible Stories for Toddlers. 2005. (Special Times Ser.). (Illus.). 32p. (J). (gr. -1-18). 9.97 *(978-0-8054-2681-6(7))* B&H Publishing Group.

—Stories That End with a Prayer. Menck, Kevin, illus. 32p. (J). (gr. k-8). 12.98 *(978-1-56919-003-6(8))* Wonder Workshop.

Encyclopaedia Britannica, Inc. Staff, compiled by. Legends, Myths, & Folktales. 2003. (Britannica Learning Library). (Illus.). (gr. 2-5). 14.95 *(978-1-59339-006-8(8),* 049907-EN-REF) Encyclopaedia Britannica, Inc.

Fitzgerald, F. Scott. Bernice Bobs Her Hair & Other Stories. Date not set. (Nelson Readers Ser.). (Illus.). 86p. (J). pap. *(978-0-17-557051-5(5))* Addison-Wesley Longman, Inc.

Foster, Elizabeth Vincent. Lyrico: The Only Horse of His Kind. Buba, Joy, illus. 2nd ed. 2004. 230p. (gr. 6-8). reprint ed. 8.95 *(978-0-930407-21-6(0))* Parabola Bks.

Franco, Eloise. Little Stories. Bredius, Rein, illus. 2003. 66p. (gr. k-5). 5.95 *(978-0-87516-384-0(X),* Devorss Pubns.) DeVorss & Co.

Gavin, Fred. Bedtime Stories. Klemek, Ryan, illus. Date not set. 64p. (J). (gr. k-3). pap. *(978-0-935668-00-1(4))* Gavin, Fred Enterprises.

Glyman, Caroline A. Forest House Firsts: Supplemental Selected Early Childhood Stories, 2 bks. Biser, Dee, illus. (J). (gr. k-3). lib. bdg. 29.90 *(978-1-56674-910-7(7))* Forest Hse. Publishing Co., Inc.

Grandma's Magical Storybook. 2003. (Illus.). 256p. (J). 12.98 *(978-1-4054-0968-1(1))* Parragon, Inc.

Hamilton, Martha & Weiss, Mitch. How & Why Stories: World Tales Kids Can Read & Tell. Lyon, Carol, illus. 2005. (World Storytelling from August House Ser.). (ENG.). 96p. (J). (gr. 1-7). pap. 15.95 *(978-0-87483-561-8(5))* August Hse. Pubs., Inc.

HarperCollins Publishers Ltd. Staff. Charming Classics Box Set No. 3: Charming Horse Library. 2003. (Charming Classics). (J). (gr. 3-7). pap. 19.99 *(978-0-06-056141-3(6))* HarperCollins Pubs.

Hetzer, Michael. Footprints on the Ceiling: Your Child's Footprint Completes the Story. Clayton, Kim, illus. 2nd ed. 2005. 32p. (J). 18.95 *(978-0-9728222-2-0(4))* Webster Henrietta Publishing.

—Footprints on the Ceiling (Collector's Edition) Your Child's Footprint Completes the Story. Clayton, Kim, illus. 2004. 32p. (J). 18.95 *(978-0-9728222-1-3(6))* Webster Henrietta Publishing.

Homer, Larona. The Shore Ghosts & Other Stories of New Jersey. Bock, William Sauts, illus. 2005. 154p. (J). (gr. 4-8). pap. *(978-0-912608-82-2(X))* Middle Atlantic Pr.

Hughes, Shirley. The Big Alfie Out of Doors Storybook. 2007. (Alfie Ser.). (Illus.). 64p. (J). (gr. -1-k). 15.95 *(978-0-09-925891-9(9),* Red Fox) Random House Children's Books GBR. Dist: Independent Pubs. Group.

Idaho Writers League Coeur d'Alene Chapter. Kaleidoscope: A Collection of Tantalizing Tales. 2003. (Illus.). (YA). (gr. 6-18). pap. 15.00 *(978-0-9740481-0-9(0))* Children's Village Foundation, Inc.

Iparraguirre, Sylvia., et al. Terminemos el Cuento. 2003. (SPA., Illus.). 128p. (YA). (gr. 9-12). 9.95 *(978-84-204-4965-4(2))* Ediciones Alfaguara ESP. Dist: Santillana USA Publishing Co., Inc.

Juliana, M., et al, eds. Treasure Box, Vol. 2. Miki, illus. 2nd l.t. rev. ed. 2009. (Treasure Box Ser.: 2). (ENG.). 32p. (J). (gr. k-2). 6.95 *(978-0-89555-552-6(2),* 1342) TAN Bks.

Kelemen, Violet. Misty Finds a Family. 2008. 92p. pap. 11.95 *(978-0-615-19128-7(2))* Violet Bks.

Lansky, Bruce & Johnson, Martha. Girls to the Rescue, Bk. 5. 108p. (J). pap. *(978-0-88166-315-0(8))* Meadowbrook Pr.

LeapFrog Schoolhouse Staff. Read-It-All Books: 2nd Grade & Up. 2003. tchr. ed. 19.95 *(978-1-59319-016-3(6),* LeapFrog Schl. Hse.) LeapFrog Enterprises, Inc.

Leeson, Robert. All the Gold in the World. 2004. (Illus.). 96p. bds. 8.95 *(978-0-7136-4059-5(6),* A&C Black) Bloomsbury Publishing Plc GBR. Dist: Consortium Bk. Sales & Distribution.

Long, Sylvia, illus. Sylvia Long's Big Book for Small Children. 2018. (Family Treasure Nature Encylopedias Ser.). (ENG.). 112p. (J). (gr. -1 — 1). 22.99 *(978-0-8118-3441-4(7))* Chronicle Bks. LLC.

Macintyre, R P. The Blue Camaro. 2006. (ENG.). 160p. pap. 13.95 *(978-1-895449-23-5(5))* Thistledown Pr., Ltd. CAN. Dist: Univ. of Toronto Pr.

Marshall, Hallie. Winnie the Pooh's Many Adventures, Set. Kurtz, John, illus. 2003. 176p. (J). 15.99 *(978-0-7868-3440-2(4))* Disney Pr.

McOmber, Rachel B., ed. McOmber Phonics Storybooks: A Trip to China. rev. ed. (Illus.). (J). *(978-0-944991-70-1(X))* Swift Learning Resources.

—McOmber Phonics Storybooks: Choose Which One - 1. rev. ed. (Illus.). (J). *(978-0-944991-67-1(X))* Swift Learning Resources.

—McOmber Phonics Storybooks: Humps & Lumps. rev. ed. (Illus.). (J). *(978-0-944991-62-6(9))* Swift Learning Resources.

—McOmber Phonics Storybooks: Kim. rev. ed. (Illus.). (J). *(978-0-944991-07-7(6))* Swift Learning Resources.

—McOmber Phonics Storybooks: Razz. rev. ed. (Illus.). (J). *(978-0-944991-06-0(8))* Swift Learning Resources.

—McOmber Phonics Storybooks: Ten in the Hut. rev. ed. (Illus.). (J). *(978-0-944991-27-5(0))* Swift Learning Resources.

—McOmber Phonics Storybooks: The Bag. rev. ed. (Illus.). (J). *(978-0-944991-03-9(3))* Swift Learning Resources.

—McOmber Phonics Storybooks: The Big Deal. rev. ed. (Illus.). (J). *(978-0-944991-47-3(5))* Swift Learning Resources.

—McOmber Phonics Storybooks: The Big Hole. rev. ed. (Illus.). (J). *(978-0-944991-38-1(6))* Swift Learning Resources.

—McOmber Phonics Storybooks: The Bon-Bon Box. rev. ed. (Illus.). (J). *(978-0-944991-14-5(9))* Swift Learning Resources.

—McOmber Phonics Storybooks: The Box Mix. rev. ed. (Illus.). (J). *(978-0-944991-15-2(7))* Swift Learning Resources.

—McOmber Phonics Storybooks: The Fumes. rev. ed. (Illus.). (J). *(978-0-944991-39-8(4))* Swift Learning Resources.

—McOmber Phonics Storybooks: The Kit. rev. ed. (Illus.). (J). *(978-0-944991-08-4(4))* Swift Learning Resources.

—McOmber Phonics Storybooks: The Land of Morning. rev. ed. (Illus.). (J). *(978-0-944991-82-4(3))* Swift Learning Resources.

—McOmber Phonics Storybooks: The Map. rev. ed. (Illus.). (J). *(978-0-944991-05-3(X))* Swift Learning Resources.

—McOmber Phonics Storybooks: The Pit Kit. rev. ed. (Illus.). (J). *(978-0-944991-09-1(2))* Swift Learning Resources.

—McOmber Phonics Storybooks: The Prize. rev. ed. (Illus.). (J). *(978-0-944991-49-7(1))* Swift Learning Resources.

—McOmber Phonics Storybooks: The Quiz Is (1) rev. ed. (Illus.). (J). *(978-0-944991-34-3(3))* Swift Learning Resources.

—McOmber Phonics Storybooks: The Quiz Is (2) rev. ed. (Illus.). (J). *(978-0-944991-35-0(1))* Swift Learning Resources.

—McOmber Phonics Storybooks: The Rope. rev. ed. (Illus.). (J). *(978-0-944991-45-9(9))* Swift Learning Resources.

—McOmber Phonics Storybooks: The Tin Lid. rev. ed. (Illus.). (J). *(978-0-944991-10-7(6))* Swift Learning Resources.

—McOmber Phonics Storybooks: Tid Bits. rev. ed. (Illus.). (J). *(978-0-944991-36-7(X))* Swift Learning Resources.

Modern Staff. Kites in Flight & Mosquito Bites. (J). 7.95 *(978-0-8136-4839-2(4))* Modern Curriculum Pr.

Monster Stories. 2003. 256p. (J). 5.98 *(978-1-4054-1008-3(6))* Parragon, Inc.

Nesbit, E. Beautiful Stories from Shakespeare for Children. Rackham, Arthur, illus. 2018. 192p. (J). (gr. 3-8). 14.99 *(978-1-63158-274-5(7),* Racehorse Publishing) Skyhorse Publishing Co., Inc.

No te dejes de Laura Sue: Social/Emotional Lap Book. (Pebble Soup Exploraciones Ser.). (SPA.). (gr. -1-18). 16.00 *(978-0-7578-1793-9(9))* Rigby Education.

Otfinoski, Steven. Our Freedom to Read Set. 2009. (Our Freedom to Read Ser.). (ENG.). (gr. 5-8). 160.00 *(978-1-60413-647-0(2),* P166843, Facts On File) Infobase Holdings, Inc.

Reading Friends Staff. Benjamin. (J). pap. *(978-0-8136-3840-9(2))* Modern Curriculum Pr.

Rothman, Cynthia Anne. A Party for Nine. l.t. ed. 2005. (Sadlier Phonics Reading Program). (Illus.). 8p. (gr. -1-1). 23.00 net. *(978-0-8215-7349-5(7))* Sadlier, William H. Inc.

Selected Children's Stories Published in Other Lands, 7 bks. (Illus.). (J). (gr. k-3). lib. bdg. 101.65 *(978-1-56674-905-3(0))* Forest Hse. Publishing Co., Inc.

Slavin, Bill. The Stone Lion, 1 vol. 2003. (ENG., Illus.). 32p. (J). (gr. 1-3). pap. 6.95 *(978-0-88995-154-9(3),* 354e7d80-4270-4d89-8848-219e051ec137) Red Deer Pr. CAN. Dist: Firefly Bks., Ltd.

Stalcup, Ann & Politi, Leo. Leo Politi: Artist of the Angels. 2004. (gr. 4). 24.95 *(978-1-893110-38-0(9))* Silver Moon Pr.

Story Rhyme Staff. Self-Esteem: Stories, Poetry & Activity Pages. Story Rhyme Staff, illus. Date not set. (Illus.). 28p. (YA). (gr. 4-9). ring bd. 19.95 *(978-1-56820-107-8(9))* Story Time Stories That Rhyme.

Taylor, Roger. Seven Silly Stories. Date not set. (Illus.). pap. 129.15 *(978-0-582-18518-0(1))* Addison-Wesley Longman, Ltd. GBR. Dist: Trans-Atlantic Pubns., Inc.

We Read More Stories. (J). tchr. ed. 4.72 *(978-0-917186-12-7(5));* Set. pap. 10.62 *(978-0-917186-11-0(7))* McQueen Publishing Co.

Weinbach, Shaindel. Cartons in the Air & Other Stories. Dershowitz, Yosef, illus. (J). 14.99 *(978-0-89906-992-0(4),* CARH) Mesorah Pubns., Ltd.

—The Friendly Persuader & Other Stories. Dershowitz, Yosef, illus. (J). 14.99 *(978-0-89906-970-8(3),* FRIH) Mesorah Pubns., Ltd.

White, E. B. E. B. White: Charlotte's Web, Stuart Little, & the Trumpet of the Swan, 3 bks., Set. 2003. (Illus.). (J). pap. 14.99 *(978-0-06-055416-3(9))* HarperCollins Pubs.

Wilder, Laura Ingalls. Little House Complete 9-Book Box Set: Books 1 To 9, Set. Williams, Garth, illus. Incl. Farmer Boy. 384p. pap. 8.99 *(978-0-06-440003-9(4));* First Four Years. 160p. pap. 9.99 *(978-0-06-440031-2(X));* Little House in the Big Woods. 256p. pap. 9.99 *(978-0-06-440001-5(8));* Little House on the Prairie. 352p. pap. 8.99 *(978-0-06-440002-2(6));* Little Town on the Prairie: A Newbery Honor Award Winner. 320p. pap. 8.99 *(978-0-06-440007-7(7));* 5. By the Shores of Silver Lake: A Newbery Honor Award Winner. 304p. pap. 9.99 *(978-0-06-440005-3(0));* (J). (gr. 3-7). 2008. (Little House Ser.). (ENG., Illus.). 2784p. 2008. reprint ed. Set pap. 80.91 *(978-0-06-440040-4(9),* HarperCollins) HarperCollins Pubs.

Young, Richard & Dockrey Young, Judy. Favorite Scary Stories of American Children. Bell, Don, illus. rev. ed. 2005. (ENG.). 128p. (J). (gr. 3-6). pap. 8.95 *(978-0-87483-563-2(1))* August Hse. Pubs., Inc.

STORIES IN RHYME

Abbot, Judi. Hugs & Kisses. Abbot, Judi, illus. 2016. (ENG., Illus.). 20p. (J). (gr. -1 — 1). bds. 7.99 *(978-1-4814-9168-6(7),* Little Simon) Little Simon.

Abery, Julie. Little Panda. Mason, Suzie, illus. 2019. (ENG.). 20p. (J). (gr. -1-k). bds. 9.99 *(978-1-68152-414-6(7),* 17591) Amicus.

—Little Tiger. 2019. (Illus.). 20p. (J). (gr. -1-k). bds. 9.99 *(978-1-68152-413-9(9),* 17590) Amicus.

Abolade, Caroline, told to. I'm Going to Be a Big Brother. 2003. 14p. 9.44 *(978-1-4116-0123-9(8))* Lulu Pr., Inc.

Accord Publishing, Accord. What Do You See? A Lift-The-Flap Book. 2014. (ENG.). 12p. (J). (-k). bds. 6.99 *(978-1-4494-4385-6(0))* Andrews McMeel Publishing.

Adams, Diane. I Can Do It Myself!, 1 vol. Hayashi, Nancy, illus. 2013. 32p. (J). (gr. -1-k). 7.99 *(978-1-56145-725-0(6))* Peachtree Publishing Co. Inc.

—Love Is: (Illustrated Story Book about Caring for Others, Book about Love for Parents & Children, Rhyming Picture Book) Keane, Claire, illus. 2017. (ENG.). 32p. (J). (gr. -1-k). 15.99 *(978-1-4521-3997-5(0))* Chronicle Bks. LLC.

—Zoom!, 1 vol. Luthardt, Kevin, illus. 2013. 32p. (J). (gr. -1-k). pap. 7.95 *(978-1-56145-683-3(7))* Peachtree Publishing Co. Inc.

Adams, Michelle Medlock. How Much Does God Love You? Keiser, Paige, illus. 2019. (ENG.). 22p. (J). (gr. -1-1). bds. 6.99 *(978-0-8249-1689-3(1),* Worthy Kids/Ideals) Worthy Publishing.

—My First Day of School. 2017. (ENG., Illus.). 20p. (J). (gr. -1-1). bds. 7.99 *(978-0-8249-1657-2(3))* Worthy Publishing.

—What Is Halloween? Wummer, Amy, illus. 2019. (ENG.). 22p. (J). (gr. -1-k). bds. 6.99 *(978-0-8249-1699-2(9),* Worthy Kids/Ideals) Worthy Publishing.

Adams, Michelle Medlock & Adams, Michelle M. Sister for Sale!, 1 vol. Brooks, Karen Stormer, illus. 2007. (I Can Read! Ser.). (ENG.). 32p. (J). (gr. -1-1). pap. 4.99 *(978-0-310-71469-9(9))* Zonderkidz.

Adeney, Anne. Five Teddy Bears. Shimmen, Cathy, illus. 2008. (Tadpoles Ser.). (ENG.). 24p. (J). (gr. -1-k). pap. *(978-0-7787-3884-8(1));* lib. bdg. *(978-0-7787-3853-4(1))* Crabtree Publishing Co.

Adler, Victoria. All of Baby, Nose to Toes. Nakata, Hiroe, illus. 2011. 30p. (J). (gr. k — 1). bds. 7.99 *(978-0-8037-3531-6(6),* Dial Bks) Penguin Young Readers Group.

Adlerman, Daniel. Rock-a-Bye Baby. Adlerman, Kimberly M., illus. 2004. 32p. (J). 15.95 *(978-1-58089-082-3(2))* Charlesbridge Publishing, Inc.

Adoff, Arnold. Black Is Brown Is Tan. McCully, Emily Arnold, illus. 2004. (ENG.). 40p. (J). (gr. -1-3). reprint ed. pap. 8.99 *(978-0-06-443644-1(6),* HarperCollins) HarperCollins Pubs.

Agee, Jon. It's Only Stanley. 2015. (J). 49.99 *(978-1-63379-786-4(4));* 14.99 *(978-1-63379-787-1(2))* Dreamscape Media, LLC.

—It's Only Stanley. 2015. (Illus.). 32p. (J). (gr. k-3). 18.99 *(978-0-8037-3907-9(9),* Dial Bks) Penguin Young Readers Group.

Agliardi, Allegra. All the Colors I See. 2018. (ENG., Illus.). 64p. (J). (gr. -1-k). 19.95 *(978-1-84976-577-0(4))* Tate Publishing, Ltd. GBR. Dist: Hachette Bk. Group.

Ahlberg, Janet & Ahlberg, Allan. Each Peach Pear Plum. 2009. 7.64 *(978-0-7848-2266-1(2),* Everbind) Marco Bk. Co.

Aigner-Clark, Julie. Baby Einstein: on the Farm. Zaidi, Nadeem, illus. 2007. (Baby Einstein Ser.). (ENG.). *(978-0-7634-2150-2(2))* Walt Disney Records.

Aiken, Zora & David. A to Z: Pick What You'll Be: Pick What You'll Be, 1 vol. 2011. (ENG., Illus.). 32p. (J). 14.99 *(978-0-7643-3701-7(7),* 4063, Schiffer Publishing Ltd) Schiffer Publishing, Ltd.

Ain, Beth. Izzy Kline Has Butterflies. 2018. (ENG.). 192p. (J). (gr. 3-7). pap. 7.99 *(978-0-399-55083-6(6),* Yearling) Random Hse. Children's Bks.

Aizen, Marina, illus. Mary Had a Little Lamb. 2012. (Classic Books with Holes Board Book Ser.). (J). 14p. spiral bd. *(978-1-84643-512-6(9));* 16p. pap. *(978-1-84643-501-0(3))* Child's Play International Ltd.

Aki. The Nature Girls. Aki, illus. 2019. (ENG., Illus.). 32p. (J). 16.99 *(978-1-62779-621-7(5),* 900156982, Holt, Henry & Co. Bks. For Young Readers) Holt, Henry & Co.

Akley, Jason. Sweet Pea & the Bumblebee. 2007. (ENG.). 36p. (J). per. 16.95 *(978-1-4327-0341-7(2))* Outskirts Pr., Inc.

Albee, Sarah. Hello, Cat, Hello, Dog. Leigh, Tom, illus. 2006. (Step-By-Step Readers Ser.). (J). pap. *(978-1-59939-054-3(X),* Reader's Digest Young Families, Inc.) Studio Fun International.

—Hic! Brannon, Tom, illus. 2006. (Step-By-Step Readers Ser.). (J). pap. *(978-1-59939-061-1(2),* Reader's Digest Young Families, Inc.) Studio Fun International.

Alborough, Jez. Billy the Goat's Big Breakfast. Alborough, Jez, illus. 2014. (ENG., Illus.). 32p. (J). 12.99 *(978-1-61067-190-3(2))* Kane Miller.

—Where's My Teddy? Alborough, Jez, illus. 2017. (ENG., Illus.). 32p. (J). (gr. -1-2). 8.99 *(978-0-7636-9871-3(7));* 25th ed. 17.99 *(978-0-7636-9816-4(4))* Candlewick Pr.

Alda, Arlene. Here a Face, There a Face. 2008. (Illus.). 32p. (J). (gr. k-k). 14.95 *(978-0-88776-845-3(8),* Tundra Bks.) Tundra Bks. CAN. Dist: Penguin Random Hse. LLC.

Aldis, Dorothy & Collins, Heather. Hiding. (FRE.). (J). pap. 7.99 *(978-0-590-24195-3(8))* Scholastic, Inc.

Alexander, Cecil Frances. All Things Bright & Beautiful. Hudson, Katy, illus. 2017. (ENG.). 20p. (J). (gr. -1-k). bds. 9.99 *(978-0-8249-1654-1(9))* Worthy Publishing.

Alexander, Kayla M. H. He Was No Magician. 2017. (ENG., Illus.). 29p. (J). pap. 13.95 *(978-1-78612-128-8(X),* 0a9a93ae-34fd-4c83-9c9a-70c55e4e77cc) Austin Macauley Pubs. Ltd. GBR. Dist: Baker & Taylor Publisher Services (BTPS).

Alexander, Kwame. Acoustic Rooster & His Barnyard Band. Bowers, Tim, illus. 2011. (ENG.). 32p. (J). (gr. 1-4). lib. bdg. 17.99 *(978-1-58536-688-0(9),* 202227) Sleeping Bear Pr.

—Booked. (Crossover Ser.). (ENG.). (J). (gr. 5-7). 2019. 336p. pap. 9.99 *(978-1-328-59630-7(3),* 1731272) 2016. 320p. 16.99 *(978-0-544-57098-6(7),* 1612557) HarperCollins Pubs. (Clarion Bks.).

—Booked. 2016. lib. bdg. 29.40 *(978-0-606-37992-2(4))* Turtleback.

—The Crossover. 2020. (ENG., Illus.). 218p. (J). (gr. 4-5). 24.19 *(978-1-64697-344-6(5))* Penworthy Co., LLC, The.

—The Crossover. 2014. lib. bdg. 29.40 *(978-0-606-37975-5(4))* Turtleback.

—The Crossover: A Newbery Award Winner. Anyabwile, Dawud, illus. (Crossover Ser.). (ENG.). (J). (gr. 3-7). 2019. 256p. pap. 10.99 *(978-0-544-93520-4(9),* 1658124) 2014. 240p. 17.99 *(978-0-544-10771-7(3),* 1540363) HarperCollins Pubs. (Clarion Bks.).

—El Crossover: Crossover (Spanish Edition), a Newbery Award Winner. Herrera, Juan Felipe, tr. Anyabwile, Dawud, illus. 2019. (Crossover Ser.). (SPA.). 256p. (J). (gr. 5-7). pap. 9.99 *(978-0-358-06473-2(2),* 1743975, Clarion Bks.) HarperCollins Pubs.

—The Door of No Return. l.t. ed. 2023. (ENG.). (J). lib. bdg. 22.99 Cengage Gale.

—The Door of No Return. 2022. (ENG., Illus.). 432p. (J). (gr. 5-17). 17.99 *(978-0-316-44186-5(4))* Little, Brown Bks. for Young Readers.

Alexander, Liza. Splish-Splash Spring! 2016. lib. bdg. 14.75 *(978-0-606-38486-5(3))* Turtleback.

S

Alinas, Marv. A Crab in the Cab. Petelinsek, Kathleen, illus. 2018. (Rhyming Word Families Ser.). (ENG.). 24p. (J). (gr. -1-2). lib. bdg. 32.79 *(978-1-5038-2348-8(2)*, 212183) Child's World, Inc, The.

—Kit's Banana Split. Petelinsek, Kathleen, illus. 2018. (Rhyming Word Families Ser.). (ENG.). 24p. (J). (gr. -1-2). lib. bdg. 32.79 *(978-1-5038-2354-9(7)*, 212187) Child's World, Inc, The.

—Ned, Ted, & the Red Shed. Petelinsek, Kathleen, illus. 2018. (Rhyming Word Families Ser.). (ENG.). 24p. (J). (gr. -1-2). lib. bdg. 32.79 *(978-1-5038-2351-8(2)*, 212189) Child's World, Inc, The.

—The Rag Bag. Petelinsek, Kathleen, illus. 2018. (Rhyming Word Families Ser.). (ENG.). 24p. (J). (gr. -1-2). lib. bdg. 32.79 *(978-1-5038-2349-5(0)*, 212194) Child's World, Inc, The.

Allen, Constance. Elmo's Mother Goose Rhymes (Sesame Street) Swanson, Maggie, illus. 2017. (Little Golden Book Ser.). 24p. (J). (-k). 4.99 *(978-1-101-93994-9(X)*, Golden Bks.) Random Hse. Children's Bks.

Allen, Kathryn Madeline. A Kiss Means I Love You. Futran, Eric, photos by. 2016. (ENG., Illus.). 16p. (J). (gr. -1 — 1). bds. 8.99 *(978-0-8075-4189-0(3)*, 0807541893) Whitman, Albert & Co.

—This Book. Doyle, Lizzy, illus. 2018. (ENG.). 24p. (J). (gr. -1 — 1). bds. 9.99 *(978-0-8075-7881-0(9)*, 807578819) Whitman, Albert & Co.

Allen, Lisa & Sharp, Julis. Time for Bed - The Secret of Shadows: Shadow Theater Inside. Johnson, Vickie, illus. 26p. (J). (gr. -1-2). pap. *(978-1-56021-355-0(8)*, 206) W.J. Fantasy, Inc.

Allman, John Robert. Boys Dance! (American Ballet Theatre) Lozano, Luciano, illus. 2020. (American Ballet Theatre Ser.). 40p. (J). (gr. -1-2). 17.99 *(978-0-593-18114-0(X))*; (ENG.). lib. bdg. 20.99 *(978-0-593-18115-7(8))* Random Hse. Children's Bks. (Doubleday Bks. for Young Readers).

Almy, Judy. My Name Is Ick: A Rhyming Story of an Alaska Caribou. 2003. 9.95 *(978-1-59433-009-4(3))* Publication Consultants.

Amato, Gaetano. Upside Right: A Children's Guide to Movement. 2010. (J). 19.95 *(978-0-615-38545-7(1))* Amato, G. J.

Amundson, Susan D. Three Little Lambs — Somewhere. Gelken, Brenda Joy, illus. 2006. 40p. (J). *(978-1-59984-002-4(2))* Bluedoor, llc.

Anastas, Margaret. A Hug for You. Winter, Susan, photos by. 2005. (ENG., Illus.). 32p. (J). (gr. -1-1). 15.99 *(978-0-06-623613-1(4))* HarperCollins Pubs.

—Mommy's Best Kisses. 2003. (ENG., Illus.). 32p. (J). (gr. -1-1). 17.99 *(978-0-06-623601-8(0)*, HarperCollins) HarperCollins Pubs.

Anderson, Airlie, illus. Cows in the Kitchen. 2009. (Classic Books with Holes US Soft Cover with CD Ser.). (ENG.). 16p. (J). *(978-1-84643-257-6(X))* Child's Play International Ltd.

—Cows in the Kitchen. 2009. (Classic Books with Holes Big Book Ser.). 16p. (J). (gr. -1-1). spiral bd. *(978-1-84643-208-8(1))* Child's Play International Ltd.

Anderson, Derek. Ten Hungry Pigs: An Epic Lunch Adventure. Anderson, Derek, illus. 2016. (ENG., Illus.). 40p. (J). (gr. -1-k). 17.99 *(978-0-545-16848-9(1))* Scholastic, Inc.

Anderson, Doug. Too Big to Dance (Paperback) Anderson, Sara, illus. 2015. (ENG.). 32p. (J). (gr. -1-2). pap. 10.95 *(978-0-9702784-9-4(7))* Sara Anderson Children's Bks.

Anderson, Georgia Lee. Bullying Is Wrong. Fox, Tom Paul, illus. 2012. (ENG.). 26p. pap. 14.95 *(978-1-57258-882-0(9)*, Aspect Bk.) TEACH Services, Inc.

Anderson, Lena & Sandin, Joan. Hedgehog, Pig, & the Sweet Little Friend. Sandin, Joan, tr. from SWE. 2007. (Illus.). 32p. (J). (gr. -1-1). 16.00 *(978-91-29-66742-4(9))* R & S Bks. SWE. Dist: Macmillan.

Anderson, M. T. The Serpent Came to Gloucester. Ibatoulline, Bagram, illus. 2005. (ENG.). 40p. (J). (gr. 1-4). 19.99 *(978-0-7636-2038-7(6))* Candlewick Pr.

Anderson, Peggy Perry. I Can Help! 2015. (Green Light Readers Ser.). (ENG., Illus.). 32p. (J). (gr. 1-4). pap. 4.99 *(978-0-544-52801-7(8)*, 1607367, Clarion Bks.) HarperCollins Pubs.

—Joe on the Go. Anderson, Peggy Perry, illus. 2012. (Green Light Readers Level 1 Ser.). (ENG., Illus.). 32p. (J). (gr. -1-3). pap. 4.99 *(978-0-547-74563-3(X)*, 1486287, Clarion Bks.) HarperCollins Pubs.

—Joe on the Go. 2012. (Green Light Readers Level 1 Ser.: 1). lib. bdg. 13.55 *(978-0-606-24018-5(7))* Turtleback.

—Let's Clean Up! Anderson, Peggy Perry, illus. 2012. (Green Light Readers Level 1 Ser.). (ENG., Illus.). 32p. (J). (gr. -1-3). pap. 4.99 *(978-0-547-74562-6(1)*, 1486286, Clarion Bks.) HarperCollins Pubs.

—Let's Clean Up! 2012. (Green Light Readers Level 1 Ser.). lib. bdg. 13.55 *(978-0-606-24024-6(1))* Turtleback.

—Out to Lunch. 2015. (Green Light Readers Ser.). (ENG., Illus.). 32p. (J). (gr. 1-4). pap. 4.99 *(978-0-544-52858-1(1)*, 1607369, Clarion Bks.) HarperCollins Pubs.

—Time for Bed, the Babysitter Said. 2012. (ENG., Illus.). 32p. (J). (gr. -1-3). pap. 5.99 *(978-0-547-85061-0(1)*, 1501045, Clarion Bks.) HarperCollins Pubs.

—To the Tub. 2012. (Green Light Readers Level 1 Ser.). (ENG., Illus.). 32p. (J). (gr. -1-3). pap. 4.99 *(978-0-547-85053-5(0)*, 1501029, Clarion Bks.) HarperCollins Pubs.

Anderson, Sara. Noisy City Day (2015 Board Book) Anderson, Sara, illus. 2015. (ENG., Illus.). 12p. (J). (gr. -1-1). bds. 10.95 *(978-1-943459-00-1(2))* Sara Anderson Children's Bks.

—Noisy City Night (2015 Board Book) Anderson, Sara, illus. 2015. (ENG., Illus.). 12p. (J). (gr. -1-1). bds. 10.95 *(978-1-943459-01-8(0))* Sara Anderson Children's Bks.

Andreae, Giles. Giraffes Can't Dance. 1 vol. Parker-Rees, Guy, illus. (J). (gr. -1-k). 2008. (ENG.). pap. 10.99 incl. audio compact disk *(978-0-545-09738-3(X))* 2007. 24.95 incl. audio *(978-0-439-02733-5(0))* Scholastic, Inc.

—Giraffes Can't Dance. Parker-Rees, Guy, illus. unabr. ed. 2011. (J). (gr. -1-1). 29.95 *(978-0-439-02734-2(9))* Weston Woods Studios, Inc.

—Heaven Is Having You. Cabban, Vanessa, illus. 2007. (Padded Board Bks.). 18p. (J). (gr. -1-1). bds. 7.95 *(978-1-58925-820-4(7))* Tiger Tales.

—I Love My Grandma. Dodd, Emma, illus. 2016. (ENG.). 32p. (J). (gr. -1-3). 16.99 *(978-1-4847-3407-0(6))* Disney Pr.

—I Love My Mommy. Dodd, Emma, illus. 2013. (ENG.). 26p. (J). (gr. -1 — 1). bds. 7.99 *(978-1-4231-6825-6(9))* Hyperion Pr.

—Keep Love in Your Heart, Little One. Vulliamy, Clara, illus. 2007. 32p. (J). (gr. -1-3). 15.95 *(978-1-58925-066-6(4))* Tiger Tales.

—Love Is a Handful of Honey. Cabban, Vanessa, illus. 2004. 32p. (J). (gr. -1-k). 5.95 *(978-1-58925-353-7(1))*; tchr. ed. 15.95 *(978-1-58925-003-1(6))* Tiger Tales.

—Rumble in the Jungle. Wojtowycz, David, illus. 2011. (ENG.). 26p. (J). (-k). bds. 9.99 *(978-1-58925-864-8(9))* Tiger Tales.

Andrews, Andy. Henry Hodges Needs a Friend, 1 vol. 2015. (ENG., Illus.). 32p. (J). 14.99 *(978-0-529-11576-8(X)*, Tommy Nelson) Nelson, Thomas Inc.

Angel, Ido. Vipo in London: The Ravens of the London Tower. 2015. (AV2 Animated Storytime Ser.). (ENG.). (J). lib. bdg. 29.99 *(978-1-4896-3911-0(X)*, AV2 by Weigl) Weigl Pubs., Inc.

Anglemyer, Jordan, illus. Grandpa's Favorites: A collection of quotes, things to ponder, stories, bits of verse, & Humor. 2007. 77p. (YA). per. 10.95 *(978-0-9796251-2-1(2))* Robertson Publishing.

Ann Scott, Lisa. Goodnight Lagoon. Sordo, Paco, illus. 2019. (ENG.). 40p. (J). (gr. -1-3). 17.99 *(978-1-4998-0845-2(3))* Little Bee Books Inc.

Ansell, Liz. The Unforgettable Snow Lady: And Other Memorable Short Stories, Songs & Rhymes. 2012. (Illus.). 40p. (-18). pap. 22.88 *(978-1-4772-3533-1(7))* AuthorHouse.

Apel, Kathryn. Bully on the Bus. 2018. (Illus.). 136p. (J). *(978-1-61067-871-1(0))* Kane Miller.

—Spinning Out on Track. 2015. 304p. (YA). (gr. 7). 12.95 *(978-0-7022-5373-7(1))* Univ. of Queensland Pr. AUS. Dist: Independent Pubs. Group.

—Too Many Friends. 2019. 208p. (J). (gr. 4-7). 12.95 *(978-0-7022-5976-0(4))* Univ. of Queensland Pr. AUS. Dist: Independent Pubs. Group.

Appelt, Kathi. Bat Jamboree. Sweet, Melissa, illus. 2004. 17.00 *(978-0-7569-4074-4(5))* Perfection Learning Corp.

—Counting Crows. Dunlavey, Rob, illus. 2015. (ENG.). 40p. (J). (gr. -1-3). 17.99 *(978-1-4424-2327-5(7))* Simon & Schuster Children's Publishing.

—Incredible Me! Karas, G. Brian, illus. 2003. (ENG.). 32p. (J). (gr. -1-3). 17.99 *(978-0-06-028622-4(9)*, HarperCollins) HarperCollins Pubs.

—Max Attacks. Dullaghan, Penelope, illus. 2019. (ENG.). 40p. (J). (gr. -1-3). 18.99 *(978-1-4814-5146-8(4)*, Atheneum/Caitlyn Dlouhy Books) Simon & Schuster Children's Publishing.

—Merry Christmas, Merry Crow. Goodell, Jon, illus. 2005. (ENG.). 32p. (J). (gr. -1-3). 16.00 *(978-0-15-202651-6(7)*, 1193419, Clarion Bks.) HarperCollins Pubs.

—Oh My Baby, Little One. Dyer, Jane, illus. 2006. (ENG.). 32p. (J). (gr. -1 — 1). pap. 5.99 *(978-0-15-206031-2(6)*, 1198114, Clarion Bks.) HarperCollins Pubs.

Appleby, Danny. Ella & the Balloons in the Sky. Pirie, Lauren, illus. 2013. 32p. (J). (gr. k-4). 15.95 *(978-1-77049-528-9(2)*, Tundra Bks.) Tundra Bks. CAN. Dist: Penguin Random Hse. LLC.

Applegate, Katherine. The One & Only Ruby. 2023. (One & Only Ser.). (ENG., Illus.). 240p. (J). (gr. 3-7). 19.99 *(978-0-06-308008-9(7)*, HarperCollins) HarperCollins Pubs.

—Sometimes You Fly. Reinhardt, Jennifer Black, illus. 2018. (ENG.). 40p. (J). (gr. -1-3). 17.99 *(978-0-547-63390-9(4)*, 1467767, Clarion Bks.) HarperCollins Pubs.

Arant, Bruce. Simpson's Sheep Just Want to Sleep! 2017. (ENG., Illus.). 32p. (J). 16.99 *(978-1-4413-2429-0(1)*, d1d43977-002e-4650-9006-9d38e13ced02) Peter Pauper Pr. Inc.

Archambault, John. By the Baobab Tree. Bender, Robert, illus. 2005. (J). *(978-1-58669-164-6(3))* Childcraft Education Corp.

—Cat in the Tree. Cooper, Stephanie, illus. 2007. (J). *(978-1-58669-230-8(5))* Childcraft Education Corp.

Archer, Peggy. A Hippy-Hoppy Toad. Wilsdorf, Anne, illus. 2018. 40p. (J). (gr. -1-2). 16.99 *(978-0-399-55676-0(1))*; (ENG.). lib. bdg. 19.99 *(978-0-399-55677-7(X))* Random Hse. Children's Bks. (Schwartz & Wade Bks.).

Arena, Jen. Salsa Lullaby. Meza, Erika, illus. 2019. (ENG.). 32p. (J). (gr. -1-2). lib. bdg. 20.99 *(978-0-525-57972-4(9)*, Knopf Bks. for Young Readers) Random Hse. Children's Bks.

Argueta, Jorge & Perez, Lucia Angela. Talking with Mother Earth / Hablando con Madre Tierra, 1 vol. 2006. (ENG., Illus.). 36p. (J). (gr. k-3). 17.95 *(978-0-88899-626-8(8))* Groundwood Bks. CAN. Dist: Publishers Group West (PGW).

Arias De Cordoba, Heather & Arias de Cordoba, Kaiya. A Year Full of Fairies. 2011. (Illus.). 28p. pap. 19.99 *(978-1-257-74775-7(4))* Lulu Pr., Inc.

Armstrong, Aldona. Every Family Is Special. 2013. (Illus.). 20p. pap. 11.59 *(978-1-4669-8913-9(0))* Trafford Publishing.

Armstrong-Ellis, Carey F. I Love You More Than Moldy Ham. 2015. (ENG., Illus.). 32p. (J). (gr. -1-3). 14.95 *(978-1-4197-1646-1(8)*, 1102101, Abrams Bks. for Young Readers) Abrams, Inc.

Armstrong, Robert W. The Big Blue Lake. Broxon, Janet, illus. 2022. (ENG.). 32p. (J). (gr. -1-k). 13.95 *(978-0-9801468-3-7(6))* All About Kids Publishing.

Arnold, Tedd. Dirty Gert. 2014. (ENG., Illus.). 32p. (J). (gr. -1-3). 7.99 *(978-0-8234-3054-3(5))* Holiday Hse., Inc.

—Even More Parts. Arnold, Tedd, illus. 2007. (Illus.). 40p. (J). (gr. -1-3). pap. 8.99 *(978-0-14-240714-1(3)*, Puffin Books) Penguin Young Readers Group.

—More Parts. 2003. (ENG., Illus.). 32p. (J). (gr. -1-3). pap. 8.99 *(978-0-14-250149-8(2)*, Puffin Books) Penguin Young Readers Group.

Arnosky, Jim. I'm a Turkey! 2009. (Illus.). (J). *(978-0-545-22631-8(7)*, Scholastic Pr.) Scholastic, Inc.

Aronson, Deborah. Dragons from Mars. Jack, Colin, illus. 2016. (ENG.). 32p. (J). (gr. -1-3). 17.99 *(978-0-06-236850-8(8)*, HarperCollins) HarperCollins Pubs.

Artell, Mike. Petite Rouge. Harris, Jim, illus. 2003. 32p. (J). (gr. k-3). 7.99 *(978-0-14-250070-5(4)*, Puffin Books) Penguin Young Readers Group.

—Petite Rouge. 2004. (J). 27.75 *(978-1-4193-1631-9(1))* Recorded Bks., Inc.

Ashburn, Boni. The Class. Gee, Kimberly, illus. 2016. (ENG.). 40p. (J). (gr. -1-3). 17.99 *(978-1-4424-2248-3(3)*, Beach Lane Bks.) Beach Lane Bks.

—The Fort That Jack Built. Helquist, Brett, illus. 2013. (ENG.). 32p. (J). (gr. -1-3). 18.95 *(978-1-4197-0795-7(7)*, 1002101, Abrams Bks. for Young Readers) Abrams, Inc.

—A Twin Is to Hug. 2019. (ENG., Illus.). 32p. (J). (gr. -1-1). 14.99 *(978-1-4197-3158-7(0)*, 1195301, Abrams Bks. for Young Readers) Abrams, Inc.

Asher, Sally. The Mermaids' Night Before Christmas. Vandiver, Melissa, illus. 2019. (J). *(978-1-946160-55-3(5))* Univ. of Louisiana at Lafayette Pr.

—Mermaids of New Orleans. Vandiver, Melissa, illus. 2018. (J). *(978-1-946160-28-7(8))* Univ. of Louisiana at Lafayette Pr.

Ashman, Linda. How to Make a Night. Tusa, Tricia, illus. Date not set. 32p. (J). (gr. -1-3). pap. 5.99 *(978-0-06-443699-1(3))* HarperCollins Pubs.

—Just Another Morning. Muñoz, Claudio, illus. 2004. (ENG.). 32p. (J). (gr. -1-3). 15.99 *(978-0-06-029053-5(6))* HarperCollins Pubs.

—Outside My Window. Christoph, Jamey, illus. 2018. (ENG.). 40p. (J). 17.00 *(978-0-8028-5465-0(6)*, Eerdmans Bks For Young Readers) Eerdmans, William B. Publishing Co.

—Take Your Pet to School Day. Kaufman, Suzanne, illus. 2019. 40p. (J). (gr. -1-2). 17.99 *(978-1-5247-6559-0(7))*; (ENG.). 20.99 *(978-1-5247-6560-6(0))* Random Hse. Children's Bks. (Random Hse. Bks. for Young Readers).

—When I Was King. McPhail, David, illus. 2008. 32p. (J). (gr. -1-3). 17.89 *(978-0-06-029052-8(8))* HarperCollins Pubs.

Ashton, Anna. Molly & Ben. 2007. (Illus.). 76p. per. *(978-1-84401-178-0(X))* Athena Pr.

Asim, Jabari. Whose Knees Are These? Pham, LeUyen, illus. 2019. (ENG.). 20p. (J). (gr. -1 — 1). bds. 7.99 *(978-0-316-45429-2(X))* Little, Brown Bks. for Young Readers.

—Whose Toes Are Those? Pham, LeUyen, illus. 2019. (ENG.). 20p. (J). (gr. -1 — 1). bds. 7.99 *(978-0-316-45432-2(X))* Little, Brown Bks. for Young Readers.

Atkins, Jeannine. Stone Mirrors: The Sculpture & Silence of Edmonia Lewis. 2018. (ENG.). 192p. (YA). (gr. 7). pap. 12.99 *(978-1-4814-5906-8(6))* Simon & Schuster Children's Publishing.

Atlas, Ron. Ten Pigs Fiddling. Flint, Stacie, illus. 2nd rev. ed. 2006. (ENG.). 32p. (J). (gr. -1-k). 17.95 *(978-0-9630243-3-6(7))* Amberwood Pr.

Atwood, Margaret. Up in the Tree, 1 vol. 2010. (ENG., Illus.). 32p. (J). (gr. k-k). 19.95 *(978-1-55498-080-2(1))* Groundwood Bks. CAN. Dist: Publishers Group West (PGW).

Aucoin, Lee & Reid, Stephanie. Todo Sobre Mí. rev. ed. 2010. (Early Literacy Ser.). (SPA., Illus.). 16p. (J). (gr. k-1). 19.99 *(978-1-4333-1943-3(8))* Teacher Created Materials, Inc.

—Todo Sobre Mi. rev. ed. 2010. (Early Literacy Ser.). (SPA., Illus.). 16p. (J). (gr. k-1). 6.99 *(978-1-4333-1942-6(X))* Teacher Created Materials, Inc.

Auerbach, Annie. Furry Bunny. Rigo, Laura, illus. 2018. (ENG.). 10p. (J). (gr. -1-k). bds. 7.99 *(978-1-4380-5011-9(9))* Sourcebooks, Inc.

—Furry Lamb. Rigo, Laura, illus. 2018. (ENG.). 10p. (J). (gr. -1-k). bds. 5.99 *(978-1-4380-5013-3(5))* Sourcebooks, Inc.

Augustine, Kristen. Can I Tell You? 2005. 9.00 *(978-0-8059-8071-4(7))* Dorrance Publishing Co., Inc.

Aulbach, Kathy. Flower Sprouts: Let's have a Fest! 2009. 29p. 15.95 *(978-0-615-21683-6(8))* Flower Sprouts.

Averiss, Corrinne. My Pet Star. Beardshaw, Ros, illus. 2020. (ENG.). 32p. (J). (gr. -1-k). pap. 10.99 *(978-1-4083-5366-0(0)*, Orchard Bks.) Hachette Children's Group GBR. Dist: Hachette Bk. Group.

Avis, Heather. Different — A Great Thing to Be! Mensinga, Sarah, illus. 2021. 40p. (J). (gr. -1-2). 12.99 *(978-0-593-23265-1(8)*, WaterBrook Pr.) Crown Publishing Group, The.

Awdry, W. A Crack in the Track (Thomas & Friends) 2004. (Bright & Early Board Books(TM) Ser.). (ENG., Illus.). 24p. (J). (— 1). bds. 4.99 *(978-0-375-82755-6(2)*, Random Hse. Bks. for Young Readers) Random Hse. Children's Bks.

—Fast Train, Slow Train (Thomas & Friends) 2014. (Big Bright & Early Board Book Ser.). (ENG., Illus.). 24p. (J). (— 1). bds. 6.99 *(978-0-385-37408-8(9)*, Random Hse. Bks. for Young Readers) Random Hse. Children's Bks.

—Go, Go, Thomas! 2013. (Thomas & Friends 8X8 Ser.). lib. bdg. 14.75 *(978-0-606-26992-6(4))* Turtleback.

—Thomas & Friends: Blue Train, Green Train (Thomas & Friends) Stubbs, Tommy, illus. 2006. (Bright & Early Books(R) Ser.). (ENG.). 36p. (J). (gr. k-k). 9.99 *(978-0-375-83463-9(X)*, Random Hse. Bks. for Young Readers) Random Hse. Children's Bks.

—Thomas & Friends: Blue Train, Green Train (Thomas & Friends) Stubbs, Tommy, illus. 2007. (Bright & Early Board Books(TM) Ser.). (ENG.). 24p. (J). (— 1). bds. 4.99 *(978-0-375-83984-9(4)*, Random Hse. Bks. for Young Readers) Random Hse. Children's Bks.

Aylesworth, Jim. Naughty Little Monkeys. Cole, Henry, illus. 2006. (ENG.). 32p. (J). (gr. -1-2). reprint ed. 7.99 *(978-0-14-240562-8(0)*, Puffin Books) Penguin Young Readers Group.

Ayres, Katherine. Up, down, & Around. Westcott, Nadine Bernard, illus. 2008. (ENG.). 32p. (J). (gr. k-k). 7.99 *(978-0-7636-4017-0(4))* Candlewick Pr.

—Up, down, & Around Big Book. Westcott, Nadine Bernard, illus. 2008. (ENG.). 32p. (J). (-k). pap. 27.99 *(978-0-7636-4018-7(2))* Candlewick Pr.

Baa, Baa Black Sheep. 2003. (J). per. *(978-1-57657-799-8(6))* Paradise Pr., Inc.

Babypants, Caspar. Ocean Motions. Endle, Kate, illus. 2018. 20p. (J). (— 1). bds. 10.99 *(978-1-63217-131-3(7)*, Little Bigfoot) Sasquatch Bks.

Bach, Annie. Night-Night, Forest Friends. 2018. (Illus.). 24p. (J). (-k). bds. 8.99 *(978-1-5247-8792-9(2)*, Grosset & Dunlap) Penguin Young Readers Group.

—Night-Night, Forest Friends. Bach, Annie, illus. 2013. (Illus.). 24p. (J). (gr. -1-k). bds. 9.99 *(978-0-8431-7278-2(9)*, Grosset & Dunlap) Penguin Young Readers Group.

Baer, Edith. Words Are Like Faces, 1 vol. Teis, Kyra, illus. 2007. (ENG.). 32p. (J). 15.95 *(978-1-59572-108-2(8))* Star Bright Bks., Inc.

Baghcheban, Samineh. Zendigiye Koodakan. 2012. 44p. pap. 12.00 *(978-0-9790573-7-3(X))* Urtext.

Baguley, Elizabeth. Just Like Brothers. Blanz, Aurélie, illus. 2018. (ENG.). 32p. (J). (gr. -1-2). 16.99 *(978-1-78285-345-9(6))* Barefoot Bks., Inc.

Baines, Andy. I Know a Goldfish That Can't Swim. 2012. 72p. (-18). pap. *(978-1-909395-50-3(1))* Legend Pr.

Bair, Sheila. Rock, Brock, & the Savings Shock. Gott, Barry, illus. 2017. (Money Tales Ser.). (ENG.). 32p. (J). (gr. -1-3). pap. 8.99 *(978-0-8075-7095-1(8)*, 807570958) Whitman, Albert & Co.

Baker, Amanda, illus. The Cheesehead Night Before Christmas. 2007. 40p. (J). per. 19.95 *(978-0-9797781-0-0(7))* Dreams 2 Wings LLC.

Baker, Keith. Hap-Pea All Year. Baker, Keith, illus. 2016. (Peas Ser.). (ENG., Illus.). 40p. (J). (gr. -1-3). 18.99 *(978-1-4814-5854-2(X)*, Beach Lane Bks.) Beach Lane Bks.

—Little Green Peas. Baker, Keith, illus. 2016. (Peas Ser.). (ENG., Illus.). 36p. (J). (gr. -1 — 1). bds. 8.99 *(978-1-4814-6248-8(2)*, Little Simon) Little Simon.

—Little Green Peas: A Big Book of Colors. Baker, Keith, illus. 2014. (Peas Ser.). (ENG., Illus.). 40p. (J). (gr. -1-3). 18.99 *(978-1-4424-7660-8(5)*, Beach Lane Bks.) Beach Lane Bks.

—LMNO Pea-Quel. Baker, Keith, illus. 2017. (Peas Ser.). (ENG., Illus.). 40p. (J). (gr. -1-3). 18.99 *(978-1-4814-5856-6(6)*, Beach Lane Bks.) Beach Lane Bks.

—LMNO Peas. Baker, Keith, illus. 2010. (Peas Ser.). (ENG., Illus.). 40p. (J). (gr. -1-3). 18.99 *(978-1-4169-9141-0(7)*, Beach Lane Bks.) Beach Lane Bks.

—LMNO Peas. Baker, Keith, illus. 2014. (Peas Ser.). (ENG., Illus.). 36p. (J). (gr. -1-k). bds. 8.99 *(978-1-4424-8978-3(2)*, Little Simon) Little Simon.

—My Octopus Arms. Baker, Keith, illus. 2013. (ENG., Illus.). 40p. (J). (gr. -1-3). 18.99 *(978-1-4424-5843-7(7)*, Beach Lane Bks.) Beach Lane Bks.

—No Two Alike. Baker, Keith, illus. 2011. (ENG., Illus.). 40p. (J). (gr. -1-2). 19.99 *(978-1-4424-1742-7(0)*, Beach Lane Bks.) Beach Lane Bks.

—1-2-3 Peas. Baker, Keith, illus. 2012. (Peas Ser.). (ENG., Illus.). 40p. (J). (gr. -1-3). 18.99 *(978-1-4424-4551-2(3)*, Beach Lane Bks.) Beach Lane Bks.

—2 Peas in a Pod! LMNO Peas; 1-2-3 Peas. Baker, Keith, illus. 2013. (ENG., Illus.). 80p. (J). (gr. -1-3). 33.99 *(978-1-4424-9991-1(5)*, Beach Lane Bks.) Beach Lane Bks.

Baker, Liza. Grandma Loves You Because You're You. McPhail, David, illus. 2018. (ENG.). 20p. (J). (gr. -1 — 1). bds. 8.99 *(978-1-338-27143-0(1)*, Cartwheel Bks.) Scholastic, Inc.

—I Love You Because You're You. McPhail, David, illus. 2008. (ENG.). 24p. (J). (gr. -1-k). bds. 8.99 *(978-0-545-02931-5(7)*, Cartwheel Bks.) Scholastic, Inc.

Baker, Ryan. How I Would Paint the World? 2006. (ENG.). 48p. per. 15.95 *(978-1-59800-969-9(9))* Outskirts Pr., Inc.

Balaam, Lisa & Balaam, Steven. Abbey the Cavi in Miami Beach. 2006. 52p. (J). 19.95 *(978-1-4196-1004-2(X))* CreateSpace Independent Publishing Platform.

Baldwin, Sherry. Santa's Tatty Old Boots. 2016. (ENG., Illus.). (J). 17.95 *(978-1-937721-37-4(X))* Randall, Peter E. Pub.

Ballard, George Anne. Flowers along the Way. Ballard, George Anne & Bolton, Georgia Helen, illus. 2012. 26p. pap. 12.00 *(978-0-9855312-2-5(3))* Bolton Publishing LLC.

Ballentine, Joyce. Nana's Nursery Rhymes 2. 2003. (J). pap. 12.00 *(978-0-8059-9211-3(1)*, RoseDog Bks.) Dorrance Publishing Co., Inc.

Balsley, Tilda. ABC Hanukkah Hunt. Poole, Helen, illus. 2013. (ENG.). 32p. (J). (gr. -1-2). E-Book 27.99 *(978-1-4677-1637-6(5)*, Kar-Ben Publishing) Lerner Publishing Group.

—Soo's Boo-Boos: She's Got 10! McNicholas, Shelagh, illus. 2013. (ENG.). 32p. (J). (gr. -1-2). 12.95 *(978-1-58925-118-2(0))* Tiger Tales.

—Ten Hungry Turkeys, 1 vol. Stott, Dorothy & Richard, Ilene, illus. 2018. (ENG.). 32p. (J). (gr. -1-3). 16.99 *(978-1-4556-2235-1(4)*, Pelican Publishing) Arcadia Publishing.

Banana-Tail. 2003. lib. bdg. 13.95 *(978-0-9727681-0-8(6))* Active Media Publishing, LLC.

Bandsuh, Jim. Helmet Hank. 2007. (Illus.). (J). per. 15.99 *(978-1-933156-19-4(8)*, Visikid Bks.) GSVQ Publishing.

Bannister, Emily, illus. Itsy Bitsy Spider. 2016. (Touch & Trace Nursery Rhymes Ser.). (ENG.). 10p. (J). (gr. -1 — 1). bds. 7.99 *(978-1-62686-764-2(X)*, Silver Dolphin Bks.) Printers Row Publishing Group.

Barad, Alexis. Puppy Love. East, Jacqueline, illus. 2013. (J). *(978-0-545-47733-8(6))* Scholastic, Inc.

Barash, Chris. Is It Hanukkah Yet? 2018. (2019 Av2 Fiction Ser.). (ENG.). 32p. (J). (gr. -1-2). lib. bdg. 34.28 *(978-1-4896-8241-3(4)*, AV2 by Weigl) Weigl Pubs., Inc.

—Is It Hanukkah Yet? Psacharopulo, Alessandra, illus. 2015. (Celebrate Jewish Holidays Ser.). (ENG.). 32p. (J). (gr. -1-3). 16.99 *(978-0-8075-3384-0(X)*, 080753384X) Whitman, Albert & Co.

—Is It Passover Yet? Psacharopulo, Alessandra, illus. 2015. (Celebrate Jewish Holidays Ser.). (ENG.). 32p. (J). (gr. -1-3). 16.99 *(978-0-8075-6330-4(7)*, 807563307) Whitman, Albert & Co.

—Is It Sukkot Yet? Psacharopulo, Alessandra, illus. 2016. (Celebrate Jewish Holidays Ser.). (ENG.). 32p. (J). (gr. -1-3). 16.99 *(978-0-8075-3388-8(2)*, 807533882) Whitman, Albert & Co.

—Jackie & Jesse & Joni & Jae. Battuz, Christine, illus. 2019. (ENG.). 24p. (J). 17.95 *(978-1-68115-550-0(8)*, c49a0776-fd1b-45cd-90ac-a5a0d78ce718, Apples & Honey Pr.) Behrman Hse., Inc.

—One Fine Shabbat. Mai-Wyss, Tatjana, illus. 2016. (ENG.). 12p. (J). (gr. -1 — 1). E-Book 23.99 *(978-1-4677-9614-9(X)*, Kar-Ben Publishing) Lerner Publishing Group.

Bardaus, Anna W. Bounce, Bounce, Baby! Grove, Christine, illus. 2013. (J). *(978-0-545-61897-7(5))* Scholastic, Inc.

—Dance, Dance, Baby! Grove, Christine, illus. 2013. (J). *(978-0-545-61899-1(1))* Scholastic, Inc.

—Reach, Reach, Baby! Grove, Christine, illus. 2013. (J). *(978-0-545-61900-4(9))* Scholastic, Inc.

—Read, Read, Baby! Grove, Christine, illus. 2013. (J). *(978-0-545-61898-4(3))* Scholastic, Inc.

Bardhan-Quallen, Sudipta. Chicks Run Wild. Jenkins, Ward, illus. 2011. (ENG.). 32p. (J). (gr. -1-1). 19.99

(978-1-4424-0673-5(9), Simon & Schuster Bks. For Young Readers) Simon & Schuster Bks. For Young Readers.
—Hampire! Fine, Howard, illus. 2011. (ENG.). 32p. (J). (gr. -1-3). 16.99 *(978-0-06-114239-0(5)*, HarperCollins) HarperCollins Pubs.
—Pirate Princess. McElmurry, Jill, illus. 2012. (ENG.). 40p. (J). (gr. -1-3). 17.99 *(978-0-06-114242-0(5)*, HarperCollins) HarperCollins Pubs.
—Snoring Beauty. Manning, Jane, illus. 2014. (J). *(978-0-06-087405-6(8))* Harper & Row Ltd.
—Snoring Beauty. Manning, Jane, illus. 2014. (ENG.). 32p. (J). (gr. -1-3). 17.99 *(978-0-06-087403-2(1)*, HarperCollins) HarperCollins Pubs.
—Tyrannosaurus Wrecks! OHora, Zachariah, illus. 2014. (ENG.). 32p. (J). (gr. -1-3). 14.95 *(978-1-4197-1035-3(4)*, 1051101, Abrams Bks. for Young Readers) Abrams, Inc.
Bardhan-Quallen, Sudipta & Kurilla, Renée. Chicks Rule! 2019. (ENG., Illus.). 40p. (J). (gr. -1-3). 16.99 *(978-1-4197-3414-4(8)*, 1210501, Abrams Bks. for Young Readers) Abrams, Inc.
Barnes, Brynne. Books Do Not Have Wings. Coelho, Rogério, illus. 2016. (ENG.). 32p. (J). (gr. k-3). 18.99 *(978-1-58536-964-5(0)*, 204112) Sleeping Bear Pr.
Barnes, Daryl. Crazy Bird Stories: Prepare Yourself for Strange Birds Behaving in Strange Ways. 2015. (ENG., Illus.). 34p. (J). pap. 20.99 *(978-1-4525-2924-0(8)*, Balboa Pr.) Author Solutions, LLC.
Barnes, Derrick D. Low-Down Bad-Day Blues. Boyd, Aaron, illus. 2004. (Just for You Ser.). (ENG.). 32p. (gr. k-1). pap. 3.99 *(978-0-439-56867-8(6)*, Teaching Resources) Scholastic, Inc.
Barnes, Peter W. Liberty Lee's Tail of Independence. Barnes, Cheryl Shaw, illus. 2012. (ENG.). 36p. (J). (gr. k-3). 16.95 *(978-1-59698-792-0(8)*, Little Patriot Pr.) Regnery Publishing.
—Marshall, the Courthouse Mouse: A Tail of the U. S. Supreme Court. Barnes, Cheryl Shaw, illus. 2012. (ENG.). 40p. (J). (gr. k). 18.99 *(978-1-59698-789-0(8)*, Little Patriot Pr.) Regnery Publishing.
—Woodrow, the White House Mouse. Barnes, Cheryl Shaw, illus. 2012. (ENG.). 40p. (J). (gr. k-3). 17.99 *(978-1-59698-788-3(X)*, Little Patriot Pr.) Regnery Publishing.
Barnes, Peter W. & Barnes, Cheryl Shaw. Woodrow for President: A Tail of Voting, Campaigns, & Elections. 2012. (ENG.). 32p. (J). (gr. k-3). 18.99 *(978-1-59698-786-9(3))* Regnery Publishing.
Barnett, Mac. The Three Billy Goats Gruff. Klassen, Jon, illus. 2022. (ENG.). 48p. (J). (gr. -1-3). 18.99 *(978-1-338-67384-5(X)*, Orchard Bks.) Scholastic, Inc.
Baron Cohen, H. V. The Story of Joe & His Magic Snout: An Operetta of Nursery Fairytales for 2 to 10 years Olds. 2009. 106p. pap. 19.27 *(978-1-4251-3582-9(X))* Trafford Publishing.
Barrow, Shelley. My Life: The Story of a NFL Child. 2007. (J). 16.99 *(978-0-9792647-0-2(7))* Mikenzi's Kardz & Bks. Llc.
Barry, Cotter. The Adventures of Morgan Morgan the Rhymester. 2010. 16p. 12.99 *(978-1-4520-0116-6(2))* AuthorHouse.
—By the Numbers. 2010. 16p. 12.99 *(978-1-4520-1476-0(0))* AuthorHouse.
—The Morgan's Family Circle. 2010. 16p. 12.99 *(978-1-4520-0114-2(6))* AuthorHouse.
—The Rhymester Morgan Morgan In: Elephants Don't Fly. 2010. 16p. 12.99 *(978-1-4520-0115-9(4))* AuthorHouse.
Barry, Debra R. Let's Go to the Market. 2012. 26p. 24.95 *(978-1-62709-916-5(6))*; 28p. pap. 24.95 *(978-1-4626-8533-2(1))* America Star Bks.
Barry, Robert. Mr. Willowby's Christmas Tree. Date not set. 32p. (J). 16.95 *(978-0-8488-2206-4(4))* Amereon Ltd.
Bartalos, Michael. Shadowville. 2013. (ENG., Illus.). 32p. (J). (gr. -1-2). 16.95 *(978-1-57687-645-9(4)*, powerHouse Bks.) powerHse. Bks.
Bartoletti, Susan Campbell. Naamah & the Ark at Night. Meade, Holly, illus. 2011. (ENG.). 32p. (J). (gr. -1-3). 16.99 *(978-0-7636-4242-6(8))* Candlewick Pr.
Barton, Jen. If Chocolate Were Purple. Matsuoka, Yoko, illus. gif. ed. 2013. (ENG.). 28p. (J). pap., instr.'s hndbk. ed. 10.89 *(978-0-615-78343-7(0)*, Flickerfawn) Barton Bks.
Bashford, Helen. Perry Panda: A Story about Parental Depression. Skinner, Russell Scott, illus. 2017. 32p. (J). 19.95 *(978-1-78592-412-5(5)*, 696669) Kingsley, Jessica Pubs. GBR. Dist: Hachette UK Distribution.
Baskwill, Jane. If Peace Is... Carter, Stephanie, illus. 2003. (J). 23p. pap. 7.95 *(978-1-59034-449-1(9))*; 24p. (gr. 11-18). 15.95 *(978-1-59034-448-4(0))* Mondo Publishing.
Bateman, Teresa. April Foolishness. Westcott, Nadine Bernard, illus. 2004. (ENG.). 32p. (J). (gr. -1-3). 8.99 *(978-0-8075-0405-5(X)*, 080750405X) Whitman, Albert & Co.
—Fluffy: Scourge of the Sea. Chesworth, Michael, illus. 2006. (ENG.). 32p. (J). (gr. -1-2). pap. 7.95 *(978-1-58089-152-3(7))* Charlesbridge Publishing, Inc.
—Ghostly Ghosts. Lamug, Ken, illus. 2019. (ENG.). 32p. (J). (gr. -1-3). 16.99 *(978-0-8075-2864-8(1)*, 807528641) Whitman, Albert & Co.
—Hunting the Daddyosaurus. Huang, Benrei, illus. 2004. 29p. (J). (gr. k-4). reprint ed. 16.00 *(978-0-7567-7796-8(8))* DIANE Publishing Co.
—A Plump & Perky Turkey, 0 vols. Shelly, Jeff, illus. 2013. (ENG.). 32p. (J). (gr. -1-3). pap. 9.99 *(978-0-7614-5188-4(9)*, 9780761451884, Two Lions) Amazon Publishing.
—Runaway Pumpkins. Coleman, Stephanie Fizer, illus. 2020. 32p. (J). (gr. -1-2). lib. bdg. 16.99 *(978-1-58089-681-8(2))* Charlesbridge Publishing, Inc.
Bauer, Marion Dane. In Like a Lion Out Like a Lamb. McCully, Emily Arnold, illus. 2012. (ENG.). 32p. (J). (gr. -1-3). pap. 7.99 *(978-0-8234-2432-0(4))* Holiday Hse., Inc.
—Little Cat's Luck. Bell, Jennifer A., illus. 2016. (ENG.). 224p. (J). (gr. 3-7). 17.99 *(978-1-4814-2488-2(2)*, Simon & Schuster Bks. For Young Readers) Simon & Schuster Bks. For Young Readers.
—My Mother Is Mine. Elwell, Peter, illus. 2009. (Classic Board Bks.). (ENG.). 36p. (J). (gr. -1-k). bds. 8.99 *(978-1-4169-6090-4(2)*, Little Simon) Little Simon.
—My Mother Is Mine. Elwell, Peter, illus. 2004. (ENG.). 40p. (J). (gr. -1-k). reprint ed. 7.99 *(978-0-689-86695-1(X)*, Simon & Schuster Bks. For Young Readers) Simon & Schuster Bks. For Young Readers.
—The Very Best Daddy of All. Wu, Leslie, illus. 2011. (Classic Board Bks.). (ENG.). 34p. (J). (gr. -1 — 1). bds. 7.99 *(978-1-4169-8517-4(4)*, Little Simon) Little Simon.
—The Very Best Daddy of All. Wu, Leslie, illus. 2007. (ENG.). 40p. (J). (gr. -1-3). 7.99 *(978-1-4169-2736-5(0)*, Simon & Schuster Bks. For Young Readers) Simon & Schuster Bks. For Young Readers.
Baum, L. Frank. Mother Goose in Prose. l.t. ed. 2005. 268p. pap. *(978-1-84637-097-7(3))* Echo Library.
Beardsley, Martyn. Five Naughty Kittens. East, Jacqueline, illus. 2005. (Reading Corner Ser.). 24p. (J). (gr. k-3). lib. bdg. 22.80 *(978-1-59771-006-0(7))* Sea-To-Sea Pubns.
Beaton, Clare. Daisy Gets Dressed. 2005. (ENG., Illus.). 24p. (J). 15.99 *(978-1-84148-794-6(5))* Barefoot Bks., Inc.
Beaton, Clare & Blackstone, Stella. Cerdota Grandota. Beaton, Clare, illus. 2006.Tr. of How Big Is a Pig. (Illus.). 24p. (J). (gr. -1-k). bds. 6.99 *(978-1-84686-018-8(0))* Barefoot Bks., Inc.
Beaty, Andrea. Aaron Slater, Illustrator. Roberts, David, illus. 2021. (Questioneers Ser.). (ENG.). 40p. (J). (gr. k-2). 18.99 *(978-1-4197-5396-1(7)*, 1730501) Abrams, Inc.
—Ada Twist, Scientist. 2016. (Questioneers Ser.). (ENG., Illus.). 32p. (J). (gr. k-2). 19.99 *(978-1-4197-2137-3(2)*, 1119001) Abrams, Inc.
—Hide & Sheep. Mayer, Bill, illus. 2011. (ENG.). 32p. (J). (gr. -1-3). 15.99 *(978-1-4169-2544-6(9)*, McElderry, Margaret K. Bks.) McElderry, Margaret K. Bks.
—Iggy Peck, Architect. 2007. (Questioneers Ser.). (ENG., Illus.). 32p. (J). (gr. k-17). 19.99 *(978-0-8109-1106-2(X)*, 05326) Abrams, Inc.
—Iggy Peck, Architect. Roberts, David, illus. 2010. (ENG.). 32p. (J). (gr. k-17). pap. 7.95 *(978-0-8109-8928-3(X))* UK Abrams Bks. for Young Readers.
—Rosie Revere, Engineer. 2013. (Questioneers Ser.). (ENG., Illus.). 32p. (J). (gr. k-2). 18.99 *(978-1-4197-0845-9(7)*, 0671201) Abrams, Inc.
—Sofia Valdez, Future Prez. 2019. (Questioneers Ser.). (ENG., Illus.). 40p. (J). (gr. k-2). 18.99 *(978-1-4197-3704-6(X)*, 1217401) Abrams, Inc.
Beaumont, Karen. Dini Dinosaur. Roode, Daniel, illus. 2012. (ENG.). 32p. (J). (gr. -1-k). 14.99 *(978-0-06-207299-3(4)*, Greenwillow Bks.) HarperCollins Pubs.
—Duck, Duck, Goose! (A Coyote's on the Loose!) Aruego, Jose & Dewey, Ariane, illus. 2004. 32p. (J). (gr. -1-2). lib. bdg. 18.89 *(978-0-06-050804-3(3))* HarperCollins Pubs.
—Duck, Duck, Goose! (a Coyote's on the Loose!) Aruego, Jose & Dewey, Ariane, illus. 2004. (ENG.). 32p. (J). (gr. -1-2). 17.99 *(978-0-06-050802-9(7)*, HarperCollins) HarperCollins Pubs.
—I Ain't Gonna Paint No More! Catrow, David, illus. 2005. (ENG.). 32p. (J). (gr. -1-3). 17.99 *(978-0-15-202488-8(3)*, 1192948, Clarion Bks.) HarperCollins Pubs.
—I Ain't Gonna Paint No More! Lap Board Book. Catrow, David, illus. 2012. (ENG.). 30p. (J). (gr. -1 — 1). bds. 12.99 *(978-0-547-87035-9(3)*, 1504857, Clarion Bks.) HarperCollins Pubs.
—I Like Myself! Catrow, David, illus. 2004. (ENG.). 32p. (J). (gr. -1-3). 18.99 *(978-0-15-202013-2(6)*, 1191551, Clarion Bks.) HarperCollins Pubs.
—I Like Myself! Lap Board Book. Catrow, David, illus. 2010. (ENG.). 32p. (J). (gr. -1 — 1). bds. 14.99 *(978-0-547-40163-8(9)*, 1427978, Clarion Bks.) HarperCollins Pubs.
—Move over, Rover! Dyer, Jane, illus. 2016. (ENG.). 40p. (J). (gr. -1-3). 7.99 *(978-0-544-80900-0(9)*, 1641299, Clarion Bks.) HarperCollins Pubs.
—Wild about Us! Stevens, Janet, illus. 2015. (ENG.). 40p. (J). (gr. -1-3). 17.99 *(978-0-15-206294-1(7)*, 1198860, Clarion Bks.) HarperCollins Pubs.
Beck, Carolyn. Richard Was a Picker, 1 vol. Hodson, Ben, illus. 2010. (ENG.). 32p. (J). (gr. -1-k). 19.95 *(978-1-55469-088-6(9))* Orca Bk. Pubs. USA.
Becker, Bonny. The Frightful Ride of Michael Mcmichael. Fearing, Mark, illus. 2018. (ENG.). 32p. (J). (gr. -1-3). 16.99 *(978-0-7636-8150-0(4))* Candlewick Pr.
Becker, Laura. The Wonder of a Summer Day. Steffen, Jennifer, illus. 2008. (ENG.). 40p. (J). (gr. -1-3). lib. bdg. *(978-1-934363-25-6(1))* Zoe Life Christian Communications.
Becker, Shelly. Even Superheroes Have Bad Days. Kaban, Eda, illus. 2016. (Superheroes Are Just Like Us Ser.). 40p. (J). (gr. -1-4). 17.99 *(978-1-4549-1394-8(0))* Sterling Publishing Co., Inc.
—Even Superheroes Make Mistakes. Kaban, Eda, illus. 2018. (Superheroes Are Just Like Us Ser.). 40p. (J). (gr. -1-4). 17.99 *(978-1-4549-2703-7(8))* Sterling Publishing Co., Inc.
Beckerman, Menucha. The Candy Kids. 2004. (My Smiling World Ser.: No. 3). (Illus.). 32p. (J). 11.95 *(978-1-931681-54-4(6))* Israel Bookshop Pubns.
Beckman, Chris & Beckman, Kelly. It's Not Scary You See... 2012. (ENG.). (J). pap. *(978-1-4675-3871-8(X))* Independent Pub.
Bee, Patricia. Try'umsee's Wings. Dunmeyer, Vernell, photos by. 2007. (ENG.). 44p. pap. 17.99 *(978-1-4257-0920-4(6))* Xlibris Corp.
Beilenson, Evelyn. The Zoo Is Closed Today! Kennedy, Anne, illus. 2014. (ENG.). 32p. (J). 16.99 *(978-1-4413-1526-7(8)*, bafefaaa-3ed9-4f39-af87-f94b55eddd8d) Peter Pauper Pr. Inc.
Beiser, Tim. Little Chicken Duck. Slavin, Bill, illus. 2013. 24p. (J). (gr. -1-2). 17.95 *(978-1-77049-392-6(1)*, Tundra Bks.) Tundra Bks. CAN. Dist: Penguin Random Hse. LLC.
Bell, Hilary & Pesenti, Antonia. Numerical Street. 2016. (Illus.). 32p. (J). (gr. -1-3). 24.99 *(978-1-74223-228-7(0)*, NewSouth) NewSouth Publishing AUS. Dist: Independent Pubs. Group.
Bell-Jackson, Sylvia. Bree's Bubble Gum Adventures: The Pajamas from the Bahamas. 2012. 36p. pap. 13.97 *(978-1-61204-299-2(6)*, Strategic Bk. Publishing) Strategic Book Publishing & Rights Agency (SBPRA).
Bell, Juliet Clare. The Kite Princess. Chapman, Laura-Kate, illus. 2012. 32p. (J). 9.99 *(978-1-84686-830-6(0))* Barefoot Bks., Inc.
Bell, Juliet Clare & Chapman, Laura Kate. The Kite Princess. 2012. (Illus.). (J). 16.99 *(978-1-84686-803-0(3))* Barefoot Bks., Inc.
Bell, Liz. Amarie & Her Family. 2011. 24p. pap. 24.95 *(978-1-4560-5430-4(9))* America Star Bks.
—Chickee Chickee Chew & Whoo Whoo Whoo. 2011. 16p. pap. 24.95 *(978-1-4626-3588-7(1))* America Star Bks.
Bell-Martin, Janelle. Head & Shoulders. 2011. (Early Literacy Ser.). (ENG.). 16p. (gr. -1-1). 19.99 *(978-1-4333-2372-0(9))*; 6.99 *(978-1-4333-2371-3(0))* Teacher Created Materials, Inc.
—Mary Had a Little Lamb. 2011. (Early Literacy Ser.). (ENG.). 16p. (gr. k-1). 19.99 *(978-1-4333-2358-4(3))*; 6.99 *(978-1-4333-2357-7(5))* Teacher Created Materials, Inc.
—Oh, Mr. Sun, 1 vol. rev. ed. 2012. (Early Literacy Ser.). (ENG.). 16p. (gr. k-1). 6.99 *(978-1-4333-3471-9(2))* Teacher Created Materials, Inc.
Bell, Philip. Jack & Boo's Dinosaur Island. Bell, Eleanor, illus. 2013. 32p. pap. *(978-0-9562980-3-4(6))* Beachy Bks.
Bell, Samantha. The Perfect Pet, 1 vol. 2013. (SPA., Illus.). 32p. (J). (gr. k-1). pap. 11.95 *(978-1-60718-701-1(9)*, 7762f99b-3f03-429d-809c-56bd3d3036bc) Arbordale Publishing.
Belloc, Hilaire. Cautionary Tales for Children. 2009. 48p. (gr. 4-7). pap. 7.75 *(978-1-60459-576-5(0))* Wilder Pubns., Corp.
Bemelmans, Ludwig. Madeline: Edicion en Espanol. Anasal, Arshes, ed. 2005. (SPA., Illus.). 44p. (J). (gr. k-4). reprint ed. 16.00 *(978-0-7567-8842-1(0))* DIANE Publishing Co.
—Madeline's Rescue. 2004. (J). (gr. -1-2). spiral bd. *(978-0-616-11864-1(3))* Canadian National Institute for the Blind/Institut National Canadien pour les Aveugles.
Ben-Gur, Naomi. The Cricket & the Ant: A Shabbat Story. Kober, Shahar, illus. 2016. (ENG.). 32p. (J). (gr. -1-3). lib. bdg. 9.99 *(978-1-4677-8935-6(6)*, 845b798c-71eb-447a-93f8-674f67360bd4, Kar-Ben Publishing) Lerner Publishing Group.
Benenfeld, Rikki. I Go to Eretz Yisroel. Benenfeld, Rikki, illus. 2017. (Toddler Experience Ser.). (ENG., Illus.). 28p. (J). 11.95 *(978-1-929628-92-6(7))* Hachai Publishing.
—I Go Visiting. 2007. (Toddler Experience Ser.). (ENG., Illus.). 32p. (J). (gr. -1-k). 11.99 *(978-1-929628-33-9(1))* Hachai Publishing.
—Let's Go to the Park. 2015. (ENG., Illus.). 36p. (J). 11.99 *(978-1-929628-82-7(X))* Hachai Publishing.
—Let's Meet Community Helpers. Benenfeld, Rikki, illus. 2013. (ENG., Illus.). 32p. (J). 11.99 *(978-1-929628-75-9(7))* Hachai Publishing.
Bennett, Artie. The Butt Book. Lester, Mike, illus. 2010. (ENG.). 32p. (J). (gr. k-2). 18.99 *(978-1-59990-311-8(3)*, 900054082, Bloomsbury USA Childrens) Bloomsbury Publishing USA.
Bennett, Elizabeth. The Biggest Pumpkin Ever! Woodruff, Liza, illus. 2007. (J). pap. *(978-0-545-00232-5(X))* Scholastic, Inc.
—It's Holiday Time! Baccala, Gladys, illus. 2012. (ENG.). 18p. (J). bds. *(978-1-58925-640-8(9))* Tiger Tales.
Benson, Nicky. I Love You More & More. Lambert, Jonny, illus. 2018. (ENG.). 24p. (J). (gr. -1-k). bds. 9.99 *(978-1-58925-227-1(6))* Tiger Tales.
Bentley, Dawn. Three Hungry Spiders & One Fat Fly! Twinem, Neecy, illus. 2010. (Stretchies Book Ser.). 16p. (J). (gr. -1-k). 8.99 *(978-0-8249-1460-8(0)*, Ideals Pubns.) Worthy Publishing.
—Three Stretchy Frogs. Wallis, Becky, illus. 2010. (Stretchies Book Ser.). 16p. (J). 8.99 *(978-0-8249-1459-2(7))* Hinkler Bks. Pty. Ltd. AUS. Dist: Ideals Pubns.
Bently, Peter. Captain Jack & the Pirates. Oxenbury, Helen, illus. 2016. (ENG.). 32p. (J). (-k). 18.99 *(978-0-525-42950-0(6)*, Dial Bks) Penguin Young Readers Group.
—The Cat, the Mouse, & the Runaway Train. Cox, Steve, illus. 2013. (J). *(978-1-4351-4968-7(8))* Barnes & Noble, Inc.
—Dustbin Dad. Ayto, Russell, illus. 2014. (ENG.). 32p. (J). 15.99 *(978-1-84738-873-5(6))* Simon & Schuster, Ltd. GBR. Dist: Simon & Schuster, Inc.
—The Great Dog Bottom Swap. Matsuoka, Mei, illus. 2011. (ENG.). 32p. (J). (gr. -1-k). pap. 12.99 *(978-1-84270-988-7(7))* Andersen Pr. GBR. Dist: Independent Pubs. Group.
—The Great Sheep Shenanigans. Matsuoka, Mei, illus. 2012. (Andersen Press Picture Bks). (ENG.). 32p. (J). (gr. -1-3). 16.95 *(978-0-7613-8990-3(3))* Lerner Publishing Group.
—Meet the Parents. Ogilvie, Sara, illus. 2014. (ENG.). 32p. (J). (gr. -1-3). 17.99 *(978-1-4814-1483-8(6)*, Simon & Schuster/Paula Wiseman Bks.) Simon & Schuster/Paula Wiseman Bks.
—The Tooth Fairy's Christmas. Parsons, Garry, illus. 2014. (J). *(978-1-4351-5739-2(7))* Barnes & Noble, Inc.
—The Yoga Ogre. Rickerty, Simon, illus. 2012. (ENG.). 32p. (J). 15.99 *(978-1-84738-902-2(3))* Simon & Schuster, Ltd. GBR. Dist: Simon & Schuster, Inc.
Berenstain, Jan & Berenstain, Mike. Let the Bible Be Your Guide. 2011. (Berenstain Bears/Living Lights Ser.). (ENG., Illus.). 40p. (J). 6.99 *(978-0-310-72714-9(6))* Zonderkidz.
Berenstain, Jan & Berenstain, Stan. The Berenstain Bears down on the Farm. Berenstain, Jan, illus. 2006. (I Can Read Level 1 Ser.). (ENG., Illus.). 32p. (J). (gr. k-3). pap. 4.99 *(978-0-06-058351-4(7)*, HarperCollins) HarperCollins Pubs.
—The Berenstain Bears Out West. Berenstain, Jan, illus. 2006. (I Can Read Level 1 Ser.). (ENG., Illus.). 32p. (J). (gr. k-3). pap. 4.99 *(978-0-06-058354-5(1)*, HarperCollins) HarperCollins Pubs.
Berenstain, Jan, et al. The Berenstain Bears Save Christmas. Berenstain, Mike, illus. 2003. (Berenstain Bears Ser.). (ENG.). 48p. (J). (gr. -1-3). 14.99 *(978-0-06-052670-2(X)*, HarperFestival) HarperCollins Pubs.
—God Made the Colors, 1 vol. 2013. (I Can Read! / Berenstain Bears / Living Lights: a Faith Story Ser.). (ENG.). 32p. (J). pap. 4.99 *(978-0-310-72507-7(0))* Zonderkidz.
Berenstain, Stan & Berenstain, Jan. The Berenstain Bears' Family Reunion. 2009. (Berenstain Bears — I Can Read Ser.). (J). lib. bdg. 13.55 *(978-0-606-04776-0(X))* Turtleback.
—The Big Book of Berenstain Bears Beginner Books. 2011. (Beginner Books(R) Ser.). (Illus.). 320p. (J). (gr. -1-2). 16.99 *(978-0-375-87366-9(X)*, Random Hse. Bks. for Young Readers) Random Hse. Children's Bks.
—We Like Kites. 2004. (Step into Reading - Level 1 Ser.). (gr. -1-2). lib. bdg. 13.55 *(978-0-613-87779-4(9))* Turtleback.
Berenstain, Stan, et al. The Berenstain Bears' Christmas Tree, 1 vol. 2009. (Berenstain Bears/Living Lights: a Faith Story Ser.). (ENG., Illus.). 72p. (J). (gr. -1-2). 12.99 *(978-0-310-71940-3(2))* Zondervan.
—The Berenstain Bears Learn to Share, 1 vol. 2010. (Berenstain Bears/Living Lights: a Faith Story Ser.). (ENG., Illus.). 40p. (J). (gr. -1-2). 6.99 *(978-0-310-71939-7(9))* Zonderkidz.
Berger, Samantha. What If... Curato, Michael, illus. 2018. (ENG.). 40p. (J). (gr. -1-3). 17.99 *(978-0-316-39096-5(8))* Little, Brown Bks. for Young Readers.
Berger, Samantha & Chanko, Pamela. It's Spring! Sweet, Melissa, illus. 2003. (ENG.). 30p. (J). (gr. -1-3). bds. 6.99 *(978-0-439-44238-1(9)*, Cartwheel Bks.) Scholastic, Inc.
—It's Spring! (a StoryPlay Book) 2017. (StoryPlay Ser.). (ENG., Illus.). 40p. (J). (gr. -1-k). 5.99 *(978-1-338-23218-9(5))* Scholastic, Inc.
Berggren, Joyce D. The Hustle & Bustle of Poor Mrs. Tustle. Muellner, Nancy, illus. 2010. 32p. pap. 12.95 *(978-0-9819860-5-0(6))* Amber Skye Publishing LLC.
Bergman, Mara. Oliver Who Would Not Sleep! Maland, Nick, illus. 2007. (J). *(978-0-439-92827-4(3)*, Levine, Arthur A. Bks.) Scholastic, Inc.
Berkes, Marianne. Marsh Music. Noreika, Robert, illus. 2011. (ENG.). 32p. (J). (gr. k-3). pap. 9.99 *(978-0-7613-7461-9(2)*, 41b5da8a-eedb-4cc9-844b-4e6ebb10f35d, Millbrook Pr.) Lerner Publishing Group.
—Over in Australia: Amazing Animals down Under, 1 vol. Dubin, Jill, illus. 2011. (Over- Dawn Pub Ser.). (ENG.). 32p. (J). (gr. -1-1). 24.94 *(978-1-58469-135-8(2))* Take Heart Pubns.
—Over in the Forest: Come & Take a Peek, 1 vol. Dubin, Jill, illus. 2012. (ENG.). 32p. (J). 16.95 *(978-1-58469-162-4(X))* Take Heart Pubns.
—Over in the Grasslands: On an African Savanna, 1 vol. Dubin, Jill, illus. 2016. (ENG.). 32p. (J). (gr. -1-2). 16.95 *(978-1-58469-567-7(6)*, Dawn Pubns.) Sourcebooks, Inc.
—Over on a Desert: Somewhere in the World, 1 vol. Dubin, Jill, illus. 2018. (ENG.). 32p. (J). (gr. -1-3). 16.95 *(978-1-58469-629-2(X)*, Dawn Pubns.) Sourcebooks, Inc.
—Over on the Farm. Morrison, Cathy, illus. 2016. (ENG.). 32p. (J). (gr. -1-2). 16.95 *(978-1-58469-548-6(X)*, Dawn Pubns.) Sourcebooks, Inc.
—The Swamp Where Gator Hides, 1 vol. Baird, Roberta, illus. 2014. (ENG.). 32p. (J). (gr. k-4). 16.95 *(978-1-58469-470-0(X))*; pap. 8.99 *(978-1-58469-471-7(8))* Sourcebooks, Inc. (Dawn Pubns.).
—The Tree That Bear Climbed, 1 vol. Rietz, Kathleen, illus. 2012. 32p. (J). (gr. -1-3). (ENG.). 17.95 *(978-1-60718-528-4(8))*; (SPA.). pap. 11.95 *(978-1-62855-426-7(6)*, 9f77be8a-74b8-4060-9de5-9f55de276c05); (ENG.). pap. 9.95 *(978-1-60718-537-6(7))* Arbordale Publishing.
Bernal, Mitchell. Skelanimals: Dead Animals Need Love Too Bernal, Mitchell, illus. l.t. ed. 2005. (Illus.). 22p. (J). per. 12.95 *(978-0-9766621-0-5(8)*, 818 554-8965) Worn Pants.
Bernstrom, Daniel. One Day in the Eucalyptus, Eucalyptus Tree. Wenzel, Brendan, illus. 2016. (ENG.). 32p. (J). (gr. -1-3). 17.99 *(978-0-06-235485-3(X)*, HarperCollins) HarperCollins Pubs.
Berry, Lynne. What Floats in a Moat? Cordell, Matthew, illus. 2013. (ENG.). 48p. (J). (gr. k-4). 19.99 *(978-1-4169-9763-4(6)*, Simon & Schuster Bks. For Young Readers) Simon & Schuster Bks. For Young Readers.
Berry, Ron. Can You Make Peter Rabbit Giggle? Sharp, Chris, illus. 2012. 10p. (J). bds. 10.99 *(978-0-8249-1418-9(X)*, Ideals Pubns.) Worthy Publishing.
Berry, Ron & Mead, David. All Aboard! Charlie the Can-Do Choo Choo. Sharp, Chris, illus. 2009. (ENG.). 8p. 12.99 *(978-0-8249-1420-2(1)*, Ideals Pubns.) Worthy Publishing.
Berthiaume, Donna M. Our Cool School Zoo Revue. Jirak, Tracey, illus. 2008. 36p. pap. 24.95 *(978-1-60672-672-3(2))* America Star Bks.
Bertram, Debbie & Bloom, Susan. The Best Book to Read. Garland, Michael, illus. 2011. 32p. (J). (gr. -1-2). pap. 7.99 *(978-0-375-87300-3(7)*, Dragonfly Bks.) Random Hse. Children's Bks.
—The Best Place to Read. Garland, Michael, illus. 2007. 32p. (J). (gr. -1-2). pap. 8.99 *(978-0-375-83757-9(4)*, Dragonfly Bks.) Random Hse. Children's Bks.
—The Best Place to Read. 2007. lib. bdg. 18.40 *(978-1-4177-9097-5(0))* Turtleback.
Bessesen, Brooke. Zachary Z. Packrat & His Amazing Collections. Campbell, Jenney, illus. 2008. 40p. (J). pap. 19.95 *(978-1-932082-83-8(2))* Arizona Highways.
Bianchini, Bob. Charlie Rides: Planes, Trains, Bikes, & More! 2017. (ENG., Illus.). 20p. (J). (gr. -1-k). bds. 8.95 *(978-1-4197-2292-9(1)*, 1156010, Abrams Appleseed) Abrams, Inc.
Bickell, Elaine. The Little Ghost Who Lost Her Boo! McGrath, Raymond, illus. 2020. (ENG.). 32p. (J). (gr. -1-3). 17.99 *(978-0-593-20215-9(5))* Flamingo Bks.
Biddulph, Rob. Happy Hatchday (Dinosaur Juniors, Book 1) 2019. (Dinosaur Juniors Ser.: 1). (ENG.). 32p. (J). 17.99 *(978-0-00-832550-3(2)*, HarperCollins Children's Bks.) HarperCollins Pubs. Ltd. GBR. Dist: HarperCollins Pubs.
—Odd Dog Out. Biddulph, Rob, illus. 2019. (ENG., Illus.). 32p. (J). (gr. -1-3). 17.99 *(978-0-06-236726-6(9)*, HarperCollins) HarperCollins Pubs.
Big Davie. The Lady & Her Cat As Told by Bigdavie: A simple easy reading bedtime story that will leave children with delightful images while drifting off to S. 2009. (Illus.). 28p. pap. 12.49 *(978-1-4389-3124-1(7))* AuthorHouse.
The Biggest Kiss. 2014. (Classic Board Bks.). (ENG., Illus.). 28p. (J). (gr. -1 — 1). bds. 7.99 *(978-1-4814-1751-8(7)*, Little Simon) Little Simon.
Bingham, Kelly. Shark Girl. 2010. (ENG., Illus.). 288p. (YA). (gr. 7). pap. 9.99 *(978-0-7636-4627-1(X))* Candlewick Pr.
Binkley, Carolyn. The Errand: And Stinkbugs & Grasshoppers Green. 2012. 24p. pap. 15.99 *(978-1-4691-6096-2(X))* Xlibris Corp.
Bird, Roy & Harp, Kim. Hark! I Hear a Meadowlark! Battis, Gwen, illus. 2013. 34p. 16.99 *(978-1-939054-08-1(7))*; 36p. pap. 10.99 *(978-1-939054-07-4(9))* Rowe Publishing.
Bird, Shelia May. My Auntie Susan. Postgate, Daniel, illus. 2008. (Tadpoles Ser.). (ENG.). 24p. (J). (gr. -1-3). pap. *(978-0-7787-3889-3(2))*; lib. bdg. *(978-0-7787-3858-9(2))* Crabtree Publishing Co.
Blabey, Aaron. Don't Call Me Bear! Blabey, Aaron, illus. 2019. (ENG., Illus.). 32p. (J). (gr. -1-k). 14.99 *(978-1-338-36002-8(7)*, Scholastic Pr.) Scholastic, Inc.

S

—Pig the Elf. 2017. (Pig the Pug Ser.). (ENG., Illus.). 32p. (J). (gr. -1-k). 14.99 (978-1-338-22122-0(1), Scholastic Pr.) Scholastic, Inc.
—Pig the Fibber. 2018. (Pig the Pug Ser.). (ENG.). 32p. (J). (gr. -1-k). 14.99 (978-1-338-29176-6(9), Scholastic Pr.) Scholastic, Inc.
—Pig the Monster. Blabey, Aaron, illus. 2021. (Pig the Pug Ser.). (ENG.). 32p. (J). (gr. -1-k). 14.99 (978-1-338-76401-7(2), Scholastic Pr.) Scholastic, Inc.
—Pig the Pug. 2016. (Pig the Pug Ser.). (ENG., Illus.). 32p. (J). (gr. -1-k). 14.99 (978-1-338-11245-0(7), Scholastic Pr.) Scholastic, Inc.
—Pig the Stinker. Blabey, Aaron, illus. 2019. (Pig the Pug Ser.). (ENG., Illus.). 32p. (J). (gr. -1-k). 14.99 (978-1-338-33754-9(8), Scholastic Pr.) Scholastic, Inc.
—Pig the Tourist. Blabey, Aaron, illus. 2020. (Pig the Pug Ser.). (ENG., Illus.). 32p. (J). (gr. -1-k). 14.99 (978-1-338-59339-6(0), Scholastic Pr.) Scholastic, Inc.
—Pig the Winner. 2017. (Pig the Pug Ser.). (ENG., Illus.). 32p. (J). (gr. -1-k). 14.99 (978-1-338-13638-8(0), Scholastic Pr.) Scholastic, Inc.
—Thelma the Unicorn. 2017. (ENG., Illus.). 28p. (J). (gr. -1-k). 14.99 (978-1-338-15842-7(2), Scholastic Pr.) Scholastic, Inc.
Blabey, Aaron, illus. Pig the Elf. 2017. 24p. (J). pap. (978-1-338-23004-8(2), Scholastic Pr.) Scholastic, Inc.
—Piranhas Don't Eat Bananas. 2019. (ENG.). 32p. (J). (gr. -1-k). 14.99 (978-1-338-29713-3(9), Scholastic Pr.) Scholastic, Inc.
Black, Joe. Afikomen Mambo. Prater, Linda, illus. 2011. (ENG.). 24p. (J). (gr. -1 — 1). pap. 8.95 (978-0-7613-5639-4(8), 65275eb0-fee4-487a-b2b1-39cb1ab217c7, Kar-Ben Publishing) Lerner Publishing Group.
Black, Michael Ian. Chicken Cheeks. Hawkes, Kevin, illus. 2009. (ENG.). 40p. (J). (gr. -1-3). 19.99 (978-1-4169-4864-3(3), Simon & Schuster Bks. For Young Readers) Simon & Schuster Bks. For Young Readers.
Black, Robyn Hood. Sir Mike. Murphy, David, illus. 2006. (Rookie Reader Skill Set Ser.). (ENG.). 32p. (J). (gr. k-2). per. 4.95 (978-0-516-25020-5(5), Children's Pr.) Scholastic Library Publishing.
Blackstone, Stella. Alligator Alphabet. Bauer, Stephanie, illus. (ENG.). (J). (gr. -1-k). 2007. 32p. bds. 9.99 (978-1-84686-073-7(3)) 2005. 48p. 16.99 (978-1-84148-494-5(6)) Barefoot Bks., Inc.
—Bear about Town / Oso en la Ciudad. Harter, Debbie, illus. 2010. (Bear Ser.). (ENG.). 24p. (J). (gr. -1-1). pap. 8.99 (978-1-84686-377-6(5)) Barefoot Bks., Inc.
—Bear at Home (Oso en Casa) Harter, Debbie, illus. 2010. 24p. (J). (gr. -1-1). pap. 7.99 (978-1-84686-422-3(4)) Barefoot Bks., Inc.
—Bear at Work. Harter, Debbie, illus. (ENG & SPA.). 24p. (J). (gr. -1-k). 2011. pap. 6.99 (978-1-84686-554-1(9)) 2008. pap. 8.99 (978-1-84686-110-9(1)) Barefoot Bks., Inc.
—Bear at Work (Oso en el Trabajo) 2012. (ENG & SPA., Illus.). 24p. (J). pap. 7.99 (978-1-84686-769-9(X)) Barefoot Bks., Inc.
—Bear in a Square / Oso en un Cuadrado. Harter, Debbie, illus. 2009. (Bear Ser.). (ENG.). 24p. (J). (gr. -1-1). pap. 8.99 (978-1-84686-387-5(2)) Barefoot Bks., Inc.
—Bear in Sunshine - Oso Bajo el Sol. Harter, Debbie, illus. 2009. (Bear Ser.). (ENG.). 24p. (J). (gr. -1-1). pap. 8.99 (978-1-84686-389-9(9)) Barefoot Bks., Inc.
—Bear on a Bike / Oso en Bicicleta. Harter, Debbie, illus. 2014. (Bear Ser.). (ENG.). 32p. (J). (gr. -1-1). pap. 8.99 (978-1-78285-079-3(1)) Barefoot Bks., Inc.
—Bear Takes a Trip. Harter, Debbie, illus. 2012. (Bear Ser.). (ENG.). 24p. (J). (gr. -1-1). bds. 8.99 (978-1-84686-757-6(6)) Barefoot Bks., Inc.
—Bear's Birthday. Harter, Debbie, illus. 2011.Tr. of El Cumpleanos de Oso. 24p. (J). (gr. -1-1). pap. 6.99 (978-1-84686-515-2(8)) Barefoot Bks., Inc.
—Bear's Busy Family / la Familia Ocupada de Oso. Harter, Debbie, illus. 2014. (Bear Ser.). (ENG.). 32p. (J). (gr. -1-1). pap. 8.99 (978-1-84686-771-2(1)) Barefoot Bks., Inc.
—Cleo in the Snow. Mockford, Caroline, illus. 2013. 24p. (J). pap. 6.99 (978-1-78285-055-7(4)); bds. 6.99 (978-1-78285-054-0(6)) Barefoot Bks., Inc.
—Cleo on the Move. Mockford, Caroline, illus. 2013. 24p. (J). bds. 6.99 (978-1-78285-056-4(2)) Barefoot Bks., Inc.
—Cleo's Color Book. Mockford, Caroline, illus. 2006. 0032p. (J). 15.99 (978-1-905236-30-5(1)) Barefoot Bks., Inc.
—A Dragon on the Doorstep. Harter, Debbie, illus. (ENG.). 32p. (J). 2006. pap. 9.99 (978-1-905236-66-4(2)) 2006. (gr. -1-k). pap. 6.99 (978-1-84686-032-4(6)) 2005. (gr. -1-1). 15.99 (978-1-84148-227-9(7)) Barefoot Bks., Inc.
—La Familia Activa de Oso. Sarfatti, Esther, tr. Harter, Debbie, illus. 2003. (Bear Ser.). (SPA.). 24p. (J). pap. 6.99 (978-1-84148-777-9(5)) Barefoot Bks., Inc.
—La Famille Active de l'Ours. 2012.Tr. of Bear's Busy Family. (FRE & ENG., Illus.). (J). pap. 6.99 (978-1-84686-772-9(X)) Barefoot Bks., Inc.
—I Dreamt I Was a Dinosaur. Beaton, Clare, illus. 2005. (ENG.). 32p. (J). (gr. -1-3). 15.99 (978-1-84148-238-5(2)) Barefoot Bks., Inc.
—I Spy the Sun in the Sky. 2009. (ENG., Illus.). (J). 14.99 (978-1-84686-276-2(0)) Barefoot Bks., Inc.
—An Island in the Sun. 2016. (ENG.). 32p. (J). (gr. -1-k). bds. 14.99 (978-1-78285-285-8(9)) Barefoot Bks., Inc.
—Jump into January. Carluccio, Maria, illus. 2004. (ENG.). 32p. (J). 15.99 (978-1-84148-629-1(9)) Barefoot Bks., Inc.
—L'Ours au Travail. 2012.Tr. of Bear at Work. (FRE & ENG.). (J). 6.99 (978-1-84686-770-5(3)) Barefoot Bks., Inc.
—My Granny Went to Market. Corr, Christopher, illus. 2006. (ENG.). 24p. (J). (gr. -1-2). pap. 9.99 (978-1-905236-62-6(X)) Barefoot Bks., Inc.
—My Granny Went to Market: A Round-the-World Counting Rhyme. Corr, Christopher, illus. 2005. (ENG.). 24p. (J). 16.99 (978-1-84148-792-2(9)) Barefoot Bks., Inc.
—On y Danse les Saisons. Carluccio, Maria, illus. 2016. (FRE.). (J). pap. (978-1-78285-298-8(0)) Barefoot Bks., Inc.
—Oso Bajo el Sol. Sarfatti, Esther, tr. Harter, Debbie, illus. 2003. (Bear Ser.). (SPA.). 24p. (J). pap. 6.99 (978-1-84148-778-6(3)) Barefoot Bks., Inc.
—Oso en Bicicleta. Sarfatti, Esther, tr. Harter, Debbie, illus. 2003. (Bear Ser.). (SPA.). 32p. (J). pap. 6.99 (978-1-84148-775-5(9)) Barefoot Bks., Inc.
—Oso en Casa. Sarfatti, Esther, tr. Harter, Debbie, illus. 2003. (Bear Ser.). (SPA.). 24p. (J). pap. 6.99 (978-1-84148-779-3(1)) Barefoot Bks., Inc.
—Oso en la Ciudad. Sarfatti, Esther, tr. Harter, Debbie, illus. 2003. (Bear Ser.). (SPA.). 24p. (J). pap. 6.99 (978-1-84148-776-2(7)) Barefoot Bks., Inc.
—Oso en un Cuadrado. Sarfatti, Esther, tr. Harter, Debbie, illus. 2003. (Bear Ser.). (SPA.). 24p. (J). pap. 6.99 (978-1-84148-774-8(0)) Barefoot Bks., Inc.
—Un Recorrido Por Los Estaciones. Carluccio, Maria, illus. 2009. (SPA.). 32p. (J). (gr. -1-2). pap. 9.99 (978-1-84686-291-5(4)) Barefoot Bks., Inc.
—Secret Seahorse. Beaton, Clare, illus. 2005. (ENG.). (J). (gr. -1-2). 24p. bds. 8.99 (978-1-905236-15-2(8)); 24p. 15.99 (978-1-84148-704-5(X)); 32p. pap. 9.99 (978-1-84148-937-7(9)) Barefoot Bks., Inc.
—Ship Shapes. Bell, Siobhan, illus. 2006. (J). 0024p. 15.99 (978-1-905236-34-3(4)); (978-1-4156-6474-2(9)) Barefoot Bks., Inc.
—Ship Shapes. 2012. lib. bdg. 17.20 (978-0-606-23826-7(3)) Turtleback.
—Skip Through the Seasons. Carluccio, Maria, illus. 2006. (ENG.). 32p. (J). (gr. -1-k). pap. 9.99 (978-1-905236-71-8(9)) Barefoot Bks., Inc.
—Talk with Me! Mockford, Caroline, illus. 2009. (ENG.). 14p. (J). (gr. -1). 7.99 (978-1-84686-180-2(2)) Barefoot Bks., Inc.
—Walk with Me! Mockford, Caroline, illus. 2009. (ENG.). 14p. (J). (gr. -1). bds. 7.99 (978-1-84686-179-6(9)) Barefoot Bks., Inc.
—Walking Through the Jungle. Harter, Debbie, illus. 2004. (ENG.). 32p. (J). (gr. -1-k). pap. 6.99 (978-1-84148-548-5(9)) Barefoot Bks., Inc.
—Walking Through the Jungle. Harter, Debbie, illus. 2004. (ENG.). 32p. (J). 9.99 (978-1-84148-182-1(3)) Barefoot Bks., Inc.
—Who Are You, Baby Kangaroo? Beaton, Clare, illus. 2004. (ENG.). 32p. (J). 14.99 (978-1-84148-217-0(X)) Barefoot Bks., Inc.
—Who Are You Baby Kangaroo? Beaton, Clare, illus. 2011. (ENG.). 32p. (J). (gr. -1-2). pap. 6.99 (978-1-84686-190-1(X)) Barefoot Bks., Inc.
Blackstone, Stella & Barefoot Books Staff. An Island in the Sun. Ceccoli, Nicoletta, illus. 2005. (ENG.). 24p. (J). pap. 6.99 (978-1-84148-079-4(7)) Barefoot Bks., Inc.
Blackstone, Stella & Bass, Jules. Hay una Vaca Entre las Coles. Beaton, Clare, illus. 2003.Tr. of There's a Cow in the Cabbage Patch. (SPA.). 32p. (J). (gr. k-2). pap. 6.99 (978-1-84148-965-0(4)) Barefoot Bks., Inc.
Blackstone, Stella & Bauer, Stephanie. Octopus Opposites. Bauer, Stephanie, illus. 2010. (Illus.). 32p. (J). (gr. -1). 16.99 (978-1-84686-328-8(7)) Barefoot Bks., Inc.
Blackstone, Stella & Harter, Debbie. Bear Takes a Trip. 2012. (Illus.). 24p. (J). (gr. -1-1). pap. 6.99 (978-1-84686-756-9(8)) Barefoot Bks., Inc.
—Who Are You? Harter, Debbie, illus. 2003. (Illus.). 24p. (J). (gr. k-2). bds. 6.99 (978-1-84148-609-3(4)) Barefoot Bks., Inc.
Blackstone, Stella & Parker, Elizabeth. L'Ours Fait un Voyage. Harter, Debbie, illus. 2013.Tr. of Bear Takes a Trip. (FRE & ENG.). 24p. (J). (gr. k-1). pap. 6.99 (978-1-84686-946-4(3)) Barefoot Bks., Inc.
Blahitka, Vira. Joad the Toad. 2013. 32p. pap. (978-1-4602-1881-5(7)) FriesenPress.
Blake, Quentin. Quentin Blake's ABC. 2014. lib. bdg. 24.50 (978-0-606-31770-2(8)) Turtleback.
Bland, Nick. The Very Cranky Bear. Bland, Nick, illus. 2014. (ENG., Illus.). 32p. (J). (gr. -1-k). 17.99 (978-0-545-61269-2(1), Orchard Bks.) Scholastic, Inc.
Blatt, Jane. Books Always Everywhere. Massini, Sarah, illus. 2013. (J). (978-0-385-37535-1(2)) Random Hse., Inc.
Blevins, James. The Crones. Whittaker, Stephen, illus. 2008. 36p. pap. 24.95 (978-1-60610-259-6(1)) America Star Bks.
Bliss, Ryan T. Mooseclumps. Bliss, Ryan T., illus. 2013. (Illus.). 58p. 15.99 (978-0-615-75521-2(6)) Artsy Bee, LLC.
Bloom, Suzanne. Number Slumber. 2016. (ENG., Illus.). 40p. (J). (gr. -1-k). 16.95 (978-1-62979-557-7(7), Astra Young Readers) Astra Publishing Hse.
Blowers, Norman. Christmas with Carly. 2008. 16p. pap. 11.50 (978-1-60693-337-4(X), Strategic Bk. Publishing) Strategic Book Publishing & Rights Agency (SBPRA).
Bloxam, Frances. Beau Beaver Goes to Town. Sollers, Jim, illus. 2009. (ENG.). 32p. (J). (gr. -1-3). 16.95 (978-0-89272-792-6(6)) Down East Bks.
Bluemle, Elizabeth. How Do You Wokka-Wokka? Cecil, Randy, illus. 2012. (ENG.). 32p. (J). (gr. -1-2). pap. 7.99 (978-0-7636-6085-7(X)) Candlewick Pr.
—Tap Tap Boom Boom. Karas, G. Brian, illus. 2014. (ENG.). 32p. (J). (gr. -1-2). 17.99 (978-0-7636-5696-6(8)) Candlewick Pr.
Blum, Denise. Anything Is Possible: The Ben Carson Story. Rea, Nathan, illus. 2015. (ENG.). 28p. (J). pap. 10.00 (978-0-9899479-1-6(2)) Mainstay Publishing.
Bock, Suzanne, illus. Meet the Angels l.t. ed. 2004. 10p. (J). bds. 12.99 (978-0-9758709-4-5(7), 13401) Journey Stone Creations, LLC.
Bodoh, Tony. Hannah's Animal Farm. 2008. 28p. pap. 14.95 (978-1-4327-2046-9(5)) Outskirts Pr., Inc.
Boedoe, Geefwee. Arrowville. Boedoe, Geefwee, illus. 2004. (Illus.). 40p. (J). (gr. -1-2). 16.89 (978-0-06-055599-3(8), Geringer, Laura Book) HarperCollins Pubs.
Bogart, Jo Ellen. Count Your Chickens. Smith, Lori Joy, illus. 2017. 32p. (J). (-k). 16.99 (978-1-77049-792-4(7), Tundra Bks.) Tundra Bks. CAN. Dist: Penguin Random Hse. LLC.
Bompart, Juanita A. Anna Pinnelope Poolah. 2011. 32p. pap. 16.95 (978-1-4497-2335-4(7), WestBow Pr.) Author Solutions, LLC.
Bond, Juliana. Pixie Tales the Wobbly Tooth. 2005. 30p. spiral bd. 12.08 (978-1-4116-6046-5(3)) Lulu Pr., Inc.
—Salad Cream. 2005. 31p. spiral bd. 12.28 (978-1-4116-6047-2(1)) Lulu Pr., Inc.
Bond, Michael. Paddington Bear Goes to Market Board Book. Alley, R. W., illus. 2014. (Paddington Ser.). (ENG.). 14p. (J). (gr. -1-3). bds. 7.99 (978-0-06-231722-3(9), HarperFestival) HarperCollins Pubs.
Boniface, William & Sullivan, Don. The Adventures of Max the Minnow. 2015. (ENG., Illus.). 26p. (J). bds. 9.99 (978-1-4494-6490-5(4)) Andrews McMeel Publishing.
Bookins, Daddy. Outsdide with Lil Boo. Piotti, Dania, illus. 2012. 38p. pap. 13.50 (978-0-9848019-3-0(6)) Inkwell Books LLC.
Boom Boom. 2014. (ENG., Illus.). 40p. (J). (gr. -1-3). 17.99 (978-1-4424-3412-7(0), Beach Lane Bks.) Beach Lane Bks.
Booth, Anne. The Christmas Fairy. Beardshaw, Rosalind, illus. 2017. (ENG.). 32p. (J). (gr. -1-2). 15.99 (978-0-7636-9629-0(3)) Candlewick Pr.
—I Want a Friend. Proud, Amy, illus. 2017. (ENG.). 32p. (J). pap. 10.99 (978-0-7459-7706-5(5), d322e2dd-abd5-495f-bf57-6714fdca9910, Lion Children's) Lion Hudson PLC GBR. Dist: Baker & Taylor Publisher Services (BTPS).
Boston Weatherford, Carole. Freedom in Congo Square. Christie, R. Gregory, illus. 2016. (ENG.). 40p. (J). (gr. -1-3). 17.99 (978-1-4998-0103-3(3)) Little Bee Books Inc.
Bostrom, Kathleen Long. Count Your Blessings. Reed, Lisa, illus. 2017. (VeggieTales Ser.). (ENG.). 20p. (J). (gr. -1-k). bds. 7.99 (978-0-8249-1664-0(6)) Worthy Publishing.
—The View at the Zoo. Francis, Guy, illus. 2019. (ENG.). 26p. (J). (gr. -1-1). bds. 7.99 (978-0-8249-1690-9(5), Worthy Kids/Ideals) Worthy Publishing.
—The View at the Zoo. 2015. (ENG., Illus.). 32p. (J). pap. 7.99 (978-0-8249-5669-1(9), Ideals Pubns.) Worthy Publishing.
Bourne, Eula E. The Conchman & the Fisherman. 2008. (ENG., Illus.). 28p. pap. 14.99 (978-1-4389-0541-9(6)) AuthorHouse.
Bousquet, Anthea. Counting St. Lucian Style: A delightfully illustrated counting rhyme set in the Caribbean island of St. Lucia. Sandiford, Ted, illus. 2011. 16p. (J). pap. (978-976-8238-01-6(1)) Maryli Pubs.
Bove, Candace Scobie. Calypso: A Day in the Life of a Puppy. 2012. 24p. 24.95 (978-1-4626-4122-2(9)) America Star Bks.
Bower, Kevin. Gilbert Grumble. 2009. (Illus.). 28p. pap. 13.99 (978-1-4490-3841-0(7)) AuthorHouse.
Bowie, C. W. Busy Fingers. Willingham, Fred, illus. 2004. (ENG.). 28p. (J). (gr. -1 — 1). bds. 7.95 (978-1-58089-048-9(2)) Charlesbridge Publishing, Inc.
Bowman, Crystal. Mommy, May I Hug the Fish?, 1 vol. Christensen, Donna, illus. 2007. (I Can Read! Ser.).Tr. of Mamá, Puedo Abrazar Al Pez? (ENG.). 32p. (J). (gr. -1-1). pap. 4.99 (978-0-310-71468-2(0)) Zonderkidz.
—My Christmas Stocking: Filled with God's Love, 1 vol. Gevry, Claudine, illus. 2015. (ENG.). 14p. (J). bds. 6.99 (978-0-310-73823-7(7)) Zonderkidz.
—My Happy Pumpkin: God's Love Shining Through Me, 1 vol. 2014. (ENG.). 14p. (J). bds. 6.99 (978-0-310-73828-2(8)) Zonderkidz.
—Thank You, God, for This Day. Fletcher, Rusty, illus. 2014. (Happy Day Ser.). (ENG.). 16p. (J). pap. 2.49 (978-1-4143-9486-2(1), 4608476, Happy Day) Tyndale Hse. Pubs.
Boynton, Colin. Tommy & the Dust Devils. 2010. 19p. 16.50 (978-0-9559931-2-1(1)) Boynton, Colin GBR. Dist: Lulu Pr., Inc.
Boynton, Sandra. Are You a Cow? Boynton, Sandra, illus. 2012. (ENG., Illus.). 16p. (J). (gr. -1-k). bds. 6.99 (978-1-4424-1733-5(1)) Simon & Schuster, Inc.
—The Going to Bed Book. Boynton, Sandra, illus. 2006. (ENG., Illus.). 14p. (J). bds. 12.95 (978-1-4169-2794-5(8), Little Simon) Little Simon.
—Hey! Wake Up! 2004. (Illus.). (J). (gr. -1-18). spiral bd., bds. (978-0-616-14611-8(6)) Canadian National Institute for the Blind/Institut National Canadien pour les Aveugles.
—Hippos Go Berserk! Boynton, Sandra, illus. 2009. (ENG., Illus.). 32p. (J). 9.99 (978-1-4169-9619-4(2), Little Simon) Little Simon.
—Little Pookie. Boynton, Sandra, illus. 2017. (Little Pookie Ser.). (ENG., Illus.). 18p. (J). (gr. -1-k). bds. 6.99 (978-1-4814-9768-8(5)) Simon & Schuster, Inc.
—Moo, Baa, La La La! braille ed. 2004. (J). (gr. 1). spiral bd., bds. (978-0-616-03082-0(7)) Canadian National Institute for the Blind/Institut National Canadien pour les Aveugles.
—Muu, Beee, ¡Así Fue! (Moo, Baa, la la La!) Boynton, Sandra, illus. 2003. (SPA., Illus.). 16p. (J). (gr. -1-k). bds. 6.99 (978-0-689-86302-8(0)) Simon & Schuster, Inc.
—Sandra Boynton's Moo, Baa, la la La! Boynton, Sandra, illus. 2009. (ENG., Illus.). 16p. (J). bds. 16.99 (978-1-4169-5035-6(4), Little Simon) Little Simon.
—What's Wrong, Little Pookie? Boynton, Sandra, illus. 2017. (Little Pookie Ser.). (ENG., Illus.). 18p. (J). (gr. -1-k). bds. 6.99 (978-1-4814-9769-5(3)) Simon & Schuster, Inc.
—Woo Hoo! You're Doing Great! 2023. (ENG., Illus.). 40p. (J). (gr. k-3). 17.99 (978-0-316-48679-8(5)) Little, Brown Bks. for Young Readers.
Bradley, Timothy J. Teddy Bear, Teddy Bear, Say Good Night. Medina, Conni & Stark, Kristy, eds. 2009. (Early Literacy Ser.). (ENG., Illus.). 16p. (gr. -1-1). 19.99 (978-1-4333-1472-8(X)) Teacher Created Materials, Inc.
—Teddy Bear, Teddy Bear, Say Good Night, 1 vol. rev. ed. 2009. (Early Literacy Ser.). (ENG., Illus.). 16p. (gr. -1-1). 6.99 (978-1-4333-1471-1(1)) Teacher Created Materials, Inc.
Brady, Karen. God Is Great: A Collection of 13 Story Book Poems, 1. l.t. ed. 2004. (Illus.). 20p. (J). 12.50 (978-0-9754169-0-7(1)) Bradybooks.biz.
Bramsen, Carin. Just a Duck? 2018. (Illus.). 34p. (J). (— 1). bds. 7.99 (978-1-5247-6600-9(3), Random Hse. Bks. for Young Readers) Random Hse. Children's Bks.
—Sleepover Duck! Bramsen, Carin, illus. 2018. (Illus.). 40p. (J). (gr. -1-2). 17.99 (978-0-385-38417-9(3), Random Hse. Bks. for Young Readers) Random Hse. Children's Bks.
Bramwell, Wendie, et al. The Friendship Alphabet. Ziegler, Michael, illus. Ziegler, Michael, photos by. 2003. 32p. (J). pap. (978-0-9741388-3-1(5)) Committee for Children.
Brannon, Pat. Has a Donkey Ever Brought You Breakfast in Bed? Demming, Karen, illus. 2012. 38p. pap. 10.00 (978-1-938634-90-1(X)) Freedom of Speech Publishing, Inc.
Braud, Alexis. Parade, 1 vol. 2016. (ENG., Illus.). 32p. (J). (gr. -1-3). 16.99 (978-1-4556-2148-4(X), Pelican Publishing) Arcadia Publishing.
Breathed, Berkeley. Edwurd Fudwupper Fibbed Big. 2003. (ENG., Illus.). 40p. (J). (gr. 1-4). pap. 10.99 (978-0-316-14425-4(8)) Little, Brown Bks. for Young Readers.
Bremmer, Patricia A. The Christmas Westie. 2007. 48p. (J). kivar 17.99 (978-0-9745884-5-2(8)) Windcall Publishing.
Bremner-Lewis, P. L. My Friend, the Unicorn. 2009. 28p. pap. 12.95 (978-1-4389-8966-2(0)) AuthorHouse.
Brennan, Eileen. Bad Astrid: Read & Listen Edition. Dunnick, Regan, illus. 2013. (ENG.). 40p. (J). (gr. -1-2). E-Book (978-0-449-81427-7(0), Random Hse. Bks. for Young Readers) Random Hse. Children's Bks.
Brennan, Linda Crotta. Marshmallow Kisses. Takabayashi, Mari, illus. 2007. (ENG.). 32p. (J). (gr. -1-3). 6.95 (978-0-618-80903-5(1), 410103, Clarion Bks.) HarperCollins Pubs.
Brennan, Martin. I Saw It in the Garden. Monroe, Michael Glenn, illus. 2006. 32p. (J). (gr. -1-3). 17.95 (978-1-58726-296-8(7), Mitten Pr.) Ann Arbor Editions LLC.
Brennan-Nelson, Denise. Buzzy the Bumblebee. Monroe, Michael Glenn, illus. 2003. (ENG.). 32p. (J). (gr. 1-4). pap. 6.95 (978-1-58536-166-3(6), 202260) Sleeping Bear Pr.
—Good Night, Forest. Bucci, Marco, illus. 2018. (ENG.). 32p. (J). (gr. -1-2). 16.99 (978-1-58536-388-9(X), 204410) Sleeping Bear Pr.
—Good Night, Reindeer. Bucci, Marco, illus. 2017. (ENG.). 32p. (J). (gr. -1-2). 16.99 (978-1-58536-370-4(7), 204329) Sleeping Bear Pr.
—He's Been a Monster All Day. Moore, Cyd, illus. 2013. (ENG.). 32p. (J). (gr. -1-1). 14.99 (978-1-58536-827-3(X), 202363) Sleeping Bear Pr.
—Teach Me to Love. 2014. (ENG., Illus.). 24p. (J). (gr. -1-1). 12.99 (978-1-58536-858-7(X), 203671) Sleeping Bear Pr.
Brennan-Nelson, Denise & Bucci, Marco. Good Night, Library. 2019. (ENG., Illus.). 32p. (J). (gr. -1-2). 16.99 (978-1-58536-406-0(1), 204658) Sleeping Bear Pr.
Brennan, Sarah. A Dirty Story. Harrison, Harry, illus. 2012. (ENG.). 24p. (J). 21.95 (978-1-937160-26-5(2)) Eliassen Creative.
—An Even Dirtier Story. Harrison, Harry, illus. 2012. (ENG.). 24p. (J). 21.95 (978-1-937160-27-2(0)) Eliassen Creative.
—The Tale of a Dark Horse. 2013. (ENG., Illus.). 32p. (J). 24.95 (978-1-937160-57-9(2)) Eliassen Creative.
—The Tale of Chester Choi. Harrison, Harry, illus. 2013. (ENG.). 32p. (J). 24.95 (978-1-937160-16-6(5)) Eliassen Creative.
—The Tale of Oswald Ox. Harrison, Harry, illus. 2012. (ENG.). 32p. (J). (978-1-937160-24-1(6)) Auspicious Times.
—The Tale of Pin Yin Panda. Harrison, Harry, illus. 2012. (ENG.). 32p. (J). 24.95 (978-1-937160-15-9(7)) Eliassen Creative.
—The Tale of Rhonda Rabbit. Harrison, Harry, illus. 2012. (ENG.). 32p. (J). 24.95 (978-1-937160-22-7(X)) Eliassen Creative.
—The Tale of Rodney Ram. Harrison, Harry, illus. 2014. (J). (978-1-937160-60-9(2)) Eliassen Creative.
—The Tale of Run Run Rat. Harrison, Harry, illus. 2012. (ENG.). 32p. (J). 24.95 (978-1-937160-25-8(4)) Eliassen Creative.
—The Tale of Temujin. Harrison, Harry, illus. 2012. (ENG.). 32p. (J). (978-1-937160-23-4(8)) Auspicious Times.
Brenner, Barbara. Good Morning, Garden. Ortakales, Denise, illus. 2004. (ENG.). 32p. (J). (gr. -1-k). 15.95 (978-1-55971-888-2(9)) Cooper Square Publishing Llc.
Brenner, Barbara & Sweet, Melissa. The Plant That Kept on Growing. 2015. (ENG., Illus.). 34p. (J). pap. 11.95 (978-1-899694-59-4(5), ipicturebooks) ibooks, Inc.
Brenner, Emily. On the First Day of Grade School. Whatley, Bruce, illus. 2004. 32p. (J). (gr. -1-1). lib. bdg. 16.89 (978-0-06-051041-1(2)) HarperCollins Pubs.
Brett, Jan. The Twelve Days of Christmas. Brett, Jan, illus. 2004. (ENG., Illus.). 32p. (J). (gr. -1 — 1). bds. 8.99 (978-0-399-24329-5(1), G.P. Putnam's Sons Books for Young Readers) Penguin Young Readers Group.
BrickHouse Education. Guess Who: Whose Silhouette Is This? 2010. (J). pap. 8.99 (978-1-59835-139-2(7)) Cambridge BrickHouse, Inc.
BrickHouse Education & Colón, Priscilla. Wild ABC's. 2009. 40p. (J). 8.99 (978-1-59835-116-3(8)) Cambridge BrickHouse, Inc.
Bridge, Chris Helene. The Same Heart. 2015. (ENG., Illus.). 32p. (J). 19.95 (978-1-942945-06-2(X), ab5ff38e-fd54-4dec-9465-debe103cfacc) Night Heron Media.
Briggs-Greenberg, Ruthie. Felicity the Dragon. 2015. (ENG., Illus.). 32p. (J). (gr. -1-2). 15.95 (978-1-63076-062-5(5)) Taylor Trade Publishing.
Bright, Rachel. The Koala Who Could. Field, Jim, illus. 2017. (ENG.). 32p. (J). (gr. -1-k). 18.99 (978-1-338-13908-2(8), Scholastic Pr.) Scholastic, Inc.
Briley, Randy W. Big Pigs & Sock Dances. 2013. 36p. pap. 10.99 (978-0-9896269-2-7(X)) Raven Mad Studios.
Brimner, Larry Dane. Monkey Math. Kulka, Joe, illus. 2007. (Rookie Reader Skill Set Ser.). (ENG.). 32p. (J). (gr. k-2). pap. 4.95 (978-0-531-13850-2(X)) Scholastic Library Publishing.
Britland, Jan. The Adventures of Rodger Dodger Dog. Swaim, Michael, illus. 2009. 40p. pap. 15.95 (978-1-936051-23-6(0)) Peppertree Pr., The.
Broach, Elise. Barnyard Baby. Doerrfeld, Cori, illus. 2013. (Baby Seasons Ser.). (ENG.). 14p. (J). (gr. -1 — 1). bds. 7.99 (978-0-316-21203-8(2)) Little, Brown Bks. for Young Readers.
Broadbent, Tom & Kosmo, Lisa. Henrietta. 2009. pap. (978-1-61623-033-3(9)) Independent Pub.
Brochmann, Holly & Bowen, Leah. A Feel Better Book for Little Tears. Ng-Benitez, Shirley, illus. 2019. (ENG.). 32p. (J). (978-1-4338-3031-0(0), Magination Pr.) American Psychological Assn.
—A Feel Better Book for Little Tempers. Ng-Benitez, Shirley, illus. 2018. 32p. (J). (978-1-4338-2817-1(0)) American Psychological Assn.
—A Feel Better Book for Little Worriers. Ng-Benitez, Shirley, illus. 2017. 32p. (J). 15.95 (978-1-4338-2718-1(2), Magination Pr.) American Psychological Assn.
Brockett, Keith. Ollie on Stage. King, Ashley, illus. 2019. (ENG.). 32p. (J). (gr. k-3). 16.99 (978-1-58536-401-5(0), 204657) Sleeping Bear Pr.
Brodsky, Kathy. A CatFish Tale. Bennett, Cameron, illus. 2012. (ENG.). (J). 19.99 (978-0-9828529-3-4(2)) Helpingwords.
—Just Sniffing Around. Bennett, Cameron, illus. 2009. (ENG.). 40p. 19.99 (978-0-578-03620-5(7)) Helpingwords.

—Mi Árbol Doblado. Bennett, Cameron, illus. 2017.Tr. of My Bent Tree. (SPA & ENG.). (J). (gr. -1-4). 1995.00 *(978-0-9977922-0-1(5))* Helpingwords.

—My Bent Tree. Bennett, Cameron, illus. 2008. (ENG.). 44p. (J). 19.95 *(978-0-615-16066-5(2))* Helpingwords.

Brody, Lazer. The Worry Worm. Shapiro, Rebecca, illus. 2007. 26p. (J). 26.95 *(978-0-9797530-1-5(5))* Kalcom Publishing.

Brooks, David. You Can Count at the Ocean. 2005. (You Can Count Ser.). (ENG., Illus.). 24p. (J). (gr. -1 — 1). bds. 7.95 *(978-1-55971-930-8(3))* Cooper Square Publishing Llc.

—You Can Count in the Jungle. 2005. (You Can Count Ser.). (ENG., Illus.). 24p. (J). (gr. -1 — 1). bds. 6.95 *(978-1-55971-931-5(1))* Cooper Square Publishing Llc.

Brooks, Susie. 5 Cheeky Monkeys. Tarbett, Debbie, illus. 2016. (J). *(978-1-84857-539-4(4))* Little Tiger Pr. Group.

Brosnan, Paris & Lerway, Paris. Billy Bee: Sugarplums & Honey. 2017. (ENG., Illus.). 27p. (J). pap. 13.95 *(978-1-78710-075-6(8),* 07536626-b42a-4a60-b991-ab346949fafb) Austin Macauley Pubs. Ltd. GBR. Dist: Baker & Taylor Publisher Services (BTPS).

Brouillard, Anne. The Bathtub Prima Donna. Brouillard, Anne, illus. 2004. (Illus.). 24p. (J). (gr. k-4). reprint ed. 13.00 *(978-0-7567-7755-5(0))* DIANE Publishing Co.

Brown, Calef. Boy Wonders. Brown, Calef, illus. 2011. (ENG., Illus.). 40p. (J). (gr. -1-3). 16.99 *(978-1-4169-7877-0(1),* Atheneum Bks. for Young Readers) Simon & Schuster Children's Publishing.

Brown, Dan. Wild Symphony. Batori, Susan, illus. 2020. (ENG.). 44p. (J). (gr. -1-2). 19.99 *(978-0-593-12384-3(0),* Rodale Kids) Random Hse. Children's Bks.

Brown, Dan. Wild Symphony. Batori, Susan, illus. 2023. (ENG.). 44p. (J). (gr. -1-2). pap. 8.99 ***(978-0-593-70423-3(1),*** Dragonfly Bks.) Random Hse. Children's Bks.

Brown, Gina Bates. Zen & Bodhi's Snowy Day. Hinder, Sarah Jane, illus. 2014. (ENG.). 24p. (J). 15.95 *(978-1-61429-165-7(9))* Wisdom Pubns.

Brown, Jahla. Nathan Is Nathan. 2009. (ENG., Illus.). 20p. (J). pap. 19.95 *(978-0-9778083-8-0(6))* Everlasting Publishing.

Brown, Jason Robert. Tickety Tock. GrandPré, Mary, illus. 2008. 32p. (J). (gr. -1-3). lib. bdg. 18.89 *(978-0-06-078753-0(8),* Geringer, Laura Book) HarperCollins Pubs.

Brown, Margaret Wise. Christmas in the Barn. Dewdney, Anna, illus. 2016. (ENG.). 40p. (J). (gr. -1-3). 17.99 *(978-0-06-237986-3(0),* HarperCollins) HarperCollins Pubs.

—Christmas in the Barn: A Christmas Holiday Book for Kids. Goode, Diane, illus. 2007. (ENG.). 32p. (J). (gr. -1-3). per. 7.99 *(978-0-06-052636-8(X),* HarperCollins) HarperCollins Pubs.

—Goodnight Moon. Hurd, Clement, illus. (ENG.). 32p. (J). (gr. -1-3). 2005. lib. bdg. 18.89 *(978-0-06-077586-5(6))* 60th anniv. ed. 2007. 18.99 *(978-0-06-077585-8(8))* HarperCollins Pubs. (HarperCollins).

—Goodnight Moon. 2007. (J). (gr. -1-2). lib. bdg. 18.40 *(978-0-8085-9386-7(2))* Turtleback.

—Goodnight Moon 123: A Counting Book. Hurd, Clement, illus. 2007. (J). (ENG.). 32p. (gr. -1-k). 16.99 *(978-0-06-112593-5(8));* 32p. (gr. -1-k). lib. bdg. 17.89 *(978-0-06-112594-2(6));* *(978-1-4287-4853-8(9))* HarperCollins Pubs.

—Goodnight Moon 123/Buenas Noches, Luna 123: A Counting Book/un Libro para Contar. Hurd, Clement, illus. 2007. (ENG & SPA.). 32p. (J). (gr. -1-k). 16.99 *(978-0-06-117325-7(8),* Rayo) HarperCollins Pubs.

—Goodnight Moon Big Book. Hurd, Clement, illus. 2007. (ENG.). 32p. (J). (gr. -1-3). pap. 24.99 *(978-0-06-111977-4(6),* HarperCollins) HarperCollins Pubs.

—Goodnight Moon Cloth Book. Hurd, Clement, illus. 2012. (ENG.). 8p. (J). (gr. -1 — 1). pap. 14.99 *(978-0-06-076224-7(1),* HarperFestival) HarperCollins Pubs.

—Sleepy ABC. Katz, Karen, illus. 2009. (ENG.). 40p. (J). (gr. -1-3). 17.99 *(978-0-06-128863-0(2),* HarperCollins) HarperCollins Pubs.

—Sleepy ABC Board Book. Katz, Karen, illus. 2016. (ENG.). 32p. (J). (gr. -1 — 1). bds. 7.99 *(978-0-06-233793-1(9),* HarperFestival) HarperCollins Pubs.

—Two Little Trains. 2003. (ENG., Illus.). 32p. (J). (gr. -1-k). pap. 8.99 *(978-0-06-443568-0(7),* HarperCollins) HarperCollins Pubs.

—Where Have You Been? Dillon, Leo and Diane, illus. 2004. (ENG.). 32p. (J). (gr. -1-1). 16.99 *(978-0-06-028378-0(5),* HarperCollins) HarperCollins Pubs.

Brown, Skila. To Stay Alive: Mary Ann Graves & the Tragic Journey of the Donner Party. (ENG.). 304p. (J). (gr. 5-9). 2018. pap. 7.99 *(978-1-5362-0369-1(6))* 2016. (Illus.). 17.99 *(978-0-7636-7811-1(2))* Candlewick Pr.

Brown, Tameka Fryer. Around Our Way on Neighbors' Day. Riley-Webb, Charlotte, illus. 2010. (ENG.). 32p. (J). (gr. k-2). 17.95 *(978-0-8109-8971-9(9),* 678101) Abrams, Inc.

—My Cold Plum Lemon Pie Bluesy Mood. Evans, Shane, illus. 2013. 32p. (J). (gr. -1-2). 18.99 *(978-0-670-01285-5(8),* Viking Books for Young Readers) Penguin Young Readers Group.

Brown-Wood, Janay. Grandma's Tiny House. Burris, Priscilla, illus. 2017. 32p. (J). (-k). lib. bdg. 17.99 *(978-1-58089-712-9(6))* Charlesbridge Publishing, Inc.

Brownlow, Michael. Ten Little Monsters. Rickerty, Simon, illus. 2016. 30p. (J). *(978-1-4351-6405-5(9))* Barnes & Noble, Inc.

—Ten Little Princesses. Rickerty, Simon, illus. 2014. (J). *(978-1-4351-5735-4(4))* Barnes & Noble, Inc.

Brownlow, Mike. Ten Little Dinosaurs. 2016. (Ten Little Ser.). (ENG., Illus.). 32p. (J). (gr. -1-k). pap. *(978-1-4083-3401-0(1),* Orchard Bks.) Hachette Children's Group GBR. Dist: Hachette Bk. Group.

—Ten Little Elves. Rickerty, Simon, illus. 2016. (J). *(978-1-4351-6404-8(0))* Barnes & Noble, Inc.

Broyles, Beverly Ashley, illus. Grandmother's Alligator/Burukenge Wa Nyanya Activity Guide. 2005. (ENG & SWA.). (J). 12.95 *(978-0-9703632-7-5(3))* Wakefield Connection, The.

Bruel, Nick. A Bad Kitty Christmas: Includes Three Ready-To-Hang Ornaments! Bruel, Nick, illus. 2011. (Bad Kitty Ser.). (ENG., Illus.). 40p. (J). (gr. -1-3). 18.99 *(978-1-59643-668-8(9),* 900070722) Roaring Brook Pr.

—Bad Kitty Christmas Storytime Set. unabr. ed. 2014. (Bad Kitty Ser.). (ENG.). 40p. (J). 12.99 *(978-1-4272-5230-2(0),* 900144186) Macmillan Audio.

Brunette, Steffan. Cough, Achoo, & Roar! 2013. 16p. pap. 7.99 *(978-1-4624-0632-6(7),* Inspiring Voices) Author Solutions, LLC.

Bruss, Deborah. Good Morning, Snowplow! Johnson, Steve & Fancher, Lou, illus. 2018. (ENG.). 32p. (J). (gr. -1 — 1). 17.99 *(978-1-338-08949-3(8),* Levine, Arthur A. Bks.) Scholastic, Inc.

Bryan, Ashley. Can't Scare Me! Bryan, Ashley, illus. 2013. (ENG., Illus.). 40p. (J). (gr. -1-3). 16.99 *(978-1-4424-7657-8(5),* Atheneum Bks. for Young Readers) Simon & Schuster Children's Publishing.

—Who Built the Stable? A Nativity Poem. Bryan, Ashley, illus. 2012. (ENG., Illus.). 40p. (J). (gr. -1-3). 19.99 *(978-1-4424-0934-7(7),* Atheneum Bks. for Young Readers) Simon & Schuster Children's Publishing.

Bryan, Sean. A Boy & His Bunny. Murphy, Tom, illus. 2011. (ENG.). 32p. (J). (gr. -1-k). 14.95 *(978-1-61145-023-1(3),* 611023, Arcade Publishing) Skyhorse Publishing Co., Inc.

—A Girl & Her Gator. Murphy, Tom, illus. 2011. (ENG.). 32p. (J). (gr. -1-k). 14.95 *(978-1-61145-032-3(2),* 611032, Arcade Publishing) Skyhorse Publishing Co., Inc.

—The Juggling Pug. Murphy, Tom, illus. (ENG.). 32p. (J). 2014. (-k). 12.95 *(978-1-62873-596-3(1))* 2011. (gr. -1-k). 12.95 *(978-1-61608-329-8(8),* 608329) Skyhorse Publishing Co., Inc. (Sky Pony Pr.).

Bryan, Sean & Murphy, Tom. A Bear & His Boy. 2011. (ENG., Illus.). 32p. (J). (gr. -1-k). 14.95 *(978-1-61145-027-9(6),* 611027, Arcade Publishing) Skyhorse Publishing Co., Inc.

Bryant, Janine. Yucky Green Beans. l.t. ed. 2005. 12p. (J). per. 5.00 *(978-0-9703474-8-0(0))* Pinnini Pubs.

Bryant, Jen. Kaleidoscope Eyes. 2010. 272p. (J). (gr. 3-7). 7.99 *(978-0-440-42190-0(X),* Yearling) Random Hse. Children's Bks.

Bryant, Laura J. Only God Can Make a Kitten, 1 vol. 2015. (ENG.). 32p. (J). 14.99 *(978-0-310-73170-2(4))* Zonderkidz.

Bryant, Phoebe. What Is That in the Air? A play date with Sayde. 2009. (Illus.). 28p. pap. 12.99 *(978-1-4490-2209-9(X))* AuthorHouse.

Buble, Brandee. O'Shae the Octopus. Liska, Eliska, illus. 2014. (ENG.). 32p. (J). (gr. -1-3). 15.95 *(978-1-927018-56-9(0))* Simply Read Bks. CAN. Dist: Ingram Publisher Services.

Buchanan, Sue & Shafer, Dana. Mud Pie Annie, 1 vol. Allen, Joy, illus. 2008. (I Can Read! Ser.). (ENG.). 32p. (J). (gr. -1-1). pap. 4.99 *(978-0-310-71572-6(5))* Zonderkidz.

Buck, Nola. A Christmas Goodnight: A Christmas Holiday Book for Kids. Wright, Sarah Jane, illus. 2011. (ENG.). 24p. (J). (gr. -1-k). 12.99 *(978-0-06-166491-5(X),* Tegen, Katherine Bks) HarperCollins Pubs.

Buckley, Richard. The Foolish Tortoise. Carle, Eric, illus. 2009. (World of Eric Carle Ser.). (ENG.). 24p. (J). (gr. -1-k). bds. 8.99 *(978-1-4169-7916-6(6),* Little Simon) Little Simon.

—The Foolish Tortoise: Book & CD. Carle, Eric, illus. 2013. (World of Eric Carle Ser.). (ENG.). 24p. (J). (gr. -1-3). pap. 10.99 *(978-1-4424-6638-8(3),* Little Simon) Little Simon.

—The Foolish Tortoise: Lap Edition. Carle, Eric, illus. 2013. (World of Eric Carle Ser.). (ENG.). 24p. (J). (gr. -1-k). bds. 12.99 *(978-1-4424-8990-5(1),* Little Simon) Little Simon.

—The Foolish Tortoise/Ready-To-Read Level 2, 1 vol. Carle, Eric, illus. 2015. (World of Eric Carle Ser.). (ENG.). 24p. (J). (gr. k-2). pap. 4.99 *(978-1-4814-3577-2(9),* 7a3ea40d-9930-41c6-98ec-71785d7c50af, Simon Spotlight) Simon Spotlight.

—The Greedy Python. 2012. (Eric Carle Ready-To-Read Ser.). lib. bdg. 13.55 *(978-0-606-26357-3(8))* Turtleback.

—The Greedy Python: Lap Edition. Carle, Eric, illus. 2013. (World of Eric Carle Ser.). (ENG.). 24p. (J). (gr. -1-k). bds. 12.99 *(978-1-4424-8991-2(X),* Little Simon) Little Simon.

—The Greedy Python/Ready-To-Read Level 1. Carle, Eric, illus. 2012. (World of Eric Carle Ser.). (ENG.). 24p. (J). (gr. -1-1). 17.99 *(978-1-4424-4577-2(7),* Simon Spotlight) Simon Spotlight.

Buckner, Andrew. Grand Poppa's Favorite Chair: No One Is As Special As You. Welker, Matthew S., illus. 2011. 48p. pap. 24.95 *(978-1-4560-8294-9(9))* America Star Bks.

Budds, Laura. Have You Ever Seen a Bear with a Purple Smile? Zimmerman, Kadie, illus. 2013. 16p. (J). 16.95 *(978-1-59152-114-3(9))* Farcountry Pr.

Budge, Robyn E. Whoda Thunkit: Rhyming Tales for the Young & Not So. 2013. 180p. pap. 15.95 *(978-1-4787-2097-3(2))* Outskirts Pr., Inc.

Budney, Blossom. N Is for Nursery, 1 vol. Bobri, Vladimir, illus. 2018. 32p. 20.00 *(978-1-85124-482-9(4))* Bodleian Library GBR. Dist: Chicago Distribution Ctr.

Buehner, Caralyn. Merry Christmas, Mr. Mouse. Buehner, Mark, illus. 2015. 40p. (J). (gr. -1-k). 17.99 *(978-0-8037-4010-5(7),* Dial Bks) Penguin Young Readers Group.

—Snowmen All Year. Buehner, Mark, illus. 2010. 32p. (J). (gr. -1-2). 17.99 *(978-0-8037-3383-1(6),* Dial Bks) Penguin Young Readers Group.

—Snowmen at Christmas. Buehner, Mark, illus. (J). (gr. -1 — 1). 2010. 28p. bds. 7.99 *(978-0-8037-3551-4(0))* 2005. 32p. 17.99 *(978-0-8037-2995-7(2))* Penguin Young Readers Group. (Dial Bks).

—Snowmen at Night. 2004. (Illus.). 26p. (J). (gr. -1 — 1). bds. 8.99 *(978-0-8037-3041-0(1),* Dial Bks) Penguin Young Readers Group.

—Snowmen at Play. Buehner, Mark, illus. 2013. 16p. (J). (gr. -1-k). 8.99 *(978-0-448-47782-4(3),* Grosset & Dunlap) Penguin Young Readers Group.

—Snowmen at Work. Buehner, Mark, illus. 2012. 32p. (J). (gr. -1-2). 18.99 *(978-0-8037-3579-8(0),* Dial Bks) Penguin Young Readers Group.

Buell, Janet. Sail Away, Little Boat. Ishida, Jui, illus. 2006. 32p. (J). 15.95 *(978-1-57505-821-4(9),* Carolrhoda Bks.) Lerner Publishing Group.

Buhlig Meister, Victoria. Tell Me a Story, Please, Mi-Mi! 2009. 36p. pap. 16.99 *(978-1-4389-2430-4(5))* AuthorHouse.

Bullard, Lisa. Not Enough Beds! A Christmas Alphabet Book. Oeltjenbruns, Joni, illus. 2004. (Picture Bks.). 32p. (J). (gr. -1-3). 15.95 *(978-1-57505-356-1(X),* Carolrhoda Bks.) Lerner Publishing Group.

Buller, Jon & Schade, Susan. I Love You, Good Night: Lap Edition. Pons, Bernadette, illus. 2013. (ENG.). 28p. (J). (gr. -1 — 1). bds. 12.99 *(978-1-4424-8539-6(6),* Little Simon) Little Simon.

Bunting, Eve. The Baby Shower. Love, Judy, illus. 2007. 28p. (J). (gr. -1-2). 15.95 *(978-1-58089-139-4(X))* Charlesbridge Publishing, Inc.

—The Bones of Fred Mcfee. Cyrus, Kurt, illus. 2005. (ENG.). 32p. (J). (gr. -1-3). pap. 7.99 *(978-0-15-205423-6(5),* 1196323, Clarion Bks.) HarperCollins Pubs.

—Flower Garden. Hewitt, Kathryn, illus. 2004. 28p. (gr. -1-2). 17.00 *(978-0-7569-4113-0(X))* Perfection Learning Corp.

—Girls a to Z. Bloom, Suzanne, illus. 2013. (ENG.). 32p. (J). (gr. k-2). pap. 7.95 *(978-1-62091-028-3(4),* Astra Young Readers) Astra Publishing Hse.

—Scary, Scary Halloween Gift Edition. Brett, Jan, illus. 2017. (ENG.). 40p. (J). (gr. -1-3). 8.99 *(978-0-544-88034-4(X),* 1651183, Clarion Bks.) HarperCollins Pubs.

—Whose Shoe? Ruzzier, Sergio, illus. 2015. (ENG.). 32p. (J). (gr. -1-3). 16.99 *(978-0-544-30210-5(9),* 1575895, Clarion Bks.) HarperCollins Pubs.

Burach, Ross. I Love My Tutu Too! (a Never Bored Book!) Burach, Ross, illus. 2020. (ENG., Illus.). 30p. (J). (gr. -1 — 1). bds. 7.99 *(978-1-338-50427-9(4),* Scholastic Pr.) Scholastic, Inc.

Burchfield, Cindy. Gimme, Gimme Moocher Marmots. Burchfield, Cindy, illus. 2007. (Illus.). 48p. per. 18.95 *(978-1-59858-457-8(X))* Dog Ear Publishing, LLC.

Burgess, Karin Whiting. It's Always a Good Day for Crabbing. 2005. (J). 16.95 *(978-0-9718303-4-9(7))* Flat Hammock Pr.

Burgess, Thornton W. The Adventures of Paddy the Beaver. 2008. 108p. per. 9.95 *(978-1-60312-502-4(7))* Aegypan.

Burkart, Jeff. Once Upon a Clear, Dark Night. 2011. (ENG.). 16p. pap. 2.49 *(978-0-7586-2579-3(0))* Concordia Publishing Hse.

Burke, Arlene Avery & Hamilton, Phyllis McAllister. Grandma's Fairy Tale Museum. 2009. 40p. pap. 21.99 *(978-1-4415-0607-8(1))* Xlibris Corp.

Burke, Zoe. CatBook. 2016. (ENG., Illus.). 24p. (J). bds. 10.95 *(978-0-7649-7371-0(1),* POMEGRANATE KIDS) Pomegranate Communications, Inc.

—Charley Harper's Animal Alphabet. Harper, Charley, illus. 2015. (ENG.). 24p. (J). bds. *(978-0-7649-7233-1(2))* Pomegranate Communications, Inc.

—Charley Harper's What's in the Coral Reef? A Nature Discovery Book. 2014. (ENG., Illus.). 34p. (J). 14.95 *(978-0-7649-6846-4(7))* Pomegranate Communications, Inc.

—Charley Harper's What's in the Rain Forest? A Nature Discovery Book. Harper, Charley, illus. 2013. 34p. (J). 14.95 *(978-0-7649-6584-5(0))* Pomegranate Communications, Inc.

—Charley Harper's What's in the Woods? A Nature Discovery Book. Harper, Charley, illus. 2013. (ENG.). 32p. (J). 14.95 *(978-0-7649-6453-4(4))* Pomegranate Communications, Inc.

—Owls & Loons. Inuit artists and printmakers of Kinngait Studios, illus. 2016. 24p. (J). bds. 10.95 *(978-0-7649-7542-4(0),* POMEGRANATE KIDS) Pomegranate Communications, Inc.

Burleigh, Robert. Clang! Clang! Beep! Beep! Listen to the City. Giacobbe, Beppe, illus. 2009. (ENG.). 32p. (J). (gr. -1-2). 19.99 *(978-1-4169-4052-4(9),* Simon & Schuster/Paula Wiseman Bks.) Simon & Schuster/Paula Wiseman Bks.

—I Love Going Through This Book. Yaccarino, Dan, illus. Date not set. 40p. (J). (gr. -1-3). pap. 5.99 *(978-0-06-443647-2(0))* HarperCollins Pubs.

—Messenger, Messenger. Root, Barry, illus. 2011. (ENG.). 32p. (J). (gr. -1-3). 17.99 *(978-1-4424-5335-7(4),* Atheneum Bks. for Young Readers) Simon & Schuster Children's Publishing.

—Night Train, Night Train. Minor, Wendell, illus. 2018. 32p. (J). (-k). lib. bdg. 16.99 *(978-1-58089-717-4(7))* Charlesbridge Publishing, Inc.

—Zoom! Zoom! Sounds of Things That Go in the City. Carpenter, Tad, illus. 2014. (ENG.). 32p. (J). (gr. -1-3). 18.99 *(978-1-4424-8315-6(6),* Simon & Schuster Bks. For Young Readers) Simon & Schuster Bks. For Young Readers.

Burnham, Janet Hayward. The Dragoness Mess. 2003. (Illus.). 32p. (J). (gr. k-1). pap. 12.95 *(978-0-9740743-1-3(4))* My Little Jessie Pr.

Burns, Joanne. Abigail Is a Big Girl Now. 2005. 20p. (J). 8.99 *(978-1-4116-2042-1(9))* Lulu Pr., Inc.

—Annibelle Is a Big Girl Now Weaning Two Year-Olds. 2005. 20p. 8.99 *(978-1-4116-2044-5(5))* Lulu Pr., Inc.

—No Says the Baby When You Say Yes, a book about the terrible Twos. 2005. 1p. 5.68 *(978-1-4116-3386-5(5))* Lulu Pr., Inc.

—What Is Heaven Like? 2005. 35p. (J). 10.99 *(978-1-4116-3360-5(1))* Lulu Pr., Inc.

Burow, Ginger. The Night That Was Christmas, 1 vol. 2009. 21p. pap. 24.95 *(978-1-4489-9842-5(5))* America Star Bks.

Burris, Priscilla. The Ants Go Marching: a Count-And-Sing Book. Burris, Priscilla, illus. 2016. (ENG., Illus.). 16p. (J). (— 1). bds. 6.99 *(978-0-545-82504-7(0),* Cartwheel Bks.) Scholastic, Inc.

Burroughs, Caleb. Good Night, Octopus (down Spc'd) An I Can Do It Book. Randall, Emma, illus. 2016. (J). bds. 0.00 *(978-1-68052-104-7(7))* Cottage Door Pr.

Burton, Jeffrey. The Itsy Bitsy Bunny. Rescek, Sanja, illus. 2016. (Itsy Bitsy Ser.). (ENG.). 16p. (J). (gr. -1 — 1). bds. 5.99 *(978-1-4814-5621-0(0),* Little Simon) Little Simon.

—The Itsy Bitsy Pilgrim. Rescek, Sanja, illus. 2016. (Itsy Bitsy Ser.). (ENG.). 16p. (J). (gr. -1 — 1). bds. 5.99 *(978-1-4814-6852-7(9),* Little Simon) Little Simon.

—The Itsy Bitsy Reindeer. Rescek, Sanja, illus. 2016. (Itsy Bitsy Ser.). (ENG.). 16p. (J). (gr. -1 — 1). bds. 5.99 *(978-1-4814-6855-8(3),* Little Simon) Little Simon.

—Jingle Bells at the Zoo. Trithart, Emma, illus. 2018. (ENG.). 14p. (J). (gr. -1 — 1). bds. 8.99 *(978-1-5344-2034-2(7),* Little Simon) Little Simon.

—My Sweet Little Megabyte. Roode, Laura, illus. 2016. (ENG.). 16p. (J). (gr. -1 — 1). bds. 5.99 *(978-1-4814-6809-1(X),* Little Simon) Little Simon.

Burton M.Sc., Kathryn Mac. Diarmid. Haley Honeybee: Finds the Magic Rose. Cox, Glendyne Dewhurst, illus. 2013. 50p. pap. *(978-0-9917941-0-2(9))* Burton, K. Publishing.

Burwitz, Patrick. Mia's Dogcow. 2009. 28p. pap. 13.00 *(978-1-4343-8580-2(9))* AuthorHouse.

Bush, Randall. The Caterbury Tails. Watson, Ben, illus. 2013. 60p. pap. 13.99 *(978-1-936670-75-8(5))* BorderStone Pr., LLC.

Bush, Zack. Made for Me. De Lauretis, Gregorio, illus. (ENG.). (J). (gr. -1-k). 2019. 20p. bds. 12.99 *(978-1-64170-200-3(1),* 550200) 2018. 32p. 16.99 *(978-1-945547-69-0(3),* 554769) Familius LLC.

Bushar, Carol. Robby the Lion Doesn't Eat Meat. 2006. 30p. 12.96 *(978-1-4116-9113-1(X))* Lulu Pr., Inc.

Butler, John. Bedtime in the Jungle, 1 vol. 2019. (ENG., Illus.). 32p. (J). (gr. -1-k). pap. 7.95 *(978-1-68263-145-4(1))* Peachtree Publishing Co. Inc.

—Can You Cuddle Like a Koala? 2005. (ENG., Illus.). 20p. (J). (gr. k-k). bds. 6.99 *(978-1-56145-347-4(1))* Peachtree Publishing Co. Inc.

—Can You Growl Like a Bear? 2012. (ENG., Illus.). 20p. (J). (-k). bds. 6.99 *(978-1-56145-667-3(5))* Peachtree Publishing Co. Inc.

Butler, John, illus. If Your Dreams Take off & Fly. 2013. (J). *(978-1-4351-4769-0(3))* Barnes & Noble, Inc.

Butler, Kristi T. A Big Surprise. Paparone, Pam, illus. 2005. (Green Light Readers Level 1 Ser.). (ENG.). 24p. (J). (gr. -1-3). pap. 5.99 *(978-0-15-205141-9(4),* 1195515, Clarion Bks.) HarperCollins Pubs.

Butler Seder, Rufus. Waddle! A Scanimation Picture Book. 2009. (Scanimation Ser.). (ENG., Illus.). 12p. (gr. -1-2). 16.95 *(978-0-7611-5112-8(5),* 15112) Workman Publishing Co., Inc.

Byous, Shawn. Because I Stubbed My Toe, 1 vol. 2014. (Fiction Picture Bks.). (ENG., Illus.). 32p. (J). (gr. k-3). pap. 6.95 *(978-1-4795-3808-9(6),* 124650, Picture Window Bks.) Capstone.

Cabral, Noel. Rachel's Four-Legged Friend. 2012. 24p. 24.95 *(978-1-4626-6089-6(4))* America Star Bks.

Cabrera, Jane. Baa, Baa, Black Sheep. 2016. (Jane Cabrera's Story Time Ser.). (ENG., Illus.). 24p. (J). (gr. -1-k). bds. 7.99 *(978-0-8234-3631-6(4))* Holiday Hse., Inc.

—The Bear Went over the Mountain. 2020. (Jane Cabrera's Story Time Ser.). (Illus.). 32p. (J). (-k). 18.99 *(978-0-8234-4653-7(0))* Holiday Hse., Inc.

—There Was an Old Woman Who Lived in a Shoe. 2017. (Jane Cabrera's Story Time Ser.). (ENG.). 32p. (J). (gr. -1-k). 7.99 *(978-0-8234-3771-9(X))* Holiday Hse., Inc.

Cali, Carol. It's a Zoo Around Here. 2012. (Illus.). 36p. pap. 8.99 *(978-1-60820-567-7(3))* MLR Pr., LLC.

Caldecott, Randolph. A Frog He Would A-Wooing Go. 2006. pap. *(978-1-4065-1224-3(9))* Dodo Pr.

Calmenson, Stephanie. Birthday at the Panda Palace. Cushman, Doug, illus. 2007. 32p. (J). (gr. -1-3). 15.99 *(978-0-06-052663-4(7))* HarperCollins Pubs.

—Jazzmatazz! Degen, Bruce, illus. 2008. 32p. (J). (gr. -1). lib. bdg. 17.89 *(978-0-06-077290-1(5))* HarperCollins Pubs.

—Late for School! 2008. (ENG., Illus.). 32p. (J). (gr. -1-2). lib. bdg. 16.95 *(978-1-57505-935-8(5))* Lerner Publishing Group.

—Look! Fish! Pinillos, Puy, illus. 2016. (Look! Ser.). (ENG.). 24p. (J). (gr. -1-1). 8.99 *(978-1-4998-0166-8(1))* Little Bee Books Inc.

Calvert, Deanna. Rookie Reader Español: Las Sombras. Lester, Mike, illus. 2005. (Rookie Reader Español Ser.). (SPA.). 32p. (J). (gr. k-2). per. 4.95 *(978-0-516-24697-0(6),* Children's Pr.) Scholastic Library Publishing.

—Shadows. Lester, Mike, illus. 2004. (Rookie Readers Ser.). 23p. (J). 12.60 *(978-0-7569-4333-2(7))* Perfection Learning Corp.

Camacho, Hector, Jr. & Warburton, Dustin. Macho Dad. Monroe, Daniel, illus. 2014. (ENG.). (J). 19.99 *(978-0-9960374-3-3(8))* Dragonbrush Arts.

Cameron, Kristy. Behind the Door of Timothy Moore. Schickle, Ian, illus. 2013. 28p. pap. *(978-0-9859790-1-0(1))* LP Publishing.

Camille, Diana, illus. A Treasury of Goops: Timeless Manners for Every Generation. 2005. Orig. Title: Goops & How to Be Them. (ENG.). 45p. (J). 19.95 *(978-0-9712368-5-1(2),* 8006811891) Goops Unlimited.

Canetti, Yanitzia. ABC's of Plants. 2010. (ENG.). 40p. (J). pap. 8.99 *(978-1-59835-118-7(4),* BrickHouse Education) Cambridge BrickHouse, Inc.

—Abecedario de Plantas. 2010. (SPA.). 40p. (J). pap. 8.99 *(978-1-59835-119-4(2),* BrickHouse Education) Cambridge BrickHouse, Inc.

—Abecedario de Profesiones y Oficios. 2009. (SPA.). 40p. (J). pap. 8.99 *(978-1-59835-122-4(2),* BrickHouse Education) Cambridge BrickHouse, Inc.

—Abecedario Nutritivo. 2009. (SPA.). 40p. (J). pap. 8.99 *(978-1-59835-115-6(X),* BrickHouse Education) Cambridge BrickHouse, Inc.

—ABeCedario Salvaje. 2009. (SPA.). 40p. (J). (gr. -1-3). pap. 7.99 *(978-1-59835-117-0(6))* Cambridge BrickHouse, Inc.

—Yummy ABC's. 2010. (ENG.). 40p. (J). pap. 8.99 *(978-1-59835-114-9(1),* BrickHouse Education) Cambridge BrickHouse, Inc.

Cannella, Nicole DeRosa. The Ribbit Exhibit: One frog's tale of a leap of Faith. 2011. 28p. pap. 13.59 *(978-1-4634-2435-0(3))* AuthorHouse.

Cannon, Sherrill S. Manner-Man. 2013. 28p. pap. 12.50 *(978-1-62212-478-7(2),* Strategic Bk. Publishing) Strategic Book Publishing & Rights Agency (SBPRA).

—Santa's Birthday Gift. 2009. 24p. pap. 11.50 *(978-1-60860-824-9(7),* Eloquent Bks.) Strategic Book Publishing & Rights Agency (SBPRA).

Cantrell, Caley. You're Bringing Me a Baby?! 2013. (Illus.). 40p. (J). 15.95 *(978-0-9859358-7-0(1),* Belle Isle Bks.) Brandylane Pubs., Inc.

Capucilli, Alyssa Satin. Biscuit's 123. Schories, Pat & Berlin, Rose Mary, illus. 2012. (Biscuit Ser.). (ENG.). 16p. (J). (gr. -1-1). bds. 6.99 *(978-0-06-162523-7(X),* HarperFestival) HarperCollins Pubs.

—Blanket of Love. Boynton-Hughes, Brooke, illus. 2017. (New Books for Newborns Ser.). (ENG.). 16p. (J). (gr. -1 — 1). bds. 7.99 *(978-1-4814-8972-0(0),* Little Simon) Little Simon.

—Good Night, My Darling Baby. Bach, Annie, illus. 2017. (New Books for Newborns Ser.). (ENG.). 16p. (J). (gr. -1 — 1). bds. 7.99 *(978-1-4814-8119-9(3),* Little Simon) Little Simon.

—Hannah Is a Big Sister. Stott, Dorothy, illus. 2014. (Hannah & Henry Ser.). 32p. (J). (gr. -1-k). 5.99 *(978-0-7641-6750-8(2))* Sourcebooks, Inc.

—Mighty Tug. Mottram, David, illus. 2018. (ENG.). 40p. (J). (gr. -1-3). 17.99 *(978-1-4814-7681-2(5),* Simon & Schuster/Paula Wiseman Bks.) Simon & Schuster/Paula Wiseman Bks.

—Monkey Play. 2012. (Step into Reading Ser.). (Illus.). 32p. (J). (gr. -1-1). pap. 5.99 *(978-0-375-86993-8(X)*, Random Hse. Bks. for Young Readers) Random Hse. Children's Bks.
—My Dad & Me. Mitchell, Susan, illus. 2009. (ENG.). 16p. (J). (gr. -1-1). 7.99 *(978-1-4169-5828-4(2)*, Little Simon) Little Simon.
—My Mom & Me. Mitchell, Susan, illus. 2009. (ENG.). 16p. (J). (gr. -1-1). 7.99 *(978-1-4169-5829-1(0)*, Little Simon) Little Simon.
—Panda Kisses. Widdowson, Kay, illus. 2008. (Step into Reading: Step 1 Ser.). (ENG.). 32p. (J). (gr. -1-1). lib. bdg. 16.19 *(978-0-375-94562-5(8))* Random House Publishing Group.
—Panda Kisses. Widdowson, Kay, illus. 2008. (Step into Reading Ser.). 32p. (J). (gr. -1-1). pap. 5.99 *(978-0-375-84562-8(3)*, Random Hse. Bks. for Young Readers) Random Hse. Children's Bks.
Carbone, Courtney. Cooking with Sam-I-Am. Brannon, Tom, illus. 2018. (Step into Reading Ser.). (ENG.). 32p. (J). (gr. -1-1). pap. 4.99 *(978-1-5247-7088-4(4)*, Random Hse. Bks. for Young Readers) Random Hse. Children's Bks.
Carigiet, Alois, illus. A Bell for Ursli: A Story from the Engadine in Switzerland, 23 vols. 2007. (ENG.). 44p. (J). *(978-0-86315-614-4(2))* Floris Bks.
Carle, Eric. My First Peek-A-Boo Animals. Carle, Eric, illus. 2017. (World of Eric Carle Ser.). (ENG., Illus.). 18p. (J). (gr. -1 — 1). bds. 7.99 *(978-1-5344-0105-1(9)*, Little Simon) Little Simon.
—The Nonsense Show. Carle, Eric, illus. 2015. (Illus.). 40p. (J). (gr. -1-2). bds. 18.99 *(978-0-399-17687-6(X)*, Philomel Bks.) Penguin Young Readers Group.
Carlson, Melody. Farmer Brown's Field Trip. Björkman, Steve, illus. 2004. 40p. (gr. -1-3). 9.99 *(978-1-58134-142-3(3))* Crossway.
—Forgive Others. Reagan, Susan Joy, illus. 2004. (Just Like Jesus Said Ser.). 32p. (J). (gr. -1-5). 12.99 *(978-0-8054-2385-3(0))* B&H Publishing Group.
—Goodnight, Angels, 1 vol. Allsopp, Sophie, illus. 2011. (ENG.). 32p. (J). 15.99 *(978-0-310-71687-7(X))* Zonderkidz.
Carlstrom, Nancy White. It's Your First Day of School, Annie Claire. Moore, Margie, illus. 2009. (ENG.). 32p. (J). (gr. k-2). 16.95 *(978-0-8109-4057-4(4)*, 639801, Abrams Bks. for Young Readers) Abrams, Inc.
Carluccio, Maria. The Sounds Around Town. Carluccio, Maria, illus. 2010. (ENG., Illus.). 13p. (J). 14.99 *(978-1-84686-362-2(7))* Barefoot Bks., Inc.
—The Sounds Around Town. 2008. (Illus.). 24p. (J). (gr. -1-k). 16.99 *(978-1-905236-28-2(X))* Barefoot Bks., Inc.
Carluccio, Maria, illus. The Sounds Around Town. 2011. 24p. (J). (gr. -1-3). pap. 7.99 *(978-1-84686-430-8(5))* Barefoot Bks., Inc.
Carney, Karin. Prince Braden's Animal Kingdom. 2011. 40p. pap. 18.95 *(978-1-4357-9406-1(0))* Lulu Pr., Inc.
—Princess Bailey & Her Animal Friends. 2011. (Illus.). 46p. pap. 18.95 *(978-0-557-95745-3(1))* Lulu Pr., Inc.
Carney, Larry, adapted by. The Three Bears Christmas. 2009. (ENG., Illus.). 24p. (J). 6.95 *(978-1-60072-112-0(5))* PC Treasures, Inc.
Carolan, Dr. Where Are My Slippers? A Book of Colors. Carolan, Joanna F., illus. 2007. 32p. 17.95 *(978-0-9715333-7-0(7))* Banana Patch Pr.
Carr, Crystal. Ram, Ham, Strawberry Jam: Identifying Nouns. 2007. 24p. per. 13.95 *(978-1-4327-0512-1(1))* Outskirts Pr., Inc.
Carson, Penny & Hess, Amy. Simon Goes Camping. 2008. 19p. 10.95 *(978-1-4357-1560-8(8))* Lulu Pr., Inc.
—Simon's Day of Rain. 2008. 17p. 10.94 *(978-1-4357-2168-5(3))* Lulu Pr., Inc.
Carta, Karla K. Chocolate in My Pocket. 2006. 21p. (J). 10.68 *(978-1-4116-9312-8(4))* Lulu Pr., Inc.
Carter, David A. Bedtime Bugs: A Pop-Up Good Night Book by David A. Carter. Carter, David A., illus. 2010. (David Carter's Bugs Ser.). (ENG., Illus.). 18p. (J). (gr. -1-2). 12.99 *(978-1-4169-9960-7(4)*, Little Simon) Little Simon.
—Bugs at the Beach: Ready-To-Read Level 1. Carter, David A., illus. 2016. (David Carter's Bugs Ser.). (ENG., Illus.). 24p. (J). (gr. -1-1). pap. 4.99 *(978-1-4814-4050-9(0)*, Simon Spotlight) Simon Spotlight.
—Busy Bug Builds a Fort: Ready-To-Read Level 1. Carter, David A., illus. 2016. (David Carter's Bugs Ser.). (ENG., Illus.). 24p. (J). (gr. -1-1). pap. 3.99 *(978-1-4814-4047-9(0)*, Simon Spotlight) Simon Spotlight.
—Colors: A Bugs Pop-Up Concept Book. Carter, David A., illus. 2010. (David Carter's Bugs Ser.). (ENG., Illus.). 16p. (J). (gr. -1-1). 10.99 *(978-1-4424-0830-2(8)*, Little Simon) Little Simon.
—Feely Bugs (Mini Edition) To Touch & Feel. Carter, David A., illus. 2005. (David Carter's Bugs Ser.). (ENG., Illus.). 14p. (J). (gr. -1-2). 12.99 *(978-1-4169-0326-0(7)*, Little Simon) Little Simon.
—Five Cars Stuck & One Big Truck: A Pop-Up Road Trip. Carter, David A., illus. 2017. (ENG., Illus.). 18p. (J). (gr. -1 — 1). bds. 15.99 *(978-1-4814-7119-0(8)*, Little Simon) Little Simon.
—A Snowy Day in Bugland! Ready-To-Read Level 1. Carter, David A., illus. 2012. (David Carter's Bugs Ser.). (ENG., Illus.). 24p. (J). (gr. -1-1). 17.99 *(978-1-4424-3895-8(9))*; pap. 3.99 *(978-1-4424-3894-1(0))* Simon Spotlight. (Simon Spotlight).
—Springtime in Bugland! Ready-To-Read Level 1. Carter, David A., illus. 2012. (David Carter's Bugs Ser.). (ENG., Illus.). 24p. (J). (gr. -1-1). 15.99 *(978-1-4424-3892-7(4))*; pap. 3.99 *(978-1-4424-3890-3(8))* Simon Spotlight. (Simon Spotlight).
Carter, Grant Matthew. The Disaster Caster. Morling, Donovan, illus. 2012. 38p. pap. 16.00 *(978-1-4349-8432-6(X)*, RoseDog Bks.) Dorrance Publishing Co., Inc.
Casale, Roberto, illus. Little Binky Bear. 2009. (ENM & ENG.). 18p. (J). 7.99 *(978-0-9825700-0-5(7))* Show N' Tell Publishing.
—El Osito Binky. 2017.Tr. of Little Binky Bear. (J). 7.99 *(978-0-9986498-0-1(5))* Show N' Tell Publishing.
Casanova, Mary. One-Dog Canoe. Hoyt, Ard, illus. 2009. (ENG.). 32p. (J). (gr. -1-1). pap. 7.99 *(978-0-312-56118-5(0)*, 900058848) Square Fish.
Cash, John Carter. Daddy Loves His Little Girl. Burckhardt, Marc, illus. 2010. (ENG.). 32p. (J). (gr. -1-3). 16.99 *(978-1-4169-7482-6(2)*, Little Simon Inspirations) Little Simon Inspirations.
Cash, M. A. Edward of Canterbury & the King of Red. Adams, Craig, illus. 2003. (J). *(978-0-9772711-0-8(2))* Jama Kids.
Caudle, P. L. The Tale of Strawberry Snow, 1 vol. 2012. (ENG., Illus.). 48p. (J). (gr. -1-3). 16.99 *(978-0-7643-4076-5(X)*, 4496) Schiffer Publishing, Ltd.
Cavanaugh, Wendy. Pumpkin in the Sky: Let's bake a pie together, you & I, with Auntie Wendy. Cavanaugh, Wendy & LeVesque, Sherry, photos by. 2011. (Illus.). 32p. (J). spiral bd. 20.00 *(978-0-9743121-1-8(8))* Eastlight Pr.
Celia, Shannon Casey. Nature's Music: Musical Colors Series 2003. (ENG., Illus.). 12p. (J). spiral bd. 10.95 *(978-1-931844-07-9(0)*, PP1019) Piano Pr.
Centeio, Tara Jaye. Mommy Loves Her Baby. Date not set. 32p. (J). (gr. -1-1). pap. 5.99 *(978-0-06-443715-8(9))* HarperCollins Pubs.
Cerf, Christopher & Peterson, Paige. Blackie: the Horse Who Stood Still: The Horse Who Stood Still. 2014. (ENG., Illus.). 64p. (J). (gr. 1-4). 16.95 *(978-1-59962-130-2(4)*, Welcome Bks) Rizzoli International Pubns., Inc.
Cervi, Isaac. Pockets. 2008. 20p. pap. 12.50 *(978-1-4389-0368-2(5))* AuthorHouse.
Cesak, Jerry. My Personal Panther. Naughton, Terry, illus. 2012. (J). *(978-0-578-10507-9(1))* Canyon Hawk Bks.
Cesler, Margaret E. The Bread Book. 2013. 12p. pap. 10.97 *(978-1-62212-527-2(4)*, Strategic Bk. Publishing) Strategic Book Publishing & Rights Agency (SBPRA).
Cesmat, Brandon. When Pigs Fall in Love & Other Stories. 2010. 150p. pap. 15.00 *(978-0-9716383-8-9(1))* Lamp Post Inc.
Chaconas, Dori. Hurry down to Derry Fair. Tyler, Gillian, illus. 2011. (ENG.). 36p. (J). (gr. -1-2). 16.99 *(978-0-7636-3208-3(2))* Candlewick Pr.
Chall, Marsha Wilson. One Pup's Up. Cole, Henry, illus. 2010. (ENG.). 32p. (J). (gr. -1 — 1). 19.99 *(978-1-4169-7960-9(3)*, McElderry, Margaret K. Bks.) McElderry, Margaret K. Bks.
—Pick a Pup. Henry, Jed, illus. 2011. (ENG.). 32p. (J). (gr. -1-k). 19.99 *(978-1-4169-7961-6(1)*, McElderry, Margaret K. Bks.) McElderry, Margaret K. Bks.
—A Secret Keeps. 2012. (Carolrhoda Picture Bks.). (Illus.). 32p. (J). (gr. k-3). lib. bdg. 16.95 *(978-0-7613-5593-9(6))* Lerner Publishing Group.
Chaltas, Thalia. Because I Am Furniture. 2010. (ENG.). 368p. (YA). (gr. 7-18). 8.99 *(978-0-14-241510-8(3)*, Speak) Penguin Young Readers Group.
Chambers, Veronica & Clampet, Jason. Papi's Bodega. Miyares, Daniel, illus. 2013. (J). *(978-1-4231-0125-3(1))* Disney Pr.
Chandler, Jeffery. The Christmas Santa Overslept. 2008. 13p. pap. 24.95 *(978-1-60703-421-6(2))* America Star Bks.
Chandler, Susan. What I Do with Vegetable Glue. Odriozola, Elena, illus. 2012. (ENG.). 24p. (J). (gr. k-3). 16.95 *(978-1-61608-661-9(0)*, 608661, Sky Pony Pr.) Skyhorse Publishing Co., Inc.
Chapman, Keith. Itsy Bitsy Spider. Tickle, Jack, illus. (Tiger Tales Ser.). (J). 2008. 24p. (gr. -1-2). pap. 6.95 *(978-1-58925-407-7(4))* 2006. 32p. 15.95 *(978-1-58925-055-0(9))* Tiger Tales.
Chapman, Mary Beth & Chapman, Steven Curtis. Shaoey & Dot: A Trip to Dr. Betterbee. 2005. 20p. (J). 6.99 *(978-1-4003-0568-1(3))* Nelson, Thomas Inc.
—Shaoey & Dot: Back in a Bug's Blink. 2005. 20p. (J). 6.99 *(978-1-4003-0569-8(1))* Nelson, Thomas Inc.
—Shaoey & Dot: Thunder & Lightning Bugs. 2005. 20p. (J). 6.99 *(978-1-4003-0570-4(5))* Nelson, Thomas Inc.
Charles, Faustin & Terry, Michael. The Selfish Crocodile Book of Nursery Rhymes. Terry, Michael, illus. 2008. (Illus.). (J). (gr. -1-k). audio compact disk 25.95 *(978-0-7475-9523-6(2))* Bloomsbury Publishing Plc GBR. Dist: Independent Pubs. Group.
Charles, Kaye Ellen. Macarthur & Martha. 2013. 56p. pap. 20.95 *(978-1-4525-8512-3(1)*, Balboa Pr.) Author Solutions, LLC.
Charlesworth, Liza. Six Silly Chicks: An Animal Friends Reader. Smith, Ian, illus. 2015. 16p. (J). pap. *(978-0-545-85966-0(2))* Scholastic, Inc.
Charley's Columbia Backyard. 2006. (J). 14.95 *(978-0-9793808-0-8(4))* Backyard Ambassador Reader Publishing Co.
Charlip, Remy. A Perfect Day. 2007. (Illus.). 40p. (J). (gr. -1). lib. bdg. 17.89 *(978-0-06-051973-5(8))* HarperCollins Pubs.
Charman, Katrina. Car, Car, Truck, Jeep. Sharratt, Nick, illus. 2018. (New Nursery Rhymes Ser.). (ENG.). 24p. (J). bds. 7.99 *(978-1-68119-895-8(9)*, 900191674, Bloomsbury Children's Bks.) Bloomsbury Publishing USA.
—Go, Go, Pirate Boat. Sharratt, Nick, illus. 2019. (New Nursery Rhymes Ser.). (ENG.). 24p. (J). bds. 8.99 *(978-1-5476-0319-0(4)*, 900211337, Bloomsbury Children's Bks.) Bloomsbury Publishing USA.
Chase, Kit, illus. Little Sweet Pea, God Loves You, 1 vol. 2019. (ENG.). 32p. (J). 15.99 *(978-0-310-76699-5(0))* Zonderkidz.
Chast, Roz. Around the Clock. Chast, Roz, illus. 2015. (ENG., Illus.). 32p. (J). (gr. -1-3). 18.99 *(978-1-4169-8476-4(3)*, Atheneum Bks. for Young Readers) Simon & Schuster Children's Publishing.
Cheetham, Stephen, illus. Off to the Park! 2014. (Tactile Bks.). 12p. (J). spiral bd. *(978-1-84643-502-7(1))* Child's Play International Ltd.
Chen, Sam. A Real Meal Table Fable. Peschel, Georgia, illus. 2007. 60p. (J). *(978-0-9800764-0-0(4))* Uncle Jim's Publishing.
Cherobin. Zoomy Boomy & the Moon: Zoomy & the Moon Learn the Strength of Love. 2009. 24p. pap. 14.99 *(978-1-4490-2069-9(0))* AuthorHouse.
—Zoomy Boomy, the Moon, & the Earth: All in its Season, & Seasons Change. 2010. 24p. pap. 14.99 *(978-1-4490-2658-5(3))* AuthorHouse.
Cherobin & Cherobin. Zoomy Boomy Lights the Night: Zoomy Conquers Shyness. 2009. 24p. pap. 14.49 *(978-1-4490-2068-2(2))* AuthorHouse.
Chichester Clark, Emma. Mimi's Book of Opposites. Chichester Clark, Emma, illus. 2004. (Illus.). 24p. (J). 9.95 *(978-1-57091-574-1(1))* Charlesbridge Publishing, Inc.
—We Are Not Fond of Rat: Band 02B/Red B (Collins Big Cat Phonics) Chichester Clark, Emma, illus. 2006. (Collins Big Cat Phonics Ser.). (ENG., Illus.). 16p. (J). (gr. -1-1). pap. 6.99 *(978-0-00-723590-2(9))* HarperCollins Pubs. Ltd. GBR. Dist: Independent Pubs. Group.
Chichester Clark, Emma, tr. & illus. Will & Squill. Chichester Clark, Emma, illus. 2006. 32p. (J). (gr. -1-k). 15.95 *(978-1-57505-936-5(3)*, Carolrhoda Bks.) Lerner Publishing Group.
Children's Press, contrib. by. The Three Little Kittens Get Dressed. 2009. (Rookie Preschool-NEW Ser.). (ENG.). 24p. (J). pap. 6.95 *(978-0-531-24579-8(9)*, Children's Pr.) Scholastic Library Publishing.
Childs, Mark. Jaloopa: Home of the Poobah Baloo. 2009. (Illus.). (J). 25.99 *(978-1-4415-0481-4(8))* Xlibris Corp.
Chilton, Mark. Stinky Dog. 2018. (ENG., Illus.). 27p. (J). 23.95 *(978-1-78629-190-5(8)*, 965ac0ee-01c3-4512-ab74-c5b73ca2b0d5); pap. 14.95 *(978-1-5289-0873-3(2)*, 7d8ac463-f8a2-459a-a983-4db2029fbbcd) Austin Macauley Pubs. Ltd. GBR. Dist: Baker & Taylor Publisher Services (BTPS).
Chin, Oliver Clyde. Harriet's Hairballs. Crawford, Gregory, tr. Crawford, Gregory, illus. 2003. 32p. (J). 15.95 *(978-1-58394-078-5(2)*, Frog Ltd.) North Atlantic Bks.
Chriscoe, Sharon. Fire Truck Dreams. Mottram, Dave, illus. 2018. (ENG.). 32p. (J). (gr. -1-3). 17.99 *(978-0-7624-6285-8(X)*, Running Pr. Kids) Running Pr.
Christelow, Eileen. Five Little Monkeys Jumping on the Bed Big Book. Christelow, Eileen, illus. 2006. (Five Little Monkeys Story Ser.). (ENG., Illus.). 32p. (J). (gr. -1-3). pap. 26.99 *(978-0-618-83682-6(9)*, 491894, Clarion Bks.) HarperCollins Pubs.
—Five Little Monkeys Jumping on the Bed Board Book. Christelow, Eileen, illus. 2017. (Five Little Monkeys Story Ser.). (ENG., Illus.). 30p. (J). (— 1). bds. 7.99 *(978-1-328-88456-5(2)*, 1698446, Clarion Bks.) HarperCollins Pubs.
—Five Little Monkeys Jumping on the Bed Padded Board Book. Christelow, Eileen, illus. 2017. (Five Little Monkeys Story Ser.). (ENG., Illus.). 30p. (J). (gr. -1 — 1). bds. 11.99 *(978-0-547-51075-0(6)*, 1443772, Clarion Bks.) HarperCollins Pubs.
—Five Little Monkeys Play Hide & Seek. Christelow, Eileen, illus. 2010. (Five Little Monkeys Story Ser.). (ENG., Illus.). 40p. (J). (gr. -1-3). pap. 9.99 *(978-0-547-33787-6(6)*, 1418278, Clarion Bks.) HarperCollins Pubs.
—Five Little Monkeys Reading in Bed Board Book. Christelow, Eileen, illus. 2014. (Five Little Monkeys Story Ser.). (ENG., Illus.). 34p. (J). (— 1). bds. 8.99 *(978-0-544-17330-9(9)*, 1552170, Clarion Bks.) HarperCollins Pubs.
—Five Little Monkeys Sitting in a Tree/Cinco Monitos Subidos a un árbol Board Bk: Bilingual English-Spanish. Christelow, Eileen, illus. 2014. (Five Little Monkeys Story Ser.). (ENG., Illus.). 28p. (J). (gr. -1 — 1). bds. 7.99 *(978-0-544-30218-1(4)*, 1577854, Clarion Bks.) HarperCollins Pubs.
—Five Little Monkeys Trick-Or-Treat. Christelow, Eileen, illus. 2018. (Five Little Monkeys Story Ser.). (ENG., Illus.). 40p. (J). (gr. -1-3). pap. 7.99 *(978-1-328-86927-2(X)*, 1696687, Clarion Bks.) HarperCollins Pubs.
—Five Little Monkeys Trick-Or-Treat Board Book. Christelow, Eileen, illus. 2015. (Five Little Monkeys Story Ser.). (ENG., Illus.). 36p. (J). (— 1). bds. 7.99 *(978-0-544-43062-4(X)*, 1595737, Clarion Bks.) HarperCollins Pubs.
—Five Little Monkeys Wash the Car. Christelow, Eileen, illus. 2004. (Five Little Monkeys Story Ser.). (ENG., Illus.). 40p. (J). (gr. -1-3). 7.99 *(978-0-618-48602-1(X)*, 100389, Clarion Bks.) HarperCollins Pubs.
Christensen, Catherine. Emily's Perfect Christmas Tree. 2015. (Illus.). (J). 14.99 *(978-1-4621-1750-5(3))* Cedar Fort, Inc./CFI Distribution.
Christie, Jacqueline. Alphabet Animals. 2012. 60p. pap. 37.37 *(978-1-4797-1567-1(0))* Xlibris Corp.
Chronicle Books & ImageBooks. Little Cat: Finger Puppet Book: (Finger Puppet Book for Toddlers & Babies, Baby Books for First Year, Animal Finger Puppets) 2014. (Little Finger Puppet Board Bks.). (ENG., Illus.). 12p. (J). (gr. -1 — 1). 7.99 *(978-1-4521-2916-7(9))* Chronicle Bks. LLC.
—Little Chick: Finger Puppet Book: (Puppet Book for Baby, Little Easter Board Book) 2015. (Little Finger Puppet Board Bks.). (ENG., Illus.). 12p. (J). (gr. -1 — 1). bds. 7.99 *(978-1-4521-2917-4(7))* Chronicle Bks. LLC.
—Little Dog: Finger Puppet Book: (Finger Puppet Book for Toddlers & Babies, Baby Books for First Year, Animal Finger Puppets) 2014. (Little Finger Puppet Board Bks.). (ENG., Illus.). 12p. (J). (gr. -1 — 1). 7.99 *(978-1-4521-2915-0(0))* Chronicle Bks. LLC.
—Little Dolphin: Finger Puppet Book: (Finger Puppet Book for Toddlers & Babies, Baby Books for First Year, Animal Finger Puppets) 2012. (Little Finger Puppet Board Bks.: FING). (ENG., Illus.). 12p. (J). (gr. -1 — 1). bds. 7.99 *(978-1-4521-0816-2(1))* Chronicle Bks. LLC.
—Little Fox: Finger Puppet Book: (Finger Puppet Book for Toddlers & Babies, Baby Books for First Year, Animal Finger Puppets) 2015. (ENG., Illus.). 12p. (J). (gr. -1 — 1). 7.99 *(978-1-4521-4230-2(0))* Chronicle Bks. LLC.
—Little Horse: Finger Puppet Book: (Finger Puppet Book for Toddlers & Babies, Baby Books for First Year, Animal Finger Puppets) 2013. (Little Finger Puppet Board Bks.). (ENG., Illus.). 12p. (J). (gr. -1 — 1). 7.99 *(978-1-4521-1249-7(5))* Chronicle Bks. LLC.
—Little Monkey: Finger Puppet Book: (Finger Puppet Book for Toddlers & Babies, Baby Books for First Year, Animal Finger Puppets) 2013. (Little Finger Puppet Board Bks.). (ENG., Illus.). 12p. (J). (gr. -1 — 1). 7.99 *(978-1-4521-1250-3(9))* Chronicle Bks. LLC.
—Little Moose: Finger Puppet Book: (Finger Puppet Book for Toddlers & Babies, Baby Books for First Year, Animal Finger Puppets) 2015. (ENG., Illus.). 12p. (J). (gr. -1 — 1). 7.99 *(978-1-4521-4231-9(9))* Chronicle Bks. LLC.
—Little Owl: Finger Puppet Book: (Finger Puppet Book for Toddlers & Babies, Baby Books for First Year, Animal Finger Puppets) 2011. (Little Finger Puppet Board Bks.). (ENG.). 12p. (J). (gr. -1 — 1). 7.99 *(978-1-4521-0221-4(X))* Chronicle Bks. LLC.
—Little Sea Turtle: Finger Puppet Book: (Finger Puppet Book for Toddlers & Babies, Baby Books for First Year, Animal Finger Puppets) 2014. (Little Finger Puppet Board Bks.). (ENG., Illus.). 12p. (J). (gr. -1 — 1). 7.99 *(978-1-4521-2913-6(4))* Chronicle Bks. LLC.
—Little Seal: Finger Puppet Book: (Finger Puppet Book for Toddlers & Babies, Baby Books for First Year, Animal Finger Puppets) 2012. (Little Finger Puppet Board Bks.: FING). (ENG., Illus.). 12p. (J). (gr. -1 — 1). 7.99 *(978-1-4521-0812-4(9))* Chronicle Bks. LLC.
—Little Shark: Finger Puppet Book: (Puppet Book for Baby, Little Toy Board Book, Baby Shark) 2013. (Little Finger Puppet Board Bks.). (ENG., Illus.). 12p. (J). (gr. -1 — 1). 7.99 *(978-1-4521-1251-0(7))* Chronicle Bks. LLC.
—Little Zebra: Finger Puppet Book: (Finger Puppet Book for Toddlers & Babies, Baby Books for First Year, Animal Finger Puppets) 2013. (Little Finger Puppet Board Bks.). (ENG., Illus.). 12p. (J). (gr. -1 — 1). bds. 6.99 *(978-1-4521-1252-7(5))* Chronicle Bks. LLC.
Chrustowski, Rick. My Little Fox. Chrustowski, Rick, illus. 2017. (ENG., Illus.). 40p. (J). (gr. -1-k). 17.99 *(978-1-4814-6961-6(4)*, Beach Lane Bks.) Beach Lane Bks.
Chukovsky, Korneï. Doctor Ouch. Seabaugh, Jan, tr. from RUS. Seabaugh, Jan, illus. 2004. (Children's International Ser.: 1). Orig. Title: Aibolit. 43p. (J). pap. 6.99 *(978-0-9740551-0-7(7))* Smith, Viveca Publishing.
Church, Caroline Jayne. Goodnight, I Love You. Church, Caroline Jayne, illus. 2012. (ENG., Illus.). 20p. (J). (gr. -1-k). bds. 8.99 *(978-0-545-39215-0(2)*, Cartwheel Bks.) Scholastic, Inc.
—I Am a Big Brother. Church, Caroline Jayne, illus. 2015. (ENG., Illus.). 24p. (J). (gr. -1 — 1). 6.99 *(978-0-545-68886-4(8)*, Cartwheel Bks.) Scholastic, Inc.
—I Am a Big Brother! / ¡Soy un Hermano Mayor! (Bilingual) (Bilingual Edition) Church, Caroline Jayne, illus. 2015. (SPA., Illus.). 24p. (J). (gr. -1 — 1). 6.99 *(978-0-545-84717-9(6)*, Scholastic en Espanol) Scholastic, Inc.
—I Am a Big Sister. Church, Caroline Jayne, illus. 2015. (ENG., Illus.). 24p. (J). (gr. -1 — 1). 6.99 *(978-0-545-68898-7(1)*, Cartwheel Bks.) Scholastic, Inc.
—I Am a Big Sister! / ¡Soy una Hermana Mayor! (Bilingual) (Bilingual Edition) Church, Caroline Jayne, illus. 2015.Tr. of ¡Soy una Hermana Mayor! (SPA., Illus.). 24p. (J). (gr. -1 — 1). 6.99 *(978-0-545-84718-6(4)*, Scholastic en Espanol) Scholastic, Inc.
—Sweet Child of Mine: a Caroline Jayne Church Treasury. Church, Caroline Jayne, illus. 2014. (ENG., Illus.). 26p. (J). (— 1). bds. 8.99 *(978-0-545-64771-7(1)*, Cartwheel Bks.) Scholastic, Inc.
Churchill, Vicki & Fuge, Charles. Sometimes I Like to Curl up in a Ball. 2003. (ENG., Illus.). 22p. (J). (gr. -1-k). bds. 8.99 *(978-1-4027-0870-1(X))* Sterling Publishing Co., Inc.
Clara & Wilson, Russell. Why Not You? Gibson, Jessica, illus. 2022. 32p. (J). (gr. -1-3). 18.99 *(978-0-593-37440-5(1))*; (ENG.). lib. bdg. 21.99 *(978-0-593-37441-2(X))* Random Hse. Children's Bks. (Random Hse. Bks. for Young Readers).
Ciundziewicki, Lech. Glupcio Zeglarz: Zbior Bajek I Wierszy. 2004. 114p. (J). per. *(978-1-59196-597-8(7))* Instant Pub.
Clarion Books, Clarion. Five Silly Ghosts Board Book. Kushnir, Hilli, illus. 2018. (ENG.). 12p. (J). (— 1). bds. 6.99 *(978-1-328-86659-2(9)*, 1696027, Clarion Bks.) HarperCollins Pubs.
Clark, Sally. Where's My Hug? 2015. (ENG., Illus.). 24p. (J). bds. 8.99 *(978-0-8249-1952-8(1)*, Ideals Pubns.) Worthy Publishing.
Clark, Seneca & Giardi, Sandy. The Yellowest Yellow Lab. Decedue, Julie, illus. 2005. 30p. (J). 11.95 *(978-0-9767276-2-0(5))* Three Bean Pr.
Clarke, Jane. Chewy Hughie: Band 07/Turquoise (Collins Big Cat) McConnell, Sarah, illus. 2006. (Collins Big Cat Ser.). (ENG.). 24p. (J). (gr. 2-2). pap. 8.99 *(978-0-00-718692-1(4))* HarperCollins Pubs. Ltd. GBR. Dist: Independent Pubs. Group.
—How to Brush Your Teeth with Snappy Crocodile. Birkett, Georgie, illus. 2017. 16p. (J). bds. 8.99 *(978-1-61067-494-2(4))* Kane Miller.
—Runny Honey. Zlatic, Tomislav, illus. 2008. (Tadpoles Ser.). (ENG.). 24p. (J). (gr. -1-3). pap. *(978-0-7787-3893-0(0))*; lib. bdg. *(978-0-7787-3862-6(0))* Crabtree Publishing Co.
Clarkson, Kelly. River Rose & the Magical Christmas. Fleming, Lucy, illus. 2017. (J). *(978-0-06-274098-4(9))* Harper & Row Ltd.
Clawson, Kimberly. Fun O' Licious. Bellomy, Gail, illus. 2007. (ENG.). 56p. per. 16.95 *(978-1-4241-5556-9(8))* America Star Bks.
Clayton, Dallas. An Awesome Book of Thanks!, 0 vols. Clayton, Dallas, illus. unabr. ed. 2010. (ENG.). 86p. (J). (gr. -1-2). 17.95 *(978-1-935597-37-7(X)*, 9781935597377, Two Lions) Amazon Publishing.
Cleary, Brian P. Crunch & Crack, Oink & Whack! An Onomatopoeia Story. Pino, Pablo, illus. 2019. (ENG.). 32p. (J). (gr. 2-5). 26.65 *(978-1-4677-8799-4(X)*, fe74533a-b23b-4109-88d5-d9414ab7877c, Millbrook Pr.) Lerner Publishing Group.
—Eight Wild Nights: A Family Hanukkah. Udovic, David, illus. 2006. 24p. (J). (gr. -1-3). lib. bdg. 16.95 *(978-1-58013-152-0(2)*, Kar-Ben Publishing) Lerner Publishing Group.
—The Sun Played Hide-And-Seek: A Personification Story. Crimmins, Carol, illus. 2017. (ENG.). 32p. (J). (gr. 2-5). lib. bdg. 26.65 *(978-1-4677-2648-1(6)*, 93e1da2d-a0f2-4ab2-91ca-8d0ff50b7076, Millbrook Pr.) Lerner Publishing Group.
—Windows, Rings, & Grapes - A Look at Different Shapes. Gable, Brian, illus. 2011. (Math Is CATegorical Ser.). pap. 39.62 *(978-0-7613-8360-4(3)*, Millbrook Pr.) Lerner Publishing Group.
Clements, Andrew. The Handiest Things in the World. Jaramillo, Raquel, illus. 2010. (ENG.). 48p. (J). (gr. -1-3). 19.99 *(978-1-4169-6166-6(6)*, Atheneum Bks. for Young Readers) Simon & Schuster Children's Publishing.
Cleofas-Moore, Ramona. Tiffany. 2008. 60p. pap. 16.95 *(978-1-60474-238-1(0))* America Star Bks.
Cleveland, Nicole K. Ode to a Fly. 2007. 56p. per. 16.95 *(978-1-4241-7977-0(7))* America Star Bks.
Clickard, Carrie. Magic for Sale. Shelley, John, illus. 2017. (ENG.). 32p. (J). (gr. -1-3). 16.95 *(978-0-8234-3559-3(8))* Holiday Hse., Inc.

—Victricia Malicia: Book-Loving Buccaneer. Meyers, Mark, illus. 2012. 32p. (J). (gr. 2-4). 16.95 *(978-1-936261-12-3(X))* Flashlight Pr.
Clough, Paige. The Jumping Orie Story. Yates, Bridget & Ward, Karen, illus. 2015. (J). *(978-1-942945-24-6(8))* Night Heron Media.
—The Jumping Orie Story. Yates, Bridget & Ward, Karen, illus. 2015. (J). *(978-0-9915511-2-5(5))* Rule 2 Bks.
Cochran, Jean M. Off I Go! Gullens, Lee M., illus. 2008. (ENG.). 32p. (J). (gr. -1-k). 16.95 *(978-0-9792035-1-0(1))* Pleasant St. Pr.
Cohen, Warren Lee. Dragon Baked Bread, 32 vols. Ssebulime, John, illus. 2005. (ENG.). 32p. (J). *(978-1-902636-70-2(8))* Clairview Bks.
Cohn, Arlen. Firsts (Eyeball Animation) Board Book Edition. Vasconcellos, Daniel, illus. gif. ed. 2004. (ENG.). 28p. (J). bds. 9.99 *(978-1-57939-168-3(0))* Andrews McMeel Publishing.
Colandro, Lucille. There Was a Cold Lady Who Swallowed Some Snow!, 1 vol. Lee, Jared, illus. unabr. ed. 2006. (ENG.). (J). (gr. -1-3). pap. 9.99 incl. audio compact disk *(978-0-439-89556-9(1))* Scholastic, Inc.
—There Was a Cold Lady Who Swallowed Some Snow! 2003. (There Was an Old Lady... Ser.). (J). (gr. k-3). lib. bdg. 17.20 *(978-0-613-72229-2(9))* Turtleback.
—There Was a Cold Lady Who Swallowed Some Snow! (a Board Book) Lee, Jared, illus. 2017. (ENG.). 32p. (J). (— 1). bds. 6.99 *(978-1-338-15187-9(8),* Cartwheel Bks.) Scholastic, Inc.
—There Was an Old Lady Who Swallowed a Bat! (Board Book) Lee, Jared, illus. 2017. (ENG.). 32p. (J). (gr. -1 — 1). bds. 6.99 *(978-1-338-13580-0(5),* Cartwheel Bks.) Scholastic, Inc.
—There Was an Old Lady Who Swallowed a Chick!, 1 vol. Lee, Jared, illus. (ENG.). (J). (gr. -1-k). 2011. pap. 10.99 incl. audio compact disk *(978-0-545-27367-1(6))* 2010. 32p. pap. 6.99 *(978-0-545-16181-7(9),* Cartwheel Bks.) Scholastic, Inc.
—There Was an Old Lady Who Swallowed a Chick! 2009. (Illus.). (J). *(978-0-545-06059-2(1))* Scholastic, Inc.
—There Was an Old Lady Who Swallowed a Chick! Lee, Jared, illus. 2010. (There Was an Old Lady... Ser.). lib. bdg. 17.20 *(978-0-606-06821-5(X))* Turtleback.
—There Was an Old Lady Who Swallowed a Frog! Lee, Jared D., illus. 2015. (J). *(978-0-545-83213-7(6))* Scholastic, Inc.
—There Was an Old Lady Who Swallowed Some Books! Lee, Jared, illus. 2012. (There Was an Old Lady... Ser.). lib. bdg. 17.20 *(978-0-606-26208-8(3))* Turtleback.
—There Was an Old Lady Who Swallowed Some Leaves! Lee, Jared, illus. 2010. (ENG.). 32p. (J). (gr. -1-k). pap. 6.99 *(978-0-545-24198-4(7),* Cartwheel Bks.) Scholastic, Inc.
Colato Lainez, René. Senor Pancho Had a Rancho. Smith, Elwood, illus. 2014. (ENG.). 32p. (J). (gr. -1-k). 7.99 *(978-0-8234-3173-1(8))* Holiday Hse., Inc.
Cole, Gina, illus. Adapt. 2005. 40p. (J). 17.00 *(978-0-9659538-3-2(1))* Soul Vision Works Publishing.
Coll, Ivar Da. Cinco Amigos. (SPA.). (J). bds. *(978-958-04-4909-6(0))* Norma S.A. COL. Dist: Lectorum Pubns., Inc.
Collins, Rachel. Fiddle Faddle Frog & Piddle Paddle Polliwog. 2010. (ENG.). 32p. pap. 16.95 *(978-0-557-53411-1(9))* Lulu Pr., Inc.
Collins, Suzanne. When Charlie McButton Lost Power. Lester, Mike, illus. 2009. 32p. 16.00 *(978-1-60686-529-3(3))* Perfection Learning Corp.
—When Charlie Mcbutton Lost Power. Lester, Mike, illus. 2007. 32p. (J). (gr. -1-3). pap. 8.99 *(978-0-14-240857-5(3),* Puffin Books) Penguin Young Readers Group.
Colors All Day. (J). 26.20 *(978-0-8136-8399-7(8))*; (gr. -1-3). 59.50 *(978-0-8136-7918-1(4))* Modern Curriculum Pr.
Comer, Brigitte Renee. The Little Hopping Frog. 2012. 24p. pap. 24.95 *(978-1-4626-8243-0(X))* America Star Bks.
Conan, Sally Anne. Sleepy Time Blessings. Rutten, Nicole, illus. 2009. (ENG.). 12p. (J). (gr. -1). bds. 8.00 *(978-0-8028-5350-9(1))* Eerdmans, William B. Publishing Co.
Coniglio, John. The Cat Who Slept All Day: What Happens While the Cat Sleeps. Key, Pamela, illus. 2006. 24p. (J). per. 2.99 *(978-1-59958-004-3(7))* Journey Stone Creations, LLC.
Connelly, Wendy. Fiona the Firefly! 2003. (Illus.). (J). 12.95 *(978-1-929039-16-6(6))* Ambassador Bks., Inc.
Connolly, C J. The Boomerang. 2010. (Illus.). 32p. (J). 16.95 *(978-0-9825559-1-0(1))* Crosswinds Pr., Inc.
—Wil, Fitz, & a Flea Named T. 2009. (Illus.). 32p. (J). 16.95 *(978-0-9825559-0-3(3))* Crosswinds Pr., Inc.
conrad, catherine. The Lemonade Stand. 2008. (Illus.). 32p. (J). lib. bdg. 16.99 *(978-0-9799065-0-3(4))* Banana Pr.
Cook, Gary. The Best Saturday Ever! Sward, Adam, illus. 2013. (Robbie's Big Adventures Ser.). (ENG.). 40p. (J). (gr. k-3). 15.95 *(978-1-938063-25-1(2),* Mighty Media Kids) Mighty Media Pr.
Cook, Julie Kidd. One Is Enough. Iwai, Melissa, illus. 2005. (Rookie Reader Skill Set Ser.). (ENG.). 24p. (J). (gr. 1-2). per. 4.95 *(978-0-516-25283-4(6),* Children's Pr.) Scholastic Library Publishing.
Cook, Marisa. The Adventures of Ollie & Ronnie: Litter. 2012. 16p. (-18). pap. 12.68 *(978-1-4669-6630-7(0))* Trafford Publishing.
Coombs, Kate. Goodnight Mr. Darcy: A BabyLit(TM) Parody Picture Book, 1 vol. 2014. (ENG., Illus.). 32p. (J). 16.99 *(978-1-4236-3670-0(8))* Gibbs Smith, Publisher.
Cooper, Susan. The Shortest Day. Ellis, Carson, illus. 2019. (ENG.). 32p. (J). (gr. k-4). 17.99 *(978-0-7636-8698-7(0))* Candlewick Pr.
Copeland, Cynthia L. & Lewis, Alexandra P. Splashy Fins, Flashy Skins: Deep-Sea Rhymes to Make You Grin. 2003. (Silly Millies Ser.: 4). (Illus.). 32p. lib. bdg. 17.90 *(978-0-7613-2906-0(4),* Millbrook Pr.) Lerner Publishing Group.
Copus, Julia. My Bed Is an Air Balloon. Jay, Alison, illus. 2018. (ENG.). 32p. 15.95 *(978-0-571-33484-1(9),* Faber & Faber Children's Bks.) Faber & Faber, Inc.
Corchin, D. J. I Feel... Awesome. 2020. (I Feel... Ser.). (Illus.). 56p. (J). (gr. -1-3). 14.99 *(978-1-7282-1973-8(6))* Sourcebooks, Inc.
Corderoy, Tracey. Whizz! Pop! Granny, Stop! Berger, Joe, illus. 2013. (ENG.). 32p. (J). (gr. -1-2). 14.99 *(978-0-7636-6551-7(7))* Candlewick Pr.
Cordsen, Carol Foskett. The Milkman. Jones, Douglas B., illus. 2007. (gr. -1-3). 17.00 *(978-0-7569-8148-8(4))* Perfection Learning Corp.
Corey, Shana. Monster Parade. Terry, Will, illus. 2009. (Step into Reading: Step 2 Ser.). (ENG.). 24p. (J). (gr. -1-1). lib. bdg. 16.19 *(978-0-375-95638-6(7))* Random House Publishing Group.
—Monster Parade. Terry, Will, illus. 2009. (Step into Reading Ser.). 24p. (J). (gr. -1-1). 5.99 *(978-0-375-85638-9(2),* Random Hse. Bks. for Young Readers) Random Hse. Children's Bks.
Corlyn, Ron. The House That Grew. 2013. 24p. pap. 24.95 *(978-1-63000-118-6(X))* America Star Bks.
Corso, Suzanne. Sammy & Sue Go Green Too! 2009. (Sammy & Sue Ser.: 0). (ENG.). 32p. 16.95 *(978-0-8253-0517-7(9))* Beaufort Bks., Inc.
Cortes, Mary. Where on Earth Did My Sock Go? 2006. (J). per. 15.95 *(978-0-9787788-3-5(9))* LUMEN-US Pubns.
Cortright, Celeste. Ready, Set, Go! Sports of All Sorts. Engel, Christiane, illus. 2020. (ENG.). 24p. (J). (gr. -1-2). 16.99 *(978-1-78285-985-7(3))*; pap. 9.99 *(978-1-78285-991-8(8))* Barefoot Bks., Inc.
Costales, Amy. Hello Night: Hola Noche. McDonald, Mercedes, illus. 2007. (ENG.). 24p. (J). (gr. -1 — 1). 14.95 *(978-0-87358-927-7(0))* Cooper Square Publishing Llc.
Coster, Simon. My Dinosaur Is More Awesome! 2015. (ENG., Illus.). 48p. (J). (gr. -1-k). 16.99 *(978-1-63220-416-5(9),* Sky Pony Pr.) Skyhorse Publishing Co., Inc.
Côté, Geneviève & Côté, Geneviève. Starring Me & You, 0 vols. Côté, Geneviève & Côté, Geneviève, illus. 2014. (Piggy & Bunny Ser.). (ENG., Illus.). 32p. (J). (gr. -1-k). 16.95 *(978-1-894786-39-3(4))* Kids Can Pr., Ltd. CAN. Dist: Hachette Bk. Group.
Cottswold, Wooley. Rose & the Bald-Headed Elephant. 2009. (Illus.). 28p. (J). 16.95 *(978-0-9779064-0-6(X))* Archie Publishing.
Cousins, Lucy. Hooray for Birds! Cousins, Lucy, illus. 2017. (ENG., Illus.). 40p. (J). (-k). 17.99 *(978-0-7636-9265-0(4))* Candlewick Pr.
—Hooray for Fish! Cousins, Lucy, illus. (ENG., Illus.). (J). (— 1). 2017. 34p. bds. 9.99 *(978-0-7636-9352-7(9))* 2005. 40p. 17.99 *(978-0-7636-2741-6(0))* Candlewick Pr.
—Maisy's First Colors: A Maisy Concept Book. Cousins, Lucy, illus. 2013. (Maisy Ser.). (ENG., Illus.). 14p. (J). (-k). bds. 7.99 *(978-0-7636-6804-4(4))* Candlewick Pr.
Cowen-Fletcher, Jane. Baby Be Kind. Cowen-Fletcher, Jane, illus. 2012. (ENG., Illus.). 18p. (J). (gr. k — 1). bds. 7.99 *(978-0-7636-5647-8(X))* Candlewick Pr.
Cowley, Joy. Freddy Bear & the Toothpaste. Webb, Philip, illus. 2017. (Freddy Bear Ser.). 20p. (J). (— 1). bds. 7.99 *(978-1-927262-97-9(6))* Upstart Pr. NZL. Dist: Independent Pubs. Group.
—Mrs. Wishy-Washy's Farm. Fuller, Elizabeth, illus. (ENG.). 32p. (J). (gr. -1-k). 2006. 8.99 *(978-0-14-240299-3(0),* Puffin Books) 2003. 17.99 *(978-0-399-23872-7(7),* Philomel Bks.) Penguin Young Readers Group.
Cox, Christine. Why the Zero Was Sad? 2008. 32p. pap. 14.49 *(978-1-4389-1056-7(8))* AuthorHouse.
Cox, Miss Karin & Cox, Karin. Pancakes on Sunday. Acar, Sinan, illus. 2012. 26p. pap. *(978-0-9873602-2-9(1))* Indelible Ink Pr.
Cox, Phil Roxbee. Fat Cat on a Mat. Tyler, Jenny, ed. Cartwright, Stephen, illus. rev. ed. 2006. (Phonics Readers Ser.). 16p. (J). (gr. -1-3). pap. 6.99 *(978-0-7945-1502-7(9),* Usborne) EDC Publishing.
—Ted's Shed. Tyler, Jenny, ed. Cartwright, Stephen, illus. rev. ed. 2006. (Phonics Readers Ser.). 16p. (J). (gr. -1-3). pap. 6.99 *(978-0-7945-1511-9(8),* Usborne) EDC Publishing.
Cox, Phil Roxbee & Cartwright, S. Goose on the Loose. 2004. (Easy Words to Read Ser.). 16p. (J). (gr. 1-18). pap. 6.95 *(978-0-7945-0036-8(6),* Usborne) EDC Publishing.
Cox, Phil Roxbee & Cartwright, Stephen. Goose on the Loose. 2004. (Phonics Board Bks.). (Illus.). 10p. (J). 4.99 *(978-0-7945-0305-5(5),* Usborne) EDC Publishing.
Coxe, Molly. Hop Frog. 2018. (Bright Owl Bks.). (Illus.). 40p. (J). (gr. -1-2). pap. 6.99 *(978-1-57565-982-4(4),* 39069031-9f08-49ff-8db6-4d6dcf3e4d5d); lib. bdg. 17.99 *(978-1-57565-981-7(6),* 501d1e26-ef1e-4b5a-a34c-7eff8c6b62b4) Astra Publishing Hse. (Kane Press).
Coyle, Carmela Lavigna. Do Princesses Become Astronauts? Gordon, Mike, illus. 2019. (Do Princesses Ser.). 32p. (J). (gr. -1-2). 15.95 *(978-1-63076-347-3(0))* Muddy Boots Pr.
—Do Princesses Have Best Friends Forever? Gordon, Mike & Gordon, Carl, illus. 2010. (ENG.). 32p. (J). E-Book *(978-1-58979-543-3(1))* Taylor Trade Publishing.
—Do Princesses Have Best Friends Forever? Gordon, Carl & Gordon, Mike, illus. 2010. (Do Princesses Ser.). (ENG.). 32p. (J). (gr. -1-3). 15.95 *(978-1-58979-542-6(3))* Taylor Trade Publishing.
—Do Princesses Make Happy Campers? Gordon, Mike, illus. 2015. (Do Princesses Ser.). 32p. (J). (gr. -1-2). 15.95 *(978-1-63076-054-0(4))* Taylor Trade Publishing.
Coyle, Carmela LaVigna. Do Princesses Really Kiss Frogs? Gordon, Mike & Gordon, Carl, illus. 2005. (Do Princesses Ser.). (ENG.). 32p. (J). (gr. -1-2). 15.95 *(978-0-87358-880-5(0))* Cooper Square Publishing Llc.
Coyle, Carmela Lavigna. Do Princesses Scrape Their Knees? 2006. (Do Princesses Ser.). (ENG., Illus.). 32p. (J). (gr. -1-2). 15.95 *(978-0-87358-909-3(2))* Cooper Square Publishing Llc.
—Do Princesses Wear Hiking Boots? Gordon, Mike & Gordon, Carl, illus. 2003. (Do Princesses Ser.). (ENG.). 32p. (J). (gr. -1-2). 15.95 *(978-0-87358-828-7(2))* Cooper Square Publishing Llc.
—Do Superheroes Have Teddy Bears? Gordon, Mike, illus. 2012. (Do Princesses Ser.). 32p. (J). (gr. -1-2). 15.95 *(978-1-58979-693-5(4))* Taylor Trade Publishing.
—The Tumbleweed Came Back. Rechin, Kevin, illus. 2013. 32p. (J). 15.95 *(978-1-933855-83-7(5),* Rio Nuevo Pubs.) Rio Nuevo Pubs.
Crabtree, Sally. Magic Train Ride. Esplugas, Sonia & Espulgas, Sonia, illus. 2007. (ENG.). 32p. (J). (gr. -1-k). 6.99 *(978-1-84686-132-1(2))* Barefoot Bks., Inc.
—Magic Train Ride. Esplugas, Sonia, illus. (Barefoot Singalongs Ser.). (J). 2007. (ENG.). 32p. (gr. -1-k). pap. 9.99 *(978-1-905236-91-6(3))* 2006. 0032p. 16.99 *(978-1-905236-52-7(2))* Barefoot Bks., Inc.
Craig, Lindsey. Dancing Feet! Brown, Marc, illus. 2012. 32p. (J). (gr. k-k). 6.99 *(978-0-307-93081-1(5),* Knopf Bks. for Young Readers) Random Hse. Children's Bks.
—Farmyard Beat. Brown, Marc, illus. 2012. 32p. (J). (gr. k-k). 6.99 *(978-0-307-93082-8(3),* Knopf Bks. for Young Readers) Random Hse. Children's Bks.
Craig, Sherryn. Midnight Madness at the Zoo, 1 vol. Jones, Karen, illus. 2016. (J). (gr. k-1). (SPA.). 39p. pap. 11.95 *(978-1-62855-744-2(3),* 9f8858c6-8461-4bd2-8a81-65b1c9987029); (ENG.). 32p. 17.95 *(978-1-62855-730-5(3))* Arbordale Publishing.
Crawford, Georgina. Archie-Parchie-Piddley-Poo. 2009. (Illus.). 24p. pap. 12.99 *(978-1-4389-7307-4(1))* AuthorHouse.
Cree, Tahara, text. Bonnie the Bee. 2012. (ENG., Illus.). 13p. pap. 5.00 *(978-0-9824964-3-5(5))* Creative Education & Publishing.
Creech, Natalee. Nothing: Nothing Can Separate You from God's Love! Cowman, Joseph, illus. 2019. (ENG.). 32p. (J). (gr. -1-3). 18.99 *(978-0-8249-5703-2(2),* Worthy Kids/Ideals) Worthy Publishing.
—When Day Is Done. Dunn, Robert, illus. 2019. 32p. (J). (gr. -1-k). 16.99 *(978-1-5064-4772-8(4),* Beaming Books) 1517 Media.
Crisp, Dan, illus. The Ants Go Marching. 2009. (Classic Books with Holes Big Book Ser.). 16p. (J). (gr. -1-1). spiral bd. *(978-1-84643-207-1(3))*; (ENG.). *(978-1-84643-256-9(1))* Child's Play International Ltd.
Cronin, Doreen. Bounce. Menchin, Scott, illus. 2007. (ENG.). 40p. (J). (gr. -1-3). 19.99 *(978-1-4169-1627-7(X),* Atheneum Bks. for Young Readers) Simon & Schuster Children's Publishing.
—Clic, Clac, Plif, Plaf: Una Aventura de Contar. Lewin, Betsy, illus. 2006. (J). (gr. -1-k). per. 6.99 *(978-1-933032-03-0(0))* Lectorum Pubns., Inc.
—Clic, Clac, Plif, Plaf: Una Aventura de Contar. Rioja, Alberto Jimenez, tr. from ENG. Lewin, Betsy, illus. 2006. (J). (gr. 5-6). 12.99 *(978-1-933032-11-5(1))* Lectorum Pubns., Inc.
—Click, Clack, Splish, Splash: A Counting Adventure, 1 vol. Lewin, Betsy, illus. 2006. (Doreen Cronin: Click-Clack & More Ser.). (ENG.). 24p. (J). (gr. k-5). lib. bdg. 31.36 *(978-1-59961-090-0(6),* 5418, Picture Bk.) Spotlight.
—Click, Clack, Splish, Splash: Click, Clack, Splish, Splash. 2006. (Click Clack Book Ser.). (ENG., Illus.). 24p. (J). (gr. -1-3). 18.99 *(978-0-689-87716-2(1),* Atheneum Bks. for Young Readers) Simon & Schuster Children's Publishing.
—Stretch. Menchin, Scott, illus. 2009. (ENG.). 40p. (J). (gr. -1-3). 19.99 *(978-1-4169-5341-8(8),* Atheneum Bks. for Young Readers) Simon & Schuster Children's Publishing.
—Wiggle. Menchin, Scott, illus. 2005. (ENG.). 40p. (J). (gr. -1-3). 19.99 *(978-0-689-86375-2(6),* Atheneum Bks. for Young Readers) Simon & Schuster Children's Publishing.
Crosby, Jeff, illus. Ten Texas Babies, 1 vol. 2014. (ENG.). 32p. (gr. k-3). 16.99 *(978-1-4556-1874-3(8),* Pelican Publishing) Arcadia Publishing.
Crossan, Sarah. One. 2015. (ENG.). 400p. (YA). (gr. 8). 17.99 *(978-0-06-211875-2(7),* Greenwillow Bks.) HarperCollins Pubs.
Crow, Kristyn. Bedtime at the Swamp. 2008. (ENG., Illus.). 32p. (J). (gr. -1-1). 16.99 *(978-0-06-083951-2(1),* HarperCollins) HarperCollins Pubs.
—Skeleton Cat. 2012. lib. bdg. 17.20 *(978-0-606-26209-5(1))* Turtleback.
—Zombelina. Idle, Molly, illus. 2013. (ENG.). 32p. (J). (gr. -1-3). 16.99 *(978-0-8027-2803-6(0),* 900081980, Bloomsbury USA Childrens) Bloomsbury Publishing USA.
—Zombelina Dances the Nutcracker. Idle, Molly, illus. 2015. (ENG.). 40p. (J). (gr. -1-3). 16.99 *(978-1-61963-640-8(9),* 900143827, Bloomsbury USA Childrens) Bloomsbury Publishing USA.
Crow, Kristyn & Aesop, Aesop. The Really Groovy Story of the Tortoise & the Hare. Forshay, Christina, illus. 2012. (J). *(978-1-61913-128-6(5))* Weigl Pubs., Inc.
Crow, Marilee & Foster, Jack. Once There Was a Monster. 2012. 20p. pap. 9.95 *(978-1-61633-331-7(6))* Guardian Angel Publishing, Inc.
Crow, Sara. Even Superheroes Have to Sleep. Record, Adam, illus. (J). (— 1). 2018. 26p. bds. 6.99 *(978-0-399-55809-2(8))* 2017. 32p. 16.99 *(978-0-399-55806-1(3))* Random Hse. Children's Bks. (Doubleday Bks. for Young Readers).
—Even Superheroes Use the Potty. Record, Adam, illus. (J). (— 1). 2019. 26p. bds. 6.99 *(978-1-5247-6599-6(6))* 2018. 32p. 16.99 *(978-0-399-55934-1(5))* Random Hse. Children's Bks. (Doubleday Bks. for Young Readers).
Crowder, Melanie. Audacity. 2016. 400p. (YA). (gr. 7). pap. 12.99 *(978-0-14-751249-9(2),* Speak) Penguin Young Readers Group.
Crowley, Peter. J T Seavey. 2012. (ENG.). 35p. (J). pap. 18.95 *(978-1-4327-8712-7(8))* Outskirts Pr., Inc.
Crown Peak Publishing. Just Be You. Crown Peak Publishing, illus. 2008. (ENG., Illus.). 40p. (J). 19.95 *(978-0-9645663-5-4(4))* Crown Peak Publishing.
Crownberry, Ethan. A Fish with a Wish. 2012. 84p. pap. 8.95 *(978-1-105-84560-4(5))* Lulu Pr., Inc.
Crozier, Lorna. More Than Balloons, 1 vol. Miller, Rachelle Anne, illus. 2017. (ENG.). 26p. (J). (gr. -1 — 1). bds. 9.95 *(978-1-4598-1028-0(7))* Orca Bk. Pubs. USA.
Crummel, Susan Stevens. All in One Hour, 0 vols. Donohue, Dorothy, illus. 2012. (ENG.). 40p. (J). (gr. k-3). pap. 9.99 *(978-0-7614-5537-0(X),* 9780761455370, Two Lions) Amazon Publishing.
—Sherlock Bones & the Missing Cheese, 0 vols. Donohue, Dorothy, illus. 2012. (ENG.). 40p. (J). (gr. 1-3). 17.99 *(978-0-7614-6186-9(8),* 9780761461869, Two Lions) Amazon Publishing.
Crystal, Billy. Grandpa's Little One. Porfirio, Guy, illus. 2006. 40p. (J). (gr. -1-k). lib. bdg. 17.89 *(978-0-06-078174-3(2))* HarperCollins Pubs.
—I Already Know I Love You. Sayles, Elizabeth, illus. (ENG.). 40p. (J). 2007. (gr. -1-3). pap. 7.99 *(978-0-06-059393-3(8),* HarperCollins) 2004. 16.99 *(978-0-06-059391-9(1))* HarperCollins Pubs.
Cuartas, Jennifer M. So Many Things. 2012. 28p. 24.95 *(978-1-4626-6328-6(1))* America Star Bks.
Cummings, Priscilla. Beetle Boddiker, 1 vol. 2009. (ENG., Illus.). 30p. (J). (gr. -1-3). 13.95 *(978-0-87033-602-7(9),* 3592, Cornell Maritime Pr./Tidewater Pubs.) Schiffer Publishing, Ltd.
Cunningham, Sheila S. Willow's Walkabout: A Children's Guide to Boston. Kelleher, Kathie, illus. 2012. (ENG.). 32p. (J). (gr. 1-3). 17.95 *(978-1-59373-096-3(9))* Bunker Hill Publishing, Inc.
Curtis, Carolyn. I Took the Moon for a Walk. Jay, Alison, illus. (ENG.). 32p. (J). 2012. (gr. -1-2). pap. 9.99 *(978-1-84148-803-5(8))* 2008. (gr. -1-2). bds. 14.99 *(978-1-84686-200-7(0))* 2004. 16.99 *(978-1-84148-611-6(6))* Barefoot Bks., Inc.
—Lleve la Luna a Pasear. Jay, Alison, illus. 2014. (SPA.). 32p. (J). (gr. -1-2). pap. 9.99 *(978-1-78285-084-7(8))* Barefoot Bks., Inc.
Curtis, Jamie Lee. Big Words for Little People. Cornell, Laura, illus. 2008. (ENG.). 40p. (J). (gr. -1-3). 18.99 *(978-0-06-112759-5(0),* HarperCollins) HarperCollins Pubs.
—I'm Gonna Like Me: Letting off a Little Self-Esteem. Cornell, Laura, illus. 2007. (ENG.). 32p. (J). (gr. -1-3). 19.99 *(978-0-06-028761-0(6),* HarperCollins) HarperCollins Pubs.
—Is There Really a Human Race? Cornell, Laura, illus. 2006. (ENG.). 40p. (J). (gr. -1-3). 17.99 *(978-0-06-075346-7(3),* HarperCollins) HarperCollins Pubs.
—It's Hard to Be Five: Learning How to Work My Control Panel. Cornell, Laura, illus. 40p. (J). (gr. -1-3). 2007. (ENG.). 18.99 *(978-0-06-008095-2(7),* HarperCollins) 2004. lib. bdg. 17.89 *(978-0-06-008096-9(5),* Cotler, Joanna Books) HarperCollins Pubs.
—My Mommy Hung the Moon: A Love Story. Date not set. 32p. (J). (gr. -1-3). pap. 6.99 *(978-0-06-443696-0(9))* HarperCollins Pubs.
—My Mommy Hung the Moon: A Love Story. Cornell, Laura, illus. 2010. (ENG.). 40p. (J). (gr. -1-3). 17.99 *(978-0-06-029016-0(1),* HarperCollins) HarperCollins Pubs.
—Today I Feel Silly & Other Moods That Make My Day. Cornell, Laura, illus. 2007. (ENG.). 40p. (J). (gr. -1-3). 18.99 *(978-0-06-024560-3(3),* HarperCollins) HarperCollins Pubs.
Cusimano Love, Maryann. You Are My I Love You. Ichikawa, Satomi, illus. 2012. 30p. (J). (gr. -1 — 1). bds. 7.99 *(978-0-399-24396-7(8),* Philomel Bks.) Penguin Young Readers Group.
—You Are My I Love You: Board Book. Ichikawa, Satomi, illus. 2010. 30p. (J). (gr. -1 — 1). bds. 6.99 *(978-0-399-24395-0(X),* Philomel Bks.) Penguin Young Readers Group.
Cuyler, Margery. Best Friends. 2017. (Step into Reading Ser.). (ENG., Illus.). 32p. (J). (gr. -1-1). pap. 5.99 *(978-0-399-55369-1(X),* Random Hse. Bks. for Young Readers) Random Hse. Children's Bks.
—The Little Dump Truck. Kolar, Bob, illus. 2014. (Little Vehicles Ser.: 1). (ENG.). 24p. (J). (gr. -1-1). bds. 8.99 *(978-0-8050-9990-4(5),* 900129326, Holt, Henry & Co. Bks. For Young Readers) Holt, Henry & Co.
—The Little Fire Truck. Kolar, Bob, illus. 2017. (Little Vehicles Ser.: 3). (ENG.). 32p. (J). 14.99 *(978-1-62779-805-1(6),* 900160047, Holt, Henry & Co. Bks. For Young Readers) Holt, Henry & Co.
—The Little Ice Cream Truck. Kolar, Bob, illus. 2018. (Little Vehicles Ser.: 4). (ENG.). 32p. (J). 17.99 *(978-1-62779-806-8(4),* 900160050, Holt, Henry & Co. Bks. For Young Readers) Holt, Henry & Co.
—The Little School Bus. Kolar, Bob, illus. 2018. (Little Vehicles Ser.: 2). (ENG.). 24p. (J). bds. 8.99 *(978-1-250-19645-3(0),* 900194112, Holt, Henry & Co. Bks. For Young Readers) Holt, Henry & Co.
—Monster Mess! Schindler, S. D., illus. 2008. (ENG.). 32p. (J). (gr. -1-1). 19.99 *(978-0-689-86405-6(1),* McElderry, Margaret K. Bks.) McElderry, Margaret K. Bks.
—Princess Bess Gets Dressed. Malone, Heather, illus. 2009. (ENG.). 32p. (J). (gr. -1-3). 18.99 *(978-1-4169-3833-0(8),* Simon & Schuster Bks. For Young Readers) Simon & Schuster Bks. For Young Readers.
—Tick Tock Clock. Neubecker, Robert, illus. 2012. (My First I Can Read Ser.). (ENG.). 32p. (J). (gr. -1 — 1). pap. 4.99 *(978-0-06-136311-5(1),* HarperCollins) HarperCollins Pubs.
Cuyler, Margery & Neubecker, Robert. Tick Tock Clock. 2012. (My First I Can Read Ser.). (ENG., Illus.). 32p. (J). (gr. -1 — 1). 16.99 *(978-0-06-136309-2(X),* HarperCollins) HarperCollins Pubs.
Cyrus, Kurt. Be a Good Dragon. Cyrus, Kurt, illus. 2018. (ENG., Illus.). 32p. (J). (gr. k-3). 16.99 *(978-1-58536-383-4(9),* 204395) Sleeping Bear Pr.
—Billions of Bricks. Cyrus, Kurt, illus. 2016. (ENG., Illus.). 32p. (J). 18.99 *(978-1-62779-273-8(2),* 900144946, Holt, Henry & Co. Bks. For Young Readers) Holt, Henry & Co.
—Shake a Leg, Egg! Cyrus, Kurt, illus. 2017. (ENG., Illus.). 32p. (J). (gr. -1-3). 17.99 *(978-1-4814-5848-1(5),* Beach Lane Bks.) Beach Lane Bks.
Czajak, Paul. Monster Needs a Christmas Tree. Grieb, Wendy, illus. 2014. (Monster & Me Ser.). (ENG.). 32p. (J). (-k). 16.95 *(978-1-938063-46-6(5),* Mighty Media Kids) Mighty Media Pr.
—Monster Needs a Costume. Grieb, Wendy, illus. (Monster & Me Ser.). (ENG.). 32p. (J). (-k). 2014. 6.99 *(978-1-938063-38-1(4))* 2013. 16.95 *(978-1-938063-09-1(0))* Mighty Media Pr. (Mighty Media Kids).
—Monster Needs a Party. Grieb, Wendy, illus. 2015. (Monster & Me Ser.). (ENG.). 32p. (J). (-k). 16.95 *(978-1-938063-55-8(4),* Mighty Media Kids) Mighty Media Pr.
—Monster Needs His Sleep. Grieb, Wendy, illus. 2014. (Monster & Me Ser.). (ENG.). 32p. (J). (-k). 16.95 *(978-1-938063-26-8(0),* Mighty Media Kids) Mighty Media Pr.
—Monster Needs Your Vote. Grieb, Wendy, illus. 2015. (Monster & Me Ser.). (ENG.). 32p. (J). (gr. -1-3). 16.95 *(978-1-938063-63-3(5),* Mighty Media Kids) Mighty Media Pr.
Dacey, Richard. Spinner McClock & the Christmas Visit. Gillett, Hallie, illus. 2004. 32p. (J). 13.95 *(978-1-929039-24-1(7))* Ambassador Bks., Inc.
Dahl, Michael. Goodnight Baseball, 1 vol. Forshay, Christina, illus. 2013. (Sports Illustrated Kids Bedtime Bks.). (ENG.). 32p. (J). (gr. -1-2). lib. bdg. 22.60 *(978-1-4048-7979-9(X),* 120852, Picture Window Bks.) Capstone.
—Goodnight Hockey. Forshay, Christina, illus. 2015. (Sports Illustrated Kids Bedtime Bks.). (ENG.). 32p. (J). (gr. -1-2). lib. bdg. 22.60 *(978-1-4795-6526-9(1),* 128515, Picture Window Bks.) Capstone.

S

—Playdate for Panda. Vidal, Oriol, illus. 2016. (Hello Genius Ser.). (ENG.). 20p. (J). (gr. -1 — 1). bds. 7.99 *(978-1-4795-8741-4(9)*, 131130, Picture Window Bks.) Capstone.

Dahl, Roald, et al. Collins Musicals - Roald Dahl's Goldilocks & the Three Bears: an Impeccably Judged Musical, 1 vol. Baiton, Janice & Daley, Michelle, eds. Blake, Quentin & Eccles, Jane, illus. 2005. (and C Black Musicals Ser.). (ENG.). 56p. (J). (gr. 2-6). pap. 42.95 *(978-0-7136-7085-1(1))* HarperCollins Pubs. Ltd. GBR. Dist: Independent Pubs. Group.

—Collins Musicals - Roald Dahl's Little Red Riding Hood & the Wolf: a Howling Hilarious Musical, 1 vol. Baiton, Janice & Daley, Michelle, eds. Blake, Quentin & Eccles, Jane, illus. 2005. (and C Black Musicals Ser.). (ENG.). 56p. (J). (gr. 2-6). pap. 42.95 incl. cd-rom *(978-0-7136-6958-9(6))* HarperCollins Pubs. Ltd. GBR. Dist: Independent Pubs. Group.

Dalmatian Press Staff. The Alphabet Song Book. 2008. (ENG.). 5p. (J). bds. 4.95 *(978-1-58117-726-8(7)*, Intervisual/Piggy Toes) Bendon, Inc.

—Mommy, Is That You? 2008. (ENG.). 5p. bds. 4.95 *(978-1-58117-714-5(3)*, Intervisual/Piggy Toes) Bendon, Inc.

Damrell, John. The Flooring Family. 2008. 40p. pap. 24.95 *(978-1-60563-007-6(1))* America Star Bks.

Dane, Dichira A. Pathway of Pebbles. 2008. 20p. pap. 24.95 *(978-1-60703-801-6(3))* America Star Bks.

Danielson, Diane K. There Is a Mouse That Is Haunting Our House. 2012. (ENG.). 28p. (J). pap. 14.99 *(978-0-9885157-0-3(9))* SDP Publishing.

Danis, Naomi. Splish-Splash, into the Bath! Kreloff, Elliot, illus. 2007. (ENG.). 16p. (J). bds. *(978-1-59354-609-0(2))* Handprint Bks.

Dannenbring, Cheryl. My Puppy Gave to Me, 1 vol. Kremsner, Cynthia, illus. 2014. (Twelve Days of Christmas Ser.). (ENG.). 32p. (J). (gr. k-3). 16.99 *(978-1-4556-1943-6(4)*, Pelican Publishing) Arcadia Publishing.

Danyi, Barb. The Maker of Heaven & Earth. 2011. 28p. (gr. -1). pap. 11.99 *(978-1-4634-1300-2(9))* AuthorHouse.

Danylyshyn, Greg. A Crash of Rhinos: And Other Wild Animal Groups. Lomp, Stephan, illus. 2016. (ENG.). 40p. (J). (gr. -1-3). 17.99 *(978-1-4814-3150-7(1)*, Little Simon) Little Simon.

Darby, Ada Claire. Skip-Come-A-Lou. 2008. (Applewood Bks.). (ENG.). 252p. pap. 17.95 *(978-1-55709-996-9(0))* Applewood Bks.

Darling, Helen. Hide-n-seek Monday. Glickstein, Jennifer, ed. Sona and Jacob, illus. 2007. (J). 10.00 *(978-0-9797674-0-1(7))* My Darling-Tots Pubns.

Darrow, Sharon. Trash. 2006. (ENG.). 160p. (YA). (gr. 7-12). 16.99 *(978-0-7636-2624-2(4))* Candlewick Pr.

Davick, Linda. I Love You, Nose! I Love You, Toes! Davick, Linda, illus. 2013. (ENG., Illus.). 32p. (J). (gr. -1-1). 19.99 *(978-1-4424-6037-9(7)*, Beach Lane Bks.) Beach Lane Bks.

—Say Hello! Davick, Linda, illus. 2015. (ENG., Illus.). 40p. (J). (gr. -1-3). 19.99 *(978-1-4814-2867-5(5)*, Beach Lane Bks.) Beach Lane Bks.

Davidge, Bud. The Mummer's Song, 1 vol. Wallace, Ian, illus. 2009. (ENG.). 32p. (J). (gr. k-k). pap. 16.95 *(978-0-88899-960-3(7))* Groundwood Bks. CAN. Dist: Publishers Group West (PGW).

Davidson, Alice Joyce. St. Francis & the Animals. Swanson, Maggie, illus. 2006. 24p. (J). 7.95 *(978-0-88271-003-7(6))* Regina Pr., Malhame & Co.

Davies, Benji, illus. Bizzy Bear: Ambulance Rescue. 2018. (Bizzy Bear Ser.). (ENG.). 8p. (J). (— 1). bds. 7.99 *(978-1-5362-0256-4(8))* Candlewick Pr.

—Bizzy Bear: Fire Rescue! 2013. (Bizzy Bear Ser.). (ENG.). 8p. (J). (— 1). bds. 7.99 *(978-0-7636-6518-0(5))* Candlewick Pr.

—Bizzy Bear: Fun on the Farm. 2011. (Bizzy Bear Ser.). (ENG.). 8p. (J). (gr. k — 1). bds. 8.99 *(978-0-7636-5879-3(0))* Candlewick Pr.

—Bizzy Bear: Let's Get to Work! 2012. (Bizzy Bear Ser.). (ENG.). 8p. (J). (gr. k — 1). bds. 7.99 *(978-0-7636-5899-1(5))* Candlewick Pr.

—Bizzy Bear: off We Go! 2012. (Bizzy Bear Ser.). (ENG.). 8p. (J). (gr. k — 1). bds. 7.99 *(978-0-7636-5900-4(2))* Candlewick Pr.

—Bizzy Bear: Pirate Adventure. 2013. (Bizzy Bear Ser.). (ENG.). 8p. (J). (— 1). bds. 7.99 *(978-0-7636-6519-7(3))* Candlewick Pr.

—Bizzy Bear: Zookeeper. 2015. (Bizzy Bear Ser.). (ENG.). 8p. (J). (— 1). bds. 7.99 *(978-0-7636-7603-2(9))* Candlewick Pr.

Davies, Kate, illus. Little Squeak School. 2014. (J). *(978-1-4351-5582-4(3))* Barnes & Noble, Inc.

—Welcome to the Mouse House. 2014. (J). *(978-1-4351-5583-1(1))* Barnes & Noble, Inc.

Davies, Kathern. Bugs, Bugs, Bugs! Sorensen, Heather, illus. 2010. 24p. pap. 12.99 *(978-1-4520-1624-5(0))* AuthorHouse.

Davies, Timothy, Sr. The Polka-Dotted Elephant. 2007. (J). per. 12.00 *(978-0-9793207-0-5(4))* Wildlife Tales Publishing.

Dávila, Valeria & López. Diary of a Fairy. Warriner, tr. Aguerrebehere, Laura, illus. 2018. (Dear Diary Ser.). 32p. (J). (gr. -1-1). 7.99 *(978-2-924786-65-9(7)*, CrackBoom! Bks.) Chouette Publishing CAN. Dist: Publishers Group West (PGW).

—Diary of a Monster. Warriner, tr. Aguerrebehere, Laura, illus. 2018. (Dear Diary Ser.). 32p. (J). (gr. -1-1). 7.99 *(978-2-924786-71-0(1)*, CrackBoom! Bks.) Chouette Publishing CAN. Dist: Publishers Group West (PGW).

—Diary of an Ogre. Warriner, tr. Aguerrebehere, Laura, illus. 2018. (Dear Diary Ser.). 32p. (J). (gr. -1-1). 7.99 *(978-2-924786-69-7(X)*, CrackBoom! Bks.) Chouette Publishing CAN. Dist: Publishers Group West (PGW).

Dávila, Valeria & López, Mónica. Diary of a Witch. Warriner, David, tr. Aguerrebehere, Laura, illus. 2018. (Dear Diary Ser.). 32p. (J). (gr. -1-1). 7.99 *(978-2-924786-67-3(3)*, CrackBoom! Bks.) Chouette Publishing CAN. Dist: Publishers Group West (PGW).

Davis, Darlene. God Made Everything. 2008. 28p. pap. 24.95 *(978-1-60672-183-4(6))* PublishAmerica, Inc.

Davis, Lindsey. The Smallest Spot of a Dot: The Little Ways We're Different, the Big Ways We're the Same. Fleming, Lucy, illus. 2023. (ENG.). 32p. (J). 18.99 *(978-0-310-74880-9(1))* Zonderkidz.

Davis, Linsey. The World Is Awake: A Celebration of Everyday Blessings, 1 vol. Fleming, Lucy, illus. 2018. (ENG.). 32p. (J). 18.99 *(978-0-310-76203-4(0))* Zonderkidz.

Davis, Terrance. Mom & Me. 2012. 24p. (-18). pap. 24.95 *(978-1-4626-9502-7(7))* America Star Bks.

Davison, Gail. Prince Alexander. PellerinUndo, Joel Ray, illus. 2016. (ENG.). 28p. (J). pap. 28.22 *(978-1-5245-1787-8(9))* Xlibris Corp.

Dawnay, Gabby. London Calls. Barrow, Alex, illus. 2015. (ENG.). 40p. (J). (gr. -1-2). 13.95 *(978-1-84976-230-4(9)*, 1669201) Tate Publishing, Ltd. GBR. Dist: Hachette Bk. Group.

Day, Nancy Raines. Baby's Firsts. Emberley, Michael, illus. 2018. 32p. (J). (— 1). lib. bdg. 14.99 *(978-1-58089-774-7(6))* Charlesbridge Publishing, Inc.

de Alba, Arlette, tr. Musica en Casa: Libro de Cuentos. 2005. (Disney Winnie the Pooh (SilverDolphin) Ser.). (SPA., Illus.). 38p. (J). (gr. -1-7). incl. audio compact disk *(978-970-718-290-5(3)*, Silver Dolphin en Español) Advanced Marketing, S. de R. L. de C. V.

de la Mare, Walter. The Ride-By-Nights. Rabei, Carolina, illus. 2019. (ENG.). 32p. pap. 9.95 *(978-0-571-30719-7(1)*, Faber & Faber Children's Bks.) Faber & Faber, Inc.

—Snow. Rabei, Carolina, illus. 2018. (Four Seasons of Walter de la Mare Ser.). (ENG.). 16p. bds. 7.95 *(978-0-571-33713-2(9)*, Faber & Faber Children's Bks.) Faber & Faber, Inc.

de Las Casas, Dianne. Dinosaur Mardi Gras, 1 vol. Gentry, Marita, illus. 2011. (ENG.). 32p. (J). (gr. k-3). 17.99 *(978-1-58980-966-6(1)*, Pelican Publishing) Arcadia Publishing.

—Mama's Bayou, 1 vol. Stone-Barker, Holly, illus. 2010. (ENG.). 32p. (J). (gr. k-k). 16.99 *(978-1-58980-787-7(1)*, Pelican Publishing) Arcadia Publishing.

Dealey, Erin. Goldie Locks Has Chicken Pox. 2004. (Illus.). (J). (gr. k-3). spiral bd. *(978-0-616-14573-9(X))*; spiral bd. *(978-0-616-14572-2(1))* Canadian National Institute for the Blind/Institut National Canadien pour les Aveugles.

—Goldie Locks Has Chicken Pox. Wakiyama, Hanako, illus. 2005. (ENG.). 40p. (J). (gr. -1-2). reprint ed. 8.99 *(978-0-689-87610-3(6)*, Aladdin) Simon & Schuster Children's Publishing.

Dean, James & Dean, Kimberly. Pete the Cat & the Bedtime Blues. Dean, James, illus. 2015. (Pete the Cat Ser.). (ENG., Illus.). 40p. (J). (gr. -1-3). 18.99 *(978-0-06-230430-8(5))*; lib. bdg. 18.89 *(978-0-06-230431-5(3))* HarperCollins Pubs. (HarperCollins).

—Pete the Cat & the Bedtime Blues. Dean, James, illus. 2023. (Pete the Cat Ser.). (ENG., Illus.). 40p. (J). (gr. -1-3). pap. 8.99 *(978-0-06-230432-2(1)*, HarperCollins) HarperCollins Pubs.

—Pete the Cat & the Cool Cat Boogie. Dean, James, illus. (Pete the Cat Ser.). (ENG., Illus.). 40p. (J). (gr. -1-3). 2023. pap. 9.99 *(978-0-06-240435-0(0))* 2017. 17.99 *(978-0-06-240434-3(2))* 2017. lib. bdg. 18.89 *(978-0-06-240909-6(3))* HarperCollins Pubs. (HarperCollins).

—Pete the Cat & the New Guy. Dean, James, illus. 2014. (Pete the Cat Ser.). (ENG., Illus.). 40p. (J). (gr. -1-3). 19.99 *(978-0-06-227560-8(7))*; lib. bdg. 18.89 *(978-0-06-227561-5(5))* HarperCollins Pubs. (HarperCollins).

—Pete the Cat & the New Guy. Dean, James, illus. 2023. (Pete the Cat Ser.). (ENG., Illus.). 40p. (J). (gr. -1-3). pap. 8.99 *(978-0-06-227562-2(3)*, HarperCollins) HarperCollins Pubs.

Dean, Kimberly. Pete the Cat & the Cool Cat Boogie. 2023. (Pete the Cat Ser.). (ENG.). 40p. (gr. -1-1). 26.19 ***(978-1-5364-7890-7(3))*** HarperCollins Pubs.

Debowski, Sharon. The Snowman, the Owl, & the Groundhog. 2007. (J). lib. bdg. 15.95 *(978-1-60227-468-6(1))*; (Illus.). 32p. (gr. -1-4). 14.95 *(978-1-60227-470-9(3))* Above the Clouds Publishing.

Decola, Diane. Butterfly. 2008. 180p. pap. 15.99 *(978-1-4389-0715-4(X))* AuthorHouse.

Degen, Bruce. Jamberry. Degen, Bruce, illus. 25th enl. anniv. ed. 2008. (ENG., Illus.). 32p. (J). (gr. -1-3). pap. 9.99 *(978-0-06-443068-5(5)*, HarperCollins) HarperCollins Pubs.

—Jamberry. 2006. (Illus.). (J). (gr. -1-3). 28.95 incl. audio compact disk *(978-1-59519-362-9(6))*; pap. 39.95 incl. audio compact disk *(978-1-59519-323-0(5))* Live Oak Media.

—Nate Likes to Skate. 2016. (I Like to Read Ser.). (ENG., Illus.). 24p. (J). (gr. -1-3). 7.99 *(978-0-8234-3543-2(1))* Holiday Hse., Inc.

Degman, Lori. Cock-A-Doodle-Oops! Zemke, Deborah, illus. 2014. (ENG.). 36p. (J). (gr. -1-3). 16.99 *(978-1-939547-07-1(5)*, cfe736e0-5259-4a08-984e-aa68e39b4859) Creston Bks.

—1 Zany Zoo. Jack, Colin, illus. 2010. (ENG.). 32p. (J). (gr. -1-2). 19.99 *(978-1-4169-8990-5(0)*, Simon & Schuster Bks. For Young Readers) Simon & Schuster Bks. For Young Readers.

deGroat, Diane. Roses Are Pink, Your Feet Really Stink. deGroat, Diane, illus. 2022. (ENG., Illus.). 32p. (J). (gr. -1-3). pap. 8.99 *(978-0-688-15220-8(1)*, HarperCollins) HarperCollins Pubs.

Deich, Cheri Bivin. The Messy Monkey Tea Party. Genth, Christina, illus. 2007. 32p. (J). (gr. -1-3). 15.95 *(978-1-60108-006-6(9))* Red Cygnet Pr.

Del Moral, Susana. Las Rimas de Bard: Un Libro con Ventanas. Zaidi, Nadeem, illus. 2005. (Baby Einstein: Libros de Carton Ser.). (SPA.). 16p. (J). (gr. -1). bds. *(978-970-718-304-9(7)*, Silver Dolphin en Español) Advanced Marketing, S. de R. L. de C. V.

del Rosario, Juleah. 500 Words or Less. 2018. (ENG., Illus.). 384p. (YA). (gr. 9). 18.99 *(978-1-5344-1044-2(9)*, Simon Pulse) Simon Pulse.

DeLand, M. Maitland. Baby Santa & the Gift of Giving. Wilson, Phil, illus. 2014. (ENG.). 36p. (J). (gr. -1-2). 14.95 *(978-1-62634-086-2(2)*, Greenleaf Book Group Pr.) Greenleaf Book Group.

DeLong, Lucianne. Mrs. Mumford's Missing. Richoll, Stephanie, illus. 2013. (Saloman Sawdust's Snappy Stories Ser.). (ENG.). 24p. (J). 4.99 *(978-0-9833237-5-4(5))* Krullstone Publishing, LLC.

Demarest, Chris. Bus. 2017. (ENG., Illus.). 16p. (J). (— 1). bds. 6.99 *(978-0-544-87087-1(5)*, 1649083, Clarion Bks.) HarperCollins Pubs.

—Plane Board Book. 2017. (ENG., Illus.). 16p. (J). (— 1). bds. 6.99 *(978-0-544-97703-7(3)*, 1663472, Clarion Bks.) HarperCollins Pubs.

—Ship Board Book. 2017. (ENG., Illus.). 16p. (J). (— 1). bds. 6.99 *(978-0-544-97702-0(5)*, 1663470, Clarion Bks.) HarperCollins Pubs.

Demas, Corinne & Roehrig, Artemis. The Grumpy Pirate. Anstee, Ashlyn, illus. 2020. (ENG.). 40p. (J). (gr. -1-k). 17.99 *(978-1-338-22297-5(X)*, Orchard Bks.) Scholastic, Inc.

Dempsey, Kristy. Me with You. Denise, Christopher, illus. 2013. 30p. (J). (gr. -1-k). bds. 7.99 *(978-0-399-16262-6(3)*, Philomel Bks.) Penguin Young Readers Group.

—Surfer Chick. Cole, Henry, illus. 2018. (ENG.). 32p. (J). (gr. -1-k). pap. 4.99 *(978-1-4197-2931-7(4)*, 689803, Abrams Bks. for Young Readers) Abrams, Inc.

—Ten Little Fingers, Two Small Hands. Massey, Jane, illus. (Mini Bee Board Bks.). (ENG.). (J). (gr. -1-k). 2018. 26p. bds. 7.99 *(978-1-4998-0671-7(X))* 2016. 32p. 16.99 *(978-1-4998-0229-0(3))* Little Bee Books Inc.

—Ten Little Toes, Two Small Feet. Massey, Jane, illus. 2016. (ENG.). 32p. (J). (gr. -1-1). 16.99 *(978-1-4998-0236-8(6))* Little Bee Books Inc.

Deneen, Brendan. Night Night, Groot. 2018. (ENG., Illus.). 30p. (J). (gr. -1-k). bds. 8.99 *(978-1-4847-8765-6(X))* Marvel Worldwide, Inc.

Denise, Anika. Monster Trucks Board Book. Wragg, Nate, illus. 2018. (ENG.). 32p. (J). (gr. -1 — 1). bds. 7.99 *(978-0-06-274162-2(4)*, HarperFestival) HarperCollins Pubs.

DePalma, Johnny. The Raindrop Keeper: (Limited Edition Hardcover) Crabapple, Molly, illus. 2006. 50p. (J). 16.50 *(978-0-9791127-8-2(8))* Umbrelly Bks.

DePalma, Kate. Let's Celebrate! Special Days Around the World. Peluso, Martina, illus. 2019. (World of Celebrations Ser.). (ENG.). 40p. (J). (gr. k-5). 17.99 *(978-1-78285-833-1(4))*; pap. 9.99 *(978-1-78285-834-8(2))* Barefoot Bks., Inc.

DePalma, Mary Newell. Bow-Wow Wiggle-Waggle. 2012. (ENG., Illus.). 32p. (J). 14.00 *(978-0-8028-5408-7(7)*, Eerdmans Bks For Young Readers) Eerdmans, William B. Publishing Co.

DePrisco, Dorothea. Lullaby & Good Night: Music & Lights. 2006. (ENG., Illus.). 12p. (gr. -1-k). 12.95 *(978-1-58117-450-2(0)*, Intervisual/Piggy Toes) Bendon, Inc.

DeRosa Bodie, Leona. One Is Fun. Davis, Catherine Baptista, illus. 2007. 30p. (J). (gr. -1). bds. 12.95 *(978-1-4243-2961-8(2))* Independent Publisher Services.

Desai, Naina. Fun Jungle. 2009. 28p. pap. 13.99 *(978-1-4490-2058-3(5))* AuthorHouse.

Dettmer, Christina. The Secret. 2017. (ENG., Illus.). (J). (gr. k-4). pap. 9.95 *(978-1-946977-54-0(3))* Yorkshire Publishing Group.

Dewane, Patrick Ryan. What If the Rain Were Bugs? Konecny, John, illus. 2013. 24p. 14.99 *(978-1-937165-39-0(6))* Orange Hat Publishing.

Dewdney, Anna. Little Excavator. 2017. (Illus.). 40p. (J). (-k). 18.99 *(978-1-101-99920-2(9)*, Viking Books for Young Readers) Penguin Young Readers Group.

—Llama Llama & the Bully Goat. 2013. (Llama Llama Ser.). (Illus.). 40p. (J). (gr. -1-k). 18.99 *(978-0-670-01395-1(1)*, Viking Books for Young Readers) Penguin Young Readers Group.

—Llama Llama Easter Egg. 2015. (Llama Llama Ser.). (Illus.). 14p. (J). (— 1). bds. 7.99 *(978-0-451-46982-3(8)*, Viking Books for Young Readers) Penguin Young Readers Group.

—Llama Llama Holiday Drama. (Llama Llama Ser.). (Illus.). (J). 2018. 36p. (— 1). bds. 14.99 *(978-1-9848-3558-1(0))* 2017. 36p. (— 1). bds. 9.99 *(978-0-425-29181-8(2))* 2010. 40p. (gr. -1-k). 18.99 *(978-0-670-01161-2(4))* Penguin Young Readers Group. (Viking Books for Young Readers).

—Llama Llama Home with Mama. 2011. (Llama Llama Ser.). (ENG., Illus.). 40p. (J). (gr. -1-k). 18.99 *(978-0-670-01232-9(7)*, Viking Books for Young Readers) Penguin Young Readers Group.

—Llama Llama Hoppity-Hop. 2012. (Llama Llama Ser.). (Illus.). 14p. (J). (gr. -1 — 1). bds. 7.99 *(978-0-670-01329-6(3)*, Viking Books for Young Readers) Penguin Young Readers Group.

—Llama Llama I Love You. 2014. (Llama Llama Ser.). (Illus.). 14p. (J). (gr. -1 — 1). bds. 6.99 *(978-0-451-46981-6(X)*, Viking Books for Young Readers) Penguin Young Readers Group.

—Llama Llama Jingle Bells. Dewdney, Anna, illus. 2014. (Llama Llama Ser.). (Illus.). 14p. (J). (— 1). bds. 6.99 *(978-0-451-46980-9(1)*, Viking Books for Young Readers) Penguin Young Readers Group.

—Llama Llama Mad at Mama. Dewdney, Anna, illus. 2007. (Llama Llama Ser.). (ENG., Illus.). 40p. (J). (gr. -1-k). 18.99 *(978-0-670-06240-9(5)*, Viking Books for Young Readers) Penguin Young Readers Group.

—Llama Llama Misses Mama. (Llama Llama Ser.). (Illus.). (J). 2019. (ENG.). 36p. (— 1). bds. 9.99 *(978-0-593-11671-5(2))* 2009. 40p. (gr. -1-k). 18.99 *(978-0-670-06198-3(0))* Penguin Young Readers Group. (Viking Books for Young Readers).

—Llama Llama Nighty-Night. 2012. (Llama Llama Ser.). (ENG., Illus.). 14p. (J). (— 1). bds. 6.99 *(978-0-670-01327-2(7)*, Viking Books for Young Readers) Penguin Young Readers Group.

—Llama Llama Red Pajama. Dewdney, Anna, illus. (Llama Llama Ser.). (ENG., Illus.). (J). 2018. 34p. (-k). bds. 15.99 *(978-0-451-48063-7(5))* 2005. 40p. (gr. -1-k). 18.99 *(978-0-670-05983-6(8))* Penguin Young Readers Group. (Viking Books for Young Readers).

—Llama Llama Red Pajama. *(978-0-439-90665-4(2))*; 2006. lp *(978-0-439-90679-1(2))* Scholastic, Inc.

—Llama Llama Red Pajama: Gift Edition. Dewdney, Anna, illus. 2014. (Llama Llama Ser.). (ENG., Illus.). 40p. (J). (gr. -1-k). 26.99 *(978-0-451-46990-8(9)*, Viking Books for Young Readers) Penguin Young Readers Group.

—Llama Llama Time to Share. 2012. (Llama Llama Ser.). (ENG., Illus.). 40p. (J). (gr. -1-k). 18.99 *(978-0-670-01233-6(5)*, Viking Books for Young Readers) Penguin Young Readers Group.

—Llama Llama Wakey-Wake. 2012. (Llama Llama Ser.). (Illus.). 14p. (J). (— 1). bds. 7.99 *(978-0-670-01326-5(9)*, Viking Books for Young Readers) Penguin Young Readers Group.

—Llama Llama's Little Library, 4 vols. 2013. (Llama Llama Ser.). (ENG., Illus.). 56p. (J). (— 1). bds. 27.96 *(978-0-670-01648-8(9)*, Viking Books for Young Readers) Penguin Young Readers Group.

—Love from Llama Llama. Dewdney, Anna, illus. 2022. (Llama Llama Ser.). 32p. (J). (gr. k-3). 9.99 *(978-0-593-52174-8(9)*, Grosset & Dunlap) Penguin Young Readers Group.

—Nelly Gnu & Daddy Too. (Illus.). (J). 2017. 36p. (-k). bds. 9.99 *(978-0-425-28977-8(X))* 2014. 32p. (gr. -1-k). 17.99 *(978-0-670-01227-5(0))* Penguin Young Readers Group. (Viking Books for Young Readers).

—Nobunny's Perfect. 2012. (ENG.). 32p. (J). (gr. -1-k). bds. 7.99 *(978-0-670-01408-8(7)*, Viking Books for Young Readers) Penguin Young Readers Group.

Un Día de Escuela de Oso. 2014. (SPA., Illus.). (J). *(978-1-78285-087-8(2))* Barefoot Bks., Inc.

Diamond, Charlotte. Slippery Fish in Hawaii. Aardema, John, illus. 2013. (ENG.). 16p. (J). (gr. -1-1). bds. 7.95 *(978-1-933067-57-5(8))* Beachhouse Publishing, LLC.

Diaz-Pimienta, Alexis. Cuentos Clasicos en Verso.Tr. of Classic Stories in Verse. (SPA.). (J). (gr. 2-4). pap. 7.98 *(978-970-643-142-4(X))* Selector, S.A. de C.V. MEX. Dist: Spanish Pubs., LLC.

Dickinson, Tom. Bob's Secret Hideaway: Band 03/Yellow. 2014. (Collins Big Cat Ser.). (ENG., Illus.). 32p. (J). (gr. k-1). pap. 7.99 *(978-0-00-753850-8(2))* HarperCollins Pubs. Ltd. GBR. Dist: Independent Pubs. Group.

Did You Know That I Love You? 2014. (ENG., Illus.). 32p. (J). (gr. -1-3). 17.99 *(978-0-06-229744-0(9)*, HarperCollins) HarperCollins Pubs.

Diesen, Deborah. The Not Very Merry Pout-Pout Fish. Hanna, Dan, illus. (Pout-Pout Fish Adventure Ser.). (ENG.). (J). 2017. 34p. bds. 8.99 *(978-0-374-30459-1(9)*, 900159459) 2015. 32p. (gr. -1-1). 17.99 *(978-0-374-35549-4(5)*, 900122565) Farrar, Straus & Giroux. (Farrar, Straus & Giroux (BYR)).

—Pippa & Percival, Pancake & Poppy: Four Peppy Puppies. Zong, Grace, illus. 2018. (ENG.). 32p. (J). (gr. -1-2). 16.99 *(978-1-58536-386-5(3)*, 204408) Sleeping Bear Pr.

—The Pout-Pout Fish. Hanna, Dan, illus. 2018. (Pout-Pout Fish Adventure Ser.: 1). (ENG.). 32p. (J). bds. 12.99 *(978-0-374-31219-0(2)*, 900199885, Farrar, Straus & Giroux (BYR)) Farrar, Straus & Giroux.

—The Pout-Pout Fish. Hanna, Dan & Hanna, Dan, illus. 2013. (Pout-Pout Fish Adventure Ser.: 1). (ENG.). 32p. (J). (gr. -1 — 1). bds. 7.99 *(978-0-374-36097-9(9)*, 900075215, Farrar, Straus & Giroux (BYR)) Farrar, Straus & Giroux.

—The Pout-Pout Fish. Hanna, Dan, illus. 2008. (Pout-Pout Fish Adventure Ser.: 1). (ENG.). 32p. (J). (gr. -1-1). 18.99 *(978-0-374-36096-2(0)*, 900031428, Farrar, Straus & Giroux (BYR)) Farrar, Straus & Giroux.

—The Pout-Pout Fish & the Bully-Bully Shark. Hanna, Dan, illus. (Pout-Pout Fish Adventure Ser.). (ENG.). 32p. (J). 2019. bds. 8.99 *(978-0-374-31222-0(2)*, 900200299) 2017. 18.99 *(978-0-374-30402-7(5)*, 900158632) Farrar, Straus & Giroux. (Farrar, Straus & Giroux (BYR)).

—The Pout-Pout Fish & the Can't-Sleep Blues. Hanna, Dan, illus. 2018. (Pout-Pout Fish Adventure Ser.). (ENG.). 32p. (J). 18.99 *(978-0-374-30403-4(3)*, 900158633, Farrar, Straus & Giroux (BYR)) Farrar, Straus & Giroux.

—The Pout-Pout Fish Book & CD Storytime Set. unabr. ed. 2013. (Pout-Pout Fish Adventure Ser.). (ENG.). (J). (gr. -1-1). 12.99 *(978-1-4272-3176-5(1)*, 900120472) Macmillan Audio.

—The Pout-Pout Fish, Far, Far from Home. Hanna, Dan, illus. (Pout-Pout Fish Adventure Ser.). (ENG.). 32p. (J). 2019. bds. 8.99 *(978-0-374-31078-3(5)*, 900194752) 2017. 16.99 *(978-0-374-30194-1(8)*, 900141733) Farrar, Straus & Giroux. (Farrar, Straus & Giroux (BYR)).

—The Pout-Pout Fish Goes to School. Hanna, Dan, illus. (Pout-Pout Fish Adventure Ser.). (ENG.). 32p. (J). 2018. bds. 7.99 *(978-0-374-30852-0(7)*, 900187130) 2014. (gr. -1-k). 18.99 *(978-0-374-36095-5(2)*, 900085614) Farrar, Straus & Giroux. (Farrar, Straus & Giroux (BYR)).

—The Pout-Pout Fish in the Big-Big Dark. Hanna, Dan, illus. (Pout-Pout Fish Adventure Ser.: 2). (ENG.). 32p. (J). (gr. -1-1). 2015. bds. 8.99 *(978-0-374-30189-7(1)*, 900141680) 2010. 18.99 *(978-0-374-30798-1(9)*, 900064075) Farrar, Straus & Giroux. (Farrar, Straus & Giroux (BYR)).

—Smile, Pout-Pout Fish. Hanna, Dan, illus. 2014. (Pout-Pout Fish Mini Adventure Ser.: 1). (ENG.). 12p. (J). (gr. -1 — 1). bds. 5.99 *(978-0-374-37084-8(2)*, 900122559, Farrar, Straus & Giroux (BYR)) Farrar, Straus & Giroux.

—You Can Do It, Pout-Pout Fish! 2019. (Pout-Pout Fish Readers Ser.). (ENG.). 24p. (J). (gr. k-1). 14.49 *(978-0-87617-547-7(7))* Penworthy Co., LLC, The.

—You Can Make a Friend, Pout-Pout Fish! 2019. (Pout-Pout Fish Readers Ser.). (ENG.). 24p. (J). (gr. k-1). 14.49 *(978-0-87617-548-4(5))* Penworthy Co., LLC, The.

Diesen, Deborah & Hanna, Dan. You Can Do It, Pout-Pout Fish! 2019. (Pout-Pout Fish Reader Ser.: 1). (ENG., Illus.). 24p. (J). pap. 5.99 *(978-1-250-06427-1(9)*, 900143686, Farrar, Straus & Giroux (BYR)) Farrar, Straus & Giroux.

—You Can Make a Friend, Pout-Pout Fish! 2019. (Pout-Pout Fish Reader Ser.: 2). (ENG., Illus.). 24p. (J). pap. 5.99 *(978-1-250-06428-8(7)*, 900143688, Farrar, Straus & Giroux (BYR)) Farrar, Straus & Giroux.

Diggs, Taye. Mixed Me! Evans, Shane W., illus. 2015. (ENG.). 40p. (J). (gr. -1-3). 17.99 *(978-1-250-04719-9(6)*, 900132069) Feiwel & Friends.

Dill, Mark. Maddie & Me: Go to the Zoo. 2012. 40p. pap. 20.99 *(978-1-4685-7481-4(7))* AuthorHouse.

Dillon-Butler, Marybeth. Myrtle the Hurdler: And Her Pink & Purple Polka-Dotted Girdle. Messing, David, illus. 2005. (ENG.). 32p. (J). (gr. -1-2). pap. 11.95 *(978-0-9785075-9-6(2)*, Ferne Pr.) Nelson Publishing & Marketing.

Dillon, Leo & Dillon, Diane. Rap a Tap Tap: Here's Bojangles - Think of That! 2005. (J). 28.95 incl. audio compact disk *(978-1-59519-369-8(3))* Live Oak Media.

Dimplechin, Lord Reginald. Does a Wuzz. 2012. 38p. 24.95 *(978-1-4626-6151-0(3))* America Star Bks.

Dingeldein, Noelle. Walter's Wheels. 2015. (ENG., Illus.). 14p. (J). (gr. -1 — 1). bds. 7.99 *(978-1-936669-36-3(6)*, 1395558) Blue Manatee Press.

DiPucchio, Kelly. Dinosnores. Goembel, Ponder, illus. 2005. 32p. (J). (gr. -1 — 1). 17.99 *(978-0-06-051577-5(5))*; lib. bdg. 16.89 *(978-0-06-051578-2(3))* HarperCollins Pubs.

—Littles: & How They Grow. Ford, A. G., illus. (J). 2019. 26p. (— 1). bds. 8.99 *(978-1-9848-2985-6(8))* 2017. 32p. (gr. -1 — 1). 17.99 *(978-0-399-55526-8(9))* Random Hse. Children's Bks. (Doubleday Bks. for Young Readers).

—Monster Makeovers. Pham, LeUyen, illus. 2006. (J). *(978-0-7868-5181-2(3))* Hyperion Bks. for Children.

—One Little Two Little Three Little Children. Lundquist, Mary, illus. 2016. (ENG.). 32p. (J). (gr. -1-3). 17.99 *(978-0-06-234866-1(3)*, Balzer & Bray) HarperCollins Pubs.

Disney & Studiomouse Staff. Give a Dog a Bone: Mother Goose. 2011. (ENG.). 20p. (J). *(978-1-59069-945-4(9))* Studio Mouse LLC.

Disney Books. Disney Baby: My First Christmas. 2017. (ENG., Illus.). 12p. (J). (gr. -1 — 1). bds. 8.99 *(978-1-368-00725-2(2)*, Disney Press Books) Disney Publishing Worldwide.

—Disney's Countdown to Christmas: A Story a Day. 2017. (ENG., Illus.). 64p. (J). (gr. 1-3). 10.99 *(978-1-4847-3052-2(6)*, Disney Press Books) Disney Publishing Worldwide.

—Olaf's Frozen Adventure: Olaf's Journey: A Light-Up Board Book. 2017. (Light-Up Board Book Ser.). (ENG., Illus.). 10p. (J). (gr. -1-k). bds. 12.99 *(978-1-368-00674-3(4)*, Disney Press Books) Disney Publishing Worldwide.

Disney, Pixar Cars, ed. Rhymes on the Go. 2009. (ENG.). 24p. 4.99 *(978-1-59069-776-4(6))* Studio Mouse LLC.

DiTerlizzi, Angela. Baby Love. Boynton-Hughes, Brooke, illus. 2015. (ENG.). 32p. (J). (gr. -1-3). 17.99 *(978-1-4424-3392-2(2)*, Beach Lane Bks.) Beach Lane Bks.

—Baby Love. Boynton-Hughes, Brooke, illus. 2018. (Classic Board Bks.). (ENG.). 36p. (J). (gr. -1 — 1). bds. 7.99 *(978-1-5344-2035-9(5)*, Little Simon) Little Simon.

—I Wanna Be a Cowgirl. Vukovic, Elizabet, illus. 2017. (ENG.). 40p. (J). (gr. -1-3). 18.99 *(978-1-4814-5299-1(1)*, Beach Lane Bks.) Beach Lane Bks.

—Just Add Glitter. Cotterill, Samantha, illus. 2018. (ENG.). 32p. (J). (gr. -1-3). 18.99 *(978-1-4814-0967-4(0)*, Beach Lane Bks.) Beach Lane Bks.

—Say What? Chou, Joey, illus. 2011. (ENG.). 32p. (J). (gr. -1-k). 19.99 *(978-1-4169-8694-2(4)*, Beach Lane Bks.) Beach Lane Bks.

—Seeking a Bunny. Smith, Allie, illus. 2017. (ENG.). 30p. (J). (gr. -1 — 1). bds. 7.99 *(978-1-4814-7672-0(6)*, Little Simon) Little Simon.

—Seeking a Santa. Smith, Allie, illus. 2016. (ENG.). 30p. (J). (gr. -1 — 1). bds. 7.99 *(978-1-4814-7674-4(2)*, Little Simon) Little Simon.

—Some Bugs. Wenzel, Brendan, illus. 2014. (ENG.). 32p. (J). (gr. -1-3). 18.99 *(978-1-4424-5880-2(1)*, Beach Lane Bks.) Beach Lane Bks.

—Some Pets. Wenzel, Brendan, illus. 2016. (ENG.). 32p. (J). (gr. -1-3). 18.99 *(978-1-4814-4402-6(6)*, Beach Lane Bks.) Beach Lane Bks.

Dixon, Dallas L. Shelby's Shoes. Williams, Nancy E., ed. Cappoen, Jennifer Tipton, illus. 2013. 24p. (J). pap. 12.98 *(978-1-938526-33-6(3))* Laurus Co., Inc., The.

Dixon, Pamela. A Windy Day Walk. Homer, Maree, illus. 2016. (ENG.). 32p. (J). (gr. 1-4). *(978-0-473-34486-3(6))* Lizzy Web Bks.

Dixon, Virginia. What Happened to Willie? Thomas, Tim, illus. 2007. 32p. (J). 16.00 *(978-0-9795386-0-5(2))* Grand Productions.

DK. I Love You Little One. 2018. (ENG.). 18p. (J). (— 1). bds. 12.99 *(978-1-4654-8016-3(1)*, DK Children) Dorling Kindersley Publishing, Inc.

—Pop-Up Peekaboo! Farm: Pop-Up Surprise under Every Flap! 2011. (Pop-Up Peekaboo! Ser.). (ENG., Illus.). 12p. (J). (gr. -1 — 1). bds. 12.99 *(978-0-7566-7172-3(8)*, DK Children) Dorling Kindersley Publishing, Inc.

—Pop-Up Peekaboo! Unicorn. 2019. (Pop-Up Peekaboo! Ser.). (ENG., Illus.). 12p. (J). (— 1). bds. 12.99 *(978-1-4654-8331-7(4)*, DK Children) Dorling Kindersley Publishing, Inc.

Dobbins, Jan. Driving My Tractor. Sim, David, illus. 2009. 32p. (J). (gr. -1-3). 16.99 *(978-1-84686-358-5(9))* Barefoot Bks., Inc.

Dobkin, Bonnie. Crazy Pizza Day. Dey, Romi, illus. 2010. (J). *(978-1-60617-150-9(X))* Teaching Strategies, LLC.

Docherty, Helen. The Snatchabook. Docherty, Thomas, illus. 2013. (ENG.). 32p. (J). (gr. -1-2). 17.99 *(978-1-4022-9082-4(9)*, 9781402290824, Sourcebooks Jabberwocky) Sourcebooks, Inc.

—The Storybook Knight. Docherty, Thomas, illus. 2016. (ENG.). 32p. (J). (gr. k-4). 17.99 *(978-1-4926-3814-8(5)*, 9781492638148, Sourcebooks Jabberwocky) Sourcebooks, Inc.

Dodd, Emma. Happy. Dodd, Emma, illus. (Emma Dodd's Love You Bks.). (ENG., Illus.). (J). (— 1). 2017. 22p. bds. 10.99 *(978-0-7636-9642-9(0))* 2015. 24p. 12.99 *(978-0-7636-8008-4(7))* Candlewick Pr.

—Wish. Dodd, Emma, illus. (Emma Dodd's Love You Bks.). (ENG., Illus.). (J). (— 1). 2017. 22p. bds. 9.99 *(978-0-7636-9643-6(9))* 2015. 24p. 14.99 *(978-0-7636-8009-1(5))* Candlewick Pr.

Dodd, Lynley. Schnitzel Von Krumm. Dogs Never Climb Trees, 1 vol. 2004. (Gold Star First Readers Ser.). (ENG., Illus.). 32p. (gr. 1-3). lib. bdg. 25.67 *(978-0-8368-4092-6(5)*, b3a88a34-ae03-454a-a7aa-ec03d4f78f85, Gareth Stevens Learning Library) Stevens, Gareth Publishing LLLP.

Dodd, Sarah J. Just Like You. Capizzi, Giusi, illus. 2019. (ENG.). 32p. (J). (gr. -1-k). pap. 10.99 *(978-0-7459-7713-3(8)*, 88a5578b-4f37-4883-89aa-e44f7ef3ec8b, Lion Children's) Lion Hudson PLC GBR. Dist: Baker & Taylor Publisher Services (BTPS).

Dodds, Dayle Ann. Full House: An Invitation to Fractions. Carter, Abby, illus. 2009. (ENG.). 32p. (J). (gr. 1-4). pap. 8.99 *(978-0-7636-4130-6(8))* Candlewick Pr.

—Minnie's Diner: A Multiplying Menu. Manders, John, illus. 2007. (ENG.). 40p. (J). (gr. k-3). pap. 8.99 *(978-0-7636-3313-4(5))* Candlewick Pr.

Doerrfeld, Cori. Little Bunny Foo Foo: The Real Story. 2016. (Illus.). 32p. (J). (-k). pap. 8.99 *(978-1-101-99774-1(5)*, Puffin Books) Penguin Young Readers Group.

Doherty, Dave, illus. There Once Was a Place Called P.O.P. 2008. 93p. (J). 61.99 *(978-1-4363-6190-3(7))* Xlibris Corp.

Dominguez, Angela. Maria Had a Little Llama / María Tenía una Llamita: Bilingual. Dominguez, Angela, illus. 2013.Tr. of Maria Had a Little Llama. (SPA., Illus.). 32p. (J). (gr. -1-2). 19.99 *(978-0-8050-9333-9(8)*, 900070912, Holt, Henry & Co. Bks. For Young Readers) Holt, Henry & Co.

Domney, Alexis. Splish, Splat!, 1 vol. Crawford, Alice, illus. 2011. (ENG.). 24p. (J). (gr. 1-3). 15.95 *(978-1-897187-88-3(2))* Second Story Pr. CAN. Dist: Orca Bk. Pubs. USA.

Donahue, Laurie. Mr. Blue a Job for You. Bryan, Hintz, illus. 2010. 32p. (J). 15.95 *(978-0-9799116-2-0(1))* LifeSong Pubs.

Donaldson, Julia. Animal Music. Sharratt, Nick, illus. 2014. (ENG.). 24p. (J). (— 1). pap. 12.99 *(978-1-4472-1095-5(6)*, 900326066, Macmillan Children's Bks.) Pan Macmillan GBR. Dist: Macmillan.

—Cave Baby, 3. Gravett, Emily, illus. 2nd ed. 2011. (ENG.). 32p. (J). (gr. -1-k). 14.99 *(978-0-330-52276-2(0)*, 900326070, Macmillan Children's Bks.) Pan Macmillan GBR. Dist: Macmillan.

—The Cook & the King. Roberts, David, illus. 2019. (ENG.). 32p. (J). (gr. -1-2). 16.99 *(978-1-4197-3757-2(0)*, 1281801) Abrams, Inc.

—The Detective Dog. Ogilvie, Sara, illus. 2018. (ENG.). 32p. (J). 19.99 *(978-1-250-15676-1(9)*, 900185100, Holt, Henry & Co. Bks. For Young Readers) Holt, Henry & Co.

—The Fish Who Cried Wolf. Scheffler, Axel, illus. (J). 2017. (ENG.). 40p. (J). (gr. -1-k). 17.99 *(978-0-439-92825-0(7))* 2008. pap. *(978-0-545-03454-8(X))* Scholastic, Inc. (Levine, Arthur A. Bks.).

—The Flying Bath. Roberts, David, illus. 2016. (ENG.). 32p. (J). (gr. -1-k). pap. 9.99 *(978-1-4472-7711-8(2)*, Macmillan Children's Bks.) Pan Macmillan GBR. Dist: Independent Pubs. Group.

—Goat Goes to Playgroup. Sharratt, Nick, illus. (ENG.). (J). 2015. 24p. (-k). bds. 12.99 *(978-1-4472-8791-9(6)*, 900326061)8. 2013. 32p. (gr. -1-k). pap. 14.99 *(978-1-4472-1094-8(8)*, 900326068) Pan Macmillan GBR. (Macmillan Children's Bks.). Dist: Macmillan.

—A Gold Star for Zog. Scheffler, Axel, illus. 2012. (ENG.). 32p. (J). (gr. -1-3). 18.99 *(978-0-545-41724-2(4)*, Levine, Arthur A. Bks.) Scholastic, Inc.

—The Gruffalo. 2006. (ENG., Illus.). 32p. (J). (gr. -1-2). pap. 7.99 *(978-0-14-240387-7(3)*, Puffin Books) Penguin Young Readers Group.

—The Gruffalo. Scheffler, Axel, illus. 2005. (ENG.). (J). (gr. -1-2). 32p. 18.99 *(978-0-8037-3109-7(4))*; 26p. bds. 8.99 *(978-0-8037-3047-2(0))* Penguin Young Readers Group. (Dial Bks).

—The Gruffalo. 2006. lib. bdg. 18.40 *(978-0-606-23141-1(2))* Turtleback.

—Gruffalo in Scots. Robertson, James, tr. Scheffler, Axel, illus. 2012. (SCO.). 32p. (J). (-k). pap. 10.99 *(978-1-84502-503-8(2))* Black and White Publishing Ltd. GBR. Dist: Independent Pubs. Group.

—The Gruffalo's Child. Scheffler, Axel, illus. 2007. (ENG.). 32p. (J). (gr. -1-2). pap. 7.99 *(978-0-14-240754-7(2)*, Puffin Books) Penguin Young Readers Group.

—The Highway Rat. Scheffler, Axel, illus. 2013. (ENG.). 32p. (J). (gr. -1-3). 17.99 *(978-0-545-47758-1(1)*, Levine, Arthur A. Bks.) Scholastic, Inc.

—The Magic Paintbrush. Stewart, Joel, illus. 2017. (ENG.). 32p. (J). (gr. -1-1). pap. 14.99 *(978-1-5098-3046-6(4)*, 900326053, Macmillan Children's Bks.) Pan Macmillan GBR. Dist: Macmillan.

—One Mole Digging a Hole. Sharratt, Nick, illus. 2015. (ENG.). 22p. (J). (-k). bds. 12.99 *(978-1-4472-8790-2(8)*, 900326060, Macmillan Children's Bks.) Pan Macmillan GBR. Dist: Macmillan.

—One Mole Digging a Hole, 2. Sharratt, Nick, illus. 2009. (ENG.). 32p. (J). (gr. k-k). pap. 14.99 *(978-0-230-70647-7(9)*, 900326072, Macmillan Children's Bks.) Pan Macmillan GBR. Dist: Macmillan.

—One Ted Falls Out of Bed. Currey, Anna, illus. 2015. (ENG.). 32p. (J). (— 1). pap. 14.99 *(978-1-4472-6614-3(5)*, 900326063, Macmillan Children's Bks.) Pan Macmillan GBR. Dist: Macmillan.

—Reiver Rat: The Highway Rat in Scots. Robertson, James, tr. from ENG. Scheffler, Axel, illus. 2015. 32p. (J). (-k). pap. 10.99 *(978-1-84502-996-8(8)*, Itchy Coo) Black and White Publishing Ltd. GBR. Dist: Independent Pubs. Group.

—Room on the Broom. Scheffler, Axel, illus. 2003. (ENG.). 32p. (J). (gr. -1-2). pap. 7.99 *(978-0-14-250112-2(3)*, Puffin Books) Penguin Young Readers Group.

—The Scarecrows' Wedding. Scheffler, Axel, illus. 2014. (ENG.). 32p. (J). (gr. -1-3). 18.99 *(978-0-545-72606-1(9)*, Levine, Arthur A. Bks.) Scholastic, Inc.

—The Snail & the Whale. 2004. (ENG., Illus.). 32p. (J). (gr. -1-2). 18.99 *(978-0-8037-2922-3(7)*, Dial Bks) Penguin Young Readers Group.

—The Snail & the Whale. Scheffler, Axel, illus. 2006. (ENG.). 32p. (J). (gr. -1-2). reprint ed. pap. 8.99 *(978-0-14-240580-2(9)*, Puffin Books) Penguin Young Readers Group.

—A Squash & a Squeeze. Scheffler, Axel, illus. 2016. (ENG.). 32p. (J). (gr. -1-k). 18.99 *(978-1-338-05220-6(9)*, Levine, Arthur A. Bks.) Scholastic, Inc.

—Stick Man. Scheffler, Axel, illus. 2009. (ENG.). 32p. (J). (gr. -1-3). 18.99 *(978-0-545-15761-2(7)*, Levine, Arthur A. Bks.) Scholastic, Inc.

—Superworm. Scheffler, Axel, illus. 2014. (ENG.). 32p. (J). (gr. -1-3). 16.99 *(978-0-545-59176-8(7)*, Levine, Arthur A. Bks.) Scholastic, Inc.

—Tabby Mctat, the Musical Cat. Scheffler, Axel, illus. 2012. (ENG.). 32p. (J). (gr. -1-3). 17.99 *(978-0-545-45168-0(X)*, Levine, Arthur A. Bks.) Scholastic, Inc.

—The Ugly Five. Scheffler, Axel, illus. 2018. (ENG.). 32p. (J). (gr. -1-3). 17.99 *(978-1-338-24953-8(3)*, Scholastic Pr.) Scholastic, Inc.

—Where's My Mom? Scheffler, Axel, illus. 2008. (ENG.). 32p. (J). (gr. -1-2). 18.99 *(978-0-8037-3228-5(7)*, Dial Bks) Penguin Young Readers Group.

—Zog & the Flying Doctors. Scheffler, Axel, illus. 2017. (ENG.). 32p. (J). (gr. -1-3). 17.99 *(978-1-338-13417-9(5)*, Levine, Arthur A. Bks.) Scholastic, Inc.

Donnelly, Rebecca. Cats Are a Liquid. Saburi, Misa, illus. 2019. (ENG.). 32p. (J). 17.99 *(978-1-250-20659-6(6)*, 900201486, Holt, Henry & Co. Bks. For Young Readers) Holt, Henry & Co.

Dopirak, Kate. Hurry Up! A Book about Slowing Down. Neal, Christopher Silas, illus. 2020. (ENG.). 40p. (J). (gr. -1-3). 18.99 *(978-1-5344-2497-5(0)*, Beach Lane Bks.) Beach Lane Bks.

—Twinkle, Twinkle, Little Car. Peterson, Mary, illus. 2018. (ENG.). 40p. (J). (gr. -1-3). 18.99 *(978-1-4814-8803-7(1)*, Beach Lane Bks.) Beach Lane Bks.

—You're My Boo. Withrow, Lesley Breen, illus. 2016. (ENG.). 40p. (J). (gr. -1-3). 17.99 *(978-1-4424-4160-6(7)*, Beach Lane Bks.) Beach Lane Bks.

Dorfman, Craig. I Knew You Could! A Book for All the Stops in Your Life. Ong, Cristina, illus. 2003. (Little Engine That Could Ser.). 32p. (J). (gr. -1-2). 12.99 *(978-0-448-43148-2(3)*, Grosset & Dunlap) Penguin Young Readers Group.

Dorman, Brandon & Murray, Marjorie Dennis. Halloween Night. 2013. (ENG., Illus.). 40p. (J). (gr. k-4). pap. 7.99 *(978-0-06-185773-7(4)*, Greenwillow Bks.) HarperCollins Pubs.

Las Dos Iguanas.Tr. of Two Iguanas. (SPA.). (J). 9.95 *(978-968-6044-78-2(7))* Corunda, Ediciones, S.A. de C.V. MEX. Dist: AIMS International Bks., Inc.

Dotlich, Rebecca Kai. You & Me. Reagan, Susan, illus. 2018. (ENG.). 14p. (J). (gr. -1-1). bds. 9.99 *(978-1-56846-321-6(9)*, 19711, Creative Editions) Creative Co., The.

Doughty, Rebecca. Before You. Doughty, Rebecca, illus. 2016. (ENG., Illus.). 32p. (J). (gr. -1-3). 14.99 *(978-0-544-46317-2(X)*, 1600264, Clarion Bks.) HarperCollins Pubs.

Douglas, Atom. Mathew's Space Ship. Douglas, Atom, . 2007. (Illus.). 32p. (J). 6.50 *(978-0-9798316-0-7(1))* JaxPublishing.net.

Douglas, Babette. Curly Hare Gets It Straight. Williams, Ted, illus. 2006. (Kiss a Me Teacher Creature Stories Ser.). (J). (gr. -1-3). *(978-1-890343-35-4(8))* Kiss A Me Productions, Inc.

—Noreen: The Real King of the Jungle. Johnson, John, illus. 2006. (Kiss a Me Teacher Creature Stories Ser.). 20p. (J). (gr. -1-3). 9.99 *(978-1-890343-25-5(0))* Kiss A Me Productions, Inc.

Downing, Johnette. Down in Mississippi, 1 vol. Zecca, Katherine, illus. 2016. (ENG.). 32p. (J). 16.99 *(978-1-4556-2098-2(X)*, Pelican Publishing) Arcadia Publishing.

—Macarooned on a Dessert Island, 1 vol. Wald, Christina, illus. 2014. (ENG.). 32p. (J). (gr. k-3). 16.99 *(978-1-4556-1936-8(1)*, Pelican Publishing) Arcadia Publishing.

—Mademoiselle Grands Doigts: A Cajun New Year's Eve Tale, 1 vol. Stanley, Heather, illus. 2018. (ENG.). 32p. (gr. -1-3). 16.99 *(978-1-4556-2393-8(8)*, Pelican Publishing) Arcadia Publishing.

—Spooky Second Line, 1 vol. 2019. (ENG., Illus.). 32p. (J). pap. 9.95 *(978-1-4556-2505-5(1)*, Pelican Publishing) Arcadia Publishing.

Downs, Jay & Downs, Jeanie. The Flutterfly. 2010. 68p. pap. 25.49 *(978-1-4520-1860-7(X))* AuthorHouse.

Downs, Mike. You See a Circus, I See... McGrory, Anik, illus. 2006. (ENG.). 32p. (J). (gr. -1-3). pap. 7.95 *(978-1-58089-155-4(1))* Charlesbridge Publishing, Inc.

Downs Webb, Michelle. What Color Is Love? 2005. 24p. 10.95 *(978-1-4116-2783-3(0))* Lulu Pr., Inc.

Doyen, Denise. The Pomegranate Witch. Moser, Barry, illus. 2013. (J). *(978-0-375-87057-6(1))*; lib. bdg. *(978-0-375-97057-3(6))* Random Hse., Inc.

—The Pomegranate Witch: (Halloween Children's Books, Early Elementary Story Books, Scary Stories for Kids) Wheeler, Eliza, illus. 2017. (ENG.). 40p. (J). (gr. k-3). 16.99 *(978-1-4521-4591-5(0))* Chronicle Bks. LLC.

Dragonwagon, Crescent. All the Awake Animals Are Almost Asleep. McPhail, David, illus. 2016. (ENG.). 30p. (J). (gr. -1 — 1). bds. 7.99 *(978-0-316-33627-7(0))* Little, Brown Bks. for Young Readers.

Dreyer, Nicole E. The Parable of the Talents. Morris, Susan, illus. 2007. (ENG.). 16p. (J). (gr. k-4). pap. 1.99 *(978-0-7586-1282-3(6))* Concordia Publishing Hse.

Drez, Jennifer & Bumstead, Robin. Goodnight Cowtown. Voight, Lisa, illus. 2012. 40p. (J). 17.95 *(978-0-615-54492-2(4))* Petit Chou Chou, LLC.

Driscoll, Laura. Disney Bunnies: Thumper Goes AThumpin' 2015. (ENG., Illus.). 12p. (J). (gr. -1 — 1). bds. 6.99 *(978-1-4847-0960-3(8)*, Disney Press Books) Disney Publishing Worldwide.

—We Are Twins. Campion, Pascal, illus. 2012. (Penguin Young Readers, Level 1 Ser.). 32p. (J). (gr. k-1). mass mkt. 4.99 *(978-0-448-46157-1(9)*, Penguin Young Readers) Penguin Young Readers Group.

—We Are Twins. 2012. (Penguin Young Readers: Level 1 Ser.). lib. bdg. 13.55 *(978-0-606-26641-3(0))* Turtleback.

Druvert, Hélène. Mary Poppins up, up & Away. 2017. (ENG., Illus.). 36p. (J). (gr. k-4). 24.95 *(978-0-500-65104-9(3)*, 565104) Thames & Hudson.

Duddle, Jonny. The Pirates Next Door. 2012. (ENG., Illus.). 44p. (J). (gr. -1-2). 17.99 *(978-0-7636-5842-7(1)*, Templar) Candlewick Pr.

—The Pirates of Scurvy Sands. Duddle, Jonny, illus. 2018. (ENG., Illus.). 44p. (J). (gr. 1-4). 16.99 *(978-0-7636-9293-3(X)*, Templar) Candlewick Pr.

Dudley, Linda. Aunt Linda's Mommy & Me Book. 2003. (J). pap. 15.99 *(978-1-4134-3830-7(X))* Borders Personal Publishing.

Duffy, Jacqueline Ann. Dillon the Dog Finds His Family. 2008. 24p. pap. 24.95 *(978-1-60563-331-2(3))* America Star Bks.

Duksta, Laura. I Love You More. Keesler, Karen, illus. 2007. 34p. (J). (gr. k-2). 17.99 *(978-1-4022-1126-3(0)*, Sourcebooks Jabberwocky) Sourcebooks, Inc.

Dunbar, Joyce. Pat-A-Cake Baby. Dunbar, Polly, illus. 2015. (ENG.). 40p. (J). (-k). 15.99 *(978-0-7636-7577-6(6))* Candlewick Pr.

Dunn, Jill. The ABC's of Going Green. Hill, Bodhi, illus. 2012. 64p. (J). 21.99 *(978-0-9852146-2-3(7))* AM Ink Publishing.

Dunphy, Madeleine. Here Is the Arctic Winter. Robinson, Alan James, illus. 2007. (Web of Life Ser.: 5). (ENG.). 32p. (J). (gr. -1-3). pap. 9.95 *(978-0-9777539-0-1(5))* Web of Life Children's Bks.

Durango, Julia. Cha-Cha Chimps. Taylor, Eleanor, illus. 2010. (ENG.). 32p. (J). (gr. -1-3). 8.99 *(978-1-4169-9574-6(9)*, Simon & Schuster Bks. For Young Readers) Simon & Schuster Bks. For Young Readers.

—Go-Go Gorillas. Taylor, Eleanor, illus. 2010. (ENG.). 32p. (J). (gr. -1-3). 19.99 *(978-1-4169-3779-1(X)*, Simon & Schuster Bks. For Young Readers) Simon & Schuster Bks. For Young Readers.

Durango, Julia & Trupiano, Katie Belle. Dream Away. Goldstrom, Robert, illus. 2011. (ENG.). 32p. (J). (gr. -1-3). 16.99 *(978-1-4169-8702-4(9)*, Simon & Schuster Bks. For Young Readers) Simon & Schuster Bks. For Young Readers.

Durso, Diana T. Did You Know That's Not My Name? Bentz, Jill M., illus. 2009. (ENG.). 50p. pap. 19.95 *(978-1-4389-3182-1(4))* AuthorHouse.

Duskey Rinker, Sherri. It's So Quiet: A Not-Quite-Going-To-Bed Book. Fucile, Tony, illus. 2021. (ENG.). 56p. (J). (gr. -1-k). 17.99 *(978-1-4521-4544-0(X))* Chronicle Bks. LLC.

Duskey Rinker, Sherri & Long, Ethan. Crane Truck's Opposites: Goodnight, Goodnight, Construction Site (Educational Construction Truck Book for Preschoolers, Vehicle & Truck Themed Board Book for 5 to 6 Year Olds, Opposite Book) 2019. (Goodnight, Goodnight Construction Site Ser.). (ENG., Illus.). 20p. (J). (gr. -1 — 1). bds. 6.99 *(978-1-4521-5317-9(5))* Chronicle Bks. LLC.

DuTemple, Leslie A. One Little Balsam Fir: A Northwoods Counting Book. Robinson, Susan, illus. 2006. 32p. (J). per. *(978-1-892384-37-9(X))* Avery Color Studios, Inc.

Dutson, Shelly. Jingle Jangle Jungle Jeepers. Christenson, Maren, illus. 2009. 24p. pap. 12.50 *(978-1-4490-1061-4(X))* AuthorHouse.

Dyer, Alyssa. When Whizzly Wanders. 2005. 15p. 6.78 *(978-1-4116-4667-4(3))* Lulu Pr., Inc.

Dwyer, Mindy. Sweet Dreams, Polar Bear. 2004. (ENG., Illus.). 32p. (J). (gr. -1-1). pap. 12.99 *(978-0-88240-555-1(1)*, Alaska Northwest Bks.) West Margin Pr.

Dyan, Penelope. Animal Rescue, Book 2, Hanauma Bay, Hawaii. Weigand, John D., photos by. 2008. (Illus.). 56p. pap. 15.95 *(978-1-935118-43-5(9))* Bellissima Publishing, LLC.

—Arianna's Shoes. Dyan, Penelope, illus. 2008. (Illus.). 44p. pap. 11.95 *(978-1-935118-33-6(1))* Bellissima Publishing, LLC.

—Ba-Ba-Ba-Bad — -The Story of One Mean Moose. Dyan, Penelope, illus. 2012. (Illus.). 34p. pap. 11.95 *(978-1-61477-053-4(0))* Bellissima Publishing, LLC.

—Baylee's Giraffes! Sometimes Only a Giraffe Will Do. Dyan, Penelope, illus. 2013. (Illus.). 34p. pap. 11.95 *(978-1-61477-085-5(9))* Bellissima Publishing, LLC.

—Ben's Adventures — -Proof Positive That Boys Will Be Boys. Dyan, Penelope, illus. 2008. (Illus.). 44p. pap. 11.95 *(978-1-935118-40-4(4))* Bellissima Publishing, LLC.

—Bunny Love! a Book about Home & Bunnies. Dyan, Penelope, illus. 2013. (Illus.). 34p. pap. 11.95 *(978-1-61477-084-8(0))* Bellissima Publishing, LLC.

—Classy Nancy — A One of a Kind Girl. Dyan, Penelope, illus. 2009. (Illus.). 48p. pap. 11.95 *(978-1-935118-45-9(5))* Bellissima Publishing, LLC.

—Courtney's Beach. Dyan, Penelope, illus. 2008. (Illus.). 44p. pap. 11.95 *(978-1-935118-35-0(8))* Bellissima Publishing, LLC.

—Eileen Green the Recycling Queen. Dyan, Penwlope, illus. 2009. 44p. pap. 11.95 *(978-1-935118-51-0(X))* Bellissima Publishing, LLC.

—The Fish That Got Away — -for Boys Only(r). Dyan, Penelope, illus. 2010. (Illus.). 34p. pap. 11.95 *(978-1-935630-29-6(6))* Bellissima Publishing, LLC.

—Frugal Frannie — and the Big Room Cleaning Day. Dyan, Penelope, illus. 2009. (Illus.). 44p. pap. 11.95 *(978-1-935118-47-3(1))* Bellissima Publishing, LLC.

—Gabriela's Dogs — -Because Happiness Really Is a Warm Puppy! Dyan, Penelope, illus. 2008. (Illus.). 44p. pap. 11.95 *(978-1-935118-37-4(4))* Bellissima Publishing, LLC.

—Grandma's Suitcase — -Where a Kid Can Always Find a Surprise! Dyan, Penelope, illus. 2008. (Illus.). 44p. pap. 11.95 *(978-1-935118-36-7(6))* Bellissima Publishing, LLC.

—I Like Football — -for Boys Only(r). Dyan, Penelope, illus. 2010. (Illus.). 34p. pap. 11.95 *(978-1-935630-27-2(X))* Bellissima Publishing, LLC.

—I Love You! Dyan, Penelope, illus. 2012. (Illus.). 34p. pap. 11.95 *(978-1-61477-050-3(6))* Bellissima Publishing, LLC.

—Jordan's Hair — -the Big Dilemm. Dyan, Penelope, illus. 2008. (Illus.). 44p. pap. 11.95 *(978-1-935118-34-3(X))* Bellissima Publishing, LLC.

—Little Miss Chris & the Incredible Red Shoes. Dyan, Penelope, illus. 2009. (Illus.). 44p. pap. 11.95 *(978-1-935118-49-7(8))* Bellissima Publishing, LLC.

—Lovely Libby. Dyan, Penelope, illus. 2010. (Illus.). 34p. pap. 11.95 *(978-1-935630-28-9(8))* Bellissima Publishing, LLC.

—Mermaids & Wishes for Tails Like Fishes. Dyan, Penelope, illus. 2009. (Illus.). 44p. pap. 11.95 *(978-1-935118-50-3(1))* Bellissima Publishing, LLC.

—Mikey & Me & the Bees, the Continuing Story of a Girl & Her Dog. Dyan, Penelope, illus. 2010. (Illus.). 48p. pap. 14.95 *(978-1-935118-90-9(0))* Bellissima Publishing, LLC.

—Mikey & Me & the Fly — -the Continuing Story of a Girl & Her Dog. Dyan, Penelope, illus. 2010. (Illus.). 50p. pap. 14.95 *(978-1-935118-94-7(3))* Bellissima Publishing, LLC.

—Mikey & Me & the Spider — -the Continuing Story of a Girl & Her Dog. Dyan, Penelope, illus. 2010. (Illus.). 50p. pap. 14.95 *(978-1-935118-95-4(1))* Bellissima Publishing, LLC.

—Mikey & Me & the Valentines — -the Continuing Story of a Girl & Her Dog. Dyan, Penelope, illus. 2010. (Illus.). 50p. pap. 14.95 *(978-1-935118-96-1(X))* Bellissima Publishing, LLC.

—Molly Moose Is on the Loose. Dyan, Penelope, illus. 2012. (Illus.). 34p. pap. 11.95 *(978-1-61477-025-1(5))* Bellissima Publishing, LLC.

—My Mother Always Says. Dyan, Penelope, illus. 2010. (Illus.). 42p. pap. 11.95 *(978-1-935118-98-5(6))* Bellissima Publishing, LLC.

—Off to School. Dyan, Penelope, illus. 2010. (Illus.). 34p. pap. 11.95 *(978-1-935630-21-0(0))* Bellissima Publishing, LLC.

—Out of Deepest Africa — -Another of Ben's Big Adventures — -for Boys Only (r). Dyan, Penelope, illus. 2010. (Illus.).

S

34p. pap. 11.95 *(978-1-935630-13-5(X))* Bellissima Publishing, LLC.

—Tammy's Left Shoe — -As Opposed to Her Right. Dyan, Penelope, illus. 2008. (Illus.). 44p. pap. 11.95 *(978-1-935118-41-1(2))* Bellissima Publishing, LLC.

—There's a Flea in My Te. Dyan, Penelope, illus. 2012. (Illus.). 34p. pap. 11.95 *(978-1-61477-047-3(6))* Bellissima Publishing, LLC.

—There's a Skunk in My Trunk. Dyan, Penelope, illus. 2012. (Illus.). 34p. pap. 11.95 *(978-1-61477-045-9(X))* Bellissima Publishing, LLC.

—There's a Teddy Bear in My Heart! Dyan, Penelope, illus. 2012. (Illus.). 34p. pap. 11.95 *(978-1-61477-048-0(4))* Bellissima Publishing, LLC.

—Three Strikes — -Doesn't Really Mean You Are Out. Dyan, Penelope, illus. 2008. (Illus.). 44p. pap. 11.95 *(978-1-935118-39-8(0))* Bellissima Publishing, LLC.

—To See or Not to See — -the Story of Kourtney's Glasses. Dyan, Penelope, illus. 2008. (Illus.). 44p. pap. 11.95 *(978-1-935118-38-1(2))* Bellissima Publishing, LLC.

—Today I Am Two! I Am Two Years Old Today! Dyan, Penelope, illus. 2010. (Illus.). 34p. pap. 11.95 *(978-1-935630-14-2(8))* Bellissima Publishing, LLC.

—Who Deserves a Giant Chocolate Chip Cookie? Dyan, Penelope, illus. 2009. (Illus.). 44p. pap. 11.95 *(978-1-935118-56-5(0))* Bellissima Publishing, LLC.

—Why Angels Sing! Dyan, Penelope, illus. 2012. (Illus.). 34p. pap. 11.95 *(978-1-61477-065-7(4))* Bellissima Publishing, LLC.

—Work It Out! Dyan, Penelope, illus. 2012. (Illus.). 34p. pap. 11.95 *(978-1-61477-056-5(5))* Bellissima Publishing, LLC.

Dyson, Nikki, illus. Flip Flap Dogs. 2018. (Flip Flap Bks.). (ENG.). 28p. (J). (gr. -1-2). 12.99 *(978-1-5362-0258-8(4))* Candlewick Pr.

Earhardt, Ainsley. I'm So Glad You Were Born: Celebrating Who You Are. Barnes, Kim, illus. 2022. (ENG.). 32p. (J). 18.99 *(978-0-310-77702-1(X))* Zonderkidz.

—Take Heart, My Child: A Mother's Dream. Kim, Jaime, illus. 2018. (ENG.). 34p. (J). (gr. -1-k). bds. 8.99 *(978-1-5344-2631-3(0)*, Little Simon) Little Simon.

—Take Heart, My Child: A Mother's Dream. Kim, Jaime, illus. 2016. (ENG.). 32p. (J). (gr. -1-3). 18.99 *(978-1-4814-6622-6(4)*, Aladdin) Simon & Schuster Children's Publishing.

Eastman, P. D. The Big Blue Book of Beginner Books. 2008. (Beginner Books(R) Ser.). (ENG., Illus.). 368p. (J). (gr. -1-2). 16.99 *(978-0-375-85552-8(1)*, Random Hse. Bks. for Young Readers) Random Hse. Children's Bks.

Eastman, P. D., et al. The Big Red Book of Beginner Books. 2010. (Beginner Books(R) Ser.). (ENG., Illus.). 344p. (J). (gr. -1-2). 16.99 *(978-0-375-86531-2(4)*, Random Hse. Bks. for Young Readers) Random Hse. Children's Bks.

Eaton, Seymour. The Roosevelt Bears, Their Travels & Adventures. 2013. (Applewood Bks.). (ENG.). 186p. pap. 17.95 *(978-1-4290-9805-2(8))* Applewood Bks.

Eberhard, Phyllis Lunde Brees. Little Miss Neat-As-A-Pin. Jacoby, Nickolina Dye, illus. 2007. (J). *(978-0-9722741-7-3(0))* Publishing Factory, The.

Ecker, Rebecca. Miss Emmalou Strain & the Hunt for Hermie. 2008. 32p. pap. 12.95 *(978-1-4327-0182-6(7))* Outskirts Pr., Inc.

Edwards, Asasimone. What's a Mimi-Saurus? 2009. (Illus.). 36p. pap. 16.99 *(978-1-4389-7919-9(3))* AuthorHouse.

Edwards, Caroline. Who Took Poppy's Skates? 2010. (ENG., Illus.). 24p. pap. *(978-1-84876-392-0(1))* Troubador Publishing Ltd.

Edwards, Nicola. You're My Little Cuddle Bug. Marshall, Natalie, illus. 2018. (You're My Little Ser.). (ENG.). 18p. (J). (gr. -1 — 1). bds. 8.99 *(978-1-68412-258-5(9)*, Silver Dolphin Bks.) Printers Row Publishing Group.

Edwards, Pamela Duncan. Four Seasons of Fun: Egg Hunts! Fireworks! Pumpkins! Reindeer! Daigneault, Sylvie, illus. 2018. (ENG.). 32p. (J). (gr. k-2). 16.99 *(978-1-58536-403-9(7)*, 204584) Sleeping Bear Pr.

—Roar! A Noisy Counting Book. Cole, Henry, illus. Date not set. 32p. (J). (gr. -1-2). pap. 5.99 *(978-0-06-443572-7(5))* HarperCollins Pubs.

Eggers, Dave. Tomorrow Most Likely (Read Aloud Family Books, Mindfulness Books for Kids, Bedtime Books for Young Children, Bedtime Picture Books) Smith, Lane, illus. 2019. (ENG.). 40p. (J). (gr. -1-k). 17.99 *(978-1-4521-7278-1(1))* Chronicle Bks. LLC.

Ehlert, Lois. Boo to You! Ehlert, Lois, illus. 2009. (ENG., Illus.). 40p. (J). (gr. -1-2). 19.99 *(978-1-4169-8625-6(1)*, Beach Lane Bks.) Beach Lane Bks.

—Lots of Spots. Ehlert, Lois, illus. 2014. (Classic Board Bks.). (ENG., Illus.). 40p. (J). (gr. -1 — 1). bds. 8.99 *(978-1-4424-8927-1(8)*, Little Simon) Little Simon.

—Oodles of Animals. Ehlert, Lois, illus. 2008. (ENG., Illus.). 56p. (J). (gr. -1-2). 18.99 *(978-0-15-206274-3(2)*, 1198806, Clarion Bks.) HarperCollins Pubs.

—Rain Fish. Ehlert, Lois, illus. 2016. (ENG., Illus.). 40p. (J). (gr. -1-3). 19.99 *(978-1-4814-6152-8(4)*, Beach Lane Bks.) Beach Lane Bks.

—The Scraps Book: Notes from a Colorful Life. Ehlert, Lois, illus. 2014. (ENG., Illus.). 72p. (J). (gr. k-5). 17.99 *(978-1-4424-3571-1(2))* Simon & Schuster Children's Publishing.

Ehrhardt, Karen. This Jazz Man. Roth, R. G., illus. 2010. (J). (gr. 1-5). 28.95 incl. audio compact disk *(978-1-4301-0740-8(5))* Live Oak Media.

Eisen, Laura. Clouds for Breakfast. Cissna, Kent, illus. 2013. 60p. pap. 14.95 *(978-0-9882113-7-7(8))* StarryBks.

Elephants, It's Raining, Martha & Me. 2018. (ENG., Illus.). 80p. (J). (gr. -1-4). 16.95 *(978-0-500-65142-1(6)*, 565142) Thames & Hudson.

Elin Hirschman, Jessica & Bright, Bonnie. The Tangle Tower. Bright, Bonnie, illus. 2006. (Illus.). 32p. (J). (gr. k-2). 14.95 *(978-0-9701155-6-0(3))* Cookie Bear Pr., Inc.

Eliot, T. S. Macavity: The Mystery Cat. Robins, Arthur, illus. 75th ed. 2016. (Old Possum Picture Bks.). (ENG.). 32p. (J). (-k). pap. 9.95 *(978-0-571-30813-2(9))* Faber & Faber, Inc.

—Macavity's Not There! A Lift-The-Flap Book. Robins, Arthur, illus. (Old Possum Picture Bks.). (ENG.). 16p. 2018. (J). bds. 8.00 *(978-0-571-33528-2(4))* 2017. 14.95 *(978-0-571-32863-5(6))* Faber & Faber, Inc.

—Skimbleshanks: The Railway Cat. Robins, Arthur, illus. 2016. (Old Possum Picture Bks.). (ENG.). 32p. (J). (-k). pap. 9.95 *(978-0-571-32483-5(5))* Faber & Faber, Inc.

Elliott, David. And Here's to You! Cecil, Randy, illus. 2009. (ENG.). 32p. (J). (gr. -1-2). pap. 7.99 *(978-0-7636-4126-9(X))* Candlewick Pr.

—Bull. (ENG.). (YA). (gr. 9). 2019. 224p. pap. 9.99 *(978-1-328-59633-8(8)*, 1731318) 2017. 200p. 17.99 *(978-0-544-61060-6(1)*, 1617400) HarperCollins Pubs. (Clarion Bks.).

—What the Grizzly Knows. Grafe, Max, illus. 2008. (ENG.). 32p. (J). (gr. -1-2). 16.99 *(978-0-7636-2778-2(X))* Candlewick Pr.

Elliott, Zetta & Strickland, Shadra. Bird, 1 vol. 2008. (ENG., Illus.). 48p. (J). (gr. 3-7). 19.95 *(978-1-60060-241-2(X))* Lee & Low Bks., Inc.

Ellis, Dianne. Rusty Rumble & His Smelly Socks. 2012. 36p. pap. 32.70 *(978-1-4691-9914-6(9))* Xlibris Corp.

—Rusty Rumble's Day at the Beach. 2012. 40p. pap. 32.70 *(978-1-4797-0360-9(5))* Xlibris Corp.

Ellis, Libby. Midge & Max's Scavenger Hunt. Jonason, Dave, illus. 2005. 12p. (J). (gr. -1-3). act. bk. ed. 14.95 *(978-1-58117-109-9(9)*, Intervisual/Piggy Toes) Bendon, Inc.

Elsohn Ross, Michael. Mama's Milk. Wolff, Ashley, illus. 2007. 32p. (J). (gr. -1-2). 12.95 *(978-1-58246-181-6(3)*, Tricycle Pr.) Random Hse. Children's Bks.

—Mama's Milk / Mamá Me Alimenta. Wolff, Ashley, illus. (J). 2016. 24p. (-k). bds. 7.99 *(978-0-553-53874-8(8))* 2008. 32p. (gr. -1-2). pap. 6.99 *(978-1-58246-245-5(3))* Random Hse. Children's Bks. (Tricycle Pr.).

Elya, Susan Middleton. Bebé Goes Shopping. Salerno, Steven, illus. 2008. (ENG.). 36p. (J). (gr. -1-3). pap. 7.99 *(978-0-15-206142-5(8)*, 1198442, Clarion Bks.) HarperCollins Pubs.

—Fire! Fuego! Brave Bomberos. Santat, Dan, illus. 2012. (ENG.). 40p. (J). (gr. -1-1). 17.99 *(978-1-59990-461-0(6)*, 900064754, Bloomsbury USA Childrens) Bloomsbury Publishing USA.

—Little Roja Riding Hood. Guevara, Susan, illus. 2014. 32p. (J). (gr. k-3). 17.99 *(978-0-399-24767-5(X)*, G.P. Putnam's Sons Books for Young Readers) Penguin Young Readers Group.

—Maya Papaya & Amigos Play Dress-Up. Mola, Maria, illus. 2018. 32p. (J). (gr. -1-2). lib. bdg. 16.99 *(978-1-58089-803-4(3))* Charlesbridge Publishing, Inc.

—Oh No, Gotta Go! Karas, G. Brian, illus. 2005. 29p. (J). (gr. k-4). reprint ed. 15.00 *(978-0-7567-8946-6(X))* DIANE Publishing Co.

—La Princesa & the Pea. Martinez-Neal, Juana, illus. 2017. 32p. (J). (gr. -1-3). 18.99 *(978-0-399-25156-6(1)*, G.P. Putnam's Sons Books for Young Readers) Penguin Young Readers Group.

—The Three Billy Goats Buenos. Ordóñez, Miguel, illus. 2020. 32p. (J). (gr. -1-3). 17.99 *(978-0-399-54739-3(8)*, G.P. Putnam's Sons Books for Young Readers) Penguin Young Readers Group.

Emmett, Jonathan. Through the Heart of the Jungle. Gomez, Elena, illus. 2003. 32p. (J). tchr. ed. 15.95 *(978-1-58925-029-1(X))*; pap. 5.95 *(978-1-58925-380-3(9))* Tiger Tales.

Emmons, Scott. The Amazing Planet Earth. Ilic, Nikolas & West, Eddie, illus. 2017. 31p. (J). *(978-1-5182-5200-6(1))* Random Hse., Inc.

—Hugo Makes a Change. Gatti, Mauro, illus. 2017. (ENG.). 32p. (J). (gr. -1-k). 13.99 *(978-1-911171-21-8(6))* Flying Eye Bks. GBR. Dist: Penguin Random Hse. LLC.

—Tyrannosaurus Rex. Ilic, Nikolas & West, Eddie, illus. 2017. 31p. (J). *(978-1-5182-5197-9(8))* Random Hse., Inc.

Emzer, Counselor. Duane, You Must be Insane. 2005. 20p. 7.97 *(978-1-4116-3091-8(2))* Lulu Pr., Inc.

Engelbreit, Mary. Mary Engelbreit's A Merry Little Christmas: Celebrate from A to Z. Engelbreit, Mary, illus. 2006. (Illus.). 40p. (J). (gr. -1-3). lib. bdg. 17.89 *(978-0-06-074159-4(7))* HarperCollins Pubs.

—Mary Engelbreit's a Merry Little Christmas: Celebrate from a to Z: a Christmas Holiday Book for Kids. Engelbreit, Mary, illus. 2010. (ENG., Illus.). 40p. (J). (gr. -1-3). pap. 7.99 *(978-0-06-074160-0(0)*, HarperCollins) HarperCollins Pubs.

—Mary Engelbreit's Nursery Tales: A Treasury of Children's Classics. Engelbreit, Mary, illus. 2008. (ENG., Illus.). 136p. (J). (gr. 4-7). 19.99 *(978-0-06-073168-7(0)*, HarperCollins) HarperCollins Pubs.

England, Brooke. Guardian Fairies. 2006. 17p. 12.00 *(978-1-4116-7923-8(7))* Lulu Pr., Inc.

Engle, Margarita. Drum Dream Girl: How One Girl's Courage Changed Music. López, Rafael & López, Rafael, illus. 2015. (ENG.). 48p. (J). (gr. -1-3). 19.99 *(978-0-544-10229-3(0)*, 1540161, Clarion Bks.) HarperCollins Pubs.

—Forest World. 2017. (ENG., Illus.). 208p. (J). (gr. 5). 19.99 *(978-1-4814-9057-3(5)*, Atheneum Bks. for Young Readers) Simon & Schuster Children's Publishing.

—Hurricane Dancers: The First Caribbean Pirate Shipwreck. 2014. (ENG.). 176p. (YA). (gr. 7-12). pap. 11.99 *(978-1-250-04010-7(8)*, 900123713) Square Fish.

—Jazz Owls: A Novel of the Zoot Suit Riots. Gutierrez, Rudy, illus. 2018. (ENG.). 192p. (YA). (gr. 7). 17.99 *(978-1-5344-0943-9(2))* Simon & Schuster Children's Publishing.

—Mountain Dog. Ivanov, Aleksey & Olga, illus. 2014. (ENG.). 240p. (J). (gr. 3-7). pap. 13.99 *(978-1-250-04424-2(3)*, 900128316) Square Fish.

—La Selva (Forest World) Romay, Alexis, tr. 2019. (SPA.). (J). (gr. 5). 224p. pap. 7.99 *(978-1-5344-2930-7(1))*; (Illus.). 208p. 17.99 *(978-1-5344-5107-0(2))* Simon & Schuster Children's Publishing. (Atheneum Bks. for Young Readers).

Engström von Alten, Sofie. Dino Does Yoga. 2019. (Illus.). 32p. (J). (gr. -1-2). 17.95 *(978-1-62317-306-7(X))* North Atlantic Bks.

Enik, Ted. Sticks 'N Stones 'N Dinosaur Bones. Newland, g. f., illus. 2013. 42p. pap. 12.99 *(978-1-939322-10-4(3))* Pixel Mouse Hse.

Epner, Paul. Herbert Hilligan & His Magical Adventure. Kuon, Vuthy & Nguyen, Duke, illus. 2003. 32p. (J). 15.95 *(978-0-9743335-0-2(6))* Imaginative Publishing, Ltd.

—Herbert Hilligan & His Magical Lunchbox. Kuon, Vuthy & Nguyen, Duke, illus. rev. ed. (Herbert Hilligan Ser.). 15.95 *(978-1-57168-549-0(9))* Eakin Pr.

—Herbert Hilligan's Lone Star Adventure. Kuon, Vuthy & Nguyen, Duke, illus. 2003. 32p. (J). 15.95 *(978-0-9743335-3-3(0))* Imaginative Publishing, Ltd.

—Herbert Hilligan's Tropical Adventure. Kuon, Vuthy & Nguyen, Duke, illus. 2003. 32p. (J). 15.95 *(978-0-9743335-2-6(2))* Imaginative Publishing, Ltd.

Erlich, Bev. Pink Roses Everywhere. gif. ed. 2004. (Illus.). 64p. (J). 14.95 *(978-0-9743913-0-4(1))* Snojoy Publishing.

Errico, Daniel. The Journey of the Marmabill. Turrill, Tiffany, illus. 2013. (ENG.). 32p. (J). (gr. -1-k). 16.95 *(978-1-62087-736-4(8)*, 620736, Sky Pony Pr.) Skyhorse Publishing Co., Inc.

—The Journey of the Noble Gnarble. Turrill, Tiffany, illus. 2013. (ENG.). 32p. (J). (gr. -1-k). 16.95 *(978-1-62087-732-6(5)*, 620732, Sky Pony Pr.) Skyhorse Publishing Co., Inc.

Esenwine, Matt Forrest & Bruss, Deborah. Don't Ask a Dinosaur. Chin, Louie, illus. 2018. (ENG.). 32p. (J). (gr. -1-2). 17.99 *(978-1-57687-841-5(4)*, powerHouse Bks.) powerHse. Bks.

Eubank, Patricia Reeder. Halloween 123. 2012. (ENG., Illus.). 22p. (J). (gr. -1 — 1). bds. 6.99 *(978-0-8249-1868-2(1)*, Ideals Pubns.) Worthy Publishing.

Evans, Nate. Bang! Boom! Roar! a Busy Crew of Dinosaurs. 2012. (ENG., Illus.). 40p. (J). (gr. -1-2). 15.99 *(978-0-06-087960-0(2)*, HarperCollins) HarperCollins Pubs.

Evans, Nate & Brown, Stephanie Gwyn. Dinosaur ABC. Santoro, Christopher, illus. 2011. (J). lib. bdg. 16.89 *(978-0-06-087962-4(9))* HarperCollins Pubs.

Evans, Ruth Todd. The Panda Who Would Not Eat. Evans, Ruth Todd, illus. 2007. (Illus.). 32p. (J). (gr. -1-3). per. 9.95 *(978-0-932653-84-0(7))* Sunbelt Pubns., Inc.

Everett, Forrest. Old MacDonald Had a Farm in Oregon. Sergeeva, Mary, illus. 2018. (Old MacDonald Had a Farm Regional Board Ser.). (ENG.). 16p. (J). (gr. k-3). bds. 12.99 *(978-1-64170-014-6(9)*, 550014) Familius LLC.

—Row, Row, Row Your Boat in Oregon. Sergeeva, Mary, illus. 2018. (Row, Row, Row Your Boat Regional Board B Ser.). (ENG.). 16p. (J). (gr. k-3). bds. 12.99 *(978-1-64170-015-3(7)*, 550015) Familius LLC.

Everett, Melissa. Do Your Ears Hang Low? Doss, Andrea, illus. 2014. (ENG.). 20p. (J). (gr. -1-2). bds. 8.99 *(978-1-4867-0358-6(5))* Flowerpot Children's Pr. Inc. CAN. Dist: Cardinal Pubs. Group.

Everson, Chance. Beginnings Vol. 2: Tales of the Mandrasaurs, Volume the Second. Geary, Steve, illus. 2004. cd-rom 9.95 *(978-0-9760303-1-7(4))* R.A.R.E. TALES.

—Discoveries: Tales of the Mandrasaurs, Volume the Third. Geary, Steve, illus. 2004. cd-rom 9.95 *(978-0-9760303-2-4(2))* R.A.R.E. TALES.

—Forever & a Day Vol. 1: Tales of the Mandrasaurs, Volume the First. Geary, Steve, illus. 2004. cd-rom 9.95 *(978-0-9760303-0-0(6))* R.A.R.E. TALES.

—Verlin's Magical Blunder: Tales of the Mandrasaurs, Volume the Seventh. Geary, Steve, illus. 2004. cd-rom 9.95 *(978-0-9760303-6-2(5))* R.A.R.E. TALES.

Ewert, Marcus. Mummy Cat. Brown, Lisa, illus. 2015. (ENG.). 48p. (J). (gr. 1-4). 16.99 *(978-0-544-34082-4(5)*, 1584824, Clarion Bks.) HarperCollins Pubs.

—She Wanted to Be Haunted. Ghahremani, Susie, illus. 2020. (ENG.). 40p. (J). 17.99 *(978-1-68119-791-3(X)*, 900187075, Bloomsbury Children's Bks.) Bloomsbury Publishing USA.

Faber, Toni Tuso. The Poodle Tales: Book One. Rudd, Benton, illus. 2012. 26p. (-18). 16.99 *(978-0-9883162-9-4(3))* Mindstir Media.

—The Poodle Tales: Book Three. Rudd, Benton, illus. 2012. 24p. 16.99 *(978-0-9886409-3-6(6))*; pap. 10.99 *(978-0-9886409-8-6(8))* Mindstir Media.

—The Poodle Tales: Book Two. Rudd, Benton, illus. 2012. 24p. 16.99 *(978-0-9885180-9-4(0))*; pap. 10.99 *(978-0-9885180-8-7(2))* Mindstir Media.

Fagan, Cary. Directed by Kaspar Snit. 2007. 160p. (J). (gr. 3-7). per. 9.95 *(978-0-88776-753-1(2)*, Tundra Bks.) Tundra Bks. CAN. Dist: Penguin Random Hse. LLC.

Fairgray, Richard & Burke, Alexander. Sweet Penny & the Lion. 2018. (ENG., Illus.). 32p. (J). (gr. -1-k). 16.99 *(978-1-5107-3484-5(8)*, Sky Pony Pr.) Skyhorse Publishing Co., Inc.

Fallon, Joe & Scarborough, Ken. Halfway Hank. Davis, Jack E., illus. 2005. 40p. (J). 15.99 *(978-0-06-623636-0(3))* HarperCollins Pubs.

Falwell, Cathryn. Mystery Vine. Falwell, Cathryn, illus. 2009. (Illus.). 32p. (J). lib. bdg. 17.89 *(978-0-06-177197-2(X)*, Greenwillow Bks.) HarperCollins Pubs.

—Turtle Splash! Countdown at the Pond. Falwell, Cathryn, illus. 2008. (ENG., Illus.). 32p. (J). (gr. -1-3). pap. 7.99 *(978-0-06-142927-9(9)*, Greenwillow Bks.) HarperCollins Pubs.

Farah, Mo, et al. Ready Steady Mo! 2017. (ENG., Illus.). 32p. (J). (gr. -1-k). pap. 8.99 *(978-1-4449-3407-6(4))* Hachette Children's Group GBR. Dist: Hachette Bk. Group.

Farley, Charlie. A T-Wit for a T-Woo. Marlow, Layn, illus. 2019. (ENG.). 32p. (J). (gr. -1-k). 14.99 *(978-1-4083-4649-5(4))*; pap. 9.99 *(978-1-4083-4650-1(8))* Hachette Children's Group GBR. (Orchard Bks.). Dist: Hachette Bk. Group.

Farnsworth-Simpson, Patricia Ann. Stories to Thrill & Delight. 2008. (ENG.). 142p. pap. 12.95 *(978-1-4357-3275-9(8))* Lulu Pr., Inc.

Farrell, Bill. Walter's Pond: The True Story of Three Brothers Who Went Fishing for Trouble. Julich, Jenniffer, illus. 2008. 16p. 8.95 *(978-0-9797790-0-8(6))* Lower Lane Publishing LLC.

Faulks, Ben. Watch Out for Muddy Puddles! Cort, Ben, illus. 2018. (ENG.). 32p. (J). 16.99 *(978-1-68119-627-5(1)*, 900179490, Bloomsbury USA Childrens) Bloomsbury Publishing USA.

Fehr, Signe. Mama Always Comes Back. 2008. 32p. pap. 14.99 *(978-1-4389-0036-0(8))* AuthorHouse.

Feierabend, John M. Kitty Alone. Echevarria, Mina, illus. 2018. (First Steps in Music Ser.). (ENG.). 32p. (J). (gr. -1-k). 17.95 *(978-1-62277-283-4(0))* G I A Pubns., Inc.

—Momma, Buy Me a China Doll. Norton, Allyssa, illus. 2017. (First Steps in Music Ser.). (ENG.). 32p. (J). (— 1). 17.95 *(978-1-62277-226-1(1))* G I A Pubns., Inc.

Fennell, Kristen & Petruccelli, Jessica, illus. A World of Hope: Written by Hope's Parents Laurie & Mike. I.t. ed. 2005. 18p. (J). per. 9.99 *(978-1-59879-069-6(2))* Lifevest Publishing, Inc.

Fenske, Jonathan. Guppy Up! Fenske, Jonathan, illus. 2013. (Penguin Young Readers, Level 1 Ser.). (ENG., Illus.). 32p. (J). (gr. k-1). mass mkt. 4.99 *(978-0-448-49646-7(1)*, Penguin Young Readers) Penguin Young Readers Group.

—Guppy Up! 2013. (Penguin Young Readers: Level 1 Ser.). lib. bdg. 13.55 *(978-0-606-28736-4(1))* Turtleback.

—A Pig, a Fox, & Stinky Socks. 2019. (ENG., Illus.). 32p. (J). (gr. k-2). 4.99 *(978-0-593-09597-3(9)*, Penguin Workshop) Penguin Young Readers Group.

—A Pig, a Fox, & Stinky Socks. 2018. (Penguin Young Readers Ser.). (ENG.). 32p. (J). (gr. -1-1). 13.89 *(978-1-64310-420-1(9))* Penworthy Co., LLC, The.

—We Need More Nuts! Fenske, Jonathan, illus. (Illus.). 32p. (J). 2019. (gr. k-2). 4.99 *(978-0-593-09599-7(5)*, Penguin Workshop) 2017. (gr. 1-2). pap. 5.99 *(978-0-515-15913-4(1)*, Penguin Young Readers) Penguin Young Readers Group.

—We Need More Nuts! 2018. (Penguin Young Readers Ser.). (ENG.). 32p. (J). (gr. -1-1). 13.89 *(978-1-64310-319-8(9))* Penworthy Co., LLC, The.

Fenton, Joe. What's under the Bed? Fenton, Joe, illus. 2008. (ENG., Illus.). 32p. (J). (gr. -1-2). 18.99 *(978-1-4169-4943-5(7)*, Simon & Schuster Bks. For Young Readers) Simon & Schuster Bks. For Young Readers.

Fernandes, Eugenie. Kitten's Summer. Fernandes, Eugenie, illus. 2013. (ENG., Illus.). 24p. (J). (gr. -1 — 1). bds. 7.95 *(978-1-55453-721-1(5))* Kids Can Pr., Ltd. CAN. Dist: Hachette Bk. Group.

Ferrari, G. m. Lake, Sky, Dragonfly. 2009. 44p. pap. 16.99 *(978-1-4490-2895-4(0))* AuthorHouse.

Ferreri, Della Ross. Precious Baby. Dong, Monique, illus. 2019. 20p. (J). (gr. -1 — 1). 7.99 *(978-1-5064-4773-5(2)*, Beaming Books) 1517 Media.

Ferry, Beth. Stick & Stone. 2017. (Stick & Stone Ser.). (ENG., Illus.). 38p. (J). (— 1). bds. 7.99 *(978-1-328-71432-9(2)*, 1673785, Clarion Bks.) HarperCollins Pubs.

—Stick & Stone. Lichtenheld, Tom, illus. 2015. (Stick & Stone Ser.). (ENG.). 48p. (J). (gr. -1-3). 19.99 *(978-0-544-03256-9(X)*, 1530246, Clarion Bks.) HarperCollins Pubs.

Ficocelli, Elizabeth. Kid Tea, 0 vols. Dibley, Glin, illus. 2013. (ENG.). 36p. (J). (gr. -1-1). pap. 9.99 *(978-1-4778-4738-1(3)*, 9781477847381, Two Lions) Amazon Publishing.

—Kid Tea. Dibley, Glin, illus. 2009. 32p. (J). (gr. -1). bds. 7.99 *(978-0-7614-5533-2(7))* Marshall Cavendish Corp.

Fineman, Kelly Ramsdell. At the Boardwalk. Armiño, Mónica, illus. 2012. (ENG.). 32p. (J). 15.95 *(978-1-58925-104-5(0))*; pap. *(978-1-58925-431-2(7))* Tiger Tales.

Finke, Margot. Kangaroo Clues. Delioglu, Mustafa, illus. 2013. 16p. pap. 9.95 *(978-1-61633-368-3(5))* Guardian Angel Publishing, Inc.

—Mama Grizzly Bear. Swan, Gloria, illus. 2012. 16p. (-18). pap. 9.95 *(978-1-61633-304-1(9))* Guardian Angel Publishing, Inc.

Finley, Ucal P. A Proper Place for Boogers. Stroud, Brenda D., illus. 2011. 54p. pap. 12.95 *(978-0-9834307-0-4(5))* G Publishing LLC.

Fischer, Kristen. Zoo Zen: A Yoga Story for Kids. 2017. (ENG., Illus.). 32p. (J). (gr. -1-2). 17.95 *(978-1-62203-891-6(6)*, 900220816) Sounds True, Inc.

Fischer, Scott M. Jump! Fischer, Scott M., illus. 2010. (ENG., Illus.). 32p. (J). (gr. -1-3). 18.99 *(978-1-4169-7884-8(4)*, Simon & Schuster Bks. For Young Readers) Simon & Schuster Bks. For Young Readers.

Fisher, Doris & Sneed, Dani. My Even Day, 1 vol. Lee, Karen, illus. 2007. (ENG.). 32p. (J). (gr. 2-3). pap. 10.95 *(978-1-934359-22-8(X)*, 9a5ad22b-185d-48b0-8049-d3ccca139144) Arbordale Publishing.

—My Even Day: Spanish, 1 vol. Lee, Karen, illus. 2007. (SPA.). 32p. (J). (gr. -1-3). 17.95 *(978-1-60718-692-2(6))* Arbordale Publishing.

—My Half Day, 1 vol. Lee, Karen, illus. 2008. (Basic Math Numbers Ser.). (ENG.). 32p. (J). (gr. -1-3). 16.95 *(978-1-934359-14-3(9))*; (gr. 2-3). pap. 9.95 *(978-1-934359-29-7(7)*, 749d829c-07c0-48dc-a6c0-7462ca3d566e) Arbordale Publishing.

—One Odd Day, 1 vol. Lee, Karen, illus. 2006. 32p. (J). (SPA.). (gr. -1-3). 17.95 *(978-1-60718-694-6(2))*; Vol. (ENG.). (gr. 2-3). pap. 11.95 *(978-1-934359-33-4(5)*, 87884c7b-5c4d-4420-944a-014b07b686b4) Arbordale Publishing.

Fisher, Rusty. Littlest Vampire's Story, 1 vol. 2014. (Story Time for Little Monsters Ser.). (ENG., Illus.). 24p. (J). (gr. -1-4). lib. bdg. 31.36 *(978-1-62402-020-9(8)*, 626, Looking Glass Library) Magic Wagon.

—Littlest Werewolf's Story, 1 vol. 2014. (Story Time for Little Monsters Ser.). (ENG.). 24p. (J). (gr. -1-4). lib. bdg. 31.36 *(978-1-62402-021-6(6)*, 628, Looking Glass Library) Magic Wagon.

—Littlest Witch's Story, 1 vol. 2014. (Story Time for Little Monsters Ser.). (ENG., Illus.). 24p. (J). (gr. -1-4). lib. bdg. 31.36 *(978-1-62402-022-3(4)*, 630, Looking Glass Library) Magic Wagon.

—Littlest Zombie's Story, 1 vol. 2014. (Story Time for Little Monsters Ser.). (ENG., Illus.). 24p. (J). (gr. -1-4). lib. bdg. 31.36 *(978-1-62402-023-0(2)*, 632, Looking Glass Library) Magic Wagon.

Fitzgerald, Paula. The ABCs of How I Love You! 2011. 16p. (J). (gr. -1-1). bds. 12.99 *(978-0-8249-1495-0(3)*, Ideals Pubns.) Worthy Publishing.

Flaxman, Jessica & Hall, Kirsten. Who Says? Becker, Wayne, illus. 2003. (My First Reader Ser.). (ENG.). 32p. (J). 18.50 *(978-0-516-22958-4(3)*, Children's Pr.) Scholastic Library Publishing.

Fleming, Candace. Oh, No! Rohmann, Eric, illus. 2018. (ENG.). 40p. (J). (gr. -1-2). 8.99 *(978-1-9848-5204-5(3)*, Dragonfly Bks.) Random Hse. Children's Bks.

—Seven Hungry Babies. Yelchin, Eugene, illus. 2010. (ENG.). 40p. (J). (gr. -1-2). 19.99 *(978-1-4169-5402-6(3)*, Atheneum Bks. for Young Readers) Simon & Schuster Children's Publishing.

Fleming, Denise. The First Day of Winter. Fleming, Denise, illus. 2012. (ENG., Illus.). 32p. (J). (gr. k-3). pap. 18.69 *(978-0-312-37138-8(1)*, 900044676) Square Fish.

—In the Small, Small Pond. Fleming, Denise, illus. 2007. (ENG., Illus.). 32p. (J). (gr. -1-k). pap. 27.99

(978-0-8050-8117-6(8), 900039664, Holt, Henry & Co. Bks. For Young Readers) Holt, Henry & Co.
—In the Tall, Tall, Grass. 2015. 32p. pap. 8.00 (978-1-61003-609-2(3)) Center for the Collaborative Classroom.
—Pumpkin Eye. 2009. (J). (gr. k-2). 27.95 incl. audio (978-0-8045-6979-8(7)) Spoken Arts, Inc.
—This Is the Nest That Robin Built. Fleming, Denise, illus. 2018. (ENG., Illus.). 32p. (J). (gr. -1-3). 18.99 (978-1-4814-3083-8(1), Beach Lane Bks.) Beach Lane Bks.
—UnderGROUND. Fleming, Denise, illus. 2012. (ENG., Illus.). 40p. (J). (gr. -1-3). 17.99 (978-1-4424-5882-6(8), Beach Lane Bks.) Beach Lane Bks.
—5 Little Ducks. Fleming, Denise, illus. 2016. (ENG., Illus.). 40p. (J). (gr. -1-3). 18.99 (978-1-4814-2422-6(X), Beach Lane Bks.) Beach Lane Bks.
Fleming, Meg. I Heart You. Wright, Sarah Jane, illus. 2016. (ENG.). 40p. (J). (gr. -1-3). 17.99 (978-1-4424-8895-3(6), Beach Lane Bks.) Beach Lane Bks.
—I Heart You. Wright, Sarah Jane, illus. 2019. (Classic Board Bks.). (ENG.). 36p. (J). (gr. -1-3). bds. 8.99 (978-1-5344-5130-8(7), Little Simon) Little Simon.
—Ready, Set, Build! Jarvis, illus. 2017. (ENG.). 32p. (J). (gr. -1-3). 16.99 (978-1-4998-0175-0(0)) Little Bee Books Inc.
—Ready, Set, Sail! Flowers, Luke, illus. 2018. (ENG.). 32p. (J). (gr. -1-3). 16.99 (978-1-4998-0533-8(0)) Little Bee Books Inc.
—Sometimes Rain. Sudyka, Diana, illus. 2018. (ENG.). 40p. (J). (gr. -1-3). 17.99 (978-1-4814-5918-1(X), Beach Lane Bks.) Beach Lane Bks.
Fletcher, Tom & Poynter, Dougie. The Dinosaur That Pooped Christmas! Parsons, Garry, illus. 2019. (Dinosaur That Ser.). (ENG.). 32p. (J). (gr. -1-3). 17.99 (978-1-4814-9872-2(X), Aladdin) Simon & Schuster Children's Publishing.
—The Dinosaur That Pooped the Bed! Parsons, Garry, illus. 2018. (Dinosaur That Ser.). (ENG.). 32p. (J). (gr. -1-3). 16.99 (978-1-4814-9870-8(3), Aladdin) Simon & Schuster Children's Publishing.
Fliess, Sue. A Dress for Me!, 0 vols. Laughead, Mike, illus. 2012. (ENG.). 24p. (J). (gr. k-3). 12.99 (978-0-7614-6148-7(5), 9780761461487, Two Lions) Amazon Publishing.
—The Earth Gives More. Engel, Christiane, illus. 2019. (ENG.). 32p. (J). (gr. -1-3). 16.99 (978-0-8075-7710-3(3), 807577103) Whitman, Albert & Co.
—Let's Build, 0 vols. Sakamoto, Miki, illus. 2014. (ENG.). 24p. (J). (gr. -1-3). 14.99 (978-1-4778-4724-4(3), 9781477847244, Two Lions) Amazon Publishing.
—Mary Had a Little Lab. Bouloubasis, Petros, illus. 2018. (ENG.). 32p. (J). (gr. -1-3). 16.99 (978-0-8075-4982-7(7), 807549827) Whitman, Albert & Co.
—Ninja Camp. Taylor, Jen, illus. 2019. (ENG.). 32p. (J). (gr. -1-3). 17.99 (978-0-7624-6331-2(7), Running Pr. Kids) Running Pr.
—The Princess & the Petri Dish. Bouloubasis, Petros, illus. 2020. (ENG.). 32p. (J). (gr. -1-3). 16.99 (978-0-8075-6644-2(6), 807566446) Whitman, Albert & Co.
Flintham, Thomas. Animal Noises. Flintham, Thomas, illus. 2016. (ENG., Illus.). 24p. (J). (gr. -1 — 1). bds. 7.99 (978-1-4814-6935-7(5), Little Simon) Little Simon.
—Animal Numbers. Flintham, Thomas, illus. 2016. (ENG., Illus.). 24p. (J). (gr. -1 — 1). bds. 7.99 (978-1-4814-6937-1(1), Little Simon) Little Simon.
Flor Ada, Alma. Celebra el Día De3 San Patricio con Samantha y Lola. Lavandeira, Sandra, illus. 2006. (Cuentos para Celebrar / Stories to Celebrate Ser.). (SPA.). 30p. (J). (gr. k-6). per. 11.95 (978-1-59820-117-8(4), Alfaguara) Santillana USA Publishing Co., Inc.
Flor Ada, Alma & Campoy, F. Isabel. Celebrate St. Patrick's Day with Samantha & Lola. Hayes, Joe & Franco, Sharon, trs. from SPA. 2006. (Stories to Celebrate Ser.). (Illus.). 30p. (J). (gr. k-6). per. 11.95 (978-1-59820-129-1(8), Alfaguara) Santillana USA Publishing Co., Inc.
Flores, Carolyn Dee. Amazing Watercolor Fish, the / el Asombroso Pez Acuarela. Flores, Carolyn Dee, illus. 2018. (ENG & SPA., Illus.). 32p. (J). (gr. -1-2). 17.95 (978-1-55885-873-2(3), Piñata Books) Arte Publico Pr.
Florian, Douglas. The Curious Cares of Bears. Sánchez, Sonia, illus. 2017. (ENG.). 32p. (J). (gr. -1-3). 16.99 (978-1-4998-0462-1(8)) Little Bee Books Inc.
—How to Draw a Dragon. Florian, Douglas, illus. 2015. (ENG., Illus.). 42p. (J). (gr. -1-3). 19.99 (978-1-4424-7399-7(1), Beach Lane Bks.) Beach Lane Bks.
—I Love My Hat, 0 vols. Keiser, Paige, illus. 2014. (ENG.). 24p. (J). (gr. -1-2). 16.99 (978-1-4778-4780-0(4), 9781477847800, Two Lions) Amazon Publishing.
Flowers, Luke. Ninja at the Firehouse (Moby Shinobi: Scholastic Reader, Level 1) Flowers, Luke, illus. 2018. (Scholastic Reader, Level 1 Ser.). (ENG., Illus.). 32p. (J). (gr. -1-3). pap. 4.99 (978-1-338-25611-6(4)) Scholastic, Inc.
—Ninja at the Pet Shop. 2018. (Scholastic Reader Level 1 Ser.). lib. bdg. 13.55 (978-0-606-41141-7(0)) Turtleback.
—Ninja in the Kitchen (Moby Shinobi: Scholastic Reader, Level 1) Flowers, Luke, illus. 2017. (Scholastic Reader, Level 1 Ser.). (ENG., Illus.). 32p. (J). (gr. -1-1). pap. 3.99 (978-0-545-93534-0(2)) Scholastic, Inc.
—Ninja on the Farm. Flowers, Luke, illus. 2016. (Scholastic Reader, Level 1 Ser.). (ENG.). 32p. (J). (gr. -1-3). pap. 3.99 (978-0-545-93537-1(7)) Scholastic, Inc.
—Ninja on the Job. Flowers, Luke, illus. 2018. (Scholastic Reader, Level 1 Ser.). (ENG., Illus.). 32p. (J). (gr. -1-3). pap. 3.99 (978-1-338-25614-7(9)) Scholastic, Inc.
—Ninja on the Job (Moby Shinobi: Scholastic Reader, Level 1) (Library Edition) Flowers, Luke, illus. 2018. (Scholastic Reader, Level 1 Ser.). (ENG., Illus.). 32p. (J). (gr. -1-1). lib. bdg. 16.99 (978-1-338-25615-4(7)) Scholastic, Inc.
—Surf's up!: an Acorn Book (Moby Shinobi & Toby, Too! #1) (Library Edition) Flowers, Luke, illus. 2019. (Moby Shinobi & Toby Too! Ser.: 1). (ENG., Illus.). 64p. (J). (gr. k-2). 23.99 (978-1-338-54753-5(4)) Scholastic, Inc.
Fluharty, Kristi and T. Lively. Fool Moon Rising. Fluharty, T. Lively, illus. 2009. (ENG.). 40p. (J). 16.99 (978-1-4335-0682-6(3)) Crossway.
Foges, Clare. Bathroom Boogie. Murphy, Al, illus. 2018. (ENG.). 32p. (J). 16.95 (978-0-571-34045-3(8), Faber & Faber Children's Bks.) Faber & Faber, Inc.
—Kitchen Disco. Murphy, Al, illus. 2017. (ENG.). 32p. (J). (-k). pap. 9.95 (978-0-571-30788-3(4)) Faber & Faber, Inc.
Foges Clare, Clare. Kitchen Disco. Murphy Al, Al, illus. 2017. (ENG.). 32p. (gr. -1-k). 16.95 (978-0-571-33697-5(3)) Faber & Faber, Inc.
Fogliano, Julie. A House That Once Was. Smith, Lane, illus. 2018. (ENG.). 48p. (J). 18.99 (978-1-62672-314-6(1), 900151167) Roaring Brook Pr.
—If I Was the Sunshine. Long, Loren, illus. 2019. (ENG.). 48p. (J). (gr. -1-3). 17.99 (978-1-4814-7243-2(7), Atheneum Bks. for Young Readers) Simon & Schuster Children's Publishing.
Follett, Ross C. Beebear 2. Sievers, Lee, illus. 2013. (ENG.). 52p. (J). (gr. -1-3). 15.95 (978-0-9881748-0-1(4), Oddlnt Media) Greenwood Hill Pr.
Fontanez, Edwin. En esta hermosa Isla. Fontanez, Edwin, illus. 2nd rev. ed. 2005. (SPA., Illus.). 32p. (J). 16.95 (978-0-9640868-7-6(5)) Exit Studio.
Foreman, Jack. Say Hello. Foreman, Michael, illus. 2012. (ENG.). 40p. (J). (gr. -1-2). pap. 8.99 (978-0-7636-6087-1(6)) Candlewick Pr.
Foreman, Jack & Foreman, Michael. Say Hello. 2015. 40p. pap. 7.00 (978-1-61003-409-8(0)) Center for the Collaborative Classroom.
Foster, Chad. Dear God: Thank-You Notes to God from Baby Boys & Girls. 2004. (J). bds. 8.99 (978-0-9644456-1-1(1)) Rising Bks.
Foster, Evelyn. Alan & the Animals. 2011. (Tadpoles Ser.). (ENG., Illus.). 24p. (J). (gr. k-2). (978-0-7787-0573-4(0)); pap. (978-0-7787-0584-0(6)) Crabtree Publishing Co.
Foster, John. Dinosaur Rap. Harter, Debbie, illus. 2016. (ENG.). 32p. (J). (gr. -1-1). 16.99 (978-1-78285-301-5(4)) Barefoot Bks., Inc.
Fox, Mem. Baby Bedtime. 2014. (ENG., Illus.). 32p. (J). (gr. -1-3). 17.99 (978-1-4814-2097-6(6), Beach Lane Bks.) Beach Lane Bks.
—Bonnie & Ben Rhyme Again. Horacek, Judy, illus. 2020. (ENG.). 32p. (J). (-3). 19.99 (978-1-5344-5352-4(0), Beach Lane Bks.) Beach Lane Bks.
—Hello Baby! Jenkins, Steve, illus. 2009. (ENG.). 32p. (J). (gr. -1-k). 17.99 (978-1-4169-8513-6(1), Beach Lane Bks.) Beach Lane Bks.
—I'm an Immigrant Too! Ghosh, Ronojoy, illus. 2018. (ENG.). 40p. (J). (gr. -1-3). 18.99 (978-1-5344-3602-2(2), Beach Lane Bks.) Beach Lane Bks.
—Let's Count Goats! Thomas, Jan, illus. 2010. (ENG.). 40p. (J). (gr. -1-3). 18.99 (978-1-4424-0598-1(8), Beach Lane Bks.) Beach Lane Bks.
—Nellie Belle. Austin, Mike, illus. 2015. (ENG.). 32p. (J). (gr. -1-3). 17.99 (978-1-4169-9005-5(4), Beach Lane Bks.) Beach Lane Bks.
—Ten Little Fingers & Ten Little Toes. Oxenbury, Helen, illus. (ENG.). 40p. (J). 2018. (— 1). pap. 26.99 (978-1-328-85225-0(3), 1694584) 2008. (gr. -1 — 1). 17.99 (978-0-15-206057-2(X), 1198193) HarperCollins Pubs. (Clarion Bks.).
—Ten Little Fingers & Ten Little Toes Lap Board Book. Oxenbury, Helen, illus. 2011. (ENG.). 38p. (J). (gr. k — 1). bds. 14.99 (978-0-547-58103-3(3), 1459676, Clarion Bks.) HarperCollins Pubs.
—Ten Little Fingers & Ten Little Toes Padded Board Book. Oxenbury, Helen, illus. 2010. (ENG.). 38p. (J). (gr. k — 1). bds. 8.99 (978-0-547-36620-3(5), 1422523, Clarion Bks.) HarperCollins Pubs.
—Ten Little Fingers & Ten Little Toes/Diez Deditos de Las Manos y Pies: Bilingual English-Spanish. Oxenbury, Helen, illus. 2012. (ENG.). 38p. (J). (gr. -1-k). bds. 8.99 (978-0-547-87006-9(X), 1504629, Clarion Bks.) HarperCollins Pubs.
—This & That. Horacek, Judy, illus. 2017. (ENG.). 32p. (J). (gr. -1-k). 17.99 (978-1-338-03780-7(3), Scholastic Pr.) Scholastic, Inc.
—Time for Bed Board Book. Dyer, Jane, illus. 2023. (ENG.). 28p. (J). (gr. -1 — 1). bds. 8.99 (978-0-15-201066-9(1), 1188713, Clarion Bks.) HarperCollins Pubs.
—Two Little Monkeys. Barton, Jill, illus. 2012. (ENG.). 32p. (J). (gr. -1-3). 16.99 (978-1-4169-8687-4(1), Beach Lane Bks.) Beach Lane Bks.
—Yoo-Hoo, Ladybug! Ljungkvist, Laura, illus. 2013. (ENG.). 32p. (J). (gr. -1-3). 19.99 (978-1-4424-3400-4(7)) Simon & Schuster Children's Publishing.
Fox, Mem & Horacek, Judy. Where Is the Green Sheep? Horacek, Judy, illus. 2004. (ENG., Illus.). 32p. (J). (gr. -1-3). 17.99 (978-0-15-204907-2(X), 1194817, Clarion Bks.) HarperCollins Pubs.
—Where Is the Green Sheep? Board Book. Horacek, Judy, illus. alt. ed. 2009. (ENG., Illus.). 32p. (J). (gr. -1 — 1). bds. 6.99 (978-0-15-206704-5(3), 1098965, Clarion Bks.) HarperCollins Pubs.
—Where Is the Green Sheep? Padded Board Book. Horacek, Judy, illus. 2019. (ENG., Illus.). 32p. (J). (— 1). bds. 8.99 (978-1-328-48266-2(9), 1715797, Clarion Bks.) HarperCollins Pubs.
—Where Is the Green Sheep?/Donde Esta la Oveja Verde? Board Book: Bilingual English-Spanish. Horacek, Judy, illus. 2010. (ENG., Illus.). 32p. (J). (gr. -1-k). bds. 5.99 (978-0-547-39694-1(5), 1427473, Clarion Bks.) HarperCollins Pubs.
Foxworthy, Jeff. Hide!!! Björkman, Steve, illus. 2010. (ENG.). 32p. (J). (gr. -1-2). 17.99 (978-0-8253-0554-2(3)) Beaufort Bks., Inc.
Frampton, David. The Whole Night Through. Frampton, David, illus. Date not set. (Illus.). 32p. (J). (gr. -1-1). pap. 5.99 (978-0-06-443652-6(7)) HarperCollins Pubs.
—The Whole Night Through: A Lullaby. Frampton, David, illus. 2004. (Illus.). 30p. (J). (gr. k-4). reprint ed. (978-0-7567-7723-4(2)) DIANE Publishing Co.
Francis, JennaKay. The Ferry Boat. Woodward II, Ed, illus. 2013. 12p. pap. 8.95 (978-1-61633-426-0(6)) Guardian Angel Publishing, Inc.
Frank, Connie. Sadie & the Night Sky. 1 vol. 2009. 24p. pap. 24.95 (978-1-60703-911-2(7)) America Star Bks.
Frank, Janet. Daddies: A Book for Dads & Kids. Gergely, Tibor, illus. 2011. (Little Golden Book Ser.). (ENG.). 24p. (J). (gr. -1-2). 5.99 (978-0-375-86130-7(0), Golden Bks.) Random Hse. Children's Bks.
Frankau, Gilbert. One of Us: A Novel in Verse. 2005. pap. 22.95 (978-1-4179-6045-3(0)) Kessinger Publishing, LLC.
Frasconi, Antonio. The House That Jack Built: A Picture Book in Two Languages. 2017. (ENG., Illus.). 32p. 14.95 (978-0-486-81646-3(X), 81646X) Dover Pubns., Inc.
—The Snow & the Sun: A South American Folk Rhyme in Two Languages. 2018. (ENG., Illus.). 32p. (gr. 1-5). 16.95 (978-0-486-81648-7(6), 816486) Dover Pubns., Inc.
Frazier, Kelly. The Red Sock Christmas. Matthes, Justice, illus. 2008. 25p. pap. 24.95 (978-1-60610-704-1(6)) America Star Bks.
Frederick, Heather Vogel. Hide-And-Squeak. Payne, C. F., illus. 2011. (ENG.). 32p. (J). (gr. -1-1). 16.99 (978-0-689-85570-2(2), Simon & Schuster Bks. For Young Readers) Simon & Schuster Bks. For Young Readers.
Fredrickson, Lane. Monster Trouble! Robertson, Michael, illus. 2015. 32p. (J). (gr. -1-2). 16.95 (978-1-4549-1345-0(2)) Sterling Publishing Co., Inc.
Freedman, Claire. Aliens in Underpants Save the World. Cort, Ben, illus. 2012. (Underpants Bks.). (ENG.). 32p. (J). (gr. -1-2). 18.99 (978-1-4424-2768-6(X), Simon & Schuster/Paula Wiseman Bks.) Simon & Schuster/Paula Wiseman Bks.
—Aliens Love Panta Claus. Cort, Ben, illus. 2011. (Underpants Bks.). (ENG.). 32p. (J). (gr. -1-2). 18.99 (978-1-4424-2830-0(9), Simon & Schuster/Paula Wiseman Bks.) Simon & Schuster/Paula Wiseman Bks.
—Cuddle Bear. Scott, Gavin, illus. 2018. (J). (978-1-61067-730-1(7)) Kane Miller.
—A Cuddle for Little Duck. Pedler, Caroline, illus. 2009. (ENG.). 20p. (J). (gr. -1-k). bds. 8.99 (978-0-545-07797-2(4), Cartwheel Bks.) Scholastic, Inc.
—Dragon Jelly. Hendra, Sue, illus. 2015. (ENG.). 32p. (J). (gr. k-3). 14.99 (978-1-61963-682-8(4), 900145471, Bloomsbury USA Childrens) Bloomsbury Publishing USA.
—I Love You, Baby! Abbot, Judi, illus. 2017. (ENG.). 32p. (J). (gr. -1-3). 17.99 (978-1-4814-9904-0(1), Simon & Schuster/Paula Wiseman Bks.) Simon & Schuster/Paula Wiseman Bks.
—Monstersaurus. Cort, Ben, illus. 2011. (ENG.). 32p. (978-1-84738-904-6(X)) Simon & Schuster, Ltd.
—Spider Sandwiches. Hendra, Sue, illus. 2014. (ENG.). 32p. (J). (gr. k-3). 15.99 (978-1-61963-364-3(7), 900134246, Bloomsbury USA Childrens) Bloomsbury Publishing USA.
Freeman, Chip. Why, Daddy, Why Are There Stars in the Sky? Perry, Lee Ann, illus. 2012. 20p. (-18). pap. 11.95 (978-1-937770-23-5(0), SPC Bks.) RPJ & Co., Inc.
Freeman, Tina, illus. Ten Little Monkeys Jumping on the Bed. 2007. (Classic Books with Holes 8x8 with CD Ser.). (ENG.). 16p. (J). (gr. -1-1). (978-1-904550-67-9(3)) Child's Play International Ltd.
French, Vivian. If I Were an Alien, 1 vol. Williams, Lisa, illus. 2009. (Get Set Readers Ser.). (ENG.). 32p. (J). (gr. 1-1). lib. bdg. 27.27 (978-1-60754-267-4(6), da869a77-0d7d-4bff-92fa-add6ed76eb48, Windmill Bks.) Rosen Publishing Group, Inc., The.
—Pig in Love. Archbold, Tim, illus. 2005. 32p. (J). lib. bdg. 9.00 (978-1-4242-0889-0(0)) Fitzgerald Bks.
Freudig, Laura. Halfway Wild, 1 vol. Barry, Kevin, illus. 2016. (ENG.). 32p. (J). 17.95 (978-1-934031-48-3(8), 73f100ad-e4d5-44ec-9395-1c31bdb64c29) Islandport Pr., Inc.
Freysinger, Karen. Adventures of Countess Pigula Her Royal Imagination. Freysinger, Karen, illus. 2006. (Illus.). (J). 15.95 (978-0-9786729-0-4(9)) Aha! Elora Danan Productions.
Friedlander, Tim. The I Like Me Dance! Edwards, W M, illus. 2007. (Playdate Kids Musical Ser.). 27p. (J). (gr. -1-3). 14.95 incl. audio compact disk (978-1-933721-07-1(3)) Playdate Kids Publishing.
Friedman, Laurie. Back-To-School Rules. Murfin, Teresa, illus. 2011. (ENG.). 32p. (J). (gr. k-3). lib. bdg. 17.99 (978-0-7613-6070-4(0), 232a5142-f743-4756-8b4d-39d5020b27e4, Carolrhoda Bks.) Lerner Publishing Group.
—Birthday Rules. Murfin, Teresa, illus. 2015. (ENG.). 32p. (J). (gr. k-3). lib. bdg. 16.99 (978-0-7613-6071-1(9), 3781be1a-340b-4a6e-a450-24de5e15dae3); E-Book 27.99 (978-1-4677-6177-2(X)) Lerner Publishing Group, (Carolrhoda Bks.).
—I'm Not Afraid of This Haunted House. Murfin, Teresa, illus. 2005. 32p. (J). (gr. k-3). 16.95 (978-1-57505-751-4(4), Carolrhoda Bks.) Lerner Publishing Group.
—Love, Ruby Valentine. Avril, Lynne, illus. 2006. (Ruby Valentine Ser.). (ENG.). 32p. (J). (gr. k-3). lib. bdg. 16.95 (978-1-57505-899-3(5), 76ef85c3-9ebb-43e3-afc4-3afa1ae7878d, Carolrhoda Bks.) Lerner Publishing Group.
—Ruby Valentine & the Sweet Surprise. Avril, Lynne, illus. 2014. (Ruby Valentine Ser.). (ENG.). 32p. (J). (gr. k-3). 16.95 (978-0-7613-8873-9(7), 7491b02d-c3ff-421c-a33c-6400cf28d745, Carolrhoda Bks.) Lerner Publishing Group.
—Ruby Valentine Saves the Day. Avril, Lynne, illus. 2010. (Ruby Valentine Ser.). (ENG.). 32p. (J). (gr. k-3). lib. bdg. 16.95 (978-0-7613-4213-7(3), 5712cf7b-cdd0-4bc4-bb02-98aa513f9e9a, Carolrhoda Bks.) Lerner Publishing Group.
Fronis, Aly. This Little Pumpkin. Flowers, Luke, illus. 2018. (ENG.). 16p. (J). (gr. -1-k). bds. 5.99 (978-1-4998-0645-8(0)) Little Bee Books Inc.
—This Little Turkey. Blanco, Migy, illus. 2016. (ENG.). 16p. (J). (gr. -1-k). bds. 5.99 (978-1-4998-0302-0(8)) Little Bee Books Inc.
Frost, Helen. Applesauce Weather. Bates, Amy June, illus. 2016. 112p. (J). (gr. 3-7). 14.99 (978-0-7636-7576-9(8)) Candlewick Pr.
—Applesauce Weather. Bates, Amy June, illus. 2018. 112p. (J). (gr. 3-7). pap. 6.99 (978-1-5362-0361-5(0)) Candlewick Pr.
—Crossing Stones. 2009. (ENG., Illus.). 192p. (YA). (gr. 7-18). 19.99 (978-0-374-31653-2(8), 900050356, Farrar, Straus & Giroux (BYR)) Farrar, Straus & Giroux.
—Hidden. 2015. (ENG.). (J). (gr. 5-9). lib. bdg. 17.60 (978-1-62765-725-9(8)) Perfection Learning Corp.
—When My Sister Started Kissing. 2017. (ENG.). 208p. (J). 16.99 (978-0-374-30303-7(7), 9780374303037, Farrar, Straus & Giroux (BYR)) Farrar, Straus & Giroux.
Frost, Maddie. Animobiles: Animals on the Mooove. 2018. (ENG., Illus.). 40p. (J). (gr. -1-3). 17.99 (978-1-4926-5671-5(2), Sourcebooks Jabberwocky) Sourcebooks, Inc.
Frost, Maddie, illus. Alfie & Bet's ABC. 2018. (J). 12.99 (978-1-61067-647-2(5)) Kane Miller.
Fry, Sonali. Where Are You, Blue? Clifton-Brown, Holly, illus. 2015. (Dot Town Ser.). (ENG.). 32p. (J). (gr. -1 — 1). bds. 8.99 (978-1-4814-3589-5(2), Little Simon) Little Simon.
Fuller, Sandy Ferguson. My Cat, Coon Cat, 1 vol. Brett, Jeannie, illus. (ENG.). (J). 2017. 32p. pap. 12.95 (978-1-944762-13-1(2), a64ab0b1-8bc9-445c-abcc-1f535f6ff3d7) 2011. 36p. 17.95 (978-1-934031-32-2(1), 2d3b0879-1c62-442a-b3b7-c5086f2cf8c1) Islandport Pr., Inc.
Fulmer, Jeffrey. My Imagination Kit. Pickering, Jimmy, tr. Pickering, Jimmy, illus. 2003. (J). 24p. 15.95 (978-1-59336-008-5(8)); 23p. pap. (978-1-59336-009-2(6)) Mondo Publishing.
Funk, Josh. Dear Dragon: A Pen Pal Tale. Montalvo, Rodolfo, illus. 2016. 40p. (J). (gr. -1-3). 18.99 (978-0-451-47230-4(6), Viking Books for Young Readers) Penguin Young Readers Group.
—Lady Pancake & Sir French Toast. Kearney, Brendan, illus. 2015. (Lady Pancake & Sir French Toast Ser.: 1). 40p. (J). (gr. -1-3). 18.99 (978-1-4549-1404-4(1), 1394148) Sterling Publishing Co., Inc.
—Lost in the Library: A Story of Patience & Fortitude. Lewis, Stevie, illus. 2018. (New York Public Library Book Ser.). (ENG.). 40p. (J). 18.99 (978-1-250-15501-6(0), 900184517, Holt, Henry & Co. Bks. For Young Readers) Holt, Henry & Co.
—Mission Defrostable. Kearney, Brendan, illus. 2018. (Lady Pancake & Sir French Toast Ser.: 3). (ENG.). 40p. (J). (gr. -1-3). 17.99 (978-1-4549-2811-9(5)) Sterling Publishing Co., Inc.
Fyleman, Rose. Mice. Ehlert, Lois, illus. 2012. (ENG.). 40p. (J). (gr. -1-k). 16.99 (978-1-4424-5684-6(1), Beach Lane Bks.) Beach Lane Bks.
Gabriel, Andrea. My Favorite Bear. 2014. 32p. pap. 8.00 (978-1-61003-310-7(8)) Center for the Collaborative Classroom.
—My Favorite Bear. Gabriel, Andrea, illus. 2004. (Illus.). 32p. (J). (-k). pap. 7.95 (978-1-58089-039-7(3)) Charlesbridge Publishing, Inc.
Gaiman, Neil. Blueberry Girl. Vess, Charles, illus. (ENG.). 32p. (J). (gr. -1-3). 2011. pap. 7.99 (978-0-06-083810-2(8)) 2009. 18.99 (978-0-06-083808-9(6)) HarperCollins Pubs. (HarperCollins).
—Blueberry Girl. 2011. (J). lib. bdg. 17.20 (978-0-606-15398-0(5)) Turtleback.
—Crazy Hair. McKean, Dave, illus. (ENG.). 40p. (J). (gr. -1-3). 2015. pap. 6.99 (978-0-06-057910-4(2)) 2009. 18.99 (978-0-06-057908-1(0)) HarperCollins Pubs. (HarperCollins).
—Crazy Hair. 2015. (J). lib. bdg. 17.20 (978-0-606-36478-2(1)) Turtleback.
—The Dangerous Alphabet. Grimly, Gris, illus. (ENG.). 32p. (J). (gr. -1-3). 2010. pap. 7.99 (978-0-06-078335-8(4)) 2008. 17.99 (978-0-06-078333-4(8)) HarperCollins Pubs. (HarperCollins).
Gaither, Doug. The Lonely Mare, 1 vol. 2010. 22p. pap. 24.95 (978-1-4489-5871-9(7)) PublishAmerica, Inc.
Galan, Alvaro & Galán, Ana. Billy Bully. Simpson, Steve, illus. 2009. (ENG.). 32p. (J). (gr. -1-3). pap. 3.99 (978-0-545-11012-9(2)) Scholastic, Inc.
Galbraith, Kathryn O. Boo, Bunny! Board Book. Mack, Jeff, illus. 2012. (ENG.). 32p. (J). (gr. -1 — 1). bds. 5.99 (978-0-547-81850-4(5), 1496581, Clarion Bks.) HarperCollins Pubs.
Galdone, Paul. Jack & the Beanstalk. Galdone, Paul, illus. 2013. (Paul Galdone Nursery Classic Ser.). (ENG., Illus.). 40p. (J). (gr. -1-3). 9.99 (978-0-544-06665-6(0), 1535016, Clarion Bks.) HarperCollins Pubs.
Gall, Chris. Substitute Creacher. 2011. (ENG., Illus.). 40p. (J). (gr. -1-3). 18.99 (978-0-316-08915-9(X)) Little, Brown Bks. for Young Readers.
Galliez, Roxane Marie. Give Me Moon. Delanssay, Cathy, illus. 2009. 44p. (J). (gr. -1-3). 14.99 (978-0-8416-7138-6(9)) Hammond World Atlas Corp.
Galloway, Fhiona, illus. Fire Engine. 2016. (J). (978-1-62885-168-7(6)) Kidsbooks, LLC.
Galvin, Laura. I Love My Mommy. 2009. (I Love My... Ser.). (ENG., Illus.). 16p. (J). 12.95 (978-1-59249-801-7(9)) Soundprints.
—I Love My Sister. 2008. (ENG., Illus.). 16p. (J). (gr. -1-k). bds. 6.95 (978-1-59249-867-3(1)) Soundprints.
Galvin, Laura, told to. I Love My Mommy. 2007. (ENG., Illus.). 16p. (J). (gr. -1-k). bds. 6.95 (978-1-59249-730-0(6)) Soundprints.
Galvin, Laura G. & Galvin, Laura. I Love My Mommy (with Download) 2011. (ENG.). 16p. (J). (978-1-60727-345-5(4)) Soundprints.
Galvin, Laura Gates. I Love My Brother. Oughton, Taylor, illus. 2008. (ENG.). 16p. (J). (gr. -1-k). bds. 6.95 (978-1-59249-866-6(3)) Soundprints.
—I Love My Daddy. 2011. (I Love My... Ser.). (ENG., Illus.). 16p. (J). (gr. -1-k). 6.95 (978-1-60727-346-2(2)) Soundprints.
—I Love My Family. 2011. (ENG.). 16p. (J). (978-1-60727-621-0(6)) Soundprints.
—I Love My Sister. Oughton, Taylor et al, illus. 2011. (I Love My... Ser.). (ENG.). 16p. (gr. -1-k). 6.95 (978-1-60727-311-0(X)) Soundprints.
—Mickey Mouse Clubhouse Fun with Numbers & Shapes. 2008. (ENG.). 20p. (J). (gr. -1-3). 9.99 (978-1-59069-655-2(7)) Studio Mouse LLC.
Gamble, Adam. Good Night Arizona. Veno, Joe, illus. 2008. (Good Night Our World Ser.). (ENG.). 20p. (J). (gr. k — 1). bds. 9.95 (978-1-60219-000-9(3)) Good Night Bks.
—Good Night California. Stevenson, Harvey, illus. 2008. (Good Night Our World Ser.). (ENG.). 24p. (J). (gr. k — 1). bds. 9.95 (978-1-60219-021-4(6)) Good Night Bks.
—Good Night Tennessee. Veno, Joe, illus. 2007. (Good Night Our World Ser.). (ENG.). 20p. (J). (gr. -1 — 1). bds. 9.95 (978-1-60219-019-1(4)) Good Night Bks.
—Good Night World. Kelly, Cooper, illus. 2009. (Good Night Our World Ser.). (ENG.). 28p. (J). (gr. -1-k). bds. 9.95 (978-1-60219-030-6(5)) Good Night Bks.

S

Gandolfi, Claudine. The Night Before Dog-Mas. Anagost, Karen, illus. 2007. (Petite Plush Kit Ser.). 64p. (J). (gr. -1-3). 9.95 *(978-1-59359-883-9(1))* Peter Pauper Pr. Inc.

Garcia, Joan. Footsteps of Angels. 2003. 52p. (J). pap. 11.95 *(978-0-7414-1602-5(6))* Infinity Publishing.

A Garden Circus. 2003. (J). 9.99 *(978-0-9740847-5-6(1))* GiGi Bks.

Garden, Randa Sue. Penny the Penguin. 2003. 48p. per. 7.95 *(978-0-615-12322-6(8))* Garden, Randa.

Gardner, Louise, illus. Five Little Easter Eggs. (ENG.). 10p. (J). 2009. (gr. -1). 5.95 *(978-1-58117-849-4(2))* 2008. 9.95 *(978-1-58117-682-7(1))* Bendon, Inc. (Intervisual/Piggy Toes).

Garland, Michael. Hooray José!, 1 vol. Garland, Michael, illus. 2007. (ENG., Illus.). 32p. (J). (gr. -1-3). 16.99 *(978-0-7614-5345-1(8))* Marshall Cavendish Corp.

Garriel, Barbara S. I Know a Shy Fellow Who Swallowed a Cello. O'Brien, John, illus. (ENG.). 32p. (J). (gr. k-2). 2012. pap. 8.99 *(978-1-59078-946-9(6))* 2004. 17.99 *(978-1-59078-043-5(4))* Astra Publishing Hse. (Astra Young Readers).

Garson, Sarah. One, Two, Cockatoo! Garson, Sarah, illus. 2012. (ENG., Illus.). 32p. (J). (gr. k — 1). pap. 10.99 *(978-1-84270-944-3(5))* Andersen Pr. GBR. Dist: Independent Pubs. Group.

Gassman, Julie. Do Not Bring Your Dragon to Recess. Elkerton, Andy, illus. 2018. (ENG.). 32p. (J). (gr. -1-2). lib. bdg. 22.65 *(978-1-5158-2843-3(3)*, 138276, Picture Window Bks.) Capstone.

—Do Not Bring Your Dragon to the Library. Elkerton, Andy, illus. 2016. (ENG.). 32p. (J). (gr. -1-2). 14.95 *(978-1-62370-651-7(3)*, 131438, Capstone Young Readers); lib. bdg. 21.32 *(978-1-4795-9175-6(0)*, 131437, Picture Window Bks.) Capstone.

—Do Not Take Your Dragon on a Field Trip. Elkerton, Andy, illus. 2019. (ENG.). 32p. (J). (gr. -1-2). lib. bdg. 16.95 *(978-1-68446-059-5(X)*, 140409, Capstone Editions) Capstone.

—Do Not Take Your Dragon to Dinner. Elkerton, Andy, illus. 2017. (Fiction Picture Bks.). (ENG.). 32p. (J). (gr. -1-2). lib. bdg. 21.32 *(978-1-4795-9888-5(7)*, 135339, Picture Window Bks.) Capstone.

Gates, Mariam. Dinosaur Yoga. 2019. (ENG., Illus.). 32p. (J). 17.95 *(978-1-68364-304-3(6)*, 900214682) Sounds True, Inc.

Gauthier, Lance C., text. The One-Eared Mouse of Pasture Hill. 2003. 55p. (J). per. 6.95 *(978-1-884540-70-7(8))* Haley's.

Gayzagian, Doris. One White Wishing Stone: A Beach Day Counting Book. 2006. (ENG., Illus.). 32p. (J). (gr. -1-2). 16.95 *(978-0-7922-5110-1(5)*, National Geographic Children's Bks.) National Geographic Society.

Gazzetta, Katherine Cutchin. Love from a Star. Gazzetta, Katherine Cutchin, illus. 2015. (ENG., Illus.). 32p. (J). (gr. -1-k). 14.99 *(978-1-58536-950-8(0)*, 204017) Sleeping Bear Pr.

Gee, Lulu. Dolly's Wonderful New Life. 2009. (Illus.). 96p. pap. 31.99 *(978-1-4389-4433-3(0))* AuthorHouse.

Gehl, Laura. And Then Another Sheep Turned Up. Adele, Amy, illus. 2015. (ENG.). 32p. (J). (gr. -1-3). E-Book 23.99 *(978-1-4677-1190-6(X)*, Kar-Ben Publishing) Lerner Publishing Group.

—Except When They Don't. Heinsz, Joshua, illus. 2019. (ENG.). 32p. (J). (gr. -1-3). 16.99 *(978-1-4998-0804-9(6))* Little Bee Books Inc.

—One Big Pair of Underwear. Lichtenheld, Tom, illus. 2018. (Classic Board Bks.). (ENG.). 36p. (J). (gr. -1-k). bds. 8.99 *(978-1-5344-2036-6(3)*, Little Simon) Little Simon.

Geiger, Lorraine Lynch. A Wild & Woolly Night. Vargo, Sharon, illus. 2007. (J). (gr. -1-3). 15.95 *(978-1-891795-25-1(2))* RGU Group, The.

Gemmen, Heather. But It's True. Lagares, Luciano, illus. 2004. (Tough Stuff for Kids Ser.). 36p. (J). (gr. 4-7). pap., pap. 5.99 *(978-0-7814-4033-2(5)*, 0781440335) Cook, David C.

Genhart, Michael. So Many Smarts! Clifton-Brown, Holly, illus. 2017. 32p. (J). *(978-1-4338-2722-8(0)*, Magination Pr.) American Psychological Assn.

The Gentleman Bat. 2014. (ENG., Illus.). 44p. (J). (gr. 7-2). 16.99 *(978-0-9913866-0-4(4))* Ripple Grove Pr.

George, Audra. Vagabonding. George, Audra, illus. 2006. (Illus.). 32p. (J). (gr. -1-3). 17.95 *(978-1-60108-010-3(7))* Red Cygnet Pr.

George, Joshua. Elepants. Poh, Jennie, illus. 2016. (J). *(978-1-4351-6486-4(5))* Barnes & Noble, Inc.

—I'm Just a Little Snowman. Green, Barry, illus. 2017. (Googley-Eye Bks.). (ENG.). 12p. (J). (gr. -1-k). bds. 7.99 *(978-1-78700-079-7(6))* Top That! Publishing PLC GBR. Dist: Independent Pubs. Group.

George, Olivia. Copy Cat. Hudson, Brett, illus. 2004. (My First Reader Ser.). (J). 18.50 *(978-0-516-24679-6(8)*, Children's Pr.) Scholastic Library Publishing.

Gerber, Carole. 10 Busy Brooms. Fleming, Michael, illus. (J). 2018. 26p. (— 1). 7.99 *(978-1-5247-6899-7(5))* 2016. 32p. (gr. -1-2). 12.99 *(978-0-553-53341-5(X))* Random Hse. Children's Bks. (Doubleday Bks. for Young Readers).

Gershator, David. Where Did the Baby Go? Gershator, Phillis, illus. 2016. (J). pap. *(978-1-934370-57-5(6))* Editorial Campana.

Gershator, Phillis. Listen, Listen. Jay, Alison, illus. (ENG.). 32p. (J). (gr. -1-2). 2008. bds. 14.99 *(978-1-84686-201-4(9))* 2007. 16.99 *(978-1-84686-084-3(9))* Barefoot Bks., Inc.

—Time for a Nap. Walker, David, illus. 2018. (Snuggle Time Stories Ser.: 9). 22p. (J). (— 1). bds. 7.95 *(978-1-4549-3130-0(2))* Sterling Publishing Co., Inc.

—Who's in the Forest? McDonald, Jill, illus. 2010. (ENG.). 13p. (J). (gr. -1-k). bds. 14.99 *(978-1-84686-476-6(3))* Barefoot Bks., Inc.

Gershator, Phillis, illus. Little Lenty. 2014. (J). pap. *(978-1-934370-48-3(7))* Editorial Campana.

Gershator, Phillis & Green, Mim. Time for a Hug. Walker, David, illus. 2013. (Snuggle Time Stories Ser.: 1). 22p. (J). (gr. -1-k). bds. 7.99 *(978-1-4549-0856-2(4))* Sterling Publishing Co., Inc.

Gershenson, Harold P. Freddy Flamingo & the Kindertown Five. Mills, Christopher, illus. 2005. 27p. (J). *(978-1-58987-070-3(0))* Kindermusik International.

—The Kindertown Fire Brigade. Mills, Christopher, illus. 2006. (J). *(978-1-58987-019-2(0))* Kindermusik International.

—Noodles from Scratch. Mills, Christopher, illus. 2006. (J). *(978-1-58987-007-9(7))* Kindermusik International.

Gerth, Melanie. Ten Little Ladybugs. Huliska-Beith, Laura, illus. 2007. (ENG.). 22p. (J). (gr. -1-3). bds. 15.95 *(978-1-58117-578-3(7)*, Intervisual/Piggy Toes) Bendon, Inc.

Gerver, Jane E. Bath Time. Ovresat, Laura, illus. 2004. (My First Reader Ser.). 31p. (J). 18.50 *(978-0-516-24677-2(1)*, Children's Pr.) Scholastic Library Publishing.

—Wait for Me! Reid, Mick, illus. (My First Reader Ser.). (J). (gr. k-1). 2005. (ENG.). 32p. pap. 3.95 *(978-0-516-25116-5(3))* 2004. 31p. 18.50 *(978-0-516-24676-5(3))* Scholastic Library Publishing. (Children's Pr.).

Ghigna, Charles. First Times, 1 vol. Smith, Lori Joy, illus. 2017. (ENG.). 32p. (J). (gr. -1-k). 19.95 *(978-1-4598-1198-0(4))* Orca Bk. Pubs. USA.

—I See Fall, 1 vol. Jatkowska, Agnieszka, illus. 2011. (I See Ser.). (ENG.). 24p. (J). (gr. -1 — 1). pap. 6.10 *(978-1-4048-6851-9(8)*, 116432, Picture Window Bks.) Capstone.

—I See Spring, 1 vol. Jatkowska, Agnieszka, illus. 2011. (I See Ser.). (ENG.). 24p. (J). (gr. -1 — 1). pap. 6.10 *(978-1-4048-6849-6(6)*, 116430, Picture Window Bks.) Capstone.

—I See Winter, 1 vol. Jatkowska, Agnieszka, illus. 2011. (I See Ser.). (ENG.). 24p. (J). (gr. -1 — 1). pap. 6.10 *(978-1-4048-6850-2(X)*, 116431, Picture Window Bks.) Capstone.

—Oh My, Pumpkin Pie! Spengler, Ken, illus. 2005. (Step into Reading Ser.). 32p. (J). (gr. -1-1). pap. 5.99 *(978-0-375-82945-1(8)*, Random Hse. Bks. for Young Readers) Random Hse. Children's Bks.

—Recycling Is Fun, 1 vol. Jatkowska, Agnieszka, illus. 2012. (My Little Planet Ser.). (ENG.). 24p. (J). (gr. -1 — 1). 6.95 *(978-1-4048-7229-5(9)*, 118111, Picture Window Bks.) Capstone.

—Snow Wonder. Woolf, Julia, illus. 2008. (Step into Reading Ser.: Vol. 2). 24p. (J). (gr. -1-1). 4.99 *(978-0-375-85586-3(6)*, Random Hse. Bks. for Young Readers) Random Hse. Children's Bks.

Ghigna, Charles & Ghigna, Debra. Barn Storm. Greenseid, Diane, illus. 2010. (Step into Reading Ser.). 32p. (J). (gr. -1-1). pap. 4.99 *(978-0-375-86114-7(9)*, Random Hse. Bks. for Young Readers) Random Hse. Children's Bks.

Gibbes, Lesley. Quick As a Wink, Fairy Pink. Acton, Sara, illus. 2019. 32p. pap. 6.99 *(978-1-921504-87-7(0)*, Working Title Pr.) HarperCollins Pubs. Australia AUS. Dist: HarperCollins Pubs.

Gibbs, Edward. Little Bee. 2012. (ENG.). 24p. (J). (gr. -1-17). bds. 8.99 *(978-0-316-12707-3(8))* Little, Brown Bks. for Young Readers.

Gibby, Bayne. You Mean the World to Me. Walker, David, illus. 2013. (ENG.). 24p. (J). (gr. -1-k). bds. 8.99 *(978-0-545-40570-6(X)*, Cartwheel Bks.) Scholastic, Inc.

Gibson, Ginger Foglesong. Tiptoe Joe. Rankin, Laura, illus. 2013. (ENG.). 32p. (J). (gr. -1-k). 17.99 *(978-0-06-177203-0(8)*, Greenwillow Bks.) HarperCollins Pubs.

Gibson, Mary, illus. Buried Treasure. 2007. 12p. (J). 5.95 *(978-0-9801269-0-7(8))* Scribe's Closet Pubns., The.

Gibson, Sherri L. In the Mind of a Child: Children's Stories. 2013. 36p. pap. 24.95 *(978-1-62709-750-5(3))* America Star Bks.

Gikow, Louise. I Can Read. Patience, John, illus. 2004. (My First Reader Ser.). 31p. (J). 18.50 *(978-0-516-24678-9(X)*, Children's Pr.) Scholastic Library Publishing.

Gilbert, Frances. Go, Girls, Go! Black, Allison, illus. 2019. (ENG.). 40p. (J). (gr. -1-3). 17.99 *(978-1-5344-2482-1(2)*, Beach Lane Bks.) Beach Lane Bks.

Gile, John. El Primer Bosque. Kohen-Klieman, Clarita, tr. 2006.Tr. of First Forest. (SPA., Illus.). 40p. per. 9.95 *(978-0-910941-15-0(7))* JGC/United Publishing Corps.

Gill, Shelley. Kiana's Iditarod. Cartwright, Shannon, illus. 2008. (Paws IV Ser.). (ENG.). 32p. (J). (gr. -1-3). pap. 10.99 *(978-1-57061-589-4(6)*, Little Bigfoot) Sasquatch Bks.

—Prickly Rose. Love, Judy, illus. 2014. 32p. (J). (gr. -1-3). pap. 7.99 *(978-1-57091-357-0(9))* Charlesbridge Publishing, Inc.

—Sitka Rose. Cartwright, Shannon, illus. 2005. (ENG.). 32p. (J). (gr. -1-3). per. 7.95 *(978-1-57091-364-8(1))* Charlesbridge Publishing, Inc.

Gilland, Gary P. The Turtle Train Troop. 2011. 24p. pap. 24.95 *(978-1-4626-3210-7(6))* America Star Bks.

Ginkel, Anne. I've Got an Elephant, 1 vol. Bynum, Janie, illus. 2013. 32p. (J). (gr. -1-3). pap. 7.99 *(978-1-56145-685-7(3))* Peachtree Publishing Co. Inc.

Giogas, Valarie. In My Backyard, 1 vol. Zecca, Katherine, illus. 2007. (ENG.). 32p. (J). (gr. -1-3). 15.95 *(978-0-9777423-1-8(8))* Arbordale Publishing.

Glass, Calliope. Star Wars: Search Your Feelings. 2018. (ENG., Illus.). 48p. (J). (gr. 1-3). 12.99 *(978-1-368-02736-6(9)*, Disney Lucasfilm Press) Disney Publishing Worldwide.

Glass, Eleri. The Red Shoes. Spires, Ashley, illus. 2017. (ENG.). 40p. (J). (gr. -1-3). 8.99 *(978-1-927018-85-9(4))* Simply Read Bks. CAN. Dist: Ingram Publisher Services.

Glassman, Bruce. Zoolidays. Kiaulevicius, Rolandas, illus. 2006. 32p. (J). (gr. -1-3). 15.95 *(978-1-60108-011-0(5))* Red Cygnet Pr.

Gliori, Debi. Goodnight World. Gliori, Debi, illus. (ENG., Illus.). (J). 2018. 26p. bds. 7.99 *(978-1-68119-789-0(8)*, 900186961, Bloomsbury Children's Bks.) 2017. 32p. 16.99 *(978-1-68119-363-2(9)*, 900171540, Bloomsbury USA Childrens) Bloomsbury Publishing USA.

—No Matter What Board Book. Gliori, Debi, illus. 2008. (ENG., Illus.). 24p. (J). (gr. -1 — 1). bds. 8.99 *(978-0-15-206343-6(9)*, 1198999, Clarion Bks.) HarperCollins Pubs.

—No Matter What Lap Board Book. Gliori, Debi, illus. 2012. (ENG., Illus.). 24p. (J). (gr. -1 — 1). bds. 12.99 *(978-0-547-71905-4(1)*, 1481812, Clarion Bks.) HarperCollins Pubs.

—Where Did That Baby Come From? Gliori, Debi, illus. 2005. (ENG., Illus.). 32p. (J). (gr. -1-3). 16.00 *(978-0-15-205373-4(5)*, 1196178, Clarion Bks.) HarperCollins Pubs.

Gloria, Truitt. Baby Jesus Is Born. 2004. (ENG., Illus.). 16p. (J). pap. 1.99 *(978-0-7586-0635-8(4))* Concordia Publishing Hse.

Glover, Clair. Fairy Penguin - the Penguin Who Loves to Play. 2013. 26p. pap. *(978-1-78222-119-7(0))* Paragon Publishing, Rothersthorpe.

Gmeyner, Elizabeth. The Key of the Kingdom: A Book of Stories & Poems for Children, 1 vol. Russell, Joyce, illus. 2004. (ENG.). 100p. (J). pap. 15.00 *(978-0-88010-549-1(6)*, Bell Pond Bks.) SteinerBooks, Inc.

Goble, Jennifer. Pop the Bubbles 1,2,3. 2011. (ENG., Illus.). 46p. (J). 15.95 *(978-0-9834645-0-1(2))* FUNdamentals/Leap In Faith.

Gobo, creator. Santa Baby. 2006. (Illus.). 10p. (gr. -1-k). 9.95 *(978-1-932915-30-3(3))* Sandvik Innovations, LLC.

Godwin, Jane. Red House, Tree House, Little Bitty Brown Mouse. Gómez, Blanca, illus. 2019. (ENG.). 40p. (J). (-k). 18.99 *(978-0-525-55381-6(9)*, Dial Bks) Penguin Young Readers Group.

Godwin, Laura. One Moon, Two Cats. Tanaka, Yoko, illus. 2011. (ENG.). 32p. (J). (gr. -1-1). 16.99 *(978-1-4424-1202-6(X)*, Atheneum Bks. for Young Readers) Simon & Schuster Children's Publishing.

Goepel, Meg. Farting Is Fun. 2010. 16p. pap. 9.99 *(978-1-4490-2346-1(0))* AuthorHouse.

Goetz, Steve. Old MacDonald Had a Boat. Kaban, Eda, illus. 2018. (ENG.). 44p. (J). (gr. -1-k). 16.99 *(978-1-4521-6505-9(X))* Chronicle Bks. LLC.

Going, K. L. Bumpety, Dunkety, Thumpety-Thump! Shin, Simone, illus. 2017. (ENG.). 48p. (J). (gr. -1-k). 17.99 *(978-1-4424-3414-1(7)*, Beach Lane Bks.) Beach Lane Bks.

Golda, Kata. Stories for Bedtime: A Keepsake Pocket & Tales to Cherish. 2011. (ENG.). 7p. (J). (gr. -1 — 1). 14.99 *(978-0-8118-7498-4(2))* Chronicle Bks. LLC.

Goldberg, Malky. What Else Do I Say? A Lift the Flap Book. Argoff, Patti, illus. 2007. (ENG.). (J). (gr. -1-k). bds. 11.99 *(978-1-929628-34-6(X))* Hachai Publishing.

Golden Books. Trains, Cranes & Troublesome Trucks (Thomas & Friends) 2015. (Big Bright & Early Board Book Ser.). (ENG., Illus.). 24p. (J). (— 1). bds. 7.99 *(978-0-385-37393-7(7)*, Random Hse. Bks. for Young Readers) Random Hse. Children's Bks.

Goldstein, Sam. Some Kids Just Can't Sit Still! Desisto, Allie, illus. 2009. (ENG.). 32p. (J). (gr. 2-4). pap. 15.95 *(978-1-886941-73-1(4))* Specialty Pr., Inc.

Gollub, Matthew. Jazz Fly 2: The Jungle Pachanga. 2010. (Jazz Fly Ser.). (ENG., Illus.). 32p. (J). (gr. k-2). 18.95 *(978-1-889910-44-4(9))* Tortuga Pr.

—Jazz Fly 2: The Jungle Pachanga. Hanke, Karen, illus. 2010. (J). *(978-1-889910-45-1(7))* Tortuga Pr.

—Ten Oni Drummers. Stone, Kazuko G., illus. 2018. (Ten Oni Drummers Ser.). (ENG.). 32p. (J). (gr. -1-k). 17.95 *(978-1-889910-51-2(1))* Tortuga Pr.

—Ten Oni Drummers / Diez Tamborileros Oni. Stone, Kazuko, illus. 2019. (Ten Oni Drummers Ser.). (SPA & ENG.). 32p. (J). (gr. -1-k). 17.95 *(978-1-889910-53-6(8))* Tortuga Pr.

Gollub, Matthew & Stone, Kazuko G. Ten Oni Drummers. 2013. (ENG., Illus.). 32p. (J). (gr. -1-3). 16.95 *(978-1-58430-011-3(6))* Lee & Low Bks., Inc.

Gonyea, Mark. One Little Monster. Gonyea, Mark, illus. 2018. (ENG., Illus.). 40p. (J). (gr. -1-3). 17.99 *(978-1-5344-0674-2(3)*, Aladdin) Simon & Schuster Children's Publishing.

Gonzalez, Maya Christina. Call Me Tree: Ll&#65533;mame &#65533;rbol, 1 vol. 2014.Tr. of Call Me Tree. (ENG.). 24p. (J). (gr. k-4). 19.95 *(978-0-89239-294-0(0)*, leelowcbp) Lee & Low Bks., Inc.

Goode, Molly. Mama Loves. McCue, Lisa, illus. 2015. (Step into Reading Ser.). 32p. (J). (gr. -1-1). 4.99 *(978-0-553-53896-0(9)*, Random Hse. Bks. for Young Readers) Random Hse. Children's Bks.

Gooderham, Chris. Even More Wicked Rhymes. 2008. 68p. pap. 13.95 *(978-1-4092-1753-4(1))* Lulu Pr., Inc.

—More Wicked Rhymes. 2008. 68p. pap. 13.95 *(978-1-4092-1663-6(2))* Lulu Pr., Inc.

—Wicked Rhymes. 2008. 68p. pap. 13.95 *(978-1-4092-1662-9(4))* Lulu Pr., Inc.

Goodman, Larry. Clean up the Glup! 2007. 24p. per. 24.95 *(978-1-4241-9141-3(6))* America Star Bks.

—The Cowboy & Other Stories. 2008. 36p. pap. 24.95 *(978-1-60813-546-2(2))* America Star Bks.

Gorey, Edward. The Wuggly Ump. Gorey, Edward, illus. 2007. (Illus.). 32p. 12.95 *(978-0-7649-4192-4(5)*, A142) Pomegranate Communications, Inc.

Gorman, Amanda. Change Sings: A Children's Anthem. Long, Loren, illus. 2021. (ENG.). 32p. (J). (gr. -1-3). 18.99 *(978-0-593-20322-4(4)*, Viking Books for Young Readers) Penguin Young Readers Group.

Gosline, Andrea Alban. Ten Little Wishes: A Baby Animal Counting Book. Bossi, Lisa Burnett, illus. 2007. 40p. (J). (gr. -1-k). 16.89 *(978-0-06-053411-0(7))* HarperCollins Pubs.

Goss, Leon. By the Light of the Moon. Luo, Shiyin Sean, illus. 2005. (J). pap. *(978-1-933156-12-5(0))*; per. 16.99 *(978-1-933156-05-7(8))* GSVQ Publishing. (VisionQuest Kids).

—I'm Good, I'm Beautiful, I'm Smart. Mailey, Maria C. & Neuburger, Jenny, illus. 2005. (J). per. *(978-1-933156-02-6(3)*, VisionQuest Kids) GSVQ Publishing.

—King for a Day. Nichols, Chris, illus. 2005. (J). pap. *(978-1-933156-09-5(0))*; per. 16.99 *(978-1-933156-01-9(5))* GSVQ Publishing. (VisionQuest Kids).

—Selfus Esteemus Personalitus Low. Tunell, Ken, illus. 2005. (J). pap. *(978-1-933156-08-8(2)*, VisionQuest Kids) GSVQ Publishing.

Goss, Leon, 3rd. Selfus Esteemus Personalitus Low. Tunell, Ken, illus. 2005. 32p. (J). per. 16.99 *(978-1-933156-00-2(7)*, VisionQuest Kids) GSVQ Publishing.

Gould, Terry. The Adventures of Sir Sniffsalot & His Friends. Proulx, Denis, illus. 2007. 48p. (gr. -1-3). pap. 15.99 *(978-0-9789057-3-6(3))* Huntington Ludlow Media Group.

—The Adventures of Sir Sniffsalot & His Friends. 2009. (Illus.). 48p. pap. 15.99 *(978-0-615-26181-2(7))* Write Away.

Gowler Greene, Rhonda. Only God Can Make a Kitten, 1 vol. Bryant, Laura J., illus. 2016. (ENG.). 28p. (J). bds. 9.99 *(978-0-310-75008-6(3))* Zonderkidz.

Grabill, Rebecca. Halloween Good Night. Okstad, Ella, illus. 2017. (ENG.). 32p. (J). (gr. -1-3). 17.99 *(978-1-4814-5061-4(1))* Simon & Schuster Children's Publishing.

Graboff, Abner. There Was an Old Lady. 2018. (Illus.). 48p. 20.00 *(978-1-85124-494-2(8))* Bodleian Library GBR. Dist: Chicago Distribution Ctr.

Grady, Karen. It's Not My Fault, She Started It. 2005. (Illus.). (J). *(978-1-59975-127-6(5))* Independent Pub.

Graegin, Stephanie. Little Fox in the Forest. Graegin, Stephanie, illus. 2017. (Illus.). 40p. (J). (gr. -1-3). 17.99 *(978-0-553-53789-5(X)*, Schwartz & Wade Bks.) Random Hse. Children's Bks.

Graham, Bobby G. Jake the Snake. 2010. 24p. pap. 16.95 *(978-1-4497-0568-8(5)*, WestBow Pr.) Author Solutions, LLC.

Grand, Robert. The Cosmic Carrot: A Journey to Wellness, Clear Vision & Good Nutrition. Webb, Ross, illus. l.t. ed. 2018. 34p. pap. 10.95 *(978-0-9967223-5-3(1))* COSMIC EDITIONS , LLC.

Grandfeather Press. Roly Poly Napoleon Discovers Colors. 2011. (ENG., Illus.). 36p. (J). pap. 6.99 *(978-0-9832355-0-7(3))* Grandfeather Pr.

Granny J. Pinky Makes a New Friend: Pinky Frink's Adventures. 2012. (ENG.). 34p. pap. 17.99 *(978-1-105-82663-4(5))* Lulu Pr., Inc.

—Pinky Visits Outer Space: Pinky Frink's Adventures. 2012. (ENG.). 36p. pap. 17.99 *(978-1-300-06064-2(6))* Lulu Pr., Inc.

Grant, Callie. Mud Puddle Hunting Day. Magee, Melanie, illus. 2013. (ENG.). 20p. (J). bds. 8.99 *(978-0-9854090-0-5(2))* Blanchard, Graham.

Grant, Holly & Campbell, K. G. Wee Sister Strange. 2017. (Illus.). 40p. (J). (gr. -1-3). 17.99 *(978-0-553-50879-6(2)*, Schwartz & Wade Bks.) Random Hse. Children's Bks.

Grant, Rick S. When I Grow Up. Alfonso, Anabel, illus. 2017. (J). pap. *(978-1-934370-67-4(3))* Editorial Campana.

—Where I Live. Sakti, Galih, illus. 2018. (J). pap. *(978-1-934370-77-3(0))* Editorial Campana.

Gravett, Emily. Bear & Hare Share! Gravett, Emily, illus. 2016. (Bear & Hare Ser.). (ENG., Illus.). 32p. (J). (gr. -1-3). 16.99 *(978-1-4814-6217-4(2)*, Simon & Schuster Bks. For Young Readers) Simon & Schuster Bks. For Young Readers.

—Cyril & Pat. Gravett, Emily, illus. 2019. (ENG., Illus.). 32p. (J). (gr. -1-3). 17.99 *(978-1-5344-3950-4(1)*, Simon & Schuster Bks. For Young Readers) Simon & Schuster Bks. For Young Readers.

—Tidy. Gravett, Emily, illus. 2017. (ENG., Illus.). 40p. (J). (gr. -1-3). 17.99 *(978-1-4814-8019-2(7)*, Simon & Schuster Bks. For Young Readers) Simon & Schuster Bks. For Young Readers.

Graw, Christine Werts. The Day I Gave My Stuff Away: The Story of Ashley Mae. 2011. 28p. pap. 13.95 *(978-1-4497-0981-5(8)*, WestBow Pr.) Author Solutions, LLC.

Gray, Kes. Frog on a Log? Field, Jim, illus. 2015. (ENG.). 32p. (J). (gr. -1-k). 17.99 *(978-0-545-68791-1(8)*, Scholastic Pr.) Scholastic, Inc.

—Nuddy Ned. Parsons, Garry, illus. 2013. (ENG.). 32p. (J). (gr. -1-k). *(978-1-4088-3659-0(9)*, 161263, Bloomsbury Children's Bks.) Bloomsbury Publishing Plc.

—Oi Cat! Field, Jim, illus. 2019. (Oi Frog & Friends Ser.). (ENG.). 32p. (J). (gr. -1-k). 16.99 *(978-1-4449-3251-5(9))*; pap. 9.99 *(978-1-4449-3252-2(7))* Hachette Children's Group GBR. Dist: Hachette Bk. Group.

Greedy Python, 1 vol. 2012. (Your Reading Path Ser.). (ENG., Illus.). 24p. (J). (gr. 3-3). pap. *(978-1-4424-4576-5(9)*, 747e8978-ed66-4776-a205-3d260273a01b, Rosen Classroom) Rosen Publishing Group, Inc., The.

Green, Andi. The Monster Who Couldn't Decide. 2010. (WorryWoo Monsters Ser.). 98p. (J). 14.99 *(978-0-9792860-3-2(4))* Monsters in My Head, LLC, The.

Green, Babs Brumer, illus. Take Her Back: An Andy-Bear Tale. 2003. 19p. (J). pap. *(978-0-9753119-0-5(5))* ATU Golden Pubns.

Green, George & Brooke, Amy/ J. George Green's, the Lion Who Couldn't Roar. 2008. (Illus.). (J). per. 16.99 *(978-1-933156-14-9(7)*, Visikid Bks.) GSVQ Publishing.

Green, Lucyna A. M., illus. Love You Little Brother. 2006. (J). *(978-1-58669-186-8(4))*; *(978-1-58669-185-1(6))* Childcraft Education Corp.

Green, M. L. Underneath My Favorite Tree. 2008. 20p. pap. 24.95 *(978-1-60474-858-1(3))* America Star Bks.

Green, Ruth. Hedgehog Holidays. 2017. (ENG., Illus.). 32p. (J). (gr. k-3). 14.95 *(978-1-84976-484-1(0)*, 1306901) Tate Publishing, Ltd. GBR. Dist: Abrams, Inc.

Greenawalt, Kelly. Princess Truly in I Am Truly. Rauscher, Amariah, illus. 2017. (Princess Truly Ser.). (ENG.). 40p. (J). (gr. -1-k). 17.99 *(978-1-338-16720-7(0)*, Orchard Bks.) Scholastic, Inc.

—Princess Truly in My Magical, Sparkling Curls. Rauscher, Amariah, illus. 2018. (Princess Truly Ser.). (ENG.). 40p. (J). (gr. -1-k). 18.99 *(978-1-338-16719-1(7)*, Orchard Bks.) Scholastic, Inc.

Greene, Rhonda. Santa's Stuck. Cole, Henry, illus. 2006. (ENG.). 32p. (J). (gr. -1-3). pap. 8.99 *(978-0-14-240686-1(4)*, Puffin Books) Penguin Young Readers Group.

Greene, Rhonda Gowler. Mail Monkeys. Bender, Robert, illus. 2006. (J). pap. *(978-1-58669-217-9(8))* Childcraft Education Corp.

—No Pirates Allowed! Said Library Lou. Ajhar, Brian, illus. 2013. (ENG.). 40p. (J). (gr. 1-3). 15.95 *(978-1-58536-796-2(6)*, 202364) Sleeping Bear Pr.

—The Very First Thanksgiving Day. Gaber, Susan, illus. 2006. (ENG.). 32p. (J). (gr. -1-1). 7.99 *(978-1-4169-1916-2(3)*, Atheneum Bks. for Young Readers) Simon & Schuster Children's Publishing.

Greenfield, Eloise. Thinker: My Puppy Poet & Me. Abdollahi, Ehsan, illus. 2019. (ENG.). 32p. (J). (gr. k-4). 15.99 *(978-1-4926-7724-6(8)*, Sourcebooks Jabberwocky) Sourcebooks, Inc.

Gregory, Manju. Jill & the Beanstalk. Anstey, David, illus. 2004. (ENG & TUR.). (J). *(978-1-84444-495-3(3))* Mantra Lingua.

Gregson, Tyler Knott & Linden, Sarah. North Pole Ninjas: MISSION: Christmas! Thibodeau, Piper, illus. 2018. 32p. (J). (gr. -1-2). 10.99 *(978-1-5247-9079-0(6)*, Penguin Workshop) Penguin Young Readers Group.

Griffis, Molly. The Buffalo in the Mall. Doner, Kim, illus. 32p. 8.95 *(978-1-57168-635-0(5))* Eakin Pr.

Griffiths, Andy. The Cat on the Mat Is Flat. Denton, Terry, illus. 2009. (ENG.). 192p. (J). (gr. -1-3). pap. 7.99 *(978-0-312-53584-1(8)*, 900054770) Square Fish.

—The Cat, the Rat, & the Baseball Bat. Denton, Terry, illus. 2013. (My Readers Ser.). (ENG.). 32p. (J). (gr. -1-1). pap. 4.99 *(978-1-250-02774-0(8)*, 900104562) Square Fish.

—Ed & Ted & Ted's Dog Fred. 2014. (My Readers: Level 2 Ser.). (J). lib. bdg. 13.55 *(978-0-606-35525-4(1))* Turtleback.

Grimes, Nikki. Danitra Brown, Class Clown. Lewis, E. B., illus. 2005. 32p. (J). lib. bdg. 17.89 *(978-0-688-17291-6(1))*; (ENG.). (gr. 3). 16.99 *(978-0-688-17290-9(3)*, HarperCollins) HarperCollins Pubs.

—Garvey's Choice. 2016. (ENG.). 120p. (J). (gr. 3-7). 16.99 *(978-1-62979-740-3(5)*, Wordsong) Highlights Pr., c/o Highlights for Children, Inc.

—Planet Middle School. (ENG., 160p. (J). 2018. Illus.). (gr. 3-6). pap. 7.99 *(978-1-61963-012-3(5)*, 900098195) 2011. 16.99 *(978-1-59990-284-5(2)*, 900051865) Bloomsbury Publishing USA. (Bloomsbury USA Childrens).

—Planet Middle School. 2019. (Penworthy Picks Middle School Ser.). (ENG.). 154p. (J). (gr. 6-8). 18.96 *(978-1-64310-917-6(0))* Penworthy Co., LLC, The.

Groover, David L. & Tchaikovsky, Peter Ilich. The Nutcracker. Sprague, Terrell Eastman, illus. 2018. (J). *(978-1-942945-63-5(9))* Night Heron Media.

Gross, S. D. Mugallumps. 2007. (Illus.). 32p. (J). per. 13.99 *(978-1-59879-303-1(9))* Lifevest Publishing, Inc.

Grossman, Bill. My Little Sister Ate One Hare. Hawkes, Kevin, illus. 2014. 32p. pap. 7.00 *(978-1-61003-374-9(4))* Center for the Collaborative Classroom.

—My Little Sister Hugged an Ape. Hawkes, Kevin, illus. 2008. (ENG.). 40p. (J). (gr. -1-2). pap. 7.99 *(978-0-385-73660-2(6)*, Dragonfly Bks.) Random Hse. Children's Bks.

Grove, Ella. A Surprise for Tommy. 2005. (Illus.). 24p. (gr. -1-5). 2.70 *(978-0-7399-2341-2(2)*, 2780) Rod & Staff Pubs., Inc.

Grover, Lorie Ann. On Pointe. 2008. (ENG.). 320p. (J). (gr. 3-7). pap. 14.99 *(978-1-4169-7826-8(7)*, McElderry, Margaret K. Bks.) McElderry, Margaret K. Bks.

Gruber, Daveda. Castle of Ice. 2008. 51p. pap. 10.94 *(978-1-4357-3251-3(0))* Lulu Pr., Inc.

Grubman, Bonnie. How Do You Get a Mouse to Smile?, 1 vol. Van Wright, Cornelius, illus. 2009. (ENG.). 32p. (J). (gr. -1-3). pap. 6.50 *(978-1-59572-167-9(3))* Star Bright Bks., Inc.

—Oy Vey! Life in a Shoe. Mottram, Dave, illus. 2019. *(978-1-68115-556-2(7)*, Apples & Honey Pr.) Behrman Hse., Inc.

—Oy Vey Life in a Shoe. Mottram, Dave, illus. 2016. (ENG.). 32p. (J). 17.95 *(978-1-68115-515-9(X)*, 59dea969-ab96-4880-8181-e7254c0178d3) Behrman Hse., Inc.

Gruhl, Jason. Everything Is Connected. Font, Ignasi, illus. 2019. 36p. (J). (gr. -1-3). 16.95 *(978-1-61180-631-1(3)*, Bala Kids) Shambhala Pubns., Inc.

Guarino, Deborah. Is Your Mama a Llama? Kellogg, Steven, illus. (ENG.). (J). (gr. -1-3). 2006. 18.95 *(978-0-439-87594-3(3))* 2004. 32p. pap. 7.99 *(978-0-439-59842-2(7)*, Scholastic Paperbacks) 2006. pap. 10.99 incl. audio compact disk *(978-0-439-87588-2(9))* Scholastic, Inc.

Guffrey, Lindsey. A Psalm for the Solar System. 2013. 24p. pap. 9.00 *(978-0-9896518-0-6(0))* Yorkshire Publishing Group.

Guidone, Thea. Drum City. Brantley-Newton, Vanessa, illus. 2015. 32p. (J). (gr. -1-2). 8.99 *(978-0-553-52350-8(3)*, Dragonfly Bks.) Random Hse. Children's Bks.

Guiffre, William. Gramma's Glasses. Pippin, Barbara, illus. 2008. 32p. (J). (gr. -1-3). pap. 9.95 *(978-1-931650-35-9(7))* Guiffre Bk. Publishing.

Guiffre, William A. Gramma's Glasses. Pippin, Barbara, illus. 2008. 32p. (J). (gr. -1-7). lib. bdg. 17.95 *(978-1-931650-19-9(5))* Guiffre Bk. Publishing.

Guile, Gill, illus. Twinkle Twinkle Little Star. 2016. (ENG.). (J). 8.95 *(978-1-58925-504-3(6))* Tiger Tales.

Gulbis, Stephen, illus. Old MacDonald Had a Barn. 2003. 22p. (YA). *(978-1-85602-453-2(9)*, Pavilion Children's Books) Pavilion Bks.

—The Wheels on the Bus. 2003. 22p. (YA). *(978-1-85602-454-9(7)*, Pavilion Children's Books) Pavilion Bks.

Gundersheimer (Mister G), Ben. Señorita Mariposa. Rivero, Marcos Almada, illus. 2019. 32p. (J). (-k). 18.99 *(978-1-5247-4070-2(5)*, Nancy Paulsen Books) Penguin Young Readers Group.

Gurewitz, Samantha & Polay, Ellyn. Marvin Mcgunk & All of His Junk. 2012. (ENG.). 27p. (J). pap. 12.95 *(978-1-4327-9705-8(0))* Outskirts Pr., Inc.

Guthrie, Arlo. Whose Moose Am I? Bradley, Cindy, illus. 2014. (ENG.). (J). 15.00 *(978-0-9915370-3-7(3))* Rising Son International, Ltd.

Guthrie, Savannah & Oppenheim, Allison. Princesses Save the World. Byrne, Eva, illus. 2018. (ENG.). 32p. (J). (gr. -1-2). 17.99 *(978-1-4197-3171-6(8)*, 1201401, Abrams Bks. for Young Readers) Abrams, Inc.

—Princesses Wear Pants. Byrne, Eva, illus. 2017. (ENG.). 32p. (J). (gr. -1-2). 18.99 *(978-1-4197-2603-3(X)*, 1186101) Abrams, Inc.

Gutierrez, Lorna. Hello, Mr. Moon. Watkins, Laura, illus. 2016. (J). *(978-1-4351-6412-3(1))* Barnes & Noble, Inc.

Gutman, Dan. Rappy Goes to Mars. Bowers, Tim, illus. 2017. (I Can Read Level 2 Ser.). (ENG.). 32p. (J). (gr. -1-3). 16.99 *(978-0-06-225269-2(0))*; pap. 4.99 *(978-0-06-225268-5(2))* HarperCollins Pubs. (HarperCollins).

—Rappy Goes to School. Bowers, Tim, illus. 2016. (ENG.). 40p. (J). (gr. -1-3). 17.99 *(978-0-06-229181-3(5)*, HarperCollins) HarperCollins Pubs.

—Rappy the Raptor. Bowers, Tim, illus. 2015. (ENG.). 40p. (J). (gr. -1-3). 17.99 *(978-0-06-229180-6(7)*, HarperCollins) HarperCollins Pubs.

Guy, Ginger Foglesong. Go Back to Bed! Bernardin, James, illus. 2006. (ENG.). 32p. (J). (gr. k-3). 16.95 *(978-1-57505-750-7(6)*, Carolrhoda Bks.) Lerner Publishing Group.

Haack, Daniel. Prince & Knight. Lewis, Stevie, illus. 2018. (ENG.). 40p. (J). (gr. -1-3). 17.99 *(978-1-4998-0552-9(7))* Little Bee Books Inc.

Haack, Daniel & Galupo, Isabel. Maiden & Princess. Human, Becca, illus. 2019. (ENG.). 40p. (J). (gr. -1-3). 17.99 *(978-1-4998-0776-9(7))* Little Bee Books Inc.

Haft, Sheryl. Goodnight Bubbala. Weber, Jill, illus. 2019. (ENG.). 32p. (J). (gr. k-k). 17.99 *(978-0-525-55477-6(7)*, Dial Bks) Penguin Young Readers Group.

Hale, Aaron. Addy Gets Made. 2008. 27p. pap. 24.95 *(978-1-60610-339-5(3))* America Star Bks.

Hall, Hannah. God Bless You & Good Night, 1 vol. 2013. (God Bless Book Ser.). (ENG.). 20p. (J). bds. 9.99 *(978-1-4003-2294-7(4)*, Tommy Nelson) Nelson, Thomas Inc.

—God Bless You & Good Night Touch & Feel, 1 vol. Whitlow, Steve, illus. 2018. (God Bless Book Ser.). (ENG.). 18p. (J). bds. 12.99 *(978-1-4002-0923-1(4)*, Tommy Nelson) Nelson, Thomas Inc.

Hall, Hannah C. Daddy Snuggles. Szmidt, Aleksandra, illus. 2019. (ENG.). 20p. (J). (gr. -1-k). bds. 7.99 *(978-0-8249-5696-7(6))* Worthy Publishing.

—God Bless Our Fall, 1 vol. Whitlow, Steve, illus. 2015. (God Bless Book Ser.). (ENG.). 20p. (J). bds. 9.99 *(978-0-529-12333-6(9)*, Tommy Nelson) Nelson, Thomas Inc.

—Mommy Cuddles. Szmidt, Aleksandra, illus. 2019. (ENG.). 20p. (J). (gr. -1-k). bds. 7.99 *(978-0-8249-5695-0(8))* Worthy Publishing.

—Sunrise, Easter Surprise! Jatkowska, Ag, illus. 2018. (ENG.). 20p. (J). (gr. -1-k). bds. 6.99 *(978-0-8249-1659-6(X))* Worthy Publishing.

Hall, Kate W. Richmond Rocks! 2009. (Illus.). (J). 14.95 *(978-1-61623-975-6(1)*, Richmondmom.com Publishing) Palari Publishing LLP.

Hall, Kirsten. Birthday Beastie: All about Counting. Luedecke, Bev, illus. 2003. (Beastieville Ser.). 32p. (J). 19.50 *(978-0-516-22891-4(9)*, Children's Pr.) Scholastic Library Publishing.

—Buried Treasure: All about Using a Map. Luedecke, Bev, illus. 2003. (Beastieville Ser.). 32p. (J). 19.50 *(978-0-516-22894-5(3)*, Children's Pr.) Scholastic Library Publishing.

—Good Times: All about the Seasons. Luedecke, Bev, illus. 2004. (Beastieville Ser.). (J). 19.50 *(978-0-516-23648-3(2)*, Children's Pr.) Scholastic Library Publishing.

—Help! All about Telling Time. Luedecke, Bev, illus. 2003. (Concept Bks.). 32p. (J). 19.50 *(978-0-516-22890-7(0)*, Children's Pr.) Scholastic Library Publishing.

—Hide-And-Seek: All about Location. Luedecke, Bev, illus. 2004. (Beastieville Ser.). (J). 19.50 *(978-0-516-23649-0(0)*, Children's Pr.) Scholastic Library Publishing.

—The Honeybee. Arsenault, Isabelle, illus. 2018. (ENG.). 48p. (J). (gr. -1-3). 18.99 *(978-1-4814-6997-5(5))* Simon & Schuster Children's Publishing.

—I'm a Princess. DeRosa, Dee, illus. 2004. (My First Reader Ser.). (ENG.). 32p. (J). (gr. k-1). pap. 3.95 *(978-0-516-24630-7(5)*, Children's Pr.) Scholastic Library Publishing.

—I'm Not Scared. Holub, Joan, illus. 2003. (My First Reader Ser.). (ENG.). 32p. (J). 18.50 *(978-0-516-22929-4(X)*, Children's Pr.) Scholastic Library Publishing.

—Let's Trade: All about Trading. Luedecke, Bev, illus. (Beastieville Ser.). (J). (gr. k-1). 2005. (ENG.). 32p. pap. 3.95 *(978-0-516-25520-0(7))* 2004. 19.50 *(978-0-516-22999-7(0))* Scholastic Library Publishing. (Children's Pr.).

—Little Lies: All about Math. Luedecke, Bev, illus. 2003. (Beastieville Ser.). 32p. (J). 19.50 *(978-0-516-22896-9(X)*, Children's Pr.) Scholastic Library Publishing.

—My New School (My First Reader) Gott, Barry, illus. 2004. (My First Reader (Reissue) Ser.). (ENG.). 32p. (J). (gr. k-1). pap. 4.95 *(978-0-516-25505-7(3)*, Children's Pr.) Scholastic Library Publishing.

—A Perfect Day: All about the Five Senses. Luedecke, Bev, illus. (Beastieville Ser.). (J). (gr. k-1). 2005. (ENG.). 32p. pap. 3.95 *(978-0-516-25521-7(5))* 2004. 19.50 *(978-0-516-24437-2(X))* Scholastic Library Publishing. (Children's Pr.).

—Slider's Pet: All about Nature. Luedecke, Bev, illus. 2004. (Beastieville Ser.). (J). 19.50 *(978-0-516-22898-3(6)*, Children's Pr.) Scholastic Library Publishing.

—Tug-of-War: All about Balance. Luedecke, Bev, illus. 2004. (Beastieville Ser.). 31p. (J). 19.50 *(978-0-516-22899-0(4)*, Children's Pr.) Scholastic Library Publishing.

—What a Mess! All about Numbers. Luedecke, Bev, illus. 2004. (Beastieville Ser.). (J). 19.50 *(978-0-516-23670-4(9)*, Children's Pr.) Scholastic Library Publishing.

Hall, Michael. Cat Tale. Hall, Michael, illus. 2012. (ENG., Illus.). 40p. (J). (gr. -1-k). 16.99 *(978-0-06-191516-1(5)*, Greenwillow Bks.) HarperCollins Pubs.

—My Heart Is Like a Zoo. 2009. (ENG., Illus.). 32p. (J). (gr. -1-3). 16.99 *(978-0-06-191510-9(6)*, Greenwillow Bks.) HarperCollins Pubs.

—My Heart Is Like a Zoo Board Book. 2013. (ENG., Illus.). 34p. (J). (gr. -1-k). bds. 7.99 *(978-0-06-191512-3(2)*, Greenwillow Bks.) HarperCollins Pubs.

Hall, Shirley. Buggy Buggy. Ledger, Faye, illus. 2010. 20p. 12.00 *(978-1-4520-6787-2(2))* AuthorHouse.

Hallinan, P. K. Brothers Forever. 2010. (ENG., Illus.). 22p. (J). (gr. -1 — 1). bds. 7.99 *(978-0-8249-1847-7(9)*, Ideals Pubns.) Worthy Publishing.

—Forever Friends! 2003. (ENG., Illus.). 28p. (J). (gr. -1-k). bds. 7.95 *(978-0-8249-5454-3(8)*, Ideals Pubns.) Worthy Publishing.

—Grandma Loves You. 2008. (ENG., Illus.). 26p. (J). (gr. -1-k). bds. 7.99 *(978-0-8249-6726-4(3)*, Ideals Pubns.) Worthy Publishing.

—Happy Birthday! 2003. (J). *(978-0-8249-6507-5(8)*, Ideals Pubns.) Worthy Publishing.

—Heartprints. 2015. (ENG., Illus.). 24p. (J). bds. 7.99 *(978-0-8249-1964-1(5)*, Ideals Pubns.) Worthy Publishing.

—How Do I Love You? 2018. (ENG., Illus.). 22p. (J). (gr. -1-k). bds. 7.99 *(978-0-8249-1682-4(4))* Worthy Publishing.

—How to Celebrate Christmas! Holiday Traditions, Rituals, & Rules in a Delightful Story. 2019. (ENG.). 24p. (J). (gr. 1-4). 12.99 *(978-1-5107-4543-8(2)*, Sky Pony Pr.) Skyhorse Publishing Co., Inc.

—How to Celebrate Thanksgiving! Holiday Traditions, Rituals, & Rules in a Delightful Story. 2019. (ENG.). 24p. (J). (gr. 1-4). 12.99 *(978-1-5107-4541-4(6)*, Sky Pony Pr.) Skyhorse Publishing Co., Inc.

—Just Open a Book. (J). 24p. 7.95 *(978-0-8249-5353-9(3))*; (ENG.). 22p. pap. 6.55 *(978-0-8249-5354-6(1))*; 24p. lib. bdg. 11.00 *(978-0-8249-5355-3(X))* Worthy Publishing. (Ideals Pubns.).

—Let's Be Friends. 2005. (ENG., Illus.). 26p. (J). (gr. -1-1). bds. 7.95 *(978-0-8249-6587-7(6)*, Ideals Pubns.) Worthy Publishing.

—Let's Learn All We Can! (ENG., Illus.). 24p. (J). pap. 6.55 *(978-0-8249-5449-9(1)*, Ideals Pubns.) Worthy Publishing.

—Let's Play As a Team. 2003. (ENG., Illus.). 28p. (J). 8.75 *(978-0-8249-5452-9(1)*, Ideals Pubns.) Worthy Publishing.

—The Looking Book. Barton, Patrice, illus. (ENG.). (J). (gr. -1-1). 2019. 26p. bds. 7.99 *(978-0-8249-1698-5(0)*, Worthy Kids/Ideals) 2009. 32p. 16.99 *(978-0-8249-5607-3(9)*, Ideals Pubns.) Worthy Publishing.

—My Mother & I: A Picture Book for Moms & Their Loving Children. 2020. (ENG.). 24p. (J). (-1). 9.99 *(978-1-5107-4546-9(7)*, Sky Pony Pr.) Skyhorse Publishing Co., Inc.

—A Rainbow of Friends. 2018. (ENG., Illus.). 22p. (J). (gr. -1-k). bds. 7.99 *(978-0-8249-1672-5(7))* Worthy Publishing.

—Sisters Forever. 2014. (ENG., Illus.). 22p. (J). bds. 7.99 *(978-0-8249-1921-4(1)*, Ideals Pubns.) Worthy Publishing.

—That's What a Friend Is! 2016. (ENG., Illus.). 22p. (J). bds. 7.99 *(978-0-8249-1969-6(6)*, Ideals Pubns.) Worthy Publishing.

Hallstrand, John & Sarah & Hawley, Karen. Zoey Helps the Mystery Dog Find a Home. 2011. 24p. pap. 11.99 *(978-1-4634-1094-0(8))* AuthorHouse.

Halsted, John David, ed. East of the Sun & West of the Moon & Other Moon Stories. 2012. (Illus.). 54p. pap. *(978-1-909302-02-0(3))* Abela Publishing.

Hamanaka, Sheila. All the Colors of the Earth. Hamanaka, Sheila, illus. 2020. (ENG., Illus.). 32p. (J). (gr. -1-3). pap. 8.99 *(978-0-688-17062-2(5)*, HarperCollins) HarperCollins Pubs.

—Grandparents Song. Hamanaka, Sheila, illus. 2003. (Illus.). 32p. (J). 15.99 *(978-0-688-17852-9(9))* HarperCollins Pubs.

Hamburg, Jennifer. Billy Bloo Is Stuck in Goo. Burach, Ross, illus. 2017. (ENG.). 32p. (J). (gr. -1-3). 16.99 *(978-0-545-88015-2(7)*, Scholastic Pr.) Scholastic, Inc.

Hamburger, Carole. The Zippity-Do-Dot: The Dot Who Dared to Pick Her Knows. Hamburger, Carole, illus. 2008. (Illus.). 40p. (J). 16.95 *(978-0-9764921-1-5(3))* Cherry Street Pr.

Hamilton, Kersten. Police Officers on Patrol. Alley, R. W., illus. 2009. 32p. (J). (gr. -1-k). 17.99 *(978-0-670-06315-4(0)*, Viking Books for Young Readers) Penguin Young Readers Group.

—Red Truck. Petrone, Valeria, illus. 2012. (Red Truck & Friends Ser.). 26p. (J). (gr. -1 — 1). bds. 8.99 *(978-0-670-01467-5(2)*, Viking Books for Young Readers) Penguin Young Readers Group.

—Yellow Copter. Petrone, Valeria, illus. 2016. (Red Truck & Friends Ser.). 26p. (J). (— 1). bds. 8.99 *(978-1-101-99796-3(6)*, Viking Books for Young Readers) Penguin Young Readers Group.

Hamlett, Martha. Bats in the Air, Bats in My Hair. Morgan, Davey, illus. 2008. (ENG.). 32p. pap. 13.99 *(978-1-4389-2358-1(9))* AuthorHouse.

Hamsa, Bobbie. Dirty Larry (Revised Edition) (a Rookie Reader) Catanese, Donna, illus. rev. ed. 2003. (Rookie Reader Ser.). (ENG.). 24p. (J). (gr. k-2). pap. 4.95 *(978-0-516-27493-5(7)*, Children's Pr.) Scholastic Library Publishing.

—Fast-Draw Freddie (Revised Edition) (a Rookie Reader) Miller, Susan, illus. rev. ed. 2003. (Rookie Reader Ser.). (ENG.). 32p. (J). (gr. k-2). pap. 4.95 *(978-0-516-27150-7(4)*, Children's Pr.) Scholastic Library Publishing.

Hankey, Sandy. Sweet Little Girl. Gay, Maria T., illus. 2004. 20p. pap. 24.95 *(978-1-4137-3329-7(8))* PublishAmerica, Inc.

Hannigan, Paula. Hugs for You. Brown, Heather, illus. 2012. (ENG.). 10p. (J). (-k). bds. 7.99 *(978-1-4494-2192-2(X))* Andrews McMeel Publishing.

Hanson, Warren. Bugtown Boogie. Johnson, Steve & Fancher, Lou, illus. 2008. 32p. (J). (gr. -1-3). 17.89 *(978-0-06-059938-6(3)*, Geringer, Laura Book) HarperCollins Pubs.

—It's Monday, Mrs. Jolly Bones! Tusa, Tricia, illus. 2013. (ENG.). 32p. (J). (gr. -1-1). 19.99 *(978-1-4424-1229-3(1)*, Beach Lane Bks.) Beach Lane Bks.

—Kiki's Hats: Our Gifts Live on & On. Hanson, Warren, illus. 2007. (ENG., Illus.). 36p. (J). (gr. -1-3). 16.95 *(978-0-931674-94-5(8)*, Waldman House Pr.) TRISTAN Publishing, Inc.

Hanton, Sophie, illus. Hugs: Tuck Each Baby into a Loving Hug. 2010. (ENG.). 12p. (J). (gr. -1 — 1). 9.99 *(978-1-60169-020-3(7))* Innovative Kids.

Hapka, Cathy, pseud. Pretend & Play Kitty: With Real Crown You Can Wear! Borlasca, Hector, illus. 2004. (Role Play Ser.). 10p. (J). (gr. -1-18). bds. 6.99 *(978-1-57151-742-5(1))* Playhouse Publishing.

Happy Birthday, Curious George (Tabbed Book) 2016. (Curious George Ser.). (ENG., Illus.). 14p. (J). (— 1). bds. 8.99 *(978-0-544-75050-0(0)*, 1633430, Clarion Bks.) HarperCollins Pubs.

Happy Halloween, Curious George Tabbed Board Book. 2008. (Curious George Ser.). (ENG., Illus.). 14p. (J). (gr. -1 — 1). bds. 7.99 *(978-0-618-91952-9(X)*, 1015625, Clarion Bks.) HarperCollins Pubs.

Happy St. Patrick's Day, Curious George: Tabbed Board Book. 2014. (Curious George Ser.). (ENG., Illus.). 14p. (J). (— 1). bds. 7.99 *(978-0-544-08888-7(3)*, 1537662, Clarion Bks.) HarperCollins Pubs.

Harley, Bill. Dirty Joe, the Pirate: A True Story. Davis, Jack E., illus. 2008. (ENG.). 32p. (J). (gr. k-3). 17.99 *(978-0-06-623780-0(7)*, HarperCollins) HarperCollins Pubs.

Harney, Jennifer. Swim Swim Sink. 2020. (ENG., Illus.). 40p. (J). (gr. -1-3). 12.99 *(978-1-368-05276-4(2))* Little, Brown Bks. for Young Readers.

—Underwear! 2019. (ENG., Illus.). 40p. (J). (gr. -1-k). 12.99 *(978-1-368-02793-9(8))* Disney Publishing Worldwide.

Harrah, Judith. Come Inside the Ark. Foster, Jack, illus. 2012. (J). pap. 17.99 *(978-1-937331-12-2(1))* ShadeTree Publishing, LLC.

Harrington, Tim. Nose to Toes, You Are Yummy! Harrington, Tim, illus. 2015. (ENG., Illus.). 32p. (J). (gr. -1-3). 17.99 *(978-0-06-232816-8(6)*, Balzer & Bray) HarperCollins Pubs.

Harris, Chris. The Alphabet's Alphabet. Santat, Dan, illus. 2020. (ENG.). 48p. (J). (gr. -1-3). 17.99 *(978-0-316-26662-8(0))* Little, Brown Bks. for Young Readers.

Harris, Christine. Four Tails: An Anthology of Four Tales for Children. 2011. (Illus.). 92p. (gr. -1). pap. 12.10 *(978-1-4520-7643-0(X))* AuthorHouse.

Harris, Jim. Dinosaur's Night Before Christmas, 1 vol. Harris, Jim, illus. 2010. (Night Before Christmas Ser.). (ENG., Illus.). 40p. (J). (gr. k-3). 16.99 *(978-1-58980-850-8(9)*, Pelican Publishing) Arcadia Publishing.

Harris, Jim & Harris, Marian. Ten Little Kittens Board Book: An Eyeball Animation Book. 2011. (ENG., Illus.). 26p. (J). (gr. -1-k). bds. 9.99 *(978-1-4494-0175-7(9))* Andrews McMeel Publishing.

Harris, Marian. Ten Little Kittens (Eyeball Animation) Harris, Jim, illus. 2010. (ENG.). 28p. (J). (gr. k). 15.99 *(978-0-7407-9197-0(4))* Andrews McMeel Publishing.

Harris, Meena. Ambitious Girl. Valdez, Marissa, illus. 2021. (Ambitious Girl Ser.: 1). (ENG.). 40p. (J). (gr. -1-3). 18.99 *(978-0-316-22969-2(5))* Little, Brown Bks. for Young Readers.

Harris, Robie H. Who?: a Celebration of Babies: A Celebration of Babies. Rosenberg, Natascha, illus. 2018. (ENG.). 20p. (J). (gr. -1 — 1). bds. 8.99 *(978-1-4197-2834-1(2)*, 1206110, Abrams Appleseed) Abrams, Inc.

Harris, Sally M. Color Me Happy. Paplinksie, Cecilia, illus. 2009. 24p. pap. 10.95 *(978-1-935137-75-7(1))* Guardian Angel Publishing, Inc.

Harris, Stephanie C. The Wonders of Monkey Mac! 2009. 302p. pap. 15.95 *(978-1-60693-257-5(8)*, Eloquent Bks.) Strategic Book Publishing & Rights Agency (SBPRA).

Harris, Trudy. The Clock Struck One: A Time-Telling Tale. Hartman, Carrie, illus. 2009. (Math Is Fun! Ser.). (ENG.). 32p. (J). (gr. k-2). 19.99 *(978-0-8225-9067-5(0)*, 96912699-1d73-456d-b3c2-39ed189e8f7a, Millbrook Pr.) Lerner Publishing Group.

—Jenny Found a Penny. Hovell, John, illus. 2007. (Math Is Fun! Ser.). (ENG.). 32p. (gr. k-3). lib. bdg. 23.93 *(978-0-8225-6725-7(3)*, Millbrook Pr.) Lerner Publishing Group.

—Over, under, in, & Ouch! Haskamp, Steve, illus. 2003. (Silly Millies Ser.). (ENG.). 32p. (gr. k-3). lib. bdg. 17.44 *(978-0-7613-2912-1(9)*, Lerner Pubns.) Lerner Publishing Group.

—Tally Cat Keeps Track. Harris, Andrew N., illus. 2010. (Math Is Fun! Ser.). (ENG.). 32p. (J). (gr. k-2). lib. bdg. 22.65 *(978-0-7613-4451-3(9)*, ce765b9f-4098-4631-8b1b-22e67647dc5e, Millbrook Pr.) Lerner Publishing Group.

Harrison, Daisy. My Grandmother Lives in a Shotgun House, 1 vol. Henriquez, Emile, illus. 2018. (ENG.). 32p. (J). (gr. -1-3). 16.99 *(978-1-4556-2302-0(4)*, Pelican Publishing) Arcadia Publishing.

Harrison, Kenny. Hide & Seek Harry on the Farm. Harrison, Kenny, illus. 2015. (ENG., Illus.). 20p. (J). (-k). bds. 6.99 *(978-0-7636-7370-3(6))* Candlewick Pr.

Harrison, Michael. Cop's Night Before Christmas, 1 vol. Miles, David, illus. 2010. (Night Before Christmas Ser.). (ENG.). 32p. (J). (gr. k-3). 16.99 *(978-1-58980-800-3(2)*, Pelican Publishing) Arcadia Publishing.

Harshman, Marc & Ryan, Cheryl. Red Are the Apples. Zahares, Wade, illus. 2007. (ENG.). 32p. (J). (gr. -1-3). pap. 7.99 *(978-0-15-206065-7(0)*, 1198217, Clarion Bks.) HarperCollins Pubs.

Hart, Caryl. Catch That Rat. McLaughlin, Tom, illus. 2013. (ENG.). 32p. (J). pap. 8.99 *(978-1-84738-931-2(7)*, Simon & Schuster Children's) Simon & Schuster, Ltd. GBR. Dist: Simon & Schuster, Inc.

—Let's Go to Playgroup. Tobia, Lauren, illus. 2017. (ENG.). 32p. (J). 11.99 *(978-1-61067-581-9(9))* Kane Miller.

Harter, Debbie. Animal Boogie. 2008. (ENG., Illus.). 32p. (J). 16.99 *(978-1-84686-231-1(0))* Barefoot Bks., Inc.

—Walking Through the Jungle. Harter, Debbie, illus. 2004. (ENG & PAN., Illus.). 32p. (J). pap. *(978-1-85269-851-5(9))* Mantra Lingua.

Harter, Debbie, illus. Walking Through the Jungle. 2004. 30p. (J). *(978-1-85269-866-9(7))*; *(978-1-85269-861-4(6))*; *(978-1-85269-846-1(2))*; (ENG & SPA.). *(978-1-85269-871-3(3))*; *(978-1-85269-876-8(4))*; *(978-1-85269-881-2(0))*; *(978-1-85269-886-7(1))*; *(978-1-85269-856-0(X))*; (GUJ.). *(978-1-85269-841-6(1))*; *(978-1-85269-831-7(4))*; *(978-1-85269-826-3(8))*; (ARA & ENG.). *(978-1-85269-811-9(X))*; *(978-1-85269-807-2(1))* Mantra Lingua.

Hartman, Brooke. Dream Flights on Arctic Nights. Zerbetz, Evon, illus. 2019. (ENG.). 32p. (J). (gr. k-3). 22.99 *(978-1-5132-6189-8(4)*, Alaska Northwest Bks.) West Margin Pr.

Hartman, Sara. When Jesus Was Born. Mitter, Kathy, illus. 2007. (ENG.). 16p. (J). (gr. k-4). pap. 1.99 *(978-0-7586-1281-6(8))* Concordia Publishing Hse.

Hartmann, Wendy. This Is the Chick. Rankin, Joan, illus. 2017. (ENG.). 32p. (J). (gr. -1-3). 17.95 *(978-1-56656-039-9(X)*, Crocodile Bks.) Interlink Publishing Group, Inc.

Hartshorne, Holly L. School Time for the Three Little Fish, 1 vol. 2009. 12p. pap. 24.95 *(978-1-60749-404-1(3))* America Star Bks.

Harvey, Jeanne Walker. My Hands Sing the Blues: Romare Bearden's Childhood Journey, 0 vols. Zunon, Elizabeth, illus. 2012. (ENG.). 40p. (J). (gr. 1-3). 17.99 *(978-0-7614-5810-4(7)*, 9780761458104, Two Lions) Amazon Publishing.

Harvey, Matt. Shopping with Dad. Latimer, Miriam, illus. 2008. 32p. (J). (gr. -1-3). 16.99 *(978-1-84686-172-7(1))* Barefoot Bks., Inc.

Haskamp, Steven, illus. Eight Silly Monkeys. 2007. (ENG.). 18p. (J). (gr. -1-3). bds. 15.95 *(978-1-58117-577-6(9)*, Intervisual/Piggy Toes) Bendon, Inc.

Hasling, Jack. Salamander the Great! 2006. (Illus.). (J). per. 10.00 *(978-0-9786988-1-2(9))* Hazel Street Productions.

Hasselbring, Janet. What Do You See, Mrs Night Heron? De Vries, Bruce, illus. 2010. 32p. pap. 12.95 *(978-1-936343-03-4(7))* Peppertree Pr., The.

S

Hatch, Morgan John. Where Dreams Are Made. 2011. 28p. pap. 24.95 *(978-1-4626-2896-4(6))* America Star Bks.
Havill, Juanita. Grow: A Novel in Verse, 1 vol. Kodman, Stanislawa, illus. 160p. (J). (gr. 3-7). 2011. pap. 7.99 *(978-1-56145-575-1(X))* 2008. 14.95 *(978-1-56145-441-9(9))* Peachtree Publishing Co. Inc.
—Jamaica's Find Book & Cd. O'Brien, Anne Sibley, illus. 2009. (ENG.). 32p. (J). (gr. -1-3). audio compact disk 10.99 *(978-0-547-11961-8(5)*, 1047233, Clarion Bks.) HarperCollins Pubs.
Haws, Ileen. Feet are Neat. 2008. 40p. pap. 18.50 *(978-1-4357-4437-0(3))* Lulu Pr., Inc.
Hay DeSimone, Corkey. Dinosaur Explore Activity & Coloring Book: Dinosaurs designed for their littlest Fans. Hay DeSimone, Corkey, illus. 2006. (Illus.). (J). 4.95 *(978-0-9777394-0-0(6))* Gentle Giraffe Pr.
—Panda Promise Activity & Coloring Book. Hay DeSimone, Corkey, illus. 2006. (Illus.). (J). 4.95 *(978-0-9747921-9-4(5))* Gentle Giraffe Pr.
Hayes, Kate. All about Poop. Garnsworthy, Mario, ed. Vaughan, Brenna, illus. 2012. (ENG.). 38p. (J). pap. 14.95 *(978-0-9854248-0-0(X))* Pinwheel Bks.
Hayles, Marsha. Bunion Burt. Davis, Jack E., illus. 2009. (ENG.). 32p. (J). (gr. -1-3). 16.99 *(978-1-4169-4132-3(0)*, McElderry, Margaret K. Bks.) McElderry, Margaret K. Bks.
Hays, Anna Jane. Here Comes Silent E! Adinolfi, JoAnn, illus. 2004. (Step into Reading Ser.). (ENG.). 32p. (J). (gr. -1-1). pap. 5.99 *(978-0-375-81233-0(4)*, Random Hse. Bks. for Young Readers) Random Hse. Children's Bks.
—Kindergarten Countdown: A Book for Kindergarteners. Davick, Linda, illus. 2013. 24p. (J). (gr. -1-2). 8.99 *(978-0-385-75371-5(3)*, Dragonfly Bks.) Random Hse. Children's Bks.
—Spring Surprises. Swearingen, Hala Wittwer, illus. 2010. (Step into Reading: Step 2 Ser.). (ENG.). 24p. (J). (gr. -1-1). lib. bdg. 16.19 *(978-0-375-95840-3(1))* Random House Publishing Group.
Hayward, Linda. It Takes Three. Koontz, Robin Michal, illus. 2003. (Silly Millies Ser.: 3). 32p. (J). (gr. 1-3). pap. 5.95 *(978-0-7613-1798-2(8))*; lib. bdg. 17.90 *(978-0-7613-2902-2(1)*, Millbrook Pr.) Lerner Publishing Group.
Hecht, Zalmy. My Very Own Letter. Judowitz, Chani, illus. 2016. (ENG.). 20p. (J). 11.95 *(978-1-929628-89-6(7))* Hachai Publishing.
Hegarty, Patricia. Everybody's Welcome. Abbott, Greg, illus. 2018. (ENG.). 32p. (J). (gr. -1-2). 16.99 *(978-1-5247-7165-2(1)*, Doubleday Bks. for Young Readers) Random Hse. Children's Bks.
Hegg, Tom & Hanson, Warren. Peef & the Baby Sister. Hegg, Tom & Hanson, Warren, illus. 2006. (ENG., Illus.). 36p. (J). (gr. -1-3). 16.95 *(978-0-931674-67-9(0)*, Waldman House Pr.) TRISTAN Publishing, Inc.
Heidenreich, Elke. Some Folk Think the South Pole's Hot: The Three Tenors Play the Antarctic. Buchholz, Quint, illus. 2004. (ENG.). 64p. (J). 17.95 *(978-1-56792-170-0(1))* Godine, David R. Pub.
Heiligman, Deborah. Cool Dog, School Dog, 0 vols. Bowers, Tim, illus. 2013. (ENG.). 32p. (J). (gr. -1-2). pap. 9.99 *(978-1-4778-1670-7(4)*, 9781477816707, Two Lions) Amazon Publishing.
—Fun Dog, Sun Dog, 0 vols. Bowers, Tim, illus. 2012. (ENG.). 34p. (J). (gr. -1-2). pap. 7.99 *(978-0-7614-5836-4(0)*, 9780761458364, Two Lions) Amazon Publishing.
Heim, Alastair. Hello, Door. Coburn, Alisa, illus. 2018. (ENG.). 32p. (J). (gr. -1-3). 16.99 *(978-1-4998-0536-9(5))* Little Bee Books Inc.
Heine, Theresa & Tavares, Victor. Star Seeker: A Journey to Outer Space. Tavares, Victor, illus. 2006. (ENG., Illus.). 32p. (J). (gr. -1-3). 16.99 *(978-1-905236-36-7(0))* Barefoot Bks., Inc.
Heinz, Brian J. Adirondack Lullaby. Henry, Maggie, illus. 2016. (ENG.). (J). bds. *(978-1-59531-053-8(3))* North Country Bks., Inc.
—The Barnyard Cat. l.t. ed. 2003. (Illus.). 32p. (J). pap. 6.96 *(978-0-936335-07-0(6))* Ballyhoo BookWorks, Inc.
—The Great North Woods. Rothman, Michael, illus. 2016. (ENG.). 32p. (J). (gr. 3-6). 18.99 *(978-1-56846-275-2(1)*, 20817, Creative Editions) Creative Co., The.
—Red Fox at McCloskey's Farm. Sheban, Chris, illus. 2006. 32p. (J). (gr. -1-3). 17.95 *(978-1-56846-195-3(X)*, Creative Editions) Creative Co., The.
Helene Bridge, Chris. Red Envelopes: Sobres Rojos. 2018. (ENG., Illus.). 32p. (J). 19.95 *(978-1-942945-65-9(5)*, a81528e3-b1fe-457c-a1d0-3c4bafb6b8d7) Night Heron Media.
Helfand, Harriet Cohen & Zager, Ellen Kahan. And There Was Evening, & There Was Morning. Zager, Ellen Kahan, illus. 2018. (ENG., Illus.). 24p. (J). (gr. -1-3). 12.99 *(978-1-5124-8364-2(8)*, 69ab789a-10a7-4075-9d3d-f314709c87df, Kar-Ben Publishing) Lerner Publishing Group.
Heling, Kathryn & Hembrook, Deborah. Ten Lucky Leprechauns. Johnson, Jay, illus. 2013. (ENG.). 24p. (J). (gr. -1-k). pap. 3.99 *(978-0-545-43648-9(6)*, Cartwheel Bks.) Scholastic, Inc.
Helmore, Jim. Letterbox Lil: A Cautionary Tale. 2006. (Illus.). (J). *(978-1-4156-4110-1(2))* Book Wholesalers, Inc.
Henderson, Robert. I See, I See. 2019. (ENG., Illus.). 48p. (J). (gr. -1-k). 17.99 *(978-1-4521-8334-3(1))* Chronicle Bks. LLC.
Henkel, Donald G. Painted Treasures or the Original 288 Tree Gnomes. Henkel, D. B., VIII, illus. 2006. (J). mass mkt. 20.50 *(978-0-9673504-1-7(7))* Quillpen.
Henning, Heather. Christmas. Bull, Nicola, ed. Chapman, Gillian, illus. 2007. (Touch & Feel Ser.). 14p. (J). (gr. -1-3). bds. 10.49 *(978-0-7586-1383-7(0))* Concordia Publishing Hse.
—Creation. Bull, Nicola, ed. Chapman, Gillian, illus. 2007. (Touch & Feel Ser.). 14p. (J). (gr. -1-3). bds. 10.49 *(978-0-7586-1384-4(9))* Concordia Publishing Hse.
Henry, Kristina. The Rat Tank, 1 vol. 2011. (ENG., Illus.). 40p. (J). (gr. -1-3). 16.99 *(978-0-7643-3842-7(0)*, 4271, Schiffer Publishing Ltd) Schiffer Publishing, Ltd.
—The Turtle Tank, 1 vol. 2011. (ENG., Illus.). 32p. (J). (gr. -1-3). 16.99 *(978-0-7643-3843-4(9)*, 4272, Schiffer Publishing Ltd) Schiffer Publishing, Ltd.
Henry, Nancy. Where's Papa? 2008. 24p. per. 24.95 *(978-1-60474-000-4(0))* America Star Bks.
Henry, Sandy. A Child's Bedtime Companion. Pavlova, Vera, illus. 2005. 26p. (J). (gr. -1-2). per. 12.95 *(978-1-929039-31-9(X))* Ambassador Bks., Inc.
Hepworth, Amelia. I Love You to the Moon & Back. Warnes, Tim, illus. 2017. (ENG.). 24p. (J). (gr. -1-k). bds. 9.99 *(978-1-68010-522-3(1))* Tiger Tales.
Herman Horatio Hornblower III. 2005. (YA). per. 5.00 *(978-1-59872-239-0(5))* Instant Pub.
Hernandez, Peter. A New Day with Rhyming Robin. 2011. 32p. pap. *(978-1-4269-5817-5(X))* Trafford Publishing (UK) Ltd.
Herrera, Juan Felipe. SkateFate. 2015. (ENG.). 128p. (YA). (gr. 8). pap. 9.99 *(978-0-06-143289-7(X)*, HarperTeen) HarperCollins Pubs.
Herzog, Pearl. The Pink Dollhouse. 2008. 112p. 29.99 *(978-1-58330-797-7(4))* Feldheim Pubs.
Hess, Megan. Claris Vol. 2: The Chicest Mouse in Paris, Volume 1. 2018. (Claris Ser.: Bk. 1). (ENG., Illus.). 48p. (J). (gr. -1-3). 17.99 *(978-1-76050-259-1(6))* Hardie Grant Bks. AUS. Dist: Hachette Bk. Group.
Hesterman, Katie. A Round of Robins. Ruzzier, Sergio, illus. 2018. 40p. (J). (gr. k-3). 16.99 *(978-0-399-54778-2(9)*, Nancy Paulsen Books) Penguin Young Readers Group.
Hewitt, Hazel & Gillett, Chrissy. A Locust Ate My Daddy's Underwears. 2008. 24p. pap. 13.95 *(978-1-84799-261-1(7))* Lulu Pr., Inc.
Heyden, Linda Vander. Hannah's Tall Order: An a to Z Sandwich. Harren, Kayla, illus. 2018. (ENG.). 32p. (J). (gr. k-2). 16.99 *(978-1-58536-382-7(0)*, 204587) Sleeping Bear Pr.
—A Horse Named Jack. Brown, Petra, illus. 2018. (ENG.). 32p. (J). (gr. -1-2). 16.99 *(978-1-58536-395-7(2)*, 204411) Sleeping Bear Pr.
Hickman, Jessica. Alligator Seder. Elissambura, illus. 2020. (ENG.). 12p. (J). (gr. -1 — 1). bds. 6.99 *(978-1-5415-6041-3(8)*, 328acd50-3eca-4a22-a925-629f27e06cde, Kar-Ben Publishing) Lerner Publishing Group.
Hicks, Barbara Jean. I Like Black & White. Prap, Lila, illus. 2006. 24p. (J). (gr. -1-3). 9.95 *(978-1-58925-056-7(7))* Tiger Tales.
—Monsters Don't Eat Broccoli. Hendra, Sue, illus. 40p. (J). (gr. -1-2). 2014. 8.99 *(978-0-385-75521-4(X)*, Dragonfly Bks.) 2009. 16.99 *(978-0-375-85686-0(2)*, Knopf Bks. for Young Readers) Random Hse. Children's Bks.
Hicks, Robert Z. Tommie Turtle's Secret. Rolseth, Ruthie, illus. 2007. (ENG.). 40p. (J). 16.95 *(978-0-9792031-0-7(4))* R.Z. Enterprises of Florida.
High, Linda Oatman. A Heart Like Ringo Starr, 1 vol. 2015. (Gravel Road Verse Ser.). (ENG.). 268p. (YA). (gr. 9-12). pap. 12.95 *(978-1-62250-963-3(4))* Saddleback Educational Publishing, Inc.
Highley, Rainey Marie. The Long Lost Tale of the Dragon & the Whale. 2013. 28p. pap. 16.95 *(978-1-4808-0151-6(8))* Archway Publishing.
Hilb, Nora, illus. Itsy Bitsy Spider. 2012. (Classic Books with Holes Board Book Ser.). (J). 14p. spiral bd. *(978-1-84643-509-6(9))*; 16p. pap. *(978-1-84643-498-3(X))* Child's Play International Ltd.
Hill, Annemarie. Meaty Treats. 2012. 16p. pap. 15.41 *(978-1-4669-3118-3(3))* Trafford Publishing.
Hill, Isabel. Building Stories, 1 vol. 2011. (ENG., Illus.). 32p. (J). 17.95 *(978-1-59572-279-9(3))*; pap. 7.95 *(978-1-59572-280-5(7))* Star Bright Bks., Inc.
Hillert, Margaret. The Cow That Got Her Wish. (J). 4.95 *(978-0-87895-694-4(8))* Modern Curriculum Pr.
—The Cow That Got Her Wish. Linda Prater, illus. 2016. (Beginning-To-Read Ser.). (ENG.). 32p. (J). (gr. k-2). pap. 13.26 *(978-1-60357-938-4(9))* Norwood Hse. Pr.
—The Cow That Got Her Wish. Prater, Linda, illus. 2016. (BeginningtoRead Ser.). (ENG.). 32p. (J). (gr. 1-2). 22.60 *(978-1-59953-797-9(4))* Norwood Hse. Pr.
—Fun Days. (J). 4.95 *(978-0-87895-678-4(6))* Modern Curriculum Pr.
—Fun Days. Roraback, Robin, illus. 2016. (BeginningtoRead Ser.). (ENG.). 32p. (J). (gr. -1-2). 22.60 *(978-1-59953-815-0(6))* Norwood Hse. Pr.
—Fun Days. Robin Roraback, illus. 2016. (Beginning-To-Read Ser.). (ENG.). 32p. (J). (gr. k-2). pap. 13.26 *(978-1-60357-977-3(X))* Norwood Hse. Pr.
—What Is It? Stalio, Ivan & Fabbrucci, Fabiano, illus. 2016. (BeginningtoRead Ser.). (ENG.). 32p. (J). (gr. k-2). 22.60 *(978-1-59953-807-5(5))* Norwood Hse. Pr.
Hilliard, Michael. Butter Bee Grows up Too Fast! 2010. 20p. pap. 12.49 *(978-1-4490-7300-8(X))* AuthorHouse.
Hills, Jodi. Hope-So. Bjornson, Barbara, illus. 2004. (ENG.). 36p. (J). 16.95 *(978-0-9726504-2-7(3))* TRISTAN Publishing, Inc.
Hilton, Jennifer & McCurry, Kristen. God Made Feelings: A Book about Emotions. Rimmington, Natasha, illus. 2017. (Frolic First Faith Ser.). 22p. (J). bds. 6.99 *(978-1-5064-1782-0(5)*, Sparkhouse Family) 1517 Media.
Hinder, Sarah Jane. Hello, Sun! A Yoga Sun Salutation to Start Your Day. 2019. (Hello, Sun! Ser.). (ENG., Illus.). 32p. (J). 17.95 *(978-1-68364-283-1(X)*, 900214679) Sounds True, Inc.
Hindley, Judy. Do Like a Duck Does! Bates, Ivan, illus. 2007. (ENG.). 40p. (J). (gr. -1-2). 5.99 *(978-0-7636-3284-7(8))* Candlewick Pr.
—Do Like a Duck Does! Bates, Ivan, illus. 2007. (gr. -1-k). 15.00 *(978-0-7569-8127-3(1))* Perfection Learning Corp.
—Do Like A Duck Does! 2007. 14.75 *(978-1-4177-8331-1(1))* Turtleback.
Hinkler Books Staff. CD Storybook: Beauty & the Beast; The Little Mermaid; Cinderella; Snow White. rev. ed. 2004. (Illus.). 128p. (J). (gr. 4-12). 14.95 incl. cd-rom *(978-1-86515-754-2(6))* Hinkler Bks. Pty. Ltd. AUS. Dist: Penton Overseas, Inc.
Hinman, Bobbie. The Fart Fairy. Adams, Mark Wayne, illus. 2010. (ENG.). 32p. (J). (gr. -1-1). 16.95 *(978-0-9786791-4-9(8))* Best Fairy Bks.
—The Knot Fairy. Bridgeman, Kristi, illus. 2010. (ENG.). 32p. (J). (gr. -1-1). 16.95 *(978-0-9786791-0-1(5))* Best Fairy Bks.
—The Sock Fairy. Bridgeman, Kristi, illus. 2008. (ENG.). 32p. (J). (gr. -1-1). 16.95 *(978-0-9786791-1-8(3))* Best Fairy Bks.
Hoberman, Mary Ann. A House Is a House for Me. 2007. (Illus.). 48p. (J). (gr. -1-1). pap. 9.99 *(978-0-14-240773-8(9)*, Puffin Books) Penguin Young Readers Group.
—The Seven Silly Eaters. Frazee, Marla, illus. 2004. (J). (gr. k-3). spiral bd. *(978-0-616-14576-0(4))* Canadian National Institute for the Blind/Institut National Canadien pour les Aveugles.
—The Sun Shines Everywhere. Lozano, Luciano, illus. 2019. (ENG.). 32p. (J). (gr. -1-3). 17.99 *(978-0-316-52384-4(4))* Little, Brown Bks. for Young Readers.
Hochman, Marisa. A Walk in Pirate's Cove, 1 vol. 2012. (ENG., Illus.). 32p. (J). *(978-0-9865679-0-2(6))* Fitzhenry & Whiteside, Ltd.
Hodgkinson, Leigh. A Place to Read. 2017. (ENG., Illus.). 32p. (J). 16.99 *(978-1-68119-323-6(X)*, 900170032, Bloomsbury USA Childrens) Bloomsbury Publishing USA.
Hodgman, Ann. Monsters Dance. Wood, Hannah, illus. 2013. (ENG.). 16p. (J). (gr. -1). bds. 8.95 *(978-1-58925-627-9(1))* Tiger Tales.
Hodgson, Mona. Bedtime in the Southwest. Graef, Renee, illus. 2004. (ENG.). 32p. (J). (gr. -1-k). 14.95 *(978-0-87358-871-3(1))* Cooper Square Publishing Llc.
Hoffman, Don. Abigail Is a Big Girl. Dakins, Todd, illus. 2nd ed. 2016. (Billy & Abby Ser.). (ENG.). 28p. (J). (gr. -1-k). pap. 3.99 *(978-1-943154-03-6(1))* Peek-A-Boo Publishing.
—Billy Is a Big Boy. Dakins, Todd, illus. 2nd ed. 2016. (Billy & Abby Ser.). (ENG.). 28p. (J). (gr. -1-k). pap. 3.99 *(978-1-943154-02-9(3))* Peek-A-Boo Publishing.
—Good Morning, Good Night Billy & Abigail. Dakins, Todd, illus. 2nd ed. 2016. (Billy & Abby Ser.). (ENG.). 24p. (J). (gr. -1-k). pap. 3.99 *(978-1-943154-09-8(0))* Peek-A-Boo Publishing.
Hoffman, Peter. A ferret in a Garret. Olson, Cindy, illus. 2008. 36p. (J). 24.99 *(978-0-9790247-6-4(5))* Artpacks.
Hoffmann, Heinrich. Slovenly Betsy: the American Struwwelpeter: From the Struwwelpeter Library. Hayn, Walter, illus. 2013. (Dover Children's Classics Ser.). (ENG.). 96p. (J). (gr. 3-8). pap. 12.99 *(978-0-486-49828-7(X)*, 49828X) Dover Pubns., Inc.
Hogan, Robb Dragon Taz. Moonlight's Spell: Rhymes for Younger Readers by TAZ. 2003. (Illus.). 61p. (J). spiral bd. 9.95 *(978-0-9742178-1-9(6))* TazTales.
Holladay, Shirley. Gail the Snail. 2009. 28p. pap. 14.99 *(978-1-4389-8744-6(7))* AuthorHouse.
Hollon, Frank Turner, et al. Glitter Girl & the Crazy Cheese. Dulemba, Elizabeth O., illus. 2006. (ENG.). 32p. (J). (gr. -1-3). *(978-1-59692-137-5(4))* MacAdam/Cage Publishing, Inc.
Holmes, Kimberly. Digibots Classroom Adventures. Lawson, Devin, illus. 2004. (J). *(978-0-9755725-0-4(4)*, 1238415) Digibots Corp.
Holt, Gretta Scott. The Reindeer Who Was Afraid to Fly. Jones, Amber & Sullivan, Allen, illus. 2008. (ENG.). 24p. pap. 11.49 *(978-1-4389-1709-2(0))* AuthorHouse.
Holt, K. A. Brains for Lunch: A Zombie Novel in Haiku?! Wilson, Gahan, illus. 2010. (ENG.). 96p. (J). (gr. 4-9). 22.99 *(978-1-59643-629-9(8)*, 900068270) Roaring Brook Pr.
—House Arrest (Young Adult Fiction, Books for Teens) 2016. (ENG.). 312p. (J). (gr. 5-17). pap. 7.99 *(978-1-4521-5648-4(4))* Chronicle Bks. LLC.
—Redwood & Ponytail: (Novels for Preteen Girls, Children's Fiction on Social Situations, Fiction Books for Young Adults, LGBTQ Books, Stories in Verse) 2019. (ENG., Illus.). 424p. (J). (gr. 5-9). 18.99 *(978-1-4521-7288-0(9))* Chronicle Bks. LLC.
Holub, Joan. Apple Countdown. Smith, Jan, illus. 2012. (J). *(978-1-61913-117-0(X))* Weigl Pubs., Inc.
—Apple Countdown. Smith, Jan, illus. 2009. (ENG.). 32p. (J). (gr. -1-3). 16.99 *(978-0-8075-0398-0(3)*, 807503983) Whitman, Albert & Co.
—Ballet Stars. McNicholas, Shelagh, illus. 2012. (Step into Reading Ser.). 24p. (J). (gr. -1-1). pap. 5.99 *(978-0-375-86909-9(3)*, Random Hse. Bks. for Young Readers) Random Hse. Children's Bks.
—Ballet Stars. 2012. (Step into Reading - Level 1 Ser.). lib. bdg. 13.55 *(978-0-606-26398-6(5))* Turtleback.
—Big Heart! A Valentine's Day Tale. Terry, Will, illus. 2007. (Ant Hill Ser.). (ENG.). 24p. (J). (gr. -1-k). lib. bdg. 13.89 *(978-1-4169-2562-0(7)*, Simon & Schuster/Paula Wiseman Bks.) Simon & Schuster/Paula Wiseman Bks.
—Big Heart! A Valentine's Day Tale (Ready-To-Read Pre-Level 1) Terry, Will, illus. 2007. (Ant Hill Ser.). (ENG.). 24p. (J). (gr. -1-k). pap. 4.99 *(978-1-4169-0957-6(5)*, Simon Spotlight) Simon Spotlight.
—Dig, Scoop, Ka-Boom! Gordon, David, illus. 2013. (Step into Reading Ser.). 24p. (J). (gr. -1-1). pap. 5.99 *(978-0-375-86910-5(7)*, Random Hse. Bks. for Young Readers) Random Hse. Children's Bks.
—Good Luck! A St. Patrick's Day Story. Terry, Will, illus. 2007. (Ant Hill Ser.). (ENG.). 24p. (J). (gr. -1-k). lib. bdg. 11.89 *(978-1-4169-2560-6(0)*, Aladdin Library) Simon & Schuster Children's Publishing.
—Good Luck! A St. Patrick's Day Story (Ready-To-Read Pre-Level 1) Terry, Will, illus. 2007. (Ant Hill Ser.). (ENG.). 24p. (J). (gr. -1-k). pap. 4.99 *(978-1-4169-0955-2(9)*, Simon Spotlight) Simon Spotlight.
—The Knights Before Christmas. Magoon, Scott, illus. 2015. (ENG.). 32p. (J). (gr. k-3). 16.99 *(978-0-8050-9932-4(8)*, 900126311, Holt, Henry & Co. Bks. For Young Readers) Holt, Henry & Co.
—Scaredy-Pants! A Halloween Story (Ready-To-Read Pre-Level 1) Terry, Will, illus. 2007. (Ant Hill Ser.). (ENG.). 24p. (J). (gr. -1-k). pap. 3.99 *(978-1-4169-0956-9(7)*, Simon Spotlight/Nickelodeon) Simon Spotlight/Nickelodeon.
—Shampoodle. Bowers, Tim, illus. 2009. (Step into Reading Ser.). 32p. (J). (gr. -1-1). pap. 5.99 *(978-0-375-85576-4(9)*, Random Hse. Bks. for Young Readers) Random Hse. Children's Bks.
—Snow Day! A Winter Tale (Ready-To-Read Pre-Level 1) Terry, Will, illus. 2008. (Ant Hill Ser.). (ENG.). 24p. (J). (gr. -1-k). pap. 4.99 *(978-1-4169-5135-3(0)*, Simon Spotlight) Simon Spotlight.
—Spring Is Here! A Story about Seeds. Terry, Will, illus. 2008. (Ant Hill Ser.). (ENG.). 24p. (J). (gr. -1-k). lib. bdg. 13.89 *(978-1-4169-5132-2(6)*, Simon & Schuster/Paula Wiseman Bks.) Simon & Schuster/Paula Wiseman Bks.
—Spring Is Here! A Story about Seeds (Ready-To-Read Pre-Level 1) Terry, Will, illus. 2008. (Ant Hill Ser.). (ENG.). 24p. (J). (gr. -1-k). pap. 4.99 *(978-1-4169-5131-5(8)*, Simon Spotlight) Simon Spotlight.
Holzer, Angela. Lovely Lily. Hansen, Angela, illus. 2009. (ENG.). 36p. (J). lib. bdg. 8.99 *(978-0-9821563-2-2(4))* Good Sound Publishing.
Hood, Susan. Lifeboat 12. 2018. (ENG., Illus.). 336p. (J). (gr. 3-8). 17.99 *(978-1-4814-6883-1(9)*, Simon & Schuster Bks. For Young Readers) Simon & Schuster Bks. For Young Readers.
—Tickly Toes. Barroux, illus. 2014. (ENG.). 24p. (J). (gr. -1 — 1). bds. 9.95 *(978-1-894786-52-2(1))* Kids Can Pr., Ltd. CAN. Dist: Hachette Bk. Group.
Hooke, R. Schuyler. Thomas' Night Before Christmas (Thomas & Friends) Courtney, Richard, illus. 2013. (Little Golden Book Ser.). (ENG.). 24p. (J). (gr. -1-k). 4.99 *(978-0-449-81663-9(X)*, Golden Bks.) Random Hse. Children's Bks.
Hooker, Renee & Jones, Karl. Life with My Family. Durst, Kathryn, illus. 2018. 32p. (J). (gr. -1-2). 17.99 *(978-1-5247-8937-4(2)*, Penguin Workshop) Penguin Young Readers Group.
Hope, Kathleen. Isiah Thomas & the Mysterious Castle Mcscary. 2012. (Illus.). 44p. pap. 24.40 *(978-1-4685-0496-5(7))* AuthorHouse.
Hopgood, Sally. A Trip to Busy Town: A Pull-The-Tab Book. Hinton, Stephanie, illus. 2014. (J). *(978-1-4351-5690-6(0))* Barnes & Noble, Inc.
Hopgood, Sally & Hinton, Stephanie. Under the Waves: A Pull-The-Tab Book. 2014. (Illus.). (J). *(978-1-4351-5691-3(9))* Barnes & Noble, Inc.
Hopkins, Ellen. Fallout. 2010. (Crank Trilogy Ser.). (ENG.). 672p. (YA). (gr. 9-18). 18.99 *(978-1-4169-5009-7(5)*, McElderry, Margaret K. Bks.) McElderry, Margaret K. Bks.
—Impulse. 2008. (ENG.). 688p. (YA). (gr. 9-12). pap. 14.99 *(978-1-4169-0357-4(7)*, McElderry, Margaret K. Bks.) McElderry, Margaret K. Bks.
—Tilt. (ENG., (YA). (gr. 9). 2014. Illus.). 624p. pap. 13.99 *(978-1-4169-8331-6(7))* 2012. 608p. 18.99 *(978-1-4169-8330-9(9))* McElderry, Margaret K. Bks. (McElderry, Margaret K. Bks.).
Hopkins, Jeanette. The Juggler. 2011. (Illus.). 32p. (J). 16.95 *(978-1-888160-58-1(6))* Ice Cube Pr., LLC.
Hopkinson, Deborah. Maria's Comet. Lanino, Deborah, illus. 2003. (ENG.). 32p. (J). (gr. -1-3). 8.99 *(978-0-689-85678-5(4)*, Simon & Schuster/Paula Wiseman Bks.) Simon & Schuster/Paula Wiseman Bks.
Hopper, Karyn. There's a Monster in My Opu. 2006. (Illus.). 24p. (J). 11.95 *(978-1-57306-244-2(8))* Bess Pr., Inc.
Hopwood, Lolly & Kusters, YoYo. Move! Flowers, Luke, illus. 2016. (ENG.). 32p. (J). (gr. -1-1). bds. 12.99 *(978-0-7611-8733-2(2)*, 18733) Workman Publishing Co., Inc.
Horacek, Judy. Yellow Is My Color Star. Horacek, Judy, illus. 2014. (ENG., Illus.). 32p. (J). (gr. -1-3). 16.99 *(978-1-4424-9299-8(6)*, Beach Lane Bks.) Beach Lane Bks.
Horacek, Petr. Jonathan & Martha. 2012. (ENG., Illus.). 40p. (gr. -1-1). 14.95 *(978-0-7148-6351-1(3))* Phaidon Pr., Inc.
Horowitz, Dave. Humpty Dumpty Climbs Again. Horowitz, Dave, illus. 2011. (ENG., Illus.). 32p. (J). (gr. -1-k). pap. 7.99 *(978-0-14-241932-8(X)*, Puffin Books) Penguin Young Readers Group.
—The Ugly Pumpkin. Horowitz, Dave, illus. (ENG., Illus.). (J). 2017. 32p. (— 1). bds. 7.99 *(978-1-5247-4084-9(5)*, Nancy Paulsen Books) 2008. 40p. (gr. -1-k). pap. 8.99 *(978-0-14-241145-2(0)*, Puffin Books) Penguin Young Readers Group.
Horsbrugh, Wilma. The Train to Glasgow. Cox, Paul, illus. 2004. (ENG.). 32p. (J). (gr. -1-3). 16.00 *(978-0-618-38143-2(0)*, 100335, Clarion Bks.) HarperCollins Pubs.
Horvath, James. Build, Dogs, Build: A Tall Tail. 2013. (ENG., Illus.). 40p. (J). (gr. -1-3). 17.99 *(978-0-06-218967-7(0)*, HarperCollins) HarperCollins Pubs.
—Work, Dogs, Work: A Highway Tail. 2014. (ENG., Illus.). 40p. (J). (gr. -1-3). 17.99 *(978-0-06-218970-7(0)*, HarperCollins) HarperCollins Pubs.
Hosford, Kate. Big Birthday. Clifton-Brown, Holly, illus. 2012. (Carolrhoda Picture Bks.). (ENG.). 32p. (J). (gr. k-2). lib. bdg. 16.95 *(978-0-7613-5410-9(7))* Lerner Publishing Group.
Hougue, Heather, ed. The Snowman Band. 2006. (Illus.). 22p. (J). spiral bd. 15.95 *(978-0-9764779-3-8(9))* Perennial Dreams Pubns.
Houran, Lori Haskins. I Will Keep You Safe & Sound. Brown, Petra, illus. 2013. (J). *(978-0-545-19752-6(X)*, Scholastic Pr.) Scholastic, Inc.
—Space Mice. Alpaugh, Priscilla, illus. 2020. (ENG.). 32p. (J). (gr. -1-3). 16.99 *(978-0-8075-7553-6(4)*, 807575534) Whitman, Albert & Co.
Houts, Amy. God's Protection Covers Me. Creighton-Pester, David, illus. 2019. 32p. (J). (gr. -1-k). 15.99 *(978-1-5064-4856-5(9)*, Beaming Books) 1517 Media.
Howard, Juliana. Catie the Copycat. 2010. 32p. (J). 17.00 *(978-1-59298-368-1(5))* Beaver's Pond Pr., Inc.
Howard, Mike. The Chronicles of Mike Bike Hall. Syder, Andrew, illus. 2016. (ENG.). (J). (gr. 1-5). pap. *(978-1-78222-488-4(2))* Paragon Publishing, Rothersthorpe.
Howard, Reginald. The Big, Big Wall. Dewey, Ariane & Aruego, Jose, illus. 2003. (Green Light Readers Level 1 Ser.). (J). (gr. -1-3). 13.50 *(978-0-613-66350-2(0))* Turtleback.
—The Big, Big Wall/No Puedo Bajar: Bilingual English-Spanish. Ada, Alma Flor & Campoy, F. Isabel, trs. Dewey, Ariane & Aruego, Jose, illus. 2009. (Green Light Readers Level 1 Ser.). (ENG.). 28p. (J). (gr. -1-3). pap. 5.99 *(978-0-547-25548-4(9)*, 1388304, Clarion Bks.) HarperCollins Pubs.
Howatt, Sandra J. Sleepyheads. Wan, Joyce, illus. 2014. (ENG.). 32p. (J). (gr. -1-3). 17.99 *(978-1-4424-2266-7(1)*, Beach Lane Bks.) Beach Lane Bks.
Howell, Julie Ann. Mrs Owl's Nest of Rhymes. LaGrange, Tiffany, illus. 2008. 24p. pap. 12.95 *(978-0-9818683-8-7(X))* Peppertree Pr., The.
Howes, Katey. Be a Maker. Vuković, Elizabet, illus. 2019. (ENG.). 32p. (J). (gr. -1-3). 18.99 *(978-1-5124-9802-8(5)*, 1bd091d0-6ed1-4210-b8ec-5ec12d9b2b5b, Carolrhoda Bks.) Lerner Publishing Group.

Hsu, Stacey W. Old Mo. Ritter, Adam, illus. 2011. (Rookie Ready to Learn — Animals Ser.). 40p. (J). (gr. -1-k). lib. bdg. 25.00 *(978-0-531-26418-8(1))*; pap. 5.95 *(978-0-531-26699-1(0))* Scholastic Library Publishing. (Children's Pr.).

Hubbard, Ben. My Very Own Kitten. Guile, Gill, illus. 2014. (ENG.). 12p. (J). (gr. -1). *(978-1-78244-602-6(8))* Top That! Publishing PLC.

—My Very Own Puppy. Guile, Gill, illus. 2014. (ENG.). 12p. (gr. -1). *(978-1-78244-603-3(6))* Top That! Publishing PLC.

Hubbell, Patricia. Black All Around! Tate, Don, illus. 2003. (ENG.). 32p. (J). 16.95 *(978-1-58430-048-9(5))* Lee & Low Bks., Inc.

—Boats: Speeding! Sailing! Cruising!, 0 vols. Halsey, Megan & Addy, Sean, illus. 2012. (ENG.). 32p. (J). (gr. -1-1). 17.99 *(978-0-7614-5524-0(8)*, 9780761455240, Two Lions) Amazon Publishing.

—Cars: Rushing! Honking! Zooming!, 0 vols. Halsey, Megan & Addy, Sean, illus. 2012. (ENG.). 32p. (J). (gr. -1-1). pap. 7.99 *(978-0-7614-5616-2(3)*, 9780761456162, Two Lions) Amazon Publishing.

—Check It Out! Reading, Finding, Helping: Reading, Finding, Helping, 0 vols. Speir, Nancy, illus. 2012. (ENG.). 32p. (J). (gr. -1-3). 16.99 *(978-0-7614-5803-6(4)*, 9780761458036, Two Lions) Amazon Publishing.

—Firefighters! Speeding! Spraying! Saving!, 0 vols. Garofoli, Viviana, illus. (ENG.). 32p. (J). (gr. -1-1). 2012. pap. 7.99 *(978-0-7614-6245-3(7)*, 9780761462453) 2009. bds. 7.99 *(978-0-7614-5615-5(5)*, 9780761456155) Amazon Publishing. (Two Lions).

—My First Airplane Ride, 0 vols. Speir, Nancy, illus. 2013. (ENG.). 40p. (J). (gr. -1-1). pap. 9.99 *(978-1-4778-1675-2(5)*, 9781477816752, Two Lions) Amazon Publishing.

—Shaggy Dogs, Waggy Dogs, 0 vols. Wu, Donald, illus. 2012. (ENG.). 32p. (J). (gr. -1-2). 17.99 *(978-0-7614-5957-6(X)*, 9780761459576, Two Lions) Amazon Publishing.

—Trains: Steaming! Pulling! Huffing!, 0 vols. Halsey, Megan & Addy, Sean, illus. 2013. (ENG.). 34p. (J). (gr. -1-1). pap. 9.99 *(978-0-7614-5593-6(0)*, 9780761455936, Two Lions) Amazon Publishing.

—Trucks: Whizz! Zoom! Rumble!, 0 vols. Halsey, Megan, illus. 2012. (ENG.). 32p. (J). (gr. -1-1). per. 9.99 *(978-0-7614-5328-4(8)*, 9780761453284, Two Lions) Amazon Publishing.

Hubery, Julia. My Daddy. Elliot, Rebecca, illus. 2014. (J). *(978-1-4351-5507-7(6))* Barnes & Noble, Inc.

Hudgens, Melica, illus. Flim Flam & Other Such Gobbledygook. 2015. (J). 14.99 *(978-1-4621-1684-3(1))* Cedar Fort, Inc./CFI Distribution.

Hudson, Cheryl Willis. Clothes I Love to Wear. 2008. (Illus.). 24p. (J). (gr. -1-3). 3.99 *(978-1-60349-004-7(3)*, Marimba Bks.) Just Us Bks., Inc.

—Hands Can. Bourke, John-Francis, photos by. 2007. (ENG., Illus.). 24p. (J). (— 1). bds. 7.99 *(978-0-7636-3292-2(9))* Candlewick Pr.

—Hands Can. Bourke, John-Francis & Bourke, John-Francis, photos by. 2003. (ENG., Illus.). 32p. (J). (gr. -1-k). 16.99 *(978-0-7636-1667-0(2))* Candlewick Pr.

—Hands Can Big Book. Bourke, John-Francis, photos by. 2012. (ENG., Illus.). 32p. (J). (gr. k-k). pap. 27.99 *(978-0-7636-5819-9(7))* Candlewick Pr.

—Las Manos. Bourke, John-Francis, illus. 2014. (SPA.). 32p. (J). (-k). pap. 5.99 *(978-0-7636-7392-5(7))* Candlewick Pr.

Hughes, Hollie. The Girl & the Dinosaur. Massini, Sarah, illus. 2020. (ENG.). 32p. (J). 17.99 *(978-1-5476-0322-0(4)*, 900211339, Bloomsbury Children's Bks.) Bloomsbury Publishing USA.

Hughes, Shirley. Alfie Weather. Hughes, Shirley, illus. 2007. (Alfie Ser.). (Illus.). 48p. (J). (gr. -1-k). pap. 15.99 *(978-0-09-940425-5(7)*, Red Fox) Random House Children's Books GBR. Dist: Independent Pubs. Group.

Hull, Rod. Dr. Potts, My Pets Have Spots! Latimer, Miriam, illus. 2017. (ENG.). 32p. (J). (gr. -1-2). pap. 9.99 *(978-1-78285-324-4(3))* Barefoot Bks., Inc.

Hulme, Joy N. Eerie Feary Feeling: A Hairy Scary Pop-up Book. Ely, Paul & Dudley, Dick, illus. 2006. 12p. (J). (gr. k-4). reprint ed. 14.00 *(978-1-4223-5171-0(8))* DIANE Publishing Co.

Hunt, Connie. Planting Love: A Tale of Love & Growing. 2012. 48p. 18.10 *(978-1-4669-0965-6(X))*; pap. 8.10 *(978-1-4669-0967-0(6))* Trafford Publishing.

Hurd, Thacher. Cat's Pajamas. 2015. (Illus.). 16p. (J). (gr. -1-k). 9.95 *(978-1-63076-030-4(7))* Taylor Trade Publishing.

Hutchins, Hazel J. I'd Know You Anywhere. 2004. (Illus.). (J). (gr. -1-18). spiral bd. *(978-0-616-14578-4(0))*; spiral bd. *(978-0-616-14577-7(2))* Canadian National Institute for the Blind/Institut National Canadien pour les Aveugles.

Hutton, John. Blanket: Baby Unplugged. Kang, Andrea, illus. 2011. (Baby Unplugged Ser.). (ENG.). 14p. (J). (— 1). bds. 7.99 *(978-1-936669-00-4(5))* Blue Manatee Press.

—Book: Baby Unplugged. Hutton, John, ed. Kang, Andrea, illus. 2012. (Baby Unplugged Ser.). (ENG.). 14p. (J). (— 1). bds. 7.99 *(978-1-936669-06-6(4))* Blue Manatee Press.

—Box: Baby Unplugged. Kang, Andrea, illus. 2012. (Baby Unplugged Ser.). (ENG.). 14p. (J). (— 1). bds. 7.99 *(978-1-936669-08-0(0))* Blue Manatee Press.

—Pets: Baby Unplugged. Kang, Andrea, illus. 2011. (Baby Unplugged Ser.). (ENG.). 14p. (J). (— 1). bds. 7.99 *(978-1-936669-02-8(1))* Blue Manatee Press.

—Yard: Baby Unplugged. Kang, Andrea, illus. 2011. (Baby Unplugged Ser.). (ENG.). 14p. (J). (— 1). bds. 7.99 *(978-1-936669-01-1(3))* Blue Manatee Press.

I Can Tie My Own Shoes. 2016. (Illus.). 13p. (J). *(978-1-4351-6291-4(9))* Barnes & Noble, Inc.

Iadonisi, Carmin & Word, Amanda. Whiny Whiny Rhino. Iadonisi, Carmin & Word, Amanda, illus. 2014. (ENG., Illus.). 32p. (J). 16.99 *(978-0-9903623-0-2(2))* Blue Blanket Publishing.

Ide, Laurie Shimizu. Okazu at the Zoo. Kanekuni, Daniel, illus. 2006. (J). *(978-1-56647-776-5(X))* Mutual Publishing LLC.

Igl, Janeane. Winter, Spring, Summer, Fall: (A Sing-Song Book) 2008. 20p. pap. 24.95 *(978-1-60563-279-7(1))* America Star Bks.

Illustratus. Ghost: Thirteen Haunting Tales to Tell (Scary Children's Books for Kids Age 9 to 12, Ghost Stories for Middle Schoolers) 2019. (ENG., Illus.). 160p. (J). (gr. 3-7). 21.99 *(978-1-4521-7128-9(9))* Chronicle Bks. LLC.

The Imaginary Zoo. 2007. (J). 16.95 *(978-0-9789880-0-5(0))* Wild About Learning, Inc.

Imbody, Amy E. & Imbody, Amy. Snug as a Bug, 1 vol. Gordon, Mike, illus. 2008. (I Can Read! Ser.). (ENG.). 32p. (J). (gr. -1-1). pap. 4.99 *(978-0-310-71575-7(X))* Zonderkidz.

Impey, Rose. Ten Little Babies. Smee, Nicola, illus. 2011. (ENG.). 32p. (J). (gr. -1-k). *(978-1-4088-1118-4(9)*, 38990, Bloomsbury Children's Bks.) Bloomsbury Publishing Plc.

Ingalls, Ann. Why Should I Walk? I Can Fly! Evans, Rebecca, illus. 2019. 32p. (J). (gr. k-3). 16.95 *(978-1-58469-638-4(9)*, Dawn Pubns.) Sourcebooks, Inc.

Ingle, L. G. Little Willy Wiggle & Johnny Amigo. 2012. 40p. pap. *(978-1-77097-479-1(2))* FriesenPress.

Innovative Kids Staff, creator. Playful Penguins. 2012. (ENG.). 6p. (J). (gr. -1 — 1). 14.99 *(978-1-60169-266-5(8))* Innovative Kids.

Intrater, Roberta Grobel. Peek-a-Boo, You! Intrater, Roberta Grobel, photos by. 2nd rev. lt. ed. 2005. (Illus.). 14p. (J). 14.99 *(978-0-9764985-0-6(2))* 1212 Pr.

Intriago, Patricia. Dot. Intriago, Patricia, illus. 2011. (ENG., Illus.). 40p. (J). (gr. -1-1). 18.99 *(978-0-374-31835-2(2)*, 900071516, Farrar, Straus & Giroux (BYR)) Farrar, Straus & Giroux.

Ipcar, Dahlov, illus. Black & White. 2015. (ENG.). 40p. (J). (gr. -1-2). 17.95 *(978-1-909263-44-4(3))* Flying Eye Bks. GBR. Dist: Penguin Random Hse. LLC.

Ipcizade, Catherine. 'Twas the Day Before Zoo Day, 1 vol. Hodson, Ben, illus. 2008. (Basic Math Operations Ser.). (ENG.). 32p. (J). (gr. -1-2). 17.95 *(978-1-60718-585-7(7))* Arbordale Publishing.

Irly, I. R. Why Crocodile Does Not Smile. 2004. (Illus.). (J). bds. *(978-0-9753075-4-0(1))* M-Graphics Publishing.

Isom, Lori Boyd. Swoosh! Wise, Noreen, ed. 2004. (Illus.). 64p. (J). per. 6.95 *(978-1-58584-560-6(4))* Gallant Gold Media LLC.

Isop, Laurie. How Do You Hug a Porcupine? Millward, Gwen, illus. 2011. (ENG.). 32p. (J). (gr. -1-1). 18.99 *(978-1-4424-1291-0(7)*, Simon & Schuster Bks. For Young Readers) Simon & Schuster Bks. For Young Readers.

Ives, Frances. Maybe the Moon. 2019. (ENG., Illus.). 32p. (J). (gr. -1-k). pap. 9.99 *(978-1-910552-84-1(4))* O'Mara, Michael Bks., Ltd. GBR. Dist: Independent Pubs. Group.

Ivinson, Yvonne. Fox & the Box. Ivinson, Yvonne, illus. 2019. (ENG., Illus.). 40p. (J). (gr. -1-3). 17.99 *(978-0-06-284287-9(0)*, Greenwillow Bks.) HarperCollins Pubs.

Ivy, Cheryl. Little Miss D: What did you SEE? 2011. 20p. pap. 11.49 *(978-1-4567-5739-7(3))* AuthorHouse.

J, Granny. Pinky Gets a New Puppy: Pinky Frink's Adventures. 2012. (ENG.). 36p. pap. 17.99 *(978-1-105-86479-7(0))* Lulu Pr., Inc.

Jackson, Ann. Rags the Recycled Doll. O'Connor, Shannon, illus. 2004. 49p. 12.95 *(978-1-57197-405-1(9))* Pentland Pr., Inc.

Jackson, Ellen. Beastly Babies. Wenzel, Brendan, illus. 2015. (ENG.). 32p. (J). (gr. -1-3). 19.99 *(978-1-4424-0834-0(0)*, Beach Lane Bks.) Beach Lane Bks.

Jackson, Ellen B. The Ballad of Booster Bogg. Carolan, Christine, illus. 2011. (J). *(978-1-934860-07-6(7))* Shenanigan Bks.

Jackson, Kathryn. Katie the Kitten. Provensen, Martin & Provensen, Alice, illus. 2018. (Little Golden Book Ser.). 24p. (J). (-k). 5.99 *(978-1-101-93925-3(7)*, Golden Bks.) Random Hse. Children's Bks.

Jackson, Kathryn, et al. A Day at the Seashore. 2010. (Little Golden Book Ser.). (Illus.). 24p. (J). (gr. -1-2). 5.99 *(978-0-375-85425-5(8)*, Golden Bks.) Random Hse. Children's Bks.

Jackson, Richard. All Ears, All Eyes. Tillotson, Katherine, illus. 2017. (ENG.). 40p. (J). (gr. -1-3). 17.99 *(978-1-4814-1571-2(9))* Simon & Schuster Children's Publishing.

—Have a Look, Says Book. Hawkes, Kevin, illus. 2016. (ENG.). 48p. (J). (gr. -1-2). 17.99 *(978-1-4814-2105-8(0))* Simon & Schuster Children's Publishing.

—Snow Scene. Vaccaro Seeger, Laura, illus. 2017. (ENG.). 40p. (J). 17.99 *(978-1-62672-680-2(9)*, 900170475) Roaring Brook Pr.

—This Beautiful Day. Lee, Suzy, illus. 2017. (ENG.). 40p. (J). (gr. -1-3). 15.99 *(978-1-4814-4139-1(6)*, Atheneum/Caitlyn Dlouhy Books) Simon & Schuster Children's Publishing.

Jacobs, Paul DuBois & Swender, Jennifer. Fire Drill. Lee, Huy Voun, illus. 2010. (ENG.). 32p. (J). (gr. -1-2). 19.99 *(978-0-8050-8953-0(5)*, 900055716, Holt, Henry & Co. Bks. For Young Readers) Holt, Henry & Co.

Jacobsen, Annie. The Terrible Troll Cat. Hanson, Susan Jo, illus. 2012. 32p. (J). 9.98 *(978-0-9778276-4-0(X))* Pickled Herring Pr.

Jacobson, Leonard. In Search of the Light. 2011. 32p. 16.99 *(978-1-890580-05-6(8))* Conscious Living Pubns.

Jaeger, Elizabeth. The Little Shepherd. Montano, Irene, illus. 2019. 32p. (J). (gr. -1-k). 16.99 *(978-1-5064-4873-2(9)*, Beaming Books) 1517 Media.

Jahn, Benny. Ah-Choo - God Bless You. Scott, Chelsey, illus. 2009. 24p. pap. 11.95 *(978-1-60844-178-5(4))* Dog Ear Publishing, LLC.

Jakary, Lin. I Lost My Sock. Olson, Ryan, illus. 2008. 40p. (J). (gr. -1-3). 16.99 *(978-1-934867-01-3(2))* Wocto Publishing.

Jakubowski, Kristan E. Paint the Town. 2008. 24p. pap. 11.85 *(978-1-4343-6912-3(9))* AuthorHouse.

Jam, Teddy. Night Cars, 1 vol. Beddows, Eric, illus. 2006. (ENG.). 32p. (J). (gr. k — 1). bds. 9.95 *(978-0-88899-748-7(5))* Groundwood Bks. CAN. Dist: Publishers Group West (PGW).

James, Dalton. The Sneakiest Pirates. 2008. 20p. pap. 10.95 *(978-1-4327-2477-1(0))* Outskirts Pr., Inc.

James, Eric. Tiny the Utah Easter Bunny. 2018. (Tiny the Easter Bunny Ser.). (ENG.). 40p. (J). (gr. k-3). 9.99 *(978-1-4926-5971-6(1)*, Hometown World) Sourcebooks, Inc.

—Tiny the West Virginia Easter Bunny. 2018. (Tiny the Easter Bunny Ser.). (ENG.). 40p. (J). (gr. k-3). 9.99 *(978-1-4926-5977-8(0)*, Hometown World) Sourcebooks, Inc.

—Tiny the Wisconsin Easter Bunny. 2018. (Tiny the Easter Bunny Ser.). (ENG.). 40p. (J). (gr. k-3). 9.99 *(978-1-4926-5978-5(9)*, Hometown World) Sourcebooks, Inc.

James, Helen Foster. Auntie Loves You! Brown, Petra, illus. 2018. (ENG.). 32p. (J). (gr. -1-1). 15.99 *(978-1-5341-1011-3(9)*, 204589) Sleeping Bear Pr.

—Daddy's Girl. Corke, Estelle, illus. 2017. (ENG.). 32p. (J). (gr. -1-2). 15.99 *(978-0-8249-5681-3(8))* Worthy Publishing.

—Grandma Loves You! Brown, Petra, illus. 2013. (ENG.). 32p. (J). (gr. -1 — 1). 15.99 *(978-1-58536-836-5(9)*, 202884) Sleeping Bear Pr.

—Grandma's Christmas Wish. Brown, Petra, illus. (ENG.). (J). (gr. -1-1). 2019. 18p. bds. 8.99 *(978-1-5341-1064-9(X)*, 204835) 2015. 32p. 15.99 *(978-1-58536-918-8(7)*, 203955) Sleeping Bear Pr.

—Grandpa Loves You! Brown, Petra, illus. 2016. (ENG.). 32p. (J). (gr. -1-1). 15.99 *(978-1-58536-940-9(3)*, 204032) Sleeping Bear Pr.

—Mommy Loves You! Brown, Petra, illus. 2017. (ENG.). 32p. (J). (gr. -1-k). 15.99 *(978-1-58536-941-6(1)*, 204232) Sleeping Bear Pr.

—Santa's Christmas Train. Bolton, Bill, illus. 2019. (ENG.). 26p. (J). (gr. -1-1). bds. 7.99 *(978-1-5460-1434-8(9)*, Worthy Kids/Ideals) Worthy Publishing.

James, Karim. The Kids Time to Rhyme: Read & Rhyme at the same Time. 2009. 16p. pap. 14.99 *(978-1-4490-0424-8(5))* AuthorHouse.

James, LeBron. I Promise. Mata, Niña, illus. 2020. (ENG.). 40p. (J). (gr. -1-3). 19.99 *(978-0-06-297106-7(9)*, HarperCollins) HarperCollins Pubs.

Jameson, Karen. Woodland Dreams. Boutavant, Marc, illus. 2020. (ENG.). 32p. (J). (gr. -1-k). 17.99 *(978-1-4521-7063-3(0))* Chronicle Bks. LLC.

Jamesson, Christine. The Adventures of Samantha the Black Racer Snake. 2005. (ENG.). 28p. per. 18.00 *(978-1-4208-1873-4(2))* AuthorHouse.

Jane, Pamela. Little Elfie One: A Christmas Holiday Book for Kids. Manning, Jane, illus. 2015. (ENG.). 32p. (J). (gr. -1-3). 17.99 *(978-0-06-220673-2(7)*, Balzer & Bray) HarperCollins Pubs.

—Little Goblins Ten. Manning, Jane, illus. 2011. (ENG.). 32p. (J). (gr. -1-3). 16.99 *(978-0-06-176798-2(0)*, HarperCollins) HarperCollins Pubs.

Jansson, Tove. The Book about Moomin, Mymble & Little My. Hannah, Sophie, tr. 2009. (Moomin Ser.). Orig. Title: Boken om Mymlan, Mumintrollet och Lilla My. (ENG., Illus.). 20p. (J). (gr. k-5). 16.95 *(978-1-897299-95-1(8)*, 900065060) Drawn & Quarterly Pubns. CAN. Dist: Macmillan.

Jantzen, Doug. Henry Hyena, Why Won't You Laugh? Claude, Jean, illus. 2015. (ENG.). 32p. (J). (gr. -1-2). 17.99 *(978-1-4814-2822-4(5)*, Aladdin) Simon & Schuster Children's Publishing.

Janvier Gibeau, Claire. Here Comes Grandpa Now. 2009. 16p. pap. 8.49 *(978-1-4490-3829-8(8))* AuthorHouse.

Jarman, Julia. Class Three at Sea. Chapman, Lynne, illus. 2008. (ENG.). 32p. (J). (gr. k-3). 16.95 *(978-0-8225-7617-4(1)*, Carolrhoda Bks.) Lerner Publishing Group.

—Class Two at the Zoo. Chapman, Lynne, illus. 2007. (Carolrhoda Picture Bks.). (ENG.). 32p. (J). (gr. k-2). 16.95 *(978-0-8225-7132-2(3)*, Carolrhoda Bks.) Lerner Publishing Group.

Jasper, Mark. Good Night Charleston. Kelly, Cooper, illus. 2007. (Good Night Our World Ser.). (ENG.). 20p. (J). (gr. k — 1). bds. 9.95 *(978-1-60219-022-1(4))* Good Night Bks.

—Good Night Florida Keys. Rosen, Anne, illus. 2008. (Good Night Our World Ser.). (ENG.). 20p. (J). (gr. -1 — 1). bds. 9.95 *(978-1-60219-020-7(8))* Good Night Bks.

Javernick, Ellen. The Birthday Pet, 0 vols. O'Malley, Kevin, illus. 2012. (ENG.). 34p. (J). (gr. -1-2). pap. 9.99 *(978-0-7614-6238-5(4)*, 9780761462385, Two Lions) Amazon Publishing.

Jeffers, Oliver. What We'll Build: Plans for Our Together Future. 2020. (ENG., Illus.). 48p. (J). (gr. -1-3). 19.99 *(978-0-593-20675-1(4)*, Philomel Bks.) Penguin Young Readers Group.

Jenkins, Barbie. The Legend of the Christmas Kiss. 2010. (ENG.). 32p. pap. 11.99 *(978-1-4391-9623-6(0)*, Howard Bks.) Howard Bks.

Jenkins, Celeste. The Lost (and Found) Balloon. Bogade, Maria, illus. 2013. (ENG.). 32p. (J). (gr. -1-3). 18.99 *(978-1-4424-6697-5(9)*, Aladdin) Simon & Schuster Children's Publishing.

Jenkins, Emily. A Greyhound, a Groundhog. Appelhans, Chris, illus. 2017. 32p. (J). (gr. -1-2). 17.99 *(978-0-553-49805-9(3)*, Schwartz & Wade Bks.) Random Hse. Children's Bks.

Jenkins-Greaves, Shenita. Raptown U. S. A. Rappers. 2013. 24p. pap. 14.95 *(978-1-4669-7717-4(5))* Trafford Publishing.

Jenkins, Ward, illus. New York, Baby! 2012. (ENG.). 24p. (J). (gr. -1 — 1). 12.99 *(978-1-4521-0619-9(3))* Chronicle Bks. LLC.

—San Francisco, Baby! 2012. (ENG.). 24p. (J). (gr. -1 — 1). 12.99 *(978-1-4521-0620-5(7))* Chronicle Bks. LLC.

Jensen, Ivan. Mary Rode to Bethlehem on Me. 2012. (ENG.). 45p. (J). pap. 17.95 *(978-1-4327-9473-6(6))* Outskirts Pr., Inc.

Jepsen, D. R. Fred's Exciting Night. 2008. 20p. pap. 24.95 *(978-1-60813-547-9(0))* America Star Bks.

Jill & the Beanstalk. 2004. (J). (ENG & TAM.). *(978-1-84444-484-7(8))*; (ENG & SPA.). *(978-1-84444-490-8(2))*; (ENG & SOM.). *(978-1-84444-487-8(2))*; (ENG & RUS.). *(978-1-84444-482-3(1))*; (ENG & POR.). *(978-1-84444-481-6(3))*; (ENG & PAN.). *(978-1-84444-494-6(5))*; (ENG & ITA.). *(978-1-84444-480-9(5))*; (ENG & GUJ.). *(978-1-84444-479-3(1))*; (ENG & FRE.). *(978-1-84444-489-2(9))*; (ENG & PER.). *(978-1-84444-491-5(0))*; (SBC & ENG.). *(978-1-84444-483-0(X))*; (CHI & ENG.). *(978-1-84444-488-5(0))*; (BEN & ENG.). *(978-1-84444-478-6(3))*; (ARA & ENG.). *(978-1-84444-486-1(4))*; (ALB & ENG.). *(978-1-84444-492-2(9))*; (ENG & VIE.). *(978-1-84444-496-0(1))*; (ENG & URD.). *(978-1-84444-485-4(6))*; E-Book incl. cd-rom *(978-1-84444-463-2(5))* Mantra Lingua.

Jin, Cindy. Catch Me If You Can. Lomp, Stephan, illus. 2017. (ENG.). 16p. (J). (gr. -1 — 1). bds. 6.99 *(978-1-4814-9218-8(7)*, Little Simon) Little Simon.

Joel, Billy. Goodnight, My Angel: A Lullabye. Gilbert, Yvonne, illus. 2004. (J). pap. *(978-0-439-55378-0(4))* Scholastic, Inc.

Johanson, Rhonda. The Great Tempo Race. 2011. 32p. pap. 21.99 *(978-1-4568-5363-1(5))* Xlibris Corp.

Johnson, Calvin. Buzzy the Vegetarian Vulture. Ciresi-Abremski, M. Kathleen, illus. 2012. 28p. pap. 12.95 *(978-1-61493-109-6(7))* Peppertree Pr., The.

Johnson, Jay, illus. Ten Little Pumpkins. 2012. (J). *(978-0-545-46862-6(0))* Scholastic, Inc.

Johnson, Kathleen A. A Voice Came to Me. 2006. lib. bdg. 17.95 *(978-0-9785623-0-4(5))* Voice of Light Pubns.

Johnson, Lindsay Lee. Ten Moonstruck Piglets. Cneut, Carll, illus. 2011. (ENG.). 32p. (J). (gr. -1-3). 16.99 *(978-0-618-86866-7(6)*, 100571, Clarion Bks.) HarperCollins Pubs.

Johnson, Stewart Martin. Bad News Belinda. 2017. (ENG., Illus.). 35p. (J). pap. 14.95 *(978-1-78554-651-8(1)*, ec331a16-035b-4526-9403-0650f1f6da1e) Austin Macauley Pubs. Ltd. GBR. Dist: Baker & Taylor Publisher Services (BTPS).

Johnston-Brown, A. M. The Chronicles of Pleasant Grove. 2006. (J). pap. 12.95 *(978-0-9760718-5-3(1))* Retriever Pr.

Johnston, Tony. Loving Hands. Bates, Amy June, illus. 2018. (ENG.). 32p. (J). (gr. -1-1). 16.99 *(978-0-7636-7993-4(3))* Candlewick Pr.

—10 Fat Turkeys. Deas, Rich, illus. (ENG.). (J). (gr. -1-k). 2009. 28p. bds. 6.99 *(978-0-545-16469-6(9))* 2004. 32p. pap. 3.99 *(978-0-439-45948-8(6))* Scholastic, Inc. (Cartwheel Bks.).

Jolley, Mike. I'll See You in the Morning. Moriuchi, Mique, illus. 2008. (ENG.). (J). (gr. -1 — 1). bds. 6.99 *(978-0-8118-6543-2(6))* Chronicle Bks. LLC.

Jones, A. Responsibility. 2011. 32p. pap. 24.95 *(978-1-4626-2167-5(8))* America Star Bks.

Jones, Ceri Wyn. Ruck in the Muck. 2015. (ENG., Illus.). 32p. (J). pap. 8.95 *(978-1-78562-067-6(3))* Gomer Pr. GBR. Dist: Casemate Pubs. & Bk. Distributors, LLC.

Jones, Gareth. The Imaginarium. 2012. 108p. 23.49 *(978-1-78035-472-9(X)*, Fastprint Publishing) Upfront Publishing Ltd. GBR. Dist: Printondemand-worldwide.com.

Jones, Gareth P. Are You the Pirate Captain? Parsons, Garry, illus. 2016. (ENG.). 32p. (J). (gr. -1-3). 16.95 *(978-1-5124-0427-2(6)*, 2997a477-7620-4034-85ae-45644aa1f9e6); E-Book 27.99 *(978-1-5124-0446-3(2))* Lerner Publishing Group.

—The Dinosaurs Are Having a Party! Parsons, Garry, illus. 2015. (ENG.). 32p. (J). (gr. -1-3). E-Book 27.99 *(978-1-4677-6317-2(9))* Lerner Publishing Group.

Jones, Kelly. Mama. Kewley, Ken, illus. 2004. 32p. (J). *(978-0-9745930-0-5(1))* Stunt Publishing.

Jones, Melanie Davis. I Can Ski! 2004. (Rookie Reader Skill Set Ser.). (ENG., Illus.). 32p. (J). (gr. k-2). pap. 4.95 *(978-0-516-27901-5(7)*, Children's Pr.) Scholastic Library Publishing.

—I Can Ski! Boles, Terry, illus. 2003. (Rookie Readers Ser.). 32p. (J). 19.50 *(978-0-516-22878-5(1)*, Children's Pr.) Scholastic Library Publishing.

Jones, Nathan Smith. The Boy Who Ate America. Nelson, Casey, illus. 2007. 32p. (J). (gr. -1-3). 16.95 *(978-1-59038-814-3(3)*, Shadow Mountain) Shadow Mountain Publishing.

Jones, Pip. Izzy Gizmo, 1 vol. Ogilvie, Sara, illus. 2018. (ENG.). 32p. (J). (gr. -1-3). 17.99 *(978-1-68263-021-1(8))* Peachtree Publishing Co. Inc.

—Squishy Mcfluff: Big Country Fair. Okstad, Ella, illus. 2018. (Squishy Mcfluff Ser.). (ENG.). 80p. (J). pap. 8.95 *(978-0-571-32070-7(8))* Faber & Faber, Inc.

—Squishy Mcfluff: Meets Mad Nana Dot. Okstad, Ella, illus. 2018. (Squishy Mcfluff Ser.). (ENG.). 80p. (J). pap. 8.95 *(978-0-571-30254-3(8)*, Faber & Faber Children's Bks.) Faber & Faber, Inc.

—Squishy Mcfluff: Seaside Rescue! Okstad, Ella, illus. 2018. (Squishy Mcfluff Ser.). (ENG.). 80p. (J). pap. 8.95 *(978-0-571-32068-4(6))* Faber & Faber, Inc.

—Squishy Mcfluff: Tea with the Queen. Okstad, Ella, illus. 2019. (Squishy Mcfluff Ser.). (ENG.). 32p. (J). 16.95 *(978-0-571-33727-9(9))* Faber & Faber, Inc.

—Squishy Mcfluff: the Invisible Cat! Okstad, Ella, illus. 2017. (Squishy Mcfluff Ser.). (ENG.). 80p. (J). (gr. k-2). pap. 8.95 *(978-0-571-30250-5(5)*, Faber & Faber Children's Bks.) Faber & Faber, Inc.

Jones, Sarah. Ears, Nose, Eyes... Surprise! 2018. (ROYGBaby Ser.). (ENG., Illus.). 14p. (J). (— 1). bds. 7.99 *(978-1-936669-62-2(5))* Blue Manatee Press.

Jones-Sorge, Jennifer Elaine. Monsters, Monsters, Monsters! The Power in Me Is Bigger Then Any Monster I've Ever Met! 2012. 48p. pap. 24.95 *(978-1-4626-7555-5(7))* America Star Bks.

Joosse, Barbara. Evermore Dragon. Cecil, Randy, illus. 2015. (Girl & Dragon Bks.). (ENG.). 32p. (J). (gr. -1-2). 15.99 *(978-0-7636-6882-2(6))* Candlewick Pr.

Jordan, Apple. Winter Wishes (Disney Princess) Marrucchi, Elisa, illus. 2006. (Step into Reading Ser.). (ENG.). 32p. (J). (gr. k-3). per. 5.99 *(978-0-7364-2409-7(1)*, RH/Disney) Random Hse. Children's Bks.

Jordan, Dana Hall. Clang Went the Cymbals: An Onomatopoeia Alphabet Book. Burma, Willingham, illus. 2008. 32p. (J). 15.99 *(978-0-9798664-0-1(5))* Capture Bks.

Jordan, Deloris. Did I Tell You I Love You Today? Evans, Shane W., illus. 2004. (ENG.). 32p. (J). (gr. -1-3). 19.99 *(978-0-689-85271-8(1)*, Simon & Schuster/Paula Wiseman Bks.) Simon & Schuster/Paula Wiseman Bks.

Jordan, Mary Ellen. Lazy Daisy, Cranky Frankie: Bedtime on the Farm. Weldon, Andrew, illus. 2013. (ENG.). 24p. (J). (gr. -1-3). 15.99 *(978-0-8075-4400-6(0)*, 807544000) Whitman, Albert & Co.

Jorden, Edwin W. Cookie Paws/Spreadin' the Sweetness. Waywell, Valerie J., illus. 2008. 32p. (J). 12.95 *(978-0-9793483-1-0(5))* Gilded Dog Enterprises LLC.

Joy, Angelica. My Cat Merigold. Bolle, Frank, illus. 2008. 56p. pap. 19.95 *(978-1-59858-591-9(6))* Dog Ear Publishing, LLC.

S

Joy, N. The Secret Olivia Told Me. Devard, Nancy, illus. 2007. 32p. (J). (gr. -1-3). 16.95 (978-1-933491-08-0(6)) Just Us Bks., Inc.

Joyce, Melanie. What Pirates Really Do. Paterson, Alex, illus. 2016. (ENG.). 32p. (J). (gr. -1-3). 16.99 (978-1-4998-0257-3(9)) Little Bee Books Inc.

Joyce, William. Sleepy Time Olie. Joyce, William, illus. 2018. (World of William Joyce Ser.). (ENG., Illus.). 40p. (J). (gr. -1-2). 17.99 (978-1-4814-8963-8(1)) Simon & Schuster Children's Publishing.

Judd, Jennifer Cole. Circus Train, 0 vols. Matthews, Melanie, illus. 2015. (ENG.). 24p. (J). (gr. -1-2). 14.99 (978-1-4778-2634-8(3), 9781477826348, Two Lions) Amazon Publishing.

Jules, Jacqueline. Goodnight Sh'ma. Hall, Melanie, illus. 2008. (ENG.). 12p. (J). (gr. -1 — 1). bds. 6.99 (978-0-8225-8945-7(1), 9f4fe877-880a-412e-aa37-60c81bb615d2, Kar-Ben Publishing) Lerner Publishing Group.

—Happy Hanukkah Lights. Shapiro, Michelle, illus. 2010. (ENG.). 12p. (J). (gr. -1 — 1). 5.95 (978-0-7613-5120-7(5), 6b1d3e67-1a45-4507-8004-6606ea176931, Kar-Ben Publishing) Lerner Publishing Group.

Jungle Limbo. l.t. ed. 2003. (Illus.). 31p. (J). spiral bd. 7.95 (978-0-9741074-0-0(9)) Catterfly Pr.

Kaczka, Fallon. What about Oysters. 2010. 24p. 13.00 (978-1-4520-2066-2(3)) AuthorHouse.

Kalban, Rachel. I Like to Be with My Family. Fruchter, Jason, illus. 2016. (Daniel Tiger's Neighborhood Ser.). (ENG.). 26p. (J). (gr. -1-k). bds. 8.99 (978-1-4814-6100-9(1), Simon Spotlight) Simon Spotlight.

Kalluk, Celina. Sweetest Kulu, 1 vol. Neonakis, Alexandria, illus. 2018. (ENG.). 36p. (J). (gr. -1 — 1). 10.95 (978-1-77227-183-6(7)) Inhabit Media Inc. CAN. Dist: Consortium Bk. Sales & Distribution.

Kalman, Bobbie. Hip-Hop Dancers. 2010. (My World Ser.). (ENG., Illus.). 16p. (J). (gr. k-2). (978-0-7787-9431-8(8)); pap. (978-0-7787-9475-2(X)) Crabtree Publishing Co.

Kaputa, Christine C. Bad Kitty! 2007. 16p. per. 9.95 (978-1-59858-478-3(2)) Dog Ear Publishing, LLC.

Karr, Lily. My Easter Bunny! Johnson, Jay, illus. 2012. (ENG.). 12p. (J). (gr. -1 — 1). bds. 4.99 (978-0-545-37117-9(1), Cartwheel Bks.) Scholastic, Inc.

—My Pumpkin. Marts, Doreen Mulryan. illus. 2014. (ENG.). 12p. (J). (gr. -1 — 1). bds. 4.99 (978-0-545-49332-1(3), Cartwheel Bks.) Scholastic, Inc.

Kass, Daniele L., ed. The City Trail: A Skip-Counting Tale. 2010. 40p. pap. 18.49 (978-1-4520-1219-3(9)) AuthorHouse.

Katz, Alan. Don't Say That Word! Catrow, David, illus. 2007. (ENG.). 32p. (J). (gr. -1-3). 19.99 (978-0-689-86971-6(1), McElderry, Margaret K. Bks.) McElderry, Margaret K. Bks.

Katz, Karen. Shake It up, Baby! Katz, Karen, illus. 2009. (ENG., Illus.). 14p. (J). (gr. -1 — 1). bds. 7.99 (978-1-4169-6737-8(0), Little Simon) Little Simon.

—Ten Tiny Babies. Katz, Karen, illus. 2011. (Classic Board Bks.). (ENG., Illus.). 32p. (J). (gr. -1-k). bds. 8.99 (978-1-4424-1394-8(8), Little Simon) Little Simon.

—Ten Tiny Babies. Katz, Karen, illus. 2008. (ENG., Illus.). 32p. (J). (gr. -1-3). 18.99 (978-1-4169-3546-9(0), McElderry, Margaret K. Bks.) McElderry, Margaret K. Bks.

Katz, Karin Jill. There's a Fly in My Soup. 2012. 16p. pap. 15.99 (978-1-4772-6331-0(4)) AuthorHouse.

Katz, Susan B. My Mama Earth. Launay, Melissa, illus. 2012. (ENG.). 24p. (J). 16.99 (978-1-84686-418-6(6)) Barefoot Bks., Inc.

—My Mama Hung the World for Me. Newey, Gail, illus. 2009. (J). (978-1-84686-269-4(8)) Barefoot Bks., Inc.

Kaufman, Jeanne. Young Henry & the Dragon. Tessler, Daria, illus. 2011. (J). (978-1-934860-11-3(5)) Shenanigan Bks.

Kavanagh, Peter. I Love My Mama. Chapman, Jane, tr. Chapman, Jane, illus. 2003. 32p. (J). 12.95 (978-1-85430-806-1(8), Simon & Schuster Bks. For Young Readers) Simon & Schuster Bks. For Young Readers.

Kay, Karin. Floppy Cat. 2009. (J). 16.95 (978-0-9823818-0-9(8)) Floppy Cat Co.

Kearney, Meg. The Girl in the Mirror: A Novel. 2012. (ENG.). 176p. (YA). (gr. 9-17). pap. 15.00 (978-0-89255-385-3(5), 255385) Persea Bks., Inc.

—When You Never Said Goodbye: An Adoptee's Search for Her Birth Mother: a Novel in Poems & Journal Entries. 2017. (ENG.). 224p. (YA). (gr. 9-17). 17.95 (978-0-89255-479-9(7), 255479) Persea Bks., Inc.

Keckler, Ben. From Here to There. Davis, Dick, illus. 2005. (Express Yourself Ser.). 42p. (J). (gr. 3-7). lib. bdg. 16.95 (978-0-9769093-0-9(8)) Eagle Creek Pubns., LLC.

—Incredibly Lonely, That's Me. Davis, Dick, illus. 2007. (Express Yourself Ser.). 42p. (J). (gr. 3-7). 17.95 (978-0-9769093-2-3(4)) Eagle Creek Pubns., LLC.

Keefer, Mikal. All Day Long, God Loves Me. Perez, Nomar, illus. 2017. (Best of Li'l Buddies Ser.). (ENG.). 16p. (J). bds. 6.99 (978-1-4707-4859-3(2)) Group Publishing, Inc.

—From Head to Toe, God Made Me. Harrington, David, illus. 2017. (Best of Li'l Buddies Ser.). (ENG.). 16p. (J). bds. 6.99 (978-1-4707-4858-6(4)) Group Publishing, Inc.

—Here's the Reason God Made Me. Becker, Paula, illus. 2017. (Best of Li'l Buddies Ser.). (ENG.). 16p. (J). bds. 6.99 (978-1-4707-4860-9(6)) Group Publishing, Inc.

—Never Fear, God Is Near. Perez, Nomar, illus. 2018. (Best of Li'l Buddies Ser.). (ENG.). 16p. bds. 6.99 (978-1-4707-5036-7(8)) Group Publishing, Inc.

Keegan, Anne. A Cat for Claire. 2008. 28p. pap. 15.00 (978-1-4389-2737-4(1)) AuthorHouse.

Keep, Richard. Clatter Bash! A Day of the Dead Celebration, 1 vol. 2008. (Illus.). 32p. (J). (gr. -1-3). pap. 8.95 (978-1-56145-461-7(3)) Peachtree Publishing Co. Inc.

Keillor, Garrison. The Old Man Who Loved Cheese. braille ed. 2004. (Illus.). (J). (gr. k-3). spiral bd. (978-0-616-01687-9(5)) Canadian National Institute for the Blind/Institut National Canadien pour les Aveugles.

Keiser, Frances R. Annie the River Otter: The Adventures of Pelican Pete. Keiser, Hugh M., illus. l.t. ed. 2006. (ENG.). 34p. (J). 19.99 (978-0-9668845-4-3(X)) Sagaponack Bks.

Keith, Donna. I Love You All the Same, 1 vol. 2014. (ENG., Illus.). 20p. (J). bds. 9.99 (978-0-529-10204-1(8), Tommy Nelson) Nelson, Thomas Inc.

—I Love You Even When, 1 vol. 2015. (ENG., Illus.). 20p. (J). bds. 9.99 (978-0-7180-3644-7(1), Tommy Nelson) Nelson, Thomas Inc.

Keller, Elinoar & Peleg Segal, Naama. Just Like I Wanted. Gordon-Noy, Aya, illus. 2015. (ENG.). 26p. (J). 17.00 (978-0-8028-5453-7(2), Eerdmans Bks For Young Readers) Eerdmans, William B. Publishing Co.

Keller, Holly. What I See. Keller, Holly, illus. 2003. (Green Light Readers Ser.). (ENG., Illus.). 24p. (J). (gr. -1-3). pap. 5.99 (978-0-15-204854-9(5), 1194657, Clarion Bks.) HarperCollins Pubs.

Kelley, Maria Felicia. Buz Words: Discovering Words in Pairs. Kelley, Maria Felicia, illus. 2007. (Illus.). 32p. (J). (gr. -1-3). 14.95 (978-0-9650918-1-7(3)) April Arts Press & Productions.

Kelley, Marty. Almost Everybody Farts. (Everybody Farts Ser.). (J). (gr. -1). 2019. 28p. bds. 8.99 (978-1-4549-3430-1(1)) 2017. (Illus.). 32p. 12.95 (978-1-4549-1954-4(X)) Sterling Publishing Co., Inc.

—The Messiest Desk. 2009. (J). (978-1-55933-319-1(7)) Zino Pr. Children's Bks.

Kelley, Marty, illus. Spring Goes Squish: A Vibrant Volume of Vociferous Vernal Verse. 2008. (J). (gr. k-2). 14.95 (978-1-55933-315-3(4)) Zino Pr. Children's Bks.

—Winter Woes. 2003. 32p. (J). 12.95 (978-1-55933-306-1(5)) Zino Pr. Children's Bks.

Kellogg, Steven. There Was an Old Woman Who Swallowed a Fly. 2003. (ENG., Illus.). (J). 16.00 (978-0-689-81703-8(7), Simon & Schuster/Paula Wiseman Bks.) Simon & Schuster/Paula Wiseman Bks.

Kellum, Rebecca L. The Conceited Little Girl. 2007. 24p. per. 24.95 (978-1-4241-9810-8(0)) America Star Bks.

Kelly, Mij. The Bump. Allan, Nicholas, illus. 2012. (ENG.). 32p. (J). (978-1-58925-107-6(5)) Tiger Tales.

—Lion's Lullaby. Clifton-Brown, Holly, illus. 2016. (ENG.). 32p. (J). (gr. -1 — 1). 16.99 (978-1-4847-2526-9(3)) Disney Pr.

Kelly, Sharon L. C. M. Coco's Vineyard Vacation: Double Fun on Martha's Vineyard. Galbraith, Alison L., illus. 2005. 40p. (J). 16.95 (978-0-9766283-0-9(9)) Secret Garden Bookworks.

Kemble, Mai S. The Moon & the Night Sweeper. Kemble, Mai S., illus. 2008. (Illus.). (J). pap. 6.95 (978-1-60108-023-3(9)) Red Cygnet Pr.

Kemble, Mai S., illus. The Moon & the Night Sweeper. 2007. 30p. (J). (gr. -1-2). 15.95 (978-1-60108-013-4(1)) Red Cygnet Pr.

Kendall, Carolyn. Phibby & Ribby. 2013. 32p. pap. (978-1-4602-0387-3(9)) FriesenPress.

Kendi, Ibram X. Antiracist Baby Board Book. Lukashevsky, Ashley, illus. 2020. 24p. (J). (— 1). bds. 8.99 (978-0-593-11041-6(2), Kokila) Penguin Young Readers Group.

—Antiracist Baby Picture Book. Lukashevsky, Ashley, illus. 2020. (ENG.). 32p. (J). (— 1). 8.99 (978-0-593-11050-8(1), Kokila) Penguin Young Readers Group.

Kennedy, Anne Vittur. One Spring Lamb, 1 vol. 2016. (ENG., Illus.). 20p. (J). bds. 8.99 (978-0-7180-8782-1(8), Tommy Nelson) Nelson, Thomas Inc.

Kennedy, Pamela. Good Night, Sleep Tight. 2019. (VeggieTales Ser.). (ENG., Illus.). 20p. (J). (gr. -1-1). bds. 7.99 (978-0-8249-1691-6(3), Worthy Kids/Ideals) Worthy Publishing.

Kenney, Cindy. Junior Asparagus. 2004. (ENG., Illus.). 100p. (J). pap. 3.99 (978-0-310-70722-6(6)) Zonderkidz.

—Laura Carrot. 2004. (ENG., Illus.). 100p. (J). pap. 3.99 (978-0-310-70723-3(4)) Zonderkidz.

Kenny, Cindy. Larry Cucumber: I Can. 2004. (ENG., Illus.). 100p. (J). pap. 3.99 (978-0-310-70721-9(8)) Zonderkidz.

Kerbel, Deborah. Before You Were Born. Del Rizzo, Suzanne, illus. 2019. (ENG.). 32p. (J). (gr. k-3). 17.95 (978-1-77278-082-6(0)) Pajama Pr. CAN. Dist: Publishers Group West (PGW).

Kerner, Susan. Always by My Side, 1 vol. Benfold Haywood, Ian P., illus. 2013. (ENG.). 32p. (J). 16.99 (978-1-59572-336-9(6)); pap. 6.99 (978-1-59572-337-6(4)) Star Bright Bks., Inc.

Kerns, Kristen. Tommy Fakes the Flu. Barrett, Casey, illus. 2013. 24p. pap. 8.99 (978-1-938768-28-6(0)) Gypsy Pubns.

Kerr, Judith. The Great Granny Gang: Band 11/Lime (Collins Big Cat) Kerr, Judith, illus. 2019. (Collins Big Cat Ser.). (ENG., Illus.). 36p. (J). (gr. k-2). pap. 9.99 (978-0-00-832090-4(X)) HarperCollins Pubs. Ltd. GBR. Dist: Independent Pubs. Group.

Ketteman, Helen. Goodnight, Little Monster, 0 vols. Leick, Bonnie, illus. 2012. (Little Monster Ser.: 1). (ENG.). 32p. (J). (gr. k-2). 16.99 (978-0-7614-5683-4(X), 9780761456834, Two Lions) Amazon Publishing.

—If Beaver Had a Fever, 0 vols. O'Malley, Kevin, illus. 2012. (ENG.). 32p. (J). (gr. -1-3). 16.99 (978-0-7614-5951-4(0), 9780761459514, Two Lions) Amazon Publishing.

Khamis, Johnny. Costi & the Raindrop Adventure. Belanger, Damon, illus. 2007. 32p. (J). (gr. -1-3). 6.95 (978-1-60005-029-9(8)) Happy About.

Khan, Aliyah. The Adventures of Solomon Spider: Solomon Sees the City. 2011. 28p. (gr. -1 — 1). pap. 14.09 (978-1-4490-1546-6(8)) AuthorHouse.

Khan, Hena. Crescent Moons & Pointed Minarets: A Muslim Book of Shapes (Islamic Book of Shapes for Kids, Toddler Book about Religion, Concept Book for Toddlers) Amini, Mehrdokht, illus. 2018. (Muslim Book of Concepts Ser.). (ENG.). 32p. (J). (gr. -1-k). 17.99 (978-1-4521-5541-8(0)) Chronicle Bks. LLC.

—Golden Domes & Silver Lanterns: A Muslim Book of Colors. Amini, Mehrdokht, illus. 2012. (Muslim Book of Concepts Ser.). (ENG.). 32p. (J). (gr. -1-2). 17.99 (978-0-8118-7905-7(4)) Chronicle Bks. LLC.

—Under My Hijab, 1 vol. Jaleel, Aaliya, illus. 2019. (ENG.). 32p. (J). (gr. -1-3). 19.95 (978-1-62014-792-4(0), leelowbooks) Lee & Low Bks., Inc.

Kiffel-Alcheh, Jamie. Can You Hear a Coo, Coo? Lumer, Marc, illus. 2018. (ENG.). 12p. (J). (gr. -1 — 1). bds. 5.99 (978-1-5124-4443-8(X), 943a2e0b-1e25-486b-a196-9b5299a360f8, Kar-Ben Publishing) Lerner Publishing Group.

—A Hoopoe Says Oop! Animals of Israel. Kuman, Ivana, illus. 2019. (ENG.). 12p. (J). (gr. -1 — 1). bds. 5.99 (978-1-5415-0049-5(0), 0715077e-df5d-44b8-b9eb-42d0f4777f59, Kar-Ben Publishing) Lerner Publishing Group.

—Kol Hakavod: Way to Go! Mercer, Sarah-Jayne, illus. 2019. (ENG.). 24p. (J). (gr. -1-1). 12.99 (978-1-5415-2211-4(7), b84a0d64-9428-41c8-bd4e-62d67e465030); pap. 7.99 (978-1-5415-3835-1(8), 7e7eff52-94d5-4a87-97c2-47a1b22118b3) Lerner Publishing Group. (Kar-Ben Publishing).

—Listen! Israel's All Around. Mack, Steve, illus. 2019. (ENG.). 12p. (J). (gr. -1 — 1). bds. 5.99 (978-1-5415-0969-6(2), a8908658-d7bb-4dd5-81b6-c57b66afe737, Kar-Ben Publishing) Lerner Publishing Group.

Kilkka, Mary. Meet the Nydees, 1 vol. 2010. 28p. 24.95 (978-1-4512-1495-6(2)) America Star Bks.

Kilpatrick, Leanne. Two by Two: Noah's Story in Rhyme. McCullough, Marilyn, illus. 2013. 28p. pap. (978-0-906672-67-9(8)) Oleander Pr., The.

Kimaya. All the Flavours of Love. 2012. 40p. pap. 13.95 (978-1-4525-0649-4(3)) Balboa Pr.

Kimla, Lenka J. I Love My Mommy. Golds, Alexandra Kimla, illus. 2008. 22p. pap. 24.95 (978-1-60703-126-0(4)) America Star Bks.

Kimmelman, Leslie. How Do I Love You? McCue, Lisa, illus. 2005. 32p. (J). lib. bdg. 16.89 (978-0-06-001201-4(3)) HarperCollins Pubs.

—Round the Turkey: A Grateful Thanksgiving. Cote, Nancy, illus. 2012. (J). 34.28 (978-1-61913-130-9(7)) Weigl Pubs., Inc.

—Trick ARRR Treat: A Pirate Halloween. Monlongo, Jorge, illus. (ENG.). 32p. (J). (gr. -1-3). 2017. pap. 7.99 (978-0-8075-8066-0(X), 080758066X) 2015. 16.99 (978-0-8075-8061-5(9), 807580619) Whitman, Albert & Co.

Kinerk, Robert. Clorinda. Kellogg, Steven, illus. 2007. (ENG.). 40p. (J). (gr. -1-3). 8.99 (978-1-4169-3964-1(4), Simon & Schuster/Paula Wiseman Bks.) Simon & Schuster/Paula Wiseman Bks.

—Clorinda Plays Baseball! Kellogg, Steven, illus. 2012. (ENG.). 40p. (J). (gr. -1-3). 16.99 (978-0-689-86865-8(0), Simon & Schuster/Paula Wiseman Bks.) Simon & Schuster/Paula Wiseman Bks.

—Clorinda Takes Flight. Kellogg, Steven, illus. 2007. (ENG.). 40p. (J). (gr. -1-3). 19.99 (978-0-689-86864-1(2), Simon & Schuster/Paula Wiseman Bks.) Simon & Schuster/Paula Wiseman Bks.

Kingsbury, Karen. Whatever You Grow up to Be, 1 vol. Docampo, Valeria, illus. rev. ed. 2014. (ENG.). 32p. (J). 17.99 (978-0-310-71646-4(2)) Zonderkidz.

Kinsman, Josephine. Ginger's New Tail. 2011. 40p. pap. 24.95 (978-1-4626-1184-3(2)) America Star Bks.

Kirk, Bill. There's a Spider in My Sink! Brown, Suzy, illus. 2008. 16p. pap. 9.95 (978-1-935137-25-2(5)) Guardian Angel Publishing, Inc.

Kirk, David. Miss Spider's Tea Party. 2018. (ENG., Illus.). 32p. (J). (gr. -1-3). 19.95 (978-0-935112-13-9(8)) Callaway Editions, Inc.

Kirk, David & Scholastic / LeapFrog. Miss Spider's Tea Party. 2008. (J). 13.99 (978-1-59319-934-0(1)) LeapFrog Enterprises, Inc.

Kirkfield, Vivian. Pippa's Passover Plate. Weber, Jill, illus. 2019. 40p. (J). (gr. -1-3). 17.99 (978-0-8234-4162-4(8)) Holiday Hse., Inc.

Kirkham, Teresa. Tattle Tom. 2003. 27p. pap. 12.95 (978-1-4137-0141-8(8)) America Star Bks.

Kittinger, Jo S. A Lunch with Punch. 2004. (Rookie Reader Español Ser.). (ENG., Illus.). 32p. (J). (gr. k-2). pap. 4.95 (978-0-516-27785-1(5), Children's Pr.) Scholastic Library Publishing.

Kitzmiller, Brenda. Muddy Mud — an Easy to Read Beginning Reader Book. 2005. 24p. 7.85 (978-1-4116-2937-0(X)) Lulu Pr., Inc.

Klay, Sharon Joy. Denny Grows a Giant Pumpkin. 2010. 28p. pap. 12.99 (978-1-4520-2871-2(0)) AuthorHouse.

Kleback, Amanda. Hoo Hoo's Song. Kleback, Amanda & Kleback, Brian, illus. 2009. 24p. pap. 12.00 (978-1-4389-1322-3(2)) AuthorHouse.

Klein-Higger, Joni. Ten Tzedakah Pennies. Leff, Tova, illus. 2005. (ENG.). 30p. (J). 11.95 (978-1-929628-19-3(6)) Hachai Publishing.

Klein, Pamela. Swing! Tanis, Joel E., illus. 2006. (ENG.). (J). 15.95 (978-1-932514-05-6(8)) College of DuPage Pr.

Kleinhenz, Sydnie Meltzer. Pleased to Eat You. 2003. (Silly Millies Ser.: 3). (Illus.). 32p. lib. bdg. 17.90 (978-0-7613-2909-1(9), Millbrook Pr.) Lerner Publishing Group.

—Trabajar y Jugar. Reasor, Mick, illus. 2006. (Rookie Reader Español Ser.). (SPA.). 23p. (J). (gr. k-2). lib. bdg. 19.50 (978-0-516-25306-0(9)) Scholastic Library Publishing.

Kleven, Elisa. The Horribly Hungry Gingerbread Boy: A San Francisco Story. 2016. (ENG., Illus.). 40p. (J). 17.00 (978-1-59714-352-3(9)) Heyday.

—Sun Bread. 2004. (gr. k-3). 17.20 (978-0-613-83005-8(9)) Turtleback.

Klug, Eric. The Monster in My Closet. Klug, Eric, illus. 2007. (Illus.). 32p. (J). (gr. -1-3). 15.95 (978-1-60108-007-3(7)) Red Cygnet Pr.

Knaggs, Robin A. I Am a Squirmy Wormy. 2012. 16p. pap. 9.99 (978-1-60911-969-0(X), Strategic Bk. Publishing) Strategic Book Publishing & Rights Agency (SBPRA).

Kneen, Maggie. The Christmas Surprise. Kneen, Maggie, illus. 2006. (Illus.). 18p. (J). (gr. k-4). reprint ed. 16.00 (978-0-7567-9837-6(X)) DIANE Publishing Co.

Kneff, Steff F. Emlyn & the Gremlin: Emlyn & the Gremlin Series. Spooner, Luke, illus. l.t. ed. 2014. (ENG.). 52p. (gr. k-3). 26.95 (978-1-62253-399-2(2)); pap. 10.95 (978-1-62253-398-5(4)) Evolved Publishing.

Knights, Nancy. Gracie's Hill. Norie, Rooney, illus. 2007. 28p. per. 7.95 (978-1-58275-192-4(7)) Black Forest Pr.

Knisley, Lucy. You Are New: (New Baby Books for Kids, Expectant Mother Book, Baby Story Book) 2019. (ENG., Illus.). 52p. (J). (gr. -1-1). 17.99 (978-1-4521-6156-3(9)) Chronicle Bks. LLC.

Knowles, Kent. Lucius & the Storm. Knowles, Kent, illus. 2007. (Illus.). 32p. (J). (gr. -1-3). 15.95 (978-1-60108-005-9(0)) Red Cygnet Pr.

Knowlton, Laurie. I Know a Librarian Who Chewed on a Word, 1 vol. Leonhard, Herb, illus. 2012. (ENG.). 32p. (J). (gr. k-3). 16.99 (978-1-58980-892-8(4), Pelican Publishing) Arcadia Publishing.

Knudsen, Michelle. Winter Is for Snowflakes. Denise & Fernando, illus. 2003. (Please Read to Me Ser.). (ENG.). 24p. (J). (gr. -1-1). 16.19 (978-0-375-82215-5(1)) Random House Publishing Group.

Koertge, Ron. Shakespeare Makes the Playoffs. 2012. (ENG., Illus.). 176p. (YA). (gr. 7). pap. 7.99 (978-0-7636-5852-6(9)) Candlewick Pr.

Kohuth, Jane. Ducks Go Vroom. Garofoli, Viviana, illus. 2011. (Step into Reading Ser.). 32p. (J). (gr. -1-1). pap. 4.99 (978-0-375-86560-2(8), Random Hse. Bks. for Young Readers) Random Hse. Children's Bks.

—Who's Got the Etrog? Elissambura, illus. 2018. (ENG.). 32p. (J). (gr. -1-2). 12.99 (978-1-5415-0966-5(8), 27e60bba-90f4-4323-b232-0f10b9b4722d, Kar-Ben Publishing) Lerner Publishing Group.

Kondrchek, Jamie. My Favorite Time of Day (Mi Hora Preferida del Dia) Vega, Eida de la, tr. from ENG. Rasemas, Joe, illus. 2009. (Day in the Life Ser.). (SPA & ENG.). 32p. (J). (gr. -1-1). lib. bdg. 25.70 (978-1-58415-837-0(9)) Mitchell Lane Pubs.

Kondrchek, Jamie & Rasemas, Joe. On My Way to School (De Camino a la Escuela) Vega, Eida de la, tr. Rasemas, Joe, illus. 2009. (Day in the Life Ser.). (SPA & ENG., Illus.). 32p. (J). (gr. -1-1). 25.70 (978-1-58415-840-0(9)) Mitchell Lane Pubs.

—What Day Is It? (Que Dia Es Hoy?) Vega, Eida de la, tr. Rasemas, Joe, illus. 2009. (Day in the Life Ser.). (SPA & ENG., Illus.). 32p. (J). (gr. -1-1). 25.70 (978-1-58415-838-7(7)) Mitchell Lane Pubs.

—What Should I Wear Today? (Que Ropa Me Pondre Hoy?) Vega, Eida de la, tr. Rasemas, Joe, illus. 2009. (Day in the Life Ser.). (ENG & SPA., Illus.). 32p. (J). (gr. -1-1). 25.70 (978-1-58415-839-4(5)) Mitchell Lane Pubs.

Koontz, Dean. Robot Santa: The Further Adventures of Santa's Twin. Parks, Phil, illus. 2004. (Santa's Twin Ser.: Bk. 2). 72p. (J). 20.89 (978-0-06-050944-6(9)) HarperCollins Pubs.

—Santa's Twin. Parks, Phil, illus. 2004. (Santa's Twin Ser.: Bk. 1). (ENG.). 64p. pap. 12.95 (978-0-06-057223-5(X), William Morrow Paperbacks) HarperCollins Pubs.

Kovalkova-McKenna, Svetlana & McKenna, Alexandra. The Fairy Book. 2009. 52p. pap. 7.58 (978-0-557-06160-0(1)) Lulu Pr., Inc.

Kovalkova-McKenna, Svetlana & McKenna, Konstantin. Oberon. 2009. 44p. pap. 7.26 (978-0-557-06114-3(8)) Lulu Pr., Inc.

Kowalski, Eli. Kushka, the Dog Named Cat. 2010. (ENG.). (J). 14.95 (978-0-9819861-4-2(5)) Toy Vey Toys.

Kralovansky, Susan. The Book That Jake Borrowed, 1 vol. Kralovansky, Susan, illus. 2018. (ENG., Illus.). 32p. (J). (gr. k-3). 19.99 (978-1-4556-2325-9(3), Pelican Publishing) Arcadia Publishing.

—Twelve Cowboys Ropin', 1 vol. Kralovansky, Susan, illus. 2015. (ENG., Illus.). 32p. (J). (gr. k-3). 16.99 (978-1-4556-2081-4(5), Pelican Publishing) Arcadia Publishing.

Kramer, Paul. Do Not Dread Wetting the Bed. 2012. (ENG & ACO.). 32p. (J). (gr. -1-3). 15.95 (978-0-9819745-0-7(3)) Aloha Wellness Pubs.

Krans, Kim. Whose Moon Is That? 2017. (Illus.). 48p. (J). (gr. -1-2). 17.99 (978-1-101-93227-8(9), Random Hse. Bks. for Young Readers) Random Hse. Children's Bks.

Krasner, Justin. Crinkle, Crinkle, Little Star. Yarlett, Emma, illus. 2017. (ENG.). 16p. (J). (gr. -1 — 1). 12.95 (978-1-5235-0120-5(0), 100120) Workman Publishing Co., Inc.

Krasnesky, Thad. Pterodactyl Show & Tell. Leonello, Tanya, illus. 2018. (ENG.). 32p. (J). (gr. k-2). 17.95 (978-1-936261-34-5(0)) Flashlight Pr.

Krebs, Chrissie. This Is a Circle. 2018. (ENG.). 32p. (J). (gr. -1-1). 16.99 (978-1-5107-3128-8(8), Sky Pony Pr.) Skyhorse Publishing Co., Inc.

Krebs, Laurie. Un Recorrido Por la Selva. Wilson, Anne, illus. 2011. (SPA.). 40p. (J). (gr. k-5). pap. 9.99 (978-1-84686-551-0(4)) Barefoot Bks., Inc.

—Riding on a Caravan. Cann, Helen, illus. 2017. (ENG.). 32p. (J). (gr. k-5). pap. 9.99 (978-1-78285-344-2(8)) Barefoot Bks., Inc.

—We're Roaming in the Rainforest. Wilson, Anne, illus. 40p. (J). 2011. (ENG.). (gr. k-5). pap. 9.99 (978-1-84686-545-9(X)) 2010. (gr. -1-5). 16.99 (978-1-84686-331-8(7)) Barefoot Bks., Inc.

—We're Sailing down the Nile: A Journey Through Egypt. Wilson, Anne, illus. 2007. (ENG.). 44p. (J). (gr. -1-1). 22.44 (978-1-84686-040-9(7)) Barefoot Bks., Ltd. GBR. Dist: Children's Plus, Inc.

—We're Sailing to Galapagos. Restelli, Grazia, illus. 2007. (ENG.). 32p. (J). (gr. k-5). pap. 9.99 (978-1-84686-102-4(0)) Barefoot Bks., Inc.

Krebs, Laurie & Cis, Valeria. The Beeman. Cis, Valeria, illus. 2008. (Illus.). 40p. (J). (gr. -1-3). 16.99 (978-1-84686-146-8(2)) Barefoot Bks., Inc.

Kreib. We're off to Find the Witch's House. Alley, R. W., illus. 2007. 32p. (J). (gr. -1-2). 7.99 (978-0-14-240854-4(9), Puffin Books) Penguin Young Readers Group.

Kremsner, Cynthia, illus. Swashbarklers of the Sea, 1 vol. 2019. (ENG.). 32p. (J). (gr. -1-3). 16.99 (978-1-4556-2414-0(4), Pelican Publishing) Arcadia Publishing.

Krensky, Stephen. Fraidy Cats. Lewin, Betsy, illus. 2015. (Scholastic Reader, Level 2 Ser.). (ENG.). 32p. (J). (gr. -1-3). pap. 3.99 (978-0-545-79966-9(X), Cartwheel Bks.) Scholastic, Inc.

—I Know a Lot! Gillingham, Sara, illus. 2013. (Empowerment Ser.). (ENG.). 12p. (J). (gr. -1 — 1). bds. 7.99 (978-1-4197-0938-8(0), 1064210, Abrams Appleseed) Abrams, Inc.

—Snack Attack: Ready-To-Read Level 1. Curtis, Stacy, illus. 2008. (Ready-To-Read Ser.). (ENG.). 32p. (J). (gr. -1-1). pap. 4.99 (978-1-4169-0238-6(4), Simon Spotlight) Simon Spotlight.

Kret, Itzah C. The Man with the Sneezes. 2003. (ENG.). 38p. per. 22.65 (978-1-4134-2895-7(9)) Xlibris Corp.

Krisher, Trudy. Bark Park! Boynton-Hughes, Brooke, illus. 2018. (ENG.). 40p. (J). (-3). 17.99 *(978-1-4814-3075-3(0),* Beach Lane Bks.) Beach Lane Bks.

Kristina Learns about Fishing. 2007. (J). *(978-0-9792728-0-6(7))* Tracepaper Bks. Inc.

Kroll, Virginia. Mosquito, 1 vol. LePlatt, Betsy, illus. 2011. (ENG.). 32p. (J). (gr. k-3). 16.99 *(978-1-58980-883-6(5),* Pelican Publishing) Arcadia Publishing.

Kroupa, Robert J. Just Like You. 2011. (J). *(978-0-9825503-4-2(0))* IGI Pr.

Kruckvich, Francis. The Blue Chequered Harlequin. 2004. (Illus.). (YA). pap. *(978-0-9746226-2-0(1))* Scribolin.

Kruckvich, Francis, text. A Hero & a Great Man. 2003. (Illus.). 33p. (YA). pap. 4.95 *(978-0-9746226-0-6(5))* Scribolin.

Krulik, Nancy. Dribble, Dribble, Drool! Blecha, Aaron, illus. 2016. (George Brown, Class Clown Ser.: 18). (ENG.). 128p. (J). (gr. 2-4). 14.75 *(978-0-606-39308-9(0))* Turtleback.

Kruil, Kathleen & Brewer, Paul. Fartiste. Kulikov, Boris, illus. 2008. (ENG.). 40p. (J). (gr. -1-3). 19.99 *(978-1-4169-2828-7(6),* Simon & Schuster Bks. For Young Readers) Simon & Schuster Bks. For Young Readers.

Kruse, Donald W. Cluck, Cluck, Cluck ... Splash! 2017. (ENG., Illus.). (J). (gr. k-5). pap. 14.95 *(978-0-9981972-9-6(7))* Zaccheus Entertainment Co.

—Cluck, Cluck, Cluck Splash! Crank, Donny, illus. 2012. 48p. pap. 12.95 *(978-1-59663-856-3(7),* Castle Keep Pr.) Rock, James A. & Co. Pubs.

—Fleas, Please. Crank, Donny, illus. 2012. 48p. pap. 12.95 *(978-1-59663-858-7(3),* Castle Keep Pr.) Rock, James A. & Co. Pubs.

—Fleas, Please! 2017. (ENG., Illus.). (J). (gr. k-5). pap. 14.95 *(978-0-9985191-0-4(3))* Zaccheus Entertainment Co.

—There's a Goof on My Roof. Crank, Donny, illus. 2012. 48p. pap. 12.95 *(978-1-59663-855-6(9),* Castle Keep Pr.) Rock, James A. & Co. Pubs.

—There's a Goof on My Roof! Crank, Donny, illus. 2017. (ENG.). (J). (gr. k-5). pap. 14.95 *(978-0-9981972-3-4(8))* Zaccheus Entertainment Co.

Krystosek, Richard. Chicken Scratch. 2013. 36p. pap. 24.95 *(978-1-63000-536-8(3))* America Star Bks.

Kuczenski, Tyler & Schumacher, Dan. Twelve Little Piggies. 2011. 28p. pap. 12.03 *(978-1-4567-5313-9(4))* AuthorHouse.

Kukla, Lauren. Being Me from a to Z. Basil, Aviel, illus. 2019. 32p. (J). (gr. -1-3). 17.99 *(978-1-5064-5259-3(0),* Beaming Books) 1517 Media.

Kulka, Joe. Vacation's Over! Return of the Dinosaurs. Kulka, Joe, illus. 2010. (Carolrhoda Picture Bks.). (ENG., Illus.). 32p. (J). (gr. k-3). lib. bdg. 17.95 *(978-0-7613-5212-9(0))* Lerner Publishing Group.

Kupchella, Rick. Girls Can! Make it Happen. Brown, Marilyn, illus. 2004. (ENG.). 40p. (J). 16.95 *(978-0-9726504-3-4(1))* TRISTAN Publishing, Inc.

—Tell Me What We Did Today. Hanson, Warren, illus. (ENG.). 32p. (J). 15.95 *(978-0-9726504-0-3(7))* TRISTAN Publishing, Inc.

Kurd, Tariq. Gordon the Goblin in Oh My! Is That a Pork Pie? Robertson, Laura, illus. 2012. 36p. pap. *(978-1-907762-10-9(8))* Malt Publishing.

Kurilovitch, Mike. Silly Sisters. 2012. 32p. pap. 18.48 *(978-1-4772-6011-1(0))* AuthorHouse.

Kurtz, Kevin. A Day in the Salt Marsh, 1 vol. Powell, Consie, illus. 2007. (Day in the Habitat Ser.). (ENG.). 32p. (J). (gr. -1-3). 15.95 *(978-0-9768823-5-0(3))* Arbordale Publishing.

Kuskin, Karla. So, What's It Like to Be a Cat? Lewin, Betsy, illus. (ENG.). (J). (gr. -1-3). 2008. 40p. 8.99 *(978-0-689-85930-4(9))* 2005. 32p. 19.99 *(978-0-689-84733-2(5))* Simon & Schuster Children's Publishing. (Atheneum Bks. for Young Readers).

Kutner, Merrily. The Zombie Nite Cafe. Long, Ethan, illus. 2007. (ENG.). 32p. (J). (gr. -1-3). 16.95 *(978-0-8234-1963-0(0))* Holiday Hse., Inc.

Kyle, Tracey. Food Fight Fiesta: A Tale about la Tomatina. Gomez, Ana, illus. 2018. 32p. (J). (gr. k-3). 16.99 *(978-1-5107-3215-5(2),* Sky Pony Pr.) Skyhorse Publishing Co., Inc.

—Gazpacho for Nacho, 0 vols. Farías, Carolina, illus. 2014. (ENG.). 32p. (J). (gr. 1-4). 16.99 *(978-1-4778-1727-8(1),* 9781477817278, Two Lions) Amazon Publishing.

—A Paintbrush for Paco. Heinsz, Joshua, illus. 2018. (ENG.). 40p. (J). (gr. -1-3). 17.99 *(978-1-4998-0544-4(6))* Little Bee Books Inc.

—Pepe & the Parade: A Celebration of Hispanic Heritage. Ortega, Mirelle, illus. 2019. (ENG.). 32p. (J). (gr. -1-3). 16.99 *(978-1-4998-0666-3(3))* Little Bee Books Inc.

Kyrja. Rupert's Tales: The Wheel of the Year - Samhain, Yule, Imbolc, & Ostara, 1 vol. 2012. (ENG., Illus.). 64p. 19.99 *(978-0-7643-3987-5(7),* 4366, Red Feather) Schiffer Publishing, Ltd.

—Rupert's Tales: The Wheel of the Year Activity Book, 1 vol. 2012. (ENG., Illus.). 40p. pap. 9.99 *(978-0-7643-4020-8(4),* 4367, Red Feather) Schiffer Publishing, Ltd.

—Rupert's Tales: a Book of Bedtime Stories: A Book of Bedtime Stories, 1 vol. Bennington Osborn, Tonia, illus. 2014. (ENG.). 64p. (J). (gr. -1-3). 19.99 *(978-0-7643-4694-1(6),* 5110, Red Feather) Schiffer Publishing, Ltd.

—Rupert's Tales: Learning Magick: Learning Magick. Osborn, Tonia Benington, illus. 2016. (Rupert's Tales Ser.: 6). (ENG.). 56p. (J). (gr. -1-3). 16.99 *(978-0-7643-4973-7(2),* 6754, Red Feather) Schiffer Publishing, Ltd.

—Rupert's Tales: the Wheel of the Year Beltane, Litha, Lammas, & Mabon: The Wheel of the Year Beltane, Litha, Lammas, & Mabon, 1 vol. 2011. (ENG., Illus.). 64p. 19.99 *(978-0-7643-3689-8(4),* 4054, Red Feather) Schiffer Publishing, Ltd.

Kysiak, Penelope Ann. You Can't Steal One's Wishes, 1 vol. 2009. 35p. pap. 24.95 *(978-1-60749-149-1(4))* America Star Bks.

Kyung, Hyewon. Bigger Than You. 2018. (ENG., Illus.). 32p. (J). (gr. -1-3). 17.99 *(978-0-06-268312-0(8),* Greenwillow Bks.) HarperCollins Pubs.

L & M Trustam. Turn Left for Christmas. 2011. (Illus.). 28p. pap. 12.19 *(978-1-4567-7084-6(5))* AuthorHouse.

La Coccinella. Look & See: Mommy, Where Are You? 2014. (Look & See! Ser.). (ENG., Illus.). 24p. (J). (gr. -1 — 1). bds. 8.95 *(978-1-4549-0615-5(4))* Sterling Publishing Co., Inc.

Lach, Will. Norman Rockwell's a Day in the Life of a Boy. Rockwell, Norman, illus. 2017. (ENG.). 60p. (J). (gr. -1-3). 16.95 *(978-0-7892-1289-4(7),* 791289, Abbeville Kids) Abbeville Pr., Inc.

—Norman Rockwell's a Day in the Life of a Girl. Rockwell, Norman, illus. 2017. (ENG.). 60p. (J). (gr. -1-3). 16.95 *(978-0-7892-1290-0(0),* 791290, Abbeville Kids) Abbeville Pr., Inc.

Lachenmeyer, Nathaniel. Octopus Escapes! Dormer, Frank W., illus. 2018. 32p. (J). (-k). lib. bdg. 16.99 *(978-1-58089-795-2(9))* Charlesbridge Publishing, Inc.

Laconi, Kristin. Karma the Kangaroo Takes the Court. 2010. 24p. pap. 12.99 *(978-1-4490-3227-2(3))* AuthorHouse.

Ladbrooke, Sheree. Big Alien School. 2011. (Illus.). 20p. pap. 12.52 *(978-1-4567-8779-0(9))* AuthorHouse.

Laden, Nina. Grow Up! 2003. (ENG., Illus.). 26p. (J). (gr. -1-7). bds. 6.99 *(978-0-8118-3761-3(0))* Chronicle Bks. LLC.

—If I Had a Little Dream. Castrillon, Melissa, illus. 2017. (ENG.). 32p. (J). (gr. -1-3). 18.99 *(978-1-4814-3924-4(3),* Simon & Schuster/Paula Wiseman Bks.) Simon & Schuster/Paula Wiseman Bks.

—Yellow Kayak. Castrillon, Melissa, illus. 2018. (ENG.). 32p. (J). (gr. -1-3). 18.99 *(978-1-5344-0194-5(6),* Simon & Schuster/Paula Wiseman Bks.) Simon & Schuster/Paula Wiseman Bks.

Lagonegro, Melissa. Friends for a Princess. 2004. (Disney Princess Step into Reading Ser.). (gr. -1-2). lib. bdg. 13.55 *(978-0-613-73713-5(X))* Turtleback.

Lai, Thanhhà. Inside Out & Back Again. 2014. (ENG.). 288p. (J). (gr. 3-7). 12.24 *(978-1-63245-350-1(9))* Lectorum Pubns., Inc.

—Inside Out & Back Again. 2009. 9.68 *(978-0-7848-3887-7(9),* Everbind) Marco Bk. Co.

—Inside Out & Back Again. 2013. 18.00 *(978-1-61383-970-6(7))* Perfection Learning Corp.

—Inside Out & Back Again. 2013. 262p. (J). lib. bdg. 18.40 *(978-0-606-27126-4(0))* Turtleback.

—Inside Out & Back Again: A Newbery Honor Award Winner. (ENG.). (J). (gr. 3-7). 2013. 288p. pap. 9.99 *(978-0-06-196279-0(1))* 2011. 272p. 16.99 *(978-0-06-196278-3(3))* HarperCollins Pubs. (HarperCollins).

—Inside Out & Back Again: a Harper Classic. 2017. (Harper Classic Ser.). (ENG.). 288p. (J). (gr. 3-7). 16.99 *(978-0-06-257402-2(7),* HarperCollins) HarperCollins Pubs.

Lakeshore Learning Materials Staff. Is Your Mama a Llama? Big Book Theme Packet. 2008. (J). pap. 44.50 *(978-1-60666-043-0(8))* Lakeshore Learning Materials.

Lakin, Patricia. Park Here (Time to Read, Level 1) Tarrant, Daniel, illus. 2020. (Time to Read Ser.). (ENG.). 32p. (J). (gr. k-2). 12.99 *(978-0-8075-6366-3(8),* 807563668) Whitman, Albert & Co.

Lamar, Gail Renfroe. Moon of the Wishing Night. Mask, Cynthia, illus. 2004. 32p. (J). 17.95 *(978-1-57966-047-5(9),* River City Kids) River City Publishing.

Lamba, Marie & Lamba, Baldev. Green Green: A Community Gardening Story. Sanchez, Sonia, illus. 2017. (ENG.). 32p. (J). 19.99 *(978-0-374-32797-2(1),* 900147768, Farrar, Straus & Giroux (BYR)) Farrar, Straus & Giroux.

Lambert, Patricia. The Blue Ribbon Chicken. 2005. 36p. (J). pap. 14.93 *(978-1-4116-6163-9(X))* Lulu Pr., Inc.

Lamont, Priscilla. Nursery Rhyme Crimes: Little Bo Peep. 2012. (Illus.). 24p. (J). pap. *(978-1-84780-354-2(7),* White Lion Publishing) Quarto Publishing Group UK.

Lampson, Rosalie. Give Mom a Minute. 2009. 32p. pap. 13.99 *(978-1-4490-1407-0(0))* AuthorHouse.

Landgraf, James, Jr. Monsters Monsters Go Away. Warrick, Jessica, illus. 2008. 40p. (J). 8.99 *(978-0-9819283-0-2(7))* Makdan Publishing.

Lang, Aubrey. Baby Sea Turtle, 1 vol. Lynch, Wayne, illus. 2007. (Nature Babies Ser.). (ENG.). 32p. (J). (gr. k-3). 16.95 *(978-1-55041-728-9(2),* 54a6db0d-f08c-4c73-8aca-630fa3a69ba8) Fitzhenry & Whiteside, Ltd. CAN. Dist: Firefly Bks., Ltd.

Lang, Gregory E. & Hill, Susanna Leonard. Why a Son Needs a Dad. Yerrill, Gail, illus. 2021. (Always in My Heart Ser.). (ENG.). 40p. (J). (gr. k-3). 10.99 *(978-1-7282-3587-5(1))* Sourcebooks, Inc.

—Why a Son Needs a Mom. Yerrill, Gail, illus. 2021. (Always in My Heart Ser.). (ENG.). 40p. (J). (gr. k-3). 10.99 *(978-1-7282-3584-4(7))* Sourcebooks, Inc.

Langcaon, Jeff, illus. My Grandpa's Battleship Missouri Tour. 2007. (J). 14.95 *(978-1-56647-831-1(6))* Mutual Publishing LLC.

Langham, Tony. Creepy Crawly Calypso. Harter, Debbie, illus. 2004. (ENG.). 32p. (J). 16.99 *(978-1-84148-699-4(X))* Barefoot Bks., Inc.

Langham, Tony & Harter, Debbie. Creepy Crawly Calypso. 2005. (ENG.). 32p. (J). pap. 9.99 *(978-1-902283-46-3(5))* Barefoot Bks., Inc.

Lapytski, Serge & Lapytski, Kristina. The Heart of a Lion! E-Hare. 2011. 84p. pap. 12.84 *(978-1-4567-4281-2(7))* AuthorHouse.

Larkin, Susan. All the Ways I Love You. East, Jacqueline, illus. 2014. (J). *(978-1-4351-5821-4(0))* Barnes & Noble, Inc.

—All the Ways I Love You. Trotter, Stuart, illus. 2012. 16p. (J). *(978-1-4351-3857-5(0))* Barnes & Noble, Inc.

Laskin, Pamela L. Ronit & Jamil. 2017. (ENG.). 192p. (YA). (gr. 8). 17.99 *(978-0-06-245854-4(X),* Tegen, Katherine Bks) HarperCollins Pubs.

Lasseter, John. Disney/Pixar a Bug's Life Read-along. 2007. (ENG., Illus.). (J). (gr. -1-3). *(978-0-7634-2180-9(4))* Walt Disney Records.

Lavender, Todd. Farmer Fred & His Hen So Red. Lavender, Todd, illus. 2012. (Illus.). 48p. pap. 9.99 *(978-0-9850410-0-7(5))* Akmaeon Publishing, LLC.

Lavin, Christine & Franco-Feeney, Betsy. Hole in the Bottom of the Sea. McHugh, Patricia & Feeney, Kathryn, eds. Franco-Feeney, Betsy, illus. 2012. (ENG., Illus.). 32p. (J). 18.95 incl. audio compact disk *(978-0-9726487-8-3(X))* Puddle Jump Pr., Ltd.

Law, Felicia. Colors. Knight, Paula, illus. 2015. (Patchwork Ser.). (ENG.). 24p. (J). (gr. k-3). lib. bdg. 22.60 *(978-1-59953-709-2(5))* Norwood Hse. Pr.

—Numbers. Knight, Paula, illus. 2015. (Patchwork Ser.). (ENG.). 24p. (J). (gr. k-3). lib. bdg. 22.60 *(978-1-59953-710-8(9))* Norwood Hse. Pr.

—Shapes. Knight, Paula, illus. 2015. (Patchwork Ser.). (ENG.). 24p. (J). (gr. k-3). lib. bdg. 22.60 *(978-1-59953-714-6(1))* Norwood Hse. Pr.

—Size. Knight, Paula, illus. 2015. (Patchwork Ser.). (ENG.). 24p. (J). (gr. k-3). pap. 11.94 *(978-1-60357-803-5(X));* lib. bdg. 22.60 *(978-1-59953-713-9(3))* Norwood Hse. Pr.

Law, Jessica. A Hole in the Bottom of the Sea. McDonald, Jill, illus. 2013. (ENG.). 24p. (J). (gr. k-3). pap. 6.99 *(978-1-84686-948-8(X))* Barefoot Bks., Inc.

Lawler, Janet. Fright School. Galletti, Chiara, illus. 2018. (ENG.). 32p. (J). (gr. -1-3). 16.99 *(978-0-8075-2553-1(7),* 807525537) Whitman, Albert & Co.

—If Kisses Were Colors Board Book. Jay, Alison, illus. 2010. (ENG.). 22p. (J). (gr. -1 — 1). bds. 7.99 *(978-0-8037-3530-9(8),* Dial Bks) Penguin Young Readers Group.

—Snowzilla, 0 vols. Haley, Amanda, illus. 2012. (ENG.). 32p. (J). (gr. -1-3). 16.99 *(978-0-7614-6188-3(4),* 9780761461883, Two Lions) Amazon Publishing.

Lawless, Mary Ann. The Proud Christmas Tree. McCool, Arlene, illus. 2006. (J). 12.95 *(978-0-9772795-0-0(2))* Tuesday's Child.

Lawrence, John. This Little Chick. Lawrence, John, illus. 2013. (ENG., Illus.). 32p. (J). (gr. -1-k). 6.99 *(978-0-7636-6350-6(6))* Candlewick Pr.

Lawson, JonArno. Leap! Bisaillon, Josée, illus. 2017. (ENG.). 32p. (J). (gr. -1-2). 16.99 *(978-1-77138-678-4(9))* Kids Can Pr., Ltd. CAN. Dist: Hachette Bk. Group.

Lawson, Robert, illus. Just for Fun: A Collection of Stories & Verses. 2013. (Dover Children's Classics Ser.). (ENG.). 64p. (gr. 2-5). pap. 6.99 *(978-0-486-49720-4(8),* 497208) Dover Pubns., Inc.

Layton, Roxanne A. Keep Goin' Owen! 2012. 24p. pap. 24.95 *(978-1-4626-6599-0(3))* America Star Bks.

Lebost, Diana. Mr. Kite & the Perilous Flight: Izzy & Daisy. Ersoz, Sahin, illus. 2013. 88p. pap. 18.95 *(978-0-9912023-5-5(X))* Pep & Olie Publishing.

LeBox, Annette. Peace Is an Offering. Graegin, Stephanie, illus. 2015. 40p. (J). (gr. -1-k). 17.99 *(978-0-8037-4091-4(3),* Dial Bks) Penguin Young Readers Group.

LeBreton, Heather. Rhyming with the Little Ones, 1 vol. LeBreton, Zachary, illus. 2009. 31p. pap. 24.95 *(978-1-60749-114-9(1))* America Star Bks.

Lebrun, Jessica. Rainbow's Mist. 2008. 17p. pap. 24.95 *(978-1-60563-242-1(2))* America Star Bks.

LeCron, Helen Cowles. The Animal Etiquette Book of Rhymes. Day, Maurice, illus. 2014. (ENG.). 64p. (J). (gr. 1-5). pap. 4.99 *(978-0-486-78234-8(4))* Dover Pubns., Inc.

Lee, Britney Winn. The Boy with Big, Big Feelings. Souva, Jacob, illus. 2019. (Big, Big Ser.). 14p. (J). (gr. -1-3). 17.99 *(978-1-5064-5450-4(X),* Beaming Books) 1517 Media.

Lee, Calee M. I Love You! Tharp, Tricia, illus. 2013. (ENG.). 32p. (J). (gr. -1-k). pap. 9.99 *(978-1-62395-471-0(1))* Xist Publishing.

Lee, Deborah Baptiste & Atcheson-Melton, Patty. In the Shade of the Spade: This Tale in a Poetry Format Takes Us on a Journey. the Illustrations Are Bright & Whimsical. You Can Almost Hear Music. Baptiste, Annette Green, illus. 2013. 48p. pap. 14.95 *(978-0-9858839-1-0(X))* Lee, Deborah I.

Lee, George Douglas. Oppy Stops the Hopping Popper. Lee, Brenda Donaloio, ed. Lee, George Douglas, illus. 2012. (Illus.). 30p. pap. 10.95 *(978-0-9848486-1-4(4))* Electric Theatre Radio Hour.

—Twyla the Truffle Pig. Lee, Brenda Donaloio, ed. Lee, George Douglas, illus. 2012. (Illus.). 34p. pap. 10.95 *(978-0-9848486-0-7(6))* Electric Theatre Radio Hour.

Lee, Jonathan. So I Could Fly Free. 2008. (ENG., Illus.). 32p. (J). *(978-1-85345-434-9(6))* Crusade for World Revival.

Lees, Caroline. Silly Sea Stories. 2010. (Illus.). 48p. pap. 19.49 *(978-1-4389-0701-7(X))* AuthorHouse.

LeFalle, Deborah. Bitty Brown Babe. Morris, Keisha, illus. 2019. 24p. (J). (gr. -1 — 1). 7.99 *(978-1-5064-4853-4(4),* Beaming Books) 1517 Media.

Lefranc, Karin & Parker, Tyler. I Want to Eat Your Books. 2015. (ENG., Illus.). 40p. (J). (gr. -1-k). 16.99 *(978-1-63450-172-9(1),* Sky Pony Pr.) Skyhorse Publishing Co., Inc.

Leiter, Richard. The Flying Hand of Marco B. Kober, Shahar, illus. 2015. (ENG.). 24p. (J). (gr. k-2). 15.99 *(978-1-58536-888-4(1),* 203813) Sleeping Bear Pr.

Leman, Nora. The Alpha Building Crew. Hartmann, April, illus. 2005. (J). *(978-1-58987-110-6(3))* Kindermusik International.

Lemke, Donald. Book-O-Beards: a Wearable Book. Lentz, Bob, illus. 2015. (Wearable Bks.). (ENG.). 12p. (J). (gr. -1-1). bds. 7.99 *(978-1-62370-183-3(X),* 127003, Capstone Young Readers) Capstone.

—Book-O-Hats: a Wearable Book. Lentz, Bob, illus. 2015. (Wearable Bks.). (ENG.). 12p. (J). (gr. -1-1). bds. 7.99 *(978-1-62370-184-0(8),* 127002, Capstone Young Readers) Capstone.

—Book-O-Teeth: a Wearable Book. Lentz, Bob, illus. 2015. (Wearable Bks.). (ENG.). 12p. (J). (gr. -1-1). bds. 7.99 *(978-1-62370-186-4(4),* 127005, Capstone Young Readers) Capstone.

Leon, Loni. Can you Imagine..., 1. Leon, Loni & Huston, Kyle, illus. 2006. 49p. (J). 21.95 *(978-0-9728556-0-0(2))* Sullivan, Kelley Enterprises.

Leonard, Marcia. El Hombre de Hojalata. Handelman, Dorothy, photos by. 2005. (ENG & SPA., Illus.). 32p. (J). (gr. -1-1). pap. 4.99 *(978-0-8225-3310-8(3))* Lerner Publishing Group.

—Me Gusta el Desorden. Translations.com Staff, tr. from ENG. Handelman, Dorothy, photos by. 2007. (Lecturas para niños de Verdad - Nivel 1 (Real Kids Readers - Level 1) Ser.).Tr. of I Like Mess. (SPA., Illus.). 32p. (gr. k-2). per. 5.95 *(978-0-8225-7800-0(X),* Ediciones Lerner) Lerner Publishing Group.

—Me Gusta el Desorden; I Like Mess. 2008. pap. 34.95 *(978-0-8225-9495-6(1))* Lerner Publishing Group.

—Mi Dia de Campamento. Translations.com Staff, tr. from ENG. Handelman, Dorothy, photos by. 2007. (Lecturas para niños de Verdad - Nivel 1 (Real Kids Readers - Level 1) Ser.).Tr. of My Camp-Out. (SPA., Illus.). 32p. (gr. k-2). per. 5.95 *(978-0-8225-7798-0(4),* Ediciones Lerner) Lerner Publishing Group.

—Mi Dia de Campamento; My Camp Out. 2008. pap. 34.95 *(978-0-8225-9496-3(X))* Lerner Publishing Group.

—Saltar, Brincar, Correr; Hop, Skip, Run. 2008. pap. 34.95 *(978-0-8225-9497-0(8))* Lerner Publishing Group.

—Trae la Pelota, Tito. Handelman, Dorothy, photos by. 2005.Tr. of Get the Ball, Slim. (Illus.). 32p. (J). (ENG & SPA.). (gr. -1-1). pap. 4.99 *(978-0-8225-3293-4(X));* (SPA., (gr. 1-1). per. 5.95 *(978-0-8225-3292-7(1),* Ediciones Lerner) Lerner Publishing Group.

Leonard, Marcia & Handelman, Dorothy. The Pet Vet. Handelman, Dorothy, illus. Leonard, Marcia, photos by. 2005. (ENG & SPA., Illus.). 32p. (J). (gr. -1-1). pap. 4.99 *(978-0-8225-3299-6(9))* Lerner Publishing Group.

Leone, Dee. Dough Knights & Dragons. Ermos, George, illus. 2017. 40p. (J). (gr. k). 16.95 *(978-1-4549-2141-7(2))* Sterling Publishing Co., Inc.

Leone, Elaine H. Grandy Goose Rhymes. 2013. (ENG.). 116p. pap. 10.99 *(978-1-4675-6477-9(X))* Independent Pub.

Lessac, Frane. Island Counting 1 2 3. Lessac, Frane, illus. 2007. (Illus.). 24p. (J). (— 1). bds. 8.99 *(978-0-7636-3518-3(5))* Candlewick Pr.

Lester, Alison. Magic Beach. 2006. (ENG., Illus.). 32p. (J). (gr. -1-k). pap. 11.99 *(978-1-74114-488-8(4))* Allen & Unwin AUS. Dist: Independent Pubs. Group.

—Noni the Pony. Lester, Alison, illus. 2012. (Noni the Pony Ser.). (ENG., Illus.). 32p. (J). (gr. -1-k). 18.99 *(978-1-4424-5959-5(X),* Beach Lane Bks.) Beach Lane Bks.

—Noni the Pony. Lester, Alison, illus. 2019. (Noni the Pony Ser.). (ENG., Illus.). 28p. (J). (gr. -1-k). bds. 7.99 *(978-1-5344-5355-5(5),* Little Simon) Little Simon.

—Noni the Pony Goes to the Beach. Lester, Alison, illus. 2015. (Noni the Pony Ser.). (ENG., Illus.). 32p. (J). (gr. -1-3). 17.99 *(978-1-4814-4625-9(8),* Beach Lane Bks.) Beach Lane Bks.

—Yikes! 25th Anniversary Edition: In Seven Wild Adventures, Who Would You Be? 75th ed. 2019. (ENG., Illus.). 32p. (J). (gr. -1-2). 19.99 *(978-1-76052-861-4(7))* Allen & Unwin AUS. Dist: Independent Pubs. Group.

Lettera, Janine Hamel. My First Day of School. 2012. 16p. pap. 7.31 *(978-1-4251-1614-9(0))* Trafford Publishing.

Lettice, Jenna. The 12 Days of Thanksgiving. Madden, Colleen, illus. 2018. (12 Days Of Ser.). 24p. (J). (gr. -1-2). pap. 4.99 *(978-1-5247-6658-0(5),* Random Hse. Bks. for Young Readers) Random Hse. Children's Bks.

Leuck, Laura. Goodnight, Baby Monster. Date not set. 32p. (J). (gr. -1-1). pap. 4.99 *(978-0-06-443723-3(X))* HarperCollins Pubs.

—My Creature Teacher. Nash, Scott, illus. 2004. (ENG.). 32p. (J). (gr. -1-1). 15.99 *(978-0-06-029694-0(1))* HarperCollins Pubs.

Levine, Abby. This Is the Dreidel. Billin-Frye, Paige, illus. 2012. (J). 34.28 *(978-1-61913-134-7(X))* Weigl Pubs., Inc.

Levine, Martha Peaslee. Stop That Nose!, 1 vol. White, Lee, illus. 2006. (ENG.). 32p. (J). (gr. -1-3). 14.95 *(978-0-7614-5280-5(X))* Marshall Cavendish Corp.

Levine, Rhoda. Three Ladies Beside the Sea. Gorey, Edward, illus. 2010. (ENG.). 40p. (J). (gr. k-4). 17.95 *(978-1-59017-354-1(6),* NYR Children's Collection) New York Review of Bks., Inc., The.

Levy, Debbie. Yiddish Saves the Day. Borlasca, Hector, illus. 2019. (ENG.). 32p. (J). 17.95 *(978-1-68115-544-9(3),* 563e41f9-3396-4de3-bb96-a74b11225faf, Apples & Honey Pr.) Behrman Hse., Inc.

Lewin, Betsy. Where Is Tippy Toes? Lewin, Betsy, illus. 2010. (ENG., Illus.). 32p. (J). (gr. -1-2). 16.99 *(978-1-4169-3808-8(7),* Atheneum Bks. for Young Readers) Simon & Schuster Children's Publishing.

Lewis, Anne Margaret. Puddle Jumpers. Cote, Nancy, illus. 2016. (ENG.). 32p. (J). (gr. -1-k). 16.99 *(978-1-63450-185-9(3),* Sky Pony Pr.) Skyhorse Publishing Co., Inc.

Lewis, Brandt. Fingers for Lunch. Doerrfeld, Cori, illus. 2016. (ENG.). 12p. (J). (gr. -1 — 1). bds. 7.99 *(978-0-316-37799-7(6))* Little, Brown Bks. for Young Readers.

Lewis, J. Patrick. What's Looking at You Kid? Graef, Renée, illus. 2012. (ENG.). 32p. (J). (gr. 1-4). 14.95 *(978-1-58536-793-1(1),* 202336) Sleeping Bear Pr.

Lewis, J. Patrick & Lewis, Leigh. It's Not the Baby. Frost, Maddie, illus. 2017. 14p. (J). (gr. -1 — 1). bds. 9.99 *(978-1-68152-194-7(6),* 14725) Amicus.

—It's Not the Puppy. Frost, Maddie, illus. 2019. 14p. (J). (gr. -1-k). bds. 9.99 *(978-1-68152-409-2(0),* 17589) Amicus.

Lewis, Jan. First Fairy Tales: Puss in Boots. 2015. (ENG., Illus.). 24p. (J). (gr. -1-12). bds. 6.99 *(978-1-86147-626-5(4),* Armadillo) Anness Publishing GBR. Dist: National Bk. Network.

—First Fairy Tales Aladdin & the Lamp. 2013. (Illus.). 24p. (J). (gr. -1-12). bds. 6.99 *(978-1-86147-337-0(0),* Armadillo) Anness Publishing GBR. Dist: National Bk. Network.

—First Fairy Tales Goldilocks & the Three Bears. 2013. (Illus.). 24p. (J). (gr. -1-12). bds. 6.99 *(978-1-86147-332-5(X),* Armadillo) Anness Publishing GBR. Dist: National Bk. Network.

—First Fairy Tales Little Red Riding Hood. 2013. (Illus.). 24p. (J). (gr. -1-12). bds. 6.99 *(978-1-86147-336-3(2),* Armadillo) Anness Publishing GBR. Dist: National Bk. Network.

—First Fairy Tales Snow White. 2013. (Illus.). 24p. (J). (gr. -1-12). bds. 6.99 *(978-1-86147-335-6(4),* Armadillo) Anness Publishing GBR. Dist: National Bk. Network.

—Princess Fairy Tales: Cinderella, the Princess & the Pea, Sleeping Beauty, the Little Mermaid. Lewis, Jan, illus. 2015. (Illus.). 48p. (J). (gr. -1-k). bds. 9.99 *(978-1-86147-423-0(7),* Armadillo) Anness Publishing GBR. Dist: National Bk. Network.

Lewis, Jan, illus. The Emperor's New Clothes. 2015. 24p. (J). (gr. -1-2). bds. 6.99 *(978-1-86147-413-1(X),* Armadillo) Anness Publishing GBR. Dist: National Bk. Network.

—First Fairy Tales: Cinderella. 2013. (ENG.). 24p. (J). (gr. -1-k). bds. 6.99 *(978-1-86147-334-9(6),* Armadillo) Anness Publishing GBR. Dist: National Bk. Network.

—First Fairy Tales: Sleeping Beauty. 2013. (ENG.). 24p. (J). (gr. -1-k). bds. 6.99 *(978-1-86147-338-7(9),* Armadillo) Anness Publishing GBR. Dist: National Bk. Network.

—First Fairy Tales: The Ugly Duckling. 2013. (ENG.). 24p. (J). (gr. -1-k). bds. 6.99 *(978-1-86147-333-2(8),* Armadillo) Anness Publishing GBR. Dist: National Bk. Network.

—First Fairy Tales: Three Little Pigs. 2013. (ENG.). 24p. (J). (gr. -1-k). bds. 6.99 *(978-1-86147-331-8(1),* Armadillo) Anness Publishing GBR. Dist: National Bk. Network.

S

—Magical Fairy Tales: Aladdin & the Lamp; the Ugly Duckling; the Emperor's New Clothes; Puss in Boots. 2016. 48p. (J). (gr. -1-12). bds. 9.99 *(978-1-86147-700-2(7)*, Armadillo) Anness Publishing GBR. Dist: National Bk. Network.
—The Princess & the Pea. 2015. 24p. (J). (gr. -1-12). bds. 6.99 *(978-1-86147-467-4(9)*, Armadillo) Anness Publishing GBR. Dist: National Bk. Network.
Lewis, Kevin. Dinosaur, Dinosaur. Kirk, Daniel, illus. 2006. (J). *(978-0-439-78228-9(7)*, Orchard Bks.) Scholastic, Inc.
—My Truck Is Stuck! Kirk, Daniel, illus. 2006. (ENG.). 30p. (J). (gr. -1-k). bds. 7.99 *(978-0-7868-3739-7(X))* Little, Brown Bks. for Young Readers.
Lewis, Michael. Cap'n Mcnasty's Pirate Guide, 1 vol. Jaskiel, Stan, illus. 2020. (ENG.). 32p. (J). (gr. 3-4). 16.99 *(978-1-4556-2525-3(6)*, Pelican Publishing) Arcadia Publishing.
—The Great Pirate Christmas Battle, 1 vol. Jaskiel, Stan, illus. 2014. (ENG.). 32p. (J). (gr. k-3). 16.99 *(978-1-4556-1934-4(5)*, Pelican Publishing) Arcadia Publishing.
—The Great Thanksgiving Food Fight, 1 vol. Jaskiel, Stan, illus. 2017. (ENG.). 32p. (J). (gr. -1-3). 16.99 *(978-1-4556-2285-6(0)*, Pelican Publishing) Arcadia Publishing.
Lewis, Rose. Sweet Dreams. Corace, Jen, illus. 2012. (ENG.). 32p. (J). (gr. -1-2). 16.95 *(978-1-4197-0189-4(4)*, 692701, Abrams Bks. for Young Readers) Abrams, Inc.
Lewison, Wendy Cheyette. Silly Milly. 2010. (Scholastic Reader Level 1 Ser.). lib. bdg. 13.55 *(978-0-606-10556-9(5))* Turtleback.
—Silly Milly (Scholastic Reader, Level 1) Westcott, Nadine Bernard, illus. 2010. (Scholastic Reader, Level 1 Ser.). (ENG.). 32p. (J). (gr. -1-3). pap. 3.99 *(978-0-545-06859-8(2))* Scholastic, Inc.
—Two Is for Twins. Nakata, Hiroe, illus. 2011. 28p. (J). (gr. -1 — 1). bds. 8.99 *(978-0-670-01310-4(2)*, Viking Books for Young Readers) Penguin Young Readers Group.
LeZotte, Ann Clare. T4. 2008. (ENG.). 112p. (J). (gr. 5-7). 14.99 *(978-0-547-04684-6(7)*, 1034970, Clarion Bks.) HarperCollins Pubs.
Liberto, Lorenzo. Matt the Rat & His Magic Cloud / Raton Mateo y Su Nube Magica: A Day at School / un Dia de Escuela. Gomez, Rocio, ed. Torres, Irving, illus. 2003. (Matt the Rat Ser. / La Serie de Ratón Mateo). (ENG & SPA.). 32p. (J). lib. bdg. 20.00 *(978-0-9743668-0-7(3))* Harvest Sun Pr., LLC.
Liberts, Jennifer. Go, Go, Trucks! Yamada, Mike, illus. 2017. (Step into Reading Ser.). 32p. (J). (gr. -1-1). 5.99 *(978-0-399-54951-9(X)*, Random Hse. Bks. for Young Readers) Random Hse. Children's Bks.
Lichtenheld, Tom. What Mess? 2012. (J). lib. bdg. 17.20 *(978-0-606-26686-4(0))* Turtleback.
Lies, Brian. Bats at the Ballgame. (Bat Book Ser.). (ENG., Illus.). 32p. (J). (gr. -1-3). 2018. pap. 7.99 *(978-1-328-88613-2(1)*, 1698494) 2010. 17.99 *(978-0-547-24970-4(5)*, 1101293) HarperCollins Pubs. (Clarion Bks.).
—Bats at the Ballgame. 2018. lib. bdg. 18.40 *(978-0-606-41004-5(X))* Turtleback.
—Bats at the Beach. 2006. (Bat Book Ser.). (ENG., Illus.). 32p. (J). (gr. -1-3). 18.99 *(978-0-618-55744-8(X)*, 529911, Clarion Bks.) HarperCollins Pubs.
—Bats at the Library. (Bat Book Ser.). (ENG., Illus.). 32p. (J). (gr. -1-3). 2014. pap. 9.99 *(978-0-544-33920-0(7)*, 1584491) 2008. 18.99 *(978-0-618-99923-1(X)*, 1027891) HarperCollins Pubs. (Clarion Bks.).
Lindahl, Ben. The World Outside My Door. 2012. 24p. pap. 15.99 *(978-1-4691-7652-9(1))* Xlibris Corp.
Lindbergh, Reeve. Nobody Owns the Sky. Paparone, Pamela, illus. 2004. 32p. (J). *(978-1-85269-347-3(9))*; *(978-1-85269-345-9(2))*; *(978-1-85269-344-2(4))*; *(978-1-85269-343-5(6))*; *(978-1-85269-342-8(8))* Mantra Lingua.
Linden, Joanne. Ben & Zip: Two Short Friends. Goldsmith, Tom, illus. 2014. (ENG.). 32p. (J). (gr. -1-k). 16.95 *(978-1-936261-28-4(6))* Flashlight Pr.
Lindsay, Elizabeth. Socks. Sharratt, Nick, illus. 2018. 32p. (J). (— 1). pap. 12.99 *(978-0-552-57221-7(7))* Transworld Publishers Ltd. GBR. Dist: Independent Pubs. Group.
Linn, Susie. Old MacDonald Had a Farm. Crisp, Dan, illus. 2019. (Counting to Ten Bks.). (ENG.). 22p. (J). 9.99 *(978-1-78700-978-3(5))* Top That! Publishing PLC GBR. Dist: Independent Pubs. Group.
—Ten Little Mermaids. Ellis, Lauren, illus. 2018. (Counting to Ten Bks.). (ENG.). 20p. (J). (gr. -1-1). bds. 10.99 *(978-1-78700-375-0(2))* Top That! Publishing PLC GBR. Dist: Independent Pubs. Group.
—Ten Little Unicorns. Hunt, Brad, illus. 2018. (Counting to Ten Bks.). (ENG.). 20p. (J). (gr. -1-1). bds. 10.99 *(978-1-78700-376-7(0))* Top That! Publishing PLC GBR. Dist: Independent Pubs. Group.
Listening with Zachary. (J). pap. 13.75 *(978-0-8136-4655-8(3))* Modern Curriculum Pr.
Lithgow, John. Carnival of the Animals. Kulikov, Boris, illus. (ENG.). 40p. (J). (gr. -1-3). 2007. 9.99 *(978-0-689-87343-0(3))* 2004. 19.99 *(978-0-689-86721-7(2))* Simon & Schuster Bks. For Young Readers. (Simon & Schuster Bks. For Young Readers).
—I'm a Manatee: (Book & CD) Hoyt, Ard, illus. 2007. (ENG.). 32p. (J). (gr. -1-3). pap. 9.99 *(978-0-689-85452-1(8)*, Little Simon) Little Simon.
—I'm a Manatee: I'm a Manatee. 2003. (ENG., Illus.). 32p. (J). (gr. -1-3). 19.99 *(978-0-689-85427-9(7)*, Simon & Schuster Bks. For Young Readers) Simon & Schuster Bks. For Young Readers.
—Mahalia Mouse Goes to College: Book & CD. Oleynikov, Igor, illus. 2007. (ENG.). 40p. (J). (gr. -1-3). 19.99 *(978-1-4169-2715-0(8)*, Simon & Schuster Bks. For Young Readers) Simon & Schuster Bks. For Young Readers.
Little Bee Books. Kisses & Cuddles. 2015. (ENG., Illus.). 16p. (J). (gr. -1 — 1). bds. 5.99 *(978-1-4998-0151-4(3))* Little Bee Books Inc.
—Our Christmas Stockings: A Touch-And-Feel Book. 2015. (ENG., Illus.). 12p. (J). (gr. -1 — 1). 6.99 *(978-1-4998-0144-6(0))* Little Bee Books Inc.
—Our Christmas Tree: A Touch-And-Feel Book. 2015. (ENG., Illus.). 12p. (J). (gr. -1 — 1). 6.99 *(978-1-4998-0145-3(9))* Little Bee Books Inc.
Little, Jean. I Know an Old Laddie. 2004. (Illus.). (J). (gr. k-3). spiral bd. *(978-0-616-01703-6(0))* Canadian National Institute for the Blind/Institut National Canadien pour les Aveugles.
Litton, Jonathan. Planet Pop-Up: Monkey on the Moon. Anderson, Nicola, illus. 2015. (Planet Pop-Up Ser.). (ENG.). 12p. (J). (gr. -1). 12.95 *(978-1-62686-372-9(5)*, Silver Dolphin Bks.) Readerlink Distribution Services, LLC.
—Planet Pop-Up: Sheep Rules the Roost! Anderson, Nicola, illus. 2015. (Planet Pop-Up Ser.). (ENG.). 12p. (J). (gr. -1). 12.95 *(978-1-62686-354-5(7)*, Silver Dolphin Bks.) Readerlink Distribution Services, LLC.
—Planet Pop-Up: Tiger Takes Off. Anderson, Nicola, illus. 2015. (Planet Pop-Up Ser.). (ENG.). 12p. (J). (gr. -1). 12.95 *(978-1-62686-373-6(3)*, Silver Dolphin Bks.) Readerlink Distribution Services, LLC.
—Roar. Galloway, Fhiona, illus. 2014. (My Little World Ser.). (ENG.). 16p. (J). (-k). bds. 7.99 *(978-1-58925-593-7(3))* Tiger Tales.
—Snap: A Peek-Through Book of Shapes. Galloway, Fhiona, illus. 2014. (My Little World Ser.). (ENG.). 16p. (J). (gr. -1-k). bds. 7.99 *(978-1-58925-566-1(6))* Tiger Tales.
—Surprise: A Book of Christmas Shapes. Galloway, Fhiona, illus. 2014. (ENG.). 16p. (J). (gr. -1-k). bds. 7.99 *(978-1-58925-567-8(4))* Tiger Tales.
Litwin, Eric. Ice Cream & Dinosaurs (Groovy Joe #1) Lichtenheld, Tom, illus. 2016. (Groovy Joe Ser.: 1). (ENG.). 40p. (J). (gr. -1-k). 17.99 *(978-0-545-88378-8(4)*, Orchard Bks.) Scholastic, Inc.
—If You're Groovy & You Know It, Hug a Friend (Groovy Joe #3) Lichtenheld, Tom, illus. 2018. (Groovy Joe Ser.: 3). (ENG.). 40p. (J). (gr. -1-k). 9.99 *(978-0-545-88380-1(6)*, Orchard Bks.) Scholastic, Inc.
—The Nuts: Bedtime at the Nut House. Magoon, Scott, illus. 2014. (ENG.). 32p. (J). (gr. -1-3). 18.99 *(978-0-316-32244-7(X))* Little, Brown Bks. for Young Readers.
—The Nuts: Keep Rolling! Magoon, Scott, illus. 2017. (ENG.). 32p. (J). (gr. -1-3). 18.99 *(978-0-316-32251-5(2))* Little, Brown Bks. for Young Readers.
—The Nuts: Sing & Dance in Your Polka-Dot Pants. Magoon, Scott, illus. 2015. (ENG.). 32p. (J). (gr. -1-3). 18.99 *(978-0-316-32250-8(4))* Little, Brown Bks. for Young Readers.
Litwin, Eric, ed. Rocking in My School Shoes. 2011. *(978-0-545-50106-4(7))* Scholastic, Inc.
Litwin, Eric & Dean, Kimberly. Pete the Cat: Rocking in My School Shoes: A Back to School Book for Kids. Dean, James, illus. 2011. (Pete the Cat Ser.). (ENG.). 40p. (J). (gr. -1-3). 19.99 *(978-0-06-191024-1(4))*; lib. bdg. 17.89 *(978-0-06-191025-8(2))* HarperCollins Pubs. (HarperCollins).
—Pete the Cat Saves Christmas. Dean, James, illus. 2012. (Pete the Cat Ser.). (ENG.). 40p. (J). (gr. -1-3). lib. bdg. 18.89 *(978-0-06-211063-3(2)*, HarperCollins) HarperCollins Pubs.
—Pete the Cat Saves Christmas: A Christmas Holiday Book for Kids. Dean, James, illus. 2019. (Pete the Cat Ser.). (ENG.). 40p. (J). (gr. -1-3). 10.99 *(978-0-06-294516-7(5)*, HarperCollins) HarperCollins Pubs.
—Pete the Cat Saves Christmas: Includes Sticker Sheet! a Christmas Holiday Book for Kids. Dean, James, illus. 2014. (Pete the Cat Ser.). (ENG.). 40p. (J). (gr. -1-3). 18.99 *(978-0-06-211062-6(4)*, HarperCollins) HarperCollins Pubs.
Livanios, Eleni. The Best Grandma in the World! Lütje, Susanne, illus. 2015. (ENG.). 16p. (J). (gr. -1-1). bds. 7.95 *(978-0-7358-4225-0(6))* North-South Bks., Inc.
—The Best Grandpa in the World! Lütje, Susanne, illus. 2015. (ENG.). 16p. (J). (gr. -1-1). bds. 7.95 *(978-0-7358-4237-3(X))* North-South Bks., Inc.
Livermore, Edward. Phebe the Blackberry Girl. 2004. reprint ed. pap. 15.95 *(978-1-4191-4126-3(0))*; pap. 1.99 *(978-1-4192-4126-0(5))* Kessinger Publishing, LLC.
Lloyd, Ashley. Red, 1 vol. Matkovich, Gregory, illus. 2009. 19p. pap. 24.95 *(978-1-61546-913-0(3))* PublishAmerica, Inc.
Lloyd-Jones, Sally. Old MacNoah Had an Ark. Newton, Jill, illus. 2008. (HarperBlessings Ser.). 32p. (J). (gr. -1-2). 17.89 *(978-0-06-055718-8(4))* HarperCollins Pubs.
—Skip to the Loo, My Darling! a Potty Book. Jeram, Anita, illus. 2016. (ENG.). 32p. (J). (-k). 11.99 *(978-0-7636-7234-8(3))* Candlewick Pr.
—Time to Say Goodnight. Chapman, Jane, illus. 2006. (ENG.). 32p. (J). (gr. -1-2). 15.99 *(978-0-06-054328-0(0))* HarperCollins Pubs.
—Tiny Bear's Bible (Girls), 1 vol. Oleynikov, Igor, illus. 2015. (ENG.). 22p. (J). bds. 16.99 *(978-0-310-74787-1(2))* Zonderkidz.
Lobel, Arnold. On Market Street: 25th Anniversary Edition. 25th anniv. ed. 2006. (ENG., Illus.). 40p. (J). (gr. -1-3). pap. 7.99 *(978-0-688-08745-6(0)*, Greenwillow Bks.) HarperCollins Pubs.
Lobel, Arnold & Lobel, Adrianne. The Frogs & Toads All Sang. Lobel, Arnold & Lobel, Adrianne, illus. 2009. (ENG., Illus.). 32p. (J). (gr. -1-2). 16.99 *(978-0-06-180022-1(8)*, HarperCollins) HarperCollins Pubs.
Lodge, Alison & Lodge, Ali. Clever Chameleon. Lodge, Alison, illus. 2005. (ENG., Illus.). 24p. (J). 15.99 *(978-1-84148-347-4(8))* Barefoot Bks., Inc.
Lomax M.Ed., L. E. A Saint Called Nicholas: The Christmas Legends Series, Vol. I. 2012. 52p. pap. 23.99 *(978-1-4582-0584-1(3)*, Abbott Pr.) Author Solutions, LLC.
Lombardi, Elizabeth L. Jonathan's Journey, 1 vol. 2012. 32p. (J). *(978-1-62148-014-3(3))* SteinerBooks, Inc.
London, Jonathan. I'm a Truck Driver. Parkins, David, illus. 2018. (ENG.). 24p. (J). bds. 7.99 *(978-1-250-17506-9(2)*, 900189297, Holt, Henry & Co. Bks. For Young Readers) Holt, Henry & Co.
Long, Ethan. Clara & Clem Take a Ride. 2012. (Penguin Young Readers: Level 1 Ser.). lib. bdg. 13.55 *(978-0-606-26639-0(9))* Turtleback.
—Clara & Clem under the Sea. Long, Ethan, illus. 2014. (Penguin Young Readers, Level 1 Ser.). (Illus.). 32p. (J). (gr. k-1). pap. 5.99 *(978-0-448-47812-8(9)*, Penguin Young Readers) Penguin Young Readers Group.
—Hi! 2015. (Animal Sounds Ser.). (ENG., Illus.). 20p. (J). (gr. -1 — 1). bds. 7.95 *(978-1-4197-1365-1(5)*, 1092710) Abrams, Inc.
—One Drowsy Dragon. 2010. (Illus.). (J). *(978-0-545-23412-2(3)*, Orchard Bks.) Scholastic, Inc.
Long, Ethan & Rinker, Sherri Duskey. Excavator's 123: Goodnight, Goodnight, Construction Site. 2019. (Goodnight, Goodnight, Construc Ser.). (ENG., Illus.). 20p. (J). (gr. -1 — 1). bds. 6.99 *(978-1-4521-5316-2(7))* Chronicle Bks. LLC.
Long, Loren. There's a Hole in the Log on the Bottom of the Lake. Long, Loren, illus. 2018. (Illus.). 40p. (J). (gr. -1-3). 17.99 *(978-0-399-16399-9(9)*, Philomel Bks.) Penguin Young Readers Group.
Lopez, Cece. Mini Munchkin Mania Mini Series Presents: Mini Munchkin in the Mirror. 2013. (ENG.). 25p. (J). pap. 13.95 *(978-1-4327-9896-3(0))* Outskirts Pr., Inc.
Lord, Jill Roman. God Made You Just Right. Wummer, Amy, illus. 2016. (ENG.). 22p. (J). bds. 7.99 *(978-0-8249-1976-4(9)*, Worthy Kids/Ideals) Worthy Publishing.
—Noisy Silent Night. 2018. (J). *(978-0-8198-5188-8(4))* Pauline Bks. & Media.
—That Grand Easter Day! Trunfio, Alessia, illus. 2018. (ENG.). 32p. (J). (gr. -1-2). 16.99 *(978-0-8249-5680-6(X))* Worthy Publishing.
Lord, John Vernon & Burroway, Janet. The Giant Jam Sandwich Board Book Board Book. Lord, John Vernon, illus. 2009. (ENG., Illus.). 28p. (J). (gr. -1-3). bds. 7.99 *(978-0-547-15077-2(6)*, 1051726, Clarion Bks.) HarperCollins Pubs.
—The Giant Jam Sandwich Book & Cd, 1 vol. Lord, John Vernon, illus. 2007. (ENG., Illus.). 32p. (J). (gr. -1-3). audio compact disk 10.99 *(978-0-618-83952-0(6)*, 419419, Clarion Bks.) HarperCollins Pubs.
Loreas, M. Neal's Frog. 2005. (ENG.). 36p. pap. 15.99 *(978-1-4134-9719-9(5))* Xlibris Corp.
The Lost Treasure of Skull Island. 2012. (Illus.). (J). *(978-1-4351-4328-9(0))* Barnes & Noble, Inc.
Lotz, Dana R. Kids' Tales. 2008. 85p. pap. 19.95 *(978-1-60672-179-7(8))* America Star Bks.
Lougheed, Cordelia. Tales of the Magpie. 2008. 36p. pap. 22.95 *(978-1-4327-2032-2(5))* Outskirts Pr., Inc.
Louise, Verna & McKinney, Doris. Tales & Rhymes for Children: Cute Little Stories for Kids. 2012. 64p. pap. 20.95 *(978-1-4497-3339-1(5)*, WestBow Pr.) Author Solutions, LLC.
Love, Maryann Cusimano. You Are My Miracle. Ichikawa, Satomi, illus. 2012. 30p. (J). (gr. -1 — 1). bds. 7.99 *(978-0-399-25791-9(8)*, Philomel Bks.) Penguin Young Readers Group.
Love, Pamela. Two Feet up, Two Feet Down. Chapman, Lynne, illus. 2005. (Rookie Reader Español Ser.). (ENG.). 32p. (J). (gr. k-2). pap. 4.95 *(978-0-516-24646-8(1)*, Children's Pr.) Scholastic Library Publishing.
Lovelace, Victoria. Animal Crackers & Alphabet Soup. 2014. (ENG.). 84p. pap. 19.95 *(978-1-4670-3532-3(7)*, b9230d6d-2918-4b50-9842-302a1082f149) AuthorHouse.
Lovett, Louise Sheppa, illus. A Happy Day. Lovett, Louise Sheppa, . 2008. 32p. (J). 18.50 *(978-0-9793419-0-8(6))* Tish & Co. LLC.
Low, Alice. Blueberry Mouse. Friend, David Michael, tr. Friend, David Michael, illus. 2004. (J). 15.95 *(978-1-59336-111-2(4))*; pap. *(978-1-59336-112-9(2))* Mondo Publishing.
Low, J. H. Lost in the Gardens. Low, J. H., illus. 2015. (ENG., Illus.). 48p. (J). 14.99 *(978-981-4677-10-3(8))* Marshall Cavendish International (Asia) Private Ltd. SGP. Dist: Independent Pubs. Group.
Lowery, Paul. Do You Know Where Sea Turtles Go? 2007. (J). 15.99 *(978-0-9792379-0-4(4))* PBL Stories LLC.
Lucado, Max. One Hand, Two Hands, 1 vol. 2010. (ENG., Illus.). 32p. (J). (gr. -1-3). 14.99 *(978-1-4003-1649-6(9)*, Tommy Nelson) Nelson, Thomas Inc.
Lucas, Sally. Dancing Dinos at the Beach. Lucas, Margeaux, illus. 2010. (Step into Reading Ser.). 32p. (J). (gr. -1-1). pap. 5.99 *(978-0-375-85640-2(4)*, Random Hse. Bks. for Young Readers) Random Hse. Children's Bks.
—Dancing Dinos Go to School. Lucas, Margeaux, illus. 2006. (Step into Reading Ser.: Vol. 1). 32p. (J). (gr. -1-1). pap. 5.99 *(978-0-375-83241-3(6)*, Random Hse. Bks. for Young Readers) Random Hse. Children's Bks.
Luebs, Robin. Please Pick Me up, Mama! Luebs, Robin, illus. 2009. (ENG., Illus.). 40p. (J). (gr. -1-k). 15.99 *(978-1-4169-7977-7(8)*, Beach Lane Bks.) Beach Lane Bks.
Lumley, Jemima. The Journey Home from Grandpa's. Fatus, Sophie, illus. 24p. (J). 2012. (gr. -1-2). 16.99 *(978-1-84686-898-6(X))* 2006. (ENG.). 6.99 *(978-1-84686-029-4(6))* 2006. (ENG.). (gr. -1-k). 9.99 *(978-1-84686-026-3(1))* 2006. (ENG.). (gr. -1-3). 16.99 *(978-1-905236-37-4(9))* Barefoot Bks., Inc.
—The Journey Home from Grandpa's. Fatus, Sophie, illus. 2010. 16p. (J). (gr. -1-3). pap. 5.99 *(978-1-84686-277-9(9))* Barefoot Bks., Inc.
Luna, James, et al. The Place Where You Live / el Lugar Donde Vives. Muraida, Thelma, illus. 2015. (SPA & ENG.). 32p. (J). (gr. k-3). 17.95 *(978-1-55885-813-8(X))* Arte Publico Pr.
Lund, Deb. All Aboard the Dinotrain. Fine, Howard, illus. 2009. (ENG.). 40p. (J). (gr. -1-3). pap. 9.99 *(978-0-547-24825-7(3)*, 1100733, Clarion Bks.) HarperCollins Pubs.
—All Aboard the Dinotrain Board Book. Fine, Howard, illus. 2011. (ENG.). 30p. (J). (gr. -1 — 1). bds. 7.99 *(978-0-547-55415-0(X)*, 1452006, Clarion Bks.) HarperCollins Pubs.
—Dinosailors. Fine, Howard, illus. 2008. (ENG.). 36p. (J). (gr. -1-3). pap. 8.99 *(978-0-15-206124-1(X)*, 1198391, Clarion Bks.) HarperCollins Pubs.
—Monsters on Machines. Neubecker, Robert, illus. 2017. (ENG.). 40p. (J). (gr. -1-3). pap. 6.99 *(978-0-544-92783-4(4)*, 1657204, Clarion Bks.) HarperCollins Pubs.
—Monsters on Machines. Neubecker, Robert, illus. 2017. (ENG.). (J). (gr. -1-3). lib. bdg. 17.20 *(978-0-606-39815-2(5))* Turtleback.
Luneau, Terri Robert & Bennett, Trevor. Big Woods Bird: An Ivory-Bill Story. 2005. (ENG., Illus.). 36p. (gr. -1-3). pap. 8.95 *(978-0-9768839-0-6(2)*, P145085) Butler Ctr. for Arkansas Studies.
Lutterbach, Johanna. Little Orly & the Cricket. Polchlopek, Mary Ann, illus. 2008. 24p. pap. 11.49 *(978-1-4389-0656-0(0))* AuthorHouse.
Lyford, Joan. Daisybelle & Dash, a Bedtime Story. 2012. 24p. pap. 14.93 *(978-1-4669-1154-3(9))* Trafford Publishing.
Lynne, Kimberlee, illus. The Frog & the Mouse. 2011. (First Steps in Music Ser.). (ENG.). 32p. (J). (gr. k-2). 17.95 *(978-1-57999-802-8(X))* G I A Pubns., Inc.
Lyon, George Ella. Planes Fly! Wiggins, Mick, illus. 2013. (ENG.). 40p. (J). (gr. -1-3). 19.99 *(978-1-4424-5025-7(8))* Simon & Schuster Children's Publishing.
—Sleepsong. Catalanotto, Peter, illus. 2008. (ENG.). 40p. (J). (gr. -1-k). 16.99 *(978-0-689-86973-0(8)*, Atheneum/Richard Jackson Bks.) Simon & Schuster Children's Publishing.
—Trucks Roll! Frazier, Craig, illus. 2007. (ENG.). 40p. (J). (gr. -1-2). 19.99 *(978-1-4169-2435-7(3)*, Atheneum/Richard Jackson Bks.) Simon & Schuster Children's Publishing.
Lyon, George Ella & Lyon, Benn. Boats Float! Wiggins, Mick, illus. 2015. (ENG.). 40p. (J). (gr. -1-3). 19.99 *(978-1-4814-0380-1(X))* Simon & Schuster Children's Publishing.
—Trains Run! Wiggins, Mick, illus. 2019. (ENG.). 40p. (J). (gr. -1-3). 17.99 *(978-1-4814-8202-8(5))* Simon & Schuster Children's Publishing.
Lyon, Tammie Speer, illus. Hickory Dickory Dock! gif. ed. 2006. 10p. (J). (gr. -1-k). bds. 10.95 *(978-1-57791-213-2(6))* Brighter Minds Children's Publishing.
—Mary Had a Little Lamb. 2006. 8p. (J). bds. 10.95 *(978-1-57791-210-1(1))* Brighter Minds Children's Publishing.
Lyons, P. J. God Is Watching over You, 1 vol. Warnes, Tim, illus. 2016. (ENG.). 16p. (J). bds. 9.99 *(978-0-310-74881-6(X))* Zonderkidz.
—Thank You, Lord, for Everything, 1 vol. Warnes, Tim, illus. 2015. (ENG.). 16p. (J). bds. 9.99 *(978-0-310-74812-0(7))* Zonderkidz.
Maccarone, Grace. Bunny Race! Long, Ethan, illus. 2009. (J). *(978-0-545-11290-1(7))* Scholastic, Inc.
—Miss Lina's Ballerinas. Davenier, Christine, illus. 2010. (Miss Lina's Ballerinas Ser.). (ENG.). 40p. (J). (gr. -1-1). 18.99 *(978-0-312-38243-8(X)*, 900051152) Feiwel & Friends.
—Six Super Easy-To-Read Stories. 2009. (Scholastic Reader Ser.). (Illus.). (J). pap. *(978-0-439-85277-7(3))* Scholastic, Inc.
MacDonald, Margaret Read. A Hen, a Chick & a String Guitar. Fatus, Sophie, illus. 2005. (ENG.). 32p. (J). 17.99 *(978-1-84148-796-0(1))* Barefoot Bks., Inc.
MacHale, D. J. The Monster Princess. Boiger, Alexandra, illus. 2010. (ENG.). 40p. (J). (gr. -1-1). 17.99 *(978-1-4169-4809-4(0)*, Aladdin) Simon & Schuster Children's Publishing.
Macht, Heather. You May Just Be a Dinosaur, 1 vol. Gillard, Jason, illus. 2015. (ENG.). 32p. (J). (gr. k-3). 16.99 *(978-1-4556-2040-1(8)*, Pelican Publishing) Arcadia Publishing.
MacIver, Juliette. Yak & Gnu. Chapman, Cat, illus. 2015. (ENG.). 32p. (J). (gr. -1-2). 14.99 *(978-0-7636-7561-5(X))* Candlewick Pr.
Mack, Harry. The Treasure Mystery Clues. 2011. 70p. pap. 19.95 *(978-1-4626-2487-4(1))* America Star Bks.
Mack, Jeff. Hush Little Polar Bear: A Picture Book. Mack, Jeff, illus. 2013. (ENG., Illus.). 36p. (J). (gr. -1-1). bds. 7.99 *(978-1-59643-945-0(9)*, 900123718) Roaring Brook Pr.
Mackall, Dandi. The Super Gifts of Spring: Easter. 2015. (Seasons Ser.). (ENG., Illus.). 32p. (J). (gr. -1-3). 9.99 *(978-1-4336-8233-9(8)*, B&H Kids) B&H Publishing Group.
Mackall, Dandi Daley. The Lost Lamb & the Good Shepherd. Manuzak, Lisa, illus. 2016. (Flipside Stories Ser.). (ENG.). 48p. (J). 14.99 *(978-1-4964-1121-1(8)*, 4612796) Tyndale Hse. Pubs.
—One Small Donkey, 1 vol. 2016. (ENG., Illus.). 32p. (J). 14.99 *(978-0-7180-8747-0(X)*, Tommy Nelson) Nelson, Thomas Inc.
MacLachlan, Patricia. The Moon's Almost Here. dePaola, Tomie, illus. 2016. (ENG.). 32p. (J). (gr. -1-3). 17.99 *(978-1-4814-2062-4(3)*, McElderry, Margaret K. Bks.) McElderry, Margaret K. Bks.
—The Poet's Dog. (ENG.). (J). (gr. 1-5). 2018. 112p. pap. 5.99 *(978-0-06-229264-3(1))* 2016. 96p. 14.99 *(978-0-06-229262-9(5))* HarperCollins Pubs. (Tegen, Katherine Bks).
Maclachlan, Patricia. Snowflakes Fall. Kellogg, Steven, illus. 2013. 32p. (J). (gr. -1-2). 17.99 *(978-0-385-37693-8(6))* Random Hse. Children's Bks.
Macnamara, Peggy & Macnamara, Katie. Rosie the Tarantula: A True Adventure in Chicago's Field Museum. 2017. (ENG., Illus.). 48p. (J). (gr. 1-6). 17.95 *(978-0-8101-3657-1(0))* Northwestern Univ. Pr.
Macnaughton, Tina. One Snowy Rescue. 2015. (ENG.). pap. *(978-0-545-92909-7(1))* Scholastic, Inc.
MacRae, Tom. When I Woke up I Was a Hippopotamus. Collins, Ross, illus. 2011. (Andersen Press Picture Books Ser.). (J). 16.95 *(978-0-7613-8099-3(X))* Andersen Pr. GBR. Dist: Lerner Publishing Group.
MacVeety, Sue Maney. Singing Sea/el Mar Que Canta. Zantay, Valerie, tr. 2005. (ENG., Illus.). 36p. per. 15.99 *(978-1-4134-7275-2(3))* Xlibris Corp.
Madden, Colleen. The Kiddie Table. 2018. (ENG., Illus.). 32p. (J). (gr. -1-2). 15.95 *(978-1-68446-002-1(6)*, 138585, Capstone Editions) Capstone.
Madison, Paul. The Purple Monkey. 2012. (Illus.). 32p. pap. 17.25 *(978-1-4669-3909-7(5))* Trafford Publishing.
Madison, Ron. Ned & the General: A Lesson about Deployment. Covolo, David, illus. 2004. 26p. (J). (gr. -1-3). *(978-1-887206-25-9(6))* Ned's Head Productions.
Madson, Trish. 10 Little Monsters Visit Texas, Volume 5. Hardyman, Nathan, illus. 2017. (10 Little Monsters Ser.: 5). (ENG.). 32p. (J). (gr. k-3). 14.99 *(978-1-945547-08-9(1)*, 554708) Familius LLC.
—12 Little Elves Visit California, Volume 3. Han, Sadie, illus. 2017. (12 Little Elves Ser.: 3). (ENG.). 32p. (J). (gr. -1-1). 16.99 *(978-1-945547-11-9(1)*, 554711) Familius LLC.
—12 Little Elves Visit Colorado, Volume 5. Kung, Chorkung, illus. 2018. (12 Little Elves Ser.: 5). (ENG.). 32p. (J). (gr. k-3). 16.99 *(978-1-64170-041-2(6)*, 550041) Familius LLC.

—12 Little Elves Visit Montana, Volume 6. Kung, Chorkung, illus. 2018. (12 Little Elves Ser.: 6). (ENG.). 32p. (J). (gr. k-3). 16.99 (978-1-64170-042-9(4), 550042) Familius LLC.

—12 Little Elves Visit Oregon, Volume 4. Han, Sadie, illus. 2017. (12 Little Elves Ser.: 4). (ENG.). 32p. (J). (gr. -1-1). 16.99 (978-1-945547-10-2(3), 554710) Familius LLC.

Mae, Darcie. Sammy & Robert. 2008. 24p. pap. 24.95 (978-1-60474-811-6(7)) America Star Bks.

—Sammy & Robert's Animal Adventures. 2008. 32p. pap. 24.95 (978-1-60703-987-7(7)) America Star Bks.

Magnus, Kellie. Little Lion Goes to School. Robinson, Michael, illus. l.t. ed. 2003. 16p. (J). 9.99 (978-0-9744211-0-0(3)) Media Magic New York.

Magsamen, Sandra. I Love You, Honey Bunny (Made with Love) Magsamen, Sandra, illus. 2016. (Made with Love Ser.). (ENG., Illus.). 14p. (J). (— 1). bds. 7.99 (978-1-338-11084-5(5), Cartwheel Bks.) Scholastic, Inc.

—I Ruff You (Made with Love) Magsamen, Sandra, illus. 2016. (Made with Love Ser.). (ENG., Illus.). 14p. (J). (gr. -1-k). bds. 7.99 (978-1-338-11082-1(9), Cartwheel Bks.) Scholastic, Inc.

—Twinkle, Twinkle, You're My Star. Magsamen, Sandra, illus. 2018. (ENG., Illus.). 10p. (J). (gr. -1 — 1). 7.99 (978-1-338-24312-3(8), Cartwheel Bks.) Scholastic, Inc.

—Whooo Loves You? Magsamen, Sandra, illus. 2017. (Made with Love Ser.). (ENG., Illus.). 10p. (J). (gr. -1 — 1). bds. 8.99 (978-1-338-11087-6(X), Cartwheel Bks.) Scholastic, Inc.

Mahoney, Liana. Forest Green: A Walk Through the Adirondack Seasons. Henry, Maggie, illus. 2014. (ENG.). (J). (978-1-59531-047-7(9)) North Country Bks., Inc.

Mahy, Margaret. The Man from the Land of Fandango. Dunbar, Polly, illus. 2012. (ENG.). 32p. (J). (gr. -1-3). 16.99 (978-0-547-81988-4(9), 1496820, Clarion Bks.) HarperCollins Pubs.

Make Believe Ideas. Five Little Monkeys & Other Counting Rhymes. Machell, Dawn, illus. 2017. (ENG.). 12p. (J). (gr. -1 — 1). 6.99 (978-1-78598-946-9(4)) Make Believe Ideas GBR. Dist: Scholastic, Inc.

Make Believe Ideas, creator. Twinkle Book & Mouse Plush. 2007. (Illus.). (J). (gr. -1-3). (978-1-84610-694-1(X)) Make Believe Ideas.

Mamakas, Stavroula & Lagoutaris, Maria Mamakas. Mama Lagoo: Bath Time Battle. 2011. 28p. pap. 14.95 (978-1-4634-1524-2(9)) AuthorHouse.

Mamma Macs. Australian Animal Walkabout. 2013. 32p. (J). pap. (978-0-9923379-0-2(9)) Karen Mc Dermott.

—Mick Mac Adoo's Australian Zoo. 2013. 30p. (J). pap. (978-0-9923379-9-5(2)) Karen Mc Dermott.

Manalang, Dan. Ambrosia. Wong, Nichole, illus. 2006. (ENG.). 32p. (J). (gr. k-2). 14.99 (978-0-9769342-0-2(5)) Flip Publishing.

Mandel, Peter. Bun, Onion, Burger. Eliopoulos, Chris, illus. 2010. (ENG.). 40p. (J). (gr. -1-1). 12.99 (978-1-4169-2466-1(3), Simon & Schuster Bks. For Young Readers) Simon & Schuster Bks. For Young Readers.

Mankita, Jay. Elar. 2013. (Illus.). 38p. (J). pap. 9.95 (978-1-935734-49-9(0)) Kitanie Bks.

Manning, L. L. Fuzz. 2010. (ENG.). 26p. pap. 15.99 (978-1-4500-5755-4(1)) Xlibris Corp.

Mansbach, Adam. Seriously, Just Go to Sleep. Cortes, Ricardo, illus. 2012. (ENG.). 36p. (gr. k-5). 15.95 (978-1-61775-078-6(6)) Akashic Bks.

Manushkin, Fran. Bamboo for Me, Bamboo for You! Hernandez, Purificacion, illus. 2017. (ENG.). 32p. (J). (gr. -1-3). 17.99 (978-1-4814-5063-8(8), Aladdin) Simon & Schuster Children's Publishing.

Manwiller, S. A. The Adventures of Jack & Max: The Truliest Meaning of Christmas. Manwiller, S. A. & Overley, Kristen V., illus. 2013. (ENG.). 38p. (J). 24.99 (978-0-9838427-7-4(9)) Sevenhorns Publishing.

Marchese, Stephen, illus. The Flights of Marceau: Week Two. 2007. (ENG.). 60p. (J). 16.95 (978-0-9797495-1-3(4)) Majestic Eagle Publishing.

Marchus, Linda. The Gorilla Who Wanted to Dance. Marchus, Linda, illus. 2003. (Illus.). 32p. (J). lib. bdg. 15.95 (978-0-9723122-1-9(8)) Wee Read Publishing.

Marciano, John Bemelmans. Madeline & the Cats of Rome. 2008. (Madeline Ser.). (ENG.). 48p. (J). (gr. 1-3). 19.99 (978-0-670-06297-3(9), Viking Books for Young Readers) Penguin Young Readers Group.

—Madeline & the Old House in Paris. 2013. (Madeline Ser.). (ENG., Illus.). 48p. (J). (gr. -1-2). 18.99 (978-0-670-78485-1(0), Viking Books for Young Readers) Penguin Young Readers Group.

—Madeline at the White House. (Madeline Ser.). (Illus.). (J). (gr. -1-2). 2020. 34p. bds. 9.99 (978-0-593-11800-9(6), Viking Books for Young Readers) 2016. 48p. pap. 9.99 (978-1-101-99780-2(X), Puffin Books) 2011. 48p. 19.99 (978-0-670-01228-2(9), Viking Books for Young Readers) Penguin Young Readers Group.

—Madeline at the White House. 2016. (Madeline Ser.). lib. bdg. 19.65 (978-0-606-38845-0(1)) Turtleback.

Margrave, David R. When Fur & Feather Get Together. Wyly, Kim, illus. 2018. (ENG.). 32p. (J). 11.99 (978-1-945507-72-4(1)) Carpenter's Son Publishing.

Mariconda, Barbara. Sort It Out!, 1 vol. Rogers, Sherry, illus. 2008. (ENG & SPA.). 32p. (J). (gr. k-1). pap. 10.95 (978-1-934359-32-7(7), 17c86867-80a5-4681-b3ea-a6a1ca86f26e); 16.95 (978-1-934359-11-2(4)) Arbordale Publishing.

—Sort It Out! Spanish. Rogers, Sherry, illus. 2008. Tr. of Sort It Out! (SPA.). 32p. (J). (gr. k-4). 17.95 (978-1-60718-695-3(0)) Arbordale Publishing.

Marinaro, Stacy. Carter the Acorn Collecting Cutie. 2008. 20p. pap. 10.50 (978-0-615-20807-7(X)) Marinaro, Stacy.

Markell, Denis. Hush, Little Monster. Iwai, Melissa, illus. 2012. (ENG.). 32p. (J). (gr. -1-1). 9.99 (978-1-4424-4195-8(X), Little Simon) Little Simon.

Markes, Julie. Shhhhh! Everybody's Sleeping. Parkins, David, illus. 32p. (J). (gr. -1-1). 2005. lib. bdg. 16.89 (978-0-06-053791-3(4)) 2004. (ENG.). 16.99 (978-0-06-053790-6(6), HarperCollins) HarperCollins Pubs.

—Thanks for Thanksgiving. Barrette, Doris, illus. (ENG.). 32p. (J). (gr. -1-3). 2008. pap. 7.99 (978-0-06-051098-5(6)) 2004. 14.99 (978-0-06-051096-1(X)) HarperCollins Pubs. (HarperCollins).

—Thanks for Thanksgiving Board Book. Barrette, Doris, illus. 2017. (ENG.). 32p. (J). (gr. -1 — 1). bds. 7.99 (978-0-06-264331-5(2), HarperFestival) HarperCollins Pubs.

Markey, Neil. Woof! Spremulli, Pam, illus. 2011. (ENG.). 34p. (J). (gr. k-k). 14.00 (978-1-935557-77-7(7)) Purple Bear Bks., Inc.

Marks, Darrell. Down on the Farm. 2013. 12p. pap. 15.99 (978-1-4817-0969-9(0)) AuthorHouse.

Marks, Nancy Freeman. Just As You Are: The Story of Leon & Sam. Buchheim, Su Jen, illus. 2003. 32p. (J). 15.00 (978-0-9722430-1-8(1)) Wave Publishing.

Markun, Alan F. New Revolution. (J). 8.95 (978-0-8022-1062-3(7)) Philosophical Library, Inc.

Marley, Bob & Marley, Cedella. Get up, Stand Up. Cabuay, John Jay, illus. 2019. (Bob Marley by Chronicle Bks.). (ENG.). 36p. (J). (gr. -1-k). 16.99 (978-1-4521-7172-2(6)) Chronicle Bks. LLC.

Marquis, Michelle. Mikey & the Mysterious Door. 2008. 32p. pap. 14.99 (978-1-4343-4823-4(7)) AuthorHouse.

Marsaw, Roy. Swim, Swam, Swum. Harris, Phyllis, illus. 2007. 32p. (J). pap. 14.95 (978-0-9744446-8-0(5)) All About Kids Publishing.

Marshall, Judy. Morning. Annelli, Nikki, illus. l.t. ed. 2005. 21p. (J). per. 9.99 (978-1-59879-050-4(1)) Lifevest Publishing, Inc.

Marshall, Linda Elovitz. Have You Ever Zeen a Ziz? Reed, Kyle, illus. 2020. (ENG.). 32p. (J). (gr. -1-3). 16.99 (978-0-8075-3173-0(1), 807531731) Whitman, Albert & Co.

—Shh ... Shh ... Shabbat. Golubeva, Evgenia, illus. 2016. (ENG.). 12p. (J). (gr. -1 — 1). bds. 5.99 (978-1-4677-5873-4(6), 3ba0a891-35f6-4c89-9695-9ac65bea93f1); E-Book 23.99 (978-1-4677-9615-6(8)) Lerner Publishing Group. (Kar-Ben Publishing).

Marshall, Natalie. Five Little Ducks: a Fingers & Toes Nursery Rhyme Book. Marshall, Natalie, illus. 2017. (Fingers & Toes Nursery Rhymes Ser.). (ENG., Illus.). 12p. (J). (gr. -1 — 1). bds. 6.99 (978-1-338-09116-8(6), Cartwheel Bks.) Scholastic, Inc.

—Five Little Pumpkins: a Fingers & Toes Nursery Rhyme Book. Marshall, Natalie, illus. 2017. (Fingers & Toes Nursery Rhymes Ser.). (ENG.). 12p. (J). (gr. -1 — 1). bds. 6.99 (978-1-338-09117-5(4), Cartwheel Bks.) Scholastic, Inc.

Martin, Bill, Jr. Baby Bear, Baby Bear, What Do You See? Carle, Eric, illus. (My First Reader Ser.). (ENG.). (J). (gr. -1-2). 2011. 40p. 9.99 (978-0-8050-9291-2(9), 900069194) 2007. 32p. 19.99 (978-0-8050-8336-1(7), 900044467) Holt, Henry & Co. (Holt, Henry & Co. Bks. For Young Readers).

—Baby Bear, Baby Bear, What Do You See? Big Book. Carle, Eric, illus. 2011. (Brown Bear & Friends Ser.). (ENG.). 32p. (J). (gr. -1-k). pap. 27.99 (978-0-8050-9345-2(1), 900072447, Holt, Henry & Co. Bks. For Young Readers) Holt, Henry & Co.

—Baby Bear, Baby Bear, What Do You See? Board Book. Carle, Eric, illus. 2009. (Brown Bear & Friends Ser.). (ENG.). 28p. (J). (gr. -1-k). bds. 8.99 (978-0-8050-8990-5(X), 900058689, Holt, Henry & Co. Bks. For Young Readers) Holt, Henry & Co.

—Brown Bear, Brown Bear, What Do You See? Carle, Eric, illus. (Brown Bear & Friends Ser.). (J). 2012. (ENG.). 28p. (gr. -1-k). bds. 12.99 (978-0-8050-9577-7(2), 900084747) 2007. 32p. pap. 7.95 (978-0-8050-8797-0(4)) 3rd anniv. ed. 2008. (ENG.). 32p. (gr. -1-k). pap. 27.95 (978-0-8050-8718-5(4), 900049190) Holt, Henry & Co. (Holt, Henry & Co. Bks. For Young Readers).

—Brown Bear, Brown Bear, What Do You See? 50th Anniversary Edition Padded Board Book. Carle, Eric, illus. 50th anniv. ed. 2016. (Brown Bear & Friends Ser.). (ENG.). 28p. (J). bds. 9.99 (978-1-62779-722-1(X), 900158726, Holt, Henry & Co. Bks. For Young Readers) Holt, Henry & Co.

—Brown Bear, Brown Bear, What Do You See? My First Reader. Carle, Eric, illus. 2010. (My First Reader Ser.). (ENG.). 40p. (J). (gr. -1-2). 8.99 (978-0-8050-9244-8(7), 900066982, Holt, Henry & Co. Bks. For Young Readers) Holt, Henry & Co.

—Oso Panda, Oso Panda, Que Ves Ahi? / Panda Bear, Panda Bear, What Do You Hear? (Spanish Edition) Mlawer, Teresa, tr. Carle, Eric, illus. 2009. (Brown Bear & Friends Ser.). Tr. of Brown Bear, Brown Bear, What Do You See? (SPA.). 26p. (J). (gr. -1-k). bds. 10.99 (978-0-8050-8756-7(7), 900049804, Holt, Henry & Co. Bks. For Young Readers) Holt, Henry & Co.

—Panda Bear, Panda Bear, What Do You See? Carle, Eric, illus. (Brown Bear & Friends Ser.). (ENG.). (J). 2014. 28p. (gr. -1-k). bds. 12.99 (978-0-8050-9950-8(6), 900127482) 2011. 40p. (gr. -1-2). 8.99 (978-0-8050-9292-9(7), 900069195) 2007. 32p. pap. 7.95 (978-0-8050-8799-4(0)) 2007. 32p. (gr. -1-k). pap. 27.99 (978-0-8050-8102-2(X), 900039555) 2006. 28p. (gr. -1-k). bds. 8.99 (978-0-8050-8078-0(3), 900038948) Holt, Henry & Co. (Holt, Henry & Co. Bks. For Young Readers).

—Panda Bear, Panda Bear, What Do You See? Slide & Find. Carle, Eric, illus. 2013. (Brown Bear & Friends Ser.). (ENG.). 22p. (J). (gr. -1 — 1). bds. 12.99 (978-0-312-51581-2(2), 900118540) St. Martin's Pr.

—Panda Bear, Panda Bear, What Do You See? 10th Anniversary Edition. Carle, Eric, illus. 2013. (Brown Bear & Friends Ser.). (ENG.). 32p. (J). (gr. -1-k). 24.99 (978-0-8050-9778-8(3), 900119353, Holt, Henry & Co. Bks. For Young Readers) Holt, Henry & Co.

—Polar Bear, Polar Bear, What Do You Hear? Carle, Eric, illus. (Brown Bear & Friends Ser.). (J). 2012. (ENG.). 28p. (gr. -1-k). bds. 14.99 (978-0-8050-9095-6(9), 900062022) 2007. 32p. 7.95 (978-0-8050-8798-7(2)) Holt, Henry & Co. (Holt, Henry & Co. Bks. For Young Readers).

—Polar Bear, Polar Bear, What Do You Hear? 20th Anniversary Edition with CD. Carle, Eric, illus. 20th anniv. ed. 2011. (Brown Bear & Friends Ser.). (ENG.). 32p. (J). (gr. -1-k). 19.99 (978-0-8050-9066-6(5), 900061041, Holt, Henry & Co. Bks. For Young Readers) Holt, Henry & Co.

—Polar Bear, Polar Bear, What Do You Hear? My First Reader. Carle, Eric, illus. 2010. (My First Reader Ser.). (ENG.). 40p. (J). (gr. -1-2). 8.99 (978-0-8050-9245-5(5), 900066985, Holt, Henry & Co. Bks. For Young Readers) Holt, Henry & Co.

—Polar Bear, Polar Bear What Do You Hear? Sound Book. Carle, Eric, illus. 2011. (Brown Bear & Friends Ser.). (ENG.). 24p. (J). (gr. -1-k). bds. 14.95 (978-0-312-51346-7(1), 900079163) St. Martin's Pr.

—Ten Little Caterpillars. Ehlert, Lois, illus. 2011. (ENG.). 40p. (J). (gr. -1-3). 18.99 (978-1-4424-3385-4(X), Beach Lane Bks.) Beach Lane Bks.

Martin, Bill, Jr. & Archambault, John. Chica Chica Bum Bum ABC (Chicka Chicka ABC) Ehlert, Lois, illus. 2011. (SPA.). 16p. (J). (gr. -1-1). bds. 7.99 (978-1-4424-2292-6(0), Libros Para Ninos) Libros Para Ninos.

—Chicka Chicka Boom Boom. Ehlert, Lois, illus. 2012. (Chicka Chicka Book Ser.). (ENG.). 36p. (J). (gr. -1 — 1). bds. 7.99 (978-1-4424-5070-7(3), Little Simon) Little Simon.

—Chicka Chicka Boom Boom: Anniversary Edition. Ehlert, Lois, illus. anniv. ed. 2009. (Chicka Chicka Book Ser.). (ENG.). 40p. (J). (gr. -1-3). 18.99 (978-1-4169-9091-8(7), Beach Lane Bks.) Beach Lane Bks.

—Chicka Chicka Boom Boom: Book & CD. Ehlert, Lois, illus. 2006. (Chicka Chicka Book Ser.). (ENG.). 40p. (J). (gr. -1-3). 10.99 (978-1-4169-2718-1(2), Little Simon) Little Simon.

—Chicka Chicka Boom Boom: Lap Edition. Ehlert, Lois, illus. 2010. (Chicka Chicka Book Ser.). (ENG.). 36p. (J). (gr. -1-1). bds. 12.99 (978-1-4169-9999-7(X), Little Simon) Little Simon.

Martin, Bill, Jr. & Sampson, Michael. Chicka Chicka 1, 2, 3. Ehlert, Lois, illus. 2014. (Chicka Chicka Book Ser.). (ENG.). 36p. (J). (gr. -1 — 1). bds. 7.99 (978-1-4814-0056-5(8), Little Simon) Little Simon.

—Chicka Chicka 1, 2, 3. Ehlert, Lois, illus. 2004. (Chicka Chicka Book Ser.). (ENG.). 40p. (J). (gr. -1-2). 18.99 (978-0-689-85881-9(7), Simon & Schuster Bks. For Young Readers) Simon & Schuster Bks. For Young Readers.

—Chicka Chicka 1, 2, 3. Ehlert, Lois, illus. 2005. (J). (gr. -1-3). 29.95 (978-0-439-76677-7(X), WHCD669) Weston Woods Studios, Inc.

—Chicka Chicka 1, 2, 3: Lap Edition. Ehlert, Lois, illus. 2013. (Chicka Chicka Book Ser.). (ENG.). 36p. (J). (gr. -1-1). bds. 12.99 (978-1-4424-6613-5(8), Little Simon) Little Simon.

Martin, Bill, Jr., et al. Chicka Chicka Boom Boom. Ehlert, Lois, illus. 2008. (J). 13.99 (978-1-59319-935-7(X)) LeapFrog Enterprises, Inc.

—Chicka Chicka Box Box! (Boxed Set) Chicka Chicka Boom Boom; Chicka Chicka 1, 2, 3. Ehlert, Lois, illus. 2013. (Chicka Chicka Book Ser.). (ENG.). 80p. (J). (gr. -1-3). 35.99 (978-1-4814-0223-1(4), Beach Lane Bks.) Beach Lane Bks.

—Kitty Cat, Kitty Cat, Are You Waking Up?, 0 vols. Bryant, Laura J., illus. 2012. (ENG.). 26p. (J). (gr. -1-1). pap. 6.99 (978-0-7614-5841-8(7), 9780761458418, Two Lions) Amazon Publishing.

Martin, David. Peep & Ducky. Walker, David M., illus. (Peep & Ducky Ser.). (ENG.). (J). (— 1). 2015. 24p. bds. 6.99 (978-0-7636-7243-0(2)) 2013. 32p. 14.99 (978-0-7636-5039-1(0)) Candlewick Pr.

—Peep & Ducky Rainy Day. Walker, David M., illus. 2018. (Peep & Ducky Ser.). (ENG.). 24p. (J). (— 1). bds. 6.99 (978-0-7636-9523-1(8)) Candlewick Pr.

—Shh! Bears Sleeping. Johnson, Steve & Fancher, Lou, illus. 2017. 28p. (J). (-k). bds. 8.99 (978-0-425-29179-5(0), Viking Books for Young Readers) Penguin Young Readers Group.

Martin-Duttmann, Robin. Zoo on the Moon. 2013. 24p. pap. 12.97 (978-1-62212-735-1(8), Strategic Bk. Publishing) Strategic Book Publishing & Rights Agency (SBPRA).

Martin, Emily Winfield. Day Dreamers: A Journey of Imagination. (Illus.). 32p. (J). 2016. (ENG.). (— 1). bds. 8.99 (978-1-101-93522-4(7)) 2014. (gr. -1-2). 18.99 (978-0-385-37670-9(7)) Random Hse. Children's Bks. (Random Hse. Bks. for Young Readers).

—Dream Animals: A Bedtime Journey. 2013. (Illus.). 32p. (J). (gr. -1-k). 18.99 (978-0-449-81080-4(1), Random Hse. Bks. for Young Readers) Random Hse. Children's Bks.

—The Wonderful Things You Will Be. 2015. (ENG., Illus.). 36p. (J). (gr. -1-2). 17.99 (978-0-385-37671-6(5)); lib. bdg. 20.99 (978-0-375-97327-7(3)) Random Hse. Children's Bks. (Random Hse. Bks. for Young Readers).

Martin, John, et al. Aesop's Fables in Rhyme for Little Philosophers. 2014. (ENG., Illus.). 96p. (J). (gr. 1-5). pap. 12.99 (978-0-486-78180-8(1), 781801) Dover Pubns., Inc.

Martin Jr, Bill. The Turning of the Year. Shed, Greg, illus. 2007. (ENG.). 28p. (J). (gr. -1-3). pap. 7.99 (978-0-15-204555-5(4), 1193717, Clarion Bks.) HarperCollins Pubs.

Martin, Mike. 365 Stories & Rhymes for Girls. (365 Stories Treasuries Ser.). 384p. (J). 9.98 (978-1-4054-1959-8(8)) Parragon, Inc.

Marzollo, Jean. I Spy Animals. 2012. (I Spy — Scholastic Ser.). lib. bdg. 13.55 (978-0-606-23968-4(5)) Turtleback.

—I Spy Little Toys. Wick, Walter, photos by. 2011. (I Spy Ser.). (ENG., Illus.). 26p. (J). (gr. -1-k). bds. 7.99 (978-0-545-22096-5(3), Cartwheel Bks.) Scholastic, Inc.

—Shanna's Lost Shoe. 2004. (ENG., Illus.). 24p. (gr. -1-1). pap. 3.99 (978-0-7868-1832-7(8), Jump at the Sun) Hyperion Bks. for Children.

Maslyn, Stacie K. B. & Maslyn, Stacie K. Mad Maddie Maxwell, 1 vol. Schettle, Jane, illus. 2007. (I Can Read! Ser.). (ENG.). 32p. (J). (gr. -1-1). pap. 4.99 (978-0-310-71467-5(2)) Zonderkidz.

Massey, Jane, illus. Potty Hero. 2016. (J). (978-0-545-92773-4(0)) Scholastic, Inc.

Massie, Rosemary. Rhymen the Rabbit: Meeting the Forest Ranger, 2011. 28p. pap. 13.95 (978-1-4634-2572-2(4)) AuthorHouse.

—Rhymen the Rabbit: Save the Forest. 2011. 28p. pap. 13.95 (978-1-4634-1597-6(4)) AuthorHouse.

Mathes, Charles. In Every Moon There Is a Face. Graston, Arlene, illus. 2003. 32p. 15.95 (978-0-9701907-4-1(3)) Illumination Arts Publishing Co., Inc.

Matheson, Christie. Tap the Magic Tree. Matheson, Christie, illus. 2013. (ENG., Illus.). 40p. (J). (gr. -1-3). 18.99 (978-0-06-227445-8(7), Greenwillow Bks.) HarperCollins Pubs.

Mau, Connie. Catch me if you Can. Lemus, Kristina, illus. l.t. ed. 2006. 28p. (J). 14.95 (978-0-9778843-0-8(9)) Mau, C. Publishing Co.

Maurer, Amy J. A Purple Hippopotamus Pillow & Pink Penguin Sheets. Smith, Rachel, illus. 2006. 52p. (J). 19.99 (978-1-59879-239-3(3)); per. 15.99 (978-1-59879-167-9(2)) Lifevest Publishing, Inc.

Maurer, Ashley, illus. Jennie Jenkins. 2015. (First Steps in Music Ser.). (ENG.). 32p. (J). (— 1). 17.95 (978-1-62277-139-4(7)) G I A Pubns., Inc.

Mauzy, Barbara. Don't Be a Schwoe: Embracing Differences, 1 vol. 2011. (ENG., Illus.). 80p. (J). (gr. -1-3). 16.99 (978-0-7643-3566-2(9), 3934) Schiffer Publishing, Ltd.

Maxwell, John C. Sometimes You Win — Sometimes You Learn for Kids. Bjorkman, Steve, illus. 2016. (ENG.). 32p. (J). (gr. -1-3). 18.99 (978-0-316-28408-0(4)) Little, Brown Bks. for Young Readers.

May, Robert L. Rudolph Shines Again. Caparo, Antonio Javier, illus. (Classic Board Bks.). (ENG.). (J). (gr. -1 — 1). 2018. 42p. bds. 7.99 (978-1-5344-1839-4(3)) 2015. 40p. 17.99 (978-1-4424-7498-7(X)) Little Simon. (Little Simon).

—Rudolph the Red-Nosed Reindeer. Caparo, Antonio Javier, illus. 2017. (Classic Board Bks.). (ENG.). 42p. (J). (gr. -1-k). bds. 7.99 (978-1-5344-0027-6(3), Little Simon) Little Simon.

Mayhew, James. Starlight Sailor. Morris, Jackie, illus. (ENG.). 24p. (J). (gr. -1-2). 2018. 7.99 (978-1-84686-750-7(9)) 2009. 16.99 (978-1-84686-185-7(3)) Barefoot Bks., Inc.

Mayo, Margaret. Emergency! Ayliffe, Alex, illus. 2003. 32p. (J). (gr. -1-1). 14.95 (978-0-87614-922-5(0), Carolrhoda Bks.) Lerner Publishing Group.

McAllen, Bob. Dirtiest Hair in the World. McClure, Tom, illus. 2008. (ENG.). 44p. (J). (gr. k-3). lib. bdg. 17.99 (978-1-934277-24-9(X)) Mam Green Publishing, Inc.

McBride, Martha J. Avery Finds Five Dollars. l.t. ed. 2004. 36p. (J). per. 19.99 (978-1-59196-434-6(2)) Instant Pub.

McCabe, Lauren A. How Many Spots Have I Got? Foulke, Nancy, illus. 2005. (J). 16.00 (978-1-893516-02-1(4)) Our Child Pr.

McCanna, Tim. Barnyard Boogie! Black, Allison, illus. 2017. (ENG.). 24p. (J). (gr. -1-k). 12.95 (978-1-4197-2346-9(4), 1163801, Abrams Appleseed) Abrams, Inc.

—Bitty Bot. Carpenter, Tad, illus. 2016. (Bitty Bot Ser.). (ENG.). 32p. (J). (gr. -1-3). 16.99 (978-1-4814-4929-8(X), Simon & Schuster Bks. For Young Readers) Simon & Schuster Bks. For Young Readers.

—Bitty Bot's Big Beach Getaway. Carpenter, Tad, illus. 2018. (Bitty Bot Ser.). (ENG.). 32p. (J). (gr. -1-3). 17.99 (978-1-4814-4931-1(1), Simon & Schuster/Paula Wiseman Bks.) Simon & Schuster/Paula Wiseman Bks.

—So Many Sounds. Miller, Andy, illus. 2018. (ENG.). 24p. (J). (gr. -1-k). 12.99 (978-1-4197-3156-3(4), 1197101, Abrams Appleseed) Abrams, Inc.

—Watersong. Smythe, Richard, illus. 2017. (ENG.). 32p. (J). (gr. -1-3). 18.99 (978-1-4814-6881-7(2), Simon & Schuster/Paula Wiseman Bks.) Simon & Schuster/Paula Wiseman Bks.

McCardell, Ken. BibleRhymes' Christmas Story, bk. 3. Chirco, Antonella, illus. ed. 2008. (BibleRhymes Ser.: 3). 28p. (J). 17.95 (978-0-9790605-2-6(4), BibleRhymes) BibleRhymes Publishing, L.L.C.

—BibleRhymes' Creation. Chirco, Antonella, illus. 2007. (BibleRhymes Ser.). 32p. (J). 17.95 (978-0-9790605-0-2(8), BibleRhymes) BibleRhymes Publishing, L.L.C.

—BibleRhymes' Noah & the Ark, bk. 2. Chirco, Antonella, illus. 2007. (BibleRhymes Ser.: 2). 28p. (J). 17.95 (978-0-9790605-1-9(6), BibleRhymes) BibleRhymes Publishing, L.L.C.

McCarthy, Michael. The Story of Daniel in the Lions' Den. Ferri, Giuliano, illus. 2003. 32p. (J). (gr. 1-3). 16.99 (978-1-84148-209-5(9)) Barefoot Bks., Inc.

McCarty, Bryan. Devyn's Gold. 2008. pap. 17.00 (978-0-8059-8640-2(5)) Dorrance Publishing Co., Inc.

McClure, Brian D. The Ants. Plumlee, Buddy, illus. 2009. (Brian D. Mcclure Childrens Book Collection). 57p. (J). (gr. -1-3). 16.95 (978-1-933426-10-5(1)) Universal Flag Publishing.

—The Birds & the Frogs. Plumlee, Buddy, illus. 2009. (Brian D. Mcclure Childrens Book Collection). 37p. (J). (gr. -1-3). 16.95 (978-1-933426-13-6(6)) Universal Flag Publishing.

—The Up down Day. Plumlee, Buddy, illus. 2009. (Brian D. Mcclure Childrens Book Collection). 47p. (J). (gr. -1-3). 14.95 (978-1-933426-07-5(1)) Universal Flag Publishing.

—Who Am I? 2006. (Illus.). 52p. (J). 12.95 (978-1-933426-03-7(9)) Universal Flag Publishing.

McColl, Pamela. Santa's Song: A Playful Holiday Sing-Along Song for Children of All Ages. 2017. (ENG., Illus.). 32p. (J). 16.95 (978-1-927979-23-5(4), 89a8aa79-6b1c-44cc-8006-796daeb68b32) Grafton and Scratch Pubs. CAN. Dist: Baker & Taylor Publisher Services (BTPS).

McConaughey, Matthew. Just Because. Kurilla, Renée, illus. 2023. (ENG.). 32p. (J). (gr. -1-3). 19.99 **(978-0-593-62203-2(0)**, Viking Books for Young Readers) Penguin Young Readers Group.

McCormick, Patricia. Sold. 2008. 263p. (J). (gr. 7-12). 19.65 (978-1-4178-1810-5(7)) Turtleback.

McCowan, Linda. Cancer Rhymes with Dancer. 2007. (Illus.). 24p. (J). (gr. -1-3). pap. 12.95 (978-0-9814596-0-8(9)) McCowan, Linda.

McCully, Emily Arnold. Late Nate in a Race. 2013. (I Like to Read Ser.). (ENG., Illus.). 24p. (J). (gr. -1-3). pap. 7.99 (978-0-8234-2755-0(2)) Holiday Hse., Inc.

McCurdie, Trevor. A Dolphin's Wish: How You Can Help Make a Difference & Save Our Oceans. Battistel, Cinzia, illus. 2020. (ENG.). 32p. (J). (gr. -1-3). 17.99 (978-1-7282-0522-9(0)) Sourcebooks, Inc.

McDaniel Rockstad, Jean. Eric Jay, Eric Jay, What Are You Gonna Do All Day? 2011. (Illus.). 24p. 16.95 (978-1-60844-941-5(6)) Dog Ear Publishing, LLC.

McDermott, Tom. Otis Steele & the Taileebone: A Southern Tall Tale, 1 vol. Crosby, Jeff, illus. 2013. (ENG.). 32p. (J). (gr. k-2). 16.99 (978-1-4556-1736-4(9), Pelican Publishing) Arcadia Publishing.

McDonald, Jill. Over in the Meadow. McDonald, Jill & Reed, Susan, illus. 2011. (ENG.). 24p. (J). (gr. 1-4). 16.99 (978-1-84686-543-5(3)) Barefoot Bks., Inc.

McDonald, Lisa. The Adventures of Penelope the Tea Cup Pig. 2012. 36p. pap. 32.70 (978-1-4771-3182-4(5)) Xlibris Corp.

McDonald, Rae A. A Fishing Surprise. Kemly, Kathleen, illus. 2007. (ENG.). 32p. (J). (gr. -1-3). 16.95 (978-1-55971-977-3(X)) Cooper Square Publishing Llc.

Mcdonnell, Patrick. Art. 2011. (J). (gr. -1-3). 29.95 (978-0-545-10697-9(4)) Weston Woods Studios, Inc.

S

McDonnell, Patrick. Art. 2006. (ENG., Illus.). 48p. (J). (gr. -1-3). 17.99 *(978-0-316-11491-2(X))* Little, Brown Bks. for Young Readers.
McDonough, Kelly. Things I Don't Like. 2012. 32p. pap. 24.95 *(978-1-4626-8177-8(8))* America Star Bks.
McDougall, Carol & LaRamee-Jones, Shanda. Baby Talk, 1 vol. 2013. (Baby Steps Ser.). (ENG., Illus.). 12p. (J). (gr. -1-k). bds. 8.95 *(978-1-77108-000-2(0),* 7f55e344-b5f4-4867-bdd1-845f1ce4f469) Nimbus Publishing, Ltd. CAN. Dist: Baker & Taylor Publisher Services (BTPS).
McGann, James, illus. The Tailor & the Mouse. 2012. (First Steps in Music Ser.). 32p. (J). (gr. -1-k). 17.95 *(978-1-57999-903-2(4))* G I A Pubns., Inc.
McGinnis, Bsn. Call My Mom!! 2013. 24p. pap. 14.99 *(978-1-4669-5595-0(3))* Trafford Publishing.
McGovern, Ann. Little Wolf. 2011. 48p. (gr. 2-4). pap. 8.95 *(978-1-4620-2711-8(3))* iUniverse, Inc.
McGranaghan, John. Saturn for My Birthday, 1 vol. Edelson, Wendy, illus. 2008. (ENG.). 32p. (J). (gr. -1-4). 16.95 *(978-1-934359-13-6(0));* pap. 8.95 *(978-1-934359-27-3(0))* Arbordale Publishing.
McGrath, Barbara Barbieri. Five Flying Penguins. Coleman, Stephanie Fizer, illus. 2018. (ENG.). 32p. (J). (gr. -1-2). lib. bdg. 12.99 *(978-1-58089-805-8(X))* Charlesbridge Publishing, Inc.
—Teddy Bear Counting. Nihoff, Tim, illus. 2010. (McGrath Math Ser.: 1). (ENG.). 32p. (J). (gr. -1-2). pap. 7.95 *(978-1-58089-216-2(7))* Charlesbridge Publishing, Inc.
McGrath, Brenda. Ding Bat Audio Book. 2006. (Illus.). 16p. (J). 13.99 *(978-0-9799050-0-1(1))* All Around Our World Publishing Co., Inc.
McGraw, Jason. Beating the Odds. 2006. (ENG.). 28p. 47.88 *(978-0-615-13681-3(8))* McGraw, Jason A.
McGregor, Janet C. Happy for a Honk & a Wave. Craft, Donna, illus. 2010. 20p. pap. 12.95 *(978-1-936343-04-1(5))* Peppertree Pr., The.
McGuckin, Mitchelle. Bullfrog Henry. 2010. 60p. pap. 23.99 *(978-1-4490-9547-5(X))* AuthorHouse.
McHenry, E. B. Poodlena. 2004. (Illus.). (J). *(978-1-58234-962-6(2))* Bloomsbury Publishing USA.
Mcintosh, Sharon. Grandma S Donut Hat. 2013. 22p. pap. 9.99 *(978-1-62697-407-4(1))* Salem Author Services.
McKee, Brett. Monsters Don't Cry. Burfoot, Ella, illus. 2012. (ENG.). 32p. (J). (gr. -1-k). 19.99 *(978-1-84939-291-4(9))* Andersen Pr. GBR. Dist: Independent Pubs. Group.
McKellar, Danica. Goodnight, Numbers. Padrón, Alicia, illus. (McKellar Math Ser.). (J). (-k). 2022. 32p. pap. 8.99 *(978-0-593-64355-6(0),* Dragonfly Bks.) 2018. (ENG.). 30p. bds. 8.99 *(978-1-101-93381-7(X),* Crown Books For Young Readers) 2017. 32p. 16.99 *(978-1-101-93378-7(X),* Crown Books For Young Readers) Random Hse. Children's Bks.
McKendry, Sam. Are You Ticklish? Mitchell, Melanie, illus. 2008. (ENG.). 12p. (J). bds. 5.95 *(978-1-58117-706-0(2),* Intervisual/Piggy Toes) Bendon, Inc.
McKenna, Mark, et al, illus. Banana Tail. 2003. 32p. (J). 12.95 *(978-0-9727681-3-9(0))* Active Media Publishing, LLC.
McKernan, Wendy. The Thing I Say I Saw Last Night: A Christmas Story. Bzymek, Izabela, illus. 2011. 32p. (J). *(978-0-9866204-0-9(8));* pap. *(978-0-9866204-1-6(6))* Little Dragon Publishing.
McKittrick, Erin. My Coyote Nose & Ptarmigan Toes: An Almost-True Alaskan Adventure. Higman, Valisa, illus. 2016. (Paws IV Ser.). 32p. (J). (gr. -1-2). pap. 10.99 *(978-1-63217-031-6(0),* Little Bigfoot) Sasquatch Bks.
McLaughlin, Julie. Hungry Mr. Gator. McKay, Ann Marie, illus. 2005. (J). 15.99 *(978-0-933101-24-1(4))* Legacy Pubns.
McLelland, Michael J. Beating the Bully. Kirk, Andrea Cope, illus. 2007. 16p. (J). 15.99 *(978-1-59955-006-0(7))* Cedar Fort, Inc./CFI Distribution.
McLeod, Kimberly. Little Mitchell Tried to Be Good, but Most of the Time He Was Misunderstood. 2012. 42p. 25.00 *(978-0-9829825-5-6(0))* Creative Energy, LLC.
McLeod, Kris Aro. Hush-a-Bye Counting: A Bedtime Book. Allyn, Virginia, illus. 2008. (ENG.). 20p. (J). (gr. -1). 14.95 *(978-1-58117-785-5(2),* Intervisual/Piggy Toes) Bendon, Inc.
McMasters, Anne. Anne's Stories for Children of All Ages. 2008. 24p. pap. 12.50 *(978-1-4343-9204-6(X))* AuthorHouse.
McMillan, Dawn. Doctor Grundy's Undies. Kinnaird, Ross, illus. 2019. (ENG.). 32p. (gr. 1-5). pap. 8.99 *(978-0-486-83248-7(1),* 832481) Dover Pubns., Inc.
McMillan, Ernest. Psalms of Passion. 2006. 48p. pap. 8.95 *(978-1-59800-224-9(4))* Outskirts Pr., Inc.
McMullan, Kate. How Do You Take a Bath? Hanson, Sydney, illus. 2018. (ENG.). 32p. (J). (gr. -1-3). 17.99 *(978-1-5247-6517-0(1),* Knopf Bks. for Young Readers) Random Hse. Children's Bks.
McMurtrie, Kevin. The Day I Was Invisible. 2013. 28p. pap. 13.55 *(978-1-4669-7976-5(3))* Trafford Publishing.
—Have You Seen My Duck? 2012. 20p. pap. 13.77 *(978-1-4669-4847-1(7))* Trafford Publishing.
McNair, Don J. Who Wants to Play?, 1 vol. 2009. 28p. pap. 24.95 *(978-1-60836-315-5(5))* America Star Bks.
McNally, Jeanne. The Girl Who Wore Many Hats. 2010. 40p. pap. 16.99 *(978-1-4490-5735-0(7))* AuthorHouse.
McNamee, Kevin. Just for Today. Movshina, Marina, illus. 2012. 16p. pap. 9.95 *(978-1-61633-314-0(6))* Guardian Angel Publishing, Inc.
—The Soggy Town of Hilltop. Ruble, Eugene, illus. 2010. 20p. pap. 10.95 *(978-1-61633-041-5(4))* Guardian Angel Publishing, Inc.
McNease, Mitzy. Chester's Presents. Cox, Kim, illus. 2006. 28p. (J). 10.95 *(978-0-9779488-0-2(3))* Blancmange Publishing LLC.
McNeely Schultz, Geri. Kristie's Excellent Adventures: A Visit to the Fridge. Bertolami, Vince, illus. 2013. (ENG.). 40p. (J). pap. 9.99 *(978-1-935766-88-9(0))* Windy City Pubs.
McPhail, David. Big Brown Bear/el Gran Oso Pardo: Bilingual English-Spanish. McPhail, David, illus. 2007. (Big Brown Bear Ser.). (ENG., Illus.). 28p. (J). (gr. -1-3). pap. 5.99 *(978-0-15-205970-5(9),* 1197929, Clarion Bks.) HarperCollins Pubs.
—I Hug You & You. 2018. (ENG., Illus.). 28p. (J). (— 1). bds. 7.99 *(978-0-8234-3994-2(1))* Holiday Hse., Inc.
McRae, G. c. Pretty Ballerina. Anderson, David, illus. 2013. 44p. pap. *(978-0-9876845-3-0(1))* Warne, MacDonald Media.
McRaven, William H. Make Your Bed with Skipper the Seal. McWilliam, Howard, illus. 2021. (ENG.). 48p. (J). (gr. -1-3). 18.99 *(978-0-316-59235-2(8))* Little, Brown Bks. for Young Readers.
Me & Dog. 2014. (ENG., Illus.). 48p. (J). (gr. -1-3). 17.99 *(978-1-4424-9413-8(1),* Simon & Schuster Bks. For Young Readers) Simon & Schuster Bks. For Young Readers.
Meachen Rau, Dana. My Special Space. Kim, Julie J., illus. 2003. (Rookie Readers Ser.). 32p. (J). 19.50 *(978-0-516-22881-5(1),* Children's Pr.) Scholastic Library Publishing.
—Stickers, Shells, & Snowglobes. 2004. (Compass Point Early Reader Ser.). (J). 18.60 *(978-0-7565-0574-5(7),* Compass Point Bks.) Capstone.
Mead, David & Berry, Ron. Who's at the Door? 2010. (Illus.). 12p. (J). (gr. -1-1). 10.99 *(978-0-8249-1431-8(7),* Ideals Pubns.) Worthy Publishing.
Meade, Holly. If I Never Forever Endeavor. Meade, Holly, illus. 2011. (Illus.). 32p. (J). (gr. -1-3). 18.99 *(978-0-7636-4071-2(9))* Candlewick Pr.
Meadows, Michelle. Hibernation Station. Cyrus, Kurt, illus. 2010. (ENG.). 40p. (J). (gr. -1-3). 18.99 *(978-1-4169-3788-3(9),* Simon & Schuster Bks. For Young Readers) Simon & Schuster Bks. For Young Readers.
—Itsy-Bitsy Baby Mouse. Cordell, Matthew, illus. 2012. (ENG.). 40p. (J). (gr. -1-2). 15.99 *(978-1-4169-3786-9(2),* Simon & Schuster Bks. For Young Readers) Simon & Schuster Bks. For Young Readers.
—Piggies in the Kitchen. Hoyt, Ard, illus. 2011. (ENG.). 32p. (J). (gr. -1-2). 14.99 *(978-1-4169-3787-6(0),* Simon & Schuster Bks. For Young Readers) Simon & Schuster Bks. For Young Readers.
—Traffic Pups. Andreasen, Dan, illus. 2011. (ENG.). 32p. (J). (gr. -1-3). 15.99 *(978-1-4169-2485-2(X),* Simon & Schuster Bks. For Young Readers) Simon & Schuster Bks. For Young Readers.
Meghan, The Duchess of Sussex, The Duchess of Sussex. The Bench. Robinson, Christian, illus. 2021. (ENG.). 40p. (J). (gr. -1-2). 18.99 *(978-0-593-43451-2(X),* Random Hse. Bks. for Young Readers) Random Hse. Children's Bks.
Meister, Cari. I Love Trees. Sirrell, Terry, illus. 2011. (Rookie Ready to Learn Ser.). 40p. (J). pap. 5.95 *(978-0-531-26733-2(4),* Children's Pr.) Scholastic Library Publishing.
—Rookie Ready to Learn en Español: Me Fascinan Los árboles. Sirrell, Terry, illus. 2011. (Rookie Ready to Learn Español Ser.). Orig. Title: Rookie Ready to Learn: I Love Trees. (SPA.). 40p. (J). pap. 5.95 *(978-0-531-26786-8(5),* Children's Pr.) Scholastic Library Publishing.
—What Can I Be? Phillips, Matt, illus. 2003. (Rookie Readers Ser.). 24p. (J). 19.50 *(978-0-516-22876-1(5),* Children's Pr.) Scholastic Library Publishing.
Meister, Victoria Buhlig. Our Playtime Friend. 2011. 28p. 13.59 *(978-1-4567-2883-0(0))* AuthorHouse.
Melcher, Mary, illus. Puppies Count. 2010. (J). *(978-1-58865-596-7(2))* Kidsbooks, LLC.
Melmed, Laura Krauss. Before We Met. Tsong, Jing Jing, illus. 2016. (ENG.). 32p. (J). (gr. -1-3). 17.99 *(978-1-4424-4156-9(9),* Beach Lane Bks.) Beach Lane Bks.
—I Love You As Much... Board Book & Picture Frame. 2003. (Illus.). 22p. (J). (gr. -1-2). 12.99 *(978-0-06-008659-6(9),* HarperFestival) HarperCollins Pubs.
Meloy, Colin. Everyone's Awake: (Read-Aloud Bedtime Book, Goodnight Book for Kids) Harris, Shawn, illus. 2020. (ENG.). 48p. (J). (gr. k-3). 17.99 *(978-1-4521-7805-9(4))* Chronicle Bks. LLC.
Meltzer Kleinhenz, Sydnie. Work & Play. Reasor, Mick, illus. 2011. (Rookie Ready to Learn Ser.). (ENG.). 32p. (J). pap. 5.95 *(978-0-531-26829-2(2),* Children's Pr.) Scholastic Library Publishing.
Melvin, Alice. The High Street. 2011. (ENG., Illus.). 52p. (J). (gr. -1-3). 15.95 *(978-1-85437-943-6(7))* Tate Publishing, Ltd. GBR. Dist: Abrams, Inc.
Merberg, Julie & Bober, Suzanne. Dreaming with Rousseau. 2007. (Mini Masters Ser.: 10). (ENG., Illus.). 22p. (J). (gr. -1 — 1). bds. 6.99 *(978-0-8118-5712-3(3))* Chronicle Bks. LLC.
—Mini French Masters Boxed Set: 4 Board Books Inside! (Books for Learning Toddler, Language Baby Book), 1 vol. 2018. (Mini Masters Ser.: 11). (ENG., Illus.). 12p. (J). (gr. -1 — 1). 19.99 *(978-1-4521-7653-6(1))* Chronicle Bks. LLC.
—Mini Masters Boxed Set (Baby Board Book Collection, Learning to Read Books for Kids, Board Book Set for Kids), 1 vol. 2006. (Mini Masters Ser.: 7). (ENG., Illus.). (J). (gr. -1 — 1). bds. 19.99 *(978-0-8118-5518-1(X))* Chronicle Bks. LLC.
—Painting with Picasso. 2006. (Mini Masters Ser.: 6). (ENG., Illus.). 22p. (J). (gr. -1 — 1). bds. 7.99 *(978-0-8118-5505-1(8))* Chronicle Bks. LLC.
—Sunday with Seurat. 2005. (Mini Masters Ser.: 8). (ENG., Illus.). 16p. (J). (gr. -1 — 1). bds. 6.99 *(978-0-8118-4758-2(6))* Chronicle Bks. LLC.
Mercer, Graham. The Secret Cave. 2009. (ENG.). 52p. pap. 10.50 *(978-1-4092-9055-1(7))* Lulu Pr., Inc.
Mermelstein, Yael. A Car That Goes Far. Rosenfeld, Dina, ed. Romanenko, Vitaliy & Romanenko, Vasilisa, illus. 2009. (ENG.). 30p. (J). (gr. 1-3). 13.99 *(978-1-929628-47-6(1))* Hachai Publishing.
Merz, Jennifer. Playground Day. 2007. 32p. 16.00 *(978-978-061-896-4(1),* Clarion Bks.) HarperCollins Pubs.
Messinger, Midge. Freddie Q. Freckle. Messinger, Robert, ed. Ferraro-Oster, Margaret, illus. unabr. ed. 2003. 40p. (gr. -1-2). 12.95 *(978-1-893237-00-1(1))* Little Mai Pr.
Messinger, Robert. I've Got Mail! Salerno, John, illus. 2003. 40p. (J). 12.95 *(978-1-893237-01-8(X))* Little Mai Pr.
Metlen, Ryan W. & Metlen, Ryan. Ewe. 2009. (J). *(978-1-58768-054-0(8),* HiddenSpring) Paulist Pr.
Metz, Chrissy & Collins, Bradley. When I Talk to God, I Talk about You. Fields, Lisa, illus. 2023. 32p. (J). (gr. -1-3). 18.99 *(978-0-593-52524-1(8))* Flamingo Bks.
Metzger, Steve. Dancing Clock. Nez, John Abbott, illus. 2011. (ENG.). 32p. 12.95 *(978-1-58925-100-7(8));* (J). pap. 7.95 *(978-1-58925-429-9(5))* Tiger Tales.
—Five Little Bunnies Hopping on a Hill. 2006. (J). *(978-0-439-80382-3(9))* Scholastic, Inc.
—Five Spooky Ghosts Playing Tricks at School. Harrald-Pilz, Marilee, illus. 2005. (J). *(978-0-439-80381-6(0))* Scholastic, Inc.
—I Love You All Year Long. Keay, Claire, illus. 2009. 20p. (J). (gr. -1-k). 8.95 *(978-1-58925-847-1(9))* Tiger Tales.
—Ice Cream King. Downing, Julie, illus. 2011. (ENG.). 32p. (J). (gr. -1-2). 15.95 *(978-1-58925-096-3(6));* pap. 7.95 *(978-1-58925-427-5(9))* Tiger Tales.
—The Turkey Train. Paillot, Jim, illus. 2013. (ENG.). 32p. (J). (gr. -1-k). 6.99 *(978-0-545-49229-4(7),* Cartwheel Bks.) Scholastic, Inc.
—Under the Apple Tree. Girasole, Alessia, illus. 2009. (J). *(978-0-545-14200-7(8))* Scholastic, Inc.
—We're Going on a Leaf Hunt. Sakamoto, Miki, illus. 2008. (ENG.). 32p. (J). (gr. -1-3). pap. 7.99 *(978-0-439-87377-2(0),* Cartwheel Bks.) Scholastic, Inc.
Meyers, Susan. Everywhere Babies. frazee, Marla, illus. 2004. (ENG.). 30p. (J). (gr. -1-k). bds. 9.99 *(978-0-15-205315-4(8),* 1196012, Clarion Bks.) HarperCollins Pubs.
—Everywhere Babies Lap Board Book. Frazee, Marla, illus. 2011. (ENG.). 30p. (J). (gr. -1 — 1). bds. 12.99 *(978-0-547-51074-3(8),* 1443771, Clarion Bks.) HarperCollins Pubs.
—This Is the Way a Baby Rides. Nakata, Hiroe, illus. 2005. (ENG.). 40p. (J). (gr. -1-1). 15.95 *(978-0-8109-5763-3(9),* Abrams Bks. for Young Readers) Abrams, Inc.
Michaels, Andie. ACHOO! ACHOO! I've Got the Flu. (ENG.). (J). 2021. pap. 14.95 *(978-1-7330663-2-7(2))* 2019. 32p. 19.95 *(978-1-7330663-0-3(6))* Mulberry Street Publishing.
Michalak, Jamie. The Coziest Place. Davis, Jon, illus. 2013. (ENG.). 32p. (J). (gr. -1-k). 14.99 *(978-1-58925-121-2(0))* Tiger Tales.
Micklos, John, Jr. & Micklos, John. One Leaf, Two Leaves, Count with Me! McFarland, Clive, illus. 2017. 32p. (J). (— 1). 16.99 *(978-0-399-54471-2(2),* Nancy Paulsen Books) Penguin Young Readers Group.
Middleton Elya, Susan. Our Celebración!, 1 vol. Aranda, Ana., illus. 2018. (ENG.). 32p. (J). (gr. k-3). 18.95 *(978-1-62014-271-4(6),* leelowbooks) Lee & Low Bks., Inc.
Mike. New Pet. Mike, illus. l.t. ed. 2005. (ENG., Illus.). 32p. (J). lib. bdg. 14.95 *(978-0-9658365-8-6(4))* Beetle Bug Bks.
Milam, Mary Kay. The Zooming Star Babies. Date not set. (J). pap. *(978-1-890622-65-7(6))* Leathers Publishing.
Miles, David W. Donuts: The Hole Story. 2018. (ENG., Illus.). 32p. (J). (gr. -1-4). 16.99 *(978-1-945547-93-5(6),* 554793) Familius LLC.
Mileto, Richard. Superbird. 2005. per. 15.50 *(978-0-8059-9658-6(3))* Dorrance Publishing Co., Inc.
Milgrim, David. Poof! a Bot! 2019. (Ready-To-Read Ser.). (ENG.). 32p. (J). (gr. k-1). 13.89 *(978-1-64310-884-1(0))* Penworthy Co., LLC, The.
—Poof! a Bot! Ready-To-Read Ready-to-Go! Milgrim, David, illus. 2019. (Adventures of Zip Ser.). (ENG., Illus.). 32p. (J). (gr. -1-k). pap. 4.99 *(978-1-5344-1102-9(X))* Simon & Schuster, Inc.
—See Zip Zap. 2019. (Ready-To-Read Ser.). (ENG.). 32p. (J). (gr. k-1). 13.89 *(978-1-64310-886-5(7))* Penworthy Co., LLC, The.
—See Zip Zap: Ready-To-Read Ready-to-Go! Milgrim, David, illus. 2018. (Adventures of Zip Ser.). (ENG., Illus.). 32p. (J). (gr. -1-k). 17.99 *(978-1-5344-1100-5(3));* pap. 4.99 *(978-1-5344-1099-2(6))* Simon Spotlight. (Simon Spotlight).
Mill, Lynda. Let's Climb the Apple Tree. 2012. 44p. pap. 17.45 *(978-1-4669-6871-4(0))* Trafford Publishing.
Millen, C. M. The Ink Garden of Brother Theophane. Wisnewski, Andrea, illus. 2010. (ENG.). 32p. (J). (gr. k-3). 18.99 *(978-1-58089-179-0(9))* Charlesbridge Publishing, Inc.
Miller, Deborah U. & Ostrove, Karen. Fins & Scales: A Kosher Tale. Ostrove, Karen, illus. 2004. (Israel Ser.). (Illus.). 32p. (J). (gr. 1-3). pap. 4.95 *(978-0-929371-25-2(9),* Kar-Ben Publishing) Lerner Publishing Group.
Miller, Janet. DuckDumB. 2010. 32p. pap. 21.95 *(978-0-557-57669-2(5))* Lulu Pr., Inc.
Miller, Joanne Fairchild & Logsdon, Clara Isabel. What If It Were Possible. 2016. (ENG., Illus.). 44p. (J). pap. 9.95 *(978-1-63047-638-0(2))* Morgan James Publishing.
Miller, Jules, illus. Ellie & the Truth about the Tooth Fairy. 2014. (ENG.). 36p. (J). (gr. -1-k). 16.95 *(978-1-62873-590-1(2),* Sky Pony Pr.) Skyhorse Publishing Co., Inc.
Miller, Pam. Wrinkles. Ostrom, Bob, illus. (Rookie Reader Skill Set Ser.). (ENG.). 32p. (J). (gr. k-2). 2006. per. 4.95 *(978-0-516-25021-2(3))* 2005. lib. bdg. 19.50 *(978-0-516-24860-8(X))* Scholastic Library Publishing. (Children's Pr.).
Miller, Pat. We're Going on a Book Hunt. Bernard Westcott, Nadine, illus. 2008. (J). (gr. -1). 17.95 *(978-1-60213-034-0(5),* Upstart Bks.) Highsmith Inc.
Miller, Pat Zietlow. Sharing the Bread: An Old-Fashioned Thanksgiving Story. McElmurry, Jill, illus. 2015. (ENG.). 32p. (J). (gr. -1-3). 18.99 *(978-0-307-98182-0(7),* Schwartz & Wade Bks.) Random Hse. Children's Bks.
Milne, A. A. Winnie the Pooh & the Wrong Bees. Shepard, E. H., illus. 2016. (ENG.). 48p. (J). 9.99 *(978-1-4052-8132-4(4))* Farshore GBR. Dist: HarperCollins Pubs.
Minor, Florence. If You Were a Panda Bear. Minor, Wendell, illus. 2013. (ENG.). 32p. (J). (gr. -1-3). 17.99 *(978-0-06-195090-2(4),* Tegen, Katherine Bks) HarperCollins Pubs.
—If You Were a Penguin. Minor, Wendell, illus. 2008. (ENG.). 32p. (J). (gr. -1-2). 19.99 *(978-0-06-113097-7(4),* Tegen, Katherine Bks) HarperCollins Pubs.
Minor, Florence F. If You Were a Penguin. Minor, Wendell, illus. 2009. 32p. (J). (gr. -1-2). lib. bdg. 18.89 *(978-0-06-113098-4(2))* HarperCollins Pubs.
Minor, Wendell. My Farm Friends. Bodett, Tom, illus. 2012. 29.95 *(978-1-4301-1096-5(1))* Live Oak Media.
—My Farm Friends. Minor, Wendell, illus. 2013. (ENG., Illus.). 28p. (J). (gr. -1-k). bds. 8.99 *(978-0-399-25799-5(3),* Nancy Paulsen Books) Penguin Young Readers Group.
Mitchell, Colleen. A Dinosaur under My Bed. Daly, Karen Anne, illus. 2013. 24p. (J). pap. 7.49 *(978-0-9853600-2-3(X))* Thistlewood Publishing.
Mitchell, Hazel. 1, 2, 3 ... by the Sea. 2013. (ENG., Illus.). 36p. (J). (gr. k-3). pap. 18.69 *(978-1-935279-94-5(7))* Kane Miller.
Mitchell, Melanie, illus. Three Craws: A Lift-The-Flap Scottish Rhyme, 30 vols. 2018. (Scottish Rhymes Ser.). 12p. (J). 9.95 *(978-1-78250-511-2(3),* Kelpies) Floris Bks. GBR. Dist: Consortium Bk. Sales & Distribution.
Mitchell, Sheena. Out of the Ark. 2012. 48p. pap. 18.41 *(978-1-4669-1489-6(0))* Trafford Publishing.
Mitton, Tony. Snowy Bear. Brown, Alison, illus. (ENG.). (J). 2016. 26p. bds. 7.99 *(978-1-68119-084-6(2),* 900158411) 2015. 32p. (gr. -1-1). 16.99 *(978-1-61963-905-8(X),* 900151395) Bloomsbury Publishing USA. (Bloomsbury USA Childrens).
—The Somethingosaur. Ayto, Russell, illus. 2014. (ENG.). 32p. (J). 17.99 *(978-0-00-758395-9(8),* HarperCollins Children's Bks.) HarperCollins Pubs. Ltd. GBR. Dist: HarperCollins Pubs.
—Terrific Trains. 2017. (Amazing Machines Ser.). (ENG.). 20p. (J). bds. 6.99 *(978-0-7534-7372-6(0),* 900178406, Kingfisher) Roaring Brook Pr.
—Twist & Hop, Minibeast Bop! 2017. (ENG., Illus.). 32p. (J). (gr. -1-k). pap. 7.99 *(978-1-4083-3687-8(1),* Orchard Bks.) Hachette Children's Group GBR. Dist: Hachette Bk. Group.
Mitton, Tony & Parker, Ant. Dazzling Diggers. 2018. (Amazing Machines Ser.). (ENG.). 20p. (J). bds. 6.99 *(978-0-7534-7394-8(1),* 900183764, Kingfisher) Roaring Brook Pr.
—Super Submarines. (Amazing Machines Ser.). (ENG.). (J). 2018. 20p. bds. 6.99 *(978-0-7534-7417-4(4),* 900187134) 2014. (Illus.). 24p. (gr. -1-k). 5.99 *(978-0-7534-7208-8(2),* 900143121) Roaring Brook Pr. (Kingfisher).
—Super Submarines. 2014. (Amazing Machines Ser.). (J). lib. bdg. 16.00 *(978-0-606-36133-0(2))* Turtleback.
Mockford, Caroline & Blackstone, Stella. Cleo's Color Book. Mockford, Caroline, illus. 2007. (Cleo Ser.). (Illus.). 24p. (J). (gr. -1-k). bds. 6.99 *(978-1-84686-060-7(1))* Barefoot Bks., Inc.
Modan, Rutu. Eddie Spaghetti. 2019. (ENG., Illus.). 24p. (J). 12.99 *(978-1-68396-177-2(3),* 683177) Fantagraphics Bks.
Mogk, Matt. That's Not Your Mommy Anymore: A Zombie Tale. Mulford, Aja, illus. 2011. (ENG.). 32p. pap. 10.00 *(978-1-56975-926-4(X))* Ulysses Pr.
Mohler, Marie. Leonard's Song. 2008. 32p. 18.95 *(978-1-4357-1372-7(9))* Lulu Pr., Inc.
Molokie, Tom. Introducing Willy Mcspry. 2011. 36p. pap. 15.65 *(978-1-4634-3697-1(1))* AuthorHouse.
Moncure, Jane Belk. My Sound Parade. Thornburgh, Rebecca, illus. 2018. (Jane Belk Moncure's Sound Box Bks.). (ENG.). 32p. (J). (gr. -1-2). 35.64 *(978-1-5038-2303-7(2),* 212158) Child's World, Inc, The.
Monroe, Colleen. A Is for Ark: Noah's Journey. Monroe, Michael Glenn, illus. 2004. 38p. (gr. -1-1). pap. 17.95 *(978-0-9754942-0-2(1))* Storytime Pr., Inc.
—A Wish to Be a Christmas Tree. Monroe, Michael Glenn, illus. 2005. (Holiday Ser.). (ENG.). 20p. (J). (gr. -1-1). bds. 9.99 *(978-1-58536-269-1(7),* 202284) Sleeping Bear Pr.
Montag, Aileen. All I Ever Wanted to Be. 2012. 28p. pap. 24.95 *(978-1-4626-8832-6(2))* America Star Bks.
Montes, Marisa. Los Gatos Black on Halloween. 2011. (SPA.). (J). (gr. -1-3). 29.95 *(978-0-545-19701-4(5))* Weston Woods Studios, Inc.
Montgomery, Margaret, illus. The Adventures of Anna Banana Shoeshine: Anna Banana Takes a Bath. 2006. 40p. (J). *(978-1-930401-49-5(3))* Central Coast Bks./Pr.
Moore, Ann C. The Colors Join Hands for A Surprise. 2010. 24p. pap. 12.79 *(978-1-4520-7572-3(7))* AuthorHouse.
Moore, Clement C. Grumpy Santa. Spiridellis, Gregg & Spiridellis, Evan, illus. 2003. (ENG.). (J). *(978-0-439-53039-2(3),* Orchard Bks.) Scholastic, Inc.
Moore, Clement Clarke. The Night Before Christmas. Price, Margaret Evans, illus. 2004. (Children's Die-Cut Shape Book Ser.). (ENG.). 16p. (J). (gr. -1-3). 10.95 *(978-1-59583-009-8(X),* 9781595830098, Green Tiger Pr.) Laughing Elephant.
Moore, Clement Clarke & Goodrich, Carter. A Creature Was Stirring. Goodrich, Carter, illus. 2006. (ENG., Illus.). 40p. (J). (gr. -1-3). 18.99 *(978-0-689-86399-8(3),* Simon & Schuster Bks. For Young Readers) Simon & Schuster Bks. For Young Readers.
Moore, Johnny Ray. But Still, We Dream: (a novel in Verse), 1 vol. 2009. 60p. pap. 16.95 *(978-1-60813-491-5(1))* America Star Bks.
Moore, Katrina. One Hug. Woolf, Julia, illus. 2019. (ENG.). 32p. (J). (gr. -1 — 1). 14.99 *(978-0-06-284954-0(9),* Tegen, Katherine Bks) HarperCollins Pubs.
Moorthy, Anita. Monkey's Drum. Sarkar, Soumitro, illus. 2003. (ENG.). 24p. pap. 3.99 *(978-81-86211-15-1(2))* Penguin Publishing Group.
Moree, Katie. Jesse's Peekaboo Safari. 2008. 20p. pap. 24.95 *(978-1-60672-473-6(8))* America Star Bks.
Moreillon, Judi. Read to Me. Teis, Kyra, illus. 2003. 24p. (J). 6.95 *(978-1-932065-49-7(0),* 1-718-784-9112) Star Bright Bks., Inc.
—Read to Me: English, 1 vol. Teis, Kyra, illus. 2004. (ENG.). 32p. (J). (gr. -1). bds. 6.95 *(978-1-59572-014-6(6))* Star Bright Bks., Inc.
Morgan, Kerry. Smile Rhymes. 2011. (Illus.). 32p. (gr. 1-2). pap. 13.99 *(978-1-4567-6339-8(3))* AuthorHouse.
Morris, Ashara. Let's Find Lucy! 2008. (Illus.). 32p. pap. 17.95 *(978-1-4327-3221-9(8))* Outskirts Pr., Inc.
Morrison, Cathy. I Want a Pet. 2012. (ENG., Illus.). 32p. (J). *(978-1-58925-113-7(X))* Tiger Tales.
Morrison, Kevin. I Can Speak Bully. Kemble, Mai S., illus. 2009. 32p. (J). 14.95 *(978-0-8091-6744-9(1),* Ambassador Bks.) Paulist Pr.
Morrison, Toni & Morrison, Slade. Peeny Butter Fudge. Cepeda, Joe, illus. 2009. (ENG.). 32p. (J). (gr. -1-3). 19.99 *(978-1-4169-8332-3(5),* Simon & Schuster/Paula Wiseman Bks.) Simon & Schuster/Paula Wiseman Bks.
Morrow, Barbara Olenyik. Mr. Mosquito Put on His Tuxedo. Goembel, Ponder, illus. 2009. (ENG.). 32p. (J). (gr. -1-3). 16.95 *(978-0-8234-2072-8(8))* Holiday Hse., Inc.
Morrow, Tara Jaye. Just Mommy & Me. Bratun, Katy, illus. 2004. 32p. (J). 13.89 *(978-0-06-000725-6(7))* HarperCollins Pubs.
Mortensen, Lori. Cindy Moo. 2012. (ENG., Illus.). 32p. (J). (gr. -1-2). 16.99 *(978-0-06-204393-1(5),* HarperCollins) HarperCollins Pubs.
—Cowpoke Clyde Rides the Range. Austin, Michael Allen, illus. 2016. (ENG.). 32p. (J). (gr. -1-3). 16.99

(978-0-544-37030-2(9), 1596763, Clarion Bks.) HarperCollins Pubs.

Mortimer, Anne. Christmas Mouse: A Christmas Holiday Book for Kids. Mortimer, Anne, illus. 2013. (ENG., Illus.). 24p. (J). (gr. -1-3). 12.99 *(978-0-06-208928-1(5)*, Tegen, Katherine Bks) HarperCollins Pubs.

Morton, Jane & Dreier, Ted. Moozie's Cow Wisdom for Loving to the "Uddermost" Royse, Jane, illus. 2003. (J). pap. 4.95 *(978-0-9662268-3-6(6))* Children's Kindness Network.

Moses, Brian. The Frog Olympics. 2017. (ENG., Illus.). 32p. (J). (gr. -1-k). pap. 9.99 *(978-0-7502-9683-0(6)*, Wayland) Hachette Children's Group GBR. Dist: Hachette Bk. Group.

Moskowitz-Sweet, Gloria & Smith, Hope Anita. It Rained Warm Bread: Moishe Moskowitz's Story of Hope. Lyon, Lea, illus. 2019. (ENG.). 160p. (J). 16.99 *(978-1-250-16572-5(5)*, 900187113, Holt, Henry & Co. Bks. For Young Readers) Holt, Henry & Co.

Moss, Lloyd. Zin! Zin! Zin! A Violin. Priceman, Marjorie, illus. 2004. (gr. -1-3). 18.00 *(978-0-7569-1919-1(3))* Perfection Learning Corp.

—Zin! Zin! Zin! A Violin. Priceman, Marjorie, illus. 2005. (Stories to Go! Ser.). (ENG.). 32p. (J). (gr. -1-3). 4.99 *(978-1-4169-0838-8(2)*, Simon & Schuster/Paula Wiseman Bks.) Simon & Schuster/Paula Wiseman Bks.

Mother Goose Staff & Studio Mouse Staff. Let's Learn. 2011. (ENG.). 10p. (J). *(978-1-59069-898-3(3))* Studio Mouse LLC.

Mother Goose Staff & Studiomouse Staff. Let's Laugh. 2011. (ENG.). 10p. (J). *(978-1-59069-897-6(5))* Studio Mouse LLC.

Moulton, Mark K. A Royal Wedding. Good, Karen H., illus. 2007. (ENG.). 32p. (J). (gr. k-3). 14.99 *(978-0-8249-8677-3(6)*, Ideals Pubns.) Worthy Publishing.

Moulton, Mark Kimball. A Cricket's Carol. Blowers, Lisa, illus. 2004. 32p. (J). 14.95 *(978-0-8249-5488-8(2)*, Ideals Pubns.) Worthy Publishing.

—Everyday Angels. Winget, Susan, illus. 2003. (ENG.). 32p. (J). 14.95 *(978-0-8249-5479-6(3)*, Ideals Pubns.) Worthy Publishing.

—Miss Sadie Mcgee Who Lived in a Tree. Good, Karen H., illus. 2008. (ENG.). 32p. (J). (gr. k-3). 16.95 *(978-0-8249-5152-8(2)*, Ideals Pubns.) Worthy Publishing.

—One Enchanted Evening. Crouch, Karen Hillard, illus. 2003. 32p. (J). 14.95 *(978-0-8249-5480-2(7)*, Ideals Pubns.) Worthy Publishing.

—Reindeer Christmas. Good, Karen Hillard, illus. 2008. (ENG.). 40p. (J). (gr. -1-3). 15.99 *(978-1-4169-6108-6(9)*, Simon & Schuster/Paula Wiseman Bks.) Simon & Schuster/Paula Wiseman Bks.

—A Snowman Named Just Bob. Hillard Good, Karen, illus. 2006. (ENG.). 16p. (J). (gr. k-3). 14.95 *(978-0-8249-1707-4(3)*, Ideals Pubns.) Worthy Publishing.

—The Visit. Winget, Susan, tr. Winget, Susan, illus. 2003. (ENG.). 56p. (J). 14.95 *(978-0-8249-5859-6(4)*, Ideals Pubns.) Worthy Publishing.

—The Visit: The Origin of the Night Before Christmas (hc), 1 vol. Winget, Susan, illus. 2013. (ENG.). 56p. (gr. 3-6). 16.99 *(978-0-7643-4575-3(3)*, 4985) Schiffer Publishing, Ltd.

—The Visit: The Origin of the Night Before Christmas (pb), 1 vol. Winget, Susan, illus. 2019. (ENG.). 52p. (gr. 3-6). pap. 9.99 *(978-0-7643-5703-9(4)*, 16397) Schiffer Publishing, Ltd.

Moulton, Mark Kimball & Chalmers, Josh. Change the World Before Bedtime, 1 vol. Good, Karen, illus. 2012. (ENG.). 32p. (J). (gr. -1-3). 16.99 *(978-0-7643-4238-7(X)*, 4551) Schiffer Publishing, Ltd.

Mucha, Mark. Adventures with Edison & His Friends Vol. 1: "Crab in a Bucket" 2008. 58p. pap. 11.95 *(978-1-934449-29-5(6))* Legacy Publishing Services, Inc.

Muecke, Anne. The Dinosaurs' Night Before Christmas. Hale, Nathan, illus. 2008. (ENG.). 36p. (J). (gr. -1-3). 18.99 *(978-0-8118-6322-3(0))* Chronicle Bks. LLC.

Mueller, Kirk Jay. Harriet Can Carry It, 1 vol. Vonthron-Laver, Sarah, illus. 2014. (ENG.). 32p. (J). 16.99 *(978-1-59572-675-9(6))* Star Bright Bks., Inc.

Muldrow, Diane E. Where Do Giggles Come From? Kennedy, Anne, illus. 2011. (Little Golden Book Ser.). 24p. (J). (gr. -1-2). 5.99 *(978-0-375-86133-8(5)*, Golden Bks.) Random Hse. Children's Bks.

Mumford, Martha. Hop Little Bunnies. 2020. (Bunny Adventures Ser.). (ENG., Illus.). 24p. (J). 17.99 *(978-1-5476-0268-1(6)*, 900209360, Bloomsbury Children's Bks.) Bloomsbury Publishing USA.

Muñoz, Mercedes. Boogie the Booger. 2008. 20p. pap. 12.95 *(978-1-4327-2211-1(5))* Outskirts Pr., Inc.

Munshey, Sana. We're off to Make 'Umrah. 2011. (ENG., Illus.). 32p. (J). (gr. -1-k). 10.95 *(978-0-86037-458-9(0))* Kube Publishing Ltd. GBR. Dist: Consortium Bk. Sales & Distribution.

—We're off to Pray. Salem, Eman, illus. 2016. (ENG.). 32p. (J). (gr. -1). 10.95 *(978-0-86037-529-6(3))* Kube Publishing Ltd. GBR. Dist: Consortium Bk. Sales & Distribution.

Munton, Gill. Who Ate All the Lettuce? Top That Publishing Staff, ed. Elliott, Rebecca, illus. 2007. 12p. (gr. -1-k). bds. *(978-1-84666-177-8(3)*, Tide Mill Pr.) Top That! Publishing PLC.

Murakami, Jon & BeachHouse Publishing. Geckos Surf. 2007. (ENG.). 16p. (J). (gr. -1-5). bds. 7.95 *(978-1-933067-22-3(5))* Beachhouse Publishing, LLC.

Murguia, Bethanie Deeney. Cockatoo, Too. 2018. (ENG., Illus.). 32p. (J). (gr. -1-1). bds. 7.99 *(978-1-4998-0579-6(9))* Little Bee Books Inc.

Murphy, Patricia J. I Need You. Bryant, Laura J., illus. 2003. (Rookie Readers Ser.). 31p. (J). (gr. 1-2). 12.60 *(978-0-7569-2065-4(5))* Perfection Learning Corp.

Murray, Alison. Hickory Dickory Dog. Murray, Alison, illus. 2014. (ENG., Illus.). 32p. (J). (-k). 16.99 *(978-0-7636-6826-6(5))* Candlewick Pr.

—The House That Zack Built. Murray, Alison, illus. 2016. (ENG., Illus.). 32p. (J). (-k). 16.99 *(978-0-7636-7844-9(9))* Candlewick Pr.

Murray, Carol. Hurry Up! Garbot, Dave, illus. 2003. (Rookie Readers Ser.). (ENG.). 32p. (J). 19.50 *(978-0-516-22585-2(5)*, Children's Pr.) Scholastic Library Publishing.

Murray, Diana. City Shapes. Collier, Bryan, illus. 2016. (ENG.). 40p. (J). (gr. -1-3). 18.99 *(978-0-316-37092-9(4))* Little, Brown Bks. for Young Readers.

—Grimelda & the Spooktacular Pet Show. Ross, Heather, illus. 2017. (ENG.). 40p. (J). (gr. -1-3). 16.99 *(978-0-06-226449-7(4)*, Tegen, Katherine Bks) HarperCollins Pubs.

—Pizza Pig. 2019. (Step into Reading Ser.). (ENG.). 31p. (J). (gr. k-1). 14.96 *(978-0-87617-968-0(5))* Penworthy Co., LLC, The.

—Pizza Pig. 2018. (Step into Reading Ser.). (Illus.). 32p. (J). (gr. -1-1). pap. 5.99 *(978-1-5247-1334-8(1)*, Random Hse. Bks. for Young Readers) Random Hse. Children's Bks.

—Summer Color! Persico, Zoe, illus. 2018. (ENG.). 40p. (J). (gr. -1-3). 18.99 *(978-0-316-37094-3(0))* Little, Brown Bks. for Young Readers.

Murray, Laura. The Gingerbread Man & the Leprechaun Loose at School. Lowery, Mike, illus. 2018. (Gingerbread Man Is Loose Ser.: 5). 32p. (J). (-k). 18.99 *(978-1-101-99694-2(3)*, G.P. Putnam's Sons Books for Young Readers) Penguin Young Readers Group.

—The Gingerbread Man Loose at Christmas. Lowery, Mike, illus. 2015. (Gingerbread Man Is Loose Ser.: 3). 32p. (J). (gr. k-k). bds. 18.99 *(978-0-399-16866-6(4)*, G.P. Putnam's Sons Books for Young Readers) Penguin Young Readers Group.

—The Gingerbread Man Loose at the Zoo. Lowery, Mike, illus. 2016. (Gingerbread Man Is Loose Ser.: 4). 32p. (J). (gr. k-3). 18.99 *(978-0-399-16867-3(2)*, G.P. Putnam's Sons Books for Young Readers) Penguin Young Readers Group.

—The Gingerbread Man Loose in the School. Lowery, Mike, illus. 2011. (Gingerbread Man Is Loose Ser.: 1). 32p. (J). (gr. k-3). 18.99 *(978-0-399-25052-1(2)*, G.P. Putnam's Sons Books for Young Readers) Penguin Young Readers Group.

—The Gingerbread Man Loose on the Fire Truck. Lowery, Mike, illus. 2013. (Gingerbread Man Is Loose Ser.: 2). 32p. (J). (gr. k-3). 18.99 *(978-0-399-25779-7(9)*, G.P. Putnam's Sons Books for Young Readers) Penguin Young Readers Group.

Murray, Marjorie Dennis. Halloween Night. 2010. (ENG., Illus.). 40p. (J). (gr. k-4). 9.99 *(978-0-06-201293-7(2)*, Greenwillow Bks.) HarperCollins Pubs.

Murray, Tamsyn. Snug as a Bug. Abbot, Judi, illus. 2013. (ENG.). 32p. (J). *(978-0-85707-108-8(4))* Barnes & Noble, Inc.

—Snug as a Bug. Abbot, Judi, illus. 2014. (ENG.). 32p. (J). (gr. -1). pap. 8.99 *(978-0-85707-109-5(2))* Simon & Schuster, Ltd. GBR. Dist: Simon & Schuster, Inc.

—Snug As a Bug. Abbot, Judi & Gaviraghi, Giuditta, illus. 2013. (ENG.). 30p. (J). *(978-1-4351-4731-7(6))* Barnes & Noble, Inc.

Musical Robot. If You're a Robot & You Know It. Carter, David A., illus. 2015. (ENG.). 14p. (J). (gr. -1-k). 16.99 *(978-0-545-81980-0(6)*, Cartwheel Bks.) Scholastic, Inc.

Muten, Burleigh. Miss Emily. Phelan, Matt, illus. 2014. (ENG.). 144p. (J). (gr. 2-5). 15.99 *(978-0-7636-5734-5(4))* Candlewick Pr.

My Amazing Pet Snail. 2013. (Illus.). (J). *(978-1-4351-4755-3(3))* Barnes & Noble, Inc.

My Crazy Christmas Catastrophe Cat. 2003. (Illus.). 22p. (J). 9.95 *(978-0-9744751-1-0(4))* Timothy Lane Pr.

My First Book of Bedtime Stories. 2003. (J). 8.99 *(978-1-59384-013-6(6))* Parklane Publishing.

Myers, Lily. This Impossible Light. 2017. 352p. (YA). (gr. 7). 17.99 *(978-0-399-17372-1(2)*, Philomel Bks.) Penguin Young Readers Group.

Myers, Tim. Looking for Luna, 0 vols. Reed, Mike, illus. 2012. (ENG.). 32p. (J). (gr. -1-3). 17.99 *(978-0-7614-5564-6(7)*, 9780761455646, Two Lions) Amazon Publishing.

Myers, Walter Dean. Jazz. Myers, Christopher, illus. 2006. (ENG.). 48p. (J). (gr. 3-7). 18.95 *(978-0-8234-1545-8(7))* Holiday Hse., Inc.

—Street Love. (ENG.). 2007. 160p. (YA). (gr. 8-18). pap. 15.99 *(978-0-06-440732-8(2))* 2006. 144p. (J). (gr. 7-18). 15.99 *(978-0-06-028079-6(4))* HarperCollins Pubs. (Amistad).

Nagai, Mariko. Under the Broken Sky. 2019. (ENG., Illus.). 304p. (J). 17.99 *(978-1-250-15921-2(0)*, 900185614, Holt, Henry & Co. Bks. For Young Readers) Holt, Henry & Co.

Nagy, Jennifer. Goats in Coats. Broughton, Ilona & Szijgyarto, Cynthia, illus. 2009. 20p. pap. 12.99 *(978-1-4389-6586-4(9))* AuthorHouse.

Namm, Diane. Guess Who? Sheldon, David, illus. 2004. (My First Reader Ser.). (ENG.). 32p. (J). (gr. k-1). pap. 3.95 *(978-0-516-25503-3(7)*, Children's Pr.) Scholastic Library Publishing.

—Little Bear. McCue, Lisa, illus. 2003. (My First Reader Ser.). (ENG.). 32p. (J). 18.50 *(978-0-516-22931-7(1)*, Children's Pr.) Scholastic Library Publishing.

—My Best Friend. Gordon, Mike, illus. 2004. (My First Reader Ser.). (ENG.). 32p. (J). 18.50 *(978-0-516-24416-7(7)*, Children's Pr.) Scholastic Library Publishing.

—My Best Friend (My First Reader) Gordon, Mike, illus. 2004. (My First Reader (Reissue) Ser.). (ENG.). 32p. (J). (gr. k-1). pap. 3.95 *(978-0-516-25504-0(5)*, Children's Pr.) Scholastic Library Publishing.

—Pick a Pet. Suárez, Maribel, illus. 2004. (My First Reader Ser.). (ENG.). 32p. (J). 18.50 *(978-0-516-24417-4(5)*, Children's Pr.) Scholastic Library Publishing.

Nance, Andrew Jordan. The Barefoot King: A Story about Feeling Frustrated. Holden, Olivia, illus. 2020. 32p. (J). (gr. -1-3). 16.95 *(978-1-61180-748-6(4)*, Bala Kids) Shambhala Pubns., Inc.

Narita, Kate. 100 Bugs! A Counting Book. Kaufman, Suzanne, illus. 2018. (ENG.). 40p. (J). 18.99 *(978-0-374-30631-1(1)*, 900175254, Farrar, Straus & Giroux (BYR)) Farrar, Straus & Giroux.

Nash, Linda. The Legend of the Lilies. 2013. (ENG.). 64p. 17.95 *(978-1-4497-8378-5(3)*, 5d3e0210-d4ce-4bc0-8578-f73738bdba87, WestBow Pr.) Author Solutions, LLC.

Nash, Margaret. My Big, New Bed. Blake, Beccy, illus. 2008. (Tadpoles Ser.). (ENG.). 24p. (J). (gr. -1-2). lib. bdg. *(978-0-7787-3859-6(0))*; pap. *(978-0-7787-3890-9(6))* Crabtree Publishing Co.

Neal, Christopher Silas. Animal Shapes. 2018. (Christopher Silas Neal Ser.). (ENG., Illus.). 40p. (J). (gr. -1-1). bds. 12.99 *(978-1-4998-0534-5(9))* Little Bee Books Inc.

Nechaev, Michelle Wagner. The Hungry Farmer. 2017. (Learn-To-Read Ser.). (ENG., Illus.). (J). pap. 3.49 *(978-1-68310-283-0(5))* Pacific Learning, Inc.

Needham, T. L. Kitty Claus. 2012. (ENG.). 27p. (J). (-18). pap. 19.95 *(978-1-4787-1788-1(2))* Outskirts Pr., Inc.

Neff, Fred. The Memory Tree. Montmeat, Jack, illus. 2008. 36p. pap. 14.99 *(978-1-59858-854-5(0))* Dog Ear Publishing, LLC.

Negroni, Jay. Emerald's Flight, 1 vol. 2008. (ENG.). 29p. pap. 24.95 *(978-1-60672-863-5(6))* America Star Bks.

Neil, Jo. Harry & the Noise in the Night. 2018. (ENG., Illus.). 28p. (J). (gr. -1-3). *(978-1-5289-2385-9(5))*; pap. *(978-1-5289-2386-6(3))* Austin Macauley Pubs. Ltd.

—Harry & the Noise in the Night. 2017. (ENG.). 26p. (J). 19.95 *(978-1-78693-316-4(0)*, 9618181d-bd90-4649-802d-e0d55be7d93b); (Illus.). pap. 11.95 *(978-1-78693-315-7(2)*, a74743cb-1279-4f72-90a6-fcad09566801) Austin Macauley Pubs. Ltd. GBR. Dist: Baker & Taylor Publisher Services (BTPS).

Neimark, Jill. The Hugging Tree: A Story about Resilience. Wong, Nicole, illus. 2015. 32p. (J). *(978-1-4338-1907-0(4)*, Magination Pr.) American Psychological Assn.

Neitzel, Shirley. Who Will I Be? A Halloween Rebus Story. Parker, Nancy Winslow, illus. 2005. 32p. (J). lib. bdg. 13.89 *(978-0-06-056068-3(1))* HarperCollins Pubs.

Nellist, Glenys. 'Twas the Evening of Christmas, 1 vol. Selivanova, Elena, illus. 2017. ('Twas Ser.). (ENG.). 32p. (J). 17.99 *(978-0-310-74553-2(5))* Zonderkidz.

—The Wonder That Is You, 1 vol. Blanz, Aurélie, illus. (ENG.). (J). 2020. 28p. bds. 9.99 *(978-0-310-76659-9(1))* 2019. 32p. 17.99 *(978-0-310-76669-8(9))* Zonderkidz.

Nelsen, Sissy. Wiggly & Giggly. 2012. 24p. pap. 17.99 *(978-1-4772-6721-9(2))* AuthorHouse.

Nelson, Joanne. When It Snows. Moore, Cyd, illus. 2012. (Discovery Phonics Ser.). (ENG.). 16p. (J). (gr. -1-3). pap. 10.47 *(978-0-8136-1087-0(7))* Modern Curriculum Pr.

Nelson, Kadir. He's Got the Whole World in His Hands. Nelson, Kadir, illus. 2005. (Illus.). 32p. (J). (gr. -1-3). 18.99 *(978-0-8037-2850-9(6)*, Dial Bks) Penguin Young Readers Group.

Nelson-Schmidt, Michelle. Cats, Cats! 2011. (ENG., Illus.). 32p. (J). pap. 5.99 *(978-1-61067-042-5(6))* Kane Miller.

—Dogs, Dogs! 2011. (ENG., Illus.). 32p. (J). pap. 5.99 *(978-1-61067-041-8(8))* Kane Miller.

NeonSeon. Life of Shouty: Food & Fitness, bk. 2. NeonSeon, illus. 2011. (Life of Shouty Ser.: 2). (ENG., Illus.). 32p. (J). 14.95 *(978-0-9842069-1-9(4))* RIXKIN.

Nestling, Rose. Bedtime Songs. Rescek, Sanja, illus. 2016. (ENG.). 12p. (J). (gr. -1-2). bds. 19.99 *(978-1-68052-123-8(3)*, 1001160) Cottage Door Pr.

Nethaway, Misty. I Know My Mommy Loves Me. 2008. 17p. pap. 24.95 *(978-1-60672-475-0(4))* America Star Bks.

Neubecker, Robert. Fall Is for School. Neubecker, Robert, illus. 2017. (ENG., Illus.). 32p. (J). (gr. -1-k). 17.99 *(978-1-4847-3254-0(5))* Disney Pr.

Neutzling, Laura. Grandpa Hugs, 1 vol. 2017. (ENG., Illus.). 20p. (J). bds. 9.99 *(978-0-7180-8940-5(5)*, Tommy Nelson) Nelson, Thomas Inc.

Nevius, Carol. Building with Dad, 0 vols. Thomson, Bill, illus. 2012. (ENG.). 32p. (J). (gr. -1-2). pap. 9.99 *(978-0-7614-5984-2(7)*, 9780761459842, Two Lions) Amazon Publishing.

—Karate Hour, 0 vols. Thomson, Bill, illus. 2012. (ENG.). 34p. (J). (gr. -1-2). pap. 9.99 *(978-0-7614-5840-1(9)*, 9780761458401, Two Lions) Amazon Publishing.

New Burlington Books, creator. The Great Big Book of Bedtime Stories & Rhyme. 2008. (Illus.). 304p. (J). *(978-1-84538-882-9(8))* New Burlington Bks.

New Players Club LLC Staff, New Players Club L. L. C. Coco Boom Boom. 2006. 32p. 12.99 *(978-1-4116-8191-0(6))* Lulu Pr., Inc.

New, William. Sam Swallow & the Riddleworld League, 1 vol. Yayo, illus. 2013. (ENG.). 144p. (J). (gr. 4-7). pap. 12.95 *(978-1-896580-98-2(X))* Tradewind Bks. CAN. Dist: Orca Bk. Pubs. USA.

Newbery, Linda. Posy. Rayner, Catherine, illus. 2008. (ENG.). 32p. (J). (gr. -1-k). 16.99 *(978-1-4169-7112-2(2)*, Atheneum Bks. for Young Readers) Simon & Schuster Children's Publishing.

Newman, Jeff. Hand Book. Newman, Jeff, illus. 2011. (ENG., Illus.). 40p. (J). (gr. -1-3). 15.99 *(978-1-4169-5013-4(3)*, Simon & Schuster Bks. For Young Readers) Simon & Schuster Bks. For Young Readers.

Newman, Lesléa. Baby's Blessings. Nakata, Hiroe, illus. 2019. (ENG.). 12p. (J). (gr. -1 — 1). bds. 5.99 *(978-1-5415-2214-5(1)*, 040e002c-9875-486d-a397-f12d98022137, Kar-Ben Publishing) Lerner Publishing Group.

Newman, Leslea. The Boy Who Cried Fabulous. Ferguson, Peter, illus. 2007. 32p. (J). (gr. -1-2). pap. 7.99 *(978-1-58246-224-0(0)*, Tricycle Pr.) Random Hse. Children's Bks.

Newman, Lesléa. Cats, Cats, Cats! Oller, Erika, illus. 2004. (ENG.). 32p. (J). (gr. -1-3). reprint ed. 9.99 *(978-0-689-86697-5(6)*, Simon & Schuster Bks. For Young Readers) Simon & Schuster Bks. For Young Readers.

Newman, Leslea. Donovan's Big Day. Dutton, Mike, illus. 2011. (ENG.). 32p. (J). (gr. -1-2). 17.99 *(978-1-58246-332-2(8)*, Tricycle Pr.) Random Hse. Children's Bks.

Newman, Lesléa. Where Is Bear? Gorbachev, Valeri, illus. 2006. (ENG.). 44p. (J). (gr. -1 — 1). pap. 7.99 *(978-0-15-205918-7(0)*, 1197770, Clarion Bks.) HarperCollins Pubs.

Newman, Tracy. Around the Passover Table. Santos, Adriana, illus. 2019. (ENG.). 32p. (J). (gr. -1-3). 17.99 *(978-0-8075-0446-8(7)*, 807504467) Whitman, Albert & Co.

—Hanukkah Is Coming! Garofoli, Viviana, illus. 2015. (ENG.). 12p. (J). (gr. -1 — 1). bds. 7.99 *(978-1-4677-5241-1(X)*, 15bdd763-55c7-4cf0-8888-5b4bc3c0046a, Kar-Ben Publishing) Lerner Publishing Group.

—Havdalah Is Coming! Garofoli, Viviana, illus. 2020. (ENG.). 12p. (J). (gr. -1 — 1). bds. 6.99 *(978-1-5415-2163-6(3)*, 701faafe-bdd8-4b76-b195-9290a39c1d77, Kar-Ben Publishing) Lerner Publishing Group.

—Passover Is Coming! Garofoli, Viviana, illus. 2016. (ENG.). 12p. (J). (gr. -1 — 1). bds. 5.99 *(978-1-4677-5242-8(8)*, 6a3273e6-8c04-4222-8780-1c92ca1c3660); E-Book 23.99 *(978-1-4677-9610-1(7))* Lerner Publishing Group. (Kar-Ben Publishing).

—Purim Is Coming! Garofoli, Viviana, illus. 2017. (ENG.). 12p. (J). (gr. -1 — 1). bds. 7.99 *(978-1-5124-0827-0(1)*, 8ce8b152-c9bb-4654-b45e-04c5bd767de7, Kar-Ben Publishing) Lerner Publishing Group.

—Rosh Hashanah Is Coming! Garofoli, Viviana, illus. 2016. (ENG.). 12p. (J). (gr. -1 — 1). E-Book 23.99 *(978-1-5124-0945-1(6)*, Kar-Ben Publishing) Lerner Publishing Group.

—Simchat Torah Is Coming! Garofoli, Viviana, illus. 2018. (ENG.). 12p. (J). (gr. -1 — 1). bds. 5.99 *(978-1-5124-2100-2(6)*, 388c65f8-ce27-4342-bcf0-20442cb0c9cf, Kar-Ben Publishing) Lerner Publishing Group.

—Sukkot Is Coming! Garofoli, Viviana, illus. 2017. (ENG.). 12p. (J). (gr. -1 — 1). bds. 6.99 *(978-1-5124-0828-7(X)*, 25c6eda2-8813-43b2-8729-5b6ad881b52a, Kar-Ben Publishing) Lerner Publishing Group.

—Tu B'Shevat Is Coming! Garofoli, Viviana, illus. 2017. (ENG.). 12p. (J). (gr. -1 — 1). bds. 5.99 *(978-1-5124-2676-2(8)*, 5e159d59-3c9d-4741-825e-df72a2d6a00e, Kar-Ben Publishing) Lerner Publishing Group.

Ng, Yvonne. The Mighty Steam Engine. Smythe, Richard, illus. 2019. 32p. (J). (gr. 1-3). 17.99 *(978-1-68152-237-1(3)*, 10864) Amicus.

Nguyen, Vincent, illus. The Crabfish. 2010. (First Steps in Music Ser.). (ENG.). 24p. (J). (gr. -1-k). 17.95 *(978-1-57999-772-4(4))* G I A Pubns., Inc.

Nicholls, Paul, illus. I Want to Be A... Pirate. 2014. (J). *(978-1-4351-5500-8(9))* Barnes & Noble, Inc.

Nicola, Robbin. Fighter Joe: The Fish of Which Dreams Are Made. Wolf, Claudia, illus. 2006. 24p. (J). per. 2.99 *(978-1-59958-001-2(2))* Journey Stone Creations, LLC.

Niemann, Christoph. Subway. Niemann, Christoph, illus. 2010. (ENG., Illus.). 40p. (J). (gr. -1-k). 19.99 *(978-0-06-157779-6(0)*, Greenwillow Bks.) HarperCollins Pubs.

The Night Before Kindergarten. 2014. (Night Before Ser.). (ENG.). 32p. (J). (gr. 7-12). 8.24 *(978-1-63245-263-4(4))* Lectorum Pubns., Inc.

Nikola-Lisa, W. My Teacher Can Teach... Anyone! Galindo, Felipe, illus. 2004. (ENG.). 32p. (J). (gr. -1-2). 16.95 *(978-1-58430-163-9(5))*; pap. 11.95 *(978-1-60060-276-4(2)*, leelowbooks) Lee & Low Bks., Inc.

Nister, Ernest, illus. Merry Magic-Go-Round: An Antique Book of Changing Pictures. 2005. 14p. (J). (gr. k-4). reprint ed. 19.00 *(978-0-7567-9156-8(1))* DIANE Publishing Co.

Nobisso, Josephine. Hot Cha Cha! Holub, Joan, illus. 2009. (ENG.). 32p. (J). (gr. k-2). 16.95 *(978-0-940112-18-6(3))* Gingerbread Hse.

—The Numbers Dance: A Counting Comedy. Ziborova, Dasha, illus. 2005. (ENG.). 32p. (J). (gr. k-2). 16.95 *(978-0-940112-11-7(6))*; pap. 8.95 *(978-0-940112-12-4(4))* Gingerbread Hse.

Nolan, Allia Zobel. Animal Parade: A Lift-The-Flap Hear-the-Sound Book. Maddocks, Maria, illus. 2011. (ENG.). 10p. (J). (gr. -1 — 1). pap. 12.99 *(978-0-547-55867-7(8)*, 1453623, Clarion Bks.) HarperCollins Pubs.

—God's Oak Tree. Chung, Chi, illus. 2007. 16p. (J). (gr. -1). 12.99 *(978-0-8254-5536-0(7))* Kregel Pubns.

Noonan, Julia. My Pumpkin. Lawson, Peter, illus. 2005. (My First Reader Ser.). (ENG.). 32p. (J). (gr. k-1). lib. bdg. 18.50 *(978-0-516-24876-9(6)*, Children's Pr.) Scholastic Library Publishing.

Northcutt, Allen. The Legend of Chris Moose: The Most Beautiful Moose in the World. 2015. (ENG.). 48p. (J). 17.95 *(978-1-938462-01-6(7)*, ab80d21c-658f-46ea-8913-8c1c1da8f348) Old Stone Pr.

Novak, Matt. A Wish for You. Novak, Matt, illus. 2010. (Illus.). 32p. (J). 16.99 *(978-0-06-155202-1(X)*, Greenwillow Bks.) HarperCollins Pubs.

Noyes, Diana. The Tickle Bug. Noyes, Diana, illus. l.t. ed. 2005. (Illus.). 20p. (J). per. 9.99 *(978-1-59879-080-1(3))* Lifevest Publishing, Inc.

Numeroff, Laura Joffe. Dogs Don't Wear Sneakers. Mathieu, Joe, illus. 2014. 40p. pap. 8.00 *(978-1-61003-344-2(2))* Center for the Collaborative Classroom.

Nutt, Robert. Amy's Light. 2010. (Illus.). 44p. (J). (gr. -1-3). 16.95 *(978-1-58469-128-0(X))*; pap. 8.95 *(978-1-58469-129-7(8))* Sourcebooks, Inc. (Dawn Pubns.).

O'Brien, Anne Sibley & Gal, Susan. Abracadabra, It's Spring! 2016. (Seasonal Magic Ser.). (ENG., Illus.). 24p. (J). (gr. -1-k). 15.99 *(978-1-4197-1891-5(6)*, 1121301, Abrams Appleseed) Abrams, Inc.

Ocker, Christ Holder. A Mouse Without a House. 2006. (J). per. *(978-1-59872-711-1(7))* Instant Pub.

O'Connell, Jennifer Barrett. It's Halloween Night! 2012. lib. bdg. 17.20 *(978-0-606-26206-4(7))* Turtleback.

O'Connor, Frankie. The Ants Go Marching One by One. Paiva, Johannah Gilman, ed. Groot, Nicole, illus. 2014. (ENG.). 32p. (J). (gr. -1-3). 7.99 *(978-1-4867-0004-2(7))* Flowerpot Children's Pr. Inc. CAN. Dist: Cardinal Pubs. Group.

October the Octopus: A Huggable Concept Book about the Months of the Year. 2014. (ENG., Illus.). 28p. (J). (gr. -1-k). 24.99 *(978-1-4814-2047-1(X)*, Simon & Schuster/Paula Wiseman Bks.) Simon & Schuster/Paula Wiseman Bks.

Odanaka, Barbara. Construction Cat. Hanson, Sydney, illus. 2018. (ENG.). 40p. (J). (gr. -1-1). 17.99 *(978-1-4814-9094-8(X)*, McElderry, Margaret K. Bks.) McElderry, Margaret K. Bks.

—Smash! Mash! Crash! There Goes the Trash! Hillenbrand, Will, illus. 2006. (ENG.). 32p. (J). (gr. -1-3). 19.99 *(978-0-689-85160-5(X)*, McElderry, Margaret K. Bks.) McElderry, Margaret K. Bks.

O'Dare, Helen. Love. O'Byrne, Nicola, illus. 2016. (ENG.). 26p. (J). (gr. -1 — 1). bds. 6.99 *(978-1-62686-677-5(5)*, Silver Dolphin Bks.) Printers Row Publishing Group.

Ode, Eric. Bigfoot Does Not Like Birthday Parties. Temairik, Jaime, illus. 2015. 40p. (J). (gr. -1-3). 16.99 *(978-1-63217-004-0(3)*, Little Bigfoot) Sasquatch Bks.

—Too Many Tomatoes. Culotta, Kent, illus. 2016. (ENG.). 32p. (J). 11.99 *(978-1-61067-400-3(6))* Kane Miller.

Odhiambo, Tori. Close to Home: The African Savannah. 2012. 32p. pap. 21.99 *(978-1-4691-9510-0(0))* Xlibris Corp.

Odom, Leslie, Jr. & Robinson, Nicolette. I Love You More Than You'll Ever Know. Ruiz, Joy Hwang, illus. 2023. (ENG.). 32p. (J). 17.99 *(978-1-250-26564-7(9)*, 900222067) Feiwel & Friends.

S

O'donnell, Tamara J. Grand Mommy's Dress up Box. 2006. (J). (978-0-9790337-1-1(3)) Crosam Pr.

O'Garden, Irene. The Scrubbly-Bubbly Car Wash. Jabar, Cynthia, illus. 2003. (ENG.). 32p. (J). (gr. -1-1). 15.99 (978-0-694-00871-1(0)) HarperCollins Pubs.

O'Hair, Margaret. Twin to Twin. Courtin, Thierry, illus. 2003. (ENG.). 32p. (J). (gr. -1-3). 17.99 (978-0-689-84494-2(8), McElderry, Margaret K. Bks.) McElderry, Margaret K. Bks.

Ohanesian, Diane. The ABCs of Thanks & Please. Chamberlain, Margaret, illus. 2011. (J). (978-0-545-37962-5(8)) Scholastic, Inc.

—Hugga Bugga Love. Flint, Gillian, illus. (ENG.). (J). (gr. -1-k). 2018. 26p. bds. 7.99 (978-1-4998-0744-8(9)) 2017. 32p. 16.99 (978-1-4998-0395-2(8)) Little Bee Books Inc.

—Snuggle down Deep. Bornoff, Emily, illus. 2018. (ENG.). 32p. (J). (gr. -1-3). 16.99 (978-1-4998-0651-9(5)) Little Bee Books Inc.

Olin, Marilyn. Mom, Mac & Cheese, Please! Pantic, Dunja, illus. 2013. (ENG.). 28p. (J). (gr. -1-k). 16.95 (978-1-62087-995-5(6), 620995, Sky Pony Pr.) Skyhorse Publishing Co., Inc.

Oliver, Ilanit. Ten Flying Brooms. Poling, Kyle, illus. 2015. (ENG.). 24p. (J). (gr. -1-k). 4.99 (978-0-545-81336-5(0), Cartwheel Bks.) Scholastic, Inc.

Olsen, Bevan. Bethlehem's Star. 2008. 16p. pap. 2.99 (978-1-59955-181-4(0)) Cedar Fort, Inc./CFI Distribution.

—The Innkeeper's Christmas. 2010. (Illus.). 12p. (J). pap. 2.99 (978-1-59955-433-4(X)) Cedar Fort, Inc./CFI Distribution.

—The Magi. 2011. (Illus.). 12p. (J). pap. 2.99 (978-1-59955-924-7(2), Bonneville Bks.) Cedar Fort, Inc./CFI Distribution.

Olsen, Jan Z. Mat Man Hats. Delaney, Molly, illus. 2008. (ENG.). 36p. stu. ed. 13.75 (978-1-891627-93-4(7)) Handwriting Without Tears.

Olson, Julie, illus. Already Asleep. 2006. (ENG.). 32p. (J). (gr. -1-3). 12.95 (978-0-9766805-6-7(4)) Keene Publishing.

Olson, Nancy. Thanksgiving at Grandma's. Marino, Michael F., illus. 2009. 24p. pap. 10.95 (978-1-4251-8909-9(1)) Trafford Publishing.

One Big Pair of Underwear. 2014. (ENG., Illus.). 40p. (J). (gr. -1-3). 19.99 (978-1-4424-5336-4(2), Beach Lane Bks.) Beach Lane Bks.

Opie, David, illus. Monkey & the Engineer. 2007. 24p. (J). 14.95 (978-0-9793972-6-4(X)) JD Publishing.

Oppenheim, Joanne. El Principe No Duerme. Latimer, Miriam, illus. 2014. (SPA.). 32p. (J). (gr. -1-2). pap. 9.99 (978-1-78285-077-9(5)) Barefoot Bks., Inc.

Oppenheim, Joanne F. The Prince's Bedtime. Latimer, Miriam, illus. 32p. (J). (gr. -1-3). 2007. pap. 7.99 (978-1-84686-106-2(3)) 2006. (ENG.). 16.99 (978-1-84148-597-3(7)) Barefoot Bks., Inc.

Oppenheim, Joanne F. & Barefoot Books Staff. The Prince's Breakfast. Latimer, Miriam, illus. 2014. 32p. (J). (gr. -1-2). 16.99 (978-1-78285-074-8(0)); 9.99 (978-1-78285-075-5(9)) Barefoot Bks., Inc.

Oppenheim, Joanne F. & Latimer, Miriam. The Prince's Bedtime. Latimer, Miriam, illus. 2007. (Illus.). 32p. (J). (gr. -1-2). 9.99 (978-1-84686-096-6(2)) Barefoot Bks., Inc.

Oppenheim, Shulamith. Where Do I End & You Begin? Felix, Monique, illus. 2015. (ENG.). 32p. (J). (gr. 1-3). 17.99 (978-1-56846-274-5(3), 20831, Creative Editions) Creative Co., The.

Organ, Betty. Peter's Christmas Eve Adventure, 1 vol. Martin, Shawn, illus. 2010. (ENG.). 32p. (J). (gr. k-3). (978-1-897174-68-5(3)) Breakwater Bks., Ltd.

Orgel, Doris. Sarah's Room. Sendak, Maurice, illus. 2005. 47p. (J). (gr. k-4). reprint ed. 15.00 (978-0-7567-9683-9(0)) DIANE Publishing Co.

Ormerod, Jan. If You're Happy & You Know It! Gardiner, Lindsey, illus. 2003. 32p. (J). (gr. -1-3). 15.95 (978-1-932065-07-7(5)); pap. 5.95 (978-1-932065-10-7(5)) Star Bright Bks., Inc.

Orodan, Mike. Peek-A-Baby: Farm: Peekaboo Flaps Inside! 2019. (Peek-A-Baby Ser.). (ENG., Illus.). 14p. (J). (gr. -1 — 1). bds. 9.99 (978-1-4521-6645-2(5)) Chronicle Bks. LLC.

—Peek-A-Baby: Ocean: Peekaboo Flaps Inside! 2019. (Peek-A-Baby Ser.). (ENG., Illus.). 14p. (J). (gr. -1 — 1). bds. 9.99 (978-1-4521-6646-9(3)) Chronicle Bks. LLC.

Orshoski, Paul. We Both Read-My Sitter Is a T-Rex! (Level 1-2) Ebbeler, Jeffrey, illus. 2011. (ENG.). 44p. (J). 9.95 (978-1-60115-253-4(1)); pap. 5.99 (978-1-60115-254-1(X)) Treasure Bay, Inc.

—We Both Read-The Mouse in My House. Ebbeler, Jeffrey, illus. 2012. 44p. (J). pap. 5.99 (978-1-60115-258-9(2)) Treasure Bay, Inc.

—We Read Phonics-I Do Not Like Greens! Ebbeler, Jeffrey, illus. 2011. (We Read Phonics: Level 4 Ser.). (ENG.). 32p. (J). (gr. 1-3). 17.44 (978-1-60115-331-9(7)) Treasure Bay, Inc.

Orshoski, Paul & Max, Dave. We Both Read-The Ant & the Pancake. 2015. (ENG., Illus.). 44p. (J). (gr. k-1). pap. 5.99 (978-1-60115-272-5(8)) Treasure Bay, Inc.

Ortiz, Estrella. A Bailar: Let's Dance. Valdivia, Paloma, illus. 2015. (ENG & SPA.). (J). (978-0-545-85368-2(0)) Scholastic, Inc.

Osmond, Jimmy. Awesome Possum Family Band. 2014. (ENG., Illus.). 40p. (J). (gr. -1-3). 16.99 (978-1-62157-211-4(0), Regnery Kids) Regnery Publishing.

Oso Se Va de Viaje. 2014. (ENG & SPA., Illus.). (J). (978-1-78285-088-5(0)) Barefoot Bks., Inc.

Osteen, Victoria. Gifts from the Heart. Palmisciano, Diane, illus. 2010. (ENG.). 32p. (J). (gr. -1-2). 19.99 (978-1-4169-5551-1(8), Little Simon Inspirations) Little Simon Inspirations.

OSullivan, Michaeleen, tr. A Monarch Universe: Children's Picture Book. 2007. (Illus.). 34p. (J). pap. 22.95 (978-0-9800222-0-9(7)) UPfirst.com Bks.

O'Toole-Freel, Judy. Aardvark, Aardvark, How Do You Do!, 1 vol. 2008. (ENG.). 31p. 24.95 (978-1-4241-6618-3(7)) America Star Bks.

Ovadia, Ron. Hank. 2013. 30p. 16.95 (978-1-60844-834-0(7)) Dog Ear Publishing, LLC.

Overton, Kim G. Nathan & Father: A Walk of Wonder. 2017. (Illus.). 32p. (J). 17.95 (978-0-9980141-0-4(9)) Flying Wren Studio.

Owen, Karen. I Could Be- Barroux, illus. 2009. (J). (978-1-84686-289-2(2)) Barefoot Bks., Inc.

—I Could Be, You Could Be. Barroux, illus. (ENG.). 32p. (J). 2012. (gr. -1-1). pap. 9.99 (978-1-84686-763-7(0)) 2010. (gr. 1-3). 16.99 (978-1-84686-405-6(4)) Barefoot Bks., Inc.

Owen, Linda. Robin's Song, 1 vol. 2009. (ENG.). 28p. (J). pap. (978-1-85345-495-0(8)) Crusade for World Revival.

Owen, Lucy. Boo-A-Bog in the Park. 2016. (ENG., Illus.). 36p. (J). pap. 8.95 (978-1-78562-169-7(6)) Gomer Pr. GBR. Dist: Casemate Pubs. & Bk. Distributors, LLC.

Owens, Lucy. My Lime Green Butterfly. 2011. 40p. pap. 22.65 (978-1-4568-7103-1(X)) Xlibris Corp.

Pace, Anne Marie. Busy-Eyed Day. Preston-Gannon, Frann, illus. 2018. (ENG.). 32p. (J). (-3). 18.99 (978-1-4814-5903-7(1), Beach Lane Bks.) Beach Lane Bks.

—Sunny's Tow Truck Saves the Day! Lee, Christopher, illus. 2019. (ENG.). 24p. (J). (gr. -1-1). 14.99 (978-1-4197-3191-4(2), 1247701) Abrams, Inc.

Pace, Dianne. Odel's Diner. 2007. (J). per. 12.95 (978-0-89315-419-6(9)) Lambert Bk. Hse., Inc.

Packard, Mary. The New Baby. Haley, Amanda, illus. 2004. (My First Reader Ser.). (ENG.). 32p. (J). (gr. k-1). pap. 3.95 (978-0-516-25506-4(1), Children's Pr.) Scholastic Library Publishing.

—Same & Different: Comparison Rhymes, 1 vol. 2004. (Rhyme Time Learning Ser.). (ENG., Illus.). 16p. (gr. k-2). lib. bdg. 24.67 (978-0-8368-4097-1(6), f21f8b0f-ab70-4722-91e1-e392529d6e47) Stevens, Gareth Publishing LLLP.

Paley-Phillips, Giles. Superchimp. Newson, Karl, illus. 2016. (J). (978-1-4351-6574-8(8)) Barnes & Noble, Inc.

Palfreman-Bunker, Claire. Can Kittens Take a Catnap? Relf, Adam, illus. 2007. (J). pap. (978-0-545-02595-9(8)) Scholastic, Inc.

Paluch, Beily. Braid the Challah: A Playful Action Rhyme. Argoff, Patti, illus. 2014. (ENG.). 12p. (J). bds. 7.99 (978-1-929628-83-4(8)) Hachai Publishing.

Pandya, Mamata. The Hare Scare: Based on the Original Gujarati Story by Gijubhai Badheka. 2004. (Illus.). 24p. (J). (978-81-291-0441-0(5)) Rupa & Co.

Pankiw, Dr Mary & Pankiw, Mary. Misilla Mouse. 2011. 32p. pap. (978-1-4269-5476-4(X)) Trafford Publishing (UK) Ltd.

Pantin, Yolanda. Splash! Faria, Rosana, illus. 2003. (SPA.). 16p. (J). (gr. -1-1). (978-980-6437-19-7(5)) Playco Editores, C.A.

Paolilli, Paul & Brewer, Dan. Nightlights. Brereton, Alice, illus. 2017. (ENG.). 32p. (J). (gr. -1-3). 16.99 (978-0-8075-5622-1(X), 080755622X) Whitman, Albert & Co.

Paquette, Ammi-Joan. Ghost in the House. Record, Adam, illus. 2019. (ENG.). 32p. (J). (gr. -1-2). 5.99 (978-0-7636-9892-8(X)) Candlewick Pr.

Parachini, Jodie. Half a Giraffe? Smythe, Richard, illus. 2018. (ENG.). 32p. (J). (gr. -1-3). 16.99 (978-0-8075-3144-0(8), 807531448) Whitman, Albert & Co.

Paraskevas, Betty. Peter Pepper's Pet Spectacular. Paraskevas, Michael, illus. 2007. 32p. (J). (gr. 2-6). pap. 14.95 (978-1-60095-257-9(7)) Carson-Dellosa Publishing, LLC.

Parenteau, Shirley. Bears on Chairs. Walker, David M., illus. 2011. (Bears on Chairs Ser.). (ENG.). 32p. (J). (gr. -1 — 1). bds. 6.99 (978-0-7636-5092-6(7)) Candlewick Pr.

Park, Barbara. Ma! There's Nothing to Do Here! a Word from Your Baby-In-Waiting. Garofoli, Viviana, illus. 2008. (Picture Book Ser.). (ENG.). 40p. (J). (gr. -1-2). 15.99 (978-0-375-83852-1(X), Random Hse. Bks. for Young Readers) Random Hse. Children's Bks.

Park, Linda Sue. Bee-Bim Bop! Lee, Ho Baek, illus. (ENG.). 32p. (J). (gr. -1-3). 2008. pap. 7.99 (978-0-547-07671-3(1), 1042030) 2005. 17.99 (978-0-618-26511-4(2), 111270) HarperCollins Pubs. (Clarion Bks.).

—What Does Bunny See? A Book of Colors & Flowers. Smith, Maggie, illus. 2018. (ENG.). 32p. (J). (gr. -1-3). pap. 7.99 (978-1-328-88611-8(5), 1698480, Clarion Bks.) HarperCollins Pubs.

—Xander's Panda Party. Phelan, Matt, illus. (ENG.). 40p. (J). (gr. -1-3). 2017. pap. 8.99 (978-1-328-74058-8(7), 1677033) 2013. 16.99 (978-0-547-55865-3(1), 1453620) HarperCollins Pubs. (Clarion Bks.).

Parker, Amy. Night Night, Daddy, 1 vol. 2016. (Night Night Ser.). (ENG., Illus.). 20p. (J). bds. 9.99 (978-0-7180-4230-1(1), Tommy Nelson) Nelson, Thomas Inc.

—A Night Night Prayer, 1 vol. 2015. (Night Night Ser.). (ENG., Illus.). 24p. (J). pap. 3.99 (978-0-7180-3652-2(2), Tommy Nelson) Nelson, Thomas Inc.

—The Plans I Have for You, 1 vol. Brantley-Newton, Vanessa, illus. 2015. (ENG.). 32p. (J). 16.99 (978-0-310-72410-0(4)) Zonderkidz.

—This Is the Day! Hernandez, Leeza, illus. 2018. (ENG.). 32p. (J). (gr. -1-3). 16.99 (978-1-338-04703-5(5), Little Shepherd) Scholastic, Inc.

Parker, Emma. At the Circus. 2010. (Illus.). 20p. pap. (978-1-877561-52-8(5)) First Edition Ltd.

—Blah the Bacteria. 2010. (Illus.). pap. (978-1-877547-46-1(8)) First Edition Ltd.

—Dancing Class. 2010. (Illus.). pap. (978-1-877561-05-4(3)) First Edition Ltd.

—Davey Dory. 2010. (Illus.). 20p. pap. (978-1-877561-58-0(4)) First Edition Ltd.

—The Fluffiest Chicken. 2010. (Illus.). pap. (978-1-877561-13-9(4)) First Edition Ltd.

—Granny Odd Legs. 2010. (Illus.). pap. (978-1-877547-86-7(7)) First Edition Ltd.

—Groat & the Coat. 2010. (Illus.). pap. (978-1-877547-99-7(9)) First Edition Ltd.

—How Many Fish? 2010. (Illus.). pap. (978-1-877561-10-8(X)) First Edition Ltd.

—How Shall I Get to School Today? 2010. (Illus.). pap. (978-1-877547-84-3(0)) First Edition Ltd.

—Karaoke Colin. 2010. (Illus.). 20p. pap. (978-1-877561-34-4(7)) First Edition Ltd.

—The Magic Show. 2010. (Illus.). pap. (978-1-877561-23-8(1)) First Edition Ltd.

—The Magic Snow Globe. 2010. (Illus.). pap. (978-1-877561-30-6(4)) First Edition Ltd.

—Missy Hip Hoppo. 2010. (Illus.). 16p. pap. (978-1-877561-56-6(8)) First Edition Ltd.

—The Monkey in the Tree. 2010. (Illus.). pap. (978-1-877547-91-1(3)) First Edition Ltd.

—Mr Grumpy Bunny. 2010. (Illus.). pap. (978-1-877561-22-1(3)) First Edition Ltd.

—Pet Day. 2010. (Illus.). pap. (978-1-877561-28-3(2)) First Edition Ltd.

—Safari Adventure. 2010. (Illus.). pap. (978-1-877561-29-0(0)) First Edition Ltd.

—Sam the Traveling Snail. 2010. (Illus.). pap. (978-1-877561-19-1(3)) First Edition Ltd.

—Skipping Sally. 2010. (Illus.). pap. (978-1-877561-24-5(X)) First Edition Ltd.

—Snafu & the Shoes. 2010. (Illus.). pap. (978-1-877561-00-9(2)) First Edition Ltd.

—The Snowman Olympics. 2010. (Illus.). 20p. pap. (978-1-877561-36-8(3)) First Edition Ltd.

—Sooty the Stink Bomb. 2010. (Illus.). pap. (978-1-877561-15-3(0)) First Edition Ltd.

—The Space Rocket. 2010. (Illus.). pap. (978-1-877547-87-4(5)) First Edition Ltd.

—The Spaghetti Tree. 2010. (Illus.). pap. (978-1-877561-02-3(9)) First Edition Ltd.

—Splat & the Hat. 2010. (Illus.). pap. (978-1-877561-04-7(5)) First Edition Ltd.

—Summer Camp. 2010. (Illus.). pap. (978-1-877561-27-6(4)) First Edition Ltd.

—There's a Bear in My Bed. 2010. (Illus.). pap. (978-1-877547-97-3(2)) First Edition Ltd.

—The Wedding Day. 2010. (Illus.). 16p. pap. (978-1-877561-51-1(7)) First Edition Ltd.

—The Wickedest Witch. 2010. (Illus.). pap. (978-1-877561-17-7(7)) First Edition Ltd.

Parker, Emma & Renaud, Marguerite. Aliens from Zen. 2010. (Illus.). 16p. pap. (978-1-877561-79-5(7)) First Edition Ltd.

—Chatterbox Caz. 2010. (Illus.). 16p. pap. (978-1-877561-77-1(0)) First Edition Ltd.

Parker, Laurie. It Really Said Christmas. Parker, Laurie, illus. 2003. (Illus.). (J). (978-0-9729615-0-9(X)) Parker, Laurie.

Parker, Marjorie Blain. I Love You near & Far. Henry, Jed, illus. 2015. 24p. (J). (gr. -1-1). 9.95 (978-1-4549-0507-3(7)) Sterling Publishing Co., Inc.

—Psst! I Love You. Hanson, Sydney, illus. (Snuggle Time Stories Ser.: 7). (J). 2018. 22p. (— 1). bds. 8.95 (978-1-4549-2705-1(4)) 2017. (ENG.). 32p. (gr. -1-k). 9.95 (978-1-4549-1721-2(0)) Sterling Publishing Co., Inc.

Parkins, Rebecca Katherine. Lilly the Little Lava Mouse. 2009. 180p. pap. 43.49 (978-1-4389-4330-5(X)) AuthorHouse.

Parkinson, Helen. How Well Can Wombats Bat? 2012. 28p. pap. 32.70 (978-1-4797-2235-8(9)) Xlibris Corp.

Partheniou Grasso, Stella. Five Busy Beavers. Battuz, Christine, illus. 2018. (ENG.). 32p. (J). (gr. -1-2). 14.99 (978-1-5107-2145-6(2), Sky Pony Pr.) Skyhorse Publishing Co., Inc.

Pastor Wil. It's Good, Okay, & Alright, 1 vol. 2010. 28p. pap. 24.95 (978-1-4489-7065-0(2)) PublishAmerica, Inc.

A Path of Clouds: The Book off Rhymes. 2013. 50p. pap. (978-965-550-241-1(4)) Contento De Semrik.

Paul, Ann Whitford. If Animals Celebrated Christmas. Walker, David, illus. (If Animals Kissed Good Night Ser.). (ENG.). (J). 2019. 24p. bds. 7.99 (978-0-374-31308-1(3), 900209754) 2018. 32p. 16.99 (978-0-374-30901-5(9), 900188209) Farrar, Straus & Giroux. (Farrar, Straus & Giroux (BYR)).

—If Animals Kissed Good Night. Walker, David, illus. 2014. (If Animals Kissed Good Night Ser.). (ENG.). 34p. (J). (gr. -1-1). bds. 7.99 (978-0-374-30021-0(6), 900129088, Farrar, Straus & Giroux (BYR)) Farrar, Straus & Giroux.

—If Animals Said I Love You. Walker, David, illus. 2017. (If Animals Kissed Good Night Ser.). (ENG.). 32p. (J). 16.99 (978-0-374-30602-1(8), 900173498, Farrar, Straus & Giroux (BYR)) Farrar, Straus & Giroux.

—If Animals Went to School. Walker, David, illus. 2019. (If Animals Kissed Good Night Ser.). (ENG.). 32p. (J). 16.99 (978-0-374-30902-2(7), 900188210, Farrar, Straus & Giroux (BYR)) Farrar, Straus & Giroux.

Paul, Ruth. Stomp! 2013. pap. (978-0-545-52940-2(9)) Scholastic, Inc.

Paul, Ruth & Lombana, J. P. Stomp! ¡a Marchar! 2013. (SPA & ENG., Illus.). (978-0-545-52795-8(3)) Scholastic, Inc.

Pauline Wall & Shelley Smith. What the Owl Saw: (a Christmas Story) 2012. 20p. pap. 15.19 (978-1-4669-2813-8(1)) Trafford Publishing.

Paulus, Kristin Harkison. There's a Lion on the Dance Floor. 2010. (Illus.). 28p. pap. 12.98 (978-1-4490-2692-9(3)) AuthorHouse.

Paxton, Tom. The Marvelous Toy. Cox, Steve, illus. 2014. 22p. (J). (gr. -1-2). bds. 7.95 (978-1-62354-043-2(7)) Charlesbridge Publishing, Inc.

Pearson, Mary E. Fast Dan. Doty, Eldon, illus. 2003. (Rookie Reader Skill Set Ser.). (ENG.). 32p. (J). (gr. k-2). pap. 4.95 (978-0-516-27494-2(5), Children's Pr.) Scholastic Library Publishing.

—Generous Me. Krejca, Gary, illus. 2011. (Rookie Ready to Learn — All about Me! Ser.). 40p. (J). (gr. -1-k). lib. bdg. 25.00 (978-0-531-26427-0(0)); (ENG.). pap. 5.95 (978-0-531-26652-6(4)) Scholastic Library Publishing. (Children's Pr.).

—I Can Do It All. Shelley, Jeff, illus. 2011. (Rookie Ready to Learn - I Can! Ser.). 32p. (J). (gr. -1-k). lib. bdg. 23.00 (978-0-531-26429-4(7), Children's Pr.) Scholastic Library Publishing.

—Rookie Ready to Learn en Español: Puedo Hacer de Todo. Shelly, Jeff, illus. 2011. (Rookie Ready to Learn Español Ser.). Orig. Title: Rookie Ready to Learn: I Can Do It All. (SPA.). 40p. (J). pap. 5.95 (978-0-531-26787-5(3), Children's Pr.) Scholastic Library Publishing.

Pearson, Mary E. & Shelly, Jeff. Puedo Hacer de Todo. Shelly, Jeff, illus. 2011. (Rookie Ready to Learn Español Ser.).Tr. of I Can Do It All. (SPA., Illus.). 40p. (J). lib. bdg. 23.00 (978-0-531-26119-4(0), Children's Pr.) Scholastic Library Publishing.

Peck, Jan. Way down Deep in the Deep Blue Sea. 2004. (ENG., Illus.). 32p. (J). (gr. -1-3). 18.99 (978-0-689-85110-0(3), Simon & Schuster Bks. For Young Readers) Simon & Schuster Bks. For Young Readers.

—Way up High in a Tall Green Tree. Petrone, Valeria, illus. 2005. (ENG.). 32p. (J). (gr. -1-3). 18.99 (978-1-4169-0071-9(3), Simon & Schuster Bks. For Young Readers) Simon & Schuster Bks. For Young Readers.

Peck, Judith. The Bright Blue Button & the Button-Hole. Stasolla, Mario, illus. 2004. 28p. (J). 18.95 (978-0-9746119-5-2(6)) Imagination Arts Pubns.

Pedlar, David Stewart. The Emu Who Knew He Could Fly! 2013. 32p. pap. 16.95 (978-1-4525-7612-1(2), Balboa Pr.) Author Solutions, LLC.

Peet, Bill. The Caboose Who Got Loose Book & Cd, 1 vol. 2008. (ENG., Illus.). 48p. (J). (gr. -1-3). audio compact disk 10.99 (978-0-618-95979-2(3), 1021923, Clarion Bks.) HarperCollins Pubs.

Pelham, David. Sam's Sandwich. Pelham, David, illus. 2015. (ENG., Illus.). 24p. (J). (gr. -1-2). 14.99 (978-0-7636-7808-1(2)) Candlewick Pr.

Pence, Charlotte. Marlon Bundo's Day in the Life of the Vice President. Pence, Karen, illus. 2018. (ENG.). 40p. (J). (gr. -1-3). 18.99 (978-1-62157-776-8(7), Regnery Kids) Regnery Publishing.

Penecale Jr., Richard P. The Luckiest Frog. 2009. 33p. (J). pap. 24.95 (978-1-4327-3023-9(1)) Outskirts Pr., Inc.

Penfold, Alexandra. All Are Welcome. Kaufman, Suzanne, illus. 2018. (ENG.). 44p. (J). (gr. -1-3). 17.99 (978-0-525-57964-9(8), Knopf Bks. for Young Readers) Random Hse. Children's Bks.

—Food Truck Fest! Dutton, Mike, illus. 2018. (ENG.). 40p. (J). 19.99 (978-0-374-30318-1(5), 900154880, Farrar, Straus & Giroux (BYR)) Farrar, Straus & Giroux.

Penn, M. W. Sidney the Silly Who Only Eats 6. Tommer, Sarah, illus. 2007. 32p. (J). (978-0-9784047-2-7(6)) Pays et Terroirs.

Penna, Natalie. Sooty the Bear: Honey Bees. 2018. (ENG., Illus.). 25p. pap. 14.95 (978-1-78823-719-2(6), 8433f32a-d76d-4edb-b813-e809bc5a01ba) Austin Macauley Pubs. Ltd. GBR. Dist: Baker & Taylor Publisher Services (BTPS).

Pepin, Rebecca. Bobby Dog & the Flying Frog. Fuller, Cari, illus. 2004. (J). (gr. 4-18). 16.99 (978-0-9760684-0-2(0)); pap. 11.99 (978-0-9760684-1-9(9)) FulloffPep Pubns.

Pepper, Lily. In the Garden at Granddad's. 2012. (Illus.). 24p. pap. 19.82 (978-1-4772-2642-1(7)) AuthorHouse.

Pereira, Chritine M. Madilynn Rose Rhyming Fairy: Volume 1, 1 vol. 2010. 44p. pap. 24.95 (978-1-61546-591-0(X)) PublishAmerica, Inc.

Perez, Irene. Rain or Shine. 2008. 16p. pap. 12.50 (978-1-4389-0873-1(3)) AuthorHouse.

Pérez-Mercado, Mary Margaret. Splat! Torrey, Rich, illus. 2011. (Rookie Ready to Learn Ser.). 40p. (J). pap. 5.95 (978-0-531-26678-6(8)); (gr. -1-k). lib. bdg. 23.00 (978-0-531-26373-0(8)) Scholastic Library Publishing. (Children's Pr.).

Perez, Olga. Sitting on Cloud 9 at the 50-Yard Line. 2012. (Illus.). 28p. pap. 19.99 (978-1-4772-9225-9(X)) AuthorHouse.

Perkins, Al. The Ear Book. Payne, Henry, illus. 2007. (Bright & Early Books(R) Ser.). 36p. (J). (gr. k-k). 9.99 (978-0-375-84251-1(9), Random Hse. Bks. for Young Readers) Random Hse. Children's Bks.

Perlman, Willa. Good Night, World. Fisher, Carolyn, illus. 2011. (ENG.). 40p. (J). (gr. -1-k). 16.99 (978-1-4424-0197-6(4), Beach Lane Bks.) Beach Lane Bks.

—Good Night, World. Fisher, Carolyn, illus. 2019. (Classic Board Bks.). (ENG.). 40p. (J). (gr. -1 — 1). bds. 8.99 (978-1-5344-4384-6(3), Little Simon) Little Simon.

Perry, Andrea. The Bickleby's' Birdbath. Angaramo, Roberta, illus. 2010. (ENG.). 40p. (J). (gr. -1-1). 19.99 (978-1-4169-0624-7(X), Atheneum Bks. for Young Readers) Simon & Schuster Children's Publishing.

Perry, Laurie. Brown Bear, 1 vol. Mackay, Hugh, illus. 2010. 22p. pap. 24.95 (978-1-4489-5702-6(8)) PublishAmerica, Inc.

Perry, Rex, illus. All Things Bright & Beautiful. 2004. 24p. (J). lib. bdg. 8.00 (978-1-4242-0638-4(3)) Fitzgerald Bks.

Perry, Robert. The Ferryboat Ride. Guzek, Greta, illus. 2017. (ENG.). 20p. (J). bds. 9.95 (978-0-88971-340-6(5), 8cdb6fe9-780a-47da-970b-f97975872ddb) Nightwood Editions CAN. Dist: Harbour Publishing Co., Ltd.

Pesca, Jodi. Angels Angels Everywhere. 2013. 20p. pap. 24.95 (978-1-63000-001-1(9)) America Star Bks.

Pesenti, Antonia. Rhyme Flies. 2018. (ENG., Illus.). 40p. (gr. -1 — 1). bds. 14.95 (978-0-7148-7639-9(9)) Phaidon Pr., Inc.

Peter, Paul & Eagle, Kim. It's Raining, It's Pouring. Davenier, Christine & Gilbert, Rob, illus. 2012. 32p. (J). (-k). 17.95 (978-1-936140-77-0(2)) Charlesbridge Publishing, Inc.

Peterson, M. S. Natasha Celeste. Polar Bear Pete's Perfect Performance. Majumder, Ankur & Soni, M. S. Ruhi, illus. 2017. (ENG.). 28p. (J). pap. (978-0-9952330-3-4(9)) Peterson, Natasha.

Petty, Dini. The Queen, the Bear & the Bumblebee. Cowles, Rose, illus. 32p. (J). 19.95 (978-1-55285-151-7(6)) Whitecap Bks., Ltd. CAN. Dist: Graphic Arts Ctr. Publishing Co.

Pfeiffer, Kathleen. Spartacus Sprout, Please Watch Out! 2011. (ENG.). 31p. 15.99 (978-1-257-50163-2(1)) Lulu Pr., Inc.

Pfister, Marcus. Questions, Questions. 2011. (ENG., Illus.). 32p. (J). (gr. -1-2). 18.95 (978-0-7358-4000-3(8)) North-South Bks., Inc.

Pfundstein, Valerie. Veterans: Heroes in Our Neighborhood. Chernesky, Felicia, ed. Anderson, Aaron, illus. 2012. (ENG.). 32p. (J). 18.95 (978-0-9837186-1-1(X)) Novanglus Publishing, LLC.

Pham, LeUyen. Big Sister, Little Sister. Pham, LeUyen, illus. 2005. (ENG., Illus.). 40p. (J). (gr. -1-3). 17.99 (978-0-7868-5182-9(1)) Little, Brown Bks. for Young Readers.

Phelan, Anne. Skydive to Hive. Rottinger, Amy, illus. 2012. 24p. pap. 11.95 (978-1-61244-098-9(3)) Halo Publishing International.

Phifer, Larry. World on a String. 2013. (ENG.). 17.95 (978-0-9886984-0-6(4)) Storytime Works.

Philips, Lyn D. Curiosity. Gadesell, Natalie, illus. 2013. 32p. pap. (978-1-904928-27-0(7)) Copeland & Wickson.

Phillips, Dee. What Can I Be? 2010. (Look at Me! Ser.). (ENG.). 5p. (J). (gr. -1-k). bds. 6.95 (978-1-84696-199-1(8), TickTock Books) Octopus Publishing Group GBR. Dist: Independent Pubs. Group.

Phillips, Dixie & Snider, K. C. Stilts the Stork. 2011. 20p. pap. 10.95 *(978-1-61633-143-6(7))* Guardian Angel Publishing, Inc.
Phillips, Jan. Just for Today. Shapiro, Alison Bonds, illus. 2005. (ENG.). 32p. (J). (gr. -1-5). 15.95 *(978-1-932073-07-2(8))* Kramer, H.J. Inc.
Phillips, Jean. The Meaning of Christmas: A Children's Story in Picture & Verse. 2005. (ENG., Illus.). 24p. pap. 7.95 *(978-0-929292-67-0(7),* 800-747-0738) Creative Properties LLC.
Phillips, Leigh Hope. Birthday Wishes. Fountain, John, illus. 2005. (J). pap. *(978-1-933156-10-4(4));* per. *(978-1-933156-03-3(1))* GSVQ Publishing. (VisionQuest Kids).
Phillips, Terrie. The Ski Trip. 2006. (Illus.). 38p. (J). lib. bdg. 12.95 *(978-0-9789449-0-2(9))* Tbooks Publishing Co.
Phyllarry (Rittmueller), Kathryn. Beauregart the Bear. 2009. (ENG., Illus.). 64p. (J). 12.95 *(978-0-943972-80-0(9))* Homestead Publishing.
Piantedosi, John J. The Cat That Purred. Maglio-Macullar, Andrea, illus. 2014. (ENG.). (J). pap. 11.95 *(978-1-56548-540-2(8))* New City Press of the Focolare.
Picayo, Mario. Fun, Fun, One Crab on the Run. Byer, Stacey, illus. 2012. (J). *(978-1-934370-27-8(4))* Editorial Campana.
—Giraffe Hears the Drum. Alfonso, Anabel, illus. 2018. (J). pap. *(978-1-934370-75-9(4))* Editorial Campana.
Pick Me up, Mama! 2014. (ENG., Illus.). 34p. (J). (gr. -1-k). bds. 6.99 *(978-1-4814-1633-7(2),* Little Simon) Little Simon.
Pierce, Craig. A Greyhound's Tale: Running for Glory, Walking for Home. Santiago, Tony, illus. 2004. (J). per. 15.00 *(978-0-9762564-0-3(1),* American Dog) Ideate Prairie.
Pierce, Terry. Jack & Jill & T-Ball Bill. 2019. (Step into Reading Ser.). (ENG.). 32p. (J). (gr. k-1). 14.96 *(978-0-87617-966-6(9))* Penworthy Co., LLC, The.
—Jack & Jill & T-Ball Bill. DiCicco, Sue, illus. 2018. (Step into Reading Ser.). 32p. (J). (gr. -1-1). pap. 4.99 *(978-1-5247-1413-0(5),* Random Hse. Bks. for Young Readers) Random Hse. Children's Bks.
—Mama Loves You So. Shin, Simone, illus. 2017. (New Books for Newborns Ser.). (ENG.). 16p. (J). (gr. -1 — 1). bds. 7.99 *(978-1-4814-8159-5(2),* Little Simon) Little Simon.
—Soccer Time! McMahon, Bob, illus. 2019. (Step into Reading Ser.). 32p. (J). (gr. -1-1). pap. 5.99 *(978-0-525-58203-8(7),* Random Hse. Bks. for Young Readers) Random Hse. Children's Bks.
—Tae Kwon Do! Bonita, Todd, illus. 2006. (Step into Reading: Step 1 Ser.). (ENG.). 32p. (J). (gr. -1-1). lib. bdg. 16.19 *(978-0-375-93448-3(0))* Random House Publishing Group.
—Tae Kwon Do! Bonita, Todd, illus. 2006. (Step into Reading Ser.). 32p. (J). (gr. -1-1). per. 5.99 *(978-0-375-83448-6(6),* Random Hse. Bks. for Young Readers) Random Hse. Children's Bks.
Piernas-Davenport, Gail. Shante Keys & the New Year's Peas. Eldridge, Marion, illus. 2017. (ENG.). 32p. (J). (gr. -1-3). pap. 8.99 *(978-0-8075-7331-0(0),* 807573310) Whitman, Albert & Co.
Pinczes, Elinor J. Inchworm & a Half. Enos, Randall, illus. 2003. (ENG.). 32p. (J). pap. 7.99 *(978-0-618-31101-9(7),* 493403, Clarion Bks.) HarperCollins Pubs.
Pinder, Eric. Counting Dinos. Bianda, Junissa, illus. 2018. (ENG.). 32p. (J). (gr. -1-3). 16.99 *(978-0-8075-1281-4(8),* 807512818) Whitman, Albert & Co.
—I'd Rather Be Riding My Bike. Cardinal, John, illus. l.t. ed. 2013. 42p. (gr. k-1). pap. 10.95 *(978-1-62253-401-2(8))* Evolved Publishing.
Pingry, Patricia A. Noses & Toes. Rose, Drew, illus. 2005. (J). *(978-0-8249-6594-5(9),* Ideals Pubns.) Worthy Publishing.
—Sounds. Rose, Drew, illus. 2005. (J). *(978-0-8249-6596-9(5),* Ideals Pubns.) Worthy Publishing.
Pinkney, Andrea Davis. The Red Pencil. Evans, Shane W., illus. 2014. (ENG.). 336p. (J). (gr. 4-17). 34.99 *(978-0-316-24780-1(4))* Little, Brown Bks. for Young Readers.
Pitman, Gayle E. A Church for All. Fournier, Laure, illus. 2018. (ENG.). 32p. (J). (gr. -1-3). 16.99 *(978-0-8075-1179-4(X),* 080751179X) Whitman, Albert & Co.
—This Day in June. Litten, Kristyna, illus. 2013. 32p. (J). *(978-1-4338-1658-1(X));* pap. *(978-1-4338-1659-8(8))* American Psychological Assn. (Magination Pr.).
Plawner, Michael A. Then & Now. 2009. 60p. pap. 10.99 *(978-0-557-08595-8(0))* Lulu Pr., Inc.
Plourde, Lynn. Only Cows Allowed!, 1 vol. Sollers, Jim & Reed, Rebecca Harrison, illus. 2011. (ENG.). 32p. (J). (gr. -1-12). 19.95 *(978-0-89272-790-2(X))* Down East Bks.
Plourde, Paulette. My Magic Pillow. 2005. (Illus.). 40p. (J). per. 8.99 *(978-1-932338-76-8(4))* Lifevest Publishing, Inc.
Plunkett, Windyann. Fiddle Me a Riddle & Bring Me the Moon. Davidson, Mary, illus. 2011. 24p. pap. 24.95 *(978-1-4626-3920-5(8))* America Star Bks.
Poer, Karla R. The Busy-Body Book of Fun-Atomy Tunes. 2008. (ENG.). 56p. pap. 21.99 *(978-1-4389-3296-5(0))* AuthorHouse.
Polacco, Patricia. G Is for Goat. Polacco, Patricia, illus. 2006. (Illus.). 32p. (J). (gr. -1-k). reprint ed. pap. 7.99 *(978-0-14-240550-5(7),* Puffin Books) Penguin Young Readers Group.
Polette, Nancy. Flying with Mother Goose. 2003. pap. 7.95 *(978-1-931334-19-8(6),* CLC0285) Pieces of Learning.
Pollock, Hal. Monster at the Bat. 2009. (ENG., Illus.). 28p. (J). (gr. 4-7). pap. 15.95 *(978-1-59687-884-6(3))* IBks., Inc.
Poltarnees, Welleran, ed. The Big Book of Christmas. 2013. (Children's Die-Cut Shape Book Ser.). (ENG., Illus.). 96p. (J). 12.95 *(978-1-59583-626-7(8))* Laughing Elephant.
Poole, Bud. Little Miss Muffet Gets Saved: A Christian Nursery Rhyme. 2012. 20p. pap. 7.95 *(978-1-4497-4170-9(3),* WestBow Pr.) Author Solutions, LLC.
Porter, Annaliese & Bancroft, Bronwyn. The Outback. 2005. (Illus.). 28p. (J). *(978-1-875641-86-4(6))* Magabala Bks.
Porter, Pamela. Yellow Moon, Apple Moon, 1 vol. James, Matt, illus. 2008. (ENG.). 32p. (J). (gr. k — 1). 17.95 *(978-0-88899-809-5(0))* Groundwood Bks. CAN. Dist: Publishers Group West (PGW).
Postgate, Daniel. Love Stinks. 2012. (J). *(978-1-61913-132-3(3))* Weigl Pubs., Inc.
Potter, Beatrix. Tickle, Tickle, Peter! A First Touch-And-Feel Book. 2012. (Peter Rabbit Ser.). (ENG.). 10p. (J). (gr. -1 — 1). bds. 9.99 *(978-0-7232-6750-8(2),* Warne) Penguin Young Readers Group.
Poulin, Ashley, illus. Risseldy, Rosseldy. 2012. (First Steps in Music Ser.). 32p. (J). (gr. k-2). 17.95 *(978-1-57999-902-5(6))* G I A Pubns., Inc.
Powell, Amy. Hope Music. Farley, Katherine, illus. 2006. 32p. (J). (gr. -1-3). per. 12.00 *(978-0-9773608-4-0(9))* Shiny Red Ball Publishing.
Prap, Lila. Daddies. 2018. (ENG., Illus.). 32p. (J). (gr. -1-k). 14.95 *(978-0-2281-0121-5(2),* a1236c95-c916-4796-b234-a38fdcf4d51a); pap. 6.95 *(978-0-2281-0166-6(2),* 87bb4328-34fe-4c2f-99b2-89d962010ec6) Firefly Bks., Ltd.
Prasadam-Halls, Smriti. I'll Never Let You Go. Brown, Alison, illus. 2015. (ENG.). 32p. (J). 16.99 *(978-1-61963-922-5(X),* 900152078, Bloomsbury USA Childrens) Bloomsbury Publishing USA.
—T. Veg: The Story of a Carrot-Crunching Dinosaur. Manolessou, Katherina, illus. 2017. (ENG.). 30p. (J). (gr. -1-3). 16.95 *(978-1-4197-2494-7(0),* 1180901, Abrams Bks. for Young Readers) Abrams, Inc.
—You Make Me Happy. 2019. (ENG., Illus.). 32p. (J). 17.99 *(978-1-68119-849-1(5),* 900189373, Bloomsbury Children's Bks.) Bloomsbury Publishing USA.
Precious Moments: Happy Harvest, 1 vol. 2016. (Precious Moments Ser.). (ENG., Illus.). 32p. (J). bds. 9.99 *(978-0-7180-3241-8(1),* Tommy Nelson) Nelson, Thomas Inc.
Prendergast, Gabrielle. Audacious, 1 vol. 2015. (ENG.). 336p. (YA). (gr. 8-12). pap. 12.95 *(978-1-4598-0264-3(0))* Orca Bk. Pubs. USA.
—Capricious, 1 vol. 2014. (ENG.). 352p. (YA). (gr. 8-12). 19.95 *(978-1-4598-0267-4(5))* Orca Bk. Pubs. USA.
Prescott, Brian. Chloe Knows Her Alphabet. 2013. 20p. pap. *(978-1-909192-51-5(1))* Beaten Track Publishing.
Press, Judy. Bubbe's Got the Beat. Hall, Mary, illus. 2017. (ENG.). 12p. (J). (gr. -1 — 1). bds. 5.99 *(978-1-5124-4763-7(3),* d4146f28-8c83-4401-8ded-078b05583b54, Kar-Ben Publishing) Lerner Publishing Group.
Price, Mary Elizabeth. Wallbaby Bumblebees. 2004. (Illus.). 40p. (J). per. 15.75 *(978-0-9715402-2-4(5),* 410-707-6686) Barnhardt & Ashe Publishing, Inc.
Price, Olivia. All Aboard Noah's Ark: A Touch & Feel Book. Mitchell, Melanie, illus. 2008. (ENG.). 12p. (J). (gr. -1). 12.95 *(978-1-58117-778-7(X),* Intervisual/Piggy Toes) Bendon, Inc.
—Bible Stories: A Touch & Feel Book. Mitchell, Melanie, illus. 2008. (ENG.). 12p. (J). (gr. -1). 12.95 *(978-1-58117-802-9(6),* Intervisual/Piggy Toes) Bendon, Inc.
Price, Roxanne M. Buckeyes Bow Ties & Sweater Vests. 2010. (Illus.). 20p. pap. *(978-1-4251-8537-4(1))* Trafford Publishing (UK) Ltd.
Priddy, Roger. Alphaprints: Sweet Heart: A Touch-And-Feel Book. 2015. (Alphaprints Ser.). (ENG., Illus.). 10p. (J). (gr. -1 — 1). bds. 7.99 *(978-0-312-51913-1(3),* 900149109) St. Martin's Pr.
—Carry-Along Tab Book: My Easter Basket. 2019. (Lift-The-Flap Tab Bks.). (ENG., Illus.). 10p. (J). bds. 8.99 *(978-0-312-52791-4(8),* 900194740) St. Martin's Pr.
—Funny Faces Santa Claus: With Lights & Sound. 2012. (Funny Faces Ser.). (ENG., Illus.). 10p. (J). (gr. -1-1). bds. 8.99 *(978-0-312-51558-4(8),* 900097399) St. Martin's Pr.
—Maze Book: Follow My Heart. 2018. (Follow Me Maze Bks.). (ENG., Illus.). 14p. (J). bds. 7.99 *(978-0-312-52763-1(2),* 900190145) St. Martin's Pr.
—Shiny Shapes: Hooray for Thanksgiving! 2018. (Shiny Shapes Ser.). (ENG., Illus.). 10p. (J). bds. 7.99 *(978-0-312-52724-2(1),* 900189781) St. Martin's Pr.
Prince, April Jones. Snowy Race. Davenier, Christine, illus. 2019. 40p. (J). (gr. -1-2). 18.99 *(978-0-8234-4141-9(5),* Margaret Ferguson Books) Holiday Hse., Inc.
Pritchard, Alicia Michele. Critter Pics. 2008. 53p. pap. 22.50 *(978-1-4357-1134-1(3))* Lulu Pr., Inc.
Prose, Francine. Rhino, Rhino, Sweet Potato. Armstrong, Matthew S., illus. 2009. 32p. (J). (gr. -1-1). lib. bdg. 18.89 *(978-0-06-008079-2(5))* HarperCollins Pubs.
Provencher, Rose-Marie. Slithery Jake. Carter, Abby, illus. 2004. (ENG.). 32p. (J). 15.99 *(978-0-06-623820-3(X))* HarperCollins Pubs.
Publications International Ltd. Staff. Mother Goose Treasury. 2007. (Illus.). 316p. 15.98 *(978-1-4127-8734-5(3))* Publications International, Ltd.
Publications International Ltd. Staff, creator. Mother Goose. 2007. (Pop-up Treasury Ser.). (Illus.). 16p. (J). (gr. -1-3). 12.98 *(978-1-4127-8833-5(1))* Publications International, Ltd.
Publications International Ltd. Staff, ed. Baby Einstein. 2007. (J). 5.98 *(978-1-4127-8481-8(6))* Phoenix International Publications, Inc.
—Baby Einstein: Look, Listen, & Discover. 2010. 14p. (J). bds. 22.98 *(978-1-4127-4517-8(9),* 1412745179) Phoenix International Publications, Inc.
—Thomas & Friends: Ding! Dong! A Visit from Thomas. 2011. 12p. (J). bds. 9.98 *(978-1-60553-985-0(6))* Phoenix International Publications, Inc.
Puckett, Gavin. Colin the Cart Horse: Fables from the Stables Book 3. Freeman, Tor, illus. 2018. (Fables from the Stables Ser.). (ENG.). 80p. (J). 8.95 *(978-0-571-31543-7(7))* Faber & Faber, Inc.
—Hayley the Hairy Horse. Freeman, Tor, illus. 2019. (Fables from the Stables Ser.). (ENG.). 80p. pap. 8.95 *(978-0-571-33780-4(5),* Faber & Faber Children's Bks.) Faber & Faber, Inc.
—Murray the Race Horse: Fables from the Stables Book 1. Freeman, Tor, illus. 2018. (Fables from the Stables Ser.). (ENG.). 80p. (J). pap. 8.95 *(978-0-571-33468-1(7))* Faber & Faber, Inc.
Pulchinski, Erin. Ethan Is Caught Blue Faced! Werrun, Anna, illus. 2013. 32p. pap. *(978-1-4602-2416-8(7))* FriesenPress.
Pulley, Kelly. The Cycling Wangdoos. Pulley, Kelly, illus. 2011. (Illus.). 32p. (J). (gr. -1-3). 16.95 *(978-0-9820812-1-1(9),* Frog Legs Ink) Gauthier Pubns. Inc.
—The Cycling Wangdoos, 1 vol. 2017. (ENG., Illus.). 32p. (J). 16.99 *(978-0-7643-5406-9(X),* 7845) Schiffer Publishing, Ltd.
—Ten Unusual Features of Lulu McDunn. Pulley, Kelly, illus. 2010. (Illus.). 32p. (J). (gr. -1). 16.95 *(978-0-9820812-7-3(8),* Frog Legs Ink) Gauthier Pubns. Inc.
Pumphrey, W. Jerome. Creepy Things Are Scaring Me! (Illus.). 32p. (J). (gr. -1-3). 5.99 *(978-0-06-443680-9(2))* HarperCollins Pubs.
Punter, Russell. There Was a Crooked Man. Semple, David, illus. 2010. (First Reading Level 2 Ser.). 32p. (J). 6.99 *(978-0-7945-2682-5(9),* Usborne) EDC Publishing.
Punter, Russell & MacKinnon, Mairi. Snail Brings the Mail. Blunt, Fred, illus. 2014. (Usborne Phonics Readers Ser.). (ENG.). (J). pap. 6.99 *(978-0-7945-3369-4(8),* Usborne) EDC Publishing.
Quaal, Jean. If Roosters Crow? 2009. 32p. pap. 14.95 *(978-1-4327-3671-2(X))* Outskirts Pr., Inc.
Quattlebaum, Mary. Jo MacDonald Saw a Pond. Bryant, Laura J., illus. 2013. 26p. (J). (gr. -1 — 1). bds. 7.95 *(978-1-58469-224-9(3),* Dawn Pubns.) Sourcebooks, Inc.
Queen Latifah. Queen of the Scene. Morrison, Frank, illus. 2006. 32p. (J). (gr. -1-3). 17.89 incl. audio compact disk *(978-0-06-077857-6(1),* Geringer, Laura Book) HarperCollins Pubs.
Quinn, David. Go to Sleep, Little Creep. Spires, Ashley, illus. 2018. 32p. (J). (-k). 17.99 *(978-1-101-93944-4(3),* Crown Books For Young Readers) Random Hse. Children's Bks.
Rabbett, Martin. Forever Buster: What a Name! What a Dog, We Exclaim! Burns, Donna, illus. 2007. (J). 13.95 *(978-0-9794649-0-4(0))* Hula Moon Pr.
Rabe, Tish. Cooking with the Grinch (Dr. Seuss) Brannon, Tom, illus. 2017. (Step into Reading Ser.). (ENG.). 32p. (J). (gr. -1-1). pap. 5.99 *(978-1-5247-1462-8(3),* Random Hse. Bks. for Young Readers) Random Hse. Children's Bks.
—Huff & Puff. Guile, Gill, illus. 2014. (My First I Can Read Ser.). (ENG.). 24p. (J). (gr. -1-3). 16.99 *(978-0-06-230502-2(6));* pap. 4.99 *(978-0-06-230501-5(8))* HarperCollins Pubs. (HarperCollins).
—Huff & Puff & the New Train. Guile, Gill, illus. 2014. (My First I Can Read Ser.). (ENG.). 24p. (J). (gr. -1-3). pap. 5.99 *(978-0-06-230503-9(4),* HarperCollins) HarperCollins Pubs.
—Huff & Puff Have Too Much Stuff! Guile, Gill, illus. 2014. (My First I Can Read Ser.). (ENG.). 24p. (J). (gr. -1-3). pap. 4.99 *(978-0-06-230505-3(0),* HarperCollins) HarperCollins Pubs.
—I Love You, Grandma! Hitch, David, illus. 2016. (Little Golden Book Ser.). (J). (-k). 24p. 5.99 *(978-1-101-93455-5(7));* *(978-1-5182-1618-3(8))* Random Hse. Children's Bks. (Golden Bks.).
—Look for the Lorax. 2012. (Step into Reading - Level 1 Ser.). lib. bdg. 13.55 *(978-0-606-23720-8(8))* Turtleback.
—Look for the Lorax (Dr. Seuss) 2012. (Step into Reading Ser.). (ENG., Illus.). 32p. (J). (gr. -1-1). pap. 4.99 *(978-0-375-86999-0(9),* Random Hse. Bks. for Young Readers) Random Hse. Children's Bks.
—Love You, Hug You, Read to You! Endersby, Frank, illus. 2015. (ENG.). 32p. (J). (gr. -1 — 1). bds. 8.99 *(978-1-101-93655-9(X),* Random Hse. Bks. for Young Readers) Random Hse. Children's Bks.
—Oh, Baby, the Places You'll Go! Seuss, illus. 2015. (ENG.). 32p. (J). (gr. 2-12). 9.99 *(978-0-553-52057-6(1),* Random Hse. Bks. for Young Readers) Random Hse. Children's Bks.
Raczka, Bob. Summer Wonders. Stead, Judy, illus. 2012. (J). 34.28 *(978-1-61913-125-5(0))* Weigl Pubs., Inc.
Raczka, Robert. Fall Mixed Up. Cameron, Chad, illus. 2011. (ENG.). 32p. (J). (gr. -1-3). lib. bdg. 19.99 *(978-0-7613-4606-7(6),* a231a1d6-f87a-4711-bd25-c1d4eb362f4a, Carolrhoda Bks.) Lerner Publishing Group.
Raden, Tammy. My Dog Blue. 2009. (ENG.). 24p. pap. 11.49 *(978-1-4490-3228-9(1))* AuthorHouse.
Radford, Tracey. Brian the Lion Goes into Space. 2018. (ENG., Illus.). 32p. (J). 16.95 *(978-1-78249-576-5(2),* 1782495762, CICO Books) Ryland Peters & Small GBR. Dist: WIPRO.
Radzinski, Kandy. What Cats Want for Christmas. Radzinski, Kandy, illus. rev. ed. 2007. (ENG., Illus.). 32p. (J). (gr. 1-4). 16.95 *(978-1-58536-340-7(5),* 202130) Sleeping Bear Pr.
—Where to Sleep. Radzinski, Kandy, illus. (ENG., Illus.). (J). (gr. 1-4). 2010. 22p. bds. 9.95 *(978-1-58536-535-7(1),* 202321) 2009. 32p. 15.95 *(978-1-58536-436-7(3),* 202164) Sleeping Bear Pr.
Rae, Jennifer. Gilbert de la Frogponde: A Swamp Story. braille ed. 2004. (Illus.). (J). (gr. k-3). spiral bd. *(978-0-616-03054-7(1));* spiral bd. *(978-0-616-04561-9(1))* Canadian National Institute for the Blind/Institut National Canadien pour les Aveugles.
Rae, Philippa. Count the Sheep to Sleep. Röhr, Stéphanie, illus. 2012. (ENG.). 28p. (J). (gr. -1-k). 12.95 *(978-1-61608-660-2(2),* 608660, Sky Pony Pr.) Skyhorse Publishing Co., Inc.
Raines Day, Nancy. Hoorade Day!, 1 vol. Van Wright, Cornelius, illus. 2018. (ENG.). 32p. (J). *(978-1-59572-807-4(4))* Star Bright Bks., Inc.
Rainey. School Is Cool. Huggens, Karin, illus. 2004. (J). *(978-0-9666199-9-7(4))* DreamDog Pr.
Rainforth, Hannah. Barnaby Bennett, 1 vol. Teo, Ali, illus. 2008. (ENG.). 32p. (J). (gr. -1-3). pap. 5.95 *(978-1-59572-156-3(8))* Star Bright Bks., Inc.
—Barnaby Bennett. Teo, Ali, illus. 2007. 32p. (J). (gr. -1-3). pap. 10.00 *(978-1-86969-232-2(2))* Univ. of Hawaii Pr.
Raisner Glass, Beth. Blue-Ribbon Dad. Moore, Margie, illus. 2011. (ENG.). 32p. (J). (gr. k-2). 15.95 *(978-0-8109-9727-1(4),* 674101, Abrams Bks. for Young Readers) Abrams, Inc.
Randall, Marilyn. Elmer the Christmas Elf. 2009. 32p. 18.95 *(978-0-557-15333-6(6))* Lulu Pr., Inc.
—A Hard Nut to Crack. 2009. 36p. pap. 18.95 *(978-0-557-15891-1(5))* Lulu Pr., Inc.
—Inside Out. 2009. 26p. 18.95 *(978-0-557-15699-3(8))* Lulu Pr., Inc.
Randles, Slim. Ol' Jimmy Dollar. Montoya, Jerry, illus. 2018. (ENG.). 52p. (J). (gr. 1-3). pap. 17.95 *(978-1-943681-24-2(4))* Nuevo Bks.
Randles, Slim & Montoya, Jerry, illus. Ol' Jimmy Dollar. 2015. 42p. (J). *(978-1-936744-40-4(6))* LPD Pr.
Rankin, Joan & Hartmann, Wendy. The African Orchestra. 2017. (ENG., Illus.). 32p. (J). (gr. 1-2). 17.95 *(978-1-56656-048-1(9),* Crocodile Bks.) Interlink Publishing Group, Inc.
Ransom, Candice. Apple Picking Day! Meza, Erika, illus. 2016. (Step into Reading Ser.). 32p. (J). (gr. -1-1). pap. 4.99 *(978-0-553-53858-8(6),* Random Hse. Bks. for Young Readers) Random Hse. Children's Bks.
—Snow Day! 2019. (Step into Reading Ser.). (ENG.). 32p. (J). (gr. k-1). 14.96 *(978-0-87617-970-3(7))* Penworthy Co., LLC, The.
—Snow Day! Meza, Erika, illus. 2018. (Step into Reading Ser.). 32p. (J). (gr. -1-1). pap. 5.99 *(978-1-5247-2037-7(2),* Random Hse. Bks. for Young Readers) Random Hse. Children's Bks.
—Tooth Fairy's Night. 2017. (Step into Reading Ser.). (Illus.). 32p. (J). (gr. -1-1). 5.99 *(978-0-399-55364-6(9),* Random Hse. Bks. for Young Readers) Random Hse. Children's Bks.
Raschka, Chris. Five for a Little One. Raschka, Chris, illus. 2006. (ENG., Illus.). 48p. (J). (gr. -1-2). 19.99 *(978-0-689-84599-4(5),* Atheneum/Richard Jackson Bks.) Simon & Schuster Children's Publishing.
—Little Black Crow. 2010. (ENG., Illus.). 40p. (J). (gr. -1-2). 19.99 *(978-0-689-84601-4(0),* Atheneum/Richard Jackson Bks.) Simon & Schuster Children's Publishing.
Rash, Andy. Agent A to Agent Z. 2004. (Illus.). (J). *(978-0-439-36883-4(9),* Levine, Arthur A. Bks.) Scholastic, Inc.
Rasmussen, Halfdan. The Ladder. Nelson, Marilyn, tr. Pratt, Pierre, illus. 2006. (ENG.). 62p. (J). (gr. -1-3). 17.99 *(978-0-7636-2282-4(6))* Candlewick Pr.
Rathmann, Peggy. The Day the Babies Crawled Away. Rathmann, Peggy, illus. 2003. (Illus.). 40p. (J). (gr. -1-k). 18.99 *(978-0-399-23196-4(X),* G.P. Putnam's Sons Books for Young Readers) Penguin Young Readers Group.
Ratnett, Michael. Dracula Steps Out. Goulding, June & Smyth, Iain, illus. 2005. 12p. (J). (gr. k-4). reprint ed. 16.00 *(978-0-7567-8585-7(5))* DIANE Publishing Co.
Ratzlaff, Aaron J. Quills. 2011. (ENG.). 40p. (J). pap. 13.99 *(978-0-8361-9509-5(4))* Herald Pr.
Rauchwerger, Diane Levin. Dinosaur on Hanukkah. Wolff, Jason, illus. 2005. (ENG.). 24p. (J). (gr. -1-1). per. 7.95 *(978-1-58013-143-8(3),* e4568a1e-54f2-40fc-8b09-8058a86a8a9f); 15.95 *(978-1-58013-145-2(X))* Lerner Publishing Group. (Kar-Ben Publishing).
Rauchwerger, Diane Levin & Levin, Diane. Dinosaur on Shabbat. Wolff, Jason, illus. 2006. (ENG.). 24p. (J). (gr. -1-1). lib. bdg. 15.95 *(978-1-58013-159-9(X),* Kar-Ben Publishing) Lerner Publishing Group.
Rauss, Ron. Can I Just Take a Nap? Shepperson, Rob, illus. 2012. (ENG.). 32p. (J). (gr. -1-1). 15.99 *(978-1-4424-3497-4(X),* Simon & Schuster/Paula Wiseman Bks.) Simon & Schuster/Paula Wiseman Bks.
Ravishankar, Anushka. Excuse Me, Is This India? Leutwiler, Anita, illus. 2003. 24p. (J). 14.95 *(978-81-86211-56-4(X))* Tara Publishing IND. Dist: Consortium Bk. Sales & Distribution.
Ray, Christie Jones & Ray, Christie Jones. Pick-A-Pick-a-Pumpkin. 2012. (Illus.). 36p. pap. 12.00 *(978-0-9853223-4-2(9))* Rose Water Cottage Pr.
Ray, J. Hamilton. Squirrels on Skis. Lemaître, Pascal, illus. 2013. (Beginner Books(R) Ser.). 64p. (J). (gr. -1-2). 9.99 *(978-0-449-81081-1(X),* Random Hse. Bks. for Young Readers) Random Hse. Children's Bks.
Ray, Mary Lyn. Go to Sleep, Little Farm Lap Board Book. Neal, Christopher Silas, illus. 2018. (ENG.). 38p. (J). (— 1). bds. 12.99 *(978-1-328-77004-2(4),* 1681070, Clarion Bks.) HarperCollins Pubs.
—Go to Sleep, Little Farm Padded Board Book. Neal, Christopher Silas, illus. 2015. (ENG.). 38p. (J). (— 1). bds. 8.99 *(978-0-544-57916-3(X),* 1613308, Clarion Bks.) HarperCollins Pubs.
Rayner, Jacqueline K. Hats Are Not for Cats! Rayner, Jacqueline K., illus. 2019. (ENG., Illus.). 32p. (J). (gr. -1-3). 17.99 *(978-1-328-96719-0(0),* 1707633, Clarion Bks.) HarperCollins Pubs.
Reade, O. K. The Little Girl & Her Shadow. 2015. (Illus.). (J). 12.99 *(978-1-4621-1618-8(3))* Cedar Fort, Inc./CFI Distribution.
Reasoner, Charles. Color Crunch! 2009. (Bite Bks.). (Illus.). (J). bds. 7.99 *(978-1-934650-15-8(3))* Just For Kids Pr., LLC.
—I'm Just a Bird. 2008. *(978-1-84666-153-2(6))* Top That! Publishing PLC.
—I'M Just a Crab! 2018. (Googley Eye Bks.). (ENG., Illus.). 12p. (J). (gr. -1-k). bds. 8.99 *(978-1-84666-157-0(9))* Top That! Publishing PLC GBR. Dist: Independent Pubs. Group.
—I'm Just a Frog. 2008. *(978-1-84666-159-4(5))* Top That! Publishing PLC.
—Inside Jolly Rodger's Pirate Ship. 2014. (Illus.). (J). *(978-1-4351-5466-7(5))* Barnes & Noble, Inc.
Reasoner, Charles, illus. Bear Hugs. 2015. (J). *(978-1-4795-5944-2(X),* Picture Window Bks.) Capstone.
—Honey Bunny. 2015. (J). *(978-1-4795-5945-9(8),* Picture Window Bks.) Capstone.
—Peep! Peep! 2015. (J). *(978-1-4795-5943-5(1),* Picture Window Bks.) Capstone.
—Puppy Love. 2015. (J). *(978-1-4795-5946-6(6),* Picture Window Bks.) Capstone.
Reasoner, Charles E. I'm Just a Fish. Reasoner, Charles E., illus. 2008. (Googley-Eye Bks.). (ENG.). 12p. (J). (gr. -1). 8.99 *(978-1-84666-155-6(2))* Top That! Publishing PLC GBR. Dist: Independent Pubs. Group.
Rebecca, Rebecca. The Turtle Who Did His Best. 2016. (ENG., Illus.). 26p. pap. 5.99 *(978-1-61984-471-1(0),* Gatekeeper Pr.) Gatekeeper Pr.
Redbank, Tennant. Tootle. DiCicco, Sue, illus. 2017. (Step into Reading Ser.). 32p. (J). (gr. -1-1). pap. 4.99 *(978-0-399-55520-6(X),* Random Hse. Bks. for Young Readers) Random Hse. Children's Bks.
Redmond, E. S. The Unruly Queen. Redmond, E. S., illus. 2012. (ENG., Illus.). 32p. (J). (gr. -1-2). 15.99 *(978-0-7636-3445-2(X))* Candlewick Pr.
Reed, Susan. Up, up, Up! Oldfield, Rachel, illus. 2010. 24p. (J). (gr. -1-2). 16.99 *(978-1-84686-369-1(4))* Barefoot Bks., Inc.
—Up, Up, Up! Oldfield, Rachel, illus. 2011. (Barefoot Singalongs Ser.). (ENG.). 24p. (J). (gr. -1-2). pap. 10.99 *(978-1-84686-550-3(6))* Barefoot Bks., Inc.
Refrrolo, C. T. Grandchild of Mine: You & I. 2006. (J). 12.00 *(978-0-8059-6845-3(8))* Dorrance Publishing Co., Inc.
Regan, Patrick. The Marvelous Monsters Talent Show. Bonson, Tom, illus. 2014. (J). *(978-1-4351-5617-3(X),* Blackbirch Pr., Inc.) Barnes & Noble, Inc.
Regier, Demar. What Time Is It? Woodruff, Liza, illus. 2005. (My First Reader Ser.). (ENG.). 32p. (J). (gr. k-1). 18.50

S

(978-0-516-25180-6(5), Children's Pr.) Scholastic Library Publishing.

Reichert, Amy. While Mama Had a Quick Little Chat. Boiger, Alexandra, illus. 2005. (ENG.). 40p. (J). (gr. -1-2). 19.99 (978-0-689-85170-4(7), Atheneum/Richard Jackson Bks.) Simon & Schuster Children's Publishing.

Reid, Carol. Spook-Ee Wook-Ee Halloween. 2012. 24p. pap. 17.99 (978-1-4772-5845-3(0)) AuthorHouse.

Reid, Rob. Comin' down to Storytime. Bernard Westcott, Nadine, illus. 2009. (J). (gr. -1-3). 17.95 (978-1-60213-039-5(6), Upstart Bks.) Highsmith Inc.

—Wave Goodbye, 1 vol. Williams, Lorraine, illus. 2013. (ENG.). 24p. (J). (gr. -1-1). pap. 10.95 (978-1-60060-341-9(6), leelowbooks) Lee & Low Bks., Inc.

Reid, Robin L. Rhyming Ricky Rutherford. Lipp, Tony, illus. 2012. 24p. pap. 24.95 (978-1-4626-8896-8(9)) America Star Bks.

Reidy, Jean. All Through My Town. Timmers, Leo, illus. (ENG.). (J). (gr. -1-k). 2015. 26p. bds. 7.99 (978-1-61963-562-3(3), 900140699) 2013. 32p. 17.99 (978-1-59990-785-7(2), 900080105) Bloomsbury Publishing USA. (Bloomsbury USA Childrens).

—Too Princessy! Leloup, Geneviève, illus. 2013. (Too! Bks.). (ENG.). 26p. (J). (gr. -1 — 1). bds. 7.99 (978-1-59990-955-4(3), 9781599909554, Bloomsbury USA Childrens) Bloomsbury Publishing USA.

Reiser, Lynn. You & Me, Baby. Gentieu, Penny, photos by. 2008. (ENG., Illus.). 32p. (J). (— 1). bds. 6.99 (978-0-375-84420-1(1), Knopf Bks. for Young Readers) Random Hse. Children's Bks.

Reiss, Mike. Santa's Eleven Months Off. 1 vol. Montgomery, Michael G., illus. 2016. 32p. (J). (gr. -1-3). pap. 7.95 (978-1-56145-962-9(3)) Peachtree Publishing Co. Inc.

Reiss, Mike & Reiss, Mike. The Boy Who Wouldn't Share. Catrow, David, illus. 2008. (ENG.). 32p. (J). (gr. 1-3). 17.99 (978-0-06-059132-8(3), HarperCollins) HarperCollins Pubs.

Resnicoff, Stan. Stanley, the Seal of Approval. 2012. (ENG.). (J). pap. (978-1-4675-1535-1(3)) Independent Pub.

Rex, Michael. Goodnight Goon: a Petrifying Parody. Rex, Michael, illus. 2012. (Illus.). 30p. (J). (gr. -1 — 1). bds. 6.99 (978-0-399-26011-7(0), G.P. Putnam's Sons Books for Young Readers) Penguin Young Readers Group.

Rex, Michael, illus. Goodnight Goon: a Petrifying Parody. 2008. 32p. (J). (gr. -1-k). 17.99 (978-0-399-24534-3(0), G.P. Putnam's Sons Books for Young Readers) Penguin Young Readers Group.

Rexroth, Sharon. America from the Sky. 2006. (J). 9.95 (978-1-57166-429-7(7)); per. 22.95 (978-1-57166-430-3(0)) Quixote Pr.

—Ohio. 2006. (ENG., Illus.). (J). per. 19.95 (978-1-57166-421-1(1)) Quixote Pr.

Rey, H. A. Curious George Pat-A-Cake. 2011. (Curious George Ser.). (ENG., Illus.). 8p. (J). (gr. k — 1). bds. 12.99 (978-0-547-51689-9(4), 1444706, Clarion Bks.) HarperCollins Pubs.

—Whose House? 2017. (ENG., Illus.). 24p. (J). (gr. -1-3). 8.99 (978-0-544-94975-1(7), 1660062, Clarion Bks.) HarperCollins Pubs.

Rey, H. A. & Rey, Margret. The H. A. Rey Treasury of Stories. 2015. (Dover Children's Classics Ser.). (ENG., Illus.). 112p. (J). (gr. 2-4). pap. 14.99 (978-0-486-78468-7(1), 784681) Dover Pubns., Inc.

Reyes, Cameron. In Your Heart. DeBroech, Sarah, illus. 2011. 28p. pap. 24.95 (978-1-4560-1009-6(3)) America Star Bks.

Reynolds, Luke. If My Love Were a Fire Truck: A Daddy's Love Song. Mack, Jeff, illus. 2018. 26p. (J). (— 1). bds. 7.99 (978-0-525-58066-9(2), Doubleday Bks. for Young Readers) Random Hse. Children's Bks.

RH Disney. Just Keep Swimming (Disney/Pixar Finding Nemo) Harchy, Atelier Philippe, illus. 2005. (Step into Reading Ser.). (ENG.). 32p. (J). (gr. k-3). pap. 4.99 (978-0-7364-2319-9(2), RH/Disney) Random Hse. Children's Bks.

Rhodes, Lou. The Phlunk's Worldwide Symphony. Elliott, Tori, illus. 2014. (ENG.). 32p. (J). pap. (978-0-9573690-2-3(6)) Strata Bks.

Rhodes, Tiffany. What I Learned This Christmas. 2013. (Illus.). 42p. pap. 15.99 (978-0-9899099-1-4(3)) Bee Creative, LLC.

Rhymes, Wriggly. No Place Like Home. 2013. (ENG., Illus.). 40p. pap. 11.00 (978-1-78035-602-0(1), Fastprint Publishing) Upfront Publishing Ltd. GBR. Dist: Printondemand-worldwide.com.

Ricci, Christine. Dora's Nursery Rhyme Adventure. Fruchter, Jason, illus. 2005. (Dora the Explorer Ser.). (J). (978-0-7172-9819-8(1)) Scholastic, Inc.

Riccobono, Michael P. Billy Balonie & the Belly Buttonie. 2010. (Illus.). 28p. pap. 19.00 (978-1-4490-3119-0(6)) AuthorHouse.

Rice, Clay. Ants 'N' Uncles. 2016. (ENG., Illus.). 32p. (J). (gr. -1-1). 16.95 (978-1-942934-68-4(9), 553468) Familius LLC.

Rice, Dona Herweck, et al. All about Me. 2009. (Early Literacy Ser.). (ENG., Illus.). 16p. (gr. k-1). 19.99 (978-1-4333-1468-1(1)) Teacher Created Materials, Inc.

Rice, James. Gaston(r) Goes to Texas, 1 vol. Rice, James, illus. 2007. (Gaston Ser.). (ENG., Illus.). 32p. (J). (gr. 1-3). 16.99 (978-1-58980-531-6(3), Pelican Publishing) Arcadia Publishing.

—Gaston(r) Lays an Offshore Pipeline, 1 vol. Rice, James, illus. 2007. (Gaston Ser.). (ENG., Illus.). 32p. (J). (gr. k-3). 16.99 (978-1-58980-510-1(0), Pelican Publishing) Arcadia Publishing.

Rice, James, illus. Gaston(r) Joins the Circus, 1 vol. 2015. (Gaston Ser.). (ENG.). 32p. (J). (gr. k-3). 16.99 (978-1-4556-2129-3(3), Pelican Publishing) Arcadia Publishing.

Richards, Arlene. That's Bingzy! Busy Building Self-Esteem. 2007. (J). per. 15.95 (978-0-9794323-2-3(4)) Bing Note, Inc.

Richmond, Marianne. Be Brave Little One. (Illus.). (J). (gr. -1-2). 2020. 26p. bds. 8.99 (978-1-7282-3060-3(8)) 2017. 40p. 9.99 (978-1-4926-5881-8(2)) Sourcebooks, Inc. (Sourcebooks Jabberwocky).

—Hooray for You! A Celebration of You-Ness. 2015. (Marianne Richmond Ser.: 0). 24p. (J). (gr. -1-2). bds. 7.99 (978-1-4926-1555-2(2), Sourcebooks Jabberwocky) Sourcebooks, Inc.

—The Night Night Book. 2011. (Marianne Richmond Ser.: 0). (Illus.). 24p. (J). (gr. -1-k). bds. 7.95 (978-1-934082-90-4(2), Sourcebooks Jabberwocky) Sourcebooks, Inc.

—You Are My Kiss Good Night. 2018. (Marianne Richmond Ser.: 0). (Illus.). 28p. (J). (gr. -1-k). bds. 8.99 (978-1-4926-7512-9(1), Sourcebooks Jabberwocky) Sourcebooks, Inc.

Rickards, Lynne. Rowan the Red Squirrel, 30 vols. Mitchell, Jon, illus. 2018. 32p. (J). 11.95 (978-1-78250-477-1(X), Kelpies) Floris Bks. GBR. Dist: Consortium Bk. Sales & Distribution.

Riddle, Waide Aaron. The Chocolate Man A Children's Horror Tale. Aragon Art Studio, illus. ed. 2010. (ENG.). 44p. pap. 15.00 (978-0-615-38560-0(5)) Waide Aaron Riddle.

Riding, Robin. Mermaids Fast Asleep. Persico, Zoe, illus. 2019. (ENG.). 32p. (J). 17.99 (978-1-250-07635-9(8), 900152143) Feiwel & Friends.

Ridley, Sharon, illus. My Wildflower Friends. Phillips, Marilyn, photos by. 2006. (J). (978-0-9786168-0-9(4)) Rio Wildflower Pubns.

Rigg, Jo. Millie Moo. 2007. (Illus.). 10p. (J). (978-1-84332-473-7(3)) Priddy Bks.

—Rocky Dog. 2007. (Illus.). 10p. (J). (978-1-84332-474-4(1)) Priddy Bks.

Riley, Kellee, illus. Tolee's Rhyme Time. 2009. (Ni Hao, Kai-Lan Ser.). (ENG.). 24p. (J). pap. 3.99 (978-1-4169-9024-6(0), Simon Spotlight/Nickelodeon) Simon Spotlight/Nickelodeon.

Rille, Lauren. I Feel Teal. Sicuro, Aimée, illus. 2018. (ENG.). 40p. (J). (gr. -1-3). 18.99 (978-1-4814-5846-7(9), Beach Lane Bks.) Beach Lane Bks.

Ringler, Matt. It's Fall! Shearing, Leonie, illus. 2006. 28p. (J). pap. (978-0-439-87146-4(8)) Scholastic, Inc.

—One Little, Two Little, Three Little Apples. Kennedy, Anne, illus. 2005. (J). pap. (978-0-439-77500-7(0)) Scholastic, Inc.

Rink, Cynthia A. Where Does the Wind Blow? Rink, Cynthia A., illus. 2004. (Sharing Nature with Children Book Ser.). (Illus.). 32p. (J). (gr. k-5). 16.95 (978-1-58469-041-2(0)) Take Heart Pubns.

Rink, Cynthia A., illus. Where Does the Wind Blow? 2004. (Sharing Nature with Children Book Ser.). 32p. (J). pap. 7.95 (978-1-58469-040-5(2)) Take Heart Pubns.

Rinker, Sherri Duskey. Buenas Noches, ConstrucciόN. Buenas Noches, DiversiόN. (Goodnight, Goodnight, Construction Site Spanish Language Edition) (Bilingual Children's Book, Spanish Books for Kids) Lazaro, Georgina, tr. Lichtenheld, Tom, illus. 2019. (Goodnight, Goodnight Construction Site Ser.). (SPA.). 32p. (J). (gr. -1 — 1). 16.99 (978-1-4521-7037-4(1)) Chronicle Bks. LLC.

—Bulldozer's Shapes: Goodnight, Goodnight, Construction Site (Kids Construction Books, Goodnight Books for Toddlers) Long, Ethan, illus. 2019. (Goodnight, Goodnight Construction Site Ser.). (ENG.). 20p. (J). (gr. -1 — 1). bds. 6.99 (978-1-4521-5321-6(3)) Chronicle Bks. LLC.

—Cement Mixer's ABC: Goodnight, Goodnight, Construction Site. Lichtenheld, Tom & Long, Ethan, illus. 2018. (Goodnight, Goodnight, Construc Ser.). (ENG.). 20p. (J). (gr. -1 — 1). bds. 6.99 (978-1-4521-5318-6(3)) Chronicle Bks. LLC.

—Construction Site: Farming Strong, All Year Long. Ford, A. G., illus. 2022. (Goodnight, Goodnight, Construc Ser.). (ENG.). 40p. (J). (gr. -1 — 1). 17.99 (978-1-7972-1387-3(3)) Chronicle Bks. LLC.

—Construction Site Mission: Demolition! Ford, AG, illus. 2024. (J). (978-1-64549-815-5(8)) Amicus Learning.

—Construction Site Mission: Demolition! Ford, A. G., illus. 2020. (Goodnight, Goodnight, Construc Ser.). (ENG.). 40p. (J). (gr. -1 — 1). 17.99 (978-1-4521-8257-5(4)) Chronicle Bks. LLC.

—Construction Site on Christmas Night: (Christmas Book for Kids, Children?s Book, Holiday Picture Book) Ford, A. G., illus. 2018. (Goodnight, Goodnight Construction Site Ser.). (ENG.). 40p. (J). (gr. -1-k). 16.99 (978-1-4521-3911-1(3)) Chronicle Bks. LLC.

—Construction Site: Road Crew, Coming Through! Ford, A. G., illus. 2021. (Goodnight, Goodnight, Construc Ser.). (ENG.). 40p. (J). (gr. -1 — 1). 17.99 (978-1-7972-0472-7(6)) Chronicle Bks. LLC.

—Dump Truck's Colors: Goodnight, Goodnight, Construction Site. Long, Ethan, illus. 2018. (Goodnight, Goodnight, Construc Ser.). (ENG.). 20p. (J). (gr. -1 — 1). bds. 6.99 (978-1-4521-5320-9(5)) Chronicle Bks. LLC.

—Goodnight, Goodnight, Construction Site. Lichtenheld, Tom, illus. 2024. (J). (978-1-64549-816-2(6)) Amicus Learning.

—Goodnight, Goodnight, Construction Site. Lichtenheld, Tom, illus. 2017. (Goodnight, Goodnight, Construc Ser.). (ENG.). 30p. (J). (gr. -1 — 1). bds. 7.99 (978-1-4521-1173-5(1)) Chronicle Bks. LLC.

—Goodnight, Goodnight, Construction Site. 2011. (Goodnight, Goodnight, Construc Ser.). (ENG., Illus.). 32p. (J). (gr. -1 — 1). 16.99 (978-0-8118-7782-4(5)) Chronicle Bks. LLC.

—Goodnight, Goodnight, Construction Site & Steam Train, Dream Train Board Books Boxed Set, 1 vol. Lichtenheld, Tom, illus. 2015. (Goodnight, Goodnight, Construc Ser.). (ENG.). 66p. (J). (gr. -1 — 1). bds. 15.99 (978-1-4521-4698-0(5)) Chronicle Bks. LLC.

—Goodnight, Goodnight, Construction Site Glow in the Dark Growth Chart. Lichtenheld, Tom, illus. 2016. (Goodnight, Goodnight Construction Site Ser.). (ENG.). 20p. (J). (gr. -1-7). 12.99 (978-1-4521-5463-3(5)) Chronicle Bks. LLC.

—Goodnight, Goodnight, Construction Site: Let's Go! (Construction Vehicle Board Books, Construction Site Books, Children's Books for Toddlers) Lichtenheld, Tom, illus. 2017. (Goodnight, Goodnight Construction Site Ser.). (ENG.). 10p. (J). (gr. -1 — 1). bds. 8.99 (978-1-4521-6476-2(2)) Chronicle Bks. LLC.

—How to Put an Octopus to Bed: (Going to Bed Book, Read-Aloud Bedtime Book for Kids) Schwarz, Viviane, illus. 2020. (ENG.). 40p. (J). (gr. -1-k). 17.99 (978-1-4521-4010-0(3)) Chronicle Bks. LLC.

—Mighty, Mighty Construction Site. Lichtenheld, Tom, illus. 2024. (J). (978-1-64549-817-9(4)) Amicus Learning.

—Mighty, Mighty Construction Site. Lichtenheld, Tom, illus. 2017. (Goodnight, Goodnight, Construc Ser.). (ENG.). 40p. (J). (gr. -1 — 1). 16.99 (978-1-4521-5216-5(0)) Chronicle Bks. LLC.

—Mighty, Mighty Construction Site. 2019. (CHI.). (gr. -1). (978-986-479-602-1(X)) Commonwealth Publishing Co., Ltd.

—Mighty, Mighty Construction Site Sound Book (Books for 1 Year Olds, Interactive Sound Book, Construction Sound Book) Lichtenheld, Tom, illus. 2019. (Goodnight, Goodnight Construction Site Ser.). (ENG.). 12p. (J). (gr. -1 — 1). bds. 12.99 (978-1-4521-6507-3(6)) Chronicle Bks. LLC.

—Steam Train, Dream Train (Books for Young Children, Family Read Aloud Books, Children's Train Books, Bedtime Stories) Lichtenheld, Tom, illus. 2018. (Goodnight, Goodnight Construction Site Ser.). (ENG.). 32p. (J). (gr. -1 — 1). bds. 7.99 (978-1-4521-5217-2(9)) Chronicle Bks. LLC.

—Steam Train, Dream Train (Easy Reader Books, Reading Books for Children) Lichtenheld, Tom, illus. 2013. (Goodnight, Goodnight Construction Site Ser.). (ENG.). 40p. (J). (gr. -1-1). 16.99 (978-1-4521-0920-6(6)) Chronicle Bks. LLC.

—Three Cheers for Kid Mcgear! (Family Read Aloud Books, Construction Books for Kids, Children's New Experiences Books, Stories in Verse) Ford, A. G., illus. 2019. (Goodnight, Goodnight, Construc Ser.). (ENG.). 40p. (J). (gr. -1 — 1). 17.99 (978-1-4521-5582-1(8)) Chronicle Bks. LLC.

—Tiny & the Big Dig. Myers, Matt, illus. 2018. (ENG.). 32p. (J). (gr. -1-k). 16.99 (978-0-545-90429-2(3), Scholastic Pr.) Scholastic, Inc.

—The 12 Sleighs of Christmas: (Christmas Book for Kids, Toddler Book, Holiday Picture Book & Stocking Stuffer) Parker, Jake, illus. 2017. (ENG.). 40p. (J). (gr. -1-k). 16.99 (978-1-4521-4514-3(8)) Chronicle Bks. LLC.

Rinker, Sherri Duskey & Lichtenheld, Tom. Goodnight, Goodnight, Construction Site. 2012. 12.95 (978-0-545-50222-1(5)) Scholastic, Inc.

Risco, Elle D. Dora Had a Little Lamb. Savitsky, Steve, illus. 2007. (Dora the Explorer Ser.). (J). (gr. -1-2). 11.65 (978-0-7569-8294-2(4)) Perfection Learning Corp.

Ritchie, Alison. Me & My Dad! Edgson, Alison, illus. 2007. (J). pap. (978-0-545-02064-0(6)) Scholastic, Inc.

Ritchie, Joseph R. Baby Looney Tunes Visit a Haunted House. Halverson, Lydia, illus. 2005. (Baby Looney Tunes Ser.). 14p. (J). (gr. -1-3). bds. 9.95 (978-0-8249-6609-6(0), Ideals Pubns.) Worthy Publishing.

—Frosty the Snowman Returns. Rose, Drew, illus. 2006. 14p. (J). (gr. -1-k). bds. 9.95 (978-0-8249-6670-6(8), Ideals Pubns.) Worthy Publishing.

—Where's Santa? Halverson, Lydia, illus. 2006. (ENG.). 14p. (J). (gr. -1-k). bds. 7.95 (978-0-8249-6673-7(2), Ideals Pubns.) Worthy Publishing.

Ritter, Philip. Tales in Rhyme from Three Little Mischief Maker's Country Time: The Escapades of Three Little Mischief Makers. 2005. (J). pap. 10.00 (978-0-8059-6928-3(4)) Dorrance Publishing Co., Inc.

Rizzi, Kathleen. What's in My Dresser?, 1 vol. Riggs, Jenna, illus. 2013. (ENG.). 32p. (J). bds. 7.99 (978-1-59572-165-5(7)) Star Bright Bks., Inc.

Rml. An Interesting Crew. 2012. 16p. (-18). pap. 15.99 (978-1-4772-8699-9(3)) AuthorHouse.

Roach, Nastashia. Dear Queens. Hernandez, Adua, illus. 2018. (ENG.). (J). 12.45 (978-1-62676-792-8(0), Melanin Origins, LLC) Grivante Pr.

Roadhouse, Patricia. Gah Reen Galoshes. 2009. 28p. pap. 16.99 (978-1-4389-7318-0(7)) AuthorHouse.

Roaring Fork Conservancy (Basalt, Colo.) Staff, contrib. by. Dee Dee the Fryingpan River Dipper. 2017. (Illus.). 48p. (J). (978-1-883551-90-2(0), Maple Corners Press) Attic Studio Publishing Hse.

Robbins, Karen. Care for Our World Play Set. 2012. (ENG.). (J). 34.95 (978-1-935414-63-6(1)) Casemate Pubs. & Bk. Distributors, LLC.

Roberts, Bethany. Thanksgiving Mice! Cushman, Doug, illus. 2005. (ENG.). 32p. (J). (gr. -1 — 1). 5.95 (978-0-618-60486-9(3)) Houghton Mifflin Harcourt Publishing Co.

Roberts, Deborah. Mr Otagiri's Promise. Ju-Young Im, Joy & Da-Young Im, Linda, illus. 2012. 40p. pap. (978-1-77067-719-7(4)) FriesenPress.

Roberts, Justin. The Smallest Girl in the Smallest Grade. Robinson, Christian, illus. 2014. 32p. (J). (gr. -1-k). 18.99 (978-0-399-25743-8(8), G.P. Putnam's Sons Books for Young Readers) Penguin Young Readers Group.

Robidoux, Annette & Sommerfeldt, Jim. Thickened Flied Lice: A Limerick in Six Chapters. Olsen, Christian, illus. 2004. (ENG.). 26p. pap. 12.99 (978-1-4134-6260-9(X)) Xlibris Corp.

Robinson, David. David Robinson: the Mushroom Picker. 2013. (ENG., Illus.). 48p. 25.00 (978-1-900828-41-3(3)) Violette Editions GBR. Dist: D.A.P./Distributed Art Pubs.

Robinson, Dierdre. I Don't Look Like You & That's Ok. 2011. 12p. (gr. 1-2). pap. 8.32 (978-1-4567-4466-3(6)) AuthorHouse.

Robinson, Hilary. Beauty & the Pea. Sanfilippo, Simona, illus. 2013. (ENG.). 32p. (J). (978-0-7787-1155-1(2)) Crabtree Publishing Co.

—Cinderella & the Beanstalk. Sanfilippo, Simona, illus. 2013. (ENG.). 32p. (J). (978-0-7787-1156-8(0)); pap. (978-0-7787-1161-2(7)) Crabtree Publishing Co.

—Croc by the Rock. Gordon, Mike, illus. 2005. 32p. (J). lib. bdg. 9.00 (978-1-4242-0885-2(8)) Fitzgerald Bks.

—A Croc Shock!, 1 vol. Gordon, Mike, illus. 2009. (Get Set Readers Ser.). (ENG.). 32p. (J). (gr. 1-1). lib. bdg. 27.27 (978-1-60754-265-0(X), 5a679107-bbd9-4f8c-8480-bf13b3c1e151, Windmill Bks.) Rosen Publishing Group, Inc., The.

—The Elves & the Emperor. Sanfilippo, Simona, illus. 2012. (ENG.). 32p. (J). (978-0-7787-8025-0(2)); pap. (978-0-7787-8036-6(8)) Crabtree Publishing Co.

—Goldilocks & the Wolf. Sanfilippo, Simona, illus. 2012. (ENG.). 32p. (J). (978-0-7787-8023-6(6)); pap. (978-0-7787-8034-2(1)) Crabtree Publishing Co.

—Hansel, Gretel, & the Ugly Duckling. Sanfilippo, Simona, illus. 2013. (ENG.). 32p. (J). (978-0-7787-1157-5(9)); pap. (978-0-7787-1166-7(8)) Crabtree Publishing Co.

—Rapunzel & the Billy Goats, 1 vol. Sanfilippo, Simona, illus. 2013. (ENG.). 32p. (J). pap. (978-0-7787-1158-2(7)) Crabtree Publishing Co.

—Snow White & the Enormous Turnip, 1 vol. Sanfilippo, Simona, illus. 2012. (ENG.). 32p. (J). pap. (978-0-7787-8035-9(X)) Crabtree Publishing Co.

—Three Pigs & a Gingerbread Man. Sanfilippo, Simona, illus. 2012. (ENG.). 32p. (J). (978-0-7787-8026-7(0)); pap. (978-0-7787-8037-3(6)) Crabtree Publishing Co.

Robinson, Michelle. And the Robot Went ... Ruzzier, Sergio, illus. 2017. (ENG.). 32p. (J). (gr. -1-3). 16.99 (978-0-544-58652-9(2), 1614145, Clarion Bks.) HarperCollins Pubs.

—Goodnight Digger: The Perfect Bedtime Book! East, Nick, illus. 2015. (Goodnight Ser.). (ENG.). 32p. (J). (gr. -1 — 1). pap. 7.99 (978-1-4380-0661-1(6)) Sourcebooks, Inc.

—Goodnight Pirate: The Perfect Bedtime Book! East, Nick, illus. 2015. (Goodnight Ser.). (ENG.). 32p. (J). (gr. -1 — 1). pap. 7.99 (978-1-4380-0662-8(4)) Sourcebooks, Inc.

—Goodnight Princess: The Perfect Bedtime Book! 2015. (Goodnight Ser.). (ENG., Illus.). 32p. (J). (gr. -1 — 1). pap. 7.99 (978-1-4380-0663-5(2)) Sourcebooks, Inc.

Robleda, Margarita. Ramon y Su Raton. Suarez, Maribel, illus. (Rana, Rema, Rimas Ser.). (SPA.). 16p. (J). (gr. k-3). 7.95 (978-1-59437-818-5(5)) Santillana USA Publishing Co., Inc.

Rocklin, Joanne. Good Guys, Bad Guys. Carpenter, Nancy, illus. 2020. (ENG.). 32p. (J). (gr. -1-3). 16.99 (978-1-4197-3417-5(2), 1138401, Abrams Bks. for Young Readers) Abrams, Inc.

Rodgers, Phillip W. When Was God Born?, 1 vol. 2008. (Discovering God Ser.). 32p. (J). 12.99 (978-0-8254-3608-6(7)) Kregel Pubns.

Rodriguez, Antonio Orlando. Mi Bicicleta es un Hada y Otros Secretos Por el Estilo. (SPA.). 68p. (J). (gr. k-2). (978-958-30-0797-2(8)) Panamericana Editorial COL. Dist: Lectorum Pubns., Inc.

Roe, Mechal Renee. Happy Hair. 2019. (Happy Hair Ser.). (ENG., Illus.). 32p. (J). (gr. -1-2). 16.99 (978-1-9848-9554-7(0), Doubleday Bks. for Young Readers) Random Hse. Children's Bks.

Rogalski, Mark. Make Me a Monster: (Juvenile Fiction, Kids Novelty Book, Children's Monster Book, Children's Lift the Flaps Book) 2019. (ENG., Illus.). 16p. (J). (gr. -1-k). bds. 14.99 (978-1-4521-6715-2(X)) Chronicle Bks. LLC.

Rogers, Anne. CAPTAIN DAN & SAILOR SAM. 2007. (ENG.). 37p. pap. 24.95 (978-1-4092-1029-0(4)) Lulu Pr., Inc.

—Sooty Wooty Is a Cat. 2008. (ENG.). 32p. pap. 23.95 (978-1-4092-2565-2(8)) Lulu Pr., Inc.

Rollins, Jack & Nelson, Steve. Frosty the Snowman Sticker Book. Thornburgh, Rebecca, illus. 2012. 24p. (J). 5.99 (978-0-8249-5646-2(X), Ideals Pubns.) Worthy Publishing.

Romagnoli, L. M. Memories of Me, 1 vol. 2009. 22p. pap. 24.95 (978-1-60836-084-0(9)) America Star Bks.

Roman, Lisa. Boots. Steckler, Megan, illus. 2009. 24p. pap. 24.95 (978-1-60749-329-7(2)) America Star Bks.

Romano, Annie Cronin. Before You Sleep: A Bedtime Book of Gratitude. Hobai, Ioana, illus. 2018. (ENG.). 40p. (J). 17.99 (978-1-62414-578-0(7), 900192299) Page Street Publishing Co.

Romero, Bernardita. Mummy, What's in Your Tummy? Romero, Bernardita, illus. 2020. (ENG., Illus.). 20p. (J). (gr. -1-k). bds. 8.99 (978-1-78285-976-5(4)) Barefoot Bks., Inc.

Roosa, Karen. Beach Day Board Book. Smith, Maggie, illus. 2018. (ENG.). 30p. (J). (— 1). bds. 7.99 (978-1-328-91069-1(5), 1701441, Clarion Bks.) HarperCollins Pubs.

Root, Phyllis. Flip, Flap, Fly! A Book for Babies Everywhere. Walker, David M., illus. 2011. (ENG.). 32p. (J). (gr. -1 — 1). bds. 7.99 (978-0-7636-5325-5(X)) Candlewick Pr.

—Looking for a Moose. Cecil, Randy, illus. 2008. (ENG.). 40p. (J). (gr. -1-2). pap. 8.99 (978-0-7636-3885-6(4)) Candlewick Pr.

—One Duck Stuck. 2003. (gr. k-3). 17.20 (978-0-613-60361-4(3)) Turtleback.

—One Duck Stuck: A Mucky Ducky Counting Book. Chapman, Jane, illus. 2003. (ENG.). 40p. (J). (gr. k-k). pap. 7.99 (978-0-7636-1566-6(8)) Candlewick Pr.

—One Duck Stuck Big Book: A Mucky Ducky Counting Book. Chapman, Jane, illus. 2008. (ENG.). 40p. (J). (gr. k-k). pap. 27.99 (978-0-7636-3817-7(X)) Candlewick Pr.

Rosario, Joann. Swiggly Swiggly Do! Rosario, Joann, illus. 2004. (Illus.). 5p. (J). (gr. -1-5). pap. 10.00 (978-0-9758746-6-0(7), 1246169) J.G.R. Enterprises.

Roscoe, Alessandra Pontes. JK, o Lobo-Guará. Oliveira, Jô, illus. 2010. (POR.). 29p. (J). (978-85-06-06063-6(X)) Companhia Melhoramentos de Sao Paulo Industrias de Papel.

Rose, Caroline Starr. Blue Birds. 2016. 400p. (J). (gr. 5). 10.99 (978-0-14-751187-4(9), Puffin Books) Penguin Young Readers Group.

—Ride on, Will Cody! A Legend of the Pony Express. Lillington, Joe, illus. 2017. (ENG.). 32p. (J). (gr. -1-3). 16.99 (978-0-8075-7068-5(0), 807570680) Whitman, Albert & Co.

Roseman-Mendoza, Natalie. Maritza's Garden Path. 2009. 32p. pap. 24.95 (978-1-60749-386-0(1)) America Star Bks.

Rosen, Wendy & End, Jackie. Chicken Fingers, Mac & Cheese... Why Do You Always Have to Say Please? Tuck-Bernstein, Cheryl, illus. 2005. 32p. (J). 14.99 (978-0-7666-1986-9(9)) Modern Publishing.

Rosenbaum, Andria Warmflash. A Grandma Like Yours: A Grandpa Like Yours. Björnson, Barbara, illus. 2006. 32p. (J). 16.95 (978-1-58013-167-4(0), Kar-Ben Publishing) Lerner Publishing Group.

—Trains Don't Sleep. Gill, Deirdre, illus. 2017. (ENG.). 40p. (J). (gr. -1-3). 16.99 (978-0-544-38074-5(6), 1591860, Clarion Bks.) HarperCollins Pubs.

Rosenberg, Madelyn. Take Care. Gregori, Giuliana, illus. 2018. (ENG.). 24p. (J). (gr. -1-3). 12.99 (978-0-8075-7732-5(4), 807577324) Whitman, Albert & Co.

Rosenthal, Amy Krouse. It's Not Fair! Lichtenheld, Tom, illus. 2008. (ENG.). 40p. (J). (gr. -1-3). 16.99 (978-0-06-115257-3(9), HarperCollins) HarperCollins Pubs.

—Little Miss, Big Sis. Reynolds, Peter H., illus. 2015. (ENG.). 40p. (J). (gr. -1-3). 19.99 (978-0-06-230203-8(5), HarperCollins) HarperCollins Pubs.

—Plant a Kiss. Reynolds, Peter H., illus. 2011. (ENG.). 40p. (J). (gr. -1-3). 15.99 (978-0-06-198675-8(5), HarperCollins) HarperCollins Pubs.

Ross, Barbara & Beatty, Nicholas. The Goops Circus: A Whimsical Telling of Do-Good Tales. Camille, Diana, illus. 2010. (Goops Ser.). 58p. (J). 19.95 incl. audio compact disk (978-0-9712368-4-4(4)) Goops Unlimited.

Rossetti-Shustak, Bernadette. I Love You Through & Through. Church, Caroline Jayne, illus. 2005. (ENG.). 24p. (J). (gr. -1 — 1). bds. 8.95 (978-0-439-67363-1(1), Cartwheel Bks.) Scholastic, Inc.

Roth, Anthony H. Little Anthony Doesn't Want to Eat His Dinner. 2012. 26p. 24.95 (978-1-4626-5776-6(1)) America Star Bks.

Roth, Carol. Here Comes the Choo Choo! Cushman, Doug, illus. 2007. (J). (978-0-15-205582-0(7)) Harcourt Trade Pubs.

—The Little School Bus. Paparone, Pamela, illus. (ENG.). 32p. (J). (gr. -1-1). 2012. 22.44 (978-0-7358-1646-6(8)) 2004. pap. 8.95 (978-0-7358-1905-4(X)) North-South Bks., Inc.

Roth, Carol & Julian, Sean. Five Little Ducklings Go to Bed. 2013. (Illus.). 32p. (J). pap. (978-0-7358-4153-6(5)) North-South Bks., Inc.

Roth-Fisch, Marla. Sensitive Sam: Sam's Sensory Adventure Has a Happy Ending! 2009. (ENG., Illus.). 29p. (J). pap. 11.95 (978-1-932565-86-7(8), P172781) Future Horizons, Inc.

Rothstein, Gloria L. Sheep Asleep. Date not set. 224p. (J). (gr. -1-1). pap. 4.99 (978-0-06-443717-2(5)) HarperCollins Pubs.

Rouss, Sylvia A. The Littlest Pair. Hannon, Holly, illus. 2005. 32p. (J). (gr. -1-1). 14.95 (978-1-930143-17-3(6), Devora Publishing) Simcha Media Group.

Rovetch, L. Bob. I Need a Kazoot! Castillon, Carly, illus. 2006. (J). (978-1-58987-055-0(7)) Kindermusik International.

—1,2,3 Octopus & Me. Gévry, Claudine, illus. 2006. (J). (978-1-58987-011-6(5)) Kindermusik International.

Rowe, Ben. Can an Alligator Drive a Nail with His Tail? 2008. 18p. pap. 24.95 (978-1-60610-625-9(2)) America Star Bks.

Rowland, Lucy. Pirate Pete & His Smelly Feet. Chambers, Mark, illus. 2017. (ENG.). 32p. (J). (gr. -1-1). 17.99 (978-1-5098-1776-4(X), Macmillan Children's Bks.) Pan Macmillan GBR. Dist: Independent Pubs. Group.

Rubin, Adam. High Five. Salmieri, Daniel, illus. 2019. 64p. (J). (-k). 19.99 (978-0-525-42889-3(5), Dial Bks) Penguin Young Readers Group.

Rubin, Susan Goldman. Jacob Lawrence in the City. 2009. (Mini Masters Modern Ser.). (ENG., Illus.). 24p. (J). (gr. -1 — 1). bds. 7.99 (978-0-8118-6582-1(7)) Chronicle Bks. LLC.

Rubinger, Ami. Big Cat, Small Cat. 2009. (ENG., Illus.). 28p. (J). (gr. -1-k). 13.95 (978-0-7892-1029-6(0), 791029, Abbeville Kids) Abbeville Pr., Inc.

—I Dream of an Elephant. 2010. (ENG., Illus.). 28p. (J). (gr. -1-k). 13.95 (978-0-7892-1058-6(4), 791058, Abbeville Kids) Abbeville Pr., Inc.

Ruble, Kam. Princess Annado Tandy's Versery Rhymes. McMullen, T. C., illus. l.t. ed. 2007. 88p. (J). per. (978-0-9779680-4-6(9)) Global Authors Pubns.

Rudi, Julie A. That's How Much I Love You. Beeke, Tiphanie, illus. 2013. (ENG.). 20p. (gr. -1). bds. 8.95 (978-1-58925-644-6(1)) Tiger Tales.

Rudolph the Red-Nosed Reindeer. 2014. (ENG., Illus.). 40p. (J). (gr. -1-1). 18.99 (978-1-4424-7495-6(5), Little Simon) Little Simon.

Rudy, Maggie & Abrams, Pam. The House That Mouse Built. Wolf, Bruce, photos by. 2011. (ENG., Illus.). 32p. (J). (gr. -1). 14.99 (978-1-935703-25-9(0)) Downtown Bookworks.

Rueda, Claudia, illus. I Know an Old Lady Who Swallowed a Fly. 2005. 14p. (J). 12.95 (978-1-58117-267-6(2), Intervisual/Piggy Toes) Bendon, Inc.

Ruelle, Karen Gray. Bark Park, 1 vol. 2014. (Illus.). 32p. (J). (gr. -1-k). pap. 7.99 (978-1-56145-773-1(6)) Peachtree Publishing Co. Inc.

Rumbaugh, Melinda. Somebunny Loves You! (ENG., Illus.). (J). 2019. 18p. (gr. -1-k). bds. 9.99 (978-0-8249-1687-9(5)) 2015. 16p. bds. 13.99 (978-0-8249-1950-4(5)) Worthy Publishing. (Worthy Kids/Ideals).

Rumble. 2014. (ENG., Illus.). 560p. (YA). (gr. 9). 21.99 (978-1-4424-8284-5(2), McElderry, Margaret K. Bks.) McElderry, Margaret K. Bks.

Rundstrom, Teressa. The Adventures of Tommy Toad. Marshall, Setsu, illus. 2004. 40p. (J). per. (978-1-932062-41-0(6)) Idea Magic Bks.

Ruurs, Margriet. A Pacific Alphabet, 1 vol. 2004. (ENG., Illus.). 32p. (J). (gr. -1-2). 9.95 (978-1-55285-264-4(4), 632f33d3-92ff-4004-bce9-2f9a85a5a64c) Whitecap Bks., Ltd. CAN. Dist: Firefly Bks., Ltd.

Ryan, Pam Muñoz. Hello Ocean. Astrella, Mark, illus. 2014. 32p. pap. 8.00 (978-1-61003-319-0(1)) Center for the Collaborative Classroom.

—Hola Mar / Hello Ocean. Astrella, Mark, illus. 2003. (Charlesbridge Bilingual Bks.).Tr. of Hello Ocean (Bilingual). 32p. (J). (gr. -1-2). pap. 7.95 (978-1-57091-372-3(2)) Charlesbridge Publishing, Inc.

Ryder, Joanne. Bear of My Heart. Moore, Margie, illus. 2009. (ENG.). 32p. (J). (gr. -1 — 1). bds. 9.99 (978-1-4169-5472-9(4), Little Simon) Little Simon.

—Won't You Be My Hugaroo? Board Book. Sweet, Melissa, illus. 2008. (ENG.). 30p. (J). (gr. -1 — 1). bds. 6.95 (978-0-15-206298-9(X), 1198872, Clarion Bks.) HarperCollins Pubs.

Rylant, Cynthia. All in a Day. McClure, Nikki, illus. (ENG.). (J). (gr. -1 — 1). 2017. 30p. bds. 9.99 (978-1-4197-2612-5(9), 647710, Abrams Appleseed) 2009. 32p. 18.95 (978-0-8109-8321-2(4), 647701, Abrams Bks. for Young Readers) Abrams, Inc.

—If You'll Be My Valentine. Kosaka, Fumi, illus. 2005. (ENG.). 32p. (J). (gr. -1-3). pap. 7.99 (978-0-06-009271-9(8), HarperCollins) HarperCollins Pubs.

—The Stars Will Still Shine. Beeke, Tiphanie, illus. 2005. 40p. (J). lib. bdg. 17.89 (978-0-06-054640-3(9)); (ENG.). (gr. -1-3). 17.99 (978-0-06-054639-7(5), HarperCollins) HarperCollins Pubs.

Sadler, Marilyn & Bollen, Roger. Money, Money, Honey Bunny! 2006. (Bright & Early Books(R) Ser.). (ENG., Illus.). 36p. (J). (gr. -1-k). 9.99 (978-0-375-83370-0(6), Random Hse. Bks. for Young Readers) Random Hse. Children's Bks.

Sáenz, Benjamin Alire. Aristotle & Dante Discover the Secrets of the Universe. 2014. lib. bdg. 23.30 (978-0-606-35117-1(5)) Turtleback.

Sagendorph, Jean. Starry Night, Hold Me Tight. Siebold, Kim, illus. 2015. (ENG.). 18p. (J). (gr. -1 — 1). bds. 6.95 (978-0-7624-5853-0(4), Running Pr. Kids) Running Pr.

Salas, Laura Purdie. A Leaf Can Be ... Dabija, Violeta, illus. 2012. (Can Be ... Bks.). (ENG.). 32p. (J). (gr. k-2). lib. bdg. 17.99 (978-0-7613-6203-6(7), c9a532c1-3829-44ad-b62b-d22a0a73b8c4, Millbrook Pr.) Lerner Publishing Group.

Salom, Andree. When the Anger Ogre Visits. Salom, Ivette, illus. 2015. (ENG.). 40p. (J). 18.95 (978-1-61429-166-4(7)) Wisdom Pubns.

Salomon, Bob & Young, Rick. Beyond the Laces. 2015. (ENG., Illus.). (J). pap. 12.95 (978-1-4951-5694-6(X)) Independent Pub.

Saltzberg, Barney. Redbird: Colors, Colors, Everywhere! 2015. (ENG., Illus.). 22p. (J). bds. (978-0-7611-8185-9(7), 18185) Workman Publishing Co., Inc.

—Twinkle, Twinkle, ABC: A Mixed-Up, Mashed-up Melody. 2017. (ENG., Illus.). 32p. (gr. -1 — 1). bds. 12.95 (978-0-7148-7507-1(4)) Phaidon Pr., Inc.

San Souci, Robert D. Cinderella Skeleton. Catrow, David, illus. 2004. (ENG.). 32p. (J). (gr. -1-3). reprint ed. pap. 7.99 (978-0-15-205069-6(8), 1195310, Clarion Bks.) HarperCollins Pubs.

Sanchez, Jenny Torres. Death, Dickinson, & the Demented Life of Frenchie Garcia. 2013. (ENG.). 272p. (YA). (gr. 7-17). pap. 15.99 (978-0-7624-4680-3(3), Running Pr. Kids) Running Pr.

Sandage, Charley. ALL AROUND ARKANSAS student Edition. 2005. (Illus.). (J). pap. (978-0-9638956-5-3(6)) Archeological Assessments, Inc.

Sandall, Ellie. Everybunny Count! Sandall, Ellie, illus. 2018. (ENG., Illus.). 32p. (J). (gr. -1-3). 17.99 (978-1-5344-0014-6(1), McElderry, Margaret K. Bks.) McElderry, Margaret K. Bks.

—Everybunny Dance! Sandall, Ellie, illus. 2017. (ENG., Illus.). 32p. (J). (gr. -1-3). 17.99 (978-1-4814-9822-7(3), McElderry, Margaret K. Bks.) McElderry, Margaret K. Bks.

—Everybunny Dream! Sandall, Ellie, illus. 2019. (ENG., Illus.). 32p. (J). (gr. -1-3). 17.99 (978-1-5344-4004-3(6), McElderry, Margaret K. Bks.) McElderry, Margaret K. Bks.

Sandburg, Carl. Rootabaga Stories. 2009. 128p. (gr. 3-18). pap. 10.95 (978-1-60664-425-6(4)) Rodgers, Alan Bks.

Sanders, Karen Nordberg. Ruth & Naomi. Rooney, Ronnie, illus. 2007. 16p. (J). (gr. k-4). 1.99 (978-0-7586-1283-0(4)) Concordia Publishing Hse.

Sandoval, Anna. Tickle a Daisy. 2007. 28p. per. 24.95 (978-1-4241-8470-5(3)) America Star Bks.

Sandra De Mos. Cleo's Playground Adventure. 2009. 40p. pap. 16.99 (978-1-4389-2049-8(0)) AuthorHouse.

Santa's Busy Christmas Eve. 2003. (J). 4.99 (978-1-59384-011-2(X)) Parklane Publishing.

Santoro, Scott. Which Way to Witch School? Santoro, Scott, illus. (ENG., Illus.). 32p. (J). (gr. -1-2). 2012. pap. 5.99 (978-0-06-078183-5(1)) 2010. 16.99 (978-0-06-078181-1(5)) HarperCollins Pubs. (HarperCollins).

Sapp, Karen. Rookie Preschool: Rookie Learn about Nauture: Who Is Sleeping? 2009. (Rookie Preschool-NEW Ser.). (ENG.). 24p. (J). pap. 6.95 (978-0-531-24586-6(1)); (gr. -1). lib. bdg. 23.00 (978-0-531-24411-1(3)) Scholastic Library Publishing. (Children's Pr.).

Sargent, Dave M., Jr. Vicious Vera, 9 vols. Huff, Jeane Lirley, illus. 2004. (Doggie Tails Ser.: 9). (J). pap. 10.95 (978-1-56763-854-7(6)) Ozark Publishing.

Sarno-Doyle, Christine. Your Inside Shape. 2012. (ENG., Illus.). 32p. (J). 17.95 (978-0-9824461-0-2(1)) SDP Publishing.

Saroyan, William & Tinkelman, Murray. Me. 2016. (ENG., Illus.). 64p. (gr. 1-3). pap. 9.99 (978-0-486-81066-9(6), 810666) Dover Pubns., Inc.

Sarta, Jon. Your Adoption Story. 2005. 20p. 9.99 (978-1-4116-6439-5(6)) Lulu Pr., Inc.

Sartell, Debra. Time for Bed, Baby Ted. Chorao, Kay, illus. 2010. (ENG.). 32p. (J). (gr. -1). 16.95 (978-0-8234-1968-5(1)) Holiday Hse., Inc.

Sassi, Laura. Goodnight, Ark, 1 vol. Chapman, Jane, illus. 2014. (ENG.). 32p. (J). bds. 16.99 (978-0-310-73784-1(2)) Zonderkidz.

—Goodnight, Manger, 1 vol. Chapman, Jane, illus. 2015. (ENG.). 32p. (J). 17.99 (978-0-310-74556-3(X)) Zonderkidz.

Sauer, Abe. Goodnight Loon. Davauer, Nathaniel, illus. 2014. (ENG.). 28p. (J). 9.95 (978-0-8166-9703-8(5)) Univ. of Minnesota Pr.

Saupé, Rick. Moses P Rose Has Broken His Nose. DeBroeck, Sarah, illus. 2012. 28p. pap. 24.95 (978-1-4626-0547-7(8)) America Star Bks.

Sauro, Joan. Does God Ever Sleep? 2005. (ENG., Illus.). 32p. (J). (gr. -1-3). 8.99 (978-1-59473-110-5(1), 0f264a4f-7d8c-4d33-857b-7367428d81a2, Skylight Paths Publishing) LongHill Partners, Inc.

Sauvageau-Smestad, Sheila. Rain, Rain, What a Pain! 2006. (Illus.). 37p. (J). per. 17.95 (978-0-9771971-6-3(6)) W & B Pubs.

Savage, Stephen. Ten Orange Pumpkins: A Counting Book. 2013. (Illus.). 48p. (J). (gr. -1-k). 17.99 (978-0-8037-3938-3(9), Dial Bks) Penguin Young Readers Group.

Sayre, April Pulley. If You're Hoppy. Urbanovic, Jackie, illus. 2011. (ENG.). 40p. (J). (gr. -1-k). 16.99 (978-0-06-156634-9(9), Greenwillow Bks.) HarperCollins Pubs.

Sayres, Brianna Caplan. Night Night, Curiosity. O'Rourke, Ryan, illus. 2020. 32p. (J). (gr. -1-2). lib. bdg. 16.99 (978-1-58089-893-5(9)) Charlesbridge Publishing, Inc.

—Where Do Diggers Celebrate Christmas? Slade, Christian, illus. (Where Do... Ser.). (J). 2019. 26p. (— 1). bds. 8.99 (978-0-525-57951-9(6)) 2018. 32p. (gr. -1-2). 16.99 (978-1-5247-7215-4(1)) Random Hse. Children's Bks. (Random Hse. Bks. for Young Readers).

—Where Do Diggers Sleep at Night? Slade, Christian, illus. (Where Do... Ser.). (J). (— 1). 2014. 26p. bds. 8.99 (978-0-385-37415-6(1)) 2012. 32p. 18.99 (978-0-375-86848-1(8)) Random Hse. Children's Bks. (Random Hse. Bks. for Young Readers).

—Where Do Jet Planes Sleep at Night? Slade, Christian, illus. 2017. (Where Do... Ser.). 32p. (J). (gr. -1-2). 16.99 (978-0-399-55448-3(3), Random Hse. Bks. for Young Readers) Random Hse. Children's Bks.

—Where Do Speedboats Sleep at Night? Slade, Christian, illus. 2019. (Where Do... Ser.). 32p. (J). (gr. -1-2). 16.99 (978-1-5247-6575-0(9), Random Hse. Bks. for Young Readers) Random Hse. Children's Bks.

—Where Do Steam Trains Sleep at Night? Slade, Christian, illus. 2017. (Where Do... Ser.). 26p. (J). (gr. -1 — 1). bds. 8.99 (978-0-553-52100-9(4), Random Hse. Bks. for Young Readers) Random Hse. Children's Bks.

Scaglione, Joanne & Small, Gail. The Big Squeal: A Wild, True, & Twisted Tail. 2005. (ENG., Illus.). 56p. pap. 47.00 (978-1-57886-256-6(6)) Rowman & Littlefield Education.

Scanlon, Cara. Where Did Grandma Go? Mattes-Ruggiero, Lynn, illus. 2008. (J). (978-1-930596-85-6(5)) Amherst Pr.

—Where Did Grandpa Go? Mattes-Ruggiero, Lynn, illus. 2008. (J). (978-1-930596-86-3(3)) Amherst Pr.

Scanlon, Liz Garton. Happy Birthday, Bunny! Graegin, Stephanie, illus. 2013. (ENG.). 32p. (J). (gr. -1-3). 19.99 (978-1-4424-0287-4(3), Beach Lane Bks.) Beach Lane Bks.

—In the Canyon. Wolff, Ashley, illus. 2015. (ENG.). 40p. (J). (gr. -1-3). 17.99 (978-1-4814-0348-1(6), Beach Lane Bks.) Beach Lane Bks.

Scelsa, Greg & Debney, John. Friends Forever. Faulkner, Stacey, ed. Mahan, Benton, illus. 2006. (J). pap. 2.99 (978-1-59198-322-4(3)) Creative Teaching Pr., Inc.

Schade, Susan. Riff Raff Sails the High Cheese. Kennedy, Anne, illus. 2014. (I Can Read Level 2 Ser.). (ENG.). 24p. (J). (gr. -1-3). pap. 3.99 (978-0-06-230509-1(3), HarperCollins) HarperCollins Pubs.

Schaefer, Lola M. An Island Grows. 2006. (ENG., Illus.). 40p. (J). (gr. -1-3). 17.99 (978-0-06-623930-9(3), Greenwillow Bks.) HarperCollins Pubs.

—Loose Tooth. Wickstrom, Sylvie K., tr. Wickstrom, Sylvie K., illus. 2004. (My First I Can Read Bks.). 32p. (J). (gr. -1-18). 14.99 (978-0-06-052776-1(5)) HarperCollins Pubs.

Schafer, Milton. I'm Big! Lew-Vriethoff, Joanne, illus. 2006. (J). (978-1-4156-8150-3(3), Dial) Penguin Publishing Group.

Schamerhorn, Ronna. Dreamy Navy Boy. 2007. 44p. per. 24.95 (978-1-4241-8372-2(3)) America Star Bks.

Schaub, Michelle. Finding Treasure: A Collection of Collections. Saldana, Carmen, illus. 2019. 32p. (J). (gr. -1-3). lib. bdg. 16.99 (978-1-58089-875-1(0)) Charlesbridge Publishing, Inc.

Schaumberg, Rose Mary & Schaumberg, Emily Rose. I'll Miss My Grandma, Wouldn't You? 2008. (Illus.). 40p. pap. 16.99 (978-1-4389-1335-3(4)) AuthorHouse.

Schertle, Alice. The Adventures of Old Bo Bear. Parkins, David, illus. 2005. (J). 16.95 (978-978-081-183-9(4)) Chronicle Bks. LLC.

—El Camioncito Azul: Little Blue Truck (Spanish Edition) McElmurry, Jill, illus. 2013.Tr. of Little Blue Truck. (SPA.). 30p. (J). (gr. -1 — 1). bds. 9.99 (978-0-547-98397-4(2), 1524121, Clarion Bks.) HarperCollins Pubs.

—Little Blue Truck. McElmurry, Jill, illus. 2008. (ENG.). 32p. (J). (gr. -1-3). 18.99 (978-0-15-205661-2(0), 1197021, Clarion Bks.) HarperCollins Pubs.

—Little Blue Truck. (J). 37.75 (978-1-4703-3557-1(3)); 194.75 (978-1-4703-3555-7(7)); 2012. 39.75 (978-1-4703-3013-2(X)); 2012. 37.75 (978-1-4703-3558-8(1)) Recorded Bks., Inc.

—Little Blue Truck Big Book. McElmurry, Jill, illus. 2010. (ENG.). 32p. (J). (gr. -1-3). pap. 26.99 (978-0-547-48248-4(5), 1439681, Clarion Bks.) HarperCollins Pubs.

—Little Blue Truck Lap Board Book. McElmurry, Jill, illus. 2015. (ENG.). 30p. (J). (— 1). bds. 12.99 (978-0-544-05685-5(X), 1533603, Clarion Bks.) HarperCollins Pubs.

—Little Blue Truck Leads the Way Big Book. McElmurry, Jill, illus. 2012. (ENG.). 40p. (J). (gr. -1-3). pap. 26.99 (978-0-547-85060-3(3), 1501044, Clarion Bks.) HarperCollins Pubs.

—Little Blue Truck Leads the Way Lap Board Book. McElmurry, Jill, illus. 2016. (ENG.). 38p. (J). (— 1). bds. 12.99 (978-0-544-70899-0(7), 1628910, Clarion Bks.) HarperCollins Pubs.

—Little Blue Truck's Christmas: A Christmas Holiday Book for Kids. McElmurry, Jill, illus. 2014. (ENG.). 24p. (J). (— 1). 18.99 (978-0-544-32041-3(7), 1582526, Clarion Bks.) HarperCollins Pubs.

—Little Blue Truck's Springtime: An Easter & Springtime Book for Kids. McElmurry, Jill, illus. 2018. (ENG.). 16p. (J). (gr. -1 — 1). bds. 13.99 (978-0-544-93809-0(7), 1658575, Clarion Bks.) HarperCollins Pubs.

—The Skeleton in the Closet. Jobling, Curtis, illus. 2003. (ENG.). 32p. (J). (gr. 1-18). 15.99 (978-0-688-17738-6(7)) HarperCollins Pubs.

—Time for School, Little Blue Truck: A Back to School Book for Kids. McElmurry, Jill, illus. 2021. (Little Blue Truck Ser.). (ENG.). 32p. (J). (gr. -1-3). 18.99 (978-0-358-41224-3(2), 1790429, Clarion Bks.) HarperCollins Pubs.

—Time for School, Little Blue Truck Big Book. McElmurry, Jill, illus. 2022. (ENG.). 32p. (J). (gr. -1-3). pap. 26.99 (978-0-358-66599-1(X), 1822616, Clarion Bks.) HarperCollins Pubs.

Scheuer, Benjamin. Hibernate with Me. Williams, Jemima, illus. 2019. (ENG.). 40p. (J). (gr. -1-3). 17.99 (978-1-5344-3217-8(5), Simon & Schuster Bks. For Young Readers) Simon & Schuster Bks. For Young Readers.

Schiller, Pam. Five Little Ducks. Newsom, Carol, illus. 2014. 19p. (J). (978-1-60128-879-0(4)) Frog Street Pr.

Schindel, John. Busy Barnyard. Holt, Steven, photos by. 2006. (Busy Book Ser.). (Illus.). 20p. (J). (— 1). 7.99 (978-1-58246-168-7(6), Tricycle Pr.) Random Hse. Children's Bks.

—Busy Kitties. Franzen, Sean, photos by. 2004. (Busy Book Ser.). (Illus.). 20p. (J). (— 1). 6.99 (978-1-58246-130-4(9), Knopf Bks. for Young Readers) Random Hse. Children's Bks.

—Busy Piggies. Holt, Steven, photos by. 2006. (Busy Book Ser.). (Illus.). 20p. (J). (gr. k — 1). 7.99 (978-1-58246-169-4(4), Tricycle Pr.) Random Hse. Children's Bks.

Schmatjen, Marc. My Giraffe Makes Me Laugh. 2010. 24p. 12.95 (978-1-4520-0941-4(4)) AuthorHouse.

Schmidt, Hans-Christian. Are You Sleeping Little One? Német, Andrea, illus. 2012. (ENG.). 18p. (J). (gr. k-k). 6.95 (978-0-7892-1120-0(3), 791120, Abbeville Kids) Abbeville Pr., Inc.

Schneider, Josh. Everybody Sleeps (but Not Fred) 2015. (ENG., Illus.). 32p. (J). (gr. -1-3). 16.99 (978-0-544-33924-8(X), 1584495, Clarion Bks.) HarperCollins Pubs.

Schnell, David. The Night Before Baseball at the Park by the Bay. Pamintuan, Macky, illus. 2013. (ENG.). 32p. 0.00 (978-0-9891043-0-2(3)) Prospect Palo Alto Publishing.

Schnitzlein, Danny. The Monster Who Ate My Peas, 1 vol. Faulkner, Matt, illus. 2010. 32p. (J). (gr. -1-3). pap. 7.95 (978-1-56145-533-1(4)) Peachtree Publishing Co. Inc.

—The Monster Who Did My Math, 1 vol. Mayer, Bill, illus. 32p. (J). (gr. -1-3). 2012. pap. 8.99 (978-1-56145-668-0(3)) 2007. 16.95 (978-1-56145-420-4(6)) Peachtree Publishing Co. Inc.

—Trick or Treat on Monster Street, 1 vol. Faulkner, Matt, illus. 2008. 32p. (J). (gr. -1-3). 16.95 (978-1-56145-465-5(6)) Peachtree Publishing Co. Inc.

Schoen, Sarah. Omar the Smiling Labrador, 1 vol. 2010. 26p. pap. 24.95 (978-1-4489-6231-0(5)) PublishAmerica, Inc.

Schoenherr, Ian. Cat & Mouse. Schoenherr, Ian, illus. 2008. (Illus.). 40p. (J). (gr. -1). lib. bdg. 17.89 (978-0-06-136314-6(6), Greenwillow Bks.) HarperCollins Pubs.

—Read It, Don't Eat It! Schoenherr, Ian, illus. 2009. (ENG., Illus.). 32p. (J). (gr. -1 — 1). 18.99 (978-0-06-172455-8(6)); lib. bdg. 18.89 (978-0-06-178034-9(0)) HarperCollins Pubs. (Greenwillow Bks.).

Scholastic, Inc. Staff. Will You Wear a Blue Hat? 2009. (Rookie Toddler Ser.). (ENG., Illus.). 14p. (J). (gr. -1 — 1). bds. 6.95 (978-0-531-24549-1(7), Children's Pr.) Scholastic Library Publishing.

Scholastic, Inc. Staff & Bermiss, Aamir Lee. I Hate to Be Sick! Wilson-Max, Ken, illus. 2004. (Just for You Ser.). (ENG.). 32p. (gr. k-3). pap. 3.99 (978-0-439-56877-7(3), Teaching Resources) Scholastic, Inc.

Scholastic Library Publishing. The Three Little Kittens Get Dressed. 2009. (Rookie Preschool Ser.). 24p. (J). (gr. -1). lib. bdg. 23.00 (978-0-531-24404-3(0), Children's Pr.) Scholastic Library Publishing.

Schomer-Wendel, Gretchen & Schomer, Adam Anthony. All Around Town, 1 vol. Renthrope, Damon, illus. 2009. (Becka & the Big Bubble Ser.). (ENG.). 32p. (J). (gr. 1-2). pap. 11.55 (978-1-60754-105-9(X), 40ba8d14-355a-4eed-8c80-5dccc55d9e6f); lib. bdg. 27.27 (978-1-60754-104-2(1), d0c1c60d-ea83-44d6-b3b9-914d5d09e595) Rosen Publishing Group, Inc., The. (Windmill Bks.).

—Becka Goes to Chicago, 1 vol. Renthrope, Damon, illus. 2009. (Becka & the Big Bubble Ser.). (ENG.). 32p. (J). (gr. 1-2). 27.27 (978-1-60754-119-6(X), e59a3a16-4f70-4398-a707-6436677d4475); pap. 11.55 (978-1-60754-120-2(3), fcacf115-09c1-4a4e-a6de-2ce94c4581bc) Rosen Publishing Group, Inc., The. (Windmill Bks.).

—Becka Goes to India, 1 vol. Renthrope, Damon, illus. 2009. (Becka & the Big Bubble Ser.). (ENG.). 32p. (J). (gr. 1-2). pap. 11.55 (978-1-60754-111-0(4), ed13b8f1-b67e-40e1-912f-9dad61ebcf1b); lib. bdg. 27.27 (978-1-60754-110-3(6), a51681e0-5005-4e43-93bb-cb63d3dee051) Rosen Publishing Group, Inc., The. (Windmill Bks.).

—Becka Goes to San Diego, 1 vol. Renthrope, Damon, illus. 2009. (Becka & the Big Bubble Ser.). (ENG.). 32p. (J). (gr. 1-2). 27.27 (978-1-60754-113-4(0), 3096e07b-9e32-40a5-aeb5-2ff400500eca); pap. 11.55 (978-1-60754-114-1(9), 6dfa7581-4d0b-4b4e-8af5-348a0418bc50) Rosen Publishing Group, Inc., The. (Windmill Bks.).

—Becka Goes to San Francisco, 1 vol. Renthrope, Damon, illus. 2009. (Becka & the Big Bubble Ser.). (ENG.). 32p. (J). (gr. 1-2). 27.27 (978-1-60754-107-3(6), 170513f4-02aa-46b8-9669-835833a908e1); pap. 11.55 (978-1-60754-108-0(4), 786c09a2-f35f-4e17-a27d-fb3874f3785c) Rosen Publishing Group, Inc., The. (Windmill Bks.).

—Becka Goes to the North Pole, 1 vol. Renthrope, Damon, illus. 2009. (Becka & the Big Bubble Ser.). (ENG.). 32p. (J). (gr. 1-2). pap. 11.55 (978-1-60754-117-2(3), c00b48e1-07cf-4ffd-b439-e3a8068d929d); lib. bdg. 27.27 (978-1-60754-116-5(5), dc207ff7-b36b-4fc4-8048-4f53104e6923) Rosen Publishing Group, Inc., The. (Windmill Bks.).

Schrader, Missy Wolgemuth & Schrader, Missy W. Hooray! I Obeyed!, 1 vol. Nuffer, Bruce, ed. 2008. (ENG., Illus.). 12p. (J). (gr. -1). bds. 3.99 (978-0-310-71396-8(X)) Zondervan.

Schroeder, Lisa. Chasing Brooklyn. 2011. (ENG.). 432p. (YA). (gr. 9). pap. 12.99 (978-1-4169-9174-8(3), Simon Pulse) Simon Pulse.

—Far from You. 2008. (ENG.). 368p. (YA). (gr. 8-18). 15.99 (978-1-4169-7506-9(3), Simon Pulse) Simon Pulse.

Schuepbach, Lynnette. Cat Time. 2006. 28p. pap. 12.95 (978-0-9759613-2-2(2)) Creative Sources.

Schulman, Janet. 10 Easter Egg Hunters. 2015. lib. bdg. 14.75 (978-0-606-36379-2(3)) Turtleback.

—10 Easter Egg Hunters: A Holiday Counting Book. Davick, Linda, illus. 2012. 26p. (J). (gr. -1 — 1). 6.99 (978-0-375-86637-1(X), Knopf Bks. for Young Readers) Random Hse. Children's Bks.

—10 Trick-Or-Treaters. Davick, Linda, illus. 2009. 26p. (J). (gr. -1-2). 7.99 (978-0-375-85347-0(2), Knopf Bks. for Young Readers) Random Hse. Children's Bks.

Schultz, Doreen. The Days of Noah. 2013. 26p. pap. 9.99 (978-1-62697-228-5(1)) Salem Author Services.

Schulz, Kathy. I Do Not Want To. Rescek, Sanja, illus. 2011. (Rookie Ready to Learn Ser.). 40p. (J). pap. 5.95 (978-0-531-26707-3(5)); (gr. -1-k). lib. bdg. 23.00 (978-0-531-26525-3(0)) Scholastic Library Publishing. (Children's Pr.).

—I Need a Little Help. Iosa, Ann, illus. 2011. (Rookie Ready to Learn — All about Me! Ser.). 32p. (J). (gr. -1-k). lib. bdg. 25.00 (978-0-531-26526-0(9), Children's Pr.) Scholastic Library Publishing.

—Rookie Ready to Learn en Español: Necesito una Ayudita. Iosa, Ann, illus. 2011. (Rookie Ready to Learn Español Ser.). Orig. Title: Rookie Ready to Learn: I Need a Little Help. (SPA.). 32p. (J). pap. 5.95 (978-0-531-26782-0(2), Children's Pr.) Scholastic Library Publishing.

Schwartz, Amy. Busy Babies. Schwartz, Amy, illus. 2019. (ENG., Illus.). 32p. (J). (gr. -1-3). 17.99 (978-1-4814-4510-8(3), Beach Lane Bks.) Beach Lane Bks.

—100 Things I Love to Do with You. 2017. (ENG., Illus.). 40p. (J). (gr. -1-k). 16.95 *(978-1-4197-2288-2(3)*, 1121401, Abrams Appleseed) Abrams, Inc.

—100 Things That Make Me Happy. 2014. (100 Things Ser.). (ENG., Illus.). 40p. (J). (gr. -1-1). 16.95 *(978-1-4197-0518-2(0)*, 1045001, Abrams Appleseed) Abrams, Inc.

Schwartz, Betty & Seresin, Lynn. Puppies, Puppies, Everywhere! A Back-And-Forth Opposites Book. Powell, Luciana Navarro, illus. 2015. (J). *(978-1-62370-236-6(4)*, Capstone Young Readers) Capstone.

Schwartz, Corey Rosen. Ninja Red Riding Hood. Santat, Dan, illus. 2014. 40p. (J). (gr. k-3). 18.99 *(978-0-399-16354-8(9)*, G.P. Putnam's Sons Books for Young Readers) Penguin Young Readers Group.

—The Three Ninja Pigs. Santat, Dan, illus. 2012. 40p. (J). (gr. k-3). 18.99 *(978-0-399-25514-4(1)*, G.P. Putnam's Sons Books for Young Readers) Penguin Young Readers Group.

—Twinderella, a Fractioned Fairy Tale. Marcero, Deborah, illus. 2017. 32p. (J). (gr. -1-3). 17.99 *(978-0-399-17633-3(0)*, G.P. Putnam's Sons Books for Young Readers) Penguin Young Readers Group.

Schwartz, Corey Rosen & Coulton, Beth. Goldi Rocks & the Three Bears. Wragg, Nate, illus. 2014. 32p. (J). (gr. k-3). 17.99 *(978-0-399-25685-1(7)*, G.P. Putnam's Sons Books for Young Readers) Penguin Young Readers Group.

Schwartz, Corey Rosen & Gomez, Rebecca J. Hensel & Gretel: Ninja Chicks. Santat, Dan, illus. 2016. 40p. (J). (gr. k-3). 18.99 *(978-0-399-17626-5(8)*, G.P. Putnam's Sons Books for Young Readers) Penguin Young Readers Group.

—Two Tough Trucks. Leung, Hilary, illus. 2019. (ENG.). 40p. (J). (gr. -1-k). 17.99 *(978-1-338-23654-5(7)*, Orchard Bks.) Scholastic, Inc.

—What about Moose? Yamaguchi, Keika, illus. 2015. (ENG.). 40p. (J). (gr. -1-3). 19.99 *(978-1-4814-0496-9(2)*, Atheneum Bks. for Young Readers) Simon & Schuster Children's Publishing.

Scieszka, Jon. Dizzy Izzy: Ready-To-Read Level 1. Shannon, David et al, illus. 2014. (Jon Scieszka's Trucktown Ser.). (ENG.). 24p. (J). (gr. -1-1). 17.99 *(978-1-4814-1460-9(7)*, Simon Spotlight) Simon Spotlight.

Scillian, Devin. Johnny Kaw: A Tall Tale. Sneed, Brad, illus. 2013. (ENG.). 32p. (J). (gr. 1-4). 15.95 *(978-1-58536-791-7(5)*, 202353) Sleeping Bear Pr.

Scott, Janine. Café Cosmos, 1 vol. Wood, Hannah, illus. 2009. (Treasure Chest Readers Ser.). (ENG.). 24p. (J). (gr. 1-1). pap. 9.15 *(978-1-60754-674-0(4)*, 1dece89f-fea7-4a4b-b784-8d6413382311); lib. bdg. 27.27 *(978-1-60754-673-3(6)*, 16ffcaf2-b162-4e05-83e0-eb19ec85efb5) Rosen Publishing Group, Inc., The. (Windmill Bks.).

—Mars Mouse, 1 vol. Wood, Hannah, illus. 2009. (Treasure Chest Readers Ser.). (ENG.). 24p. (J). (gr. 1-1). pap. 9.15 *(978-1-60754-677-1(9)*, 91ae73ab-a879-4fb8-9c38-fd87648aaf30); lib. bdg. 27.27 *(978-1-60754-676-4(0)*, c87bb159-35dd-4473-a072-85a046b4d8b0) Rosen Publishing Group, Inc., The. (Windmill Bks.).

Scott, Joanna I. Stanley the Moose: Book One of the Woodsie Tails Series. 2009. (Illus.). 40p. (J). 19.95 net. *(978-0-9795678-1-0(5))* Cherakota Publishing.

Scribens, Sunny. Baby Dream. 2019. (ENG., Illus.). 16p. (J). (gr. -1-k). bds. 7.99 *(978-1-78285-729-7(X))* Barefoot Bks., Inc.

—Baby Dream / Soñando con Bebé. 2019. (ENG., Illus.). 16p. (J). (gr. -1-k). bds. 7.99 *(978-1-78285-737-2(0))* Barefoot Bks., Inc.

—My Friend Robot! Skipp, Hui, illus. 2017. (ENG.). 32p. (J). (gr. -1-1). 16.99 *(978-1-78285-322-0(7))* Barefoot Bks., Inc.

Scudamore, Angelika, illus. Little Puppy's Busy Day. 2016. (J). *(978-1-62885-142-7(2))* Kidsbooks, LLC.

Sears, Gale. The Missing Christmas Treasure. Johnson, Meredith, illus. 2012. (J). *(978-1-60861-283-3(X))* Covenant Communications, Inc.

Seaworthy, Oscar. Port Side Pirates. 2008. (ENG., Illus.). 32p. (J). 6.99 *(978-1-84686-205-2(1))*; 9.99 *(978-1-84686-153-6(5))* Barefoot Bks., Inc.

Seder, Rufus Butler. AL Galope! 2009. (Scanimation Ser.). (SPA., Illus.). 12p. (J). (gr. -1-3). 12.95 *(978-0-7611-5415-0(9)*, 15415) Workman Publishing Co., Inc.

Seeger, Laura Vaccaro. Green. 2015. (CHI.). 40p. (J). *(978-7-5568-0145-9(4))* 21st Century Publishing Hse.

—Green. 2014. (KOR.). 36p. (J). *(978-89-7938-085-9(2))* Dasan Publishing Hse.

Seigerman, Michelle. A Christmastime Book of Rhymes. 2005. 35p. pap. 13.08 *(978-1-4116-4960-6(5))* Lulu Pr., Inc.

Selbert, Kathryn, illus. Ally Bally Bee: A Lift-The-flap Book, 30 vols. 2022. (Scottish Rhymes Ser.). 12p. (J). 9.95 *(978-1-78250-439-9(7)*, Kelpies) Floris Bks. GBR. Dist: Consortium Bk. Sales & Distribution.

Self, Timothy. Davy the Dolphin. Lt. ed. 2003. (Illus.). 22p. (J). per. 8.99 *(978-1-932338-30-0(6))* Lifevest Publishing, Inc.

Seltzer, Eric. Arf! Buzz! Cluck! A Rather Noisy Alphabet. Creighton-Pester, David, illus. 2018. (ENG.). 24p. (J). (gr. -1 — 1). bds. 7.99 *(978-1-5344-1297-2(2)*, Little Simon) Little Simon.

—Bake, Mice, Bake! Rosenberg, Natascha, illus. 2012. (Penguin Young Readers, Level 1 Ser.). 32p. (J). (gr. k-1). mass mkt. 4.99 *(978-0-448-45763-5(6)*, Penguin Young Readers) Penguin Young Readers Group.

—Bake, Mice, Bake! 2012. (Penguin Young Readers: Level 1 Ser.). lib. bdg. 13.55 *(978-0-606-23625-6(2))* Turtleback.

—Dog on His Bus. Braun, Sebastien, illus. 2012. (Penguin Young Readers, Level 2 Ser.). 32p. (J). (gr. 1-2). pap. 5.99 *(978-0-448-45904-2(3)*, Penguin Young Readers) Penguin Young Readers Group.

—Doodle Dog: Ready-To-Read Level 1. 2005. (Doodle Dog Ser.). (ENG., Illus.). 32p. (J). (gr. -1-1). pap. 4.99 *(978-0-689-85910-6(4)*, Simon Spotlight) Simon Spotlight.

—Granny Doodle Day: Ready-To-Read Level 1. Seltzer, Eric, illus. 2006. (Doodle Dog Ser.). (ENG., Illus.). 32p. (J). (gr. -1-1). pap. 4.99 *(978-0-689-85911-3(2)*, Simon & Schuster/Paula Wiseman Bks.) Simon & Schuster/Paula Wiseman Bks.

—Party Pigs! 2019. (Ready-To-Read Ser.). (ENG.). 32p. (J). (gr. k-1). 13.96 *(978-0-87617-998-7(7))* Penworthy Co., LLC, The.

—Party Pigs! Ready-To-Read Pre-Level 1. Disbury, Tom, illus. 2019. (Ready-To-Read Ser.). (ENG.). 32p. (J). (gr. -1-k). 17.99 *(978-1-5344-2879-9(8))*; pap. 4.99 *(978-1-5344-2878-2(X))* Simon Spotlight. (Simon Spotlight).

—Space Cows. 2019. (Ready-To-Read Ser.). (ENG.). 32p. (J). (gr. k-1). 13.89 *(978-1-64310-887-2(5))* Penworthy Co., LLC, The.

—Space Cows: Ready-To-Read Pre-Level 1. Disbury, Tom, illus. 2018. (Ready-To-Read Ser.). (ENG.). 32p. (J). (gr. -1-k). 17.99 *(978-1-5344-2876-8(3))*; pap. 4.99 *(978-1-5344-2875-1(5))* Simon Spotlight. (Simon Spotlight).

Seltzer, Eric & Hall, Kirsten. Dog on His Bus. Braun, Sébastien, illus. 2012. (Penguin Young Readers Level 2 Ser.). lib. bdg. 13.55 *(978-0-606-25815-9(9))* Turtleback.

Sendak, Maurice. Bumble-Ardy. Sendak, Maurice, illus. 2011. (ENG., Illus.). 40p. (J). 17.95 *(978-0-06-205198-1(9)*, HarperCollins) HarperCollins Pubs.

—One Was Johnny Board Book: A Counting Book. Sendak, Maurice, illus. 2017. (ENG., Illus.). 46p. (J). (gr. -1-3). bds. 7.95 *(978-0-06-266809-7(9)*, HarperCollins) HarperCollins Pubs.

Senior, Suzy. Teddy Bear Says Good Night. Mitchell, Melanie, illus. 2014. (Teddy Bear Says Ser.). (ENG.). 12p. (J). (— 1). bds. 6.99 *(978-0-7459-6436-2(2)*, 9c45181d-511c-4096-98c0-033b661f8d29, Lion Children's) Lion Hudson PLC GBR. Dist: Baker & Taylor Publisher Services (BTPS).

Senir, Mirik & Shubow, Mary Jane. When I First Held You: A Lullaby from Israel. 2009. (J). lib. bdg. 17.95 *(978-0-7613-5096-5(9)*, Kar-Ben Publishing) Lerner Publishing Group.

Sensel, Joni. Bears Barge In. Bivins, Christopher, illus. 2003. 32p. (J). (gr. -1-18). 14.95 *(978-0-9701195-0-6(X))* Dream Factory Bks.

Serfozo, Mary. Plumply, Dumply Pumpkin. Petrone, Valeria, illus. 2006. (Classic Board Bks.). (ENG.). 28p. (J). (gr. -1-1). bds. 7.99 *(978-0-689-86277-9(6)*, Little Simon) Little Simon.

—Plumply, Dumply Pumpkin. Petrone, Valeria, illus. 2004. (ENG.). 32p. (J). (gr. -1-3). 8.99 *(978-0-689-87135-1(X)*, Aladdin) Simon & Schuster Children's Publishing.

Sesame Street Staff. Fairy Furry 2 bk Rhyming Rapunzel Rosita & Beanstalk. 2007. 15.99 *(978-1-59069-624-8(7))* Studio Mouse LLC.

Sesame Workshop. Just One You! 2015. (Sesame Street Scribbles Ser.: 0). (ENG.). 32p. (J). (gr. -1-3). 10.99 *(978-1-4022-9735-9(1))* Sourcebooks, Inc.

Seuss. The Big Orange Book of Beginner Books. 2015. (Beginner Books(R) Ser.). (ENG., Illus.). 240p. (J). (gr. -1-2). 16.99 *(978-0-553-52425-3(9)*, Random Hse. Bks. for Young Readers) Random Hse. Children's Bks.

—The Bippolo Seed & Other Lost Stories. 2011. (Classic Seuss Ser.). (ENG., Illus.). 72p. (J). (gr. k-4). 16.99 *(978-0-375-86435-3(0)*, Random Hse. Bks. for Young Readers) Random Hse. Children's Bks.

—The Cat in the Hat. Seuss, illus. 2010. (ENG., Illus.). 64p. pap. *(978-0-00-734869-5(X)*, HarperCollins Children's Bks.) HarperCollins Pubs. Ltd.

—The Cat in the Hat/el Gato Ensombrerado (the Cat in the Hat Spanish Edition) Bilingual Edition. 2015. (Classic Seuss Ser.).Tr. of Cat in the Hat/el Gato Ensombrerado. (Illus.). 72p. (J). (gr. -1-2). 16.99 *(978-0-553-52443-7(7)*, Random Hse. Bks. for Young Readers) Random Hse. Children's Bks.

—Come over to My House. Kath, Katie, illus. 2016. (Beginner Books(R) Ser.). (ENG.). 64p. (J). (gr. -1-2). 9.99 *(978-0-553-53665-2(6)*, Random Hse. Bks. for Young Readers) Random Hse. Children's Bks.

—Daisy-Head Mayzie. 2016. (Classic Seuss Ser.). (ENG., Illus.). 64p. (J). (gr. k-4). 17.99 *(978-0-553-53900-4(0)*, Random Hse. Bks. for Young Readers) Random Hse. Children's Bks.

—Dr. Seuss's Book of Animals. 2018. (Bright & Early Books(R) Ser.). (ENG., Illus.). 36p. (J). (-k). 9.99 *(978-1-5247-7055-6(8)*, Random Hse. Bks. for Young Readers) Random Hse. Children's Bks.

—The Eye Book. abr. ed. 2016. (Big Bright & Early Board Book Ser.). (ENG., Illus.). 24p. (J). (gr. -1 — 1). bds. 6.99 *(978-0-553-53631-7(1)*, Random Hse. Bks. for Young Readers) Random Hse. Children's Bks.

—The Foot Book. abr. ed. 2016. (Big Bright & Early Board Book Ser.). (ENG., Illus.). 24p. (J). (gr. -1 — 1). bds. 6.99 *(978-0-553-53630-0(3)*, Random Hse. Bks. for Young Readers) Random Hse. Children's Bks.

—Fox in Socks. 2015. (Big Bright & Early Board Book Ser.). (ENG., Illus.). 24p. (J). (— 1). bds. 7.99 *(978-0-553-51336-3(2)*, Random Hse. Bks. for Young Readers) Random Hse. Children's Bks.

—Fox in Socks: Dr. Seuss's Book of Tongue Tanglers. 2011. (Bright & Early Board Books(TM) Ser.). (ENG., Illus.). 24p. (J). (gr. -1 — 1). bds. 5.99 *(978-0-307-93180-1(3)*, Random Hse. Bks. for Young Readers) Random Hse. Children's Bks.

—El Gato Ensombrerado (the Cat in the Hat Spanish Edition) 2015. (Beginner Books(R) Ser.). (SPA., Illus.). 72p. (J). (gr. -1-2). lib. bdg. 13.99 *(978-0-553-50980-9(2)*, Random Hse. Bks. for Young Readers) Random Hse. Children's Bks.

—Happy Birthday to You! Great Big Flap Book. 2017. (ENG., Illus.). 12p. (J). (-k). bds. 12.99 *(978-1-5247-1460-4(7)*, Random Hse. Bks. for Young Readers) Random Hse. Children's Bks.

—Hop on Pop. (Big Bright & Early Board Book Ser.). (ENG., Illus.). 24p. (J). (— 1). 2015. bds. 6.99 *(978-0-553-49679-6(4))* 2004. bds. 5.99 *(978-0-375-82837-9(0))* Random Hse. Children's Bks. (Random Hse. Bks. for Young Readers).

—Horton & the Kwuggerbug & More Lost Stories. 2014. (Classic Seuss Ser.). (ENG., Illus.). 56p. (J). (gr. -1-3). 16.99 *(978-0-385-38298-4(7)*, Random Hse. Bks. for Young Readers) Random Hse. Children's Bks.

—How the Grinch Stole Christmas! Grow Your Heart Edition: Grow Your Heart 3-D Cover Edition. 2017. (Classic Seuss Ser.). (ENG., Illus.). 64p. (J). (gr. k-4). 19.99 *(978-1-5247-1461-1(5)*, Random Hse. Bks. for Young Readers) Random Hse. Children's Bks.

—Huevos Verdes con Jamón (Green Eggs & Ham Spanish Edition) 2019. (Beginner Books(R) Ser.). (SPA., Illus.). 72p. (J). (gr. -1-2). 9.99 *(978-0-525-70723-3(9)*, Random Hse. Bks. for Young Readers) Random Hse. Children's Bks.

—The Lorax. Seuss, illus. 2010. (ENG., Illus.). 24p. bds. *(978-0-00-732618-1(1)*, HarperCollins Children's Bks.) HarperCollins Pubs. Ltd.

—El lórax (the Lorax Spanish Edition) 2019. (Classic Seuss Ser.). (SPA.). 72p. (J). (gr. 1-4). 16.99 *(978-0-525-70731-8(X))*; lib. bdg. 19.99 *(978-0-525-70732-5(8))* Random Hse. Children's Bks. (Random Hse. Bks. for Young Readers).

—Mr. Brown Can Moo! Can You? 2014. (Big Bright & Early Board Book Ser.). (ENG., Illus.). 24p. (J). (-k). bds. 6.99 *(978-0-385-38712-5(1)*, Random Hse. Bks. for Young Readers) Random Hse. Children's Bks.

—Oh, Baby! Go, Baby! 2010. (Dr. Seuss Nursery Collection). (ENG., Illus.). 14p. (J). (gr. -1 — 1). 11.99 *(978-0-375-85738-6(9)*, Random Hse. Bks. for Young Readers) Random Hse. Children's Bks.

—¡Oh, Cúan Lejos Llegarás! (Oh, the Places You'll Go! Spanish Edition) 2019. (Classic Seuss Ser.). (SPA., Illus.). 56p. (J). (gr. 2-12). 18.99 *(978-0-525-70733-2(6)*, Random Hse. Bks. for Young Readers) Random Hse. Children's Bks.

—Oh, the Thinks You Can Think! (Big Bright & Early Board Book Ser.). (ENG., Illus.). 24p. (J). 2014. (-k). bds. 7.99 *(978-0-385-38713-2(X))* 2009. (gr. -1 — 1). bds. 5.99 *(978-0-375-85794-2(X))* Random Hse. Children's Bks. (Random Hse. Bks. for Young Readers).

—Un Pez Dos Peces Pez Rojo Pez Azul (One Fish Two Fish Red Fish Blue Fish Spanish Edition) 2019. (Beginner Books(R) Ser.). (SPA., Illus.). 72p. (J). (gr. -1-2). 9.99 *(978-0-525-70729-5(8)*, Random Hse. Bks. for Young Readers) Random Hse. Children's Bks.

—What Pet Should I Get? (Beginner Books(R) Ser.). (ENG.). (J). (gr. -1-2). 2019. 40p. lib. bdg. 12.99 *(978-0-525-70736-3(0))* 2019. (Illus.). 40p. 9.99 *(978-0-525-70735-6(2))* 2015. (Illus.). 48p. 17.99 *(978-0-553-52426-0(7))* Random Hse. Children's Bks. (Random Hse. Bks. for Young Readers).

—What Was I Scared Of? 2009. (ENG., Illus.). 32p. (J). (gr. k-4). 12.99 *(978-0-375-85342-5(1)*, Random Hse. Bks. for Young Readers) Random Hse. Children's Bks.

Seuss, et al. The Big Aqua Book of Beginner Books. Lopshire, Robert & Cummings, Art, illus. 2017. (Beginner Books(R) Ser.). (ENG.). 256p. (J). (gr. -1-2). 16.99 *(978-1-5247-6442-5(6)*, Random Hse. Bks. for Young Readers) Random Hse. Children's Bks.

Seuss, Dr. Hay un Molillo en Mi Bolsillo! Canetti, Yanitzia, tr. from ENG. 2007.Tr. of There's a Wocket in my Pocket! (SPA., Illus.). 26p. (J). (gr. k-3). 8.99 *(978-1-933032-25-2(1))* Lectorum Pubns., Inc.

—Oh, the Places You'll Go! Seuss, Dr., illus. 2003. (Dr Seuss - Yellow Back Book Ser.). (ENG., Illus.). 48p. pap. *(978-0-00-715852-2(1)*, HarperCollins Children's Bks.) HarperCollins Pubs. Ltd.

—Oh, the Places You'll Go! 2003. 7.95 *(978-1-56890-373-6(1))* Peaceable Kingdom Pr.

—Un Pez, Dos Peces, Pez Rojo. Canetti, Yanitzia, tr. from ENG. 2005. 64p. (J). 8.99 *(978-1-930332-83-6(1))* Lectorum Pubns., Inc.

—What Pet Should I Get? 2015. 48p. (J). lib. bdg. 30.60 *(978-0-606-37381-4(0))* Turtleback.

—Y Pensar Que lo Vi Por la Calle Porvenir, 1. Canetti, Yanitzia James, tr. from ENG. 2006.Tr. of And to Think That I Saw It on Mulberry Street. (SPA., Illus.). (J). (gr. -1-3). 14.99 *(978-1-933032-07-8(3))* Lectorum Pubns., Inc.

—Yoruga la Tortuga y Otros Cuentos, 1. Canetti, Yanitzia, tr. from ENG. 2008.Tr. of Yertle the Turtle & Other Stories. (SPA., Illus.). 76p. (J). (gr. 2-3). 15.99 *(978-1-933032-41-2(3))* Lectorum Pubns., Inc.

Seuss, Dr., illus. Poisson Un - Poisson Deux - Poisson Rouge - Poisson Bleu. 2011. (FRE.). 64p. (J). (gr. -1-3). 12.95 *(978-1-61243-029-4(5))* Ulysses Pr.

Seuss, Dr. & Berger, Sholem. [Eyn Fish, Tsvey Fish, Royter Fish, Bloyer Fish. 2007. (YID., Illus.). 62p. (J). *(978-0-9726939-3-6(9))* Twenty-fourth Street Bks, LLC.

Seuss, Dr., et al. Virent Ova! Viret Perna! 2003.Tr. of Green Eggs & Ham. (ENG., Illus.). 72p. (J). 50.00 *(978-0-86516-555-7(6))* Bolchazy-Carducci Pubs.

Shaber, Mark. Animals & Stuff. LaGrange, Tiffany, illus. 2008. 32p. pap. 12.95 *(978-1-934246-10-8(7))* Peppertree Pr., The.

Shamberger, Lindsey. I, I, I for iguan. 2012. 44p. pap. 24.95 *(978-1-4626-7536-4(0))* America Star Bks.

Shanker, Myrna Gelman. Lazar, the Good Deed Dog. Robinson, Linda, illus. 2010. (J). *(978-0-9829273-0-4(4))* IGI Pr.

Shankman, Ed. I Met a Moose in Maine One Day. O'Neill, Dave, illus. 2008. (Shankman & O'Neill Ser.). (ENG.). 32p. (J). (gr. -1-3). 17.99 *(978-1-933212-77-7(2)*, Commonwealth Editions) Applewood Bks.

shapouri, naiyer. Sweet Dreams Buggy. 2009. 32p. pap. 13.60 *(978-0-557-04866-3(4))* Lulu Pr., Inc.

Sharp, Lani. Has Anyone Seen the Creature? 2016. (ENG., Illus.). 24p. pap. 9.95 *(978-1-78554-396-8(2)*, 2b175d46-ee31-4189-8e2c-2bdce7d4690c) Austin Macauley Pubs. Ltd. GBR. Dist: Baker & Taylor Publisher Services (BTPS).

Sharp, Michael. Captain Tristan Am I. Van Tine, Laura, illus. 2009. 20p. (J). pap. *(978-1-897455-10-4(0))* Avatar Pubns., Inc.

—Vayda Jane Bean. 2007. (J). *(978-1-897455-68-5(2))* Avatar Pubns., Inc.

Sharp, Paul. Rookie Ready to Learn en Español: Pablo el Lanzador. Sharp, Paul, illus. 2011. (Rookie Ready to Learn Español Ser.). Orig. Title: Rookie Ready to Learn: Paul the Pitcher. (SPA., Illus.). 40p. (J). pap. 5.95 *(978-0-531-26781-3(4)*, Children's Pr.) Scholastic Library Publishing.

—Rookie Ready to Learn: Paul the Pitcher. Sharp, Paul, illus. 2011. (Rookie Ready to Learn Ser.). (ENG., Illus.). 40p. (J). pap. 5.95 *(978-0-531-26651-9(6)*, Children's Pr.) Scholastic Library Publishing.

Sharp, Paul, illus. Paul the Pitcher. 2011. (Rookie Ready to Learn: All about Me! Ser.). (ENG.). 40p. (J). (gr. -1-1). lib. bdg. 18.69 *(978-0-531-26426-3(2)*, Children's Pr.) Scholastic Library Publishing.

Shaskan, Stephen. Toad on the Road: A Cautionary Tale. Shaskan, Stephen, illus. 2017. (ENG., Illus.). 32p. (J). (gr. -1-3). 17.99 *(978-0-06-239347-0(2)*, HarperCollins) HarperCollins Pubs.

—Toad on the Road: Mama & Me. 2018. (ENG., Illus.). 32p. (J). (gr. -1-3). 17.99 *(978-0-06-239349-4(9)*, HarperCollins) HarperCollins Pubs.

Shattil, Wendy, et al, photos by. Sierra Babies. 2013. (Illus.). 26p. (J). 8.95 *(978-1-56037-557-9(4))* Farcountry Pr.

Shaw, Calvin. Snowy Farm. Lu, Oamul, illus. 2019. (ENG.). 32p. (J). (gr. -1-3). 17.99 *(978-1-5344-1047-3(3)*, Simon & Schuster/Paula Wiseman Bks.) Simon & Schuster/Paula Wiseman Bks.

Shaw, Nancy E. Sheep Blast Off! Apple, Margot, illus. 2011. (Sheep in a Jeep Ser.). (ENG.). 32p. (J). (gr. -1-3). pap. 6.99 *(978-0-547-52025-4(5)*, 1445464, Clarion Bks.) HarperCollins Pubs.

—Sheep Go to Sleep. Apple, Margot, illus. (Sheep in a Jeep Ser.). (ENG.). 32p. (J). (gr. -1-3). 2019. pap. 7.99 *(978-1-328-60368-5(7)*, 1732077) 2015. 16.99 *(978-0-544-30989-0(8)*, 1581244) HarperCollins Pubs. (Clarion Bks.).

—Sheep Go to Sleep Board Book. Apple, Margot, illus. 2016. (Sheep in a Jeep Ser.). (ENG.). 30p. (J). (gr. -1-3). bds. 7.99 *(978-0-544-64053-5(5)*, 1620828, Clarion Bks.) HarperCollins Pubs.

—Sheep in a Jeep. Apple, Margot, illus. 2013. (Sheep in a Jeep Ser.). (ENG.). 32p. (J). (gr. -1-3). pap. 26.99 *(978-0-547-99383-6(8)*, 1525236, Clarion Bks.) HarperCollins Pubs.

—Sheep in a Jeep Book & Cd, 1 vol. Apple, Margot, illus. 2006. (Sheep in a Jeep Ser.). (ENG.). 32p. (J). (gr. -1-3). audio compact disk 10.99 *(978-0-618-69522-5(2)*, 441919, Clarion Bks.) HarperCollins Pubs.

—Sheep in a Shop Board Book. Apple, Margot, illus. 2017. (Sheep in a Jeep Ser.). (ENG.). 28p. (J). (— 1). bds. 7.99 *(978-1-328-70286-9(3)*, 1672394, Clarion Bks.) HarperCollins Pubs.

—Sheep Out to Eat Board Book. Apple, Margot, illus. 2005. (Sheep in a Jeep Ser.). (ENG.). 28p. (J). (gr. k — 1). bds. 6.99 *(978-0-618-58339-3(4)*, 587642, Clarion Bks.) HarperCollins Pubs.

Shaw, Stephanie. A Cookie for Santa. Robert, Bruno, illus. 2014. (ENG.). 32p. (J). (gr. 1-4). 17.99 *(978-1-58536-883-9(0)*, 203675) Sleeping Bear Pr.

Shea, Bob. Race You to Bed. Shea, Bob, illus. 2010. (ENG., Illus.). 40p. (J). (gr. -1-2). 16.99 *(978-0-06-170417-8(2)*, Tegen, Katherine Bks) HarperCollins Pubs.

Shear, Dani. The Foodie Club. Weinstein, Holly, illus. 2013. (ENG.). 50p. (J). 16.99 *(978-1-61053-027-9(6))* Blackbird Bks.

Sheehan, Monica. Love Is You & Me. Sheehan, Monica, illus. 2013. (ENG., Illus.). 48p. (J). (gr. -1-3). 14.99 *(978-1-4424-3607-7(7)*, Little Simon) Little Simon.

Shelton, Jayne C. In Grandma's Arms. Katz, Karen, illus. 2008. (ENG.). 24p. (J). (gr. -1-k). bds. 7.99 *(978-0-545-06868-0(1))* Scholastic, Inc.

Shepherd, Donna J. Bradybug. Grady, Kit, illus. 2010. 20p. pap. 10.95 *(978-1-61633-071-2(6))* Guardian Angel Publishing, Inc.

—Chizzy's Topsy Tale. Collier, Kevin Scott, illus. 2008. 20p. pap. 10.95 *(978-1-935137-10-8(7))* Guardian Angel Publishing, Inc.

Shepherd, Donna J. & Foster, Jack. Where Is Salami. 2011. (Illus.). 16p. pap. 9.95 *(978-1-61633-147-4(X))* Guardian Angel Publishing, Inc.

Sheppard, Markette. My Rainy Day Rocket Ship. Palmer, Charly, illus. 2020. (ENG.). 32p. (J). (gr. -1-3). 17.99 *(978-1-5344-6177-2(9)*, Simon & Schuster Bks. For Young Readers) Simon & Schuster Bks. For Young Readers.

—What Is Light? Johnson, Cathy Ann, illus. 2020. (ENG.). 32p. (J). (gr. -1-3). 19.99 *(978-1-5344-7651-6(2))* Simon & Schuster, Inc.

Sherwood, Lance. Grandpa Tales. 2012. 54p. pap. 14.95 *(978-0-615-72525-3(2))* Spitzer, Lance.

Shields, Carol Diggory. Saturday Night at the Dinosaur Stomp. Nash, Scott, illus. 2008. (ENG.). 32p. (J). (gr. -1-3). pap. 7.99 *(978-0-7636-3887-0(0))* Candlewick Pr.

Shields, Gillian. When the World Is Ready for Bed (padded Board) Currey, Anna, illus. 2010. (ENG.). 26p. (J). (gr. -1 — 1). bds. 7.99 *(978-1-59990-533-4(7)*, 900068691, Bloomsbury USA Childrens) Bloomsbury Publishing USA.

—When the World Was Waiting for You. Currey, Anna, illus. 2012. (ENG.). 26p. (J). (gr. -1 — 1). bds. 8.99 *(978-1-59990-849-6(2)*, 900081566, Bloomsbury USA Childrens) Bloomsbury Publishing USA.

Shirtliffe, Leanne. The Change Your Name Store. Kügler, Tina & Kügler, Tina, illus. 2014. (ENG.). 32p. (J). (gr. -1-k). 16.95 *(978-1-62873-608-3(9)*, Sky Pony Pr.) Skyhorse Publishing Co., Inc.

—No More Beige Food. Kugler, Tina, illus. 2016. (ENG.). 32p. (J). (gr. -1-k). 16.99 *(978-1-63450-180-4(2)*, Sky Pony Pr.) Skyhorse Publishing Co., Inc.

Shively, Julie. What Belongs? Kurtz, John, illus. 2004. (Baby Looney Toons Ser.). (ENG.). 16p. (J). 6.95 *(978-0-8249-6561-7(2)*, Ideals Pubns.) Worthy Publishing.

Shoopman, Jim. Zachary Hamm in the Land of Eggs. 2012. 82p. pap. 14.95 *(978-0-9846558-1-6(6))* Taylor and Seale Publishing.

Shulman, Lisa. Old MacDonald Had a Woodshop. Wolff, Ashley, illus. 2004. 32p. (J). (gr. -1-k). reprint ed. pap. 7.99 *(978-0-14-240186-6(2)*, Puffin Books) Penguin Young Readers Group.

Shulman, Mark. Gorilla Garage, 0 vols. Nguyen, Vincent, illus. 2013. (ENG.). 42p. (J). (gr. -1-3). pap. 9.99 *(978-1-4778-1663-9(1)*, 9781477816639, Two Lions) Amazon Publishing.

Sickler, Jonas. Indestructibles: Humpty Dumpty: Chew Proof · Rip Proof · Nontoxic · 100% Washable (Book for Babies, Newborn Books, Safe to Chew) 2010. (Indestructibles Ser.). (ENG., Illus.). 12p. (J). (gr. -1 — 1). pap. 5.95 *(978-0-7611-5861-5(8)*, 15861) Workman Publishing Co., Inc.

Siddals, Mary McKenna. Compost Stew: An a to Z Recipe for the Earth. Wolff, Ashley, illus. 2010. 40p. (J). (gr. -1-2). 18.99 *(978-1-58246-316-2(6)*, Tricycle Pr.) Random Hse. Children's Bks.

Sidman, Joyce. Before Morning. Krommes, Beth, illus. 2016. (ENG.). 48p. (J). (gr. -1-3). 17.99 *(978-0-547-97917-5(7),* 1523509, Clarion Bks.) HarperCollins Pubs.

Sierra, Judy. Ballyhoo Bay. Anderson, Derek, illus. 2009. (ENG.). 40p. (J). (gr. -1-3). 19.99 *(978-1-4169-5888-8(6),* Simon & Schuster/Paula Wiseman Bks.) Simon & Schuster/Paula Wiseman Bks.

—Everyone Counts. Brown, Marc, illus. 2019. 40p. (J). (gr. -1-2). 17.99 *(978-0-525-64620-4(5),* Knopf Bks. for Young Readers) Random Hse. Children's Bks.

—Make Way for Readers. Karas, G. Brian, illus. 2016. (ENG.). 32p. (J). (gr. -1-3). 17.99 *(978-1-4814-1851-5(3),* Simon & Schuster Bks. For Young Readers) Simon & Schuster Bks. For Young Readers.

—The Secret Science Project That Almost Ate the School. Gammell, Stephen, illus. 2006. (ENG.). 32p. (J). (gr. 1-4). 19.99 *(978-1-4169-1175-3(8),* Simon & Schuster/Paula Wiseman Bks.) Simon & Schuster/Paula Wiseman Bks.

—Suppose You Meet a Dinosaur: a First Book of Manners. Bowers, Tim, illus. 2016. 40p. (J). (gr. -1-2). 7.99 *(978-1-101-93250-6(3),* Dragonfly Bks.) Random Hse. Children's Bks.

—What Time Is It, Mr. Crocodile? Cushman, Doug, illus. 2007. (ENG.). 32p. (J). (gr. -1-3). pap. 7.99 *(978-0-15-205850-0(8),* 1197570, Clarion Bks.) HarperCollins Pubs.

—Wild about Books. Brown, Marc, illus. 2004. (ENG.). 40p. (J). (gr. -1-2). 18.99 *(978-0-375-82538-5(X),* Knopf Bks. for Young Readers) Random Hse. Children's Bks.

Signorino, Slug, illus. I Know an Old Lady Who Swallowed a Fly: A Traditional Rhyme. 2004. 16p. (J). (gr. k-4). reprint ed. pap. 10.00 *(978-0-7567-9066-0(2))* DIANE Publishing Co.

Sileo, Frank J. Bee Calm: The Buzz on Yoga. Keay, Claire, illus. 2019. (ENG.). 32p. (J). *(978-1-4338-2957-4(6),* Magination Pr.) American Psychological Assn.

—Bee Still: An Invitation to Meditation. Keay, Claire, illus. 2018. 32p. (J). *(978-1-4338-2870-6(7),* Magination Pr.) American Psychological Assn.

—Did You Hear? A Story about Gossip. Zivoin, Jennifer, illus. 2017. 32p. (J). *(978-1-4338-2720-4(4),* Magination Pr.) American Psychological Assn.

—A World of Pausabilities: An Exercise in Mindfulness. Zivoin, Jennifer, illus. 2017. 32p. (J). *(978-1-4338-2323-7(3),* Magination Pr.) American Psychological Assn.

Sill, Cathryn. About Mollusks: A Guide for Children. 1 vol. Sill, John, illus. 2008. (About... Ser.: 9). 40p. (J). (gr. -1-2). pap. 7.95 *(978-1-56145-406-8(0))* Peachtree Publishing Co. Inc.

Silver, Skye. Baby Play. 2019. (ENG., Illus.). 16p. (J). (gr. -1-k). bds. 7.99 *(978-1-78285-728-0(1))* Barefoot Bks., Inc.

—Baby Play / Jugando con Bebé. 2019. (ENG., Illus.). 16p. (J). (gr. -1-k). bds. 7.99 *(978-1-78285-736-5(2))* Barefoot Bks., Inc.

Silverman, Erica. The Hanukkah Hop! D'Amico, Steven, illus. 2011. (ENG.). 32p. (J). (gr. -1-3). 12.99 *(978-1-4424-0604-9(6),* Simon & Schuster Bks. For Young Readers) Simon & Schuster Bks. For Young Readers.

—Wake up, City! Fournier, Laure, illus. 2016. (ENG.). 32p. (J). (gr. -1-3). 16.99 *(978-1-4998-0173-6(4))* Little Bee Books Inc.

Silverstein, Shel. A Giraffe & a Half. Silverstein, Shel, illus. 40th anniv. ed. 2014. (ENG., Illus.). 48p. (J). (gr. -1-3). 18.99 *(978-0-06-025655-5(9),* HarperCollins) HarperCollins Pubs.

Silvestri, Linda. Clementina & the Hooey-Phooey Circus Troupe. 2007. (ESP., Illus.). (YA). 12.95 *(978-0-9710696-8-8(9))* Jorlan Publishing, Inc.

Simmons, Andra. What Anna Loves. Capaldi, Gina, illus. 2006. 24p. (J). (gr. -1-3). 15.95 *(978-1-59714-044-7(9))* Heyday.

Simon, Charnan. Lodo! Handelman, Dorothy, photos by. 2005.Tr. of Mud! (ENG & SPA., Illus.). 32p. (J). (gr. -1-1). pap. 4.99 *(978-0-8225-3295-8(6))* Lerner Publishing Group.

—Lodo! Nivel 1. Handelman, Dorothy, photos by. 2005. (Lecturas para Niños de Verdad (Real Kids Readers) Ser.).Tr. of Mud! (SPA., Illus.). 32p. (J). (gr. 1-1). per. 5.95 *(978-0-8225-3294-1(8),* Ediciones Lerner) Lerner Publishing Group.

—Me Gusta Ganar! Translations.com Staff, tr. from ENG. Handelman, Dorothy, photos by. 2007. (Lecturas para niños de Verdad - Nivel 1 (Real Kids Readers - Level 1) Ser.).Tr. of I Like to Win! (SPA., Illus.). 32p. (J). (gr. k-2). per. 5.95 *(978-0-8225-7801-7(8),* Ediciones Lerner) Lerner Publishing Group.

—Me Gusta Ganar; I Like to Win. 2008. pap. 34.95 *(978-0-8225-9499-4(4))* Lerner Publishing Group.

Simon, Francesca. Hack & Whack. Cotterill, Charlotte, illus. 2017. (ENG.). 32p. (gr. -1-k). 16.95 *(978-0-571-32871-0(7),* Faber & Faber Children's Bks.) Faber & Faber, Inc.

Sims, Lesley. Spider in a Glider. 2019. (Phonics Readers Ser.). (ENG.). 24ppp. (J). pap. 6.99 *(978-0-7945-4362-4(6),* Usborne) EDC Publishing.

Sing to Baby Jesus. 2013. (Illus.). 32p. (J). 14.99 *(978-1-62108-071-8(4))* Covenant Communications, Inc.

Singer, Marilyn. Float, Flutter. 2019. (Ready-To-Read Ser.). (ENG.). 32p. (J). (gr. k-1). 13.96 *(978-0-87617-994-9(4))* Penworthy Co., LLC, The.

—Float, Flutter: Ready-To-Read Pre-Level 1. Durst, Kathryn, illus. 2019. (Ready-To-Read Ser.). (ENG.). 32p. (J). (gr. -1-k). pap. 4.99 *(978-1-5344-2129-5(7),* Simon Spotlight) Simon Spotlight.

—What Is Your Dog Doing? Habbley, Kathleen, illus. 2011. (ENG.). 32p. (J). (gr. -1-2). 12.99 *(978-1-4169-7931-9(X),* Atheneum Bks. for Young Readers) Simon & Schuster Children's Publishing.

—What's a Banana? Pizzoli, Greg, illus. 2016. (ENG.). 24p. (J). (gr. -1-k). 12.95 *(978-1-4197-2139-7(9),* 1114201, Abrams Appleseed) Abrams, Inc.

Sinke, Grandma Janet Mary. Grandma's Christmas Tree. Pennington, Craig, illus. l.t. ed. 2004. (Grandma Janet Mary Ser.). 50p. (J). *(978-0-9742732-1-1(X))* My Grandma & Me Pubs.

Sipe, Kelly. What It Takes to Be a Hero. 2012. 24p. pap. 12.45 *(978-1-4624-0326-4(3),* Inspiring Voices) Author Solutions, LLC.

Siwak, Brenda S. Counting on the Bay. Dodge, Barbara A., illus. 2006. (J). per. 14.95 *(978-0-9790906-0-8(1))* Pleasant Plains Pr.

Siy, Alexandra. One Tractor. Rogers, Jacqueline, illus. 2018. (I Like to Read Ser.). (ENG.). 32p. (J). (gr. -1-3). 6.99 *(978-0-8234-4015-3(X))* Holiday Hse., Inc.

Skalak, Daniel. All Summer's Fun. Skalak, Daniel, illus. 2006. (Illus.). 32p. (J). (gr. -1-3). 15.95 *(978-1-60108-000-4(X))* Red Cygnet Pr.

Skillen, Roy. The Three Wise Men. 2010. 24p. pap. 11.50 *(978-1-60911-107-6(9),* Eloquent Bks.) Strategic Book Publishing & Rights Agency (SBPRA).

Skotnicki, Jill. Ham & Beans: Have You Seen the Color Green? 2010. 28p. pap. 12.49 *(978-1-4520-6452-9(0))* AuthorHouse.

Slack, Rebecca Kai Dotlich; illustrations by Michael. Race Car Count. 2017. (ENG., Illus.). 32p. (J). bds. 10.99 *(978-1-62779-934-8(6),* 900163126, Holt, Henry & Co. Bks. For Young Readers) Holt, Henry & Co.

Slate, Joseph. Miss Bindergarten Has a Wild Day in Kindergarten. Wolff, Ashley, illus. 2006. 40p. (J). (gr. -1-k). reprint ed. pap. 8.99 *(978-0-14-240709-7(7),* Puffin Books) Penguin Young Readers Group.

Slater, David Michael. The Boy & the Book: [a Wordless Story]. Kolar, Bob, illus. 2015. 32p. (J). (-k). lib. bdg. 16.95 *(978-1-58089-562-0(X))* Charlesbridge Publishing, Inc.

Slater, Teddy. The Luckiest St. Patrick's Day Ever! Long, Ethan, illus. 2007. (J). *(978-0-439-86648-4(0))* Scholastic, Inc.

—Tim Feels Scared. Rescek, Sanja, illus. 2011. (J). *(978-0-545-35179-9(0))* Scholastic, Inc.

Slaton, Donna F. Ben Beagle Plays. 2016. (Illus.). 32p. (J). (gr. -1-1). 18.99 *(978-1-937008-43-7(6))* Heart to Heart Publishing, Inc.

SLAY, Jenette. ABBY, the Easter Chicken. 2008. 29p. 13.96 *(978-1-4357-1062-7(2))* Lulu Pr., Inc.

Slayton, Fran Cannon. Snowball Moon. Bishop, Tracy, illus. (ENG.). (J). (gr. -1-k). 2019. 26p. bds. 7.99 *(978-1-4998-0991-6(3))* 2017. 32p. 16.99 *(978-1-4998-0495-9(4))* Little Bee Books Inc.

Sloat, Teri. Zip! Zoom! on a Broom. Bonnet, Rosalinde, illus. (ENG.). (J). (gr. -1 — 1). 2019. 24p. bds. 7.99 *(978-0-316-25672-8(2))* 2017. 40p. 16.99 *(978-0-316-25673-5(0))* Little, Brown Bks. for Young Readers.

Slonim, David. I Loathe You. Slonim, David, illus. (ENG., Illus.). 24p. (J). (gr. -1-3). 2018. 7.99 *(978-1-5344-3311-3(2))* 2012. 15.99 *(978-1-4424-2244-5(0))* Simon & Schuster Children's Publishing. (Aladdin).

Smallman, Steve. Smelly Peter: The Great Pea Eater. Dreidemy, Joëlle, illus. 2008. 32p. (J). (gr. 4-7). 15.95 *(978-1-58925-076-5(1))* Tiger Tales.

Smart Kidz, creator. The ABC's of How I Love You: You're My Alphabet of Love! 2013. (Parent Love Letters Ser.). (ENG., Illus.). 12p. (gr. -1). bds. 12.99 *(978-1-891100-30-7(0),* Smart Kids) Penton Overseas, Inc.

Smart Kidz Media, creator. O Christmas Tree! 2013. (ENG., Illus.). 12p. (J). bds. 12.99 *(978-1-939658-05-0(5),* Smart Kids) Penton Overseas, Inc.

—Silent Night. 2013. (ENG., Illus.). 12p. (J). bds. 12.99 *(978-1-939658-01-2(2),* Smart Kids) Penton Overseas, Inc.

Smart Kidz Media Studios Staff, ed. It's Bedtime! 2011. 16p. 7.99 *(978-1-891100-78-9(5),* Smart Kids) Penton Overseas, Inc.

Smerek, Kim. What Is Zazu?, 1 bk. Smerek, Kim, illus. 2003. (Illus.). 24p. (J). bds. 7.95 *(978-0-9745116-0-3(9))* Sunshine Bks. for Children.

Smethurst, Julia. Fincluck from Kentucky: A Picture Book. 2013. (Illus.). 39p. (J). *(978-1-938905-36-0(9))* Acclaim Pr., Inc.

Smiley, Jess Smart. 10 Little Monsters Visit New York City, Volume 5. Hardyman, Nathan, illus. 2016. (10 Little Monsters Ser.: 5). (ENG.). 32p. (J). (gr. k-3). 16.95 *(978-1-942934-67-7(X),* 553467) Familius LLC.

Smiley, Jess Smart, abr. 12 Little Elves Visit Washington, Volume 2. 2016. (12 Little Elves Ser.: 2). (ENG., Illus.). 32p. (J). (gr. k-3). 16.95 *(978-1-942934-71-4(8),* 553471) Familius LLC.

Smith, Ben Bailey. Bear Moves. Akyuz, Sav, illus. 2018. (ENG.). 40p. (J). (-k). 15.99 *(978-0-7636-9831-7(8),* Candlewick Entertainment) Candlewick Pr.

Smith, Bill O. Chickadees At Night. Murphy, Charles R., illus. 2012. 32p. *(978-0-615-56972-7(2))* Smith, Bill O.

Smith, C. Michelle. Skeeter Sneeter Doodlebop. Foreman, A., illus. 2009. 24p. pap. 15.63 *(978-1-934840-54-2(8))* Nimble Bks. LLC.

Smith, Craig. The Dinky Donkey (a Wonky Donkey Book) Cowley, Katz, illus. 2019. (ENG.). 24p. (J). (gr. -1-k). pap. 7.99 *(978-1-338-60063-4(4))* Scholastic, Inc.

Smith, Craig & Thomson, Maureen. Willbee the Bumblebee. Cowley, Katz, illus. 2019. (ENG.). 32p. (J). (gr. -1-k). pap. 7.99 *(978-1-338-57521-7(X))* Scholastic, Inc.

Smith, Danna. The Hawk of the Castle: A Story of Medieval Falconry. Ibatoulline, Bagram, illus. 2017. (ENG.). 40p. (J). (gr. -1-3). 19.99 *(978-0-7636-7992-7(5))* Candlewick Pr.

—Springtime Babies. Fisher, Takako, illus. 2018. (Little Golden Book Ser.). 24p. (J). (-k). 4.99 *(978-1-5247-1516-8(6),* Golden Bks.) Random Hse. Children's Bks.

—Swallow the Leader. Sherry, Kevin, illus. 2016. (ENG.). 32p. (J). (gr. -1-3). 16.99 *(978-0-544-10518-8(4),* 1540594, Clarion Bks.) HarperCollins Pubs.

—Two at the Zoo/Dos en el Zoologico Board Book: Bilingual English-Spanish. Petrone, Valeria, illus. 2011.Tr. of Two at the Zoo - A Counting Book. (ENG.). 30p. (J). (gr. -1-k). bds. 5.99 *(978-0-547-58137-8(8),* 1459824, Clarion Bks.) HarperCollins Pubs.

Smith, Ian & Julian, Sean. Rooster's Alarm. Smith, Ian, illus. 2009. (Tadpoles Ser.). (ENG., Illus.). 24p. (J). (gr. -1-2). pap. *(978-0-7787-3905-0(8));* (gr. k-2). lib. bdg. *(978-0-7787-3874-9(4))* Crabtree Publishing Co.

Smith, Icy. Daddy, My Favorite Guy. 2013. 28p. 16.95 *(978-0-9856237-9-1(9))* East West Discovery Pr.

Smith, Jennifer Lynne. Things I Wonder. Perez, Angela J., ed. Gray, Angela M., illus. 2007. 36p. (J). 14.95 *(978-0-9778328-5-9(6))* His Work Christian Publishing.

Smith Jr., Charles R. I Am the World. 2013. (ENG., Illus.). 48p. (J). (gr. -1-2). 17.99 *(978-1-4424-2302-2(1))* Simon & Schuster Children's Publishing.

Smith, Loretta. Bela & the Gold Medallion. Marconi, Gloria, illus. Preston, James, photos by. 2012. 32p. pap. 13.00 *(978-1-930357-27-3(3))* Do The Write Thing Foundation of DC.

Smith, Michael. My Ducky Buddy. Oliva, Octavio, illus. 2011. 23p. (J). *(978-0-9821675-4-0(7))* East West Discovery Pr.

—My Ducky Buddy. Oliva, Octavio, illus. 2015. (ARA & ENG.). 23p. (J). *(978-0-9913454-3-4(6))* East West Discovery Pr.

Smith, Michael & Oliva, Octavio. Grasshopper Buddy. Oliva, Octavio, illus. 2012. (SPA & ENG., Illus.). (J). *(978-0-9856237-0-8(5))* East West Discovery Pr.

Smith, Richard G. When the Moon Fell Down. Date not set. 32p. (J). (gr. -1-18). pap. 4.99 *(978-0-06-443550-5(4))* HarperCollins Pubs.

Smith, Shoham. An after Bedtime Story. Tsarfati, Einat, illus. 2016. (ENG.). 48p. (J). (gr. k-2). 16.95 *(978-1-4197-1873-1(8),* 1121501, Abrams Bks. for Young Readers) Abrams, Inc.

Sneison, Doug. Who's Got the Face? 2007. (Illus.). 48p. (J). 16.95 *(978-0-9777811-0-2(0))* Petalous Publishing, LLC.

Snow, Pegeen. Eat Your Peas, Louise! Venezia, Mike, illus. 2011. (Rookie Ready to Learn - My Family & Friends Ser.). 40p. (J). (gr. -1-k). lib. bdg. 23.00 *(978-0-531-26527-7(7),* Children's Pr.) Scholastic Library Publishing.

—Eat Your Peas, Louise! (Rookie Ready to Learn - My Family & Friends) Venezia, Mike, illus. 2011. (Rookie Ready to Learn Ser.). (ENG.). 40p. (J). (gr. -1-k). pap. 5.95 *(978-0-531-26709-7(1),* Children's Pr.) Scholastic Library Publishing.

Snow, Peggy. My Favorite Places from a to Z. Barber, Brian, illus. 2007. (My Favorites Ser.). (ENG.). 32p. (J). (gr. -1). lib. bdg. 15.99 *(978-1-934277-03-4(7))* Mam Green Publishing, Inc.

—My Favorite Sounds from a to Z. 2007. (ENG.). 32p. (J). lib. bdg. 15.99 *(978-1-934277-02-7(9))* Mam Green Publishing, Inc.

Snow, Virginia B. Summer Walk, 1 vol. (ENG.). 32p. (J). (gr. -1-3). 2019. 8.99 *(978-1-4236-5394-3(7))* 2016. (Illus.). 16.99 *(978-1-4236-4215-2(5))* Gibbs Smith, Publisher.

Snowden, Gary. Hank & Kale Visit the Aquarium. Smith, William E., illus. 2012. 24p. pap. 8.99 *(978-1-938768-05-7(1))* Gypsy Pubns.

Snyder, Betsy, illus. I Can Dream: (Baby Board Book, Book for Learning, Toddler Book. 2018. (I Can Ser.). (ENG.). 14p. (J). (gr. -1 — 1). bds. 8.99 *(978-1-4521-6214-0(X))* Chronicle Bks. LLC.

—I Can Play. 2015. (I Can Interactive Board Bks.). (ENG.). 14p. (J). (gr. -1 — 1). bds. 8.99 *(978-1-4521-2905-1(3))* Chronicle Bks. LLC.

Snyder, Betsy E., illus. Lily's Potty. 2010. 16p. (J). bds. *(978-1-60906-001-5(6))* Begin Smart LLC.

Snyder, Sally. If It's to Be, It's up to Me! The ABC's of Character Building. Snyder, Sally, illus. 2008. (ENG., Illus.). 59p. (J). (gr. -1-3). 22.50 *(978-1-933197-57-9(9))* Orange Frazer Pr.

Snyder, Susan. There's a Frog Trapped in the Bathroom. Johanson, Anna, illus. 2005. 23p. (J). (gr. 1-3). 9.95 *(978-0-9715411-0-8(8))* Kotzig Publishing, Inc.

—The Very Stubborn Centipede. Johanson, Anna, illus. 2005. 24p. (J). (gr. 2-4). 9.95 *(978-0-9767163-0-3(5))* Kotzig Publishing, Inc.

Snyder, Susan E. Shivers & Shakes. 2006. (Illus.). 31p. (J). (gr. k-2). 9.95 *(978-0-9767163-5-8(6))* Kotzig Publishing, Inc.

Soban Biniashvili, Freidele Galya. There Is a Reason Why. Zimmer, Glenn, illus. 2016. (ENG.). 38p. (J). 13.99 *(978-1-929628-90-2(0))* Hachai Publishing.

Sobel, June. B Is for Bulldozer: A Construction ABC. Iwai, Melissa, illus. 2006. (ENG.). 32p. (J). (gr. -1-3). pap. 7.99 *(978-0-15-205774-9(9),* 1197355, Clarion Bks.) HarperCollins Pubs.

—B Is for Bulldozer: A Construction ABC. Iwai, Melissa, illus. 2006. 28p. (gr. -1-k). 17.00 *(978-0-7569-7037-6(7))* Perfection Learning Corp.

—B Is for Bulldozer Board Book: A Construction ABC. Iwai, Melissa, illus. 2013. (ENG.). 32p. (J). (— 1). bds. 7.99 *(978-0-544-10808-0(6),* 1540731, Clarion Bks.) HarperCollins Pubs.

—B Is for Bulldozer Lap Board Book: A Construction ABC. Iwai, Melissa, illus. 2018. (ENG.). 32p. (J). (— 1). bds. 12.99 *(978-1-328-77052-3(4),* 1681071, Clarion Bks.) HarperCollins Pubs.

—The Goodnight Train. Huliska-Beith, Laura, illus. (Goodnight Train Ser.). (ENG.). 32p. (J). (gr. -1-3). 2017. pap. 7.99 *(978-1-328-74002-1(1),* 1677042) 2006. 17.99 *(978-0-15-205436-6(7),* 1196359) HarperCollins Pubs. (Clarion Bks.).

—Shiver Me Letters: A Pirate ABC. Cole, Henry, illus. (ENG.). 32p. (J). (gr. -1-3). 2009. pap. 8.99 *(978-0-15-206679-6(9),* 1199768) 2006. 17.99 *(978-0-15-216732-5(3),* 1201748) HarperCollins Pubs. (Clarion Bks.).

Sobel, June & Huliska-Beith, Laura. The Goodnight Train Rolls On! Huliska-Beith, Laura, illus. 2018. (Goodnight Train Ser.). (ENG., Illus.). 32p. (J). (gr. -1-3). 17.99 *(978-1-328-50019-9(5),* 1717900, Clarion Bks.) HarperCollins Pubs.

Sones, Sonya. What My Girlfriend Doesn't Know. 2013. (ENG., Illus.). 320p. (YA). (gr. 7). pap. 12.99 *(978-1-4424-9384-1(4),* Simon & Schuster Bks. For Young Readers) Simon & Schuster Bks. For Young Readers.

—What My Mother Doesn't Know. 2004. 259p. (gr. 7-12). 19.00 *(978-0-7569-4268-7(3))* Perfection Learning Corp.

—What My Mother Doesn't Know. 2013. (ENG., Illus.). 288p. (YA). (gr. 7). pap. 12.99 *(978-1-4424-9385-8(2),* Simon & Schuster Bks. For Young Readers) Simon & Schuster Bks. For Young Readers.

Soprano, Sophie, illus. Laughing All the Way. 2008. (J). *(978-1-59811-642-7(8))* Covenant Communications.

Soule, Jean Conder. Never Tease a Weasel. Booth, George, illus. 2011. 40p. (J). (gr. -1-2). pap. 8.99 *(978-0-375-87285-3(X),* Dragonfly Bks.) Random Hse. Children's Bks.

Spangler, Lois. Fort on Fourth Street, the: a Story about the Six Simple Machines, 1 vol. Wald, Christina, illus. 2013. (ENG.). 32p. (J). (gr. 2-3). pap. 10.95 *(978-1-60718-632-8(2),* 3251b480-d1c0-4b93-9f0f-9102cce9cf79) Arbordale Publishing.

—The Fort on Fourth Street, the: a Story about the Six Simple Machines, 1 vol. Wald, Christina, illus. 2013. (ENG.). 32p. (J). (gr. 1-4). 17.95 *(978-1-60718-620-5(9))* Arbordale Publishing.

Sparkes, Amy. Ellie's Magic Wellies. East, Nick, illus. 2017. (ENG.). 32p. (J). (gr. -1-k). pap. 7.99 *(978-1-4052-7379-4(8))* Farshore GBR. Dist: HarperCollins Pubs.

Sparks, Evan. Freddy's Tale. 2006. 44p. pap. 14.88 *(978-1-4116-7427-1(8))* Lulu Pr., Inc.

Sparrow, Leilani. My New Shoes. Taylor, Dan, illus. (Mini Bee Board Bks.). (ENG.). (J). (gr. -1-1). 2018. 24p. bds. 7.99 *(978-1-4998-0729-5(5))* 2016. 32p. 16.99 *(978-1-4998-0363-1(X))* Little Bee Books Inc.

Spencer, Jamie. The Train to Maine. Reed, Rebecca, illus. 2008. (ENG.). 32p. (J). (gr. -1-3). 15.95 *(978-0-89272-767-4(5))* Down East Bks.

Sperring, Mark. Little Hugs from Little Loves. Frost, Maddie, illus. 2019. (ENG.). 24p. (J). (gr. -1 — 1). bds. 7.99 *(978-0-316-48433-6(4))* Little, Brown Bks. for Young Readers.

—The Littlest Things Give the Loveliest Hugs. Frost, Maddie, illus. 2018. (ENG.). 32p. (J). (gr. -1-3). 17.99 *(978-0-316-48434-3(2))* Little, Brown Bks. for Young Readers.

—The Shape of My Heart. Paterson, Alys, illus. 2015. (ENG.). 32p. (J). (gr. -1-1). bds. 8.99 *(978-1-68119-017-4(6),* 900155505, Bloomsbury USA Childrens) Bloomsbury Publishing USA.

Sperring, Mark & Teckentrup, Britta. Your Hand in My Hand. 2015. (ENG., Illus.). 32p. (J). (gr. -1-k). 15.99 *(978-0-545-80642-8(9),* Scholastic Pr.) Scholastic, Inc.

S

Spinelli, Eileen. Another Day As Emily. Lew-Vriethoff, Joanne, illus. 2015. 240p. (J). (gr. 3-7). 8.99 *(978-0-449-80989-1(7),* Yearling) Random Hse. Children's Bks.

—Bath Time, 1 vol. Pedersen, Janet, illus. 2003. (ENG.). 32p. (J). 14.95 *(978-0-7614-5117-4(X))* Marshall Cavendish Corp.

—Birdie. 2019. (ENG., Illus.). 208p. (J). *(978-0-8028-5513-8(X),* Eerdmans Bks For Young Readers) Eerdmans, William B. Publishing Co.

—Do You Have a Cat? Valério, Geraldo & Valério, Geraldo, illus. 2010. (ENG.). 32p. (J). (gr. -1-3). 16.00 *(978-0-8028-5351-6(X),* Eerdmans Bks For Young Readers) Eerdmans, William B. Publishing Co.

—Do You Have a Dog? Valério, Geraldo & Valério, Geraldo, illus. 2011. (ENG.). 26p. (J). 16.00 *(978-0-8028-5387-5(0),* Eerdmans Bks For Young Readers) Eerdmans, William B. Publishing Co.

—Hug a Bug. Andreasen, Dan, illus. 2009. 32p. (J). (gr. -1-3). lib. bdg. 17.89 *(978-0-06-051833-2(2))* HarperCollins Pubs.

—I Know It's Autumn. Hayashi, Nancy, tr. Hayashi, Nancy, illus. 2004. 32p. (J). (gr. -1-2). lib. bdg. 17.89 *(978-0-06-029423-6(X))* HarperCollins Pubs.

—I Know It's Autumn. Hayashi, Nancy, illus. 2004. (ENG.). 32p. (J). (gr. -1-2). 16.99 *(978-0-06-029422-9(1),* HarperCollins) HarperCollins Pubs.

—Love You Always. Flint, Gillian, illus. 2018. (ENG.). 22p. (J). (gr. -1-k). bds. 7.99 *(978-0-8249-1667-1(0))* Worthy Publishing.

—Silly Tilly, 0 vols. Slonim, David, illus. 2012. (ENG.). 32p. (J). (gr. -1-2). pap. 9.99 *(978-0-7614-5990-3(1),* 9780761459903, Two Lions) Amazon Publishing.

—Thankful, 1 vol. Preston, Archie, illus. 2018. (ENG.). 20p. (J). bds. 8.99 *(978-0-310-76782-4(2))* Zonderkidz.

—Thankful, 1 vol. 2015. (ENG., Illus.). 32p. (J). 16.99 *(978-0-310-00088-4(2))* Zonderkidz.

—When No One Is Watching. Johnson, David, illus. 2013. 26p. (J). 16.00 *(978-0-8028-5303-5(X),* Eerdmans Bks For Young Readers) Eerdmans, William B. Publishing Co.

—When Papa Comes Home Tonight. McPhail, David, illus. 2009. (ENG.). 32p. (J). (gr. -1-k). 16.99 *(978-1-4169-1028-2(X),* Simon & Schuster Bks. For Young Readers) Simon & Schuster Bks. For Young Readers.

Spink, Matt. Some Birds. 2016. (ENG., Illus.). 32p. (J). (gr. -1-k). 15.95 *(978-1-4197-2070-3(8),* 1140701, Abrams Appleseed) Abrams, Inc.

Sprenkle, Connie L. My Shining Star. 2011. 24p. pap. 15.99 *(978-1-4568-2168-5(7))* Xlibris Corp.

Spruill, Edward L. & Spruill, Sonya. Jordan's Hair. Peringer, Stephen Mercer, illus. 2005. 16p. (J). (gr. -1-3). 8.00 *(978-0-8170-1484-1(5))* Judson Pr.

Spurr, Elizabeth. At the Beach, 1 vol. Oliphant, Manelle, illus. 2013. 22p. (J). (gr. -1 — 1). bds. 6.99 *(978-1-56145-583-6(0))* Peachtree Publishing Co. Inc.

—Happy Sparkling Hanukkah. Madden, Colleen, illus. 2011. (J). *(978-1-4027-9660-9(9))* Sterling Publishing Co., Inc.

—In the Garden, 1 vol. Oliphant, Manelle, illus. 2012. 22p. (J). (— 1). bds. 6.99 *(978-1-56145-581-2(4))* Peachtree Publishing Co. Inc.

—In the Rain, 1 vol. Oliphant, Manelle, illus. 2018. (In the Weather Ser.). (ENG.). 22p. (J). (gr. -1 — 1). bds. 7.99 *(978-1-56145-853-0(8))* Peachtree Publishing Co. Inc.

—In the Snow, 1 vol. Oliphant, Manelle, illus. 2017. (In the Weather Ser.). 22p. (J). (gr. -1 — 1). bds. 6.99 *(978-1-56145-855-4(4))* Peachtree Publishing Co. Inc.

—In the Wind, 1 vol. Oliphant, Manelle, illus. 2016. (In the Weather Ser.). 22p. (J). (gr. -1 — 1). bds. 6.99 *(978-1-56145-854-7(6))* Peachtree Publishing Co. Inc.

—In the Woods, 1 vol. Oliphant, Manelle, illus. 2012. 22p. (J). (— 1). bds. 6.95 *(978-1-56145-582-9(2))* Peachtree Publishing Co. Inc.

—Monsters, Mind Your Manners! Scales, Simon, illus. 2012. (J). 34.28 *(978-1-61913-124-8(2))* Weigl Pubs., Inc.

Squillace, Elisa, illus. Down in the Jungle. 2005. (Classic Books with Holes Board Book Ser.). 14p. (J). (gr. -1-1). spiral bd. *(978-1-904550-61-7(4))* Child's Play International Ltd.

Staake, Bob. Can You See Me? 2019. (Beginner Books(R) Ser.). (ENG., Illus.). 40p. (J). (gr. -1-2). lib. bdg. 12.99 *(978-0-375-97197-6(1),* Random Hse. Bks. for Young Readers) Random Hse. Children's Bks.

—The Red Lemon. Staake, Bob, illus. 2012. (Illus.). 32p. (J). (gr. -1-3). pap. 7.99 *(978-0-307-97846-2(X),* Dragonfly Bks.) Random Hse. Children's Bks.

—The Red Lemon. 2012. lib. bdg. 18.40 *(978-0-606-26785-4(9))* Turtleback.

Stainton, Sue. I Love Dogs. Truesdell, Sue, illus. 2010. (J). lib. bdg. 15.89 *(978-0-06-117058-4(5))* HarperCollins Pubs.

—I Love Dogs! 2014. (ENG., Illus.). 32p. (J). (gr. -1-3). 14.99 *(978-0-06-117057-7(7),* Tegen, Katherine Bks) HarperCollins Pubs.

Stair, Karen Smith. Glasses, Glasses Oh What Do I See. 2004. (Illus.). 32p. 14.95 (978-0-9755407-1-8(8)) Bk. Pubs. Network.

Stanley, Robert. Nelly Goes Out to Sea, 1 vol. 2010. 46p. pap. 24.95 (978-1-4489-8828-0(4)) PublishAmerica, Inc.

Stanton, Andy. Danny Mcgee Drinks the Sea. Layton, Neal, illus. 2017. (ENG.). 32p. (J). (gr. -1-3). 17.99 (978-1-5247-1736-0(3), Schwartz & Wade Bks.) Random Hse. Children's Bks.

Starnes, Allison. Bernadette the Brave. 2016. (ENG., Illus.). (J). 18.95 (978-0-9913761-2-4(9)) Book M Publishing.

Stead, Judy, illus. Mister Sun. 2006. (J). (978-1-58987-097-0(2)) Kindermusik International.

Steer, Dugald A. Snappy Little Halloween. Matthews, Derek, illus. 2004. 20p. (J). (gr. k-4). reprint ed. 13.00 (978-0-7567-7403-5(9)) DIANE Publishing Co.

Steig, Jeanne. Tales from Gizzard's Grill. Turner, Sandy, illus. 2004. 80p. (J). 17.89 (978-0-06-000960-1(8), Cotler, Joanna Books) HarperCollins Pubs.

Stein, Gertrude. To Do: A Book of Alphabets & Birthdays. 2011. (ENG., Illus.). 128p. 30.00 (978-0-300-17097-9(1)) Yale Univ. Pr.

Stein, Kristen. The Vegetarian Lion. 2006. 36p. (J). pap. 13.28 (978-1-4116-6459-3(0)) Lulu Pr., Inc.

Stein, Peter. The Boy & the Bear. 2019. (Illus.). 40p. (J). (gr. -1-2). 17.99 (978-0-8234-4095-5(8)) Holiday Hse., Inc.

—Bugs Galore. Staake, Bob, illus. 2013. (ENG.). 32p. (J). (— 1). bds. 8.99 (978-0-7636-6220-2(8)) Candlewick Pr.

—Trucks Galore. Staake, Bob, illus. 2017. (ENG.). 32p. (J). (gr. -1-3). 17.99 (978-0-7636-8978-0(5)) Candlewick Pr.

Steinberg, D. J. Kindergarten, Here I Come! Chambers, Mark, illus. 2012. (Here I Come! Ser.). 32p. (J). (gr. -1-k). pap. 5.99 (978-0-448-45624-9(9), Grosset & Dunlap) Penguin Young Readers Group.

—Second Grade, Here I Come! Wood, Laura, illus. 2017. (Here I Come! Ser.). 32p. (J). (gr. k-2). pap. 5.99 (978-0-515-15808-3(9), Grosset & Dunlap) Penguin Young Readers Group.

Steinberg, Laya. All Around Me, I See. Arbo, Cris, illus. 2005. (Sharing Nature with Children Book Ser.). 32p. (J). 16.95 (978-1-58469-068-9(2)); pap. 8.95 (978-1-58469-069-6(0)) Take Heart Pubns.

—Thesaurus Rex Finds a Friend. Harter, Debbie, illus. 2006. (J). (978-1-905236-48-0(4)) Barefoot Bks., Inc.

Steiner, Nancy. On This Night: The Steps of the Seder in Rhyme. Leff, Tova, illus. 2013. (ENG.). 32p. (J). 11.99 (978-1-929628-51-3(X)) Hachai Publishing.

Stenton, Murray, illus. My Brother Is Special: A Sibling with Cerebral Palsy. 2016. (J). pap. (978-1-61599-309-3(6)) Loving Healing Pr., Inc.

Stephenson, Midji. Whose Tail on the Trail at Grand Canyon. Spengler, Kenneth, illus. 2012. (J). (978-1-934656-55-6(0)) Grand Canyon Conservancy.

Sterer, Gideon. From Ed's to Ned's. Cummins, Lucy Ruth, illus. 2020. (ENG.). 48p. (J). (gr. -1-2). 20.99 (978-0-525-64807-9(0), Knopf Bks. for Young Readers) Random Hse. Children's Bks.

Sterling Children's, Sterling. Look & See: What Sound Do You Make? 2014. (Look & See! Ser.). (Illus.). 24p. (J). (gr. -1 — 1). bds. 8.95 (978-1-4549-0642-1(1)) Sterling Publishing Co., Inc.

Sterling Publishing Co., Inc. Staff. Garage. Finn, Rebecca, illus. 2015. (Busy Bks.). (ENG.). 10p. (J). (— 1). bds. 8.95 (978-1-4549-1734-2(2)) Sterling Publishing Co., Inc.

Sternberg, Julie. Like Pickle Juice on a Cookie. Cordell, Matthew, illus. (Eleanor Ser.). (ENG.). (J). 2016. 144p. (gr. 1-4). pap. 7.99 (978-1-4197-2050-5(3), 658803) 2011. 128p. (gr. 3-5). 15.95 (978-0-8109-8424-0(5), 658801) Abrams, Inc. (Amulet Bks.).

Sterner, Wendy L. Seymore Monster. 2008. 32p. pap. 24.95 (978-1-60441-748-7(X)) America Star Bks.

Stevens, Cat. Peace Train. Reynolds, Peter H., illus. 2021. (ENG.). 40p. (J). (gr. -1-3). 18.99 (978-0-06-305399-1(3), HarperCollins) HarperCollins Pubs.

Stevens, Gary J. If I Called You a Hippopotamus! Stead, April-Nicole, illus. 2010. 24p. pap. 11.50 (978-1-60911-280-6(6), Eloquent Bks.) Strategic Book Publishing & Rights Agency (SBPRA).

Stevens, K. T. Stories for Children. 2012. 22p. pap. 16.95 (978-1-4626-9031-2(9)) America Star Bks.

Stewart, Sarah. The Library. Small, David, illus. pap. 35.95 incl. audio compact disk (978-1-59519-010-9(4)); 2004. (J). (gr. -1-2). 28.95 incl. audio compact disk (978-1-59519-011-6(2)) Live Oak Media.

Stewart, Wilson N. Cock-a-Doodle-Who? 2007. (ENG., Illus.). 6p. (J). 15.99 (978-0-7868-0826-7(8)) Hyperion Bks. for Children.

Stiegemeyer, Julie. Seven Little Bunnies, 0 vols. Bryant, Laura J., illus. 2012. (ENG.). 34p. (J). (gr. -1-1). 15.99 (978-0-7614-5600-1(7), 9780761456001, Two Lions) Amazon Publishing.

Stockham, Jess, illus. Down by the Station. 2007. (Classic Books with Holes 8x8 with CD Ser.). (ENG.). 16p. (J). (gr. -1-1). (978-1-904550-68-6(1)) Child's Play International Ltd.

Stofko, Michael D. The Tale of Taylor the Tailor. 2012. 30p. pap. 19.99 (978-1-4772-0238-8(2)) AuthorHouse.

—A Visit from the Zoo. 2011. 32p. pap. 12.77 (978-1-4567-2968-4(3)) AuthorHouse.

Stohs, Anita Reith. Oh, Come, Little Children. Huang, Benrei, illus. 2006. 22p. (J). (gr. -1-3). 14.99 (978-0-7586-1215-1(X)) Concordia Publishing Hse.

Stolz, Donald R. Classroom Times: Charactoons & Rhymes. Thornton, Barbara, illus. 2011. 266p. 76.95 (978-1-60976-951-2(1), Strategic Bk. Publishing) Strategic Book Publishing & Rights Agency (SBPRA).

Stone, Kate. Bunnies for Tea. 2013. (ENG., Illus.). 10p. (J). bds. 8.99 (978-1-4494-2887-7(8)) Andrews McMeel Publishing.

Stone, Tanya Lee. T Is for Turkey. Kelley, Gerald, illus. 2009. 24p. (J). (gr. -1-k). mass mkt. 6.99 (978-0-8431-2570-2(5), Price Stern Sloan) Penguin Young Readers Group.

Stone, Tiffany. Teatime. Van Der Linde, Jori, illus. 2017. 32p. (J). 15.95 (978-1-927018-67-5(6)) Simply Read Bks. CAN. Dist: Ingram Publisher Services.

Storad, Conrad J. Rattlesnake Rules. Jensen, Nathaniel P., illus. 2012. (ENG.). 40p. (J). (gr. 1-4). pap. 10.50 (978-1-58985-211-2(7), Story Monsters Pr.) Story Monsters LLC.

Storm, Raen. God's Palette. 2007. 16p. per. 24.95 (978-1-4137-1793-8(4)) America Star Bks.

Story Time Book: Rhyme Time & Story Time. 2004. reprint ed. pap. 15.95 (978-1-4191-1380-2(1)) Kessinger Publishing, LLC.

Storybots. The Amazing Planet Earth (StoryBots) 2017. (Step into Reading Ser.). (Illus.). 32p. (J). (gr. -1-1). pap. 4.99 (978-1-5247-1857-2(2), Random Hse. Bks. for Young Readers) Random Hse. Children's Bks.

—Tyrannosaurus Rex (StoryBots) 2017. (Step into Reading Ser.). (Illus.). 32p. (J). (gr. -1-1). pap. 4.99 (978-1-5247-1866-4(1), Random Hse. Bks. for Young Readers) Random Hse. Children's Bks.

Straker, Bethany, illus. The Funny Bunny Fly. 2014. (ENG.). 32p. (J). (gr. -1-k). 14.95 (978-1-62914-610-2(2), Sky Pony Pr.) Skyhorse Publishing Co., Inc.

Stranaghan, Crystal. The 13th Floor: Colouring Outside the Lines. Bzymek, Izabela, illus. 2012. 34p. (-18). (978-1-926691-25-1(3)) Gumboot Bks.

Stranaghan, Crystal J. Then It Rained. Espadaler, Rosa, illus. 2007. 24p. (J). (978-0-9784047-8-9(5)) Pays et Terroirs.

Stratford, Anne Margaret. My Daddy Is A Soldier. 2008. (Illus.). 40p. (J). 17.99 (978-0-9817933-0-1(0)) Diamond Fly Publishing, Inc.

Strelitz Haber, Tiffany. The Monster Who Lost His Mean. Edmunds, Kirstie, illus. 2012. (ENG.). 40p. (J). (gr. -1-3). 18.99 (978-0-8050-9375-9(3), 900073740, Holt, Henry & Co. Bks. For Young Readers) Holt, Henry & Co.

Strong, Cynda. Where Do Angels Sleep? Denos, Julia, illus. 2007. 24p. (J). (gr. -1-3). 14.99 (978-0-7586-1298-4(2)) Concordia Publishing Hse.

Strouss, Jessica & Strouss, Stephen. There's a Dog at My Feet when I Eat. 2010. 36p. 15.49 (978-1-4269-4342-3(3)) Trafford Publishing.

Stuart, Pamela Haught. Just like my Papa. 2008. 40p. per. 16.99 (978-1-4343-5369-6(9)) AuthorHouse.

Studio Mouse, creator. Rhymes on the Go! rev. ed. 2008. (ENG., Illus.). 36p. (J). 12.99 (978-1-59069-614-9(X)) Studio Mouse LLC.

Sturges, Philemon. I Love Bugs! Halpern, Shari, illus. 2005. (ENG.). 32p. (J). (gr. -1-3). 19.99 (978-0-06-056168-0(8), HarperCollins) HarperCollins Pubs.

—I Love School! Halpern, Shari, illus. 2014. 32p. pap. 7.00 (978-1-61003-329-9(9)) Center for the Collaborative Classroom.

—I Love School! Halpern, Shari, illus. 32p. (J). (gr. -1-1). 2004. lib. bdg. 14.89 (978-0-06-009285-6(8)) 2006. (ENG.). reprint ed. pap. 9.99 (978-0-06-009286-3(6), HarperCollins) HarperCollins Pubs.

—I Love Tools! Halpern, Shari, illus. 2006. 24p. (J). (gr. -1-1). 14.89 (978-0-06-009288-7(2)) HarperCollins Pubs.

—I Love Trains. Halpern, Shari, illus. 2003. (ENG.). 32p. (J). (gr. -1-1). pap. 7.99 (978-0-06-443667-0(5), HarperCollins) HarperCollins Pubs.

—I Love Trains! Board Book. Halpern, Shari, illus. 2006. (ENG.). 28p. (J). (gr. -1-1). bds. 6.99 (978-0-06-083774-7(8), HarperFestival) HarperCollins Pubs.

Sturtevant, Karen. The Adventures of Gert & Stu & Zippy Too. 2012. 36p. pap. 18.99 (978-1-4772-9360-7(4)) AuthorHouse.

Stutson, Caroline. Blue Corn Soup. Weidner, Teri, illus. 2017. (ENG.). 32p. (J). (gr. k-2). 16.99 (978-1-58536-967-6(5), 204325) Sleeping Bear Pr.

—By the Light of the Halloween Moon, 0 vols. Hawkes, Kevin, illus. 2012. (ENG.). 32p. (J). (gr. -1-3). pap. 7.99 (978-0-7614-6244-6(9), 9780761462446, Two Lions) Amazon Publishing.

—My Family Four Floors Up. Krampien, Celia, illus. 2018. (ENG.). 32p. (J). (gr. -1-2). 16.99 (978-1-58536-991-1(8), 204406) Sleeping Bear Pr.

—Prairie Primer: A to Z. Lamb, Susan Condie, illus. 2006. 29p. (J). (gr. -1-2). reprint ed. 16.00 (978-1-4223-5585-5(3)) DIANE Publishing Co.

StVil, Yves Lola. Girls Like Me. (ENG.). 320p. (YA). (gr. 7). 2018. pap. 8.99 (978-1-328-90102-6(5), 1700156) 2016. 17.99 (978-0-544-70674-3(9), 1628646) HarperCollins Pubs. (Clarion Bks.).

Suarez, Maribel, illus. Rebecca. (Rowing Frog's Rhymes Ser.). 16p. (J). (gr. k-3). 7.95 (978-1-59437-840-9(1)) Santillana USA Publishing Co., Inc.

Suen, Anastasia. Subway. Katz, Karen, illus. 2008. 24p. (J). (gr. -1-k). bds. 7.99 (978-0-670-01109-4(6), Viking Books for Young Readers) Penguin Young Readers Group.

Sullivan, Kevin. The Best Hawaiian Style Mother Goose Ever! Aoki, Deb, illus. 2006. 40p. 16.95 incl. cd-rom (978-0-9644149-6-9(1)) Hawaya, Inc.

Sullivan, Licsw. Mindfully Me! 2012. 12p. pap. 10.99 (978-1-105-46639-7(6)) Lulu Pr., Inc.

Surgal, Jon. Have You Seen My Dinosaur? Mathieu, Joe, illus. 2010. (Beginner Books(R) Ser.). (ENG.). 48p. (J). (gr. -1-2). 9.99 (978-0-375-85639-6(0), Random Hse. Bks. for Young Readers) Random Hse. Children's Bks.

Surplice, Holly. I Love You, Little One. Surplice, Holly, illus. 2019. (ENG., Illus.). 24p. (J). (-k). bds. 9.99 (978-1-5362-0578-7(8)) Candlewick Pr.

—Peek-A-Boo Bunny: An Easter & Springtime Book for Kids. Surplice, Holly, illus. 2014. (ENG., Illus.). 32p. (J). (gr. -1-3). 9.99 (978-0-06-224265-5(2), HarperCollins) HarperCollins Pubs.

Suter, Janine. Noah's Floating Animal Park. Gunther, Richard, illus. 2009. 32p. (J). 10.99 (978-0-89051-576-1(X), Master Books) New Leaf Publishing Group.

Sutherland, Marc. The Waiting Place. Sutherland, Marc, illus. 2004. (Illus.). 24p. (J). (gr. k-4). reprint ed. 15.00 (978-0-7567-8382-2(8)) DIANE Publishing Co.

Sutton, Kay. Nan & Grandad's Book of Short Stories. 2009. (Illus.). 52p. pap. 20.49 (978-1-4490-0575-7(6)) AuthorHouse.

Sutton, Sally. Demolicion. Lovelock, Brian, illus. 2014. (Construction Crew Ser.). (SPA.). 22p. (J). (-k). bds. 8.99 (978-0-7636-7031-3(6)) Candlewick Pr.

—Demolition. Lovelock, Brian, illus. 2014. (Construction Crew Ser.). (ENG.). 22p. (J). (-k). bds. 8.99 (978-0-7636-6493-0(6)) Candlewick Pr.

—Farmer John's Tractor. Belton, Robyn, illus. 2013. (ENG.). 32p. (J). (gr. -1-2). 15.99 (978-0-7636-6430-5(8)) Candlewick Pr.

Sweeney, Linda Booth. When the Snow Falls. Christy, Jana, illus. 2017. 32p. (J). (-k). 16.99 (978-0-399-54720-1(7), G.P. Putnam's Sons Books for Young Readers) Penguin Young Readers Group.

Sweet Dreams, Pout-Pout Fish. 2015. (Pout-Pout Fish Mini Adventure Ser.: 3). (ENG., Illus.). 12p. (J). (gr. -1 — 1). bds. 6.99 (978-0-374-38010-6(4), 900122563, Farrar, Straus & Giroux (BYR)) Farrar, Straus & Giroux.

Swenson, Jamie A. A Fall Ball for All. Fedele, Chiara, illus. 2018. (ENG.). 32p. (J). (gr. k-2). 19.99 (978-1-5124-9803-5(3), 58a720c8-25c5-494b-baa5-616ae97cfa71, Millbrook Pr.) Lerner Publishing Group.

Swerling, Lisa & Lazar, Ralph. The Sky Is the Limit: A Celebration of All the Things You Can Do (Graduation Book for Kids, Preschool Graduation Gift, Toddler Book) 2020. (ENG., Illus.). 60p. (J). (gr. -1-17). 14.99 (978-1-4521-7982-7(4)) Chronicle Bks. LLC.

Swift, Ginger. All God's Creatures (Little Sunbeams) Cottage Door Press, ed. Sosa, Daniela, illus. 2019. (Little Sunbeams Ser.). (ENG.). 12p. (J). (gr. -1 — 1). bds. 7.99 (978-1-68052-523-6(9), 1003790) Cottage Door Pr.

—Good Morning, God. Cottage Door Press, ed. Sosa, Daniela, illus. 2018. (Little Sunbeams Ser.). (ENG.). 12p. (J). (gr. -1 — 1). bds. 7.99 (978-1-68052-377-5(5), 1003420) Cottage Door Pr.

—Good Night, God. Cottage Door Press, ed. Sosa, Daniela, illus. 2018. (Little Sunbeams Ser.). (ENG.). 12p. (J). (gr. -1 — 1). bds. 7.99 (978-1-68052-375-1(9), 1003400) Cottage Door Pr.

—Little Blue Boat. Cottage Door Press, ed. Persico, Zoe, illus. 2016. (ENG.). 12p. (J). (gr. -1 — 1). bds. 7.99 (978-1-68052-077-4(6), 1000800) Cottage Door Pr.

—Little Green Frog. Cottage Door Press, ed. Demidova, Olga, illus. 2016. (ENG.). 12p. (J). (gr. -1 — 1). bds. 7.99 (978-1-68052-082-8(2), 1000650) Cottage Door Pr.

—Little Yellow Bee. Cottage Door Press, ed. Longhi, Katya, illus. 2016. (ENG.). 12p. (J). (gr. -1 — 1). bds. 7.99 (978-1-68052-083-5(0), 1000660) Cottage Door Pr.

Swinburne, Stephen R. Safe in a Storm. Bell, Jennifer, illus. 2016. (J). (978-0-545-66987-0(1)) Scholastic, Inc.

Symes, Sally. Funny Face, Sunny Face. Beardshaw, Rosalind, illus. 2015. (ENG.). 32p. (J). (-k). 14.99 (978-0-7636-7606-3(3)) Candlewick Pr.

Tabby, Abigail. Monsters Munch Lunch! 2013. (Step into Reading - Level 1 Ser.). lib. bdg. 13.55 (978-0-606-26983-4(5)) Turtleback.

—Welcome Home, Baby! Williams, Sam, illus. 2017. (New Books for Newborns Ser.). (ENG.). 16p. (J). (— 1). bds. 8.99 (978-1-5344-0103-7(2), Little Simon) Little Simon.

Tafolla, Carmen. What Can You Do with a Rebozo? / ¿Qué Puedes Hacer con un Rebozo? Cordova, Amy, illus. 2009. 32p. (J). (gr. -1-2). pap. 8.99 (978-1-58246-271-4(2), Tricycle Pr.) Random Hse. Children's Bks.

Taft, Jean. Worm Weather. Hunt, Matt, illus. 2015. 32p. (J). (-k). bds. 5.99 (978-0-448-48740-3(3), Grosset & Dunlap) Penguin Young Readers Group.

Tango-Hampton, Doreen. I Like Gum. Pfleegor, Gina, illus. 2007. (ENG.). 32p. (J). (gr. -1-3). 15.95 (978-0-9726614-2-3(5)) Shenanigan Bks.

Tara, Stephanie L. Gwynne, Fair & Shining. Fodi, Lee Edward, illus. 2006. (J). (gr. -1-3). 16.95 (978-1-933285-62-7(1)) Brown Books Publishing Group.

Tarbett, Debbie, illus. 5 Stomping Elephants. 2016. (J). (978-1-84857-542-4(4)) Little Tiger Pr.

Tarpley, Todd. Ten Tiny Toes. 2018. (ENG., Illus.). 28p. (J). (gr. -1 — 1). bds. 7.99 (978-0-316-43580-2(5)) Little, Brown Bks. for Young Readers.

Tarter, Mildred. Alexis Sets up Search Groups. 2013. 26p. pap. 16.49 (978-1-4389-6881-0(7)) AuthorHouse.

—Rexis! Where Are You! 2010. 24p. pap. 16.49 (978-1-4389-6874-2(4)) AuthorHouse.

Taxali, Gary. This Is Silly! 2010. (J). (978-0-439-71837-0(6), Scholastic Pr.) Scholastic, Inc.

Taylor, Bonnie Highsmith. Simon Can't Say Hippopotamus. Hornung, Phyllis, tr. Hornung, Phyllis, illus. 2003. 24p. (J). 14.95 (978-1-59336-017-7(7)); pap. (978-1-59336-018-4(5)) Mondo Publishing.

Taylor-Butler, Christine. Ah-Choo. Koeller, Carol, illus. 2005. (My First Reader Ser.). (ENG.). 32p. (J). (gr. k-1). 18.50 (978-0-516-25175-2(9), Children's Pr.) Scholastic Library Publishing.

Taylor, C. Brian. Atop the Tree Top: A Christmas Story. Butler, Sharon, illus. 2003. (J). 15.95 (978-0-9747054-0-8(3)) Rilly Silly Bk. Co., The.

Taylor, Dorothea. There's a Dragon in My Closet. Palmer, Charly, illus. 2020. (ENG.). 32p. (J). (gr. -1-3). 17.99 (978-1-5344-7646-2(6)) Simon & Schuster, Inc.

Taylor, Martin. The Lost Treasure of the Sunken City. Catling, Andy, illus. 2012. (J). (978-1-4351-4330-2(2)) Barnes & Noble, Inc.

Taylor, Thomas. The Pets You Get. Reynolds, Adrian, illus. 2013. (ENG.). 32p. (J). (gr. -1-3). 16.95 (978-1-4677-1143-2(8), 6b92e368-27d7-4535-bc74-f4d91d824681) Lerner Publishing Group.

Taylor, Yvonne. Hartlie: The Streak. Taylor, Yvonne, ed. (Hartlie: Vol. 1). (Illus.). 32p. (J). 10.99 (978-0-9709187-0-3(4)) Peaceable Productions.

Teckentrup, Britta. Moon: a Peek-Through Picture Book. 2018. (ENG., Illus.). 32p. (J). (gr. -1-2). 17.99 (978-1-5247-6966-6(5), Doubleday Bks. for Young Readers) Random Hse. Children's Bks.

Tedesco, Tina. The Stork Dropped Your Here for a Reason. 2006. (J). pap. 8.00 (978-0-8059-7233-7(1)) Dorrance Publishing Co., Inc.

Temple, Kate. Room on Our Rock. Baynton, Terri Rose, illus. 2019. (J). 12.99 (978-1-61067-902-2(4)) Kane Miller.

Templeton, Donna L. Mother's Surprise. Berlinger, Nancy A., illus. 2009. (ENG.). 32p. (J). pap. 9.99 (978-0-9764336-6-8(4)) MJS Publishing Group LLC.

Tenney, Yevet. I Never Got to Say Goodbye. 2013. 24p. pap. 9.99 (978-0-9889595-1-4(8)) Mindstir Media.

Teraskai, Stanley Todd. Ghosts for Breakfast, 1 vol. Shinjo, Shelly, illus. 2017. (ENG.). 32p. (J). (gr. k-4). pap. 10.95 (978-1-62014-350-6(X), leelowbooks) Lee & Low Bks., Inc.

Testa, Joseph Anthony. Are Cat Ears Made of Chocolate? A Children's Rhyme. 2012. 28p. pap. 17.99 (978-1-4772-7977-9(6)) AuthorHouse.

Testa, Maggie. Buddy & Pals. 2018. (Ready-To-Read Ser.). (ENG.). 32p. (J). (gr. -1-1). 13.89 (978-1-64310-678-6(3)) Penworthy Co., LLC, The.

Testa, Maria. Becoming Joe Dimaggio. Hunt, Scott, illus. 2005. (ENG.). 64p. (J). (gr. 5-9). reprint ed. pap. 7.99 (978-0-7636-2444-6(6)) Candlewick Pr.

Tey, Priscilla. In-Between Things. Tey, Priscilla, illus. 2018. (ENG., Illus.). 40p. (J). (gr. -1-3). 16.99 (978-0-7636-8983-4(1)) Candlewick Pr.

Themerson, Franciszka & Themerson, Franciszka. My First Nursery Book. 2009. (ENG., Illus.). 72p. (J). (gr. -1-2). 16.95 (978-0-8109-7978-9(0), 660401, Abrams Bks. for Young Readers) Abrams, Inc.

Theron Elkins, J. A Christmas Gift for Santa: A Bedtime Book, 1 vol. Jatkowska, Ag, illus. 2019. (ENG.). 32p. (J). 17.99 (978-0-310-72961-7(0)) Zonderkidz.

Thimble The Fairy. Thimble the Fairy's Acorns & Tea. Patch, Sebastion, illus. 2011. (ENG.). 48p. (J). 8.99 (978-0-9827304-0-9(3)) Eleve Publishing.

Thomas, Deborah Kadiar. Cemetery Jamboree, 1 vol. Thomas, Deborah Kadiar, illus. 2016. (ENG., Illus.). 32p. (J). (gr. k-5). pap. 9.95 (978-1-4556-2239-9(7), Pelican Publishing) Arcadia Publishing.

Thomas, Jan. Rhyming Dust Bunnies. Thomas, Jan, illus. 2009. (ENG., Illus.). 40p. (J). (gr. -1-3). 17.99 (978-1-4169-7976-0(X), Beach Lane Bks.) Beach Lane Bks.

Thomas, Martin. My Mom Is There. Jatkowska, Ag, illus. 2018. (ENG.). 20p. (gr. -1 — 1). bds. 8.99 (978-1-5107-3616-0(6), Sky Pony Pr.) Skyhorse Publishing Co., Inc.

Thomas Nelson Community College Staff. God's Love in My Heart, 1 vol. 2014. (ENG.). 24p. bds. 9.99 (978-0-529-11141-8(1), Tommy Nelson) Nelson, Thomas Inc.

Thompson, Chad. Yankee Doodle. 2011. (Early Literacy Ser.). (ENG.). 16p. (gr. k-1). 19.99 (978-1-4333-2365-2(6)); 6.99 (978-1-4333-2364-5(8)) Teacher Created Materials, Inc.

Thompson, Chad J. Rhymes with Doug. Thompson, Chad J., illus. 2016. (ENG., Illus.). 40p. (J). (gr. -1-3). 16.99 (978-1-4814-7095-7(7), Aladdin) Simon & Schuster Children's Publishing.

Thompson, Kim Mitzo. Five Little Monkeys Jumping on the Bed. Girouard, Patrick, illus. 2010. (Padded Board Book W/CD Ser.). 8p. (J). (gr. k-2). bds. 10.99 incl. audio compact disk (978-1-59922-581-4(6)) Twin Sisters IP, LLC.

—The Wheels on the Bus. Holm, Sharon Lane, illus. 2010. (Padded Board Book W/CD Ser.). 8p. (J). (gr. k-2). bds. 10.99 incl. audio compact disk (978-1-59922-580-7(8)) Twin Sisters IP, LLC.

Thompson, Lauren. Chew, Chew, Gulp! Krosoczka, Jarrett J., illus. 2011. (ENG.). 32p. (J). (gr. -1-k). 18.99 (978-1-4169-9744-3(X), McElderry, Margaret K. Bks.) McElderry, Margaret K. Bks.

—Good Night, Bunny. Yue, Stephanie, illus. 2018. (ENG.). 32p. (J). (gr. -1-k). 16.99 (978-0-545-60335-5(8), Orchard Bks.) Scholastic, Inc.

—Hop, Hop, Jump! Krosoczka, Jarrett J., illus. 2012. (ENG.). 32p. (J). (gr. -1-3). 18.99 (978-1-4169-9745-0(8), McElderry, Margaret K. Bks.) McElderry, Margaret K. Bks.

—Leap Back Home to Me. Cordell, Matthew, illus. 2011. (ENG.). 32p. (J). (gr. -1-3). 19.99 (978-1-4169-0664-3(9), McElderry, Margaret K. Bks.) McElderry, Margaret K. Bks.

—One Starry Night. Bean, Jonathan, illus. (ENG.). 32p. (J). 2011. (gr. -1-3). lib. bdg. 17.99 (978-0-689-82851-5(9)) 2003. 6.99 (978-0-689-84215-3(5)) McElderry, Margaret K. Bks. (McElderry, Margaret K. Bks.).

Thompson, Richard. The Follower, 1 vol. Springett, Martin, illus. 2003. (ENG.). 32p. (J). (gr. 1-3). pap. 7.95 (978-1-55041-880-4(7), f8727bf0-bf98-46d5-9fd8-544bd1cbf8bb) Fitzhenry & Whiteside, Ltd. CAN. Dist: Firefly Bks., Ltd.

Thompson, Shannon Raines. Mad about Miller. Stone, Kathrine Thompson, ed. Shehan, Terece, illus. 2006. 24p. (YA). 12.95 (978-1-59971-853-8(7)) Aardvark Global Publishing.

—Nuts about Neal. Stone, Kathrine Thompson, ed. Shehan, Terece, illus. 2006. 24p. (YA). 12.95 (978-1-59971-852-1(9)) Aardvark Global Publishing.

Thomson, Sarah L. Pirates, Ho!, 0 vols. Gilpin, Stephen, illus. 2012. (ENG.). 32p. (J). (gr. -1-3). pap. 7.99 (978-0-7614-6247-7(3), 9780761462477, Two Lions) Amazon Publishing.

Thong, Roseanne. Red Is a Dragon: A Book of Colors. Lin, Grace, illus. 2008. (ENG.). 40p. (J). (gr. -1-17). pap. 7.99 (978-0-8118-6481-7(2)) Chronicle Bks. LLC.

—Round Is a Tortilla: A Book of Shapes. Parra, John, illus. 2015. (Latino Book of Concepts Ser.). (ENG.). 40p. (J). (gr. -1-k). 7.99 (978-1-4521-4568-6(7)) Chronicle Bks. LLC.

Thong, Roseanne Greenfield. Green Is a Chile Pepper: A Book of Colors. 2014. (Multicultural Shapes & Colors Ser.). (Illus.). 40p. (J). lib. bdg. 28.50 (978-1-60753-707-6(9)) Amicus Learning.

—Green Is a Chile Pepper: A Book of Colors. Parra, John, illus. (Latino Book of Concepts Ser.). (ENG.). 40p. (J). (gr. -1-k). 2016. 7.99 (978-1-4521-5645-3(X)) 2014. 16.99 (978-1-4521-0203-0(1)) Chronicle Bks. LLC.

—One Is a Drummer: A Book of Numbers. 2014. (Multicultural Shapes & Colors Ser.). (Illus.). 40p. (J). lib. bdg. 28.50 (978-1-60753-567-6(X)) Amicus Learning.

—One Is a Pinata: a Book of Numbers (Learn to Count Books, Numbers Books for Kids, Preschool Numbers Book) Parra, John, illus. 2019. (Latino Book of Concepts Ser.). (ENG.). 40p. (J). (gr. -1-k). 16.99 (978-1-4521-5584-5(4)) Chronicle Bks. LLC.

—Red Is a Dragon. Lin, Grace, illus. 2014. 40p. pap. 7.00 (978-1-61003-333-6(7)) Center for the Collaborative Classroom.

—Red Is a Dragon: A Book of Colors. 2014. (Multicultural Shapes & Colors Ser.). (Illus.). 40p. (J). lib. bdg. 28.50 (978-1-60753-565-2(3)) Amicus Learning.

—Round Is a Mooncake: A Book of Shapes. 2014. (Multicultural Shapes & Colors Ser.). (Illus.). 40p. (J). lib. bdg. 28.50 *(978-1-60753-564-5(5))* Amicus Learning.
—Round Is a Tortilla: A Book of Shapes. 2014. (Multicultural Shapes & Colors Ser.). (Illus.). 40p. (J). lib. bdg. 28.50 *(978-1-60753-566-9(1))* Amicus Learning.
—Round Is a Tortilla: A Book of Shapes. Parra, John, illus. 2013. (Latino Book of Concepts Ser.). (ENG.). 40p. (J). (gr. -1-k). 16.99 *(978-1-4521-0616-8(9))* Chronicle Bks. LLC.
Thornton, E. J. I Have a Secret: Do I Keep It? 2004. (Illus.). 24p. per. 8.95 *(978-1-932344-66-0(7))* Thornton Publishing, Inc.
Thrasher, Grady. Tim & Sally's Beach Adventure. Rabon, Elaine Hearn, illus. 2008. (ENG.). 48p. (J). (gr. -1-3). 18.95 *(978-1-58818-161-9(8))* Hill Street Pr., LLC.
Ticktock Media, Ltd. Staff. At the Beach with the Snappy Little Crab. 2009. (Touch & Feel Fun Ser.). (ENG.). 10p. (J). (gr. k — 1). bds. 5.95 *(978-1-84696-809-9(7),* TickTock Books) Octopus Publishing Group GBR. Dist: Independent Pubs. Group.
—In the Garden with the Hungry Little Snail. 2009. (Touch & Feel Fun Ser.). (ENG.). 10p. (J). (gr. k — 1). bds. 5.95 *(978-1-84696-810-5(0),* TickTock Books) Octopus Publishing Group GBR. Dist: Independent Pubs. Group.
—Under the Ocean with the Little Yellow Submarine. 2009. (Touch & Feel Fun Ser.). (ENG.). 10p. (J). (gr. k — 1). bds. 5.95 *(978-1-84696-811-2(9),* TickTock Books) Octopus Publishing Group GBR. Dist: Independent Pubs. Group.
—Zoom into Space with the Shiny Red Rocket. 2009. (Touch & Feel Fun Ser.). (ENG.). 10p. (J). (gr. k — 1). bds. 5.95 *(978-1-84696-812-9(7),* TickTock Books) Octopus Publishing Group GBR. Dist: Independent Pubs. Group.
Tietz, Heather. Yes, Jesus Loves You. Miller, Nancy, illus. 2009. 20p. (J). (gr. k-4). 14.95 *(978-0-8091-6743-2(3),* Ambassador Bks.) Paulist Pr.
Tiger Tales. Baby's First Bunny. 1 vol. Ward, Sarah, illus. 2016. (To Baby with Love Ser.). (ENG.). 10p. (J). (gr. -1 — 1). bds. 14.99 *(978-1-58925-213-4(6))* Tiger Tales.
—Five Little Pumpkins. Mantle, Ben, illus. 2010. (ENG.). 24p. (J). (gr. -1-k). bds. 8.95 *(978-1-58925-856-3(8))* Tiger Tales.
—I Love You, Grandma. Tyger, Rory, illus. 2017. (ENG.). 28p. (J). (gr. -1-k). bds. 7.99 *(978-1-68010-524-7(8))* Tiger Tales.
—Ten Splishy, Splashy Fish. Tarbett, Debbie, illus. 2017. (ENG.). 26p. (J). (gr. -1-k). mass mkt. 4.99 *(978-1-68010-412-7(8))* Tiger Tales.
Tillis, Dionne. Willameana Whitney White & the Magical Butterfly. 2012. 24p. pap. 17.99 *(978-1-4685-7286-5(5))* AuthorHouse.
Tillman, Nancy. I Knew You Could Do It! 2019. (ENG., Illus.). 32p. (J). 17.99 *(978-1-250-11377-1(6),* 900171050) Feiwel & Friends.
—On the Night You Were Born. (ENG., Illus.). 32p. (J). 2017. bds. 9.99 *(978-1-250-16401-8(X),* 900186655) 2010. bds. 7.99 *(978-0-312-60155-3(7),* 900064146) Feiwel & Friends.
—On the Night You Were Born. Tillman, Nancy, illus. 2006. (ENG., Illus.). 32p. (J). (gr. -1 — 1). 18.99 *(978-0-312-34606-5(9),* 900041898) Feiwel & Friends.
—On the Night You Were Born. 1 vol., Set. unabr. ed. 2012. (ENG., Illus.). 32p. (J). (— 1). pap. 12.99 *(978-1-4272-2646-4(6),* 900087155) Macmillan Audio.
—The Spirit of Christmas. Tillman, Nancy, illus. 2009. (ENG., Illus.). 32p. (J). (gr. -1-3). 17.99 *(978-0-312-54965-7(2),* 900055822) Feiwel & Friends.
—Wherever You Are: My Love Will Find You. Tillman, Nancy, illus. (ENG., Illus.). 32p. (J). (gr. -1-3). 2012. bds. 8.99 *(978-1-250-01797-0(1),* 900087504) 2010. 18.99 *(978-0-312-54966-4(0),* 900055823) Feiwel & Friends.
—You Are Loved Collection. Tillman, Nancy, illus. 2012. (ENG., Illus.). 96p. (J). (gr. k-1). 53.97 *(978-1-250-01135-0(3),* 900084994) Feiwel & Friends.
—You're Here for a Reason. (ENG., Illus.). (J). 2017. 16p. bds. 8.99 *(978-1-250-10650-6(8),* 900164479) 2015. 32p. (gr. -1-3). 18.99 *(978-1-250-05626-9(8),* 900138737) Feiwel & Friends.
Tillman, Nancy & Metaxas, Eric. It's Time to Sleep, My Love: Illustrated by Nancy Tillman. Tillman, Nancy, illus. 2011. (ENG., Illus.). 34p. (J). (— 1). bds. 7.99 *(978-0-312-67336-9(1),* 900072514) Feiwel & Friends.
Timbaland & Myers, Christopher. Nighttime Symphony. Myers, Christopher & Kaa Illustration, illus. 2019. (ENG.). 32p. (J). (gr. -1-3). 17.99 *(978-1-4424-1208-8(9),* Atheneum Bks. for Young Readers) Simon & Schuster Children's Publishing.
Timmers, Leo. Gus's Garage. Timmers, Leo, illus. 2017. (ENG., Illus.). 32p. (gr. -1-k). (J). 16.99 *(978-1-77657-092-8(8),* 972546ee-c75c-40e3-b578-20e22695b85e); 9.99 *(978-1-77657-094-2(4))* Gecko Pr. NZL. Dist: Lerner Publishing Group.
Tinsley, Jillian. Wally the Warthog. Wood, Douglas, illus. 2012. 24p. (J). pap. 10.99 *(978-1-61254-782-4(6))* Small Pr., The.
Tischler, Tracey. Heroes in the Sandbox. 2009. 28p. pap. 13.95 *(978-1-4490-5502-8(8))* AuthorHouse.
To Be Perfectly Honest: A Novel Based on an Untrue Story. 2014. (ENG., Illus.). 496p. (YA). (gr. 7). pap. 11.99 *(978-0-689-87605-9(X),* Simon & Schuster Bks. For Young Readers) Simon & Schuster Bks. For Young Readers.
Todd, Mark. Food Trucks! 2014. (ENG., Illus.). 32p. (J). (gr. -1-3). 17.99 *(978-0-544-15784-2(2),* 1550624, Clarion Bks.) HarperCollins Pubs.
Todd, Traci N. Wiggle, Waggle, Loop-De-Loo! Barner, Bob, illus. 2006. (J). *(978-1-58987-009-3(3))* Kindermusik International.
Toht, Patricia. Pick a Pine Tree. Jarvis, illus. 2017. (ENG.). 40p. (J). (gr. -1-2). 17.99 *(978-0-7636-9571-2(8))* Candlewick Pr.
Tolstoy, Aleksei, et al. The Gigantic Turnip. 2009. (Illus.). (J). 16.99 *(978-1-84686-298-4(1))* Barefoot Bks., Inc.
Tomlin, Chris. Good Good Father for Little Ones. 1 vol. 2017. (ENG., Illus.). 24p. (J). bds. 9.99 *(978-0-7180-8697-8(X),* Tommy Nelson) Nelson, Thomas Inc.
Tomlinson, Jill. The Gorilla Who Wanted to Grow Up. Howard, Paul, illus. 2014. (ENG.). 112p. (J). (gr. -1-2). pap. 5.99 *(978-1-4052-7195-0(7))* Farshore GBR. Dist: HarperCollins Pubs.
Top That Publishing Staff, ed. The Midnight Fairies. Atkins, Alison, illus. 2007. (Sparkling Jigsaw Book Ser.). 10p. (J). (gr. -1). bds. *(978-1-84666-278-2(8),* Tide Mill Pr.) Top That! Publishing PLC.
—There Were Ten Bears in a Bed: A Count-and-Feel Book. Atkins, Alison, illus. 2007. (Story Book Ser.). 22p. (J). (gr. -1). bds. *(978-1-84666-130-3(7),* Tide Mill Pr.) Top That! Publishing PLC.
Toral, Miguel A. Babu Goes Back to the Zoo. 2009. 32p. pap. 15.70 *(978-1-4389-6330-3(0))* AuthorHouse.
Torres, J. Checkers & Dot at the Beach. Lum, J., illus. 2013. (Checkers & Dot Ser.: 4). 16p. (J). (— 1). bds. 7.95 *(978-1-77049-444-2(8),* Tundra Bks.) Tundra Bks. CAN. Dist: Penguin Random Hse. LLC.
—Checkers & Dot at the Zoo. Lum, J., illus. 2012. (Checkers & Dot Ser.: 2). 16p. (J). (gr. k — 1). bds. 7.95 *(978-1-77049-442-8(1),* Tundra Bks.) Tundra Bks. CAN. Dist: Penguin Random Hse. LLC.
—Checkers & Dot on the Farm. Lum, J., illus. 2013. (Checkers & Dot Ser.: 3). 16p. (J). (— 1). bds. 7.95 *(978-1-77049-443-5(X),* Tundra Bks.) Tundra Bks. CAN. Dist: Penguin Random Hse. LLC.
Tougas, Chris. Dojo Daycare. 2014. (Dojo Ser.: 1). (ENG., Illus.). 32p. (J). (gr. -1-3). 16.95 *(978-1-77147-057-5(7),* Owlkids) Owlkids Bks. Inc. CAN. Dist: Publishers Group West (PGW).
—Dojo Surprise. 2016. (Dojo Ser.: 3). (ENG., Illus.). 32p. (J). (gr. -1-3). 16.95 *(978-1-77147-143-5(3),* Owlkids) Owlkids Bks. Inc. CAN. Dist: Publishers Group West (PGW).
Tran-Davies, N. Daddy Is a Conundrum! 2012. 40p. (-18). pap. *(978-1-4602-0043-8(8))* FriesenPress.
Trapani, Iza. Gabe & Goon. Trapani, Iza, illus. 2016. (Illus.). 32p. (J). (gr. -1-1). lib. bdg. 16.95 *(978-1-58089-640-5(5))* Charlesbridge Publishing, Inc.
—Haunted Party. Trapani, Iza, illus. (Illus.). 28p. (J). 2010. (gr. -1-2). pap. 7.95 *(978-1-58089-247-6(7))* 2009. (ENG., (gr. k-3). 22.44 *(978-1-58089-246-9(9))* Charlesbridge Publishing, Inc.
Trasler, Janee. Bathtime for Chickies. 2015. (Chickies Ser.). (ENG., Illus.). 24p. (J). (gr. -1 — 1). bds. 8.99 *(978-0-06-234229-4(0),* HarperFestival) HarperCollins Pubs.
—Big Chickie, Little Chickie. 2016. (ENG., Illus.). 24p. (J). (gr. -1 — 1). bds. 8.99 *(978-0-06-234231-7(2),* HarperFestival) HarperCollins Pubs.
—A New Chick for Chickies: An Easter & Springtime Book for Kids. Trasler, Janee, illus. 2014. (Chickies Ser.). (ENG., Illus.). 24p. (J). (gr. -1 — 1). bds. 8.99 *(978-0-06-227471-7(6),* HarperFestival) HarperCollins Pubs.
Tregay, Sarah. Love & Leftovers. 2011. (ENG.). 448p. (YA). (gr. 8). 17.99 *(978-0-06-202358-2(6),* Tegen, Katherine Bks) HarperCollins Pubs.
Treml, Renee. Wombat Big, Puggle Small. 2020. 24p. (J). (gr. -1-k). bds. 11.99 *(978-1-76089-055-1(3),* Picture Puffin) Penguin Random Hse. AUS. Dist: Independent Pubs. Group.
Trent, Shanda. Farmers' Market Day. Dippold, Jane, illus. 2013. (ENG.). 32p. (J). (gr. -1-1). 12.95 *(978-1-58925-115-1(6))* Tiger Tales.
Treyes, Jill. Brooke & Brandon Welcome Brandon. 2010. 28p. pap. 12.99 *(978-1-4389-1939-3(5))* AuthorHouse.
Trinco, Trish. The Leaf That Wouldn't Leave. Langdo, Bryan, illus. 2008. (ENG.). 32p. (J). 16.95 *(978-0-931674-90-7(5),* Waldman House Pr.) TRISTAN Publishing, Inc.
Trumbauer, Lisa. The Great Reindeer Rebellion. Ho, Jannie, illus. 2014. 32p. (J). (gr. -1). pap. 6.95 *(978-1-4549-1356-6(8))* Sterling Publishing Co., Inc.
—Rookie Ready to Learn en Español: un Diente Está Flojo. Gray, Steve, illus. 2011. (Rookie Ready to Learn Español Ser.). Orig. Title: Rookie Ready to Learn: a Tooth Is Loose. (SPA.). 32p. (J). pap. 5.95 *(978-0-531-26785-1(7),* Children's Pr.) Scholastic Library Publishing.
—A Tooth Is Loose. Gray, Steve, illus. (Rookie Ready to Learn Ser.). (J). 2011. 32p. pap. 5.95 *(978-0-531-26735-6(0))* 2005. (ENG.). 24p. pap. 4.95 *(978-0-516-25841-6(9))* Scholastic Library Publishing. (Children's Pr.).
Tsitoukis, Kristen L. The Tooth Song. 2008. 16p. pap. 8.50 *(978-1-4343-9539-9(1))* AuthorHouse.
Tucker, Kathy. Do Pirates Take Baths? 2015. (Illus.). 27p. (J). *(978-1-4896-3861-8(X))* Weigl Pubs., Inc.
Tucker, Lindy. Oddvark & the Yellow Kazoo. 2013. 94p. pap. 12.95 *(978-1-4575-2083-9(4))* Dog Ear Publishing, LLC.
Tucker Slingsby Ltd., Staff. My Big Book of Fairy Tales in Rhyme! Lewis, Jan, illus. 2004. 224p. (J). *(978-1-902272-31-3(5))* Tucker Slingsby, Ltd.
Tucker, Stephen. The Three Billy Goats Gruff. 2 vols. Sharratt, Nick, illus. 2017. (Lift-The-Flap Fairy Tales Ser.). (ENG.). 24p. (J). (gr. -1-k). 10.99 *(978-1-5098-2978-1(4))* Pan Macmillan GBR. Dist: Independent Pubs. Group.
—The Three Little Pigs. 2 vols. Sharratt, Nick, illus. 2016. (Lift-The-Flap Fairy Tales Ser.). (ENG.). 24p. (J). (gr. -1-k). bds. 11.99 *(978-1-5098-1713-9(1))* Pan Macmillan GBR. Dist: Independent Pubs. Group.
Tudor, Tasha. Around the Year. Tudor, Tasha, illus. 2004. (ENG., Illus.). 64p. (J). (gr. -1-3). 8.99 *(978-0-689-87350-8(6),* Aladdin) Simon & Schuster Children's Publishing.
Tuell, Todd. Ninja, Ninja, Never Stop! Carpenter, Tad, illus. 2014. (ENG.). 32p. (J). (gr. -1-1). 14.95 *(978-1-4197-1027-8(3),* 1070901, Abrams Appleseed) Abrams, Inc.
Tugwood, Wendy. I Love You Too, I Love You Three. McGraw, Sheila & McGraw, Sheila, illus. 2016. (ENG.). 24p. (J). (gr. -1-1). 14.95 *(978-1-77085-784-1(2),* c8159125-9b73-4780-bdf1-62f545bb9ceb) Firefly Bks., Ltd.
Turnbull, Elizabeth. Bonnwit Kabrit. Vaganos, Erin, illus. 2013. 36p. 17.95 *(978-1-61153-073-5(3))* Light Messages Publishing.
Turner, Jennifer. My Name Is Jake. Bell, Susan, illus. 2012. 32p. (J). 14.99 *(978-1-938032-04-2(7));* pap. 7.99 *(978-1-938032-05-9(5))* Peaks Pr. LLC.
Turner, Marie. God Made the Animals. Romero, Naomi, illus. 2017. 22p. (J). 6.99 *(978-1-5064-2185-8(7),* Sparkhouse Family) 1517 Media.
Tutu Nene - Hawaiian Mother Goose Rhymes. 2004. (J). audio compact disk 14.99 *(978-0-931548-60-4(8))* Island Heritage Publishing.
Tuzee, John & Tuzee, Diane. Charlie Canoe & Other Boats, Too. Kasun, Mike, illus. 2006. (J). *(978-0-9755348-2-3(3))* Kids Life Pr.
Twin Sister Produtions. Sesame Street What Did Elmo Say? 2008. (ENG.). 20p. (J). (gr. -1-3). 9.99 *(978-1-59069-657-6(3))* Studio Mouse LLC.
Twin Sisters(r) Staff. Five Little Skunks. 2010. (J). (gr. k-2). pap. 4.99 *(978-1-59922-509-8(3))* Twin Sisters IP, LLC.
Tyler, Jenny & Hawthorn, Phillip. Who's Making That Noise? 2008. (Luxury Flap Bks). 16p. (J). 9.99 *(978-0-7945-1695-6(5),* Usborne) EDC Publishing.
—Who's Making That Smell? Cartwright, Stephen, illus. 2007. (Luxury Flap Bks). 16p. (J). (gr. -1-3). 9.99 *(978-0-7945-1696-3(3),* Usborne) EDC Publishing.
Uhlig, Elizabeth. I Want to Be. Uhlig, Elizabeth, illus. 2008. (ENG., Illus.). (J). pap. 12.95 *(978-0-9815345-1-0(1))* Marble Hse. Editions.
Ulz, Ivan. Fire Truck! Kaida, Garrett, illus. 2013. 36p. 19.00 *(978-0-9896231-0-0(6))* Temple Street Pr.
Underwood, Deborah. Interstellar Cinderella: (Princess Books for Kids, Books about Science) Hunt, Meg, illus. 2015. (Future Fairy Tales Ser.). (ENG.). 40p. (J). (gr. -1-k). 17.99 *(978-1-4521-2532-9(5))* Chronicle Bks. LLC.
—Ogilvy. McBeth, T. L., illus. 2019. (ENG.). 40p. (J). 18.99 *(978-1-250-15176-6(7),* 900183400, Holt, Henry & Co. Bks. For Young Readers) Holt, Henry & Co.
Union, Gabrielle & Wade, Dwyane. Shady Baby. Whitaker, Tara Nicole, illus. 2021. (ENG.). 32p. (J). (gr. -1-3). 18.99 *(978-0-06-305403-5(5),* HarperCollins) HarperCollins Pubs.
Unser, Virginia. The Night Before Cat-Mas. Anagost, Karen, illus. 2007. (Petite Plush Kit Ser.). 64p. (J). (gr. -1-3). 9.95 *(978-1-59359-882-2(3))* Peter Pauper Pr. Inc.
Unwin, Shelly. You're Five! Battersby, Katherine, illus. 2018. (ENG.). 32p. (J). (-k). 9.99 *(978-1-76029-131-0(5))* Allen & Unwin AUS. Dist: Independent Pubs. Group.
—You're Four! Battersby, Katherine, illus. 2018. (ENG.). 32p. (J). (-k). 9.99 *(978-1-76029-130-3(7))* Allen & Unwin AUS. Dist: Independent Pubs. Group.
—You're Two! Battersby, Katherine, illus. 2019. (ENG.). 26p. (J). (— 1). bds. 7.99 *(978-1-9848-9247-8(9),* Doubleday Bks. for Young Readers) Random Hse. Children's Bks.
Up above & down Below. 2008. (Illus.). 42p. (J). lib. bdg. 14.95 *(978-0-9795400-1-1(1))* NANUQ Publishing.
Upton, Elizabeth. Maxi the Little Taxi. Cole, Henry, illus. 2016. (ENG.). 32p. (J). (gr. -1-k). 17.99 *(978-0-545-79860-0(4),* Scholastic Pr.) Scholastic, Inc.
Vaccaro Seeger, Laura. Blue. 2018. (ENG., Illus.). 40p. (J). 18.99 *(978-1-62672-066-4(5),* 900134217) Roaring Brook Pr.
—Green. 2012. (ENG., Illus.). 36p. (J). (gr. -1-1). 18.99 *(978-1-59643-397-7(3),* 900051551) Roaring Brook Pr.
Valko, Danna. Dee & Maya Are Best Friends. 2013. (Illus.). *(978-1-62563-112-1(X)); (978-1-62510-726-8(9))* Tate Publishing, Ltd.
Vamos, Samantha R. Alphabet Trains. O'Rourke, Ryan, illus. 2015. 32p. (J). (gr. -1-2). lib. bdg. 15.99 *(978-1-58089-592-7(1))* Charlesbridge Publishing, Inc.
—The Piñata That the Farm Maiden Hung. Serra, Sebastià & Serra, Sebastià, illus. 2019. 32p. (J). (gr. -1-3). lib. bdg. 18.99 *(978-1-58089-796-9(7))* Charlesbridge Publishing, Inc.
Van Buren, David. I Love You As Big As the World. Warnes, Tim, illus. 2013. (ENG.). 22p. (J). (-k). bds. 8.95 *(978-1-58925-603-3(4))* Tiger Tales.
Van Dusen, Chris. A Camping Spree with Mr. Magee: (Read Aloud Books, Series Books for Kids, Books for Early Readers) 2003. (Mr. Magee Ser.: MCGE). (ENG., Illus.). 36p. (J). (gr. -1-7). 16.99 *(978-0-8118-3603-6(7))* Chronicle Bks. LLC.
—The Circus Ship. Van Dusen, Chris, illus. 2015. (ENG., Illus.). 40p. (J). (gr. -1-3). 8.99 *(978-0-7636-5592-1(9))* Candlewick Pr.
—Down to the Sea with Mr. Magee: (Kids Book Series, Early Reader Books, Best Selling Kids Books) 2006. (Mr. Magee Ser.). (ENG., Illus.). 36p. (J). (gr. -1-7). pap. 8.99 *(978-0-8118-5225-8(3))* Chronicle Bks. LLC.
—If I Built a Car. 2007. (If I Built Ser.). (Illus.). 40p. (J). (gr. k-k). pap. 8.99 *(978-0-14-240825-4(5),* Puffin Books) Penguin Young Readers Group.
—If I Built a Car. Van Dusen, Chris, illus. 2005. (If I Built Ser.). (ENG., Illus.). 32p. (J). (gr. -1-k). 17.99 *(978-0-525-47400-5(5),* Dutton Books for Young Readers) Penguin Young Readers Group.
—If I Built a Car. Van Dusen, Chris, illus. 2007. (Illus.). (gr. -1-3). lib. bdg. 17.00 *(978-0-7569-8149-5(2))* Perfection Learning Corp.
—If I Built a House. (If I Built Ser.). (Illus.). (J). (-k). 2019. 40p. pap. 8.99 *(978-1-9848-1484-5(2),* Puffin Books) 2012. 32p. 18.99 *(978-0-8037-3751-8(3),* Dial Bks) Penguin Young Readers Group.
—If I Built a School. Van Dusen, Chris, illus. 2019. (If I Built Ser.). (Illus.). 32p. (J). (gr. k-3). 18.99 *(978-0-525-55291-8(X),* Dial Bks) Penguin Young Readers Group.
—King Hugo's Huge Ego. 2011. (ENG., Illus.). 40p. (J). (gr. -1-2). 18.99 *(978-0-7636-5004-9(8))* Candlewick Pr.
—Learning to Ski with Mr. Magee: (Read Aloud Books, Series Books for Kids, Books for Early Readers) 2010. (Mr. Magee Ser.). (ENG., Illus.). 36p. (J). (gr. -1-3). 16.99 *(978-0-8118-7495-3(8))* Chronicle Bks. LLC.
—Randy Riley's Really Big Hit. Van Dusen, Chris, illus. 2012. (ENG., Illus.). 32p. (J). (gr. -1-3). 17.99 *(978-0-7636-4946-3(5))* Candlewick Pr.
Van Dusen, Ross, illus. Crocka Dog in the Evil Forest. 2015. (J). *(978-1-936744-54-1(6),* Rio Grande Bks.) LPD Pr.
—How Crocka Dog Came to Be. 2015. (J). *(978-1-936744-39-8(2))* LPD Pr.
—Lyle Got Stuck in a Tree & Became an Honorary Fireman. 2015. (J). *(978-1-936744-45-9(7),* Rio Grande Bks.) LPD Pr.
—What Makes a Rainbow? 2015. (J). *(978-1-936744-32-9(5),* Rio Grande Bks.) LPD Pr.
—What Makes a Snowflake? 2015. (J). *(978-1-936744-48-0(1),* Rio Grande Bks.) LPD Pr.
—What Makes the Lightning? 2016. (J). *(978-1-943681-03-7(1),* Rio Grande Bks.) LPD Pr.
Van Fleet, Mara. Little Color Fairies. Van Fleet, Mara, illus. 2012. (ENG., Illus.). 16p. (J). (gr. -1-1). 15.99 *(978-1-4424-3434-9(1),* Simon & Schuster/Paula Wiseman Bks.) Simon & Schuster/Paula Wiseman Bks.
—Night-Night, Princess. Van Fleet, Mara, illus. 2014. (ENG., Illus.). 16p. (J). (gr. -1-1). 14.99 *(978-1-4424-8646-1(5),* Simon & Schuster/Paula Wiseman Bks.) Simon & Schuster/Paula Wiseman Bks.
—Three Little Mermaids. Van Fleet, Mara, illus. 2011. (ENG., Illus.). 16p. (J). (gr. -1-k). 17.99 *(978-1-4424-1286-6(0),* Simon & Schuster/Paula Wiseman Bks.) Simon & Schuster/Paula Wiseman Bks.
Van Fleet, Matthew. Chomp Goes the Alligator. Van Fleet, Matthew, illus. 2018. (ENG., Illus.). 26p. (J). (gr. -1). 19.99 *(978-1-5344-2677-1(9),* Simon & Schuster/Paula Wiseman Bks.) Simon & Schuster/Paula Wiseman Bks.
—Color Dog. 2015. (ENG., Illus.). 22p. (J). (gr. -1-k). 24.99 *(978-1-4814-4986-1(9),* Simon & Schuster Bks. For Young Readers) Simon & Schuster Bks. For Young Readers.
—Lick! Mini Board Book. Van Fleet, Matthew, illus. 2013. (ENG., Illus.). 14p. (J). (gr. -1-1). 12.99 *(978-1-4424-6049-2(0),* Simon & Schuster/Paula Wiseman Bks.) Simon & Schuster/Paula Wiseman Bks.
—Tails. 2017. (ENG., Illus.). 20p. (J). (— 1). bds. 14.99 *(978-1-328-88685-9(9),* 1699384, Clarion Bks.) HarperCollins Pubs.
Van Lemon, M. Champions of the Garden Games: Winter Fun for Everyone. 2009. 48p. pap. 20.95 *(978-1-4490-3580-8(9))* AuthorHouse.
Vandever, Daniel W. Fall in Line, Holden. Frank, LaFrenda, ed. Vandever, Daniel W., illus. 2017. (Illus.). 32p. (J). *(978-1-893354-50-0(4))* Salina Bookshelf Inc.
Vantrease, Norma. Ants in My Pants. Cox, Steve, illus. 2004. (Rookie Readers Ser.). 31p. (J). 12.60 *(978-0-7569-4280-9(2))* Perfection Learning Corp.
Varon, Sara. Hold Hands. 2019. (ENG., Illus.). 40p. (J). 17.99 *(978-1-59643-588-9(7),* 900064858, First Second Bks.) Roaring Brook Pr.
Vassallo, Rebecca. Listen to Luther. 2006. 24p. (J). 10.87 *(978-1-4116-8169-9(X))* Lulu Pr., Inc.
Vaughn, C. L. I See Aliens. 2007. 15p. 10.95 *(978-1-4357-0117-5(8))* Lulu Pr., Inc.
Vazov, George D. The Other Side of the Mushroom. 2006. 12.00 *(978-0-8059-9018-6(6))* Dorrance Publishing Co., Inc.
Velazquez, Catherine. Dirty Birdie. 2012. 32p. pap. 18.48 *(978-0-578-10152-1(1))* Jiovanie.
Velde, Marie. Laundry Day. 2007. (Illus.). (J). bds. 22.95 *(978-1-933156-17-0(1),* Visikid Bks.) GSVQ Publishing.
Verburg, Bonnie. The Tree House That Jack Built. Teague, Mark, illus. 2014. (ENG.). 40p. (J). (gr. -1-k). 17.99 *(978-0-439-85338-5(9),* Orchard Bks.) Scholastic, Inc.
Verde, Susan. The Museum. Reynolds, Peter H., illus. 2013. (ENG.). 32p. (J). (gr. -1-2). 17.99 *(978-1-4197-0594-6(6),* 1048601, Abrams Bks. for Young Readers) Abrams, Inc.
—Rock 'n' Roll Soul. Cordell, Matthew, illus. 2018. (ENG.). 32p. (J). (gr. k-2). 16.99 *(978-1-4197-2849-5(0),* 697701, Abrams Bks. for Young Readers) Abrams, Inc.
—You & Me. Reynolds, Peter H., illus. 2015. (ENG.). 32p. (J). (gr. k-17). 14.95 *(978-1-4197-1197-8(0),* 1085501, Abrams Bks. for Young Readers) Abrams, Inc.
Verdick, Elizabeth. Peep Leap. 0 vols. Bendall-Brunello, John, illus. 2013. (ENG.). 32p. (J). (gr. -1-2). 16.99 *(978-1-4778-1640-0(2),* 9781477816400, Two Lions) Amazon Publishing.
—Small Walt. Rosenthal, Marc, illus. 2017. (ENG.). 40p. (J). (gr. -1-3). 17.99 *(978-1-4814-4845-1(5),* Simon & Schuster Bks. For Young Readers) Simon & Schuster Bks. For Young Readers.
Verdick, Elizabeth & Lisovskis, Marjorie. Cuddle: A Board Book about Snuggling. 2013. (Happy Healthy Baby(r) Ser.). (ENG., Illus.). 24p. (J). (— 1). bds. 7.99 *(978-1-57542-423-1(1))* Free Spirit Publishing Inc.
—Cuddle / Abrazos y Mimos: A Board Book about Snuggling/un Libro de Carton Sobre Afectos y Sentimientos. 2019. (Happy Healthy Baby(r) Ser.). (ENG., Illus.). 24p. (J). (— 1). bds. 7.99 *(978-1-63198-448-8(9),* 84488) Free Spirit Publishing Inc.
—Move: A Board Book about Movement. 2013. (Happy Healthy Baby(r) Ser.). (ENG., Illus.). 24p. (J). (— 1). bds. 7.99 *(978-1-57542-422-4(3),* 24224) Free Spirit Publishing Inc.
Viau, Nancy. City Street Beat. 2015. (Illus.). 32p. (J). *(978-1-4896-3855-7(5))* Weigl Pubs., Inc.
—First Snow. Shipman, Talitha, illus. 2018. (ENG.). 32p. (J). (gr. -1-3). 16.99 *(978-0-8075-2440-4(9),* 807524409) Whitman, Albert & Co.
—Storm Song. 0 vols. Gynux, illus. 2013. 24p. (gr. k-3). (ENG.). (J). 12.99 *(978-1-4778-1646-2(1),* 9781477816462, Two Lions); pap. 12.99 *(978-1-4778-6646-7(9))* Amazon Publishing.
—Today Is a Beach Day! Alder, Charlie, illus. 2020. (ENG.). 32p. (J). (gr. -1-3). 16.99 *(978-0-8075-9396-7(6),* 807593966) Whitman, Albert & Co.
Vigneault, Gilles. A Gift for Sophie. Jorisch, Stéphane & Jorisch, Stéphane, illus. 2013. (ENG.). 44p. (J). (gr. k-2). 16.95 *(978-2-923163-98-7(2))* La Montagne Secrete CAN. Dist: Independent Pubs. Group.
Virjan, Emma J. What This Story Needs Is a Pig in a Wig. 2015. (Pig in a Wig Book Ser.). (ENG., Illus.). 40p. (J). (gr. -1-3). 10.99 *(978-0-06-232724-6(0),* HarperCollins) HarperCollins Pubs.
Vision, Mutiya Sahar. Disabilities. Alcantara, Ignacio, illus. 2009. 32p. 17.00 *(978-0-9659538-9-4(0))* Von Curtis Publishing.
Viswanath, Shobha. The Blue Jackal. Joshi, Dileep, illus. 2016. (ENG.). 34p. (J). 15.00 *(978-0-8028-5466-7(4),* Eerdmans Bks For Young Readers) Eerdmans, William B. Publishing Co.
Von Feder, Rosa. Babies Love Halloween. Cottage Door Press, ed. Peterson, Stacy, illus. 2016. (Babies Love Ser.). (ENG.). 12p. (J). (gr. -1 — 1). bds. 7.99 *(978-1-68052-115-3(2),* 1001081) Cottage Door Pr.
von Olfers, Sibylle. Mother Earth & Her Children: A Quilted Fairy Tale. Zipes, Jack, tr. Schoen-Smith, Sieglinde, illus. 2015. (ENG.). 32p. (J). (— 1). 12.95 *(978-1-933308-50-0(8))* Breckling Pr.
—Mother Earth & Her Children Coloring Book: Color the Wonderful World of Nature As You See It! 24 Magical, Mythical Coloring Scenes. Zipes, Jack, tr. Schoen-Smith, Sieglinde, illus. 2015. (ENG.). 24p. (J). (gr. 2-4). pap. 6.95 *(978-1-933308-54-8(0))* Breckling Pr.

S

von Rosenberg, Byron. Dale the Uniclyde: An adventure in Friendship. Parrott, Heather, illus. 2007. 22p. (J). 11.95 *(978-0-9759858-6-1(8))* Red Mountain Creations.
VonFeder, Rosa. Trick or Treat. Cottage Door Press, ed. Dale-Scott, Lindsay, illus. 2017. (ENG.). 12p. (J). (gr. -1-k). bds. 10.99 *(978-1-68052-197-9(7),* 1001950) Cottage Door Pr.
Wagenbach, Debbie. The Grouchies. Mack, Steve, illus. 2009. 32p. (J). (gr. -1-3). pap. 9.95 *(978-1-4338-0553-0(7),* Magination Pr.) American Psychological Assn.
—The Grouchies. Mack, Steve, illus. 2009. 32p. (J). (gr. -1-3). 14.95 *(978-1-4338-0543-1(X),* Magination Pr.) American Psychological Assn.
Wagner, Linda. Lady Flatterley. 2008. 44p. pap. 22.95 *(978-1-4327-3233-2(1))* Outskirts Pr., Inc.
Wahl, Jan. Elf Night. Weevers, Peter, illus. 2005. (Picture Bks.). 32p. (gr. k-2). 15.25 *(978-1-57505-512-1(0))* Lerner Publishing Group.
—I Met a Dinosaur. Sheban, Chris, illus. 2015. 32p. (J). (gr. 1-3). 17.99 *(978-1-56846-233-2(6),* 21098, Creative Editions) Creative Co., The.
Waites, Joan, illus. An Artist's Night Before Christmas, 1 vol. 2017. (Night Before Christmas Ser.). (ENG.). 32p. (J). (gr. -1-3). 16.99 *(978-1-4556-2205-4(2),* Pelican Publishing) Arcadia Publishing.
Walden, Libby. Bear Hugs. Riley, Vicky, illus. 2017. (ENG.). 18p. (J). (gr. -1-k). bds. 7.99 *(978-1-68010-519-3(1))* Tiger Tales.
Walker, Anna. I Love My Mom. Walker, Anna, illus. 2010. (ENG., Illus.). 32p. (J). (gr. -1-1). 9.99 *(978-1-4169-8318-7(X),* Simon & Schuster Bks. For Young Readers) Simon & Schuster Bks. For Young Readers.
—I Love to Dance. Walker, Anna, illus. 2011. (ENG., Illus.). 32p. (J). (gr. -1-1). 9.99 *(978-1-4169-8323-1(6),* Simon & Schuster Bks. For Young Readers) Simon & Schuster Bks. For Young Readers.
—I Love to Sing. Walker, Anna, illus. 2011. (ENG., Illus.). 32p. (J). (gr. -1-1). 9.99 *(978-1-4169-8322-4(8),* Simon & Schuster Bks. For Young Readers) Simon & Schuster Bks. For Young Readers.
—I Love Vacations. Walker, Anna, illus. 2011. (ENG., Illus.). 32p. (J). (gr. -1-1). 9.99 *(978-1-4169-8321-7(X),* Simon & Schuster Bks. For Young Readers) Simon & Schuster Bks. For Young Readers.
Walker, Joni. Tell Me What God Made. Walker, Joni, illus. 2007. (Illus.). 20p. (J). (gr. -1-3). bds. 6.49 *(978-0-7586-1247-2(8))* Concordia Publishing Hse.
Walker, Joni, illus. Jesus Hears Me. 2008. 20p. (J). (gr. -1). bds. 6.49 *(978-0-7586-1508-4(6))* Concordia Publishing Hse.
Wallace, Adam. How to Catch a Gingerbread Man. Elkerton, Andy, illus. 2021. (How to Catch Ser.). (ENG.). 40p. (J). (gr. k-3). 10.99 *(978-1-7282-0935-7(8))* Sourcebooks, Inc.
—How to Catch a Leprechaun. Elkerton, Andy, illus. 2016. (How to Catch Ser.). (ENG.). 32p. (J). (gr. k-6). 10.99 *(978-1-4926-3291-7(0),* 9781492632917) Sourcebooks, Inc.
—How to Catch a Mermaid. Elkerton, Andy, illus. 2018. (How to Catch Ser.: 0). (ENG.). 40p. (J). (gr. k-5). 10.99 *(978-1-4926-6247-1(X))* Sourcebooks, Inc.
—How to Catch a Snowman. Elkerton, Andy, illus. 2018. (How to Catch Ser.). (ENG.). 40p. (J). (gr. k-5). 17.99 *(978-1-4926-8055-0(9))* Sourcebooks, Inc.
—How to Catch a Turkey. Elkerton, Andy, illus. 2018. (How to Catch Ser.: 0). 40p. (J). (gr. k-6). 10.99 *(978-1-4926-6435-2(9))* Sourcebooks, Inc.
—How to Catch a Unicorn. Elkerton, Andy, illus. 2019. (How to Catch Ser.: 0). (ENG.). 40p. (J). (gr. k-6). 10.99 *(978-1-4926-6973-9(3))* Sourcebooks, Inc.
—How to Catch an Elf. Elkerton, Andy, illus. (J). 2020. *(978-1-7282-2274-5(5))* 2016. (ENG.). 32p. 10.99 *(978-1-4926-4631-0(8),* 9781492646310) Sourcebooks, Inc.
—How to Catch the Easter Bunny. Elkerton, Andy, illus. 2017. (How to Catch Ser.: 3). (ENG.). 40p. (J). (gr. k-6). 10.99 *(978-1-4926-3817-9(X),* 9781492638179) Sourcebooks, Inc.
Wallace, Adam & Wallace, Adam. How to Catch a Monster. Elkerton, Andy, illus. 2017. (How to Catch Ser.: 0). (ENG.). 40p. (J). (gr. k-3). 10.99 *(978-1-4926-4894-9(9))* Sourcebooks, Inc.
—How to Catch the Tooth Fairy. Elkerton, Andy, illus. 2016. (How to Catch Ser.: 0). (ENG.). 32p. (J). (gr. k-6). 10.99 *(978-1-4926-3733-2(5),* 9781492637332) Sourcebooks, Inc.
Wallingford, Stephanie & Rynders, Dawn. A Day at the Lake. Villnave, Erica Pelton, illus. 2013. (ENG.). 32p. (-k). pap. 10.95 *(978-1-938063-03-9(1),* Mighty Media Kids) Mighty Media Pr.
Walsh, Joanna. The Biggest Kiss. Abbot, Judi, illus. 2011. (ENG.). 32p. (J). (gr. -1-3). 14.99 *(978-1-4424-2769-3(8),* Simon & Schuster/Paula Wiseman Bks.) Simon & Schuster/Paula Wiseman Bks.
—I Love Mom. Abbot, Judi, illus. 2019. (Classic Board Bks.). (ENG.). 28p. (J). (gr. -1 — 1). bds. 7.99 *(978-1-5344-3900-9(5),* Little Simon) Little Simon.
—I Love Mom. Abbot, Judi, illus. 2014. (ENG.). 32p. (J). (gr. -1-3). 16.99 *(978-1-4814-2808-8(X),* Simon & Schuster/Paula Wiseman Bks.) Simon & Schuster/Paula Wiseman Bks.
—The Perfect Hug. Abbot, Judi, illus. 2012. (ENG.). 32p. (J). (gr. -1-3). 14.99 *(978-1-4424-6606-7(5),* Simon & Schuster/Paula Wiseman Bks.) Simon & Schuster/Paula Wiseman Bks.
Walsh, Liza Gardner. How Do Fairies Have Fun in the Sun? Mitchell, Hazel, illus. 2019. 22p. (J). (gr. -1 — 1). 8.95 *(978-1-60893-661-8(9))* Down East Bks.
Walstead, Alice. How to Catch a Daddysaurus. Elkerton, Andy, illus. 2023. (How to Catch Ser.). (ENG.). 40p. (J). (gr. k-5). 10.99 *(978-1-7282-6618-3(1))* Sourcebooks, Inc.
—How to Catch a Witch. Joyce, Megan, illus. 2022. (How to Catch Ser.). 40p. (J). (gr. k-5). 10.99 *(978-1-7282-1035-3(6))* Sourcebooks, Inc.
Walters, Virginia. Are We There Yet, Daddy? Schindler, S. D., illus. 2005. 27p. (J). (gr. k-4). reprint ed. 16.00 *(978-0-7567-9708-9(X))* DIANE Publishing Co.
Walton, A. E. What Should I Do with My Love for You? 2009. 24p. pap. 11.49 *(978-1-4389-8532-9(0))* AuthorHouse.
Walton, Mildred D. Spring Reborn. 2012. 28p. pap. 21.99 *(978-1-4691-2556-5(0))* Xlibris Corp.
Walton, Rick. Bunny Christmas: A Family Celebration. Miglio, Paige, illus. 2004. 32p. (J). (ENG.). 15.99 *(978-0-06-008415-8(4));* lib. bdg. 16.89 *(978-0-06-008416-5(2))* HarperCollins Pubs.
—So Many Bunnies Board Book: A Bedtime ABC & Counting Book: an Easter & Springtime Book for Kids. Miglio, Paige, illus. 2018. (ENG.). 32p. (J). (gr. -1 — 1). bds. 7.99 *(978-0-688-17364-7(0),* HarperFestival) HarperCollins Pubs.
—10 Little Monsters Visit Oregon. Smiley, Jess Smart, illus. 2014. (ENG.). 32p. (J). (gr. -1-3). 16.95 *(978-1-939629-29-6(2),* 552929) Familius LLC.
Walvoord, Linda. Razzamadaddy, 1 vol. Yoshikawa, Sachiko, tr. Yoshikawa, Sachiko, illus. 2004. (ENG.). 32p. (J). 14.95 *(978-0-7614-5158-7(7))* Marshall Cavendish Corp.
Walz, Susan. Balloons to the Moon. 2008. 29p. pap. 24.95 *(978-1-60474-586-3(X))* America Star Bks.
Wan, Joyce. You Are My Magical Unicorn. Wan, Joyce, illus. 2018. (ENG., Illus.). 14p. (J). (gr. -1-k). bds. 6.99 *(978-1-338-33410-4(7),* Cartwheel Bks.) Scholastic, Inc.
Wang, Margaret. Eency Weency Spider. Rueda, Claudia, illus. 2006. (ENG.). 12p. (J). (gr. -1-3). bds. 10.95 *(978-1-58117-418-2(7),* Intervisual/Piggy Toes) Bendon, Inc.
—Who Stole the Cookie from the Cookie Jar? Schneider, Christine, illus. 2006. (ENG.). 12p. (J). (gr. -1-3). 4.95 *(978-1-58117-429-8(2),* Intervisual/Piggy Toes) Bendon, Inc.
Ward, B. J. Farty Marty. Kellogg, Steven, illus. 2013. (ENG.). 32p. (J). (gr. -1-3). 16.99 *(978-1-4424-3901-6(7),* Simon & Schuster Bks. For Young Readers) Simon & Schuster Bks. For Young Readers.
Ward, Jennifer. Because You Are My Baby. Long, Sylvia, illus. 2007. (ENG.). 32p. (J). (gr. -1-1). 15.95 *(978-0-87358-911-6(4))* Cooper Square Publishing Llc.
—The Busy Tree, 0 vols. Falkenstern, Lisa, illus. 2012. (ENG.). 32p. (J). (gr. -1-2). 17.99 *(978-0-7614-5550-9(7),* 9780761455509, Two Lions) Amazon Publishing.
—The Seed & the Giant Saguaro. Rangner, Mike K., illus. 2003. (ENG.). 32p. (J). (gr. -1-3). 15.95 *(978-0-87358-845-4(2))* Cooper Square Publishing Llc.
—The Sunhat. Sisson, Stéphanie Roth, illus. 2013. (ENG.). (J). 15.95 *(978-1-933855-78-3(9).* Rio Nuevo Pubs.) Rio Nuevo Pubs.
—Way up in the Arctic. Spengler, Kenneth J., illus. 2007. (ENG.). 32p. (J). (gr. -1-3). 15.95 *(978-0-87358-928-4(9))* Cooper Square Publishing Llc.
Ward, Sarah, illus. My Little Storybook: Little Duck Learns to Swim. 2016. (ENG.). 12p. (J). (gr. -1 — 1). bds. 4.99 *(978-1-4998-0190-3(4))* Little Bee Books Inc.
Wargin, Kathy-jo. Moose on the Loose. Bendall-Brunello, John, illus. 2009. (ENG.). 32p. (J). (gr. 1-4). 16.99 *(978-1-58536-427-5(4),* 202158) Sleeping Bear Pr.
—Otter Out of Water. Bendall-Brunello, John, illus. 2014. (ENG.). 32p. (J). (gr. k-3). 15.95 *(978-1-58536-431-2(2),* 203005) Sleeping Bear Pr.
—P Is for Pumpkin: God's Harvest Alphabet, 1 vol. Pang, YaWen Ariel, illus. 2008. (ENG.). 40p. (J). (gr. -1-3). 15.99 *(978-0-310-71180-3(0))* Zonderkidz.
—Scare a Bear. Bendall-Brunello, John, illus. 2010. (ENG.). 32p. (J). (gr. 1-4). 15.95 *(978-1-58536-430-5(4),* 202161) Sleeping Bear Pr.
Warner, Michael N. Tales to Make You Scream for Your Momma. Warner, Robert, illus. 2018. 208p. (J). pap. 11.95 *(978-0-9963756-1-0(9))* All About Kids Publishing.
Warnes, Tim. Daddy Hug. Chapman, Jane, illus. 2008. (ENG.). 32p. (J). (gr. -1-k). 17.99 *(978-0-06-058950-9(7),* HarperCollins) HarperCollins Pubs.
Warnes, Tim, illus. Sweet Dreams, Little Bear. 2013. (ENG.). 18p. (gr. -1). bds. 8.95 *(978-1-58925-604-0(2))* Tiger Tales.
Warnes, Tim, et al. My Little Box of Bedtime Stories: Can't You Sleep, Puppy?/Time to Sleep, Little Bear!/What Are You Doing in My Bed?/Sleep Tight, Giner Kitten/Good Night, Emily!/Don't Be Afraid, Little Ones. Pedler, Caroline & Massey, Jane, illus. 2013. (ENG.). (J). (gr. -1-1). pap. 8.95 *(978-1-58925-442-8(2))* Tiger Tales.
Warnock, Chris. Toys Overboard!, 1 vol. 2009. (ENG.). 48p. 24.95 *(978-1-60672-197-1(6))* America Star Bks.
Watson, Clyde. Midnight Moon. Natti, Susanna, illus. 2006. (ENG.). 24p. (J). (gr. -1-k). *(978-1-59692-162-7(5))* MacAdam/Cage Publishing, Inc.
Wax, Wendy. City Witch, Country Switch, 0 vols. Gibala-Broxholm, Scott, illus. 2013. (ENG.). 42p. (J). (gr. -1-3). pap. 9.99 *(978-1-4778-1676-9(3),* 9781477816769, Two Lions) Amazon Publishing.
—What Do You Say? Please & Thank You. Dillard, Sarah, illus. 2005. (J). *(978-1-58987-108-3(1))* Kindermusik International.
Weatherford, Carole Boston. Sugar Hill: Harlem's Historic Neighborhood. Christie, R. Gregory, illus. 2014. (ENG.). 32p. (J). (gr. -1-3). 16.99 *(978-0-8075-7650-2(6),* 807576506) Whitman, Albert & Co.
Weathers, R. F. Jill's Joyful Surprise. 2005. 32p. pap. 18.00 *(978-1-4208-5263-9(9))* AuthorHouse.
Webb, Steve. City Kitty Cat. Le Huche, Magali, illus. 2015. (ENG.). 32p. (J). (gr. -1-3). 17.99 *(978-1-4814-4331-9(3),* Simon & Schuster Bks. For Young Readers) Simon & Schuster Bks. For Young Readers.
—Happy Zappa Cat. Le Huche, Magali, illus. 2014. (ENG.). 32p. 15.99 *(978-0-85707-620-5(5),* Simon & Schuster Children's) Simon & Schuster, Ltd. GBR. Dist: Simon & Schuster, Inc.
Weeks, Sarah. Baa-Choo! Manning, Jane, illus. 2006. (I Can Read Level 1 Ser.). (ENG.). 32p. (J). (gr. k-3). pap. 4.99 *(978-0-06-443740-0(X),* HarperCollins) HarperCollins Pubs.
—Catfish Kate & the Sweet Swamp Band. Smith, Elwood H., illus. 2009. (ENG.). 32p. (J). (gr. -1-3). 19.99 *(978-1-4169-4026-5(X),* Atheneum Bks. for Young Readers) Simon & Schuster Children's Publishing.
—If I Were a Lion. Solomon, Heather M., illus. 2004. (ENG.). 40p. (J). (gr. -1-3). 19.99 *(978-0-689-84836-0(6),* Atheneum Bks. for Young Readers) Simon & Schuster Children's Publishing.
—Mac & Cheese. Manning, Jane, illus. 2010. (I Can Read Level 1 Ser.). (ENG.). 32p. (J). (gr. -1-3). 16.99 *(978-0-06-117079-9(8));* pap. 5.99 *(978-0-06-117081-2(X))* HarperCollins Pubs. (HarperCollins).
—Mac & Cheese & the Perfect Plan. Manning, Jane, illus. 2012. 32p. (J). lib. bdg. 17.89 *(978-0-06-117083-6(6));* (ENG.). 17.99 *(978-0-06-117082-9(8),* HarperCollins); (ENG.). pap. 4.99 *(978-0-06-117084-3(4),* HarperCollins) HarperCollins Pubs.
—Pip Squeak. Manning, Jane, illus. 2008. (I Can Read Level 1 Ser.). (ENG.). 32p. (J). (gr. k-3). pap. 4.99 *(978-0-06-075638-3(1),* HarperCollins) HarperCollins Pubs.
—Pip Squeak. Manning, Jane, illus. 2007. (I Can Read Bks.). 32p. (J). (gr. -1-3). lib. bdg. 16.89 *(978-0-06-075637-6(3),* Geringer, Laura Book) HarperCollins Pubs.
Wegwerth, A. L. Little Bo Peep & Her Bad, Bad Sheep: A Mother Goose Hullabaloo. Flowers, Luke, illus. 2016. (Fiction Picture Bks.). (ENG.). 40p. (J). (gr. -1-2). lib. bdg. 22.65 *(978-1-4795-6483-5(4),* 128336, Picture Window Bks.) Capstone.
Weidknecht, Lisa. E Is for Emotions. 2009. 56p. pap. 21.99 *(978-1-4343-9260-2(0))* AuthorHouse.
Weimer, Heidi. You're My Little Love Bug! 2013. (ENG., Illus.). 12p. (gr. -1). bds. 12.99 *(978-1-891100-29-1(7),* Smart Kids) Penton Overseas, Inc.
Weimer, Heidi R. Happy Birthday to You! 2007. (ENG., Illus.). 14p. (gr. -1-k). bds. 12.99 *(978-0-8249-6699-7(6),* Ideals Pubns.) Worthy Publishing.
—How Do I Kiss You? Sharp, Chris, illus. 2008. (ENG.). 18p. (J). (gr. -1-k). bds. 12.99 *(978-0-8249-1814-9(2),* Ideals Pubns.) Worthy Publishing.
—Love from My Heart: To a Precious Sweet Little Girl. 2005. (ENG., Illus.). 14p. (J). (gr. -1-3). bds. 12.99 *(978-0-8249-6655-3(4),* Ideals Pubns.) Worthy Publishing.
—Love from My Heart: To a Snuggly Cuddly Little Boy. 2005. (Parent Love Letters Ser.). (ENG., Illus.). 14p. (J). (gr. -1-3). bds. 12.99 *(978-0-8249-6654-6(6),* Ideals Pubns.) Worthy Publishing.
Weinberger, Kimberly. Dolphin's Big Leap. Ziss, Debra, illus. 2003. (Hello Reader! Ser.). 30p. (J). *(978-0-439-44159-9(5))* Scholastic, Inc.
Weinshall Liberman, Judith. Ice Cream Snow. 2012. (Illus.). 34p. (J). 18.99 *(978-1-4575-1578-1(4))* Dog Ear Publishing, LLC.
Weinstone, David. Music Class Today! Vogel, Vin, illus. 2015. (ENG.). 40p. (J). (gr. -1 — 1). 19.99 *(978-0-374-35131-1(7),* 900138002, Farrar, Straus & Giroux (BYR)) Farrar, Straus & Giroux.
Weiser, Florence, illus. Twinkle, Twinkle, Little Star: A Light-Up Bedtime Book. 2017. (ENG.). 10p. (J). (gr. -1 — 1). bds. 10.99 *(978-0-7624-6182-0(9),* Running Pr. Kids) Running Pr.
Weiss, Ellen. Twins in the Park: Ready-To-Read Pre-Level 1. Williams, Sam, illus. 2003. (Ready-To-Read Ser.). (ENG.). 24p. (J). (gr. -1-k). pap. 4.99 *(978-0-689-85742-3(X),* Simon Spotlight) Simon Spotlight.
—Whatever You Do, I Love You. Williams, Sam, illus. 2010. (ENG.). 16p. (J). (gr. -1 — 1). bds. 7.99 *(978-1-4424-0809-8(X),* Little Simon) Little Simon.
Wekelo, Kerry. Audrey's Journey: Round & Round Yoga. 2012. 16p. pap. 15.99 *(978-1-4685-9645-8(4))* AuthorHouse.
Welch, Willy. Grumbly Bunnies. Lyon, Tammie Speer, illus. 2004. 32p. (J). 15.95 *(978-1-58089-086-1(5))* Charlesbridge Publishing, Inc.
Wells, Philip. Daddy Island. Daly, Niki, illus. 2015. 24p. (J). (gr. -1-k). pap. 7.99 *(978-1-84148-198-2(X))* Barefoot Bks., Inc.
Wells, Rosemary. Hand in Hand. Wells, Rosemary, illus. 2016. (ENG., Illus.). 32p. (J). 17.99 *(978-1-62779-434-3(4),* 900150563, Holt, Henry & Co. Bks. For Young Readers) Holt, Henry & Co.
—Love Waves. Wells, Rosemary, illus. 2011. (ENG., Illus.). 32p. (J). (gr. -1-2). 15.99 *(978-0-7636-4989-0(9))* Candlewick Pr.
—Love Waves: Midi Edition. Wells, Rosemary, illus. 2012. (ENG., Illus.). 32p. (J). (gr. k — 1). 8.99 *(978-0-7636-6224-0(0))* Candlewick Pr.
—Max's Bug. Grey, Andrew, illus. 2017. (Max & Ruby Ser.). 32p. (J). (gr. 1-2). pap. 5.99 *(978-0-515-15740-6(6),* Penguin Young Readers) Penguin Young Readers Group.
—Max's Lunch. Grey, Andrew, illus. 2017. (Max & Ruby Ser.). 32p. (J). (gr. 1-2). pap. 4.99 *(978-0-515-15737-6(6),* Penguin Young Readers) Penguin Young Readers Group.
—Noisy Nora. Wells, Rosemary, illus. 2007. (Illus.). 28p. (gr. -1-2). 17.00 *(978-0-7569-7870-9(X))* Perfection Learning Corp.
—Read to Your Bunny: with a Note from T. Berry Brazelton, M. D. Wells, Rosemary, illus. 2003. (ENG., Illus.). 14p. (J). (gr. -1). bds. 7.99 *(978-0-439-54337-8(1),* Cartwheel Bks.) Scholastic, Inc.
—Sleep, My Bunny. Wells, Rosemary, illus. 2018. (ENG., Illus.). 24p. (J). (-k). 14.99 *(978-0-7636-9262-9(X))* Candlewick Pr.
Welsh, Karen Leis. Frolicking Friends. 2012. (Illus.). 44p. pap. 21.99 *(978-1-4685-6422-8(6))* AuthorHouse.
Welton, Jude. Tomas Loves... A Rhyming Book about Fun, Friendship - & Autism. Telford, Jane, illus. 2015. 32p. 17.95 *(978-1-84905-544-4(0),* 693420) Kingsley, Jessica Pubs. GBR. Dist: Hachette UK Distribution.
Wendel, Gretchen Schomer & Schomer, Adam Anthony. Becka & the Big Bubble: Becka Goes to San Diego. Renthrope, Damon, illus. 2008. 32p. (J). (gr. -1-3). 11.99 *(978-1-933754-51-2(6))* Waterside Pr.
Wendel, Gretchen Schomer & Schomer, Adam Anthony. Becka Goes to Chicago. Renthrope, Damon, illus. 2008. (ENG.). 36p. (J). (gr. -1-3). 11.99 *(978-1-933754-52-9(4))* Waterside Publishing.
Wenjen, Mia. Sumo Joe, 1 vol. Iwata, Nat, illus. 2019. (ENG.). 40p. (J). (gr. k-3). 20.95 *(978-1-62014-802-0(1),* leelowbooks) Lee & Low Bks., Inc.
Wenz, Graham D. The Day a Cockroach Crawled under My Door: This Book Won't Be a Bore! 2012. 44p. pap. 21.99 *(978-1-4797-0761-4(9))* Xlibris Corp.
Wenzel, Brendan, illus. Hello Hello (Books for Preschool & Kindergarten, Poetry Books for Kids) 2018. (ENG.). 52p. (J). (gr. -1-k). 17.99 *(978-1-4521-5014-7(1))* Chronicle Bks. LLC.
—A Stone Sat Still. 2019. (ENG.). 56p. (J). (gr. -1-k). 17.99 *(978-1-4521-7318-4(4))* Chronicle Bks. LLC.
Western, Colleen. Why Elephants Don't Ride School Buses. 2011. 16p. (gr. 1-2). pap. 10.67 *(978-1-4269-6865-5(5))* Trafford Publishing.
Westheimer, Ruth K. Leopold. (ENG., Illus.). 2017. 36p. pap. 11.99 *(978-1-68336-709-3(X))* 2015. 34p. (J). 24.95 *(978-1-63026-918-0(2))* Turner Publishing Co.
Weston Woods Staff, creator. Each Peach Pear Plum. 2011. 38.75 *(978-0-439-77214-3(1));* 18.95 *(978-0-439-77212-9(5));* 29.95 *(978-0-439-77213-6(3))* Weston Woods Studios, Inc.
—Goodnight Moon. 2011. 18.95 *(978-0-439-72684-9(0));* 38.75 *(978-0-439-72686-3(7));* 29.95 *(978-0-439-73472-1(X))* Weston Woods Studios, Inc.
—How Do Dinosaurs Eat Their Food? 2011. 18.95 *(978-0-439-02748-9(9));* 38.75 *(978-0-439-02740-3(3))* Weston Woods Studios, Inc.
—How Do Dinosaurs Get Well Soon? 2011. 18.95 *(978-0-439-84621-9(8));* 29.95 *(978-0-439-76689-0(3));* 38.75 *(978-0-439-84622-6(6))* Weston Woods Studios, Inc.
—How Do Dinosaurs Go to School? 2011. 38.75 *(978-0-545-19712-0(0))* Weston Woods Studios, Inc.
—In the Small, Small Pond. 2011. 38.75 *(978-0-439-84578-6(5))* Weston Woods Studios, Inc.
—Johnny Appleseed. 2011. 18.95 *(978-0-439-72731-0(6));* 38.75 *(978-0-439-72733-4(2))* Weston Woods Studios, Inc.
—Madeline's Rescue. 2011. 18.95 *(978-0-439-72770-9(7));* 29.95 *(978-0-439-73488-2(6));* 38.75 *(978-0-439-72772-3(3))* Weston Woods Studios, Inc.
—May I Bring a Friend? 2011. 18.95 *(978-0-439-72783-9(9));* 29.95 *(978-0-439-73490-5(8));* 38.75 *(978-0-439-72836-2(3))* Weston Woods Studios, Inc.
Wetzel, JoAnne Stewart. Mermaid School. Swaney, Julianna, illus. 2018. (ENG.). 32p. (J). (gr. -1-2). 18.99 *(978-0-399-55716-3(4),* Knopf Bks. for Young Readers) Random Hse. Children's Bks.
Whatley, Bruce. That Magnetic Dog. 2015. (Illus.). 32p. (J). (gr. -1-3). pap. 9.99 *(978-0-207-18420-8(8),* HarperCollins) HarperCollins Pubs.
Wheeler, Lisa. Babies Can Sleep Anywhere. Búzio, Carolina, illus. 2019. (ENG.). 22p. (J). (gr. -1 — 1). bds. 7.99 *(978-1-4197-3492-2(X),* 1166810, Abrams Appleseed) Abrams, Inc.
—Babies Can Sleep Anywhere. Buzio, Carolina, illus. 2017. (ENG.). 32p. (J). (gr. -1-k). 14.95 *(978-1-4197-2536-4(X),* 1166801, Abrams Appleseed) Abrams, Inc.
—Boogie Knights. Siegel, Mark, illus. 2008. (ENG.). 40p. (J). (gr. -1-3). 16.99 *(978-0-689-87639-4(4),* Atheneum/Richard Jackson Bks.) Simon & Schuster Children's Publishing.
—Bubble Gum, Bubble Gum. Huliska-Beith, Laura, illus. 2019. (ENG.). 32p. (J). 18.95 *(978-1-948959-09-4(7))* Purple Hse. Pr.
—Castaway Cats. Goembel, Ponder, illus. 2006. (ENG.). 32p. (J). (gr. -1-2). 19.99 *(978-0-689-86232-8(6),* Atheneum/Richard Jackson Bks.) Simon & Schuster Children's Publishing.
—Dino-Baseball. Gott, Barry, illus. 2010. (Dino-Sports Ser.). (ENG.). 32p. (J). (gr. k-3). lib. bdg. 18.99 *(978-0-7613-4429-2(2),* ca81637a-1288-4003-9492-c5d3bdd41808, Carolrhoda Bks.) Lerner Publishing Group.
—Dino-Basketball. Gott, Barry, illus. 2011. (Dino-Sports Ser.). (ENG.). 32p. (J). (gr. k-3). 18.99 *(978-0-7613-6393-4(9),* 9855baa7-c0eb-4df2-9a3b-256ee4bb7848, Carolrhoda Bks.) Lerner Publishing Group.
—Dino-Boarding. Gott, Barry, illus. 2014. (Dino-Sports Ser.). (ENG.). 32p. (J). (gr. k-3). lib. bdg. 18.99 *(978-1-4677-0213-3(7),* bcd54035-8bbe-467e-91aa-4138cbcaaa41, Carolrhoda Bks.) Lerner Publishing Group.
—Dino-Christmas. Gott, Barry, illus. 2018. (Dino-Holidays Ser.). (ENG.). 32p. (J). (gr. k-3). 18.99 *(978-1-5124-0315-2(6),* 2b1e3a2e-5863-41a2-8996-3b48c8f63a65, Carolrhoda Bks.) Lerner Publishing Group.
—Dino-Dancing. Gott, Barry, illus. 2017. (Dino-Sports Ser.). (ENG.). 32p. (J). (gr. k-3). lib. bdg. 18.99 *(978-1-5124-0316-9(4),* 7f8b0cdb-2c6c-402b-bbf8-92d27532e350, Carolrhoda Bks.) Lerner Publishing Group.
—Dino-Football. Gott, Barry, illus. 2012. (Dino-Sports Ser.). (ENG.). 32p. (J). (gr. k-3). lib. bdg. 18.99 *(978-0-7613-6394-1(7),* 7fb1d8f1-ba7a-4535-86f0-2150f5f6187b, Carolrhoda Bks.) Lerner Publishing Group.
—Dino-Halloween. Gott, Barry, illus. 2019. (Dino-Holidays Ser.). Orig. Title: Dino-Halloween. (ENG.). 32p. (J). (gr. k-3). 18.99 *(978-1-5124-0317-6(2),* fb634b77-1851-4760-8184-8331ade2603f, Carolrhoda Bks.) Lerner Publishing Group.
—Dino-Hockey. Gott, Barry, illus. 2007. (Dino-Sports Ser.). (ENG.). 32p. (J). (gr. k-3). 18.99 *(978-0-8225-6191-0(3),* 626a35f9-4b11-4014-adcf-91acd236d1a0, Carolrhoda Bks.) Lerner Publishing Group.
—Dino-Racing. Gott, Barry, illus. 2016. (Dino-Sports Ser.). (ENG.). 32p. (J). (gr. k-3). lib. bdg. 18.99 *(978-1-5124-0314-5(8),* f463a43f-a77d-48fd-8820-d8f09b31699b); E-Book 35.99 *(978-1-5124-0886-7(7))* Lerner Publishing Group. (Carolrhoda Bks.).
—Dino-Soccer. Gott, Barry, illus. 2009. (Dino-Sports Ser.). (ENG.). 32p. (J). (gr. k-3). 18.99 *(978-0-8225-9028-6(X),* 3a7e422c-294d-4475-b765-8a7f45376638, Carolrhoda Bks.) Lerner Publishing Group.
—Dino-Swimming. Gott, Barry, illus. 2015. (Dino-Sports Ser.). (ENG.). 32p. (J). (gr. k-3). lib. bdg. 18.99 *(978-1-4677-0214-0(5),* f3f77eea-4055-4d94-ae5a-31a30899e91b, Carolrhoda Bks.) Lerner Publishing Group.
—Dino-Thanksgiving. Gott, Barry, illus. 2020. (Dino-Holidays Ser.). (ENG.). 32p. (J). (gr. k-3). 18.99 *(978-1-5124-0318-3(0),* 967cec8a-0a13-4116-a015-3be1da5e4709, Carolrhoda Bks.) Lerner Publishing Group.
—Even Monsters Go to School. Van Dusen, Chris, illus. 2019. (ENG.). 32p. (J). (gr. -1-3). 17.99 *(978-0-06-236642-9(4),* Balzer & Bray) HarperCollins Pubs.
—Farmer Dale's Red Pickup Truck Board Book. Bates, Ivan, illus. 2014. (ENG.). 32p. (J). (— 1). bds. 7.99 *(978-0-544-24765-9(5),* 1566128, Clarion Bks.) HarperCollins Pubs.
—Jazz Baby. Christie, R. Gregory, illus. 2007. (ENG.). 40p. (J). (gr. -1-3). 18.99 *(978-0-15-202522-9(7),* 1193042, Clarion Bks.) HarperCollins Pubs.
—People Don't Bite People. Idle, Molly, illus. 2018. (People Bks.). (ENG.). 40p. (J). (gr. -1-3). 17.99

(978-1-4814-9082-5(6), Atheneum Bks. for Young Readers) Simon & Schuster Children's Publishing.

—People Share with People. Idle, Molly, illus. 2019. (People Bks.). (ENG.). 40p. (J). (gr. -1-3). 17.99 (978-1-5344-2559-0(4), Atheneum Bks. for Young Readers) Simon & Schuster Children's Publishing.

—The Pet Project: Cute & Cuddly Vicious Verses. OHora, Zachariah, illus. 2013. (ENG.). 40p. (J). (gr. -1-3). 19.99 (978-1-4169-7595-3(0), Atheneum Bks. for Young Readers) Simon & Schuster Children's Publishing.

—Seadogs: An Epic Ocean Operetta. Siegel, Mark, illus. 2006. (ENG.). 40p. (J). (gr. 2-5). reprint ed. 8.99 (978-1-4169-4103-3(7), Atheneum Bks. for Young Readers) Simon & Schuster Children's Publishing.

—Uncles & Antlers. Floca, Brian, illus. 2014. (ENG.). 40p. (J). (gr. -1-3). 17.99 (978-1-4814-3018-0(1), Atheneum Bks. for Young Readers) Simon & Schuster Children's Publishing.

Where Does the Sun Go? 2006. (Illus.). 40p. (J). (gr. -1-3). 14.95 (978-0-9786813-0-2(4)) Elora Pr.

Whincup, Sara. The St John's Cross Spider. Yapsangco, Kenn, illus. 2015. (ENG.). 28p. (J). pap. 28.22 (978-1-5035-0985-6(0)) Xlibris Corp.

Whitaker, Kent. Big Mo's Tennis Ball Hunt. 2007. (Illus.). (J). (978-0-9779053-8-6(1)) Great American Pubs.

White, Dianne. Blue on Blue. Krommes, Beth, illus. 2014. (ENG.). 48p. (J). (gr. k-3). 19.99 (978-1-4424-1267-5(4), Beach Lane Bks.) Beach Lane Bks.

White, Dianne & Wiseman, Daniel. Goodbye Brings Hello: A Book of Firsts. 2018. (ENG., Illus.). 40p. (J). (gr. -1-3). 17.99 (978-0-544-79875-5(9), 1640192, Clarion Bks.) HarperCollins Pubs.

White, Kathryn. El Hermanito de Ruby. Latimer, Miriam, illus. 2013. 32p. (J). pap. 8.99 (978-1-78285-026-7(0)) Barefoot Bks., Inc.

—Ruby's Baby Brother. Latimer, Miriam, illus. 2013. 32p. (J). 16.99 (978-1-84686-864-1(5)); (ENG.). (gr. -1-2). pap. 8.99 (978-1-84686-950-1(1)) Barefoot Bks., Inc.

—Ruby's School Walk. Latimer, Miriam, illus. 2010. 32p. (J). (gr. -1-2). 16.99 (978-1-84686-275-5(2)) Barefoot Bks., Inc.

—Ruby's Sleepover. Latimer, Miriam, illus. (ENG.). 32p. (J). 2013. (gr. -1-2). pap. 8.99 (978-1-84686-758-3(4)) 2012. 16.99 (978-1-84686-593-0(X)) Barefoot Bks., Inc.

—The Tickle Test. Reynolds, Adrian, illus. 2017. (ENG.). 32p. (J). (gr. -1-3). 17.99 (978-1-5124-8126-6(2), d1c8fd07-3e9a-42d4-951c-c5b526566cbe) Lerner Publishing Group.

White, Kimberly. Mood Music: Musical Colors Series Axford, Elizabeth C., ed. 2003. (Musical Colors Rhyming Story Coloring Book Ser.). (ENG., Illus.). 16p. (J). spiral bd. 10.95 (978-1-931844-06-2(2), PP1018) Piano Pr.

White, Loricia. Little Tail's Rhyming Roots. 2012. 74p. pap. 19.95 (978-1-4626-6885-4(2)) America Star Bks.

Whitehouse, Ben, illus. Dinner for Dinos: Gulp, Guzzle, Chomp, Chew, 1 vol. 2018. (ENG.). 20p. (J). bds. 9.99 (978-1-4003-1214-6(0), Tommy Nelson) Nelson, Thomas Inc.

Whiteside, Andy. Valentino Finds a Home, 1 vol. Hnatov, Catherine, illus. 2012. (ENG.). (J). 32p. 15.95 (978-1-59572-284-3(X)); 24p. pap. 5.95 (978-1-59572-286-7(6)) Star Bright Bks., Inc.

Whitlow, Steve. God Bless You & Good Night, 1 vol. 2018. (God Bless Book Ser.). (ENG., Illus.). 32p. (J). 16.99 (978-1-4003-0897-2(6), Tommy Nelson) Nelson, Thomas Inc.

Whybrow, Ian. Faraway Farm. Ayliffe, Alex, illus. 2006. (ENG.). 32p. (J). (gr. -1-2). lib. bdg. 15.95 (978-1-57505-938-9(X), Carolrhoda Bks.) Lerner Publishing Group.

—Say Boo to the Animals! Warnes, Tim, illus. 2017. (J). (978-1-4351-6509-0(8)) Barnes & Noble, Inc.

—Say Goodnight to the Sleepy Animals! Eaves, Edward, illus. 2017. (J). (978-1-4351-6510-6(1)) Barnes & Noble, Inc.

—Say Hello to the Animals! Warnes, Tim, illus. 2017. 20p. (J). (978-1-4351-6512-0(8)) Barnes & Noble, Inc.

—Say Hello to the Baby Animals! Eaves, Edward, illus. 2017. (J). (978-1-4351-6513-7(6)) Barnes & Noble, Inc.

—Say Hello to the Jungle Animals! Eaves, Edward, illus. 2017. (J). (978-1-4351-6511-3(X)) Barnes & Noble, Inc.

—Say Hello to the Snowy Animals! Eaves, Edward, illus. 2012. (J). (978-0-7607-9675-7(0)) Barnes & Noble, Inc.

—Where's Tim's Ted? It's Time for Bed! Ayto, Russell, illus. 2014. (ENG.). 32p. (J). 17.99 (978-0-00-755929-9(1), HarperCollins Children's Bks.) HarperCollins Pubs. Ltd. GBR. Dist: HarperCollins Pubs.

Whyte, Hugh, illus. Rock Steady: A Story of Noah's Ark. 2006. 28p. (J). (gr. k-4). reprint ed. 17.00 (978-1-4223-5556-5(X)) DIANE Publishing Co.

Widgen, Susan. A Caring Deed for Becky. Novak, Steven, illus. 2012. 36p. pap. 8.99 (978-1-60820-579-0(7)) MLR Pr., LLC.

Wieder, Stefanie Paige. Baby Food. 2019. (ENG., Illus.). 16p. (J). (gr. -1-k). bds. 7.99 (978-1-78285-730-3(3)) Barefoot Bks., Inc.

Wiersum, Gale. The Animals' Christmas Eve. 2007. (Little Golden Book Ser.). (Illus.). 24p. (J). (gr. -1-k). 4.99 (978-0-375-83923-8(2), Golden Bks.) Random Hse. Children's Bks.

Wigden, Susan. I Want to Learn to Dance. Franzese, Nora Tapp, illus. 2012. 36p. pap. 11.99 (978-1-60820-725-1(0)) MLR Pr., LLC.

Wiggins, Leah Holder. My Neighbor Is Gone. Wiggins, Margaret W., illus. 2006. 28p. (J). per. 17.99 (978-0-9768579-5-2(2)) eVision, LLC.

Wilcox, Leah. Waking Beauty. Monks, Lydia, illus. 2011. 32p. (J). (gr. -1-k). pap. 7.99 (978-0-14-241538-2(3), Puffin Books) Penguin Young Readers Group.

Wild, Margaret. This Little Piggy Went Dancing. Niland, Deborah, illus. 2014. (ENG.). 24p. (J). (-k). 15.99 (978-1-74331-511-8(2)) Allen & Unwin AUS. Dist: Independent Pubs. Group.

Wilde, Gloria. Lucifer: Good Angel Gone Bad. Bauer, John, illus. 2007. 36p. 14.95 (978-1-57258-462-4(9), 945-6323) TEACH Services, Inc.

Wilden, Beverley. Who Said Monsters Don't Exist? 2010. (Illus.). 32p. pap. 12.99 (978-1-4490-7313-8(1)) AuthorHouse.

Wilder, Ben. Big & Small, God Made Them All. Carin, Siegfried, ed. Watson, Laura, illus. 2016. (ENG.). 34p. (J). (gr. k-2). pap. 14.95 (978-0-9909865-7-7(8)) Thorpe, Betsy Literary Services.

Wilder, Beth. Bugs in Shoes, 1 vol. 2012. (ENG., Illus.). 64p. (J). 14.99 (978-0-7643-3967-7(2), 4351) Schiffer Publishing, Ltd.

Wildman, Dale. Do You Know the Way to Find an A? A Rhyming ABC Book. Sisung, Peter, illus. 2006. 24p. (J). per. 2.99 (978-1-59958-002-9(0)) Journey Stone Creations, LLC.

Wilhelm, Hans. Pigs in a Blanket (Board Books for Toddlers, Bedtime Stories, Goodnight Board Book) Salcedo, Erica, illus. 2019. (Pigs in A Ser.). (ENG.). 14p. (J). (gr. -1 — 1). bds. 9.99 (978-1-4521-6451-9(7)) Chronicle Bks. LLC.

Wilkinson, Thomas M. A Forest Through the Trees. 2009. (ENG.). 87p. pap. 12.99 (978-0-557-17693-9(X)) Lulu Pr., Inc.

Wilkinson, William L. Glorious Praise. Blackmon, Kim, illus. 2012. 32p. pap. 10.00 (978-1-62050-019-4(1)) Angels of Agape.

Wilks, Mike. The Weather Works. Wilks, Mike, illus. 2016. (ENG., Illus.). 32p. (J). 17.95 (978-0-7649-7538-7(2)) Pomegranate Communications, Inc.

Willard, Nancy. A Starlit Snowfall. Pinkney, Jerry, illus. 2011. (ENG.). 32p. (J). (gr. -1-3). 6.99 (978-0-316-18366-6(0)) Little, Brown Bks. for Young Readers.

Willems, Mo. Nanette's Baguette. Willems, Mo, illus. 2016. (ENG., Illus.). 40p. (J). (gr. -1-k). 17.99 (978-1-4847-2286-2(8), Hyperion Books for Children) Disney Publishing Worldwide.

Williams, Becky. Ten Little Mermaids. East, Jacqueline, illus. 2007. (Story Book Ser.). 22p. (J). (gr. -1). bds. (978-1-84666-375-8(X), Tide Mill Pr.) Top That! Publishing PLC.

Williams, Brenda. Millie's Chickens. Cis, Valeria, illus. 40p. (J). 2015. (ENG.). (gr. -1-2). pap. 9.99 (978-1-78285-083-0(X)) 2014. 16.99 (978-1-78285-082-3(1)) Barefoot Bks., Inc.

—Outdoor Opposites. Oldfield, Rachel, illus. 2015. (Barefoot Singalongs Ser.). (ENG.). 32p. (J). (gr. -1-2). pap. 10.99 (978-1-78285-095-3(3)) Barefoot Bks., Inc.

Williams, Carol Lynch. Glimpse. (ENG., (YA). (gr. 9). 2012. Illus.). 512p. pap. 13.99 (978-1-4169-9731-3(8)) 2010. 496p. 16.99 (978-1-4169-9730-6(X)) Simon & Schuster/Paula Wiseman Bks. (Simon & Schuster/Paula Wiseman Bks.).

Williams, David K. The Picnic. Ovresat, Laura, illus. 2006. (Green Light Readers Level 1 Ser.). (ENG.). 24p. (J). (gr. -1-3). pap. 4.99 (978-0-15-205782-4(X), 1197377, Clarion Bks.) HarperCollins Pubs.

—The Picnic. Ovresat, Laura, illus. 2006. (Green Light Readers Level 1 Ser.). (gr. -1-1). 13.95 (978-0-7569-7209-7(4)) Perfection Learning Corp.

—Tick Tock. Ovresat, Laura, illus. 2006. (Green Light Readers Level 1 Ser.). (ENG.). 24p. (J). (gr. -1-3). pap. 5.99 (978-0-15-205605-6(X), 1196859, Clarion Bks.) HarperCollins Pubs.

Williams, Dawn. Very Little Venus & the Very Friendly Fly. Chou, Joey, illus. 2007. 48p. (J). 15.00 (978-0-9770783-2-5(9)) SunriseHouse Pubs.

Williams, Delphine. Freckles with All the Speckles. 2008. 36p. pap. 24.95 (978-1-60703-402-5(6)) America Star Bks.

Williams, Harland, illus. The Kid with Too Many Nightmares. 2004. (J). (978-0-8431-1582-6(3), Price Stern Sloan) Penguin Publishing Group.

Williams, Lisa E. The Christmas Hippo. 2012. (Illus.). 28p. pap. 16.95 (978-1-4497-2474-0(4), WestBow Pr.) Author Solutions, LLC.

Williams, Maggy. Celia & the Glue Man: A Girl's Journey to Becoming Gluten-Free & Happy. Agresta, Elizabeth, illus. 2018. (J). pap. (978-1-61599-390-1(8)) Loving Healing Pr., Inc.

—"I'm Mixed!" Agresta, Elizabeth, illus. 2018. 38p. (J). pap. (978-1-61599-359-8(2)) Loving Healing Pr., Inc.

Williams, Rozanne. A Picnic. 2017. (Learn-To-Read Ser.). (ENG., Illus.). (J). pap. 3.49 (978-1-68310-322-6(X)) Pacific Learning, Inc.

Williams, Rozanne Lanczak. Purple Snerd. 2003. (Green Light Readers Level 2 Ser.). (gr. k-3). lib. bdg. 13.50 (978-0-613-66373-1(X)) Turtleback.

Williams, Sam. Snack Time. Williams, Sam, illus. 2016. (Noah's Park Ser.: 3). (ENG., Illus.). 14p. (J). (gr. -1-k). bds. 7.99 (978-1-4814-4263-3(5), Little Simon) Little Simon.

Williams, Sandra. Look with Me. 2012. (Illus.). 40p. pap. 20.99 (978-1-4772-1318-6(X)) AuthorHouse.

Williams, Sue. I Went Walking. Vivas, Julie, illus. 2014. 32p. pap. 27.00 (978-1-61003-230-8(6)) Center for the Collaborative Classroom.

—I Went Walking. Vivas, Julie, illus. 2004. (J). (gr. -1-2). audio compact disk 28.95 (978-1-59112-720-8(3)) 2003. pap. 39.95 incl. audio compact disk (978-1-59112-721-5(1)) Live Oak Media.

—Let's Go Visiting Board Book. Vivas, Julie, illus. 2003. (ENG.). 32p. (J). (gr. k — 1). bds. 7.99 (978-0-15-204638-5(0), 1193973, Clarion Bks.) HarperCollins Pubs.

Williams, Vera B. Amber Was Brave, Essie Was Smart. Williams, Vera B., illus. 2004. (ENG., Illus.). 72p. (J). (gr. 2-7). reprint ed. pap. 7.99 (978-0-06-057182-5(9), Greenwillow Bks.) HarperCollins Pubs.

Willis, Jeanne. The Cow Tripped over the Moon: a Nursery Rhyme Emergency. Stewart, Joel, illus. 2015. (ENG.). 32p. (J). (gr. -1-2). 15.99 (978-0-7636-7402-1(8)) Candlewick Pr.

—Don't Go There! Bragadottir, Hrefna, illus. 2019. (ENG.). 32p. (J). (gr. -1-k). 17.99 (978-1-5415-5508-2(2), 89fc0478-8b00-4f74-9ce9-c2c90363b4b8) Lerner Publishing Group.

—Hippospotamus. Ross, Tony, illus. 2012. (Andersen Press Picture Bks). (ENG.). 32p. (J). (gr. -1-3). 16.95 (978-1-4677-0316-1(8)) Lerner Publishing Group.

—I'm in Charge! Jarvis, illus. 2018. (ENG.). 32p. (J). (-k). 16.99 (978-1-5362-0259-5(2)) Candlewick Pr.

—I'M Sure I Saw a Dinosaur. Reynolds, Adrian, illus. 2011. (Andersen Press Picture Books Ser.). (ENG.). 32p. 16.95 (978-0-7613-8093-1(0)) Andersen Pr. GBR. Dist: Lerner Publishing Group.

—Not Just a Book. Ross, Tony, illus. 2018. (ENG.). 32p. (J). (gr. -1-3). 17.99 (978-1-5415-3569-5(3), c9aec5ae-67e5-4131-b776-42d35de242a5) Lerner Publishing Group.

—Slug Needs a Hug! Ross, Tony, illus. 2015. (ENG.). 32p. (J). (gr. -1-3). 17.99 (978-1-4677-9309-4(4), 7f9d8f68-27c2-42e6-aeaf-961d4351753a); E-Book 27.99 (978-1-4677-9317-9(5)) Lerner Publishing Group.

—The T-Rex Who Lost His Specs! Ross, Tony, illus. 2018. (ENG.). 32p. (J). (gr. -1-3). 17.99 (978-1-5415-1456-0(4), a2b03f79-23c6-43dc-b9ed-63f4b8bdfd0f) Lerner Publishing Group.

—The Tale of Georgie Grub. Chamberlain, Margaret, illus. 2012. (ENG.). 32p. (J). (gr. -1-k). pap. 12.99 (978-1-84939-065-1(7)) Andersen Pr. GBR. Dist: Independent Pubs. Group.

—Upside down Babies. Reynolds, Adrian, illus. 2014. (ENG.). 32p. (J). (gr. -1-3). 16.95 (978-1-4677-3424-0(1), 2e46e88c-1ead-4934-b5c4-8599ee20187c) Lerner Publishing Group.

—We're Going to a Party! Ross, Tony, illus. 2015. (ENG.). 16p. (J). (-k). pap. 14.99 (978-1-84939-456-7(3)) Andersen Pr. GBR. Dist: Independent Pubs. Group.

—Who's in the Loo? Reynolds, Adrian, illus. 10th ed. 2016. (ENG.). 12p. (J). (— 1). bds. 9.99 (978-1-78344-420-5(7)) Andersen Pr. GBR. Dist: Independent Pubs. Group.

Willson, Sarah. Do Not Wake Jake. Johnson, Meredith, illus. 2006. (Step-By-Step Readers Ser.). (J). (978-1-59939-059-8(0), Reader's Digest Young Families, Inc.) Studio Fun International.

Wilson, Andrew. Sophie & the Heidelberg Cat. Garcia, Helena Perez, illus. 2019. (ENG.). 36p. 12.99 (978-1-4335-6418-5(1)) Crossway.

Wilson, Bob. Stanley Bagshaw & the Twenty Two Ton Whale. 2006. (Stanley Bagshaw Ser.). (Illus.). 32p. (J). (gr. k-2). pap. 6.95 (978-1-903015-50-6(2)) Barn Owl Bks, London GBR. Dist: Independent Pubs. Group.

Wilson, Karma. Animal Strike at the Zoo. It's True! Spengler, Margaret, illus. 2006. (ENG.). 32p. (J). (gr. -1-1). 16.99 (978-0-06-057502-1(6), HarperCollins) HarperCollins Pubs.

—Bear Can't Sleep. Chapman, Jane, illus. 2018. (Bear Bks.). (ENG.). 40p. (J). (gr. -1-3). 18.99 (978-1-4814-5973-0(2), McElderry, Margaret K. Bks.) McElderry, Margaret K. Bks.

—Bear Counts. Chapman, Jane, illus. 2015. (Bear Bks.). (ENG.). 32p. (J). (gr. -1-2). 18.99 (978-1-4424-8092-6(0), McElderry, Margaret K. Bks.) McElderry, Margaret K. Bks.

—Bear Feels Scared. Chapman, Jane, illus. 2011. (Bear Bks.). (ENG.). 34p. (J). (gr. -1 — 1). bds. 7.99 (978-1-4424-2755-6(8), Little Simon) Little Simon.

—Bear Feels Scared. Chapman, Jane, illus. 2008. (Bear Bks.). (ENG.). 40p. (J). (gr. -1-3). 18.99 (978-0-689-85986-1(4), McElderry, Margaret K. Bks.) McElderry, Margaret K. Bks.

—Bear Feels Sick. Chapman, Jane, illus. 2012. (Bear Bks.). (ENG.). 34p. (J). (gr. -1-2). bds. 8.99 (978-1-4424-4093-7(7), Little Simon) Little Simon.

—Bear Feels Sick. Chapman, Jane, illus. 2007. (Bear Bks.). (ENG.). 40p. (J). (gr. -1-3). 19.99 (978-0-689-85985-4(6), McElderry, Margaret K. Bks.) McElderry, Margaret K. Bks.

—Bear Sees Colors. Chapman, Jane, illus. 2014. (Bear Bks.). (ENG.). 32p. (J). (gr. -1-3). 18.99 (978-1-4424-6536-7(0), McElderry, Margaret K. Bks.) McElderry, Margaret K. Bks.

—Bear Snores On. Chapman, Jane, illus. 2005. (Bear Bks.). (ENG.). 34p. (J). (gr. -1-k). bds. 7.99 (978-1-4169-0272-0(4), Little Simon) Little Simon.

—Bear Stays up for Christmas. Chapman, Jane, illus. 2011. (Bear Bks.). (ENG.). 34p. (J). (gr. -1 — 1). bds. 8.99 (978-1-4424-2790-7(6), Little Simon) Little Simon.

—Bear Stays up for Christmas. Chapman, Jane, illus. 2004. (Bear Bks.). (ENG.). 40p. (J). (gr. -1-3). 17.99 (978-0-689-85278-7(9), McElderry, Margaret K. Bks.) McElderry, Margaret K. Bks.

—Bear Wants More. Chapman, Jane, illus. 2008. (Bear Bks.). (ENG.). 34p. (J). (gr. -1-2). bds. 8.99 (978-1-4169-4922-0(4), Little Simon) Little Simon.

—Bear Wants More. Chapman, Jane, illus. 2003. (Bear Bks.). (ENG.). 40p. (J). (gr. -1-3). 18.99 (978-0-689-84509-3(X), McElderry, Margaret K. Bks.) McElderry, Margaret K. Bks.

—Bear's Loose Tooth. Chapman, Jane, illus. 2014. (Bear Bks.). (ENG.). 34p. (J). (gr. -1-k). bds. 8.99 (978-1-4424-8936-3(7), Little Simon) Little Simon.

—Bear's Loose Tooth. Chapman, Jane, illus. 2011. (Bear Bks.). (ENG.). 40p. (J). (gr. -1-3). 18.99 (978-1-4169-5855-0(X), McElderry, Margaret K. Bks.) McElderry, Margaret K. Bks.

—Bear's New Friend. Chapman, Jane, illus. 2009. (Bear Bks.). (ENG.). 34p. (J). (gr. -1-2). bds. 7.99 (978-1-4169-5438-5(4), Little Simon) Little Simon.

—Bear's New Friend. Chapman, Jane, illus. 2006. (Bear Bks.). (ENG.). 40p. (J). (gr. -1-3). 18.99 (978-0-689-85984-7(8), McElderry, Margaret K. Bks.) McElderry, Margaret K. Bks.

—Big Bear, Small Mouse. Chapman, Jane, illus. 2016. (Bear Bks.). (ENG.). 32p. (J). (gr. -1-3). 18.99 (978-1-4814-5971-6(6), McElderry, Margaret K. Bks.) McElderry, Margaret K. Bks.

—The Cow Loves Cookies. Hall, Marcellus, illus. 2010. (ENG.). 40p. (J). (gr. -1-3). 18.99 (978-1-4169-4206-1(8), McElderry, Margaret K. Bks.) McElderry, Margaret K. Bks.

—A Dog Named Doug. Myers, Matt, illus. 2018. (ENG.). 40p. (J). (gr. -1-3). 17.99 (978-1-4424-4931-2(4), McElderry, Margaret K. Bks.) McElderry, Margaret K. Bks.

—Duddle Puck: The Puddle Duck. Hall, Marcellus, illus. 2015. (ENG.). 40p. (J). (gr. -1-3). 17.99 (978-1-4424-4927-5(6), McElderry, Margaret K. Bks.) McElderry, Margaret K. Bks.

—A Frog in the Bog. Rankin, Joan, illus. (ENG.). 32p. (J). (gr. -1-3). 2007. 8.99 (978-1-4169-2727-3(1)) 2003. 18.99 (978-0-689-84081-4(0)) McElderry, Margaret K. Bks. (McElderry, Margaret K. Bks.).

—Hilda Must Be Dancing. Watts, Suzanne, illus. 2004. (ENG.). 32p. (J). (gr. -1-3). 19.99 (978-0-689-84788-2(2), McElderry, Margaret K. Bks.) McElderry, Margaret K. Bks.

—Hilda Must Be Dancing. Watts, Suzanne, illus. 2008. (ENG.). 32p. (J). (gr. -1-3). 7.99 (978-1-4169-5083-7(4)) Simon & Schuster, Inc.

—Hogwash! McMullan, Jim, illus. 2011. (ENG.). 40p. (J). (gr. -1-3). 18.99 (978-0-316-98840-7(5)) Little, Brown Bks. for Young Readers.

—How to Bake an American Pie. 2007. (ENG., Illus.). 40p. (J). (gr. -1-3). 19.99 (978-0-689-86506-0(6), McElderry, Margaret K. Bks.) McElderry, Margaret K. Bks.

—Mama Always Comes Home. Dyer, Brooke, illus. 32p. (J). (gr. -1-1). 2007. (ENG.). pap. 6.99 (978-0-06-057507-6(7), Harper Trophy) 2005. 15.99 (978-0-06-057505-2(0)) HarperCollins Pubs.

—Mama, Why? Mendez, Simon, illus. 2011. (ENG.). 40p. (J). (gr. -1-2). 16.99 (978-1-4169-4205-4(X), McElderry, Margaret K. Bks.) McElderry, Margaret K. Bks.

—Moose Tracks! 2006. (ENG., Illus.). 32p. (J). (gr. -1-2). 19.99 (978-0-689-83437-0(3), McElderry, Margaret K. Bks.) McElderry, Margaret K. Bks.

—Princess Me. Unzner, Christa, illus. 2007. (ENG.). 32p. (J). (gr. -1-3). 19.99 (978-1-4169-4098-2(7), McElderry, Margaret K. Bks.) McElderry, Margaret K. Bks.

—Sleepyhead. Segal, John, illus. 2012. (Classic Board Bks.). (ENG.). 32p. (J). (gr. -1-3). bds. 8.99 (978-1-4424-3433-2(3), Little Simon) Little Simon.

—Sleepyhead. Segal, John, illus. 2006. (ENG.). 32p. (J). (gr. -1-3). 19.99 (978-1-4169-1241-5(X), McElderry, Margaret K. Bks.) McElderry, Margaret K. Bks.

—Whopper Cake. 2007. (ENG., Illus.). 32p. (J). (gr. -1-3). 19.99 (978-0-689-83844-6(1), McElderry, Margaret K. Bks.) McElderry, Margaret K. Bks.

Wilson, Kip. White Rose. 2019. (ENG.). 368p. (YA). (gr. 7). 17.99 (978-1-328-59443-3(2), 1730256, Versify) HarperCollins Pubs.

Wilson, Kris E. & Maurer, Toby. How Putter Learned His ABC's: An alphabet Book for Your Littlest Golfer. 2010. 17.00 (978-0-578-05153-6(2)) Sandy Putter Pr.

Wilson, Land. The Girl Who Spoke to the Moon: A Story about Friendship & Loving Our Earth. Cornelison, Sue, illus. 2nd rev. ed. 2020. (ENG.). 40p. (J). (gr. k-2). 17.99 (978-1-4926-9873-9(3), Little Pickle Pr.) Sourcebooks, Inc.

—Sofia's Dream. Cornelison, Sue, illus. 2010. (ENG.). 40p. (J). (gr. -1-2). 18.95 (978-0-9829938-1-1(1), Little Pickle Pr.) Sourcebooks, Inc.

Wilson, Porcia D. My Pink Friend: A Rhyming Love Story. 2012. 44p. pap. 18.99 (978-1-4685-6852-3(3)) AuthorHouse.

Wilson Sanger, Amy. A Little Bit of Soul Food. Wilson Sanger, Amy, illus. 2004. (World Snacks Ser.). (Illus.). 20p. (J). (— 1). 7.99 (978-1-58246-109-0(0), Tricycle Pr.) Random Hse. Children's Bks.

—Yum Yum Dim Sum. Wilson Sanger, Amy, illus. 2003. (World Snacks Ser.). (Illus.). 22p. (J). (gr. -1 — 1). 7.99 (978-1-58246-108-3(2), Knopf Bks. for Young Readers) Random Hse. Children's Bks.

Wilson, Zachary. A Circle in the Sky. Adinolfi, JoAnn, illus. (Rookie Ready to Learn Ser.). (ENG.). (J). 2011. 40p. pap. 5.95 (978-0-531-26746-2(6)) 2006. 32p. lib. bdg. 19.50 (978-0-531-12570-0(X)) Scholastic Library Publishing. (Children's Pr.).

—Rookie Ready to Learn en Español: un Circulo en el Cielo. Adinolfi, JoAnn, illus. 2011. (Rookie Ready to Learn Español Ser.). Orig. Title: Rookie Ready to Learn: a Circle in the Sky. (SPA.). 40p. (J). pap. 5.95 (978-0-531-26791-2(1), Children's Pr.) Scholastic Library Publishing.

Wilson, Zachary & Adinolfi, JoAnn. Un Circulo en el Cielo. Adinolfi, JoAnn, illus. 2011. (Rookie Ready to Learn Español Ser.). (SPA., Illus.). 40p. (J). lib. bdg. 23.00 (978-0-531-26123-1(9), Children's Pr.) Scholastic Library Publishing.

Winburn, William B. Hide-And-Peek. 2010. (J). (978-85-312-5235-8(0)) Children's Pr., Ltd.

Windolph, Maria Theresa. Sugar Bear. 2008. 16p. pap. 24.95 (978-1-60474-813-0(3)) America Star Bks.

Wing, Natasha. The Night Before Class Picture Day. 2016. (Night Before Ser.). lib. bdg. 14.75 (978-0-606-38834-4(6)) Turtleback.

—The Night Before First Grade. Zemke, Deborah, illus. 2005. (Night Before Ser.). 32p. (J). (gr. k-1). pap. 4.99 (978-0-448-43747-7(3), Grosset & Dunlap) Penguin Young Readers Group.

—The Night Before Hanukkah. Wummer, Amy, illus. 2014. (Night Before Ser.). (ENG.). 32p. (J). (gr. -1-k). 4.99 (978-0-448-48140-1(5), Grosset & Dunlap) Penguin Young Readers Group.

—The Night Before Hanukkah. 2014. (Night Before Ser.). lib. bdg. 13.55 (978-0-606-36160-6(X)) Turtleback.

—The Night Before Kindergarten. Durrell, Julie, illus. 2014. (Night Before Ser.). 32p. (J). (gr. -1-k). 12.99 (978-0-448-48255-2(X), Grosset & Dunlap) Penguin Young Readers Group.

—The Night Before Kindergarten Graduation. Wummer, Amy, illus. 2019. (Night Before Ser.). 32p. (J). (gr. -1-1). pap. 5.99 (978-1-5247-9001-1(X), Grosset & Dunlap) Penguin Young Readers Group.

—The Night Before My Birthday. Wummer, Amy, illus. 2014. (Night Before Ser.). 32p. (J). (gr. -1-k). 5.99 (978-0-448-48000-8(X), Grosset & Dunlap) Penguin Young Readers Group.

—The Night Before My Birthday. 2014. (Night Before Ser.). lib. bdg. 14.75 (978-0-606-34133-2(1)) Turtleback.

—The Night Before My First Communion. Wummer, Amy, illus. 2018. (Night Before Ser.). 32p. (J). (-k). pap. 5.99 (978-1-5247-8619-9(5), Grosset & Dunlap) Penguin Young Readers Group.

—The Night Before Preschool. Wummer, Amy, illus. 2011. (Night Before Ser.). 32p. (J). (gr. -1-k). pap. 4.99 (978-0-448-45451-1(3), Grosset & Dunlap) Penguin Young Readers Group.

—The Night Before St. Patrick's Day. Wummer, Amy, illus. 2009. (Night Before Ser.). (ENG.). 32p. (J). (gr. -1-3). pap. 5.99 (978-0-448-44852-7(1), Grosset & Dunlap) Penguin Young Readers Group.

—The Night Before the Fourth of July. Wummer, Amy, illus. 2015. (Night Before Ser.). 32p. (J). (gr. -1-k). bds. 4.99 (978-0-448-48712-0(8), Grosset & Dunlap) Penguin Young Readers Group.

—The Night Before the Snow Day. Wummer, Amy, illus. 2016. (Night Before Ser.). 32p. (J). (-k). pap. 4.99 (978-0-399-53942-8(5), Grosset & Dunlap) Penguin Young Readers Group.

—The Night Before the Tooth Fairy. Johansen Newman, Barbara, illus. 2003. (Night Before Ser.). 32p. (J). (gr. -1-3). pap. 5.99 (978-0-448-43252-6(8), Grosset & Dunlap) Penguin Young Readers Group.

Winn, L. B. Butterpod Jerome & the Planet of Gabool. Winn, L. B., illus. 2007. (Illus.). (J). pap. 18.95 (978-0-9791884-0-4(7)) Winn, Lynnette.

Winnette, Sandy. A Snow Angel Story Book: Little Beth & the Snow Angel. 2008. 108p. pap. 11.99 *(978-1-4343-8133-0(1))* AuthorHouse.

Winslow, Tim, illus. The Kingdom of Avalon. 2005. 48p. (J). *(978-0-9748505-0-4(0))* Winslow's Art.

Winter, Milo, illus. The Three Little Kittens: Shape Book. 2009. (Children's Die-Cut Shape Book Ser.). (ENG.). 16p. (J). (gr. -1-1). 10.95 *(978-1-59583-374-7(9),* 9781595833747) Laughing Elephant.

Winters, Kari-Lynn. No-Matter-What Friend, 1 vol. Pratt, Pierre, illus. 2014. (ENG.). 32p. (J). (gr. 1-3). 16.95 *(978-1-896580-83-8(1))* Tradewind Bks. CAN. Dist: Orca Bk. Pubs. USA.

—Stinky Skunk Mel. Opal, Paola, illus. 2014. (ENG.). 32p. (J). (gr. -1-3). 15.95 *(978-1-897476-83-3(3))* Simply Read Bks. CAN. Dist: Ingram Publisher Services.

Winthrop, Elizabeth. Dancing Granny, 1 vol. Murdocca, Sal, illus. 2003. (ENG.). 32p. (J). 16.95 *(978-0-7614-5141-9(2))* Marshall Cavendish Corp.

Wise, William. Ten Sly Piranhas. Chess, Victoria, illus. 2004. 32p. (J). (gr. -1-k). pap. 7.99 *(978-0-14-240074-6(2),* Puffin Books) Penguin Young Readers Group.

Wishinsky, Frieda. Jennifer Jones Won't Leave Me Alone. Layton, Neal, illus. 2005. (Carolrhoda Picture Bks.). 32p. (J). (gr. -1-3). per. 6.95 *(978-1-57505-921-1(5));* (gr. k-2). 15.95 *(978-0-87614-921-8(2))* Lerner Publishing Group.

Wisnewski, Andrea. Little Old Farm Folk. 2017. (ENG., Illus.). 34p. (J). bds. 8.95 *(978-1-56792-594-4(4))* Godine, David R. Pub.

Wissinger, Tamera Will. Gone Camping: A Novel in Verse. Cordell, Matthew, illus. (ENG.). 112p. (J). (gr. 1-4). 2019. pap. 7.99 *(978-1-328-59634-5(6),* 1731320) 2017. 15.99 *(978-0-544-63873-0(5),* 1620560) HarperCollins Pubs. (Clarion Bks.).

—Gone Fishing: A Novel in Verse. Cordell, Matthew, illus. 2015. (ENG.). 128p. (J). (gr. 1-4). pap. 6.99 *(978-0-544-43931-3(7),* 1596830, Clarion Bks.) HarperCollins Pubs.

—This Old Band. Loveridge, Matt, illus. 2014. (ENG.). 32p. (J). (gr. -1-k). 16.95 *(978-1-62873-595-6(3),* Sky Pony Pr.) Skyhorse Publishing Co., Inc.

Witte, Anna. El Loro Tico Tango. Witte, Anna, illus. 2011. (SPA., Illus.). 24p. (J). (gr. -1-1). 9.99 *(978-1-84686-670-8(7))* Barefoot Bks., Inc.

—The Parrot Tico Tango. 2005. (ENG., Illus.). 24p. (J). (gr. -1-3). pap. 6.99 *(978-1-905236-11-4(5))* Barefoot Bks., Inc.

—The Parrot Tico Tango. Witte, Anna, illus. 2005. (ENG., Illus.). 24p. (J). (gr. k-3). 15.99 *(978-1-84148-243-9(9))* Barefoot Bks., Inc.

Witte, Anna & Amador, Brian. The Parrot Tico Tango. Witte, Anna, illus. 2011. (Illus.). 24p. (J). (gr. -1-2). 9.99 *(978-1-84686-669-2(3))* Barefoot Bks., Inc.

Wojtusik, Elizabeth. Kitty Up! Yoshikawa, Sachiko, illus. 2008. (J). *(978-0-8037-3045-8(4),* Dial) Penguin Publishing Group.

Wolf, Allan. New Found Land: Lewis & Clark's Voyage of Discovery. 2007. (ENG., Illus.). 512p. (YA). (gr. 7-9). per. 19.99 *(978-0-7636-3288-5(0))* Candlewick Pr.

Wolf, Linda. Cozy Kitty, 1 vol. 2009. 43p. pap. 24.95 *(978-1-61546-636-8(3))* America Star Bks.

Wolf, Maria. Maggy Cans. 2012. 52p. (gr. 4-6). pap. 11.95 *(978-1-4772-8093-5(6))* AuthorHouse.

Wolf, Sallie. Truck Stuck. Davies, Andy Robert, illus. (J). (— 1). 2017. 28p. bds. 7.99 *(978-1-58089-781-5(9))* 2009. 32p. pap. 7.95 *(978-1-58089-257-5(4))* Charlesbridge Publishing, Inc.

Wolfe, Greg. Shmelf the Hanukkah Elf. McWilliam, Howard, illus. 2016. (ENG.). 32p. (J). 17.99 *(978-1-61963-521-0(6),* 900139020, Bloomsbury USA Childrens) Bloomsbury Publishing USA.

Wolff, Virginia Euwer. True Believer. 2004. (Make Lemonade Trilogy: No. 2). 272p. (J). (gr. 7-18). pap. 38.00 incl. audio *(978-0-8072-2283-6(6),* Listening Library) Random Hse. Audio Publishing Group.

Wood, Audrey. A Dog Needs a Bone! 2007. (J). pap. *(978-0-545-00006-2(8))* Blue Sky Pr.

—Piggy Pie Po. Wood, Audrey & Wood, Don, illus. (ENG.). 32p. (J). (gr. -1-3). 2018. pap. 9.99 *(978-1-328-88612-5(3),* 1698482) 2010. 17.99 *(978-0-15-202494-9(8),* 1192966) HarperCollins Pubs. (Clarion Bks.).

—Silly Sally. braille ed. 2004. (J). (gr. 1). spiral bd., bds. *(978-0-616-01864-4(9))* Canadian National Institute for the Blind/Institut National Canadien pour les Aveugles.

—Silly Sally Lap-Sized Board Book. 2007. (ENG., Illus.). 30p. (J). (gr. -1-3). bds. 11.99 *(978-0-15-205902-6(4),* 1197722, Clarion Bks.) HarperCollins Pubs.

—Ten Little Fish. Wood, Bruce, illus. 2004. (ENG.). 40p. (J). (gr. -1-k). 18.99 *(978-0-439-63569-1(1),* Blue Sky Pr., The) Scholastic, Inc.

Wood, Carol. Grandma Carol's Book of Stories in Rhyme. 2009. (Illus.). 48p. pap. 19.49 *(978-1-4389-5413-4(1))* AuthorHouse.

Woodend, Rosetta. Sammy Salmon's Big Adventure: The lifecycle of a Salmon, 1. 2005. (Illus.). 12p. (J). per. 9.95 *(978-0-9760342-0-9(4))* Animal Tracks Pr.

Woodruff, Liza, illus. What Time Is It? 2005. (My First Reader Ser.). (ENG.). 32p. (J). (gr. k-4). per. 3.95 *(978-0-516-25279-7(8),* Children's Pr.) Scholastic Library Publishing.

Woodward, Caroline. A West Coast Summer. Evans, Carol, illus. 2018. (ENG.). 32p. (J). *(978-1-55017-843-2(1),* 3de1bfb6-1c7a-473c-8e3e-04342b2609c9) Harbour Publishing Co., Ltd.

Woolf, Julia. Jack's Room (Rookie Preschool - My First Rookie Reader) 2009. (Rookie Preschool Ser.). (ENG.). 24p. (J). (gr. -1 — 1). pap. 6.95 *(978-0-531-24575-0(6),* Children's Pr.) Scholastic Library Publishing.

—Rookie Preschool: My First Rookie Reader: Jack's Room. 2009. (Rookie Preschool Ser.). (ENG.). 24p. (J). (gr. -1). 23.00 *(978-0-531-24400-5(8),* Children's Pr.) Scholastic Library Publishing.

Worth, Bonnie. The Cat in the Hat: Cooking with the Cat (Dr. Seuss) Moroney, Christopher, illus. 2003. (Step into Reading Ser.). (ENG.). 32p. (J). (gr. -1-1). pap. 5.99 *(978-0-375-82494-4(4),* 53560581, Random Hse. Bks. for Young Readers) Random Hse. Children's Bks.

Worthen, Diane. Oliver's Wish: A Tale from the Garden. 2012. 36p. pap. 20.99 *(978-1-4685-4005-5(X))* AuthorHouse.

Wright, Blanche Fisher, illus. The Real Mother Goose. 2017. (First Avenue Classics (tm) Ser.). (ENG.). 214p. (J). (gr. -1-4). E-Book 19.99 *(978-1-5124-6673-7(5),* 9781512466737, First Avenue Editions) Lerner Publishing Group.

Wright, Maureen. Earth Day, Birthday!, 0 vols. Kim, Violet, illus. 2012. (ENG.). 32p. (J). (gr. -1-2). 17.99 *(978-0-7614-6109-8(4),* 9780761461098, Two Lions) Amazon Publishing.

—Sleep, Big Bear, Sleep!, 0 vols. Hillenbrand, Will, illus. 2012. (ENG.). 32p. (J). (gr. -1-2). 16.99 *(978-0-7614-5560-8(4),* 9780761455608, Two Lions) Amazon Publishing.

—Sneeze, Big Bear, Sneeze!, 0 vols. Hillenbrand, Will, illus. 2012. (ENG.). 32p. (J). (gr. -1-2). 16.99 *(978-0-7614-5959-0(6),* 9780761459590, Two Lions) Amazon Publishing.

Wright, Michael. Jake Starts School. Wright, Michael, illus. 2010. (ENG., Illus.). 48p. (J). (gr. -1-1). 21.19 *(978-0-312-60884-2(5),* 900065180) Square Fish.

Wuehr, Tina L. Field Dance. Brown, Mari, illus. 2005. 18p. (J). (gr. -1-3). *(978-0-9739962-0-3(X))* Wuehr, Tina.

—Neela Potts Has Lots of Knots. Brown, Mari, illus. 2008. 30p. (J). (gr. -1-3). *(978-0-9739962-3-4(4))* Wuehr, Tina.

Wundram, Bill. Finnius: The Tale of a Lost Little Elephant. Tucker, Eric, illus. 2003. (J). *(978-1-59152-011-5(8),* Sweetgrass Bks.) Farcountry Pr.

Xiong, Kim, illus. Paper Horse. 2008. (ENG & CHI.). 37p. (J). 18.95 *(978-1-60603-003-5(5))* Better Chinese LLC.

Yaccarino, Dan. Five Little Pumpkins Came Back Board Book. Yaccarino, Dan, illus. 2018. (ENG., Illus.). 16p. (J). (gr. -1 — 1). bds. 6.99 *(978-0-06-284021-9(5),* HarperFestival) HarperCollins Pubs.

Yackle, Deanne. Jenny & Me. 2005. (J). lib. bdg. *(978-0-9725485-4-0(8))* Waterfall Ridge.

Yankovic, Al, pseud. My New Teacher & Me! Hargis, Wes, illus. 2013. (ENG.). 40p. (J). (gr. -1-3). 18.99 *(978-0-06-219203-5(5),* HarperCollins) HarperCollins Pubs.

—When I Grow Up. Hargis, Wes, illus. 2011. (ENG.). 32p. (J). (gr. -1-3). 19.99 *(978-0-06-192691-4(4),* HarperCollins) HarperCollins Pubs.

Yarrow, Peter & Lipton, Lenny. Puff, the Magic Dragon. Puybaret, Eric, illus. 2007. (ENG.). 24p. (J). 16.95 *(978-1-4027-5279-7(2));* 16.95 *(978-1-4027-5219-3(9))* Sterling Publishing Co., Inc.

Yates, Gene. The Dragon Opposites Book. 2005. (Illus.). 14p. (J). *(978-1-58865-283-6(1))* Kidsbooks, LLC.

Yates, Gene, illus. The Chameleon Colors Book. 2006. (J). *(978-1-58865-361-1(7))* Kidsbooks, LLC.

—The Dragon Opposites Book. 2006. (J). *(978-1-58865-362-8(5))* Kidsbooks, LLC.

—The Giraffe Numbers Book. 2006. (J). *(978-1-58865-364-2(1))* Kidsbooks, LLC.

Yates, Gene & Frank, Thomas. What Can Simon Be? Yates, Gene, illus. 2006. (Illus.). (J). *(978-1-58865-366-6(8))* Kidsbooks, LLC.

Yee, Wong Herbert. Fireman Small: Fire down Below! Yee, Wong Herbert, illus. 2004. (ENG., Illus.). 32p. (J). (gr. -1-3). pap. 6.99 *(978-0-618-49492-7(8),* 498899, Clarion Bks.) HarperCollins Pubs.

—A Small Christmas. 2007. (ENG., Illus.). 32p. (J). (gr. -1-3). 6.95 *(978-0-618-91534-7(6),* 1014889, Clarion Bks.) HarperCollins Pubs.

—Summer Days & Nights. Yee, Wong Herbert, illus. 2012. (ENG., Illus.). 32p. (J). (gr. -1-1). 19.99 *(978-0-8050-9078-9(9),* 900061501, Holt, Henry & Co. Bks. For Young Readers) Holt, Henry & Co.

—Tracks in the Snow. Yee, Wong Herbert, illus. 2007. (ENG., Illus.). 32p. (J). (gr. -1-1). per. 8.99 *(978-0-312-37134-0(9),* 900044662) Square Fish.

Yeoman, John. All the Year Round. Blake, Quentin, illus. 2019. (ENG.). 32p. (J). (gr. k-2). pap. 16.99 *(978-1-78344-613-1(7))* Andersen Pr. GBR. Dist: Independent Pubs. Group.

Yeomans, Ellen. Some Snow Is... Offermann, Andrea, illus. 2019. 32p. (J). (gr. -1-3). 17.99 *(978-0-399-54754-6(1),* G.P. Putnam's Sons Books for Young Readers) Penguin Young Readers Group.

Ying, Jonathan. Lost & Found, What's That Sound? Board Book. Ying, Victoria, illus. 2018. (ENG.). 28p. (J). (gr. -1 — 1). bds. 7.99 *(978-0-06-238069-2(9),* HarperFestival) HarperCollins Pubs.

Yolen, Jane. A Bear Sat on My Porch Today: (Story Books for Kids, Childrens Books with Animals, Friendship Books, Inclusivity Book) Alexander, Rilla, illus. 2018. (ENG.). 32p. (J). (gr. -1-k). 17.99 *(978-1-4521-0249-8(X))* Chronicle Bks. LLC.

—¿Cómo Aprenden los Colores los Dinosaurios? Teague, Mark, illus. 2006.Tr. of How Do Dinosaurs Learn Their Colors? (SPA.). 6p. (J). (gr. -1-k). bds. 6.99 *(978-0-439-87192-1(1),* Scholastic en Espanol) Scholastic, Inc.

—¿Cómo Dicen Estoy Enojado Los Dinosaurios? (How Do Dinosaurs Say I'm Mad?) Teague, Mark, illus. 2014. Orig. Title: (How Do Dinosaurs Say I'm Mad?). (SPA.). 40p. (J). (gr. -1-k). pap. 6.99 *(978-0-545-62780-1(X),* Scholastic en Espanol) Scholastic, Inc.

—Creepy Monsters, Sleepy Monsters. Murphy, Kelly, illus. 2013. (ENG.). 32p. (J). (gr. -1-2). 8.99 *(978-0-7636-6283-7(6))* Candlewick Pr.

—Friendship on the High Seas: Ready-To-Read Level 1. Moran, Mike, illus. 2019. (School of Fish Ser.). (ENG.). 32p. (J). (gr. -1-1). pap. 4.99 *(978-1-5344-3891-0(2),* Simon Spotlight) Simon Spotlight.

—How Do Dinosaurs Choose Their Pets? Teague, Mark, illus. 2016. (ENG.). 40p. (J). (gr. -1-k). 18.99 *(978-1-338-03278-9(X),* Blue Sky Pr., The) Scholastic, Inc.

—How Do Dinosaurs Clean Their Room? Teague, Mark, illus. 2004. (ENG.). 6p. (J). (gr. -1-k). bds. 7.99 *(978-0-439-64950-6(1),* Blue Sky Pr., The) Scholastic, Inc.

—How Do Dinosaurs Count to Ten? Teague, Mark, illus. 2004. (ENG.). 12p. (J). (gr. -1-k). bds. 7.99 *(978-0-439-64949-0(8),* Blue Sky Pr., The) Scholastic, Inc.

—How Do Dinosaurs Eat Their Food? Teague, Mark, illus. 2005. (ENG.). 40p. (J). (gr. -1-k). 18.99 *(978-0-439-24102-1(2),* Blue Sky Pr., The) Scholastic, Inc.

—How Do Dinosaurs Get Well Soon? Teague, Mark, illus. 2003. (ENG.). 40p. (J). (gr. -1-3). 18.99 *(978-0-439-24100-7(6),* Blue Sky Pr., The) Scholastic, Inc.

—How Do Dinosaurs Go to School? Teague, Mark, illus. 2007. (ENG.). 40p. (J). (gr. -1-k). 18.99 *(978-0-439-02081-7(6),* Blue Sky Pr., The) Scholastic, Inc.

—How Do Dinosaurs Go to School? Teague, Mark, illus. 2011. (J). (gr. -1-3). 29.95 *(978-0-545-19700-7(7));* 18.95 *(978-0-545-19707-6(4))* Weston Woods Studios, Inc.

—How Do Dinosaurs Go to Sleep? Teague, Mark, illus. 2016. (ENG.). 12p. (J). (— 1). bds. 7.99 *(978-0-545-94120-4(2),* Blue Sky Pr., The) Scholastic, Inc.

—How Do Dinosaurs Learn Their Colors? Teague, Mark, illus. 2006. (ENG.). 12p. (J). (gr. -1-k). bds. 7.99 *(978-0-439-85653-9(1),* Blue Sky Pr., The) Scholastic, Inc.

—How Do Dinosaurs Learn to Read? Teague, Mark, illus. 2018. (ENG.). 40p. (J). (gr. -1-k). 18.99 *(978-1-338-23301-8(7),* Blue Sky Pr., The) Scholastic, Inc.

—How Do Dinosaurs Love Their Cats? Teague, Mark, illus. 2010. (ENG.). 14p. (J). (gr. -1-k). bds. 7.99 *(978-0-545-15354-6(9),* Blue Sky Pr., The) Scholastic, Inc.

—How Do Dinosaurs Love Their Dogs? Teague, Mark, illus. 2010. (ENG.). 14p. (J). (gr. -1-k). bds. 7.99 *(978-0-545-15352-2(2),* Blue Sky Pr., The) Scholastic, Inc.

—How Do Dinosaurs Play with Their Friends? Teague, Mark, illus. 2006. (ENG.). 6p. (J). (gr. -1-k). bds. 7.99 *(978-0-439-85654-6(X),* Blue Sky Pr., The) Scholastic, Inc.

—How Do Dinosaurs Say Good Night?, 1 vol. Teague, Mark, illus. 2008. (ENG.). (J). (gr. -1-3). pap. 10.99 incl. audio compact disk *(978-0-545-09319-4(8))* Scholastic, Inc.

—How Do Dinosaurs Say Happy Birthday? Teague, Mark, illus. 2011. (ENG.). 12p. (J). (gr. -1-k). bds. 7.99 *(978-0-545-15353-9(0),* Blue Sky Pr., The) Scholastic, Inc.

—How Do Dinosaurs Say Happy Chanukah? Teague, Mark, illus. (ENG.). (J). (gr. -1 — 1). 2019. 34p. bds. 7.99 *(978-1-338-33032-8(2))* 2012. 40p. 16.99 *(978-0-545-41677-1(9))* Scholastic, Inc. (Blue Sky Pr., The).

—How Do Dinosaurs Say I Love You? Teague, Mark, illus. (J). 2020. (ENG.). 34p. (gr. -1 — 1). bds. 7.99 *(978-1-338-71282-7(9),* Cartwheel Bks.) 2011. pap. *(978-0-545-33076-3(9))* 2009. (ENG.). 40p. (gr. -1 — 1). 17.99 *(978-0-545-14314-1(4),* Blue Sky Pr., The) Scholastic, Inc.

—How Do Dinosaurs Say I'm MAD? Teague, Mark, illus. 2013. (ENG.). 40p. (J). (gr. -1-k). 18.99 *(978-0-545-14315-8(2),* Blue Sky Pr., The) Scholastic, Inc.

—How Do Dinosaurs Say Merry Christmas? Teague, Mark, illus. (ENG.). (J). (gr. -1 — 1). 2019. 34p. bds. 7.99 *(978-1-338-33043-4(8))* 2012. 40p. 18.99 *(978-0-545-41678-8(7))* Scholastic, Inc. (Blue Sky Pr., The).

—How Do Dinosaurs Stay Friends? Teague, Mark, illus. 2016. (ENG.). 40p. (J). (gr. -1-k). 18.99 *(978-0-545-82934-2(8),* Blue Sky Pr., The) Scholastic, Inc.

—How Do Dinosaurs Stay Safe? Teague, Mark, illus. 2015. (ENG.). 40p. (J). (gr. -1-k). 18.99 *(978-0-439-24104-5(9),* Blue Sky Pr., The) Scholastic, Inc.

—My Father Knows the Names of Things. Jorisch, Stéphane, illus. 2010. (ENG.). 32p. (J). (gr. -1-3). 19.99 *(978-1-4169-4895-7(3),* Simon & Schuster Bks. For Young Readers) Simon & Schuster Bks. For Young Readers.

—The Scarecrow's Dance. Ibatoulline, Bagram, illus. 2009. (ENG.). 32p. (J). (gr. -1-3). 19.99 *(978-1-4169-3770-8(6),* Simon & Schuster Bks. For Young Readers) Simon & Schuster Bks. For Young Readers.

—School of Fish: Ready-To-Read Level 1. Moran, Mike, illus. 2019. (School of Fish Ser.). (ENG.). 32p. (J). (gr. -1-1). 17.99 *(978-1-5344-3889-7(0));* pap. 4.99 *(978-1-5344-3888-0(2))* Simon Spotlight. (Simon Spotlight).

—Sing a Season Song. Ashlock, Lisel, illus. 2015. (ENG.). 48p. (J). (gr. 1-3). 22.95 *(978-1-56846-255-4(7),* 20829, Creative Editions) Creative Co., The.

—Waking Dragons. Anderson, Derek, illus. 2012. (ENG.). 32p. (J). (gr. -1-3). 19.99 *(978-1-4169-9032-1(1),* Simon & Schuster Bks. For Young Readers) Simon & Schuster Bks. For Young Readers.

—What to Do with a Box. Sheban, Chris, illus. (ENG.). (J). 2018. 14p. (gr. -1-1). bds. 8.99 *(978-1-56846-320-9(0),* 19702) 2016. 32p. (gr. 1-3). 18.99 *(978-1-56846-289-9(1),* 19704) Creative Co., The. (Creative Editions).

—What to Do with a String. Payne, C. F., illus. 2019. 32p. (J). (gr. 1-3). 18.99 *(978-1-56846-322-3(7),* 18910, Creative Editions) Creative Co., The.

—Where Have the Unicorns Gone? Sanderson, Ruth, illus. 2003. (ENG.). 32p. (J). (gr. -1-3). 9.99 *(978-0-689-86359-2(4),* Simon & Schuster/Paula Wiseman Bks.) Simon & Schuster Bks. For Young Readers.

Yolen, Jane, narrated by. How Do Dinosaurs Eat Their Food? 2011. (J). (gr. -1-2). 29.95 *(978-0-439-02746-5(2))* Weston Woods Studios, Inc.

Yolen, Jane & Stemple, Heidi E. Y. Not All Princesses Dress in Pink. Lanquetin, Anne-Sophie, illus. 2010. (ENG.). 32p. (J). (gr. -1-3). 17.99 *(978-1-4169-8018-6(0),* Simon & Schuster Bks. For Young Readers) Simon & Schuster Bks. For Young Readers.

—Sleep, Black Bear, Sleep. Dyer, Brooke, illus. 2007. 32p. (J). (gr. -1-1). (ENG.). 15.99 *(978-0-06-081560-8(4),* HarperCollins); lib. bdg. 16.89 *(978-0-06-081561-5(2))* HarperCollins Pubs.

—You Nest Here with Me. Sweet, Melissa, illus. 2019. 28p. (J). (— 1). bds. 7.99 *(978-1-68437-371-0(9),* Astra Young Readers) Astra Publishing Hse.

Yoon, Salina. Humpty Dumpty. Yoon, Salina, illus. 2012. (ENG., Illus.). 18p. (J). (gr. -1 — 1). bds. 7.99 *(978-1-4424-1411-2(1),* Little Simon) Little Simon.

—Jack & Jill: A Halloween Nursery Rhyme. Yoon, Salina, illus. 2012. (ENG., Illus.). 18p. (J). (gr. -1 — 1). bds. 5.99 *(978-1-4424-1410-5(3),* Little Simon) Little Simon.

—Old MacDonald Had a Farm. 2008. (Salina Yoon Bks.). (Illus.). 12p. (J). (gr. -1-k). bds. 9.99 *(978-0-8431-2817-8(8),* Price Stern Sloan) Penguin Young Readers Group.

York Lumbard, Alexis. Angels. Weedn, Flavia, illus. 2013. 28p. (J). (gr. -1-1). 14.95 *(978-1-937786-15-1(3),* Wisdom Tales) World Wisdom, Inc.

You Can Be Anything! 2006. (Illus.). 32p. (J). 14.95 *(978-0-9786813-1-9(2))* Elora Pr.

Young, Ed. Seven Blind Mice. Young, Ed, illus. 2007. (Illus.). pap. 14.95 incl. audio *(978-0-439-02784-7(5));* (J). 24.95 incl. audio *(978-0-439-02782-3(9))* Scholastic, Inc.

—Seven Blind Mice. Young, Ed, illus. 2011. (Illus.). 18.95 *(978-0-439-02785-4(3));* (J). 29.95 *(978-0-439-02783-0(7))* Weston Woods Studios, Inc.

Young, Jessica. Pet This Book. Wiseman, Daniel, illus. 2018. (ENG.). 32p. (J). 15.99 *(978-1-68119-507-0(0),* 900175607, Bloomsbury Children's Bks.) Bloomsbury Publishing USA.

—Play This Book. Wiseman, Daniel, illus. 2018. (ENG.). 32p. (J). 15.99 *(978-1-68119-506-3(2),* 900175599, Bloomsbury Children's Bks.) Bloomsbury Publishing USA.

Young, Karen. A Chimpanzee Tale. 2009. (Illus.). 36p. pap. 16.99 *(978-1-4389-2448-9(8))* AuthorHouse.

Young, Samantha. I Can't Wait. 2012. (ENG.). 24p. pap. 15.99 *(978-1-4772-6013-5(7))* AuthorHouse.

Young, Shelley. Doc Broc's Cave Adventure. Young, Shelley, illus. 2005. (Illus.). 44p. 19.95 *(978-1-58054-406-1(1))* Woodland Publishing, Inc.

You're One! 2014. (Year-By-Year Bks.). (ENG., Illus.). 16p. (J). (— 1). bds. 7.95 *(978-1-934649-46-6(5))* Bailiwick Pr.

Zabel, Alanna. A Chair in the Air. 2006. 35p. pap. 16.00 *(978-1-4116-7436-3(7))* Lulu Pr., Inc.

Zaglada, Vladimir. Gymmy the Owl & His Friends. 2012. 52p. pap. 24.99 *(978-1-4772-0226-5(9))* AuthorHouse.

—Gymmy the Owl & His Friends: Tales in Rhyme about the Animal Kingdom's Natural Gymnasts. 2012. 52p. pap. 24.99 *(978-1-4685-6011-4(5))* AuthorHouse.

Zaibak, Bushra. I am Not Afraid. 2007. (Illus.). 37p. (J). mass mkt. *(978-0-9787849-7-3(9))* Lucent Interpretations, LLC.

Zalesny, Michele. The Elves' Surprise. 2008. (ENG., Illus.). 20p. (J). pap. 9.25 *(978-1-935125-06-8(0))* Robertson Publishing.

The Zany Zanimal Zoo. 2005. (Illus.). 40p. (J). 14.95 *(978-0-9769738-0-5(4))* Redel, Nicole.

Zaring, Laurie. Who Could You Be at the Zoo? Barlup, Jessica, illus. 2013. 24p. pap. 12.95 *(978-1-61244-175-7(0))* Halo Publishing International.

Zeeh, Shawn. Tucker Farm: Under the Big Top. 2012. 36p. pap. 21.99 *(978-1-4771-2685-1(6))* Xlibris Corp.

Zelaya, Carol. Caring for Emily's Family. 2008. (Illus.). 24p. (J). (gr. 2-3). 14.95 *(978-0-9796265-1-7(X))* Richlee Publishing.

—Emily Waits for Her Family. Metcalf, Kristin, illus. 2007. (Emily the Chickadee Ser.). 32p. (J). (gr. 2-3). 14.95 *(978-0-9796265-0-0(1))* Richlee Publishing.

—Emily's New Home: Emily the Chickadee. 2008. (Illus.). 36p. (J). (gr. 2-3). 14.95 *(978-0-9796265-2-4(8))* Richlee Publishing.

Zenz, Aaron. The Hiccupotamus, 0 vols. Zenz, Aaron, illus. 2012. (Hiccupotamus & Friends Ser.: 1). (ENG., Illus.). 32p. (J). (gr. -1-1). 12.99 *(978-0-7614-5622-3(8),* 9780761456223, Two Lions) Amazon Publishing.

Zettler, Andrew. The Teeniest Tiniest Yawn. Zettler, Andrew, illus. l.t. ed. 2014. (ENG., Illus.). 36p. (J). 17.99 *(978-0-9912370-0-5(5))* Royal Penny Pr., The.

Ziarnik, Natalie. A Lullaby of Summer Things. Valentine, Madeline, illus. 2018. 40p. (J). (gr. -1-3). 17.99 *(978-1-101-93552-1(9),* Schwartz & Wade Bks.) Random Hse. Children's Bks.

Ziefert, Harriet. Messy Bessie: Where's My Homework? De Muth, Roger, illus. 2007. (J). *(978-1-4287-4707-4(9))* Handprint Bks.

Zimmer, Tracie Vaughn. 42 Miles. 2008. (ENG., Illus.). 80p. (J). (gr. 5-7). 16.00 *(978-0-618-61867-5(8),* 100453, Clarion Bks.) HarperCollins Pubs.

Zimmerman, Kwanza A. What Day Is It? 2008. 16p. per. 24.95 *(978-1-4241-9954-9(9))* America Star Bks.

Zinner, Gennieve. The UFB's of Bugsville, Florida USA, 1 vol. Ballinger, Carolyn, illus. 2010. 48p. pap. 24.95 *(978-1-4489-7977-6(3))* PublishAmerica, Inc.

Zobel-Nolan, Allia. Mrs. McGee's Coconut. Cottrill, Peter, illus. 2009. 32p. (J). (gr. -1-2). 15.95 *(978-1-58925-079-6(6));* pap. 6.95 *(978-1-58925-414-5(7))* Tiger Tales.

Zoellick, Todd. Daniel Harrington Fairbanks the Third & a Day on the Farm. 2012. 40p. pap. 18.58 *(978-1-4772-8408-7(7))* AuthorHouse.

—Daniel Harrington Fairbanks the Third & the Dog That Wouldn't Bark. 2009. 52p. pap. 20.49 *(978-1-4490-1047-8(4))* AuthorHouse.

Zoss, Lori. A Bed for Fred. 2013. 24p. 15.95 *(978-1-936449-52-1(8))* Hugo House Publishers, Ltd.

Zschock, Martha. Hello, Rockies! 2014. (Hello Ser.). (ENG., Illus.). 16p. (J). (gr. -1-k). bds. 9.99 *(978-1-938700-21-7(X),* 9781938700217, Commonwealth Editions) Applewood Bks.

Zuckerman, Linda. The Day Is Waiting, 1 vol. Freeman, Don, illus. 2015. (ENG.). 32p. (J). 9.99 *(978-0-310-74054-4(1))* Zonderkidz.

Zvetkoff, Kathleen Charnes. The Adventures of Willy the Monkey. 2008. 40p. pap. *(978-0-9784909-5-9(9))* Soul Asylum Poetry.

365 Stories & Rhymes for Boys. (365 Stories Treasuries Ser.). 384p. (J). 9.98 *(978-1-4054-1958-1(X))* Parragon, Inc.

STORIES WITHOUT WORDS

Alexander, Jed. Red. 2018. (ENG., Illus.). 32p. (J). (gr. -1-3). 15.95 *(978-1-944903-11-4(9),* 1313501, Cameron Kids) Cameron + Co.

Alonso, Cynthia. Aquarium: (Aquarium Books for Kids, Picture Book about Marine Animals, Nature Books) 2018. (ENG., Illus.). 40p. (J). (gr. -1-k). 17.99 *(978-1-4521-6875-3(X))* Chronicle Bks. LLC.

Andersen, Hans Christian. Wild Swans. Maguire, Thomas Aquinas, illus. 2012. (ENG.). 104p. (J). pap. 24.95 *(978-1-897476-36-9(1))* Simply Read Bks. CAN. Dist: Ingram Publisher Services.

Anderson, Hans Christian. Los Cisnes Salvajes.Tr. of Wild Swans. (SPA., Illus.). 48p. (J). (gr. 3-5). 9.56 *(978-84-241-5524-7(6))* Everest Editora ESP. Dist: Lectorum Pubns., Inc.

Anno, Mitsumasa & Kobayashi, Miki. Anno's Denmark. 2018. (Illus.). (J). *(978-1-893103-75-7(7))* Beautiful Feet Bks.

Ardizzone, Edward. The Wrong Side of the Bed. 2017. (ENG., Illus.). 32p. (J). (gr. -1-1). 13.99 *(978-0-14-137027-9(0))* Penguin Bks., Ltd. GBR. Dist: Independent Pubs. Group.

Baker, Jeannie. Mirror. Baker, Jeannie, illus. 2010. (ENG., Illus.). 48p. (J). (gr. k-4). 21.99 *(978-0-7636-4848-0(5))* Candlewick Pr.

Baker, Liza. Harold & the Purple Crayon: Under the Sea. 2003. (Festival Reader Ser.). (ENG., Illus.). 32p. (J). (gr. -1-2). pap. 3.99 *(978-0-06-000178-0(X),* HarperFestival) HarperCollins Pubs.

Banyai, Istvan. The Other Side. Banyai, Istvan, illus. 2005. (ENG., Illus.). 44p. (J). (gr. k-2). 18.69 *(978-0-8118-4608-0(3)*, Chronicle Bks.) Chronicle Bks. LLC.
Bartlett, T. C. Tuba Lessons. Felix, Monique, illus. 2010. (ENG.). 32p. (J). (gr. k-3). 17.95 *(978-1-56846-209-7(3)*, 22071, Creative Editions) Creative Co., The.
Becker, Aaron. Journey. Becker, Aaron, illus. 2013. (ENG., Illus.). 40p. (J). (gr. -1-3). 17.99 *(978-0-7636-6053-6(1))* Candlewick Pr.
—Quest. Becker, Aaron, illus. 2014. (ENG., Illus.). 40p. (J). (gr. -1-3). 17.99 *(978-0-7636-6595-1(9))* Candlewick Pr.
—Quest. 2015. (CHI.). 40p. (J). *(978-7-5133-1677-4(5))* New Star Publishing Hse.
—Return. Becker, Aaron, illus. 2016. (ENG., Illus.). 40p. (J). (gr. -1-3). 17.99 *(978-0-7636-7730-5(2))* Candlewick Pr.
—A Stone for Sascha. Becker, Aaron, illus. 2018. (ENG., Illus.). 48p. (J). (gr. k-4). 17.99 *(978-0-7636-6596-8(7))* Candlewick Pr.
Boyd, Lizi. Flashlight: (Picture Books, Wordless Books for Kids, Camping Books for Kids, Bedtime Story Books, Children's Activity Books, Children's Nature Books) 2014. (ENG., Illus.). 40p. (J). (gr. -1-1). 16.99 *(978-1-4521-1894-9(9))* Chronicle Bks. LLC.
Boynton-Hughes, Brooke. Brave Molly: (Empowering Books for Kids, Overcoming Fear Kids Books, Bravery Books for Kids) 2019. (ENG., Illus.). 48p. (J). (gr. k-3). 16.99 *(978-1-4521-6100-6(3))* Chronicle Bks. LLC.
Carmi, Giora. A Circle of Friends, 1 vol. (ENG., Illus.). 32p. (J). (gr. k-9). 2006. pap. 5.95 *(978-1-59572-060-3(X))* 2003. 15.95 *(978-1-932065-00-8(8))* Star Bright Bks., Inc.
Cole, Henry. Spot & Dot. Cole, Henry, illus. 2019. (ENG., Illus.). 32p. (J). (gr. -1-3). 17.99 *(978-1-5344-2555-2(1)*, Little Simon) Little Simon.
—Spot, the Cat. Cole, Henry, illus. 2016. (ENG., Illus.). 32p. (J). (gr. -1-3). 18.99 *(978-1-4814-4225-1(2)*, Little Simon) Little Simon.
Cordell, Matthew. Wolf in the Snow. 2017. (ENG., Illus.). 48p. (J). 18.99 *(978-1-250-07636-6(6)*, 900152144) Feiwel & Friends.
—Wolf in the Snow. 2018. (CHI.). (gr. -1-1). *(978-986-189-861-2(1))* Grimm Cultural Ent., Co., Ltd.
dePaola, Tomie. Pancakes for Breakfast. 2018. lib. bdg. 18.40 *(978-0-606-41211-7(5))* Turtleback.
Diamond, Donna. The Shadow. Diamond, Donna, illus. 2010. (ENG., Illus.). 32p. (J). (gr. k-3). 15.99 *(978-0-7636-4878-7(7))* Candlewick Pr.
Donovan, Jane Monroe. Small, Medium & Large. Donovan, Jane Monroe, illus. 2010. (ENG., Illus.). 32p. (J). (gr. 1-4). 15.95 *(978-1-58536-447-3(9)*, 202172) Sleeping Bear Pr.
Drummond, Sarah, illus. Raven & the Red Ball. 2013. (ENG.). 28p. (J). 9.95 *(978-0-7649-6609-5(X))* Pomegranate Communications, Inc.
Dudley, Rebecca. Hank Finds an Egg. Dudley, Rebecca, photos by. 2013. (ENG., Illus.). 40p. (J). 16.99 *(978-1-4413-1158-0(0)*, 302680cb-33e6-46cb-8a69-8d52946a6a7b) Peter Pauper Pr. Inc.
Edwards, Wallace. Woodrow at Sea. Edwards, Wallace, illus. 2018. (ENG., Illus.). 32p. (J). (gr. -1-k). 16.95 *(978-1-77278-029-1(4))* Pajama Pr. CAN. Dist: Publishers Group West (PGW).
The Farmer & the Clown. 2014. (Farmer Bks.). (ENG., Illus.). 32p. (J). (gr. -1-3). 18.99 *(978-1-4424-9744-3(0)*, Beach Lane Bks.) Beach Lane Bks.
Feelings, Tom. The Middle Passage: White Ships / Black Cargo. 2018. (Illus.). 80p. (YA). (gr. 7). 29.99 *(978-0-525-55244-4(8)*, Dial Bks) Penguin Young Readers Group.
Félix, Monique. The Alphabet. 2015. (J). pap. *(978-1-62832-262-0(4)*, Creative Paperbacks) Creative Co., The.
Felix, Monique. Mouse Book: the Colors. Felix, Monique, illus. 2013. (ENG., Illus.). 32p. (J). (gr. -1-k). 12.99 *(978-1-56846-234-9(4)*, 21757, Creative Editions) Creative Co., The.
Felix, Monique, illus. The Alphabet. 2012. (Mouse Book Ser.). 32p. (J). (gr. -1-k). 12.99 *(978-1-56846-226-4(3)*, 22054, Creative Editions) Creative Co., The.
—Mouse Book: the Numbers. 2013. 32p. (J). (gr. -1-k). 12.99 *(978-1-56846-235-6(2)*, 21759, Creative Editions) Creative Co., The.
—The Wind. 2012. (Mouse Book Ser.). (ENG.). 32p. (J). (gr. -1-k). 12.99 *(978-1-56846-227-1(1)*, 22055, Creative Editions) Creative Co., The.
Furie, Matt. The Night Riders. 2013. (Illus.). 48p. (J). (gr. -1-3). 8.95 *(978-1-938073-72-4(X)*, 54da59fb-b496-483f-a5f6-41367ed7cd06) McSweeney's Publishing.
Garoche, Camille. The Snow Rabbit. 2015. (Illus.). 56p. (J). (gr. -1-3). 16.95 *(978-1-59270-181-0(7))* Enchanted Lion Bks., LLC.
Gebhardt, Joelle. Mr. Buttonman & the Great Escape. 2020. (ENG., Illus.). 40p. (J). (gr. -1-3). 16.95 *(978-1-77229-028-8(9))* Simply Read Bks. CAN. Dist: Ingram Publisher Services.
Geisert, Arthur, creator. Ice. 2011. (Stories Without Words Ser.). (ENG., Illus.). 32p. (J). (gr. -1-2). 14.95 *(978-1-59270-098-1(5))* Enchanted Lion Bks., LLC.
—Thunderstorm. (ENG., Illus.). (J). 2015. 34p. (gr. k). 60.00 *(978-1-59270-170-4(1))* 2013. 32p. (gr. -1). 17.95 *(978-1-59270-133-9(7))* Enchanted Lion Bks., LLC.
Genhart, Michael. I See You: A Story for Kids about Homelessness & Being Unhoused. Lew-Vriethoff, Joanne, illus. 2017. 40p. (J). 15.95 *(978-1-4338-2758-7(1)*, Magination Pr.) American Psychological Assn.
Goldstyn, Jacques. Letters to a PrisonerLe Prisonnier Sans Frontières. Keenlyside, Angela, tr. from FRE. 2017. Orig. Title: Le Prisonnier Sans Frontières. (ENG., Illus.). 48p. (J). (gr. 4). 18.95 *(978-1-77147-251-7(0))* Owlkids Bks. Inc. CAN. Dist: Publishers Group West (PGW).
Hare, John. Field Trip to the Moon. 2019. (Field Trip Adventures Ser.). (ENG., Illus.). 40p. (J). (gr. -1-3). 17.99 *(978-0-8234-4253-9(5)*, Margaret Ferguson Books) Holiday Hse., Inc.
—Field Trip to the Ocean Deep. 2020. (Field Trip Adventures Ser.). (ENG., Illus.). 40p. (J). (gr. -1-3). 17.99 *(978-0-8234-4630-8(1)*, Margaret Ferguson Books) Holiday Hse., Inc.
Hegbrook, Thomas. Imaginature: 100 Stories Without Words, 1 vol. 2016. (ENG., Illus.). 64p. (J). *(978-1-84857-480-9(0)*, 360 Degrees) Tiger Tales.
Hillenbrand, Will. Snowman's Story, 0 vols. 2014. (ENG., Illus.). 32p. (J). (gr. -1-2). 16.99 *(978-1-4778-4787-9(1)*, 9781477847879, Two Lions) Amazon Publishing.
Himler, Ronald. Dancing Boy, 1 vol. 2005. (ENG., Illus.). 32p. (J). (gr. -1-k). 15.95 *(978-1-59572-020-7(0))* Star Bright Bks., Inc.
Hussenot, Victor. The Land of Lines. 2015. (ENG., Illus.). 44p. (J). (gr. 1-4). 12.99 *(978-1-4521-4282-1(3))* Chronicle Bks. LLC.
Hutch Matthews, Kristina. The Cat Flap: A Tale of Harmony & Balance. Hutch Matthews, Kristina, illus. 2014. (Illus.). 44p. (J). 18.95 *(978-0-9914513-1-9(7))* BrightShadow Publishing.
Idle, Molly. Flora & the Flamingo. 2013. (Flora Ser.). (ENG., Illus.). 44p. (J). (gr. -1-1). 18.99 *(978-1-4521-1006-6(9))* Chronicle Bks. LLC.
—Flora & the Peacocks. 2016. (Flora & Friends Ser.). (ENG., Illus.). 40p. (J). (gr. -1-k). 17.99 *(978-1-4521-3816-9(8))* Chronicle Bks. LLC.
Jay, Alison, illus. Bee & Me. 2017. (J). *(978-0-605-97081-6(5))* Candlewick Pr.
Jocelyn, Marthe. One Patch of Blue, 1 vol. 2019. (ENG., Illus.). 24p. (J). (gr. -1 — 1). bds. 9.95 *(978-1-4598-2073-9(8))* Orca Bk. Pubs. USA.
—One Piece of String, 1 vol. 2017. (ENG., Illus.). 24p. (J). (gr. -1 — 1). bds. 10.95 *(978-1-4598-1318-2(9))* Orca Bk. Pubs. USA.
—One Red Button, 1 vol. 2017. (ENG., Illus.). 24p. (J). (gr. -1 — 1). bds. 9.95 *(978-1-4598-1315-1(4))* Orca Bk. Pubs. USA.
—One Yellow Ribbon, 1 vol. 2019. (ENG., Illus.). 24p. (J). (gr. -1 — 1). bds. 9.95 *(978-1-4598-2076-0(2))* Orca Bk. Pubs. USA.
Johnson, Mariana Ruiz. While You Are Sleeping: (Bedtime Books for Kids, Wordless Bedtime Stories for Kids) 2018. (ENG., Illus.). 36p. (J). (gr. -1-k). 16.99 *(978-1-4521-6599-8(8))* Chronicle Bks. LLC.
Kastelic, Maja. A Boy & a House. 2018. (ENG., Illus.). 32p. (J). (gr. k-2). 9.95 *(978-1-77321-054-4(8))* Annick Pr., Ltd. CAN. Dist: Publishers Group West (PGW).
Kerascoët & Kerascoët. I Walk with Vanessa: A Picture Book Story about a Simple Act of Kindness. 2018. (Illus.). 40p. (J). (gr. -1-3). 17.99 *(978-1-5247-6955-0(X))* Random Hse. Children's Bks.
Kuhlmann, Torben. Moletown. 2015. (ENG., Illus.). 32p. (J). (gr. -1-2). 17.95 *(978-0-7358-4208-3(6))* North-South Bks., Inc.
Kumon. What Does Baby See? 2008. (Illus.). 12p. (J). bds. *(978-1-934618-27-1(6))* Begin Smart LLC.
Laidlaw, Sarah. Through the Seasons, 30 vols. 2018. (Illus.). 12p. (J). 9.95 *(978-1-78250-469-6(9))* Floris Bks. GBR. Dist: Consortium Bk. Sales & Distribution.
Lam, Thao. Skunk on a String. 2016. (ENG., Illus.). 40p. (J). (gr. -1-2). 18.95 *(978-1-77147-131-2(X)*, Owlkids) Owlkids Bks. Inc. CAN. Dist: Publishers Group West (PGW).
—Wallpaper. 2018. (ENG., Illus.). 32p. (J). (gr. -1-3). 18.95 *(978-1-77147-283-8(9))* Owlkids Bks. Inc. CAN. Dist: Publishers Group West (PGW).
Lanan, Jessica. The Fisherman & the Whale. Lanan, Jessica, illus. 2019. (ENG., Illus.). 48p. (J). (gr. -1-3). 17.99 *(978-1-5344-1574-4(2)*, Simon & Schuster Bks. For Young Readers) Simon & Schuster Bks. For Young Readers.
Lawson, JonArno. Sidewalk Flowers, 1 vol. Smith, Sydney, illus. 2015. (ENG.). 32p. (J). (gr. -1-2). 17.99 *(978-1-55498-431-2(9))* Groundwood Bks. CAN. Dist: Publishers Group West (PGW).
Lee, Jihyeon. Door: (Wordless Children's Picture Book, Adventure, Friendship) 2018. (ENG., Illus.). 56p. (J). (gr. -1-k). 17.99 *(978-1-4521-7142-5(4))* Chronicle Bks. LLC.
Lee, Suzy. Lines: (Wordless Kids Books, Children's Winter Books, Ice Skating Story for Kids) 2017. (ENG., Illus.). 40p. (J). (gr. -1-k). 17.99 *(978-1-4521-5665-1(4))* Chronicle Bks. LLC.
—Mirror. 2010. (ENG., Illus.). 48p. (J). (gr. -1). 15.95 *(978-1-934734-39-1(X))* Seven Footer Pr.
—Wave: (Books about Ocean Waves, Beach Story Children's Books) 2008. (ENG., Illus.). 40p. (J). (gr. -1-17). 15.99 *(978-0-8118-5924-0(X))* Chronicle Bks. LLC.
Lehman, Barbara. Museum Trip. (ENG., Illus.). 40p. (J). (gr. -1-3). 2017. pap. 9.99 *(978-1-328-74051-9(X)*, 1677019) 2006. 17.99 *(978-0-618-58125-2(1)*, 592181) HarperCollins Pubs. (Clarion Bks.).
—Rainstorm. 2007. (ENG., Illus.). 32p. (J). (gr. -1-3). 17.99 *(978-0-618-75639-1(6)*, 519814, Clarion Bks.) HarperCollins Pubs.
—Trainstop. 2008. (ENG., Illus.). 32p. (J). (gr. -1-3). 17.99 *(978-0-618-75640-7(X)*, 569198, Clarion Bks.) HarperCollins Pubs.
Lehrer, Damon. Rocket Boy. 2016. (ENG., Illus.). 32p. (J). 17.95 *(978-1-56792-587-6(1))* Godine, David R. Pub.
Lemke, Donald. The Awakening, 1 vol. Glass House Graphics, illus. 2011. (Good vs Evil Ser.). (ENG.). 48p. (J). (gr. 5-9). lib. bdg. 23.99 *(978-1-4342-2089-9(3)*, 102835, Stone Arch Bks.) Capstone.
—Diver Down, 1 vol. Glass House Graphics, illus. 2011. (Good vs Evil Ser.). (ENG.). 48p. (J). (gr. 5-9). lib. bdg. 23.99 *(978-1-4342-2092-9(3)*, 102838, Stone Arch Bks.) Capstone.
Lever, Jill. The Worm Who Knew Karate! Denton, Terry, illus. 2019. 32p. (J). (gr. k-3). 15.99 *(978-0-14-350602-7(1)*, Puffin) Penguin Bks., Ltd. GBR. Dist: Independent Pubs. Group.
Logan, Laura. Little Butterfly. Logan, Laura, illus. 2016. (ENG., Illus.). 32p. (J). (gr. -1-3). 14.99 *(978-0-06-228126-5(7)*, Balzer & Bray) HarperCollins Pubs.
Lupano, Wilfred. A Sea of Love. 2020. (ENG., Illus.). 224p. (YA). 24.99 *(978-1-942367-45-1(7)*, 9cbb732c-4cf0-40cd-8e84-7459b0d9a466) Magnetic Pr.
Luthardt, Kevin. Peep!, 1 vol. (Illus.). 36p. (J). (gr. -1-k). 2012. pap. 7.95 *(978-1-56145-682-6(9))* 2003. 15.95 *(978-1-56145-046-6(4))* Peachtree Publishing Co. Inc.
MacKay, Elly. Waltz of the Snowflakes. 2017. (ENG., Illus.). 32p. (J). (gr. -1-3). 16.99 *(978-0-7624-5338-2(9)*, Running Pr. Kids) Running Pr.
Martin Vidal, Beatriz. Bird. 2015. (Illus.). 32p. (J). 16.95 *(978-1-927018-64-4(1))* Simply Read Bks. CAN. Dist: Ingram Publisher Services.
Mayer, Mercer. Frog Goes to Dinner. Mayer, Mercer, illus. 2003. (Boy, a Dog, & a Frog Ser.). (Illus.). 32p. (J). (gr. -1-k). 7.99 *(978-0-8037-2884-4(0)*, Dial Bks) Penguin Young Readers Group.
—Octopus Soup, 0 vols. Mayer, Mercer, illus. 2012. (ENG., Illus.). 24p. (J). (gr. -1-2). 16.99 *(978-0-7614-5812-8(3)*, 9780761458128, Two Lions) Amazon Publishing.
McClure, Nikki. The Great Chicken Escape. 2018. (ENG., Illus.). 40p. (J). (gr. -1-3). 16.95 *(978-1-944903-22-0(4)*, 1313201, Cameron Kids) Cameron + Co.
McCully, Emily Arnold. Picnic. McCully, Emily Arnold, illus. 2003. (Illus.). 32p. (J). (gr. -1-k). 16.89 *(978-0-06-623855-5(2))* HarperCollins Pubs.
—Picnic. 2003. (ENG., Illus.). 32p. (J). (gr. -1-k). 17.99 *(978-0-06-623854-8(4)*, HarperCollins) HarperCollins Pubs.
—School. McCully, Emily Arnold, illus. 2005. (Illus.). 32p. (J). lib. bdg. 16.89 *(978-0-06-623857-9(9))* HarperCollins Pubs.
Merveille, David. Mr. Hulot at the Beach. 2016. (ENG., Illus.). 32p. (J). 18.95 *(978-0-7358-4254-0(X))* North-South Bks., Inc.
Miyares, Daniel. Float. Miyares, Daniel, illus. 2015. (ENG., Illus.). 48p. (J). (gr. -1-3). 18.99 *(978-1-4814-1524-8(7)*, Simon & Schuster Bks. For Young Readers) Simon & Schuster Bks. For Young Readers.
Newgarden, Mark & Cash, Megan Montague. Bow-Wow's Colorful Life. 2009. (ENG., Illus.). 18p. (J). (gr. k — 1). bds. 4.99 *(978-0-15-206564-5(4)*, 1098976, Clarion Bks.) HarperCollins Pubs.
Newman, Jeff. The Boys. Newman, Jeff, illus. 2010. (ENG., Illus.). 40p. (J). (gr. -1-2). 19.99 *(978-1-4169-5012-7(5)*, Simon & Schuster Bks. For Young Readers) Simon & Schuster Bks. For Young Readers.
—Found. Day, Larry, illus. 2018. (ENG.). 48p. (J). (gr. -1-3). 19.99 *(978-1-5344-1006-0(6)*, Simon & Schuster Bks. For Young Readers) Simon & Schuster Bks. For Young Readers.
Nordling, Lee. Andrew the Seeker. Roberts, Scott, illus. 2017. (Game for Adventure Ser.). (ENG.). 32p. (J). (gr. k-3). 25.32 *(978-1-5124-1330-4(5)*, 4f77d2e5-2cdc-4d1d-823e-a3c0a48f5399, Graphic Universe™) Lerner Publishing Group.
—Chavo the Invisible. Silva, Flávio B., illus. 2018. (Game for Adventure Ser.). (ENG.). 40p. (J). (gr. k-3). pap. 7.99 *(978-1-5415-1046-3(1)*, 2d737fb1-4fa6-4648-a810-c0adc9a0297c, Graphic Universe™) Lerner Publishing Group.
ón, Raúl. Draw! ón, Raúl, illus. 2014. (ENG., Illus.). 40p. (J). (gr. -1-3). 17.99 *(978-1-4424-9492-3(1)*, Simon & Schuster/Paula Wiseman Bks.) Simon & Schuster/Paula Wiseman Bks.
—Imagine! ón, Raúl, illus. 2018. (ENG., Illus.). 48p. (J). (gr. -1-3). 17.99 *(978-1-4814-6273-0(3)*, Simon & Schuster/Paula Wiseman Bks.) Simon & Schuster/Paula Wiseman Bks.
Oswald, Pete. Hike. Oswald, Pete, illus. 2020. (ENG., Illus.). 40p. (J). (gr. -1-3). 18.99 *(978-1-5362-0157-4(X))* Candlewick Pr.
Otoshi, Kathryn. Draw the Line. 2017. (ENG., Illus.). 48p. (J). 18.99 *(978-1-62672-563-8(2)*, 900161308) Roaring Brook Pr.
Parda, Piotr. Graduation Day. 2017. (ENG., Illus.). 52p. (J). (gr. k-2). 18.99 *(978-0-9913866-7-3(1))* Ripple Grove Pr.
Pett, Mark. The Boy & the Airplane. Pett, Mark, illus. 2013. (ENG., Illus.). 40p. (J). (gr. -1). 18.99 *(978-1-4424-5123-0(8)*, Simon & Schuster Bks. For Young Readers) Simon & Schuster Bks. For Young Readers.
—The Girl & the Bicycle. Pett, Mark, illus. 2014. (ENG., Illus.). 40p. (J). (gr. -1). 18.99 *(978-1-4424-8319-4(9)*, Simon & Schuster Bks. For Young Readers) Simon & Schuster Bks. For Young Readers.
Pham, LeUyen. The Bear Who Wasn't There. 2016. (ENG., Illus.). 40p. (J). 19.99 *(978-1-59643-970-2(X)*, 900126977) Roaring Brook Pr.
Pinkney, Jerry. The Lion & the Mouse. 2011. 29.95 *(978-0-545-29677-9(3))* Weston Woods Studios, Inc.
—The Lion & the Mouse. 2018. (CHI.). (J). (gr. k-3). *(978-7-5340-6246-9(2))* Zehjiang People's Fine Arts Publishing Hse.
—The Lion & the Mouse (Caldecott Medal Winner) 2009. (ENG., Illus.). 40p. (J). (gr. -1-3). 18.99 *(978-0-316-01356-7(0))* Little, Brown Bks. for Young Readers.
Prendergast, Kate. Dog on a Digger. Prendergast, Kate, illus. 2018. (ENG., Illus.). 32p. (J). (gr. -1-1). 16.99 *(978-1-5362-0041-6(7))* Candlewick Pr.
Raschka, Chris. A Ball for Daisy. 2012. (CHI & ENG.). 32p. (J). (gr. -1-2). *(978-986-189-345-7(8))* Grimm Cultural Ent., Co., Ltd.
—A Ball for Daisy. 2013. (CHI.). 48p. (J). (gr. -1-2). *(978-7-5414-5730-2(2))* Yunnan Juvenile and Children's Bks. Pr.
—A Ball for Daisy: (Caldecott Medal Winner) Raschka, Chris, illus. (Illus.). (J). (gr. -1-2). 2015. 36p. bds. 8.99 *(978-0-553-53723-9(7))* 2011. 32p. 18.99 *(978-0-375-85861-1(X))* Random Hse. Children's Bks.
Ray, Lynn E. Hallelujah. 2010. (Illus.). 32p. (J). (gr. k-3). 12.95 *(978-1-897476-07-9(8))* Simply Read Bks. CAN. Dist: Ingram Publisher Services.
Rey, H. A. & Rey, Margret. The H. A. Rey Treasury of Stories. 2015. (Dover Children's Classics Ser.). (ENG., Illus.). 112p. (J). (gr. 2-4). pap. 14.99 *(978-0-486-78468-7(1)*, 784681) Dover Pubns., Inc.
Riphagen, Loes, illus. Animals Home Alone. 2011. (ENG.). 32p. (J). (gr. -1-3). 15.95 *(978-1-934734-55-1(1))* Seven Footer Pr.
Robinson, Christian. Another. Robinson, Christian, illus. 2019. (ENG., Illus.). 56p. (J). (gr. -1-3). 17.99 *(978-1-5344-2167-7(X)*, Atheneum Bks. for Young Readers) Simon & Schuster Children's Publishing.
Runton, Andy. Owly & Wormy, Bright Lights & Starry Nights. Runton, Andy, illus. 2012. (ENG., Illus.). 40p. (J). (gr. -1-3). 19.99 *(978-1-4169-5775-1(8)*, Atheneum Bks. for Young Readers) Simon & Schuster Children's Publishing.
—Owly & Wormy, Friends All Aflutter! Runton, Andy, illus. 2011. (ENG., Illus.). 40p. (J). (gr. -1-2). 17.99 *(978-1-4169-5774-4(X)*, Atheneum Bks. for Young Readers) Simon & Schuster Children's Publishing.
Savage, Stephen. Sign Off. Savage, Stephen, illus. 2019. (ENG., Illus.). 56p. (J). (gr. -1-3). 17.99 *(978-1-5344-1210-1(7)*, Beach Lane Bks.) Beach Lane Bks.
Shin, Ami. Mice in the City: London. 2018. (Mice in the City Ser.: 0). (Illus.). 32p. (J). (gr. k-5). 19.95 *(978-0-500-65129-2(9)*, 565129) Thames & Hudson.
—Mice in the City: New York. 2018. (Mice in the City Ser.: 0). (Illus.). 32p. (J). (gr. k-5). 19.95 *(978-0-500-65128-5(0)*, 565128) Thames & Hudson.
Sickler, Jonas, illus. Indestructibles: Frere Jacques: Chew Proof · Rip Proof · Nontoxic · 100% Washable (Book for Babies, Newborn Books, Safe to Chew) 2011. (Indestructibles Ser.). (ENG.). 12p. (J). (gr. -1 — 1). pap. 5.95 *(978-0-7611-5923-0(1)*, 15923) Workman Publishing Co., Inc.
—Indestructibles: Hickory Dickory Dock: Chew Proof · Rip Proof · Nontoxic · 100% Washable (Book for Babies, Newborn Books, Safe to Chew) 2011. (Indestructibles Ser.). (ENG.). 12p. (J). (gr. -1 — 1). pap. 5.95 *(978-0-7611-5921-6(5)*, 15921) Workman Publishing Co., Inc.
Sim, Stephanie. Copycat. 2016. (Illus.). 32p. (J). (gr. -1-2). 16.95 *(978-1-927018-76-7(5))* Simply Read Bks. CAN. Dist: Ingram Publisher Services.
Sima, Jessie. Spencer's New Pet. Sima, Jessie, illus. 2019. (ENG., Illus.). 56p. (J). (gr. -1-3). 17.99 *(978-1-5344-1877-6(6)*, Simon & Schuster Bks. For Young Readers) Simon & Schuster Bks. For Young Readers.
Staake, Bob. Bluebird. Staake, Bob, illus. 2013. (Illus.). 40p. (J). (gr. -1-3). 17.99 *(978-0-375-87037-8(7)*, Schwartz & Wade Bks.) Random Hse. Children's Bks.
Sturm, James. Birdsong: A Story in Pictures. 2016. (Illus.). 60p. (J). (gr. k-1). 12.95 *(978-1-935179-94-8(2)*, TOON Books) Astra Publishing Hse.
Tan, Shaun. The Arrival. Tan, Shaun, illus. 2007. (ENG., Illus.). 128p. (J). (gr. 7-12). 21.99 *(978-0-439-89529-3(4)*, Levine, Arthur A. Bks.) Scholastic, Inc.
—The Arrival. 2007. (J). *(978-0-439-89530-9(8)*, Levine, Arthur A. Bks.) Scholastic, Inc.
Tanaka, Shinsuke, illus. Wings. 2006. (ENG.). 80p. (J). (gr. -1). 14.95 *(978-1-933327-19-8(7))* Purple Bear Bks., Inc.
Tanaka, Yoko. Dandelion's Dream. Tanaka, Yoko, illus. 2020. (ENG., Illus.). 40p. (J). (gr. -1-2). 16.99 *(978-1-5362-0453-7(6))* Candlewick Pr.
Thomson, Bill. Chalk, 0 vols. Thomson, Bill, illus. 2012. (ENG., Illus.). 40p. (J). (gr. -1-2). 15.99 *(978-0-7614-5526-4(4)*, 9780761455264, Two Lions) Amazon Publishing.
Timmers, Leo. Monkey on the Run. Timmers, Leo, illus. 2019. (ENG., Illus.). 32p. (J). (gr. -1-k). 17.99 *(978-1-77657-250-2(5)*, e8b6aeda-6b84-4a21-8ff1-5de56aa08dfb) Gecko Pr. NZL. Dist: Lerner Publishing Group.
Turkowski, Einar, illus. Houses Floating Home. 2016. (ENG.). 32p. (J). (gr. -1-3). 16.95 *(978-1-59270-183-4(3))* Enchanted Lion Bks., LLC.
Ukhova, Tatiana, illus. Grasshopper. 2021. (Aldana Libros Ser.). 56p. (J). (gr. -1-2). 18.95 *(978-1-77164-692-5(6)*, Greystone Kids) Greystone Books Ltd. CAN. Dist: Publishers Group West (PGW).
Valério, Geraldo. Blue Rider, 1 vol. 2018. (Illus.). 44p. (J). (gr. -1-2). 19.95 *(978-1-55498-981-2(7))* Groundwood Bks. CAN. Dist: Publishers Group West (PGW).
—Turn on the Night, 1 vol. 2016. (ENG., Illus.). 40p. (J). (gr. -1). 19.99 *(978-1-55498-841-9(1))* Groundwood Bks. CAN. Dist: Publishers Group West (PGW).
Valério, Geraldo & Valério, Geraldo. Blue Rider. Valério, Geraldo & Valério, Geraldo, illus. 2018. (ENG., Illus.). 44p. E-Book *(978-1-55498-982-9(5))* Groundwood Bks.
Van den Ende, Peter. The Wanderer. 2020. (ENG., Illus.). 96p. (J). (gr. 3-9). 21.99 *(978-1-64614-017-6(6))* Levine Querido.
Varon, Sara. Robot Dreams. Varon, Sara, illus. 2016. (ENG., Illus.). 224p. (J). pap. 14.99 *(978-1-250-07350-1(2)*, 900150780) Square Fish.
Wiesner, David. Free Fall. Wiesner, David, illus. 2008. (ENG., Illus.). 32p. (J). (gr. -1-3). 17.99 *(978-0-06-156741-4(8)*, HarperCollins) HarperCollins Pubs.
—I Got It! Wiesner, David, illus. 2018. (ENG., Illus.). 32p. (J). (gr. -1-3). 17.99 *(978-0-544-30902-9(2)*, 1581567, Clarion Bks.) HarperCollins Pubs.
Young, Cybèle. Out the Window, 1 vol. 2013. (ENG., Illus.). 30p. (J). (gr. -1 — 1). bds. 12.95 *(978-1-55498-370-4(3))* Groundwood Bks. CAN. Dist: Publishers Group West (PGW).
Zoboli, Giovanna. Professional Crocodile: (Wordless Kids Books, Alligator Children's Books, Early Elemetary Story Books) Di Giorgio, Mariachiara, illus. 2017. (ENG.). 32p. (J). (gr. k-3). 17.99 *(978-1-4521-6506-6(8))* Chronicle Bks. LLC.

STORKS

Best, Arthur. Storks, 1 vol. 2018. (Migrating Animals Ser.). (ENG.). 24p. (J). (gr. 1-1). 27.36 *(978-1-5026-3721-5(9)*, e0e00784-e9b8-43fc-ba12-503f75d11476) Cavendish Square Publishing LLC.
Gish, Melissa. Storks. (Living Wild Ser.). (ENG.). 48p. (J). 2016. (gr. 5-9). pap. 12.00 *(978-1-62832-172-2(5)*, 20902, Creative Paperbacks) 2015. (Illus.). (gr. 4-7). *(978-1-60818-571-9(0)*, 20901, Creative Education) Creative Co., The.
Otfinoski, Steven. Cranes & Storks, 1 vol. 2010. (Animals, Animals Ser.). (ENG.). 48p. (gr. 5-5). 32.64 *(978-0-7614-3973-8(0)*, 46445512-9ff9-442e-8ace-27011c6e973d) Cavendish Square Publishing LLC.
Riggs, Kate. Amazing Animals: Storks. 2017. (Amazing Animals Ser.). (ENG., Illus.). 24p. (J). (gr. 1-3). pap. 9.99 *(978-1-62832-366-5(3)*, 20048, Creative Paperbacks) Creative Co., The.
—Storks. 2017. (Amazing Animals Ser.). (ENG., Illus.). 24p. (J). (gr. 1-4). *(978-1-60818-758-4(6)*, 20050, Creative Education) Creative Co., The.
World Book, Inc. Staff, contrib. by. Storks & Other Large Wading Birds. 2005. (World Book's Animals of the World Ser.). (Illus.). 64p. (J). *(978-0-7166-1267-4(4))* World Bk., Inc.

—World Book's Animals of the World Set 4. 2005. (World Book's Animals of the World Ser.). (Illus.). 64p. (gr. 2-8). 189.00 (978-0-7166-1261-2(5)) World Bk., Inc.

STORKS—FICTION

Award, Anna, et al. The Fox & the Stork & the Man, His Son & the Donkey. 2014. (ENG.). 24p. (J). pap. 6.95 (978-1-84135-955-7(6)) Award Pubns. Ltd. GBR. Dist: Parkwest Pubns., Inc.

Drescher, Henrik. The Strange Appearance of Howard Cranebill. 2006. (ENG., Illus.). 32p. (J). (gr. -1-1). (978-1-59692-134-4(X)) MacAdam/Cage Publishing, Inc.

Frisch, Wilhelmine. The Storks of Lillegaard. Jauss, Anne Marie, illus. 2011. 230p. 46.95 (978-1-258-08105-8(9)) Literary Licensing, LLC.

McDermott, Gerald. The Fox & the Stork. McDermott, Gerald, illus. 2003. (ENG., Illus.). 24p. (J). (gr. -1-3). pap. 4.99 (978-0-15-204837-2(5), 1194607, Clarion Bks.) HarperCollins Pubs.

Penovi, Celina. The Clumsy Stork - la Cigüeña Despistad. 2009. 32p. pap. 17.50 (978-1-4490-2746-9(6)) AuthorHouse.

Phillips, Dixie & Snider, K. C. Stilts the Stork. 2011. 20p. pap. 10.95 (978-1-61633-143-6(7)) Guardian Angel Publishing, Inc.

Tedesco, Tina. The Stork Dropped Your Here for a Reason. 2006. (J). pap. 8.00 (978-0-8059-7233-7(1)) Dorrance Publishing Co., Inc.

STORMS

see also Hurricanes; Meteorology; Rain and Rainfall; Snow; Thunderstorms; Tornadoes; Winds

also other kinds of storms

Aarons, Jacob. Stormy Weather. 2005. (Illus.). 20p. (J). (978-0-328-13452-6(X), Scott Foresman) Addison-Wesley Educational Pubs., Inc.

Aboff, Marcie. Tornadoes!, 1 vol. Sotirovski, Aleksandar, illus. 2012. (First Graphics: Wild Earth Ser.). (ENG.). 24p. (J). (gr. k-3). lib. bdg. 24.65 (978-1-4296-7608-3(6), 117205) Capstone.

Ahearn, Dan & Ahearn, Janet. Storm Chasers. 2011. (Navigators Ser.). (J). pap. (978-1-61672-961-5(9)) Benchmark Education Co.

Amidon Lusted, Marcia, ed. Extreme Weather Events, 1 vol. 2017. (Global Viewpoints Ser.). (ENG.). 224p. (gr. 10-12). pap. 32.70 (978-1-5345-0112-6(6), ea23cf0a-6adb-4fa8-b89b-df88a318fa2a); lib. bdg. 47.83 (978-1-5345-0114-0(2), 2c6cd297-67f1-4e18-802c-0baca96f0b89) Greenhaven Publishing LLC.

Appleby, Alex. It's Stormy!, 1 vol. 2013. (What's the Weather? Ser.). (Illus.). 24p. (J). (gr. k-k). (ENG.). pap. 9.15 (978-1-4339-9405-0(4), dac5a8a5-20d7-4865-af7e-bac5a4525e1e); (ENG., lib. bdg. 25.27 (978-1-4339-9404-3(6), af3958a4-fa27-4cb9-bb36-d2c567bf69ba); pap. 48.90 (978-1-4339-9406-7(2)) Stevens, Gareth Publishing LLLP.

—It's Stormy! / ¡Es una Tormenta!, 1 vol. 2013. (What's the Weather? / ¿Qué Tiempo Hace? Ser.). (ENG & SPA., Illus.). 24p. (J). (gr. k-k). lib. bdg. 25.27 (978-1-4339-9456-2(9), 881e49f6-4583-44dd-911a-54ab9d049a5b) Stevens, Gareth Publishing LLLP.

Ball, Jacqueline A. Blizzard! The 1888 Whiteout. 2005. (X-Treme Disasters That Changed America Ser.). (Illus.). 32p. (J). (gr. 2-5). lib. bdg. 25.27 (978-1-59716-006-3(7)) Bearport Publishing Co., Inc.

Benchmark Education Company. The Power of Storms (Teacher Guide) 2005. (978-1-4108-4636-5(9)) Benchmark Education Co.

Benchmark Education Company, LLC Staff, compiled by. Storms: Theme Set. 2006. (J). 109.00 (978-1-4108-7080-3(4)) Benchmark Education Co.

Berger, Melvin & Berger, Gilda. Hurricanes Have Eyes but Can't See: And Other Amazing Facts about Wild Weather. 2003. (Illus.). 48p. (J). (978-0-439-54980-6(9)) Scholastic, Inc.

Blizzards. 3rd ed. 2018. (J). (978-0-7166-9929-3(X)) World Bk., Inc.

Bowman, Chris. Survive a Blizzard. 2016. (Survival Zone Ser.). (ENG., Illus.). 24p. (J). (gr. 3-7). 26.95 (978-1-62617-441-2(5), Torque Bks.) Bellwether Media.

—Survive a Tornado. 2016. (Survival Zone Ser.). (ENG., Illus.). 24p. (J). (gr. 3-7). 26.95 (978-1-62617-444-3(X), Torque Bks.) Bellwether Media.

Brannon, Barbara. Discover Storms. 2005. (J). pap. (978-1-4108-5124-6(9)) Benchmark Education Co.

Brinker, Spencer. A Stormy Day. 2018. (Weather Watch Ser.). (ENG., Illus.). 16p. (J). (gr. -1-1). 6.99 (978-1-64280-137-8(2)); 16.96 (978-1-64280-000-5(7)) Bearport Publishing Co., Inc.

Bryan, Dale-Marie. Tornadoes. 2013. (Earth in Action Ser.). (ENG., Illus.). 48p. (J). (gr. 4-8). pap. 18.50 (978-1-62403-005-5(X), 8680) ABDO Publishing Co.

Bullard, Lisa. Blizzards. 2015. (Pull Ahead Books — Forces of Nature Ser.). (ENG., Illus.). 32p. (J). (gr. k-3). E-Book 46.65 (978-1-5124-1047-1(0), Lerner Pubns.) Lerner Publishing Group.

Bundey, Nikki. Storms & People. 2005. (Science of Weather Ser.). (Illus.). 32p. (gr. 4-6). lib. bdg. 21.27 (978-1-57505-499-5(X)) Lerner Publishing Group.

Cain, Marie Mowery. Storm Watch. 2013. (Big Books, Red Ser.). (ENG & SPA., Illus.). 16p. pap. 33.00 (978-1-59246-214-8(6)) Big Books, by George!

Canavan, Roger. You Wouldn't Want to Live Without Extreme Weather! 2015. (You Wouldn't Want to Live Without Ser.). lib. bdg. 20.80 (978-0-606-36711-0(X)) Turtleback.

—You Wouldn't Want to Live Without Extreme Weather! (You Wouldn't Want to Live Without...) Bergin, Mark, illus. 2015. (You Wouldn't Want to Live Without... Ser.). (ENG.). 32p. (J). (gr. 3). pap. 9.95 (978-0-531-21408-4(7), Watts, Franklin) Scholastic Library Publishing.

Canizares, Susan & Chessen, Betsey. Storms: Tormentas. 2004. (Science Emergent Readers Ser.). (ENG & SPA., Illus.). (J). (978-0-439-66392-2(X)) Scholastic, Inc.

Cernak, Linda. The Science of a Tornado. 2015. (21st Century Skills Library: Disaster Science Ser.). (ENG., Illus.). 32p. (J). (gr. 4-8). 32.07 (978-1-63362-482-5(X), 206836) Cherry Lake Publishing.

Challen, Paul. Hurricane & Typhoon Alert! 3rd rev. ed. 2011. (Disaster Alert! Ser.: No. 17). (ENG., Illus.). 32p. (J). (gr. 3-6). pap. (978-0-7787-1626-6(0)) Crabtree Publishing Co.

Connell, Kate. Hoping for Rain: The Dust Bowl Adventures of Patty & Earl Buckler. 2004. (I Am American Ser.). (Illus.). 40p. (J). (gr. 3-7). pap. 6.99 (978-0-7922-6903-8(9), National Geographic Children's Bks.) Disney Publishing Worldwide.

David, Alex. Swept Away: Escalating Storms & Disasters, 1 vol. 2019. (Taking Action on Climate Change Ser.). (ENG.). 64p. (gr. 6-6). pap. 16.28 (978-1-5026-5234-8(X), c9264b2c-3909-4e41-8ad4-3650193a872a) Cavendish Square Publishing LLC.

Davies, Jon. Storm Chasers! on the Trail of Twisters. Rath, Robert, illus. Davies, Jon & Reed, Jim, photos by. 2007. 48p. (J). (gr. 3-7). pap. 12.95 (978-1-56037-407-7(1)) Farcountry Pr.

Donnelly, Karen. Storms of the Past & the Future. 2009. (Earth's Changing Weather & Climate Ser.). 24p. (gr. 4-4). 42.50 (978-1-61512-250-9(8), PowerKids Pr.) Rosen Publishing Group, Inc., The.

Doudna, Kelly. It Is Stormy, 1 vol. 2003. (Weather Ser.). (ENG., Illus.). 24p. (J). (gr. k-3). lib. bdg. 24.21 (978-1-57765-776-7(4), SandCastle) ABDO Publishing Co.

Doudna, Kelly & Craig, Diane. Winter Storm or Blizzard?, 1 vol. 2015. (This or That? Weather Ser.). (ENG., Illus.). 24p. (J). (gr. k-4). 32.79 (978-1-62403-958-4(8), 19572, Super SandCastle) ABDO Publishing Co.

Dougherty, Terri. The Worst Tornadoes of All Time, 1 vol. 2012. (Epic Disasters Ser.). (ENG.). 32p. (J). (gr. 3-9). pap. 8.29 (978-1-4296-8015-8(6), 118347); lib. bdg. 28.65 (978-1-4296-7660-1(4), 117257) Capstone. (Capstone Pr.).

Dreier, David. Be a Storm Chaser. 2008. (Scienceworks! Ser.). (Illus.). 32p. (gr. 3-5). lib. bdg. 26.00 (978-0-8368-8929-1(0)) Stevens, Gareth Publishing LLLP.

Dreier, David Louis. Be a Storm Chaser. 2008. (Scienceworks! Ser.). 32p. pap. 8.95 (978-0-8368-8936-9(3)) Stevens, Gareth Publishing LLLP.

Faidley, Warren, Jr. How to Survive Any Storm: Severe Weather Handbook. 2003. (Illus.). 213p. spiral bd. 17.95 (978-0-9728107-0-8(6)) Weatherstock, Inc.

Fleisher, Paul. Lightning, Hurricanes, & Blizzards: The Science of Storms. 2010. (Weatherwise Ser.). (ENG., Illus.). 48p. (J). (gr. 4-8). lib. bdg. 29.27 (978-0-8225-7536-8(1)) Lerner Publishing Group.

Furgang, Adam. Adapting to Intense Storms, 1 vol. 2012. (Science to the Rescue: Adapting to Climate Change Ser.). (ENG.). 64p. (YA). (gr. 5-5). lib. bdg. 37.13 (978-1-4488-6848-3(3), c045314e-926b-4937-bc06-968d50fa9119, Rosen Reference) Rosen Publishing Group, Inc., The.

Garbe, Suzanne. Threatening Skies: History's Most Dangerous Weather, 1 vol. 2013. (Dangerous History Ser.). (ENG.). 32p. (J). (gr. 3-9). 28.65 (978-1-4765-0128-4(9), 122205, Capstone Pr.) Capstone.

Garland, Sherry. Voices of the Dust Bowl, 1 vol. Hierstein, Judith, illus. 2012. (Voices of History Ser.). (ENG.). 40p. (J). (gr. 3-3). 19.99 (978-1-58980-964-2(5), Pelican Publishing) Arcadia Publishing.

Gifford, Clive. Chasing the World's Most Dangerous Storms. 2010. (Extreme! Ser.). (ENG.). 32p. (gr. 3-4). pap. 47.70 (978-1-4296-5123-3(7), Capstone Pr.) Capstone.

Gleason, Carrie. Ocean Storm Alert! 2004. (Disaster Alert! Ser.). (ENG., Illus.). 32p. (J). pap. (978-0-7787-1611-2(2)) Crabtree Publishing Co.

Goin, Miriam Busch. National Geographic Readers: Storms! 2009. (Readers Ser.). (ENG., Illus.). 32p. (J). (gr. -1-k). lib. bdg. 14.90 (978-1-4263-0395-1(5), National Geographic Children's Bks.) Disney Publishing Worldwide.

—Storms. 2009. (Readers Ser.). (Illus.). 32p. (J). (gr. -1-k). 5.99 (978-1-4263-0394-4(7), National Geographic Kids) Disney Publishing Worldwide.

—Storms (1 Hardcover/1 CD) 2016. (National Geographic Readers: Pre-Reader Ser.). (ENG.). (J). (978-1-4301-2125-1(4)) Live Oak Media.

—Storms (1 Paperback/1 CD) 2016. (National Geographic Readers: Pre-Reader Ser.). (ENG.). (J). pap. (978-1-4301-2124-4(6)) Live Oak Media.

Gray, Susan H. Storm Chaser. 2015. (21st Century Skills Library: Cool STEAM Careers Ser.). (ENG., Illus.). 32p. (J). (gr. 4-7). 32.07 (978-1-63362-565-5(6), 206444) Cherry Lake Publishing.

Group/McGraw-Hill, Wright. Savage Storms: Tornadoes & Hurricanes, 6 vols. (Book2WebTM Ser.). (gr. 4-8). 36.50 (978-0-322-04424-1(3)) Wright Group/McGraw-Hill.

Hamen, Susan E. The 12 Worst Hurricanes of All Time. 2019. (All-Time Worst Disasters Ser.). (ENG., Illus.). 32p. (J). (gr. 3-6). 32.80 (978-1-63235-538-6(8), 13912, 12-Story Library) Bookstaves, LLC.

Harcourt School Publishers Staff. When Storm Library Book Grade K: Harcourt School Publishers Storytown. 2009. pap. 8.75 (978-0-15-352482-0(0)) Harcourt Schl. Pubs.

Hardyman, Robyn. Snow & Blizzards, 1 vol. 2010. (Weatherwise Ser.). (ENG.). 32p. (gr. 4-4). (J). pap. 11.60 (978-1-61532-276-3(0), 2d8ff99c-cf67-4dd0-ab0d-11cdede007be, PowerKids Pr.); (Illus.). (YA). lib. bdg. 30.27 (978-1-61532-264-0(7), fbb7146e-10e9-4997-905e-daed24d6bd1f) Rosen Publishing Group, Inc., The.

—Wind & Storms, 1 vol. 2010. (Weatherwise Ser.). (ENG.). 32p. (gr. 4-4). (J). pap. 11.60 (978-1-61532-282-4(5), 451a6f1b-4ce1-4d0e-8b3c-b843c3234799, PowerKids Pr.); (Illus.). (YA). lib. bdg. 30.27 (978-1-61532-267-1(1), a27bc644-0045-4ae3-83f3-85c6303f9421) Rosen Publishing Group, Inc., The.

Honders, Christine. Chasing Extreme Weather, 1 vol. 2018. (Spotlight on Weather & Natural Disasters Ser.). (ENG.). 24p. (gr. 4-6). 27.93 (978-1-5081-6876-8(8), 096b4c8a-990e-4504-9cd3-edb0ab25b6ce, PowerKids Pr.) Rosen Publishing Group, Inc., The.

Hurricanes, Typhoons, & Other Tropical Cyclones. 2nd ed. 2009. (Illus.). 47p. (J). (978-0-7166-9824-1(2)) World Bk., Inc.

Jeffrey, Gary. Hurricane Hunters & Tornado Chasers. 2009. (Graphic Careers Ser.). (ENG.). 48p. (YA). (gr. 5-5). 58.50 (978-1-61512-885-3(9), Rosen Reference) Rosen Publishing Group, Inc., The.

—Hurricane Hunters & Tornado Chasers, 1 vol. Garofalo, Gianluca, illus. 2008. (Graphic Careers Ser.). (ENG.). 48p. (gr. 5-5). per. 14.05 (978-1-4042-1459-0(3), d963ad23-fe8f-4c78-8a53-dcb6c4522b93); (YA). lib. bdg. 37.13 (978-1-4042-1458-3(5), 3486897e-4cf0-4e1a-83f8-3b59a796e2cf) Rosen Publishing Group, Inc., The.

—Tornadoes & Superstorms. 2007. (Graphic Natural Disasters Ser.). (ENG.). 48p. (YA). 58.50 (978-1-4488-1667-5(X), Rosen Reference) Rosen Publishing Group, Inc., The.

—Tornadoes & Superstorms, 1 vol. Riley, Terry, illus. 2007. (Graphic Natural Disasters Ser.). (ENG.). 48p. (gr. 5-5). (J). lib. bdg. 37.13 (978-1-4042-1993-9(5), 341abb57-9639-4eda-b52c-cd55d0121d81); pap. 14.05 (978-1-4042-1985-4(4), 47b4b752-3b70-4880-a791-75d17e2d453d) Rosen Publishing Group, Inc., The.

Jensen, Belinda. A Snowstorm Shows Off: Blizzards. Kurilla, Renée, illus. 2016. (Bel the Weather Girl Ser.). (ENG.). 24p. (J). (gr. -1-3). 25.32 (978-1-4677-7961-6(X), a318c34f-545c-4d7f-aede-2411c622631b, Millbrook Pr.) Lerner Publishing Group.

—Spinning Wind & Water: Hurricanes. Kurilla, Renée, illus. 2016. (Bel the Weather Girl Ser.). (ENG.). 24p. (J). (gr. -1-3). 25.32 (978-1-4677-7962-3(8), f8fc79b6-57bb-436f-8756-f114371a326a, Millbrook Pr.) Lerner Publishing Group.

Johnson, Robin. What Is a Blizzard? 2016. (ENG., Illus.). 24p. (J). (978-0-7787-2395-0(X)) Crabtree Publishing Co.

Kallio, Jamie. 12 Things to Know about Wild Weather. 2015. (Today's News Ser.). (ENG., Illus.). 32p. (J). (gr. 3-6). 32.80 (978-1-63235-035-0(1), 11613, 12-Story Library) Bookstaves, LLC.

Kesselring, Susan. With Weather. 2018. (J). pap. (978-1-4896-9980-0(5), AV2 by Weigl) Weigl Pubs., Inc.

Kliman, Gilbert, et al. My Personal Story about Tropical Storm Stan: A Guided Activity Workbook for Children, Adolescents & Families. 2006. (Illus.). spiral bd. 19.00 (978-0-9790846-8-3(7)) Children's Psychological Health Ctr., Inc., The.

KociendaGenevieve. BLIZZARDS: KILLER SNOWSTORM BEGINNING BOOK WITH ONLINE ACCESS, 1 vol. 2014. (ENG., Illus.). 24p. pap., E-Book 9.50 (978-1-107-62164-0(X)) Cambridge Univ. Pr.

Koontz, Robin. The Science of a Tsunami. 2015. (21st Century Skills Library: Disaster Science Ser.). (ENG., Illus.). 32p. (J). (gr. 4-8). 32.07 (978-1-63362-483-2(8), 206840) Cherry Lake Publishing.

Kosara, Tori. Wild Weather Around the World. 2010. (Illus.). 46p. (J). pap. (978-0-545-32147-1(6)) Scholastic, Inc.

Kostigen, Thomas M. Extreme Weather: Surviving Tornadoes, Sandstorms, Hailstorms, Blizzards, Hurricanes, & More! 2014. (Illus.). 112p. (J). (gr. 3-7). pap. 12.99 (978-1-4263-1811-5(1), National Geographic Kids) Disney Publishing Worldwide.

Krajnik, Elizabeth. Clouds & Precipitation, 1 vol. 2018. (Spotlight on Weather & Natural Disasters Ser.). (ENG.). 24p. (gr. 4-6). 27.93 (978-1-5081-6886-7(5), 1c1c38a9-e9f6-484e-9104-c5b221ce6723, PowerKids Pr.) Rosen Publishing Group, Inc., The.

Levey, Richard H. Dust Bowl! The 1930s Black Blizzards. 2005. (X-Treme Disasters That Changed America Ser.). 32p. (J). lib. bdg. 28.50 (978-1-59716-007-0(5)) Bearport Publishing Co., Inc.

Levy, Janey. World's Worst Hurricanes, 1 vol. 2008. (Deadly Disasters Ser.). (ENG., Illus.). 24p. (J). (gr. 2-3). lib. bdg. 26.27 (978-1-4042-4511-2(1), 04f06595-bdd4-4033-8951-c9130def6779, PowerKids Pr.) Rosen Publishing Group, Inc., The.

Lew, Kristi. Hurricanes, 1 vol. 2018. (Nature's Mysteries Ser.). (ENG.). 32p. (gr. 2-3). pap. 13.90 (978-1-5081-0650-0(9), 35b43dfc-7643-4172-a88f-8a1d53ed96aa, Britannica Educational Publishing) Rosen Publishing Group, Inc., The.

Linde, Barbara M. The Power of Storms. 2005. (J). pap. (978-1-4108-4588-7(5)) Benchmark Education Co.

—When Floods Flow, 1 vol. 2015. (Eye on the Sky Ser.). (ENG., Illus.). 32p. (J). (gr. 3-4). pap. 11.50 (978-1-4824-2880-3(6), 32262a6d-ba82-4adb-9013-f4ae0e9c21ce) Stevens, Gareth Publishing LLLP.

Lusted, Marcia Amidon. The 12 Worst Tornadoes of All Time. 2019. (All-Time Worst Disasters Ser.). (ENG., Illus.). 32p. (J). (gr. 3-6). 32.80 (978-1-63235-541-6(8), 13915, 12-Story Library) Bookstaves, LLC.

MacAulay, Kelley & Kalman, Bobbie. Cambios del Estado del Tiempo: Las Tormentas. 2006. (Libro de Bobbie Kalman Ser.). (SPA & ENG., Illus.). 32p. (J). (gr. 3-7). pap. (978-0-7787-8390-9(1)); lib. bdg. (978-0-7787-8376-3(6)) Crabtree Publishing Co.

—Changing Weather: Storms, 1 vol. 2006. (Nature's Changes Ser.). (ENG., Illus.). 32p. (J). (gr. 4-7). pap. (978-0-7787-2314-1(3)) Crabtree Publishing Co.

—Les Tempêtes. Briere, Marie-Josee, tr. from ENG. 2007. (Petit Monde Vivant Ser.). (FRE., Illus.). 32p. (J). (gr. 4-7). pap. 9.95 (978-2-89579-166-9(X)) Bayard Canada Livres CAN. Dist: Crabtree Publishing Co.

Maloof, Torrey. Extreme Weather, 1 vol. 2015. (Science: Informational Text Ser.). (ENG., Illus.). 32p. (J). (gr. 3-4). pap. 11.99 (978-1-4807-4647-3(9)) Teacher Created Materials, Inc.

Manolis, Kay. Blizzards. 2008. (Extreme Weather Ser.). (ENG., Illus.). 24p. (J). (gr. 2-5). lib. bdg. 26.95 (978-1-60014-183-6(8)) Bellwether Media.

Markovics, Joyce. Blizzard. 2014. (It's a Disaster! Ser.). 24p. (J). (gr. -1-3). lib. bdg. 26.99 (978-1-62724-125-0(6)) Bearport Publishing Co., Inc.

Markovics, Joyce L. Blitzed by a Blizzard! 2010. (Disaster Survivors Ser.). (Illus.). 32p. (YA). (gr. 4-7). lib. bdg. 28.50 (978-1-936087-54-9(5)) Bearport Publishing Co., Inc.

—Tormenta de Nieve. 2014. (Pedacitos Primeros Lectores: Que Desastre! Ser.). (SPA., Illus.). 24p. (J). (gr. -1-2). lib. bdg. 26.99 (978-1-62724-245-5(7)) Bearport Publishing Co., Inc.

Marquardt, Meg. The Science of a Flood. 2015. (21st Century Skills Library: Disaster Science Ser.). (ENG., Illus.). 32p. (J). (gr. 4-8). 32.07 (978-1-63362-479-5(X), 206824) Cherry Lake Publishing.

Marrin, Albert. Years of Dust: The Story of the Dust Bowl. 2013. (Illus.). 128p. (J). (gr. 5-8). 26.19 (978-0-525-42077-4(0), Dutton) Penguin Publishing Group.

Mattern, Joanne. The Science of Blizzards. 2019. (Science of Natural Disasters Ser.). (ENG.). 32p. (J). (gr. 3-3). 63.48 (978-1-5026-4639-2(0)) Cavendish Square Publishing LLC.

Maurer, Daniel D. Do You Really Want to Drive in a Blizzard? A Book about Predicting Weather. Alberini, Teresa, illus. 2016. (Adventures in Science Ser.). (ENG.). 24p. (J). (gr. 1-4). lib. bdg. 20.95 (978-1-60753-959-9(4), 15630) Amicus.

McAneney, Caitie. Slammed by Tsunamis, 1 vol. 2017. (Natural Disasters: How People Survive Ser.). (ENG.). 32p. (J). (gr. 4-5). 27.93 (978-1-5383-2565-0(9), 333a1fdc-e3f0-4fcd-8396-16a0f865798f, PowerKids Pr.) Rosen Publishing Group, Inc., The.

Meister, Cari. Blizzards. 2015. (Illus.). 24p. (J). lib. bdg. (978-1-62031-223-0(9)) Jump! Inc.

Mezzanotte, Jim. Dust Storms, 1 vol. (Wild Weather Ser.). (ENG.). 24p. 2009. (J). (gr. 1-1). pap. 9.15 (978-1-4339-2360-9(2), 0bd55f2d-5da4-40e7-b594-752bf4f94b0a) 2009. (J). (gr. 1-1). lib. bdg. 24.67 (978-1-4339-2346-3(7), b5328a0c-7870-4ee9-912d-029bea16e20e) 2007. (Illus.). (gr. 2-4). pap. 9.15 (978-0-8368-7918-6(X), 11063505-9ed7-4520-8bc7-419d6ed29936) 2007. (Illus.). (gr. 2-4). lib. bdg. 24.67 (978-0-8368-7911-7(2), 3e416a46-3806-4131-8a3d-9dfa87234e7f) Stevens, Gareth Publishing LLLP. (Weekly Reader Leveled Readers).

—Granizadas (Hailstorms), 1 vol. 2009. (Tiempo Extremo (Wild Weather) Ser.). (SPA.). 24p. (J). (gr. 1-1). pap. 9.15 (978-1-4339-2367-8(X), 97909ca7-3a7b-4e66-b729-635f28b2ca28); lib. bdg. 24.67 (978-1-4339-2353-1(X), cae0619f-6e67-4427-875e-e848e798b2b8) Stevens, Gareth Publishing LLLP. (Weekly Reader Leveled Readers).

—Hailstorms, 1 vol. (Wild Weather Ser.). (ENG.). 24p. 2009. (J). (gr. 1-1). pap. 9.15 (978-1-4339-2361-6(0), 1147c993-a3c4-4271-96c1-6b29805cb104) 2009. (J). (gr. 1-1). lib. bdg. 24.67 (978-1-4339-2347-0(5), ae9ec1b6-6cb0-4c62-b901-0863cacbc0b8) 2007. (Illus.). (gr. 2-4). pap. 9.15 (978-0-8368-7919-3(8), 3391e91e-6f87-4a69-9e5f-f8508ea34863) 2007. (Illus.). (gr. 2-4). lib. bdg. 24.67 (978-0-8368-7912-4(0), f29d489b-6b47-48f2-8e3d-357b0ea206b7) Stevens, Gareth Publishing LLLP. (Weekly Reader Leveled Readers).

—Snowstorms, 1 vol. (Wild Weather Ser.). (ENG.). 24p. 2009. (J). (gr. 1-1). pap. 9.15 (978-1-4339-2363-0(7), 3caa3f09-31a3-4aed-afd2-604dbdb6f6db) 2009. (J). (gr. 1-1). lib. bdg. 24.67 (978-1-4339-2349-4(1), 452d2527-346c-46dd-95a0-1e051f1b8e0c) 2007. (Illus.). (gr. 2-4). pap. 9.15 (978-0-8368-7921-6(X), 84092193-a3c6-4663-8686-7064682cc6fd) 2007. (Illus.). (gr. 2-4). lib. bdg. 24.67 (978-0-8368-7914-8(7), 6ffa4e36-9b6d-417e-8b7d-4150850e2d31) Stevens, Gareth Publishing LLLP. (Weekly Reader Leveled Readers).

—Tormentas de Nieve (Snowstorms), 1 vol. (Tiempo Extremo (Wild Weather) Ser.). (SPA.). 24p. 2009. (J). (gr. 1-1). pap. 9.15 (978-1-4339-2369-2(6), d12b2498-a5c3-46d1-8990-2dfd74749352) 2009. (J). (gr. 1-1). lib. bdg. 24.67 (978-1-4339-2355-5(6), 065511a9-3387-48eb-a35c-0e8fc55b40cc) 2007. (Illus.). (gr. 2-4). pap. 9.15 (978-0-8368-8079-3(X), 94231bdb-ce11-45b6-bb73-c0c0f9af9754) 2007. (Illus.). (gr. 2-4). lib. bdg. 24.67 (978-0-8368-8072-4(2), 131659b7-ab35-44f7-b822-7405b2e3b596) Stevens, Gareth Publishing LLLP. (Weekly Reader Leveled Readers).

—Tormentas de Polvo (Dust Storms), 1 vol. (Tiempo Extremo (Wild Weather) Ser.). (SPA.). 24p. 2009. (J). (gr. 1-1). pap. 9.15 (978-1-4339-2370-8(X), 4fe9557f-572c-4c06-a99d-aac329d3a13a) 2009. (J). (gr. 1-1). lib. bdg. 24.67 (978-1-4339-2356-2(4), e7fa52f7-4460-4f17-b88d-39b30ca14a17) 2007. (Illus.). (gr. 2-4). pap. 9.15 (978-0-8368-8080-9(3), 49c222a9-6e06-4494-a71a-dbb46d7b19f6) 2007. (Illus.). (gr. 2-4). lib. bdg. 24.67 (978-0-8368-8073-1(0), df04998f-0d01-4268-9530-fc34160df517) Stevens, Gareth Publishing LLLP. (Weekly Reader Leveled Readers).

National Geographic Learning. Reading Expeditions (Science: Earth Science): Extreme Weather. 2007. (ENG., Illus.). 32p. (J). pap. 18.95 (978-0-7922-4575-9(X)) CENGAGE Learning.

Osborne, Mary Pope. Twisters & Other Terrible Storms: A Nonfiction Companion to Magic Tree House #23: Twister on Tuesday. Osborne, Will & Murdocca, Sal, illus. 2003. (Magic Tree House (R) Fact Tracker Ser.: 8). 128p. (J). (gr. 2-5). 6.99 (978-0-375-81358-0(6), Random Hse. Bks. for Young Readers) Random Hse. Children's Bks.

Pattison, Darcy. Prairie Storms, 1 vol. Rietz, Kathleen, illus. 2011. (ENG.). 32p. (J). (gr. -1-4). 16.95 (978-1-60718-129-3(0)); pap. 8.95 (978-1-60718-139-2(8)) Arbordale Publishing.

Peppas, Lynn. Severe Storm & Blizzard Alert! 2004. (Disaster Alert! Ser.). (ENG., Illus.). 32p. (J). pap. (978-0-7787-1605-1(8)); lib. bdg. (978-0-7787-1573-3(6)) Crabtree Publishing Co.

Perdew, Laura. The 12 Worst Floods of All Time. 2019. (All-Time Worst Disasters Ser.). (ENG., Illus.). 32p. (J). (gr. 3-6). 32.80 (978-1-63235-536-2(1), 13910, 12-Story Library) Bookstaves, LLC.

Perish, Patrick. Survive a Hurricane. 2016. (Survival Zone Ser.). (ENG., Illus.). 24p. (J). (gr. 3-7). 26.95 (978-1-62617-443-6(1), Torque Bks.) Bellwether Media.

—Survive a Tsunami. 2016. (Survival Zone Ser.). (ENG., Illus.). 24p. (J). (gr. 3-7). 26.95 (978-1-62617-445-0(8), Torque Bks.) Bellwether Media.

Pettiford, Rebecca. Ice Storms. 2020. (Natural Disasters Ser.). (ENG.). 24p. (J). (gr. k-3). lib. bdg. 26.95 (978-1-64487-152-2(1), Blastoff! Readers) Bellwether Media.

Portman, Michael. Blinding Blizzards, 1 vol. 2012. (Angry Earth Ser.). (ENG.). 32p. (gr. 3-4). (J). pap. 11.50 (978-1-4339-6531-9(3), eb9ea03f-20dd-4155-bd12-413d4464b129, Gareth Stevens Learning Library); (YA). lib. bdg. 29.27 (978-1-4339-6529-6(1), 186a103e-9515-4051-a747-8621ab236ed6) Stevens, Gareth Publishing LLLP.

Rajczak, Michael. Deadly Droughts. 2016. (Where's the Water? Ser.). (ENG.). 24p. (J). (gr. -1-3). 18.95 *(978-1-5311-8605-0(X))* Perfection Learning Corp.
—Deadly Droughts, 1 vol. 2016. (Where's the Water? Ser.). (ENG., Illus.). 24p. (J). (gr. 2-3). pap. 9.15 *(978-1-4824-4680-7(4),* bd1edc76-aa0c-433b-8894-5a405dc5050a); lib. bdg. 24.27 *(978-1-4824-4682-1(0),* 8af761d3-980a-473f-855d-d7b9150f95ee) Stevens, Gareth Publishing LLLP.
Ransom, Candice. The Day of the Black Blizzard. Harden, Laurie, illus. 2016. (On My Own History Ser.). (ENG.). 48p. (J). (gr. 2-4). pap. 8.99 *(978-1-5124-1152-2(3),* 252ccb81-066d-47f7-883f-7efc7bbd8fd9, First Avenue Editions) Lerner Publishing Group.
Rathburn, Betsy. Blizzards. 2019. (Natural Disasters Ser.). (ENG., Illus.). 24p. (J). (gr. k-3). pap. 7.99 *(978-1-61891-745-4(5),* 12314, Blastoff! Readers) Bellwether Media.
Raum, Elizabeth. Blizzard! 2016. (Natural Disasters Ser.). (ENG., Illus.). 32p. (J). (gr. 2-5). lib. bdg. 20.95 *(978-1-60753-988-9(8),* 15786) Amicus.
—Can You Survive Storm Chasing? An Interactive Survival Adventure, 1 vol. 2011. (You Choose: Survival Ser.). (ENG., 112p. (J). (gr. 3-7). Illus.). lib. bdg. 32.65 *(978-1-4296-6587-2(4),* 115709); pap. 6.95 *(978-1-4296-7347-1(8),* 116885) Capstone. (Capstone Pr.).
Rea, Amy C. Perspectives on the Dust Bowl. 2018. (Perspectives on US History Ser.). (ENG., Illus.). 32p. (J). (gr. 3-6). 32.80 *(978-1-63235-399-3(7),* 13721, 12-Story Library) Bookstaves, LLC.
Rice, William B. Las Inundaciones y las Ventiscas. rev. ed. 2010. (Science: Informational Text Ser.).Tr. of Floods & Blizzards. (SPA., Illus.). 32p. (gr. 3-5). pap. 11.99 *(978-1-4333-2157-3(2))* Teacher Created Materials, Inc.
—Los Tornados. rev. ed. 2010. (Science: Informational Text Ser.). (SPA., Illus.). 32p. (gr. 3-5). pap. 11.99 *(978-1-4333-2155-9(6))* Teacher Created Materials, Inc.
Rigby. When Day Turned to Night. 2014. (Rigby Literacy Ser.). (ENG.). 32p. (gr. 4-4). pap. 12.55 *(978-0-7578-2002-1(6))* Rigby Education.
Roker, Al. Al Roker's Extreme Weather: Tornadoes, Typhoons, & Other Weather Phenomena. 2017. (ENG., Illus.). 48p. (J). (gr. 3-7). 16.99 *(978-0-06-248499-4(0),* HarperCollins) HarperCollins Pubs.
Royston, Angela. Storms!, 1 vol. 2011. (Eyewitness Disaster Ser.). (ENG.). 32p. (gr. 3-3). 31.21 *(978-1-60870-004-2(6),* 6ef7e207-5c05-443f-b768-0408d15585a3) Cavendish Square Publishing LLC.
Roza, Greg. Severe Storms: Measuring Velocity, 1 vol. (Math for the REAL World Ser.). 32p. (gr. 5-5). 2009. (ENG., Illus.). pap. 10.00 *(978-1-4042-6085-6(4),* 0b31cbfb-c655-4696-96cc-52fbb0356a3b) 2009. 47.90 *(978-1-60851-365-9(3),* PowerKids Pr.) 2006. (ENG., Illus.). (YA). lib. bdg. 28.93 *(978-1-4042-3366-9(0),* 8be3ba0f-3d3f-44cf-a60b-868b2ada3ce4) Rosen Publishing Group, Inc., The.
Rudolph, Jessica. Erased by a Tornado! 2010. (Disaster Survivors Ser.). (Illus.). 32p. (YA). (gr. 4-7). lib. bdg. 28.50 *(978-1-936087-52-5(9))* Bearport Publishing Co., Inc.
Salzmann, Mary Elizabeth. Biggest, Baddest Book of Storms, 1 vol. 2015. (Biggest, Baddest Bks.). (ENG.). 24p. (J). (gr. k-4). 32.79 *(978-1-62403-519-7(1),* 16689, Super SandCastle) ABDO Publishing Co.
Sandler, Michael. Catastrophic Storms: Set Of 6. 2011. (Navigators Ser.). (J). pap. 48.00 net. *(978-1-4108-5082-9(X))* Benchmark Education Co.
Schuetz, Kristin. Severe Weather. 2015. (Understanding Weather Ser.). (ENG., Illus.). 24p. (J). (gr. k-3). lib. bdg. 26.95 *(978-1-62617-254-8(4),* Blastoff! Readers) Bellwether Media.
Schuh, Mari C. Tsunamis [Scholastic]. 2010. (Earth in Action Ser.). (ENG.). 24p. pap. 0.49 *(978-1-4296-5802-7(9),* Capstone Pr.) Capstone.
Schwartz, Heather E. Tracking a Storm. rev. ed. 2018. (Smithsonian: Informational Text Ser.). (ENG., Illus.). 32p. (J). (gr. 3-5). pap. 11.99 *(978-1-4938-6704-2(0))* Teacher Created Materials, Inc.
Shea, Therese M. When Blizzards Blow, 1 vol. 2015. (Eye on the Sky Ser.). (ENG., Illus.). 32p. (J). (gr. 3-4). pap. 11.50 *(978-1-4824-2876-6(8),* 7a7b9a24-7353-4dd5-906d-63f6ab7b64de) Stevens, Gareth Publishing LLLP.
Shoals, James. Extreme Weather. 2019. (Illus.). 48p. (J). *(978-1-4222-4355-8(9))* Mason Crest.
Shulman, Mark & Meredith Books Staff. Super Storms That Rocked the World: Hurricanes, Tsunamis, & Other Disasters. 2008. (Illus.). 40p. (J). (gr. 4-7). per. 6.99 *(978-0-696-23978-6(7))* Meredith Bks.
Spilsbury, Louise & Claybourne, Anna. The Complete Guide to Extreme Weather. 2016. (Illus.). 144p. (J). *(978-1-4351-6354-6(0))* Barnes & Noble, Inc.
Steele, Philip & Morris, Neil. Inside Hurricanes & Tornadoes, 1 vol. 2006. (Inside Nature's Disasters Ser.). (ENG., Illus.). 36p. (gr. 4-6). lib. bdg. 28.67 *(978-0-8368-7249-1(5),* ed4e4ac3-8aa8-4a67-a288-eea3e56c40b7, Gareth Stevens Learning Library) Stevens, Gareth Publishing LLLP.
Stein, Paul. Storms of the Future. 2009. (Library of Future Weather & Climate Ser.). 64p. (gr. 5-5). 58.50 *(978-1-60853-651-1(3))* Rosen Publishing Group, Inc., The.
Stewart, Mark. Blizzards & Winter Storms, 1 vol. 2008. (Ultimate 10: Natural Disasters Ser.). (ENG.). 48p. (YA). (gr. 3-3). lib. bdg. 33.67 *(978-0-8368-9150-8(3),* 9550c152-1cbb-4db1-a2f5-7dd71c58b1b2) Stevens, Gareth Publishing LLLP.
Stoltman, Joan. Following Extreme Weather with a Storm Chaser, 1 vol. 2018. (Get to Work! Ser.). (ENG.). 24p. (gr. 2-3). pap. 9.15 *(978-1-5382-1229-5(3),* e250c222-bef2-4ad9-9560-6d0a39b47719) Stevens, Gareth Publishing LLLP.
Storm: Level Q, 6 vols. (Wonder Worldtm Ser.). 48p. 39.95 *(978-0-7802-2953-2(3))* Wright Group/McGraw-Hill.
Storm Trackers: Six-Pack. (Greetings Ser.: Vol. 3). (gr. 3-5). 31.00 *(978-0-7635-2076-2(4))* Rigby Education.
Storms, 10 vols. 2007. (Storms Ser.). (ENG.). 24p. (gr. 2-4). lib. bdg. 123.35 *(978-0-8368-7910-0(4),* b798aabc-5a27-4992-b652-aea85003e7d2, Weekly Reader Leveled Readers) Stevens, Gareth Publishing LLLP.
Strain Trueit, Trudi. Stormy Days, 1 vol. 2010. (Weather Watch Ser.). (ENG.). 24p. (gr. k-1). 25.50 *(978-0-7614-4016-1(X),* 6024ae98-d454-46fb-90a1-06a60b28470a) Cavendish Square Publishing LLC.
Temple, Bob. Ice Storm! The 1998 Freeze. 2006. (X-Treme Disasters That Changed America Ser.). (Illus.). 32p. (YA). (gr. 2-5). lib. bdg. 28.50 *(978-1-59716-275-3(2))* Bearport Publishing Co., Inc.
Thomas, Rick & Picture Window Books Staff. Eye of the Storm: A Book about Hurricanes, 1 vol. Shea, Denise, illus. 2005. (Amazing Science: Weather Ser.). (ENG.). 24p. (J). (gr. -1-3). per. 8.95 *(978-1-4048-1845-3(6),* 93087, Picture Window Bks.) Capstone.
Thompson, Tamara, ed. Solar Storms, 1 vol. 2012. (At Issue Ser.). (ENG.). 104p. (gr. 10-12). pap. 28.80 *(978-0-7377-6206-8(3),* 98b7d1c6-cf21-435b-b4ed-233f00b6353a); lib. bdg. 41.03 *(978-0-7377-6205-1(5),* 6bf0a18d-2a43-4eca-ad6f-3ef227ff272c) Greenhaven Publishing LLC. (Greenhaven Publishing).
Thunderstorms. 3rd ed. 2018. (J). *(978-0-7166-9939-2(7))* World Bk., Inc.
Time for Kids Magazine Staff, ed. Storms! 2006. (Time for Kids Science Scoops Ser.). (Illus.). 32p. (gr. 1-3). 14.00 *(978-0-7569-6674-4(4))* Perfection Learning Corp.
Tormentas (Storms), 8 vols. 2007. (Tormentas (Storms) Ser.). (SPA.). 24p. (gr. 2-4). lib. bdg. 98.68 *(978-0-8368-8069-4(2),* b7ac67bc-e351-44d2-a6ae-11def84d14dd, Weekly Reader Leveled Readers) Stevens, Gareth Publishing LLLP.
Tras las Tormentas: 6 Small Books. (Saludos Ser.: Vol. 3). (SPA.). (gr. 3-5). 31.00 *(978-0-7635-2082-3(9))* Rigby Education.
Way, Jennifer & Gaffney, Timothy R. Severe-Storm Scientists: Chasing Tornadoes & Hurricanes, 1 vol. 2015. (Extreme Science Careers Ser.). (ENG., Illus.). 128p. (gr. 7-7). 38.93 *(978-0-7660-6968-8(0),* 2133208f-6fb7-4dce-9047-f1a91154d0b7) Enslow Publishing, LLC.
Webster, Christine. Storms. (Illus.). 24p. (J). 2013. *(978-1-61913-542-0(6))* 2012. (ENG., (gr. 4-7). lib. bdg. 27.13 *(978-1-61913-540-6(X),* AV2 by Weigl) 2006. (gr. 3-7). lib. bdg. 24.45 *(978-1-59036-412-3(0))* 2006. pap. 8.95 *(978-1-59036-418-5(X))* Weigl Pubs., Inc.
Wendorff, Anne. Ice Storms. 2008. (Extreme Weather Ser.). (ENG., Illus.). 24p. (J). (gr. 2-5). lib. bdg. 26.95 *(978-1-60014-186-7(2))* Bellwether Media.
Westcott, Jim. Natural Disasters. 2017. (Rank It! Ser.). (ENG., Illus.). 32p. (J). (gr. 4-6). lib. bdg. *(978-1-68072-175-1(5),* 10534, Bolt) Black Rabbit Bks.
Wetterer, Margaret K. & Wetterer, Charles M. Caminando Bajo la Nieve. Young, Mary O'Keefe, illus. 2007. (Yo Solo Historia Ser.). 48p. (J). (gr. 4-7). per. 6.95 *(978-0-8225-7789-8(5))* Lerner Publishing Group.
Wind & Storms: 6 Each of 1 Student Book, 6 vols. (Sunshinetm Science Ser.). 24p. (gr. 1-2). 41.95 *(978-0-7802-1376-0(9))* Wright Group/McGraw-Hill.
Wind & Storms: Big Book. (Sunshinetm Science Ser.). 24p. (gr. 1-2). 37.50 *(978-0-7802-1377-7(7))* Wright Group/McGraw-Hill.
Woods, Michael & Woods, Mary B. Blizzards. 2008. (Disasters up Close Ser.). (ENG., Illus.). 64p. (gr. 4-8). lib. bdg. 27.93 *(978-0-8225-6575-8(7),* Lerner Pubns.) Lerner Publishing Group.
—Hurricanes. 2006. (Disasters up Close Ser.). (Illus.). 64p. (J). (gr. 3-7). lib. bdg. 27.93 *(978-0-8225-4710-5(4),* Lerner Pubns.) Lerner Publishing Group.
World Book, Inc. Staff, contrib. by. Blizzards. (J). 2007. *(978-0-7166-9802-9(1))* 2nd ed. 2009. (Illus.). 47p. *(978-0-7166-9818-0(8))* World Bk., Inc.
—Ice Storms. (J). 2nd ed. 2009. (Illus.). 47p. *(978-0-7166-9825-8(0))* 3rd ed. 2018. *(978-0-7166-9936-1(2))* World Bk., Inc.
Yomtov, Nel. The Children's Blizzard Of 1888: A Cause-And-Effect Investigation. 2016. (Cause-And-Effect Disasters Ser.). (ENG., Illus.). 40p. (J). (gr. 4-6). E-Book 46.65 *(978-1-5124-1129-4(9),* Lerner Pubns.) Lerner Publishing Group.
Zoehfeld, Kathleen Weidner. What Makes a Blizzard? Frost, Maddie, illus. 2018. (Let's-Read-And-Find-Out Science 2 Ser.). (ENG.). 40p. (J). (gr. -1-3). 17.99 *(978-0-06-248473-4(7));* pap. 6.99 *(978-0-06-248472-7(9))* HarperCollins Pubs. (HarperCollins).

STORMS—FICTION

Asare, Meshack. Sosu's Call. Asare, Meshack, illus. 2006. (ENG., Illus.). 40p. (J). (gr. k-4). 11.99 *(978-1-929132-21-8(2))* Kane Miller.
Bailey, David J. The Storm. 2016. (ENG.). 190p. (J). pap. 11.95 *(978-1-78554-826-0(3),* 117c8019-8df2-4fc5-9774-fbb9e767038b) Austin Macauley Pubs. Ltd. GBR. Dist: Baker & Taylor Publisher Services (BTPS).
Banks, Kate. El Pajaro, el Mono y la Serpiente en la Selva. Bogacki, Tomek, illus. (SPA.). 24p. (J). (gr. k-2). *(978-84-261-3129-4(8),* JV2823) Juventud, Editorial ESP. Dist: Lectorum Pubns., Inc.
Barthe, Raquel M. Rigoberta y la Tormenta. 2018. 40p. (J). pap. 18.99 *(978-607-746-386-3(8))* Progreso, Editorial, S. A. MEX. Dist: Lectorum Pubns., Inc.
Bates, Sonya Spreen. Thunder Creek Ranch, 1 vol. Charko, Kasia, illus. 2013. (Orca Echoes Ser.). (ENG.). 64p. (J). (gr. 1-3). pap. 7.95 *(978-1-4598-0112-7(1))* Orca Bk. Pubs. USA.
Bell, Lucy. Rufus & the Scary Storm: A Book about Being Brave. Garton, Michael, illus. 2018. (Frolic First Faith Ser.). 32p. (J). (gr. -1-3). 12.99 *(978-1-5064-3971-6(3),* Sparkhouse Family) 1517 Media.
Benson, Donna. Ghost Finds 100ct Diamond in Little Rock. 2012. 36p. 19.95 *(978-1-4626-6892-2(5))* America Star Bks.
Bentley, Sue. Sunshine Shimmers. 2014. (Magic Puppy Ser.: 12). lib. bdg. 14.75 *(978-0-606-34141-7(2))* Turtleback.
Beveridge, Cathy. Stormstruck. 2006. (ENG., Illus.). 214p. (J). pap. *(978-1-55380-041-5(9))* Ronsdale Pr.
Bodett, Tom. Williwaw! unabr. ed. 2004. 208p. (J). (gr. 5-9). pap. 38.00 incl. audio *(978-0-8072-8226-7(X),* LL0169, Listening Library) Random Hse. Audio Publishing Group.
Bolme, Edward Sarah. Jesus Stops a Storm. Gillette, Tim, illus. l.t. ed. 2003. 20p. (J). bds. 6.99 *(978-0-9725546-3-3(7))* CREST Pubns.
Bridwell, Norman. Clifford the Big Red Dog. Bridwell, Norman, illus. 2018. (ENG., Illus.). 32p. (J). (gr. -1-k). 16.99 *(978-1-338-30473-2(9))* Scholastic, Inc.
—Clifford the Big Red Dog (Classic Storybook), 1 vol. Bridwell, Norman, illus. 2010. (ENG., Illus.). 32p. (J). (gr. -1-3). pap. 5.99 *(978-0-545-21578-7(1),* Cartwheel Bks.) Scholastic, Inc.
Caban, Connie. Don't Be Afraid of the Storm. Page, illus. 2011. 32p. pap. 12.95 *(978-1-936343-97-3(5))* Peppertree Pr., The.
Caine, Rachel, pseud. Lord of Misrule. 2009. (Morganville Vampires Ser.: Bk. 5). 352p. (YA). lib. bdg. 20.00 *(978-1-4242-4704-2(7))* Fitzgerald Bks.
—Lord of Misrule: The Morganville Vampires, Book 5. 2009. (Morganville Vampires Ser.: 5). (ENG.). 256p. (YA). (gr. 9-18). mass mkt. 7.99 *(978-0-451-22572-6(4),* Berkley) Penguin Publishing Group.
Carroll, Mona. Jacob's Storm, 1 vol. 2010. 22p. 24.95 *(978-1-4489-8069-7(0))* PublishAmerica, Inc.
Caught in the Storm: Individual Title Six-Packs. (gr. k-1). 23.00 *(978-0-7635-9046-8(0))* Rigby Education.
Chriscoe, Sharon. Scary Weather, Scaredy Cat, 1 vol. 2008. (ENG.). 48p. 24.95 *(978-1-60474-143-8(0))* America Star Bks.
Crawford, Ruth. Squirrel Boy & Brad: The Storm. 2010. 24p. pap. 12.99 *(978-1-4490-1611-1(1))* AuthorHouse.
Crummel, Susan Stevens. Ten-Gallon Bart Beats the Heat, 0 vols. Donohue, Dorothy, illus. 2012. (ENG.). 40p. (J). (gr. 1-3). 17.99 *(978-0-7614-5634-6(1),* 9780761456346, Two Lions) Amazon Publishing.
Dahl, Michael. Dragonblood: Claws in the Snow. Vue, Tou, illus. 2010. (Dragonblood Ser.). (ENG.). 40p. (J). (gr. 4-8). pap. 6.25 *(978-1-4342-2308-1(6),* 103177, Stone Arch Bks.) Capstone.
D'Amico, Carmela & D'Amico, Steven. Ella Sets Sail. 2008. (J). *(978-0-439-83156-7(3),* Levine, Arthur A. Bks.) Scholastic, Inc.
Daniel, Zoe. Angel: Through My Eyes - Natural Disaster Zones. White, Lyn, ed. 2019. (Through My Eyes Ser.). (ENG.). 192p. (J). (gr. 6-9). pap. 15.99 *(978-1-76011-377-3(8))* Allen & Unwin AUS. Dist: Independent Pubs. Group.
Davis, Ashley. The Big Storm, 1 vol. 2006. (Neighborhood Readers Ser.). (ENG.). 16p. (gr. 1-2). pap. 6.50 *(978-1-4042-7192-0(9),* acd57e4e-3518-4d62-8b03-069c49727692, Rosen Classroom) Rosen Publishing Group, Inc., The.
Dearen, Patrick. When the Sky Rained Dust. 2004. 132p. (J). pap. 14.95 *(978-1-57168-830-9(7),* Eakin Pr.) Eakin Pr.
Dionne, Erin. Captain's Log: Snowbound. Ebbeler, Jeffrey, illus. 2018. (ENG.). 32p. (J). (gr. -1-3). lib. bdg. 17.99 *(978-1-58089-825-6(4))* Charlesbridge Publishing, Inc.
Dudgeon and Oxenham, Dudgeon and Oxenham. Cyclones & Shadows. 2017. (Illus.). 168p. (J). (gr. 1-5). 9.95 *(978-1-925164-76-3(4))* Fremantle Pr. AUS. Dist: Independent Pubs. Group.
Edwards, Carol. Jacy Meets Betsy: Jacy's Search for Jesus Book 2. Frey, Daniel, illus. 2006. 32p. (J). 15.95 *(978-0-9755314-1-9(7))* Majestic Publishing, LLC.
Erickson, Mary Ellen. Snowstorm. 2005. (J). *(978-0-9765453-3-0(0))* Dr. Mary's Bks.
Erin, Bethany. The Wind & the Blows. 2010. 24p. pap. 11.99 *(978-1-4490-7569-9(X))* AuthorHouse.
Ering, Timothy Basil. The Unexpected Love Story of Alfred Fiddleduckling. Ering, Timothy Basil, illus. 2017. (ENG., Illus.). 48p. (J). (-k). 16.99 *(978-0-7636-6432-9(4))* Candlewick Pr.
Falk, Barbara Bustetter. Gardener Pig. 2007. (ENG.). 38p. pap. 15.99 *(978-1-4257-2957-8(6))* Xlibris Corp.
Fane, Judy B. Paddy the Pelican Survives the Storm. Alden, Carol, illus. 2010. 48p. pap. 16.50 *(978-1-60911-448-0(5),* Eloquent Bks.) Strategic Book Publishing & Rights Agency (SBPRA).
Fernandez, Joy C. Rockman. 2010. 36p. pap. 16.45 *(978-1-4520-6751-3(1))* AuthorHouse.
The Fisherman. 2013. (Illus.). 16p. pap. 9.95 *(978-1-61633-446-8(0))* Guardian Angel Publishing, Inc.
Friedman, Laurie. Ruby Valentine Saves the Day. Avril, Lynne, illus. 2010. (Ruby Valentine Ser.). (ENG.). 32p. (J). (gr. k-3). lib. bdg. 16.95 *(978-0-7613-4213-7(3),* 5712cf7b-cdd0-4bc4-bb02-98aa513f9e9a, Carolrhoda Bks.) Lerner Publishing Group.
Fudge, Keith. The Rainy Day Discovery. 2006. (J). per. 11.95 *(978-1-889743-37-0(2))* Robbie Dean Pr.
Gaskins, Terry & Treigle, Jimmy. The Very Big Storm: Created by Terry Gaskins Inspired by Jimmy Treigle. 2009. 28p. pap. 13.99 *(978-1-4389-4220-9(6))* AuthorHouse.
Geisert, Arthur, creator. Thunderstorm. (ENG., Illus.). (J). 2015. 34p. (gr. k). 60.00 *(978-1-59270-170-4(1))* 2013. 32p. (gr. -1). 17.95 *(978-1-59270-133-9(7))* Enchanted Lion Bks., LLC.
Gillespie, Gary Franklin. Storytime with Grandp. 2011. 60p. pap. 31.99 *(978-1-4653-3598-2(6))* Xlibris Corp.
Giulieri, Anne. Little Sea Horse & the Big Storm. Aranda, Omar, illus. 2012. (Engage Literacy Blue Ser.). (ENG.). 16p. (J). (gr. k-2). pap. 36.94 *(978-1-4296-8993-9(5),* 18393, Capstone Pr.) Capstone.
Gohmann, Johanna. A Spooky Day at Sea. Innerebner, Jessika von, illus. 2017. (Pirate Kids Ser.). (ENG.). 32p. (J). (gr. -1-3). lib. bdg. 32.79 *(978-1-5321-3040-3(6),* 27042, Calico Chapter Bks) Magic Wagon.
Gonzales Betrand, Diane. The Story Circle / el Circulo de Cuentos. Martin, Wendy, illus. 2016. (ENG, MUL & SPA.). 32p. (J). (gr. k-3). 17.95 *(978-1-55885-826-8(1),* Piñata Books) Arte Publico Pr.
Gramatky, Hardie. Little Toot. Gramatky, Hardie, illus. 2007. (Little Toot Ser.). (Illus.). 104p. (J). (gr. -1-2). 17.99 *(978-0-399-24713-2(0),* G.P. Putnam's Sons Books for Young Readers) Penguin Young Readers Group.
Graves, Susan Elaine. Lily the Lucky Ducky, 1 vol. 2010. 44p. 24.95 *(978-1-4489-4433-0(3))* PublishAmerica, Inc.
Gray, P. J. The Lab Book 3, 1 vol. 2014. (Trippin' Ser.). (ENG.). 64p. (YA). (gr. 9-12). pap. 10.75 *(978-1-62250-933-1(1))* Saddleback Educational Publishing, Inc.
Green, John, et al. Let It Snow: Three Holiday Romances. 2008. (ENG.). 358p. (YA). (gr. 7-18). pap. 12.99 *(978-0-14-241214-5(7),* Speak) Penguin Young Readers Group.
Hale, Bruce. Syd Hoff's Danny & the Dinosaur & the Big Storm. Cutting, David, illus. 2017. (J). *(978-1-5182-4495-7(5))* HarperCollins Pubs. Ltd.
Hall, Rose. After the Storm. Jazvic, Beryl, illus. 2005. (J). bds. 19.95 *(978-0-9770503-0-7(0))* Institute For Behavior Change Incorporated The.
Hatfield, Ruth. The Book of Storms. Call, Greg, illus. 2016. (Book of Storms Trilogy Ser.). (ENG.). 384p. (J). (gr. 5-9). 18.40 *(978-0-606-39364-5(1))* Turtleback.
Haughton, Emma. Rainy Day. Rinaldi, Angelo, illus. (Carolrhoda Picture Books Ser.). 32p. (J). 2004. pap. 6.95 *(978-1-57505-668-5(2))* 2003. (gr. -1-3). 6.95 *(978-1-57505-452-0(3),* Carolrhoda Bks.) Lerner Publishing Group.
Horacek, Petr. Puffin Peter. Horacek, Petr, illus. 2013. (ENG., Illus.). 40p. (J). (gr. -1-2). 17.99 *(978-0-7636-6572-2(X))* Candlewick Pr.
Jax, T. L. Fraidy-Frieda's Light Show. Jax, T. L., illus. l.t. ed. 2004. (Illus.). 30p. (J). 9.95 *(978-0-9743890-2-8(1))* Flaxenfluff Pr., LLC.
Jennings, Arleen Naish. God Is in the Rain. 2012. 64p. (gr. 1-2). pap. 8.95 *(978-1-4759-3292-8(8))* iUniverse, Inc.
Johnson, D. B. Henry Works. 2019. (Henry Book Ser.). (ENG., Illus.). 32p. (J). (gr. -1-3). pap. 7.99 *(978-0-358-11207-5(9),* 1749865, Clarion Bks.) HarperCollins Pubs.
—Henry Works. 2004. 32p. (J). (gr. k-3). 15.00 *(978-0-618-55204-7(9))* Houghton Mifflin Harcourt Trade & Reference Pubs.
Johnson, Kristin. Black Blizzard. 2017. (Day of Disaster Ser.). (ENG.). 112p. (YA). (gr. 6-12). 26.65 *(978-1-5124-2774-5(8),* 17c8644d-c2b1-4cf1-8ab2-8023ed5185d3); E-Book 39.99 *(978-1-5124-3506-1(6),* 9781512435061) Lerner Publishing Group. (Darby Creek).
Johnson, Kristin F. Black Blizzard. 2017. (Day of Disaster Ser.). (ENG.). 112p. (YA). (gr. 6-12). E-Book 6.99 *(978-1-5124-3507-8(4),* 9781512435078, Darby Creek) Lerner Publishing Group.
Johnson, Terry Lynn. Dust Storm! Orban, Jani, illus. 2018. (Survivor Diaries). (ENG.). 128p. (J). (gr. 1-5). 9.99 *(978-0-544-97098-4(5),* 1662531, Clarion Bks.) HarperCollins Pubs.
K/H (Pathways). Kindergarten Stepping Stones: Kindergarten the Bravest Dog Ever - The True Story of Balto Trade Book. rev. ed. 2010. (ENG.). 48p. pap. 9.00 *(978-0-7575-8646-0(5))* Kendall Hunt Publishing Co.
Kapica, Dan. Mangrove Seed Chronicles: Learning to Trust. 2007. (Illus.). 64p. 24.95 *(978-0-9797158-0-8(6),* Mangrove Seed Expressions) Mangrove Seed, Inc.
Kehret, Peg. The Flood Disaster. 2008. (ENG.). 160p. (J). (gr. 3-7). pap. 8.99 *(978-1-4169-9109-0(3),* Simon & Schuster/Paula Wiseman Bks.) Simon & Schuster/Paula Wiseman Bks.
Lance, Scott. Pourman's Library. 2003. 108p. (YA). pap. 10.95 *(978-0-595-30148-5(7))* iUniverse, Inc.
Lasser, Jessica. Stormy the Cloud. 2012. 24p. pap. 17.99 *(978-1-4685-6214-9(2))* AuthorHouse.
Leeson, Christine. Molly & the Storm. Hansen, Gaby, illus. 2003. 32p. (J). (gr. k-2). tchr. ed. 15.95 *(978-1-58925-027-7(3))* Tiger Tales.
Lepp, Royden. Barnabas Helps a Friend, 1 vol. Lepp, Royden, illus. 2008. (I Can Read! / Barnabas Ser.). (ENG., Illus.). 32p. (J). (gr. -1-1). pap. 4.99 *(978-0-310-71585-6(7))* Zonderkidz.
Little, Judy. Yody & Bippy the Boo: Friends for Life. 2010. 28p. pap. 12.49 *(978-1-4389-7145-2(1))* AuthorHouse.
London, Lewis. Wesley Owl. 2010. (Illus.). 36p. (J). pap. 16.99 *(978-1-4490-6122-7(2))* AuthorHouse.
Lyon, Nathan W. & Ellis, Kevin L. Sam the Clam. 2010. 28p. pap. 14.95 *(978-1-4520-7784-0(3))* AuthorHouse.
Maguire, Gregory. What-the-Dickens: The Story of a Rogue Tooth Fairy. 2007. (ENG.). 304p. (J). (gr. 4-8). 24.80 *(978-1-4287-6555-9(7),* Follettbound) Follett School Solutions.
Manushkin, Fran. Stocking up for the Storm. Zarrin, Laura, illus. 2019. (Katie Woo's Neighborhood Ser.). (ENG.). 32p. (J). (gr. k-2). 21.32 *(978-1-5158-4455-6(2),* 140567, Picture Window Bks.) Capstone.
Maria, Miss Yvonne. Beautiful Black Mermaids of the Bayou, 1 vol. 2009. 48p. pap. 16.95 *(978-1-60836-236-3(1))* America Star Bks.
Matsakis, Cynthia. Sister Sun, Brother Storm. Silver, Jane, illus. 2012. 32p. 24.95 *(978-1-4575-0768-7(4))* Dog Ear Publishing, LLC.
Maurer, Tracy Nelson. Storm Codes. Rodriguez, Christina, illus. 2007. (ENG.). 40p. (J). pap. 8.95 *(978-0-89317-064-6(X),* WW-064X); (gr. 1-7). lib. bdg. 17.95 *(978-0-89317-063-9(1),* WW-0631) Finney Co., Inc. (Windward Publishing).
May, Maggie. Pilot, Swaydy & Friends. Larade, April, illus. 2011. 30p. pap. 24.95 *(978-1-4560-8499-8(2))* America Star Bks.
Mayer, Mercer. Just a Big Storm. 2013. (Little Critter Ser.). (J). lib. bdg. 13.55 *(978-0-606-27153-0(8))* Turtleback.
Maylin, Grace B. There Will Come Another: A Lesson from the Trees. Maylin, Grace B., photos by. 2007. (Illus.). per. *(978-0-9792384-0-6(4))* Maylin, Grace.
McElligott, Matthew. Mad Scientist Academy: the Weather Disaster. 2018. (Mad Scientist Academy Ser.: 2). (Illus.). 40p. (J). (gr. k-3). 8.99 *(978-0-553-52381-2(3),* Dragonfly Bks.) Random Hse. Children's Bks.
McPhail, David. The Searcher & Old Tree. McPhail, David, illus. 2011. (ENG., Illus.). 32p. (J). (gr. -1-2). pap. 7.95 *(978-1-58089-224-7(8))* Charlesbridge Publishing, Inc.
Messenger, Shannon. Let the Storm Break. 2014. (Sky Fall Ser.: 2). (ENG., Illus.). 400p. (YA). (gr. 7). 17.99 *(978-1-4424-5044-8(4),* Simon Pulse) Simon Pulse.
Messier, Mireille. The Branch. Pratt, Pierre, illus. 2016. (ENG.). 32p. (J). (gr. -1-2). 16.95 *(978-1-77138-564-0(2))* Kids Can Pr., Ltd. CAN. Dist: Hachette Bk. Group.
Milgrim, David. Look Out! a Storm! Ready-To-Read Pre-Level 1. Milgrim, David, illus. 2019. (Adventures of Otto Ser.). (ENG., Illus.). 32p. (J). (gr. -1-k). 17.99 *(978-1-5344-4197-2(2));* pap. 4.99 *(978-1-5344-4196-5(4))* Simon Spotlight. (Simon Spotlight).
Milway, Alex. Operation Robot Storm: The Mythical 9th Division. 2013. (ENG., Illus.). 224p. (J). pap. 5.99 *(978-1-61067-074-6(4))* Kane Miller.

Montes, Hugo & Montes, Michelle. Young Eagles Armor Academy: Caught in the Storm, V02. 2010. 76p. (J). pap. 5.99 *(978-1-60683-022-2(8))* Harrison House Pubs.

Montgomery, R. A. Island of Time. Louie, Wes & Cannella, Marco, illus. 2009. (ENG.). 144p. (J). (gr. 4-8). pap. 6.99 *(978-1-933390-28-4(X))* Chooseco LLC.

Moore, Marcia. Wind & Oyster Jack, 1 vol. Crow, Heather, illus. 2017. (ENG.). 32p. (J). 14.99 *(978-0-7643-5422-9(1),* 7745) Schiffer Publishing, Ltd.

Moss, Marissa. Rose's Journal: The Story of a Girl in the Great Depression. 2004. (Young American Voice Bks.). (Illus.). (gr. 3-7). 17.00 *(978-0-7569-4230-4(6))* Perfection Learning Corp.

Munoz, Norma. Los Cuentos de la Casa del Arbol. Olson, John & Olson, Johan, illus. rev. ed. 2005. (Castillo de la Lectura Blanca Ser.). (SPA & ENG.). 72p. (J). (gr. -1-3). pap. 6.95 *(978-970-20-0124-9(2))* Castillo, Ediciones, S. A. de C. V. MEX. Dist: Macmillan.

Murray, Eva. Island Birthday, 1 vol. Hogan, Jamie, illus. 2015. (ENG.). 32p. (J). (gr. 1-7). 16.95 *(978-0-88448-425-7(4),* 884425) Tilbury Hse. Pubs.

Nevis, Lance. Animal Rain. Laible MBA, Steve William, ed. Piper, Tom, illus. 2012. 36p. pap. 10.99 *(978-0-9850142-7-8(X))* Kodel Group, LLC, The.

Nielsen, Jennifer A. Wrath of the Storm. 2018. (Mark of the Thief Ser.: 3). lib. bdg. 18.40 *(978-0-606-41136-3(4))* Turtleback.

Parker, Emma. The Lightning Game. 2010. (Illus.). 24p. pap. *(978-1-877561-55-9(X))* First Edition Ltd.

Pearson, Iris & Merrill, Mike. The Adventures of Lady: The Big Storm. Pearson, Iris, ed. Project Firefly Animation Studios, illus. rev. ed. 2007. 34p. (J). 11.99 *(978-0-9789984-2-4(1))* Adventures of Lady LLC, The.

—The Adventures of Lady: The Big Storm Coloring Book. Pearson, Iris, ed. Project Firefly Animation Studios, illus. 2007. 34p. (J). pap. 5.49 *(978-0-9789984-3-1(X))* Adventures of Lady LLC, The.

Pfister, Marcus. Rainbow Fish Finds His Way. 2006. (Rainbow Fish Ser.). (ENG., Illus.). 32p. (J). (gr. -1-2). 19.95 *(978-0-7358-2084-5(8))* North-South Bks., Inc.

Pova, Rosie J. Sunday Rain. Rauscher, Amariah, illus. 2021. (ENG.). 32p. (J). (gr. -1-2). 17.99 *(978-1-911373-97-1(8),* 928035d7-9430-4a5f-984c-e353b2131e12) Lantana Publishing GBR. Dist: Lerner Publishing Group.

Preus, Margi. Storm's Coming! Geister, David, illus. 2016. (ENG.). 32p. (J). 16.95 *(978-1-68134-018-0(6))* Minnesota Historical Society Pr.

Randolph, Joanne. Stormy: a Storm Cloud's Story, 1 vol. 2009. (Nature Stories Ser.). (ENG., Illus.). 24p. (J). (gr. 1-2). lib. bdg. 27.27 *(978-1-60754-092-2(4),* 142ee8c3-dd4d-4709-9be4-7c3b114fc8b3, Windmill Bks.) Rosen Publishing Group, Inc., The.

Regan, Dian. The Snow Blew Inn. Cushman, Doug, illus. 2011. (ENG.). 32p. (J). 16.95 *(978-0-8234-2351-4(4))* Holiday Hse., Inc.

Reinoso, Carlos. Little Ducky Jr. & the Whirlwind Storm: A Tale of Loss, Hope,and Renewal. Reinoso, Carlos, illus. l.t. ed. 2005. (Illus.). 50p. (J). 8.99 *(978-0-9777672-0-5(5))* Behavioral Health & Human Development Ctr.

Rivers, Phoebe. A Perfect Storm. 2013. (Saranormal Ser.: 10). (ENG., Illus.). 160p. (J). (gr. 3-7). 15.99 *(978-1-4424-8959-2(6));* pap. 5.99 *(978-1-4424-8958-5(8))* Simon Spotlight. (Simon Spotlight).

Rixon, Denise. The Owl That Barked: Tammy, 1 vol. 2009. 203p. pap. 24.95 *(978-1-4489-8472-5(6))* America Star Bks.

Robertson, Charmaine. The Worst Storm, 1 vol. 2016. (Rosen REAL Readers: STEM & STEAM Collection). (ENG.). 12p. (gr. k-1). pap. 6.33 *(978-1-5081-2640-9(2),* 406c0382-6ba2-4660-81d1-c5828a6c33c9, Rosen Classroom) Rosen Publishing Group, Inc., The.

Rocco, John. Blizzard. Rocco, John, illus. 2014. (ENG., Illus.). 40p. (J). (gr. -1-k). 18.99 *(978-1-4231-7865-1(3))* Little, Brown Bks. for Young Readers.

Rossi, Joyce & Rising Moon Editors. The Gullywasher: El Chaparron Torrencial. 2004. (ENG., Illus.). 32p. (J). (gr. k-3). pap. 7.95 *(978-0-87358-728-0(6))* Cooper Square Publishing Llc.

Rowland, Joanna. Stay Through the Storm. Tu, Lorian, illus. 2019. 32p. (J). (gr. -1-3). 16.99 *(978-1-5064-5058-2(X),* Beaming Books) 1517 Media.

Rylant, Cynthia. Annie & Snowball & the Wintry Freeze: Ready-To-Read Level 2. Stevenson, Suçie & Stevenson, Suçie, illus. (Annie & Snowball Ser.: 8). (ENG.). 40p. (J). (gr. k-2). 2011. pap. 4.99 *(978-1-4169-7206-8(4))* 2010. 17.99 *(978-1-4169-7205-1(6))* Simon Spotlight. (Simon Spotlight).

—The Storm. McDaniels, Preston, illus. 2003. (Lighthouse Family Ser.: 1). (ENG.). 80p. (J). (gr. 1-5). pap. 5.99 *(978-0-689-84882-7(X),* Simon & Schuster Bks. For Young Readers) Simon & Schuster Bks. For Young Readers.

—The Storm. 2003. (Lighthouse Family Ser.: 1). (gr. 3-6). 16.00 *(978-0-613-87052-8(2))* Turtleback.

Saddleback Educational Publishing Staff, ed. Crash, 1 vol. unabr. ed. 2010. (Heights Ser.). (ENG.). 50p. (gr. 4-8). pap. 9.75 *(978-1-61651-283-5(0))* Saddleback Educational Publishing, Inc.

Sargent, Dave & Sargent, Pat. The Chuck Wagon: Don't Be Stubborn, 10 vols., Vol. 7. Lenoir, Jane, illus. 2005. (Colorado Cowboys Ser.: 10). 32p. (J). pap. 10.95 *(978-1-59381-099-3(7));* lib. bdg. 23.60 *(978-1-59381-098-6(9))* Ozark Publishing.

—The Colorado Blizzard: Be Determined, 10 vols., Vol. 8. Lenoir, Jane, illus. 2005. (Colorado Cowboys Ser.: 10). 32p. (J). pap. 10.95 *(978-1-59381-027-5(X))* Ozark Publishing.

—The Drought: Have Faith, 10 vols., Vol. 9. Lenoir, Jane, illus. 2005. (Colorado Cowboys Ser.: 10). 32p. (J). pap. 10.95 *(978-1-59381-103-7(9));* lib. bdg. 23.60 *(978-1-59381-102-0(0))* Ozark Publishing.

Schwabach, Karen. The Storm Before Atlanta. 2012. (ENG.). 320p. (J). (gr. 4-6). lib. bdg. 21.19 *(978-0-375-95866-3(5),* Yearling) Random Hse. Children's Bks.

Seaman, Kathleen. Annycole, 1 vol. 2009. 49p. pap. 16.95 *(978-1-4489-1970-3(3))* America Star Bks.

Simmons, Derek. Flash of Life. 2006. 85p. pap. 16.95 *(978-1-4241-3890-6(6))* PublishAmerica, Inc.

Simpson, Dana. Phoebe & Her Unicorn in the Magic Storm. 2017. (Phoebe & Her Unicorn Ser.: Vol. 6). (ENG., Illus.). 157p. (J). (gr. 3-6). 33.99 *(978-1-4494-9450-6(1))* Andrews McMeel Publishing.

—Phoebe & Her Unicorn in the Magic Storm. 2017. (Phoebe & Her Unicorn Ser.: 6). lib. bdg. 20.85 *(978-0-606-40512-6(7))* Turtleback.

Simpson, Dana, illus. Phoebe & Her Unicorn in the Magic Storm. 2017. 157p. (J). *(978-1-5182-5085-9(8))* Andrews McMeel Publishing.

Skogen, Jennifer. Shattered. 2017. (Survive Ser.). (ENG.). 192p. (YA). (gr. 5-12). lib. bdg. 31.42 *(978-1-68076-734-6(8),* 25402, Epic Escape) EPIC Pr.

Sniegoski, Thomas E. Monstrous. (Savage Ser.). (ENG.). 448p. (YA). (gr. 9). 2018. pap. 12.99 *(978-1-4814-7719-2(6))* 2017. (Illus.). 18.99 *(978-1-4814-7718-5(8))* Simon Pulse. (Simon Pulse).

Snyder, Maria V. Storm Watcher. 2013. 228p. (gr. 4-8). pap. 9.99 *(978-1-61603-033-9(X))* Leap Bks.

Spradlin, Michael P. Denali Storm: A 4D Book. Karkavelas, Spiros, illus. 2018. (Pararescue Corps Ser.). (ENG.). 128p. (J). (gr. 4-8). lib. bdg. 27.32 *(978-1-4965-5203-7(2),* 136213, Stone Arch Bks.) Capstone.

—Sandstorm Blast: A 4D Book. Karkavelas, Spiros, illus. 2018. (Pararescue Corps Ser.). (ENG.). 128p. (J). (gr. 4-8). lib. bdg. 27.32 *(978-1-4965-5159-7(1),* 136172, Stone Arch Bks.) Capstone.

Steig, William. Brave Irene Storytime Set. unabr. ed. 2013. (Macmillan Young Listeners Story Time Sets Ser.). (ENG., Illus.). (J). (gr. -1-3). 12.99 *(978-1-4272-3780-4(8),* 900129806) Macmillan Audio.

Stolz, Mary. Storm in the Night. Cummings, Pat, illus. 2020. (ENG.). 32p. (J). (gr. -1-3). pap. 8.99 *(978-0-06-443256-6(4),* HarperCollins) HarperCollins Pubs.

A Stormy Adventure: Facing the Fear of Storms. 2004. (J). 6.99 *(978-0-9753870-3-0(0))* Write On!

Swinburne, Stephen R. Safe in a Storm. Bell, Jennifer, illus. 2016. (J). *(978-0-545-66987-0(1))* Scholastic, Inc.

Swinney, Kay. Marty Moose & the Mystical Reunion, 1 vol. 2009. 73p. pap. 19.95 *(978-1-61546-867-6(6))* America Star Bks.

Tafuri, Nancy. The Big Storm: A Very Soggy Counting Book. Tafuri, Nancy, illus. 2013. (Classic Board Bks.). (ENG., Illus.). 34p. (J). (gr. -1 — 1). bds. 7.99 *(978-1-4424-8179-4(X),* Little Simon) Little Simon.

—The Big Storm: A Very Soggy Counting Book. Tafuri, Nancy, illus. 2009. (ENG., Illus.). 32p. (J). (gr. -1-2). 18.99 *(978-1-4169-6795-8(8),* Simon & Schuster Bks. For Young Readers) Simon & Schuster Bks. For Young Readers.

Tate, Elizabeth Dawn. There's a Storm Brewing Outside. 2009. 24p. pap. 15.50 *(978-1-60693-239-1(X),* Eloquent Bks.) Strategic Book Publishing & Rights Agency (SBPRA).

Tekavec, Heather. Storm Is Coming! Spengler, Margaret, illus. 2004. 32p. (J). (gr. -1-3). reprint ed. pap. 7.99 *(978-0-14-240070-8(X),* Puffin Books) Penguin Young Readers Group.

Viau, Nancy. Storm Song, 0 vols. Gynux, illus. 2013. 24p. (gr. k-3). (ENG.). (J). 12.99 *(978-1-4778-1646-2(1),* 9781477816462, Two Lions); pap. 12.99 *(978-1-4778-6646-7(9))* Amazon Publishing.

Ward, Jennifer. The Sunhat. Sisson, Stéphanie Roth, illus. 2013. (ENG.). (J). 15.95 *(978-1-933855-78-3(9),* Rio Nuevo Pubs.) Rio Nuevo Pubs.

Welsh, Karen Leis. Frolicking Friends. 2012. (Illus.). 44p. pap. 21.99 *(978-1-4685-6422-8(6))* AuthorHouse.

Weston Woods Staff, creator. Brave Irene. 2011. 29.95 *(978-0-439-73468-4(1));* 18.95 *(978-0-439-72665-8(4));* 38.75 *(978-0-439-72666-5(2))* Weston Woods Studios, Inc.

White, Dianne. Blue on Blue. Krommes, Beth, illus. 2014. (ENG.). 48p. (J). (gr. k-3). 19.99 *(978-1-4424-1267-5(4),* Beach Lane Bks.) Beach Lane Bks.

Williams, Teresa Ann. Friends of Wildwood, 1 vol. 2009. 48p. pap. 16.95 *(978-1-4489-9419-9(5))* America Star Bks.

Willis, Jeanne. La Tormenta Monstruosa. (Cotton Cloud Ser.). (SPA.). (J). (gr. 1-3). pap. *(978-84-480-0180-3(X))* Timun Mas, Editorial S.A. ESP. Dist: Lectorum Pubns., Inc.

Wozniak, Paul. Stranded in a Snowstorm! Webber, Mike, illus. 2014. 82p. pap. 11.95 *(978-1-63047-173-6(9))* Morgan James Publishing.

Xiong, Kim, illus. Paper Horse. 2008. (ENG & CHI.). 37p. (J). 18.95 *(978-1-60603-003-5(5))* Better Chinese LLC.

Yoon, Salina. Stormy Night. (ENG., Illus.). (J). 2016. 32p. bds. 9.99 *(978-1-68119-165-2(2),* 900161159) 2015. 40p. (gr. -1-1). 14.99 *(978-0-8027-3780-9(3),* 900139076) Bloomsbury Publishing USA. (Bloomsbury USA Childrens).

Zappa, Shana Muldoon, et al. Tessa's Lost & Found, 9. 2016. (Star Darlings Ser.). (ENG.). 176p. (J). (gr. 3-6). 21.19 *(978-1-4844-8193-6(3))* Disney Pr.

STORYTELLING

Bicknell, Joanna. Build a Story Book. 2007. (Illus.). 20p. (J). (gr. k-5). pap. *(978-1-84610-426-8(2))* Make Believe Ideas.

Boston, David, illus. Wonder Tales from Around the World. 2006. (World Storytelling from August House Ser.). (ENG.). 158p. (J). (gr. 3-7). pap. 19.95 *(978-0-87483-422-2(8),* AH228) August Hse. Pubs., Inc.

Brown, Roberta Simpson. Queen of the Cold-Blooded Tales. Hall, Wendell E., illus. 2005. (American Storytelling Ser.). (ENG.). 175p. (J). (gr. 5-17). pap. 9.95 *(978-0-87483-408-6(2))* August Hse. Pubs., Inc.

Career Building Through Using Digital Story Tools. 2013. (Digital Career Building Ser.). 64p. (YA). (gr. 7-12). pap. 77.70 *(978-1-4777-1736-3(6))* Rosen Publishing Group, Inc., The.

Charlesworth, Liza. Punctuation Tales. 2009. (ENG.). (gr. 2-5). 36.99 *(978-0-545-11401-1(2))* Scholastic, Inc.

Doyle, Alfreda C. Story Time Literacy Coach: Literacy, Storytelling & Rhyme. unabr. ed. 2005. (Alfreda's Radio Ser.: Vol. 1). (gr. 5-9). spiral bd. 39.95 *(978-1-56820-305-8(5))* Story Time Stories That Rhyme.

Edupress, creator. My Story Book: Primary. 2009. 32p. pap. 1.99 *(978-1-56472-944-6(3))* Edupress, Inc.

Glaser, Jason. Career Building Through Using Digital Story Tools, 1 vol. 2013. (Digital Career Building Ser.). (ENG.). 64p. (YA). (gr. 6-6). 37.13 *(978-1-4777-1722-6(6),* c7326c3e-cb83-413a-959e-86dddb6d4050); pap. 13.95 *(978-1-4777-1735-6(8),* 7ee48943-6f1a-418b-9371-40cf05a92d34) Rosen Publishing Group, Inc., The.

Hamilton, Martha & Weiss, Mitch. Through the Grapevine: World Tales Kids Can Read & Tell. Lyon, Carol, illus. 2006. (ENG.). 128p. (J). (gr. 1-6). pap. 15.95 *(978-0-87483-624-0(7))* August Hse. Pubs., Inc.

—Through the Grapevine: World Tales Kids Can Read & Tell. Lyon, Carol, illus. 2005. (ENG.). 128p. (J). (gr. 1-6). 24.95 *(978-0-87483-625-7(5))* August Hse. Pubs., Inc.

How Rabbit Caught the Sun: Individual Title Six-Packs. (Story Steps Ser.). (gr. k-2). 32.00 *(978-0-7635-9811-2(9))* Rigby Education.

How the Geese Saved Rome: Individual Title Six-Packs. (Story Steps Ser.). (gr. k-2). 32.00 *(978-0-7635-9801-3(1))* Rigby Education.

Johnson, Robin. How Do Artists Tell Stories? 2019. (Full STEAM Ahead! - Arts in Action Ser.). (Illus.). 24p. (J). (gr. 1-1). *(978-0-7787-6211-9(4));* pap. *(978-0-7787-6270-6(X))* Crabtree Publishing Co.

K/H (Pathways). Pathways: Grade 6 Dr. Rabbit Trade Book. rev. ed. 2011. (ENG.). 30p. pap. 11.00 *(978-0-7575-4840-6(7))* Kendall Hunt Publishing Co.

Langston-George, Rebecca, et al. Encounter: Narrative Nonfiction Stories. 2018. (Encounter: Narrative Nonfiction Stories Ser.). (ENG.). (J). (gr. 3-7). 188.58 *(978-1-5435-1394-3(8),* 27974, Capstone Pr.) Capstone.

Madden-Lunsford, Kerry. Nothing Fancy about Kathryn & Charlie. Madden-Lunsford, Lucy, illus. 2013. (ENG.). 36p. (J). pap. 14.95 *(978-0-9828528-0-4(0))* Mockingbird Publishing.

Matthews, John & Matthews, Caitlin. Storyworld: Create a Story Kit. 2010. (Illus.). *(978-0-7636-5319-4(5))* Templar Publishing.

Neuburger, Emily K. Show Me a Story: 40 Craft Projects & Activities to Spark Children's Storytelling. 2012. (ENG., Illus.). 144p. (J). (gr. k-7). pap. 16.95 *(978-1-60342-988-7(3),* 62988) Storey Publishing, LLC.

Packard, Mary. The Storyteller. Land Eagle, illus. 2009. 196p. (J). *(978-1-4351-1557-6(0))* Metro Bks.

Reid, Rob. Storytime Slam: 15 Lesson Plans for Preschool & Primary Story Programs. 2006. (Illus.). 85p. pr. 16.95 *(978-1-932146-52-3(0),* Upstart Bks.) Highsmith Inc.

Set of 7 StoryTellers. (Classic Storytellers Ser.). (Illus.). (gr. 4-8). lib. bdg. *(978-1-58415-321-4(0))* Mitchell Lane Pubs.

Snedeker, Gus. Tell Me a Story: Family Folklore. 2013. (Illus.). 48p. (J). pap. *(978-1-4222-2499-1(6))* Mason Crest.

—Tell Me a Story: Family Folklore. Jabbour, Alan, ed. 2012. (North American Folklore for Youth Ser.). (Illus.). 48p. (J). (gr. 4). 19.95 *(978-1-4222-2488-5(0))* Mason Crest.

A Storyteller's Journey, 6 Pack. (Bookweb Ser.). 32p. (gr. 4-18). 34.00 *(978-0-7635-3738-8(1))* Rigby Education.

Stotter, Ruth. A Loop of String: String Stories & String Stunts: Traditional & Original String Figures & Stories. Coffey, Kevin, illus. 2009. 110p. (J). pap. 22.95 *(978-1-58790-170-6(6))* Regent Pr.

The Tug of War: Individual Title Six-Pack. (Story Steps Ser.). (gr. k-2). 23.00 *(978-0-7635-9620-0(5))* Rigby Education.

Watts, Eleanor. Oxford Basics: Storytelling. 2006. (Oxford Applied Linguistics Ser.). (ENG., Illus.). 88p. 14.30 *(978-0-19-441976-5(2))* Oxford Univ. Pr., Inc.

Welsh, Anne Marie & Tuchman, Laura. A World of Girls. Garcia, Helena, illus. 2010. 40p. (J). *(978-0-88441-750-7(6))* Girl Scouts of the USA.

Whelon, Chuck. Word Play: Write Your Own Crazy Comics, No. 1. 2011. (Dover Kids Activity Bks.). (ENG., Illus.). 64p. (J). (gr. 3-5). pap. 5.99 *(978-0-486-48165-4(4),* 481654) Dover Pubns., Inc.

—Word Play! - Write Your Own Crazy Comics, No. 2. 2011. (Dover Kids Activity Bks.). (ENG., Illus.). 64p. (J). (gr. 3-5). pap. 6.99 *(978-0-486-48166-1(2),* 481662) Dover Pubns., Inc.

STORYTELLING—COLLECTIONS

DeSpain, Pleasant. Sweet Land of Story: Thirty-Six American Tales to Tell. (ENG., Illus.). 176p. (J). (gr. 3-7). 2006. 19.95 *(978-0-87483-569-4(0))* 2005. pap. 12.95 *(978-0-87483-600-4(X))* August Hse. Pubs., Inc.

Hamilton, Martha, et al. Noodlehead Stories: World Tales Kids Can Read & Tell. 2006. (ENG., Illus.). 96p. (J). (gr. 1-6). pap. 14.95 *(978-0-87483-585-4(2))* August Hse. Pubs., Inc.

Lil Gems & Black, Magenta. Tutu's Lil Gems. 2012. 60p. pap. 8.95 *(978-0-9885632-3-0(1))* Pink Kiss Publishing Co.

Young, Richard & Young, Judy D. African-American Folktales. 2006. (American Storytelling Ser.). (ENG.). 176p. (J). (gr. 3-7). pap. 12.95 *(978-0-87483-309-6(4))* August Hse. Pubs., Inc.

STORYTELLING—FICTION

Abbott, Jacob. Stories Told to Rollo's Cousin Lucy. 2005. pap. 22.95 *(978-1-4179-5651-7(8))* Kessinger Publishing, LLC.

Adams, W. Royce. Raid on Rairarubi. 2008. 148p. (gr. 4-7). pap. 10.95 *(978-0-9712206-8-3(9))* Rairarubia Bks.

Akbarpour, Ahmad. That Night's Train, 1 vol. Saghafi, Majid, tr. Arsenault, Isabelle, illus. 2012. (ENG.). 96p. (J). (gr. 3-4). 14.95 *(978-1-55498-169-4(7))* Groundwood Bks. CAN. Dist: Publishers Group West (PGW).

Alary, Laura. Mira & the Big Story. Todd, Sue, illus. 2012. (ENG.). 36p. (J). 12.00 *(978-1-55896-693-2(5),* Skinner Hse. Bks.) Unitarian Universalist Assn.

Aliki. Marianthe's Story: Painted Words & Spoken Memories. Aliki, illus. 2019. (ENG., Illus.). 64p. (J). (gr. k-5). pap. 8.99 *(978-0-06-185774-4(2),* Greenwillow Bks.) HarperCollins Pubs.

Auxier, Jonathan. The Night Gardener. (ENG.). 2015. 384p. (YA). (gr. 3-7). pap. 9.99 *(978-1-4197-1531-0(3),* 1076503) 2014. 368p. (J). (gr. 5-17). 19.99 *(978-1-4197-1144-2(X),* 1076501, Amulet Bks.) Abrams, Inc.

—The Night Gardener. 2015. (J). lib. bdg. 19.60 *(978-0-606-36891-9(4))* Turtleback.

BAtey, Kathey. Exaggeration Aggravation. 2006. (J). per. 15.00 *(978-0-9790017-1-0(4))* Spirited Presentations.

—Exaggeration Aggravation. GEbhard, Andy, illus. 2006. (J). 8.00 *(978-0-9790017-0-3(6))* Spirited Presentations.

Beck, Ian. The Secret History of Tom Trueheart. 2007. (Illus.). 352p. (J). (gr. 3-7). 16.99 *(978-0-06-115210-8(2));* lib. bdg. 17.89 *(978-0-06-115211-5(0))* HarperCollins Pubs.

Beharrell, Gayle. The Adventures of Charlie. 2008. 36p. pap. 16.99 *(978-1-4389-2546-2(8))* AuthorHouse.

Benton, Jim. The End (Almost) 2014. (Illus.). (J). *(978-0-545-67536-9(7),* Scholastic Pr.) Scholastic, Inc.

Black, Holly. How the King of Elfhame Learned to Hate Stories. Cai, Rovina, illus. 2020. (Folk of the Air Ser.). (ENG.). 192p. (YA). (gr. 9-17). 17.99 *(978-0-316-54088-9(9))* Little, Brown Bks. for Young Readers.

Blakemore, Megan Frazer. The Story Web. 2019. (ENG.). 336p. (J). 16.99 *(978-1-68119-525-4(9),* 900176198, Bloomsbury Children's Bks.) Bloomsbury Publishing USA.

Blubaugh, Penny. Serendipity Market. 2011. (ENG.). 304p. (YA). (gr. 8). pap. 8.99 *(978-0-06-146877-3(0),* HarperTeen) HarperCollins Pubs.

Blume, Lesley M. M. Cornelia & the Audacious Escapades of the Somerset Sisters. 2008. 272p. (J). (gr. 3-7). 8.99 *(978-0-440-42110-8(1),* Yearling) Random Hse. Children's Bks.

Bowling, Joyce E. & Sester, Richard. A Path of Stitches, 1 vol. 2010. 22p. pap. 24.95 *(978-1-4489-6426-0(1))* PublishAmerica, Inc.

Brown, Sharon. Nana, Tell Me a Story. 2009. 58p. pap. 15.99 *(978-1-4415-4478-0(X))* Xlibris Corp.

Broyles, Beverly Ashley, illus. Grandmother's Alligator/Burukenge Wa Nyanya Activity Guide. 2005. (ENG & SWA.). (J). 12.95 *(978-0-9703632-7-5(3))* Wakefield Connection, The.

Burford, Lorrimer. A Jamaican Storyteller's Tale. 2005. (ENG., Illus.). 197p. pap. 7.99 *(978-976-8184-84-9(1))* Penguin Publishing Group.

Cahill, Byron. The Legend of Skywoman. 2005. (J). pap. *(978-1-4108-4232-9(0))* Benchmark Education Co.

Cajoleas, Jimmy. The Rambling. 2019. (ENG.). 304p. (J). (gr. 3-7). 16.99 *(978-0-06-249878-6(9),* HarperCollins) HarperCollins Pubs.

Cardno, Anthony R. The Firflake: A Christmas Story. Cornue, Don, illus. 2008. 56p. pap. 8.95 *(978-0-595-52468-6(0))* iUniverse, Inc.

Catalanotto, Peter. Ivan the Terrier. Catalanotto, Peter, illus. 2007. (ENG., Illus.). 32p. (J). (gr. -1-3). 19.99 *(978-1-4169-1247-7(9),* Atheneum/Richard Jackson Bks.) Simon & Schuster Children's Publishing.

Cazet, Denys. Grandpa Spanielson's Chicken Pox Stories No. 1: The Octopus. Cazet, Denys, illus. 2005. (I Can Read Bks.). (Illus.). 48p. (J). (gr. -1-3). lib. bdg. 16.89 *(978-0-06-051089-3(7))* HarperCollins Pubs.

—The Octopus. Cazet, Denys, illus. 2008. (Grandpa Spanielson's Chicken Pox Stories Ser.). (Illus.). (J). (gr. -1-3). pap. 16.95 incl. audio *(978-1-4301-0455-1(4));*Set. pap. 31.95 incl. audio compact disk *(978-1-4301-0460-5(0));*Set. pap. 29.95 incl. audio *(978-1-4301-0457-5(0))* Live Oak Media.

—The Shrunken Head. 2007. (I Can Read Bks.: No. 3). (Illus.). 48p. (J). (gr. -1-3). lib. bdg. 16.89 *(978-0-06-073014-7(5))* HarperCollins Pubs.

—A Snout for Chocolate. 2006. (I Can Read Bks.). (Illus.). (J). (gr. -1-3). (ENG.). 48p. 15.99 *(978-0-06-051093-0(5));* 47p. lib. bdg. 16.89 *(978-0-06-051094-7(3))* HarperCollins Pubs.

—A Snout for Chocolate. Cazet, Denys, illus. 2008. (Grandpa Spanielson's Chicken Pox Stories Ser.). (Illus.). (J). (gr. -1-3). pap. 16.95 incl. audio *(978-1-4301-0463-6(5));*Set. pap. 29.95 incl. audio *(978-1-4301-0465-0(1));*Set. pap. 31.95 incl. audio compact disk *(978-1-4301-0468-1(6))* Live Oak Media.

—A Snout for Chocolate. 2007. (I Can Read Bks.). (Illus.). 48p. (gr. -1-3). 15.00 *(978-0-7569-8056-6(9))* Perfection Learning Corp.

Church, Alfred J. Three Greek Children. 2008. (Illus.). 160p. pap. 9.95 *(978-1-59915-081-9(6))* Yesterday's Classics.

Clayton, Colleen. What Happens Next. 2013. (ENG.). 320p. (YA). (gr. 10-17). pap. 17.99 *(978-0-316-19869-1(2),* Poppy) Little, Brown Bks. for Young Readers.

Connelly, Valerie. Goosh Gosh from the Lilac Kitchen & Other Childhood Stories. 2013. (Illus.). 42p. pap. 14.95 *(978-1-935993-49-0(6))* Nightengale Pr.

Connolly, Brian A. Hawk. 2007. 156p. 20.95 *(978-1-60264-030-6(0));* 160p. per. 13.95 *(978-1-60264-029-0(7))* Virtualbookworm.com Publishing, Inc.

Contreras, Kathleen. Braids - Trencitas. Lindmark, Margaret, illus. 2009. (ENG & SPA.). 32p. (J). (gr. -1-3). 16.99 *(978-1-933032-27-6(8))* Lectorum Pubns., Inc.

Cooke, Trish. Look Back! Binch, Caroline, illus. 2017. (ENG.). 32p. (J). (gr. 1-2). pap. 8.95 *(978-1-56656-099-3(3),* Crocodile Bks.) Interlink Publishing Group, Inc.

Cooper, Bernice Soroka. The Little Elf-Frog. 2012. 24p. pap. 17.99 *(978-1-4772-9525-0(9))* AuthorHouse.

Cooper, Susan. The Word Pirates. Kellogg, Steven, illus. 2019. 40p. (J). (gr. -1-3). 18.99 *(978-0-8234-4359-8(0),* Neal Porter Bks) Holiday Hse., Inc.

Coppo, Marianna. A Very Late Story. 2018. (ENG., Illus.). 48p. (J). (-k). 17.95 *(978-1-911171-66-9(6))* Flying Eye Bks. GBR. Dist: Penguin Random Hse. LLC.

Cornelia, Funke. CORAZÓN DE TINTA. 2006. (SPA., Illus.). 598p. (J). *(978-84-7844-235-5(9))* Siruela, Ediciones S.A.

Cowley, Joy. Big Bear & Little Bear: Story. Lam, Amy, illus. 2013. (ENG.). 8p. pap. *(978-1-927186-23-7(4),* Joy Cowley Club) Flying Start Bks.

Dadey, Debbie. Treasure in Trident City. Avakyan, Tatevik, illus. 2014. (Mermaid Tales Ser.: 8). (ENG.). 128p. (J). (gr. 1-4). pap. 6.99 *(978-1-4424-8266-1(4),* Aladdin) Simon & Schuster Children's Publishing.

Dadey, Debby & Dadey, Debbie. Treasure in Trident City, Bk. 8. Avakyan, Tatevik, illus. 2015. (Mermaid Tales Ser.). (ENG.). 120p. (J). (gr. 1-4). 31.36 *(978-1-61479-329-8(8),* 17151, Chapter Bks.) Spotlight.

Davis, Kathy Ellen. Ta-Da! Juanita, Kaylani, illus. 2018. (ENG.). 40p. (J). (gr. -1-k). 16.99 *(978-1-4521-4513-6(X))* Chronicle Bks. LLC.

Derubertis, Barbara. Eddie Elephant's Exciting Egg-Sitting. 2010. pap. 45.32 *(978-0-7613-6507-5(9))* Astra Publishing Hse.

deRubertis, Barbara. Maxwell Moose's Mountain Monster. Alley, R. W., illus. 2011. (Animal Antics A to Z Ser.). 32p. (J). pap. 45.32 *(978-0-7613-7659-0(3));* (ENG.). lib. bdg. 22.60 *(978-1-57565-334-1(6))* Astra Publishing Hse.

deRubertis, Barbara & DeRubertis, Barbara. Eddie Elephant's Exciting Egg-Sitting. Alley, R. W., illus. 2012. (Animal Antics A to Z Ser.). 32p. (J). (gr. 2 — 1). cd-rom 7.95 *(978-1-57565-398-3(2))* Astra Publishing Hse.

—Maxwell Moose's Mountain Monster. Alley, R. W., illus. 2012. (Animal Antics A to Z Ser.). 32p. (J). (gr. 2 — 1). cd-rom 7.95 *(978-1-57565-406-5(7))* Astra Publishing Hse.
DiSalvo-Ryan, DyAnne. The Sloppy Copy Slipup. 2006. (ENG., Illus.). 103p. (J). (gr. 2-4). 22.44 *(978-0-8234-1947-0(9))* Holiday Hse., Inc.
Dokey, Cameron. The Storyteller's Daughter: A Retelling of "the Arabian Nights" 2007. (Once upon a Time Ser.). (ENG., Illus.). 240p. (YA). (gr. 9). mass mkt. 8.99 *(978-1-4169-3776-0(5)*, Simon Pulse) Simon Pulse.
Donald, Alison. The New Libearian. Willmore, Alex, illus. 2018. (ENG.). 32p. (J). (gr. -1-3). 16.99 *(978-0-544-97365-7(8)*, 1663219, Clarion Bks.) HarperCollins Pubs.
Donaldson, Julia. The Fish Who Cried Wolf. Scheffler, Axel, illus. (J). 2017. (ENG.). 40p. (gr. -1-k). 17.99 *(978-0-439-92825-0(7))* 2008. pap. *(978-0-545-03454-8(X))* Scholastic, Inc. (Levine, Arthur A. Bks.).
Dubison, Valentine. Willington Woods. 2008. 52p. pap. 7.95 *(978-1-4327-2153-4(4))* Outskirts Pr., Inc.
Durst, Sarah Beth. The Stone Girl's Story. (ENG.). 336p. (J). (gr. 5-7). 2019. pap. 7.99 *(978-1-328-60391-3(1)*, 1732110) 2018. 16.99 *(978-1-328-72945-3(1)*, 1675344) HarperCollins Pubs. (Clarion Bks.).
Eagar, Lindsay. Hour of the Bees. 368p. (J). (gr. 5-9). 2017. (ENG.). pap. 9.99 *(978-0-7636-9120-2(8))* 2016. 16.99 *(978-0-7636-7922-4(4))* Candlewick Pr.
Falatko, Julie. No Boring Stories! Santoso, Charles, illus. 2018. 48p. (J). (gr. -1-3). 17.99 *(978-0-451-47682-1(4)*, Viking Books for Young Readers) Penguin Young Readers Group.
—Snappsy the Alligator (Did Not Ask to Be in This Book) Miller, Tim J., illus. 2016. 40p. (J). (gr. -1-3). 18.99 *(978-0-451-46945-8(3)*, Viking Books for Young Readers) Penguin Young Readers Group.
Fenske, Jonathan. Wake up, Crabby!: an Acorn Book (a Crabby Book #3) Fenske, Jonathan, illus. 2019. (Crabby Book Ser.: 3). (ENG., Illus.). 48p. (J). (gr. -1-1). pap. 4.99 *(978-1-338-28161-3(5))* Scholastic, Inc.
—Wake up, Crabby!: an Acorn Book (a Crabby Book #3) (Library Edition) Fenske, Jonathan, illus. 2019. (Crabby Book Ser.: 3). (ENG., Illus.). 48p. (J). (gr. -1-1). 23.99 *(978-1-338-28163-7(1))* Scholastic, Inc.
Fox, Mem. This & That. Horacek, Judy, illus. 2017. (ENG.). 32p. (J). (gr. -1-k). 17.99 *(978-1-338-03780-7(3)*, Scholastic Pr.) Scholastic, Inc.
Fraillon, Zana. The Bone Sparrow. 2016. (ENG.). 240p. (J). (gr. 4-7). 16.99 *(978-1-4847-8151-7(1))* Little, Brown Bks. for Young Readers.
Gilmore, Rachna. The Sower of Tales. 1 vol. (ENG., 348p. (J). (gr. 4-6). 2017. Illus.). per. 7.95 *(978-1-55041-590-2(5)*, ff655c1a-3901-4995-a80e-2f1d9cb38660) 2005. 10.95 *(978-1-55041-945-0(5)*, 977e3866-99b9-420d-96d9-b9b314d1ca94) Trifolium Bks., Inc. CAN. Dist: Firefly Bks., Ltd.
Gonzales Betrand, Diane. The Story Circle / el Circulo de Cuentos. Martin, Wendy, illus. 2016. (ENG, MUL & SPA.). 32p. (J). (gr. k-3). 17.95 *(978-1-55885-826-8(1)*, Piñata Books) Arte Publico Pr.
Griffiths, Andy. The 39-Story Treehouse: Mean Machines & Mad Professors! Denton, Terry, illus. 2015. (Treehouse Bks.: 3). (ENG.). 352p. (J). (gr. 1-5). 15.99 *(978-1-250-02692-7(X)*, 900098157) Feiwel & Friends.
—The 39-Story Treehouse: Mean Machines & Mad Professors! Denton, Terry, illus. 2016. (Treehouse Bks.: 3). (ENG.). 368p. (J). pap. 8.99 *(978-1-250-07511-6(4)*, 900151529) Square Fish.
Gutsche, Brigitte. The Intruder. 2006. (J). pap. *(978-0-88092-743-7(7))* Royal Fireworks Publishing Co.
Hadley, Caroline. Woodside; or, Look, Listen & Learn. 2007. (ENG., Illus.). 80p. per. *(978-1-4065-1557-2(4))* Dodo Pr.
Hanson, Mary. How to Save Your Tail* *if You Are a Rat Nabbed by Cats Who Really Like Stories about Magic Spoons, Wolves with Snout-Warts, Big, Hairy Chimney Trolls ... & Cookies, Too. 2008. (ENG., Illus.). 112p. (J). (gr. 1-4). 5.99 *(978-0-440-42228-0(0)*, Yearling) Random Hse. Children's Bks.
Hartnett, Sonya. The Silver Donkey. Spudvilas, Anne, illus. 2004. viii, 193p. (J). *(978-0-670-04240-1(4)*, Viking Adult) Penguin Publishing Group.
Hedman, Jack. The Gift of Gab: A Collection of Recollections. 2012. 48p. pap. 21.88 *(978-1-4669-1021-8(6))* Trafford Publishing.
Heidicker, Christian McKay. Scary Stories for Young Foxes. Wu, Junyi, illus. 2019. (Scary Stories for Young Foxes Ser.: 1). (ENG.). 320p. (J). 16.99 *(978-1-250-18142-8(9)*, 900190382, Holt, Henry & Co. Bks. For Young Readers) Holt, Henry & Co.
—Scary Stories for Young Foxes. Wu, Junyi, illus. 2021. (Scary Stories for Young Foxes Ser.: 1). (ENG.). 336p. (J). pap. 8.99 *(978-1-250-25044-5(7)*, 900190383) Square Fish.
Higgins, Ryan T. Bruce & the Legend of Soggy Hollow. 2023. (Mother Bruce Ser.). 48p. (J). (gr. -1-k). 18.99 ***(978-1-368-05958-9(9)***, Disney-Hyperion) Disney Publishing Worldwide.
Hughes, V. I. Aziz the Story Teller. Czernecki, Stefan, illus. 2006. 29p. (J). (gr. k-4). reprint ed. 17.00 *(978-1-4223-5298-4(6))* DIANE Publishing Co.
Hunter, Todd H. Elf Night: A Christmas Story. Gavrilovskiy, Olga, illus. 2006. 52p. (J). (gr. -1-7). 16.95 *(978-0-9788085-0-1(9))* Tetoca Pr.
Isabel, Delgado Maria. Chave's Memories / Los Recuerdos de Chave. Yvonne, Symank, illus. 2008. 32p. (J). pap. 7.95 *(978-1-55885-244-0(1)*, Piñata Books) Arte Publico Pr.
Johnston, Tony. My Abuelita. Morales, Yuyi, illus. 2009. (ENG.). 32p. (J). (gr. -1-3). 17.99 *(978-0-15-216330-3(1)*, 1200683, Clarion Bks.) HarperCollins Pubs.
Jones, Lloyd. Mister Pip. 2010. 256p. 21.85 *(978-0-7569-9114-2(5))* Perfection Learning Corp.
Keller, Tae. When You Trap a Tiger. 2020. 304p. (J). *(978-0-593-17534-7(4))* Random Hse., Inc.
—When You Trap a Tiger: (Newbery Medal Winner) (J). (gr. 3-7). 2023. 320p. pap. 8.99 *(978-1-5247-1573-1(5)*, Yearling) 2020. (ENG.). 304p. 17.99 *(978-1-5247-1570-0(0)*, Random Hse. Bks. for Young Readers) 2020. (ENG.). 304p. lib. bdg. 19.99 *(978-1-5247-1571-7(9)*, Random Hse. Bks. for Young Readers) Random Hse. Children's Bks.
Kinelski, Marilyn D. Am I Important? 2011. 28p. pap. 13.59 *(978-1-4634-1965-3(1))* AuthorHouse.
Kirby, Matthew J. Icefall. 2013. (ENG.). 336p. (J). (gr. 3-7). pap. 10.99 *(978-0-545-27425-8(7)*, Scholastic Paperbacks) Scholastic, Inc.
Koksal, Erin. Bedtime for Abbie. 2010. 23p. (J). pap. 11.95 *(978-1-4327-5693-2(1))* Outskirts Pr., Inc.
Kroll, Steven. The Tyrannosaurus Game, 0 vols. Schindler, S. D., illus. 2012. (ENG.). 32p. (J). (gr. -1-3). 17.99 *(978-0-7614-5603-2(1)*, 9780761456032, Two Lions) Amazon Publishing.
Kurtz, Jane. In the Small, Small Night. Isadora, Rachel, illus. 2005. (ENG.). 32p. (J). (gr. k-5). 17.99 *(978-0-06-623814-2(5)*, Greenwillow Bks.) HarperCollins Pubs.
Lang, Heidi. Wrong Way Summer. 2020. (ENG., Illus.). 288p. (J). (gr. 3-7). 16.99 *(978-1-4197-3693-3(0)*, 1219301) Abrams, Inc.
LaRochelle, David. It's a Tiger! Tankard, Jeremy, illus. 2012. (ENG.). 36p. (J). (gr. -1-k). 17.99 *(978-0-8118-6925-6(3))* Chronicle Bks. LLC.
Lawrence, Iain. The Giant-Slayer. 2012. (ENG.). 304p. (J). (gr. 4-6). lib. bdg. 18.69 *(978-0-385-90393-6(6)*, Delacorte Pr.) Random Hse. Children's Bks.
Lehrhaupt, Adam. Idea Jar. Pilutti, Deb, illus. 2018. (ENG.). 40p. (J). (gr. -1-3). 18.99 *(978-1-4814-5166-6(9)*, Simon & Schuster/Paula Wiseman Bks.) Simon & Schuster/Paula Wiseman Bks.
—This Is a Good Story. Le Huche, Magali, illus. 2017. (ENG.). 40p. (J). (gr. k-3). 18.99 *(978-1-4814-2935-1(3)*, Simon & Schuster/Paula Wiseman Bks.) Simon & Schuster/Paula Wiseman Bks.
Lewis, Gill. A Story Like the Wind. Weaver, Jo, illus. 2018. (ENG.). 80p. (J). 16.00 *(978-0-8028-5514-5(8)*, Eerdmans Bks For Young Readers) Eerdmans, William B. Publishing Co.
Lin, Grace. Starry River of the Sky. 2014. (ENG., Illus.). 320p. (J). (gr. 3-7). pap. 11.99 *(978-0-316-12597-0(0))* Little, Brown Bks. for Young Readers.
—Starry River of the Sky. 2014. (J). lib. bdg. 20.85 *(978-0-606-32277-5(9))* Turtleback.
—When the Sea Turned to Silver. 2017. (J). lib. bdg. 20.85 *(978-0-606-40629-1(8))* Turtleback.
—When the Sea Turned to Silver (National Book Award Finalist) (ENG.). (J). (gr. 3-7). 2017. 400p. pap. 11.99 *(978-0-316-12594-9(6))* 2016. (Illus.). 384p. 18.99 *(978-0-316-12592-5(X))* Little, Brown Bks. for Young Readers.
Little, Jean & de Vries, Maggie. Once upon a Golden Apple: 25th Anniversary Edition. Gilman, Phoebe, illus. 25th ed. 2016. (ENG.). 26p. (J). (— 1). bds. 7.99 *(978-0-670-07007-7(6)*, Puffin Canada) PRH Canada Young Readers CAN. Dist: Penguin Random Hse. LLC.
Lobel, Arnold. Historias de Ratones. 2003. (SPA.). 64p. *(978-84-95123-95-4(9)*, KA7695) Kalandraka Editora, S.L. ESP. Dist: Lectorum Pubns., Inc.
Lodding, Linda Ravin. Little Red Riding Sheep. Atkinson, Cale, illus. 2017. (ENG.). 40p. (J). (gr. -1-3). 17.99 *(978-1-4814-5748-4(9))* Simon & Schuster Children's Publishing.
Lois, Lowry. Gooney Bird Greene. Middy Chilman, Thomas, illus. 2004. (Gooney Bird Ser.: No. 1). 88p. (gr. 2-5). 16.00 *(978-0-7569-2583-3(5))* Perfection Learning Corp.
Lyon, George Ella. My Friend, the Starfinder. Gammell, Stephen, illus. 2008. (ENG.). 40p. (J). (gr. -1-2). 19.99 *(978-1-4169-2738-9(7)*, Atheneum/Richard Jackson Bks.) Simon & Schuster Children's Publishing.
Maguire, Gregory. What-The-Dickens: The Story of a Rogue Tooth Fairy. 2008. (ENG., Illus.). 304p. (gr. 4-7). pap. 10.99 *(978-0-7636-4147-4(2))* Candlewick Pr.
—What-the-Dickens: The Story of a Rogue Tooth Fairy. 2007. (ENG.). 304p. (J). (gr. 4-8). 24.80 *(978-1-4287-6555-9(7)*, Follettbound) Follett School Solutions.
Manley, Craig. The Rammarg Files. 2006. (J). lib. bdg. *(978-0-88092-742-0(9))* Royal Fireworks Publishing Co.
Manushkin, Fran. Katie's Spooky Sleepover. Lyon, Tammie, illus. 2016. (Katie Woo Ser.). (ENG.). 32p. (J). (gr. k-2). lib. bdg. 21.32 *(978-1-4795-9640-9(X)*, 131859, Picture Window Bks.) Capstone.
Martins, E. V. Cookie Nana's Story Book: Featuring " Grumpy Granddad " 2009. (Illus.). 40p. pap. 16.99 *(978-1-4389-2325-3(2))* AuthorHouse.
Matthews, Dave & Smith, Clete. If We Were Giants. Caparo, Antonio, illus. 2021. 48p. (J). (gr. 3-7). pap. 7.99 *(978-1-368-01869-2(6)*, Disney-Hyperion) Disney Publishing Worldwide.
Matthews, John and Caitlin. StoryWorld: Christmas Tales: Create-A-Story Kit. 2011. (Storyworld Ser.). (ENG., Illus.). 24p. (J). (gr. 4-7). 9.99 *(978-0-7636-5573-0(2)*, Templar) Candlewick Pr.
—StoryWorld: Tales from the Haunted House: Create-A-Story Kit. 2011. (Storyworld Ser.). (ENG., Illus.). 24p. (J). (gr. 4-7). 9.99 *(978-0-7636-5568-6(6)*, Templar) Candlewick Pr.
McCleery, William. Wolf Story. Chappell, Warren, illus. 2012. 88p. (J). (gr. k-4). 16.95 *(978-1-59017-589-7(1)*, NYR Children's Collection) New York Review of Bks., Inc., The.
McLaughlin, Tom. The Story Machine. 2015. (ENG., Illus.). 32p. (J). (gr. -1-1). 12.99 *(978-1-4088-3934-8(2)*, 234931, Bloomsbury Children's Bks.) Bloomsbury Publishing Plc GBR. Dist: Macmillan.
Montgomery, Ross. Christmas Dinner of Souls. 2017. (ENG., Illus.). 240p. (J). 12.50 *(978-0-571-31797-4(9)*, Faber & Faber Children's Bks.) Faber & Faber, Inc.
Moser, Fiadhnait. The Serendipity of Flightless Things. 2019. (ENG.). 320p. (J). (gr. 4-9). 16.99 *(978-1-4998-0843-8(7)*, Yellow Jacket) Bonnier Publishing USA.
Muth, Jon J. Addy's Cup of Sugar: Based on a Buddhist Story of Healing (a Stillwater & Friends Book) Muth, Jon J., illus. 2020. (ENG., Illus.). 32p. (J). (gr. -1-3). 17.99 *(978-0-439-63428-1(8)*, Scholastic Pr.) Scholastic, Inc.
—Zen Ghosts (a Stillwater & Friends Book) Muth, Jon J., illus. 2010. (ENG., Illus.). 40p. (J). (gr. -1-3). 18.99 *(978-0-439-63430-4(X)*, Scholastic Pr.) Scholastic, Inc.
—Zen Shorts, 1 vol. Muth, Jon J., illus. 2010. (ENG.). (J). (gr. -1-3). audio compact disk 18.99 *(978-0-545-22760-5(7))* Scholastic, Inc.
—Zen Shorts (a Stillwater & Friends Book), 1 vol. Muth, Jon J., illus. 2005. (ENG., Illus.). 40p. (J). (gr. -1-3). 17.99 *(978-0-439-33911-7(1)*, Scholastic Pr.) Scholastic, Inc.
—Zen Socks (a Stillwater & Friends Book) Muth, Jon J., illus. 2015. (ENG., Illus.). 40p. (J). (gr. -1-3). 17.99 *(978-0-545-16669-0(1)*, Scholastic Pr.) Scholastic, Inc.
Nance, Andrew. Return to Daemon Hall: Evil Roots. Polhemus, Coleman, illus. 2011. (ENG.). 256p. (YA). (gr. 7-12). 21.99 *(978-0-8050-8748-2(6)*, 900049739, Holt, Henry & Co. Bks. For Young Readers) Holt, Henry & Co.
Nash, Scott. Tuff Fluff: The Case of Duckie's Missing Brain. Nash, Scott, illus. 2004. (Illus.). (J). 101.94 *(978-0-7636-2503-0(5))*; (ENG., 40p. (gr. 1-4). 17.99 *(978-0-7636-1882-7(9))* Candlewick Pr.
Niemi, Renee. Because Gage Believed. 2013. 20p. pap. 24.95 *(978-1-62709-730-7(9))* America Star Bks.
Oppenheim, Joanne F. The Prince's Bedtime. Latimer, Miriam, illus. 2007. 32p. (J). (gr. -1-3). pap. 7.99 *(978-1-84686-106-2(3))* Barefoot Bks., Inc.
Paulsen, Gary. Fishbone's Song. 2016. (ENG., Illus.). 160p. (J). (gr. 5). 18.99 *(978-1-4814-5226-7(6)*, Simon & Schuster Bks. For Young Readers) Simon & Schuster Bks. For Young Readers.
Peacock, Thomas. The Forever Sky. Lee, Annette S., illus. 2019. (ENG.). 32p. (J). 17.95 *(978-1-68134-098-2(4))* Minnesota Historical Society Pr.
Pearl, Alexa. Tales of Sasha 9: the Disappearing History. Sordo, Paco, illus. 2018. (Tales of Sasha Ser.: 9). (ENG.). 112p. (J). (gr. k-3). 16.99 *(978-1-4998-0607-6(8))*; pap. 5.99 *(978-1-4998-0606-9(X))* Little Bee Books Inc.
Porte, Barbara Ann. Beauty & the Serpent: Thirteen Tales of Unnatural Animals. Covey, Rosemary Felt, illus. 2008. (ENG.). 128p. (YA). (gr. 7). pap. 7.99 *(978-1-4169-7579-3(9)*, Simon & Schuster/Paula Wiseman Bks.) Simon & Schuster/Paula Wiseman Bks.
Porter, Rhonda. Brody Meets a Bully. 2008. 16p. pap. 24.95 *(978-1-60610-311-1(3))* America Star Bks.
Resman, Michael. The Villagers. Senelwa, Fred, tr. Gathigo, Cyrus Ngatia, illus. 2012. 40p. pap. *(978-976-8142-41-2(3))* Producciones de la Hamaca.
Rosenthal, Eileen. I'll Save You Bobo! Rosenthal, Marc, illus. 2012. (ENG.). 40p. (J). (gr. -1-1). 19.99 *(978-1-4424-0378-9(0)*, Atheneum Bks. for Young Readers) Simon & Schuster Children's Publishing.
Say, Allen. Kamishibai Man. 2005. (ENG., Illus.). 32p. (J). (gr. -1-3). 17.99 *(978-0-618-47954-2(6)*, 598441, Clarion Bks.) HarperCollins Pubs.
Schami, Rafik. The Storyteller of Damascus. Knorr, Peter, illus. 2018. (ENG.). 48p. (J). 18.95 *(978-1-62371-971-5(2)*, Crocodile Bks.) Interlink Publishing Group, Inc.
Schmidt, Gary D. Mara's Stories: Glimmers in the Darkness. 2008. (ENG.). 160p. (YA). (gr. 5-9). per. 15.99 *(978-0-312-37388-7(0)*, 900045532) Square Fish.
Schow, Betsy. Banished. 2018. (Storymakers Ser.: 3). (ENG.). 336p. (YA). (gr. 6-12). pap. 10.99 *(978-1-4926-3602-1(9))* Sourcebooks, Inc.
Sidney, Margaret. Polly Pepper's Book. 2011. 316p. 50.95 *(978-1-258-10539-6(X))* Literary Licensing, LLC.
Small, Lily. Mia the Mouse: Fairy Animals of Misty Wood. 2015. (Fairy Animals of Misty Wood Ser.: 4). (ENG., Illus.). 144p. (J). (gr. k-3). pap. 6.99 *(978-1-62779-144-1(2)*, 900137177, Holt, Henry & Co. Bks. For Young Readers) Holt, Henry & Co.
Spinner, Stephanie. It's a Miracle! A Hanukkah Storybook. McElmurry, Jill, illus. 2007. (ENG.). 48p. (J). (gr. -1-3). 7.99 *(978-1-4169-5001-1(X)*, Aladdin) Simon & Schuster Children's Publishing.
Stahl, Jon. The Dragons Eat Noodles on Tuesdays. Bentley, Tadgh, illus. 2019. (ENG.). 40p. (J). (gr. -1-3). 17.99 *(978-1-338-12551-1(6)*, Scholastic Pr.) Scholastic, Inc.
Stauffacher, Sue. The Space Between Before & After. 2019. 288p. (J). (gr. 4-7). 17.99 *(978-0-8234-4148-8(2)*, Margaret Ferguson Books) Holiday Hse., Inc.
Stead, Philip C. Bear Has a Story to Tell. 2013. (CHI & ENG.). 32p. (J). (gr. -1-2). 29.99 *(978-7-5391-8389-3(6))* 21st Century Publishing Hse.
—Bear Has a Story to Tell. Stead, Erin E., illus. 2012. (ENG.). 32p. (J). (gr. -1-1). 19.99 *(978-1-59643-745-6(6)*, 900077930) Roaring Brook Pr.
Stein, David Ezra. Interrupting Chicken. Stein, David Ezra, illus. (Interrupting Chicken Ser.). (ENG., Illus.). (J). 2019. 34p. (-k). bds. 8.99 *(978-1-5362-0672-2(5))* 2016. 40p. (gr. -1-3). 7.99 *(978-0-7636-8903-2(3))* 2010. 40p. (gr. -1-3). 17.99 *(978-0-7636-4168-9(5))* Candlewick Pr.
—Interrupting Chicken. 2016. (ENG.). 38p. (J). (gr. -1-2). 19.36 net. *(978-1-64310-039-5(4))* Penworthy Co., LLC, The.
—Interrupting Chicken & the Elephant of Surprise. Stein, David Ezra, illus. 2018. (Interrupting Chicken Ser.). (ENG., Illus.). 40p. (J). (gr. -1-3). 17.99 *(978-0-7636-8842-4(8))* Candlewick Pr.
Stewart, Paul. Far-Flung Adventures: Hugo Pepper. 2012. (Far-Flung Adventures Ser.). (ENG.). 272p. (J). (gr. 3-7). 7.99 *(978-0-385-75223-7(7)*, Yearling) Random Hse. Children's Bks.
Tanner, Lian. Battlesong: Book Three in the Icebreaker Trilogy. 2018. (Icebreaker Trilogy Ser.: 3). (ENG.). 304p. (J). pap. 15.99 *(978-1-250-15871-0(0)*, 900185527) Square Fish.
Theroux, Phyllis. Serefina under the Circumstances. Priceman, Marjorie, illus. 2004. 30p. (J). (gr. k-4). reprint ed. *(978-0-7567-7756-2(9))* DIANE Publishing Co.
Tonti, Mat. The Book of Secrets. Tonti, Mat, illus. 2020. (ENG., Illus.). 208p. (J). (gr. 3-5). 19.99 *(978-1-5415-7825-8(2)*, 19dcb295-d07f-4fda-99fb-7d14d5741f18, Kar-Ben Publishing) Lerner Publishing Group.
Turk, Evan. The Storyteller. Turk, Evan, illus. 2016. (ENG., Illus.). 48p. (J). (gr. -1-3). 18.99 *(978-1-4814-3518-5(3))* Simon & Schuster Children's Publishing.
Velasquez, Eric. Octopus Stew. 2019. (Illus.). 40p. (J). (gr. -1-3). 17.99 *(978-0-8234-3754-2(X))* Holiday Hse., Inc.
Venable, Colleen AF. Amy the Red Panda Is Writing the Best Story in the World. Chan, Ruth, illus. 2017. (ENG.). 40p. (J). (gr. -1-3). 17.99 *(978-0-06-233848-8(X)*, Greenwillow Bks.) HarperCollins Pubs.
Vincent, Harris T. & Brewer, Mary. When Grandmother Was A Little Girl. 2010. 40p. 23.99 *(978-1-4520-7728-4(2))* AuthorHouse.
Virjan, Emma J. What This Story Needs Is a Pig in a Wig. 2015. (Pig in a Wig Book Ser.). (ENG., Illus.). 40p. (J). (gr. -1-3). 10.99 *(978-0-06-232724-6(0)*, HarperCollins) HarperCollins Pubs.
Wade, Maryam. Bently & the Silver Wings. 2011. 24p. pap. 24.95 *(978-1-4560-7503-3(9))* America Star Bks.
Waide, Christine. The Candy Darlings. 2006. (ENG.). 310p. (YA). (gr. 9-12). per. 18.95 *(978-0-618-58969-2(4)*, 497559, Clarion Bks.) HarperCollins Pubs.
Watkins, Rowboat. Big Bunny: (Funny Bedtime Read Aloud Book for Kids, Bunny Book) 2018. (ENG., Illus.). 40p. (J). (gr. -1-k). 16.99 *(978-1-4521-6390-1(1))* Chronicle Bks. LLC.
Watt, Mélanie & Watt, Mélanie. Chester's Back! Watt, Mélanie & Watt, Mélanie, illus. 2013. (Chester Ser.). (ENG., Illus.). 32p. (J). (gr. -1-3). 9.99 *(978-1-55453-461-6(5))* Kids Can Pr., Ltd. CAN. Dist: Hachette Bk. Group.
Weston Woods Staff, creator. A Story-A Story. 2011. 18.95 *(978-0-439-72891-1(6))*; 29.95 *(978-0-439-73521-6(1))* Weston Woods Studios, Inc.
—A Story-Astory. 2011. 38.75 *(978-0-439-72892-8(4))* Weston Woods Studios, Inc.
Wiggin, Kate Douglas. Polly Oliver's Problem. 2007. 108p. per. 9.95 *(978-1-60312-369-3(5))*; 22.95 *(978-1-60312-707-3(0))* Aegypan.
—Polly Oliver's Problem. 2016. (ENG., Illus.). (J). 24.95 *(978-1-357-78791-2(X))* Creative Media Partners, LLC.
Wiggin, Kate Douglas Smith. Polly Oliver's Problem. 2017. (ENG., Illus.). (J). 22.95 *(978-1-374-96499-0(9))* Capital Communications, Inc.
Willems, Mo. I Broke My Trunk!-An Elephant & Piggie Book. 2011. (Elephant & Piggie Book Ser.). (ENG., Illus.). 64p. (J). (gr. -1-k). 9.99 *(978-1-4231-3309-4(9)*, Hyperion Books for Children) Disney Publishing Worldwide.
Wolfson, Jill. What I Call Life. 2008. (ENG.). 288p. (J). (gr. 5-9). pap. 19.99 *(978-0-312-37752-6(5)*, 900049142) Square Fish.
Wooding, Chris. Poison. 2006. 1.00 *(978-1-4237-9048-8(0))* Recorded Bks., Inc.
Woodruff, Liza. A Quieter Story. 2019. (Illus.). 40p. (J). (gr. -1-1). 18.99 *(978-0-8234-4164-8(4)*, Margaret Ferguson Books) Holiday Hse., Inc.
Wyeth, Sharon Dennis. The Granddaughter Necklace. Ibatoulline, Bagram, illus. (J). 2013. (ENG.). 32p. (gr. -1-3). 18.99 *(978-0-545-08125-2(4))* 2012. pap. *(978-0-545-23983-7(4))* Scholastic, Inc. (Levine, Arthur A. Bks.).
Yaccarino, Dan. I Am a Story. Yaccarino, Dan, illus. 2016. (ENG., Illus.). 40p. (J). (gr. -1-3). 17.99 *(978-0-06-241106-8(3)*, HarperCollins) HarperCollins Pubs.
Zarins, Kim. Sometimes We Tell the Truth. 2016. *(978-1-4814-7554-9(1))* Simon & Schuster, Inc.
—Sometimes We Tell the Truth. 2017. (ENG.). 448p. (YA). (gr. 9). pap. 12.99 *(978-1-4814-6500-7(7)*, Simon Pulse) Simon Pulse.
Zusak, Markus. The Book Thief. 2014. (ENG.). 576p. (YA). 17.24 *(978-1-63245-052-4(6))* Lectorum Pubns., Inc.
—The Book Thief. 2009. 12.64 *(978-0-7848-1941-8(6)*, Everbind) Marco Bk. Co.
—The Book Thief. 2008. 552p. (gr. 7-12). 23.00 *(978-0-7569-8440-3(8))* Perfection Learning Corp.
—The Book Thief. (ENG., Illus.). (YA). (gr. 7-12). 2007. 608p. pap. 14.99 *(978-0-375-84220-7(9))* 2013. 592p. pap. 14.99 *(978-0-385-75472-9(8))* Random Hse. Children's Bks. (Knopf Bks. for Young Readers).
—The Book Thief. l.t. ed. 2006. (ENG.). 552p. 23.99 *(978-1-4104-6806-2(2))*; 757p. (YA). (gr. 7-12). 24.95 *(978-0-7862-9021-5(8))* Thorndike Pr.
—The Book Thief. 2008. (ENG., Illus.). 560p. pap. *(978-0-552-77389-8(1)*, Black Swan) Transworld Publishers Ltd.
—The Book Thief. 2007. 552p. lib. bdg. 24.50 *(978-1-4177-9738-7(X))* 2013. lib. bdg. 24.50 *(978-0-606-34656-6(2))* Turtleback.
—The Book Thief (Anniversary Edition) anniv. ed. 2016. (ENG., Illus.). 592p. (YA). (gr. 7-12). 22.99 *(978-1-101-93418-0(2)*, Knopf Bks. for Young Readers) Random Hse. Children's Bks.

STOVES—FICTION

Fussell, Bonnie. More Than a Stove. Sadler, Dale, illus. l.t. ed. 2004. 32p. (J). pap. 7.99 *(978-0-615-12702-6(9))* Blackberry Pubs.

STOWE, HARRIET BEECHER, 1811-1896

Elliot, Henry. Harriet Beecher Stowe: The Voice of Humanity in White America, 1 vol. 2009. (Voices for Freedom Ser.). (ENG., Illus.). 64p. (J). (gr. 5-8). pap. *(978-0-7787-4837-3(5))*; lib. bdg. *(978-0-7787-4821-2(9))* Crabtree Publishing Co.
Griffiths, Katie. Harriet Beecher Stowe: Author & Abolitionist, 1 vol. 2016. (Great American Thinkers Ser.). (ENG., Illus.). 128p. (J). (gr. 9-9). 47.36 *(978-1-5026-1930-3(X)*, e0837d98-e85e-4f42-b472-bf45f0e02b37) Cavendish Square Publishing LLC.
Griskey, Michele. Harriet Beecher Stowe. 2005. (Classic Storytellers Ser.). (Illus.). 48p. (J). (gr. 4-8). lib. bdg. 29.95 *(978-1-58415-375-7(X))* Mitchell Lane Pubs.
Haugen, Brenda. Harriet Beecher Stowe: The Inspiring Life Story of the Abolition Advocate. 2016. (Inspiring Stories Ser.). (ENG., Illus.). 112p. (J). (gr. 5-7). lib. bdg. 38.65 *(978-0-7565-5164-3(1)*, 128792, Compass Point Bks.) Capstone.
Marsh, Carole. Harriet Beecher Stowe. 2003. 12p. (gr. k-4). 2.95 *(978-0-635-02356-8(3))* Gallopade International.
Rau, Dana Meachen. Who Was Harriet Beecher Stowe? Copeland, Gregory, illus. 2015. (Who Was-? Chapters Ser.). (ENG.). 112p. (J). (gr. 3-6). 21.19 *(978-1-4844-5253-0(4)*, Penguin Workshop) Penguin Young Readers Group.
—Who Was Harriet Beecher Stowe? 2015. (Who Was... ? Ser.). (Illus.). 105p. (J). lib. bdg. 16.00 *(978-0-606-36598-7(2))* Turtleback.
Rau, Dana Meachen & Who HQ. Who Was Harriet Beecher Stowe? Copeland, Gregory, illus. 2015. (Who Was? Ser.). 112p. (J). (gr. 3-7). 6.99 *(978-0-448-48301-6(7)*, Penguin Workshop) Penguin Young Readers Group.

STRATEGIC MATERIALS

see Materials

STRATIGRAPHIC GEOLOGY

see Geology, Stratigraphic

STRATOSPHERE

Jakubiak, David J. What Can We Do about Ozone Loss? (Illus.). 24p. 2012. (J). 49.50 *(978-1-4488-5379-3(6)*,

S

PowerKids Pr.) 2011. (ENG., (J). (gr. 2-3). pap. 9.25 *(978-1-4488-5118-8(1),* d0aa2715-5485-4a5c-933d-40226ab9b9b3, PowerKids Pr.) 2011. (ENG., (YA). (gr. 2-3). lib. bdg. 26.27 *(978-1-4488-4985-7(3),* 494e0409-76a1-48cb-bb22-467fe2ffc786) Rosen Publishing Group, Inc., The.

STRAVINSKY, IGOR, 1882-1971

Stringer, Lauren. When Stravinsky Met Nijinsky: Two Artists, Their Ballet, & One Extraordinary Riot. Stringer, Lauren, illus. 2013. (ENG., Illus.). 32p. (J). (gr. -1-3). 16.99 *(978-0-547-90725-3(7),* 1512512, Clarion Bks.) HarperCollins Pubs.

Whiting, Jim. The Life & Times of Igor Stravinsky. 2004. (Masters of Music Ser.). (Illus.). 48p. (gr. 4-8). lib. bdg. 20.95 *(978-1-58415-277-4(X))* Mitchell Lane Pubs.

STRAWBERRY SHORTCAKE (FICTITIOUS CHARACTER)—FICTION

Ball, Georgia. Volume 1: the Baby Berrykin Baking Challenge Part 1. Mebberson, Amy, illus. 2017. (Strawberry Shortcake Ser.). (ENG.). 24p. (J). (gr. 2-8). lib. bdg. 31.36 *(978-1-5321-4029-7(0),* 25461, Graphic Novels) Spotlight.

—Volume 2: the Baby Berrykin Baking Challenge Part 2. Mebberson, Amy, illus. 2017. (Strawberry Shortcake Ser.). (ENG.). 24p. (J). (gr. 2-8). lib. bdg. 31.36 *(978-1-5321-4030-3(4),* 25462, Graphic Novels) Spotlight.

Ball, Georgia & Mebberson, Amy. Strawberry Shortcake, Vol. 1. 2013. (ENG., Illus.). 104p. (J). (gr. 4-8). pap. 14.99 *(978-1-937676-61-2(7),* 9781937676612) Ape Entertainment.

Bryant, Megan E. Rapunzel. Huxtable, Tonja & Huxtable, John, illus. 2007. (Berry Fairy Tales Ser.). (J). *(978-1-4287-4159-1(3),* Grosset & Dunlap) Penguin Publishing Group.

Jacobs, Lana. A Brand-New Look. 2013. (Penguin Young Readers Level 2 Ser.). lib. bdg. 13.55 *(978-0-606-29293-1(4))* Turtleback.

—Lost & Found. 2012. (Penguin Young Readers Level 2 Ser.). lib. bdg. 13.55 *(978-0-606-23626-3(0))* Turtleback.

—Show-And-Tell. 2013. (Penguin Young Readers Level 2 Ser.). (Illus.). 31p. (J). lib. bdg. 13.55 *(978-0-606-31694-1(9))* Turtleback.

Matheis, Mickie. The Butterfly Parade. 2016. (Penguin Young Readers Level 2 Ser.). lib. bdg. 13.55 *(978-0-606-38429-2(4))* Turtleback.

Okaty, Nicole. Orange Blossom's Fruity Fun Book: A Juicy Orange Adventure. 2004. (Illus.). 39p. *(978-0-439-70466-3(9))* Scholastic, Inc.

Strawberry Shortcake Activity Book Collection. 2005. (J). *(978-1-59487-137-5(X))* Artist Studios, Ltd.

Strawberry Shortcake Berry Loveable Diary. 2005. 7.95 *(978-1-59487-083-5(7))* Artist Studios, Ltd.

STREAMLINING

see Aerodynamics

STREET TRAFFIC

see Traffic Regulations

STREETS

see also Roads

Mara, Wil. What Should I Do? near a Busy Street. 2011. (Community Connections: What Should I Do? Ser.). (ENG., Illus.). 24p. (J). (gr. 2-5). lib. bdg. 29.21 *(978-1-61080-051-8(6),* 201044) Cherry Lake Publishing.

Our Street: Big Book: Level D. Group 1. (Sunshine Ser.). 8p. 20.95 *(978-0-7802-5732-0(4))* Wright Group/McGraw-Hill.

Stewart, Kara. A City Street, 1 vol. 2008. (Real Life Readers Ser.). (ENG.). 8p. (gr. k-1). pap. 5.15 *(978-1-4042-7961-2(X),* 09a7e009-9f6f-4134-a701-085731a8ad30, Rosen Classroom) Rosen Publishing Group, Inc., The.

STRINGED INSTRUMENTS

see also names of stringed instruments, e.g. Guitar; etc.

Dick, William & Scott, Laurie. Mastery for Strings, 3 vols. 2004. 109p. spiral bd. 15.95 *(978-0-9753919-0-7(9))* Mastery For Strings Pubns.

Ganeri, Anita. Stringed Instruments. 2011. (ENG., Illus.). 32p. (J). pap. 10.95 *(978-1-77092-032-3(3))* Saunders Bk. Co. CAN. Dist: RiverStream Publishing.

Kenney, Karen Latchana. Swaying Strings. Heinsz, Joshua, illus. 2019. (Physics of Music Ser.). (ENG.). 24p. (J). (gr. k-2). lib. bdg. 33.99 *(978-1-68410-344-7(4),* 140264) Cantata Learning.

Kreutzer, Rudolph. Forty-Two Studies for Violin. Singer, Edmund, ed. (Carl Fischer Music Library: No. 120). 73p. (J). pap. 10.95 *(978-0-8258-0025-2(0))* Fischer, Carl LLC.

Lillywhite, Rosalind & Marshall, Andrew. Abracadabra Strings - Abracadabra Double Bass Book 1, 1 vol. Moss, Carla & Sebba, Jane, eds. Parks, Paul et al, illus. 2005. (Abracadabra Ser.). (ENG.). 64p. (J). pap. 24.95 incl. audio compact disk *(978-0-7136-7097-4(5))* HarperCollins Pubs. Ltd. GBR. Dist: Independent Pubs. Group.

Nunn, Daniel. Strings, 1 vol. 2011. (Instruments & Music Ser.). (ENG.). 24p. (J). (gr. -1-1). pap. 6.29 *(978-1-4329-5069-9(X),* 115122, Heinemann) Capstone.

Smith, Erica. Making Music with Stringed Instruments. 2009. (Reading Room Collection 2 Ser.). 24p. (gr. 3-4). 42.50 *(978-1-60851-979-8(1),* PowerKids Pr.) Rosen Publishing Group, Inc., The.

Stevens, Kathryn. Cellos. 2019. (Musical Instruments Ser.). (ENG.). 24p. (J). (gr. 3-6). lib. bdg. 32.79 *(978-1-5038-3187-2(6),* 213314) Child's World, Inc, The.

Storey, Rita. The Violin & Other Stringed Instruments. 2010. (J). 28.50 *(978-1-59920-212-9(3))* Black Rabbit Bks.

Wearing, Katie & Scott, Elaine. Abracadabra Strings Beginners - Abracadabra Viola Beginner (Pupil's Book + CD), 1 vol. rev. ed. 2007. (Abracadabra Ser.). (ENG., Illus.). 32p. (J). pap. 11.95 *(978-0-7136-7839-0(9))* HarperCollins Pubs. Ltd. GBR. Dist: Independent Pubs. Group.

STRINGED INSTRUMENTS—FICTION

Baker, Keith. Just How Long Can a Long String Be? 2009. (J). pap. *(978-0-545-08662-2(0),* Levine, Arthur A. Bks.) Scholastic, Inc.

Meadows, Daisy. Victoria the Violin Fairy #6. 2010. (ENG.). 80p. (J). lib. bdg. 15.39 *(978-1-4242-4735-6(7))* Fitzgerald Bks.

STRUCTURAL BOTANY

see Plant Anatomy

STRUCTURAL DRAFTING

see Mechanical Drawing

STUDENT ACTIVITIES

see also College and School Journalism; School Sports

Abrams, Pam. Finger Fun: PACK-Tivities. 2011. (PACKtivities Ser.: 2). (ENG.). 48p. (J). (gr. -1-3). 9.99 *(978-1-935703-37-2(4))* Downtown Bookworks.

Accord Publishing, Accord. Go Fun! Doodle: Summer Fun. 2012. (ENG.). 72p. (J). pap. 4.99 *(978-1-4494-1735-2(3))* Andrews McMeel Publishing.

—Go Fun! Dot-To-Dot: Summer Fun. 2012. (ENG.). 72p. (J). pap. 4.99 *(978-1-4494-1814-4(7))* Andrews McMeel Publishing.

—Zoo Babies. 2010. (ENG., Illus.). 12p. (J). (gr. -1). 9.99 *(978-0-7407-9201-4(6))* Andrews McMeel Publishing.

Adam, Sarah E., illus. Abby in Vermont Coloring & Activity Book. 2008. 32p. (J). 4.95 *(978-0-9793790-1-7(6))* Howard Printing, Inc.

Adventures in Suburbia-Boston. 2nd ed. 2003. (J). per. 19.95 *(978-0-9743319-1-1(0))* Kiwi Media Group, Inc.

Aguinaco, Carmen F. Amigos de Jesús 2009: A Bilingual Catechetical Program. un Programa Catequético BilingüE. Advent 2008 - November 2009. Petersen, William, illus. 2008.Tr. of Friends of Jesus 2009. (ENG & SPA.). 408p. (J). pap. 99.00 *(978-0-89570-503-7(6))* Claretian Pubns.

Ahearn, Dan. Time for Kids Readers. 2003. (Time for Kids Readers Ser.). (ENG.). pap. 84.96 *(978-0-15-340566-2(X))* Harcourt Schl. Pubs.

Akhila Rajan And Ananya Rajan. Crafabets Adventure. 2011. 56p. pap. 31.99 *(978-1-4568-3197-4(6))* Xlibris Corp.

Al-Muzher, Engineer Khalid Mohammed. Smart Boy Diary: How smartly can you keep your innovative ideas? 2011. 32p. pap. 19.67 *(978-1-4567-8299-3(1))* AuthorHouse.

Alderson, Phil. Busy Kids Dinosaurs Magnetic Playbook. 2007. (Busy Kids Ser.). (Illus.). 10p. (J). (gr. -1-3). bds. *(978-1-84610-552-4(8))* Make Believe Ideas.

Allain, Moose. Fill-Me-In. Allain, Moose, illus. 2016. (ENG., Illus.). 96p. (J). (gr. 1-4). 16.99 *(978-0-7636-8532-4(1),* Big Picture Press) Candlewick Pr.

Allen, Heather. BOOST Earth Day Is Every Day! Activity Book. 2013. (Dover Kids Activity Books: Nature Ser.). (ENG.). 48p. (J). (gr. 3-5). pap. 5.99 *(978-0-486-49433-3(0),* 494330) Dover Pubns., Inc.

Altmann, Scott. Guitar Rock Star Sticker Activity Book. 2008. (Dover Little Activity Bks.). (ENG.). 4p. (J). (gr. -1-5). pap. 1.50 *(978-0-486-46790-0(2))* Dover Pubns., Inc.

Amery, Heather. Cinderella Kid Kit with Pop Out Coach. Cartwright, Stephen, illus. 2006. (Usborne First Stories Ser.). 16p. (J). (gr. -1-3). pap. 8.99 *(978-1-58086-877-8(0),* Usborne) EDC Publishing.

Aminah's World: An Activity Book & Children's Guide about Artist Aminah Brenda Lynn Robinson. 2018. (ENG.). 60p. (J). (gr. 3-8). 24.95 *(978-0-918881-35-9(8))* Ohio Univ. Pr.

Anastasio, Dina. Mask Making Around the World. 2011. (Early Connections Ser.). (J). *(978-1-61672-588-4(5))* Benchmark Education Co.

Anderson, Airlie. What to Doodle? Jr. - Princesses, Fairies, Mermaids & More! 2013. (Dover Doodle Bks.). (ENG.). 128p. (J). (gr. k-3). pap. 4.99 *(978-0-486-49951-2(0))* Dover Pubns., Inc.

Andreae, Giles. Captain Flinn & the Pirate Dinosaurs: Missing Treasure! Ayto, Russell, illus. 2008. (Captain Flinn & the Pirate Dinosaurs Ser.). (ENG.). 32p. (J). (gr. -1-3). 17.99 *(978-1-4169-6745-3(1),* McElderry, Margaret K. Bks.) McElderry, Margaret K. Bks.

Andrew, Edwards & Fleur, Thornton. Footsteps of the Past: William Booth. 2005. (Footsteps of the Past Ser.). pap. 5.00 *(978-1-903087-83-1(X))* DayOne Pubns. GBR. Dist: Send The Light Distribution LLC.

Andrews, Jackie. On the Farm. 2012. (ENG., Illus.). 24p. (J). pap. 6.50 *(978-1-84135-354-8(X))* Award Pubns. Ltd. GBR. Dist: Parkwest Pubns., Inc.

Anholt, Laurence. Anholt's Artists Activity Book. 2012. (ENG.). 48p. (J). (gr. k-3). pap. 11.99 *(978-1-4380-0114-2(2))* Sourcebooks, Inc.

Anorak Press Staff & Olmedillas, Cathy, compiled by. Anorak: The Happy Mag For Kids. 2012. (ENG., Illus.). 64p. (J). pap. 9.99 *(978-1-4236-3317-4(2),* Anorak Pr.) Gibbs Smith, Publisher.

Anton, Carrie, ed. Go for It! Start Smart, Have Fun, & Stay Inspired in Any Activity. Laskey, Shannon, illus. 2008. (American Girl Library). (ENG.). 64p. (YA). (gr. 3-18). pap. 9.95 *(978-1-59369-423-4(7))* American Girl Publishing, Inc.

Archie Superstars. Archie's Fun 'n' Games Activity Book. 2013. (Illus.). 192p. (J). (gr. 4-7). 6.99 *(978-1-936975-51-8(3))* Archie Comic Pubns., Inc.

Arciniega Bailey, Yvette. Squiggly Wiggly Lines. 2013. 34p. pap. 7.99 *(978-1-4575-2390-8(6))* Dog Ear Publishing, LLC.

Arcturus Publishing Staff. Paper Planes. 2013. (ENG.). 96p. (J). pap. 12.95 *(978-1-78212-289-0(3),* 0b5f0e38-39f7-4c60-8084-7b5e91af1c65) Arcturus Publishing GBR. Dist: Baker & Taylor Publisher Services (BTPS).

Armadillo. Supersticker Fun! Numbers, Colours, Sizes, Opposites. 2017. (ENG., Illus.). 64p. (J). (gr. -1-12). pap. 8.99 *(978-1-86147-773-6(2),* Armadillo) Anness Publishing GBR. Dist: National Bk. Network.

Armadillo Publishing Staff & Armadillo Press Saff. 200 Stickers! Playtime, Dressing Up, Party, Food & Drink: An Entertaining Play & Learn Book. 2017. (Illus.). 64p. (J). (gr. -1-12). pap. 8.99 *(978-1-86147-772-9(4),* Armadillo) Anness Publishing GBR. Dist: National Bk. Network.

Artz, Tracy. The Sneaky Leprechaun. 2011. 41p. pap. 10.95 *(978-1-4327-6324-4(5))* Outskirts Pr., Inc.

Aryal, Naren. Hello, Beaker! Morehead State University. Schartup, Adam, illus. 2013. (ENG.). (J). 14.95 *(978-1-62086-151-6(8))* Amplify Publishing Group.

AWARD & Award, Anna. Dot to Dot: Butterfly. 2015. (ENG.). 16p. (J). pap. 3.99 *(978-1-78270-122-4(2))* Award Pubns. Ltd. GBR. Dist: Parkwest Pubns., Inc.

Award, Anna. English. Burton, Terry, illus. 2012. (ENG.). 36p. (J). pap. 8.25 *(978-1-84135-801-7(0))* Award Pubns. Ltd. GBR. Dist: Parkwest Pubns., Inc.

—English/French. Burton, Terry, illus. 2012. (ENG.). 36p. (J). pap. 8.25 *(978-1-84135-802-4(9))* Award Pubns. Ltd. GBR. Dist: Parkwest Pubns., Inc.

Award Publications Staff. ABC. 2012. (ENG., Illus.). 24p. (J). 6.50 *(978-1-84135-552-8(6))* Award Pubns. Ltd. GBR. Dist: Parkwest Pubns., Inc.

—Ballerina Lisa: Glitter Paper Doll. 2012. (ENG.). 12p. (J). 6.50 *(978-1-84135-629-7(8))* Award Pubns. Ltd. GBR. Dist: Parkwest Pubns., Inc.

—Fairy Belle. 2012. (ENG., Illus.). 12p. (J). 6.50 *(978-1-84135-631-0(X))* Award Pubns. Ltd. GBR. Dist: Parkwest Pubns., Inc.

—My First Alphabet: Activities in Key Skills, Parent Tips. 2012. (ENG., Illus.). 24p. (J). pap. 4.95 *(978-1-84135-573-3(9))* Award Pubns. Ltd. GBR. Dist: Parkwest Pubns., Inc.

—My First Words. 2012. (ENG., Illus.). 24p. (J). pap. 4.95 *(978-1-84135-574-0(7))* Award Pubns. Ltd. GBR. Dist: Parkwest Pubns., Inc.

—My First Writing. 2012. (ENG., Illus.). 24p. (J). pap. 4.95 *(978-1-84135-572-6(0))* Award Pubns. Ltd. GBR. Dist: Parkwest Pubns., Inc.

—Princess Sophia: Glitter Paper Doll. 2017. (ENG.). 20p. (J). 5.99 *(978-1-84135-630-3(1))* Award Pubns. Ltd. GBR. Dist: Parkwest Pubns., Inc.

—123. 2012. (ENG., Illus.). 24p. (J). 6.50 *(978-1-84135-553-5(4))* Award Pubns. Ltd. GBR. Dist: Parkwest Pubns., Inc.

Award Staff & Award, Anna. Sticker Fun & Activity. 2015. (ENG.). 48p. (J). pap. 7.99 *(978-1-78270-013-5(7))* Award Pubns. Ltd. GBR. Dist: Parkwest Pubns., Inc.

Ayers, Chris. MY Daily Zoo: A Drawing Activity Book for All Ages. 2011. (ENG., Illus.). 96p. pap. 9.95 *(978-1-933492-63-6(5))* Design Studio Pr.

AZ Books. Bright Colors. 2013. (Matching Pictures Ser.). (ENG.). 20p. (J). (gr. -1-k). bds. 5.95 *(978-1-61889-310-9(6))* AZ Bks. LLC.

AZ Books, creator. Lion & His Kingdom. 2013. (Amusing Stories Ser.). (ENG., Illus.). 10p. (J). (gr. -1-k). bds. 7.95 *(978-1-61889-306-2(8))* AZ Bks. LLC.

—Meeting Friends. 2013. (Velvet Fantasy Ser.). (ENG., Illus.). 16p. (J). (gr. 1-3). pap. 4.95 *(978-1-61889-295-9(9))* AZ Bks. LLC.

—Sea Adventures. 2013. (Spot In! Ser.). (ENG., Illus.). 10p. (J). (gr. 1-3). 15.95 *(978-1-61889-314-7(9))* AZ Bks. LLC.

—Space Adventures. 2013. (Spot In! Ser.). (ENG., Illus.). 10p. (J). (gr. 1-3). 15.95 *(978-1-61889-313-0(0))* AZ Bks. LLC.

—Stylish Gifts. 2013. (Velvet Fantasy Ser.). (ENG., Illus.). 16p. (J). (gr. 1-3). pap. 4.95 *(978-1-61889-296-6(7))* AZ Bks. LLC.

AZ Books Staff. Fast Cars. Tulup, Natasha, ed. 2012. (Workshop Ser.). (ENG.). 10p. (J). (gr. -1-k). bds. 10.95 *(978-1-61889-161-7(8))* AZ Bks. LLC.

—Flying Planes. Tulup, Natasha, ed. 2012. (Workshop Ser.). (ENG.). 10p. (J). (gr. -1-k). 10.95 *(978-1-61889-159-4(6))* AZ Bks. LLC.

—Happy Holidays. 2013. (Velvet Fantasy Ser.). (ENG., Illus.). 16p. (J). (gr. 1-3). pap. 4.95 *(978-1-61889-294-2(0))* AZ Bks. LLC.

—Making Machines. Sisoj, Natalja, ed. 2012. (Modeling Clay Bks.). (ENG.). 12p. (J). (gr. -1-2). bds. 10.95 *(978-1-61889-198-3(7))* AZ Bks. LLC.

—Making the Farm. Sisoj, Natalja, ed. 2012. (Modeling Clay Bks.). (ENG.). 12p. (J). (gr. -1-2). bds. 10.95 *(978-1-61889-197-6(9))* AZ Bks. LLC.

—Making the Forest. Sisoj, Natalja, ed. 2012. (Modeling Clay Bks.). (ENG.). 12p. (J). (gr. -1-2). bds. 10.95 *(978-1-61889-199-0(5))* AZ Bks. LLC.

—Sailing Ships. Tulup, Natasha, ed. 2012. (Workshop Ser.). (ENG.). 10p. (J). (gr. -1-k). bds. 10.95 *(978-1-61889-162-4(6))* AZ Bks. LLC.

—Shapes. Slusar, Julia, ed. 2012. (Pull It Out Ser.). (ENG.). 10p. (J). (— 1). 7.95 *(978-1-61889-194-5(4))* AZ Bks. LLC.

—Stylish Girls. 2013. (Velvet Fantasy Ser.). (ENG., Illus.). 16p. (J). (gr. 1-3). pap. 4.95 *(978-1-61889-292-8(4))* AZ Bks. LLC.

AZ Books Staff & Evans, Olivia. Making the Zoo. Sisoj, Natalja, ed. 2012. (Modeling Clay Bk Ser.). (ENG., Illus.). 12p. (J). (gr. -1-2). bds. 10.95 *(978-1-61889-196-9(0))* AZ Bks. LLC.

Babsky, Irene. Let's Play with Words: Fun Activities, Games & Write-In Word Puzzles. 2015. (Illus.). 64p. (J). (gr. k-3). 7.99 *(978-1-86147-294-6(3))* Anness Publishing GBR. Dist: National Bk. Network.

Bailey, Ellen. The London Activity Book: With Palaces, Puzzles & Pictures to Colour. Pinder, Andrew & Mosedale, Julian, illus. 2013. (ENG.). 64p. (J). (gr. 2-4). pap. 8.99 *(978-1-78055-095-4(2))* O'Mara, Michael Bks., Ltd. GBR. Dist: Independent Pubs. Group.

Baines, Becky. Nat Geo Action Journal: Talk Like a Pirate, Analyze Your Dreams, Fingerprint Your Friends, Rule Your Own Country, & Other Wild Things to Do to Be Yourself. 2010. 176p. (J). (gr. 5-9). pap. 12.95 *(978-1-4263-0748-5(9),* National Geographic Kids) Disney Publishing Worldwide.

Baker, Sandy. Colorea Mi Jardin: Un Libro para Colorear Pájaros, Abejas, Mariposas y Bichos. Thiessen, Carolyn, tr. 2013. 32p. pap. 7.00 *(978-0-9832383-8-6(3))* Black Garnet Pr.

Baker, Yaba. Princess Briana. 2004. (Illus.). 72p. (J). 17.99 *(978-1-928889-05-2(0),* 262-002) Just Like Me, Inc.

Balcom, Katherine. Waterpark. 2014. pap. 11.66 *(978-1-4896-2243-3(8))* Weigl Pubs., Inc.

Balkan, Gabrielle. The 50 States: Activity Book: Maps of the 50 States of the USA, Volume 2. Linero, Sol, illus. 2016. (50 States Ser.: 2). (ENG.). 32p. (J). (gr. 3-6). pap., act. bk. ed. 11.99 *(978-1-84780-862-2(X),* 311627, Wide Eyed Editions) Quarto Publishing Group UK GBR. Dist: Hachette UK Distribution.

Ball, Liz, illus. A Standardbred Star: Learn about Harness Racing with Star & Friends. 2007. (YA). 3.95 *(978-0-9793891-0-8(0))* United States Trotting Association.

Barbaresi, Nina. Glitter Rubber Duckies Stickers. 2008. (ENG., Illus.). 4p. (J). (gr. -1-5). 1.50 *(978-0-486-46842-6(9))* Dover Pubns., Inc.

Barefoot Books. Build-A-Story Cards: Magical Castle. Latimer, Miriam, illus. 2018. (Barefoot Books Build-A-Story Cards Ser.). (ENG.). 36p. (J). (gr. k-5). 12.99 *(978-1-78285-383-1(9))* Barefoot Bks., Inc.

Barefoot Books, et al. Dotty Spotty Doodles. 2008. (Illus.). 24p. (J). pap. 6.99 *(978-1-84686-232-8(9))* Barefoot Bks., Inc.

—Pirates Fun Activities. 2008. (ENG., Illus.). 16p. (J). pap. 4.99 *(978-1-84686-217-5(5))* Barefoot Bks., Inc.

Barefoot Books Staff, et al. Zig Zag Zebra. 2008. (Illus.). 24p. (J). pap., act. bk. ed. 6.99 *(978-1-84686-233-5(7))* Barefoot Bks., Inc.

Barkan, Joanne. A Western Activity Book: Set Of 6. 2011. (Navigators Ser.). (J). pap. 50.00 net. *(978-1-4108-2579-7(5))* Benchmark Education Co.

Barnabas Fund, Trustees Staff. Brothers & Sisters: Loving Our Persecuted Family. 2012. (ENG., Illus.). 38p. (gr. 1-7). pap. 10.00 *(978-0-9853109-7-4(9))* Isaac Publishing.

Barner, Bob. Animals! Matching Game. 2011. (ENG.). 72p. (J). (gr. -1-17). 16.99 *(978-1-4521-0055-5(1))* Chronicle Bks. LLC.

—Dinosaurs! Matching Game. 2009. (ENG.). 72p. (J). (gr. -1-17). 16.99 *(978-0-8118-6980-5(6))* Chronicle Bks. LLC.

Barnhart, Norm, et al. My First Guides. 2017. (My First Guides). (ENG., Illus.). 24p. (J). (gr. 1-3). 167.94 *(978-1-5157-3595-3(8),* 25435, Capstone Pr.) Capstone.

Barry, Ron & Fitzgerald, Paula. Me 'n Mom: A Keepsake Scrapbook Journal. Sharp, Chris, illus. 2009. (ENG.). 33p. pap. 14.99 *(978-0-8249-1435-6(X),* Ideals Pubns.) Worthy Publishing.

Battaglioli, Peter. What to Doodle? Crazy Faces. 2013. (Dover Doodle Bks.). (ENG.). 48p. (J). (gr. 2-5). pap. 4.99 *(978-0-486-49100-4(5))* Dover Pubns., Inc.

Baur, Becky. Dotty's First Book: Colours, Shapes, Numbers. 2017. (ENG., Illus.). 16p. (J). (gr. -1-k). bds. 12.95 *(978-0-500-65107-0(8),* 565107) Thames & Hudson.

Beathard, Patricia. Schools of Yesteryear: History of the One-Room School. 2012. (Illus.). 68p. (gr. 4-6). pap. 27.68 *(978-1-4669-7024-3(3))* Trafford Publishing.

Beaty, Andrea. Iggy Peck's Big Project Book for Amazing Architects. Roberts, David, illus. 2017. (Questioneers Ser.). (ENG.). 96p. (J). (gr. k-2). pap. 14.99 *(978-1-4197-1892-2(4),* 1126707) Abrams, Inc.

Beaumont, Chris. Amazing Cubeecraft Paper Models: 16 Never-Before-Seen Paper Models. 2013. (ENG., Illus.). 32p. (J). (gr. 3-6). 9.99 *(978-0-486-49272-8(9),* 492729) Dover Pubns., Inc.

Beausoliel, Loyan & Wells, Leah. Games That Sing: 25 Activities to Keep Children on Their Toes. 2011. (Illus.). 52p. pap. 16.95 incl. audio compact disk *(978-1-4291-2116-3(5))* Heritage Music Pr.

Beecroft, Simon & Harvey, Guy. The Tintin & Snowy Big Activity Book. 2011. (ENG., Illus.). 96p. (J). pap. 19.95 *(978-0-86719-761-7(7))* Last Gasp of San Francisco.

The Beginner's Bible Super Girls of the Bible Sticker & Activity, 1 vol. 2015. (Beginner's Bible Ser.). (ENG.). 16p. (J). pap. 7.99 *(978-0-310-75118-2(7))* Zonderkidz.

Beilenson, Suzanne. Quiz Book: Who R U? 2008. (Activity Book Ser.). 160p. (J). (gr. k-5). spiral bd. 12.99 *(978-1-59359-807-5(6))* Peter Pauper Pr. Inc.

Bell, Robin. My Adventure with Pirates: Advanced My Adventure. 2009. (ENG.). 44p. (J). 8.99 *(978-1-59092-462-4(2))* Blue Forge Pr.

Benchmark Education Company, LLC Staff, compiled by. Sort & Classify. 2006. (J). 204.00 *(978-1-4108-7051-3(0))* Benchmark Education Co.

Bender, Albert C. More 'Kids in the Alley' Tales. 2011. (Illus.). 200p. pap. 16.95 *(978-1-4327-7174-4(4))* Outskirts Pr., Inc.

Berenstain, Jan & Berenstain, Stan. The Berenstain Bears' Christmas Coloring & Activity Book. 2014. (Dover Christmas Activity Books for Kids Ser.). (ENG.). 256p. (J). (gr. k-3). pap. 12.99 *(978-0-486-79209-5(9),* 792099) Dover Pubns., Inc.

—The Berenstain Bears(r)' First Time Do-It! Book. 2014. (Dover Kids Activity Bks.). (ENG., Illus.). 112p. (J). (gr. k-3). pap. 12.99 *(978-0-486-78179-2(8),* 781798) Dover Pubns., Inc.

—The Berenstain Bears Giant Coloring & Activity Book. 2013. (Dover Kids Activity Bks.). (ENG.). 272p. (J). (gr. -1-2). pap. 9.99 *(978-0-486-49341-1(5),* 493415) Dover Pubns., Inc.

Bernard, Stephanie & Goff, Amber. Using Cursive Today, 1 vol. rev. ed. 2015. (Classroom Resource Ser.). (ENG., Illus.). 80p. (gr. 2-5). mass mkt. 9.99 *(978-1-4258-1544-8(8))* Shell Educational Publishing.

Bernd & Richter, Susan. I See You Through My Heart. 2008. bds. 8.95 *(978-1-931353-44-1(1))* Saddle Pal Creations, Inc.

Beylon, Cathy. Shiny Dinosaurs Stickers. 2004. (Dover Little Activity Books Stickers Ser.). (ENG., Illus.). 2p. (J). (gr. -1-5). 1.50 *(978-0-486-43536-7(9))* Dover Pubns., Inc.

Big Picture Press. Where Did They Go? Bornoff, Emily, illus. 2016. (ENG.). 32p. (J). (-k). 14.99 *(978-0-7636-8920-9(3),* Big Picture Press) Candlewick Pr.

Biggs, Kathy. Dragonflies of North America: A Color & Learn Book for All Ages, with Activities. Manolis, Tim, illus. l.t. ed. 2007. (ENG.). 48p. (J). *(978-0-9677934-4-3(0))* Azalea Creek Publishing.

—Dragonflies of North America: A Color & Learn Book for All Ages, with Activities. Manolis, Tim, illus. l.t. ed. 2007. 48p. (J). cd-rom *(978-0-9677934-5-0(9))* Azalea Creek Publishing.

Billet, Marion. I Love Music: My First Sound Book. Billet, Marion, illus. 2016. (ENG., Illus.). 16p. (J). (gr. -1 — 1). 9.99 *(978-1-338-03261-1(5),* Cartwheel Bks.) Scholastic, Inc.

Bird, Grace. Beetles Ahoy! 2009. 48p. pap. *(978-1-84923-423-8(X))* YouWriteOn.

Birney, Betty G. Humphrey's Book of Fun Fun Fun. 2013. (Humphrey Ser.). (ENG.). 240p. (J). (gr. 3-7). pap. 8.99 *(978-0-14-750951-2(3),* Puffin Books) Penguin Young Readers Group.

Bixley, Donovan. My First Board Book: Things That Go! 2022. (My First Board Book Ser.). (ENG., Illus.). 24p. (J). (gr. -1-k). bds. 13.99 *(978-1-86971-348-5(6))* Hachette New Zealand NZL. Dist: Hachette Bk. Group.

Blackbird Publishing Staff. Mr. HookWorm Coloring Book. 2007. (Illus.). 32p. (J). per. 1.50 *(978-0-9789798-7-4(7))* Blackbird's World Publishing Co.

Blair, Beth L. & Ericsson, Jennifer A. The Everything Kids' Hanukkah Puzzle & Activity Book: Games, Crafts, Trivia, Songs, & Traditions to Celebrate the Festival of Lights! 2008. (Everything(r) Kids Ser.). (ENG., Illus.). 144p. pap., act. bk. ed. 9.99 *(978-1-59869-788-9(9),* Everything) Adams Media Corp.

—The Everything Kids' More Amazing Mazes Book: Wind Your Way Through Hours of Adventurous Fun! 2010. (Everything(r) Kids Ser.). (ENG., Illus.). 144p. pap. 16.99 *(978-1-4405-0150-0(5),* Everything) Adams Media Corp.

Blake, Rose. Meet the Artist: David Hockney. 2017. (ENG., Illus.). 32p. (J). (gr. 3-7). pap. 12.95 *(978-1-84976-446-9(8)*, 1307103) Tate Publishing, Ltd. GBR. Dist: Hachette Bk. Group.

Bloomenstein, Susan. Make Your Own Flower Bouquet Sticker Activity Book. 2016. (Dover Little Activity Books Stickers Ser.). (ENG.). 8p. (J). (gr. -1-2). pap. 2.50 *(978-0-486-80589-4(1)*, 805891) Dover Pubns., Inc.

Bloomsbury. My Snowman Activity & Sticker Book. 2014. (ENG., Illus.). 32p. (J). (gr. -1-1). pap. 4.99 *(978-1-61963-312-4(4)*, 900132533, Bloomsbury Activity Bks.) Bloomsbury Publishing USA.

—My Spooky Halloween Activity & Sticker Book. 2014. (Sticker Activity Bks.). (ENG.). 32p. (J). (gr. -1-1). pap. 4.99 *(978-1-61963-332-2(9)*, 900132597, Bloomsbury Activity Bks.) Bloomsbury Publishing USA.

Bloomsbury USA. I'm a Flower Girl! Activity & Sticker Book. 2016. (ENG., Illus.). 32p. (J). pap. 5.99 *(978-1-61963-993-5(9)*, 900154241, Bloomsbury Activity Bks.) Bloomsbury Publishing USA.

—My Activity Books for Girls. 2014. (Sticker Activity Bks.). (ENG.). 192p. (J). (gr. -1-3). pap. 12.99 *(978-1-61963-638-5(7)*, 900143856, Bloomsbury USA Childrens) Bloomsbury Publishing USA.

—My Animals Activity & Sticker Book. 2015. (ENG.). 112p. (J). (gr. k-3). pap. 12.99 *(978-1-61963-762-7(6)*, 900147927, Bloomsbury Activity Bks.) Bloomsbury Publishing USA.

Boardworks Learning Centers: I've Got It! 2006. (J). bds. *(978-0-9755252-8-9(X))* Evergreen Pr. of Brainerd, LLC.

Bohn, Kendall. Abstract Adventure. 2009. (Kaleidoscopia Coloring Book Ser.). (Illus.). (J). 8.95 *(978-0-929636-98-6(8))* Itasca Bks.

Bohn, Kendall, creator. Prehistoric Adventure: A Kaleidoscopia Coloring Book. 2005. (Illus.). 56p. pap. 8.95 *(978-0-929636-37-5(6))* Syren Bk. Co.

Bokor, Dina. Alphabet: In the World of Things. 2013. (ENG.). 18p. (J). pap. 11.95 *(978-1-4787-0031-9(9))* Outskirts Pr., Inc.

Bone, Emily & Pratt, Leonie. Recycling Things to Make & Do. 2010. (Activity Book Ser.). 32p. (J). pap. 6.99 *(978-0-7945-2675-7(6)*, Usborne) EDC Publishing.

Boodey, Erin. Work Your Body Grow Your Brain. Konecny, John, illus. 2012. 26p. 13.99 *(978-1-937165-23-9(X))* Orange Hat Publishing.

Books, Carlton. Kate & Pippa Dress-Up Sticker Book: Create Stylish Outfits & Design Your Own Accessories! 2013. (Y Ser.). (ENG., Illus.). 24p. (gr. 1-3). pap. 7.95 *(978-1-78097-147-6(8))* Carlton Bks., Ltd. GBR. Dist: Two Rivers Distribution.

Boozarjomehri, Keon Arasteh. 3D Printing at School & Makerspaces, 1 vol. 2017. (Project Learning with 3D Printing Ser.). (ENG.). 128p. (YA). (gr. 9-9). 47.36 *(978-1-5026-3148-0(2)*, 2cee843c-6b84-445c-8c2a-b63b6f52524b); pap. 22.16 *(978-1-5026-3426-9(0)*, 59513437-7243-40ed-8230-a657c733a167) Cavendish Square Publishing LLC.

Bordessa, Kris. Great Medieval Projects. Braley, Shawn, illus. 2008. (Build It Yourself Ser.). (ENG.). 128p. (J). (gr. 3-7). 21.95 *(978-1-934670-26-2(X)*, 130793b0-e254-4536-98b3-18b7b3ddc2a2) Nomad Pr.

—Great Medieval Projects: You Can Build Yourself. Braley, Shawn, illus. 2008. (Build It Yourself Ser.). 128p. (J). (gr. 3-7). pap. 15.95 *(978-0-9792268-0-9(5)*, c3df102a-d618-4f50-a0cf-6a719c3b857a) Nomad Pr.

Boreal, Carole. I Love Paris, Rome, Berlin, London: Doodle Your Way Across Europe! 2015. (ENG., Illus.). 152p. (J). (gr. 7-12). pap. 14.99 *(978-1-4521-3516-8(9))* Chronicle Bks. LLC.

Borja, Richard. Flash! Alphabet Enigma. 2009. 48p. pap. 14.92 *(978-1-84728-659-8(3))* Lulu Pr., Inc.

Bork, Rhoda. Pioneering: Activities to Live History. 2007. (J). *(978-0-9786018-6-7(6))* Sparrow Media Group, Inc.

Boutan, Mila. Rousseau: Art Activity Pack. 2005. (Illus.). 22p. (J). (gr. 4-8). pap. 10.00 *(978-0-7567-9413-2(7))* DIANE Publishing Co.

Bowman, Crystal. Our Daily Bread for Kids. 2015. (Our Daily Bread for Kids Ser.). (ENG.). 48p. (-3). 3.99 *(978-1-62707-482-7(1))* Discovery Hse. Pubs.

Bowman, Lucy. Drawing, Doodling & Coloring Book Girls. 2012. (Activity Cards Ser.). 128p. (J). pap. 13.99 *(978-0-7945-3297-0(7)*, Usborne) EDC Publishing.

—Girl's Activity Book. 2013. (Doodle Bks). 96p. (J). pap. 12.99 *(978-0-7945-3172-0(5)*, Usborne) EDC Publishing.

Bowman, Lucy & MacLaine, James. The Usborne Little Girls' Activity Book. Watt, Fiona, ed. Harrison, Erica et al, illus. 2014. (ENG.). 64p. (J). pap. 9.99 *(978-0-7945-2790-7(6)*, Usborne) EDC Publishing.

Brack, Amanda. Sticker Your Bricks: Style Your Building Brick Masterpieces with Reusable Stickers. 2016. (ENG., Illus.). 96p. (J). (gr. k). 12.99 *(978-1-5107-0722-1(0)*, Sky Pony Pr.) Skyhorse Publishing Co., Inc.

Brack, Susan. Mommy & Me Stickers. 2011. (Dover Little Activity Books Stickers Ser.). (ENG.). 8p. (J). (gr. k-3). pap. 1.50 *(978-0-486-48233-0(2))* Dover Pubns., Inc.

Bradford, Valerie Ann. Activites Makes Learning Fun. 2011. 54p. 24.99 *(978-1-4653-3771-9(7))*; pap. 15.99 *(978-1-4653-3770-2(9))* Xlibris Corp.

—Activities Makes Learning Fun: Volume II. 2011. 52p. 24.99 *(978-1-4653-4707-7(0))*; pap. 15.99 *(978-1-4653-4706-0(2))* Xlibris Corp.

Brandt, DeAnna Ortiz & Brandt, Daniel P. Bug Log Kids. 2017. (Nature Journals). (ENG., Illus.). 88p. (J). (gr. k-7). spiral bd. 11.95 *(978-1-59193-727-2(2)*, Adventure Pubns.) AdventureKEEN.

Bree, Loris & Bree, Marlin. Kid's Travel Fun Book: Draw. Make Stuff. Play Games. Have Fun for Hours! 2nd ed. 2007. (Kid's Travel Ser.). (ENG., Illus.). 96p. (J). (gr. 4-7). per. 8.99 *(978-1-892147-13-4(0))* Marlor Pr., Inc.

Bright & Beyond - 1 Ano. 2007. (J). 9.95 *(978-0-9763648-3-2(2))* Pal Toys, LLC.

Bright & Beyond - 2 Anos. 2007. (SPA.). (J). 9.95 *(978-0-9763648-4-9(0))* Pal Toys, LLC.

Bright & Beyond - Preescolar: Anos 3 To 5. 2007. Orig. Title: Bright & Beyond - Preschool. (SPA.). (J). 9.95 *(978-0-9763648-5-6(9))* Pal Toys, LLC.

Briley, Randy William. Sketchboy. 2013. 104p. pap. 23.00 *(978-0-9896269-1-0(1))* Raven Mad Studios.

Broadbent, Paul. Being A Cartoonist. 2007. (Trackers-Math Ser.). (gr. 2-5). pap. 5.00 *(978-1-59055-937-6(1))* Pacific Learning, Inc.

—Beneath Our Feet. 2007. (Trackers-Math Ser.). (gr. 2-5). pap. 5.00 *(978-1-59055-929-1(0))* Pacific Learning, Inc.

Brooks, Felicity. Getting Dressed Magnet Book. Widdowson, Kay, illus. 2009. (Magnet Bks). 10p. (J). bds. 19.99 *(978-0-7945-2356-5(0)*, Usborne) EDC Publishing.

Brooks, Felicity & Fearn, Katrina. First Dot-To-Dot Animals. 2013. (First Dot-To-Dot Ser.). 16p. (J). pap. 5.99 *(978-0-7945-3198-0(9)*, Usborne) EDC Publishing.

—First Dot-To-Dot Things That Go. 2013. (First Dot-To-Dot Ser.). 16p. (J). pap. 5.99 *(978-0-7945-3162-1(8)*, Usborne) EDC Publishing.

Broom, Jenny. Animalium Poster Book. Scott, Katie, illus. 2017. (Welcome to the Museum Ser.). (ENG.). 56p. (J). (gr. 2-4). pap. 22.00 *(978-0-7636-9318-3(9)*, Big Picture Press) Candlewick Pr.

—ArtCards: Accessorize. Haworth, Hennie, illus. 2013. (ENG.). 72p. (J). (gr. 1-4). pap. 17.99 *(978-0-7636-6892-1(3)*, Big Picture Press) Candlewick Pr.

—Artcards: Fashion. Haworth, Hennie, illus. 2014. (ENG.). 72p. (J). (gr. 1-4). pap. 17.99 *(978-0-7636-7519-6(9)*, Big Picture Press) Candlewick Pr.

Brown, Kyle. My Wedding Activity Book. 2009. (ENG.). 48p. pap. 9.95 *(978-0-557-06217-1(9))* Lulu Pr., Inc.

Brown, Peggy & Lovett, Nate. The Everything Girls Super Cute Kawaii Fun Book: Tons of Creative, Fun Kawaii Activities — Doodles, Games, Crafts, & More! 2014. (Everything(r) Kids Ser.). (ENG.). 128p. pap. 14.99 *(978-1-4405-7700-0(5))* Adams Media Corp.

Bryan, Sarah Jane & Bellenson, Suzanne. Mega Magna Forms Princess. McGregor, Barbara, illus. 2008. (Activity Book Ser.). 48p. (J). (gr. -1-3). spiral bd. 19.95 *(978-1-59359-808-2(4))* Peter Pauper Pr. Inc.

—Mega Magna Forms Safari Adventure. Klug, David, illus. 2008. (Activity Book Ser.). 48p. (J). (gr. -1-3). spiral bd. 19.95 *(978-1-59359-809-9(2))* Peter Pauper Pr. Inc.

Bugbird, Tim. Beat the Book. 2016. (ENG.). 70p. (J). (gr. 1-5). 14.99 *(978-1-78598-074-9(2))* Make Believe Ideas GBR. Dist: Scholastic, Inc.

Build It Yourself. 2011. (Build It Yourself Ser.). (ENG.). 32p. (gr. 3-4). pap. 190.80 *(978-1-4296-6432-5(0)*, Capstone Pr.) Capstone.

Build Your Own Superheroes Sticker Book. 2017. (Build Your Own Sticker Bks.). (ENG.). (J). pap. 8.99 *(978-0-7945-3877-4(0)*, Usborne) EDC Publishing.

Bumpers, Katrina. Alphabet Fun, Book 2: Coloring & Activity Book. 2008. (Illus.). 64p. (gr. -1-3). pap. 10.95 *(978-0-9797208-1-9(8))* K's Kids Publishing.

Bunnell, Jacinta. Sometimes the Spoon Runs Away with Another Spoon Coloring Book. Kusinitz, Nathaniel, illus. 2010. (Reach & Teach Ser.). (ENG.). 32p. pap. 10.00 *(978-1-60486-329-1(3))* PM Pr.

Bunton, M. Catherine. The Little Maestro: A Forest Club Activity Book. 2010. 90p. pap. 9.95 *(978-1-60594-392-3(4)*, Llumina Pr.) Aeon Publishing Inc.

Burke, Fatti & Burke, John. Irelandopedia Activity Book. 2016. (ENG., Illus.). 32p. (J). pap. 18.00 *(978-0-7171-7149-1(3))* Gill Bks. IRL. Dist: Casemate Pubs. & Bk. Distributors, LLC.

Burlew, Rich, creator. The Order of the Stick Coloring Book. 2012. (Illus.). 32p. (YA). pap. 4.99 *(978-0-9854139-0-3(5))* Giant in the Playground.

Burnett, Gretel. The A-B-C Smarts: Book 2. 2009. 84p. pap. 28.99 *(978-1-4490-4575-3(8))* AuthorHouse.

Bush-Retherford, Dody & Clark, Paul. Lil Witches Wheel of the Year Coloring Book. 2009. (ENG.). 69p. pap. 9.00 *(978-0-557-09779-1(7))* Lulu Pr., Inc.

Buster Books. I Heart Lists. 2017. (I Heart Pocket Colouring Ser.). (ENG.). 128p. (J). (gr. 2). pap. 8.99 *(978-1-78055-450-1(8))* O'Mara, Michael Bks., Ltd. GBR. Dist: Independent Pubs. Group.

Busy Kids Horses & Ponies Sticker Activity Book. 2008. (Busy Kids Ser.). (Illus.). 12p. (J). (gr. -1-3). pap. *(978-1-84610-722-1(9))* Make Believe Ideas.

But I Don't Know: Women's Ministry. 2005. mass mkt. 6.50 *(978-1-59317-001-1(7))* Warner Pr., Inc.

Butterfield, M. & Edom, H. Science with Air. rev. ed. 2008. (Science Activities Ser.). 24p. (J). pap. 5.99 *(978-0-7945-2331-2(5)*, Usborne) EDC Publishing.

Butz, Steve. Year Round Project-Based Activities for STEM Grd 2-3. 2013. (ENG.). 112p. pap. 14.99 *(978-1-4206-3027-5(X))* Teacher Created Resources, Inc.

Cabanillas, Laura Sabin. The Abc's of Character. Sebastian, illus. 2009. 60p. pap. 12.95 *(978-0-9818488-2-2(6))* Ajoyin Publishing, Inc.

Calliella, Trisha. I Have, Who Has? Language Arts, Grades 3-4: 38 Interactive Card Games, Vol. 2206. Hamaguchi, Carla, ed. Hillam, Corbin, illus. 2006. (I Have, Who Has? Ser.). 204p. (J). (gr. 3-4). per. 19.99 *(978-1-59198-228-9(6)*, 2206) Creative Teaching Pr., Inc.

—I Have, Who Has? Language Arts, Grades 5-6: 38 Interactive Card Games. Hamaguchi, Carla, ed. Hillam, Corbin, illus. 2006. (I Have, Who Has? Ser.). 204p. (J). (gr. 5-6). per. 19.99 *(978-1-59198-229-6(4))* Creative Teaching Pr., Inc.

Calma, Jocelyn. Little Malia's Big Poi Idea. Robinson, Don, illus. 2009. 28p. (J). 12.99 *(978-1-59524-328-7(3))* Giddy Up, LLC.

Calver, Paul & Award, Anna. My Favourite Rescuers Sticker Book. 2015. (ENG., Illus.). 20p. (J). pap. 7.99 *(978-1-907604-21-8(9))* Award Pubns. Ltd. GBR. Dist: Parkwest Pubns., Inc.

Campoy, F. Isabel. My Day from A to Z. 2008. (Alphabet Bks.). (ENG.). 32p. (gr. -1-1). 33.69 *(978-1-60396-324-4(3))* Santillana USA Publishing Co., Inc.

Candle Books, creator. More 365 Activities for Kids, 1 vol. 2005. (Illus.). 366p. (J). (gr. -1-3). spiral bd. 13.99 *(978-0-8254-7292-3(X)*, Candle Bks.) Lion Hudson PLC GBR. Dist: Kregel Pubns.

Candlewick Press Staff. Harry Potter: Winter at Hogwarts: a Magical Coloring Set, Set. 2016. (Harry Potter Ser.). (ENG.). 48p. (J). (gr. 3-7). 15.99 *(978-0-7636-9589-7(0))* Candlewick Pr.

Carluccio, Maria. Sounds Around Town. Carluccio, Maria, illus. 2016. (ENG., Illus.). 32p. (J). (gr. -1-k). bds. 14.99 *(978-1-78285-281-0(6))* Barefoot Bks., Inc.

Carole Marsh. Los Angeles Coloring & Activity Book. 2004. (City Bks.). 24p. (gr. k-5). pap. 3.95 *(978-0-635-02229-5(X))* Gallopade International.

—San Francisco Coloring & Activity Book. 2004. (City Bks.). 24p. (J). (gr. k-5). pap., act. bk. ed. 3.95 *(978-0-635-02228-8(1))* Gallopade International.

Carson Dellosa Education, compiled by. Everyday Words in Spanish: Photographic. 2004. (ENG.). 104p. (gr. -1-8). 7.99 *(978-1-936022-83-0(4)*, 3924) Carson-Dellosa Publishing, LLC.

—First Grade Skills. 2010. (Home Workbooks Ser.: 4). (ENG.). 64p. (gr. 1-1). pap. 4.49 *(978-1-60418-784-7(0)*, 104353) Carson-Dellosa Publishing, LLC.

—Phonics for Kindergarten, Grade K. 2010. (Home Workbooks Ser.: 12). (ENG.). 64p. (gr. k-k). pap. 4.49 *(978-1-60418-774-8(3)*, 104343) Carson-Dellosa Publishing, LLC.

—Scissors Skills, Grades PK - 1. 2010. (Home Workbooks Ser.: 17). (ENG.). 64p. (gr. -1-1). pap. 4.49 *(978-1-60418-766-3(2)*, 104335) Carson-Dellosa Publishing, LLC.

Carson-Dellosa Publishing Staff. All about Me, Grades Pk - 1. 2010. (Home Workbooks Ser.: 1). (ENG.). 64p. (gr. -1-1). pap. 4.49 *(978-1-60418-767-0(0)*, 104336) Carson-Dellosa Publishing, LLC.

—Beginning Reading, Grades K. 2010. (Home Workbooks Ser.: 3). (ENG.). 64p. (gr. k-k). pap. 4.49 *(978-1-60418-773-1(5)*, 104342) Carson-Dellosa Publishing, LLC.

—Get Ready for Kindergarten. 2010. (Home Workbooks Ser.: 5). (ENG.). 64p. (gr. k-k). pap. 4.49 *(978-1-60418-771-7(9)*, 104340) Carson-Dellosa Publishing, LLC.

—Hidden Pictures, Grades PK - 1. 2010. (Home Workbooks Ser.: 6). (ENG.). 64p. (gr. -1-1). pap. 4.49 *(978-1-60418-770-0(0)*, 104339) Carson-Dellosa Publishing, LLC.

—Letters & Sounds, Grades K - 1. 2010. (Home Workbooks Ser.: 7). (ENG.). 64p. (gr. k-1). pap. 4.49 *(978-1-60418-779-3(4)*, 104348) Carson-Dellosa Publishing, LLC.

—Mazes,Grades PK - 1. 2010. (Home Workbooks Ser.: 9). (ENG.). 64p. (gr. -1-1). pap. 4.49 *(978-1-60418-769-4(7)*, 104338) Carson-Dellosa Publishing, LLC.

—Numbers 0-30, Grades K - 1. 2010. (Home Workbooks Ser.: 10). (ENG.). 64p. (gr. k-1). pap. 4.49 *(978-1-60418-783-0(2)*, 104352) Carson-Dellosa Publishing, LLC.

—Phonics for First Grade. 2010. (Home Workbooks Ser.: 11). (ENG.). 64p. (gr. 1-1). pap. 4.49 *(978-1-60418-785-4(9)*, 104354) Carson-Dellosa Publishing, LLC.

—Printing Practice for Beginners. 2010. (Home Workbooks Ser.: 13). (ENG.). 64p. (gr. k-1). pap. 4.49 *(978-1-60418-780-9(8)*, 104349) Carson-Dellosa Publishing, LLC.

—Puzzles & Games for Math, Grade 1. 2010. (Home Workbooks Ser.: 14). (ENG.). 64p. (gr. 1-1). pap. 4.49 *(978-1-60418-791-5(3)*, 104360) Carson-Dellosa Publishing, LLC.

Carson-Dellosa Publishing Staff, compiled by. Puzzles & Games for Math, Grade 2. 2010. (Home Workbooks Ser.: 15). (ENG.). 64p. (gr. 2-2). pap. 4.49 *(978-1-60418-798-4(0)*, 104367) Carson-Dellosa Publishing, LLC.

Cedar Fort. Hooray for Mom! Drawing My Favorite Moments with Mom. 2017. (ENG.). (J). 14.99 *(978-1-4621-1990-5(5))* Cedar Fort, Inc./CFI Distribution.

Ceol, Cheryl. Can You Picture This? You Draw It / You Say It / You Find It / You Write It. 2012. 44p. pap. 20.99 *(978-1-4525-6422-7(1))* Balboa Pr.

Cernek, Kim. Preschool Songs & Fingerplays: Building Language Experience Through Rhythm & Movement. 2006. (Early Learning Ser.). (Illus.). 128p. (J). (gr. -1-1). per. 13.99 *(978-1-59198-223-4(5))* Creative Teaching Pr., Inc.

Chakrabarti, Nina. Hello Nature: Draw, Collect, Make & Grow. 2016. (ENG.). 224p. (J). (gr. 2-6). pap. 18.99 *(978-1-78067-735-4(9)*, King, Laurence Publishing) Orion Publishing Group, Ltd. GBR. Dist: Hachette Bk. Group.

Chakrabarti, Nina, illus. Hello Nature Activity Cards: 30 Activities. 2018. (ENG.). 173p. (J). (gr. 2-6). 13.99 *(978-1-78627-185-3(0)*, King, Laurence Publishing) Orion Publishing Group, Ltd. GBR. Dist: Hachette Bk. Group.

Chambers, Jo. Caring for Wild Animals. 2007. (Trackers-Math Ser.). (gr. 2-5). pap. 5.00 *(978-1-59055-933-8(9))* Pacific Learning, Inc.

Chaney, Scott. Christian Warriors: Games, Gear, Gospel - Especially for Christian Youth. 2009. (Illus.). 144p. (J). 49.95 *(978-1-58117-938-5(3)*, Intervisual/Piggy Toes) Bendon, Inc.

Charlesbridge, ed. Sir Cumference Classroom Activities. 2015. (Sir Cumference Ser.). 32p. (J). (gr. 3-7). pap. 9.95 *(978-1-58089-724-2(X))* Charlesbridge Publishing, Inc.

Charlesworth, Liza. Punctuation Tales. 2009. (ENG.). (gr. 2-5). 36.99 *(978-0-545-11401-1(2))* Scholastic, Inc.

Cherry, Meri. Play, Make, Create, a Process-Art Handbook: With over 40 Art Invitations for Kids * Creative Activities & Projects That Inspire Confidence, Creativity, & Connection. 2019. (ENG., Illus.). 160p. (J). (gr. -1-7). pap. 25.99 *(978-1-63159-716-9(7)*, 307352, Quarry Bks.) Quarto Publishing Group USA.

Chihuly Art Kit. 2006. (Chihuly Ser.). (J). (gr. -1). 28.00 *(978-1-57684-157-0(X))* Chihuly Workshop, Inc.

Child, Lauren. Charlie & Lola: Charlie & Lola a Very Shiny Wipe-Clean Letters Activity Book. 2019. (Charlie & Lola Ser.). (ENG.). 16p. (J). (gr. -1-1). pap. 9.99 *(978-1-4083-5056-0(4)*, Orchard Bks.) Hachette Children's Group GBR. Dist: Hachette Bk. Group.

Chilek, Laurie. ¡Qué miedo! ¡un tobogán! (the Scary Slide) 2007. (Lecturas del barrio (Neighborhood Readers) Ser.). (SPA.). 8p. 29.95 *(978-1-4042-7291-0(7)*, Rosen Classroom) Rosen Publishing Group, Inc., The.

Chlebowski, Rachel. Better Together! (Shimmer & Shine) Cespedes-Alicea, Marcela, illus. 2017. (ENG.). 128p. (J). (gr. -1-2). pap. 9.99 *(978-0-399-55793-4(8)*, Golden Bks.) Random Hse. Children's Bks.

—Color Your World! (Sunny Day) Workman, Lisa, illus. 2018. (ENG.). 128p. (J). (gr. -1-2). pap. 7.99 *(978-0-525-57770-6(X)*, Golden Bks.) Random Hse. Children's Bks.

Chorba, April & Editors of Klutz. Dot Jewelry: Make Pretty Paper Bracelets & Necklaces. 2013. (ENG.). 56p. (J). (gr. 3). 19.99 *(978-0-545-49278-2(5))* Klutz.

Chorba, April & Murphy, Pat. The Book of Impossible Objects: 25 Eye-Popping Projects to Make, See & Do. 2013. (ENG.). 48p. (J). (gr. 3). 19.99 *(978-0-545-49647-6(0))* Klutz.

Chronicle Books. The World of Eric Carle(TM) the Very Hungry Caterpillar(TM) Lacing Cards: (Occupational Therapy Toys, Lacing Cards for Toddlers, Fine Motor Skills Toys, Lacing Cards for Kids) 2012. (World of Erice Carle Activities for Little Ones Ser.). (ENG., Illus.). 10p. (J). (gr. -1-17). 18.99 *(978-1-4521-0819-3(6))* Chronicle Bks. LLC.

Ciminera, Siobhan. Stuck on Christmas! A Mega Sticker Book. Collection/Jupiterimages Unlimited, illus. 2008. (ENG.). 48p. (J). (gr. -1-2). 12.99 *(978-1-4169-6784-2(2)*, Simon Scribbles) Simon Scribbles.

Citylit Kids. Write On! 2012. 68p. pap. 10.00 *(978-1-936328-10-9(0))* CityLit Pr.

Civardi, Anne. Moving House Sticker Book. 2009. (First Experiences Sticker Bks). 18p. (J). pap. 6.99 *(978-0-7945-2430-2(3)*, Usborne) EDC Publishing.

—New Baby Sticker Book. 2008. (First Experiences Sticker Bks). (Illus.). 16p. (J). pap. 6.99 *(978-0-7945-2181-3(9)*, Usborne) EDC Publishing.

Clanton, Ben, ed. Drawn to Color: A Pacific Northwest Coloring Book. 2017. (ENG., Illus.). 64p. (J). pap. 15.99 *(978-1-63217-109-2(0)*, Little Bigfoot) Sasquatch Bks.

Clark, Ruth E. Airport Mouse Activity Fun Book 1. Jones, Phil, illus. 2010. 16p. (J). pap. 5.99 *(978-0-9792963-6-9(6))* Hibiscus Publishing.

—Airport Mouse Becomes a VIP/VIM World Traveler Activity Fun Book 4. Jones, Phil, illus. 2010. 16p. (J). pap. 5.99 *(978-0-9792963-9-0(0))* Hibiscus Publishing.

—Airport Mouse Explores on Opening Day Activity Fun Book 3. Jones, Phil, illus. 2010. 16p. (J). pap. 5.99 *(978-0-9792963-8-3(2))* Hibiscus Publishing.

—Airport Mouse Works the Night Shift Activity Fun Book 2. Jones, Phil, illus. 2010. 16p. (J). pap. 5.99 *(978-0-9792963-7-6(4))* Hibiscus Publishing.

Clarke, Catriona. 50 Things to Do on Vacation. Meredith, Samantha, illus. 2007. (Activity Cards Ser.). 50p. (J). (gr. 4-7). 9.99 *(978-0-7945-1704-5(8)*, Usborne) EDC Publishing.

Classroom Complete Press, creator. High Frequency Picture Words, Grades PK-2. 2011. (Literacy Skills Ser.). (ENG.). 39.95 *(978-1-55319-514-6(0)*, Classroom Complete Pr.) Rainbow Horizons Publishing, Inc.

—High Frequency Sight Words, Grades PK-2. 2011. (Literacy Skills Ser.). (ENG.). 39.95 *(978-1-55319-513-9(2)*, Classroom Complete Pr.) Rainbow Horizons Publishing, Inc.

—Sight & Picture Words, Grades PK-2. 2011. (Literacy Skills Ser.). (ENG.). 54.95 *(978-1-55319-515-3(9)*, Classroom Complete Pr.) Rainbow Horizons Publishing, Inc.

Cline, Mike & Yi-Cline, Nancy. Franky Fox's Fun with English Activity Book, Level A1. Yi-Cline, Nancy, ed. Cline, Mike, illus. 2007. (Illus.). 62p. pap. 7.99 *(978-0-9777419-1-5(5)*, SIAB) Lingo Pr. LLC.

—Franky Fox's Fun with English Level A1. Yi-Cline, Nancy, ed. Cline, Mike, illus. 2007. (Illus.). 65p. 14.99 *(978-0-9777419-0-8(7)*, SITB) Lingo Pr. LLC.

Clineff, Jeff. Too Many Kitties. Movshina, Marina, illus. 2007. (ESK.). 24p. (J). 9.95 *(978-1-933090-10-8(3))* Guardian Angel Publishing, Inc.

Clover, Forever & Bell, Holly. Forever Clover: Forever Friends Sticker & Activity Book. 2015. (Forever Clover Ser.). (ENG., Illus.). 64p. (J). (gr. k-4). pap. 7.99 *(978-1-921894-42-8(3))* Little Hare Bks. AUS. Dist: Independent Pubs. Group.

Cloyd, Nancy J. & Wach, Delia Bowman. Teddy Bear's Favorite Pictures: A Quiet Time Sharing Book. Wach, Delia Bowman, illus. 2007. (Illus.). 32p. (J). (gr. -1). 15.95 *(978-0-929915-75-3(5))* Headline Bks., Inc.

Coan, Sharon. Special Me, 1 vol. 2009. (Early Literacy Ser.). (ENG., Illus.). 16p. (gr. k-1). 6.99 *(978-1-4333-1469-8(X))* Teacher Created Materials, Inc.

—Yo Soy Especial. rev. ed. 2010. (Early Literacy Ser.).Tr. of Special Me. (SPA., Illus.). 16p. (gr. k-1). 19.99 *(978-1-4333-1945-7(4))*; 6.99 *(978-1-4333-1944-0(6))* Teacher Created Materials, Inc.

Cohen, Liz Zoller & Dicillo, Mike. My Interactive Point-And-Play 10-Book Library, 10 vols. 2011. (Illus.). (J). *(978-1-60553-886-0(8))* Publications International, Ltd.

Colich, Abby & Ventura, Marne. Go-To Guides. 2017. (Go-To Guides). (ENG.). 32p. (J). (gr. 3-9). 122.60 *(978-1-5157-3670-7(9)*, 25461, Capstone Pr.) Capstone.

Colleen, Marcie. Love, Triangle. Shea, Bob, illus. 2017. (ENG.). 32p. (J). (gr. -1-3). 17.99 *(978-0-06-241084-9(9)*, Balzer & Bray) HarperCollins Pubs.

Collins Easy Learning. First Words Age 3-5 Wipe Clean Activity Book: Ideal for Home Learning. 2017. (Collins Easy Learning Preschool Ser.). (ENG.). 24p. (J). (gr. -1-k). 7.95 *(978-0-00-821293-3(7))* HarperCollins Pubs. Ltd. GBR. Dist: Independent Pubs. Group.

—Telling the Time Wipe Clean Activity Book: Ideal for Home Learning (Collins Easy Learning KS1) 2018. (Collins Easy Learning KS1 Ser.). (ENG.). 24p. (J). (gr. -1-k). 7.95 *(978-0-00-827538-9(6))* HarperCollins Pubs. Ltd. GBR. Dist: Independent Pubs. Group.

Collins, Elaine Banks. See What I Can Do. Floyd, John, Jr., illus. 2006. 10p. (J). (gr. -1). bds. 5.95 *(978-0-9752860-4-3(8))* OurRainbow Pr., LLC.

Coloring Fun: Coloring/Activity Book (English/Spanish) Low Price Point. 2006. (Illus.). (J). 2.99 *(978-0-9770455-9-4(5))* Mighty Kids Media.

Compendium Inc, creator. My Artwork. 2011. 64p. (J). pap. 5.95 *(978-1-932319-98-9(0))* Compendium, Inc., Publishing & Communications.

—My Writing. 2011. (ENG.). 64p. (J). pap. 5.95 *(978-1-932319-97-2(2))* Compendium, Inc., Publishing & Communications.

Conlon, Mara. Brainiac's Go Green! Activity Book. Klug, David, illus. 2008. (Activity Book Ser.). 127p. (J). (gr. k-5). 12.99 *(978-1-59359-806-8(8))* Peter Pauper Pr. Inc.

—Butterflies & Friends: An Art Activity Book for Adventurous Artists of All Ages. Zschock, Martha Day, illus. 2009. (Scratch & Sketch Ser.). 64p. (J). (gr. 1). spiral bd., act. bk. ed. 12.99 *(978-1-59359-841-9(6))* Peter Pauper Pr. Inc.

—Ready, Set, Draw... under the Sea! Steckler, Kerren Barbas, illus. 2009. (Activity Bks). 40p. (J). spiral bd. 15.99 (978-1-59359-837-2(8)) Peter Pauper Pr. Inc.

Connery-Boyd, Peg. Totally Michigan! 2016. (Hawk's Nest Activity Bks.: 0). (ENG.). 64p. (J). (gr. k-3). pap. 8.99 (978-1-4926-4191-9(X), 9781492641919) Sourcebooks, Inc.

—Totally New England! 2016. (Hawk's Nest Activity Bks.: 0). (ENG.). 64p. (J). pap. 12.99 (978-1-4926-3379-2(8), 9781492633792) Sourcebooks, Inc.

—Totally Pacific Northwest! 2016. (Hawk's Nest Activity Bks.: 0). (ENG.). 64p. (J). (gr. k-3). pap. 8.99 (978-1-4926-3969-5(9), 9781492639695) Sourcebooks, Inc.

Conway, Laurence. Sing & Learn! 2009. 92p. pap. 30.00 (978-1-60693-543-9(7), Eloquent Bks.) Strategic Book Publishing & Rights Agency (SBPRA).

Cook, David C., 3rd. Mary & Martha. 2008. (Pencil Fun Bks). 16p. (J). pap. 9.90 (978-1-4347-6816-2(3)) Cook, David C.

Cook, Deanna F. & Craig, Katie. Horse Play! 25 Crafts, Party Ideas & Activities for Horse-Crazy Kids. 2016. (ENG., Illus.). 68p. (J). (gr. 3-7). spiral bd., act. bk. ed. 12.95 (978-1-61212-759-0(2), 622759) Storey Publishing, LLC.

Cookie Jar Entertainment Inc Staff. ABC Doodlebops. 2007. 32p. mass mkt. 4.99 (978-1-60095-270-8(4), Doodlebops) Cookie Jar.

—Doodlebops Count to Ten. 2007. 32p. mass mkt. 4.99 (978-1-60095-356-9(5), Doodlebops) Cookie Jar.

—Doodlebops Rock. 2007. 32p. (J). mass mkt. 4.99 (978-1-60095-269-2(0), Doodlebops) Cookie Jar.

Cool Things Press. 75 Cool Things to Color. 2008. 80p. pap. 12.95 (978-0-615-20795-7(2)) Cool Things Pr.

—75 Cool Things to Cut Out. 2008. 152p. pap. 15.95 (978-0-615-20796-4(0)) Cool Things Pr.

Cool Toys & Games, 6 vols. 2015. (Cool Toys & Games Ser.: 6). (ENG.). 32p. (J). (gr. 3-6). lib. bdg. 205.32 (978-1-68078-044-4(1), 19093, Checkerboard Library) ABDO Publishing Co.

Coon, Cyndi, illus. Art That Pops! How to Make Wacky 3-D Creations That Jump, Spin, & Spring! 2006. 48p. (J). pap. (978-0-439-81337-2(9)) Scholastic, Inc.

Copeland, Peter F. Scenes of Olde New York Coloring Book. 2009. (Dover American History Coloring Bks.). (ENG.). 48p. (gr. 3-8). pap. 5.99 (978-0-486-47494-6(1), 474941) Dover Pubns., Inc.

Corr, Christopher. Whole World: Fun Eco Activities. 2008. (Illus.). 24p. (J). pap. 4.99 (978-1-84686-220-5(5)) Barefoot Bks., Inc.

Cosmic City Blast off! Preschool Guide. 2007. (Vacation Bible School Ser.). 112p. (J). (gr. 3-5). pap. 9.99 (978-1-4347-9963-0(8)) Cook, David C.

Cosneau, Géraldine & Cosneau, Géraldine. All Around the World: Sports & Games. 2016. (ENG., Illus.). 48p. (J). (gr. -1-2). pap. 16.95 (978-1-84976-410-0(7), 1673003) Tate Publishing, Ltd. GBR. Dist: Hachette Bk. Group, Abrams, Inc.

Cosneau, Olivia. At the Seashore: My Nature Sticker Activity Book (Ages 5 & up, with 120 Stickers, 24 Activities & 1 Quiz) My Nature Sticker Activity Book. 2016. (ENG., Illus.). 24p. (J). (gr. k-3). 9.99 (978-1-61689-461-0(X)) Princeton Architectural Pr.

—Butterflies of the World: My Nature Sticker Activity Book. 2016. (ENG., Illus.). 24p. (J). (gr. k-3). 9.99 (978-1-61689-465-8(2)) Princeton Architectural Pr.

—Garden Insects & Bugs: My Nature Sticker Activity Book. 2018. (ENG.). (J). (gr. -1-1). pap. 9.99 (978-1-61689-664-5(7)) Princeton Architectural Pr.

Costanzo, Beth. A Day at the Beach. 2009. 28p. pap. 12.49 (978-1-4389-8180-2(5)) AuthorHouse.

Cowling, Dan. Color Yourself Smart: Geography. Franklin, Mark, illus. 2012. (Color Yourself Smart Ser.). (ENG.). 128p. 19.95 (978-1-60710-216-8(1), Thunder Bay Pr.) Readerlink Distribution Services, LLC.

Crabtree Publishing, creator. Green Team, Set. 2008. (ENG.). 32p. (J). (978-0-7787-4094-0(3)) Crabtree Publishing Co.

Crane, Cheryl L. Facing Lions, Giants & Other Big Dudes: A Bible Study Workbook on Courage for Ages 6-12. 2008. 112p. pap. 17.95 (978-1-4401-0609-5(6)) iUniverse, Inc.

—Pressing on When the Pressure's On: A Bible Study Workbook on Perseverance for Ages 6-12. 2009. 112p. pap. 10.95 (978-1-4401-5830-8(4)) iUniverse, Inc.

Creative Kids, 12 vols. 2016. (Creative Kids Ser.). 32p. (gr. 3-3). (ENG.). 181.62 (978-1-4994-8097-9(0), 101428e6-e1c6-4ea4-8955-a6e142370129); pap. 70.50 (978-1-4994-8117-4(9)) Rosen Publishing Group, Inc., The. (Windmill Bks.).

Creative Writing Book IR. 2017. (Write Your Own Bks.). (ENG.). (J). spiral bd. 14.99 (978-0-7945-3874-3(6), Usborne) EDC Publishing.

Crossling, Nick & Creative Haven. Creative Haven Alhambra Designs. 2013. (Adult Coloring Books: World & Travel Ser.). (ENG., Illus.). 64p. (gr. 3). pap. 6.99 (978-0-486-49316-9(4), 493164) Dover Pubns., Inc.

CrossStaff Publishing, creator. The Ten Commandments Movie Coloring Book: Part 1. 2007. (Epic Stories of the Bible Ser.). (Illus.). 32p. (J). (gr. -1-3). 5.99 (978-0-9743876-1-1(4)) CrossStaff Publishing.

Cryan, Mary Beth. My Christmas Tree. 2014. (ENG.). 24p. (J). (gr. 2-5). 9.99 (978-0-486-77775-7(8), 777758) Dover Pubns., Inc.

Cuban, Mark. Let's Go Mavs! 2007. (978-1-932888-72-0(1)) Amplify Publishing Group.

Curious George Super Sticker Activity Book. 2009. (Curious George Ser.). (ENG., Illus.). 124p. (J). (gr. -1-3). act. bk. ed. 12.99 (978-0-547-23896-8(7), 1084376, Clarion Bks.) HarperCollins Pubs.

Currie, Lisa. Me, You, Us: A Book to Fill Out Together. 2014. (ENG., Illus.). 186p. (gr. k-12). pap. 16.00 (978-0-399-16794-2(3), TarcherPerigee) Penguin Publishing Group.

Currie, Robin. The Baby Bible ABCs, 1 vol. Basaluzzo, Constanza, illus. 2009. (Baby Bible Ser.). (ENG.). 48p. (J). bds. 12.99 (978-1-4347-6542-0(3), 106166) Cook, David C.

Curry, Don, ed. Madagascar, Kit, Bk. 2. 2008. 32p. (J). act. bk. ed. 14.99 (978-0-696-23489-7(0)) Meredith Bks.

Cutting, David. Toy Doctor Sticker Paper Doll. 2015. (ENG.). 4p. (J). (gr. k-3). pap. 1.50 (978-0-486-79098-5(3), 790983) Dover Pubns., Inc.

Cuxart, Bernadette. Modeling Clay Animals: Easy-To-Follow Projects in Simple Steps. 2010. (ENG.). 96p. (J). (gr. 2-7). pap. 12.99 (978-0-7641-4579-7(7)) Sourcebooks, Inc.

Dahl, Michael. Hello Genius Milestone Box. Vidal, Oriol, illus. 2016. (Hello Genius Ser.). (ENG.). 24p. (J). (gr. 1-2). pap., pap., pap. 11.99 (978-1-4795-9838-0(0), 134969, Picture Window Bks.) Capstone.

Dahlen, Noelle. I Love Dogs & Cats! 2019. (Dover Kids Activity Books: Animals Ser.). (ENG.). 96p. (J). (gr. 1-3). pap. 7.99 (978-0-486-83320-0(8), 833208) Dover Pubns., Inc.

—Owls Coloring Book. 2014. (Dover Animal Coloring Bks.). (ENG.). 32p. (J). (gr. k). pap. 3.99 (978-0-486-78033-7(3), 780333) Dover Pubns., Inc.

Dailey, Joanna. The Catholic Children's Bible Activity Booklet. 2013. (ENG.). 100p. (gr. 1-5). spiral bd. 31.95 (978-1-59982-181-8(8)) Saint Mary's Press of Minnesota.

Danks, Fiona, et al. Nature's Playground: Activities, Crafts, & Games to Encourage Children to Get Outdoors. 2007. (ENG., Illus.). 192p. (J). (gr. 2-4). pap. 19.95 (978-1-55652-723-4(3)) Chicago Review Pr., Inc.

David C Cook. Noah's Park Children's Church Craft Book, Red Edition. 2007. (Children's Church Kit Ser.). (ENG.). 112p. (J). pap. 14.99 (978-0-7814-4492-7(6), 105095) Cook, David C.

—Noah's Park Children's Church Leader's Guide, Red Edtion. 2007. (Children's Church Kit Ser.). (ENG.). 272p. (J). pap. 49.99 (978-0-7814-4494-1(2), 105097) Cook, David C.

—Noah's Park Children's Church Snacks & Games, Red Edition. 2007. (Children's Church Kit Ser.). (ENG.). 112p. (J). pap. 14.99 (978-0-7814-4491-0(8), 105094) Cook, David C.

—Ooze & Awes in God's Creation, 1 vol. 2009. (Bible Funstuff Ser.). (ENG.). 112p. (J). pap. 19.99 (978-1-4347-6720-2(5), 106038) Cook, David C.

David C. Cook Publishing Company Staff. Blast off! Preschool Student Book. 2007. (Vacation Bible School Ser.). 24p. (J). (gr. 3-5). pap. 2.99 (978-1-4347-9956-2(5)) Cook, David C.

—Cosmic City Elementary Student Book. 2007. (Vacation Bible School Ser.). 24p. (J). (gr. 6-12). pap. 2.99 (978-1-4347-9955-5(7)) Cook, David C.

—Jesus & Me: BOZ's Big Book of Bible Fun. 2008. (Boz the Bear Ser.). 236p. (J). pap. 14.99 (978-1-4347-6789-9(2)) Cook, David C.

—Jesus Feeds 5000. 2008. (Pencil Fun Bks). 16p. (J). pap. 9.90 (978-0-7814-4900-7(6)) Cook, David C.

—Lazarus Lives, 10, Pack. 2008. (Pencil Fun Bks). 16p. (J). pap. 9.90 (978-1-4347-6820-9(1)) Cook, David C.

—Let the Children Come 2009. (Pencil Fun Bks). 16p. (J). pap. 9.90 (978-1-4347-6815-5(5)) Cook, David C.

—The Lord's Prayer. 2008. (Pencil Fun Bks). 16p. (J). pap. 9.90 (978-0-7814-4901-4(4)) Cook, David C.

—Outer Limits Mission Log Upper Elementary Student Book. 2007. (Vacation Bible School Ser.). 24p. (YA). (gr. 9-12). pap. 2.99 (978-1-4347-9954-8(9)) Cook, David C.

—Pencil Fun Book: Jesus Is Alive. 2007. (Pencil Fun Books Ser.). 16p. (J). (gr. 3-7). 9.90 (978-0-7814-4521-4(3)) Cook, David C.

—Pencil Fun Book: Joeseph Saves His Family. 2007. (Pencil Fun Books Ser.). 16p. (J). (gr. 3-7). 9.90 (978-0-7814-4522-1(1)) Cook, David C.

—Pencil Fun Book: Noah Builds an Ark. 2007. (Pencil Fun Books Ser.). 16p. (J). (gr. 3-7). 9.90 (978-0-7814-4523-8(X)) Cook, David C.

—Ring, Robe & Shoes, 10, Pack. 2008. (Pencil Fun Bks). 16p. (J). pap. 9.90 (978-1-4347-6822-3(8)) Cook, David C.

—Scripture Pictures - Miracles & Parables of Jesus. 2005. 106p. 29.99 (978-0-7814-4201-5(X), 078144201X) Cook, David C.

David C. Cook Publishing Company Staff, creator. Classy, Flashy Bible Dramas. 2008. (Bible Fun Stuff for Tweens Ser.). (Illus.). 112p. (J). (gr. 4-5). pap. 16.99 (978-1-4347-6858-2(9)) Cook, David C.

—Full Tilt Wacky Games. 2008. (Bible Fun Stuff for Middle School Ser.). (Illus.). 112p. (J). (gr. 6-8). pap. 19.99 (978-1-4347-6855-1(4)) Cook, David C.

—Memory Maker Bible Crafts. 2008. (Bible Fun Stuff for 2nd-3rd Grades Ser.). (Illus.). 112p. (J). (gr. 2-3). pap. 19.99 (978-1-4347-6859-9(7)) Cook, David C.

—Score with Scripture Games. 2008. (Bible Fun Stuff for K-1 Ser.). (Illus.). 112p. (J). (gr. k-1). pap. 19.99 (978-1-4347-6861-2(9)) Cook, David C.

—Stick'em up Bible Crafts. 2008. (Bible Fun Stuff for Preschool Ser.). (Illus.). 112p. (J). (gr. -1-k). pap. 19.99 (978-1-4347-6864-3(3)) Cook, David C.

—Through-the-Bible Crafts. 2008. (Bible Fun Stuff for K-1 Ser.). (Illus.). 112p. (J). (gr. k-1). pap. 19.99 (978-1-4347-6862-9(7)) Cook, David C.

David, Juliet. Candle Bible for Toddlers. Prole, Helen, illus. 2006. (Candle Bible for Toddlers Ser.). (ENG.). 400p. (J). (gr. -1-k). 12.99 (978-1-85985-602-4(0), d048b2a6-5b58-4316-9dea-36ab05e118a2, Candle Bks.) Lion Hudson PLC GBR. Dist: Baker & Taylor Publisher Services (BTPS).

—Dot to Dot Coloring & Stickers Bk. 1, 1 vol., 1. Smith, Jan, illus. 2008. (Candle Activity Fun Ser.). 24p. (J). (gr. 4-7). pap. 6.99 (978-0-8254-7360-9(8), Candle Bks.) Lion Hudson PLC GBR. Dist: Kregel Pubns.

Davies, Hannah. The Big Fabulous Colouring Book. 2017. (ENG.). 48p. (J). (gr. 3). pap. 14.99 (978-1-78055-452-5(4)) O'Mara, Michael Bks., Ltd. GBR. Dist: Independent Pubs. Group.

Davis, Mary J. Spur of the Moment Preschool Activities. 2005. (Bible Funstuff Ser.). (ENG.). 112p. pap. 16.99 (978-0-7814-4230-5(3), 104153) Cook, David C.

Dawnay, Gabby. London Calls Sticker Book. Barrow, Alex, illus. 2017. (ENG.). 20p. (J). (gr. k-17). pap. 11.95 (978-1-84976-384-4(4), 1648103) Tate Publishing, Ltd. GBR. Dist: Hachette Bk. Group.

Daynes, Katie & Watt, Fiona, eds. Baby Scrapbook. 2008. (Baby Scrapbook Ser.). (Illus.). 32p. (J). bds. 19.99 (978-0-7945-1957-5(1), Usborne) EDC Publishing.

de Klerk, Roger, illus. Foxy Learns Colors, 1 vol. 2009. (Foxy Learns Ser.). (ENG.). 16p. (J). pap. 4.95 (978-1-59496-181-6(6)) Teora USA LLC.

—Foxy Learns Shapes, 1 vol. 2009. (Foxy Learns Ser.). (ENG.). 16p. (J). pap. 4.95 (978-1-59496-179-3(4)) Teora USA LLC.

—Foxy Learns to Add, 1 vol. 2009. (Foxy Learns Ser.). (ENG.). 16p. (J). pap. 4.95 (978-1-59496-178-6(6)) Teora USA LLC.

—Foxy Learns to Tell Time, 1 vol. 2009. (Foxy Learns Ser.). (ENG.). 16p. (J). pap. 4.95 (978-1-59496-180-9(8)) Teora USA LLC.

De Lopez, Jacqueline Salazar. Little Hands, Busy Minds. 2012. 162p. pap. 39.95 (978-0-9853094-8-0(2)) Warren Publishing, Inc.

de Sturtz, Maria Ester H. Milagros en la Bibla. Fernandez, Lucia, illus. 2007. (Manos a la Obra Ser.). 32p. (J). (gr. -1-4). per. 7.99 (978-0-7586-1458-2(6)) Concordia Publishing Hse.

de Sturtz, Marie Ester H. Por Las Aguas De la Biblia (God & Water in the Bible) 2011. 32p. pap. 1.99 (978-0-7586-2677-6(0)) Concordia Publishing Hse.

—Por Las Aguas De La Biblia (God & Water in the Bible) - Bilingual. 2011. 32p. pap. 1.99 (978-0-7586-2679-0(7)) Concordia Publishing Hse.

—Reyes y Profetas (Kings & Prophets) 2011. 32p. pap. 1.99 (978-0-7586-2676-9(2)) Concordia Publishing Hse.

—Reyes y profetas (Kings & Prophets) - Bilingual. 2011. 32p. pap. 1.99 (978-0-7586-2678-3(9)) Concordia Publishing Hse.

Dean, Arlan & Ward, Kay. The California Mission Activity Book, 1 vol. 2003. (Missions of California Ser.). (ENG., Illus.). 144p. (gr. 4-4). pap. 19.95 (978-0-404-28506-7(6), c56eb104-7c06-46b3-b4b9-22553edc11f6, Rosen Classroom) Rosen Publishing Group, Inc., The.

Dean, James & Dean, Kimberly. Pete the Cat: My First I Can Draw. Dean, James, illus. 2016. (Pete the Cat Ser.). (ENG., Illus.). 160p. (J). (gr. -1-3). pap. 9.99 (978-0-06-230443-8(7), HarperFestival) HarperCollins Pubs.

—Pete the Cat's Big Doodle & Draw Book. Dean, James, illus. 2015. (Pete the Cat Ser.). (ENG., Illus.). 128p. (J). (gr. -1-3). pap. 12.99 (978-0-06-230442-1(9), HarperFestival) HarperCollins Pubs.

DeNinno, Joanne & Gill, Kim. The Question Challenge Card Game Fun Sheets. 2012. 34.95 net. (978-1-60723-023-6(2)) Super Duper Pubns.

Denmark-Allen, Eva. I Was, I Am, i Will Be! - Yo Fui! Yo soy! Yo Sere! 2007. (ENG & SPA., Illus.). 56p. (J). per. 12.00 (978-0-9792016-8-4(3)) Professional Publishing Hse. LLC.

Dent, Sabrina. Proverbs Kids Fun Activity Book. 2006. (Illus.). 40p. (J). 5.99 (978-0-9796148-0-4(5)) Joint Heir Multimedia.

deRubertis, Barbara & Roser, Nancy. Let's Read Together: Resource Guide. 2005. (Let's Read Together Ser.). (Illus.). 56p. pap. 12.95 (978-1-57565-139-2(4)) Astra Publishing Hse.

Desalle, Nicole. Safe at Play. 2011. pap. 39.95 (978-0-7664-3752-4(3)) Abrams & Co. Pubs., Inc.

DeShazer, Dennis & Green, Jon, creators. Music Is for Children: Kit B Advanced, Level 6. 2007. (Boz: the Green Bear Next Door Ser.). (J). (gr. -1-3). stu. ed. 5.95 (978-0-7814-4973-1(1), 83725) Cook, David C.

Desjardins, Margaret M. Murky, Quirky, Beserky Math. Bohart, Lisa, illus. 2013. 24p. pap. 13.95 (978-1-61493-210-9(7)) Peppertree Pr., The.

Desso, Karen. Early Learning Reading Games: Levels A-D. 2007. 119p. spiral bd. 15.99 (978-0-9793576-8-8(3)) New Learning Publishing.

Deuchars, Marion. Draw Paint Print Like the Great Artists: Marion Deuchars' Book of Great Artists. 2014. (ENG., Illus.). 224p. (J). (gr. 3-7). pap. 19.95 (978-1-78067-281-6(0), King, Laurence Publishing) Orion Publishing Group, Ltd. GBR. Dist: Hachette Bk. Group.

Deuchars, Marion, illus. Art Play. 2016. (ENG.). 224p. (J). (gr. 2-6). pap. 19.99 (978-1-78067-877-1(0), King, Laurence Publishing) Orion Publishing Group, Ltd. GBR. Dist: Hachette Bk. Group.

Deveny, Mary Alice. Pockets: Book: Nonfiction_Juvenile, The Molly Brave Preschool Series Vol. 1. Sweetman, Gary W., photos by. 2011. (Illus.). 40p. (J). pap. 14.95 (978-1-61245-000-1(8)) Molly Brave.

Devos, Sarah. I Am Never Bored: the Best Ever Craft & Activity Book for Kids: 100 Great Ideas for Kids to Do When There Is Nothing to Do. Thyssen, Emma, illus. 2018. (ENG.). 144p. (J). (gr. k-4). pap. 15.99 (978-1-63159-468-7(0), 301938, Quarry Bks.) Quarto Publishing Group USA.

DeVries Sokol, Dawn. The Doodle Circle: A Fill-In Journal for BFFs to Share. 2013. (ENG.). 160p. (J). (gr. 3-7). pap. 12.95 (978-1-61769-053-2(8), 1052703, Amulet Bks.) Abrams, Inc.

Deyes, Alfie. Pointless Book 2 Bk. 2: Continued by Alfie Deyes Finished by You. 2015. (ENG., Illus.). 192p. (gr. 3-17). pap. 19.99 (978-0-7624-5920-9(4), Running Pr.) Running Pr.

Diamant-Cohen, Betsy. Mother Goose on the Loose — Here, There, & Everywhere. 2019. (ENG.). 160p. pap. 69.99 (978-0-8389-1647-6(3)) American Library Assn.

Dickason, Chris. The Planes, Trains & Cars Colouring Book. Dickason, Chris, illus. 2017. (ENG., Illus.). 64p. (J). (gr. k-2). pap. 6.99 (978-1-78055-251-4(3)) O'Mara, Michael Bks., Ltd. GBR. Dist: Independent Pubs. Group.

Diehn, Andi. Explore Poetry! With 25 Great Projects. Stone, Bryan, illus. 2015. (Explore Your World Ser.). (ENG.). 96p. (J). (gr. 1-5). 19.95 (978-1-61930-279-2(9), 638b125b-17a6-4e15-b179-9722a3dbfeba) Nomad Pr.

Dischler, Patricia. Tea Party Celebrations! 2012. (ENG.). pap. 19.95 (978-1-4675-3709-4(8)) Independent Pub.

Disney Enterprises Inc. Staff, creator. Disney's Lilo & Stitch Time for Fun! Bath Time Bubble Book. 2007. (Disney Bath Time Bubble Bks.). (Illus.). (J). (gr. -1-k). 4.99 (978-0-7666-2553-2(2)) Modern Publishing.

Disney Modern Publishing & Greenwald, Todd J., creators. Wizards of Waverly Place: A Day in the Life. 2009. (Illus.). (J). pap. 4.99 (978-0-7666-3301-8(2)) Modern Publishing.

DK. Baby Touch Your Nose. 2016. (Baby Sparkle Ser.). (ENG., Illus.). 14p. (J). (— 1). bds. 6.99 (978-1-4654-5071-5(8), DK Children) Dorling Kindersley Publishing, Inc.

—Colors with Ladybug. 2018. (Learn with a Ladybug Ser.). (ENG., Illus.). 14p. (J). (— 1). bds. 9.99 (978-1-4654-6842-0(0), DK Children) Dorling Kindersley Publishing, Inc.

—LEGO(r) NINJAGO: Build Your Own Adventure: With Lloyd Minifigure & Exclusive Ninja Merch, Book Includes More Than 50 Buil. 2015. (LEGO Build Your Own Adventure Ser.). (ENG.). 80p. (J). (gr. 2-5). 24.99 (978-1-4654-3590-3(5), DK Children) Dorling Kindersley Publishing, Inc.

—My Best Pop-Up Noisy Train Book. 2017. (Noisy Pop-Up Bks.). (ENG., Illus.). 18p. (J). (-k). bds. 15.99 (978-1-4654-6173-5(6), DK Children) Dorling Kindersley Publishing, Inc.

—My Encyclopedia of Very Important Things: For Little Learners Who Want to Know Everything. 2016. (My Very Important Encyclopedias Ser.). (ENG., Illus.). 224p. (J). (gr. k-4). 18.99 (978-1-4654-4968-9(X), DK Children) Dorling Kindersley Publishing, Inc.

—Pop-Up Peekaboo! Bedtime: Pop-Up Surprise under Every Flap! 2014. (Pop-Up Peekaboo! Ser.). (ENG.). 12p. (J). (gr. -1 — 1). bds. 12.99 (978-1-4654-2035-0(5), DK Children) Dorling Kindersley Publishing, Inc.

—Pop-Up Peekaboo! Tractor: Pop-Up Surprise under Every Flap! 2014. (Pop-Up Peekaboo! Ser.). (ENG., Illus.). 12p. (J). (gr. -1 — 1). bds. 12.99 (978-1-4654-1665-0(X), DK Children) Dorling Kindersley Publishing, Inc.

—Sophie la Girafe: ABC Flashcards. 2017. (Sophie la Girafe Ser.). (ENG.). 26p. (J). (— 1). 12.99 (978-1-4654-5702-8(X), DK Children) Dorling Kindersley Publishing, Inc.

—Sophie la Girafe: Good Night, Sophie: A Touch & Feel Book. 2017. (Sophie la Girafe Ser.). (ENG., Illus.). 12p. (J). (— 1). bds. 7.99 (978-1-4654-5625-0(2), DK Children) Dorling Kindersley Publishing, Inc.

—Ultimate Sticker Book: Disney Moana. 2016. (Ultimate Sticker Book Ser.). (ENG.). 16p. (J). (gr. k-4). pap. 6.99 (978-1-4654-5260-3(5), DK Children) Dorling Kindersley Publishing, Inc.

—Ultimate Sticker Book: Disney Pixar Coco. 2017. (Ultimate Sticker Book Ser.). (ENG.). 16p. (J). (gr. k-3). pap. 6.99 (978-1-4654-5574-1(4), DK Children) Dorling Kindersley Publishing, Inc.

—Ultimate Sticker Collection: American Girl. 2016. (Ultimate Sticker Collection). (ENG.). 96p. (J). (gr. k-3). pap. 12.99 (978-1-4654-4922-1(1), DK Children) Dorling Kindersley Publishing, Inc.

—Ultimate Sticker Collection: DC Comics Super Heroes. 2016. (Ultimate Sticker Collection). (ENG.). 96p. (J). (gr. 1-4). pap. 12.99 (978-1-4654-4549-0(8), DK Children) Dorling Kindersley Publishing, Inc.

—Ultimate Sticker Collection: Disney Pixar Finding Dory. 2016. (Ultimate Sticker Collection). (ENG., Illus.). 96p. (J). (gr. -1-1). pap. 12.99 (978-1-4654-4979-5(5), DK Children) Dorling Kindersley Publishing, Inc.

—Ultimate Sticker Collection: Marvel: Heroes Unite! More Than 1,000 Reusable Full-Color Stickers. 2014. (Ultimate Sticker Collection). (ENG.). 96p. (J). (gr. k-2). pap. 12.99 (978-1-4654-1684-1(6), DK Children) Dorling Kindersley Publishing, Inc.

—100 First Words. 2017. (100 First Ser.). (ENG., Illus.). 16p. (J). (— 1). bds. 10.99 (978-1-4654-5700-4(3), DK Children) Dorling Kindersley Publishing, Inc.

Do It Yourself Set Of 15. 2014. (ENG.). pap. 134.85 (978-1-4846-2352-7(5), Heinemann) Capstone.

Doherty, Gillian. 1001 Animals to Spot. 2010. (1001 Things to Spot Ser.). 32p. (J). 9.99 (978-0-7945-2704-4(3), Usborne) EDC Publishing.

—1001 Things to Spot Long Ago. Gower, Teri, illus. rev. ed. 2006. (1001 Things to Spot Ser.). 32p. (J). (gr. -1-3). pap. 6.99 (978-0-7945-0716-9(6), Usborne) EDC Publishing.

Donahue, Peter. Not-Your-Average Superhero Mazes. 2009. (Dover Kids Activity Books: Fantasy Ser.). (ENG.). 48p. (J). (gr. 1-4). pap. 4.99 (978-0-486-47039-9(3), 470393) Dover Pubns., Inc.

—Not-Your-Average Superhero Stickers. 2009. (Dover Little Activity Books Stickers Ser.). (ENG., Illus.). 4p. (J). (gr. -1-2). pap. 1.50 (978-0-486-47040-5(7)) Dover Pubns., Inc.

—What to Doodle? Jr. - Superheroes & Robots! 2013. (Dover Doodle Bks.). (ENG.). 128p. (J). (gr. 1-5). pap. 4.99 (978-0-486-49954-3(5), 499545) Dover Pubns., Inc.

Donaldson, Julia. My First Animal Fun Sticker Book. Sharratt, Nick, illus. 2016. (ENG.). 30p. (J). (gr. -1-2). pap. 8.99 (978-1-5098-1622-4(4)) Pan Macmillan GBR. Dist: Independent Pubs. Group.

—Room on the Broom Big Activity Book. Scheffler, Axel, illus. 2015. (ENG.). 48p. (J). (gr. -1-3). pap. 12.99 (978-0-448-48944-5(9), Grosset & Dunlap) Penguin Young Readers Group.

Donner, Candie. Easter Activity Book. Kinney, Cyndi, ed. 2013. (J). pap. 22.99 (978-1-61625-617-3(6)); cd-rom 12.99 (978-1-61625-616-6(8)) Knowledge Box Central.

Doodlewire. 2010. 40p. (J). (gr. 3). 14.99 (978-1-59174-843-4(7)) Klutz.

Dorling Kindersley Publishing Staff. Leaf it to Cubs. 2008. 16p. (J). (gr. k-5). 2.49 (978-0-7566-3324-0(9)) Dorling Kindersley Publishing, Inc.

Dot-to-Dot 1-100+ Spanish Version. 2007. (J). per. (978-1-58232-163-9(9)) ECS Learning Systems, Inc.

Doughty, Sarah. Flippin' Awesome: Water Bottle Flip Games, Tricks & Stunts for Everyone! 2016. (ENG., Illus.). 64p. (J). (gr. 4-4). pap. 14.99 (978-1-63158-169-4(4), Racehorse Publishing) Skyhorse Publishing Co., Inc.

Dover. Bugs Activities Dover Chunky Book. 2009. (Dover Little Activity Bks.). (ENG., Illus.). 320p. (J). (gr. -1-5). 6.99 (978-0-486-47425-0(9)) Dover Pubns., Inc.

—Cool Construction Site Stickers. 2016. (Dover Little Activity Books Stickers Ser.). (ENG.). 4p. (J). (gr. -1-3). 2.50 (978-0-486-80316-6(3), 803163) Dover Pubns., Inc.

—Moustache Stickers. 2014. (ENG.). 4p. (J). (gr. k-3). 2.50 (978-0-486-78036-8(8), 780368) Dover Pubns., Inc.

—On the Go Activities Dover Chunky Book. 2009. (Dover Little Activity Bks.). (ENG., Illus.). 320p. (J). (gr. -1-5). pap. 6.99 (978-0-486-47430-4(5), 474305) Dover Pubns., Inc.

—Spot the Differences: Art Masterpieces, Bk. 3. 2012. (Dover Kids Activity Bks.). (ENG., Illus.). 64p. (J). (gr. 3-5). pap. 10.99 (978-0-486-48085-5(2), 480852) Dover Pubns., Inc.

—Spot the Differences Bk. 4: Art Masterpiece Mysteries, Bk .4. 2013. (Dover Kids Activity Bks.). (ENG., Illus.). 64p. (J). (gr. 3-5). pap. 10.99 (978-0-486-48086-2(0), 480860) Dover Pubns., Inc.

Dover & Merrell, Patrick. Game on! MORE Awesome Activities for Clever Kids. 2019. (Dover Kids Activity Bks.). (ENG.). 144p. (J). (gr. 3-6). pap. 12.99 (978-0-486-82467-3(5), 824675) Dover Pubns., Inc.

Dover & Printworks KMG Staff. Sea Life Field Guide. 2013. (Dover Science for Kids Ser.). (ENG.). 48p. (J). (gr. 3-8). pap. 5.99 (978-0-486-49157-8(9), 491579) Dover Pubns., Inc.

Dover & Tattoos. Moustache Tattoos: For Your Face or Finger! 2013. (Dover Tattoos Ser.). (ENG., Illus.). 2p. (J). (gr. 3-4). pap. 3.50 (978-0-486-49329-9(6), 493296) Dover Pubns., Inc.

Dover Publications Inc. Staff, ed. Revolutionary War, Kit. 2009. (ENG.). 4p. (J). (gr. 5). 19.99 (978-0-486-47356-7(2)) Dover Pubns., Inc.

Dover Staff. Spectacular Scales & Nifty Notes Tattoos. 2011. (Dover Tattoos Ser.). (ENG.). 4p. (J). (gr. 1-4). pap. 1.99 (978-0-486-48191-3(3)) Dover Pubns., Inc.

Dover Staff & Printworks KMG Staff. Dinosaurs Field Guide. 2013. (Dover Science for Kids Ser.). (ENG.). 48p. (J). (gr. 3-8). pap. 5.99 (978-0-486-49156-1(0), 491560) Dover Pubns., Inc.

Dowley, Tim. Bible People Activity Fun, 1 vol. 2017. (Activity Fun Ser.). (ENG.). 64p. (J). pap. 3.99 (978-1-78128-328-8(1), 2ea70717-f6ca-4fae-834e-e0520c17ee28, Candle Bks.) Lion Hudson PLC GBR. Dist: Baker & Taylor Publisher Services (BTPS).

Down, Heather. Postcards from Space: The Chris Hadfield Story. 2013. 50p. pap. (978-1-894813-65-5(0)) Wintertickle Pr.

Doyle, James. The Superhero Handbook: 20 Super Activities to Help You Save the World! Ford, Jason, illus. 2017. (ENG.). 144p. (J). (gr. 2-6). pap. 12.99 (978-1-78067-974-7(2), King, Laurence Publishing) Orion Publishing Group, Ltd. GBR. Dist: Hachette Bk. Group.

Doyle, Lizzy. Color by Numbers. 2017. (ENG.). 96p. (J). (gr. 1-7). pap. 9.99 (978-1-78428-469-5(6), 7d88a7b2-b953-4503-9b59-68e2e33202f1) Arcturus Publishing GBR. Dist: Baker & Taylor Publisher Services (BTPS).

Draught Associates, Draught. Visual Aid Doodling Book for Creative Kids. 2012. (ENG.). 96p. (J). (gr. k-6). pap. 11.95 (978-1-907317-70-5(8)) Black Dog Publishing Ltd. GBR. Dist: Consortium Bk. Sales & Distribution.

Dudziuk, Kasia, et al. My First Activity Book. 2018. (ENG.). 256p. (J). pap. 14.99 (978-1-78828-303-8(1), fc75b1f1-8027-4cf0-95a5-902b2012a5b6) Arcturus Publishing GBR. Dist: Baker & Taylor Publisher Services (BTPS).

Duke, Nell K., et al. Engaging Families in Children's Literacy Development: A Guide for Leading Successful Workshops, Including - Ready-to-Show Videos * Step-by-Step Plans & Schedules * Easy-to-Prepare Workshop Activities * Read-Aloud Trade Book Pack. 2014. (ENG., Illus.). 48p. pap. 149.99 (978-0-545-56148-8(5), Teaching Resources) Scholastic, Inc.

Dunn, Justine. Hey! There's Science in My Literature! Grades 1-2. Radtke, Becky, illus. 2007. (Rigby Best Teachers Press Ser.). 96p. per. 13.99 (978-1-4190-2848-9(0)) Houghton Mifflin Harcourt Supplemental Pubs.

Dunn, Mary. My Adventure in the Southeast: Advanced My Adventure. 2007. 44p. (J). pap. 8.99 (978-1-59092-436-5(3)) Blue Forge Pr.

—My Adventure on a Dinosaur Dig. 2006. 44p. (J). 8.99 (978-1-59092-281-1(6)) Blue Forge Pr.

—My Adventure with Mozart. 2006. 44p. (J). 8.99 (978-1-59092-459-4(2)) Blue Forge Pr.

—My Adventure with Rembrandt. 2006. 44p. (J). 8.99 (978-1-59092-463-1(0)) Blue Forge Pr.

Dutton, Michael. Amusement Park Science Activity Book. 2015. (Dover Science for Kids Ser.). (ENG.). 48p. (J). (gr. 3). pap. 4.99 (978-0-486-78035-1(X), 78035X) Dover Pubns., Inc.

Dworkin, Motoko. A Year in Japan: Folktales, Songs & Art for the Classroom. 2nd ed. 2012. (Illus.). 151p. pap. 26.95 (978-0-9836716-1-9(3)) Paradise Copies, Inc.

Dyan, Penelope. Sticks — the for Boys Only Version — Because Sticks Are Also People. Dyan, Penelope, illus. 2008. (Illus.). 52p. pap. 11.95 (978-1-935118-13-8(7)) Bellissima Publishing, LLC.

Dziengel, Ana. STEAM Play & Learn: 20 Fun Step-By-step Preschool Projects about Science, Technology, Engineering, Art, & Math! 2018. (ENG., Illus.). 80p. (J). (gr. -1-k). pap. 15.95 (978-1-63322-526-8(7), 301714, Walter Foster Jr) Quarto Publishing Group USA.

—STEAM Play & Learn: Fun Step-By-step Projects to Teach Kids about STEAM. 2019. (Little Engineers Ser.). (ENG., Illus.). 32p. (J). (gr. -1-2). 26.65 (978-1-942875-77-2(0), 9a5a584b-10ee-45cb-a76e-7f2c88302c0c, Walter Foster Jr) Quarto Publishing Group USA.

Early Concepts, 10 vols. 2017. (Early Concepts Ser.). 24p. (ENG.). (gr. 1-1). 126.35 (978-1-5081-6249-0(2), 37c3ce03-efc1-469b-81b7-ecfc03fbf84b); (gr. 4-6). pap. 41.25 (978-1-5081-6252-0(2)) Rosen Publishing Group, Inc., The. (PowerKids Pr.).

Eckel, Jessie. The Boys' Coloring Book. 2013. (ENG.). 128p. (J). (gr. -1-2). pap. 8.95 (978-1-4549-0716-9(9)) Sterling Publishing Co., Inc.

Editors of Brain Quest. Brain Quest America: 850 Questions & Answers to Challenge the Mind. Teacher-Approved! 4th rev. ed. 2013. (Brain Quest Smart Cards Ser.). (ENG.). 152p. (J). (gr. 4-7). 11.95 (978-0-7611-7239-0(4), 17239) Workman Publishing Co., Inc.

—Brain Quest for the Car: 1,100 Questions & Answers All about America. 4th rev. ed. 2013. (Brain Quest Smart Cards Ser.). (ENG.). 152p. (J). (gr. 2-7). 11.95 (978-0-7611-7401-1(X), 17401) Workman Publishing Co., Inc.

Editors of Klutz. Create Your Own Quote Art: 11 Wall Art Projects to Foil, Color & Stencil, 1 vol. 2016. (ENG.). (J). (gr. 3-7). 19.99 (978-0-545-90651-7(2)) Klutz.

—The Encyclopedia of My Immaturity: Your Own Personal Diary-Ah. 2011. (ENG.). (J). (gr. 3-7). 16.99 (978-1-59174-923-3(9)) Klutz.

—Fashionably Me: A Journal That's Just My Style. 2013. (ENG., Illus.). 100p. (J). (gr. 3). 16.99 (978-0-545-56165-5(5)) Klutz.

—Fingerprint Fabulous. Editors of Klutz & Burton, Bonnie, eds. 2010. (ENG.). 40p. (J). (gr. 1). 14.95 (978-1-59174-748-2(1)) Klutz.

—Friendship Pixies. 2011. (ENG.). (J). (gr. 3-3). 16.99 (978-1-59174-917-2(4)) Klutz.

—Glossy Bands: Stretchy Bracelets to Share with Your Friends. Editors of Klutz, ed. 2010. (ENG.). (J). (gr. 3-18). 19.95 (978-1-59174-730-7(9)) Klutz.

—Klutz: 101 Outrageously Fun Things to Do, 1 vol. 2017. (ENG.). 80p. (J). (gr. 3-7). 19.99 (978-1-338-10640-4(6)) Klutz.

—The Klutz Book of Inventions. 2010. (ENG.). 200p. (J). (gr. 3-18). 19.99 (978-1-59174-879-3(8)) Klutz.

—Make Your Own Mini Erasers, 1 vol. 2016. (ENG.). 48p. (J). (gr. 3-7). 21.99 (978-1-338-03750-0(1)) Klutz.

—Marker Everything. 2016. (ENG.). 48p. (J). (gr. 3-7). 19.99 (978-0-545-85851-9(8)) Klutz.

—The Marvelous Book of Magical Horses: Dress up Paper Horses & Their Fairy Friends. 2011. (ENG.). 50p. (J). (gr. 1-1). 19.99 (978-1-59174-926-4(3)) Klutz.

—The Marvelous Book of Magical Mermaids: Dress up Paper Mermaids & Their Seahorse Friends. 2014. (ENG.). 50p. (J). (gr. 1). 19.99 (978-0-545-69214-4(8)) Klutz.

—My Egg Carton Animals. 2017. (Klutz Jr Ser.). (ENG.). 28p. (J). 12.99 (978-0-545-93244-8(0)) Scholastic, Inc.

—My Hand Art. 2017. (Klutz Jr Ser.). (ENG.). 20p. (J). 12.99 (978-0-545-93246-2(7)) Scholastic, Inc.

—My Twinkly Tiaras. 2017. (Klutz Jr Ser.). (ENG.). 20p. (J). 14.99 (978-0-545-93249-3(1)) Scholastic, Inc.

—Neon Chalk Lettering. 2016. (ENG.). 76p. (J). (gr. 3-7). 18.99 (978-1-338-03754-8(4)) Scholastic, Inc.

—Potholders & Other Loopy Projects. 2013. (ENG.). 40p. (J). (gr. 2-5). 19.99 (978-0-545-44943-4(X)) Klutz.

—Safety Pin Bracelets. 2011. (ENG.). (J). (gr. 3-7). 19.99 (978-1-59174-932-5(8)) Klutz.

—Sew Mini Treats: More Than 18 Food Plushies to Stitch & Stuff. 2016. (ENG.). 48p. (J). (gr. 3-7). 21.99 (978-0-545-90652-4(0)) Klutz.

—Shimmer Art. 2016. (ENG.). (J). (gr. 7). 21.99 (978-0-545-90650-0(4)) Klutz.

—Star Wars Thumb Doodles. Editors of Klutz, ed. 2013. (ENG.). 40p. (J). (gr. 3). 16.99 (978-0-545-49284-3(X)) Klutz.

—Sticker Design Studio. 2011. (ENG.). 54p. (J). (gr. 3-7). 16.99 (978-1-59174-935-6(2)) Klutz.

—Toolbox Jewelry. 2013. (ENG.). 60p. (J). (gr. 3). 21.99 (978-0-545-56134-1(5)) Klutz.

Editors of Klutz & Nichols, Kaitlyn. Make Clay Charms. 2013. (ENG.). 60p. (J). (gr. 3). 21.99 (978-0-545-49856-2(2)) Klutz.

Editors of Klutz & Phillips, Karen. It's All about Us (... Especially Me!) 2013. (ENG.). 126p. (J). (gr. 3). 16.99 (978-0-545-49280-5(7)) Klutz.

Editors of Klutz & Scholastic. Coloring Crush, 1 vol. 2015. (ENG.). 72p. (J). (gr. 3-7). 16.99 (978-0-545-93097-0(9)) Klutz.

Educational Adventures, creator. Blazin' Hot: Coloring/Activity Book (Spanish) w/ Snipe. 2006. (SPA., Illus.). (J). 2.99 (978-0-9770455-5-6(2)) Mighty Kids Media.

Edupress, creator. My Story Book: Primary. 2009. 32p. pap. 1.99 (978-1-56472-944-6(3)) Edupress, Inc.

Edwards, Andrew & Thornton, Fleur. Wilberforce: 24 Ready to Use Lesson Plans: an Activity Book. 2007. (Illus.). 32p. (J). (gr. 3-7). pap. 4.99 (978-0-89221-672-7(7)) New Leaf Publishing Group.

Einhorn, Kama. Letter of the Week Flip Chart. 2010. (ENG.). 26p. (gr. -1-1). pap. 27.99 (978-0-545-22417-8(9), Teaching Resources) Scholastic, Inc.

Eisbruch, Emily. Curious Kids Activity Guide to Michigan. 2007. pap. 9.95 (978-0-9789140-0-4(7)) Curious Kids Guides.

Eisenberg, Rebecca & Kjesbo, Rynette. Cool in School Communication Game: Gb362. Lefebvre, Patrick, photos by. 2011. (Illus.). (J). 64.95 net. (978-1-58650-994-1(2)) Super Duper Pubns.

Elder, Jeremy. Animal Kaleidoscope Designs Coloring Book. 2017. (Dover Animal Coloring Bks.). (ENG., Illus.). 32p. (J). (gr. 3-6). pap. 3.99 (978-0-486-80883-3(1), 808831) Dover Pubns., Inc.

—ComicQuest ZOMBIES UNLEASHED. 2013. (Dover Children's Activity Bks.). (ENG.). 48p. (J). (gr. 3-8). pap. 4.99 (978-0-486-49943-7(X)) Dover Pubns., Inc.

—Japanese Tattoo Art Stained Glass Coloring Book. 2010. (Dover Design Coloring Bks.). (ENG., Illus.). 32p. (J). (gr. 1-5). pap. 7.99 (978-0-486-47533-2(6), 475336) Dover Pubns., Inc.

—Monsters Destroyed My City! Sticker Activity Book. 2012. (Dover Little Activity Books Stickers Ser.). (ENG.). 4p. (J). (gr. 1-5). pap. 1.50 (978-0-486-48878-3(0), 488780) Dover Pubns., Inc.

—Pinball Mazes Activity Book: Can You Top the High Score? 2012. (Dover Children's Activity Bks.). (ENG.). 48p. (J). (gr. 3-8). pap. 4.99 (978-0-486-49003-8(3)) Dover Pubns., Inc.

Elliot, Rachel. Seek & Find Princess: Find a Charm Book. Regan, Lisa, illus. 2014. (Seek & Find Bks.). (ENG.). 32p. (J). (gr. -1-1). 9.99 (978-0-7641-6697-6(2)) Sourcebooks, Inc.

Ellis, Colette. Credo: I Believe. Avakoff, Caroline, ed. Pelicano, Christopher J., illus. 2009. (Faith & Life Ser.). 121p. (J). pap. 7.95 (978-0-89870-898-1(2)) Ignatius Pr.

Ellis, Paula. Arizona Activity Book, 1 vol. Nitzsche, Shane, illus. 2012. (Color & Learn Ser.). (ENG.). 64p. (J). (gr. k-5). pap. 6.95 (978-1-59193-288-8(2), Adventure Pubns.) AdventureKEEN.

—Great Lakes Activity Book, 1 vol. Christenson, Anna & Nitzsche, Shane, illus. 2015. (Color & Learn Ser.). (ENG.). 64p. (J). (gr. 3-7). pap. 6.95 (978-1-59193-526-1(1), Adventure Pubns.) AdventureKEEN.

—Great Smoky Mountains Activity Book, 1 vol. Nitzsche, Shane, illus. 2015. (Color & Learn Ser.). (ENG.). 64p. (J). (gr. k-5). pap. 6.95 (978-1-59193-455-4(9), Adventure Pubns.) AdventureKEEN.

—Minnesota Activity Book, 1 vol. Nitzsche, Shane, illus. 2013. (Color & Learn Ser.). (ENG.). 64p. (J). (gr. k-5). pap. 6.95 (978-1-59193-377-9(3), Adventure Pubns.) AdventureKEEN.

—Texas Activity Book, 1 vol. Nitzsche, Shane, illus. 2012. (Color & Learn Ser.). (ENG.). 64p. (J). (gr. k-5). pap. 6.95 (978-1-59193-376-2(5), Adventure Pubns.) AdventureKEEN.

—Yosemite Activity Book, 1 vol. Nitzsche, Shane, illus. 2013. (Color & Learn Ser.). 64p. (J). (gr. 2-3). pap. 5.95 (978-1-59193-299-4(8), Adventure Pubns.) AdventureKEEN.

Elrod, Julie. Splitting Hares. 2008. 36p. pap. 16.50 (978-1-60693-484-5(8), Eloquent Bks.) Strategic Book Publishing & Rights Agency (SBPRA).

Engelbreit, Mary. Mary Engelbreit's Color ME Christmas Book of Postcards: A Christmas Holiday Book for Kids. Engelbreit, Mary, illus. 2017. (ENG., Illus.). 20p. (J). (gr. -1). pap. 9.99 (978-0-06-266327-6(5), HarperCollins) HarperCollins Pubs.

—Mary Engelbreit's Color Me Christmas Coloring Book. 2016. (ENG., Illus.). 96p. (J). (gr. -1-3). pap. 16.99 (978-0-06-256260-9(6), HarperCollins) HarperCollins Pubs.

Enyancha. Legends of the Garden: Faeries & Herbs: A Child's Activity Book for Exploring the Worlds of Faeries & Herbs. 2013. (ENG.). 56p. pap. 24.95 (978-1-4327-9080-6(3)) Outskirts Pr., Inc.

Enz, Tammy. Build It Yourself, 4 vols., Set. Incl. Build Your Own Mini Golf Course, Lemonade Stand, & Other Things to Do. (ENG.). 32p. (J). (gr. 3-9). 2010. lib. bdg. 28.65 (978-1-4296-5438-8(4), 113850, Capstone Pr.); (Build It Yourself Ser.). (ENG.). 32p. 2010. 85.95 o.p. (978-1-4296-5440-1(6), 170566, Capstone Pr.) Capstone.

Enz, Tammy & Grant, Rachel. Junior Makers 4D, 4 vols. Brizuela, Dario, illus. 2018. (Junior Makers 4D Ser.). (ENG.). 48p. (J). (gr. 3-9). 135.96 (978-1-5157-9504-9(7), 27386, Capstone Classroom) Capstone.

Epstein, Len. Presidents Facts & Fun Activity Book. 2012. (Dover Kids Activity Books: U. S. A. Ser.). (ENG.). 48p. (J). (gr. 3-5). pap. 4.99 (978-0-486-48277-4(4), 482774) Dover Pubns., Inc.

Estellon, Pascale. Photo Finish. 2010. (ENG., Illus.). 64p. (J). (gr. k). pap. 10.95 (978-1-934734-54-4(3)) Seven Footer Pr.

—Picture This. 2010. (ENG., Illus.). 64p. (J). (gr. k). pap. 10.95 (978-1-934734-53-7(5)) Seven Footer Pr.

Etringer, Kathy. Mrs. E's Extraordinary Number Activities. Mitchell, Judy & Sussman, Ellen, eds. Rojas, Mary Galan, illus. 2006. 128p. (J). pap. 13.95 (978-1-57310-506-4(6)) Teaching & Learning Co.

Evan-Moor Educational Publishers. The Never-Bored Kid Book 2 Ages 6-7, Vol. 2. 2006. (Never-Bored Kid Book Ser.). (ENG., Illus.). 144p. (J). (gr. 1-2). pap., tchr. ed. 10.99 (978-1-59673-158-5(3), EMC 6309) Evan-Moor Educational Pubs.

—The Never-Bored Kid Book 2 Ages 7-8, Vol. 2. 2006. (Never-Bored Kid Book Ser.). (ENG., Illus.). 144p. (J). (gr. 2-3). pap., tchr. ed. 10.99 (978-1-59673-159-2(1), EMC6310) Evan-Moor Educational Pubs.

—The Never-Bored Kid Book 2 Ages 8-9, Vol. 2. 2006. (Never-Bored Kid Book Ser.). (ENG., Illus.). 144p. (J). (gr. 3-4). pap., tchr. ed. 10.99 (978-1-59673-160-8(5), EMC 6311) Evan-Moor Educational Pubs.

—The Never-Bored Kid Book Ages 5-6. 2006. (Never-Bored Kid Book Ser.). (ENG., Illus.). 160p. (J). (gr. k-1). pap., tchr. ed. 10.99 (978-1-59673-154-7(0), EMC 6303) Evan-Moor Educational Pubs.

—The Never-Bored Kid Book Ages 7-8. 2006. (Never-Bored Kid Book Ser.). (ENG., Illus.). (J). (gr. 2-3). pap., tchr. ed. 10.99 (978-1-59673-155-4(9), EMC 6304) Evan-Moor Educational Pubs.

Falligant, Erin, ed. 3-D Studio. Laskey, Shannon, illus. 2008. 48p. (J). 17.95 (978-1-59369-414-2(8)) American Girl Publishing, Inc.

Feelings Garden Coloring & Activity Book. 2005. (J). (978-0-9768827-2-5(8)) Prevention Through Puppetry, Inc.

Feldman, Jean. Dr Jean Variety Pack. 2007. (J). (gr. -1-3). pap. 56.87 incl. audio compact disk (978-1-59198-719-2(9)) Creative Teaching Pr., Inc.

—Highway Letters, Numbers & Shapes: PreK-1. 2010. 80p. pap. 22.99 (978-1-61601-036-2(3)) Creative Teaching Pr., Inc.

—Sing along & Read along with Dr. Jean All-in-One Pack (with Lap Books) 2009. pap. 58.86 incl. audio compact disk (978-1-60689-163-6(4)) Youngheart Music.

Ferri, Francesca, illus. Duck & Friends: A Soft & Fuzzy Book Just for Baby! 2017. (Friends Cloth Bks.). (ENG.). 8p. (J). (gr. -1-k). 12.99 (978-1-4380-0975-9(5)) Sourcebooks, Inc.

First Look & Find: Scooby Doo. 2013. 18p. (J). bds. 9.98 (978-1-4508-6369-8(8), 1450863698) Phoenix International Publications, Inc.

First Sticker Learning Book. 2008. (Photographic Sticker Fun Learning Ser.). 48p. pap. (978-1-4054-9555-4(3)) Parragon, Inc.

Fish, Sandra Palmer. Peace by Piece. 2012. (ENG.). pap. 19.05 (978-1-4675-2679-1(7)) Independent Pub.

Fisher, Verna. Explore Colonial America! 25 Great Projects, Activities, Experiments. Stone, Bryan, illus. 2009. (Explore Your World Ser.). (ENG.). 96p. (J). (gr. k-4). pap. 12.95 (978-1-934670-37-8(5), bfa636d5-34f8-4952-bc10-af6976bc8446) Nomad Pr.

Fitchett, Jilda, 4th. Aunt Molly's Transition — Seeing Death in A New Light. 2006. (Illus.). 91p. (J). per. 15.95 (978-0-9773244-0-8(0)) Light Line.

Fitzsimmons, Christy. Krissy & the Indians, 1 vol. Steckler, Megan, illus. 2009. 28p. pap. 24.95 (978-1-61546-206-3(6)) America Star Bks.

Flynn, Riley. Asking Questions & Finding Solutions. 2016. (Science & Engineering Practices Ser.). (ENG., Illus.). 24p. (J). (gr. -1-2). lib. bdg. 27.32 (978-1-5157-0947-3(7), 132267, Capstone Pr.) Capstone.

Fogle, Robin. A Christmas Story. 2006. (J). pap. 1.79 (978-1-59317-159-9(5)) Warner Pr., Inc.

Ford, Jason, illus. Stickyscapes Superheroes. 2018. (ENG.). 297p. (J). (gr. -1-2). 10.99 (978-1-78627-203-4(2), King, Laurence Publishing) Orion Publishing Group, Ltd. GBR. Dist: Hachette Bk. Group.

Ford, Jessie. My First Toolbox: Press Out & Play. 2018. (Press-Out & Play Ser.). (ENG., Illus.). 10p. (J). (gr. -1-k). bds. 14.99 (978-1-4197-2929-4(2), 1211310, Abrams Appleseed) Abrams, Inc.

Forthun, Angela. Joozu! Activities for Beginners. 2004. (JPN.). 80p. (J). 49.95 (978-1-86366-717-3(2)) Education Services Australia Ltd. AUS. Dist: Cheng & Tsui Co.

Fowler, Eleri. Bold Springtime to Color. 2017. (ENG., Illus.). 96p. (J). (gr. -1). pap. 15.99 (978-0-06-256996-7(1), HarperCollins) HarperCollins Pubs.

Franceschelli, Christopher. Cityblock (an Abrams Block Book) 2016. (Abrams Block Book Ser.). (ENG., Illus.). 96p. (J). (gr. -1-k). bds. 16.95 (978-1-4197-2189-2(5), 1146210) Abrams, Inc.

Frank, Lisa. A Magical World! Giant Coloring & Activity Book. 2010. (Lisa Frank Ser.). (Illus.). 96p. (J). 2.49 (978-0-7666-3777-1(8)) Modern Publishing.

French, Cathy. Make a Necklace. 2011. (Early Connections Ser.). (J). (978-1-61672-235-7(5)) Benchmark Education Co.

—Make an Animal Mobile. 2011. (Early Connections Ser.). (J). (978-1-61672-559-4(1)) Benchmark Education Co.

—Make an Island. 2011. (Early Connections Ser.). (J). (978-1-61672-560-0(5)) Benchmark Education Co.

French, Felicity. Kids Unplugged Animal Adventures Activity Book. 2016. (Kids Unplugged Ser.). (ENG., Illus.). 64p. (J). pap. 7.99 (978-1-4413-1996-8(4), deffba45-5f17-4838-835f-e6b6bde97f32) Peter Pauper Pr. Inc.

Friedman, Pamela & Bauer, Larry. Activites de Fin d'Annee Scolaire. (FRE.). pap. (978-0-439-98519-2(6)) Scholastic Canada, Ltd.

From Trash to Treasure. 2013. (From Trash to Treasure Ser.). 32p. (J). (gr. 3-6). pap. 423.00 (978-1-4777-2704-1(3)); (gr. 3-6). pap. 70.50 (978-1-4777-2703-4(5)); (ENG.). (gr. 4-5). 181.02 (978-1-4777-1539-0(8), dc838c5c-f5b7-485f-bf23-4818daf07fad) Rosen Publishing Group, Inc., The. (PowerKids Pr.).

Frost, Adam. The Book of Me. Ray, Sarah, illus. 2017. (ENG.). 160p. (J). pap. (978-1-4088-7681-7(7), 297453, Bloomsbury Children's Bks.) Bloomsbury Publishing Plc.

Fulcher, Roz. Science Around the House: Simple Projects Using Household Recyclables. 2010. (Dover Science for Kids Ser.). (ENG., Illus.). 80p. (J). (gr. 3-5). pap. 6.99 (978-0-486-47645-2(6), 476456) Dover Pubns., Inc.

Fun to Learn Activity Book - Blue. 2005. (J). per. (978-1-933581-50-7(6)) Byeway Bks.

Fun to Learn Activity Book - Red. 2005. (J). per. (978-1-933581-49-1(2)) Byeway Bks.

Gaffney, Sean Kevin & Activity Books. AREA 51 UFO Maintenance & Repair Manual Activity Book. 2012. (Dover Kids Activity Books: Fantasy Ser.). (ENG., Illus.). 48p. (J). (gr. 3-5). 7.99 (978-0-486-49035-9(1), 490351) Dover Pubns., Inc.

Galloway, Fhiona, illus. Busy Day Sticker Book. 2014. (My Little World Ser.). (ENG.). 14p. (J). pap. 3.99 (978-1-58925-446-6(5)) Tiger Tales.

Galvin, Laura. The Big Wide World. 2006. (ENG., Illus.). 48p. (J). (gr. -1-2). pap., act. bk. ed. 3.99 (978-1-59249-469-9(2), 1C100) Soundprints.

Galvin, Laura Gates & Studio Mouse Editorial. Animals & Nature. 2006. (Peep & the Big Wide Worldtm Ser.). (ENG., Illus.). 48p. (J). (gr. -1-2). pap. 3.99 (978-1-59249-470-5(6), 1C101) Soundprints.

Gandolfi, Claudine. Scratch & Sketch Vikings: An Art Activity Book for Legendary Artists & Explorers of All Ages. Zschock, Martha Day, illus. 2015. (Scratch & Sketch Ser.). (ENG.). 64p. (J). spiral bd. 12.99 (978-1-4413-1813-8(5), 2ef4d3c7-8369-434f-a18e-6838f73d0fdb) Peter Pauper Pr. Inc.

Gaspas, Diane & Creative Haven Staff. Creative Haven Chinese Designs Coloring Book. 2013. (Creative Haven Coloring Bks.). (ENG., Illus.). 64p. (gr. 3). pap. 5.99 (978-0-486-49313-8(X), 49313X) Dover Pubns., Inc.

George, Joshua. Ancient Romans Sticker Book: Create Riotous Roman Sticker Scenes! Myer, Ed, illus. 2017. (Sticker History Ser.). (ENG.). 38p. (J). (gr. k-6). pap. 8.99 (978-1-78445-872-0(4)) Top That! Publishing PLC GBR. Dist: Independent Pubs. Group.

—Ice Age. Myer, Ed, illus. 2016. (Sticker History Ser.). (ENG.). 38p. (J). (gr. 2-6). pap. 8.99 (978-1-78445-860-7(0)) Top That! Publishing PLC GBR. Dist: Independent Pubs. Group.

—Tracing: Early Learning Through Art. Stanley, Mandy, illus. 2017. (Arty Mouse Creativity Bks.). (ENG.). 48p. (J). (gr. -1-k). pap. 6.99 (978-1-78445-624-5(1)) Top That! Publishing PLC GBR. Dist: Independent Pubs. Group.

Gibeau, Claire Janvier. Active Alphabet. 2009. 16p. pap. 8.49 (978-1-4490-3828-1(X)) AuthorHouse.

Gibson, Karen Bush. Native American History for Kids: With 21 Activities. 2010. (For Kids Ser.: 35). (ENG., Illus.). 144p. (J). (gr. 4-18). pap. 18.99 (978-1-56976-280-6(5)) Chicago Review Pr., Inc.

Giddy Up Staff. Littlest Pet Shop Color N Carry II. 2009. act. bk. ed. 5.99 (978-1-59524-267-9(8)) Giddy Up, LLC.

—Littlest Pet Shop ColorBlast. 2009. act. bk. ed. 7.99 (978-1-59524-268-6(6)) Giddy Up, LLC.

—Transformers Color N Carry II. 2009. (J). act. bk. ed. 6.99 (978-1-59524-269-3(4)) Giddy Up, LLC.

Giddy Up Staff, contrib. by. Blendy Pen Small Blister Kit. 2009. 6.99 (978-0-9770652-8-8(6)) Giddy Up, LLC.

—Hannah Montana Surprize Ink Book. 2009. (J). 6.99 (978-1-59524-430-7(1)) Giddy Up, LLC.

—High School Musical Surprize Ink Book. 2009. (J). 6.99 (978-1-59524-435-2(2)) Giddy Up, LLC.

—Littlest Pet Shop Rub N Color Mini Book. 2009. 4.99 (978-1-59524-322-5(4)) Giddy Up, LLC.

—Littlest Pet Shop Surprize Ink Book. 2009. (J). 6.99 (978-1-59524-222-8(8)) Giddy Up, LLC.

—Littlest Pet Shop Surprize Ink Book 2. 2009. (J). 6.99 (978-1-59524-287-7(2)) Giddy Up, LLC.

—Littlest Pet Shop Water Wow Book. 2009. 6.99 (978-1-59524-223-5(6)) Giddy Up, LLC.

—Littlests Pet Shop Color Blast Mini. 2009. 4.99 (978-1-59524-280-8(5)) Giddy Up, LLC.

—Mickey Color Blast Mini. 2009. 4.99 (978-1-59524-317-1(8)) Giddy Up, LLC.

—Mickey Surprize Ink Book. 2009. 6.99 (978-1-59524-293-8(7)) Giddy Up, LLC.

—Mickey Water Wow Book. 2009. 6.99 (978-1-59524-304-1(6)) Giddy Up, LLC.

—My Little Pony Color Blast Mini. 2009. 4.99 (978-1-59524-120-7(5)) Giddy Up, LLC.

—My Little Pony Surprize Ink Book 3. 2009. 6.99 (978-1-59524-101-6(9)) Giddy Up, LLC.

—Princess Pop Beads How to Book. 2009. (J). 15.99 (978-1-59524-407-9(7)) Giddy Up, LLC.

—Princess Water Wow Book. 2009. 14.14 (978-1-159-52429-6(7)) General Bks. LLC.

—Sesame Street Surprize Ink Book 2. 2009. 6.99 (978-1-59524-072-9(1)) Giddy Up, LLC.

—Spiderman Blendy Pen Poster Book. 2009. (J). 12.99 (978-1-59524-457-4(3)) Giddy Up, LLC.

—Spiderman Color Blast Mini. 2009. 4.99 (978-1-59524-488-8(3)) Giddy Up, LLC.

—Spiderman Surprize Ink Book. 2009. (J). 6.99 (978-1-59524-036-1(5)) Giddy Up, LLC.

—Spiderman Surprize Ink Book2. 2009. 6.99 (978-1-59524-100-9(0)) Giddy Up, LLC.

—Spiderman Water Wow Book. 2009. 6.99 *(978-1-59524-273-0(2))* Giddy Up, LLC.
—Sponge Bob Rub N Color Mini. 2009. 4.99 *(978-1-59524-443-7(3))* Giddy Up, LLC.
—SpongeBob Surprize Ink Book 4. 2009. 6.99 *(978-1-59524-205-1(8))* Giddy Up, LLC.
—Thomas Tank Rub N Color Mini Book. 2009. 4.99 *(978-1-59524-321-8(6))* Giddy Up, LLC.
—Thomas Tank Surprize Ink Book. 2009. 6.99 *(978-1-59524-288-4(0))* Giddy Up, LLC.
—Thomas Tank Water Wow Book. 2009. 6.99 *(978-1-59524-290-7(2))* Giddy Up, LLC.
—Tigger & Pooh Surprize Ink Book. 2009. (J). 6.99 *(978-1-59524-289-1(9))* Giddy Up, LLC.
—Transformers Animated Water Wow Book. 2009. 6.99 *(978-1-59524-434-5(4))* Giddy Up, LLC.
Giglio, Judy. Third Grade Scholar. Boyer, Robin, illus. 2005. (ENG.). 32p. (J). pap. 2.99 *(978-1-58947-458-1(9))* School Zone Publishing Co.
Gilkerson, Patricia. My Adventure in the Desert. 2006. 44p. (J). 8.99 *(978-1-59092-278-1(6))* Blue Forge Pr.
—My Adventure Inside a Volcano. 2006. 44p. (J). 8.99 *(978-1-59092-443-3(6))* Blue Forge Pr.
—My Adventure on a Ranch. 2006. 44p. (J). 8.99 *(978-1-59092-282-8(4))* Blue Forge Pr.
—My Adventure Scuba Diving. 2006. (My Adventure Ser.). 44p. (J). (gr. -1-3). pap. 8.99 *(978-1-59092-286-6(7))* Blue Forge Pr.
—My Adventure with Dogs. 2009. (ENG.). 44p. (J). 8.99 *(978-1-59092-451-8(7))* Blue Forge Pr.
—My Adventure with Eagles. 2009. (ENG.). 44p. (J). 8.99 *(978-1-59092-453-2(3))* Blue Forge Pr.
—My Adventure with Owls. 2009. (ENG.). 44p. (J). 8.99 *(978-1-59092-460-0(6))* Blue Forge Pr.
—My Adventure with Sea Horses. 2009. (ENG.). 44p. (J). 8.99 *(978-1-59092-465-5(7))* Blue Forge Pr.
—My Adventure with Sea Turtles. 2009. (ENG.). 44p. (J). 8.99 *(978-1-59092-466-2(5))* Blue Forge Pr.
—My Adventure with Sharks. 2009. (ENG.). 44p. (J). 8.99 *(978-1-59092-468-6(1))* Blue Forge Pr.
—My Adventure with Squirrels. 2009. (ENG.). 44p. (J). 8.99 *(978-1-59092-470-9(3))* Blue Forge Pr.
—My Adventure with Whales. 2009. (ENG.). 44p. (J). 8.99 *(978-1-59092-475-4(4))* Blue Forge Pr.
—My Adventure with Wild Horses. 2006. 44p. (J). 8.99 *(978-1-59092-312-2(X))* Blue Forge Pr.
—My Adventure with Wolves. 2009. (ENG.). 44p. (J). 8.99 *(978-1-59092-476-1(2))* Blue Forge Pr.
Gill, Mickey & Gill, Cheryl. Dude Diary 2. 2011. (ENG., Illus.). (J). (gr. 4-7). 10.99 *(978-1-892951-53-3(3))* GO Publishing Co.
—Dude Diary 4: Write Stuff, Draw Randomly, Destroy If Needed! 2013. (ENG., Illus.). (J). pap. 10.99 *(978-1-892951-65-6(7))* GO Publishing Co.
—New! Girl Diary: Your Days, Your Way! 2013. (ENG., Illus.). (J). 10.99 *(978-1-892951-68-7(1))* GO Publishing Co.
Gillespie, L. Sticker Dressing Warriors. Ordas, Emi, illus. 2013. (Sticker Dressing Ser.). 34p. (J). pap. 8.99 *(978-0-7945-3353-3(1))*, Usborne) EDC Publishing.
Gillespie, Lisa Jane. Sticker Dressing Extreme Sports. Ordas, Emi, illus. 2014. (Usborne Activities Ser.). (ENG.). 24p. (J). (gr. -1-3). 8.99 *(978-0-7945-3164-5(4))*, Usborne) EDC Publishing.
Gilpen, Rebecca. Boy's Activity Book. 2013. (Doodle Bks). 96p. (J). pap. 12.99 *(978-0-7945-3171-3(7))*, Usborne) EDC Publishing.
—Christmas Activity Book. 2012. (Activity Bks). 100p. (J). pap. 12.99 *(978-0-7945-3321-2(3))*, Usborne) EDC Publishing.
Gilpin, Rebecca. Amazing Activity Book (formerly Boys' Activity Book) 2015. (Doodle Bks.). (ENG.). 96+ 4p. (J). (gr. k-5). pap. 12.99 *(978-0-7945-3527-8(5))*, Usborne) EDC Publishing.
—Cosas de Hadas. 2005. (Titles in Spanish Ser.). (SPA.). 32p. (J). pap. 8.95 *(978-0-7460-6393-4(8))*, Usborne) EDC Publishing.
—Travel Activity Book. 2013. (Doodle Bks). 96p. (J). pap. 12.99 *(978-0-7945-3287-1(X))*, Usborne) EDC Publishing.
Gingold, Janet. My Adventure on a Lake: Advanced My Adventure. 2009. (ENG.). 72p. (J). pap. 9.99 *(978-1-59092-442-6(8))* Blue Forge Pr.
—My Adventure with Arthropods: Advanced My Adventure. 2007. 44p. (J). pap. 8.99 *(978-1-59092-447-1(9))* Blue Forge Pr.
—My Adventure with Reptiles: Advanced My Adventure. 2009. (ENG.). 72p. (J). pap. 9.99 *(978-1-59092-464-8(9))* Blue Forge Pr.
Giulieri, Anne. Make Two Crocodiles. 2012. (Engage Literacy Blue Ser.). (ENG.). 16p. (J). (gr. k-2). pap. 36.94 *(978-1-4296-8987-8(0))*, 18390, Capstone Pr.) Capstone.
Gleisner, Jenna Lee. A Trip to the Pumpkin Patch. 2017. (Welcoming the Seasons Ser.). (ENG.). 24p. (J). (gr. -1-2). lib. bdg. 32.79 *(978-1-5038-1664-0(8))*, 211494) Child's World, Inc, The.
Golden Books. Numbers, Letters, & More! (PAW Patrol) Golden Books, illus. 2017. (ENG., Illus.). 64p. (J). (gr. -1-2). pap. 6.99 *(978-1-5247-6930-7(4))*, Golden Bks.) Random Hse. Children's Bks.
—Pat the Zoo (Pat the Bunny) LV Studio, illus. 2012. (Touch-And-Feel Ser.). 16p. (J). (gr. k — 1). spiral bd. 14.99 *(978-0-307-97797-7(8))*, Golden Bks.) Random Hse. Children's Bks.
—PAW Patrol Super Sticker Fun! (Paw Patrol) Golden Books, illus. 2018. (ENG., Illus.). 48p. (J). (gr. -1-2). pap. 9.99 *(978-0-525-57788-1(2))*, Golden Bks.) Random Hse. Children's Bks.
—Rubble on the Double! (Paw Patrol) Lovett, Nate, illus. 2016. (ENG.). 48p. (J). (gr. -1-2). pap. 4.99 *(978-1-101-93699-3(1))*, Golden Bks.) Random Hse. Children's Bks.
—Ruff-Ruff Rescues! (Paw Patrol) Golden Books, illus. 2015. (ENG., Illus.). 128p. (J). (gr. -1-2). pap. 9.99 *(978-0-553-52080-4(6))*, Golden Bks.) Random Hse. Children's Bks.
Golden Books Staff & Artful Doodlers Limited Staff. Blue's Quilt. 2005. (Illus.). 32p. (J). (gr. -1-2). pap. 0.48 *(978-0-375-87512-0(3))*, Golden Bks.) Random Hse. Children's Bks.
Golding, Elizabeth & Gray, Dean. A Moonlight Book: Christmas Hide-And-Seek. 2016. (ENG., Illus.). 12p. (J). (gr. -1-3). 10.95 *(978-0-7624-5965-0(4))*, Running Pr. Kids) Running Pr.
Golliher, Bill & Vaughan, Jack, illus. Webber Interactive WH Questions Level 2: Whcd22. 2006. (J). cd-rom 49.99 *(978-1-58650-647-6(1))* Super Duper Pubns.
Gonzales, Sharon, illus. Airport Explorers: 2008 Activity Book. 2008. 32p. (J). 6.95 *(978-0-9745294-2-4(7))* San Diego County Regional Airport Authority.
Good Attitudes Make You SHine. 2007. (Illus.). 48p. (J). pap. 15.00 *(978-0-9799440-0-0(7))* Artists On Video, LLC / (d/b/a) MN Productions.
Goodridge, Teresa. Glitter Magical Unicorns Stickers. 2019. (Dover Little Activity Books Stickers Ser.). (ENG., Illus.). 2p. (J). (gr. k). 2.99 *(978-0-486-83324-8(0))*, 833240) Dover Pubns., Inc.
—Happy Christmas Stickers. 2016. (Dover Little Activity Books Stickers Ser.). (ENG., Illus.). 4p. (J). (gr. k-3). pap. 1.99 *(978-0-486-80774-4(6))*, 807746) Dover Pubns., Inc.
Goodwin, Brenda L., concept. The Mangoes & the Kids: Teach A Child, Change the World. 2007. (Illus.). 37p. 10.00 *(978-0-9745861-2-0(9))* Science & God, Inc.
Gordon, Lynn. Cool Tricks for Kids. 2008. (ENG., Illus.). 54p. (gr. 8-17). 6.95 *(978-0-8118-6374-2(3))* Chronicle Bks. LLC.
—52 Fun Things to Do in the Car. rev. ed. 2009. (ENG., Illus.). 54p. (J). (gr. -1-17). 6.95 *(978-0-8118-6371-1(9))* Chronicle Bks. LLC.
—52 Fun Things to Do on the Plane. rev. ed. 2009. (ENG., Illus.). 54p. (J). (gr. -1-17). 6.95 *(978-0-8118-6372-8(7))* Chronicle Bks. LLC.
Graham, Ian. Build Your Own Cool Cars. 2004. (Illus.). 48p. *(978-0-439-67662-5(2))* Scholastic, Inc.
Graham, Oakley. Funny Animals Sticker Fun: Mix & Match the Stickers to Make Funny Animals. Green, Barry, illus. 2019. (Dover Sticker Bks.). (ENG.). 64p. (J). (gr. -1-3). pap. 9.99 *(978-0-486-83288-3(0))*, 832880) Dover Pubns., Inc.
—Funny Faces Sticker Fun: Mix & Match the Stickers to Make Funny Faces. Green, Barry, illus. 2019. (Dover Sticker Bks.). (ENG.). 64p. (J). (gr. -1-3). pap. 9.99 *(978-0-486-83287-6(2))*, 832872) Dover Pubns., Inc.
Granhold, Adriana. Mattie Knowsmath & the Great Shape Hunt. 2012. 32p. pap. 24.95 *(978-1-4626-7202-8(7))* America Star Bks.
Gray, Leon. Discovery Globe: Build-Your-Own Globe Kit. Edmonds, Sarah, illus. 2018. (ENG.). 48p. (J). (gr. 3-7). 22.99 *(978-0-7636-9748-8(6))* Candlewick Pr.
Green, John. Great Scenes from Horror Stories. 2012. (Dover Horror Coloring Bks.). (ENG.). 32p. (gr. 3-5). pap. 3.99 *(978-0-486-48840-0(3))*, 488403) Dover Pubns., Inc.
Green, John & Appelbaum, Stanley. Life in Old Japan Coloring Book. 2008. (Dover World History Coloring Bks.). (ENG.). 48p. (J). (gr. 1-5). pap. 4.99 *(978-0-486-46883-9(6))*, 468836) Dover Pubns., Inc.
Green, John & Blaisdell, Bob. Great Scenes from Dickens' Novels. 2005. (Dover Classic Stories Coloring Book Ser.). (ENG., Illus.). 32p. (J). (gr. 3-8). pap. 3.95 *(978-0-486-43985-3(2))* Dover Pubns., Inc.
Green, John & Drawing Staff. How to Draw Horses. 2009. (Dover How to Draw Ser.). (ENG., Illus.). 64p. (J). (gr. 1-4). pap. 5.99 *(978-0-486-46759-7(7))*, 467597) Dover Pubns., Inc.
Greenwald, Todd J., contrib. by. Wizards of Waverly Place Sticker Activity Book. 2009. (Wizards of Waverly Place Ser.). (Illus.). (J). pap. 4.99 *(978-0-7666-3308-7(X))* Modern Publishing.
Groeneweg, Nicole. Interactive Projects & Displays: Ideas for a Student-Created Learning Environment. F, Stacey, ed. Yamada, Jane, illus. 2006. (J). pap. 13.99 *(978-1-59198-315-6(0))* Creative Teaching Pr., Inc.
Guckian, Mara Ellen & Teacher Created Resources Staff. Alphabet Mystery Pictures. PreK-1. 2012. (Start to Finish (Teacher Created Resources) Ser.). (ENG., Illus.). 64p. pap. 6.99 *(978-1-4206-2787-9(2))* Teacher Created Resources, Inc.
—Number Mystery Pictures, Prek-1. 2012. (Start to Finish (Teacher Created Resources) Ser.). (ENG., Illus.). 64p. pap. 6.99 *(978-1-4206-2788-6(0))* Teacher Created Resources, Inc.
Gul, Hasibe, et al. My Wonderful Body. 2011. (ENG.). 16p. (J). (gr. -1 — 1). pap. 3.95 *(978-1-59784-241-9(9))*, Tughra Bks.) Blue Dome, Inc.
—Nutritious Vegetables. 2011. (ENG., Illus.). 16p. (J). (gr. -1 — 1). pap. 3.95 *(978-1-59784-239-6(7))*, Tughra Bks.) Blue Dome, Inc.
Gunes, Aysenur. Makkah & Madinah Activity Book. Polat, Ercan, illus. 2015. (Discover Islam Sticker Activity Bks.). (ENG.). 32p. (J). 5.95 *(978-0-86037-544-9(7))* Kube Publishing Ltd. GBR. Dist: Consortium Bk. Sales & Distribution.
—Mosques of the World Activity Book. Polat, Ercan, illus. 2015. (Discover Islam Sticker Activity Bks.). (ENG.). 32p. (J). 5.95 *(978-0-86037-539-5(0))* Kube Publishing Ltd. GBR. Dist: Consortium Bk. Sales & Distribution.
Gunnell, Beth, et al. Girls' Gorgeous World. Gunnell, Beth et al, illus. 2015. (ENG.). 128p. (J). (gr. 2). pap. 12.99 *(978-1-78055-151-7(7))* O'Mara, Michael Bks., Ltd. GBR. Dist: Independent Pubs. Group.
Gurrea, Susana, illus. A Super Scotland Activity Book: Games, Puzzles, Drawing, Stickers & More, 30 vols. 2018. (Super Scotland Ser.). 40p. (J). 9.95 *(978-1-78250-479-5(6))*, Kelpies) Floris Bks. GBR. Dist: Consortium Bk. Sales & Distribution.
Haas, Trisha & Haas, Charlotte. Slime! Do-It-Yourself Projects to Make at Home. 2017. (ENG., Illus.). 64p. (J). pap. 7.99 *(978-1-63158-216-5(X))*, Racehorse Publishing) Skyhorse Publishing Co., Inc.
Hadley, Suzanne. Faithgirlz Handbook: How to Let Your Faith Shine Through. 2009. (Faithgirlz! Ser.). (ENG., Illus.). 96p. (J). (gr. 4-7). pap. 9.99 *(978-0-310-71966-3(6))* Zonderkidz.
Hamaguchi, Carla. Letters, Numbers, Color & Shape Learning Centers. 2006. (Early Learning Ser.). (Illus.). 96p. (J). (gr. -1-1). pap. 20.99 *(978-1-59198-214-2(6))*, 2228) Creative Teaching Pr., Inc.
—Letters, Numbers, Colors & Shapes Activity Pages. 2006. (Illus.). 144p. (J). (gr. -1-1). per. 15.99 *(978-1-59198-225-8(1))*, 2227) Creative Teaching Pr., Inc.
Hamlet: Activity Pack. 2003. 133p. (YA). pap. *(978-1-58049-622-3(9))*, PA0121) Prestwick Hse., Inc.
Hammah, Aisha. The Image Game. Stubblefield, Linda, ed. Hammah, Aisha, illus. 2013. (Illus.). 192p. pap. *(978-0-9810759-3-8(2))*; pap. *(978-0-9810759-8-3(3))* WTL International.
Handford, Martin. Where's Waldo? the Treasure Hunt: Activity Book. Handford, Martin, illus. 2016. (Where's Waldo? Ser.). (ENG., Illus.). 96p. (J). (gr. 2-5). pap. 12.99 *(978-0-7636-8811-0(8))* Candlewick Pr.
Hanson, Anders Mann & Mann, Elissa. Cool String Art: Creative Activities That Make Math & Science Fun for Kids! 2013. (Cool Art with Math & Science Ser.). (ENG.). 32p. (gr. 3-6). lib. bdg. 34.21 *(978-1-61783-824-8(1))*, 4594, Checkerboard Library) ABDO Publishing Co.
—Cool Structures: Creative Activities That Make Math & Science Fun for Kids! 2013. (Cool Art with Math & Science Ser.). (ENG.). 32p. (J). (gr. 3-6). lib. bdg. 34.21 *(978-1-61783-825-5(X))*, 4596, Checkerboard Library) ABDO Publishing Co.
—Cool Tessellations: Creative Activities That Make Math & Science Fun for Kids! 2013. (Cool Art with Math & Science Ser.). (ENG.). 32p. (J). (gr. 3-6). lib. bdg. 34.21 *(978-1-61783-826-2(8))*, 4598, Checkerboard Library) ABDO Publishing Co.
Hanson, P. H. My Mommy's Tote. 2013. (ENG.). 16p. (J). (gr. -1-1). 19.99 *(978-0-7611-7740-1(X))*, 17740) Workman Publishing Co., Inc.
Harding, James. From Wibbleton to Wobbleton: Adventures with the Elements of Music & Movement. Noyes, Eli, illus. 2014. (Pentatonic Press Integrated Learning Ser.: 3). (ENG.). 201p. pap. 32.00 *(978-0-9773712-5-9(5))* Pentatonic Pr.
Hargrove, Julia. Tomb of the Unknowns. 2003. (Historic Monuments Ser.). (Illus.). 48p. (J). pap. 6.95 *(978-1-57310-405-0(1))* Teaching & Learning Co.
Harper, Valentina. Creative Coloring Animals: Art Activity Pages to Relax & Enjoy! 2014. (Creative Coloring Book Ser.: 9). (ENG., Illus.). 72p. pap. 9.99 *(978-1-57421-971-5(5))*, DO5506, Design Originals) Fox Chapel Publishing Co., Inc.
Harrison, Paul. Collins Big Cat Phonics for Letters & Sounds - down the River: Band 02B/Red B, Bd. 2B. 2018. (Collins Big Cat Ser.). (ENG., Illus.). 16p. (J). pap. 6.99 *(978-0-00-823023-4(4))* HarperCollins Pubs. Ltd. GBR. Dist: Independent Pubs. Group.
Hasibe, Gul, et al. Delicious Fruits. 2011. (ENG.). 16p. (J). (gr. -1 — 1). pap. 3.95 *(978-1-59784-240-2(0))*, Tughra Bks.) Blue Dome, Inc.
Hattenhauer, Ina, illus. Dollhouse Sticker Book. 2012. (Sticker Activity Book Ser.). 24p. (J). pap. 8.99 *(978-0-7945-2944-4(5))*, Usborne) EDC Publishing.
Haugen-McLane, Janie. Real-World Picture Words Software - Household Words. 2004. (J). cd-rom 69.95 *(978-1-58804-374-0(6))* P C I Education.
—Real-World Picture Words Software - Kitchen/Bathroom Words. 2004. (J). cd-rom 69.95 *(978-1-58804-375-7(4))* P C I Education.
Haws, Ileen. Nothin' 2 Do. 2008. 67p. pap. 9.90 *(978-1-4357-3654-2(0))* Lulu Pr., Inc.
Haynes, Betsy. My Adventure Panning for Gold. 2007. 44p. (J). 8.99 *(978-1-59092-444-0(4))* Blue Forge Pr.
Haynes-Mayes, Ingrid. A Recipe of Ideas for Phonemic Awareness & Phonics: Hands-on Activities for Primary Grades. 2006. (J). per. *(978-1-59872-635-0(8))* Instant Pub.
Headway Level A Thinking Book. (J). *(978-0-89688-280-5(2))*, 88-280) Open Court Publishing Co.
Hecht, Kristina. A Bird & a Bee, 1 vol. 2009. 16p. pap. 24.95 *(978-1-60836-408-4(9))* America Star Bks.
Hedde, Rebecca. Science with Magnets. rev. ed. 2008. (Science Activities Ser.). 24p. (J). pap. 5.99 *(978-0-7945-1406-8(5))*, Usborne) EDC Publishing.
Heimberg, Justin. The Spirit Glass: A Book of Magically Hidden Images. 2011. (ENG., Illus.). 32p. (J). (gr. 2). 16.95 *(978-1-934734-49-0(7))* Seven Footer Pr.
Hendrickson Publishers, creator. The Explorer Bible. 2006. (Illus.). 190p. (J). (gr. -1-3). pap. 12.95 *(978-1-59856-042-8(5))* Hendrickson Pubs. Marketing, LLC.
Henig, Sherry. Group Rules! The Social Skills & Ground Rules for Children's Groups. 2008. (Illus.). 32p. (J). pap. *(978-0-9777203-5-4(7))* Brenner Publishing, LLC.
Herbert, Janis. Abraham Lincoln for Kids: His Life & Times with 21 Activities. 2007. (For Kids Ser.: 23). (ENG., Illus.). 160p. (J). (gr. 4-7). pap. 18.99 *(978-1-55652-656-5(3))* Chicago Review Pr., Inc.
Hewitt, Angie. First Numbers: Touch-And-Trace Early Learning Fun! 2017. (Little Groovers Ser.). (ENG., Illus.). 12p. (J). (— 1). bds. 7.99 *(978-1-5107-0838-9(3))*, Sky Pony Pr.) Skyhorse Publishing Co., Inc.
Hickerson, Brandy. My Brother & Me. 2008. 60p. pap. 31.99 *(978-1-4363-1635-4(9))* Xlibris Corp.
Highlights, creator. Jumbo Pad of Puzzling Fun. 2016. (Highlights Jumbo Books & Pads Ser.). (ENG.). 256p. (J). (gr. 1-4). pap. 12.99 *(978-1-62979-617-8(4))*, Highlights) Highlights Pr., c/o Highlights for Children, Inc.
—101 Bananas. 2018. (Highlights Hidden Pictures 101 Activity Bks.). 144p. (J). (gr. 1-4). pap. 9.99 *(978-1-62979-942-1(4))*, Highlights) Highlights Pr., c/o Highlights for Children, Inc.
—101 Socks. 2018. (Highlights Hidden Pictures 101 Activity Bks.). (Illus.). 144p. (J). (gr. 1-4). pap. 9.99 *(978-1-68437-170-9(8))*, Highlights) Highlights Pr., c/o Highlights for Children, Inc.
Highlights Learning, creator. Kindergarten Big Fun Workbook. 2017. (Highlights Big Fun Activity Workbooks Ser.). (ENG.). 256p. (J). (gr. -1-1). pap. 12.99 *(978-1-62979-763-2(4))*, Highlights) Highlights Pr., c/o Highlights for Children, Inc.
—Preschool Big Fun Workbook. 2017. (Highlights Big Fun Activity Workbooks Ser.). (ENG.). 256p. (J). (gr. -1-k). pap. 12.99 *(978-1-62979-762-5(6))*, Highlights) Highlights Pr., c/o Highlights for Children, Inc.
Hill, Kevin. A - Z Animal Coloring & Activity Book: English & Spanish. 2012. 60p. (gr. -1). pap. 12.95 *(978-1-4772-0407-8(5))* AuthorHouse.
Hinkler Books, creator. Pop Diva Make-Up Kit. 2014. (Glamour Girl Ser.). (ENG., Illus.). (J). (gr. 4-7). *(978-1-74352-899-0(X))* Hinkler Bks. Pty, Ltd.
—Princess Make-Up Kit. 2014. (Glamour Girl Ser.). (ENG., Illus.). (J). (gr. 4-7). *(978-1-74352-898-3(1))* Hinkler Bks. Pty, Ltd.
Hinkler Books, ed. My Amazing Sticker Activity Book. 2012. 48p. (J). 10.99 *(978-1-74308-633-9(4))* Hinkler Bks. Pty, Ltd. AUS. Dist: Ideals Pubns.
—My Pretty Pink Tea Party. 2012. 40p. (J). 19.99 *(978-1-74308-981-1(3))* Hinkler Bks. Pty, Ltd. AUS. Dist: Ideals Pubns.
Hirschmann, Kris. 100 Screen Free Ways to Beat Boredom! Paganelli, Elisa, illus. 2018. (ENG.). 96p. (J). (gr. 2-5). pap. 8.99 *(978-1-4380-1149-3(0))* Sourcebooks, Inc.
Hodgson, Julie. Fun with Number Rhymes for the Early Years. 2005. (Illus.). 96p. pap. *(978-1-903853-72-6(9))* Brilliant Pubns.
Hoerner, L. Cat & Dog Dress up Sticker Paper Dolls. 2015. (Dover Little Activity Books Paper Dolls Ser.). (ENG.). 4p. (J). (gr. k-3). pap. 2.50 *(978-0-486-79371-9(0))*, 793710) Dover Pubns., Inc.
—Fanciful Fairies & Dazzling Dragons Coloring Book. 2013. (Dover Fantasy Coloring Bks.). (ENG.). 32p. (gr. 3-6). pap. 3.99 *(978-0-486-49979-6(0))*, 499790) Dover Pubns., Inc.
Hoffman, Joan. Tracing Trails Pre-Writing Skills. 2019. (ENG.). 32p. (J). (gr. -1-k). pap. 4.49 *(978-1-60159-117-3(9))*, a6d13a4f-fa3a-48b4-b0ad-a64b6f93add0) School Zone Publishing Co.
Holdaway, Chelsea. The Sabbath Is a Special Day: A Sacrament Meeting Activity Book. 2017. (ENG.). (J). (gr. -1-k). pap. 5.99 *(978-1-4621-2105-2(5))* Cedar Fort, Inc./CFI Distribution.
Holden, Pam. Make a Scarecrow, 1 vol. Storey, Jim, illus. 2015. (ENG.). 16p. (-1). pap. *(978-1-77654-133-1(2))*, Red Rocket Readers) Flying Start Bks.
Holland, Beth. Webber HearBuilder Following Directions Fun Sheets: Hbbk55. Ink, Bruce & Golliher, Bill, illus. 2011. 216p. (J). spiral bd. 34.95 net. *(978-1-58650-992-7(6))* Super Duper Pubns.
Hollihan, Kerrie Logan. Theodore Roosevelt for Kids: His Life & Times, 21 Activities. 2010. (For Kids Ser.: 33). (ENG., Illus.). 144p. (J). (gr. 4-18). pap. 16.95 *(978-1-55652-955-9(4))*, 1311179) Chicago Review Pr., Inc.
Holt, William T. Brand New Shoes Coloring & Activity Book. 2013. (Illus.). 66p. pap. 5.75 *(978-0-9895062-1-2(5))* SearlStudio Publishing.
Honig, Bruce. In Pursuit of the Aha! & Ha! Ha! Ha!: Games & Activities for Kids & Their Parents. 2009. 97p. pap. 12.90 *(978-1-4116-2959-2(0))* Lulu Pr., Inc.
—The Pursuit of the Aha & Ha! Ha! Ha!: Games & Activities That Support, Challenge & Use Creative Thinking (Divergent) in the Classroom. 2009. 97p. pap. 12.92 *(978-1-4116-3052-9(1))* Lulu Pr., Inc.
Hopscotch Set C Add-On Package. 2013. pap. 85.50 *(978-1-61391-264-5(1))* Pacific Learning, Inc.
Hourglass Press, Hourglass & Sauza, Saul. The Super-Deluxe, Epic Journal of Awesomeness. 2015. (Dover Kids Activity Bks.). (ENG.). 64p. (J). (gr. 1-7). pap. 5.99 *(978-0-486-78328-4(6))*, 783286) Dover Pubns., Inc.
House, Katherine L. Lighthouses for Kids: History, Science, & Lore with 21 Activities. 2008. (For Kids Ser.: 26). (ENG., Illus.). 128p. (J). (gr. 4-7). pap. 16.99 *(978-1-55652-720-3(9))* Chicago Review Pr., Inc.
Hruby, Patrick. Natural Wonders: A Patrick Hruby Coloring Book. 2011. (ENG.). 32p. pap. 9.95 *(978-1-934429-71-6(6))* AMMO Bks., LLC.
Hughes, Mónica. Stripes. 2005. (Big Cat Ser.). (gr. k-2). pap. 6.50 *(978-1-60457-021-2(0))* Pacific Learning, Inc.
Huskmitnavn, illus. The Family Fun Coloring Book. 2018. (ENG.). 64p. pap. 14.95 *(978-1-58423-674-0(4))*, cd8e9611-5eda-45ef-97e3-47fff20a34e8) Gingko Pr., Inc.
Ikids. Fashion Girls Around the World. 2010. (ENG., Illus.). 10p. (J). (gr. -1-1). 19.99 *(978-1-58476-960-6(2))* Innovative Kids.
Information Explorer (Set), 16 vols., Set. Incl. Creating a Digital Portfolio. Rabbat, Suzy. 2011. lib. bdg. 32.07 *(978-1-61080-121-8(0))*, 201128); Find the Right Site. Truesdell, Ann. 2010. lib. bdg. 32.07 *(978-1-60279-638-6(6))*, 200341); Find Your Way Online. Rabbat, Suzy. 2010. lib. bdg. 32.07 *(978-1-60279-639-3(4))*, 200342); Get Ready for a Winning Science Project. Buczynski, Sandra. 2011. lib. bdg. 32.07 *(978-1-61080-124-9(5))*, 201134); Go Straight to the Source. Fontichiaro, Kristin. 2010. lib. bdg. 32.07 *(978-1-60279-640-9(8))*, 200343); Hit the Books. Rabbat, Suzy. 2010. lib. bdg. 32.07 *(978-1-60279-641-6(6))*, 200344); Make the Grade. Gordon, Carol A. 2010. lib. bdg. 32.07 *(978-1-60279-642-3(4))*, 200345); Online Etiquette & Safety. Cornwall, Phyllis. 2010. lib. bdg. 32.07 *(978-1-60279-956-1(3))*, 200637); Podcasting 101. Fontichiaro, Kristin. 2010. lib. bdg. 32.07 *(978-1-60279-953-0(9))*, 200631); Put It All Together. Cornwall, Phyllis. 2010. lib. bdg. 32.07 *(978-1-60279-643-0(2))*, 200346); Shooting Video to Make Learning Fun. Green, Julie. 2010. lib. bdg. 32.07 *(978-1-60279-955-4(5))*, 200635); Social Studies Projects That Shine. Wilkie, Sara. 2011. lib. bdg. 32.07 *(978-1-61080-123-2(7))*, 201132); Team up Online. Pascaretti, Vicki & Wilkie, Sara. 2010. lib. bdg. 32.07 *(978-1-60279-644-7(0))*, 200347); Using Digital Images. Rabbat, Suzy. 2010. lib. bdg. 32.07 *(978-1-60279-954-7(7))*, 200633); Write It Down. Green, Julie. 2010. lib. bdg. 32.07 *(978-1-60279-645-4(9))*, 200348); Your Fascinating Family History. Johnson, Mary J. 2011. lib. bdg. 32.07 *(978-1-61080-122-5(9))*, 201130); 32p. (gr. 4-8). (Explorer Library: Information Explorer Ser.). (ENG., Illus.). 2011. 456.00 *(978-1-61080-149-2(0))*, 201014) Cherry Lake Publishing.
Ingram, Zoe. America the Beautiful to Color: Road Trip Adventures to Color. Ingram, Zoe, illus. 2017. (ENG., Illus.). 96p. (J). (gr. -1). pap. 15.99 *(978-0-06-256990-5(2))*, HarperCollins Pubs.
Ingram, Zoë, illus. Press Out & Color: Butterflies. 2017. (ENG.). 20p. (J). (gr. 5). 15.99 *(978-0-7636-9506-4(8))* Candlewick Pr.
Isaacs, Connie. Mix & Match Animals: Over 100 Animals to Create! Green, Barry, illus. 2019. (Dover Kids Activity Books: Animals Ser.). (ENG.). 12p. (J). (gr. -1-3). bds. 9.99 *(978-0-486-83289-0(9))*, 832899) Dover Pubns., Inc.

It's Cool to Learn about Countries (Set), 4 vols., Set. Incl. It's Cool to Learn about Countries: Egypt. Marsico, Katie. lib. bdg. 34.93 *(978-1-61080-100-3(8)*, 201094); It's Cool to Learn about Countries: Ethiopia. Somervill, Barbara A. lib. bdg. 34.93 *(978-1-61080-099-0(0)*, 201092); It's Cool to Learn about Countries: Germany. Franchino, Vicky. lib. bdg. 34.93 *(978-1-61080-098-3(2)*, 201090); It's Cool to Learn about Countries: Vietnam. Rau, Dana Meachen. lib. bdg. 34.93 *(978-1-61080-097-6(4)*, 201088); 48p. (gr. 4-8). (Explorer Library: Social Studies Explorer Ser.). (ENG., Illus.). 2011. 125.44 *(978-1-61080-148-5(2)*, 201010) Cherry Lake Publishing.

Jacobson, John, et al. Say Hello Wherever You Go: Music Strategies, Songs & Activities for Grades K-2. 2010. (ENG.). 40p. pap. 19.99 incl. audio compact disk *(978-1-4234-8824-8(5)*, 09971397) Leonard, Hal Corp.

Jacobson, Ryan. Constellations Activity Book, 1 vol. Nitzsche, Shane, illus. 2012. (ENG.). 64p. (J). (gr. k-5). pap. 6.95 *(978-1-59193-325-0(0)*, Adventure Pubns.) AdventureKEEN.

Jan, Young. The Orange Slipknot Curriculum Unit. 2008. 138p. spiral bd. *(978-0-9772525-6-5(6))* Raven Publishing Inc. of Montana.

Jaramillo, Gloria. Busy Kids' Colors, Shapes & Sizes. Poirier, Nadine, illus. 2008. (Busy Kids Ser.). 36p. (J). (gr. -1-k). bds. 12.99 *(978-2-7641-1677-7(2))* Gardner Pubns.

Jarrow, Gail. Fatal Fever: Tracking down Typhoid Mary. 2014. (Deadly Diseases Ser.). (ENG., Illus.). 192p. (J). (gr. 5-12). E-Book *(978-1-62979-060-2(5)*, Calkins Creek) Highlights Pr., c/o Highlights for Children, Inc.

Jensen, Pamela. Reverently, Quietly: Sacrament Meeting Activity Book. 2014. pap. 5.99 *(978-1-4621-1215-9(3)*, Horizon Pubs.) Cedar Fort, Inc./CFI Distribution.

Jerome, Kate B. Lucky to Live in Texas. 2017. (Arcadia Kids Ser.). (ENG., Illus.). 32p. (J). 16.99 *(978-0-7385-2769-7(6))* Arcadia Publishing.

Jiang, Helga. Clay Charm Magic! 25 Amazing, Teeny-Tiny Projects to Make with Polymer Clay. 2014. (ENG.). 128p. (J). (gr. k). 12.95 *(978-1-63220-398-4(7)*, Sky Pony Pr.) Skyhorse Publishing Co., Inc.

Joel's Library Jam, 1 VHS cassette. 2005. (J). VHS, cd-rom *(978-0-9744419-1-7(0)*, CET) Greater Cincinnati TV Educational Foundation.

Johnson, Dirk, illus. Purdue University Coloring & Activity Adventure Book. 2007. 52p. (J). pap. *(978-0-9790923-0-5(2))* DirkDesigns, LLC.

Johnson, Robin. Toys & Games in Different Places. 2017. (Learning about Our Global Community Ser.). (Illus.). 24p. (J). (gr. 2-2). *(978-0-7787-3662-2(8))*; pap. *(978-0-7787-3666-0(0))* Crabtree Publishing Co.

Johnstone, Michael. Fun Time Teddy Bear Stickers: Sticker & Colour-In Playbook with over 200 Reusable Stickers. Tulip, Jenny, illus. 2017. (ENG.). 72p. (J). (gr. -1-12). pap. 8.99 *(978-1-86147-771-2(6)*, Armadillo) Anness Publishing GBR. Dist: National Bk. Network.

Jones, Rebecca, illus. The Coloring Book of Cards & Envelopes: Summertime. 2017. (ENG.). 74p. (J). (gr. 2-5). pap. 10.99 *(978-0-7636-9340-4(5))* Candlewick Pr.

Joseph, Patricia L. This Is Bb. 2008. 20p. pap. 24.95 *(978-1-60672-351-7(0))* PublishAmerica, Inc.

K 1001 Learning Activities. 2013. (gr. k-k). spiral bd. 12.99 *(978-1-4508-5666-9(7)*, 1450856667) Phoenix International Publications, Inc.

Kagan, Miguel. Match Mine: Language Builder. 2008. per. 19.00 *(978-1-879097-21-6(4))* Kagan Publishing.

Kalman, Bobbie. Fun Ways to Learn. 2017. (My World Ser.). (Illus.). 24p. (J). (gr. 1-1). *(978-0-7787-9595-7(0))*; pap. *(978-0-7787-9603-9(5))* Crabtree Publishing Co.

—I Can Do It! 2011. (ENG.). 16p. (J). *(978-1-4271-1015-2(8))* Crabtree Publishing Co.

Kampia, Judy. God's Great Book: A Complete Collection of Bible Stories & Activities for All Ages. 2007. 596p. 36.99 *(978-1-4257-4890-6(2))* Xlibris Corp.

Kann, Victoria. Pinkalicious: Goldidoodles. Kann, Victoria, illus. 2013. (Pinkalicious Ser.). (ENG., Illus.). 128p. (J). (gr. -1-3). pap. 12.99 *(978-0-06-223334-9(3)*, HarperFestival) HarperCollins Pubs.

—Pinkalicious: Pinkadoodles. Kann, Victoria, illus. 2011. (Pinkalicious Ser.). (ENG., Illus.). 128p. (J). (gr. -1-7). pap. 12.99 *(978-0-06-202265-3(2)*, HarperFestival) HarperCollins Pubs.

—Pinkalicious: Pinkafy Your World: a Reusable Sticker Book. Kann, Victoria, illus. 2013. (Pinkalicious Ser.). (ENG., Illus.). 12p. (J). (gr. -1-3). 6.99 *(978-0-06-223333-2(5)*, HarperFestival) HarperCollins Pubs.

Kavanagh, James & Waterford Press Staff. Mammals Nature Activity Book. Leung, Raymond, illus. 2nd ed. 2011. (Nature Activity Book Ser.). (ENG.). 32p. (J). (gr. -1-12). pap. 6.95 *(978-1-58355-581-1(1))* Waterford Pr., Inc.

—My First Arctic: Nature Activity Book. Leung, Raymond, illus. 2011. (Nature Activity Book Ser.). (ENG.). 32p. (J). (gr. -1-8). pap., act. bk. ed. 6.95 *(978-1-58355-586-6(2))* Waterford Pr., Inc.

—My First Grasslands Nature: Nature Activity Book. Leung, Raymond, illus. 2011. (Nature Activity Book Ser.). (ENG.). 32p. (J). (gr. -1-6). pap., act. bk. ed. 6.95 *(978-1-58355-589-7(7))* Waterford Pr., Inc.

—My First Seashores: Nature Activity Book. Leung, Raymond, illus. 2013. (Nature Activity Book Ser.). (ENG.). 32p. (J). (gr. -1-12). pap., act. bk. ed. 6.95 *(978-1-58355-590-3(0))* Waterford Pr., Inc.

—My First Wetlands Nature. Leung, Raymond, illus. 2011. (Nature Activity Book Ser.). (ENG.). 32p. (J). (gr. 2-4). act. bk. ed. 6.95 *(978-1-58355-591-0(9))* Western National Parks Assn.

—Seashore Wildlife: Nature Activity Book. Leung, Raymond, illus. 2nd ed. 2013. (Nature Activity Book Ser.). (ENG.). 32p. (J). (gr. -1-8). pap., act. bk. ed. 6.95 *(978-1-58355-584-2(6))* Waterford Pr., Inc.

Kaye, Megan. Do You Know Who You Are? Singer, Allison, ed. 2014. (ENG., Illus.). 192p. (YA). (gr. 8-12). pap. 15.99 *(978-1-4654-1649-0(8)*, DK Children) Dorling Kindersley Publishing, Inc.

Kenney, Sean. Cool Creations in 101 Pieces. 2014. (Sean Kenney's Cool Creations Ser.). (ENG., Illus.). 32p. (J). (gr. -1-4). 15.99 *(978-1-62779-017-8(9)*, 900130257, Holt, Henry & Co. Bks. For Young Readers) Holt, Henry & Co.

—Cool Creations in 35 Pieces. Kenney, Sean, illus. 2013. (Sean Kenney's Cool Creations Ser.). (ENG., Illus.). 32p. (J). (gr. -1-3). 17.99 *(978-0-8050-9692-7(2)*, 900096223, Holt, Henry & Co. Bks. For Young Readers) Holt, Henry & Co.

Key Porter Books, creator. Face Painting: Enchanting Designs for Faces & Bodies. rev. ed. 2007. (Gymboree Play & Music Ser.). (ENG., Illus.). 36p. (J). (gr. -1-2). bds. *(978-1-55263-962-7(2))* Magma.

—Music Play: Inspired Ways to Explore Music. rev. ed. 2007. (Gymboree Play & Music Ser.). (ENG., Illus.). 36p. (J). (gr. -1-2). bds. *(978-1-55263-964-1(9))* Magma.

Key Porter Books Staff. Gymboree in a Princess Castle. rev. ed. 2007. (ENG., Illus.). 1p. (J). *(978-1-55263-923-8(1))* Magma.

—Gymboree on a Pirate Ship. rev. ed. 2007. (ENG., Illus.). 1p. (J). *(978-1-55263-921-4(5))* Magma.

Khan, Sarah. Dinosaur Quiz Cards. 2012. (Activity Cards Ser.). 50p. (J). 9.99 *(978-0-7945-3262-8(4)*, Usborne) EDC Publishing.

Kids: Watershed Protection. 2003. (J). *(978-1-888631-29-6(5))* Project WET Foundation.

Kids Can Do It!, 12 vols. 2017. (Kids Can Do It! Ser.). 32p. (ENG.). (gr. 3-3). 181.62 *(978-1-4994-8268-3(X)*, 5aaf8ff5-262e-44b1-a281-4c073143e6ad); (gr. 8-8). pap. 70.50 *(978-1-4994-8378-9(3))* Rosen Publishing Group, Inc., The. (Windmill Bks.).

Kids, National Geographic. Things That Go Sticker Activity Book. 2019. 56p. (J). (gr. -1-k). pap. 6.99 *(978-1-4263-3537-2(7)*, National Geographic Kids) Disney Publishing Worldwide.

Killam, Catherine D. The Sweeet Old Lady Coloring & Activity Book. Svensson, Richard, illus. 2013. 62p. pap. 6.99 *(978-0-9910700-4-6(6))* Enchanted Forest Publishing.

—The Sweeet Old Lady down the Street. Svensson, Richard, illus. 2013. 42p. pap. 9.99 *(978-0-9910700-2-2(X))* Enchanted Forest Publishing.

King, Sharon. Junior Alien Zone: Creative Experiences for Hands of All Ages! 2009. (Illus.). 51p. pap. 14.95 *(978-1-4327-1162-7(8))* Outskirts Pr., Inc.

Kings, Gary & Ginger, Richard. Funky Junk: Recycle Rubbish into Art! Green, Barry, illus. 2012. (Dover Children's Activity Bks.). (ENG.). 64p. (J). (gr. 3-5). pap. 9.99 *(978-0-486-49022-9(X)*, 49022X) Dover Pubns., Inc.

Kirkby, Joanne & Cooper, Sharon, illus. Mosaic Picture Sticker Book. 2015. (Mosaic Sticker Bks.). (ENG.). 24+12p. (J). (gr. k-5). pap. 10.99 *(978-0-7945-3015-0(X)*, Usborne) EDC Publishing.

Kitch, Anne E. What We Do in Lent: A Child's Activity Book. Perez, Dorothy Thompson, illus. 2007. (ENG.). 48p. (J). pap. 11.95 *(978-0-8192-2278-7(X)*, 1ced57e3-eb23-4bcd-8d16-139996b90359) Church Publishing, Inc.

Klawitter, Pamela Amick. Centers on the Go: Fun, Creative Activity Folders to Take to Your Seat. VanBlaricum, Pam, ed. Armstrong, Bev & Baker, Don, illus. 2005. 192p. pap. 19.99 *(978-0-88160-378-1(3)*, LW435, Learning Works, The) Creative Teaching Pr., Inc.

Kliman, Gilbert. My Personal Story about Hurricanes Katrina & Rita: A Guided Activity Workbook for Middle & High School Students. 2005. (YA). spiral bd. 19.00 *(978-0-9790846-9-0(5))* Children's Psychological Health Ctr., Inc., The.

Kliman, Gilbert, et al. My Personal Story about Tropical Storm Stan: A Guided Activity Workbook for Children, Adolescents & Families. 2006. (Illus.). spiral bd. 19.00 *(978-0-9790846-8-3(7))* Children's Psychological Health Ctr., Inc., The.

Kline, Trish & Donev, Mary. The Busy Preschooler's Guide to Learning. 2007. (Illus.). 128p. (J). per. 60.00 *(978-1-934307-17-5(3))* Ghost Hunter Productions.

—Celebration of Letters A & B: Busy Preschoolers. 2007. (Illus.). 16p. (J). per. 20.00 *(978-1-934307-04-5(1))* Ghost Hunter Productions.

—Celebration of Letters C & D: Busy Preschoolers. 2007. (Illus.). 16p. (J). per. 20.00 *(978-1-934307-05-2(X))* Ghost Hunter Productions.

—Celebration of Letters E & F: Busy Preschoolers. 2007. (Illus.). 16p. (J). per. 20.00 *(978-1-934307-06-9(8))* Ghost Hunter Productions.

—Celebration of Letters G & H: Busy Preschoolers. 2007. (Illus.). 16p. (J). per. 20.00 *(978-1-934307-07-6(6))* Ghost Hunter Productions.

—Celebration of Letters I & J: Busy Preschoolers. 2007. (Illus.). 16p. (J). per. 20.00 *(978-1-934307-08-3(4))* Ghost Hunter Productions.

—Celebration of Letters K & L: Busy Preschoolers. 2007. (Illus.). 16p. (J). per. 20.00 *(978-1-934307-09-0(2))* Ghost Hunter Productions.

—Celebration of Letters M & N: Busy Preschoolers. 2007. (Illus.). 16p. (J). per. 20.00 *(978-1-934307-10-6(6))* Ghost Hunter Productions.

—Celebration of Letters O & Q: Busy Preschoolers. 2007. (Illus.). 16p. (J). per. 20.00 *(978-1-934307-11-3(4))* Ghost Hunter Productions.

—Celebration of Letters P & R: Busy Preschoolers. 2007. (Illus.). 16p. (J). per. 20.00 *(978-1-934307-12-0(2))* Ghost Hunter Productions.

—Celebration of Letters S & T: Busy Preschoolers. 2007. (Illus.). 16p. (J). per. 20.00 *(978-1-934307-13-7(0))* Ghost Hunter Productions.

—Celebration of Letters U & V: Busy Preschoolers. 2007. (Illus.). 16p. (J). per. 20.00 *(978-1-934307-14-4(9))* Ghost Hunter Productions.

—Celebration of Letters W & X: Busy Preschoolers. 2007. (Illus.). 16p. (J). per. 20.00 *(978-1-934307-15-1(7))* Ghost Hunter Productions.

—Celebration of Letters Y & Z: Busy Preschoolers. 2007. (Illus.). 16p. (J). per. 20.00 *(978-1-934307-16-8(5))* Ghost Hunter Productions.

Klug, Kirsten. Oregon Is Fun! Rain or Sun! Skorpen, Neal, illus. 2011. 20p. (J). pap. 7.95 *(978-0-9798173-3-5(1))* Bamboo River Pr.

Klutz Editors. El libro del body Crayon. 2004. (SPA., Illus.). 42p. (J). spiral bd. 17.95 *(978-968-5528-02-3(0))* Klutz Latino MEX. Dist: Independent Pubs. Group.

—The Many Moods of Me Journal. 2015. (ENG.). 76p. (J). (gr. 3-7). 16.99 *(978-0-545-80546-9(5))* Klutz.

Klutz Editors, contrib. by. Paper Fashions Fancy. 2008. (ENG., Illus.). 58p. (J). (gr. 3-18). 21.95 *(978-1-59174-519-8(5))* Klutz.

Klutz Editors & Dzwonik, Cristian. De las 1000 y una Actividades. 2005. (SPA., Illus.). 120p. (J). spiral bd. 15.95 *(978-968-5528-17-7(9))* Klutz Latino MEX. Dist: Independent Pubs. Group.

Knighton, Kate. 50 Easter Things to Make & Do. 2009. (50 Easter Things to Make & Do Ser.). 104p. (J). (gr. 1). spiral bd. 9.99 *(978-0-7945-2206-3(8)*, Usborne) EDC Publishing.

Koerner, Sandy, et al. Water Adventures Around the World, 10 vols. 2008. (ENG.). 30p. (J). (gr. 3-5). pap. 25.00 *(978-1-58321-558-6(1))* American Water Works Assn.

Kohl, MaryAnn F. Making Make-Believe: Hands-On Projects for Play & Pretend. 2nd ed. 2018. (Bright Ideas for Learning Ser.: 6). (ENG., Illus.). 192p. (J). (gr. -1-3). pap. 16.99 *(978-0-914090-48-9(8))* Chicago Review Pr., Inc.

Kontzias, Bill. Read & See. 2018. (I Like to Read Ser.). (ENG.). 32p. (J). (gr. -1-3). 6.99 *(978-0-8234-3983-6(6))* Holiday Hse., Inc.

Kramer, Lance. Great Ancient China Projects: You Can Build Yourself. Weinberg, Steven, illus. 2008. (Build It Yourself Ser.). (ENG.). 128p. (J). (gr. 3-7). pap. 21.95 *(978-1-934670-02-6(2)*, 4cdd6ed0-4313-441e-823c-ba6431242 4f6) Nomad Pr.

Krause, Maria. Coloring Book Hokusai. 2015. (Coloring Bks.). (ENG.). 32p. (J). (gr. 1-4). pap. 8.95 *(978-3-7913-7215-0(7))* Prestel Verlag GmbH & Co KG. DEU. Dist: Penguin Random Hse. LLC.

Kronheimer, Ann. The Peter Pan Colouring Book. 2017. (ENG.). 32p. (J). (gr. 1-4). pap. 7.99 *(978-1-78055-435-8(4))* O'Mara, Michael Bks., Ltd. GBR. Dist: Independent Pubs. Group.

—The Princess Colouring Book. Kronheimer, Ann, illus. 2014. (ENG., Illus.). 64p. (J). (gr. 1). pap. 10.99 ***(978-1-78055-342-9(0)***, Buster Bks.) O'Mara, Michael Bks., Ltd. GBR. Dist: Independent Pubs. Group.

Kronheimer, Ann. The Wonderful Wizard of Oz Colouring Book. 2017. (ENG.). 32p. (J). (gr. 1-4). pap. 8.99 *(978-1-78055-436-5(2))* O'Mara, Michael Bks., Ltd. GBR. Dist: Independent Pubs. Group.

Kurowski, Kathryn. Year Round Project-Based Activities for STEM PreK-K. 2013. (ENG.). 112p. pap. 14.99 *(978-1-4206-3024-4(5))* Teacher Created Resources, Inc.

Kurtz, John. FLIP OUTS — Funny Farm: Color Your Own Cartoon! 2015. (ENG., Illus.). 64p. (J). (gr. k-3). pap. 1.99 *(978-0-486-79483-9(0)*, 794830) Dover Pubns., Inc.

—Ice Palace Sticker Activity Book. 2016. (Dover Little Activity Books Stickers Ser.). (ENG.). 4p. (J). (gr. k-2). pap. 1.99 *(978-0-486-80528-3(X)*, 80528X) Dover Pubns., Inc.

—Santa Claus Christmas Paper Dolls. 2013. (Dover Paper Dolls Ser.). (ENG.). 32p. (J). (gr. 1-5). 9.99 *(978-0-486-49424-1(1)*, 494241) Dover Pubns., Inc.

Kyle, Margaret. The Family Story Bible Colouring Book. 2013. (ENG., Illus.). 28p. (J). (gr. 10-10). 5.95 *(978-1-77064-570-7(5))* Wood Lake Publishing, Inc. CAN. Dist: Westminster John Knox Pr.

Ladybird. A History of Ferrari Activity Book - Ladybird Readers Level 3. 2019. (Ladybird Readers Ser.). (ENG., Illus.). 16p. (J). (gr. -1-2). pap. 5.99 *(978-0-241-36521-2(X))* Penguin Random Hse. AUS. Dist: Independent Pubs. Group.

Laliberte, Mario, illus. Match, Sort & Play. 2007. (Hands-on Bks.). 48p. (J). (gr. -1-k). spiral bd. 9.99 *(978-2-7641-1936-5(4))* Tormont Pubns.

Lamb, Stacey, et al, illus. My First Christmas Activity Book. 2013. (ENG.). 50p. (J). pap. 11.99 *(978-0-7945-3182-9(2)*, Usborne) EDC Publishing.

Lamb, Stacey, illus. Wipe-Clean Dot-To-Dot. 2013. (Wipe-Clean Bks). 20p. (J). pap. 7.99 *(978-0-7945-3278-9(0)*, Usborne) EDC Publishing.

Lambert, Nat. Beep-Beep! Magnetic First Words. 2018. (Play & Learn Ser.). (ENG.). 10p. (J). (gr. -1-1). bds. 7.99 *(978-1-78700-385-9(X))* Top That! Publishing PLC GBR. Dist: Independent Pubs. Group.

—Rainy Day Activity Book. 2017. (ENG.). 96p. (J). (gr. 2-4). pap. 9.99 *(978-1-78445-695-5(0))* Top That! Publishing PLC GBR. Dist: Independent Pubs. Group.

—3D Shark Attack! Make a Hungry Shark Smash Through Your Wall. Smith, Mark, illus. 2015. (Press Out & Build Wall Model Ser.). (ENG.). 24p. (J). (gr. 2). 19.99 *(978-1-78244-973-7(6))* Top That! Publishing PLC GBR. Dist: Independent Pubs. Group.

Lane, Leena. Christmas Fun: Bible Activity Book. Bishop, Roma, illus. 2015. (J). pap. 9.95 *(978-0-8198-1651-1(5))* Pauline Bks. & Media.

—Easter Days: My First Bible Activity Book. 2008. (Illus.). 31p. (J). pap. 6.95 *(978-0-59325-123-9(8))* Word Among Us Pr.

Langeler, Gerard. Let's Make Faces. Grindell, Joan & Grindell, Mark, illus. 2009. (ENG.). 24p. (J). (gr. -1-3). spiral bd. 14.95 *(978-1-932565-63-8(9)*, P172770) Future Horizons, Inc.

Language Arts Explorer (Set), 26 vols., Set. Incl. Save the Planet: Compost It. Barker, David M. 2010. lib. bdg. 32.07 *(978-1-60279-656-0(4)*, 200349); Save the Planet: Growing Your Own Garden. Hirsch, Rebecca. 2010. lib. bdg. 32.07 *(978-1-60279-657-7(2)*, 200350); Save the Planet: Helping Endangered Animals. Hirsch, Rebecca. 2010. lib. bdg. 32.07 *(978-1-60279-658-4(0)*, 200351); Save the Planet: Keeping Water Clean. Farrell, Courtney. 2010. lib. bdg. 32.07 *(978-1-60279-659-1(9)*, 200352); Save the Planet: Local Farms & Sustainable Foods. Vogel, Julia. 2010. lib. bdg. 32.07 *(978-1-60279-660-7(2)*, 200353); Save the Planet: Protecting Our Natural Resources. Hirsch, Rebecca. 2010. lib. bdg. 32.07 *(978-1-60279-661-4(0)*, 200354); Save the Planet: Reduce, Reuse, & Recycle. Minden, Cecilia. 2010. lib. bdg. 32.07 *(978-1-60279-662-1(9)*, 200355); Save the Planet: Using Alternative Energies. Farrell, Courtney. 2010. lib. bdg. 32.07 *(978-1-60279-663-8(7)*, 200356); Set. History Digs (Set) 2011. 320.70 *(978-1-61080-243-7(8)*, 201030); Set. Science Lab (Set) 2011. 256.56 *(978-1-61080-245-1(4)*, 201032); 32p. (gr. 4-8). (Explorer Library: Language Arts Explorer Ser.). (ENG., Illus.). 2011. 741.00 *(978-1-61080-239-0(X)*, 201026) Cherry Lake Publishing.

Larson, Jennifer. Category Cut-Ups Workbook with CD-ROM: Bk335. Prince, Audrey & Webber, Thomas, eds. 2006. (J). 26.95 *(978-1-58650-635-3(8))* Super Duper Pubns.

Lasseter, John, frwd. Designing with Pixar: 45 Activities to Create Your Own Characters, Worlds, & Stories. 2016. (ENG., Illus.). 80p. (J). (gr. 1-7). pap. 14.99 *(978-1-4521-5505-0(4))* Chronicle Bks. LLC.

LeCompte, David & Padrick, Kendell. Eugene Stillwell Wants to Know! Part III. 2009. (Eugene Stillwell Wants to Know! Ser.). (ENG.). 96p. (J). (gr. 4-6). pap. 4.95 *(978-1-929945-91-7(4))* Big Guy Bks., Inc.

Leisure Arts, creator. Scrapbooking with Your Kids: The Ultimate Guide to Kid-Friendly Crafting. 2008. (ENG., Illus.). 196p. pap. 22.95 *(978-1-60140-525-8(1))* Leisure Arts, Inc.

Lester, Stephanie. Year Round Project-Based Activities for STEM Grd 1-2. 2013. (ENG.). 112p. pap. 14.99 *(978-1-4206-3025-1(3))* Teacher Created Resources, Inc.

Levin, Freddie. Glitter Hanukkah Stickers. 2009. (Dover Little Activity Books Stickers Ser.). (ENG., Illus.). 2p. (J). (gr. 1-4). 2.99 *(978-0-486-47018-4(0)*, 470180) Dover Pubns., Inc.

—Outer Space Activity Book. 2009. (Dover Little Activity Bks.). (ENG.). 64p. (J). (gr. k-3). pap. 2.99 *(978-0-486-47389-5(9)*, 473899) Dover Pubns., Inc.

Levin, Michael. Start to Finish: Word Searches. 2006. (ENG.). 64p. pap. 6.99 *(978-1-4206-5994-8(4))* Teacher Created Resources, Inc.

Levin, Michael H. Start to Finish - Word Searches, Grades 3-4. 2006. (Start to Finish (Lerner) Ser.). (ENG., Illus.). 64p. (gr. 3-5). per. 6.99 *(978-1-4206-5995-5(2))* Teacher Created Resources, Inc.

Levy, Talia. Scratch & Sketch Trace-Along Doodle Mania: An Art Activity Book for Imaginative Artists of All Ages. Zschock, Martha Day, illus. 2015. (Scratch & Sketch Trace-Along Ser.). (ENG.). 64p. (J). (gr. k). spiral bd. 14.99 *(978-1-4413-1727-8(9)*, 06a77e73-08a2-4612-bc06-4caf416892d8) Peter Pauper Pr. Inc.

Lew-McCabe, Minette, illus. Make Your Own Hawaii Landmarks. 2007. *(978-1-59700-381-0(6))* Island Heritage Publishing.

Lewis, Jan, illus. My Busy Day. 2017. 14p. (J). (gr. -1-12). pap. 11.99 *(978-1-86147-723-1(6))* Anness Publishing, Inc.

Lierman, Jane. Cursive Writing Practice: Inspiring Quotes. 2009. (ENG.). 48p. (gr. 3-6). pap. 10.99 *(978-0-545-09437-5(2)*, Teaching Resources) Scholastic, Inc.

Life Changing Miracles: 30+ Powerful Fun Hands-on Learning Activities for Kids for Remarkable Improvement in Life Choices & Actions. 2006. (J). ring bd. 19.95 *(978-0-9786034-0-3(0)*, LCMRingbound); cd-rom 19.95 *(978-0-9786034-1-0(9))* Insight Services, Inc. (Children's Insight).

Light, Steve. Cars Go. 2016. (Vehicles Go! Ser.: 4). (ENG., Illus.). 16p. (J). (gr. -1 — 1). bds. 9.99 *(978-1-4521-5067-3(2))* Chronicle Bks. LLC.

Liguori Publications, creator. Every Day of Advent & Christmas, Year C: A Book of Activities for Chidlren. 2006. (Illus.). 31p. pap. 2.95 *(978-0-7648-1541-6(5))* Liguori Pubns.

Lil' Bratz 5 in 1 Superly Duperly. 2005. 52p. pap. 3.99 *(978-0-7666-2251-7(7))* Modern Publishing.

Linn, Susie. Copying: Early Learning Through Art. Stanley, Mandy, illus. 2017. (Arty Mouse Creativity Bks.). (ENG.). 48p. (J). (gr. -1-k). pap. 6.99 *(978-1-78445-626-9(8))* Top That! Publishing PLC GBR. Dist: Independent Pubs. Group.

—Pasting: Early Learning Through Art. 2017. (Arty Mouse Creativity Bks.). (ENG.). 48p. (J). (gr. -1-k). pap. 6.99 *(978-1-78700-039-1(7))* Top That! Publishing PLC GBR. Dist: Independent Pubs. Group.

Litchfield, Jo, illus. Baby Brother Look & Say. 2008. (Look & Say Board Bks). 12p. (J). bds. 7.99 *(978-0-7945-2101-1(0)*, Usborne) EDC Publishing.

Little & Large Sticker Activity Bk - Monster Machines. 2008. 24p. pap. *(978-1-84810-059-6(0))* Miles Kelly Publishing, Ltd.

Little & Large Sticker Activity Bugs. 2008. 24p. pap. *(978-1-84810-057-2(4))* Miles Kelly Publishing, Ltd.

Little & Large Sticker Activity Dinosaurs. 2008. 24p. pap. *(978-1-84810-058-9(2))* Miles Kelly Publishing, Ltd.

Little & Large Sticker Activity on the Farm. 2008. 24p. pap. *(978-1-84810-060-2(4))* Miles Kelly Publishing, Ltd.

Little & Large Sticker Activity Pirates. 2008. 24p. pap. *(978-1-84810-061-9(2))* Miles Kelly Publishing, Ltd.

Little & Large Sticker Activity Sharks. 2008. 24p. pap. *(978-1-84810-062-6(0))* Miles Kelly Publishing, Ltd.

Little & Large Sticker Activity Space. 2008. 24p. pap. *(978-1-84810-063-3(9))* Miles Kelly Publishing, Ltd.

Little & Large Sticker Activity Whales & Dolphins. 2008. 24p. pap. *(978-1-84810-064-0(7))* Miles Kelly Publishing, Ltd.

Little Children's Dinosaur Activity Book. 2017. (Activity Books for Little Children Ser.). (ENG.). (J). pap. 9.99 *(978-0-7945-3796-8(0)*, Usborne) EDC Publishing.

Litton, Jonathan. I Spy Learn & Go. Galloway, Fhiona, illus. 2015. (My Little World Ser.). (ENG.). 48p. (J). (gr. -1-2). 9.99 *(978-1-58925-313-1(2))* Tiger Tales.

—I Spy on the Farm. Galloway, Fhiona, illus. 2015. (My Little World Ser.). (ENG.). 48p. (J). (gr. -1-2). 9.99 *(978-1-58925-312-4(4))* Tiger Tales.

Ljungkvist, Laura. Search & Spot: Go! 2016. (Search & Spot Book Ser.). (ENG., Illus.). 40p. (J). (gr. -1-3). 16.99 *(978-0-544-57042-9(1)*, 1612568, Clarion Bks.) HarperCollins Pubs.

Lluch, Alex A. Let's Leap Ahead Kindergarten. 2013. 250p. (J). (gr. -1). spiral bd. 9.95 *(978-1-936061-84-6(8))* WS Publishing.

—Let's Leap Ahead Kindergarten School Games. 2014. (Illus.). 50p. (J). (gr. -1-k). spiral bd. 9.95 *(978-1-61351-081-0(0))* WS Publishing.

—Let's Leap Ahead Kindergarten Wipe-Off. 2013. 80p. (J). (gr. k). bds. 12.95 *(978-1-61351-013-1(6))* WS Publishing.

—Let's Leap Ahead Pre-K. 2013. 250p. (J). (gr. -1). spiral bd. 9.95 *(978-1-936061-83-9(X))* WS Publishing.

—Let's Leap Ahead: Pre-K Fun Pad: Pre-K Fun Pad. 2013. 80p. (J). (gr. -1). pap. 3.95 *(978-1-61351-020-9(9))* WS Publishing.

—Let's Leap Ahead Pre-K School Games. 2014. 50p. (J). (gr. -1-k). spiral bd. 9.95 *(978-1-61351-080-3(2))* WS Publishing.

—Let's Leap Ahead Pre-K Wipe-Off. 2013. 80p. (J). (gr. -1). bds. 12.95 *(978-1-61351-012-4(8))* WS Publishing.

Lluch, Isabel B. & Lluch, Emily. B. F. F. Quizzes. 2013. 128p. (J). (gr. 6). pap. 7.95 *(978-1-61351-030-8(6))* WS Publishing.

S

Lobdell-Bulson, Jodi. The Toddler Room: Free Play. 2013. 16p. pap. 7.95 *(978-1-4582-1256-6(4),* Abbott Pr.) Author Solutions, LLC.

Loman, Sam, illus. Magical Unicorn Christmas Activity Book. 2019. (Dover Christmas Activity Books for Kids Ser.). (ENG.). 96p. (J). (gr. 1-4). pap. 10.99 *(978-0-486-83226-5(0),* 832260) Dover Pubns., Inc.

—Magical Unicorn Spot the Differences. 2019. (Dover Kids Activity Books: Fantasy Ser.). (ENG.). 96p. (J). (gr. -1-3). pap. 10.99 *(978-0-486-83229-6(5),* 832295) Dover Pubns., Inc.

Loman, Sam & Regan, Lisa. Magical Mermaid Activity Book. 2018. (ENG., Illus.). 96p. (J). pap., act. bk. ed. 9.99 *(978-1-78888-156-2(7),* 22172d25-81f7-45df-adb6-442d48ef3f07) Arcturus Publishing GBR. Dist: Baker & Taylor Publisher Services (BTPS).

Lombardo, Michelle. The OrganWise Guys Pepto's Place Activity Book. Herron, Mark, illus. 2003. (J). pap., act. bk. ed. 4.95 *(978-1-931212-52-6(X))* OrganWise Guys Inc., The.

Longhi, Phoebe. The Steampunk Coloring & Activity Book: Containing Illustrations, Recipes, Formulas & Other Activities to Entertain & Entice Creativity for the Prevention of Ennui & General Malaise among the Youth of Today & Their Progenitors. 2012. (ENG., Illus.). 64p. pap. 11.95 *(978-1-933149-63-9(9))* Manic D Pr.

Longoria, Dora. Beans a la Charr. 2009. 28p. pap. 15.49 *(978-1-4389-4028-1(9))* AuthorHouse.

Lu, Nick, illus. Bumper-To-Bumper Stroller Cars. 2017. (Bumper-To-Bumper Ser.). (ENG.). 10p. (J). 9.99 *(978-1-4521-5504-3(6))* Chronicle Bks. LLC.

Lucero, Jaime. Bilingual Bingo. 2008. (SPA.). 80p. (gr. k-3). pap. 12.99 *(978-0-439-70067-2(1),* Teaching Resources) Scholastic, Inc.

Lumsden, Colin, illus. Apostles. 2003. (Bible Colour & Learn Ser.). 32p. pap. 2.50 *(978-1-903087-51-0(1))* DayOne Pubns. GBR. Dist: Send The Light Distribution LLC.

Lunis, Natalie. Making a Weather Station. 2011. (Early Connections Ser.). (J). *(978-1-61672-613-3(X))* Benchmark Education Co.

MacKenzie, Carine. Bible Heroes Elijah. 2005. (Bible Art Ser.). (ENG.). 16p. (J). act. bk. ed. 2.50 *(978-1-84550-089-4(X),* 69cd6d17-ddc7-4276-b7f8-a3950156b0d6) Christian Focus Pubns. GBR. Dist: Baker & Taylor Publisher Services (BTPS).

MacKinnon, Mairi. The Usborne Animal Alphabet Activity Book. Home, Sarah & Barker, Vicky, illus. 2014. (ENG.). (J). pap. 9.99 *(978-0-7945-3274-1(8),* Usborne) EDC Publishing.

Maclaine, James. Drawing, Doodling & Coloring Book Boys. 2012. (Activity Cards Ser.). 128p. (J). pap. 13.99 *(978-0-7945-3296-3(9),* Usborne) EDC Publishing.

MacLaine, James & Bowman, Lucy. The Usborne Little Boys' Activity Book. Watt, Fiona, ed. Harrison, Erica et al, illus. 2014. (ENG.). 64p. (J). pap. 9.99 *(978-0-7945-2888-1(0),* Usborne) EDC Publishing.

Mad Libs. All I Want for Christmas Is Mad Libs: World's Greatest Word Game. 2013. (Mad Libs Ser.). 240p. (J). (gr. 3-7). pap. 6.99 *(978-0-8431-7666-7(0),* Mad Libs) Penguin Young Readers Group.

Madema, Victoria. Bacon Stickers. 2016. (Dover Little Activity Books Stickers Ser.). (ENG.). 8p. (J). (gr. k-3). 1.99 *(978-0-486-80443-9(7),* 804437) Dover Pubns., Inc.

—Look & Find Letters to Color. 2013. (Dover Alphabet Coloring Bks.). (ENG., Illus.). 32p. (J). (gr. -1-2). pap. 3.99 *(978-0-486-48702-1(4),* 487024) Dover Pubns., Inc.

—Look & Find Numbers to Color. 2014. (Dover Kids Activity Bks.). (ENG.). 48p. (J). (gr. k-5). pap. 4.99 *(978-0-486-49464-7(0),* 494640) Dover Pubns., Inc.

—Look & Find Opposites to Color. 2014. (ENG.). 48p. (J). (gr. k-5). pap. 4.99 *(978-0-486-49463-0(2))* Dover Pubns., Inc.

—Strawberry Stickers. 2016. (Dover Little Activity Books Stickers Ser.). (ENG.). 8p. (J). (gr. k-3). pap. 1.99 *(978-0-486-80317-3(1),* 803171) Dover Pubns., Inc.

Mahon, Elaine. Preparing for First Reconciliation: A Guide for Families. 2013. (ENG., Illus.). 32p. (J). pap. 8.95 *(978-1-84730-400-1(1))* Veritas Pubns. IRL. Dist: Casemate Pubs. & Bk. Distributors, LLC.

Mai. Many Hands. 2012. 24p. pap. 15.99 *(978-1-4771-4246-2(0))* Xlibris Corp.

Make Believe Ideas. Christmas Cheer, 1 vol. Ede, Lara, illus. 2016. (ENG.). 54p. (J). (gr. -1-7). pap. 6.99 *(978-1-78598-447-1(0))* Make Believe Ideas GBR. Dist: Scholastic, Inc.

—Dino Explorer. Make Believe Ideas, illus. 2018. (ENG.). 24p. (J). (gr. 1-5). 9.99 *(978-1-78692-913-6(9))* Make Believe Ideas GBR. Dist: Scholastic, Inc.

—Farmyard Fun. Ede, Lara, illus. 2016. (ENG.). 86p. (J). (gr. -1-6). pap. 9.99 *(978-1-78598-146-3(3))* Make Believe Ideas GBR. Dist: Scholastic, Inc.

—I Love Christmas Activity Book, 1 vol. 2016. (ENG.). 48p. (J). (gr. -1-7). bds. 8.99 *(978-1-78598-446-4(2))* Make Believe Ideas GBR. Dist: Scholastic, Inc.

—I Love Unicorns. Ede, Lara, illus. 2018. (ENG.). 86p. (J). (gr. -1-7). 9.99 *(978-1-78692-860-3(4))* Make Believe Ideas GBR. Dist: Scholastic, Inc.

—Magical Unicorn Craft Kit. Make Believe Ideas, illus. 2018. (ENG.). 24p. (J). (gr. 1-5). 9.99 *(978-1-78692-914-3(7))* Make Believe Ideas GBR. Dist: Scholastic, Inc.

—My First Copy & Color. Lane, Charly, illus. 2017. (ENG.). 56p. (J). (gr. -1-7). pap. 6.99 *(978-1-78598-952-0(9))* Make Believe Ideas GBR. Dist: Scholastic, Inc.

—My First Sticker Dot-To-Dot. Lane, Charly, illus. 2016. (ENG.). 56p. (J). (gr. -1-7). pap. 6.99 *(978-1-78598-483-9(7))* Make Believe Ideas GBR. Dist: Scholastic, Inc.

—My Pretty Pink Sticker Purse. Machell, Dawn, illus. 2015. (ENG.). 96p. (J). (gr. -1-7). pap. 9.99 *(978-1-78393-764-6(5))* Make Believe Ideas GBR. Dist: Scholastic, Inc.

—My Super Sparkly Sticker Purse. Machell, Dawn, illus. 2016. (ENG.). 96p. (J). (gr. -1-7). pap. 9.99 *(978-1-78598-147-0(1))* Make Believe Ideas GBR. Dist: Scholastic, Inc.

—Ultimate Sticker File: Dinosaurs. Abbott, John A., illus. 2014. (ENG.). 96p. (J). pap. 6.99 *(978-1-78393-115-6(9))* Make Believe Ideas GBR. Dist: Scholastic, Inc.

—1000 Christmas Stickers. Make Believe Ideas, illus. 2013. (ENG.). 56p. (J). pap. 6.99 *(978-1-78235-572-4(3))* Make Believe Ideas GBR. Dist: Scholastic, Inc.

—1000 Stickers: I Love Hearts. Make Believe Ideas, illus. 2014. (ENG.). 28p. (J). pap. 6.99 *(978-1-78235-896-1(X))* Make Believe Ideas GBR. Dist: Scholastic, Inc.

—1000 Stickers Sweet Treats. Make Believe Ideas, illus. 2013. (ENG.). 56p. (J). pap. 6.99 *(978-1-78235-485-7(9))* Make Believe Ideas GBR. Dist: Scholastic, Inc.

Make Believe Ideas, creator. My Princess Dress up Book. 2007. (Illus.). 12p. (J). (gr. -1-3). *(978-1-84610-529-6(3))* Make Believe Ideas.

Mallett, Lisa, illus. Forty-Eight Funny Faces: Use the Cling-On Stickers to Make Funny Faces! 2015. (ENG.). 56p. (J). (gr. -1-2). pap. 8.99 *(978-1-4380-0599-7(7))* Sourcebooks, Inc.

Malone, Sydney. For Me & U! Fun for BFFs. May, Kyla, illus. 2014. (ENG.). 112p. (J). (gr. 1-4). pap. 8.99 *(978-0-545-73297-0(2),* Scholastic Nonfiction) Scholastic, Inc.

Mancini-Wilson, Debbie. Color My World: An Interactive Poetry Book for Kids of All Ages. 2007. (Illus.). 80p. (J). 19.99 *(978-0-9787586-0-8(9))* Harmony Pubns., LLC.

Manualidades y Otro Actividades. 2006. 32p. (J). pap. 8.99 *(978-0-7460-6647-8(3),* Usborne) EDC Publishing.

Marie-France, Marcie & Lebuis, Peter. Divisions Chansons et Activités, 1 vol. 2013. (FRE.). 64p. 19.95 *(978-1-55386-235-2(X),* 9781553862352) Jordan, Sara Publishing.

—Multiplications Chansons et Activités, 2 vols. 2013. (FRE.). 64p. 19.95 *(978-1-55386-229-1(5),* 9781553862291) Jordan, Sara Publishing.

—Soustractions Chansons et Activités, 2 vols. 2013. (FRE.). 64p. 19.95 *(978-1-55386-232-1(5),* 9781553862321) Jordan, Sara Publishing.

Marinaro, Stacy. If I Became a U. S. Marine. 2009. 46p. 24.95 *(978-0-615-21988-2(8))* Marinaro, Stacy.

Marrero, Alba. Diego's Busy Week: Learn the days of the week as you tag along with a boy named Diego. 2009. 20p. pap. 10.99 *(978-1-4389-5201-7(5))* AuthorHouse.

Marsh, Carole. America's National Parks Coloring & Activity Book. 2016. (Non-State Ser.). (ENG., Illus.). (J). pap. 5.99 *(978-0-635-12460-9(2))* Gallopade International.

—The Big Florida Reproducible Activity Book! 2004. (Florida Experience Ser.). (Illus.). 96p. pap. 12.95 *(978-0-635-06408-0(1))* Gallopade International.

—The Big New Hampshire Reproducible Activity Book-New Version. 2015. (New Hampshire Experience Ser.). (ENG.). (J). pap. 12.95 *(978-0-635-06491-2(X))* Gallopade International.

—The Big Oklahoma Reproducible Activity Book! 2008. (Oklahoma Experience Ser.). (Illus.). 96p. pap. 12.95 *(978-0-635-06402-8(2))* Gallopade International.

—Electricity: Common Core Lessons & Activities. 2013. (Common Core Ser.). (ENG., Illus.). 24p. (J). (gr. 4-7). pap. 4.99 *(978-0-635-10614-8(0))* Gallopade International.

—Quit Bossing Us Around! The Declaration of Independence. 2004. (American Milestones Ser.). (Illus.). 28p. (J). (gr. 4-12). pap. 5.95 *(978-0-635-02680-4(5))* Gallopade International.

Marsham, Liz. Coloring & Creativity Book (Fantastic Beasts & Where to Find Them) 2016. (Fantastic Beasts & Where to Find Them Ser.). (ENG.). 80p. (J). (gr. 3-7). pap. 8.99 *(978-1-338-11680-9(0))* Scholastic, Inc.

Martin, Jorge. Fingerprint Fun: Add Painty Prints. Martin, Jorge, illus. 2016. (ENG., Illus.). 32p. (J). (gr. -1-1). 7.99 *(978-1-78055-304-7(8))* O'Mara, Michael Bks., Ltd. GBR. Dist: Independent Pubs. Group.

Martinez, Kathleen & Edwards, Sue. Colossal Clubs: Activities-Based Curriculum for School-Age Programs. Edwards, Mark, illus. 2006. per. 29.95 *(978-0-917505-39-3(5),* School Age Notes) Gryphon Hse., Inc.

Masters, Neil. Butterflies Coloring Book. 2013. (ENG.). 34p. 12.07 *(978-1-62884-656-0(9),* Baby Professor (Education Kids)) Speedy Publishing LLC.

Masterson, Josephine. A Nest for Robin, 1 vol. 2015. (Rosen REAL Readers: STEM & STEAM Collection). (ENG.). 12p. (gr. k-1). pap. 6.33 *(978-1-4994-9511-9(0),* a2b50ef7-72ea-4f45-8b3f-f119c28513bc, Rosen Classroom) Rosen Publishing Group, Inc., The.

Math Puzzle Pad (was Math Games Pad) 2017. (Tear-Off Pads Ser.). (ENG.). (J). pap. 5.99 *(978-0-7945-3805-7(3),* Usborne) EDC Publishing.

Matheis, Mickie. Peanuts Mad Libs: World's Greatest Word Game. 2015. (Peanuts Ser.). (ENG.). 48p. (J). (gr. 3-7). pap. 4.99 *(978-0-8431-8331-3(4),* Mad Libs) Penguin Young Readers Group.

Matthews, John & Matthews, Caitlin. Storyworld: Create a Story Kit. 2010. (Illus.). *(978-0-7636-5319-4(5))* Templar Publishing.

Matz, Rita T. What Can I Do Today? 2013. 118p. (gr. -1-6). pap. 12.19 *(978-1-4669-8324-3(8))* Trafford Publishing.

May, Darcy. Glitter Christmas Fairy Sticker Paper Doll. 2008. (Dover Little Activity Books Paper Dolls Ser.). (ENG., Illus.). 2p. (J). (gr. 1-4). 2.99 *(978-0-486-46536-4(5),* 465365) Dover Pubns., Inc.

Mayhew, James. Katie: Discover Art with Katie: A National Gallery Sticker Activity Book. 150th anniv. ed. 2017. (Katie Ser.). (ENG.). 16p. (J). (gr. -1-k). pap. 6.99 *(978-1-4083-4982-3(5),* Orchard Bks.) Hachette Children's Group GBR. Dist: Hachette Bk. Group.

—Katie: Get Colouring with Katie: A National Gallery Book. 2017. (Katie Ser.). (ENG.). 16p. (J). (gr. -1-k). pap. 6.99 *(978-1-4083-4981-6(7),* Orchard Bks.) Hachette Children's Group GBR. Dist: Hachette Bk. Group.

Mazurkiewicz, Jessica. Butterfly Fun Activity Book. 2009. (Dover Little Activity Bks.). (ENG., Illus.). 64p. (J). (gr. k-3). 2.99 *(978-0-486-47198-3(5),* 471985) Dover Pubns., Inc.

—Forever Inspired Coloring Book: Fairyworld. 2016. (Forever Inspired Coloring Bks.). (ENG., Illus.). 96p. (J). (gr. 3-7). pap. 7.99 *(978-1-944686-23-9(1),* Racehorse Publishing) Skyhorse Publishing Co., Inc.

—Forever Inspired Coloring Book: Unicorns & Mystical Creatures. 2016. (Forever Inspired Coloring Bks.). (ENG., Illus.). 96p. (J). (gr. 3-7). pap. 7.99 *(978-1-944686-22-2(3),* Racehorse Publishing) Skyhorse Publishing Co., Inc.

—Haunted House Activity Book. 2010. (Dover Little Activity Bks.). (ENG., Illus.). 64p. (J). (gr. k-3). 2.50 *(978-0-486-47522-6(0),* 475220) Dover Pubns., Inc.

—Psalms Stained Glass Coloring Book. 2011. (Dover Religious Coloring Book Ser.). (ENG., Illus.). 32p. (J). (gr. 2-5). pap. 7.99 *(978-0-486-47834-0(3),* 478343) Dover Pubns., Inc.

—Santa's Workshop Stained Glass Coloring Book. 2008. (Dover Christmas Coloring Bks.). (ENG., Illus.). 32p. (J). (gr. 3-5). pap. 6.99 *(978-0-486-46937-9(9),* 469379) Dover Pubns., Inc.

—Treasure Hunt. 2009. (Dover Little Activity Bks.). (ENG.). 64p. (J). (gr. k-3). pap., act. bk. ed. 2.50 *(978-0-486-47042-9(3),* 470423) Dover Pubns., Inc.

Mazurkiewicz, Jessica & Dutton, Michael. 3-D Coloring Book — Abstractions. 2014. (Dover Design Coloring Bks.). (ENG., Illus.). 32p. (J). (gr. 3-5). pap. 5.99 *(978-0-486-48416-7(5),* 484165) Dover Pubns., Inc.

Mazurkiewicz, Jessica & Noble, Marty. 3-D Coloring Book - Christmas Designs. 2013. (Dover Christmas Coloring Bks.). (ENG.). 128p. (J). (gr. 3-12). pap. 9.99 *(978-0-486-49343-5(1),* 493431) Dover Pubns., Inc.

McArdle, Thaneeya. The Everything Girls Ultimate Body Art Book: 50+ Cool Doodle Tattoos to Create & Wear! 2014. (Everything(r) Kids Ser.). (ENG.). 128p. pap. 14.99 *(978-1-4405-7351-4(4))* Adams Media Corp.

McCarthy, Pat. Heading West: Life with the Pioneers, 21 Activities. 2009. (For Kids Ser.: 31). (ENG., Illus.). 144p. (J). (gr. 4-7). pap. 16.95 *(978-1-55652-809-5(4))* Chicago Review Pr., Inc.

McCumbee, Stephie. The Garden in My Mind Activity Guide: Lessons for Social Skill & Common Core Development. Griffin, Lisa M., illus. unabr. ed. 2014. (ENG.). 48p. (gr. k-6). pap. 20.95 *(978-1-934490-55-6(5))* Boys Town Pr.

McIntyre, Laura. The Everything Girls Ultimate Sleepover Party Book: 100+ Ideas for Sleepover Games, Goodies, Makeovers, & More! 2014. (Everything(r) Kids Ser.). (ENG.). 160p. pap. 16.99 *(978-1-4405-7393-4(X),* Everything) Adams Media Corp.

McKay, Jodi. Where Are the Words? 2018. (2019 Av2 Fiction Ser.). (ENG.). (J). (gr. -1-2). lib. bdg. 34.28 *(978-1-4896-8283-3(X),* AV2 by Weigl) Weigl Pubs., Inc.

—Where Are the Words? Holmes, Denise, illus. 2016. (ENG.). 32p. (J). (gr. -1-3). 16.99 *(978-0-8075-8733-1(8),* 807587338) Whitman, Albert & Co.

McLaughlin, Kari Massie. My Adventure with Dragonflies. 2009. 44p. (J). 8.99 *(978-1-59092-452-5(5))* Blue Forge Pr.

—My Adventure with Flamingos. 2009. 44p. (J). 8.99 *(978-1-59092-454-9(1))* Blue Forge Pr.

—My Adventure with Ladybugs. 2009. (ENG.). 44p. (J). 8.99 *(978-1-59092-457-0(6))* Blue Forge Pr.

—My Adventure with Penguins. 2009. (ENG.). 44p. (J). 8.99 *(978-1-59092-461-7(4))* Blue Forge Pr.

—My Adventure with the Cherokee. 2007. 44p. (J). 8.99 *(978-1-59092-446-4(0))* Blue Forge Pr.

—My Adventure with the Wright Brothers. 2007. 44p. (J). 8.99 *(978-1-59092-471-6(1))* Blue Forge Pr.

—My Adventure with Thomas Edison. 2007. 44p. (J). 8.99 *(978-1-59092-472-3(X))* Blue Forge Pr.

McManaman, Yelena & Droujkova, Maria. Moebius Noodles: Adventurous Math for the Playground Crowd. 2013. (Natural Math Ser.: 3). (ENG., Illus.). 88p. pap. 24.00 *(978-0-9776939-5-5(3))* Delta Stream Media.

McNamara, Margaret. The Pumpkin Patch. Gordon, Mike, illus. 2008. (Robin Hill School Ser.). (J). (gr. -1-1). pap. 16.95 *(978-1-4301-0622-7(0))* Live Oak Media.

McNeil, Niki, et al. HOCPP 1053 Narnia. 2005. spiral bd. 15.50 *(978-1-60308-053-8(8))* In the Hands of a Child.

—HOCPP 1072 Katy's Big Snow Day. 2006. spiral bd. 15.50 *(978-1-60308-072-9(4))* In the Hands of a Child.

—HOCPP 1073 Charlotte & Wilbur. 2006. spiral bd. 24.50 *(978-1-60308-073-6(2))* In the Hands of a Child.

McNutt, Nan. The Spindle Whorl: A Story & Activity Book for Ages 8 - 10. Roger, Fernandes, illus. 2nd ed. 2011. (Native American Art Activity Book Ser.). (ENG.). 56p. (J). (gr. 3-5). pap. 9.95 *(978-0-88240-762-3(7),* West Winds Pr.) West Margin Pr.

McNutt, Nan & Miller, Bruce ""subiyay"". The Twined Basket: A Story & Activity Book for Ages 10 - 12. Youso, Justin & Kaino, Kim, illus. 2011. (Native American Art Activity Book Ser.). (ENG.). 56p. (J). (gr. 5-7). pap. 9.95 *(978-0-88240-760-9(0),* West Winds Pr.) West Margin Pr.

McSweeney's. The Goods: Volume 1. 2013. (ENG., Illus.). 96p. (J). (gr. 2-4). pap. 22.99 *(978-0-7636-6894-5(X),* Big Picture Press) Candlewick Pr.

Meloche, Renee Taft. Heroes for Young Readers Activity Guide for Books 1-4: Educational & Character-Building Lessons for Children. 2006. (Heroes for Young Readers Ser.). (Illus.). 90p. per. 12.99 *(978-1-57658-367-8(8))* YWAM Publishing.

—Heroes for Young Readers Activity Guide for Books 13-16: Educational & Character-Building Lessons for Children. 2006. (ENG., Illus.). 85p. pap. 12.99 *(978-1-57658-370-8(8))* YWAM Publishing.

Meltzer, Brad. I Am...: a Journal for Extraordinary Kids. Eliopoulos, Chris, illus. 2019. (Ordinary People Change the World Ser.). 40p. (J). (gr. k-4). 14.99 *(978-0-525-57700-3(9),* Clarkson Potter) Potter/Ten Speed/Harmony/Rodale.

Menten, Ted. Steampunk Vixens Paper Dolls. 2014. (ENG.). 32p. (gr. 6-12). pap. 9.99 *(978-0-486-78340-6(5),* 783405) Dover Pubns., Inc.

Meredith, Samantha & Wyk, Hanri van, illus. Weddings Sticker Color Book. 2011. (First Sticker Coloring Bks). 20p. (J). pap. 5.99 *(978-0-7945-3108-9(3),* Usborne) EDC Publishing.

Merrill, Yvonne Y. America Vol. 3: Art Activities about Lewis & Clark, Pioneers, & Plains Indians. Simpson, Mary, illus. 2009. (Hands-on Ser.: 3). (ENG.). 82p. (gr. k-10). pap. 25.00 *(978-0-9778797-1-7(2))* KK.

Michaels, Sarah, et al. Extra Ring Bling Rings: Rb67. 2013. 9.95 *(978-1-60723-093-9(3))* Super Duper Pubns.

—Ring Bling Extra Hands: Rb69. 2013. pap. 14.95 *(978-1-60723-092-2(5))* Super Duper Pubns.

Michele, Tracey. Make a String Phone. 2011. (Learn-Abouts Ser.). (Illus.). 16p. (J). pap. 7.95 *(978-1-59920-607-3(2))* Black Rabbit Bks.

—Make a Treasure Map. 2011. (Illus.). 16p. (J). pap. 7.95 *(978-1-59920-606-6(4))* Black Rabbit Bks.

Micheletti, Judy. Snibbles: Really Creative Problem Solving Lessons & Mind-Stimulating Exercises for Gifted Students & Their Teachers, Ages 5 through Really Old! 2005. (Illus.). 70p. *(978-0-910609-50-0(0))* Gifted Education Pr.

Micronations: Invent Your Own Country & Culture with 25 Projects. 2014. (Build It Yourself Ser.). (ENG., Illus.). 128p. (J). (gr. 3-7). 21.95 *(978-1-61930-218-1(7),* 4abb41ae-a126-4e65-8b4e-fa03e4c4412d) Nomad Pr.

Midgley, Elizabeth Cole. Daily Discoveries for August. Mitchell, Judith, ed. Guymon, Jennette King, illus. 2005. 192p. (J). pap. 12.95 *(978-1-57310-452-4(3))* Teaching & Learning Co.

—Daily Discoveries for October. Mitchell, Judith, ed. Guymon, Jennette King, illus. 2005. 192p. (J). pap. 12.95 *(978-1-57310-454-8(X))* Teaching & Learning Co.

—Daily Discoveries for September. Mitchess, Judith, ed. Guymon, Jennette King, illus. 2005. 192p. (J). pap. 12.95 *(978-1-57310-453-1(1))* Teaching & Learning Co.

Miles, David. Wild about the Bible Sticker & Activity Book, 1 vol. 2016. (Adventure Bible Ser.). (ENG., Illus.). 32p. (J). pap. 6.99 *(978-0-310-75405-3(4))* Zonderkidz.

Miller, Eileen Rudisill. Fashion Models Paper Dolls. 2013. (Dover Paper Dolls Ser.). (ENG.). 32p. (J). (gr. 2-5). pap. 7.99 *(978-0-486-48877-6(2))* Dover Pubns., Inc.

—Glitter Princess Stickers. 2008. (Dover Little Activity Books Stickers Ser.). (ENG., Illus.). 2p. (J). (gr. 1-4). 2.99 *(978-0-486-46577-7(2),* 465772) Dover Pubns., Inc.

—Glitter Snow Princess Sticker Paper Doll. 2009. (Dover Little Activity Books Paper Dolls Ser.). (ENG.). 2p. (J). (gr. 1-4). pap. 2.99 *(978-0-486-47138-9(1),* 471381) Dover Pubns., Inc.

—Happy Easter Stained Glass Coloring Book. 2010. (Dover Holiday Coloring Book Ser.). (ENG., Illus.). 32p. (J). (gr. -1-8). pap. 6.99 *(978-0-486-47296-6(5),* 472965) Dover Pubns., Inc.

—Nutcracker Ballet Paper Dolls with Glitter! 2011. (Dover Paper Dolls Ser.). (ENG.). 32p. (J). (gr. 1-4). pap. 12.99 *(978-0-486-48390-0(8))* Dover Pubns., Inc.

Minden, Cecilia & Roth, Kate. Language Arts Explorer Junior (Set), 10 vols., Set. Incl. How to Write a Journal. lib. bdg. 29.21 *(978-1-60279-994-3(6),* 200988); How to Write a Letter. lib. bdg. 29.21 *(978-1-60279-991-2(1),* 200982); How to Write a Poem. lib. bdg. 29.21 *(978-1-60279-995-0(4),* 200990); How to Write a Report. lib. bdg. 29.21 *(978-1-61080-105-8(9),* 201112); How to Write about Your Adventure. lib. bdg. 29.21 *(978-1-61080-106-5(7),* 201114); How to Write an Ad. lib. bdg. 29.21 *(978-1-61080-107-2(5),* 201116); How to Write an E-Mail. lib. bdg. 29.21 *(978-1-60279-993-6(8),* 200986); How to Write an Interview. lib. bdg. 29.21 *(978-1-60279-996-7(2),* 200992); How to Write & Give a Speech. lib. bdg. 29.21 *(978-1-61080-108-9(3),* 201118); 24p. (J). (gr. 1-4). (Explorer Junior Library: Language Arts Explorer Junior Ser.). (ENG., Illus.). 2011. 256.40 *(978-1-61080-153-9(9),* 201024) Cherry Lake Publishing.

—Writing a Poem. 2019. (Write It Right Ser.). (ENG., illus.). 24p. (J). (gr. 1-4). pap. 12.79 *(978-1-5341-3941-1(9),* 212593); lib. bdg. 30.64 *(978-1-5341-4285-5(1),* 212592) Cherry Lake Publishing.

Miner, Julie Dobson. EEK! Mini Monsters Tattoos. 2016. (Dover Little Activity Bks.). (ENG.). 4p. (J). (gr. -1-2). pap. 3.50 *(978-0-486-80586-3(7),* 805867) Dover Pubns., Inc.

—EEK! Monsters Coloring Book. 2017. (Dover Fantasy Coloring Bks.). (ENG., Illus.). 32p. (J). (gr. -1-2). pap. 3.99 *(978-0-486-81441-4(6),* 814416) Dover Pubns., Inc.

Mitton, Tony. Amazing Machines Cool Cars Activity Book. Parker, Ant, illus. 2017. (Amazing Machines Ser.). (ENG.). 24p. (J). pap. 5.99 *(978-0-7534-7296-5(1),* 900161205, Kingfisher) Roaring Brook Pr.

Miyamoto, Tetsuya & KenKen Puzzle, LLC. Will Shortz Presents I Can KenKen! Volume 1 Vol. 1: 75 Puzzles for Having Fun with Math. 2008. (ENG.). 112p. (J). pap. 14.99 *(978-0-312-54641-0(6),* 900055743, St. Martin's Griffin) St. Martin's Pr.

—Will Shortz Presents I Can KenKen! Volume 2 Vol. 2: 75 Puzzles for Having Fun with Math. 2008. (ENG.). 112p. (J). pap. 18.99 *(978-0-312-54642-7(4),* 900055745, St. Martin's Griffin) St. Martin's Pr.

—Will Shortz Presents I Can KenKen! Volume 3 Vol. 3: 75 Puzzles for Having Fun with Math. 2008. (ENG.). 112p. (J). pap. 18.99 *(978-0-312-54643-4(2),* 900055747, St. Martin's Griffin) St. Martin's Pr.

Modern Publishing, creator. Smurfs & Smiles! Giant Coloring & Activity Book. 2010. (Smurf Ser.). (Illus.). 96p. (J). 2.49 *(978-0-7666-3746-7(8))* Modern Publishing.

—The Smurfs Super Coloring & Activity Bk. 2010. (Smurf Ser.). (Illus.). (J). 3.99 *(978-0-7666-3774-0(3))* Modern Publishing.

—A Smurfy Day! Giant Coloring & Activity Book. 2010. (Smurf Ser.). (Illus.). 96p. (J). 2.49 *(978-0-7666-3745-0(X))* Modern Publishing.

—Way to Go, Wildcats! 2009. (Disney High School Musical 3: Senior Year Ser.). (Illus.). (J). (gr. 4-7). pap. 2.99 *(978-0-7666-3233-2(4))* Modern Publishing.

Modern Publishing Staff. Angry Birds Giant Coloring & Activity Book-Big Surprise! 2013. pap. *(978-1-55993-451-0(4))* PSI & Assocs.

—Ariel's World! 2007. (Disney Bath Time Bubble Bks.). (J). (gr. -1-k). 4.99 *(978-0-7666-2554-9(0))* Modern Publishing.

—Colors! 2007. (Disney Bath Time Bubble Bks.). (Illus.). (J). (gr. -1-k). 4.99 *(978-0-7666-2552-5(4))* Modern Publishing.

—Feelings! 2007. (Disney Bath Time Bubble Bks.). (Illus.). (J). (gr. -1-k). 4.99 *(978-0-7666-2550-1(8))* Modern Publishing.

—Fisher-Price Laugh, Smile & Learn. 2009. 96p. (J). (gr. -1). pap. 2.99 *(978-0-7666-3488-6(4))* Modern Publishing.

—Fisher Price Little People Kindergarten, Vol. 1. 2013. pap., wbk. ed. *(978-0-7666-2817-5(5))* Modern Publishing.

—Fisher-Price Precious Planet. 2010. (Color by Number Bks.). (J). 64p. pap. 2.99 *(978-0-7666-3727-6(1));* 112p. (gr. -1). pap. 4.99 *(978-0-7666-3755-9(7))* Modern Publishing.

—Fisher-Price Spike. 2010. (Super Coloring & Activity Bks.). 112p. (J). (gr. -1). pap. 4.99 *(978-0-7666-3756-6(5))* Modern Publishing.

—Fisher-Price Spike the Ultra Dinosaur. 2009. (Giant Coloring & Activity Bks.). 96p. (J). (gr. -1). pap. 2.99 *(978-0-7666-3491-6(4))* Modern Publishing.

—Lisa Frank Super Coloring & Activity Book with Handle: A Colorful World! 2010. 96p. pap. 5.99 *(978-0-7666-3807-5(3))* Modern Publishing.

—Opposites! 2007. (Disney Bath Time Bubble Bks.). (Illus.). (J). (gr. -1-k). 4.99 *(978-0-7666-2556-3(7))* Modern Publishing.

—Toys! 2007. (Disney Bath Time Bubble Bks.). (Illus.). (J). (gr. -1-k). 4.99 *(978-0-7666-2549-5(4))* Modern Publishing.
—Zhu Zhu Pets Giant Coloring & Activity Book: Furry Friends! 2010. 96p. (J). pap. 2.99 *(978-0-7666-3764-1(6))* Modern Publishing.
—Zhu Zhu Pets Giant Coloring & Activity Book: Happy Hamsters! 2010. 96p. (J). pap. 2.99 *(978-0-7666-3765-8(4))* Modern Publishing.
Modern Publishing Staff, ed. Lots of Fun in Care a Lot. 2005. 12p. pap. 3.99 *(978-0-7666-1868-8(4))* Modern Publishing.
—Record Breaking Racers. 2005. 32p. pap. 2.99 *(978-0-7666-1909-8(5))* Modern Publishing.
—Sun & Fun in Care a Lot. 2005. 12p. pap. 3.99 *(978-0-7666-1869-5(2))* Modern Publishing.
—Tuned up Challengers. 2005. 12p. pap. 2.99 *(978-0-7666-1908-1(7))* Modern Publishing.
Modern Publishing Staff & Disney Staff, contrib. by. A Day in the Life. 2007. 39p. pap. 4.99 *(978-0-7666-2811-3(6))* Modern Publishing.
Moench, Megan Hansen. Know Your State Activity Book Washington. 1 vol. 2015. (ENG., Illus.). 272p. (J). pap. 14.99 *(978-1-4236-4059-2(4))* Gibbs Smith, Publisher.
Moerbeek, Kees, illus. & des. Space. Moerbeek, Kees, des. 2008. (Roly Poly Box Bks.). 24p. (J). (gr. -1-1). spiral bd. *(978-1-84643-246-0(4))* Child's Play International Ltd.
Moffatt, Frances. My Fashion Doodles & Designs: 200 Activities to Sketch, Color & Create. 2015. (ENG., Illus.). 208p. (J). (gr. 2). pap. 16.95 *(978-1-61243-434-6(7))* Ulysses Pr.
Monet, Claude & Noble, Marty. Colorier Vos Propres Tableaux de Monet. 2013. (Dover Bilingual Books for Kids Ser.). (ENG.). 64p. (gr. 3-12). pap. 5.99 *(978-0-486-49328-2(8),* 493288) Dover Pubns., Inc.
MoonRattles. Heritage Holiday Activity Guide: Chinese New Year 2007. 1 vol. 2006. (Illus.). 52p. (J). spiral bd. *(978-0-9790920-0-8(0))* MoonRattles.
—Heritage Holiday Activity Guide: Seventh Lunar Month. 2007. (Illus.). 52p. (J). spiral bd. *(978-0-9790920-5-3(1))* MoonRattles.
Morris, Linda Loper. No Yellow Horse, If You Please. 2011. 28p. pap. 15.99 *(978-1-4628-4628-3(9))* Xlibris Corp.
Mother Goose Programs, prod. What's the BIG Idea? Shapes & Spaces Librarian Manual. 2008. 70p. pap. *(978-0-9753985-9-3(8))* Mother Goose Programs.
Mugford, Simon. Collins Big Cat Phonics for Letters & Sounds - Art Is Fun!: Band 03/Yellow. 2018. (Collins Big Cat Ser.). (ENG., Illus.). 16p. (J). pap. 6.99 *(978-0-00-823025-8(0))* HarperCollins Pubs. Ltd. GBR. Dist: Independent Pubs. Group.
Multicultural Activities Blackline Masters. (Greetings Ser.). (gr. 3-5). 21.00 *(978-0-7635-2230-8(9))*; 21.00 *(978-0-7635-2231-5(7))* Rigby Education.
Mummakay. Flying Free: Meditations for Kids in Star Language. 2013. (Illus.). 36p. pap. 16.95 *(978-1-4525-0905-1(0),* Balboa Pr.) Author Solutions, LLC.
Music. ABCs & Much More Activity & Coloring Book. 2008. (Illus.). 177p. (J). pap. 14.95 *(978-0-9818635-1-1(5))* Music, Movement & Magination Bks.
Mussler-Wright, Richard & Baran, Laura. PCS Edventures! Bricklab Grade 3. 2007. (Illus.). spiral bd. *(978-0-9753193-5-2(3))* PCS Edventures, Inc.
—PCS Edventures! Bricklab Grade 4. 2006. spiral bd. *(978-0-9753193-6-9(1))* PCS Edventures, Inc.
My Puptatl Book. 2006. (J). spiral bd. 8.00 *(978-0-9786947-0-8(8))* Puptattle Pr., Inc.
My Puptatl Youth Book. 2006. (J). spiral bd. 8.00 *(978-0-9786947-1-5(6))* Puptattle Pr., Inc.
My Very Own Activity Pages: Summer 2004. 2004. (J). pap. 1.79 *(978-1-59317-067-7(X))* Warner Pr., Inc.
My Weird School Classroom Activity Sheet. (J). *(978-0-06-072730-7(6))* HarperCollins Pubs.
Nance, Andrew Jordan. Puppy Mind. Durk, Jim, illus. 2016. 32p. (J). (gr. -1-2). 18.95 *(978-1-941529-44-7(5),* Plum Blossom Bks.) Parallax Pr.
Nancy Giorgio-Kupiec. Nanje's Imagination or Is It ? 2009. 20p. pap. 10.49 *(978-1-4389-7068-4(4))* AuthorHouse.
National Geographic. National Geographic Kids: Animal: Creativity Book. 2013. 80p. (J). (gr. 1-3). pap. 12.99 *(978-1-4263-1402-5(7),* National Geographic Kids) Disney Publishing Worldwide.
National Geographic Kids. Get Outside Creativity Book: Cutouts, Games, Stencils, Stickers. 2016. 80p. (J). (gr. 1-3). pap. 12.99 *(978-1-4263-2326-3(3),* National Geographic Kids) Disney Publishing Worldwide.
—Junior Ranger Activity Book: Puzzles, Games, Facts, & Tons More Fun Inspired by the U. S. National Parks! 2016. (Illus.). 160p. (J). (gr. 3-7). pap., act. bk. ed. 14.99 *(978-1-4263-2304-1(2),* National Geographic Kids) Disney Publishing Worldwide.
—National Geographic Kids Amazing Pets Sticker Activity Book: Over 1,000 Stickers! 2014. (Illus.). 56p. (J). (gr. -1-k). pap. 6.99 *(978-1-4263-1555-8(4),* National Geographic Kids) Disney Publishing Worldwide.
—National Geographic Kids Cool Animals Sticker Activity Book: Over 1,000 Stickers! 2013. (Illus.). 56p. (J). (gr. -1-k). pap. 6.99 *(978-1-4263-1113-0(3),* National Geographic Kids) Disney Publishing Worldwide.
—National Geographic Kids Creepy Crawly: Sticker Activity Book. 2016. (NG Sticker Activity Bks.). 56p. (J). (gr. -1-k). pap., act. bk. ed. 6.99 *(978-1-4263-2425-3(1),* National Geographic Kids) Disney Publishing Worldwide.
—National Geographic Kids Cutest Animals Sticker Activity Book: Over 1,000 Stickers! 2013. (Illus.). 56p. (J). (gr. -1-k). pap. 6.99 *(978-1-4263-1112-3(5),* National Geographic Kids) Disney Publishing Worldwide.
—National Geographic Kids Dinos Sticker Activity Book: Over 1,000 Stickers! 2014. (NG Sticker Activity Bks.). 56p. (J). (gr. -1-k). pap. 6.99 *(978-1-4263-1773-6(5),* National Geographic Kids) Disney Publishing Worldwide.
—National Geographic Kids In My Backyard: Sticker Activity Book. 2016. (NG Sticker Activity Bks.). 56p. (J). (gr. -1-k). pap., act. bk. ed. 6.99 *(978-1-4263-2403-1(0),* National Geographic Kids) Disney Publishing Worldwide.
—National Geographic Kids: In the Jungle: Sticker Activity Book. 2015. (NG Sticker Activity Bks.). 56p. (J). (gr. -1-k). pap. 6.99 *(978-1-4263-2056-9(6),* National Geographic Kids) Disney Publishing Worldwide.
—National Geographic Kids Look & Learn: Colors! 2012. (Illus.). 24p. (J). (gr. -1-k). bds. 6.99 *(978-1-4263-0929-8(5),* National Geographic Kids) Disney Publishing Worldwide.
—National Geographic Kids Look & Learn: Look Up. 2016. (Look & Learn Ser.). (Illus.). 24p. (J). (gr. -1-k). bds. 6.99 *(978-1-4263-2454-3(5),* National Geographic Kids) Disney Publishing Worldwide.
—National Geographic Kids Look & Learn: Opposites! 2012. (Look & Learn Ser.). (Illus.). 24p. (J). (gr. -1-k). bds. 6.99 *(978-1-4263-1043-0(9),* National Geographic Kids) Disney Publishing Worldwide.
—National Geographic Kids Look & Learn: Patterns! 2013. (Look & Learn Ser.). 24p. (J). (gr. -1-k). bds. 6.99 *(978-1-4263-1123-9(0),* National Geographic Kids) Disney Publishing Worldwide.
—National Geographic Kids Look & Learn: Same & Different. 2012. (Illus.). 24p. (J). (gr. -1-k). bds. 6.99 *(978-1-4263-0928-1(7),* National Geographic Kids) Disney Publishing Worldwide.
—National Geographic Kids Look & Learn: Shapes! 2012. (Look & Learn Ser.). (Illus.). 24p. (J). (gr. -1-k). bds. 6.99 *(978-1-4263-1042-3(0),* National Geographic Kids) Disney Publishing Worldwide.
—National Geographic Kids On Safari: Sticker Activity Book. 2016. (NG Sticker Activity Bks.). 56p. (J). (gr. -1-k). pap. 6.99 *(978-1-4263-2402-4(2),* National Geographic Kids) Disney Publishing Worldwide.
—National Geographic Kids Super Space Sticker Activity Book: Over 1,000 Stickers! 2014. (Illus.). 56p. (J). (gr. -1-k). pap. 6.99 *(978-1-4263-1556-5(2),* National Geographic Kids) Disney Publishing Worldwide.
—Weird but True Sticker Doodle Book: Outrageous Facts, Awesome Activities, Plus Cool Stickers for Tons of Wacky Fun! 2016. (Weird but True Ser.: 3). (Illus.). 160p. (J). (gr. 3-7). pap. 12.99 *(978-1-4263-2456-7(1),* National Geographic Kids) Disney Publishing Worldwide.
National Geographic Staff. National Geographic Kids Weird but True! 2014. (Weird but True Ser.). lib. bdg. 24.50 *(978-0-606-35578-0(2))* Turtleback.
National Marine Fisheries Service (U.S.), ed. Understanding Marine Debris: Games & Activities for Kids of All Ages. 2009. (ENG., Illus.). 22p. 2.50 *(978-0-16-083974-0(2),* 003-017-00558-5, National Marine Fisheries Service) United States Government Printing Office.
National Oceanic and Atmospheric Administration (U.S.) & National Marine Fisheries Service (U.S.), compiled by. Chesapeake Bay Activity Book. 2008. (ENG., Illus.). 24p. (gr. 3-6). pap. 3.50 *(978-0-16-081321-4(2),* National Marine Fisheries Service) United States Government Printing Office.
National Park Service Staff, ed. Junior Paleontologist Activity Book: Ages 5 to 12: Explore, Learn, Protect. Wood, Ethan, illus. rev. ed. 2012. (ENG.). 22p. (gr. k-6). 6.00 *(978-0-16-090846-0(9))* National Park Service Div. of Pubns.
Naylor, Amy. Whoosh! Easy Paper Airplanes for Kids: Color, Fold & Fly! 2013. (Dover Kids Activity Bks.). (ENG.). 48p. (J). (gr. -1-3). pap. 6.99 *(978-0-486-49231-5(1),* 492311) Dover Pubns., Inc.
Neal, Angie & Kjesbo, Rynette. Simply Social 7 at School. Bristol, Mark, illus. 2011. 216p. (J). spiral bd. 34.95 net. *(978-1-60723-005-2(4))* Super Duper Pubns.
Nemmers, Lee. Monsters: An Art Activity Book for Creative Kids of All Ages. Zschock, Martha Day, illus. 2013. (Scratch & Sketch Ser.). (ENG.). 64p. (J). (gr. k). spiral bd. 12.99 *(978-1-4413-1154-2(8))* Peter Pauper Pr. Inc.
—Scratch & Sketch Trace-Along Constellations: An Art Activity Book for Artistic Stargazers of All Ages. Zschock, Martha Day, illus. 2015. (Scratch & Sketch Trace-Along Ser.). (ENG.). 64p. (J). (gr. k). spiral bd. 14.99 *(978-1-4413-1726-1(0),* e6fbee8a-24d3-4f0a-8535-666440ead174) Peter Pauper Pr. Inc.
—Scratch & Sketch Trace-Along Robots: An Art Activity Book for Artistic Inventors of All Ages. Wheeler, David Cole, illus. 2015. (Scratch & Sketch Trace-Along Ser.). (ENG.). 64p. (J). spiral bd. 14.99 *(978-1-4413-1812-1(7),* 4f92aadd-8db5-4339-a48d-0bbda5620acc) Peter Pauper Pr. Inc.
Nemmers, Tom. Knights Scratch & Sketch: For Brave Artists & Loyal Subjects of All Ages. Barbas Steckler, Kerren, illus. 2007. (Scratch & Sketch sER.). 80p. (J). 12.99 *(978-1-59359-877-8(7))* Peter Pauper Pr. Inc.
Nesworthy, Lauren. Darth Vader, Rebel Hunter! 2016. (Star Wars DK Readers Level 2 Ser.). lib. bdg. 13.55 *(978-0-606-38713-2(7))* Turtleback.
Newland, Sonya. Doodle Yourself Smart... Physics. 2012. (Doodle Bks.). (ENG., Illus.). 128p. pap. 12.95 *(978-1-60710-439-1(3),* Thunder Bay Pr.) Readerlink Distribution Services, LLC.
Newman-D'Amico, Fran. Birthday Activity Book. 2006. (Dover Little Activity Bks.). (ENG., Illus.). 64p. (J). (gr. k-3). act. bk. ed. 1.99 *(978-0-486-44441-3(4))* Dover Pubns., Inc.
—Christmas Fun Activity Book. 2015. (Dover Christmas Activity Books for Kids Ser.). (ENG.). 48p. (J). (gr. -1-2). pap. 4.99 *(978-0-486-79183-8(1),* 791831) Dover Pubns., Inc.
—Design Your Own Ugly Christmas Sweater Sticker Activity Book. 2015. (Dover Little Activity Bks.). (ENG., Illus.). 4p. (J). (gr. k-3). 1.99 *(978-0-486-80104-9(7),* 801047) Dover Pubns., Inc.
—Glitter Decorate a Christmas Tree Sticker Activity Book. 2009. (Dover Little Activity Books Stickers Ser.). (ENG., Illus.). 2p. (J). (gr. 1-4). 2.99 *(978-0-486-47127-3(6),* 471276) Dover Pubns., Inc.
—Glitter Decorate Christmas Cookies Sticker Activity Book. 2019. (Dover Little Activity Books Stickers Ser.). (ENG., Illus.). 8p. (J). (gr. k-2). 2.99 *(978-0-486-83414-6(X),* 83414X) Dover Pubns., Inc.
—Make Your Own Pizza:Sticker Activity Book. 2006. (Dover Little Activity Books Stickers Ser.). (ENG., Illus.). 4p. (J). (gr. k-3). act. bk. ed. 1.99 *(978-0-486-45224-1(7),* 452247) Dover Pubns., Inc.
—My Busy Backyard Activity Book. 2016. (Dover Little Activity Bks.). (ENG.). 64p. (J). (gr. k-3). pap. 2.50 *(978-0-486-81034-8(8),* 810348) Dover Pubns., Inc.
—Vacation Fun Activity Book. 2007. (Dover Kids Activity Bks.). (ENG., Illus.). 64p. (J). (gr. -1-2). per. 5.99 *(978-0-486-45896-0(2),* 458962) Dover Pubns., Inc.
Nicholls, Paul. Wind-up Race Cars. 2010. (Wind-up Bks). 14p. (J). bds. 29.99 *(978-0-7945-2657-3(8),* Usborne) EDC Publishing.
Nichols, Travis. Maze Quest: (Adventure Books for Kids, Children?s Fantasy Books, Interactive Kids Books, Activity Book for Kids) 2018. (ENG., Illus.). 64p. (J). (gr. 1-7). pap. 12.99 *(978-1-4521-6989-7(6))* Chronicle Bks. LLC.
Nicholson, Sue & Robins, Deri. The Great Big Art Activity Book. 2008. (Illus.). 240p. (J). *(978-1-84538-618-4(3))* New Burlington Bks.
Noble, Marty. Fanciful Butterflies Stained Glass Coloring Book. 2012. (Dover Butterfly Coloring Bks.). (ENG., Illus.). 32p. (gr. 3-5). pap. 7.99 *(978-0-486-48649-9(4),* 486494) Dover Pubns., Inc.
—Impressionist Art. 2009. (Dover Stained Glass Coloring Book Ser.). (ENG., Illus.). 32p. (gr. 6-8). pap. 6.99 *(978-0-486-46538-8(1))* Dover Pubns., Inc.
—Mandalas GemGlow Stained Glass Coloring Book. 2010. (Dover Mandala Coloring Bks.). (ENG., Illus.). 32p. (J). (gr. 1-5). pap. 7.99 *(978-0-486-47478-6(X),* 47478X) Dover Pubns., Inc.
Noble, Marty & Creative Haven. Creative Haven African Designs Coloring Book. 2013. (Adult Coloring Books: World & Travel Ser.). (ENG., Illus.). 64p. (gr. 3). pap. 5.99 *(978-0-486-49309-1(1),* 493091) Dover Pubns., Inc.
Noble, Marty & Creative Haven Staff. Creative Haven Day of the Dead Coloring Book. 2013. (Adult Coloring Books: Holidays & Celebrations Ser.). (ENG., Illus.). 64p. (gr. 3). pap. 6.99 *(978-0-486-49213-1(3),* 492133) Dover Pubns., Inc.
Noodoll. A Day in Ricetown: A Ricemonster Activity Book. 2017. (Illus.). 48p. (J). (gr. -1-5). pap. 14.95 *(978-0-500-65102-5(7),* 565102) Thames & Hudson.
Northcott, Richard. In the Mountains. 2013. (ENG., Illus.). 40p. pap. 11.00 *(978-0-19-464687-1(4))* Oxford Univ. Pr., Inc.
O'Connon, Jane & Harper Collins/Leap Frog. LeapReader Book, Fancy Nancy Explorer Extraordinaire! Glasser, Robin Preiss, illus. 2017. (J). (gr. -1-7). pap. 13.99 *(978-1-60685-272-9(8))* LeapFrog Enterprises, Inc.
O'Dowd, Chris & Murphy, Nick Vincent. Moone Boy & the Marvellous Activity Manual. 2017. (ENG., Illus.). 144p. (J). (gr. 3-7). 9.99 *(978-1-5098-3259-0(9))* Pan Macmillan GBR. Dist: Independent Pubs. Group.
The OH Book. 2007. (Illus.). 12p. (J). 14.99 *(978-0-9793506-1-0(1))* Sportime International.
Okido, Okido. Color Me In! An Activity Book. 2013. (Illus.). 128p. (J). (gr. k-3). pap. 14.95 *(978-0-500-65017-2(9),* 565017) Thames & Hudson.
Olabi, Adriana. Fine Motor Activities. 2012. 84p. pap. 26.50 *(978-1-61897-712-0(1),* Strategic Bk. Publishing) Strategic Book Publishing & Rights Agency (SBPRA).
Olmedillas, Cathy, compiled by. Anorak. 2013. (ENG., Illus.). 64p. (J). pap. 9.99 *(978-1-4236-3340-2(7),* Anorak Pr.) Gibbs Smith, Publisher.
Olsen, Jan Z., creator. Color Print & Number Wall Cards. 2013. (ENG.). tchr. ed. 18.95 *(978-1-934825-11-2(5))* Handwriting Without Tears.
Omoth, Tyler. Busting Boredom with Technology. 2017. (Boredom Busters Ser.). (ENG., Illus.). 32p. (J). (gr. 3-9). lib. bdg. 28.65 *(978-1-5157-4705-5(0),* 134344, Capstone Pr.) Capstone.
Omoth, Tyler & Swanson, Jennifer. Boredom Busters. 2017. (Boredom Busters Ser.). (ENG., Illus.). 32p. (J). (gr. 3-9). 122.60 *(978-1-5157-4718-5(2),* 25888, Capstone Pr.) Capstone.
O'Neal, Claire. Washington, D. C. 2009. (Class Trip Ser.). (Illus.). 48p. (J). (gr. 2-5). lib. bdg. 29.95 *(978-1-58415-809-7(3))* Mitchell Lane Pubs.
O'Reilly, Wenda. Art Ditto. 2007. 24.95 *(978-1-889613-56-7(8))* Birdcage Pr.
Orloff, Karen Kaufman. Mystery at the Aquarium (a Nightlight Detective Book) Smith, Jamie, illus. 2014. (ENG.). 26p. (J). 12.99 *(978-1-4413-1615-8(9),* 9781441316158) Peter Pauper Pr. Inc.
Ortac, Arda. Sharp Kids Activity. Ortac, Feride, illus. 2009. 80p. Bk. 1. pap. 9.00 *(978-1-60743-151-0(3))*Bk. 02. pap. 9.00 *(978-1-60743-152-7(1))* Independent Pub.
Ortiz, Associate Professor Enrique. Ten Elephants & a Spider's Web: A Traditional Latin American Counting Rhyme & Other Activities: Spanish/English. 2009. 20p. 10.80 *(978-0-615-26124-9(8))* Ortiz, Enrique Publishing.
Ortler, Brett. Animal Tracks Activity Book. 1 vol. Nitzsche, Shane & Christenson, Anna, illus. 2015. (Color & Learn Ser.). (ENG.). 64p. (J). (gr. 3-7). pap. 6.95 *(978-1-59193-538-4(5),* Adventure Pubns.) AdventureKEEN.
—Outer Space Activity Book. Juliano, Phil, illus. 2017. (Color & Learn Ser.). (ENG.). 64p. (J). (gr. k-5). pap. 6.95 *(978-1-59193-708-1(6),* Adventure Pubns.) AdventureKEEN.
Osborne, Mary Pope & Boyce, Natalie Pope. Games & Puzzles from the Tree House: Over 200 Challenges! Murdocca, Sal, illus. 2010. (Magic Tree House (R) Ser.). 256p. (J). (gr. 1-4). act. bk. ed. 6.99 *(978-0-375-86216-8(1),* Random Hse. Bks. for Young Readers) Random Hse. Children's Bks.
Osborne, Nancy. Rhyming Words: Cut & Paste. l.t. ed. 2007. (Illus.). 52p. ring bd. 9.95 *(978-1-928856-07-8(1))* Osborne Pr.
O'Shay, Alex. Ten Acts of Kindess: An Alex Story. 2011. 44p. pap. 16.59 *(978-1-4634-2027-7(7))* AuthorHouse.
Osteen, Victoria. My Happy Heart Books (Boxed Set) A Touch-And-Feel Book Boxed Set. Day, Betsy, illus. 2009. (ENG.). 66p. (J). (gr. -1-k). bds. 19.99 *(978-1-4169-5549-8(6),* Little Simon Inspirations) Little Simon Inspirations.
Over 100 Things to Do on a Plane. 2017. (Activity Puzzle Bks.). (ENG.). (J). pap. 5.99 *(978-0-7945-3966-5(1),* Usborne) EDC Publishing.
P. I. Kids. Disney Junior Lots of Look & Finds. 2015. (ENG.). 192p. (J). pap. *(978-1-4508-9408-1(9),* 1450894089) Publications International, Ltd.
—Look Find Activity Pad Stickers - O/P. 2014. (ENG.). 64p. (J). pap. *(978-1-4508-8557-7(8),* 1450885578) Phoenix International Publications, Inc.
—Look Find Activity Pad Stickers Mi-O/P. 2014. (ENG.). 64p. (J). pap. *(978-1-4508-8556-0(X),* 145088556X) Phoenix International Publications, Inc.
—Planes Fire & Rescue Look & Find - O/P. 2014. (ENG.). 24p. (J). 7.98 *(978-1-4508-8350-4(8),* 1450883508) Phoenix International Publications, Inc.
Pacheco, Luis Gabriel & Pacheco, Alma Rosa, illus. Juegos Recreativos para Ninos. 2003. (SPA.). 182p. (J). pap. *(978-970-651-625-1(5))* Editorial Oceano De Mexico, S.A. DE C.V.
Paddington 2: Sticker Activity Book: Movie Tie-In. 2017. (ENG.). 48p. (J). 7.99 *(978-0-00-825445-2(1),* HarperCollins Children's Bks.) HarperCollins Pubs. Ltd. GBR. Dist: HarperCollins Pubs.
Pal Toys, creator. Bright & Beyond - Age 1 English. 2007. (J). 9.95 *(978-0-9763648-7-0(5))* Pal Toys, LLC.
—Bright & Beyond - Age 2 English. 2007. (J). 9.95 *(978-0-9763648-8-7(3))* Pal Toys, LLC.
—Bright & Beyond - Baby English. 2007. (J). 9.95 *(978-0-9763648-6-3(7))* Pal Toys, LLC.
—Bright & Beyond - Bebes. 2007. (J). 9.95 *(978-0-9763648-2-5(4))* Pal Toys, LLC.
—Bright & Beyond - Preschool English. 2007. (J). 9.95 *(978-0-9763648-9-4(1))* Pal Toys, LLC.
Palomares, Susanna, et al. Hearts & Minds: An Afterschool Program for Developing Reading Literacy & Emotional Intelligence. 2012. 158p. pap. 28.95 *(978-1-56499-084-6(2))* Innerchoice Publishing.
Panaccione, Nancy. Mine! Diary: My Ideas Need Expressing. 2013. (ENG., Illus.). (J). (gr. 4-7). 12.95 *(978-1-892951-67-0(3))* GO Publishing Co.
Panchyk, Richard. Franklin Delano Roosevelt for Kids: His Life & Times with 21 Activities. 2007. (For Kids Ser.: 24). (ENG., Illus.). 160p. (J). (gr. 4-8). pap. 14.95 *(978-1-55652-657-2(1))* Chicago Review Pr., Inc.
Pang, Ophelia. Ophelia Pang's Interactive Art Book. 2017. (Colouring Bks.). (ENG., Illus.). 96p. pap. 14.95 *(978-1-84994-382-6(6),* Batsford) Pavilion Bks. GBR. Dist: Penguin Random Hse. LLC.
Parkes, Lois. Paper Sport: Activities, Games & Puzzles for Sporty Kids. 2012. 44p. pap. 21.99 *(978-1-4771-2582-3(5))* Xlibris Corp.
Parr, todd. Planet Color by Todd Parr Jumbo Journal Save the Blue. 2009. (Todd Parr by Chronicle Bks.). (ENG.). 160p. (J). (gr. -1-3). 9.99 *(978-0-8118-7153-2(3))* Chronicle Bks. LLC.
Parsons, Sandra J. What Could a Kid Do? 2011. 24p. pap. 15.99 *(978-1-4628-8733-0(3))* Xlibris Corp.
Paulding, Barbara. Circus Scratch & Sketch: An Art Activity Book. Zschock, Martha Day, illus. 2009. (Scratch & Sketch Ser.). 64p. (J). (gr. -1). spiral bd. 14.99 *(978-1-59359-832-7(7))* Peter Pauper Pr. Inc.
—Water Magic. Steckler, Kerren Barbas, illus. 2009. (Young Artist Ser.). 24p. (J). (gr. -1). 15.99 *(978-1-59359-842-6(4))* Peter Pauper Pr. Inc.
PC Treasures Staff, ed. Barney's Giant Coloring & Activity Book. 2009. (ENG., Illus.). 384p. (J). pap. 3.99 *(978-1-60072-220-2(2))* PC Treasures, Inc.
Pearlstein, Don. Make Your Own Laptop: Color & Build Your Own Computer! Stillerman, Robbie, illus. 2011. (Dover Children's Activity Bks.). (ENG.). 24p. (J). (gr. k-3). pap. 9.99 *(978-0-486-48532-4(3))* Dover Pubns., Inc.
Pedigree Books. Angry Birds Star Wars Super Interactive Annual 2014. 2013. 80p. (J). 12.99 *(978-1-908152-05-3(2))* Pedigree Bks., Ltd. GBR. Dist: Diamond Bk. Distributors.
—Angry Birds Super Interactive Annual 2014. 2013. 80p. (J). 12.99 *(978-1-908152-04-6(4))* Pedigree Bks., Ltd. GBR. Dist: Diamond Bk. Distributors.
—Annoying Orange Super Interactive Annual 2014. 2013. 80p. (J). 12.99 *(978-1-908152-06-0(0))* Pedigree Bks., Ltd. GBR. Dist: Diamond Bk. Distributors.
—Barbie Annual 2014. 2013. 80p. (J). 12.99 *(978-1-907602-72-6(0))* Pedigree Bks., Ltd. GBR. Dist: Diamond Bk. Distributors.
—Cut the Rope Super Interactive Annual 2014. 2013. 80p. (J). 12.99 *(978-1-908152-08-4(7))* Pedigree Bks., Ltd. GBR. Dist: Diamond Bk. Distributors.
—Dreamworks Heroes Annual 2014. 2013. (Illus.). 80p. (J). 12.99 *(978-1-907602-99-3(2))* Pedigree Bks., Ltd. GBR. Dist: Diamond Bk. Distributors.
—Family Guy Annual 2014. 2013. 80p. (J). 12.99 *(978-1-907602-73-3(9))* Pedigree Bks., Ltd. GBR. Dist: Diamond Bk. Distributors.
—Olly Murs Special by Smash Hits Annual 2014. 2013. 80p. (J). 12.99 *(978-1-907602-90-0(9))* Pedigree Bks., Ltd. GBR. Dist: Diamond Bk. Distributors.
—One Direction Special by Smash Hits Annual 2014. 2013. 80p. (J). 12.99 *(978-1-907602-89-4(5))* Pedigree Bks., Ltd. GBR. Dist: Diamond Bk. Distributors.
—Pokemon Annual 2014. 2013. 80p. (J). 12.99 *(978-1-907602-74-0(7))* Pedigree Bks., Ltd. GBR. Dist: Diamond Bk. Distributors.
—Shoot Annual 2014. 2013. 80p. (J). 12.99 *(978-1-907602-75-7(5))* Pedigree Bks., Ltd. GBR. Dist: Diamond Bk. Distributors.
—Smurfs 2 Annual 2014. 2013. 80p. (J). 12.99 *(978-1-907602-91-7(7))* Pedigree Bks., Ltd. GBR. Dist: Diamond Bk. Distributors.
—Sonic the Hedgehog Super Interactive Annual 2014. 2013. 80p. (J). 12.99 *(978-1-908152-07-7(9))* Pedigree Bks., Ltd. GBR. Dist: Diamond Bk. Distributors.
—South Park Annual 2014. 2013. 80p. (J). 12.99 *(978-1-907602-94-8(1))* Pedigree Bks., Ltd. GBR. Dist: Diamond Bk. Distributors.
—Star Wars Annual 2014. 2013. 80p. (J). 12.99 *(978-1-907602-84-9(4))* Pedigree Bks., Ltd. GBR. Dist: Diamond Bk. Distributors.
—Star Wars: the Clone Wars Annual 2014: The Clone Wars Annual 2014. 2013. 80p. (J). 12.99 *(978-1-907602-95-5(X))* Pedigree Bks., Ltd. GBR. Dist: Diamond Bk. Distributors.
—Tatty Teddy & Blue Nose Friends Annual 2014. 2013. 80p. (J). 12.99 *(978-1-907602-92-4(5))* Pedigree Bks., Ltd. GBR. Dist: Diamond Bk. Distributors.
—Turbo Annual 2014. 2013. 80p. (J). 12.99 *(978-1-907602-93-1(3))* Pedigree Bks., Ltd. GBR. Dist: Diamond Bk. Distributors.

S

Peek Inside the Jungle. 2017. (Peek Inside BDs Ser.). (ENG.). (J). bds. 11.99 *(978-0-7945-3920-7(3)*, Usborne) EDC Publishing.

Peek, Patsy. Reading Comprehension Practice: Grades 2-8 Practice Worksheets Featuring Story Webs, Newspaper Ads, Fliers. 2012. 64p. (gr. 2-4). pap. 13.95 *(978-1-4772-4933-8(8))* AuthorHouse.

Peirce, Lincoln. Big Nate: Fun Blaster: Cheezy Doodles, Crazy Comix, & Loads of Laughs! Peirce, Lincoln, illus. 2015. (Big Nate Activity Book Ser.: 2). (ENG., Illus.). 224p. (J). (gr. 3-7). pap. 7.99 *(978-0-06-234951-4(1)*, Balzer & Bray) HarperCollins Pubs.

—Big Nate Super Scribbler. Peirce, Lincoln, illus. 2015. (Big Nate Activity Book Ser.: 5). (ENG., Illus.). 224p. (J). (gr. 3-7). pap. 6.99 *(978-0-06-234922-4(8)*, Balzer & Bray) HarperCollins Pubs.

Pencil Fun Book: Jesus Is Born. 2007. (Pencil Fun Books Ser.). 16p. (J). (gr. 3-7). 9.90 *(978-0-7814-4520-7(5))* Cook, David C.

Penovi, Celina. Guess It If You Can! — ¿Adivinarás Quizás? Volume I - School Time! — Volumen I - Hora de ir a la Escuela! 2009. 24p. pap. 15.99 *(978-1-4490-2744-5(X))* AuthorHouse.

Perchyonok, Tamara. Chemistry & Fun for Kids of All Ages: Billingual Book. 2007. pap. 9.00 *(978-0-8059-8606-8(5))* Dorrance Publishing Co., Inc.

Percy, Tasha. The Official Irb Rugby World Cup 2015 Activity Book. 2015. (Y Ser.). (ENG., Illus.). 56p. (J). (gr. 2-7). pap. 9.95 *(978-1-78312-123-6(8))* Carlton Kids GBR. Dist: Two Rivers Distribution.

Pereira, Diego Jourdan. FLIP OUTS — Fairy Fun: Color Your Own Cartoon! 2015. (ENG., Illus.). 64p. (J). (gr. k-3). pap. 1.99 *(978-0-486-79487-7(3)*, 794873) Dover Pubns., Inc.

Perkins, Miss Quinn. I Know When the Rainbow Comes. Perkins, Terrell D., illus. 2013. 28p. pap. 9.95 *(978-0-9851628-0-1(5))* Soulful Storytellers, Inc.

Perry, Phyllis J. Colorado Fun: Activities for on the Road & at Home. Tarr, Lisa M., illus. 2007. 80p. (J). (gr. 1-7). pap. 12.95 *(978-1-55566-402-2(4)*, Johnson Bks.) Bower Hse.

Peter Pauper Press, Inc., creator. Kids Unplugged: Ocean Quest. 2016. (Kids Unplugged Ser.). (ENG., Illus.). 64p. (J). pap. 7.99 *(978-1-4413-1997-5(2)*, 36afadf0-cc08-41b9-a84a-b4bdad24b518) Peter Pauper Pr. Inc.

—Kids Unplugged Fashion Activity Book. 2017. (ENG.). (J). pap. 7.99 *(978-1-4413-2278-4(7))* Peter Pauper Pr. Inc.

—Scratch & Sketch Horses (Trace-Along) An Art Activity Book for Artistic Horse Lovers of All Ages. 2017. (Scratch & Sketch Trace-Along Ser.). (ENG., Illus.). 64p. (J). spiral bd. 14.99 *(978-1-4413-2251-7(5)*, e73c6d46-764f-4216-915d-ad53f0bb1cd7) Peter Pauper Pr. Inc.

—Scratch & Sketch National Parks (Trace-Along) An Art Activity Book for Artistic Rangers of All Ages. 2017. (Scratch & Sketch Trace-Along Ser.). (ENG., Illus.). 64p. (J). spiral bd. 14.99 *(978-1-4413-2271-5(X)*, 48e67508-02fc-4dd5-bf56-22e404e0a377) Peter Pauper Pr. Inc.

—Scratch & Sketch Take Flight (Trace-Along) An Art Activity Book for Artistic Aviators of All Ages. 2017. (Scratch & Sketch Trace-Along Ser.). (ENG., Illus.). 64p. (J). spiral bd. 14.99 *(978-1-4413-2250-0(7)*, 373559c2-0438-4fd8-b7a0-d8bc7ccf4163) Peter Pauper Pr. Inc.

Peter Pauper Press Staff, creator. America: An Art Activity Book for Patriotic Artists & Explorers of All Ages. 2008. (Activity Book Ser.). (Illus.). 64p. (J). (gr. k-5). 12.99 *(978-1-59359-802-0(5))* Peter Pauper Pr. Inc.

—Garden Fairies: Scratch & Sketch: an Art Activity Book. 2007. (Activity Book Ser.). (Illus.). 64p. (J). (gr. 3-7). 12.99 *(978-1-59359-870-9(X))* Peter Pauper Pr. Inc.

Petruccio, Steven James. Create Your Own Dream Car Sticker Activity Book. 2006. (Dover Little Activity Books Stickers Ser.). (ENG., Illus.). 4p. (J). (gr. k-3). 1.99 *(978-0-486-44737-7(5)*, 447375) Dover Pubns., Inc.

—Create Your Own Fire Truck. 2010. (Dover Little Activity Books Stickers Ser.). (ENG., Illus.). 4p. (J). (gr. 1-4). 2.50 *(978-0-486-47548-6(4)*, 475484) Dover Pubns., Inc.

—Create Your Own Robot. 2006. (Dover Little Activity Books Stickers Ser.). (ENG., Illus.). 4p. (J). (gr. k-3). act. bk. ed. 1.99 *(978-0-486-44878-7(9)*, 448789) Dover Pubns., Inc.

—Let's Build a House! Coloring Book. 2017. (Dover Kids Coloring Bks.). (ENG.). 32p. (J). (gr. 1-4). pap. 3.99 *(978-0-486-81213-7(8)*, 812138) Dover Pubns., Inc.

Pfister, Marcus. Rainbow Fish Classroom Companion. 2017. (ENG., Illus.). 48p. (J). (gr. -1-3). pap., tchr. ed. 14.95 *(978-0-7358-4290-8(6))* North-South Bks., Inc.

Phillips, Dee. Big Zoo. 2009. (Flip Flap Fun Bks.). (ENG.). 5p. (J). (gr. -1-k). bds. 5.95 *(978-1-84696-086-4(X)*, TickTock Books) Octopus Publishing Group GBR. Dist: Independent Pubs. Group.

Phillips, Jillian. The World Around Us! Seeing. 2010. (Dover Science for Kids Coloring Bks.). (ENG., Illus.). 32p. (J). (gr. k-3). pap. 4.99 *(978-0-486-47731-2(2)*, 477312) Dover Pubns., Inc.

Phillips, Karen. Doodle Journal: My Life in Scribbles. 2010. (Illus.). 76p. (J). (gr. 3-18). 16.95 *(978-1-59174-736-9(8))* Klutz.

—The Truth about My Name: And What It Reveals about Me! 2010. 50p. (J). (gr. 3-18). 16.99 *(978-1-59174-855-7(0))* Klutz.

Phillips, Karen, ed. My All-Time Top 5: Make the Lists of Your Life. 2008. (Illus.). 60p. (J). (gr. 3-18). 16.95 *(978-1-59174-516-7(0))* Klutz.

Phoenix Books Staff, illus. Sofia the First Royal Picnic - Little Sound Book. 2014. 12p. (J). bds. 9.98 *(978-1-4508-7487-8(8)*, 0b73a7ef-ea68-4afb-b340-9a4f6fc740c0) Phoenix International Publications, Inc.

—Thomas' Piano Book. 2014. 14p. (J). bds. 12.98 *(978-1-4508-6584-5(4)*, 1450865844) Phoenix International Publications, Inc.

Phoenix International Staff, illus. Doc Mcstuffins the Doc Is in. 2014. 10p. (J). bds. 17.98 *(978-1-4508-8186-9(6)*, 1450881866) Phoenix International Publications, Inc.

—Thomas & the Telescope. 2014. 12p. (J). bds. 17.98 *(978-1-4508-7993-4(4)*, 1450879934) Phoenix International Publications, Inc.

PI Kids. Disney: Disney Junior Jake & the Neverland Pirates Sound Book. 2014. (ENG.). 6p. (J). bds. 7.99 *(978-1-4508-7763-3(X)*, 1605, PI Kids) Phoenix International Publications, Inc.

PI, Kids. Disney Junior Look & Find O/P. 2014. (ENG., Illus.). 24p. (J). 7.98 *(978-1-4508-8491-4(1)*, 1450884911) Phoenix International Publications, Inc.

PI Kids. Disney Minnie: Best Friends First Look & Find. Phillipson, Patricia, illus. 2014. (ENG.). 16p. (J). bds. 12.99 *(978-1-4508-7919-4(5)*, 1608, PI Kids) Phoenix International Publications, Inc.

—Disney Minnie: Best Friends Little First Look & Find. 2014. (ENG.). 24p. (J). bds. 5.99 *(978-1-4508-8351-1(6)*, 1638, PI Kids) Phoenix International Publications, Inc.

PI, Kids. LPIANO Little Piano Book Dora - O/P. 2014. (ENG.). 12p. (J). *(978-1-4508-7593-6(9)*, 1450875939) Publications International, Ltd.

PI Kids. Me Reader Disney Princess Me Reader: Electronic Reader & 8-Book Library. The Disney Storybook Art Team, illus. 2013. (ENG.). 192p. (J). (gr. k-4). 34.99 *(978-1-4508-6873-0(8)*, 1558, PI Kids) Phoenix International Publications, Inc.

—Nickelodeon Bubble Guppies: Little First Look & Find. Moore, Harry, illus. 2014. (ENG.). 24p. (J). bds. 5.99 *(978-1-4508-8347-4(8)*, 1636, PI Kids) Phoenix International Publications, Inc.

PI, Kids. Sesame Street at the Zoo Look & Fi- O/P. 2014. (ENG., Illus.). 24p. (J). 7.98 *(978-1-4508-8417-4(2)*, 1450884172) Phoenix International Publications, Inc.

PI Kids. Sesame Street: Elmo's Big Fire Truck Sound Book. Berry, Bob & Goldberg, Barry, illus. 2014. (ENG.). 12p. (J). bds. 23.99 *(978-1-4508-7442-7(8)*, 1583, PI Kids) Phoenix International Publications, Inc.

—Sesame Street: I Can Do It! First Look & Find. 2009. (ENG.). 16p. (J). bds. 12.99 *(978-1-4127-1706-9(X)*, 1349, PI Kids) Phoenix International Publications, Inc.

—Sesame Street: Trick or Treat with Elmo Sound Book. McGee, Warner & Goldberg, Barry, illus. 2009. (ENG.). 12p. (J). bds. 14.99 *(978-1-4127-7896-1(4)*, 12530, PI Kids) Phoenix International Publications, Inc.

Piano, Maureen. My Adventure to the Wonders of the World. 2006. 44p. (J). 8.99 *(978-1-59092-445-7(2))* Blue Forge Pr.

—My Adventure with Tidepools. 2009. (ENG.). 44p. (J). 8.99 *(978-1-59092-473-0(8))* Blue Forge Pr.

Pickett, Cheryl. Creation Inspirations: A New View of Your Neighborhood. 2013. 126p. pap. 14.95 *(978-0-9841855-1-1(8))* Brighter Day Publishing.

Picthall, Chez. My Bike. Gunzi, Christiane, ed. 2015. (ENG., Illus.). 20p. (J). pap. 6.50 *(978-1-906572-54-9(2))* Award Pubns. Ltd. GBR. Dist: Parkwest Pubns., Inc.

—My Favourite Racers Sticker Book. Rayner, Katy, ed. 2015. (Illus.). 20p. (J). pap. 7.99 *(978-1-906572-65-5(8))* Award Pubns. Ltd. GBR. Dist: Parkwest Pubns., Inc.

Pikachu Press, . Pokémon Super Activity Book: Do You Know Unova? 2012. (Pokemon Pikachu Press Ser.). (ENG.). 200p. (J). (gr. 3-6). act. bk. ed. 12.99 *(978-1-60438-156-6(6))* Pokemon, USA, Inc.

Pincock, Amy. Quiet Book Patterns. 2013. 14.99 *(978-1-4621-1245-6(5)*, Horizon Pubs.) Cedar Fort, Inc./CFI Distribution.

Pinder, Andrew, illus. The Boys' Doodle Book: Amazing Pictures to Complete & Create. 2008. (ENG.). 128p. (J). (gr. -1-17). pap. 12.95 *(978-0-7624-3506-7(2)*, Running Pr. Kids) Running Pr.

—The Girls' Doodle Book: Amazing Pictures to Complete & Create. 2008. (ENG.). 128p. (J). (gr. -1-17). pap. 12.95 *(978-0-7624-3505-0(4)*, Running Pr. Kids) Running Pr.

Pinestein Press. Abcs of Language & Literacy. Carroll, Raymond, illus. 2007. 180p. per. 19.99 *(978-0-9795364-4-1(8))* Chowder Bay Bks.

—Pre-K Prep! Carroll, Raymond, illus. 2007. 180p. per. 19.99 *(978-0-9795364-3-4(X))* Chowder Bay Bks.

Pinnington, Andrea. Creativity on the Go: Dragons. 2018. (Creativity on the Go Ser.). (ENG.). 80p. (J). (gr. 1-3). pap. 12.95 *(978-1-78312-173-1(4))* Carlton Kids GBR. Dist: Two Rivers Distribution.

—Creativity on the Go: Pirates. 2018. (Creativity on the Go Ser.). (ENG.). 80p. (J). (gr. 1-3). pap. 12.95 *(978-1-78312-176-2(9))* Carlton Kids GBR. Dist: Two Rivers Distribution.

Pitamic, Maja & Laidlaw, Jill. Fine Art Adventures: 36 Creative, Hands-On Projects Inspired by Classic Masterpieces. 2017. (Art Adventures Ser.). (ENG., Illus.). 144p. (J). (gr. 1). pap. 19.99 *(978-0-912777-04-7(4))* Chicago Review Pr., Inc.

Pitches, Neale & Hollingsworth, Toni. CSI Comprehensive Strategies Instruction Kit: Grade 6. 2008. (CSI). (gr. 6). 895.00 *(978-1-60457-111-0(X))* Pacific Learning, Inc.

Pivard, Gilles. Where Is Turold. 2012. (Illus.). 20p. *(978-2-8151-0107-3(6))* OREP Edition & Communication.

Pixton, Amy. Indestructibles: Things That Go! Chew Proof · Rip Proof · Nontoxic · 100% Washable (Book for Babies, Newborn Books, Vehicle Books, Safe to Chew) Lomp, Stephan, illus. 2017. (Indestructibles Ser.). (ENG.). 12p. (J). (gr. -1 — 1). pap. 5.99 *(978-0-7611-9362-3(6)*, 19362) Workman Publishing Co., Inc.

Playmobil & Buster Books Staff. The Official Playmobil Activity Book. 2014. (ENG.). 64p. (J). (gr. k-2). pap. 8.99 *(978-1-78055-302-3(1))* O'Mara, Michael Bks., Ltd. GBR. Dist: Independent Pubs. Group.

Plum, Joan Ensor & Plum, Paul S. I Am Special: Jesus Is Our Friend. Most, Andee, illus. 5th ed. 2007. 112p. (J). (gr. k-1). per. 11.95 *(978-1-59276-296-5(4))* Our Sunday Visitor, Publishing Div.

Polette, Nancy. A-Z Activities for the K-2 Student. 2005. (J). pap. 19.95 *(978-1-931334-71-6(4))* Pieces of Learning.

Polsky, Cheryl. Libby & Her Friends Explore Los Angeles, Californi. 2012. 28p. pap. 17.99 *(978-1-4772-2125-9(5))* AuthorHouse.

Poole, Helen, illus. My Jolly Red Santa Activity & Sticker Book. 2015. (ENG.). 32p. (J). (gr. -1-3). pap. 4.99 *(978-1-61963-791-7(X)*, 900148770, Bloomsbury Activity Bks.) Bloomsbury Publishing USA.

Poston, Valerie Williams, illus. ArbeZ ZebrA Teaches A to Z, 3 vols., Vol. 1. 2007. 33p. (J). spiral bd. 39.99 *(978-0-9779063-0-7(2))* Gain Literacy Skills / Lynette Gain Williams.

Potter, William. Dinosaur Activity Book. 2017. (ENG.). 96p. (J). pap. 9.99 *(978-1-78828-367-0(8)*, 9781788283670) Arcturus Publishing GBR. Dist: Baker & Taylor Publisher Services (BTPS).

Pratt, Leonie. Mermaid Things to Make & Do Kid Kit. 2005. 32p. (J). 15.99 *(978-1-58086-842-6(8)*, Usborne) EDC Publishing.

Press, Pikachu. Pokemon Felties: How to Make 16 of Your Favorite Pokemon. 2013. (ENG.). 80p. (J). (gr. 3-6). 14.99 *(978-1-60438-177-1(9))* Pokemon, USA, Inc.

Prestel. Botticelli: Coloring Book, 1 vol. 2016. (Coloring Bks.). (ENG.). 32p. (J). (gr. 1-4). pap. 8.95 *(978-3-7913-7227-3(0))* Prestel Verlag GmbH & Co KG. DEU. Dist: Penguin Random Hse. LLC.

Prestel Publishing, ed. Coloring Book Turner. 2012. (Coloring Bks.). (ENG.). 32p. (J). (gr. 1-4). pap. 8.95 *(978-3-7913-7090-3(1))* Prestel Verlag GmbH & Co KG. DEU. Dist: Penguin Random Hse. LLC.

Price, Roger & Stern, Leonard. Dance Mania Mad Libs: World's Greatest Word Game. 2009. (Mad Libs Ser.). 48p. (J). (gr. 3-7). 5.99 *(978-0-8431-3712-5(6)*, Mad Libs) Penguin Young Readers Group.

—Happily Ever Mad Libs: World's Greatest Word Game. 2010. (Mad Libs Ser.). 48p. (J). (gr. 3-7). 5.99 *(978-0-8431-9962-8(8)*, Mad Libs) Penguin Young Readers Group.

—Holly, Jolly Mad Libs: World's Greatest Word Game. 2009. (Mad Libs Ser.). (Illus.). 224p. (J). (gr. 3-7). 6.99 *(978-0-8431-8950-6(9)*, Mad Libs) Penguin Young Readers Group.

—Mad Libs Forever: World's Greatest Word Game. 2013. (Mad Libs Ser.). 240p. (J). (gr. 3-7). pap. 6.99 *(978-0-8431-7667-4(9)*, Mad Libs) Penguin Young Readers Group.

—Peace, Love, & Mad Libs: World's Greatest Word Game. 2009. (Mad Libs Ser.). 48p. (J). (gr. 3-7). 4.99 *(978-0-8431-8930-8(4)*, Mad Libs) Penguin Young Readers Group.

—The Wizard of Oz Mad Libs: World's Greatest Word Game. 2013. (Mad Libs Ser.). (ENG.). 48p. (J). (gr. 3-7). 5.99 *(978-0-8431-8017-6(X)*, Mad Libs) Penguin Young Readers Group.

Priddy, Roger. Alphaprints: Create Your Own: A Sticker & Doodle Activity Book. 2018. (Alphaprints Ser.). (ENG., Illus.). 78p. (J). spiral bd. 12.99 *(978-0-312-52544-6(3)*, 900180397) St. Martin's Pr.

—Busy Babies Words. 2010. 8p. (J). bds. 4.99 *(978-0-312-50854-8(9)*, Priddy Bks.) St. Martin's Pr.

—Dot to Dot for Tiny Tots Wipe Clean Activity Book. 2014. (Dot to Dot Ser.). (ENG.). 56p. (J). (gr. -1 — 1). spiral bd. 12.99 *(978-0-312-51772-4(6)*, 900137837) St. Martin's Pr.

—First 100 Stickers: First Numbers, Colors, Shapes. 2017. (First 100 Ser.). (ENG.). 80p. (J). pap. 9.99 *(978-0-312-52063-2(8)*, 900160377) St. Martin's Pr.

—First 100 Stickers: Trucks & Things That Go: Sticker Book, with over 500 Stickers. 2016. (First 100 Ser.). (ENG.). 80p. (J). pap. 9.99 *(978-0-312-52145-5(6)*, 900165282) St. Martin's Pr.

—Lift-The-tab: I Love You. 2015. (Lift-The-Flap Tab Bks.). (ENG., Illus.). 16p. (J). bds. 8.99 *(978-0-312-52032-8(8)*, 900158947) St. Martin's Pr.

—Mo Chéad Foclóir. Ó' Murchadha, Niall, tr. 2013. (GLE.). 10p. (J). 20.00 *(978-0-7171-5807-2(1))* M.H. Gill & Co. U. C. IRL. Dist: Dufour Editions, Inc.

—My Big Seek-And-Find Book: With Wipe-Clean Pen! 2018. (Seek-And-Find Ser.). (ENG., Illus.). 56p. (J). spiral bd. 12.99 *(978-0-312-52224-7(X)*, 900175689) St. Martin's Pr.

—My Giant Seek-And-Find Activity Book: More Than 200 Activities: Match It, Puzzles, Searches, Dot-To-Dot, Coloring, Mazes, & More! 2016. (Seek-And-Find Ser.). (ENG., Illus.). 200p. (J). pap. 11.99 *(978-0-312-52065-6(4)*, 900161688) St. Martin's Pr.

—Preschool Color & Activity Book: With Pictures to Color, Puzzle Fun, & More! 2011. (Color & Activity Bks.). (ENG., Illus.). 84p. (J). (gr. -1-k). pap. 6.99 *(978-0-312-51317-7(8)*, 900079572) St. Martin's Pr.

—Puzzle Play Set: MY PLAY FARM: Three Chunky Books & a Giant Jigsaw Puzzle! 2017. (First Learning Play Sets Ser.). (ENG., Illus.). 10p. (J). bds. 18.99 *(978-0-312-52662-7(8)*, 900186526) St. Martin's Pr.

—See, Touch, Feel: A First Sensory Book. 2018. (See, Touch, Feel Ser.). (ENG., Illus.). 16p. (J). bds. 12.99 *(978-0-312-52759-4(4)*, 900189944) St. Martin's Pr.

—Sticker Activity Animals: Over 100 Stickers with Coloring Pages. 2018. (Sticker Activity Fun Ser.). (ENG., Illus.). 32p. (J). pap. 5.99 *(978-0-312-52250-6(9)*, 900175594) St. Martin's Pr.

—Sticker Doodle Boo! Things That Go Boo! with over 200 Stickers. 2013. (Sticker Doodle Ser.). (ENG.). 120p. (J). (gr. k-3). pap. 6.99 *(978-0-312-51614-7(2)*, 900120433) St. Martin's Pr.

—Sticker Doodle I Love You: Awesome Things to Do, with over 200 Stickers. 2013. (Sticker Doodle Ser.). (ENG.). 120p. (J). (gr. k-3). pap. 6.99 *(978-0-312-51647-5(9)*, 900121774) St. Martin's Pr.

—Sticker Friends: Christmas: Over 300 Reusable Stickers. 2016. (Sticker Friends Ser.). (ENG.). 24p. (J). pap. 5.99 *(978-0-312-52050-2(6)*, 900159784) St. Martin's Pr.

—Stickerpedia: Packed with Fascinating Facts, Absorbing Activities & over 8000 Stickers! 2015. (Sticker Activity Fun Ser.). (ENG.). 148p. (J). (gr. k-3). pap. 12.99 *(978-0-312-51911-7(7)*, 900149115) St. Martin's Pr.

—Wipe Clean: Early Learning Activity Book. 2007. (Wipe Clean Activity Bks.). (ENG., Illus.). 56p. (J). (— 1). spiral bd. 12.95 *(978-0-312-49922-8(1)*, 900044254) St. Martin's Pr.

—Wipe Clean: My Big Activity Workbook. 2008. (Wipe Clean Ser.). (ENG., Illus.). 56p. (J). (gr. -1-k). spiral bd., wbk. ed. 12.99 *(978-0-312-50214-0(1)*, 900051303) St. Martin's Pr.

—Wipe Clean Workbook Numbers 1-20. 2010. (Wipe Clean Learning Bks.). (ENG.). 28p. (J). (gr. -1-1). spiral bd., wbk. ed. 7.99 *(978-0-312-50869-2(7)*, 900067917) St. Martin's Pr.

—Wipe Clean Workbook Tracing & Pen Control: Includes Wipe-Clean Pen. 2010. (Wipe Clean Learning Bks.). (ENG.). 26p. (J). (gr. -1-1). spiral bd., wbk. ed. 7.99 *(978-0-312-50870-8(0)*, 900067918) St. Martin's Pr.

Prothero, Tiffany. Let's Go Green! An Earth-Friendly Coloring Book. 2009. (Dover Nature Coloring Book Ser.). (ENG., Illus.). 32p. (J). (gr. -1-2). pap. 3.99 *(978-0-486-46817-4(8)*, 468178) Dover Pubns., Inc.

Pruett, Jason. Seek & Find: Book of Mormon Stories (Board Book) 2017. (ENG., Illus.). (gr. -1). bds. 12.99 *(978-1-4621-2099-4(7))* Cedar Fort, Inc./CFI Distribution.

Pruett, Mary, illus. Color the Western Birds: Discover the Great Outdoors. 2010. (Pruett Ser.). (ENG.). 32p. (J). pap. 5.99 *(978-0-87108-957-1(2)*, West Winds Pr.) West Margin Pr.

Publications International Ltd. Staff. Marvel Heroes Extreme Look & Find. 2014. 24p. (J). 9.98 *(978-1-4508-7263-8(8)*, 1450872638) Phoenix International Publications, Inc.

—Sesame Street: Say Cheese Elmo: Play-A-Sound Camera Book. 2013. 12p. (J). (gr. k-3). bds. 16.99 *(978-1-4508-3228-1(8)*, 72cb51f4-311b-45cb-87a5-a5d14e7b6c62) Phoenix International Publications, Inc.

—1St Look & Find Spiderman. 2009. 16p. (J). bds. 9.98 *(978-1-4127-7770-4(4))* Phoenix International Publications, Inc.

—1St Look & Find What's Different Tigger & Pooh. 2013. 12p. (J). (gr. -1-1). bds. 7.98 *(978-1-4127-1880-6(5)*, b9d2cf07-a5f4-4865-8cf4-66ad1cd9b1bf) Phoenix International Publications, Inc.

Publications International Ltd. Staff, creator. Disney Princess: the Little Mermaid: Play-A-Sound Book. 2013. (Illus.). 12p. (J). (gr. k-4). bds. 10.99 *(978-1-4508-6773-3(1)*, 18a3bf8b-49b6-41ec-8af3-9adb0da6460f) Phoenix International Publications, Inc.

—Look & Find: Disney Princess: the Little Mermaid. 2013. 24p. (J). (gr. 1-3). 7.98 *(978-1-4508-6996-6(3)*, 23104826-4b2a-459d-8edc-2f0362eaf16d) Phoenix International Publications, Inc.

—Sesame Street ABCs & 123s Wipe-off Activity Kit. 2007. (Wipe off Activity Kit Ser.). 14.98 *(978-1-4127-7442-0(X))* Publications International, Ltd.

—Tonka Wipe-off Activity Kit: ABCs And 123s. 2007. (Wipe off Activity Kit Ser.). 14.98 *(978-1-4127-7443-7(8))* Publications International, Ltd.

Publications International Ltd. Staff, ed. Abby Cadabby Fairy Tale Fun. 2009. 16p. (J). bds. 9.98 *(978-1-4127-1720-5(5)*, PIL Kids) Publications International, Ltd.

—Baby Einstein. 2007. (J). 9.98 *(978-1-4127-6695-1(8))* Phoenix International Publications, Inc.

—Dena Designs: My Doodles. 2011. 100p. (J). spiral bd. 13.98 *(978-1-4508-0990-0(1))* Publications International, Ltd.

—Disney Big Hero 6 Look & Find. 2014. 24p. (J). 7.98 *(978-1-4508-8381-8(8)*, 1450883818) Publications International, Ltd.

—Disney Classics Shaped Books. 2011. 8p. (J). bds. 4.98 *(978-1-4508-0909-2(X))* Publications International, Ltd.

—Disney Fairies: Best Friends Forever Scrapbook. 2011. 48p. (J). spiral bd. 11.98 *(978-1-60553-468-8(4))* Publications International, Ltd.

—Disney Jr. Sound Storybook Treasury. 2014. (Play-A-Sound Ser.). (ENG.). 36p. (J). bds. *(978-1-4508-7597-4(1)*, 07aff99a-94d0-4fb5-a4af-79dede796146) Phoenix International Publications, Inc.

—Disney(r) Junior Look & Find(r) Treasury: 4 Look & Find Books & 1 Big Volume. 2014. 72p. (J). *(978-1-4508-8355-9(9)*, 1450883559) Phoenix International Publications, Inc.

—Disney(r) Mickey Mouse Clubhouse Let's Explore: Take a Closer Look! a Magnifying Glass & Sound Book. 2014. 14p. (J). *(978-1-4508-7599-8(8)*, 1450875998) Phoenix International Publications, Inc.

—Disney(r) Mickey Mouse Clubhouse Silly Sing-Along: Sing High! Sing Low! Sing with an Echo! 2014. 14p. (J). *(978-1-4508-7604-9(8)*, ae256d2e-eb06-4361-9ac8-2e21277a9d86) Phoenix International Publications, Inc.

—Disney Minnie Let's Have a Tea Party: Play-A-Sound Book & Cuddly Minnie. 2014. 6p. (J). bds. 19.98 *(978-1-4508-7453-3(3)*, 3ed17924-bf5b-4c7a-b781-4089274afc8c) Phoenix International Publications, Inc.

—Disney Pixar. 2010. 64p. (J). pap. 10.98 *(978-1-60553-357-5(2)*, PIL Kids) Publications International, Ltd.

—Disney Pixar:Planes: 12 Board Book Block Set. 2014. 10p. (J). bds. 9.98 *(978-1-4508-7362-8(6)*, 1450873626) Phoenix International Publications, Inc.

—Disney Princess My Charming Life Deluxe Scrapbook. 2011. 48p. (J). spiral bd. 11.98 *(978-1-60553-469-5(2))* Publications International, Ltd.

—Disney(r) Sofia the First the Perfect Party: A Flashlight Adventure Sound Book. 2014. 14p. (J). 16.98 *(978-1-4508-7476-2(2)*, 31bc99fe-fde1-4d89-9e76-09c40bd0ccb5) Phoenix International Publications, Inc.

—Disney(r) Super Look & Find(r) Activity Pad: 100's of Find 'ems, Best-Loved Characters! Hidden Pictures! More Than 50 Stickers! 2014. 64p. (J). *(978-1-4508-8558-4(6)*, 1450885586) Publications International, Ltd.

—Dora the Explorer Ballerina Songs: Play-A-Sound Book & Huggable Dora. 2014. 6p. (J). bds. 19.98 *(978-1-4508-7449-6(5)*, 8127d4c1-9e76-4d4f-80b8-6c35da23c50a) Phoenix International Publications, Inc.

—Electronic Time for Learning: States. 2010. 120p. 18.98 *(978-1-4127-9853-2(1)*, PIL Kids) Publications International, Ltd.

—Hello Kitty(r); Hello Kitty's Guitar. 2014. 12p. (J). bds. 17.98 *(978-1-4508-7603-2(X)*, 145087603X) Phoenix International Publications, Inc.

—I Can Be a Princess: Picture Book. 2014. 22p. (J). bds. 4.98 *(978-1-4508-8582-9(9)*, 1450885829) Publications International, Ltd.

—Look & Find: Disney Princess: Winter Dreams. 2013. 24p. (J). (gr. 1-3). 7.99 *(978-1-4127-7695-0(3)*, 6d2a82ab-c0bb-4992-b098-a59561ffbf42) Phoenix International Publications, Inc.

—Mickey & Friends Look & Find Extreme. 2014. 24p. (J). 9.98 *(978-1-4508-8775-5(9)*, 1450887759) Publications International, Ltd.

—Mickey Mouse Clubhouse, What's Different? 2009. 24p. (J). 7.98 *(978-1-4127-1876-9(7),* PIL Kids) Publications International, Ltd.
—Minnie Mouse: Surprise, Surprise! Play-A-Sound Book. 2012. 10p. (J). (gr. k-3). bds. 7.99 *(978-1-4508-6848-8(7),* 0897e306-d7d1-4df0-a08f-afd88e1cfa82) Phoenix International Publications, Inc.
—My First Wipe-off: A to Z Animals Dictionary. 2010. 28p. (J). spiral bd. 7.98 *(978-1-4127-9386-5(6))* Phoenix International Publications, Inc.
—My Little Treasury Cuddle up Stories. 2014. 160p. (J). bds. *(978-1-4508-7282-9(4),* 1450872824) Phoenix International Publications, Inc.
—My Little Treasury My First Bible Stories. 2014. (Illus.). 160p. (J). bds. *(978-1-4508-7298-0(0),* 1450872980) Phoenix International Publications, Inc.
—Nickelodeon Dora the Explorer: Follow the Music: Piano Book. 2013. 14p. (J). bds. 16.98 *(978-1-4508-6380-3(9),* 355bc6ba-2b76-413c-bb3d-3975072deb9b) Phoenix International Publications, Inc.
—Out & About. 2010. 18p. (J). bds. 12.98 *(978-1-4127-4466-9(0),* PIL Kids) Publications International, Ltd.
—Sesame Write & Erase Board Book. 2014. 28p. (J). bds. 9.98 *(978-1-4508-8130-2(0),* 1450881300) Phoenix International Publications, Inc.
—Spongebob Squarepants. 2007. (J). 9.98 *(978-1-4127-6481-0(5))* Phoenix International Publications, Inc.
—Spongebob Squarepants Sea Mail. 2014. 6p. (J). bds. 19.98 *(978-1-4508-7454-0(1),* dcd91ed2-9e34-4ce7-b781-6a9ed2ae624a) Phoenix International Publications, Inc.
—Sunshine Doodle Book. Designs, Dena, illus. 2016. 80p. (J). spiral bd. *(978-1-68022-410-8(7),* 1680224107, PIL Kids) Publications International, Ltd.
—Super Fun Sticker Activities: More Than 1,000 Stickers! 2014. 64p. (J). pap. *(978-1-4508-3188-8(5),* 1450831885) Publications International, Ltd.
—Thomas Celebration Pop Up Sound. 2010. 14p. 19.98 *(978-1-4127-4513-0(6))* Publications International, Ltd.
—Write-And-Erase Look & Find(r) Disney Minnie: Packed with 'find 'ems & Picture Puzzles! Look, Circle, Wipe Clean, & Play Again! 2014. 28p. (J). bds. 9.98 *(978-1-4508-7918-7(7),* 1450879187) Phoenix International Publications, Inc.
Publishing, Autumn. I Want to Color BIG Pictures. 2009. 80p. pap. 12.99 *(978-1-60095-389-7(1))* Carson-Dellosa Publishing, LLC.
Puffin. 100 Iconic Postcards. 2019. 100p. 29.95 *(978-0-241-35196-3(0))* Penguin Random Hse. AUS. Dist: Independent Pubs. Group.
Pulley, Kelly. The Beginner's Bible a Christmas Celebration Sticker & Activity Book, 1 vol. 2015. (Beginner's Bible Ser.). (ENG.). 16p. (J). pap. 8.99 *(978-0-310-74670-6(1))* Zonderkidz.
—The Beginner's Bible Super Heroes of the Bible Sticker & Activity, 1 vol. 2015. (Beginner's Bible Ser.). (ENG., Illus.). 16p. (J). pap. 7.99 *(978-0-310-74751-2(1))* Zonderkidz.
Racknor & Morrow. Wordszart. 2011. 92p. pap. 29.99 *(978-0-557-55589-5(2))* Lulu Pr., Inc.
Radtke, Becky. Fairy Tales. 2004. (Dover Little Activity Bks.). (ENG., Illus.). 64p. (J). (gr. 3-5). pap., act. bk. ed. 1.50 *(978-0-486-43854-2(6))* Dover Pubns., Inc.
—Going Green! Activity Book. 2009. (Dover Little Activity Bks.). (ENG.). 64p. (J). (gr. 3-5). pap. 1.99 *(978-0-486-46810-5(0))* Dover Pubns., Inc.
—Keep the Scene Green! Earth-Friendly Activities. 2010. (Dover Children's Activity Bks.). (ENG., Illus.). 30p. (J). (gr. 1-5). pap. 3.99 *(978-0-486-47534-9(4))* Dover Pubns., Inc.
—Trains Activity Book. 2007. (Dover Little Activity Bks.). (ENG., Illus.). 64p. (J). (gr. k-3). per. 2.50 *(978-0-486-45683-6(8),* 456838) Dover Pubns., Inc.
Radtke, Becky J. All about Marvelous Me! A Draw & Write Journal. 2014. (Dover Kids Activity Bks.). (ENG.). 64p. (J). (gr. 1-4). pap. 5.99 *(978-0-486-78626-1(9),* 786269) Dover Pubns., Inc.
—BOOST Keep the Scene Green! Earth-Friendly Activities. 2013. (Dover Kids Activity Books: Nature Ser.). (ENG.). 32p. (J). (gr. 1-2). pap. 4.99 *(978-0-486-49417-3(9),* 494179) Dover Pubns., Inc.
—Christmas Color by Number. 2015. (Dover Christmas Coloring Bks.). (ENG.). 32p. (J). (gr. -1-2). pap. 3.99 *(978-0-486-80051-6(2),* 800512) Dover Pubns., Inc.
—Four Seasons of Fun Activity Book. 2013. (ENG.). 48p. (J). (gr. 1-4). pap. 4.99 *(978-0-486-49894-2(8))* Dover Pubns., Inc.
—Hooray for the USA! Activity Book. 2016. (Dover Little Activity Bks.). (ENG.). 64p. (J). (gr. -1-3). pap. 1.99 *(978-0-486-80780-5(0),* 807800) Dover Pubns., Inc.
—Unicorns Awesome Activity Book. 2018. (Dover Kids Activity Books: Fantasy Ser.). (ENG.). 48p. (J). (gr. 1-4). pap. 4.99 *(978-0-486-82807-7(7),* 828077) Dover Pubns., Inc.
Rand McNally, creator. Kids' Backseat Travel Kit. 2015. (ENG.). (J). (gr. 4-7). pap. 19.99 *(978-0-528-01327-0(0))* Rand McNally.
Random House. My Blue Railway Box Box (Thomas & Friends) 2017. (Bright & Early Board Books(TM) Ser.). (ENG., Illus.). 96p. (J). (— 1). bds. 14.99 *(978-1-5247-7224-6(0),* Random Hse. Bks. for Young Readers) Random Hse. Children's Bks.
Rankie, Barbara. Subtraction Unplugged, 2 vols. 2nd ed. 2013. (ENG.). 64p. 19.95 *(978-1-55386-217-8(1),* 1553862171) Jordan, Sara Publishing.
Ransom, Sharon L., ed. Cocurricular Activities: Their Values & Benefits, 11 vols. 2005. (Illus.). 64p. (YA). lib. bdg. 219.45 *(978-1-59084-888-3(8))* Mason Crest.
Ranson, Erin. Under the Sea. Green, Barry, illus. 2007. (Magnetic Story & Play Scene Ser.). (ENG.). 8p. (J). (gr. -1-1). 9.99 *(978-1-84666-089-4(0))* Top That! Publishing PLC GBR. Dist: Independent Pubs. Group.
Rasinski, Timothy V. Daily Word Ladders: Grades 1-2 Grades 1-2. 2008. (ENG.). 176p. (gr. 1-2). pap. 19.99 *(978-0-545-07476-6(2),* Teaching Resources) Scholastic, Inc.
Rasmussen, R. Kent. World War I for Kids: A History with 21 Activities. 2014. (For Kids Ser.: 50). (ENG., Illus.). 192p. (J). (gr. 4). pap. 19.99 *(978-1-61374-556-4(7))* Chicago Review Pr., Inc.
Reader, Jenny. Girl 2 Girl: The Swap Book You Share with Your Friends. Martin, Caroline & Davies, Nic, illus. 2003. 96p. (J). pap. *(978-0-439-56743-5(2))* Scholastic, Inc.
Regan, Lisa & Webb, Trudi. Caveman Capers Activity Fun. Green, Barry, illus. 2019. (Dover Kids Activity Bks.). (ENG.). 48p. (J). (gr. 1-4). pap. 7.99 *(978-0-486-83291-3(0),* 832910) Dover Pubns., Inc.
—Magical Fairies Activity Fun. Green, Barry, illus. 2019. (Dover Children's Activity Bks.). (ENG.). 48p. (J). (gr. 1-4). pap. 7.99 *(978-0-486-83292-0(9),* 832929) Dover Pubns., Inc.
—Pirates Ahoy! Activity Fun. Green, Barry, illus. 2019. (Dover Kids Activity Books: Fantasy Ser.). (ENG.). 48p. (J). (gr. 1-4). pap. 7.99 *(978-0-486-83293-7(7),* 832937) Dover Pubns., Inc.
—Playful Ponies Activity Fun. Green, Barry, illus. 2019. (Dover Kids Activity Books: Animals Ser.). (ENG.). 48p. (J). (gr. 1-4). pap. 7.99 *(978-0-486-83297-5(X),* 83297X) Dover Pubns., Inc.
Reilly, Kathleen M. Cities: Discover How They Work. Casteel, Tom, illus. 2014. (Build It Yourself Ser.). (ENG.). 128p. (J). (gr. 3-7). 21.95 *(978-1-61930-213-6(6),* 3bf37164-7d80-4de7-89dc-d2661fce5554) Nomad Pr.
Rettore, Kenny. At the Beach. Ferri, Francesca, illus. 2018. 8p. (J). (gr. -1 — 1). 6.99 *(978-1-4380-7862-5(5))* Sourcebooks, Inc.
Reynolds, Peter H. Big Screen Books: For Big Fans of Story Sharing: the Dot Download: the Dot - Download. 2011. (J). cd-rom 29.95 *(978-1-891405-71-6(3))* FableVision Pr.
—The Dot: Make Your Mark Kit, 2 vols. Reynolds, Peter H., illus. 2013. (Creatrilogy Ser.). (ENG., Illus.). 56p. (J). (gr. k-4). 24.99 *(978-0-7636-6978-2(4))* Candlewick Pr.
Rhatigan, Joe. All You Need Is a Pencil: the Totally Hilarious All about America Activity Book. 2016. (All You Need Is a Pencil Ser.: 3). (Illus.). 144p. (J). (gr. 2-5). pap. 7.95 *(978-1-62354-076-0(3))* Charlesbridge Publishing, Inc.
—All You Need Is a Pencil: the Weird, Wacky, & Unusual Activity Book. 2016. (All You Need Is a Pencil Ser.: 4). (Illus.). 144p. (J). (gr. 2-5). pap. 7.95 *(978-1-62354-077-7(1))* Charlesbridge Publishing, Inc.
Rhodes, Immacula A. Little Learners Packets: Basic Concepts. 2018. (Little Learner Packets Ser.). (ENG.). 96p. (gr. -1-k). pap. 12.99 *(978-1-338-23031-4(X))* Scholastic, Inc.
Rhodes, Karen. Do You Know Jesus? 2005. (J). pap. 1.79 *(978-1-59317-111-7(0))* Warner Pr., Inc.
Richardson, Sarah. Art in a Box. 2011. (ENG., Illus.). 20p. (J). (gr. k-6). 21.95 *(978-1-85437-927-6(5))* Tate Publishing, Ltd. GBR. Dist: Abrams, Inc.
richmond, keli. Literacy Speaks 2. 2008. (J). pap. 197.00 *(978-0-9799245-5-2(3))* Northern Speech Services.
Riley, Margaret. Crafty Parties for Kids: Creative Ideas, Invitations, Games, Favors, & More. 2013. (ENG., Illus.). 32p. pap. 9.99 *(978-1-57421-353-9(9),* DO3476, Design Originals) Fox Chapel Publishing Co., Inc.
Rising Moon, creator. The Great Colorado Activity Book. 2007. (ENG., Illus.). 56p. (J). (gr. 1-5). pap. 7.95 *(978-0-87358-921-5(1))* Cooper Square Publishing Llc.
Rivera, Mirabelle. What is your favorite Color? 2008. 20p. pap. 24.95 *(978-1-4241-8454-5(1))* America Star Bks.
Rivers-Moore, Debbie & Davis, Caroline. In the Ocean. 2017. (ENG.). 8p. (J). (gr. -1 — 1). 5.99 *(978-1-4380-7828-1(5))* Sourcebooks, Inc.
RiverStream Readers - Level 1. 2013. (RiverStream Readers Ser.: 1). 124p. (gr. -1-2). 11.49 *(978-1-62588-901-0(1))* Black Rabbit Bks.
RiverStream Readers - Level 2. 2013. (RiverStream Readers Ser.: 2). 124p. (gr. -1-2). 11.49 *(978-1-62588-902-7(X))* Black Rabbit Bks.
RiverStream Readers - Level 3. 2013. (RiverStream Readers Ser.: 3). 124p. (gr. -1-2). 11.49 *(978-1-62588-903-4(8))* Black Rabbit Bks.
RiverStream Readers - Pre-1. 2013. (RiverStream Readers Ser.: PK). 124p. (gr. -1-2). 11.49 *(978-1-62588-900-3(3))* Black Rabbit Bks.
Robertson, Robbin Davis. The Sneaky Shoe Bug. Sexton, Jessa R., ed. Keaggy, Sarah, illus. 2012. 44p. 16.00 *(978-0-9860150-4-5(0))* O'More Publishing.
Robles Echeverria, Maria De Jesus & ALONSO CURIEL, Jorge David. Paisaje de Risas. DIVINCENZO, Yoselem G., illus. 2013. 72p. pap. 14.99 *(978-1-61196-924-5(7))* Pintos, Yoselem G.
Robson, Kirsteen. Aliens Sticker Book. Burnett, Seb, illus. 2014. (Usborne Activities Ser.). (ENG.). 22p. (J). 8.99 *(978-0-7945-3101-0(6),* Usborne) EDC Publishing.
—Wipe-Clean Pirate Activities. 2015. (Wipe-Clean Bks.). (ENG.). 22p. (J). (gr. k-5). pap. 7.99 *(978-0-7945-3543-8(7),* Usborne) EDC Publishing.
—Wipe-Clean Vacation Activities. 2015. (Wipe-Clean Bks.). (ENG.). 22p. (J). (gr. k-5). pap. 7.99 *(978-0-7945-3480-6(5),* Usborne) EDC Publishing.
Robson, Kirsten. Big Maze Book. 2013. (Doodle Bks). 64p. (J). pap. 9.99 *(978-0-7945-3345-8(0),* Usborne) EDC Publishing.
Rock Spring Elementary. Roadrunner Writing Rocks! 2013. 210p. pap. 15.00 *(978-0-9859367-2-3(X))* Pen & Publish, LLC.
Roeder, Annette. The Art Coloring Book. 2018. (Coloring Bks.). (ENG.). 128p. (J). (gr. -1-3). pap. 12.95 *(978-3-7913-7362-1(5))* Prestel Verlag GmbH & Co KG. DEU. Dist: Penguin Random Hse. LLC.
—Coloring Book Vincent Van Gogh. 2009. (Coloring Bks.). (ENG.). 32p. (J). (gr. 1-4). pap. 8.95 *(978-3-7913-4331-0(9))* Prestel Verlag GmbH & Co KG. DEU. Dist: Penguin Random Hse. LLC.
Rogers, Kirsteen. Haunted House Sticker Book. 2012. (Sticker Activity Book Ser.). 24p. (J). pap. 8.99 *(978-0-7945-3163-8(6),* Usborne) EDC Publishing.
—Monsters Sticker Book. 2012. (Sticker Activity Book Ser.). 34p. (J). pap. 8.99 *(978-0-7945-3325-0(6),* Usborne) EDC Publishing.
Rogge, Robie. Peekaboo! Stroller Cards: in the Forest. White, Teagan, illus. 2017. (ENG.). 10p. (J). (gr. -1 — 1). 9.99 *(978-1-4521-5384-1(1))* Chronicle Bks. LLC.
Romeo & Juliet: Activity Pack. 2003. 130p. (YA). pap. *(978-1-58049-621-6(0),* PA0126) Prestwick Hse., Inc.
Romero, Kyle & Padron, Maria Lorena. Herbert Hoover Junior Ranger Activity Book. National Park Service Staff & Herbert Hoover National Historic Site (U.S), eds. 2013. (ENG., Illus.). 15p. (J). 6.00 *(978-0-16-092067-7(1))* National Park Service Div. of Pubns.
Rookie Ready to Learn - All about Me!, 5 vols., Set. Incl. Being Me. Broski, Julie. Vigla, Vincent, illus. 40p. lib. bdg. 23.00 *(978-0-531-26428-7(9));* Generous Me. Pearson, Mary E. Krejca, Gary, illus. 40p. lib. bdg. 25.00 *(978-0-531-26427-0(0));* I Need a Little Help. Schulz, Kathy. Iosa, Ann, illus. 32p. lib. bdg. 25.00 *(978-0-531-26526-0(9));* Just Like Me. Neasi, Barbara J. Hantel, Johanna, illus. 40p. lib. bdg. 25.00 *(978-0-531-26371-6(1));* Paul the Pitcher. Sharp, Paul, illus. 40p. lib. bdg. 18.69 *(978-0-531-26426-3(2));* (J). (gr. -1-1). 2011. (Rookie Ready to Learn Ser.). 2011. Set lib. bdg. 115.00 *(978-0-531-28350-9(X),* Children's Pr.) Scholastic Library Publishing.
Ross, Suzanne. BOOST Rain Forest Activity Book. 2013. (Dover Kids Activity Books: Nature Ser.). (ENG.). 48p. (J). (gr. 1-2). pap. 5.99 *(978-0-486-49413-5(6),* 494136) Dover Pubns., Inc.
Rouss, Sylvia A. Sammy Spider's Shabbat Fun Book. Kahn, Katherine Janus, illus. 2006. (ENG.). 24p. (J). (gr. -1-3). pap. 4.95 *(978-1-58013-147-6(6),* eb304561-bd0d-4f76-bed1-71868397c6cb, Kar-Ben Publishing) Lerner Publishing Group.
Roytman, Arkady. Secret Agent Sticker Activity. 2009. (Dover Little Activity Books Stickers Ser.). (ENG., Illus.). 4p. (J). (gr. k-3). 1.50 *(978-0-486-47136-5(5),* 471365) Dover Pubns., Inc.
—Treasures of King Tut's Tomb Stained Glass Coloring Book. 2009. (Dover Stained Glass Coloring Book Ser.). (ENG., Illus.). 32p. (J). (gr. -1-5). pap. 6.99 *(978-0-486-46996-6(4))* Dover Pubns., Inc.
Roytman, Arkady, et al. Build a 3-D Poster Coloring Book — Outer Space. 2012. (Dover 3-D Coloring Book Ser.). (ENG.). 16p. (J). (gr. 3-5). pap. 5.99 *(978-0-486-49831-7(X),* 49831X) Dover Pubns., Inc.
Running Press, ed. Frozen: Melting Olaf the Snowman Kit. Running Press, . 2015. (RP Minis Ser.). (ENG., Illus.). 32p. pap. 12.95 *(978-0-7624-5740-3(6),* Running Pr. Minature Editions) Running Pr.
—Scratch & Stencil: Ponies. Running Press, . 2013. (ENG.). 24p. (J). (gr. -1-17). pap. 12.95 *(978-0-7624-5215-6(3),* Running Pr. Kids) Running Pr.
Rupp, Cecelia, ed. How to Be #1 Kid at Table Manners: Activity Book. 2012. (ENG.). pap. 44.95 *(978-1-4675-3185-6(5))* Independent Pub.
Ruth, Angie. My Adventure Bug Collecting. 2006. 44p. (J). 8.99 *(978-1-59092-448-8(7))* Blue Forge Pr.
—My Adventure in the Snow. 2006. 44p. (J). 8.99 *(978-1-59092-435-8(5))* Blue Forge Pr.
Sabatino, Chris. City Doodles: Boston. 2013. (ENG., Illus.). 240p. (J). pap. 9.99 *(978-1-4236-3207-8(9))* Gibbs Smith, Publisher.
—Pocketdoodles for Boys, 1 vol. 2010. (ENG.). 272p. (J). (gr. 1). 9.99 *(978-1-4236-0756-4(2))* Gibbs Smith, Publisher.
—Superhero Doodles for Kids, 1 vol. 2012. (ENG., Illus.). 272p. (J). pap. 9.99 *(978-1-4236-2483-7(1))* Gibbs Smith, Publisher.
Sachse, Dina, illus. My Body: 12 Lift-N-Learn Flashcards about the Human Body, 12 vols. 2013. (Early Start Singles Ser.). (ENG.). 12p. (J). *(978-1-77132-070-2(2))* SpiceBox Products Ltd.
—My Clothes: 12 Lift-N-Learn Flashcards about Clothes, 26 vols. 2013. (Early Start Singles Ser.). (ENG.). 12p. (J). *(978-1-77132-101-3(6))* SpiceBox Products Ltd.
—My Food: 12 Lift-N-Learn Flashcards about Food!, 26 vols. 2013. (Early Start Singles Ser.). (ENG.). 12p. (J). *(978-1-77132-102-0(4))* SpiceBox Products Ltd.
Sage, Alison. Stop That Robot!: Band 00/Lilac (Collins Big Cat) Dunn, Gary, illus. 2007. (Collins Big Cat Ser.). (ENG.). 16p. (J). (gr. -1-k). pap. 6.99 *(978-0-00-718678-5(9))* HarperCollins Pubs. Ltd. GBR. Dist: Independent Pubs. Group.
Saint Mary's Press Staff. Lesson in a Bag-Reconciliation Lesson 6. 2012. (ENG.). 26.99 *(978-1-59982-403-1(5))* Saint Mary's Press of Minnesota.
—Lesson in a Bag-Reconciliation Lesson 7. 2012. (ENG.). 26.99 *(978-1-59982-404-8(3))* Saint Mary's Press of Minnesota.
—Lesson in a Bag-Reconciliation Lesson 8. 2012. (ENG.). 26.99 *(978-1-59982-405-5(1))* Saint Mary's Press of Minnesota.
Salch, Megan. 100+ Activities for Houston Kids 2006. 2005. (Illus.). 40p. pap. 19.95 *(978-0-9776154-0-7(5))* Salch, Megan F.
Salzmann, Mary Elizabeth. Money for School, 1 vol. 2010. (Your Piggy Bank: a Guide to Spending & Saving for Kids! Ser.). (ENG.). 24p. (J). (gr. k-4). 31.36 *(978-1-61641-031-5(0),* 15844, Looking Glass Library) Magic Wagon.
Sanchez, John Joseph P. Illuminating the Legacy: A Coloring & Activity Book of the CNMI's History. Ogo, Luis S., illus. 2006. 106p. (J). (gr. 4-5). pap. *(978-1-878453-89-1(0))* Univ. of Guam, Micronesian Area Research Ctr.
Samat, Marjorie. Creative Cats Stickers. 2016. (Dover Little Activity Bks.). (ENG., Illus.). 4p. 1.99 *(978-0-486-80703-4(7),* 807037) Dover Pubns., Inc.
Sayre, April Pulley. The Slowest Book Ever. Murphy, Kelly, illus. 2016. (ENG.). 176p. (J). (gr. 3-7). 16.95 *(978-1-62091-783-1(1),* Astra Young Readers) Astra Publishing Hse.
Sazaklis, John. Design & Draw. 2012. (Dark Knight Rises Ser.). (ENG.). 64p. (J). (gr. -1-3). pap., act. bk. ed. 6.99 *(978-0-06-213226-0(1),* HarperFestival) HarperCollins Pubs.
Schab, Lisa M. Cool, Calm, Confident: A Workbook to Help Kids Learn Assertiveness Skills. 2009. (ENG.). 184p. (J). (gr. k-5). pap. 18.95 *(978-1-57224-630-0(8),* 6300, Instant Help Books) New Harbinger Pubns.
Schmitt, Conrad. ¡Así Se Dice! 2009. (Glencoe Spanish Ser.). (SPA.). 160p. (gr. 6-12). pap., wbk. ed. 23.20 *(978-0-07-892935-9(0),* 0078929350) McGraw-Hill Education.
—Asi Se Dice 2009, Level 1A. 2009. (Glencoe Spanish Ser.). (SPA.). 160p. (gr. 6-12). pap., wbk. ed. 23.20 *(978-0-07-892934-2(2),* 0078929342) McGraw-Hill Education.
Scholastic. Accents: Color Your Classroom! 2017. (Color Your Classroom Ser.). (ENG.). (gr. -1-6). 6.99 *(978-1-338-12796-6(9))* Teacher's Friend Pubns., Inc.
—Color Your Classroom! Birthdays. 2017. (Color Your Classroom Ser.). (ENG.). (gr. -1-6). 3.49 *(978-1-338-12800-0(0))* Teacher's Friend Pubns., Inc.
—Color Your Classroom! Welcome. 2017. (Color Your Classroom Ser.). (ENG.). (gr. -1-6). 3.49 *(978-1-338-12799-7(3))* Teacher's Friend Pubns., Inc.
—Early Learning: Ready to Read. 2018. (ENG.). 256p. (gr. -1-1). pap. 9.99 *(978-1-338-32317-7(2))* Scholastic, Inc.
—Early Learning Sticker Workbook. 2015. (Scholastic Early Learners Ser.). (ENG.). 104p. (J). (gr. -1-k). 9.99 *(978-0-545-90335-6(1),* Cartwheel Bks.) Scholastic, Inc.
—First Grade Wipe-Clean Workbook: Scholastic Early Learners (Wipe-Clean) 2015. (Scholastic Early Learners Ser.). (ENG.). 56p. (J). (gr. k-2). bds. 9.99 *(978-0-545-90327-1(0),* Cartwheel Bks.) Scholastic, Inc.
—Get Ready for Pre-K Jumbo Workbook: Scholastic Early Learners (Jumbo Workbook) 2018. (Scholastic Early Learners Ser.). (ENG.). 240p. (J). (gr. -1-k). pap. 12.99 *(978-1-338-29179-7(3),* Cartwheel Bks.) Scholastic, Inc.
—Harry Potter Magical Creatures Postcard Coloring Book. 2016. (ENG.). 40p. (J). (gr. 3). pap. 9.99 *(978-1-338-05459-0(7))* Scholastic, Inc.
—Harry Potter Magical Places & Characters Coloring Book: The Official Coloring Book. 2016. (ENG.). 96p. (J). (gr. 3). pap. 15.99 *(978-1-338-03001-3(9))* Scholastic, Inc.
—Harry Potter Magical Places & Characters Poster Coloring Book. 2016. (ENG.). 40p. (J). (gr. 3). pap. 24.99 *(978-1-338-13292-2(X))* Scholastic, Inc.
—Kindergarten Jumbo Workbook: Scholastic Early Learners (Jumbo Workbook) 2018. (Scholastic Early Learners Ser.). (ENG.). 240p. (J). (gr. -1-3). pap. 12.99 *(978-1-338-29216-9(1),* Cartwheel Bks.) Scholastic, Inc.
—Kindergarten Wipe-Clean Workbook: Scholastic Early Learners (Wipe-Clean Workbook) 2015. (Scholastic Early Learners Ser.). (ENG.). 56p. (J). (gr. -1 — 1). bds., wbk. ed. 9.99 *(978-0-545-90326-4(2),* Cartwheel Bks.) Scholastic, Inc.
—Pre-K Wipe-Clean Workbook: Scholastic Early Learners (Wipe-Clean) 2015. (Scholastic Early Learners Ser.). Tr. of Included Wipe Clean Pen. (ENG.). 56p. (J). (gr. -1 — 1). bds., wbk. ed. 9.99 *(978-0-545-90324-0(6),* Cartwheel Bks.) Scholastic, Inc.
—Sight Word Tales, 1 vol. 2008. (ENG.). (gr. k-2). pap., pap., pap. 82.99 *(978-0-545-01642-1(8))* Scholastic, Inc.
—Weekly Reader: Summer Express: Between Grades 1 And 2, 1 vol. 2017. (Weekly Reader: Summer Express Ser.). (ENG., Illus.). 144p. (J). (gr. 1-2). pap., pap., pap. 12.99 *(978-1-338-10890-3(5))* Scholastic, Inc.
—Weekly Reader: Summer Express: Between Grades 2 And 3, 1 vol. 2017. (Weekly Reader: Summer Express Ser.). (ENG., Illus.). 144p. (J). (gr. 2-3). pap., wbk. ed. 12.99 *(978-1-338-10891-0(3))* Scholastic, Inc.
—Weekly Reader: Summer Express: Between Grades 3 And 4, 1 vol. 2017. (Weekly Reader: Summer Express Ser.). (ENG., Illus.). 144p. (J). (gr. 3-4). pap., pap. 12.99 *(978-1-338-10892-7(1))* Scholastic, Inc.
—Weekly Reader: Summer Express: Between Grades K And 1, 1 vol. 2017. (Weekly Reader: Summer Express Ser.). (ENG., Illus.). 144p. (J). (gr. k-1). pap., pap., pap. 12.99 *(978-1-338-10889-7(1))* Scholastic, Inc.
—Weekly Reader: Summer Express: Between Grades PreK & K, 1 vol. 2017. (Weekly Reader: Summer Express Ser.). (ENG., Illus.). 144p. (J). (gr. -1-k). pap., pap., pap. 12.99 *(978-1-338-10888-0(3))* Scholastic, Inc.
—Write & Wipe ABC 123: Scholastic Early Learners (Write & Wipe) 2015. (Scholastic Early Learners Ser.). (ENG.). 28p. (J). (gr. -1-k). bds. 8.99 *(978-0-545-90640-1(7),* Cartwheel Bks.) Scholastic, Inc.
Scholastic Early Learners Staff. Lift the Flap: Look Who's Talking! 2018. (Scholastic Early Learners Ser.). (ENG.). 14p. (J). (gr. -1 — 1). bds. 14.99 *(978-1-338-28396-9(0),* Cartwheel Bks.) Scholastic, Inc.
Scholastic Early Learners Staff & Scholastic. Trace, Play, & Learn: ABC 123 (Scholastic Early Learners) 2015. (Scholastic Early Learners Ser.). (ENG.). 12p. (J). (gr. -1 — 1). 12.99 *(978-0-545-90313-4(0),* Cartwheel Bks.) Scholastic, Inc.
Scholastic, Inc. Staff. Clifford Forever Friends. 2008. 29.99 *(978-0-439-93520-3(2))* Scholastic, Inc.
Scholastic Library Publishing. Rookie Ready to Learn, 30 vols., Set. Incl. Set. Rookie Ready to Learn - All about Me! (gr. -1-k). lib. bdg. 115.00 *(978-0-531-28350-9(X));* Set. Rookie Ready to Learn - Animals. (gr. k-3). lib. bdg. 115.00 *(978-0-531-27450-7(0));* Set. Rookie Ready to Learn - First Science: Me & My World. (gr. -1-k). lib. bdg. 115.00 *(978-0-531-23850-9(4));* Set. Rookie Ready to Learn - I Can! (gr. -1-k). lib. bdg. 115.00 *(978-0-531-25150-8(0));* Set. Rookie Ready to Learn - My Family & Friends. (gr. -1-k). lib. bdg. 115.00 *(978-0-531-24450-0(4));* Set. Rookie Ready to Learn - Numbers & Shapes. (gr. -1-k). lib. bdg. 115.00 *(978-0-531-24300-8(1));* Set. Rookie Ready to Learn - Out & About: In My Community. (gr. -1-k). lib. bdg. 115.00 *(978-0-531-25905-4(6));* Set. Rookie Ready to Learn - Seasons & Weather. (gr. -1-k). lib. bdg. 115.00 *(978-0-531-26724-0(5));* (J). 2011. 2011. Set lib. bdg. 920.00 *(978-0-531-29149-8(9),* Children's Pr.) Scholastic Library Publishing.
—A True Book-Experiments. 2011. (True Book-Experiments Ser.). (J). 174.00 *(978-0-531-20912-7(1),* Children's Pr.) Scholastic Library Publishing.
—A True Book-Physical Science. 2011. (True Book-Physical Science Ser.). (J). 174.00 *(978-0-531-25935-1(8),* Children's Pr.) Scholastic Library Publishing.
Scholastic Teaching Resources. Preschool Basic Skills: Fine-Motor & Scissor Skills. 2012. (Preschool Basic Skills Ser.). (ENG., Illus.). 48p. (gr. -1 — 1). pap. 6.99 *(978-0-545-42966-5(8))* Teacher's Friend Pubns., Inc.
School Activities: Actividades Escolares, 10 vols. 2003. (School Activities / Actividades Escolares Ser.). (ENG & SPA., Illus.). (J). (gr. 1-2). lib. bdg. 131.35 *(978-0-8239-6910-4(X),* 135b4c6f-cc6b-4302-96b5-dbc288d50f9f, Editorial Buenas Letras) Rosen Publishing Group, Inc., The.
School, Blue Mountain. Colored Pencils. 2013. 26p. pap. 6.99 *(978-1-61720-891-1(4))* Wilder Pubns., Corp.

S

School Zone. Animal Alphabet. 2008. (ENG.). 26p. (J). 5.99 (978-1-58947-932-6(7)) School Zone Publishing Co.

School Zone Interactive Staff. Dot-to-Dots. Boyer, Robin, illus. 2006. (ENG.). 64p. (J). (gr. 1-2). 7.99 (978-1-58947-302-7(7)) School Zone Publishing Co.

—Hidden Pictures. Sullivan, Mary, illus. rev. ed. 2006. (ENG.). 64p. (J). (gr. 1-2). 7.99 (978-1-58947-301-0(9)) School Zone Publishing Co.

School Zone Staff. Big Hidden Pictures & More. 2019. (ENG.). 320p. (J). (gr. k-2). pap. 13.99 (978-1-60159-258-3(2), 3280724e-3904-4601-88f6-cd53873b8ceb) School Zone Publishing Co.

Schuler, Kimberly B. I Will Remember You: My Catholic Guide Through Grief. 2011. 144p. (J). (gr. 2-6). pap. 10.95 (978-0-8198-3704-2(0)) Pauline Bks. & Media.

Schulz, Charles M., creator. Peanuts: Snoopy Loves to Doodle: Create & Complete Pictures with the Peanuts Gang. 2011. (ENG.). 64p. (J). (gr. -1-17). pap. 7.95 (978-0-7624-4378-9(2), Running Pr. Kids) Running Pr.

Science Explorer Junior (Set), 20 vols., Set. Incl. Junior Scientists: Experiment with Bugs. Gray, Susan H. (gr. 3-6). 2010. lib. bdg. 32.07 (978-1-60279-842-7(7), 200550); Junior Scientists: Experiment with Heat. Lockwood, Sophie. (gr. 3-6). 2010. lib. bdg. 32.07 (978-1-60279-843-4(5), 200552); Junior Scientists: Experiment with Liquids. Mullins, Matt. (gr. 3-6). 2010. lib. bdg. 32.07 (978-1-60279-846-5(X), 200558); Junior Scientists: Experiment with Magnets. Taylor-Butler, Christine. (gr. 3-6). 2010. lib. bdg. 32.07 (978-1-60279-844-1(3), 200554); Junior Scientists: Experiment with Plants. Gray, Susan H. (gr. 3-6). 2010. lib. bdg. 32.07 (978-1-60279-839-7(7), 200544); Junior Scientists: Experiment with Rocks. Lockwood, Sophie. (gr. 3-6). 2010. lib. bdg. 32.07 (978-1-60279-836-6(2), 200538); Junior Scientists: Experiment with Seeds. Gray, Susan H. (gr. 3-6). 2010. lib. bdg. 32.07 (978-1-60279-835-9(4), 200536); Junior Scientists: Experiment with Soil. Franchino, Vicky. (gr. 3-6). 2010. lib. bdg. 32.07 (978-1-60279-837-3(0), 200540); Junior Scientists: Experiment with Solar Energy. Taylor-Butler, Christine. (gr. 3-6). 2010. lib. bdg. 32.07 (978-1-60279-840-3(0), 200546); Junior Scientists: Experiment with Solids. Gregory, Josh. (gr. 3-6). 2010. lib. bdg. 32.07 (978-1-60279-845-8(1), 200556); Junior Scientists: Experiment with Water. Simon, Charnan & Kazunas, Ariel. (gr. 3-6). 2010. lib. bdg. 32.07 (978-1-60279-838-0(9), 200542); Junior Scientists: Experiment with Weather. Orr, Tamra B. (gr. 3-6). 2010. lib. bdg. 32.07 (978-1-60279-841-0(9), 200548); Set. Think Like a Scientist (Set) (gr. 4-8). 2011. 256.56 (978-1-61080-249-9(7), 201036); (Explorer Junior Library: Science Explorer Junior Ser.). (ENG., Illus.). 32p. 2011. 641.40 (978-1-61080-247-5(0), 201034) Cherry Lake Publishing.

Scollen, Chris. Busy Kids Sticker Storybook Sleeping Beauty. 2008. (Illus.). 12p. (J). (gr. -1-3). pap. (978-1-84610-807-5(1)) Make Believe Ideas.

Scott, Ellen. Design Your Own Teddy Bears Sticker Activity Book. 2017. (Dover Little Activity Bks.). (ENG., Illus.). 4p. (gr. k-3). pap. 2.50 (978-0-486-81866-5(7), 818667) Dover Pubns., Inc.

—Glitter Flamingos Stickers. 2019. (Dover Little Activity Books Stickers Ser.). (ENG.). 2p. (gr. k). 2.99 (978-0-486-83398-9(4), 833984) Dover Pubns., Inc.

Scott, James. The Indian in the Cupboard: Activity Pack. 2003. 138p. (YA). pap. (978-1-58049-625-4(3), PA0124) Prestwick Hse., Inc.

Scott, Xavier. Great Diary Planner for Teens: Diary. 2013. (ENG.). 50p. 14.77 (978-1-62884-694-2(1), Speedy Kids (Children's Fiction)) Speedy Publishing LLC.

Scotton, Rob. Splat the Cat: Doodle & Draw: a Coloring & Activity Book. 2013. (Splat the Cat Ser.). (ENG., Illus.). 64p. (J). (gr. -1-3). 6.99 (978-0-06-211607-9(X), HarperFestival) HarperCollins Pubs.

Scraper, Katherine, et al. Boredom Busters! Try This! Free & Inexpensive Things to Make & Do. 2011. (J). pap. (978-1-4509-5325-2(5)) Benchmark Education Co.

Seddon, Wayne & Seddon, Leigh. Scribbles: Using your eyes to see with your Mind. 2008. 44p. pap. 20.00 (978-1-59858-559-9(2)) Dog Ear Publishing, LLC.

Seed, Karen Gordon. In the Jungle: Create Amazing Pictures One Sticker at a Time! Buxton, Michael, illus. 2018. (Sticka-Pix Ser.). (ENG.). 36p. (J). (gr. 2-5). pap. 6.99 (978-1-4380-1138-7(5)) Sourcebooks, Inc.

—In the Ocean: Create Amazing Pictures One Sticker at a Time! Buxton, Michael, illus. 2018. (Sticka-Pix Ser.). (ENG.). 36p. (J). (gr. 2-5). pap. 6.99 (978-1-4380-1139-4(3)) Sourcebooks, Inc.

Seek-and-Find Fun. 2010. (Spot It Ser.). 32p. 77.97 (978-1-4296-5198-1(9), Capstone Pr.) Capstone.

Seifert, Sheila & Naylor, Beth. Stepping up, Stepping Out. 2008. (Discipleship Junction Ser.). (ENG., Illus.). 112p. (J). (gr. 1-6). pap. 14.99 (978-0-7814-4562-7(0), 105437) Cook, David C.

Selber, Danielle. Pope Francis Bobblehead. 2015. (RP Minis Ser.). (ENG., Illus.). 32p. pap. 9.95 (978-0-7624-5692-5(2), Running Pr. Minature Editions) Running Pr.

Serrano, Shea. Bun B's Rapper Coloring & Activity Book. 2013. (ENG.). 48p. pap., act. bk. ed. 14.99 (978-1-4197-1041-4(9), 1070703, Abrams Image) Abrams, Inc.

Sesame Workshop Staff. I Am a Friend. 2011. (J). (gr. k-1). pap. 3.99 (978-1-59922-884-6(X)) Twin Sisters IP, LLC.

—I Like School. 2011. (J). (gr. k-1). pap. 3.99 (978-1-59922-885-3(8)) Twin Sisters IP, LLC.

—Sesame Play-N-Learn 123S. 2011. (J). (gr. k-1). bds. 3.99 (978-1-59545-896-4(4)) Twin Sisters IP, LLC.

—Sesame Play-N-Learn Abcs. 2011. (J). (gr. k-1). bds. 3.99 (978-1-59545-895-7(6)) Twin Sisters IP, LLC.

—Sesame Play-N-Learn Dot to Dots. 2011. (J). (gr. k-1). bds. 3.99 (978-1-59545-897-1(2)) Twin Sisters IP, LLC.

—Sesame Play-N-Learn Mazes. 2011. (J). (gr. k-1). bds. 3.99 (978-1-59545-898-8(0)) Twin Sisters IP, LLC.

Sesame Workshop Staff, ed. ABC Sesame Street Flash Cards. 2009. (ENG.). 30p. 9.95 (978-1-74185-997-3(2), Ideals Pubns.) Worthy Publishing.

—Pets Elmos World Flash Cards. 2009. (ENG.). 30p. 9.95 (978-1-74185-995-9(6), Ideals Pubns.) Worthy Publishing.

—Your Body Elmos World Flash Cards. 2009. (ENG.). 15p. 9.95 (978-1-74185-994-2(8), Ideals Pubns.) Worthy Publishing.

Seuss. The Little Blue Boxed Set of Bright & Early Board Books by Dr. Seuss: Hop on Pop; Oh, the Thinks You Can Think!; Ten Apples up on Top!; the Shape of Me & Other Stuff, 4 vols. 2012. (Bright & Early Board Books(TM) Ser.). (ENG., Illus.). 24p. (J). (— 1). bds. 19.96 (978-0-307-97586-7(X), Random Hse. Bks. for Young Readers) Random Hse. Children's Bks.

—My Book about Christmas by ME, Myself: With Some Help from the Grinch & Dr. Seuss. 2016. (ENG., Illus.). 64p. (J). (gr. -1-3). 16.99 (978-0-553-52446-8(1), Random Hse. Bks. for Young Readers) Random Hse. Children's Bks.

—Oh, the Places You'll Go! the Read It! Write It! 2-Book Boxed Set Collection: Dr. Seuss's Oh, the Places You'll Go!; Oh, the Places I'll Go! by ME, Myself, 2 vols. 2016. (ENG., Illus.). 120p. (J). (gr. -1-3). 35.98 (978-0-553-53872-4(1), Random Hse. Bks. for Young Readers) Random Hse. Children's Bks.

Sévigny, Eric, illus. Caillou - The Little Artist. 2011. (Activity Bks.). (ENG.). 96p. (J). (gr. -1-1). 7.95 (978-2-89450-809-1(3)) Caillouet, Gerry.

Shaffer, Christy. Glow-In-the-Dark Snowflakes Stickers. 2009. (Dover Little Activity Books Stickers Ser.). (ENG., Illus.). 2p. (J). (gr. 1-4). pap. 1.99 (978-0-486-47062-7(8), 470628) Dover Pubns., Inc.

—Learning about Mythical Creatures. 2005. (Dover Little Activity Bks.). (ENG., Illus.). 16p. (J). (gr. 3-5). pap. 1.50 (978-0-486-44047-7(8)) Dover Pubns., Inc.

Shanddaramon. A Pagan Book of ABCs. 2009. (ENG.). 60p. pap. (978-0-557-09532-2(8)) Lulu Pr., Inc.

—The 12 Days of Yule. 2008. 33p. 16.95 (978-0-615-26465-3(4)) Astor Pr.

Share Time with Me. 2004. (J). per. 5.95 (978-0-9760282-0-8(4)) RAPC - Sparkle & Shine Project.

Shaw-Russell, Susan. Coral Reef Fish Friends Sticker Activity Book. 2016. (Dover Little Activity Books Stickers Ser.). (ENG.). 8p. (J). (gr. -1-3). 2.50 (978-0-486-80775-1(4), 807754) Dover Pubns., Inc.

—Make Your Own Bookmark Sticker Activity Book: Monsters, Robots & More! 2014. (ENG.). 8p. (J). (gr. k-3). 1.99 (978-0-486-78142-6(9), 781429) Dover Pubns., Inc.

—Make Your Own Bookmark Sticker Activity Book: Princesses, Mermaids & More! 2014. (ENG.). 8p. (J). (gr. k-3). pap. 1.99 (978-0-486-78141-9(0), 781410) Dover Pubns., Inc.

—Robots Activity Book. 2009. (Dover Little Activity Bks.). (ENG., Illus.). 64p. (J). (gr. k-3). pap. 2.50 (978-0-486-47227-0(2), 472272) Dover Pubns., Inc.

—Seek, Sketch & Color — Alphabet. 2013. (Dover Kids Activity Bks.). (ENG.). 64p. (J). (gr. 1-3). pap. 5.99 (978-0-486-49772-3(0), 497720) Dover Pubns., Inc.

—Seek, Sketch & Color — Animals. 2013. (Dover Kids Activity Books: Animals Ser.). (ENG.). 64p. (J). (gr. 1-3). pap. 5.99 (978-0-486-49773-0(9), 497739) Dover Pubns., Inc.

—Smiley Robot Tattoos. 2011. (Dover Tattoos Ser.). (ENG., Illus.). 4p. (J). (gr. 1-4). pap. 1.50 (978-0-486-48190-6(5), 481905) Dover Pubns., Inc.

—The Three Bears Activity Book. 2009. (Dover Little Activity Bks.). (ENG., Illus.). 64p. (J). (gr. -1-5). pap. 1.99 (978-0-486-47059-7(8)) Dover Pubns., Inc.

Shaw-Russell, Susan, et al. Animals on Parade Find & Color. 2012. (Dover Kids Activity Books: Animals Ser.). (ENG.). 48p. (J). (gr. k-6). pap. 4.99 (978-0-486-48938-4(8), 489388) Dover Pubns., Inc.

Shepherd-Guenette, C. Lost & Found. 2005. pap. (978-1-84401-531-3(9)) Athena Pr.

Sherman, Michael & Klutz Editors. Me vs. You: Head to Head Pencil Puzzles! 2011. 50p. (J). (gr. 3-7). 10.99 (978-1-59174-929-5(8)) Klutz.

Shulman, Mark. Are You "Normal"? More Than 100 Questions That Will Test Your Weirdness. 2011. (Illus.). 176p. (J). (gr. 3-7). pap. 12.95 (978-1-4263-0837-6(X), National Geographic Kids) Disney Publishing Worldwide.

Signoretti, Brenda. Freddie the Frog & Friends. REVILLE, TONI-ANN, illus. 2011. 32p. pap. 12.99 (978-1-4634-4633-8(0)) AuthorHouse.

Simon & Schuster UK. Colour in One Direction! 2014. (ENG.). 32p. (J). pap. 5.99 (978-1-4711-1867-8(3), Simon & Schuster Children's) Simon & Schuster, Ltd. GBR. Dist: Simon & Schuster, Inc.

Simon and Schuster UK Staff. Colour in 5 SOS! 2014. (ENG.). 32p. (J). 5.99 (978-1-4711-2469-3(X), Simon & Schuster Children's) Simon & Schuster, Ltd. GBR. Dist: Simon & Schuster, Inc.

—Ultimate Boy Band Pack! 2014. (ENG.). 48p. (J). 8.99 (978-1-4711-2473-0(8), Simon & Schuster Children's) Simon & Schuster, Ltd. GBR. Dist: Simon & Schuster, Inc.

Simon, M. Ed. Parrots 2 Peacocks Pattern Book. 2005. pap. 34.65 (978-1-4010-6134-0(6)) Xlibris Corp.

Simon, Mary Manz. Countdown to Christmas. Hartley, Brian, illus. 2019. 52p. (J). (gr. -1-k). 14.99 (978-1-5064-4854-1(2), Beaming Books) 1517 Media.

Siuda, Erik & Creative Haven. Creative Haven Modern Tattoo Designs Coloring Book. 2013. (Adult Coloring Books: Art & Design Ser.). (ENG., Illus.). 64p. (J). (gr. 6). pap. 6.99 (978-0-486-49326-8(1), 493261) Dover Pubns., Inc.

Siwa, JoJo. JoJo's Guide to Making Your Own Fun: #DoItYourself. 2018. (ENG., Illus.). 192p. (J). (gr. 3-7). 18.99 (978-1-4197-3208-9(0), 1250203, Amulet Bks.) Abrams, Inc.

Skiles, Janet. Happy Birthday! Tattoos. 2016. (Dover Little Activity Bks.). (ENG., Illus.). 2p. (J). (gr. 1-3). 1.99 (978-0-486-81070-6(4), 810704) Dover Pubns., Inc.

Slam! Activity Pack. 2003. 172p. (YA). pap. (978-1-58049-624-7(5), PA0123) Prestwick Hse., Inc.

Sloyer, Sarah. Dumpling Cats Coloring Book with Stickers. 2019. (Dover Animal Coloring Bks.). (ENG.). 32p. pap. 7.99 (978-0-486-82917-3(0), 829170) Dover Pubns., Inc.

Small World Creations. Busy Bee's Garden! Bathtime Fun with Rattly Rings & a Friendly Bug Pal. Haines, Emma, illus. 2018. (ENG.). 8p. (J). (gr. -1 — 1). 6.99 (978-1-4380-7905-9(2)) Sourcebooks, Inc.

Smart Kids Publishing Staff. My Snuggle up Bedtime Book. Smart Kids Publishing Staff, illus. 2007. (Illus.). 16p. 14.99 (978-0-8249-6695-9(3), Ideals Pubns.) Worthy Publishing.

SmartLab, creator. Custom Car Design Shop. 2011. (SmartLAB Ser.). (J). 7.99 (978-1-60380-123-2(5), SmartLab) becker&mayer! books.

—Fashion Designer. 2011. (SmartLAB Ser.). (J). 7.99 (978-1-60380-122-5(7), SmartLab) becker&mayer! books.

—Fashion Studio. 2011. (SmartLAB Ser.). (J). (gr. 2). 24.99 (978-1-60380-127-0(8), SmartLab) becker&mayer! books.

—Glitter Spa Lab. 2011. (SmartLAB Ser.). (J). 7.99 (978-1-60380-118-8(9), SmartLab) becker&mayer! books.

—It's Alive! T. Rex. 2011. (SmartLAB Ser.). (J). (gr. 1). 14.99 (978-1-60380-066-2(2), SmartLab) becker&mayer! books.

—Secret Formula Lab. 2011. (SmartLAB Ser.). (J). 7.99 (978-1-60380-120-1(0), SmartLab) becker&mayer! books.

SMARTLAB Creative Team. Indoor Outdoor Science Lab. 2010. 12p. mass mkt. 39.99 (978-1-60380-051-8(4)) becker&mayer! books.

—Inside Out! the Human Body. 2010. 12p. mass mkt. 39.99 (978-1-60380-052-5(2)) becker&mayer! books.

Smiley, Jess Smart. Rumpus on the Run: A Monster Look-N-Find Book. 2013. (ENG., Illus.). 22p. (J). (gr. -1-3). 14.95 (978-1-62086-444-9(4)) Amplify Publishing Group.

Smith, A. G. Tallest Building in the World - Burj Khalifa: Cut & Assemble. 2011. (Dover Children's Activity Bks.). (ENG., Illus.). 20p. (gr. 3-6). pap. 9.99 (978-0-486-48235-4(9)) Dover Pubns., Inc.

Smith, A. g. & Smith, A. G. The White House Cut & Assemble. 2010. (Dover Children's Activity Bks.). (ENG., Illus.). 20p. (J). (gr. 3-6). pap. 9.99 (978-0-486-47681-0(2), 476812) Dover Pubns., Inc.

Smith, Kimberly. Monkeying Around: Meet Chippey & His Friends. Goris, Laura, illus. 2012. 44p. (J). pap. 14.98 (978-0-9843166-6-3(3)) Artists' Orchard, LLC, The.

Smith, Naniloa. The Children Are Happy Activity Book with Animals from the Southwest. 2003. (J). 11.00 (978-0-9744005-0-1(5)) In the Desert.

Smith, Nikki. Five Little Speckled Frogs Activity Guide. 2010. 66p. pap. 10.00 (978-0-557-36823-5(5)) Lulu Pr., Inc.

Smith, Sherri Graves. Bully's Game Day Rules. Danielson, Damon, illus. 2013. (ENG.). (J). 14.95 (978-1-62086-334-3(0)) Amplify Publishing Group.

—Cimarron's Game Day Rules. Danielson, Damon, illus. 2013. (ENG.). (J). 14.95 (978-1-62086-230-8(1)) Amplify Publishing Group.

—Cocky's Game Day Rules. Danielson, Damon, illus. 2013. (ENG.). (J). 14.95 (978-1-62086-085-4(6)) Amplify Publishing Group.

—Nittany Lion's Game Day Rules. Danielson, Damon, illus. 2013. (ENG.). (J). 14.95 (978-1-62086-233-9(6)) Amplify Publishing Group.

—Reveille's Game Day Rules. Danielson, Damon, illus. 2013. (ENG.). (J). (gr. -1-3). 14.95 (978-1-62086-350-3(2)) Amplify Publishing Group.

—Tiger's Game Day Rules. Danielson, Damon, illus. 2013. (ENG.). (J). (gr. -1-3). 14.95 (978-1-62086-086-1(4)) Amplify Publishing Group.

Snape, Charles & Snape, Juliet. Brain Busters: Games, Puzzles & More! 2012. (Dover Kids Activity Bks.). (ENG., Illus.). 64p. (J). (gr. 3-5). pap. 9.99 (978-0-486-48779-3(2), 487792) Dover Pubns., Inc.

Snellenberger, Earl & Snellenberger, Bonita. Dinosaur Activity Book: The Wonder's of God's World. Snellenberger, Earl & Snellenberger, Bonita, illus. 2008. (ENG., Illus.). 128p. (J). (gr. 4-6). per. 9.99 (978-0-89051-515-0(8), Master Books) New Leaf Publishing Group.

—Noah's Ark Pre-School Activity Book. Snellenberger, Earl & Snellenberger, Bonita, illus. 2014. (ENG., Illus.). 98p. (J). (gr. -1-3). pap. 8.99 (978-0-89051-832-8(7), Master Books) New Leaf Publishing Group.

Snow, Philip. Animals of the Bible. Snow, Philip, illus. 2005. (Bible Discover & Colour Ser.). (Illus.). 32p. (J). (gr. -1-7). 4.00 (978-1-903087-88-6(0)) DayOne Pubns. GBR. Dist: Send The Light Distribution LLC.

—Birds of the Bible. Snow, Philip, illus. 2005. (Bible Discover & Colour Ser.). (Illus.). 32p. (J). (gr. -1-7). 4.00 (978-1-903087-89-3(9)) DayOne Pubns. GBR. Dist: Send The Light Distribution LLC.

Snozek, Lee Anne & Coloring Books for Adults. Outrageous Octagons. 2009. (Dover Design Coloring Bks.). (ENG., Illus.). 32p. (gr. 3-8). pap. 3.99 (978-0-486-47301-7(5), 473015) Dover Pubns., Inc.

So, Patty. So Simple at-Home A Month of Ideas: 31 Fun & Simple Activities to Reinforce Your Child's Reading Success! 2007. 36p. (J). spiral bd. (978-0-9772158-5-0(7)) So Simple Learning.

Social Studies Explorer (Set), 21 vols., Set. Incl. It's Cool to Learn about Countries: Bangladesh. Orr, Tamra B. 2010. lib. bdg. 34.93 (978-1-60279-829-8(X), 200524); It's Cool to Learn about Countries: Brazil. Franchino, Vicky. 2010. lib. bdg. 34.93 (978-1-60279-827-4(3), 200520); It's Cool to Learn about Countries: China. Raatma, Lucia. 2010. lib. bdg. 34.93 (978-1-60279-823-6(0), 200512); It's Cool to Learn about Countries: India. Raatma, Lucia. 2010. lib. bdg. 34.93 (978-1-60279-824-3(9), 200514); It's Cool to Learn about Countries: Indonesia. Orr, Tamra B. 2010. lib. bdg. 34.93 (978-1-60279-826-7(5), 200518); It's Cool to Learn about Countries: Japan. Somervill, Barbara A. 2010. lib. bdg. 34.93 (978-1-60279-832-8(X), 200530); It's Cool to Learn about Countries: Mexico. Somervill, Barbara A. 2010. lib. bdg. 34.93 (978-1-60279-833-5(8), 200532); It's Cool to Learn about Countries: Nigeria. Rau, Dana Meachen. 2010. lib. bdg. 34.93 (978-1-60279-830-4(3), 200526); It's Cool to Learn about Countries: Pakistan. Labrecque, Ellen. 2010. lib. bdg. 34.93 (978-1-60279-828-1(1), 200522); It's Cool to Learn about Countries: Philippines. Franchino, Vicky. 2010. lib. bdg. 34.93 (978-1-60279-834-2(6), 200534); It's Cool to Learn about Countries: Russia. Marsico, Katie. 2010. lib. bdg. 34.93 (978-1-60279-831-1(1), 200528); It's Cool to Learn about Countries: United States. Marsico, Katie. 2010. lib. bdg. 34.93 (978-1-60279-825-0(7), 200516); Set. It's Cool to Learn about the United States (Set) 2011. 174.65 (978-1-61080-191-1(1), 201012); 48p. (gr. 4-8). (Explorer Library: Social Studies Explorer Ser.). (ENG., Illus.). 2011. 658.56 (978-1-61080-253-6(5), 201008) Cherry Lake Publishing.

Soffer, Ruth. Animal Illustrations to Paint or Color. 2007. (Dover Animal Coloring Bks.). (ENG., Illus.). 48p. (J). (gr. 3-8). 5.99 (978-0-486-45696-6(X), 45696X) Dover Pubns., Inc.

Sood, Sana Hoda. Diwali: A Cultural Adventure. Hoda, Rubina, illus. 2013. (ENG.). (J). (gr. -1-3). 14.95 (978-1-62086-396-1(0)) Amplify Publishing Group.

Sosa, Carlos. Celebrations. 2007. (Familia Banderas Ser.). (Illus.). 48p. (J). (gr. 3-7). per. 9.95 (978-1-933669-11-3(X)) Literary Architects, LLC.

—Cultures. 2007. (Familia Banderas Ser.). (Illus.). 48p. (J). (gr. 3-7). per. 9.95 (978-1-933669-12-0(8)) Literary Architects, LLC.

Sovak, Jan. Build a Giant Poster Coloring Book — Under the Sea. 2013. (Dover Sea Life Coloring Bks.). (ENG., Illus.). 48p. (J). (gr. 2-6). pap. 4.99 (978-0-486-49139-4(0), 491390) Dover Pubns., Inc.

—Mega Dinosaurs Coloring Book. 2019. (Dover Dinosaur Coloring Bks.). (ENG.). 48p. (J). (gr. 3-6). pap. 5.99 (978-0-486-83396-5(8), 833968) Dover Pubns., Inc.

Sovak, Jan, et al. Build a 3-D Poster Coloring Book — Fairies. 2012. (Dover Fantasy Coloring Bks.). (ENG.). 16p. (J). (gr. 3-5). pap. 5.99 (978-0-486-49830-0(1), 498301) Dover Pubns., Inc.

Spear, Kevin. My Very Own Activity Pages: Spring 2004. 2004. (Illus.). (J). pap. 1.79 (978-1-59317-077-6(7)) Warner Pr., Inc.

Speechmark. Who, What, When, Where Colorcards. 2009. (Colorcards Ser.). (ENG.). 36p. (C). 54.95 (978-1-909301-13-9(2), Y330215) Routledge.

Spohn, Rebecca. Ready, Set, Create! A Kid's Guide to Crafting. 2012. (ENG., Illus.). 92p. pap. 19.95 (978-1-59647-425-3(4)) Good Year Bks.

Squires, Patricia. Enter Here. 2008. 62p. (J). 41.99 (978-1-4257-7867-5(4)) Xlibris Corp.

Stadler, Charlotte. Making Patterns. Adams, Alison, ed. 2011. (Early Connections Ser.). (ENG.). (J). (gr. 2). 8.00 net. (978-1-61672-640-9(7)) Benchmark Education Co.

Stanford, Elisa & Basaluzzo, Constanza. The Baby Bible 1,2,3, 1 vol. 2009. (Baby Bible Ser.). (ENG.). 48p. (J). bds. 12.99 (978-1-4347-6540-6(7), 106168) Cook, David C.

Stanley, Mandy, illus. Arty Words: Early Learning Through Art. 2016. (Arty Mouse Wipe Clean with Pen Ser.). (ENG.). 24p. (J). (gr. -1-2). pap. 7.99 (978-1-78445-858-4(9)) Top That! Publishing PLC GBR. Dist: Independent Pubs. Group.

Stansbie, Stephanie. Dinosaurs: A Busy Sticker Activity Book. Nowowiejska, Kasia, illus. 2016. (Little Snappers Ser.). (ENG.). 96p. (J). (gr. -1-2). 9.99 (978-1-58925-319-3(1)) Tiger Tales.

The Star-Spangled Workbook. 2006. per. 34.95 (978-0-9787820-1-6(1)) King, Joel.

Stardoll. Sticker Holiday Dress Up. 2013. (Stardoll Ser.). 24p. (J). (gr. 2-4). pap. 8.99 (978-0-85751-177-5(7)) Transworld Publishers Ltd. GBR. Dist: Independent Pubs. Group.

Staying Focused. 2007. (J). per. 10.00 (978-0-9788937-2-9(7)) Amani Publishing, LLC.

Steck-Vaughn Staff. Three Cheers for November. 2004. (Three Cheers For... ! Ser.). (ENG., Illus.). 96p. (gr. -1 — 1). pap. 12.99 (978-0-7398-9310-4(6)) Houghton Mifflin Harcourt Publishing Co.

Steck-Vaughn Staff, creator. Sensational Seasons: Spring. 2007. (Sensational Seasons Ser.). (Illus.). 96p. per. 13.99 (978-1-4190-3393-3(X)) Steck-Vaughn.

Steele-Saccio, Eva. Headbands & Hairstyles: Make & Wear Super Stylish Headbands. 2010. (ENG.). 60p. (J). (gr. 3-18). 19.99 (978-1-59174-864-9(X)) Klutz.

Stella, Heather. Get Ready for Kindergarten: Letters & Sight Words: 247 Fun Exercises for Mastering Skills for Success in School. 2013. (Get Ready for School Ser.). (ENG.). 128p. (J). (gr. -1-2). pap. 7.95 (978-1-57912-937-8(4), 81937, Black Dog & Leventhal Pubs. Inc.) Hachette Bks.

—Get Ready for School First Grade Laptop Workbook: Sight Words, Beginning Reading, Handwriting, Vowels & Consonants, Word Families. 2014. (Get Ready for School Ser.). (ENG.). 193p. (J). (gr. -1-17). spiral bd. 13.95 (978-1-57912-975-0(7), 81975, Black Dog & Leventhal Pubs. Inc.) Hachette Bks.

—Get Ready for School Pre-Kindergarten Laptop Workbook: Uppercase Letters, Tracing, Beginning Sounds, Writing, Patterns. 2014. (Get Ready for School Ser.). (ENG.). 194p. (J). (gr. -1-17). spiral bd. 13.95 (978-1-57912-973-6(0), 81973, Black Dog & Leventhal Pubs. Inc.) Hachette Bks.

Stephens, Edna Cucksey. Core Democratic Values with Rock U. S. A. Herrick, Mark J., illus. 2004. (Connect-It Ser.). 62p. (J). (gr. -1-3). pap. 24.95 (978-0-9749412-0-2(4)) EDCO Publishing, Inc.

Stephens, Sarah Hines & Mann, Bethany. Do It Now! Tricks: Rad Stunts & Sneaky Pranks. 2012. (ENG.). 80p. (J). pap. 6.99 (978-1-61628-391-9(2)) Weldon Owen, Inc.

Stevenson, May. Brilliant Activities for Reading Non-Fiction: Comprehension Activities for 7-11 Year Olds. 2006. (Illus.). 128p. pap. (978-1-903853-46-7(X)) Brilliant Pubns.

Stevenson-Spurgon, Barbara J. Old Silent One & Fresh Water Fishing: This Is a Bitty Book. 2008. 40p. pap. 17.99 (978-1-4343-7790-6(3)) AuthorHouse.

Stewart, Whitney. Mindful Kids. Braun, Mina, illus. 2017. (Barefoot Books Activity Decks Ser.). (ENG.). 58p. (J). (gr. k-5). 16.99 (978-1-78285-327-5(8)) Barefoot Bks., Inc.

Sticker It Up! 2013. (Imagine It! Ser.). (ENG., Illus.). 40p. (J). (gr. 3-7). (978-1-77132-069-6(9)) SpiceBox Products Ltd.

Stillerman, Robbie. Glitter Jewelry Sticker Activity Book. 2008. (Dover Little Activity Books Stickers Ser.). (ENG., Illus.). 2p. (J). (gr. 1-4). 1.50 (978-0-486-46576-0(4)) Dover Pubns., Inc.

—Monster Mix & Match Sticker Activity Book. 2007. (Dover Little Activity Bks.). (ENG., Illus.). 4p. (J). (gr. -1-5). pap. 1.50 (978-0-486-45663-8(3)) Dover Pubns., Inc.

Stilson, Linda J. Sew Easy Felt Puppets. 2005. (Illus.). 118p. 23.25 (978-0-9770043-8-6(4)) New Global Publishing.

Stohs, Anita Reith. Praise God with Paper Cups: 45 Easy Bible Crafts; Grades 1-5. Koehler, Ed, illus. 2005. (CPH Teaching Resource Ser.). 64p. pap. 10.99 (978-0-7586-0842-0(X)) Concordia Publishing Hse.

Stone, Sandra J. Playing: A Kid's Curriculum. Kizer, Fran, illus. 2nd ed. 2005. 234p. (Orig.). per. 18.95 (978-1-59647-003-3(8)) Good Year Bks.

Strait, Mark, et al, creators. Webber Interactive WH Questions Level 1: Whcd11. 2006. (J). cd-rom 49.95 (978-1-58650-642-1(0)) Super Duper Pubns.

Strauss, Elizabeth. Beginning Reading 1-2. 2008. (ENG.). 32p. (J). pap. 2.99 (978-0-88743-756-4(7)) School Zone Publishing Co.

Strickland, Tessa & DePalma, Kate. Barefoot Books Children of the World. Dean, David, illus. 2016. (ENG.). 64p. (J). (gr. k-5). 19.99 *(978-1-78285-296-4(4))* Barefoot Bks., Inc.
Studio Mouse. Sesame Street Celebrates School: Learn & Carry 4 Books with CD. rev. ed. 2007. (ENG.). 4x20p. 14.99 *(978-1-59069-565-4(8))* Studio Mouse LLC.
Sun, Ming-Ju. Creative Haven Japanese Kimono Designs Coloring Book. 2013. (Adult Coloring Books: World & Travel Ser.). (ENG., Illus.). 64p. (gr. 3). pap. 6.99 *(978-0-486-49344-2(X),* 49344X) Dover Pubns., Inc.
Sunflower Education Staff. A Golden Thread. 2012. 54p. pap. 11.95 *(978-1-937166-13-7(9))* Sunflower Education.
Super Duper Publications Staff. Electronic Spinner 1-6: Spin267. 2007. (J). 10.95 *(978-1-58650-744-2(3))* Super Duper Pubns.
Suzuki, Genevieve A. & Murakami, Jon J. The Original Poi Cats on Oahu. 2005. 24p. (J). pap. 5.95 *(978-1-56647-731-4(X))* Mutual Publishing LLC.
Swanson, Maggie. Floral Fantasies Stained Glass Coloring Book. 2013. (Dover Flower Coloring Bks.). (ENG., Illus.). 32p. (gr. 3-8). pap. 7.99 *(978-0-486-49807-2(7),* 498077) Dover Pubns., Inc.
—My Backyard Color by Number. 2017. (Dover Kids Coloring Bks.). (ENG.). 32p. (J). (gr. -1-2). pap. 3.99 *(978-0-486-81461-2(0),* 814610) Dover Pubns., Inc.
—My Storybook Paper Dolls. 2013. (Dover Paper Dolls Ser.). (ENG., Illus.). 32p. (J). (gr. 1). pap. 9.99 *(978-0-486-48989-6(2),* 489892) Dover Pubns., Inc.
—Spark - Sun, Moon & Stars Coloring Book. 2015. (Dover Space Coloring Bks.). (ENG., Illus.). 64p. (J). (gr. 1-4). pap. 6.99 *(978-0-486-80216-9(7),* 802167) Dover Pubns., Inc.
Swanson Sateren, Shelley. Max & Zoe: the Very Best Art Project, 1 vol. Sullivan, Mary, illus. 2013. (Max & Zoe Ser.). (ENG.). 32p. (J). (gr. k-2). pap. 5.19 *(978-1-4795-2329-0(1),* 124367, Picture Window Bks.) Capstone.
Swanson, Tom, illus. Twas the Night Before Christmas. 2011. (Recordable Bks). 12p. (J). ring bd. 24.99 *(978-1-60130-261-8(4),* Usborne) EDC Publishing.
Sykes, Andy. The Hexjibber Colouring & Activity Book. 2007. 84p. pap. 14.95 *(978-1-4303-2817-9(7))* Lulu Pr., Inc.
Sylvan Learning. Pre-K Page per Day: Letters: Alphabet Recognition, Uppercase Letters, Lowercase Letters, Writing Letters. 2012. (Sylvan Page per Day Series, Language Arts Ser.). 64p. (J). (gr. -1-2). pap. 6.99 *(978-0-307-94455-9(7),* Sylvan Learning Publishing) Random Hse. Children's Bks.
Szpirglas, Jeff & Saint-Onge, Danielle. Train Your Brain: How Your Brain Learns Best. 2017. (Exploring the Brain Ser.). (Illus.). 48p. (J). (gr. 5-6). *(978-0-7787-3498-7(6))* Crabtree Publishing Co.
Taib, Saadah. Prophet Ibrahim & the Little Bird Activity Book. Rosli, Shazana, illus. 2020. (Prophets of Islam Activity Bks.). 16p. (J). pap. 3.95 *(978-0-86037-740-5(7))* Kube Publishing Ltd. GBR. Dist: Consortium Bk. Sales & Distribution.
—Prophet Ismail & the ZamZam Well Activity Book. Rosli, Shazana, illus. 2020. (Prophets of Islam Activity Bks.). 16p. (J). pap. 3.95 *(978-0-86037-745-0(8))* Kube Publishing Ltd. GBR. Dist: Consortium Bk. Sales & Distribution.
Talhamy, Sarah. Children's Workbook. 2005. (J). ring bd. *(978-0-615-12907-5(2))* SLG.
Tallarico, Tony, Sr. Little Hidden Pictures. 2008. (Dover Little Activity Bks.). (ENG., Illus.). 64p. (J). (gr. 3-5). pap. 2.50 *(978-0-486-46581-4(0),* 465810) Dover Pubns., Inc.
Tallarico, Tony, Sr. & Activity Books Staff. More Little Hidden Pictures. 2013. (Dover Little Activity Bks., Illus.). 64p. (J). (gr. k-3). pap. 2.50 *(978-0-486-49337-4(7),* 493377) Dover Pubns., Inc.
Tallarico, Tony, Sr. & Tallarico, Tony J., Jr. Cars & Trucks Mazes. 2013. (Dover Kids Activity Bks.). (ENG., Illus.). 48p. (J). (gr. 2-5). pap. 4.99 *(978-0-486-49890-4(5),* 498905) Dover Pubns., Inc.
Tallarico, Tony J., Jr. Baseball Facts & Fun Activity Book. 2017. (Dover Kids Activity Bks.). (ENG.). 48p. (J). (gr. 1-4). pap. 4.99 *(978-0-486-81442-1(4),* 814424) Dover Pubns., Inc.
—Famous Firsts Activity Book. 2013. (Dover Children's Activity Bks.). (ENG.). 48p. (J). (gr. 3-8). pap. 4.99 *(978-0-486-48839-4(X))* Dover Pubns., Inc.
—Presidents Activity Book. 2009. (Dover Little Activity Bks.). (ENG., Illus.). 64p. (J). (gr. k-3). pap. 1.99 *(978-0-486-47388-8(0),* 473880) Dover Pubns., Inc.
Taplin, Sam. Diggers Sticker Book. 2008. (Sticker Bks). (Illus.). 16p. (J). pap. 6.99 *(978-0-7945-2109-7(6),* Usborne) EDC Publishing.
—Farm Sticker Book. 2008. (Sticker Bks). (Illus.). 16p. (J). pap. 6.99 *(978-0-7945-2110-3(X),* Usborne) EDC Publishing.
—Zoo (First Sticker Book) Johansson, Cecilia, illus. 2011. (First Sticker Book Ser.). 24p. (J). pap. 6.99 *(978-0-7945-2927-7(5),* Usborne) EDC Publishing.
Tauber, Sabine. Hieronymus Bosch: Coloring Book. 2014. (Coloring Bks.). (ENG., Illus.). 32p. (J). (gr. 1-4). pap. 8.95 *(978-3-7913-7176-4(2))* Prestel Verlag GmbH & Co KG. DEU. Dist: Penguin Random Hse. LLC.
Taylor, Adam. George in the UK: The Unknown Kingdom. Taylor, Adam & West, Jeannette, eds. 2011. (Illus.). 28p. (J). 8.99 *(978-0-9766062-9-1(1))* Higher Ground Pr.
Taylor, Jeremy. Strength of Love. 2012. 32p. pap. 24.95 *(978-1-4626-7083-3(0))* America Star Bks.
Taylor, Jo. Back to School Sticker Paper Dolls. 2014. (ENG.). 4p. (J). (gr. k-3). 1.50 *(978-0-486-78140-2(2),* 781402) Dover Pubns., Inc.
—Sneaker Designs Coloring Book. 2017. (Dover Design Coloring Bks.). (ENG.). 32p. (J). (gr. 1-4). pap. 3.99 *(978-0-486-80935-9(8),* 809358) Dover Pubns., Inc.
Taylor, Lindsay & Smith, Suzanne. Doodle Girl Summer Sticker Activity. Maurri, Marnie, illus. 2018. (ENG.). 24p. (J). 9.99 *(978-1-4711-2320-7(0),* Simon & Schuster Children's) Simon & Schuster, Ltd. GBR. Dist: Simon & Schuster, Inc.
Taylor Trade Publish. Meet Ranger Rick Jr: Critter Crafts & Recipes. 2016. (Ranger Rick: Animal Fun for Young Children Ser.). (Illus.). 32p. (J). (gr. -1-1). pap. 5.99 *(978-1-63076-210-0(5))* Taylor Trade Publishing.
Thames & Hudson. This Book Thinks You're a Scientist: Imagine · Experiment · Create. Russell, Harriet, illus. 2016. (ENG.). 96p. (J). (gr. 2-5). pap. 14.95 *(978-0-500-65081-3(0),* 565081) Thames & Hudson.
The Broons. The Broons Colouring Book. 2016. (ENG., Illus.). 64p. (J). pap. 11.99 *(978-1-910230-36-7(7))* Black and White Publishing Ltd. GBR. Dist: Independent Pubs. Group.
The Editors at Michael O'Mara. The Big Book of Amazing Activities. 2017. (ENG., Illus.). 128p. (J). (gr. k). pap. 12.99 *(978-1-62686-733-8(X),* Silver Dolphin Bks.) Printers Row Publishing Group.
The Learning Company, The Learning. Achieve! Grade 1: Think. Play. Achieve! 2014. (Achieve! Ser.). (ENG., Illus.). 320p. (J). (gr. -1-3). pap. 12.99 *(978-0-544-37261-0(1),* 1590910, Clarion Bks.) HarperCollins Pubs.
—Achieve! Grade 2: Think. Play. Achieve! 2014. (Achieve! Ser.). (ENG., Illus.). 320p. (J). (gr. -1-3). pap. 12.99 *(978-0-544-37251-1(4),* 1590911, Clarion Bks.) HarperCollins Pubs.
—Achieve! Grade 3: Think. Play. Achieve! 2014. (Achieve! Ser.). (ENG., Illus.). 320p. (J). (gr. 3-7). pap. 12.99 *(978-0-544-37241-2(7),* 1590912, Clarion Bks.) HarperCollins Pubs.
—Achieve!: Kindergarten: Building Skills for School Success. 2012. (Achieve! Ser.). (ENG., Illus.). 320p. (J). (gr. -1-3). pap. 12.99 *(978-0-547-79108-1(9),* 1492964, Clarion Bks.) HarperCollins Pubs.
—Achieve!: Pre-Kindergarten: Building Skills for School Success. 2012. (Achieve! Ser.). (ENG., Illus.). 320p. (J). (gr. -1-3). pap. 12.99 *(978-0-547-79107-4(0),* 1492963, Clarion Bks.) HarperCollins Pubs.
—Learning with Curious George Kindergarten Math. 2012. (Learning with Curious George Ser.). (ENG., Illus.). 64p. (J). (gr. -1-3). pap. 6.99 *(978-0-547-79097-8(X),* 1492955, Clarion Bks.) HarperCollins Pubs.
—Learning with Curious George Kindergarten Reading. 2012. (Learning with Curious George Ser.). (ENG., Illus.). 64p. (J). (gr. -1-3). pap. 6.99 *(978-0-547-79096-1(1),* 1492954, Clarion Bks.) HarperCollins Pubs.
—Learning with Curious George Pre-K Math. 2012. (Learning with Curious George Ser.). (ENG., Illus.). 64p. (J). (gr. -1-3). pap. 6.99 *(978-0-547-79055-8(4),* 1492952, Clarion Bks.) HarperCollins Pubs.
—Learning with Curious George Pre-K Reading. 2012. (Learning with Curious George Ser.). (ENG., Illus.). 64p. (J). (gr. -1-3). pap. 6.99 *(978-0-547-79054-1(6),* 1492951, Clarion Bks.) HarperCollins Pubs.
Theodore, Elizabeth. Lily's Lollipop Moments. 2006. (Illus.). 60p. (J). ring bd. 22.50 *(978-0-9792472-2-4(5))* Lily Wish Factory.
Think Like a Scientist (Set), 8 vols., Set. Incl. Think Like a Scientist at the Beach. Rau, Dana Meachen. lib. bdg. 32.07 *(978-1-61080-168-3(7),* 201106); Think Like a Scientist in the Backyard. Mullins, Matt. lib. bdg. 32.07 *(978-1-61080-167-6(9),* 201104); Think Like a Scientist in the Car. Mullins, Matt. lib. bdg. 32.07 *(978-1-61080-164-5(4),* 201098); Think Like a Scientist in the Classroom. Hindman, Susan. lib. bdg. 32.07 *(978-1-61080-170-6(9),* 201110); Think Like a Scientist in the Garden. Mullins, Matt. lib. bdg. 32.07 *(978-1-61080-166-9(0),* 201102); Think Like a Scientist in the Gym. Taylor-Butler, Christine. lib. bdg. 32.07 *(978-1-61080-163-8(6),* 201096); Think Like a Scientist in the Kitchen. Mullins, Matt. lib. bdg. 32.07 *(978-1-61080-165-2(2),* 201100); Think Like a Scientist on the Playground. Rau, Dana Meachen. lib. bdg. 32.07 *(978-1-61080-169-0(5),* 201108); (gr. 4-8). (Explorer Junior Library: Science Explorer Junior Ser.). (ENG., Illus.). 32p. 2011. 256.56 *(978-1-61080-249-9(7),* 201036) Cherry Lake Publishing.
Thomas, Becky & Sweeney, Monica. Loom Magic Creatures!: 25 Awesome Animals & Mythical Beings for a Rainbow of Critters. 2014. (ENG., Illus.). 128p. (J). (gr. k). 12.95 *(978-1-62914-795-6(8),* Sky Pony Pr.) Skyhorse Publishing Co., Inc.
Thomas, Danita & Thomas, John E. Inventos y Experimentos para Ninos: Una Nueva Coleccion de Inventos y Experimentos un Poco Locos y Chiflados. 2007. (Kid Concoctions - Spanish Ser.). (Illus.). 80p. (J). per. 9.99 *(978-0-8054-4498-8(X),* B&H Bks.) B&H Publishing Group.
Thomas, Vernada. Pre-Handwriting Book. 2008. 200p. 29.99 *(978-1-4363-8001-0(4));* pap. 19.99 *(978-1-4363-8000-3(6))* Xlibris Corp.
Ticktock Media, Ltd. Staff. Birthday Party. 2009. (Busy Tots Ser.). (ENG.). 10p. (J). (gr. -1-k). bds. 6.95 *(978-1-84696-801-3(1),* TickTock Books) Octopus Publishing Group GBR. Dist: Independent Pubs. Group.
—Guess What? Everyday Things. 2008. (Mini Flap Ser.). (ENG.). 10p. (J). (gr. k — 1). bds. 5.95 *(978-1-84696-818-1(6),* TickTock Books) Octopus Publishing Group GBR. Dist: Independent Pubs. Group.
—Little Helper. 2009. (Busy Tots Ser.). (ENG.). 10p. (J). (gr. -1-k). bds. 6.95 *(978-1-84696-798-6(8),* TickTock Books) Octopus Publishing Group GBR. Dist: Independent Pubs. Group.
—My Fairy Garden. 2008. (Sparkle Bks.). (ENG.). 10p. (J). (gr. -1-k). bds. 6.95 *(978-1-84696-802-0(X),* TickTock Books) Octopus Publishing Group GBR. Dist: Independent Pubs. Group.
—My Night-Time Animals. 2008. (Sparkle Bks.). (ENG.). 10p. (J). (gr. -1-k). bds. 6.95 *(978-1-84696-803-7(8),* TickTock Books) Octopus Publishing Group GBR. Dist: Independent Pubs. Group.
—My Ocean Creatures. 2008. (Sparkle Bks.). (ENG.). 10p. (J). (gr. -1-k). bds. 6.95 *(978-1-84696-804-4(6),* TickTock Books) Octopus Publishing Group GBR. Dist: Independent Pubs. Group.
—My Space Adventure. 2008. (Sparkle Bks.). (ENG.). 10p. (J). (gr. -1-k). bds. 6.95 *(978-1-84696-805-1(4),* TickTock Books) Octopus Publishing Group GBR. Dist: Independent Pubs. Group.
—My World: Opposites. 2008. (Tab Bks.). (ENG.). 10p. (J). (gr. -1-k). bds. 4.95 *(978-1-84696-823-5(2),* TickTock Books) Octopus Publishing Group GBR. Dist: Independent Pubs. Group.
—Shopping Day. 2009. (Busy Tots Ser.). (ENG.). 10p. (J). (gr. -1-k). bds. 6.95 *(978-1-84696-799-3(6),* TickTock Books) Octopus Publishing Group GBR. Dist: Independent Pubs. Group.
—Summer Vacation. 2009. (Busy Tots Ser.). (ENG.). 10p. (J). (gr. -1-k). bds. 6.95 *(978-1-84696-800-6(3),* TickTock Books) Octopus Publishing Group GBR. Dist: Independent Pubs. Group.
—What Am I? Animal Moms & Babies. 2008. (Mini Flap Ser.). (ENG.). 10p. (J). (gr. k — 1). bds. 5.95 *(978-1-84696-817-4(8),* TickTock Books) Octopus Publishing Group GBR. Dist: Independent Pubs. Group.
Tierney, Tom. Fashions of the Roaring Twenties Coloring Book. 2013. (Dover Fashion Coloring Book Ser.). (ENG., Illus.). 32p. (gr. 3-12). pap. 4.99 *(978-0-486-49950-5(2),* 499502) Dover Pubns., Inc.
Tiger Tales. Christmas Sticker Activities. Ordas, Emi, illus. 2014. (My First Ser.). (ENG.). 40p. (J). (gr. -1-2). 7.99 *(978-1-58925-307-0(8))* Tiger Tales.
—Funny Faces Sticker Fun! (Blue) Tiger Tales, illus. 2014. (ENG., Illus.). 14p. (J). (gr. -1-k). pap. 3.99 *(978-1-58925-304-9(3))* Tiger Tales.
—Halloween Sticker Activities. Ordas, Emi, illus. 2014. (My First Ser.). (ENG.). 40p. (J). (gr. -1-2). 6.99 *(978-1-58925-306-3(X))* Tiger Tales.
Tillman, Nancy. You Are Loved: Welcome Wishes for New Babies. 2018. (ENG., Illus.). 32p. (J). 17.99 *(978-1-250-18297-5(2),* 900190690) Feiwel & Friends.
Tincknell, Cathy. Amazing Things for Boys to Make & Do. Kelly, John, illus. 2013. (Dover Kids Activity Bks.). (ENG.). 32p. (J). (gr. 3-5). 6.99 *(978-0-486-49723-5(2),* 497232) Dover Pubns., Inc.
—Amazing Things for Girls to Make & Do. Kelly, John, illus. 2013. (Dover Kids Activity Bks.). (ENG.). 32p. (J). (gr. 3-5). 6.99 *(978-0-486-49722-8(4),* 497224) Dover Pubns., Inc.
Tnt. God's Miracle Maker: Elisha. 2007. (On the Way Ser.). (ENG.). 96p. (J). pap. 17.99 *(978-1-84550-291-1(4),* a642cba5-04c3-49ef-b65c-fd48b2aff738) Christian Focus Pubns. GBR. Dist: Baker & Taylor Publisher Services (BTPS).
Todd, Richard E. Baptism: A Bible Study Wordbook for Kids. 2009. (ENG., Illus.). 32p. (gr. 4-7). pap. 7.99 *(978-1-60066-194-5(7),* WingSpread Pubs.) Moody Pubs.
—Church: A Bible Study Wordbook for Kids. 2009. (ENG., Illus.). 32p. (gr. 4-7). pap. 6.99 *(978-1-60066-196-9(3),* WingSpread Pubs.) Moody Pubs.
—Communion: A Bible Study Wordbook for Kids. 2009. (ENG., Illus.). 32p. (gr. 4-7). pap. 7.99 *(978-1-60066-195-2(5),* WingSpread Pubs.) Moody Pubs.
—Giving: A Bible Study Wordbook for Kids. 2009. (ENG., Illus.). 32p. (gr. 4-7). pap. 7.99 *(978-1-60066-197-6(1),* WingSpread Pubs.) Moody Pubs.
The Toddler Room: Free Play. 2013. 16p. pap. 7.95 *(978-1-4582-1259-7(9),* Abbott Pr.) Author Solutions, LLC.
Tonges, Wilshire, et al. Slurping Soup & Other Confusions. 2nd ed. 2013. (Illus.). 82p. pap. *(978-1-909193-22-2(4))* Summertime Publishing.
Tonka 5 in 1 Superly Duperly. 2005. 52p. pap. 3.99 *(978-0-7666-2249-4(5))* Modern Publishing.
Top That. Let's Stencil Things That Go. 2008. *(978-1-84666-584-4(1))* Top That! Publishing PLC.
Top That Publishing Staff, ed. Funny Monsters. 2005. 12p. *(978-1-84510-734-5(9))* Top That! Publishing PLC.
Top That!, creator. Roald Dahl Build Your Own Willy Wonka's Chocolate Factory. 2005. (Press Out & Build Ser.). (Illus.). 12p. (J). pap. *(978-1-905359-58-5(6))* Top That! Publishing PLC.
Top That! Kids, creator. Magnetic Silly Faces. 2007. (Illus.). 10p. (J). *(978-1-84666-345-1(8))* Top That! Publishing PLC.
Torres, Laura & Sherman, Michael. Limpiapipas de Locura. 2004. (SPA., Illus.). 46p. (J). spiral bd. 15.95 *(978-968-5528-09-2(8))* Klutz Latino MEX. Dist: Independent Pubs. Group.
Toufexis, George. Alexander Hamilton Activity Book. 2017. (Dover Kids Activity Books: U. S. A. Ser.). (ENG.). 48p. (J). (gr. 4-7). pap. 4.99 *(978-0-486-81852-8(7),* 818527) Dover Pubns., Inc.
—Big Apple Brain Busters Activity Book. 2016. (Dover Kids Activity Books: U. S. A. Ser.). (ENG.). 48p. (J). (gr. 2-5). 5.99 *(978-0-486-79926-1(3),* 799263) Dover Pubns., Inc.
—Chicago Challenge Activity Book. 2016. (Dover Kids Activity Books: U. S. A. Ser.). (ENG.). 48p. (J). (gr. 2-5). 4.99 *(978-0-486-79927-8(1),* 799271) Dover Pubns., Inc.
—Glitter Tattoos Day of the Dead. 2014. (ENG.). 2p. (J). (gr. 1-4). pap. 1.99 *(978-0-486-78014-6(7),* 780147) Dover Pubns., Inc.
—Monster Matrix Activity Book. 2013. (Dover Children's Activity Bks.). (ENG.). 48p. (J). (gr. 3-8). pap. 4.99 *(978-0-486-49963-5(4))* Dover Pubns., Inc.
—The Outrageous Human Body Activity Book. 2013. (Dover Children's Science Bks.). (ENG.). 48p. (J). (gr. 3-8). pap. 4.99 *(978-0-486-49116-5(1))* Dover Pubns., Inc.
—U. S. A. Facts & Fun Activity Book. 2017. (Dover Kids Activity Books: U. S. A. Ser.). (ENG.). 48p. (J). (gr. 3-6). pap. 4.99 *(978-0-486-81379-0(7),* 813797) Dover Pubns., Inc.
—Ultimate Horse-Athon Facts & Activity Book. 2013. (Dover Kids Activity Books: Animals Ser.). (ENG.). 48p. (J). (gr. 3-8). pap. 4.99 *(978-0-486-49184-4(6),* 491846) Dover Pubns., Inc.
Tracey, Andrée. Marvelous Me! a Personalized Coloring Book. 2016. (Dover Coloring Bks.). (ENG.). 32p. (J). (gr. -1-3). pap. 4.99 *(978-0-486-80758-4(4),* 807584) Dover Pubns., Inc.
Trafford, Adrienne. Tarot Designs Coloring Book. 2014. (Dover Design Coloring Bks.). (ENG., Illus.). 32p. (J). (gr. 6-8). pap. 3.99 *(978-0-486-49460-9(8),* 494608) Dover Pubns., Inc.
Trembinsky, Laverne Gray. A Friend Sent from Heaven for Andrew: A Little Boy Finds His Self Experiencing Loneliness Because His Family Had to Move Because of Financial Hardsh. 2009. 45p. (J). pap. 10.95 *(978-1-4327-3458-9(X))* Outskirts Pr., Inc.
Tsukamoto, Allen. Somethin Fishy for the Small Fry. 2006. 28p. (J). pap. 5.95 *(978-0-944462-50-8(2))* Hawaii Fishing News.
Tuchman, Gail & Gray, Margaret. AddUps My Day! Griego, Tony, illus. 2012. (Dover Little Activity Bks.). (ENG.). 32p. (J). (gr. k-3). pap. 1.50 *(978-0-486-49862-1(X),* 49862X) Dover Pubns., Inc.
Tucker, Angel. Four Pals on a Field Trip: An Adventure with Friends Who Are Different. Pileggi, Steve, illus. 2013. (Four Pals Ser.). (ENG.). 34p. (J). (gr. -1-3). pap. 8.95 *(978-1-62086-487-6(8))* Amplify Publishing Group.
Tudhope, Simon. Build Your Own Motorcycles Sticker Book. 2015. (Build Your Own Sticker Bks.). (ENG.). 24+10p. (J). (gr. k-5). pap. 8.99 *(978-0-7945-3546-9(1),* Usborne) EDC Publishing.
Tullet, Hervé & Tullet, Hervé. The Giant Game of Sculpture. 2014. (ENG., Illus.). 16p. (gr. k-3). 29.95 *(978-0-7148-6800-4(0))* Phaidon Pr., Inc.
Tunnell, Amber. The Night Sky: Stories of the Stars (Bedtime Shadow Book) Zschock, Martha Day, illus. 2014. (Bedtime Shadow Bks.). (ENG.). 7p. (J). spiral bd. 12.99 *(978-1-4413-1581-6(0),* 05f84944-6b2a-4d63-b9be-adbaaa743f0c) Peter Pauper Pr. Inc.
Tupera, Tupera. Make Faces: Doodle & Sticker Book with 52 Faces + 6 Sticker Sheets. 2015. (ENG., Illus.). 52p. (J). (gr. 1-4). pap. 12.95 *(978-1-4521-3930-2(X))* Chronicle Bks. LLC.
Twin Sisters(r) Staff. Learning with Elmo: Animals. 2010. (J). (gr. k-2). 9.99 *(978-1-59922-402-2(X))* Twin Sisters IP, LLC.
Twin Sisters(r) Staff, creator. Gross & Annoying Songs. 2005. (Illus.). 95p. (J). pap. 12.99 incl. audio compact disk *(978-1-57583-821-2(4))* Twin Sisters IP, LLC.
Tyrtania, Joachim & Hemrich-Skomer, Denise. Together Time: Cycle A. 2007. (Illus.). 80p. per. 10.95 *(978-0-9787087-2-6(5))* Bound by Grace Pr., LLC.
Ultman, Suzy, illus. Masha's World: Coloring & Activity Book (Interactive Kids Books, Arts & Crafts Books for Kids) 2018. (ENG.). 48p. (J). (gr. -1-k). 14.99 *(978-1-4521-6644-5(7))* Chronicle Bks. LLC.
Usborne Books Staff, creator. Usborne Doodle Pad for Boys. 2014. (ENG., Illus.). (J). pap. 5.99 *(978-0-7945-3291-8(8),* Usborne) EDC Publishing.
—Usborne Doodle Pad for Girls. 2014. (ENG., Illus.). (J). pap. 5.99 *(978-0-7945-3189-8(X),* Usborne) EDC Publishing.
—50 Travel Games & Activities. 2006. (Activity Cards Ser.). 50p. (J). 9.99 *(978-0-7945-1319-1(0),* Usborne) EDC Publishing.
Valencia, Vanessa. Mamma's Planet Earth. 2011. 24p. pap. 10.95 *(978-1-4525-3921-8(9))* Balboa Pr.
Valois, Rob. Intergalactic Adventure. 2008. (Star Wars). (ENG.). 32p. (J). (gr. 1-3). pap., act. bk. ed. 4.99 *(978-0-448-44997-5(8))* Penguin Publishing Group.
Van Leeuwen, Michele D., creator. Summer Bridge Activities: Grades PK to K. 2012. (Summer Bridge Activities Ser.). (ENG., Illus.). 150p. pap. 14.95 *(978-1-60996-440-5(3))* Carson-Dellosa Publishing, LLC.
Van Leeuwen, Wendy. The Ten Commandments Activity Book. 2007. (Illus.). 16p. (J). pap. 1.89 *(978-1-59317-210-7(9))* Warner Pr., Inc.
Vandergrift, Adam. Slime Sorcery: 97 Magical Concoctions Made from Almost Anything - Including Fluffy, Galaxy, Crunchy, Magnetic, Color-Changing, & Glow-in-the-Dark Slime. 2017. (ENG., Illus.). 128p. (J). pap. 29.95 *(978-1-61243-754-5(0))* Ulysses Pr.
Verma, Dinesh, et al. Hindi Alphabet Activity Book International Edition. 2009. (ENG.). 112p. pap. 25.00 *(978-0-557-10678-3(8))* Lulu Pr., Inc.
Virden, William & Borg, Mary. My Colorado Teacher Guide. 2010. 43p. pap. 3.95 *(978-1-59363-656-2(3))* Prufrock Pr.
Virges, Audrey M. A Day in Kindergarten. 2012. 60p. pap. 24.99 *(978-1-4772-8168-0(1))* AuthorHouse.
Vision, David & Vision, Mutiya. What Makes Me Beautiful? ¿Qué Es lo Que Me Hace Hermoso? 2013.Tr. of ¿Qué Es lo Que Me Hace Hermoso? (Illus.). 24p. (J). 17.00 *(978-0-9816254-1-6(X),* Vision Works Publishing) Soul Vision Works Publishing.
Vogt, Janet. Music Brain Teasers. 2006. pap. 19.95 *(978-0-89328-248-6(0))* Lorenz Corp., The.
Volke, Gordon. Big World Activity Sticker Book, Vol. 2. 2004. (Illus.). 16p. 7.25 *(978-1-84161-130-3(1))* Ravette Publishing, Ltd. GBR. Dist: Parkwest Pubns., Inc.
Waldron, Hannah, illus. Pirate Adventure Dice. 2014. (ENG.). 16p. (J). (gr. 1-4). 14.95 *(978-1-85669-938-9(2),* King, Laurence Publishing) Orion Publishing Group, Ltd. GBR. Dist: Hachette Bk. Group.
Walker, Gloria. Stop & Go Safety. 2008. 24p. (J). pap. 14.95 *(978-1-883589-91-2(6))* Clark Publishing, Inc.
Walker, Sylvia. My Sleepover Coloring Book. 2010. (Dover Kids Coloring Bks.). (ENG., Illus.). 32p. (J). (gr. -1-4). pap. 3.99 *(978-0-486-47656-8(1),* 476561) Dover Pubns., Inc.
—Our New Baby Coloring Book. 2014. (Dover Kids Coloring Bks.). (ENG.). 32p. (J). (gr. -1-2). pap. 3.99 *(978-0-486-49462-3(4),* 494624) Dover Pubns., Inc.
Wallace, Melissa. It's Great to Be a Baton Rouge Kid: An a-Z Coloring Book, 1 vol. 2017. (It's Great to Be Ser.). (ENG., Illus.). 32p. pap. 4.95 *(978-1-4556-2373-0(3),* Pelican Publishing) Arcadia Publishing.
Ward, Ellie. Vacation Doodles. 2010. (Y Ser.). (ENG., Illus.). 96p. (J). (gr. 3). pap. 7.95 *(978-1-84732-652-2(8))* Carlton Bks., Ltd. GBR. Dist: Two Rivers Distribution.
Warner Press, creator. The Best Christmas Gift Ever: Coloring & Activity Book. 2008. (J). (gr. -1-3). pap. 11.34 *(978-1-59317-324-1(5))* Warner Pr., Inc.
—Bible Sports Heroes: Great Lessons You Can Learn from God's Favorite Athletes Activity Book. 2008. (J). (gr. -1-3). pap. 11.34 *(978-1-59317-325-8(3))* Warner Pr., Inc.
—Don't You Wonder about This World? 2008. (Illus.). (J). pap. 11.34 *(978-1-59317-321-0(0))* Warner Pr., Inc.
—Learning the Lord's Prayer: Coloring & Activity Book. 2008. (J). (gr. -1-3). pap. 11.34 *(978-1-59317-323-4(7))* Warner Pr., Inc.
—Zacchaeus Climbs a Tree Coloring Book. 2009. (ENG., Illus.). 16p. (J). (gr. -1-k). pap. 11.34 *(978-1-59317-337-1(7))* Warner Pr., Inc.
Warner Press Kids, creator. The First Christmas. 2008. (Illus.). 16p. (J). (gr. 1-5). pap. 11.34 *(978-1-59317-326-5(1))* Warner Pr., Inc.
—The Jelly Bean Prayer Coloring & Activity Book. 2009. (Illus.). (J). (gr. -1-2). 11.34 *(978-1-59317-348-7(2))* Warner Pr., Inc.
—The Jelly Bean Witness. 2009. 16p. (J). (gr. 1-5). pap. 11.34 *(978-1-59317-350-0(4))* Warner Pr., Inc.
—Jesus Is Born: Coloring Book. 2008. 16p. (J). (gr. -1-3). pap. 11.34 *(978-1-59317-322-7(9))* Warner Pr., Inc.
—Paul, a Servant of Jesus: Activity Book. 2008. 16p. (J). (gr. -1-3). pap. 11.34 *(978-1-59317-327-2(X))* Warner Pr., Inc.
—Queen Esther. 2008. (Illus.). 16p. (J). (gr. -1-2). pap. 11.34 *(978-1-59317-220-6(6))* Warner Pr., Inc.
Wasikhongo, Odalo Magruder. My First Book of Numbers. Wasikhongo, Odalo Magruder, illus. 2012. (Illus.). 24p. pap. 5.00 *(978-0-9845203-2-9(5))* WasiWorks Studio LLC.
Watkins, Courtney. Dream It! Draw It! Think It! Do It! Activities to Ignite Creativity. 2016. (ENG., Illus.). 96p. (J). pap. 9.99 *(978-1-4494-8034-9(9))* Andrews McMeel Publishing.

S

Watt, Fiona. Big Dinosaur Sticker Book. 2013. (Sticker Activity Bks). 34p. (J). pap. 8.99 *(978-0-7945-3373-1(6),* Usborne) EDC Publishing.
—Big Doodling Book. 2012. (Activity Bks). 96p. (J). bds. 11.99 *(978-0-7945-3269-7(1),* Usborne) EDC Publishing.
—Big Drawing Book. Thompson, Josephine & Day, Caroline, illus. 2013. (Doodle Bks). 95p. (J). pap. 11.99 *(978-0-7945-3365-6(5),* Usborne) EDC Publishing.
—Lots of Things to Find & Color. 2011. 96p. pap. 12.99 *(978-0-7945-2963-5(1),* Usborne) EDC Publishing.
—Monster Doodles. 2010. (Doodle Cards Ser.). 50p. (J). 9.99 *(978-0-7945-2550-7(4),* Usborne) EDC Publishing.
—Rubber Stamp Activities. 2017. (Stamp Activities* Ser.). (ENG.). 64p. (J). 19.99 *(978-0-7945-4007-4(4),* Usborne) EDC Publishing.
—Spooky Sticker Book. 2008. (Sticker Bks). (Illus.). 32p. (J). pap. 8.99 *(978-0-7945-2342-8(0),* Usborne) EDC Publishing.
—Sticker Dolly Dressing Costumes Around the World. 2013. (Sticker Dolly Dressing Ser.). 34p. (J). pap. 8.99 *(978-0-7945-3382-3(5),* Usborne) EDC Publishing.
—Sticker Dolly Dressing Parties. Moore, Jo, illus. 2013. (Sticker Dolly Dressing Ser.). 34p. (J). pap. 8.99 *(978-0-7945-3370-0(1),* Usborne) EDC Publishing.
—Sticker Dressing Explorers. 2013. (Sticker Dressing Ser.). 34p. (J). pap. 8.99 *(978-0-7945-3374-8(4),* Usborne) EDC Publishing.
—Winter Wonderland Sticker Book. 2012. (Sticker Activity Bks). 34p. (J). pap. 8.99 *(978-0-7945-3320-5(5),* Usborne) EDC Publishing.
Weber, Amy & Creative Haven Staff. Creative Haven Curious Creatures Coloring Book. 2013. (Adult Coloring Books: Animals Ser.). (ENG., Illus.). 64p. (gr. 3). pap. 6.99 *(978-0-486-49269-8(9),* 492699) Dover Pubns., Inc.
Weisburd, Claudia & Sniad, Tamara. Afterschool Style Guide: Graffitiwall. 2006. 79p. spiral bd. 29.95 incl. cd-rom *(978-0-9797125-2-4(1))* Foundation, Inc.
—Global GraffitiWall. 2008. (Illus.). 76p. spiral bd. 24.95 *(978-0-9797125-3-1(X))* Foundation, Inc.
Weisburd, Claudia, et al. Afterschool Style in Practice: 25 Skill-Building Meetngs for Staff. 2007. (Illus.). 182p. spiral bd. 59.95 *(978-0-9797125-0-0(5))* Foundation, Inc.
Wellington, Monica. Color & Cook CHRISTMAS COOKIES. 2009. (Dover Christmas Activity Books for Kids Ser.). (ENG., Illus.). 32p. (J). (gr. -1-3). pap. 4.99 *(978-0-486-47448-9(8),* 474488) Dover Pubns., Inc.
—My Garden. 2011. (Dover Sticker Bks.). (ENG., Illus.). 6p. (J). (gr. k-5). 7.99 *(978-0-486-48381-8(9))* Dover Pubns., Inc.
—My Garden Stickers. 2011. (Dover Sticker Bks.). (ENG., Illus.). 4p. (J). (gr. k-3). pap. 5.99 *(978-0-486-48374-0(6))* Dover Pubns., Inc.
—Night House Bright House Find & Color. 2013. (Dover Kids Activity Bks.). (ENG.). 32p. (J). (gr. -1-2). pap. 3.99 *(978-0-486-49162-2(5),* 491625) Dover Pubns., Inc.
Wells, Jason & Wells, Jeff. Albert Is Our Mascot. Carlson, Patrick, illus. 2013. (That's Not Our Mascot Ser.). (ENG.). (J). 14.95 *(978-1-62086-283-4(2))* Amplify Publishing Group.
—Aubie Is Our Mascot. Carlson, Patrick, illus. 2013. (That's Not Our Mascot Ser.). (ENG.). (J). 14.95 *(978-1-62086-292-6(1))* Amplify Publishing Group.
—Big Al Is Our Mascot. Carlson, Patrick, illus. 2013. (That's Not Our Mascot Ser.). (ENG.). (J). 14.95 *(978-1-62086-290-2(5))* Amplify Publishing Group.
—Big Red Is Our Mascot. Carlson, Patrick, illus. 2013. (That's Not Our Mascot Ser.). (ENG.). (J). 14.95 *(978-1-62086-291-9(3))* Amplify Publishing Group.
—Bully Is Our Mascot. Carlson, Patrick, illus. 2013. (That's Not Our Mascot Ser.). (ENG.). (J). 14.95 *(978-1-62086-294-0(8))* Amplify Publishing Group.
—Cocky Is Our Mascot. Carlson, Patrick, illus. 2013. (That's Not Our Mascot Ser.). (ENG.). (J). 14.95 *(978-1-62086-287-2(5))* Amplify Publishing Group.
—Hairy Dawg Is Our Mascot. Carlson, Patrick, illus. 2013. (That's Not Our Mascot Ser.). (ENG.). (J). 14.95 *(978-1-62086-284-1(0))* Amplify Publishing Group.
—Mike the Tiger Is Our Mascot. Carlson, Patrick, illus. 2013. (That's Not Our Mascot Ser.). (ENG.). (J). 14.95 *(978-1-62086-293-3(X))* Amplify Publishing Group.
—Rebel Is Our Mascot. 2013. (ENG., Illus.). (J). (gr. -1-3). 14.95 *(978-1-62086-295-7(6))* Amplify Publishing Group.
—Reveille Is Our Mascot. Carlson, Patrick, illus. 2013. (That's Not Our Mascot Ser.). (ENG.). (J). 14.95 *(978-1-62086-296-4(4))* Amplify Publishing Group.
—Scratch Is Our Mascot. Carlson, Patrick, illus. 2013. (That's Not Our Mascot Ser.). (ENG.). (J). 14.95 *(978-1-62086-285-8(9))* Amplify Publishing Group.
—Smokey Is Our Mascot. Carlson, Patrick, illus. 2013. (That's Not Our Mascot Ser.). (ENG.). (J). 14.95 *(978-1-62086-288-9(3))* Amplify Publishing Group.
—Truman Is Our Mascot. Carlson, Patrick, illus. 2013. (That's Not Our Mascot Ser.). (ENG.). (J). 14.95 *(978-1-62086-286-5(7))* Amplify Publishing Group.
Wells, Rachel, illus. That's Not My Sticker Book Christmas. rev. ed. 2012. (That's Not My . . Sticker Bks). 28p. (J). pap. 4.99 *(978-0-7945-3318-2(3),* Usborne) EDC Publishing.
Wells, Robin. So Many Classes. Piworski, Marcin, illus. 2017. (School Days Ser.). (ENG.). 24p. (gr. -1-2). pap. 9.95 *(978-1-68342-773-5(4),* 9781683427735) Rourke Educational Media.
Wesleyan Publishing House, creator. Knowing God's Truth: 52 Reproducible in-Class Activities & Family Devotionals. 2006. (Building Kids Faith Ser.). (Illus.). 100p. per. 15.99 *(978-0-89827-342-7(0))* Wesleyan Publishing Hse.
The Western Hemisphere Through the Five Themes of Geography Map Activities Book plus 5 Transparencies. 2005. (Western Hemisphere Through the Five Themes of Geography Ser.). 16p. 55.95 *(978-1-4042-5159-5(6),* Rosen Classroom) Rosen Publishing Group, Inc., The.
Westing, Jemma. Out of the Box: 25 Cardboard Engineering Projects for Makers. 2017. (DK Activity Lab Ser.). (ENG., Illus.). 144p. (J). (gr. 2-5). 19.99 *(978-1-4654-5896-4(4),* DK Children) Dorling Kindersley Publishing, Inc.
What Is a Tangaroo. 2007. (Illus.). 32p. (J). pap. 24.99 *(978-0-9793506-2-7(X))* Sportime International.
What Would You Choose?, 8 vols. 2016. (What Would You Choose? Ser.). (ENG.). 00032p. (J). (gr. 4-5). lib. bdg. 113.08 *(978-1-4824-6073-5(4),* 4a7daead-fec7-4f2d-9aa3-5e056aedafa5) Stevens, Gareth Publishing LLLP.
Whelon, Chuck. Create Your Own Dinosaurs Sticker Activity Book. 2015. (Dover Little Activity Books Stickers Ser.). (ENG.). 4p. (J). (gr. k-3). 2.50 *(978-0-486-78957-6(8),* 789578) Dover Pubns., Inc.
—FLIP OUTS — Dinosaurs: Color Your Own Cartoon! 2015. (ENG., Illus.). 64p. (J). (gr. k-3). pap. 1.99 *(978-0-486-79486-0(5),* 794865) Dover Pubns., Inc.
—Sea Animals Finger Tattoos. 2014. (ENG.). 1p. (J). (gr. 1-4). pap. 3.50 *(978-0-486-78440-3(1),* 784401) Dover Pubns., Inc.
—What to Doodle? Fantastic Fantasy! 2009. (Dover Doodle Bks.). (ENG., Illus.). 64p. (J). (gr. 2-5). pap. 5.99 *(978-0-486-47044-3(X),* 47044X) Dover Pubns., Inc.
—What to Doodle? Things That Go! 2009. (Dover Doodle Bks.). (ENG., Illus.). 64p. (J). (gr. -1-2). pap. 5.99 *(978-0-486-47045-0(8),* 470458) Dover Pubns., Inc.
—Zoo Animals Finger Tattoos. 2014. (ENG.). 2p. (J). (gr. 1-4). 3.50 *(978-0-486-78439-7(8),* 784398) Dover Pubns., Inc.
White, Mia. CAREFUL, YOU Could HURT the DOLPHINS - Zoe's World Dr. Mia White. White, Mia, illus. 2007. (Illus.). per. 24.00 *(978-1-60361-710-9(8))* Belle Media International, Inc. Div of True News.
Wick, Walter. Can You See What I See? Once upon a Time: Picture Puzzles to Search & Solve. Wick, Walter, photos by. 2006. (Can You See What I See? Ser.). (ENG., Illus.). 40p. (J). (gr. -1-3). 13.99 *(978-0-439-61777-2(4),* Cartwheel Bks.) Scholastic, Inc.
Wiemeier, Aaron. My Feelings Workbook. Trapp, Karla, illus. 2011. 104p. (J). pap. 19.95 *(978-1-59850-095-0(3))* Youthlight, Inc.
Wiggles 5 in 1 Superfy Duperly. 2005. 52p. pap. 3.99 *(978-0-7666-2252-4(5))* Modern Publishing.
Wik, John & Creative Haven Staff. Creative Haven Tessellation Patterns Coloring Book. 2013. (Adult Coloring Books: Art & Design Ser.). (ENG., Illus.). 64p. (J). (gr. 3). pap. 6.99 *(978-0-486-49165-3(X),* 49165X) Dover Pubns., Inc.
Wildot Press. Jacob's Back Yard. 2006. (Illus.). 42p. (J). spiral bd. 14.95 *(978-0-9789043-9-5(7))* Wildot Pr.
—Jacob's Front Yard. 2006. (Illus.). 39p. (J). spiral bd. 15.95 *(978-0-9789043-8-8(9))* Wildot Pr.
Wildwood Forest Customizable Outdoor Banner. 2009. (Vacation Bible School Ser.). (J). 35.00 *(978-2-608-00908-1(5))* Cook, David C.
Williams, Christine M. Building a Sight Vocabulary with Comprehension: The It Family. 2012. 24p. pap. 17.99 *(978-1-4772-8498-8(2))* AuthorHouse.
Williams, Colleen Madonna Flood. My Adventure in the Mesozoic Period: Advanced My Adventure. 2009. (ENG.). 44p. (J). pap. 8.99 *(978-1-59092-437-2(1))* Blue Forge Pr.
—My Adventure in the Wild West. 2007. 44p. (J). 8.99 *(978-1-59092-439-6(8))* Blue Forge Pr.
—My Adventure on April Fool's Day. 2009. (ENG.). 44p. (J). 8.99 *(978-1-59092-544-7(0))* Blue Forge Pr.
—My Adventure on Christmas. 2006. 44p. (J). 8.99 *(978-1-59092-545-4(9))* Blue Forge Pr.
—My Adventure on Easter. 2007. 44p. (J). 8.99 *(978-1-59092-546-1(7))* Blue Forge Pr.
—My Adventure on Father's Day. 2007. 44p. (J). 8.99 *(978-1-59092-547-8(5))* Blue Forge Pr.
—My Adventure on Groundhog Day. 2009. (ENG.). 44p. (J). 8.99 *(978-1-59092-548-5(3))* Blue Forge Pr.
—My Adventure on Halloween. 2006. 44p. (J). 8.99 *(978-1-59092-549-2(1))* Blue Forge Pr.
—My Adventure on Martin Luther King Jr. Day. 2009. (ENG.). 44p. (J). 8.99 *(978-1-59092-551-5(3))* Blue Forge Pr.
—My Adventure on Mother's Day. 2007. 44p. (J). 8.99 *(978-1-59092-552-2(1))* Blue Forge Pr.
—My Adventure on My Birthday. 2009. 44p. (J). 8.99 *(978-1-59092-553-9(X))* Blue Forge Pr.
—My Adventure on New Year's Day. 2006. 44p. (J). 8.99 *(978-1-59092-554-6(8))* Blue Forge Pr.
—My Adventure on President's Day. 2007. 44p. (J). 8.99 *(978-1-59092-555-3(6))* Blue Forge Pr.
—My Adventure on St. Patrick's Day. 2007. 44p. (J). 8.99 *(978-1-59092-556-0(4))* Blue Forge Pr.
—My Adventure on Thanksgiving Day. 2006. 44p. (J). 8.99 *(978-1-59092-557-7(2))* Blue Forge Pr.
—My Adventure on the Fourth of July. 2009. (ENG.). 44p. (J). 8.99 *(978-1-59092-560-7(2))* Blue Forge Pr.
—My Adventure on Valentine's Day. 2009. (ENG.). 44p. (J). 8.99 *(978-1-59092-558-4(0))* Blue Forge Pr.
—My Adventure on Veteran's Day. 2006. 44p. (J). 8.99 *(978-1-59092-559-1(9))* Blue Forge Pr.
—My Adventure with Knights. 2009. (ENG.). 44p. (J). 8.99 *(978-1-59092-456-3(8))* Blue Forge Pr.
—My Adventure with Leonardo da Vinci. 2009. (ENG.). 44p. (J). 8.99 *(978-1-59092-458-7(4))* Blue Forge Pr.
—My Adventure with Shakespeare. 2009. (ENG.). 44p. (J). 8.99 *(978-1-59092-467-9(3))* Blue Forge Pr.
—My Adventure with Vikings. 2009. (ENG.). 44p. (J). 8.99 *(978-1-59092-474-7(6))* Blue Forge Pr.
—Schooling Day-by-day in May. 2007. 44p. (J). 8.99 *(978-1-59092-521-8(1))* Blue Forge Pr.
Williams, Lynette Gain. Handwriting Begins with Art: The Partner Book to ArbeZ ZebrA Teaches A to Z. 2007. 165p. (J). spiral bd. 19.99 *(978-0-9779063-1-4(0))* Gain Literacy Skills / Lynette Gain Williams.
Williams, Rozanne Lanczak. Sing & Read with Greg & Steve All-in-One Pack. 2009. pap. 58.86 *(978-1-60689-164-3(2))* Youngheart Music.
Wilson, Becky. Lonely Planet Kids Sticker World - Museum 1. Basil, Aviel, illus. 2018. (Lonely Planet Kids Ser.). (ENG.). 40p. (J). (gr. 1-3). 6.99 *(978-1-78701-135-9(6),* 5697) Lonely Planet Global Ltd. IRL. Dist: Hachette Bk. Group.
Wilson, CeCe. The Thunder Cloud Cookies, 1 vol. 2015. (Rosen REAL Readers: STEM & STEAM Collection). (ENG.). 12p. (gr. k-1). pap. 6.33 *(978-1-4994-9523-2(4),* ccfbe911-ca38-4cd3-a9c6-ebc7974360df, Rosen Classroom) Rosen Publishing Group, Inc., The.
Winslow, Jeremy. Hours of Coloring Fun with Shapes & Patterns. 2011. 182p. 30.99 *(978-1-4568-8227-3(9));* pap. 20.99 *(978-1-4568-8226-6(0))* Xlibris Corp.
Wipe-Clean Action Words to Copy. 2017. (Wipe-Clean Bks.). (ENG.). (J). pap. 7.99 *(978-0-7945-3938-2(6),* Usborne) EDC Publishing.
Wipe-Clean Dinosaur Activities. 2017. (Wipe-Clean Activity Books* Ser.). (ENG.). (J). pap. 7.99 *(978-0-7945-3987-0(4),* Usborne) EDC Publishing.
Withers, Margaret. Welcome to the Lord's Table: A Practical Course for Preparing Children to Receive Holy Communion. 3rd rev. ed. 2013. (ENG., Illus.). 96p. pap. *(978-1-84101-734-1(5),* Barnabas for Children) Bible Reading Fellowship.
Wojciechowska, Maia. Shadow of a Bull. 2007. 151p. (gr. 3-7). 17.00 *(978-0-7569-7999-7(4))* Perfection Learning Corp.
Wolf, Laurie Goldrich. Boy-Made: Green & Groovy. 2012. (Green & Groovy Ser.: 3). (ENG.). 64p. (J). (gr. 1). 16.99 *(978-1-935703-28-0(5))* Downtown Bookworks.
Wood, Anita. BFF Journal, 1 vol. Kalis, Jennifer, illus. 2011. (ENG.). 144p. (J). (gr. 1). spiral bd. 12.99 *(978-1-4236-1814-0(9))* Gibbs Smith, Publisher.
—Doodle Your Day, 1 vol. Kalis, Jennifer, illus. 2013. (ENG.). 224p. (J). pap. 16.99 *(978-1-4236-2368-7(1))* Gibbs Smith, Publisher.
—Travel Doodles for Kids, 1 vol. Sabatino, Chris, illus. 2012. (ENG.). 272p. (J). pap. 9.99 *(978-1-4236-2454-7(8))* Gibbs Smith, Publisher.
Wood, Kristen. Find Albert Alberta Too. 2009. 36p. 19.95 *(978-1-935159-11-7(9))* My Campus Adventure, Inc.
—Find Big Al. 2009. 36p. 19.95 *(978-1-935159-10-0(0))* My Campus Adventure, Inc.
—Find Reveille. 2009. 36p. 19.95 *(978-1-935159-08-7(9))* My Campus Adventure, Inc.
—Find Uga Hairy Dawg Too. 2009. 36p. 19.95 *(978-1-935159-09-4(7))* My Campus Adventure, Inc.
Wood, Mark. Beyond Classroom Enrichment: Creative Units for Gifted Students. 2004. (Illus.). 80p. *(978-0-910609-48-7(9))* Gifted Education Pr.
Woodworth, Viki. United States Maze Craze. 2009. (Dover Kids Activity Books: U. S. A. Ser.). (ENG., Illus.). 64p. (J). (gr. 3-4). pap. 5.99 *(978-0-486-46831-0(3),* 468313) Dover Pubns., Inc.
—The 50 States: Facts & Fun. 2010. (Dover Little Activity Bks.). (ENG., Illus.). 64p. (J). (gr. 1-5). pap. 2.50 *(978-0-486-47524-0(7),* 475247) Dover Pubns., Inc.
Woram, Catherine & Youngs, Clare. Rainy Day Book of Things to Make & Do. 2012. (ENG., Illus.). 160p. pap. *(978-1-84975-272-5(9))* Ryland Peters & Small.
Workman Publishing. Eyelike Stickers: Space. 2014. (Eyelike Stickers Ser.). (ENG.). 12p. (J). pap. 6.95 *(978-0-7611-7965-8(8),* 17965) Workman Publishing Co., Inc.
—Paint by Sticker Kids, the Original: Create 10 Pictures One Sticker at a Time! (Kids Activity Book, Sticker Art, No Mess Activity, Keep Kids Busy) 2016. (Paint by Sticker Ser.). (ENG., Illus.). 34p. (J). (gr. k-4). 9.95 *(978-0-7611-8941-1(6),* 18941) Workman Publishing Co., Inc.
—Paint by Sticker Kids: under the Sea: Create 10 Pictures One Sticker at a Time! 2017. (Paint by Sticker Ser.). (ENG., Illus.). 44p. (J). (gr. k-4). 9.95 *(978-1-5235-0038-3(7),* 100038) Workman Publishing Co., Inc.
—Paint by Sticker Kids: Zoo Animals: Create 10 Pictures One Sticker at a Time! 2016. (Paint by Sticker Ser.). (ENG., Illus.). 44p. (J). (gr. k-7). 9.95 *(978-0-7611-8960-2(2),* 18960) Workman Publishing Co., Inc.
Workman Publishing, et al. Summer Brain Quest: Between Grades 1 And 2. Yan, Edison & Dukes, Rachel, illus. 2017. (Summer Brain Quest Ser.). (ENG.). 160p. (J). (gr. 1-2). pap. 12.99 *(978-0-7611-8917-6(3),* 18917) Workman Publishing Co., Inc.
—Summer Brain Quest: Between Grades 2 And 3. Yan, Edison & Cummings, Matt, illus. 2017. (Summer Brain Quest Ser.). (ENG.). 160p. (J). (gr. 2-3). pap. 12.99 *(978-0-7611-8918-3(1),* 18918) Workman Publishing Co., Inc.
—Summer Brain Quest: Between Grades 3 And 4. Yan, Edison, illus. 2017. (Summer Brain Quest Ser.). (ENG.). 160p. (J). (gr. 3-4). pap. 12.99 *(978-0-7611-8919-0(X),* 18919) Workman Publishing Co., Inc.
—Summer Brain Quest: Between Grades 4 And 5. Yan, Edison & Thomas, Chad, illus. 2017. (Summer Brain Quest Ser.). (ENG.). 160p. (J). (gr. 4-5). pap. 12.99 *(978-0-7611-8920-6(3),* 18920) Workman Publishing Co., Inc.
—Summer Brain Quest: Between Grades 5 And 6. Yan, Edison & Pietch, Carey, illus. 2017. (Summer Brain Quest Ser.). (ENG.). 160p. (J). (gr. 5-6). pap. 12.99 *(978-0-7611-9328-9(6),* 19328) Workman Publishing Co., Inc.
—Summer Brain Quest: Between Grades K And 1. Yan, Edison & Wicks, Maris, illus. 2017. (Summer Brain Quest Ser.). (ENG.). 160p. (J). (gr. k-1). pap. 12.95 *(978-0-7611-8916-9(5),* 18916) Workman Publishing Co., Inc.
World Book, Inc. Staff, contrib. by. Fun with Painting & Sculpture. 2011. (J). *(978-0-7166-0226-2(1))* World Bk., Inc.
The World of Eric Carle My Alphabet Activity Kit. 2007. (J). 16.99 *(978-0-9794445-0-0(0))* Loew-Cornell, Inc.
The World of Eric Carle My Animals Activity Kit. 2007. (J). 16.99 *(978-0-9794445-4-8(3))* Loew-Cornell, Inc.
The World of Eric Carle My Numbers Activity Kit. 2007. (J). 16.99 *(978-0-9794445-1-7(9))* Loew-Cornell, Inc.
The World of Eric Carle My Shapes Activity Kit. 2007. (J). 16.99 *(978-0-9794445-3-1(5))* Loew-Cornell, Inc.
Wright, Natalie. Slime 101: How to Make Stretchy, Fluffy, Glittery & Colorful Slime! 2017. (ENG., Illus.). 48p. (gr. 1-6). pap. 6.99 *(978-0-486-82091-0(2),* 820912) Dover Pubns., Inc.
Wynne, Patricia J. Butterfly Activity Book. 2007. (Dover Kids Activity Books: Animals Ser.). (ENG., Illus.). 48p. (J). (gr. -1-2). 4.95 *(978-0-486-45692-8(7),* 456927) Dover Pubns., Inc.
—Creative Haven SeaScapes Coloring Book. 2013. (Adult Coloring Books: Sea Life Ser.). (ENG.). 64p. (J). (gr. 3). pap. 5.99 *(978-0-486-49423-4(3),* 494233) Dover Pubns., Inc.
—Glow-in-the-Dark Skeleton Stickers. 2009. (Dover Little Activity Books Stickers Ser.). (ENG., Illus.). 2p. (J). (gr. 1-4). 2.99 *(978-0-486-47129-7(2),* 471292) Dover Pubns., Inc.
—Wild Animals Activity Book. 2008. (Dover Kids Activity Books: Animals Ser.). (ENG., Illus.). 48p. (J). (gr. k-3). pap. 4.95 *(978-0-486-46564-7(0),* 465640) Dover Pubns., Inc.
Wynne, Patricia J. & Whelon, Chuck. 3-D Mazes — Dinosaurs. 2012. (Dover Kids Activity Books: Dinosaurs Ser.). (ENG.). 32p. (J). (gr. 1-6). 5.99 *(978-0-486-49015-1(7),* 490157) Dover Pubns., Inc.
Yasuda, Anita. Explore Ancient Chinese Myths! With 25 Great Projects. Casteel, Tom, illus. 2017. (Explore Your World Ser.). (ENG.). 96p. (J). (gr. 3-4). pap. 14.95 *(978-1-61930-611-0(5),* d9bdc34e-3c81-4911-bed0-b7f120c808b7) Nomad Pr.
—Explore Water! 25 Great Projects, Activities, Experiments. Stone, Bryan, illus. 2011. (Explore Your World Ser.). (ENG.). 96p. (J). (gr. k-4). pap. 12.95 *(978-1-936313-42-6(1),* baedaabf-fa86-4ca2-858d-88d225cdef2a) Nomad Pr.
Yates, Irene. Christmas Activities for ks1 Maths. 2005. pap. *(978-1-903853-68-9(0))* Brilliant Pubns.
—Christmas Activities for Ks2 Maths. 2005. (Illus.). 64p. pap. *(978-1-903853-69-6(9))* Brilliant Pubns.
—Christmas Activities for Language & L. 2007. *(978-1-903853-67-2(2))* Brilliant Pubns.
Young, Helen Ann. Your World Discovery Scrapbook. Young, Tim Blair, illus. 2013. 40p. pap. *(978-1-908353-03-0(1))* Young Editions.
Yteane Milliona Devalt. Princess Million: All about Me & Activity Book. 2009. 32p. pap. 12.99 *(978-1-4389-2526-4(3))* AuthorHouse.
Zelinski, E. J. Pensar a lo Grande: Ejercicios Simples y Divertidos para Potenciar la Creatividad. (SPA.). 212p. *(978-84-95456-79-3(6),* 87420) Ediciones Oniro S.A.
Zhu, Ping, illus. Stickyscapes at the Museum. 2018. (Magma for Laurence King Ser.). (ENG.). (J). (gr. 1-4). pap. 10.99 *(978-1-78067-972-3(6),* King, Laurence Publishing) Orion Publishing Group, Ltd. GBR. Dist: Hachette Bk. Group.
Zimmerman, Bill. Pocketdoodles for Young Artists, 1 vol. 2010. (ENG., Illus.). 272p. (J). (gr. 1). 9.99 *(978-1-4236-0466-2(0))* Gibbs Smith, Publisher.
Zommer, Yuval. The Big Sticker Book of the Blue. 2018. (Big Book Ser.: 10). (ENG., Illus.). 56p. (J). (gr. -1-5). pap. 14.95 *(978-0-500-65180-3(9),* 565180) Thames & Hudson.
ZOO, La. Incredible Stickers! An Activity Book with Stickers. Miyakoshi, Junko, tr. 2010. (King of Play Ser.). (ENG., Illus.). 52p. (J). (gr. -1). pap. 7.95 *(978-1-934734-38-4(1))* Seven Footer Pr.
—Let's Color! A Coloring Book Like No Other. 2009. (King of Play Ser.). (ENG.). 128p. (gr. -1). pap. 12.95 *(978-1-934734-02-5(0))* Seven Footer Pr.
—Squiggles! A Drawing Book. Oku, Makiko, tr. 2009. (King of Play Ser.). (ENG., Illus.). 64p. (J). (gr. -1). pap. 7.95 *(978-1-934734-13-1(6))* Seven Footer Pr.
—Stickers! An Activity Book with Stickers. Miyakoshi, Junko, tr. 2010. (King of Play Ser.). (ENG., Illus.). 52p. (J). (gr. -1). pap. 7.95 *(978-1-934734-37-7(3))* Seven Footer Pr.
Zook, Melinda. L-E-t-t-e-r-s. 2012. 24p. pap. 24.95 *(978-1-4626-7175-5(6))* America Star Bks.
Zourelias, Diana. Build a Giant Poster Coloring Book — United States Map. 2013. (Dover Kids Coloring Bks.). (ENG., Illus.). 48p. (J). (gr. 3-5). pap. 4.99 *(978-0-486-49152-3(8),* 491528) Dover Pubns., Inc.
—Find & Color the Impostor Activity Book. 2018. (Dover Kids Activity Bks.). (ENG.). 128p. (J). (gr. 1-4). pap. 9.99 *(978-0-486-82975-3(8),* 829758) Dover Pubns., Inc.
—My Awesome Superhero Journal: A Fun Fill-In Book for Kids. 2018. (Dover Kids Activity Bks.). (ENG.). 96p. (J). (gr. 1-4). pap. 7.99 *(978-0-486-82412-3(8),* 824128) Dover Pubns., Inc.
—My Fantastic Vacation Journal: A Fun Fill-In Book for Kids. 2019. (Dover Children's Activity Bks.). (ENG.). 96p. (J). (gr. 1-4). pap. 7.99 *(978-0-486-82415-4(2),* 824152) Dover Pubns., Inc.
—SPARK Silly Sea Life Find It! Color It! 2016. (Dover Kids Activity Books: Animals Ser.). (ENG.). 64p. (J). (gr. 1-4). pap. 5.99 *(978-0-486-81095-9(X),* 81095X) Dover Pubns., Inc.
Zschock, Martha Day, illus. Spooky Scratch & Sketch: For Spooky Artists & Trick-or-Treaters of All Ages. 2007. (Scratch & Sketch Ser.). (ENG.). 64p. (J). spiral bd. 12.99 *(978-1-59359-881-5(5),* 7c2b78bf-bdeb-4e78-8a9d-0a69d7a65302) Peter Pauper Pr. Inc.

STUDENT AID

see Scholarships; Student Loans

STUDENT GUIDANCE

see Educational Counseling; Vocational Guidance

STUDENT LIFE AND CUSTOMS

see Students

STUDENT LOANS

see also Scholarships

Aresty, Reecy. Getting into College & Paying for It: Solutions for High School & College Families Guaranteed to Cut the Cost! I.t. ed. 2003.Tr. of Superando Americano: Como Ingresar a la Universidad Y Pagar Los Mas Bajos Costos! (SPA., Illus.). 258p. (YA). per. 27.95 *(978-0-9760251-1-5(6))* College Assistance, Inc.
Bryfonski, Dedria, ed. Student Loans, 1 vol. 2011. (At Issue Ser.). (ENG.). 120p. (gr. 10-12). 41.03 *(978-0-7377-5600-5(4),* 4e6f75ed-5590-4f28-9d10-b74ef5442b25, Greenhaven Publishing) Greenhaven Publishing LLC.
Hamilton, Robert M. Should a College Education Be Free?, 1 vol. 2018. (Points of View Ser.). (ENG.). 24p. (gr. 3-3). pap. 9.25 *(978-1-5345-2781-2(8),* 5a85dd3f-3201-4bf8-a1ed-1aff68aeb559, KidHaven Publishing) Greenhaven Publishing LLC.
Merino, Noël, ed. Student Loans, 1 vol. 2016. (At Issue Ser.). (ENG.). 88p. (gr. 10-12). 41.03 *(978-0-7377-7410-8(X),* e795ced2-090a-475b-b11e-6e7b42ce3d30, Greenhaven Publishing) Greenhaven Publishing LLC.
Rugg, Frederick E. Financial Aid in Less Than 3000 Words. 6p. (YA). 9th rev. ed. 2003. pap. 6.95 *(978-1-883062-51-4(9))* 10th rev. ed. 2004. pap. 6.95 *(978-1-883062-57-6(8))* Rugg's Recommendations.
—Thirty Questions & Answers on the Colleges. (YA). 9th rev. ed. 2003. 20p. pap. 9.95 *(978-1-883062-52-1(7))* 10th rev. ed. 2004. 20p. pap. 9.95 *(978-1-883062-56-9(X))* 11th rev. ed. 2005. 21p. pap. 9.95 *(978-1-883062-61-3(6))* Rugg's Recommendations.
A Student's Guide to Financial Empowerment. 2013. (Student's Guide to Financial Empowerment Ser.). 64p. (YA).

(gr. 7-12). pap. 77.70 *(978-1-4777-2693-8(4))*; pap. 466.20 *(978-1-4777-2694-5(2))*; (ENG.). 222.72 *(978-1-4488-9362-1(3)*, 49c73184-7af4-40ee-b165-facfd59573d5) Rosen Publishing Group, Inc., The.

STUDENT MOVEMENTS

see Youth Movement

STUDENT PROTESTS

see Youth Movement

STUDENT REVOLT

see Youth Movement

STUDENTS

Ahlberg, Janet & Ahlberg, Allan. Starting School. 2004. (J). (gr. k-3). spiral bd. *(978-0-616-11861-0(9))* Canadian National Institute for the Blind/Institut National Canadien pour les Aveugles.

Alpine, Rachele. Friday Night Stage Lights. 2018. (Mix Ser.). (ENG.). 352p. (J). (gr. 4-8). 17.99 *(978-1-5344-0459-5(7))*; (Illus.). pap. 8.99 *(978-1-5344-0458-8(9))* Simon & Schuster Children's Publishing. (Aladdin).

Bily, Cynthia A., ed. Dress Codes in Schools, 1 vol. 2014. (Issues That Concern You Ser.). (ENG., Illus.). 104p. (gr. 7-10). lib. bdg. 43.63 *(978-0-7377-6930-2(0)*, fadff5e5-e30e-4b9b-a649-b7d0ff704687, Greenhaven Publishing) Greenhaven Publishing LLC.

Brindell Fradin, Dennis. Turning Points in History, 12 vols., Group 4. Incl. First Lunar Landing. 34.07 *(978-0-7614-4256-1(1)*, 2a64a349-32a7-41c4-9b47-d4ecef34bf16); Hurricane Katrina. Bloom Fradin, Judith. 34.07 *(978-0-7614-4261-5(8)*, 516d2f6d-7f79-4ec9-b419-2220b5bdeb93); Louisiana Purchase. 34.07 *(978-0-7614-4257-8(X)*, 53cdb14d-b8e2-418d-8921-ceb098a75c1e); Montgomery Bus Boycott. 34.07 *(978-0-7614-4258-5(8)*, 0d3787c1-13eb-4d62-aab1-b3d95ad87102); Stamp Act Of 1765. (Illus.). 34.07 *(978-0-7614-4260-8(X)*, ebda7934-06c6-4918-bac9-93a066b6efcd); 9/11/01. 34.07 *(978-0-7614-4259-2(6)*, 75002057-d3bf-4e16-9278-148fda1efa7d); 48p. (gr. 4-4). (Turning Points in U. S. History Ser.). (ENG.). 2010. Set lib. bdg. 204.42 *(978-0-7614-4255-4(3)*, 1c6e051b-4576-4b2a-9335-6d08323f0a30, Cavendish Square) Cavendish Square Publishing LLC.

Bullard, Lisa. Who Works at Hannah's School? Becker, Paula J., illus. 2017. (Cloverleaf Books (tm) — off to School Ser.). (ENG.). 24p. (J). (gr. k-2). pap. 8.99 *(978-1-5124-5581-6(4)*, ad42b7b5-083b-4e5a-b490-9a462732911b, Millbrook Pr.) Lerner Publishing Group.

Collins, Anna. Student Rights in a New Age of Activism, 1 vol. annot. ed. 2019. (Hot Topics Ser.). (ENG.). 104p. (gr. 7-7). pap. 20.99 *(978-1-5345-6816-7(6)*, 1436407c-9732-41af-bc24-a22a844c782f); lib. bdg. 41.03 *(978-1-5345-6817-4(4)*, eca42a66-856f-4390-8ad2-5fb09080a7f4) Greenhaven Publishing LLC. (Lucent Pr.).

Crockett, Kyle A. Nutrition for Achievement in Sports & Academics. Borus, Joshua, ed. 2013. (Understanding Nutrition: a Gateway to Physical & Mental Health Ser.). (Illus.). 48p. (J). (gr. 5-18). pap. 9.95 *(978-1-4222-2990-3(4))*; 19.95 *(978-1-4222-2884-5(3))* Mason Crest.

De Jesús, Ada. El Baile de Octavo y Otros Recuerdos / the Eighth Grade Dance & Other Memories. 2019. (ENG & SPA., Illus.). 64p. (J). (gr. 6-9). pap. 9.95 *(978-1-55885-885-5(7))* Arte Publico Pr.

Dudley Gold, Susan. Tinker V. des Moines: Free Speech for Students, 1 vol. 2007. (Supreme Court Milestones Ser.). (ENG., Illus.). 128p. (YA). (gr. 8-8). lib. bdg. 45.50 *(978-0-7614-2142-9(4)*, 50a15397-ed35-4b8d-b27b-01c21a7b756d) Cavendish Square Publishing LLC.

Elliott, Tommy. I Don't Want To: Go to School. 2009. 24p. pap. 13.49 *(978-1-4389-5123-2(X))* AuthorHouse.

Fry, Ron. Surefire Tips to Improve Your Memory Skills, 1 vol., 1. 2015. (Surefire Study Success Ser.). (ENG.). 144p. (YA). (gr. 7-8). 38.80 *(978-1-5081-7089-1(4)*, e6a7ce85-aa68-4893-8d97-02a5116b0159, Rosen Young Adult) Rosen Publishing Group, Inc., The.

—Surefire Tips to Improve Your Reading Skills, 1 vol., 1. 2015. (Surefire Study Success Ser.). (ENG.). 144p. (YA). (gr. 7-8). 38.80 *(978-1-5081-7094-5(0)*, f782fa03-8732-441e-86ec-7b6b95573862, Rosen Young Adult) Rosen Publishing Group, Inc., The.

Gitlin, Martin, ed. Student Protests, 1 vol. 2019. (Introducing Issues with Opposing Viewpoints Ser.). (ENG.). 120p. (gr. 7-10). 43.63 *(978-1-5345-0574-2(1)*, 448b618d-b505-4f53-8a10-6e797143b3f3) Greenhaven Publishing LLC.

Glasser, Debbie & Schenck, Emily. New Kid, New Scene: A Guide to Moving & Switching Schools. 2011. (Illus.). 112p. (J). pap. 9.95 *(978-1-4338-1038-1(7)*, Magination Pr.) American Psychological Assn.

Glasser, Debbie, et al. New Kid, New Scene: A Guide to Moving & Switching Schools. 2011. (Illus.). 112p. (J). 14.95 *(978-1-4338-1039-8(5)*, Magination Pr.) American Psychological Assn.

Hartzler, Aaron. Rapture Practice: A True Story about Growing up Gay in an Evangelical Family. 2014. (ENG.). 416p. (YA). (gr. 10-17). pap. 11.99 *(978-0-316-09464-1(1))* Little, Brown Bks. for Young Readers.

Haugen, David M. & Musser, Susan, eds. Discipline & Punishment, 1 vol. 2012. (Teen Rights & Freedoms Ser.). (ENG., Illus.). 176p. (gr. 10-12). lib. bdg. 43.63 *(978-0-7377-6401-7(5)*, fc7ae1d0-60e3-43c0-941a-70e94836c8dc, Greenhaven Publishing) Greenhaven Publishing LLC.

Havemeyer, Janie. Should Kids Wear School Uniforms? 2018. (Shape Your Opinion Ser.). (ENG., Illus.). 48p. (J). (gr. 1-3). 26.60 *(978-1-59953-929-4(2))* Norwood Hse. Pr.

Heing, Bridey. The White Rose Movement: Nonviolent Resistance to the Nazis, 1 vol. 2017. (Peaceful Protesters Ser.). (ENG.). 112p. (YA). (gr. 9-9). 44.50 *(978-1-5026-3120-6(2)*, b7763320-44c0-475a-8fc9-26bd2d75ff10); pap. 20.99 *(978-1-5026-3397-2(3)*, aef5139a-cc72-4bd3-ad59-f7267365adb5) Cavendish Square Publishing LLC.

Hudson, David L. Rights of Students. (Point/Counterpoint: Issues in Contemporary American Society Ser.). (gr. 9-13). 2004. (ENG., Illus.). 110p. 35.00 *(978-0-7910-7920-1(1)*, P114073) 2nd rev. ed. 2010. 112p. (C). 35.00 *(978-1-60413-692-0(8))* Infobase Holdings, Inc. (Facts On File).

Hurt, Avery Elizabeth, ed. Student Rights, 1 vol. 2017. (Issues That Concern You Ser.). (ENG.). 112p. (YA). (gr. 7-10). 43.63 *(978-1-5345-0225-3(4)*, 61f15bf6-72fc-498f-aa83-c936c9538be3); pap. 29.30 *(978-1-5345-0280-2(7)*, bfed5f19-a96f-4575-adcc-3977cee308d0) Greenhaven Publishing LLC.

Jacobsen, Aryelle. A Is for Awkward: A Guide to Surviving Middle School. 2017. (ENG., Illus.). (J). (gr. 5-6). 18.95 *(978-1-63051-443-3(8))*; (gr. 7-12). pap. 7.95 *(978-1-63051-442-6(X))* Chiron Pubns.

Jeffrey, Gary. The Little Rock Nine & the Fight for Equal Education, 1 vol. 2012. (Graphic History of the Civil Rights Movement Ser.). (ENG., Illus.). 24p. (J). (gr. 3-3). lib. bdg. 26.60 *(978-1-4339-7483-0(5)*, f8b2bcb2-4bfd-4b07-8022-90f9173c2140) Stevens, Gareth Publishing LLLP.

Lindin, Emily. UnSlut: A Diary & a Memoir. 2015. (ENG., Illus.). 272p. (YA). (gr. 9-12). 14.99 *(978-1-942186-00-7(2)*, 5d5e5227-8b5d-4bd2-b66e-fbbc818a2dbe, Zest Bks.) Lerner Publishing Group.

Lucas, Eileen. The Little Rock Nine Stand up for Their Rights. Gustavson, Adam, illus. 2011. (History Speaks: Picture Books Plus Reader's Theater Ser.). 48p. pap. 56.72 *(978-0-7613-7634-7(8))* Lerner Publishing Group.

Marcovitz, Hal. Teens & Career Choices. Developed in Association with the Gallup Organization Staff, ed. 2013. (Gallup Youth Survey: Major Issues & Trends Ser.: 14). 112p. (J). (gr. 7-18). 24.95 *(978-1-4222-2950-7(5))* Mason Crest.

Mattern, Joanne. After School / Después de la Escuela, 1 vol. 2006. (My Day at School / Mi día en la Escuela Ser.). (ENG & SPA., Illus.). 24p. (gr. k-2). pap. 9.15 *(978-0-8368-7364-1(5)*, 477ec2e4-61d9-458c-8599-8cad8ed5c846); lib. bdg. 24.67 *(978-0-8368-7357-3(2)*, 454a7af5-7e24-484e-bb1b-f791d58f6066) Stevens, Gareth Publishing LLLP. (Weekly Reader Leveled Readers).

McCarney, Rosemary. The Way to School, 1 vol. 2015. (Plan International Canada Bks.: 3). (ENG., Illus.). 32p. (J). (gr. 1-3). 18.95 *(978-1-927583-78-4(0))* Second Story Pr. CAN. Dist: Orca Bk. Pubs. USA.

Mcpherson, Stephanie Sammartino. Stressed Out in School? Learning to Deal with Academic Pressure, 1 vol. 2010. (Issues in Focus Today Ser.). (ENG., Illus.). 112p. (gr. 6-7). lib. bdg. 35.93 *(978-0-7660-3069-5(5)*, b8b74d97-b350-4df4-9058-a7ba12f3f96b) Enslow Publishing, LLC.

Meet Our New Student, 8 vols., Set. Incl. Meet Our New Student from Australia. Weil, Ann. (Illus.). 47p. (J). (gr. 3-7). 2008. lib. bdg. 29.95 *(978-1-58415-652-9(X))*; Meet Our New Student from China. Orr, Tamra. (Illus.). 48p. (YA). (gr. 2-5). 2008. lib. bdg. 29.95 *(978-1-58415-647-5(3))*; Meet Our New Student from Colombia. Murcia, Rebecca Thatcher. (Illus.). 48p. (J). (gr. 1-5). 2008. lib. bdg. 29.95 *(978-1-58415-650-5(3))*; Meet Our New Student from Great Britain. Orr, Tamra. (Illus.). 48p. (J). (gr. 4-7). 2008. lib. bdg. 29.95 *(978-1-58415-648-2(1))*; Meet Our New Student from Haiti. Torres, John A. (Illus.). 48p. (YA). (gr. 2-5). 2008. lib. bdg. 29.95 *(978-1-58415-653-6(8))*; Meet Our New Student from India. Ejaz, Khadija. (Illus.). 48p. (J). (gr. 2-5). 2009. lib. bdg. 25.70 *(978-1-58415-779-3(8))*; Meet Our New Student from Israel. Saul, Laya. (Illus.). 48p. (J). (gr. 3-7). 2008. lib. bdg. 29.95 *(978-1-58415-651-2(1))*; Meet Our New Student from Japan. McManus, Lori. 48p. (J). (gr. 2-5). 2009. 29.95 *(978-1-58415-780-9(1))*; Meet Our New Student from Korea. Kjelle, Marylou Morano. (Illus.). 48p. (YA). (gr. 2-5). 2008. lib. bdg. 29.95 *(978-1-58415-649-9(X))*; Meet Our New Student from Malaysia. Weil, Ann. (Illus.). 48p. (J). (gr. 1-5). 2008. lib. bdg. 29.95 *(978-1-58415-654-3(6))*; Meet Our New Student from Mali. Ogunnaike, Oludamini. (Illus.). 48p. (J). (gr. 2-5). 2009. lib. bdg. 25.70 *(978-1-58415-734-2(8))*; Meet Our New Student from Mexico. Orr, Tamra. (Illus.). 48p. (YA). (gr. 2-5). 2008. lib. bdg. 29.95 *(978-1-58415-646-8(5))*; Meet Our New Student from New Zealand. Weil, Ann. (Illus.). 48p. (J). (gr. 2-5). 2008. lib. bdg. 29.95 *(978-1-58415-657-4(0))*; Meet Our New Student from Nicaragua. Torres, John Albert. 48p. (J). (gr. 2-5). 2009. 29.95 *(978-1-58415-824-0(X))*; Meet Our New Student from Nigeria. Ogunnaike, Anna M. (Illus.). 47p. (YA). (gr. 2-5). 2008. lib. bdg. 29.95 *(978-1-58415-655-0(4))*; Meet Our New Student from Quebec. Weil, Ann. 48p. (J). (gr. 2-5). 2009. 29.95 *(978-1-58415-778-6(X))*; Meet Our New Student from South Africa. Koosman, Melissa. (Illus.). 47p. (J). (gr. 2-5). 2009. lib. bdg. 29.95 *(978-1-58415-781-6(X))*; Meet Our New Student from Tanzania. Weil, Ann. 48p. (YA). (gr. 2-5). 2008. lib. bdg. 29.95 *(978-1-58415-656-7(2))*; Meet Our New Student from Zambia. Torres, John Albert. 48p. (J). (gr. 2-5). 2010. 29.95 *(978-1-58415-735-9(6))*; 2010. Set lib. bdg. 599.00 *(978-1-58415-783-0(6))* Mitchell Lane Pubs.

Messina, Noreen E. Teenwork: Four Teens Tell All: A Guide for Finding Jobs. 2005. (Illus.). 126p. (gr. 6-12). per. 12.75 *(978-1-59070-598-8(X))* Goodheart-Willcox Pub.

Meyer, Terry. Navigating a New School, 1 vol. 2012. (Middle School Survival Handbook Ser.). (ENG., Illus.). 64p. (YA). (gr. 6-6). lib. bdg. 37.13 *(978-1-4488-8312-7(1)*, 9b81aa29-13f3-4354-82a9-1482d6f6933c, Rosen Reference) Rosen Publishing Group, Inc., The.

Meyer, Terry Teague. Navigating a New School, 1 vol. 2012. (Middle School Survival Handbook Ser.). (ENG., Illus.). 64p. (YA). (gr. 6-6). pap. 13.95 *(978-1-4488-8319-6(9)*, 675a53a3-9051-45bc-a25a-e8477b4abf5f, Rosen Reference) Rosen Publishing Group, Inc., The.

Miller, Jake. Who's Who in a School Community, 1 vol. 2004. (Exploring Community Ser.). (ENG., Illus.). 24p. (gr. 2-3). pap. 8.25 *(978-1-4042-5030-7(1)*, df81e871-3fc6-4b7c-947c-7c66a9c31786, PowerKids Pr.) Rosen Publishing Group, Inc., The.

—Who's Who in School Community, 1 vol. 2004. (Communities at Work Ser.). (ENG., Illus.). 24p. (J). (gr. 2-2). lib. bdg. 26.27 *(978-1-4042-2788-0(1)*, 57e4dcff-b4be-43db-9323-6ef723536649, PowerKids Pr.) Rosen Publishing Group, Inc., The.

Miller, Karen, ed. Student Life, 1 vol. 2011. (Opposing Viewpoints Ser.). (ENG.). 216p. (gr. 10-12). 50.43 *(978-0-7377-4990-8(3)*, 61351b34-03fc-4915-bef1-285712ef761b); pap. 34.80 *(978-0-7377-4991-5(1)*, 80a53deb-65bf-45c1-a1b8-2138abe97888) Greenhaven Publishing LLC. (Greenhaven Publishing).

Newsom, Tony. High School Student Safety Tips. 2007. (ENG., Illus.). 95p. (YA). pap. 8.99 *(978-0-9787143-5-2(0))* Carrington Bks.

—Middle School Student Safety Tips. 2007. (ENG., Illus.). 43p. (YA). pap. 8.99 *(978-0-9787143-4-5(2))* Carrington Bks.

—Student Safety Tips: 45 that Every 3rd - 5th Grader Must Know!, 2 vols., Spanish Edition. 2nd ed. 2007. (ENG., Illus.). 52p. pap. 6.99 *(978-0-9787143-2-1(6))* Carrington Bks.

Oakley, Barbara, et al. Learning How to Learn: How to Succeed in School Without Spending All Your Time Studying; a Guide for Kids & Teens. 2018. (Illus.). 256p. (gr. 5). pap. 17.00 *(978-0-14-313254-7(7)*, TarcherPerigee) Penguin Publishing Group.

Oestreicher, Mark. My School, 1 vol. 2007. (Middle School Survival Ser.). (ENG., Illus.). 192p. (YA). (gr. 7-9). pap. 9.99 *(978-0-310-27882-5(1))* Zondervan.

Ogle, Rex. Free Lunch. 2019. (ENG.). 208p. (J). (gr. 6-9). 17.95 *(978-1-324-00360-1(X)*, 340360, Norton Young Readers) Norton, W. W. & Co., Inc.

Orr, Tamra B. September 11 & Terrorism in America. 2017. (Perspectives Library: Modern Perspectives Ser.). (ENG., Illus.). 32p. (J). (gr. 4-7). lib. bdg. 32.07 *(978-1-63472-858-4(0)*, 209858) Cherry Lake Publishing.

Pearsall, Shelley. All of the Above. Steptoe, Javaka, illus. 2007. 234p. (gr. 3-7). 18.00 *(978-0-7569-8144-0(1))* Perfection Learning Corp.

Reid, Stephanie. School. 2011. (Early Literacy Ser.). (ENG.). 16p. (gr. k-1). 19.99 *(978-1-4333-2354-6(0))*; 6.99 *(978-1-4333-2353-9(2))* Teacher Created Materials, Inc.

Rice, Dona Herweck. Big Kid School, 1 vol. 2011. (Early Literacy Ser.). (ENG.). 16p. (gr. k-1). 6.99 *(978-1-4333-2355-3(9))*; 19.99 *(978-1-4333-2356-0(7))* Teacher Created Materials, Inc.

Rogers, Amy B. What Are Student Rights?, 1 vol. 2019. (What's the Issue? Ser.). (ENG.). 24p. (gr. 3-3). lib. bdg. 26.23 *(978-1-5345-3219-9(6)*, 8c861193-734b-47f6-9751-6749512e8797, KidHaven Publishing) Greenhaven Publishing LLC.

Ruurs, Margriet. My School in the Rain Forest: How Children Attend School Around the World. 2009. (ENG., Illus.). 32p. (J). (gr. k-k). 17.99 *(978-1-59078-601-7(7)*, Astra Young Readers) Astra Publishing Hse.

Seigel, Rachel. The Debate about School Uniforms. 2018. (Pros & Cons Ser.). (ENG., Illus.). 48p. (J). (gr. 5-6). pap. 11.95 *(978-1-63517-597-4(6)*, 1635175976); lib. bdg. 34.21 *(978-1-63517-525-7(9)*, 1635175259) North Star Editions. (Focus Readers).

—The Debate about School Uniforms. 2018. 48p. (J). *(978-1-4896-9612-0(1)*, AV2 by Weigl) Weigl Pubs., Inc.

Shea, John M. Self-Injury & Cutting: Stopping the Pain, 1 vol. 2013. (Helpline: Teen Issues & Answers Ser.). (ENG., Illus.). 80p. (YA). (gr. 5-6). lib. bdg. 38.41 *(978-1-4488-9448-2(4)*, 6ad61855-2f3d-4de8-93cc-633919557690, Rosen Classroom) Rosen Publishing Group, Inc., The.

Smith, Sarah. School, Vol. 7. 2018. (Etiquette for Success Ser.). 64p. (J). (gr. 7). 31.93 *(978-1-4222-3972-8(1))* Mason Crest.

Swim, Luann. Cracking the System. 2012. 60p. pap. 29.95 *(978-1-937065-00-3(6))* B & B Educational Advancement & Pubns., Inc.

Twin Talk: Advice from a TV Talk Show. 2005. (Illus.). 37p. *(978-0-439-12406-5(9))* Scholastic, Inc.

Vizzini, Ned. Teen Angst? Naaah ... 2010. 272p. (YA). (gr. 7-12). 9.99 *(978-0-385-73945-0(1)*, Delacorte Pr.) Random Hse. Children's Bks.

Whyte, Donna. What Makes a Good Teacher? Here's What the Kids Say! Garamella, Joyce Orchard, illus. 2003. 32p. (J). 6.95 *(978-1-884548-59-8(8)*, Crystal Springs Bks.) Staff Development for Educators.

Words for All Time: Students Letters to Holocaust Survivors. 2008. (YA). mass mkt. 19.95 *(978-0-9793771-6-7(1))* ComteQ Publishing.

Wright, Pamela. Rant Room. 2011. 82p. pap. 19.95 *(978-1-4560-9428-7(9))* America Star Bks.

STUDENTS—EMPLOYMENT

Messina, Noreen E. Teenwork: Four Teens Tell All: A Guide for Finding Jobs. 2005. (Illus.). 126p. (gr. 6-12). per. 12.75 *(978-1-59070-598-8(X))* Goodheart-Willcox Pub.

Troutman, Kathryn K. Creating Your High School Resume, Second Edition: A Step-by-Step Guide to Preparing an Effective Resume for Jobs, College & Training Programs. 2nd ed. 2003. (Illus.). 160p. pap. 10.95 *(978-1-56370-902-9(3)*, JIST Works) JIST Publishing.

STUDENTS—FICTION

Abramsen, Ruth M. Akeelah's Spider. 2008. 36p. per. 13.95 *(978-1-59800-440-3(9))* Outskirts Pr., Inc.

Achi, Taro. Mamoru the Shadow Protector Volume 1. 2008. (ENG., Illus.). 176p. (YA). pap. 9.95 *(978-1-59796-183-7(3))* DrMaster Pubns. Inc.

Albertalli, Becky. Leah on the off Beat. 2019. (ENG.). (YA). (gr. 9). lib. bdg. 21.80 *(978-1-6636-2843-5(2))* Perfection Learning Corp.

—Leah on the Offbeat. (ENG.). 368p. (YA). (gr. 9). 2019. pap. 10.99 *(978-0-06-264381-0(9))* 2018. 17.99 *(978-0-06-264380-3(0))* HarperCollins Pubs. (Balzer & Bray).

Alegria, Malin. Cruzar el Limite (Crossing the Boundary) 2012. (Border Town (Spanish) Ser.: 1). (SPA.). lib. bdg. 16.00 *(978-0-606-26239-2(3))* Turtleback.

Alexander, Shannon Lee. Life after Juliet. 2016. (ENG.). 304p. (YA). 16.99 *(978-1-63375-323-5(9)*, 900159056) Entangled Publishing, LLC.

Alfonsi, Alice. Freaked Out. 2004. 148p. (J). lib. bdg. 16.92 *(978-1-4242-0687-2(1))* Fitzgerald Bks.

Allen-Vath, Ami. Liars & Losers Like Us. 2016. (ENG.). 240p. (J). (gr. 8-8). 16.99 *(978-1-63450-184-2(5)*, Sky Pony Pr.) Skyhorse Publishing Co., Inc.

Alpine, Rachele. Operation Pucker Up. 2015. (Mix Ser.). (ENG., Illus.). 256p. (J). (gr. 4-8). 17.99 *(978-1-4814-3236-8(2)*, Aladdin) Simon & Schuster Children's Publishing.

Anna, Jennifer. Yen Shei & the American Bonsai. 2009. (ENG., Illus.). 88p. (YA). pap. 14.99 *(978-1-59092-153-1(4))* Blue Forge Pr.

Anonymous. The Book of David. 2014. (Anonymous Diaries). (ENG., Illus.). 288p. (YA). (gr. 9). pap. 9.99 *(978-1-4424-8985-1(5)*, Simon Pulse) Simon Pulse.

Baker, Mary. Christmas Annie. 2009. 70p. pap. 7.96 *(978-0-557-17289-4(6))* Lulu Pr., Inc.

Banim, Lisa. Hands off My Crush-Boy! 2004. 125p. (J). lib. bdg. 16.92 *(978-1-4242-0684-1(7))* Fitzgerald Bks.

Bargiel, Nina G. & Amsterdam, Shane. Fintastic Friends Forever. 2016. (Illus.). 32p. (J). *(978-1-5182-1661-9(7))* Little Brown & Co.

Barnholdt, Lauren. Heat of the Moment. 2015. (Moment of Truth Ser.: 1). (ENG.). 304p. (YA). (gr. 8). pap. 9.99 *(978-0-06-232139-8(0)*, HarperTeen) HarperCollins Pubs.

—One Moment in Time. 2015. (Moment of Truth Ser.: 2). (ENG.). 304p. (YA). (gr. 8). pap. 9.99 *(978-0-06-232141-1(2)*, HarperTeen) HarperCollins Pubs.

Bean, Raymond. Sweet Farts #1, 0 vols. unabr. ed. 2012. (Sweet Farts Ser.: 1). (ENG.). 138p. (J). (gr. 2-6). pap. 9.95 *(978-1-61218-250-6(X)*, 9781612182506, Two Lions) Amazon Publishing.

—Sweet Farts #2: Rippin' It Old School, 0 vols. unabr. ed. 2010. (Sweet Farts Ser.: 2). (ENG.). 184p. (J). (gr. 2-6). pap. 9.95 *(978-1-935597-08-7(6)*, 9781935597087, Two Lions) Amazon Publishing.

—Sweet Farts #3: Blown Away, 0 vols. unabr. ed. 2012. (Sweet Farts Ser.: 3). (ENG.). 172p. (J). (gr. 2-6). pap. 9.95 *(978-1-61218-251-3(8)*, 9781612182513, Two Lions) Amazon Publishing.

Beck, Ricky. A Puzzled Heart. 2008. 85p. pap. 19.95 *(978-1-60441-385-4(9))* America Star Bks.

Benjamin, Ali. The Next Great Paulie Fink. 2019. (ENG., Illus.). 368p. (J). (gr. 3-7). 16.99 *(978-0-316-38088-1(1))* Little, Brown Bks. for Young Readers.

Bennett, W. J., Jr. Sydney & Garrett's Great Arkansas Adventury. 2005. (J). pap. *(978-0-9794044-6-7(0))* Archeological Assessments, Inc.

Benoit, Charles. You. 2012. (ENG.). 256p. (YA). (gr. 8). pap. 8.99 *(978-0-06-194706-3(7)*, HarperTeen) HarperCollins Pubs.

Benton, Jim. Nobody's Perfect. I'm As Close As It Gets. 2013. (Dear Dumb Diary: Year Two Ser.: 3). lib. bdg. 16.00 *(978-0-606-31535-7(7))* Turtleback.

Binder, John. The Girl Who Applied Everywhere. 2011. 160p. (YA). 17.99 *(978-1-936679-02-7(7))* Wicker Park Pr., Ltd.

Bittmann, Suzy. Life with Molly Mcgee - Sports Chick: Caught in a Pickle. 2010. 211p. pap. 15.99 *(978-0-557-46339-8(4))* Lulu Pr., Inc.

Blanda, Dominick. The Super Duper Kid Fantastic. 2009. 32p. pap. 14.99 *(978-1-4389-4566-8(3))* AuthorHouse.

Blitt, Natalie. Carols & Crushes. 2016. 243p. (J). pap. *(978-1-338-08780-2(0))* Scholastic, Inc.

—Snow One Like You. 2017. 258p. (J). pap. *(978-1-338-17474-8(6))* Scholastic, Inc.

Bow, James. The Young City: The Unwritten Books. 2008. (Unwritten Bks.: 3). (ENG.). 264p. (YA). (gr. 7). pap. 12.99 *(978-1-55002-846-1(4))* Dundurn Pr. CAN. Dist: Publishers Group West (PGW).

Bradley, Kimberly Brubaker. Fighting Words. 2020. (ENG.). 272p. (J). (gr. 5-7). 17.99 *(978-1-9848-1568-2(7)*, Dial Bks) Penguin Young Readers Group.

Brian, Kate, pseud. Cruel Love. 2011. (Privilege Ser.). (ENG.). 224p. (YA). (gr. 9). pap. 9.99 *(978-1-4424-0788-6(3)*, Simon & Schuster Bks. For Young Readers) Simon & Schuster Bks. For Young Readers.

—Sweet Deceit. 2010. (Privilege Ser.: Bk. 4). (ENG.). 224p. (YA). (gr. 9-18). pap. 9.99 *(978-1-4169-6762-0(1)*, Simon & Schuster Bks. For Young Readers) Simon & Schuster Bks. For Young Readers.

Bristow, Catherine. My Strange & Terrible Malady. 2008. (YA). pap. 15.95 *(978-1-934575-19-2(4))* Autism Asperger Publishing Co.

Brown, Teri. Read My Lips. 2008. (ENG.). 256p. (YA). (gr. 9-12). pap. 8.99 *(978-1-4169-5868-0(1)*, Simon Pulse) Simon Pulse.

Bryant, Ann. School Friends - Drama at Silver Spires. 2013. pap. 5.99 *(978-0-7945-3147-8(4)*, Usborne) EDC Publishing.

—School Friends - Welcome to Silver Spires. 2013. pap. 5.99 *(978-0-7945-3146-1(6)*, Usborne) EDC Publishing.

Bryant, Jen. Ringside 1925. 2009. 240p. (J). (gr. 5). 7.99 *(978-0-440-42189-4(6)*, Yearling) Random Hse. Children's Bks.

Buckley, Kate. Choices: A Novel. 2009. 208p. (J). pap. 14.95 *(978-1-935359-12-8(6))* Bk. Pubs. Network.

Burke, Morgan. Get It Started. 2010. (Party Room Ser.: 1). (ENG.). 272p. (J). (gr. 11). pap. 12.99 *(978-1-4424-1420-4(0)*, Simon Pulse) Simon Pulse.

Burleigh, Cyril. The Hilltop Boys on Lost Island. 2017. (ENG., Illus.). (J). pap. 12.95 *(978-1-374-85209-9(0))* Capital Communications, Inc.

—The Hilltop Boys on the River. 2005. 26.95 *(978-1-4218-0327-2(5)*, 1st World Library - Literary Society) 1st World Publishing, Inc.

Cabot, Meg. The Princess Diaries, Volume VII: Party Princess, Vol. VII. 2008. (Princess Diaries: 7). (ENG.). 320p. (YA). (gr. 8). pap. 9.99 *(978-0-06-154374-6(8)*, HarperTeen) HarperCollins Pubs.

Caine, Rachel, pseud. Fall of Night: The Morganville Vampires. 2013. (Morganville Vampires Ser.: 14). (ENG.). 368p. (YA). (gr. 9). pap. 9.99 *(978-0-451-41426-7(8)*, Berkley) Penguin Publishing Group.

Calame, Don. Swim the Fly. 2010. (ENG., Illus.). 352p. (YA). (gr. 9). pap. 11.99 *(978-0-7636-4776-6(4))* Candlewick Pr.

Cali, Davide & Chaud, Benjamin. The Truth about My Unbelievable School ... 2018. (Funny Thing Happened Ser.). (ENG., Illus.). 44p. (J). (gr. 1-4). 12.99 *(978-1-4521-5594-4(1))* Chronicle Bks. LLC.

Cannon, Chris. Blackmail Boyfriend. 2015. (ENG., Illus.). 260p. (J). pap. 16.99 *(978-1-943892-03-7(2))* Entangled Publishing, LLC.

Carolina Esquivel Rael. Anthony P the Talker. 2009. 44p. pap. 16.99 *(978-1-4389-5861-3(7))* AuthorHouse.

S

Carter, Aimée. The Goddess Test. 2011. (Goddess Test Ser.: 1). lib. bdg. 20.85 *(978-0-606-26943-8(6))* Turtleback.

Carter, Aimée & Carter, Aimée. The Goddess Test. 2011. (Goddess Test Novel Ser.: 1). (ENG.). 304p. (YA). (gr. 9-18). pap. 11.99 *(978-0-373-21026-8(4)*, Harlequin Teen) Harlequin Enterprises ULC CAN. Dist: HarperCollins Pubs.

Carter, Brooke. Learning Seventeen, 1 vol. 2018. (Orca Soundings Ser.). (ENG.). 144p. (YA). (gr. 8-12). pap. 9.95 *(978-1-4598-1553-7(X))* Orca Bk. Pubs. USA.

Chapman, Allen. Frank Roscoes Secret or the Darewell Chu. 2007. pap. *(978-1-4065-1431-5(4))* Dodo Pr.

Charbonneau, Joelle. Need. 2017. (ENG.). 352p. (YA). (gr. 7). pap. 9.99 *(978-0-544-93883-0(6)*, 1658459, Clarion Bks.) HarperCollins Pubs.

Cheng, Haw. Sixth Grade Was a Nightmare, & Seventh Is Worse: A 12-Year Old Speaks Out. Thurman, Joann M., ed. Costner, Howard, illus. Date not set. 128p. (J). (gr. 3-9). 11.95 *(978-0-89896-335-9(4))* Larksdale.

Clark-Elliott, Mary. The Day Ms. Qualbaum Came to Visit. 2013. 44p. pap. 20.72 *(978-1-4907-0921-5(5))* Trafford Publishing.

Clark, Sherryl & Perry, Ellyse. Ellyse Perry: Winning Touch. 2017. (Ellyse Perry Ser.: 3). 160p. (J). (gr. 4-7). 13.99 *(978-0-14-378128-8(6))* Random Hse. Australia AUS. Dist: Independent Pubs. Group.

Clements, Andrew. Frindle. Selznick, Brian, illus. 105p. (J). (gr. 3-5). pap. 4.50 *(978-0-8072-1522-7(8)*, Listening Library) Random Hse. Audio Publishing Group.

—Frindle. unabr. ed. 2004. (Middle Grade Cassette Librariestm Ser.). 105p. (J). (gr. 3-7). pap. 29.00 incl. audio *(978-0-8072-7994-6(3)*, S YA 961 SP, Listening Library) Random Hse. Audio Publishing Group.

—Jake Drake, Class Clown. Pedersen, Janet, illus. 2007. (Jake Drake Ser.: Bk. 4). (ENG.). 96p. (J). (gr. 2-5). pap. 5.99 *(978-1-4169-4912-1(7)*, Atheneum Bks. for Young Readers) Simon & Schuster Children's Publishing.

—Jake Drake, Teacher's Pet. Pedersen, Janet, illus. 2007. (Jake Drake Ser.: 3). (ENG.). 96p. (J). (gr. 2-5). pap. 5.99 *(978-1-4169-3932-0(6)*, Atheneum Bks. for Young Readers) Simon & Schuster Children's Publishing.

Cleveland, Marie. Jason's Giant Dilemma: A Storybook Land Adventure. 2007. 76p. per. 19.95 *(978-1-4241-7811-7(8))* America Star Bks.

Cole, Cathy. The New Girl. 2015. 210p. (YA). *(978-0-545-87876-0(4))* Scholastic, Inc.

—The Trouble with Love. 2015. 200p. (J). *(978-0-545-87877-7(2))* Scholastic, Inc.

Colfer, Chris. Struck by Lightning: The Carson Phillips Journal. (Land of Stories Ser.). (ENG., Illus.). 272p. (YA). (gr. 10-17). 2013. pap. 10.99 *(978-0-316-23293-7(9))* 2012. 17.99 *(978-0-316-23295-1(5))* Little, Brown Bks. for Young Readers.

Constantine, Robin. The Promise of Amazing. 2015. (ENG.). 400p. (YA). (gr. 9). pap. 9.99 *(978-0-06-227949-1(1)*, Balzer & Bray) HarperCollins Pubs.

Cook, Eileen. Getting Revenge on Lauren Wood. 2010. (ENG.). (YA). (gr. 9). 288p. pap. 9.99 *(978-1-4424-0976-7(2))*; 272p. 15.99 *(978-1-4169-7433-8(4))* Simon Pulse. (Simon Pulse).

Cooper, T. & Glock-Cooper, Allison. Changers Book One: Drew. 2014. (Changers Ser.). (ENG., Illus.). 288p. (gr. 6). pap. 11.95 *(978-1-61775-195-0(2)*, Black Sheep) Akashic Bks.

—Changers Book Two: Oryon. 2015. (Changers Ser.). (ENG., Illus.). 288p. (J). (gr. 6). pap. 11.95 *(978-1-61775-307-7(6)*, Black Sheep) Akashic Bks.

Crane, Cheri J. Moment of Truth: A Novel. 2005. 238p. (YA). *(978-1-59156-727-1(0))* Covenant Communications.

Craw, Gloria. Atlantis Quest. 2016. (Atlantis Rising Ser.: 2). (ENG.). 356p. (YA). 16.99 *(978-1-63375-283-2(6)*, 9781633752832) Entangled Publishing, LLC.

Crilley, Mark. Miki Falls: Autumn. Crilley, Mark, illus. 2007. (Miki Falls Ser.: 3). (ENG., Illus.). 176p. (J). (gr. 8-12). pap. 9.99 *(978-0-06-084618-3(6)*, HarperCollins) HarperCollins Pubs.

Cross II, Cecil R. Next Semester. 2009. (ENG., Illus.). 256p. (YA). pap. 12.99 *(978-0-373-83145-6(5)*, Harlequin Kimani TRU) Harlequin Enterprises ULC CAN. Dist: HarperCollins Pubs.

Cummings, C. R. The Cadet Under-Officer: The Army Cadets. 2nd ed. 2013. 368p. pap. *(978-0-9875975-5-7(8))* DoctorZed Publishing.

Danziger, Paula. It's a Fair Day, Amber Brown. Ross, Tony, illus. 2003. (Readalongs for Beginning Readers Ser.). (J). 25.95 incl. audio *(978-1-59112-246-3(5))*; pap. 29.95 incl. audio *(978-1-59112-247-0(3))* Live Oak Media.

Danzinger, Paula. Get Ready for Second Grade, Amber Brown. Ross, Tony, illus. 2003. (Readalongs for Beginning Readers Ser.). (J). 25.95 incl. audio *(978-1-59112-234-0(1))*; pap. 29.95 incl. audio *(978-1-59112-235-7(X))* Live Oak Media.

David, Christopher. Denholme & the Skeleton Mystery. 2006. 274p. pap. 22.52 *(978-1-4120-8014-9(2))* Trafford Publishing.

Day, Nick. Surprised? 2017. (Summer Road Trip Ser.). (ENG.). 184p. (YA). (gr. 5-12). 31.42 *(978-1-68076-726-1(7)*, 27441, Epic Escape) EPIC Pr.

de Campi, Alex. Kat & Mouse: Tripped, Vol.2. Manfredi, Federica, illus. 2007. (Kat & Mouse Manga Ser.: 2). (ENG.). 96p. (J). (gr. 4-1). pap. 5.99 *(978-1-59816-549-4(6)*, e6390ae8-e307-44cd-8793-cc66156010f7, TOKYOPOP Manga) TOKYOPOP, Inc.

De Pauw, Linda Grant. In Search of Molly Pitcher. 164p. 2008. pap. 12.00 *(978-1-4357-0607-1(2))* 2007. 30.00 *(978-1-4303-1345-8(5))* Lulu Pr., Inc.

DeCesare, Leah. Forks, Knives, & Spoons: A Novel. 2017. (ENG.). 408p. pap. 17.95 *(978-1-943006-10-6(5))* SparkPr. (a Bks.parks Imprint).

Delsol, Wendy. Flock. 2013. (ENG.). 400p. (YA). (gr. 7). pap. 8.99 *(978-0-7636-6467-1(7))* Candlewick Pr.

deVos, Kelly. Fat Girl on a Plane. 2018. (ENG.). 384p. (YA). 18.99 *(978-0-373-21253-8(4)*, Harlequin Teen) Harlequin Enterprises ULC CAN. Dist: HarperCollins Pubs.

Divine, L. Hustlin' 2009. (Drama High Ser.: 7). lib. bdg. 26.95 *(978-0-606-00156-4(5))* Turtleback.

Don, Lari. Wolf Notes & Other Musical Mishaps, 24 vols. 2nd rev. ed. 2014. (Fabled Beasts Chronicles Ser.: 2). (Illus.). 272p. (J). 9.95 *(978-1-78250-138-1(X)*, Kelpies) Floris Bks. GBR. Dist: Consortium Bk. Sales & Distribution.

Donbavand, Tommy. EDGE: Tommy Donbavand's Funny Shorts: Dinner Ladies of Doooooom! Myers, Kevin, illus. 2018. (EDGE: Tommy Donbavand's Funny Shorts Ser.). (ENG.). 64p. (J). (gr. 2-4). 12.99 *(978-1-4451-5385-8(8)*, Franklin Watts) Hachette Children's Group GBR. Dist: Hachette Bk. Group.

Donovan, Rebecca. Out of Breath, 0 vols. unabr. ed. 2013. (Breathing Ser.: 3). (ENG.). 432p. (YA). (gr. 7-12). pap. 9.99 *(978-1-4778-1718-6(2)*, 9781477817186, Skyscape) Amazon Publishing.

Duncan, Lois. Killing Mr. Griffin. 223p. (YA). (gr. 7-18). pap. 4.50 *(978-0-8072-1373-5(X)*, Listening Library) Random Hse. Audio Publishing Group.

Eagar, Kirsty. Summer Skin. 2018. (ENG.). 352p. (YA). pap. 17.99 *(978-1-250-14600-7(3)*, 900181144) Feiwel & Friends.

Eggleston, Edward. The Hoosier School-Boy. 2017. (ENG., Illus.). (J). 22.95 *(978-1-374-98615-2(1))*; pap. 12.95 *(978-1-374-98614-5(3))* Capital Communications, Inc.

—The Hoosier School-Boy. (ENG., Illus.). (J). 2017. pap. 12.95 *(978-1-375-40372-6(9))* 2015. 22.95 *(978-1-296-63732-3(8))* Creative Media Partners, LLC.

—The Hoosier Schoolboy. 2013. (Collected Works of Edward Eggleston). 425p. reprint ed. lthr. 79.00 *(978-0-7812-1178-9(6))* Reprint Services Corp.

—The Schoolmaster's Stories for Boys & Girls. 2013. (Collected Works of Edward Eggleston). 279p. reprint ed. lthr. 79.00 *(978-0-7812-1176-5(X))* Reprint Services Corp.

Ennis, Ryan R. The Thursday Surprise: A Story about Kids & Autism. Stroud, Brenda, illus. 2011. 86p. pap. 9.95 *(978-0-9843426-7-9(2))* G Publishing LLC.

Esham, Barbara. Last to Finish: A Story about the Smartest Boy in Math Class. Gordon, Mike, illus. 2008. 32p. (J). (gr. k-18). 16.95 *(978-1-60336-456-0(0)*, Adventures of Everyday Geniuses, The) Mainstream Connections Publishing.

Fairchild Hawks, Lyn. How Wendy Redbird Dancing Survived the Dark Ages of Nought. 2013. (ENG.). 286p. (C). pap. 16.99 *(978-0-9888837-2-7(4))* Hawks, Lyn.

Faris, Stephanie. Piper Morgan in Charge! Fleming, Lucy, illus. 2016. (Piper Morgan Ser.: 2). (ENG.). 112p. (J). (gr. 1-4). pap. 6.99 *(978-1-4814-5711-8(X)*, Aladdin) Simon & Schuster Children's Publishing.

—Piper Morgan Joins the Circus. Fleming, Lucy, illus. 2016. (Piper Morgan Ser.: 1). (ENG.). 112p. (J). (gr. 1-4). 16.99 *(978-1-4814-5709-5(8)*, Simon & Schuster/Paula Wiseman Bks.) Simon & Schuster/Paula Wiseman Bks.

—Piper Morgan Plans a Party. Fleming, Lucy, illus. 2017. (Piper Morgan Ser.: 5). (ENG.). 96p. (J). (gr. 1-4). 16.99 *(978-1-5344-0386-4(8))*; pap. 5.99 *(978-1-5344-0385-7(X))* Simon & Schuster Children's Publishing. (Aladdin).

Farley, Robin. Mia & the Girl with a Twirl. 2013. (Mia I Can Read Bks.). (J). lib. bdg. 13.55 *(978-0-606-31811-2(9))* Turtleback.

Feder, Aliza & Sofer, Rochel. We Need to Talk. 2008. 250p. 18.95 *(978-1-934440-30-8(2)*, Devora Publishing) Simcha Media Group.

Fergus, Maureen. Recipe for Disaster. 2009. 256p. (J). (gr. 5-9). 18.95 *(978-1-55453-319-0(8))* Kids Can Pr., Ltd. CAN. Dist: Hachette Bk. Group.

Ferguson, Donald. The Chums of Scranton High at Ice Hockey. 2007. 124p. per. *(978-1-4065-2361-4(5))* Dodo Pr.

—Chums of Scranton High at Ice Hockey. 2006. 25.95 *(978-1-4218-2936-4(3))*; pap. 10.95 *(978-1-4218-3036-0(1))* 1st World Publishing, Inc.

—Chums of Scranton High on the Cinder Pat. 2006. 25.95 *(978-1-4218-2937-1(1))*; pap. 10.95 *(978-1-4218-3037-7(X))* 1st World Publishing, Inc.

—The Chums of Scranton High on the Cinder Path. 2007. 124p. per. *(978-1-4065-2363-8(1))* Dodo Pr.

—The Chums of Scranton High, or, Hugh Morgan's Uphill Fight. 2007. 136p. per. *(978-1-4065-2362-1(3))* Dodo Pr.

—Chums of Scranton High Out for the Penna. 2006. 25.95 *(978-1-4218-2938-8(X))*; pap. 10.95 *(978-1-4218-3038-4(8))* 1st World Publishing, Inc.

—The Chums of Scranton High Out for the Pennant, or, in the Three Town League. 2007. 124p. per. *(978-1-4065-2364-5(X))* Dodo Pr.

Ferguson, Jo Ann. The Cabinet of Souls. 2016. lib. bdg. 17.20 *(978-0-606-38787-3(0))* Turtleback.

Ferguson, John B. Cindy Before. 2003. (YA). per. 10.95 *(978-0-9728144-4-7(2))* Caslon Pr.

Figueroa, Acton. So Not the Drama. 2005. (Illus.). 79p. (J). *(978-1-4156-3929-0(9))* Disney Pr.

Finn, Ann-Marie, illus. Gus, the Asparagus. 2017. (ENG.). (J). pap. *(978-0-9945570-6-3(X))* Riveted Pr.

Finn, Perdita. Stealing the Show. Moran, Mike, illus. 2006. (Time Flyers Ser.: Vol. 1). 109p. (J). pap. *(978-0-439-74433-1(4))* Scholastic, Inc.

Fischer, JoAnn. Our Teacher Is A Fish! 2008. (ENG.). 34p. pap. 10.00 *(978-1-4196-7477-8(3))* CreateSpace Independent Publishing Platform.

Fischer, Nancy Richardson. When Elephants Fly. 2018. (ENG.). 400p. (YA). 18.99 *(978-1-335-01236-4(2)*, Harlequin Teen) Harlequin Enterprises ULC CAN. Dist: HarperCollins Pubs.

Flower, Graham Jessie. Grace Harlowe's Return to Overton Campus. 2004. reprint ed. 1.99 *(978-1-4192-2222-1(8))*; pap. 20.95 *(978-1-4191-2222-4(3))* Kessinger Publishing, LLC.

—Grace Harlowe's Second Year at Overton College. 2004. reprint ed. pap. 20.95 *(978-1-4191-2223-1(1))*; pap. 1.99 *(978-1-4192-2223-8(6))* Kessinger Publishing, LLC.

Flower, Jessie Graham. Grace Harlowe's Return to Overton Campus. 2007. 260p. 29.95 *(978-1-4344-9674-4(0))*; per. 19.95 *(978-1-4344-9673-7(2))* Wildside Pr., LLC.

—Grace Harlowe's Second Year at Overton Campus. 2007. 252p. 29.95 *(978-1-4344-9676-8(7))*; per. 19.95 *(978-1-4344-9675-1(9))* Wildside Pr., LLC.

—Grace Harlowe's Sophomore Year at High School. 2007. 256p. 29.95 *(978-1-4344-9678-2(3))*; per. 19.95 *(978-1-4344-9677-5(5))* Wildside Pr., LLC.

—Grace Harlowe's Third Year at Overton College. 2007. 252p. 29.95 *(978-1-4344-9680-5(5))*; per. 19.95 *(978-1-4344-9679-9(1))* Wildside Pr., LLC.

Foglia, Auttem. The Big Picture. 2010. 48p. pap. 10.59 *(978-1-4520-6681-3(7))* AuthorHouse.

Foglio, Kaja & Foglio, Phil. Agatha Heterodyne & the Clockwork Princess: A Gaslamp Fantasy with Adventure, Romance & Mad Science. Foglio, Kaja & Foglio, Phil, eds. 2013. (ENG., Illus.). 112p. (YA). pap. 25.00 *(978-1-890856-39-7(8)*, 719d9e51-00a4-403d-a8c3-a1cb570e83ef) Studio Foglio, LLC.

Frank, E. R. Friction. 2004. (ENG.). 208p. (YA). (gr. 7). reprint ed. pap. 10.99 *(978-0-689-85385-2(8)*, Simon Pulse) Simon Pulse.

Freeman, Hilary. The Boy from France. 2012. 192p. (YA). (gr. 8). pap. 11.99 *(978-1-84812-301-4(9))* Bonnier Publishing GBR. Dist: Independent Pubs. Group.

Fujinari, Yuuki. Ugly Duckling's Love Revolution, Vol. 3, Vol. 3. 2011. (Ugly Duckling's Love Revolution Ser.: 3). (ENG., Illus.). 192p. (gr. 8-17). pap. 11.99 *(978-0-7595-3177-2(3))* Yen Pr. LLC.

Gayle, Emi. Night & Day. 2014. 132p. (YA). *(978-1-937744-55-7(8))* J. Taylor Publishing.

Gibsen, Cole. Life Unaware. 2015. 284p. (YA). *(978-1-62844-152-9(6))* Entangled Publishing, LLC.

Glass, George. Black-Tie Spy. 2013. 94p. (J). pap. *(978-0-545-47271-5(7))* Scholastic, Inc.

Goode, John. End of the Innocence. 2016. (ENG., Illus.). (J). 29.99 *(978-1-63533-008-3(4)*, Harmony Ink Pr.) Dreamspinner Pr.

Goodwin, Vincent. Body-Snatcher, 1 vol. 2014. (Graphic Horror Ser.). (ENG.). 32p. (J). (gr. 5-8). lib. bdg. 32.79 *(978-1-62402-013-1(5)*, 9096, Graphic Planet - Fiction) Magic Wagon.

Gottesfeld, Jeff. Choices. 2014. (Campus Confessions Ser.: 3). (YA). lib. bdg. 20.80 *(978-0-606-34000-7(9))* Turtleback.

—Frenemies. 2014. (Campus Confessions Ser.: 2). (YA). lib. bdg. 20.80 *(978-0-606-33999-5(X))* Turtleback.

Grabenstein, Chris. I Funny: A Middle School Story. Patterson, James, ed. Park, Laura, illus. 2012. 303p. (J). 11.99 *(978-0-316-22638-7(6)*, 1351607) Little Brown & Co.

Grant, Robert. Jack in the Bush or A Summer on a Salmon River. 2005. pap. 33.95 *(978-1-4179-5573-2(2))* Kessinger Publishing, LLC.

Gray, Laurie. Maybe I Will. 2013. 212p. pap. 14.95 *(978-1-935462-72-9(5))* Luminis Bks., Inc.

Greene, Janice. The 75-Cent Son, 1 vol. unabr. ed. 2010. (Q Reads Ser.). (ENG.). 32p. (YA). (gr. 9-12). pap. 8.50 *(978-1-61651-186-9(9))* Saddleback Educational Publishing, Inc.

Greer, Hannah. The Gift of Re, the Adventures of the Whiz Kids. 2009. 200p. 24.50 *(978-1-60860-466-1(7)*, Eloquent Bks.) Strategic Book Publishing & Rights Agency (SBPRA).

Gregorio, I. W. None of the Above. 2015. (ENG.). 352p. (YA). (gr. 9). 17.99 *(978-0-06-233531-9(6)*, Balzer & Bray) HarperCollins Pubs.

Gutman, Dan. Mayor Hubble Is in Trouble! 2012. (My Weirder School Ser.: 6). (J). lib. bdg. 14.75 *(978-0-606-26525-6(2))* Turtleback.

Hancock, H. Irving. The High School Boys' Fishing Trip: Or, Dick & Co. 's Rivals in the Wilderness. 2017. (ENG., Illus.). (J). 23.95 *(978-1-374-93026-1(1))* Capital Communications, Inc.

—The High School Captain of the Team. rev. ed. 2006. 212p. 27.95 *(978-1-4218-1740-8(3))*; pap. 12.95 *(978-1-4218-1840-5(X))* 1st World Publishing, Inc. (1st World Library - Literary Society).

—The High School Captain of the Team. 2007. 176p. per. *(978-1-4065-1987-7(1))* Dodo Pr.

—The High School Freshmen. rev. ed. 2006. 212p. 27.95 *(978-1-4218-1741-5(1))*; pap. 12.95 *(978-1-4218-1841-2(8))* 1st World Publishing, Inc. (1st World Library - Literary Society).

—The High School Freshmen. 2007. 180p. per. *(978-1-4065-1988-4(X))* Dodo Pr.

—The High School Freshmen: Or, Dick & Co. 's First Year Pranks & Sports. 2017. (ENG., Illus.). (J). 23.95 *(978-1-374-93030-8(X))*; pap. 13.95 *(978-1-374-93029-2(6))* Capital Communications, Inc.

—The High School Freshmen: Or, Dick & Co. 's First Year Pranks & Sports. 2017. (ENG., Illus.). (J). pap. *(978-0-649-60244-5(7))* Trieste Publishing Pty Ltd.

—The High School Freshmen; or, Dick & Co. 's First Year Pranks & Sports. 2017. (ENG., Illus.). (J). pap. *(978-0-649-14431-0(7))* Trieste Publishing Pty Ltd.

—The High School Left End. rev. ed. 2006. 212p. 27.95 *(978-1-4218-1742-2(X))*; pap. 12.95 *(978-1-4218-1842-9(6))* 1st World Publishing, Inc. (1st World Library - Literary Society).

—The High School Left End. 2007. 176p. per. *(978-1-4065-1989-1(8))* Dodo Pr.

—The High School Pitcher. 2007. 176p. per. *(978-1-4065-1990-7(1))* Dodo Pr.

Hapka, Catherine, pseud. Friends 4 Ever? 2008. (High School Musical Stories from East High Ser.). 124p. (J). (gr. 3-7). 12.65 *(978-0-7569-8820-3(9))* Perfection Learning Corp.

Harris, Tim. Mr. Bambuckle's Remarkables. 2019. (Mr. Bambuckle Ser.: 1). (ENG., Illus.). 240p. (J). (gr. 3-7). pap. 7.99 *(978-1-4926-8558-6(5))* Sourcebooks, Inc.

Heard, B. R. If. 2007. (ENG.). 176p. pap. 15.95 *(978-0-615-16192-1(8))* Lulu Pr., Inc.

Heydt, Scott. Mice Don't Taste Like Chicken. Aaron, Rich, illus. 2011. 188p. pap. 13.00 *(978-0-9830109-2-0(7))* Helm Publishing.

Holder, Nancy, et al. Wicked 2: Legacy & Spellbound. 2008. (Wicked Ser.). (ENG.). 672p. (YA). (gr. 9). pap. 13.99 *(978-1-4169-7117-7(3)*, Simon Pulse) Simon Pulse.

Holm, Jennifer L. Middle School Is Worse Than Meatloaf: A Year Told Through Stuff. Castaldi, Elicia, illus. 2011. (ENG.). 128p. (J). (gr. 3-7). pap. 9.99 *(978-1-4424-3663-3(8)*, Atheneum Bks. for Young Readers) Simon & Schuster Children's Publishing.

Hunt, Leo. Eight Rivers of Shadow. 2017. (ENG.). 368p. (YA). (gr. 9). pap. 9.99 *(978-0-7636-9457-9(6))* Candlewick Pr.

Hurwitz, Kathleen A. Timothy's Tic. Mc Kelvey, Shawn, illus. 2008. 40p. (gr. -1 — 1). 16.99 *(978-1-4389-1924-9(7))* AuthorHouse.

Ignatow, Amy. The Popularity Papers: Book Four: the Rocky Road Trip of Lydia Goldblatt & Julie Graham-Chang. 2012. (ENG., Illus.). 208p. (J). (gr. 4-8). 16.95 *(978-1-4197-0182-5(7)*, 1003701, Amulet Bks.) Abrams, Inc.

—The Popularity Papers Bk. 2: Book Two: the Long-Distance Dispatch Between Lydia Goldblatt & Julie Graham-Chang. 2012. (Popularity Papers). (ENG., Illus.). 208p. (J). (gr. 3-7). pap. 9.95 *(978-1-4197-0183-2(5)*, 675603, Amulet Bks.) Abrams, Inc.

—The Popularity Papers: Book Two: The Long-Distance Dispatch Between Lydia Goldblatt & Julie Graham-Chang. 2011. (ENG., Illus.). 208p. (J). (gr. 4-8). 16.95 *(978-0-8109-9724-0(X)*, 675601, Amulet Bks.) Abrams, Inc.

Immenschuh, Marilyn Y. Samantha & the Kids of Room 220. 2007. 148p. per. 11.95 *(978-0-595-46842-3(X))* iUniverse, Inc.

Inches, Alison. School Gyrls POW Scrapbook. 2010. (School Gyrls Ser.). (ENG.). 64p. (J). pap. 7.99 *(978-1-4424-0865-4(0)*, Simon Spotlight) Simon Spotlight.

Izumi, Kaneyoshi. Seiho Boys' High School!, Vol. 3. 2010. (Seiho Boys' High School! Ser.: 3). (ENG., Illus.). 192p. pap. 9.99 *(978-1-4215-3733-7(8))* Viz Media.

Jackson, Tiffany D. Monday's Not Coming. (ENG.). (YA). (gr. 8). 2019. 464p. pap. 12.99 *(978-0-06-242268-2(5))* 2018. 448p. 18.99 *(978-0-06-242267-5(7))* HarperCollins Pubs. (Tegen, Katherine Bks).

Jager, Hartmut. The Secret of the Green Paint: Annette Vetter Adventure #2. 2007. (Illus.). 196p. (YA). pap. 9.95 *(978-0-944851-28-9(2))* Earth Star Pubns.

James, Steven. Blur, 0 vols. 2014. (Blur Trilogy Ser.: 1). (ENG.). 368p. (YA). (gr. 7-12). pap. 9.99 *(978-1-4778-4727-5(8)*, 9781477847275, Skyscape) Amazon Publishing.

Jeremiah, Omari. Paper Boy Four: L. O. E. P. S. Worst Nightmare. Rollins, Berni, illus. 2007. 96p. (YA). (gr. 7-12). pap. 12.99 *(978-1-929188-15-4(3))* Morton Bks.

Jones, Jasmine, adapted by. Just Like Lizzie. 2003. (Lizzie Mcguire Ser.). (Illus.). 153p. (J). 12.65 *(978-0-7569-2720-2(X))* Perfection Learning Corp.

—Lizzie Loves Ethan. 2003. (Lizzie Mcguire Ser.). (Illus.). 152p. (J). 12.65 *(978-0-7569-2721-9(8))* Perfection Learning Corp.

—Oh, Brother! 2005. 146p. (J). lib. bdg. 16.92 *(978-1-4242-0682-7(0))* Fitzgerald Bks.

Kadence, Sam. Unicorns & Rainbow Poop. (J). 2016. (ENG., Illus.). 27.99 *(978-1-63477-988-3(6)*, Harmony Ink Pr.) 2014. 246p. pap. *(978-1-63216-417-9(5))* Dreamspinner Pr.

Kalicky, Anne. My Life in Smiley (Book 1 in Smiley Series) It's All Good. 2018. (My Life in Smiley Ser.). (ENG., Illus.). 208p. (J). 13.99 *(978-1-4494-8987-8(7))* Andrews McMeel Publishing.

—My Life in Smiley (Book 3 in Smiley Series) Save Me! 2019. (My Life in Smiley Ser.). (ENG., Illus.). 208p. (J). 13.99 *(978-1-4494-9572-5(9))* Andrews McMeel Publishing.

Kane, Kim. Pip: The Story of Olive. 2010. (ENG.). 256p. (J). (gr. 3-6). lib. bdg. 22.44 *(978-0-385-75172-8(9)*, David Fickling Bks.) Random Hse. Children's Bks.

Kate, Lauren. Passion. (Fallen Ser.: 3). (ENG.). (YA). (gr. 7). 2012. 448p. pap. 13.99 *(978-0-385-73917-7(6)*, Ember) 2011. 432p. 18.99 *(978-0-385-73916-0(8)*, Delacorte Pr.) Random Hse. Children's Bks.

—Passion. 2012. (Fallen Ser.: 3). lib. bdg. 22.10 *(978-0-606-26410-5(8))* Turtleback.

Katschke, Judy. First Grade Feast!/By Judy Katschke; Illustrated by Clare Elsom. Elsom, Clare, illus. 2014. 32p. (J). pap. *(978-0-545-75844-4(0))* Scholastic, Inc.

Kaye, Marilyn. Speak No Evil, 6. 2011. (Gifted Ser.). (ENG.). 208p. (YA). (gr. 6-8). pap. 22.44 *(978-0-7534-6564-6(7)*, 9780753465646) Kingfisher Publications, plc GBR. Dist: Children's Plus, Inc.

Kelly, Jamie & Benton, Jim. Never Underestimate Your Dumbness. 2008. (Dear Dumb Diary Ser.). (Illus.). 150p. (gr. 4-7). 16.00 *(978-0-7569-8814-2(4))* Perfection Learning Corp.

Kelm, Tracy Martin. Light. 2011. 116p. pap. 11.95 *(978-1-4327-6308-4(3))* Outskirts Pr., Inc.

Kenneally, Miranda. Catching Jordan. (Hundred Oaks Ser.: 1). (YA). 2011. (ENG.). 288p. (gr. 7-12). pap. 14.99 *(978-1-4022-6227-2(2))* 2nd ed. 2020. 384p. (gr. 8-12). pap. 10.99 *(978-1-7282-1061-2(5))* Sourcebooks, Inc.

—Stealing Parker. 2012. (Hundred Oaks Ser.: 2). 256p. (YA). (gr. 7-12). pap. 10.99 *(978-1-4022-7187-8(5))* Sourcebooks, Inc.

Kerick, Mia. Not Broken, Just Bent [Library Edition]. 2014. 180p. pap. 14.99 *(978-1-62798-529-1(8)*, Harmony Ink Pr.) Dreamspinner Pr.

Kern, Peggy. The Test. 2011. (Bluford Ser.: 18). 139p. (YA). (gr. k-12). pap. 4.95 *(978-1-59194-234-4(9))* Townsend Pr.

King, A. S. I Crawl Through It. 2016. (YA). lib. bdg. 22.10 *(978-0-606-38333-2(6))* Turtleback.

Kiyuduki, Satoko, creator. GA: Geijutsuka Art Design Class, Vol. 7, Vol. 7. 2016. (GA: Geijutsuka Art Design Class Ser.: 7). (ENG., Illus.). 128p. (J). (gr. 8-17). pap. 17.00 *(978-0-316-54536-5(8))* Yen Pr. LLC.

Klein, Abby. A Little Bit Lucky (Ready, Freddy! 2nd Grade #7) McKinley, John, illus. 2009. (39 Clues Ser.: 7). (ENG.). 96p. (J). (gr. 4-7). E-Book 13.99 *(978-0-545-93218-9(1))* Scholastic, Inc.

Klein, J. M. New School, New Me!, 1 vol. 2018. (Totally Secret Diary of Dani D. Ser.). (ENG.). 64p. (YA). (gr. 2-3). 23.25 *(978-1-5383-8196-0(6)*, 765fbfc3-1486-4ed4-94b5-27d0895051d1); pap. 13.35 *(978-1-5383-8195-3(8)*, ca0db874-610c-4d21-a737-ad4327ae802c) Enslow Publishing, LLC.

Knowles, Jo. Still a Work in Progress. 2019. (ENG.). 320p. (J). (gr. 5-9). pap. 7.99 *(978-1-5362-0737-8(3))* Candlewick Pr.

Komura, Ayumi. Mixed Vegetables, Vol. 8. 2010. (Mixed Vegetables Ser.: 8). (ENG., Illus.). 208p. pap. 9.99 *(978-1-4215-3235-6(2))* Viz Media.

Korman, Gordon. Born to Rock. rev. ed. 2017. (ENG.). 240p. (YA). (gr. 7-17). pap. 8.99 *(978-1-4847-9841-6(4))* Hyperion Bks. for Children.

Koss, Amy Goldman. The Not-So-Great Depression. 2010. (ENG.). 272p. (YA). (gr. 7-18). pap. 19.99 *(978-1-59643-613-8(1))* Roaring Brook Pr.

Krulik, Nancy. How I Survived Middle School: Madame President. 2006. 104p. pap. *(978-0-439-90090-4(5))* Scholastic, Inc.

Langan, John. Search for Safety. 2012. (Bluford High — Scholastic Ser.: 13). lib. bdg. 16.00 *(978-0-606-26204-0(0))* Turtleback.
Langan, Paul. Promises to Keep, 19. 2013. (Bluford Ser.: 19). 151p. pap. 5.95 *(978-1-59194-303-7(5))* Townsend Pr.
—Survivor, 20. 2013. (Bluford Ser.: 20). pap. 5.95 *(978-1-59194-304-4(3))* Townsend Pr.
Langhorne Folan, Karyn & Langan, Paul. Breaking Point. 2011. (Bluford Ser.: 16). (J). (gr. k-12). pap. 4.95 *(978-1-59194-232-0(2))* Townsend Pr.
Laughton, Geoff. By the Creek. 2016. (ENG., Illus.). (J). 24.99 *(978-1-63477-945-6(2),* Harmony Ink Pr.) Dreamspinner Pr.
Lay, Kathryn. Time Under the Sea. Bardin, Dave, illus. 2016. (Time Twisters Ser.). (ENG.). 112p. (J). (gr. 2-5). lib. bdg. 38.50 *(978-1-62402-180-0(8),* 24539, Calico Chapter Bks.) ABDO Publishing Co.
Leach, Sara. Warm Up, 1 vol. 2014. (Orca Limelights Ser.). (ENG.). 128p. (J). (gr. 4-7). pap. 9.95 *(978-1-4598-0428-9(7))* Orca Bk. Pubs. USA.
Lezin, Katya. Knight Swam. 2010. 138p. pap. 14.99 *(978-0-557-20384-0(8))* Lulu Pr., Inc.
Li, August. Fox-Hat & Neko. 2016. (ENG., Illus.). (YA). 29.99 *(978-1-63533-018-2(1),* Harmony Ink Pr.) Dreamspinner Pr.
Liang, Kuan & Yung, Kao. Magic Lover's Tower, Vol. 1. 2008. (ENG., Illus.). 176p. (YA). pap. 9.95 *(978-1-59796-153-0(1))* DrMaster Pubns. Inc.
Lockwood, Cara. The Scarlet Letterman. 2007. (Bard Academy Ser.: 2). (ENG.). 272p. (YA). (gr. 9-12). pap. 17.99 *(978-1-4165-2490-8(8))* Pocket Books.
Lorimer, Janet. The Bad Luck Play, 1 vol. unabr. ed. 2010. (Q Reads Ser.). (ENG.). 32p. (YA). (gr. 9-12). pap. 8.50 *(978-1-61651-198-2(2))* Saddleback Educational Publishing, Inc.
—Student Bodies, 1 vol. unabr. ed. 2010. (Q Reads Ser.). (ENG.). 32p. (YA). (gr. 9-12). pap. 8.50 *(978-1-61651-219-4(9))* Saddleback Educational Publishing, Inc.
Lynne, Zoe. That Witch! (ENG., 2016. Illus.). (J). 24.99 *(978-1-63477-959-3(2))* 2013. 204p. (YA). pap. 14.99 *(978-1-62380-692-7(5))* Dreamspinner Pr. (Harmony Ink Pr.).
—That Witch! [Library Edition]. 2013. 204p. pap. 14.99 *(978-1-62380-927-0(4),* Harmony Ink Pr.) Dreamspinner Pr.
Madigan, L. K. Flash Burnout. 2010. (ENG.). 336p. (YA). (gr. 9). pap. 7.99 *(978-0-547-40493-6(X),* 1428346, Clarion Bks.) HarperCollins Pubs.
Marrs, Christie, creator. The Perfect Gift: I B Hoofinit's Horse Tales. I.t. ed. 2004. (Illus.). 57p. (J). mass mkt. 5.99 *(978-1-928890-19-5(9))* I. B. Hoofinit Co.
Marsh, Carole. Adventure to the Planet Mars! 2007. (Field Trips (Gallopade International) Ser.). (Illus.). 114p. (J). (gr. 2-9). 14.95 *(978-0-635-06392-2(1))* Gallopade International.
Maschari, Jennifer. Things That Surprise You. 2017. (ENG.). 288p. (J). (gr. 3-7). 16.99 *(978-0-06-243892-8(1),* Balzer & Bray) HarperCollins Pubs.
Mathews, Temple. The Sword of Armaggeddon. 2010. ix, 291p. *(978-1-935618-17-1(2))* BenBella Bks.
Mayfield, Jamie. A Broken Kind of Life. 2016. (ENG., Illus.). (YA). (gr. 9-12). 24.99 *(978-1-63477-926-5(6),* Harmony Ink Pr.) Dreamspinner Pr.
McClintock, Norah. From Above, 1 vol. 2016. (Riley Donovan Ser.: 2). (ENG.). 240p. (YA). (gr. 8-12). pap. 10.95 *(978-1-4598-0933-8(5))* Orca Bk. Pubs. USA.
McCormick, Wilfred. Quick Kick: A Bronc Burnett Story. 2011. 192p. 42.95 *(978-1-258-10149-7(1))* Literary Licensing, LLC.
McEwan, Jamie. Rufus the Scrub Does Not Wear a Tutu. Margeson, John, illus. 2006. 64p. (J). (gr. 2-3). 14.95 *(978-1-58196-060-0(3),* Darby Creek) Lerner Publishing Group.
—Scrubs Forever! Margeson, John, illus. 2008. (Darby Creek Exceptional Titles Ser.). (ENG.). 64p. (J). (gr. 2-5). lib. bdg. 14.95 *(978-1-58196-069-3(7),* Darby Creek) Lerner Publishing Group.
Mcgill, Leslie. Fighter. 2014. (Cap Central Ser.: 1). (YA). lib. bdg. 20.80 *(978-0-606-35737-1(8))* Turtleback.
—Hacker. 2014. (Cap Central Ser.: 3). (YA). lib. bdg. 20.80 *(978-0-606-35739-5(4))* Turtleback.
—Running Scared. 2014. (Cap Central Ser.: 2). (YA). lib. bdg. 20.80 *(978-0-606-35738-8(6))* Turtleback.
McGinnis, Mindy. The Female of the Species. (ENG.). (YA). (gr. 9). 2017. 368p. pap. 10.99 *(978-0-06-232090-2(4))* 2016. 352p. 17.99 *(978-0-06-232089-6(0))* HarperCollins Pubs. (Tegen, Katherine Bks).
McGovern, Cammie. A Step Toward Falling. 2016. (ENG.). 384p. (YA). (gr. 9). pap. 9.99 *(978-0-06-227114-3(8),* HarperTeen) HarperCollins Pubs.
—A Step Toward Falling. 2016. (YA). lib. bdg. 20.85 *(978-0-606-39483-3(4))* Turtleback.
Meade, L. T. The Rebel of the School. 2007. (ENG.). 272p. pap. 21.99 *(978-1-4346-4869-3(9))* Creative Media Partners, LLC.
Medina, Meg. Merci Suárez Changes Gears. (Merci Suárez Ser.: 1). (ENG.). 368p. (J). (gr. 4-7). 2020. pap. 8.99 *(978-1-5362-1258-7(X))* 2018. 18.99 *(978-0-7636-9049-6(X))* Candlewick Pr.
Michaels, Robbie. Caught in the Middle. 2016. (Caught in the ACT Ser.: Vol. 2). (ENG., Illus.). (YA). 24.99 *(978-1-63477-951-7(7),* Harmony Ink Pr.) Dreamspinner Pr.
Miglis, Jenny. New Student Starfish. Martinez, Heather, illus. 2003. (SpongeBob SquarePants Ser.). (ENG.). 64p. (J). pap. 3.99 *(978-0-689-86164-2(8),* Simon Spotlight/Nickelodeon) Simon Spotlight/Nickelodeon.
Millman, Selena. Anyone Can Make A Difference. 2006. 109p. (YA). per. *(978-0-9793058-6-3(1))* Millman, Selena.
Money, Mo. Little Sister. 2011. (School Gyrls Ser.). (ENG.). 112p. (J). pap. 5.99 *(978-1-4424-0879-1(0),* Simon & Schuster/Paula Wiseman Bks.) Simon & Schuster/Paula Wiseman Bks.
Moore, Carolyn. Christmas Holly. 2010. (ENG.). 24p. pap. 15.99 *(978-1-4535-1273-9(X))* Xlibris Corp.
Moore, Stephanie Perry. Always Upbeat/All That. 2012. (Lockwood Lions Ser.). (YA). lib. bdg. 26.90 *(978-0-606-26492-1(2))* Turtleback.
Mori, Kotaro. Stray Little Devil. (Stray Little Devil Ser.). (ENG., Illus.). (YA). Vol. 1. 2006. 200p. pap. 9.95 *(978-1-59796-043-4(8))* Vol. 2. 2006. 200p. pap. 9.95 *(978-1-59796-044-1(6))* Vol. 3. 2006. 200p. pap. 9.95 *(978-1-59796-045-8(4))* Vol. 4. 2007. 208p. pap. 9.95 *(978-1-59796-046-5(2))* DrMaster Pubns. Inc.
Morpurgo, Michael. The War of Jenkins' Ear. 2nd ed. 2011. (ENG.). 192p. (J). (gr. 5-7). pap. 7.99 *(978-1-4052-2672-1(2))* Farshore GBR. Dist: HarperCollins Pubs.
Morton, Scott. An Encyclopedia for My Son, 1 vol. 2010. 46p. 24.95 *(978-1-4489-4748-5(0))* PublishAmerica, Inc.
Moses, Jennifer Anne. Tales from My Closet. 2014. 298p. (J). pap. *(978-0-545-66811-8(5),* Scholastic Pr.) Scholastic, Inc.
Myers, Marion P. "Never That" Belly up... & Bully Down! Brevard, Pierre, illus. 2007. (ENG.). 34p. per. 21.99 *(978-1-4257-7005-1(3))* Xlibris Corp.
Nayeri, Daniel. Everything Sad Is Untrue: (a True Story) 2020. (ENG., Illus.). 368p. (J). (gr. 7-12). 18.99 *(978-1-64614-000-8(1))* Levine Querido.
Noel, Alyson. Shadowland: The Immortals. 2010. (Immortals Ser.: 3). (ENG.). 368p. (YA). (gr. 7-12). pap. 15.00 *(978-0-312-65005-6(1),* 900069209, St. Martin's Griffin) St. Martin's Pr.
Norton, Tamra. Comfortable in My Own Genes: A Novel. 2004. 175p. (J). pap. 15.95 *(978-1-55517-772-0(7))* Cedar Fort, Inc./CFI Distribution.
Now I'll Tell You Everything. 2014. (Alice Ser.: 25). (ENG., Illus.). 544p. (YA). (gr. 9). pap. 12.99 *(978-1-4424-4591-8(2),* Atheneum Bks. for Young Readers) Simon & Schuster Children's Publishing.
Nurse, Holly. Meridian Brown Goes to School. 2009. (Illus.). 60p. pap. *(978-1-84748-535-9(9))* Athena Pr.
Oboh, Rolic. Treasure Hunt. 2006. 108p. pap. 7.99 *(978-1-84426-318-9(5))* Upfront Publishing Ltd. GBR. Dist: Printondemand-worldwide.com.
O'Keeffe, Frank. Harry Flammable: A Novel (Large Print 16pt) 2013. 240p. pap. *(978-1-4596-6316-9(0))* ReadHowYouWant.com, Ltd.
Optic, Oliver, pseud. Outward Bound. 2007. 180p. (gr. 4-7). per. *(978-1-4068-4343-9(1))* Echo Library.
—Outward Bound: Or Young America Afloat. I.t. ed. 2007. (ENG.). 274p. pap. 23.99 *(978-1-4264-9153-5(0))* Creative Media Partners, LLC.
Park, Barbara. Junie B., First Grader: Cheater Pants. 2004. (Junie B. Jones Ser.: 21). (gr. k-3). lib. bdg. 14.75 *(978-0-613-85713-0(5))* Turtleback.
Pascal, Francine. Una Larga Noche.Tr. of All Night Long. (SPA.). 128p. (J). 7.95 *(978-84-272-3875-6(4))* Molino, Editorial ESP. Dist: AIMS International Bks., Inc.
—Peligrosa Tentacion.Tr. of Dangerous Love. (SPA., Illus.). 136p. (J). 7.95 *(978-84-272-3876-3(2))* Molino, Editorial ESP. Dist: AIMS International Bks., Inc.
—Querida Hermana.Tr. of Dear Sister. (SPA., Illus.). 168p. (J). 7.95 *(978-84-272-3877-0(0))* Molino, Editorial ESP. Dist: AIMS International Bks., Inc.
Paterson, Katherine. Marvin One Too Many. Clark Brown, Jane, illus. 2003. (Readalongs for Beginning Readers Ser.). (J). pap. 29.95 incl. audio *(978-1-59112-255-5(4))* Live Oak Media.
Patterson, James. Ali Cross. (Ali Cross Ser.: 1). (ENG.). (J). (gr. 5-9). 2020. 336p. pap. 8.99 *(978-0-316-70568-4(3))* 2019. 320p. 16.99 *(978-0-316-53041-5(7))* Little Brown & Co. (Jimmy Patterson).
Patterson, James & Grabenstein, Chris. I Funny: A Middle School Story. Park, Laura, illus. (I Funny Ser.: 1). (ENG.). 320p. (J). (gr. 3-7). 2015. pap. 8.99 *(978-0-316-20692-1(X))* 2013. 13.99 *(978-0-316-32200-3(8))* 2012. 34.99 *(978-0-316-20693-8(8),* 1351607) Little Brown & Co. (Jimmy Patterson).
Patterson, James & Tebbetts, Chris. Middle School: Get Me Out of Here! Park, Laura, illus. (Middle School Ser.: 2). (ENG.). 288p. (J). (gr. 3-7). 2018. pap. 9.99 *(978-0-316-20669-3(5))* 2014. 13.99 *(978-0-316-32201-0(6))* 2012. 32.99 *(978-0-316-20671-6(7))* Little Brown & Co. (Jimmy Patterson).
Patterson, Matthew. Shake Them up, Mrs Nut. 2008. 104p. per. 9.95 *(978-1-4327-2008-7(2))* Outskirts Pr., Inc.
Paul, Naomi. Code Name Komiko, 1 vol. 2014. (Scarlet Voyage Ser.). (ENG., Illus.). 288p. (YA). (gr. 6-7). pap. 13.88 *(978-1-62324-024-0(7),* a02dff69-e522-4a70-91d2-a35c68e2aad9) Enslow Publishing, LLC.
Pavey, Stephen. Free RollinApos. 2005. pap. 24.95 *(978-1-4137-0890-5(0))* PublishAmerica, Inc.
Payne, K. E. 365 Days. 2011. (ENG.). 280p. (YA). (gr. 7). pap. 13.95 *(978-1-60282-540-6(8))* Bold Strokes Bks.
Peirce, Lincoln. Big Nate — Mr. Popularity. 2014. (Big Nate Graphic Novels Ser.: 4). (J). lib. bdg. 20.85 *(978-0-606-35482-0(4))* Turtleback.
—Big Nate Goes for Broke. Peirce, Lincoln, illus. (Big Nate Ser.: 4). (ENG., Illus.). 224p. (J). (gr. 3-7). 2016. pap. 7.99 *(978-0-06-236753-2(6))* 2012. 15.99 *(978-0-06-199661-0(0))* 2012. lib. bdg. 14.89 *(978-0-06-199662-7(9))* HarperCollins Pubs. (HarperCollins).
—Big Nate Goes for Broke. 2016. (Big Nate Ser.: 4). 224p. (J). lib. bdg. 17.20 *(978-0-606-38137-6(6))* Turtleback.
—Big Nate: I Can't Take It! 2013. (Big Nate Ser.: 7). (ENG., Illus.). 224p. (J). pap. 11.99 *(978-1-4494-2937-9(8))* Andrews McMeel Publishing.
—Big Nate: Mr. Popularity. Peirce, Lincoln, illus. 2014. (Big Nate Comix Ser.: 4). (ENG., Illus.). 224p. (J). (gr. 3-7). pap. 9.99 *(978-0-06-208700-3(2),* HarperCollins) HarperCollins Pubs.
Pennypacker, Sara. Clementine's Letter. Frazee, Marla, illus. 2009. (Clementine Ser.: 3). (ENG.). 160p. (J). (gr. 1-5). pap. 5.99 *(978-0-7868-3885-1(X))* Little, Brown Bks. for Young Readers.
Perry, Fred. Grossery Games. 2012. (ENG., Illus.). 128p. (J). (gr. 4-7). pap. 10.99 *(978-0-9850925-5-9(6),* baf71806-dc15-4c9c-a7f7-67e5a6bd9621) Antarctic Pr., Inc.
—Playing Dead. 2012. (ENG., Illus.). 128p. (J). pap. 10.99 *(978-0-9850925-4-2(8),* fd0c2d86-94c4-479a-ada8-c3f0d61fbb76) Antarctic Pr., Inc.
Perry, Hailey. On the Move. 2010. 188p. pap. 12.00 *(978-1-60844-428-1(7))* Dog Ear Publishing, LLC.
Philips, Fleur. Crumble. 2013. 168p. (YA). pap. 8.99 *(978-0-9889299-0-6(2))* Philips, Fleur.
Phillips, Lyda. Mr Touchdown. 2008. 184p. 23.95 *(978-1-4401-0976-8(1));* pap. 13.95 *(978-1-60528-029-5(1))* iUniverse, Inc. (iUniverse Star).
Phillips, Rebecca. These Things I've Done. 2018. (ENG.). 368p. (YA). (gr. 9). 9.99 *(978-0-06-257091-8(9),* HarperTeen) HarperCollins Pubs.
Pilumeli, Tanya. The Dragonfly Keeper. 2008. 264p. (J). per. 12.95 *(978-0-9801396-0-0(0))* FAVA Pr.
Plath, Sylvia. The Bell Jar. 2005. (ENG.). 240p. (J). 12.95 *(978-0-571-22616-0(7),* Faber & Faber Children's Bks.) Faber & Faber, Inc.
Potter, Ryan. Perennial, 0 vols. 2014. (ENG.). 296p. (YA). (gr. 7-9). pap. 9.99 *(978-1-4778-1818-3(9),* 9781477818183, Skyscape) Amazon Publishing.
Poulsen, David A. Blind Date. 2nd rev. ed. 2008. (Lawrence High Yearbook Ser.). (ENG.). 96p. (J). (gr. 2-7). pap. *(978-1-55263-933-7(9))* Me to We.
—Wild Thing. 2008. (Lawrence High Yearbook Ser.). (ENG.). 96p. (gr. 2-7). pap. *(978-1-55263-931-3(2))* Me to We.
Prendergast, Gabrielle. Capricious, 1 vol. 2014. (ENG.). 352p. (YA). (gr. 8-12). 19.95 *(978-1-4598-0267-4(5))* Orca Bk. Pubs. USA.
Pugin-Rodas, M. C. The Eight Ball Club: Ocean of Fire. 2007. (ENG., Illus.). 144p. pap. 15.95 *(978-0-9793761-2-2(2))* ESOL Publishing.
Rain, Mandy. Rock 'n' Roll. 2011. (School Gyrls Ser.). (ENG.). 128p. (J). pap. 5.99 *(978-1-4424-0878-4(2),* Simon & Schuster/Paula Wiseman Bks.) Simon & Schuster/Paula Wiseman Bks.
Ramirez, D. a. & Ramirez, D. A. Kingdom of Glass. 2012. 336p. pap. 12.99 *(978-0-9834198-8-4(4))* Vinspire Publishing LLC.
Ramos, Dania. Who's Ju? 2015. (ENG.). 174p. (J). pap. 9.95 *(978-1-937997-61-8(8))* Northampton Hse.
Ramsey, Jo. Blue Jeans & Sweatshirts. 2016. (ENG., Illus.). (J). 24.99 *(978-1-63477-942-5(8),* Harmony Ink Pr.) Dreamspinner Pr.
Ramsey, R. M. The Browser Bunch: The Browser Files Presents... the Big Lie. 2006. (J). pap. 8.00 *(978-0-8059-7172-9(6))* Dorrance Publishing Co., Inc.
Redgate, Riley. Seven Ways We Lie. 2017. (ENG.). 368p. (YA). (gr. 8-17). pap. 9.95 *(978-1-4197-2348-3(0),* 1132503, Amulet Bks.) Abrams, Inc.
Redmond, E. S. Bug Blonsky & His Very Long List of Don'ts. Redmond, E. S., illus. 2018. (ENG., Illus.). 80p. (J). (gr. 1-4). 15.99 *(978-0-7636-8935-3(1))* Candlewick Pr.
Regan, Dian. Cyberpals According to Kaley. 2006. (Illus.). 128p. (J). (gr. 3-7). 15.95 *(978-1-58196-051-8(4),* Darby Creek) Lerner Publishing Group.
Richards, Natalie D. We All Fall Down. 2017. (ENG.). 368p. (YA). (gr. 8-12). pap. 10.99 *(978-1-4926-5438-4(8))* Sourcebooks, Inc.
Robbins, Maureen & Steinkraus, Kyla. Ready, Set, Race! Reese, Bob, illus. 2011. (Little Birdie Readers Ser.). (ENG.). 24p. (gr. 2-3). pap. 9.95 *(978-1-61236-033-1(5),* 9781612360331) Rourke Educational Media.
Roberts, Dw. Pep Squad Mysteries Book: Trouble on Avalance Mountain. 2008. (ENG., Illus.). 101p. pap. 8.99 *(978-0-557-16575-9(X))* Lulu Pr., Inc.
Robins, Eleanor. Art Show Mystery, 1 vol. unabr. ed. 2011. (Carter High Mysteries Ser.). (ENG.). 48p. (YA). (gr. 9-12). 9.75 *(978-1-61651-560-7(0))* Saddleback Educational Publishing, Inc.
—Aztec Ring Mystery, 1 vol. unabr. ed. 2011. (Carter High Mysteries Ser.). (ENG.). 48p. (YA). (gr. 9-12). 9.75 *(978-1-61651-561-4(9))* Saddleback Educational Publishing, Inc.
—Boy of Their Dreams, 1 vol. unabr. ed. 2010. (Carter High Chronicles Ser.). (ENG.). 52p. (YA). (gr. 9-12). pap. 9.75 *(978-1-61651-305-4(5))* Saddleback Educational Publishing, Inc.
—Break All Rules, 1 vol. unabr. ed. 2011. (Choices Ser.). (ENG.). 52p. (YA). (gr. 5-12). 9.75 *(978-1-61651-590-4(2))* Saddleback Educational Publishing, Inc.
—Broken Promise, 1 vol. unabr. ed. 2011. (Choices Ser.). (ENG.). 52p. (YA). (gr. 5-12). 9.75 *(978-1-61651-591-1(0))* Saddleback Educational Publishing, Inc.
—Don't Get Caught, 1 vol. unabr. ed. 2011. (Choices Ser.). (ENG.). 52p. (YA). (gr. 5-12). 9.75 *(978-1-61651-592-8(9))* Saddleback Educational Publishing, Inc.
—Easy Pass, 1 vol. unabr. ed. 2011. (Choices Ser.). (ENG.). 52p. (YA). (gr. 5-12). 9.75 *(978-1-61651-596-6(1))* Saddleback Educational Publishing, Inc.
—Friend or Foe?, 1 vol. unabr. ed. 2011. (Choices Ser.). (ENG.). 52p. (YA). (gr. 5-12). 9.75 *(978-1-61651-593-5(7))* Saddleback Educational Publishing, Inc.
—It Does Matter, 1 vol. unabr. ed. 2010. (Carter High Senior Year Ser.). (ENG.). 52p. (YA). (gr. 9-12). pap. 9.75 *(978-1-61651-324-5(1))* Saddleback Educational Publishing, Inc.
—It Is Not a Date, 1 vol. unabr. ed. 2010. (Carter High Chronicles Ser.). (ENG.). 52p. (YA). (gr. 9-12). pap. 9.75 *(978-1-61651-309-2(8))* Saddleback Educational Publishing, Inc.
—Just Be Yourself, 1 vol. unabr. ed. 2010. (Carter High Senior Year Ser.). (ENG.). 52p. (YA). (gr. 9-12). pap. 9.75 *(978-1-61651-325-2(X))* Saddleback Educational Publishing, Inc.
—The Last Time, 1 vol. unabr. ed. 2010. (Carter High Senior Year Ser.). (ENG.). 52p. (YA). (gr. 9-12). pap. 9.75 *(978-1-61651-326-9(8))* Saddleback Educational Publishing, Inc.
—Library Book Mystery, 1 vol. unabr. ed. 2011. (Carter High Mysteries Ser.). (ENG.). 48p. (YA). (gr. 9-12). 9.75 *(978-1-61651-564-5(3))* Saddleback Educational Publishing, Inc.
—One Date Too Many, 1 vol. unabr. ed. 2010. (Carter High Chronicles Ser.). (ENG.). 52p. (YA). (gr. 9-12). pap. 9.75 *(978-1-61651-310-8(1))* Saddleback Educational Publishing, Inc.
—One More Chance, 1 vol. unabr. ed. 2010. (Carter High Senior Year Ser.). (ENG.). 52p. (YA). (gr. 9-12). pap. 9.75 *(978-1-61651-327-6(6))* Saddleback Educational Publishing, Inc.
—Pay Back, 1 vol. unabr. ed. 2011. (Choices Ser.). (ENG.). 52p. (YA). (gr. 5-12). 9.75 *(978-1-61651-594-2(5))* Saddleback Educational Publishing, Inc.
—Someone to Count, 1 vol. unabr. ed. 2010. (Carter High Senior Year Ser.). (ENG.). 52p. (YA). (gr. 9-12). pap. 9.75 *(978-1-61651-328-3(4))* Saddleback Educational Publishing, Inc.
—Time to Move On, 1 vol. unabr. ed. 2010. (Carter High Senior Year Ser.). (ENG.). 52p. (YA). (gr. 9-12). pap. 9.75 *(978-1-61651-329-0(2))* Saddleback Educational Publishing, Inc.
—Too Late, 1 vol. unabr. ed. 2010. (Carter High Chronicles Ser.). (ENG.). 52p. (YA). (gr. 9-12). pap. 9.75 *(978-1-61651-312-2(8))* Saddleback Educational Publishing, Inc.
—Trust Me, 1 vol. unabr. ed. 2011. (Choices Ser.). (ENG.). 52p. (YA). (gr. 5-12). 9.75 *(978-1-61651-599-7(6))* Saddleback Educational Publishing, Inc.
—The Worst Year Ever, 1 vol. unabr. ed. 2010. (Carter High Senior Year Ser.). (ENG.). 52p. (YA). (gr. 9-12). pap. 9.75 *(978-1-61651-330-6(6))* Saddleback Educational Publishing, Inc.
Rose, Deborah Lee. The Spelling Bee Before Recess. Armstrong-Ellis, Carey, illus. 2013. (ENG.). 32p. (J). (gr. k-4). 16.95 *(978-1-4197-0847-3(3),* 698701, Abrams Bks. for Young Readers) Abrams, Inc.
Rose, Sue. Jinxed! 2006. (Unfabulous! Ser.). (Illus.). 118p. (J). *(978-1-4156-5170-4(1))* Scholastic, Inc.
Ryan, Hugh. Spy Academy: Mission Twinpossible. 2012. 93p. (J). pap. *(978-0-545-37173-5(2))* Scholastic, Inc.
Ryan, Tom. Pop Quiz, 1 vol. 2017. (Orca Limelights Ser.). (ENG.). 128p. (J). (gr. 4-7). pap. 9.95 *(978-1-4598-1222-2(0))* Orca Bk. Pubs. USA.
Rylander, Chris. Crisis Zero. 2016. (Codename Conspiracy Ser.: 3). (ENG.). 400p. (J). (gr. 3-7). 16.99 *(978-0-06-232747-5(X),* Walden Pond Pr.) HarperCollins Pubs.
Salvatierra, Dante. Latchkey Kids & the Fight for A Free F. 2006. (ENG.). 236p. pap. 13.95 *(978-1-4303-0969-7(5))* Lulu Pr., Inc.
Schraff, Anne. A Boy Called Twister, 1 vol. unabr. ed. 2010. (Urban Underground Ser.). (ENG.). 180p. (YA). (gr. 9-12). pap. 11.95 *(978-1-61651-002-2(1))* Saddleback Educational Publishing, Inc.
—The Experiment, 1 vol. unabr. ed. 2010. (Q Reads Ser.). (ENG.). 32p. (YA). (gr. 9-12). pap. 8.50 *(978-1-61651-181-4(8))* Saddleback Educational Publishing, Inc.
—If You Were Mine, 1 vol. 2013. (Urban Underground Ser.). (ENG.). 195p. (YA). (gr. 9-12). pap. 11.95 *(978-1-62250-041-3(5))* Saddleback Educational Publishing, Inc.
—Leap of Faith, 1 vol. unabr. ed. 2011. (Urban Underground Ser.). (ENG.). 201p. (YA). (gr. 9-12). pap. 11.95 *(978-1-61651-588-1(0))* Saddleback Educational Publishing, Inc.
—Outrunning the Darkness, 1 vol. unabr. ed. 2010. (Urban Underground Ser.). (ENG.). 191p. (YA). (gr. 9-12). pap. 11.95 *(978-1-61651-000-8(5))* Saddleback Educational Publishing, Inc.
—Shadows of Guilt, 1 vol. unabr. ed. 2010. (Urban Underground Ser.). (ENG.). 179p. (YA). (gr. 9-12). pap. 11.95 *(978-1-61651-001-5(3))* Saddleback Educational Publishing, Inc.
—The Water's Edge. unabr. ed. 2011. (Urban Underground Ser.). (ENG.). 197p. (YA). (gr. 9-12). pap. 11.95 *(978-1-61651-589-8(9))* Saddleback Educational Publishing, Inc.
Schraff, Anne E. Don't Think about Tomorrow. 2012. (Urban Underground — Harriet Tubman High School Ser.: 23). (YA). lib. bdg. 20.80 *(978-0-606-23796-3(8))* Turtleback.
—Hurting Time. 2012. (Urban Underground — Cesar Chavez High School Ser.: 27). (YA). lib. bdg. 20.80 *(978-0-606-26597-3(X))* Turtleback.
—If You Were Mine. 2013. (Urban Underground — Harriet Tubman High School Ser.). (YA). lib. bdg. 20.80 *(978-0-606-31581-4(0))* Turtleback.
—The One for Me. 2013. (Urban Underground — Harriet Tubman High School Ser.). lib. bdg. 20.80 *(978-0-606-31582-1(9))* Turtleback.
—Out of Love for You. 2012. (Urban Underground — Harriet Tubman High School Ser.: 24). (YA). lib. bdg. 20.80 *(978-0-606-23797-0(6))* Turtleback.
—The Outcasts. 2012. (Urban Underground — Harriet Tubman High School Ser.: 21). (YA). lib. bdg. 20.80 *(978-0-606-23794-9(1))* Turtleback.
—The Rescuers. 2012. (Urban Underground — Harriet Tubman High School Ser.: 25). (YA). lib. bdg. 20.80 *(978-0-606-23798-7(4))* Turtleback.
—See No Evil. 2012. (Urban Underground — Harriet Tubman High School Ser.: 22). (YA). lib. bdg. 20.80 *(978-0-606-23795-6(X))* Turtleback.
Schuck, Philip. A Ricochet from Circumstance. 2005. (YA). 19.95 *(978-0-9764670-0-7(3))* Smithfield Capital Corp.
Schweizer, Chris. The Creeps: Book 2: the Trolls Will Feast! 2016. (Creeps Ser.). (ENG., Illus.). 128p. (J). (gr. 3-7). 17.95 *(978-1-4197-1882-3(7),* 1093301, Amulet Bks.) Abrams, Inc.
Scott, Elizabeth. Something, Maybe. 2010. (ENG.). 240p. (YA). (gr. 9). pap. 9.99 *(978-1-4169-5356-2(6),* Simon Pulse) Simon Pulse.
Sherman, Deborah. Triple Chocolate Brownie Genius, 1 vol. 2007. (ENG.). 120p. (J). (gr. 4-5). pap. 9.95 *(978-1-55455-035-7(1),* ae076da6-d6d5-4794-8b3b-44055be2c7ce) Fitzhenry & Whiteside, Ltd. CAN. Dist: Firefly Bks., Ltd.
The Shoe Grabber: Individual Title Six-Pack. (Story Steps Ser.). (gr. k-2). 23.00 *(978-0-7635-9832-7(1))* Rigby Education.
Simon, Coco. Alexis: The Icing on the Cupcake. 2014. (Cupcake Diaries: 20). lib. bdg. 17.20 *(978-0-606-35786-9(6))* Turtleback.
—Alexis & the Perfect Recipe. 2013. (Cupcake Diaries: 4). (ENG., Illus.). 160p. (J). (gr. 3-7). 17.99 *(978-1-4424-7493-2(9),* Simon Spotlight) Simon Spotlight.
—Alexis the Icing on the Cupcake. 2014. (Cupcake Diaries: 20). (ENG., Illus.). 160p. (J). (gr. 3-7). pap. 7.99 *(978-1-4814-0468-6(7),* Simon Spotlight) Simon Spotlight.
—Katie & the Cupcake Cure. 2011. (Cupcake Diaries: 1). (ENG.). 160p. (J). (gr. 3-7). pap. 7.99 *(978-1-4424-2275-9(0),* Simon Spotlight) Simon Spotlight.

S

—Katie & the Cupcake War. 2014. (Cupcake Diaries: 9). (ENG., Illus.). 160p. (J). (gr. 3-7). 17.99 *(978-1-4424-9609-5(6)*, Simon Spotlight) Simon Spotlight.

—Katie & the Cupcake War. 2012. (Cupcake Diaries: 9). lib. bdg. 17.20 *(978-0-606-26335-1(7))* Turtleback.

—Katie Sprinkled Secrets. 2015. (Cupcake Diaries: 25). (ENG., Illus.). 160p. (J). (gr. 3-7). pap. 7.99 *(978-1-4814-2919-1(1)*, Simon Spotlight) Simon Spotlight.

Slater, Calvin. Game On. 2015. 332p. (YA). *(978-1-4806-9396-8(0))* Kensington Publishing Corp.

Smith, Tiana. Match Me If You Can. 2020. (ENG.). 304p. (YA). pap. 17.99 *(978-1-250-23345-5(3)*, 900187739) Square Fish.

St. Mark Kindergarten. Kindergarten Goes to Outer Space for the Day. 2009. 28p. pap. 12.49 *(978-1-4490-0587-0(X))* AuthorHouse.

Standish, Burt L. Frank Merriwell's Pupils. Rudman, Jack, ed. 2003. (Frank Merriwell Ser.). pap. 9.95 *(978-0-8373-9133-5(4))* Merriwell, Frank Inc.

Stapleton, Rhonda. Flirting with Disaster. 2010. (ENG.). 256p. (YA). (gr. 7-18). pap. 9.99 *(978-1-4169-7465-9(2)*, Simon Pulse) Simon Pulse.

Step Up 2 - The Streets. 2008. 160p. pap. 4.99 *(978-1-4231-1319-5(5))* Disney Pr.

Stephens, Sarah Hines. Spring Break-Up. 2006. (Zoey 101 Ser.). 103p. (J). *(978-1-4156-8963-9(6))* Scholastic, Inc.

Stilton, Thea. Thea Stilton & the Blue Scarab Hunt. 2012. (Thea Stilton Ser.: 11). lib. bdg. 19.65 *(978-0-606-26183-8(4))* Turtleback.

Stine, R. L. Fear Street Super Thriller: Nightmares: (2 Books in 1: the Dead Boyfriend; Give Me a K-I-L-L) 2017. (Fear Street Ser.). (ENG.). 576p. (YA). pap. 12.99 *(978-1-250-13424-0(2)*, 900177785, St. Martin's Griffin) St. Martin's Pr.

—The Rottenest Angel. Park, Trip, illus. (Rotten School Ser.: Bk. 10). 4.99 *(978-0-06-078829-2(1))* HarperCollins Pubs.

—The Rottenest Angel, Set. Park, Trip, illus. 2011. (Rotten School Ser.: No. 10). (ENG.). 128p. (J). (gr. 2-6). 31.36 *(978-1-59961-834-0(6)*, 13137, Chapter Bks.) Spotlight.

Stratemeyer, Edward. The Rover Boys at College or the Right R. 2004. reprint ed. pap. 22.95 *(978-1-4191-8114-6(9))* Kessinger Publishing, LLC.

—The Rover Boys at College or the Right Road & the Wrong. 2004. reprint ed. pap. 1.99 *(978-1-4192-8114-3(3))* Kessinger Publishing, LLC.

Sullivan, Michael. Escapade Johnson & the Witches of Belknap County. Kolitsky, Joy, illus. 2008. (Escapade Johnson Ser.). (ENG.). 99p. (J). (gr. 2-4). pap. 3.95 *(978-1-929945-90-0(6))* Big Guy Bks., Inc.

Tackett, Wendy. The Snow Wish. 2011. 100p. (gr. 4-6). 19.95 *(978-1-4620-2608-1(7))*; pap. 9.95 *(978-1-4620-2606-7(0))* iUniverse, Inc.

Taddonio, Lea. Book 3: First Fight. Price, Mina, illus. 2016. (Head over Heels Ser.). (ENG.). 48p. (J). (gr. 3-7). lib. bdg. 34.21 *(978-1-62402-194-7(8)*, 24567, Spellbound) Magic Wagon.

Taylor, Chloē. Cute As a Button. Zhang, Nancy, illus. 2014. (Sew Zoey Ser.: 5). (ENG.). 176p. (J). (gr. 3-7). pap. 5.99 *(978-1-4814-0248-4(X)*, Simon Spotlight) Simon Spotlight.

—Dressed to Frill. Zhang, Nancy, illus. 2015. (Sew Zoey Ser.: 12). (ENG.). 176p. (J). (gr. 3-7). pap. 7.99 *(978-1-4814-2930-6(2)*, Simon Spotlight) Simon Spotlight.

Taylor, Chloe. On Pins & Needles. Zhang, Nancy, illus. 2013. (Sew Zoey Ser.: 2). (ENG.). 160p. (J). (gr. 3-7). pap. 6.99 *(978-1-4424-7936-4(1)*, Simon Spotlight) Simon Spotlight.

—Ready to Wear. Zhang, Nancy, illus. 2013. (Sew Zoey Ser.: 1). (ENG.). 176p. (J). (gr. 3-7). pap. 7.99 *(978-1-4424-7933-3(7)*, Simon Spotlight) Simon Spotlight.

Tennant, Kim. Thin Club. 2007. 52p. per. 10.00 *(978-1-4257-2619-5(4))* Xlibris Corp.

Thaler, Mike. The Class Picture Day from the Black Lagoon. Lee, Jared D., illus. 2012. 64p. (J). pap. *(978-0-545-47666-9(6))* Scholastic, Inc.

There's No Room for You, Maddie Morrison. 2006. (J). per. 6.99 *(978-0-9786117-0-5(5))* Neal Morgan Publishing.

Thomas, Debbie. Class Act. 2015. (ENG.). 224p. (J). pap. 9.99 *(978-1-78117-262-9(5))* Mercier Pr., Ltd., The IRL. Dist: Casemate Pubs. & Bk. Distributors, LLC.

Thomas, Paul R., reader. The Reeve's Tale. 2006. pap. 10.00 *(978-0-8425-2667-8(6))* Brigham Young Univ.

Thomas, Teri. The Barge Ghost, 1 vol. unabr. ed. 2010. (Q Reads Ser.). (ENG.). 32p. (YA). (gr. 9-12). pap. 8.50 *(978-1-61651-211-8(3))* Saddleback Educational Publishing, Inc.

Thompson, Brian. Reject High. 2013. 270p. pap. 11.95 *(978-0-9891056-0-6(1))* Great Nation Publishing.

Time, Nicholas O. Houston, We Have a Klutz! 2016. (In Due Time Ser.: 4). (ENG., Illus.). 160p. (J). (gr. 3-7). 17.99 *(978-1-4814-7237-1(2)*, Simon Spotlight) Simon Spotlight.

Tolman, Stacia. The Spaces Between Us. 2020. (ENG.). 304p. (YA). pap. 10.99 *(978-1-250-25091-9(9)*, 900189272) Square Fish.

Tomlinson, Everett T. Winning His W. 2006. pap. *(978-1-4068-1194-0(7))* Echo Library.

Uncle Tom's Cabin: Response Journal. 2003. 48p. (YA). *(978-1-58049-983-5(X)*, RJ83) Prestwick Hse., Inc.

von Ziegesar, Cecily. Gossip Girl: I Will Always Love You: A Gossip Girl Novel. 2010. (Gossip Girl Ser.: 12). (ENG.). 400p. (YA). (gr. 10-17). pap. 19.99 *(978-0-316-04359-5(1)*, Poppy) Little, Brown Bks. for Young Readers.

Waite, Judy. Shopaholic. 2015. (ENG., Illus.). 224p. (YA). (gr. 7). pap. 10.99 *(978-1-4814-7506-8(1)*, Atheneum Bks. for Young Readers) Simon & Schuster Children's Publishing.

Walters, Eric. Stuffed, 1 vol. 2006. (Orca Soundings Ser.). (ENG.). 108p. (YA). (gr. 9-12). 26.19 *(978-1-55143-519-0(5))* Orca Bk. Pubs. USA.

Warner, Susan. Daisy in the Field. 2017. (ENG., Illus.). (J). 26.95 *(978-1-374-97071-7(9))* Capital Communications, Inc.

Warner, Susan & Wetherell, Elizabeth. Daisy in the Field. 2011. 272p. 29.95 *(978-1-4638-9964-6(5))*; pap. 16.95 *(978-1-4638-0163-2(7))* Rodgers, Alan Bks.

Weatherly, L. A. Them. 2013. (ENG.). 80p. (YA). (gr. 6-12). pap. 6.95 *(978-1-78112-185-6(0))*; lib. bdg. 22.60 *(978-1-78112-184-9(2))* Lerner Publishing Group.

Webster, Jean. Daddy-Long-Legs. 2004. reprint ed. pap. 19.95 *(978-1-4191-1490-8(5))*; pap. 1.99 *(978-1-4192-1490-5(X))* Kessinger Publishing, LLC.

Wells, Robison. Dark Energy. 2016. (ENG.). 288p. (YA). (gr. 8). 17.99 *(978-0-06-227505-9(4)*, HarperTeen) HarperCollins Pubs.

Weston, Alan & Gempko, Gloria. The Girl from Keelonia. 2003. (J). pap. 7.95 *(978-0-9742808-0-6(1))* Lill-Till Pr.

White, Sarah. Our Broken Pieces. 2017. (ENG.). 288p. (YA). (gr. 9). pap. 9.99 *(978-0-06-247313-4(1)*, HarperTeen) HarperCollins Pubs.

Whitesides, Tyler. Curse of the Broomstaff. 2013. (Janitors Ser.: 3). (ENG., Illus.). 384p. (J). (gr. 5). 18.99 *(978-1-60907-605-4(2)*, 5107237, Shadow Mountain) Shadow Mountain Publishing.

—Janitors. 2011. (Janitors Ser.: Bk. 1). pap. 34.99 *(978-1-60908-075-4(0))* Deseret Bk. Co.

—Janitors. (Janitors Ser.: 1). (ENG., Illus.). (J). (gr. 5). 2012. 320p. pap. 9.99 *(978-1-60907-065-6(8)*, 5078581) 2011. 312p. 17.99 *(978-1-60908-056-3(4)*, 5057487) Shadow Mountain Publishing. (Shadow Mountain).

—Secrets of New Forest Academy. 2013. (Janitors Ser.: 2). (ENG., Illus.). 368p. (J). (gr. 5). pap. 8.99 *(978-1-60907-546-0(3)*, 5105035, Shadow Mountain) Shadow Mountain Publishing.

Whittemore, Jo. Confidentially Yours #3: Heather's Crush Catastrophe. 2016. (Confidentially Yours Ser.: 3). (ENG.). 288p. (J). (gr. 3-7). 6.99 *(978-0-06-235897-4(9)*, HarperCollins) HarperCollins Pubs.

Wilkes, Nita. Stalking Bailey. 2010. 185p. pap. 10.95 *(978-1-4327-4862-3(9))* Outskirts Pr., Inc.

Williams, Nicole. Clash, 2. 2012. (Crash Ser.: 2). (ENG.). 288p. (YA). (gr. 11). pap. 9.99 *(978-0-06-226715-3(9)*, HarperCollins) HarperCollins Pubs.

—Crash, 1. 2012. (Crash Ser.: 1). (ENG.). 384p. (YA). (gr. 11). pap. 9.99 *(978-0-06-226714-6(0)*, HarperCollins) HarperCollins Pubs.

—Crush, 3. 2013. (Crash Ser.: 3). (ENG.). 400p. (YA). (gr. 11). pap. 9.99 *(978-0-06-226717-7(5)*, HarperCollins) HarperCollins Pubs.

Winfield, Arthur M. The Mystery at Putnam Hall. 2007. 272p. 26.95 *(978-1-4218-4130-4(4))*; per. 11.95 *(978-1-4218-4228-8(9))* 1st World Publishing, Inc. (1st World Library - Literary Society).

—Rover Boys at College or the Right Road. 2006. pap. 30.95 *(978-1-4286-4106-8(8))* Kessinger Publishing, LLC.

—Rover Boys at School. 2006. pap. *(978-1-4068-3129-0(8))* Echo Library.

—The Rover Boys down East or the Struggle for the Stanhope Fortune. 2006. (ENG.). 316p. per. 30.95 *(978-1-4286-4113-6(0))* Kessinger Publishing, LLC.

—Rover Boys in Alaska or Lost in the Fiel. 2006. pap. 30.95 *(978-1-4286-4107-5(6))* Kessinger Publishing, LLC.

—The Rover Boys in Business or the Search for the Missing Bonds. 2006. (ENG.). 316p. per. 30.95 *(978-1-4286-4098-6(3))* Kessinger Publishing, LLC.

—The Rover Boys in the Air or from College Campus to the Clouds. 2006. (ENG.). 316p. per. 30.95 *(978-1-4286-4103-7(3))* Kessinger Publishing, LLC.

—Rover Boys on A Tour or Last Days at Bri. 2006. pap. 31.95 *(978-1-4286-4389-5(3))* Kessinger Publishing, LLC.

Yang, Gene Luen. Animal Crackers: A Gene Luen Yang Collection. 2012. (ENG., Illus.). 216p. (YA). pap. 14.95 *(978-1-59362-183-4(3)*, 1ea5f6ba-5e7c-42c4-953c-459bccf52a55) Slave Labor Bks.

Young, Karen Romano. Doodlebug: A Novel in Doodles. 2012. (ENG., Illus.). 128p. (J). (gr. 3-7). pap. 15.99 *(978-1-250-01020-9(9)*, 900084757) Square Fish.

Yung, Kao & Liang, Kuan. Magic Lover's Tower, Vol. 2. 2008. (Magic Lover's Tower Ser.). (ENG., Illus.). 176p. (YA). (gr. 8). pap. 9.95 *(978-1-59796-154-7(X))* DrMaster Pubns. Inc.

Yunisa. Schoolaholic Princess 1: the Miracle Boys. 2008. 242p. pap. 15.88 *(978-1-4357-6026-4(3))* Lulu Pr., Inc.

—Schoolaholic Princess 3: Simfoni Cinta. 2008. 220p. pap. 14.88 *(978-1-4357-6045-5(X))* Lulu Pr., Inc.

Zielinski, Valerie & Skaletski, Roslyn. The Adventures of Bella. 2011. 48p. pap. 14.00 *(978-1-4634-2018-5(8))* AuthorHouse.

Zurchin, Cynthia, et al. The Whale Done School: Transforming a School's Culture by Catching Students Doing Things Right. 2012. 124p. pap. 14.95 *(978-1-4685-9536-9(9))* AuthorHouse.

STUDENTS—PERSONNEL WORK

see Educational Counseling

STUDY, METHOD OF

see Study Skills

STUDY SKILLS

see also Self-Culture

also subjects with the subdivision Study and Teaching, e.g. Art—Study and Teaching, etc.

Anhalt, Edward. Raise Your GPA 1 Full Grade. 2003. 265p. (YA). pap. 19.95 *(978-0-595-24645-8(1)*, Writers Club Pr.) iUniverse, Inc.

Beck, Isabel. Questioning the Author: An Approach for Enhancing Student Engagement with Text. 122p. 84.95 incl. DVD *(978-0-322-04355-8(7))* Wright Group/McGraw-Hill.

Berry, Joy. A Fun & Easy Way to Do Your Homework. Bartholomew, illus. 2010. (Fun & Easy Way Ser.). (ENG.). 48p. (J). (gr. 1-5). pap. 7.95 *(978-1-60577-320-9(4))* Berry, Joy Enterprises.

—A Fun & Easy Way to Get Good Grades. Bartholomew, illus. 2010. (Fun & Easy Way Ser.). (ENG.). 48p. (J). (gr. 1-5). pap. 7.95 *(978-1-60577-321-6(2))* Berry, Joy Enterprises.

—Get Good Grades. 2009. (Fun & Easy Way Ser.). (ENG.). 52p. (J). (gr. 2-5). pap. 7.95 *(978-1-60577-311-7(5))* Berry, Joy Enterprises.

Bidaisee, Sharlini. Toddler's Basic Knowledge. 2006. 13p. (J). 10.30 *(978-1-4116-6849-2(9))* Lulu Pr., Inc.

Black, Howard, et al. Learning on Purpose: A Self-Management Approach to Study Skills. 2006. (Learning on Purpose Ser.). 320p. (gr. 7-12). pap. 14.99 *(978-0-89455-753-8(X))* Critical Thinking Co., The.

Burling, Alexis. Strengthening Test Preparation Skills, 1 vol. 2017. (Skills for Success Ser.). (ENG., Illus.). 64p. (J). (gr. 7-7). 36.13 *(978-1-5081-7574-2(8)*, 20b75611-a174-491b-95c0-162b7d50b2be, Rosen Young Adult) Rosen Publishing Group, Inc., The.

Caillou: Thinking Skills. 2003. 32p. pap., wbk. ed. 14.95 incl. cd-rom *(978-1-57791-030-5(3))* Brighter Minds Children's Publishing.

Cali, Charlene C. The Nature of Study Skills: Hardworking Helen K Honeybee Study Skills 3. Norcross, Harry, illus. 56p. (J). (gr. 8-9). 14.95 *(978-1-57543-101-7(7))* MAR*CO Products, Inc.

Cassel, Katrina L. The Middle School Survival Manual. 2010. 128p. (J). (gr. 6-18). pap. 8.99 *(978-0-7586-1790-3(9))* Concordia Publishing Hse.

Childs, Mattie S. Lesson Helpers. 2004. 74p. (YA). per. 19.99 *(978-1-4116-0948-8(4))* Lulu Pr., Inc.

Creative Imaging. 2nd ed. 2004. 116p. (YA). pap. *(978-0-938465-01-0(5))* Zo Publishing.

Doherty, Edith J. S. Primary Independent. 60p. (J). pap., stu. ed. 14.95 *(978-0-945984-06-1(5)*, Zephyr Pr.) Chicago Review Pr., Inc.

DynaNotes Test Taking Tips. 2006. (J). pap. *(978-1-933854-37-3(5))* DynaStudy, Inc.

DynaNotes Test Taking Tips Transparency Set. 2006. (J). trans. *(978-1-933854-38-0(3))* DynaStudy, Inc.

Everett, Reese. Homework, Yes or No. 2016. (Seeing Both Sides Ser.). (ENG.). 32p. (gr. 3-6). 32.79 *(978-1-68191-380-3(1)*, 9781681913803) Rourke Educational Media.

Fetty, Margaret, ed. The Ultimate Book of Second Grade Skills: Grade 2. Hierstein, Judy & Boyer, Lyn, illus. 2009. (Ultimate Book of Skills Ser.). 224p. pap. 16.99 *(978-1-4190-9953-3(1))* Steck-Vaughn.

Fry, Ron. Surefire Tips to Improve Your Memory Skills, 1 vol., 1. 2015. (Surefire Study Success Ser.). (ENG.). 144p. (YA). (gr. 7-8). 38.80 *(978-1-5081-7089-1(4)*, e6a7ce85-aa68-4893-8d97-02a5116b0159, Rosen Young Adult) Rosen Publishing Group, Inc., The.

—Surefire Tips to Improve Your Reading Skills, 1 vol., 1. 2015. (Surefire Study Success Ser.). (ENG.). 144p. (YA). (gr. 7-8). 38.80 *(978-1-5081-7094-5(0)*, f782fa03-8732-441e-86ec-7b6b95573862, Rosen Young Adult) Rosen Publishing Group, Inc., The.

—Surefire Tips to Improve Your Study Skills, 1 vol., 1. 2015. (Surefire Study Success Ser.). (ENG.). 256p. (J). (gr. 7-8). 38.80 *(978-1-5081-7098-3(3)*, d88afc7a-44e0-4d10-8e12-e5453d05d0d2, Rosen Young Adult) Rosen Publishing Group, Inc., The.

Future Ready Project Skills. 2017. (Future Ready Project Skills Ser.). 48p. (gr. 3-4). pap. 70.20 *(978-0-7660-8809-2(X))* Enslow Publishing, LLC.

Gehret, Jeanne. The Don't-Give-Up Kid: And Learning Differences. DePauw, Sandra A., illus. 2nd rev. ed. 2003. 40p. (J). (gr. 1-5). 13.95 *(978-0-9625136-3-3(6))* Verbal Images Pr.

Girard, Vanessa P. High School Survival Guide: United in Diversity. 2008. (Illus.). 72p. (YA). pap. 11.95 *(978-0-939479-33-7(8)*, Backintyme) Backintyme Publishing.

Goldhammer, Richard. Gotta Do Homework! Elephant Notes - Study Tips You'll Never Forget. 2003. (Elephant Notes Ser.). (YA). (gr. 6-8). spiral bd. *(978-0-9716873-0-1(7))* ElephantSide Pr.

Hamilton, Robert M. Should Students Have to Take Tests?, 1 vol. 2017. (Points of View Ser.). (ENG.). 24p. (gr. 3-3). pap. 9.25 *(978-1-5345-2344-9(8)*, f0e81684-7a30-45cc-9e60-10725f401241); lib. bdg. 26.23 *(978-1-5345-2346-3(4)*, 1919674e-cb74-4911-9972-c397fbf4e6da) Greenhaven Publishing LLC.

Hands-On Literacy Center - Farm Set. (J). (gr. -1-1). pap. 149.00 *(978-0-9673268-9-4(3))* Learning Fasten-Ations, Inc.

Heiderer, Conrad. Alpha-Blocke: Alpha-Blocke.com Learning Forum Animals, Art & the Alphabet Series with Case & Talking CD. 2004. (Illus.). 32p. spiral bd. 39.95 incl. audio compact disk *(978-0-9746699-0-8(3))* Heiderer, Conrad.

Holt, Rinehart and Winston Staff. Holt Science & Technology: Directed Reading Answer Key. 4th ed. 2004. (Illus.). pap. 11.20 *(978-0-03-037018-2(3))* Holt McDougal.

—Holt Science & Technology: Directed Reading Worksheets. 4th ed. 2004. pap. 15.00 *(978-0-03-036992-6(4))*; pap. 15.00 *(978-0-03-036993-3(2))*; pap. 15.00 *(978-0-03-036994-0(0))* Holt McDougal.

HOP, LLC. Hooked on Kindergarten. 2006. 99.99 *(978-1-933863-88-7(9))* HOP, LLC.

—Hooked on Pre-K. 2006. 99.99 *(978-1-933863-89-4(7))* HOP, LLC.

—Sylvan School Success. 2006. 199.99 *(978-1-931020-76-3(0))* HOP, LLC.

I Can Do It!, 6 vols. 2004. (I Can Do It! Ser.). (ENG.). 24p. (gr. k-2). lib. bdg. 71.01 *(978-0-8368-4322-4(3)*, bb8b7b95-f27c-4fd8-9b71-6189b1042a85, Weekly Reader Leveled Readers) Stevens, Gareth Publishing LLLP.

Lambert, Monica & Algozzine, Bob. Strategies That Make Learning Fun. 2nd ed. 2003. (Illus.). 184p. (gr. k-12). 36.95 *(978-1-57035-915-6(6)*, 211LEARN) Cambium Education, Inc.

Learning Company Books Staff, ed. Reader Rabbit 1st Grade Workbook. 2003. (Illus.). 320p. (J). (gr. 1-18). pap., wbk. ed. *(978-0-7630-7543-9(4))* Magma.

—Reader Rabbit Kindergarten Workbook. 2003. (Illus.). 320p. (J). (gr. k-18). pap., wbk. ed. *(978-0-7630-7542-2(6))* Magma.

—Reader Rabbit Preschool Workbook. 2003. (Illus.). 320p. (J). (gr. -1-18). pap., wbk. ed. *(978-0-7630-7541-5(8))* Magma.

Machajewski, Sarah. Interpreting Data about the Thirteen Colonies, 1 vol. 2018. (Project Learning Through American History Ser.). (ENG.). 32p. (gr. 4-5). 27.93 *(978-1-5383-3067-8(9)*, c9e55879-4df6-4eb6-87ac-f7c284624232); pap. 11.00 *(978-1-5383-3068-5(7)*, 232307c5-08d9-454e-a7eb-709c824eb45a) Rosen Publishing Group, Inc., The. (PowerKids Pr.).

Modi, Narendra. Exam Warriors. 2019. (ENG., Illus.). 208p. pap. 14.95 *(978-0-14-344150-2(7)*, Penguin Enterprise) Penguin Bks. India PVT, Ltd IND. Dist: Independent Pubs. Group.

Moore, Gary W. Becoming a Master Student: Keys to Student Success. 2004. 305p. 38.00 *(978-0-9760939-0-9(1)*, 0-9760939-0-1) Tudor Assocs. Pr.

Morris, Daphne. Trevor Romain's How to Do Homework Without Throwing up DVD Educator Kit. 2007. (J). 69.99 *(978-1-934365-00-7(9))* Romain, Trevor Co., The.

—Trevor Romain's How to Do Homework Without Throwing up VHS Educator Kit. 2007. (J). 69.99 *(978-1-934365-01-4(7))* Romain, Trevor Co., The.

Moss, Marissa. Amelia's Book of Notes & Note Passing. Moss, Marissa, illus. 2006. (Amelia Ser.). (ENG., Illus.). 80p. (J). (gr. 4-7). 14.99 *(978-0-689-87446-8(4)*, Simon & Schuster/Paula Wiseman Bks.) Simon & Schuster/Paula Wiseman Bks.

Moss, Wendy L. & Deluca-Acconi, Robin. School Made Easier: A Kid's Guide to Study Strategies & Anxiety-Busting Tools. (Illus.). 128p. 2014. pap. *(978-1-4338-1336-8(X))* 2013. (ENG., 14.95 *(978-1-4338-1335-1(1))* American Psychological Assn. (Magination Pr.).

Newsom, Mary T. & Jones, Joy. The Homework Survival Kit. (J). *(978-0-9637644-2-3(X))* Spoken Word, The.

Osborne, Corinne. Picture Book Learning, Vol. 1. 2004. (ENG & AFA.). 60p. per. 11.99 *(978-0-9760725-0-8(5)*, PBLSSV1P) Picture Bk. Learning, Inc.

Percival, Simon. The Practical Guide to Revision Techniques. 2005. (Practical Guides). (ENG., Illus.). 72p. per. *(978-1-85539-201-4(1)*, Network Continuum Education) Bloomsbury Publishing Plc.

Rosenberg, Gary, et al. Jon & Jayne's Guide to Getting Through School. 2009. (Jon & Jayne Doe Ser.: No. 3). (ENG., Illus.). 128p. (YA). (gr. 7-11). pap. 9.95 *(978-0-7573-0735-5(3)*, HCI Teens) Health Communications, Inc.

Rozakis, Laurie. Get Test Smart! The Ultimate Guide to Middle School Standardized Tests. 2007. 144p. (J). *(978-1-4287-1884-5(2)*, Scholastic Reference) Scholastic, Inc.

School Zone Publishing Company Staff. Following Directions. (Illus.). (J). 19.99 incl. audio compact disk *(978-0-88743-930-8(6))* School Zone Publishing Co.

Scott, John, suppl. How to Study. 2004. (YA). 30.00 *(978-1-879498-80-8(4))* SportAmerica.

Shannon, Rosemarie, et al, adapted by. Dot-To-Dot Stories. 2004. (Kids Can Learn with Franklin Ser.). (ENG., Illus.). 32p. (J). (gr. 1-3). 3.95 *(978-1-55337-600-2(5))* Kids Can Pr., Ltd. CAN. Dist: Hachette Bk. Group.

—Measurement. 2003. (Kids Can Learn with Franklin Ser.). (ENG., Illus.). 32p. (J). (gr. k-1). 3.95 *(978-1-55337-595-1(5))* Kids Can Pr., Ltd. CAN. Dist: Hachette Bk. Group.

Sirotowitz, Sandi, et al. Study Strategies for Early School Success: Seven Steps to Improve Your Learning. 2003. (Seven Steps Family Guides). (ENG., Illus.). 146p. pap. 18.00 *(978-1-886941-55-7(6))* Specialty Pr., Inc.

Steck-Vaughn, creator. Using Information Resources, Grade 2. 2009. (Using Information Resources Ser.). (Illus.). 64p. pap. 9.99 *(978-1-4190-9937-3(X))* Steck-Vaughn.

—Using Information Resources, Grade 3. 2009. (Using Information Resources Ser.). (Illus.). 64p. pap. 9.99 *(978-1-4190-9938-0(8))* Steck-Vaughn.

—Using Information Resources, Grade 4. 2009. (Using Information Resources Ser.). (Illus.). 64p. pap. 9.99 *(978-1-4190-9939-7(6))* Steck-Vaughn.

—Using Information Resources, Grade 5. 2009. (Using Information Resources Ser.). (Illus.). 64p. pap. 9.99 *(978-1-4190-9940-3(X))* Steck-Vaughn.

—Using Information Resources, Grade 6. 2009. (Using Information Resources Ser.). (Illus.). 64p. pap. 9.99 *(978-1-4190-9941-0(8))* Steck-Vaughn.

Stern, Judith M. & Ben-Ami, Uzi. Many Ways to Learn: A Kid's Guide to LD. Chesworth, Michael & Pearce, Carl, illus. 2nd rev. ed. 2010. 112p. (J). (gr. 3-8). 14.95 *(978-1-4338-0739-8(4))*; pap. 9.95 *(978-1-4338-0740-4(8))* American Psychological Assn. (Magination Pr.).

Study Skills & Strategies for Students in High School. 2005. spiral bd. 40.00 *(978-0-9745999-4-6(8))* Mangrum-Strichart Learning Resources.

Study Skills Fun. 2003. 34.95 *(978-1-57543-115-4(7))* MAR*CO Products, Inc.

Summer School Program: Grade 1 Complete Package. (gr. 1-18). 650.00 *(978-0-7578-3236-9(9))* Rigby Education.

Summer School Program: Grade 2 Complete Package. (gr. 2-18). 750.00 *(978-0-7578-3237-6(7))* Rigby Education.

Summer School Program: Grade 3 Complete Package. (gr. 3-18). 750.00 *(978-0-7578-3238-3(5))* Rigby Education.

Summer School Program: Grade 4 Complete Package. (gr. 4-18). 750.00 *(978-0-7578-3239-0(3))* Rigby Education.

Summer School Program: Grade 5 Complete Package. (gr. 5-18). 650.00 *(978-0-7578-3240-6(7))* Rigby Education.

Summer School Program: Grade 6 Complete Package. (gr. 6-18). 725.00 *(978-0-7578-3241-3(5))* Rigby Education.

Summer School Program: Grade 7 Complete Package. (gr. 7-18). 725.00 *(978-0-7578-3242-0(3))* Rigby Education.

Summer School Program: Grade 8 Complete Package. (gr. 8-18). 725.00 *(978-0-7578-3243-7(1))* Rigby Education.

Summer School Program: Grade K Complete Package. (gr. k-18). 650.00 *(978-0-7578-3235-2(0))* Rigby Education.

Swim, Luann. Cracking the System. 2012. 60p. pap. 29.95 *(978-1-937065-00-3(6))* B & B Educational Advancement & Pubns., Inc.

Teacher Created Resources Staff. Mastering Fifth Grade Skills. 2006. (ENG.). 240p. (gr. 5). pap. 19.99 *(978-1-4206-3941-4(2))* Teacher Created Resources, Inc.

ThemeMaker Student Tool. 2005. 4.90 *(978-0-9769527-9-4(3))* Mindwing Concepts, Inc.

Walsh, Brian Everard. Thinking, Reading, Remembering: Brain-Friendly Tips & Techniques for a Student's Enriched Learning. 2013. 76p. pap. *(978-0-9917463-5-4(X))* Walsh Seminars, Ltd.

Watkins, Dewhite. Quick & Dirty Secrets of College Success: A Professor Tells It All. 2004. 128p. (YA). per. 14.95 *(978-0-9742632-1-2(4))* Blue Boy Publishing Co.

The Weaver Curriculum. 2004. (gr. k-12). Vol. 1. 145.00 *(978-1-58095-842-4(7)*, WV001, Weaver) Vol. 2. 145.00 *(978-1-58095-843-1(5)*, WV002, Weaver) Vol. 3. 145.00 *(978-1-58095-844-8(3)*, WV003, Lifepac) Vol. 4. 145.00 *(978-1-58095-845-5(1)*, WV004, Lifepac) Vol. 5. 145.00 *(978-1-58095-846-2(X)*, WV005, Weaver) Alpha Omega Pubns., Inc.

Whitney, Brooks. How to Master the School Universe: Homework, Teachers, Tests, Bullies, & Other Ways to Survive the Classroom. Kennedy, Kelly, illus. 2004. 80p. (J). pap. *(978-0-439-57902-5(3))* Scholastic, Inc.

Willis, Mariaemma & Kindle Hodson, Victoria. Mid-life Crisis Begins in Kindergarten: How we learn the habit of settling for

Less. 2004. spiral bd. 10.00 *(978-0-9772350-0-1(9))* LearningSuccess Pr.

STUNT PERFORMERS

Brown Bear Books. Stunt Crews: Death-Defying Feats. 2012. (Mission Impossible Ser.). (ENG., Illus.). 32p. (J). (gr. 4-6). lib. bdg. 31.35 *(978-1-936333-30-1(9),* 16754) Brown Bear Bks.

Cohn, Jessica & Kuligowski, Stephanie. Fearless! Stunt People, 1 vol. 2nd rev. ed. 2013. (TIME for KIDS(r): Informational Text Ser.). (ENG.). 64p. (gr. 4-8). pap. 14.99 *(978-1-4333-4941-6(8))* Teacher Created Materials, Inc.

Gonzalez, Lissette. Stunt Performers & Stunt Doubles. (Dangerous Jobs Ser.). 24p. (gr. 2-3). 2009. 42.50 *(978-1-61512-136-6(6))* 2007. (ENG., Illus.). (J). lib. bdg. 26.27 *(978-1-4042-3780-3(1),* a35f5d10-88f2-4d9f-8aa8-d8a79b490fc7) Rosen Publishing Group, Inc., The. (PowerKids Pr.).

Green, Sara. Stunts. 2018. (Movie Magic Ser.). (ENG., Illus.). 32p. (J). (gr. 3-8). lib. bdg. 27.95 *(978-1-62617-850-2(X),* Blastoff! Discovery) Bellwether Media.

Hamilton, S. L. Daredevil. 2015. (Xtreme Jobs Ser.). (ENG., Illus.). 32p. (J). (gr. 3-9). 32.79 *(978-1-62403-757-3(7),* 17748, Abdo & Daughters) ABDO Publishing Co.

—Stunt Performer. 2015. (Xtreme Jobs Ser.). (ENG., Illus.). 32p. (J). (gr. 3-9). 32.79 *(978-1-62403-760-3(7),* 17754, Abdo & Daughters) ABDO Publishing Co.

Horn, Geoffrey M. Movie Stunts & Special Effects, 1 vol. 2006. (Making Movies Ser.). (ENG., Illus.). 32p. (gr. 3-3). lib. bdg. 28.67 *(978-0-8368-6840-1(4),* d29d6744-d7b6-4b9a-9907-97faad8280d2) Stevens, Gareth Publishing LLLP.

Kuligowski, Stephanie & Cohn, Jessica. Fearless! Stunt People, 1 vol. 2nd rev. ed. 2013. (TIME for KIDS(r): Informational Text Ser.). (ENG., Illus.). 64p. (J). (gr. 4-8). lib. bdg. 31.96 *(978-1-4333-7440-1(4))* Teacher Created Materials, Inc.

Monnig, Alex. Stunt Performers in Action. 2017. (Dangerous Jobs in Action Ser.). (ENG.). 32p. (J). (gr. 3-6). lib. bdg. 35.64 *(978-1-5038-1633-6(8),* 211149) Child's World, Inc, The.

Ormoth, Tyler, et al. Wild Stunts. 2015. (Wild Stunts Ser.). (ENG.). 32p. (J). (gr. 3-4). 122.60 *(978-1-4914-6666-7(9),* 22908, Capstone Pr.) Capstone.

Rauf, Don. Extreme Movie Stunts, 1 vol. 2019. (Extreme Sports & Stunts Ser.). (ENG.). 48p. (gr. 5-5). 33.47 *(978-1-7253-4737-3(7),* bef8877f-d2aa-4599-82af-800ac4bbb8d1) Rosen Publishing Group, Inc., The.

Rechner, Amy. Stunt Performer. 2019. (Cool Careers Ser.). (ENG., Illus.). 24p. (J). (gr. 3-7). lib. bdg. 26.95 *(978-1-64487-065-5(7),* Torque Bks.) Bellwether Media.

Richard, Stephen. Stunt Man. 2008. (321 Go! Ser.). (ENG., Illus.). 32p. pap. *(978-1-84167-784-2(1))* Ransom Publishing Ltd.

Ridley, Frances. Stunt Pros. 2009. (ENG., Illus.). 32p. (J). (gr. 4-7). lib. bdg. *(978-0-7787-3779-7(9))* Crabtree Publishing Co.

Tougas, Joe. Mind-Blowing Movie Stunts. 2015. (Wild Stunts Ser.). (ENG., Illus.). 32p. (J). (gr. 3-9). lib. bdg. 28.65 *(978-1-4914-4256-2(5),* 128674, Capstone Pr.) Capstone.

Wood, Alix. Stunt Performer, 1 vol., 1. 2014. (World's Coolest Jobs Ser.). (ENG.). 32p. (J). (gr. 4-4). 28.93 *(978-1-4777-5999-8(9),* 25b15336-237e-404e-a7ef-ef154b2f9d0c, PowerKids Pr.) Rosen Publishing Group, Inc., The.

STUYVESANT, PETER, 1592-1672

Krizner, L. J. Peter Stuyvesant: New Amsterdam, & the Origins of New York. 2009. (Library of American Lives & Times Ser.). 112p. (gr. 5-5). 69.20 *(978-1-60853-498-2(7))* Rosen Publishing Group, Inc., The.

Whiting, Jim. Peter Stuyvesant. 2007. (Profiles in American History Ser.). (Illus.). 48p. (J). (gr. 3-7). lib. bdg. 29.95 *(978-1-58415-526-3(4))* Mitchell Lane Pubs.

STYLE, LITERARY

see also Criticism; Letter Writing; Literature—History and Criticism; Rhetoric

Bodden, Valerie. Imagery & Description. 2016. (Odysseys in Prose Ser.). (ENG., Illus.). 80p. (J). (gr. 7-10). *(978-1-60818-728-7(4),* 20685, Creative Education) Creative Co., The.

—Wording & Tone. (Odysseys in Prose Ser.). (ENG., Illus.). 80p. (J). (gr. 7-11). 2017. pap. 14.99 *(978-1-62832-326-9(4),* 20689, Creative Paperbacks) 2016. *(978-1-60818-730-0(6),* 20691, Creative Education) Creative Co., The.

Donovan, Sandy. Bored Bella Learns about Fiction & Nonfiction, 1 vol. Hernandez, Leeza, illus. 2010. (In the Library). (ENG.). 24p. (J). (gr. k-4). lib. bdg. 27.32 *(978-1-4048-5758-2(3),* 102495, Picture Window Bks.) Capstone.

STYLE IN DRESS

see Costume; Fashion

SU DOKU

see Sudoku

SUBMARINE DIVING

see Deep Diving

SUBMARINE EXPLORATION

see Underwater Exploration

SUBMARINE GEOLOGY

Meredith, Susan. Undersea Life to Color. Cooper, Jenny, illus. 2014. (ENG.). (J). pap. 5.99 *(978-0-7945-2854-6(6),* Usborne) EDC Publishing.

SUBMARINE WARFARE

see also Submarines (Ships)

Nardo, Don. In the Water: Strategies & Tactics. 2014. (J). *(978-1-59935-464-4(0))* Reynolds, Morgan Inc.

—In the Water: Torpedoes, Missiles, & Dive-Bombs. 2014. (ENG.). (J). 27.45 *(978-1-59935-460-6(8))* Reynolds, Morgan Inc.

West, Krista. Underwater Warfare of the Future. 2009. (Library of Future Weaponry Ser.). 64p. (gr. 6-6). 58.50 *(978-1-60853-642-9(4))* Rosen Publishing Group, Inc., The.

SUBMARINES (SHIPS)

Allen, Kenny. Submarines, 1 vol. 2012. (Monster Machines Ser.). (ENG., Illus.). 24p. (J). (gr. 1-2). pap. 9.15 *(978-1-4339-7180-8(1),* 15fab9a0-9092-49f8-bd8a-c13db35cf449); lib. bdg. 25.27 *(978-1-4339-7179-2(8),* ff38bfe9-89b5-4ac4-8799-035f436b319e) Stevens, Gareth Publishing LLLP.

Aloian, Molly. Deep-Diving Submarines. 2011. (ENG.). 32p. (J). *(978-0-7787-2728-6(9));* (Vehicles on the Move Ser.: No. 14). pap. *(978-0-7787-2735-4(1))* Crabtree Publishing Co.

Amato, William. Nuclear Submarines. 2009. (High-Tech Vehicles Ser.). 24p. (gr. 2-3). 42.50 *(978-1-61513-306-2(2),* PowerKids Pr.) Rosen Publishing Group, Inc., The.

—Submarinos nucleares (Nuclear Submarines) 2009. (Vehículos de alta tecnología (High-Tech Vehicles) Ser.). (SPA.). 24p. (gr. 2-3). 42.50 *(978-1-60854-720-3(5),* Editorial Buenas Letras) Rosen Publishing Group, Inc., The.

Boatner, Kay. National Geographic Kids Funny Fill-in: My Ocean Adventure. 2013. (Illus.). 48p. (J). (gr. 3-7). pap. 4.99 *(978-1-4263-1643-2(7),* National Geographic Kids) Disney Publishing Worldwide.

Bodden, Valerie. Submarines. 2012. (Illus.). 23p. (J). 25.65 *(978-1-60818-128-5(6),* Creative Education) Creative Co., The.

Bow, James. Water Vehicles. 2018. (Vehicles on the Job Ser.). (ENG.). 24p. (J). (gr. 1-3). 25.27 *(978-1-59953-946-1(2))* Norwood Hse. Pr.

Brody, Walt. How Submarines Work. 2019. (Lightning Bolt Books (r) — Military Machines Ser.). (ENG., Illus.). 24p. (J). (gr. 1-3). 29.32 *(978-1-5415-5568-6(6),* 3110d309-1fb0-4ebd-ac78-9e5055989ea1); pap. 9.99 *(978-1-5415-7458-8(3),* 9e2e135a-b9c6-454c-8a1e-14da4bfb2f30) Lerner Publishing Group. (Lerner Pubns.).

Brook, Henry. True Sea Stories. 2005. (True Adventure Stories Ser.). (Illus.). 154p. (J). (gr. 5). lib. bdg. 12.95 *(978-1-58086-693-4(X))* EDC Publishing.

Cooke, Tim. Submarines. 2012. (Ultimate Military Machines Ser.). (Illus.). 32p. (gr. 4-7). lib. bdg. 31.35 *(978-1-59920-822-0(9))* Black Rabbit Bks.

Dellaccio, Tanya. How a Submarine Is Built, 1 vol. 2020. (Engineering Our World Ser.). (ENG.). 24p. (gr. 2-3). pap. 9.15 *(978-1-5382-4715-0(1),* 26a9ea62-b88f-44e3-b85d-6ff8226100e6) Stevens, Gareth Publishing LLLP.

Diedrick, Noah. Submarines: Use Place Value Understanding & Properties of Operations to Perform Multi-Digit Arithmetic, 1 vol. 2014. (Rosen Math Readers Ser.). (ENG.). 24p. (J). (gr. 3-3). pap. 8.25 *(978-1-4777-4936-4(5),* c91cfc34-e716-4c47-9457-f4138f1d2197, PowerKids Pr.) Rosen Publishing Group, Inc., The.

Doeden, Matt. Submarines. 2005. (Pull Ahead Books — Mighty Movers Ser.). (ENG., Illus.). 32p. (J). (gr. k-3). per. 7.99 *(978-0-8225-2900-2(9),* 28c09ff1-db14-4c6d-8f93-ce51fdd7d072, First Avenue Editions) Lerner Publishing Group.

Doyle, Kevin. Submarines. 2004. (Military Hardware in Action Ser.). (Illus.). 48p. (J). (gr. 4-9). lib. bdg. 25.26 *(978-0-8225-4704-4(X))* Lerner Publishing Group.

Ellis, Catherine. Submarines. (Mega Military Machines Ser.). 24p. (gr. 1-1). 2009. 42.50 *(978-1-61514-638-3(5),* PowerKids Pr.) 2007. (ENG., Illus.). (J). lib. bdg. 26.27 *(978-1-4042-3665-3(1),* 4cfc3986-ff68-4e6c-88e2-e9cebe9f068d) Rosen Publishing Group, Inc., The.

—Submarines/Submarinos. 2009. (Mega Military Machines/Megamáquinas militares Ser.). (ENG & SPA.). 24p. (gr. 1-1). 42.50 *(978-1-61514-643-7(1),* Editorial Buenas Letras) Rosen Publishing Group, Inc., The.

—Submarines/Submarinos, 1 vol. Brusca, María Cristina, tr. 2007. (Mega Military Machines / Megamáquinas Militares Ser.). (SPA & ENG., Illus.). 24p. (J). (gr. 1-1). lib. bdg. 26.27 *(978-1-4042-7620-8(3),* a8fe313b-54d3-4d59-94e8-f271e97615b5) Rosen Publishing Group, Inc., The.

Frith, Alex. Submarines II. 2011. (Submarines Ser.). 80p. (J). pap. 8.99 *(978-0-7945-2557-6(1),* Usborne) EDC Publishing.

Garcia, Adam. Inside Submarines: Use Place Value Understanding & Properties of Operations to Perform Multi-Digit Arithmetic, 1 vol. 2014. (InfoMax Math Readers Ser.). (ENG.). 24p. (J). (gr. 3-3). pap. 8.25 *(978-1-4777-4627-1(7),* 1a3a2d23-38bc-4851-bb3e-edec1467b00a, Rosen Classroom) Rosen Publishing Group, Inc., The.

Harasymiw, Mark J. Life on a Submarine, 1 vol. 2013. (Extreme Jobs in Extreme Places Ser.). (ENG., Illus.). 32p. (gr. 3-4). pap. 11.50 *(978-1-4339-8503-4(9),* f9317cea-c990-418a-815e-a516039cf994); lib. bdg. 29.27 *(978-1-4339-8502-7(0),* 403feb4e-ae9e-497e-8be9-c63103ab983b) Stevens, Gareth Publishing LLLP.

Jackson, Kay. Navy Submarines in Action. 2009. (Amazing Military Vehicles Ser.). 24p. (gr. 3-3). 42.50 *(978-1-61511-324-8(X),* PowerKids Pr.); (ENG.). (J). pap. 9.25 *(978-1-4358-3161-2(6),* 5719c62c-48fa-4d6a-81e6-92de9c55a180, PowerKids Pr.); (ENG.). (YA). lib. bdg. 26.27 *(978-1-4358-2751-6(1),* e22fa1c6-a616-4a79-a880-93c3e08bdaa7) Rosen Publishing Group, Inc., The.

Kiland, Taylor Baldwin & Teitelbaum, Michael. Military Submarines: Sea Power, 1 vol. 2015. (Military Engineering in Action Ser.). (ENG., Illus.). 48p. (gr. 6-6). 29.60 *(978-0-7660-6918-3(4),* 399bfcaa-0f0c-45cf-b446-0caa09228e4a); pap. 12.70 *(978-0-7660-7069-1(7),* 587a4539-b0d8-4781-8601-b0015f58a2e7) Enslow Publishing, LLC.

Langley, Andrew. Submarines. 2010. (Machines on the Move Ser.). 32p. (J). 28.50 *(978-1-60753-062-6(7))* Amicus Learning.

—Submarines. 2012. (ENG., Illus.). 32p. (gr. 1-3). pap. 8.95 *(978-1-926722-72-6(8))* Saunders Bk. Co. CAN. Dist: RiverStream Publishing.

Mahaney, Ian F. Extreme Submarines, 1 vol. 2015. (Extreme Machines Ser.). (ENG.). 32p. (J). (gr. 3-4). pap. 11.00 *(978-1-4994-1188-1(X),* c8f1ddf3-ffac-4d4c-aff5-b68e5137855c, PowerKids Pr.) Rosen Publishing Group, Inc., The.

Mallard, Neil. Submarine. 2003. (ENG., Illus.). 64p. (J). (gr. k-6). 15.99 *(978-0-7894-9501-3(5),* Prentice Hall) Savvas Learning Co.

Miles, John C. Fighting Forces of World War II at Sea. 2019. (Fighting Forces of World War II Ser.). (ENG., Illus.). 32p. (J). (gr. 3-9). lib. bdg. 28.65 *(978-1-5435-7481-4(5),* 141002) Capstone.

Murray, Stuart. Submarines. 2014. (Illus.). 48p. (J). *(978-1-4351-5371-4(5))* Barnes & Noble, Inc.

—Submarines, 1 vol., 1. 2015. (What's Inside? Ser.). (ENG.). 48p. (J). (gr. 3-4). pap. 12.75 *(978-1-5081-4615-5(2),* f2a7c5e1-4028-47b7-92fc-030c59239593, PowerKids Pr.) Rosen Publishing Group, Inc., The.

Nardo, Don. In the Water: Strategies & Tactics. 2014. (J). *(978-1-59935-464-4(0))* Reynolds, Morgan Inc.

—In the Water: Submarines. 2014. (J). *(978-1-59935-458-3(6))* Reynolds, Morgan Inc.

Nelson, Drew. Submarines & Submersibles, 1 vol. 2013. (Military Machines Ser.). (ENG., Illus.). 32p. (J). (gr. 3-4). pap. 11.50 *(978-1-4339-8478-5(4),* d5cf2071-7911-48e9-bafe-d9fa90062e23); lib. bdg. 29.27 *(978-1-4339-8477-8(6),* 48b7309d-b9cd-4186-aa89-609f578500b5) Stevens, Gareth Publishing LLLP.

Parker, Steve. Ships & Submarines. 2010. (How It Works Ser.). 40p. (J). (gr. 3-18). lib. bdg. 19.95 *(978-1-4222-1798-6(1))* Mason Crest.

Rice Jr., Earle. The Virginia Class Submarines. 2018. lib. bdg. 29.95 *(978-1-68020-174-1(3))* Mitchell Lane Pubs.

Ross, David. The World's Most Powerful Submarines, 1 vol. 2016. (World's Most Powerful Machines Ser.). (ENG., Illus.). 224p. (J). (gr. 9-9). 46.80 *(978-1-4994-6586-0(6),* 077135fb-e889-4b63-aa85-f1aec0d4618d) Rosen Publishing Group, Inc., The.

Ruck, Colleen. Submarines. 2011. (My Favorite Machines Ser.). (ENG.). 24p. (J). (gr. 1-4). 28.50 *(978-1-59920-678-3(1),* 17351) Black Rabbit Bks.

Sirota, Lyn A. Ships & Subs. 2017. (Rank It! Ser.). (ENG.). 32p. (J). (gr. 4-6). pap. 9.99 *(978-1-64466-213-7(2),* 11480); (Illus.). lib. bdg. *(978-1-68072-179-9(8),* 10542) Black Rabbit Bks. (Bolt).

Stefoff, Rebecca. Submarines, 1 vol. 2007. (Great Inventions Ser.). (ENG., Illus.). 128p. (YA). (gr. 8-8). lib. bdg. 45.50 *(978-0-7614-2229-7(3),* 91a70dbf-d58a-432d-bc27-75f24541c815) Cavendish Square Publishing LLC.

Stone, Lynn M. Submarines. 2005. (Fighting Forces Ser.). (Illus.). 32p. (J). (gr. 4-8). lib. bdg. 28.50 *(978-1-59515-466-8(3),* 1244408) Rourke Educational Media.

Walker, Sally M. Shipwreck Search: Discovery of the H. L. Hunley. Verstraete, Elaine, illus. (On My Own Science Ser.). (ENG.). 48p. (gr. 2-4). 2007. (J). per. 7.99 *(978-0-8225-6449-2(1),* c091eaf0-8595-4cc4-81dd-f04fe879a8c7, First Avenue Editions) 2006. lib. bdg. 25.26 *(978-1-57505-878-8(2),* Millbrook Pr.) Lerner Publishing Group.

Weller, George. The Story of Submarines. 2003. 210p. pap. 29.00 *(978-0-7581-4985-5(9))* Textbook Pubs.

West, David. Modern Warships & Submarines, 1 vol. Pang, Alex, illus. 2011. (Machines Close-Up Ser.). (ENG.). 32p. (gr. 4-4). 31.21 *(978-1-60870-110-0(7),* 4bec0be5-c9bd-4986-8690-2b3f3a283437) Cavendish Square Publishing LLC.

—Submarines. (What's Inside? Ser.). (ENG., Illus.). 24p. (J). (gr. k-3). 2017. 28.50 *(978-1-62588-405-3(2),* 19390) 2015. 27.10 *(978-1-62588-068-0(5),* 19320) Black Rabbit Bks. (Smart Apple Media).

—Submarines. West, David, illus. 2019. (War Machines Ser.). (ENG., Illus.). 32p. (J). (gr. 5-6). pap. *(978-0-7787-6683-4(7),* e2401d4c-7356-431e-8524-cfe7bc9870f8); lib. bdg. *(978-0-7787-6668-1(3),* 3354c6de-69f0-4203-8467-4344c8b33dd3) Crabtree Publishing Co.

West, Krista. Underwater Warfare of the Future. 2009. (Library of Future Weaponry Ser.). 64p. (gr. 6-6). 58.50 *(978-1-60853-642-9(4))* Rosen Publishing Group, Inc., The.

Zuehlke, Jeffrey. Indonesia in Pictures. 2nd ed. 2005. (Visual Geography Series, Second Ser.). (Illus.). 80p. (YA). (gr. 7-12). lib. bdg. 27.93 *(978-0-8225-2074-0(5))* Lerner Publishing Group.

SUBMARINES (SHIPS)—FICTION

Appleton, Victor. Into the Abyss. 2007. (Tom Swift, Young Inventor Ser.). (ENG.). 160p. (gr. 3-7). 27.07 *(978-1-59961-350-5(6))* Spotlight.

—Tom Swift & His Submarine Boat or Unde. 2006. pap. *(978-1-4065-0908-3(6))* Dodo Pr.

Blaine, John. The Boy Scouts on a Submarine. 2018. (ENG., Illus.). 116p. (YA). (gr. 7-12). pap. *(978-93-5297-262-3(7))* Alpha Editions.

—Boy Scouts on A Submarine. 2006. 25.95 *(978-1-4218-2969-2(X));* pap. 10.95 *(978-1-4218-3069-8(8))* 1st World Publishing, Inc.

Brunellière, Lucie. Deep in the Ocean. 2019. (ENG., Illus.). 14p. (J). (gr. -1-k). bds. 15.99 *(978-1-4197-3356-7(7),* 1254910, Abrams Appleseed) Abrams, Inc.

Carlson, Drew. Attack of the Turtle. Johnson, David A., illus. 2008. (ENG.). 157p. (YA). (gr. 4-6). pap. 22.44 *(978-0-8028-5338-7(2),* Eerdmans Bks For Young Readers) Eerdmans, William B. Publishing Co.

Cummings, Mary. And the Baker's Boy Went to Sea. 2006. (Illus.). 195p. (YA). 16.95 *(978-0-9774855-0-5(1))* Sparkling Pr.

de Lesseps, Ferdinand Zoticus. Oceanology: The True Account of the Voyage of the Nautilus. Hawkins, Emily, ed. 2009. (Ologies Ser.: 8). (ENG., Illus.). 32p. (J). (gr. 3-7). 29.99 *(978-0-7636-4290-7(8))* Candlewick Pr.

Dickinson, Peter. Emma Tupper's Diary. 2014. (ENG.). 212p. (J). (gr. 4). pap. 12.00 *(978-1-61873-063-3(0),* Big Mouth Hse.) Small Beer Pr.

Drake, Robert L. The Boy Allies under the Sea. 2005. 27.95 *(978-1-4218-1083-6(2));* 244p. pap. 12.95 *(978-1-4218-1183-3(9))* 1st World Publishing, Inc. (1st World Library - Literary Society).

—The Boy Allies under the Sea. 2018. (ENG., Illus.). 188p. (YA). (gr. 7-12). pap. *(978-93-5297-244-9(9))* Alpha Editions.

—The Boy Allies under the Sea. 2017. (ENG., Illus.). (J). 23.95 *(978-1-374-95915-6(4))* Capital Communications, Inc.

Driscoll, James R. The Brighton Boys with the Submarine Fleet. 2005. 26.95 *(978-1-59540-819-8(3),* 1st World Library - Literary Society) 1st World Publishing, Inc.

Durham, Victor G. Submarine Boys & the Spies. 2006. 27.95 *(978-1-4218-3008-7(6));* pap. 12.95 *(978-1-4218-3108-4(2))* 1st World Publishing, Inc.

—Submarine Boys for the Flag. 2006. 27.95 *(978-1-4218-3009-4(4));* pap. 12.95 *(978-1-4218-3109-1(0))* 1st World Publishing, Inc.

—Submarine Boys Lightning Cruise. 2006. 27.95 *(978-1-4218-3010-0(8));* pap. 12.95 *(978-1-4218-3110-7(4))* 1st World Publishing, Inc.

—Submarine Boys on Duty. 2006. 27.95 *(978-1-4218-3011-7(6));* pap. 12.95 *(978-1-4218-3111-4(2))* 1st World Publishing, Inc.

—Submarine Boys Trial Trip. 2006. 26.95 *(978-1-4218-3012-4(4));* pap. 11.95 *(978-1-4218-3112-1(0))* 1st World Publishing, Inc.

Falls, Kat. Rip Tide. 2011. 314p. (J). pap. *(978-0-545-43175-0(1),* Scholastic Pr.) Scholastic, Inc.

Fleming, Candace. Papa's Mechanical Fish. Kulikov, Boris, illus. 2013. (ENG.). 40p. (J). (gr. k-3). 19.99 *(978-0-374-39908-5(5),* 900050960, Farrar, Straus & Giroux (BYR)) Farrar, Straus & Giroux.

Gardner, Charlie. The Beatles Yellow Submarine. Edelmann, Heinz, illus. 2006. 37p. (J). (gr. 4-8). reprint ed. 18.00 *(978-1-4223-5184-0(X))* DIANE Publishing Co.

Gibson, Jamie. Thirteen Ways to Sink a Sub. (J). 4.50 *(978-0-8072-1387-2(X),* Listening Library) Random Hse. Audio Publishing Group.

Larry, H. I. Zac Power #2: Deep Waters: 24 Hours to Save the World ... & Finish His Homework. 2. Oswald, Ash, illus. 2008. (Zac Power Ser.: 2). (ENG.). 96p. (J). (gr. 2-4). pap. 6.99 *(978-0-312-34655-3(7),* 900042756) Square Fish.

Lerangis, Peter. Max Tilt: 80 Days or Die. 2018. (Max Tilt Ser.: 2). (ENG., Illus.). 400p. (J). (gr. 3-7). 17.99 *(978-0-06-244103-4(5),* HarperCollins) HarperCollins Pubs.

—Max Tilt: 80 Days or Die. 2019. (Max Tilt Ser.: 2). (ENG.). 416p. (J). (gr. 3-7). pap. 6.99 *(978-0-06-244104-1(3),* HarperCollins) HarperCollins Pubs.

McOmber, Rachel B., ed. McOmber Phonics Storybooks: The Sub. rev. ed. (Illus.). (J). *(978-0-944991-22-0(X))* Swift Learning Resources.

Mitton, Tony & Parker, Ant. Super Submarines. (Amazing Machines Ser.). (ENG.). (J). 2018. 20p. bds. 6.99 *(978-0-7534-7417-4(4),* 900187134) 2014. (Illus.). 24p. (gr. -1-k). 5.99 *(978-0-7534-7208-8(2),* 900143121) Roaring Brook Pr. (Kingfisher).

—Super Submarines. 2014. (Amazing Machines Ser.). (J). lib. bdg. 16.00 *(978-0-606-36133-0(2))* Turtleback.

My Day in a Submarine. 2004. (J). ring bd. 3.25 *(978-0-9762740-3-2(5),* Flat Kids) Smart Smiles Co., The.

Osborne, Mary Pope. Das magische Baumhaus 09. Der Ruf der Delfine. 18.95 *(978-3-7855-4185-2(6))* Loewe Verlag GmbH DEU. Dist: Distribooks, Inc.

Prestwood, Donna. Center World. 2006. 120p. per. 10.95 *(978-1-59824-206-5(7))* E-BookTime LLC.

Ralphson, G. Harvey. Boy Scouts in a Submarine. 2018. (ENG., Illus.). 146p. (YA). (gr. 7-12). pap. *(978-93-5297-275-3(9))* Alpha Editions.

—Boy Scouts in a Submarine. 2007. 104p. per. *(978-1-4068-3726-1(1))* Echo Library.

Rockwood, Roy. Under the Ocean to the South Pole. 2007. 120p. per. *(978-1-4068-3972-2(8))* Echo Library.

—Under the Ocean to the South Pole. 2009. 152p. 24.95 *(978-1-60664-626-7(5));* pap. 12.95 *(978-1-60664-365-5(7))* Rodgers, Alan Bks.

—Under the Ocean to the South Pole: Or, the Strange Cruise of the Submarine Wonder. 2017. (ENG., Illus.). (J). 23.95 *(978-1-374-84548-0(5))* Capital Communications, Inc.

—Under the Ocean to the South Pole or the Strange Cruise of the Submarine Wonder. 2007. 180p. 95.99 *(978-1-4280-7589-4(5));* per. 89.99 *(978-1-4280-7588-7(7))* IndyPublish.com.

Roddy, Lee. Secret of the Sunken Sub. 2006. (Ladd Family Adventure Ser.: Vol. 5). (Illus.). 132p. (Orig.). (J). (gr. 4-7). per. 7.99 *(978-0-88062-254-7(7))* Mott Media.

Roy, Philip. Journey to Atlantis. 2009. (ENG., Illus.). 224p. pap. 10.95 *(978-1-55380-076-7(1))* Ronsdale Pr. CAN. Dist: SPD-Small Pr. Distribution.

—Submarine Outlaw. 2008. (ENG., Illus.). 254p. pap. 10.95 *(978-1-55380-058-3(3))* Ronsdale Pr. CAN. Dist: SPD-Small Pr. Distribution.

Steinkraus, Kyla. Under the Sea. Brown, Alan, illus. 2016. (Paisley Atoms Ser.). (ENG.). 64p. (gr. 2-5). 28.50 *(978-1-68191-713-9(0),* 9781681917139) Rourke Educational Media.

Swann, Stephen. Where's Our Submarine. 2009. 58p. pap. 21.50 *(978-1-4452-3146-4(8))* Lulu Pr., Inc.

Trowell, Michelle. Pilot Your Own Deep-Sea Submarine. Dronsfield, Paul, illus. 2007. 22p. (J). (gr. -1-3). *(978-1-84666-352-9(0),* Tide Mill Pr.) Top That! Publishing PLC.

Vern, Jules. Twenty Thousand Leagues under the Sea. abr. ed. 2019. (ENG.). (J). 232p. 19.95 *(978-1-61895-531-9(4));* 230p. pap. 12.95 *(978-1-61895-530-2(6))* Bibliotech Pr.

—Twenty Thousand Leagues under the Sea. 2018. (ENG., Illus.). 170p. (J). (gr. 5). pap. 7.99 *(978-1-9779-9837-8(2))* CreateSpace Independent Publishing Platform.

—Twenty Thousand Leagues under the Sea. (ENG., Illus.). (J). 2017. (gr. 5). pap. 17.95 *(978-1-376-13408-7(X))* 2015. (gr. 3-7). 27.95 *(978-1-296-82308-5(3))* Creative Media Partners, LLC.

—Twenty Thousand Leagues under the Sea. 2019. (ENG.). 238p. (J). (gr. 5). pap. *(978-1-989201-88-6(1))* East India Publishing Co.

—Twenty Thousand Leagues under the Sea. Lt. ed. 2006. 592p. pap. *(978-1-84702-222-6(7))* Echo Library.

—Twenty Thousand Leagues under the Sea. 2019. (ENG.). 662p. (J). (gr. 3-7). pap. 25.99 *(978-1-7033-4221-5(6))* Independently Published.

—Twenty Thousand Leagues under the Sea. 2020. (ENG.). 230p. (J). (gr. 3-7). 19.95 *(978-1-64439-407-6(3))* IndoEuropeanPublishing.com.

—Twenty Thousand Leagues under the Sea. 2018. (ENG., Illus.). 254p. (J). (gr. 5). *(978-3-7326-2412-6(9))* Klassik Literatur. ein Imprint der Salzwasser Verlag GmbH.

S

—Twenty Thousand Leagues under the Sea. 2018. (ENG., Illus.). 388p. (J). (gr. 5). pap. 16.95 *(978-0-940075-35-1(0))* Quillquest Books.

—Twenty Thousand Leagues under the Sea. 2016. (ENG.). 376p. (J). (gr. 3-7). pap. *(978-93-5304-941-6(5))* Rupa & Co.

—Veinte Mil Leguas de Viaje Submarino Tr. of Twenty Thousand Leagues under the Sea. (SPA., Illus.). 160p. (YA). 11.95 *(978-84-7281-075-4(5)*, AF1075) Auriga, Ediciones S.A. ESP. Dist: Continental Bk. Co., Inc.

—20,000 Leagues under the Sea. 2008. (Bring the Classics to Life Ser.). (ENG., Illus.). 72p. (gr. 4-12). pap., act. bk. ed. 10.95 *(978-1-55576-091-5(0)*, EDCTR405B) EDCON Publishing Group.

—20,000 Leagues under the Sea, 1 vol. Fisher, Eric Scott, illus. 2011. (Calico Illustrated Classics Ser.: No. 3). (ENG.). 112p. (J). (gr. 2-5). 38.50 *(978-1-61641-110-7(4)*, 4027, Calico Chapter Bks.) ABDO Publishing Co.

Verne, Julio & Vern, Jules. Veinte Mil Leguas de Viaje Submarino. 2019. (Brújula y la Veleta Ser.).Tr. of Twenty Thousand Leagues under the Sea. (SPA.). 64p. (J). (gr. 2-4). pap. 9.95 *(978-987-718-566-9(0))* Ediciones Lea S.A. ARG. Dist: Independent Pubs. Group.

Zajonc, Taylor. The Iron Island. Rodriguez, Geraldine, illus. 2018. (Adventures of Samuel Oliver Ser.). (ENG.). 48p. (J). (gr. 3-7). lib. bdg. 34.21 *(978-1-5321-3373-2(1)*, 31169, Spellbound) Magic Wagon.

SUBSTANCE ABUSE

see also Alcoholism; Drug Abuse; Tobacco Habit

Abramovitz, Melissa. Understanding Addiction. 2017. (Understanding Psychology Ser.). (ENG.). 80p. (YA). (gr. 5-12). 39.93 *(978-1-68282-271-5(0))* ReferencePoint Pr., Inc.

Ambrose, Marylou & Deisler, Veronica. Investigate Cocaine & Crack, 1 vol. 2014. (Investigate Drugs Ser.). (ENG., Illus.). 112p. (gr. 5-6). lib. bdg. 34.93 *(978-0-7660-4255-1(3)*, 26bf4da1-40d0-4636-af64-bf4244b6a90c) Enslow Publishing, LLC.

—Investigate Methamphetamine, 1 vol. 2014. (Investigate Drugs Ser.). (ENG., Illus.). 112p. (gr. 5-6). lib. bdg. 34.93 *(978-0-7660-4254-4(5)*, d0347aa4-e64c-4105-974a-237912a301c6) Enslow Publishing, LLC.

Benson, Alana. Crack & Cocaine Abuse, 1 vol. 2018. (Overcoming Addiction Ser.). (ENG., Illus.). 64p. (J). (gr. 7-7). 36.13 *(978-1-5081-7939-9(5)*, bd5e102d-c95b-40bf-9f98-3891c24ebb0b) Rosen Publishing Group, Inc., The.

Berry, Joy. Substance Abuse. 2009. (ENG.). 52p. (J). (gr. k-7). pap. 7.95 *(978-1-60577-502-9(9))* Berry, Joy Enterprises.

Bestor, Sheri Mabry. Substance Abuse: The Ultimate Teen Guide. 2015. (It Happened to Me Ser.: 36). (Illus.). 208p. pap. 40.00 *(978-1-4422-5662-0(1))* Rowman & Littlefield Publishers, Inc.

—Substance Abuse: The Ultimate Teen Guide. 2013. (It Happened to Me Ser.: 36). (ENG., Illus.). 208p. 69.00 *(978-0-8108-8558-5(1))* Scarecrow Pr., Inc.

Bigelow, Barbara C. & Edgar, Kathleen J. The UXL Encyclopedia of Drugs & Addictive Substances, 5 vols. 2005. (Illus.). (J). *(978-1-4144-0446-2(8))*; *(978-1-4144-0448-6(4))*; *(978-1-4144-0447-9(6))*; *(978-1-4144-0449-3(2))*; *(978-1-4144-0445-5(X))* Cengage Gale.

Brinkerhoff, Shirley. Drug Therapy & Substance-Related Disorders. 2004. (Encyclopedia of Psychiatric Drugs & Their Disorders Ser.). (Illus.). 128p. (YA). lib. bdg. 24.95 *(978-1-59084-577-6(3))* Mason Crest.

Bryan, Bethany. Methamphetamine & Stimulant Abuse, 1 vol. 2018. (Overcoming Addiction Ser.). (ENG.). 64p. (gr. 7-7). 36.13 *(978-1-5081-7940-5(9)*, 173dc4b1-bdde-4c1c-8b02-920b5925680b) Rosen Publishing Group, Inc., The.

Burlingame, Jeff. Crystal Meth, 1 vol. 2013. (Dangerous Drugs Ser.). (ENG.). 64p. (gr. 6-6). pap. 16.28 *(978-1-62712-059-3(9)*, a757e32e-7e4a-4af5-8ab1-2a9dddcc5011) Cavendish Square Publishing LLC.

Centore, Michael. Intervention & Recovery, Vol. 13. Becker, Sara, ed. 2016. (Drug Addiction & Recovery Ser.). (Illus.). 64p. (J). (gr. 7). 23.95 *(978-1-4222-3605-5(6))* Mason Crest.

Connolly, Sean. Inhalants. 2006. (Straight Talking Ser.). (Illus.). 46p. (YA). (gr. 4-7). lib. bdg. 32.80 *(978-1-58340-648-9(4))* Black Rabbit Bks.

—Inhalants. 2009. (Straight Talking Ser.). (ENG., Illus.). 48p. (YA). (gr. 8-12). pap. *(978-1-895058-53-6(8))* Saunders Bk. Co.

Cross, Carrie L. & Iorizzo, Carrie. Crystal Meth. 2011. (ENG., Illus.). 48p. (J). pap. *(978-0-7787-5514-2(2)*, 1331588); (gr. 4-7). lib. bdg. *(978-0-7787-5507-4(X)*, 1331588) Crabtree Publishing Co.

Curriculum in a Box: Substance Abuse. 2005. (YA). 924.95 incl. DVD *(978-1-55548-256-5(2)*, 377dv) Human Relations Media.

DeCarlo, Carolyn. Inhalant, Whippet, & Popper Abuse, 1 vol. 2018. (Overcoming Addiction Ser.). (ENG., Illus.). 64p. (J). (gr. 7-7). 36.13 *(978-1-5081-7945-0(X)*, 38ca8157-55e1-40c0-87cc-156d3af20bd7) Rosen Publishing Group, Inc., The.

Eben Field, Jon & Field, Jon Eben. Dealing with Drugs Inhalants & Solvents. 2011. (ENG.). 48p. (J). pap. *(978-0-7787-5515-9(0))*; (gr. 4-7). lib. bdg. *(978-0-7787-5508-1(8))* Crabtree Publishing Co.

Esherick, Joan. Drug - & Alcohol-Related Health Issues. McDonnell, Mary Ann & Forman, Sara, eds. 2013. (Young Adult's Guide to the Science of Health Ser.: 15). 128p. (J). (gr. 7-18). 24.95 *(978-1-4222-2808-1(8))* Mason Crest.

Espejo, Roman, ed. Chemical Dependency, 1 vol. 2011. (Opposing Viewpoints Ser.). (ENG.). 216p. (gr. 10-12). (J). pap. 34.80 *(978-0-7377-5216-8(5)*, bd992ba8-eb74-4099-bb60-4ed654494697); lib. bdg. 50.43 *(978-0-7377-5215-1(7)*, 3d4b805c-5032-426b-9cb7-474bb947b807) Greenhaven Publishing LLC. (Greenhaven Publishing).

Flath, Camden. 21st-Century Counselors: New Approaches to Mental Health & Substance Abuse. 2010. (New Careers for the 21st Century Ser.). 64p. (YA). (gr. 7-18). pap. 9.95 *(978-1-4222-2046-7(X))*; (Illus.). lib. bdg. 22.95 *(978-1-4222-1825-9(2))* Mason Crest.

Flynn, Noa. Inhalants & Solvents: Sniffing Disaster. 2009. (Illicit & Misused Drugs Ser.). (Illus.). 128p. (YA). (gr. 7-18). lib. bdg. 24.95 *(978-1-4222-0157-2(0))* Mason Crest.

Gordon, Sherri Mabry. Teens & Addiction. 2018. (Teen Health & Safety Ser.). (ENG.). 80p. (YA). (gr. 6-12). 39.93 *(978-1-68282-503-7(5))* ReferencePoint Pr., Inc.

Gottfried, Ted. The Facts about Marijuana, 1 vol. 2006. (Facts about Drugs Ser.). (ENG.). 128p. (gr. 6-6). 45.50 *(978-0-7614-1806-1(7)*, 622f8f5e-8691-4526-a4c2-dce63c5b0c2d) Cavendish Square Publishing LLC.

Hamen, Susan E. Heroin & Its Dangers. 2019. (Drugs & Their Dangers Ser.). (ENG.). 80p. (YA). (gr. 6-12). 41.27 *(978-1-68282-707-9(0)*, BrightPoint Pr.) ReferencePoint Pr., Inc.

Harrow, Jeremy. Crystal Meth, 1 vol. 2007. (Incredibly Disgusting Drugs Ser.). (ENG., Illus.). 48p. (YA). (gr. 5-8). lib. bdg. 34.47 *(978-1-4042-1953-3(6)*, f20b2e17-308c-4e87-bf14-8799ec207efc) Rosen Publishing Group, Inc., The.

Hasan, Heather. Caffeine & Nicotine: A Dependent Society. 2009. (Drug Abuse & Society Ser.). 64p. (gr. 6-6). 58.50 *(978-1-61512-218-9(4))* Rosen Publishing Group, Inc., The.

Haugen, David M. & Musser, Susan, eds. Addiction, 1 vol. 2013. (Introducing Issues with Opposing Viewpoints Ser.). (ENG., Illus.). 128p. (gr. 7-10). 43.63 *(978-0-7377-4164-3(3)*, 97f96491-4e4e-4ceb-b429-e16a059e2eab, Greenhaven Publishing) Greenhaven Publishing LLC.

Henneberg, Susan. Defeating Addiction & Alcoholism, 1 vol., 1. 2015. (Effective Survival Strategies Ser.). (ENG., Illus.). 64p. (J). (gr. 6-6). 36.13 *(978-1-4994-6179-4(8)*, 05044ba7-f32b-4373-9e0c-40faa2f5f85b, Rosen Young Adult) Rosen Publishing Group, Inc., The.

Human Relations Media, prod. Clued in! on Addiction & Your Brain. 2005. (ENG.). (J). pap. 4.95 *(978-1-55548-050-9(0)*, 674) Human Relations Media.

Hunter, David. Thousands of Deadly Chemicals: Smoking & Health. 2008. (J). pap. 26.95 *(978-1-4222-1334-6(X))* Mason Crest.

Information Plus Alcohol & Tobacco November 2005, Vol. 2005. 2005. 49.00 *(978-1-4144-0405-9(0))* Cengage Gale.

Ingram, Scott. Marijuana. 2008. (Junior Drug Awareness Ser.). (ENG., Illus.). 110p. (gr. 5-8). lib. bdg. 30.00 *(978-0-7910-9695-6(5)*, P145754, Facts On File) Infobase Holdings, Inc.

Jacobson, Robert. Illegal Drugs America's Anguish. 2005. (Information Plus Reference: Illegal Drugs Ser.). 168p. (J). per. 49.00 *(978-1-4144-0419-6(0))* Cengage Gale.

Juzwiak, Rich. Addictive Personality. 2009. (Teen Mental Health Ser.). 48p. (gr. 5-6). 53.00 *(978-1-60853-292-6(5))* Rosen Publishing Group, Inc., The.

Juzwiak, Richard. Addictive Personality, 1 vol. 2008. (Teen Mental Health Ser.). (ENG., Illus.). 48p. (YA). (gr. 5-6). lib. bdg. 34.47 *(978-1-4042-1802-4(5)*, 38d603c5-5160-43e4-87b6-a4b63c7c74ad) Rosen Publishing Group, Inc., The.

Koellhoffer, Tara. Inhalants & Solvents. 2008. (Junior Drug Awareness Ser.). (ENG.). 112p. (gr. 5-8). 30.00 *(978-0-7910-9698-7(X)*, P145664, Facts On File) Infobase Holdings, Inc.

Krajnik, Elizabeth. Why Are Drugs & Alcohol Bad for Me?, 1 vol. 2018. (Help Me Understand Ser.). (ENG., Illus.). 24p. (J). (gr. 3-3). 25.27 *(978-1-5081-6722-8(2)*, 81f90c58-c314-4004-8a40-58a447e6b09d, PowerKids Pr.) Rosen Publishing Group, Inc., The.

Krasner, Barbara, ed. Harm Reduction: Public Health Strategies, 1 vol. 2018. (Opposing Viewpoints Ser.). (ENG.). 176p. (gr. 10-12). 50.43 *(978-1-5345-0413-4(3)*, db19734f-a4c6-431b-a7e2-626d22d0890a) Greenhaven Publishing LLC.

Kuhar, Michael J. & Howard, Charles. Substance Abuse, Addiction, & Treatment, 1 vol. 2012. (Substance Abuse, Addiction, & Treatment Ser.). (ENG.). 320p. (YA). (gr. 8-8). 88.36 *(978-0-7614-7943-7(0)*, 409aaf3e-594a-41c3-9dc2-a8422a60aedc) Cavendish Square Publishing LLC.

Landau, Jennifer, ed. Teens Talk about Drugs & Alcohol. 2017. (Teen Voices: Real Teens Discuss Real Problems Ser.). (Illus.). 64p. (J). (gr. 12-17). 77.70 *(978-1-5081-7634-3(5))* Rosen Publishing Group, Inc., The.

Latta, Sara L. Investigate Steroids & Performance Drugs, 1 vol. 2014. (Investigate Drugs Ser.). (ENG., Illus.). 112p. (gr. 5-6). lib. bdg. 34.93 *(978-0-7660-4240-7(5)*, d1c7a737-a701-4cdf-8fa6-46b3e06c89f9) Enslow Publishing, LLC.

Leonard, Basia & Roberts, Jeremy. The Truth about Prescription Drugs, 1 vol. 2011. (Drugs & Consequences Ser.). (ENG., Illus.). 64p. (YA). (gr. 5-5). lib. bdg. 37.13 *(978-1-4488-4642-9(0)*, 3f0e25a0-d679-412b-b41d-2c3fe7d3741c) Rosen Publishing Group, Inc., The.

Libal, Autumn. The FDA & Psychiatric Drugs: Drugs & Psychology for the Mind & Body, 19 vols., Set. 2004. (Psychiatric Disorders Ser.). (Illus.). 128p. (J). lib. bdg. *(978-1-59084-559-2(5))* Mason Crest.

Libal, Joyce. Drug Therapy an Substance-Related Disorders. 2003. (Psychiatric Disorders: Drugs & Psychology for the Mind & Bod Ser.). (Illus.). 124p. (YA). (gr. 8-12). pap. 14.95 *(978-1-4222-0401-6(4))* Mason Crest.

—Substance-Related Disorders. McDonnell, Mary Ann & Esherick, Donald, eds. 2013. (State of Mental Illness & Its Therapy Ser.: 19). (Illus.). 128p. (J). (gr. 7-18). 24.95 *(978-1-4222-2838-8(X))* Mason Crest.

Marcovitz, Hal. Drug Abuse, 1 vol. 2008. (Hot Topics Ser.). (ENG., Illus.). 112p. (gr. 7-7). lib. bdg. 41.03 *(978-1-4205-0081-3(3)*, 411f86b0-dd76-461f-be84-2595bd27f1ed, Lucent Pr.) Greenhaven Publishing LLC.

Mason, Paul. Know the Facts about Drinking & Smoking. 2009. (J). 70.50 *(978-1-4358-5463-5(2)*, Rosen Reference) Rosen Publishing Group, Inc., The.

Medina, Sarah. Know the Facts about Drugs. 2009. 48p. (J). 70.50 *(978-1-4358-5459-8(4)*, Rosen Reference); (ENG.). (YA). (gr. 5-6). pap. 12.75 *(978-1-4358-5458-1(6)*, 3bb1dcc6-8dd2-4faa-a143-007560729278, Rosen Reference); (ENG., Illus.). (YA). (gr. 5-6). lib. bdg. 34.47 *(978-1-4358-5337-9(7)*, 169a591a-acc8-41fc-9891-ecae523a20cf) Rosen Publishing Group, Inc., The.

Mooney, Carla. The Dangers of Marijuana. 2016. (ENG., Illus.). 80p. (J). (gr. 5-12). *(978-1-68282-020-9(3))* ReferencePoint Pr., Inc.

Nelson, Julie. Marijuana's Harmful Effects on Youth, Vol. 5. 2018. (Marijuana Today Ser.). 80p. (J). (gr. 7). lib. bdg. 33.27 *(978-1-4222-4107-3(6))* Mason Crest.

Parks, Peggy J. Smoking. rev. ed. 2014. (Matters of Opinion Ser.). (ENG.). 64p. (J). (gr. 4-6). lib. bdg. 27.93 *(978-1-59953-602-6(1))* Norwood Hse. Pr.

—Teens & Substance Abuse. 2015. (ENG., Illus.). 80p. (J). lib. bdg. *(978-1-60152-832-2(9))* ReferencePoint Pr., Inc.

Petersen, Christine. Inhalants, 1 vol. 2013. (Dangerous Drugs Ser.). (ENG.). 64p. (gr. 6-6). 36.93 *(978-1-60870-824-6(1)*, bdb65ccb-5e87-4724-804f-8f52e230bc26); pap. 16.28 *(978-1-62712-060-9(2)*, 0863c101-c3e2-4e94-8d82-b3d5e29a642f) Cavendish Square Publishing LLC.

Poole, H. W. Alcohol & Tobacco, Vol. 13. Becker, Sara, ed. 2016. (Drug Addiction & Recovery Ser.). (Illus.). 64p. (J). (gr. 7). 23.95 *(978-1-4222-3599-7(8))* Mason Crest.

Prentzas, G. S. (Scott). The Truth about Inhalants, 1 vol. 2013. (Drugs & Consequences Ser.). (ENG., Illus.). 64p. (J). (gr. 5-5). 37.13 *(978-1-4777-1893-3(1)*, 0f72900d-6f52-4d4b-9fee-47a2008efbb6) Rosen Publishing Group, Inc., The.

Rebman, Renée C. Are You Doing Risky Things? Cutting, Bingeing, Snorting, & Other Dangers, 1 vol. 2014. (Got Issues? Ser.). (ENG., Illus.). 112p. (gr. 6-7). lib. bdg. 38.93 *(978-0-7660-5996-2(0)*, c00544f9-c869-4ae2-9b1f-9a3418fd830e) Enslow Publishing, LLC.

Robinson, Matthew. Inhalant Abuse. 2009. (Incredibly Disgusting Drugs Ser.). 48p. (gr. 5-8). 53.00 *(978-1-61513-501-1(4)*, Rosen Reference) Rosen Publishing Group, Inc., The.

Roffé Menhard, Francha & Purdie Salas, Laura. Inhalants, 1 vol. 2010. (Drug Facts Ser.). (ENG., Illus.). 32p. (gr. 5-5). 31.21 *(978-0-7614-4350-6(9)*, 2f0e7a73-40a8-4df7-8aff-8bd25142f6e5) Cavendish Square Publishing LLC.

Sanna, E. J. Heroin & Other Opioids: Poppies' Perilous Children. Henningfield, Jack E., ed. 2012. (Illicit & Misused Drugs Ser.). 128p. (J). (gr. 7). 24.95 *(978-1-4222-2433-5(3))*; pap. 14.95 *(978-1-4222-2452-6(X))* Mason Crest.

Schaefer, Wyatt, ed. Addiction, 1 vol. 2007. (Social Issues Firsthand Ser.). (ENG., Illus.). 128p. (gr. 10-12). lib. bdg. 39.93 *(978-0-7377-2494-3(3)*, dba0cbec-8fdc-4e90-bf0f-3c1b5c6fdaf1, Greenhaven Publishing) Greenhaven Publishing LLC.

Schwartzenberger, Tina, ed. Substance Use & Abuse. 2006. (Understanding Global Issues Ser.). (Illus.). 56p. (J). (gr. 3-7). lib. bdg. 28.50 *(978-1-59036-232-7(2))* Weigl Pubs., Inc.

Sharp, Katie John. Teenagers & Tobacco: Nicotine & the Adolescent Brain. 2008. (Illus.). 112p. (J). pap. 26.95 *(978-1-4222-1333-9(1))* Mason Crest.

Sheff, David & Sheff, Nic. High: Everything You Want to Know about Drugs, Alcohol, & Addiction. 2019. (ENG., Illus.). 272p. (J). (gr. 5). 16.99 *(978-0-544-64434-2(4)*, 1621300, Clarion Bks.) HarperCollins Pubs.

Sherry, Clifford J. Inhalants. 2009. (Drug Abuse Prevention Library). 64p. (gr. 5-5). 58.50 *(978-1-60853-430-2(8))* Rosen Publishing Group, Inc., The.

Skancke, Jennifer. Addicted to Opioids. 2019. (Addicted Ser.). (ENG.). 80p. (YA). (gr. 6-12). 41.27 *(978-1-68282-571-6(X))* ReferencePoint Pr., Inc.

Sommers, Michael. Cocaine. 2009. (Incredibly Disgusting Drugs Ser.). 48p. (gr. 5-8). 53.00 *(978-1-61513-493-9(X)*, Rosen Reference) Rosen Publishing Group, Inc., The.

Spilsbury, Louise. Drinking & Drugs? Skills to Avoid 'Em & Stay Cool, 1 vol. 2018. (Life Skills Ser.). (ENG.). 48p. (gr. 5-5). lib. bdg. 30.93 *(978-0-7660-9971-5(7)*, 810996e9-69d4-444a-b4d2-4849143948d9) Enslow Publishing, LLC.

Steffens, Bradley. Is Marijuana Harmful? 2016. (ENG.). 80p. (J). (gr. 5-12). lib. bdg. *(978-1-68282-097-1(1))* ReferencePoint Pr., Inc.

Thomas, Amy N. Burning Money: The Cost of Smoking. 2007. (Tobacco: the Deadly Drug Ser.). (Illus.). 112p. (YA). (gr. 3-7). pap. 12.95 *(978-1-4222-0808-3(7))* Mason Crest.

Tina, Schwartzenberger. Substance Use & Abuse. 2007. (Understanding Global Issues Ser.). 56p. (J). pap. 11.95 *(978-1-59036-506-9(2))* Weigl Pubs., Inc.

Triggle, David J., ed. Inhalants. 2004. (Drugs: the Straight Facts Ser.). (ENG., Illus.). 112p. lib. bdg. 30.00 *(978-0-7910-7636-1(9)*, P113931, Facts On File) Infobase Holdings, Inc.

Turner, Amanda. Helping Those with Addictions. 2019. (Careers Making a Difference Ser.). (Illus.). 80p. (J). (gr. 12). lib. bdg. 34.60 *(978-1-4222-4258-2(7))* Mason Crest.

Uhl, Xina M. Who Is Using Opioids & Opiates? 2017. (Opioids & Opiates: the Silent Epidemic* Ser.: Vol. 5). (ENG., Illus.). 64p. (YA). (gr. 7-12). 23.95 *(978-1-4222-3827-1(X))* Mason Crest.

SUBSTANCE ABUSE—FICTION

Anonymous. Breaking Bailey. 2019. (Anonymous Diaries). (ENG.). 384p. (YA). (gr. 9). 19.99 *(978-1-5344-3308-3(2))*; (Illus.). pap. 11.99 *(978-1-5344-3309-0(0))* Simon Pulse. (Simon Pulse).

Cohn, Rachel. You Know Where to Find Me. 2009. (ENG.). 224p. (YA). (gr. 7). pap. 8.99 *(978-0-689-87860-2(5)*, Simon & Schuster Bks. For Young Readers) Simon & Schuster Bks. For Young Readers.

—You Know Where to Find Me. 2008. (ENG.). 204p. (YA). (gr. 7-12). 22.44 *(978-0-689-87859-6(1))* Simon & Schuster, Inc.

Gibson, Sylvia Scott & Gibson, James E. Latawnya the Naughty Horse Two, 1 vol. Gibson, Gregory V., illus. 2010. 22p. 24.95 *(978-1-4489-7859-5(9))* PublishAmerica, Inc.

Harvey, Sarah N. & Stevenson, Robin. Blood on the Beach, 1 vol. 2017. (ENG.). 272p. (YA). (gr. 8-12). pap. 14.95 *(978-1-4598-1293-2(X))* Orca Bk. Pubs. USA.

Iversen, Jeremy. Rush. 2011. (ENG.). 272p. (YA). (gr. 9). pap. 11.99 *(978-1-4424-2400-5(1)*, Simon Pulse) Simon Pulse.

—21. 2005. (ENG.). 272p. (YA). pap. 6.99 *(978-0-689-87623-3(8)*, Simon Pulse) Simon Pulse.

Kiely, Brendan. The Gospel of Winter. 2015. (ENG., Illus.). 320p. (YA). (gr. 9). pap. 12.99 *(978-1-4424-8490-0(X)*, McElderry, Margaret K. Bks.) McElderry, Margaret K. Bks.

Lancett, Peter. Gun Dog. 2008. (Cutting Edge Ser.). (ENG.). 200p. pap. *(978-1-84167-713-2(2))* Ransom Publishing Ltd.

Marie, Jessica. Keeping Broken Promises, 1 vol. 2010. 182p. pap. 24.95 *(978-1-4489-5273-1(5))* America Star Bks.

Millar, Martin. Lonely Werewolf Girl. 2008. (ENG.). 560p. per. 16.95 *(978-0-9796636-6-6(0)*, Soft Skull Pr.) Counterpoint Pr.

Nayeri, Daniel & Nayeri, Dina. Another Jekyll, Another Hyde. 2012. (ENG., Illus.). 400p. (YA). (gr. 9). 17.99 *(978-0-7636-5261-6(X))* Candlewick Pr.

Smith-Leckie, Nina. The Fall & Rise of Abuse-a-Saurus Rex. Gordon, Danny, illus. 2003. 28p. (YA). (gr. 5-18). pap. 6.95 *(978-0-9725382-0-6(8))* Prairie Arts, Inc.

Tharp, Tim. The Spectacular Now. 2010. (ENG.). 304p. (YA). (gr. 9). pap. 9.99 *(978-0-375-86502-2(0)*, Knopf Bks. for Young Readers) Random Hse. Children's Bks.

SUBURBAN HOMES

see Architecture, Domestic

SUBURBAN LIFE

Bodden, Valerie. A Suburb. 2007. (My First Look at: Communities Ser.). (Illus.). 24p. (J). (gr. -1-3). lib. bdg. 24.25 *(978-1-58341-514-6(9)*, Creative Education) Creative Co., The.

Flatt, Lizann. Life in a Suburban City. 2010. (Learn about Urban Life Ser.). (ENG., Illus.). 32p. (J). (gr. 3-6). lib. bdg. *(978-0-7787-7394-8(9))*; (gr. 4-9). pap. *(978-0-7787-7404-4(X))* Crabtree Publishing Co.

National Geographic Learning. Reading Expeditions (Social Studies: American Communities Across Time): a Suburban Community of The 1950s. 2007. (ENG., Illus.). 24p. (J). pap. 15.95 *(978-0-7922-8691-2(X))* CENGAGE Learning.

Rogers, Amy B. American Communities: We Live in a Suburb, 1 vol., 1. 2015. (American Communities Ser.). (ENG.). 24p. (J). (gr. 1-1). pap. 9.25 *(978-1-5081-4200-3(9)*, 9855f206-47f7-41e8-a265-0624e49da3e6, PowerKids Pr.) Rosen Publishing Group, Inc., The.

Sterling, Kristin. Living in Suburban Communities. 2008. pap. 34.95 *(978-0-8225-9479-6(X))*; (ENG., Illus.). 24p. lib. bdg. 23.93 *(978-0-8225-8598-5(7)*, Lerner Pubns.) Lerner Publishing Group.

Summers, Portia. My School Community, 1 vol. 2016. (Zoom in on Communities Ser.). (ENG.). 24p. (gr. 2-2). pap. 10.95 *(978-0-7660-7824-6(8)*, 90cee62a-8ea6-4fc3-a806-feb3bb068157) Enslow Publishing, LLC.

—My Suburban Community, 1 vol. 2016. (Zoom in on Communities Ser.). (ENG.). 24p. (gr. 2-2). pap. 10.95 *(978-0-7660-7833-8(7)*, dc3a686a-d881-46df-b927-9a08f36a42f6) Enslow Publishing, LLC.

SUBWAYS

Conley, Kate. Engineering the London Underground. 2017. (Building by Design Set 2 Ser.). (ENG., Illus.). 48p. (J). (gr. 4-8). lib. bdg. 35.64 *(978-1-5321-1374-1(9)*, 27672) ABDO Publishing Co.

Kenney, Karen Latchana. Building a Highway. 2020. (Sequence Amazing Structures Ser.). (ENG.). 32p. (J). (gr. 2-5). pap. 12.00 *(978-1-68152-560-0(7)*, 10761) Amicus.

Lassieur, Allison. Subways in Action. 2012. (Transportation Zone Ser.). (ENG.). 24p. (gr. 1-2). pap. 41.70 *(978-1-4296-8395-1(3))*; (Illus.). (J). pap. 7.29 *(978-1-4296-7967-1(0)*, 118299) Capstone. (Capstone Pr.).

Leighton, Christina. City Trains. 2017. (Amazing Trains Ser.). (ENG., Illus.). 24p. (J). (gr. k-3). lib. bdg. 26.95 *(978-1-62617-669-0(8)*, Blastoff! Readers) Bellwether Media.

—Subway Trains. 2017. (Amazing Trains Ser.). (ENG., Illus.). 24p. (J). (gr. k-3). lib. bdg. 26.95 *(978-1-62617-674-4(4)*, Blastoff! Readers) Bellwether Media.

McCarthy, Cecilia Pinto. Engineering the NYC Subway System. 2017. (Building by Design Ser.). (ENG., Illus.). 48p. (J). (gr. 4-8). lib. bdg. 35.64 *(978-1-5321-1168-6(1)*, 25912) ABDO Publishing Co.

Miller, Heather Lynne. Subway Ride. Rama, Sue, illus. 2011. (ENG.). 32p. (J). (gr. -1-3). pap. 7.95 *(978-1-58089-112-7(8))* Charlesbridge Publishing, Inc.

New York Tansit Museum. New York City Subway Trains: 12 Classic Punch-and-Build Trains, 1 vol. 2003. (ENG., Illus.). 48p. (J). (gr. 2-3). pap. 19.99 *(978-1-58685-324-2(4))* Gibbs Smith, Publisher.

Peters, Elisa. Let's Ride the Subway! 2014. (Public Transportation Ser.). 24p. (J). (gr. k-2). pap. 49.50 *(978-1-4777-6516-6(6))*; (ENG.). (gr. 1-2). 25.27 *(978-1-4777-6521-0(2)*, 8587211b-d63f-4c61-9023-9ddb73a6f5a2) Rosen Publishing Group, Inc., The. (PowerKids Pr.).

Peters, Elisa & Eida, de la Vega. Let's Ride the Subway! (¡Vamos a Tomar el Metro!), 1 vol. de la Vega, Eida, ed. 2014. (Transporte Público / Public Transportation Ser.). (SPA & ENG.). 24p. (J). (gr. 1-2). lib. bdg. 25.27 *(978-1-4777-6785-6(1)*, 09bfa8a1-a6af-4d62-ae01-74bc337ad51d, PowerKids Pr.) Rosen Publishing Group, Inc., The.

Ponzi, Emiliano. The Great New York Subway Map. 2018. (ENG., Illus.). 36p. (J). 19.95 *(978-1-63345-025-7(2)*, 1653501) Museum of Modern Art.

Raum, Elizabeth. The Life of Harriet Tubman. 2019. (Sequence Change Maker Biographies Ser.). (ENG.). 32p. (J). (gr. 2-5). lib. bdg. *(978-1-68151-676-9(4)*, 10808) Amicus.

Reis, Ronald A. The New York City Subway System. 2009. (ENG., Illus.). 144p. (gr. 5-8). 35.00 *(978-1-60413-046-1(6)*, P162091, Facts On File) Infobase Holdings, Inc.

Rose, Simon. Underground Transportation Systems. 2018. (Underground Worlds Ser.). (Illus.). 32p. (J). (gr. 4-4). *(978-0-7787-6127-3(4))* Crabtree Publishing Co.

Ryan, Phillip. Subways, 1 vol. 2010. (All Aboard! Ser.). (ENG.). 24p. (J). (gr. 1-2). pap. 9.25 *(978-1-4488-1213-4(5)*, 200864d0-f0e9-4d6e-97f5-cefbae50c478); lib. bdg. 26.27 *(978-1-4488-0636-2(4)*, bd0e98b4-6ac4-4e74-9f74-a6c4794c3f3b) Rosen Publishing Group, Inc., The.

Santella, Andrew. Cornerstones of Freedom: Building the New York Subway. 2007. (Cornerstones of Freedom Ser.). (ENG.,

Illus.). 48p. (J). (gr. 4-6). 26.00 (978-0-516-23638-4(5), Children's Pr.) Scholastic Library Publishing.
Williams, John Matthew. Trains Go!, 1 vol. 2017. (Ways to Go Ser.). (ENG.). 24p. (J). (gr. k-k). pap. 9.15 (978-1-5382-1025-3(8), 836ea712-da86-4ed7-961c-9d770f2d5ca1) Stevens, Gareth Publishing LLLP.
Winget, Mary. Subways. 2007. (Pull Ahead Books — Mighty Movers Ser.). (ENG., Illus.). 32p. (gr. k-3). (J). per. 7.99 (978-0-8225-6424-9(6), 261d6fc3-5932-4661-91cb-1b7d82adab30, First Avenue Editions); lib. bdg. 22.60 (978-0-8225-6418-8(1), Lerner Pubns.) Lerner Publishing Group.

SUBWAYS—FICTION

Bluemle, Elizabeth. Tap Tap Boom Boom. Karas, G. Brian, illus. 2014. (ENG.). 32p. (J). (gr. -1-2). 17.99 (978-0-7636-5696-6(8)) Candlewick Pr.
Cohen, Miriam. Down in the Subway, 1 vol. Hope Greenberg, Melanie, illus. 2003. (ENG.). 32p. (J). (gr. k-3). pap. 6.99 (978-1-932065-24-4(5)); 16.99 (978-1-932065-08-4(3)) Star Bright Bks., Inc.
de la Peña, Matt. Milo Imagines the World. Robinson, Christian, illus. 2021. (ENG.). 40p. (J). (gr. -1-3). 18.99 (978-0-399-54908-3(0), G.P. Putnam's Sons Books for Young Readers) Penguin Young Readers Group.
Derrick, Patricia & O'Neil, Shirley. Rathbone the Rat. Martinez, J-P Loppo, illus. 2007. 32p. (J). (gr. -1-3). 18.95 incl. audio compact disk (978-1-933818-17-7(4)) Animalations.
Holman, Felice. Slake's Limbo. unabr. ed. 2004. 117p. (J). (gr. 7-18). pap. 29.00 incl. audio (978-0-8072-8744-6(X), YA254SP, Listening Library) Random Hse. Audio Publishing Group.
Niemann, Christoph. Subway. Niemann, Christoph, illus. 2010. (ENG., Illus.). 40p. (J). (gr. -1-k). 19.99 (978-0-06-157779-6(0), Greenwillow Bks.) HarperCollins Pubs.
Novel Units. Slake's Limbo Novel Units Student Packet. 2019. (ENG.). (J). pap., stu. ed., wbk. ed. 13.99 (978-1-58130-749-8(7), Novel Units, Inc.) Classroom Library Co.
Potter, Ellen. Olivia Kidney Secret Beneath City. 2009. (ENG.). 336p. (J). (gr. 3-7). 9.99 (978-0-14-241263-3(5), Puffin Books) Penguin Young Readers Group.
Reid, Barbara. The Subway Mouse. Reid, Barbara, illus. (Illus.). 2017. 40p. (gr. 1-2). pap. 7.95 (978-0-439-78917-2(6)) 2005. (J). (978-0-439-77430-7(6)) Scholastic, Inc.
Rusu, Meredith. C Train: A New Beginning. Atuesta, Angela, illus. 2023. (ENG & SPA.). 32p. (J). 18.99 Circle Tales, The.
Shusterman, Neal. Downsiders. 2009. (ENG.). 272p. (YA). (gr. 7). pap. 12.99 (978-1-4169-9747-4(4), Simon & Schuster Bks. For Young Readers) Simon & Schuster Bks. For Young Readers.
Spiegelman, Nadja. Lost in NYC: A Subway Adventure. Sánchez, Sergio García, illus. 2016. (Toon Graphics Ser.). (ENG.). 52p. (J). (gr. 3-6). lib. bdg. 34.21 (978-1-61479-499-8(5), 21435, Graphic Novels) Spotlight.
—Lost in NYC: a Subway Adventure: A TOON Graphic. Garcia Sanchez, Sergio, illus. 2015. 52p. (J). (gr. 3-7). 16.99 (978-1-935179-81-8(0), TOON Books) Astra Publishing Hse.
Stilton, Gerónimo. The Phantom of the Subway. Wolf, Matt, illus. 2004. (Geronimo Stilton Ser.: No. 13). 112p. (J). lib. bdg. 10.00 (978-1-4242-0282-9(5)) Fitzgerald Bks.
Suen, Anastasia. Subway. Katz, Karen, illus. 2008. 24p. (J). (gr. -1-k). bds. 7.99 (978-0-670-01109-4(6), Viking Books for Young Readers) Penguin Young Readers Group.
Tan, Sheri. Follow That Map!, 1 vol. Ng-Benitez, Shirley, illus. 2019. (Confetti Kids Ser.: 7). (ENG.). 32p. (J). (gr. k-2). 14.95 (978-1-62014-569-2(3), leelowbooks); pap. 10.95 (978-1-62014-570-8(7), leelowbooks) Lee & Low Bks., Inc.

SUCCESS

see also Business; Leadership; Life Skills

The Action Principles: Armed Service Tribute Edition. 2nd ed. 2003. mass mkt. 20.00 (978-1-884864-19-3(8)) American Success Institute, Inc.
Adler, Mia Sharon. Essential Proteen, Student Journal: A Life Skills Program for Helping Teens Succeed. 2006. (ENG.). 48p. pap. 14.99 (978-0-87822-582-8(X), P466760) Research Pr.
Antill, Sara. Grit, 1 vol. 2013. (Character Strength Ser.). 24p. (J). (ENG.). (gr. 2-3). pap. 9.25 (978-1-4488-9814-5(5), 8dc93072-3744-44a9-9b9b-040091ea4a96); (ENG.). (gr. 2-3). lib. bdg. 26.27 (978-1-4488-9678-3(9), a63c2462-963e-44f1-bffb-c264fd692ceb); (gr. 3-6). pap. 49.50 (978-1-4488-9815-2(3)) Rosen Publishing Group, Inc., The. (PowerKids Pr.).
—Zest, 1 vol. 2013. (Character Strength Ser.). 24p. (J). (ENG.). (gr. 2-3). pap. 9.25 (978-1-4488-9812-1(9), 5b0fa2f8-4d9e-4867-ba81-390cd42525b4); (ENG.). (gr. 2-3). lib. bdg. 26.27 (978-1-4488-9677-6(0), 9c904f5d-c84c-4e83-a409-ba48349687ac); (gr. 3-6). pap. 49.50 (978-1-4488-9813-8(7)) Rosen Publishing Group, Inc., The. (PowerKids Pr.).
Berman, Ron. Who's Got Next? Future Leaders of America. 2013. (Av2 Audio Chapter Bks.). (ENG., Illus.). 92p. (J). (gr. 4-7). lib. bdg. 27.13 (978-1-62127-998-3(7), AV2 by Weigl) Weigl Pubs., Inc.
Bernstein, Ben. Stressed Out! for Teens. 2014. (ENG., Illus.). xi, 254p. (J). 34.95 (978-1-942672-54-8(3)) Familius LLC.
Berry, Joy. You Can... Work It! Being Smart, Being Creative, Being Assertive, Being in Control, Getting Organized & Attaining Goals! 2009. (ENG.). 304p. (J). (gr. 5-7). pap. 12.95 (978-1-60577-602-6(5)) Berry, Joy Enterprises.
Bishop, John. Goal Setting for Students: Winner of three national parenting book Awards. 2003. (Illus.). (YA). pap. 11.95 (978-0-9743700-0-2(2)) Accent On Success.
Black, Donnette. Madam C. J. Walker's Road to Success. 2010. 36p. pap. 17.50 (978-1-4520-2443-1(X)) AuthorHouse.
Conway, Hollis. Grasshopper: The Hollis Conway Story. 2004. 30p. (J). per. (978-1-59196-584-8(5)) Instant Pub.
Covey, Sean. The 6 Most Important Decisions You'll Ever Make: A Guide for Teens: Updated for the Digital Age. 2017. (ENG., Illus.). 336p. pap. 18.99 (978-1-5011-5713-4(2), Touchstone) Touchstone.
Crockett, Kyle A. Nutrition for Achievement in Sports & Academics. Borus, Joshua, ed. 2013. (Understanding Nutrition: a Gateway to Physical & Mental Health Ser.). (Illus.). 48p. (J). (gr. 5-18). pap. 9.95 (978-1-4222-2990-3(4)); 19.95 (978-1-4222-2884-5(3)) Mason Crest.
Crow, Gary & Crow, Marissa. The Success Train. 2003. (Illus.). 73p. (J). pap. 9.95 (978-0-9741685-5-5(6)) Koenisha Pubns.
Davis, Sampson, et al. We Beat the Street: How a Friendship Pact Led to Success. 2006. (Illus.). 208p. (J). (gr. 5-18). 9.99 (978-0-14-240627-4(9), Puffin Books) Penguin Young Readers Group.
Dugan, Christine. From Rags to Riches, 1 vol. 2nd rev. ed. 2013. (TIME for KIDS(r): Informational Text Ser.). (ENG., Illus.). 64p. (J). (gr. 4-8). pap. 14.99 (978-1-4333-4910-2(8)) Teacher Created Materials, Inc.
Dyer, Wayne & Dyer, Summer. 10 Secrets for Success & Inner Peace for Teens. 2004. 12.95 (978-1-4019-0270-4(7), 2707, Hay Hse. Lifestyles) Hay Hse., Inc.
Fiszer, Edward P. Thoughts to Inspire: Daily Messages for Young People. 2004. (ENG.). 176p. pap. 60.00 (978-1-57886-124-8(1)) Scarecrow Pr., Inc.
Flemmings, Tyrone. Home Schooled Boss. 2011. 12p. pap. 12.99 (978-1-4567-5157-9(3)) AuthorHouse.
Gareth Guides to an Extraordinary Life: Set 2, 12 vols. 2018. (Gareth Guides to an Extraordinary Life Ser.). (ENG.). 32p. (gr. 4-5). lib. bdg. 177.60 (978-1-5382-2184-6(5), e86ca806-0f87-4516-9b9c-e2d07fb4726d) Stevens, Gareth Publishing LLLP.
Graham, Stedman. Move Without the Ball: Put Your Skills & Your Magic to Work for You. 2004. (ENG., Illus.). 208p. pap. 15.99 (978-0-7432-3440-5(5), Touchstone) Touchstone.
Hansen, Mark & Ferber, Kevin S. Success 101 for Teens: Dollars & Sense for a Winning Financial Life. 2012. (ENG.). 176p. pap. 12.95 (978-1-55778-901-3(0), 5e304a18-9516-4718-a318-b52a07c05a38) Paragon Hse. Pubs.
Harrington, Paul. The Secret to Teen Power. 2010. (JPN., Illus.). 254p. (YA). (978-4-04-791630-2(7)) Fukuinkan Shoten.
—The Secret to Teen Power. 2009. (ENG., Illus.). 192p. (YA). (gr. 7-18). 19.99 (978-1-4169-9498-5(X)) Simon Pulse/Beyond Words.
Harris, Laurie Lanzen. Biography for Beginners: African-American Leaders. 2007. (J). lib. bdg. 30.00 (978-1-931360-35-7(9)) Favorable Impressions.
Honders, Christine. Why Should I Listen to My Parents?, 1 vol. 2019. (Listening to Leaders Ser.). (ENG.). 24p. (gr. 2-2). pap. 9.25 (978-1-5383-4168-1(9), 8270b24a-00f6-49d6-8e73-bdfe04395f89, PowerKids Pr.) Rosen Publishing Group, Inc., The.
Howat, Irene. Ten Boys Who Used Their Talents. rev. ed. 2006. (Lightkeepers Ser.). (ENG., Illus.). 160p. (J). (gr. 3-7). per. 8.99 (978-1-84550-146-4(2), f52e4002-6476-4170-a087-931bf34b73de) Christian Focus Pubns. GBR. Dist: Baker & Taylor Publisher Services (BTPS).
—Ten Girls Who Used Their Talents. rev. ed. 2006. (Lightkeepers Ser.). (ENG., Illus.). 160p. (J). (gr. 3-7). per. 8.99 (978-1-84550-147-1(0), 48f9a641-4ed8-4a03-be87-a6ef262de680) Christian Focus Pubns. GBR. Dist: Baker & Taylor Publisher Services (BTPS).
Hunt, Christopher. Victory after High School: Survive or Thrive —-You Choose! 2005. 144p. (YA). per. 16.95 (978-0-9765973-4-6(9)) Adjust Communications.
Islam, Sabirul. The World at Your Feet: Three Strikes to a Successful Entrepreneurial Life. 2010. (Illus.). 120p. pap. (978-0-462-09952-1(0)) Marshall Cavendish.
Kiefer, Jeanne. Jobs for Kids: A Smart Kid's Q & A Guide. Green, Anne Canevari, illus. 2003. (Single Titles Ser.). 112p. (gr. 5-8). lib. bdg. 25.90 (978-0-7613-2611-3(1), Millbrook Pr.) Lerner Publishing Group.
Leslie, Roger. Success Express for Teens: 50 Life-Changing Activities. 2003. (ENG., Illus.). 224p. pap. 14.95 (978-1-886298-09-5(2), e24462f5-7a31-4d3d-acca-7c030d252ceb) Bayou Publishing.
Lewis, Carole. Pathway to Success. 2004. (First Place Bible Studies). 240p. pap. 19.99 (978-0-8307-2927-2(5), Gospel Light) Gospel Light Pubns.
Lilly, Karen. The Failure Book. 2020. (ENG., Illus.). 96p. (J). pap. 14.95 (978-0-87441-977-1(8), 06bd437d-c372-4fbd-828d-632e5f738e9f) Behrman Hse., Inc.
Lüsted, Marcia Amidon. The Most Influential Women in Business, 1 vol. 2018. (Breaking the Glass Ceiling: the Most Influential Women Ser.). (ENG., Illus.). 112p. (J). (gr. 8-8). 40.13 (978-1-5081-7967-2(0), aeb5ae19-8a78-4f9f-85be-5941a3cabdea) Rosen Publishing Group, Inc., The.
Mandino, Og. Og Mandino's Great Trilogy: The Greatest Salesman in the World, the Greatest Secret in the World & the Greatest Miracle in the World. 2008. 420p. (J). (978-0-8119-0428-5(8)) Lifetime Bks.
Marcovitz, Hal. Puerto Ricans. 2009. (Successful Americans Ser.). 64p. (YA). (gr. 9-12). 22.95 (978-1-4222-0516-7(9)) Mason Crest.
—Russian Americans. 2007. (Successful Americans Ser.). (Illus.). 64p. (YA). (gr. 7-18). pap. 9.95 (978-1-4222-0868-7(0)) Mason Crest.
McAneney, Caitie. The Most Powerful Words about the American Dream, 1 vol. 2019. (Words That Shaped America Ser.). (ENG.). 32p. (gr. 4-5). pap. 11.50 (978-1-5382-4803-4(4), 7618d8fa-c086-40c3-8a3c-d766a8d1b28d) Stevens, Gareth Publishing LLLP.
McDuffie, Daryl L. ABC's to Unlimited Success: How to Turn All Your Dreams into Reality. 2003. (YA). per. 9.97 (978-0-9727582-0-8(8)) G Publishing LLC.
Mitchell-Tulloss, Delores. ABCs of Character for People Around the World. Hardison, Brian, illus. 2007. 32p. (J). pap. (978-0-9670712-6-8(7)) zReyomi Publishing.
Mr. Blue. From Underdog to Wonderdog: Top Ten Tricks to Lead Your Pack. 2012. (ENG., Illus.). 52p. (J). (gr. 1-5). pap. 14.95 (978-1-936354-26-9(8), Tremendous Leadership) Tremendous Life Bks.
Norris, David A. Lasting Success: Quality Decisions, Relationships & Untamed Emotions. 2003. (Illus.). 256p. per. (978-0-943177-12-0(X), 0-943177-12-x) Heartland Foundation, Inc.
Novak, Robby & Montague, Brad. Kid President's Guide to Being Awesome. 2016. (ENG., Illus.). 256p. (J). (gr. 3-7). pap. 12.99 (978-0-06-243871-3(9), HarperCollins) HarperCollins Pubs.
Nussbaum, Ben. Fantastic Lives: Against All Odds (Level 8) 2018. (TIME(r): Informational Text Ser.). (ENG., Illus.). 48p. (J). (gr. 7-8). pap. 11.99 (978-1-4258-5012-8(X)) Teacher Created Materials, Inc.
O'Connor, Frances. Frequently Asked Questions about Academic Anxiety. 2009. (FAQ: Teen Life Ser.). 64p. (gr. 5-6). 58.50 (978-1-61512-560-9(4)) Rosen Publishing Group, Inc., The.
Orr, Tamra. Zest. 2013. (7 Character Strengths of Highly Successful Students Ser.). (Illus.). 64p. (J). (gr. 5-8). pap. 77.70 (978-1-4488-9568-7(5)) Rosen Publishing Group, Inc., The.
Orr, Tamra B. Zest, 1 vol. 2013. (7 Character Strengths of Highly Successful Students Ser.). (ENG., Illus.). 64p. (J). (gr. 6-6). 37.12 (978-1-4488-9541-0(3), 447beb6b-b583-4a73-b221-21eabdbcfdb5); pap. 13.95 (978-1-4488-9567-0(7), 9781fb8c-fe30-425d-867e-36c1fac7297b) Rosen Publishing Group, Inc., The.
Ortega, Julian G. Warrior Inspiration. 2010. 152p. pap. 11.95 (978-1-59330-659-5(8)) Aventine Pr.
Paxson, Jillip Naysinthe, told to. The First Thirty. anniv. ed. 2015. (ENG.). 96p. (YA). (gr. 5-16). pap. 10.00 (978-0-9758794-1-2(3)) IdeaList Enterprises, Inc.
Paxson, Jillip Naysinthe & Siegman, Greg Forbes. The First Thirty. 2005. 96p. (YA). pap. 10.00 (978-0-9758794-0-5(5)) IdeaList Enterprises, Inc.
Preparing for School Success. 2017. (978-1-59723-348-4(X)) Active Parenting Pubs.
Rameck, Hunt, et al. We Beat the Street: How a Friendship Pact Led to Success. 2014. (ENG.). 208p. (J). 12.24 (978-1-63245-093-7(3)) Lectorum Pubns., Inc.
Rayel, Michael G. A 31-Day Success Principles for Kids & Teens. 2006. 64p. (J). pap. (978-0-9737070-3-8(8)) Soar Dime, Limited/Oikos Global.
Reber, Deborah. Doable: The Girls' Guide to Accomplishing Just about Anything. 2015. (ENG., Illus.). 208p. (YA). (gr. 7). pap. 12.99 (978-1-58270-466-1(X), Simon Pulse) Simon Pulse.
Reynolds, Luke. Fantastic Failures: True Stories of People Who Changed the World by Falling down First. 2018. (ENG., Illus.). 304p. (J). (gr. 3-7). 21.99 (978-1-58270-664-1(6)); pap. 12.99 (978-1-58270-665-8(4)) Aladdin/Beyond Words.
Richards-Ross, Sanya. Right on Track: Run, Race, Believe, 1 vol. 2018. (ENG.). 224p. (YA). 18.99 (978-0-310-76090-0(9)) Zondervan.
Richardson, Dot. Go for It: Conversations on Being You. 2004. (Girls Explore, Reach for the Stars Ser.). (Illus.). 140p. (J). 20.00 (978-0-9749456-0-6(9), Girls Explore) Girls Explore LLC.
Ross, Margaret. Casey & the Amazing Good Finder: Teaching Adults & Children How to Succeed in School, Work, Life & Relationships. l.t. ed. 2005. (Illus.). 32p. (J). 9.99 (978-0-9715713-5-8(X)) Kamaron Institute Pr.
Rossi, Debra M. No Horsing Around: Kick off to Success in School. 2004. (Illus.). 32p. (J). 5.95 (978-0-9758982-0-8(5)) Rossi, Debra.
Scott, John, text. Juniors: How to Make the Team. 2004. (YA). 30.00 (978-1-879498-78-5(2)) SportAmerica.
Shaffer, Jody Jensen. You Can Too! Success after Failure (Level 5) 2017. (TIME for KIDS(r): Informational Text Ser.). (ENG., Illus.). 48p. (gr. 4-8). pap. 13.99 (978-1-4258-4990-0(3)) Teacher Created Materials, Inc.
Shelton, C. H. & Shelton, C. H. A Kid's Guide to Being a Winner. Gillespie, Greg G., illus. 2011. 38p. (J). (gr. 2-8). 9.99 (978-0-9841910-4-8(6)) Choice PH.
Shepherd, Jodie. Perseverance: I Have Grit! 2015. (Rookie Talk about It Ser.). (ENG., Illus.). 32p. (J). pap. 5.95 (978-0-531-21379-7(X), Children's Pr.) Scholastic Library Publishing.
Siddoway, Ramona. Grit. 2013. (7 Character Strengths of Highly Successful Students Ser.). (Illus.). 64p. (J). (gr. 5-8). pap. 77.70 (978-1-4488-9560-1(X)); (ENG., (gr. 6-6). 37.12 (978-1-4488-9540-3(5), efa36d12-2ea1-4354-ad4e-e6693ca0c518); (ENG., (gr. 6-6). pap. 13.95 (978-1-4488-9559-5(6), a2f7459f-eacd-47d6-8d3d-e33a3fb37575) Rosen Publishing Group, Inc., The.
Silverman, Robin L. & Silverman, Robin Landew. Reaching Your Goals. 2004. (Life Balance Ser.). (ENG.). 80p. (J). 20.50 (978-0-531-12342-3(1), Watts, Franklin) Scholastic Library Publishing.
Skills for Success, 10 vols. 2017. (Skills for Success Ser.). (ENG.). 64p. (gr. 7-7). 180.65 (978-1-4994-6636-2(6), 475cfaa2-b41e-4d3a-afcf-9e1eefa227b2, Rosen Young Adult) Rosen Publishing Group, Inc., The.
Smith, Charles R., Jr. 28 Days: Moments in Black History That Changed the World. Evans, Shane W., illus. 2015. (ENG.). 56p. (J). (gr. -1-5). 19.99 (978-1-59643-820-0(7), 900087175) Roaring Brook Pr.
Smith, Sarah. Etiquette for Success: Social Media & Online Manners, Vol. 7. 2018. (Etiquette for Success Ser.). 64p. (J). (gr. 7). lib. bdg. 31.93 (978-1-4222-3973-5(X)) Mason Crest.
—Etiquette for Success: Workplace, Vol. 7. 2018. (Etiquette for Success Ser.). 64p. (J). (gr. 7). lib. bdg. 31.93 (978-1-4222-3976-6(4)) Mason Crest.
Tebow, Tim. Shaken: Young Reader's Edition: Fighting to Stand Strong No Matter What Comes Your Way. 2020. (ENG.). 208p. (YA). (gr. 5). pap. 12.99 (978-0-525-65350-9(3), WaterBrook Pr.) Crown Publishing Group, The.
Ward, Lesley. Showdown: Underdogs (Level 7) 2018. (TIME(r): Informational Text Ser.). (ENG., Illus.). 48p. (J). (gr. 6-8). pap. 11.99 (978-1-4258-5007-4(3)) Teacher Created Materials, Inc.
Wilson, Nolan. The Teen's Guide to Getting Ahead: How to Succeed in High School & Beyond. 2008. 192p. (YA). (gr. 8-11). pap. 15.95 (978-1-897073-92-6(5)) Lobster Pr. CAN. Dist: Orca Bk. Pubs. USA.
Wong, Tyrus. Work/School Lives: Let's Talk Champ! Wong, Tyrus, ed. 2023. (ENG., Illus.). 114p. (J). (gr. 6-18). pap., act. bk. ed. 11.99 (978-0-9829466-5-7(1)) Golf Machine, Ltd.!
The 7 Character Strengths of Highly Successful Students. 2013. (7 Character Strengths of Highly Successful Students Ser.). 64p. (J). (gr. 5-8). pap. 543.90 (978-1-4777-1242-9(9)); (gr. 5-8). pap. 90.65 (978-1-4777-1241-2(0)); (ENG.). (gr. 6-6). 259.84 (978-1-4488-9554-0(5), e73cf5d7-ef99-4201-9924-ddfdd93a08a0) Rosen Publishing Group, Inc., The.

SUDOKU

Bloom, Jonathan. The Must Have Sudoku Holiday Gift 480 Puzzles. 2012. 278p. pap. (978-0-9814261-5-0(8)) Sudokids.Com.
Chisholm, Alastair. The Kids' Book of Sudoku 1. 2018. (Buster Puzzle Bks.). (ENG.). 192p. (J). (gr. 3-7). pap. 4.99 (978-1-78055-501-0(6)) O'Mara, Michael Bks., Ltd. GBR. Dist: Independent Pubs. Group.
—The Kids' Book of Sudoku 2. 2018. (Buster Puzzle Bks.). (ENG.). 192p. (J). (gr. 3-7). pap. 5.99 (978-1-78055-503-4(2)) O'Mara, Michael Bks., Ltd. GBR. Dist: Independent Pubs. Group.
Granny, Smith. Granny Smith's Sudoku Solver: For Beginners & Other Wise People. 2010. 100p. pap. 12.95 (978-1-4520-0287-3(8)) AuthorHouse.
Griffiths-Jones, Sam & Moog, Bob. Sudoku for Kids. 2006. (Spinner Books for Kids Ser.). (ENG.). 158p. (J). (gr. 4-7). pap. 6.95 (978-1-57528-963-2(6)) Univ. Games.
Kattan, Peter & Kattan, Nicola. Kindergarten Sudoku: 4x4 Sudoku Puzzles for Kids. 2007. (ENG.). 48p. pap. 7.50 (978-0-615-15334-6(8)) Kattan, Peter I.
Longo, F. Sudoku Puzzles for Vacation. 2018. (Puzzlewright Junior Sudoku Ser.: 3). (ENG.). 96p. (J). (gr. 3). pap. 7.95 (978-1-4549-2959-8(6), Puzzlewright) Sterling Publishing Co., Inc.
Molski, Carol. Bible Word Suduko. Koehler, Ed, illus. 2007. (CPH Teaching Resource Ser.). (ENG.). 64p. pap. 10.99 (978-0-7586-1344-8(X)) Concordia Publishing Hse.
Moog, Bob. Do You Sudoku? Spicy: Over 200 Puzzles for Experienced Sudoku Solvers. 2006. (Spinner Bks.). (ENG.). 264p. per. 9.95 (978-1-57528-899-4(0)) Univ. Games.
Pazzelli, John. A First Sudoku Book. Zourelias, Diana, illus. 2006. (Dover Kids Activity Bks.). (ENG.). 64p. (J). (gr. 3-8). per. 3.95 (978-0-486-45074-2(0), 450740) Dover Pubns., Inc.
Shortz, Will. Will Shortz Presents Math Masters Sudoku: 150 Puzzles for Clever Kids: Sudoku for Kids Volume 1. 2017. (Sudoku for Kids Ser.: 1). (ENG.). 176p. (J). pap. 17.99 (978-1-250-15017-2(5), 900182497, St. Martin's Griffin) St. Martin's Pr.
Shortz, Will, intro. Will Shortz Presents the Monster Book of Sudoku for Kids: 150 Fun Puzzles. 2006. (ENG., Illus.). 176p. (J). (gr. 3-7). pap. 9.99 (978-0-312-36842-5(9), 900042516, St. Martin's Griffin) St. Martin's Pr.
Sirkis, Rafael. Wacky Facts. 2007. (Apple Paperbacks Ser.). (ENG., Illus.). 144p. (J). (gr. 4-7). pap. 4.99 (978-0-439-02280-4(0)) Scholastic, Inc.
Stickels, Terry & Immanuvel, Anthony. Go!Games Sudoku. 2010. (Go!Games Ser.). (ENG.). 288p. pap. 8.99 (978-1-936140-08-4(X), Imagine Publishing) Charlesbridge Publishing, Inc.
Teora, creator. Picture Sudoku, 1 vol. 2008. (ENG., Illus.). 12p. (J). (gr. -1-3). pap. 4.95 (978-1-59496-166-3(2)) Teora USA LLC.
—Sudoku 1: 42 Puzzles for Kids, 1 vol. 2005. (ENG., Illus.). 24p. (J). pap. 3.95 (978-1-59496-126-7(3)) Teora USA LLC.
—Sudoku 2: 42 Puzzles for Kids, 1 vol. 2005. (ENG., Illus.). 24p. (J). pap. 3.95 (978-1-59496-127-4(1)) Teora USA LLC.
The Puzzle Society, The Puzzle. Pocket Posh Girl Sudoku 2 Vol. 2: 100 Puzzles. 2011. (ENG.). 128p. pap. 7.99 (978-1-4494-0738-4(2)) Andrews McMeel Publishing.

SUEZ CANAL (EGYPT)

Bodden, Valerie. Suez Canal. 2006. (Modern Wonders of the World Ser.). (Illus.). 32p. (J). 18.95 (978-1-58341-441-5(X), Creative Education) Creative Co., The.
Fiscus, James. The Suez Crisis. 2009. (War & Conflict in the Middle East Ser.). 64p. (gr. 5-5). 58.50 (978-1-60854-741-8(8)) Rosen Publishing Group, Inc., The.
Fiscus, James W. The Suez Crisis, 1 vol. 2003. (War & Conflict in the Middle East Ser.). (ENG., Illus.). 64p. (gr. 5-5). lib. bdg. 37.13 (978-0-8239-4550-4(2), d1679606-94b2-4bb1-8825-577f100388fe) Rosen Publishing Group, Inc., The.
Riggs, Kate. Suez Canal. 2009. (Now That's Big Ser.). 24p. (J). (gr. 1-5). lib. bdg. 24.25 (978-1-58341-706-5(0), Creative Education) Creative Co., The.

SUFFRAGE

see also classes of people with the subdivision Suffrage, e.g. Women—Suffrage; etc.

Acks, Alex. Key Voting Laws, 1 vol. 2019. (Laws That Changed History Ser.). (ENG.). 80p. (gr. 7-7). pap. 18.65 (978-1-5026-5535-6(7), 911629d3-6ccc-4d83-95d0-b54699e3db27); lib. bdg. 37.36 (978-1-5026-5536-3(5), b599657d-bcea-440c-b1ed-9443c31306c3) Cavendish Square Publishing LLC.
—Key Voting Laws. 2019. (J). pap. (978-1-9785-1446-1(8)) Enslow Publishing, LLC.
Almasy, Kip. Why Voting Matters, 1 vol. 2017. (Spotlight on Civic Action Ser.). (ENG.). 32p. (J). (gr. 4-5). 27.93 (978-1-5081-6395-4(2), f21c0c6e-970b-41dd-9bc9-05ab37cce721, PowerKids Pr.) Rosen Publishing Group, Inc., The.
Berlatsky, Noah, ed. Voting Rights, 1 vol. 2015. (Opposing Viewpoints Ser.). (ENG.). 248p. (gr. 10-12). pap. 34.80 (978-0-7377-7301-9(4), 1b57b9d6-c45b-442a-b2e1-397dc60fb40b, Greenhaven Publishing) Greenhaven Publishing LLC.
Burgan, Michael. The Voting Rights Act Of 1965: An Interactive History Adventure. 2015. (You Choose: History Ser.). (ENG., Illus.). 112p. (J). (gr. 3-7). pap. 6.95 (978-1-4914-1805-5(2), 127252, Capstone Pr.) Capstone.
Diesen, Deborah. Equality's Call: The Story of Voting Rights in America. Mora, Magdalena, illus. 2020. (ENG.). 48p. (J). (gr. -1-3). 17.99 (978-1-5344-3958-0(7), Beach Lane Bks.) Beach Lane Bks.

S

Eboch, M. M., ed. Voting Rights & Voter ID Laws, 1 vol. 2018. (Introducing Issues with Opposing Viewpoints Ser.). (ENG.). 120p. (gr. 7-10). 43.63 *(978-1-5345-0365-6(X),* e7df2a10-eb0c-4fe7-915d-6c1cdfddced2) Greenhaven Publishing LLC.

Egan, Tracie. Voting, 1 vol. 2003. (Primary Source Library of American Citizenship Ser.). (ENG., Illus.). 32p. (YA). (gr. 5-5). lib. bdg. 29.13 *(978-0-8239-4479-8(4),* 35a51c2f-3c04-49e5-979f-67a24ea08675, Rosen Reference) Rosen Publishing Group, Inc., The.

Isler, Claudia. The Right to Vote. 2009. (Individual Rights & Civic Responsibility Ser.). 128p. (gr. 7-12). 63.90 *(978-1-61513-516-5(2))* Rosen Publishing Group, Inc., The.

Lansford, Tom. Political Participation & Voting Rights, Vol. 8. Lansford, Tom, ed. 2016. (Foundations of Democracy Ser.). (Illus.). 64p. (J). (gr. 7). 23.95 *(978-1-4222-3631-4(5))* Mason Crest.

Miller, Derek. Voter Disenfranchisement, 1 vol. 2019. (Dilemmas in Democracy Ser.). (ENG.). 80p. (gr. 7-7). pap. 18.64 *(978-1-5026-4509-8(2),* ee83eed4-0dd0-4ff9-901e-f2cb1af136db) Cavendish Square Publishing LLC.

Orr, Tamra. A History of Voting Rights. 2012. (J). lib. bdg. 29.95 *(978-1-61228-262-6(8))* Mitchell Lane Pubs.

Quinlan, Julia J. Everything You Need to Know about Voting Rights & Voter Disenfranchisement, 1 vol. 2018. (Need to Know Library). (ENG.). 64p. (J). (gr. 6-6). 36.13 *(978-1-5081-7921-4(2),* 74a5341f-9a38-4c9c-b29c-ce8a7e2216f6); pap. 13.95 *(978-1-5081-7930-6(1),* 866623fd-8368-442f-8746-be9d44ebc63b) Rosen Publishing Group, Inc., The. (Rosen Young Adult).

Quinn, Barbara & Isler, Claudia. Understanding Your Right to Vote, 1 vol. 2011. (Personal Freedom & Civic Duty Ser.). (ENG., Illus.). 144p. (YA). (gr. 7-7). lib. bdg. 39.80 *(978-1-4488-4665-8(X),* 0e9c07bd-85cf-44f4-a616-ea73fbdd37a8) Rosen Publishing Group, Inc., The.

Rajczak Nelson, Kristen. What Is Voting?, 1 vol. 2018. (Why Voting Matters Ser.). (ENG.). 24p. (gr. 2-2). 25.27 *(978-1-5383-3011-1(3),* 70f30c05-d5b6-48d0-ac6a-1beb6e2624df, PowerKids Pr.) Rosen Publishing Group, Inc., The.

—Who Can Vote?, 1 vol. 2018. (Why Voting Matters Ser.). (ENG.). 24p. (gr. 2-2). 25.27 *(978-1-5383-3015-9(6),* b00a2f78-27f0-42c2-acab-dda800dca647, PowerKids Pr.) Rosen Publishing Group, Inc., The.

SUFFRAGETTES

see Suffragists

SUFFRAGISTS

Adiletta, Dawn. Elizabeth Cady Stanton: Women's Suffrage & the First Vote. (Library of American Lives & Times Ser.). 112p. (gr. 5-5). 2009. 69.20 *(978-1-60853-479-1(0))* 2004. (ENG., Illus.). (J). lib. bdg. 38.27 *(978-1-4042-2647-0(8),* c7dcb355-12ad-4a2b-9bd6-5e815734870e) Rosen Publishing Group, Inc., The.

Baskes Litwin, Laura. Susan B. Anthony: Social Reformer & Feminist, 1 vol. 2016. (Heroes of the Women's Suffrage Movement Ser.). (ENG., Illus.). 128p. (gr. 6-6). 38.93 *(978-0-7660-7888-8(4),* 9937aa3a-d7e8-460d-9069-21ceca68976f) Enslow Publishing, LLC.

Bjornlund, Lydia D. Women of the Suffrage Movement. 2003. (Women in History Ser.). (ENG., Illus.). 112p. (J). 33.45 *(978-1-59018-173-7(5),* Lucent Bks.) Cengage Gale.

Bohannon, Lisa Frederiksen. Failure is Impossible: The Story of Susan B. Anthony. 2004. (Feminist Voices Ser.). (Illus.). 112p. (YA). (gr. 6-12). 23.95 *(978-1-883846-77-0(3),* First Biographies) Reynolds, Morgan Inc.

Boothroyd, Jennifer. Susan B. Anthony: A Life of Fairness. 2006. (Pull Ahead Bks.). (Illus.). 32p. (J). (gr. 3-7). lib. bdg. 22.60 *(978-0-8225-3479-2(7),* Lerner Pubns.) Lerner Publishing Group.

—Susan B. Anthony: Una Vida de Igualdad. Translations.com Staff, tr. 2006. (Libros para Avanzar-Biografías (Pull Ahead Books-Biographies) Ser.). (ENG & SPA., Illus.). 32p. (gr. k-3). lib. bdg. 22.60 *(978-0-8225-6234-4(0))* Lerner Publishing Group.

Brown, Don. A Voice from the Wilderness: The Story of Anna Howard Shaw. 2010. 32p. (J). (gr. k-3). pap. 5.95 *(978-0-618-58544-1(3))* Houghton Mifflin Harcourt Trade & Reference Pubs.

Carson, Mary Kay. Who Was Susan B. Anthony Vote? And Other Questions about Women's Suffrage. 2015. (Good Question! Ser.). (ENG., Illus.). 32p. (J). (gr. 2). pap. 5.95 *(978-1-4549-1242-2(1))* Sterling Publishing Co., Inc.

Chambers, Veronica & The Staff of The New York Times, The Staff. Finish the Fight! The Brave & Revolutionary Women Who Fought for the Right to Vote. The Staff of The New York Times, The Staff, illus. 2020. (ENG., Illus.). 144p. (J). (gr. 3-7). 18.99 *(978-0-358-40830-7(X),* 1789830, Versify) HarperCollins Pubs.

Connors, Kathleen. Life of Susan B. Anthony. 2014. (Famous Lives (Gareth Stevens Paperback) Ser.). (ENG.). 24p. (J). (gr. 2-4). 18.95 *(978-1-5311-8606-7(8))* Perfection Learning Corp.

—The Life of Susan B. Anthony, 1 vol., Vol. 1. 2013. (Famous Lives Ser.). (ENG.). 24p. (J). (gr. 1-2). 25.27 *(978-1-4824-0425-8(7),* acaba0c6-f2f2-4657-ad3c-0f0ca3e168d0) Stevens, Gareth Publishing LLLP.

Cooper, Meghan. The Women's Suffrage Movement, 1 vol. 2017. (Interwar Years Ser.). (ENG., Illus.). 128p. (YA). (gr. 9-9). 47.36 *(978-1-5026-2711-7(6),* 9fba2995-9bb5-4c20-8af0-ef0382acad3f) Cavendish Square Publishing LLC.

Day, Meredith & Adams, Colleen. A Primary Source Investigation of Women's Suffrage, 1 vol. 2015. (Uncovering American History Ser.). (ENG., Illus.). 64p. (J). (gr. 5-6). 36.13 *(978-1-4994-3519-1(3),* 660575d3-b2a5-4086-afca-025534c3c917, Rosen Central) Rosen Publishing Group, Inc., The.

Frey, Wendy. Citizen Heroes. 2007. (Illus.). 68p. (J). *(978-1-4105-0887-4(0)); (978-1-4105-0888-1(9))* Building Wings LLC.

Gaines, Alison. Mary Edwards Walker: The Only Female Medal of Honor Recipient, 1 vol. 2017. (Fearless Female Soldiers, Explorers, & Aviators Ser.). (ENG.). 128p. (YA). (gr. 9-9). 47.36 *(978-1-5026-2745-2(0),* 4f3af724-2a96-4315-a3da-8590d2a2d372) Cavendish Square Publishing LLC.

Gillibrand, Kirsten. Bold & Brave: Ten Heroes Who Won Women the Right to Vote. Kalman, Maira, illus. 40p. (J). (gr. 1-4). 2020. pap. 8.99 *(978-0-593-30266-8(4),* Dragonfly Bks.) 2018. 18.99 *(978-0-525-57901-4(X),* Knopf Bks. for Young Readers) 2018. (ENG.). lib. bdg. 21.99 *(978-0-525-57902-1(8),* Knopf Bks. for Young Readers) Random Hse. Children's Bks.

Goddu, Krystyna Poray. What's Your Story, Susan B. Anthony? 2016. (Cub Reporter Meets Famous Americans Ser.). (ENG., Illus.). 32p. (J). (gr. k-3). 26.65 *(978-1-4677-8785-7(X),* 199ae9d8-e2ff-4af1-8a22-f4579b2b7584, Lerner Pubns.) Lerner Publishing Group.

Havelin, Kate. Victoria Woodhull: Fearless Feminist. 2006. (Trailblazer Biographies Ser.). (ENG., Illus.). 112p. (gr. 5-9). lib. bdg. 31.93 *(978-0-8225-5986-3(2),* Lerner Pubns.) Lerner Publishing Group.

Heroes of the Women's Suffrage Movement, 12 vols. 2016. (Heroes of the Women's Suffrage Movement Ser.). (ENG.). 128p. (gr. 6-6). lib. bdg. 233.58 *(978-0-7660-7507-8(9),* 1559d9d3-c207-45a2-a632-b3d10cd66cd2) Enslow Publishing, LLC.

Herweck, Dona. Susan B. Anthony, 1 vol. 2nd rev. ed. 2014. (TIME for KIDS(r): Informational Text Ser.). (ENG., Illus.). 28p. (J). (gr. 2-3). lib. bdg. 23.96 *(978-1-4807-1063-4(6))* Teacher Created Materials, Inc.

Hicks, Peter. Documenting Women's Suffrage, 1 vol. (Documenting History Ser.). (ENG., Illus.). 48p. (gr. 7-7). 2010. (YA). lib. bdg. 34.47 *(978-1-4358-9672-7(6),* 64e2f741-0196-4463-9572-81ba734a002c) 2009. (J). pap. 12.75 *(978-1-4358-9675-8(0),* 8051fc89-f56d-4c1d-93b0-cc7f216609cf, Rosen Reference) Rosen Publishing Group, Inc., The.

Hollihan, Kerrie Logan. Rightfully Ours: How Women Won the Vote, 21 Activities. 2012. (For Kids Ser.: 43). (ENG., Illus.). 144p. (J). (gr. 4). pap. 18.99 *(978-1-883052-89-8(0))* Chicago Review Pr., Inc.

Hopkinson, Deborah. Susan B. Anthony: Fighter for Women's Rights. Bates, Amy, illus. 2005. 32p. (J). lib. bdg. 15.00 *(978-1-4242-1563-8(3))* Fitzgerald Bks.

—Susan B. Anthony: Fighter for Women's Rights (Ready-To-Read Level 3) Bates, Amy June, illus. 2005. (Ready-To-Read Stories of Famous Americans Ser.). (ENG.). 32p. (J). (gr. 1-3). pap. 4.99 *(978-0-689-86909-9(6),* Simon Spotlight) Simon Spotlight.

Jones, Naomi E. Ida B. Wells-Barnett: Suffragette & Social Activist, 1 vol. 2019. (African American Trailblazers Ser.). (ENG.). 128p. (gr. 9-9). pap. 22.16 *(978-1-5026-4560-9(2),* cb519ffa-ab7a-438d-b1e0-9a25e98d89c7) Cavendish Square Publishing LLC.

Kanefield, Teri. Susan B. Anthony: The Making of America #4. 2019. (Making of America Ser.). (ENG., Illus.). 240p. (J). (gr. 5-9). 16.99 *(978-1-4197-3401-4(6),* 1263701, Abrams Bks. for Young Readers) Abrams, Inc.

Kendall, Martha E. Susan B. Anthony: Fighter for Women's Voting Rights, 1 vol. 2014. (Legendary American Biographies Ser.). (ENG.). 96p. (gr. 6-6). 29.60 *(978-0-7660-6500-0(6),* 5b91bb09-ca37-4a55-b789-c3bd37a03e6e); pap. 13.88 *(978-0-7660-6501-7(4),* 3d2c3346-79bf-45c6-8cc5-a3ad33f1d8cf) Enslow Publishing, LLC.

Kennedy, Nancy B. Women Win the Vote! 19 for the 19th Amendment. 2020. (ENG., Illus.). 128p. (J). (gr. 5-9). 19.95 *(978-1-324-00414-1(2),* 340414, Norton Young Readers) Norton, W. W. & Co., Inc.

Kent, Deborah. Elizabeth Cady Stanton: Founder of the Women's Suffrage Movement, 1 vol. 2016. (Heroes of the Women's Suffrage Movement Ser.). (ENG.). 128p. (gr. 6-6). 38.93 *(978-0-7660-7889-5(2),* 05025743-f964-4f6c-8e70-67989020d66a) Enslow Publishing, LLC.

—Elizabeth Cady Stanton: Woman Knows the Cost of Life, 1 vol. 2008. (Americans: the Spirit of a Nation Ser.). (ENG., Illus.). 128p. (gr. 5-6). lib. bdg. 35.93 *(978-0-7660-3357-3(0),* a08165a5-32e5-45ad-8cb3-d3e3ffca7805) Enslow Publishing, LLC.

Kulling, Monica. Susan B. Anthony: Her Fight for Equal Rights. Plenzke, Maike, illus. 2020. (Step into Reading Ser.). 32p. (J). (gr. -1-1). pap. 4.99 *(978-0-593-11982-2(7),* Random Hse. Bks. for Young Readers) Random Hse. Children's Bks.

Lynch, Seth. Women's Suffrage, 1 vol. 2018. (Look at U. S. History Ser.). (ENG.). 32p. (gr. 2-2). 28.27 *(978-1-5382-2135-8(7),* 325fee0c-fff5-468c-8535-021f02d59803) Stevens, Gareth Publishing LLLP.

Mattern, Joanne. Elizabeth Cady Stanton & Susan B. Anthony: Fighting Together for Women's Rights. 2009. (Women Who Shaped History Ser.). 24p. (gr. 2-3). 42.50 *(978-1-60854-818-7(X),* PowerKids Pr.) Rosen Publishing Group, Inc., The.

McPherson, Stephanie Sammartino. Susan B. Anthony. 2006. (History Maker Bios Ser.). (Illus.). 48p. (J). (gr. 3-7). lib. bdg. 26.60 *(978-0-8225-5938-2(2),* Lerner Pubns.) Lerner Publishing Group.

Mosley, Shelley & Charles, John. The Suffragists in Literature for Youth: The Fight for the Vote. annot. ed. 2006. (Literature for Youth Ser.: 10). (ENG.). 342p. (gr. 3-7). per. 87.00 *(978-0-8108-5372-0(8))* Scarecrow Pr., Inc.

National Geographic Learning. Language, Literacy & Vocabulary - Reading Expeditions (U. S. History & Life): Women Work for Change. 2006. (Avenues Ser.). (ENG., Illus.). 36p. (J). pap. 20.95 *(978-0-7922-5456-0(2))* CENGAGE Learning.

—Reading Expeditions (Social Studies: People Who Changed America): Votes for Women. 2007. (ENG., Illus.). 40p. (J). pap. 21.95 *(978-0-7922-8626-4(X))* CENGAGE Learning.

Ohlin, Nancy. Women's Suffrage. Simó, Roger, illus. 2018. (Blast Back! Ser.). (ENG.). 112p. (J). (gr. 2-5). 16.99 *(978-1-4998-0619-9(1));* pap. 5.99 *(978-1-4998-0618-2(3))* Little Bee Books Inc.

Orr, Tamra B. The Life & Times of Susan B. Anthony. 2006. (Profiles in American History Ser.). (Illus.). 48p. (J). (gr. 3-7). lib. bdg. 29.95 *(978-1-58415-445-7(4))* Mitchell Lane Pubs.

Penne, Barbra. Susan B. Anthony: Pioneering Leader of the Women's Rights Movement, 1 vol. 2015. (Britannica Beginner Bios Ser.). (ENG.). 32p. (J). (gr. 2-3). 26.06 *(978-1-62275-951-4(6),* 0f247e64-5aaa-4ae5-bd39-166dccba8de4, Britannica Educational Publishing) Rosen Publishing Group, Inc., The.

Pollack, Pam, et al. Who Was Susan B. Anthony? Lacey, Mike, illus. 2014. (Who Was? Ser.). (ENG.). 112p. (J). (gr. 3-7). 6.99 *(978-0-448-47963-7(X),* Penguin Workshop) Penguin Young Readers Group.

Rappaport, Doreen. Elizabeth Started All the Trouble. Faulkner, Matt, illus. 2016. (ENG.). 40p. (J). (gr. -1-3). 18.99 *(978-0-7868-5142-3(2))* Disney Pr.

Raum, Elizabeth. The Life of Susan B. Anthony. 2019. (Sequence Change Maker Biographies Ser.). (ENG.). 32p. (J). (gr. 2-5). lib. bdg. *(978-1-68151-681-3(0),* 10813) Amicus.

Roberts, David. Suffragette: the Battle for Equality. Roberts, David, illus. 2019. (ENG., Illus.). 128p. (J). (gr. 2-5). 25.00 *(978-1-5362-0841-2(8))* Candlewick Pr.

Sjonger, Rebecca. Susan B. Anthony: On a Woman's Right to Vote. 2019. (Deconstructing Powerful Speeches Ser.). 48p. (J). (gr. 6-6). pap. *(978-0-7787-5255-4(0))* Crabtree Publishing Co.

Slade, Suzanne. Friends for Freedom: The Story of Susan B. Anthony & Frederick Douglass. Tadgell, Nicole, illus. 2014. (ENG.). 40p. (J). (gr. 1-4). 16.95 *(978-1-58089-568-2(9))* Charlesbridge Publishing, Inc.

—Friends for Freedom: The Story of Susan B. Anthony & Frederick Douglass. 2014. (Illus.). 39p. *(978-1-60734-651-7(6))* Charlesbridge Publishing, Inc.

Somervill, Barbara A. Votes for Women! The Story of Carrie Chapman Catt. 2004. (Feminist Voices Ser.). (Illus.). 128p. (YA). (gr. 6-12). 23.95 *(978-1-883846-96-1(X),* First Biographies) Reynolds, Morgan Inc.

Spiller, Sara. Susan B. Anthony. Bane, Jeff, illus. 2019. (My Early Library: My Itty-Bitty Bio Ser.). (ENG.). 24p. (J). (gr. k-1). pap. 12.79 *(978-1-5341-3923-7(0),* 212521); lib. bdg. 30.64 *(978-1-5341-4267-1(3),* 212520) Cherry Lake Publishing.

Stoltman, Joan. Elizabeth Cady Stanton, 1 vol. 2018. (Little Biographies of Big People Ser.). (ENG.). 24p. (gr. 1-2). 24.27 *(978-1-5382-1836-5(4),* c624885d-3665-4dee-b5d7-777942743dfd) Stevens, Gareth Publishing LLLP.

Stone, Tanya Lee. Elizabeth Leads the Way: Elizabeth Cady Stanton & the Right to Vote. Gibbon, Rebecca, illus. 2010. (ENG.). 32p. (J). (gr. 1-5). pap. 8.99 *(978-0-312-60236-9(7),* 900064232) Square Fish.

Van Meter, Larry A. Women Win the Vote: The Hard-Fought Battle for Women's Suffrage, 1 vol. 2008. (America's Living History Ser.). (ENG., Illus.). 128p. (gr. 5-6). lib. bdg. 35.93 *(978-0-7660-2940-8(9),* e2ef301e-36a7-40e3-aecf-b97a243931c4) Enslow Publishing, LLC.

Vink, Amanda. Suffragists & Those Who Opposed Them, 1 vol. 2019. (Opponents in American History Ser.). (ENG.). 32p. (gr. 4-5). 27.93 *(978-1-5383-4371-5(1),* 58d951df-193e-49d1-93ed-d1f796e00309, PowerKids Pr.) Rosen Publishing Group, Inc., The.

White, Linda Arms. I Could Do That! Esther Morris Gets Women the Vote. Carpenter, Nancy, illus. 2005. (ENG.). 40p. (J). (gr. 2-4). 18.99 *(978-0-374-33527-4(3),* 900022004, Farrar, Straus & Giroux (BYR)) Farrar, Straus & Giroux.

—I Could Do That! Esther Morris Gets Women the Vote. unabr. ed. 2006. (J). (gr. 2-4). 29.95 *(978-0-439-90582-4(6),* WHCD692) Weston Woods Studios, Inc.

Zimet, Susan & Hasak-Lowy, Todd. Roses & Radicals: The Epic Story of How American Women Won the Right to Vote. 2020. 176p. (J). (gr. 5). pap. 9.99 *(978-0-425-29146-7(4),* Puffin Books) Penguin Young Readers Group.

SUGAR

Allard, Mario, illus. Caillou at the Sugar Shack. 2018. (Clubhouse Ser.). (ENG.). 24p. (J). (gr. -1-1). 3.99 *(978-2-89718-467-4(1))* Caillouet, Gerry.

Aronson, Marc & Budhos, Marina. Sugar Changed the World: A Story of Magic, Spice, Slavery, Freedom, & Science. 2010. (ENG., Illus.). 176p. (YA). (gr. 7-18). 21.99 *(978-0-618-57492-6(1),* 100422, Clarion Bks.) HarperCollins Pubs.

Braithwaite, Jill. From Cane to Sugar. 2004. (Start to Finish Ser.). (Illus.). 24p. (J). (gr. k-2). lib. bdg. 18.60 *(978-0-8225-0940-0(7))* Lerner Publishing Group.

Eagen, Rachel. The Biography of Sugar. 2005. (How did That Get There? Ser.). (ENG., Illus.). 32p. (J). (gr. 4-5). pap. *(978-0-7787-2521-3(9))*; lib. bdg. *(978-0-7787-2485-8(9))* Crabtree Publishing Co.

Friesen, Helen Lepp. Maple Syrup. 2011. 24p. (YA). (gr. 2-4). *(978-1-77071-660-5(2));* pap. *(978-1-77071-666-7(1))* Weigl Educational Pubs. Ltd.

Furgang, Adam. Salty & Sugary Snacks: The Incredibly Disgusting Story, 1 vol. 2011. (Incredibly Disgusting Food Ser.). (ENG., Illus.). 48p. (YA). (gr. 5-8). pap. 12.75 *(978-1-4488-2283-6(1),* d0080215-01f4-44f5-929a-f81e27126a17, Rosen Reference); lib. bdg. 34.47 *(978-1-4488-1267-7(4),* d5bb4c7d-9142-436e-8f91-6cb697ad4aa8) Rosen Publishing Group, Inc., The.

Hayes, Amy. Turning Sap into Maple Syrup, 1 vol. 2015. (Step-By-Step Transformations Ser.). (ENG., Illus.). 24p. (gr. 1-1). pap. 9.23 *(978-1-5026-0457-6(4),* e8c1d030-cdc8-47ef-b33b-a3c916a2329a) Cavendish Square Publishing LLC.

Laforest, Carine. Caillou at the Sugar Shack. 2018. (Caillou 8x8 Bks). (ENG.). 24p. (J). (gr. -1-k). 13.89 *(978-1-64310-218-4(4))* Penworthy Co., LLC, The.

O'Ryan, Ellie. The Sugary Secrets Behind Candy: Ready-To-Read Level 3. McClurkan, Rob, illus. 2015. (Science of Fun Stuff Ser.). (ENG.). 48p. (J). (gr. 1-3). pap. 4.99 *(978-1-4814-5626-5(1),* Simon Spotlight) Simon Spotlight.

Owings, Lisa. From Sugar Beet to Sugar. 2015. (Start to Finish, Second Ser.). (ENG., Illus.). 24p. (J). (gr. k-3). lib. bdg. 23.99 *(978-1-4677-6020-1(X),* 865a434f-c17d-42f1-a80a-0ccee55f76da); E-Book 35.99 *(978-1-4677-6290-8(3))* Lerner Publishing Group. (Lerner Pubns.).

Perritano, John. Sugar & Sweeteners. 2017. (Illus.). 64p. (J). *(978-1-4222-3744-1(3))* Mason Crest.

Schuh, Mari. Sugars & Fats. 2012. (What's on Myplate? Ser.). (ENG.). 24p. (J). (gr. k-1). pap. 43.74 *(978-1-4296-9423-0(8),* 18616, Capstone Pr.) Capstone.

WalkerTheo. SUGAR: OUR GUILTY PLEASURE LOW INTERMEDIATE BOOK WITH ONLINE ACCESS, 1 vol. 2014. (ENG., Illus.). 28p. (J). pap., E-Book 9.50 *(978-1-107-68146-0(4))* Cambridge Univ. Pr.

World Book, Inc. Staff, contrib. by. Sugar. 2019. (Illus.). 48p. (J). *(978-0-7166-2865-1(1))* World Bk., Inc.

SUGARCANE

Eagen, Rachel. The Biography of Sugar. 2005. (How Did That Get Here? Ser.). (ENG., Illus.). 32p. (J). (gr. 4-5). lib. bdg. *(978-0-7787-2485-8(9))* Crabtree Publishing Co.

SUICIDE

see also Assisted Suicide; Right to Die

Bleuel, Amy. Project Semicolon: Your Story Isn't Over. 2017. (ENG., Illus.). 352p. (YA). (gr. 9). pap. 9.99 *(978-0-06-246652-5(6),* HarperCollins) HarperCollins Pubs.

Cafferty Lerner, Alicia & Wilmoth Lerner, Adrienne, eds. Suicide in Arthur Miller's Death of a Salesman, 1 vol. 2008. (Social Issues in Literature Ser.). (ENG., Illus.). 200p. (gr. 10-12). pap. 33.00 *(978-0-7377-4019-6(1),* 4da78d2c-4f5e-4645-8a33-13f1e73d4ee8); lib. bdg. 48.03 *(978-0-7377-4018-9(3),* b2e75a2b-fa46-44c5-9033-56d098e7bd1d) Greenhaven Publishing LLC. (Greenhaven Publishing).

Cartlidge, Cherese. Teens & Suicide. 2017. (Teen Mental Health Ser.). (ENG., Illus.). 80p. (J). (gr. 5-12). *(978-1-68282-131-2(5))* ReferencePoint Pr., Inc.

Chandler, Matt. Understanding Suicide. 2019. (21st Century Skills Library: Upfront Health Ser.). (ENG., Illus.). 32p. (J). (gr. 4-8). pap. 14.21 *(978-1-5341-5086-7(2),* 213651); lib. bdg. 32.07 *(978-1-5341-4800-0(0),* 213650) Cherry Lake Publishing.

Eagen, Rachel. Suicide. 2010. (ENG.). 48p. (J). pap. *(978-0-7787-2138-3(8))*; lib. bdg. *(978-0-7787-2131-4(0))* Crabtree Publishing Co.

Esherick, Joan. The Silent Cry: Teen Suicide & Self-Destructive Behaviors. 2006. (Science of Health Ser.). (Illus.). 128p. (YA). lib. bdg. 24.95 *(978-1-59084-851-7(9))* Mason Crest.

Goldsmith, Connie. Understanding Suicide: A National Epidemic. 2016. (ENG., Illus.). 112p. (YA). (gr. 7-12). 35.99 *(978-1-4677-8570-9(9),* 6d06d18a-af10-42f0-953e-91d7410b74fe, Twenty-First Century Bks.) Lerner Publishing Group.

Huddle, Lorena & Schleifer, Jay. Teen Suicide, 1 vol. 2011. (Teen Mental Health Ser.). (ENG., Illus.). 48p. (YA). (gr. 5-6). lib. bdg. 34.47 *(978-1-4488-4586-6(6),* d95d7194-8901-4ee2-925c-400d4de402c1) Rosen Publishing Group, Inc., The.

Kahn, Robert, et al. Bobby & Mandee's Too Solid for Suicide. 2017. (ENG., Illus.). (YA). pap. 9.95 *(978-1-947825-28-4(3))* Yorkshire Publishing Group.

Knightsmith, Pooky. Can I Tell You about Self-Harm? A Guide for Friends, Family & Professionals. Evans, Elise, illus. 2018. (Can I Tell You About...? Ser.). 72p. (J). pap. 15.95 *(978-1-78592-428-6(1),* 696716) Kingsley, Jessica Pubs. GBR. Dist: Hachette UK Distribution.

Libal, Joyce. Antidepressants & Suicide: When Treatment Kills. (Antidepressants Ser.). (Illus.). 112p. (YA). (gr. 7-18). 2008. lib. bdg. 24.95 *(978-1-4222-0099-5(X))* 2007. pap. 14.95 *(978-1-4222-0407-8(3))* Mason Crest.

Marcovitz, Hal. Teens & Suicide. Developed in Association with the Gallup Organization Staff, ed. 2013. (Gallup Youth Survey: Major Issues & Trends Ser.: 14). 112p. (J). (gr. 7-18). 24.95 *(978-1-4222-2958-3(0))* Mason Crest.

—Teens & Suicide. 2008. (Gallup Youth Survey, Major Issues & Trends Ser.). (Illus.). 112,128p. (YA). (gr. 7-9). lib. bdg. 22.95 *(978-1-59084-724-4(5))* Mason Crest.

Pack-Jordan, Erin. Everything You Need to Know about Suicide & Self-Harm, 1 vol. 2018. (Need to Know Library). (ENG.). 64p. (J). (gr. 6-6). pap. 13.95 *(978-1-5081-8354-9(6),* c914db63-ccba-4ec3-89d0-cc54af2859b1, Rosen Young Adult) Rosen Publishing Group, Inc., The.

Parks, Peggy J. How Can Suicide Be Reduced? 2014. (In Controversy Ser.). (ENG., Illus.). 96p. (J). lib. bdg. *(978-1-60152-662-5(8))* ReferencePoint Pr., Inc.

Peters, Jennifer, ed. Critical Perspectives on Assisted Suicide, 1 vol. 2019. (Analyzing the Issues Ser.). (ENG.). 232p. (gr. 8-8). 50.93 *(978-1-9785-0327-4(X),* a8777e67-b3f0-4f42-a70b-fcf07d72619f) Enslow Publishing, LLC.

Peterson, Judy Monroe. I'm Suicidal, Now What?, 1 vol. 2015. (Teen Life 411 Ser.). (ENG., Illus.). 112p. (J). (gr. 7-7). 38.80 *(978-1-4994-6136-7(4),* a8b7a6fd-9500-4f9c-befb-9ea9f6b496e4, Rosen Young Adult) Rosen Publishing Group, Inc., The.

Powell, Jillian. Self-Harm & Suicide, 1 vol. 2008. (Emotional Health Issues Ser.). (ENG., Illus.). 48p. (YA). (gr. 5-6). lib. bdg. 33.67 *(978-0-8368-9202-4(X),* 8da98a51-125a-42a6-abc7-8aba982b6538) Stevens, Gareth Publishing LLLP.

Salomon, Ron. Suicide. 2007. (Psychological Disorders Ser.). (ENG., Illus.). 109p. (gr. 7-12). lib. bdg. 37.50 *(978-0-7910-9007-7(8),* P126121, Facts On File) Infobase Holdings, Inc.

Smid, Emmi. Luna's Red Hat: An Illustrated Storybook to Help Children Cope with Loss & Suicide. Smid, Emmi, illus. 2015. (Illus.). 34p. (J). 21.95 *(978-1-84905-629-8(3),* 693789) Kingsley, Jessica Pubs. GBR. Dist: Hachette UK Distribution.

Steffens, Bradley. The Suicide Epidemic. 2019. (ENG.). 80p. (J). (gr. 6-12). 41.27 *(978-1-68282-741-3(0))* ReferencePoint Pr., Inc.

—Thinking Critically: Teen Suicide. 2018. (Thinking Critically Ser.). (ENG.). 80p. (YA). (gr. 6-12). 39.93 *(978-1-68282-447-4(0))* ReferencePoint Pr., Inc.

Teen Mental Health: Set 2, 12 vols. 2011. (Teen Mental Health Ser.). (ENG., Illus.). 48p. (J). (gr. 5-6). 206.82 *(978-1-4488-4873-7(3),*

2c86fe20-8343-4ec8-a443-3bbb661d5466) Rosen Publishing Group, Inc., The.

Thiele, Christine. What Catholic Teens Should Know about Suicide. Larkin, Jean K., ed. 2004. (What Catholic Teens Should Know Ser.). (Illus.). 8p. (YA). 7.95 *(978-0-89837-240-3(2)*, 441110) Pflaum Publishing Group.

Wahl, Elizabeth. Do You Have a Friend Who Is Suicidal?, 1 vol. 2015. (Got Issues? Ser.). (ENG., Illus.). 112p. (gr. 7-8). lib. bdg. 38.93 *(978-0-7660-7191-9(X)*, b6022bb2-cd6e-43e7-8cfc-34595c1b41a8) Enslow Publishing, LLC.

Zadunajsky, Donna M. Talk to Me. Stevens, Deborah Bowman, ed. 2018. (Help Me! Ser.: Vol. 2). (ENG., Illus.). 122p. (YA). 23.99 *(978-1-938037-73-3(1))* Zadunajsky, Donna M.

SUICIDE—FICTION

Allison, Jennifer. Gilda Joyce, Psychic Investigator. 2006. (Gilda Joyce Ser.: 1). (ENG.). 336p. (J). (gr. 5-18). reprint ed. 9.99 *(978-0-14-240698-4(8)*, Puffin Books) Penguin Young Readers Group.

Anonymous. Jay's Journal. Sparks, Beatrice, ed. (Anonymous Diaries). (ENG.). 240p. (YA). 2012. (gr. 9). 17.99 *(978-1-4424-8094-0(7))* 2010. (gr. 7). pap. 11.99 *(978-1-4424-1993-3(8))* Simon Pulse. (Simon Pulse).

Asher, Jay. Thirteen Reasons Why. 2014. (ENG.). 336p. (YA). 15.24 *(978-1-63245-099-9(2))* Lectorum Pubns., Inc.

—Thirteen Reasons Why. 2009. 11.72 *(978-0-7848-3782-5(1)*, Everbind) Marco Bk. Co.

—Thirteen Reasons Why. (ENG.). (YA). (gr. 7-18). 2011. 336p. pap. 11.99 *(978-1-59514-188-0(X))* 2007. 320p. 18.99 *(978-1-59514-171-2(5))* Penguin Young Readers Group. (Razorbill).

—Thirteen Reasons Why. 2011. (ENG.). (YA). (gr. 7-12). lib. bdg. 21.60 *(978-1-60686-991-8(4))* Perfection Learning Corp.

—Thirteen Reasons Why. 2011. (CHI & ENG.). 304p. (YA). (gr. 7-12). pap. *(978-986-6345-81-4(5))* Spring International Pubs.

—Thirteen Reasons Why. 2011. lib. bdg. 22.10 *(978-0-606-15085-9(4))* Turtleback.

—Thirteen Reasons Why 10th Anniversary Edition. 10th anniv. ed. 2016. (ENG.). 352p. (YA). (gr. 7). 18.99 *(978-1-59514-788-2(8)*, Razorbill) Penguin Young Readers Group.

—13 Reasons Why. 2017. (ENG., Illus.). 320p. (YA). (gr. 7). pap. 11.99 *(978-0-451-47829-0(0)*, Razorbill) Penguin Young Readers Group.

Balog, Cyn. That Night. 2019. (ENG.). 320p. (YA). (gr. 8-12). pap. 12.99 *(978-1-4926-7904-2(6))* Sourcebooks, Inc.

Banting, Celia. I only said I couldn't Cope. 2006. (Illus.). 240p. (YA). per. 14.99 *(978-0-9786648-2-4(5))* Wighita Pr.

—I Only Said Yes So That They'd Like Me. 2006. (Illus.). 224p. (YA). per. 14.99 *(978-0-9786648-1-7(7))* Wighita Pr.

Bernard, Romily. Remember Me. 2014. (Find Me Ser.: 2). (ENG.). 368p. (YA). (gr. 8). 17.99 *(978-0-06-222906-9(0)*, HarperTeen) HarperCollins Pubs.

Borris, Albert. Crash into Me. (ENG.). 272p. (YA). (gr. 9). 2010. pap. 9.99 *(978-1-4169-9827-3(6))* 2009. 16.99 *(978-1-4169-7435-2(0))* Simon Pulse. (Simon Pulse).

Bradley, Kimberly Brubaker. Fighting Words. 2020. (ENG.). 272p. (J). (gr. 5-7). 17.99 *(978-1-9848-1568-2(7)*, Dial Bks) Penguin Young Readers Group.

Brewer, Zac. Madness. 2017. (ENG.). 304p. (YA). (gr. 9). 17.99 *(978-0-06-245785-1(3)*, HarperTeen) HarperCollins Pubs.

Butcher, Kristin. The Hemingway Tradition. 2004. 92p. 19.95 *(978-0-7569-4299-1(3))* Perfection Learning Corp.

Carlson, Melody. Beyond Reach. 2007. (Secret Life of Samantha Mcgregor Ser.: 2). 256p. (J). (gr. 7-12). per. 15.99 *(978-1-59052-693-4(7)*, Multnomah Bks.) Crown Publishing Group, The.

Chalifour, Francis. After. 2005. 144p. (YA). (gr. 7). pap. 7.95 *(978-0-88776-705-0(2)*, Tundra Bks.) Tundra Bks. CAN. Dist: Penguin Random Hse. LLC.

—Le Fils du Pendu. 2006. 168p. (YA). (gr. 7). per. 7.95 *(978-0-88776-795-1(8))* Tundra Bks. CAN. Dist: Penguin Random Hse. LLC.

Chapman, Elsie. Along the Indigo. 2018. (ENG.). 392p. (gr. 8-17). 17.99 *(978-1-4197-2531-9(9)*, Amulet Bks.) Abrams, Inc.

Chapman, Erica M. Teach Me to Forget. 2016. (ENG.). 288p. (YA). 17.99 *(978-1-4405-9457-1(0)*, Simon Pulse) Simon Pulse.

Chayil, Eishes. Hush. 2012. (ENG.). 368p. (YA). (gr. 9-12). pap. 10.99 *(978-0-8027-2332-1(2)*, 900076205, Bloomsbury USA Childrens) Bloomsbury Publishing USA.

Cohn, Rachel. You Know Where to Find Me. 2009. (ENG.). 224p. (YA). (gr. 7). pap. 8.99 *(978-0-689-87860-2(5)*, Simon & Schuster Bks. For Young Readers) Simon & Schuster Bks. For Young Readers.

—You Know Where to Find Me. 2008. (ENG.). 204p. (YA). (gr. 7-12). 22.44 *(978-0-689-87859-6(1))* Simon & Schuster, Inc.

Connelly, Neil. Into the Hurricane. 2017. (ENG.). 240p. (YA). (gr. 9). 17.99 *(978-0-545-85381-1(8)*, Levine, Arthur A. Bks.) Scholastic, Inc.

Cross, Mimi. Before Goodbye, 0 vols. 2016. (ENG.). 399p. (YA). (gr. 8-12). pap. 9.99 *(978-1-5039-4972-0(9)*, 9781503949720, Skyscape) Amazon Publishing.

Crutcher, Chris. Chinese Handcuffs. 2004. (ENG.). 304p. (YA). (gr. 9). pap. 9.99 *(978-0-06-059839-6(5)*, Greenwillow Bks.) HarperCollins Pubs.

Davis, Lane. I Swear. (ENG., Illus.). 288p. (YA). (gr. 9). 2013. pap. 10.99 *(978-1-4424-3507-0(0))* 2012. 16.99 *(978-1-4424-3506-3(2))* Simon & Schuster Bks. For Young Readers. (Simon & Schuster Bks. For Young Readers).

Deal, Paul. Lighting Candles. 2003. 122p. (YA). 20.95 *(978-0-595-65804-6(0))*; pap. 10.95 *(978-0-595-28457-3(4))* iUniverse, Inc.

Deuker, Carl. High Heat. 2005. (ENG.). 352p. (J). (gr. 8-18). pap. 8.99 *(978-0-06-057248-8(5)*, HarperTeen) HarperCollins Pubs.

Donley, Jan. The Side Door. 2010. (ENG.). 288p. (J). (gr. 9). pap. 14.95 *(978-1-935226-12-3(6))* Spinsters Ink Bks.

Dunn, Pintip. The Darkest Lie. 2016. viii, 292p. (YA). *(978-1-5182-2703-5(1)*, Kensington Bks.) Kensington Publishing Corp.

Ella, Sara. Coral, 1 vol. 2019. (ENG.). 384p. (YA). 18.99 *(978-0-7852-2445-7(9))* Nelson, Thomas Inc.

Ford, Michael Thomas. Suicide Notes. (ENG.). (YA). (gr. 9). 2019. 320p. pap. 15.99 *(978-0-06-284551-1(9)*, HarperCollins) 2010. 304p. pap. 9.99 *(978-0-06-073757-3(3)*, HarperTeen) HarperCollins Pubs.

Forman, Gayle. I Was Here. l.t. ed. 2015. 420p. 24.99 *(978-1-4104-8255-6(3))* Cengage Gale.

—I Was Here. 2016. (ENG.). 304p. (YA). (gr. 9). pap. 10.99 *(978-0-14-751403-5(7)*, Speak) Penguin Young Readers Group.

—I Was Here. 2016. lib. bdg. 22.10 *(978-0-606-38404-9(9))* Turtleback.

Fortunati, Karen. The Weight of Zero. 2018. (ENG.). 400p. (YA). (gr. 9). 11.99 *(978-1-101-93892-8(7)*, Ember) Random Hse. Children's Bks.

Freymann-Weyr, Garret. Stay with Me. 2007. (ENG.). 320p. (YA). (gr. 9-12). pap. 17.99 *(978-0-618-88404-9(1)*, 487146, Clarion Bks.) HarperCollins Pubs.

Gallier, Laura. The Delusion: We All Have Our Demons. 2017. (Delusion Ser.: 1). (ENG.). 336p. (YA). 22.99 *(978-1-4964-2236-1(8)*, 20_29568, Wander) Tyndale Hse. Pubs.

Giles, Gail. What Happened to Cass McBride? 2007. 211p. 18.00 *(978-0-7569-8178-5(6))* Perfection Learning Corp.

—What Happened to Cass Mcbride? 2007. (ENG.). 240p. (J). (gr. 10-17). per. 13.99 *(978-0-316-16639-3(1))* Little, Brown Bks. for Young Readers.

—What Happened to Cass McBride? A Novel. 2006. (ENG.). 224p. pap. *(978-0-00-639197-5(4)*, Harper Trophy) HarperCollins Pubs.

Going, K. L. Fat Kid Rules the World. 2004. (ENG.). 224p. (YA). (gr. 7-18). reprint ed. pap. 10.99 *(978-0-14-240208-5(7)*, Penguin Books) Penguin Young Readers Group.

Gonzales, S. The Law of Inertia. 2018. (ENG.). 353p. (YA). pap. 19.99 *(978-1-944995-87-4(0))* Amberjack Publishing Co.

Goobie, Beth. Who Owns Kelly Paddik?, 1 vol. 2003. (Orca Soundings Ser.). (ENG.). 128p. (YA). (gr. 8-12). pap. 9.95 *(978-1-55143-239-7(0))* Orca Bk. Pubs. USA.

—Who Owns Kelly Paddik? 2004. (Orca Soundings Ser.). 89p. 19.95 *(978-0-7569-4358-5(2))* Perfection Learning Corp.

Gormally, Eleanor. The Little Flower Bulb: Helping Children Bereaved by Suicide. Loki, #VALUE! & Splink, illus. 2011. (ENG.). 32p. (J). (gr. -1-3). pap. 21.95 *(978-1-84730-260-1(2))* Veritas Pubns. IRL. Dist: Casemate Pubs. & Bk. Distributors, LLC.

Hand, Cynthia. The Last Time We Say Goodbye. (ENG.). 400p. (YA). (gr. 8). 2016. pap. 15.99 *(978-0-06-231848-0(9))* 2015. 17.99 *(978-0-06-231847-3(0))* HarperCollins Pubs. (HarperTeen).

—The Last Time We Say Goodbye. 2016. (YA). lib. bdg. 20.85 *(978-0-606-38130-7(9))* Turtleback.

Healey, Karen. The Shattering. 2013. (ENG.). 336p. (YA). (gr. 7-17). pap. 8.99 *(978-0-316-12573-4(3))* Little, Brown Bks. for Young Readers.

Hodkin, Michelle. The Becoming of Noah Shaw. (Shaw Confessions Ser.: 1). (ENG.). (YA). (gr. 9). 2018. 400p. pap. 12.99 *(978-1-4814-5644-9(X))* 2017. (Illus.). 384p. 18.99 *(978-1-4814-5643-2(1))* Simon & Schuster Bks. For Young Readers. (Simon & Schuster Bks. For Young Readers).

—The Reckoning of Noah Shaw. 2018. (Shaw Confessions Ser.: 2). (ENG., Illus.). 400p. (YA). (gr. 9). 19.99 *(978-1-4814-5646-3(6)*, Simon & Schuster Bks. For Young Readers) Simon & Schuster Bks. For Young Readers.

Holtz-Bacha, Christina. Second Chance. 2007. 96p. 8.95 *(978-0-9773082-6-2(X))* LBF Bks., LLC.

Hopkins, Ellen. Impulse. (ENG.). (YA). (gr. 9-12). 2008. 688p. pap. 14.99 *(978-1-4169-0357-4(7))* 2007. 672p. 24.99 *(978-1-4169-0356-7(9))* McElderry, Margaret K. Bks. (McElderry, Margaret K. Bks.).

—Rumble. 2016. lib. bdg. 24.50 *(978-0-606-38277-9(1))* Turtleback.

Hubbard, Jennifer. Try Not to Breathe. 2013. (ENG.). 256p. (YA). (gr. 9). pap. 8.99 *(978-0-14-242387-5(4)*, Speak) Penguin Young Readers Group.

Johnston, Jeffry W. Fragments. 2007. (ENG.). 208p. (YA). (gr. 7). per. 9.99 *(978-1-4169-2486-9(8)*, Simon Pulse) Simon Pulse.

Kaulen, Diane Bouman. In the Wake of Suicide: A Child's Journey. McAdoo, Grami & McAdoo, O'Pa, illus. 2008. (J). (gr. 3-5). 14.95 *(978-0-9764026-5-7(3))* Longhorn Creek Pr.

Kirby, Jessi. Moonglass. (ENG.). (YA). (gr. 7). 2012. 256p. pap. 11.99 *(978-1-4424-1695-6(5))* 2011. 240p. 16.99 *(978-1-4424-1694-9(7))* Simon & Schuster Bks. For Young Readers. (Simon & Schuster Bks. For Young Readers).

Konen, Leah. The after Girls. 2013. (ENG.). 304p. (YA). 17.95 *(978-1-4405-6108-5(7)*, Simon Pulse) Simon Pulse.

LaCour, Nina. Hold Still. 2019. (ENG.). 272p. (YA). (gr. 7). pap. 11.99 *(978-0-525-55608-4(7)*, Penguin Books) Penguin Young Readers Group.

Lecesne, James. Trevor: A Novella. (Illus.). (J). (gr. 5-9). 2013. 112p. pap. 9.95 *(978-1-60980-487-9(2))* 2012. (ENG., 114p. 14.95 *(978-1-60980-420-6(1))* Seven Stories Pr. (Triangle Square).

Leveen, Tom. Random. 2014. (ENG., Illus.). 224p. (YA). (gr. 9). 17.99 *(978-1-4424-9956-0(7)*, Simon Pulse) Simon Pulse.

Lynch, Chris. Freewill. 2006. 148p. (YA). (gr. 7-10). reprint ed. 16.00 *(978-0-7567-9869-7(8))* DIANE Publishing Co.

Maguire, Eden. Arizona. 2010. (Beautiful Dead Ser.: 2). (ENG.). 288p. (YA). (gr. 8-12). pap. 11.99 *(978-1-4022-3945-8(9))* Sourcebooks, Inc.

Maynard, Joyce. The Cloud Chamber. 2006. (ENG.). 288p. (YA). (gr. 7-7). pap. 13.99 *(978-1-4169-2699-3(2)*, Simon Pulse) Simon Pulse.

McDaniel, Lurlene. Breathless. 2010. (ENG.). 176p. (YA). (gr. 7). mass mkt. 7.99 *(978-0-440-24016-7(6)*, Delacorte Bks. for Young Readers) Random Hse. Children's Bks.

McDaniel, Lurlene N. So Much to Live For: The Dawn Rochelle Series, Book Three. 2003. (Lurlene Mcdaniel Bks.: No. 3). (ENG., Illus.). 160p. (YA). (gr. 7-12). reprint ed. pap. 7.99 *(978-1-58196-005-1(0)*, e0f6edb2-6bcb-48fe-95d5-a1143197d53a, Darby Creek) Lerner Publishing Group.

McGhee, Alison. What I Leave Behind. (ENG.). (YA). (gr. 9). 2019. 224p. pap. 11.99 *(978-1-4814-7657-7(2))* 2018. (Illus.). 208p. 18.99 *(978-1-4814-7656-0(4))* Simon & Schuster Children's Publishing. (Atheneum Bks. for Young Readers).

Messer, Celeste M. A Message from Teddy. Hoeffner, Deb, illus. 2004. 82-92p. 4.95 *(978-0-9702171-5-8(3))* AshleyAlan Enterprises.

Mickle, Shelley Fraser. The Turning Hour. 2004. 264p. (YA). pap. 16.95 *(978-1-57966-008-6(8))* River City Publishing.

Mitchell, Todd. Backwards. 2013. (ENG.). 288p. (YA). (gr. 7). 17.99 *(978-0-7636-6277-6(1))* Candlewick Pr.

Moon, Sarah. Sparrow. 2019. (ENG.). 272p. (YA). (gr. 7-7). pap. 10.99 *(978-1-338-31286-7(3)*, Levine, Arthur A. Bks.) Scholastic, Inc.

Niven, Jennifer. All the Bright Places. 2015. 432p. pap. *(978-0-14-135703-4(7))* Penguin Bks., Ltd.

—All the Bright Places. (ENG.). (YA). (gr. 9). 2016. 416p. pap. 10.99 *(978-0-385-75591-7(0)*, Ember) 2015. 400p. 19.99 *(978-0-385-75588-7(0)*, Knopf Bks. for Young Readers) Random Hse. Children's Bks.

—All the Bright Places. 2016. lib. bdg. 22.10 *(978-0-606-38876-4(1))* Turtleback.

Pan, Emily X. R. The Astonishing Color of After. 2019. (ENG.). 480p. (YA). (gr. 7-17). pap. 11.99 *(978-0-316-46401-7(5))* Little, Brown Bks. for Young Readers.

Peters, Julie Anne. By the Time You Read This, I'll Be Dead. 2011. (ENG.). 240p. (J). (gr. 5-9). pap. 11.99 *(978-1-4231-3021-5(9))* Little, Brown Bks. for Young Readers.

Pitcher, Chelsea. The S-Word. 2013. (ENG.). 320p. pap. 19.99 *(978-1-4516-9516-8(0)*, Gallery Bks.) Gallery Bks.

Rodriguez, Cindy L. When Reason Breaks. 2015. (ENG.). 304p. (YA). (gr. 7-12). 17.99 *(978-1-61963-412-1(0)*, 900135717, Bloomsbury USA Childrens) Bloomsbury Publishing USA.

Sanchez, Jenny Torres. Death, Dickinson, & the Demented Life of Frenchie Garcia. 2013. (ENG.). 272p. (YA). (gr. 7-17). pap. 15.99 *(978-0-7624-4680-3(3)*, Running Pr. Kids) Running Pr.

Schoenbohm, Ann. Rising above Shepherdsville. 2019. (ENG., Illus.). 320p. (J). (gr. 3-7). 17.99 *(978-1-4814-5283-0(5)*, Beach Lane Bks.) Beach Lane Bks.

Self, Jeffery. A Very, Very Bad Thing. 2017. (ENG.). 240p. (YA). (gr. 9). 17.99 *(978-1-338-11840-7(4)*, PUSH) Scholastic, Inc.

Summers, Courtney. Fall for Anything. 2010. (ENG.). 240p. (YA). (gr. 9-12). 15.99 *(978-0-312-65673-7(4)*, 900069752, St. Martin's Griffin) St. Martin's Pr.

Thompson, Holly. Orchards. 2012. 336p. (YA). (gr. 7-12). (ENG.). lib. bdg. 26.19 *(978-0-385-90806-1(7)*, Delacorte Pr.); pap. 10.99 *(978-0-385-73978-8(8)*, Ember) Random Hse. Children's Bks.

Thrash, Maggie. We Know It Was You. 2016. (Strange Ser.). (ENG., Illus.). 352p. (YA). (gr. 9). 17.99 *(978-1-4814-6200-6(8)*, Simon Pulse) Simon Pulse.

Trueman, Terry. Inside Out. 128p. 2003. (J). lib. bdg. 16.89 *(978-0-06-623963-7(X))* 2004. (ENG.). (YA). (gr. 9). reprint ed. pap. 9.99 *(978-0-06-447376-7(7)*, HarperTeen) HarperCollins Pubs.

—No Right Turn. 2009. (ENG.). 176p. (YA). (gr. 9). pap. 8.99 *(978-0-06-057493-2(3)*, HarperTeen) HarperCollins Pubs.

Warga, Jasmine. My Heart & Other Black Holes. 2015. (ENG.). 320p. (YA). (gr. 9). 17.99 *(978-0-06-232467-2(5)*, Balzer & Bray) HarperCollins Pubs.

Weingarten, Lynn. Suicide Notes from Beautiful Girls. (ENG., Illus.). 336p. (YA). (gr. 9). 2016. pap. 12.99 *(978-1-4814-1858-4(0))* 2015. 19.99 *(978-1-4814-1853-9(X))* Simon Pulse. (Simon Pulse).

—Suicide Notes from Beautiful Girls. 2016. (ENG.). (YA). (gr. 9). lib. bdg. 22.10 *(978-0-606-39882-4(1))* Turtleback.

Williams, Carol Lynch. Glimpse. (ENG., (YA). (gr. 9). 2012. Illus.). 512p. pap. 13.99 *(978-1-4169-9731-3(8))* 2010. 496p. 16.99 *(978-1-4169-9730-6(X))* Simon & Schuster/Paula Wiseman Bks. (Simon & Schuster/Paula Wiseman Bks.).

Young, Suzanne. The Epidemic. 2016. (Program Ser.: 4). (ENG., Illus.). 384p. (YA). (gr. 9). 19.99 *(978-1-4814-4470-5(0)*, Simon Pulse) Simon Pulse.

—The Program. (Program Ser.: 1). (ENG., Illus.). (YA). (gr. 9). 2014. 432p. pap. 12.99 *(978-1-4424-4581-9(5))* 2013. 416p. 19.99 *(978-1-4424-4580-2(7))* Simon Pulse. (Simon Pulse).

—The Treatment. (Program Ser.: 2). (ENG., Illus.). (YA). (gr. 9). 2015. 368p. pap. 12.99 *(978-1-4424-4584-0(X))* 2014. 352p. 19.99 *(978-1-4424-4583-3(1))* Simon Pulse. (Simon Pulse).

SUKKOT

Fishman, Cathy Goldberg. On Sukkot & Simchat Torah. Hall, Melanie, illus. 2006. (ENG.). 32p. (J). (gr. -1-4). lib. bdg. 17.95 *(978-1-58013-165-0(4)*, Kar-Ben Publishing) Lerner Publishing Group.

Kropf, Latifa Berry. It's Sukkah Time. Cohen, Tod, illus. Cohen, Tod, photos by. 2003. (Sukkot & Simchat Torah Ser.). (ENG.). 24p. (J). (gr. -1-1). 12.95 *(978-1-58013-084-4(4)*, Kar-Ben Publishing) Lerner Publishing Group.

Miller, Reagan. Sukkot, 1 vol. 2010. (ENG., Illus.). 32p. (J). pap. *(978-0-7787-4784-0(0))*; (gr. 1-3). *(978-0-7787-4766-6(2))* Crabtree Publishing Co.

SUKKOT—FICTION

Cohen, Deborah Bodin. Engineer Ari & the Sukkah Express. Kober, Shahar, illus. 2010. (Sukkot & Simchat Torah Ser.). (ENG.). 32p. (J). (gr. k-3). lib. bdg. 17.95 *(978-0-7613-5126-9(4)*, Kar-Ben Publishing) Lerner Publishing Group.

Kohuth, Jane. Who's Got the Etrog? Elissambura, illus. 2018. (ENG.). 32p. (J). (gr. -1-2). 12.99 *(978-1-5415-0966-5(8)*, 27e60bba-90f4-4323-b232-0f10b9b4722d, Kar-Ben Publishing) Lerner Publishing Group.

Korngold, Jamie S. Sadie's Sukkah Breakfast. Fortenberry, Julie, illus. 2011. (Sukkot & Simchat Torah Ser.). (ENG.). 24p. (J). (gr. -1-1). lib. bdg. 16.95 *(978-0-7613-5647-9(9)*, Kar-Ben Publishing) Lerner Publishing Group.

Lepon, Shoshana. Hillel Builds a House. Ruiz, Ángeles, illus. 2020. (ENG.). 32p. (J). (gr. -1-3). 17.99 *(978-1-5415-4402-4(1)*, 8fa8284d-6dbf-42d7-9020-18bb71a86656, Kar-Ben Publishing) Lerner Publishing Group.

Newman, Tracy. Sukkot Is Coming! Garofoli, Viviana, illus. 2017. (ENG.). 12p. (J). (gr. -1 — 1). bds. 6.99 *(978-1-5124-0828-7(X)*, 25c6eda2-8813-43b2-8729-5b6ad881b52a, Kar-Ben Publishing) Lerner Publishing Group.

Ofanansky, Allison. Sukkot Treasure Hunt. Alpern, Eliyahu, illus. Alpern, Eliyahu, photos by. 2009. (Sukkot & Simchat Torah Ser.). (ENG.). 32p. (J). (gr. -1-5). 15.95 *(978-0-8225-8763-7(7)*, Kar-Ben Publishing) Lerner Publishing Group.

Rouss, Sylvia A. Sammy Spider's First Sukkot. Kahn, Katherine Janus, illus. 2004. (ENG.). 32p. (J). (gr. -1-3). 17.95 *(978-1-58013-142-1(5)*, Kar-Ben Publishing) Lerner Publishing Group.

—Sammy Spider's First Sukkot. Kahn, Katherine Janus, illus. 2004. (ENG.). 32p. (J). (gr. -1-3). pap. 8.99 *(978-1-58013-083-7(6)*, 30089e0a-abc2-4e86-8e0f-4cc8ea2d1fd6, Kar-Ben Publishing) Lerner Publishing Group.

Terwilliger, Kelly. Bubbe Isabella & the Sukkot Cake. Hornung, Phyllis, illus. 2005. 24p. (J). (gr. 3-8). per. 6.95 *(978-1-58013-128-5(X)*, Kar-Ben Publishing) Lerner Publishing Group.

Weilerstein, Sadie Rose. K'tonton's Sukkot Adventure. 2016. (ENG., Illus.). 32p. pap. 11.95 *(978-0-8276-1268-6(0))* Jewish Pubn. Society.

SULLIVAN, ANNIE, 1866-1936

Adams, Colleen. The Courage of Helen Keller. 2009. (Reading Room Collection 2 Ser.). 24p. (gr. 3-4). 42.50 *(978-1-60851-992-7(9)*, PowerKids Pr.) Rosen Publishing Group, Inc., The.

Butler, Darren J. Helen Keller: Leader Without Sight or Sound. 2012. (Illus.). 108p. (J). pap. *(978-1-59421-083-9(7))* Seacoast Publishing, Inc.

Delano, Marfe Ferguson. Helen's Eyes: A Photobiography of Annie Sullivan, Helen Keller's Teacher. 2015. (Photobiographies Ser.). (Illus.). 64p. (J). (gr. 5-9). pap. 7.99 *(978-1-4263-2222-8(4)*, National Geographic Kids) Disney Publishing Worldwide.

Hollingsworth, Tamara. Helen Keller: A New Vision, 1 vol. 2nd rev. ed. 2013. (TIME for KIDS(r): Informational Text Ser.). (ENG., Illus.). 48p. (J). (gr. 4-5). lib. bdg. 29.96 *(978-1-4807-1115-0(2))* Teacher Created Materials, Inc.

Lambert, Joseph. Annie Sullivan & the Trials of Helen Keller. Lambert, Joseph, illus. 2018. (Center for Cartoon Studies Presents Ser.). (ENG., Illus.). 96p. (J). (gr. 5-9). 17.99 *(978-1-368-02230-9(8))* Little, Brown Bks. for Young Readers.

MacLeod, Elizabeth. Helen Keller. Krystoforski, Andrej, illus. 2007. (Kids Can Read Ser.). 32p. (J). (gr. 1-3). 14.95 *(978-1-55337-999-7(3))* Kids Can Pr., Ltd. CAN. Dist: Hachette Bk. Group.

O'Brien, John A. Who Was Helen Keller? Harrison, Nancy, illus. 2003. (Who Was...? Ser.). 107p. (J). (gr. 3-7). 12.65 *(978-0-7569-1596-4(1))* Perfection Learning Corp.

Rappaport, Doreen. Helen's Big World: The Life of Helen Keller. Tavares, Matt, illus. 2012. (Big Words Book Ser.: 6). (ENG.). 48p. (J). (gr. 1-3). 18.99 *(978-0-7868-0890-8(X))* Little, Brown Bks. for Young Readers.

SUMMER

Aloian, Molly. How Do We Know It Is Summer? 2013. (ENG., Illus.). 24p. (J). *(978-0-7787-0960-2(4))*; (gr. 2-2). pap. *(978-0-7787-0964-0(7))* Crabtree Publishing Co.

Appleby, Alex. ¿Qué Sucede en Verano? / What Happens in Summer?, 1 vol., Vol. 1. 2013. (Cuatro Estaciones Estupendas / Four Super Seasons Ser.). (SPA & ENG.). 24p. (J). (gr. k-k). 25.27 *(978-1-4824-0128-8(2)*, e493c895-3347-4056-8e4d-deacb496bd98) Stevens, Gareth Publishing LLLP.

—What Happens in Summer?, 1 vol., Vol. 1. 2013. (Four Super Seasons Ser.). (ENG.). 24p. (J). (gr. k-k). 25.27 *(978-1-4824-0109-7(6)*, 1e49cd4d-7698-45ad-be38-5419f1ec2e3a) Stevens, Gareth Publishing LLLP.

Barklem, Jill. Cuento de Verano.Tr. of Summer Story. (J). pap. 8.95 *(978-84-233-2619-8(5))* Ediciones Destino ESP. Dist: Planeta Publishing Corp.

Barnham, Kay. Summer, 1 vol. 2010. (Seasons Ser.). (ENG.). 24p. (J). (gr. 1-1). lib. bdg. 26.27 *(978-1-61532-570-2(0)*, bb9b5953-79df-496f-ab9b-bc96f30ef16c, PowerKids Pr.) Rosen Publishing Group, Inc., The.

Baxter, Nicola. Summer. 2009. (J). 24.25 *(978-1-59771-122-7(5))* Sea-To-Sea Pubns.

Brush, Jim. Extreme Summer Sports. 2013. (ENG., Illus.). 46p. (J). 35.65 *(978-1-59771-407-5(0))* Sea-To-Sea Pubns.

Butterworth Moira. Summer. James, Helen, illus. 2005. (Seasons (Smart Apple Media) Ser.). 32p. (YA). (gr. 2-4). lib. bdg. 27.10 *(978-1-58340-615-1(8))* Black Rabbit Bks.

Carr, Aaron. Summer. 2013. 25.00 *(978-1-62127-494-0(2))* Weigl Pubs., Inc.

Casado, Dami & Casado, Alicia. El Verano. 2005. (Brujita Mo y las Cuatro Estaciones Ser.). (SPA & ESP., Illus.). 14p. (J). (gr. k-4). per., bds. 7.99 *(978-84-272-6235-5(3))* Molino, Editorial ESP. Dist: Santillana USA Publishing Co., Inc.

Collinson, Clare. Summer. 2010. (Thinking about the Seasons Ser.). 32p. 28.50 *(978-1-59771-261-3(2))* Sea-To-Sea Pubns.

Dawson, Emily C. Summer & Winter. 2011. (Amicus Readers. Let's Compare (Level A) Ser.). (ENG.). 24p. (J). (gr. -1-2). lib. bdg. 25.65 *(978-1-60753-003-9(1)*, 17024) Amicus.

DeGezelle, Terri. Exploring Summer, 1 vol. 2012. (Exploring the Seasons Ser.). (ENG.). 24p. (J). (gr. -1-2). pap. 7.29 *(978-1-4296-7912-1(3)*, 118244); (J). (gr. -1-2). lib. bdg. 27.32 *(978-1-4296-7698-4(1)*, 117295); (gr. k-1). pap. 41.70 *(978-1-4296-8352-4(X))* Capstone. (Capstone Pr.).

Early Macken, JoAnn. Summer, 1 vol. 2005. (Seasons of the Year Ser.). (ENG., Illus.). 16p. (gr. k-1). pap. 6.30 *(978-0-8368-6360-4(7)*, 0c77ae9d-7f04-4eaf-b818-7a1d88dc6576); lib. bdg. 21.67 *(978-0-8368-6355-0(0)*, b5f9e655-81d1-42f7-9790-e38e6d3f9b0c) Stevens, Gareth Publishing LLLP. (Weekly Reader Leveled Readers).

—Summer / Verano, 1 vol. 2005. (Seasons of the Year / Las Estaciones Del Año Ser.). (Illus.). 16p. (gr. k-1). (SPA & ENG.). pap. 6.30 *(978-0-8368-6539-4(1)*, 86151e66-541c-4b7f-953c-be0241c024b1); (ENG & SPA., lib. bdg. 21.67 *(978-0-8368-6534-9(0)*, 8baf3972-9a27-4641-abc1-91a56b493a17) Stevens, Gareth Publishing LLLP. (Weekly Reader Leveled Readers).

Endres, Hollie J. The Letter Ss Set: Spring & Summer, 6 vols. 2004. (Letter Bks.). (ENG.). 8p. (gr. k-1). pap. 29.70 *(978-0-7368-4118-4(0))* Capstone.

Enslow, Brian. Summer Colors, 1 vol. 2011. (All about Colors of the Seasons Ser.). (ENG., Illus.). 24p. (gr. -1-1). pap. 10.35 (978-1-59845-266-2(5), 0f4538f4-27fe-4d18-863d-e607d3432113, Enslow Publishing) Enslow Publishing, LLC.
Eystad, Janet Lynn. What I Got into Last Summer. 2012. 28p. 24.95 (978-1-4626-5316-4(2)) America Star Bks.
Felix, Rebecca. How's the Weather in Summer? 2014. (21st Century Basic Skills Library: Let's Look at Summer Ser.). (ENG., Illus.). 24p. (J). (gr. k-3). 26.35 (978-1-63137-596-5(2), 205167) Cherry Lake Publishing.
—Keeping Cool in Summer. 2014. (21st Century Basic Skills Library: Let's Look at Summer Ser.). (ENG., Illus.). 24p. (J). (gr. k-3). 26.35 (978-1-63137-597-2(0), 205171) Cherry Lake Publishing.
—Visiting the Beach in Summer. 2014. (21st Century Basic Skills Library: Let's Look at Summer Ser.). (ENG., Illus.). 24p. (J). (gr. k-3). 26.35 (978-1-63137-598-9(9), 205175) Cherry Lake Publishing.
—What Do Bees Do in Summer? 2014. (21st Century Basic Skills Library: Let's Look at Summer Ser.). (ENG., Illus.). 24p. (J). (gr. k-3). pap. 12.79 (978-1-63137-646-7(2), 205188) Cherry Lake Publishing.
—What Do People Do in Summer? 2014. (21st Century Basic Skills Library: Let's Look at Summer Ser.). (ENG., Illus.). 24p. (J). (gr. k-3). 26.35 (978-1-63137-602-3(0), 205191) Cherry Lake Publishing.
—What Happens to Plants in Summer? 2014. (21st Century Basic Skills Library: Let's Look at Summer Ser.). (ENG., Illus.). 24p. (J). (gr. k-3). 26.35 (978-1-63137-603-0(9), 205195) Cherry Lake Publishing.
Flatt, Lizann. Shaping up Summer. Barron, Ashley, illus. 2018. (Math in Nature Ser.: 4). (ENG.). 32p. (J). (gr. k-4). pap. 8.95 (978-1-77147-163-3(8)) Owlkids Bks. Inc. CAN. Dist: Publishers Group West (PGW).
Gamble, Adam & Jasper, Mark. Good Night Summer. Blackmore, Katherine, illus. 2017. (Good Night Our World Ser.). 20p. (J). (— 1). bds. 9.95 (978-1-60219-440-3(8)) Good Night Bks.
George, Jean Craighead. Summer Moon. 2003. (J). (gr. 3-7). 20.75 (978-0-8446-7243-4(2)) Smith, Peter Pub., Inc.
Glaser, Rebecca. Summer. 2012. (ENG., Illus.). 24p. (J). lib. bdg. 25.65 (978-1-62031-015-1(5)) Jump! Inc.
Here Comes Summer! 2003. (J). per. (978-1-57657-969-5(7)) Paradise Pr., Inc.
Herriges, Ann. Summer. 2006. (Seasons Ser.). (ENG., Illus.). 24p. (J). (gr. k-3). lib. bdg. 26.95 (978-1-60014-032-7(7)) Bellwether Media.
—Summer. 2011. (Blastoff! Readers Ser.). 24p. (J). pap. 5.95 (978-0-531-26248-1(0), Children's Pr.) Scholastic Library Publishing.
Herrington, Lisa M. How Do You Know It's Summer? 2013. (ENG.). 32p. (J). 23.00 (978-0-531-29948-7(1)) Scholastic Library Publishing.
Hinman, Bonnie. Get Outside in Summer. 2019. (Get Outside Ser.). (ENG., Illus.). 32p. (J). (gr. 2-3). 31.35 (978-1-64185-333-0(6), 1641853336, Focus Readers) North Star Editions.
Jackson, Ellen B. The Summer Solstice. 2003. (Illus.). 32p. (J). (gr. 3-6). pap. 7.95 (978-0-7613-1965-6(9), Millbrook Pr.) Lerner Publishing Group.
Jeffries, Joyce. Dinosaurs in the Summer, 1 vol. 2014. (Dinosaur School Ser.). (ENG.). 24p. (J). (gr. k-k). 25.27 (978-1-4824-0714-3(0), a34011ea-f226-4d0d-8d0d-5c6f8d28048b) Stevens, Gareth Publishing LLLP.
Kalz, Jill. Summer. 2005. (My First Look at Seasons Ser.). (Illus.). 24p. (J). (gr. k-3). lib. bdg. 15.95 (978-1-58341-364-7(2), Creative Education) Creative Co., The.
Latham, Irene. When the Sun Shines on Antarctica: And Other Poems about the Frozen Continent. Wadham, Anna, illus. 2016. (ENG.). 32p. (J). (gr. 3-6). E-Book 30.65 (978-1-4677-9729-0(4), Millbrook Pr.) Lerner Publishing Group.
Latta, Sara L. Why Is It Summer?, 1 vol. 2012. (Why Do We Have Seasons? Ser.). (ENG., Illus.). 24p. (gr. k-2). pap. 10.35 (978-1-59845-390-4(4), aab9d43d-370e-4c92-99c6-11018ca4bca1, Enslow Elementary) Enslow Publishing, LLC.
Lim, Annalees. 10-Minute Seasonal Crafts for Summer, 1 vol. 2014. (10-Minute Seasonal Crafts Ser.). (ENG., Illus.). 24p. (J). (gr. 2-3). lib. bdg. 28.93 (978-1-4777-9210-0(4), d69b2367-d887-4c2c-9c80-7a584ced0ba1, Windmill Bks.) Rosen Publishing Group, Inc., The.
Lindeen, Mary. Summer! 2015. (BeginningtoRead Ser.). (ENG., Illus.). 32p. (J). (gr. k-2). lib. bdg. 22.60 (978-1-59953-680-4(3)) Norwood Hse. Pr.
—Summer. 2015. (Beginning-To-Read Ser.). (ENG., Illus.). 32p. (J). (gr. k-2). pap. 13.26 (978-1-60357-740-3(8)) Norwood Hse. Pr.
Macken, JoAnn Early. What We Do in Summer. 2018. (Seasons Can Be Fun (LOOK! Books (tm)) Ser.). (ENG., Illus.). 24p. (J). (gr. -1-3). lib. bdg. 25.32 (978-1-63440-307-8(X), a62b08f2-5c39-4b4c-b1e7-044123c4e5ce) Red Chair Pr.
Madinabeitia Manso, Susana. In Summer/en Verano. Hanako Momohara, Emily, illus. 2018. (Seasons/Estaciones Ser.). (ENG.). 14p. (J). (— 1). bds. 7.99 (978-1-936669-64-6(1)) Blue Manatee Press.
McGee, Randel. Fun & Festive Summer Crafts: Tie-Dyed Shirts, Bug Cages, & Sand Castles, 1 vol. 2014. (Fun & Festive Crafts for the Seasons Ser.). (ENG., Illus.). 48p. (gr. 3-3). lib. bdg. 26.93 (978-0-7660-4319-0(3), 7be22054-08ab-4b02-92b8-fd5c4695775f, Enslow Elementary) Enslow Publishing, LLC.
Meister, Cari. Summer Is Super. Lingenfelter, Jim, illus. 2010. (First Graphics: Seasons Ser.). (ENG.). 24p. (gr. 1-2). pap. 35.70 (978-1-4296-5694-8(8)); (J). lib. bdg. 24.65 (978-1-4296-4730-4(2), 103274) Capstone.
Mercado, Nancy E. Boredom Busters! Activities to Do for Kids Like You! 2003. (Illus.). 38p. (J). (978-0-439-52312-7(5)) Scholastic, Inc.
Minden, Cecilia. What Can I See in the Summer? 2018. (Seasons Ser.). (ENG.). 16p. (J). (gr. -1-2). pap. 11.36 (978-1-5341-2875-0(1), 211546, Cherry Blossom Press) Cherry Lake Publishing.
Moon, Walt K. ¡el Verano Es Divertido! (Summer Is Fun!) 2017. (Bumba Books (r) en Español — Diviértete con Las Estaciones (Season Fun) Ser.). (SPA., Illus.). 24p. (J). (gr. -1-1). 26.65 (978-1-5124-2862-9(0), 1353f998-bcca-449a-968a-524c8282993d, Ediciones Lerner) Lerner Publishing Group.
Murray, Julie. Summer, 1 vol. 2015. (Seasons Ser.). (ENG., Illus.). 24p. (J). (gr. -1-2). 31.36 (978-1-62970-921-5(2), 18300, Abdo Kids) ABDO Publishing Co.
Owen, Ruth. How Do You Know It's Summer? (Signs of the Seasons Ser.). 24p. (J). 2016. (ENG., Illus.). (gr. k-3). pap. 7.99 (978-1-944998-50-9(0)) 2012. (gr. -1-3). lib. bdg. 26.99 (978-1-61772-399-5(1)) Bearport Publishing Co., Inc.
Peters, Katie. We Like the Summer. 2019. (Seasons All Around Me (Pull Ahead Readers — Nonfiction) Ser.). (ENG., Illus.). 16p. (J). (gr. -1-1). pap. 8.99 (978-1-5415-7346-8(3), 58d5867c-6574-4f91-bb56-574cd3e7e71a, Lerner Pubns.) Lerner Publishing Group.
Pettiford, Rebecca. Summer. 2018. (Seasons of the Year Ser.). (ENG., Illus.). 24p. (J). (gr. k-3). pap. 7.99 (978-1-61891-303-6(4), 12099, Blastoff! Readers) Bellwether Media.
Publications International Ltd. Staff, ed. Staying Smart in Summer: Entering 1st Grade. 2011. 128p. (J). 7.98 (978-1-4508-1421-8(2)) Phoenix International Publications, Inc.
—Staying Smart in Summer: Entering 2nd Grade. 2011. 128p. (J). 7.98 (978-1-4508-1420-1(4)) Phoenix International Publications, Inc.
—Staying Smart in Summer: Entering Kindergarten. 2011. 128p. (J). 7.98 (978-1-4508-1422-5(0)) Phoenix International Publications, Inc.
Ross, Kathy. Crafts to Make in the Summer. Enright, Vicky, illus. 2003. (Crafts for All Seasons Ser.: 3). (ENG.). 64p. (gr. k-3). pap. 9.95 (978-0-7613-0334-3(0), First Avenue Editions) Lerner Publishing Group.
Rustad, Martha E. H. Today Is a Sunny Day. 2017. (What Is the Weather Today? Ser.). (ENG., Illus.). 24p. (J). (gr. k-2). pap. 6.29 (978-1-4966-0943-4(3), 134530, Pebble) Capstone.
Schuette, Sarah L. Let's Look at Summer: A 4D Book. rev. ed. 2018. (Investigate the Seasons Ser.). (ENG., Illus.). 24p. (J). (gr. -1-2). pap. 6.95 (978-1-5435-0875-8(8), 137614); lib. bdg. 29.32 (978-1-5435-0859-8(6), 137610) Capstone. (Capstone Pr.).
Schuh, Mari. L'été. 2019. (Spot les Saisons Ser.). (FRE.). 16p. (J). (gr. -1-2). (978-1-77092-440-6(X), 14535) Amicus.
—Summer. 2019. (Spot Seasons Ser.). (ENG.). 16p. (J). (gr. -1-2). lib. bdg. (978-1-68151-551-9(2), 14512) Amicus.
—El Verano. 2019. (Estaciones Ser.). (SPA.). 16p. (J). (gr. -1-2). lib. bdg. (978-1-68151-627-1(6), 18667) Amicus.
Smith, Kim. Sunny Summer Lapbook. Kinney, Cyndi, ed. 2013. (J). pap. 25.99 (978-1-61625-542-8(0)); cd-rom 19.99 (978-1-61625-541-1(2)) Knowledge Box Central.
—Sunny Summer Lapbook: Assembled. Kinney, Cyndi, ed. 2013. (J). pap. 35.99 (978-1-61625-544-2(7)) Knowledge Box Central.
Smith, Sian. What Can You See in Summer?, 1 vol. 2014. (Seasons Ser.). (ENG.). 24p. (J). (gr. -1-1). pap. 5.99 (978-1-4846-0355-0(9), 126441, Heinemann) Capstone.
Spalding, Maddie. Animals in Summer. 2018. (Welcoming the Seasons Ser.). (ENG.). 24p. (J). (gr. -1-2). lib. bdg. 32.79 (978-1-5038-2377-8(6), 212220) Child's World, Inc, The.
—Plants in Summer. 2018. (Welcoming the Seasons Ser.). (ENG.). 24p. (J). (gr. -1-2). lib. bdg. 32.79 (978-1-5038-2381-5(4), 212224) Child's World, Inc, The.
—Summer Solstice. 2018. (Welcoming the Seasons Ser.). (ENG.). 24p. (J). (gr. -1-2). lib. bdg. 32.79 (978-1-5038-2382-2(2), 212225) Child's World, Inc, The.
—A Trip to the Beach. 2018. (Welcoming the Seasons Ser.). (ENG.). 24p. (J). (gr. -1-2). lib. bdg. 32.79 (978-1-5038-2376-1(8), 212219) Child's World, Inc, The.
—Weather in Summer. 2018. (Welcoming the Seasons Ser.). (ENG.). 24p. (J). (gr. -1-2). lib. bdg. 32.79 (978-1-5038-2383-9(0), 212226) Child's World, Inc, The.
Spalding, Maddie & Willis, John. Animals. 2018. (Illus.). 24p. (J). pap. (978-1-4896-9678-6(4), AV2 by Weigl) Weigl Pubs., Inc.
—Plants. 2018. (Illus.). 24p. (J). (978-1-4896-9681-6(4), AV2 by Weigl) Weigl Pubs., Inc.
Storey, Rita. Art for Summer, 1 vol. 2017. (Outdoor Art Room Ser.). (ENG., Illus.). 32p. (J). (gr. 3-3). 30.27 (978-1-5081-9419-4(X), 5136f20a-dabe-4745-a646-f0d2d05b91d0); pap. 12.75 (978-1-5081-9468-2(8), 44a1c5fc-9be3-4cee-bcc7-8370fb11441f) Rosen Publishing Group, Inc., The. (Windmill Bks.).
Thayer, Tanya. Summer. 2005. (First Step Nonfiction Ser.). (Illus.). 24p. (gr. k-2). lib. bdg. 17.27 (978-0-8225-1984-3(4)) Lerner Publishing Group.
Ticktock Media, Ltd. Staff. Summer Vacation. 2009. (Busy Tots Ser.). (ENG.). 10p. (J). (gr. -1-k). bds. 6.95 (978-1-84696-800-6(3), TickTock Books) Octopus Publishing Group GBR. Dist: Independent Pubs. Group.
Turnbull, Stephanie. Summer. 2013. (Seasons Ser.). (Illus.). 24p. (J). (gr. 1-4). 25.65 (978-1-59920-848-0(2)) Black Rabbit Bks.
Ventura, Marne & Peschke, Marci. Kylie Jean Summer Camp Craft Queen, 1 vol. Mourning, Tuesday, illus. 2014. (Kylie Jean Craft Queen Ser.). (ENG.). 32p. (J). (gr. 1-3). lib. bdg. 27.32 (978-1-4795-2193-7(0), 124031, Picture Window Bks.) Capstone.
Winnick, Nick. Summer. 2010. (World of Wonder Ser.). 24p. (J). (gr. 2-4). lib. bdg. 25.70 (978-1-61690-047-2(4)) Weigl Pubs., Inc.
—Summer: Wow Study of Day & Seasons. 2010. (J). pap. 9.95 (978-1-61690-051-9(2)); (978-1-61690-055-7(5)) Weigl Pubs., Inc.

SUMMER—FICTION

Acosta, Margarita. Summer at Grandma's. 2013. 36p. pap. 14.95 (978-1-60594-983-3(3), Llumina Pr.) Aeon Publishing Inc.
Alley, R. W. Gretchen over the Beach. 2016. (ENG., Illus.). 32p. (J). (gr. -1-3). 14.99 (978-0-547-90708-6(7), 1512358, Clarion Bks.) HarperCollins Pubs.
Alpine, Rachele. You Throw Like a Girl. 2017. (Mix Ser.). (ENG., Illus.). 272p. (J). (gr. 4-8). pap. 8.99 (978-1-4814-5984-6(8), Simon & Schuster/Paula Wiseman Bks.) Simon & Schuster/Paula Wiseman Bks.
Alvarez, Julia. De Como Tia Lola Salvo el Verano (How Aunt Lola Saved the Summer Spanish Edition) 2012. (Tia Lola Stories Ser.: 3). (SPA.). 192p. (J). (gr. 3-7). 7.99 (978-0-307-93023-1(8), Yearling) Random Hse. Children's Bks.
Anderson, D. M. Killer Cows. 2010. 274p. (YA). pap. 13.99 (978-1-59080-686-9(7), Quake) Echelon Press Publishing.
Anne, Paula. Sultry Smith. 2009. 80p. pap. 9.99 (978-1-60860-970-3(7), Eloquent Bks.) Strategic Book Publishing & Rights Agency (SBPRA).
Applegate, Katherine. Sun-Kissed Christmas. 2010. (Summer Ser.). (ENG.). 208p. (YA). (gr. 9-18). pap. 8.99 (978-1-4169-9397-1(5), Simon Pulse) Simon Pulse.
Aronskind, Ofer. That Same Summer. 2008. 156p. pap. 12.95 (978-0-595-50605-7(4)) iUniverse, Inc.
Austin, Heather. Boatyard Ducklings. Austin, Heather, illus. 2008. (ENG., Illus.). 32p. (J). (gr. -1-3). 15.95 (978-0-89272-663-9(6)) Down East Bks.
Baier, Hiltrud. Greta in Schweden. 2009. 114p. pap. (978-3-8391-2523-6(5)) Books on Demand GmbH.
Bailey, Mary. Vhan Zeely & the Time Prevaricators. 2009. 192p. 25.50 (978-1-60693-477-7(5), Eloquent Bks.) Strategic Book Publishing & Rights Agency (SBPRA).
Baker, Mary. Amy's Apple Butter Granny. 2009. 48p. pap. 16.95 (978-1-61582-032-0(9)) America Star Bks.
Barbour, Ralph Henry. The Lilac Girl. 2017. (ENG., Illus.). (J). (gr. -1-7). 22.95 (978-1-374-97707-5(1)); pap. 12.95 (978-1-374-97706-8(3)) Capital Communications, Inc.
—The Lilac Girl. 2006. (Illus.). pap. (978-1-4065-0778-2(4)) Dodo Pr.
Barclay, Jane. How Hot Was It? Cole, Kathryn, ed. Donato, Janice, illus. (ENG.). 24p. (J). 14.95 (978-1-894222-70-9(9)) Lobster Pr. CAN. Dist: Univ. of Toronto Pr.
Becker, Laura. The Wonder of a Summer Day. Steffen, Jennifer, illus. 2008. (ENG.). 40p. (J). (gr. -1-3). lib. bdg. (978-1-934363-25-6(1)) Zoe Life Christian Communications.
Beckford, Lois. The Interesting Pen Pal. 2010. 44p. pap. 21.99 (978-1-4415-0678-2(3)) Xlibris Corp.
Bee, Clair. No Hitter: A Chip Hilton Sports Story. 2011. 192p. (gr. 3-8). 42.95 (978-1-258-09702-8(8)) Literary Licensing, LLC.
Beil, Michael D. Summer at Forsaken Lake. Kneen, Maggie, illus. 2013. (ENG.). 336p. (J). (gr. 5). pap. 10.99 (978-0-375-86496-4(2), Yearling) Random Hse. Children's Bks.
Bell, Hilary & Pesenti, Antonia. Summer Time. 2020. (Illus.). 44p. (J). 24.99 (978-1-74223-607-0(3), NewSouth) NewSouth Publishing AUS. Dist: Independent Pubs. Group.
Benson, Donna. Spotlight on the Cupcakes: The Cupcakes Club #3. 2008. (ENG.). 115p. (J). pap. 7.95 (978-0-9799159-2-5(9)) Pink Lemonade, LLC.
Benson, Irene Elliott. Ethel Hollister's Second Summer As a Campfire Girl. 2018. (ENG., Illus.). 80p. (YA). (gr. 7-12). pap. (978-93-5297-310-1(0)) Alpha Editions.
BentleyMarla. Summer Sounds Level 1 Beginner/Elementary. 2010. (Cambridge Experience Readers Ser.). (ENG., Illus.). 46p. pap. 14.75 (978-84-8323-995-7(7)) Cambridge Univ. Pr.
Benton, Jim. The Worst Things in Life Are Also Free (Dear Dumb Diary #10) Benton, Jim, illus. 2010. (Dear Dumb Diary Ser.: 10). (ENG., Illus.). 160p. (J). (gr. 4-7). pap. 7.99 (978-0-545-11614-5(7), Scholastic Paperbacks) Scholastic, Inc.
Berner, Rotraut Susanne. All Around Bustletown: Summer. 2020. (All Around Bustletown Ser.). (ENG., Illus.). 14p. (J). (-k). bds. 14.95 (978-3-7913-7420-8(6)) Prestel Verlag GmbH & Co KG. DEU. Dist: Penguin Random Hse. LLC.
Bice, Charles. What Lies Beneath. 2009. 208p. pap. 16.50 (978-0-578-03340-2(2)) Wimabi Pr.
Black, Allyson. Crushed, Bk. 5. Spaziante, Patrick & Riley, Kellee, illus. 2011. (Scarlett & Crimson Ser.). (ENG.). 112p. (J). pap. 6.99 (978-1-4169-9648-4(6), Simon Spotlight) Simon Spotlight.
Blackwell-Burke, Melissa & Kunkel, Kristen. Summertime Surprise. 2003. (J). spiral bd. 14.95 (978-1-58605-956-9(4), LeapFrog Schl. Hse.) LeapFrog Enterprises, Inc.
Blume, Judy. Otherwise Known As Sheila the Great. 2004. (ENG.). 160p. (J). (gr. 3-7). 6.99 (978-0-425-19380-8(2), Berkley) Penguin Publishing Group.
Bracken- Murphy, Julie. Sammy's Summer Vacation. 2007. 52p. per. 13.95 (978-1-4327-0615-9(2)) Outskirts Pr., Inc.
Bradford, Michael. Button Hill, 1 vol. 2015. (ENG.). 264p. (J). (gr. 4-7). pap. 12.95 (978-1-4598-0755-6(3)) Orca Bk. Pubs. USA.
Branch, Dianne. Summer Fun. 2012. 12p. pap. 15.99 (978-1-4772-1108-3(X)) AuthorHouse.
Brennan, Linda Crotta. Marshmallow Kisses. Takabayashi, Mari, illus. 2007. (ENG.). 32p. (J). (gr. -1-3). 6.95 (978-0-618-80903-5(1), 410103, Clarion Bks.) HarperCollins Pubs.
Brenner, Tom. And Then Comes Summer. Kim, Jaime, illus. 2017. (And Then Comes Ser.). (ENG.). 32p. (J). (gr. -1-3). 17.99 (978-0-7636-6071-0(X)) Candlewick Pr.
Brody, Jessica. Boys of Summer. 2016. (ENG., Illus.). 352p. (J). (gr. 9). 17.99 (978-1-4814-6349-2(7), Simon Pulse) Simon Pulse.
Brogle, Jennifer. The Adventures of Jennifer & Sherry: Summertime. 2013. 60p. pap. 25.36 (978-1-4669-7560-6(1)) Trafford Publishing.
Buffie, Margaret. Who Is Frances Rain? 20th ed. 2007. 184p. (J). (gr. 7-9). 7.95 (978-1-55453-209-4(4)) Kids Can Pr., Ltd. CAN. Dist: Hachette Bk. Group.
Bunting, Eve. The Best Summer Ever. Masse, Josée, illus. 2012. (I AM a READER!: Frog & Friends Ser.). (ENG.). 48p. (J). (gr. 1-2). pap. 3.99 (978-1-58536-691-0(9), 202377); lib. bdg. 9.95 (978-1-58536-550-0(5), 202223) Sleeping Bear Pr.
Burk, Josh. The Summer of Saint Nick. 2007. (ENG.). 152p. (YA). per. 12.95 (978-0-9768042-2-2(0)) Maven Of Memory Publishing.
Burningham, John. Picnic. Burningham, John, illus. 2014. (ENG., Illus.). 32p. (J). (-k). 17.99 (978-0-7636-6945-4(8)) Candlewick Pr.
Burns, A. M. & Ricci, Caitlin. Running with the Pack. 2017. (ENG., Illus.). (YA). 25.99 (978-1-64080-359-6(9), Harmony Ink Pr.) Dreamspinner Pr.
Bush, Laura. Our Great Big Backyard. Rogers, Jacqueline, illus. 2018. (ENG.). 40p. (J). (gr. -1-3). pap. 8.99 (978-0-06-246841-3(3), HarperCollins) HarperCollins Pubs.
Bush, Laura & Hager, Jenna Bush. Our Great Big Backyard. Rogers, Jacqueline, illus. 2016. (ENG.). 40p. (J). (gr. -1-3). 18.99 (978-0-06-246835-2(9), HarperCollins) HarperCollins Pubs.
Buyea, Rob. Mr. Terupt Falls Again. 2013. (Mr. Terupt Ser.: 2). 400p. (J). (gr. 3-7). 8.99 (978-0-307-93046-0(7), Yearling) Random Hse. Children's Bks.
—Mr. Terupt Falls Again. 2013. lib. bdg. 18.40 (978-0-606-32236-2(1)) Turtleback.
Calame, Don. Swim the Fly. 2010. (ENG., Illus.). 352p. (YA). (gr. 9). pap. 11.99 (978-0-7636-4776-6(4)) Candlewick Pr.
Castanga, Felicity. The Incredible Here & Now. l.t. ed. 2013. 212p. pap. (978-1-4596-7083-9(3)) ReadHowYouWant.com, Ltd.
Chapman, Brenda. Where Trouble Leads: A Jennifer Bannon Mystery. 2007. (Jennifer Bannon Mystery Ser.: 3). (ENG., Illus.). 136p. (YA). (gr. 5-18). per. 9.95 (978-1-894917-44-5(8), Napoleon & Co.) Dundurn Pr. CAN. Dist: Publishers Group West (PGW).
Cheney, Cora. The Doll of Lilac Valley. Cassidy, Nancy White, illus. 2003. 128p. 11.95 (978-0-9714612-5-3(2)) Green Mansion Pr. LLC.
Child's Play. Summer. Busby, Ailie, illus. 2015. (Seasons Ser.: 4). 12p. (J). (gr. 1-1). spiral bd. (978-1-84643-742-7(3)) Child's Play International Ltd.
Christensen, Gerda. Troll Peter Discovers the Bog-Woman's Secret & Other Stories. 2010. 40p. pap. 18.27 (978-1-4251-8822-1(2)) Trafford Publishing.
Clark, Catherine. The Summer of Everything: Picture Perfect & Wish You Were Here. 2016. (ENG., Illus.). 448p. (YA). (gr. 8). pap. 9.99 (978-0-06-235922-3(3), HarperTeen) HarperCollins Pubs.
Combs, Sarah. Breakfast Served Anytime. 2014. (ENG.). 272p. (YA). (gr. 7). 16.99 (978-0-7636-6791-7(9)) Candlewick Pr.
Compagnucci, Veronica M. Emily Finds Her Voice. 2013. 40p. pap. 24.95 (978-1-63004-288-2(9)) America Star Bks.
Coppens, Katie. The Acadia Files: Book Two, Autumn Science, 1 vol. Hatam, Holly, illus. 2018. (Acadia Science Ser.: 2). (ENG.). 80p. (J). (gr. 4-7). 13.95 (978-0-88448-604-6(4), 884604) Tilbury Hse. Pubs.
Coteau Books. The Ghost in the Machine. 2005. (ENG.). 222p. (J). (gr. 6-9). pap. 7.95 (978-1-55050-227-5(1)) Coteau Bks. CAN. Dist: Fitzhenry & Whiteside, Ltd.
Cramer, Michelle Ann. The Chasers. 2006. (ENG.). 118p. pap. 9.74 (978-1-84728-998-8(3)) Lulu Pr., Inc.
Creech, Sharon. Absolutely Normal Chaos. 2012. 230p. (J). (gr. 4-7). lib. bdg. 18.40 (978-0-613-02936-0(4)) Turtleback.
Crowley, Kieran Mark. Colm & the Lazarus Key. 2009. (ENG., Illus.). 224p. (J). pap. 14.95 (978-1-85635-646-6(9)) Mercier Pr., Ltd., The IRL. Dist: Dufour Editions, Inc.
Cruea, Kim. Summer Falls Junior Rangers: The First Adventures. 2008. 73p. pap. 19.95 (978-1-60474-552-8(5)) America Star Bks.
Curious George & the Ice Cream Surprise. 2011. (Curious George Ser.). (ENG., Illus.). 24p. (J). (gr. -1-3). pap. 4.99 (978-0-547-24285-9(9), 1099394, Clarion Bks.) HarperCollins Pubs.
Dagostino, Argus. Belcher Bomb. 2008. 53p. pap. 16.95 (978-1-60441-596-4(7)) America Star Bks.
Dalton, Michelle. Swept Away. 2015. (Sixteenth Summer Ser.). (ENG., Illus.). 320p. (YA). (gr. 7). pap. 10.99 (978-1-4814-3608-3(2), Simon Pulse) Simon Pulse.
Dangerous Summer 2. 2006. (J). (978-1-933343-19-8(2)) Stabenfeldt Inc.
Daniels, Darla. Carrie Goes Camping. 2011. 24p. pap. 16.95 (978-1-4626-0642-9(3)) America Star Bks.
Darling, Angela. Maddie's Camp Crush. 2013. (Crush Ser.: 2). (ENG.). 160p. (J). (gr. 3-7). pap. 5.99 (978-1-4424-8334-7(2), Simon Spotlight) Simon Spotlight.
D'Ath, Justin. Pool. 2009. 297p. (Orig.). (YA). (978-1-876462-51-2(5)) Ford Street Publishing Pty, Limited.
Davidson, Thomas A. Penny Found in Willowbrooke. 2009. 40p. pap. 14.75 (978-1-60693-774-7(X), Strategic Bk. Publishing) Strategic Book Publishing & Rights Agency (SBPRA).
Day, Karen. A Million Miles from Boston. 2012. (ENG.). 224p. (J). (gr. 4-6). lib. bdg. 21.19 (978-0-385-90763-7(X), Lamb, Wendy Bks.) Random Hse. Children's Bks.
Dearie, Anne Crofton. Ginger Cat. 2011. (Illus.). 92p. pap. 12.10 (978-1-4567-7484-4(0)) AuthorHouse.
DeFelice, Cynthia. Fort. 2016. (ENG.). 224p. (J). pap. 12.99 (978-1-250-07973-2(X), 900154609) Square Fish.
—Fort. 2016. (J). lib. bdg. 17.20 (978-0-606-38552-7(5)) Turtleback.
dePaola, Tomie. Four Friends in Summer. dePaola, Tomie, illus. 2003. (ENG., Illus.). 32p. (J). (gr. -1-3). reprint ed. 19.99 (978-0-689-85693-8(8), Simon & Schuster Bks. For Young Readers) Simon & Schuster Bks. For Young Readers.
Dessen, Sarah. That Summer. 2004. (ENG.). 224p. (YA). (gr. 7-7). 10.99 (978-0-14-240172-9(2), Speak) Penguin Young Readers Group.
Dolsingh, Kanisha. Once upon a Time: In London Town with Minnie Drew. 2011. 28p. pap. 16.99 (978-1-4567-5731-1(8)) AuthorHouse.
Dorling Kindersley Publishing Staff. Summer Adventures. 2013. (DK Reader Level 3 Ser.). lib. bdg. 13.55 (978-0-606-31476-3(8)) Turtleback.
Doyle, Patrick H. T. Edgar Font's Hunt for a House to Haunt: Adventure One: the Castle Tower Lighthouse. 2006. (Illus.). 213p. (J). (gr. -1). per. 6.99 (978-0-9786132-0-4(1)) Armadillo Bks.
—Edgar Font's Hunt for a House to Haunt: Adventure Two: the Fakersville Power Station. Doyle, Patrick H. T., illus. 2007. (Edgar Font's Hunt for a House to Haunt Ser.). (Illus.). 303p. (J). (gr. 4-7). per. 7.99 (978-0-9786132-1-1(X)) Armadillo Bks.
DuVall, Nell. Summer Day. Weltner, Dave, illus. l.t. ed. 2003. 13p. 7.95 (978-0-9706654-6-1(6)) Sprite Pr.
Ellis, Amanda & Block, Maggie. Jwenlapaix in the Bateyes. 2009. 52p. pap. 24.00 (978-1-4389-4391-6(1)) AuthorHouse.

Emzer, Counselor. The Day Before Summer Vacation. 2004. 31p. pap. 24.95 *(978-1-4137-2680-0(1))* PublishAmerica, Inc.

Engle, Dawn A. Ella's Golden Heart Goes to Camp. 2011. 40p. pap. 14.95 *(978-1-60911-392-6(6)*, Eloquent Bks.) Strategic Book Publishing & Rights Agency (SBPRA).

English, Karen. Hot Day on Abbott Avenue. Steptoe, Javaka, illus. 2019. (ENG.). 32p. (J). (gr. -1-3). pap. 7.99 *(978-1-328-50006-9(3)*, 1718045, Clarion Bks.) HarperCollins Pubs.

Enright, Elizabeth. Thimble Summer. unabr. ed. 2004. 136p. (J). (gr. 3-7). pap. 36.00 incl. audio *(978-0-8072-0671-3(7)*, Listening Library) Random Hse. Audio Publishing Group.

—Thimble Summer. Enright, Elizabeth, illus. 2008. (ENG., Illus.). 144p. (J). (gr. 3-7). pap. 8.99 *(978-0-312-38002-1(X)*, 900050525) Square Fish.

Everett, Clare. Henrietta - a Rabbit's Tale of Summer Time Fun. 2012. 116p. pap. *(978-1-84914-296-0(3))* CompletelyNovel.com.

Falken, L. C. Snuggle Bunnies. McCue, Lisa, illus. 2018. (ENG.). 18p. (J). (gr. -1 — 1). bds. 6.99 *(978-0-7944-4069-5(X)*, Studio Fun International) Printers Row Publishing Group.

Faris, Stephanie. Piper Morgan Summer of Fun Collection Books 1-4 (Boxed Set) Piper Morgan Joins the Circus; Piper Morgan in Charge!; Piper Morgan to the Rescue; Piper Morgan Makes a Splash. Fleming, Lucy, illus. 2017. (Piper Morgan Ser.). (ENG.). 432p. (J). (gr. 1-4). pap. 23.99 *(978-1-4814-9978-1(5)*, Aladdin) Simon & Schuster Children's Publishing.

Ferrer, Caridad. When the Stars Go Blue: A Novel. 2010. (ENG.). 336p. (YA). (gr. 9-18). pap. 22.99 *(978-0-312-65004-9(3)*, 900069171, St. Martin's Griffin) St. Martin's Pr.

Firestone, Carrie. The Unlikelies. (ENG.). (YA). (gr. 9-17). 2018. 352p. pap. 10.99 *(978-0-316-38289-2(2))* 2017. 336p. 17.99 *(978-0-316-38286-1(8))* Little, Brown Bks. for Young Readers.

Fisher, Rick. Unknown Heroes. 2007. (ENG., Illus.). 32p. (J). per. 14.95 *(978-1-59800-899-9(4))* Outskirts Pr., Inc.

Fitzgerald-Tracy, Kathleen. For the Love of Butter. 2009. (ENG.). 26p. pap. 21.99 *(978-1-4500-0124-3(6))* Xlibris Corp.

Fitzhugh, Percy K. Pee-Wee Harris. 2004. reprint ed. pap. 1.99 *(978-1-4192-4057-7(9))*; pap. 15.95 *(978-1-4191-4057-0(4))* Kessinger Publishing, LLC.

Flaggert, Candy. Ok, Said Carrie Katherine, 1 vol. Chipka, Sandy, illus. 2008. (ENG.). 25p. 24.95 *(978-1-60563-502-6(2))* America Star Bks.

Freeman, Lisa. Riptide Summer. 2017. (ENG.). 304p. (J). (gr. 8-8). 17.99 *(978-1-5107-1167-9(8)*, Sky Pony Pr.) Skyhorse Publishing Co., Inc.

Furgang, Kathy. A Happy Summer Day & un día feliz de Verano: 6 English, 6 Spanish Adaptations. 2011. (ENG & SPA.). (J). 75.00 net. *(978-1-4108-5656-2(9))* Benchmark Education Co.

Galante, Cecilia. The Summer of May. 2011. (ENG., Illus.). 256p. (J). (gr. 4-8). 16.99 *(978-1-4169-8023-0(7)*, Aladdin) Simon & Schuster Children's Publishing.

—The Summer of May. 2012. (ENG., Illus.). 256p. (J). (gr. 4-8). pap. 7.99 *(978-1-4169-8304-0(X)*, Simon & Schuster/Paula Wiseman Bks.) Simon & Schuster/Paula Wiseman Bks.

Galbraith, Kathryn O. Summer Babies, 1 vol. Pons, Adela, illus. 2019. (Babies in the Park Ser.). 20p. (J). (gr. -1 — 1). bds. 6.99 *(978-1-68263-069-3(2))* Peachtree Publishing Co. Inc.

Gale, Emily. The Other Side of Summer. 2017. (ENG.). 336p. (J). (gr. 3-7). 16.99 *(978-0-06-265674-2(0)*, HarperCollins) HarperCollins Pubs.

Garcia, Cristina. Dreams of Significant Girls. (ENG.). 256p. (YA). (gr. 9). 2012. pap. 8.99 *(978-1-4169-7930-2(1))* 2011. 16.99 *(978-1-4169-7920-3(4))* Simon & Schuster Bks. For Young Readers. (Simon & Schuster Bks. For Young Readers).

The Gauntlet. (J). 14.00 *(978-1-931555-16-6(8))* Our Lady of Victory Schl.

George, J. A. Camp Aconyte. 2008. 65p. pap. 19.95 *(978-1-60610-631-0(7))* America Star Bks.

George, Kallie. Home Again. 2018. (Heartwood Hotel Ser.: 4). (J). lib. bdg. 16.00 *(978-0-606-40973-5(4))* Turtleback.

Germain, Kerry. Kimo's Summer Vacation. Montes, Keoni, illus. 2003. 52p. (J). 12.95 *(978-0-9705889-4-4(1))* Island Paradise Publishing.

Ghigna, Charles. I See Summer, 1 vol. Jatkowska, Agnieszka, illus. 2011. (I See Ser.). (ENG.). 24p. (J). (gr. -1 — 1). pap. 6.10 *(978-1-4048-6852-6(6)*, 116433, Picture Window Bks.) Capstone.

Gifford, Peggy. Moxy Maxwell Does Not Love Stuart Little. Fisher, Valorie, photos by. 2008. (Moxy Maxwell Ser.: 1). (ENG., Illus.). 112p. (J). (gr. 2-5). 6.99 *(978-0-440-42230-3(2)*, Yearling) Random Hse. Children's Bks.

Gill, Amber. Joseph's Summer. 2006. 71p. pap. 16.95 *(978-1-4241-0122-1(0))* PublishAmerica, Inc.

Giordano, Anthony. Another Boring Summer... Again! 2009. 154p. (YA). pap. 11.25 *(978-1-60695-077-7(0))* Cacoethes Publishing Hse., LLC.

Golden Books. Keep Styling! (Sunny Day) Workman, Lisa A., illus. 2018. (ENG.). 128p. (J). (gr. -1-2). pap. 7.99 *(978-1-5247-6854-6(5)*, Golden Bks.) Random Hse. Children's Bks.

Gonzales, Andrea & Houser, Sophie. Girl Code: Gaming, Going Viral, & Getting It Done. 2018. (ENG., Illus.). 304p. (YA). (gr. 8). pap. 9.99 *(978-0-06-247247-2(X)*, HarperCollins) HarperCollins Pubs.

Goode, Suzi. The Lost Wizard Series Bk 1. 2007. pap. 11.95 *(978-1-59374-817-3(5))* Whiskey Creek Pr., LLC.

Gow, Kailin. Loving Summer. 2012. 250p. (-18). pap. 9.99 *(978-1-59748-044-4(4)*, The Edge) Sparklesoup LLC.

Grant, Katy. Tug-Of-War. 2010. (Summer Camp Secrets Ser.). (ENG.). 256p. (J). (gr. 3-7). pap. 7.99 *(978-1-4169-9161-8(1)*, Aladdin) Simon & Schuster Children's Publishing.

Greeley, David. Seven Friends, 1 vol. Marquis, KariAnn, illus. 2010. 38p. 24.95 *(978-1-4489-4101-8(6))* PublishAmerica, Inc.

Green, Holly G. Don't Slam the Door. Scott, Sarah Chamberlin, illus. 2005. (ENG.). 39p. (J). (gr. 2-7). 19.95 *(978-0-9744803-7-4(1))* PublishingWorks.

Greenberg, Lauren Abbey. The Battle of Junk Mountain. 2018. (ENG.). 224p. (J). (gr. 3-7). 16.99 *(978-0-7624-6295-7(7)*, Running Pr. Kids) Running Pr.

Greenwald, Lisa. Dog Beach Unleashed: The Seagate Summers Book Two. 2015. (Seagate Summers Ser.). (ENG., Illus.). 36p. (J). (gr. 5-9). 15.95 *(978-1-4197-1481-8(3)*, 1072001, Amulet Bks.) Abrams, Inc.

—Dog Beach Unleashed (the Seagate Summers #2) 2016. (ENG.). 256p. (J). (gr. 3-7). pap. 7.95 *(978-1-4197-2056-7(2)*, 1072003, Amulet Bks.) Abrams, Inc.

Greer, Hannah. The Castle Ivengless: The Velvet Bag Memoirs, Bk. 3. 2009. 145p. pap. 24.95 *(978-1-60749-105-7(2))* America Star Bks.

Grund, Carol A. Anna Mei, Escape Artist. 2011. 168p. (J). (gr. 4-7). pap. 8.95 *(978-0-8198-0794-6(X))* Pauline Bks. & Media.

Gundel, Jean. The Mystery Key at Camp Green Meadow. Robertson, R. H., illus. 2011. (J). pap. 14.95 *(978-1-59571-730-6(7))* Word Association Pubs.

Gutman, Dan. Back to School, Weird Kids Rule! 2014. (My Weird School Ser.). (J). lib. bdg. 16.00 *(978-0-606-35502-5(2))* Turtleback.

Hall, Donald. Lucy's Summer. McCurdy, Michael, illus. 2015. (ENG.). 40p. (J). (gr. 1-18). pap. 14.95 *(978-1-56792-348-3(8))* Godine, David R. Pub.

Han, Jenny. The Complete Summer I Turned Pretty Trilogy (Boxed Set) The Summer I Turned Pretty; It's Not Summer Without You; We'll Always Have Summer. 2013. (Summer I Turned Pretty Ser.). (ENG., Illus.). 928p. (YA). (gr. 7). pap. 35.99 *(978-1-4424-9832-7(3)*, Simon & Schuster Bks. For Young Readers) Simon & Schuster Bks. For Young Readers.

—It's Not Summer Without You. (Summer I Turned Pretty Ser.). (ENG.). (YA). (gr. 7). 2011. 320p. pap. 11.99 *(978-1-4169-9556-2(0))* 2010. 288p. 19.99 *(978-1-4169-9555-5(2))* 2022. (Illus.). 320p. pap. 11.99 *(978-1-6659-3799-3(8))* Simon & Schuster Bks. For Young Readers. (Simon & Schuster Bks. For Young Readers).

—The Summer I Turned Pretty. (Summer I Turned Pretty Ser.). (ENG.). (YA). (gr. 7). 2010. 304p. pap. 11.99 *(978-1-4169-6829-0(6))* 2009. 288p. 19.99 *(978-1-4169-6823-8(7))* Simon & Schuster Bks. For Young Readers. (Simon & Schuster Bks. For Young Readers).

—The Summer I Turned Pretty. 2010. lib. bdg. 22.10 *(978-0-606-14529-9(X))* Turtleback.

Harrison, Lisi, creator. Alicia. 2008. (Clique Summer Collection: 3). (ENG., Illus.). 144p. (YA). (gr. 7-17). pap. 10.99 *(978-0-316-02753-3(7)*, Poppy) Little, Brown Bks. for Young Readers.

Hartgraves, Richard. Little Cedar. 2006. 130p. pap. 24.95 *(978-1-4241-4603-1(8))* PublishAmerica, Inc.

Hawthorne, Rachel. Island Girls & Boys. 2005. (ENG.). 336p. (YA). (gr. 9). pap. 8.99 *(978-0-06-075546-1(6)*, HarperTeen) HarperCollins Pubs.

Hayes, Karel. The Summer Visitors, 10 vols. Hayes, Karel, illus. 2011. (ENG., Illus.). 32p. (J). (gr. -1-12). 17.95 *(978-0-89272-918-0(X))* Down East Bks.

Hearst, Allyson. White Pajamas: A Karate Story. 2011. 68p. pap. 19.95 *(978-1-4626-3871-0(6))* America Star Bks.

Heflin, Ronald. Caddo Lake. 2011. 156p. pap. 24.95 *(978-1-4626-0093-9(X))* America Star Bks.

Heidtke, John. A Summer's Passage on Sutter's Bay. 2005. (J). per. *(978-0-9748426-6-0(4)*, Accent Pubns.) Ajoyin Publishing, Inc.

Hemmerle, Jamie. The Lost & Found Summer. 2010. (Illus.). 312p. pap. 15.95 *(978-1-4327-6268-1(0))* Outskirts Pr., Inc.

Henkes, Kevin. Summer Song. Dronzek, Laura, illus. 2020. (ENG.). 40p. (J). (gr. -1-3). 18.99 *(978-0-06-286613-4(3))*; lib. bdg. 19.89 *(978-0-06-286614-1(1))* HarperCollins Pubs. (Greenwillow Bks.).

—Summer Song Board Book. Dronzek, Laura, illus. 2021. (ENG.). 36p. (J). (gr. -1 — 1). bds. 8.99 *(978-0-06-286616-5(8)*, Greenwillow Bks.) HarperCollins Pubs.

Hesse, Karen. Come on, Rain! 2004. (J). (gr. k-3). 29.95 *(978-1-55592-500-0(6))* Weston Woods Studios, Inc.

Hillert, Margaret. It's Summer, Dear Dragon. Schimmell, David, illus. 2009. (BeginningtoRead Ser.). 32p. (J). (gr. k-2). lib. bdg. 22.60 *(978-1-59953-313-1(8))* Norwood Hse. Pr.

Ho, Jannie, illus. Violet Rose & the Summer Campout. 2017. (Violet Rose Ser.). (ENG.). 52p. (J). (gr. -1-3). 8.99 *(978-0-7636-9333-6(2))* Candlewick Pr.

Hobbs, Olivia. The Summer of Violet. 2011. 56p. pap. 15.99 *(978-1-4653-3539-5(0))* Xlibris Corp.

Hogan, Jamie. Seven Days of Daisy, 1 vol. Hogan, Jamie, illus. 2011. (ENG., Illus.). 32p. (J). (gr. -1-12). 14.95 *(978-0-89272-919-7(8))* Down East Bks.

Hopkinson, Deborah. Pioneer Summer. Farcy, Patrick, illus. 2005. 74p. (J). lib. bdg. 15.00 *(978-1-59054-911-7(2))* Fitzgerald Bks.

Hordos, Sandra. Marissa Plans a Princess Tea Party. Allen, Joshua, illus. 2010. 28p. pap. 12.49 *(978-1-4520-2557-5(6))* AuthorHouse.

Horsfall, S. J. Jodie & Lilly... & the Fake Mansion. 2009. 58p. pap. 7.50 *(978-0-557-12474-9(3))* Lulu Pr., Inc.

Horvath, Polly. My One Hundred Adventures. 2010. (My One Hundred Adventures Ser.: 1). (Illus.). 272p. (J). (gr. 3-7). 8.99 *(978-0-375-85526-9(2)*, Yearling) Random Hse. Children's Bks.

Houts, Michelle. Sea Glass Summer. Ibatoulline, Bagram, illus. 2019. 32p. (J). (gr. -1-3). 16.99 *(978-0-7636-8443-3(0))* Candlewick Pr.

Howell, Hayley L. Sammy's Two Left Feet: Groovin' with Mr. Smooth: Discovering How to Believe in Yourself. 2010. 32p. pap. 15.95 *(978-1-4520-5733-0(8))* AuthorHouse.

Howington, C. D. Aunt Cindy's House. 2011. 96p. pap. 19.95 *(978-1-4626-1113-3(3))* America Star Bks.

Howland, Leila. The Forget-Me-Not Summer. Kim, Ji-Hyuk, illus. 2016. (Silver Sisters Ser.: 1). (ENG.). 368p. (J). (gr. 3-7). pap. 7.99 *(978-0-06-231870-1(5)*, HarperCollins) HarperCollins Pubs.

Hurst, Elva. Summer on the Farm. 2014. (Farm Life Ser.). 80p. pap. 6.99 *(978-0-7369-6091-5(0))* Harvest Hse. Pubs.

Innocenti, Jane. Aunt Jane's Summer Garden. 2012. 20p. pap. 24.95 *(978-1-62709-103-9(3))* America Star Bks.

Irvine, Kitty & MacPherson-Irvine, Julie. Mysterious Moorings with Mouse. 2017. (ENG.). 96p. (J). pap. 11.95 *(978-1-78693-220-4(2)*, b4497a1c-0581-417e-a47b-bb389a574432) Austin Macauley Pubs. Ltd. GBR. Dist: Baker & Taylor Publisher Services (BTPS).

Irwin, Inez Haynes. Maida's Little House. 2004. reprint ed. pap. 27.95 *(978-1-4179-4236-7(3))* Kessinger Publishing, LLC.

Irwin, Ms. Judy. What Did You Say? 2012. 78p. pap. *(978-0-9877088-5-4(6))* Irwin, Judy.

Jackson, Kathryn, et al. A Day at the Seashore. 2010. (Little Golden Book Ser.). (Illus.). 24p. (J). (gr. -1-2). 5.99 *(978-0-375-85425-5(8)*, Golden Bks.) Random Hse. Children's Bks.

Jain, Rohan. Summertime for Me. 2017. (Text Connections Guided Close Reading Ser.). (J). (gr. k). *(978-1-4900-1765-5(8))* Benchmark Education Co.

Jardine Stoddart, Heidi. East to the Sea, 1 vol. 2006. (ENG., Illus.). 32p. (J). (gr. -1-3). pap. 11.95 *(978-1-55109-577-6(7)*, 3cfbcb0f-f867-4d00-a28a-91cd0f76dc07) Nimbus Publishing, Ltd. CAN. Dist: Baker & Taylor Publisher Services (BTPS).

Jocelyn, Marthe. Mayfly. 2004. (Illus.). 32p. (J). (gr. -1-k). 14.95 *(978-0-88776-676-3(5)*, Tundra Bks.) Tundra Bks. CAN. Dist: Penguin Random Hse. LLC.

—Ready for Summer. 2008. (Ready for Ser.). (Illus.). 16p. (J). (gr. -1-k). 7.95 *(978-0-88776-860-6(1)*, Tundra Bks.) Tundra Bks. CAN. Dist: Penguin Random Hse. LLC.

—Would You. 2008. (ENG.). 176p. (J). (gr. 4-7). 19.99 *(978-0-88776-816-3(4)*, Tundra Bks.) Tundra Bks. CAN. Dist: Penguin Random Hse. LLC.

Johnson, James Ray. Timmy Wee Pee & Castle Friends. 2009. 28p. pap. 24.95 *(978-1-60836-886-0(6))* America Star Bks.

Johnson, Mary Victoria. Golden. 2017. (Summer Road Trip Ser.). (ENG.). 184p. (YA). (gr. 5-12). 31.42 *(978-1-68076-722-3(4)*, 27437, Epic Escape) EPIC Pr.

Johnston, E. K. Exit, Pursued by a Bear. 2017. lib. bdg. 22.10 *(978-0-606-39797-1(3))* Turtleback.

Joseph, Curtis M. Max Baxter. 2008. 57p. pap. 16.95 *(978-1-60610-206-0(0))* America Star Bks.

—Order of Godalming: Max Baxter, 1 vol. 2009. 64p. pap. 19.95 *(978-1-60836-525-8(5))* America Star Bks.

Julius, Jessica. Olaf's Perfect Day (Disney Frozen) The Disney Storybook Art Team, illus. 2015. (Little Golden Book Ser.). (ENG.). 24p. (J). (-k). 5.99 *(978-0-7364-3356-3(2)*, Golden/Disney) Random Hse. Children's Bks.

June, Christina. It Started with Goodbye, 1 vol. 2017. (ENG.). 272p. (YA). pap. 12.99 *(978-0-310-75866-2(1))* Blink.

Katz, Karen. Baby Loves Summer! A Karen Katz Lift-The-Flap Book. Katz, Karen, illus. 2012. (ENG., Illus.). 14p. (J). (gr. -1 — 1). bds. 7.99 *(978-1-4424-2746-4(9)*, Little Simon) Little Simon.

—Where Is Baby's Beach Ball? A Lift-The-Flap Book. Katz, Karen, illus. 2009. (ENG., Illus.). 14p. (J). (gr. -1 — 1). bds. 7.99 *(978-1-4169-4962-6(3)*, Little Simon) Little Simon.

Kaur, K. S. The Horncastles & the Magnopeus Medicine. Kaur, Bal, illus. 2012. 154p. pap. *(978-1-78148-023-6(0))* Grosvenor Hse. Publishing Ltd.

Keefer, Nick T. Pear-A-Dise. Bowser, Sean T., illus. 2013. 28p. pap. 12.95 *(978-0-9894814-6-5(8))* Warren Publishing, Inc.

Kelly, Katy. Melonhead & the Big Stink. 2011. (Melonhead Ser.: 2). 224p. (J). (gr. 3-7). 7.99 *(978-0-375-84527-7(5)*, Yearling) Random Hse. Children's Bks.

Kerber, Purnima & Mead, Purnima. Bibia Tells Her Story! Kerber, Kathy, illus. 2010. (ENG.). 24p. pap. 14.50 *(978-1-4490-4753-5(X))* AuthorHouse.

Kinney, Jeff. Dog Days. (Diary of a Wimpy Kid Ser.: 4). (J). 2011. 75.75 *(978-1-4407-7756-1(X))* 2010. (SPA.). 181.75 *(978-1-4407-7748-6(9))* 2010. 54.75 *(978-1-4407-7747-9(0))* 2010. 44.75 *(978-1-4407-7753-0(5))* 2010. 46.75 *(978-1-4407-7751-6(9))* 2009. 52.75 *(978-1-4407-7749-3(7))* 2009. 1.25 *(978-1-4407-7755-4(1))* Recorded Bks., Inc.

—Dog Days. 2009. (Diary of a Wimpy Kid Ser.: 4). (J). lib. bdg. 25.70 *(978-0-606-23665-2(1))* Turtleback.

Kinton, P. D. Wishing for Wizards & Chips for Te. 2010. 28p. pap. *(978-1-907211-26-3(8))* Grosvenor Hse. Publishing Ltd.

Kirby, Stan. Captain Awesome Takes a Dive. O'Connor, George, illus. 2012. (Captain Awesome Ser.: 4). (ENG.). 128p. (J). (gr. k-4). 17.99 *(978-1-4424-4203-0(4))*; pap. 6.99 *(978-1-4424-4202-3(6))* Little Simon. (Little Simon).

—Captain Awesome Takes a Dive. 2012. (Captain Awesome Ser.: 4). lib. bdg. 14.75 *(978-0-606-26325-2(X))* Turtleback.

Koraido, Beth S. Summers with Grampa Gus. 2008. 63p. pap. 19.95 *(978-1-60703-384-4(4))* America Star Bks.

Korda, Lerryn. It's Vacation Time: Playtime with Little Nye. Korda, Lerryn, illus. 2010. (Playtime with Little Nye Ser.). (ENG., Illus.). 26p. (J). (— 1). 8.99 *(978-0-7636-4813-8(2))* Candlewick Pr.

Kraft, Erik P. Lenny & Mel's Summer Vacation. Kraft, Erik P., illus. 2012. (Ready-For-Chapters Ser.). (ENG., Illus.). 64p. (J). (gr. 2-5). pap. 6.99 *(978-0-689-86874-0(X)*, Simon & Schuster/Paula Wiseman Bks.) Simon & Schuster/Paula Wiseman Bks.

Kreitzer, Dora. Summer in Connecticut. 2012. 18p. pap. 16.95 *(978-1-4626-8665-0(6))* America Star Bks.

LaBree Stute, Lela. Summer Pugs. 2010. (ENG.). 44p. pap. 19.99 *(978-0-557-41763-6(5))* Lulu Pr., Inc.

Lacy, Sandy Allbee. Pepe & Lupita & the Great Yawn Jar. Schrom, Garren, illus. 2013. 36p. pap. 10.95 *(978-1-60494-923-0(6))* Wheatmark, Inc.

Larry Sweitzer. The Ghost, the Eggheads, & Babe Ruth's Piano: A Novel. 2009. 180p. 23.95 *(978-1-4401-7103-1(3))*; pap. 13.95 *(978-1-4401-7104-8(1))* iUniverse, Inc.

Le Blanc, Lennie. The Minnesota Summer. 2011. 116p. (gr. 4-6). pap. 10.95 *(978-1-4620-3887-9(5))* iUniverse, Inc.

Leoni, Nancy. Toby Goes to Camp, 1 vol. Leoni, Nancy, illus. 2009. (Illus.). 21p. pap. 24.95 *(978-1-61546-417-3(4))* America Star Bks.

Lester, James D. Corn Flower: A Girl of the Great Plains. 2018. (Illus.). 103p. (J). pap. *(978-1-63293-219-8(9))* Sunstone Pr.

Levy, Dana Alison. The Family Fletcher Takes Rock Island. 2017. (Family Fletcher Ser.: 2). (ENG.). 272p. (J). (gr. 4-7). 7.99 *(978-0-553-52133-7(0)*, Yearling) Random Hse. Children's Bks.

Lewis, Kevin. Kj's Adventures. 2011. 28p. pap. 15.99 *(978-1-4653-3573-9(0))* Xlibris Corp.

Lewis, Linda. Loving Two Is Hard to Do. 2008. (ENG.). 160p. (YA). (gr. 7). pap. 8.95 *(978-1-4169-7534-2(9)*, Simon Pulse) Simon Pulse.

Lowery, Rae. Charlie & the Case of the Big Bully: The Adventures of Charlie #4, 1 vol. 2010. 108p. pap. 19.95 *(978-1-4489-5558-9(0))* America Star Bks.

Lowry, Brigid. Things You Either Hate or Love: A Novel. 2007. (ENG.). 192p. (YA). (gr. 8-12). pap. 18.99 *(978-0-312-36308-6(7)*, 900040880, St. Martin's Griffin) St. Martin's Pr.

Lubar, David. Dog Days. 80p. (J). (gr. 4-8). 2011. (ENG.). per. 7.99 *(978-1-58196-025-9(5)*, 6d9bb1e0-1830-48ed-a543-0f23f1ac5e48) 2004. 15.95 *(978-1-58196-013-6(1))* Lerner Publishing Group. (Darby Creek).

Luciani, Brigitte. How Will We Get to the Beach? Tharlet, Eve, illus. 2003. (ENG.). 32p. (J). (gr. -1). pap. 7.95 *(978-0-7358-1783-8(9))* North-South Bks., Inc.

Luxa, Sue. One Golden Summer. 2004. (Illus.). 80p. (J). pap. 8.95 *(978-1-890437-99-2(9)*, 1234248) Western Reflections Publishing Co.

Mac a'Bháird, Natasha. Hannah in the Spotlight: Star Club Book 1. 2016. (Star Club Ser.: 1). (ENG.). 192p. (J). pap. 15.00 *(978-1-84717-845-9(6))* O'Brien Pr., Ltd., The IRL. Dist: Dufour Editions, Inc.

Mack, Winnie. After All, You're Callie Boone. 2013. (ENG.). 192p. (J). (gr. 4-7). pap. 14.99 *(978-1-250-02735-1(7)*, 900098307) Square Fish.

MacPherson, Lorry. Lynne Woke Up! Alexander, Yvonne Rabdau, illus. 2007. 20p. per. 24.95 *(978-1-4137-2536-0(8))* America Star Bks.

Malik, Katherine. Giselle's Magical World, 1 vol. 2009. 150p. pap. 24.95 *(978-1-4489-1902-4(9))* America Star Bks.

Maloney, Peter. Here Comes Summer! 2004. (Illus.). 32p. pap. *(978-0-439-55363-6(6))* Scholastic, Inc.

Mara, Nichole. All Aboard! the Airport Train (an Abrams Extend-A-Book) Kolb, Andrew, illus. 2019. (Abrams Extend-A-Book Ser.). (ENG.). 10p. (J). (gr. -1 — 1). bds. 9.99 *(978-1-4197-3678-0(7)*, 1257610) Abrams, Inc.

The Marsh Runners. 2004. (J). per. 14.95 *(978-0-9761178-0-3(0))* Maritime Kids Quest Pr.

Martin, Amy. As You Wake. 2013. 294p. pap. 10.93 *(978-0-9882051-2-3(2))* Martin, Amy.

Martin, Ann M. Ten Good & Bad Things about My Life (So Far) 2013. (ENG.). 288p. (J). (gr. 4-7). pap. 8.99 *(978-1-250-03413-7(2)*, 900120583) Square Fish.

Martin-Fluet, Marie T. The Fairies' Century Celebration. 2011. 40p. pap. 18.62 *(978-1-4567-2477-1(0))* AuthorHouse.

Martin, Laura. Float. (Float Ser.: 1). (ENG.). (J). (gr. 3-7). 2019. 368p. pap. 7.99 *(978-0-06-280378-8(6))* 2018. 352p. 16.99 *(978-0-06-280376-4(X))* HarperCollins Pubs. (HarperCollins).

Maskame, Estelle. Did I Mention I Need You? 2016. (Did I Mention I Love You (DIMILY) Ser.: 2). (ENG.). 384p. (YA). (gr. 8-12). pap. 10.99 *(978-1-4926-3218-4(X)*, 9781492632184) Sourcebooks, Inc.

Maunder, Roger. Mundy Pond. 2006. (ENG.). 195p. per. *(978-1-897174-09-8(8))* Breakwater Bks., Ltd.

Mayfield, Holly. Melvin: A True Story with a Happy Ending. Gilman, Sara, illus. 2013. 38p. pap. 9.99 *(978-0-9892711-9-6(6))* Mindstir Media.

Mazer, Anne. The Best Is Yet to Come. 2004. (Amazing Days of Abby Hayes Ser.: No. 1). 109p. (J). lib. bdg. 16.92 *(978-1-4242-1197-5(2))* Fitzgerald Bks.

—That's the Way the Cookie Crumbles. 2005. (Amazing Days of Abby Hayes Ser.: Bk. 16). (Illus.). 119p. (J). (gr. 3-7). 12.65 *(978-0-7569-6480-1(6))* Perfection Learning Corp.

McBroom, Jill D. Here Comes Bobbyblob! 2008. 16p. pap. 7.76 *(978-1-4251-7174-2(5))* Trafford Publishing.

McCoy, Mary. Camp So-And-So. 2017. (ENG.). 424p. (YA). (gr. 8-12). E-Book 9.99 *(978-1-5124-3428-6(0)*, 9781512434286); E-Book 27.99 *(978-1-5124-3429-3(9)*, 9781512434293) Lerner Publishing Group. (Carolrhoda Lab™).

McDonald, Megan. Judy Moody & the NOT Bummer Summer. Reynolds, Peter H., illus. 2018. (Judy Moody Ser.: 10). (ENG.). 208p. (J). (gr. 1-4). pap. 5.99 *(978-1-5362-0084-3(0))* Candlewick Pr.

Mcdonald, Megan. Judy Moody & the Not Bummer Summer. 2012. (Judy Moody Ser.: 10). lib. bdg. 16.00 *(978-0-606-23800-7(X))* Turtleback.

Mcdonald, Megan & Michalak, Jamie. Judy Moody & the Poop Picnic (Judy Moody Movie Tie-In) Reynolds, Peter H. & Candlewick Press Staff, illus. 2011. (Judy Moody Ser.). (ENG.). 48p. (J). (gr. k-3). pap. 3.99 *(978-0-7636-5553-2(8))* Candlewick Pr.

McLean, Matthew. A Bewitching Summer, 1 vol. 2009. 100p. pap. 19.95 *(978-1-60836-686-6(3))* America Star Bks.

McMullan, Kate. Pearl & Wagner: Five Days till Summer. Alley, R. W., illus. 2014. (Pearl & Wagner Ser.: 5). 48p. (J). (gr. 1-3). pap. 4.99 *(978-0-448-48137-1(5)*, Penguin Young Readers) Penguin Young Readers Group.

McPhail, J. A. Dawn of Day. Battis, Gwen, illus. 2012. 200p. 17.99 *(978-0-9851196-2-1(4))* Rowe Publishing.

Meadows, Daisy. Joy the Summer Vacation Fairy. Ripper, Georgie, illus. 2007. (Rainbow Magic — Special Edition Ser.). 177p. (gr. -1-3). lib. bdg. 17.20 *(978-1-4177-7081-6(3))* Turtleback.

Meddaugh, Susan. Pool Party. 2011. (Martha Speaks Ser.). (ENG., Illus.). 24p. (J). (gr. -1-3). pap. 3.99 *(978-0-547-43882-5(6))* Houghton Mifflin Harcourt Publishing Co.

Meister, Cari. Tiny Goes to the Movies. 2016. (Penguin Young Readers Level 2 Ser.). lib. bdg. 13.55 *(978-0-606-38851-1(6))* Turtleback.

Menefee, Angelo K. Billy's First Summer Vacation. 2007. (Illus.). (J). per. 16.95 *(978-1-60002-249-4(9))* Mountain Valley Publishing, LLC.

Meredith, Susan Markowitz. A Happy Summer Day: Set Of 6. 2010. (Early Connections Ser.). (J). 37.00 net. *(978-1-4108-1371-8(1))* Benchmark Education Co.

Meyer, C. The Very First Unicorn. 2013. 24p. pap. 24.95 *(978-1-63004-317-9(6))* America Star Bks.

Michalak, Jamie. Judy Moody & the Thrill Points Race (Judy Moody Movie Tie-In) Candlewick Press, illus. 2011. (Judy

S

Moody Ser.). (ENG.). 48p. (J). (gr. k-3). pap. 3.99 *(978-0-7636-5552-5(X))* Candlewick Pr.
Michels, Anna. 26 Kisses. 2016. (ENG.). (YA). (gr. 9). pap. 12.99 *(978-1-4814-8515-9(6))* Simon & Schuster.
Middleton Elya, Susan. Our Celebración!, 1 vol. Aranda, Ana., illus. 2018. (ENG.). 32p. (J). (gr. k-3). 18.95 *(978-1-62014-271-4(6),* leelowbooks) Lee & Low Bks., Inc.
Montague, Chester. Timmy's Vacation. 2008. 40p. pap. 24.95 *(978-1-60441-225-3(9))* America Star Bks.
Montgomery, E. j. Hailey Walker & the Mystery of the Absent Professor. 2013. 180p. pap. 13.95 *(978-1-4575-2068-6(0))* Dog Ear Publishing, LLC.
Morah, Chizoba. The Anderson Twins. 2007. 76p. per. 19.95 *(978-1-60441-015-0(9))* America Star Bks.
Morgan, Melissa J. Suddenly Last Summer #20. 2008. (Camp Confidential Ser.: 20). 160p. (J). (gr. 3-7). pap. 4.99 *(978-0-448-44881-7(5),* Grosset & Dunlap) Penguin Young Readers Group.
Morgan, Retta & Morgan, Kris. Love Hates. 2011. 152p. pap. 11.99 *(978-1-4567-1448-2(1))* AuthorHouse.
Morris, Susan. Fritha's Summer. 2009. (Illus.). 251p. (J). pap. *(978-0-9551886-6-4(0))* M Pr.
Mostoller, Marcia. Emma's Summer Camp Dilemm. 2011. 64p. pap. 19.95 *(978-1-4626-2814-8(1))* America Star Bks.
Mun-Ensor, Michelle. Aloh. 2011. 32p. pap. 24.95 *(978-1-4560-9848-3(9))* America Star Bks.
Murray, Diana. Summer Color! Persico, Zoe, illus. 2018. (ENG.). 40p. (J). (gr. -1-3). 18.99 *(978-0-316-37094-3(0))* Little, Brown Bks. for Young Readers.
Mutrie, Matthew. Brady O'Brian Saves the Day. Morales, Andrew, illus. 2007. 37p. pap. 24.95 *(978-1-4241-9009-6(6))* America Star Bks.
Neely, Judith. And Even More. 2009. 24p. pap. 11.49 *(978-1-4389-5649-7(5))* AuthorHouse.
Newman, Constance. Summer Fruits. Fiorentino, Chiara, illus. 2017. (Seasons Around Me Ser.). (ENG.). 24p. (gr. -1-2). pap. 9.95 *(978-1-68342-753-7(X),* 9781683427537) Rourke Educational Media.
Nicholas, Nicki. Peter & Lil's Summer Day Adventure. 2011. 24p. pap. 15.50 *(978-1-4269-5358-3(5))* Trafford Publishing.
Night, P. J. Home, Sweet Haunt. 2013. (Creepover Ser.: 15). lib. bdg. 16.00 *(978-0-606-32047-4(4))* Turtleback.
Noel, Alyson. Cruel Summer. 2008. (ENG.). 240p. (YA). (gr. 8-12). pap. 17.99 *(978-0-312-35511-1(4),* 900038147, St. Martin's Griffin) St. Martin's Pr.
—Forever Summer. 2011. (ENG.). 464p. (YA). (gr. 8-12). pap. 29.99 *(978-0-312-60439-4(4),* 900076464, St. Martin's Griffin) St. Martin's Pr.
Nolan, Allia Zobel. God's Light, Shining Bright. Bryant, Laura J., illus. 2006. 8p. (J). 12.99 *(978-0-8254-5527-8(8))* Kregel Pubns.
Novel Units. Summer of the Monkeys Novel Units Teacher Guide. 2019. (ENG.). (J). pap. 12.99 *(978-1-56137-065-8(7),* Novel Units, Inc.) Classroom Library Co.
Ockler, Sarah. Twenty Boy Summer. 2010. (ENG.). 320p. (YA). (gr. 7-17). pap. 17.99 *(978-0-316-05158-3(6))* Little, Brown Bks. for Young Readers.
Older, Daniel José. Shadowshaper. 2016. (ENG.). 297p. (YA). (gr. 9). 20.85 *(978-0-606-39124-5(X))* Turtleback.
Olsen, Alana. It's Summer, 1 vol. 2016. (Four Seasons Ser.). (ENG., Illus.). 24p. (gr. 1-1). pap. 9.25 *(978-1-5081-5187-6(3),* b1948dad-5778-49b1-9019-95773aaba471, PowerKids Pr.) Rosen Publishing Group, Inc., The.
One, Hitoshi. Fireworks, Should We See It from the Side or the Bottom? (light Novel) 2018. (ENG., Illus.). 208p. (YA). (gr. 8-17). 20.00 *(978-1-9753-5326-1(9),* 9781975353261, Yen Pr.) Yen Pr. LLC.
Ormondroyd, Edward. Castaways on Long Ago. 2003. (Illus.). 188p. (J). (gr. 5-18). 12.95 *(978-0-9714612-8-4(7))* Green Mansion Pr. LLC.
Packard, Diane. Batina & Croakus. 2013. 36p. pap. 20.99 *(978-1-4817-0420-5(6))* AuthorHouse.
Pak, Kenard. Goodbye Summer, Hello Autumn. Pak, Kenard, illus. 2016. (ENG., Illus.). 32p. (J). 18.99 *(978-1-62779-415-2(8),* 900149957, Holt, Henry & Co. Bks. For Young Readers) Holt, Henry & Co.
Palmer, Robin. Wicked Jealous: A Love Story. 2012. (ENG.). 272p. (YA). (gr. 6-8). 26.19 *(978-0-14-241894-9(3))* Penguin Young Readers Group.
Panini Publishing, creator. Scooby Doo! Summer Annual. 2011. (Illus.). 63p. (J). (gr. 4-7). pap. *(978-1-84653-145-3(4))* Panini Publishing.
Pantelo, Amber. The Totally Meaningless Summer. 2004. 75p. (YA). pap. 12.95 *(978-0-7414-1914-9(9))* Infinity Publishing.
Papademetriou, Lisa & Minsky, Terri. A Very Lizzie Summer. 2005. (Lizzie Mcguire Super Special Ser.). (Illus.). 265p. (J). *(978-1-4155-9625-8(5))* Disney Pr.
Parish, Herman. Amelia Bedelia Digs In. 2018. (Amelia Bedelia Chapter Book Ser.: 12). (J). lib. bdg. 14.75 *(978-0-606-40061-9(3))* Turtleback.
Parr, Letitia. When Sea & Sky Are Blue. Watts, John, illus. 32p. (J). (gr. -1-3). 13.95 *(978-0-87592-059-7(4))* Scroll Pr., Inc.
Patterson, C. Marie. Little Dinky's Love for Basketball. 2009. 24p. pap. 15.99 *(978-1-4415-1255-0(1))* Xlibris Corp.
Perez, Angela J. Zack Attack! Hazard, Andrea, illus. 2007. 36p. (J). 17.95 *(978-0-9778328-9-7(9))* His Work Christian Publishing.
Phelan, Matt. Bluffton: My Summers with Buster. Phelan, Matt, illus. 2017. (ENG., Illus.). (J). (gr. 4-7). lib. bdg. 24.50 *(978-0-606-39837-4(6))* Turtleback.
—Bluffton: My Summers with Buster Keaton. Phelan, Matt, illus. 2017. (ENG., Illus.). 232p. (J). (gr. 4-7). pap. 14.99 *(978-0-7636-8706-9(5))* Candlewick Pr.
—Pignic: A Springtime Book for Kids. Phelan, Matt, illus. 2018. (ENG., Illus.). 32p. (J). (gr. -1-3). 17.99 *(978-0-06-244339-7(9),* Greenwillow Bks.) HarperCollins Pubs.
Philbin, Joanna. Rules of Summer. 2014. (Rules of Summer Ser.: 1). (ENG.). 368p. (YA). (gr. 10-17). pap. 18.99 *(978-0-316-21204-5(0),* Poppy) Little, Brown Bks. for Young Readers.
Pittar, Gill. Milly, Molly & Special Friends (book W/dolls) 2006. 28p. pap. *(978-1-86972-104-6(7))* Milly Molly Bks.
Polak, Monique. Forensics Squad Unleashed, 1 vol. 2016. (ENG.). 208p. (J). (gr. 4-7). pap. 10.95 *(978-1-4598-0979-6(3))* Orca Bk. Pubs. USA.
Posner, Renee & Quinton, Sasha. Suzy Season Loves Summer. D'Argo, Laura, illus. (Be Mine Bears Ser.). (J). bds. 4.99 *(978-1-58209-351-2(2))* Bks. Are Fun, Ltd.
Price, Jennifer L. Half Moon: Phases of the Moon: Book 2, 1 vol. 2009. 252p. pap. 27.95 *(978-1-4489-2193-5(7))* PublishAmerica, Inc.
Pyne, Jane. Tommy's Secret. 2009. 86p. pap. 10.49 *(978-1-4389-9102-3(9))* AuthorHouse.
Rabe, Tish. On the First Day of Summer Vacation. Jennings, Sarah, illus. 2019. (ENG.). 32p. (J). (gr. -1-3). 9.99 *(978-0-06-266852-3(8),* HarperCollins) HarperCollins Pubs.
Raczka, Bob. Summer Wonders. Stead, Judy, illus. 2012. (J). 34.28 *(978-1-61913-125-5(0))* Weigl Pubs., Inc.
Rad, Charles J. The Boy they called a Snowball. 2007. (ENG.). 140p. pap. 20.95 *(978-1-84753-461-3(9))* Lulu Pr., Inc.
Ramirez, Terry. Growing up with Olivi: The Beguiling Blue-Haired Beauty of Boysenberry Lane. 2009. 96p. pap. 9.95 *(978-0-595-47668-8(6))* iUniverse, Inc.
Ramos, Ramona J. A Summer with Kaitlyn & Lexi. 2011. 48p. pap. 16.95 *(978-1-4626-1890-3(1))* America Star Bks.
Rayner, Shoo. Roman Brit: 06: Dead Heat. 2016. (History of Britain In 12... Ser.). (ENG., Illus.). 64p. (J). (gr. k-2). pap. 7.99 *(978-1-4083-3463-8(1),* Orchard Bks.) Hachette Children's Group GBR. Dist: Hachette Bk. Group.
Rebello, Kevin. Julia & Mckinley's Day at the Beach. 2009. 32p. pap. 12.99 *(978-1-4389-7330-2(6))* AuthorHouse.
Reimiller, Diane L. A Duck Named Quackers, 1 vol. Jastrzebski, Brandy, illus. 2009. 12p. pap. 24.95 *(978-1-60836-771-9(1))* America Star Bks.
Reynolds Naylor, Phyllis. Boys Rock! 2007. (Boy/Girl Battle Ser.: 11). (ENG.). 144p. (J). (gr. 3-7). 5.99 *(978-0-440-41990-7(5),* Yearling) Random Hse. Children's Bks.
—The Grooming of Alice. 2012. (Alice Ser.: 12). (ENG., Illus.). 240p. (J). (gr. 5-9). pap. 7.99 *(978-1-4424-3496-7(1),* Atheneum Bks. for Young Readers) Simon & Schuster Children's Publishing.
—Intensely Alice. 2009. (Alice Ser.: 21). (ENG.). 288p. (YA). (gr. 9-18). 16.99 *(978-1-4169-7551-9(9),* Atheneum Bks. for Young Readers) Simon & Schuster Children's Publishing.
Richardson, Bernard. Freddy Weller's Holiday. 2011. 50p. 24.99 *(978-1-4628-9548-9(4));* pap. 15.99 *(978-1-4628-9547-2(6))* Xlibris Corp.
Richens, Carol & Smith, Lori. Lori's Summer Fun with Tamara! 2009. 33p. 16.40 *(978-1-4357-1113-6(0))* Lulu Pr., Inc.
Ritchie, Polly. A Pocket Full of Frogs. 2007. 124p. pap. 10.00 *(978-0-9795103-2-8(5))* Ascended Ideas.
Roberts, Johanna Lonsdorf. Summer at the Cabin. Shaggy Dog Press, ed. Challoner, Audrey, illus. 2007. 32p. (J). per. *(978-0-9722007-2-1(X))* Shaggy Dog Pr.
Robinson, Stephen. The Duke of Cork. 2011. 86p. pap. 19.95 *(978-1-4560-3340-8(9))* America Star Bks.
Rodgers, Mary. Summer Switch. 224p. (J). (gr. 4-6). pap. 4.95 *(978-0-8072-1550-0(3),* Listening Library) Random Hse. Audio Publishing Group.
Romer, Ruth. The Great Lemonade Standoff. 2005. (J). pap. *(978-1-4108-4200-8(2))* Benchmark Education Co.
Rue, Nancy N. Lucy's Perfect Summer, 1 vol. 2016. (Faithgirlz / a Lucy Novel Ser.: 3). (ENG.). 192p. (J). pap. 7.99 *(978-0-310-75504-3(2))* Zonderkidz.
Rylant, Cynthia. Annie & Snowball & the Book Bugs Club. 2012. (Annie & Snowball Ready-To-Read Ser.). lib. bdg. 13.55 *(978-0-606-23692-8(9))* Turtleback.
—Annie & Snowball & the Book Bugs Club: Ready-To-Read Level 2. Stevenson, Suçie & Stevenson, Suçie, illus. (Annie & Snowball Ser.: 9). (ENG.). 40p. (J). (gr. k-2). 2012. pap. 4.99 *(978-1-4169-7201-3(3))* 2011. 17.99 *(978-1-4169-7199-3(8))* Simon Spotlight. (Simon Spotlight).
—Cobble Street Cousins Complete Collection (Boxed Set) In Aunt Lucy's Kitchen; a Little Shopping; Special Gifts; Some Good News; Summer Party; Wedding Flowers. Halperin, Wendy Anderson, illus. 2018. (Cobble Street Cousins Ser.). (ENG.). 400p. (J). (gr. 2-5). pap. 34.99 *(978-1-5344-1633-8(1),* Aladdin) Simon & Schuster Children's Publishing.
—Mr. Putter & Tabby Clear the Decks. Howard, Arthur, illus. alt. ed. 2011. (Mr. Putter & Tabby Ser.). (ENG.). 44p. (J). (gr. 1-4). pap. 5.99 *(978-0-547-57695-4(1),* 1458450, Clarion Bks.) HarperCollins Pubs.
Sadd, Kenn. Crazy Cracked Pots. 2009. 144p. pap. 24.95 *(978-1-61546-673-3(8))* America Star Bks.
Sam's Last Summer. 2006. (J). per. 5.95 *(978-0-9790796-3-4(2))* PJR Assocs., Ltd.
Schraff, Anne. One Amazing Summer. 2017. (Red Rhino Ser.). lib. bdg. 18.40 *(978-0-606-40324-5(8))* Turtleback.
Schronk, Julie. The Grass Grows Green. 2007. 208p. per. 24.95 *(978-1-60441-057-0(4))* America Star Bks.
Schwartz, Joanne. Pinny in Summer, 1 vol. Malenfant, Isabelle, illus. 2016. (ENG.). 32p. (J). (gr. -1-2). 16.95 *(978-1-55498-782-5(2))* Groundwood Bks. CAN. Dist: Publishers Group West (PGW).
Sevigny, Alisha. Summer Constellations. 2018. (ENG.). 264p. (J). (gr. 9-12). 17.99 *(978-1-77138-929-7(X))* Kids Can Pr., Ltd. CAN. Dist: Hachette Bk. Group.
Shanahan, Lisa. The Grand, Genius Summer of Henry Hoobler. 2018. (ENG.). 224p. (J). (gr. 2-6). pap. 11.99 *(978-1-76029-301-7(6))* Allen & Unwin AUS. Dist: Independent Pubs. Group.
Sheckels, Astrid, illus. Nic & Nellie, 1 vol. 2013. (ENG.). 36p. (J). (gr. 1-4). 17.95 *(978-1-934031-52-0(6),* d981927c-4686-4ef6-bbee-9d134ce68c96) Islandport Pr., Inc.
Simms, Abigail & Gabrielle. Let's Turn Our World Upside Down. 2013. 28p. pap. 16.09 *(978-1-4669-8156-0(3))* Trafford Publishing.
Simon, Coco. Emma All Stirred Up! (Cupcake Diaries: 7). (ENG.), 160p. (J). (gr. 3-7). 2013. Illus.). 17.99 *(978-1-4424-8567-9(1))* 2012. pap. 6.99 *(978-1-4424-5078-3(9))* Simon Spotlight. (Simon Spotlight).
—Emma All Stirred Up! 2012. (Cupcake Diaries: 7). lib. bdg. 17.20 *(978-0-606-26309-2(8))* Turtleback.
Simoneau, Shelly. The Cows Came Running & the Horses Did Too! 2011. 28p. pap. 14.99 *(978-1-4567-3107-6(6))* AuthorHouse.
Sinclair, Gardine. Stageschool by the Sea. 2013. 176p. (J). pap. *(978-1-78299-389-6(4))* FeedARead.com.
Sioux Rose. Cassandra's Tale: Invitation to the Circle. 2010. 200p. pap. 16.95 *(978-1-4401-9510-5(2))* iUniverse, Inc.
Sís, Peter. Ice Cream Summer. Sís, Peter, illus. 2015. (ENG., Illus.). 40p. (J). (gr. -1-3). 18.99 *(978-0-545-73161-4(5),* Scholastic Pr.) Scholastic, Inc.
Skalak, Daniel. All Summer's Fun. Skalak, Daniel, illus. 2006. (Illus.). 32p. (J). (gr. -1-3). 15.95 *(978-1-60108-000-4(X))* Red Cygnet Pr.
Sloan, L. Bridges. 2005. 164p. 22.99 *(978-1-58832-123-7(1));* per. 12.99 *(978-1-58832-122-0(3))* Unlimited Publishing LLC.
Smith Jr., Charles R. Chameleon. 2010. (ENG., Illus.). 384p. (YA). (gr. 7). pap. 7.99 *(978-0-7636-4660-8(1))* Candlewick Pr.
Smoot, Madeline, compiled by. Summer Shorts: A Short Story Collection. 2005. (ENG., Illus.). 360p. (J). (gr. 2-7). pap. 8.95 *(978-0-9769417-5-0(9))* Blooming Tree Pr.
Smythe, Katie. The Summer Picnic, 1 vol. 2015. (Rosen REAL Readers: STEM & STEAM Collection). (ENG.). 8p. (gr. k-1). pap. 5.46 *(978-1-4994-9557-7(9),* 4f01c03b-4d63-44a7-8e71-9fbfe3d720ec, Rosen Classroom) Rosen Publishing Group, Inc., The.
Snow, Virginia B. Summer Walk, 1 vol. (ENG.). 32p. (J). (gr. -1-3). 2019. 8.99 *(978-1-4236-5394-3(7))* 2016. (Illus.). 16.99 *(978-1-4236-4215-2(5))* Gibbs Smith, Publisher.
Snyder, Laurel. My Jasper June. (ENG.). 304p. (J). (gr. 3-7). 2021. pap. 9.99 *(978-0-06-283663-2(3))* 2019. 16.99 *(978-0-06-283662-5(5))* 2019. E-Book *(978-0-06-283664-9(1),* 9780062836649) HarperCollins Pubs. (Waldon Pond Pr.).
Sommer, Sharon. The Adventures of Summer Hills: Rowdy Red's Lesson. 2008. 28p. per. 24.95 *(978-1-4241-9374-5(5))* America Star Bks.
Spinelli, Eileen. Now It Is Summer. DePalma, Mary, illus. 2011. (ENG.). 36p. (YA). (gr. -1-3). 16.00 *(978-0-8028-5340-0(4),* Eerdmans Bks For Young Readers) Eerdmans, William B. Publishing Co.
—Summerhouse Time. Lew-Vriethoff, Joanne, illus. 2009. (ENG.). 224p. (J). (gr. 3-7). 8.99 *(978-0-440-42224-2(8),* Yearling) Random Hse. Children's Bks.
Sprenger, Luke. Sommer in Canvas Bay. 2008. (GER.). 92p. pap. 13.95 *(978-1-4092-3213-1(1))* Lulu Pr., Inc.
Spruill, Beverle. The Dream Box. 2009. 24p. pap. 13.50 *(978-1-4490-3783-3(6))* AuthorHouse.
Staffen, Julie. Krista Kay Summer Adventures. 2010. 156p. pap. 10.95 *(978-1-60920-005-3(5))* Ajoyin Publishing, Inc.
Stanek, Robert, pseud. Bugville Critters Start Summer Vacation. 2011. (Illus.). 32p. pap. 4.99 *(978-1-57545-257-9(X),* Reagent Pr. Bks. for Young Readers) RP Media.
—Start Summer Vacation. 2010. (Illus.). 32p. pap. 8.99 *(978-1-57545-174-9(3),* Reagent Pr. Bks. for Young Readers) RP Media.
Stein, David Ezra. Honey. Stein, David Ezra, illus. 2018. (ENG., Illus.). 32p. (J). (-k). 16.99 *(978-1-5247-3786-3(0),* Nancy Paulsen Books) Penguin Young Readers Group.
Stevens, Michael J. Silver Spitfire. 2010. 164p. pap. *(978-1-907652-13-4(2))* Grosvenor Hse. Publishing Ltd.
Stewart, A. W. Rooktime. 2010. 284p. pap. 15.49 *(978-1-4520-1460-9(4))* AuthorHouse.
Stewart, Dianne C. Longitude - Zero Degrees. 2009. (ENG.). 200p. pap. 8.95 *(978-0-9667359-4-9(3),* BeanPole Bks.) OH Industries.
Stewart, Kiera. The Summer of Bad Ideas. 2017. (ENG.). 304p. (J). (gr. 3-7). 16.99 *(978-0-06-236021-2(3),* HarperCollins) HarperCollins Pubs.
Stine, R. L. Attack of the Jack. 2017. (Goosebumps SlappyWorld Ser.: 2). lib. bdg. 17.20 *(978-0-606-40169-2(5))* Turtleback.
—Temptation: Goodnight Kiss; Goodnight Kiss 2; "the Vampire Club" 2012. (ENG.). 416p. (YA). (gr. 7). pap. 11.99 *(978-1-4424-5068-4(1),* Simon Pulse) Simon Pulse.
Strasser, Todd & Thacker, Nola. The Shore: Shirt & Shoes Not Required; LB (Laguna Beach) 2011. (ENG.). 480p. (YA). (gr. 9). pap. 9.99 *(978-1-4424-1970-4(9),* Simon Pulse) Simon Pulse.
Stratton, Erin. There's Nothing Wrong with Boys. Gregeory, Vicki, illus. 2010. 26p. pap. 12.00 *(978-1-60911-021-5(8),* Eloquent Bks.) Strategic Book Publishing & Rights Agency (SBPRA).
Summer Fun: Individual Title Six-Packs. (Literatura 2000 Ser.). (gr. -1-1). 28.00 *(978-0-7635-0064-1(X))* Rigby Education.
Swayne Tidwell, Deborah. Magic Eraser & Camp Real. 2009. 16p. pap. 8.50 *(978-1-4343-8916-9(2))* AuthorHouse.
Tamaki, Mariko. This One Summer. Tamaki, Jillian, illus. 2014. (ENG.). 320p. (YA). (gr. 7). 22.99 *(978-1-62672-094-7(0),* 900135617, First Second Bks.) Roaring Brook Pr.
—This One Summer. Tamaki, Jillian, illus. 2014. (ENG.). 320p. (YA). (gr. 7). pap. 18.99 *(978-1-59643-774-6(X),* 900081621, First Second Bks.) Roaring Brook Pr.
Tan, Shaun. Rules of Summer. Tan, Shaun, illus. 2014. (ENG.). 48p. (J). (gr. -1-3). 19.99 *(978-0-545-63912-5(3),* Levine, Arthur A. Bks.) Scholastic, Inc.
Tashjian, Janet. My Life As a Book. Tashjian, Jake, illus. 2011. (My Life Ser.: 1). (ENG.). 240p. (J). (gr. 4-7). pap. 7.99 *(978-0-312-67289-8(6),* 900072374) Square Fish.
Taylor, Chloe. Knot Too Shabby! Zhang, Nancy, illus. 2014. (Sew Zoey Ser.: 7). (ENG.). 176p. (J). (gr. 3-7). pap. 5.99 *(978-1-4814-1398-5(8),* Simon Spotlight) Simon Spotlight.
—Swatch Out! Zhang, Nancy, illus. 2014. (Sew Zoey Ser.: 8). (ENG.). 176p. (J). (gr. 3-7). pap. 5.99 *(978-1-4814-1535-4(2),* Simon Spotlight) Simon Spotlight.
Thaler, Mike. The Summer Camp from the Black Lagoon. Lee, Jared, illus. 2016. (Black Lagoon Adventures Set 4 Ser.). (ENG.). 64p. (J). (gr. 2-6). lib. bdg. 31.36 *(978-1-61479-608-4(4),* 24341, Chapter Bks.) Spotlight.
—The Summer Vacation from the Black Lagoon. Lee, Jared D., illus. 2010. 62p. (J). *(978-0-545-07224-3(7))* Scholastic, Inc.
—The Summer Vacation from the Black Lagoon, 1 vol. Lee, Jared, illus. 2012. (Black Lagoon Adventures Ser.: No. 2). (ENG.). 64p. (J). (gr. 2-6). 31.36 *(978-1-59961-964-4(4),* 3608, Chapter Bks.) Spotlight.
Thompson, Kay & Knight, Hilary. Eloise Ready-To-Read Value Pack: Eloise's Summer Vacation; Eloise at the Wedding; Eloise & the Very Secret Room; Eloise Visits the Zoo; Eloise Throws a Party!; Eloise's Pirate Adventure, Pack. 2012. (Eloise Ser.). (ENG.). 192p. (J). (gr. -1-1). pap. 17.96 *(978-1-4424-4949-7(7),* Simon Spotlight) Simon Spotlight.
Thompson, Lauren. Mouse Loves Summer: Ready-To-Read Pre-Level 1. Erdogan, Buket, illus. 2018. (Mouse Ser.). (ENG.). 32p. (J). (gr. -1-k). 17.99 *(978-1-5344-2057-1(6));* pap. 4.99 *(978-1-5344-2056-4(8))* Simon Spotlight. (Simon Spotlight).
—Mouse's First Summer. Erdogan, Buket, illus. 2013. (Classic Board Bks.). (ENG.). 34p. (J). (gr. -1 — 1). bds. 8.99 *(978-1-4424-5842-0(9),* Little Simon) Little Simon.
—Mouse's First Summer. Erdogan, Buket, illus. 2014. (J). *(978-1-4351-5506-0(8))* Simon & Schuster.
Thomson, Sarah L. Feel the Summer. Yamada, Kana, illus. 2006. (ENG.). 32p. (J). (gr. -1-3). 14.95 *(978-1-59687-174-8(1))* IBks., Inc.
Toska, Mary Lou. Ernest's Dream: A Young Boy Wanting to Spend the Summer in the High Alps. 2012. 20p. pap. 24.95 *(978-1-4626-8662-9(1))* America Star Bks.
Treanor, H. T. The Sun Stone. Tarnowski, Mark, illus. 2012. 16p. pap. 10.00 *(978-1-60976-125-7(1),* Strategic Bk. Publishing) Strategic Book Publishing & Rights Agency (SBPRA).
Turner, Julie Anne. A Tale of Summerland. 2007. (Illus.). 72p. pap. *(978-1-84401-902-1(0))* Athena Pr.
Ulrich, Paulina. Flightless Bird. 2011. (ENG.). 424p. pap. 11.99 *(978-1-4565-3438-7(6))* CreateSpace Independent Publishing Platform.
Usher, Sam. Sun. Usher, Sam, illus. 2018. (Seasons Quartet Ser.). (ENG., Illus.). 40p. (J). (gr. -1-2). 16.99 *(978-0-7636-9949-9(7),* Templar) Candlewick Pr.
Vail, Rachel. Justin Case: Shells, Smells, & the Horrible Flip-Flops of Doom, 2. Cordell, Matthew, illus. 2013. (Justin Case Ser.: 2). (ENG.). 208p. (J). (gr. 2-4). pap. 7.99 *(978-1-250-02723-8(3),* 900098294) Square Fish.
Valentin, Karen. Block Party. 2009. 32p. (J). (gr. -1-3). 6.95 *(978-1-60349-017-7(5),* Marimba Bks.) Just Us Bks., Inc.
Van Name, Sarah. The Goodbye Summer. 2019. 352p. (YA). (gr. 8-12). pap. 10.99 *(978-1-4926-7703-1(5))* Sourcebooks, Inc.
Velez, Edia L. Jessica's Summer Vacation - Las Vacaciones de Verano de Jéssic. 2011. 44p. pap. 18.49 *(978-1-4490-2301-0(0))* AuthorHouse.
Viva, Frank. Sea Change: A TOON Graphic. 2016. (Illus.). 120p. (J). (gr. 3-7). 18.95 *(978-1-935179-92-4(6),* Toon Books) Astra Publishing Hse.
Vivian, Siobhan. Stay Sweet. (ENG.). 368p. (YA). (gr. 9). 2019. pap. 11.99 *(978-1-4814-5233-5(9))* 2018. (Illus.). 17.99 *(978-1-4814-5232-8(0))* Simon & Schuster Bks. For Young Readers. (Simon & Schuster Bks. For Young Readers).
—Stay Sweet. 2018. (ENG.). 368p. (YA). (gr. 9). pap. 12.99 *(978-1-5344-0503-5(8))* Simon & Schuster, Inc.
Voake, Steve. Daisy Dawson on the Farm. Meserve, Jessica, illus. 2013. (Daisy Dawson Ser.). (ENG.). 96p. (J). (gr. 1-4). pap. 7.99 *(978-0-7636-6340-7(9))* Candlewick Pr.
Vogel, Vin. The Thing about Yetis. 2015. (Illus.). 32p. (J). (gr. -1-k). 16.99 *(978-0-8037-4170-6(7),* Dial Bks) Penguin Young Readers Group.
Walker, Melissa. Lovestruck Summer. 2009. (ENG.). 272p. (J). (gr. 9-18). pap. 5.99 *(978-0-06-171586-0(7),* HarperTeen) HarperCollins Pubs.
Wallace, Bonny. The Raymond Wikins' Adventures, Children of Straw. 2009. 70p. pap. 9.95 *(978-1-60860-699-3(6),* Eloquent Bks.) Strategic Book Publishing & Rights Agency (SBPRA).
WALSH, Mitchell. How Do Fairies Have Fun in The. 2018. (Illus.). 32p. (J). (gr. -1-2). 17.95 *(978-1-60893-993-0(6))* Down East Bks.
Waters, Cassie. Cool Down. 2012. (Pool Girls Ser.: 3). (ENG.). 160p. (J). (gr. 3-7). 15.99 *(978-1-4424-5377-7(X));* pap. 5.99 *(978-1-4424-4709-7(5))* Simon Spotlight. (Simon Spotlight).
—Heat Wave. 2012. (Pool Girls Ser.: 2). (ENG.). 160p. (J). (gr. 3-7). pap. 5.99 *(978-1-4424-4146-0(1),* Simon Spotlight) Simon Spotlight.
Weetman, Nova. A Hot Cold Summer: Choose Your Own Ever After. 2016. (ENG.). 256p. (J). pap. 5.99 *(978-1-61067-354-9(9))* Kane Miller.
Weihrich, Carroll. On Jim Street. 2003. 144p. 24.50 *(978-1-932621-19-8(9));* per. 15.00 *(978-1-932621-18-1(0))* Open Bk. Publishing.
Welles, Lee. Enter the Earth. Hameister, Ann, illus. 2006. (Gaia Girls Ser.: 1). (ENG.). 336p. (YA). (gr. 4-7). 18.95 *(978-1-933609-00-3(1))* Chelsea Green Publishing.
Wells, Carolyn. Patty's Butterfly Days. 2005. 28.95 *(978-1-4218-0309-8(7),* 1st World Library - Literary Society) 1st World Publishing, Inc.
Wells, Naomi. Jada's Summer Project: Organizing Data, 1 vol. 2017. (Computer Kids: Powered by Computational Thinking Ser.). (ENG., Illus.). 24p. (J). (gr. 3-4). 25.27 *(978-1-5383-2404-2(0),* e1770724-7fa0-4d05-bbea-700f3fe2f65a, PowerKids Pr.); pap. *(978-1-5081-3788-7(9),* c3dc7985-bb88-40bf-9cfc-6d86fc9fbd9e, Rosen Classroom) Rosen Publishing Group, Inc., The.
Wells, Rosemary. Ivy Takes Care. LaMarche, Jim, illus. (ENG.). 208p. (J). (gr. 3-7). 2015. pap. 6.99 *(978-0-7636-7660-5(8))* 2013. 15.99 *(978-0-7636-5352-1(7))* Candlewick Pr.
White, Alexis. Three Peas in a Pod. 2008. 56p. pap. 11.95 *(978-1-4327-1869-5(X))* Outskirts Pr., Inc.
Wiebe, Kathleen. Willow Creek Summer. 2005. 217p. (J). (gr. 7-12). 7.95 *(978-1-55050-169-8(0))* Coteau Bks. CAN. Dist: Fitzhenry & Whiteside, Ltd.
Wiersbitzky, Shannon. What Flowers Remember. 2014. 158p. (J). 18.95 *(978-1-60898-166-3(5))* namelos llc.
Wiggin, Kate Douglas. A Summer in a Canyon. 2007. 140p. 24.95 *(978-1-60312-626-7(0))* Aegypan.
Wilkins, Phil Cole. Dragog & the Seven Weeks of Summer. 2012. 164p. (gr. -1). pap. 15.60 *(978-1-4567-8998-5(8))* AuthorHouse.
Williams, Alan. Archy the Flying Dolphin & the Vampire's Curse. 2007. pap. 15.38 *(978-1-4251-3151-7(4))* Trafford Publishing.
Williams, Billie A. Fourteen Is Too Many: The Survivors. 2013. 24p. pap. 24.95 *(978-1-63004-179-3(3))* America Star Bks.
Wines, Michael P. Stupid Alabama: A Laugh-So-Hard-You-Will-Snot about Growing up to Discover Not All Things Are Stupid but a Lot of Them Are. Gierhart, Steve, ed. Floyd, Claire, illus. 2013. (ENG.). 244p. (gr. 5-12).

pap. 19.95 *(978-1-938667-13-8(1))* Ardent Writer Pr., LLC, The.

Winkler, Henry & Oliver, Lin. Summer School! What Genius Thought That Up? 2006. (Hank Zipzer Ser.: No. 8). (Illus.). 157p. (J). (gr. 3-9). lib. bdg. 24.21 *(978-1-59961-107-5(4))* Spotlight.

Wishinsky, Frieda. Camp Disaster, 1 vol. 2016. (Orca Currents Ser.). (ENG.). 120p. (J). (gr. 4-7). pap. 9.95 *(978-1-4598-1114-0(3))* Orca Bk. Pubs. USA.

Wittman, Kathy A. Raina's Vision Quest, 1 vol. 2010. 78p. pap. 19.95 *(978-1-61582-656-8(4))* America Star Bks.

Wolf, Maria. Maggy Cans. 2012. 52p. (gr. 4-6). pap. 11.95 *(978-1-4772-8093-5(6))* AuthorHouse.

Wong, Janet S. & Cote, Genevieve. Minn & Jake's Almost Terrible Summer. 2008. (ENG., Illus.). 112p. (J). (gr. 2-5). 16.99 *(978-0-374-34977-6(0)*, 900044565, Farrar, Straus & Giroux (BYR)) Farrar, Straus & Giroux.

Yee, Wong Herbert. Summer Days & Nights. Yee, Wong Herbert, illus. 2012. (ENG., Illus.). 32p. (J). (gr. -1-1). 19.99 *(978-0-8050-9078-9(9)*, 900061501, Holt, Henry & Co. Bks. For Young Readers) Holt, Henry & Co.

Young, Marlene Lauster. Before Summer's End. 2012. 36p. (-18). pap. 20.99 *(978-1-4772-6810-0(3))* AuthorHouse.

Zappone, Melanie Lippincott. The Sounds of Summer Sank in the Sea. 2011. 24p. (gr. -1). 12.68 *(978-1-4567-3856-3(9))* AuthorHouse.

Ziarnik, Natalie. A Lullaby of Summer Things. Valentine, Madeline, illus. 2018. 40p. (J). (gr. -1-3). 17.99 *(978-1-101-93552-1(9)*, Schwartz & Wade Bks.) Random Hse. Children's Bks.

SUMMER—POETRY

Carpenter, Stephen, illus. What I Did on My Summer Vacation: Kids' Favorite Funny Summer Vacation Poems. 2009. (Giggle Poetry Ser.). (ENG.). 80p. (J). (gr. 1-9). pap. 18.99 *(978-1-4169-7047-7(9)*, Running Pr.) Running Pr.

Forman, Ruth. Young Cornrows Callin Out the Moon. Bayoc, Cbabi, illus. 2007. (ENG.). 24p. (J). (gr. -1-3). lib. bdg. 16.95 *(978-0-89239-218-6(5))* Lee & Low Bks., Inc.

Lansky, Bruce. What I Did on My Summer Vacation: Kids' Favorite Funny Poems about Summer Vacation. Carpenter, Stephen, illus. 2009. *(978-0-88166-539-0(8))* Meadowbrook Pr.

SUMMER HOMES

see Architecture, Domestic; Houses

SUMMER RESORTS—FICTION

Doktorski, Jennifer. The Summer after You & Me. 2015. 304p. (YA). (gr. 8-12). pap. 12.99 *(978-1-4926-1903-1(5))* Sourcebooks, Inc.

Saldin, Erin. The Dead Enders. (ENG.). 448p. (YA). (gr. 9). 2019. pap. 12.99 *(978-1-4814-9041-2(9))* 2018. (Illus.). 18.99 *(978-1-4814-9033-7(8))* Simon Pulse. (Simon Pulse).

SUMMER THEATER—FICTION

Knudsen, Michelle. Revenge of the Evil Librarian. (ENG.). 288p. (gr. 9). 2019. (J). pap. 8.99 *(978-0-7636-9739-6(7))* 2017. (YA). 16.99 *(978-0-7636-8828-8(2))* Candlewick Pr.

SUN

see also Solar Energy; Solar System

Adamson, Thomas K. The Sun [Scholastic]. 2011. (Exploring the Galaxy Ser.). 24p. pap. 0.50 *(978-1-4296-6290-1(5)*, Capstone Pr.) Capstone.

Anderson, Michael. The Sun, Stars, & Galaxies, 1 vol. 2011. (Solar System Ser.). (ENG., Illus.). 96p. (J). (gr. 8-8). lib. bdg. 35.29 *(978-1-61530-519-3(X)*, 4da0729d-9c90-488b-b525-d7146a1edaa8) Rosen Publishing Group, Inc., The.

Appleby, Alex. It's Sunny!, 1 vol. 2013. (What's the Weather? Ser.). 24p. (J). (gr. k-k). (ENG.). pap. 9.15 *(978-1-4339-9409-8(7)*, f49b7ca5-5325-4950-8c3c-e713362a2050); pap. 48.90 *(978-1-4339-9410-4(0))*; (ENG., Illus.). lib. bdg. 25.27 *(978-1-4339-9408-1(9)*, 31813962-5f96-414b-92f3-7e80d26cfd59) Stevens, Gareth Publishing LLLP.

—It's Sunny! / ¡Está Soleado!, 1 vol. 2013. (What's the Weather? / ¿Qué Tiempo Hace? Ser.). (SPA & ENG., Illus.). 24p. (J). (gr. k-k). 25.27 *(978-1-4339-9454-8(2)*, 8520c099-825c-40d9-9a9e-704fd347d662) Stevens, Gareth Publishing LLLP.

Asch, Frank. The Sun Is My Favorite Star. Asch, Frank, illus. 2008. (ENG., Illus.). 32p. (J). (gr. -1-3). pap. 9.99 *(978-0-15-206397-9(8)*, 1199150, Clarion Bks.) HarperCollins Pubs.

Aspen-Baxter, Linda & Kissock, Heather. El Sol. 2012. (Mirando Al Cielo Ser.). (SPA., Illus.). 24p. (J). (gr. k-2). 27.13 *(978-1-61913-219-1(2)*, AV2 by Weigl) Weigl Pubs., Inc.

Asselin, Kristine Carlson. Our Sun. 2010. (Solar System & Beyond Ser.). (ENG.). 32p. (J). (gr. 3-4). pap. 48.60 *(978-1-4296-6409-7(6)*, 16155, Capstone Pr.); (Illus.). pap. 8.10 *(978-1-4296-6238-3(7)*, 115390) Capstone.

Bang, Molly & Chisholm, Penny. Living Sunlight: How Plants Bring the Earth to Life. Bang, Molly, illus. 2009. (ENG., Illus.). 40p. (J). (gr. -1-3). 19.99 *(978-0-545-04422-6(7)*, Blue Sky Pr., The) Scholastic, Inc.

—Rivers of Sunlight: How the Sun Moves Water Around the Earth. Bang, Molly, illus. 2017. (ENG., Illus.). 48p. (J). (gr. -1-3). 19.99 *(978-0-545-80541-4(4)*, Blue Sky Pr., The) Scholastic, Inc.

Bartlett, Melissa. What Makes the Sun So Hot?, 1 vol. 2013. (Rosen Readers Ser.). (ENG.). 24p. (J). (gr. 3-3). pap. 8.25 *(978-1-4777-2542-9(3)*, c08f84b7-688c-4ca9-a94e-9a590b882711); pap. 49.50 *(978-1-4777-2543-6(1))* Rosen Publishing Group, Inc., The. (Rosen Classroom).

Bath, Louella. Mysteries of the Sun. 2013. (InfoMax Readers Ser.). (ENG.). 24p. (J). (gr. 3-4). pap. 49.50 *(978-1-4777-2595-5(4))*; (Illus.). pap. 8.25 *(978-1-4777-2593-1(8)*, 77522ede-2816-4609-9b39-c2cdae917585) Rosen Publishing Group, Inc., The. (Rosen Classroom).

Bauer, Marion Dane. Sun: Ready-To-Read Level 1. Wallace, John, illus. 2016. (Weather Ready-To-Reads Ser.). (ENG.). 32p. (J). (gr. -1-1). pap. 4.99 *(978-1-4814-6339-3(X)*, Simon Spotlight) Simon Spotlight.

Bell, Cassie. The Hot Sun. 2016. (Spring Forward Ser.). (J). (gr. k). *(978-1-4900-3734-9(9))* Benchmark Education Co.

Bell, Trudy E. The Sun: Our Nearest Star. 2003. (New Solar System Ser.). (J). lib. bdg. 28.50 *(978-1-58340-286-3(1))* Black Rabbit Bks.

Benchmark Education Co., LLC. Fun in the Sun Big Book. 2014. (Shared Reading Foundations Ser.). (J). (gr. -1). *(978-1-4509-9439-2(3))* Benchmark Education Co.

Benson, Jodyanne. The Sun & Earth's Surface, 1 vol. 2019. (Power of the Sun Ser.). (ENG.). 32p. (gr. 3-3). pap. 11.58 *(978-1-5026-4666-8(8)*, 0724a52e-3b08-4485-b63e-31ff0e5b074d) Cavendish Square Publishing LLC.

Blaisdell, Molly. Our Sun. 2008. (Discovering & Exploring Science Ser.). (Illus.). 16p. (J). (gr. -1-3). 12.95 *(978-0-7569-8257-7(X))* Perfection Learning Corp.

Boothroyd, Jennifer. What Does Sunlight Do? 2014. (First Step Nonfiction — Let's Watch the Weather Ser.). (ENG., Illus.). 24p. (J). (gr. k-2). pap. 6.99 *(978-1-4677-4496-6(4)*, f6fd0111-3633-4f80-ba8a-1606c2b85dfe); lib. bdg. 23.99 *(978-1-4677-3921-4(9)*, cff3eea9-7a81-44f3-96ce-e88baf7a15d1, Lerner Pubns.) Lerner Publishing Group.

Bow, James. Understanding Our Sun. 2019. (Mission: Space Science Ser.). (Illus.). 48p. (J). (gr. 5-5). *(978-0-7787-5395-7(6))*; pap. *(978-0-7787-5406-0(5))* Crabtree Publishing Co.

Branley, Franklyn M. Sunshine Makes the Seasons. Rex, Michael, illus. 2005. (Let's-Read-And-Find-Out Science 2 Ser.). (ENG.). 40p. (J). (gr. k-4). pap. 5.99 *(978-0-06-059205-9(2)*, Collins) HarperCollins Pubs.

Branley, Franklyn Mansfield. Sunshine Makes the Seasons. Rex, Michael, illus. 2005. (Let's-Read-and-Find-Out-Science Ser.). (ENG.). 40p. (J). (gr. -1 — 1). 15.99 *(978-0-06-059203-5(6))* HarperCollins Pubs.

Bredeson, Carmen & Dyson, Marianne. Exploring the Sun, 1 vol. 2015. (Launch into Space! Ser.). (ENG.). 32p. (gr. 3-4). pap. 11.52 *(978-0-7660-6833-9(1)*, 91c2fc22-2dec-4f14-ac52-ee9a4990b4f0); (Illus.). 26.93 *(978-0-7660-6835-3(8)*, cf9b91d6-8f0c-4990-9d3d-e6075861a5d7) Enslow Publishing, LLC.

Brennan, Linda Crotta. There Is Day & Night. 2014. (Tell Me Why Library). (ENG., Illus.). 24p. (J). (gr. 2-5). 29.21 *(978-1-63188-007-0(1)*, 205435) Cherry Lake Publishing.

Brinker, Spencer. A Sunny Day. 2018. (Weather Watch Ser.). (ENG.). 16p. (J). (gr. -1-1). 6.99 *(978-1-64280-134-7(8))*; (Illus.). 16.96 *(978-1-64280-001-2(5))* Bearport Publishing Co., Inc.

Brinkman, Patricia. Discover the Sun. 2006. (J). pap. *(978-1-4108-6477-2(4))* Benchmark Education Co.

—The Sun. 2006. (J). pap. *(978-1-4108-6474-1(X))* Benchmark Education Co.

Budd Josselin. The Sun Is Not a Yellow Balloon: Fun with the Sun for Kids. 2013. 28p. pap. 9.74 *(978-1-63022-159-1(7)*, Baby Professor (Education Kids)) Speedy Publishing LLC.

Burton, Margie, et al. Our Sun. 2011. (Early Connections Ser.). (J). *(978-1-61672-532-7(X))* Benchmark Education Co.

Capaccio, George. The Sun, 1 vol. 2010. (Space! Ser.). (ENG.). 64p. (gr. 5-5). lib. bdg. 35.50 *(978-0-7614-4242-4(1)*, 54a401fd-eeaa-45a0-b8fa-49625e4a1261) Cavendish Square Publishing LLC.

Carson, Mary Kay. Far-Out Guide to the Sun, 1 vol. 2010. (Far-Out Guide to the Solar System Ser.). (ENG., Illus.). 48p. (gr. 4-6). 27.93 *(978-0-7660-3179-1(9)*, d196138e-e746-4a4e-ad8b-fe4084661cfa); pap. 11.53 *(978-1-59845-180-1(4)*, 4782d60f-ea5c-4554-b13e-75df8985cb22, Enslow Elementary) Enslow Publishing, LLC.

Chrismer, Melanie. The Sun (Scholastic News Nonfiction Readers: Space Science) 2008. (Scholastic News Nonfiction Readers Ser.). (ENG., Illus.). 24p. (J). (gr. 1-2). pap. 6.95 *(978-0-531-14768-9(1)*, Children's Pr.) Scholastic Library Publishing.

Coan, Sharon. Lo Que Puede Hacer el Sol. 2nd rev. ed. 2016. (TIME for KIDS(r): Informational Text Ser.). (SPA., Illus.). 12p. (gr. -1-k). 7.99 *(978-1-4938-2962-0(9))* Teacher Created Materials, Inc.

—What the Sun Can Do. 2nd rev. ed. 2015. (TIME for KIDS(r): Informational Text Ser.). (ENG., Illus.). 12p. (gr. -1-k). 7.99 *(978-1-4938-2053-5(2))* Teacher Created Materials, Inc.

Crabtree Editor & Miller, Reagan. The Sun. 2012. (Journey Through Space Ser.). (ENG.). 24p. (J). (gr. 3-6). lib. bdg. *(978-0-7787-5309-4(3))* Crabtree Publishing Co.

Crane, Cody. The Sun. 2018. (Getting to Know the World's Greatest Composers Ser.). (J). lib. bdg. 116.00 *(978-0-531-22982-8(3)*, Children's Pr.) Scholastic Library Publishing.

DeCristofano, Carolyn Cinami. The Sun & the Moon. Morley, Taia, illus. 2016. (Let's-Read-And-Find-Out Science 1 Ser.). (ENG.). 40p. (J). (gr. -1-3). pap. 7.99 *(978-0-06-233803-7(X)*, HarperCollins) HarperCollins Pubs.

Demuth, Patricia Brennan. The Sun: Our Amazing Star. 2016. (Illus.). 32p. (J). (gr. -1-1). pap. 4.99 *(978-0-448-48828-8(0)*, Grosset & Dunlap) Penguin Young Readers Group.

Dickmann, Nancy. Exploring the Sun, 1 vol. 2015. (Spectacular Space Science Ser.). (ENG., Illus.). 48p. (J). (gr. 5-6). 33.47 *(978-1-4994-3621-1(1)*, e7f40830-a875-4da6-96a8-c427e888e045, Rosen Central) Rosen Publishing Group, Inc., The.

—The Sun & the Solar System, 1 vol. 2018. (Space Facts & Figures Ser.). (ENG.). 32p. (gr. 2-3). 28.93 *(978-1-5081-9522-1(6)*, 2e87bdaa-6b4b-4f46-ab7b-8c23b3685cf3, Windmill Bks.) Rosen Publishing Group, Inc., The.

Dobeck, Maryann. Circling the Sun. 2004. (Reading PowerWorks Ser.). (Illus.). 16p. (gr. 1-3). pap. 6.10 *(978-0-7608-8917-6(1))* Sundance/Newbridge Educational Publishing.

Doudna, Kelly. It Is Sunny, 1 vol. 2003. (Weather Ser.). (Illus.). 24p. (J). (gr. k-3). lib. bdg. 24.21 *(978-1-57765-777-4(2)*, SandCastle) ABDO Publishing Co.

Duffey, Gary. Windows. 2012. 16p. pap. 7.95 *(978-1-4582-0512-4(6)*, Abbott Pr.) Author Solutions, LLC.

Duling, Kaitlyn. The Sun & Renewable Energy, 1 vol. 2019. (Power of the Sun Ser.). (ENG.). 32p. (J). (gr. 3-3). lib. bdg. 30.21 *(978-1-5026-4680-4(3)*, 872e0106-0a92-42dc-ad2a-c3589d713072) Cavendish Square Publishing LLC.

Eckart, Edana. Watching the Sun. 2004. (Welcome Bks.). (ENG., Illus.). 24p. (J). (gr. -1-2). pap. 4.95 *(978-0-516-25939-0(3)*, Children's Pr.) Scholastic Library Publishing.

Edison, Erin. Sunlight, 1 vol. 2011. (Weather Basics Ser.). (ENG.). 24p. (J). (gr. -1-2). pap. 7.29 *(978-1-4296-7081-4(9)*, 116757); (gr. k-1). pap. 44.74 *(978-1-4296-7087-6(8)*, 16680, Capstone Pr.) Capstone.

Elish, Dan. The Sun, 1 vol. 2007. (Kaleidoscope: Space Ser.). (ENG., Illus.). 48p. (gr. 4-4). lib. bdg. 32.64 *(978-0-7614-2048-4(7)*, 667aed39-e166-4330-9f9f-e25201fd813e) Cavendish Square Publishing LLC.

Faulkner, Nicholas & Gregersen, Erik. The Sun & the Origins of the Solar System, 1 vol. 2018. (Universe & Our Place in It Ser.). (ENG.). 128p. (gr. 10-10). pap. 20.95 *(978-1-5081-0604-3(5)*, f7416183-e1f7-4006-a8d8-5502f3dd64e5, Britannica Educational Publishing) Rosen Publishing Group, Inc., The.

Flynn, Claire E. A Trip to the Sun, 1 vol. 2014. (Fantastic Science Journeys Ser.). (ENG.). 32p. (J). (gr. 2-3). pap. 11.50 *(978-1-4824-2014-2(7)*, ea0c5bfe-7bec-4495-a1cf-7c21107351de) Stevens, Gareth Publishing LLLP.

Ganeri, Anita. Sunshine, 1 vol. 2004. (Weather Around You Ser.). (ENG., Illus.). 24p. (gr. 2-4). lib. bdg. 24.67 *(978-0-8368-4301-9(0)*, b10d4ac8-11ed-401d-bdcb-8bf677e5103c, Weekly Reader Leveled Readers) Stevens, Gareth Publishing LLLP.

Garbe, Suzanne. The Science Behind Wonders of the Sun: Sun Dogs, Lunar Eclipses, & Green Flash. 2016. (Science Behind Natural Phenomena Ser.). (ENG., Illus.). 32p. (J). (gr. 3-9). lib. bdg. 28.65 *(978-1-5157-0778-3(4)*, 132118, Capstone Pr.) Capstone.

Gardener, Ryan. Thank You God for Making the Sun. 2008. 28p. pap. 12.95 *(978-1-4389-1488-6(1))* AuthorHouse.

Gardner, Robert. Science Fair Projects about the Sun & the Moon, 1 vol. 2016. (Hands-On Science Ser.). (ENG.). 48p. (gr. 4-4). pap. 12.70 *(978-0-7660-8215-1(6)*, ca703e88-3c77-48ff-9f01-4cc20ad03da7) Enslow Publishing, LLC.

Gendell, Megan & Connolly, Rachel. Your Home in Space: Everything You Wanted to Know about Earth, the Sun, & the Moon. 2008. (Illus.). 32p. (J). *(978-0-545-04457-8(X))* Scholastic, Inc.

Gifford, Clive. Stars, Galaxies, & the Milky Way. 2015. (Watch This Space! Ser.). (ENG., Illus.). 32p. (J). (gr. 4-5). lib. bdg. *(978-0-7787-2022-5(5))* Crabtree Publishing Co.

Glaser, Chaya. El Sol: Una Superestrella. 2015. (Fuera de Este Mundo Ser.). (SPA., Illus.). 24p. (J). (gr. -1-3). lib. bdg. 26.99 *(978-1-62724-597-5(9))* Bearport Publishing Co., Inc.

—The Sun: A Super Star. 2015. (Out of This World Ser.). (ENG.). 24p. (J). (gr. -1-3). lib. bdg. 26.99 *(978-1-62724-569-2(3))* Bearport Publishing Co., Inc.

Goldstein, Margaret. The Sun. 2009. pap. 6.95 *(978-0-8225-4760-0(0))* Lerner Publishing Group.

Goldstein, Margaret J. The Sun. 2003. (Our Universe Ser.). (ENG., Illus.). 32p. (gr. 2-4). lib. bdg. 22.60 *(978-0-8225-4647-4(7))* Lerner Publishing Group.

Graham, Ian. Our Sun. 2015. (Space Ser.). (ENG., Illus.). 24p. (J). (gr. 1-3). lib. bdg. 28.50 *(978-1-62588-210-3(6)*, 17404) Black Rabbit Bks.

Gregoire, Maryellen. Our Sun, 1 vol. 2011. (Wonder Readers Emergent Level Ser.). (ENG.). 16p. (gr. -1-1). (J). pap. 6.25 *(978-1-4296-7868-1(2)*, 118200); pap. 35.94 *(978-1-4296-8136-0(5))* Capstone. (Capstone Pr.).

Hansen, Grace. The Sun. 2017. (Our Galaxy Ser.). (ENG., Illus.). 24p. (J). (gr. -1-2). lib. bdg. 32.79 *(978-1-5321-0054-3(X)*, 25182, Abdo Kids) ABDO Publishing Co.

Hantula, Richard & Asimov, Isaac. El Sol (the Sun), 1 vol. 2003. (Isaac Asimov's Biblioteca Del Universo Del Siglo XXI (Isaac Asimov's 21st Century Library of the Universe) Ser.).Tr. of Sun. (SPA., Illus.). 32p. (gr. 3-5). lib. bdg. 28.67 *(978-0-8368-3861-9(0)*, 9f699839-5c2c-4a78-add1-2139c0ea36ea, Gareth Stevens Learning Library) Stevens, Gareth Publishing LLLP.

Harman, Alice. Sun, 1 vol., 1. 2015. (Fact Finders: Space Ser.). (ENG., Illus.). 24p. (J). (gr. 2-2). pap. 9.25 *(978-1-5081-9137-7(9)*, 2a64be47-53bb-4c44-9bfc-f0e028d0b3a5, Windmill Bks.) Rosen Publishing Group, Inc., The.

Hawksett, David. Our Sun: Can You Figure Out Its Mysteries?, 1 vol. 2017. (Be a Space Scientist! Ser.). (ENG.). 48p. (J). (gr. 5-5). pap. 12.75 *(978-1-5383-2300-7(1)*, ea3cd831-5d3b-4f81-a9b1-b1c25b513be5); (Illus.). 31.93 *(978-1-5383-2207-9(2)*, 5f53eea8-0383-4690-ab0a-81be0c3c7560) Rosen Publishing Group, Inc., The. (PowerKids Pr.).

Hicks, Terry Allan. Why Does the Sun Set?, 1 vol. 2010. (Tell Me Why, Tell Me How Ser.). (ENG.). 32p. (gr. 3-3). 32.64 *(978-0-7614-3993-6(5)*, dbac377f-8741-4b5f-b064-c5ae72121529) Cavendish Square Publishing LLC.

Hudak, Heather C. The Sun. 2016. (Exploring Our Universe Ser.). (ENG., Illus.). 32p. (J). (gr. 3-6). lib. bdg. 32.79 *(978-1-68078-409-1(9)*, 23677, Checkerboard Library) ABDO Publishing Co.

Hutson, Matt. The Inside Story of the Sun. 2006. (J). 7.80 *(978-1-933798-06-6(8))* Sally Ride Science.

James, Lincoln. The Sun, 1 vol. 2010. (Our Solar System Ser.). (ENG.). 24p. (J). (gr. k-2). pap. 9.15 *(978-1-4339-3849-8(9)*, 89a527af-1040-4677-9359-162a6b9d968e); (Illus.). lib. bdg. 25.27 *(978-1-4339-3848-1(0)*, 3564f120-176e-43d8-9cd0-7e402666bade) Stevens, Gareth Publishing LLLP.

Jefferis, David. The Sun: Our Local Star. 2008. (Exploring Our Solar System Ser.). (ENG., Illus.). 32p. (J). (gr. 3-7). pap. *(978-0-7787-3749-0(7))* Crabtree Publishing Co.

Jemison, Mae & Rau, Dana Meachen. Exploring Our Sun. 2013. (True Book: Space Revised Ser.). (ENG., Illus.). 48p. (J). (gr. 3-5). lib. bdg. 21.19 *(978-0-531-25502-5(6)*, Children's Pr.) Scholastic Library Publishing.

Kalman, Bobbie. La Tierra y el Sol. 2009. (SPA.). 32p. (J). *(978-0-7787-8241-4(7))*; pap. *(978-0-7787-8258-2(1))* Crabtree Publishing Co.

Kalman, Bobbie & MacAulay, Kelley. Earth & the Sun, 1 vol. 2008. (Looking at Earth Ser.). (ENG., Illus.). 32p. (J). (gr. 3-7). pap. *(978-0-7787-3212-9(6))*; lib. bdg. *(978-0-7787-3202-0(9))* Crabtree Publishing Co.

Kelly, Harold G. Inside the Sun. 2009. (Reading Room Collection 2 Ser.). 24p. (gr. 3-4). 42.50 *(978-1-60851-974-3(0)*, PowerKids Pr.) Rosen Publishing Group, Inc., The.

—El Sol por dentro (Inside the Sun) 2009. (Reading Room Collection: Spanish Ser.). (SPA.). 24p. (gr. 3-4). 42.50 *(978-1-60854-177-5(0)*, Editorial Buenas Letras) Rosen Publishing Group, Inc., The.

Kerrod, Robin & Posada, Mia. Dandelions: Stars in the Grass. 2003. (Illus.). 32p. (J). pap. 6.95 *(978-1-57505-399-8(3))* Lerner Publishing Group.

Kissock, Heather. Sun. 2011. (J). *(978-1-61690-953-6(6))*; *(978-1-61690-599-6(9))* Weigl Pubs., Inc.

Klepeis, Alicia Z. The Sun & the Weather. 2019. (Power of the Sun Ser.). (ENG.). 32p. (gr. 3-3). 63.48 *(978-1-5026-4671-2(4))* Cavendish Square Publishing LLC.

Koehler, Max. Journey to the Sun, 1 vol. 2014. (Spotlight on Space Science Ser.). (ENG., Illus.). 32p. (J). (gr. 5-5). pap. 12.75 *(978-1-4994-0378-7(X)*, 8837b69f-c25d-4b52-bd31-43542ed4fef7, PowerKids Pr.) Rosen Publishing Group, Inc., The.

Labrecque, Ellen. The Sun & Stars. 2019. (Our Place in the Universe Ser.). (ENG., Illus.). 24p. (J). (gr. 1-3). 25.99 *(978-1-9771-0847-0(4)*, 140465, Pebble) Capstone.

Lee, Sally. Sunny Weather: A 4D Book. 2018. (All Kinds of Weather Ser.). (ENG., Illus.). 24p. (J). (gr. -1-2). lib. bdg. 24.65 *(978-1-9771-0185-3(2)*, 138710, Pebble) Capstone.

Lilly, Melinda. Sun & Moon. Thompson, Scott M., photos by. 2005. (Rourke Discovery Library). (Illus.). 24p. (J). (gr. 1-4). lib. bdg. 14.95 *(978-1-59515-405-7(1)*, 1244276) Rourke Educational Media.

Lindeen, Mary. Sun & Shade. 2017. (Beginning-To-Read Ser.). (ENG.). 32p. (J). (gr. k-2). pap. 13.26 *(978-1-68404-091-9(4))*; (Illus.). 22.60 *(978-1-59953-872-3(5))* Norwood Hse. Pr.

Lockyer, John. The Sun, 1 vol. 2018. (ENG., Illus.). 21p. (J). pap. *(978-1-77654-257-4(6)*, Red Rocket Readers) Flying Start Bks.

MacDonald, Margaret. Energy from the Sun. 2011. (Learn-Abouts Ser.). (Illus.). 16p. (J). pap. 7.95 *(978-1-59920-634-9(X))* Black Rabbit Bks.

Martin, Justin McCory. The Sun. 2007. (Illus.). 16p. (J). 3.95 *(978-0-545-00730-6(5))* Scholastic, Inc.

Mason Crest. Sun, Vol. 7. 2016. (Solar System Ser.: Vol. 7). (ENG., Illus.). 48p. (J). (gr. 5-8). 20.95 *(978-1-4222-3553-9(X))* Mason Crest.

Mattern, Joanne. The Sun & Animals. 2019. (Power of the Sun Ser.). (ENG.). 32p. (gr. 3-3). 63.48 *(978-1-5026-4663-7(3))* Cavendish Square Publishing LLC.

McAnulty, Stacy. Sun! One in a Billion. Lewis, Stevie, illus. 2018. (Our Universe Ser.: 2). (ENG.). 40p. (J). 18.99 *(978-1-250-19932-4(8)*, 900194804, Holt, Henry & Co. Bks. For Young Readers) Holt, Henry & Co.

McNeil, Niki, et al. HOCPP 1124 the Sun. 2006. spiral bd. 16.00 *(978-1-60308-124-5(0))* In the Hands of a Child.

Miller, Reagan. The Sun. 2012. (ENG.). 24p. (J). pap. *(978-0-7787-5314-8(X))* Crabtree Publishing Co.

Miller, Violet. Why Does the Sun Set?, 1 vol. 2013. (Nature's Super Secrets Ser.). (ENG., Illus.). 24p. (J). (gr. 1-2). 25.27 *(978-1-4339-8180-7(7)*, 14472636-0935-4640-aa6e-8ba4d9e18009); pap. 9.15 *(978-1-4339-8181-4(5)*, 70ebbba7-28ef-4d13-b77d-087a2703a9ea) Stevens, Gareth Publishing LLLP.

Mitchell, Melanie. Sun. 2004. (First Step Nonfiction). (J). lib. bdg. 17.76 *(978-0-8225-0187-9(2)*, Lerner Pubns.); (ENG., Illus.). 24p. lib. bdg. 23.93 *(978-0-8225-5139-3(X))* Lerner Publishing Group.

Mitchell, Melanie S. The Sun. 2003. (First Step Nonfiction Ser.). (Illus.). 22p. (J). pap. 5.95 *(978-0-8225-3593-5(9)*, Lerner Pubns.) Lerner Publishing Group.

Moon, Walt K. Let's Explore the Sun. 2017. (Bumba Books (r) — a First Look at Space Ser.). (ENG., Illus.). 24p. (J). (gr. -1-1). 26.65 *(978-1-5124-3348-7(9)*, bf4e5509-c75e-448e-bed0-2fd49a703f9e, Lerner Pubns.) Lerner Publishing Group.

Moore, David. National Geographic Science 1-2 (Earth Science: Sun, Moon, & Stars): Explore on Your Own: the Sun Shines. 2009. (C). pap. 8.95 *(978-0-7362-5591-2(5))* National Geographic School Publishing, Inc.

Morey, Allan. Solar Storm. 2019. (It's the End of the World! Ser.). (ENG., Illus.). 24p. (J). (gr. 3-7). lib. bdg. 26.95 *(978-1-64487-084-6(3)*, Torque Bks.) Bellwether Media.

Morgan, Emily. Next Time You See a Sunset. 2012. (Next Time You See Ser.). (ENG., Illus.). 32p. (J). (gr. -1-k). pap. 12.95 *(978-1-936959-16-7(X)*, P218555) National Science Teachers Assn.

—La Próxima Vez Que Veas una Puesta Del Sol. 2016. (Next Time You See Ser.). (SPA., Illus.). 32p. (J). (gr. 2-4). pap. 13.99 *(978-1-68140-282-6(3))* National Science Teachers Assn.

Murphy, Patricia J. Why Is the Sun So Hot? (Library of Why Ser.). 24p. (gr. 3-4). 2009. 42.50 *(978-1-60853-966-6(0)*, PowerKids Pr.) 2003. (ENG., Illus.). (J). lib. bdg. 26.27 *(978-0-8239-6235-8(0)*, 31f503ff-974f-4b0b-ba36-8c61f653f6c3) Rosen Publishing Group, Inc., The.

Nadeau, Isaac. Learning about the Movement of the Sun & Other Stars with Graphic Organizers, 1 vol. (Graphic Organizers in Science & Social Studies). (ENG., Illus.). 24p. (gr. 4-5). 2005. pap. 8.25 *(978-1-4042-5040-6(9)*, 9fcb7273-1f54-4d12-b835-cf44a401dfc6) 2004. (J). 25.27 *(978-1-4042-2805-4(5)*, 2f750e05-dfdc-4cf6-b853-f1c2f6caf1ff) Rosen Publishing Group, Inc., The. (PowerKids Pr.).

National Geographic Learning. Language, Literacy & Vocabulary - Reading Expeditions (Earth Science): Stars. 2007. (ENG., Illus.). 36p. (J). pap. 20.95 *(978-0-7922-5433-1(3))* CENGAGE Learning.

—Reading Expeditions (Science: Earth Science): Earth, Sun, Moon. 2007. (ENG., Illus.). 32p. (J). pap. 18.95 *(978-0-7922-4573-5(3))* CENGAGE Learning.

S

Nations, Susan. Hace Sol (Let's Read about Sun), 1 vol. 2007. (¿Qué Tiempo Hace? (Let's Read about Weather) Ser.). (SPA., Illus.). 12p. (J). (gr. k-1). lib. bdg. 17.67 (978-0-8368-8111-0(7), 74ac7fdc-d671-4182-8bab-fcf9f072897c) Stevens, Gareth Publishing LLLP.

—Let's Read about Sun, 1 vol. 2007. (Let's Read about Weather Ser.). (ENG., Illus.). 12p. (gr. k-1). pap. 5.10 (978-0-8368-7812-7(4), 8fa2e217-69d9-4c0b-ba3d-7f2c4c758015); lib. bdg. 17.67 (978-0-8368-7807-3(8), 7a78d14a-d2ec-4f6b-91af-6aa121c3a36c) Stevens, Gareth Publishing LLLP. (Weekly Reader Leveled Readers).

Nations, Susan & Boyett, Suzi. Hace Sol (Let's Read about Sun), 1 vol. 2007. (¿Qué Tiempo Hace? (Let's Read about Weather) Ser.). (SPA., Illus.). 12p. (J). (gr. k-1). pap. 5.10 (978-0-8368-8116-5(8), c4aa0bbf-c7a9-493d-a1ca-f2ef8f37860e, Weekly Reader Leveled Readers) Stevens, Gareth Publishing LLLP.

Nelson, Robin. Un Día Soleado (A Sunny Day) 2006. (Mi Primer Paso al Mundo Real Ser.). (Illus.). 23p. (J). (gr. -1-3). per. 5.95 (978-0-8225-6552-9(8), Ediciones Lerner) Lerner Publishing Group.

—Sunny. (First Step Nonfiction — Kinds of Weather Ser.). (ENG., Illus.). 8p. (J). (gr. k-2). 2005. pap. 5.99 (978-0-8225-5367-0(8), 91fdb989-c04e-429f-9c43-b408b17f886a) 2015. E-Book 23.99 (978-1-5124-1039-6(X)) Lerner Publishing Group.

—A Sunny Day. 2005. (First Step Nonfiction Ser.). (Illus.). 24p. (gr. k-2). lib. bdg. 17.27 (978-0-8225-0176-3(7)) Lerner Publishing Group.

Nuestra Estrella: El Sol. (SPA.). (J). 10.00 (978-84-342-1470-5(9)) Parramon Ediciones S.A. ESP. Dist: Distribuidora Norma, Inc.

Olien, Rebecca. Exploring the Sun. (Objects in the Sky Ser.). 24p. (gr. 3-3). 2009. 42.50 (978-1-60851-142-6(1)) 2007. (ENG., Illus.). (J). lib. bdg. 26.27 (978-1-4042-3464-2(0), b8eed2ba-a2e8-4d34-9503-ec495cb7fd65) Rosen Publishing Group, Inc., The. (PowerKids Pr.).

Orme, Helen & Orme, David. Let's Explore the Sun, 1 vol. 2007. (Space Launch! Ser.). (ENG., Illus.). 24p. (gr. 2-4). lib. bdg. 25.67 (978-0-8368-7948-3(1), 4359697d-75bf-431f-81e9-dc478d045050, Gareth Stevens Learning Library) Stevens, Gareth Publishing LLLP.

Orr, Tamra. I Spy in the Sky the Sun. 2011. (Randy's Corner Ser.). (Illus.). 32p. (J). (gr. k-3). lib. bdg. 25.70 (978-1-58415-972-8(3)) Mitchell Lane Pubs.

Our Friend the Sun. 2004. (J). pap. 14.95 (978-1-932762-07-5(8)) Elderberry Press, Inc.

Owen, Ruth. The Sun, 1 vol. 2013. (Explore Outer Space Ser.). (ENG.). 32p. (J). (gr. 2-3). pap. 11.00 (978-1-61533-757-6(1), ca652064-34e3-46ab-8365-5755a88dcaaf); lib. bdg. 29.93 (978-1-61533-720-0(2), 6070d6d6-8976-4f6b-9ac4-54450be0c2f4) Rosen Publishing Group, Inc., The. (Windmill Bks.).

—The Sun. 2013. (Explore Outer Space Ser.). 32p. (J). (gr. 3-6). pap. 60.00 (978-1-61533-758-3(X)) Windmill Bks.

Oxlade, Chris. Space Watch: The Sun. 2010. (Eye on Space Ser.). 24p. (J). pap. 8.25 (978-1-61532-550-4(6), PowerKids Pr.); (ENG.). (gr. 1-1). lib. bdg. 26.27 (978-1-61532-543-6(3), 8c49acef-9257-4f16-b0ad-883f41c43021) Rosen Publishing Group, Inc., The.

Parker, Steve. The Sun, 1 vol. 2007. (Earth & Space Ser.). (ENG., Illus.). 48p. (YA). (gr. 6-6). lib. bdg. 34.47 (978-1-4042-3737-7(2), 6d319b6f-3236-445a-8e45-f1dec803a8e4) Rosen Publishing Group, Inc., The.

Peters, Elisa. The Sun, 1 vol. 2012. (PowerKids Readers: the Universe Ser.). (ENG., Illus.). 24p. (J). (gr. k-k). pap. 9.25 (978-1-4488-7465-1(3), 3fdc92e1-ba31-42bb-a540-a57d279730cc); lib. bdg. 26.27 (978-1-4488-7385-2(1), e4c357f4-79bc-48cd-aca5-bd0984eafd41) Rosen Publishing Group, Inc., The. (PowerKids Pr.).

—The Sun: El Sol, 1 vol. 2012. (PowerKids Readers: el Universo / the Universe Ser.). (SPA & ENG., Illus.). 24p. (J). (gr. k-k). lib. bdg. 26.27 (978-1-4488-7821-5(7), ad47ea4c-c9b4-4f66-b4fa-297cd43ef736, PowerKids Pr.) Rosen Publishing Group, Inc., The.

Peters, Katie. The Sun Shines Everywhere. 2019. (Let's Look at Weather (Pull Ahead Readers — Nonfiction) Ser.). (ENG., Illus.). 16p. (J). (gr. -1-1). pap. 8.99 (978-1-5415-7325-3(0), d85b8b82-d262-4284-abf2-2c8b033f8b43); lib. bdg. 27.99 (978-1-5415-5837-3(5), ac652e28-538a-4c55-b992-3989c72d4990) Lerner Publishing Group. (Lerner Pubns.).

Peterson, Cris. Seed, Soil, Sun: Earth's Recipe for Food. Lundquist, David R., photos by. (ENG., Illus.). 32p. (J). (gr. k-3). 2012. pap. 8.99 (978-1-59078-947-6(4)) 2010. 17.95 (978-1-59078-713-7(7)) Astra Publishing Hse. (Astra Young Readers).

Picray, Michael E. The Sun with Code. 2012. (Sky Science Ser.). (ENG., Illus.). 24p. (J). (gr. 4-7). lib. bdg. 27.13 (978-1-61913-097-5(1), AV2 by Weigl) Weigl Pubs., Inc.

Ponka, Katherine. Math on the Sun, 1 vol. 2016. (Solve It! Math in Space Ser.). (ENG., Illus.). 24p. (J). (gr. 2-3). 24.27 (978-1-4824-4936-5(6), 9edb76bc-2ee6-414b-a9cb-643c637177ba) Stevens, Gareth Publishing LLLP.

Portillo, Athena Yvette. Sun & Moon. 2007. (Illus.). 32p. (J). pap. 8.00 (978-0-8059-7278-8(1)) Dorrance Publishing Co., Inc.

Rathburn, Betsy. The Sun. 2018. (Space Science Ser.). (ENG., Illus.). 24p. (J). (gr. 3-7). lib. bdg. 26.95 (978-1-62617-862-5(3), Torque Bks.) Bellwether Media.

Reilly, Carmel. The Sun, 1 vol. 2012. (Sky Watching Ser.). (ENG.). 32p. (gr. 5-5). 31.21 (978-1-60870-584-9(6), a686cbf1-b154-4c64-87b8-8e560581fce1) Cavendish Square Publishing LLC.

Rhythms of the Sun. 2004. lib. bdg. 30.00 net. (978-0-9749364-0-6(5)) Chuttani, Kabir.

Rice, Dona & Otterman, Joseph. Powered by the Sun. rev. ed. 2019. (Smithsonian: Informational Text Ser.). (ENG., Illus.). 24p. (J). (gr. 1-2). pap. 8.99 (978-1-4938-6658-8(3)) Teacher Created Materials, Inc.

Rice, Dona Herweck. Here Comes the Sun, 1 vol. rev. ed. 2014. (Science: Informational Text Ser.). (ENG., Illus.). 24p. (gr. -1-1). pap. 9.99 (978-1-4807-4529-2(4)) Teacher Created Materials, Inc.

Rice, William. Our Sun, 1 vol. rev. ed. (Science: Informational Text Ser.). (ENG., Illus.). 24p. (gr. 1-2). 2015. lib. bdg. 22.96 (978-1-4938-1157-1(6)) 2014. pap. 9.99 (978-1-4807-4570-4(7)) Teacher Created Materials, Inc.

Riggs, Kate. The Sun. 2015. (Across the Universe Ser.). (ENG.). 24p. (J). (gr. 1-4). pap. 9.99 (978-1-62832-085-5(0), 21129, Creative Paperbacks); (978-1-60818-485-9(4), 21128, Creative Education) Creative Co., The.

Roberts, Jeremy. Benito Mussolini. 2005. (First Step Nonfiction Ser.). (Illus.). 112p. (J). (gr. 3-7). lib. bdg. 29.27 (978-0-8225-2648-3(4), Lerner Pubns.) Lerner Publishing Group.

Robertson, Charmaine. All about Sunlight, 1 vol. 2016. (Rosen REAL Readers: STEM & STEAM Collection). (ENG.). 8p. (gr. k-1). pap. 5.46 (978-1-5081-2410-8(8), 82d2aa4c-a133-47b9-94eb-fcde3cc169c7, Rosen Classroom) Rosen Publishing Group, Inc., The.

Rogers, Kate. Exploring the Sun. 2017. (Journey Through Our Solar System Ser.). 24p. (gr. 1-2). 49.50 (978-1-5345-2250-3(6), KidHaven Publishing); (ENG.). pap. 9.25 (978-1-5345-2292-3(1), 611a0926-9c45-472d-9e30-e9bc899efabf); (ENG.). lib. bdg. 26.23 (978-1-5345-2278-7(6), da469c1d-6116-442b-87af-cc70cd3d4fb3) Greenhaven Publishing LLC.

Rosenberg, Pam. Sunny Weather Days. 2006. (Scholastic News Nonfiction Readers Ser.). (ENG., Illus.). 24p. (J). (gr. 1-2). lib. bdg. 22.00 (978-0-531-16770-0(4)) Scholastic Library Publishing.

Rossiter, Brienna. Sun. 2019. (Weather Ser.). (ENG., Illus.). 16p. (J). (gr. k-1). 25.64 (978-1-64185-792-5(7), 1641857927, Focus Readers) North Star Editions.

Roumanis, Alexis. The Sun. 2016. (Illus.). 24p. (J). (978-1-5105-0983-2(6)) SmartBook Media, Inc.

Rushworth, Gary. Our Solar System the Sun: Set Of 6. 2011. (Navigators Ser.). (J). pap. 44.00 net. (978-1-4108-6220-4(8)) Benchmark Education Co.

—Our Solar System: the Sun: Text Pairs. 2008. (Bridges/Navigators Ser.). (J). (gr. 3). 89.00 (978-1-4108-8371-1(X)) Benchmark Education Co.

Rustad, Martha E. H. El Sol/the Sun. 2012. (En el Espacio/Out in Space Ser.). (MUL.). 24p. (gr. k-1). pap. 35.70 (978-1-4296-8557-3(3)); (J). (gr. -1-2). pap. 5.95 (978-1-4296-8556-6(5), 118527) Capstone.

—The Sun. 2016. (Space Ser.). (ENG., Illus.). 24p. (J). (gr. -1-2). lib. bdg. 22.65 (978-1-4914-8324-4(5), 130797, Capstone Pr.) Capstone.

—The Sun: Revised Edition. rev. ed. 2008. (Out in Space Ser.). (ENG., Illus.). 24p. (J). (gr. -1-2). pap. 6.29 (978-1-4296-2837-2(5), 95334, Capstone Pr.) Capstone.

—The Sun [Scholastic]. 2009. (Out in Space Ser.). 24p. (gr. k-1). pap. 2.50 (978-1-4296-4052-7(9), Pebble) Capstone.

—Today Is a Sunny Day. 2017. (What Is the Weather Today? Ser.). (ENG., Illus.). 24p. (J). (gr. -1-2). lib. bdg. 24.65 (978-1-5157-4920-2(7), 134536, Pebble) Capstone.

Ryback, Carol. The Sun, 1 vol. 2005. (In the Sky Ser.). (ENG., Illus.). 24p. (gr. 2-4). pap. 9.15 (978-0-8368-6351-2(8), a75fe222-451e-44e0-8b63-125fbe31525d); lib. bdg. 24.67 (978-0-8368-6346-8(1), 74f75f3b-e0cb-4e98-b88f-31d3323d973e) Stevens, Gareth Publishing LLLP. (Weekly Reader Leveled Readers).

Sabatino, Michael. How Long Will the Sun Last?, 1 vol. 2013. (Space Mysteries Ser.). 32p. (J). (gr. 2-3). (ENG.). 29.27 (978-1-4339-9223-0(X), edeef2e8-e504-436e-bfa6-09a00f413806); (ENG.). pap. 11.50 (978-1-4339-9224-7(8), cefa69a7-2f23-46db-b352-02156409aff0); pap. 63.00 (978-1-4339-9225-4(6)) Stevens, Gareth Publishing LLLP.

Sasso, Sandy Eisenberg. Adam & Eve's New Day. Rothenberg, Joani Keller, illus. 2006. (ENG.). 24p. (gr. -1). bds. 7.99 (978-1-59473-205-8(1), 316f8644-7638-4472-b248-c71e33b4d423, Skylight Paths Publishing) LongHill Partners, Inc.

Schatz, Dennis & Fraknoi, Andrew. Solar Science: Exploring Sunspots, Seasons, Eclipses, & More. 2016. (ENG., Illus.). 360p. pap. 73.99 (978-1-941316-07-8(7)) National Science Teachers Assn.

Schuh, Mari. Where Does Light Come From? 2019. (Let's Look at Light Ser.). (ENG., Illus.). 24p. (J). (gr. -1-2). pap. 6.95 (978-1-9771-1042-8(8), 141118, Pebble) Capstone.

Schwabacher, Martin. The Sun, 1 vol. 2003. (Blastoff! Ser.). (ENG., Illus.). 64p. (gr. 5-5). 34.07 (978-0-7614-1402-5(9), 9b64aca7-9416-4556-bf9d-634999156223f) Cavendish Square Publishing LLC.

Seluk, Nick. The Sun Is Kind of a Big Deal. Seluk, Nick, illus. 2018. (ENG., Illus.). 40p. (J). (gr. -1-3). 17.99 (978-1-338-16697-2(2), Orchard Bks.) Scholastic, Inc.

Sexton, Colleen. The Sun. 2010. (Exploring Space Ser.). (ENG., Illus.). 24p. (J). (gr. k-3). lib. bdg. 26.95 (978-1-60014-400-4(4), Blastoff! Readers) Bellwether Media.

Shepherd, Jodie. To the Sun! Becker, Paula J., illus. 2017. (Cloverleaf Books (tm) — Space Adventures Ser.). (ENG.). 24p. (J). (gr. k-2). E-Book 38.65 (978-1-5124-2835-3(3)); E-Book 38.65 (978-1-5124-3899-4(5), 9781512438994) Lerner Publishing Group. (Millbrook Pr.).

Sikkens, Crystal. Day & Night. 2019. (Full STEAM Ahead! - Science Starters Ser.). (Illus.). 24p. (J). (gr. 1-1). (978-0-7787-6187-7(8)) Crabtree Publishing Co.

Simon, Seymour. The Sun. 2015. (J). lib. bdg. 17.20 (978-0-606-37729-4(8)) Turtleback.

—The Sun: Revised Edition. rev. ed. 2015. (ENG., Illus.). 32p. (J). (gr. 1-5). pap. 7.99 (978-0-06-234505-9(2), HarperCollins) HarperCollins Pubs.

Sohn, Emily. Solar Energy. 2019. (IScience Ser.). (ENG., Illus.). 48p. (J). (gr. 5-6). pap. 13.26 (978-1-68404-407-8(3)) Norwood Hse. Pr.

—Sun, Moon, & Stars. 2019. (IScience Ser.). (ENG., Illus.). 32p. (J). (gr. 3-4). pap. 13.26 (978-1-68404-386-6(7)) Norwood Hse. Pr.

Sparrow, Giles. Destination the Sun, 1 vol. 2009. (Destination Solar System Ser.). (ENG., Illus.). 32p. (J). (gr. 3-4). pap. 11.00 (978-1-4358-3467-5(4), d27cbcd8-1aec-4a22-90f7-783eb312a87c); lib. bdg. 28.93 (978-1-4358-3448-4(8), 60de3b7d-ceb9-46ab-bad6-48962a1d2bfc) Rosen Publishing Group, Inc., The. (PowerKids Pr.).

Steffoff, Rebecca. The Sun & the Earth, 1 vol. 2014. (Is It Science? Ser.). (ENG.). 48p. (gr. 5-5). lib. bdg. 32.64 (978-1-62712-521-5(3), 8ffef77a-d267-4117-b9de-0752c5657e06) Cavendish Square Publishing LLC.

Stewart, Tobi Stanton. Solar Storms. 2009. (Reading Room Collection 2 Ser.). 24p. (gr. 3-4). 42.50 (978-1-60851-987-3(2), PowerKids Pr.) Rosen Publishing Group, Inc., The.

Storad, Conrad J. Day & Night. 2011. (My Science Library). (ENG., Illus.). 24p. (gr. k-1). pap. 9.95 (978-1-61741-926-3(5), 9781617419263) Rourke Educational Media.

—Our Sun Brings Life. 2011. (My Science Library). (ENG., Illus.). 24p. (gr. k-1). pap. 9.95 (978-1-61741-925-6(7), 9781617419256) Rourke Educational Media.

Stott, Carole. Mission: Space: Explore the Galaxy. 2016. (Illus.). 128p. (J). (978-1-4654-5376-1(8)) Dorling Kindersley Publishing, Inc.

Strain Trueit, Trudi. Sunny Days, 1 vol. 2010. (Weather Watch Ser.). (ENG.). 24p. (gr. k-1). 25.50 (978-0-7614-4017-8(8), 0889ffa8-06e7-4c03-8a44-ff6a8a34cb94) Cavendish Square Publishing LLC.

The Sun: Level L, 6 vols. (Wonder Worldtm Ser.). 16p. 34.95 (978-0-7802-4607-2(1)) Wright Group/McGraw-Hill.

The Sun & Other Stars Instructional Guide. 2009. (Grade 8: Science Exit Project Kits Ser.). spiral bd. (978-1-4042-4026-1(8), Rosen Classroom) Rosen Publishing Group, Inc., The.

Sundance/Newbridge LLC Staff. Circling the Sun. 2004. (Reading PowerWorks Ser.). (gr. 1-3). 37.50 (978-0-7608-8916-9(3)) Sundance/Newbridge Educational Publishing.

—Our Sun, Our Weather. 2007. (Early Science Ser.). (gr. k-3). 18.95 (978-1-4007-6531-7(5)); pap. 6.10 (978-1-4007-6527-0(7)) Sundance/Newbridge Educational Publishing.

Taylor-Butler, Christine. The Sun. 2014. (True Book(tm), A — Space Ser.). (ENG.). 48p. (J). lib. bdg. 31.00 (978-0-531-21157-1(6)) Scholastic Library Publishing.

Terp, Gail. El Sol y Otras Estrellas. 2018. (Descubrimiento Del Espacio Profundo Ser.). (SPA.). 32p. (J). (gr. 4-6). lib. bdg. (978-1-68072-974-0(8), 12459, Bolt) Black Rabbit Bks.

—The Sun & Other Stars. 2018. (Deep Space Discovery Ser.). (ENG.). 32p. (gr. 2-7). 9.95 (978-1-68072-718-0(4)); (J). (gr. 4-6). pap. 9.99 (978-1-64466-271-7(X), 12337); (Illus.). (J). (gr. 4-6). lib. bdg. (978-1-68072-424-0(X), 12336) Black Rabbit Bks. (Bolt).

Tomecek, Steve. Jump into Science!: Sun. 2016. (Jump into Science Ser.). (Illus.). 32p. (J). (gr. -1-k). pap. 7.99 (978-1-4263-2368-3(9), National Geographic Kids) Disney Publishing Worldwide.

Turnbull, Stephanie. Sun, Moon & Stars. Chen, Kuo Kang & Mayer, Uwe, illus. 2006. (Beginners Nature: Level 2 Ser.). 32p. (J). (gr. 1-3). 4.99 (978-0-7945-1399-3(9), Usborne) EDC Publishing.

Waxman, Laura Hamilton. The Sun. 2010. (Early Bird Astronomy Ser.). (ENG.). 48p. (gr. 2-5). lib. bdg. 26.60 (978-0-7613-3871-0(3)) Lerner Publishing Group.

Wells, Robert E. Why Do Elephants Need the Sun? 2012. (J). 34.28 (978-1-61913-142-2(0)) Weigl Pubs., Inc.

—Why Do Elephants Need the Sun? Wells, Robert E., illus. 2012. (Wells of Knowledge Science Ser.). (ENG., Illus.). 32p. (J). (gr. -1-3). pap. 8.99 (978-0-8075-9082-9(7), 807590827) Whitman, Albert & Co.

What Is a Sun?, 1 vol. 2014. (Let's Find Out! Space Science Ser.). (ENG.). 32p. (J). (gr. 2-3). 26.06 (978-1-62275-461-8(1), a7b0de08-7633-4361-bce9-a70c6d108003) Rosen Publishing Group, Inc., The.

Wilkins, Mary-Jane. The Sun. 2017. (Our Solar System Ser.). (ENG., Illus.). 24p. (J). (gr. 2-4). 28.50 (978-1-78121-363-6(1), 16657) Brown Bear Bks.

World Book, Inc. Staff, contrib. by. The Sun & Other Stars. (J). 2010. (Illus.). 64p. (978-0-7166-9539-4(1)) 2006. 63p. (978-0-7166-9501-1(4)) 2nd ed. 2006. (Illus.). 64p. (978-0-7166-9521-9(9)) World Bk., Inc.

SUN—FICTION

Aesop, Aesop. The Wind & the Sun. 2012. (J). 29.99 (978-1-61913-108-8(0)) Weigl Pubs., Inc.

Arrington, Linda. Purple Time. 2012. 36p. pap. 24.95 (978-1-4626-9613-0(9)) America Star Bks.

Asch, Frank. Moonbear's Sunrise. Asch, Frank, illus. 2014. (Moonbear Ser.). (ENG., Illus.). 32p. (J). (gr. -1-3). 16.99 (978-1-4424-6647-0(2), Aladdin) Simon & Schuster Children's Publishing.

Bailey, Jacqui. Sun up, Sun Down: The Story of Day & Night, 1 vol. Lilly, Matthew, illus. 2004. (Science Works). (ENG.). 32p. (J). (gr. 3-6). per. 7.95 (978-1-4048-1128-7(1), 92526, Picture Window Bks.) Capstone.

Bell, Cassie; Grudzina. The Boy & the Sun. Grudzina, Rebecca, ed. 2016. (Spring Forward Ser.). (ENG.). (J). (gr. k). 6.84 net. (978-1-4900-6011-8(1)) Benchmark Education Co.

Bell-Martin, Janelle. Oh, Mr. Sun. 2012. (Early Literacy Ser.). (ENG.). 16p. (gr. k-1). 19.99 (978-1-4333-3472-6(0)); 6.99 (978-1-4333-3471-9(2)) Teacher Created Materials, Inc.

Belle, Deborah A. The Day the Sun Called Out Sick!!! Collenberger, Chris, illus. 2013. 30p. pap. 12.99 (978-0-9853406-0-5(6)) Scribez, Scarebz & Vibez.

Boles, Rhonda G. Why Does the Sun Set, Mommy? 2009. 24p. pap. 10.99 (978-1-4389-8112-3(0)) AuthorHouse.

Bondestam, Linda, illus. My Little Small. 2018. (ENG.). 52p. (J). (gr. -1-3). 15.95 (978-1-59270-209-1(0)) Enchanted Lion Bks., LLC.

Brewer, Michelle. Sunrise in My Cup. 2011. 28p. (gr. -1). pap. 13.99 (978-1-4567-3995-9(6)) AuthorHouse.

Brinkley, Inez. Rainbows & Promises. 2006. 43p. (J). 15.98 (978-1-4116-9579-5(8)) Lulu Pr., Inc.

Bronn, Charles Heil. The Sun, the Moon, & the Gardener's Son. Kami, Y. Z., illus. 2006. 30p. (J). (gr. 4-12). reprint ed. 16.00 (978-1-4223-5222-9(6)) DIANE Publishing Co.

Brown, Betisa Garagozlu. Sister Sun & Sister Moon. 2012. 28p. pap. 13.95 (978-1-4525-4635-3(5)) Balboa Pr.

Bruchac, Joseph. How Chipmunk Got His Stripes. 2003. (gr. k-3). lib. bdg. 17.20 (978-0-613-61631-7(6)) Turtleback.

Butler, Andrea. El Senor Sol y el Senor Mar, Level 3. Flor Ada, Alma, tr. Hong, Lily T., illus. 2003. (Dejame Leer Ser.). (SPA.). 16p. (J). (gr. -1-3). 6.50 (978-0-673-36302-2(3), Good Year Bks.) Celebration Pr.

Carrington, Samala. Sally Sunshine Mandy Moon. 2011. 20p. (gr. -1). pap. 12.99 (978-1-4567-6708-2(9)) AuthorHouse.

Clifford, Kathryn & Renn, Chantal. George the Sun Safe Superstar. 2012. (ENG., Illus.). 26p. pap. 11.00 (978-1-78035-317-3(0), Fastprint Publishing) Upfront Publishing Ltd. GBR. Dist: Printondemand-worldwide.com.

Climent, Elena. Triste Historia del Sol con Final Feliz. (SPA.). (J). (gr. k-3). pap. 4.76 net. (978-0-8136-1521-9(6), TR4081) Modern Curriculum Pr.

Cunningham, Matthew. Abigail & the Birth of the Sun. Sarah Wilkins, illus. 2019. 32p. (J). (gr. -1-k). 17.99 (978-0-14-377270-5(8)) Penguin Group New Zealand, Ltd. NZL. Dist: Independent Pubs. Group.

Dalton, Kippy. Groundhog & the Sun. Czernichowska, Joanna, illus. 2016. (Spring Forward Ser.). (J). (gr. 1). (978-1-4900-9369-7(9)) Benchmark Education Co.

Davis, Darren. Atlas Gt Planets. 2006. (ENG.). 16p. (J). (gr. -1-12). bds. 5.99 (978-1-59559-103-6(6)) Left Field,Angel Gate.

Denver, John. Sunshine on My Shoulders, 1 vol. Canyon, Christopher, illus. 2003. 32p. (J). (gr. -1 — 1). pap. 8.99 (978-1-58469-050-4(X), Dawn Pubns.) Sourcebooks, Inc.

Dewdney, Anna. Llama Llama Sand & Sun: A Touch & Feel Book. 2015. (Llama Llama Ser.). (Illus.). 10p. (J). (gr. -1 — 1). bds. 12.99 (978-0-448-49639-9(9), Grosset & Dunlap) Penguin Young Readers Group.

di Chiara, Francesca, illus. The Sun & the Wind. 2007. (First Reading Level 1 Ser.). 32p. (J). (gr. -1-3). 8.99 (978-0-7945-1811-0(7), Usborne) EDC Publishing.

Eagle, Golden. Father Sun & Luis the Lizard. l.t. ed. 2005. (Illus.). 22p. (J). per. 12.99 (978-1-59879-026-9(9)) Lifevest Publishing, Inc.

Esteban, Angel. Pablo, Pablo en Busca del Sol. 2003. (SPA.). 48p. (978-84-263-1408-6(2), LV1312) Vives, Luis Editorial (Edelvives) ESP. Dist: Lectorum Pubns., Inc.

Fischer, Kelly. The Moon Throws a Birthday Party. Duckworth, Michelle, illus. 2011. 32p. (J). 19.50 (978-1-58385-237-8(9)) ktf-writers-studio.

Gay, Marie-Louise. Mademoiselle Moon, 1 vol. 2006. (ENG., Illus.). 32p. (J). (gr. k-2). pap. 7.95 (978-1-55005-134-6(2), ba7c0bef-e090-42f1-bc8b-ebc662fbd603) Fitzhenry & Whiteside, Ltd. CAN. Dist: Firefly Bks., Ltd.

Gerstein, Mordicai. The Night World. 2015. (ENG., Illus.). 40p. (J). (gr. -1-3). 18.99 (978-0-316-18822-7(0)) Little, Brown Bks. for Young Readers.

Glickman, Claudia. Skin Sense. 2007. (Illus.). 16p. (J). (978-0-615-16242-3(8)) L.G. Publishing.

Goins, Debra Lynn. One Day I Tried to Catch the Sun. 2011. 24p. (gr. 1-2). pap. 11.32 (978-1-4634-1872-4(8)) AuthorHouse.

Graham, Bob. How the Sun Got to Coco's House. Graham, Bob, illus. 2015. (ENG., Illus.). 40p. (J). (gr. -1-1). 18.99 (978-0-7636-8109-8(1)) Candlewick Pr.

Guess What the Sun Saw? Individual Title Six-Packs. (gr. -1-2). 23.00 (978-0-7635-8808-3(3)) Rigby Education.

Handa, Nimret. Good Night Stories. 2004. (Illus.). 20p. (J). (978-81-291-0373-4(7)) Rupa & Co.

Hardesty, Michael. Who Made the Sun, Mommy? 2011. 28p. 15.95 (978-1-4520-7721-5(5)) AuthorHouse.

Hello, Sunny Day! 2012. (ENG.). 36p. pap. 20.99 (978-1-4490-0244-2(7)) AuthorHouse.

Henson, Dwayne. Mr. Sunny Sunshine#8482; Fun Smiles. 2007. (ENG.). 28p. 15.99 (978-1-4257-5929-2(7)); pap. 13.99 (978-1-4257-4403-6(5)) Xlibris Corp.

Heo, Yumi. Sun & Moon Have a Tea Party. Stoop, Naoko, illus. 2020. 40p. (J). (gr. -1-2). 17.99 (978-0-385-39033-0(5), Schwartz & Wade Bks.) Random Hse. Children's Bks.

Hija del Sol y de Luna (Daughter of Sun & Moon) (SPA.). 24p. (J). 4.95 (978-84-246-1610-6(3)) La Galera, S.A. Editorial ESP. Dist: AIMS International Bks., Inc.

Hoberman, Mary Ann. The Sun Shines Everywhere. Lozano, Luciano, illus. 2019. (ENG.). 32p. (J). (gr. -1-3). 17.99 (978-0-316-52384-4(4)) Little, Brown Bks. for Young Readers.

Hofmeister, Alan, et al. Mat in the Sun. (Reading for All Learners Ser.). (Illus.). (J). pap. (978-1-56861-094-8(7)) Swift Learning Resources.

Hooten, K. J. The Egg Nanny Tales. 2008. 98p. pap. 19.95 (978-1-60563-722-8(X)) America Star Bks.

Hopkins, Leslie. A World Apart. 2012. 20p. pap. 17.99 (978-1-4772-6783-7(2)) AuthorHouse.

Hougasian, Amy. The Big Foot Sun. 2008. 36p. pap. 16.99 (978-1-4343-3920-1(3)) AuthorHouse.

Jasmine, Jean-Pierre. It's Raining Uber. 2013. 166p. (J). pap. 13.99 (978-1-4808-0122-6(4)) Archway Publishing.

Jefferson, Patti Brassard. How Long Will You Love Me? Jefferson, Patti Brassard, illus. 2013. (Illus.). 28p. pap. 12.95 (978-1-61244-178-8(5)) Halo Publishing International.

Johnson, Angela. A Cool Moonlight. 2005. (ENG.). 144p. (J). (gr. 3-7). reprint ed. 6.99 (978-0-14-240284-9(2), Puffin Books) Penguin Young Readers Group.

Johnson, Anne & Mortenson. Catch the Sun. 2013. 11.50 (978-1-59298-983-6(7)) Beaver's Pond Pr., Inc.

Kleven, Elisa. Sun Bread. 2004. (gr. k-3). 17.20 (978-0-613-83005-8(9)) Turtleback.

Kuracka, Vicki. When the Sun Sleeps. 2010. 16p. pap. 9.99 (978-1-60911-509-8(0), Eloquent Bks.) Strategic Book Publishing & Rights Agency (SBPRA).

Lawrence, Maggie. An Element of Fun. 2008. 76p. pap. 27.95 (978-1-4092-4969-6(7)) Lulu Pr., Inc.

Lenhardt, Lisa M. Good Morning Son. 2012. 16p. pap. 15.99 (978-1-4772-1647-7(2)) AuthorHouse.

—Good Morning Sun. 2012. 16p. pap. 15.99 (978-1-4772-1651-4(0)) AuthorHouse.

Leslie, Lindsay. Nova the Star Eater. Kim, John Taesoo, illus. 2019. (ENG.). 32p. (J). 17.99 (978-1-62414-693-0(7), 900197961) Page Street Publishing Co.

Lewis, Kelly. Where Is the Sun? 2016. (Spring Forward Ser.). (J). (gr. 1). (978-1-4900-3726-4(8)) Benchmark Education Co.

Llewellyn, Claire. The Sun Is up. Cambridge Reading Adventures. Pink a Band. Lopez, Ayesha, illus. 2016. (Cambridge Reading Adventures Ser.). (ENG.). 16p. pap. 7.95 *(978-1-107-54987-6(6))* Cambridge Univ. Pr.
Mack, Karen. The Magical Adventures of Sun Beams. 2009. 42p. 31.99 *(978-1-4415-3636-5(1))* Xlibris Corp.
Matsakis, Cynthia. Sister Sun, Brother Storm. Silver, Jane, illus. 2012. 32p. 24.95 *(978-1-4575-0768-7(4))* Dog Ear Publishing, LLC.
McCluire, Brian D. The Sun & the Moon. 2006. (Illus.). 36p. (J). 14.95 *(978-1-933426-09-9(8))* Universal Flag Publishing.
Mill, Fran. Harriet's Hunt for the Sun. 2010. 28p. pap. 12.49 *(978-1-4520-1491-3(4))* AuthorHouse.
Miller, Jules, illus. When Night Became Day. 2015. (ENG.). 32p. (J). (gr. -1-k). 16.95 *(978-1-62914-632-4(3))*, Sky Pony Pr.) Skyhorse Publishing Co., Inc.
Mutuku, E. M. When the Sun Challenged the Moon. 2012. 20p. pap. 15.50 *(978-1-4634-4718-2(3))* AuthorHouse.
Neher, Anna-Luise. A Tale from the Trunk No. 2: With Words! Words! Words! 2009. 56p. pap. 10.82 *(978-1-4251-8284-7(4))* Trafford Publishing.
Newton, Maria. Sol the Sun. 2011. 24p. pap. 28.03 *(978-1-4568-5420-1(8))* Xlibris Corp.
Nieto, Terry. Sun Go Away. 2010. 24p. pap. 15.99 *(978-1-4535-3543-1(8))* Xlibris Corp.
Nix, Pamela. Tummel the Tumbleweed. Barnes, Trisha, ed. Paulson, Arlie & Nix, Pamela, illus. 2011. 26p. (J). pap. 7.99 *(978-0-9815914-9-0(3))* River Canyon Pr.
Nolan, Allia Zobel. When God Tucks in the Day. Chung, Chi, illus. 2005. 16p. (J). 12.99 *(978-0-8254-5524-7(3))* Kregel Pubns.
O'Day, Joseph E. I Like Sunshine! Foster, Ron, illus. 2007. (J). *(978-1-929039-41-8(7))* Ambassador Bks., Inc.
Paratore, Coleen Murtagh. Catching the Sun. 2010. (J). *(978-0-618-45780-9(1))* Houghton Mifflin Harcourt Publishing Co.
Pittis, Arthur M. Sun So Hot I Froze to Death: A Waldorf Reader for Advanced Fourth Grade. Mitchell, David S., ed. Peacock, Ausa M., illus. 2005. (ENG.). (J). bds. 12.00 *(978-1-888365-65-8(X))* Waldorf Publications.
Pugliano-Martin, Carol. How Davy Crockett Moved the Sun: An American Tall Tale. 2006. (J). pap. *(978-1-4108-6168-9(6))* Benchmark Education Co.
Rankin, Hollie. When the Sun Fell Out of the Sky. 2019. (ENG., Illus.). 17p. pap. 13.95 *(978-1-138-36044-0(9))*, K396234) Routledge.
Rihani, Ina. Song to the Sun. 2012. 56p. pap. 31.99 *(978-1-4653-1123-8(8))* Xlibris Corp.
Ritz, Lee F. The Sun & the Wind. Hale, Randy, illus. 2013. 62p. 23.99 *(978-1-940840-00-0(7))* Ritz, Lee Pubns.
Rodenbur, Susan. The Boy Who Captured the Sun. Kirkpatrick, Karen, illus. 2007. 32p. per. 12.95 *(978-1-59858-515-5(0))* Dog Ear Publishing, LLC.
Rodricks, Marie. Razzle the Sunbeam. 2008. 68p. pap. 10.49 *(978-1-4343-9651-8(7))* AuthorHouse.
Rosario, Joann. Where Did Sabrina Go? Rosario, Joann, illus. 2004. (Illus.). 13p. (J). (gr. -1-5). pap. 10.00 *(978-0-9758746-1-5(6))* J.G.R. Enterprises.
Santillo, LuAnn. The Sun. Santillo, LuAnn, ed. 2003. (Half-Pint Kids Readers Ser.). (Illus.). 7p. (J). (gr. -1-1). pap. 1.00 *(978-1-59256-047-9(4))* Half-Pint Kids, Inc.
Seda, Gus. Prohex the Cat. 2012. 44p. pap. 24.95 *(978-1-4626-7704-7(5))* America Star Bks.
Shaposhnik, Alina. A Warm Yellow Pancake, 1 vol. 2010. 22p. 24.95 *(978-1-4489-7067-4(9))* PublishAmerica, Inc.
Sharpe, Katie & Sharpe, Tony. Wake up Sun. 2008. (ENG.). 26p. pap. 14.99 *(978-1-4389-2897-5(1))* AuthorHouse.
Sijercic, Hedina. An Unusual Family: A Romani Folktale. Greven, Doris, illus. 2009. 28p. pap. *(978-0-9781707-7-6(6))* Magoria Bks.
Sinois, Latrice J. You Are My Sunshine. 2012. 20p. pap. 17.99 *(978-1-4772-5731-9(4))* AuthorHouse.
Smale, Denise L. What If the Sun Didn't Rise. Smale, Denise L. & Blowars, Ryan, illus. 2011. 32p. pap. 24.95 *(978-1-4560-5032-0(X))* America Star Bks.
Sparks, Shanti. Honey & the Sunset. 2008. (Illus.). 38p. (J). pap. 9.00 *(978-0-8059-7553-6(5))* Dorrance Publishing Co., Inc.
Stead, Judy, illus. Mister Sun. 2006. (J). *(978-1-58987-097-0(2))* Kindermusik International.
The Sun in the Sky. 2003. lib. bdg. 12.99 *(978-0-9740997-0-5(8))* Lisa The Weather Wonder Inc.
The Sun's Story. 2013. (Illus.). 36p. pap. 14.99 *(978-1-940426-01-3(4))* Love Ink LLC.
Swarbrick, David E. Peggy's Play House. 2011. 24p. pap. 24.95 *(978-1-4626-1989-4(4))* America Star Bks.
Sweeney, Monica. How the Crayons Saved the Rainbow. Parker-Thomas, Feronia, illus. 2016. (How the Crayons Saved Ser.: 1). 32p. (J). (gr. -1-k). 16.99 *(978-1-5107-0583-8(X)*, Sky Pony Pr.) Skyhorse Publishing Co., Inc.
Thomas, Leigh Maria. Ray & the Rainbow. 2003. (ENG., Illus.). 24p. pap. 11.00 *(978-1-4120-1490-8(5))* Trafford Publishing.
Thompson, Carol. Sun. Thompson, Carol, illus. 2014. (Whatever the Weather Ser.). (Illus.). 12p. (J). (gr. k-k). spiral bd. *(978-1-84643-680-2(X))* Child's Play International Ltd.
Tomos, Angharad. Diffodd Yr Haul. 2005. (WEL., Illus.). 48p. pap. *(978-0-86243-080-1(1))* Y Lolfa.
Tsinajinnie, Veronica. Johonaa'ei: Bringer of Dawn. Thomas, Peter A., tr. from NAV. Singer, Ryan, illus. 2007. (ENG & NAV.). 32p. (J). (gr. -1-3). 17.95 *(978-1-893354-54-8(7))* Salina Bookshelf Inc.
Veil, Karney. Sun & Moon Play Hide & Seek: A Children's Story. 2012. 24p. (-18). pap. 24.95 *(978-1-4626-9401-3(2))* America Star Bks.
Waller, C. L. Lady Sun & the Man in the Moon. 2008. 16p. per. 24.95 *(978-1-4241-8670-9(6))* America Star Bks.
Where Does the Sun Go? 2006. (Illus.). 40p. (J). (gr. -1-3). 14.95 *(978-0-9786813-0-2(4))* Elora Pr.
Wilhelm, Hans. Hello, Sun! Wilhelm, Hans, illus. 2005. (Illus.). 32p. (gr. k-2). 15.25 *(978-1-57505-348-6(9))* Lerner Publishing Group.
Yankey, Lindsey. Sun & Moon. 2015. (Illus.). 32p. (J). (gr. -1-3). 16.95 *(978-1-927018-60-6(9))* Simply Read Bks. CAN. Dist: Ingram Publisher Services.

SUN-DIALS
see Sundials

SUN GLASSES
see Eyeglasses

SUNDAY
see Sabbath

SUNDIALS

Bryson, Theresa. Make a Sundial. 2011. (Early Connections Ser.). (J). *(978-1-61672-558-7(3))* Benchmark Education Co.

SUNFLOWERS

Bellavia, Rebecca. Planting Sunflowers: Represent & Interpret Data, 1 vol. 2014. (Math Masters: Measurement & Data Ser.). (ENG.). 24p. (J). (gr. 2-2). 25.27 *(978-1-4777-6408-4(9)*, 9a9fa10b-1ade-48fc-8b47-2370205927b3); pap. 8.25 *(978-1-4777-4825-1(3)*, b353be4c-39ef-4ca3-afda-76d866d2e919) Rosen Publishing Group, Inc., The. (Rosen Classroom).
Berger, Melvin & Berger, Gilda. A Sunflower Grows Up. 2008. (Illus.). 32p. (J). *(978-0-439-02530-0(3))* Scholastic, Inc.
Cooper, Jason. Sunflower. 2003. (Life Cycles II Ser.). (Illus.). 24p. (J). lib. bdg. 27.07 *(978-1-58952-708-9(9))* Rourke Educational Media.
De la Bédoyère, Camilla. Seed to Sunflower. 2012. (ENG., Illus.). 24p. (J). (gr. 1-3). pap. 7.95 *(978-1-926853-40-6(7))* Saunders Bk. Co. CAN. Dist: RiverStream Publishing.
—Seed to Sunflower. 2013. (Illus.). 24p. (J). *(978-1-4351-4710-2(3))* Barnes & Noble, Inc.
Diary of a Sunflower: Individual Title Six-Packs. (Story Steps Ser.). (gr. k-2). 32.00 *(978-0-7635-9839-6(9))* Rigby Education.
Dickmann, Nancy. A Sunflower's Life, 1 vol. 2010. (Watch It Grow Ser.). (ENG., Illus.). 24p. (J). (gr. -1-1). 25.32 *(978-1-4329-4144-4(5)*, 113271); pap. 6.29 *(978-1-4329-4153-6(4)*, 113279) Capstone. (Heinemann).
—La Vida Del Girasol. 2011. (¡Mira Cómo Crece! Ser.). (SPA.). 24p. (J). (gr. -1-1). pap. 6.29 *(978-1-4329-5289-1(7)*, 116015, Heinemann) Capstone.
Dunn, Mary R. A Sunflower's Life Cycle. 2017. (Explore Life Cycles Ser.). (ENG., Illus.). 24p. (J). (gr. -1-2). pap. 6.95 *(978-1-5157-7056-5(7)*, 135486); lib. bdg. 27.32 *(978-1-5157-7050-3(8)*, 135480) Capstone. (Capstone Pr.).
Franks, Katie. Sunflowers up Close. (Nature up Close Ser.). 24p. 2009. (gr. k-1). 42.50 *(978-1-61514-829-5(9))* 2007. (ENG., Illus.). (J). (gr. 1-1). lib. bdg. 26.27 *(978-1-4042-4141-1(8)*, 5968a44e-3b1d-48a8-9b36-323b90a531ac) Rosen Publishing Group, Inc., The. (PowerKids Pr.).
—Sunflowers up Close / Los Girasoles. 2009. (Nature up Close / la naturaleza de cerca Ser.). (ENG & SPA.). 24p. (gr. k-1). 42.50 *(978-1-61514-835-6(3)*, Editorial Buenas Letras) Rosen Publishing Group, Inc., The.
—Sunflowers up Close/Los Girasoles, 1 vol. Sanz, Pilar, tr. 2007. (Nature up Close / la Naturaleza de Cerca Ser.). (ENG & SPA., Illus.). 24p. (J). (gr. 1-1). lib. bdg. 26.27 *(978-1-4042-7680-2(7)*, dd148d32-9c7f-4cbe-b211-1375495ab307, Editorial Buenas Letras) Rosen Publishing Group, Inc., The.
Hipp, Andrew. El Girasol: Por Dentro y Por Fuera, 1 vol. Brusca, Maria Cristina, tr. di Gaudesi, Andrea Ricciardi, illus. 2003. (Explora la Naturaleza (Getting into Nature) Ser.). (SPA.). 32p. (J). (gr. 3-4). lib. bdg. 28.93 *(978-1-4042-2868-9(3)*, 9e68b24a-1e6b-46b9-8d3f-9d04410ca17e) Rosen Publishing Group, Inc., The.
—El Girasol: Por dentro y por fuera (Sunflower:Inside & Out) 2009. (Explora la Naturaleza (Getting into Nature) Ser.). (SPA.). 32p. (gr. 3-4). 47.90 *(978-1-61512-336-0(9)*, Editorial Buenas Letras) Rosen Publishing Group, Inc., The.
—Sunflower, 1 vol. 2004. (Getting into Nature Ser.). (ENG., Illus.). 32p. (J). (gr. 3-4). lib. bdg. 28.93 *(978-0-8239-4210-7(4)*, c54db81d-dd65-4eee-828a-27cbaa379cba) Rosen Publishing Group, Inc., The.
—Sunflowers: Inside & Out. 2009. (Getting into Nature Ser.). 32p. (gr. 3-4). 47.90 *(978-1-61512-726-9(7)*, PowerKids Pr.) Rosen Publishing Group, Inc., The.
Life Cycles - from Seed to Sunflower. 2005. (J). per. 8.95 *(978-1-59566-145-6(X))* QEB Publishing Inc.
Markovics, Joyce L. Sunflower. 2015. (See It Grow Ser.). (ENG.). 24p. (J). (gr. -1-3). lib. bdg. 26.99 *(978-1-62724-843-3(9))* Bearport Publishing Co., Inc.
Massie, Elizabeth. Looking at a Sunflower. 2016. (Spring Forward Ser.). (J). (gr. 1). *(978-1-4900-2234-5(1))* Benchmark Education Co.
Nelson, Robin. Sunflowers. 2009. pap. 34.95 *(978-0-7613-4122-2(6))* Lerner Publishing Group.
Peters, Elisa. It's a Sunflower! (Everyday Wonders Ser.). 24p. (gr. 1-1). 2009. 42.50 *(978-1-61512-324-7(5))* 2008. (ENG., Illus.). (J). lib. bdg. 26.27 *(978-1-4042-4458-0(1)*, f0aea2b8-8481-478e-84e4-e6406c29da11) Rosen Publishing Group, Inc., The. (PowerKids Pr.).
—It's a Sunflower! Es un Girasol!, 1 vol. 2008. (Everyday Wonders / Maravillas de Todos Los Días Ser.). (SPA & ENG.). 24p. (J). (gr. 1-1). lib. bdg. 26.27 *(978-1-4358-2523-9(3)*, 74646381-dea6-4b25-8d76-662e476fb2ec) Rosen Publishing Group, Inc., The.
—It's a Sunflower! / ¡Es un Girasol! 2009. (Everyday Wonders / Maravillas de todos los días Ser.). (ENG & SPA.). 24p. (gr. 1-1). 42.50 *(978-1-61512-330-8(X)*, Editorial Buenas Letras) Rosen Publishing Group, Inc., The.
Peters, Katie. Let's Look at Sunflowers. 2020. (Plant Life Cycles (Pull Ahead Readers — Nonfiction) Ser.). (ENG., Illus.). 16p. (J). (gr. -1-1). 27.99 *(978-1-5415-9022-9(8)*, 973dbfe9-0fb4-45a4-a543-5f387024b2c7, Lerner Pubns.) Lerner Publishing Group.
Phelps, Bonnie. The Life Cycle of a Sunflower, 1 vol. 2015. (Watch Them Grow! Ser.). (ENG.). 24p. (J). (gr. 1-1). pap. 9.25 *(978-1-4994-0684-9(3)*, 87b2282e-76fc-45d9-be3c-f62756e5b8e3, PowerKids Pr.) Rosen Publishing Group, Inc., The.
Reid, Barbara. Seed to Sunflower: A First Look Board Book. Crysler, Ian, photos by. 2004. (Illus.). 12p. (J). (gr. k-2). reprint ed. 10.00 *(978-0-7567-7853-8(0))* DIANE Publishing Co.
Riggs, Kate. Sunflower. (Grow with Me Ser.). (ENG.). 32p. (J). (gr. 3-6). 2013. pap. 9.99 *(978-0-89812-771-3(8)*, 21982, Creative Paperbacks) 2012. (Illus.). 19.95 *(978-1-60818-218-3(5)*, 21976, Creative Education) Creative Co., The.
Smith, Ian. How Does it Grow? From Seed to Sunflower. 2004. (Illus.). 24p. (J). lib. bdg. 15.95 *(978-1-59566-016-9(X))* QEB Publishing Inc.
Stewart, David. How a Seed Grows into a Sunflower. Franklin, Carolyn, illus. 2008. (Amaze Ser.). (ENG.). 32p. (J). (gr. k-3). 27.00 *(978-0-531-20442-9(1)*, Children's Pr.) Scholastic Library Publishing.
Sunflowers. 2009. (First Step Nonfiction - Plant Life Cycles Ser.). (gr. k-2). 21.27 *(978-0-7613-4072-0(6)*, Lerner Pubns.) Lerner Publishing Group.
Thomson, Ruth. A Sunflower's Life Cycle. 2010. (Let's Look at Life Cycles Ser.). 24p. (J). (gr. k-2). lib. bdg., E-Book 42.50 *(978-1-4488-0360-6(8))*; (ENG.). (gr. 2-2). pap. 9.25 *(978-1-61532-230-5(2)*, 6e13df5b-1606-4121-b680-eb4876de55d9, PowerKids Pr.); (ENG., Illus.). (gr. 2-2). lib. bdg. 26.27 *(978-1-61532-219-0(1)*, 5cc10af6-f27e-4ba8-9539-c722ce95c5fb, PowerKids Pr.) Rosen Publishing Group, Inc., The.
Watts, Barrie. Sunflower. 2003. 32p. (J). lib. bdg. 24.25 *(978-1-58340-232-0(2))* Black Rabbit Bks.

SUNFLOWERS—FICTION

Brown, Ruth. Ten Seeds. Brown, Ruth, illus. 2013. (ENG., Illus.). 24p. (J). (gr. -1-k). 10.99 *(978-1-84939-251-8(X))* Andersen Pr. GBR. Dist: Independent Pubs. Group.
Higgs, Liz Curtis. The Sunflower Parable, 1 vol. Munger, Nancy, illus. 10th anniv. ed. 2007. (Parable Ser.). (ENG.). 32p. (J). (gr. -1-2). 7.99 *(978-1-4003-0845-3(3)*, Tommy Nelson) Nelson, Thomas Inc.
I Am a Wish. 2013. 36p. pap. 16.99 *(978-1-4808-0094-6(5))* Archway Publishing.
John, Jory. The Bad Seed Presents: the Good, the Bad, & the Spooky: Over 150 Spooky Stickers Inside. a Halloween Book for Kids. Oswald, Pete, illus. 2021. (Food Group Ser.). (ENG.). 32p. (J). (gr. -1-3). 12.99 *(978-0-06-295454-1(7)*, HarperCollins) HarperCollins Pubs.
Kaider, Azi Sabi. Angela's Sunflower. 2012. 24p. pap. 16.95 *(978-1-4772-9703-2(0))* AuthorHouse.
Kosinski, Colleen Rowan, illus. Lilla's Sunflowers. 2016. (ENG.). 32p. (J). (gr. -1-k). 16.99 *(978-1-5107-0464-0(7)*, Sky Pony Pr.) Skyhorse Publishing Co., Inc.
Maile's Sunflower. 2nd ed. 2006. (J). *(978-0-9787864-0-3(8))* Picket Press.
Mockford, Caroline. What's This? A Seed's Story. Mockford, Caroline, illus. 2007. (ENG., Illus.). 32p. (J). (gr. -1-2). pap. 7.99 *(978-1-84686-071-3(7))* Barefoot Bks., Inc.
Monroe, Darrell. Sammy Sunflower. 2012. 32p. pap. 19.99 *(978-1-4772-6891-9(X))* AuthorHouse.
My Sunflowers. 2003. (J). per. *(978-1-57657-897-1(6))* Paradise Pr., Inc.
Ochiltree, Dianne. Sunflowers Measure Up! 2003. (Hello Math Reader Ser.). (Illus.). (J). *(978-0-439-24228-8(2))* Scholastic, Inc.
Parton, Paula. I Always Wondered. Parton, Paula, illus. 2009. (Illus.). 44p. pap. 11.95 *(978-1-935118-48-0(X))* Bellissima Publishing, LLC.
Post, Cynthia W. Carrie Flower: Goes to Camp. 2011. pap. 15.95 *(978-0-7414-6462-0(4))* Infinity Publishing.
—Carrie Flower: Goes to the Hospital. 2011. pap. 12.95 *(978-0-7414-6461-3(6))* Infinity Publishing.
—Carrie Flower: Meet Carrie Flower. 2011. pap. 10.95 *(978-0-7414-6463-7(2))* Infinity Publishing.
Powell, Jillian. Sam's Sunflower. Boccardo, Johanna, illus. 2008. (Tadpoles Ser.). (ENG.). 24p. (J). (gr. -1-3). pap. *(978-0-7787-3895-4(7))*; lib. bdg. *(978-0-7787-3864-0(7))* Crabtree Publishing Co.
Tazewell, Lora A. Jelly Bread & Water Juice. 2009. 48p. pap. 17.49 *(978-1-4389-1973-7(5))* AuthorHouse.
Wagner, Larry. The Adventures of Sally Sunflower. 2004. 23p. pap. 24.95 *(978-1-4137-4009-7(X))* PublishAmerica, Inc.

SUNKEN CITIES
see Extinct Cities

SUNKEN TREASURE
see Buried Treasure

SUPERIOR, LAKE—FICTION

Erdrich, Louise. Chickadee. Erdrich, Louise, illus. 2012. (Birchbark House Ser.: 4). (ENG., Illus.). 208p. (J). (gr. 3-7). 16.99 *(978-0-06-057790-2(8)*, HarperCollins) HarperCollins Pubs.
Wargin, Kathy-jo. The Voyageur's Paddle. Geister, David, illus. rev. ed. 2007. (Myths, Legends, Fairy & Folktales Ser.). (ENG.). 40p. (J). (gr. 1-4). 19.99 *(978-1-58536-007-9(4)*, 201942) Sleeping Bear Pr.

SUPERMAN (FICTITIOUS CHARACTER)—FICTION

Aptekar, Devan. Darkseid's Revenge. Gordon, Eric A. & Gordon, Steven E., illus. 2012. (ENG.). 24p. (J). (gr. -1-3). pap. 3.99 *(978-0-06-188533-4(9)*, HarperFestival) HarperCollins Pubs.
—Darkseid's Revenge. Gordon, Eric A. & Gordon, Steven E., illus. 2012. (Justice League Classic 8X8 Ser.). (J). lib. bdg. 13.55 *(978-0-606-23566-2(3))* Turtleback.
Baltazar, Art & Aureliani, Franco. And Now... Braniac!, 1 vol. 2014. (Superman Family Adventures Ser.). (ENG., Illus.). 32p. (J). (gr. 1-3). 22.60 *(978-1-4342-6478-7(5)*, 124160, Stone Arch Bks.) Capstone.
Batman vs. Superman: Their Greatest Battles. 2015. lib. bdg. 20.85 *(978-0-606-37886-4(3))* Turtleback.
Bird, Benjamin. Day of the Bizarros! Levins, Tim, illus. 2015. (Amazing Adventures of Superman! Ser.). (ENG.). 32p. (J). (gr. k-2). pap. 3.95 *(978-1-4795-6522-1(9)*, 128512, Stone Arch Bks.) Capstone.
—Magic Monsters! Levins, Tim, illus. 2015. (Amazing Adventures of Superman! Ser.). (ENG.). 32p. (J). (gr. k-2). pap. 3.95 *(978-1-4795-6525-2(3)*, 128514, Stone Arch Bks.) Capstone.
—Supergirl's Pet Problem! Levins, Tim, illus. 2015. (Amazing Adventures of Superman! Ser.). (ENG.). 32p. (J). (gr. k-2). pap. 3.95 *(978-1-4795-6523-8(7)*, 128511, Stone Arch Bks.) Capstone.
Black, Jake & Meredith Books Staff. Robo Monster. Stewart, Scott, illus. 2008. 22p. (J). pap. 3.99 *(978-0-696-23957-1(4))* Meredith Bks.
Bond, Gwenda. Double Down. 2016. (Lois Lane Ser.). (ENG.). 384p. (YA). (gr. 9-12). 16.95 *(978-1-63079-038-7(9)*, 130898, Switch Pr.) Capstone.
—Fallout. (Lois Lane Ser.). (ENG.). 304p. (YA). (gr. 9-12). 2016. pap. 9.95 *(978-1-63079-006-6(0)*, 127340) 2015. 16.95 *(978-1-63079-005-9(2)*, 127326) Capstone. (Switch Pr.).
—Triple Threat. (Lois Lane Ser.). (ENG.). 360p. (YA). (gr. 9-12). 2018. pap. 9.95 *(978-1-63079-084-4(2)*, 134777) 2017. 16.95 *(978-1-63079-082-0(6)*, 134776) Capstone. (Switch Pr.).
Bright, J. E. The Man of Steel: Cyborg Superman. Levins, Tim, illus. 2013. (Man of Steel Ser.). (ENG.). 88p. (J). (gr. 3-7). pap. 5.95 *(978-1-4342-4219-8(6)*, 120277, Stone Arch Bks.) Capstone.
Dahl, Michael. A Buried Starship. Levins, Tim & Vecchio, Luciano, illus. 2017. (Superman Tales of the Fortress of Solitude Ser.). (ENG.). 40p. (J). (gr. 4-8). lib. bdg. 24.65 *(978-1-4965-4395-0(5)*, 134635, Stone Arch Bks.) Capstone.
—Good Morning, Superman! Lozano, Omar, illus. 2017. (DC Super Heroes Ser.). (ENG.). 32p. (J). (gr. -1-2). lib. bdg. 23.99 *(978-1-5158-0970-8(6)*, 134754, Stone Arch Bks.) Capstone.
—Last Son of Krypton. Delaney, John, illus. 2009. (Superman Ser.). (ENG.). 56p. (J). (gr. 3-6). pap. 4.95 *(978-1-4342-1370-9(6)*, 95667); lib. bdg. 26.65 *(978-1-4342-1155-2(X)*, 95369) Capstone. (Stone Arch Bks.).
—The Museum Monsters. Schoening, Dan, illus. 2009. (Superman Ser.). (ENG.). 56p. (J). (gr. 3-6). pap. 4.95 *(978-1-4342-1372-3(2)*, 95669, Stone Arch Bks.) Capstone.
—Rays of Doom. Levins, Tim & Vecchio, Luciano, illus. 2017. (Superman Tales of the Fortress of Solitude Ser.). (ENG.). 40p. (J). (gr. 4-8). lib. bdg. 24.65 *(978-1-4965-4396-7(3)*, 134636, Stone Arch Bks.) Capstone.
—Superman Tales of the Fortress of Solitude. 2017. (Superman Tales of the Fortress of Solitude Ser.). (ENG.). 40p. (J). (gr. 4-8). 101.28 *(978-1-4965-4414-8(5)*, 26073, Stone Arch Bks.) Capstone.
DC Comics Staff. Superman. 2013. (Stand-Up Mover Ser.: 1). (ENG.). 10p. (J). bds. 8.99 *(978-0-7944-2839-6(8))* Reader's Digest Assn., Inc., The.
DC Comics Staff, et al. Death of Superman. Kahan, Bob, ed. rev. ed. 2011. (Superman Ser.). (ENG., Illus.). 168p. (YA). pap. 12.99 *(978-1-56389-097-0(6))* DC Comics.
de la Peña, Matt. Superman: Dawnbreaker. 2019. (DC Icons Ser.). (ENG.). 336p. (YA). (gr. 7). lib. bdg. 21.99 *(978-0-399-54966-3(8)*, Random Hse. Bks. for Young Readers) Random Hse. Children's Bks.
Harper, Benjamin, adapted by. Superman Returns the Movie Storybook. movie tie-in ed. 2006. (ENG., Illus.). 48p. (J). (gr. k-3). 22.44 *(978-0-696-22901-5(3))* Meredith Bks.
Hoena, Blake A. Under the Red Sun, 1 vol. Schoening, Dan, illus. 2009. (Superman Ser.). (ENG.). 56p. (J). (gr. 3-6). pap. 4.95 *(978-1-4342-1375-4(7)*, 95672); lib. bdg. 27.32 *(978-1-4342-1159-0(2)*, 95373) Capstone. (Stone Arch Bks.).
Katz, David Bar. My First Superman Book: Touch & Feel. 2011. (DC Super Heroes Ser.). (ENG.). 12p. (J). bds. 11.99 *(978-1-935703-00-6(5))* Downtown Bookworks.
King, Trey. Race Around the World! Wang, Sean, illus. 2016. (LEGO DC Super Heroes Ser.). (ENG.). 24p. (J). (gr. -1-3). pap. 3.99 *(978-0-545-86797-9(5))* Scholastic, Inc.
Korté, Steve. The Man of Steel: Superman vs. Mr. Mxyzptlk. Levins, Tim, illus. 2013. (Man of Steel Ser.). (ENG.). 88p. (J). (gr. 3-7). pap. 5.95 *(978-1-4342-4826-8(7)*, 121742, Stone Arch Bks.) Capstone.
Korte, Steve. Race to Save the Day! 2018. (Justice League Classic 8X8 Ser.). (J). lib. bdg. 13.55 *(978-0-606-41043-4(0))* Turtleback.
Korté, Steve. Superman & the Invasion of Earth: A Solar System Adventure. Schigiel, Gregg, illus. 2018. (Superman Solar System Adventures Ser.). (ENG.). 32p. (J). (gr. 4-8). lib. bdg. 27.99 *(978-1-5435-1565-7(7)*, 137923, Capstone Pr.) Capstone.
—Superman & the Menace on Mercury: A Solar System Adventure. Brizuela, Dario, illus. 2018. (Superman Solar System Adventures Ser.). (ENG.). 32p. (J). (gr. 4-8). lib. bdg. 27.99 *(978-1-5435-1567-1(3)*, 137925, Capstone Pr.) Capstone.
—Superman & the Mischief on Mars: A Solar System Adventure. Schigiel, Gregg, illus. 2018. (Superman Solar System Adventures Ser.). (ENG.). 32p. (J). (gr. 4-8). lib. bdg. 27.99 *(978-1-5435-1563-3(0)*, 137922, Capstone Pr.) Capstone.
—Superman & the Nightmare on Neptune: A Solar System Adventure. Brizuela, Dario, illus. 2018. (Superman Solar System Adventures Ser.). (ENG.). 32p. (J). (gr. 4-8). lib. bdg. 27.99 *(978-1-5435-1574-9(6)*, 137929, Capstone Pr.) Capstone.
—Superman & the Trials of Jupiter: A Solar System Adventure. Schigiel, Gregg, illus. 2018. (Superman Solar System Adventures Ser.). (ENG.). 32p. (J). (gr. 4-8). lib. bdg. 27.99 *(978-1-5435-1571-8(1)*, 137926, Capstone Pr.) Capstone.
—Superman & the Utopia on Uranus: A Solar System Adventure. Brizuela, Dario, illus. 2018. (Superman Solar System Adventures Ser.). (ENG.). 32p. (J). (gr. 4-8). lib. bdg. 27.99 *(978-1-5435-1573-2(8)*, 137928, Capstone Pr.) Capstone.
—Superman & the Villains on Venus: A Solar System Adventure. Brizuela, Dario, illus. 2018. (Superman Solar System Adventures Ser.). (ENG.). 32p. (J). (gr. 4-8). lib. bdg. 27.99 *(978-1-5435-1566-4(5)*, 137924, Capstone Pr.) Capstone.
—Superman Day Disaster. Brizuela, Dario, illus. 2018. (You Choose Stories: Superman Ser.). (ENG.). 112p. (J). (gr. 2-6). lib. bdg. 32.65 *(978-1-4965-5824-4(3)*, 136912, Stone Arch Bks.) Capstone.
Lemke, Donald. Bizarro's Last Laugh. 2017. (Justice League Classic: I Can Read! Ser.). (Illus.). 31p. (J). lib. bdg. 13.55 *(978-0-606-39632-5(2))* Turtleback.
—Superman: A Giant Attack. 2015. (Justice League Classic: I Can Read! Ser.). (J). lib. bdg. 13.55 *(978-0-606-36955-8(4))* Turtleback.

S

—Superman - A Giant Attack. Ferguson, Lee, illus. 2015. (I Can Read Level 2 Ser.). (ENG.). 32p. (J). (gr. -1-3). pap. 3.99 (978-0-06-234488-5(9)) HarperCollins Pubs.

—Superman Classic: Pranking News. Spaziante, Patrick, illus. 2016. (I Can Read Level 2 Ser.). 32p. (J). (gr. -1-3). pap. 3.99 (978-0-06-236085-4(X)) HarperCollins Pubs.

—Superman Versus the Silver Banshee. 2013. (Justice League Classic: I Can Read! Ser.). (J). lib. bdg. 13.55 (978-0-606-27156-1(2)) Turtleback.

—Superman vs. the Silver Banshee. Smith, Andy, illus. 2013. (I Can Read Level 2 Ser.). (ENG.). 32p. (J). (gr. -1-3). pap. 3.99 (978-0-06-188524-2(X)) HarperCollins Pubs.

Lemke, Donald B. Bizarro's Last Laugh. Spaziante, Patrick, illus. 2017. 31p. (J). (978-1-5182-3834-5(3)) Harper & Row Ltd.

Man Of Steel. 2013. (Man of Steel Ser.). (ENG.). 88p. (gr. 2-3). 106.60 (978-1-4342-4812-1(7)); pap. 23.80 (978-1-4342-4864-0(X)) Capstone. (Stone Arch Bks.).

The Man of Steel. 2013. (Man of Steel Ser.). (ENG.). 88p. (J). (gr. 2-3). 109.28 (978-1-4342-4811-4(9), 172079, Stone Arch Bks.) Capstone.

Manning, Matthew K. Apokolips Invasion. Brizuela, Dario, illus. 2018. (You Choose Stories: Superman Ser.). (ENG.). 112p. (J). (gr. 2-6). lib. bdg. 32.65 (978-1-4965-5825-1(1), 136913, Stone Arch Bks.) Capstone.

—The Poisoned Planet, 1 vol. Vecchio, Luciano, illus. 2012. (Man of Steel Ser.). (ENG.). 88p. (J). (gr. 3-7). lib. bdg. 26.65 (978-1-4342-4091-0(6), 119810, Stone Arch Bks.) Capstone.

—Superman: An Origin Story. Vecchio, Luciano, illus. 2015. (DC Super Heroes Origins Ser.). (ENG.). 48p. (J). (gr. k-2). lib. bdg. 23.99 (978-1-4342-9728-0(4), 127060, Stone Arch Bks.) Capstone.

—Superman Battles the Billionaire Bully. Beavers, Ethen, illus. 2017. (DC Super Hero Stories Ser.). (ENG.). 56p. (J). (gr. 1-3). lib. bdg. 25.32 (978-1-4965-4634-0(2), 134875, Stone Arch Bks.) Capstone.

Manning, Matthew K., et al. You Choose Stories: Superman. Brizuela, Dario, illus. 2018. (You Choose Stories: Superman Ser.). (ENG.). 112p. (J). (gr. 2-6). 130.60 (978-1-4965-5828-2(6), 27469, Stone Arch Bks.) Capstone.

McCLOUD, Scott. Be Careful What You Wish For... Burchett, Rick & Austin, Terry, illus. 2012. (Superman Adventures Ser.). (ENG.). 32p. (J). (gr. 2-5). lib. bdg. 22.60 (978-1-4342-4550-2(0), 120510, Stone Arch Bks.) Capstone.

—Distant Thunder, 1 vol. Burchett, Rick & Austin, Terry, illus. 2012. (Superman Adventures Ser.). (ENG.). 32p. (J). (gr. 2-5). 22.60 (978-1-4342-4551-9(9), 120511, Stone Arch Bks.) Capstone.

Rosen, Lucy. Friends & Foes. Gordon, Steven E. & Gordon, Eric A., illus. 2013. (I Can Read Level 2 Ser.). (ENG.). 32p. (J). (gr. -1-3). pap. 3.99 (978-0-06-223595-4(8)) HarperCollins Pubs.

—Parasite City. Gordon, Steven E. & Gordon, Eric A., illus. 2011. (ENG.). 24p. (J). (gr. -1-3). pap. 3.99 (978-0-06-188532-7(0), HarperFestival) HarperCollins Pubs.

—Superman's Superpowers. Tong, Andie, illus. 2013. (I Can Read Level 2 Ser.). (ENG.). 32p. (J). (gr. -1-3). pap. 3.99 (978-0-06-223597-8(4)) HarperCollins Pubs.

Sazaklis, John. Battle in Metropolis. 2013. (Justice League Classic 8X8 Ser.). lib. bdg. 13.55 (978-0-606-31827-3(5)) Turtleback.

—Day of Doom. 2013. (Justice League Classic: I Can Read! Ser.). (J). lib. bdg. 13.55 (978-0-606-32162-4(4)) Turtleback.

—The Fate of Krypton. Roberts, Jeremy, illus. 2013. (Man of Steel Ser.). (ENG.). 24p. (J). (gr. -1-3). pap. 3.99 (978-0-06-223593-0(1), HarperFestival) HarperCollins Pubs.

—Man of Steel. 2013. (Man of Steel Ser.). (ENG.). 12p. (J). (gr. -1-3). pap. 6.99 (978-0-06-223605-0(9), HarperFestival) HarperCollins Pubs.

—Superman: Escape from the Phantom Zone. Gordon, Steven E., illus. 2011. (I Can Read Level 2 Ser.). (ENG.). 32p. (J). (gr. -1-3). pap. 3.99 (978-0-06-188519-8(3)) HarperCollins Pubs.

—Superman Saves Smallville. Roberts, Jeremy, illus. 2013. (Man of Steel Ser.). (ENG.). 24p. (J). (gr. -1-3). pap. 3.99 (978-0-06-223603-6(2), HarperFestival) HarperCollins Pubs.

Sazaklis, John & Farley, John. Attack of the Toyman. 2012. (Justice League Classic 8X8 Ser.). (J). lib. bdg. 13.55 (978-0-606-26859-2(6)) Turtleback.

Scholastic, Inc. Staff & Kogge, Michael. Cross Fire. 2016. (Batman vs. Superman: Dawn of Justice Ser.). (ENG.). 144p. (J). (gr. 2-5). lib. bdg. 16.00 (978-0-606-38097-3(3)) Turtleback.

Siegel, Jerry, et al. Adventures of Superman. Gordon, Steven E. et al, illus. 2013. 125p. (J). (978-1-4351-5063-8(5)) Barnes & Noble, Inc.

Simonson, Louise. Lex Luthor's Power Grab! Vecchio, Luciano, illus. 2015. (Superman: Comic Chapter Bks.). (ENG.). 88p. (J). (gr. 3-7). lib. bdg. 21.32 (978-1-4965-0508-8(5), 128581, Stone Arch Bks.) Capstone.

Sonneborn, Scott. The Man of Steel: Superman vs. the Moon Bandits. Cavallaro, Mike, illus. 2013. (Man of Steel Ser.). (ENG.). 88p. (J). (gr. 3-7). 26.65 (978-1-4342-4093-4(2), 119812); pap. 5.95 (978-1-4342-4223-5(4), 120281) Capstone. (Stone Arch Bks.).

Steele, Michael Anthony. Metallo Attacks! Brizuela, Dario, illus. 2018. (You Choose Stories: Superman Ser.). (ENG.). 112p. (J). (gr. 2-6). lib. bdg. 32.65 (978-1-4965-5826-8(X), 136914, Stone Arch Bks.) Capstone.

Stephens, Sarah Hines. Metropolis Mayhem. Brizuela, Dario, illus. 2018. (You Choose Stories: Superman Ser.). (ENG.). 112p. (J). (gr. 2-6). lib. bdg. 32.65 (978-1-4965-5827-5(8), 136915, Stone Arch Bks.) Capstone.

—Superman Classic: Superman & the Mayhem of Metallo. Mada Design Staff, illus. 2010. (Superman Classics). (ENG.). 24p. (J). (gr. -1-3). pap. 3.99 (978-0-06-188529-7(0), HarperFestival) HarperCollins Pubs.

Stevens, Eric. The Menace of Metallo, 1 vol. McManus, Shawn, illus. 2009. (Superman Ser.). (ENG.). 56p. (J). (gr. 3-6). pap. 4.95 (978-1-4342-1371-6(4), 95668, Stone Arch Bks.) Capstone.

Stewart, Yale. Escape from Future World!, 1 vol. Stewart, Yale, illus. 2014. (Amazing Adventures of Superman! Ser.). (ENG., Illus.). 32p. (J). (gr. k-2). lib. bdg. 25.32 (978-1-4795-5732-5(3), 126752, Stone Arch Bks.) Capstone.

Sudduth, Brent. I Am Superman! Edwards, Tommy Lee, illus. 2006. (Superman Returns Ser.). 24p. (J). (gr. 4-7). pap. 3.99 (978-0-696-22905-3(6)) Meredith Bks.

Sudduth, Brent & Meredith Books Staff. Doom in a Box. Panosian, Dan, illus. 2008. 22p. (J). pap. 3.99 (978-0-696-23956-4(6)) Meredith Bks.

Sudeith, Alaina. Superman Classic: The Superman Reusable Sticker Book. 2011. (ENG.). 12p. (J). (gr. -1-3). pap. 6.99 (978-0-06-188538-9(X), HarperFestival) HarperCollins Pubs.

Superman: Comic Chapter Books, 1 vol. 2014. (Superman: Comic Chapter Bks.). (ENG.). 88p. (gr. 3-7). pap. 11.90 (978-1-4342-9535-4(4), Stone Arch Bks.) Capstone.

Sutton, Laurie S. The Demons of Deep Space. Vecchio, Luciano, illus. 2012. (Man of Steel Ser.). (ENG.). 88p. (J). (gr. 3-7). lib. bdg. 26.65 (978-1-4342-4098-9(3), 119817, Stone Arch Bks.) Capstone.

—Going Ape. Gordon, Eric A. & Gordon, Steven E., illus. 2012. (I Can Read Level 2 Ser.). (ENG.). 32p. (J). (gr. -1-3). pap. 3.99 (978-0-06-188522-8(3)) HarperCollins Pubs.

—Going Ape. 2012. (Justice League Classic: I Can Read! Ser.). (J). lib. bdg. 13.55 (978-0-606-26260-6(1)) Turtleback.

—The Man of Steel: Superman vs. the Doomsday Army, 1 vol. Levins, Tim & Vecchio, Luciano, illus. 2013. (Man of Steel Ser.). (ENG.). 88p. (J). (gr. 3-7). 26.65 (978-1-4342-4487-1(3), 120486); pap. 5.95 (978-1-4342-4827-5(5), 121744) Capstone. (Stone Arch Bks.).

—The Planet Collector, 1 vol. Vecchio, Luciano, illus. 2014. (Superman: Comic Chapter Bks.). (ENG.). 88p. (J). (gr. 3-7). 21.32 (978-1-4342-9133-2(2), 125579, Stone Arch Bks.) Capstone.

Sutton, Laurie S. & Sutton, Laurie. The Man of Steel: Superman vs. the Demons of Deep Space. Vecchio, Luciano, illus. 2012. (Man of Steel Ser.). (ENG.). 88p. (J). (gr. 3-7). pap. 5.95 (978-1-4342-4220-4(X), 120278, Stone Arch Bks.) Capstone.

Teitelbaum, Michael. I Am Superman. Farley, Rick, illus. 2009. (I Can Read Level 2 Ser.). (ENG.). 32p. (J). (gr. -1-3). pap. 3.99 (978-0-06-187857-2(X)) HarperCollins Pubs.

—I Am Superman. 2009. (Justice League Classic: I Can Read! Ser.). (J). lib. bdg. 13.55 (978-0-606-06951-9(8)) Turtleback.

—Meet the Super Heroes. 2009. (Justice League Classic: I Can Read! Ser.). (J). lib. bdg. 13.55 (978-0-606-06941-0(0)) Turtleback.

—Superman Versus Mongul. Mada Design Staff, illus. 2011. (I Can Read Level 2 Ser.). (ENG.). 32p. (J). (gr. -1-3). pap. 3.99 (978-0-06-188518-1(5)) HarperCollins Pubs.

Weissburg, Paul. The Man of Steel: Superman & the Man of Gold. Levins, Tim, illus. 2012. (Man of Steel Ser.). (ENG.). 88p. (J). (gr. 3-7). pap. 5.95 (978-1-4342-4222-8(6), 120280, Stone Arch Bks.) Capstone.

Wrecks, Billy. Bizarro Day! 2013. (Step into Reading Level 2 Ser.). lib. bdg. 13.55 (978-0-606-26971-1(1)) Turtleback.

—Bizarro Day! (DC Super Friends) Legramandi, Francesco, illus. 2013. (Step into Reading Ser.). (ENG.). 32p. (J). (gr. k-3). pap. 4.99 (978-0-307-98119-6(3), Random Hse. Bks. for Young Readers) Random Hse. Children's Bks.

—Superman! (DC Super Friends) Beavers, Ethen, illus. 2013. (Little Golden Book Ser.). (ENG.). 24p. (J). (-k). 4.99 (978-0-307-93195-5(1), Golden Bks.) Random Hse. Children's Bks.

Yang, Gene Luen. Superman, Volume 1: Before Truth. 2016. lib. bdg. 29.40 (978-0-606-39485-7(0)) Turtleback.

SUPERMARKETS

Cohen, Marina. 3-D Shapes. 2010. (My Path to Math Ser.). (ENG.). 24p. (J). (gr. k-3). (978-0-7787-6779-4(5)); pap. (978-0-7787-6788-6(4)) Crabtree Publishing Co.

Colby, Jennifer. Grocery Store. 2016. (21st Century Junior Library: Explore a Workplace Ser.). (ENG., Illus.). 24p. (J). (gr. 2-5). 29.21 (978-1-63471-073-2(8), 208371) Cherry Lake Publishing.

Craats, Rennay. Le Magasin Général: Le Début de la Colonie. Karvonen, Tanjah, tr. from ENG. 2011. (FRE., Illus.). 24p. (gr. 3-6). (978-1-77071-420-5(0)) Weigl Educational Pubs. Ltd.

Holden, Pam. At the Supermarket, 1 vol. 2017. (ENG., Illus.). 17p. (J). pap. (978-1-77654-216-1(9), Red Rocket Readers) Flying Start Bks.

Hutchings, Amy. What Happens at a Supermarket?, 1 vol. 2009. (Where People Work Ser.). (ENG.). 24p. (gr. 1-1). (J). lib. bdg. 24.67 (978-1-4339-0069-3(6), 188a0615-8f36-48b5-80b7-7d3b0a051f79); pap. 9.15 (978-1-4339-0133-1(1), 71528cbd-9de3-4aa7-9f32-2b76ff5ff15f) Stevens, Gareth Publishing LLLP. (Weekly Reader Leveled Readers).

—What Happens at a Supermarket? / ¿Qué Pasa en un Supermercado?, 1 vol. 2009. (Where People Work / ¿dónde Trabaja la Gente? Ser.). (SPA & ENG.). 24p. (gr. 1-1). (J). lib. bdg. 24.67 (978-1-4339-0077-8(7), 297ff9dc-bbac-4e90-9aaf-efd5cca899c5); pap. 9.15 (978-1-4339-0141-6(2), 76fe191a-924c-4d46-b407-aca53d320379) Stevens, Gareth Publishing LLLP. (Weekly Reader Leveled Readers).

Keogh, Josie. A Trip to the Grocery Store, 1 vol. 2012. (PowerKids Readers: My Community Ser.). (ENG., Illus.). 24p. (J). (gr. k-k). 26.27 (978-1-4488-7403-3(3), 7cc8fa8d-fd5f-4bac-8aa1-a41f790bab09); pap. 9.25 (978-1-4488-7482-8(3), 62d0588e-f7d1-431a-b519-4be2c26d25ff) Rosen Publishing Group, Inc., The. (PowerKids Pr.).

—A Trip to the Grocery Store: De Visita en la Tienda, 1 vol. 2012. (PowerKids Readers: Mi Comunidad / My Community Ser.). (SPA & ENG., Illus.). 24p. (J). (gr. k-k). lib. bdg. 26.27 (978-1-4488-7827-7(6), f2825186-817a-4c7d-8919-eb0fca64c674, PowerKids Pr.) Rosen Publishing Group, Inc., The.

Marsico, Katie. Working at a Grocery Store. 2008. (21st Century Junior Library: Careers Ser.). (ENG., Illus.). 24p. (gr. 2-5). lib. bdg. 29.21 (978-1-60279-265-4(8), 200170) Cherry Lake Publishing.

Mattern, Joanne. I Use Math at the Store, 1 vol. 2005. (I Use Math Ser.). (ENG., Illus.). 24p. (gr. k-2). pap. 9.15 (978-0-8368-4863-2(2), 90724d4b-858e-4ec1-bf3a-b0471bdb89d7); lib. bdg. 24.67 (978-0-8368-4856-4(X), a6387fab-6a72-48d7-9f26-874adfcef86b) Stevens, Gareth Publishing LLLP. (Weekly Reader Leveled Readers).

—I Use Math at the Store / Uso Las Matemáticas en la Tienda, 1 vol. 2005. (I Use Math / Uso Las Matemáticas Ser.). (ENG & SPA., Illus.). 24p. (gr. k-2). lib. bdg. 24.67 (978-0-8368-6001-6(2), 22f6304f-f8c1-42e6-a009-f3e04dc15654, Weekly Reader Leveled Readers) Stevens, Gareth Publishing LLLP.

The Super Supermarket Plan: Individual Title Six-Packs. (gr. k-1). 23.00 (978-0-7635-8844-1(X)) Rigby Education.

SUPERMARKETS—FICTION

Benavides, Desiree. Little Henry's Adventures: Henry's Trip to the Supermarket. 2008. 24p. pap. 24.95 (978-1-60563-011-3(X)) America Star Bks.

Elya, Susan Middleton. Bebé Goes Shopping. Salerno, Steven, illus. 2008. (ENG.). 36p. (J). (gr. -1-3). pap. 7.99 (978-0-15-206142-5(8), 1198442, Clarion Bks.) HarperCollins Pubs.

Food from the Farm: Individual Title Six-Packs. (gr. -1-2). 23.00 (978-0-7635-8994-3(2)) Rigby Education.

Gutman, Dan. Rappy Goes to the Supermarket. Bowers, Tim, illus. 2017. (I Can Read Level 2 Ser.). (ENG.). 32p. (J). (gr. -1-3). 4.99 (978-0-06-225262-3(3), HarperCollins) HarperCollins Pubs.

Herman, Alison & Grossman, Lynne. Dolly Goes to the Supermarket. Eve, Lealand, illus. 2007. 22p. (J). 24.96 (978-0-9746153-0-1(7)) DMH Pr., Inc.

In the Supermarket: Individual Title, 6 Packs. (Chiquilibros Ser.). (gr. k-1). 23.00 (978-0-7635-0453-3(X)) Rigby Education.

Meredith Books Staff. Foodfight! Curry, Don, ed. 2008. (I Can Find It Ser.). 22p. (J). 7.99 (978-0-696-23425-5(4)) Meredith Bks.

—Foodfight! Deluxe Sound Storybook. Curry, Don, ed. 2008. 22p. (J). 15.95 (978-0-696-23424-8(6)) Meredith Bks.

Neill, Joan Walmer. The Amazing Tale of Bub the Trier. 2012. 36p. pap. 20.00 (978-1-4772-6240-5(7)) AuthorHouse.

Rockwell, Anne. At the Supermarket. Rockwell, Anne, illus. 2015. (ENG., Illus.). 30p. (J). (gr. -1-k). bds. 8.99 (978-1-62779-315-5(1), 900146218, Holt, Henry & Co. Bks. For Young Readers) Holt, Henry & Co.

Snell, Gordon. The Supermarket Ghost. Askin, Corrina & Byrne, Bob, illus. 2007. (ENG.). 80p. (J). pap. 10.95 (978-1-84717-049-1(8)) O'Brien Pr., Ltd., The IRL. Dist: Dufour Editions, Inc.

Spitzer, Linda & Myers, Sarah. Tales of the Paper Bag Fairies/Color Version. 2005. 54p. (J). pap. 14.95 (978-1-4116-4095-5(0)) Lulu Pr., Inc.

When Dad Got Lost: Individual Title, 6 packs. (gr. -1-2). 27.00 (978-0-7635-9484-8(9)) Rigby Education.

Williams, Rozanne. The World in a Supermarket. 2017. (Learn-To-Read Ser.). (ENG., Illus.). (J). pap. 3.49 (978-1-68310-243-4(6)) Pacific Learning, Inc.

SUPERNATURAL

see also Spirits

Chmielewski, Gary. The Ghost Zone: Jokes, Riddles, Tongue Twisters & Daffynitions. Caputo, Jim, illus. rev. ed. 2009. (Funny Zone Ser.). (ENG.). 24p. (J). (gr. 2-4). lib. bdg. 22.60 (978-1-59953-297-4(2)) Norwood Hse. Pr.

Cox, Barbara & Forbes, Scott. Beyond the Grave, 1 vol., Vol. 1. 2014. (Creepy Chronicles Ser.). (ENG., Illus.). 32p. (J). (gr. 5-6). 29.27 (978-1-4824-0226-1(2), b31805b5-ea17-4efe-9dc3-194774bd20bc) Stevens, Gareth Publishing LLLP.

—Maniacal Monsters & Bizarre Beasts, 1 vol., Vol. 1. 2014. (Creepy Chronicles Ser.). (ENG., Illus.). 32p. (J). (gr. 5-6). 29.27 (978-1-4824-0236-0(X), d0e08db8-243d-4e51-844b-6ac5f6038fbe) Stevens, Gareth Publishing LLLP.

Day, Jon. Arswyd Mawr! Yr Anhygoel A'r Anesboniadwy. 2005. (WEL., Illus.). 32p. pap. (978-0-86381-415-0(8)) Gwasg Carreg Gwalch.

—Supernatural. 2004. (Illus.). 32p. pap. (978-1-904516-01-9(7), Pavilion Children's Books) Pavilion Bks.

Ganeri, Anita & West, David. Supernatural Creatures. (Illus.). 32p. 2012. 70.50 (978-1-4488-5233-8(1)) 2011. (ENG., (gr. 4-5). pap. 12.75 (978-1-4488-5232-1(3), 56c4a09f-9807-4ecc-af96-e879d984970f) 2011. (ENG., (gr. 4-5). lib. bdg. 30.27 (978-1-4488-5197-3(1), 3a308f88-80f8-434b-a57b-5a38ef5cac64) Rosen Publishing Group, Inc., The. (PowerKids Pr.).

Howard, Ian T. One Love, Two Worlds. Bishop, Tracey, illus. 2010. 36p. pap. 14.75 (978-1-60911-771-9(9), Eloquent Bks.) Strategic Book Publishing & Rights Agency (SBPRA).

Kroll, Jennifer. The Science of Superpowers. 2016. (Time for Kids Nonfiction Readers Ser.). (ENG.). (J). (gr. 5-8). lib. bdg. 22.10 (978-0-606-39544-1(X)) Turtleback.

Kuligowski, Stephanie. Unsolved! Mysterious Events, 1 vol. 2nd rev. ed. 2013. (TIME for KIDS(r): Informational Text Ser.). (ENG., Illus.). 48p. (J). (gr. 4-5). lib. bdg. 29.96 (978-1-4807-1103-7(9)) Teacher Created Materials, Inc.

—Unsolved! Mysterious Places, 1 vol. 2nd rev. ed. 2013. (TIME for KIDS(r): Informational Text Ser.). (ENG., Illus.). 48p. (J). (gr. 4-5). lib. bdg. 29.96 (978-1-4807-1104-4(7)) Teacher Created Materials, Inc.

Loh-Hagan, Virginia. Witching Hour Hacks. 2019. (Could You Survive? Ser.). (ENG., Illus.). 32p. (J). (gr. 4-8). pap. 14.21 (978-1-5341-5070-6(6), 213587); lib. bdg. 32.07 (978-1-5341-4784-3(5), 213586) Cherry Lake Publishing. (45th Parallel Press).

Mariolle, Mathieu. Even for A Dreamer Like Me. 3rd rev. ed. 2010. pap. 56.72 (978-0-7613-6960-8(0)) Lerner Publishing Group.

Omoth, Tyler & McCollum, Sean. Paranormal Handbooks. 2016. (Paranormal Handbooks Ser.). (ENG.). 32p. (J). (gr. 3-9). 122.60 (978-1-5157-1325-8(3), 24841, Capstone Pr.) Capstone.

Rauf, Don. Faith. 2017. (Freaky Phenomena Ser.: Vol. 8). (ENG., Illus.). 48p. (J). (gr. 5-8). 20.95 (978-1-4222-3774-8(5)) Mason Crest.

Steinberg, Lewis M. Investigating Miracles, 1 vol. 2016. (Understanding the Paranormal Ser.). (ENG.). 48p. (J). (gr. 5-5). lib. bdg. 28.41 (978-1-5081-0223-6(6), d457ae97-405c-4e03-8a2c-3987f4e002a6, Britannica Educational Publishing) Rosen Publishing Group, Inc., The.

Stevens, C. J. The Supernatural Side of Maine. 2003. (YA). 12.00 (978-1-882425-16-7(2)) Wade, John Pub.

Walker, Kathryn. Mysterious Healing. 2009. (Unsolved! Ser.). (ENG., Illus.). 32p. (J). (gr. 3-5). pap. (978-0-7787-4163-3(X)); (gr. 4-6). lib. bdg. (978-0-7787-4150-3(8)) Crabtree Publishing Co.

World Book, Inc. Staff, contrib. by. Tales of Mystery & the Unknown: A Supplement to Childcraft — the How & Why Library. 2006. (Illus.). 208p. (J). (978-0-7166-0616-1(X)) World Bk., Inc.

SUPERNATURAL—FICTION

Adamchuk, Rachelle G. Disappearance: The First Part of Trickery & Honest Deception. 2006. 169p. pap. 16.99 (978-1-4120-8991-3(3)) Trafford Publishing.

Afterglow. 2014. (ENG., Illus.). 336p. (YA). (gr. 9). pap. 11.99 (978-1-4424-5038-7(X), Simon & Schuster Bks. For Young Readers) Simon & Schuster Bks. For Young Readers.

Ahdieh, Renée. The Beautiful. (Beautiful Quartet Ser.: 1). (ENG.). (YA). (gr. 7). 2021. 480p. pap. 5.99 (978-1-5247-3819-8(0), Penguin Books) 2021. 480p. pap. 12.99 (978-0-593-46266-9(1), G.P. Putnam's Sons Books for Young Readers) 2019. 448p. 18.99 (978-1-5247-3817-4(4), G.P. Putnam's Sons Books for Young Readers) Penguin Young Readers Group.

Alender, Katie. As Dead As It Gets. 2013. (Bad Girls Don't Die Ser.: 3). (ENG.). 448p. (J). (gr. 5-9). pap. 9.99 (978-1-4231-3778-8(7)) Hyperion Pr.

—From Bad to Cursed. 2012. (Bad Girls Don't Die Ser.: 2). (ENG.). 448p. (YA). (gr. 5-9). pap. 11.99 (978-1-4231-3777-1(9)) Hyperion Pr.

Alexander, William. A Festival of Ghosts. Murphy, Kelly, illus. 2018. (ENG.). 272p. (J). (gr. 3-7). 17.99 (978-1-4814-6918-0(5), McElderry, Margaret K. Bks.) McElderry, Margaret K. Bks.

—A Properly Unhaunted Place. Murphy, Kelly, illus. 2017. (ENG.). 192p. (J). (gr. 3-7). 16.99 (978-1-4814-6915-9(0), McElderry, Margaret K. Bks.) McElderry, Margaret K. Bks.

—A Properly Unhaunted Place. 2019. (Penworthy Picks Middle School Ser.). (ENG.). 182p. (J). (gr. 4-5). 18.96 (978-1-64310-942-8(1)) Penworthy Co., LLC, The.

Allende, Isabel. City of the Beasts. 2009. (P. S. Ser.: Bk. 1). (ENG.). 448p. pap. 14.99 (978-0-06-182511-8(5), Harper Perennial) HarperCollins Pubs.

—City of the Beasts. Peden, Margaret Sayers, tr. from SPA. 2004. (City of the Beasts Ser.: Bk. 1). (ENG.). 432p. (J). (gr. 5-18). reprint ed. pap. 7.99 (978-0-06-053503-2(2), Rayo) HarperCollins Pubs.

Almond, David. Clay. 2008. (ENG.). 272p. (YA). (gr. 7-12). pap. 8.99 (978-0-440-42013-2(X), Delacorte Bks. for Young Readers) Random Hse. Children's Bks.

Alston, B. B. Amari & the Great Game. (Supernatural Investigations Ser.). (ENG.). 432p. 2023. (gr. 4-7). 28.69 **(978-1-5364-8191-4(2))** 2023. (J). (gr. 3-7). pap. 10.99 **(978-0-06-297520-1(X))** 2022. (Illus.). (J). (gr. 3-7). 18.99 (978-0-06-297519-5(6)) HarperCollins Pubs. (Balzer & Bray).

—Amari & the Night Brothers. (Supernatural Investigations Ser.: 1). (ENG.). 2022. 432p. (J). (gr. 3-7). pap. 11.99 (978-0-06-297517-1(X)) 2021. (Illus.). 416p. (J). (gr. 3-7). 17.99 (978-0-06-297516-4(1))1. 2022. 432p. (gr. 4-7). 29.94 (978-1-5364-7242-4(5)) HarperCollins Pubs. (Balzer & Bray).

Alston, B. B. Amari y Los Hermanos de la Noche / Amari & the Night Brothers. 2023. (Amari Ser.). (SPA.). 448p. (J). (gr. 4-7). pap. 14.95 **(978-1-64473-875-7(9))** Penguin Random House Grupo Editorial ESP. Dist: Penguin Random Hse. LLC.

Altebrando, Tara. The Possible. 2018. (ENG.). 320p. (YA). pap. 10.99 (978-1-68119-700-5(6), 900182280, Bloomsbury Young Adult) Bloomsbury Publishing USA.

Anderson, Jodi Lynn. My Diary from the Edge of the World. 2015. (ENG., Illus.). 432p. (J). (gr. 3-7). 18.99 (978-1-4424-8387-3(3), Aladdin) Simon & Schuster Children's Publishing.

—My Diary from the Edge of the World. 2017. (ENG., Illus.). 448p. (J). (gr. 3-7). pap. 9.99 (978-1-4424-8388-0(1), Simon & Schuster/Paula Wiseman Bks.) Simon & Schuster/Paula Wiseman Bks.

Anderson, Maree. Freaks in the City, Bk.2. 2015. (ENG., Illus.) 290p. pap. (978-0-9941160-2-4(0)) Anderson, Maree.

Anderson, R. J. Spell Hunter. 2009. (Faery Rebels Ser.). (ENG.). 336p. (J). (gr. 8-18). 16.99 (978-0-06-155474-2(X)) HarperCollins Pubs.

—Wayfarer. 2010. (ENG.). 304p. (J). (gr. 8-18). 16.99 (978-0-06-155477-3(4), HarperTeen) HarperCollins Pubs.

Angelini, Josephine. Dreamless. 2013. (Starcrossed Trilogy Ser.: 2). (ENG.). 512p. (YA). (gr. 8). pap. 10.99 (978-0-06-201202-9(9), HarperTeen) HarperCollins Pubs.

—Goddess. 2013. (Starcrossed Trilogy Ser.: 3). (ENG.). 432p. (YA). (gr. 8). 17.99 (978-0-06-201203-6(7), HarperTeen) HarperCollins Pubs.

—Starcrossed. 2012. (Starcrossed Trilogy Ser.: 1). (ENG.). 512p. (YA). (gr. 8). pap. 10.99 (978-0-06-201200-5(2), HarperTeen) HarperCollins Pubs.

Anthony, Horowitz. Evil Star. 2007. (Gatekeepers Ser.: 2). 318p. lib. bdg. 19.65 (978-1-4177-7663-4(3)) Turtleback.

—Necropolis, 9 vols. 2009. (Gatekeepers Ser.: 4). (J). 92.75 (978-1-4407-0430-7(9)); 122.75 (978-1-4407-0434-5(1)); 120.75 (978-1-4407-0436-9(8)); 90.75 (978-1-4407-0432-1(5)); 254.75 (978-1-4407-0431-4(7)); 1.25 (978-1-4407-0439-0(2)) Recorded Bks., Inc.

—Necropolis. 2009. 400p. pap. (978-1-4063-2108-1(7)) Walker Bks., Ltd.

—Oblivion. 2014. (Gatekeepers Ser.: 5). lib. bdg. 20.85 (978-0-606-36035-7(2)) Turtleback.

—Raven's Gate. 2005. (SWE.). 288p. pap. (978-1-84428-619-5(3)) Walker Bks., Ltd.

—The Switch. 2009. (ENG.). 256p. (YA). (gr. 6-8). 22.44 (978-0-399-25062-0(X)) Penguin Young Readers Group.

Appelbaum, Susannah. Divah. 2016. (ENG.). 400p. (J). (gr. 6-6). 17.99 (978-1-63450-674-8(X), Sky Pony Pr.) Skyhorse Publishing Co., Inc.

Appelt, Kathi & McGhee, Alison. Maybe a Fox. 2016. (ENG., Illus.). 272p. (J). (gr. 5-9). 18.99 (978-1-4424-8242-5(7), Atheneum/Caitlyn Dlouhy Books) Simon & Schuster Children's Publishing.

Applegate, Katherine. The Capture. 2012. (Animorphs Ser.: 6). lib. bdg. 17.20 (978-0-606-26194-4(X)) Turtleback.

Arden, Katherine. Small Spaces. (Small Spaces Quartet Ser.: 1). (J). (gr. 5). 2019. 256p. 8.99 *(978-0-525-51504-3(6),* Puffin Books) 2018. 224p. 16.99 *(978-0-525-51502-9(X),* G.P. Putnam's Sons Books for Young Readers) Penguin Young Readers Group.
—Small Spaces. Lt. ed. 2019. (ENG.). 290p. (YA). *(978-1-4328-6589-4(7))* Thorndike Pr.
Armstrong, K. L. & Marr, Melissa. Loki's Wolves. 2014. (Blackwell Pages Ser.: 1). (ENG.). 374p. (J). (gr. 3-7). pap. 8.99 *(978-0-316-20497-2(8))* Little, Brown Bks. for Young Readers.
Armstrong, Kelley. The Awakening. (Darkest Powers Ser.: 2). (ENG.). (YA). (gr. 8-18). 2009. 368p. 17.99 *(978-0-06-166276-8(3))*2. 2010. 384p. pap. 11.99 *(978-0-06-145055-6(3))* HarperCollins Pubs. (HarperCollins).
—The Awakening, 7 vols. 2009. (Darkest Powers Ser.: 2). (YA). 133.75 *(978-1-4407-3103-7(9))*; 103.75 *(978-1-4407-3099-3(7))* Recorded Bks., Inc.
—The Calling. 2013. (Darkness Rising Ser.: 2). (ENG.). 352p. (YA). (gr. 8). pap. 10.99 *(978-0-06-179706-4(5),* HarperCollins) HarperCollins Pubs.
—The Calling: Number 2 in Series. 2012. (Darkness Rising Ser.: Bk. 2). (ENG.). 336p. pap. *(978-1-907410-47-5(3))* Atom Pr.
—The Gathering. (Darkness Rising Ser.: 1). (ENG.). (YA). (gr. 8). 2012. 384p. pap. 9.99 *(978-0-06-179703-3(0))* 2011. 368p. 17.99 *(978-0-06-179702-6(2))* HarperCollins Pubs. (HarperCollins).
—The Gathering. (Darkness Rising Ser.: Bk. 1). (YA). 1.25 *(978-1-4498-6189-6(X))*; 100.75 *(978-1-4498-6186-5(5))*; 2013. 102.75 *(978-1-4498-6184-1(9))* Recorded Bks., Inc.
—The Reckoning. (Darkest Powers Ser.: 3). (ENG.). (YA). (gr. 8). 2011. 416p. pap. 10.99 *(978-0-06-145056-3(1))* 2010. 400p. 17.99 *(978-0-06-166283-6(6))* HarperCollins Pubs. (HarperCollins).
—Sea of Shadows. (Age of Legends Trilogy Ser.: 1). (ENG.). (YA). (gr. 8). 2015. 432p. pap. 9.99 *(978-0-06-207125-5(4))* 2014. 416p. 17.99 *(978-0-06-207124-8(6))* HarperCollins Pubs. (HarperCollins).
—Sea of Shadows. 2015. (Age of Legends Ser.: 1). (YA). lib. bdg. 20.85 *(978-0-606-36511-6(7))* Turtleback.
—The Summoning. 2009. (Darkest Powers Ser.: 1). (ENG.). 416p. (YA). (gr. 8). pap. 10.99 *(978-0-06-145054-9(5),* HarperCollins) HarperCollins Pubs.
—The Summoning, 7 vols. 2009. (Darkest Powers Ser.: 1). (J). 243.75 *(978-1-4361-9718-2(X))*; 81.75 *(978-1-4361-9717-5(1))* Recorded Bks., Inc.
Arnett, Dee. Gifted. 2008. 240p. pap. 18.95 *(978-1-4092-0442-8(1))* Lulu Pr., Inc.
Arnett, Mindee. The Nightmare Affair. 2014. (Arkwell Academy Ser.: 1). (ENG.). 400p. (YA). (gr. 9-12). pap. 19.99 *(978-0-7653-3336-0(8),* 900084947, Tor Teen) Doherty, Tom Assocs., LLC.
—The Nightmare Dilemma. 2015. (Arkwell Academy Ser.: 2). (ENG.). 400p. (YA). (gr. 8-12). pap. 10.99 *(978-0-7653-3337-7(6),* 900084950, Tor Teen) Doherty, Tom Assocs., LLC.
Arnold, Shari. Mystique. 2012. (YA). *(978-1-4521-0363-1(1))* Chronicle Bks. LLC.
Arroyo, Raymond. Will Wilder #2: the Lost Staff of Wonders. 2018. (Will Wilder Ser.: 2). 368p. (J). (gr. 3-7). 8.99 *(978-0-553-53970-7(1),* Yearling) Random Hse. Children's Bks.
Arsenault, Emily. The Leaf Reader. 2018. 256p. (YA). (gr. 9). pap. 10.99 *(978-1-61695-907-4(X),* Soho Teen) Soho Pr., Inc.
Ashby, Amanda. Fairy Bad Day. 2011. (ENG.). 352p. (YA). (gr. 7-12). 22.44 *(978-0-14-241259-6(7))* Penguin Young Readers Group.
Ashton, Brodi. Everbound. 2013. (Evermeath Ser.: 2). (ENG.). 384p. (YA). (gr. 8). pap. 9.99 *(978-0-06-207117-0(3),* Balzer & Bray) HarperCollins Pubs.
—Everneath. 2012. (Everneath Ser.: 1). (ENG.). 400p. (YA). (gr. 9). pap. 9.99 *(978-0-06-207114-9(9),* Balzer & Bray) HarperCollins Pubs.
—Evertrue. 2014. (Everneath Ser.: 3). (ENG.). 368p. (YA). (gr. 9). 17.99 *(978-0-06-207119-4(X),* Balzer & Bray) HarperCollins Pubs.
Atwater-Rhodes, Amelia. Persistence of Memory. 2010. (Den of Shadows Ser.: 5). (ENG.). 224p. (YA). (gr. 7). pap. 8.99 *(978-0-440-24004-4(2),* Delacorte Pr.) Random Hse. Children's Bks.
—Poison Tree. 2013. 240p. (YA). (gr. 7). pap. 8.99 *(978-0-385-73755-5(6),* Ember) Random Hse. Children's Bks.
—Token of Darkness. 2011. (Den of Shadows Ser.: 6). (ENG.). 208p. (YA). (gr. 7). pap. 8.99 *(978-0-385-73751-7(3),* Ember) Random Hse. Children's Bks.
Atwood, M. C. The Devils You Know. 2018. (ENG.). 288p. (YA). (gr. 9). pap. 10.99 *(978-1-61695-933-3(9),* Soho Teen) Soho Pr., Inc.
Atwood, Megan. The Bridge of Death, No. 4. 2012. (Paranormalists Ser.: 4). (ENG.). 104p. (YA). (gr. 6-12). lib. bdg. 27.99 *(978-0-7613-8335-2(2),* 0970d7ee-50a1-4e52-92fa-dcc199cc5a36, Darby Creek) Lerner Publishing Group.
—The Cursed Ballet, No. 3. 2013. (Dario Quincy Academy of Dance Ser.: 3). (ENG.). 104p. (YA). (gr. 6-12). pap. 7.95 *(978-1-4677-1485-3(2),* 9b7e4fb0-5041-4fd2-8080-8f0ddaa654e5); lib. bdg. 27.99 *(978-1-4677-0932-3(8),* 0f81794f-3a51-4d9a-ba11-1fb3f11e032d) Lerner Publishing Group. (Darby Creek).
—Leaping at Shadows, No. 1. 2013. (Dario Quincy Academy of Dance Ser.: 1). (ENG.). 112p. (YA). (gr. 6-12). lib. bdg. 27.99 *(978-1-4677-0930-9(1),* 2cf7be7a-40e7-4265-9a58-dc426f02267d, Darby Creek) Lerner Publishing Group.
—The Mayhem on Mohawk Avenue, No. 3. 2012. (Paranormalists Ser.: 3). (ENG.). 104p. (YA). (gr. 6-12). lib. bdg. 27.99 *(978-0-7613-8334-5(4),* ab0f8f59-4398-49c1-b326-72fe33f0066a, Darby Creek) Lerner Publishing Group.
—Stolen Luck, No. 2. 2013. (Dario Quincy Academy of Dance Ser.: 2). (ENG.). 112p. (YA). (gr. 6-12). pap. 7.95 *(978-1-4677-1484-6(4),* bd0cba15-31f6-464e-99f5-780d648c879c); lib. bdg. 27.99 *(978-1-4677-0931-6(X),* a04bd39a-478b-412f-a97e-a1d2f008b4e2) Lerner Publishing Group. (Darby Creek).
Baer, Marianna. The Inconceivable Life of Quinn. 2017. (ENG.). 384p. (YA). (gr. 8-17). 18.95 *(978-1-4197-2302-5(2),* 1158201) Abrams, Inc.
Balog, Cyn. Sleepless. 2010. (ENG.). 240p. (YA). (gr. 7-12). 22.44 *(978-0-385-73848-4(X))* Random House Publishing Group.
Barnes, Jennifer Lynn. Fate. 2009. (Tattoo Ser.). (ENG.). 368p. (YA). (gr. 7-18). pap. 8.99 *(978-0-385-73537-7(5),* Delacorte Bks. for Young Readers) Random Hse. Children's Bks.
—Tattoo. 2007. (Tattoo Ser.). (ENG.). 272p. (J). (gr. 7-12). pap. 9.99 *(978-0-385-73347-2(X),* Delacorte Bks. for Young Readers) Random Hse. Children's Bks.
Barnes, Vivi. Paper or Plastic. 2015. (Entangled Teen Ser.). (ENG.). 352p. (YA). pap. 9.99 *(978-1-62266-521-1(X),* 9781622665211) Entangled Publishing, LLC.
Bast, Michael. Death's Academy. 2014. (J). pap. 14.99 *(978-1-4621-1380-4(X),* Horizon Pubs.) Cedar Fort, Inc./CFI Distribution.
Bastian, Kimberlee Ann. The Orphan, the Soulcatcher, & the Black Blizzard. 2012. 258p. pap. 22.50 *(978-1-105-06633-7(9))* Lulu.com GBR. Dist: Lulu Pr., Inc.
Bauer, Marion Dane. The Red Ghost. Ferguson, Peter, illus. 2009. (Stepping Stone Book(TM) Ser.). 96p. (J). (gr. 1-4). 4.99 *(978-0-375-84082-1(6),* Random Hse. Bks. for Young Readers) Random Hse. Children's Bks.
Beatty, Robert. Serafina & the Black Cloak. 2016. (Serafina Ser.: 1). (J). lib. bdg. 18.40 *(978-0-606-38336-3(0))* Turtleback.
—Serafina & the Black Cloak-The Serafina Series Book 1. (ENG.). (J). (gr. 3-7). 2016. (Serafina Ser.: 1). 320p. pap. 8.99 *(978-1-4847-1187-3(4))* 2015. 304p. 16.99 *(978-1-4847-0901-6(2))* Disney Publishing Worldwide. (Disney-Hyperion).
—Serafina & the Seven Stars-The Serafina Series Book 4. 2019. (Serafina Ser.: 4). (ENG., Illus.). 352p. (J). (gr. 3-7). 16.99 *(978-1-368-00759-7(7),* Disney-Hyperion) Disney Publishing Worldwide.
—Serafina & the Splintered Heart. 2018. (Serafina Ser.: 3). (J). lib. bdg. 18.40 *(978-0-606-40962-9(9))* Turtleback.
—Serafina & the Splintered Heart-The Serafina Series Book 3. (Serafina Ser.: 3). (ENG.). (J). (gr. 3-7). 2018. 384p. pap. 8.99 *(978-1-4847-7805-0(7))* 2017. 368p. 16.99 *(978-1-4847-7504-2(X))* Disney Publishing Worldwide. (Disney-Hyperion).
—Serafina & the Twisted Staff. 2017. (Serafina Ser.: 2). (J). lib. bdg. 18.40 *(978-0-606-39977-7(1))* Turtleback.
—Serafina & the Twisted Staff-The Serafina Series Book 2. (Serafina Ser.: 2). (ENG.). (J). (gr. 3-7). 2017. 400p. pap. 8.99 *(978-1-4847-7806-7(5))* 2016. 384p. 16.99 *(978-1-4847-7503-5(1))* Disney Publishing Worldwide. (Disney-Hyperion).
—Willa of Dark Hollow. (Willa of the Wood Ser.). (ENG.). (J). (gr. 3-7). 2022. 384p. pap. 7.99 *(978-1-368-00948-5(4))* 2021. (Illus.). 368p. 17.99 *(978-1-368-00760-3(0))* Disney Publishing Worldwide. (Disney-Hyperion).
—Willa of the Wood: Willa of the Wood, Book 1. 2019. (Willa of the Wood Ser.: 1). (ENG.). 400p. (J). (gr. 3-7). pap. 7.99 *(978-1-368-00947-8(6),* Disney-Hyperion) Disney Publishing Worldwide.
The Beautiful & the Damned. 2014. (ENG., Illus.). 288p. (YA). (gr. 7). pap. 11.99 *(978-1-4424-8836-6(0),* Simon Pulse) Simon Pulse.
Bedford, Martyn. Flip. 2012. (ENG.). 272p. (YA). (gr. 7-12). 24.94 *(978-0-385-90808-5(3),* Lamb, Wendy Bks.); pap. 9.99 *(978-0-375-86552-7(7),* Ember) Random Hse. Children's Bks.
Behrens, Kathryn J. Breakdown. 2016. (Atlas of Cursed Places Ser.). (ENG.). 96p. (YA). (gr. 6-12). lib. bdg. 26.65 *(978-1-5124-1323-6(2),* db301279-6588-4513-88e6-fa63ae4be1cc, Darby Creek) Lerner Publishing Group.
Bellairs, John. The Ghost in the Mirror - the House with a Clock in Its Walls 4. 2019. (House with a Clock in Its Walls Ser.: 4). (ENG., Illus.). 256p. (J). (gr. 4-7). pap. 11.99 *(978-1-84812-816-3(9))* Bonnier Publishing GBR. Dist: Independent Pubs. Group.
—The House with a Clock in Its Walls. Gorey, Edward, illus. 2004. (Lewis Barnavelt Ser.: Bk. 1). (ENG.). 192p. (J). (gr. 3-7). pap. 7.99 *(978-0-14-240257-3(5),* Puffin Books) Penguin Young Readers Group.
—The House with a Clock in Its Walls. Gorey, Edward, illus. 2004. (John Bellairs Mysteries Ser.). 179p. (J). (gr. 3-7). 13.65 *(978-0-7569-5257-0(3))* Perfection Learning Corp.
—The House with a Clock in Its Walls. (Lewis Barnavelt Ser.: Bk. 1). 179p. (J). (gr. 4-6). pap. 4.50 *(978-0-8072-1423-7(X),* Listening Library) Random Hse. Audio Publishing Group.
—The House with a Clock in Its Walls. 2004. 17.20 *(978-1-4176-3513-9(4))* Turtleback.
—The Revenge of the Wizard's Ghost (A Johnny Dixon Mystery: Book Four) 2011. 108p. pap. 14.95 *(978-1-61756-336-2(6))* Open Road Integrated Media, Inc.
Benson, Amber. Among the Ghosts. Grace, Sina, illus. 2011. (ENG.). 256p. (J). (gr. 3-7). pap. 6.99 *(978-1-4169-9426-8(2),* Aladdin) Simon & Schuster Children's Publishing.
Benz, Derek & Lewis, J. S. Grey Griffins: the Brimstone Key. 2011. (Grey Griffins: the Clockwork Chronicles Ser.: 1). (ENG.). 400p. (J). (gr. 3-7). pap. 19.99 *(978-0-316-04521-6(7))* Little, Brown Bks. for Young Readers.
Bérubé, Amelinda. The Dark Beneath the Ice. 2019. (ENG.). 336p. (YA). (gr. 8-12). pap. 10.99 *(978-1-4926-7878-6(3))* Sourcebooks, Inc.
Berube, Amelinda. Here There Are Monsters. 2019. (ENG., Illus.). 352p. (YA). (gr. 8-12). pap. 10.99 *(978-1-4926-7101-5(0))* Sourcebooks, Inc.
Betterton, Jerry W. The Adventures of Hot Rolls. 2013. 44p. pap. 24.99 *(978-1-4797-8184-3(3))* Xlibris Corp.
Bick, Ilsa J. Draw the Dark. (ENG.). 344p. (YA). (gr. 9-12). 2011. pap. 9.95 *(978-0-7613-8131-0(7),* 308f22d6-6abe-45af-b28c-b962f2cb5485) 2010. 16.95 *(978-0-7613-5686-8(X))* Lerner Publishing Group. (Carolrhoda Lab™).
Billingsley, Franny. Chime. 2011. (Playaway Young Adult Ser.). (YA). 59.99 *(978-1-61707-143-0(9))* Findaway World, LLC.
—Chime. 2012. (ENG.). 320p. (YA). (gr. 7-12). 26.19 *(978-0-8037-3552-1(9),* Dial) Penguin Publishing Group.
—Chime. 2012. (ENG.). 384p. (YA). (gr. 7-18). 8.99 *(978-0-14-242092-8(1),* Speak) Penguin Young Readers Group.
Black, Holly. Ironside: A Modern Faerie Tale. 2020. (Modern Faerie Tales Ser.). (ENG.). 288p. (YA). (gr. 9). 19.99 *(978-1-5344-8455-9(8))*; pap. 11.99 *(978-1-5344-8454-2(X))* McElderry, Margaret K. Bks. (McElderry, Margaret K. Bks.).
—Tithe: A Modern Faerie Tale. 2020. (Modern Faerie Tales Ser.). (ENG.). 272p. (YA). (gr. 9). 19.99 *(978-1-5344-8450-4(7))*; pap. 11.99 *(978-1-5344-8451-1(5))* McElderry, Margaret K. Bks. (McElderry, Margaret K. Bks.).
Block, Francesca Lia. Blood Roses. 2008. 144p. (J). (gr. 9-18). 15.99 *(978-0-06-076384-8(1),* Cotler, Joanna Books) HarperCollins Pubs.
—Teen Spirit. 2014. (ENG.). 240p. (YA). (gr. 9). 17.99 *(978-0-06-200809-1(9),* HarperTeen) HarperCollins Pubs.
Blomfield, Alan. The Pendant of Epoch. 2008. 128p. *(978-1-86950-714-5(2))* HarperCollins Pubs. Australia.
Blue Moon. 2014. (Dead City Ser.: 2). (ENG., Illus.). 336p. (J). (gr. 4-8). pap. 8.99 *(978-1-4424-4132-3(1),* Aladdin) Simon & Schuster Children's Publishing.
Blumenthal, Deborah. The Lifeguard. (ENG.). 288p. (YA). (gr. 8-12). 2013. 9.99 *(978-0-8075-4536-2(8),* 807545368) 2012. 16.99 *(978-0-8075-4535-5(X),* 080754535X) Whitman, Albert & Co.
Blythe, Daniel. Shadow Breakers. 2013. (J). *(978-0-545-47980-6(0),* Chicken Hse., The) Scholastic, Inc.
Boles, Jim. Ivan the Invacar & the Cave. Cunningham, Bob, illus. 2013. 52p. pap. 19.95 *(978-0-9858052-2-7(6))* People Ink Pr.
Bondor-Stone, Annabeth & White, Connor. Jaclyn Hyde. 2019. (ENG.). 240p. (J). (gr. 3-7). 16.99 *(978-0-06-267145-5(6),* HarperCollins) HarperCollins Pubs.
Boone, Martina. Illusion. 2016. (Heirs of Watson Island Ser.). (ENG., Illus.). 480p. (YA). (gr. 9). 17.99 *(978-1-4814-1128-8(4),* Simon Pulse) Simon Pulse.
Bostick, B. k. Huber Hill & the Dead Man's Treasure. 2011. (J). *(978-1-59955-911-7(0),* Bonneville Bks.) Cedar Fort, Inc./CFI Distribution.
Bosworth, Jennifer. The Killing Jar. 2016. (ENG.). 352p. (YA). 34.99 *(978-0-374-34137-4(0),* 900126267, Farrar, Straus & Giroux (BYR)) Farrar, Straus & Giroux.
Bourbeau, Julie. The Wednesdays. Beene, Jason, illus. 2013. (ENG.). 256p. (J). (gr. 2-5). pap. 7.99 *(978-0-375-87286-0(8),* Yearling) Random Hse. Children's Bks.
Bourne, Tracey. Not Just a Dream! 2009. (Illus.). 52p. pap. 11.49 *(978-1-4389-4819-5(0))* AuthorHouse.
Bouton, Warren Hussey. The Captain's Return: A Spooky Tale from Nantucket. Locke, Barbara Kauffmann, illus. 2004. (J). per. 5.95 *(978-0-9700555-4-5(4))* Hither Creek Pr.
Bowvayne. A Spell Behind Bars. Snow, Alan, illus. 2006. (Misadventures of Danny Cloke Ser.). 208p. (J). (gr. 6). lib. bdg. 12.99 *(978-1-58086-926-3(2),* Usborne) EDC Publishing.
Bracegirdle, P. J. Sinister Scenes. (Joy of Spooking Ser.). (ENG.). 320p. (J). (gr. 3-7). 2012. pap. 6.99 *(978-1-4169-3421-9(9))* 2011. 15.99 *(978-1-4169-3420-2(0))* McElderry, Margaret K. Bks. (McElderry, Margaret K. Bks.).
—Unearthly Asylum. (Joy of Spooking Ser.). (ENG.). (J). (gr. 3-7). 2011. 320p. pap. 5.99 *(978-1-4169-3419-6(7))* 2010. 304p. 15.99 *(978-1-4169-3418-9(9))* McElderry, Margaret K. Bks. (McElderry, Margaret K. Bks.).
Braswell, Liz. The Fallen. movie tie-in ed. 2011. (Nine Lives of Chloe King Ser.: 1). (ENG.). 256p. (YA). (gr. 9). pap. 8.99 *(978-1-4424-4134-7(8),* Simon Pulse) Simon Pulse.
—The Nine Lives of Chloe King: The Fallen; the Stolen; the Chosen. 2011. (Nine Lives of Chloe King Ser.). (ENG.). 784p. (YA). (gr. 9). pap. 14.99 *(978-1-4424-3570-4(4),* Simon Pulse) Simon Pulse.
—The Nine Lives of Chloe King: The Fallen; the Stolen; the Chosen. 2011. lib. bdg. 25.75 *(978-0-606-23293-7(1))* Turtleback.
Bray, Libba. A Great & Terrible Beauty. 2005. (Gemma Doyle Trilogy Ser.: 1). (ENG.). 432p. (YA). (gr. 7). reprint ed. pap. 10.99 *(978-0-385-73231-4(7),* Ember) Random Hse. Children's Bks.
—Lair of Dreams: A Diviners Novel. 2015. (Diviners Ser.: 2). (ENG.). 624p. (YA). (gr. 7-17). E-Book 45.00 *(978-0-316-36488-1(6))* Little, Brown Bks. for Young Readers.
—Rebel Angels. 2006. (Gemma Doyle Trilogy Ser.: 2). (ENG.). 576p. (YA). (gr. 7-12). pap. 16.99 *(978-0-385-73341-0(0),* Ember) Random Hse. Children's Bks.
—The Sweet Far Thing. 2009. (Gemma Doyle Trilogy Ser.: 3). (ENG.). 848p. (YA). (gr. 7). pap. 14.99 *(978-0-440-23777-8(7),* Ember) Random Hse. Children's Bks.
Bredeson, Michelle. Legends. 2012. 220p. pap. *(978-1-61706-158-5(1))* Roxby Media Ltd.
Brennan, Herbie. The Faeman Quest, 5. 2012. (Faerie Wars Chronicles Ser.). (ENG.). 368p. (YA). (gr. 7-12). 26.19 *(978-1-59990-476-4(4),* 900065985) Bloomsbury Publishing USA.
—Faerie Lord. 2009. 1.00 *(978-1-4074-4311-9(9))* Recorded Bks., Inc.
—Faerie Wars, 1. 2012. (Faerie Wars Chronicles Ser.). (ENG., Illus.). 367p. (YA). (gr. 7-12). 24.94 *(978-1-58234-810-0(3),* 900019989) Bloomsbury Publishing USA.
—Faerie Wars. 1.00 *(978-1-4074-5906-6(6))* Recorded Bks., Inc.
Brewer, Heather. The Cemetery Boys. 2016. (YA). lib. bdg. 20.85 *(978-0-606-38741-5(2))* Turtleback.
Brezenoff, Steve. Burning Secrets, 1 vol. Vue, Tou, illus. 2008. (Vortex Bks.). (ENG.). 112p. (J). (gr. 5-9). pap. 7.19 *(978-1-59889-920-7(1),* 94322, Stone Arch Bks.) Capstone.
—Curses for Sale, 1 vol. Percival, Tom, illus. 2012. (Ravens Pass Ser.). (ENG.). 96p. (J). (gr. 3-6). pap. 6.15 *(978-1-4342-4209-9(9),* 120266, Stone Arch Bks.) Capstone.
—New in Town, 1 vol. Percival, Tom, illus. 2012. (Ravens Pass Ser.). (ENG.). 96p. (J). (gr. 3-6). pap. 6.15 *(978-1-4342-4210-5(2),* 120268); lib. bdg. 25.32 *(978-1-4342-3793-4(1),* 117092) Capstone. (Stone Arch Bks.).
Brodey, Lisette. Mystical High. 2013. (ENG.). 264p. (YA). pap. 13.95 *(978-0-9815836-8-6(7))* Saberlee Bks.
Brodien-Jones, Chris. The Dreamkeepers. 2009. (ENG.). 148p. (YA). (gr. 7). pap. 8.99 *(978-1-4424-0221-8(0),* Simon & Schuster Bks. For Young Readers) Simon & Schuster Bks. For Young Readers.
—The Glass Puzzle. 2013. (Illus.). 319p. (J). *(978-0-385-74298-6(3),* Delacorte Pr) Random House Publishing Group.
Brown, Merry. Gold Manor Ghost House. 2013. 328p. pap. 13.99 *(978-0-615-79766-3(0))* YA Bks.
Brown, Roberta Simpson. The Walking Trees & Other Scary Stories. 2006. (ENG.). 140p. (J). (gr. 6-9). pap. 11.95 *(978-0-87483-143-6(1))* August Hse. Pubs., Inc.
Bruchac, Joseph. Wolf Mark, 1 vol. 2011. (ENG.). 392p. (YA). (gr. 7-12). 20.95 *(978-1-60060-661-8(X),* leelowtu, Tu Bks.) Lee & Low Bks., Inc.
Buckingham, Royce. Demonkeeper. 2007. 216p. (J). *(978-1-4287-4608-4(0))* Penguin Publishing Group.
—Demonkeeper. 2007. (ENG.). 216p. (J). (gr. 6-8). 22.44 *(978-0-399-24649-4(5))* Penguin Young Readers Group.
Buckley-Archer, Linda. The Many Lives of John Stone. 2015. (ENG., Illus.). 544p. (YA). (gr. 7). 17.99 *(978-1-4814-2637-4(0))* Simon & Schuster Children's Publishing.
Burne, Cristy. Takeshita Demons: Monster Matsuri. 2012. (Illus.). 128p. (J). pap. *(978-1-84780-137-1(4),* White Lion Publishing) Quarto Publishing Group UK.
Burnham, Erik. The New Ghostbusters. 2016. lib. bdg. 30.60 *(978-0-606-38722-4(6))* Turtleback.
Burns, Laura J. & Metz, Melinda. Sacrifice. 2011. (ENG.). 272p. (YA). (gr. 9). 17.99 *(978-1-4424-3900-9(9),* Simon & Schuster Bks. For Young Readers) Simon & Schuster Bks. For Young Readers.
Butler, Erin. Blood Hex. 2013. 260p. pap. *(978-1-77130-351-4(4))* Evernight Publishing.
Cabot, Meg. Haunted. 2007. (Mediator Ser.: No. 5). 263p. 18.00 *(978-0-7569-7831-0(9))* Perfection Learning Corp.
Cach, Lisa. Wake unto Me. 2011. 320p. (YA). (gr. 7-18). 8.99 *(978-0-14-241436-1(0),* Speak) Penguin Young Readers Group.
Caine, Rachel, pseud. Bite Club: The Morganville Vampires, 10 vols. 2011. (Morganville Vampires Ser.: 10). (ENG.). 368p. (YA). (gr. 9). pap. 9.99 *(978-0-451-23468-1(5),* Berkley) Penguin Publishing Group.
—Bitter Blood: The Morganville Vampires. 2013. (Morganville Vampires Ser.: 13). (ENG.). 432p. (YA). (gr. 9). pap. 9.99 *(978-0-451-41424-3(1),* Berkley) Penguin Publishing Group.
—Black Dawn: The Morganville Vampires. 2012. (Morganville Vampires Ser.: 12). (ENG.). 400p. (YA). (gr. 9). pap. 9.99 *(978-0-451-23793-4(5),* Berkley) Penguin Publishing Group.
—Ghost Town: The Morganville Vampires, 9 vols. 2011. (Morganville Vampires Ser.: 9). (ENG.). 368p. (YA). (gr. 9-18). 9.99 *(978-0-451-23291-5(7),* Berkley) Penguin Publishing Group.
—Last Breath: The Morganville Vampires, 11 vols. 2012. (Morganville Vampires Ser.: 11). (ENG.). 368p. (YA). (gr. 9). 9.99 *(978-0-451-23580-0(0),* Berkley) Penguin Publishing Group.
—Lord of Misrule. 2009. (Morganville Vampires Ser.: Bk. 5). 352p. (YA). lib. bdg. 20.00 *(978-1-4242-4704-2(7))* Fitzgerald Bks.
—Lord of Misrule: The Morganville Vampires, Book 5. 2009. (Morganville Vampires Ser.: 5). (ENG.). 256p. (YA). (gr. 9-18). mass mkt. 7.99 *(978-0-451-22572-6(4),* Berkley) Penguin Publishing Group.
—Midnight Alley. 2007. (Morganville Vampires Ser.: Bk. 3). 256p. (YA). lib. bdg. 20.00 *(978-1-4242-4705-9(5))* Fitzgerald Bks.
—Midnight Alley: The Morganville Vampires, Book III. 2007. (Morganville Vampires Ser.: 3). (ENG.). 256p. (YA). (gr. 9-18). mass mkt. 7.99 *(978-0-451-22238-1(5),* Berkley) Penguin Publishing Group.
—Midnight Bites: Stories of the Morganville Vampires. 2016. (Morganville Vampires Ser.). (ENG.). 512p. (YA). (gr. 9). pap. 12.00 *(978-1-101-98978-4(5),* Berkley) Penguin Publishing Group.
—Paper & Fire. 2017. (Great Library: 2). (ENG.). 400p. (YA). (gr. 9). pap. 12.00 *(978-0-451-47314-1(0),* Berkley) Penguin Publishing Group.
—Paper & Fire. 2017. (Great Library: 2). lib. bdg. 20.85 *(978-0-606-40361-0(2))* Turtleback.
Cameron, Erica. Sing Sweet Nightingale. 2014. (Dream War Saga Ser.: 1). (ENG.). 369p. (YA). (gr. 7-9). pap. 9.95 *(978-1-937053-96-3(2))* Spencer Hill Pr.
Campbell, D. Andrew. Catharsis. 2013. 340p. pap. 12.50 *(978-0-9897522-0-6(8))* Broviak Publishing.
Campbell, K. G. A Small Zombie Problem. 2019. (Zombie Problems Ser.: 1). (Illus.). 240p. (J). (gr. 3-7). 16.99 *(978-0-553-53955-4(8),* Knopf Bks. for Young Readers) Random Hse. Children's Bks.
Cannon, Sarah. Oddity. 2019. (ENG.). 320p. (J). pap. 7.99 *(978-1-250-17906-7(8),* 900174055) Square Fish.
Carman, Patrick. Thirteen Days to Midnight. 2011. (ENG.). 304p. (J). (gr. 7-17). pap. 16.99 *(978-0-316-00404-6(9))* Little, Brown Bks. for Young Readers.
Carroll, Jenny, pseud & Cabot, Meg. Shadowland, 5 vols. unabr. ed. 2005. (Mediator Ser.: 1). (YA). (gr. 3-7). 69.75 *(978-1-4193-4144-1(8),* 42055) Recorded Bks., Inc.
Casella, Jody. Thin Space. 2013. (ENG.). 256p. (YA). (gr. 7). 16.99 *(978-1-58270-435-7(X))*; pap. 10.99 *(978-1-58270-392-3(2))* Simon Pulse. (Simon Pulse).
Cashore, Kristin. Jane, Unlimited. 2018. (Illus.). 480p. (YA). (gr. 9). pap. 10.99 *(978-0-14-751310-6(3),* Speak) Penguin Young Readers Group.
Cast, P. C. & Cast, Kristin. Burned: A House of Night Novel. (House of Night Novels Ser.: 7). (ENG.). 336p. (YA). (gr. 7-12). 2011. pap. 13.00 *(978-0-312-38796-9(2),* 900054119) 2010. 22.00 *(978-0-312-60616-9(8),* 900059356) St. Martin's Pr. (St. Martin's Griffin).
—Destined: A House of Night Novel. 2013. (House of Night Novels Ser.: 9). (ENG.). 336p. (YA). (gr. 7-12). pap. 12.99 *(978-0-312-38798-3(9),* 900054121, St. Martin's Griffin) St. Martin's Pr.

S

—Neferet's Curse: A House of Night Novella. 2013. (House of Night Novellas Ser.: 3). (ENG., Illus.). 160p. (YA). (gr. 7). 14.99 *(978-1-250-00025-5(4)*, 900078258, St. Martin's Griffin) St. Martin's Pr.

—Untamed. I.t. ed. 2009. (House of Night Ser.: Bk. 4). (ENG.). 510p. (YA). 23.95 *(978-1-4104-1965-1(7))* Thorndike Pr.

—Untamed: A House of Night Novel. (House of Night Novels Ser.: 4). (ENG.). 352p. (YA). 2009. (gr. 7-12). 21.99 *(978-0-312-59630-9(8)*, 900063092) 2008. (gr. 8-12). pap. 11.99 *(978-0-312-37983-4(8)*, 900050334, St. Martin's Griffin) St. Martin's Pr.

Chadda, Sarwat. The City of Death. 2013. (J). pap. *(978-0-545-38519-0(9))* Scholastic, Inc.

Chandler, Elizabeth. The Back Door of Midnight. 2010. (Dark Secrets Ser.: Vol. 5). (ENG.). 320p. (YA). (gr. 7-18). pap. 9.99 *(978-1-4424-0626-1(7)*, Simon Pulse) Simon Pulse.

Cho, Kat. Wicked Fox. 2019. 448p. (YA). (gr. 7). 18.99 *(978-1-9848-1234-6(3)*, G.P. Putnam's Sons Books for Young Readers) Penguin Young Readers Group.

Chokshi, Roshani. Aru Shah & the City of Gold: A Pandava Novel Book 4. I.t. ed. 2021. (Pandava Novel Ser.: 4). (ENG.). lib. bdg. 22.99 *(978-1-4328-8689-9(4))* Thorndike Pr.

—Aru Shah & the End of Time. 1. 2019. (Pandava Ser.). (ENG.). 376p. (gr. 4-6). 24.94 *(978-1-5364-5430-7(3)*, Riordan, Rick) Disney Pr.

—Aru Shah & the End of Time. 2022. (Pandava Ser.). (ENG.). 126p. (J). (gr. 4-5). 24.46 ***(978-1-68505-435-9(8))*** Penworthy Co., LLC, The.

—Aru Shah & the End of Time. 2019. (Pandava Ser.: Vol. 1). (ENG.). 384p. lib. bdg. 19.80 *(978-1-6636-2563-2(8))* Perfection Learning Corp.

—Aru Shah & the Nectar of Immortality. I.t. ed. 2022. (Pandava Ser.: 5). (ENG.). lib. bdg. 22.99 *(978-1-4328-9739-0(X))* Cengage Gale.

—Aru Shah & the Song of Death, 2. 2020. (Pandava Ser.). (ENG.). 400p. (gr. 4-6). 22.44 *(978-1-5364-6224-1(1)*, Riordan, Rick) Disney Pr.

—Aru Shah & the Tree of Wishes, 3. 2021. (Pandava Ser.). (ENG.). 416p. (gr. 4-6). 22.44 *(978-1-5364-6778-9(2)*, Riordan, Rick) Disney Pr.

—Rick Riordan Presents Aru Shah & the City of Gold: A Pandava Novel Book 4. 2021. (Pandava Ser.: 4). (ENG.). 400p. (J). (gr. 3-7). 16.99 *(978-1-368-01386-4(4)*, Riordan, Rick) Disney Publishing Worldwide.

—Rick Riordan Presents Aru Shah & the City of Gold (a Pandava Novel, Book 4) A Pandava Novel Book 4. 2022. (Pandava Ser.: 4). (ENG.). 416p. (J). (gr. 3-7). pap. 8.99 *(978-1-368-02358-0(4)*, Riordan, Rick) Disney Publishing Worldwide.

—Rick Riordan Presents Aru Shah & the End of Time (a Pandava Novel, Book 1) 2018. (Pandava Ser.: 1). (ENG.). 368p. (J). (gr. 3-7). 16.99 *(978-1-368-01235-5(3)*, Riordan, Rick) Disney Publishing Worldwide.

—Rick Riordan Presents Aru Shah & the End of Time (a Pandava Novel Book 1) 2019. (Pandava Ser.: 1). (ENG.). 384p. (J). (gr. 3-7). pap. 8.99 *(978-1-368-02356-6(8)*, Riordan, Rick) Disney Publishing Worldwide.

—Rick Riordan Presents Aru Shah & the Nectar of Immortality (a Pandava Novel, Book 5) A Pandava Novel Book 5. 2022. (Pandava Ser.: 5). (ENG.). 384p. (J). (gr. 3-7). 16.99 *(978-1-368-05544-4(3)*, Riordan, Rick) Disney Publishing Worldwide.

—Rick Riordan Presents Aru Shah & the Song of Death (a Pandava Novel Book 2) (Pandava Ser.: 2). (ENG.). 400p. (J). (gr. 3-7). 2020. pap. 7.99 *(978-1-368-02355-9(X))* 2019. 16.99 *(978-1-368-01384-0(8))* Disney Publishing Worldwide. (Riordan, Rick).

—Rick Riordan Presents Aru Shah & the Tree of Wishes (a Pandava Novel Book 3) (Pandava Ser.: 3). (ENG.). (J). (gr. 3-7). 2021. 416p. pap. 7.99 *(978-1-368-02357-3(6))* 2020. 400p. 16.99 *(978-1-368-01385-7(6))* Disney Publishing Worldwide. (Riordan, Rick).

Christopher, Neil. The Hidden: A Compendium of Arctic Giants, Dwarves, Gnomes, Trolls, Faeries & Other Strange Beings from Inuit Oral History, 1 vol. Austin, Mike, illus. 2014. (ENG.). 194p. (YA). (gr. 8-12). 29.95 *(978-1-927095-59-1(X))* Inhabit Media Inc. CAN. Dist: Consortium Bk. Sales & Distribution.

Clare, Cassandra. City of Ashes. 2008. (Mortal Instruments Ser.: Bk. 2). (YA). (gr. 9). 64.99 *(978-1-60640-964-0(6))* Findaway World, LLC.

—City of Ashes. 2008. (YA). (Mortal Instruments Ser.: 2). (ENG.). 464p. (gr. 9-12). 24.99 *(978-1-4169-1429-7(3))*; 416p. pap. *(978-1-4063-1849-4(3))* McElderry, Margaret K. Bks. (McElderry, Margaret K. Bks.).

—City of Bones. (Mortal Instruments Ser.: 1). (ENG., Illus.). (YA). (gr. 9). 2015. 544p. pap. 14.99 *(978-1-4814-5592-3(3))* 2007. 496p. 24.99 *(978-1-4169-1428-0(5))* McElderry, Margaret K. Bks. (McElderry, Margaret K. Bks.).

—City of Bones. 2008. (Mortal Instruments Ser.: Bk. 1). 485p. (gr. 9-12). 23.00 *(978-1-60686-361-9(4))* Perfection Learning Corp.

—City of Bones. 2018. (Mortal Instruments Ser.: 1). (ENG., Illus.). 720p. (gr. 9). mass mkt. 9.99 *(978-1-5344-3178-2(0))* Pocket Books.

—City of Bones, 12 vols. 2007. (Mortal Instruments Ser.: 1). (YA). 131.75 *(978-1-4281-5454-4(X))*; 133.75 *(978-1-4281-5452-0(3))*; 122.75 *(978-1-4281-5448-3(5))*; 286.75 *(978-1-4281-5449-0(3))*; 1.25 *(978-1-4281-5445-2(0))*; 120.75 *(978-1-4281-5450-6(7))* Recorded Bks., Inc.

—City of Bones. 2013. (The Mortal Instruments Ser.: Bk. 1). pap. *(978-1-4424-9306-3(2))* Simon & Schuster, Inc.

—City of Bones. I.t. ed. 2008. (Mortal Instruments Ser.: 1). (ENG.). 503p. (YA). 31.95 *(978-1-4104-0958-4(9))* Thorndike Pr.

—City of Bones. 2015. (Mortal Instruments Ser.: Bk. 1). (Illus.). 544p. (YA). lib. bdg. 25.75 *(978-0-606-37731-7(X))* Turtleback.

—City of Fallen Angels. 2011. (Mortal Instruments Ser.: 4). (ENG.). 432p. (YA). (gr. 9-18). 24.99 *(978-1-4424-0354-3(3)*, McElderry, Margaret K. Bks.) McElderry, Margaret K. Bks.

—City of Fallen Angels, 11 vols. (Mortal Instruments Ser.: 4). (YA). 2012. 133.75 *(978-1-4618-0638-7(0))* 2011. 135.75 *(978-1-4618-0637-0(2))* 2011. 133.75 *(978-1-4618-0641-7(0))* 2011. 1.25 *(978-1-4640-2483-2(9))* 2011. 317.75 *(978-1-4618-0642-4(9))* Recorded Bks., Inc.

—City of Glass. (Mortal Instruments Ser.: 3). (ENG., (YA). (gr. 9). 2015. Illus.). 592p. pap. 14.99 *(978-1-4814-5598-5(2))* 2009. 560p. 24.99 *(978-1-4169-1430-3(7))* McElderry, Margaret K. Bks. (McElderry, Margaret K. Bks.).

—City of Glass. 2010. 23.00 *(978-1-60686-827-0(6))* Perfection Learning Corp.

—City of Glass. 2009. pap. *(978-1-4424-9308-7(9))* Simon & Schuster.

—City of Glass. 2015. (Mortal Instruments Ser.: Bk. 3). (Illus.). 592p. (J). lib. bdg. 25.75 *(978-0-606-37733-1(6))* Turtleback.

—City of Heavenly Fire. 2014. (Mortal Instruments Ser.: 6). (ENG., Illus.). 752p. (YA). (gr. 9). 24.99 *(978-1-4424-1689-5(0)*, McElderry, Margaret K. Bks.) McElderry, Margaret K. Bks.

—City of Lost Souls. (Mortal Instruments Ser.: 5). (ENG., (YA). (gr. 9). 2015. Illus.). 592p. pap. 14.99 *(978-1-4814-5600-5(8))* 2012. 544p. 24.99 *(978-1-4424-1686-4(6))* McElderry, Margaret K. Bks. (McElderry, Margaret K. Bks.).

—City of Lost Souls, 16 vols. 2012. (Mortal Instruments Ser.: Bk. 5). (YA). 135.75 *(978-1-4640-3948-5(8))*; 133.75 *(978-1-4640-3951-5(8))*; 317.75 *(978-1-4640-3949-2(6))*; 133.75 *(978-1-4640-3952-2(6))* Recorded Bks., Inc.

—City of Lost Souls. 2015. (Mortal Instruments Ser.: Bk. 5). 592p. (YA). lib. bdg. 25.75 *(978-0-606-37736-2(0))* Turtleback.

—City of Lost Souls. 2012. 512p. pap. *(978-1-4063-3760-0(9))* Walker Bks., Ltd.

—Clockwork Angel. (Infernal Devices Ser.: 1). (ENG., Illus.). (YA). (gr. 9). 2015. 544p. pap. 14.99 *(978-1-4814-5602-9(4))* 2010. 496p. 24.99 *(978-1-4169-7586-1(1))* McElderry, Margaret K. Bks. (McElderry, Margaret K. Bks.).

—Clockwork Angel. 2013. (CHI & ENG.). 240p. (YA). (gr. 8-17). pap. *(978-986-6000-84-3(2))* Spring International Pubs.

—Clockwork Angel. 2015. (Infernal Devices Ser.: Bk. 1). 544p. (YA). lib. bdg. 25.75 *(978-0-606-37737-9(9))* 2012. (Infernal Devices Graphic Novel Ser.: 1). lib. bdg. 24.55 *(978-0-606-32257-7(4))* Turtleback.

—Clockwork Prince. (Infernal Devices Ser.: 2). (YA). 2015. (ENG., Illus.). 560p. (gr. 9). pap. 14.99 *(978-1-4814-5601-2(6))* 2011. (ENG., Illus.). 528p. (gr. 9-18). 24.99 *(978-1-4169-7588-5(8))* 2011. 502p. *(978-1-4424-5174-2(2))* McElderry, Margaret K. Bks. (McElderry, Margaret K. Bks.).

—Clockwork Prince. 2015. (Infernal Devices Ser.: Bk. 2). 560p. (YA). lib. bdg. 25.75 *(978-0-606-37895-6(2))* 2013. (Infernal Devices Graphic Novel Ser.: 2). lib. bdg. 24.55 *(978-0-606-32258-4(2))* Turtleback.

—Clockwork Princess. 2013. (YA). (Infernal Devices Ser.: 3). (ENG., Illus.). 592p. (gr. 9). 24.99 *(978-1-4169-7590-8(X))*; 570p. *(978-1-4424-8541-9(8))* McElderry, Margaret K. Bks. (McElderry, Margaret K. Bks.).

—The Dark Artifices, the Complete Collection: Lady Midnight; Lord of Shadows; Queen of Air & Darkness. 2019. (Dark Artifices Ser.). (ENG., Illus.). 2288p. (YA). (gr. 9). 74.99 *(978-1-5344-4954-1(X)*, McElderry, Margaret K. Bks.) McElderry, Margaret K. Bks.

—The Infernal Devices: Clockwork Angel; Clockwork Prince; Clockwork Princess. 2013. (Infernal Devices Ser.: Bks. 1-3). (ENG.). 1520p. (YA). (gr. 9). 74.99 *(978-1-4424-8372-9(5)*, McElderry, Margaret K. Bks.) McElderry, Margaret K. Bks.

—The Infernal Devices: Clockwork Angel. 2012. (Infernal Devices Ser.: 1). (ENG.). 240p. (gr. 8-17). pap. 13.00 *(978-0-316-20098-1(0)*, Yen Pr.) Yen Pr. LLC.

—Lady Midnight. 2016. (Dark Artifices Ser.: 1). (ENG., Illus.). 688p. (YA). (gr. 9-12). 24.99 *(978-1-4424-6835-1(1)*, McElderry, Margaret K. Bks.) McElderry, Margaret K. Bks.

—Lady Midnight. 2017. lib. bdg. 26.95 *(978-0-606-40535-5(6))* Turtleback.

—Lord of Shadows. (YA). 2018. (Dark Artifices Ser.: 2). (ENG., Illus.). 752p. (gr. 9). pap. 14.99 *(978-1-4424-6841-2(6))* 2017. (Dark Artifices Ser.: 2). (ENG., Illus.). 720p. (gr. 9). 24.99 *(978-1-4424-6840-5(9))* 2017. 699p. *(978-1-5344-0617-9(4))* McElderry, Margaret K. Bks. (McElderry, Margaret K. Bks.).

—Queen of Air & Darkness. 2018. (Dark Artifices Ser.: 3). (ENG., Illus.). 912p. (YA). (gr. 9). 24.99 *(978-1-4424-6843-6(2))*; E-Book *(978-1-4424-6845-0(9))* McElderry, Margaret K. Bks. (McElderry, Margaret K. Bks.).

Clare, Cassandra & Lewis, Joshua. The Shadowhunter's Codex. 2013. (Mortal Instruments Ser.). (ENG., Illus.). 288p. (YA). (gr. 9). 24.99 *(978-1-4424-1692-5(0))*; 49.99 *(978-1-4424-9682-8(7))* McElderry, Margaret K. Bks. (McElderry, Margaret K. Bks.).

Clare, Cassandra, et al. The Bane Chronicles. Clare, Cassandra, ed. 2014. (Bane Chronicles Ser.). (ENG., Illus.). 528p. (YA). (gr. 9). 24.99 *(978-1-4424-9599-9(5)*, McElderry, Margaret K. Bks.) McElderry, Margaret K. Bks.

—Tales from the Shadowhunter Academy. (Tales from the Shadowhunter Academy Ser.). (ENG.). (YA). (gr. 9). 2017. 704p. pap. 14.99 *(978-1-4814-4326-5(7))* 2016. (Illus.). 672p. 24.99 *(978-1-4814-4325-8(9))* McElderry, Margaret K. Bks. (McElderry, Margaret K. Bks.).

Clewarth, John. Firestorm Rising. 2012. (Illus.). 200p. pap. *(978-1-4710-3681-1(2))* Lulu.com.

—Firestorm Rising. 2018. (ENG., Illus.). 216p. (J). (gr. 4-6). pap. *(978-1-912513-70-3(6))* Silver Quill Publishing.

Climer, Steven Lee. Young of Heart. 2006. (YA). pap. *(978-0-9790649-5-1(3))* Mardi Gras Publishing, LLC.

Cochran, Molly. Legacy, 1. 2011. (Legacy Ser.). (ENG.). 432p. (YA). (gr. 9-12). 17.99 *(978-1-4424-1739-7(0))* Simon & Schuster, Inc.

—Poison. 2012. (Legacy Ser.). (ENG.). 368p. (YA). (gr. 9). 17.99 *(978-1-4424-5050-9(9)*, Simon & Schuster/Paula Wiseman Bks.) Simon & Schuster/Paula Wiseman Bks.

Cody, Matthew. The Dead Gentleman. 2012. 288p. (J). (gr. 5). 7.99 *(978-0-375-84490-4(2)*, Yearling) Random Hse. Children's Bks.

—Powerless. 2011. 288p. (J). (Supers of Noble's Green Ser.: 1). (gr. 3-7). 8.99 *(978-0-375-84489-8(9)*, Yearling);1. (Supers of Noble Green Ser.). (ENG.). (gr. 4-6). lib. bdg. 18.69 *(978-0-375-95595-2(X)*, Knopf Bks. for Young Readers) Random Hse. Children's Bks.

—Super. 2014. (Supers of Noble's Green Ser.: 2). (ENG.). 304p. (J). (gr. 3-7). 9.99 *(978-0-375-87291-4(4)*, Yearling) Random Hse. Children's Bks.

—Villainous. 2015. (Supers of Noble's Green Ser.: 3). (ENG.). 320p. (J). (gr. 3-7). 8.99 *(978-0-385-75492-7(2)*, Yearling) Random Hse. Children's Bks.

Cole, Kresley. Dead of Winter. 2015. (Arcana Chronicles Ser.). (ENG.). 320p. (YA). (gr. 9). pap. 13.99 *(978-1-4814-2346-5(0))*; (Illus.). 18.99 *(978-1-4814-2345-8(2))* Simon & Schuster Bks. For Young Readers. (Simon & Schuster Bks. For Young Readers).

—Endless Knight. 2013. (Arcana Chronicles Ser.: 2). (YA). 246.75 *(978-1-4703-8090-8(0))*; 116.75 *(978-1-4703-8957-4(6))*; 116.75 *(978-1-4703-8987-1(8))*; 118.75 *(978-1-4703-8997-0(5))*; 1.25 *(978-1-4703-8070-0(6))* Recorded Bks., Inc.

—Endless Knight. 2013. (Arcana Chronicles Ser.). (ENG., Illus.). 336p. (YA). (gr. 9). 18.99 *(978-1-4424-3667-1(0)*, Simon & Schuster Bks. For Young Readers) Simon & Schuster Bks. For Young Readers.

—Poison Princess. 2013. (Arcana Chronicles Ser.: 1). (YA). 1.25 *(978-1-4703-8731-0(X))* Recorded Bks., Inc.

—Poison Princess. (Arcana Chronicles Ser.). (ENG., (YA). (gr. 9). 2013. Illus.). 400p. pap. 13.99 *(978-1-4424-3665-7(4))* 2012. 384p. 18.99 *(978-1-4424-3664-0(6))* Simon & Schuster Bks. For Young Readers. (Simon & Schuster Bks. For Young Readers).

Columbus, Chris & Vizzini, Ned. House of Secrets. 2015. (House of Secrets Ser.: Vol. 1). (KOR.). 580p. (J). *(978-89-491-7127-2(9))* Biryongso Publishing Co.

—House of Secrets. Call, Greg, illus. (House of Secrets Ser.: 1). (J). 2014. (ENG.). 512p. (gr. 3-7). pap. 7.99 *(978-0-06-219247-9(7)*, Balzer & Bray) 2013. (ENG.). 496p. (gr. 3-7). 17.99 *(978-0-06-219246-2(9)*, Balzer & Bray) 2013. 490p. *(978-0-06-225964-6(4))* HarperCollins Pubs.

—House of Secrets. 2014. (House of Secrets Ser.: 1). (J). lib. bdg. 18.40 *(978-0-606-35070-9(5))* Turtleback.

—House of Secrets: Battle of the Beasts. Call, Greg, illus. 2014. (House of Secrets Ser.: 2). (ENG.). 480p. (J). (gr. 3-7). 17.99 *(978-0-06-219249-3(3)*, Balzer & Bray) HarperCollins Pubs.

Condie, Ally & Reichs, Brendan. The Beast. 2019. (Darkdeep Ser.). (ENG.). 336p. (J). 16.99 *(978-1-5476-0203-2(1)*, 900203288, Bloomsbury Children's Bks.) Bloomsbury Publishing USA.

—The Darkdeep. (Darkdeep Ser.). (ENG.). (J). 2019. 288p. pap. 7.99 *(978-1-5476-0248-3(1)*, 900207570) 2018. 272p. 16.99 *(978-1-5476-0046-5(2)*, 900196366) Bloomsbury Publishing USA. (Bloomsbury Children's Bks.).

Condie, Allyson Braithwaite & Reichs, Brendan. The Darkdeep. 2018. 261p. (J). *(978-1-5476-0215-5(5))* Bloomsbury Publishing USA.

Conway, K. R. Stormfront, vol. 2. 2014. (The Undertow Ser.). 428p. (YA). (gr. 7-17). pap. 15.95 *(978-0-9897763-4-9(4))* Conway, Kathleen R.

Cook, Kristi. Haven. 2012. (ENG.). 448p. (YA). (gr. 9). pap. 12.99 *(978-1-4424-0761-9(1)*, Simon Pulse) Simon Pulse.

—Mirage. (ENG., (YA). (gr. 9). 2013. Illus.). 416p. pap. 12.99 *(978-1-4424-4300-6(6))* 2012. 384p. 16.99 *(978-1-4424-4299-3(9))* Simon Pulse. (Simon Pulse).

Cooper, Susan. The Boggart & the Monster. 2018. (Boggart Ser.). (ENG.). 224p. (J). (gr. 3-7). pap. 7.99 *(978-1-5344-2012-0(6)*, McElderry, Margaret K. Bks.) McElderry, Margaret K. Bks.

Coppel, Alfred Jr. & Coppel, Alfred. The Peacemaker. 2011. 24p. pap. 6.95 *(978-1-4638-0006-2(1))* Rodgers, Alan Bks.

Córdova, Zoraida. Bruja Born. 2019. (Brooklyn Brujas Ser.: 2). (ENG.). 352p. (YA). (gr. 8-12). pap. 10.99 *(978-1-7282-0986-9(2))* Sourcebooks, Inc.

—Labyrinth Lost. 2017. (Brooklyn Brujas Ser.: 1). (ENG.). 352p. (YA). (gr. 8-12). pap. 10.99 *(978-1-4926-2316-8(4))* Sourcebooks, Inc.

Cordova, Zoraida. The Savage Blue: A Vicious Deep Novel. 2014. (Vicious Deep Ser.: 2). (ENG.). 416p. (YA). (gr. 7-12). pap. 14.99 *(978-1-4926-0124-1(1))* Sourcebooks, Inc.

Córdova, Zoraida. The Vast & Brutal Sea: A Vicious Deep Novel. 2015. (Vicious Deep Ser.: 3). (ENG.). 336p. (YA). (gr. 8-12). pap. 9.99 *(978-1-4926-0867-7(X))* Sourcebooks, Inc.

Cordova, Zoraida. The Vicious Deep. 2012. (Vicious Deep Ser.: 1). (ENG.). 384p. (YA). (gr. 7-12). pap. 13.99 *(978-1-4022-7441-1(6))* Sourcebooks, Inc.

Cormier, Robert. Fade. 2004. (ENG.). 320p. (YA). (gr. 9-17). pap. 8.99 *(978-0-385-73134-8(5)*, Delacorte Bks. for Young Readers) Random Hse. Children's Bks.

Cosper, Andy. The Adventures of Drew Kreeger: Book 1. 2008. 56p. pap. 14.95 *(978-1-4327-3320-9(6))* Outskirts Pr., Inc.

Coville, Bruce. Always October. 2012. (ENG.). 384p. (J). (gr. 3-7). 16.99 *(978-0-06-089095-7(9)*, HarperCollins) HarperCollins Pubs.

Cowing, Sue. Call Me Drog. 2014. (ENG.). 320p. (J). 13.99 *(978-0-00-757804-7(0))* HarperCollins Pubs. Ltd. GBR. Dist: Independent Pubs. Group.

Craddock, Erik. Dragon Boogie. 2012. (Stone Rabbit Ser.: 7). lib. bdg. 17.20 *(978-0-606-23868-7(9))* Turtleback.

Cremer, Andrea. Bloodrose. 2012. (Nightshade Ser.: 3). lib. bdg. 22.10 *(978-0-606-26635-2(6))* Turtleback.

—Rift. 2013. (Nightshade Novels Ser.). (ENG.). 464p. (YA). (gr. 8-12). 26.19 *(978-0-399-25613-4(X))* Penguin Young Readers Group.

—Snakeroot. 2014. (Nightshade Ser.: 4). (ENG.). 352p. (YA). (gr. 9). pap. 10.99 *(978-0-14-750860-7(6)*, Speak) Penguin Young Readers Group.

Cross, Kady. Sisters of Blood & Spirit. 2016. (Sisters of Blood & Spirit Ser.: 1). (ENG.). 272p. (YA). pap. 9.99 *(978-0-373-21188-3(0)*, Harlequin Teen) Harlequin Enterprises ULC CAN. Dist: HarperCollins Pubs.

—Sisters of Salt & Iron. 2016. (Sisters of Blood & Spirit Ser.: 2). (ENG.). 352p. (YA). 18.99 *(978-0-373-21176-0(7)*, Harlequin Teen) Harlequin Enterprises ULC CAN. Dist: HarperCollins Pubs.

Cross, Mimi. Shining Sea, 0 vols. 2016. (ENG.). 432p. (YA). (gr. 9-12). pap. 9.99 *(978-1-5039-3553-2(1)*, 9781503935532, Skyscape) Amazon Publishing.

Crowley, Kieran Mark. Colm & the Ghost's Revenge. 2012. (ENG.). 320p. (J). pap. 13.95 *(978-1-85635-997-9(2))* Mercier Pr., Ltd., The IRL. Dist: Dufour Editions, Inc.

Cusick, Richie Tankersley. Blood Brothers. 2006. (Unseen Ser.: 3). (ENG.). 272p. (YA). (gr. 7-18). 8.99 *(978-0-14-240583-3(3)*, Speak) Penguin Young Readers Group.

—The Unseen Volume 2: Blood Brothers/Sin & Salvation. 2012. (Unseen Ser.: 2). (ENG.). 640p. (YA). (gr. 7). pap. 7.99 *(978-0-14-242337-0(8)*, Speak) Penguin Young Readers Group.

Dahl, Michael. Dark Tower Rising, 1 vol. Kovar, Ben, illus. 2012. (Troll Hunters Ser.). (ENG.). 112p. (J). (gr. 5-9). lib. bdg. 25.32 *(978-1-4342-3308-0(1)*, 116272, Stone Arch Bks.) Capstone.

—Fallen Star, 1 vol. Kovar, Ben, illus. 2012. (Troll Hunters Ser.). (ENG.). 112p. (J). (gr. 5-9). lib. bdg. 25.32 *(978-1-4342-3310-3(3)*, 116274, Stone Arch Bks.) Capstone.

—Skyfall, 1 vol. Kovar, Ben, illus. 2012. (Troll Hunters Ser.). (ENG.). 112p. (J). (gr. 5-9). lib. bdg. 25.32 *(978-1-4342-3307-3(3)*, 116271, Stone Arch Bks.) Capstone.

—Troll Hunters, 1 vol. Kovar, Ben, illus. 2012. (Troll Hunters Ser.). (ENG.). 320p. (J). (gr. 4-6). 12.95 *(978-1-4342-4590-8(X)*, 120539, Stone Arch Bks.) Capstone.

Damico, Gina. Wax. 2016. (ENG.). 368p. (YA). (gr. 7). 17.99 *(978-0-544-63315-5(6)*, 1619758, Clarion Bks.) HarperCollins Pubs.

Davies, Anna. Wrecked. 2013. (ENG., Illus.). 336p. (YA). (gr. 9). pap. 9.99 *(978-1-4424-3279-6(9)*, Simon & Schuster Bks. For Young Readers) Simon & Schuster Bks. For Young Readers.

Davies, Jocelyn. A Beautiful Dark. 2012. (ENG.). 416p. (YA). (gr. 8). pap. 9.99 *(978-0-06-199066-3(3)*, HarperTeen) HarperCollins Pubs.

—Fractured Light. 2013. (ENG.). 368p. (YA). (gr. 8). pap. 9.99 *(978-0-06-199068-7(X)*, HarperTeen) HarperCollins Pubs.

—A Radiant Sky. 2014. (ENG.). 384p. (YA). (gr. 8). pap. 9.99 *(978-0-06-199070-0(1)*, HarperTeen) HarperCollins Pubs.

Davis, Bryan. Beyond the Gateway (Reapers Trilogy V2) 2015. (ENG.). 384p. (YA). pap. 12.99 *(978-0-9898122-4-5(3))* Scrub Jay Journeys.

Dawson, Delilah S. Servants of the Storm. 2014. (ENG., Illus.). 384p. (YA). (gr. 9). 17.99 *(978-1-4424-8378-1(4)*, Simon Pulse) Simon Pulse.

De Haven, Tom. The Orphan's Tent. 2005. (Illus.). 192p. mass mkt. 5.99 *(978-0-7434-9772-5(4))* ibooks, Inc.

De Lint, Charles. Waifs & Strays. 2004. (ENG.). 416p. (YA). (gr. 7-18). 8.99 *(978-0-14-240158-3(7)*, Firebird) Penguin Young Readers Group.

Degrado, Louis Paul. The Questors' Adventures: The Round House & the Moaning Walls. 2012. 326p. 29.95 *(978-1-4759-4469-3(1))*; pap. 19.95 *(978-1-4759-4470-9(5))* iUniverse, Inc.

Del Negro, Janice M. Passion & Poison: Tales of Shape-Shifters, Ghosts, & Spirited Women, 0 vols. Natale, Vince, illus. 2013. (ENG.). 64p. (YA). (gr. 7-12). pap. 9.99 *(978-1-4778-1685-1(2)*, 9781477816851, Skyscape) Amazon Publishing.

Delaney, Joseph. Ghost Prison. 2014. (ENG.). 112p. (YA). (gr. 6-12). pap. 8.99 *(978-1-4926-0174-6(8))* Sourcebooks, Inc.

—The Last Apprentice: a Coven of Witches. Arrasmith, Patrick, illus. (Last Apprentice Short Fiction Ser.: 2). (ENG.). 240p. (YA). (gr. 8). 2011. pap. 10.99 *(978-0-06-196040-6(3))* 2010. 16.99 *(978-0-06-196038-3(1))* HarperCollins Pubs. (Greenwillow Bks.).

—The Last Apprentice: Attack of the Fiend (Book 4) Arrasmith, Patrick, illus. 2009. (Last Apprentice Ser.: 4). (ENG.). 576p. (YA). (gr. 8-18). pap. 9.99 *(978-0-06-089129-9(7)*, Greenwillow Bks.) HarperCollins Pubs.

—The Last Apprentice: Clash of the Demons (Book 6) Arrasmith, Patrick, illus. (Last Apprentice Ser.: 6). (ENG.). (YA). (gr. 8-18). 2009. 416p. 17.99 *(978-0-06-134462-6(1))*Bk. 6. 2010. 432p. pap. 10.99 *(978-0-06-134464-0(8))* HarperCollins Pubs. (Greenwillow Bks.).

—The Last Apprentice: Curse of the Bane (Book 2) (Last Apprentice Ser.: 2). (ENG., Illus.). (YA). (gr. 8-9). 2007. 496p. pap. 9.99 *(978-0-06-076623-8(9))* 2006. 480p. 18.99 *(978-0-06-076621-4(2))* HarperCollins Pubs. (Greenwillow Bks.).

—The Last Apprentice: Fury of the Seventh Son (Book 13), Bk. 13. Arrasmith, Patrick, illus. (Last Apprentice Ser.: 13). (ENG.). 480p. (YA). (gr. 8). 2015. pap. 10.99 *(978-0-06-219232-5(9))* 2014. 17.99 *(978-0-06-219231-8(0))*, HarperCollins Pubs. (Greenwillow Bks.).

—The Last Apprentice: Night of the Soul Stealer (Book 3), Bk. 3. 2008. (Last Apprentice Ser.: 3). (ENG.). 528p. (YA). (gr. 8-18). pap. 9.99 *(978-0-06-076626-9(3)*, Greenwillow Bks.) HarperCollins Pubs.

—The Last Apprentice: Rage of the Fallen (Book 8) Bk. 8. Arrasmith, Patrick, illus. 2012. (Last Apprentice Ser.: 8). (ENG.). 416p. (YA). (gr. 8). pap. 10.99 *(978-0-06-202758-0(1)*, Greenwillow Bks.) HarperCollins Pubs.

—The Last Apprentice: Revenge of the Witch (Book 1), Bk. 1. Arrasmith, Patrick, illus. (Last Apprentice Ser.: 1). (ENG.). (YA). (gr. 8). 2005. 368p. 18.99 *(978-0-06-076618-4(2))* 2006. 384p. reprint ed. pap. 10.99 *(978-0-06-076620-7(4))* HarperCollins Pubs. (Greenwillow Bks.).

—The Last Apprentice: Rise of the Huntress (Book 7) Bk. 7, Bk. 7. Arrasmith, Patrick, illus. 2011. (Last Apprentice Ser.: 7). (ENG.). 464p. (YA). (gr. 8). pap. 10.99 *(978-0-06-171512-9(3)*, Greenwillow Bks.) HarperCollins Pubs.

—The Last Apprentice: Slither (Book 11), Bk. 11. 2013. (Last Apprentice Ser.: 11). (ENG.). 416p. (YA). (gr. 8). 17.99 *(978-0-06-219234-9(5)*, Greenwillow Bks.) HarperCollins Pubs.

—The Last Apprentice: the Spook's Bestiary: The Guide to Creatures of the Dark. Heller, Julek, illus. 2011. (Last Apprentice Short Fiction Ser.: 3). (ENG.). 240p. (YA). (gr. 8). 16.99 *(978-0-06-208114-8(4)*, Greenwillow Bks.) HarperCollins Pubs.

—The Last Apprentice: the Spook's Tale: And Other Horrors. (Last Apprentice Short Fiction Ser.: 1). (ENG.). 176p. (YA). (gr. 8-18). 2010. pap. 9.99 *(978-0-06-173031-3(9))* 2009. 16.99 *(978-0-06-173028-3(9))* HarperCollins Pubs. (Greenwillow Bks.).

—The Last Apprentice: Wrath of the Bloodeye (Book 5) (Last Apprentice Ser.: 5). (ENG., (YA). (gr. 8-18). 2009. Illus.). 544p. pap. 10.99 *(978-0-06-134461-9(3))*Bk. 5. 2008. 528p.

17.99 *(978-0-06-134459-6(1))* HarperCollins Pubs. (Greenwillow Bks.).
—A New Darkness. 2014. (ENG.). 352p. (YA). (gr. 8). 17.99 *(978-0-06-233453-4(0)*, Greenwillow Bks.) HarperCollins Pubs.
Delsol, Wendy. Flock. 2013. (ENG.). 400p. (YA). (gr. 7). pap. 8.99 *(978-0-7636-6467-1(7))* Candlewick Pr.
—Frost. (ENG., Illus.). 384p. (YA). (gr. 7). 2012. pap. 8.99 *(978-0-7636-6249-3(6))* 2011. 15.99 *(978-0-7636-5386-6(1))* Candlewick Pr.
—Stork. (ENG., Illus.). 368p. (YA). (gr. 7). 2011. pap. 8.99 *(978-0-7636-5687-4(9))* 2010. 15.99 *(978-0-7636-4844-2(2))* Candlewick Pr.
Despain, Bree. The Lost Saint. 2011. (ENG.). 416p. (J). (gr. 7). pap. 9.99 *(978-1-60684-235-5(8)*, Carolrhoda Lab™) Lerner Publishing Group.
Desrochers, Lisa. Original Sin. 2011. (Personal Demons Ser.: 2). (ENG.). 400p. (YA). (gr. 9-18). pap. 19.99 *(978-0-7653-2809-0(7)*, 900070223, Tor Teen) Doherty, Tom Assocs., LLC.
DeStefano, Lauren. Dreaming Dangerous. 2018. (ENG.). 208p. (J). 16.99 *(978-1-68119-447-9(3)*, 900172801, Bloomsbury Children's Bks.) Bloomsbury Publishing USA.
Disney Books. Gravity Falls: Pining Away. 2014. (Gravity Falls Chapter Book Ser.: 1). (ENG., Illus.). 112p. (J). (gr. 1-3). pap. 4.99 *(978-1-4847-1139-2(4)*, Disney Press Books) Disney Publishing Worldwide.
DiTerlizzi, Tony & Black, Holly. Lucinda's Secret. l.t. ed. 2006. (Spiderwick Chronicles: Bk. 3). (Illus.). 142p. (J). (gr. 4-7). 23.95 *(978-0-7862-8585-3(0))* Thorndike Pr.
Diver, Lucienne. Fangtabulous. 2017. (Vamped Ser.: Vol. 4). (ENG., Illus.). (YA). pap. 14.95 *(978-1-62268-121-1(5))* Bella Rosa Bks.
d'Lacey, Chris. The Fire Eternal. 2010. (Last Dragon Chronicles Ser.: 4). lib. bdg. 19.65 *(978-0-606-12558-1(2))* Turtleback.
—Fire Star (the Last Dragon Chronicles #3) 2007. (Last Dragon Chronicles Ser.: 3). (ENG.). 560p. (J). (gr. 4-7). 9.99 *(978-0-439-90185-7(5)*, Scholastic Paperbacks) Scholastic, Inc.
—The Fire Within (the Last Dragon Chronicles #1) 2007. (Last Dragon Chronicles Ser.: 1). (ENG.). 352p. (J). (gr. 3-7). pap. 9.99 *(978-0-439-67244-3(9)*, Orchard Bks.) Scholastic, Inc.
—Fire World. 2012. (Last Dragon Chronicles Ser.: 6). lib. bdg. 19.65 *(978-0-606-23967-7(7))* Turtleback.
—Icefire (the Last Dragon Chronicles #2) 2007. (Last Dragon Chronicles Ser.: 2). (ENG.). 432p. (J). (gr. 3-7). pap. 9.99 *(978-0-439-67246-7(5)*, Orchard Bks.) Scholastic, Inc.
Dorset, Skylar. The Boy with the Hidden Name: Otherworld Book Two. 2014. (Otherworld Ser.: 2). (ENG.). 320p. (YA). (gr. 7-12). pap. 9.99 *(978-1-4022-9256-9(2)*, 9781402292569) Sourcebooks, Inc.
—The Girl Who Never Was. 2014. (Otherworld Ser.: 1). (ENG.). 304p. (YA). (gr. 7-12). pap. 9.99 *(978-1-4022-9253-8(8)*, 9781402292538) Sourcebooks, Inc.
Doyle, Catherine. The Storm Keeper's Island. (Storm Keeper's Island Ser.: 1). (ENG.). (J). 2020. 336p. pap. 7.99 *(978-1-5476-0253-7(8)*, 900210114) 2019. 304p. (gr. 3-6). E-Book 11.89 *(978-1-5476-0011-3(X))* 2019. 320p. 16.99 *(978-1-68119-959-7(9)*, 900194404) Bloomsbury Publishing USA. (Bloomsbury Children's Bks.).
Duff, Hilary. Devoted: An Elixir Novel. 2012. (Elixir Ser.). (ENG.). 368p. (YA). (gr. 9). pap. 9.99 *(978-1-4424-0856-2(1)*, Simon & Schuster Bks. For Young Readers) Simon & Schuster Bks. For Young Readers.
—Elixir. 2011. (Playaway Young Adult Ser.). (YA). 59.99 *(978-1-4417-7416-3(5))* Findaway World, LLC.
—Elixir. 2011. (Elixir Ser.). (ENG.). 336p. (YA). (gr. 9). pap. 12.99 *(978-1-4424-0854-8(5)*, Simon & Schuster Bks. For Young Readers) Simon & Schuster Bks. For Young Readers.
—True: An Elixir Novel. (Elixir Ser.). (ENG., 304p. (YA). (gr. 7). 2014. Illus.). pap. 12.99 *(978-1-4424-0858-6(8))* 2013. 17.99 *(978-1-4424-0857-9(X))* Simon & Schuster Bks. For Young Readers. (Simon & Schuster Bks. For Young Readers).
Duncan, Lois. Down a Dark Hall. 2011. (ENG.). 240p. (YA). (gr. 7-17). pap., pap. 13.99 *(978-0-316-09898-4(1))* Little, Brown Bks. for Young Readers.
—Down a Dark Hall. 181p. (YA). (gr. 7-18). pap. 4.99 *(978-0-8072-1370-4(5)*, Listening Library) Random Hse. Audio Publishing Group.
Dunning, John Harris & Singh, Nikhil. Salem Brownstone: All along the Watchtowers. Singh, Nikhil, illus. 2010. (ENG., Illus.). 96p. (YA). (gr. 7-18). 18.99 *(978-0-7636-4735-3(7))* Candlewick Pr.
Durst, Sarah Beth. Ice. 2010. (ENG.). 336p. (YA). (gr. 7). pap. 8.99 *(978-1-4169-8644-7(8)*, McElderry, Margaret K. Bks.) McElderry, Margaret K. Bks.
Edge, Christopher. Twelve Minutes to Midnight. 2014. (Penelope Tredwell Mysteries Ser.: 1). (ENG.). 256p. (J). (gr. 3-7). 16.99 *(978-0-8075-8133-9(X)*, 080758133X) Whitman, Albert & Co.
Eggers, Dave. The Lifters. (ENG., Illus.). 352p. (J). (gr. 3-7). 2019. pap. 9.99 *(978-1-5247-6419-7(1)*, Yearling) 2018. lib. bdg. 20.99 *(978-1-5247-6417-3(5)*, Knopf Bks. for Young Readers) Random Hse. Children's Bks.
Endless Knight. 2014. (Arcana Chronicles Ser.). (ENG., Illus.). 336p. (YA). (gr. 9). pap. 12.99 *(978-1-4424-3668-8(9)*, Simon & Schuster Bks. For Young Readers) Simon & Schuster Bks. For Young Readers.
Ernshaw, Shea. The Wicked Deep. (ENG.). (YA). (gr. 9). 2019. 336p. pap. 12.99 *(978-1-4814-9735-0(9))* 2018. (Illus.). 320p. 19.99 *(978-1-4814-9734-3(0))* Simon Pulse. (Simon Pulse).
Evans, Neil, illus. Spine Shivers. 2016. (Spine Shivers Ser.). (ENG.). 128p. (gr. 3-4). pap. 13.90 *(978-1-4965-3083-7(7)*, Stone Arch Bks.) Capstone.
Fallon, Leigh. Carrier of the Mark. 2011. (Carrier of the Mark Ser.: 1). (ENG.). 352p. (YA). (gr. 8). pap. 8.99 *(978-0-06-202787-0(5)*, HarperTeen) HarperCollins Pubs.
—Shadow of the Mark. 2013. (Carrier of the Mark Ser.: 2). (ENG.). 320p. (YA). (gr. 8). pap. 9.99 *(978-0-06-212800-3(0)*, HarperTeen) HarperCollins Pubs.
Fama, Elizabeth. Monstrous Beauty. 2013. (ENG.). 352p. (YA). (gr. 7-12). pap. 17.99 *(978-1-250-03425-0(6)*, 900120598) Square Fish.
Farley, Christina. Gilded. 0 vols. 2014. (Gilded Ser.: 1). (ENG.). 352p. (YA). (gr. 7-12). pap. 9.99 *(978-1-4778-1097-2(8)*, 9781477810972, Skyscape) Amazon Publishing.
Farley, Steven. And the Shape-Shifter. 2009. (Black Stallion Ser.). (ENG.). 272p. (J). (gr. 4-6). lib. bdg. 21.19 *(978-0-375-96531-9(9)*, Yearling) Random Hse. Children's Bks.
—The Black Stallion & the Shape-Shifter. 2010. (Black Stallion Ser.). (ENG.). 272p. (J). (gr. 3-7). 8.99 *(978-0-375-84532-1(1)*, Yearling) Random Hse. Children's Bks.
Feil, Hila. Blue Moon. 2007. (ENG., Illus.). 272p. (YA). (gr. 7). pap. 17.99 *(978-0-15-205933-0(4)*, 1197811, Clarion Bks.) HarperCollins Pubs.
Ferguson, Jo Ann. The Cabinet of Souls. 2016. lib. bdg. 17.20 *(978-0-606-38787-3(0))* Turtleback.
Fewer, Patrick W. Sammy the Snow Snake: A Halloween Haunting Yukon Style. 2009. 24p. pap. 11.49 *(978-1-4490-2075-0(5))* AuthorHouse.
Fitzpatrick, Becca. The Complete Hush, Hush Saga (Boxed Set) Hush, Hush; Crescendo; Silence; Finale. 2012. (Hush, Hush Saga Ser.: Bks. 1-4). (ENG.). 1744p. (YA). (gr. 9). 87.99 *(978-1-4424-7372-0(X)*, Simon & Schuster Bks. For Young Readers) Simon & Schuster Bks. For Young Readers.
—Crescendo. 2011. (Hush, Hush Saga: Bk. 2). (SPA.). 408p. (YA). pap. 20.95 *(978-84-666-4639-0(6))* Ediciones B ESP. Dist: Spanish Pubs., LLC.
—Crescendo. (Hush, Hush Saga Ser.: Bk. 2). (ENG.). (YA). (gr. 9). 2012. 464p. pap. 13.99 *(978-1-4169-8944-8(7))* 2010. 432p. 21.99 *(978-1-4169-8943-1(9))* Simon & Schuster Bks. For Young Readers. (Simon & Schuster Bks. For Young Readers).
—Crescendo (Spanish Edition) 2019. (Hush, Hush Ser.: 2). (SPA.). 408p. (J). (gr. 8-12). pap. 16.95 *(978-84-204-3424-7(8)*, Alfaguara) Penguin Random House Grupo Editorial ESP. Dist: Penguin Random Hse. LLC.
—Finale. (Hush, Hush Saga Ser.). (ENG., (YA). (gr. 9). 2013. Illus.). 480p. pap. 13.99 *(978-1-4424-2668-9(3))* 2012. 464p. 21.99 *(978-1-4424-2667-2(5))* Simon & Schuster Bks. For Young Readers. (Simon & Schuster Bks. For Young Readers).
—Hush, Hush. 2010. (Hush, Hush Saga: Bk. 1). (SPA.). 368p. (YA). pap. 20.95 *(978-84-666-4417-4(2))* Ediciones B ESP. Dist: Spanish Pubs., LLC.
—Hush, Hush. 3 vols. Ruiz, Derek, ed. 2012. (Hush, Hush Saga: Bk. 1). (Illus.). 120p. (YA). 19.95 *(978-0-9836131-1-4(7))* Sea Lion Bks.
—Hush, Hush. (Hush, Hush Saga Ser.: Bk. 1). (ENG.). (YA). (gr. 9-18). 2010. 432p. pap. 13.99 *(978-1-4169-8942-4(0))* 2009. 400p. 21.99 *(978-1-4169-8941-7(2))* Simon & Schuster Bks. For Young Readers. (Simon & Schuster Bks. For Young Readers).
—Silence. (Hush, Hush Saga Ser.: Bk. 3). (ENG.). (YA). (gr. 9). 2013. 464p. pap. 13.99 *(978-1-4424-2665-8(9))* 2011. 448p. 21.99 *(978-1-4424-2664-1(0))* Simon & Schuster Bks. For Young Readers. (Simon & Schuster Bks. For Young Readers).
Fletcher, Brenden. Yearbook. 2016. (Gotham Academy Ser.: 3). lib. bdg. 29.40 *(978-0-606-39222-8(X))* Turtleback.
Frost, Heather. Guardians. 2013. (Seers - Trilogy Ser.: Vol. 3). (ENG.). 424p. (J). (gr. 8-12). pap. 17.99 *(978-1-4621-1035-3(5)*, Sweetwater Bks.) Cedar Fort, Inc./CFI Distribution.
G. Nadel, H. Eternal. l.t. ed. 2013. 194p. pap. *(978-1-4596-6748-8(4))* ReadHowYouWant.com, Ltd.
Gaiman, Neil. Coraline. 2003. (FRE.). (J). (gr. 5-8). pap. *(978-2-226-14019-7(0))* Albin-Michel, Editions.
—Coraline. 3rd ed. 2003. (SPA., Illus.). 160p. *(978-84-7888-579-4(X)*, 1952) Emece Editores.
—Coraline. (ENG.). 2021. 176p. pap. 18.99 *(978-0-06-308823-8(1))* 2006. (Illus.). 192p. (gr. 6-8). pap. 13.99 *(978-0-06-113937-6(8))* HarperCollins Pubs. (William Morrow Paperbacks).
—Coraline. McKean, Dave, illus. 2004. (ENG.). 224p. (J). (gr. 3-7). pap. 9.99 *(978-0-06-057591-5(3)*, HarperCollins) HarperCollins Pubs.
—Coraline, 12 Copies. 2003. (J). pap. 71.88 *(978-0-06-057152-8(7))*; pap. 71.88 *(978-0-06-056895-5(X))* HarperCollins Pubs.
—Coraline. McKean, Dave, illus. movie tie-in ed. 2008. (ENG.). 176p. (J). (gr. 3). pap. 6.99 *(978-0-06-164969-1(4)*, HarperFestival) HarperCollins Pubs.
—Coraline. 2019. (ENG.). 176p. lib. bdg. 29.40 *(978-1-6636-3455-9(6))* 2003. 162p. (gr. 7-9). 17.00 *(978-0-7569-1568-1(6))* Perfection Learning Corp.
—Coraline, Vol. 1. 2009. (SPA.). 188p. (YA). 20.95 *(978-84-92429-74-5(7))* Roca Editorial ESP. Dist: Spanish Pubs., LLC.
—Coraline. McKean, Dave, illus. 2007. 151p. (J). (gr. 6-8). 60.00 *(978-1-59606-147-7(2))* Subterranean Pr.
—Coraline. 2012. (J). (gr. 5-8). lib. bdg. 18.40 *(978-0-613-67322-8(0))* Turtleback.
—Coraline: Reading Group Guide. McKean, Dave, illus. *(978-0-06-056878-8(X))* HarperCollins Pubs.
—Coraline 10th Anniversary Edition. McKean, Dave, illus. 10th anniv. ed. 2012. (ENG.). 208p. (J). (gr. 3-7). pap. 9.99 *(978-0-380-80734-5(3)*, HarperCollins) HarperCollins Pubs.
—Coraline (Spanish Edition) 2009. (SPA.). 160p. (J). (gr. 3-7). pap. 12.95 *(978-84-9838-237-2(8))* Publicaciones y Ediciones Salamandra, S.A. ESP. Dist: Penguin Random Hse. LLC.
—The Graveyard Book. 2009. (CHI.). 304p. (J). (gr. 5-8). pap. *(978-957-33-2574-1(8))* Crown Publishing Co., Ltd.
—The Graveyard Book. McKean, Dave, illus. (J). 2018. (ENG.). 368p. (gr. 5). pap. 10.99 *(978-0-06-053094-5(4)*, HarperCollins) 2008. 552p. pap. 17.99 *(978-0-06-170912-8(3))* 2008. (ENG.). 368p. (gr. 5-7). 17.99 *(978-0-06-053092-1(8)*, HarperCollins) 2008. (ENG.). 320p. (gr. 5-7). lib. bdg. 18.89 *(978-0-06-053093-8(6)*, HarperCollins) HarperCollins Pubs.
—The Graveyard Book. 2009. 19.00 *(978-1-60686-823-2(3))* Perfection Learning Corp.
—The Graveyard Book. 2011. (Literature Kit Ser.). (ENG., Illus.). 55p. pap. 12.95 *(978-1-55319-559-7(0)*, Classroom Complete Pr.) Rainbow Horizons Publishing, Inc.
—The Graveyard Book, 7 vols. 2008. (J). 256.75 *(978-1-4361-5882-4(6))*; 100.75 *(978-1-4361-5887-9(7)*, Recorded Bks., Inc.
—The Graveyard Book. l.t. ed. 2009. (ENG.). 373p. (YA). 23.95 *(978-1-4104-1441-0(8))* Thorndike Pr.
—The Graveyard Book. 2010. (J). lib. bdg. 19.65 *(978-0-606-14883-2(3))* Turtleback.
—The Graveyard Book Commemorative Edition. McKean, Dave, illus. 2014. (ENG.). 352p. (J). (gr. 5-7). pap. 9.99 *(978-0-06-234918-7(X)*, HarperCollins) HarperCollins Pubs.
Gaiman, Neil & Russell, P. Craig. The Graveyard Book Graphic Novel: Volume 1, Vol. 1. Russell, P. Craig, illus. 2014. (ENG., Illus.). 192p. (J). (gr. 3-7). 19.99 *(978-0-06-219481-7(X)*, Quill Tree Bks.) HarperCollins Pubs.
—The Graveyard Book Graphic Novel: Volume 2, Vol. 2. Russell, P. Craig, illus. 2014. (ENG., Illus.). 176p. (J). (gr. 3-7). 19.99 *(978-0-06-219483-1(6)*, Quill Tree Bks.) HarperCollins Pubs.
Garcia, Kami & Stohl, Margaret. Beautiful Chaos. 2012. (Beautiful Creatures Ser.: 3). (ENG.). 528p. (YA). (gr. 7-17). pap. 16.99 *(978-0-316-12351-8(X))* Little, Brown Bks. for Young Readers.
—Beautiful Creatures. 2010. (Beautiful Creatures Ser.: 1). (ENG.). 592p. (YA). (gr. 7-17). pap. 16.99 *(978-0-316-07703-3(8))* Little, Brown Bks. for Young Readers.
Garcia, Kami & Stohl, Margaret. Beautiful Creatures. 2010. (Beautiful Creatures Ser.: 1). (YA). lib. bdg. 23.30 *(978-0-606-26699-4(2))* Turtleback.
Garcia, Kami & Stohl, Margaret. The Beautiful Creatures Complete Paperback Collection. 2013. (Beautiful Creatures Ser.: Bks. 1-4). (ENG.). 2272p. (YA). (gr. 7-17). pap. 64.00 *(978-0-316-25090-0(2))* Little, Brown Bks. for Young Readers.
García, Kami & Stohl, Margaret. Beautiful Darkness. 2010. (Beautiful Creatures Ser.: Bk. 2). (YA). 59.99 *(978-1-60941-036-0(X))* Findaway World, LLC.
—Beautiful Darkness. 2010. (Beautiful Creatures Ser.: Bk. 2). 512p. pap. 17.99 *(978-0-316-09861-8(2))* Little, Brown Bks. for Young Readers.
Garcia, Kami & Stohl, Margaret. Beautiful Darkness. 2011. (Beautiful Creatures Ser.: 2). (ENG.). 528p. (YA). (gr. 7-17) pap. 15.99 *(978-0-316-07704-0(6))* Little, Brown Bks. for Young Readers.
Garcia, Kami & Stohl, Margaret. Beautiful Darkness. 2011. (Beautiful Creatures Ser.: 2). (YA). lib. bdg. 24.50 *(978-0-606-26700-7(X))* Turtleback.
—Beautiful Redemption. 2012. (Beautiful Creatures Ser.: Bk. 4). (ENG.). 576p. (YA). (gr. 7-17). pap. 9.99 *(978-0-316-22519-9(3))* Little, Brown Bks. for Young Readers.
Garcia, Kami & Stohl, Margaret. Beautiful Redemption. 2013. (Beautiful Creatures Ser.: 4). (ENG.). 496p. (YA). (gr. 7-17). pap. 15.99 *(978-0-316-12356-3(0))* Little, Brown Bks. for Young Readers.
Garcia, Kami & Stohl, Margaret. Beautiful Redemption. 2013. (Beautiful Creatures Ser.: 4). (YA). lib. bdg. 24.50 *(978-0-606-32282-9(5))* Turtleback.
—Dangerous Creatures. 2014. 327p. (YA). *(978-0-316-37626-6(4))* Little, Brown Bks. for Young Readers.
Garcia, Kami & Stohl, Margaret. Dangerous Creatures. 2015. (ENG.). 400p. (J). (gr. 7-17). pap. 19.99 *(978-0-316-37032-5(0))* Little, Brown Bks. for Young Readers.
Garcia McCall, Guadalupe. Summer of the Mariposas. 2012. (ENG.). 352p. (YA). 19.95 *(978-1-60060-900-8(7)*, Tu Bks.) Lee & Low Bks., Inc.
Gates, J. Gabriel & Keel, Charlene. Ghost Crown. 2012. (Tracks Ser.). (ENG.). 456p. (YA). (gr. 6-12). pap. 9.95 *(978-0-7573-1594-7(1)*, HCI Teens) Health Communications, Inc.
Geragotelis, Brittany. Life's a Witch. 2013. (Life's a Witch Ser.). (ENG., Illus.). 320p. (YA). (gr. 9). 16.99 *(978-1-4424-6655-5(3)*, Simon & Schuster Bks. For Young Readers) Simon & Schuster Bks. For Young Readers.
Germano, Yveta. Bring Me Back. 2013. 298p. 27.99 *(978-1-938516-75-7(3))*; 318p. pap. 13.99 *(978-1-938516-17-7(6))* Midnight Hologram, LLC.
Ghost, Derek The. Scary School. Fischer, Scott M., illus. (Scary School Ser.: 1). (ENG.). (J). (gr. 3-7). 2012. 272p. pap. 6.99 *(978-0-06-196094-9(2))* 2011. 256p. 16.99 *(978-0-06-196092-5(6))* HarperCollins Pubs. (HarperCollins).
—Scary School #2: Monsters on the March. Fischer, Scott M., illus. 2013. (Scary School Ser.: 2). (ENG.). 272p. (J). (gr. 3-7). pap. 6.99 *(978-0-06-196097-0(7)*, HarperCollins) HarperCollins Pubs.
—Scary School #3: the Northern Frights. Fischer, Scott M., illus. 2013. (Scary School Ser.: 3). (ENG.). 272p. (J). (gr. 3-7). 16.99 *(978-0-06-196098-7(5)*, HarperCollins) HarperCollins Pubs.
Giles, Lamar. The Last Last-Day-Of-Summer. Adeola, Dapo, illus. 2019. (Legendary Alston Boys Adventure Ser.). (ENG.). 304p. (J). (gr. 3-7). 17.99 *(978-1-328-46083-7(5)*, 1712835, Versify) HarperCollins Pubs.
Gleason, Colleen. The Spiritglass Charade: A Stoker & Holmes Novel. 2014. (Stoker & Holmes Ser.: 2). (ENG., Illus.). 360p. (YA). (gr. 7-12). 17.99 *(978-1-4521-1071-4(9))* Chronicle Bks. LLC.
Golden, Christopher & Lebbon, Tim. The Sea Wolves Bk. 2, Bk. 2. Ruth, Greg, illus. 2012. (Secret Journeys of Jack London Ser.: 2). (ENG.). 400p. (YA). (gr. 8). 16.99 *(978-0-06-186320-2(3)*, HarperTeen) HarperCollins Pubs.
—The Wild. Ruth, Greg, illus. 2011. (Secret Journeys of Jack London Ser.: 1). (ENG.). 368p. (YA). (gr. 5-18). 15.99 *(978-0-06-186317-2(3)*, HarperTeen) HarperCollins Pubs.
Golding, Julia. The Chimera's Curse, 0 vols. 2013. (Companions Quartet Ser.: 4). (ENG.). 320p. (J). (gr. 4-8). pap. 9.99 *(978-0-7614-5726-8(7)*, 9780761457268, Two Lions) Amazon Publishing.
—The Gorgon's Gaze, 0 vols., Bk. 2. 2013. (Companions Quartet Ser.: 2). (ENG.). 320p. (J). (gr. 4-8). pap. 9.99 *(978-0-7614-5653-7(8)*, 9780761456537, Two Lions) Amazon Publishing.
—Mines of the Minotaur, 0 vols., Bk. 3. unabr. ed. 2013. (Companions Quartet Ser.: 3). (ENG., Illus.). 288p. (J). (gr. 4-6). pap. 9.99 *(978-0-7614-5796-1(8)*, 9780761457961, Two Lions) Amazon Publishing.
—Secret of the Sirens, 0 vols. 2012. (Companions Quartet Ser.: 1). (ENG.). 368p. (J). (gr. 4-8). pap. 9.99 *(978-0-7614-5617-9(1)*, 9780761456179, Two Lions) Amazon Publishing.
Grant, Donna. Hungrige Begierde. 2014.Tr. of The Hunger. (GER.). pap. 5.99 *(978-1-942017-15-8(4))* DL Grant, LLC.
Grant, Michael. Gone. (Gone Ser.: 1). (Illus.). 576p. 2014. (ENG.). (YA). (gr. 8). pap. 15.99 *(978-0-06-144878-2(8)*, Tegen, Katherine Bks) 2008. (J). (gr. 7-18). lib. bdg. 18.89 *(978-0-06-144877-5(X)*, HarperTeen) 2008. (ENG., (YA). (gr. 8-18). 19.99 *(978-0-06-144876-8(1)*, Tegen, Katherine Bks) HarperCollins Pubs.
—Hunger. (Gone Ser.: 2). (ENG., Illus.). 608p. (YA). (gr. 8-18). 2014. pap. 12.99 *(978-0-06-144908-6(3))* 2009. 18.99 *(978-0-06-144906-2(7))* HarperCollins Pubs. (Tegen, Katherine Bks).
—Lies. (Gone Ser.: 3). (ENG., Illus.). 464p. (YA). (gr. 8). 2014. pap. 11.99 *(978-0-06-144911-6(3))* 2010. 17.99 *(978-0-06-144909-3(1))* HarperCollins Pubs. (Tegen, Katherine Bks).
—Light. 2013. (Gone Ser.: 6). (ENG., Illus.). 432p. (YA). (gr. 9). 18.99 *(978-0-06-144918-5(0)*, Tegen, Katherine Bks) HarperCollins Pubs.
—Messenger of Fear. 2014. (Messenger of Fear Ser.: 1). (ENG.). 272p. (YA). (gr. 9). 17.99 *(978-0-06-220740-1(7)*, Tegen, Katherine Bks) HarperCollins Pubs.
—Plague. (Gone Ser.: 4). (ENG.). (YA). (gr. 8). 2014. 528p. pap. 12.99 *(978-0-06-144914-7(8))* 2011. 512p. 17.99 *(978-0-06-144912-3(1))* HarperCollins Pubs. (Tegen, Katherine Bks).
—The Tattooed Heart. 2015. (Messenger of Fear Ser.: 2). (ENG.). 400p. (YA). (gr. 9). 17.99 *(978-0-06-220743-2(1)*, Tegen, Katherine Bks) HarperCollins Pubs.
Gratton, Tessa. Blood Magic. 2012. (Blood Journals). (ENG.). 416p. (YA). (gr. 8-12). lib. bdg. 26.19 *(978-0-375-96733-7(8))* Random House Publishing Group.
—Blood Magic. 2011. 408p. (YA). pap. *(978-0-375-86486-5(5))* Random Hse. Children's Bks.
Gratton, Tessa, et al. The Curiosities: A Collection of Stories. 2014. (ENG.). 304p. (YA). (gr. 7-12). pap. 11.95 *(978-1-4677-1623-9(5)*, fc308abd-51e8-46a0-b22d-eb5831170362, Carolrhoda Lab™) Lerner Publishing Group.
Gray, Claudia. Fateful. 2012. (ENG.). 352p. (YA). (gr. 9). pap. 9.99 *(978-0-06-200621-9(5)*, HarperTeen) HarperCollins Pubs.
—Sorceress. 2016. (Spellcaster Ser.: 3). (ENG.). 368p. (YA). (gr. 8). pap. 9.99 *(978-0-06-196125-0(6)*, HarperTeen) HarperCollins Pubs.
Green, Dawn A. Marianne Wellman's School for Girls. 2011. 236p. pap. 24.95 *(978-1-4626-0715-0(2))* America Star Bks.
Greenfield, Amy Butler. Chantress Alchemy. 2015. (Chantress Ser.). (ENG., Illus.). 368p. (YA). (gr. 7). pap. 10.99 *(978-1-4424-5708-9(2)*, McElderry, Margaret K. Bks.) McElderry, Margaret K. Bks.
Gregory, Philippa. Changeling, 10 vols. 2012. (Order of Darkness Ser.). (YA). 92.75 *(978-1-4640-4583-7(6))*; 90.75 *(978-1-4640-4587-5(9))*; 90.75 *(978-1-4640-4586-8(0))*; 265.75 *(978-1-4640-4584-4(4))* Recorded Bks., Inc.
—Changeling. van Deelen, Fred & Taylor, Sally, illus. (Order of Darkness Ser.: 1). (ENG.). (YA). (gr. 9). 2013. 352p. pap. 9.99 *(978-1-4424-5345-6(1))* 2012. 272p. 18.99 *(978-1-4424-5344-9(3))* Simon Pulse. (Simon Pulse).
—Fools' Gold. van Deelen, Fred, illus. 2014. (Order of Darkness Ser.: 3). (ENG.). 384p. (YA). (gr. 9). 19.99 *(978-1-4424-7690-5(7)*, Simon Pulse) Simon Pulse.
—Stormbringers. van Deelen, Fred, illus. 2013. (Order of Darkness Ser.: 2). (ENG.). 336p. (YA). (gr. 9). pap. 9.99 *(978-1-4424-7688-2(5))*; 17.99 *(978-1-4424-7687-5(7))* Simon Pulse. (Simon Pulse).
Griswold-Ford, Valerie. Last Rites. 2013. 322p. pap. *(978-1-897492-66-6(9))* Dragon Moon Pr.
Guterson, Ben. The Secrets of Winterhouse. Bristol, Chloe, illus. 2019. (Winterhouse Ser.: 2). (ENG.). 400p. (J). pap. 9.99 *(978-1-250-23352-3(6)*, 900174324) Square Fish.
—Winterhouse. Bristol, Chloe, illus. 2018. (Winterhouse Ser.: 1). (ENG.). 400p. (J). pap. 8.99 *(978-1-250-29419-7(3)*, 900174321) Square Fish.
Gutman, Dan. Houdini & Me. 2021. (ENG., Illus.). 224p. (J). (gr. 3-7). 16.99 *(978-0-8234-4515-8(1))* Holiday Hse., Inc.
Haddix, Margaret Peterson. Greystone Secrets #1: the Strangers. Lambelet, Anne, illus. (Greystone Secrets Ser.: 1). (ENG.). (J). (gr. 3-7). 2020. 432p. pap. 9.99 *(978-0-06-283838-4(5))* 2019. 416p. 17.99 *(978-0-06-283837-7(7))* 2019. 432p. E-Book *(978-0-06-283839-1(3)*, 9780062838391) HarperCollins Pubs. (Tegen, Katherine Bks).
—Greystone Secrets #2: the Deceivers. (Greystone Secrets Ser.: 2). (ENG.). (J). (gr. 3-7). 2021. 464p. pap. 10.99 *(978-0-06-283841-4(5))* 2020. (Illus.). 448p. 17.99 *(978-0-06-283840-7(7))* HarperCollins Pubs. (Tegen, Katherine Bks).
Hammond, Andrew. Crypt 2: Traitor's Revenge. 2012. (ENG.). 352p. (YA). (gr. 7-17). pap. 8.99 *(978-0-7553-7822-7(9))* Headline Publishing Group GBR. Dist: Hachette Bk. Group.
—Crypt 3: Mask of Death. 2012. (ENG.). 352p. (YA). (gr. 7-17). pap. 8.99 *(978-0-7553-7823-4(7))* Headline Publishing Group GBR. Dist: Hachette Bk. Group.
—CRYPT: Guardians' Reckoning: Book 5. 2014. (ENG.). 368p. (YA). (gr. 7-12). pap. 8.99 *(978-0-7553-7825-8(3))* Headline Publishing Group GBR. Dist: Hachette Bk. Group.
Hand, Cynthia. Boundless. 2013. (Unearthly Ser.: 3). (ENG.). 448p. (YA). (gr. 8). pap. 9.99 *(978-0-06-199621-4(1)*, HarperTeen) HarperCollins Pubs.
—Hallowed: An Unearthly Novel. 2012. (Unearthly Ser.: 2). (ENG.). 432p. (YA). (gr. 8). pap. 10.99 *(978-0-06-199619-1(X)*, HarperTeen) HarperCollins Pubs.
—Unearthly. 2011. (Unearthly Ser.: 1). (ENG.). 464p. (YA). (gr. 8). pap. 9.99 *(978-0-06-199617-7(3)*, HarperTeen) HarperCollins Pubs.
Hand, Cynthia, et al. My Plain Jane. (Lady Janies Ser.). (ENG.). (YA). (gr. 8). 2019. 480p. pap. 10.99 *(978-0-06-265278-2(8))* 2018. 464p. 17.99 *(978-0-06-265277-5(X))* HarperCollins Pubs. (HarperTeen).

S

Hanlon, Jennifer. A Shadow's Tale. 2014. (ENG., Illus.). 274p. (J). (gr. -1-12). pap. 12.95 *(978-1-78279-136-2(1),* Our Street Bks.) Hunt, John Publishing Ltd. GBR. Dist: National Bk. Network.

Hardinge, Frances. Cuckoo Song. 2016. (ENG.). 432p. (YA). (gr. 8-17). pap. 12.99 *(978-1-4197-1939-4(4),* 1096603, Amulet Bks.) Abrams, Inc.

—Cuckoo Song. 2016. lib. bdg. 20.80 *(978-0-606-38211-3(9))* Turtleback.

Harold & I. 2007. (ENG., Illus.). 291p. (J). (gr. 3-8). per. 13.99 *(978-0-7684-2432-4(1))* Send The Light Distribution LLC.

Harrison, Kim, pseud. Early to Death, Early to Rise. 2011. (Madison Avery Ser.: 2). (ENG., Illus.). 256p. (YA). (gr. 9). pap. 8.99 *(978-0-06-144169-1(4),* HarperCollins) HarperCollins Pubs.

—Once Dead, Twice Shy. 2009. (Madison Avery Ser.: Bk. 1). 240p. (YA). lib. bdg. 17.89 *(978-0-06-171820-5(3));* (gr. 9-18). 16.99 *(978-0-06-171816-8(5))* HarperCollins Pubs. (HarperTeen).

—Once Dead, Twice Shy: A Novel. 2010. (Madison Avery Ser.: 1). (ENG.). 256p. (YA). (gr. 8). pap. 8.99 *(978-0-06-144168-4(6),* HarperCollins) HarperCollins Pubs.

Harrold, A. F. The Afterwards. Gravett, Emily, illus. 2019. (ENG.). 208p. (J). 17.99 *(978-1-5476-0044-1(6),* 900196151, Bloomsbury Children's Bks.) Bloomsbury Publishing USA.

—The Imaginary. Gravett, Emily, illus. 2015. (ENG.). 240p. (J). (gr. 3-6). 16.99 *(978-0-8027-3811-0(7),* 900141005, Bloomsbury USA Childrens) Bloomsbury Publishing USA.

—The Song from Somewhere Else. Pinfold, Levi, illus. 2017. (ENG.). 240p. (J). 16.99 *(978-1-68119-401-1(5),* 900172517, Bloomsbury USA Childrens) Bloomsbury Publishing USA.

—The Song from Somewhere Else. 2018. (J). lib. bdg. 19.65 *(978-0-606-41074-8(0))* Turtleback.

Hautman, Pete. The Cydonian Pyramid. 2014. (Klaatu Diskos Ser.: 2). (ENG.). 368p. (YA). (gr. 7). pap. 8.99 *(978-0-7636-6933-1(4))* Candlewick Pr.

Havard, Amanda. The Survivors. 2011. (ENG.). (YA). 294p. 21.99 *(978-0-9833190-0-9(6));* 300p. pap. 11.99 *(978-0-9833190-2-3(2))* Chafie Pr., LLC.

Hawkins, Rachel. Demonglass, 2. 2012. (Hex Hall Novel Ser.: 2). (ENG.). 384p. (J). (gr. 5-9). pap. 8.99 *(978-1-4231-2844-1(3))* Hyperion Bks. for Children.

—Spell Bound, 3. 2013. (Hex Hall Novel Ser.: 3). (ENG.). 352p. (J). (gr. 7-17). pap. 10.99 *(978-1-4231-2140-4(6))* Hyperion Bks. for Children.

Hawthorne, Rachel. Dark Guardian #4: Shadow of the Moon. 2010. (Dark Guardian Ser.: 4). (ENG.). 256p. (YA). (gr. 9-18). pap. 8.99 *(978-0-06-196290-5(2),* HarperTeen) HarperCollins Pubs.

Hayes, Gwen. Dreaming Awake. 2012. (Falling under Novel Ser.). (ENG.). 336p. (YA). (gr. 7-18). 9.99 *(978-0-451-23554-1(1),* Berkley) Penguin Publishing Group.

—Falling Under. 2011. (Falling under Novel Ser.: 1). (ENG.). 336p. (YA). (gr. 7-18). 9.99 *(978-0-451-23268-7(2),* Berkley) Penguin Publishing Group.

Haynes, Gibby. Me & Mr. Cigar. Haynes, Gibby, illus. 2020. (ENG., Illus.). 256p. (YA). (gr. 9). 18.99 *(978-1-61695-812-1(X),* Soho Teen) Soho Pr., Inc.

Healey, Karen. The Shattering. 2013. (ENG.). 336p. (YA). (gr. 7-17). pap. 8.99 *(978-0-316-12573-4(3))* Little, Brown Bks. for Young Readers.

Hearn, Julie. The Minister's Daughter. 2006. (ENG.). 272p. (YA). (gr. 7-12). pap. 7.99 *(978-0-689-87691-2(2),* Atheneum Bks. for Young Readers) Simon & Schuster Children's Publishing.

Helget, Nicole. Wonder at the Edge of the World. 2015. (ENG., Illus.). 384p. (J). (gr. 3-7). 17.00 *(978-0-316-24510-4(0))* Little, Brown Bks. for Young Readers.

Henderson, Jason. Alex Van Helsing: The Triumph of Death. 2012. (Alex Van Helsing Ser.: 3). (ENG.). 320p. (YA). (gr. 8). 17.99 *(978-0-06-195103-9(X),* HarperTeen) HarperCollins Pubs.

—Alex Van Helsing: Vampire Rising. (Alex Van Helsing Ser.: 1). (ENG.). (YA). (gr. 8). 2011. 272p. pap. 8.99 *(978-0-06-195100-8(5))* 2010. 256p. 16.99 *(978-0-06-195099-5(8))* HarperCollins Pubs. (HarperTeen).

Henry, April. The Lonely Dead. 2020. (ENG.). 240p. (YA). pap. 14.99 *(978-1-250-23376-9(3),* 900185223) Square Fish.

Henry, Pam. Cold Call. 2011. 200p. pap. *(978-1-84903-065-6(0))* Schiel & Denver Publishing Ltd.

Hensley, Nathaniel. The Strange Tale of Hector & Hannah Crowe. 2015. (ENG.). 222p. (J). (gr. 8-18). 13.95 *(978-1-937240-49-3(5))* Casa de Snapdragon LLC.

Hibbs, Sasha. Black Amaranth. 2013. 286p. pap. *(978-1-77130-526-6(6))* Evernight Publishing.

Higgins, Simon. Moonshadow: the Nightmare Ninja. 2012. (Moonshadow Ser.: 2). (ENG.). 384p. (J). (gr. 3-7). pap. 19.99 *(978-0-316-05534-5(4))* Little, Brown Bks. for Young Readers.

Hightman, J. P. Spirit. 2008. 224p. (gr. 7-18). (ENG.). (J). 16.99 *(978-0-06-085063-0(9));* (YA). lib. bdg. 17.89 *(978-0-06-085064-7(7))* HarperCollins Pubs. (HarperTeen).

Hill, Will. Department 19: First Edition, 1. 2012. (Department Nineteen Ser.: 1). (ENG.). 544p. (YA). (gr. 9-12). pap. 9.99 *(978-1-59514-485-0(4),* Razorbill) Penguin Young Readers Group.

Hirsch, Alex. Gravity Falls:: Journal 3. 2016. (ENG., Illus.). 288p. (J). (gr. 3-7). 19.99 *(978-1-4847-4669-1(4),* Disney Press Books) Disney Publishing Worldwide.

—Gravity Falls:: Lost Legends: 4 All-New Adventures! 2018. (ENG., Illus.). 144p. (J). (gr. 3-7). 19.99 *(978-1-368-02142-5(5),* Disney Press Books) Disney Publishing Worldwide.

Hite, Kenneth. Where the Deep Ones Are. 2009. 32p. 19.95 *(978-1-58978-103-0(1),* Atlas Games) Trident, Inc.

Hoban, Russell. A Birthday for Frances. Hoban, Lillian, illus. 2012. (I Can Read Level 2 Ser.). (ENG.). 48p. (J). (gr. k-3). pap. 4.99 *(978-0-06-083797-6(7),* HarperCollins) HarperCollins Pubs.

Hocking, Amanda. Ascend. l.t. ed. 2012. (Trylle Trilogy: Bk. 3). (ENG.). 412p. (J). (gr. 8-12). 23.99 *(978-1-4104-5014-2(7))* Thorndike Pr.

—Ascend: A Trylle Novel. 2012. (Trylle Novel Ser.: 3). (ENG.). 336p. (YA). (gr. 7). pap. 13.99 *(978-1-250-00633-2(3),* 900081191, St. Martin's Griffin) St. Martin's Pr.

—Switched, 1. 2012. (Trylle Novel Ser.: 1). (ENG.). 336p. (YA). (gr. 9-12). pap. 13.99 *(978-1-250-00631-8(7),* 900081189, St. Martin's Griffin) St. Martin's Pr.

—Switched. l.t. ed. 2012. (Trylle Trilogy: Bk. 1). (ENG.). 408p. (gr. 7-12). 23.99 *(978-1-4104-4865-1(7))* Thorndike Pr.

—Tidal. 2014. (Watersong Novel Ser.: 3). (ENG.). 352p. (YA). (gr. 7). pap. 25.99 *(978-1-250-00566-3(3),* 900080970, St. Martin's Griffin) St. Martin's Pr.

—Torn. 2012. (Trylle Novel Ser.: 2). (ENG.). 336p. (YA). (gr. 7-12). pap. 20.00 *(978-1-250-00632-5(5),* 900081190, St. Martin's Griffin) St. Martin's Pr.

—Torn. l.t. ed. 2012. (Trylle Trilogy: Bk. 2). (ENG.). 450p. (J). (gr. 7-12). 23.99 *(978-1-4104-5013-5(9))* Thorndike Pr.

—Wake. 2013. (Watersong Novel Ser.: 1). (ENG.). 320p. (YA). (gr. 7). pap. 23.99 *(978-1-250-00564-9(7),* 900080965, St. Martin's Griffin);1. (gr. 8-12). 26.19 *(978-1-250-00812-1(3),* 9781250008121) St. Martin's Pr.

Hodkin, Michelle. The Becoming of Noah Shaw. (Shaw Confessions Ser.: 1). (ENG.). (YA). (gr. 9). 2018. 400p. pap. 12.99 *(978-1-4814-5644-9(X))* 2017. (Illus.). 384p. 18.99 *(978-1-4814-5643-2(1))* Simon & Schuster Bks. For Young Readers. (Simon & Schuster Bks. For Young Readers).

—The Evolution of Mara Dyer. (Mara Dyer Trilogy Ser.: 2). (ENG., Illus.). (YA). (gr. 9). 2013. 560p. pap. 14.99 *(978-1-4424-2180-6(0))* 2012. 544p. 19.99 *(978-1-4424-2179-0(7))* Simon & Schuster Bks. For Young Readers. (Simon & Schuster Bks. For Young Readers).

—The Reckoning of Noah Shaw. 2018. (Shaw Confessions Ser.: 2). (ENG., Illus.). 400p. (YA). (gr. 9). 19.99 *(978-1-4814-5646-3(6),* Simon & Schuster Bks. For Young Readers) Simon & Schuster Bks. For Young Readers.

—The Retribution of Mara Dyer. 2014. (Mara Dyer Trilogy Ser.: 3). (ENG., Illus.). 480p. (YA). (gr. 9). 18.99 *(978-1-4424-8423-8(3),* Simon & Schuster Bks. For Young Readers) Simon & Schuster Bks. For Young Readers.

—The Unbecoming of Mara Dyer. (Mara Dyer Trilogy Ser.: 1). (ENG., Illus.). (YA). (gr. 9). 2012. 480p. pap. 14.99 *(978-1-4424-2177-6(0))* 2011. 464p. 24.99 *(978-1-4424-2176-9(2))* Simon & Schuster Bks. For Young Readers. (Simon & Schuster Bks. For Young Readers).

Hoffmann, Alice. Nightbird. 2016. lib. bdg. 18.40 *(978-0-606-38451-3(0))* Turtleback.

Hogan, Edward. Daylight Saving. 2012. (ENG., Illus.). 224p. (YA). (gr. 7). 16.99 *(978-0-7636-5913-4(4))* Candlewick Pr.

Holder, Nancy & Viguie, Debbie. Unleashed. 2012. (Wolf Spring Chronicles Ser.: 1). (ENG.). 400p. (YA). (gr. 7). pap. 9.99 *(978-0-385-74099-9(9),* Ember) Random Hse. Children's Bks.

Holder, Nancy, et al. Crusade. (Crusade Ser.). (ENG.). (YA). (gr. 9). 2011. 496p. pap. 9.99 *(978-1-4169-9803-7(9))* 2010. 480p. 16.99 *(978-1-4169-9802-0(0))* Simon Pulse. (Simon Pulse).

—Damned. 2011. (Crusade Ser.). (ENG.). 544p. (YA). (gr. 9). pap. 9.99 *(978-1-4169-9805-1(5),* Simon Pulse) Simon Pulse.

—Vanquished. 2012. (Crusade Ser.). (ENG.). 496p. (YA). (gr. 9). 16.99 *(978-1-4169-9806-8(3));* pap. 9.99 *(978-1-4169-9807-5(1))* Simon Pulse. (Simon Pulse).

Holt, Catherine. Midnight Reynolds & the Agency of Spectral Protection. 2018. (Midnight Reynolds Ser.: 2). (ENG.). 264p. (J). (gr. 3-7). 14.99 *(978-0-8075-5128-8(7),* 807551287) Whitman, Albert & Co.

—Midnight Reynolds & the Phantom Circus. 2019. (Midnight Reynolds Ser.: 3). 272p. (J). (gr. 3-6). pap. 9.99 *(978-0-8075-5132-5(5),* 807551325) Whitman, Albert & Co.

—Midnight Reynolds & the Spectral Transformer. 2017. (Midnight Reynolds Ser.: 1). 272p. (J). (gr. 3-7). (ENG.). 14.99 *(978-0-8075-5125-7(2),* 807551252); pap. 9.99 *(978-0-8075-5126-4(0),* 807551260) Whitman, Albert & Co.

Holt, Simon. Soulstice, 2. 2009. (Devouring Ser.). (ENG.). 288p. (YA). (gr. 7-12). 22.44 *(978-0-316-03571-2(8))* Little Brown & Co.

—Soulstice. 2010. (Devouring Ser.: 2). (ENG.). 288p. (J). (gr. 7-17). pap. 15.99 *(978-0-316-03574-3(2))* Little, Brown Bks. for Young Readers.

Holub, Joan & Williams, Suzanne. Cassandra the Lucky. 2013. (Goddess Girls Ser.: 12). (ENG., Illus.). 256p. (J). (gr. 3-7). 16.99 *(978-1-4424-8818-2(2));* pap. 7.99 *(978-1-4424-8817-5(4))* Simon & Schuster Children's Publishing. (Aladdin).

Hopkinson, Nalo. The Chaos. (ENG., 256p. (YA). (gr. 9). 2013. Illus.). pap. 11.99 *(978-1-4424-5926-7(3))* 2012. 16.99 *(978-1-4169-5488-0(0))* McElderry, Margaret K. Bks. (McElderry, Margaret K. Bks.).

Horning, Mandy Cha'rae. The Defenders: Rise of the Perfected. 2012. 118p. (gr. 10-12). 23.99 *(978-1-4772-5327-4(0));* pap. 14.95 *(978-1-4772-5328-1(9))* AuthorHouse.

Horowitz, Anthony. Return to Groosham Grange: The Unholy Grail. 2010. (ENG.). 224p. (J). (gr. 5-18). 7.99 *(978-0-14-241571-9(5),* Puffin Books) Penguin Young Readers Group.

—The Switch. 2010. (ENG.). 192p. (J). (gr. 5-18). 7.99 *(978-0-14-241547-4(2),* Puffin Books) Penguin Young Readers Group.

Horvath, Polly. Very Rich. 2018. 304p. (J). (gr. 3-7). 17.99 *(978-0-8234-4028-3(1),* Margaret Ferguson Books) Holiday Hse., Inc.

Houck, Colleen. Recreated. 2017. (Reawakened Ser.: 2). (ENG.). 416p. (YA). (gr. 9). pap. 14.99 *(978-0-385-37663-1(4),* Ember) Random Hse. Children's Bks.

—Reunited. (Reawakened Ser.: 3). (ENG.). (YA). (gr. 9). 2018. 480p. pap. 11.99 *(978-0-399-55571-8(4),* Ember) 2017. 464p. 17.99 *(978-0-399-55568-8(4),* Delacorte Pr.) Random Hse. Children's Bks.

—Tiger's Quest. 2013. (Tiger's Curse Ser.: 2). (ENG.). 512p. (J). (gr. 7). pap. 11.95 *(978-1-4549-0358-1(9))* Sterling Publishing Co., Inc.

Howard, A. G. Ensnared. 2015. (Splintered Ser.). (ENG.). 384p. (YA). (gr. 9-17). pap. 8.95 *(978-1-4197-1504-4(6))* Abrams, Inc.

—Ensnared (Splintered Series #3) 2015. (ENG.). 416p. (J). (gr. 9-17). 17.95 *(978-1-4197-1229-6(2),* 1079501, Amulet Bks.) Abrams, Inc.

—Ensnared (Splintered Series #3) Splintered Book Three. 2015. (Splintered Ser.). (ENG.). 416p. (YA). (gr. 8-17). pap. 10.99 *(978-1-4197-1675-1(1),* 1079503, Amulet Bks.) Abrams, Inc.

—Splintered. 2013. (Splintered Ser.). (ENG.). 384p. (YA). (gr. 8-17). pap. 8.95 *(978-1-4197-0627-1(6))* Abrams, Inc.

—Splintered. 2014. (Splintered Ser.: 1). (J). lib. bdg. 19.60 *(978-0-606-35235-2(X))* Turtleback.

—Unhinged. 2014. (Splintered Ser.). (ENG.). 384p. (YA). (gr. 8-17). pap. 8.95 *(978-1-4197-1047-6(8))* Abrams, Inc.

—Unhinged. 2015. (Splintered Ser.: 2). (J). lib. bdg. 19.60 *(978-0-606-36565-9(6))* Turtleback.

—Unhinged (Splintered Series #2) 2015. (Splintered Ser.). (ENG.). 416p. (YA). (gr. 8-17). pap. 10.99 *(978-1-4197-1373-6(6),* 1036403) Abrams, Inc.

Howe, James. Howie Monroe & the Doghouse of Doom. Helquist, Brett, illus. 2003. (Tales from the House of Bunnicula Ser.: 3). (ENG.). 112p. (J). (gr. 2-5). pap. 6.99 *(978-0-689-83952-8(9),* Atheneum Bks. for Young Readers) Simon & Schuster Children's Publishing.

Hueller, P. W. The Friend. 2016. (Tartan House Ser.). (ENG.). 96p. (J). (gr. 3-6). *(978-1-63235-162-3(5),* 11893, 12-Story Library) Bookstaves, LLC.

Hulme-Cross, Benjamin. The House of Memories. Evergreen, Nelson, illus. 2015. (Dark Hunter Ser.). (ENG.). 64p. (J). (gr. 4-8). pap. 4.99 *(978-1-4677-8085-8(5),* dc2a87ce-8f71-42e9-b061-e920ab07c356, Darby Creek) Lerner Publishing Group.

—The Marsh Demon. Evergreen, Nelson, illus. 2015. (Dark Hunter Ser.). (ENG.). 64p. (J). (gr. 4-8). E-Book 34.65 *(978-1-4677-8658-4(6),* Darby Creek) Lerner Publishing Group.

—Ship of Death. Evergreen, Nelson, illus. 2015. (Dark Hunter Ser.). (ENG.). 64p. (J). (gr. 4-8). pap. 4.99 *(978-1-4677-8090-2(1),* 82a3aab9-b7a0-4867-a530-ce2eba732b58, Darby Creek) Lerner Publishing Group.

—The Stone Witch. Evergreen, Nelson, illus. 2015. (Dark Hunter Ser.). (ENG.). 64p. (J). (gr. 4-8). pap. 4.99 *(978-1-4677-8089-6(8),* ba40e2dd-741d-4adb-87c8-e2b4d6162eea, Darby Creek) Lerner Publishing Group.

Hunter, C. C. Almost Midnight. 2016. (Shadow Falls: after Dark Ser.). (ENG.). 416p. (YA). pap. 16.00 *(978-1-250-08100-1(9),* 900154290, St. Martin's Griffin) St. Martin's Pr.

—Awake at Dawn. 2011. (Shadow Falls Novel Ser.: 2). (ENG.). 400p. (YA). (gr. 7-12). pap. 14.99 *(978-0-312-62468-2(9),* 900066453, St. Martin's Griffin) St. Martin's Pr.

—Born at Midnight. 2011. (Shadow Falls Novel Ser.: 1). (ENG.). 416p. (YA). (gr. 7-12). pap. 12.99 *(978-0-312-62467-5(0),* 900066452, St. Martin's Griffin) St. Martin's Pr.

—Chosen at Nightfall. 2013. (Shadow Falls Novel Ser.: 5). (ENG.). 416p. (YA). (gr. 7). pap. 12.99 *(978-1-250-01289-0(9),* 900084503, St. Martin's Griffin) St. Martin's Pr.

—Eternal. unabr. ed. 2014. (Shadow Falls: after Dark Ser.: 2). (ENG.). 400p. (YA). (gr. 7-12). 19.99 *(978-1-250-05630-6(6),* 900138741, St. Martin's Griffin) St. Martin's Pr.

—Eternal: Shadow Falls: after Dark. 2014. (Shadow Falls: after Dark Ser.: 2). (ENG.). 400p. (YA). (gr. 7-12). pap. 12.99 *(978-1-250-04461-7(8),* 900127030, St. Martin's Griffin) St. Martin's Pr.

—Reborn. 2014. (Shadow Falls: after Dark Ser.: 1). (ENG.). 400p. (YA). (gr. 7). pap. 14.99 *(978-1-250-03591-2(0),* 900121850, St. Martin's Griffin) St. Martin's Pr.

—Shadow Falls: the Next Chapter: Taken at Dusk & Whispers at Moonrise, 2 bks. in 1. 2014. (Shadow Falls Novel Ser.). (ENG.). 784p. (YA). (gr. 8-12). pap. 13.99 *(978-1-250-06695-4(6),* 900146059, St. Martin's Griffin) St. Martin's Pr.

—Taken at Dusk. 2012. (Shadow Falls Novel Ser.: 3). (ENG.). 400p. (YA). (gr. 7-12). pap. 14.00 *(978-0-312-62469-9(7),* 900066454, St. Martin's Griffin) St. Martin's Pr.

—Whispers at Moonrise. 2012. (Shadow Falls Novel Ser.: 4). (ENG.). 400p. (YA). (gr. 7-12). pap. 14.99 *(978-1-250-01191-6(4),* 900084501, St. Martin's Griffin) St. Martin's Pr.

Hunter, Erin. Moonrise. 2015. (Warriors — the New Prophecy Ser.: 2). (J). lib. bdg. 18.40 *(978-0-606-36501-7(X))* Turtleback.

Hutchinson, Emily, retold by. Nathaniel Hawthorne, 1 vol. 2004. (Great American Short Stories Ser.). (ENG., Illus.). 80p. (gr. 4-6). lib. bdg. 26.67 *(978-0-8368-4252-4(9),* 7bd58e61-a59d-403d-9c43-845718f4279b, Gareth Stevens Learning Library) Stevens, Gareth Publishing LLLP.

In a World Just Right. 2015. (ENG., Illus.). 432p. (YA). (gr. 7). 18.99 *(978-1-4814-1660-3(X))* Simon & Schuster Children's Publishing.

Jacobs, John Hornor. The Conformity. 2015. (Twelve-Fingered Boy Trilogy Ser.). (ENG.). 312p. (YA). (gr. 9-12). E-Book 27.99 *(978-1-4677-6182-6(6),* Carolrhoda Lab™) Lerner Publishing Group.

James, Syrie & James, Ryan M. Forbidden. 2012. (Forbidden Ser.: 1). (ENG.). 416p. (YA). (gr. 8). pap. 9.99 *(978-0-06-202789-4(1),* HarperTeen) HarperCollins Pubs.

Jarvis, Robin. Dancing Jax. 2012. (ENG., Illus.). 576p. (YA). 8.99 *(978-0-00-745341-2(8),* HarperCollins Children's Bks.) HarperCollins Pubs. Ltd. GBR. Dist: HarperCollins Pubs.

Jay, Stacey. Juliet Immortal. 2012. (Juliet Immortal Ser.: 1). 320p. (YA). (gr. 9). pap. 9.99 *(978-0-385-74017-3(4),* Ember) Random Hse. Children's Bks.

—Romeo Redeemed. 2013. (Juliet Immortal Ser.). 384p. (YA). (gr. 9). pap. 10.99 *(978-0-385-74019-7(0),* Ember) Random Hse. Children's Bks.

Jinks, Catherine. The Last Bogler. 2017. (How to Catch a Bogle Ser.: 3). (ENG.). 336p. (J). (gr. 5-7). pap. 7.99 *(978-0-544-81309-0(X),* 1641901, Clarion Bks.) HarperCollins Pubs.

Johnson, Christine. Nocturne. 2011. (ENG.). 368p. (YA). (gr. 7). 16.99 *(978-1-4424-0776-3(X),* Simon Pulse) Simon Pulse.

—Nocturne: A Claire de Lune Novel. 2012. (ENG.). 384p. (YA). (gr. 7). pap. 9.99 *(978-1-4424-0777-0(8),* Simon Pulse) Simon Pulse.

Jolley, Dan. Five Elements #1: the Emerald Tablet. 2017. (Five Elements Ser.: 1). (ENG., Illus.). 320p. (J). (gr. 3-7). pap. 7.99 *(978-0-06-241166-2(7),* HarperCollins) HarperCollins Pubs.

Jordan, Sophie. Hidden. 2012. (Firelight Ser.: 3). (ENG.). 272p. (YA). (gr. 8). 17.99 *(978-0-06-193512-1(3),* HarperCollins) HarperCollins Pubs.

Kagawa, Julie. Rogue. 2015. (Talon Saga Ser.: 2). (ENG.). 464p. (YA). (gr. 9-12). 17.99 *(978-0-373-21146-3(5),* Harlequin Teen) Harlequin Enterprises ULC CAN. Dist: HarperCollins Pubs.

Karchut, Darby. Griffin Rising. 2011. 176p. (YA). pap. 15.95 *(978-1-60619-210-8(8))* Twilight Times Bks.

Kassner, Heather. The Bone Garden. Saunders, Matt, illus. 2020. (ENG.). 288p. (J). pap. 7.99 *(978-1-250-25053-7(6),* 900195831) Square Fish.

Kate, Lauren. Fallen. (Fallen Ser.: 1). (ENG.). (YA). (gr. 7). 2010. 480p. pap. 12.99 *(978-0-385-73913-9(3),* Ember) 2009. 464p. 18.99 *(978-0-385-73893-4(5),* Delacorte Pr.) Random Hse. Children's Bks.

—Fallen. 2010. (Fallen Ser.: 1). lib. bdg. 22.10 *(978-0-606-15168-9(0))* Turtleback.

—Fallen in Love. 2012. (Fallen Ser.). (ENG.). 224p. (YA). (gr. 7). pap. 10.99 *(978-0-385-74262-7(2),* Ember) Random Hse. Children's Bks.

—Passion. (Fallen Ser.: 3). (ENG.). (YA). (gr. 7). 2012. 448p. pap. 13.99 *(978-0-385-73917-7(6),* Ember) 2011. 432p. 18.99 *(978-0-385-73916-0(8),* Delacorte Pr.) Random Hse. Children's Bks.

—Passion. 2012. (Fallen Ser.: 3). lib. bdg. 22.10 *(978-0-606-26410-5(8))* Turtleback.

—Rapture. (Fallen Ser.: 4). (ENG.). (YA). (gr. 7). 2014. 480p. pap. 10.99 *(978-0-385-73919-1(2),* Ember) 2012. 464p. 17.99 *(978-0-385-73918-4(4),* Delacorte Pr.) Random Hse. Children's Bks.

—Torment. (Fallen Ser.: 2). (ENG.). (YA). (gr. 7). 2011. 480p. pap. 10.99 *(978-0-385-73915-3(X),* Ember) 2010. 464p. 17.99 *(978-0-385-73914-6(1),* Delacorte Pr.) Random Hse. Children's Bks.

—Torment. 2011. (Fallen Ser.: 2). lib. bdg. 22.10 *(978-0-606-22247-1(2))* Turtleback.

—Unforgiven. 2016. (Fallen Ser.). (ENG.). 368p. (YA). (gr. 7). pap. 10.99 *(978-0-385-74264-1(9),* Ember) Random Hse. Children's Bks.

Kavanagh, Herminie Templeton. Darby O'Gill & the Crocks of Gold: And Other Irish Tales. Schluenderfritz, Ted, illus. 2003. ix, 155p. (J). pap. 14.95 *(978-1-928832-85-0(7))* Sophia Institute Pr.

Kaye, Marilyn. Here Today, Gone Tomorrow, 3. 2011. (Gifted Ser.). (ENG.). 224p. (YA). (gr. 6-8). pap. 22.44 *(978-0-7534-6310-9(5),* 9780753463109) Kingfisher Publications, plc GBR. Dist: Children's Plus, Inc.

—Now You See Me, 5. 2010. (Gifted Ser.). (ENG.). 224p. (YA). (gr. 5-8). pap. 22.44 *(978-0-7534-3046-0(0),* 9780753430460) Kingfisher Publications, plc GBR. Dist: Children's Plus, Inc.

—Speak No Evil, 6. 2011. (Gifted Ser.). (ENG.). 208p. (YA). (gr. 6-8). pap. 22.44 *(978-0-7534-6564-6(7),* 9780753465646) Kingfisher Publications, plc GBR. Dist: Children's Plus, Inc.

Keaton, Kelly. A Beautiful Evil. (ENG.). (YA). (gr. 9). 2013. 320p. pap. 11.99 *(978-1-4424-0928-6(2))* 2. 2012. 304p. 17.99 *(978-1-4424-0927-9(4))* Simon Pulse. (Simon Pulse).

—Darkness Becomes Her. (ENG.). (YA). (gr. 9). 2012. 320p. pap. 12.99 *(978-1-4424-0925-5(8))* 2011. 288p. 16.99 *(978-1-4424-0924-8(X))* Simon Pulse. (Simon Pulse).

—The Wicked Within. (ENG., Illus.). 288p. (YA). (gr. 9). 2014. pap. 9.99 *(978-1-4424-9316-2(X))* 2013. 17.99 *(978-1-4424-9315-5(1))* Simon Pulse. (Simon Pulse).

Keats, Israel. The Team Curse. 2019. (League of the Paranormal Ser.). (ENG.). 112p. (YA). (gr. 6-12). pap. 7.99 *(978-1-5415-7298-0(X),* 431daf2b-6574-4977-9bff-536f112edaf6); lib. bdg. 26.65 *(978-1-5415-5683-6(6),* 5a3b27db-aa65-4a6f-a274-e4bf7fdfe6cc) Lerner Publishing Group. (Darby Creek).

Keeble, Helen. Fang Girl. 2012. (ENG.). 352p. (YA). (gr. 8). pap. 9.99 *(978-0-06-208225-1(6),* HarperTeen) HarperCollins Pubs.

Keil, Michelle Ruiz. All of Us with Wings. 2019. (ENG., Illus.). 360p. (YA). (gr. 11). 18.99 *(978-1-64129-034-0(X),* Soho Teen) Soho Pr., Inc.

Kemmerer, Brigid. Sacrifice. 2014. (Elemental Ser.: 5). (ENG.). 336p. (YA). (gr. 13). pap. 16.95 *(978-0-7582-9439-5(5))* Kensington Publishing Corp.

Kenyon, Sherrilyn. The Dark-Hunters: Infinity, Vol. 1, Vol. 1. 2013. (Dark-Hunters Ser.: 1). (ENG., Illus.). 240p. (gr. 11-17). 13.00 *(978-0-316-19053-4(5),* Yen Pr.) Yen Pr. LLC.

—Infamous: Chronicles of Nick, 4 vols. 2013. (Chronicles of Nick Ser.: 3). (ENG.). 480p. (YA). (gr. 7). pap. 16.00 *(978-1-250-00285-3(0),* 900079521, St. Martin's Griffin) St. Martin's Pr.

—Inferno: Chronicles of Nick. 2014. (Chronicles of Nick Ser.: 4). (ENG.). 464p. (YA). (gr. 7). pap. 14.99 *(978-1-250-00286-0(9),* 900079522, St. Martin's Griffin) St. Martin's Pr.

—Infinity: Chronicles of Nick. 2011. (Chronicles of Nick Ser.: 1). (ENG.). 480p. (YA). (gr. 7-18). pap. 14.00 *(978-0-312-60304-5(5),* 900064303, St. Martin's Griffin) St. Martin's Pr.

—Invincible: The Chronicles of Nick. (Chronicles of Nick Ser.: 2). (ENG.). 432p. (YA). (gr. 7). 2012. pap. 15.00 *(978-0-312-60327-4(4),* 900064304) 2011. 27.99 *(978-0-312-59906-5(4),* 900063529) St. Martin's Pr. (St. Martin's Griffin).

Keswick, Kitty. Freaksville. Cox, Val, illus. 2010. 328p. (YA). (gr. 8-12). pap. 16.99 *(978-1-61603-001-8(1))* Leap Bks.

Kibuishi, Kazu. Escape from Lucien, 6. 2018. (Amulet Ser.). (ENG.). 213p. (J). (gr. 4-5). 23.96 *(978-1-64310-260-3(5))* Penworthy Co., LLC, The.

—Escape from Lucien. 2014. (Amulet Ser.: 6). lib. bdg. 24.50 *(978-0-606-36039-5(5))* Turtleback.

—Escape from Lucien: a Graphic Novel (Amulet #6) Kibuishi, Kazu, illus. (Amulet Ser.: 6). (ENG., Illus.). 224p. (J). (gr. 3-7). 2015. 24.99 *(978-0-545-84899-2(7))* 6. 2014. pap. 12.99 *(978-0-545-43315-0(0))* Scholastic, Inc. (Graphix).

—Firelight, 7. 2018. (Amulet Ser.). (ENG.). 197p. (J). (gr. 4-5). 23.96 *(978-1-64310-261-0(3))* Penworthy Co., LLC, The.

—Firelight. 2016. (Amulet Ser.: 7). (ENG., Illus.). 224p. (J). (gr. 3-7). lib. bdg. 24.50 *(978-0-606-38070-6(1))* Turtleback.

—Firelight: a Graphic Novel (Amulet #7) Kibuishi, Kazu, illus. 2016. (Amulet Ser.: 7). (ENG., Illus.). 208p. (J). (gr. 3-7).

24.99 (978-0-545-83966-2(1)); pap. 12.99 (978-0-545-43316-7(9)) Scholastic, Inc. (Graphix).

—The Last Council, 4. 2018. (Amulet Ser.). (ENG.). 207p. (J). (gr. 4-5). 23.96 (978-1-64310-258-0(3)) Penworthy Co., LLC, The.

—The Last Council. 2011. (Amulet Ser.: 4). lib. bdg. 24.50 (978-0-606-23209-8(5)) Turtleback.

—The Last Council: a Graphic Novel (Amulet #4) 2015. (Amulet Ser.: 4). (ENG.). 224p. (J). (gr. 3-7). 24.99 (978-0-545-20886-4(6), Graphix) Scholastic, Inc.

—The Last Council: a Graphic Novel (Amulet #4) Kibuishi, Kazu, illus. 2011. (Amulet Ser.: 4). (ENG., Illus.). 224p. (J). (gr. 4-7). pap. 12.99 (978-0-545-20887-1(4), Graphix) Scholastic, Inc.

—The Stonekeeper's Curse. 2009. (Amulet Ser.: 2). lib. bdg. 24.50 (978-0-606-10671-9(5)) Turtleback.

—The Stonekeeper's Curse: a Graphic Novel (Amulet #2) Kibuishi, Kazu, illus. (Amulet Ser.: 2). (ENG., Illus.). 224p. (J). 2015. (gr. 3-7). 24.99 (978-0-439-84682-0(X)) 2009. (gr. 4-7). pap. 12.99 (978-0-439-84683-7(8)) Scholastic, Inc. (Graphix).

Kibuishi, Kazu, illus. Firelight. 2016. 197p. (J). (978-1-4806-9909-0(8)) Baker & Taylor, CATS.

Kidd, Ronald. Room of Shadows. (ENG.). 256p. (J). (gr. 3-7). 2018. pap. 9.99 (978-0-8075-6807-1(4), 807568074) 2017. 16.99 (978-0-8075-6805-7(8), 807568058) Whitman, Albert & Co.

Kimmel, Elizabeth Cody. Suddenly Supernatural: Crossing Over. 2011. (Suddenly Supernatural Ser.: 4). (ENG.). 256p. (J). (gr. 3-7). pap. 14.99 (978-0-316-13345-6(0)) Little, Brown Bks. for Young Readers.

—Suddenly Supernatural: Scaredy Kat. 2010. (Suddenly Supernatural Ser.: 2). (ENG.). 272p. (J). (gr. 3-7). pap. 15.99 (978-0-316-08745-2(9)) Little, Brown Bks. for Young Readers.

—Suddenly Supernatural: School Spirit. 2010. (Suddenly Supernatural Ser.: 1). (ENG.). 336p. (J). (gr. 3-7). pap. 17.99 (978-0-316-07821-4(2)) Little, Brown Bks. for Young Readers.

Kindl, Patrice. Owl in Love. 2004. (ENG.). 224p. (YA). (gr. 7-18). pap. 14.95 (978-0-618-43910-2(2)) Houghton Mifflin Harcourt Publishing Co.

Kinney, Jeff. Rowley Jefferson's Awesome Friendly Spooky Stories. 2021. (ENG., Illus.). 224p. (J). (gr. 3-7). 14.99 (978-1-4197-5697-9(4), 1748601) Abrams, Inc.

Klause, Annette Curtis. Freaks: Alive, on the Inside! (ENG.). 336p. (YA). 2007. (gr. 9). pap. 15.99 (978-0-689-87038-5(8)) 2006. (Illus.). (gr. 8-18). 16.95 (978-0-689-87037-8(X)) McElderry, Margaret K. Bks. (McElderry, Margaret K. Bks.).

Knight, Karsten. Afterglow. 2013. (ENG., Illus.). 336p. (YA). (gr. 9). 17.99 (978-1-4424-5037-0(1), Simon & Schuster Bks. For Young Readers) Simon & Schuster Bks. For Young Readers.

—Embers & Echoes. (ENG., (YA). (gr. 9). 2013. Illus.). 496p. pap. 9.99 (978-1-4424-5035-6(5)) 2012. 480p. 16.99 (978-1-4424-5030-1(4)) Simon & Schuster Bks. For Young Readers. (Simon & Schuster Bks. For Young Readers).

—Wildefire. 2011. (ENG.). 400p. (YA). (gr. 9-18). 16.99 (978-1-4424-2117-2(7), Simon & Schuster Bks. For Young Readers) Simon & Schuster Bks. For Young Readers.

Kogler, Jennifer. The Otherworldlies. 2008. 400p. (J). lib. bdg. 17.89 (978-0-06-073960-7(6)); (ENG.). (gr. 5-18). 16.99 (978-0-06-073959-1(2)) HarperCollins Pubs. (Eos).

Konen, Leah. The after Girls. 2013. (ENG.). 304p. (YA). 17.95 (978-1-4405-6108-5(7), Simon Pulse) Simon Pulse.

Korman, Gordon. The Dragonfly Effect. 2016. (Hypnotists Ser.: 3). lib. bdg. 17.20 (978-0-606-38813-9(3)) Turtleback.

—The Hypnotists. 2014. (Hypnotists Ser.: 1). lib. bdg. 17.20 (978-0-606-35808-8(0)) Turtleback.

—The Hypnotists (the Hypnotists, Book 1), Bk. 1. 2014. (Hypnotists Ser.: 1). (ENG.). 240p. (J). (gr. 3-7). pap. 7.99 (978-0-545-50325-9(6), Scholastic Paperbacks) Scholastic, Inc.

—Memory Maze. 2015. (Hypnotists Ser.: 2). lib. bdg. 17.20 (978-0-606-37016-5(1)) Turtleback.

Kotecki, Nathan. The Suburban Strange. (Suburban Strange Ser.). (ENG.). (YA). (gr. 9). 2013. 384p. pap. 8.99 (978-0-544-10479-2(X), 1540788) 2012. 368p. 16.99 (978-0-547-72996-1(0), 1483969) HarperCollins Pubs. (Clarion Bks.).

Kozlowsky, M. P. The Dyerville Tales. Thompson, Brian, illus. 2014. (ENG.). 336p. (J). (gr. 3-7). 16.99 (978-0-06-199871-3(0), Waldon Pond Pr.) HarperCollins Pubs.

—Juniper Berry. Madrid, Erwin, illus. 2012. (ENG.). 240p. (J). (gr. 3-7). pap. 7.99 (978-0-06-199870-6(2), Waldon Pond Pr.) HarperCollins Pubs.

Kreie, Chris. Blood Moon. 2017. (Midnight Ser.). (ENG.). 96p. (YA). (gr. 4-4). E-Book (978-1-5124-3483-5(3), 9781512434835); (gr. 6-12). E-Book 39.99 (978-1-5124-3482-8(5), 9781512434828) Lerner Publishing Group. (Darby Creek).

Krovatin, Christopher. Gravediggers: Terror Cove. 2013. (Gravediggers Ser.: 2). (ENG.). 368p. (J). (gr. 3-7). 16.99 (978-0-06-207743-1(0), Tegen, Katherine Bks) HarperCollins Pubs.

—Gravediggers: Mountain of Bones. 2013. (Gravediggers Ser.: 1). (ENG.). 352p. (J). (gr. 3-7). pap. 6.99 (978-0-06-207741-7(4), Tegen, Katherine Bks) HarperCollins Pubs.

Kurtagich, Dawn. And the Trees Crept In. 2017. (ENG.). 368p. (YA). (gr. 10-17). pap. 9.99 (978-0-316-29871-1(9)) Little, Brown Bks. for Young Readers.

Laar-Yond C.T. Six Fingers & the Blue Warrior. Playcrib, illus. 2013. 36p. pap. 14.00 (978-1-62212-177-9(5), Strategic Bk. Publishing) Strategic Book Publishing & Rights Agency (SBPRA).

Lackey, Mercedes & Edghill, Rosemary. Shadow Grail #2: Conspiracies: Conspiracies. 2011. (Shadow Grail Ser.: 2). (ENG.). 352p. (YA). (gr. 8-12). pap. 18.99 (978-0-7653-1762-9(1), 900041774, Tor Teen) Doherty, Tom Assocs., LLC.

—Shadow Grail #3: Sacrifices. 2013. (Shadow Grail Ser.: 3). (ENG.). 304p. (YA). (gr. 8-12). pap. 17.99 (978-0-7653-1763-6(X), 900041776, Tor Teen) Doherty, Tom Assocs., LLC.

LaFevers, Robin. Mortal Heart. 2018. (His Fair Assassin Ser.: 3). (ENG., Illus.). 496p. (YA). (gr. 9). pap. 15.99 (978-1-328-56767-3(2), 1726824, Clarion Bks.) HarperCollins Pubs.

LaFleur, Suzanne. Listening for Lucca. 2015. (ENG.). 240p. (J). (gr. 4-7). pap. 8.99 (978-0-307-98030-4(8), Yearling) Random Hse. Children's Bks.

Lanang, Vanessa. The Paranormal Playbook. 2019. (League of the Paranormal Ser.). (ENG.). 120p. (YA). (gr. 6-12). pap. 7.99 (978-1-5415-7296-6(3), 6b4f93ce-323d-4c62-adeb-c2d05fd3162e); lib. bdg. 26.65 (978-1-5415-5682-9(8), 1d3d20df-0c81-4016-b779-72f2b63f646d) Lerner Publishing Group. (Darby Creek).

Langer, Dana. Siren Sisters. 2017. (ENG., Illus.). 256p. (J). (gr. 4-8). 17.99 (978-1-4814-6686-8(0), Simon & Schuster/Paula Wiseman Bks.) Simon & Schuster/Paula Wiseman Bks.

Langrish, Katherine. The Shadow Hunt. 2010. 322p. lib. bdg. (978-0-06-111678-0(5)) HarperCollins Pubs.

—Troll Blood. 2008. (ENG., Illus.). 352p. (J). (gr. 5-8). 16.99 (978-0-06-111674-2(2), HarperCollins) HarperCollins Pubs.

—Troll Blood. Stevens, Tim & Wyatt, David, illus. 2008. 352p. (YA). (gr. 5-8). lib. bdg. 17.89 (978-0-06-111675-9(0), Eos) HarperCollins Pubs.

—Troll Mill. 2008. (ENG., Illus.). 336p. (YA). (gr. 7). pap. 7.99 (978-0-06-058309-5(6), Eos) HarperCollins Pubs.

Latta, Ruth. The Revenant & Other Stories for Hallowe'en. 2004. 54p. (978-0-9683382-8-5(3)) Latta, Roger K.

Leake, Jessica. Through the White Wood. 2019. (ENG.). 416p. (YA). (gr. 9). 17.99 (978-0-06-266629-1(0), HarperTeen) HarperCollins Pubs.

Lee, Kathy. The Runaway Train. 2011. 144p. pap. (978-1-84427-505-2(1)) Scripture Union.

Lee, Mackenzi. This Monstrous Thing. 2015. (ENG.). 384p. (YA). (gr. 8). 17.99 (978-0-06-238277-1(2), Tegen, Katherine Bks) HarperCollins Pubs.

Lee, Stan. The Dragon's Return. 2017. (Zodiac Legacy Ser.: 2). (J). lib. bdg. 20.85 (978-0-606-39500-7(8)) Turtleback.

—The Zodiac Legacy: the Dragon's Return. 2017. (Zodiac Ser.). (ENG., Illus.). 448p. (J). (gr. 3-7). pap. 9.99 (978-1-4847-5255-5(4), Disney Press Books) Disney Publishing Worldwide.

Lemke, Donald. The Awakening, 1 vol. Glass House Graphics, illus. 2011. (Good vs Evil Ser.). (ENG.). 48p. (J). (gr. 5-9). lib. bdg. 23.99 (978-1-4342-2089-9(3), 102835, Stone Arch Bks.) Capstone.

Lewis, Richard. The Demon Queen. 2012. (ENG.). 240p. (YA). (gr. 7). pap. 11.99 (978-1-4169-3590-2(8), Simon & Schuster Bks. For Young Readers) Simon & Schuster Bks. For Young Readers.

—Monster's Proof. 2009. (ENG.). 288p. (YA). (gr. 7-18). 15.99 (978-1-4169-3591-9(6), Simon & Schuster Bks. For Young Readers) Simon & Schuster Bks. For Young Readers.

Lindsey, Mary. Shattered Souls. 2012. (ENG.). 336p. (YA). (gr. 9). pap. 8.99 (978-0-14-242190-1(1), Speak) Penguin Young Readers Group.

Linko, Gina. Flower Moon. 2018. (ENG.). 256p. (J). (gr. 4-8). 15.99 (978-1-5107-2274-3(2), Sky Pony Pr.) Skyhorse Publishing Co., Inc.

Liparulo, Robert. Gatekeepers, 1 vol. 2009. (Dreamhouse Kings Ser.: 3). (ENG.). 320p. (YA). pap. 14.99 (978-1-59554-729-3(0)) Nelson, Thomas Inc.

—House of Dark Shadows, 1 vol. 2009. (Dreamhouse Kings Ser.: 1). (ENG.). 304p. (YA). pap. 9.99 (978-1-59554-727-9(4)) Nelson, Thomas Inc.

—Whirlwind, 1 vol. 2010. (Dreamhouse Kings Ser.: 5). (ENG.). 320p. (YA). pap. 14.99 (978-1-59554-892-4(0)) Nelson, Thomas Inc.

Littlefield, Sophie. Banished. 2011. (ENG.). 304p. (J). (gr. 8-12). lib. bdg. 24.94 (978-0-385-90735-4(4)) Random House Publishing Group.

Livingston, Lesley. Descendant. 2013. (Starling Trilogy Ser.: 2). (ENG.). 336p. (YA). (gr. 8). 17.99 (978-0-06-206310-6(3), HarperTeen) HarperCollins Pubs.

Lloyd-Jones, Emily. The Hearts We Sold. 2019. (ENG., Illus.). 416p. (YA). (gr. 9-17). pap. 10.99 (978-0-316-31455-8(2)) Little, Brown Bks. for Young Readers.

London, J. A. After Daybreak: A Darkness Before Dawn Novel. 2013. (Darkness Before Dawn Ser.: 3). (ENG., Illus.). 336p. (YA). (gr. 9). pap. 9.99 (978-0-06-202067-3(6), HarperTeen) HarperCollins Pubs.

Long, Loren & Bildner, Phil. Blastin' the Blues. Long, Loren, illus. 2011. (Sluggers Ser.: 5). (ENG., Illus.). 448p. (J). (gr. 3-7). pap. 8.99 (978-1-4169-1891-2(4), Simon & Schuster Bks. For Young Readers) Simon & Schuster Bks. For Young Readers.

—Home of the Brave. Long, Loren, illus. (Sluggers Ser.: 6). (ENG., Illus.). 336p. (J). (gr. 3-7). 2011. pap. 9.99 (978-1-4169-1892-9(2)) 2010. 15.99 (978-1-4169-1868-4(X)) Simon & Schuster Bks. For Young Readers. (Simon & Schuster Bks. For Young Readers).

—Magic in the Outfield. Long, Loren, illus. 2009. (Sluggers Ser.: 1). (ENG., Illus.). 160p. (J). (gr. 3-7). pap. 9.99 (978-1-4169-1884-4(1), Simon & Schuster Bks. For Young Readers) Simon & Schuster Bks. For Young Readers.

—Water, Water Everywhere. Long, Loren, illus. (Sluggers Ser.: 4). (ENG., Illus.). (J). (gr. 3-7). 2010. 288p. pap. 9.99 (978-1-4169-1890-5(6)) 2009. 272p. 14.99 (978-1-4169-1866-0(3)) Simon & Schuster Bks. For Young Readers. (Simon & Schuster Bks. For Young Readers).

Love, Damien. Monstrous Devices. 2019. (ENG., Illus.). 368p. (J). (gr. 3-7). 8.99 (978-0-451-47859-7(2), Puffin Books) Penguin Young Readers Group.

Lu, Marie. The Midnight Star. l.t. ed. 2016. (Young Elites Ser.). (ENG.). 408p. 22.99 (978-1-4104-9438-2(1)) Cengage Gale.

—The Midnight Star. (Young Elites Ser.). (ENG.). (YA). (gr. 7). 2017. 368p. pap. 12.99 (978-0-14-751170-6(4), Speak) 2016. (Illus.). 336p. 18.99 (978-0-399-16785-0(4), G.P. Putnam's Sons Books for Young Readers) Penguin Young Readers Group.

—The Rose Society. (Young Elites Ser.: 2). (ENG.). (YA). (gr. 7). 2016. 448p. pap. 11.99 (978-0-14-751169-0(0), Speak) 2015. (Illus.). 416p. 18.99 (978-0-399-16784-3(6), G.P. Putnam's Sons Books for Young Readers) Penguin Young Readers Group.

—The Rose Society. l.t. ed. 2015. (Young Elites Ser.). (ENG.). 22.99 (978-1-4104-8465-9(3)) Thorndike Pr.

—The Rose Society. 2016. (Young Elites Ser.: 2). (ENG.). 432p. (YA). (gr. 7). 22.10 (978-0-606-39314-0(5)) Turtleback.

—The Young Elites. (Young Elites Ser.: 1). (ENG., Illus.). (YA). (gr. 7). 2015. 400p. pap. 11.99 (978-0-14-751168-3(2), Speak) 2014. 368p. 18.99 (978-0-399-16783-6(8), G.P. Putnam's Sons Books for Young Readers) Penguin Young Readers Group.

—The Young Elites. 2015. (ENG.). (YA). (gr. 7). lib. bdg. 21.60 (978-1-68065-052-5(1)) Perfection Learning Corp.

—The Young Elites. 2015. (Young Elites Ser.: 1). lib. bdg. 22.10 (978-0-606-37575-7(9)) Turtleback.

Lubar, David. Teeny Weenies: Freestyle Frenzy: And Other Stories. Mayer, Bill, illus. 2019. (Teeny Weenies Ser.: 2). (ENG.). 128p. (J). 12.99 (978-1-250-17350-8(7), 900188883, Starscape) Doherty, Tom Assocs., LLC.

—Teeny Weenies: the Intergalactic Petting Zoo: And Other Stories. Mayer, Bill, illus. 2019. (Teeny Weenies Ser.: 1). (ENG.). 128p. (J). 12.99 (978-1-250-17342-3(6), 900188882, Starscape) Doherty, Tom Assocs., LLC.

Lynne, Zoe. Carnival - Decatur. 2016. (ENG., Illus.). (J). 24.99 (978-1-63477-948-7(7), Harmony Ink Pr.) Dreamspinner Pr.

Maberry, Jonathan. The Orphan Army. 2015. (Nightsiders Ser.: 1). (ENG., Illus.). 400p. (J). (gr. 3-7). 16.99 (978-1-4814-1575-0(1), Simon & Schuster Bks. For Young Readers) Simon & Schuster Bks. For Young Readers.

—The Orphan Army. 2016. (Nightsiders Ser.: 1). lib. bdg. 18.40 (978-0-606-38959-4(8)) Turtleback.

—Vault of Shadows. (Nightsiders Ser.: 2). (ENG.). 464p. (J). (gr. 3-7). 2017. pap. 8.99 (978-1-4814-1579-8(4)) 2016. (Illus.). 16.99 (978-1-4814-1578-1(6)) Simon & Schuster Bks. For Young Readers. (Simon & Schuster Bks. For Young Readers).

MacHale, D. J. The Black. (Morpheus Road Ser.: 2). (ENG.). (J). (gr. 5-9). 2012. 432p. pap. 10.99 (978-1-4169-6520-6(3)) 2011. 416p. 18.99 (978-1-4169-6517-6(3)) Simon & Schuster Children's Publishing. (Aladdin).

—Black Moon Rising (the Library Book 2) (Library: 2). 304p. (J). (gr. 3-7). 2018. pap. 7.99 (978-1-101-93260-5(0), Yearling) 2017. 16.99 (978-1-101-93257-5(0), Random Hse. Bks. for Young Readers) Random Hse. Children's Bks.

—The Blood. (Morpheus Road Ser.: 3). (ENG.). 384p. (J). (gr. 5-9). 2013. pap. 11.99 (978-1-4169-6521-3(1)) 2012. 19.99 (978-1-4169-6518-3(1)) Simon & Schuster Children's Publishing. (Aladdin).

—Curse of the Boggin (the Library Book 1) 2016. (Library: 1). 256p. (J). (gr. 3-7). 16.99 (978-1-101-93253-7(8), Random Hse. Bks. for Young Readers) Random Hse. Children's Bks.

—The Light. (Morpheus Road Ser.: 1). (ENG.). 352p. (J). 2010. (gr. 5-9). pap. 10.99 (978-1-4169-6519-0(X))1. 2011. (gr. 6-8). 22.44 (978-1-4169-6516-9(5)) Simon & Schuster Children's Publishing. (Aladdin).

—Oracle of Doom (the Library Book 3) 2018. (Library: 3). 304p. (J). (gr. 3-7). 16.99 (978-1-101-93261-2(9), Random Hse. Bks. for Young Readers) Random Hse. Children's Bks.

MacKey, Cindy. Hannah's Day of Revelations. 2013. 46p. pap. 13.99 (978-0-9892699-4-0(9)) Cyrano Bks.

MacKnight, Wendy McLeod. The Frame-Up. Schoenherr, Ian, illus. (ENG.). (J). (gr. 3-7). 2019. 400p. pap. 7.99 (978-0-06-266831-8(5)) 2018. 384p. 16.99 (978-0-06-266830-1(7)) HarperCollins Pubs. (Greenwillow Bks.).

Maguire, Eden. Arizona. 2010. (Beautiful Dead Ser.: 2). (ENG.). 288p. (YA). (gr. 8-12). pap. 11.99 (978-1-4022-3945-8(9)) Sourcebooks, Inc.

Maizel, Rebecca. Stolen Nights: A Vampire Queen Novel. 2013. (Vampire Queen Ser.: 2). (ENG.). 320p. (YA). (gr. 7-12). pap. 16.99 (978-0-312-64992-0(4), 900069067, St. Martin's Griffin) St. Martin's Pr.

Malkin, Nina. Swear. (ENG.). 480p. (YA). (gr. 11). 2012. pap. 9.99 (978-1-4424-2111-0(8)) 2011. 17.99 (978-1-4424-2110-3(X)) Simon Pulse. (Simon Pulse).

—Swoon. 2010. (ENG.). 432p. (YA). (gr. 11). pap. 9.99 (978-1-4169-9801-3(2), Simon Pulse) Simon Pulse.

Maloney, Andrew. The Master Song. 2014. (Blue Time Ser.: 1). (ENG., Illus.). 352p. (gr. 7). pap. 15.99 (978-1-62911-176-6(7), 770172) Whitaker Hse.

—Verse of Valor. 2015. (Blue Time Ser.: 2). (ENG.). 288p. (gr. 7). pap. 15.99 (978-1-62911-357-9(3), 770306) Whitaker Hse.

Marillier, Juliet. Cybele's Secret. 2011. (Wildwood Dancing Ser.: 2). (ENG.). 448p. (YA). (gr. 7). pap. 9.99 (978-0-553-49486-0(4), Knopf Bks. for Young Readers) Random Hse. Children's Bks.

—Wildwood Dancing. 2008. (Wildwood Dancing Ser.: 1). (ENG.). 432p. (YA). (gr. 7). pap. 16.99 (978-0-375-84474-4(0), Knopf Bks. for Young Readers) Random Hse. Children's Bks.

Mariolle, Mathieu. Changing Moon. rev. ed. 2010. pap. 56.72 (978-0-7613-6953-0(8)) Lerner Publishing Group.

—Even for a Dreamer Like Me. MiniKim et al, illus. 2010. (Nola's Worlds Ser.: 3). (ENG.). 128p. (J). (gr. 6-9). 30.60 (978-0-7613-6505-1(2)) Lerner Publishing Group.

—Ferrets & Ferreting Out. MiniKim et al, illus. 2010. (Nola's Worlds Ser.: 2). (ENG.). 136p. (J). (gr. 6-9). 30.60 (978-0-7613-6504-4(4)) Lerner Publishing Group.

—Nola's Worlds, 3 vols., Set. MiniKim et al, illus. Incl. Even for a Dreamer Like Me. 128p. 30.60 (978-0-7613-6505-1(2)); Ferrets & Ferreting Out. 136p. 30.60 (978-0-7613-6504-4(4)); (Illus.). (J). (gr. 6-9). 2010. Set lib. bdg. 91.80 (978-0-7613-6500-6(1), Graphic Universe™) Lerner Publishing Group.

Markell, Denis. The Game Masters of Garden Place. 2019. (Illus.). 304p. (J). (gr. 5). 7.99 (978-1-101-93194-3(9), Yearling) Random Hse. Children's Bks.

Marr, Melissa & Pratt, Tim, eds. Rags & Bones: New Twists on Timeless Tales. 2015. (ENG.). 368p. (YA). (gr. 10-17). pap. 17.99 (978-0-316-21293-9(8)) Little, Brown Bks. for Young Readers.

Marr Osb, Andrew. From Beyond to Here: Merendael's Gift & Other Stories. 2012. 320p. (gr. 4-6). 29.95 (978-1-4759-3460-1(2)); pap. 19.95 (978-1-4759-3458-8(0)) iUniverse, Inc.

Martin, R. T. Dark Star. 2017. (Midnight Ser.). (ENG.). 96p. (YA). (gr. 6-12). 26.65 (978-1-5124-2769-1(1), 8eeb8a61-2d0b-4e89-bb5c-bc1bee46c19d); E-Book 39.99 (978-1-5124-3485-9(X), 9781512434859) Lerner Publishing Group. (Darby Creek).

Marz, Ron. Witchblade Redemption, Vol. 4. 2012. (ENG., Illus.). 160p. pap. 19.99 (978-1-60706-424-4(3), 12a49951-f938-438c-9d58-a3c76bfa591f) Image Comics.

Mass, Wendy. The Last Present: a Wish Novel. 2015. (ENG.). 256p. (J). (gr. 3-7). pap. 7.99 (978-0-545-31017-8(2)) Scholastic, Inc.

—13 Gifts. 2013. (Willow Falls Ser.: 3). lib. bdg. 17.20 (978-0-606-31957-7(3)) Turtleback.

—13 Gifts: a Wish Novel. 2013. (ENG.). 352p. (J). (gr. 3-7). pap. 7.99 (978-0-545-31004-8(0)) Scholastic, Inc.

Matas, Carol. The Freak. rev. ed. 2008. (Freak (Key Porter Books) Ser.). (ENG.). 128p. (J). (gr. 5-18). pap. (978-1-55263-930-6(4)) Magma.

—Tales of a Reluctant Psychic: The Freak, Visions, & Far. 2009. (ENG.). 424p. (YA). (gr. 7-18). pap. (978-1-55470-203-9(8)) Me to We.

Mather, Adriana. Haunting the Deep. (ENG.). (YA). (gr. 7). 2018. 368p. pap. 9.99 (978-0-553-53954-7(X), Ember) 2017. 352p. lib. bdg. 20.99 (978-0-553-53952-3(3), Knopf Bks. for Young Readers) Random Hse. Children's Bks.

Matthews, John. Henry Hunter & the Cursed Pirates: Henry Hunter Series #2. 2017. (Henry Hunter Ser.). (ENG., Illus.). 240p. (J). (gr. 2-7). 15.99 (978-1-5107-1039-9(6), Sky Pony Pr.) Skyhorse Publishing Co., Inc.

McCall, Guadalupe García. El Verano de Las Mariposas, 1 vol. Bowles, David, tr. 2018. Orig. Title: Summer of the Mariposas. (SPA.). 384p. (YA). (gr. 6-12). pap. 16.95 (978-1-62014-786-3(6), leelowtu, Tu Bks.) Lee & Low Bks., Inc.

McCarry, Sarah. All Our Pretty Songs: A Novel. 2013. (Metamorphoses Trilogy Ser.: 1). (ENG.). 240p. (YA). (gr. 8-12). pap. 19.99 (978-1-250-02708-5(X), 900098096, St. Martin's Griffin) St. Martin's Pr.

—Dirty Wings: A Novel. 2014. (Metamorphoses Trilogy Ser.: 2). (ENG.). 288p. (YA). (gr. 8-12). 24.99 (978-1-250-04938-4(5), 900098104, St. Martin's Griffin) St. Martin's Pr.

McCaughan, Timothy. Crimson Soul. 2005. 200p. per. 12.95 (978-1-58961-438-3(0)) PageFree Publishing, Inc.

McClellan, Rachel. Fractured Truth. 2014. 16.99 (978-1-4621-1392-7(3), Horizon Pubs.) Cedar Fort, Inc./CFI Distribution.

McCormack, Devon. Hideous. 2016. (ENG., Illus.). (J). 24.99 (978-1-63533-028-1(9), Harmony Ink Pr.) Dreamspinner Pr.

McCracken, Connie. Indigo Boy & Crystalline Girl. Craig, Chris, illus. 2009. 24p. pap. 10.95 (978-1-4269-0423-3(1)) Trafford Publishing.

McEntire, K. D. Reaper. 2012. (Lightbringer Ser.: 2). (ENG.). 342p. (YA). (gr. 7). 16.95 (978-1-61614-632-0(X), Pyr) Start Publishing LLC.

McGann, Oisín. Under Fragile Stone, Vol. 2. 2005. (ENG., Illus.). 384p. (J). pap. 12.95 (978-0-86278-835-3(8)) O'Brien Pr., Ltd., The IRL. Dist: Dufour Editions, Inc.

McKenzie, Paige. The Haunting of Sunshine Girl. 2016. (Haunting of Sunshine Girl Ser.: Vol. 1). (ENG.). 320p. (YA). (gr. 7-17). lib. bdg. 21.80 (978-1-5311-8307-3(7)) Perfection Learning Corp.

—The Haunting of Sunshine Girl: Book One. 2016. (Haunting of Sunshine Girl Ser.: 1). (ENG.). 320p. (YA). (gr. 7-17). pap. 10.99 (978-1-60286-302-6(4)) Hachette Bk. Group.

—The Haunting of Sunshine Girl: Book One. 2015. (Haunting of Sunshine Girl Ser.: 1). (ENG.). 304p. (YA). (gr. 7-17). 16.00 (978-1-60286-272-2(9)) Hachette Bks.

—The Sacrifice of Sunshine Girl. 2018. (Haunting of Sunshine Girl Ser.: 3). (ENG.). 336p. (YA). (gr. 7-17). pap. 9.99 (978-1-60286-335-4(0)) Hachette Bk. Group.

McLelland, Brad & Sylvester, Louis. The Fang of Bonfire Crossing: Legends of the Lost Causes. 2020. (Legends of the Lost Causes Ser.: 2). (ENG.). 400p. (J). pap. 20.99 (978-1-250-23360-8(7), 900174394) Square Fish.

McMann, Lisa. Bang. (Visions Ser.: 2). (ENG., (YA). (gr. 9). 2014. Illus.). 272p. pap. 9.99 (978-1-4424-6628-9(6)) 2013. 256p. 16.99 (978-1-4424-6625-8(1)) Simon Pulse. (Simon Pulse).

—Crash. 2013. (Visions Ser.: 1). (ENG.). 256p. (YA). (gr. 9). 19.99 (978-1-4424-0391-8(8), Simon Pulse) Simon Pulse.

—Cryer's Cross. 2011. (ENG.). (YA). (gr. 9). 256p. pap. 9.99 (978-1-4169-9482-4(3)); (Illus.). 240p. 16.99 (978-1-4169-9481-7(5)) Simon Pulse. (Simon Pulse).

—Map of Flames (the Forgotten Five, Book 1) 2022. (Forgotten Five Ser.: 1). (J). (gr. 3-7). (ENG.). 400p. 9.99 (978-0-593-32542-1(7)); 384p. 17.99 (978-0-593-32540-7(0)) Penguin Young Readers Group. (G.P. Putnam's Sons Books for Young Readers).

McNally, Janet. The Looking Glass. 2018. (ENG., Illus.). 336p. (YA). (gr. 8). 17.99 (978-0-06-243627-6(9), HarperTeen) HarperCollins Pubs.

McNamee, Graham. Bonechiller. 2012. (ENG.). 304p. (YA). (gr. 7). pap. 11.99 (978-0-307-97593-5(2), Ember) Random Hse. Children's Bks.

McNeal, Tom. Far Far Away. 2014. (ENG.). 400p. (YA). (gr. 7). pap. 10.99 (978-0-375-84329-7(9), Ember) Random Hse. Children's Bks.

McTiernan, Deborah. Lilly Noble & Actual Magic. 2013. (ENG.). 318p. (YA). pap. 14.99 (978-0-9891807-0-2(0)) Actual Magic Enterprises, LLC.

Mead, Richelle. Blood Promise. 2010. (Vampire Academy Ser.: 4). lib. bdg. 20.85 (978-0-606-14565-7(6)) Turtleback.

—Blood Promise: A Vampire Academy Novel. 2010. (Vampire Academy Ser.: 4). (ENG.). 528p. (YA). (gr. 7-18). pap. 13.99 (978-1-59514-310-5(6), Razorbill) Penguin Young Readers Group.

—The Golden Lily: A Bloodlines Novel. 2013. (Bloodlines Ser.: 2). (ENG.). 448p. (YA). (gr. 7). pap. 12.99 (978-1-59514-602-1(4), Razorbill) Penguin Young Readers Group.

—Last Sacrifice: A Vampire Academy Novel. 2011. (Vampire Academy Ser.: 6). (ENG.). 608p. (YA). (gr. 7-18). 13.99 (978-1-59514-440-9(4), Razorbill) Penguin Young Readers Group.

—Midnight Jewel. 2017. (Glittering Court Ser.: 2). (ENG.). 416p. (YA). (gr. 7). 19.99 (978-1-59514-843-8(4), Razorbill) Penguin Young Readers Group.

—Spirit Bound: A Vampire Academy Novel. 2011. (Vampire Academy Ser.: 5). (ENG.). 512p. (YA). (gr. 7-18). 13.99 (978-1-59514-366-2(1), Razorbill) Penguin Young Readers Group.

Mebus, Scott. Gods of Manhattan 2: Spirits in the Park, Vol. 2. 2010. (ENG.). 400p. (J). (gr. 3-7). 8.99 *(978-0-14-241645-7(2),* Puffin Books) Penguin Young Readers Group.
Meldrum, Christina. Madapple. 2010. 416p. (YA). (gr. 9-18). pap. 10.99 *(978-0-375-85177-3(1),* Knopf Bks. for Young Readers) Random Hse. Children's Bks.
Melissa Strangway. Abigail's Mirror. 2010. 316p. pap. 18.95 *(978-1-4401-6176-6(3))* iUniverse, Inc.
Messenger, Shannon. Let the Sky Fall. 2013. (Sky Fall Ser.: 1). (ENG., (YA). (gr. 7). Illus.). 432p. pap. 12.99 *(978-1-4424-5042-4(8));* 416p. 17.99 *(978-1-4424-5041-7(X))* Simon Pulse. (Simon Pulse).
—Let the Storm Break. 2014. (Sky Fall Ser.: 2). (ENG., Illus.). 400p. (YA). (gr. 7). 17.99 *(978-1-4424-5044-8(4),* Simon Pulse) Simon Pulse.
—Let the Wind Rise. (Sky Fall Ser.: 3). (ENG., Illus.). (YA). (gr. 7). 2017. 432p. pap. 12.99 *(978-1-4814-4655-6(X))* 2016. 416p. 19.99 *(978-1-4814-4654-9(1))* Simon Pulse. (Simon Pulse).
Messer, Celeste M. Andi's Choice. Hoeffner, Deb, illus. 2004. 82-92p. 4.95 *(978-0-9702171-6-5(1))* AshleyAlan Enterprises.
—The Boy Who Cried Wolf. Hoeffner, Deb, illus. 2004. 82-92p. 4.95 *(978-0-9702171-9-6(6))* AshleyAlan Enterprises.
Messner, Kate. All the Answers. 2016. (ENG.). 272p. (J). pap. 8.99 *(978-1-68119-020-4(6),* 900156128, Bloomsbury USA Childrens) Bloomsbury Publishing USA.
Metcalf, Dawn. Indelible. 2013. (Twixt Ser.: 1). (ENG.). 384p. (YA). pap. 9.99 *(978-0-373-21073-2(6),* Harlequin Teen) Harlequin Enterprises ULC CAN. Dist: HarperCollins Pubs.
Metz, Melinda. Raven's Point. 2005. pap. *(978-0-06-052373-2(5))* HarperCollins Canada, Ltd.
Meyer, Stephenie. Breaking Dawn. 2008. (Twilight Saga Ser.: 4). (ENG.). 768p. (YA). (gr. 7-17). 24.99 *(978-0-316-06792-8(X))* Little, Brown Bks. for Young Readers.
—Breaking Dawn. 2010. (Twilight Saga Ser.: 4). (YA). lib. bdg. 29.40 *(978-0-606-23108-4(0))* Turtleback.
—The Twilight Saga Collection Set, 4 vols. 2008. (ENG.). 2560p. (YA). (gr. 7-17). 92.00 *(978-0-316-03184-4(4))* Little, Brown Bks. for Young Readers.
Meyer, Stephenie, et al. Prom Nights from Hell. 2010. (ENG.). 336p. (YA). (gr. 9). pap. 9.99 *(978-0-06-197600-1(8),* HarperTeen) HarperCollins Pubs.
Meyer, William. The Search for the Lost Prophecy. (Horace J. Edwards & the Time Keepers Ser.). (ENG.). 240p. (J). (gr. 3-6). 2018. pap. 9.99 *(978-1-58536-983-6(7),* 204332) 2017. (Illus.). 16.99 *(978-1-58536-982-9(9),* 204317) Sleeping Bear Pr.
Mientus, Andy. The Backstagers & the Ghost Light (Backstagers #1) Sygh, Rian, illus. 2018. (Backstagers Ser.). (ENG.). 208p. (J). (gr. 5-9). 14.99 *(978-1-4197-3120-4(3),* 1220801, Amulet Bks.) Abrams, Inc.
—The Backstagers & the Theater of the Ancients (Backstagers #2) Sygh, Rian & BOOM! Studios, illus. 2019. (Backstagers Ser.). (ENG.). 192p. (YA). (gr. 5-9). 14.99 *(978-1-4197-3365-9(6),* 1262501, Amulet Bks.) Abrams, Inc.
Miles, Elizabeth. Envy. 2013. (Fury Ser.: 2). (ENG., Illus.). 416p. (YA). (gr. 9). pap. 9.99 *(978-1-4424-2222-3(X),* Simon Pulse) Simon Pulse.
—Eternity. 2013. (Fury Ser.: 3). (ENG., Illus.). 336p. (YA). (gr. 9). 17.99 *(978-1-4424-2227-8(0));* pap. 9.99 *(978-1-4424-2228-5(9))* Simon Pulse. (Simon Pulse).
—Fury, 11 vols. 2012. (YA). 110.75 *(978-1-4640-3957-7(7));* 271.75 *(978-1-4640-3955-3(0));* 126.75 *(978-1-4640-3958-4(5));* 112.75 *(978-1-4640-3954-6(2))* Recorded Bks., Inc.
—Fury. 2012. (Fury Ser.: 1). (ENG.). 400p. (YA). (gr. 9). pap. 9.99 *(978-1-4424-2225-4(4),* Simon Pulse) Simon Pulse.
Milford, Kate. Bluecrowne: A Greenglass House Story. (Greenglass House Ser.). (ENG., Illus.). (J). (gr. 5-7). 2020. 288p. pap. 9.99 *(978-0-358-09754-9(1),* 1747616) 2018. 272p. 17.99 *(978-1-328-46688-4(4),* 1713526) HarperCollins Pubs. (Clarion Bks.).
—The Boneshaker. Offermann, Andrea, illus. 2011. (ENG.). 384p. (J). (gr. 5-7). pap. 7.99 *(978-0-547-55004-6(9),* 1450216, Clarion Bks.) HarperCollins Pubs.
Miranda, Megan. Fracture. 2013. (ENG.). 304p. (YA). (gr. 7-12). pap. 11.99 *(978-0-8027-3431-0(6),* 900088180, Bloomsbury USA Childrens) Bloomsbury Publishing USA.
—Fracture, 1. 2013. (Fracture Ser.). (ENG.). 272p. (YA). (gr. 8-12). 26.19 *(978-0-8027-2309-3(6),* 9780802723093) Walker & Co.
Mitchell, Briar Lee & Keely, Jack. The Whistlebrass Storm Watcher. 2016. (Whistlebrass Mysteries Ser.: 2). (ENG.). 272p. (YA). pap. 12.95 *(978-1-68261-268-2(6))* Simon & Schuster.
Mitchell, Saundra. The Elementals. 2014. (ENG.). 304p. (YA). (gr. 7). pap. 16.99 *(978-0-544-30239-6(7),* 1578442, Clarion Bks.) HarperCollins Pubs.
—The Springsweet. 2013. (ENG.). 304p. (YA). (gr. 7). pap. 16.99 *(978-0-544-00327-9(6),* 1525369, Clarion Bks.) HarperCollins Pubs.
Monahan, Hillary. Mary: the Summoning. 2015. (Bloody Mary Ser.: 1). (ENG.). 272p. (J). (gr. 7-12). pap. 9.99 *(978-1-4231-8693-9(1))* Hyperion Bks. for Children.
Montgomery, R. A. Return to Haunted House. Newton, Keith, illus. 2010. (ENG.). 80p. (J). (gr. 2-2). pap. 7.99 *(978-1-933390-40-6(9))* Chooseco LLC.
Montgomery, Ross. Max & the Millions. 2018. 265p. (J). pap. *(978-1-5247-1887-9(4))* Earthscan Canada.
—Max & the Millions. 2018. (ENG.). 272p. (J). (gr. 3-7). 16.99 *(978-1-5247-1884-8(X),* Lamb, Wendy Bks.) Random Hse. Children's Bks.
Moody, Patrick. The Gravedigger's Son. Carter, Graham, illus. 2017. 304p. (J). (gr. 2-7). 16.99 *(978-1-5107-1073-3(6),* Sky Pony Pr.) Skyhorse Publishing Co., Inc.
Moore, Alice. Touched by Darkness. 2011. 208p. 24.95 *(978-1-4502-9095-1(7));* pap. 14.95 *(978-1-4502-9096-8(5))* iUniverse, Inc.
Moore, Kelly, et al. Neverwas. 2014. (YA). pap. *(978-0-545-43419-5(X))* Scholastic, Inc.
Moore, Stuart, et al. The Dragon's Return. 2016. *(978-1-4847-7415-1(9))* Disney Publishing Worldwide.
Moreci, Michael & Seeley, Steve. Murder, Death, & the Devil, Vol. 1. 2012. (ENG., Illus.). 160p. (YA). pap. 14.99 *(978-1-60706-657-6(2),* 70092e64-7d87-495a-961b-ecc1c0456b8d) Image Comics.
Morgan, Melissa J. Charmed Forces #19: Super Special. 2008. (Camp Confidential Ser.: 19). 256p. (J). (gr. 3-7). pap. 5.99 *(978-0-448-44722-3(3),* Grosset & Dunlap) Penguin Young Readers Group.
Morin, James F. Rothshield Chasing Shadows. 2006. pap. 14.95 *(978-1-59330-422-5(6))* Aventine Pr.
Moskowitz, Hannah. Teeth. 2013. (ENG.). 288p. (YA). (gr. 9-12). 17.99 *(978-1-4424-6532-9(8),* Simon Pulse) Simon Pulse.
—Zombie Tag. 2011. (ENG.). 240p. (J). (gr. 4-7). 27.99 *(978-1-59643-720-3(0),* 900075383) Roaring Brook Pr.
Mosley, Walter. When the Thrill Is Gone: A Leonid Mcgill Mystery, 3 vols. 2012. (Leonid Mcgill Mystery Ser.: 3). (ENG.). 384p. (gr. 12). 16.00 *(978-0-451-23565-7(7),* Berkley) Penguin Publishing Group.
Moulton, Courtney Allison. Shadows in the Silence. 2014. (Angelfire Ser.: 3). (ENG.). 480p. (YA). (gr. 9). pap. 9.99 *(978-0-06-200241-9(4),* Tegen, Katherine Bks) HarperCollins Pubs.
Mull, Brandon. Grip of the Shadow Plague. Dorman, Brandon, illus. 2009. (Fablehaven Ser.: 3). (ENG.). 512p. (J). (gr. 3-8). pap. 9.99 *(978-1-4169-8603-4(0),* Aladdin) Simon & Schuster Children's Publishing.
Murdock, Catherine Gilbert. Wisdom's Kiss. 2013. (ENG.). 320p. (YA). (gr. 7). pap. 8.99 *(978-0-547-85540-0(0),* 1501132, Clarion Bks.) HarperCollins Pubs.
Murgia, Jennifer. Forest of Whispers. 2014. (Hedge Witch Ser.: 1). (ENG., Illus.). 270p. (gr. 7-9). pap. 9.95 *(978-1-937053-56-7(3))* Spencer Hill Pr.
Murphy, Emily Bain. The Disappearances. (ENG.). 400p. (YA). (gr. 7). 2018. pap. 11.99 *(978-1-328-90407-2(5),* 1700752) 2017. 17.99 *(978-0-544-87936-2(8),* 1650974) HarperCollins Pubs. (Clarion Bks.).
Murphy, Jill. A Bad Spell for the Worst Witch. Murphy, Jill, illus. 2014. (Worst Witch Ser.: 2). (ENG., Illus.). 128p. (J). (gr. 3-7). pap. 6.99 *(978-0-7636-7252-2(1))* Candlewick Pr.
Myers, Bill. The Chamber of Lies, 1 vol. 2009. (Elijah Project Ser.: 4). (ENG.). 128p. (J). (gr. 4-7). pap. 6.99 *(978-0-310-71196-4(7))* Zonderkidz.
—The Enemy Closes In, 1 vol., 2. 2009. (Elijah Project Ser.). (ENG.). 128p. (J). (gr. 4-7). pap. 6.99 *(978-0-310-71194-0(0))* Zonderkidz.
Myers, Bill & Riordan, James. On the Run, 1 vol., 1. 2009. (Elijah Project Ser.). (ENG.). 128p. (J). (gr. 4-7). pap. 4.99 *(978-0-310-71193-3(2))* Zonderkidz.
Myers, Walter Dean. Dope Sick. 2010. (ENG.). 208p. (YA). (gr. 9). pap. 11.99 *(978-0-06-121479-0(5),* Amistad) HarperCollins Pubs.
Naughton, Sarah. The Blood List. 2014. (ENG.). 304p. (YA). pap. 9.99 *(978-0-85707-866-7(6),* Simon & Schuster Children's) Simon & Schuster, Ltd. GBR. Dist: Simon & Schuster, Inc.
—The Hanged Man Rises. 2013. (ENG., Illus.). 240p. (J). pap. 6.99 *(978-0-85707-864-3(X),* Simon & Schuster Children's) Simon & Schuster, Ltd. GBR. Dist: Simon & Schuster, Inc.
Nayeri, Daniel & Nayeri, Dina. Another Jekyll, Another Hyde. 2012. (ENG., Illus.). 400p. (YA). (gr. 9). 17.99 *(978-0-7636-5261-6(X))* Candlewick Pr.
Neill, Chloe. Charmfall: A Novel of the Dark Elite. 2012. (Dark Elite Ser.: 3). (ENG.). 288p. (YA). (gr. 9). 9.99 *(978-0-451-23080-5(9),* Berkley) Penguin Publishing Group.
Neilsen, David. Beyond the Doors. 2017. 368p. (J). (gr. 3-7). 16.99 *(978-1-101-93582-8(0),* Crown Books For Young Readers) Random Hse. Children's Bks.
Newsome, Richard. The Emerald Casket. Duddle, Jonny, illus. 2012. (ENG.). 384p. (J). (gr. 3-7). pap. 6.99 *(978-0-06-194493-2(9),* Waldon Pond Pr.) HarperCollins Pubs.
—The Mask of Destiny, 3. Duddle, Jonny, illus. 2013. (ENG.). 384p. (J). (gr. 3-7). pap. 6.99 *(978-0-06-194495-6(5),* Waldon Pond Pr.) HarperCollins Pubs.
Night, P. J. You Can't Come in Here!, 2. 2011. (You're Invited to a Creepover Ser.: 2). (ENG.). 160p. (J). (gr. 3-7). pap. 7.99 *(978-1-4424-2095-3(2),* Simon Spotlight) Simon & Schuster Children's Publishing.
—You Can't Come in Here! 2018. (You're Invited to a Creepover Ser.: 2). (ENG.). 160p. (J). (gr. 3-7). 17.99 *(978-1-5344-1658-1(7),* Simon Spotlight) Simon Spotlight.
—You Can't Come in Here!, 1 vol. 2013. (You're Invited to a Creepover Ser.). (ENG.). 160p. (J). (gr. 3-6). lib. bdg. 31.36 *(978-1-61479-066-2(3),* 15854, Chapter Bks.) Spotlight.
Nishi, Yoshiyuki. Muhyo & Roji's Bureau of Supernatural Investigation, Vol. 18. 2010. (Muhyo & Roji's Bureau of Supernatural Investigation Ser.: 18). (ENG., Illus.). 192p. pap. 9.99 *(978-1-4215-2840-3(1))* Viz Media.
Noël, Alyson. Blue Moon. 2009. (Immortals Ser.: 2). (YA). lib. bdg. 20.85 *(978-0-606-07221-2(7))* Turtleback.
Noel, Alyson. Blue Moon: The Immortals. 2009. (Immortals Ser.: 2). (ENG.). 304p. (YA). (gr. 7-12). pap. 12.99 *(978-0-312-53276-5(8),* 900054353, St. Martin's Griffin) St. Martin's Pr.
—Dark Flame: A Novel. 2012. (Immortals Ser.: 4). (ENG.). 336p. (YA). (gr. 7-12). pap. 15.00 *(978-0-312-58375-0(3),* 900075111, St. Martin's Griffin) St. Martin's Pr.
—Everlasting: A Novel. 2013. (Immortals Ser.: 6). (ENG.). 352p. (YA). (gr. 7-12). pap. 13.99 *(978-1-250-02517-3(6),* 900097463, St. Martin's Griffin) St. Martin's Pr.
Noël, Alyson. Evermore. 2009. (Immortals Ser.: 1). (YA). lib. bdg. 22.10 *(978-0-606-10569-9(7))* Turtleback.
Noel, Alyson. Evermore: The Immortals. 2009. (Immortals Ser.: 1). (ENG.). 320p. (YA). (gr. 7-12). pap. 12.99 *(978-0-312-53275-8(X),* 900054351, St. Martin's Griffin) St. Martin's Pr.
—Mystic. 2013. (Soul Seekers Ser.: 3). (ENG.). 320p. (YA). (gr. 7). pap. 24.00 *(978-0-312-57567-0(X),* 900075091, St. Martin's Griffin) St. Martin's Pr.
—Shadowland: The Immortals. 2010. (Immortals Ser.: 3). (ENG.). 368p. (YA). (gr. 7-12). pap. 15.00 *(978-0-312-65005-6(1),* 900069209, St. Martin's Griffin) St. Martin's Pr.
Nolan, Han. Dancing on the Edge. 2007. (ENG., Illus.). 272p. (YA). (gr. 7-12). pap. 20.99 *(978-0-15-205884-5(2),* 1197666, Clarion Bks.) HarperCollins Pubs.
Nomura, Mizuki. Book Girl & the Corrupted Angel (light Novel), Volume 4. 2012. (Book Girl Ser.: 4). (ENG., Illus.). 248p. (YA). (gr. 8-17). pap. 13.00 *(978-0-316-07694-4(5),* Yen Pr.) Yen Pr. LLC.
—Book Girl & the Scribe Who Faced God, Part 1 (light Novel), Volume 7. 2013. (Book Girl Ser.: 7). (ENG.). 232p. (YA). (gr. 8-17). 13.00 *(978-0-316-07697-5(X),* Yen Pr.) Yen Pr. LLC.
—Book Girl & the Scribe Who Faced God, Part 2 (light Novel), Volume 8. 2014. (Book Girl Ser.: 8). (ENG., Illus.). 264p. (YA). (gr. 8-17). pap. 11.99 *(978-0-316-07698-2(8),* Yen Pr.) Yen Pr. LLC.
Noyes, Deborah. The Ghosts of Kerfol. (ENG., Illus.). 176p. (YA). (gr. 9). 2010. pap. 7.99 *(978-0-7636-4825-1(6))* 2008. 22.44 *(978-0-7636-3000-3(4))* Candlewick Pr.
—Plague in the Mirror. 2013. (ENG.). 272p. (YA). (gr. 9). 16.99 *(978-0-7636-5980-6(0))* Candlewick Pr.
Ogburn, Jacqueline. The Unicorn in the Barn. Green, Rebecca, illus. (ENG.). 304p. (J). (gr. 3-7). 2019. pap. 7.99 *(978-1-328-59585-0(4),* 1730758) 2017. 16.99 *(978-0-544-76112-4(X),* 1634613) HarperCollins Pubs. (Clarion Bks.).
O'Hara, Mo. My Big Fat Zombie Goldfish. Jagucki, Marek, illus. 2013. (My Big Fat Zombie Goldfish Ser.: 1). (ENG.). 192p. (J). (gr. 2-5). 13.99 *(978-1-250-02919-5(8),* 900118405) Feiwel & Friends.
Okorafor, Nnedi. Akata Warrior. 2018. (Nsibidi Scripts Ser.: 2). (ENG.). 512p. (YA). (gr. 7). pap. 12.99 *(978-0-14-242585-5(0),* Speak) Penguin Young Readers Group.
—Akata Witch. (Nsibidi Scripts Ser.: 1). (ENG.). (YA). (gr. 7). 2017. 384p. pap. 11.99 *(978-0-14-242091-1(3),* Speak) 2011. 368p. 18.99 *(978-0-670-01196-4(7),* Viking Books for Young Readers) Penguin Young Readers Group.
—Akata Witch. 2017. (Akata Witch Ser.: 1). lib. bdg. 22.10 *(978-0-606-40101-2(6))* Turtleback.
—Akata Woman. 2022. (Nsibidi Scripts Ser.: 3). (Illus.). 416p. (J). (gr. 7). 18.99 *(978-0-451-48058-3(9),* Viking Books for Young Readers) Penguin Young Readers Group.
Older, Daniel José. Shadowshaper (the Shadowshaper Cypher, Book 1) 2016. (Shadowshaper Cypher Ser.: 1). (ENG.). 320p. (YA). (gr. 9-9). pap. 12.99 *(978-1-338-03247-5(X))* Scholastic, Inc.
Omololu, C. J. Transcendence. 2012. (ENG.). 336p. (YA). (gr. 8-12). 26.19 *(978-0-8027-2370-3(5),* 9780802723703) Walker & Co.
Oppel, Kenneth. The Nest. Klassen, Jon, illus. (ENG.). (J). (gr. 5). 2016. 272p. pap. 8.99 *(978-1-4814-3233-7(8))* 2015. 256p. 19.99 *(978-1-4814-3232-0(X))* Simon & Schuster Bks. For Young Readers. (Simon & Schuster Bks. For Young Readers).
—Such Wicked Intent: The Apprenticeship of Victor Frankenstein, Book Two. (ENG., 320p. (YA). (gr. 7). 2012. Illus.). 16.99 *(978-1-4424-0318-5(7))*Bk. 2. 2013. pap. 12.99 *(978-1-4424-0319-2(5))* Simon & Schuster Bks. For Young Readers. (Simon & Schuster Bks. For Young Readers).
Ormsbee, K. E. The House in Poplar Wood: (Fantasy Middle Grade Novel, Mystery Book for Middle School Kids) 2018. (ENG., Illus.). 344p. (J). (gr. 3-7). 16.99 *(978-1-4521-4986-8(0))* Chronicle Bks. LLC.
Ormsbee, Kathryn. The Great Unknowable End. 2019. (ENG., Illus.). 400p. (YA). (gr. 7). 19.99 *(978-1-5344-2050-2(9),* Simon & Schuster Bks. For Young Readers) Simon & Schuster Bks. For Young Readers.
Ortega, Claribel A. Ghost Squad. 2020. (ENG.). 256p. (J). (gr. 3-7). 17.99 *(978-1-338-28012-8(0),* Scholastic Pr.) Scholastic, Inc.
Owens, Jeanette. The Nature Spirits. 2012. (Illus.). 44p. pap. 24.40 *(978-1-4772-4283-4(X))* AuthorHouse.
Page, Nathan. The Montague Twins: the Witch's Hand: (a Graphic Novel) Shannon, Drew, illus. 2020. (Montague Twins Ser.: 1). 352p. (YA). (gr. 7). pap. 17.99 *(978-0-525-64677-8(9),* Knopf Bks. for Young Readers) Random Hse. Children's Bks.
Pan, Emily X. R. The Astonishing Color of After. 2019. (ENG.). 480p. (YA). (gr. 7-17). pap. 11.99 *(978-0-316-46401-7(5))* Little, Brown Bks. for Young Readers.
Parker, Daniel. April. 2014. (Countdown Ser.: 4). (ENG.). 144p. (YA). (gr. 7). pap. 13.99 *(978-1-4814-2589-6(7),* Simon Pulse) Simon Pulse.
—August. 2014. (Countdown Ser.: 8). (ENG.). 144p. (YA). (gr. 7). pap. 13.99 *(978-1-4814-2593-3(5),* Simon Pulse) Simon Pulse.
—February. 2014. (Countdown Ser.: 2). (ENG.). 144p. (J). (gr. 7). pap. 13.99 *(978-1-4814-2587-2(0),* Simon Pulse) Simon Pulse.
—January. 2014. (Countdown Ser.: 1). (ENG.). 144p. (YA). (gr. 7). pap. 13.99 *(978-1-4814-2586-5(2),* Simon Pulse) Simon Pulse.
—July. 2014. (Countdown Ser.: 7). (ENG.). 144p. (YA). (gr. 7). pap. 13.99 *(978-1-4814-2592-6(7),* Simon Pulse) Simon Pulse.
—June. 2014. (Countdown Ser.: 6). (ENG.). 144p. (YA). (gr. 7). pap. 13.99 *(978-1-4814-2591-9(9),* Simon Pulse) Simon Pulse.
—March. 2014. (Countdown Ser.: 3). (ENG.). 144p. (YA). (gr. 7). pap. 13.99 *(978-1-4814-2588-9(9),* Simon Pulse) Simon Pulse.
—May. 2014. (Countdown Ser.: 5). (ENG.). 144p. (YA). (gr. 7). pap. 13.99 *(978-1-4814-2590-2(0),* Simon Pulse) Simon Pulse.
—November. 2014. (Countdown Ser.: 11). (ENG.). 144p. (YA). (gr. 7). pap. 13.99 *(978-1-4814-2596-4(X),* Simon Pulse) Simon Pulse.
—October. 2014. (Countdown Ser.: 10). (ENG.). 144p. (YA). (gr. 7). pap. 13.99 *(978-1-4814-2595-7(1),* Simon Pulse) Simon Pulse.
—September. 2014. (Countdown Ser.: 9). (ENG.). 144p. (YA). (gr. 7). pap. 13.99 *(978-1-4814-2594-0(3),* Simon Pulse) Simon Pulse.
Parker, Natalie C. Behold the Bones. 2016. (Beware the Wild Ser.: 2). (ENG.). 368p. (YA). (gr. 8). 17.99 *(978-0-06-224155-9(9),* HarperTeen) HarperCollins Pubs.
Parlato, Steven. The Precious Dreadful: A Novel. 2018. (ENG., Illus.). 352p. (YA). (gr. 9). 18.99 *(978-1-5072-0277-7(6),* Simon Pulse) Simon Pulse.
Patten, E. J. The Legend Thief. Rocco, John, illus. 2013. (Hunter Chronicles Ser.: 2). (ENG.). 384p. (J). (gr. 3-7). 16.99 *(978-1-4424-2035-9(9),* Simon & Schuster Bks. For Young Readers) Simon & Schuster Bks. For Young Readers.
—Return to Exile. Rocco, John, illus. (Hunter Chronicles Ser.: 1). (ENG.). 512p. (J). (gr. 3-7). 2013. pap. 7.99 *(978-1-4424-2033-5(2))* 2011. 16.99 *(978-1-4424-2032-8(4))* Simon & Schuster Bks. For Young Readers. (Simon & Schuster Bks. For Young Readers).
Paulson, Ingrid. Valkyrie Rising. 2012. (ENG.). 352p. (YA). (gr. 8). 17.99 *(978-0-06-202572-2(4),* HarperTeen) HarperCollins Pubs.
Peacock, Kathleen. Willowgrove. 2016. (Shifters Novel Ser.: 3). (ENG.). 384p. (YA). (gr. 9). pap. 9.99 *(978-0-06-204872-1(4),* Tegen, Katherine Bks) HarperCollins Pubs.
Pearce, Jackson. Fathomless. 2013. (Fairy Tale Retelling Ser.). (ENG.). 320p. (YA). (gr. 10-17). pap. 8.99 *(978-0-316-20777-5(2))* Little, Brown Bks. for Young Readers.
—Sisters Red. 2011. (Fairy Tale Retelling Ser.). (ENG.). 352p. (YA). (gr. 10-17). pap. 18.99 *(978-0-316-06867-3(5))* Little, Brown Bks. for Young Readers.
—Sweetly. 2012. (Fairy Tale Retelling Ser.). (ENG.). 336p. (YA). (gr. 10-17). pap. 17.99 *(978-0-316-06866-6(7))* Little, Brown Bks. for Young Readers.
Penn, Mw. The Pe'lerin of the Orb. 2013. 228p. pap. 11.95 *(978-0-9840425-4-8(7))* MathWord Pr., LLC.
Perales, Alonso M. Brujas, Lechuzas y Espantos/Witches, Owls & Spooks. Pluecker, John, tr. from SPA. 2008. (ENG & SPA., Illus.). 96p. (J). (gr. 3-7). pap. 9.95 *(978-1-55885-512-0(2),* Piñata Books) Arte Publico Pr.
Peretti, Frank E. The Deadly Curse of Toco-Rey. Life Publishers International Staff, tr. from ENG. 2005. (RUS., Illus.). 156p. (J). *(978-0-7361-0347-3(3))* Life Pubs. International.
Peretti, Frank E. & Thomas Nelson Publishing Staff. The Secret of the Desert Stone, 1 vol., 5. 2005. (Cooper Kids Adventure Ser.: 5). (ENG.). 160p. (J). pap. 6.99 *(978-1-4003-0574-2(8),* Tommy Nelson) Nelson, Thomas Inc.
Perez, Marlene. Dead Is a Battlefield. 2012. (Dead Is Ser.: 6). (ENG.). 240p. (YA). (gr. 7). pap. 7.99 *(978-0-547-60734-4(2),* 1463411, Clarion Bks.) HarperCollins Pubs.
—Dead Is a Battlefield. 2012. (Dead Is Ser.: 6). lib. bdg. 18.40 *(978-0-606-24759-7(9))* Turtleback.
—Dead Is a Killer Tune. 2012. (Dead Is Ser.: 7). lib. bdg. 18.40 *(978-0-606-26623-9(2))* Turtleback.
—Dead Is a State of Mind. 2009. (Dead Is Ser.: 2). (ENG., Illus.). 192p. (YA). (gr. 7-18). pap. 7.99 *(978-0-15-206210-1(6),* 1063350, Clarion Bks.) HarperCollins Pubs.
—Dead Is Just a Dream. 2014. (Dead Is Ser.: 8). lib. bdg. 18.40 *(978-0-606-35990-0(7))* Turtleback.
—Dead Is Not an Option. 2011. (Dead Is Ser.: 5). (ENG.). 256p. (YA). (gr. 7-18). pap. 7.99 *(978-0-547-34593-2(3),* 1419607, Clarion Bks.) HarperCollins Pubs.
—Dead Is the New Black. 2008. (Dead Is Ser.: 1). (ENG., Illus.). 208p. (YA). (gr. 7-18). pap. 8.99 *(978-0-15-206408-2(7),* 1199183, Clarion Bks.) HarperCollins Pubs.
Peterfreund, Diana. Ascendant. 2012. (Killer Unicorns Ser.: 2). (ENG.). 416p. (YA). (gr. 9). pap. 8.99 *(978-0-06-149005-7(9),* HarperTeen) HarperCollins Pubs.
Peterson, Shelley. Sundancer: The Saddle Creek Series. 2017. (Saddle Creek Ser.: 2). (ENG.). 408p. (YA). pap. 12.99 *(978-1-4597-3948-2(5))* Dundurn Pr. CAN. Dist: Publishers Group West (PGW).
Peterson, Will. Triskellion 3: the Gathering. 2010. (Triskellion Ser.: 3). (ENG., Illus.). 384p. (J). (gr. 9-18). 16.99 *(978-0-7636-4847-3(7))* Candlewick Pr.
Pierce, Tamora. Emperor Mage. 2015. (Immortals Ser.: 3). (ENG., Illus.). 368p. (YA). (gr. 7). pap. 12.99 *(978-1-4814-4026-4(8))* Simon & Schuster Children's Publishing.
—The Realms of the Gods. 2005. (Immortals Ser.: No. 4). 347p. (gr. 7-12). 18.00 *(978-0-7569-5775-9(3))* Perfection Learning Corp.
—The Realms of the Gods. 2015. (Immortals Ser.: 4). (ENG., Illus.). 352p. (YA). (gr. 7). pap. 12.99 *(978-1-4814-4028-8(4))* Simon & Schuster Children's Publishing.
—Wild Magic. 2005. (Immortals Ser.: No. 1). (Illus.). 362p. (gr. 7-12). 18.00 *(978-0-7569-5508-3(4))* Perfection Learning Corp.
—Wild Magic. 2015. (Immortals Ser.: 1). (ENG., Illus.). 368p. (YA). (gr. 7). pap. 12.99 *(978-1-4814-4022-6(5))* Simon & Schuster Children's Publishing.
Pietron, Barbara. Thunderstone. 2013. (Legacy in Legend Ser.: 1). (ENG.). 262p. (YA). (gr. 7). pap. 12.99 *(978-1-940368-91-7(X))* Scribe Publishing Co.
Pike, Christopher, pseud. Black Knight. 2014. (Witch World Ser.: 2). (ENG., Illus.). 464p. (YA). (gr. 9). 19.99 *(978-1-4424-6733-0(9));* pap. 11.99 *(978-1-4424-6734-7(7))* Simon Pulse. (Simon Pulse).
—Red Queen. 2014. (Witch World Ser.: 1). (ENG., Illus.). 560p. (YA). (gr. 9). pap. 11.99 *(978-1-4424-3029-7(X),* Simon Pulse) Simon Pulse.
—Strange Girl. 2015. (ENG., Illus.). 432p. (YA). (gr. 9). pap. 12.99 *(978-1-4814-5058-4(1),* Simon Pulse) Simon Pulse.
—Thirst (Boxed Set) Thirst No. 1; Thirst No. 2; Thirst No. 3, 3 vols. 2013. (Thirst Ser.). (ENG.). 1744p. (YA). (gr. 9). pap. 30.99 *(978-1-4424-8375-0(X),* Simon Pulse) Simon Pulse.
—Thirst No. 1: The Last Vampire, Black Blood, Red Dice. 2009. (Thirst Ser.: 1). (ENG., Illus.). 624p. (YA). (gr. 9). pap. 14.99 *(978-1-4169-8308-8(2),* Simon Pulse) Simon Pulse.
—Thirst No. 2 No. 2: Phantom, Evil Thirst, Creatures of Forever, Bk. 2. 2010. (Thirst Ser.: 2). (ENG.). 608p. (YA). (gr. 9). pap. 14.99 *(978-1-4169-8309-5(0),* Simon Pulse) Simon Pulse.
—Thirst No. 3: The Eternal Dawn. 2010. (Thirst Ser.: 3). (ENG.). 512p. (YA). (gr. 9-18). pap. 14.99 *(978-1-4424-1317-7(4),* Simon Pulse) Simon Pulse.
—Thirst No. 4: The Shadow of Death, 4. 2011. (Thirst Ser.: 4). (ENG., Illus.). 528p. (YA). (gr. 9). pap. 10.99 *(978-1-4424-1319-1(0),* Simon Pulse) Simon Pulse.
—Thirst No. 5: The Sacred Veil. 2013. (Thirst Ser.: 5). (ENG., Illus.). 512p. (YA). (gr. 7). pap. 14.99 *(978-1-4424-6731-6(2),* Simon Pulse) Simon Pulse.

—Witch World. 2012. (Witch World Ser.: 1). (ENG.). 528p. (YA). (gr. 9). 17.99 *(978-1-4424-3028-0(1)*, Simon Pulse) Simon Pulse.

Plum, Amy. Die for Me. (Die for Me Ser.: 1). (ENG.). (YA). (gr. 9). 2012. 368p. pap. 8.99 *(978-0-06-200402-4(6))* 2011. 352p. 17.99 *(978-0-06-200401-7(8))* HarperCollins Pubs. (HarperTeen).

—Until I Die. 2013. (Die for Me Ser.: 2). (ENG.). 384p. (YA). (gr. 9). pap. 10.99 *(978-0-06-200405-5(0)*, HarperTeen) HarperCollins Pubs.

Plum-Ucci, Carol. Fire Will Fall. 2011. (ENG.). 492p. (YA). (gr. 9). pap. 25.99 *(978-0-547-55007-7(3)*, 1450217, Clarion Bks.) HarperCollins Pubs.

—Fire Will Fall. 2011. (ENG.). 496p. (YA). (gr. 9-12). 24.94 *(978-0-15-216562-8(2))* Houghton Mifflin Harcourt Publishing Co.

Poblocki, Dan. The Nightmarys. 2011. 336p. (J). (gr. 3-7). pap. 8.99 *(978-0-375-84257-3(8)*, Yearling) Random Hse. Children's Bks.

—The Stone Child. 2010. 288p. (J). (gr. 3-7). pap. 8.99 *(978-0-375-84255-9(1)*, Yearling) Random Hse. Children's Bks.

Pon, Cindy. Silver Phoenix. 2011. (Silver Phoenix Ser.: 1). (ENG.). 368p. (YA). (gr. 9). pap. 8.99 *(978-0-06-173024-5(6)*, Greenwillow Bks.) HarperCollins Pubs.

Ponti, James. Dark Days. 2015. (Dead City Ser.: 3). (ENG., Illus.). 304p. (J). (gr. 4-8). 18.99 *(978-1-4814-3636-6(8)*, Aladdin) Simon & Schuster Children's Publishing.

—Dead City. (Dead City Ser.: 1). (ENG., Illus.). (J). (gr. 4-8). 2013. 304p. pap. 8.99 *(978-1-4424-4130-9(5))* 2012. 288p. 19.99 *(978-1-4424-4129-3(1))* Simon & Schuster Children's Publishing. (Aladdin).

Poole, Gabriella. Darke Academy 02: Blood Ties. 2010. (Darke Academy Ser.). (ENG.). 304p. (YA). (gr. 7-17). pap. 9.99 *(978-0-340-98925-8(4))* Hachette Children's Group GBR. Dist: Hachette Bk. Group.

Popescu, Petru. Weregirls: Birth of the Pack: Birth of the Pack. rev. ed. 2007. (ENG.). 352p. (YA). (gr. 8-12). pap. 18.99 *(978-0-7653-1641-7(2)*, 900039012, Tor Teen) Doherty, Tom Assocs., LLC.

Porte, Barbara Ann. Beauty & the Serpent: Thirteen Tales of Unnatural Animals. Covey, Rosemary Feit, illus. 2008. (ENG.). 128p. (YA). (gr. 7). pap. 7.99 *(978-1-4169-7579-3(9)*, Simon & Schuster/Paula Wiseman Bks.) Simon & Schuster/Paula Wiseman Bks.

Porter, Sarah. The Twice Lost. 2014. (Lost Voices Trilogy Ser.: 3). (ENG.). 480p. (YA). (gr. 7). pap. 9.99 *(978-0-547-48255-2(8)*, 1439698, Clarion Bks.) HarperCollins Pubs.

—Waking Storms. 2013. (Lost Voices Trilogy Ser.: 2). (ENG.). 416p. (YA). (gr. 7). pap. 8.99 *(978-0-547-48254-5(X)*, 1439697, Clarion Bks.) HarperCollins Pubs.

Priestley, Chris. Through Dead Eyes. 2014. (ENG.). 240p. (J). (gr. 7). pap. *(978-1-4088-1107-8(3)*, 31012, Bloomsbury Children's Bks.) Bloomsbury Publishing Plc.

Prm, Katherine & Dee, Stacy. The Veil. 2010. 233p. (YA). pap. 15.95 *(978-1-59705-540-6(9))* Wings ePress, Inc.

Randall, Thomas. The Waking: A Winter of Ghosts. 2011. (YA). pap. 9.99 *(978-1-59990-252-4(4)*, Bloomsbury USA Childrens) Bloomsbury Publishing USA.

Raney, Renee Simmons. Hairy, Scary, but Mostly Merry Fairies! Curing Nature Deficiency Through Folklore, Imagination, & Creative Activities. Crowe, Carolyn Walker, illus. 2017. (ENG.). 128p. pap. 15.95 *(978-1-58838-328-0(8)*, 8814, NewSouth Bks.) NewSouth, Inc.

Raymond, Roger & Savoy, Darryl. Ralph Filmore: Paranormal Investigator. O'Reilly, Sean Patrick, ed. 2012. (Illus.). 78p. (J). pap. 14.95 *(978-1-926914-31-2(7))* Arcana Studio, Inc.

Reber, Kelseyleigh. If I Fall: The Circle & Cross: Book One. 2013. (ENG.). 238p. (J). pap. 14.99 *(978-0-9889351-3-6(9))* Aperture Pr., LLC.

Reed, Bliss & Reed, Sinclair. This Summer I Plan to Rule the World. rev. ed. 2009. (ENG., Illus.). 100p. (J). (gr. k-7). pap. *(978-0-9822200-2-3(2))* Temmen, Edition, Horst Temmen.

Reeves, Dia. Bleeding Violet. 2010. (ENG.). 480p. (YA). (gr. 9). pap. 20.99 *(978-1-4169-8619-5(7)*, Simon Pulse) Simon Pulse.

—Slice of Cherry. 2011. (ENG.). (YA). (gr. 9). 528p. pap. 14.99 *(978-1-4169-8621-8(9))*; 512p. 16.99 *(978-1-4169-8620-1(0))* Simon Pulse. (Simon Pulse).

Reger, Rob & Gruner, Jessica. Emily the Strange: Dark Times. Reger, Rob & Parker, Buzz, illus. 2011. (Emily the Strange Ser.: 3). (ENG.). 248p. (YA). (gr. 8). pap. 10.99 *(978-0-06-145237-6(8)*, HarperCollins) HarperCollins Pubs.

Regin, Andrew. Guardians: Volume 1. 2012. 286p. pap. 27.95 *(978-1-4626-8856-2(X))* America Star Bks.

Reichs, Kathy. Virals. 2014. lthr. 79.00 *(978-1-62715-582-3(1))* Leatherbound Bestsellers.

—Virals. 2011. (Virals Ser.: 1). (ENG.). 480p. (J). (gr. 5-18). 11.99 *(978-1-59514-426-3(9)*, Puffin Books) Penguin Young Readers Group.

—Virals. 2011. 20.00 *(978-1-61383-226-4(5))* Perfection Learning Corp.

Reichs, Kathy & Reichs, Brendan. Trace Evidence. 2016. (Virals Ser.). lib. bdg. 20.85 *(978-0-606-38400-1(6))* Turtleback.

—Virals. 2011. (Virals Ser.: 1). lib. bdg. 20.85 *(978-0-606-23069-8(6))* Turtleback.

Reiss, Kathryn. Pale Phoenix. 2003. (ENG., Illus.). 336p. (J). (gr. 5-7). pap. 15.95 *(978-0-15-204927-0(4)*, 1194878, Clarion Bks.) HarperCollins Pubs.

Renae, Cameo. Hidden Wings. 2013. 270p. pap. 13.99 *(978-1-939769-21-3(3))* Crushing Hearts and Black Butterfly Publishing.

Richards, Justin. The Chaos Code. 2007. (ENG.). 400p. (YA). (gr. 7-12). 17.95 *(978-1-59990-124-4(2)*, 9781599901244, Bloomsbury USA Childrens) Bloomsbury Publishing USA.

Richardson, Tracy. The Field. unabr. ed. 2013. (ENG.). 200p. (YA). (gr. 7-12). pap. 11.95 *(978-1-935462-82-8(2))* Luminis Bks., Inc.

Riggs, Ransom. Hollow City. Riggs, Ransom, illus. 2015. (Miss Peregrine's Peculiar Children Ser.: 2). (Illus.). lib. bdg. 22.10 *(978-0-606-36394-5(7))* Turtleback.

—Hollow City: The Second Novel of Miss Peregrine's Peculiar Children. 2015. (Miss Peregrine's Peculiar Children Ser.: 2). (Illus.). 416p. (YA). (gr. 9). pap. 14.99 *(978-1-59474-735-9(0))* Quirk Bks.

—Hollow City: The Second Novel of Miss Peregrine's Peculiar Children. Riggs, Ransom, illus. 2014. (Miss Peregrine's Peculiar Children Ser.: 2). (Illus.). 352p. (YA). (gr. 9). 18.99 *(978-1-59474-612-3(5))* Quirk Bks.

—Hollow City: the Graphic Novel: The Second Novel of Miss Peregrine's Peculiar Children. 2016. (Miss Peregrine's Peculiar Children: the Graphic Novel Ser.: 2). (ENG., Illus.). 272p. (YA). (gr. 8-17). 20.00 *(978-0-316-30679-9(7))* Yen Pr. LLC.

—Library of Souls. 2017. (Miss Peregrine's Peculiar Children Ser.: 3). (ENG.). (YA). (gr. 9). lib. bdg. 23.30 *(978-0-606-39808-4(2))* Turtleback.

—Library of Souls: The Third Novel of Miss Peregrine's Peculiar Children. 2015. (Miss Peregrine's Peculiar Children Ser.: 3). (Illus.). 400p. (YA). (gr. 9). 18.99 *(978-1-59474-758-8(X))* Quirk Bks.

—A Map of Days. 2018. (Miss Peregrine's Peculiar Children Ser.: 4). (ENG.). 496p. (YA). (gr. 7). 22.99 *(978-0-7352-3214-3(8)*, Dutton Books for Young Readers) Penguin Young Readers Group.

—Miss Peregrine's Home for Peculiar Children. (Miss Peregrine's Peculiar Children Ser.: 1). (Illus.). (YA). (gr. 9). 2013. 384p. pap. 14.99 *(978-1-59474-603-1(6))* 2011. 352p. 18.99 *(978-1-59474-476-1(9))* Quirk Bks.

—Miss Peregrine's Home for Peculiar Children. l.t. ed. 2012. (ENG.). 484p. (J). (gr. 8-12). 23.99 *(978-1-4104-5023-4(6))* Thorndike Pr.

—Miss Peregrine's Home for Peculiar Children. 2013. (Miss Peregrine's Peculiar Children Ser.: 1). (SWE.). lib. bdg. 22.10 *(978-0-606-32081-8(4))* Turtleback.

—Miss Peregrine's Home for Peculiar Children (Movie Tie-In Edition) 2016. (Miss Peregrine's Peculiar Children Ser.: 1). (Illus.). 392p. (YA). (gr. 9). pap. 11.99 *(978-1-59474-902-5(7))* Quirk Bks.

—Miss Peregrine's Peculiar Children Boxed Set, 3 vols. 2015. (Miss Peregrine's Peculiar Children Ser.). (Illus.). 1216p. (YA). (gr. 9). 44.97 *(978-1-59474-890-5(X))* Quirk Bks.

Riggs, Ransom, et al. Miss Peregrine's Home for Peculiar Children. 2011. pap. *(978-1-59474-574-4(9))* Quirk Bks.

Ritter, William. Beastly Bones. 2016. (Jackaby Ser.: 2). lib. bdg. 20.80 *(978-0-606-39017-0(0))* Turtleback.

Rivers, Phoebe. Moment of Truth, 5. 2012. (Saranormal Ser.: 5). (ENG.). 160p. (J). (gr. 3-7). 15.99 *(978-1-4424-6127-7(6)*, Simon Spotlight) Simon & Schuster Children's Publishing.

—Moment of Truth. 2012. (Saranormal Ser.: 5). (ENG.). 160p. (J). (gr. 3-7). pap. 7.99 *(978-1-4424-6125-3(X)*, Simon Spotlight) Simon Spotlight.

—Spirits of the Season. 2012. (Saranormal Ser.: 4). (ENG.). 160p. (J). (gr. 3-7). 15.99 *(978-1-4424-5379-1(6))*; pap. 6.99 *(978-1-4424-5223-7(4))* Simon Spotlight. (Simon Spotlight).

—Yesterday & Today. 2013. (Saranormal Ser.: 11). (ENG., Illus.). 160p. (J). (gr. 3-7). 15.99 *(978-1-4424-8962-2(6))*; pap. 5.99 *(978-1-4424-8961-5(8))* Simon Spotlight. (Simon Spotlight).

Rivers, Rae. The Keepers: Declan (the Keepers, Book 2), Book 2. 2014. (Keepers Ser.: 2). (ENG.). 336p. pap. 11.99 *(978-0-00-810443-6(3)*, One More Chapter) HarperCollins Pubs. Ltd. GBR. Dist: HarperCollins Pubs.

Robertson, Andrea. Bloodrose: A Nightshade Novel. 2012. (Nightshade Ser.: 3). (ENG.). 432p. (YA). (gr. 9). pap. 12.99 *(978-0-14-242370-7(X)*, Speak) Penguin Young Readers Group.

—Nightshade: Book 1. 2011. (Nightshade Ser.: 1). (ENG.). 496p. (YA). (gr. 9-18). pap. 12.99 *(978-0-14-241980-9(X)*, Speak) Penguin Young Readers Group.

Robinson, Gary. Billy Buckhorn Abnormal. 2014. (Billy Buckhorn Ser.: 1). (ENG.). 172p. (YA). (gr. 8-12). pap. 9.95 *(978-1-939053-07-7(2)*, 7th Generation) BPC.

—Billy Buckhorn Paranormal. 2015. (Billy Buckhorn Ser.: 2). (ENG.). 120p. (YA). (gr. 8-12). pap. 9.95 *(978-1-939053-08-4(0)*, 7th Generation) BPC.

—Billy Buckhorn Supranormal. 2015. (Billy Buckhorn Ser.: 3). (ENG.). 128p. (YA). (gr. 8-12). pap. 9.95 *(978-1-939053-12-1(9)*, 7th Generation) BPC.

Robison, Dan. Death Chant: Kimo's Battle with the Shamanic Forces. 2006. 194p. (J). pap. *(978-0-922993-52-9(1))* Marquette Bks.

Rollins, Danielle. Burning. 2017. (ENG.). 368p. (YA). pap. 9.99 *(978-1-68119-205-5(5)*, 900162857, Bloomsbury USA Childrens) Bloomsbury Publishing USA.

Rosati, Gina. Auracle. 2014. (ENG.). 304p. (YA). (gr. 7-12). pap. 17.99 *(978-1-250-04006-0(X)*, 900123709) Square Fish.

Rose, Imogen. Initiation: Japanese Language Edition. Galeano, Tomomi, tr. 2013. 482p. pap. 16.99 *(978-1-940015-04-0(9))* Imogen Rose.

Rosen, Jonathan. Night of the Living Cuddle Bunnies: Devin Dexter #1. (Devin & Dexter Ser.: 1). (ENG.). (J). (gr. 2-7). 2018. 304p. pap. 9.99 *(978-1-5107-3487-6(2))* 2017. 256p. 15.99 *(978-1-5107-1523-3(1))* Skyhorse Publishing Co., Inc. (Sky Pony Pr.).

Rosenberg, Madelyn & Crockett, Mary. Dream Boy. 2014. 336p. (YA). (gr. 7-12). pap. 9.99 *(978-1-4022-9583-6(9)*, 9781402295836) Sourcebooks, Inc.

Rosoff, Meg. There Is No Dog. l.t. ed. 2012. (ENG.). 392p. (J). (gr. 7-12). 23.99 *(978-1-4104-4707-4(3))* Thorndike Pr.

Roux, Madeleine. Asylum. (Asylum Ser.: 1). (ENG.). (YA). (gr. 9). 2014. 336p. pap. 15.99 *(978-0-06-222097-4(7))* 2013. (Illus.). 320p. 17.99 *(978-0-06-222096-7(9))* HarperCollins Pubs. (HarperCollins).

—Asylum. 2015. (SPA.). 320p. (YA). (gr. 9-12). pap. 20.99 *(978-987-612-778-3(0))* V&R Editoras.

—Catacomb. 2015. (Asylum Ser.: 3). (ENG.). 336p. (YA). (gr. 9). 17.99 *(978-0-06-236405-0(7)*, HarperCollins) HarperCollins Pubs.

—Sanctum. 2014. (Illus.). 343p. (YA). *(978-0-06-235182-1(6))* Harper & Row Ltd.

—Sanctum. 2014. (Asylum Ser.: 2). (ENG., Illus.). 352p. (YA). (gr. 9). 17.99 *(978-0-06-222099-8(3)*, HarperCollins) HarperCollins Pubs.

—Tomb of Ancients. Compiet, Iris, illus. 2019. (House of Furies Ser.: 3). (ENG.). 384p. (YA). (gr. 9). 17.99 *(978-0-06-249873-1(8)*, HarperTeen) HarperCollins Pubs.

Rubinstein, Gillian. Under the Cat's Eye: A Tale of Morph & Mystery. 2017. (ENG.). 208p. (J). (gr. 3-7). pap. 13.99 *(978-1-5344-2935-2(2)*, Aladdin) Simon & Schuster Children's Publishing.

Russell, Randy. Dead Rules. 2011. (ENG.). 384p. (YA). (gr. 8-18). 16.99 *(978-0-06-198670-3(4)*, HarperTeen) HarperCollins Pubs.

Sabatini, Kimberly. Touching the Surface. 2013. (ENG., Illus.). 352p. (YA). (gr. 9). pap. 9.99 *(978-1-4424-4003-6(1)*, Simon Pulse) Simon Pulse.

Sak., M. J. The Stone Summons. 2007. 141p. pap. 15.95 *(978-1-84799-791-3(0))* Lulu Pr., Inc.

Samms, Olivia. Sketchy. 2013. pap. *(978-1-4778-6650-4(7))* Amazon Publishing.

Sands, Kevin. The Assassin's Curse. 2017. (Blackthorn Key Ser.: 3). (ENG., Illus.). 544p. (J). (gr. 5-9). 19.99 *(978-1-5344-0523-3(2)*, Aladdin) Simon & Schuster Children's Publishing.

—The Assassin's Curse. 2018. (Blackthorn Key Ser.: 3). (ENG., Illus.). 560p. (J). (gr. 5-9). pap. 9.99 *(978-1-5344-0524-0(0)*, Simon & Schuster/Paula Wiseman Bks.) Simon & Schuster/Paula Wiseman Bks.

—The Blackthorn Key. (Blackthorn Key Ser.: 1). (ENG., Illus.). (J). (gr. 5-9). 2016. 400p. pap. 8.99 *(978-1-4814-4652-5(5))* 2015. 384p. 19.99 *(978-1-4814-4651-8(7))* Simon & Schuster Children's Publishing. (Aladdin).

—The Blackthorn Key. 2016. lib. bdg. 18.40 *(978-0-606-38966-2(0))* Turtleback.

—Call of the Wraith. (Blackthorn Key Ser.: 4). (ENG.). 512p. (J). (gr. 5-9). 2019. pap. 9.99 *(978-1-5344-2848-5(8))* 2018. (Illus.). 19.99 *(978-1-5344-2847-8(X))* Simon & Schuster Children's Publishing. (Aladdin).

—Mark of the Plague. (Blackthorn Key Ser.: 2). (ENG.). (J). (gr. 5-9). 2017. 560p. pap. 9.99 *(978-1-4814-4675-4(4))* 2016. (Illus.). 544p. 19.99 *(978-1-4814-4674-7(6))* Simon & Schuster Children's Publishing. (Aladdin).

Saunders, Kate. The Land of Neverendings. 2017. (ENG.). 336p. (J). 14.50 *(978-0-571-31084-5(2)*, Faber & Faber Children's Bks.) Faber & Faber, Inc.

Savage, J. Scott. Case File 13: Zombie Kid. Holgate, Doug, illus. 2013. (Case File 13 Ser.: 1). (ENG.). 304p. (J). (gr. 3-7). pap. 7.99 *(978-0-06-213327-4(6)*, HarperCollins) HarperCollins Pubs.

Schaeffer, Rebecca. Only Ashes Remain. 2019. (Market of Monsters Ser.: 2). (ENG.). 432p. (YA). (gr. 9). 17.99 *(978-1-328-86355-3(7)*, 1694451, Clarion Bks.) HarperCollins Pubs.

Schaenen, Inda. All the Cats of Cairo. 2007. 225p. (J). (gr. -1-10). per. 8.95 *(978-0-9768126-5-4(7))* Brown Barn Bks.

Schreiber, Ellen. Full Moon Kisses. 2013. (Full Moon Ser.: 3). (ENG.). 224p. (YA). (gr. 8). pap. 9.99 *(978-0-06-198654-3(2)*, Tegen, Katherine Bks) HarperCollins Pubs.

—Magic of the Moonlight, 2. 2012. (Full Moon Ser.: 2). (ENG.). 256p. (YA). (gr. 8-12). pap. 9.99 *(978-0-06-198656-7(9)*, Tegen, Katherine Bks) HarperCollins Pubs.

—Once in a Full Moon. 2011. (Full Moon Ser.: 1). (ENG.). 320p. (YA). (gr. 8). pap. 9.99 *(978-0-06-198652-9(6)*, Tegen, Katherine Bks) HarperCollins Pubs.

—Vampire Kisses 9: Immortal Hearts, 9. 2013. (Vampire Kisses Ser.: 9). (ENG.). 272p. (YA). (gr. 8-12). pap. 10.99 *(978-0-06-207009-8(6)*, Tegen, Katherine Bks) HarperCollins Pubs.

Schwab, V. E. The near Witch. 2020. 320p. pap. 16.99 *(978-1-78909-114-4(4))* 2019. 360p. 19.99 *(978-1-78909-112-0(8))* Titan Bks. Ltd. GBR. (Titan Bks.). Dist: Penguin Random Hse. LLC.

Schwab, Victoria. The Archived. 2014. (Archived Ser.). (ENG., Illus.). 352p. (J). (gr. 7-12). pap. 10.99 *(978-1-4231-7108-9(X))* Little, Brown Bks. for Young Readers.

Schwab, Victoria & Schwab, V. E. Tunnel of Bones (City of Ghosts #2) 2019. (City of Ghosts Ser.: 2). (ENG., Illus.). 304p. (J). (gr. 4-7). 17.99 *(978-1-338-11104-0(3)*, Scholastic Pr.) Scholastic, Inc.

Scott, Michael. The Alchemyst. 2009. (ENG., Illus.). 375p. (gr. 6-10). 19.00 *(978-1-60686-514-9(5))* Perfection Learning Corp.

—The Alchemyst. (Secrets of the Immortal Nicholas Flamel Ser.: 1). (ENG.). 400p. (YA). (gr. 7). 2008. pap. 11.99 *(978-0-385-73600-8(2)*, Ember) 2007. (Illus.). 18.99 *(978-0-385-73357-1(7)*, Delacorte Bks. for Young Readers) Random Hse. Children's Bks.

—The Enchantress. 2013. (Secrets of the Immortal Nicholas Flamel Ser.: 6). (ENG.). 528p. (YA). (gr. 7). pap. 10.99 *(978-0-385-73536-0(7)*, Ember) Random Hse. Children's Bks.

—The Enchantress. 2013. (Secrets of the Immortal Nicholas Flamel Ser.: 6). lib. bdg. 22.10 *(978-0-606-31947-8(6))* Turtleback.

—The Magician. 2009. (Secrets of the Immortal Nicholas Flamel Ser.: 2). (ENG.). 496p. (YA). (gr. 7). pap. 11.99 *(978-0-385-73728-9(9)*, Ember) Random Hse. Children's Bks.

—The Necromancer. 2011. (Secrets of the Immortal Nicholas Flamel Ser.: 4). (ENG.). 416p. (YA). (gr. 7). pap. 11.99 *(978-0-385-73532-2(4)*, Ember) Random Hse. Children's Bks.

—The Necromancer. l.t. ed. 2010. (Secrets of the Immortal Nicholas Flamel Ser.). (ENG.). 690p. pap. 23.99 *(978-1-4104-2851-6(6))* Thorndike Pr.

—The Sorceress. 2010. (Secrets of the Immortal Nicholas Flamel Ser.: 3). (ENG.). 512p. (YA). (gr. 7-18). pap. 11.99 *(978-0-385-73530-8(8)*, Ember) Random Hse. Children's Bks.

—The Sorceress. 2010. (Secrets of the Immortal Nicholas Flamel Ser.: 3). lib. bdg. 22.10 *(978-0-606-14133-8(2))* Turtleback.

—The Sorceress the Secrets of the Immortal Nicholas Flamel. l.t. ed. 2009. (Secrets of the Immortal Nicholas Flamel Ser.). (ENG.). 614p. (YA). 23.95 *(978-1-4104-2092-3(2))* Thorndike Pr.

—The Warlock. 2012. (Secrets of the Immortal Nicholas Flamel Ser.: 5). (ENG.). 400p. (YA). (gr. 7). pap. 11.99 *(978-0-385-73534-6(0)*, Ember) Random Hse. Children's Bks.

—The Warlock. l.t. ed. 2011. (Secrets of the Immortal Nicholas Flamel Ser.). (ENG.). 545p. 23.99 *(978-1-4104-4157-7(1))* Thorndike Pr.

—The Warlock. 2012. (Secrets of the Immortal Nicholas Flamel Ser.: 5). lib. bdg. 22.10 *(978-0-606-26411-2(6))* Turtleback.

Seabrooke, Brenda. Cemetery Street. 2008. 144p. (J). (gr. 3-7). 16.95 *(978-0-8234-2115-2(5))* Holiday Hse., Inc.

Seduction. 2014. (Legacy Ser.). (ENG., Illus.). 416p. (YA). (gr. 9). 17.99 *(978-1-4814-0023-7(1)*, Simon & Schuster/Paula Wiseman Bks.) Simon & Schuster/Paula Wiseman Bks.

Seeley, Tim. Rebirth, Vol. 2. 2012. (ENG., Illus.). 160p. (YA). pap. 16.99 *(978-1-60706-637-8(8)*, 8ac2a50c-3087-4b31-9464-2e0b38e1756b) Image Comics.

Shanker, Tarun & Zekas, Kelly. These Vicious Masks. 2016. (These Vicious Masks Ser.: 1). (ENG.). 320p. (YA). pap. 15.99 *(978-1-250-07389-1(8)*, 900150894) Feiwel & Friends.

Sheff, Nic. Harmony House. 2016. (ENG.). 304p. (YA). (gr. 9). 17.99 *(978-0-06-233709-2(2)*, HarperTeen) HarperCollins Pubs.

Shields, Gillian. Eternal. 2012. (Immortal Ser.: 3). (ENG.). 384p. (YA). (gr. 8). pap. 9.99 *(978-0-06-200040-8(3)*, Tegen, Katherine Bks) HarperCollins Pubs.

—Immortal. 2010. (Immortal Ser.: 1). (ENG.). 384p. (YA). (gr. 8-12). pap. 8.99 *(978-0-06-137583-5(7)*, Tegen, Katherine Bks) HarperCollins Pubs.

Shirvington, Jessica. Corruption. 2017. (Disruption Ser.: 02). 448p. 9.99 *(978-1-4607-5219-7(8)*, HarperCollins) HarperCollins Pubs.

—Emblaze. 2013. (Embrace Ser.: 3). (ENG.). 464p. (YA). (gr. 7-12). pap. 14.99 *(978-1-4022-7131-1(X))* Sourcebooks, Inc.

—Endless. 2014. (Embrace Ser.: 4). (ENG.). 480p. (YA). (gr. 7-12). pap. 15.99 *(978-1-4022-8945-3(6))* Sourcebooks, Inc.

—Entice. 2013. (Embrace Ser.: 2). (ENG.). 464p. (YA). (gr. 7-12). pap. 16.99 *(978-1-4022-7128-1(X))* Sourcebooks, Inc.

Showalter, Gena. Alice in Zombieland. 2013. (White Rabbit Chronicles Ser.: 1). (ENG.). 416p. pap. 10.99 *(978-0-373-21089-3(2)*, Harlequin Teen) Harlequin Enterprises ULC CAN. Dist: HarperCollins Pubs.

—Alice in Zombieland. 2013. (J). lib. bdg. 20.85 *(978-0-606-31712-2(0))* Turtleback.

—The Queen of Zombie Hearts. 2014. (White Rabbit Chronicles Ser.: 3). (ENG.). 464p. (YA). 18.99 *(978-0-373-21131-9(7)*, Harlequin Teen) Harlequin Enterprises ULC CAN. Dist: HarperCollins Pubs.

—Through the Zombie Glass. 2014. (White Rabbit Chronicles Ser.: 2). (ENG.). 480p. (YA). pap. 12.99 *(978-0-373-21129-6(5)*, Harlequin Teen) Harlequin Enterprises ULC CAN. Dist: HarperCollins Pubs.

Shull, Megan. The Swap. (ENG.). 400p. (J). (gr. 5-9). 2016. pap. 7.99 *(978-0-06-231170-2(0))* 2014. 16.99 *(978-0-06-231169-6(7))* HarperCollins Pubs. (Tegen, Katherine Bks).

Shulman, Polly. The Poe Estate. 2015. 272p. (J). (gr. 5). 17.99 *(978-0-399-16614-3(9)*, Nancy Paulsen Books) Penguin Young Readers Group.

Shusterman, Neal. Bruiser. 2010. (ENG.). 336p. (YA). (gr. 9-18). 17.99 *(978-0-06-113408-1(2)*, Quill Tree Bks.) HarperCollins Pubs.

—Dread Locks #1. 2006. (Dark Fusion Ser.: 1). 176p. (YA). (gr. 7-18). 7.99 *(978-0-14-240599-4(X)*, Speak) Penguin Young Readers Group.

—Duckling Ugly. 2007. (Dark Fusion Ser.: 2). 224p. (YA). (gr. 7-18). 8.99 *(978-0-14-240684-7(8)*, Speak) Penguin Young Readers Group.

—Red Rider's Hood. 2006. (Dark Fusion Ser.: 3). (ENG.). 192p. (YA). (gr. 7-18). 7.99 *(978-0-14-240678-6(3)*, Speak) Penguin Young Readers Group.

—Scorpion Shards. 2013. (Star Shards Chronicles Ser.: 1). (ENG., Illus.). (YA). (gr. 7). 240p. 17.99 *(978-1-4424-5836-9(4))*; 256p. pap. 12.99 *(978-1-4424-5114-8(9))* Simon & Schuster Bks. For Young Readers. (Simon & Schuster Bks. For Young Readers).

—Shattered Sky. 2013. (Star Shards Chronicles Ser.: 3). (ENG., Illus.). 544p. (YA). (gr. 7). 17.99 *(978-1-4424-5835-2(6))*; pap. 9.99 *(978-1-4424-5117-9(3))* Simon & Schuster Bks. For Young Readers. (Simon & Schuster Bks. For Young Readers).

—Thief of Souls. 2013. (Star Shards Chronicles Ser.: 2). (ENG., Illus.). (YA). (gr. 7). 304p. 17.99 *(978-1-4424-5837-6(2))*; 320p. pap. 12.99 *(978-1-4424-5112-4(2))* Simon & Schuster Bks. For Young Readers. (Simon & Schuster Bks. For Young Readers).

Sierra, Judy. Never Kick a Ghost & Other Silly Chillers. Constantin, Pascale, illus. 2011. (I Can Read Level 2 Ser.). (ENG.). 32p. (J). (gr. k-3). pap. 5.99 *(978-0-06-143521-8(X)*, HarperCollins) HarperCollins Pubs.

Simmons, Derek. Flash of Life. 2006. 85p. pap. 16.95 *(978-1-4241-3890-6(6))* PublishAmerica, Inc.

Sinclair, Alison. Lightborn. 2011. (Darkborn Trilogy Ser.: 2). (Illus.). 320p. (gr. 12). 7.99 *(978-0-451-46358-6(7)*, Ace) Penguin Publishing Group.

Singleton, Linda Joy. Don't Die, Dragonfly. Karre, Andrew, ed. 2004. (Seer Ser.: 1). (ENG.). 288p. (YA). pap. 9.95 *(978-0-7387-0526-2(8))* Llewellyn Pubns.

—Last Dance. 2005. (Seer Ser.: 2). (ENG.). 264p. (YA). pap. 9.95 *(978-0-7387-0638-2(8)*, Flux) Llewellyn Pubns.

Skelton, Matthew. The Story of Cirrus Flux. 2012. (ENG., Illus.). 304p. (J). (gr. 4-6). lib. bdg. 21.19 *(978-0-385-90398-1(7))* Random House Publishing Group.

Slade, Arthur G. The Hunchback Assignments, 1. 2010. (Hunchback Assignments Ser.). (ENG.). 288p. (YA). (gr. 7-12). lib. bdg. 24.94 *(978-0-385-90694-4(3))* Random House Publishing Group.

Slater, Adam. The Shadowing - Hunted, 1. 2012. (Shadowing Ser.). (ENG.). 208p. (gr. 7-12). 24.94 *(978-1-60684-261-4(7))* Farshore GBR. Dist: Children's Plus, Inc.

—The Shadowing #2: Skinned. 2012. (ENG.). 256p. (J). (gr. 7-7). 16.99 *(978-1-60684-262-1(5)*, Carolrhoda Lab™) Lerner Publishing Group.

Smith, Cynthia Leitich. Blessed. 2011. (Tantalize Ser.: 3). (ENG., Illus.). 480p. (YA). (gr. 9-18). 17.99 *(978-0-7636-4326-3(2))* Candlewick Pr.

—Diabolical. 2012. (Tantalize Ser.: 4). (ENG., Illus.). 368p. (YA). (gr. 9-12). 17.99 *(978-0-7636-5118-3(4))* Candlewick Pr.

—Feral Curse. 2014. (Feral Ser.: 2). (ENG., Illus.). 272p. (YA). (gr. 9). 17.99 *(978-0-7636-5910-3(X))* Candlewick Pr.

—Tantalize. 2008. (Tantalize Ser.: 1). (ENG., Illus.). 336p. (YA). (gr. 9). pap. 9.99 *(978-0-7636-4059-0(X))* Candlewick Pr.

Smith, Jennifer E. The Storm Makers. Helquist, Brett, illus. 2013. (ENG.). 384p. (J). (gr. 3-7). pap. 19.99

(978-0-316-17959-1(0)) Little, Brown Bks. for Young Readers.

Smith, L. J. Dark Visions: The Strange Power; the Possessed; the Passion. 2009. (Dark Visions Ser.: Bks 1-3). (ENG.). 752p. (YA). (gr. 7). pap. 15.99 *(978-1-4169-8956-1(0)*, Simon Pulse) Simon Pulse.

—The Fury & Dark Reunion. 2007. (Vampire Diaries: 3). (YA). lib. bdg. 20.85 *(978-0-606-07135-2(0))* Turtleback.

—The Secret Circle: the Temptation. 2014. (Secret Circle Ser.: 6). (ENG.). 304p. (YA). (gr. 8). pap. 9.99 *(978-0-06-213045-7(5)*, HarperTeen) HarperCollins Pubs.

—The Vampire Diaries: the Fury & Dark Reunion, 2 vols. 2007. (Vampire Diaries: Nos. 3-4). (ENG.). 528p. (YA). (gr. 8-12). pap. 12.99 *(978-0-06-114098-3(8)*, HarperTeen) HarperCollins Pubs.

—The Vampire Diaries: the Hunters: Moonsong Vol. 9. 2013. (Vampire Diaries: the Hunters Ser.: 2). (ENG.). 416p. (YA). (gr. 9). pap. 10.99 *(978-0-06-201771-0(3)*, HarperTeen) HarperCollins Pubs.

—The Vampire Diaries: the Hunters: Phantom. (Vampire Diaries: the Hunters Ser.: 1). (ENG.). (YA). (gr. 9). 2012. 432p. pap. 10.99 *(978-0-06-201769-7(1))* 2011. 416p. 17.99 *(978-0-06-201768-0(3))* HarperCollins Pubs. (HarperTeen).

—The Vampire Diaries: the Return: Midnight. 2012. (Vampire Diaries: the Return Ser.: 3). (ENG.). 592p. (YA). (gr. 8). pap. 10.99 *(978-0-06-172086-4(0)*, HarperTeen) HarperCollins Pubs.

—The Vampire Diaries: the Return: Nightfall. 2010. (Vampire Diaries: the Return Ser.: 1). (ENG.). 608p. (YA). (gr. 8). pap. 11.99 *(978-0-06-172080-2(1)*, HarperTeen) HarperCollins Pubs.

—The Vampire Diaries: the Return: Shadow Souls. 2011. (Vampire Diaries: the Return Ser.: 2). (ENG.). 624p. (YA). (gr. 8). pap. 11.99 *(978-0-06-172083-3(6)*, HarperTeen) HarperCollins Pubs.

Smith, L. J. & Clark, Aubrey. The Salvation: Unseen, 1. 2013. (Vampire Diaries: 1). (ENG.). 306p. (YA). (gr. 7-12). pap. 9.99 *(978-1-4778-0967-9(8)*, 9781477809679, 47North) Amazon Publishing.

Smith, L. J. & Kevin Williamson & Julie Plec, Kevin Williamson. The Vampire Diaries: Stefan's Diaries #4: the Ripper, 4. 2011. (Vampire Diaries: Stefan's Diaries: 4). (ENG.). 256p. (YA). (gr. 9-12). pap. 11.99 *(978-0-06-211393-1(3)*, HarperTeen) HarperCollins Pubs.

—The Vampire Diaries: Stefan's Diaries #5: the Asylum. 2012. (Vampire Diaries: Stefan's Diaries: 5). (ENG.). 256p. (YA). (gr. 9). pap. 11.99 *(978-0-06-211395-5(X)*, HarperTeen) HarperCollins Pubs.

Smith, Lane. Return to Augie Hobble. 2017. (J). lib. bdg. 18.40 *(978-0-606-38550-3(9))* Turtleback.

Smith-Ready, Jeri. Shade. (ENG.). (YA). (gr. 9). 2011. 336p. pap. 9.99 *(978-1-4169-9407-7(6))* 2010. 320p. 17.99 *(978-1-4169-9406-0(8))* Simon Pulse. (Simon Pulse).

—Shift. (ENG.). (YA). (gr. 9). 2012. 400p. pap. 9.99 *(978-1-4169-9409-1(2))* 2011. 384p. 17.99 *(978-1-4169-9408-4(4))* Simon Pulse. (Simon Pulse).

—Shine. 2012. (ENG.). 416p. (YA). (gr. 9). pap. 9.99 *(978-1-4424-3946-7(7)*, Simon Pulse) Simon Pulse.

Smith, Ronald L. The Mesmerist. 2019. (ENG., Illus.). 288p. (J). (gr. 5-7). pap. 9.99 *(978-1-328-49800-7(X)*, 1717857, Clarion Bks.) HarperCollins Pubs.

Smith, Sarah. The Other Side of Dark. 2010. (ENG.). 320p. (YA). (gr. 7-18). 16.99 *(978-1-4424-0280-5(6)*, Atheneum Bks. for Young Readers) Simon & Schuster Children's Publishing.

Snaith, Simone. Between the Water & the Woods. Kipin, Sara, illus. 2019. 320p. (YA). (gr. 7). 18.99 *(978-0-8234-4020-7(6))* Holiday Hse., Inc.

Sniegoski, Thomas E. The Fallen 1: The Fallen & Leviathan, 1. 2010. (Fallen Ser.: 1). (ENG.). 544p. (YA). (gr. 11-12). pap. 14.99 *(978-1-4424-0862-3(6)*, Simon Pulse) Simon Pulse.

—The Fallen 2: Aerie & Reckoning. 2010. (Fallen Ser.: 2). (ENG.). 576p. (YA). (gr. 11-18). pap. 13.99 *(978-1-4424-0863-0(4)*, Simon Pulse) Simon Pulse.

—The Fallen 3 Vol. 3: End of Days. 2011. (Fallen Ser.: 3). (ENG.). 384p. (YA). (gr. 9). pap. 9.99 *(978-1-4424-2349-7(8)*, Simon Pulse) Simon Pulse.

—The Fallen 4: Forsaken. 2012. (Fallen Ser.: 4). (ENG.). 416p. (YA). (gr. 9). pap. 13.99 *(978-1-4424-4699-1(4)*, Simon Pulse) Simon Pulse.

—The Fallen 5: Armageddon. 2013. (Fallen Ser.: 5). (ENG., Illus.). 592p. (YA). (gr. 9). pap. 13.99 *(978-1-4424-6005-8(9)*, Simon Pulse) Simon Pulse.

Snyder, Maria V., et al. Spirited. 2012. (Illus.). 332p. (J). (gr. 8-12). pap. 16.99 *(978-1-61603-020-9(8))* Leap Bks.

Snyder, Zilpha Keatley. The Egypt Game. Raible, Alton, illus. 2009. (ENG.). 240p. (J). (gr. 3-7). pap. 8.99 *(978-1-4169-9051-2(8)*, Atheneum Bks. for Young Readers) Simon & Schuster Children's Publishing.

—The Unseen. 2005. 199p. 16.00 *(978-0-7569-5670-7(6))* Perfection Learning Corp.

Spradlin, Michael P. Live & Let Shop. 2005. (Spy Goddess Ser.: Bk. 1). (ENG., Illus.). 224p. (gr. 7-18). 15.99 *(978-0-06-059407-7(1))* HarperCollins Pubs.

Springer, Nancy. Possessing Jessie. 2010. (ENG.). 128p. (YA). (gr. 7-18). pap. 16.95 *(978-0-8234-2259-3(3))* Holiday Hse., Inc.

St. Crow, Lili. Betrayals, 10 vols. 2010. (Strange Angels Ser.: 2). (YA). 95.75 *(978-1-4407-7156-9(1))* Recorded Bks., Inc.

—Betrayals. 2009. (Strange Angels Ser.: 2). lib. bdg. 20.85 *(978-0-606-09020-9(7))* Turtleback.

—Betrayals: A Strange Angels Novel, 2. 2009. (Strange Angels Ser.: 2). (ENG., Illus.). 304p. (YA). (gr. 7-18). pap. 26.19 *(978-1-59514-252-8(5)*, Razorbill) Penguin Young Readers Group.

—Defiance, 4. 2011. (Strange Angels Ser.: 4). (ENG.). 304p. (YA). (gr. 7-18). 26.19 *(978-1-59514-392-1(0)*, Razorbill) Penguin Young Readers Group.

—Jealousy, 10 vols. 2010. (Strange Angels Ser.: 3). (J). 86.75 *(978-1-4498-2774-8(8))*; 209.75 *(978-1-4498-2772-4(1))*; 1.25 *(978-1-4498-2777-9(2))*; 68.75 *(978-1-4498-2773-1(X))*; 83.75 *(978-1-4498-2776-2(4))* Recorded Bks., Inc.

—Jealousy. 2010. (Strange Angels Ser.: 3). lib. bdg. 20.85 *(978-0-606-14566-4(4))* Turtleback.

—Jealousy: A Strange Angels Novel. 2010. (Strange Angels Ser.: 3). (ENG.). 320p. (YA). (gr. 7-18). 9.99 *(978-1-59514-290-0(8)*, Razorbill) Penguin Young Readers Group.

—Strange Angels, 9 vols. 2009. (Strange Angels Ser.: 1). (J). 181.75 *(978-1-4407-6194-2(9))*; 117.75 *(978-1-4407-6197-3(3))*; 84.75 *(978-1-4407-6195-9(7))*; 87.75 *(978-1-4407-6193-5(0))*; 114.75 *(978-1-4407-6199-7(X))* Recorded Bks., Inc.

—Strange Angels. 2009. (Strange Angels Ser.: 1). lib. bdg. 20.85 *(978-0-606-08957-9(8))* Turtleback.

Stahler, David, Jr. Doppelganger. (YA). 2008. (ENG.). 272p. (gr. 8). pap. 8.99 *(978-0-06-087234-2(9)*, HarperTeen) 2006. (Illus.). 272p. (gr. 7-12). 16.99 *(978-0-06-087232-8(2))* 2006. (Illus.). 258p. (gr. 7-12). lib. bdg. 17.89 *(978-0-06-087233-5(0))* HarperCollins Pubs.

Staniszewski, Anna. Finders Reapers. 2016. (Switched at First Kiss Ser.: 2). 272p. (J). (gr. 5-8). pap. 7.99 *(978-1-4926-1549-1(8))* Sourcebooks, Inc.

—I'm with Cupid. 2015. (Switched at First Kiss Ser.: 1). 240p. (J). (gr. 5-8). pap. 7.99 *(978-1-4926-1546-0(3)*, 9781492615460) Sourcebooks, Inc.

—Match Me If You Can. 2017. (Switched at First Kiss Ser.: 3). 240p. (J). (gr. 5-8). pap. 12.99 *(978-1-4926-1552-1(8)*, 9781492615521) Sourcebooks, Inc.

Stayer, Elizabeth. Santa's Magic Stardust. 2009. 40p. pap. 18.49 *(978-1-4490-2884-8(5))* AuthorHouse.

Stegmaier, Laura J. Ling-Ling Turner, Ppi: Mystery of the Rising Island. 2013. 92p. pap. 10.95 *(978-1-4575-2363-2(9))* Dog Ear Publishing, LLC.

Stemple, Adam & Yolen, Jane. Sanctuary: Book 2. Zangara, Orion, illus. 2018. (Stone Man Mysteries Ser.). (ENG.). 88p. (YA). (gr. 7-12). pap. 8.99 *(978-1-5415-1043-2(7)*, 56cb1424-a16d-418a-a0c5-52e2dda42a46);No. 2. 29.32 *(978-1-4677-4197-2(3)*, 96ca54a0-3352-4fc3-8226-178cee1ddbb1) Lerner Publishing Group. (Graphic Universe™).

—Stone Cold: Book 1, No. 1. Zangara, Orion, illus. 2016. (Stone Man Mysteries Ser.: 1). (ENG.). 80p. (YA). (gr. 7-12). pap. 8.99 *(978-1-5124-1155-3(8)*, f2275e16-f0aa-4e03-9423-302d12617e07); lib. bdg. 29.32 *(978-1-4677-4196-5(5)*, 1ced9530-2931-4585-8c9c-adff2d2724ca) Lerner Publishing Group. (Graphic Universe™).

Stentiford, Tyler Michael. A Darker Secret. 2009. (ENG.). 128p. (YA). pap. 9.99 *(978-1-60138-315-0(0))* Atlantic Publishing Group, Inc.

Stevenson, Robert Louis. Dr. Jekyll & Mr. Hyde. 2008. (Bring the Classics to Life Ser.). (ENG., Illus.). 72p. (gr. 4-12). pap., act. bk. ed. 10.95 *(978-0-931334-50-4(0)*, EDCTR-402B) EDCON Publishing Group.

Stiefvater, Maggie. Blue Lily, Lily Blue (the Raven Cycle, Book 3), 1 vol. 2014. (Raven Cycle Ser.: 3). (ENG.). 400p. (YA). (gr. 9-9). 21.99 *(978-0-545-42496-7(8)*, Scholastic Pr.) Scholastic, Inc.

—Blue Lily, Lily Blue (the Raven Cycle, Book 3) (Unabridged Edition), 1 vol. unabr. ed. 2014. (Raven Cycle Ser.: 3). (ENG.). 2p. (YA). (gr. 7). audio compact disk 39.99 *(978-0-545-64907-0(2))* Scholastic, Inc.

—The Dream Thieves. 2014. (Raven Cycle Ser.: 2). lib. bdg. 20.85 *(978-0-606-36029-6(8))* Turtleback.

—The Dream Thieves (the Raven Cycle, Book 2) (Raven Cycle Ser.: 2). (ENG.). 448p. (YA). (gr. 9). 2014. pap. 12.99 *(978-0-545-42495-0(X)*, Scholastic Paperbacks) 2013. 19.99 *(978-0-545-42494-3(1)*, Scholastic Pr.) Scholastic, Inc.

—The Dream Thieves (the Raven Cycle, Book 2) (Unabridged Edition), 1 vol. unabr. ed. 2013. (Raven Cycle Ser.: 2). (ENG.). 2p. (YA). (gr. 9). audio compact disk 39.99 *(978-0-545-60039-2(1))* Scholastic, Inc.

—Forever. l.t. ed. 2011. (Shiver Trilogy: Bk. 3). (ENG.). 597p. 23.99 *(978-1-4104-3606-1(3))* Thorndike Pr.

—Forever. 2014. (Wolves of Mercy Falls Ser.: 3). lib. bdg. 20.85 *(978-0-606-36649-6(0))* Turtleback.

—Forever (Shiver, Book 3) 2014. (Shiver Ser.: 3). (ENG.). 416p. (YA). (gr. 9). pap. 10.99 *(978-0-545-68280-0(0))* Scholastic, Inc.

—Forever (Shiver, Book 3) (Unabridged Edition), 1 vol. unabr. ed. 2011. (Shiver Ser.: 3). (ENG.). 5p. (YA). (gr. 8). audio compact disk 79.99 *(978-0-545-31555-5(7))* Scholastic, Inc.

—Hunted (Spirit Animals, Book 2), Bk. 2. 2014. (Spirit Animals Ser.: 2). (ENG., Illus.). 192p. (J). (gr. 3-7). 13.99 *(978-0-545-52244-1(7)*, Scholastic Pr.) Scholastic, Inc.

—Lament: The Faerie Queen's Deception. 2008. (Lament Novel Ser.: 1). (ENG., Illus.). 336p. (YA). (gr. 9-12). pap. 9.95 *(978-0-7387-1370-0(8)*, 0738713708, Flux) North Star Editions.

—Linger. 2014. (Shiver Ser.). (ENG.). (YA). (gr. 9). lib. bdg. 20.60 *(978-1-68065-091-4(2))* Perfection Learning Corp.

—Linger. l.t. ed. 2011. (Shiver Trilogy: Bk. 2). (ENG.). 488p. pap. 23.99 *(978-1-4104-3447-0(8))* Thorndike Pr.

—Linger (Shiver, Book 2), 1 vol. 2014. (Shiver Ser.: 2). (ENG.). 384p. (YA). (gr. 9). pap. 10.99 *(978-0-545-68279-4(7))* Scholastic, Inc.

—The Raven King (the Raven Cycle, Book 4) 2016. (Raven Cycle Ser.: 4). (ENG.). 448p. (YA). (gr. 9-9). 18.99 *(978-0-545-42498-1(4)*, Scholastic Pr.) Scholastic, Inc.

—The Raven King (the Raven Cycle, Book 4) (Unabridged Edition), 1 vol. unabr. ed. 2016. (Raven Cycle Ser.: 4). (ENG.). 1p. (YA). (gr. 7). audio compact disk 39.99 *(978-0-545-64908-7(0))* Scholastic, Inc.

—Shiver. 2011. (Shiver Trilogy: Bk. 1). 9.64 *(978-0-7848-3572-2(1)*, Everbind) Marco Bk. Co.

—Shiver. (ENG.). (gr. 9). 2014. (Shiver Ser.). (YA). lib. bdg. 20.60 *(978-1-68065-090-7(4))* 2010. (Shiver Trilogy: Bk. 1). 392p. 20.00 *(978-1-60686-750-1(4))* Perfection Learning Corp.

—Shiver. l.t. ed. 2010. (Shiver Trilogy: Bk. 1). (ENG.). 506p. 23.95 *(978-1-4104-2667-3(X))* Thorndike Pr.

—Shiver. 2014. (Wolves of Mercy Falls Ser.: 1). lib. bdg. 20.85 *(978-0-606-36647-2(4))* Turtleback.

—Shiver (Shiver, Book 1), 1 vol. 2014. (Shiver Ser.: 1). (ENG.). 416p. (YA). (gr. 9). pap. 12.99 *(978-0-545-68278-7(9))* Scholastic, Inc.

—Sinner (Shiver) 2015. (Shiver Ser.). (ENG.). 368p. (YA). (gr. 9). pap. 12.99 *(978-0-545-65459-3(9))* Scholastic, Inc.

Stine, R. L. Dangerous Girls #2: the Taste of Night. 2005. (Dangerous Girls Ser.: 2). (ENG.). 288p. (YA). (gr. 8-18). pap. 8.99 *(978-0-06-059618-7(X)*, HarperTeen) HarperCollins Pubs.

—The Horror at Chiller House (Goosebumps HorrorLand #19) 2011. (Goosebumps Horrorland Ser.: 19). (ENG., Illus.). 160p. (J). (gr. 3-7). pap. 6.99 *(978-0-545-16200-5(9)*, Scholastic Paperbacks) Scholastic, Inc.

—Revenge of the Lawn Gnomes (Classic Goosebumps #19) 2011. (Classic Goosebumps Ser.: 19). (ENG.). 160p. (J). (gr. 3-7). pap. 7.99 *(978-0-545-29835-3(0)*, Scholastic Paperbacks) Scholastic, Inc.

—The Taste of Night. 2004. (Dangerous Girls Ser.: No. 2). (ENG.). 240p. (J). (gr. 7-18). 14.99 *(978-0-06-059616-3(3))* HarperCollins Pubs.

—Temptation: Goodnight Kiss; Goodnight Kiss 2; "the Vampire Club" 2012. (ENG.). 416p. (YA). (gr. 7). pap. 11.99 *(978-1-4424-5068-4(1)*, Simon Pulse) Simon Pulse.

Strange, Jason. The Demon Card, 1 vol. Kendall, Bradford & Evergreen, Nelson, illus. 2012. (Jason Strange Ser.). (ENG.). 72p. (J). (gr. 3-6). pap. 6.25 *(978-1-4342-3884-9(9)*, 118065, Stone Arch Bks.) Capstone.

—The Demon Card, 1 vol. Evergreen, Nelson & Kendall, Bradford, illus. 2012. (Jason Strange Ser.). (ENG.). 72p. (J). (gr. 3-6). lib. bdg. 25.32 *(978-1-4342-3296-0(4)*, 116259, Stone Arch Bks.) Capstone.

—The Graveyard Plot, 1 vol. Evergreen, Nelson & Kendall, Bradford, illus. 2012. (Jason Strange Ser.). (ENG.). 72p. (J). (gr. 3-6). pap. 6.25 *(978-1-4342-3886-3(5)*, 118067, Stone Arch Bks.) Capstone.

Strom, Yale. The Wedding That Saved a Town. Prosmitsky, Jenya, illus. 2008. (J). (gr. -1). 17.95 *(978-0-8225-7376-0(8)*, Kar-Ben Publishing) Lerner Publishing Group.

Strong, Karen. Just South of Home. 2019. (ENG., Illus.). 320p. (J). (gr. 3-7). 17.99 *(978-1-5344-1938-4(1)*, Simon & Schuster Bks. For Young Readers) Simon & Schuster Bks. For Young Readers.

Stroud, Jonathan. Buried Fire. 2004. 332p. (J). pap. *(978-0-7818-5794-9(5))* Hippocrene Bks., Inc.

—Lockwood & Co.: the Creeping Shadow. 2016. (Lockwood & Co Ser.: 4). (ENG., Illus.). 464p. (J). (gr. 5-9). 16.99 *(978-1-4847-0967-2(5))* Little, Brown Bks. for Young Readers.

—Lockwood & Co.: the Empty Grave. (Lockwood & Co Ser.: 5). (ENG.). (J). (gr. 5-9). 2018. 480p. pap. 8.99 *(978-1-4847-9006-9(5))* 2017. (Illus.). 448p. 16.99 *(978-1-4847-7872-2(3))* Little, Brown Bks. for Young Readers.

—Lockwood & Co.: the Hollow Boy. (Lockwood & Co Ser.: 3). (ENG.). (J). (gr. 5-9). 2016. 416p. pap. 8.99 *(978-1-4847-1189-7(0))* 2015. 400p. 37.99 *(978-1-4847-0968-9(3))* Little, Brown Bks. for Young Readers.

—Lockwood & Co.: the Screaming Staircase. 2013. (Lockwood & Co Ser.: 1). (ENG.). 400p. (J). (gr. 5-9). 16.99 *(978-1-4231-6491-3(1))* Hyperion Pr.

—Lockwood & Co.: the Screaming Staircase. 2014. (Lockwood & Co Ser.: 1). (ENG., Illus.). 416p. (J). (gr. 5-9). pap. 9.99 *(978-1-4231-8692-2(3))* Little, Brown Bks. for Young Readers.

—Lockwood & Co.: the Whispering Skull. (Lockwood & Co Ser.: 2). (ENG.). (J). (gr. 5-9). 2015. 464p. pap. 9.99 *(978-1-4231-9462-0(4))* 2014. 448p. 17.99 *(978-1-4231-6492-0(X))* Little, Brown Bks. for Young Readers.

Sublime. 2014. (ENG., Illus.). 336p. (YA). (gr. 9). 17.99 *(978-1-4814-1368-8(6)*, Simon & Schuster Bks. For Young Readers) Simon & Schuster Bks. For Young Readers.

Sullivan, Laura L. Under the Green Hill, 1. 2010. (Green Hill Novels Ser.). (ENG.). 320p. (J). (gr. 4-6). 22.44 *(978-0-8050-8984-4(5)*, 9780805089844, Holt, Henry & Co.) Holt, Henry & Co.

—Under the Green Hill. 2011. (ENG.). 336p. (J). (gr. 4-8). pap. 17.99 *(978-0-312-55149-0(5)*, 900074427) Square Fish.

Suma, Nova Ren. Imaginary Girls. 2012. (ENG.). 352p. (YA). (gr. 9-18). pap. 8.99 *(978-0-14-242143-7(X)*, Speak) Penguin Young Readers Group.

—The Walls Around Us. 2016. (ENG.). 336p. (YA). (gr. 9-12). pap. 9.95 *(978-1-61620-590-4(3)*, 73590) Algonquin Young Readers.

—The Walls Around Us. 2016. lib. bdg. 20.80 *(978-0-606-37957-1(6))* Turtleback.

Sun, Amanda. Storm. 2015. (Paper Gods Ser.: 5). (ENG.). 304p. (YA). pap. 9.99 *(978-0-373-21174-6(0)*, Harlequin Teen) Harlequin Enterprises ULC CAN. Dist: HarperCollins Pubs.

Sundell, Joanne. Arctic Shadow. 2015. (Watch Eyes Trilogy Ser.: 2). (ENG.). 278p. (YA). 25.95 *(978-1-4328-3008-3(2)*, Five Star Trade) Cengage Gale.

—Arctic Will. 2016. (ENG.). 326p. (YA). 25.95 *(978-1-4328-3175-2(5)*, Five Star) Cengage Gale.

Sunseri, Heather. Mindsiege. 2013. (ENG.). 374p. (YA). pap. 14.00 *(978-0-9887153-5-6(X))* Sunseri, Heather.

Talkington, Amy. Liv, Forever. 2015. (Illus.). 288p. (YA). (gr. 9). pap. 10.99 *(978-1-61695-479-6(5)*, Soho Teen) Soho Pr., Inc.

Tanigawa, Nagaru. The Boredom of Haruhi Suzumiya (light Novel) 2010. (Haruhi Suzumiya Ser.: 3). (ENG., Illus.). 224p. (YA). (gr. 10-17). 24.00 *(978-0-316-03886-7(5)*, Yen Pr.) Yen Pr. LLC.

—The Melancholy of Suzumiya Haruhi-Chan, Vol. 6. 2012. (Melancholy of Suzumiya Haruhi-Chan Ser.: 6). (ENG., Illus.). 160p. (gr. 11-17). pap. 11.99 *(978-0-316-22914-2(8))* Yen Pr. LLC.

—The Sigh of Haruhi Suzumiya. 2009. (Haruhi Suzumiya Ser.: Bk. 1). (ENG., Illus.). 208p. (YA). (gr. 10-18). 14.99 *(978-0-316-03881-2(4))* Hachette Bk. Group.

Taylor, G. P. The Shadowmancer Returns: The Curse of Salamander Street. 2007. (Shadowmancer; 04 Ser.). 240p. (J). *(978-1-4287-4670-1(6)*, Putnam Juvenile) Penguin Publishing Group.

Taylor, Laini. Daughter of Smoke & Bone. 2023. (YA). 75.00 *(978-1-955876-21-6(5))* LitJoy Crate.

—Daughter of Smoke & Bone. (Daughter of Smoke & Bone Ser.: 1). (ENG.). (YA). (gr. 10-17). 2020. 448p. pap. 12.99 *(978-0-316-45918-1(6))* 2012. 624p. pap. 26.99 *(978-0-316-22435-2(9))* Little, Brown Bks. for Young Readers.

—Daughter of Smoke & Bone. 2012. (Daughter of Smoke & Bone Ser.: 1). (YA). lib. bdg. 24.50 *(978-0-606-26704-5(2))* Turtleback.

—Days of Blood & Starlight. l.t. ed. 2012. (Daughter of Smoke & Bone Ser.: 2). (ENG.). 688p. (YA). (gr. 10-17). 47.99 *(978-0-316-22433-8(2))* Little, Brown Bks. for Young Readers.

—Lips Touch: Three Times. Di Bartolo, Jim, illus. 2011. (ENG.). 288p. (YA). (gr. 7-7). pap. 14.99 *(978-0-545-05586-4(5)*, Levine, Arthur A. Bks.) Scholastic, Inc.

Teitelbaum, Michael. The Phantom Pharaoh. 2015. (Cold Whispers Ser.). (ENG., Illus.). 32p. (J). (gr. 2-6). lib. bdg. 28.50 *(978-1-62724-810-5(2))* Bearport Publishing Co., Inc.

Terrell, Heather. Eternity: A Fallen Angel Novel. 2011. (Fallen Angel Ser.: 2). (ENG.). 304p. (YA). (gr. 8). pap. 8.99 *(978-0-06-196571-5(5)*, HarperTeen) HarperCollins Pubs.

The Story Pirates & West, Jacqueline. The Story Pirates Present. Aly, Hatem, illus. 2019. (Story Pirates Ser.: 2). 288p. (J). (gr. 3-7). 13.99 *(978-1-63565-091-4(7)*, 9781635650914, Random Hse. Bks. for Young Readers) Random Hse. Children's Bks.

Thomas, Novene. The Enchanted Opera: Supernaturally Enchanting & Spiritually Enlightening. 2013. 192p. pap. 13.95 *(978-1-62212-986-7(5)*, Strategic Bk. Publishing) Strategic Book Publishing & Rights Agency (SBPRA).

Thompson, Kate. Midnight's Choice. unabr. ed. 2004. (Switchers Ser.: Vol. 2). 240p. (J). (gr. 5-9). pap. 38.00 incl. audio *(978-0-8072-8769-9(5)*, Listening Library) Random Hse. Audio Publishing Group.

Thomson, Sarah L. Deadly Wish: A Ninja's Journey. 2017. (Ninja's Journey Ser.). (ENG.). 240p. (J). (gr. 5-9). 17.95 *(978-1-62979-777-9(4)*, Astra Young Readers) Astra Publishing Hse.

—Mercy: The Last New England Vampire, 1 vol. 2011. (ENG.). 178p. (J). pap. 16.95 *(978-1-934031-36-0(4)*, 53a309a3-c71e-4f20-bdd3-f4fe46e103af) Islandport Pr., Inc.

Ticktock Media, Ltd. Staff. The Unexplained: Encounters with Ghosts, Monsters, & Aliens. 2008. (ENG.). 96p. (J). (gr. 2-4). pap. 9.95 *(978-1-84696-807-5(0)*, TickTock Books) Octopus Publishing Group GBR. Dist: Independent Pubs. Group.

Tiernan, Cate. Darkest Fear. 2014. (Birthright Ser.: 1). (ENG., Illus.). 368p. (YA). (gr. 9). pap. 9.99 *(978-1-4424-8245-6(1)*, Simon Pulse) Simon Pulse.

Towell, Katy. Skary Childrin & the Carousel of Sorrow. 2013. 272p. (J). (ENG.). (gr. 8-12). lib. bdg. 24.94 *(978-0-375-96860-0(1))*; (gr. 3-7). pap. 8.99 *(978-0-375-87240-2(X))* Random Hse. Children's Bks. (Knopf Bks. for Young Readers).

Trapani, Iza. Haunted Party. Trapani, Iza, illus. (Illus.). 28p. (J). 2010. (gr. -1-2). pap. 7.95 *(978-1-58089-247-6(7))* 2009. (ENG., (gr. k-3). 22.44 *(978-1-58089-246-9(9))* Charlesbridge Publishing, Inc.

Trivas, Tracy. The Wish Stealers. 2011. (ENG.). 288p. (J). (gr. 3-7). pap. 8.99 *(978-1-4169-8726-0(6)*, Aladdin) Simon & Schuster Children's Publishing.

Troupe, Thomas Kingsley. Darling Doll. Faber, Rudy, illus. 2016. (Hauntiques Ser.). (ENG.). 128p. (J). (gr. 4-6). lib. bdg. 25.32 *(978-1-4965-3548-1(0)*, 132657, Stone Arch Bks.) Capstone.

—Ghostly Goalie. Faber, Rudy, illus. 2016. (Hauntiques Ser.). (ENG.). 128p. (J). (gr. 4-6). lib. bdg. 25.32 *(978-1-4965-3544-3(8)*, 132654, Stone Arch Bks.) Capstone.

—Hauntiques, 4 vols. 2016. (Hauntiques Ser.). (ENG., Illus.). 128p. (J). (gr. 4-6). 106.60 *(978-1-4965-3561-0(8)*, 25039, Stone Arch Bks.) Capstone.

—Phantom's Favorite. Faber, Rudy, illus. 2016. (Hauntiques Ser.). (ENG.). 128p. (J). (gr. 4-6). lib. bdg. 25.32 *(978-1-4965-3546-7(4)*, 132655, Stone Arch Bks.) Capstone.

—Wandering Wagon. Faber, Rudy, illus. 2016. (Hauntiques Ser.). (ENG.). 128p. (J). (gr. 4-6). lib. bdg. 25.32 *(978-1-4965-3547-4(2)*, 132656, Stone Arch Bks.) Capstone.

Tubb, Kristin O'Donnell. The 13th Sign. 2014. (ENG.). 288p. (J). (gr. 5-9). pap. 21.99 *(978-1-250-05059-5(6)*, 900134114) Square Fish.

Turner, Suzy. The Ghost of Josiah Grimshaw: A Morgan Sisters Novel. 2013. 286p. pap. *(978-989-97348-6-9(1))* Turner, Suzanne.

—The Temporal Stone: A Morgan Sisters Novel. 2013. 288p. pap. *(978-989-98351-0-8(2))* Turner, Suzanne.

Turnquist, Myrtle Moose. How Do Dandelions Grow. 2011. 48p. pap. 20.50 *(978-1-4634-3776-3(5))* AuthorHouse.

Uehashi, Nahoko. The Beast Player. Hirano, Cathy, tr. 2019. (ENG., Illus.). 352p. (YA). 19.99 *(978-1-250-30746-0(5)*, 900198010, Holt, Henry & Co. Bks. For Young Readers) Holt, Henry & Co.

Valentine, Nicole. A Time Traveler's Theory of Relativity. 2019. (ENG., Illus.). 352p. (J). (gr. 4-8). 17.99 *(978-1-5415-5538-9(4)*, 2b60b16e-6e91-4b27-b7dd-76c86cce49dc, Carolrhoda Bks.) Lerner Publishing Group.

van Arsdale, Peternelle. The Beast Is an Animal. (ENG.). 352p. (YA). (gr. 9). 2018. pap. 11.99 *(978-1-4814-8842-6(2))* 2017. (Illus.). 17.99 *(978-1-4814-8841-9(4))* McElderry, Margaret K. Bks. (McElderry, Margaret K. Bks.).

Vande Velde, Vivian. All Hallows' Eve: 13 Stories. 2010. (ENG., Illus.). 240p. (YA). (gr. 7). pap. 8.99 *(978-0-15-206473-0(7)*, 1199331, Clarion Bks.) HarperCollins Pubs.

Verano, M. Book of Shadows. (Diary of a Haunting Ser.). (ENG.). (YA). (gr. 9). 2018. 304p. pap. 12.99 *(978-1-4814-9203-4(9))* 2017. (Illus.). 288p. 17.99 *(978-1-4814-9202-7(0))* Simon Pulse. (Simon Pulse).

—Diary of a Haunting. (Diary of a Haunting Ser.). (ENG., Illus.). (YA). (gr. 9). 2016. 336p. pap. 10.99 *(978-1-4814-3068-5(8))* 2015. 320p. 17.99 *(978-1-4814-3069-2(6))* Simon Pulse. (Simon Pulse).

—Possession. 2016. (Diary of a Haunting Ser.). (ENG., Illus.). 352p. (YA). (gr. 9). 17.99 *(978-1-4814-6441-3(8)*, Simon Pulse) Simon Pulse.

Verday, Jessica. The Beautiful & the Damned. 2013. (ENG., Illus.). 272p. (YA). (gr. 7). 17.99 *(978-1-4424-8835-9(2)*, Simon Pulse) Simon Pulse.

—The Hidden. (ENG.). 400p. (YA). (gr. 9). 2012. pap. 14.99 *(978-1-4169-7898-5(4))* 2011. 17.99 *(978-1-4169-7897-8(6))* Simon Pulse. (Simon Pulse).

—The Hollow. (ENG.). (YA). (gr. 7). 2010. 528p. pap. 14.99 *(978-1-4169-7894-7(1))*No. 1. 2009. 544p. 17.99 *(978-1-4169-7893-0(3))* Simon Pulse. (Simon Pulse).

Vernick, Shirley Reva. The Black Butterfly, 1 vol. 2014. (ENG.). 226p. (J). (gr. 8-12). 19.95 *(978-1-935955-79-5(9),* 23353382, Cinco Puntos Press) Lee & Low Bks., Inc.
Verstraete, Majanka. The Doll Maker: Weirdville. l.t. ed. 2013. (ENG.). 86p. (gr. 2-6). pap. 9.95 *(978-1-62253-065-6(9))* Evolved Publishing.
Volk, Gretchen. The Amazing Adventures of Tristy Ruth, Raisin Girl. 2012. 258p. pap. *(978-1-105-51531-6(1))* Lulu.com.
Wade, Rebecca. The Theft & the Miracle. 2007. 351p. (J). (gr. 4-7). lib. bdg. 17.89 *(978-0-06-077495-0(9))* HarperCollins Pubs.
Walker, Melissa. Dust to Dust. 2016. (ENG.). 320p. (YA). (gr. 8). pap. 9.99 *(978-0-06-207738-7(4),* Tegen, Katherine Bks) HarperCollins Pubs.
Wallace, Kali. Shallow Graves. 2017. (ENG.). 384p. (YA). (gr. 9). pap. 9.99 *(978-0-06-236621-4(1),* Tegen, Katherine Bks) HarperCollins Pubs.
Walsh, Sara. The Dark Light. 2013. (ENG., Illus.). 512p. (YA). (gr. 9). pap. 9.99 *(978-1-4424-3458-5(9),* Simon Pulse) Simon Pulse.
Walters, Ednah. Awakened: Book One of the Guardian Legacy. 2010. 272p. (YA). pap. 12.99 *(978-1-61706-038-0(0))* Pill Hill Pr.
Waters, Daniel. Break My Heart 1,000 Times. 2013. (ENG., Illus.). 352p. (J). (gr. 7-17). pap. 9.99 *(978-1-4231-2228-9(3))* Hyperion Pr.
Watson, Andi. Princess Decomposia & Count Spatula. 2015. (ENG., Illus.). 176p. (YA). (gr. 8). 19.99 *(978-1-62672-275-0(7),* 900148323, First Second Bks.) Roaring Brook Pr.
Watts, Julia. Free Spirits. 2009. (ENG.). 176p. (J). (gr. 1). pap. 8.95 *(978-0-9667359-2-5(7),* BeanPole Bks.) OH Industries.
Watts, Leander. Beautiful City of the Dead. 2007. (ENG.). 256p. (YA). (gr. 7-12). pap. 14.99 *(978-0-618-59499-3(X),* 474084, Clarion Bks.) HarperCollins Pubs.
Weatherly, L. A. Angel Burn. 2011. (Angel Ser.: 1). (ENG., Illus.). 464p. (YA). (gr. 9). pap. 9.99 *(978-0-7636-5846-5(4));* 17.99 *(978-0-7636-5652-2(6))* Candlewick Pr.
—Angel Fire. 2012. (Angel Ser.: 2). (ENG., Illus.). 656p. (YA). (gr. 9). 17.99 *(978-0-7636-5679-9(8))* Candlewick Pr.
Weiss, Sonya. Reckoning. 2016. (ENG., Illus.). 210p. (J). pap. 15.00 *(978-1-60183-730-1(5))* Kensington Publishing Corp.
Wells, Charity. The Trouble with the Supernatural, 1 vol. 2010. 84p. pap. 19.95 *(978-1-4489-2117-1(1))* America Star Bks.
Wells, Robison. Blackout. 2014. (Blackout Ser.: 1). (ENG.). 448p. (YA). (gr. 8). pap. 9.99 *(978-0-06-202613-2(5),* HarperTeen) HarperCollins Pubs.
—Dead Zone. (Blackout Ser.: 2). (ENG.). (YA). (gr. 8). 2015. 400p. pap. 10.99 *(978-0-06-227503-5(8))* 2014. 384p. 17.99 *(978-0-06-227502-8(X))* HarperCollins Pubs. (HarperTeen).
Welvaert, Scott R. The Mosquito King: An Agate & Buck Adventure, 1 vol. Garvey, Brann, illus. 2007. (Agate & Buck Adventure Ser.). (ENG.). 112p. (J). (gr. 5-9). 26.65 *(978-1-59889-857-6(4),* 94254, Stone Arch Bks.) Capstone.
—The Mosquito King: An Agate & Buck Adventure, 1 vol. Garvey, Brann, illus. 2008. (Vortex Bks.). (ENG.). 112p. (J). (gr. 2-3). pap. 6.95 *(978-1-59889-923-8(6),* 94325, Stone Arch Bks.) Capstone.
West, Carly Anne. The Bargaining. 2015. (ENG., Illus.). 416p. (YA). (gr. 9). 17.99 *(978-1-4424-4182-8(8),* Simon Pulse) Simon Pulse.
—The Murmurings. (ENG., 384p. (YA). (gr. 9). 2014. Illus.). pap. 13.99 *(978-1-4424-4180-4(1))* 2013. 16.99 *(978-1-4424-4179-8(8))* Simon Pulse. (Simon Pulse).
West, Jacqueline. Last Things. 2019. (ENG.). 416p. (YA). (gr. 8). 17.99 *(978-0-06-287506-8(X),* Greenwillow Bks.) HarperCollins Pubs.
West, Kasie. Pivot Point. 2013. (Pivot Point Ser.: 1). (ENG.). 384p. (YA). (gr. 8). pap. 9.99 *(978-0-06-211736-6(X),* HarperTeen) HarperCollins Pubs.
—Split Second. 2014. (Pivot Point Ser.: 2). (ENG.). 368p. (YA). (gr. 8). 17.99 *(978-0-06-211738-0(6),* HarperTeen) HarperCollins Pubs.
Westover, Steve. Crater Lake: Battle for Wizard Island. 2012. pap. 14.99 *(978-1-59955-960-5(9))* Cedar Fort, Inc./CFI Distribution.
—Return of the Mystic Gray. 2013. 15.99 *(978-1-4621-1187-9(4))* Cedar Fort, Inc./CFI Distribution.
White, Kiersten. Endlessly. 2013. (Paranormalcy Ser.: 3). (ENG.). 416p. (YA). (gr. 8). pap. 10.99 *(978-0-06-198589-8(9),* HarperTeen) HarperCollins Pubs.
—Paranormalcy. 2011. (Paranormalcy Ser.: 1). (ENG.). 368p. (YA). (gr. 8). pap. 9.99 *(978-0-06-198585-0(6),* HarperTeen) HarperCollins Pubs.
—Supernaturally. 2012. (Paranormalcy Ser.: 2). (ENG.). 368p. (YA). (gr. 8). pap. 9.99 *(978-0-06-198587-4(2),* HarperTeen) HarperCollins Pubs.
Whitten, A. J. The Cellar. 2011. (ENG.). 288p. (YA). (gr. 7-18). pap. 16.99 *(978-0-547-23253-9(5),* 1082798, Clarion Bks.) HarperCollins Pubs.
—The Well. 2009. (ENG., Illus.). 336p. (YA). (gr. 7-18). pap. 18.95 *(978-0-547-23229-4(2),* 1082742, Clarion Bks.) HarperCollins Pubs.
Whyte, Elana. My Gift: A Book about a Child Who Sees Spirit. 2013. 32p. pap. 13.95 *(978-1-4525-8724-0(8),* Balboa Pr.) Author Solutions, LLC.
Wiebe, Joanna. The Wicked Awakening of Anne Merchant: Book Two of the V Trilogy. 2015. 320p. (J). (gr. 7). pap. 12.95 *(978-1-940363-29-5(2))* BenBella Bks.
Wilde, Oscar. The Picture of Dorian Gray, 1 vol. Fisher, Eric Scott, illus. 2011. (Calico Illustrated Classics Ser.: No. 4). (ENG.). 112p. (J). (gr. 2-5). 38.50 *(978-1-61641-618-8(1),* 4051, Calico Chapter Bks.) ABDO Publishing Co.
Williams, Carol Lynch. Messenger. 2017. (ENG.). 288p. (YA). (gr. 7). pap. 10.99 *(978-1-4814-5777-4(2),* Simon & Schuster/Paula Wiseman Bks.) Simon & Schuster/Paula Wiseman Bks.
Willocks, Tim. Doglands. 2012. (ENG.). 336p. (YA). (gr. 7). pap. 9.99 *(978-0-375-85818-5(0),* Ember) Random Hse. Children's Bks.
Wilson, Norah & Doherty, Heather. Embrace the Night. 2013. 226p. pap. *(978-1-927651-09-4(3),* Something Shiny Pr.) Wilson, Norah.
Winter, Isobelle. Weather. Odgers, Sally, ed. Kelsey, Amanda, illus. 2013. 236p. (J). pap. 23.25 *(978-1-61572-946-3(1))* Damnation Bks.
Winters, Cat. The Cure for Dreaming. 2016. (ENG., Illus.). 384p. (YA). (gr. 8-17). pap. 9.95 *(978-1-4197-1941-7(6),* 1075303, Amulet Bks.) Abrams, Inc.
—The Raven's Tale. 2019. (ENG., Illus.). 368p. (gr. 7-17). 17.99 *(978-1-4197-3362-8(1),* 1153101, Amulet Bks.) Abrams, Inc.
Wrede, Patricia C. & Stevermer, Caroline. The Grand Tour: Being a Revelation of Matters of High Confidentiality & Greatest Importance, Including Extracts from the Intimate Diary of a Noblewoman & the Sworn Testimony of a Lady of Quality. 2006. (ENG., Illus.). 480p. (YA). (gr. 7-12). pap. 21.95 *(978-0-15-205556-1(8),* 1196709, Clarion Bks.) HarperCollins Pubs.
—The Mislaid Magician or Ten Years After: Being the Private Correspondence Between Two Prominent FamiliesRegarding a Scandal Touching the Highest Levels of Government & TheSecurity of the Realm. 2009. (ENG., Illus.). 336p. (YA). (gr. 7). pap. 18.95 *(978-0-15-206209-5(2),* 1099016, Clarion Bks.) HarperCollins Pubs.
Yancey, Rick. The Curse of the Wendigo. 2011. (Monstrumologist Ser.: 2). (ENG.). 464p. (YA). (gr. 9). pap. 13.99 *(978-1-4169-8451-1(8),* Simon & Schuster Bks. For Young Readers) Simon & Schuster Bks. For Young Readers.
—The Final Descent. 2013. (Monstrumologist Ser.: 4). (ENG., Illus.). 320p. (YA). (gr. 9). 18.99 *(978-1-4424-5153-7(X),* Simon & Schuster Bks. For Young Readers) Simon & Schuster Bks. For Young Readers.
—The Isle of Blood. (Monstrumologist Ser.: 3). (ENG.). 560p. (YA). (gr. 9). 2012. pap. 13.99 *(978-1-4169-8453-5(4))* 2011. (Illus.). 18.99 *(978-1-4169-8452-8(6))* Simon & Schuster Bks. For Young Readers. (Simon & Schuster Bks. For Young Readers).
—The Monstrumologist. 2010. (Monstrumologist Ser.: 1). (ENG.). 464p. (YA). (gr. 9). pap. 13.99 *(978-1-4169-8449-8(6),* Simon & Schuster Bks. For Young Readers) Simon & Schuster Bks. For Young Readers.
Yates, Alexander. The Winter Place. 2015. (ENG., Illus.). 448p. (YA). (gr. 9). 17.99 *(978-1-4814-1981-9(1))* Simon & Schuster Children's Publishing.
Young, Suzanne. Hotel for the Lost. 2016. (ENG., Illus.). 304p. (YA). (gr. 9). pap. 10.99 *(978-1-4814-2301-4(0),* Simon Pulse) Simon Pulse.
—Hotel Ruby. 2015. (ENG., Illus.). 288p. (YA). (gr. 9). 17.99 *(978-1-4814-2300-7(2),* Simon Pulse) Simon Pulse.
Yovanoff, Brenna. The Replacement. 2011. (ENG.). 368p. (YA). (gr. 7-18). 8.99 *(978-1-59514-381-5(5),* Razorbill) Penguin Young Readers Group.
Zafon, Carlos. Marina. 2011. (FRE.). (YA). (gr. 8-12). pap. *(978-2-266-21302-8(4))* Le Robert.
Zafon, Carlos Ruiz. Marina. 2014. (ENG.). 336p. (YA). (gr. 7-17). 34.99 *(978-0-316-04471-4(7))* Little, Brown Bks. for Young Readers.
—The Prince of Mist. 2011. (ENG.). 256p. (YA). (gr. 7-17). pap., pap. 14.99 *(978-0-316-04480-6(6))* Little, Brown Bks. for Young Readers.
—The Watcher in the Shadows. (ENG.). (YA). (gr. 7-17). 2014. 288p. pap. 15.99 *(978-0-316-04475-2(X))* 2013. 272p. 18.00 *(978-0-316-04476-9(8))* Little, Brown Bks. for Young Readers.
Zink, Michelle. Circle of Fire. 2012. (Prophecy of the Sisters Ser.: 3). (ENG.). 368p. (YA). (gr. 7-17). pap. 19.99 *(978-0-316-03446-3(0))* Little, Brown Bks. for Young Readers.
—Guardian of the Gate. 2011. (Prophecy of the Sisters Ser.: 2). (ENG.). 368p. (YA). (gr. 7-17). pap. 18.99 *(978-0-316-02740-3(5))* Little, Brown Bks. for Young Readers.
—Prophecy of the Sisters. 2010. (Prophecy of the Sisters Ser.: 1). (ENG.). 368p. (YA). (gr. 7-17). pap. 18.99 *(978-0-316-02741-0(3))* Little, Brown Bks. for Young Readers.
Zuravicky, Orli. Dear Diary: Monster House. 2006. (Illus.). 32p. (J). lib. bdg. 15.00 *(978-1-4242-1561-4(7))* Fitzgerald Bks.

SUPERSONIC AERODYNAMICS

see Aerodynamics, Supersonic

SUPERSONIC WAVES

see Ultrasonic Waves

SUPERSTITION

see also Alchemy; Apparitions; Astrology; Charms; Divination; Dreams; Fairies; Folklore; Fortune-Telling; Ghosts; Occultism; Vampires; Witchcraft

Loh-Hagan, Virginia. Super Superstitions. 2018. (Stranger Than Fiction Ser.). (ENG., Illus.). 32p. (J). (gr. 4-8). lib. bdg. 32.07 *(978-1-5341-2933-7(2),* 211776, 45th Parallel Press) Cherry Lake Publishing.
Rigby Education Staff. Keep Tradition. (Greetings Ser.). (Illus.). (gr. 3-5). 21.00 *(978-0-7635-2229-2(5))* Rigby Education.
Sanna, Ellyn. Folk Customs. 2004. (North American Folklore Ser.). (Illus.). 112p. (J). (gr. 7-18). lib. bdg. 22.95 *(978-1-59084-336-9(3))* Mason Crest.
Stewart, Sheila. The Psychology of Our Dark Side: Humans' Love Affair with Vampires & Werewolves. 2010. (Making of a Monster Ser.). (Illus.). 64p. (YA). (gr. 7-18). pap. 9.95 *(978-1-4222-1960-7(7));* lib. bdg. 22.95 *(978-1-4222-1807-5(4))* Mason Crest.

SUPERSTITION—FICTION

Applegate, Katherine. Never Race a Runaway Pumpkin. Biggs, Brian, illus. 2009. (Roscoe Riley Rules Ser.: 7). (ENG.). 96p. (J). (gr. 1-5). pap. 4.99 *(978-0-06-178370-8(6))* HarperCollins Pubs.
—Never Race a Runaway Pumpkin. 2009. (Roscoe Riley Rules Ser.: 7). (J). lib. bdg. 14.75 *(978-0-606-06090-5(1))* Turtleback.
—Roscoe Riley Rules #7: Never Race a Runaway Pumpkin. Biggs, Brian, illus. 2009. (Roscoe Riley Rules Ser.: 7). (ENG.). 96p. (J). (gr. 1-5). 15.99 *(978-0-06-178372-2(2),* HarperCollins) HarperCollins Pubs.
The Bad Luck of King Fred: Individual Title Six-Packs. (Action Packs Ser.). 104p. (gr. 3-5). 44.00 *(978-0-7635-8408-5(8))* Rigby Education.
Bowen, Fred. Lucky Enough, 1 vol. 2018. (Fred Bowen Sports Story Ser.: 22). 144p. (J). (gr. 2-6). pap. 6.99 *(978-1-56145-958-2(5))* Peachtree Publishing Co. Inc.
Brodeur, Tom. Regina Silsby's Secret War. 2004. 248p. (J). 7.49 *(978-1-59166-235-8(4))* BJU Pr.
Brown, Marc. Arthur & the Bad-Luck Brain. 2003. (Marc Brown Arthur Chapter Bks.). (Illus.). 55p. (gr. 2-4). 14.25 *(978-0-7569-1701-2(8))* Perfection Learning Corp.
Chan, Crystal. Bird. (ENG.). (J). (gr. 3-7). 2015. 320p. pap. 8.99 *(978-1-4424-5091-2(6))* 2014. (Illus.). 304p. 16.99 *(978-1-4424-5089-9(4),* Atheneum Bks. for Young Readers) Simon & Schuster Children's Publishing.
Christopher, Matt. Shadow over Second. Dewdney, Anna, illus. 2009. (New Peach Street Mudders Sports Library). 64p. (J). (gr. 2-4). lib. bdg. 23.93 *(978-1-59953-320-9(0))* Norwood Hse. Pr.
Hairston, Lisa Lee & Graham, Joanne. The Luckiest Girl in Luckyville. 2013. 36p. pap. 15.50 *(978-1-4669-8192-8(X))* Trafford Publishing.
Haven, Paul. The Seven Keys of Balabad. Zug, Mark, illus. 2010. (ENG.). 288p. (J). (gr. 4-6). lib. bdg. 21.19 *(978-0-375-93350-9(6))* Random House Publishing Group.
—Two Hot Dogs with Everything. 2007. (ENG., Illus.). 320p. (J). (gr. 3-7). per. 9.99 *(978-0-375-83349-6(8),* Yearling) Random Hse. Children's Bks.
Nelson, Suzanne. Dead in the Water. 2013. 171p. (J). pap. *(978-0-545-54302-6(9))* Scholastic, Inc.
Nervelle, Rosemarie. The Witch of Beaver Creek Mine. 2007. (ENG.). 160p. (J). (gr. 3-7). 14.95 *(978-0-89272-741-4(1));* 2nd ed. pap. 9.95 *(978-0-89272-763-6(2))* Down East Bks.
O'Connor, Jane. Just My Luck! 2013. (Fancy Nancy - I Can Read! Ser.). (J). lib. bdg. 13.55 *(978-0-606-35044-0(6))* Turtleback.
Parish, Herman. Amelia Bedelia Tries Her Luck. 2013. (Amelia Bedelia: I Can Read! Ser.). (J). lib. bdg. 13.55 *(978-0-606-32445-8(3))* Turtleback.
Sullivan, Laura L. Under the Green Hill, 1. 2010. (Green Hill Novels Ser.). (ENG.). 320p. (J). (gr. 4-6). 22.44 *(978-0-8050-8984-4(5),* 9780805089844, Holt, Henry & Co.) Holt, Henry & Co.
—Under the Green Hill. 2011. (ENG.). 336p. (J). (gr. 4-8). pap. 17.99 *(978-0-312-55149-0(5),* 900074427) Square Fish.
Villanueva, Gail D. My Fate According to the Butterfly. 2019. (ENG.). 240p. (J). (gr. 3-7). 17.99 *(978-1-338-31050-4(X),* Scholastic Pr.) Scholastic, Inc.
Westergard, Tim. The Jesus Box, 1 vol. 2009. 16p. pap. 24.95 *(978-1-60749-694-6(1))* America Star Bks.

SURF

see Ocean Waves

SURFING

Abdo, Kenny. Windsurfing. 2017. (Action Sports (Fly!) Ser.). (ENG., Illus.). 24p. (J). (gr. 2-8). lib. bdg. 31.36 *(978-1-5321-2097-8(4),* 26780, Abdo Zoom-Fly) ABDO Publishing Co.
Bass, Scott. Extreme Sports: Surf! Your Guide to Longboarding, Shortboarding, Tubing, Aerials, Hanging Ten & More. 2003. (Extreme Sports Ser.). (ENG., Illus.). 64p. (J). (gr. 4-7). pap. 8.95 *(978-0-7922-5108-8(3),* National Geographic Children's Bks.) National Geographic Society.
Buckley, Jim. Big Wave Surfing. 2015. (Intense Sports Ser.). (ENG.). 48p. (gr. 4-8). 35.64 *(978-1-63430-438-2(1),* 9781634304382) Rourke Educational Media.
Carr, Aaron. Surf. 2013. (ENG & SPA.). (J). *(978-1-62127-637-1(6))* Weigl Pubs., Inc.
—Surfing. (Illus.). (J). 2013. 32p. 27.13 *(978-1-61913-515-4(9))* 2012. (ENG., 24p. pap. 12.95 *(978-1-61913-521-5(3),* AV2 by Weigl) Weigl Pubs., Inc.
Cassriel, Betsy R. Kiteboarding. 2015. (Intense Sports Ser.). (ENG.). 48p. (gr. 4-8). 35.64 *(978-1-63430-439-9(X),* 9781634304399) Rourke Educational Media.
Crossingham, John & Kalman, Bobbie. Extreme Surfing, 1 vol. 2003. (Extreme Sports - No Limits Ser.). (ENG., Illus.). 32p. (J). (gr. 3). pap. *(978-0-7787-1715-7(1));* lib. bdg. *(978-0-7787-1669-3(4))* Crabtree Publishing Co.
De Macedo, Joao. How to Be a Surfer. 2007. (Illus.). 176p. (J). pap. 24.95 *(978-1-84126-201-7(3))* Meyer & Meyer Sport, Ltd. GBR. Dist: Cardinal Pubs. Group.
DeLa Vega, Timothy T., et al. 200 Years of Surfing Literature: An Annotated Bibliography. 2004. (Illus.). 108p. per. 19.95 *(978-0-9754328-0-8(X))* DeLaVega, T.
Dugan, Christine. Hang Ten! Surfing, 1 vol. 2nd rev. ed. (TIME for KIDS(r): Informational Text Ser.). (ENG., 48p. (gr. 4-5). 2013. Illus.). (J). lib. bdg. 29.96 *(978-1-4807-1107-5(1))* 2012. pap. 13.99 *(978-1-4333-4831-0(4))* Teacher Created Materials, Inc.
Fitzpatrick, Jim. Surfing. 2007. (21st Century Skills Library: Healthy for Life Ser.). (ENG., Illus.). 32p. (gr. 4-8). lib. bdg. 32.07 *(978-1-60279-019-3(1),* 200036) Cherry Lake Publishing.
Goldish, Meish. Surf Dog Miracles. 2012. (Dog Heroes Ser.). 32p. (J). (gr. 2-7). lib. bdg. 28.50 *(978-1-61772-577-7(3))* Bearport Publishing Co., Inc.
Goranson, Christopher D. Danny Harf: Wakeboarding Superstar. 2009. (Extreme Sports Biographies Ser.). 64p. (gr. 3-4). 58.50 *(978-1-61512-461-9(6),* Rosen Reference) Rosen Publishing Group, Inc., The.
Hamilton, Bethany. Ask Bethany [Updated Edition], 1 vol. rev. ed. 2014. (Faithgirlz / Soul Surfer Ser.). (ENG., Illus.). 192p. (J). 9.99 *(978-0-310-74572-3(1))* Zonderkidz.
—Be Unstoppable: The Art of Never Giving Up, 1 vol. 2018. (ENG., Illus.). 128p. (YA). 16.99 *(978-0-310-76485-4(8))* Zondervan.
Hamilton, Bethany & Bundschuh, Rick. Soul Surfer: A True Story of Faith, Family, & Fighting to Get Back on the Board. 2006. (ENG., Illus.). 240p. (YA). (gr. 9). pap. 16.00 *(978-1-4165-0346-0(3),* MTV Bks.) MTV Books.
Kocienda, Genevieve. Catch a Wave: the Story of Surfing Beginning Book with Online Access, 1 vol. 2014. (ENG., Illus.). 24p. (J). pap., E-Book, E-Book 9.50 *(978-1-107-65191-3(3))* Cambridge Univ. Pr.
Laval, Anne-Marie. Windsurfing & Kite Surfing. 2012. (Adrenaline Rush Ser.). 32p. (gr. 4-7). lib. bdg. 31.35 *(978-1-59920-683-7(8))* Black Rabbit Bks.
MacDonald, Steele Lisa. The Science of Waves & Surfboards. rev. ed. 2018. (Smithsonian: Informational Text Ser.). (ENG., Illus.). 32p. (J). (gr. 3-5). pap. 11.99 *(978-1-4938-6705-9(9))* Teacher Created Materials, Inc.
Mahaney, Ian F. Danny Harf: Wakeboarding Champion. 2009. (Extreme Sports Biographies Ser.). 24p. (gr. 3-4). 42.50 *(978-1-61512-462-6(4),* PowerKids Pr.) Rosen Publishing Group, Inc., The.
Marsico, Katie. Surviving a Shark Attack: Bethany Hamilton. 2019. (They Survived (Alternator Books (r)) Ser.). (ENG., Illus.). 32p. (J). (gr. 3-6). lib. bdg. 29.32 *(978-1-5415-2353-1(9),* 219854b2-a068-4315-bcbd-4a8a3f071a8e, Lerner Pubns.) Lerner Publishing Group.
Mason, Paul. Surfing, 1 vol. 2012. (To the Limit Ser.). (ENG., Illus.). 32p. (J). (gr. 3-6). pap. 11.00 *(978-1-4488-7070-7(4),* 336ec72d-d553-449c-b7b0-a010ca24e904); lib. bdg. 28.93 *(978-1-4488-7030-1(5),* 4bb25fd9-2f72-4122-a9ce-374ec7d8e9c7) Rosen Publishing Group, Inc., The. (PowerKids Pr.).
Mattern, Joanne. Kiteboarding. 2008. (Illus.). 24p. (J). lib. bdg. *(978-1-60472-396-0(3))* Rourke Educational Media.
McClellan, Ray. Surfing. 2008. (Action Sports Ser.). (ENG., Illus.). 24p. (J). (gr. 3-7). lib. bdg. 26.95 *(978-1-60014-145-4(5))* Bellwether Media.
McFee, Shane. Surfing, 1 vol. 2008. (Living on the Edge Ser.). (ENG., Illus.). 24p. (J). (gr. 2-3). lib. bdg. 26.27 *(978-1-4042-4219-7(8),* ed95b607-d458-4f1c-81b9-bfd190fa3537) Rosen Publishing Group, Inc., The.
Merlin, Hope & Green, Naima. An Insider's Guide to Surfing, 1 vol. 2014. (Sports Tips, Techniques, & Strategies Ser.). (ENG.). 48p. (YA). (gr. 6-6). 33.47 *(978-1-4777-8081-7(5),* 482d0459-9ee1-4674-81b8-3f920d4cfe09, Rosen Reference) Rosen Publishing Group, Inc., The.
Nardo, Don. Surfing, 1 vol. 2014. (Science Behind Sports Ser.). (ENG., Illus.). 104p. (gr. 7-7). lib. bdg. 41.03 *(978-1-4205-1156-7(4),* ac31bb01-5b52-4d14-ab26-a1bd2d1bbad6, Lucent Pr.) Greenhaven Publishing LLC.
Orr, Tamra B. Extreme Skysurfing, 1 vol. 2013. (Sports on the Edge Ser.). (ENG.). 48p. (gr. 4-4). 32.64 *(978-1-60870-232-9(4),* 5abc5d18-036d-48ab-a6f9-3a0f17b7cc57) Cavendish Square Publishing LLC.
Otfinoski, Steven. Extreme Surfing, 1 vol. 2012. (Sports on the Edge Ser.). (ENG., Illus.). 48p. (gr. 4-4). 32.64 *(978-1-60870-231-2(6),* b746b7c6-c09c-426f-88b6-a162665fe3cc) Cavendish Square Publishing LLC.
Pierce, Terry. Surfing A to Z Coloring Book. Kofsky, Kristen, illus. 2004. 24p. pap. 4.95 *(978-1-57306-178-0(6))* Bess Pr., Inc.
Poolos, Jamie. Surfing & Wind Surfing, 1 vol. 2015. (Sports to the Extreme Ser.). (ENG., Illus.). 48p. (J). (gr. 5-6). 33.47 *(978-1-4994-3573-3(8),* 9e2a3881-7888-43bc-8e2e-c89244665438, Rosen Central) Rosen Publishing Group, Inc., The.
Reed, Kevin. The Dog's Guide to Surfing: Hanging Ten with Man's Best Friend. Crump, A. K., ed. 2005. (ENG., Illus.). 128p. (gr. 5-18). pap. *(978-0-9674898-7-2(3))* Temmen, Edition, Horst Temmen.
Rusch, Elizabeth. Gidget the Surfing Dog: Catching Waves with a Small but Mighty Pug. 2020. (Illus.). 48p. (J). (gr. 2-5). 18.99 *(978-1-63217-271-6(2),* Little Bigfoot) Sasquatch Bks.
Sandler, Michael. Super Surfers. (X-Moves Ser.). 24p. 2018. (ENG.). (J). (gr. 1-6). 7.99 *(978-1-64280-094-4(5))* 2009. (Illus.). (YA). (gr. 2-5). lib. bdg. 26.99 *(978-1-59716-953-0(6))* Bearport Publishing Co., Inc.
Scherer, Randy. Kelly Slater, 1 vol. 2012. (People in the News Ser.). (ENG., Illus.). 104p. (gr. 7-7). lib. bdg. 41.03 *(978-1-4205-0757-7(5),* 0ceb3183-39b2-45ab-b410-2706276c33f2, Lucent Pr.) Greenhaven Publishing LLC.
Smalley, Carol Parenzan. Ride the Giant Waves with Garrett Mcnamara. 2006. (Extreme Sports Ser.). (Illus.). 32p. (J). (gr. 1-4). lib. bdg. 25.70 *(978-1-58415-486-0(1))* Mitchell Lane Pubs.
Smith, Ryan A. Surfboards. 2006. 32p. (gr. 3-5). 22.45 *(978-1-4103-0719-4(0),* Blackbirch Pr., Inc.) Cengage Gale.
—Surfboards: From Start to Finish. Howard, Devon, photos by. 2006. (Made in the U. S. A. Ser.). (ENG., Illus.). 32p. (J). (gr. 3-7). lib. bdg. 25.65 *(978-1-4103-0728-6(X),* Blackbirch Pr., Inc.) Cengage Gale.
Surfing. 2004. (I-Quest Ser.). (J). *(978-1-84229-743-8(0))* Top That! Publishing PLC.
Wiseman, Blaine. Surfing. 2015. (J). *(978-1-4896-4299-8(4))* Weigl Pubs., Inc.
—Surfing: X Games. 2008. (Extreme Ser.). (Illus.). 32p. (J). (gr. 4-6). pap. 9.95 *(978-1-59036-917-3(3));* lib. bdg. 26.00 *(978-1-59036-916-6(5))* Weigl Pubs., Inc.
Yomtov, Nel. The Science of a Cutback. 2015. (21st Century Skills Library: Full-Speed Sports Ser.). (ENG., Illus.). 32p. (J). (gr. 4-7). 32.07 *(978-1-63362-581-5(8),* 206508) Cherry Lake Publishing.

SURFING—FICTION

Alexander, Kwame. Surf's Up. Miyares, Daniel, illus. (ENG.). (J). (— 1). 2018. 24p. bds. 7.95 *(978-0-7358-4313-4(9))* 2016. 32p. 18.95 *(978-0-7358-4220-5(5))* North-South Bks., Inc.
Allen, J. Kent. Embritt Waters & the Mark of the Rattlesnake. 2006. 229p. (J). pap. 14.95 *(978-0-7414-2769-4(9))* Infinity Publishing.
Apte, Sunita. Ride the Whale: A Surfer Tall Tale. Reed, Kyle, illus. 2006. 16p. (J). pap. *(978-0-439-74638-0(8))* Scholastic, Inc.
The Beach by the Bay: Tanner & Kai Go Surfing. 2007. (Illus.). 24p. (J). 15.95 *(978-0-9796039-0-7(0))* Sandbridge Sons Publishing.
Bo, Ben. Skullcrack. 207p. (J). pap. *(978-0-7475-4220-9(1))* Bloomsbury Publishing Plc GBR. Dist: Penguin Canada.
—Skullcrack. 2003. (ENG.). 168p. (YA). (gr. 5-12). pap. 6.95 *(978-0-8225-3311-5(1))* Lerner Publishing Group.
Bundschuh, Rick. Burned: A Novel, 1 vol. 2014. (Faithgirlz / Soul Surfer Ser.: 2). (ENG.). 128p. (J). pap. 7.99 *(978-0-310-74555-6(1))* Zonderkidz.
—Clash: A Novel, 1 vol. 2014. (Faithgirlz / Soul Surfer Ser.: 1). (ENG.). 128p. (J). pap. 7.99 *(978-0-310-74582-2(9))* Zonderkidz.
Choyce, Lesley. Wave Warrior, 1 vol. 2007. (Orca Soundings Ser.). (ENG.). (YA). (gr. 8-12). 112p. 14.95 *(978-1-55143-649-4(3));* 128p. per. 9.95 *(978-1-55143-647-0(7))* Orca Bk. Pubs. USA.

Christopher, Matt. Catching Waves. 2006. (ENG.). 128p. (J). (gr. 3-7). per. 9.99 (978-0-316-05848-3(3)) Little, Brown Bks. for Young Readers.

Condon, Bill. Pipeline News, 1 vol. rev. ed. 2013. (Literary Text Ser.). (ENG., Illus.). 32p. (J). (gr. 3-4). pap. 11.99 (978-1-4333-5635-3(X)) Teacher Created Materials, Inc.

Connor, James. Surfing Summer. 2011. 138p. 22.99 (978-1-4568-8368-3(2)); pap. 15.99 (978-1-4568-8367-6(4)) Xlibris Corp.

—Surfing Summers. 2011. 138p. 22.99 (978-1-4568-9545-7(1)); pap. 15.99 (978-1-4568-9544-0(3)) Xlibris Corp.

Dalton, Michelle. Pulled Under. 2014. (Sixteenth Summer Ser.). (ENG., Illus.). 288p. (YA). (gr. 7). pap. 9.99 (978-1-4814-0700-7(7), Simon Pulse) Simon Pulse.

Dean, James & Dean, Kimberly. Pete the Cat: Pete at the Beach. Dean, James, illus. 2013. (My First I Can Read Ser.). (ENG., Illus.). 32p. (J). (gr. -1-3). 17.99 (978-0-06-211073-2(X), HarperCollins) HarperCollins Pubs.

deGroat, Diane. Gilbert, the Surfer Dude. deGroat, Diane, illus. 2010. (I Can Read Level 2 Ser.). (ENG., Illus.). 32p. (J). (gr. k-3). pap. 4.99 (978-0-06-125213-6(1), HarperCollins) HarperCollins Pubs.

—Gilbert, the Surfer Dude. 2009. (Illus.). 31p. (J). lib. bdg. 18.89 (978-0-06-125212-9(3)) HarperCollins Pubs.

Dirks, Adam. Unstoppable Me, 1 vol. Guile, Gill, illus. 2018. (ENG.). 26p. (J). bds. 9.99 (978-0-310-76497-7(1)) Zonderkidz.

Freeman, Lisa. Riptide Summer. 2017. (ENG.). 304p. (J). (gr. 8-8). 17.99 (978-1-5107-1167-9(8), Sky Pony Pr.) Skyhorse Publishing Co., Inc.

Garcia, Jeffrey. Santa Claus & the Molokai Mules. 2009. 32p. 17.95 (978-0-9840942-0-2(2)) Garcia, Jeffrey.

Germain, Kerry. Kimo's Surfing Lesson. Moore, Nicolette, illus. 2007. 48p. (gr. k-5). (J). 12.95 (978-0-9705889-5-1(X)); pap. 12.95 (978-0-9705889-3-7(3)) Island Paradise Publishing.

Gorman, Chris. Indi Surfs. 2015. (ENG., Illus.). 40p. (J). (gr. -1-3). 16.95 (978-1-57687-765-4(5), powerHouse Bks.) powerHse. Bks.

Hall, Susan & Hall, Susan, illus. Surf That Wave! 2006. (Backyardigans Ser.). (ENG.). 24p. (J). (gr. -1-3). pap. 3.99 (978-1-4169-1482-2(X), Simon Spotlight/Nickelodeon) Simon Spotlight/Nickelodeon.

Harvey, Paul. Level 1: Surfer! 2nd ed. 2008. (Pearson English Graded Readers Ser.). (ENG.). 32p. pap. 11.99 (978-1-4058-6969-0(0), Pearson ELT) Pearson Education.

Hemphill, Rick, illus. The Adventures of Kirra & Rincon: Li'l Kids, Big Waves. 2005. 32p. (J). 17.99 (978-0-9766408-0-6(5)) Kerr, Justin & Shelley.

Hoeffner, Karol Ann. Surf Ed. 2010. (ENG.). 288p. (YA). (gr. 9). pap. 13.99 (978-1-4424-1418-1(9), Simon Pulse) Simon Pulse.

Irwin, Bindi & Black, Jess. Surfing with Turtles: Bindi Wildlife Adventures, 8. 2013. (Bindi's Wildlife Adventures Ser.: 8). (ENG.). 112p. (J). (gr. 3-6). pap. 8.99 (978-1-4022-8094-8(7), Sourcebooks Jabberwocky) Sourcebooks, Inc.

Kearins, Krit. Surf's up Penny. 2009. (978-1-61658-332-3(0)) Independent Pub.

Kuperman, Marina. Turtle Feet, Surfer's Beat. 2007. 164p. (J). pap. 9.99 (978-0-9801109-0-6(4)) Kuperman, Marina.

La Rose, Melinda. Surfin' Turf. 2019. (Illus.). 31p. (J). (978-1-4242-5739-3(5)) Disney Publishing Worldwide.

Larose, Melinda. Surfin' Turf. 2014. (World of Reading Ser.). (Illus.). 31p. (J). lib. bdg. 13.55 (978-0-606-34108-0(0)) Turtleback.

Leblanc, A. J. Donnie & His First Surf Lesson. 2012. 20p. pap. 24.95 (978-1-4626-8646-9(X)) PublishAmerica, Inc.

Leibold, Jay. Surf Monkeys. Utomo, Gabhor, illus. 2017. (ENG.). 144p. (J). (gr. 4-8). pap. 6.99 (978-1-937133-24-5(9)) Chooseco LLC.

MacPherson, D. R. The First Wave. 2009. 68p. pap. 21.00 (978-1-60860-456-2(X), Eloquent Bks.) Strategic Book Publishing & Rights Agency (SBPRA).

—The Sport of Kings. 2011. 92p. pap. 25.00 (978-1-60911-294-3(6), Strategic Bk. Publishing) Strategic Book Publishing & Rights Agency (SBPRA).

Maddox, Jake. Beach Bully. Aburto, Jesus, illus. 2013. (Jake Maddox Sports Stories Ser.). (ENG.). 72p. (J). (gr. 2-3). pap. 35.70 (978-1-4342-6234-9(0), 20039); (gr. 3-6). pap. 5.95 (978-1-4342-6206-6(5), 123504); (gr. 3-6). lib. bdg. 25.99 (978-1-4342-5973-8(0), 122930) Capstone. (Stone Arch Bks.).

—Shark Attack! A Survive! Story. Tiffany, Sean, illus. 2009. (Jake Maddox Sports Stories Ser.). (ENG.). 72p. (J). (gr. 3-6). 25.99 (978-1-4342-1210-8(6), 95406, Stone Arch Bks.) Capstone.

—Storm Surfer, 1 vol. Mourning, Tuesday, illus. 2008. (Jake Maddox Girl Sports Stories Ser.). (ENG.). 72p. (J). (gr. 3-6). lib. bdg. 25.32 (978-1-4342-0471-4(5), 94419); per. 5.95 (978-1-4342-0521-6(5), 94461) Capstone. (Stone Arch Bks.).

Marie, Cynthia. Sister Aggie Goes Surfing. 2012. 50p. pap. 20.95 (978-1-4497-5404-4(X), WestBow Pr.) Author Solutions, LLC.

Martin, R. T. Riptide. 2019. (To the Limit Ser.). (ENG.). 104p. (YA). (gr. 6-12). 26.65 (978-1-5415-4036-1(0), 13d54020-f345-4b90-8213-09d1d5ea8f63, Darby Creek) Lerner Publishing Group.

McIntosh, Kenneth. Close-Up: Forensic Photography. 2009. (J). pap. 24.95 (978-1-4222-1455-8(9)) Mason Crest.

—Close-Up: Forensic Photography, 5 vols. Sanborn, Casey, illus. 2007. (Crime Scene Club Ser.: Bk. 5). 144p. (YA). (gr. 9-12). lib. bdg. 24.95 (978-1-4222-0251-7(8)) Mason Crest.

McKinley, Ryan. The Pirate Bride. 2010. 105p. 21.95 (978-1-4327-5546-1(3)); (Illus.). pap. 14.95 (978-1-4327-5545-4(5)) Outskirts Pr., Inc.

Mindes, Erin. Missy Moo, Where Are You off to? Surfing Adventure. Harston, David, illus. 2011. (J). 14.95 (978-0-9841558-8-0(0)) Tasty Minstrel Games.

Morecroft, Judith. Malu Kangaroo. Bancroft, Bronwyn, illus. 2008. (ENG.). 40p. (J). (gr. k-2). pap. 13.95 (978-1-921272-51-6(1)) Little Hare Bks. AUS. Dist: Independent Pubs. Group.

Murakami, Jon & BeachHouse Publishing. Geckos Surf. 2007. (ENG.). 16p. (J). (gr. -1-5). bds. 7.95 (978-1-933067-22-3(5)) Beachhouse Publishing, LLC.

Nagler, Michelle H. Scooby-Doo in Lost at Sea, 1 vol. Sur, Duendes del, illus. 2016. (Scooby-Doo Early Reading Adventures Ser.). (ENG.). 24p. (J). (gr. -1-2). lib. bdg. 31.36 (978-1-61479-476-9(6), 21389) Spotlight.

Neri, G. Surf Mules. 2014. (ENG.). 288p. (YA). (gr. 8-12). pap. 9.95 (978-1-4677-4238-2(4), 64a82165-dd2a-4063-b230-c2f1004aaf15, Carolrhoda Lab™) Lerner Publishing Group.

Noel, Alyson. Forever Summer. 2011. (ENG.). 464p. (YA). (gr. 8-12). pap. 29.99 (978-0-312-60439-4(4), 900076464, St. Martin's Griffin) St. Martin's Pr.

—Laguna Cove: A Novel. 2006. (ENG.). 224p. (YA). (gr. 8-13). pap. 16.99 (978-0-312-34869-4(X), 900031658, St. Martin's Griffin) St. Martin's Pr.

Novel Units. The Big Wave Novel Units Teacher Guide. 2019. (ENG.). (YA). pap. 12.99 (978-1-56137-120-4(3), Novel Units, Inc.) Classroom Library Co.

Priebe, Val. I Only Surf Online, 1 vol. Santillan, Jorge, illus. 2011. (Sports Illustrated Kids Victory School Superstars Ser.). (ENG.). 56p. (J). (gr. 1-3). pap. 5.95 (978-1-4342-3394-3(4), 116407, Stone Arch Bks.) Capstone.

Publications International Ltd. Staff. Interactive Sound Surfs Up. 2007. 24p. (J). 16.98 (978-1-4127-6829-0(2), PIL Kids) Publications International, Ltd.

Renaud, Andrea. Sammy the Surfing Pelican Meets Steve the Surf Guru. l.t. ed. 2003. (Illus.). 32p. (J). per. (978-0-9717041-3-8(9)) A Happy Friend, Inc.

Reynolds, Aaron. Dude! Santat, Dan, illus. 2018. (ENG.). 40p. (J). 17.99 (978-1-62672-603-1(5), 900162895) Roaring Brook Pr.

Roddy, Lee. The Mystery of the Wild Surfer. 2006. (Ladd Family Adventure Ser.: Vol. 6). (Illus.). 135p. (J). (gr. 4-7). per. 7.99 (978-0-88062-255-4(5)) Mott Media.

Ross, Jeff. Dawn Patrol, 1 vol. 2012. (Orca Sports Ser.). (ENG.). 160p. (J). (gr. 4-7). pap. 9.95 (978-1-4598-0062-5(1)) Orca Bk. Pubs. USA.

Starfall Education. Surfer Girl. Starfall Education, ed. 2004. (ENG., Illus.). 8p. (J). pap. (978-1-59577-014-1(3)) Starfall Education.

Stilton, Gerónimo. Surfing for Secrets. 2015. (Geronimo Stilton Cavemice Ser.: 8). lib. bdg. 17.20 (978-0-606-37058-5(7)) Turtleback.

Terrell, Brandon. Riptide Pride, 1 vol. Cano, Fernando, illus. 2011. (Sports Illustrated Kids Graphic Novels Ser.). (ENG.). 56p. (J). (gr. 3-8). pap. 7.19 (978-1-4342-3399-8(5), 116412); lib. bdg. 26.65 (978-1-4342-2238-1(1), 103101) Capstone. (Stone Arch Bks.).

Toms, Suzette. Surfing Surprise, 1 vol. 2018. (ENG., Illus.). 21p. (J). pap. (978-1-77654-248-2(7), Red Rocket Readers) Flying Start Bks.

Tsong, Jing Jing. Sam Surfs. 2010. 20p. (J). pap. 7.95 (978-1-933067-33-9(0)) Beachhouse Publishing, LLC.

Wahn, Udo. Cabo & Coral Go Surfing! Lyn, Jami, illus. 2007. 48p. (J). pap. 17.95 (978-0-615-17598-0(8)) Caboandcoral.com.

SURGEONS

Bankston, John. Joseph Lister & the Story of Antiseptics. 2004. (Uncharted, Unexplored, & Unexplained Ser.). (Illus.). 48p. (J). (gr. 4-8). lib. bdg. 29.95 (978-1-58415-262-0(1)) Mitchell Lane Pubs.

Benge, Janet & Benge, Geoff. Heroes of History - Ben Carson: A Chance at Life. 2014. (ENG., Illus.). 192p. (YA). pap. 11.99 (978-1-62486-034-8(6)) Emerald Bks.

—Paul Brand: Helping Hands. 2011. (ENG.). (YA). pap. 11.99 (978-1-57658-536-8(0)) YWAM Publishing.

Hooks, Gwendolyn. Tiny Stitches: The Life of Vivien Thomas, 1 vol. Bootman, Colin, illus. 2016. (ENG.). 32p. (J). (gr. 2-8). 19.95 (978-1-62014-156-4(6), leelowbooks) Lee & Low Bks., Inc.

Lewis, Deborah Shaw & Lewis, Gregg. Gifted Hands: The Ben Carson Story [Revised Kids Edition], 1 vol. rev. ed. 2014. (ZonderKidz Biography Ser.). (ENG., Illus.). 176p. (J). pap. 7.99 (978-0-310-73830-5(X)) Zonderkidz.

Lim, Bridget & Ramen, Fred. Albucasis: The Father of Modern Surgery, 1 vol. 2016. (Physicians, Scientists, & Mathematicians of the Islamic World Ser.). (ENG.). 112p. (gr. 6-6). 38.80 (978-1-5081-7140-9(8), ba3e970d-391d-4ae9-979e-46d783ada49f) Rosen Publishing Group, Inc., The.

Marsh, Carole. Antonia C. Novello: First Female U. S. Surgeon General: First Female U. S. Surgeon General. 2003. 12p. (gr. k-4). 2.95 (978-0-635-02139-7(0)) Gallopade International.

—Charles Drew: Dedicated Doctor. 2004. (1000 Readers Ser.). (Illus.). 12p. (J). (gr. k-4). per. 2.95 (978-0-635-02528-9(0)) Gallopade International.

Marsico, Katie. Charles Drew. Bane, Jeff, illus. 2018. (My Early Library: My Itty-Bitty Bio Ser.). (ENG.). 24p. (J). (gr. k-1). lib. bdg. 30.64 (978-1-5341-2879-8(4), 211560) Cherry Lake Publishing.

Ramen, Fred. Albucasis (Abu al-Qasim Al-Zahrawi) Renowned Muslim Surgeon of the Tenth Century. 2009. (Great Muslim Philosophers & Scientists of the Middle Ages Ser.). 112p. (gr. 6-6). 66.50 (978-1-61513-178-5(7), Rosen Reference) Rosen Publishing Group, Inc., The.

Saxby, Claire. Meet Weary Dunlop. Lord, Jeremy, illus. 2015. (Meet... Ser.). (ENG.). 32p. (J). (gr. -1-k). 21.99 (978-0-85798-536-1(1)) Random Hse. Australia AUS. Dist: Independent Pubs. Group.

—Meet... Weary Dunlop. Lord, Jeremy, illus. 2016. 36p. (J). (gr. k-2). 15.99 (978-0-85798-587-3(6)) Random Hse. Australia AUS. Dist: Independent Pubs. Group.

Schraff, Anne. The Life of Dr. Charles Drew: Blood Bank Innovator, 1 vol. 2014. (Legendary African Americans Ser.). (ENG.). 96p. (gr. 6-6). 31.61 (978-0-7660-6265-8(1), a6ebcc05-3228-41ba-8257-509692c261e8); pap. 13.88 (978-0-7660-6266-5(X), f765a6d6-f3b4-4a57-b398-79f2ba079082) Enslow Publishing, LLC.

Spitz, Michael. Life As a Doctor in the Civil War, 1 vol. 2017. (Life As... Ser.). (ENG.). 32p. (gr. 3-3). pap. 11.58 (978-1-5026-3035-3(4), e11411b3-38c4-4f65-a99a-a2e86b7df7dd) Cavendish Square Publishing LLC.

Stoltman, Joan. Gareth's Guide to Becoming a Brain Surgeon. 2017. (Gareth Guides to an Extraordinary Life Ser.). 32p. (J). (gr. 4-5). pap. 63.00 (978-1-5382-0334-7(0)) Stevens, Gareth Publishing LLLP.

Venezia, Mike. Charles Drew: Doctor Who Got the World Pumped up to Donate Blood. Venezia, Mike, illus. 2009. (Getting to Know the World's Greatest Inventors & Scientists Ser.). (ENG., Illus.). 32p. (J). (gr. 2-5). 28.00 (978-0-531-23725-0(7)) Scholastic Library Publishing.

—Charles Drew: Doctor Who Got the World Pumped up to Donate Blood (Getting to Know the World's Greatest Inventors & Scientists) Venezia, Mike, illus. 2009. (Getting to Know the World's Greatest Inventors & Scientists Ser.). (ENG., Illus.). 32p. (J). (gr. 3-4). pap. 6.95 (978-0-531-21334-6(X), Children's Pr.) Scholastic Library Publishing.

Wyckoff, Edwin Brit. The African-American Heart Surgery Pioneer: The Genius of Vivien Thomas, 1 vol. 2013. (Genius Inventors & Their Great Ideas Ser.). (ENG.). 48p. (gr. 3-3). pap. 11.53 (978-1-4644-0210-4(8), 2b8ef94c-a9ea-46db-8f27-258b06589a23); (Illus.). 27.93 (978-0-7660-4140-0(9), 29aa2b19-9222-4a9d-a7af-cb14c12bc2ff) Enslow Publishing, LLC. (Enslow Elementary).

SURGERY

Alagna, Magdalena. Everything You Need to Know about the Dangers of Cosmetic Surgery. 2009. (Need to Know Library). 64p. (gr. 5-5). 58.50 (978-1-60854-093-8(6)) Rosen Publishing Group, Inc., The.

Alter, Judy. Surgery. 2008. (21st Century Skills Innovation Library: Innovation in Medicine Ser.). (ENG., Illus.). 32p. (gr. 4-8). lib. bdg. 32.07 (978-1-60279-224-1(0), 200155) Cherry Lake Publishing.

Apel, Melanie Ann. Let's Talk about When You Have to Get Stitches. 2009. (Let's Talk Library). 24p. (gr. 2-3). 42.50 (978-1-60853-447-0(2), PowerKids Pr.) Rosen Publishing Group, Inc., The.

Bankston, John. Joseph Lister & the Story of Antiseptics. 2004. (Uncharted, Unexplored, & Unexplained Ser.). (Illus.). 48p. (J). (gr. 4-8). lib. bdg. 29.95 (978-1-58415-262-0(1)) Mitchell Lane Pubs.

Cobb, Allan B. The Bionic Human. 2009. (Library of Future Medicine Ser.). 64p. (gr. 5-5). 58.50 (978-1-60853-631-3(9)) Rosen Publishing Group, Inc., The.

Colby, Jennifer. Lamprey Eels to Robots. 2019. (21st Century Junior Library: Tech from Nature Ser.). (ENG., Illus.). 24p. (J). (gr. 2-5). pap. 12.79 (978-1-5341-3953-4(2), 212641) Cherry Lake Publishing.

—Lampreys to Robots. 2019. (21st Century Junior Library: Tech from Nature Ser.). (ENG., Illus.). 24p. (J). (gr. 2-5). lib. bdg. 30.64 (978-1-5341-4297-8(5), 212640) Cherry Lake Publishing.

Furstinger, Nancy. Unstoppable: True Stories of Amazing Bionic Animals. 2017. (ENG., Illus.). 128p. (J). (gr. 3-7). 16.99 (978-0-544-87966-9(X), 1650975, Clarion Bks.) HarperCollins Pubs.

Gagne, Tammy. Artificial Organs. 2019. (Engineering the Human Body Ser.). (ENG.). 32p. (J). (gr. 3-5). 31.35 (978-1-64185-762-8(5), 1641857625, Focus Readers) North Star Editions.

Giddens, Sandra. Future Techniques in Surgery. 2009. (Library of Future Medicine Ser.). 64p. (gr. 5-5). 58.50 (978-1-60853-630-6(0)) Rosen Publishing Group, Inc., The.

Harris, Michael C. Spare Parts for People, 1 vol. 2011. (Cool Science Ser.). (ENG.). 48p. (gr. 4-4). 31.21 (978-1-60870-080-6(1), 889f7953-eb8c-4238-96ee-0d497a50a76d) Cavendish Square Publishing LLC.

Herrington, Lisa M. I Need Stitches (Rookie Read-About Health) (Library Edition) 2015. (Rookie Read-About Health Ser.). (ENG., Illus.). 32p. (J). (gr. 1-2). lib. bdg. 25.00 (978-0-531-21039-0(1), Children's Pr.) Scholastic Library Publishing.

Libal, Autumn. Can I Change the Way I Look? A Teen's Guide to the Health Implications of Cosmetic Surgery, Makeovers, & Beyond. 2006. (Science of Health Ser.). (Illus.). 128p. (YA). 24.95 (978-1-59084-843-2(8)) Mason Crest.

May, Erica. Emerson Learns about Surgery. Millward, Hayley, illus. 2013. (ENG.). (J). (gr. -1-3). 14.95 (978-1-62086-279-7(4)) Amplify Publishing Group.

Nargi, Lela. Karl's New Beak: 3-D Printing Builds a Bird a Better Life. Popham, Harriet, illus. 2019. (ENG.). 32p. (gr. -1-2). 17.95 (978-1-68446-026-7(3), 139699, Capstone Editions) Capstone.

Silverstein, Virginia & Silverstein Nunn, Laura. Handy Health Guide to Bites & Stings, 1 vol. 2013. (Handy Health Guides). (ENG.). 48p. (gr. 5-6). pap. 11.53 (978-1-4644-0485-6(2), 73cbc9ed-87cb-4eea-bb03-fe53daf73882) Enslow Publishing, LLC.

—Handy Health Guide to Burns & Blisters, 1 vol. 2013. (Handy Health Guides). (ENG.). 48p. (gr. 5-6). pap. 11.53 (978-1-4644-0487-0(9), 34d79567-fe09-4261-b356-7afb36a13a61) Enslow Publishing, LLC.

Stearman, Kaye. The Debate about Cosmetic Surgery, 1 vol. 2010. (Ethical Debates Ser.). (ENG.). 48p. (YA). (gr. 6-6). lib. bdg. 34.47 (978-1-4358-9650-5(5), 8f609d1e-76aa-458b-960f-1a89fc900e8c, Rosen Reference) Rosen Publishing Group, Inc., The.

SURGERY—VOCATIONAL GUIDANCE

Bailey, Diane. Brain Surgeons, 1 vol. 2008. (Extreme Careers Ser.). (ENG., Illus.). 64p. (YA). (gr. 5-5). lib. bdg. 37.13 (978-1-4042-1787-4(8), e4fe0185-1f69-45a1-9420-c425ffa8649f) Rosen Publishing Group, Inc., The.

Ellis, Catherine. Planes, 1 vol. 2007. (Mega Military Machines Ser.). (ENG., Illus.). 24p. (J). (gr. 1-1). lib. bdg. 26.27 (978-1-4042-3667-7(8), b1e40b2a-8cb3-469a-a164-9be2bb0d9df3) Rosen Publishing Group, Inc., The.

SURINAME

Streissguth, Thomas. Suriname in Pictures. 2009. (Visual Geography Series, Second Ser.). (ENG.). 80p. (gr. 5-12). 31.93 (978-1-57505-964-8(9)) Lerner Publishing Group.

Williams, Colleen Madonna Flood & Flood Williams, Colleen Madonna. Suriname. 2009. (South America Today Ser.). (Illus.). 63p. (J). (gr. 4-7). 21.95 (978-1-4222-0641-6(6)) Mason Crest.

SURVEYING

Marsico, Katie. Levels. 2013. (21st Century Junior Library: Basic Tools Ser.). (ENG.). 24p. (J). (gr. 2-5). pap. 12.79 (978-1-62431-304-2(3), 203010); (Illus.). 29.21 (978-1-62431-172-7(5), 203008) Cherry Lake Publishing.

Merrill, Amy French. A Day in the Life of a Colonial Surveyor. 2009. (Library of Living & Working in Colonial Times Ser.). 24p. (gr. 3-3). 42.50 (978-1-60853-740-2(4), PowerKids Pr.) Rosen Publishing Group, Inc., The.

Petersen, Christine. The Surveyor, 1 vol. 2011. (Colonial People Ser.). (ENG.). 48p. (gr. 4-4). 34.07 (978-0-7614-4805-1(5), f1d2b84e-a0e8-4249-b423-ef731729c885) Cavendish Square Publishing LLC.

SURVEYS, SOCIAL

see Social Surveys

SURVIVAL

see also Wilderness Survival

Abdo, Kenny. How to Survive a Flood. 2018. (How to Survive Ser.). (ENG., Illus.). 24p. (J). (gr. 2-8). lib. bdg. 31.36 (978-1-5321-2325-2(6), 28417, Abdo Zoom-Fly) ABDO Publishing Co.

—How to Survive a Hurricane. 2018. (How to Survive Ser.). (ENG., Illus.). 24p. (J). (gr. 2-8). lib. bdg. 31.36 (978-1-5321-2326-9(4), 28419, Abdo Zoom-Fly) ABDO Publishing Co.

—How to Survive a Tornado. 2018. (How to Survive Ser.). (ENG., Illus.). 24p. (J). (gr. 2-8). lib. bdg. 31.36 (978-1-5321-2327-6(2), 28421, Abdo Zoom-Fly) ABDO Publishing Co.

Bailey, Diane. Survival Skills, Vol. 10. 2016. (Great Outdoors! Ser.). (Illus.). 48p. (J). (gr. 5). 20.95 (978-1-4222-3574-4(2)) Mason Crest.

Bell, Samantha. Being Lost at Sea. 2018. 24p. (J). (978-1-4896-9773-8(X), AV2 by Weigl) Weigl Pubs., Inc.

—How to Survive Being Lost at Sea. 2015. (Survival Guides). (ENG.). 24p. (J). (gr. 2-5). 32.79 (978-1-60973-159-5(X), 208795) Child's World, Inc, The.

Benge, Janet & Benge, Geoff. Heroes of History - Louis Zamperini: Redemption. 2014. (ENG.). 218p. (J). pap. 11.99 (978-1-62486-049-2(4)) Emerald Bks.

Blake, Kevin. Lost in the Antarctic. 2014. (Stranded! Ser.). (ENG.). 32p. (J). (gr. 2-7). lib. bdg. 28.50 (978-1-62724-289-9(9)) Bearport Publishing Co., Inc.

Borgenicht, David. Weird Junior Edition. 2014. (Worst-Case Scenario Survival Handbook Ser.). (ENG.). 128p. (J). (gr. 4-7). 41.35 (978-1-59920-974-6(8), 19407, Smart Apple Media) Black Rabbit Bks.

Borgenicht, David, et al. Gross Junior Edition. 2014. (Worst-Case Scenario Survival Handbook Ser.). (ENG., Illus.). 128p. (J). (gr. 4-7). 41.35 (978-1-59920-975-3(6), 19404, Smart Apple Media) Black Rabbit Bks.

Braun, Eric. Fighting to Survive in the Wilderness: Terrifying True Stories. 2019. (Fighting to Survive Ser.). (ENG., Illus.). 64p. (J). (gr. 4-9). pap. 8.95 (978-0-7565-6234-2(1), 140934); lib. bdg. 35.32 (978-0-7565-6187-1(6), 140667) Capstone. (Compass Point Bks.).

Braun, Eric Mark & Raum, Elizabeth. Fighting to Survive Space Disasters: Terrifying True Stories. 2019. (Fighting to Survive Ser.). (ENG., Illus.). 64p. (J). (gr. 4-9). pap. 8.95 (978-0-7565-6233-5(3), 140935); lib. bdg. 35.32 (978-0-7565-6186-4(8), 140665) Capstone. (Compass Point Bks.).

Brown, Alex. Secret Missions. 2009. (Difficult & Dangerous Ser.). (J). 28.50 (978-1-59920-159-7(3)) Black Rabbit Bks.

Brush, Jim & Scarborough, Kate. Extreme Survival. 2012. (Fast Facts Ser.). (ENG., Illus.). 32p. (gr. 4-6). pap. 28.50 (978-1-59771-325-2(2)) Sea-To-Sea Pubns.

Butterfield, Moira. Survive & Thrive: A Pocket Guide to Wilderness Safety Skills, Plus 16 Quick-Check Skill Cards. 2016. (ENG., Illus.). 112p. (J). (gr. 3-7). pap. 11.99 (978-1-4380-0842-4(2)) Sourcebooks, Inc.

Campbell, Guy. Survival: How to Survive Anything, Anywhere. 2019. (Buster Know-How Ser.). (ENG., Illus.). 128p. (J). (gr. 4-6). pap. 16.99 (978-1-78055-509-6(1)) O'Mara, Michael Bks., Ltd. GBR. Dist: Independent Pubs. Group.

Champion, Neil. Finding Food & Water. 2012. (ENG., Illus.). 32p. (gr. 3-7). pap. 8.95 (978-1-926722-55-9(8)) Saunders Bk. Co. CAN. Dist: RiverStream Publishing.

—Fire & Cooking. 2010. (Survive Alive Ser.). (ENG., Illus.). 32p. (J). (gr. 3-7). pap. 8.95 (978-1-926722-57-3(4), 17223) Amicus.

—In an Emergency. 2012. (ENG., Illus.). 32p. (gr. 3-7). pap. 8.95 (978-1-926722-58-0(2)) Saunders Bk. Co. CAN. Dist: RiverStream Publishing.

Colson, Rob. Ultimate Survival Guide for Kids. 2015. (ENG., Illus.). 96p. (J). (gr. 5-8). pap. 9.95 (978-1-77085-619-6(6), 9479530c-c7f2-4ec2-8d9e-517ea66bb885) Firefly Bks., Ltd.

Cook, Peter & Salariya, David. Sail on a 19th-Century Whaling Ship! Grisly Tasks You'd Rather Not Do. Antram, David, illus. 2004. (You Wouldn't Want to Ser.). (ENG.). (J). 29.00 (978-0-531-12356-0(1)) Scholastic Library Publishing.

Currie, Stephen. Escapes from Man-Made Disasters. 2003. (Great Escapes Ser.). (ENG., Illus.). 112p. (J). pap. 30.85 (978-1-59018-277-2(4)) Cengage Gale.

—Escapes from Natural Disasters. 2004. (Great Escapes Ser.). (ENG., Illus.). 112p. (J). 30.85 (978-1-59018-278-9(2), Lucent Bks.) Cengage Gale.

Dakota, Heather. Jurassic Survival Guide. 2014. (Illus.). 96p. (J). (978-0-545-80815-6(4)) Scholastic, Inc.

Dakota, Heather, et al. Monster: Survival Guide. Castro, Ali, illus. 2015. 128p. (J). (978-0-545-85166-4(1), Tangerine Pr.) Scholastic, Inc.

Doeden, Matt. Can You Survive the Desert? An Interactive Survival Adventure. 2012. (You Choose: Survival Ser.). (ENG.). 112p. (gr. 3-4). pap. 41.70 (978-1-4296-8479-8(8), Capstone Pr.) Capstone.

—You Choose: Survival. 2012. (You Choose: Survival Ser.). (ENG.). 112p. (gr. 3-4). pap. 250.20 (978-1-4296-8482-8(8), Capstone Pr.) Capstone.

Doeden, Matt & Penn, Jim. Can You Survive the Jungle? An Interactive Survival Adventure, 1 vol. 2011. (You Choose: Survival Ser.). (ENG., Illus.). 112p. (J). (gr. 3-7). lib. bdg. 32.65 (978-1-4296-6588-9(2), 115711); pap. 6.95 (978-1-4296-7349-5(4), 116886) Capstone. (Capstone Pr.).

Dowswell, P. True Survival Stories. 2004. (True Adventure Stories Ser.). 144p. (J). lib. bdg. 12.95 *(978-1-58086-457-2(0))* EDC Publishing.

Dowswell, Paul. Survival. rev. ed. 2012. (Usborne True Stories Ser.). (Illus.). 144p. (J). (gr. 4-7). per. 4.99 *(978-0-7945-1843-1(5)*, Usborne) EDC Publishing.

Dugan, Christine. Struggle for Survival. 2nd rev. ed. 2016. (TIME(r): Informational Text Ser.). (ENG., Illus.). 48p. (J). (gr. 5-8). pap. 13.99 *(978-1-4938-3605-5(6))* Teacher Created Materials, Inc.

Earl, C. F. & Vanderhoof, Gabrielle. Army Rangers. 2010. (Special Forces Ser.). (Illus.). 64p. (YA). (gr. 7-18). lib. bdg. 22.95 *(978-1-4222-1838-9(4))* Mason Crest.

Eggleton, Jill. Living to Tell the Tale. 2007. (Connectors Ser.). (gr. 2-5). pap. *(978-1-877453-15-1(3))* Global Education Systems Ltd.

Felix, Rebecca. Duct Tape Survival Gear. 2017. (Create with Duct Tape Ser.). (ENG., Illus.). 32p. (J). (gr. 2-5). 26.65 *(978-1-5124-2666-3(0)*, fea61926-d718-4de2-861e-2f1f33c89d26); E-Book 39.99 *(978-1-5124-3854-3(5)*, 9781512438543); E-Book 6.99 *(978-1-5124-3855-0(3)*, 9781512438550); E-Book 39.99 *(978-1-5124-2763-9(2))* Lerner Publishing Group. (Lerner Pubns.).

Fink, Courtney. Wings, Shells, & Fur: Surviving in the Wild, 1 vol. 2013. (InfoMax Readers Ser.). (ENG.). 24p. (J). (gr. 3-3). pap. 8.25 *(978-1-4777-2519-1(9)*, ed00961e-00ac-4920-8594-773123ce232d); pap. 49.50 *(978-1-4777-2520-7(2))* Rosen Publishing Group, Inc., The. (Rosen Classroom).

Goldish, Meish. Lost in a Desert. 2015. (Illus.). 32p. (J). lib. bdg. 28.50 *(978-1-62724-285-1(6))* Bearport Publishing Co., Inc.

—Lost on a Mountain. 2015. (Illus.). 32p. (J). lib. bdg. 28.50 *(978-1-62724-292-9(9))* Bearport Publishing Co., Inc.

Green, Jen & Belinda, Gallagher. Survival Handbook - Jungle: Could You Get Out Alive? Kelly, Richard, ed. 2017. (Illus.). 220p. pap. 9.99 *(978-1-78209-434-0(2))* Miles Kelly Publishing, Ltd. GBR. Dist: Parkwest Pubns., Inc.

Green, Jen & Kelly, Miles. Extreme Survival. Kelly, Richard, ed. 2017. (Illus.). 48p. (J). pap. 9.95 *(978-1-84810-307-8(7))* Miles Kelly Publishing, Ltd. GBR. Dist: Parkwest Pubns., Inc.

Hanel, Rachael. Can You Survive Antarctica? An Interactive Survival Adventure, 1 vol. 2011. (You Choose: Survival Ser.). (ENG., 112p. (J). (gr. 3-7). Illus.). lib. bdg. 32.65 *(978-1-4296-6589-6(0)*, 115710); pap. 41.70 *(978-1-4296-7346-4(X)*, 16839); pap. 6.95 *(978-1-4296-7345-7(1)*, 116884) Capstone. (Capstone Pr.).

Hanel, Rachael, et al. You Choose: Can You Survive Collection. 2017. (You Choose: Survival Ser.). (ENG., Illus.). 328p. (J). (gr. 3-7). pap., pap., pap. 9.99 *(978-1-5157-6198-3(3)*, 135048, Capstone Pr.) Capstone.

—You Choose: Survival Classroom Collection. 2013. (You Choose: Survival Ser.). (ENG.). 112p. (J). (gr. 3-4). pap., pap. 376.30 *(978-1-62065-715-7(5)*, 19309, Capstone Pr.) Capstone.

Hoena, B. A. Can You Survive an Alien Invasion? An Interactive Doomsday Adventure. Fisher-Johnson, Paul, illus. 2015. (You Choose: Doomsday Ser.). (ENG.). 112p. (J). (gr. 3-7). lib. bdg. 32.65 *(978-1-4914-5853-2(4)*, 128816, Capstone Pr.) Capstone.

Hofer, Charles. Washed Away by Floods, 1 vol. 2017. (Natural Disasters: How People Survive Ser.). (ENG.). 32p. (J). (gr. 4-5). 27.93 *(978-1-5383-2569-8(1)*, 43c66e57-bc9a-4563-b3c8-d5dc0a19ac49, PowerKids Pr.) Rosen Publishing Group, Inc., The.

Howell, John. The Life & Adventures of Alexander Selkirk, the Real Robinson Crusoe: A Narrative Founded on Facts. unabr. ed. 2012. (Illus.). 94p. 39.99 *(978-1-4622-8912-7(6))* Repressed Publishing LLC.

Hubbard, Ben. Tornado: Perspectives on Tornado Disasters, 1 vol. 2014. (Disaster Dossiers Ser.). (ENG., Illus.). 56p. (J). (gr. 6-10). pap. 9.49 *(978-1-4846-0189-1(0)*, 126170, Heinemann) Capstone.

Jeffrey, Gary. Defying Death at Sea. Riley, Terry, illus. 2010. (Graphic Survival Stories Ser.). 48p. (YA). 58.50 *(978-1-61532-897-0(1))*; (ENG.). (gr. 5-5). 37.13 *(978-1-4358-3530-6(1)*, 831b4e33-37f6-4b47-819a-c4d20f53fbb3); (ENG.). (gr. 5-5). pap. 15.05 *(978-1-61532-863-5(7)*, 06ba29f2-027c-4b17-a7f6-5cabbedb5bce) Rosen Publishing Group, Inc., The. (Rosen Reference).

Klepeis, Alicia Z. Space Survival: Keeping People Alive in Space. 2019. (Future Space Ser.). (ENG., Illus.). 32p. (J). (gr. 3-9). pap. 7.95 *(978-1-5435-7521-7(8)*, 141052); lib. bdg. 28.65 *(978-1-5435-7265-0(0)*, 140596) Capstone.

Krajnik, Elizabeth. Twisted by Tornadoes, 1 vol. 2017. (Natural Disasters: How People Survive Ser.). (ENG.). 32p. (J). (gr. 4-5). 27.93 *(978-1-5383-2567-4(5)*, 5a1de1f3-739d-4e2b-b896-146c9a1e418e, PowerKids Pr.) Rosen Publishing Group, Inc., The.

Kras, Sara Louise. The Hunted: Polar Prey, 1 vol. 2014. (Speeding Star Ser.). (ENG.). 64p. (J). (gr. 3-3). 30.60 *(978-1-62285-080-8(7)*, 6b8034df-1966-44ce-994b-8542c045df01) Enslow Publishing, LLC.

Lake, G. G. Take Your Pick of Survival Situations. 2017. (Take Your (Equally Horrible) Pick! Ser.). (ENG., Illus.). 32p. (J). (gr. 3-9). lib. bdg. 27.32 *(978-1-5157-4473-3(6)*, 134175, Capstone Pr.) Capstone.

Lassieur, Allison. Can You Survive Being Lost at Sea? An Interactive Survival Adventure. 2013. (You Choose: Survival Ser.). (ENG.). 112p. (J). (gr. 3-4). pap. 41.70 *(978-1-62065-712-6(0)*, 19306, Capstone Pr.) Capstone.

—Can You Survive the Titanic? An Interactive Survival Adventure, 1 vol. 2011. (You Choose: Survival Ser.). (ENG., 112p. (J). (gr. 3-7). Illus.). lib. bdg. 32.65 *(978-1-4296-6586-5(6)*, 115708); pap. 6.95 *(978-1-4296-7351-8(6)*, 116887) Capstone. (Capstone Pr.).

Law, Felicia & Bailey, Gerry. Caught in the Rapids. Noyes, Leighton, illus. 2015. (Science to the Rescue Ser.). (ENG.). 32p. (J). (gr. 4-4). *(978-0-7787-1674-7(0))* Crabtree Publishing Co.

Lewis, Brenda Ralph. Wilderness Rescue with the U. S. Search & Rescue Task Force. 2004. (Rescue & Prevention Ser.). (Illus.). 96p. (YA). (gr. 7-18). lib. bdg. 22.95 *(978-1-59084-404-5(1))* Mason Crest.

Lewis, Simon. Survival at Sea. 2009. (Difficult & Dangerous Ser.). (ENG.). 32p. (J). (gr. 3-6). 28.50 *(978-1-59920-160-3(7)*, 19268, Smart Apple Media) Black Rabbit Bks.

—Survival at Sea. 2009. (Difficult & Dangerous Ser.). (ENG., Illus.). 32p. (J). (gr. 3-7). pap. *(978-1-897563-27-4(2))* Saunders Bk. Co.

Lloyd Kyi, Tanya. When the Worst Happens: Extraordinary Stories of Survival. Parkins, David, illus. 2014. (ENG.). 128p. (J). (gr. 5-8). pap. 14.95 *(978-1-55451-682-7(X)*, 9781554516827) Annick Pr., Ltd. CAN. Dist: Publishers Group West (PGW).

Loh-Hagan, Virginia. AI Uprising Hacks. 2019. (Could You Survive? Ser.). (ENG.). 32p. (J). (gr. 4-8). pap. 14.21 *(978-1-5341-5068-3(4)*, 213579); (Illus.). lib. bdg. 32.07 *(978-1-5341-4782-9(9)*, 213578) Cherry Lake Publishing. (45th Parallel Press).

—Alien Invasion Hacks. 2019. (Could You Survive? Ser.). (ENG., Illus.). 32p. (J). (gr. 4-8). pap. 14.21 *(978-1-5341-5067-6(6)*, 213575); lib. bdg. 32.07 *(978-1-5341-4781-2(0)*, 213574) Cherry Lake Publishing. (45th Parallel Press).

—Aron Ralston: Trapped in the Desert. 2018. (True Survival Ser.). (ENG.). 32p. (J). (gr. 4-8). pap. 14.21 *(978-1-5341-0872-1(6)*, 210852); (Illus.). lib. bdg. 32.07 *(978-1-5341-0773-1(8)*, 210851) Cherry Lake Publishing. (45th Parallel Press).

—Harrison Okene: Sixty Hours Underwater. 2019. (True Survival Ser.). (ENG., Illus.). 32p. (J). (gr. 4-8). pap. 14.21 *(978-1-5341-3986-2(9)*, 212773); lib. bdg. 32.07 *(978-1-5341-4330-2(0)*, 212772) Cherry Lake Publishing. (45th Parallel Press).

—Hunted by Predators Hacks. 2019. (Could You Survive? Ser.). (ENG., Illus.). 32p. (J). (gr. 4-8). pap. 14.21 *(978-1-5341-5072-0(2)*, 213595); lib. bdg. 32.07 *(978-1-5341-4786-7(1)*, 213594) Cherry Lake Publishing. (45th Parallel Press).

—Lost in Space Hacks. 2019. (Could You Survive? Ser.). (ENG.). 32p. (J). (gr. 4-8). pap. 14.21 *(978-1-5341-5069-0(2)*, 213583); (Illus.). lib. bdg. 32.07 *(978-1-5341-4783-6(7)*, 213582) Cherry Lake Publishing. (45th Parallel Press).

—Michael Benson: Trapped in a Volcano. 2019. (True Survival Ser.). (ENG., Illus.). 32p. (J). (gr. 4-8). pap. 14.21 *(978-1-5341-3985-5(0)*, 212769); lib. bdg. 32.07 *(978-1-5341-4329-6(7)*, 212768) Cherry Lake Publishing. (45th Parallel Press).

—Nuclear Explosion Hacks. 2019. (Could You Survive? Ser.). (ENG.). 32p. (J). (gr. 4-8). pap. 14.21 *(978-1-5341-5071-3(4)*, 213591); (Illus.). lib. bdg. 32.07 *(978-1-5341-4785-0(3)*, 213590) Cherry Lake Publishing. (45th Parallel Press).

—The Robertson Family: Attacked by Orcas. 2019. (True Survival Ser.). (ENG., Illus.). 32p. (J). (gr. 4-8). pap. 14.21 *(978-1-5341-3987-9(7)*, 212777); lib. bdg. 32.07 *(978-1-5341-4331-9(9)*, 212776) Cherry Lake Publishing. (45th Parallel Press).

—Witching Hour Hacks. 2019. (Could You Survive? Ser.). (ENG., Illus.). 32p. (J). (gr. 4-8). pap. 14.21 *(978-1-5341-5070-6(6)*, 213587); lib. bdg. 32.07 *(978-1-5341-4784-3(5)*, 213586) Cherry Lake Publishing. (45th Parallel Press).

—Zombie Apocalypse Hacks. 2019. (Could You Survive? Ser.). (ENG., Illus.). 32p. (J). (gr. 4-8). pap. 14.21 *(978-1-5341-5065-2(X)*, 213567); lib. bdg. 32.07 *(978-1-5341-4779-9(9)*, 213566) Cherry Lake Publishing. (45th Parallel Press).

Long, David. Survivors: Blue Peter Award Winner. Hyndman, Kerry, illus. 2017. (ENG.). 192p. (J). pap. 13.95 *(978-0-571-33966-2(2)*, Faber & Faber Children's Bks.) Faber & Faber, Inc.

Mack, Molly. Finding Food in the Wild, 1 vol., 1. 2015. (Wilderness Survival Skills Ser.). (ENG., Illus.). 24p. (J). (gr. 3-4). pap. 9.25 *(978-1-5081-4307-9(2)*, 603c04ca-22f4-4714-acd6-3ce276082a0c, PowerKids Pr.) Rosen Publishing Group, Inc., The.

Makerspace Survival, 12 vols. 2017. (Makerspace Survival Ser.). 48p. (ENG.). (gr. 5-5). 191.58 *(978-1-4994-3405-7(7)*, 3bf7f305-39fb-4ba1-8cca-28f5cd1678cb); (gr. 9-10). pap. 70.50 *(978-1-4994-3410-1(3))* Rosen Publishing Group, Inc., The. (PowerKids Pr.).

Markle, Sandra. Rescues! 2006. (ENG., Illus.). 88p. (gr. 3-8). lib. bdg. 25.26 *(978-0-8225-3413-6(4))* Lerner Publishing Group.

Marsico, Katie. Surviving a Canyon: Aron Ralston. 2019. (They Survived (Alternator Books (r)) Ser.). (ENG., Illus.). 32p. (J). (gr. 3-6). 29.32 *(978-1-5415-2351-7(2)*, 25cbef04-4875-4507-a597-0f782f7e1392, Lerner Pubns.) Lerner Publishing Group.

McCarthy, Tom. Survival: True Stories. 2016. (Mystery & Mayhem Ser.). (ENG., Illus.). 128p. (J). (gr. 3-6). 19.95 *(978-1-61930-476-5(7)*, fb526cb1-9ffa-49d0-a34f-6c37ff16af39) Nomad Pr.

McCollum, Sean. Fighting to Survive Airplane Crashes: Terrifying True Stories. 2019. (Fighting to Survive Ser.). (ENG., Illus.). 64p. (J). (gr. 4-9). pap. 8.95 *(978-0-7565-6230-4(9)*, 140931); lib. bdg. 35.32 *(978-0-7565-6183-3(3)*, 140662) Capstone. (Compass Point Bks.).

McCumiskey, Gavin. Shackleton the Voyage of the James Caird: A Graphic Account. 2016. (ENG., Illus.). 96p. (J). pap. 12.99 *(978-1-84889-281-1(0)*, Collins Pr., The) M.H. Gill & Co. U. C. IRL. Dist: Casemate Pubs. & Bk. Distributors, LLC.

McGee, Brenda Holt & Keiser, Debbie Triska. High-Interest Nonfiction: Survivors 3-5. Hoelscher, Wolfgang, ed. 2003. (Skills for Success Ser.). 128p. (gr. 3-5). pap. 16.99 *(978-0-88724-950-1(7)*, CD-4320) Carson-Dellosa Publishing, LLC.

McNab, Chris. Survival at Sea. Carney, John, ed. 2014. (Extreme Survival in the Military Ser.: 12). 64p. (J). (gr. 7-18). lib. bdg. 23.95 *(978-1-4222-3084-8(8))* Mason Crest.

—Surviving Captivity. Carney, John, ed. 2014. (Extreme Survival in the Military Ser.: 12). 64p. (J). (gr. 7-18). lib. bdg. 23.95 *(978-1-4222-3089-3(9))* Mason Crest.

—Surviving the World's Extreme Regions: Desert, Arctic, Mountains, & Jungle. Carney, John, ed. 2014. (Extreme Survival in the Military Ser.: 12). (Illus.). 64p. (J). (gr. 7-18). lib. bdg. 23.95 *(978-1-4222-3092-3(9))* Mason Crest.

Naber, Therese. The Science of Survival, 1 vol. 2016. (Super-Awesome Science Ser.). (ENG., Illus.). 48p. (J). (gr. 4-8). lib. bdg. 35.64 *(978-1-68078-252-3(5)*, 22105) ABDO Publishing Co.

Ogden, Charlie. Surviving a Killer Virus, 1 vol. 2017. (Surviving the Impossible Ser.). (ENG.). 32p. (J). (gr. 4-5). pap. 11.50 *(978-1-5382-1463-3(6)*, bb460d1f-1a1c-4044-8731-a8f9256903c8); lib. bdg. 28.27 *(978-1-5382-1416-9(4)*, 4fc77c36-6c97-4317-a434-1da64444d4d1) Stevens, Gareth Publishing LLLP.

—Surviving a Robot Revolution, 1 vol. 2017. (Surviving the Impossible Ser.). (ENG.). 32p. (J). (gr. 4-5). pap. 11.50 *(978-1-5382-1459-6(8)*, 5f07cf4d-1416-475e-92ae-51f6bc23b70b); lib. bdg. 28.27 *(978-1-5382-1420-6(2)*, f7089ea5-e4f4-430a-bf59-31b425f1888b) Stevens, Gareth Publishing LLLP.

—Surviving a Zombie Apocalypse, 1 vol. 2017. (Surviving the Impossible Ser.). (ENG.). 32p. (J). (gr. 4-5). pap. 11.50 *(978-1-5382-1499-2(7)*, f4d2c47f-2331-49ac-8496-ceeda62eff7f); lib. bdg. 28.27 *(978-1-5382-1422-0(9)*, edb32f43-b2de-4f29-b50a-20991cb0fa25) Stevens, Gareth Publishing LLLP.

—Surviving an Alien Invasion, 1 vol. 2017. (Surviving the Impossible Ser.). (ENG.). 32p. (J). (gr. 4-5). pap. 11.50 *(978-1-5382-1461-9(X)*, c126945c-8069-437d-aaf2-06c344e8512a); lib. bdg. 28.27 *(978-1-5382-1418-3(0)*, 8c31df68-1a13-4c51-8fdd-51c3b8c7ed67) Stevens, Gareth Publishing LLLP.

—Surviving in a World Without Power, 1 vol. 2017. (Surviving the Impossible Ser.). (ENG.). 32p. (J). (gr. 4-5). pap. 11.50 *(978-1-5382-1457-2(1)*, f8e36ebe-4c34-4da0-8f9b-32d89b6550b6); lib. bdg. 28.27 *(978-1-5382-1424-4(5)*, 157ad5d9-bb3c-43b4-b688-264191b6018b) Stevens, Gareth Publishing LLLP.

—Surviving the Yellowstone Supervolcano, 1 vol. 2017. (Surviving the Impossible Ser.). (ENG.). 32p. (J). (gr. 4-5). pap. 11.50 *(978-1-5382-1455-8(5)*, 276510a3-dc80-4a05-9a0a-86ee47d954b7); lib. bdg. 28.27 *(978-1-5382-1426-8(1)*, c9deeb4b-5194-49e9-8841-ca52ee35aeff) Stevens, Gareth Publishing LLLP.

Oliver, Martin. Boys Only: How to Survive Anything! Ecob, Simon, illus. 2012. (Best at Everything Ser.). (ENG.). 64p. (J). (gr. 3-7). pap. 6.99 *(978-0-545-43096-8(8)*, Scholastic Paperbacks) Scholastic, Inc.

Olson, Tod. Lost in the Amazon: a Battle for Survival in the Heart of the Rainforest (Lost #3) 2018. (Lost Ser.: 3). (ENG., Illus.). 176p. (J). (gr. 3-7). pap. 7.99 *(978-0-545-92827-4(3)*, Scholastic Nonfiction) Scholastic, Inc.

—Lost in the Pacific, 1942: Not a Drop to Drink. 2016. (J). *(978-0-545-92808-3(7))* Scholastic, Inc.

Owen, Ruth. Jungle Survival Guide. 2010. (ENG., Illus.). 32p. (J). pap. *(978-0-7787-7555-3(0))*; lib. bdg. *(978-0-7787-7533-1(X))* Crabtree Publishing Co.

Oxlade, Chris. Be an Explorer. Sassin, Eva, illus. 2015. (Go Wild Ser.). (ENG.). 32p. (J). (gr. 3-6). E-Book 42.65 *(978-1-4677-7223-5(2)*, Hungry Tomato (r)) Lerner Publishing Group.

Perish, Patric. Survive an Earthquake. 2017. (Survival Zone Ser.). (ENG., Illus.). 24p. (J). (gr. 3-7). lib. bdg. 26.95 *(978-1-62617-584-6(5)*, Torque Bks.) Bellwether Media.

Perish, Patrick. Survive a Fire. 2017. (Survival Zone Ser.). (ENG., Illus.). 24p. (J). (gr. 3-7). lib. bdg. 26.95 *(978-1-62617-581-5(0)*, Torque Bks.) Bellwether Media.

—Survive a Plane Crash. 2017. (Survival Zone Ser.). (ENG., Illus.). 24p. (J). (gr. 3-7). lib. bdg. 26.95 *(978-1-62617-582-2(9)*, Torque Bks.) Bellwether Media.

—Survive an Avalanche. 2017. (Survival Zone Ser.). (ENG., Illus.). 24p. (J). (gr. 3-7). lib. bdg. 26.95 *(978-1-62617-583-9(7)*, Torque Bks.) Bellwether Media.

—Survive on a Desert Island. 2016. (Survival Zone Ser.). (ENG., Illus.). 24p. (J). (gr. 3-7). 26.95 *(978-1-62617-448-1(2)*, Torque Bks.) Bellwether Media.

Philbrick, Nathaniel. In the Heart of the Sea (Young Readers Edition) The True Story of the Whaleship Essex. 2015. (Illus.). 208p. (J). (gr. 3-7). 8.99 *(978-1-101-99776-5(1)*, Puffin Books) Penguin Young Readers Group.

Porterfield, Jason. Shipwreck: True Stories of Survival. (Survivor Stories Ser.). 48p. (gr. 5-5). 2009. 53.00 *(978-1-60853-256-8(9)*, Rosen Reference) 2007. (ENG., Illus.). (YA). lib. bdg. 34.47 *(978-1-4042-1000-4(8)*, 9ba7d99f-743b-45f4-b41a-c009cdda42cd) Rosen Publishing Group, Inc., The.

Prentzas, G. S. Lost at Sea. 2015. (Illus.). 32p. (J). lib. bdg. 28.50 *(978-1-62724-290-5(2))* Bearport Publishing Co., Inc.

Rice, William B. Struggle for Survival. 2nd rev. ed. 2016. (TIME(r): Informational Text Ser.). (ENG.). 48p. (J). (gr. 5-8). pap. 11.99 *(978-1-4938-3603-1(X))* Teacher Created Materials, Inc.

—Struggle for Survival: Shelter. 2016. (Time for Kids Nonfiction Readers Ser.). (ENG.). (J). (gr. 5-8). lib. bdg. 20.85 *(978-0-606-39540-3(7))* Turtleback.

Ridley, Frances. Lost at Sea. 2008. (Crabtree Contact Ser.). (ENG., Illus.). 32p. (J). (gr. 3-7). lib. bdg. *(978-0-7787-3809-1(4))* Crabtree Publishing Co.

Russo, Kristin J. Survival Facts or Fibs. 2018. (Facts or Fibs? Ser.). (ENG., Illus.). 32p. (J). (gr. 3-9). lib. bdg. 28.65 *(978-1-5435-0206-0(7)*, 137128, Capstone Pr.) Capstone.

Searl, Duncan. Trapped! 2005. (Illus.). 48p. (J). *(978-0-669-51413-1(6))* Great Source Education Group, Inc.

Spalding, Frank. Plane Crash: True Stories of Survival. (Survivor Stories Ser.). 48p. (gr. 5-5). 2009. 53.00 *(978-1-60853-255-1(0)*, Rosen Reference) 2007. (ENG., Illus.). (YA). lib. bdg. 34.47 *(978-1-4042-0999-2(9)*, 47e2d75e-9f33-43b1-b07a-735e58ee2771) Rosen Publishing Group, Inc., The.

Spilsbury, Richard & Spilsbury, Louise. The Cave of Shadows. 2015. (Science Adventures Ser.). (ENG., Illus.). 32p. (J). (gr. 3-7). 31.35 *(978-1-62588-147-2(9))* Black Rabbit Bks.

—Crushed! 2015. (Science Adventures Ser.). (ENG., Illus.). 32p. (J). (gr. 3-7). 31.35 *(978-1-62588-145-8(2))* Black Rabbit Bks.

—A Cry in the Dark. 2015. (Science Adventures Ser.). (ENG., Illus.). 32p. (J). (gr. 3-7). 31.35 *(978-1-62588-144-1(4))* Black Rabbit Bks.

—Escape the Volcano. 2015. (Science Adventures Ser.). (ENG., Illus.). 32p. (J). (gr. 3-7). 31.35 *(978-1-62588-146-5(0))* Black Rabbit Bks.

—Shipwrecked. 2015. (Science Adventures Ser.). (ENG., Illus.). 32p. (J). (gr. 3-7). 31.35 *(978-1-62588-149-6(5))* Black Rabbit Bks.

—Shipwrecked: Explore Floating & Sinking & Use Science to Survive. 2016. (Illus.). 30p. (J). pap. *(978-1-62588-399-5(4))* Black Rabbit Bks.

—Sparks, Shocks, & Secrets: Explore Electricity & Use Science to Survive. 2016. (Illus.). 30p. (J). pap. *(978-1-62588-400-8(1))* Black Rabbit Bks.

Stride, Lottie & Oliver, Martin. Girls Only: How to Survive Anything! Geremia, Daniela & Ecob, Simon, illus. 2012. (Best at Everything Ser.). (ENG.). 64p. (J). (gr. 3-7). pap. 6.99 *(978-0-545-43095-1(X)*, Scholastic Paperbacks) Scholastic, Inc.

Sumerak, Marc. Survival Handbook: An Essential Companion to the Great Outdoors. 2019. (ENG., Illus.). 140p. (J). (gr. 2-4). pap. 16.99 *(978-0-7603-6435-2(4)*, 306803) becker&mayer! books.

Surviving Disaster. 2015. (Surviving Disaster Ser.). (ENG.). 48p. (J). (gr. 5-6). pap., pap., pap. 423.00 *(978-1-4777-8627-7(9)*, Rosen Central) Rosen Publishing Group, Inc., The.

Survivors: Ordinary People, Extraordinary Circumstances, 13 vols., Set. Incl. Danger in the Deep: Surviving Shark Attacks. Zoldak, Joyce. (YA). 24.95 *(978-1-4222-0511-2(8))*; Enemy Within: Overcoming Cancer & Other Life-Threatening Diseases. Therrien, Patricia. (YA). 24.95 *(978-1-4222-0450-4(2))*; In Defense of Our Country: Survivors of Military Conflict. Nelson, Sheila. (YA). 24.95 *(978-1-4222-0452-8(9))*; Nature's Wrath: Surviving Natural Disasters. Sanna, Ellyn. (YA). 24.95 *(978-1-4222-0454-2(5))*; Never Again: Survivors of the Holocaust. Nelson, Sheila. (J). 24.95 *(978-1-4222-0459-7(6))*; Those Who Remain: What It Means to Be a Survivor. Sanna, Ellyn. (Illus.). (J). 24.95 *(978-1-4222-0457-3(X))*; When Danger Hits Home: Survivors of Domestic Violence. Zoldak, Joyce. (YA). 24.95 *(978-1-4222-0460-3(X))*; 128p. (gr. 7-12). 2010. 2009. Set lib. bdg. 324.35 *(978-1-4222-0449-8(9))* Mason Crest.

Tarshis, Lauren. I Survived Collector's Toolbox (I Survived) 2015. (I Survived Ser.). (ENG.). (J). (gr. 3-7). 49.90 *(978-0-545-86101-4(2))* Scholastic, Inc.

—Nature Attacks! 2015. (Illus.). 157p. (J). *(978-0-545-90802-3(7)*, Scholastic Pr.) Scholastic, Inc.

—Nature Attacks! (I Survived True Stories #2) 2015. (I Survived True Stories Ser.: 2). (ENG., Illus.). 176p. (J). (gr. 2-5). 12.99 *(978-0-545-85231-9(5)*, Scholastic Paperbacks) Scholastic, Inc.

Teen Survival Guide, 12 vols. 2017. (Teen Survival Guide Ser.). (ENG.). (J). (gr. 6-6). lib. bdg. 177.60 *(978-0-7660-9195-5(3)*, 4499b6cb-742d-437f-bc53-b79174900b5f) Enslow Publishing, LLC.

Troupe, Thomas Kingsley. Surviving on a Desert Island. 2018. (Survival Guides You Didn't Know You Needed Ser.). (ENG., Illus.). 24p. (J). (gr. 4-6). 28.50 *(978-1-68072-342-7(1)*, 12137, Hi Jinx) Black Rabbit Bks.

Tunby, Benjamin. Surviving a Space Disaster: Apollo 13. 2019. (They Survived (Alternator Books (r)) Ser.). (ENG., Illus.). 32p. (J). (gr. 3-6). 29.32 *(978-1-5415-2350-0(4)*, ab165ec4-a23d-4f4c-889b-fa9cfccea128, Lerner Pubns.) Lerner Publishing Group.

Tyler, Madeline. Surviving a Megatsunami, 1 vol. 2018. (Surviving the Impossible Ser.). (ENG.). 32p. (gr. 4-5). pap. 11.50 *(978-1-5382-3506-5(4)*, 1020e8d5-fbbd-4c5b-bdad-5d447acd68ef) Stevens, Gareth Publishing LLLP.

—Surviving a Vampire Invasion, 1 vol. 2018. (Surviving the Impossible Ser.). (ENG.). 32p. (gr. 4-5). pap. 11.50 *(978-1-5382-3514-0(5)*, b0222e30-095b-4d27-8fe1-71e30fd2666a) Stevens, Gareth Publishing LLLP.

—Surviving an Ice Age, 1 vol. 2018. (Surviving the Impossible Ser.). (ENG.). 32p. (gr. 4-5). pap. 11.50 *(978-1-5382-3518-8(8)*, 956a8a0c-d6ca-47db-9ead-45dd2cc741c6) Stevens, Gareth Publishing LLLP.

—Surviving in a World Without Water, 1 vol. 2018. (Surviving the Impossible Ser.). (ENG.). 32p. (gr. 4-5). pap. 11.50 *(978-1-5382-3522-5(6)*, 2acc52d8-fb9c-4a1f-8eaa-dc78bf6cb414) Stevens, Gareth Publishing LLLP.

—Surviving the Rise of the Mummies, 1 vol. 2018. (Surviving the Impossible Ser.). (ENG.). 32p. (gr. 4-5). pap. 11.50 *(978-1-5382-3526-3(9)*, 3e3de852-3379-4781-86b3-ba463c26bf83) Stevens, Gareth Publishing LLLP.

Tylers, Michael. Surviving a Nuclear War, 1 vol. 2018. (Surviving the Impossible Ser.). (ENG.). 32p. (gr. 4-5). pap. 11.50 *(978-1-5382-3510-2(2)*, 61d325dc-6886-4f9f-a63d-709305d07e0e) Stevens, Gareth Publishing LLLP.

Vale, Janice. True Life Survival: Band 12/Copper (Collins Big Cat) Wademan, Spike, illus. 2007. (Collins Big Cat Ser.). (ENG.). 32p. (J). (gr. 2-4). pap. 9.99 *(978-0-00-723078-5(8))* HarperCollins Pubs. Ltd. GBR. Dist: Independent Pubs. Group.

Ventura, Marne. Floods. 2018. (J). pap. *(978-1-4896-9786-8(1)*, AV2 by Weigl) Weigl Pubs., Inc.

—How to Survive a Tornado. 2015. (Survival Guides). (ENG.). 24p. (J). (gr. 2-5). 32.79 *(978-1-60973-161-8(1)*, 208792) Child's World, Inc, The.

—How to Survive an Animal Attack. 2015. (Survival Guides). (ENG.). 24p. (J). (gr. 2-5). 32.79 *(978-1-60973-163-2(8)*, 208794) Child's World, Inc, The.

—Tsunamis. 2018. (J). *(978-1-4896-9793-6(4)*, AV2 by Weigl) Weigl Pubs., Inc.

S

Verstraete, Larry. Surviving the Hindenburg. Geister, David, illus. 2012. (ENG.). 32p. (J). (gr. 1-4). 16.95 *(978-1-58536-787-0(7)*, 202228) Sleeping Bear Pr.

Wacholtz, Anthony. Can You Survive a Zombie Apocalypse? An Interactive Doomsday Adventure. Southall, James & Southall, James, illus. 2015. (You Choose: Doomsday Ser.). (ENG.). 112p. (J). (gr. 3-7). pap. 6.95 *(978-1-4914-5925-6(5)*, 128845, Capstone Pr.) Capstone.

Werther, Scott P. Alive! Airplane Crash in the Andes Mountains. 2003. (Survivor Ser.). (Illus.). 48p. (J). 24.50 *(978-0-516-24329-0(2)*, Children's Pr.) Scholastic Library Publishing.

Wilson, Patrick. Surviving by Trapping, Fishing, & Eating Plants. Carney, John, ed. 2014. (Extreme Survival in the Military Ser.: 12). (Illus.). 64p. (J). (gr. 7-18). lib. bdg. 23.95 *(978-1-4222-3088-6(0))* Mason Crest.

—Surviving Natural Disasters. Carney, John, ed. 2014. (Extreme Survival in the Military Ser.: 12). 64p. (J). (gr. 7-18). lib. bdg. 23.95 *(978-1-4222-3091-6(0))* Mason Crest.

Woolf, Alex. The Science of Natural Disasters: the Devastating Truth about Volcanoes, Earthquakes, & Tsunamis (the Science of the Earth) (Library Edition) Rowland, Andy, illus. 2018. (Science Of... Ser.). (ENG.). 32p. (J). (gr. 3-7). lib. bdg. 29.00 *(978-0-531-22766-4(9)*, Watts, Franklin) Scholastic Library Publishing.

Wulffson, Don L. The Upside-Down Voyage. Lyall, Dennis, illus. 2005. (J). *(978-1-59336-334-5(6))*; pap. *(978-1-59336-335-2(4))* Mondo Publishing.

Yomtov, Nel. The Unbreakable Zamperini: A World War II Survivor's Brave Story. Szlapa, Rafal, illus. 2019. (Amazing World War II Stories Ser.). (ENG.). 32p. (J). (gr. 3-9). pap. 7.95 *(978-1-5435-7548-4(X)*, 141080); lib. bdg. 34.65 *(978-1-5435-7313-8(4)*, 140618) Capstone.

Yomtov, Nelson. Terrors from the Deep: True Tales of Surviving Shark Attacks. 2015. (True Stories of Survival Ser.). (ENG., Illus.). 32p. (J). (gr. 3-9). lib. bdg. 31.32 *(978-1-4914-6573-8(5)*, 129053, Capstone Pr.) Capstone.

You Choose: Survival. 2011. (You Choose: Survival Ser.). (ENG.). 112p. (gr. 3-4). 127.96 *(978-1-4296-6590-2(4))*; pap. 166.80 *(978-1-4296-7354-9(0))*; pap. 27.80 *(978-1-4296-7353-2(2))* Capstone. (Capstone Pr.).

Zullo, Allan. Miracle Pets: True Tales of Courage & Survival. 2011. 122p. *(978-0-545-25507-3(4))* Scholastic, Inc.

SURVIVAL—FICTION

Aaron, Chester. An American Ghost. 2011. (YA). pap. *(978-1-936144-28-0(X))* Zumaya Pubns. LLC.

—Gideon. 2009. (ENG., Illus.). 190p. (YA). pap. 12.99 *(978-1-934841-62-4(5)*, Zumaya Thresholds) Zumaya Pubns. LLC.

Abdo, Kenny. Camp Terror. 2017. (Survive Ser.). (ENG.). 192p. (YA). (gr. 5-12). lib. bdg. 31.42 *(978-1-68076-729-2(1)*, 25392, Epic Escape) EPIC Pr.

Acton, Vanessa. Aftershock. 2017. (Day of Disaster Ser.). (ENG.). 112p. (YA). (gr. 6-12). E-Book 39.99 *(978-1-5124-3500-9(7)*, 9781512435009, Darby Creek) Lerner Publishing Group.

—Backfire. 2017. (Day of Disaster Ser.). (ENG.). 112p. (YA). (gr. 6-12). 26.65 *(978-1-5124-2775-2(6)*, 65f1861b-fdfc-4ecb-ac4a-beb3f6360b27); E-Book 6.99 *(978-1-5124-3504-7(X)*, 9781512435047); E-Book 39.99 *(978-1-5124-3503-0(1)*, 9781512435030) Lerner Publishing Group. (Darby Creek).

—Vortex. 2017. (Day of Disaster Ser.). (ENG.). 104p. (YA). (gr. 6-12). E-Book 6.99 *(978-1-5124-3513-9(9)*, 9781512435139); E-Book 39.99 *(978-1-5124-3512-2(0)*, 9781512435122); E-Book 39.99 *(978-1-5124-2780-6(2))* Lerner Publishing Group. (Darby Creek).

Adams, Carolyn Lee. Ruthless. 2015. (ENG., Illus.). 256p. (YA). (gr. 9). 17.99 *(978-1-4814-2262-8(6)*, Simon Pulse) Simon Pulse.

Aguirre, Ann. Enclave. 2012. (Razorland Trilogy Ser.: 1). (ENG.). 288p. (YA). (gr. 7). pap. 10.99 *(978-0-312-55137-7(1)*, 900074423) Square Fish.

—Horde. 2014. (Razorland Trilogy Ser.: 3). (ENG.). 464p. (YA). (gr. 7). pap. 18.99 *(978-1-250-05077-9(4)*, 900134148) Square Fish.

—Outpost. 2013. (Razorland Trilogy Ser.: 2). (ENG.). 352p. (YA). (gr. 7). pap. 13.99 *(978-1-250-03418-2(3)*, 900120590) Square Fish.

Alderson, Sarah. Losing Lila. 2013. (ENG.). 352p. (J). pap. 10.00 *(978-0-85707-197-2(1)*, Simon & Schuster Children's) Simon & Schuster, Ltd. GBR. Dist: Simon & Schuster, Inc.

Alexander, Kwame. The Door of No Return. l.t. ed. 2023. (ENG.). (J). lib. bdg. 22.99 Cengage Gale.

—The Door of No Return. 2022. (ENG., Illus.). 432p. (J). (gr. 5-17). 17.99 *(978-0-316-44186-5(4))* Little, Brown Bks. for Young Readers.

Alikhan, Salima. Emmi in the City: A Great Chicago Fire Survival Story. Trunfio, Alessia, illus. 2019. (Girls Survive Ser.). (ENG.). 112p. (J). (gr. 3-7). lib. bdg. 26.65 *(978-1-4965-7851-8(1)*, 139369, Stone Arch Bks.) Capstone.

Allison, Samuel B. An American Robinson Crusoe. 2005. 136p. pap. 10.95 *(978-1-4218-0186-5(8))*; 26.95 *(978-1-4218-0086-8(1))* 1st World Publishing, Inc. (1st World Library - Literary Society).

—An American Robinson Crusoe. 2004. reprint ed. pap. 15.95 *(978-1-4191-0613-2(9))*; pap. 1.99 *(978-1-4192-0613-9(3))* Kessinger Publishing, LLC.

Anderson, M. T. Landscape with Invisible Hand. (ENG.). 160p. (gr. 9). 2019. (J). pap. 8.99 *(978-0-7636-9950-5(0))* 2017. (YA). 16.99 *(978-0-7636-8789-2(8))* Candlewick Pr.

Anderson, T. Neill. City of the Dead: Galveston Hurricane 1900. 2013. (J). pap. 16.95 *(978-1-58089-515-6(8))* Charlesbridge Publishing, Inc.

—Horrors of History: City of the Dead: Galveston Hurricane 1900. 2013. (Horrors of History Ser.). (Illus.). 144p. (J). (gr. 5). 16.95 *(978-1-58089-514-9(X))* Charlesbridge Publishing, Inc.

Appelfeld, Aharon. Adam & Thomas. Green, Jeffrey M., tr. Dumas, Philippe, illus. 2017. 160p. (J). (gr. 3-7). pap. 14.95 *(978-1-60980-744-3(8)*, Triangle Square) Seven Stories Pr.

—Long Summer Nights. Green, Jeffrey, tr. Mintzi, Vali, illus. 2019. (ENG.). 160p. (J). (gr. 5-9). 18.95 *(978-1-60980-898-3(3)*, Triangle Square) Seven Stories Pr.

Appelt, Kathi. The Underneath. 2012. (CHI.). 272p. (J). (gr. 4-7). pap. *(978-7-5442-5040-5(7))* Nanhai Publishing Co.

—The Underneath. Small, David, illus. 2010. (KOR.). 395p. (YA). pap. *(978-89-527-5767-8(X))* Sigongsa Co., Ltd.

—The Underneath. Small, David, illus. (ENG.). (J). (gr. 5-9). 2010. 336p. pap. 8.99 *(978-1-4169-5059-2(1))* 2008. 320p. 19.99 *(978-1-4169-5058-5(3))* Simon & Schuster Children's Publishing. (Atheneum Bks. for Young Readers).

—The Underneath. 2010. lib. bdg. 19.65 *(978-0-606-14504-6(4))* Turtleback.

Appleton, Victor. Tom Swift & his Wireless Message. 2005. 26.95 *(978-1-4218-1506-0(0))*; 196p. pap. 11.95 *(978-1-4218-1606-7(7))* 1st World Publishing, Inc. (1st World Library - Literary Society).

—Tom Swift & His Wireless Message or Th. 2006. pap. *(978-1-4065-0911-3(6))* Dodo Pr.

Arden, Katherine. Small Spaces. (Small Spaces Quartet Ser.: 1). (J). (gr. 5). 2019. 256p. 8.99 *(978-0-525-51504-3(6)*, Puffin Books) 2018. 224p. 16.99 *(978-0-525-51502-9(X)*, G.P. Putnam's Sons Books for Young Readers) Penguin Young Readers Group.

—Small Spaces. l.t. ed. 2019. (ENG.). 290p. (YA). *(978-1-4328-6589-4(7))* Thorndike Pr.

Armentrout, Jennifer L. Lux: Opposition: Special Collector's Edition. collector's ed. 2014. (Lux Novel Ser.: 5). (ENG.). 500p. (YA). 19.99 *(978-1-62266-733-8(6)*, 900146176) Entangled Publishing, LLC.

—Opposition. 2013. (Lux Ser.: Bk. 5). (ENG.). (J). pap. 9.99 *(978-1-62266-026-1(9)*, Entangled Teen) Entangled Publishing, LLC.

—Origin. 2013. (ENG.). (Lux Ser.: Bk. 4). (J). pap. 9.99 *(978-1-62061-280-4(1))*; (Lux Novel Ser.: 4). 400p. (YA). (gr. 7-12). pap. 10.99 *(978-1-62266-075-9(7)*, 900128407) Entangled Publishing, LLC.

Armstrong, Kelley. The Calling. 2013. (Darkness Rising Ser.: 2). (ENG.). 352p. (YA). (gr. 8). pap. 10.99 *(978-0-06-179706-4(5)*, HarperCollins) HarperCollins Pubs.

—The Calling: Number 2 in Series. 2012. (Darkness Rising Ser.: Bk. 2). (ENG.). 336p. pap. *(978-1-907410-47-5(3))* Atom Pr.

Arvidson, Douglas. Brothers of the Fire Star. Scarborough, Rob, illus. 2012. 207p. (YA). pap. 15.95 *(978-1-890109-91-2(6)*, Cross Time) Crossquarter Publishing Group.

Asai, Carrie. The Book of the Shadow. Alarcão, Renato, illus. 2013. (Samurai Girl Ser.: 2). (ENG.). 224p. (YA). (gr. 11). pap. 13.99 *(978-1-4814-1540-8(9)*, Simon Pulse) Simon Pulse.

Ashley, Bernard. Solitaire. 2012. (Fiction Ser.). 338p. (J). pap. 6.99 *(978-0-7945-3031-0(1)*, Usborne) EDC Publishing.

Avalos, Francisco. Amazon Tale. 2013. 124p. 29.99 *(978-1-4797-6689-5(5))*; pap. 19.99 *(978-1-4797-6688-8(7))* Xlibris Corp.

Ayder, Earl. The Longest Shortcut. McGrellis, Cynthia, illus. 2005. 40p. pap. 8.53 *(978-0-7578-9857-0(2))* Rigby Education.

Bacigalupi, Paolo. The Drowned Cities. 2013. (ENG.). 464p. (J). (gr. 10-17). pap. 12.99 *(978-0-316-05622-9(7))* 2012. 448p. (YA). 17.99 *(978-0-316-20037-0(9))* Little, Brown Bks. for Young Readers.

—The Drowned Cities. 2012. 352p. *(978-1-59606-506-2(0))* Subterranean Pr.

—The Drowned Cities. 2013. (J). lib. bdg. 22.10 *(978-0-606-31749-8(X))* Turtleback.

—Tool of War. (Ship Breaker Ser.). (ENG.). 384p. (YA). 2018. (gr. 9-17). pap. 19.99 *(978-0-316-22081-1(7))* 2017. (gr. 10-17). 17.99 *(978-0-316-22083-5(3))* Little, Brown Bks. for Young Readers.

Bailey, Em. The Special Ones. 2018. (ENG.). 304p. (YA). (gr. 7). pap. 15.99 *(978-1-328-90106-4(8)*, 1700164, Clarion Bks.) HarperCollins Pubs.

—The Special Ones. 2018. lib. bdg. 20.85 *(978-0-606-40993-3(9))* Turtleback.

Barbieri, Kara. White Stag: A Permafrost Novel. 2019. (ENG.). 368p. (YA). pap. *(978-1-250-22619-8(8)*, Wednesday Bks.) St. Martin's Pr.

Barclay, Linwood. Escape: Book 2. 2019. (Chase Ser.). 240p. (J). (gr. 4-7). 10.99 *(978-1-5101-0221-7(3)*, Orion Children's Bks.) Hachette Children's Group GBR. Dist: Hachette Bk. Group.

Barnes, Jennifer Lynn. The Lovely & the Lost. 2019. (ENG.). 336p. (YA). (gr. 7-17). 17.99 *(978-1-4847-7620-9(8))* Hyperion Pr.

Barr, Ellisa. Outage, 0 vols. 2015. (Powerless Nation Ser.: 1). (ENG.). 218p. (YA). (gr. 7-12). pap. 9.99 *(978-1-4778-2994-3(6)*, 9781477829943, Skyscape) Amazon Publishing.

Bauer, Joan. Backwater. 2005. 185p. 18.00 *(978-0-7569-5779-7(6))* Perfection Learning Corp.

Bennett, Jenn. Starry Eyes. 2018. (ENG.). 432p. (YA). (gr. 9). pap. 12.99 *(978-1-5344-2570-5(5))*; (Illus.). 17.99 *(978-1-4814-7880-9(X)*, Simon Pulse) Simon Pulse.

Berquist, Emma. Devils unto Dust. 2018. (ENG.). 496p. (YA). (gr. 8). 17.99 *(978-0-06-264278-3(2)*, Greenwillow Bks.) HarperCollins Pubs.

Beveridge, Cathy. Stormstruck. 2006. (ENG., Illus.). 214p. (J). pap. *(978-1-55380-041-5(9))* Ronsdale Pr.

Bick, Ilsa J. Ashes. 2012. (Ashes Trilogy Ser.: Bk. 1). (ENG.). 480p. (YA). (gr. 9-12). pap. 17.99 *(978-1-60684-385-7(0)*, 49a7f184-e32c-49cf-ac7d-91c59f25b4dc, Carolrhoda Lab™) Lerner Publishing Group.

—Monsters. 2014. (Ashes Trilogy Ser.). (ENG.). 688p. (YA). (gr. 9-12). pap. 17.99 *(978-1-60684-544-8(6)*, 7d912f36-8c5b-416f-8a24-12a20a671761, Carolrhoda Lab™) Lerner Publishing Group.

—Shadows. 2013. (Ashes Trilogy Ser.: Bk. 2). (ENG.). 528p. (YA). (gr. 9-12). pap. 17.99 *(978-1-60684-445-8(8)*, 2bf296e8-9263-4946-aaf1-1b28a02600de, Carolrhoda Lab™) Lerner Publishing Group.

Black Ice. 2014. (ENG., Illus.). 400p. (YA). (gr. 9). 19.99 *(978-1-4424-7426-0(2)*, Simon & Schuster Bks. For Young Readers) Simon & Schuster Bks. For Young Readers.

Blizzard: Colorado 1886. 2014. (Survivors Ser.). (ENG., Illus.). 160p. (J). (gr. 3-7). pap. 7.99 *(978-1-4814-0969-8(7)*, Aladdin) Simon & Schuster Children's Publishing.

Bodeen, S. A. The Compound. 2011. 9.46 *(978-0-7848-3490-9(3)*, Everbind) Marco Bk. Co.

—The Compound. 2009. (Compound Ser.: 1). (ENG.). 272p. (YA). (gr. 7-12). pap. 10.99 *(978-0-312-57860-2(1)*, 900061807) Square Fish.

—Found: Book 4 of the Shipwreck Island Series. 2018. (Shipwreck Island Ser.: 4). (ENG.). 160p. (J). pap. 9.99 *(978-1-250-02784-9(5)*, 900104992) Square Fish.

—The Raft. 2013. (ENG.). 256p. (YA). (gr. 7-12). pap. 11.99 *(978-1-250-02739-9(X)*, 900098311) Square Fish.

Boorman, Kate A. Darkthaw: A Winterkill Novel. 2015. (Winterkill Ser.). (ENG.). 336p. (YA). (gr. 7-17). 17.95 *(978-1-4197-1663-8(8)*, 1106301, Amulet Bks.) Abrams, Inc.

—Heartfire: A Winterkill Novel. 2016. (Winterkill Ser.: 3). (ENG.). 336p. (YA). (gr. 7-17). 17.95 *(978-1-4197-2124-3(0)*, 1106401, Amulet Bks.) Abrams, Inc.

Borgenicht, David & Khan, Hena. Amazon: You Decide How to Survive! 2015. (Worst-Case Scenario Ultimate Adventure Ser.). (ENG., Illus.). 204p. (J). (gr. 3-8). 47.10 *(978-1-59920-980-7(2)*, 19400, Smart Apple Media) Black Rabbit Bks.

Borgenicht, David & Lurie, Alexander. Deadly Seas: You Decide How to Survive! 2015. (WorstCase Scenario Ultimate Adventure Ser.). (ENG., Illus.). 204p. (gr. 3-8). 47.10 *(978-1-59920-981-4(0))* Black Rabbit Bks.

Bowen, Carl. Bone Yard. Lee, Marc, illus. 2016. (Firestormers Ser.). (ENG.). 112p. (J). (gr. 4-8). lib. bdg. 27.32 *(978-1-4965-3306-7(2)*, 132447, Stone Arch Bks.) Capstone.

Bradford, Chris. Bodyguard: Survival (Book 6), Bk. 6. 2017. (Bodyguard Ser.: 6). (ENG.). 272p. (J). (gr. 5). pap. 8.99 *(978-1-5247-3707-8(0)*, Philomel Bks.) Penguin Young Readers Group.

Bradman, Tony. Alien. 2012. (Stoke Books Titles Ser.). 64p. (J). (gr. 5-8). pap. 45.32 *(978-0-7613-9214-9(9))* Stoke Bks.

Brallier, Max. The Last Kids on Earth. Holgate, Douglas, illus. 2015. (Last Kids on Earth Ser.: 1). (ENG.). 256p. (J). (gr. 3-7). 13.99 *(978-0-670-01661-7(6)*, Viking Books for Young Readers) Penguin Young Readers Group.

—The Last Kids on Earth & the Cosmic Beyond. Holgate, Douglas, illus. 2017. 257p. (J). pap. *(978-0-425-28872-6(2)*, Viking Books for Young Readers) Penguin Young Readers Group.

—The Last Kids on Earth & the Cosmic Beyond. 2015. *(978-1-338-03913-9(X))* Scholastic, Inc.

—The Last Kids on Earth & the Nightmare King. Holgate, Douglas, illus. 2017. (Last Kids on Earth Ser.: 3). (ENG.). 272p. (J). (gr. 3-7). 13.99 *(978-0-425-28871-9(4)*, Viking Books for Young Readers) Penguin Young Readers Group.

—The Last Kids on Earth & the Zombie Parade. Holgate, Douglas, illus. 2016. (Last Kids on Earth Ser.: 2). (ENG.). 320p. (J). (gr. 3-7). 13.99 *(978-0-670-01662-4(4)*, Viking Books for Young Readers) Penguin Young Readers Group.

—The Last Kids on Earth: the Monster Box (books 1-3), 3 vols., Set. Holgate, Douglas, illus. 2018. (Last Kids on Earth Ser.). (ENG.). 816p. (J). (gr. 3-7). 41.97 *(978-0-451-48108-5(9)*, Viking Books for Young Readers) Penguin Young Readers Group.

Brallier, Max & Holgate, Douglas. The Last Kids on Earth & the Cosmic Beyond. 2018. (Last Kids on Earth Ser.: 4). (ENG., Illus.). 288p. (J). (gr. 3-7). 13.99 *(978-0-425-29208-2(8)*, Viking Books for Young Readers) Penguin Young Readers Group.

Braun, Melinda. Avalanche. 2016. (ENG., Illus.). 272p. (YA). (gr. 9). 17.99 *(978-1-4814-3822-3(0)*, Simon Pulse) Simon Pulse.

—Stranded. 2015. (ENG., Illus.). 272p. (YA). (gr. 9). 17.99 *(978-1-4814-3819-3(0)*, Simon Pulse) Simon Pulse.

Bray, Libba. Beauty Queens. 2012. (ENG.). 400p. (YA). (gr. 8). pap. 10.99 *(978-0-439-89598-9(7)*, Scholastic Paperbacks) Scholastic, Inc.

Brown, Frank. Among the Pandemoniumous Mismaides: A Fantasy. 2008. 148p. 22.95 *(978-0-595-71458-2(7))* iUniverse, Inc.

Brown, Peter. The Wild Robot. (Wild Robot Ser.: 1). (ENG., Illus.). (J). (gr. 3-7). 2020. 320p. pap. 8.99 *(978-0-316-38200-7(0))* 2016. 288p. 17.99 *(978-0-316-38199-4(3))* Little, Brown Bks. for Young Readers.

—The Wild Robot. 2019. (J). lib. bdg. 18.40 *(978-0-606-40625-7(8))* Turtleback.

—The Wild Robot, 1. 2020. (Wild Robot Ser.). (ENG.). 304p. (gr. 3-6). 24.94 *(978-1-5364-3507-8(4))* Little, Brown Bks. for Young Readers.

—The Wild Robot Escapes. (Wild Robot Ser.: 2). (ENG.). 288p. (J). (gr. 3-7). 2020. pap. 8.99 *(978-0-316-47926-4(8))* 2018. (Illus.). 17.99 *(978-0-316-38204-5(3))* Little, Brown Bks. for Young Readers.

—The Wild Robot Escapes, 2. 2020. (Wild Robot Ser.). (ENG.). 288p. (gr. 3-6). 24.94 *(978-1-5364-6223-4(3))* Little, Brown Bks. for Young Readers.

Brown, Peter, illus. The Wild Robot Escapes. 2018. 279p. (J). *(978-0-316-45375-2(7))* Little Brown & Co.

Bruchac, Joseph. Arrow of Lightning, 1 vol. 2017. (Killer of Enemies Ser.: 3). (ENG.). 400p. (YA). (gr. 7-12). 19.95 *(978-1-62014-330-8(5)*, leelowtu, Tu Bks.) Lee & Low Bks., Inc.

—Killer of Enemies, 1 vol. 2013. (Killer of Enemies Ser.: 1). (ENG.). 400p. (YA). (gr. 6-12). pap. 12.95 *(978-1-62014-276-9(7)*, leelowtu); 19.95 *(978-1-62014-143-4(4)*, 1620141434) Lee & Low Bks., Inc. (Tu Bks.).

—The Long Run. 2016. (PathFinders Ser.). (ENG.). 116p. (YA). (gr. 8-12). pap. 9.95 *(978-1-939053-09-1(9)*, 7th Generation) BPC.

—Trail of the Dead, 1 vol. 2015. (Killer of Enemies Ser.: 2). (ENG.). 400p. (YA). (gr. 7-12). 19.95 *(978-1-62014-261-5(9)*, leelowtu) Lee & Low Bks., Inc.

Brunson, Emma. Survivor Spirit Book: Megan's Ark. 2010. 204p. pap. 13.50 *(978-1-60911-834-1(0)*, Eloquent Bks.) Strategic Book Publishing & Rights Agency (SBPRA).

Buckley, Michael. Undertow. (Undertow Trilogy Ser.). (ENG.). (YA). (gr. 7). 2016. 400p. pap. 10.99 *(978-0-544-81319-9(7)*, 1641921) 2015. 384p. 18.99 *(978-0-544-34825-7(7)*, 1585834) HarperCollins Pubs. (Clarion Bks.).

Burgess, Thornton W. Whitefoot the Woodmouse. 2011. 118p. 23.95 *(978-1-4638-9567-9(4))* Rodgers, Alan Bks.

Burt, Jake. Cleo Porter & the Body Electric. 2020. (ENG., Illus.). 288p. (J). 16.99 *(978-1-250-23655-5(X)*, 900210567) Feiwel & Friends.

—Cleo Porter & the Body Electric. 2022. (ENG., Illus.). 288p. (J). pap. 7.99 *(978-1-250-80272-9(5)*, 900210568) Square Fish.

Byler, Linda. The Homestead: The Dakota Series, Book 1. 2017. (Dakota Ser.: 1). (ENG.). 368p. pap. 14.99 *(978-1-68099-213-7(9)*, Good Bks.) Skyhorse Publishing Co., Inc.

Caine, Rachel, pseud & Aguirre, Ann. Honor Bound. (Honors Ser.: 2). (ENG.). (YA). (gr. 8). 2020. 496p. pap. 12.99 *(978-0-06-257103-8(6))* 2019. (Illus.). 480p. 17.99 *(978-0-06-257102-1(8))* HarperCollins Pubs. (Tegen, Katherine Bks).

Calkhoven, Laurie. G. I. Dogs: Judy, Prisoner of War (G. I. Dogs #1) 2018. (ENG., Illus.). 128p. (J). (gr. 2-5). pap. 5.99 *(978-1-338-18523-2(3))* Scholastic, Inc.

Capetta, Amy Rose. Unmade. 2016. (ENG.). 384p. (YA). (gr. 9). pap. 9.99 *(978-0-544-54258-7(4)*, 1608916, Clarion Bks.) HarperCollins Pubs.

Carey, Anna. Eve. (Eve Ser.: 1). (ENG.). (YA). (gr. 8). 2012. 352p. pap. 9.99 *(978-0-06-204851-6(1))* 2011. 336p. 17.99 *(978-0-06-204850-9(3))* HarperCollins Pubs. (HarperCollins).

—Eve. 2012. (SPA.). 224p. (YA). pap. 20.95 *(978-84-9918-434-0(0))* Roca Editorial ESP. Dist: Spanish Pubs., LLC.

Casanova, Mary. When Eagles Fall. 2014. (Fesler-Lampert Minnesota Heritage Ser.). (ENG.). 160p. pap. 9.95 *(978-0-8166-9211-8(4))* Univ. of Minnesota Pr.

Cawthon, Scott & Breed-Wrisley, Kira. Five Nights at Freddy's Collection: an AFK Series, 1 vol. 2018. (Five Nights at Freddy's Ser.). (ENG.). 2112p. (YA). (gr. 7-7). pap., pap., pap. 29.97 *(978-1-338-32302-3(4))* Scholastic, Inc.

—The Fourth Closet. 2018. 304p. *(978-1-74299-848-0(8))* Scholastic, Inc.

—The Fourth Closet: Five Nights at Freddy's (Original Trilogy Book 3) 3rd ed. 2018. (Five Nights at Freddy's Ser.: 3). (ENG.). 352p. (YA). (gr. 7-7). pap. 9.99 *(978-1-338-13932-7(0))* Scholastic, Inc.

—The Silver Eyes. 2016. 389p. (J). *(978-1-338-14418-5(9))*; *(978-1-5182-3111-7(X))* Scholastic, Inc.

—The Silver Eyes. 2016. (Five Nights at Freddy's Ser.: bk.1). (YA). lib. bdg. 20.85 *(978-0-606-39982-1(8))* Turtleback.

—The Silver Eyes: Five Nights at Freddy's (Original Trilogy Book 1), Vol. 1. 2016. (Five Nights at Freddy's Ser.: 1). (ENG.). 400p. (YA). (gr. 7-7). pap. 9.99 *(978-1-338-13437-7(X))* Scholastic, Inc.

—The Twisted Ones. 2017. (Five Nights at Freddy's Ser.: 2). lib. bdg. 20.85 *(978-0-606-40155-5(5))* Turtleback.

—The Twisted Ones: Five Nights at Freddy's (Original Trilogy Book 2), Vol. 2. Aguirre, Claudia, illus. 2017. (Five Nights at Freddy's Ser.: 2). (ENG.). 304p. (J). (gr. 7-7). pap. 9.99 *(978-1-338-13930-3(4))* Scholastic, Inc.

Chabert, Jack. Poptropica: Book 1: Mystery of the Map, Bk. 1. 2016. (Poptropica Ser.). (ENG., Illus.). 112p. (J). (gr. 1-4). 9.95 *(978-1-4197-2067-3(8)*, 1140201, Amulet Bks.) Abrams, Inc.

Chabot, Jason. Above: Broken Sky Chronicles, Book 2. 2017. (Broken Sky Chronicles Ser.: 2). (ENG.). 384p. (YA). pap. 19.95 *(978-1-68162-604-8(7))* Turner Publishing Co.

—Below: Broken Sky Chronicles, Book 1. 2016. (Broken Sky Chronicles Ser.: 1). (ENG.). 308p. (YA). 29.95 *(978-1-68162-602-4(0))*; pap. 16.95 *(978-1-68162-601-7(2)*, Turner Publishing Co.

—Beyond: Broken Sky Chronicles, Book 3. 2017. (Broken Sky Chronicles Ser.: 3). (ENG.). 432p. (YA). 35.99 *(978-1-68162-608-6(X))*; pap. 19.99 *(978-1-68162-607-9(1))* Turner Publishing Co.

Chandler, Kristen. Wolves, Boys & Other Things That Might Kill Me. 2011. (ENG.). 283p. (YA). (gr. 7-12). 24.94 *(978-0-670-01142-1(8))* Penguin Young Readers Group.

Chapman, Elsie. Divided (Dualed Sequel) 2015. (Dualed Ser.: 2). (ENG.). 336p. (YA). (gr. 7). pap. 9.99 *(978-0-449-81298-3(7)*, Ember) Random Hse. Children's Bks.

Charbonneau, Joelle. Graduation Day. 2015. (Testing Ser.: 3). (ENG.). 304p. (YA). (gr. 7). pap. 15.99 *(978-0-544-54120-7(0)*, 1608879, Clarion Bks.) HarperCollins Pubs.

—Independent Study. 2015. (Testing Ser.: 2). lib. bdg. 20.85 *(978-0-606-36832-2(9))* Turtleback.

—Independent Study: The Testing, Book 2. (Testing Ser.: 2). (ENG.). (YA). (gr. 7). 2015. 336p. pap. 15.99 *(978-0-544-43945-0(7)*, 1596844) 2014. 320p. 17.99 *(978-0-547-95920-7(6)*, 1520240) HarperCollins Pubs. (Clarion Bks.).

Charman, Katrina. Survival Tails: Endurance in Antarctica. 2018. (Survival Tails Ser.: 2). (ENG.). 272p. (J). (gr. 3-7). 16.99 *(978-0-316-47789-5(3))* Little, Brown Bks. for Young Readers.

—The Survival Tails: the Titanic. 2018. (Survival Tails Ser.: 1). (ENG., Illus.). 224p. (J). (gr. 3-7). pap. 7.99 *(978-0-316-47783-3(4))* Little, Brown Bks. for Young Readers.

—Titanic. 2018. (Survival Tails Ser.: 1). (J). lib. bdg. 18.40 *(978-0-606-40981-0(5))* Turtleback.

Choyce, Lesley. Breaking Point, 1 vol. 2012. (Orca Soundings Ser.). (ENG.). 128p. (YA). (gr. 8-12). pap. 9.95 *(978-1-4598-0128-8(8))* Orca Bk. Pubs. USA.

Christopher, John. Empty World. 2015. (ENG., Illus.). 256p. (J). (gr. 5-9). pap. 8.99 *(978-1-4814-2000-6(3)*, Aladdin) Simon & Schuster Children's Publishing.

Clark, Samantha M. The Boy, the Boat, & the Beast. (ENG.). 256p. (J). (gr. 3-7). 2019. pap. 8.99 *(978-1-5344-1256-9(5))* 2018. (Illus.). 17.99 *(978-1-5344-1255-2(7))* Simon & Schuster/Paula Wiseman Bks. (Simon & Schuster/Paula Wiseman Bks.).

Cole, Gwen. Ride On. 2018. (ENG.). 280p. (YA). (gr. 6-12). 16.99 *(978-1-5107-2993-3(3)*, Sky Pony Pr.) Skyhorse Publishing Co., Inc.

Collins, Suzanne. The Ballad of Songbirds & Snakes (a Hunger Games Novel) (Unabridged Edition), 2 vols. unabr. ed. 2020. Orig. Title: Untitled Panem Novel (Audio): a Hunger Games Novel. (ENG.). (YA). (gr. 7-7). audio compact disk 44.99 *(978-1-338-63519-5(0))* Scholastic, Inc.

—Catching Fire. 2009. (Hunger Games Trilogy: Bk. 2). (YA). 74.99 *(978-1-61574-572-2(6))* Findaway World, LLC.
—Catching Fire. 2009. 12.04 *(978-0-7848-3842-6(9),* Everbind) Marco Bk. Co.
—Catching Fire. 2011. (ENG.). 448p. pap. *(978-1-4071-3209-9(1))* Scholastic.
—Catching Fire. l.t. ed. (Hunger Games Trilogy: 2). (ENG.). (YA). 2012. 498p. (gr. 7-12). pap. 14.99 *(978-1-59413-585-9(1),* Large Print Pr.) 2009. 499p. 23.95 *(978-1-4104-2044-2(2))* Thorndike Pr.
—Catching Fire. 2013. (Hunger Games Trilogy Ser.: 2). lib. bdg. 24.50 *(978-0-606-32025-2(3))* Turtleback.
—Catching Fire. 2011. (Hunger Games Trilogy: Bk. 2). (CHI.). 344p. (YA). (gr. 7-12). pap. *(978-7-5063-5566-7(3))* Writers' Publishing Hse.
—Catching Fire (Hunger Games, Book Two), 1 vol. (Hunger Games Ser.: 2). (ENG.). 400p. (gr. 7). 2013. (YA). pap. 14.99 *(978-0-545-58617-7(8))* 2009. (J). pap. 22.99 *(978-0-439-02349-8(1))* Scholastic, Inc. (Scholastic Pr.).
—En llamas (los Juegos del Hambre 2), Bk. 2. 2010. (Hunger Games Trilogy: Bk. 2). (SPA.). 416p. (J). (gr. 8-12). pap. 19.99 *(978-84-272-0000-5(5))* Lectorum Pubns., Inc.
—En llamas (los Juegos del Hambre 2) 2012. (Hunger Games Trilogy: Bk. 2). (SPA.). 416p. (gr. 8-12). pap. 21.99 *(978-84-272-0213-9(X))* Molino, Editorial ESP. Dist: Lectorum Pubns., Inc.
—The Hunger Games. 2009. (Hunger Games Trilogy: Bk. 1). 10.85 *(978-0-7848-3801-3(1),* Everbind) Marco Bk. Co.
—The Hunger Games. 2010. (Hunger Games Trilogy: Bk. 1). (ENG.). 374p. (gr. 7-12). 21.00 *(978-1-60686-581-1(1))* Perfection Learning Corp.
—The Hunger Games. Fournier, Guillaume, tr. 2011. (Hunger Games Trilogy: Bk. 1). (FRE.). 398p. (YA). (gr. 7-12). pap. *(978-2-266-18269-0(2))* Presses Pocket.
—The Hunger Games. 2011. (Hunger Games Trilogy: 1). (YA). 69.75 *(978-1-4561-3196-8(6))* Recorded Bks., Inc.
—The Hunger Games. 2009. (Hunger Games Trilogy: Bk. 1). (ENG., Illus.). 448p. pap. *(978-1-4071-0908-4(1),* Scholastic) Scholastic, Inc.
—The Hunger Games. l.t. ed. (Hunger Games Trilogy: Bk. 1). (ENG.). (YA). 2012. 484p. (gr. 7-12). pap. 14.99 *(978-1-59413-587-3(8),* Large Print Pr.) 2009. 485p. 23.95 *(978-1-4104-1986-6(X))* Thorndike Pr.
—The Hunger Games. 2010. (Hunger Games Trilogy Ser.: 1). (SWE.). lib. bdg. 22.10 *(978-1-4178-3173-9(1))* Turtleback.
—The Hunger Games. 2010. (Hunger Games Trilogy: Bk. 1). (CHI.). 324p. (YA). (gr. 7-12). pap. *(978-7-5063-5153-9(6))* Writers' Publishing Hse.
—The Hunger Games (Hunger Games, Book One), 1 vol. (Hunger Games Ser.: 1). (ENG.). 384p. (J). (gr. 7-18). 2010. pap. 14.99 *(978-0-439-02352-8(1))* 2008. 22.99 *(978-0-439-02348-1(3))* Scholastic, Inc. (Scholastic Pr.).
—The Hunger Games (Hunger Games, Book One) (Unabridged Edition), 9 vols., Vol. 1. unabr. ed. 2018. (Hunger Games Ser.: 1). (ENG.). 2p. (YA). (gr. 7). audio compact disk 44.99 *(978-1-338-33492-0(1))* Scholastic, Inc.
—Hunger Games Trilogy Boxed Set: Paperback Classic Collection. 2014. (Hunger Games Ser.). (ENG.). (J). (gr. 7-7). 36.97 *(978-0-545-67031-9(4),* Scholastic Pr.) Scholastic, Inc.
—The Hunger Games Trilogy Boxed Set Set. 2010. (Hunger Games Ser.: 1). (ENG.). (J). (gr. 7-7). 53.97 *(978-0-545-26535-5(5),* Scholastic Pr.) Scholastic, Inc.
—Los Juegos del Hambre. 2012. (Hunger Games Trilogy Spanish Ser.: 1).Tr. of Hunger Games. (SPA.). lib. bdg. 33.05 *(978-0-606-26447-1(7))* Turtleback.
—Los Juegos del Hambre (los Juegos del Hambre 1) 2012. (Hunger Games Trilogy: Bk. 1). (SPA.). 400p. (gr. 8-12). pap. 21.99 *(978-84-272-0212-2(1))* Molino, Editorial ESP. Dist: Lectorum Pubns., Inc.
—Mockingjay. 2011. (Hunger Games Trilogy: Bk. 3). (CHI.). 435p. (YA). (gr. 7-12). pap. *(978-986-213-216-6(7))* Locus Publishing Co.
—Mockingjay. (Hunger Games Trilogy: 3). (YA). 2011. 77.75 *(978-1-4561-3203-3(2))* 2010. 75.75 *(978-1-4561-3205-7(9))* 2010. 1.25 *(978-1-4640-2636-2(X))* Recorded Bks., Inc.
—Mockingjay. 2011. (Hunger Games Ser.: Vol. 3). (ENG.). 448p. (YA). (gr. 8-12). pap. *(978-1-4071-3210-5(5))* Scholastic Canada, Ltd.
—Mockingjay. 2010. pap. *(978-0-439-02354-2(8),* Scholastic Pr.) Scholastic, Inc.
—Mockingjay. l.t. ed. (Hunger Games Trilogy: Bk. 3). (ENG.). (YA). 2012. 502p. (gr. 7-12). pap. 14.99 *(978-1-59413-586-6(X),* Large Print Pr.) 2010. 503p. 23.99 *(978-1-4104-2841-7(9))* Thorndike Pr.
—Mockingjay. 2014. (Hunger Games Trilogy Ser.: 3). lib. bdg. 24.50 *(978-0-606-36328-0(9))*; lib. bdg. 24.50 *(978-0-606-35133-1(7))* Turtleback.
—Mockingjay (Hunger Games, Book Three), 1 vol. (Hunger Games Ser.: 3). (ENG.). 400p. (J). (gr. 7). 2014. pap. 14.99 *(978-0-545-66326-7(1))* 2010. 19.99 *(978-0-439-02351-1(3))* Scholastic, Inc. (Scholastic Pr.).
—Sinsajo. 2012. (Hunger Games Trilogy Spanish Ser.: 3).Tr. of Mockingjay. (SPA.). lib. bdg. 33.05 *(978-0-606-26449-5(3))* Turtleback.
—Sinsajo (los Juegos del Hambre 3) (Hunger Games Trilogy: Bk. 3). (SPA.). 424p. (gr. 8-12). 2012. pap. 21.99 *(978-84-272-0214-6(8))* 2010. (J). pap. 19.99 *(978-84-272-0038-8(2))* Molino, Editorial ESP. Dist: Lectorum Pubns., Inc.
Condon, Bill. How to Survive in the Jungle by the Person Who Knows, 1 vol. rev. ed. 2013. (Literary Text Ser.). (ENG., Illus.). 28p. (J). (gr. 2-3). pap. 10.99 *(978-1-4333-5599-8(X))*; lib. bdg. 19.96 *(978-1-4807-1721-3(5))* Teacher Created Materials, Inc.
Connell, Richard Edward. The Most Dangerous Game. 2010. (Creative Short Stories Ser.). (Illus.). 48p. (J). (gr. 5-18). 19.95 *(978-1-58341-920-5(9),* Creative Education) Creative Co., The.
Connelly, Neil. Into the Hurricane. 2017. (ENG.). 240p. (YA). (gr. 9). 17.99 *(978-0-545-85381-1(8),* Levine, Arthur A. Bks.) Scholastic, Inc.
Cook, Trish. Outward Blonde. 2016. (ENG.). 279p. (YA). pap. 9.99 *(978-1-945293-04-7(7))* Adaptive Studios.
Cooper, Sari. The Horse of the River: A Camp Canyon Falls Adventure. 2019. (ENG., Illus.). 176p. (J). pap. *(978-1-55017-877-7(6),* 18796128-afbf-4804-b0b6-15dc52dd3f3d) Harbour Publishing Co., Ltd.
Cooper, Susan. Ghost Hawk. 2013. (ENG.). 336p. (J). (gr. 5-9). 16.99 *(978-1-4424-8141-1(2),* McElderry, Margaret K. Bks.) McElderry, Margaret K. Bks.
Courage, Nick. Storm Blown. 2019. (ENG.). 352p. (J). (gr. 4-7). 16.99 *(978-0-525-64596-2(9),* Delacorte Bks. for Young Readers) Random Hse. Children's Bks.
Crawford, Brian. The Evil Wind. 2017. (Survive Ser.). (ENG.). 192p. (YA). (gr. 5-12). lib. bdg. 31.42 *(978-1-68076-732-2(1),* 25398, Epic Escape) EPIC Pr.
Cremer, Andrea. The Inventor's Secret. 2015. (Inventor's Secret Ser.: 1). (ENG.). 416p. (YA). (gr. 7). pap. 10.99 *(978-0-14-751438-7(X),* Speak) Penguin Young Readers Group.
Crewe, Megan. The Lives We Lost. 2018. (Fallen World Ser.: Vol. 2). (ENG., Illus.). 292p. (YA). (gr. 7-12). pap. 11.99 *(978-0-9952169-8-3(3))* Another World Pr.
—The Way We Fall. 2018. (Fallen World Ser.: Vol. 1). (ENG., Illus.). 336p. (YA). (gr. 7-12). pap. 11.99 *(978-0-9952169-4-5(0))* Another World Pr.
—The Way We Fall. 1. 2013. (Fallen World Trilogy Ser.). (ENG.). 336p. (YA). (gr. 8-12). 24.94 *(978-1-4231-4631-5(X))* Hyperion Bks. for Children.
—The Worlds We Make. 2018. (Fallen World Ser.: Vol. 3). (ENG., Illus.). 298p. (YA). (gr. 7-12). pap. 11.99 *(978-0-9952169-9-0(1))* Another World Pr.
Crockett, S. D. After the Snow. 2013. (After the Snow Ser.: 1). (ENG.). 320p. (YA). (gr. 7-12). pap. 13.99 *(978-1-250-01676-8(2),* 900087090) Square Fish.
Crossan, Sarah. Breathe. (Breathe Ser.: 1). (ENG.). (YA). (gr. 9). 2013. 400p. pap. 11.99 *(978-0-06-211870-6(6))* 2012. 384p. 17.99 *(978-0-06-211869-1(2))* HarperCollins Pubs. (Greenwillow Bks.).
Crowder, Melanie. Parched. 2014. (ENG.). 160p. (J). (gr. 5-7). pap. 7.99 *(978-0-544-33631-5(3),* 1584177, Clarion Bks.) HarperCollins Pubs.
Cummings, Lindsay. The Murder Complex #2: the Death Code. 2016. (Murder Complex Ser.: 2). (ENG.). 512p. (YA). (gr. 9). pap. 9.99 *(978-0-06-222004-2(7),* Greenwillow Bks.) HarperCollins Pubs.
Curtis, Robert. Blackberries. 2013. 130p. pap. *(978-1-74335-111-6(9))* D Publishing.
Curtis, Simon. Boy Robot. 2016. (ENG., Illus.). 432p. (YA). (gr. 9). 17.99 *(978-1-4814-5929-7(5),* Simon Pulse) Simon Pulse.
Cushman, Karen. Rodzina. 2020.Tr. of Rodzina. (ENG.). 240p. (J). (gr. 3-7). pap. 7.99 *(978-0-358-09751-8(7),* 1747610, Clarion Bks.) HarperCollins Pubs.
Dafoe, Daniel. Aventuras de Robinson Crusoe. 2003. (Advanced Reading Ser.: Vol. 73).Tr. of Adventures of Robinson Crusoe. (SPA., Illus.). 118p. (J). (gr. 4-7). *(978-84-239-9043-6(5))* Espasa Calpe, S.A.
—Robinson Crusoe. 2012. 338p. pap. 10.99 *(978-1-61382-256-2(1))* Simon & Brown.
—Robinson Crusoe: With a Discussion of Resourcefulness. Landgraf, Kenneth, illus. 2003. (Values in Action Illustrated Classics Ser.). 190p. (J). *(978-1-59203-035-4(1))* Learning Challenge, Inc.
Dafoe, Daniel, et al. Robinson Crusoe. (Classics Illustrated Ser.). (Illus.). 52p. (YA). pap. 4.95 *(978-1-57209-021-7(9))* Classics International Entertainment, Inc.
Dahlstrom, S. J. Black Rock Brothers. 2018. (Adventures of Wilder Good Ser.: 5). (ENG., Illus.). 210p. (J). (gr. 3-6). pap. 9.95 *(978-1-58988-127-3(3))* Dry, Paul Bks., Inc.
Dando-Collins, Stephen. Caesar the War Dog: Operation Black Shark. 2016. (Caesar the War Dog Ser.: 5). 304p. (J). (gr. 4-6). pap. 11.99 *(978-0-85798-863-8(8))* Random Hse. Australia AUS. Dist: Independent Pubs. Group.
Darke, J. A. & Terrell, Brandon. Sasquatch Island. Evans, Neil, illus. 2018. (Spine Shivers Ser.). (ENG.). 128p. (J). (gr. 4-6). lib. bdg. 26.65 *(978-1-4965-6432-0(4),* 138272, Stone Arch Bks.) Capstone.
Dashner, James. The Death Cure. 2013. (Maze Runner Ser.: 3). lib. bdg. 20.85 *(978-0-606-27005-2(1))* Turtleback.
—The Death Cure (Maze Runner, Book Three) (Maze Runner Ser.: 3). (ENG.). (YA). (gr. 7). 2013. 368p. pap. 10.99 *(978-0-385-73878-1(1))* 2011. 352p. 19.99 *(978-0-385-73877-4(3))* Random Hse. Children's Bks. (Delacorte Pr.).
—The Fever Code. 2018. (Maze Runner Ser.: 0.5). lib. bdg. 22.10 *(978-0-606-40948-3(3))* Turtleback.
—The Fever Code (Maze Runner, Book Five; Prequel) 2016. (Maze Runner Ser.: 5). (ENG.). 384p. (YA). (gr. 7). 18.99 *(978-0-553-51309-7(5),* Delacorte Pr.) Random Hse. Children's Bks.
—The Kill Order. 2014. (Maze Runner Ser.: 0). lib. bdg. 20.85 *(978-0-606-35572-8(3))* Turtleback.
—The Kill Order (Maze Runner, Book Four; Origin) Book Four; Origin. 2014. (Maze Runner Ser.: 4). (ENG.). 384p. (YA). (gr. 7). pap. 10.99 *(978-0-385-74289-4(4),* Delacorte Pr.) Random Hse. Children's Bks.
—The Maze Runner: Virus Letal. 2013. 362p. (YA). pap. 15.99 *(978-987-612-565-9(6))* V&R Editoras.
—The Scorch Trials. 2011. (Maze Runner Ser.: 2). lib. bdg. 20.85 *(978-0-606-23430-6(6))* Turtleback.
—The Scorch Trials (Maze Runner, Book Two) (Maze Runner Ser.: 2). (ENG.). (YA). (gr. 7). 2011. 400p. pap. 10.99 *(978-0-385-73876-7(5))* 2010. 384p. 19.99 *(978-0-385-73875-0(7))* Random Hse. Children's Bks. (Delacorte Pr.).
Davenport, Roger. Wanderer. (ENG.). 2016. 268p. (J). (gr. 6-6). pap. 8.99 *(978-1-5107-0389-6(6))* 2013. 288p. (YA). (gr. 8-12). 16.95 *(978-1-62087-541-4(1),* 620541) Skyhorse Publishing Co., Inc. (Sky Pony Pr.).
Davies, Stephen. Outlaw. 2011. (ENG.). 304p. (YA). (gr. 7). 16.99 *(978-0-547-39017-8(3))* Houghton Mifflin Harcourt Publishing Co.
Dawson, Delilah S. Strike. 2016. (ENG., Illus.). 480p. (YA). (gr. 9). 17.99 *(978-1-4814-2342-7(8),* Simon Pulse) Simon Pulse.
de la Peña, Matt. The Living. 2015. (Living Ser.). (ENG.). 336p. (YA). (gr. 9). pap. 10.99 *(978-0-385-74121-7(9),* Ember) Random Hse. Children's Bks.
Deborah, Ellis. The Breadwinner. 2014. (ENG.). 176p. (J). 13.20 *(978-1-63245-145-3(X))* Lectorum Pubns., Inc.
Defoe, Daniel. Classic Starts(r): Robinson Crusoe: Retold from the Daniel Defoe Original. Akib, Jamel, illus. 2006. (Classic Starts(r) Ser.). 160p. (J). (gr. 2-4). 6.95 *(978-1-4027-2664-4(3))* Sterling Publishing Co., Inc.
—Robinson Crusoe Level 4 Intermediate Book with CD-ROM & Audio CD, 1 vol. 2009. (ENG.). 96p. pap. 13.00 incl. cd-rom, audio compact disk *(978-84-8323-550-8(1))* Cambridge Univ. Pr.
DefoeDaniel. Robinson Crusoe: Paperback Student Book Without Answers. 2009. (Cambridge Experience Readers Ser.). (ENG.). 96p. pap. 14.75 *(978-84-8323-553-9(6))* Cambridge Univ. Pr.
DeStefano, Lauren. Sever. 2013. (Chemical Garden Trilogy Ser.: 3). (ENG.). 400p. (YA). (gr. 9). pap. 9.99 *(978-1-4424-0910-1(X))* Simon & Schuster.
—Sever. 2013. (Chemical Garden Trilogy Ser.: 3). (ENG.). 384p. (YA). (gr. 9). 17.99 *(978-1-4424-0909-5(6),* Simon & Schuster Bks. For Young Readers) Simon & Schuster Bks. For Young Readers.
Dixon, John. Phoenix Island. 2014. (ENG.). 320p. pap. 17.99 *(978-1-4767-3865-9(3),* Gallery Bks.) Gallery Bks.
Doeden, Matt. Can You Survive a Global Blackout? An Interactive Doomsday Adventure. Nathan, James, illus. 2015. (You Choose: Doomsday Ser.). (ENG.). 112p. (J). (gr. 3-7). lib. bdg. 32.65 *(978-1-4914-5850-1(X),* 128813, Capstone Pr.) Capstone.
—Can You Survive an Artificial Intelligence Uprising? An Interactive Doomsday Adventure. Fisher-Johnson, Paul, illus. 2016. (You Choose: Doomsday Ser.). (ENG.). 112p. (J). (gr. 3-7). lib. bdg. 32.65 *(978-1-4914-8107-3(2),* 130598, Capstone Pr.) Capstone.
—Can You Survive an Asteroid Strike? An Interactive Doomsday Adventure. Davidson, Paul, illus. 2016. (You Choose: Doomsday Ser.). (ENG.). 112p. (J). (gr. 3-7). lib. bdg. 32.65 *(978-1-4914-8109-7(9),* 130600, Capstone Pr.) Capstone.
Doyle, Bill & Borgenicht, David. Everest: You Decide How to Survive! 2015. (Worst-Case Scenario Ultimate Adventure Ser.). (ENG., Illus.). 204p. (J). (gr. 3-8). 47.10 *(978-1-59920-978-4(0),* 19401, Smart Apple Media) Black Rabbit Bks.
Dragon, Laura. Hurricane Boy, 1 vol. 2014. (ENG., Illus.). 160p. (J). (gr. 3-7). pap. 14.95 *(978-1-4556-1916-0(7),* Pelican Publishing) Arcadia Publishing.
Drake, Raelyn. Off Road. 2019. (To the Limit Ser.). (ENG.). 96p. (YA). (gr. 6-12). 26.65 *(978-1-5415-4035-4(2),* 5ffab555-1567-4bbb-bce2-8c0095679256, Darby Creek) Lerner Publishing Group.
—On Edge. 2019. (To the Limit Ser.). (ENG.). 104p. (YA). (gr. 6-12). 26.65 *(978-1-5415-4038-5(7),* f4eab6d3-de77-4267-8203-8d9d4bd9d376, Darby Creek) Lerner Publishing Group.
Duey, Kathleen & Bale, Karen A. Earthquake: San Francisco 1906. 2014. (Survivors Ser.). (ENG., Illus.). 160p. (J). (gr. 3-7). pap. 7.99 *(978-1-4814-0079-4(7),* Aladdin) Simon & Schuster Children's Publishing.
—Fire: Chicago 1871. 2014. (Survivors Ser.). (ENG., Illus.). 176p. (J). (gr. 3-7). pap. 7.99 *(978-1-4424-9054-3(3),* Aladdin) Simon & Schuster Children's Publishing.
—Fire: Chicago 1871. 2014. (Survivors Ser.). (ENG., Illus.). 176p. (J). (gr. 3-7). 16.99 *(978-1-4424-9055-0(1),* Simon & Schuster/Paula Wiseman Bks.) Simon & Schuster/Paula Wiseman Bks.
—Flood: Mississippi 1927. 2015. (Survivors Ser.). (ENG., Illus.). 176p. (J). (gr. 3-7). pap. 7.99 *(978-1-4814-1642-9(1),* Aladdin) Simon & Schuster Children's Publishing.
—Titanic: April 1912. 2014. (Survivors Ser.). (ENG., Illus.). 192p. (J). (gr. 3-7). 15.99 *(978-1-4424-9052-9(7),* Simon & Schuster/Paula Wiseman Bks.) Simon & Schuster/Paula Wiseman Bks.
—Train Wreck: Kansas 1892. 2016. (Survivors Ser.). (ENG., Illus.). 160p. (J). (gr. 3-7). 17.99 *(978-1-4814-6801-5(4),* Simon & Schuster/Paula Wiseman Bks.) Simon & Schuster/Paula Wiseman Bks.
Duncan, Alexandra. Blight. 2017. (ENG.). 400p. (YA). (gr. 8). 17.99 *(978-0-06-239699-0(4),* Greenwillow Bks.) HarperCollins Pubs.
Dunivan, Dennis W. Escape from Communist Heaven. 2013. (ENG., Illus.). 392p. (J). (gr. -1-12). 17.99 *(978-1-59181-229-6(1))* Sentient Pubns.
Durst, Sarah Beth. Vessel. (ENG., Illus.). 432p. (YA). (gr. 7). 2013. pap. 9.99 *(978-1-4424-2377-0(3))* 2012. 16.99 *(978-1-4424-2376-3(5))* McElderry, Margaret K. Bks. (McElderry, Margaret K. Bks.).
Duyvis, Corinne. On the Edge of Gone. 2016. (ENG.). 464p. (J). (gr. 8-17). 17.95 *(978-1-4197-1903-5(3),* 1104701, Amulet Bks.) Abrams, Inc.
Eames, Brian. The Dagger X. 2013. (Dagger Chronicles Ser.). (ENG.). 368p. (J). (gr. 3-7). 15.99 *(978-1-4424-6855-9(6),* Simon & Schuster Bks. For Young Readers) Simon & Schuster Bks. For Young Readers.
—The Dagger X. 2013. (Dagger Chronicles Ser.). (ENG., Illus.). 368p. (J). (gr. 3-7). pap. 6.99 *(978-1-4424-6856-6(4),* Simon & Schuster/Paula Wiseman Bks.) Simon & Schuster/Paula Wiseman Bks.
Ellis, Deborah. The Breadwinner. 2013. 164p. pap. *(978-1-4596-6483-8(3))* ReadHowYouWant.com, Ltd.
—The Breadwinner. 2015. (Breadwinner Ser.: 1). lib. bdg. 20.80 *(978-0-606-37232-9(6))* Turtleback.
—The Breadwinner (movie Tie-In Edition), 1 vol. 2017. (Breadwinner Ser.: 1). (ENG., Illus.). 160p. (J). (gr. 5-9). pap. 10.99 *(978-1-77306-071-2(6))* Groundwood Bks. CAN. Dist: Publishers Group West (PGW).
—Parvana's Journey, 1 vol. 2015. (Breadwinner Ser.: 2). (ENG., Illus.). 200p. (J). (gr. 5-9). pap. 10.99 *(978-1-55498-770-2(9))* Groundwood Bks. CAN. Dist: Publishers Group West (PGW).
Emerson, Kevin. The Shores Beyond Time. (Chronicle of the Dark Star Ser.: 3). (ENG.). 512p. (J). (gr. 3-7). 2020. pap. 8.99 *(978-0-06-230678-4(2))* 2019. 16.99 *(978-0-06-230677-7(4))* HarperCollins Pubs. (Walden Pond Pr.).
Ender, Wylie. Crash. 2017. (Survive Ser.). (ENG.). 192p. (YA). (gr. 5-12). lib. bdg. 31.42 *(978-1-68076-730-8(5),* 25394, Epic Escape) EPIC Pr.
Eshbaugh, Julie. Obsidian & Stars. 2018. (ENG.). 368p. (YA). (gr. 9). pap. 9.99 *(978-0-06-239929-8(2),* HarperTeen) HarperCollins Pubs.
Fane, Judy B. Paddy the Pelican Survives the Storm. Alden, Carol, illus. 2010. 48p. pap. 16.50 *(978-1-60911-448-0(5),* Eloquent Bks.) Strategic Book Publishing & Rights Agency (SBPRA).
Farrant, Natasha. A Talent for Trouble. 2019. (ENG.). 272p. (J). (gr. 5-7). 16.99 *(978-1-328-58078-8(4),* 1728482, Clarion Bks.) HarperCollins Pubs.
Finke, M. e. Taconi & Claude: Double Trouble. 2011. 102p. pap. 8.95 *(978-1-61633-130-6(5))* Guardian Angel Publishing, Inc.
Fiona Fox Staff, ed. The Swiss Family Robinson. 2012. (ENG., Illus.). 224p. (J). 15.00 *(978-1-84135-839-0(8))* Award Pubns. Ltd. GBR. Dist: Parkwest Pubns., Inc.
Fleming, Bryn. Cassie & Jasper: Kidnapped Cattle. 2016. (Range Riders Ser.). (ENG.). 147p. (J). 24.99 *(978-1-943328-66-6(8))*; pap. 10.99 *(978-1-941821-95-4(2))* West Margin Pr. (West Winds Pr.).
Fountain, Ele. Refugee 87. 2020. (ENG.). 256p. (J). (gr. 3-7). pap. 8.99 *(978-0-316-42301-4(7))* Little, Brown Bks. for Young Readers.
Frey, James. Endgame: the Complete Training Diaries: Volumes 1, 2, And 3. 2015. (Endgame: the Training Diaries: Nos. 1-3). (ENG.). 416p. (YA). (gr. 9). pap. 9.99 *(978-0-06-233276-9(7),* HarperCollins) HarperCollins Pubs.
—Endgame: the Complete Zero Line Chronicles. 2016. (Endgame: the Zero Line Chronicles Ser.). (ENG.). 288p. (YA). (gr. 9). pap. 9.99 *(978-0-06-233277-6(5),* HarperCollins) HarperCollins Pubs.
Frey, James & Johnson-Shelton, Nils. Endgame: Sky Key. 2015. (Endgame Ser.: 2). (ENG., Illus.). 512p. (YA). (gr. 9). 19.99 *(978-0-06-233261-5(9),* HarperCollins) HarperCollins Pubs.
—Endgame: the Calling. (Endgame Ser.: 1). (ENG.). (YA). (gr. 9). 2015. 496p. pap. 10.99 *(978-0-06-233259-2(7))* 2014. 480p. 19.99 *(978-0-06-233258-5(9))* HarperCollins Pubs. (HarperCollins).
Fukuda, Andrew. The Hunt. 2012. (Hunt Trilogy Ser.: 1). (ENG.). 304p. (YA). (gr. 7). pap. 12.99 *(978-1-250-00529-8(9),* 900080955, St. Martin's Griffin) St. Martin's Pr.
—The Prey. 2013. (Hunt Trilogy Ser.: 2). (ENG.). 336p. (YA). (gr. 7-12). pap. 16.99 *(978-1-250-00530-4(2),* 900080956, St. Martin's Griffin) St. Martin's Pr.
Garner, Em. Mercy Mode. 2014. (Contaminated Ser.). (ENG.). 341p. (YA). (gr. 7-12). 17.99 *(978-1-60684-356-7(7),* 2128b0bf-02fc-4d42-8da7-4a7424292054, Carolrhoda Lab™) Lerner Publishing Group.
Gary, Paulsen. Hatchet. 2014. (ENG.). 192p. (J). (gr. 3-3). 12.24 *(978-1-63245-105-7(0))* Lectorum Pubns., Inc.
Gemeinhart, Dan. Scar Island. 2017. (ENG.). 256p. (J). (gr. 3-7). 16.99 *(978-1-338-05384-5(1),* Scholastic Pr.) Scholastic, Inc.
George, Jean Craighead. Julie. Minor, Wendell, illus. 2019. (Julie of the Wolves Ser.: 2). (ENG.). 256p. (J). (gr. 3-7). pap. 9.99 *(978-0-06-288431-2(X),* HarperCollins) HarperCollins Pubs.
—Julie of the Wolves. l.t. ed. 2004. (Beeler Mystery Ser.). 32.95 *(978-1-58118-121-0(3))* LRS.
—Julie of the Wolves: A Newbery Award Winner. Schoenherr, John, illus. (Julie of the Wolves Ser.: 1). (ENG.). (J). (gr. 8-18). 2019. 224p. pap. 9.99 *(978-0-06-440058-9(1))* 2003. 208p. pap. 8.99 *(978-0-06-054095-1(8))* HarperCollins Pubs. (HarperCollins).
Gibbs, Stuart. Spy Camp. (Spy School Ser.). (ENG., Illus.). (J). (gr. 3-7). 2014. 352p. pap. 8.99 *(978-1-4424-5754-6(6))* 2013. 336p. 18.99 *(978-1-4424-5753-9(8))* Simon & Schuster Bks. For Young Readers. (Simon & Schuster Bks. For Young Readers).
Giff, Patricia Reilly. Island War. 208p. (J). (gr. 3-7). 2020. pap. 7.99 *(978-0-8234-4540-0(2))* 2018. 16.99 *(978-0-8234-3954-6(2))* Holiday Hse., Inc.
Gillespie, Hollis. We Will Be Crashing Shortly. 2015. (ENG.). 240p. (YA). 17.99 *(978-1-4405-6770-4(0),* Simon Pulse) Simon Pulse.
Gilman, David. Blood Sun. 2012. (Danger Zone Ser.: 3). (ENG.). 432p. (YA). (gr. 7). pap. 10.99 *(978-0-440-42241-9(8),* Ember) Random Hse. Children's Bks.
Gilmore, Grace. Lost in the Blizzard. Brown, Petra, illus. 2015. (Tales from Maple Ridge Ser.: 5). (ENG.). 128p. (J). (gr. k-4). pap. 6.99 *(978-1-4814-4749-2(1),* Little Simon) Little Simon.
Glasgow, Kathleen. Girl in Pieces. 2018. (ENG.). 448p. (YA). (gr. 9). pap. 10.99 *(978-1-101-93474-6(3),* Ember) Random Hse. Children's Bks.
Gleitzman, Morris. Once. 2013. (Once Ser.: 1). (ENG.). 192p. (YA). (gr. 7). pap. 10.99 *(978-0-312-65304-0(2),* 900069444) Square Fish.
—Then. 2013. (Once Ser.: 2). (ENG.). 224p. (YA). (gr. 7). pap. 11.99 *(978-1-250-00341-6(5),* 900079882) Square Fish.
Golden, Christopher & Lebbon, Tim. The Wild. Ruth, Greg, illus. 2011. (Secret Journeys of Jack London Ser.: 1). (ENG.). 368p. (YA). (gr. 5-18). 15.99 *(978-0-06-186317-2(3),* HarperTeen) HarperCollins Pubs.
Gott, Robert. Jinxed. 2007. 96p. (YA). pap. *(978-1-4207-0732-8(9))* Sundance/Newbridge Educational Publishing.
Grant, Donna. Hungrige Begierde. 2014.Tr. of The Hunger. (GER.). pap. 5.99 *(978-1-942017-15-8(4))* DL Grant, LLC.
Grant, Michael. Gone. (Gone Ser.: 1). (Illus.). 576p. 2014. (ENG.). (YA). (gr. 8). pap. 15.99 *(978-0-06-144878-2(8),* Tegen, Katherine Bks) 2008. (J). (gr. 7-18). lib. bdg. 18.89 *(978-0-06-144877-5(X),* HarperTeen) 2008. (ENG.). (YA). (gr. 8-18). 19.99 *(978-0-06-144876-8(1),* Tegen, Katherine Bks) HarperCollins Pubs.
—Hunger. (Gone Ser.: 2). (ENG., Illus.). 608p. (YA). (gr. 8-18). 2014. pap. 12.99 *(978-0-06-144908-6(3))* 2009. 18.99 *(978-0-06-144906-2(7))* HarperCollins Pubs. (Tegen, Katherine Bks).
—Lies. (Gone Ser.: 3). (ENG., Illus.). 464p. (YA). (gr. 8). 2014. pap. 11.99 *(978-0-06-144911-6(3))* 2010. 17.99 *(978-0-06-144909-3(1))* HarperCollins Pubs. (Tegen, Katherine Bks).

S

—Light. 2013. (Gone Ser.: 6). (ENG., Illus.). 432p. (YA). (gr. 9). 18.99 (978-0-06-144918-5(0), Tegen, Katherine Bks) HarperCollins Pubs.
—Plague. (Gone Ser.: 4). (ENG.). (YA). (gr. 8). 2014. 528p. pap. 12.99 (978-0-06-144914-7(8)) 2011. 512p. 17.99 (978-0-06-144912-3(1)) HarperCollins Pubs. (Tegen, Katherine Bks).
Gratz, Alan. Grenade. (ENG.). 288p. E-Book 17.99 (978-1-338-24571-4(6)); 2018. (Illus.). (J). (gr. 4-7). 17.99 (978-1-338-24569-1(4)) Scholastic, Inc. (Scholastic Pr.).
—Grenade. l.t. ed. 2020. (ENG.). lib. bdg. 22.99 (978-1-4328-7747-7(X)) Thorndike Pr.
—Ground Zero, 1 vol. 2021. (ENG., Illus.). 336p. (J). (gr. 4-7). 17.99 (978-1-338-24575-2(9), Scholastic Pr.) Scholastic, Inc.
—Refugee, 1 vol. 2017. (ENG.). 352p. (J). (gr. 4-7). 17.99 (978-0-545-88083-1(1), Scholastic Pr.) Scholastic, Inc.
—Two Degrees. 2022. (ENG.). 384p. (J). (gr. 3-7). 17.99 (978-1-338-73567-3(5), Scholastic Pr.) Scholastic, Inc.
Gregg, Stacy. The Diamond Horse. 2017. (ENG.). 272p. (J). 6.99 (978-0-00-824384-5(0), HarperCollins Children's Bks.) HarperCollins Pubs. Ltd. GBR. Dist: HarperCollins Pubs.
Griffin, Paul. Adrift. 2015. 228p. (YA). (978-0-545-87195-2(6), Scholastic Pr.) Scholastic, Inc.
—Skyjacked. 2019. (ENG.). 240p. (YA). (gr. 7-7). 17.99 (978-1-338-04741-7(8), Scholastic Pr.) Scholastic, Inc.
Grylls, Bear. The Blizzard Challenge. McCann, Emma, illus. 2017. 117p. (J). pap. (978-1-61067-763-9(3)) Kane Miller.
—The Desert Challenge. McCann, Emma, illus. 2017. 115p. (J). pap. (978-1-61067-764-6(1)) Kane Miller.
—The Earthquake Challenge. McCann, Emma, illus. 2019. 117p. (J). pap. (978-1-61067-930-5(X)) Kane Miller.
—The Jungle Challenge. McCann, Emma, illus. 2017. 117p. (J). (978-1-61067-768-4(4)) Kane Miller.
—The River Challenge. McCann, Emma, illus. 2019. 117p. (J). pap. 4.99 (978-1-61067-929-9(6)) Kane Miller.
—The Sea Challenge. McCann, Emma, illus. 2017. 118p. (J). pap. (978-1-61067-769-1(2)) Kane Miller.
—The Volcano Challenge. McCann, Emma, illus. 2019. 131p. (J). pap. 4.99 (978-1-61067-935-0(0)) Kane Miller.
Gunderson, Jessica. Carrie & the Great Storm: A Galveston Hurricane Survival Story. Forsyth, Matt, illus. 2019. (Girls Survive Ser.). (ENG.). 112p. (J). (gr. 3-7). pap. 7.95 (978-1-4965-8447-2(3), 140972); lib. bdg. 26.65 (978-1-4965-8385-7(X), 140681) Capstone. (Stone Arch Bks.).
—Passage to Fortune: Searching for Saguenay. Kurtz, Rory, illus. 2016. (Discovering the New World Ser.). (ENG.). 96p. (J). (gr. 3-5). lib. bdg. 26.65 (978-1-4965-3481-1(6), 132579, Stone Arch Bks.) Capstone.
—Passage to Fortune: Searching for Saguenay. Kurtz, Rory, illus. 2016. (Discovering the New World Ser.). (ENG.). 96p. (J). (gr. 3-5). pap. 7.95 (978-1-4965-3482-8(4), 132581, Stone Arch Bks.) Capstone.
Gutman, Dan. Getting Air. 2008. (ENG.). 240p. (J). (gr. 3-7). pap. 7.99 (978-0-689-87681-3(5), Simon & Schuster Bks. For Young Readers) Simon & Schuster Bks. For Young Readers.
Halse Anderson, Laurie. Fever 1793. 2014. (ENG.). 272p. (J). 12.24 (978-1-63245-124-8(7)) Lectorum Pubns., Inc.
Hannon, Rose. Finding Agate: An Epic Story of a Poodle's Heart & His Will to Survive. 2010. 268p. pap. 16.99 (978-1-4490-8986-3(0)) AuthorHouse.
Harvey, Sarah N. & Stevenson, Robin. Blood on the Beach, 1 vol. 2017. (ENG.). 272p. (YA). (gr. 8-12). pap. 14.95 (978-1-4598-1293-2(X)) Orca Bk. Pubs. USA.
Hashimoto, Meika. The Trail. (ENG.). 240p. (J). (gr. 3-7). 2018. pap. 8.99 (978-1-338-03587-2(8)) 2017. 16.99 (978-1-338-03586-5(X), Scholastic Pr.) Scholastic, Inc.
Havard, Amanda. The Survivors. 2011. (ENG.). (YA). 294p. 21.99 (978-0-9833190-0-9(6)); 300p. pap. 11.99 (978-0-9833190-2-3(2)) Chafie Pr., LLC.
—The Survivors: Body & Blood. 2013. 458p. (YA). 23.99 (978-0-9833190-8-5(1)) Chafie Pr., LLC.
Heard, Margaret. It's Water Time. 2012. (ENG.). 41p. pap. 16.99 (978-1-105-86035-5(3)) Lulu Pr., Inc.
Heidicker, Christian McKay. Scary Stories for Young Foxes. Wu, Junyi, illus. 2019. (Scary Stories for Young Foxes Ser.: 1). (ENG.). 320p. (J). 16.99 (978-1-250-18142-8(9), 900190382, Holt, Henry & Co. Bks. For Young Readers) Holt, Henry & Co.
—Scary Stories for Young Foxes. Wu, Junyi, illus. 2021. (Scary Stories for Young Foxes Ser.: 1). (ENG.). 336p. (J). pap. 8.99 (978-1-250-25044-5(7), 900190383) Square Fish.
Heltzel, Anne. Circle Nine. 2011. (ENG.). 272p. (YA). (gr. 9). 16.99 (978-0-7636-5333-0(0)) Candlewick Pr.
Hicks, Faith Erin. The Nameless City 2016. (Nameless City Ser.: 1). (ENG., Illus.). 240p. (J). pap. 16.99 (978-1-62672-156-2(4), 900140614, First Second Bks.) Roaring Brook Pr.
Higson, Charlie. The End. (Enemy Novel Ser.: 7). (ENG.). 512p. (YA). (gr. 9-17). 2017. pap. 10.99 (978-1-4847-3291-5(X)) 2016. 17.99 (978-1-4847-1695-3(7)) Hyperion Bks. for Children.
—The Fallen. 2015. (Enemy Novel Ser.: 5). (ENG.). 560p. (YA). (gr. 9-17). pap. 9.99 (978-1-4231-6636-8(1)) Hyperion Bks. for Children.
—The Fear. rev. ed. 2014. (Enemy Novel Ser.: 3). (ENG.). 496p. (YA). (gr. 9-17). pap. 9.99 (978-1-4847-2144-5(6)) Hyperion Bks. for Children.
—The Hunted. 2015. (Enemy Novel Ser.: 6). (ENG.). 464p. (YA). (gr. 9-17). 17.99 (978-1-4231-6567-5(5)) Hyperion Bks. for Children.
Hill, Will. After the Fire. 2018. (ENG.). 464p. (YA). (gr. 8-12). 17.99 (978-1-4926-6979-1(2)) Sourcebooks, Inc.
—After the Fire. 2019. (ENG.). 464p. (YA). (gr. 8-12). pap. 15.99 (978-1-4926-7880-9(5)) Sourcebooks, Inc.
Hirsch, Jeff. The Darkest Path. 2013. (YA). pap. (978-0-545-51224-4(7), Scholastic Pr.) Scholastic, Inc.
—Unnatural Disasters. 2019. (ENG.). 352p. (YA). (gr. 7). 17.99 (978-0-544-99916-9(9), 1666807, Clarion Bks.) HarperCollins Pubs.
Hobbs, Will. Crossing the Wire. 2007. (Illus.). 216p. (gr. 5-9). 17.00 (978-0-7569-8053-5(4)) Perfection Learning Corp.
—Downriver. 2012. (ENG., Illus.). 208p. (J). (gr. 5-9). pap. 7.99 (978-1-4424-4547-5(5), Atheneum Bks. for Young Readers) Simon & Schuster Children's Publishing.
—Wild Man Island. 2003. (ENG.). 192p. (J). (gr. 5-18). pap. 6.99 (978-0-380-73310-1(2), HarperCollins) HarperCollins Pubs.
Hoena, Blake. Can You Survive a Supervolcano Eruption? An Interactive Doomsday Adventure. Vanzo, Filippo, illus. 2016. (You Choose: Doomsday Ser.). (ENG.). 112p. (J). (gr. 3-7). lib. bdg. 32.65 (978-1-4914-8108-0(0), 130599, Capstone Pr.) Capstone.
—Could You Escape a Deserted Island? An Interactive Survival Adventure. 2019. (You Choose: Can You Escape? Ser.). (ENG., Illus.). 112p. (J). (gr. 3-7). pap. 6.95 (978-1-5435-7560-6(9), 141092); lib. bdg. 32.65 (978-1-5435-7395-4(9), 140691) Capstone.
Holyoke, Polly. The Neptune Challenge. 2016. (ENG.). 352p. (J). (gr. 5-9). pap. 18.99 (978-1-4847-1571-0(3)) Hyperion Bks. for Children.
Hood, Susan. Lifeboat 12. 2018. (ENG., Illus.). 336p. (J). (gr. 3-8). 17.99 (978-1-4814-6883-1(9), Simon & Schuster Bks. For Young Readers) Simon & Schuster Bks. For Young Readers.
Howling, Eric. Plunge, 1 vol. 2017. (Orca Sports Ser.). (ENG.). 160p. (J). (gr. 4-7). pap. 9.95 (978-1-4598-1419-6(3)) Orca Bk. Pubs. USA.
Hughes, Alison. Lost in the Backyard, 1 vol. 2015. (ENG.). 144p. (J). (gr. 4-7). pap. 10.95 (978-1-4598-0794-5(4)) Orca Bk. Pubs. USA.
Hughes, Mark Peter. A Crack in the Sky. (Greenhouse Chronicles Ser.). (ENG.). 416p. (J). 2011. (gr. 3-7). 9.99 (978-0-385-73709-8(2))1. 2012. (gr. 7-12). lib. bdg. 22.44 (978-0-385-90645-6(5)) Random Hse. Children's Bks. (Yearling).
Hunter, Erin. Darkness Falls. 2014. (Survivors Ser.: 3). (J). lib. bdg. 18.40 (978-0-606-35496-7(4)) Turtleback.
—Dead of Night. 2017. (Survivors Gathering Darkness Ser.: 2). (J). lib. bdg. 18.40 (978-0-606-39621-9(7)) Turtleback.
—The Empty City. 2013. (Survivors Ser.: 1). (J). lib. bdg. 18.40 (978-0-606-31803-7(8)) Turtleback.
—A Hidden Enemy. 2014. (Survivors Ser.: 2). (J). lib. bdg. 18.40 (978-0-606-35056-3(X)) Turtleback.
—Red Moon Rising. 2018. (Survivors Gathering Darkness Ser.: 4). (J). lib. bdg. 18.40 (978-0-606-41371-8(5)) Turtleback.
—Survivors #1: the Empty City. (Survivors Ser.: 1). (ENG.). (J). (gr. 3-7). 2013. 304p. pap. 9.99 (978-0-06-210258-4(3)) 2012. 288p. 16.99 (978-0-06-210256-0(7)) 2012. 288p. lib. bdg. 17.89 (978-0-06-210257-7(5)) HarperCollins Pubs. (HarperCollins).
—Survivors #2: a Hidden Enemy. (Survivors Ser.: 2). (ENG.). (J). (gr. 3-7). 2014. 304p. pap. 9.99 (978-0-06-210262-1(1)) 2013. 288p. lib. bdg. 17.89 (978-0-06-210261-4(3)) HarperCollins Pubs. (HarperCollins).
—Survivors #3: Darkness Falls. 2014. (Survivors Ser.: 3). (ENG.). 320p. (J). (gr. 3-7). pap. 7.99 (978-0-06-210266-9(4), HarperCollins) HarperCollins Pubs.
—Survivors #4: the Broken Path. 2014. (Survivors Ser.: 4). (ENG.). 320p. (J). (gr. 3-7). lib. bdg. 17.89 (978-0-06-210269-0(9), HarperCollins) HarperCollins Pubs.
—Survivors #5: the Endless Lake. 2014. (Survivors Ser.: 5). (ENG.). 320p. (J). (gr. 3-7). 16.99 (978-0-06-210272-0(9), HarperCollins) HarperCollins Pubs.
—Survivors #6: Storm of Dogs. 2015. (Survivors Ser.: 6). (ENG.). 304p. (J). (gr. 3-7). pap. 9.99 (978-0-06-210278-2(8), HarperCollins) HarperCollins Pubs.
—Survivors: Tales from the Packs. 2015. (Survivors Ser.). (ENG.). 320p. (J). (gr. 3-7). pap. 7.99 (978-0-06-229154-7(8), HarperCollins) HarperCollins Pubs.
—Survivors: the Empty City & a Hidden Enemy. 2014. (ENG.). 592p. (J). (gr. 3-7). pap. 7.99 (978-0-06-232146-6(3), HarperCollins) HarperCollins Pubs.
—Survivors: the Gathering Darkness #2: Dead of Night. Kubinyi, Laszlo & Green, Julia, illus. 2016. (Survivors: the Gathering Darkness Ser.: 2). (ENG.). 304p. (J). (gr. 3-7). 16.99 (978-0-06-234337-6(8), HarperCollins) HarperCollins Pubs.
—Survivors: the Gathering Darkness #6: the Final Battle. Kubinyi, Laszlo & Green, Julia, illus. 2019. (Survivors: the Gathering Darkness Ser.: 6). (ENG.). (J). (gr. 3-7). 352p. pap. 7.99 (978-0-06-234355-0(6)); 336p. 16.99 (978-0-06-234353-6(X)); 336p. lib. bdg. 17.89 (978-0-06-234354-3(8)) HarperCollins Pubs. (HarperCollins).
—Warriors: Dawn of the Clans #4: the Blazing Star. 4th ed. 2014. (Warriors: Dawn of the Clans Ser.: 4). (ENG., Illus.). 320p. (J). (gr. 3-7). 16.99 (978-0-06-206358-8(8), HarperCollins) HarperCollins Pubs.
Hurwitz, Gregg. The Rains: A Novel. 2017. (Rains Brothers Ser.: 1). (ENG.). 368p. (YA). pap. 18.99 (978-0-7653-8268-9(7), 900152373, Tor Teen) Doherty, Tom Assocs., LLC.
Hutchinson, Shaun David, et al. Feral Youth. (ENG., Illus.). (YA). (gr. 9). 2018. 336p. pap. 12.99 (978-1-4814-9112-9(1)) 2017. 320p. 17.99 (978-1-4814-9111-2(3)) Simon Pulse. (Simon Pulse).
Ireland, Justina. Dread Nation. (ENG.). (YA). (gr. 9). 2019. 480p. pap. 11.99 (978-0-06-257061-1(7)) 2018. 464p. 17.99 (978-0-06-257060-4(9)) HarperCollins Pubs. (Balzer & Bray).
Isbell, Tom. The Capture. 2016. (Prey Trilogy Ser.: 2). (ENG.). 448p. (YA). (gr. 8). 17.99 (978-0-06-221605-2(8), HarperTeen) HarperCollins Pubs.
—The Prey. 2015. (Prey Trilogy Ser.: 1). (ENG.). 416p. (YA). (gr. 8). 17.99 (978-0-06-221601-4(5), HarperTeen) HarperCollins Pubs.
Island of the Blue Dolphins. 2011. 9.00 (978-0-7848-3655-2(8), Everbind) Marco Bk. Co.
Jane, Sarah. Maiden Voyage: a Titanic Story. 2018. (ENG.). 256p. (J). (gr. 7-7). pap. 9.99 (978-1-338-22665-2(7), Scholastic Pr.) Scholastic, Inc.
Jenkins, Jerry B. Crash at Cannibal Valley, 1 vol. 2006. (AirQuest Adventures Ser.: 1). (ENG.). 160p. (J). (gr. 3-7). pap. 6.99 (978-0-310-71347-0(1)) Zonderkidz.
Jinks, Catherine. Living Hell. 2011. (ENG.). 264p. (YA). (gr. 7). pap. 14.99 (978-0-547-54998-9(9), 1450165, Clarion Bks.) HarperCollins Pubs.
Johnson, Kristin. Black Blizzard. 2017. (Day of Disaster Ser.). (ENG.). 112p. (YA). (gr. 6-12). 26.65 (978-1-5124-2774-5(8), 17c8644d-c2b1-4cf1-8ab2-8023ed5185d3); E-Book 39.99 (978-1-5124-3506-1(6), 9781512435061) Lerner Publishing Group. (Darby Creek).
—Deep Freeze. 2017. (Day of Disaster Ser.). (ENG.). 104p. (YA). (gr. 6-12). 26.65 (978-1-5124-2776-9(4), 3aba1100-6d46-4bf9-bdd4-e098edba4172); E-Book 39.99 (978-1-5124-3509-2(0), 9781512435092); E-Book 39.99 (978-1-5124-2783-7(7)) Lerner Publishing Group. (Darby Creek).
—Wall of Water. 2017. (Day of Disaster Ser.). (ENG.). 112p. (YA). (gr. 6-12). E-Book 39.99 (978-1-5124-3515-3(5), 9781512435153); E-Book 39.99 (978-1-5124-2786-8(1)) Lerner Publishing Group. (Darby Creek).
Johnson, Kristin F. Black Blizzard. 2017. (Day of Disaster Ser.). (ENG.). 112p. (YA). (gr. 6-12). E-Book 6.99 (978-1-5124-3507-8(4), 9781512435078, Darby Creek) Lerner Publishing Group.
—Deep Freeze. 2017. (Day of Disaster Ser.). (ENG.). 104p. (YA). (gr. 6-12). E-Book 6.99 (978-1-5124-3510-8(4), 9781512435108, Darby Creek) Lerner Publishing Group.
—Wall of Water. 2017. (Day of Disaster Ser.). (ENG.). 112p. (YA). (gr. 6-12). E-Book 6.99 (978-1-5124-3516-0(3), 9781512435160, Darby Creek) Lerner Publishing Group.
Johnson, Terry Lynn. Avalanche! Orban, Jani, illus. 2018. (Survivor Diaries). (ENG.). 112p. (J). (gr. 1-5). pap. 6.99 (978-1-328-51906-1(6), 1720632); 9.99 (978-0-544-97039-7(X), 1662544) HarperCollins Pubs. (Clarion Bks.).
—Dog Driven. 2019. (ENG., Illus.). 240p. (J). (gr. 5). 17.99 (978-1-328-55159-7(8), 1724778, Clarion Bks.) HarperCollins Pubs.
—Dust Storm! Orban, Jani, illus. 2018. (Survivor Diaries). (ENG.). 128p. (J). (gr. 1-5). 9.99 (978-0-544-97098-4(5), 1662531, Clarion Bks.) HarperCollins Pubs.
—Falcon Wild. 2017. 176p. (J). (gr. 5). lib. bdg. 16.99 (978-1-58089-788-4(6)) Charlesbridge Publishing, Inc.
—Lost! Orban, Jani, illus. 2018. (Survivor Diaries). (ENG.). 112p. (J). (gr. 1-5). 9.99 (978-0-544-97118-9(3), 1662530); pap. 6.99 (978-1-328-51907-8(4), 1720643) HarperCollins Pubs. (Clarion Bks.).
—Lost! 2018. (Survivor Diaries). lib. bdg. 16.00 (978-0-606-41210-0(7)) Turtleback.
—Overboard! Orban, Jani, illus. (Survivor Diaries). (ENG.). 112p. (J). (gr. 1-5). 2018. pap. 8.99 (978-1-328-51905-4(8), 1720631) 2017. 9.99 (978-0-544-97010-6(1), 1662447) HarperCollins Pubs. (Clarion Bks.).
—Overboard! 2018. (Survivor Diaries). lib. bdg. 16.00 (978-0-606-41208-7(5)) Turtleback.
Jonsberg, Barry. Pandora Jones: Reckoning. 2016. (Pandora Jones Ser.). (ENG.). 336p. (YA). (gr. 8). pap. 12.99 (978-1-74331-813-3(8)) Allen & Unwin AUS. Dist: Independent Pubs. Group.
Kadohata, Cynthia. A Million Shades of Gray. 2011. (ENG., Illus.). 240p. (J). (gr. 5-9). pap. 8.99 (978-1-4424-2919-2(4), Atheneum Bks. for Young Readers) Simon & Schuster Children's Publishing.
Karr, Kathleen. Worlds Apart, 0 vols. unabr. ed. 2013. (ENG.). 208p. (J). (gr. 4-6). pap. 9.99 (978-1-4778-1710-0(7), 9781477817100, Two Lions) Amazon Publishing.
Karwoski, Gail Langer. When Hurricane Katrina Hit Home. Marshall, Julia, illus. 2013. Orig. Title: When Hurricane Katrina Hit Home. (ENG.). 192p. (gr. 4-7). 29.99 (978-1-62619-083-2(6), History Pr., The) Arcadia Publishing.
Kaufman, Amie & Spooner, Meagan. Their Fractured Light. 2016. (Starbound Trilogy Ser.: 3). (ENG.). 432p. (YA). (gr. 7-12). pap. 19.99 (978-1-4847-4783-4(6)) Hyperion Pr.
Keats, Israel. Deserted. 2018. (Attack on Earth Ser.). (ENG.). 112p. (YA). (gr. 6-12). pap. 7.99 (978-1-5415-2629-7(5), a3bd9e3a-6897-4bd1-8082-d17df4bbe7d2); lib. bdg. 26.65 (978-1-5415-2574-0(4), 2cea1cb0-09ce-4573-ba9a-ff8596e35033) Lerner Publishing Group. (Darby Creek).
Kehret, Peg. Secret Journey. 2008. (ENG.). 144p. (J). (gr. 3-7). pap. 8.99 (978-1-4169-9112-0(3), Simon & Schuster/Paula Wiseman Bks.) Simon & Schuster/Paula Wiseman Bks.
Kelley, Jane. Nature Girl. 2011. (ENG., Illus.). 256p. (J). (gr. 3-7). pap. 7.99 (978-0-375-85635-8(8), Yearling) Random Hse. Children's Bks.
Kennedy, Katie. What Goes Up. 2018. (ENG.). 352p. (YA). pap. 10.99 (978-1-61963-914-0(9), 900151484, Bloomsbury Young Adult) Bloomsbury Publishing USA.
Kennedy, Marlane. Blizzard Night (Disaster Strikes #3) Madrid, Erwin, illus. 2014. (Disaster Strikes Ser.: 3). (ENG.). 128p. (J). (gr. 2-5). pap. 4.99 (978-0-545-53048-4(2), Scholastic Paperbacks) Scholastic, Inc.
—Earthquake Shock. 2014. (Disaster Strikes Ser.: 1). lib. bdg. 14.75 (978-0-606-35827-9(7)) Turtleback.
—Tornado Alley. 2014. (Disaster Strikes Ser.: 2). lib. bdg. 14.75 (978-0-606-35828-6(5)) Turtleback.
—Volcano Blast (Disaster Strikes #4) Madrid, Erwin, illus. 2015. (Disaster Strikes Ser.: 4). (ENG.). 128p. (J). (gr. 2-5). pap. 4.99 (978-0-545-53047-7(4), Scholastic Paperbacks) Scholastic, Inc.
Kephart, Beth. This Is the Story of You. 2016. (ENG., Illus.). 264p. (YA). (gr. 7-12). 17.99 (978-1-4521-4284-5(X)) Chronicle Bks. LLC.
Kerr, Gordon. Story of Robinson Crusoe. 2006. 100p. per. (978-1-4067-2131-7(X), Hesperides Pr.) Read Bks.
Key, Watt. Deep Water. 2019. (ENG.). 288p. (J). pap. 7.99 (978-1-250-29439-5(8), 900177053) Square Fish.
Keyser, Amber J. The Way Back from Broken. (ENG.). 216p. (YA). (gr. 6-12). 2018. pap. 9.99 (978-1-5415-1488-1(2), 053f47d3-53bb-4099-bb59-532f84376fbd) 2015. E-Book 27.99 (978-1-4677-8817-5(1)) Lerner Publishing Group. (Carolrhoda Lab™).
King, Emily R. The Hundredth Queen. 2017. (Hundredth Queen Ser.: 1). (YA). (ENG.). 300p. (gr. 10-13). pap. 9.99 (978-1-5039-4365-0(8), 9781503943650, Skyscape); (978-1-5039-9865-0(7)) Amazon Publishing.
Kizer, Amber. A Matter of Days. 2016. (ENG.). 288p. (YA). (gr. 7). pap. 9.99 (978-0-385-73974-0(5), Ember) Random Hse. Children's Bks.
—A Matter of Days. 2016. lib. bdg. 20.85 (978-0-606-38875-7(3)) Turtleback.
Klein, Glasko. The Fallout. 2018. (Attack on Earth Ser.). (ENG.). 104p. (YA). (gr. 6-12). 26.65 (978-1-5415-2577-1(9), 83f6c253-cd01-42b2-80d2-20ff18c76b91, Darby Creek) Lerner Publishing Group.
Klimo, Kate. Dog Diaries #14: Sunny. Jessell, Tim, illus. 2019. (Dog Diaries: 14). 160p. (J). (gr. 2-5). pap. 7.99 (978-0-525-64823-9(2), Random Hse. Bks. for Young Readers) Random Hse. Children's Bks.
Kloepfer, John. Sludgment Day. 2012. (Zombie Chasers Ser.: 3). (J). lib. bdg. 16.00 (978-0-606-26867-7(7)) Turtleback.
—The Zombie Chasers #2: Undead Ahead. Wolfhard, Steve, illus. 2011. (Zombie Chasers Ser.: 2). (ENG.). 224p. (J). (gr. 3-7). 16.99 (978-0-06-185307-4(0), HarperCollins) HarperCollins Pubs.
—The Zombie Chasers #3: Sludgment Day. Wolfhard, Steve, illus. 2012. (Zombie Chasers Ser.: 3). (ENG.). 224p. (J). (gr. 3-7). 16.99 (978-0-06-185310-4(0), HarperCollins) HarperCollins Pubs.
—The Zombie Chasers #5: Nothing Left to Ooze. DeGrand, David, illus. 2014. (Zombie Chasers Ser.: 5). (ENG.). 224p. (J). (gr. 3-7). 16.99 (978-0-06-223098-0(0), HarperCollins) HarperCollins Pubs.
—The Zombie Chasers #7: World Zombination. 2015. (Zombie Chasers Ser.: 7). (ENG., Illus.). 240p. (J). (gr. 3-7). 16.99 (978-0-06-229027-4(4), HarperCollins) HarperCollins Pubs.
Kloepfer, John & Wolfhard, Steve. Zombie Chasers: Undead Ahead. 2nd ed. 2011. (Zombie Chasers Ser.: 2). (ENG., Illus.). 224p. (J). (gr. 3-7). pap. 9.99 (978-0-06-185308-1(9), HarperCollins) HarperCollins Pubs.
—The Zombie Chasers #3: Sludgment Day. 3rd ed. 2012. (Zombie Chasers Ser.: 3). (ENG., Illus.). 224p. (J). (gr. 3-7). pap. 8.99 (978-0-06-185311-1(9), HarperCollins) HarperCollins Pubs.
Kolby, Janel. Winterfolk. 2018. (ENG.). 320p. (YA). (gr. 8). 17.99 (978-0-06-248700-1(0), HarperTeen) HarperCollins Pubs.
Korman, Gordon. Escape. 2008. (Island (Playaway Audio) Ser.). (J). 34.99 (978-1-60514-854-0(7)) Findaway World, LLC.
Kras, Sara Louise. The Hunted: Polar Prey, 1 vol. 2014. (Speeding Star Ser.). (ENG.). 64p. (J). (gr. 3-3). pap. 12.71 (978-1-62285-081-5(5), baa834c0-d2c1-4270-b412-c916778748dc) Enslow Publishing, LLC.
Kreie, Chris. Take Shelter. 2018. (Attack on Earth Ser.). (ENG.). 112p. (YA). (gr. 6-12). pap. 7.99 (978-1-5415-2631-0(7), f97b38d8-1c87-40b0-8b19-ebd5c2f36aaf); lib. bdg. 26.65 (978-1-5415-2578-8(7), d2b53f7d-5a7e-42ff-a7fb-3a6c8be8e7ef) Lerner Publishing Group. (Darby Creek).
Kurtz, Jane. River Friendly, River Wild. Brennan, Neil, illus. 2007. (ENG.). 40p. (J). (gr. -1-3). 8.99 (978-1-4169-3487-5(1), Simon & Schuster/Paula Wiseman Bks.) Simon & Schuster/Paula Wiseman Bks.
LaFleur, Suzanne. Beautiful Blue World. 2017. (ENG., Illus.). 240p. (J). (gr. 3-7). pap. 8.99 (978-0-307-98032-8(4), Yearling) Random Hse. Children's Bks.
Lake, Nick. Hostage Three. 2013. (ENG.). 320p. (gr. 7). E-Book 7.99 (978-1-61963-149-6(0), Bloomsbury USA Childrens) Bloomsbury Publishing USA.
—In Darkness. 2014. (ENG.). 368p. (YA). (gr. 9). pap. 10.99 (978-1-61963-122-9(9), 900120824, Bloomsbury USA Childrens) Bloomsbury Publishing USA.
Lamana, Julie T. Upside down in the Middle of Nowhere. 2015. (ENG.). 328p. (J). (gr. 4-7). pap. 7.99 (978-1-4521-2880-1(4)) Chronicle Bks. LLC.
Lamb, Charles, et al. Tales from Shakespeare: "Twelfth Night" Strang, Kay, ed. rev. ed. 2005. (Illus.). 40p. pap. 4.95 (978-0-9542905-7-3(7)) Capercaillie Bks., Ltd GBR. Dist: Gatewood Pr.
Lanang, Vanessa. Whiteout. 2019. (To the Limit Ser.). (ENG.). 112p. (YA). (gr. 6-12). pap. 7.99 (978-1-5415-4556-4(7), 201b6a88-8b09-4d65-b8b4-68f5d8a9cd4c, Darby Creek) Lerner Publishing Group.
LaRoche, Jannette. Stranded. 2020. (Road Trip Ser.). (ENG.). 104p. (YA). (gr. 6-12). 26.65 (978-1-5415-5686-7(0), 5f1e1a01-5a60-4ca3-aafe-abf01abe09e2, Darby Creek) Lerner Publishing Group.
Lasky, Kathryn. Star Wolf. 2014. (Wolves of the Beyond Ser.: 6). (ENG.). 256p. (J). (gr. 3-7). pap. 7.99 (978-0-545-27972-7(0), Scholastic Paperbacks) Scholastic, Inc.
Law, Felicia & Way, Steve. A Storm at Sea: Sorting, Mapping, & Grids in Action, 1 vol. Spoor, Mike, illus. 2009. (Mandrill Mountain Math Mysteries Ser.). (ENG.). 32p. (J). (gr. 2-3). 27.27 (978-1-60754-815-7(1), 8ef36f64-756f-4e9e-ba11-50de241ce395); pap. 11.55 (978-1-60754-820-1(8), 97b78dc7-e6a6-4efd-9acc-1d62e87eeaf2) Rosen Publishing Group, Inc., The. (Windmill Bks.).
Lawrence, Iain. The Skeleton Tree. 2016. 288p. (J). (gr. 5-7). 16.99 (978-0-385-73378-6(X), Delacorte Bks. for Young Readers) Random Hse. Children's Bks.
Laybourne, Emmy. Monument 14. 2013. (Monument 14 Ser.: 1). (ENG., Illus.). 352p. (YA). (gr. 8-13). pap. 11.99 (978-1-250-02738-2(1), 900098310) Square Fish.
—Monument 14: Sky on Fire. 2014. (Monument 14 Ser.: 2). (ENG.). 272p. (YA). (gr. 8-13). pap. 12.99 (978-1-250-04432-7(4), 900128326) Square Fish.
—Sky on Fire. 2013. (Monument 14 Ser.: Bk. 2). (ENG.). vi, 217p. (YA). (978-1-4449-1765-9(X)) Feiwel & Friends.
Lee, Stacey. Outrun the Moon. 2017. lib. bdg. 22.10 (978-0-606-40097-8(4)) Turtleback.
Lehman, Theodore H. Defying Odds. 2014. (YA). pap. (978-1-935604-63-1(5)) Gaon Bks.
Leitich Smith, Greg. Borrowed Time. 2015. (ENG., Illus.). 192p. (J). (gr. 5-7). 16.99 (978-0-544-23711-7(0), 1564706, Clarion Bks.) HarperCollins Pubs.
Leveen, Tom. Mercy Rule. 2018. (ENG.). 456p. (YA). (gr. 9-9). 17.99 (978-1-5107-2698-7(5), Sky Pony Pr.) Skyhorse Publishing Co., Inc.
Liggett, Kim. The Grace Year: A Novel. (ENG., Illus.). 416p. (YA). 2020. pap. 11.99 (978-1-250-14545-1(7), 900181039) 2019. 16.99 (978-1-250-14544-4(9), 900181038) St. Martin's Pr. (Wednesday Bks.).
—The Unfortunates. 2019. (ENG.). 224p. (YA). pap. 9.99 (978-0-7653-8101-9(X), 900146849, Tor Teen) Doherty, Tom Assocs., LLC.
Locke, Elsie. A Canoe in the Mist. 2005. (ENG.). 224p. (978-1-86950-568-4(9)) HarperCollins Pubs. Australia.
Lorentz, Dayna. No Safety in Numbers. 2013. (No Safety in Numbers Ser.: 1). 288p. (YA). (gr. 7). pap. 10.99

(978-0-14-242597-8(4), Speak) Penguin Young Readers Group.

Lowden, Stephanie. Time of the Eagle: A Story of an Ojibwe Winter. 2004. 128p. (J). pap. 12.00 *(978-1-883953-34-8(0))* Great Lakes Literary, LLC.

Luper, Eric. The Risky Rescue (Key Hunters #6) 2017. (Key Hunters Ser.: 6). (ENG., Illus.). 128p. (J). (gr. 2-5). pap. 5.99 *(978-1-338-21229-7(X)*, Scholastic Paperbacks) Scholastic, Inc.

Maberry, Jonathan. Bits & Pieces. 2015. (Rot & Ruin Ser.: 5). (ENG., Illus.). 592p. (YA). (gr. 7). 24.99 *(978-1-4814-4418-7(2))* Simon & Schuster Children's Publishing.

—Dust & Decay. (Rot & Ruin Ser.: 2). (ENG.). (YA). (gr. 7). 2012. 544p. pap. 13.99 *(978-1-4424-0236-2(9))* 2011. 528p. 24.99 *(978-1-4424-0235-5(0))* Simon & Schuster Bks. For Young Readers. (Simon & Schuster Bks. For Young Readers).

—Fire & Ash. (Rot & Ruin Ser.: 4). (ENG., Illus.). 544p. (YA). (gr. 7). 2014. pap. 13.99 *(978-1-4424-3993-1(9))* 2013. 24.99 *(978-1-4424-3992-4(0))* Simon & Schuster Bks. For Young Readers. (Simon & Schuster Bks. For Young Readers).

—Flesh & Bone. (Rot & Ruin Ser.: 3). (ENG., (YA). (gr. 7). 2013. Illus.). 496p. pap. 13.99 *(978-1-4424-3990-0(4))* 2012. 480p. 17.99 *(978-1-4424-3989-4(0))* Simon & Schuster Bks. For Young Readers. (Simon & Schuster Bks. For Young Readers).

—Rot & Ruin, 11 vols. 2010. (Rot & Ruin Ser.: 1). (J). 122.75 *(978-1-4498-3356-5(X))*; 90.75 *(978-1-4498-3354-1(3))*; 1.25 *(978-1-4498-3360-2(8))*; 120.75 *(978-1-4498-3358-9(6))*; 256.75 *(978-1-4498-3353-4(5))* Recorded Bks., Inc.

—Rot & Ruin. (Rot & Ruin Ser.: 1). (ENG.). (YA). (gr. 7). 2011. 480p. pap. 13.99 *(978-1-4424-0233-1(4))* 2010. 464p. 17.99 *(978-1-4424-0232-4(6))* Simon & Schuster Bks. For Young Readers. (Simon & Schuster Bks. For Young Readers).

—Rot & Ruin. 2011. (Rot & Ruin Ser.: 1). lib. bdg. 23.30 *(978-0-606-23292-0(3))* Turtleback.

Mac, Carrie. Wildfire. 2020. (ENG.). 272p. (YA). (gr. 9). 17.99 *(978-0-399-55629-6(X)*, Knopf Bks. for Young Readers) Random Hse. Children's Bks.

Manale, Shizumi & Marshall, Richard. Running with Cosmos Flowers: The Children of Hiroshima, 1 vol. 2014. (ENG., Illus.). 152p. (YA). (gr. 8-8). 16.99 *(978-1-4556-1966-5(3)*, Pelican Publishing) Arcadia Publishing.

Marman, Richard. Mcalister's Spark. Marman, Richard, illus. 2013. (Illus.). 364p. pap. *(978-1-909302-21-1(X))* Abela Publishing.

Marryat, Frederick. Masterman Ready. l.t. ed. 2006. 276p. pap. 23.99 *(978-1-4264-0573-0(1))* Creative Media Partners, LLC.

Marsden, John. Tomorrow, When the War Began (Tomorrow #1) 2006. (Tomorrow Ser.: 1). (ENG.). 304p. (J). (gr. 7-7). 12.99 *(978-0-439-82910-6(0)*, Scholastic Paperbacks) Scholastic, Inc.

Martin, Laura. The Ark Plan. DesChamps, Eric, illus. 2017. (Edge of Extinction Ser.: 1). (ENG.). (J). (gr. 3-7). lib. bdg. 17.20 *(978-0-606-40046-6(X))* Turtleback.

—Edge of Extinction #2: Code Name Flood. Deschamps, Eric, illus. 2018. (Edge of Extinction Ser.: 2). (ENG.). 368p. (J). (gr. 3-7). pap. 7.99 *(978-0-06-241626-1(X)*, HarperCollins) HarperCollins Pubs.

Martin, R. T. The Field Trip. 2018. (Attack on Earth Ser.). (ENG.). 112p. (YA). (gr. 6-12). 26.65 *(978-1-5415-2573-3(6)*, 06e260b9-f5cb-42f2-80c8-692f0c9fe067, Darby Creek) Lerner Publishing Group.

—Riptide. 2019. (To the Limit Ser.). (ENG.). 104p. (YA). (gr. 6-12). 26.65 *(978-1-5415-4036-1(0)*, 13d54020-f345-4b90-8213-09d1d5ea8f63, Darby Creek) Lerner Publishing Group.

—Safe Zone. 2017. (Level Up Ser.). (ENG.). 112p. (YA). (gr. 6-12). pap. 7.99 *(978-1-5124-5360-7(9)*, 4b340d12-02d0-489e-a9cd-c0f80ec63dde); lib. bdg. 26.65 *(978-1-5124-3986-1(X)*, 239c2cad-d57a-4415-85bc-2ab2fc7ecf43) Lerner Publishing Group. (Darby Creek).

—Spinning Out. 2020. (Road Trip Ser.). (ENG.). 104p. (YA). (gr. 6-12). 26.65 *(978-1-5415-5685-0(2)*, dc154f5c-66c5-4d54-ad67-f485c28db03c, Darby Creek) Lerner Publishing Group.

Mason, Prue. Camel Rider. 2011. 9.49 *(978-0-7848-3618-7(3)*, Everbind) Marco Bk. Co.

Mass, Wendy. Voyagers: the Seventh Element (Book 6) 2016. (Voyager Ser.: 6). 208p. (J). (gr. 3-7). 12.99 *(978-0-385-38673-9(7)*, Random Hse. Bks. for Young Readers) Random Hse. Children's Bks.

Massey, David. Taken. 2014. (ENG.). 320p. (YA). E-Book *(978-0-545-66129-4(3))*; (gr. 9). 18.99 *(978-0-545-66128-7(5)*, Chicken Hse., The) Scholastic, Inc.

Matthews, L. S. Fish. 2006. 183p. (gr. 5-9). 16.50 *(978-0-7569-6626-3(4))* Perfection Learning Corp.

Mayer, Shannon & Breene, K. F. Shadowspell Academy: the Culling Trials. 2019. 576p. (YA). (gr. 9-12). 16.99 *(978-1-5107-5510-9(1)*, Sky Pony Pr.) Skyhorse Publishing Co., Inc.

McCaffrey, Laura Williams. Marked. 2017. (ENG.). 368p. (YA). (gr. 7). pap. 9.99 *(978-0-544-93884-7(4)*, 1658461, Clarion Bks.) HarperCollins Pubs.

McCaughrean, Geraldine. The White Darkness. (YA). 2008. (ENG.). 400p. (gr. 8-12). pap. 9.99 *(978-0-06-089037-7(1))* 2007. 373p. (gr. 7-12). 18.89 *(978-0-06-089036-0(3))* HarperCollins Pubs. (HarperTeen).

McClintock, Norah. Taken, 1 vol. 2009. (ENG.). 176p. (YA). (gr. 8-12). pap. 14.95 *(978-1-55469-152-4(4))* Orca Bk. Pubs. USA.

McDougall, Sophia. Mars Evacuees. (ENG.). (J). (gr. 3-7). 2016. 432p. pap. 7.99 *(978-0-06-229400-5(8))* 2015. 416p. 16.99 *(978-0-06-229399-2(0))* HarperCollins Pubs. (HarperCollins).

McGinnis, Mindy. Not a Drop to Drink. 2013. (ENG.). 320p. (YA). (gr. 9). 17.99 *(978-0-06-219850-1(5)*, Tegen, Katherine Bks) HarperCollins Pubs.

McGoran, Jon. Spiked. 2020. (Spliced Ser.: 3). 352p. (YA). (gr. 9). 18.99 *(978-0-8234-4091-7(5))* Holiday Hse., Inc.

—Spliced. (Spliced Ser.: 1). (YA). 2019. 416p. (gr. 7). pap. 9.99 *(978-0-8234-4234-8(9))* 2017. (ENG.). 400p. (gr. 9). 18.95 *(978-0-8234-3855-6(4))* Holiday Hse., Inc.

—Splintered. 2019. (Spliced Ser.: 2). 352p. (YA). (gr. 9). 18.99 *(978-0-8234-4090-0(7))* Holiday Hse., Inc.

Mikaelsen, Ben. Red Midnight. 2003. (ENG.). 224p. (J). (gr. 3-7). pap. 6.99 *(978-0-380-80561-7(8))* HarperCollins Español.

—Red Midnight. 2003. 212p. (gr. 5-9). 17.00 *(978-0-7569-1550-6(3))* Perfection Learning Corp.

Monninger, Joseph. Flood. 2014. (Stay Alive Ser.: 4). lib. bdg. 16.00 *(978-0-606-36065-4(4))* Turtleback.

Montgomery, R. A. Silver Wings. Semionov, Vladimir, illus. 2007. (ENG.). 144p. (J). (gr. 4-8). pap. 7.99 *(978-1-933390-23-9(9))* Chooseco LLC.

Moore, Stephanie Perry. Getting Home. 2018. (Attack on Earth Ser.). (ENG.). 104p. (YA). (gr. 6-12). pap. 7.99 *(978-1-5415-2628-0(7)*, 6c7038c6-4bf9-4551-b3f6-a8e5fdd1c3f5); lib. bdg. 26.65 *(978-1-5415-2575-7(2)*, 300dbd6a-844a-436f-b919-a2b2b67e6f26) Lerner Publishing Group. (Darby Creek).

More Than This. 2014. (ENG.). 480p. (YA). (gr. 9). pap. 12.00 *(978-0-7636-7620-9(9))* Candlewick Pr.

Morgan, Kass. Day 21. (100 Ser.: 2). (ENG.). 320p. (YA). (gr. 10-17). 2015. pap. 12.99 *(978-0-316-23457-3(5))* 2014. 18.00 *(978-0-316-23455-9(9))* Little, Brown Bks. for Young Readers.

—Homecoming. 2015. (100 Ser.: 3). (ENG.). 352p. (YA). (gr. 10-17). pap. 12.99 *(978-0-316-38196-3(9))* Little, Brown Bks. for Young Readers.

Morphew, Chris. The Phoenix Files, Contact. 2013. 320p. (YA). pap. 6.99 *(978-1-61067-092-0(2))* Kane Miller.

Mullin, Mike. Ashen Winter. 2013. (Ashfall Ser.). (ENG.). 580p. (YA). (gr. 6). pap. 13.99 *(978-1-933718-98-9(6))* Tanglewood Pr.

—Ashfall. (Ashfall Ser.). (ENG.). 476p. (gr. 8). 2012. (YA). pap. 13.99 *(978-1-933718-74-3(9))* 2011. (J). 17.95 *(978-1-933718-55-2(2))* Tanglewood Pr.

Myers, Edward. Climb or Die. 2nd ed. 2016. 154p. (J). pap. *(978-1-932727-12-8(4))* Montemayor Pr.

—Solos en la Montaña. 2016. (SPA.). 157p. (J). pap. *(978-1-932727-18-0(3))* Montemayor Pr.

Nagai, Mariko. Under the Broken Sky. 2019. (ENG., Illus.). 304p. (J). 17.99 *(978-1-250-15921-2(0)*, 900185614, Holt, Henry & Co. Bks. For Young Readers) Holt, Henry & Co.

Napoli, Donna Jo. Storm. 2014. (ENG., Illus.). 368p. (YA). (gr. 9). 17.99 *(978-1-4814-0302-3(8)*, Simon & Schuster/Paula Wiseman Bks.) Simon & Schuster/Paula Wiseman Bks.

Nelson, O. T. The Girl Who Owned a City: Graphic Novel. Delk, Chrissy, illus. 2012. (Single Titles Ser.). (ENG.). 128p. (YA). (gr. 5-12). lib. bdg. 29.27 *(978-0-7613-4903-7(0)*, Graphic Universe™) Lerner Publishing Group.

Nelson, O. T. (Terry). The Girl Who Owned a City. 2012. (ENG.). 208p. (YA). (gr. 5-12). pap. 9.99 *(978-0-7613-5086-6(1)*, 7994c097-e4ac-4e65-a42b-ee32768ba735, Carolrhoda Bks.) Lerner Publishing Group.

Nielsen, Jennifer A. Iceberg. 2023. (ENG.). 352p. (J). (gr. 3-7). 17.99 *(978-1-338-79502-8(3)*, Scholastic Pr.) Scholastic, Inc.

Northrop, Michael. Trapped. 2011. (ENG.). 240p. (J). (gr. 7-10). 17.99 *(978-0-545-21012-6(7)*, Scholastic Pr.) Scholastic, Inc.

Novel Units. Lord of the Flies Novel Units Teacher Guide. 2019. (ENG.). (YA). (gr. 9-12). pap. 12.99 *(978-1-56137-383-3(4)*, BK8384, Novel Units, Inc.) Classroom Library Co.

Nuri, Alya & Nuri, Alya. Amr's Adventure in Europe. 2013. 68p. pap. *(978-1-935948-29-2(6))* Roxby Media Ltd.

O'Dell, Scott. Island of the Blue Dolphins. 184p. (J). (gr. 3-5). pap. 5.99 *(978-0-8072-8327-1(4))*; 2004. (gr. 5-9). pap. 36.00 incl. audio *(978-0-8072-8326-4(6)*, YA163SP) Random Hse. Audio Publishing Group. (Listening Library).

—Island of the Blue Dolphins. l.t. ed. 2005. (ENG.). 223p. pap. 10.95 *(978-0-7862-7254-9(6)*, Large Print Pr.) Thorndike Pr.

—Island of the Blue Dolphins. 2010. lib. bdg. 18.40 *(978-0-606-10724-2(X))* Turtleback.

—Island of the Blue Dolphins: A Newbery Award Winner. Lewin, Ted, illus. 2010. (ENG.). 192p. (J). (gr. 3-7). pap. 8.99 *(978-0-547-32861-4(3)*, 1416953, Clarion Bks.) HarperCollins Pubs.

—Island of the Blue Dolphins: And Related Readings. 2006. (McDougal Littell Literature Connections Ser.). (ENG., Illus.). 208p. (gr. 6-8). 18.50 *(978-0-395-87473-8(4)*, 2-70833) Great Source Education Group, Inc.

O'Guilin, Peadar. The Invasion (the Call, Book 2) 2018. (ENG.). 336p. (J). (gr. 7-7). 18.99 *(978-1-338-04562-8(8))* Scholastic, Inc.

Olsen, Erik. Cobble Cavern. 2012. (J). pap. 16.99 *(978-1-4621-1009-4(6))* Cedar Fort, Inc./CFI Distribution.

Olson, Kayla. The Sandcastle Empire. 2018. (ENG.). 480p. (YA). (gr. 9). pap. 9.99 *(978-0-06-248488-8(5))* 2017. 455p. *(978-0-06-269312-9(3))* HarperCollins Pubs. (HarperTeen).

Onyebuchi, Tochi. War Girls. 2019. (ENG.). 464p. (YA). (gr. 7). 18.99 *(978-0-451-48167-2(4)*, Razorbill) Penguin Young Readers Group.

Ormand, Kate. Dark Days. (ENG.). (gr. 6-12). 2018. 272p. pap. 8.99 *(978-1-5107-1710-7(2))* 2014. 256p. (J). 16.95 *(978-1-62873-594-9(5))* Skyhorse Publishing Co., Inc. (Sky Pony Pr.).

Osa, Nancy. The Battle of Zombie Hill: Defenders of the Overworld #1. 2015. (Defenders of the Overworld Ser.). (ENG.). 272p. (J). (gr. 6-6). pap. 9.99 *(978-1-63450-996-1(X)*, Sky Pony Pr.) Skyhorse Publishing Co., Inc.

Paley, Jane. Hooper Finds a Family: A Hurricane Katrina Dog's Survival Tale. 2018. (ENG.). 144p. (J). (gr. 3-7). pap. 6.99 *(978-0-06-201105-3(7)*, HarperCollins) HarperCollins Pubs.

Palmer, Ingrid. All Out of Pretty. 2018. (ENG.). 344p. (YA). (gr. 7-12). 16.99 *(978-1-939547-48-4(2)*, 8fe2a0c1-3f0e-4034-be6e-b825aed9d232) Creston Bks.

Park, Linda Sue. A Long Walk to Water: Based on a True Story. (ENG., Illus.). 128p. (J). (gr. 5-7). 2011. pap. 9.99 *(978-0-547-57731-9(1)*, 1458533) 2010. 18.99 *(978-0-547-25127-1(0)*, 1101512) HarperCollins Pubs. (Clarion Bks.).

—A Long Walk to Water: Based on a True Story. 2009. 8.32 *(978-0-7848-3885-3(2)*, Everbind) Marco Bk. Co.

—A Long Walk to Water: Based on a True Story. 2011. 18.00 *(978-1-61383-124-3(2))* Perfection Learning Corp.

—A Long Walk to Water: Based on a True Story. 2011. lib. bdg. 18.40 *(978-0-606-23406-1(3))* Turtleback.

Parks, Kathy. The Lifeboat Clique. 2018. (ENG.). 352p. (YA). (gr. 8). pap. 9.99 *(978-0-06-239398-2(7)*, Tegen, Katherine Bks) HarperCollins Pubs.

Parry, Rosanne. A Horse Named Sky. Fagan, Kirbi, illus. 2023. (Voice of the Wilderness Novel Ser.). (ENG.). 272p. (J). (gr. 3-7). 18.99 **(978-0-06-299595-7(2)**, Greenwillow Bks.) HarperCollins Pubs.

Paterson, Katherine. Bread & Roses, Too. (ENG.). 288p. (J). 2008. (gr. 5-7). pap. 7.99 *(978-0-547-07651-5(7)*, 1042025) 2006. (gr. 4-6). 22.44 *(978-0-618-65479-6(8))* HarperCollins Pubs. (Clarion Bks.).

Patterson, James. Crazy House. 2019. (Crazy House Ser.: 1). (ENG.). 352p. mass mkt. 8.99 *(978-1-5387-1406-5(X))* Grand Central Publishing.

—Crazy House. 2018. (Crazy House Ser.: 1). (ENG.). 384p. (YA). (gr. 9-17). pap. 9.99 *(978-0-316-51499-6(3)*, Jimmy Patterson) Little Brown & Co.

Patterson, James & Tebbetts, Chris. Middle School: Save Rafe! Park, Laura, illus. 2014. (Middle School Ser.: 6). (ENG.). 288p. (J). (gr. 3-7). 13.99 *(978-0-316-32212-6(1)*, Jimmy Patterson) Little Brown & Co.

Patterson, James & Tebbetts, Christopher. Save Rafe! Park, Laura, illus. 2014. 269p. (J). *(978-0-316-28629-9(X))* Little Brown & Co.

Paulsen, Gary. Brian's Return. 2012. (Hatchet Adventure Ser.: 4). (ENG.). 160p. (YA). (gr. 5). pap. 10.99 *(978-0-307-92960-0(4)*, Ember) Random Hse. Children's Bks.

—Brian's Winter. 2012. (Hatchet Adventure Ser.: 3). (ENG.). 176p. (YA). (gr. 5). pap. 10.99 *(978-0-307-92958-7(2)*, Ember) Random Hse. Children's Bks.

—Brian's Winter. 2012. lib. bdg. 20.85 *(978-0-606-23879-3(4))* Turtleback.

—Hatchet. 2003. (ENG.). 160p. (J). mass mkt. 9.99 *(978-0-330-31045-1(3)*, Pan) Pan Macmillan GBR. Dist: Trafalgar Square Publishing.

—Hatchet. 2006. 18.40 *(978-1-4177-6883-7(5))* Turtleback.

—Hatchet: 20th Anniversary Edition. Willis, Drew, illus. 20th anniv. ed. 2007. (ENG.). 192p. (J). (gr. 5-9). 19.99 *(978-1-4169-2508-8(2)*, Simon & Schuster Bks. For Young Readers) Simon & Schuster Bks. For Young Readers.

—Hatchet: 30th Anniversary Edition. Willis, Drew, illus. 30th ed. 2017. (ENG.). 224p. (J). (gr. 5-9). pap. 9.99 *(978-1-4814-8629-3(2)*, Simon & Schuster Bks. For Young Readers) Simon & Schuster Bks. For Young Readers.

—Northwind. 2022. (ENG.). 256p. (J). 18.99 *(978-0-374-31420-0(9)*, 900225846, Farrar, Straus & Giroux (BYR)) Farrar, Straus & Giroux.

—Northwind. 2024. (ENG.). 256p. (gr. 6-8). 24.94 ***(978-1-5364-8333-8(8))*** Square Fish.

Paulsen, Gary. The River. 2012. (Hatchet Adventure Ser.: 2). (ENG.). 176p. (YA). (gr. 5). pap. 9.99 *(978-0-307-92961-7(2)*, Ember) Random Hse. Children's Bks.

—The River. 2012. lib. bdg. 20.85 *(978-0-606-23880-9(8))* Turtleback.

Paulson, Gary. Hatchet. unabr. ed. 2004. 195p. (J). (gr. 5-9). pap. 36.00 incl. audio *(978-0-8072-8319-6(3)*, YA161SP, Listening Library) Random Hse. Audio Publishing Group.

Pearson, Mary E. The Beauty of Darkness: The Remnant Chronicles, Book Three. 2017. (Remnant Chronicles Ser.: 3). (ENG.). 688p. (YA). pap. 14.99 *(978-1-250-11531-7(0)*, 900157585) Square Fish.

—The Fox Inheritance, 2. 2013. (Jenna Fox Chronicles Ser.: 2). (ENG.). 320p. (YA). (gr. 7-12). pap. 12.99 *(978-1-250-01032-2(2)*, 900084770) Square Fish.

Peretti, Frank E. Trapped at the Bottom of the Sea. 2004. 144p. (Cooper Kids Adventure Ser.: No. 4). (gr. 4-7). 5.99 *(978-0-89107-594-3(1))*; Vol. 4. (Cooper Kids Adventure Ser.: 4). (ENG.). (J). (gr. 3-6). pap. 6.99 *(978-1-58134-621-3(2))* Crossway.

Peretti, Frank E. & Thomas Nelson Publishing Staff. Mayday at Two Thousand Five Hundred, 1 vol., 8. 2005. (Cooper Kids Adventure Ser.: 8). (ENG.). 160p. (J). pap. 6.99 *(978-1-4003-0577-3(2)*, Tommy Nelson) Nelson, Thomas Inc.

Perkins, Lynne Rae. Nuts to You. Perkins, Lynne Rae, illus. 2014. (ENG., Illus.). 272p. (J). (gr. 3-7). 16.99 *(978-0-06-009275-7(0)*, Greenwillow Bks.) HarperCollins Pubs.

Perry, Michael. The Scavengers. (ENG.). 336p. (J). (gr. 3-7). 2015. pap. 9.99 *(978-0-06-202617-0(8))* 2014. 16.99 *(978-0-06-202616-3(X))* HarperCollins Pubs. (HarperCollins).

Pfeffer, Susan Beth. The Dead & the Gone. 2010. (Life As We Knew It Ser.: 2). (ENG.). 336p. (YA). (gr. 7-12). pap. 9.99 *(978-0-547-25855-3(0)*, 1402120, Clarion Bks.) HarperCollins Pubs.

—The Dead & the Gone. 2010. (Last Survivors Ser.: 2). 321p. lib. bdg. 19.65 *(978-0-606-14464-3(1))* Turtleback.

—This World We Live In, Bk. 3. 2011. (Life As We Knew It Ser.: 3). (ENG.). 256p. (YA). (gr. 7). pap. 9.99 *(978-0-547-55028-2(6)*, 1450237, Clarion Bks.) HarperCollins Pubs.

Phelan, James. Survivor, 2. 2013. (Alone Ser.). (ENG.). 256p. (YA). (gr. 9-12). 26.19 *(978-0-7582-8068-8(8))* Kensington Publishing Corp.

Philbrick, Rodman. The Big Dark. 2019. (Penworthy Picks Middle School Ser.). (ENG.). 178p. (J). (gr. 4-5). 17.96 *(978-1-64310-933-6(2))* Penworthy Co., LLC, The.

—The Big Dark. 2017. (ENG.). 192p. (J). (gr. 3-7). pap. 6.99 *(978-0-545-78976-9(1)*, Blue Sky Pr., The) Scholastic, Inc.

—Wildfire (the Wild Series) A Novel. 2019. (ENG.). 208p. (J). (gr. 3-7). 17.99 *(978-1-338-26690-0(X)*, Blue Sky Pr., The) Scholastic, Inc.

—Zane & the Hurricane: a Story of Katrina. 2015. (ENG.). 192p. (J). (gr. 5-9). pap. 8.99 *(978-0-545-34239-1(2)*, Blue Sky Pr., The) Scholastic, Inc.

Phillips, Dee. Titanic. 2014. (Yesterday's Voices Ser.). (YA). lib. bdg. 19.60 *(978-0-606-35583-4(9))* Turtleback.

Pipe, Jim. How to Survive on a Desert Island, 1 vol. 2012. (Tough Guides). (ENG., Illus.). 32p. (J). (gr. 4-5). pap. 11.00 *(978-1-4488-7935-9(3)*, 2573f758-7322-46f5-be26-8dba06231ae9, PowerKids Pr.) Rosen Publishing Group, Inc., The.

Platt, Randall. The Girl Who Wouldn't Die. 2017. (ENG.). 368p. (J). (gr. 8-8). 16.99 *(978-1-5107-0809-9(X)*, Sky Pony Pr.) Skyhorse Publishing Co., Inc.

Pohl, Laura. The Last 8. (Last 8 Ser.: 1). (YA). (gr. 8-12). 2020. 384p. pap. 10.99 *(978-1-4926-9156-3(9))* 2019. (ENG.). 368p. 17.99 *(978-1-4926-6989-0(X))* Sourcebooks, Inc.

Pon, Cindy. Ruse. 2019. (ENG., Illus.). 304p. (YA). (gr. 9). 18.99 *(978-1-5344-1992-6(6)*, Simon Pulse) Simon Pulse.

—Want. (ENG.). (YA). (gr. 9). 2019. 352p. pap. 12.99 *(978-1-4814-8923-2(2))* 2017. (Illus.). 336p. 19.99 *(978-1-4814-8922-5(4))* Simon Pulse. (Simon Pulse).

Prasad, Chandra. Damselfly: A Novel. 2018. (ENG.). 272p. (YA). (gr. 7-7). 18.99 *(978-0-545-90792-7(6)*, Scholastic Pr.) Scholastic, Inc.

Pratchett, Terry. Nation. 2008. 504p. (J). pap. 16.99 *(978-0-06-170913-5(1))*; (ENG.). 384p. (YA). (gr. 8-18). 17.99 *(978-0-06-143301-6(2)*, Clarion Bks.) HarperCollins Pubs.

Preller, James. Blood Mountain. 2019. (ENG.). 240p. (J). 16.99 *(978-1-250-17485-7(6)*, 900189253) Feiwel & Friends.

Prendergast, G. S. Cold Falling White. (Nahx Invasions Ser.: 2). (ENG.). 576p. (YA). (gr. 9). 2020. pap. 13.99 *(978-1-4814-8188-5(6))* 2019. 19.99 *(978-1-4814-8187-8(8))* Simon & Schuster Bks. For Young Readers. (Simon & Schuster Bks. For Young Readers).

—Cold Falling White. 2019. (ENG.). 368p. (YA). *(978-1-5011-4714-2(5))* Simon & Schuster Children's Publishing.

—Zero Repeat Forever. 2017. (ENG.). (YA). (gr. 9). pap. 12.99 *(978-1-5344-1808-0(3))* Simon & Schuster.

—Zero Repeat Forever. (Nahx Invasions Ser.: 1). (ENG.). (YA). (gr. 9). 2019. 512p. pap. 13.99 *(978-1-4814-8185-4(1))* 2017. (Illus.). 496p. 17.99 *(978-1-4814-8184-7(3))* Simon & Schuster Bks. For Young Readers. (Simon & Schuster Bks. For Young Readers).

Pressler, Mirjam. Malka. Murdoch, Brian, tr. 2005. 280p. (YA). (gr. 7-12). 13.65 *(978-0-7569-5217-4(4))* Perfection Learning Corp.

Probst, Jeff & Tebbetts, Chris. Stranded. 2013. (Stranded Ser.: 1). lib. bdg. 17.20 *(978-0-606-36788-2(8))* Turtleback.

Probst, Jeff & Tebbetts, Christopher. Desperate Measures. 2016. (Stranded, Shadow Island Ser.: 3). 172p. (J). lib. bdg. 17.20 *(978-0-606-37562-7(7))* Turtleback.

—Shadow Island: Desperate Measures. 2016. (Stranded Ser.: 6). (ENG.). 192p. (J). (gr. 3-7). 6.99 *(978-0-14-751390-8(1)*, Puffin Books) Penguin Young Readers Group.

—Shadow Island: the Sabotage. 2015. (Stranded Ser.: 5). (ENG.). 224p. (J). (gr. 3-7). 6.99 *(978-0-14-751389-2(8)*, Puffin Books) Penguin Young Readers Group.

—Stranded. 2013. (Stranded Ser.: 1). (ENG.). 208p. (J). (gr. 3-7). pap. 8.99 *(978-0-14-242424-7(2)*, Puffin Books) Penguin Young Readers Group.

—Trial by Fire. 2013. 174p. (J). *(978-0-14-751195-9(X))* Penguin Publishing Group.

—Trial by Fire. 2013. (Stranded Ser.: 2). (ENG.). 208p. (J). (gr. 3-7). pap. 8.99 *(978-0-14-242425-4(0)*, Puffin Books) Penguin Young Readers Group.

Proimos III, James, Jr. Apocalypse Meow Meow. Proimos III, James, Jr., illus. 2015. (ENG., Illus.). 224p. (J). (gr. 3-6). 15.99 *(978-1-61963-472-5(4)*, 900137802, Bloomsbury USA Childrens) Bloomsbury Publishing USA.

Pyron, Bobbie. A Dog's Way Home. 2012. (ENG.). 336p. (J). (gr. 3-7). pap. 6.99 *(978-0-06-198672-7(0)*, Tegen, Katherine Bks) HarperCollins Pubs.

R. M. Ballantyne. The Coral Island. 2007. 316p. per. 14.95 *(978-1-4218-4004-8(9)*, 1st World Library - Literary Society) 1st World Publishing, Inc.

Raver-Lampman, Greg. Adrift: Lost in Life, Marooned at Sea. 2006. 132p. 14.95 *(978-1-888842-32-6(6))* Absey & Co.

Reichs, Brendan. Chrysalis. 2019. (Project Nemesis Ser.: 3). (ENG.). 416p. (YA). (gr. 7). 18.99 *(978-0-525-51705-4(7)*, G.P. Putnam's Sons Books for Young Readers) Penguin Young Readers Group.

—Genesis. 2019. (Project Nemesis Ser.: 2). (ENG.). 528p. (YA). (gr. 7). pap. 10.99 *(978-0-399-54497-2(6)*, Penguin Books) Penguin Young Readers Group.

—Nemesis. 2018. (Project Nemesis Ser.: 1). (ENG.). 480p. (YA). (gr. 7). pap. 12.99 *(978-0-399-54494-1(1)*, Penguin Books) Penguin Young Readers Group.

Reid, Roger. Longleaf: A Novel. 2015. (ENG.). 136p. (J). (gr. 4-7). pap. 14.95 *(978-1-58838-311-2(3)*, 8884, NewSouth Bks.) NewSouth, Inc.

Revis, Beth. Shades of Earth. 2013. (Across the Universe Trilogy: 3). lib. bdg. 20.85 *(978-0-606-32117-4(9))* Turtleback.

—Shades of Earth: An Across the Universe Novel. 2013. (Across the Universe Ser.: 3). (ENG.). 448p. (YA). (gr. 9). pap. 10.99 *(978-1-59514-615-1(6)*, Razorbill) Penguin Young Readers Group.

Reynolds Naylor, Phyllis. Roxie & the Hooligans. Boiger, Alexandra, illus. 2007. 115p. (gr. 2-5). 16.00 *(978-0-7569-8284-3(7))* Perfection Learning Corp.

Rhodes, Jewell Parker. Ninth Ward. 2012. (J). lib. bdg. 18.40 *(978-0-606-26158-6(3))* Turtleback.

Richards, Natalie D. One Was Lost. (ENG., (YA). (gr. 7-12). 2017. Illus.). 23.99 *(978-1-4926-6232-7(1))* 2016. 320p. pap. 12.99 *(978-1-4926-1574-3(9)*, 9781492615743) Sourcebooks, Inc.

Roberts, Jeyn. Dark Inside. (ENG.). (YA). (gr. 9). 2012. 352p. pap. 12.99 *(978-1-4424-2352-7(8))* 2011. 336p. 17.99 *(978-1-4424-2351-0(X))* Simon & Schuster Bks. For Young Readers. (Simon & Schuster Bks. For Young Readers).

—Rage Within. (ENG., 368p. (YA). (gr. 9). 2013. Illus.). pap. 11.99 *(978-1-4424-2355-8(2))* 2012. 17.99 *(978-1-4424-2354-1(4))* Simon & Schuster Bks. For Young Readers. (Simon & Schuster Bks. For Young Readers).

Rorby, Ginny. Lost in the River of Grass. 2012. (ENG.). 264p. (YA). (gr. 7-12). pap. 9.99 *(978-0-7613-8498-4(7)*, 12ae2bd5-22e5-4761-8bde-ed56322fd477, Carolrhoda Lab™) Lerner Publishing Group.

Rosenblum, Gregg. Revolution 19. 2013. (Revolution 19 Ser.: 1). (ENG.). 272p. (YA). (gr. 8). 17.99 *(978-0-06-212595-8(8)*, HarperTeen) HarperCollins Pubs.

Ross, Joel. The Fog Diver. (Fog Diver Ser.: 1). (ENG.). (J). (gr. 3-7). 2016. 352p. pap. 7.99 *(978-0-06-235294-1(6))* 2015. 336p. 16.99 *(978-0-06-235293-4(8))* HarperCollins Pubs. (HarperCollins).

—The Lost Compass. (Fog Diver Ser.: 2). (ENG.). (J). (gr. 3-7). 2017. 368p. pap. 9.99 *(978-0-06-235309-2(8))* 2016. 352p. 16.99 *(978-0-06-235297-2(0))* HarperCollins Pubs. (HarperCollins).

—The Lost Compass. 2017. (Fog Diver Ser.: Vol. 2). (ENG.). (J). (gr. 3-7). lib. bdg. 17.20 *(978-0-606-40052-7(4))* Turtleback.

Roth, Veronica. Carve the Mark. 2017. (Carve the Mark Ser.: 1). (ENG.). (YA). (gr. 9). 512p. pap. 12.99 *(978-0-06-234864-7(7))*; (Illus.). 480p. 22.99 *(978-0-06-234863-0(9))* HarperCollins Pubs. (Tegen, Katherine Bks).

—Carve the Mark. 2018. (YA). lib. bdg. 24.50 *(978-0-606-41030-4(9))* Turtleback.

—The Fates Divide. Lt. ed. 2018. (ENG.). 602p. (YA). lib. bdg. 24.99 *(978-1-4328-5197-2(7))* Cengage Gale.

—The Fates Divide. 2019. (Carve the Mark Ser.: 2). (ENG.). 480p. (YA). (gr. 9). pap. 14.99 *(978-0-06-242696-3(6))* 2018. (ENG.). 464p. (J). *(978-0-00-819220-4(0))* 2018. (Illus.). 443p. (J). *(978-0-06-284238-1(2))*Bk. 2. 2018. (Carve the Mark Ser.: 2). (ENG., Illus.). 464p. (YA). (gr. 9). 21.99 *(978-0-06-242695-6(8))* HarperCollins Pubs. (Tegen, Katherine Bks).

Rundell, Katherine. The Explorer. (ENG.). (J). (gr. 3-7). 2018. 352p. pap. 8.99 *(978-1-4814-1946-8(3))* 2017. (Illus.). 336p. 16.99 *(978-1-4814-1945-1(5))* Simon & Schuster Bks. For Young Readers. (Simon & Schuster Bks. For Young Readers).

Saddleback Educational Publishing Staff, ed. River, 1 vol. unabr. ed. 2010. (Heights Ser.). (ENG.). 50p. (gr. 4-8). pap. 9.75 *(978-1-61651-281-1(4))* Saddleback Educational Publishing, Inc.

Sage, Angie. Maximillian Fly. 2019. (ENG.). 384p. (J). (gr. 3-7). 16.99 *(978-0-06-257116-8(8))*, Tegen, Katherine Bks) HarperCollins Pubs.

Salote, Ana. Oy Yew. 2013. 276p. pap. *(978-1-78299-659-0(1))* FeedARead.com.

Saltzwedel, Hans H. Hans' Journal: A Young German's Memories of His Family's Survival During Germany's Darkest Days. 2003. (Illus.). 234p. per. 19.95 net. *(978-1-931934-17-6(7))* Back Yard Pub.

Sangster, Caitlin. Last Star Burning. (Last Star Burning Ser.). (ENG.). (YA). (gr. 7). 2018. 416p. pap. 12.99 *(978-1-4814-8614-9(4))* 2017. (Illus.). 400p. 19.99 *(978-1-4814-8613-2(6))* Simon Pulse. (Simon Pulse).

—Shatter the Suns. (Last Star Burning Ser.). (ENG.). (YA). (gr. 7). 2019. 544p. pap. 12.99 *(978-1-4814-8617-0(9))* 2018. (Illus.). 528p. 19.99 *(978-1-4814-8616-3(0))* Simon Pulse. (Simon Pulse).

Savit, Gavriel. Anna & the Swallow Man. 2016. (CHI.). 272p. (YA). (gr. 7). pap. *(978-957-33-3251-0(5))* Crown Publishing Co., Ltd.

—Anna & the Swallow Man. 2017. (ENG.). 256p. (YA). (gr. 7). pap. 9.99 *(978-0-553-52208-2(6)*, Ember) Random Hse. Children's Bks.

—Anna & the Swallow Man. 2017. lib. bdg. 20.85 *(978-0-606-39876-3(7))* Turtleback.

Scarrow, Alex. Plague Land. 2017. (Plague Land Ser.: 1). (ENG.). 384p. (YA). (gr. 8-12). pap. 10.99 *(978-1-4926-5210-6(5))* Sourcebooks, Inc.

—Plague Land: Reborn. 2018. (Plague Land Ser.: 2). (ENG.). 416p. (YA). (gr. 8-12). pap. 10.99 *(978-1-4926-6023-1(X))* Sourcebooks, Inc.

Schaaf, Ron. BearClaw: Finding Courage Within. 2007. (J). *(978-0-9787555-1-5(0))* Hickory Tales Publishing.

Schroeder, Lisa. Far from You. 2010. (ENG.). 384p. (YA). (gr. 9). pap. 12.99 *(978-1-4169-7507-6(1)*, Simon Pulse) Simon Pulse.

Schwarz, S. L. Treasure at Lure Lake. 2016. (Illus.). 185p. (J). pap. 12.99 *(978-1-4621-1790-1(2))*; *(978-1-4621-2600-2(6))* Cedar Fort, Inc./CFI Distribution.

Schwebel, Sara L. & O'Dell, Scott. Island of the Blue Dolphins: The Complete Reader's Edition. 2016. (ENG., Illus.). 224p. 29.95 *(978-0-520-28937-6(4))* Univ. of California Pr.

Scott, Elizabeth. Miracle. 2013. (ENG., Illus.). 240p. (YA). (gr. 9). pap. 9.99 *(978-1-4424-1707-6(2)*, Simon Pulse) Simon Pulse.

Sepetys, Ruta. Ashes in the Snow (Movie Tie-In) 2018. (ENG.). 384p. (YA). (gr. 7). pap. 11.99 *(978-1-9848-3674-8(9)*, Penguin Books) Penguin Young Readers Group.

—Between Shades of Gray. 2012. (ENG & JPN.). 398p. (YA). (gr. 7). pap. *(978-4-00-115651-5(2))* Iwanami Shoten.

—Between Shades of Gray. 2009. 10.36 *(978-0-7848-3779-5(1)*, Everbind) Marco Bk. Co.

—Between Shades of Gray. (ENG., (YA). (gr. 7-18). 2012. Illus.). 384p. pap. 12.99 *(978-0-14-242059-1(X)*, Penguin Books) 2011. 352p. 19.99 *(978-0-399-25412-3(9)*, Philomel Bks.) Penguin Young Readers Group.

—Between Shades of Gray. Lt. ed. (ENG.). 2020. lib. bdg. 22.99 *(978-1-4328-7360-8(1))* 2011. 432p. (YA). 23.99 *(978-1-4104-4083-9(4))* Thorndike Pr.

—Between Shades of Gray. 2012. lib. bdg. 20.85 *(978-0-606-26089-3(7))* Turtleback.

Sherman, M. Zachary. Damage Control, 1 vol. Cage, Josef, illus. 2012. (Bloodlines Ser.). (ENG.). 88p. (J). (gr. 4-8). lib. bdg. 27.32 *(978-1-4342-3765-1(6)*, 117026, Stone Arch Bks.) Capstone.

Shimose Poe, Mayumi. Alice on the Island: A Pearl Harbor Survival Story. Forsyth, Matt, illus. 2019. (Girls Survive Ser.). (ENG.). 112p. (J). (gr. 3-7). pap. 7.95 *(978-1-4965-8012-2(5)*, 139979, Stone Arch Bks.) Capstone.

Shusterman, Neal. UnSouled. (Unwind Dystology Ser.: 3). (ENG., Illus.). (YA). (gr. 7). 2014. 432p. pap. 12.99 *(978-1-4424-2370-1(6))* 2013. 416p. 19.99 *(978-1-4424-2369-5(2))* Simon & Schuster Bks. For Young Readers. (Simon & Schuster Bks. For Young Readers).

—Unsouled. 2014. (Unwind Dystology Ser.: 3). lib. bdg. 23.30 *(978-0-606-36107-1(3))* Turtleback.

—UnWholly. (Unwind Dystology Ser.: 2). (ENG.). 416p. (YA). (gr. 7). 2013. pap. 12.99 *(978-1-4424-2367-1(6)*, Simon & Schuster Bks. For Young Readers) 2012. 19.99 *(978-1-4424-2366-4(8))* Simon & Schuster Bks. For Young Readers.

—UnWholly. 2013. (Unwind Dystology Ser.: 2). lib. bdg. 23.30 *(978-0-606-32336-9(8))* Turtleback.

—Unwind. 2011. 10.36 *(978-0-7848-3496-1(2)*, Everbind) Marco Bk. Co.

—Unwind. (Unwind Dystology Ser.: 1). (ENG., Illus.). (YA). 2009. 384p. (gr. 8). pap. 12.99 *(978-1-4169-1205-7(3))* 2007. 352p. (gr. 7-12). 19.99 *(978-1-4169-1204-0(5))* Simon & Schuster Bks. For Young Readers. (Simon & Schuster Bks. For Young Readers).

—Unwind. 2009. (Unwind Dystology Ser.: 1). lib. bdg. 23.30 *(978-0-606-10700-6(2))* Turtleback.

Shusterman, Neal & Elfman, Eric. I Am the Walrus. 2023. (N. O. A. H Files Ser.: 1). (ENG.). 400p. (J). (gr. 5-9). 17.99 *(978-0-7595-5524-2(9))* Little, Brown Bks. for Young Readers.

Shusterman, Neal & Shusterman, Jarrod. Dry. (ENG.). (YA). (gr. 7). 2019. 416p. pap. 12.99 *(978-1-4814-8197-7(5))* 2018. (Illus.). 400p. 19.99 *(978-1-4814-8196-0(7))* Simon & Schuster Bks. For Young Readers. (Simon & Schuster Bks. For Young Readers).

Sigler, Scott. Alight: Book Two of the Generations Trilogy. 2016. (Generations Trilogy Ser.: 2). 448p. (gr. 9). pap. 12.00 *(978-0-553-39317-0(0)*, Del Rey) Random Hse. Worlds.

—Alive. 2016. (Generations Trilogy Ser.: 1). 384p. (gr. 9). pap. 14.00 *(978-0-553-39312-5(X)*, Del Rey) Random House Publishing Group.

—Alone. 2017. (Generations Trilogy Ser.: 3). 560p. (YA). (gr. 9). pap. 15.00 *(978-0-553-39321-7(9)*, Del Rey) Random Hse. Worlds.

Skogen, Jennifer. Shattered. 2017. (Survive Ser.). (ENG.). 192p. (YA). (gr. 5-12). lib. bdg. 31.42 *(978-1-68076-734-6(8)*, 25402, Epic Escape) EPIC Pr.

Smelcer, John. The Trap. 2007. (ENG.). 176p. (YA). (gr. 7-9). per. 10.99 *(978-0-312-37755-7(X)*, 900049151) Square Fish.

Smith, Andrew. Exile from Eden: Or, after the Hole. Smith, Andrew, illus. 2019. (ENG., Illus.). 368p. (YA). (gr. 9). 18.99 *(978-1-5344-2223-0(4)*, Simon & Schuster Bks. For Young Readers) Simon & Schuster Bks. For Young Readers.

—Grasshopper Jungle. 2015. (ENG.). 416p. (YA). (gr. 9). pap. 11.99 *(978-0-14-242500-8(1)*, Speak) Penguin Young Readers Group.

Smith, Caighlan. Children of Icarus. 2016. (ENG.). 312p. (YA). (gr. 9-12). 16.95 *(978-1-63079-057-8(5)*, 132186, Switch Pr.) Capstone.

Smith, Dan. Boy X. 2017. 274p. (J). *(978-1-338-17150-1(X))* Scholastic, Inc.

Smith, Duane. Heritage Revealed Series, 3. (J). (gr. 2-9). pap. 13.95 *(978-1-886218-00-0(5))* Azimuth Pr.

Smith, Nikki Shannon. Noelle at Sea: A Titanic Survival Story. Forsyth, Matt, illus. 2019. (Girls Survive Ser.). (ENG.). 112p. (J). (gr. 3-7). lib. bdg. 25.99 *(978-1-4965-7850-1(3)*, 139368, Stone Arch Bks.) Capstone.

Smith, Roland. Ascent. 2018. (Peak Marcello Adventure Ser.: 3). (ENG.). 240p. (YA). (gr. 7). 17.99 *(978-0-544-86759-8(9)*, 1648549, Clarion Bks.) HarperCollins Pubs.

—The Edge. 2016. (Peak Marcello Adventure Ser.: 2). (ENG.). 240p. (YA). (gr. 7). pap. 7.99 *(978-0-544-81354-0(5)*, 1641953, Clarion Bks.) HarperCollins Pubs.

—Peak. 2008. (Peak Marcello Adventure Ser.: 1). (ENG., Illus.). 256p. (YA). (gr. 7). pap. 9.99 *(978-0-15-206268-2(8)*, 1198787, Clarion Bks.) HarperCollins Pubs.

—The Surge. 2011. (Storm Runners Ser.: Bk. 2). 133p. (J). pap. *(978-0-545-39462-8(7)*, Scholastic Pr.) Scholastic, Inc.

Sniegoski, Thomas E. Monstrous. (Savage Ser.). (ENG.). 448p. (YA). (gr. 9). 2018. pap. 12.99 *(978-1-4814-7719-2(6))* 2017. (Illus.). 18.99 *(978-1-4814-7718-5(8))* Simon Pulse. (Simon Pulse).

—Savage. (Savage Ser.). (ENG.). (YA). (gr. 9). 2017. 432p. pap. 9.99 *(978-1-4814-4374-6(7))* 2016. (Illus.). 416p. 17.99 *(978-1-4814-4373-9(9))* Simon Pulse. (Simon Pulse).

Sorrells/Sorrells. Scratch. 2006. 222p. (J). lib. bdg. 23.08 *(978-1-4242-2214-8(1))* Fitzgerald Bks.

Speare, Elizabeth George. The Sign of the Beaver. 135p. (J). (gr. 4-6). pap. 4.99 *(978-0-8072-1517-3(1)*, Listening Library) Random Hse. Audio Publishing Group.

—The Sign of the Beaver: A Newbery Honor Award Winner. 2011. (ENG.). 144p. (J). (gr. 5-7). pap. 9.99 *(978-0-547-57711-1(7)*, 1458459, Clarion Bks.) HarperCollins Pubs.

Sperry, Armstrong. Call It Courage. 2008. 17.20 *(978-1-4178-1178-6(1))* Turtleback.

Spinale, Wendy. Everland (the Everland Trilogy, Book 1) 2016. (Everland Ser.: 1). (ENG.). 320p. (YA). (gr. 7). 17.99 *(978-0-545-83694-4(8)*, Scholastic Pr.) Scholastic, Inc.

—Ozland (the Everland Trilogy, Book 3) 2018. (Everland Ser.: 3). (ENG.). 288p. (YA). (gr. 7-7). 17.99 *(978-0-545-95322-1(7)*, Scholastic Pr.) Scholastic, Inc.

—Umberland (the Everland Trilogy, Book 2) 2017. (Everland Ser.: 2). (ENG.). 288p. (YA). (gr. 7). 17.99 *(978-0-545-95318-4(9)*, Scholastic Pr.) Scholastic, Inc.

Spooner, Meagan. Lark Ascending. 2014. (Skylark Trilogy Ser.). (ENG.). 328p. (YA). (gr. 7-12). 17.95 *(978-0-7613-8867-8(2)*, 9c8b3bbe-4f94-42e2-a78b-3a8870d6a56c, Carolrhoda Lab™) Lerner Publishing Group.

—Shadowlark. 2013. (Skylark Trilogy Ser.). (ENG.). 336p. (YA). (gr. 7-12). E-Book 27.99 *(978-1-4677-1664-2(2)*, Carolrhoda Lab™) Lerner Publishing Group.

—Skylark. 2012. (Skylark Trilogy Ser.). (ENG.). 344p. (YA). (gr. 7-12). 17.95 *(978-0-7613-8865-4(6)*, e83334e5-216e-4448-b5ff-af0d5f446791, Carolrhoda Lab™) Lerner Publishing Group.

Spradlin, Michael P. Into the Killing Seas. 2015. (J). (ENG.). 224p. (gr. 3-7). 16.99 *(978-0-545-72602-3(6)*, Scholastic Pr.); 185p. *(978-0-545-83764-4(2))* Scholastic, Inc.

—Pararescue Corps. Karkavelas, Spiros, illus. 2019. (Pararescue Corps Ser.). (ENG.). 240p. (J). (gr. 4-8). pap., pap., pap. 9.95 *(978-1-4965-8105-1(9)*, 140248, Stone Arch Bks.) Capstone.

—Viper Strike: A 4D Book. Karkavelas, Spiros, illus. 2018. (Pararescue Corps Ser.). (ENG.). 128p. (J). (gr. 4-8). lib. bdg. 27.32 *(978-1-4965-5202-0(4)*, 136214, Stone Arch Bks.) Capstone.

Stasse, Lisa M. The Defiant: The Forsaken Trilogy. 2014. (ENG., Illus.). 352p. (YA). (gr. 7). 17.99 *(978-1-4424-3271-0(3)*, Simon & Schuster Bks. For Young Readers) Simon & Schuster Bks. For Young Readers.

—The Defiant: The Forsaken Trilogy. 2015. (ENG., Illus.). 352p. (YA). (gr. 7). pap. 10.99 *(978-1-4424-3272-7(1))* Simon & Schuster Children's Publishing.

—The Forsaken: The Forsaken Trilogy. (ENG., (YA). (gr. 7). 2013. Illus.). 400p. pap. 11.99 *(978-1-4424-3266-6(7))* 2012. 384p. 16.99 *(978-1-4424-3265-9(9))* Simon & Schuster Bks. For Young Readers. (Simon & Schuster Bks. For Young Readers).

—The Uprising: The Forsaken Trilogy. (ENG., (YA). (gr. 7). 2014. Illus.). 400p. pap. 9.99 *(978-1-4424-3269-7(1))* 2013. 384p. 16.99 *(978-1-4424-3268-0(3))* Simon & Schuster Bks. For Young Readers. (Simon & Schuster Bks. For Young Readers).

Steig, William. Abel's Island. 2007. (Newbery Award & Honor Bks.). (Illus.). 117p. (gr. 3-7). 17.00 *(978-0-7569-8290-4(1))* Perfection Learning Corp.

—Abel's Island. 2007. (Illus.). 117p. (J). (gr. 4-7). 17.20 *(978-1-4177-9383-9(X))* Turtleback.

Stevens, Courtney. Four Three Two One. 2018. (ENG.). 400p. (YA). (gr. 9). 17.99 *(978-0-06-239854-3(7)*, HarperTeen) HarperCollins Pubs.

Stohl, Margaret. Icons. 2014. (Icons Ser.: 1). (ENG.). 464p. (YA). (gr. 7-17). pap. 21.99 *(978-0-316-20519-1(2))* Little, Brown Bks. for Young Readers.

Stolarz, Laurie Faria. Jane Anonymous: A Novel. 2020. (ENG.). 320p. (YA). 18.99 *(978-1-250-30370-7(2)*, 900197163, Wednesday Bks.) St. Martin's Pr.

Sullivan, Annie. Tiger Queen, 1 vol. 2019. (ENG.). 336p. (YA). 17.99 *(978-0-310-76877-7(2))* Blink.

Sullivan, Tara. Golden Boy. 2014. 384p. (J). (gr. 5). pap. 8.99 *(978-0-14-242450-6(1)*, Puffin Books) Penguin Young Readers Group.

Summers, Courtney. This Is Not a Test. 2012. (ENG.). 336p. (YA). (gr. 8). pap. 14.00 *(978-0-312-65674-4(2)*, 900069754, St. Martin's Griffin) St. Martin's Pr.

Sundell, Joanne. Arctic Shadow. 2015. (Watch Eyes Trilogy Ser.: 2). (ENG.). 278p. (YA). 25.95 *(978-1-4328-3008-3(2)*, Five Star Trade) Cengage Gale.

—Arctic Will. 2016. (ENG.). 326p. (YA). 25.95 *(978-1-4328-3175-2(5)*, Five Star) Cengage Gale.

Sutton, Laurie S. Stranded. Nathan, James, illus. 2017. (Bug Team Alpha Ser.). (ENG.). 112p. (J). (gr. 3-6). lib. bdg. 26.65 *(978-1-4965-5185-6(0)*, 136188, Stone Arch Bks.) Capstone.

Suzanne, Collins. Los juegos del hambre. 2009. (Hunger Games Trilogy: Bk. 1). (SPA.). pap. 19.99 *(978-84-9867-539-9(1))* RBA Libros, S.A. ESP. Dist: Lectorum Pubns., Inc.

Sylvester, Kevin. MiNRS. (MiNRS Ser.: 1). (ENG., Illus.). (J). (gr. 3-7). 2016. 352p. pap. 8.99 *(978-1-4814-4040-0(3))* 2015. 336p. 18.99 *(978-1-4814-4039-4(X))* McElderry, Margaret K. Bks. (McElderry, Margaret K. Bks.).

—MiNRS 2. 2016. (MiNRS Ser.: 2). (ENG., Illus.). 352p. (J). (gr. 3-7). 17.99 *(978-1-4814-4042-4(X)*, McElderry, Margaret K. Bks.) McElderry, Margaret K. Bks.

Tait, Chris & Wyss, Johann David. The Swiss Family Robinson. Akib, Jamel, illus. 2007. 151p. (J). *(978-1-4287-4213-0(1))* Sterling Publishing Co., Inc.

Tarshis, Lauren. I Survived Hurricane Katrina 2005. 2011. (I Survived Ser.: No. 3). lib. bdg. 14.75 *(978-0-606-23743-7(7))* Turtleback.

—I Survived Hurricane Katrina, 2005 (I Survived #3) Dawson, Scott, illus. 2011. (I Survived Ser.: 3). (ENG.). 112p. (J). (gr. 2-5). pap. 5.99 *(978-0-545-20696-9(0)*, Scholastic Paperbacks) Scholastic, Inc.

—I Survived the American Revolution, 1776 (I Survived #15), Vol .15. 2017. (I Survived Ser.: 15). (ENG., Illus.). 144p. (J). (gr. 2-5). pap. 4.99 *(978-0-545-91973-9(8)*, Scholastic Paperbacks) Scholastic, Inc.

—I Survived the Attacks of September 11, 2001. 2012. (I Survived Ser.: No. 6). lib. bdg. 14.75 *(978-0-606-26205-7(9))* Turtleback.

—I Survived the Attacks of September 11th, 2001 (I Survived #6) Dawson, Scott, illus. 2012. (I Survived Ser.: 6). (ENG.). 112p. (J). (gr. 3-7). pap. 5.99 *(978-0-545-20700-3(2)*, Scholastic Paperbacks) Scholastic, Inc.

—I Survived the Battle of Gettysburg 1863. 2013. (I Survived Ser.: No. 7). lib. bdg. 14.75 *(978-0-606-31530-2(6))* Turtleback.

—I Survived the Battle of Gettysburg, 1863 (I Survived #7) 2013. (I Survived Ser.: 7). (ENG., Illus.). 112p. (J). (gr. 2-5). pap. 5.99 *(978-0-545-45936-5(2)*, Scholastic Pr.) Scholastic, Inc.

—I Survived the Bombing of Pearl Harbor 1941. 2011. (I Survived Ser.: No. 4). lib. bdg. 14.75 *(978-0-606-23744-4(5))* Turtleback.

—I Survived the Bombing of Pearl Harbor, 1941 (I Survived #4), 1 vol. Dawson, Scott, illus. 2011. (I Survived Ser.: 4). (ENG.). 112p. (J). (gr. 2-5). pap. 5.99 *(978-0-545-20698-3(7)*, 49b44782-3a49-4716-a4c4-75402e52d8fb, Scholastic Paperbacks) Scholastic, Inc.

—I Survived the Children's Blizzard, 1888 (I Survived #16) 2018. (I Survived Ser.: 16). (ENG.). 144p. (J). (gr. 2-5). pap. 4.99 *(978-0-545-91977-7(0)*, Scholastic Paperbacks) Scholastic, Inc.

—I Survived the Children's Blizzard, 1888 (I Survived #16) (Library Edition) 2018. (I Survived Ser.: 16). (ENG., Illus.). 144p. (J). (gr. 2-5). lib. bdg. 25.99 *(978-0-545-91978-4(9)*, Scholastic Paperbacks) Scholastic, Inc.

—I Survived the Destruction of Pompeii, 79 A. D. 2014. (I Survived Ser.: No. 10). (Illus.). 95p. (J). lib. bdg. 14.75 *(978-0-606-36067-8(0))* Turtleback.

—I Survived the Destruction of Pompeii, AD 79. Dawson, Scott, illus. 2014. 95p. (J). *(978-0-545-77568-7(X)*, Scholastic Pr.) Scholastic, Inc.

—I Survived the Destruction of Pompeii, AD 79 (I Survived #10) 2014. (I Survived Ser.: 10). (ENG., Illus.). 112p. (J). (gr. 2-5). pap. 5.99 *(978-0-545-45939-6(7))* Scholastic, Inc.

—I Survived the Eruption of Mount St. Helens, 1980 (I Survived #14) 2016. (I Survived Ser.: 14). (ENG., Illus.). 112p. (J). (gr. 2-5). pap. 5.99 *(978-0-545-65852-2(7)*, Scholastic Paperbacks) Scholastic, Inc.

—I Survived the Hindenburg Disaster, 1937 (I Survived #13) 2016. (I Survived Ser.: 13). (ENG.). 112p. (J). (gr. 2-5). pap. 5.99 *(978-0-545-65850-8(0)*, Scholastic Paperbacks) Scholastic, Inc.

—I Survived the Japanese Tsunami 2011. 2013. (I Survived Ser.: No. 8). lib. bdg. 14.75 *(978-0-606-32390-1(2))* Turtleback.

—I Survived the Japanese Tsunami, 2011 (I Survived #8) 2013. (I Survived Ser.: 8). (ENG., Illus.). 112p. (J). (gr. 2-5). pap. 5.99 *(978-0-545-45937-2(0)*, Scholastic Paperbacks) Scholastic, Inc.

—I Survived the Joplin Tornado, 2011 (I Survived #12) Dawson, Scott, illus. 2015. (I Survived Ser.: 12). (ENG.). 112p. (J). (gr. 2-5). pap. 5.99 *(978-0-545-65848-5(9)*, Scholastic Paperbacks) Scholastic, Inc.

—I Survived the Nazi Invasion 1944. 2014. (I Survived Ser.: No. 9). lib. bdg. 14.75 *(978-0-606-35397-7(6))* Turtleback.

—I Survived the Nazi Invasion, 1944 (I Survived #9) 2014. (I Survived Ser.: 9). (ENG., Illus.). 112p. (J). (gr. 3-7). pap. 5.99 *(978-0-545-45938-9(9))* Scholastic, Inc.

—I Survived the San Francisco Earthquake 1906. 2012. (I Survived Ser.: No. 5). lib. bdg. 14.75 *(978-0-606-23936-3(7))* Turtleback.

—I Survived the San Francisco Earthquake, 1906 (I Survived #5) Dawson, Scott, illus. 2012. (I Survived Ser.: 5). (ENG.). 112p. (J). (gr. 2-5). pap. 5.99 *(978-0-545-20699-0(5)*, Scholastic Paperbacks) Scholastic, Inc.

—I Survived the Shark Attacks of 1916. 2010. (I Survived Ser.: No. 2). lib. bdg. 14.75 *(978-0-606-23742-0(9))* Turtleback.

—I Survived the Shark Attacks of 1916 (I Survived #2) Dawson, Scott, illus. 2010. (I Survived Ser.: 2). (ENG.). 112p. (J). (gr. 2-5). pap. 5.99 *(978-0-545-20695-2(2)*, Scholastic Paperbacks) Scholastic, Inc.

—I Survived the Sinking of the Titanic 1912. 2010. (I Survived Ser.: No. 1). lib. bdg. 14.75 *(978-0-606-23741-3(0))* Turtleback.

—I Survived the Sinking of the Titanic, 1912 (I Survived #1) Dawson, Scott, illus. 2010. (I Survived Ser.: 1). (ENG.). 112p. (J). (gr. 2-5). 4.99 *(978-0-545-20694-5(4)*, Scholastic Paperbacks) Scholastic, Inc.

Taylor, Theodore. The Cay. 2003. (ENG.). 160p. (J). (gr. 5-7). mass mkt. 7.99 *(978-0-440-22912-4(X)*, Laurel Leaf) Random Hse. Children's Bks.

Taylor, Theodore & Taylor, Theodore. The Cay. 2003. (gr. 5-8). lib. bdg. 17.20 *(978-0-613-72282-7(5))* Turtleback.

Thomas, Lex. The Burnouts. 2016. (Quarantine Ser.: 3). (ENG.). 296p. (YA). (gr. 9-12). pap. 9.99 *(978-1-5124-0419-7(5)*, e71b4da5-69dd-42c0-af43-1a1b573637a4, Carolrhoda Lab™) Lerner Publishing Group.

—The Giant. (Quarantine Ser.). (ENG.). 352p. (YA). (gr. 9-12). 2018. pap. 9.99 *(978-1-5415-3846-7(3)*, ba896617-e02e-4086-8dbc-3a543f00f30a) 2016. E-Book 27.99 *(978-1-5124-0159-2(5))* Lerner Publishing Group. (Carolrhoda Lab™).

—The Loners. (Quarantine Ser.: No. 1). (ENG.). 416p. (gr. 9). 2012. 17.99 *(978-1-60684-329-1(X))*Bk. 1. 2013. (YA). pap. 9.99 *(978-1-60684-438-0(5)*, a4290b32-f23c-40fb-9b34-385c9b02c589) Lerner Publishing Group. (Carolrhoda Lab™).

—The Saints. Bk. 2. 2014. (Quarantine Ser.: No. 2). (ENG.). 416p. (YA). (gr. 9-12). pap. 9.99 *(978-1-60684-540-0(3)*, 9b2df3a0-3933-41db-aeb0-259ae3dfdc73, Carolrhoda Lab™) Lerner Publishing Group.

Thompson, Paul B. Lost Republic, 1 vol. 2015. (Scarlet Voyage Ser.). (ENG.). 256p. (J). (gr. 6-7). 23.61 *(978-1-62324-000-4(X)*, 7d18d20e-88c8-4879-b024-02bdf91c8627) Enslow Publishing, LLC.

Treggiari, Jo. Ashes, Ashes. (ENG.). 352p. (YA). (gr. 7). 2013. pap. 9.99 *(978-0-545-25564-6(3)*, Scholastic Paperbacks) 2011. 17.99 *(978-0-545-25563-9(5)*, Scholastic Pr.) Scholastic, Inc.

Troupe, Thomas Kingsley. Blizzard - A Tale of Snow-Blind Survival. Fagan, Kirbi, illus. 2016. (Survive! Ser.). (ENG.). 56p. (J). (gr. 4-8). lib. bdg. 25.32 *(978-1-4965-2554-3(X)*, 130513, Stone Arch Bks.) Capstone.

—Flight Down. 2016. (Tartan House Ser.). (ENG.). 96p. (J). (gr. 3-6). *(978-1-63235-161-6(7)*, 11892, 12-Story Library) Bookstaves, LLC.

—Lost - A Wild Tale of Survival. Fagan, Kirbi, illus. 2016. (Survive! Ser.). (ENG.). 56p. (J). (gr. 4-8). lib. bdg. 25.32 *(978-1-4965-2557-4(4)*, 130516, Stone Arch Bks.) Capstone.

—Survive! 2016. (Survive! Ser.). (ENG., Illus.). 56p. (J). (gr. 4-8). 101.28 *(978-1-4965-2575-8(2)*, 23953, Stone Arch Bks.) Capstone.

Tullson, Diane. The Darwin Expedition, 1 vol. 2007. (Orca Soundings Ser.). (ENG.). 128p. (YA). (gr. 8-12). per. 9.95 *(978-1-55143-676-0(0))* Orca Bk. Pubs. USA.

Turner, Tracey. Lost in the Desert of Dread. 2014. (LOST: Can You Survive? Ser.). (ENG., Illus.). 128p. (J). (gr. 6-6). *(978-0-7787-0725-7(3))* Crabtree Publishing Co.

—Lost in the Jungle of Doom. 2014. (LOST: Can You Survive? Ser.). (ENG., Illus.). 128p. (J). (gr. 6-6). *(978-0-7787-0727-1(X))* Crabtree Publishing Co.

Uhlberg, Myron. A Storm Called Katrina, 1 vol. Bootman, Colin, illus. 40p. (J). (gr. 2-5). 2015. pap. 8.99 *(978-1-56145-887-5(2))* 2011. 17.95 *(978-1-56145-591-1(1))* Peachtree Publishing Co. Inc.

—A Storm Called Katrina. 2015. lib. bdg. 19.60 *(978-0-606-37467-5(1))* Turtleback.

Van Draanen, Wendelin. Runaway. 2012. (ENG.). 272p. (YA). (gr. 5). pap. 9.99 *(978-0-307-97597-3(5)*, Ember) Random Hse. Children's Bks.

—Wild Bird. 2019. (ENG.). 336p. (YA). (gr. 7). pap. 10.99 *(978-1-101-94047-1(6)*, Ember) Random Hse. Children's Bks.

Van Dusen, Chris. The Circus Ship. Van Dusen, Chris, illus. 2015. (ENG., Illus.). 40p. (J). (gr. -1-3). 8.99 *(978-0-7636-5592-1(9))* Candlewick Pr.

Van Tol, Alex. Knifepoint, 1 vol. 2010. (Orca Soundings Ser.). (ENG.). 128p. (YA). (gr. 9-12). lib. bdg. 26.19 *(978-1-55469-306-1(3))*; (gr. 8-12). pap. 9.95 *(978-1-55469-305-4(5))* Orca Bk. Pubs. USA.

—A Punta de Cuchillo, 1 vol. 2011. (Spanish Soundings Ser.). (SPA.). 136p. (YA). (gr. 8-12). pap. 9.95 *(978-1-55469-863-9(4))* Orca Bk. Pubs. USA.

Vanasse, Patricia. Resilient. Shalaby, Asharaf, illus. 2013. (ENG.). 328p. (YA). pap. 13.99 *(978-0-9860373-2-0(X))* Pants On Fire Pr.

Vincent, Rachel. 99 Lies. 2018. (100 Hours Ser.: 2). (ENG.). 416p. (YA). (gr. 9). 17.99 *(978-0-06-241159-4(4)*, Tegen, Katherine Bks) HarperCollins Pubs.
—100 Hours. 2018. (100 Hours Ser.: 1). (ENG.). 384p. (YA). (gr. 9). pap. 9.99 *(978-0-06-241157-0(8)*, Tegen, Katherine Bks) HarperCollins Pubs.
Voorhees, Coert. On the Free. 2017. (ENG.). 280p. (YA). (gr. 9-12). 17.99 *(978-1-5124-2913-8(9)*, 43e96ca4-2df6-49e1-b581-bfb0ae0a00f1, Carolrhoda Lab™) Lerner Publishing Group.
Walden, Mark. Aftershock. 2014. (H. I. V. E. Ser.: 7). (ENG., Illus.). 304p. (J). (gr. 3-7). 19.99 *(978-1-4424-9467-1(0)*, Simon & Schuster Bks. For Young Readers) Simon & Schuster Bks. For Young Readers.
—Deadlock. 2015. (H. I. V. E. Ser.: 8). (ENG., Illus.). 304p. (J). (gr. 3-7). 18.99 *(978-1-4424-9470-1(0)*, Simon & Schuster Bks. For Young Readers) Simon & Schuster Bks. For Young Readers.
—Earthfall. 2013. (Earthfall Trilogy Ser.: 1). (ENG., Illus.). 272p. (J). (gr. 3-7). 16.99 *(978-1-4424-9415-2(8)*, Simon & Schuster Bks. For Young Readers) Simon & Schuster Bks. For Young Readers.
—Redemption. 2018. (Earthfall Trilogy Ser.: 3). (ENG., Illus.). 304p. (J). (gr. 3-7). 17.99 *(978-1-4424-9421-3(2)*, Simon & Schuster Bks. For Young Readers) Simon & Schuster Bks. For Young Readers.
—Retribution. 2015. (Earthfall Trilogy Ser.: 2). (ENG., Illus.). 272p. (J). (gr. 3-7). 17.99 *(978-1-4424-9418-3(2)*, Simon & Schuster Bks. For Young Readers) Simon & Schuster Bks. For Young Readers.
Wallace, Brandon. The Journey Home. (Wilder Boys Ser.). (ENG., Illus.). 208p. (J). 2017. (gr. 4-8). pap. 8.99 *(978-1-4814-3266-5(4))* 2016. (gr. 3-7). 17.99 *(978-1-4814-3267-2(2))* Simon & Schuster Children's Publishing. (Aladdin).
—Wilder Boys. 2017. (Wilder Boys Ser.). (ENG.). 256p. (J). (gr. 4-8). pap. 8.99 *(978-1-4814-3263-4(X)*, Simon & Schuster/Paula Wiseman Bks.) Simon & Schuster/Paula Wiseman Bks.
Wallenfels, Stephen. Pod. 2012. (ENG.). 304p. (gr. 12). 7.99 *(978-1-937007-43-0(X)*, Ace) Penguin Publishing Group.
Walters, Eric. Fourth Dimension. 2018. (Neighborhood Ser.: 4). (ENG.). 384p. (YA). (gr. 7). 17.99 *(978-0-14-319844-4(0)*, Penguin Teen) PRH Canada Young Readers CAN. Dist: Penguin Random Hse. LLC.
—The Rule of Three: Fight for Power. 2015. (Rule of Three Ser.: 2). (ENG.). 352p. (YA). (gr. 7). 27.99 *(978-0-374-30179-8(4)*, 900140944, Farrar, Straus & Giroux (BYR)) Farrar, Straus & Giroux.
Watkins, Steve. On Blood Road (a Vietnam War Novel) 2018. (ENG.). 288p. (YA). (gr. 7-7). 18.99 *(978-1-338-19701-3(0)*, Scholastic Pr.) Scholastic, Inc.
Weissman, D. S. Crown the King #2. 2016. (ENG., Illus.). 216p. (J). (gr. 8-12). pap. 12.99 *(978-1-68076-681-3(3)*, Epic Pr.) ABDO Publishing Co.
Weitz, Chris. The Revival. 2016. (Young World Ser.: 3). (ENG.). 272p. (YA). (gr. 10-17). 18.99 *(978-0-316-22634-9(3))* Little, Brown Bks. for Young Readers.
—The Young World. 2015. (Young World Ser.: 1). (ENG.). 400p. (YA). (gr. 10-17). pap. 19.99 *(978-0-316-22628-8(9))* Little, Brown Bks. for Young Readers.
Wells, Dan. Partials. (ENG.). (YA). 2013. (Partials Sequence Ser.: 1). 528p. (gr. 9). pap. 11.99 *(978-0-06-207105-7(X)*, Balzer & Bray) 2012. (Partials Sequence Ser.: 1). 480p. (gr. 9). 17.99 *(978-0-06-207104-0(1)*, Balzer & Bray) 2012. 496p. pap. 9.99 *(978-0-06-213569-8(4))* HarperCollins Pubs.
Wells, Robison. Feedback. (ENG.). (YA). 2013. (Variant Ser.: 2). 336p. (gr. 8). pap. 10.99 *(978-0-06-202611-8(9))* 2012. 320p. pap. 9.99 *(978-0-06-222830-7(7))* HarperCollins Pubs. (HarperTeen).
Westerfeld, Scott. Impostors, 1 vol. (Impostors Ser.). (ENG.). 416p. (YA). (gr. 7-7). 2021. 12.99 *(978-1-338-75790-3(3))* 2018. 18.99 *(978-1-338-15151-0(7)*, Scholastic Pr.) Scholastic, Inc.
—Shatter City (Impostors, Book 2) 2019. (Impostors Ser.: 2). (ENG.). 416p. (YA). (gr. 7-7). 18.99 *(978-1-338-15041-4(3)*, Scholastic Pr.) Scholastic, Inc.
Westerfeld, Scott & Lanagan, Margo. Swarm. 2018. (Zeroes Ser.: 2). lib. bdg. 24.50 *(978-0-606-40832-5(0))* Turtleback.
Westerfeld, Scott, et al. Swarm. (Zeroes Ser.: 2). (ENG.). (YA). (gr. 9). 2018. 480p. pap. 12.99 *(978-1-4814-4340-1(2))* 2016. (Illus.). 464p. 19.99 *(978-1-4814-4339-5(9))* Simon Pulse. (Simon Pulse).
White, Ellen Emerson. Voyage on the Great Titanic. 2010. (Dear America Ser.). (ENG., Illus.). 208p. (J). (gr. 3-9). 12.99 *(978-0-545-23834-2(X)*, Scholastic Pr.) Scholastic, Inc.
Wiggins, Bethany. Stung. 2014. (ENG.). 320p. (YA). (gr. 9). pap. 10.99 *(978-0-8027-3589-8(4)*, 900123276, Bloomsbury USA Childrens) Bloomsbury Publishing USA.
Williams, M. C. No where to be Found: Time Is Short. l.t. ed. 2006. 38p. per. 3.65 *(978-1-59879-099-3(4))* Lifevest Publishing, Inc.
Williams, Michael. Diamond Boy. 2014. (ENG., Illus.). 400p. (YA). (gr. 7-17). 18.00 *(978-0-316-32069-6(2))* Little, Brown Bks. for Young Readers.
—Now Is the Time for Running. 2013. (ENG.). 240p. (YA). (gr. 7-17). pap. 10.99 *(978-0-316-07788-0(7))* Little, Brown Bks. for Young Readers.
Williamson, Joshua. Disney Kingdoms: the Haunted Mansion #1. Coelho, Jorge & Beaulieu, Jean-François, illus. 2016. (Disney Kingdoms: the Haunted Mansion Ser.). (ENG.). 24p. (J). (gr. 1-5). lib. bdg. 31.36 *(978-1-61479-587-2(8)*, 24368, Graphic Novels) Spotlight.
—Disney Kingdoms: the Haunted Mansion #2. Coelho, Jorge & Beaulieu, Jean-François, illus. 2016. (Disney Kingdoms: the Haunted Mansion Ser.). (ENG.). 24p. (J). (gr. 1-5). lib. bdg. 31.36 *(978-1-61479-588-9(6)*, 24369, Graphic Novels) Spotlight.
—Disney Kingdoms: the Haunted Mansion #3. Coelho, Jorge & Beaulieu, Jean-François, illus. 2016. (Disney Kingdoms: the Haunted Mansion Ser.). (ENG.). 24p. (J). (gr. 1-5). lib. bdg. 31.36 *(978-1-61479-589-6(4)*, 24370, Graphic Novels) Spotlight.
—Disney Kingdoms: the Haunted Mansion #4. Coelho, Jorge & Beaulieu, Jean-François, illus. 2016. (Disney Kingdoms: the Haunted Mansion Ser.). (ENG.). 24p. (J). (gr. 1-5). lib. bdg. 31.36 *(978-1-61479-590-2(8)*, 24371, Graphic Novels) Spotlight.
—Disney Kingdoms: the Haunted Mansion #5. Coelho, Jorge & Beaulieu, Jean-François, illus. 2016. (Disney Kingdoms: the Haunted Mansion Ser.). (ENG.). 24p. (J). (gr. 1-5). lib. bdg. 31.36 *(978-1-61479-591-9(6)*, 24372, Graphic Novels) Spotlight.
Wilson, Diane Lee. Raven Speak. 2011. (ENG.). 256p. (YA). (gr. 7). pap. 11.99 *(978-1-4169-8654-6(5)*, McElderry, Margaret K. Bks.) McElderry, Margaret K. Bks.
Windover, Liz. Blood Island. Utomo, Gabhor, illus. 2014. (ENG.). 144p. (J). (gr. 4-8). mass mkt. 6.99 *(978-1-937133-46-7(X))* Chooseco LLC.
Winfield, Arthur M. The Rover Boys on Land & Sea or the Crusoes of Seven Islands. 2006. (ENG.). 284p. per. 28.95 *(978-1-4286-4097-9(5))* Kessinger Publishing, LLC.
Wolff, Tracy. Book 4: Arrival. Kinsella, Pat, illus. 2016. (Mars Bound Ser.). (ENG.). 48p. (J). (gr. 3-7). lib. bdg. 34.21 *(978-1-62402-200-5(6)*, 24579, Spellbound) Magic Wagon.
Wood, Gail. Lizzie, Light Feather & the Quarry Bluff Storm. 2015. (Illus.). viii, 88p. (J). pap. *(978-1-57249-415-2(8)*, White Mane Kids) White Mane Publishing Co., Inc.
Woods, Brenda. Saint Louis Armstrong Beach. 2012. lib. bdg. 16.00 *(978-0-606-26661-1(5))* Turtleback.
Woolley, Justin. A City Called Smoke: the Territory 2. 2015. (Territory Ser.: Bk. 2). (ENG., Illus.). 286p. (YA). pap. *(978-1-76030-089-0(6))* Momentum.
—A Town Called Dust: the Territory 1. 2015. (Territory Ser.: Bk. 1). (ENG., Illus.). 302p. (YA). pap. *(978-1-76030-037-1(3))* Momentum.
—A World of Ash: the Territory 3. 2016. (Territory Ser.: Bk. 3). (ENG., Illus.). 324p. (YA). pap. *(978-1-76030-245-0(7))* Momentum.
Wyss, Johann D. The Swiss Family Robinson (Abridged Edition) Abridged Edition. 2009. (Puffin Classics Ser.). 496p. (J). (gr. 5-7). pap. 8.99 *(978-0-14-132530-9(5)*, Puffin Books) Penguin Young Readers Group.
Wyss, Johann David. The Swiss Family Robinson. Monahan, Liz, illus. 2014. 46p. (J). *(978-1-4351-5826-9(1))* Barnes & Noble, Inc.
—The Swiss Family Robinson: Critical Reading Series. (Young Collector's Illustrated Classics Ser.). (Illus.). 192p. (J). (gr. 3-7). 9.95 *(978-1-56156-459-0(1))* Kidsbooks, LLC.
—Swiss Family Robinson: With a Discussion of Teamwork. Butterfield, Ned, illus. 2003. (Values in Action Illustrated Classics Ser.). 191p. (J). *(978-1-59203-036-1(X))* Learning Challenge, Inc.
Wyss, Johann David, illus. The Swiss Family Robinson. 2004. reprint ed. pap. 30.95 *(978-1-4191-5012-8(X))*; pap. 1.99 *(978-1-4192-5012-5(4))* Kessinger Publishing, LLC.
Wyss, Johann David & Kingston, William Henry Giles. The Swiss Family Robinson: A Translation from the Original German. 2016. (J). pap. *(978-1-5124-2612-0(1))* Lerner Publishing Group.
Yancey, Rick. The Infinite Sea. 2015. (5th Wave Ser.: 2). lib. bdg. 22.10 *(978-0-606-38204-5(6))* Turtleback.
—The Infinite Sea: The Second Book of the 5th Wave. 2015. (5th Wave Ser.: 2). (ENG.). 352p. (YA). (gr. 9-12). pap. 12.99 *(978-1-101-99698-0(6)*, Penguin Books) Penguin Young Readers Group.
—The Last Star. 2017. (5th Wave Ser.: 3). lib. bdg. 22.10 *(978-0-606-40098-5(2))* Turtleback.
—The Last Star: The Final Book of the 5th Wave. 2016. (5th Wave Ser.: 3). (ENG.). 352p. (YA). (gr. 9). 18.99 *(978-0-399-16243-5(7)*, G.P. Putnam's Sons Books for Young Readers) Penguin Young Readers Group.
—The 5th Wave. 2015. (5th Wave Ser.: Vol. 1). (ENG.). (YA). (gr. 9). lib. bdg. 21.60 *(978-1-62765-623-8(5))* Perfection Learning Corp.
—The 5th Wave. l.t. ed. 2016. (5th Wave Ser.: 1). 630p. pap. 12.99 *(978-1-59413-981-9(4)*, Large Print Pr.) Thorndike Pr.
—The 5th Wave. 2015. (5th Wave Ser.: 1). lib. bdg. 22.10 *(978-0-606-36640-3(7))*; lib. bdg. 22.10 *(978-0-606-37680-8(1))* Turtleback.
—The 5th Wave: The First Book of the 5th Wave Series. 2015. (5th Wave Ser.: 1). (ENG.). 512p. (YA). (gr. 9). pap. 12.99 *(978-0-14-242583-1(4)*, Penguin Books) Penguin Young Readers Group.
—The 5th Wave Collection, 3 vols. 2017. (5th Wave Ser.). (ENG.). (YA). (gr. 9). pap., pap., pap. 35.97 *(978-0-425-29032-3(8)*, Speak) Penguin Young Readers Group.
Yates, Alexander. How We Became Wicked. 2019. (ENG., Illus.). 368p. (YA). (gr. 9). 19.99 *(978-1-4814-1984-0(6)*, Atheneum Bks. for Young Readers) Simon & Schuster Children's Publishing.
Yolen, Jane. Trash Mountain. Monroe, Chris, illus. 2015. (ENG.). 184p. (J). (gr. 3-6). E-Book 27.99 *(978-1-4677-7170-2(8)*, Carolrhoda Bks.) Lerner Publishing Group.
Zeiss, Joyce Burns. Out of the Dragon's Mouth. 2015. (ENG., Illus.). 240p. (YA). (gr. 9-12). pap. 11.99 *(978-0-7387-4196-3(5)*, 0738741965, Flux) North Star Editions.

SURVIVAL AFTER AIRPLANE ACCIDENTS, SHIPWRECKS, ETC.
see Survival

SURVIVAL OF THE FITTEST
see Natural Selection

SUSPENSION BRIDGES
see Bridges

SUTTER, JOHN AUGUSTUS, 1803-1880

Dunn, Joe & National Geographic Learning Staff. The California Gold Rush, 1 vol. Dunn, Ben, illus. 2007. (Graphic History Ser.). (ENG.). 32p. (J). (gr. 3-8). 32.79 *(978-1-60270-076-5(1)*, 9038, Graphic Planet - Fiction) Magic Wagon.
Hayhurst, Chris. John Sutter: California Pioneer. (Primary Sources of Famous People in American History Ser.). 32p. 2009. (gr. 2-3). 47.90 *(978-1-60851-696-4(2))* 2003. (ENG., Illus.). (gr. 3-4). pap. 10.00 *(978-0-8239-4186-5(8)*, aff37eda-1381-403a-b5a9-85b6e6f409bf) 2003. (ENG., Illus.). (gr. 3-4). lib. bdg. 29.13 *(978-0-8239-4114-8(0)*, b82a395f-eb6e-4082-9b75-6930abc41d53, Rosen Reference) Rosen Publishing Group, Inc., The.
—John Sutter: California Pioneer = Pionero de California, 1 vol. 2003. (Famous People in American History / Grandes Personajes en la Historia de los Estados Unidos Ser.). (ENG & SPA., Illus.). 32p. (gr. 2-3). lib. bdg. 29.13 *(978-0-8239-4162-9(0)*, eda2d0cf-650b-4eb6-874a-1f34a319e096, Editorial Buenas Letras) Rosen Publishing Group, Inc., The.
—John Sutter: California Pioneer / Pionero de California. 2009. (Famous People in American History/Grandes personajes en la historia de los Estados Unidos Ser.). (ENG & SPA.). 32p. (gr. 2-3). 47.90 *(978-1-61512-549-4(3)*, Editorial Buenas Letras) Rosen Publishing Group, Inc., The.
—John Sutter: Pionero de California, 1 vol. 2003. (Grandes Personajes en la Historia de los Estados Unidos (Famous People in American History) Ser.). (SPA., Illus.). 32p. (gr. 3-4). lib. bdg. 29.13 *(978-0-8239-4138-4(8)*, 7d2240bd-1bb0-4be6-b4ce-4f1e9e94aa23, Editorial Buenas Letras) Rosen Publishing Group, Inc., The.
—John Sutter: Pionero de California (John Sutter: California Pioneer) 2009. (Grandes personajes en la historia de los Estados Unidos (Famous People in American History) Ser.). (SPA.). 32p. (gr. 2-3). 47.90 *(978-1-61512-803-7(4)*, Editorial Buenas Letras) Rosen Publishing Group, Inc., The.
Katirgis, Jane & Hayhurst, Chris. Meet John Sutter: California Gold Rush Pioneer, 1 vol. 2019. (Introducing Famous Americans Ser.). (ENG.). 32p. (gr. 3-4). pap. 11.53 *(978-1-9785-1142-2(6)*, f7a55a55-7f7b-419c-9ced-c5f1585fc501) Enslow Publishing, LLC.
Mattern, Joanne. America's Gold Rush: John Sutter & the Discovery of Gold in California. 2009. (Great Moments in American History Ser.). 32p. (gr. 3-3). 47.90 *(978-1-61513-139-6(6))* Rosen Publishing Group, Inc., The.

SUTTER'S FORT (SACRAMENTO, CALIF.)

Mattern, Joanne. America's Gold Rush: John Sutter & the Discovery of Gold in California. 2009. (Great Moments in American History Ser.). 32p. (gr. 3-3). 47.90 *(978-1-61513-139-6(6))* Rosen Publishing Group, Inc., The.

SWALLOWS

Savage, Stephen. Swallow, 1 vol. 2008. (Animal Neighbors Ser.). (ENG.). 32p. (gr. 3-3). pap. 11.60 *(978-1-4042-4576-1(6)*, 602b7345-1c9e-4c42-8a11-d23498b94586, Rosen Classroom); (Illus.). (J). lib. bdg. 28.93 *(978-1-4358-4999-0(X)*, 84cb058f-4507-4d25-bc73-fab685f1cbdd, PowerKids Pr.) Rosen Publishing Group, Inc., The.

SWALLOWS—FICTION

Collins, Rachel. Sidney Swallow Sings. 2010. 32p. pap. 15.95 *(978-0-557-44696-4(1))* Lulu Pr., Inc.
Howie, Vicki. The Easter Swallows. Grudina, Paola Bertolini, illus. 2007. 32p. (J). 10.95 *(978-0-8198-2360-1(0))* Pauline Bks. & Media.
Morpurgo, Michael. Dear Olly. Birmingham, Christian, illus. 2007. (ENG.). 128p. (gr. 4-7). mass mkt. 7.99 *(978-0-00-675333-9(7)*, HarperCollins Children's Bks.) HarperCollins Pubs. Ltd. GBR. Dist: HarperCollins Pubs.
Politi, Leo. Song of the Swallows. 2009. (ENG., Illus.). 32p. (J). (gr. 1). 16.95 *(978-0-89236-989-8(2))* Oxford Univ. Pr., Inc.
Rouss, Sylvia & Avalone, C. The Littlest Fish. 2008. 32p. 12.95 *(978-1-934440-53-7(1)*, Pitspopany Pr.) Simcha Media Group.
Wilde, Oscar. Le Prince Hereux. (FRE.). (J). pap. 15.95 *(978-2-07-051629-2(6))* Gallimard, Editions FRA. Dist: Distribooks, Inc.

SWAMPS
see Marshes

SWANS

Banks, Rosie. Nasty Swans. 2017. (Cutest Animals... That Could Kill You! Ser.). 24p. (J). (gr. 2-3). 48.90 *(978-1-5382-1088-8(6))* Stevens, Gareth Publishing LLLP.
Bodden, Valerie. Swans. 2012. (Amazing Animals Ser.). (ENG.). 24p. (J). (gr. 1-4). 24.25 *(978-1-58341-719-5(2)*, 22093, Creative Education) Creative Co., The.
Gray, Leon. Trumpeter Swan: The World's Largest Waterbird. 2013. (Even More SuperSized! Ser.). 24p. (J). (gr. k-3). lib. bdg. 26.99 *(978-1-61772-734-4(2))* Bearport Publishing Co., Inc.
Helget, Nicole Lea. Swans. 2009. (Living Wild Ser.). (ENG., Illus.). 48p. (J). (gr. 5-8). 22.95 *(978-1-58341-659-4(5)*, 22197, Creative Education) Creative Co., The.
Hoff, Mary King. Swans. 2005. (Wild World of Animals (Creative Education) Ser.). (Illus.). 32p. (J). (gr. 2-5). lib. bdg. 18.95 *(978-1-58341-354-8(5)*, Creative Education) Creative Co., The.
Meister, Cari. Do You Really Want to Meet a Swan? Fabbri, Daniele, illus. 2014. (Do You Really Want to Meet ... ? Ser.). (ENG.). 24p. (J). (gr. 1-4). lib. bdg. 27.10 *(978-1-60753-458-7(4)*, 15900) Amicus.
Meyer, Therese. The Little Ballerina & Her Friends the Swans. 2004. (Illus.). 52p. *(978-0-9750325-0-3(X))* Baby Swan.
—La Petite Ballerine et Ses Amis les Cygnes (The Little Ballerina & Her Friends the Swans) Meyer, Therese, illus. 2004. (FRE., Illus.). 52p. *(978-0-9750325-1-0(8))* Baby Swan.
Stewart, Melissa. Swans, 1 vol. 2008. (Animals, Animals Ser.). (ENG., Illus.). 48p. (gr. 5-5). lib. bdg. 32.64 *(978-0-7614-2530-4(6)*, 30893100-0484-48bf-b3d2-c341a43e684e) Cavendish Square Publishing LLC.

SWANS—FICTION

Andersen, Hans Christian. The Wild Swans. Lewis, Naomi, tr. Gilbert, Yvonne, illus. 2005. (ENG.). 48p. (J). 17.99 *(978-1-84148-164-7(5))* Barefoot Bks., Inc.
Anderson, Hans Christian. The Wild Swans: A Tale of Persistence. Lohmann, Renate, illus. 2006. (J). *(978-1-59939-093-2(0)*, Reader's Digest Young Families, Inc.) Studio Fun International.
Bradman, Tony. The Ugly Duckling Returns, 1 vol. Warburton, Sarah, illus. 2014. (After Happily Ever After Ser.). (ENG.). 56p. (J). (gr. 3-6). lib. bdg. 25.99 *(978-1-4342-7953-8(7)*, 124702, Stone Arch Bks.) Capstone.
Consugar, Beth. Swanee Day. Rottinger, Amy, illus. 2013. 24p. pap. 12.95 *(978-1-61244-176-4(9))* Halo Publishing International.
Dougherty, John. Bansi O'Hara & the Bloodline Prophecy. 2008. (Bansi O'Hara Ser.: 1). (ENG., Illus.). 288p. (J). (gr. 4-6). 22.44 *(978-0-440-86787-6(8))* Transworld Publishers Ltd. GBR. Dist: Children's Plus, Inc.
Duncan Edwards, Pamela. Honk! Cole, Henry, illus. 2014. 32p. pap. 8.00 *(978-1-61003-226-1(8))* Center for the Collaborative Classroom.
Dunn, Lynette. The Swans of Spindrift Lake. 2016. (ENG.). 117p. (J). pap. 10.95 *(978-1-78455-580-1(0)*, f11867fa-b455-4863-aaad-22663d23b107) Austin Macauley Pubs. Ltd. GBR. Dist: Baker & Taylor Publisher Services (BTPS).
Furukawa, Masumi, illus. The Ugly Duckling. 2007. (Flip-Up Fairy Tales Ser.). 24p. (J). (gr. -1-2). *(978-1-84643-095-4(X))* Child's Play International Ltd.
Grant, Cj. The Princess & the Swan. 2012. 48p. pap. 21.88 *(978-1-4669-1594-7(3))* Trafford Publishing.
Gulla, Rosemarie. On the Wings of the Swan. Undercuffler, Gary, illus. 2008. (Treasury of the Lost Scrolls Ser.). (ENG.). 32p. (J). (gr. 1-4). 17.99 *(978-0-9793000-0-4(2)*, Alazar Pr.) Royal Swan Enterprises, Inc.
Harvey, Tom. Guido, the Swan with an Attitude. 2011. 44p. (gr. -1). pap. 17.99 *(978-1-4269-6855-6(8))* Trafford Publishing.
Lane, Jessica E. The Secret of the Swans. 2009. 52p. pap. 31.99 *(978-1-4415-5517-5(X))* Xlibris Corp.
Leonard, Barry, ed. The Ugly Duckling. 2003. (Illus.). 12p. (J). (gr. k-4). reprint ed. 17.00 *(978-0-7567-6858-4(6))* DIANE Publishing Co.
Lewis, Karianna. Gladyus & the Voodoo Priestess. 2012. (ENG.). 21p. 15.99 *(978-1-300-00528-5(9))* Lulu Pr., Inc.
London, Jonathan. Little Swan, 0 vols. Rodanas, Kristina, illus. 2012. (ENG.). 32p. (J). (gr. -1-3). 17.99 *(978-0-7614-5523-3(X)*, 9780761455233, Two Lions) Amazon Publishing.
Martin, Rafe. Birdwing. 2007. (ENG.). 384p. (J). (gr. 7-12). pap. 7.99 *(978-0-439-21168-0(9)*, Levine, Arthur A. Bks.) Scholastic, Inc.
McGuire, Sarah. The Flight of Swans. 2018. (ENG.). 448p. (J). (gr. 4-8). 18.99 *(978-1-5124-4027-0(2)*, 9fb6e720-cb31-4131-933c-4199722cb62f, Carolrhoda Bks.) Lerner Publishing Group.
McLemore, Anna-Marie. Blanca & Roja. 2020. (ENG.). 400p. (YA). pap. 14.99 *(978-1-250-21163-7(8)*, 900186385) Square Fish.
McNamee, Barbara Oakley. Kelsey & Seattle. 2007. (J). pap. 15.00 *(978-0-8059-7428-7(8))* Dorrance Publishing Co., Inc.
Meadows, Daisy. Sophia the Snow Swan Fairy. 2012. (Illus.). 65p. (J). *(978-0-545-42600-8(6))* Scholastic, Inc.
Mini Cuentos: Atletas se Entrenan, Zorro y la Ciguena.Tr. of Mini Fairy Tales: Fox & the Swan. (SPA.). (J). (gr. k-4). 4.98 *(978-970-607-621-2(2))* Larousse, Ediciones, S. A. de C. V. MEX. Dist: Continental Bk. Co., Inc.
Novel Units. The Trumpet of the Swan Novel Units Student Packet. 2019. (ENG.). (J). pap. 13.99 *(978-1-56137-710-7(4)*, Novel Units, Inc.) Classroom Library Co.
—The Trumpet of the Swan Novel Units Teacher Guide. 2019. (ENG.). (J). pap. 12.99 *(978-1-56137-067-2(3)*, Novel Units, Inc.) Classroom Library Co.
Olsen, Kaki. Swan & Shadow: A Swan Lake Story. 2016. (ENG.). 299p. (YA). pap. 18.99 *(978-1-4621-1814-4(3)*, Sweetwater Bks.) Cedar Fort, Inc./CFI Distribution.
Parrish, Edith E. Sara the Purple Goose & Susan the Black Swan. 2010. 24p. pap. 17.99 *(978-1-4490-8879-8(1))* AuthorHouse.
Phillips, Vivian A. Swan. Date not set. (Illus.). 20p. (Orig.). (J). pap. *(978-1-888413-02-1(6))* Seasoning Quilting (Arts & Crafts).
Spudvilas, Anne. Swan Lake. 2019. (ENG.). 48p. (J). (gr. 5-9). 19.99 *(978-1-74331-845-4(6))* Allen & Unwin AUS. Dist: Independent Pubs. Group.
Tafuri, Nancy. Whose Chick Are You? 2007. (ENG., Illus.). 40p. (J). (gr. -1-k). 16.99 *(978-0-06-082514-0(6)*, Greenwillow Bks.) HarperCollins Pubs.
—Whose Chick Are You? Board Book: An Easter & Springtime Book for Kids. Tafuri, Nancy, illus. 2019. (ENG., Illus.). 38p. (J). (gr. -1 — 1). bds. 7.99 *(978-0-06-285739-2(8)*, Greenwillow Bks.) HarperCollins Pubs.
Weis, Ms. Jane. Silas the Special Swan. 2010. 28p. pap. 12.99 *(978-1-4500-3494-4(2))* Xlibris Corp.
Welsh, Lisa. Sammy Swan: The Big Storm. 2010. 24p. pap. 14.49 *(978-1-4490-7234-6(8))* AuthorHouse.
White, E. B. The Trumpet of the Swan. unabr. ed. 2004. 210p. (J). (gr. 4-7). pap. 38.00 incl. audio *(978-0-8072-8710-1(5)*, YA243SP, Listening Library) Random Hse. Audio Publishing Group.
—The Trumpet of the Swan 50th Anniversary. Marcellino, Fred, illus. 2020. (ENG.). 272p. (J). (gr. 3-7). pap. 9.99 *(978-0-06-440867-7(1)*, HarperCollins) HarperCollins Pubs.
Wood, David & Wood, Aimee. The Beautiful Swan. 2008. 24p. pap. 14.95 *(978-1-59858-624-4(6))* Dog Ear Publishing, LLC.
Zahler, Diane. Princess of the Wild Swans. 2013. (ENG., Illus.). 240p. (J). (gr. 3-7). pap. 6.99 *(978-0-06-200495-6(6)*, HarperCollins) HarperCollins Pubs.

SWEDEN

Ainsley, Dominic J. Sweden, Vol. 16. 2018. (European Countries Today Ser.). (Illus.). 96p. (J). (gr. 7). 34.60 *(978-1-4222-3992-6(6))* Mason Crest.
Anderson, Margaret J. Carl Linnaeus: Father of Classification, 1 vol. 2009. (Great Minds of Science Ser.). (ENG., Illus.). 128p. (gr. 5-6). lib. bdg. 35.93 *(978-0-7660-3009-1(1)*, b4a47fe9-85d9-4947-b0ad-cdbcc62f40db) Enslow Publishing, LLC.
—Carl Linnaeus: Genius of Classification, 1 vol. 2014. (Genius Scientists & Their Genius Ideas Ser.). (ENG.). 96p. (gr. 5-5). (J). 29.60 *(978-0-7660-6540-6(5)*, 83c9f646-5d58-49d7-b4fb-cf0e34a75de2); pap. 13.88 *(978-0-7660-6541-3(3)*, f46de9af-6872-45da-aa5e-e0751b90bbce) Enslow Publishing, LLC.
Barber, Nicola. Focus on Sweden, 1 vol. 2007. (World in Focus Ser.). (ENG., Illus.). 64p. (gr. 5-8). pap. 15.05 *(978-0-8368-6746-6(7)*, 83076e3e-bced-4a38-8f2d-76ba650b48eb); lib. bdg. 36.67 *(978-0-8368-6739-8(4)*,

S

ec62254c-d3ed-41a2-be8d-960c689fc31e) Stevens, Gareth Publishing LLLP. (Gareth Stevens Secondary Library).

Blomquist, Christopher. A Primary Source Guide to Sweden. (Countries of the World). 24p. (gr. 2-3). 2009. 42.50 (978-1-61512-046-8(7)) 2004. (ENG., Illus.). (J). lib. bdg. 26.27 (978-1-4042-2758-3(X), e65b0a40-4729-4814-9462-8829569c330b) Rosen Publishing Group, Inc., The. (PowerKids Pr.).

Devera, Czeena. Alfred Nobel. Bane, Jeff, illus. 2018. (My Early Library: My Itty-Bitty Bio Ser.). (ENG.). 24p. (J). (gr. k-1). lib. bdg. 30.64 (978-1-5341-2885-9(9), 211584) Cherry Lake Publishing.

Docalavich, Heather. Sweden. 2007. (European Union Ser.). (Illus.). 88p. (YA). (gr. 3-7). lib. bdg. 21.95 (978-1-4222-0063-6(9)) Mason Crest.

Docalavich, Heather & Indovino, Shaina C. Sweden. Bruton, John, ed. 2012. (Major European Union Nations Ser.). 64p. (J). (gr. 7). 22.95 (978-1-4222-2260-7(8)) Mason Crest.

Docalavich, Heather & Indovino, Shaina Carmel. Sweden. 2012. (J). pap. (978-1-4222-2291-1(8)) Mason Crest.

Dyan, Penelope. This Is Sweden — -A Kid's Guide to Stockholm, Swedem. Weigand, John D., photos by. 2011. (Illus.). 34p. pap. 11.95 (978-1-61477-003-9(4)) Bellissima Publishing, LLC.

Enderlein, Cheryl L. Christmas in Sweden, 1 vol. 2013. (Christmas Around the World Ser.). (ENG., Illus.). 24p. (J). (gr. 1-3). lib. bdg. 27.99 (978-1-62065-140-7(8), 120830, Capstone Pr.) Capstone.

Gofen, Ethel Caro, et al. Sweden, 1 vol. 3rd rev. ed. 2014. (Cultures of the World (Third Edition)(r) Ser.). (ENG., Illus.). 144p. (gr. 5-5). lib. bdg. 48.79 (978-1-5026-0074-5(9), 1baa17ef-96cb-4ea0-9622-5c013348820f) Cavendish Square Publishing LLC.

Grahame, Deborah. Sweden, 1 vol. 2007. (Discovering Cultures Ser.). (ENG., Illus.). 48p. (gr. 3-4). lib. bdg. 31.21 (978-0-7614-1985-3(3), 44b1f1a0-b948-4bb4-976a-0f5dc6b887ec) Cavendish Square Publishing LLC.

Hogan, Edward Patrick & Hogan, Joan Marie. Sweden. 2nd rev. ed. 2011. (ENG., Illus.). 128p. (gr. 6-12). 35.00 (978-1-61753-048-7(4), P197764, Facts On File) Infobase Holdings, Inc.

Hyde, Natalie. Cultural Traditions in Sweden. 2015. (Cultural Traditions in My World Ser.). (ENG., Illus.). 32p. (J). (gr. 2-3). (978-0-7787-8064-9(3)) Crabtree Publishing Co.

Johnson, Allen LeRoy. Sweden through the Eyes of a Six-year-old: Adventures with Grandchildren 2005. (Illus.). 180p. 15.00 (978-1-880675-06-9(4)) Creative Enterprises.

Kohen, Elizabeth, et al. Spain, 1 vol. 3rd rev. ed. 2013. (Cultures of the World (Third Edition)(r) Ser.). (ENG.). 144p. (gr. 5-5). 48.79 (978-1-60870-871-0(3), 26a9338f-9da3-4ea5-9d69-2a761b5a4bcf) Cavendish Square Publishing LLC.

Larsson, Carl. A Family: Paintings from a Bygone Age, 24 vols. 2007. (ENG., Illus.). 30p. (J). (gr. 1). (978-0-86315-583-3(9)) Floris Bks.

Lomberg, Michelle. Sweden. 2018. (Illus.). 32p. (J). (978-1-4896-7504-0(3), AV2 by Weigl) Weigl Pubs., Inc.

Mattern, Joanne. Sweden, 1 vol. 2017. (Exploring World Cultures (First Edition) Ser.). (ENG.). 32p. (gr. 3-3). pap. 12.16 (978-1-5026-3027-8(3), f8c94381-1487-4ac8-a181-61d331125007) Cavendish Square Publishing LLC.

McKenna, Amy, ed. Denmark, Finland, & Sweden, 4 vols. 2013. (Britannica Guide to Countries of the European Union Ser.). (ENG.). 256p. (YA). (gr. 10-10). 113.18 (978-1-61530-996-2(9), a450b3a6-a0da-42be-879a-6860b2350e8f); (Illus.). lib. bdg. 56.59 (978-1-61530-969-6(1), 89024dab-40d5-49f3-a4a8-9e74a86cfecb) Rosen Publishing Group, Inc., The.

Miles, Liz. Linnaeus Organising Nature: Band 18/Pearl. 2017. (Collins Big Cat Ser.). (ENG., Illus.). 80p. (J). pap. 12.99 (978-0-00-820897-4(2)) HarperCollins Pubs. Ltd. GBR. Dist: Independent Pubs. Group.

Murray, Julie. Sweden, 1 vol. 2014. (Explore the Countries Ser.). (ENG.). 40p. (J). (gr. 2-5). lib. bdg. 35.64 (978-1-62403-347-6(4), 1370, Big Buddy Bks.) ABDO Publishing Co.

Porterfield, Jason. Niklas Zennstrom & Skype, 1 vol. 2013. (Internet Biographies Ser.). (ENG., Illus.). 128p. (YA). (gr. 7-7). lib. bdg. 39.80 (978-1-4488-9527-4(8), 1b15dd92-9da4-4a93-b89e-31bc844a66a1, Rosen Classroom) Rosen Publishing Group, Inc., The.

—Sweden: A Primary Source Cultural Guide, 1 vol. 2003. (Primary Sources of World Cultures Ser.). (ENG., Illus.). 128p. (gr. 4-5). lib. bdg. 43.60 (978-0-8239-3841-4(7), c6b9fc19-f345-49a9-99c3-b8e8e0dba339) Rosen Publishing Group, Inc., The.

Rechner, Amy. Sweden. 2018. (Country Profiles Ser.). (ENG., Illus.). 32p. (J). (gr. 3-8). lib. bdg. 27.95 (978-1-62617-735-2(X), Blastoff! Discovery) Bellwether Media.

Rydaker, Ewa. Lucia Morning in Sweden. Lewis, Anne Gillespie, ed. Stahlberg, Carina, illus. 2014. (ENG.). 35p. (J). (gr. -1-3). pap. 8.99 (978-1-935666-65-3(7)) Nodin Pr.

Sexton, Colleen. Sweden. 2010. (Exploring Countries Ser.). (ENG., Illus.). 32p. (J). (gr. 3-7). lib. bdg. 27.95 (978-1-60014-490-5(X), Blastoff! Readers) Bellwether Media.

Zocchi, Judy. In Sweden. Brodie, Neale, illus. 2005. (Global Adventures II Ser.). 32p. (J). pap. 10.95 (978-1-59646-176-5(4)); lib. bdg. 21.65 (978-1-59646-087-4(3)); per. 10.95 (978-1-59646-177-2(2)) Dingles & Co.

—In Sweden/en Suecia. Brodie, Neale, illus. 2005. (Global Adventures I Ser.).Tr. of En Japón. (ENG & SPA.). 32p. (J). pap. 10.95 (978-1-59646-178-9(0)); lib. bdg. 21.65 (978-1-59646-088-1(1)); per. 10.95 (978-1-59646-179-6(9)) Dingles & Co.

SWEDEN—FICTION

Anderson, Hans Christian. Pictures of Sweden. 2006. pap. (978-1-4065-0860-4(8)) Dodo Pr.

Baier, Hiltrud. Greta in Schweden. 2009. 114p. pap. (978-3-8391-2523-6(5)) Books on Demand GmbH.

Dines, Carol. The Queen's Soprano. 2007. (ENG., Illus.). 336p. (YA). (gr. 9). pap. 18.95 (978-0-15-206102-9(9)) Houghton Mifflin Harcourt Publishing Co.

Gripe, Maria. The Glassblower's Children. Gripe, Harald, illus. 2019. (ENG.). 176p. (J). (gr. 3-7). pap. 11.99 (978-1-68137-378-2(5), NYRB Kids) New York Review of Bks., Inc., The.

Howard, Velma Swanston, tr. Wonderful Adventures of Nils. 2013. 354p. pap. (978-1-78139-369-7(9)) Benediction Classics.

Lagerlöf, Selma. The Further Adventures of Nils. 2005. pap. 31.95 (978-1-4179-9042-9(2)) Kessinger Publishing, LLC.

—The Further Adventures of Nils. Howard, Velma Swanston, tr. 2003. 284p. pap. 14.95 (978-1-59224-320-4(7)); 32.95 (978-1-59224-541-3(2)) Wildside Pr., LLC.

—The Wonderful Adventures of Nils. Howard, Velma Swanston, tr. 2007. 440p. per. (978-1-4065-2572-4(3)) Dodo Pr.

—The Wonderful Adventures of Nils. 2004. reprint ed. pap. 34.95 (978-1-4191-8845-9(3)); pap. 1.99 (978-1-4192-8845-6(8)) Kessinger Publishing, LLC.

—The Wonderful Adventures of Nils. 2009. 360p. (gr. 4-7). pap. 10.99 (978-1-60459-624-3(4)) Wilder Pubns., Corp.

—The Wonderful Adventures of Nils. Howard, Velma Swanston, tr. 2003. 284p. pap. 14.95 (978-1-59224-322-8(3)) Wildside Pr., LLC.

—The Wonderful Adventures of Nils. 2003. 32.95 (978-1-59224-745-5(8)) Wildside Pr., LLC.

Lewis, Beverly & Querin, Pamela. Annika's Secret Wish. 2006. (Illus.). 32p. (J). (gr. k-4). reprint ed. 15.00 (978-0-7567-9876-5(0)) DIANE Publishing Co.

Lindgren, Astrid. Pippi Longstocking. 2013. (Puffin Chalk Ser.). (ENG.). 160p. (J). (gr. 3-7). pap. 7.99 (978-0-14-242752-1(7), Puffin Books) Penguin Young Readers Group.

Lindgren, Astrid & Crampton, Patricia. The Red Bird. Tornqvist, Marit, illus. 2005. (J). 5.99 (978-0-439-62797-9(4), Levine, Arthur A. Bks.) Scholastic, Inc.

Lindman. Flicka, Ricka, Dicka & the Little Dog. Lindman, illus. 2013. (Flicka, Ricka, Dicka Ser.). (ENG., Illus.). 32p. (J). (gr. -1-3). 9.99 (978-0-8075-2509-8(X), 080752509X) Whitman, Albert & Co.

—Flicka, Ricka, Dicka & the New Dotted Dresses. Lindman, illus. 2012. (Flicka, Ricka, Dicka Ser.). (ENG., Illus.). 32p. (J). (gr. -1-3). 9.99 (978-0-8075-2484-8(0), 807524840) Whitman, Albert & Co.

—Flicka, Ricka, Dicka & the Strawberries. Lindman, illus. 2013. (Flicka, Ricka, Dicka Ser.). (ENG., Illus.). 32p. (J). (gr. -1-3). 9.99 (978-0-8075-2512-8(X), 080752512X) Whitman, Albert & Co.

—Flicka, Ricka, Dicka & the Three Kittens. Lindman, illus. 2013. (Flicka, Ricka, Dicka Ser.). (ENG., Illus.). 32p. (J). (gr. -1-3). 9.99 (978-0-8075-2515-9(4), 807525154) Whitman, Albert & Co.

—Flicka, Ricka, Dicka & Their New Skates. Lindman, illus. 2011. (Flicka, Ricka, Dicka Ser.). (ENG., Illus.). 32p. (J). (gr. -1-3). 9.99 (978-0-8075-2491-6(3), 807524913) Whitman, Albert & Co.

—Flicka, Ricka, Dicka Bake a Cake. Lindman, illus. 2013. (Flicka, Ricka, Dicka Ser.). (ENG., Illus.). 32p. (J). (gr. -1-3). 9.99 (978-0-8075-2506-7(5), 807525065) Whitman, Albert & Co.

—Flicka, Ricka, Dicka Go to Market. Lindman, illus. 2012. (Flicka, Ricka, Dicka Ser.). (ENG., Illus.). 32p. (J). (gr. -1-3). 9.99 (978-0-8075-2478-7(6), 807524786) Whitman, Albert & Co.

Lindman, Maj. Flicka, Ricka, Dicka & the New Dotted Dresses. 2012. (J). (978-0-8075-2495-4(6)) Whitman, Albert & Co.

Lois, Lowry. Number the Stars: And Related Readings. 2006. (Literature Connections Ser.). 172p. (gr. 6-12). (978-0-395-88457-7(8), 2-70863) Holt McDougal.

Mankell, Henning. A Bridge to the Stars. 2009. (Joel Gustafsson Ser.: No. 1). (ENG.). 176p. (YA). (gr. 7). pap. 7.99 (978-0-440-24042-6(5), Delacorte Bks. for Young Readers) Random Hse. Children's Bks.

—Journey to the End of the World. 2011. (Joel Gustafsson Ser.: No. 4). (ENG.). 208p. (YA). (gr. 7). pap. 8.99 (978-0-385-73498-1(0), Delacorte Bks. for Young Readers) Random Hse. Children's Bks.

—When the Snow Fell. 2011. (Joel Gustafsson Ser.: No. 3). (ENG.). 256p. (YA). (gr. 7). pap. 8.99 (978-0-440-24044-0(1), Delacorte Bks. for Young Readers) Random Hse. Children's Bks.

Oldfield, Matt. Zlatan: From the Playground to the Pitch. 2018. (Ultimate Football Heroes Ser.). (ENG., Illus.). 176p. (J). (gr. 2-7). pap. 11.99 (978-1-78606-810-1(9)) Blake, John Publishing, Ltd. GBR. Dist: Independent Pubs. Group.

Popper, Carol. David, Mormor, Horno & the Yak: An Alphabet Mystery. 2008. 24p. pap. 24.95 (978-1-4241-8772-0(9)) America Star Bks.

Thor, Annika. A Faraway Island. Schenck, Linda, tr. 2011. (Faraway Island Ser.: 1). 256p. (J). (gr. 3-7). 7.99 (978-0-375-84495-9(3), Yearling) Random Hse. Children's Bks.

—The Lily Pond. Schenck, Linda, tr. (Faraway Island Ser.). 224p. (J). (gr. 4-7). 2012. 7.99 (978-0-385-74040-1(9), Yearling)2. 2013. (ENG.). lib. bdg. 21.19 (978-0-385-90838-2(5), Delacorte Pr.) Random Hse. Children's Bks.

Uncle Markie. Piglett é & Bobo Have Visitors. 2003. (YA). ring bd. 9.95 (978-1-933129-12-9(3)) Studio 403.

SWEDES—UNITED STATES

Gunderson, Cory Gideon. Swedish Americans. 2003. (Immigrants in America Ser.). (ENG., Illus.). 112p. (gr. 6-12). 30.00 (978-0-7910-7131-1(6), P113738, Facts On File) Infobase Holdings, Inc.

SWEDES—UNITED STATES—FICTION

Shaw, Janet. Kirsten's Short Story Collection. Lewis, Kim & Graef, Renee, illus. 2006. (American Girls Collection). 213p. (J). (gr. 3-8). 12.95 (978-1-59369-323-7(0)) American Girl Publishing, Inc.

SWEDISH LANGUAGE

Modéré, Armelle & Hokenson, Linda. My First English/Swedish Dictionary of Sentences. 2008. (SWE & ENG.). 128p. (978-1-57534-049-4(6)) Skandisk, Inc.

SWIFT, JONATHAN, 1667-1745

Aykroyd, Clarissa. Savage Satire: The Story of Jonathan Swift. 2006. (World Writers Ser.). (Illus.). 160p. (J). (gr. 3-7). lib. bdg. 27.95 (978-1-59935-027-1(0)) Reynolds, Morgan Inc.

SWIFT, TOM (FICTITIOUS CHARACTER)—FICTION

ABDO Publishing Company Staff. Tom Swift, Young Inventor - 4 Titles. 2007. (Tom Swift, Young Inventor Ser.). (ENG.). 165p. 108.28 (978-1-59961-349-9(2)) Spotlight.

Appleton, Victor. The Adventures of Tom Swift. 2007. 456p. per. 19.95 (978-1-4344-9982-0(0)) Wildside Pr., LLC.

—The Alien Probe. (Tom Swift Ser.). (J). (gr. 3-7). 20.95 (978-0-88411-464-2(3)) Amereon Ltd.

—The City in the Stars. (Tom Swift Ser.). (J). (gr. 3-7). 20.95 (978-0-88411-463-5(5)) Amereon Ltd.

—Into the Abyss. 2007. (Tom Swift, Young Inventor Ser.). (ENG.). 160p. (gr. 3-7). 27.07 (978-1-59961-350-5(6)) Spotlight.

—The Rescue Mission. (Tom Swift Ser.). (J). (gr. 3-7). 20.95 (978-0-88411-458-1(9)) Amereon Ltd.

—The Robot Olympics, 2. 2006. (Tom Swift, Young Inventor Ser.: 2). (ENG.). 176p. (J). (gr. 3-7). pap. 7.99 (978-1-4169-1361-0(0)) Simon & Schuster, Inc.

—The Robot Olympics. 2007. (Tom Swift, Young Inventor Ser.). (ENG.). 160p. (gr. 4-7). 27.07 (978-1-59961-351-2(4)) Spotlight.

—Rocket Racers. 2007. (Tom Swift, Young Inventor Ser.: 4). (ENG.). 160p. (J). (gr. 3-7). pap. 6.99 (978-1-4169-3488-2(X), Aladdin) Simon & Schuster Children's Publishing.

—The Space Hotel. 2006. (Tom Swift, Young Inventor Ser.: 3). (ENG.). 160p. (J). (gr. 3-7). pap. 6.99 (978-1-4169-1751-9(9), Aladdin) Simon & Schuster Children's Publishing.

—The Space Hotel. 2007. (Tom Swift, Young Inventor Ser.). (ENG.). 160p. (gr. 4-7). 27.07 (978-1-59961-353-6(0)) Spotlight.

—Terror on the Moons of Jupiter. (Tom Swift Ser.). (J). (gr. 3-7). 20.95 (978-0-88411-460-4(0)) Amereon Ltd.

—Tom Swift among the Diamond Makers. 2005. 26.95 (978-1-4218-1086-7(7)); 196p. pap. 11.95 (978-1-4218-1186-4(3)) 1st World Publishing, Inc. (1st World Library - Literary Society).

—Tom Swift among the Diamond Makers. 2007. 224p. 29.95 (978-1-4344-9458-0(6)); per. 19.95 (978-1-4344-9457-3(8)) Wildside Pr., LLC.

—Tom Swift among the Diamond Makers or Th. 2006. pap. (978-1-4065-0892-5(6)) Dodo Pr.

—Tom Swift among the Fire Fighters. 2005. 27.95 (978-1-4218-1088-1(3)); 204p. pap. 12.95 (978-1-4218-1188-8(X)) 1st World Publishing, Inc. (1st World Library - Literary Society).

—Tom Swift among the Fire Fighters. 2006. (ENG.). pap. (978-1-4068-0726-4(5)) Echo Library.

—Tom Swift among the Fire Fighters. 2004. reprint ed. pap. 1.99 (978-1-4192-9047-3(9)); pap. 20.95 (978-1-4191-9047-6(4)) Kessinger Publishing, LLC.

—Tom Swift among the Fire Fighters or Bat. 2006. pap. (978-1-4065-0893-2(4)) Dodo Pr.

—Tom Swift & His Aerial Warship. 2005. 27.95 (978-1-4218-1092-8(1)); 212p. pap. 12.95 (978-1-4218-1192-5(8)) 1st World Publishing, Inc. (1st World Library - Literary Society).

—Tom Swift & His Aerial Warship. 2004. reprint ed. pap. 1.99 (978-1-4192-8451-9(7)) Kessinger Publishing, LLC.

—Tom Swift & His Aerial Warship or the. 2006. pap. (978-1-4065-0894-9(2)) Dodo Pr.

—Tom Swift & his Air Glider. 2005. 26.95 (978-1-4218-1500-8(1), 1st World Library - Literary Society) 1st World Publishing, Inc.

—Tom Swift & His Air Glider. 2004. reprint ed. pap. 20.95 (978-1-4191-8452-9(0)); pap. 1.99 (978-1-4192-8452-6(5)) Kessinger Publishing, LLC.

—Tom Swift & His Air Glider or Seeking. 2006. pap. (978-1-4065-0895-6(0)) Dodo Pr.

—Tom Swift & His Air Scout. 2005. 27.95 (978-1-4218-1091-1(3)); 208p. pap. 12.95 (978-1-4218-1191-8(X)) 1st World Publishing, Inc. (1st World Library - Literary Society).

—Tom Swift & His Air Scout. 2004. reprint ed. pap. 1.99 (978-1-4192-9048-0(7)); pap. 20.95 (978-1-4191-9048-3(2)) Kessinger Publishing, LLC.

—Tom Swift & His Air Scout or Uncle Sam. 2006. pap. (978-1-4065-0896-3(9)) Dodo Pr.

—Tom Swift & His Airship. 2005. 27.95 (978-1-59540-801-3(0), 1st World Library - Literary Society) 1st World Publishing, Inc.

—Tom Swift & His Airship. 2006. pap. (978-1-4065-0897-0(7)) Dodo Pr.

—Tom Swift & His Airship. 2007. 224p. 29.95 (978-1-4344-9460-3(8)); per. 19.95 (978-1-4344-9459-7(4)) Wildside Pr., LLC.

—Tom Swift & His Big Tunnel. 2005. 27.95 (978-1-4218-1093-5(X)); 216p. pap. 12.95 (978-1-4218-1193-2(6)) 1st World Publishing, Inc. (1st World Library - Literary Society).

—Tom Swift & His Big Tunnel. 2004. reprint ed. pap. 20.95 (978-1-4191-8454-3(7)); pap. 1.99 (978-1-4192-8454-0(1)) Kessinger Publishing, LLC.

—Tom Swift & His Big Tunnel or the Hidd. 2006. pap. (978-1-4065-0898-7(5)) Dodo Pr.

—Tom Swift & His Electric Locomotive. 2005. 27.95 (978-1-4218-1087-4(5)); 200p. pap. 12.95 (978-1-4218-1187-1(1)) 1st World Publishing, Inc. (1st World Library - Literary Society).

—Tom Swift & His Electric Locomotive: Or Two Miles a Minute on the Rails. 2007. (ENG.). 136p. pap. 18.99 (978-1-4346-1490-2(5)) Creative Media Partners, LLC.

—Tom Swift & His Electric Locomotive or. 2006. pap. (978-1-4065-0899-4(3)) Dodo Pr.

—Tom Swift & His Electric Rifle. 2005. 26.95 (978-1-59540-802-0(9), 1st World Library - Literary Society) 1st World Publishing, Inc.

—Tom Swift & His Electric Rifle. 2006. pap. (978-1-4065-0900-7(0)) Dodo Pr.

—Tom Swift & His Electric Runabout. 2004. reprint ed. pap. 20.95 (978-1-4191-8455-0(5)); pap. 1.99 (978-1-4192-8455-7(X)) Kessinger Publishing, LLC.

—Tom Swift & His Electric Runabout. 2007. 224p. 29.95 (978-1-4344-9462-7(4)); per. 19.95 (978-1-4344-9461-0(6)) Wildside Pr., LLC.

—Tom Swift & His Electric Runabout or T. 2006. pap. (978-1-4065-0901-4(9)) Dodo Pr.

—Tom Swift & His Electronic Electroscope. (J). (gr. 5-6). 20.95 (978-0-88411-462-8(7)) Amereon Ltd.

—Tom Swift & His Giant Cannon. 2005. 27.95 (978-1-4218-1089-8(1)); 204p. pap. 12.95 (978-1-4218-1189-5(8)) 1st World Publishing, Inc. (1st World Library - Literary Society).

—Tom Swift & His Giant Cannon. 2004. reprint ed. pap. 20.95 (978-1-4191-8456-7(3)); pap. 1.99 (978-1-4192-8456-4(8)) Kessinger Publishing, LLC.

—Tom Swift & His Giant Cannon or the Io. 2006. pap. (978-1-4065-0902-1(7)) Dodo Pr.

—Tom Swift & His Great Searchlight. 2005. 204p. pap. 12.95 (978-1-4218-1190-1(1), 1st World Library - Literary Society) 1st World Publishing, Inc.

—Tom Swift & his Great Searchlight. 2005. 27.95 (978-1-4218-1090-4(5), 1st World Library - Literary Society) 1st World Publishing, Inc.

—Tom Swift & His Great Searchlight. 2004. reprint ed. pap. 1.99 (978-1-4192-8457-1(6)); pap. 20.95 (978-1-4191-8457-4(1)) Kessinger Publishing, LLC.

—Tom Swift & His Great Searchlight or O. 2006. pap. (978-1-4065-0903-8(5)) Dodo Pr.

—Tom Swift & his Motor-Boat. 2005. 26.95 (978-1-4218-1501-5(X)); 196p. pap. 11.95 (978-1-4218-1600-5(8)); 192p. pap. 11.95 (978-1-4218-1601-2(6)) 1st World Publishing, Inc. (1st World Library - Literary Society).

—Tom Swift & his Motor-Cycle. 2005. 26.95 (978-1-4218-1502-2(8)); 192p. pap. 11.95 (978-1-4218-1602-9(4)) 1st World Publishing, Inc. (1st World Library - Literary Society).

—Tom Swift & His Motor Cycle. 2004. reprint ed. pap. 1.99 (978-1-4192-8459-5(2)) Kessinger Publishing, LLC.

—Tom Swift & His Motor-Cycle, Tom Swift & His Motor-Boat, Tom Swift & His Airship. 2007. 292p. per. 12.99 (978-1-60459-097-5(1)) Wilder Pubns., Corp.

—Tom Swift & His MotorBoat or the Rival. 2006. pap. (978-1-4065-0904-5(3)) Dodo Pr.

—Tom Swift & his Photo Telephone. 2005. 27.95 (978-1-4218-1503-9(6)); 204p. pap. 12.95 (978-1-4218-1603-6(2)) 1st World Publishing, Inc. (1st World Library - Literary Society).

—Tom Swift & His Photo Telephone or the. 2006. pap. (978-1-4065-0906-9(X)) Dodo Pr.

—Tom Swift & his Sky Racer. 2005. 26.95 (978-1-4218-1504-6(4)); 192p. pap. 11.95 (978-1-4218-1604-3(0)) 1st World Publishing, Inc. (1st World Library - Literary Society).

—Tom Swift & His Sky Racer. 2004. reprint ed. pap. 1.99 (978-1-4192-8461-8(4)) Kessinger Publishing, LLC.

—Tom Swift & His Sky Racer or the Quick. 2006. pap. (978-1-4065-0907-6(8)) Dodo Pr.

—Tom Swift & His Submarine Boat. 2004. reprint ed. pap. 20.95 (978-1-4191-8462-8(8)); pap. 1.99 (978-1-4192-8462-5(2)) Kessinger Publishing, LLC.

—Tom Swift & His Submarine Boat or Unde. 2006. pap. (978-1-4065-0908-3(6)) Dodo Pr.

—Tom Swift & His Triphibian Atomicar. (Tom Swift Ser.). (J). (gr. 5-6). 20.95 (978-0-88411-459-8(7)) Amereon Ltd.

—Tom Swift & His Undersea Search. 2007. 228p. 29.95 (978-1-4344-8363-8(0)); per. 17.95 (978-1-4344-8362-1(2)) Wildside Pr., LLC.

—Tom Swift & His Undersea Search or the. 2006. pap. (978-1-4065-0909-0(4)) Dodo Pr.

—Tom Swift & his War Tank. 2005. 27.95 (978-1-4218-1505-3(2)); 212p. pap. 12.95 (978-1-4218-1605-0(9)) 1st World Publishing, Inc. (1st World Library - Literary Society).

—Tom Swift & His War Tank. 2004. reprint ed. pap. 1.99 (978-1-4192-9054-1(1)); pap. 20.95 (978-1-4191-9054-4(7)) Kessinger Publishing, LLC.

—Tom Swift & His War Tank or Doing His. 2006. pap. (978-1-4065-0910-6(8)) Dodo Pr.

—Tom Swift & His Wireless Message. 2007. 220p. 24.95 (978-1-4344-9231-9(1)); per. 14.95 (978-1-4344-9137-4(4)) Wildside Pr., LLC.

—Tom Swift & his Wireless Message. 2005. 26.95 (978-1-4218-1506-0(0)); 196p. pap. 11.95 (978-1-4218-1606-7(7)) 1st World Publishing, Inc. (1st World Library - Literary Society).

—Tom Swift & His Wireless Message or Th. 2006. pap. (978-1-4065-0911-3(6)) Dodo Pr.

—Tom Swift & his Wizard Camera. 2005. 26.95 (978-1-4218-1507-7(9)); 196p. pap. 11.95 (978-1-4218-1607-4(5)) 1st World Publishing, Inc. (1st World Library - Literary Society).

—Tom Swift & His Wizard Camera or Thril. 2006. pap. (978-1-4065-0912-0(4)) Dodo Pr.

—Tom Swift & the Electronic Hydrolung. l.t. ed. 2007. (ENG.). 132p. pap. 19.99 (978-1-4346-3073-5(0)) Creative Media Partners, LLC.

—Tom Swift & the Visitor from Planet X. 2006. pap. (978-1-4065-0913-7(2)) Dodo Pr.

—Tom Swift Circling the Globe. 2007. 224p. 29.95 (978-1-4344-9464-1(0)); per. 19.95 (978-1-4344-9463-4(2)) Wildside Pr., LLC.

—Tom Swift in Captivity. 2005. 27.95 (978-1-4218-1508-4(7)); 200p. pap. 12.95 (978-1-4218-1608-1(3)) 1st World Publishing, Inc. (1st World Library - Literary Society).

—Tom Swift in Captivity. 2004. reprint ed. pap. 20.95 (978-1-4191-9056-8(3)); pap. 1.99 (978-1-4192-9056-5(8)) Kessinger Publishing, LLC.

—Tom Swift in Captivity or A Daring Escap. 2006. pap. (978-1-4065-0914-4(0)) Dodo Pr.

—Tom Swift in the Caves of Ice. 2005. 27.95 (978-1-4218-1509-1(5)); 204p. pap. 12.95 (978-1-4218-1609-8(1)) 1st World Publishing, Inc. (1st World Library - Literary Society).

—Tom Swift in the Caves of Ice or the Wre. 2006. pap. (978-1-4065-0915-1(9)) Dodo Pr.

—Tom Swift in the City of Gold. 2005. 27.95 (978-1-4218-1510-7(9)); 204p. pap. 12.95

(978-1-4218-1610-4(5)) 1st World Publishing, Inc. (1st World Library - Literary Society).
—Tom Swift in the City of Gold or Marvelo. 2006. pap. (978-1-4065-0916-8(7)) Dodo Pr.
—Tom Swift in the Land of Wonders. 2005. 27.95 (978-1-4218-1511-4(7)); 204p. pap. 12.95 (978-1-4218-1611-1(3)) 1st World Publishing, Inc. (1st World Library - Literary Society).
—Tom Swift in the Land of Wonders. 2004. reprint ed. pap. 20.95 (978-1-4191-9057-5(1)); pap. 1.99 (978-1-4192-9057-2(6)) Kessinger Publishing, LLC.
—Tom Swift in the Land of Wonders or the. 2006. pap. (978-1-4065-0917-5(5)) Dodo Pr.
—The Tom Swift Omnibus #1: Tom Swift & his Motor-Cycle, Tom Swift & His Motor-Boat, Tom Swift & His Airship. 2007. 292p. 24.95 (978-1-60459-098-2(X)) Wilder Pubns., Corp.
—The Tom Swift Omnibus #2: Tom Swift & His Submarine Boat, Tom Swift & His Electric Runabout, Tom Swift & His Wireless Message. 2007. 296p. per. 12.99 (978-1-60459-099-9(8)) Wilder Pubns., Corp.
—Tom Swift Omnibus #3: Tom Swift among the Diamond Makers, Tom Swift in the Caves of Ice, Tom Swift & His Sky Racer. 2007. 296p. per. 12.99 (978-1-60459-101-9(3)); per. 12.99 (978-1-60459-102-6(1)) Wilder Pubns., Corp.
—Tom Swift Omnibus #4: Tom Swift & His Electric Rifle, Tom Swift in the City of Gold, Tom Swift & His Air Glider. 2007. 304p. 24.95 (978-1-60459-103-3(X)); per. 12.99 (978-1-60459-104-0(8)) Wilder Pubns., Corp.
—Tom Swift Omnibus #5: Tom Swift in Captivity, Tom Swift & His Wizard Camera, Tom Swift & His Great Searchlight. 2007. 312p. 24.95 (978-1-60459-106-4(4)); per. 12.99 (978-1-60459-105-7(6)) Wilder Pubns., Corp.
—The Tom Swift Omnibus #6: Tom Swift & His Giant Cannon, Tom Swift & His Photo Telephone, Tom Swift & His Aerial Warship. 2007. 296p. 24.95 (978-1-60459-109-5(9)); per. 12.99 (978-1-60459-108-8(0)) Wilder Pubns., Corp.
—The Tom Swift Omnibus #7: Tom Swift & His Big Tunnel, Tom Swift in the Land of Wonders, Tom Swift & His War Tank. 2007. 312p. 24.99 (978-1-60459-111-8(0)); per. 12.99 (978-1-60459-110-1(2)) Wilder Pubns., Corp.
—The Tom Swift Omnibus #8: Tom Swift & His Air Scout, Tom Swift & His Undersea Search, Tom Swift among the Fire Fighters, Tom Swift & His Electri. 2007. 420p. per. 14.99 (978-1-60459-112-5(9)) Wilder Pubns., Corp.
—The Tom Swift Omnibus #8: Tom Swift & His Air Scout, Tom Swift & His Undersea Search, Tom Swift among the Fire Fighters,Tom Swift & His Electric. 2007. 420p. 29.99 (978-1-60459-113-2(7)) Wilder Pubns., Corp.
—The Tom Swift Treasury. 2007. 540p. per. 29.99 (978-1-934451-09-0(6)); 600p. per. 29.99 (978-1-934451-10-6(X)) Wilder Pubns., Corp.
Appleton, Victor & Appleton, Victor, II. Under the Radar. 2007. (Tom Swift, Young Inventor Ser.: 6). (ENG.). 160p. (J). (gr. 3-7). pap. 6.99 (978-1-4169-3644-2(0), Simon & Schuster/Paula Wiseman Bks.) Simon & Schuster/Paula Wiseman Bks.

SWIMMING

see also Diving

Abery, Julie. Yusra Swims. Deng, Sally, illus. 2020. 32p. (J). (gr. 1-3). 19.99 (978-1-56846-329-2(4), 18373, Creative Editions) Creative Co., The.
Adler, David A. America's Champion Swimmer: Gertrude Ederle. Widener, Terry, illus. 2005. (ENG.). 32p. (J). (gr. -1-3). reprint ed. pap. 11.99 (978-0-15-205251-5(8), 1195820, Clarion Bks.) HarperCollins Pubs.
Barr, Linda. The Water Patrol: Saving Surfers' Lives in Big Waves. 2005. (High Five Reading - Blue Ser.). (ENG., Illus.). 48p. (gr. 3-4). per. 9.00 (978-0-7368-5749-9(4)) Capstone.
Barth, Katrin & Dietze, Jurgen. Swimming: Training. 2004. (Illus.). 152p. pap. 14.95 (978-1-84126-145-4(9)) Meyer & Meyer Sport, Ltd. GBR. Dist: Lewis International, Inc.
Boudreau, Hélène. Swimming Science. 2008. (Sports Science Ser.). (ENG., Illus.). 32p. (J). (gr. 4-6). pap. (978-0-7787-4555-6(4)); lib. bdg. (978-0-7787-4538-9(4)) Crabtree Publishing Co.
Buckey, A. W. Women in Swimming. 2020. (She's Got Game Ser.). (ENG., Illus.). 32p. (J). (gr. 3-5). pap. 9.95 (978-1-64493-143-1(5), 1644931435); lib. bdg. 31.35 (978-1-64493-064-9(1), 1644930641) North Star Editions. (Focus Readers).
Buckley, James. Katie Ledecky. 2017. (Amazing Americans: Olympians Ser.). (ENG.). 24p. (J). (gr. -1-3). 26.99 (978-1-68402-240-3(1)) Bearport Publishing Co., Inc.
Bussiere, Desireé. Swimming by the Numbers, 1 vol. 2013. (Sports by the Numbers Ser.). (ENG.). 24p. (J). (gr. k-3). lib. bdg. 29.93 (978-1-61783-846-0(2), 13706, SandCastle) ABDO Publishing Co.
Capucilli, Alyssa Satin. My First Swim Class: Ready-To-Read Pre-Level 1. Wachter, Jill, photos by. 2018. (My First Ser.). (ENG., Illus.). 32p. (J). (gr. -1-k). 17.99 (978-1-5344-0488-5(0)); pap. 3.99 (978-1-5344-0487-8(2)) Simon Spotlight. (Simon Spotlight).
Crossingham, John. La Natation. 2009. (Sans Limites Ser.). (FRE., Illus.). 32p. (J). pap. 9.95 (978-2-89579-231-4(3)) Bayard Canada Livres CAN. Dist: Crabtree Publishing Co.
Crowe, Ellie. The Story of Olympic Swimmer Duke Kahanamoku, 1 vol. Waldrep, Richard, illus. 2019. (Story Of Ser.). (ENG.). 80p. (J). (gr. 4-8). 10.95 (978-1-62014-852-5(8), leelowbooks) Lee & Low Bks., Inc.
Davis, Marcia. Teach Your Child to Swim the Gentle Way: With Positive Reinforcement. 2011. 84p. pap. 19.95 (978-1-4626-0268-1(1)) America Star Bks.
Fishman, Jon M. Katie Ledecky. 2020. (Sports All-Stars (Lerner (tm) Sports) Ser.). (ENG., Illus.). 32p. (J). (gr. 2-5). 29.32 (978-1-5415-9750-1(8), 32a444bc-57c0-49f9-8263-7f9d3d9a6721, Lerner Pubns.) Lerner Publishing Group.
Flynn, Brendan. ¡Hora de Natación! (Swimming Time!) 2017. (Bumba Books (r) en Español — ¡Hora de Deportes! (Sports Time!) Ser.). (SPA., Illus.). 24p. (J). (gr. -1-1). 26.65 (978-1-5124-2875-9(2), f981954c-3b92-4d45-bbcb-bb5b80883de4, Ediciones Lerner) Lerner Publishing Group.
—Swimming Time! 2016. (Bumba Books (r) — Sports Time! Ser.). (ENG., Illus.). 24p. (J). (gr. -1-1). lib. bdg. 26.65 (978-1-5124-1435-6(2), a0a07b47-3499-4edd-8f79-f6b344561d55, Lerner Pubns.) Lerner Publishing Group.
Fox, Martha Capwell. Swimming. 2003. (History of Sports Ser.). (ENG., Illus.). 104p. (J). 30.85 (978-1-59018-073-0(9), Lucent Bks.) Cengage Gale.
Giff, Patricia Reilly. Horas de Sol.Tr. of Sunny Side Up. (SPA.). (J). 3.95 (978-0-922852-52-9(9)) AIMS International Bks., Inc.
Gifford, Clive. Swimming, 1 vol. 2010. (Tell Me about Sports Ser.). (ENG., Illus.). 32p. (gr. 4-4). 31.21 (978-0-7614-4462-6(9), 69c73e57-5015-492c-88fe-6e5fa7ffac2e) Cavendish Square Publishing LLC.
—Swimming, 1 vol. 2008. (Personal Best Ser.). (ENG., Illus.). 32p. (YA). (gr. 4-4). lib. bdg. 30.27 (978-1-4042-4443-6(3), 6b5a69a3-2755-4287-bb9e-64add0cdbd5d) Rosen Publishing Group, Inc., The.
—Swimming & Diving. 2011. (Olympic Sports Ser.). (ENG.). 32p. (J). (gr. 4-8). lib. bdg. 19.95 (978-1-60753-192-0(5), 17107) Amicus.
—Swimming & Diving. 2011. (ENG., Illus.). 32p. (J). pap. 10.95 (978-1-77092-039-2(0)) Saunders Bk. Co. CAN. Dist: RiverStream Publishing.
Goldish, Meish. Michael Phelps: Anything Is Possible! 2009. (Defining Moments Ser.). (Illus.). 32p. (YA). (gr. 2-5). lib. bdg. 28.50 (978-1-59716-855-7(6)) Bearport Publishing Co., Inc.
Grudzina, Rebecca. Tim's Swim. Piwowarski, Marcin, illus. 2017. (Text Connections Guided Close Reading Ser.). (J). (gr. k). (978-1-4900-1766-2(6)) Benchmark Education Co.
Hardman, Lizabeth. Swimming, 1 vol. 2011. (Science Behind Sports Ser.). (ENG., Illus.). 104p. (gr. 7-7). 41.03 (978-1-4205-0273-2(5), 8b7a3250-2748-4d14-b294-5927b08d0c8e, Lucent Pr.) Greenhaven Publishing LLC.
Heos, Bridget. Be Safe Around Water. Baroncelli, Silvia, illus. 2014. (Be Safe! Ser.). (ENG.). 24p. (J). (gr. 1-4). lib. bdg. 25.65 (978-1-60753-448-8(7), 15873) Amicus.
Herman, Gail. Make-A-Splash Writing Rules, 1 vol. 2009. (Grammar All-Stars: Writing Tools Ser.). (ENG.). 32p. (J). (gr. 2-4). pap. 11.50 (978-1-4339-2136-0(7), c15ed5fd-914d-4224-8a50-acb23bb541c7); lib. bdg. 28.67 (978-1-4339-1943-5(5), ab7445df-a43b-49bd-91ae-08f75610f86a) Stevens, Gareth Publishing LLLP. (Gareth Stevens Learning Library).
Hoena, Blake. Swimming. 2015. (J). lib. bdg. 25.65 (978-1-62031-182-0(8), Bullfrog Bks.) Jump! Inc.
Holden, Pam. Learning to Swim, 1 vol. 2015. (ENG., Illus.). 16p. (-1). pap. (978-1-77654-081-5(6), Red Rocket Readers) Flying Start Bks.
—Watch Me Swim, 1 vol. Hansen, Christine, illus. 2009. (Red Rocket Readers Ser.). (ENG.). 16p. (gr. -1-1). pap. (978-1-877363-31-3(6), Red Rocket Readers) Flying Start Bks.
Kear, Angela A. Mommy & Me Go to Swimming Lessons. 2012. 30p. pap. 15.95 (978-1-60594-929-1(9)) Aeon Publishing Inc.
Kehm, Greg. Olympic Swimming & Diving. (Great Moments in Olympic History Ser.). 48p. (gr. 5-6). 2009. 53.00 (978-1-61513-162-4(0), Rosen Reference) 2007. (ENG., Illus.). (YA). lib. bdg. 34.47 (978-1-4042-0970-1(0), f230c654-7ef6-4adb-bc81-9080dc33cd67) Rosen Publishing Group, Inc., The.
Kennedy, Mike. Michael Phelps, 1 vol. 2009. (People We Should Know (Second Series) Ser.). (ENG.). 48p. (J). (gr. 3-5). pap. 11.50 (978-1-4339-2151-3(0), c10eb56c-5cde-4362-a61e-2c47cff7d4b5); lib. bdg. 33.67 (978-1-4339-1950-3(8), 9c4d1374-f328-4c9d-9fa4-58c0d6e8c863) Stevens, Gareth Publishing LLLP. (Gareth Stevens Learning Library).
Kesselring, Susan. Around Water. 2018. (978-1-4896-9955-8(4), AV2 by Weigl) Weigl Pubs., Inc.
Knowlton, MaryLee. Safety Around Water. 2008. (Staying Safe Ser.). (ENG.). 32p. (J). (gr. -1-3). lib. bdg. (978-0-7787-4315-6(2)) Crabtree Publishing Co.
Lanser, Amanda. The Science Behind Swimming, Diving, & Other Water Sports. 2016. (Science of the Summer Olympics Ser.). (ENG., Illus.). 32p. (J). pap. 48.70 (978-1-4914-8169-1(2), 23985) Capstone.
LeBoutillier, Nate. Swimming. 2012. (J). 35.65 (978-1-60818-211-4(8), Creative Education) Creative Co., The.
Long, Jessica. Unsinkable: From Russian Orphan to Paralympic Swimming World Champion. 2018. (ENG., Illus.). 112p. (J). (gr. 5-7). 16.99 (978-1-328-70725-3(3), 1672841, Clarion Bks.) HarperCollins Pubs.
MacCallum, Jess. Swimming with the Fishes. 5th rev. ed. 2004. per. 5.95 (978-0-9749673-0-1(0)) In Ardua Tendit Pr.
Macy, Sue. Trudy's Big Swim: How Gertrude Ederle Swam the English Channel & Took the World by Storm. Collins, Matt, illus. 2019. 40p. (J). (gr. 1-4). pap. 8.99 (978-0-8234-4189-1(X)) Holiday Hse., Inc.
Manley, Claudia B. Ultra Swimming. 2009. (Ultra Sports Ser.). 64p. (gr. 5-8). 58.50 (978-1-60854-610-7(1), Rosen Reference) Rosen Publishing Group, Inc., The.
Mara, Wil. What Should I Do? at the Pool. 2011. (Community Connections: What Should I Do? Ser.). (ENG., Illus.). 24p. (gr. 2-5). lib. bdg. 29.21 (978-1-61080-056-3(7), 201054) Cherry Lake Publishing.
Markovics, Joyce L. Michael Phelps. 2017. (Amazing Americans: Olympians Ser.). (ENG., Illus.). 24p. (J). (gr. -1-3). 26.99 (978-1-68402-239-7(8)) Bearport Publishing Co., Inc.
Mason, Paul. How to Improve at Swimming. 2007. (How to Improve At- Ser.). (ENG., Illus.). 48p. (J). (gr. 3-7). pap. (978-0-7787-3592-2(3)); lib. bdg. (978-0-7787-3570-0(2)) Crabtree Publishing Co.
Minden, Cecilia. Jump In the Pool. 2018. (Little Blossom Stories Ser.). (ENG.). 16p. (J). (gr. -1-2). pap. 11.36 (978-1-5341-2864-4(6), 211513, Cherry Blossom Press) Cherry Lake Publishing.
—Swimming. 2008. (21st Century Skills Library: Real World Math Ser.). (ENG., Illus.). 32p. (gr. 4-8). lib. bdg. 32.07 (978-1-60279-246-3(1), 200197) Cherry Lake Publishing.
Morey, Allan. Swimming & Diving. 2015. (Summer Olympic Sports Ser.). (ENG., Illus.). 32p. (J). (gr. 2-4). 19.95 (978-1-60753-809-7(1)) Amicus Learning.
Nagle, Jeanne. What Happens to Your Body When You Swim, 1 vol. 2009. (How & Why of Exercise Ser.). (ENG., Illus.). 48p. (YA). (gr. 5-6). 34.47 (978-1-4358-5309-6(1), 5e299e4e-3890-4064-b215-9557e7d5e8f2) Rosen Publishing Group, Inc., The.
Nelson, Robin. Swimming Is Fun! 2013. (First Step Nonfiction — Sports Are Fun! Ser.). (ENG., Illus.). 24p. (J). (gr. k-2). pap. 6.99 (978-1-4677-1539-3(5), 42c94fd7-1ef2-4ed0-b11d-b8471d06523a) Lerner Publishing Group.
Orr, Tamra B. The Science of a Flip Turn. 2015. (21st Century Skills Library: Full-Speed Sports Ser.). (ENG., Illus.). 32p. (J). (gr. 4-7). 32.07 (978-1-63362-583-9(4), 206516) Cherry Lake Publishing.
Osborne, M. K. La Natación y Los Saltos Ornamentales. 2020. (Deportes Olímpicos de Verano Ser.). (SPA.). 32p. (J). (gr. 2-5). lib. bdg. (978-1-68151-898-5(8), 10702) Amicus.
Page, Jason. Swimming, Diving, & Other Water Sports. 2008. (Olympic Sports Ser.). (ENG., Illus.). 32p. (J). (gr. 3-7). pap. (978-0-7787-4036-0(6)); lib. bdg. (978-0-7787-4019-3(6)) Crabtree Publishing Co.
Peterson, Christine. The Science Behind Swimming, Diving, & Other Water Sports. 2016. (Science of the Summer Olympics Ser.). (ENG., Illus.). 32p. (J). (gr. 3-9). pap. 7.95 (978-1-4914-8161-5(7), 130640); lib. bdg. 28.65 (978-1-4914-8157-8(9), 130636) Capstone. (Capstone Pr.).
Rebman, Nick. Swimming. 2018. (Sports Ser.). (ENG., Illus.). 16p. (J). (gr. k-1). pap. 7.95 (978-1-64185-025-4(6), 1641850256); lib. bdg. 25.64 (978-1-63517-923-1(8), 1635179238) North Star Editions. (Focus Readers).
Rodomista, Kim. 101 Cool Pool Games for Children: Fun & Fitness for Swimmers of All Levels. Patterson, Robin, illus. 2006. (SmartFun Activity Bks.). (ENG.). 160p. (J). (gr. -1). per. 17.99 (978-0-89793-483-1(0), Hunter Hse.) Turner Publishing Co.
Romanek, Trudee. Splash It Swimming. 2012. (ENG., Illus.). 32p. (J). pap. (978-0-7787-3163-4(4)) Crabtree Publishing Co.
Ryan, Emma. Surprising Swimmers (Scholastic Reader, Level 2) 2013. (Scholastic Reader, Level 2 Ser.). (ENG.). 32p. (J). (gr. 1-3). pap. 3.99 (978-0-545-55266-0(4)) Scholastic, Inc.
Scheff, Matt. Simone Manuel. 2016. (Olympic Stars Ser.). (ENG., Illus.). 32p. (J). (gr. 3-9). lib. bdg. 32.79 (978-1-68078-560-9(5), 23803, SportsZone) ABDO Publishing Co.
Schuh, Mari. Swimming. 2019. (Spot Sports Ser.). (ENG.). 16p. (J). (gr. -1-1). pap. 7.99 (978-1-68152-439-9(2), 11025) Amicus.
Schwartz, Heather E. Simone Manuel: Swimming Star. 2018. (Women Sports Stars Ser.). (ENG., Illus.). 32p. (J). (gr. 3-9). lib. bdg. 28.65 (978-1-5157-9707-4(4), 136855, Capstone Pr.) Capstone.
Sheen, Barbara. Michael Phelps, 1 vol. 2010. (People in the News Ser.). (ENG.). 96p. (gr. 7-7). 41.03 (978-1-4205-0282-4(4), baa1dc84-fa5c-4cf4-a1db-87fa9a125f47, Lucent Pr.) Greenhaven Publishing LLC.
—Natalie Coughlin, 1 vol. 2013. (People in the News Ser.). (ENG., Illus.). 96p. (gr. 7-7). lib. bdg. 41.03 (978-1-4205-0998-4(5), 9ee2b0d3-5fb0-4f71-8489-cf3a897d2d94, Lucent Pr.) Greenhaven Publishing LLC.
Shofner, Melissa Raé. Let's Go Swimming, 1 vol. 2017. (Let's Get Active! Ser.). (ENG.). 24p. (J). (gr. 1-1). 25.27 (978-1-5081-6389-3(8), 16a5b107-c228-4991-8264-96d8b6c9bf05, PowerKids Pr.) Rosen Publishing Group, Inc., The.
Skinner, Tina. Hot Tubs & Spas: An Inspirational Design Guide, 1 vol. 2003. (ENG., Illus.). 144p. (gr. 10-13). pap. 24.95 (978-0-7643-1841-2(1), 2216) Schiffer Publishing, Ltd.
Spence, Kelly. Yusra Mardini: Refugee Hero & Olympic Swimmer. 2018. (Remarkable Lives Revealed Ser.). (ENG., Illus.). 32p. (J). (gr. 3-3). (978-0-7787-4711-6(5)); pap. (978-0-7787-4726-0(3)) Crabtree Publishing Co.
Timblin, Stephen. Swimming. 2008. (21st Century Skills Innovation Library: Innovation in Sports Ser.). (ENG., Illus.). 32p. (gr. 4-8). lib. bdg. 32.07 (978-1-60279-258-6(5), 200125) Cherry Lake Publishing.
Torsiello, David P. Michael Phelps: Swimming for Olympic Gold, 1 vol. 2009. (Hot Celebrity Biographies Ser.). (ENG., Illus.). 48p. (gr. 5-7). lib. bdg. 27.93 (978-0-7660-3591-1(3), ac24e243-5636-4b37-b61f-51163b4b62ec) Enslow Publishing, LLC.
Wendorff, Anne. Swimming. 2009. (My First Sports Ser.). (ENG., Illus.). 24p. (J). (gr. 2-5). lib. bdg. 26.95 (978-1-60014-326-7(1), Blastoff! Readers) Bellwether Media.
Wilson, CeCe. Baby Seal Learns to Swim, 1 vol. 2015. (Rosen REAL Readers: STEM & STEAM Collection). (ENG.). 8p. (gr. k-1). pap. 5.46 (978-1-4994-9580-5(3), ea3401d5-0759-4820-a347-45082fb1d5db, Rosen Classroom) Rosen Publishing Group, Inc., The.
Wood, Alix. You Can Be a Swimmer, 1 vol., Vol. 1. 2013. (Let's Get Moving! Ser.). (ENG.). 32p. (J). (gr. 3-4). 29.27 (978-1-4824-0287-2(4), dbd1c26c-ab1d-499a-bde2-71b8baf1d6ba); pap. 11.50 (978-1-4824-0288-9(2), 2294c06e-580b-4af6-aae5-3383e0933c73) Stevens, Gareth Publishing LLLP.
Zuehlke, Jeffrey. Michael Phelps (Revised Edition) 2009. pap. 40.95 (978-0-7613-4777-4(1)) Lerner Publishing Group.

SWIMMING—FICTION

Applegate, Katherine. Roscoe Riley Rules #4: Never Swim in Applesauce. Biggs, Brian, illus. 2016. (Roscoe Riley Rules Ser.: 4). (ENG.). 128p. (J). (gr. 1-5). pap. 6.99 (978-0-06-239251-0(4), HarperCollins) HarperCollins Pubs.
Ashby, Gaylene. STORY TIME A Collection of Three Children's Stories. 2008. 28p. 14.95 (978-1-4357-1929-3(8)) Lulu Pr., Inc.
Atkins, Jeannine. Preparadas... Listas... Ya! 2004. (SPA., Illus.). (J). (gr. k-3). spiral bd. (978-0-616-07274-5(0)) Canadian National Institute for the Blind/Institut National Canadien pour les Aveugles.
Atkins, Jill. Toad Swims for his Life! Mostyn, David, illus. 2004. (ENG.). 24p. (J). lib. bdg. 23.65 (978-1-59646-712-5(6)) Dingles & Co.
Battiste, Alyse. Super Sally's Fantastic Fun Day. 2007. (Illus.). 68p. (J). pap. 15.97 (978-0-9798217-1-4(1)) Candalyse Publishing.
Beinstein, Phoebe. ¡A nadar, Boots! (Swim, Boots, Swim!) Roper, Robert, illus. 2009. (Dora la Exploradora Ser.). (SPA.). 24p. (J). pap. 3.99 (978-1-4169-7939-5(5), Libros Para Ninos) Libros Para Ninos.
—Swim, Boots, Swim! Roper, Robert, illus. 2009. (Dora the Explorer Ser.: 29). (ENG.). 24p. (J). (gr. -1-2). pap. 3.99 (978-1-4169-7195-5(5), Simon Spotlight/Nickelodeon) Simon Spotlight/Nickelodeon.
Bentley, Sue. A Splash of Forever. 2014. (Magic Kitten Ser.: 14). lib. bdg. 16.00 (978-0-606-35684-8(3)) Turtleback.
—A Splash of Forever #14. Swan, Angela, illus. 2014. (Magic Kitten Ser.: 14). (ENG.). 128p. (J). (gr. 1-3). 6.99 (978-0-448-46797-9(6), Grosset & Dunlap) Penguin Young Readers Group.
Brigham, Marilyn. Swim!, 0 vols. Velasquez, Eric, illus. 2012. (ENG.). 24p. (J). (gr. -1-k). 7.99 (978-0-7614-6253-8(8), 9780761462538, Two Lions) Amazon Publishing.
Bringsvaerd, Tor Age. Ruffen: The Escape to Loch Ness. Hansen, Thore, illus. 2009. (Ruffen Ser.). 72p. (J). (gr. 1-4). 16.95 (978-0-9815761-2-1(5)) Mackenzie Smiles, LLC.
—Ruffen: The Sea Serpent Who Couldn't Swim. Hansen, Thore, illus. 2008. (Ruffen Ser.). 64p. (J). (gr. -1-3). 16.95 (978-0-9790347-9-4(5)) Mackenzie Smiles, LLC.
Brown, Kathryn. Freddy the Brave. 2010. (ENG.). 43p. pap. 12.50 (978-1-4461-2959-3(4)) Lulu Pr., Inc.
Bruna, Dick. Miffy Goes Swimming. 2004. (Illus.). 12p. bds. 5.99 (978-1-59226-204-5(X)) Big Tent Entertainment, Inc.
—Miffy va a Nadar/Miffy Goes Swimming. 2004. (SPA., Illus.). 12p. (J). bds. 5.99 (978-1-59226-209-0(0)) Big Tent Entertainment, Inc.
Bulion, Leslie. Uncharted Waters, 1 vol. 2009. 192p. (J). (gr. 3-7). pap. 7.95 (978-1-56145-485-3(0)) Peachtree Publishing Co. Inc.
Calame, Don. Swim the Fly. 2010. (ENG., Illus.). 352p. (YA). (gr. 9). pap. 11.99 (978-0-7636-4776-6(4)) Candlewick Pr.
Capdevila, Roser & Vendrell, Maria Martinez. El Agua Inquieta. 2003.Tr. of Rough Water. (SPA.). 24p. (J). 7.95 (978-84-233-1742-4(0)) Ediciones Destino ESP. Dist: Planeta Publishing Corp.
Carbone, Courtney. This Makes Me Scared: Dealing with Feelings. Kushnir, Hilli, illus. 2019. (Rodale Kids Curious Readers/Level 2 Ser.: 5). 32p. (J). (gr. -1-1). pap. 4.99 (978-1-63565-080-8(1), 9781635650808, Rodale Kids) Random Hse. Children's Bks.
Carpenter, Nancy, illus. Queen Victoria's Bathing Machine. 2014. (ENG.). 40p. (J). (gr. k-3). 18.99 (978-1-4169-2753-2(0), Simon & Schuster/Paula Wiseman Bks.) Simon & Schuster/Paula Wiseman Bks.
Caruso, D. A. Cool by the Pool. 2005. pap. 19.99 (978-0-9765953-0-4(3)) Mighty Kids Media.
Cassano, Carol E. A Journey to the Bottom of the Ocean: Heavenly Adventures Volume 2. 2011. 20p. pap. (978-1-4269-7335-2(7)) Trafford Publishing (UK) Ltd.
Chaconas, Dori. The Swimming Lesson. McCue, Lisa, illus. 2014. (Cork & Fuzz Ser.: 7). 32p. (J). (gr. 1-3). pap. 5.99 (978-0-448-48051-0(4), Penguin Young Readers) Penguin Young Readers Group.
Clement, Gary. Swimming, Swimming, 1 vol. 2015. (ENG., Illus.). 48p. (J). (gr. -1-2). 18.95 (978-1-55498-449-7(1)) Groundwood Bks. CAN. Dist: Publishers Group West (PGW).
Cornwall, Gaia. Jabari Jumps. Cornwall, Gaia, illus. 2017. (ENG., Illus.). 32p. (J). (gr. -1-3). 17.99 (978-0-7636-7838-8(4)) Candlewick Pr.
Cousins, Lucy. Maisy Learns to Swim: A Maisy First Experience Book. Cousins, Lucy, illus. 2015. (Maisy Ser.). (ENG., Illus.). 32p. (J). (-k). 7.99 (978-0-7636-7749-7(3)) Candlewick Pr.
Craig, Deborah Anne. Paddle, the Extraordinary Duck. Glueck, Michael Wells, ed. Karcz, Katherine, illus. 2011. 42p. pap. 19.95 (978-1-4583-6916-1(1)) Lulu Pr., Inc.
Crays, Lettie L. Timmy the Turtle Learns to Swim. Rollins, Joe, illus. 2011. 44p. (J). pap. 11.95 (978-1-937089-06-1(1)) Truth Bk. Pubs.
Crossan, Sarah. The Weight of Water. 2018. (ENG., Illus.). 240p. (J). pap. 10.99 (978-1-68119-954-2(8), 900194338, Bloomsbury Young Adult) Bloomsbury Publishing USA.
—The Weight of Water. 2018. (J). lib. bdg. 22.10 (978-0-606-41077-9(5)) Turtleback.
Crouse, Donna J. The Ruby Ring: The Whispering Cove Kids Club. 2005. 114p. pap. 12.99 (978-0-9765339-0-0(1)) Crouse, Donna J.
Crutcher, Chris. Whale Talk. (ENG.). (YA). 2018. 352p. (gr. 9). pap. 11.99 (978-0-06-268775-3(1)) 2009. 304p. (gr. 8). pap. 9.99 (978-0-06-177131-6(7)) HarperCollins Pubs. (Greenwillow Bks.).
—Whale Talk. 2004. 224p. (J). (gr. 7-18). pap. 38.00 incl. audio (978-0-8072-2289-8(5), Listening Library) Random Hse. Audio Publishing Group.
Curr, Martin. Sharp Claws Learns to Swim. 2010. 26p. pap. 21.99 (978-1-4535-1414-6(7)) Xlibris Corp.
Dale, Jay. Our Special Rock Pool. Everitt-Stewart, Andrew, illus. 2012. (Engage Literacy Green Ser.). (ENG.). 16p. (J). (gr. k-2). pap. 36.94 (978-1-4296-9011-9(9), 18400, Capstone Pr.) Capstone.
Dale, Jay & Scott, Kay. Our Special Rock Pool, 1 vol. Everitt-Stewart, Andrew, illus. 2012. (Engage Literacy Green Ser.). (ENG.). 16p. (J). (gr. k-2). pap. 6.99 (978-1-4296-9009-6(7), 120013, Capstone Pr.) Capstone.
D'Ath, Justin. Pool. 2009. 297p. (Orig.). (YA). (978-1-876462-51-2(5)) Ford Street Publishing Pty, Limited.
Degman, Lori. Norbert's Big Dream. Bucci, Marco, illus. 2016. (ENG.). 32p. (J). (gr. k-3). 16.99 (978-1-58536-959-1(4), 204108) Sleeping Bear Pr.
Devoles, Margaret. My Aunt Calls Me Saree. 2007. 88p. per. 19.95 (978-1-4241-7579-6(8)) America Star Bks.
Dewdney, Anna. Llama Llama Learns to Swim. 2018. (Llama Llama 8X8 Ser.). lib. bdg. 14.75 (978-0-606-41334-3(0)) Turtleback.
Dewdney, Anna, creator. Llama Llama Learns to Swim. 2018. (Llama Llama Ser.). (Illus.). 24p. (J). (gr. -1-1). pap. 5.99 (978-1-5247-8719-6(1), Penguin Young Readers Licenses) Penguin Young Readers Group.

S

Diersch, Sandra. False Start, 1 vol. 2005. (Lorimer Sports Stories Ser.: 78). (ENG.). 104p. (J). (gr. 4-8). 8.95 (978-1-55028-872-8(5), 872); (gr. 3-7). 17.44 (978-1-55028-873-5(3), 873) James Lorimer & Co. Ltd., Pubs. CAN. Dist: Formac Lorimer Bks. Ltd., Children's Plus, Inc.

Dipinto, Michael J. The Princess Mermaid & the Missing Sea Shells. Marsh, Bobbie, illus. 2013. 36p. pap. 15.95 (978-1-61493-151-5(8)) Peppertree Pr., The.

Doty, M. Surviving High School. 2012. (Surviving High School Ser.: 1). (ENG.). 224p. (YA). (gr. 7-17). pap. 13.99 (978-0-316-22015-6(9), Poppy) Little, Brown Bks. for Young Readers.

Dubose, Sarah. Uncharted Waters. 2013. 440p. pap. (978-1-4596-6282-7(2)) ReadHowYouWant.com, Ltd.

Dubovoy, Silvia. Turquesita. (SPA.). (J). pap. (978-968-6465-18-1(9)) Casa de Estudios de Literatura y Talleres Artisticos Amaquemecan A.C. MEX. Dist: Lectorum Pubns., Inc.

Dyan, Penelope. Courtney's Beach. Dyan, Penelope, illus. 2008. (Illus.). 44p. pap. 11.95 (978-1-935118-35-0(8)) Bellissima Publishing, LLC.

—Summer Surfs the Olympic Trials. 2008. 168p. pap. 11.95 (978-1-935118-06-0(4)) Bellissima Publishing, LLC.

East, Vastine. I Swam with an Angel. 2011. 52p. pap. 31.99 (978-1-4653-5059-6(4)) Xlibris Corp.

Elliott, Rebecca. Eva at the Beach: a Branches Book (Owl Diaries #14) Elliott, Rebecca, illus. 2021. (Owl Diaries: 14). (ENG., Illus.). 80p. (J). (gr. k-2). pap. 5.99 (978-1-338-29879-6(8)) Scholastic, Inc.

—Eva at the Beach: a Branches Book (Owl Diaries #14) (Library Edition) Elliott, Rebecca, illus. 2021. (Owl Diaries: 14). (ENG., Illus.). 80p. (J). (gr. k-2). lib. bdg. 24.99 (978-1-338-29881-9(X)) Scholastic, Inc.

Faris, Stephanie. Piper Morgan Makes a Splash. Fleming, Lucy, illus. 2017. (Piper Morgan Ser.: 4). (ENG.). 96p. (J). (gr. 1-4). pap. 5.99 (978-1-4814-5717-0(9), Simon & Schuster/Paula Wiseman Bks.) Simon & Schuster/Paula Wiseman Bks.

Feinstein, John. Rush for the Gold: Mystery at the Olympics (the Sports Beat, 6) 2013. (Sports Beat Ser.: 6). 320p. (J). (gr. 5). pap. 10.99 (978-0-375-87168-9(3), Yearling) Random Hse. Children's Bks.

Fenn, G. Manville. Brownsmith's Boy. 2008. 260p. pap. 15.95 (978-1-60664-154-5(9)) Aegypan.

Figiel, Lisa. Swimming Is Fun! 2010. 24p. pap. 11.49 (978-1-4490-5520-2(6)) AuthorHouse.

Gallagher, Diana G. Pool Problem: The Complicated Life of Claudia Cristina Cortez, 1 vol. Garvey, Brann, illus. 2009. (Claudia Cristina Cortez Ser.). (ENG.). 88p. (J). (gr. 4-8). 27.32 (978-1-4342-1577-2(6), 95750, Stone Arch Bks.) Capstone.

Galvin, Laura Gates. Baby Polar Bear Learns to Swim. 2008. (Smithsonian Baby Animals Ser.). (ENG., Illus.). 16p. (gr. -1-k). 13.95 (978-1-59249-786-7(1)); (J). 6.95 (978-1-59249-785-0(3)) Soundprints.

Garis, Howard Roger. Sammie & Susie Littletail. 2005. 26.95 (978-1-4218-1465-0(X), 1st World Library - Literary Society) 1st World Publishing, Inc.

Garratt, Irene Joyce. Andrew's Activities: Two in One Stories. 2009. (Illus.). 20p. pap. 10.49 (978-1-4389-4235-3(4)) AuthorHouse.

Garton, Sam. Otter: Let's Go Swimming! Garton, Sam, illus. 2017. (My First I Can Read Ser.). (ENG., Illus.). 32p. (J). (gr. -1-3). pap. 4.99 (978-0-06-236663-4(7), Balzer & Bray) HarperCollins Pubs.

Garton, Sam, illus. Otter: Let's Go Swimming! 2017. 32p. (J). (978-1-5182-4207-6(3), Balzer & Bray) HarperCollins Pubs.

Glover, Darryl. The Pirate Kitty. Austin, Britta, ed. Kosir, Ana, illus. 2008. 24p. (J). 16.95 (978-0-9821387-0-0(9)) MagicStar Inc.

Going Swimming: KinderConcepts Individual Title Six-Packs. (Kinderstarters Ser.). 8p. (gr. -1-1). 21.00 (978-0-7635-8731-4(1)) Rigby Education.

Gottschalk, Bre. The Lucky Necklace. 2011. 24p. pap. 11.99 (978-1-4389-8725-5(0)) AuthorHouse.

Gough, Simon. I Can'T Fly & I Can'T Swim. 2011. (Illus.). 24p. pap. 11.44 (978-1-4567-8063-0(8)) AuthorHouse.

Green, Poppy. Forget-Me-Not Lake. Bell, Jennifer A., illus. 2015. (Adventures of Sophie Mouse Ser.: 3). (ENG.). 128p. (J). (gr. k-4). 17.99 (978-1-4814-3000-5(9), Little Simon) Little Simon.

—Forget-Me-Not Lake. Bell, Jennifer A., illus. 2017. (Adventures of Sophie Mouse Ser.). (ENG.). 128p. (J). (gr. k-4). lib. bdg. 31.36 (978-1-5321-4112-6(2), 26985, Chapter Bks.) Spotlight.

Greve, Meg. Swim for It! DuFalla, Anita, illus. 2011. (Little Birdie Readers Ser.). (ENG.). 24p. (gr. k-1). 28.50 (978-1-61741-805-1(6), 9781617418051) Rourke Educational Media.

Hambleton, Laura. Chameleon Swims, 1 vol. Choudhury, Dorbesh, tr. 2005. (Chameleon Ser.). (ENG., Illus.). 16p. (J). (gr. -1). bds. 8.95 (978-1-84059-437-9(3)) Milet Publishing.

Hancock, H. Irving. The Grammar School Boys in Summer Athletics. rev. ed. 2006. 216p. 27.95 (978-1-4218-1748-4(9)); pap. 12.95 (978-1-4218-1848-1(5)) 1st World Publishing, Inc. (1st World Library - Literary Society).

—The Grammar School Boys in Summer Athletics. 2018. (ENG., Illus.). 174p. (YA). (gr. 7-12). pap. (978-93-5297-410-8(7)) Alpha Editions.

—The Grammar School Boys in Summer Athletics. 2007. 184p. per. (978-1-4065-1982-2(0)) Dodo Pr.

—The Grammar School Boys in Summer Athletics: Or, Dick & Co. Make Their Fame Secure. 2017. (ENG., Illus.). (J). 23.95 (978-1-374-93018-6(0)); pap. 13.95 (978-1-374-93017-9(2)) Capital Communications, Inc.

—The Grammar School Boys in Summer Athletics: Or, Dick & Co. Make Their Fame Secure. 2017. (ENG., Illus.). (J). pap. (978-0-649-59640-9(4)); pap. (978-0-649-10906-7(6)) Trieste Publishing Pty Ltd.

Haslett, Katherine A. The Day Amy Met the Prime Minister & Mrs. Blair. 2007. (Illus.). 32p. (J). pap. 8.00 (978-0-8059-7353-2(2)) Dorrance Publishing Co., Inc.

Herbertson, Lisa. Swimming Along. Kennedy, Catherine, illus. 2011. 26p. pap. 12.00 (978-1-60976-293-3(2), Eloquent Bks.) Strategic Book Publishing & Rights Agency (SBPRA).

Hicks, Betty. Swimming with Sharks / Track Attack: Two Books in One. McCauley, Adam, illus. 2010. (Gym Shorts Ser.). (ENG.). 128p. (J). (gr. 2-4). pap. 16.99 (978-0-312-60237-6(5), 900064236) Square Fish.

Hofmeister, Alan, et al. Swim with Us. (Reading for All Learners Ser.). (Illus.). (J). pap. (978-1-56861-140-2(4)) Swift Learning Resources.

Holm, Jennifer L. & Holm, Matthew. Babymouse #20: Babymouse Goes for the Gold. Holm, Jennifer L. & Holm, Matthew, illus. 2016. (Babymouse Ser.: 20). (ENG., Illus.). 96p. (J). (gr. 2-5). pap. 6.99 (978-0-307-93163-4(3)) Penguin Random Hse. LLC.

—The Power of the Parasite. 2012. (Squish Ser.: 3). lib. bdg. 17.20 (978-0-606-26405-1(1)) Turtleback.

—Squish #3: the Power of the Parasite. Holm, Jennifer L. & Holm, Matthew, illus. 2012. (Squish Ser.: 3). (Illus.). 96p. (J). (gr. 2-5). pap. 6.99 (978-0-375-84391-4(4), Random Hse. Bks. for Young Readers) Random Hse. Children's Bks.

Howells, Amanda. The Summer of Skinny Dipping. (YA). 2019. 320p. (gr. 8-12). pap. 10.99 (978-1-4926-9671-1(4)) 2010. (ENG.). 304p. (gr. 7-12). pap. 9.99 (978-1-4022-3862-8(2)) Sourcebooks, Inc.

I love to Swim. 2004. (J). per. (978-1-57657-473-7(3)) Paradise Pr., Inc.

Isabel, Michelle. Murtle the Sea Turtle. Isabel, Michelle & Thomas, Franselica, illus. 2011. 24p. pap. 24.95 (978-1-4626-0114-1(6)) America Star Bks.

James, Simon. Querido Salvatierra. de la Vega, Eida, tr. from ENG. 2003.Tr. of Dear Mr. Blueberry. (SPA.). (J). (gr. k-2). pap. 8.99 (978-1-930332-45-4(9)) Lectorum Pubns., Inc.

Jansson, Tove. Moomin's Winter Follies. 2012. (Moomin Ser.). (ENG., Illus.). 48p. (J). (gr. 4-7). pap. 9.95 (978-1-77046-098-0(5), 900087417) Drawn & Quarterly Pubns. CAN. Dist: Macmillan.

Jennie Lyon Wood. Bath Time Bears Have So Much Fun. Kristie Kryssing, illus. 2009. 24p. pap. 12.99 (978-1-4389-4420-3(9)) AuthorHouse.

Jentsch, R. D. Froggy & Friends Go to the Creek, 1 vol. Jentsch, Joyce Harp, illus. 2009. 41p. pap. 24.95 (978-1-60836-966-9(8)) America Star Bks.

Johnson, Grace. The Little Fish Who Was Afraid to Swim. 2008. 36p. pap. 15.49 (978-1-4389-2262-1(0)) AuthorHouse.

Kang, Anna. Can I Tell You a Secret? Weyant, Christopher, illus. 2016. (ENG.). 40p. (J). (gr. -1-3). 17.99 (978-0-06-239684-6(6), HarperCollins) HarperCollins Pubs.

Kemp, Dane. Imaginary Tales. 2011. 186p. pap. 24.95 (978-1-4560-4686-6(1)) America Star Bks.

Kessler, Liz. The Tail of Emily Windsnap. Gibb, Sarah, illus. 2012. (Emily Windsnap Ser.: 1). (ENG.). 224p. (J). (gr. 3-7). pap. 6.99 (978-0-7636-6020-8(5)) Candlewick Pr.

—The Tail of Emily Windsnap. 2012. (Emily Windsnap Ser.: Bk. 1). lib. bdg. 16.00 (978-0-606-25544-8(3)) Turtleback.

Kim, YunYeong. Brown Bear's Dream. Kim, KyeMahn, illus. rev. ed. 2014. (MySELF Bookshelf Ser.). (ENG.). 32p. (J). (gr. k-2). pap. 11.94 (978-1-60357-655-0(X)); lib. bdg. 25.27 (978-1-59953-646-0(3)) Norwood Hse. Pr.

Kirby, Stan. Captain Awesome Takes a Dive. O'Connor, George, illus. 2012. (Captain Awesome Ser.: 4). (ENG.). 128p. (J). (gr. k-4). 17.99 (978-1-4424-4203-0(4)); pap. 6.99 (978-1-4424-4202-3(6)) Little Simon. (Little Simon).

—Captain Awesome Takes a Dive. 2012. (Captain Awesome Ser.: 4). lib. bdg. 14.75 (978-0-606-26325-2(X)) Turtleback.

Knudsen, Michelle. Fish & Frog Big Book: Brand New Readers. Petrone, Valeria, illus. 2010. (Brand New Readers Ser.). (ENG.). 48p. (J). (gr. -1-3). pap. 24.99 (978-0-7636-4810-7(8)) Candlewick Pr.

Koerner, Miranda Pike. Blue Mermaid. 2013. 210p. pap. 12.99 (978-1-62237-202-7(6)) Turquoise Morning Pr.

Koffsky, Ann. Noah's Swim-A-Thon. 2016. (ENG.). 32p. (J). pap. 9.95 (978-1-68115-519-7(2), 52caebb3-d65b-4e90-b35e-d0a856084982, Apples & Honey Pr.) Behrman Hse., Inc.

Koffsky, Ann D. Noah's Swim-A-Thon. 2010. (J). (978-0-8074-1168-1(X)) URJ Pr.

Kovalski, Maryann. Omar on Board, 1 vol. (ENG., Illus.). 32p. (J). (gr. k-2). 2007. 6.95 (978-1-55455-033-3(5), 3004aa42-52a5-46f1-8a96-10ede06c1961) 2005. 9.95 (978-1-55041-918-4(8), 7d9c1192-3556-42ca-98d3-6d2aa997bf2f) Trifolium Bks., Inc. CAN. Dist: Firefly Bks., Ltd.

Lach, Will. Norman Rockwell's a Day in the Life of a Girl. Rockwell, Norman, illus. 2017. (ENG.). 60p. (J). (gr. -1-3). 16.95 (978-0-7892-1290-0(0), 791290, Abbeville Kids) Abbeville Pr., Inc.

Larsen, Alison. Thomas the Turtle. 2006. (Illus.). 21p. (J). per. 14.95 (978-1-60002-097-1(6), 3961) Mountain Valley Publishing, LLC.

Leaf, Autumn. Coto, Child of the Ocean. 2008. 122p. pap. 19.95 (978-1-60703-843-6(9)) America Star Bks.

Lepp, Royden. Barnabas Goes Swimming, 1 vol. Lepp, Royden, illus. 2008. (I Can Read! / Barnabas Ser.). (ENG., Illus.). 32p. (J). (gr. -1-1). pap. 4.99 (978-0-310-71584-9(9)) Zonderkidz.

Lewis, Edwina. Who Swims? Parker, Ant, illus. 2003. (Who... Ser.). 16p. (YA). (978-1-85602-448-8(2), Pavilion Children's Books) Pavilion Bks.

The Long Legged Turtle. 2013. 44p. pap. 16.99 (978-1-4808-0460-9(6)) Archway Publishing.

Long, Tammy J. Like a Fish. 2010. (J). pap. 7.95 (978-1-932715-81-1(9)) UMI (Urban Ministries, Inc.).

Luebbe, Tara & Cattie, Becky. Shark Nate-O. Duncan, Daniel, illus. 2018. (ENG.). 40p. (J). (gr. -1-3). 17.99 (978-1-4998-0496-6(2)) Little Bee Books Inc.

Lyles, Tanya. The Frog That Needed an Umbrella. 2006. 17.00 (978-0-8059-9906-8(X)) Dorrance Publishing Co., Inc.

MacGregor, Jill. Swim Safe Little Seals. 2006. (Illus.). 31p. (J). 14.95 (978-0-9774062-0-3(2)) Seal Publishing, LLC.

Mack, Winnie. After All, You're Callie Boone. 2013. (ENG.). 192p. (J). (gr. 4-7). pap. 14.99 (978-1-250-02735-1(7), 900098307) Square Fish.

Maddox, Jake. Diving off the Edge, 1 vol. Tiffany, Sean, illus. 2009. (Jake Maddox Sports Stories Ser.). (ENG.). 72p. (J). (gr. 3-6). lib. bdg. 25.99 (978-1-4342-1205-4(X), 95402, Stone Arch Bks.) Capstone.

—Pool Panic. Wood, Katie, illus. 2016. (Jake Maddox Girl Sports Stories Ser.). (ENG.). 72p. (J). (gr. 3-6). lib. bdg. 25.32 (978-1-4965-2618-2(X), 131174, Stone Arch Bks.) Capstone.

Maddox, Jake & Maddox, Jake. Gold Medal Swim, 1 vol. Garcia, Eduardo, illus. 2012. (Jake Maddox Sports Stories Ser.). (ENG.). 72p. (J). (gr. 3-6). pap. 5.95 (978-1-4342-3902-0(0), 118087); lib. bdg. 25.99 (978-1-4342-3288-5(3), 116252) Capstone. (Stone Arch Bks.).

Martin, Ann M. Jessi's Gold Medal (the Baby-Sitters Club #55) 2017. (Scholastic Reader, Level 1 Ser.: 55). (ENG.). 160p. (J). (gr. -1-k). E-Book 4.99 (978-0-545-69049-2(8)) Scholastic, Inc.

Mayer, Mercer. Just a Day at the Pond. Mayer, Mercer, illus. 2008. (Little Critter Ser.). (ENG., Illus.). 24p. (J). (gr. -1-2). pap. 3.99 (978-0-06-053961-0(5), HarperFestival) HarperCollins Pubs.

McBride, Anthony. The Fish That Was Afraid to Swim. 2013. (ENG.). 52p. pap. 21.88 (978-1-4669-9388-4(X)) Trafford Publishing.

McCarthy, Jenna & Evans, Carolyn. Maggie Malone Makes a Splash. 2015. (Maggie Malone Ser.: 3). (ENG.). 192p. (J). (gr. 4-7). pap. 8.99 (978-1-4022-9312-2(7)) Sourcebooks, Inc.

Mcdonald, Megan. Stink & the Freaky Frog Freakout. Reynolds, Peter H., illus. 2019. (Stink Ser.). (ENG.). 160p. (J). (gr. 1-5). lib. bdg. 31.36 (978-1-5321-4331-1(1), 31861, Chapter Bks.) Spotlight.

McDonald, Megan. Stink & the Freaky Frog Freakout. Reynolds, Peter H., illus. 2013. (Stink Ser.: 8). (ENG.). 160p. (J). (gr. 1-4). 15.99 (978-0-7636-6140-3(6)) Candlewick Pr.

Mcdonald, Megan. Stink & the Freaky Frog Freakout. 2014. (Stink Ser.: 8). lib. bdg. 14.75 (978-0-606-35164-5(7)) Turtleback.

McFarlane, Susannah. Making Waves: EJ12 Girl Hero. 2017. 128p. (J). pap. 5.99 (978-1-61067-508-6(8)) Kane Miller.

McGhee, Patti Gray. Ducky Bill's Great Race. Vermillion, Danny, illus. 2013. 46p. 24.95 (978-1-63000-424-8(3)); 48p. pap. 24.95 (978-1-62709-522-8(5)) America Star Bks.

McQuinn, Anna. Leo Can Swim. Hearson, Ruth, illus. 2016. (Leo Can! Ser.). (ENG.). 24p. (J). (— 1). lib. bdg. 9.95 (978-1-58089-725-9(8)) Charlesbridge Publishing, Inc.

McVoy, Terra Elan. In Deep. 2014. (ENG., Illus.). 304p. (YA). (gr. 9). 17.99 (978-1-4814-0136-4(X), Simon Pulse) Simon Pulse.

Metzger, Steve. Five Little Sharks Swimming in the Sea. Bryant, Laura, illus. 2004. (J). (978-0-439-66139-3(0)); pap. (978-0-439-59228-4(3)) Scholastic, Inc.

Molski, Carol. Swimming Sal. DePalma, Mary Newell, illus. 2009. 36p. (J). (gr. -1-3). 17.00 (978-0-8028-5327-1(7), Eerdmans Bks For Young Readers) Eerdmans, William B. Publishing Co.

Montgomery, Lewis B. The Case of the Purple Pool. Wummer, Amy, illus. 2011. (Milo & Jazz Mysteries Ser.). pap. 39.62 (978-0-7613-8358-1(1));No. 7. 96p. (J). lib. bdg. 22.60 (978-1-57565-343-3(5)) Astra Publishing Hse.

—The Case of the Purple Pool (Book 7), No. 7. Wummer, Amy, illus. 2011. (Milo & Jazz Mysteries Ser.). 96p. (J). (gr. 2-6). pap. 6.99 (978-1-57565-342-6(7), 3b6d083b-f85b-48d6-aeec-cf0f69f8882b, Kane Press) Astra Publishing Hse.

Morpurgo, Michael. Mairi's Mermaid. 2006. (Blue Bananas Ser.). (ENG., Illus.). 48p. (J). (gr. -1-3). lib. bdg. (978-0-7787-0851-3(9)) Crabtree Publishing Co.

Morrison, Laurie. Up for Air. 2019. (ENG., Illus.). 288p. (YA). (gr. 5-9). 16.99 (978-1-4197-3366-6(4), 1215601, Amulet Bks.) Abrams, Inc.

Muller, Hildegard. The Cowboy. 2015. (I Like to Read Ser.). (ENG., Illus.). 24p. (J). (gr. -1-3). 7.99 (978-0-8234-3316-2(1)) Holiday Hse., Inc.

Nickelodeon. Swim, Boots, Swim! 2013. (Dora the Explorer 8X8 Ser.). lib. bdg. 13.55 (978-0-606-31933-1(6)) Turtleback.

Northrop, Michael. Surrounded by Sharks. 2014. (ENG.). 224p. (YA). (gr. 4-7). 18.99 (978-0-545-61545-7(3), Scholastic Pr.) Scholastic, Inc.

Ntihemuka, Patty Froese. Hyacinth Doesn't Grow Up: And Hyacinth Doesn't Drown. 2010. (J). pap. 10.99 (978-0-8163-2386-9(0)) Pacific Pr. Publishing Assn.

Oliver, Helen. Ellen's First Swim. 2009. 32p. pap. 16.49 (978-1-4389-9828-2(7)) AuthorHouse.

O'Ryan, Ray. Drake Makes a Splash! Jack, Colin, illus. 2014. (Galaxy Zack Ser.: 8). (ENG.). 128p. (J). (gr. k-4). pap. 6.99 (978-1-4424-9360-5(7), Little Simon) Little Simon.

Panckridge, Michael & Harvey, Pam. In the Deep End. 2007. (ENG.). 220p. (978-0-207-20064-9(5)) HarperCollins Pubs. Australia.

Pants Makes the Swim Team. 2004. (J). per. 7.99 (978-0-9755959-2-3(X)) Girl Named Pants, Inc., A.

PeachMoon Publishing. The Adventures of Lucky the Lizard Las aventuras del lagarto Lucky. 2008. (ENG & SPA., Illus.). 100p. (J). pap. 19.95 (978-0-9795831-4-8(4)) PeachMoon Publishing.

Petersen, Pat. The Turtle Who Couldn't Swim. Pham, Xuan, illus. 2012. 28p. 24.95 (978-1-4626-8615-5(X)); pap. 24.95 (978-1-4626-4847-4(9)) America Star Bks.

Polak, Monique. Flip Turn, 1 vol. 2004. (Lorimer Sports Stories Ser.: 67). (ENG.). 104p. (J). (gr. 4-8). 16.95 (978-1-55028-819-3(9), 819) James Lorimer & Co. Ltd., Pubs. CAN. Dist: Formac Lorimer Bks. Ltd.

Qualey, Marsha. Gracie Laroo at Pig Jubilee. Litten, Kristyna, illus. 2017. (Gracie Laroo Ser.). (ENG.). 40p. (J). (gr. k-2). lib. bdg. 21.32 (978-1-5158-1442-9(4), 135712, Picture Window Bks.) Capstone.

—Gracie Laroo Goes to School. Litten, Kristyna, illus. 2017. (Gracie Laroo Ser.). (ENG.). 40p. (J). (gr. k-2). lib. bdg. 21.32 (978-1-5158-1440-5(8), 135710, Picture Window Bks.) Capstone.

—Gracie Laroo Sets Sail. Litten, Kristyna, illus. 2017. (Gracie Laroo Ser.). (ENG.). 40p. (J). (gr. k-2). lib. bdg. 21.32 (978-1-5158-1439-9(4), 135709, Picture Window Bks.) Capstone.

—The Marvelous, Amazing, Pig-Tastic Gracie Laroo! Litten, Kristyna & Litten, Kristyna, illus. 2018. (Gracie Laroo Ser.). (ENG.). 128p. (J). (gr. k-2). pap., pap., pap. 5.95 (978-1-5158-1458-0(0), 135717, Picture Window Bks.) Capstone.

Random House. Hide-And-Go-Swim! (Bubble Guppies) MJ Illustrations, illus. 2014. (ENG.). 12p. (J). (— 1). bds. 5.99 (978-0-385-38515-2(3), Random Hse. Bks. for Young Readers) Random Hse. Children's Bks.

—Swim, Boots, Swim! (Dora the Explorer) Random House, illus. 2013. (Pictureback(R) Ser.). (ENG., Illus.). 24p. (J). (gr. -1-2). 3.99 (978-0-449-81850-3(0), Random Hse. Bks. for Young Readers) Random Hse. Children's Bks.

Ratto, Linda Lee. Perfection. 2004. (YA). per. 16.95 (978-0-9748508-3-2(7)) Power Pr.

Reed, Lynn Rowe. Swim to the Moon. 2009. 32p. pap. 12.99 (978-1-4389-4980-2(4)) AuthorHouse.

Reh, Rusalka. The Secret of the Water Knight, 0 vols. Derbyshire, Katy, tr. unabr. ed. 2011. (ENG.). 100p. (J). (gr. 4-7). pap. 9.95 (978-1-61109-006-2(7), 9781611090062, Two Lions) Amazon Publishing.

Reis, Jason & Hurley, Meagan. The Adventures of Burt: Burt & the Big Race. 2012. 28p. pap. 19.99 (978-1-4634-4126-5(6)) AuthorHouse.

Reynolds Naylor, Phyllis. Alice the Brave. 2011. (Alice Ser.: 7). (ENG., Illus.). 176p. (J). (gr. 5-9). pap. 7.99 (978-1-4424-2851-5(1)) Simon & Schuster, Inc.

RH Disney. Just Keep Swimming (Disney/Pixar Finding Nemo) Harchy, Atelier Philippe, illus. 2005. (Step into Reading Ser.). (ENG.). 32p. (J). (gr. k-3). pap. 4.99 (978-0-7364-2319-9(2), RH/Disney) Random Hse. Children's Bks.

Rippin, Sally. The Deep End. Fukuoka, Aki, illus. 2016. (ENG.). 48p. (J). pap. 4.99 (978-1-61067-390-7(5)) Kane Miller.

Rocco, John & Primiano, Jay. Swim That Rock. Rocco, John, illus. 2017. (ENG., Illus.). 304p. (J). (gr. 7). pap. 7.99 (978-0-7636-9447-0(9)) Candlewick Pr.

Rockwell, Anne. Katie Catz Makes a Splash. Meisel, Paul, illus. 2003. (Good Sports Ser.). 40p. (J). (gr. -1-1). 15.99 (978-0-06-028441-1(2)) HarperCollins Pubs.

Rosen, Robert. Not Yet! Grott, Isabella, illus. 2017. (Play Time Ser.) (ENG.). 24p. (J). (gr. -1-2). pap. 9.95 (978-1-68342-766-7(1), 9781683427667) Rourke Educational Media.

Rylant, Cynthia. Brownie & Pearl Take a Dip. Biggs, Brian, illus. 2011. (Brownie & Pearl Ser.). (ENG.). 24p. (J). (gr. -1-3). 16.99 (978-1-4169-8638-6(3), Beach Lane Bks.) Beach Lane Bks.

Scholastic, Inc. Staff. Peppa Goes Swimming. 2015. (Peppa Pig 8X8 Ser.). lib. bdg. 13.55 (978-0-606-37082-0(X)) Turtleback.

Schuurmans, Hilde. Sidney Won't Swim. Schuurmans, Hilde, illus. (Illus.). pap. 6.95 (978-1-57091-515-4(6)) Charlesbridge Publishing, Inc.

Scotton, Rob. Splish, Splash, Splat! Scotton, Rob, illus. 2011. (Splat the Cat Ser.). (ENG., Illus.). 40p. (J). (gr. -1-3). 16.99 (978-0-06-197868-5(X), HarperCollins) HarperCollins Pubs.

Seuling, Barbara. Robert Goes to Camp. Brewer, Paul, illus. 2007. (Robert Bks.). (ENG.). 160p. (J). (gr. k-4). 16.95 (978-0-8126-2753-4(9)) Cricket Bks.

Skinner, Vicky. How to Breathe Underwater. 2019. (ENG.). 352p. (YA). pap. 10.99 (978-1-250-30924-2(7), 900198436) Square Fish.

Smith Dinbergs, Holly. Pool Pals. Maddock, Monika, illus. 2005. (Girlz Rock! Ser.). (J). pap. (978-1-59336-705-3(8)) Mondo Publishing.

Snider, Ann. The Giant Sea & Me. 2008. (Illus.). 24p. pap. 14.99 (978-1-4389-1720-7(1)) AuthorHouse.

Spalding, Andrea. Seal Song, 1 vol. Milelli, Pascal, illus. 2011. (ENG.). 32p. (J). (gr. -1-k). 19.95 (978-1-55469-242-2(3)) Orca Bk. Pubs. USA.

Stroke of Luck (Swimming) 64p. (YA). (gr. 6-12). pap. 10.95 (978-0-8224-6482-2(9)) Globe Fearon Educational Publishing.

Sue-A-Quan, Goomatie. A Seal Fascination at Sea: A Fascinating Seal. 2008. (Illus.). 38p. (J). pap. 19.00 (978-0-8059-7517-8(9)) Dorrance Publishing Co., Inc.

Swimming Lessons with Stewie the Duck. 2005. (J). 9.95 (978-0-9668611-3-6(2)) Kimberly Pr., LLC.

Terada, Junzo. Animal Friends: Swimming Hole Party! (Animal Books for Toddlers, Jungle Animal Board Book) 2017. (Animal Friends Ser.). (ENG., Illus.). 10p. (J). bds. 9.99 (978-1-4521-4983-7(6)) Chronicle Bks. LLC.

Thaler, Mike. The Pool Party from the Black Lagoon. Lee, Jared D., illus. 2016. 64p. (J). pap. (978-0-545-85073-5(8)) Scholastic, Inc.

Thomas, Cameron. Mystery of the Lake. Krystoforski, Andrej, illus. 2004. (Jungle of Utt Ser.). 40p. (J). 16.95 (978-0-921800-02-6(9)) MGT Developments, Ltd. CAN. Dist: Independent Pubs. Group.

Trueit, Trudi. Mom, There's a Dinosaur in Beeson's Lake. Paillot, Jim, illus. 2011. (Secrets of a Lab Rat Ser.). (ENG.). 160p. (J). (gr. 3-7). pap. 6.99 (978-1-4169-6112-3(7), Aladdin) Simon & Schuster Children's Publishing.

—Mom, There's a Dinosaur in Beeson's Lake, 2. Paillot, Jim, illus. 2010. (Secrets of a Lab Rat Ser.). (ENG.). 160p. (J). (gr. 3-7). 14.99 (978-1-4169-7593-9(4)) Simon & Schuster, Inc.

Walker, Anna. Lottie & Walter. Walker, Anna, illus. 2019. (ENG., Illus.). 40p. (J). (gr. -1-3). 17.99 (978-1-328-47038-6(5), 1714020, Clarion Bks.) HarperCollins Pubs.

Ward, M. The Evergreens Get Wet: The Evergreens. 2009. (Illus.). 28p. pap. 12.49 (978-1-4389-8960-0(1)) AuthorHouse.

Ward, Sarah, illus. My Little Storybook: Little Duck Learns to Swim. 2016. (ENG.). 12p. (J). (gr. -1 — 1). bds. 4.99 (978-1-4998-0190-3(4)) Little Bee Books Inc.

Waters, Cassie. Heat Wave. 2012. (Pool Girls Ser.: 2). (ENG.). 160p. (J). (gr. 3-7). pap. 5.99 (978-1-4424-4146-0(1), Simon Spotlight) Simon Spotlight.

Wells, Rosemary. Eduardo: Cumpleanos en la Piscina. 2003. Orig. Title: Edward's Big Splash. (SPA., Illus.). 22p. (J). (gr. -1-k). 12.95 (978-1-56014-664-3(8)) Santillana USA Publishing Co., Inc.

Wheeler, Lisa. Dino-Swimming. Gott, Barry, illus. 2015. (Dino-Sports Ser.). (ENG.). 32p. (J). (gr. k-3). lib. bdg. 18.99 (978-1-4677-0214-0(5), f3f77eea-4055-4d94-ae5a-31a30899e91b); E-Book 35.99 (978-1-4677-8809-0(0)) Lerner Publishing Group. (Carolrhoda Bks.).

Wildsmith, Brian. The Little Wood Duck, 1 vol. Wildsmith, Brian, illus. (ENG., Illus.). 32p. (J). 2007. (gr. -1-3). 16.95 (978-1-59572-042-9(1)) 2006. pap. 6.95 (978-1-59572-049-8(9)) Star Bright Bks., Inc.

Williams, Carol Lynch. Signed, Skye Harper. 2014. (ENG., Illus.). 304p. (YA). (gr. 7). 17.99 *(978-1-4814-0032-9(0),* Simon & Schuster/Paula Wiseman Bks.) Simon & Schuster/Paula Wiseman Bks.

Wilson, Karma. Don't Be Afraid, Little Pip. Chapman, Jane, illus. 2009. (ENG.). 40p. (J). (gr. -1-2). 17.99 *(978-0-689-85987-8(2),* McElderry, Margaret K. Bks.) McElderry, Margaret K. Bks.

Winton, Tim. The Deep. Louise, Karen, illus. 32p. (YA). pap. 13.95 *(978-1-86368-210-7(4))* Fremantle Pr. AUS. Dist: Independent Pubs. Group.

Yasuda, Anita. The Swim Race, 1 vol. Harpster, Steve, illus. 2012. (My First Graphic Novel Ser.). (ENG.). 32p. (J). (gr. k-2). pap. 6.25 *(978-1-4342-3864-1(4),* 118046, Stone Arch Bks.) Capstone.

Yum, Hyewon. Saturday Is Swimming Day. Yum, Hyewon, illus. 2018. (ENG., Illus.). 40p. (J). (gr. -1-1). 17.99 *(978-0-7636-9117-2(8))* Candlewick Pr.

SWINE

see Pigs

SWITZERLAND

Brown, Anne K. Roger Federer, 1 vol. 2011. (People in the News Ser.). (ENG., Illus.). 112p. (gr. 7-7). lib. bdg. 41.03 *(978-1-4205-0611-2(0),* 1e627f53-c132-4e1c-a187-ede777f85aa1, Lucent Pr.) Greenhaven Publishing LLC.

Carr, Simonetta. John Calvin. Taglietti, Emanuele, illus. 2008. (ENG.). 63p. (J). 18.00 *(978-1-60178-055-3(9))* Reformation Heritage Bks.

Delessert, Etienne. Night Circus. 2015. (ENG., Illus.). 32p. (J). (gr. 2-4). 19.99 *(978-1-56846-277-6(8),* 21106, Creative Editions) Creative Co., The.

Glaser, Jason. Roger Federer, 1 vol. 2011. (Today's Sports Greats Ser.). (ENG., Illus.). 32p. (gr. 4-5). (J). pap. 11.50 *(978-1-4339-5872-4(4),* 094ca5e8-3481-4fd8-b0c3-9f94c219d40d, Gareth Stevens Learning Library); (YA). lib. bdg. 29.27 *(978-1-4339-5870-0(8),* fdc15776-68f4-4e78-a0f9-5f4b56b8f379) Stevens, Gareth Publishing LLLP.

Hammond, Paula. Italy & Switzerland. 2004. (Cultures & Costumes Ser.). (Illus.). 64p. (YA). (gr. 7-18). lib. bdg. 19.95 *(978-1-59084-438-0(6))* Mason Crest.

Juettner Fernandes, Bonnie. The Large Hadron Collider. 2014. (Great Idea Ser.). (ENG., Illus.). 48p. (J). (gr. 4-6). lib. bdg. 26.60 *(978-1-59953-600-2(5))* Norwood Hse. Pr.

Klepeis, Alicia Z. Switzerland, 1 vol. 2019. (Exploring World Cultures (First Edition) Ser.). (ENG.). 32p. (gr. 3-3). pap. 12.16 *(978-1-5026-5168-6(8),* ca471c33-46de-4f98-adfa-a3418146d74c) Cavendish Square Publishing LLC.

Levy, Patricia & Lord, Richard. Switzerland, 1 vol. 2nd rev. ed. 2005. (Cultures of the World (Second Edition)(r) Ser.). (ENG., Illus.). 144p. (gr. 5-5). 49.79 *(978-0-7614-1850-4(4),* 5b13effa-ebff-4baf-8224-54169dfbfdce) Cavendish Square Publishing LLC.

Levy, Patricia, et al. Switzerland, 1 vol. 3rd rev. ed. 2015. (Cultures of the World (Third Edition)(r) Ser.). (ENG., Illus.). 144p. (gr. 5-5). lib. bdg. 48.79 *(978-1-5026-0344-9(6),* f41d8bb1-5673-4801-940d-795b531e2653) Cavendish Square Publishing LLC.

Rechner, Amy. Switzerland. 2019. (Country Profiles Ser.). (ENG., Illus.). 32p. (J). (gr. 3-8). lib. bdg. 27.95 *(978-1-62617-964-6(6),* Blastoff! Discovery) Bellwether Media.

Rowell, Rebecca. Switzerland, 1 vol. 2013. (Countries of the World Set 2 Ser.). (ENG., Illus.). 144p. (YA). (gr. 6-12). lib. bdg. 42.79 *(978-1-61783-638-1(9),* 4900, Essential Library) ABDO Publishing Co.

Van Cleaf, Kristin. Switzerland. 2008. (Countries Set 6 Ser.). 40p. (gr. k-6). 27.07 *(978-1-59928-786-7(2),* Checkerboard Library) ABDO Publishing Co.

Zobel, Derek. Switzerland. 2011. (Illus.). 32p. (J). *(978-0-531-20959-2(8));* (ENG., (gr. 3-7). lib. bdg. 27.95 *(978-1-60014-577-3(9),* Blastoff! Readers) Bellwether Media.

Zocchi, Judy. In Switzerland. Brodie, Neale, illus. 2005. (Global Adventures I Ser.). 32p. (J). pap. 10.95 *(978-1-59646-156-7(X));* lib. bdg. 21.65 *(978-1-59646-006-5(7));* per. 10.95 *(978-1-59646-157-4(8))* Dingles & Co.

—In Switzerland/en Suiza. Brodie, Neale, illus. 2005. (Global Adventures I Ser.).Tr. of En Suiza. (ENG & SPA.). 32p. (J). pap. 10.95 *(978-1-59646-158-1(6));* lib. bdg. 21.65 *(978-1-59646-007-2(5));* per. 10.95 *(978-1-59646-159-8(4))* Dingles & Co.

SWITZERLAND—FICTION

Angel, Ido. Vipo in Switzerland: A Swiss Skiing Adventure. 2015. (AV2 Animated Storytime Ser.). (ENG.). (J). lib. bdg. 29.99 *(978-1-4896-3925-7(X),* AV2 by Weigl) Weigl Pubs., Inc.

Berg, Jean Horton. Pierre, the Young Watchmaker. D'Adamo, Anthony, illus. 2011. 190p. 42.95 *(978-1-258-08171-3(7))* Literary Licensing, LLC.

Cage, Elizabeth. Spy Girls Are Forever. 2013. (Spy Girls Ser.: 4). (ENG., Illus.). 192p. (YA). (gr. 7). pap. 13.99 *(978-1-4814-2082-2(8),* Simon Pulse) Simon Pulse.

Campbell, Angella. Angel & Turkish. 2011. 32p. pap. 14.99 *(978-1-4634-0372-0(0))* AuthorHouse.

—Engel und Turkish. 2012. 32p. pap. 19.99 *(978-1-4772-2556-1(0))* AuthorHouse.

Carigiet, Alois, illus. A Bell for Ursli: A Story from the Engadine in Switzerland, 23 vols. 2007. (ENG.). 44p. (J). *(978-0-86315-614-4(2))* Floris Bks.

Chatterton, Martin. Brain Full of Holes. 2008. 208p. *(978-1-921272-28-8(7))* Little Hare Bks. AUS. Dist: HarperCollins Pubs. Australia.

Creech, Sharon. Bloomability. 2012. (ENG., Illus.). 272p. (J). (gr. 3-7). pap. 7.99 *(978-0-06-440823-3(X),* HarperCollins) HarperCollins Pubs.

—Bloomability. unabr. ed. 2004. 273p. (J). (gr. 4-7). pap. 38.00 incl. audio *(978-0-8072-8754-5(7),* YA257SP, Listening Library) Random Hse. Audio Publishing Group.

—Bloomability. 2012. (J). (gr. 3-6). 17.20 *(978-0-613-22826-8(X))* Turtleback.

—The Unfinished Angel. 2013. (ENG.). 160p. (J). (gr. 3-7). pap. 7.99 *(978-0-06-143097-8(8),* HarperCollins) HarperCollins Pubs.

Dalmatian Press Staff, adapted by. Heidi. (SPA., Illus.). (YA). 11.95 *(978-84-7281-082-2(8),* AF1082) Auriga, Ediciones S.A. ESP. Dist: Continental Bk. Co., Inc.

—Heidi. (Young Collector's Illustrated Classics Ser.). (Illus.). 192p. (J). (gr. 3-7). 9.95 *(978-1-56156-455-2(9))* Kidsbooks, LLC.

Dunseith, Peter. Bird of Heaven: The Story of a Swazi Sangoma. 2010. (Illus.). 257p. pap. *(978-0-624-04557-1(9))* NB Pubs. Ltd.

Evatt, Harriet. The Mystery of the Alpine Castle. 2011. 242p. 46.95 *(978-1-258-08839-2(8))* Literary Licensing, LLC.

Fisher, Leonard Everett. William Tell. Fisher, Leonard Everett, illus. 2006. (Illus.). 28p. (J). reprint ed. 16.00 *(978-0-7567-9880-2(9))* DIANE Publishing Co.

Furlong, C. T. Killer Strangelets. 2011. (Arctic6 Ser.). 208p. (J). pap. *(978-0-9562315-6-7(X))* Inside Pocket Publishing, Ltd.

Garcia, Cristina. Dreams of Significant Girls. (ENG.). 256p. (YA). (gr. 9). 2012. pap. 8.99 *(978-1-4169-7930-2(1))* 2011. 16.99 *(978-1-4169-7920-3(4))* Simon & Schuster Bks. For Young Readers. (Simon & Schuster Bks. For Young Readers).

A Gift to Share. 2005. (J). 17.00 *(978-0-9721457-1-8(0))* Silent Moon Bks.

Haddix, Margaret Peterson. Caught. 2012. (Missing Ser.: 5). (ENG.). 352p. (J). (gr. 3-7). 16.99 *(978-1-4169-8982-0(X),* Simon & Schuster Bks. For Young Readers) Simon & Schuster Bks. For Young Readers.

—Caught. 2013. (Missing Ser.: 5). lib. bdg. 18.40 *(978-0-606-27045-8(0))* Turtleback.

Hawking, Stephen & Hawking, Lucy. George & the Big Bang. Parsons, Garry, illus. (George's Secret Key Ser.). (ENG.). (J). (gr. 3-7). 2013. 304p. pap. 13.99 *(978-1-4424-4006-7(6))* 2012. 336p. 22.99 *(978-1-4424-4005-0(8))* Simon & Schuster Bks. For Young Readers. (Simon & Schuster Bks. For Young Readers).

Hedij, Charles. Fields of Discovery. 2006. 220p. pap. 24.95 *(978-1-4241-0605-9(2))* PublishAmerica, Inc.

Henderson, Jason. Alex Van Helsing: Vampire Rising. 2010. (Alex Van Helsing Ser.: 1). (ENG.). 256p. (YA). (gr. 8-18). 16.99 *(978-0-06-195099-5(8),* HarperTeen) HarperCollins Pubs.

Hergé. The Calculus Affair. (Illus.). 62p. (J). 19.95 *(978-0-8288-5014-8(3))* French & European Pubns., Inc.

Kleinman, Estelle. Bloomability. Friedland, Joyce & Kessler, Rikki, eds. 2009. (Novel-Ties Ser.). (Illus.). 41p. pap. 16.95 *(978-0-7675-4276-0(2))* Learning Links Inc.

Klimo, Kate. Barry. 2013. (Dog Diaries: 3). lib. bdg. 18.40 *(978-0-606-32455-7(0))* Turtleback.

Krulik, Nancy. Nice Snowing You! 2014. (Magic Bone Ser.: 4). lib. bdg. 14.75 *(978-0-606-34145-5(5))* Turtleback.

—Nice Snowing You! #4. Braun, Sebastien, illus. 2014. (Magic Bone Ser.: 4). 128p. (J). (gr. 1-3). 6.99 *(978-0-448-46446-6(2),* Grosset & Dunlap) Penguin Young Readers Group.

Krulik, Nancy E. Nice Snowing You! Braun, Sébastien, illus. 2014. 108p. (J). *(978-1-62565-236-2(4),* Grosset & Dunlap) Penguin Publishing Group.

Lee, Mackenzi. This Monstrous Thing. 2015. (ENG.). 384p. (YA). (gr. 8). 17.99 *(978-0-06-238277-1(2),* Tegen, Katherine Bks) HarperCollins Pubs.

McCall Smith, Alexander. Max & Maddy & the Chocolate Money Mystery. Pamintuan, Macky, illus. 2008. (Max & Maddy Ser.). (ENG.). 72p. (J). (gr. 3-6). 17.44 *(978-1-59990-036-0(X),* 9781599900360) Bloomsbury Publishing USA.

Mitchell, George. The Marmots of Lenk & the Long Sleep. 2011. 66p. pap. 20.95 *(978-1-4476-2895-8(0))* Lulu Pr., Inc.

Montgomery, R. A. Behind the Wheel. Sundaravej, Sittisan, illus. 2010. (ENG.). 144p. (J). (gr. 4-8). pap. 7.99 *(978-1-933390-35-2(2))* Chooseco LLC.

Oppel, Kenneth. This Dark Endeavor: The Apprenticeship of Victor Frankenstein. 2011. (Apprenticeship of Victor Frankenstein Ser.: Bk. 1). (ENG.). (YA). (gr. 7-12). 64.99 *(978-1-4558-2316-1(3))* Findaway World, LLC.

—This Dark Endeavor: The Apprenticeship of Victor Frankenstein. (ENG., (YA). (gr. 7). 2012. Illus.). 320p. pap. 12.99 *(978-1-4424-0316-1(0))* 2011. 304p. lib. bdg. 17.99 *(978-1-4424-0315-4(2))* Simon & Schuster Bks. For Young Readers. (Simon & Schuster Bks. For Young Readers).

Osborne, Mary Pope. Dogs in the Dead of Night, Bk. 18. Murdocca, Sal, illus. 2013. (Magic Tree House (R) Merlin Mission Ser.: 18). 144p. (J). (gr. 2-5). 6.99 *(978-0-375-86796-5(1),* Random Hse. Bks. for Young Readers) Random Hse. Children's Bks.

—Dogs in the Dead of Night. 2013. (Magic Tree House Merlin Missions Ser.: 18). lib. bdg. 16.00 *(978-0-606-31939-3(5))* Turtleback.

Perkins, Lucy Fitch. The Swiss Twins. 2004. reprint ed. pap. 1.99 *(978-1-4192-8467-0(3));* pap. 15.95 *(978-1-4191-8467-3(9))* Kessinger Publishing, LLC.

Rose, Imogen. Initiation: Japanese Language Edition. Galeano, Tomomi, tr. 2013. 482p. pap. 16.99 *(978-1-940015-04-0(9))* Imogen Rose.

Spyri, Johanna. Heidi. (J). 24.95 *(978-0-8488-1179-2(8))* Amereon Ltd.

—Heidi. 2014. (ENG.). 345p. 17.50 *(978-1-78270-044-9(7))* Award Pubns. Ltd. GBR. Dist: Parkwest Pubns., Inc.

—Heidi. 2017. (GER., Illus.). (J). pap. *(978-3-7448-7494-6(X))* Books on Demand GmbH.

—Heidi. Smith, Briony May, illus. 2020. (ENG.). 96p. (J). (gr. k-4). 17.99 *(978-1-5362-1422-2(1))* Candlewick Pr.

—Heidi. 2017. (ENG., Illus.). (J). pap. 15.95 *(978-1-374-82311-2(2));* (gr. 3-7). 25.95 *(978-1-374-82312-9(0))* Capital Communications, Inc.

—Heidi. 2013. 425p. reprint ed. lthr. 69.00 *(978-0-7426-1047-7(0))* Classic Bks.

—Heidi. (ENG., Illus.). (J). 2016. (gr. 3-7). 26.95 *(978-1-358-32517-5(0))* 2015. (gr. 4-7). 26.95 *(978-1-340-18081-2(2))* 2015. (gr. 4-7). 26.95 *(978-1-340-63493-3(7))* Creative Media Partners, LLC.

—Heidi. Carsey, Alice, illus. 2019. (ENG.). 204p. (J). (gr. 4-7). pap. 7.99 *(978-1-4209-6135-5(7))* Digireads.com Publishing.

—Heidi. 2008. (Bring the Classics to Life Ser.). (Illus.). 72p. (gr. 1-12). pap., act. bk. ed. 10.95 *(978-1-55576-178-3(X),* EDCTR-107B) EDCON Publishing Group.

—Heidi. 2003. pap. *(978-1-84637-585-9(1))* Echo Library.

—Heidi. (ENG.). (J). 2019. 348p. (gr. 3-7). pap. 36.99 *(978-1-7078-1133-5(4))* 2019. 216p. (gr. 3-7). pap. 12.43 *(978-1-7107-1933-8(8))* 2019. 346p. (gr. 3-7). pap. 14.99 *(978-1-6999-8529-8(4))* 2019. 178p. (gr. 3-7). pap. 9.99 *(978-1-7025-0578-9(2))* 2019. 348p. (gr. 4-7). pap. 19.99 *(978-1-6967-9837-2(X))* 2019. 348p. (gr. 4-7). pap. 19.99 *(978-1-6910-9020-4(4))* 2019. 348p. (gr. 4-7). pap. 19.99 *(978-1-6949-7494-5(4))* 2019. 178p. (gr. 4-7). pap. 14.99 *(978-1-6962-6581-2(9))* 2019. 118p. (gr. 4-7). pap. 8.99 *(978-1-6896-7508-6(X))* 2019. 376p. (gr. 4-7). pap. 25.99 *(978-1-0825-2695-4(9))* 2019. 354p. (gr. 4-7). pap. 19.99 *(978-1-0974-8597-0(8))* 2019. 354p. (gr. 4-7). pap. 19.99 *(978-1-0704-9842-3(4))* 2019. 614p. (gr. 4-7). pap. 35.99 *(978-1-0958-8729-5(7))* 2019. 354p. (gr. 4-7). pap. 20.99 *(978-1-0934-3792-8(8))* 2018. (Illus.). 166p. (gr. 4-7). pap. 12.99 *(978-1-7919-2096-8(9))* Independently Published.

—Heidi. 2017. (ENG.). 288p. (J). (gr. 3-7). pap. *(978-93-86348-79-1(9))* Jaico Publishing Hse.

—Heidi. Kirk, Maria L., illus. 2015. (First Avenue Classics (tm) Ser.). (ENG.). 192p. (YA). (gr. 3-8). E-Book 19.99 *(978-1-4677-5846-8(9),* First Avenue Editions) Lerner Publishing Group.

—Heidi. l.t. ed. 2004. (Large Print Ser.). 433p. 26.00 *(978-1-58287-666-5(5))* North Bks.

—Heidi. 2017. (ENG., Illus.). 372p. 12.99 *(978-1-5098-4292-6(6),* 900183857, Collector's Library, The) Pan Macmillan GBR. Dist: Macmillan.

—Heidi. 2020. (Be Classic Ser.). (Illus.). 272p. (J). (gr. 3-7). pap. 7.99 *(978-0-593-20316-3(X),* Puffin Books) Penguin Young Readers Group.

—Heidi. Bond, Anna, illus. 2014. (Puffin in Bloom Ser.). 336p. (J). (gr. 3-7). 17.00 *(978-0-14-751402-8(9),* Puffin Books) Penguin Young Readers Group.

—Heidi. (ENG., Illus.). (J). 2018. 178p. (gr. 4-7). 24.76 *(978-1-7317-0690-4(1))* 2018. 178p. (gr. 4-7). 12.68 *(978-1-7317-0345-3(7))* 2018. 178p. (gr. 4-7). pap. 12.69 *(978-1-7317-0691-1(X))* 2018. 178p. (gr. 4-7). pap. 5.89 *(978-1-7317-0346-0(5))* 2018. 178p. (gr. 4-7). pap. 5.89 *(978-1-61382-387-3(8))* 2011. (gr. 3-7). 14.99 *(978-1-61382-679-9(6))* 2011. (gr. 3-7). 14.99 *(978-1-61382-680-5(X))* Simon & Brown.

—Heidi. 2013. (ENG., Illus.). 336p. (J). (gr. 2-7). 14.95 *(978-1-62087-686-2(8),* 620686, Sky Pony Pr.) Skyhorse Publishing Co., Inc.

—Heidi. 2018. (Classics with Ruskin Ser.: Vol. 4). (ENG., Illus.). 256p. (YA). (gr. 7-12). pap. *(978-93-87693-85-2(6))* Speaking Tiger Publishing.

—Heidi. 2008. (ENG., Illus.). (J). 18.99 *(978-1-4341-1623-9(9),* Waking Lion Press); 260p. 18.99 *(978-1-4341-1622-2(0),* Classic Bks. Library) The Editorium, LLC.

—Heidi. 2017. (ENG., Illus.). (J). (gr. 3-7). pap. *(978-0-649-60078-6(9));* pap. *(978-0-649-00846-9(4))* Trieste Publishing Pty Ltd.

—Heidi. 2018. (ENG., Illus.). 184p. (J). 19.99 *(978-1-5154-3799-4(X))* Wilder Pubns., Corp.

—Heidi: With a Discussion of Optimism. Clift, Eva, illus. 2003. (Values in Action Illustrated Classics Ser.). 190p. (J). *(978-1-59203-030-9(0))* Learning Challenge, Inc.

—Heidi: Lessons at Home & Abroad. Bowman, Peter James, tr. from GER. Hellard, Susan, illus. 2017. (Alma Junior Classics Ser.). (ENG.). 288p. (J). pap. 11.00 *(978-1-84749-665-2(2),* 367214) Alma Classics GBR. Dist: Bloomsbury Publishing Plc.

—What Sami Sings with the Birds. 2010. 48p. pap. *(978-1-4076-5301-3(6))* HardPr.

Spyri, Johanna & Blaisdell, Robert. Heidi: Adapted for Young Readers. Kliros, Thea, illus. 2011. (Dover Children's Thrift Classics Ser.). (ENG.). 80p. (J). (gr. 3-8). pap. 4.00 *(978-0-486-40166-9(9),* 401669) Dover Pubns., Inc.

Spyri, Johanna & Carsey, Alice. Heidi. 2018. (ENG., Illus.). 262p. (J). pap. 15.95 *(978-1-296-79739-3(2))* Creative Media Partners, LLC.

Spyri, Johanna & Lacey, Mike. Heidi, 1 vol. 2011. (Calico Illustrated Classics Ser.: No. 4). (ENG., Illus.). 112p. (J). (gr. 2-5). 38.50 *(978-1-61641-613-3(0),* 4041, Calico Chapter Bks.) ABDO Publishing Co.

Titus, Eve. Basil & the Lost Colony. Galdone, Paul, illus. 2017. (Great Mouse Detective Ser.: 5). (ENG.). 96p. (J). (gr. 1-4). pap. 6.99 *(978-1-4814-6413-0(2),* Aladdin) Simon & Schuster Children's Publishing.

Wells, Helen. Cherry Ames, Ski Nurse Mystery. 2007. (Cherry Ames Nurse Stories Ser.). 224p. (J). (gr. 3-7). 14.95 *(978-0-8261-0437-3(1))* Springer Publishing Co., Inc.

Zahn, Muriel. Grimsel: The Story of A Valiant Saint Bernard & Three Boys in the Swiss Alps. Walsh, William, illus. 2011. 178p. 42.95 *(978-1-258-07805-8(8))* Literary Licensing, LLC.

SYMBIOSIS

see Plant Ecology

SYMBOLISM

see also Christian Art and Symbolism; Heraldry

Adams, Michelle Medlock. What Is America? Wummer, Amy, illus. 2019. (What Is... ? Ser.). (ENG.). 22p. (J). (gr. -1-1). bds. 7.99 *(978-0-8249-1695-4(6),* Worthy Kids/Ideals) Worthy Publishing.

Bateman, Teresa. Red, White, Blue & Uncle Who? The Stories Behind Some of America's Patriotic Symbols. O'Brien, John, illus. 2003. (ENG.). 64p. (J). (gr. 3-7). pap. 8.99 *(978-0-8234-1784-1(0))* Holiday Hse., Inc.

Baxter, Pam. A Cup of Light: All about the Flaming Chalice. 2010. (J). pap. 5.00 *(978-1-55896-575-1(0),* Skinner Hse. Bks.) Unitarian Universalist Assn.

Cesky, Brittany. The Bald Eagle. 2018. (US Symbols Ser.). (ENG., Illus.). 24p. (J). (gr. 1-1). pap. 8.95 *(978-1-63517-833-3(9),* 1635178339) North Star Editions.

—The Bald Eagle. 2018. (US Symbols Ser.). (ENG., Illus.). 24p. (J). (gr. k-3). lib. bdg. 31.36 *(978-1-5321-6045-5(3),* 28722, Pop! Cody Koala) Pop!

Douglas, Lloyd G. The Bald Eagle. 2003. (Welcome Bks.). 24p. (J). 19.00 *(978-0-516-25851-5(6));* (ENG.). (gr. -1-2). pap. 4.95 *(978-0-516-27874-2(6))* Scholastic Library Publishing. (Children's Pr.).

Herrington, Lisa M. The Bald Eagle (Rookie Read-About American Symbols) 2014. (Rookie Read-About American Symbols Ser.). (ENG., Illus.). 32p. (J). (gr. 1-2). pap. 5.95 *(978-0-531-21837-2(6),* Children's Pr.) Scholastic Library Publishing.

Love, Mary A. Learning Through Symbolism & Celebrations. Flournoy, L. Diana, illus. 2nd rev. ed. 2011. (ENG.). 168p. pap. 24.00 *(978-1-929548-00-2(1))* Love's Creative Resources.

Marcovitz, Hal. Bald Eagle: The Story of Our National Bird. Moreno, Barry, ed. 2014. (Patriotic Symbols of America Ser.: 20). 48p. (J). (gr. 4-18). 20.95 *(978-1-4222-3120-3(8))* Mason Crest.

Patrick, Joseph. Our National Symbols, 1 vol. 2008. (Real Life Readers Ser.). (ENG.). 16p. (gr. 2-3). pap. 7.05 *(978-1-4358-0049-6(4),* 24e1c988-469e-4b30-87f6-e332c2ace6be, Rosen Classroom) Rosen Publishing Group, Inc., The.

Rookie Read-About(r) American Symbols (Set Of 7) 2014. (Rookie Read-About(r) American Symbols Ser.). (J). *(978-0-531-24360-2(5))* Scholastic Library Publishing.

Schuh, Mari. The Bald Eagle. 2018. (Symbols of American Freedom Ser.). (ENG., Illus.). 24p. (J). (gr. k-3). lib. bdg. 26.95 *(978-1-62617-883-0(6),* Blastoff! Readers) Bellwether Media.

SYMMETRY

Alaina, Maria. Both Sides are the Same. 2011. (Wonder Readers Early Level Ser.). (ENG.). 16p. (gr. -1-1). pap. 35.94 *(978-1-4296-8072-1(5),* Capstone Pr.) Capstone.

Bellos, Alex & Harriss, Edmund. Patterns of the Universe: A Coloring Adventure in Math & Beauty. 2015. (ENG., Illus.). 144p. pap. 14.95 *(978-1-61519-323-3(5),* 779323) Experiment LLC, The.

—Visions of the Universe: A Coloring Journey Through Math's Great Mysteries. 2016. (ENG., Illus.). 144p. pap. 14.95 *(978-1-61519-367-7(7),* 779367) Experiment LLC, The.

Canavan, Thomas. Shapes & Symmetry: 50 Math Super Puzzles, 1 vol. 2011. (Math Standards Workout Ser.). (ENG., Illus.). 48p. (YA). (gr. 5-5). pap. 12.75 *(978-1-4488-6683-0(9),* 2b0eec55-5545-4658-a254-4a03e92130c9, Rosen Reference) Rosen Publishing Group, Inc., The.

Feldman, Sarah. Symmetry in Our World. 2011. (Early Connections Ser.). (J). *(978-1-61672-671-3(7))* Benchmark Education Co.

Kalman, Bobbie. What Is Symmetry in Nature? 2010. (Looking at Nature Ser.). (ENG., Illus.). 24p. (J). (gr. -1-2). lib. bdg. *(978-0-7787-3327-0(0))* Crabtree Publishing Co.

Leedy, Loreen. Seeing Symmetry. 2013. (ENG., Illus.). 32p. (J). (gr. 1-4). pap. 7.99 *(978-0-8234-2762-8(5))* Holiday Hse., Inc.

Moskal, Greg. Modern Buildings: Identifying Bilateral & Rotational Symmetry & Transformations. 2009. (PowerMath: Proficiency Ser.). 32p. (gr. 4-5). 47.90 *(978-1-60851-397-0(1),* PowerKids Pr.) Rosen Publishing Group, Inc., The.

SYNAGOGUES

Hoffman, Lawrence A. & Wolfson, Ron. What You Will See Inside a Synagogue. Aron, Bill, photos by. 2008. (What You Will See Inside ... Ser.). (ENG., Illus.). 32p. (J). pap. 8.99 *(978-1-59473-256-0(6),* 0206b87d-4ecf-4a43-af2c-3d2eaf77e346, Skylight Paths Publishing) LongHill Partners, Inc.

Person, Hara & Lewy, Faye Tillis. My Synagogue Scrapbook. Schoenberg-Lam, Dahlia, illus. 2006. pap. 11.95 *(978-0-8074-0990-9(1),* 164065) URJ Pr.

SYNTHETIC PRODUCTS

see also Plastics

also names of snythetic products, e.g. Rubber, Artificial; etc.

Carr, Aaron. Natural o Hecho Por el Hombre. 2013. (SPA., Illus.). 24p. (J). *(978-1-62127-607-4(4))* Weigl Pubs., Inc.

Is It Natural or Human-Made? 2014. (What's the Matter? Ser.). (ENG., Illus.). 24p. (J). (gr. 1-2). *(978-0-7787-0535-2(8))* Crabtree Publishing Co.

SYRIA

Behnke, Alison. Syria in Pictures. 2005. (Visual Geography Series, Second Ser.). (ENG., Illus.). 80p. (gr. 5-12). 31.93 *(978-0-8225-2396-3(5))* Lerner Publishing Group.

Berlatsky, Noah, ed. Syria, 1 vol. 2014. (Opposing Viewpoints Ser.). (ENG., Illus.). 232p. (gr. 10-12). lib. bdg. 50.43 *(978-0-7377-7006-3(6),* eda4c9e0-e7fb-483c-b4f6-b9e3ae642f8a, Greenhaven Publishing) Greenhaven Publishing LLC.

Brown, Don. The Unwanted: Stories of the Syrian Refugees. Brown, Don, illus. 2018. (ENG., Illus.). 112p. (J). (gr. 7). 18.99 *(978-1-328-81015-1(1),* 1688847, Clarion Bks.) HarperCollins Pubs.

Capek, Michael. The Syrian Conflict. 2016. (Special Reports Set 2 Ser.). (ENG., Illus.). 112p. (J). (gr. 6-12). lib. bdg. 41.36 *(978-1-68078-398-8(X),* 23561, Essential Library) ABDO Publishing Co.

—Understanding Syria Today. 2014. (Illus.). 63p. (J). (gr. 3-6). 33.95 *(978-1-61228-646-4(1))* Mitchell Lane Pubs.

Dicker, Katie. The Syrian Civil War, 1 vol. 2017. (I Witness War Ser.). (ENG.). 48p. (gr. 5-6). pap. 13.93 *(978-1-5026-3432-0(5),* 0fd2ad5a-9231-4f57-97f5-af292d70ed1a); lib. bdg. 33.07 *(978-1-5026-3254-8(3),* be601bc2-1572-4a0e-986d-122e2ead595b) Cavendish Square Publishing LLC.

Draper, Allison Stark. A Historical Atlas of Syria. 2009. (Historical Atlases of South Asia, Central Asia, & the Middle East Ser.). 64p. (gr. 6-6). 61.20 *(978-1-61513-329-1(1))* Rosen Publishing Group, Inc., The.

Etheredge, Laura. Syria, Lebanon, & Jordan, 1 vol. 2011. (Middle East: Region in Transition Ser.). (ENG., Illus.). 248p. (YA). (gr. 10-10). lib. bdg. 43.59 *(978-1-61530-329-8(4),* b19482da-7bc4-4f09-9f95-b00cd6590743) Rosen Publishing Group, Inc., The.

Fansa, Khaldoun. Explore the Old City of Aleppo: Come with Tamim to a World Heritage Site. Asaad, Abdalla, illus. 2020. (ENG.). 152p. (J). 25.00 *(978-1-951082-15-4(X),* Cune Pr. Classics) Rare Bird Bks.

Gelfand, Dale Evva. Syria, 1 vol. 2013. (Countries of the World Set 2 Ser.). (ENG.). 144p. (YA). (gr. 6-12). lib. bdg. 42.79 *(978-1-61783-639-8(7),* 4902, Essential Library) ABDO Publishing Co.

S

Heing, Bridey. Cultural Destruction by ISIS, 1 vol. 2017. (Crimes of ISIS Ser.). (ENG.). 104p. (gr. 8-8). pap. 20.95 (978-0-7660-9583-0(5), 24fb96b3-8cc0-4e73-81a6-e2d0fb5c97af) Enslow Publishing, LLC.

Kummer, Patricia K. Syria. 2005. (Enchantment of the World Ser.). (ENG., Illus.). 144p. (YA). (gr. 5-9). 39.00 (978-0-516-23677-3(6)) Scholastic Library Publishing.

Mason, Helen. A Refugee's Journey from Syria, 1 vol. 2017. (Leaving My Homeland Ser.). (ENG., Illus.). 32p. (J). (gr. 4-4). pap. (978-0-7787-3184-9(7)) Crabtree Publishing Co.

Murray, Julie. Syria. 2017. (Explore the Countries Set 4 Ser.). (ENG., Illus.). 40p. (J). (gr. 2-5). lib. bdg. 35.64 (978-1-5321-1052-8(9), 25680, Big Buddy Bks.) ABDO Publishing Co.

Orr, Tamra. Syrian Heritage. 2018. (21st Century Junior Library: Celebrating Diversity in My Classroom Ser.). (ENG., Illus.). 24p. (J). (gr. 2-4). lib. bdg. 30.64 (978-1-5341-2907-8(3), 211672) Cherry Lake Publishing.

Shoup, John A. The History of Syria, 1 vol. 2018. (Greenwood Histories of the Modern Nations Ser.). (ENG., Illus.). 256p. (C). 70.00 (978-1-4408-5834-5(9), 795772, Greenwood) Bloomsbury Publishing USA.

Skinner, Patricia. Syria, 1 vol. 2004. (Countries of the World Ser.). (ENG., Illus.). 96p. (gr. 6-8). lib. bdg. 33.67 (978-0-8368-3118-4(7), 2e5072b5-8fef-4fc2-ad47-04faa34856ad) Stevens, Gareth Publishing LLLP.

South, Coleman & Jermyn, Leslie. Syria, 1 vol. 2nd rev. ed. 2006. (Cultures of the World (Second Edition)(r) Ser.). (ENG., Illus.). 144p. (gr. 5-5). lib. bdg. 49.79 (978-0-7614-2054-5(1), a62781c6-802d-4847-8e5d-20bc52015b54) Cavendish Square Publishing LLC.

South, Coleman, et al. Syria, 1 vol. 3rd rev. ed. 2016. (Cultures of the World (Third Edition)(r) Ser.). (ENG., Illus.). 144p. (gr. 5-5). lib. bdg. 48.79 (978-1-5026-1703-3(X), ece237dd-013a-4170-b8e7-20ea02053d30) Cavendish Square Publishing LLC.

Spence, Kelly. Yusra Mardini: Refugee Hero & Olympic Swimmer. 2018. (Remarkable Lives Revealed Ser.). (ENG., Illus.). 32p. (J). (gr. 3-3). (978-0-7787-4711-6(5)); pap. (978-0-7787-4726-0(3)) Crabtree Publishing Co.

Stark Draper, Allison. A Historical Atlas of Syria, 1 vol. 2003. (Historical Atlases of South Asia, Central Asia, & the Middle East Ser.). (ENG., Illus.). 64p. (gr. 6-6). lib. bdg. 37.13 (978-0-8239-3983-1(9), e7b09c5c-4db8-475d-87db-d32893b35b62) Rosen Publishing Group, Inc., The.

Sullivan, Anne Marie. Syria. (Major Muslim Nations Ser.). 2010. 126p. (YA). (gr. 5-18). lib. bdg. 25.95 (978-1-4222-1382-7(X)) Vol. 13. 2015. (Illus.). 128p. (J). (gr. 7). lib. bdg. 25.95 (978-1-4222-3451-8(7)) Mason Crest.

Thiel, Kristin. True Teen Stories from Syria: Surviving Civil War, 1 vol. 2018. (Surviving Terror: True Teen Stories from Around the World Ser.). (ENG.). 112p. (YA). (gr. 8-8). 45.93 (978-1-5026-3541-9(0), 2eeee78a-55f8-4749-8b4f-bf490be5c502) Cavendish Square Publishing LLC.

Yomtov, Nel. Enchantment of the World, Second Series: Syria. 2013. (ENG., Illus.). 144p. (J). 40.00 (978-0-531-23679-6(X)) Scholastic Library Publishing.

Zahler, Kathy A. The Assads' Syria. 2009. (Dictatorships Ser.). (ENG.). 160p. (gr. 9-12). 38.60 (978-0-8225-9095-8(6)) Lerner Publishing Group.

SYSTEMS ENGINEERING

see also Bionics

Lerner, K. Lee, et al. U-X-L Doomed: The Science Behind Disasters. 2015. (Illus.). (J). (978-1-4103-1777-3(3)) Cengage Gale.

Mara, Wil. Robotics Engineer. 2015. (21st Century Skills Library: Cool STEAM Careers Ser.). (ENG., Illus.). 32p. (J). (gr. 4-7). pap. 14.21 (978-1-63362-045-2(X), 205937) Cherry Lake Publishing.

U X L, ed. UXL Man-Made Disasters, 3 vols. 2015. (U-X-L Man-Made Disasters Ser.). (ENG., Illus.). 348.00 (978-1-4103-1774-2(9), UXL) Cengage Gale.

Winchester, Jim. World's Worst Aircraft. 2009. (World's Worst: from Innovation to Disaster Ser.). 80p. (gr. 8-8). 61.20 (978-1-60854-857-6(0)) Rosen Publishing Group, Inc., The.

T

TACOMA NARROWS BRIDGE (TACOMA, WASH.)—FICTION

Hartinger, Brent. Project Sweet Life. 2009. (J). lib. bdg. 17.89 (978-0-06-082412-9(3), HarperTeen) HarperCollins Pubs.

TADPOLES

Anderson, Judith. Once There Was a Tadpole. Gordon, Mike, illus. 2010. (Nature's Miracles Ser.). (ENG.). 32p. (J). (gr. k-3). 18.69 (978-0-7641-4496-7(0), B.E.S. Publishing) Peterson's.

Bailer, Darice. How Do Tadpoles Become Frogs?, 1 vol. 2011. (Tell Me Why, Tell Me How Ser.). (ENG.). 32p. (gr. 3-3). 32.64 (978-0-7614-4824-2(1), 3e0c2be7-7e58-4316-be53-b927b8fd93c3) Cavendish Square Publishing LLC.

Bekkering, Annalise. Frogs. 2010. pap. 9.95 (978-1-60596-926-8(5)); 24p. (J). (gr. 2-4). lib. bdg. 25.70 (978-1-60596-925-1(7)) Weigl Pubs., Inc.

Berger, Melvin & Berger, Gilda. A Tadpole Grows Up. 2008. (Illus.). 32p. (J). (978-0-439-02528-7(1)) Scholastic, Inc.

Evans, Shira. National Geographic Readers: Tadpole to Frog (L1/Coreader) 2018. (Readers Ser.). (Illus.). 48p. (J). (gr. -1-k). pap. 4.99 (978-1-4263-3203-6(3), National Geographic Kids) Disney Publishing Worldwide.

Ganeri, Anita. Frogs & Tadpoles. Axworthy, Anni, illus. 2010. (Animal Families Ser.). (ENG.). 14p. (J). bds. 10.99 (978-1-84089-642-8(6)) Evans Brothers, Ltd. GBR. Dist: Independent Pubs. Group.

Gold, Annabelle. A Tadpole Grows Up, 1 vol. 2012. (InfoMax Readers Ser.). (ENG., Illus.). 24p. (J). (gr. 1-1). pap. 8.25 (978-1-4488-8983-9(9), 9aaa45e4-16bf-4926-9d33-05d5ce777d25, Rosen Classroom) Rosen Publishing Group, Inc., The.

Hayes, Amy. A Tadpole Becomes a Frog, 1 vol. 2015. (Transformations in Nature Ser.). (ENG.). 24p. (gr. 1-1). pap. 9.23 (978-1-5026-0818-5(9), 37777f70-e7fa-4fc6-b73b-2cf799d5c7e5) Cavendish Square Publishing LLC.

Herrington, Lisa M. Tadpole to Frog (Rookie Read-About Science: Life Cycles) (Library Edition) 2014. (Rookie Read-About Science Ser.). (ENG.). 32p. (J). (gr. 1-2). lib. bdg. 25.00 (978-0-531-21057-4(X), Children's Pr.) Scholastic Library Publishing.

Ho, Cammie. Tadpole Tadpole. 2016. (Life Cycle Bks.). (ENG., Illus.). 31p. (J). (gr. k-2). pap. 7.99 (978-1-943241-01-9(5)) Phonic Monic.

Hommedieu, Arthur John. Egg, Tadpole, Frog. 2006. (Metamorphoses Ser.). (Illus.). 16p. (J). (gr. 1-5). spiral bd. (978-1-84643-012-1(7)) Child's Play International Ltd.

Kalman, Bobbie. Tadpoles to Frogs, 1 vol. 2008. (It's Fun to Learn about Baby Animals Ser.). (ENG., Illus.). 24p. (J). (gr. k-3). pap. (978-0-7787-3975-3(9)) Crabtree Publishing Co.

Keeping Tadpoles Alive! Individual Title Six-Packs. (Discovery World Ser.). 24p. (gr. 1-2). 33.00 (978-0-7635-8476-4(2)) Rigby Education.

Milbourne, A. Tadpoles & Frogs. 2004. (Beginners Ser.). 32p. (J). (gr. 1-18). lib. bdg. 12.95 (978-1-58086-465-7(1)) EDC Publishing.

Milbourne, Anna. Tadpoles & Frogs. Donaera, Patrizia & Wray, Zoe, illus. 2007. (Usborne Beginners Ser.). 32p. (J). 4.99 (978-0-7945-1345-0(X), Usborne) EDC Publishing.

Osburn, Mary Rose. Two-Digit Numbers with Tadpoles, 1 vol. 2017. (Animal Math Ser.). (ENG.). 24p. (J). (gr. 1-2). pap. 9.15 (978-1-5382-0860-1(1), 2659691e-c545-4502-ab2f-98da7becb46c) Stevens, Gareth Publishing LLLP.

Royston, Angela. Tadpole Story. 2011. (ENG., Illus.). 24p. (J). pap. (978-0-7787-7881-3(9)); (gr. 3-6). (978-0-7787-7859-2(2)) Crabtree Publishing Co.

Stewart, David. How a Tadpole Grows into a Frog. Franklin, Carolyn, illus. 2008. (Amaze Ser.). (ENG.). 32p. (J). (gr. k-3). pap. 8.95 (978-0-531-20454-2(5)); 24.94 (978-0-531-20443-6(X)) Scholastic Library Publishing. (Children's Pr.).

Tonkin, Rachel. Egg to Frog. Fizer Coleman, Stephanie, illus. 2019. (Follow the Life Cycle Ser.). (ENG.). 24p. (J). (gr. 2-2). lib. bdg. (978-0-7787-6386-4(2), f4073435-d8a2-40e4-84c1-cb89728d0ef7) Crabtree Publishing Co.

Zemlicka, Shannon. The Story of a Frog: It Starts with a Tadpole. 2021. (Step by Step Ser.). (ENG., Illus.). 24p. (J). (gr. -1-2). 26.65 (978-1-5415-9724-2(9), c7c3c8b4-d67f-48c4-bcd5-b8e95228de87, Lerner Pubns.) Lerner Publishing Group.

Zoehfeld, Kathleen Weidner. From Tadpole to Frog (Scholastic Reader, Level 1) 2011. (Scholastic Reader, Level 1 Ser.). (ENG.). 32p. (J). (gr. -1-1). pap. 3.99 (978-0-545-27337-4(4), Scholastic Paperbacks) Scholastic, Inc.

TADPOLES—FICTION

and Film Studio, Shanghai Animation & Tang, Sanmu. Tadpoles Looking for Their Mother. Xiaozhen, Wu, tr. 2010. (Favorite Childrens Cartoons from China Ser.). (ENG., Illus.). 32p. (gr. -1-3). pap. 5.95 (978-1-60220-972-5(3)) Shanghai Pr.

Asch, Frank. Moonbear's Pet. Asch, Frank, illus. 2014. (Moonbear Ser.). (ENG., Illus.). 32p. (J). (gr. -1-3). 18.99 (978-1-4424-9430-5(1), Simon & Schuster/Paula Wiseman Bks.) Simon & Schuster/Paula Wiseman Bks.

Azore, Barbara. Wanda & the Frogs. Graham, Georgia, illus. 2007. 32p. (J). (gr. -1-1). 18.95 (978-0-88776-761-6(3), Tundra Bks.) Tundra Bks. CAN. Dist: Penguin Random Hse. LLC.

Bickta, Brenda L. Tad's Life in the Lily Pond. 2008. 74p. pap. 19.95 (978-1-60672-647-1(1)) America Star Bks.

Bronson, Tammy Carter. Polliwog. Bronson, Tammy Carter, illus. 2006. (ENG & SPA., Illus.). (J). 7.99 (978-0-9678167-5-3(0)) Bookaroos Publishing, Inc.

—Polliwog. Davi, Annou, tr. Bronson, Tammy Carter, illus. 2004. (SPA & ENG., Illus.). 32p. (J). lib. bdg. 17.00 (978-0-9678167-4-6(2)) Bookaroos Publishing, Inc.

Cain, Sheridan. The Teeny Weeny Tadpole. Tickle, Jack, illus. 2005. 32p. (J). 15.95 (978-1-58925-047-5(8)) Tiger Tales.

Carter, Denzel T. Tadpole Grows Up, 1 vol. 2015. (Rosen REAL Readers: STEM & STEAM Collection). (ENG.). 12p. (gr. k-1). pap. 6.33 (978-1-4994-9520-1(X), d0e84949-b24c-4062-948d-c408218eaf30, Rosen Classroom) Rosen Publishing Group, Inc., The.

Clarke, Jane. Only Tadpoles Have Tails. Gray, Jane, illus. 2003. (Flying Foxes Ser.). (ENG.). 48p. (J). lib. bdg. (978-0-7787-1484-2(5)) Crabtree Publishing Co.

Curious George Tadpole Trouble. 2007. (Curious George Ser.). (ENG., Illus.). 24p. (J). (gr. -1-3). 4.99 (978-0-618-77712-9(1), 463157, Clarion Bks.) HarperCollins Pubs.

E.C., Nanci. I Just Might! Meade, Gregory S., illus. 2007. 20p. per. 9.95 (978-1-59858-548-3(7)) Dog Ear Publishing, LLC.

Farfan, Flores & Antonio, Jose. Axolotl: El Ajolote. Celestino, Cleofas Ramirez, illus. 2003. (SPA.). 40p. (J). (978-968-411-569-9(5)) Ediciones Era.

Greene, Stephanie. Owen Foote, Mighty Scientist. Smith, Catharine Bowman, illus. 2004. (ENG.). 96p. (J). (gr. 1-4). tchr. ed. 15.00 (978-0-618-43016-1(4), 100349, Clarion Bks.) HarperCollins Pubs.

Jefferson, E. Louis. The Little Tadpole-A Story of Friendship: Companion Coloring Book. 2012. 48p. pap. 7.00 (978-1-105-61123-0(X)) Lulu.com GBR. Dist: Lulu Pr., Inc.

—Terry-The Little Tadpole-Making New Friends. 2013. (ENG.). 89p. pap. 35.00 (978-1-300-61843-0(4)) Lulu Pr., Inc.

Kent, Jack. The Caterpillar & the Polliwog. Kent, Jack, illus. 2018. (Classic Board Bks.). (ENG., Illus.). 34p. (J). (gr. -1-k). bds. 7.99 (978-1-5344-1377-1(4), Little Simon) Little Simon.

Kimura, Ken & Murakami, Yasunari. 999 Tadpoles. 2011. (ENG., Illus.). 40p. (J). (gr. -1-3). 17.95 (978-0-7358-4013-3(X)) North-South Bks., Inc.

La Beree, Brian, illus. Herbert the Tadpole in the Big Change: Color-Me Version. 2007. 48p. (J). 6.95 (978-0-9800736-0-7(X)) Sophrose Entertainment Inc.

Lobel, Arnold & Lobel, Adrianne. The Frogs & Toads All Sang. Lobel, Arnold & Lobel, Adrianne, illus. 2009. (ENG., Illus.). 32p. (J). (gr. -1-2). 16.99 (978-0-06-180022-1(8), HarperCollins) HarperCollins Pubs.

Mese, John R. & Kelsey, Dawn M. On the Flippy Side. Holden, Chanler, illus. 2009. 30p. (J). 10.95 (978-0-9725853-1-6(1)) Mosscovered Gumbo Barn.

Milbourne, Anna. In the Pond. 2007. 24p. (J). 9.99 (978-0-7945-1544-7(4), Usborne) EDC Publishing.

Narváez, Concha López & Salmeron, Carmelo. Tomas Es Distinto a los Demas.Tr. of Tomas Is Different from the Others. (SPA.). 64p. (J). (gr. 2-4). (978-84-216-3432-5(1)) Bruño, Editorial ESP. Dist: Lectorum Pubns., Inc.

Rice, Cindy & Stolarski, Jerry. Mr. Mahaffy on Wisdom Pond: The Beginning. 2007. (ENG.). 84p. per. 19.95 (978-1-4241-3097-9(2)) America Star Bks.

Rosenthal, Michele Marie. The Frog & the Tadpole's Great Swamp Adventure, 1 vol. 2009. 22p. pap. 24.95 (978-1-61546-178-3(7)) America Star Bks.

Sargent, Dave & Sargent, Pat. Little Tadpole, 10. Robinson, Laura, illus. 2004. (Learn to Read Ser.: 10). 18p. (J). 20. lib. bdg. 9.95 (978-1-56763-836-3(8)) Vol. 20. lib. bdg. 20.95 (978-1-56763-835-6(X)) Ozark Publishing.

—Little Tadpole/el Renacuajo Pequeño, 10 vols. Robinson, Laura, illus. 2004. (Learn to Read Ser.: 10). (ENG & SPA.). 18p. (J). pap. 10.95 (978-1-56763-567-6(9)); lib. bdg. 20.95 (978-1-56763-999-5(2)) Ozark Publishing.

Shorty. Tad, the Sad Tadpole, 1 vol. Evans, Margaret, illus. 2009. 29p. pap. 19.95 (978-1-4489-2458-5(8)) PublishAmerica, Inc.

Sommer, Carl. King of the Pond. Budwine, Greg, illus. 2014. (J). pap. (978-1-57537-956-2(2)) Advance Publishing, Inc.

—King of the Pond(El Rey Del Estanque) Budwine, Greg, illus. 2009. (Another Sommer-Time Story Bilingual Ser.). (SPA & ENG.). 48p. (J). lib. bdg. 16.95 (978-1-57537-156-6(1)) Advance Publishing, Inc.

Sparks, Evan. Freddy's Tale. 2006. 44p. pap. 14.88 (978-1-4116-7427-1(8)) Lulu Pr., Inc.

There's a Rainbow in the River: Individual Title Six-Packs. (gr. k-1). 23.00 (978-0-7635-8850-2(4)) Rigby Education.

Tiny Tiny Tadpole. 2005. (J). bds. 7.99 (978-1-933200-17-0(0)) Family Bks. at Home.

Ward, Nick. The Tadpole Prince. 2003. (Illus.). 32p. (YA). (978-1-84365-016-4(9), Pavilion Children's Books) Pavilion Bks.

Weston Woods Staff, creator. The Caterpillar & the Polliwog. 2011. 18.95 (978-0-439-73152-2(6)); 38.75 (978-0-439-73154-6(2)) Weston Woods Studios, Inc.

Willis, Jeanne. Tadpole's Promise. 15th ed. 2018. (ENG., Illus.). 32p. (J). (—1). pap. 14.99 (978-1-78344-586-8(6)) Andersen Pr. GBR. Dist: Independent Pubs. Group.

Wilson, Kevin. Brown Spot. 2006. 60p. (J). pap. 12.00 (978-1-4116-8059-3(6)) Lulu Pr., Inc.

Wrucke, Mary. Timmy the Tadpole, 1 vol. Cooke, Bev., illus. 2009. 25p. pap. 24.95 (978-1-60813-776-3(7)) America Star Bks.

TAE KWON DO

Adamson, Thomas K. & Heather. Tae Kwon Do, 1 vol. 2015. (Inside Martial Arts Ser.). (ENG., Illus.). 48p. (J). (gr. 3-6). lib. bdg. 34.21 (978-1-62403-606-4(6), 17079, SportsZone) ABDO Publishing Co.

Chandler, Matthew Allan. Tae Kwon Do: A Guide for Athletes & Fans. 2019. (Sports Zone Ser.). (ENG., Illus.). 32p. (J). (gr. 3-6). pap. 7.95 (978-1-5435-7462-3(9), 140902); lib. bdg. 27.99 (978-1-5435-7431-9(9), 140715) Capstone.

Chesterman, Barnaby. Taekwondo: Winning Ways. James, Adam, ed. 2015. (Mastering Martial Arts Ser.). (Illus.). 96p. (J). (gr. 5). lib. bdg. 24.95 (978-1-4222-3245-3(X)) Mason Crest.

Falk, Laine. Let's Talk Tae Kwon Do (Scholastic News Nonfiction Readers: Sports Talk) 2008. (Scholastic News Nonfiction Readers Ser.). (ENG.). 24p. (J). (gr. 1-2). pap. 6.95 (978-0-531-20428-3(6), Children's Pr.) Scholastic Library Publishing.

Schuh, Mari. Tae Kwon Do. 2019. (Spot Sports Ser.). (ENG.). 16p. (J). (gr. -1-1). pap. 7.99 (978-1-68152-440-5(6), 11026) Amicus.

Wells, Garrison. Tae Kwon Do: Korean Foot & Fist Combat. 2012. (Martial Arts Sports Zone Ser.). (ENG., Illus.). 32p. (gr. 4-8). lib. bdg. 26.60 (978-0-7613-8458-8(8), Lerner Pubns.) Lerner Publishing Group.

Wood, Alix. Tae Kwon Do, 1 vol. 2013. (Kid's Guide to Martial Arts Ser.). (ENG., Illus.). 32p. (J). (gr. 2-3). pap. 12.75 (978-1-4777-0354-0(3), de924f05-314e-441b-b5c5-2bc55672bcbb); lib. bdg. 30.27 (978-1-4777-0316-8(0), 7f072470-4e45-47d9-8131-6392ecd6b73b) Rosen Publishing Group, Inc., The. (PowerKids Pr.).

TAFT, WILLIAM H. (WILLIAM HOWARD), 1857-1930

Benson, Michael. William H. Taft. 2004. (Presidential Leaders Ser.). (ENG., Illus.). 112p. (gr. 6-12). 29.27 (978-0-8225-0849-6(4), Lerner Pubns.) Lerner Publishing Group.

Randolph, Ryan P. How to Draw the Life & Times of William Howard Taft, 1 vol. 2005. (Kid's Guide to Drawing the Presidents of the United States of America Ser.). (ENG., Illus.). 32p. (YA). (gr. 4-4). 30.27 (978-1-4042-3003-3(3), 04d8ccfb-589a-48c8-833e-ad21ebc569b3) Rosen Publishing Group, Inc., The.

Rumsch, BreAnn. William Taft, 1 vol. 2016. (United States Presidents *2017 Ser.). (ENG., Illus.). 40p. (J). (gr. 2-5). lib. bdg. 35.64 (978-1-68078-117-5(0), 21851, Big Buddy Bks.) ABDO Publishing Co.

Venezia, Mike. William Howard Taft: Twenty-Seventh President. Venezia, Mike, illus. 2007. (Getting to Know the U. S. Presidents Ser.). (Illus.). 32p. (J). (gr. 3-7). pap. 7.95 (978-0-516-25239-1(9), Children's Pr.) Scholastic Library Publishing.

Wilson, Natashya. How to Draw the Life & Times of William Howard Taft. 2009. (Kid's Guide to Drawing the Presidents of the United States of America Ser.). 32p. (gr. 4-4). 50.50 (978-1-61511-165-7(4), PowerKids Pr.) Rosen Publishing Group, Inc., The.

TAHITI

NgCheong-Lum, Roseline. Tahiti, 1 vol. (Cultures of the World (Third Edition)(r) Ser.). (ENG.). 144p. (gr. 5-5). 2017. lib. bdg. 48.79 (978-1-5026-2741-4(8), 9b2ca89e-2d3f-4554-8ef5-514bc0ce1af9) 2nd rev. ed. 2008. lib. bdg. 49.79 (978-0-7614-2089-7(4), 478ad83a-72bc-49c5-9ad3-e38d186950e8) Cavendish Square Publishing LLC.

TAHITI—FICTION

Jensen, Kathryn. Splash! 2012. 194p. 29.95 (978-1-4489-6574-8(8)) America Star Bks.

Lumry, Amanda & Hurwitz, Laura. Adventures of Riley: Dolphins in Danger. McIntyre, Sarah, illus. 2005. 36p. (J). 15.95 (978-0-9748411-1-3(0)) Eaglemont Pr.

TAILORING

Here are entered works on the cutting and making of men's, or men's and women's clothing. Works limited to the cutting and making of women's clothes are entered under Dressmaking.

see also Dressmaking

Fontichiaro, Kristin. A Better Backpack. 2019. (21st Century Skills Innovation Library: Design a Better World Ser.). (ENG., Illus.). 32p. (J). (gr. 4-7). pap. 14.21 (978-1-5341-3973-2(7), 212721); lib. bdg. 32.07 (978-1-5341-4317-3(3), 212720) Cherry Lake Publishing.

TAILORS

Petersen, Christine. The Tailor, 1 vol. 2012. (Colonial People Ser.). (ENG.). 48p. (gr. 4-4). 34.07 (978-1-60870-417-0(3), 1af62c56-8259-4630-bcb2-11ab51657959) Cavendish Square Publishing LLC.

TAILORS—FICTION

Andersen, Hans Christian. The Emperor's New Clothes. Burton, Virginia Lee, illus. 2014. (Folk Tale Classics Ser.). (ENG.). 48p. (J). (gr. -1-3). 9.99 (978-0-544-15952-5(7), 1550259, Clarion Bks.) HarperCollins Pubs.

Bright, J. E. The Brave Little Tailor: A Grimm & Gross Retelling. Banks, Timothy, illus. 2018. (Michael Dahl Presents: Grimm & Gross Ser.). (ENG.). 64p. (J). (gr. 3-5). lib. bdg. 21.99 (978-1-4965-7315-5(3), 138919, Stone Arch Bks.) Capstone.

Brown, Jason Robert. Tickety Tock. GrandPré, Mary, illus. 2008. 32p. (J). (gr. -1-3). lib. bdg. 18.89 (978-0-06-078753-0(8), Geringer, Laura Book) HarperCollins Pubs.

Giff, Patricia Reilly. A House of Tailors. 2006. (ENG.). 160p. (J). (gr. 3-7). 6.99 (978-0-440-23800-3(5), Yearling) Random Hse. Children's Bks.

Luxbacher, Irene. Mr. Frank, 1 vol. 2014. (ENG., Illus.). 32p. (J). (gr. k-3). 16.95 (978-1-55498-435-0(1)) Groundwood Bks. CAN. Dist: Publishers Group West (PGW).

McGann, James, illus. The Tailor & the Mouse. 2012. (First Steps in Music Ser.). 32p. (J). (gr. -1-k). 17.95 (978-1-57999-903-2(4)) G I A Pubns., Inc.

McGuire, Sarah. Valiant. (ENG.). 384p. (J). (gr. 5-12). 2018. pap. 9.99 (978-1-5415-1487-4(4), ae71f656-e91b-41c2-bf3e-bd9727f98f3d) 2015. E-Book 27.99 (978-1-5124-0198-1(6)) Lerner Publishing Group. (Carolrhoda Bks.).

Perez, Marlene. Princess Rock & the Royal Inches. 2004. (Shared Connections Ser.). (J). pap. 27.00 (978-1-4108-1633-7(8)); instr.'s gde. ed. 27.00 (978-1-4108-1609-2(5)) Benchmark Education Co.

Stofko, Michael D. The Tale of Taylor the Tailor. 2012. 30p. pap. 19.99 (978-1-4772-0238-8(2)) AuthorHouse.

Toledo, Eymard. The Best Tailor in Pinbauê. 2017. (Illus.). 32p. (J). (gr. k-3). 18.95 (978-1-60980-804-4(5), Triangle Square) Seven Stories Pr.

TAIWAN

Behnke, Alison. Taiwan in Pictures. 2007. (Visual Geography (Lerner) Ser.). (Illus.). 80p. (YA). (gr. 7-12). lib. bdg. 31.93 (978-0-8225-7148-3(X)) Twenty First Century Bks.

Hsu, Yi Ling. Typhoon Holidays: Taiwan. Kwag, Jin-yeong, illus. 2015. (Global Kids Storybooks Ser.). (ENG.). 32p. (J). (gr. 1-4). pap. 8.99 (978-1-925233-43-8(X), 2d596315-36c6-4d6d-82c0-3f783f079161, Big and SMALL) ChoiceMaker Pty. Ltd., The AUS. Dist: Lerner Publishing Group.

King, David C. & Orr, Tamra B. Taiwan. 2006. (Enchantment of the World Ser.). (ENG., Illus.). 144p. (J). (gr. 5-9). 37.00 (978-0-516-24856-1(1), Children's Pr.) Scholastic Library Publishing.

Moiz, Azra & Wu, Janice. Taiwan, 1 vol. 2nd rev. ed. 2007. (Cultures of the World (Second Edition)(r) Ser.). (ENG., Illus.). 144p. (gr. 5-5). lib. bdg. 49.79 (978-0-7614-2069-9(X), e2b6e016-acdc-4d9d-9580-d24874bb9c96) Cavendish Square Publishing LLC.

Moiz, Azra, et al. Taiwan, 1 vol. 3rd rev. ed. 2016. (Cultures of the World (Third Edition)(r) Ser.). (ENG., Illus.). 144p. (gr. 5-5). lib. bdg. 48.79 (978-1-5026-1846-7(X), 268d711d-3ae5-4ddf-9423-1c86dcbe4ba0) Cavendish Square Publishing LLC.

Owings, Lisa. Taiwan. 2014. (Exploring Countries Ser.). (ENG., Illus.). 32p. (J). (gr. 3-7). lib. bdg. 27.95 (978-1-62617-070-4(3), Blastoff! Readers) Bellwether Media.

Ryan, Michaela. Taiwan, 1 vol. 2003. (Countries of the World Ser.). (ENG., Illus.). 96p. (gr. 6-8). lib. bdg. 33.67 (978-0-8368-2368-4(0), bfebbbeb-3966-4a42-8ca2-9c3a459beb34) Stevens, Gareth Publishing LLLP.

Salter, Christopher L. Taiwan. 2004. (Modern World Nations Ser.). (ENG., Illus.). 144p. (gr. 6-12). lib. bdg. 35.00 (978-0-7910-7914-0(7), P114068, Facts On File) Infobase Holdings, Inc.

Somervill, Barbara A. Taiwan. 2014. (Enchantment of the World Ser.: 2). (ENG.). 144p. (J). lib. bdg. 40.00 (978-0-531-22018-4(4)) Scholastic Library Publishing.

Wan, Vanessa. Welcome to Taiwan, 1 vol. 2004. (Welcome to My Country Ser.). (ENG., Illus.). 48p. (gr. 2-4). lib. bdg. 29.67 (978-0-8368-3122-1(5), b4e44d67-21b1-4dea-905d-26c89f19e75b) Stevens, Gareth Publishing LLLP.

Williams, Heather DiLorenzo. Taiwan. 2019. (Countries We Come From Ser.). (ENG., Illus.). 32p. (J). (gr. k-3). 19.95 (978-1-64280-191-0(7)) Bearport Publishing Co., Inc.

TAIWAN—FICTION

Evans, Richard Paul. Michael Vey 4: Hunt for Jade Dragon. 2014. (Michael Vey Ser.: 4). (ENG., Illus.). 336p. (YA). (gr. 7). 19.99 *(978-1-4814-2438-7(6)*, Simon Pulse/Mercury Ink) Simon Pulse/Mercury Ink.

Hsu, Yi Ling. Typhoon Holidays: Taiwan. Cowley, Joy, ed. Kwag, Jin-yeong, illus. 2015. (Global Kids Storybooks Ser.). (ENG.). 32p. (gr. 1-4). 26.65 *(978-1-925246-04-9(3))*; 7.99 *(978-1-925246-56-8(6))*; 26.65 *(978-1-925246-30-8(2))* ChoiceMaker Pty. Ltd., The AUS. (Big and SMALL). Dist: Lerner Publishing Group.

Huang, SuHua. A Faithful Reading Partner: A Story from a Hakka Village. 2012. 28p. pap. 19.99 *(978-1-4685-6267-5(3))* AuthorHouse.

Itoh, Shimpei. Hyper Dolls, Vol. 5. 2003. (Illus.). 208p. pap. 15.95 *(978-1-929090-67-9(6))* International Comics & Entertainment L.L.C.

Lin, Grace. Dumpling Days. 2019. (Pacy Lin Novel Ser.: 3). (ENG., Illus.). 272p. (J). (gr. 3-7). pap. 7.99 *(978-0-316-53133-7(2))* Little, Brown Bks. for Young Readers.

Pan, Emily X. R. The Astonishing Color of After. 2019. (ENG.). 480p. (YA). (gr. 7-17). pap. 11.99 *(978-0-316-46401-7(5))* Little, Brown Bks. for Young Readers.

Pon, Cindy. Want. (ENG.). (YA). (gr. 9). 2019. 352p. pap. 12.99 *(978-1-4814-8923-2(2))* 2017. (Illus.). 336p. 19.99 *(978-1-4814-8922-5(4))* Simon Pulse. (Simon Pulse).

TALES

see Fables; Fairy Tales; Folklore; Legends

TALISMANS

see Charms

TALKING

see Speech

TALKING PICTURES

see Motion Pictures

TALL TALES

see also American Wit and Humor; Folklore; Legends

Cali, Davide & Chaud, Benjamin. The Truth about My Unbelievable Summer ... 2016. (ENG., Illus.). 44p. (J). (gr. 1-4). 12.99 *(978-1-4521-4483-2(4))* Chronicle Bks. LLC.

Case, Maggie. A Squirrel's Tale. 2011. 24p. (gr. -1). pap. 11.32 *(978-1-4567-5118-0(2))* AuthorHouse.

Coyle, Carmela Lavigna. The Tumbleweed Came Back. Rechin, Kevin, illus. 2013. 32p. (J). 15.95 *(978-1-933855-83-7(5)*, Rio Nuevo Pubs.) Rio Nuevo Pubs.

Day, Karen. Tall Tales. 2007. (ENG.). 229p. (J). (gr. 4-6). lib. bdg. 18.69 *(978-0-375-93773-6(0)*, Lamb, Wendy Bks.) Random Hse. Children's Bks.

Enderle, Dotti. The Cotton Candy Catastrophe at the Texas State Fair, 1 vol. Galey, Chuck, illus. 2004. (ENG.). 32p. (J). (gr. k-3). 19.99 *(978-1-58980-189-9(X)*, Pelican Publishing) Arcadia Publishing.

—Gingerbread Man Superhero!, 1 vol. Kulka, Joe, illus. 2009. (ENG.). 32p. (J). (gr. k-3). 16.99 *(978-1-58980-521-7(6)*, Pelican Publishing) Arcadia Publishing.

Garretson, Jerri. Kansas Tall Tales: Tenth Anniversary Anthology. Garretson, Jerri & Dollar, Diane A., illus. 2008. 106p. (J). pap. 19.95 *(978-0-9659712-7-0(9))* Ravenstone Pr.

Gill, Shelley. Prickly Rose. Love, Judy, illus. 2014. 32p. (J). (gr. -1-3). pap. 7.99 *(978-1-57091-357-0(9))* Charlesbridge Publishing, Inc.

—Sitka Rose. Cartwright, Shannon, illus. 2005. (ENG.). 32p. (J). (gr. -1-3). per. 7.95 *(978-1-57091-364-8(1))* Charlesbridge Publishing, Inc.

Hayes, Joe. The Lovesick Skunk, 1 vol. Castro L., Antonio, illus. 2016. (ENG.). 32p. (J). (gr. k-7). 7.95 *(978-1-941026-04-5(4)*, 8d7d164e-2331-4b4d-9c16-177daac6c8e2, Cinco Puntos Press) Lee & Low Bks., Inc.

Hopkinson, Deborah. Apples to Oregon. 2014. 17.00 *(978-1-63419-642-0(2))* Perfection Learning Corp.

—Apples to Oregon: Being the (Slightly) True Narrative of How a Brave Pioneer Father Brought Apples, Peaches, Pears, Plums, Grapes, & Cherries (and Children) Across the Plains. Carpenter, Nancy, illus. 2004. (ENG.). 40p. (J). (gr. -1-3). 19.99 *(978-0-689-84769-1(6))* Simon & Schuster, Inc.

Hurston, Zora Neale & Thomas, Joyce Carol. Lies & Other Tall Tales. Myers, Christopher, illus. 2015. (ENG.). 40p. (J). (gr. -1-3). pap. 7.99 *(978-0-06-000657-0(9)*, HarperCollins) HarperCollins Pubs.

Irving, Washington. The Devil & Tom Walker. 2007. (Tale Blazers: American Literature Ser.). 37p. (J). (gr. 4-7). pap. 3.30 *(978-0-89598-665-8(5))* Perfection Learning Corp.

Jacques, Brian. The Tale of Urso Brunov: Little Father of All Bears. Natchev, Alexi, illus. 2003. (ENG.). 48p. (J). (gr. -1-1). 21.19 *(978-0-399-23762-1(3))* Penguin Young Readers Group.

Jenkins, Amanda. Pecos Bill & Sluefoot Sue: An American Tall Tale. 2006. (J). pap. *(978-1-4108-7158-9(4))* Benchmark Education Co.

Johnston, Tony. Levi Strauss Gets a Bright Idea: A Fairly Fabricated Story of a Pair of Pants. Innerst, Stacy, illus. 2011. (ENG.). 32p. (J). (gr. -1-3). 17.99 *(978-0-15-206145-6(2)*, 1198451, Clarion Bks.) HarperCollins Pubs.

Jones, Nathan Smith. The Boy Who Ate America. Nelson, Casey, illus. 2007. 32p. (J). (gr. -1-3). 16.95 *(978-1-59038-814-3(3)*, Shadow Mountain) Shadow Mountain Publishing.

Kaplan, Bruce Eric. Meaniehead. Kaplan, Bruce Eric, illus. 2014. (ENG., Illus.). 40p. (J). (gr. -1-3). 17.99 *(978-1-4424-8542-6(6)*, Simon & Schuster Bks. For Young Readers) Simon & Schuster Bks. For Young Readers.

Kellogg, Steven. Paul Bunyan. 2004. (J). (gr. k-3). 17.20 *(978-0-8085-6790-5(X))* Turtleback.

Kimmel, Eric. Big Sam: a Rosh Hashanah Tall Tale. Starr, Jim, illus. 2017. (ENG.). 32p. (J). 17.95 *(978-1-68115-525-8(7)*, b57d0cd4-3605-4b00-8051-5d5c5cd9a780) Behrman Hse., Inc.

Kimmel, Eric A. The Great Texas Hamster Drive, 0 vols. Whatley, Bruce, illus. 2012. (ENG.). 40p. (J). (gr. -1-3). 16.99 *(978-0-7614-5357-4(1)*, 9780761453574, Two Lions) Amazon Publishing.

Krensky, Stephen. John Henry. Oldroyd, Mark, illus. 2006. (On My Own Folklore Ser.). (ENG.). 48p. (J). (gr. 2-4). lib. bdg. 25.26 *(978-1-57505-887-0(1)*, Millbrook Pr.) Lerner Publishing Group.

Manos, John. Big Ben Helps the Town. 2006. (Early Explorers Ser.). (J). pap. *(978-1-4108-6119-1(8))* Benchmark Education Co.

McClurkan, Rob. Aw, Nuts! 2014. (ENG., Illus.). 32p. (J). (gr. -1-3). 17.99 *(978-0-06-231729-2(6)*, HarperCollins) HarperCollins Pubs.

McDermott, Tom. Otis Steele & the Talleebone: A Southern Tall Tale, 1 vol. Crosby, Jeff, illus. 2013. (ENG.). 32p. (J). (gr. k-2). 16.99 *(978-1-4556-1736-4(9)*, Pelican Publishing) Arcadia Publishing.

McKissack, Patricia. Porch Lies: Tales of Slicksters, Tricksters, & Other Wily Characters. Carrilho, Andre, illus. 2006. (ENG.). 160p. (J). (gr. 3-7). 19.99 *(978-0-375-83619-0(5)*, Schwartz & Wade Bks.) Random Hse. Children's Bks.

Meredith, Susan Markowitz. Tall Tales of the Bunyans. 2016. (Spring Forward Ser.). (J). (gr. 2). *(978-1-4900-9430-4(X))* Benchmark Education Co.

Nolen, Jerdine. Big Jabe. Nelson, Kadir, illus. 2003. (ENG.). 32p. (J). (gr. k-5). pap. 7.99 *(978-0-06-054061-6(3)*, Amistad) HarperCollins Pubs.

—Thunder Rose. Nelson, Kadir, illus. 2007. (ENG.). 32p. (J). (gr. k-3). pap. 8.99 *(978-0-15-206006-0(5)*, 1198036, Clarion Bks.) HarperCollins Pubs.

—Thunder Rose. Nelson, Kadir, illus. 2007. (gr. k-3). 17.00 *(978-0-7569-8199-0(9))* Perfection Learning Corp.

Oppel, Kenneth. Peg & the Whale. 2004. (Illus.). (J). (gr. k-3). spiral bd. *(978-0-616-07245-5(7))* Canadian National Institute for the Blind/Institut National Canadien pour les Aveugles.

Orback, Craig, illus. Paul Bunyan. 2006. (On My Own Folklore Ser.). 48p. (J). (gr. -1-3). lib. bdg. 25.26 *(978-1-57505-888-7(X)*, Millbrook Pr.) Lerner Publishing Group.

Petruccio, Steven James. American Legends & Tall Tales. 2011. (Dover Classic Stories Coloring Book Ser.). (ENG., Illus.). 32p. (J). (gr. 3-6). pap. 3.99 *(978-0-486-47786-2(X)*, 47786X) Dover Pubns., Inc.

Rossi, Joyce & Rising Moon Editors. The Gullywasher: El Chaparron Torrencial. 2004. (ENG., Illus.). 32p. (J). (gr. k-3). pap. 7.95 *(978-0-87358-728-0(6))* Cooper Square Publishing Llc.

Rozier, Lucy Margaret. Jackrabbit Mccabe & the Electric Telegraph. Espinosa, Leo, illus. 2015. 40p. (J). (gr. -1-3). 18.99 *(978-0-385-37843-7(2)*, Schwartz & Wade Bks.) Random Hse. Children's Bks.

San Souci, Robert D. Cut from the Same Cloth: American Women of Myth, Legend, & Tall Tale. Pinkney, Brian, illus. 2005. 140p. 17.00 *(978-0-7569-6284-5(6))* Perfection Learning Corp.

Schnetzler, Pattie L. Widdermaker. Sealock, Rick, illus. 2005. 32p. (gr. k-2). 15.95 *(978-0-87614-647-7(7))* Lerner Publishing Group.

Scillian, Devin. Johnny Kaw: A Tall Tale. Sneed, Brad, illus. 2013. (ENG.). 32p. (J). (gr. 1-4). 15.95 *(978-1-58536-791-7(5)*, 202353) Sleeping Bear Pr.

Smith, Andrea P. Paul Bunyan. (Illus.). 24p. (J). 2012. 63.60 *(978-1-4488-5221-5(8))* 2011. (ENG., (gr. 2-3). pap. 11.60 *(978-1-4488-5220-8(X)*, cabeaddb-c060-4697-81df-84aba6c25c44) 2011. (ENG., (gr. 2-3). lib. bdg. 28.93 *(978-1-4488-5191-1(2)*, 566b9213-22a9-4dfe-90f7-f01931a4d7f7) Rosen Publishing Group, Inc., The. (PowerKids Pr.).

Smith, Ken. Tales from My Welsh Village. 2019. (ENG.). 384p. pap. 18.00 *(978-1-78461-525-3(0))* Y Lolfa GBR. Dist: Casemate Pubs. & Bk. Distributors, LLC.

Sowash, Rick. Ripsnorting Whoppers! A Book of Ohio Tall Tales. 2003. (J). 19.95 *(978-0-9762412-1-8(8))*; pap. 11.95 *(978-0-9762412-0-1(X))* Sowash, Rick Publishing Co.

Stone Arch Books Staff. The Tall Tale of Paul Bunyan. Blecha, Aaron, illus. 2010. (Graphic Spin Ser.). (ENG.). 40p. (J). (gr. 3-6). pap. 5.95 *(978-1-4342-2268-8(3)*, 103131, Stone Arch Bks.) Capstone.

Strauss, Kevin. Pecos Bill Invents the Ten-Gallon Hat, 1 vol. Harrington, David, illus. 2012. (ENG.). 32p. (J). (gr. k-3). 17.99 *(978-1-4556-1502-5(1)*, Pelican Publishing) Arcadia Publishing.

Tong, Paul, illus. Pecos Bill. 2006. (On My Own Folklore Ser.). 48p. (J). (gr. -1-3). lib. bdg. 25.26 *(978-1-57505-889-4(8)*, Millbrook Pr.) Lerner Publishing Group.

Webb, Lois. Tall Tales. 2007. (J). per. *(978-0-9791550-4-8(5))* About Time Publishing.

Weber, Lisa K., illus. Pecos Bill, Colossal Cowboy: The Graphic Novel. 2010. (Graphic Spin Ser.). (ENG.). 40p. (J). (gr. 3-6). pap. 5.95 *(978-1-4342-2267-1(5)*, 103130); lib. bdg. 25.32 *(978-1-4342-1896-4(1)*, 102355) Capstone. (Stone Arch Bks.).

Weidt, Maryann. Mama Loved to Worry. Balsaitis, Rachael, illus. 2016. (ENG.). 32p. (J). (gr. -1-1). 16.95 *(978-0-87351-994-6(9))* Minnesota Historical Society Pr.

Welling, Peter J. Darlene Halloween & the Great Chicago Fire, 1 vol. Welling, Peter J., illus. 2007. (ENG., Illus.). 32p. (J). (gr. k-3). 16.99 *(978-1-58980-479-1(1)*, Pelican Publishing) Arcadia Publishing.

Willey, Margaret. Clever Beatrice & the Best Little Pony. Solomon, Heather M., illus. 2004. (ENG.). 40p. (J). (gr. -1-3). 18.99 *(978-0-689-85339-5(4)*, Atheneum Bks. for Young Readers) Simon & Schuster Children's Publishing.

Wood, Audrey. Bunyans. 2014. 17.00 *(978-1-63419-650-5(3))* Perfection Learning Corp.

Yeager, Anne H. American Tall Tales. 2017. (Text Connections Guided Close Reading Ser.). (J). (gr. 2). *(978-1-4900-1839-3(5))* Benchmark Education Co.

TALLCHIEF, MARIA, 1925-2013

Gourley, Catherine. Who Is Maria Tallchief? Taylor, Val Paul, illus. 2003. (Who Was...? Ser.). 103p. 15.00 *(978-0-7569-1592-6(9))* Perfection Learning Corp.

TAMPA BAY RAYS (BASEBALL TEAM)

Epstein, Brad. Tampa Bay Rays 101: My First Team-Board-book. 2008. (ENG., Illus.). 22p. (J). pap. *(978-1-932530-78-0(9)*, 101 Bk.) Michaelson Entertainment.

Kennedy, Mike & Stewart, Mark. Meet the Rays. 2010. (Smart about Sports Ser.). 24p. (J). (gr. k-3). lib. bdg. 22.60 *(978-1-59953-374-2(X))* Norwood Hse. Pr.

LeBoutillier, Nate. The Story of the Tampa Bay Rays. 2011. (J). 35.65 *(978-1-60818-057-8(3)*, Creative Education) Creative Co., The.

Shofner, Shawndra. The Story of the Tampa Bay Devil Rays. 2007. (Baseball, the Great American Game Ser.). (Illus.). 48p. (YA). (gr. 4-7). lib. bdg. 32.80 *(978-1-58341-501-6(7))* Creative Co., The.

Stewart, Mark. The Tampa Bay Rays. 2012. (Team Spirit Ser.). 48p. (J). (gr. 3-6). lib. bdg. 29.27 *(978-1-59953-498-5(3))* Norwood Hse. Pr.

TANKS (MILITARY SCIENCE)

Adams, Simon. Tanks. 2009. (War Machines Ser.). (YA). (gr. 5-9). 28.50 *(978-1-59920-224-2(7))* Black Rabbit Bks.

Alvarez, Carlos. M109A6 Paladins. 2009. (Military Machines Ser.). (ENG., Illus.). 24p. (J). (gr. 3-7). lib. bdg. 26.95 *(978-1-60014-283-3(4))* Bellwether Media.

Bodden, Valerie. Tanks. 2012. (Illus.). 23p. (J). 25.65 *(978-1-60818-129-2(4)*, Creative Education) Creative Co., The.

Boutland, Craig. Attack Vehicles on Land: Tanks & Armored Fighting Vehicles. 2019. (Military Machines in the War on Terrorism Ser.). (ENG., Illus.). 32p. (J). (gr. 3-9). lib. bdg. 28.65 *(978-1-5435-7380-0(0)*, 140669) Capstone.

Brody, Walt. How Tanks Work. 2019. (Lightning Bolt Books (r) — Military Machines Ser.). (ENG., Illus.). 24p. (J). (gr. 1-3). 29.32 *(978-1-5415-5566-2(X)*, e0c1dba1-d645-42cc-a3b0-b2dd20bb6bdf); pap. 9.99 *(978-1-5415-7459-5(1)*, ea040484-e0fe-4b5a-bd05-bc3abc4cdf26) Lerner Publishing Group. (Lerner Pubns.).

Brook, Henry. Tanks. 2011. (Discovery Adventures Ser.). 80p. (J). pap. 8.99 *(978-0-7945-2137-0(1)*, Usborne) EDC Publishing.

Challen, Paul C. Mighty Tanks, 1 vol. 2010. (Vehicles on the Move Ser.). (ENG., Illus.). 32p. (J). (gr. k-3). pap. *(978-0-7787-3063-7(8))*; lib. bdg. *(978-0-7787-3049-1(2))* Crabtree Publishing Co.

Colson, Rob Scott. Tanks & Military Vehicles, 1 vol. 2013. (Ultimate Machines Ser.). (ENG., Illus.). 24p. (J). (gr. 5-5). pap. 9.25 *(978-1-4777-0119-5(2)*, 2095d0fa-a36e-4626-b302-7f178df433e9); lib. bdg. 26.27 *(978-1-4777-0067-9(6)*, 87a019d5-ad03-401d-94ac-b4844a0da467) Rosen Publishing Group, Inc., The. (PowerKids Pr.).

Cooke, Tim. Tanks. 2012. (Ultimate Military Machines Ser.). (Illus.). 32p. (J). (gr. 4-7). lib. bdg. 31.35 *(978-1-59920-823-7(7))* Black Rabbit Bks.

Cornish, Geoff. Tanks. 2003. (Military Hardware in Action Ser.). (ENG., Illus.). 48p. (J). (gr. 5-9). lib. bdg. 25.26 *(978-0-8225-4701-3(5))* Lerner Publishing Group.

David, Jack. Abrams Tanks. 2007. (Military Machines Ser.). (ENG., Illus.). 24p. (J). (gr. 3-7). lib. bdg. 26.95 *(978-1-60014-101-0(3))* Bellwether Media.

David West. Tank. 2006. (Illus.). 32p. (J). pap. *(978-1-4109-2566-4(8))* Steck-Vaughn.

Dieker, Wendy Strobel. Tanks. 2019. (Spot Mighty Machines Ser.). (ENG.). 16p. (J). (gr. -1-2). *(978-1-68151-648-6(9)*, 10780) Amicus.

Dougherty, Martin J. Tanks of World War II up Close, 1 vol., 1. Pearson, Colin, illus. 2015. (Military Technology: Top Secret Clearance Ser.). (ENG.). 224p. (YA). (gr. 7-8). 46.80 *(978-1-5081-7086-0(X)*, ba99d0bc-7c0f-4334-913a-da6201606697, Rosen Young Adult) Rosen Publishing Group, Inc., The.

Ellis, Catherine. Tanks/Tanques. 2009. (Mega Military Machines/Megamaquinas militares Ser.). (ENG & SPA.). 24p. (J). (gr. 1-1). 42.50 *(978-1-61514-644-4(X)*, Editorial Buenas Letras) Rosen Publishing Group, Inc., The.

—Tanks/Tanques, 1 vol. Brusca, Maria Cristina, tr. 2007. (Mega Military Machines / Megamaquinas Militares Ser.). (SPA & ENG., Illus.). 24p. (J). (gr. 1-1). lib. bdg. 26.27 *(978-1-4042-7619-2(X)*, d11d2fe9-1bb7-49ce-9b64-248fcc92f54c) Rosen Publishing Group, Inc., The.

Harvey, Ian & Chasemore, Richard. Tanks. (Illus.). 32p. (J). mass mkt. 8.99 *(978-0-590-24940-9(1))* Scholastic, Inc.

Haskew, Michael E. Tanks: Inside & Out, 1 vol. 2011. (Weapons of War Ser.). (ENG., Illus.). 160p. (J). (gr. 7-7). lib. bdg. 47.80 *(978-1-4488-5980-1(8)*, d66fd16e-4557-4f89-8424-054b953ca693) Rosen Publishing Group, Inc., The.

—The World's Most Powerful Tanks, 1 vol. 2016. (World's Most Powerful Machines Ser.). (ENG., Illus.). 224p. (J). (gr. 9-9). 46.80 *(978-1-4994-6558-7(0)*, b4bedfe0-be48-4f1e-a0d8-58dabb19572d) Rosen Publishing Group, Inc., The.

Jackson, Kay. Military Tanks in Action. 2009. (Amazing Military Vehicles Ser.). 24p. (gr. 3-3). 42.50 *(978-1-61511-318-7(5)*, PowerKids Pr.); (ENG.). (YA). lib. bdg. 26.27 *(978-1-4358-2749-3(X)*, 382e6516-5e19-4803-847a-a8a2e19c2ab3); (ENG., Illus.). (J). pap. 9.25 *(978-1-4358-3159-9(4)*, 3ef15006-2050-402f-a0d8-ba09424190f6, PowerKids Pr.) Rosen Publishing Group, Inc., The.

Jackson, Robert. 101 Great Tanks, 1 vol. 2010. (101 Greatest Weapons of All Times Ser.). (ENG., Illus.). 112p. (YA). (gr. 10-10). lib. bdg. 39.80 *(978-1-4358-3595-5(6)*, baffb633-ab21-4909-9b67-6e2899b82c94) Rosen Publishing Group, Inc., The.

LaFontaine, Bruce. Tanks & Armored Vehicles. 2013. (Dover Planes Trains Automobiles Coloring Ser.). (ENG., Illus.). 48p. (J). (gr. 3-8). pap. 5.99 *(978-0-486-41317-4(9)*, 413179) Dover Pubns., Inc.

Mavrikis, Peter. Tanks. 2014. (Illus.). 48p. (J). *(978-1-4351-5365-3(0))* Barnes & Noble, Inc.

—Tanks, 1 vol., 1. 2015. (What's Inside? Ser.). (ENG.). 48p. (J). (gr. 3-4). pap. 12.75 *(978-1-5081-4619-3(5)*, fd973b04-4adf-43a9-ab4e-53f73b1d0b41, PowerKids Pr.) Rosen Publishing Group, Inc., The.

Morey, Allan. Tanks. 2014. (Illus.). 24p. (J). lib. bdg. 25.65 *(978-1-62031-106-6(2)*, Bullfrog Bks.) Jump! Inc.

Murray, Laura K. Tanks. 2016. (Seedlings Ser.). (Illus.). 24p. (J). 28.50 *(978-1-60818-665-5(2)*, Creative Education); (ENG., (gr. -1-k). pap. 7.99 *(978-1-62832-250-7(0)*, 22681, Creative Paperbacks) Creative Co., The.

Murrell, Deborah. Knights & Armor, 1 vol. 2008. (Medieval Warfare Ser.). (ENG.). 32p. (gr. 3-3). (J). lib. bdg. 28.67 *(978-0-8368-9210-9(0)*, 70d52ad7-e696-42e3-a36b-adcd12a89f22, Gareth Stevens Secondary Library); pap. 11.50 *(978-0-8368-9337-3(9)*, 4cf7c546-a668-4647-9ac4-ca8964c9e443) Stevens, Gareth Publishing LLLP.

Nagelhout, Ryan. Tanks, 1 vol. 2014. (Mighty Military Machines Ser.). (ENG.). 32p. (J). (gr. 1-1). pap. 11.50 *(978-1-4824-2126-2(7)*, 9f8dac5a-0425-4e9c-9e66-ce8652095e60) Stevens, Gareth Publishing LLLP.

Riggs, Kate. FV101 Scorpion. 2018. (Now That's Fast! Ser.). (ENG.). 24p. (J). (gr. 1-4). pap. 8.99 *(978-1-62832-586-7(0)*, 19855, Creative Paperbacks) Creative Co., The.

Scheff, Matt. Tanks: A 4D Book. 2018. (Mighty Military Machines Ser.). (ENG., Illus.). 24p. (J). (gr. -1-2). lib. bdg. 24.65 *(978-1-9771-0111-2(9)*, 138302, Pebble) Capstone.

Souter, Gerry & Kiland, Taylor Baldwin. Armored Tanks: Battlefield Dominance, 1 vol. 2015. (Military Engineering in Action Ser.). (ENG., Illus.). 48p. (gr. 6-6). 29.60 *(978-0-7660-6908-4(7)*, b87b3960-6fc1-4af6-97e2-ecacb2f14c65); pap. 12.70 *(978-0-7660-7059-2(X)*, eba82e7c-f3cb-46af-8633-546f75735e97) Enslow Publishing, LLC.

Tanks. 2003. (Illus.). 32p. (YA). pap. *(978-1-904516-34-7(3)*, Pavilion Children's Books) Pavilion Bks.

West, David. Tanks. (What's Inside? Ser.). (ENG., Illus.). 24p. (J). (gr. k-3). 2017. 28.50 *(978-1-62588-406-0(0)*, 19391) 2015. 27.10 *(978-1-62588-069-7(3)*, 19321) Black Rabbit Bks. (Smart Apple Media).

—Tanks. West, David, illus. 2019. (War Machines Ser.). (ENG., Illus.). 32p. (J). (gr. 5-6). pap. *(978-0-7787-6684-1(5)*, 02674d78-310a-4f84-b7f0-dadef7336ce3); lib. bdg. *(978-0-7787-6669-8(1)*, c69f6e5e-e82d-415e-8f60-575babfdce9e) Crabtree Publishing Co.

West, David, illus. Tanks. 2017. (What's Inside? Ser.). 24p. (gr. k-3). lib. bdg. 28.50 *(978-1-62588-402-2(8))* Black Rabbit Bks.

Zuehlke, Jeffrey. Tanks. 2005. (Pull Ahead Books-Mighty Movers Ser.). (ENG., Illus.). 32p. (gr. k-3). lib. bdg. 22.60 *(978-0-8225-2865-4(7)*, Lerner Pubns.) Lerner Publishing Group.

TANZANIA

Here are entered works on the jurisdiction of Tanzania formed in 1964 by the merger of Tanganyika and Zanzibar for all periods and subjects. Works on the island of Zanzibar for all periods are entered under Zanzibar. Works limited in subject coverage to the historical, political or cultural aspects of Tanganyika for the period before the merger in 1964 are entered under Tanganyika. Works on other subjects relating to Tanganyika for any pre-merger period are entered under the name of the present jurisdiction, Tanzania.

Cavallo, Anna. Tanzania. 2011. (Country Explorers Ser.). 48p. pap. 51.02 *(978-0-7613-7627-9(5))* Lerner Publishing Group.

Doak, Robin S. Jane Goodall: Chimpanzee Protector, 1 vol. 2014. (Women in Conservation Ser.). (ENG., Illus.). 48p. (J). (gr. 3-6). pap. 8.99 *(978-1-4846-0474-8(1)*, 126604, Heinemann) Capstone.

Edwards, Roberta. Who Is Jane Goodall? 2012. (Who Is...? Ser.). lib. bdg. 16.00 *(978-0-606-26651-2(8))* Turtleback.

Ferguson, Amanda. The Attack Against the U. S. Embassies in Kenya & Tanzania. 2009. (Terrorist Attacks Ser.). 64p. (gr. 5-5). 58.50 *(978-1-60853-309-1(3))* Rosen Publishing Group, Inc., The.

Guidi, Victoria. Who on Earth Is Jane Goodall? Champion for the Chimpanzees, 1 vol. 2009. (Scientists Saving the Earth Ser.). (ENG., Illus.). 112p. (gr. 5-6). lib. bdg. 35.93 *(978-1-59845-119-1(7)*, 3bf4bd2e-0f8b-4d4f-91f8-096c6440187a) Enslow Publishing, LLC.

Hand, Carol. Jane Goodall, 1 vol. 2014. (Great Science Writers Ser.). (ENG., Illus.). 112p. (J). (gr. 7-7). 38.80 *(978-1-4777-7685-8(0)*, 1e07e3f0-5d47-4a5c-a94d-856fb2601132) Rosen Publishing Group, Inc., The.

Heale, Jay & Wong, Winnie. Tanzania, 1 vol. 2nd rev. ed. 2009. (Cultures of the World (Second Edition)(r) Ser.). (ENG.). 144p. (gr. 5-5). lib. bdg. 49.79 *(978-0-7614-3417-7(8)*, c41e1b84-8b9a-48d6-8db2-33b9fb2b6624) Cavendish Square Publishing LLC.

Heale, Jay, et al. Tanzania, 1 vol. 2018. (Cultures of the World (Third Edition)(r) Ser.). (ENG.). 144p. (gr. 5-5). lib. bdg. 48.79 *(978-1-5026-3632-4(8)*, 87da3671-1c12-4ccf-a266-0d5d23e0f979) Cavendish Square Publishing LLC.

Hyde, Natalie. Serengeti Research Journal. 2018. (Ecosystems Research Journal Ser.). (Illus.). 32p. (J). (gr. 4-5). *(978-0-7787-4660-7(7))* Crabtree Publishing Co.

K. Williams, Megan. Maddy's Amazing African Birthday, 1 vol. Vallecchi, Alessandro & Vallecchi Williams, Maddalena, photos by. 2009. (ENG., Illus.). 32p. (J). (gr. 1-4). pap. 12.95 *(978-1-897187-47-0(5))* Second Story Pr. CAN. Dist: Orca Bk. Pubs. USA.

Krebs, Laurie. We All Went on Safari: A Counting Journey Through Tanzania. Cairns, Julia, illus. 2003. (ENG.). 32p. (J). (gr. k-3). 16.99 *(978-1-84148-478-5(4))* Barefoot Bks., Inc.

Leathers, Dan. The Snows of Kilimanjaro. 2007. (On the Verge of Extinction Ser.). (Illus.). 32p. (YA). (gr. 2-5). lib. bdg. 25.70 *(978-1-58415-584-3(1))* Mitchell Lane Pubs.

MacDonald, Joan Vos. Tanzania. Rotberg, Robert I., ed. 2012. (Evolution of Africa's Major Nations Ser.). (Illus.). 88p. (J). (gr. 7). 22.95 *(978-1-4222-2186-0(5))* Mason Crest.

—Tanzania. 2011. (J). pap. *(978-1-4222-2214-0(4))* 2006. (Illus.). 85p. (YA). lib. bdg. 21.95 *(978-1-59084-813-5(6))* Mason Crest.

Mailu, David G. Julius Nyerere: Father of Ujamaa. 2005. (Lion Book Ser.). (Illus.). ix, 81p. (J). *(978-9966-951-32-8(6))* Sasa Sema Publications Ltd.

Oachs, Emily Rose. Tanzania. 2016. (Exploring Countries Ser.). (ENG., Illus.). 32p. (J). (gr. 3-7). 27.95 *(978-1-62617-405-4(9)*, Blastoff! Readers) Bellwether Media.

Pritchett, Bev. Tanzania in Pictures. 2nd ed. 2008. (Visual Geography (Lerner) Ser.). (Illus.). 80p. (YA). (gr. 7-12). lib.

TUV

bdg. 30.60 *(978-0-8225-8571-8(5))* Twenty First Century Bks.
Pugliano-Martin, Carol. Cats of the Serengeti. 2011. (Early Connections Ser.). (J). *(978-1-61672-575-4(3))* Benchmark Education Co.
Rice, Dona. El Serengueti. rev. ed. 2019. (Mathematics in the Real World Ser.). (SPA.). 20p. (J). (gr. k-1). 8.99 *(978-1-4258-2818-9(3))* Teacher Created Materials, Inc.
Wairagala, Wakabi. Tanzania, 1 vol. 2004. (Countries of the World Ser.). (ENG., Illus.). 96p. (gr. 6-8). lib. bdg. 33.67 *(978-0-8368-3119-1(5),* 8d6e2cde-c15e-45aa-896f-f2f5ea6d80c2) Stevens, Gareth Publishing LLLP.
Watson, Galadriel Findlay. Mount Kilimanjaro. (J). 2013. 28.55 *(978-1-62127-476-6(4))* 2013. pap. 13.95 *(978-1-62127-482-7(9))* 2008. (Illus.). 32p. (gr. 5-6). pap. 9.95 *(978-1-59036-935-7(1))* 2008. (Illus.). 32p. (gr. 5-6). lib. bdg. 26.00 *(978-1-59036-934-0(3))* Weigl Pubs., Inc.
Weil, Ann. Meet Our New Student from Tanzania. 2008. (Meet Our New Student Ser.). 48p. (YA). (gr. 2-5). lib. bdg. 29.95 *(978-1-58415-656-7(2))* Mitchell Lane Pubs.
Winter, Jeanette. The Watcher: Jane Goodall's Life with the Chimps. Winter, Jeanette, illus. 2011. (ENG., Illus.). 48p. (J). (gr. -1-3). 18.99 *(978-0-375-86774-3(0),* Schwartz & Wade Bks.) Random Hse. Children's Bks.

TANZANIA—FICTION

Archambault, John. By the Baobab Tree. Bender, Robert, illus. 2005. (J). *(978-1-58669-164-6(3))* Childcraft Education Corp.
Burgess, Lisa Maria. Juma & Little Sungura. Gugu, Abdul M., illus. 2013. 32p. 19.95 *(978-1-939604-06-4(0));* pap. 9.99 *(978-1-939604-02-6(8))* Barranca Pr.
—Juma Cooks Chapati. Gugu, Abdul M., illus. 2013. 32p. 19.95 *(978-1-939604-08-8(7));* pap. 9.99 *(978-1-939604-04-0(4))* Barranca Pr.
—Juma on Safari. Gugu, Abdul M., illus. 2013. 32p. 19.95 *(978-1-939604-07-1(9));* pap. 9.99 *(978-1-939604-03-3(6))* Barranca Pr.
—Juma's Dhow Race. Gugu, Abdul M., illus. 2013. 32p. 19.95 *(978-1-939604-09-5(5));* pap. 9.99 *(978-1-939604-05-7(2))* Barranca Pr.
Carlson, Martin D. Rfaud Tastes Wisdom. Oketch, Alphonce Omondi, illus. 2013. 36p. pap. 11.00 *(978-0-9848791-2-0(9))* BoCook Publishing.
Krebs, Laurie. We All Went on Safari. Cairns, Julia, illus. 2004. (ENG.). 32p. (J). (gr. k-5). pap. 9.99 *(978-1-84148-119-7(X))* Barefoot Bks., Inc.
—We All Went on Safari: A Counting Journey Through Tanzania. Cairns, Julia, illus. 2010. (J). 18.10 *(978-0-7569-9319-1(9))* Perfection Learning Corp.
Krulik, Nancy. Super Special: Two Tales, One Dog. Braun, Sebastien, illus. 2016. (Magic Bone Ser.: 12). 192p. (J). (gr. 1-3). 6.99 *(978-0-448-48877-6(9),* Grosset & Dunlap) Penguin Young Readers Group.
Matthews, T. J. The Canoeing Safari. Rheburg, Judy, illus. 2004. (J). *(978-0-938978-35-0(7))* Wycliffe Bible Translators.
—The Village Safari. Rheburg, Judy, illus. 2005. (J). *(978-0-938978-36-7(5))* Wycliffe Bible Translators.
Meyrick, Rich. Jaspa's Journey 2: The Pride of London. 2016. (ENG., Illus.). (J). (gr. 4-6). pap. 15.95 *(978-1-62815-315-6(6))* Speaking Volumes, LLC.
Milway, Katie Smith. The Banana-Leaf Ball: How Play Can Change the World. Milway, Katie Smith, illus. 2017. (CitizenKid Ser.). (ENG., Illus.). 32p. (J). (gr. 3-7). 18.99 *(978-1-77138-331-8(3))* Kids Can Pr., Ltd. CAN. Dist: Hachette Bk. Group.
Mollel, Tololwa M. My Rows & Piles of Coins. Lewis, E. B., illus. 2019. (ENG.). 32p. (J). (gr. -1-3). pap. 8.99 *(978-0-358-12447-4(6),* 1753728, Clarion Bks.) HarperCollins Pubs.
Mwamgwirani, Juma Mwakimatu & Mwakimatu, Juma Mwamgwirani. The Choice. 2015. (ENG., Illus.). 148p. (J). pap. *(978-9987-08-162-2(2))* Mkuki na Nyoka Pubs.
Newman, Gwill York. Bingo Bear Was Here: A Toy Bear's Climb to the Top of Africa's Highest Mountain. Babcock, Jeff, illus. 2003. 48p. (J). pap. 8.95 *(978-0-86534-395-5(0))* Sunstone Pr.
Pennels, Geraldine M. The School Shenanigans of Amy & Nontand: Volume Two Fifth Grade. 2010. 144p. pap. 11.50 *(978-1-60911-848-8(0),* Eloquent Bks.) Strategic Book Publishing & Rights Agency (SBPRA).
Popescu, Petru. Footprints in Time. 2008. 256p. (J). (gr. 5). lib. bdg. 17.89 *(978-0-06-088400-0(2),* Geringer, Laura Book) HarperCollins Pubs.
Quirk, Katie. A Girl Called Problem. 2013. (ENG., Illus.). 256p. (J). pap. 8.50 *(978-0-8028-5404-9(4),* Eerdmans Bks For Young Readers) Eerdmans, William B. Publishing Co.
Schwalbach, Pamela. The Happiest Day for Simeon & Sula. 2011. 28p. (gr. 4-6). pap. 15.00 *(978-1-4567-5062-6(3))* AuthorHouse.
Serengeti Safari: Animal Adventures in Africa. 2010. 64p. pap. 6.00 *(978-81-7806-191-7(0))* Unicorn Bks. Pvt Ltd. IND. Dist: Mahal, Pustak Pubs., Booksellers & Order Suppliers.
Stuve-Bodeen, Stephanie. Babu's Song. Boyd, Aaron, illus. 2003. (ENG.). 32p. (J). 16.95 *(978-1-58430-058-8(2))* Lee & Low Bks., Inc.
—Elizabeti's Doll, 1 vol. 2009. (Elizabeti Ser.). (ENG., Illus.). (J). (gr. -1-2). 32p. pap. 11.95 *(978-1-58430-081-6(7),* leelowbooks); 34p. 16.95 *(978-1-880000-70-0(9))* Lee & Low Bks., Inc.
—La Muneca de Elizabeti. Sarfatti, Esther, tr. Hale, Christy, illus. braille ed. 2004. (SPA.). (J). (gr. k-3). spiral bd. *(978-0-616-08966-8(X))* Canadian National Institute for the Blind/Institut National Canadien pour les Aveugles.
—La Muñeca de Elizabeti (Spanish Edition), 1 vol. 2009. (Elizabeti Ser.). (SPA., Illus.). 32p. (J). (gr. -1-2). pap. 11.95 *(978-1-58430-001-4(9),* leelowbooks) Lee & Low Bks., Inc.
Sullivan, Tara. Golden Boy. 2014. 384p. (J). (gr. 5). pap. 8.99 *(978-0-14-242450-6(1),* Puffin Books) Penguin Young Readers Group.
Weston Woods Staff, creator. Elizabeti's Doll. 2011. 38.75 *(978-0-439-84574-8(2));* 18.95 *(978-0-439-73629-9(3))* Weston Woods Studios, Inc.
White, Paul. Jungle Doctor in Slippery Places. 2011. (Flamingo Fiction 9-13s Ser.). (ENG., Illus.). 160p. (J). (gr. 4-7). pap. 8.99 *(978-1-84550-298-0(1),* 2d5341c8-b7a7-41d9-9f98-f018ae7cd7c8) Christian Focus Pubns. GBR. Dist: Baker & Taylor Publisher Services (BTPS).
—Jungle Doctor Meets a Lion. 2011. (Flamingo Fiction 9-13s Ser.). (ENG., Illus.). 176p. (J). 8.99 *(978-1-84550-392-5(9),* 0590f404-45d7-4593-b5b3-7e20994a2ae9) Christian Focus Pubns. GBR. Dist: Baker & Taylor Publisher Services (BTPS).
—Jungle Doctor on the Hop. 2015. (Flamingo Fiction 9-13s Ser.). (ENG., Illus.). 160p. (J). (gr. 4-7). per. 8.99 *(978-1-84550-297-3(3),* d66d650a-5d06-4ed6-9f8e-bb803656ca4a) Christian Focus Pubns. GBR. Dist: Baker & Taylor Publisher Services (BTPS).
—Jungle Doctor Pulls a Leg. rev. ed. 2008. (Flamingo Fiction 9-13s Ser.). (ENG., Illus.). 176p. (J). 8.99 *(978-1-84550-389-5(9),* 202e638e-2686-475c-9905-e26560541b03) Christian Focus Pubns. GBR. Dist: Baker & Taylor Publisher Services (BTPS).
—Jungle Doctor Spots a Leopard. rev. ed. 2008. (Flamingo Fiction 9-13s Ser.). (ENG., Illus.). 176p. (J). (gr. 5-7). per. 8.99 *(978-1-84550-301-7(5),* 19e1be96-5b42-4620-a898-bc67dd924342) Christian Focus Pubns. GBR. Dist: Baker & Taylor Publisher Services (BTPS).
—Jungle Doctor Stings a Scorpion. rev. ed. 2008. (Flamingo Fiction 9-13s Ser.). (ENG., Illus.). 160p. (J). 8.99 *(978-1-84550-390-1(2),* 365d3eb7-29af-4f22-ba6a-32a6c0f815de) Christian Focus Pubns. GBR. Dist: Baker & Taylor Publisher Services (BTPS).

TAOISM

Hartz, Paula R. Daoism. 3rd. ed. 2009. (World Religions Ser.). (ENG., Illus.). 144p. (gr. 6-12). 40.00 *(978-1-60413-115-4(2),* P163099, Facts On File) Infobase Holdings, Inc.
McGinnis, Mark W. The Show-Off Monkey & Other Taoist Tales. 2017. (Illus.). 80p. (J). (gr. k-4). 19.95 *(978-1-61180-347-1(0))* Shambhala Pubns., Inc.

TAPE RECORDERS

see Magnetic Recorders and Recording

TAPESTRY

Noble, Marty. Medieval Tapestries Coloring Book. 2004. (Dover Fashion Coloring Book Ser.). (ENG., Illus.). 32p. (gr. 6-8). pap. 3.99 *(978-0-486-43686-9(1),* 436861) Dover Pubns., Inc.

TAPESTRY—FICTION

Hinrichs, Alexandra S. D. Thérèse Makes a Tapestry. Graef, Renée, illus. 2016. (ENG.). 40p. (J). (gr. 1). 19.95 *(978-1-60606-473-3(8),* J. Paul Getty Museum) Getty Pubns.
Perkins, T. J. Image in the Tapestry: A Kim & Kelly Mystery. 2005. (Illus.). 155p. (YA). 10.99 *(978-0-9777538-3-3(2))* GumShoe Press.
Polacco, Patricia. Christmas Tapestry. 2008. (ENG.). 48p. (J). (gr. 1-4). pap. 8.99 *(978-0-14-241165-0(5),* Puffin Books) Penguin Young Readers Group.

TARBELL, IDA M. (IDA MINERVA), 1857-1944

McCully, Emily Arnold. Ida M. Tarbell: The Woman Who Challenged Big Business — And Won! 2014. (ENG., Illus.). 288p. (YA). (gr. 7). 18.99 *(978-0-547-29092-8(6),* 1412369, Clarion Bks.) HarperCollins Pubs.
Somervill, Barbara A. Ida Tarbell: Pioneer Investigative Reporter. 2004. (World Writers Ser.). (Illus.). 112p. (YA). (gr. 6-12). 23.95 *(978-1-883846-87-9(0),* First Biographies) Reynolds, Morgan Inc.

TARZAN (FICTITIOUS CHARACTER)—FICTION

Briggs, Andy. Tarzan: The Greystoke Legacy. 2011. (ENG.). 304p. pap. *(978-0-571-27238-9(X))* Faber & Faber, Ltd.
Burroughs, Edgar. Tarzan of the Apes. (ENG.). (J). 2020. 254p. (gr. 3-7). pap. 9.99 *(978-1-6550-6992-5(6))* 2019. 282p. pap. 30.99 *(978-1-7074-2950-9(2))* Independently Published.
—Tarzan of the Apes. 2019. (Tarzan Ser.: Vol. 1). (ENG.). 214p. (J). 12.99 *(978-1-5154-4344-5(2));* pap. 6.99 *(978-1-5154-4345-2(0))* Wilder Pubns., Corp.
—The Tarzan Twins. Grant, Douglas, illus. 2011. 126p. 40.95 *(978-1-258-05126-6(5))* Literary Licensing, LLC.
San Souci, Robert D. & Burroughs, Edgar. Tarzan. McCurdy, Michael, illus. 2004. 31p. (J). (gr. k-4). reprint ed. 16.00 *(978-0-7567-7576-6(0))* DIANE Publishing Co.

TASMANIA

Markle, Sandra. Tasmanian Devils. 2006. (Animal Scavengers Ser.). (Illus.). 39p. (J). (gr. 3-7). pap. 7.95 *(978-0-8225-3470-9(3),* First Avenue Editions) Lerner Publishing Group.

TASMANIA—FICTION

Conolan, Emily. Break Your Chains: the Freedom Finders. 2019. (Freedom Finders Ser.). (ENG., Illus.). 288p. (J). (gr. 4-8). pap. 10.99 *(978-1-76029-491-5(8))* Allen & Unwin AUS. Dist: Independent Pubs. Group.
Johnson, Gillian. Thora & the Incredible Crystals. 2007. (Illus.). 272p. *(978-0-207-20017-5(3))* HarperCollins Pubs. Australia.
Nowra, Louis. Into That Forest. 0 vols. 2013. (ENG.). 160p. (YA). (gr. 7-9). 16.99 *(978-1-4778-1725-4(5),* 9781477817254, Skyscape); 162p. 16.99 *(978-1-4778-6725-9(2))* Amazon Publishing.
Parker, Richard. Voyage to Tasmani. Seward, Prudence, illus. 2011. 128p. 40.95 *(978-1-258-08572-8(0))* Literary Licensing, LLC.
Roy, James. Billy Mack's War. 2004. 245p. (J). pap. *(978-0-7022-3479-8(6))* Univ. of Queensland Pr.
Russon, Penni. Breathe. 2007. (ENG., Illus.). 368p. (YA). (gr. 9-18). 16.99 *(978-0-06-079393-7(7))* HarperCollins Pubs.

TAVERNS (INNS)

see also Hotels, Motels, etc.; Restaurants

The Life of a Colonial Innkeeper. 2013. (Jr. Graphic Colonial America Ser.). 24p. (J). (gr. 3-6). pap. 63.60 *(978-1-4777-1436-2(7),* PowerKids Pr.) Rosen Publishing Group, Inc., The.
Pelleschi, Andrea. The Life of a Colonial Innkeeper, 1 vol. 2013. (Jr. Graphic Colonial America Ser.). (ENG.). 24p. (J). (gr. 2-3). 28.93 *(978-1-4777-1309-9(3),* 8718f95d-1bae-43b9-9fba-2f81dc3b8f62); pap. 11.60 *(978-1-4777-1435-5(9),* 88f89634-3149-413e-aebb-13fdcc77ed10) Rosen Publishing Group, Inc., The. (PowerKids Pr.).

TAXATION

Colby, Jennifer. Money in the Community. Bane, Jeff, illus. 2018. (My Early Library: My Guide to Money Ser.). (ENG.). 24p. (J). (gr. k-1). lib. bdg. 30.64 *(978-1-5341-2901-6(4),* 211648) Cherry Lake Publishing.
Crayton, Lisa A. & La Bella, Laura. Taxes: What They Are & How They Work, 1 vol. 2015. (Economics in the 21st Century Ser.). (ENG.). 96p. (gr. 8-8). 36.27 *(978-0-7660-7376-0(9),* 62dab4df-8ac2-45ac-888b-0827d512b022) Enslow Publishing, LLC.
Engdahl, Sylvia, ed. Taxation, 1 vol. 2010. (Issues on Trial Ser.). (ENG.). 184p. (gr. 10-12). 49.93 *(978-0-7377-4492-7(8),* 67e03631-0939-4653-abc1-f3131ff4c39e, Greenhaven Publishing) Greenhaven Publishing LLC.
Gagne, Tammy. Teen Guide to Earning Income. 2014. (ENG., Illus.). 48p. (gr. 4-6). lib. bdg. 29.95 *(978-1-61228-470-5(1))* Mitchell Lane Pubs.
Harmon, Julian. My Dad Pays Taxes. 2013. (InfoMax Readers Ser.). (ENG.). 24p. (J). (gr. 2-3). pap. 49.50 *(978-1-4777-2442-2(7));* (Illus.). pap. 8.25 *(978-1-4777-2440-8(0),* 3013e971-d61d-49b1-b056-ca1ce64f37e5) Rosen Publishing Group, Inc., The. (Rosen Classroom).
Hiber, Amanda, ed. Do Tax Breaks Benefit the Economy?, 1 vol. 2009. (At Issue Ser.). (ENG.). 120p. (gr. 10-12). 41.03 *(978-0-7377-4298-5(4),* 5c17a888-270d-4052-beee-a240e48939d2); pap. 28.80 *(978-0-7377-4297-8(6),* 4bf337c7-a9bc-4607-b721-cf8266184400) Greenhaven Publishing LLC. (Greenhaven Publishing).
Lankford, Ronald D., Jr., ed. Should the Rich Pay Higher Taxes?, 1 vol. 2014. (At Issue Ser.). (ENG.). 112p. (gr. 10-12). pap. 28.80 *(978-0-7377-6859-6(2),* e032a72b-98d7-4c48-9150-3ebf5a7f7a9d); lib. bdg. 41.03 *(978-0-7377-6858-9(4),* 7086b5c5-e0df-4fe4-ac49-bbec314de2bd) Greenhaven Publishing LLC. (Greenhaven Publishing).

TAXATION—UNITED STATES

Arbus, Abby. Why Do We Pay Taxes?, 1 vol. 2013. (Rosen Readers Ser.). (ENG.). 24p. (J). (gr. 2-2). pap. 8.25 *(978-1-4777-2296-1(3),* a68186dd-6c83-44d5-9e69-d1998d1c33d1); pap. 49.50 *(978-1-4777-2297-8(1))* Rosen Publishing Group, Inc., The. (Rosen Classroom).
Barousse, Jason. The Internal Revenue Service: Why U. S. Citizens Pay Taxes, 1 vol. 2017. (Landmarks of Democracy: American Institutions Ser.). (ENG.). 24p. (J). (gr. 3-3). pap. 9.25 *(978-1-5081-6139-4(9),* 7abe7069-8568-4393-8316-427d00f9c5c7, PowerKids Pr.) Rosen Publishing Group, Inc., The.
Bedesky, Baron & Bedesky, Baron. What Are Taxes? 2008. (ENG., Illus.). 32p. (J). (gr. 3-7). pap. *(978-0-7787-4262-3(8))* Crabtree Publishing Co.
Bissinger, Caleb, ed. Taxes & Society's Priorities, 1 vol. 2017. (Introducing Issues with Opposing Viewpoints Ser.). (ENG.). 120p. (YA). (gr. 7-10). 43.63 *(978-1-5345-0192-8(4),* bfe2bd96-c565-4c8e-8972-3e03f3b979b3) Greenhaven Publishing LLC.
Brennan, Linda Crotta. Understanding Taxes. 2015. (21st Century Skills Library: Real World Math Ser.). (ENG., Illus.). 32p. (J). (gr. 4-7). 32.07 *(978-1-63362-577-8(X),* 206492) Cherry Lake Publishing.
Brezina, Corona. What You Need to Know about Taxes, 1 vol. 2020. (Teen Guide to Adulting: Gaining Financial Independence Ser.). (ENG.). 80p. (gr. 6-7). pap. 16.30 *(978-1-7253-4071-8(2),* 4d6111af-be47-4fec-9808-e10beff4e3a4) Rosen Publishing Group, Inc., The.
Brindell Fradin, Dennis. The Stamp Act Of 1765, 1 vol. 2010. (Turning Points in U. S. History Ser.). (ENG., Illus.). 48p. (gr. 4-4). 34.07 *(978-0-7614-4260-8(X),* ebda7934-06c6-4918-bac9-93a066b6efcd) Cavendish Square Publishing LLC.
Clifton, Gillian. How Are Taxes Used? Understanding Citizenship, 1 vol. 2018. (Civics for the Real World Ser.). (ENG.). 16p. (gr. 2-3). pap. *(978-1-5383-6545-8(6),* 84862e4b-bc45-4a16-8c68-70d368cc6573, Rosen Classroom) Rosen Publishing Group, Inc., The.
De Capua, Sarah. Paying Taxes. 2012. (True Books: Civics (Paperback) Ser.). (ENG.). 48p. (J). (gr. 2-4). 17.75 *(978-1-5311-7649-5(6))* Perfection Learning Corp.
Forest, Christopher. The Rebellious Colonists & the Causes of the American Revolution. 2012. (Story of the American Revolution Ser.). (ENG.). 32p. (J). (gr. 3-4). pap. 48.60 *(978-1-4296-9291-5(X),* 18525, Capstone Pr.) Capstone.
Kowalski, Kathiann M. Taxes, 1 vol. 2007. (Open for Debate Ser.). (ENG., Illus.). 144p. (YA). (gr. 8-8). lib. bdg. 45.50 *(978-0-7614-1887-0(3),* 895cfd0a-fdd4-42af-94f1-3f712dad7f51) Cavendish Square Publishing LLC.
La Bella, Laura. How Taxation Works, 1 vol. 2010. (Real World Economics Ser.). (ENG., Illus.). 80p. (YA). (gr. 6-6). lib. bdg. 38.47 *(978-1-4358-9463-1(4),* 02e98f43-4ff7-4c72-959b-8355de13c593) Rosen Publishing Group, Inc., The.
Mapua, Jeff. Taxation: Interpreting the Constitution, 1 vol. 2014. (Understanding the United States Constitution Ser.). (ENG., Illus.). 112p. (J). (gr. 7-7). 38.80 *(978-1-4777-7504-2(8),* 2278c8a7-a4f1-4e64-a990-24f3fb5e8620) Rosen Publishing Group, Inc., The.
Mara, Wil. Taxes at Work. 2016. (21st Century Skills Library: a Citizen's Guide Ser.). (ENG., Illus.). 32p. (J). (gr. 4-7). 32.07 *(978-1-63471-067-1(3),* 208347) Cherry Lake Publishing.
Merino, Noël, ed. Tax Reform, 1 vol. 2011. (Opposing Viewpoints Ser.). (ENG.). 216p. (gr. 10-12). lib. bdg. 50.43 *(978-0-7377-5241-0(6),* 434506bc-7809-4ee2-a210-50880b22be17, Greenhaven Publishing) Greenhaven Publishing LLC.
—Tax Reform, 1 vol. 2011. (Opposing Viewpoints Ser.). (ENG.). 216p. (gr. 10-12). pap. 34.80 *(978-0-7377-5242-7(4),* e1c624b4-624c-4b6e-a2fe-c8ec94b952ff, Greenhaven Publishing) Greenhaven Publishing LLC.
Miller, Derek. Collecting Taxes, 1 vol. 2018. (How Government Works). (ENG.). 64p. (gr. 5-5). pap. 16.28 *(978-1-5026-4029-1(5),* 876381f9-8cf9-45ce-80b6-98528ce0ad0a) Cavendish Square Publishing LLC.
Minden, Cecilia. Understanding Taxes. 2009. (21st Century Skills Library: Real World Math Ser.). (ENG.). 32p. (gr. 4-8). lib. bdg. 32.07 *(978-1-60279-311-8(5),* 200207) Cherry Lake Publishing.
Nichols, Clive & Bussing-Burks, Marie. Taxes & Government Spending, 1 vol. 2011. (Dollars & Sense: a Guide to Financial Literacy Ser.). (ENG.). 64p. (gr. 5-5). (J). pap. 13.95 *(978-1-4488-4725-9(7),* 0b124fc1-9faa-43ec-a87d-5d96c4d4523b); (YA). lib. bdg. 37.13 *(978-1-4488-4714-3(1),* 9eab23e2-7d57-4362-9cdf-2d4ecf0026cc) Rosen Publishing Group, Inc., The.
Roxburgh, Ellis. The Whiskey Rebellion. 2017. (Rebellions, Revolts, & Uprisings Ser.). 48p. (gr. 5-5). pap. 84.30 *(978-1-5382-0757-4(5))* Stevens, Gareth Publishing LLLP.
Sebree, Chet'la. Understanding Taxation, 1 vol. 2019. (21st-Century Economics Ser.). (ENG.). 80p. (gr. 8-8). pap. 18.64 *(978-1-5026-4614-9(5),* ecee4a31-a2fb-4059-826c-cea33b66926d) Cavendish Square Publishing LLC.
Steinberg, Lynnae D. What Are Taxes?, 1 vol. 2015. (Let's Find Out! Government Ser.). (ENG.). 32p. (J). (gr. 2-3). 26.06 *(978-1-62275-981-1(8),* 353051e2-524d-4b6c-a380-2a6c66ede6f1, Britannica Educational Publishing) Rosen Publishing Group, Inc., The.
Townsend, Chris. What Does a Taxpayer Do?, 1 vol. 2018. (What Does a Citizen Do? Ser.). (ENG.). 48p. (gr. 5-5). 30.93 *(978-0-7660-9875-6(3),* 5ed1a856-e796-45ea-a62e-684ef76d5a50) Enslow Publishing, LLC.

TAXIDERMY

Little & Large Sticker Activity Baby Animals. 2008. 24p. pap. *(978-1-84810-055-8(8))* Miles Kelly Publishing, Ltd.

TAYLOR, SUSIE KING, 1848-1912

Dell, Pamela. Memoir of Susie King Taylor: A Civil War Nurse. 2017. (First-Person Histories Ser.). (ENG., Illus.). 32p. (J). (gr. 3-6). lib. bdg. 27.99 *(978-1-5157-3354-6(8),* 133346, Capstone Pr.) Capstone.

TAYLOR, ZACHARY, 1784-1850

Elston, Heidi. Zachary Taylor, 1 vol. 2016. (United States Presidents *2017 Ser.). (ENG., Illus.). 40p. (J). (gr. 2-5). lib. bdg. 35.64 *(978-1-68078-118-2(9),* 21853, Big Buddy Bks.) ABDO Publishing Co.
Kops, Deborah. Encyclopedia of Presidents: Zachary Taylor. 2004. (Encyclopedia of Presidents Ser.). (ENG., Illus.). 112p. (YA). (gr. 5-9). 34.00 *(978-0-516-23442-7(0))* Scholastic Library Publishing.
Otfinoski, Steven. Zachary Taylor, 1 vol. 2012. (Presidents & Their Times Ser.). (ENG., Illus.). 96p. (gr. 6-6). 36.93 *(978-1-60870-187-2(5),* 593983e0-e8e3-4513-8e82-b2c01b88c1ca) Cavendish Square Publishing LLC.
Roberts, Jeremy. Zachary Taylor. 2005. (Presidential Leaders Ser.). (Illus.). 112p. (J). (gr. 3-7). lib. bdg. 29.27 *(978-0-8225-1397-1(8))* Lerner Publishing Group.
Schmidt, Roderic. How to Draw the Life & Times of Zachary Taylor. (Kid's Guide to Drawing the Presidents of the United States of America Ser.). 32p. (gr. 4-4). 2009. 50.50 *(978-1-61511-169-5(7),* PowerKids Pr.) 2005. (ENG.). (YA). 30.27 *(978-1-4042-2989-1(2),* 6b491a5a-bc35-437b-8c04-cf49a647ecd2) Rosen Publishing Group, Inc., The.
Venezia, Mike. Zachary Taylor: Twelfth President, 1849-1850. Venezia, Mike, illus. 2005. (Getting to Know the U. S. Presidents Ser.). (ENG., Illus.). 32p. (J). (gr. 3-4). 28.00 *(978-0-516-22617-0(7),* Children's Pr.) Scholastic Library Publishing.

TCHAIKOVSKY, PETER ILICH, 1840-1893

Orchid Publishing, prod. The Sleeping Beauty Ballet by Aleksandra. 2011. (ENG., Illus.). 36p. (J). 19.95 *(978-0-9831641-2-8(6))* Orchid Publishing, Inc.
Venezia, Mike. Peter Tchaikovsky (Revised Edition) (Getting to Know the World's Greatest Composers) Venezia, Mike, illus. 2018. (Getting to Know the World's Greatest Composers Ser.). (ENG., Illus.). 40p. (J). (gr. 3-4). pap. 7.95 *(978-0-531-23371-9(5),* Children's Pr.) Scholastic Library Publishing.

TEA

Clarke, Zoë. Collins Big Cat Phonics for Letters & Sounds - Sip It: Band 01A/Pink A, Bd. 1A. 2018. (Collins Big Cat Phonics Ser.). (ENG., Illus.). 16p. (J). (gr. -1-k). pap. 6.99 *(978-0-00-825134-5(7))* HarperCollins Pubs. Ltd. GBR. Dist: Independent Pubs. Group.
Gleason, Carrie. The Biography of Tea. 2007. (How Did That Get Here? Ser.). (ENG., Illus.). 32p. (J). (gr. 3-7). lib. bdg. *(978-0-7787-2493-3(X));* (gr. 2-9). pap. *(978-0-7787-2529-9(4))* Crabtree Publishing Co.
Sato, Shozo. Tea Ceremony: Explore the Unique Japanese Tradition of Sharing Tea. 2017. (Asian Arts & Crafts for Creative Kids Ser.). (ENG., Illus.). 64p. (J). (gr. 2-6). 9.95 *(978-0-8048-4988-3(9))* Tuttle Publishing.

TEA ROOMS

see Restaurants

TEACH, EDWARD, -1718

Buckley, James, Jr. & Who HQ. Who Was Blackbeard? Qiu, Joseph J. M., illus. 2015. (Who Was? Ser.). 112p. (J). (gr. 3-7). 6.99 *(978-0-448-48308-5(4),* Penguin Workshop) Penguin Young Readers Group.
Buckley, James. Who Was Blackbeard? 2015. (Who Was... ? Ser.). lib. bdg. 16.00 *(978-0-606-37556-6(2))* Turtleback.
Caldwell, Stella. Blackbeard's Pirateworld: Cut-Throats of the Caribbean. 2011. (Y Ser.). (ENG., Illus.). 80p. (J). (gr. 3-7). 19.95 *(978-1-84732-973-8(X))* Carlton Bks., Ltd. GBR. Dist: Two Rivers Distribution.
Cooke, Tim. Blackbeard: A Notorious Pirate in the Caribbean, 1 vol. 2015. (Wanted! Famous Outlaws Ser.). (ENG., Illus.). 48p. (J). (gr. 6-8). pap. 15.05 *(978-1-4824-4247-2(7),*

8f808262-5a79-4559-b632-e546660fb970) Stevens, Gareth Publishing LLLP.
Sullivan, Laura L. Blackbeard. 2015. (J). lib. bdg. *(978-1-62713-525-2(1))* Cavendish Square Publishing LLC.

TEACH, EDWARD, -1718—FICTION

Castroman, Nicole. Blacksouls. (ENG.). 400p. (YA). (gr. 9). 2018. pap. 11.99 *(978-1-4814-9106-8(7))* 2017. (Illus.). 17.99 *(978-1-4814-9105-1(9))* Simon Pulse. (Simon Pulse).
Marsh, Carole. The Mystery of Blackbeard the Pirate. Marsh, Carole, photos by. 2009. (Real Kids, Real Places Ser.). (Illus.). 150p. (J). 18.99 *(978-0-635-06992-4(X))*, Marsh, Carole Mysteries) Gallopade International.
O'Donnell, Liam. Blackbeard's Sword: The Pirate King of the Carolinas. Spoor, Mike, illus. 2007. (Historical Fiction Ser.). (ENG.). 56p. (J). (gr. 3-6). pap. 6.25 *(978-1-59889-404-2(8)*, 93551, Stone Arch Bks.) Capstone.
Penn, Audrey. Blackbeard & the Gift of Silence. 2009. (ENG.). 350p. (J). (gr. 2-7). pap. 8.95 *(978-1-933718-32-3(3))* Tanglewood Pr.
—Blackbeard & the Sandstone Pillar: When Lightning Strikes. 2009. (ENG.). 350p. (J). (gr. 2-7). pap. 8.95 *(978-1-933718-31-6(5))* Tanglewood Pr.
Pyle, Howard. The Story of Jack Ballister's Fortunes: Being the Narrative of the Adventures of a Young Gentleman of Good Family, Who Was Kidnapped in the Year 1719 & Carried to the Plantations of the Continent of Virginia, Where He Fell in with That Famous Pirate Captain Edward Teach, or Blackbeard; of His Escape from the Pirates & the Rescue of a Young Lady from Out Their Hands. unabr. ed. 2012. (Illus.). 436p. 49.99 *(978-1-4622-8858-8(8))* Repressed Publishing LLC.

TEACHER-STUDENT RELATIONSHIPS—FICTION

Alexander, Carol. Class Clown. Friedland, Joyce & Kessler, Rikki, eds. 2007. (Novel-Ties Ser.). (Illus.). 24p. pap. 16.95 *(978-0-7675-1014-1(3))* Learning Links Inc.
Anderson, John David. Ms. Bixby's Last Day. 2016. (ENG.). 320p. (J). (gr. 3-7). 17.99 *(978-0-06-233817-4(X)*, Walden Pond Pr.) HarperCollins Pubs.
Anderson, Laurie Halse. Teacher's Pet. 2009. (Vet Volunteers Ser.: 7). (ENG.). 160p. (J). (gr. 3-7). 7.99 *(978-0-14-241252-7(X)*, Puffin Books) Penguin Young Readers Group.
Avi. Don't You Know There's a War On? 2nd ed. 2003. 208p. (J). pap. *(978-0-439-53096-5(2)*, HarperCollins) HarperCollins Pubs.
—Don't You Know There's a War On? 2003. 193p. (gr. 3-7). 18.00 *(978-0-7569-1383-0(7))* Perfection Learning Corp.
Barnard, Sara. Goodbye, Perfect. 2019. (ENG.). 384p. (YA). (gr. 9). 19.99 *(978-1-5344-0244-7(6)*, Simon Pulse) Simon Pulse.
Buyea, Rob. Because of Mr. Terupt. (J). (gr. 3-7). 2011. (Mr. Terupt Ser.: 1). 336p. 8.99 *(978-0-375-85824-6(5)*, Yearling) 2010. 288p. 17.99 *(978-0-385-73882-8(X)*, Delacorte Bks. for Young Readers) Random Hse. Children's Bks.
—Mr. Terupt Falls Again. 2013. (Mr. Terupt Ser.: 2). 400p. (J). (gr. 3-7). 8.99 *(978-0-307-93046-0(7)*, Yearling) Random Hse. Children's Bks.
—Mr. Terupt Falls Again. 2013. lib. bdg. 18.40 *(978-0-606-32236-2(1))* Turtleback.
Clements, Andrew. Frindle. 2014. (ENG.). 112p. (J). 11.24 *(978-1-63245-158-3(1))* Lectorum Pubns., Inc.
—Head of the Class (Boxed Set) Frindle; the Landry News; the Janitor's Boy. Selznick, Brian, illus. 2007. (ENG.). 416p. (J). (gr. 3-7). pap. 23.99 *(978-1-4169-4974-9(7)*, Atheneum Bks. for Young Readers) Simon & Schuster Children's Publishing.
—Jake Drake, Teacher's Pet. 2007. (Jake Drake Ser.: 3). lib. bdg. 16.00 *(978-1-4177-9035-7(0))* Turtleback.
DeClements, Barthe. Sixth Grade Can Really Kill You. 2008. 160p. (J). (gr. 3-7). 5.99 *(978-0-14-241380-7(1)*, Puffin Books) Penguin Young Readers Group.
deGroat, Diane. No More Pencils, No More Books, No More Teacher's Dirty Looks! deGroat, Diane, illus. (Gilbert Ser.). (Illus.). 32p. (J). (gr. -1-3). 2009. (ENG.). pap. 7.99 *(978-0-06-079116-2(0)*, HarperCollins) 2006. 15.99 *(978-0-06-079114-8(4))* 2006. (ENG., lib. bdg. 18.89 *(978-0-06-079115-5(2)*, HarperCollins) HarperCollins Pubs.
Devargas, Casey Anthony. The Kindergarten Treasure. 2012. 44p. pap. 7.00 *(978-0-9859042-0-3(8))* CD Publishing.
Donaldson, Jennifer. Lies You Never Told Me. 2019. 336p. (YA). (gr. 9). pap. 9.99 *(978-1-59514-853-7(1)*, Razorbill) Penguin Young Readers Group.
Donohoe, Helen. Birdy Flynn. 2017. (ENG.). 384p. (J). pap. 11.99 *(978-1-78074-939-6(2)*, 1780749392, Rock the Boat) Oneworld Pubns. GBR. Dist: Grantham Bk. Services.
Foglia, Auttem. The Big Picture. 2010. 48p. pap. 10.59 *(978-1-4520-6681-3(7))* AuthorHouse.
Freeman, Martha. Fourth-Grade Weirdo. 2004. (Illus.). 147p. (gr. 4-7). 15.50 *(978-0-7569-4117-8(2))* Perfection Learning Corp.
Gingras, Charlotte. Pieces of Me. Ouriou, Susan, tr. 2009. 144p. (J). (gr. 7-9). 17.95 *(978-1-55453-242-1(6))* Kids Can Pr., Ltd. CAN. Dist: Hachette Bk. Group.
Grover, Lorie Ann. Hit, 1 vol. 2015. (ENG.). 224p. (YA). pap. 8.99 *(978-0-310-72938-9(6))* Blink.
Jackson, Marcus. Because My Teacher Said I Can. 2011. 24p. pap. 13.86 *(978-1-4567-6492-0(6))* AuthorHouse.
Jakobitz, Marilee. Martha Lu & the Whobegots. 2008. 32p. pap. 24.95 *(978-1-60441-482-0(0))* America Star Bks.
Johnson, Sandi. My Teacher Is an Alien. Durant, Sybrina, ed. Sturgen, Bobbi, illus. 2014. (ENG.). 30p. (J). (gr. k-5). pap. 12.99 *(978-1-929063-75-8(X)*, 285) Moons & Stars Publishing For Children.
Korman, Gordon. The Unteachables. 2019. (ENG.). (J). (gr. 3-7). 304p. pap. 9.99 *(978-0-06-256390-3(4))*; 288p. 18.99 *(978-0-06-256388-0(2))*; 288p. lib. bdg. 17.89 *(978-0-06-256389-7(0))* HarperCollins Pubs. (Balzer & Bray).
Laird, Judie. Lori Takes Piano Lessons. 2009. 20p. pap. 10.95 *(978-1-4490-1205-2(1))* AuthorHouse.
Layne, Steven L., et al. T Is for Teachers: A School Alphabet. Ettlinger, Doris, illus. 2005. (ENG.). 40p. (J). (gr. 1-4). 16.95 *(978-1-58536-159-5(3)*, 202019) Sleeping Bear Pr.
McLellan, Gretchen Brandenburg. Mrs. Mcbee Leaves Room 3, 1 vol. Zong, Grace, illus. 2017. 32p. (J). (gr. -1-3). 16.95 *(978-1-56145-944-5(5))* Peachtree Publishing Co. Inc.
Meyerhoff, Jenny. A Squirmy, Wormy Surprise. Chatelain, Éva, illus. 2017. (Friendship Garden Ser.: 6). (ENG.). 128p. (J). (gr. 2-5). 16.99 *(978-1-4814-7055-1(8))*; pap. 5.99 *(978-1-4814-7054-4(X))* Simon & Schuster Children's Publishing. (Aladdin).
Morgan, Amanda K. Such a Good Girl. (ENG.). (YA). (gr. 9). 2018. 304p. pap. 11.99 *(978-1-4814-4958-8(3))* 2017. (Illus.). 288p. 17.99 *(978-1-4814-4957-1(5))* Simon Pulse. (Simon Pulse).
Muluka, B. Kandu & the Lake. 2004. (Illus.). 44p. pap. *(978-9966-25-165-7(0))* Heinemann Kenya, Limited (East African Educational Publishers Ltd E.A.E.P.) KEN. Dist: Michigan State Univ. Pr.
Newmann, Ed, illus. Marvin Monster's Teacher Jitters. 2006. (ENG.). 48p. (J). (gr. 4-7). per. 6.95 *(978-0-9766805-3-6(X))* Keene Publishing.
Oates, Joyce Carol. Sexy. 2005. 272p. (J). (gr. 7-18). 16.99 *(978-0-06-054149-1(0)*, HarperTeen) HarperCollins Pubs.
Ohlin, Nancy. Consent. 2015. (ENG., Illus.). 288p. (YA). (gr. 9). 17.99 *(978-1-4424-6490-2(9)*, Simon Pulse) Simon Pulse.
Polacco, Patricia. An a from Miss Keller. Polacco, Patricia, illus. 2015. (Illus.). 40p. (J). (gr. k-3). bds. 18.99 *(978-0-399-16691-4(2)*, G.P. Putnam's Sons Books for Young Readers) Penguin Young Readers Group.
Quick, Matthew. Every Exquisite Thing. 2016. (ENG.). 272p. (YA). (gr. 10-17). 17.99 *(978-0-316-37959-5(X))* Little, Brown Bks. for Young Readers.
Rathmann, Peggy. Ruby the Copycat. Rathmann, Peggy, illus. 2006. (Scholastic Bookshelf Ser.). (ENG., Illus.). 32p. (J). (gr. -1-3). per. 7.99 *(978-0-439-47228-9(8)*, Teaching Resources) Scholastic, Inc.
Regan, Dian. The World According to Kaley. 2005. (ENG., Illus.). 112p. (J). (gr. 2-5). 14.99 *(978-1-58196-039-6(5)*, Darby Creek) Lerner Publishing Group.
Rentas, Donna. Leticia Goes to School. 2008. 16p. pap. 24.95 *(978-1-4241-8966-3(7))* America Star Bks.
Reynolds Naylor, Phyllis. The Agony of Alice. 2011. (Alice Ser.: 1). (ENG.). 176p. (J). (gr. 5-9). pap. 7.99 *(978-1-4424-2363-3(3)*, Atheneum Bks. for Young Readers) Simon & Schuster Children's Publishing.
Ruby, Laura. Bad Apple. 2011. (ENG.). 272p. (YA). (gr. 8). pap. 10.99 *(978-0-06-124333-2(7)*, HarperTeen) HarperCollins Pubs.
Rue, Nancy N. Totally Unfair, 1 vol., 4. 2005. ('Nama Beach High Ser.). (ENG.). 160p. (YA). pap. 6.99 *(978-0-310-25183-5(4))* Zondervan.
Sanders, Jennifer. My Student Teacher's Last Day. 2009. 32p. pap. 12.99 *(978-1-4389-4417-3(9))* AuthorHouse.
Schraff, Anne. The Petition. 2008. (Passages Ser.). 103p. (J). (gr. 4-6). lib. bdg. 13.95 *(978-0-7569-8391-8(6))* Perfection Learning Corp.
Seevers, Tim. Love, Grandp. 2009. 28p. pap. 14.99 *(978-1-4389-3507-2(2))* AuthorHouse.
Standiford, Natalie. Breaking up Is Really, Really Hard to Do. 2005. (Dating Game Ser.: 2). (ENG.). 224p. (YA). (gr. 7-17). pap. 13.99 *(978-0-316-11041-9(8))* Little, Brown Bks. for Young Readers.
—The Dating Game, No. 1. 2005. (Dating Game Ser.: 1). (ENG.). 224p. (J). (gr. 7-17). pap. 13.99 *(978-0-316-11040-2(X))* Little, Brown Bks. for Young Readers.
Toten, Teresa. Beware That Girl. 2018. (ENG.). 336p. (YA). (gr. 9). pap. 9.99 *(978-0-553-50793-5(1)*, Ember) Random Hse. Children's Bks.
Williams, Lorraine. Poor Dan. Felton, Richard, illus. 2008. 36p. per. 24.95 *(978-1-60441-170-6(8))* America Star Bks.
Winkler, Henry & Oliver, Lin. Always Watch Out for the Flying Potato Salad! #9. Garrett, Scott, illus. 2017. (Here's Hank Ser.: 9). 128p. (J). (gr. 1-3). 6.99 *(978-1-101-99583-9(1)*, Penguin Workshop) Penguin Young Readers Group.
Wright, Kiyah. Joshua's Surprise. 2010. 28p. pap. 16.95 *(978-1-4490-8234-5(3))* AuthorHouse.

TEACHER TRAINING

see Teachers—Training of

TEACHERS

see also Educators; Teaching

Alarcon, Roben. Teachers Then & Now, 1 vol. rev. ed. 2006. (Social Studies: Informational Text Ser.). (ENG.). 32p. (gr. 2-3). pap. 11.99 *(978-0-7439-9375-3(6))* Teacher Created Materials, Inc.
Ames, Michelle. Teachers in Our Community, 1 vol. 2009. (On the Job Ser.). (ENG., Illus.). 24p. (J). (gr. 1-1). pap. 9.25 *(978-1-4358-2456-0(3)*, 0207a023-139e-4a0a-9a3e-52cd8687027f); lib. bdg. 26.27 *(978-1-4042-8069-4(3)*, 5a85b6b0-ff4f-4df9-842b-4ddec3fddef9) Rosen Publishing Group, Inc., The. (PowerKids Pr.).
Anthony, David. Teachers on the Job, 1 vol. 2016. (Jobs in Our Community Ser.). (ENG.). 24p. (J). (gr. 1-1). lib. bdg. 26.23 *(978-1-5345-2147-6(X)*, d6f20b27-8e02-459f-bb33-a70dfa6b7012, KidHaven Publishing) Greenhaven Publishing LLC.
Arnold, Quinn M. Les Enseignants. 2017. (Graines de Savoir Ser.). (FRE., Illus.). 24p. (J). (gr. -1-k). *(978-1-77092-389-8(6)*, 20429) Creative Co., The.
—Teachers. 2017. (Seedlings Ser.). (ENG., Illus.). 24p. (J). (gr. -1-k). *(978-1-60818-875-8(2)*, 20360, Creative Education) Creative Co., The.
Askew, Amanda & Crowson, Andrew. Teacher. 2012. (ENG., Illus.). 24p. (gr. 1-3). pap. 7.95 *(978-1-926853-50-5(4))* Saunders Bk. Co. CAN. Dist: RiverStream Publishing.
Bao, Julie. A Loving Teacher Forever: A True Story of Loving Children, Defying Fate & Achieving Teaching Excellence. 2004. (Illus.). 32p. (J). 15.00 *(978-0-9748890-0-9(8))* Dings Bks.
Barth, Daisy. Thank You, Teacher, Because... 2008. (ENG., Illus.). 64p. (J). (gr. 4-7). pap. 9.95 *(978-1-933176-19-2(9))* Red Rock Pr., Inc.
Bell, Samantha. Teacher. Bane, Jeff, illus. 2017. (My Early Library: My Friendly Neighborhood Ser.). (ENG.). 24p. (J). (gr. k-1). lib. bdg. 30.64 *(978-1-63472-828-7(9)*, 209738) Cherry Lake Publishing.
Boothroyd, Jennifer. All about Teachers. 2020. (Sesame Street (r) Loves Community Helpers Ser.). (ENG., Illus.). 32p. (J). (gr. -1-2). 29.32 *(978-1-5415-8994-0(7)*, bfdebc0d-202f-4ef3-989a-02612fe10df7, Lerner Pubns.) Lerner Publishing Group.
Brooks, Felicity. Tessa the Teacher. Litchfield, Jo, illus. 2006. 24p. (J). per. 6.99 *(978-0-7945-0937-8(1)*, Usborne) EDC Publishing.
Bryant, Jen. Six Dots: a Story of Young Louis Braille. Kulikov, Boris, illus. 2016. 40p. (J). (gr. -1-3). 18.99 *(978-0-449-81337-9(1)*, Knopf Bks. for Young Readers) Random Hse. Children's Bks.
Clasky, Leonard. Teachers Are Important! Roles in My Community, 1 vol. 2018. (Civics for the Real World Ser.). (ENG.). 8p. (gr. k-1). pap. *(978-1-5383-6358-4(5)*, 6663a42c-ffd9-4a39-ab64-676b3a9aa69b, Rosen Classroom) Rosen Publishing Group, Inc., The.
Crane, Natalie. I Go to Work as a Teacher. 2003. (I Go to Work As Ser.). (Illus.). (J). pap. *(978-1-58417-106-5(5))*; lib. bdg. *(978-1-58417-043-3(3))*; lib. bdg. *(978-1-58417-044-0(1))* Lake Street Pubs.
Cunningham, Kevin. Teacher. 2008. (21st Century Skills Library: Cool Careers Ser.). (ENG., Illus.). 32p. (gr. 4-8). lib. bdg. 32.07 *(978-1-60279-298-2(4)*, 200137) Cherry Lake Publishing.
de Nijs, Erika. A Teacher's Job, 1 vol. 2015. (Community Workers Ser.). (ENG., Illus.). 24p. (gr. 1-1). lib. bdg. 25.93 *(978-1-5026-0431-6(0)*, c89dd02f-774a-4bdd-b7ec-c19f02524e96) Cavendish Square Publishing LLC.
Deedrick, Tami. Teachers Help, 1 vol. 2014. (Our Community Helpers Ser.). (ENG., Illus.). 24p. (J). (gr. -1-2). pap. 6.29 *(978-1-4765-5153-1(7)*, 124472); lib. bdg. 24.65 *(978-1-4765-3949-2(9)*, 123949) Capstone. (Pebble).
Demi. Confucius: The Heart of China, 1 vol. 2018. (ENG., Illus.). 48p. (J). (gr. 3-12). 21.00 *(978-1-62014-193-9(0)*, leelowshens) Lee & Low Bks., Inc.
Dent, Jenny. Great Teachers. 2003. (Spiritual Teachings for Children Ser.). (Illus.). 32p. (gr. k-9). 17.95 *(978-0-85487-054-7(7))* White Eagle Publishing Trust GBR. Dist: DeVorss & Co.
Donaldson, Madeline. Louis Braille. 2008. pap. 52.95 *(978-0-8225-9393-5(9))* Lerner Publishing Group.
Early Macken, JoAnn. Teachers, 1 vol. 2010. (People in My Community (Second Edition) Ser.). (ENG., Illus.). 24p. (gr. k-2). pap. 9.15 *(978-1-4339-3348-6(9)*, e00cd7cc-f89d-4484-9310-c7e273b27d86); (J). 25.27 *(978-1-4339-3347-9(0)*, 67197f32-ddc4-4201-934c-84344cf39571) Stevens, Gareth Publishing LLLP.
—Teachers / Maestros, 1 vol. 2010. (People in My Community / Mi Comunidad Ser.). (SPA & ENG., Illus.). 24p. (gr. k-2). pap. 9.15 *(978-1-4339-3766-8(2)*, 96dde7f4-8a3e-4bdf-a3b9-7bd2ea7a44b6) Stevens, Gareth Publishing LLLP.
Franco, Michou. I Can Be a Teacher, 1 vol. 2017. (I Can Be Anything! Ser.). (ENG.). 24p. (gr. k-k). pap. 9.15 *(978-1-4824-6333-0(4)*, 0014868a-dc83-44ea-935e-1a115cac0f62) Stevens, Gareth Publishing LLLP.
Freed, Kira. Teachers Are Important. 2017. (Text Connections Guided Close Reading Ser.). (J). (gr. k). *(978-1-4900-1780-8(1))* Benchmark Education Co.
Freeman, Dallas. Mirth & Misery: Memoirs of a Midwestern Maverick. 2003. 267p. per. 14.95 net. *(978-1-931934-22-0(3))* Back Yard Pub.
Gaertner, Meg. Teachers. 2018. (Community Workers Ser.). (ENG., Illus.). 24p. (J). (gr. 1-1). pap. 8.95 *(978-1-63517-810-4(X)*, 163517810X) North Star Editions.
—Teachers. 2018. (Community Workers Ser.). (ENG., Illus.). 24p. (J). (gr. k-3). lib. bdg. 31.36 *(978-1-5321-6015-8(1)*, 28662, Pop! Cody Koala) Pop!
Given-Wilson, Rachel & Silivanch, Annalise. Your Future As a Teacher, 1 vol. 2019. (High-Demand Careers Ser.). (ENG., Illus.). 80p. (J). (gr. 7-7). 37.47 *(978-1-5081-8795-0(9)*, bec46db0-40a0-4d9f-a3f4-0e2989fcdb02, Rosen Young Adult) Rosen Publishing Group, Inc., The.
Graham, Patti. And That Is Why We Teach: A Celebration of Teachers. Wellman, Megan D., illus. 2008. (ENG.). 32p. (J). (gr. 4-7). 17.95 *(978-1-933916-23-1(0))* Nelson Publishing & Marketing.
Harper, Clay. Are You Sure That Was a Rabbit?, 1 vol. 2012. (ENG., Illus.). 32p. (J). (gr. -1-3). 12.99 *(978-0-7643-4007-9(7)*, 4426) Schiffer Publishing, Ltd.
Heos, Bridget. Let's Meet a Teacher. Poling, Kyle, illus. 2013. (Cloverleaf Books (tm) — Community Helpers Ser.). (ENG.). 24p. (J). (gr. 2). pap. 8.99 *(978-1-4677-0805-0(4)*, 53b51c6f-8a45-48bd-a392-b42797101950, Millbrook Pr.) Lerner Publishing Group.
—Teachers in My Community. Poling, Kyle, illus. 2018. (Meet a Community Helper (Early Bird Stories (tm)) Ser.). (ENG.). 24p. (J). (gr. k-2). 29.32 *(978-1-5415-2022-6(X)*, 666fabac-6b17-4386-9d1a-a4a745e8da77, Lerner Pubns.) Lerner Publishing Group.
Honders, Christine. Why Should I Listen to My Teachers?, 1 vol. 2019. (Listening to Leaders Ser.). (ENG.). 24p. (gr. 2-2). pap. 9.25 *(978-1-5383-4172-8(7)*, 7ec409a6-987f-4582-bb27-838100d90a3b, PowerKids Pr.) Rosen Publishing Group, Inc., The.
Jackson, Garnet N. Shirley Chisholm, Congresswoman. 2012. (ENG., Illus.). (J). (gr. 1-4). pap. 7.47 net. *(978-0-8136-5247-4(2)*, Modern Curriculum Pr.) Savvas Learning Co.
Jeffries, Joyce. Meet the Teacher, 1 vol. 2012. (People Around Town Ser.). (Illus.). 24p. (gr. k-k). (ENG.). (J). 25.27 *(978-1-4339-7340-6(5)*, bc4315b0-0562-4e7e-a3e8-e976f1330a90); (ENG., (J). pap. 9.15 *(978-1-4339-7341-3(3)*, b6e3052b-e101-4cc8-8310-e7f58afe9d60); 69.20 *(978-1-4339-8063-3(0))* Stevens, Gareth Publishing LLLP.
—Meet the Teacher / Te Presento a Los Maestros, 1 vol. 2012. (People Around Town / Gente de Mi Ciudad Ser.). (SPA & ENG., Illus.). 24p. (J). (gr. k-k). 25.27 *(978-1-4339-7392-5(8)*, b2f54639-2e93-44e7-8dc3-9c21a4410b90) Stevens, Gareth Publishing LLLP.
Kawa, Katie. A Day with a Teacher. 2020. (J). *(978-1-5026-5337-6(0))* Cavendish Square Publishing LLC.
Kelly, Sheila M. & Rotner, Shelley. School Days. Rotner, Shelley, photos by. 2020. (ENG., Illus.). 32p. (J). (gr. -1-2). 26.65 *(978-1-5415-5776-5(X)*, 02383e8d-5fe8-4935-9616-e5b47e2a2329, Millbrook Pr.) Lerner Publishing Group.
Kidde, Rita. What Do Teachers Do?, 1 vol. 2014. (Jobs in My School Ser.). (ENG.). 24p. (J). (gr. 1-2). lib. bdg. 25.27 *(978-1-4777-6556-2(5)*, 3032e037-150b-4488-a9db-551206933cd7, PowerKids Pr.) Rosen Publishing Group, Inc., The.
—What Do Teachers Do? (¿Qué Hacen los Maestros?), 1 vol. de la Vega, Eida, ed. 2014. (Oficios en Mi Escuela / Jobs in My School Ser.). (SPA & ENG.). 24p. (J). (gr. 1-2). lib. bdg. 25.27 *(978-1-4777-6798-6(3)*, e3af1ec7-56ee-45f6-8a1a-956e23f0b828, PowerKids Pr.) Rosen Publishing Group, Inc., The.
Lawson, Sabina. Taking Action to Improve Schools. 2016. (Who's Changing the World? Ser.). (ENG., Illus.). 48p. (J). (gr. 4-6). 33.32 *(978-1-4677-9393-3(0)*, e2dd84a6-75c0-4e11-9896-1559914feae0); E-Book 50.65 *(978-1-4677-9666-8(2))* Lerner Publishing Group. (Lerner Pubns.).
Leaf, Christina. Teachers. 2018. (Community Helpers Ser.). (ENG., Illus.). 24p. (J). (gr. k-3). pap. 7.99 *(978-1-61891-310-4(7)*, 12096, Blastoff! Readers) Bellwether Media.
Leake, Diyan. Teachers, 1 vol. 2008. (People in the Community Ser.). (ENG., Illus.). 24p. (gr. -1-1). 21.99 *(978-1-4329-1191-1(0)*, Heinemann) Capstone.
Leigh, Autumn. My Teacher, 1 vol. 2008. (Real Life Readers Ser.). (ENG.). 8p. (gr. k-1). pap. 5.15 *(978-1-4042-7975-9(X)*, adc40ba9-50a6-40b5-bdb7-87e31a7d7ce3, Rosen Classroom) Rosen Publishing Group, Inc., The.
Lesinski, Jeanne M. Bill Gates. 2005. (First Step Nonfiction Ser.). (Illus.). 112p. (J). (gr. 3-7). lib. bdg. 27.93 *(978-0-8225-2642-1(5)*, Lerner Pubns.) Lerner Publishing Group.
Less, Emma. Teachers. 2018. (Real-Life Superheroes Ser.). (ENG.). 16p. (J). (gr. k-2). pap. 7.99 *(978-1-68152-281-4(0)*, 14921) Amicus.
Levin, Daniel, et al. Becoming a Responsive Science Teacher: Focusing on Student Thinking in Secondary Science. 2013. (ENG.). 270p. pap. 29.95 *(978-1-936959-05-1(4)*, P218225) National Science Teachers Assn.
Liebman, Dan & Liebman, Dan. I Want to Be a Teacher. 2nd rev. ed. 2018. (I Want to Be Ser.). (ENG., Illus.). 24p. (J). (gr. -1-2). pap. 3.99 *(978-0-2281-0102-4(6)*, 62e6d9b6-000a-4c19-8ac8-13f5a65bdbab) Firefly Bks., Ltd.
Lohse, Joyce B. Emily Griffith: Opportunity's Teacher. 2005. (Now You Know Bio Ser.). (Illus.). 50p. (J). pap. 8.95 *(978-0-86541-077-0(1))* Filter Pr., LLC.
Mara, Wil. The Schoolmaster, 1 vol. 2011. (Colonial People Ser.). (ENG.). 48p. (gr. 4-4). 34.07 *(978-0-7614-4801-3(2)*, a4a1cebd-de00-4ad7-8468-880c7ef3dc47) Cavendish Square Publishing LLC.
Markowitz, Siri. HELP with RAISING YOUR NURSERY or PRESCHOOL CHILDREN - 26 great ideas for parents & preschool Teachers. 2009. 44p. pap. 19.99 *(978-0-557-09610-7(3))* Lulu Pr., Inc.
McDonnell, Peter. Helping Others: The Story of Fanny Jackson Coppin. 2005. (Illus.). 16p. (J). *(978-0-7367-2901-7(1))* Zaner-Bloser, Inc.
Mckissack, Patricia & Mckissack, Fredrick. Mary Mcleod Bethune: Woman of Courage, 1 vol. 2013. (Famous African Americans Ser.). (ENG., Illus.). 24p. (J). (gr. k-2). 25.27 *(978-0-7660-4103-5(4)*, bb51f675-6c66-4402-8dd2-b86f5e19eeeb) Enslow Publishing, LLC.
Mellor, C. Michael. Louis Braille: A Touch of Genius. 2006. (Illus.). 144p. (J). 35.00 *(978-0-939173-70-9(0))* National Braille Pr.
Meltzer, Mirta. My Hands Mis Manos. 2013. 32p. pap. 12.99 *(978-1-61286-157-9(1))* Avid Readers Publishing Group.
Miller, Connie Colwell. I'll Be a Teacher. Baroncelli, Silvia, illus. 2018. (When I Grow Up Ser.). (ENG.). 24p. (J). (gr. 1-4). pap. 8.99 *(978-1-68152-319-4(1)*, 15060); lib. bdg. *(978-1-68151-399-7(4)*, 15054) Amicus.
Mitchell, Melanie. Teachers. 2005. (Pull Ahead Bks.). (Illus.). 32p. (J). lib. bdg. 22.60 *(978-0-8225-1696-5(9))* Lerner Publishing Group.
montell, alicia. Our Friend Oso. 2008. 206p. pap. 24.95 *(978-1-4241-7732-5(4))* America Star Bks.
Murray, Aaron R. Teachers Help Us, 1 vol. 2012. (All about Community Helpers Ser.). (ENG., Illus.). 24p. (gr. -1-1). 25.27 *(978-0-7660-4045-8(3)*, 157d85fb-c2e0-4dae-9e3c-22c759fef6fd, Enslow Publishing) Enslow Publishing, LLC.
Murray, Julie. Maestros. 2016. (Trabajos en Mi Comunidad Ser.). (SPA.). 24p. (J). (gr. -1-2). pap. 7.95 *(978-1-4966-0727-0(9)*, 131752, Capstone Classroom) Capstone.
—Teachers, 1 vol. 2015. (My Community: Jobs Ser.). (ENG., Illus.). 24p. (J). (gr. -1-2). 31.36 *(978-1-62970-917-8(4)*, 18292, Abdo Kids) ABDO Publishing Co.
Nelid, Piper. My Father Teaches Overseas, 1 vol., 1. 2015. (Rosen REAL Readers: Social Studies Nonfiction / Fiction: Myself, My Community, My World Ser.). (ENG.). 12p. (J). (gr. k-1). pap. 6.33 *(978-1-5081-1734-6(9)*, d4266005-f8eb-42c4-85d4-9a30481b04c5, Rosen Classroom) Rosen Publishing Group, Inc., The.
Nicholson, Dorinda Makanaonalani. The School the Aztec Eagle Built, 1 vol. 2016. (ENG., Illus.). 40p. (J). (gr. 3-7). 18.95 *(978-1-60060-440-9(4)*, leelowbooks) Lee & Low Bks., Inc.
Paderewski, Elliot. We Respect Our Teachers, 1 vol. 2016. (Rosen REAL Readers: Social Studies Nonfiction / Fiction: Myself, My Community, My World Ser.). (ENG.). 8p. (gr. k-1). pap. 5.46 *(978-1-5081-2296-8(2)*, 9107e608-3d3d-4981-97fd-dbed2f9d4922, Rosen Classroom) Rosen Publishing Group, Inc., The.
Parkes, Elle. Hooray for Teachers! 2016. (Bumba Books (r) — Hooray for Community Helpers! Ser.). (ENG., Illus.). 24p. (J). (gr. -1-1). 26.65 *(978-1-5124-1437-0(9)*, 28879ca3-58f1-4a8a-8886-3c30b347cd8a, Lerner Pubns.) Lerner Publishing Group.
—¡Que Vivan Los Maestros! (Hooray for Teachers!) 2017. (Bumba Books (r) en Español — ¡Que Vivan Los Ayudantes Comunitarios! (Hooray for Community Helpers!) Ser.). (SPA., Illus.). 24p. (J). (gr. -1-1). 26.65 *(978-1-5124-4132-1(5)*, 6aee9fb1-52d4-4afd-8519-f435c18360f6, Ediciones Lerner) Lerner Publishing Group.
Pressberg, Dava. A Teacher's Tools, 1 vol. 2015. (Community Helpers & Their Tools Ser.). (ENG., Illus.). 24p. (J). (gr. 2-3). pap. 9.25 *(978-1-4994-0855-3(2)*,

TUV

386e477a-def5-4567-b05b-aaaab04aae0a, PowerKids Pr.) Rosen Publishing Group, Inc., The.

Raatma, Lucia. Shirley Chisholm, 1 vol. 2011. (Leading Women Ser.). (ENG., Illus.). 96p. (J). (gr. 7-7). 42.64 *(978-0-7614-4953-9(1),* 76e44034-3809-4585-b09c-6019d0e95e1c) Cavendish Square Publishing LLC.

Randolph, Ryan P. Frontier Schools & Schoolteachers. 2009. (Library of the Westward Expansion Ser.). 24p. (gr. 3-4). 42.50 *(978-1-60853-935-2(0),* PowerKids Pr.) Rosen Publishing Group, Inc., The.

Riggs, Kate. Seedlings: Teachers. 2017. (Seedlings Ser.). (ENG., Illus.). 24p. (J). (gr. -1-1). pap. 8.99 *(978-1-62832-490-7(2),* 20361, Creative Paperbacks) Creative Co., The.

Rivera, Sheila. Teacher. 2005. (First Step Nonfiction — Work People Do Ser.). (ENG., Illus.). 8p. (J). (gr. k-2). pap. 5.99 *(978-0-8225-5361-8(9),* d875a484-662c-4500-9c59-69c98406ac2f) Lerner Publishing Group.

Rogers, Seth. Maestros: Tiempo. rev. ed. 2019. (Mathematics in the Real World Ser.). (SPA., Illus.). 24p. (J). (gr. 1-2). pap. 9.99 *(978-1-4258-2853-0(1))* Teacher Created Materials, Inc.

—On the Job: Teachers: Time (Grade 1) rev. ed. 2018. (Mathematics in the Real World Ser.). (ENG., Illus.). 24p. (J). (gr. 1-2). pap. 9.99 *(978-1-4258-5691-5(8))* Teacher Created Materials, Inc.

Sanna, Ellyn. Special Education Teacher. Riggs, Ernestine G. & Gholar, Cheryl, eds. 2013. (Careers with Character Ser.: 18). 96p. (J). (gr. 7-18). 22.95 *(978-1-4222-2767-1(7))* Mason Crest.

Schraff, Anne. Jaime Escalante: Inspirational Math Teacher, 1 vol. 2009. (Latino Biography Library). (ENG., Illus.). 128p. (gr. 6-7). lib. bdg. 35.93 *(978-0-7660-2967-5(0),* b2b936df-cb29-48fd-b9de-507270c61963) Enslow Publishing, LLC.

Schwartz, Heather E. Mary McLeod Bethune: Education & Equality. rev. ed. 2016. (Social Studies: Informational Text Ser.). (ENG., Illus.). 32p. (J). (gr. 4-8). pap. 11.99 *(978-1-4938-3545-4(9))* Teacher Created Materials, Inc.

—NASA Mathematician Katherine Johnson. 2017. (STEM Trailblazer Bios Ser.). (ENG., Illus.). 32p. (J). (gr. 2-5). 26.65 *(978-1-5124-5703-2(5),* 4b873c43-8f8b-4233-b212-0f0ee2d34fe9, Lerner Pubns.) Lerner Publishing Group.

Shava, Ryder. Mr. Ramirez Is My Teacher, 1 vol., 1. 2015. (Rosen REAL Readers: Social Studies Nonfiction / Fiction: Myself, My Community, My World Ser.). (ENG.). 8p. (J). (gr. k-1). pap. 5.46 *(978-1-5081-1710-0(1),* 547d12e6-f150-4590-8eea-b69a6136296c, Rosen Classroom) Rosen Publishing Group, Inc., The.

Siemens, Jared. Teachers. 2016. 24p. (J). *(978-1-5105-2111-7(9))* SmartBook Media, Inc.

—Teachers. 2015. 24p. (J). *(978-1-4896-3657-7(9))* Weigl Pubs., Inc.

Stewart, Tobi. Colonial Teachers. 2009. (Reading Room Collection 1 Ser.). 16p. (gr. 2-3). 37.50 *(978-1-60851-942-2(2),* PowerKids Pr.) Rosen Publishing Group, Inc., The.

Stewart, Tobi Stanton. Colonial Teachers, 1 vol. 2005. (Reading Room Collection 1 Ser.). (ENG., Illus.). 16p. (J). (gr. 2-3). lib. bdg. 22.27 *(978-1-4042-3351-5(2),* 5573687f-bc12-4143-97ed-f2d20a8fdea6, PowerKids Pr.) Rosen Publishing Group, Inc., The.

Stratton, Connor. Working at a School. 2020. (People at Work Ser.). (ENG.). 16p. (J). (gr. k-1). pap. 7.95 *(978-1-64493-095-3(1),* 1644930951); lib. bdg. 25.64 *(978-1-64493-016-8(1),* 1644930161) North Star Editions. (Focus Readers).

Sunseri, Sophia Natasha. Working As a Teacher in Your Community, 1 vol. 2015. (Careers in Your Community Ser.). (ENG., Illus.). 80p. (J). (gr. 7-8). 37.47 *(978-1-4994-6117-6(8),* d8c7020d-02b6-4ef7-bb3a-2b5510c2280b, Rosen Young Adult) Rosen Publishing Group, Inc., The.

Trent, Tererai. The Girl Who Buried Her Dreams in a Can: A True Story. Gilchrist, Jan Spivey, illus. 2015. 40p. (J). (gr. 1-3). 18.99 *(978-0-670-01654-9(3),* Viking Books for Young Readers) Penguin Young Readers Group.

Vogel, Elizabeth. Meet My Teacher. 2009. (My School Ser.). 24p. (gr. 1-2). 37.50 *(978-1-61514-704-5(7),* PowerKids Pr.) Rosen Publishing Group, Inc., The.

Walsh, Barbara E. The Poppy Lady: Moina Belle Michael & Her Tribute to Veterans. Johnson, Layne, illus. 2012. (ENG.). 40p. (J). (gr. 2-5). 18.99 *(978-1-59078-754-0(4),* Calkins Creek) Highlights Pr., c/o Highlights for Children, Inc.

Whyte, Donna. What Makes a Good Teacher? Here's What the Kids Say! Garamella, Joyce Orchard, illus. 2003. 32p. (J). 6.95 *(978-1-884548-59-8(8),* Crystal Springs Bks.) Staff Development for Educators.

Wigu Publishing. When I Grow up I Want to Be... a Teacher! Carlee Learns a Surprising Lesson! 2013. (When I Grow Up I Want To Be....Ser.). (Illus.). 62p. pap. 12.95 *(978-1-939973-08-5(2),* Wigu Publishing) Wigu Publishing.

Winter, Jeanette. Biblioburro: A True Story from Colombia. Winter, Jeanette, illus. 2010. (ENG., Illus.). 32p. (J). (gr. 1-4). 18.99 *(978-1-4169-9778-8(4),* Beach Lane Bks.) Beach Lane Bks.

Wolfe, Helen. Terrific Women Teachers, 1 vol. 2011. (Women's Hall of Fame Ser.: 17). (ENG., Illus.). 118p. (J). (gr. 4-8). pap. 10.95 *(978-1-897187-86-9(6))* Second Story Pr. CAN. Dist: Orca Bk. Pubs. USA.

Wyckoff, Edwin Brit. Sign Language Man: Thomas H. Gallaudet & His Incredible Work, 1 vol. 2010. (Genius at Work! Great Inventor Biographies Ser.). (ENG., Illus.). 32p. (gr. 3-3). lib. bdg. 26.60 *(978-0-7660-3447-1(X),* 2ce6028a-0fed-4805-8569-cb8f5cab6e58) Enslow Publishing, LLC.

TEACHERS—FICTION

Abramsen, Ruth M. Akeelah's Spider. 2008. 36p. per. 13.95 *(978-1-59800-440-3(9))* Outskirts Pr., Inc.

Adler, David A. School Trouble for Andy Russell. Hillenbrand, Will, illus. 2005. (Andy Russell Ser.: Bk. 3). (ENG.). 128p. (J). (gr. 1-4). pap. 9.95 *(978-0-15-205428-1(6),* 1196335, Clarion Bks.) HarperCollins Pubs.

—School Trouble for Andy Russell. Hillenbrand, Will, illus. 2007. (Andy Russell Ser.: Bk. 3). 118p. pap. 6.60 *(978-1-4189-5227-3(3))* Houghton Mifflin Harcourt Supplemental Pubs.

—School Trouble for Andy Russell. Hillenbrand, Will, illus. 2008. (Andy Russell Ser.: Bk. 3). (J). (gr. 2-5). pap. 28.95 incl. audio compact disk *(978-1-4301-0484-1(8));* pap. 24.95 incl. audio *(978-1-4301-0483-4(X))* Live Oak Media.

—Young Cam Jansen & the Substitute Mystery, No. 11. Natti, Susanna, illus. 2006. (Young Cam Jansen Ser.: 11). (ENG.). 32p. (J). (gr. 1-3). mass mkt. 4.99 *(978-0-14-240660-1(0),* Penguin Young Readers) Penguin Young Readers Group.

Aikawa, Yu. Dark Edge. 2005. (Dark Edge Ser.). (ENG., Illus.). 200p. (YA). Vol. 3. pap. 9.95 *(978-1-59796-030-4(6))* Vol. 4. pap. 9.95 *(978-1-59796-024-3(1))* DrMaster Pubns. Inc.

Akbarpour, Ahmad. That Night's Train, 1 vol. Saghafi, Majid, tr. Arsenault, Isabelle, illus. 2012. (ENG.). 96p. (J). (gr. 3-4). 14.95 *(978-1-55498-169-4(7))* Groundwood Bks. CAN. Dist: Publishers Group West (PGW).

Alfonsi, Alice, adapted by. 'Rents: Lizzie Mcguire. 2005. 134p. (J). lib. bdg. 16.92 *(978-1-4242-0689-6(8))* Fitzgerald Bks.

Alger, Horatio. Strive & Succeed. 2007. 172p. 24.95 *(978-1-4344-8359-1(2));* per. 14.95 *(978-1-4344-8358-4(4))* Wildside Pr., LLC.

Allard, Harry & Marshall, James. Miss Nelson Has a Field Day. 2015. 32p. pap. 7.00 *(978-1-61003-506-4(2))* Center for the Collaborative Classroom.

Allard, Harry G., Jr. Miss Nelson Has a Field Day Book & CD, 1 vol. Marshall, James, illus. 2012. (ENG.). 32p. (J). (gr. -1-3). audio 10.99 *(978-0-547-75376-8(4),* 1487728, Clarion Bks.) HarperCollins Pubs.

—Miss Nelson Is Back Book & CD, 1 vol. Marshall, James, illus. 2011. (ENG.). 32p. (J). (gr. -1-3). audio 10.99 *(978-0-547-57718-0(4),* 1458493, Clarion Bks.) HarperCollins Pubs.

Allard, Harry G., Jr. & Marshall, James. The Miss Nelson Collection: 3 Complete Books In 1! Miss Nelson Is Missing, Miss Nelson Is Back, & Miss Nelson Has a Field Day. 2014. (ENG., Illus.). 112p. (J). (gr. 1-4). 18.99 *(978-0-544-08222-9(2),* 1537237, Clarion Bks.) HarperCollins Pubs.

Amato, Mary. Edgar Allan's Official Crime Investigation Notebook. 2010. (ENG.). 176p. (J). (gr. 4-6). 21.19 *(978-0-8234-2271-5(2))* Holiday Hse., Inc.

—Our Teacher Is a Vampire & Other (Not) True Stories. Long, Ethan, illus. (ENG.). 256p. (J). (gr. 3-7). 2017. pap. 6.99 *(978-0-8234-3769-6(8))* 2016. 16.95 *(978-0-8234-3553-1(9))* Holiday Hse., Inc.

Anderson, John David. Ms. Bixby's Last Day. 2016. (ENG.). 320p. (J). (gr. 3-7). 17.99 *(978-0-06-233817-4(X),* Walden Pond Pr.) HarperCollins Pubs.

Andrews, Julie & Hamilton, Emma Walton. The Very Fairy Princess: Teacher's Pet. 2013. (Passport to Reading Level 1 Ser.). (J). lib. bdg. 14.75 *(978-0-606-31741-2(4))* Turtleback.

Anna, Jennifer. Yen Shei & the American Bonsai. 2009. (ENG., Illus.). 88p. (YA). pap. 14.99 *(978-1-59092-153-1(4))* Blue Forge Pr.

Avi. The Secret School. 2003. 157p. (J). (gr. 3-7). 13.60 *(978-0-7569-1625-1(9))* Perfection Learning Corp.

Ayres, Katherine. Family Tree. 2012. 116p. pap. 7.99 *(978-1-936495-21-4(X))* BookPartners, LLC.

Barnes, Phil. My Teacher's a Robot! 2015. (ENG.). 63p. (J). (gr. 1-2). mass mkt. 8.95 *(978-1-78455-935-9(0),* 2e43b527-f3de-4545-b9e1-d6f75c93f153) Austin Macauley Pubs. Ltd. GBR. Dist: Baker & Taylor Publisher Services (BTPS).

—My Teacher's a Spy! 2017. (ENG.). 66p. (J). pap. 10.95 *(978-1-78629-497-5(4),* 718f7420-02c0-4e75-ab7b-c2d3d49bf9ff) Austin Macauley Pubs. Ltd. GBR. Dist: Baker & Taylor Publisher Services (BTPS).

Barnholdt, Lauren & Beaky, Suzanne. Hailey Twitch & the Great Teacher Switch. 2010. (Hailey Twitch Ser.: 2). (Illus.). 176p. (J). (gr. 2-4). pap. 10.99 *(978-1-4022-2445-4(1),* Sourcebooks Jabberwocky) Sourcebooks, Inc.

Barns, Crosby H. Who Programmed the Species? The Theory of Scientific Coincidence. 2008. 36p. pap. 16.99 *(978-1-4389-0727-7(3))* AuthorHouse.

Baxter, Alice L. Adam's Atomic Adventures. 2007. 76p. per. 8.95 *(978-0-595-45616-1(2))* iUniverse, Inc.

Beasley, Cheryl. Piano Paradise: My Piano Has a Big Secret. 2006. (ENG.). 52p. per. 16.95 *(978-1-4241-4590-4(2))* PublishAmerica, Inc.

Beck, Ricky. A Puzzled Heart. 2008. 85p. pap. 19.95 *(978-1-60441-385-4(9))* America Star Bks.

Becker, Bonny. The Magical Ms. Plum. Portnoy, Amy, illus. 2011. (ENG.). 112p. (J). (gr. 1-4). 7.99 *(978-0-375-84760-8(X),* Yearling) Random Hse. Children's Bks.

Beckford, Lois. The Interesting Pen Pal. 2010. 44p. pap. 21.99 *(978-1-4415-0878-2(3))* Xlibris Corp.

Bellamy, Diane. But I Will Teach You. 2004. (YA). pap. 15.00 *(978-1-56411-297-2(7))* UBUS Communications Systems.

Bellingham, Brenda. Lilly in the Middle, 1 vol. Owen, Elizabeth, illus. 2003. (Formac First Novels Ser.: 25). (ENG.). 64p. (J). (gr. 1-5). 4.95 *(978-0-88780-589-9(2),* 589); 14.95 *(978-0-88780-590-5(6),* 590) Formac Publishing Co., Ltd. CAN. Dist: Formac Lorimer Bks. Ltd.

Bickel, Karla. Teacher's Remarkable Secret. Bickel, Karla, illus. l.t. ed. 2004. (Illus.). 16p. (J). (gr. -1-6). pap. 5.00 *(978-1-891452-09-3(6),* 2) Heart Arbor Bks.

Bildner, Phil. A Whole New Ballgame. 2016. (Rip & Red Ser.: 1). (J). lib. bdg. 17.20 *(978-0-606-38553-4(3))* Turtleback.

Birney, Betty G. Mysteries According to Humphrey. 2013. (According to Humphrey Ser.: 8). lib. bdg. 16.00 *(978-0-606-31699-6(X))* Turtleback.

Blane, Francisco. Little Jack Horner. Price, Nick, illus. 2010. (Rising Readers Ser.). (J). 3.49 *(978-1-60719-701-0(4))* Newmark Learning LLC.

Boné, Thomas H., illus. The Teacher Who Would Not Retire Becomes a Movie Star. 2012. (J). *(978-0-9792918-6-9(0))* Blue Marlin Pubns.

—The Teacher Who Would Not Retire Discovers a New Planet. 2009. (J). 17.95 *(978-0-9792918-3-8(6))* Blue Marlin Pubns.

—The Teacher Who Would Not Retire Retires. 2017. (J). *(978-0-9885295-7-1(2))* Blue Marlin Pubns.

Borden, Louise. The Last Day of School. Gustavson, Adam, illus. 2006. (ENG.). 40p. (J). (gr. 2-5). 19.99 *(978-0-689-86869-6(3),* McElderry, Margaret K. Bks.) McElderry, Margaret K. Bks.

Braxton, Simone. Miss Tina Is My Teacher: Roles in My Community, 1 vol. 2018. (Civics for the Real World Ser.). (ENG.). 8p. (gr. k-1). pap. *(978-1-5383-6355-3(0),* 5cd37d40-c594-422e-88cf-1bbbbbf03894, Rosen Classroom) Rosen Publishing Group, Inc., The.

Brenner, Emily. On the First Day of Grade School. Whatley, Bruce, illus. 2004. 32p. (J). (gr. -1-1). lib. bdg. 16.89 *(978-0-06-051041-1(2))* HarperCollins Pubs.

Brezenoff, Steve. Cheaters. 2013. (Ravens Pass Ser.). (ENG.). 96p. (J). (gr. 2-3). pap. 36.90 *(978-1-4342-6291-2(X),* 20262, Stone Arch Bks.) Capstone.

—Cheaters, 1 vol. Pinelli, Amerigo, illus. 2013. (Ravens Pass Ser.). (ENG.). 96p. (J). (gr. 3-6). lib. bdg. 25.32 *(978-1-4342-4616-5(7),* 120605, Stone Arch Bks.) Capstone.

—Witch Mayor, 1 vol. Percival, Tom, illus. 2012. (Ravens Pass Ser.). (ENG.). 96p. (J). (gr. 3-6). lib. bdg. 25.32 *(978-1-4342-3791-0(5),* 117090, Stone Arch Bks.) Capstone.

Brink, LeeAnn. The Stuff in the Back of the Desk. Cratty, Aaron, illus. 2006. 24p. (J). per. 10.95 *(978-1-934246-05-4(0))* Peppertree Pr., The.

Broad, Michael. Zombie Cows!, 2 vols., No. 2. Broad, Michael, illus. 2011. (Agent Amelia Ser.: 2). (ENG., Illus.). 144p. (J). (gr. 2-5). lib. bdg. 22.65 *(978-0-7613-8057-3(4),* 6ab86559-2b7d-4b2e-bf35-1cbee740a7c1, Darby Creek) Lerner Publishing Group.

—#2 Zombie Cows! 2011. (Agent Amelia Ser.). pap. 33.92 *(978-0-7613-8342-0(5),* Darby Creek) Lerner Publishing Group.

—#3 Hypno Hounds! 2011. (Agent Amelia Ser.). pap. 33.92 *(978-0-7613-8343-7(3),* Darby Creek) Lerner Publishing Group.

Brown, Jeffrey. My Teacher Is a Robot. 2019. (Illus.). 40p. (J). (gr. -1-2). 17.99 *(978-0-553-53451-1(3));* (ENG., lib. bdg. 20.99 *(978-0-553-53452-8(1))* Random Hse. Children's Bks. (Crown Books For Young Readers).

Brown, Marc. Arthur's Teacher Trouble. 2004. (Arthur Adventure Ser.). (J). (gr. k-3). spiral bd. *(978-0-616-00406-7(0));* spiral bd. *(978-0-616-01603-9(4))* Canadian National Institute for the Blind/Institut National Canadien pour les Aveugles.

—La Visita del Senor Rataquemada. Sarfatti, Esther, tr. from ENG. 2003.Tr. of Arthur's Teacher Moves In. (SPA.). (J). (gr. k-2). pap. 6.95 *(978-1-930332-41-6(6))* Lectorum Pubns., Inc.

Brown, Peter. My Teacher Is a Monster! (No, I Am Not.) 2014. (ENG., Illus.). 40p. (J). (gr. -1-3). 18.99 *(978-0-316-07029-4(7))* Little, Brown Bks. for Young Readers.

Burns, Jane. My Sister's My Teacher! 2017. (ENG.). 182p. (J). pap. 14.95 *(978-1-78612-482-1(3),* aab81ec6-e7a5-4641-b583-7cdbe7df8e23) Austin Macauley Pubs. Ltd. GBR. Dist: Baker & Taylor Publisher Services (BTPS).

Buyea, Rob. Because of Mr. Terupt. (J). (gr. 3-7). 2011. (Mr. Terupt Ser.: 1). 336p. 8.99 *(978-0-375-85824-6(5),* Yearling) 2010. 288p. 17.99 *(978-0-385-73882-8(X),* Delacorte Bks. for Young Readers) Random Hse. Children's Bks.

Byler, Linda. Big Decisions: A Novel Based on True Experiences from an Amish Writer!, 1 vol. 2011. (ENG.). 345p. pap. 13.99 *(978-1-56148-700-4(7),* Good Bks.) Skyhorse Publishing Co., Inc.

—Little Amish Matchmaker: A Christmas Romance. 2012. (ENG.). 187p. 14.95 *(978-1-56148-776-9(7),* Good Bks.) Skyhorse Publishing Co., Inc.

—When Strawberries Bloom: A Novel Based on True Experiences from an Amish Writer! 2010. (ENG.). 297p. pap. 13.99 *(978-1-56148-699-1(X),* Good Bks.) Skyhorse Publishing Co., Inc.

Caldwell, Daisy L. Sarah the Oh So Silly, but Shy Stegosaurus, 1 vol. 2009. 24p. pap. 24.95 *(978-1-61546-319-0(4))* America Star Bks.

Callen, Sharon. Ms. Wilde & Oscar, 1 vol. rev. ed. 2013. (Literary Text Ser.). (ENG., Illus.). 32p. (J). (gr. 2-3). pap. 10.99 *(978-1-4333-5611-7(2));* lib. bdg. 19.96 *(978-1-4807-1733-6(9))* Teacher Created Materials, Inc.

Calmenson, Stephanie & Cole, Joanna. Teacher's Pets. Ross, Heather, illus. 2015. (Ready, Set, Dogs! Ser.: 2). (ENG.). 144p. (J). (gr. 1-4). pap. 11.99 *(978-1-250-05705-1(1),* 900139115) Square Fish.

Carle, Eric. Thank You, Teacher from the Very Hungry Caterpillar. Carle, Eric, illus. 2021. (Illus.). 32p. (J). (-k). 9.99 *(978-0-593-22618-6(6))* Penguin Young Readers Group.

Cartee, Mary. Go Forth My Angels. 2011. 82p. pap. 19.95 *(978-1-4626-4058-4(3))* America Star Bks.

Cassidy, Sara. Seeing Orange, 1 vol. Meissner, Amy, illus. 2012. (Orca Echoes Ser.). (ENG.). 64p. (J). (gr. 1-3). pap. 6.95 *(978-1-55469-991-9(6))* Orca Bk. Pubs. USA.

Chabert, Jack. Sam Battles the Machine! 2017. (Eerie Elementary — Branches Ser.: bk.6). (ENG.). (J). lib. bdg. 14.75 *(978-0-606-40191-3(1))* Turtleback.

Chambers, Jerry. The Cat Who Became a Teacher. 2013. 40p. pap. 24.95 *(978-1-63000-040-0(X))* America Star Bks.

Chan, Marty. The Mystery of the Mad Science Teacher. 2008. (ENG.). 127p. (J). (gr. 2-7). pap. 10.95 *(978-1-897235-38-6(0))* Thistledown Pr., Ltd. CAN. Dist: Univ. of Toronto Pr.

Chatterton, Martin. The Brain Finds a Leg. 2007. 207p. *(978-1-921049-79-8(0))* Little Hare Bks. AUS. Dist: HarperCollins Pubs. Australia.

Chriscoe, Sharon. Scary Weather, Scaredy Cat. 1 vol. 2008. (ENG.). 48p. 24.95 *(978-1-60474-143-8(0))* America Star Bks.

Clark-Elliott, Mary. The Day Ms. Qualbaum Came to Visit. 2013. 44p. pap. 20.72 *(978-1-4907-0921-5(5))* Trafford Publishing.

Cleary, Beverly. Querido Senor Henshaw. 2003. (Ramona Quimby Ser.).Tr. of Dear Mr. Henshaw. (SPA.). 136p. (J). 9.95 *(978-84-239-9013-9(3))* Espasa Calpe, S.A. ESP. Dist: Planeta Publishing Corp.

Clements, Andrew. Frindle. Selznick, Brian, illus. 105p. (J). (gr. 3-5). pap. 4.50 *(978-0-8072-1522-7(8),* Listening Library) Random Hse. Audio Publishing Group.

—Frindle. unabr. ed. 2004. (Middle Grade Cassette Librariestm Ser.). 105p. (J). (gr. 3-7). pap. 29.00 incl. audio *(978-0-8072-7994-6(3),* S YA 961 SP, Listening Library) Random Hse. Audio Publishing Group.

—Head of the Class (Boxed Set) Frindle; the Landry News; the Janitor's Boy. Selznick, Brian, illus. 2007. (ENG.). 416p. (J). (gr. 3-7). pap. 23.99 *(978-1-4169-4974-9(7),* Atheneum Bks. for Young Readers) Simon & Schuster Children's Publishing.

—Jake Drake, Class Clown. Pedersen, Janet, illus. 2007. (Jake Drake Ser.: Bk. 4). (ENG.). 96p. (J). (gr. 2-5). pap. 5.99 *(978-1-4169-4912-1(7),* Atheneum Bks. for Young Readers) Simon & Schuster Children's Publishing.

—Jake Drake, Teacher's Pet. Pedersen, Janet, illus. 2007. (Jake Drake Ser.: 3). (ENG.). 96p. (J). (gr. 2-5). pap. 5.99 *(978-1-4169-3932-0(6),* Atheneum Bks. for Young Readers) Simon & Schuster Children's Publishing.

—El Periodico Landry. Selznick, Brian, illus. 2004.Tr. of Landry News. (SPA.). (YA). pap. 9.99 *(978-84-241-7886-4(6))* Everest Editora ESP. Dist: Lectorum Pubns., Inc.

Cooper, Barbara. Emma Exclamation Point, 1 vol. 2004. (Meet the Puncs: a Remarkable Punctuation Family Ser.). (ENG., Illus.). 32p. (gr. 2-4). lib. bdg. 28.67 *(978-0-8368-4225-8(1),* 1ff31e5a-6e3d-4dbf-a748-25f18d0aa66b, Gareth Stevens Learning Library) Stevens, Gareth Publishing LLLP.

Coppock, Phil & Bower's 2008-2009 4th Grade Class. Rubber Tuesday. 2010. 70p. pap. 12.95 *(978-1-4327-5751-9(2))* Outskirts Pr., Inc.

Coville, Bruce. My Teacher Is an Alien. (My Teacher Is an Alien Ser.: Bk. 1). 123p. (J). (Illus.). (gr. 4-7). pap. 4.50 *(978-0-8072-1528-9(7));* 2004. (gr. 3-6). pap. 29.00 incl. audio *(978-0-8072-8029-4(1),* S YA 971 SP) Random Hse. Audio Publishing Group. (Listening Library).

Cox, Judy. Don't Be Silly, Mrs. Millie!, 0 vols. Mathieu, Joe, illus. 2012. (ENG.). 34p. (J). (gr. -1-2). pap. 6.99 *(978-0-7614-5727-5(5),* 9780761457275, Two Lions) Amazon Publishing.

—Happy Birthday, Mrs. Millie!, 0 vols. Mathieu, Joe, illus. 2012. (ENG.). 32p. (J). (gr. -1-2). 16.99 *(978-0-7614-6126-5(4),* 9780761461265, Two Lions) Amazon Publishing.

—Mrs. Millie Goes to Philly!, 0 vols. Mathieu, Joe, illus. 2013. (ENG.). 32p. (J). (gr. -1-2). pap. 9.99 *(978-1-4778-1680-6(1),* 9781477816806, Two Lions) Amazon Publishing.

Crane, Carol. Handkerchief Quilt. Palmer, Gary, illus. 2010. (ENG.). 32p. (J). (gr. 1-4). 15.95 *(978-1-58536-344-5(8),* 202134) Sleeping Bear Pr.

Creech, Sharon. A Fine, Fine School. 2004. (Illus.). (J). (gr. k-3). spiral bd. *(978-0-616-11107-9(X))* Canadian National Institute for the Blind/Institut National Canadien pour les Aveugles.

—A Fine, Fine School. Bliss, Harry, illus. 2004. (J). (gr. k-3). spiral bd. *(978-0-616-11106-2(1))* Canadian National Institute for the Blind/Institut National Canadien pour les Aveugles.

—A Fine, Fine School. Bliss, Harry, illus. 2003. (ENG.). 32p. (J). (gr. -1-3). pap. 8.99 *(978-0-06-000728-7(1),* HarperCollins) HarperCollins Pubs.

Crisanaz, Catherine M. The Best House for Molly. 2008. 36p. per. 24.95 *(978-1-4241-9093-5(2))* America Star Bks.

Crow, P. For the Love of Miss Bard. 2010. 222p. pap. 18.00 *(978-0-9802257-9-2(5))* Peddlers Group.

Cuchna, Reid. Out of Love, 1 vol. 2009. 327p. pap. 29.95 *(978-1-60836-345-2(7))* America Star Bks.

Curious George Race Day (Reader Level 1) 2010. (Curious George TV Ser.). (ENG., Illus.). 24p. (J). (gr. -1-3). pap. 4.99 *(978-0-547-39361-2(X),* 1426984, Clarion Bks.) HarperCollins Pubs.

Dahl, Roald. Matilda. 2007.Tr. of Matilda. 18.40 *(978-1-4177-8613-8(2))* Turtleback.

Danneberg, Julie. Field-Trip Fiasco. Love, Judy, illus. 2015. (Jitters Ser.: 5). 32p. (J). (gr. k-3). 16.95 *(978-1-58089-671-9(5))* Charlesbridge Publishing, Inc.

—First Year Letters. Love, Judy, illus. 2014. 32p. pap. 7.00 *(978-1-61003-320-6(5))* Center for the Collaborative Classroom.

—Last Day Blues. Love, Judy, illus. 2006. (Jitters Ser.: 2). (ENG.). 32p. (J). (gr. k-3). 7.99 *(978-1-58089-104-2(7))* Charlesbridge Publishing, Inc.

Deal, Sarah E. The Spotless Ladybug. 2008. 31p. pap. 24.95 *(978-1-60672-964-9(0))* America Star Bks.

Dean, James, illus. Pete the Cat & the Surprise Teacher. 2017. 32p. (J). *(978-1-5182-3399-9(6))* Harper & Row Ltd.

Dean, James & Dean, Kimberly. Pete the Cat & the Surprise Teacher. Dean, James, illus. 2017. (My First I Can Read Ser.). (ENG., Illus.). 32p. (J). (gr. -1-3). 4.99 *(978-0-06-240428-2(8),* HarperCollins) HarperCollins Pubs.

DeBray, Sherry. The Teacher's Gift. Cauthen, Tommy, illus. 2004. 30p. *(978-1-59421-007-5(1))* Seacoast Publishing, Inc.

Decker, Wendy. The Bedazzling Bowl. 2006. pap. 13.99 *(978-1-60034-468-8(2))* Salem Author Services.

DeClements, Barthe. Fourth Grade Wizards. 2008. 128p. (J). (gr. 3-7). 5.99 *(978-0-14-241348-7(8),* Puffin Books) Penguin Young Readers Group.

Depken, Kristen L. Driving School. 2013. (Cars Step into Reading Ser.). lib. bdg. 13.55 *(978-0-606-31932-4(8))* Turtleback.

Derby, Sally. Whoosh Went the Wind!, 0 vols. Nguyen, Vincent, illus. 2013. (ENG.). 32p. (J). (gr. -1-3). pap. 9.99 *(978-1-4778-1677-6(1),* 9781477816776, Two Lions) Amazon Publishing.

Diesen, Deborah. Pout-Pout Fish: Back to School. Hanna, Dan, illus. 2019. (Pout-Pout Fish Paperback Adventure Ser.). (ENG.). 24p. (J). 5.99 *(978-0-374-31047-9(5),* 900193159, Farrar, Straus & Giroux (BYR)) Farrar, Straus & Giroux.

Diroma, Joseph. Pinuccio. Jones, Bob, illus. 2009. 24p. pap. 14.99 *(978-1-60844-036-8(2))* Dog Ear Publishing, LLC.

du Bois, William Pène. Twenty-One Balloons. du Bois, William Pène, illus. 2005. (Illus.). 180p. (J). lib. bdg. 15.00 *(978-1-4242-2270-4(2))* Fitzgerald Bks.

Duncan, Alice Faye. Memphis, Martin, & the Mountaintop: The Sanitation Strike Of 1968. Christie, R. Gregory, illus. 2018. (ENG.). 40p. (J). (gr. 2-5). 17.99 *(978-1-62979-718-2(9),* Calkins Creek) Highlights Pr., c/o Highlights for Children, Inc.

dyer, kc. Ms. Zephyr's Notebook. 2007. (ENG., Illus.). 206p. (YA). (gr. 7). pap. 12.99 *(978-1-55002-691-7(7))* Dundurn Pr. CAN. Dist: Publishers Group West (PGW).

Earl, David G. Koala Koala, I'm Not a Bear, I'm a Koala. Gentry, T. Kyle, illus. 2009. 32p. pap. 12.95 *(978-1-936051-22-9(2))* Peppertree Pr., The.

Eaton, Kelly Toole. Kellina Makes Her Dreams Come True. 2011. 40p. pap. 21.99 *(978-1-4568-8824-4(2))* Xlibris Corp.
Ecton, Anne Massey. Passing Through Camelot. 2006. (J). *(978-0-88092-620-1(1))* Royal Fireworks Publishing Co.
Edwards, Wysteria. Bethany Bubbles Makes a Mistake. Abbott, Jason, illus. 2011. 34p. pap. 14.50 *(978-1-60911-353-7(5),* Strategic Bk. Publishing) Strategic Book Publishing & Rights Agency (SBPRA).
Elliott, Rebecca. A Woodland Wedding. 2016. (Owl Diaries: 3). (ENG.). 80p. (J). (gr. k-2). lib. bdg. 14.75 *(978-0-606-38068-3(X))* Turtleback.
—A Woodland Wedding: a Branches Book (Owl Diaries #3) (Library Edition), Vol. 3. Elliott, Rebecca, illus. 2016. (Owl Diaries: 3). (ENG., Illus.). 80p. (J). (gr. k-2). 24.99 *(978-0-545-82558-0(X))* Scholastic, Inc.
Enderle, Dotti. Tell No One!, 1 vol. McWilliam, Howard, illus. 2009. (Ghost Detectors Ser.: No. 1). (ENG.). 80p. (J). (gr. 2-5). 35.64 *(978-1-60270-692-7(1),* 8804, Calico Chapter Bks.) ABDO Publishing Co.
English, Karen. Nikki & Deja: Substitute Trouble. Freeman, Laura, illus. 2014. (Nikki & Deja Ser.). (ENG.). 112p. (J). (gr. 1-4). pap. 6.99 *(978-0-544-22388-2(8),* 1563368, Clarion Bks.) HarperCollins Pubs.
—Nikki & Deja: Wedding Drama. Freeman, Laura, illus. 2013. (Nikki & Deja Ser.). (ENG.). 112p. (J). (gr. 1-4). pap. 6.99 *(978-0-544-00324-8(1),* 1526366, Clarion Bks.) HarperCollins Pubs.
—Pizza Party: The Carver Chronicles, Book Six. Freeman, Laura, illus. 2019. (Carver Chronicles Ser.: 6). (ENG.). 128p. (J). (gr. 1-4). pap. 7.99 *(978-0-358-09747-1(9),* 1747602, Clarion Bks.) HarperCollins Pubs.
Esham, Barbaraa. Mrs. Gorski, I Think I Have the Wiggle Fidgets. Gordon, Mike, illus. 2008. (ENG, SPA & FRE.). 32p. (J). (gr. k-18). 16.95 *(978-1-60336-469-0(2),* Adventures of Everyday Geniuses, The) Mainstream Connections Publishing.
Eulberg, Elizabeth. The Great Shelby Holmes Meets Her Match. 2017. (ENG., Illus.). 240p. (J). 16.99 *(978-1-68119-054-9(0),* 900157431, Bloomsbury USA Childrens) Bloomsbury Publishing USA.
Evans, Stephanie. Steven James: I Just Can't Pay Attention. 2011. 28p. 12.03 *(978-1-4567-2707-9(9))* AuthorHouse.
Feder, Aliza & Sofer, Rochel. We Need to Talk. 2008. 250p. 18.95 *(978-1-934440-30-8(2),* Devora Publishing) Simcha Media Group.
Figley, Marty Rhodes. The Prairie Adventure of Sarah & Annie, Blizzard Survivors. Hammond, Ted & Carbajal, Richard Pimentel, illus. 2011. (History's Kid Heroes Set III Ser.). pap. 51.02 *(978-0-7613-8621-6(1),* Graphic Universe™) Lerner Publishing Group.
—The Prairie Adventure of Sarah & Annie, Blizzard Survivors. Carbajal, Richard & Hammond, Ted, illus. 2011. (History's Kid Heroes Ser.). (ENG.). 32p. (J). (gr. 3-5). pap. 9.99 *(978-0-7613-7808-2(1),* d4c7e7ff-1ce6-47c5-8250-3453ef99ba72, Graphic Universe™) Lerner Publishing Group.
—The Schoolchildren's Blizzard. Haas, Shelly O., illus. 2004. (On My Own History Ser.). (ENG.). 48p. (J). (gr. 2-4). pap. 8.99 *(978-1-57505-619-7(4),* a675f403-7243-488e-ad5b-fbd615d20ef5, First Avenue Editions) Lerner Publishing Group.
Finchler, Judy & O'Malley, Kevin. Congratulations, Miss Malarkey! O'Malley, Kevin, illus. 2011. (Miss Malarkey Ser.). (ENG., Illus.). 32p. (J). (gr. k-2). 21.19 *(978-0-8027-9836-7(5),* 9780802798367) Walker & Co.
—Miss Malarkey's Field Trip. O'Malley, Kevin, illus. 2004. (Miss Malarkey Ser.). (ENG., Illus.). 32p. (J). (gr. k-2). 21.19 *(978-0-8027-8913-6(7),* 9780802789136) Walker & Co.
Finley, Leah. Ms T. 2007. 108p. (J). per. 8.95 *(978-0-9794815-1-2(1))* Bellissima Publishing, LLC.
—The One & Only Mr C. 2009. 82p. pap. 8.95 *(978-1-935118-75-6(7))* Bellissima Publishing, LLC.
Fischer, JoAnn. Our Teacher Is A Fish! 2008. (ENG.). 34p. pap. 10.00 *(978-1-4196-7477-8(3))* CreateSpace Independent Publishing Platform.
Flake, Sharon G. The Skin I'm In. 2007. (J). lib. bdg. 19.65 *(978-1-4178-0860-1(8))* Turtleback.
Fleischman, Paul. The Dunderheads. Roberts, David, illus. 2012. (ENG.). 56p. (J). (gr. 1-4). pap. 8.99 *(978-0-7636-5239-5(3))* Candlewick Pr.
Fleming, Candace. The Fabled Fifth Graders of Aesop Elementary School. 2012. (Aesop Elementary School Ser.: 2). 176p. (J). (gr. 2-5). 8.99 *(978-0-375-87187-0(X),* Yearling) Random Hse. Children's Bks.
—The Fabled Fourth Graders of Aesop Elementary School. (Aesop Elementary School Ser.: 1). 192p. (J). 2009. (gr. 2-5). 7.99 *(978-0-440-42229-7(9))*1. 2007. (ENG.). (gr. 4-6). lib. bdg. 18.69 *(978-0-375-93672-2(6))* Random Hse. Children's Bks. (Yearling).
Fletcher, Ralph. Flying Solo. 2008. (ENG.). 144p. (J). (gr. 5-7). pap. 7.99 *(978-0-547-07652-2(5),* 1042026, Clarion Bks.) HarperCollins Pubs.
Fox, Alex. Windsock Wesley & His Wild & Wonderful Weather MacHine, Living in Cloud. Bazzoni, Lainie M. A., illus. 2010. 48p. pap. 16.50 *(978-1-60911-873-0(1),* Eloquent Bks.) Strategic Book Publishing & Rights Agency (SBPRA).
Francis, Pauline, retold by. The Turn of the Screw, 1 vol. 2010. (Essential Classics - Horror Ser.). (ENG., Illus.). 48p. pap. *(978-0-237-54110-1(6))* Evans Brothers, Ltd.
Frank, E. R. Friction. 2004. (ENG.). 208p. (YA). (gr. 7). reprint ed. pap. 10.99 *(978-0-689-85385-2(8),* Simon Pulse) Simon Pulse.
Friedrich, Joachim. The Disappearing Bio Teacher. Date not set. (Illus.). 144p. (J). (gr. 3-7). 14.99 *(978-0-7868-0700-0(8))* Hyperion Pr.
Frost, Helen. Room 214: a Year in Poems. 2014. (ENG., Illus.). 128p. (J). (gr. 5-9). pap. 8.99 *(978-1-250-04009-1(4),* 900123712) Square Fish.
Funny, Ania. The Power of Ania to Change the World of Bullying. 2012. 28p. pap. 15.99 *(978-1-4797-4599-9(5))* Xlibris Corp.
Galante, Cecilia. The Summer of May. 2012. (ENG., Illus.). 256p. (J). (gr. 4-8). pap. 7.99 *(978-1-4169-8304-0(X),* Simon & Schuster/Paula Wiseman Bks.) Simon & Schuster/Paula Wiseman Bks.
Gall, Chris. Substitute Creacher. 2011. (ENG., Illus.). 40p. (J). (gr. -1-3). 18.99 *(978-0-316-08915-9(X))* Little, Brown Bks. for Young Readers.
Gao, Charlie. Children City & Teacher Town. 2009. 80p. pap. 10.49 *(978-1-4389-7547-4(3))* AuthorHouse.
Garland, Michael. Miss Smith & the Haunted Library. 2012. 32p. (J). (gr. -1-2). 7.99 *(978-0-14-242122-2(7),* Puffin Books) Penguin Young Readers Group.
—Miss Smith Reads Again! 2006. (Illus.). (J). *(978-1-4156-8098-8(1),* Dutton Juvenile) Penguin Publishing Group.
—Miss Smith's Incredible Storybook. Garland, Michael, illus. 2005. (Illus.). 32p. (J). (gr. -1-2). pap. 8.99 *(978-0-14-240282-5(6),* Puffin Books) Penguin Young Readers Group.
—Miss Smith's Incredible Storybook. 2007. 27.95 incl. audio *(978-0-8045-6945-3(2));* 29.95 incl. audio compact disk *(978-0-8045-4159-6(0))* Spoken Arts, Inc.
Gelenius, Deb. My Mom, My Teacher. 2013. 28p. pap. 11.95 *(978-1-61244-135-1(1))* Halo Publishing International.
Gensler, Sonia. The Revenant. (gr. 7). 2013. 352p. (YA). pap. 9.99 *(978-0-375-86139-0(4),* Ember) 2011. (ENG.). 336p. (J). lib. bdg. 26.19 *(978-0-375-96701-6(X),* Knopf Bks. for Young Readers) Random Hse. Children's Bks.
Gilbert, Frances. Today the Teacher Changed Our Seats. 2012. (Illus.). 24p. pap. 17.99 *(978-1-4772-9905-0(X))* AuthorHouse.
Glennon, Michelle. My Big Green Teacher: Don't Rock the Boat: Saving Our Oceans. Glennon, Michelle, illus. 2008. (Illus.). 32p. (J). 19.95 *(978-0-9796625-2-2(4))* GDG Publishing.
—My Big Green Teacher: Please Turn off the Lights. Glennon, Michelle, illus. 2008. (ENG., Illus.). 32p. (J). 19.95 *(978-0-9796625-3-9(2))* GDG Publishing.
—My Big Green Teacher: Seven Generations from Now. Glennon, Michelle, illus. 2008. (Illus.). (J). 19.95 *(978-0-9797952-1-3(4))* GDG Publishing.
—My Big Green Teacher: Take a Deep Breath: Saving Our Rainforests. Glennon, Michelle, illus. 2008. (ENG., Illus.). 32p. (J). 19.95 *(978-0-9797952-0-6(6))* GDG Publishing.
—My Big Green Teacher: Taking the Green Road. Glennon, Michelle, illus. 2008. (Illus.). 32p. (J). 19.95 *(978-0-9796625-7-7(5))* GDG Publishing.
—My Big Green Teacher: Recycling: It's Easy Being Green. Glennon, Michelle, illus. 2007. (Illus.). 32p. (J). 19.95 *(978-0-9796625-6-0(7))* GDG Publishing.
Grant, Vicki. Cochonnet, 1 vol. 2011. (Orca Currents en Français Ser.). (FRE.). 112p. (J). (gr. 4-7). pap. 9.95 *(978-1-4598-0006-9(0))* Orca Bk. Pubs. USA.
Greene, Stephanie. Princess Posey & the Monster Stew, 4 vols. Roth Sisson, Stephanie, illus. 2012. (Princess Posey, First Grader Ser.: 4). 96p. (J). (gr. k-3). pap. 5.99 *(978-0-14-242105-5(7),* Puffin Books) Penguin Young Readers Group.
—Princess Posey & the Perfect Present: Book 2, Bk. 2. Roth Sisson, Stephanie, illus. 2011. (Princess Posey, First Grader Ser.: 2). 96p. (J). (gr. k-3). 6.99 *(978-0-14-241828-4(5),* Puffin Books) Penguin Young Readers Group.
—Princess Posey & the Tiny Treasure. Roth Sisson, Stephanie, illus. 2013. (Princess Posey, First Grader Ser.: 5). 96p. (J). (gr. k-3). pap. 5.99 *(978-0-14-242415-5(3),* Puffin Books) Penguin Young Readers Group.
Griffiths, Andy. Treasure Fever! 2008. (Schooling Around Ser.: No. 1). 198p. (J). pap. *(978-0-545-09222-7(1))* Scholastic, Inc.
Guest, Elissa Haden. Iris & Walter & the Substitute Teacher. Davenier, Christine, illus. 2006. (Iris & Walter Ser.). 44p. (gr. 1-4). 15.95 *(978-0-7569-7122-9(5))* Perfection Learning Corp.
Gutman, Dan. Miss Kraft Is Daft! Paillot, Jim, illus. 2012. (My Weirder School Ser.: 7). (J). lib. bdg. 14.75 *(978-0-606-27125-7(2))* Turtleback.
—Miss Laney Is Zany! 2010. (My Weird School Daze Ser.: 8). (J). lib. bdg. 14.75 *(978-0-606-10112-7(8))* Turtleback.
—Miss Newman Isn't Human! Paillot, Jim, illus. 2018. 105p. (J). *(978-1-5182-5371-3(7))* Harper & Row Ltd.
—Mr. Cooper Is Super! Paillot, Jim, illus. 2015. (My Weirdest School Ser.: 1). (J). lib. bdg. 14.75 *(978-0-606-36482-9(X))* Turtleback.
—Mr. Jack Is a Maniac! 2014. (My Weirder School Ser.: 10). (J). lib. bdg. 13.55 *(978-0-606-35066-2(7))* Turtleback.
—Mrs. Lizzy Is Dizzy! 2010. (My Weird School Daze Ser.: 9). (J). lib. bdg. 14.75 *(978-0-606-10113-4(6))* Turtleback.
—Mrs. Master Is a Disaster! 2017. (My Weirdest School Ser.: 8). (Illus.). 105p. (J). lib. bdg. 14.75 *(978-0-606-40078-7(8))* Turtleback.
—Mrs. Meyer Is on Fire! Paillot, Jim, illus. 2016. 105p. (J). *(978-1-4806-9926-7(8))* Harper & Row Ltd.
—Mrs. Yonkers Is Bonkers! Paillot, Jim, illus. 2007. (My Weird School Ser.: 18). (J). 14.75 *(978-1-4177-8222-2(6))* Turtleback.
—Ms. Cuddy Is Nutty! Paillot, Jim, illus. 2015. 106p. (J). *(978-1-4242-6518-3(5))* Harper & Row Ltd.
—My Weird School #1: Miss Daisy Is Crazy!, 1 vol. Paillot, Jim, illus. 2004. (My Weird School Ser.: 1). (ENG.). 96p. (J). (gr. 1-5). pap. 5.99 *(978-0-06-050700-8(4),* cd7f67f8-4d4e-4aec-9bc9-50817b6dc3f9, HarperCollins) HarperCollins Pubs.
—My Weird School #10: Mr. Docker Is off His Rocker! Paillot, Jim, illus. 2006. (My Weird School Ser.: 10). (ENG.). 112p. (J). (gr. 1-5). pap. 5.99 *(978-0-06-082227-9(9),* HarperCollins) HarperCollins Pubs.
—My Weird School #14: Miss Holly Is Too Jolly! A Christmas Holiday Book for Kids. Paillot, Jim, illus. 2006. (My Weird School Ser.: 14). (ENG.). 112p. (J). (gr. 1-5). pap. 5.99 *(978-0-06-085382-2(4),* HarperCollins) HarperCollins Pubs.
—My Weird School #17: Miss Suki Is Kooky! Paillot, Jim, illus. 2007. (My Weird School Ser.: 17). (ENG.). 112p. (J). (gr. 1-5). pap. 5.99 *(978-0-06-123473-6(7),* HarperCollins) HarperCollins Pubs.
—My Weird School #18: Mrs. Yonkers Is Bonkers! Paillot, Jim, illus. 2007. (My Weird School Ser.: 18). (ENG.). 112p. (J). (gr. 1-5). pap. 4.99 *(978-0-06-123475-0(3),* HarperCollins) HarperCollins Pubs.
—My Weird School #21: Ms. Krup Cracks Me Up! Paillot, Jim, illus. 2008. (My Weird School Ser.: 21). (ENG.). 112p. (J). (gr. 1-5). pap. 4.99 *(978-0-06-134605-7(5),* HarperCollins) HarperCollins Pubs.
—My Weird School #4: Ms. Hannah Is Bananas! Paillot, Jim, illus. 2004. (My Weird School Ser.: 4). (ENG.). 96p. (J). (gr. 1-5). pap. 4.99 *(978-0-06-050706-0(3),* HarperCollins) HarperCollins Pubs.
—My Weird School Daze! Paillot, Jim, illus. 2007. (J). *(978-1-4287-4814-9(8))* HarperCollins Pubs.
—My Weird School Daze #1: Mrs. Dole Is Out of Control! Paillot, Jim, illus. 2008. (My Weird School Daze Ser.: 1). (ENG.). 112p. (J). (gr. 1-5). pap. 4.99 *(978-0-06-134607-1(1),* HarperCollins) HarperCollins Pubs.
—My Weird School Daze #10: Miss Mary Is Scary! Paillot, Jim, illus. 2010. (My Weird School Daze Ser.: 10). (ENG.). 112p. (J). (gr. 1-5). pap. 4.99 *(978-0-06-170397-3(4),* HarperCollins) HarperCollins Pubs.
—My Weird School Daze #11: Mr. Tony Is Full of Baloney! Paillot, Jim, illus. 2010. (My Weird School Daze Ser.: 11). (ENG.). 112p. (J). (gr. 1-5). pap. 4.99 *(978-0-06-170399-7(0));* lib. bdg. 15.89 *(978-0-06-170400-0(8))* HarperCollins Pubs. (HarperCollins).
—My Weird School Daze 12-Book Box Set: Books 1-12, 12 vols. Paillot, Jim, illus. 2013. (My Weird School Daze Ser.). (ENG.). 500p. (J). (gr. 1-5). pap. 58.88 *(978-0-06-228891-2(1),* HarperCollins) HarperCollins Pubs.
—My Weird School Daze #12: Ms. Leakey Is Freaky! No. 12. Paillot, Jim, illus. 2011. (My Weird School Daze Ser.: 12). (ENG.). 112p. (J). (gr. 1-5). pap. 4.99 *(978-0-06-170402-4(4),* HarperCollins) HarperCollins Pubs.
—My Weird School Daze #2: Mr. Sunny Is Funny! Paillot, Jim, illus. 2008. (My Weird School Daze Ser.: 2). (ENG.). 112p. (J). (gr. 1-5). pap. 4.99 *(978-0-06-134609-5(8));*No. 2. lib. bdg. 15.89 *(978-0-06-134610-1(1))* HarperCollins Pubs. (HarperCollins).
—My Weird School Daze #3: Mr. Granite Is from Another Planet!, No. 3. Paillot, Jim, illus. 2008. (My Weird School Daze Ser.: 3). (ENG.). 112p. (J). (gr. 1-5). pap. 4.99 *(978-0-06-134611-8(X),* HarperCollins) HarperCollins Pubs.
—My Weird School Daze #8: Miss Laney Is Zany! Paillot, Jim, illus. 2010. (My Weird School Daze Ser.: 8). (ENG.). 112p. (J). (gr. 1-5). pap. 4.99 *(978-0-06-155415-5(4),* HarperCollins) HarperCollins Pubs.
—My Weird School Daze #9: Mrs. Lizzy Is Dizzy! Paillot, Jim, illus. 2010. (My Weird School Daze Ser.: 9). (ENG.). 112p. (J). (gr. 1-5). pap. 4.99 *(978-0-06-155416-2(2));* lib. bdg. 15.89 *(978-0-06-155418-6(9))* HarperCollins Pubs. (HarperCollins).
—My Weird School Special: Back to School, Weird Kids Rule! Paillot, Jim, illus. 2014. (My Weird School Special Ser.). (ENG.). 144p. (J). (gr. 1-5). pap. 5.99 *(978-0-06-220685-5(0),* HarperCollins) HarperCollins Pubs.
—My Weird School Special: Oh, Valentine, We've Lost Our Minds! Paillot, Jim, illus. 2014. (My Weird School Special Ser.). (ENG.). 144p. (J). (gr. 1-5). pap. 6.99 *(978-0-06-228403-7(7),* HarperCollins) HarperCollins Pubs.
—My Weirder School #10: Mr. Jack Is a Maniac! Paillot, Jim, illus. 2014. (My Weirder School Ser.: 10). (ENG.). 112p. (J). (gr. 1-5). pap. 4.99 *(978-0-06-219841-9(6),* HarperCollins) HarperCollins Pubs.
—My Weirder School #5: Ms. Beard Is Weird! Paillot, Jim, illus. 2012. (My Weirder School Ser.: 5). (ENG.). 112p. (J). (gr. 1-5). pap. 6.99 *(978-0-06-204209-5(2),* HarperCollins) HarperCollins Pubs.
—My Weirdest School #1: Mr. Cooper Is Super! Paillot, Jim, illus. 2015. (My Weirdest School Ser.: 1). (ENG.). 112p. (J). (gr. 1-5). pap. 4.99 *(978-0-06-228421-1(5),* HarperCollins) HarperCollins Pubs.
—My Weirdest School #10: Miss Newman Isn't Human! Paillot, Jim, illus. 2018. (My Weirdest School Ser.: 10). (ENG.). 112p. (J). (gr. 1-5). pap. 4.99 *(978-0-06-242939-1(6));* lib. bdg. 16.89 *(978-0-06-242940-7(X))* HarperCollins Pubs. (HarperCollins).
—My Weirdest School #2: Ms. Cuddy Is Nutty! Paillot, Jim, illus. 2015. (My Weirdest School Ser.: 2). (ENG.). 112p. (J). (gr. 1-5). pap. 5.99 *(978-0-06-228424-2(X));* lib. bdg. 15.89 *(978-0-06-228425-9(8))* HarperCollins Pubs. (HarperCollins).
—My Weirdest School #3: Miss Brown Is Upside Down! Paillot, Jim, illus. 2015. (My Weirdest School Ser.: 3). (ENG.). 112p. (J). (gr. 1-5). pap. 5.99 *(978-0-06-228427-3(4),* HarperCollins) HarperCollins Pubs.
—My Weirdest School #6: Mr. Nick Is a Lunatic! Paillot, Jim, illus. 2016. (My Weirdest School Ser.: 6). (ENG.). 112p. (J). (gr. 1-5). pap. 5.99 *(978-0-06-228436-5(3),* HarperCollins) HarperCollins Pubs.
—My Weirdest School #8: Mrs. Master Is a Disaster! Paillot, Jim, illus. 2017. (My Weirdest School Ser.: 8). (ENG.). 112p. (J). (gr. 1-5). pap. 5.99 *(978-0-06-242933-9(7),* HarperCollins) HarperCollins Pubs.
—Oh, Valentine, We've Lost Our Minds! 2014. (My Weird School Ser.). (J). lib. bdg. 16.00 *(978-0-606-36460-7(9))* Turtleback.
Haberdasher, Violet. Knightley Academy. 2011. (ENG.). 512p. (J). (gr. 3-7). pap. 5.99 *(978-1-4169-9144-1(1),* Aladdin) Simon & Schuster Children's Publishing.
Hambrick, Sharon. Brain Games. 2009. (J). 8.99 *(978-1-59166-954-8(5))* BJU Pr.
Handwerk, Marina. Hey Cool, I've Never Seen a Teacher with His Head Cut off Before! 2007. 284p. per. 11.95 *(978-1-4327-0332-5(3))* Outskirts Pr., Inc.
Harley, Bill. Charlie Bumpers vs. the Teacher of the Year, 1 vol. Gustavson, Adam, illus. (Charlie Bumpers Ser.: 1). 160p. (J). (gr. 2-5). 2014. pap. 7.99 *(978-1-56145-824-0(4))* 2013. 14.95 *(978-1-56145-732-8(9))* Peachtree Publishing Co. Inc.
Harney, D. G. Meet Mr. Ugly, 1 vol. 2010. 133p. pap. 24.95 *(978-1-4489-5191-8(7))* America Star Bks.
Harper, Charise Mericle. Still Just Grace. 2009. (Just Grace Ser.: 2). (ENG., Illus.). 160p. (J). (gr. 1-4). pap. 7.99 *(978-0-618-93482-9(0),* 1018125, Clarion Bks.) HarperCollins Pubs.
Harper, Jamie. Miss Mingo & the Fire Drill. Harper, Jamie, illus. 2012. (Miss Mingo Ser.). (ENG., Illus.). 40p. (J). (gr. -1-3). pap. 7.99 *(978-0-7636-6086-4(8))* Candlewick Pr.
—Miss Mingo & the First Day of School. 2006. (Illus.). 26p. (J). *(978-1-4156-9174-8(6))* Candlewick Pr.
—Miss Mingo Weathers the Storm. Harper, Jamie, illus. (Miss Mingo Ser.). (ENG., Illus.). 40p. (J). (gr. -1-3). 2017. 6.99 *(978-0-7636-9514-9(9))* 2012. 15.99 *(978-0-7636-4931-9(7))* Candlewick Pr.
Harris, Tim. Mr. Bambuckle's Remarkables. 2019. (Mr. Bambuckle Ser.: 1). (ENG., Illus.). 240p. (J). (gr. 3-7). pap. 7.99 *(978-1-4926-8558-6(5))* Sourcebooks, Inc.
Harris, Valerie F. & Jones, Eula V. My Teacher Doesn't Like Me. Date not set. 22p. (J). (gr. k-6). pap. *(978-1-889654-00-3(0))* Enricharamics, Inc.
Harriton, Maxine. A School Trip to the Fruit Planet, 1. l.t. ed. 2006. 34p. (J). (gr. -1-1). lib. bdg. 18.95 *(978-0-9787248-0-1(1),* 00-01-851-447X) UpTree Publishing.
Hayes, Carolyn. School Starts Today: The Mccool School Series. 2011. 28p. pap. 13.59 *(978-1-4520-6747-6(3))* AuthorHouse.
Henkes, Kevin. El Gran día de Lily: Lily's Big Day (Spanish Edition), 1 vol. Henkes, Kevin, illus. 2008. (SPA., Illus.). 40p. (J). (gr. -1-3). 17.99 *(978-0-06-136316-0(2))* HarperCollins Español.
—Lilly's Big Day. Henkes, Kevin, illus. 2006. (ENG., Illus.). 40p. (J). (gr. -1-3). 18.99 *(978-0-06-074236-2(4));* lib. bdg. 18.89 *(978-0-06-074237-9(2))* HarperCollins Pubs. (Greenwillow Bks.).
—Lilly's Big Day. 2014. (J). lib. bdg. 17.20 *(978-0-606-35472-1(7))* Turtleback.
—Lilly's Purple Plastic Purse. Henkes, Kevin, illus. 10th anniv. ed. 2006. (ENG., Illus.). 40p. (J). (gr. -1-4). 19.99 *(978-0-688-12897-5(1),* Greenwillow Bks.) HarperCollins Pubs.
—Lilly's Purple Plastic Purse. Henkes, Kevin, illus. (Illus.). pap. 18.95 incl. audio compact disk *(978-1-59112-347-7(X));* pap. 16.95 incl. audio *(978-0-87499-686-9(4));* pap. incl. audio compact disk *(978-1-59112-557-0(X));* pap. incl. audio *(978-0-87499-688-3(0))* Live Oak Media.
—Lilly's Purple Plastic Purse 20th Anniversary Edition. Henkes, Kevin, illus. 20th ed. 2016. (ENG., Illus.). 40p. (J). (gr. -1-3). 17.99 *(978-0-06-242419-8(X),* Greenwillow Bks.) HarperCollins Pubs.
—Lily y Su Bolso de Plastico Morado. 2017.Tr. of Lilly's Purple Plastic Purse. (SPA.). (J). pap. 9.99 *(978-1-63245-667-0(2))* Lectorum Pubns., Inc.
Hiaasen, Carl. Scat. 2011. 10.54 *(978-0-7848-3574-6(8),* Everbind) Marco Bk. Co.
—Scat. 2010. 19.00 *(978-1-60686-585-9(4))* Perfection Learning Corp.
—Scat. (ENG.). 400p. (J). (gr. 5). 2012. 8.99 *(978-0-440-42104-7(7),* Yearling) 2010. pap. 9.99 *(978-0-375-83487-5(7),* Ember) Random Hse. Children's Bks.
—Scat. 2012. lib. bdg. 18.40 *(978-0-606-26532-4(5))* Turtleback.
Higbee, Heidi. It Could Happen... on the Bus. Hezlep, Amber, illus. 2012. 32p. (J). pap. 16.95 *(978-0-9882940-0-4(1))* Bryson Taylor Publishing.
Hill, Kirkpatrick. The Year of Miss Agnes. 2003. (Aladdin Historical Fiction Ser.). 115p. (gr. 3-7). 17.00 *(978-0-7569-1407-3(8))* Perfection Learning Corp.
Hitchcock, Shannon. Ruby Lee & Me. 2018. (ENG.). 224p. (J). (gr. 3-7). pap. 7.99 *(978-0-545-78231-9(7),* Scholastic Pr.) Scholastic, Inc.
Hobbs, Leigh. Freaks on the Loose: The Whole Scary Story. 2018. (ENG., Illus.). 240p. (J). (gr. 2-6). pap. 13.99 *(978-1-76029-431-1(4))* Allen & Unwin AUS. Dist: Independent Pubs. Group.
Hobbs, Valerie. Minnie Mcclary Speaks Her Mind. 2013. (ENG.). 240p. (J). (gr. 4-8). pap. 17.99 *(978-1-250-03408-3(6),* 900120578) Square Fish.
Hoffman, James. The Fabulous Principal Pie, Level 3. Hoffman, Joan, ed. Brooks, Nan, illus. 3rd ed. 2011. (ENG.). 16p. (J). (gr. -1-2). pap. 3.49 *(978-0-88743-266-8(2),* c1ff05b1-3fbe-4c16-82f2-ee8d4269cb86) School Zone Publishing Co.
Holmes, Sara. Operation Yes. 2009. 234p. (J). pap. *(978-0-545-20418-7(6))* Scholastic, Inc.
Hopkinson, Deborah. A Letter to My Teacher: A Teacher Appreciation Gift. Carpenter, Nancy, illus. 2017. 40p. (J). (gr. -1-3). 18.99 *(978-0-375-86845-0(3),* Schwartz & Wade Bks.) Random Hse. Children's Bks.
Horn, Lorri. Dewey Fairchild, Sibling Problem Solver. 2019. (Dewey Fairchild Ser.: 3). (ENG.). 256p. (J). (gr. 4-7). 13.99 *(978-1-948705-41-7(9))* Amberjack Publishing Co.
—Dewey Fairchild, Teacher Problem Solver. 2018. (Dewey Fairchild Ser.: 2). (ENG., Illus.). 286p. (J). (gr. 4-7). 13.99 *(978-1-944995-85-0(4))* Amberjack Publishing Co.
Horton, Elizabeth. Pick Me, Pick Me. Kinsley, Sean, illus. 2008. (ENG.). 32p. (J). 14.95 *(978-0-9797460-0-0(0))* Lerue Pr., LLC.
Hortten, Jacqueline Faye. Pu Beach. l.t. ed. 2004. (Illus.). 27p. (J). pap. 14.95 *(978-0-9728393-0-3(5))* Children's Bookshoppe Stop, The.
Houdek, Andrea. Mice in My Tummy. Collier, Kevin Scott, illus. 2012. 16p. pap. 9.95 *(978-1-61633-219-8(0))* Guardian Angel Publishing, Inc.
Howell, Heather. Emily's Ballet Recital. 2010. 32p. pap. 12.99 *(978-1-4490-8457-8(5))* AuthorHouse.
Hrdlitschka, Shelley. Kat's Fall. 2005. 168p. 18.95 *(978-0-7569-6315-6(X))* Perfection Learning Corp.
Hudgins, Larry. My Dog Spike, 1 vol. 2009. 55p. pap. 16.95 *(978-1-60836-421-3(6))* America Star Bks.
Huelin, Jodi. Alvin & the Chipmunks: Alvin & the Substitute Teacher. Artful Doodlers Limited Staff, illus. 2013. (I Can Read Level 2 Ser.). 32p. (J). (gr. -1-3). pap. 3.99 *(978-0-06-225223-4(2),* HarperFestival) HarperCollins Pubs.
—Alvin & the Substitute Teacher. 2013. (I Can Read! Level 2 Ser.). (J). lib. bdg. 13.55 *(978-0-606-32462-5(3))* Turtleback.
Hunsaker, Debbie. Reading Rug. 2012. 28p. pap. 19.99 *(978-1-4678-7018-4(8))* AuthorHouse.
Hutt, Aletha. Mama & Baba's First Chinese Words. 2011. 16p. 12.68 *(978-1-4269-5076-6(4))* Trafford Publishing.
Ingalls, Ann & Gallion, Sue Lowell. Tip & Tucker Road Trip. Ceolin, André, illus. 2019. (Tip & Tucker Ser.). (ENG.). 32p. (J). (gr. k-2). 9.99 *(978-1-5341-1006-9(2),* 204653); pap. 4.99 *(978-1-5341-1007-6(0),* 204661) Sleeping Bear Pr.
Jane, Pamela. Milo & the Flapjack Fiasco! Johnson, Meredith, ed. Johnson, Meredith, tr. 2004. (Illus.). 32p. (J). 13.95 *(978-1-59336-113-6(0));* pap. *(978-1-59336-114-3(9))* Mondo Publishing.

TUV

Jarvis, Mary Rowles. Dick Lionheart. 2007. (Illus.). 76p. per. (978-1-4065-2709-4(2)) Dodo Pr.

Jocelyn, Marthe. Mable Riley: A Reliable Record of Humdrum, Peril, & Romance. 2007. 279p. (gr. 4-7). 17.00 (978-0-7569-8183-9(2)) Perfection Learning Corp.

Johns, Eric. Mindreaders. 2007. 184p. pap. 16.95 (978-1-4357-0121-2(6)) Lulu Pr., Inc.

Jones, A. Responsibility. 2011. 32p. pap. 24.95 (978-1-4626-2167-5(8)) America Star Bks.

Judd, Merlynne. Circle of Friendship. 2010. 76p. pap. 24.99 (978-1-4520-6783-4(X)) AuthorHouse.

Julie, Danneberg. First Day Jitters. 2014. (Mrs. Hartwell's Class Adventures Ser.). (ENG.). 32p. (J). (gr. k-3). 11.20 (978-1-63245-322-8(3)) Lectorum Pubns., Inc.

Katar, Al. Captain Scratch: Island of Simanj. 2007. (J). 21.99 (978-1-934035-31-3(9)) Trent's Prints.

Katschke, Judy. Teacher's Pet. Geddes, Serena, illus. 2017. (Marguerite Henry's Misty Inn Ser.: 7). (ENG.). 128p. (J). (gr. 2-5). pap. 5.99 (978-1-4814-6991-3(6), Aladdin) Simon & Schuster Children's Publishing.

Katz, T. Miss L'eau. 2007. 44p. (YA). pap. 14.99 (978-1-59092-404-4(5)) Blue Forge Pr.

Kelly, Erin Entrada. We Dream of Space: A Newbery Honor Award Winner. 2020. (ENG., Illus.). 400p. (J). (gr. 3-7). 16.99 (978-0-06-274730-3(4), Greenwillow Bks.) HarperCollins Pubs.

Kelm, Tracy Martin. Light. 2011. 116p. pap. 11.95 (978-1-4327-6308-4(3)) Outskirts Pr., Inc.

Kenah, Katharine. The Best Teacher in Second Grade. Carter, Abby, illus. 2007. (I Can Read Level 2 Ser.). (ENG.). 48p. (J). (gr. k-3). pap. 4.99 (978-0-06-053566-7(0), HarperCollins) HarperCollins Pubs.

—The Best Teacher in Second Grade. Carter, Abby, illus. 2007. (I Can Read Bks.). 48p. (gr. -1-3). 14.00 (978-0-7569-8105-1(0)) Perfection Learning Corp.

Kendall, Sydney. A Turn for de Wurst. 318p. (J). (gr. 3-5). 9.99 (978-0-88092-461-0(6)) Royal Fireworks Publishing Co.

Kindl, Patrice. Owl in Love. 2004. (ENG.). 224p. (YA). (gr. 7-18). pap. 14.95 (978-0-618-43910-2(2)) Houghton Mifflin Harcourt Publishing Co.

King, Seth David. The Substitute Teacher Named Mr King. Clark, Matthew Levi, illus. 2005. 24p. (gr. 2-6). 12.00 (978-0-9640837-6-9(0)) Ascension Education.

Kingsley, Kate. Everything but the Truth. 2010. (Young, Loaded, & Fabulous Ser.: 2). (ENG.). 304p. (YA). (gr. 9-18). pap. 9.99 (978-1-4169-9400-8(9), Simon Pulse) Simon Pulse.

Kirby, Stan. Captain Awesome vs. the Sinister Substitute Teacher. O'Connor, George, illus. 2016. (Captain Awesome Ser.: 16). (ENG.). 128p. (J). (gr. k-4). pap. 5.99 (978-1-4814-5858-0(2), Little Simon) Little Simon.

Kline, Suzy. Horrible Harry & the June Box. Wummer, Amy, illus. 2012. (Horrible Harry Ser.: 27). 80p. (J). (gr. 2-4). pap. 4.99 (978-0-14-242185-7(5), Puffin Books) Penguin Young Readers Group.

—Horrible Harry & the Wedding Spies. 2016. (Horrible Harry Ser.: 32). lib. bdg. 14.75 (978-0-606-38389-9(1)) Turtleback.

—Horrible Harry Takes the Cake. Remkiewicz, Frank, illus. 2007. (Horrible Harry Ser.: 19). 64p. (J). (gr. 2-4). 4.99 (978-0-14-240939-8(1), Puffin Books) Penguin Young Readers Group.

—Horrible Harry Takes the Cake. Remkiewicz, Frank, illus. 2007. (Horrible Harry Ser.). 45p. (gr. 2-5). 14.00 (978-0-7569-8158-7(1)) Perfection Learning Corp.

Knowles, Jo. Read Between the Lines. 2015. (ENG.). 336p. (YA). (gr. 9). 16.99 (978-0-7636-6387-2(5)) Candlewick Pr.

Kolczynski, Sean. The Night Before Middle School! 2012. 28p. pap. 21.99 (978-1-4771-4794-8(2)) Xlibris Corp.

Konigsburg, E. L. The View from Saturday. 280p. (YA). (gr. 5-18). pap. 4.95 (978-0-8072-1511-1(2), Listening Library) Random Hse. Audio Publishing Group.

Kremer, Kevin. Santa's Our Substitute Teacher. Ely, Dave, illus. 2006. 150p. (gr. 4-7). per. 5.99 (978-0-9663335-4-1(3), 703-001) Snow In Sarasota Publishing.

Krosoczka, Jarrett J. Lunch Lady & the Author Visit Vendetta: Lunch Lady #3. 2009. (Lunch Lady Ser.: 3). (ENG.). 96p. (J). (gr. 2-5). pap. 6.99 (978-0-375-86094-2(0), Knopf Bks. for Young Readers) Random Hse. Children's Bks.

Krulik, Nancy. Doggone It! #8. John and Wendy, illus. 8th ed. 2006. (Katie Kazoo, Switcheroo Ser.: 8). (ENG.). 80p. (J). (gr. 2-4). 6.99 (978-0-448-43172-7(6), Grosset & Dunlap) Penguin Young Readers Group.

—Flower Power. John and Wendy Staff, illus. 2008. (Katie Kazoo, Switcheroo Ser.). 78p. (gr. 2-5). 14.00 (978-0-7569-8806-7(3)) Perfection Learning Corp.

Kuroda, Yosuke & Hayashiya, Shizuru. Onegai Teacher, No. 2. 2003. 120p. pap. 9.95 (978-1-58899-179-9(2)) ComicsOne Corp./Dr. Masters.

Laminack, Lester L. Snow Day!, 1 vol. Gustavson, Adam, illus. 2007. 32p. (J). (gr. -1-3). 17.99 (978-1-56145-418-1(4)) Peachtree Publishing Co. Inc.

Langdale, Mark Roland. Professor Doppelganger & the Fantastical Cloud Factory. 2012. 106p. pap. (978-1-78003-267-2(6)) Pen Pr. Pubs., Ltd.

Larsen, Angela Sage. Broken Record, Bk. 4. 2013. (Fifties Chix Ser.: 4). (ENG., Illus.). 200p. (YA). pap. 9.95 (978-1-60746-446-4(2), Premiere) FastPrncil, Inc.

—Keeping Secrets, Bk. 2. 2012. (Fifties Chix Ser.: 2). (ENG.). 220p. (YA). pap. 9.95 (978-1-60746-367-2(9), Premiere) FastPrncil, Inc.

—Till the End of Time. 2013. (Fifties Chix Ser.: 5). (ENG.). 200p. (YA). pap. 9.95 (978-1-60746-468-6(3), Premiere) FastPrncil, Inc.

Lauren, Whitney. Vanessa & Johnny: The Cabinets. 2011. 84p. pap. 9.99 (978-1-4269-5827-4(7)) Trafford Publishing.

Lay, Kathryn. The Substitutes: An Up2U Action Adventure, 1 vol. Calo, Marcos, illus. 2015. (Up2U Adventures Ser.). (ENG.). 80p. (J). (gr. 2-5). 35.64 (978-1-62402-095-7(X), 17359, Calico Chapter Bks.) ABDO Publishing Co.

LeapFrog Staff. Ozzie & Mack. 2008. (J). pap. 39.99 (978-1-59319-976-0(7)); pap. 49.99 (978-1-59319-924-1(4)) LeapFrog Enterprises, Inc.

Lee, Mary Ellen. Danny & Life on Bluff Point: Blizzard of '95 revised Edition. 2009. 160p. (gr. 4-7). pap. 12.95 (978-0-595-53308-4(6)) iUniverse, Inc.

Leppard, Lois Gladys. The Mysterious Teacher. 2003. 160p. (J). mass mkt. 4.99 (978-1-889893-98-3(6), Ambassador-Emerald, International) Emerald Hse. Group, Inc.

Leuck, Laura. My Creature Teacher. Nash, Scott, illus. 2004. (ENG.). 32p. (J). (gr. -1-1). 15.99 (978-0-06-029694-0(1)) HarperCollins Pubs.

Limbaugh, Rush. Rush Revere & the Brave Pilgrims: Time-Travel Adventures with Exceptional Americans. 2013. (Rush Revere Ser.: 1). (ENG., Illus.). 224p. 21.00 (978-1-4767-5586-1(8), Threshold Editions) Threshold Editions.

—Rush Revere & the First Patriots: Time-Travel Adventures with Exceptional Americans. 2014. (Rush Revere Ser.: 2). (ENG., Illus.). 256p. 21.00 (978-1-4767-5588-5(4), Threshold Editions) Threshold Editions.

Limbaugh, Rush & Adams Limbaugh, Kathryn. Rush Revere & the American Revolution: Time-Travel Adventures with Exceptional Americans. 2014. (Rush Revere Ser.: 3). (ENG.). 256p. 21.00 (978-1-4767-8987-3(8), Threshold Editions) Threshold Editions.

Limbaugh, Rush H., III & Limbaugh, Kathryn Adams. Rush Revere & the American Revolution. Hiers, Christopher, illus. 2014. 244p. (J). pap. (978-1-4767-8989-7(4), Threshold Editions) Threshold Editions.

Liz Collard. Jeremiah, the Schoolhouse Dog. 2009. 28p. pap. 12.79 (978-1-4269-0990-0(X)) Trafford Publishing.

Lockard, Lynn. Gone Batty!!! 2009. 40p. pap. 16.99 (978-1-4389-8516-9(9)) AuthorHouse.

Loever, Charmaine. David's Big Break. Bohman, Natasha, illus. 2008. 52p. pap. 22.99 (978-1-4389-3173-9(5)) AuthorHouse.

Luddy, Karon. Spelldown: The Big-Time Dreams of a Small-Town Word Whiz. 2008. (Mix Ser.). (ENG.). 224p. (J). (gr. 4-8). pap. 10.99 (978-1-4169-5452-1(X), Simon & Schuster/Paula Wiseman Bks.) Simon & Schuster/Paula Wiseman Bks.

Luning, Barbara. The Quilted Zoo. 2008. 28p. pap. 15.99 (978-1-4363-1778-8(9)) Xlibris Corp.

Lynch, Janet Nichols. Messed Up. 2009. (ENG.). 320p. (YA). (gr. 7-18). 17.95 (978-0-8234-2185-5(6)) Holiday Hse., Inc.

—Peace Is a Four-Letter Word. 2005. 158p. (YA). (gr. 8-12). per. 9.95 (978-1-59714-014-0(7), Great Valley Bks.) Heyday.

Magee, Helen. What's French for Help, George? Lt. ed. 2007. pap. (978-1-905665-68-6(7)) Pollinger In Print.

Mahy, Margaret. The Very Wicked Headmistress. Chamberlain, Margaret, illus. 2006. 94p. (J). (gr. 2-4). pap. 6.95 (978-1-903015-46-9(4)) Barn Owl Bks, London GBR. Dist: Independent Pubs. Group.

Maltby, Robert I. Diquan & the Book Monster, 1 vol. 2009. 39p. pap. 24.95 (978-1-61546-964-2(8)) America Star Bks.

Manell, Keane. Hall Pass to the Tenth Dimension. 2009. 56p. pap. 10.95 (978-1-4389-7401-9(9)) AuthorHouse.

Manushkin, Fran. Katie & the Fancy Substitute, 1 vol. Lyon, Tammie, illus. 2014. (Katie Woo Ser.). (ENG.). 32p. (J). (gr. k-2). 21.32 (978-1-4795-5138-0(0), 125542, Picture Window Bks.) Capstone.

Manzak, Bonnie. The Big Red Cat. 2011. 32p. pap. 21.99 (978-1-4568-6607-5(9)) Xlibris Corp.

Marshall, Catherine. The Angry Intruder, 1 vol. 2018. (Christy of Cutter Gap Ser.: 3). 112p. (J). pap. 7.99 (978-1-68370-161-3(5)) Evergreen Farm.

—The Bridge to Cutter Gap, 1 vol. 2018. (Christy of Cutter Gap Ser.: 1). 112p. (J). pap. 7.99 (978-1-68370-157-6(7)) Evergreen Farm.

—Silent Superstitions, 1 vol. 2018. (Christy of Cutter Gap Ser.: 2). 112p. (J). pap. 7.99 (978-1-68370-159-0(3)) Evergreen Farm.

Matsuura, Richard & Matsuura, Ruth. Angels Masquerading on Earth. Chao, Linus, illus. (J). 7.95 (978-1-887916-07-3(5)) Orchid Isle Publishing Co.

Mayhew, James. Ella Bella Ballerina & the Magic Toyshop. 2017. (ENG., Illus.). 32p. (J). (gr. -1-3). 14.99 (978-1-4380-5005-8(4), Sourcebooks Jabberwocky) Sourcebooks, Inc.

McClintock, Norah. Shadow of Doubt, No. 5. 2012. (Robyn Hunter Mysteries Ser.: 5). (ENG.). 232p. (YA). (gr. 6-12). lib. bdg. 27.99 (978-0-7613-8315-4(8), b6e28dab-7e3e-402e-87c0-8fa43f0097ef, Darby Creek) Lerner Publishing Group.

McDaniel, Lurlene. Prey. (ENG.). 208p. (YA). 2010. (gr. 7). mass mkt. 7.99 (978-0-440-24015-0(8), Laurel Leaf) 2008. (gr. 9-12). lib. bdg. 21.19 (978-0-385-90457-5(6), Delacorte Pr.) Random Hse. Children's Bks.

McDonald, Megan. Judy Moody Goes to College. Reynolds, Peter H., illus. 2018. (Judy Moody Ser.: 8). (ENG.). 176p. (J). (gr. 1-4). pap. 5.99 (978-1-5362-0078-2(6)) Candlewick Pr.

Mcdonald, Megan. Judy Moody Goes to College. (Judy Moody Ser.: 8). 2018. lib. bdg. 16.00 (978-0-606-41198-1(4)) 2010. lib. bdg. 16.00 (978-0-606-12352-5(0)) 2009. lib. bdg. 16.00 (978-0-606-01313-0(X)) Turtleback.

McDonald, Megan. Judy Moody Goes to College, Bk. 8. Reynolds, Peter H., illus. 2010. (Judy Moody Ser.: 8). (ENG.). 144p. (J). (gr. 1-4). 16.99 (978-0-7636-4856-5(6)) Candlewick Pr.

Mcghee, Alison. Mrs. Watson Wants Your Teeth. Bliss, Harry, illus. 2007. 32p. (J). reprint ed. 16.00 (978-1-4223-6777-3(0)) DIANE Publishing Co.

—Mrs. Watson Wants Your Teeth. Bliss, Harry, illus. unabr. ed. 2007. (Picture Book Readalong Ser.). (J). (gr. -1-2). 28.95 incl. audio compact disk (978-1-59519-902-7(0)) Live Oak Media.

McGroary, Mary Beth. My Teacher Hates Me. 2012. 24p. 24.95 (978-1-4626-6012-4(6)) America Star Bks.

McKissack, Robert. Try Your Best. Cepeda, Joe, illus. 2004. (ENG.). 24p. (J). (gr. -1-3). pap. 4.99 (978-0-15-205090-0(6), 1195368, Clarion Bks.) HarperCollins Pubs.

McKissack, Robert L. Try Your Best. Cepeda, Joe, illus. 2005. (Green Light Readers Level 2 Ser.). (gr. k-2). 13.95 (978-0-7569-5630-1(7)) Perfection Learning Corp.

McMullan, Kate. Pearl & Wagner: Five Days till Summer. 2014. (Penguin Young Readers: Level 3 Ser.). lib. bdg. 13.55 (978-0-606-35727-2(0)) Turtleback.

McNamara, Margaret. Summer Treasure: Ready-To-Read Level 1. Gordon, Mike, illus. 2012. (Robin Hill School Ser.). (ENG.). 32p. (J). (gr. -1-1). 17.99 (978-1-4424-3646-6(8)); pap. 4.99 (978-1-4424-3645-9(X)) Simon Spotlight. (Simon Spotlight).

Mendenhall, Gaylee. My Teacher is Bald! 2011. 28p. pap. 14.99 (978-1-4634-5032-8(X)) AuthorHouse.

Michie, Brandon J. Ollie the Octopus: Animal Lessons. 2011. 20p. 13.49 (978-1-4567-4782-4(7)) AuthorHouse.

Miller, Sarah. Miss Spitfire: Reaching Helen Keller. (ENG.). (J). (gr. 5-7). 2010. 256p. pap. 8.99 (978-1-4424-0851-7(0)) 2007. 240p. 17.99 (978-1-4169-2542-2(2)) Simon & Schuster Children's Publishing. (Atheneum Bks. for Young Readers).

Millman, Selena. Anyone Can Make A Difference. 2006. 109p. (YA). per. (978-0-9793058-6-3(1)) Millman, Selena.

Millsap, Ella. A Portrait of a Church in Stone: The Keeper of the Honeybees. 2013. 62p. (J). pap. 12.00 (978-0-9891960-3-1(8)) Professional Publishing Hse. LLC.

Mitter, Kathryn, illus. Eloise Has a Lesson: Ready-To-Read Level 1. 2005. (Eloise Ser.). (ENG.). 32p. (J). (gr. -1-1). pap. 4.99 (978-0-689-87367-6(0), Simon Spotlight) Simon Spotlight.

A Monkey Ate My Homework. 2007. 32p. pap. 4.50 (978-0-8341-2287-1(1), 083-412-2871) Beacon Hill Pr. of Kansas City.

Montgomery, L. M. Anne of Avonlea. 2018. (ENG., Illus.). 250p. (J). (gr. 3-7). pap. (978-93-5297-101-5(9)) Alpha Editions.

—Anne of Avonlea. (ENG., Illus.). (J). 2018. 400p. pap. 17.95 (978-1-376-49928-5(2)) 2015. 27.95 (978-1-297-91573-4(9)) Creative Media Partners, LLC.

—Anne of Avonlea. 2005. pap. (978-1-905432-15-8(1)) Dodo Pr.

—Anne of Avonlea. 2011. 214p. (gr. 4-7). pap. 15.95 (978-1-4638-0054-3(1)) Rodgers, Alan Bks.

—Anne of Avonlea. 2005. (Aladdin Classics Ser.). (ENG., Illus.). 416p. (J). (gr. 4-7). pap. 5.99 (978-1-4169-0328-4(3), Aladdin) Simon & Schuster Children's Publishing.

—Anne of Avonlea. 2018. (Anne of Green Gables: the Complete Collection: 2). (ENG.). 336p. (J). (gr. 6-12). 8.99 (978-1-78226-444-6(2), 5ab6e735-475a-4e0f-a18b-99628df1f473) Sweet Cherry Publishing GBR. Dist: Baker & Taylor Publisher Services (BTPS).

—Anne of Avonlea. 2018. (ENG., Illus.). 276p. (YA). 24.99 (978-1-5287-0644-5(7), Classic Bks. Library) The Editorium, LLC.

—Anne of Avonlea. 2019. (ENG.). 262p. (J). pap. 11.89 (978-1-7278-8486-9(8)) CreateSpace Independent Publishing Platform.

—Anne of Avonlea. (ENG.). 2019. 268p. (J). pap. 12.99 (978-1-7018-6034-6(1)) 2019. 386p. (J). pap. 22.99 (978-1-0899-1022-0(3)) 2019. 386p. (J). pap. 22.99 (978-1-0830-1790-1(X)) 2019. 546p. (J). pap. 36.99 (978-1-0825-6163-4(0)) 2019. 386p. (J). pap. 22.99 (978-1-0807-5704-6(X)) 2019. 546p. (J). pap. 35.99 (978-1-0800-7977-3(7)) 2019. 818p. (J). pap. 46.99 (978-1-0781-0625-2(8)) 2019. 544p. (J). pap. 35.99 (978-1-0780-6471-2(7)) 2019. 546p. (J). pap. 31.99 (978-1-0753-6837-0(5)) 2019. 386p. (YA). pap. 22.99 (978-1-0726-8331-5(8)) 2019. 546p. (YA). pap. 30.99 (978-1-0707-5140-5(5)) 2019. 268p. (YA). pap. 18.99 (978-1-0705-9376-0(1)) 2019. 568p. (YA). pap. 33.99 (978-1-0987-6527-9(3)) 2019. 364p. (YA). pap. 19.99 (978-1-0968-7536-9(5)) 2019. 268p. (YA). pap. 16.99 (978-1-0954-6547-9(3)) 2019. 546p. (YA). pap. 34.99 (978-1-0916-4683-4(X)) 2019. 506p. (YA). pap. 29.99 (978-1-7965-5870-8(2)) 2019. (Illus.). 546p. (YA). pap. 34.99 (978-1-7929-7537-0(6)) 2018. (Illus.). 240p. (YA). pap. 15.99 (978-1-7919-1487-5(X)) Independently Published.

—Anne of Avonlea. 2019. (ENG.). 252p. (J). pap. 27.99 (978-1-7077-7448-7(X)) Independently Published.

—Anne of Avonlea. 2012. (World Classics Ser.). (ENG.). 228p. pap. 19.99 (978-1-909438-94-1(4), Sovereign) Bollinger, Max GBR. Dist: Gardners Bks. Ltd., Lightning Source UK, Ltd.

—Anne of Avonlea. Lt. ed. 2006. (ENG.). pap. (978-1-4068-3173-3(5)) Echo Library.

—Kilmeny of the Orchard. 2018. (ENG., Illus.). 118p. (J). (gr. 4-7). pap. (978-93-5297-106-0(X)) Alpha Editions.

—Kilmeny of the Orchard. 2010. 146p. pap. 16.95 (978-1-60444-108-6(9)) IndoEuropeanPublishing.com.

—Kilmeny of the Orchard. 2018. (ENG., Illus.). 124p. (J). (gr. 4-7). 14.99 (978-1-5154-3231-9(9)) Wilder Pubns., Corp.

—Kilmeny of the Orchard. 2019. (ENG.). (J). 122p. pap. 7.99 (978-1-7018-6677-5(3)); 248p. pap. 11.99 (978-1-6999-8624-0(X)); 248p. pap. 15.99 (978-1-6967-9912-6(0)); 248p. pap. 15.99 (978-1-6949-7534-8(7)); 248p. pap. 15.99 (978-1-6910-9073-0(5)); 332p. pap. 19.99 (978-1-6862-7332-2(0)); 376p. pap. 25.00 (978-1-0895-1503-6(0)); 332p. pap. 19.99 (978-1-0776-9765-2(1)); 252p. pap. 18.99 (978-1-0784-0836-3(X)); 122p. pap. 9.99 (978-1-0805-1773-2(1)); 252p. pap. 15.99 (978-1-0803-9449-4(4)); 332p. pap. 19.99 (978-1-0859-0762-0(7)); 252p. pap. 18.99 (978-1-0830-6207-9(7)); 252p. pap. 15.99 (978-1-0761-2348-0(1)); 334p. pap. 19.99 (978-1-0727-4932-5(7)); 166p. pap. 12.99 (978-1-0705-1744-5(5)); 376p. pap. 22.99 (978-1-0997-7222-1(2)); 230p. pap. 13.99 (978-1-0989-2774-5(5)); 252p. pap. 15.99 (978-1-0974-8816-2(0)); 252p. pap. 15.99 (978-1-0934-3789-8(8)); 252p. pap. 16.99 (978-1-0917-4648-0(6)); 252p. pap. 14.99 (978-1-7969-7320-4(3)) Independently Published.

—Kilmeny of the Orchard. 2019. (ENG.). (J). 112p. pap. 15.99 (978-1-7077-9097-5(3)); 84p. pap. 5.99 (978-1-7036-1459-6(3)) Independently Published.

Montgomery, Lucy Maud. Anne of Avonlea. 2019. (ENG.). (J). (gr. 3-7). 276p. pap. 12.95 (978-0-368-78940-3(3)); 96p. pap. 12.71 (978-0-368-28129-7(9)) Blurb, Inc.

—Anne of Avonlea. (ENG.). (gr. 3-7). 2020. 170p. (YA). pap. 9.99 (978-1-6594-8477-9(4)) 2018. (Illus.). 594p. (J). pap. 34.99 (978-1-7916-6454-1(7)) Independently Published.

—Anne of Avonlea. Blake, Sheba, ed. 2020. (ENG.). 254p. (YA). (gr. 3-7). pap. 14.99 (978-1-222-29341-8(2)) Indy Pub.

—Anne of Avonlea. 2008. (Illus.). 268p. (J). (gr. 3-7). 18.99 (978-1-4341-1489-1(9), Waking Lion Press) The Editorium, LLC.

—Kilmeny of the Orchard. 2019. (ENG.). 264p. (J). (gr. 4-7). 25.95 (978-0-469-78399-7(0)); pap. 15.95 (978-0-469-78398-0(2)) Creative Media Partners, LLC. (Wentworth Pr.).

Montgomery, Lucy Maud & Grandma's Treasures. Anne of Avonlea. 2019. (ENG.). 252p. (YA). (gr. 3-7). (978-1-7948-2437-9(5)) Lulu Pr., Inc.

Montgomery, Lucy Maud & Treasures, Grandma's. Anne of Avonlea. 2019. (ENG.). 252p. (YA). (gr. 3-7). pap. (978-1-7948-2462-1(6)) Lulu Pr., Inc.

Morgan, Winter. Hidden in the Chest. 2017. (Unofficial Minecrafters Academy Ser.: 5). lib. bdg. 18.40 (978-0-606-40310-8(8)) Turtleback.

Morrison, Jaydene & Peterson, Russell. I Hate You, Miss Bliss. 2012. 36p. pap. 20.99 (978-1-4772-9740-7(5)) AuthorHouse.

Moss, Marissa. Amelia's 6th-Grade Notebook. Moss, Marissa, illus. 2005. (Amelia Ser.). (ENG., Illus.). 80p. (J). (gr. 4-7). 14.99 (978-0-689-87040-8(X), Simon & Schuster/Paula Wiseman Bks.) Simon & Schuster/Paula Wiseman Bks.

Mrs Bold, 6 Packs. (Literatura 2000 Ser.). (gr. 1-2). 28.00 (978-0-7635-0101-3(8)) Rigby Education.

Mrs Keen: Individual Title Six-Packs. (gr. -1-2). 27.00 (978-0-7635-9462-6(8)) Rigby Education.

My Teacher Glows in the Dark. 2014. (My Teacher Bks.: 3). (ENG., Illus.). 192p. (J). (gr. 3-7). 17.99 (978-1-4814-0432-7(6), Simon & Schuster/Paula Wiseman Bks.) Simon & Schuster/Paula Wiseman Bks.

Myracle, Lauren. Oopsy Daisy: A Flower Power Book. 2012. (Flower Power Ser.). (ENG.). 368p. (YA). (gr. 4-8). pap. 8.95 (978-1-4197-0418-5(4), 694303, Amulet Bks.) Abrams, Inc.

Naegele, K. Z. The Chatty Hat. 2011. 36p. pap. 24.95 (978-1-4626-3652-5(7)) America Star Bks.

Newton-Perry, Linda. Eye of the Beast. 2009. 62p. pap. 7.98 (978-0-557-06333-8(7)) Lulu Pr., Inc.

Nikola-Lisa, W. My Teacher Can Teach... Anyone! Galindo, Felipe, illus. 2004. (ENG.). 32p. (J). (gr. -1-2). 16.95 (978-1-58430-163-9(5)); pap. 11.95 (978-1-60060-276-4(2), leelowbooks) Lee & Low Bks., Inc.

Novel Units. Miss Nelson Is Back / Miss Nelson Is Missing Novel Units Teacher Guide. 2019. (Miss Nelson Ser.). (ENG.). (J). (gr. -1-3). pap. 12.99 (978-1-56137-032-0(0), Novel Units, Inc.) Classroom Library Co.

—The View from Saturday Novel Units Student Packet. 2019. (ENG.). (J). pap. 13.99 (978-1-56137-936-1(0), Novel Units, Inc.) Classroom Library Co.

Nurse, Holly. Meridian Brown Goes to School. 2009. (Illus.). 60p. pap. (978-1-84748-535-9(9)) Athena Pr.

Oceanak, Karla. Dumbstruck. Spanjer, Kendra, illus. 2011. (Aldo Zelnick Comic Novel Ser.: 4). (ENG.). 160p. (J). (gr. 3-7). 12.95 (978-1-934649-16-9(3)) Bailiwick Pr.

O'Connor, Jane. Fancy Nancy at the Museum. 2008. (I Can Read Level 1 Ser.). (ENG., Illus.). 32p. (J). (gr. -1-3). pap. 4.99 (978-0-06-123607-5(1), HarperCollins) HarperCollins Pubs.

—Fancy Nancy at the Museum. Glasser, Robin Preiss, illus. 2008. (I Can Read Level 1 Ser.). (ENG.). 32p. (J). (gr. -1-3). 17.99 (978-0-06-123608-2(X), HarperCollins) HarperCollins Pubs.

O'Connor, Jane & Harper Collins / LeapFrog. Fancy Nancy at the Museum. Glasser, Robin Preiss, illus. 2008. (Fancy Nancy Ser.). (J). 13.99 (978-1-59319-940-1(6)) LeapFrog Enterprises, Inc.

Oliver, Ilanit. Olivia & the Best Teacher Ever. 2012. (Olivia 8x8 Ser.). lib. bdg. 13.55 (978-0-606-26367-2(5)) Turtleback.

O'Malley, Kevin & Finchler, Judy. Miss Malarkey Leaves No Reader Behind. O'Malley, Kevin, illus. 2010. (Miss Malarkey Ser.). (ENG., Illus.). 32p. (J). (gr. k-3). pap. 8.99 (978-0-8027-2098-6(6), 900066992, Bloomsbury USA Childrens) Bloomsbury Publishing USA.

Pace, Anne Marie. A Teacher for Bear. Wohnoutka, Mike, illus. 2011. (J). (978-0-545-37776-8(5)) Scholastic, Inc.

Pallotta, Jerry. What I Saw in the Teachers' Lounge. McWilliam, Howard, illus. 2012. (J). (978-0-545-38472-8(9)) Scholastic, Inc.

Papell, David. Harlem Awakenings. 2007. (ENG.). 48p. pap. 12.95 (978-0-615-17531-7(7)) Papell, David.

Parbi, Eunice Efiba Asare. Yum! Yum! Yum! Trust Us! We Will Blow It! Series 1. 2012. (Illus.). 28p. pap. 21.35 (978-1-4772-4719-8(X)) AuthorHouse.

Parish, Peggy. Teach Us, Amelia Bedelia. Sweat, Lynn, illus. 2005. (Amelia Bedelia Ser.). 58p. (gr. -1-3). 14.00 (978-0-7569-4804-7(5)) Perfection Learning Corp.

Parker, Robert. Edenville Owls. 2008. 194p. (gr. 4-6). 18.00 (978-0-7569-8920-0(5)) Perfection Learning Corp.

Parr, todd. Teachers Rock! 2016. (ENG., Illus.). 32p. (J). (gr. -1-1). 18.99 (978-0-316-26512-6(8)) Little, Brown Bks. for Young Readers.

Parton, Matthew R. My Closet Monster Ate My Homework, 1 vol. 2009. (ENG.). 30p. 24.95 (978-1-60836-184-7(5)) America Star Bks.

Passen, Lisa. The Attack of the 50-Foot Teacher. 2005. (Illus.). 28p. (J). (gr. k-4). reprint ed. 16.00 (978-0-7567-9665-5(2)) DIANE Publishing Co.

Patterson, Matthew. Shake Them up, Mrs Nut. 2008. 104p. per. 9.95 (978-1-4327-2008-7(2)) Outskirts Pr., Inc.

Pattou, Edith. Mrs. Spitzer's Garden: [Gift Edition]. Tusa, Tricia, illus. gif. ed. 2007. (ENG.). 32p. (J). (gr. -1-3). 12.99 (978-0-15-205802-9(8), 1197433, Clarion Bks.) HarperCollins Pubs.

Peck, Richard. The Teacher's Funeral. 2006. (ENG.). 224p. (J). (gr. 3-7). reprint ed. 8.99 (978-0-14-240507-9(8), Puffin Books) Penguin Young Readers Group.

Pef. Belle lisse poire du prince De. pap. 16.95 (978-2-07-054806-4(6)) Gallimard, Editions FRA. Dist: Distribooks, Inc.

Peirce, Lincoln. Big Nate Strikes Again. 2015. (Big Nate Ser.: 2). (J). lib. bdg. 17.20 (978-0-606-36504-8(4)) Turtleback.

Penner, Stephen. Professor Barrister's Dinosaur Mysteries #1: The Case of the Truncated Troodon. Penner, Stephen, illus. 2010. (Illus.). 44p. pap. 19.25 (978-1-60888-005-8(2)) Nimble Bks. LLC.

Pennypacker, Sara. Clementine's Letter. Frazee, Marla, illus. 2009. (Clementine Ser.: 3). (ENG.). 160p. (J). (gr. 1-5). pap. 5.99 (978-0-7868-3885-1(X)) Little, Brown Bks. for Young Readers.

Perelstein, Jennifer. Who Moved the Masterpieces? A Visit to the Mcnay Art Museum. 2010. 30p. pap. 15.99 *(978-1-60844-585-1(2))* Dog Ear Publishing, LLC.
Pilkey, Dav. Captain Underpants & the Attack of the Talking Toilets. 2004. (Captain Underpants Ser.: No. 2). (J). lib. bdg. 19.95 *(978-0-439-68436-1(6),* Scholastic, Inc.) Scholastic, Inc.
—Captain Underpants & the Perilous Plot of Professor Poopypants. 2004. (Captain Underpants Ser.: No. 4). (J). lib. bdg. 19.95 *(978-0-439-68440-8(4),* Scholastic, Inc.) Scholastic, Inc.
—Captain Underpants & the Wrath of the Wicked Wedgie Woman. 2004. (Captain Underpants Ser.: No. 5). (J). lib. bdg. 19.95 *(978-0-439-68441-5(2),* Scholastic, Inc.) Scholastic, Inc.
Polacco, Patricia. The Art of Miss Chew. Polacco, Patricia, illus. 2012. (Illus.). 40p. (J). (gr. k-3). 18.99 *(978-0-399-25703-2(9),* G.P. Putnam's Sons Books for Young Readers) Penguin Young Readers Group.
—Gracias, Senor Falker. 2006. (SPA., Illus.). 34p. (J). (gr. 2-3). per. 9.99 *(978-1-933032-02-3(2),* LC34004) Lectorum Pubns., Inc.
—The Junkyard Wonders. Polacco, Patricia, illus. 2010. (ENG., Illus.). 48p. (J). (gr. 1-4). 18.99 *(978-0-399-25078-1(6),* Philomel Bks.) Penguin Young Readers Group.
—The Lemonade Club. Polacco, Patricia, illus. 2007. (Illus.). 48p. (J). (gr. 1-4). 18.99 *(978-0-399-24540-4(5),* Philomel Bks.) Penguin Young Readers Group.
—Mr. Wayne's Masterpiece. Polacco, Patricia, illus. 2014. (Illus.). 40p. (J). (gr. k-3). 18.99 *(978-0-399-16095-0(7),* G.P. Putnam's Sons Books for Young Readers) Penguin Young Readers Group.
—Thank You, Mr. Falker. Polacco, Patricia, illus. 2012. (Illus.). 40p. (J). (gr. k-3). 15.99 *(978-0-399-25762-9(4),* Philomel Bks.) Penguin Young Readers Group.
Pollard, Mary Jean. Octrina the Octopus. 2011. 28p. pap. 15.99 *(978-1-4568-4778-4(3))* Xlibris Corp.
Poulsen, David A. Numbers. 2nd ed. 2015. (ENG.). 200p. (YA). pap. 12.99 *(978-1-4597-3248-3(0))* Dundurn Pr. CAN. Dist: Publishers Group West (PGW).
—Numbers. 2008. (ENG.). 232p. (YA). (gr. 6-18). *(978-1-55470-095-0(7))* Me to We.
Primavera, Elise. Louise the Big Cheese & the Back-To-School Smarty-Pants. Goode, Diane, illus. 2011. (ENG.). 40p. (J). (gr. k-3). 16.99 *(978-1-4424-0600-1(3),* Simon & Schuster/Paula Wiseman Bks.) Simon & Schuster/Paula Wiseman Bks.
—Making Mistakes on Purpose. 2017. (Ms. Rapscott's Girls Ser.: 2). (Illus.). 384p. (J). (gr. 3-7). 8.99 *(978-0-14-751768-5(0),* Puffin Books) Penguin Young Readers Group.
Prinz, Yvonne. Still There, Clare. 2005. (ENG.). 4p. (J). pap., tchr. ed. *(978-1-55192-821-0(3))* Raincoast Bk. Distribution CAN. Dist: Publishers Group West (PGW).
Profilet, Cynthia. Maggie's Golden Moment. Barron, Ann, illus. 2005. (J). *(978-0-9637735-1-7(8))* Sterling Pr., Inc.
Ramesh, Serita. Jason & the Ingenious Number Trick: A Story about Patterns. 2010. 28p. pap. 15.49 *(978-1-4490-4740-5(8))* AuthorHouse.
Ransom, Jeanie Franz. Don't Squeal Unless It's a Big Deal: A Tale of Tattletales. Urbanovic, Jackie, illus. 2005. 32p. (J). (ENG.). 14.95 *(978-1-59147-239-1(3));* (gr. -1-3). pap. 9.95 *(978-1-59147-240-7(7))* American Psychological Assn. (Magination Pr.).
Reagan, Jean. How to Get Your Teacher Ready. Wildish, Lee, illus. 2017. (How to Ser.). (ENG.). 32p. (J). (gr. -1-3). 18.99 *(978-0-553-53825-0(X),* Knopf Bks. for Young Readers) Random Hse. Children's Bks.
Red & Green Choices by Green Irene: Niki's Next Grade. 2003. (J). per. 14.50 *(978-0-9742280-1-3(X))* Green Irene.
Rentala, Sita Kanaka Valli. Ocean Flows: In Prose: Zcumby's Judo (on Global Warming) 2010. 44p. (J). pap. 19.99 *(978-1-4490-8780-7(9))* AuthorHouse.
Repka, Janice. The Clueless Girl's Guide to Being a Genius. 2011. (ENG.). 176p. (J). (gr. 4-6). 21.19 *(978-0-525-42333-1(8))* Penguin Young Readers Group.
Robins, Eleanor. Where Is Mr. Zane?, 1 vol. unabr. ed. 2011. (Carter High Mysteries Ser.). (ENG.). 48p. (YA). (gr. 9-12). 9.75 *(978-1-61651-569-0(4))* Saddleback Educational Publishing, Inc.
Rogers, Blessing. Gabby & Ralph Meet Their New Teacher. 2010. 24p. 11.49 *(978-1-4520-5447-6(9))* AuthorHouse.
Rogers, Kelly. Buyer Beware, 1 vol. Peterschmidt, Betsy, illus. 2016. (Rm. 201 Ser.). (ENG.). 48p. (J). (gr. 3-7). lib. bdg. 34.21 *(978-1-62402-167-1(0),* 21581, Spellbound) Magic Wagon.
—The House Sitters, 1 vol. Peterschmidt, Betsy, illus. 2016. (Rm. 201 Ser.). (ENG.). 48p. (J). (gr. 3-7). lib. bdg. 34.21 *(978-1-62402-168-8(9),* 21583, Spellbound) Magic Wagon.
—The Key, 1 vol. Peterschmidt, Betsy, illus. 2016. (Rm. 201 Ser.). (ENG.). 48p. (J). (gr. 3-7). lib. bdg. 34.21 *(978-1-62402-169-5(7),* 21585, Spellbound) Magic Wagon.
—Study Group. Peterschmidt, Betsy, illus. 2016. (Rm. 201 Ser.). (ENG.). 48p. (J). (gr. 3-7). lib. bdg. 34.21 *(978-1-62402-170-1(0),* 21587, Spellbound) Magic Wagon.
Rolle Williams, Joyce. Chris's Story: A Family Voting Secret Revealed. 2008. 24p. pap. 12.99 *(978-1-4389-4258-2(3))* AuthorHouse.
Rose, Nancy. The Secret Life of Squirrels: Back to School! 2018. (ENG., Illus.). 32p. (J). (gr. -1-3). 17.99 *(978-0-316-50621-2(4))* Little, Brown Bks. for Young Readers.
Rosenthal, Paris. Dear Teacher, A Celebration of People Who Inspire Us. Hatam, Holly, illus. 2021. (ENG.). 40p. (J). (gr. -1-3). 18.99 *(978-0-06-301274-5(X),* HarperCollins) HarperCollins Pubs.
Roy, James. Max Quigley, Technically Not a Bully. 2009. (ENG., Illus.). 208p. (J). (gr. 3-7). 14.99 *(978-0-547-15263-9(9),* 1051980, Clarion Bks.) HarperCollins Pubs.
Roy, Ron. Calendar Mysteries #9: September Sneakers. Gurney, John Steven, illus. 2013. (Calendar Mysteries Ser.: 9). (ENG.). 80p. (J). (gr. 1-4). 7.99 *(978-0-375-86887-0(9),* Random Hse. Bks. for Young Readers) Random Hse. Children's Bks.
—September Sneakers. 2013. (Calendar Mysteries Ser.: 9). lib. bdg. 14.75 *(978-0-606-32231-7(0))* Turtleback.
Rutland, Mirium. Miss Pistachios Big Day. 2007. (Illus.). 48p. pap. *(978-1-58690-063-2(3))* Mould, Paul Publishing.
Ryan, Carol. A Bridge Through Time, 1 vol. 2010. 276p. pap. 27.95 *(978-1-4489-4254-1(3))* PublishAmerica, Inc.
Sawaski, James H. The Next Chess Team: A Novel. 2012. 120p. (gr. 10-12). pap. 10.95 *(978-1-4759-2425-1(9))* iUniverse, Inc.
Scanlon, Rachel. Operation Reverse April Fools' 2008. 56p. pap. 16.95 *(978-1-60441-649-7(1))* America Star Bks.
Scheerger, Sarah. Operation Frog Effect. 2020. 320p. (J). (gr. 3-7). pap. 8.99 *(978-0-525-64415-6(6),* Yearling) Random Hse. Children's Bks.
Schmatz, Pat. Bluefish. (ENG.). 240p. (YA). (gr. 7). 2013. pap. 9.99 *(978-0-7636-6341-4(7))* 2011. (Illus.). 15.99 *(978-0-7636-5334-7(9))* Candlewick Pr.
Schraff, Anne. The Haunting of Hawthorne. 2008. (Passages Ser.). 125p. (YA). (gr. 7-9). lib. bdg. 13.95 *(978-0-7569-8379-6(7))* Perfection Learning Corp.
—The Hero at Crow's Crossing, 1 vol. 2015. (Red Rhino Ser.). (ENG.). 68p. (J). (gr. 4-7). pap. 9.95 *(978-1-62250-943-0(9))* Saddleback Educational Publishing, Inc.
—The Petition. 2008. (Passages Ser.). 103p. (J). (gr. 4-6). lib. bdg. 13.95 *(978-0-7569-8391-8(6))* Perfection Learning Corp.
—The Quality of Mercy. 2011. (Urban Underground — Harriet Tubman High School Ser.). (YA). lib. bdg. 20.80 *(978-0-606-14800-9(0))* Turtleback.
Schraff, Anne E. The Hero at Crow's Crossing. 2015. (Red Rhino Ser.). (J). lib. bdg. 18.40 *(978-0-606-36844-5(2))* Turtleback.
Sherrard, Valerie. Speechless. 2007. (ENG.). 176p. (YA). (gr. 6). pap. 12.99 *(978-1-55002-701-3(8))* Dundurn Pr. CAN. Dist: Publishers Group West (PGW).
Shipton, Paul. Clown School. Blake, Beccy, illus. 2005. (ENG.). 24p. (J). lib. bdg. 23.65 *(978-1-59646-752-1(5))* Dingles & Co.
The Shoe Grabber: Individual Title Six-Pack. (Story Steps Ser.). (gr. k-2). 23.00 *(978-0-7635-9832-7(1))* Rigby Education.
Shubert Sees the Best. 2004. (J). 9.00 *(978-1-889609-23-2(4))* Loving Guidance, Inc.
Skidmore, Marlene. In Trouble Again! 2010. 24p. pap. 9.99 *(978-0-9845208-9-3(9))* Faithful Life Pubs.
Slate, Joseph. Miss Bindergarten Celebrates the Last Day of Kindergarten. Wolff, Ashley, illus. 2008. 40p. (J). (gr. -1-k). pap. 8.99 *(978-0-14-241060-8(8),* Puffin Books) Penguin Young Readers Group.
Snyder, Susan E. Shivers & Shakes. 2006. (Illus.). 31p. (J). (gr. k-2). 9.95 *(978-0-9767163-5-8(6))* Kotzig Publishing, Inc.
Solomons, David. My Gym Teacher Is an Alien Overlord. 2017. lib. bdg. 18.40 *(978-0-606-40090-9(7))* Turtleback.
Sommerdorf, Norma. Red River Girl. 2006. (ENG., Illus.). 192p. (J). (gr. 3-7). 16.95 *(978-0-8234-1903-6(7))* Holiday Hse., Inc.
Spanyol, Jessica. Clive Is a Teacher. Spanyol, Jessica, illus. 2017. (Clive's Jobs Ser.: 4). (Illus.). 14p. (J). spiral bd. *(978-1-84643-990-2(6))* Child's Play International Ltd.
Sparks, Kerry. Jen & the Frosted Friends: Book #2 of the Get Frosted Series. 2010. 84p. pap. 10.99 *(978-1-4520-5349-3(9))* AuthorHouse.
Spurling, Wesley. Books for Jacob. 2009. 24p. pap. 14.79 *(978-1-4389-2231-7(0))* AuthorHouse.
—Gerry the Giraffe. 2009. 36p. pap. 16.99 *(978-1-4389-4223-0(0))* AuthorHouse.
Spyri, Johanna. Rico & Stineli. 2006. 148p. (gr. 4-7). per. 11.95 *(978-1-59818-873-8(9))* Aegypan.
Stamper, Judith Bauer. Rocky Road Trip. Gangloff, Hope, illus. 2004. (Magic School Bus Science Chapter Bks.). 89p. (gr. 2-5). lib. bdg. 15.00 *(978-0-7569-3093-6(6))* Perfection Learning Corp.
Stanley, Malaika Rose. Miss Bubble's Troubles. Smith, Jan, illus. 2010. 40p. (J). (gr. 2-4). pap. 10.99 *(978-1-84853-024-9(2))* Transworld Publishers Ltd. GBR. Dist: Independent Pubs. Group.
Steinke, Aron Nels. Mr. Wolf's Class: a Graphic Novel (Mr. Wolf's Class #1) 2018. (Mr. Wolf's Class Ser.: 1). (ENG., Illus.). 160p. (J). (gr. 2-5). pap. 9.99 *(978-1-338-04768-4(X));* Vol. 1. 18.99 *(978-1-338-04769-1(8))* Scholastic, Inc. (Graphix).
Stilton, Geronimo. Thea Stilton & the Dragon's Code. 2009. (Geronimo Stilton Special Edition Ser.: No. 1). (Illus.). 158p. 18.00 *(978-1-60686-420-3(3))* Perfection Learning Corp.
—Thea Stilton & the Dragon's Code. 2009. (Thea Stilton Ser.: 1). lib. bdg. 19.65 *(978-0-606-00231-8(6))* Turtleback.
Stilton, Geronimo & Stilton, Thea. Thea Stilton & the Ghost of the Shipwreck. 2010. (Thea Stilton Ser.: 3). lib. bdg. 19.65 *(978-0-606-06843-7(0))* Turtleback.
Stilton, Thea. Thea Stilton & the Dragon's Code (Thea Stilton #1) A Geronimo Stilton Adventure. 2009. (Thea Stilton Ser.: 1). (ENG., Illus.). 176p. (J). (gr. 2-5). pap. 8.99 *(978-0-545-10367-1(3),* Scholastic Paperbacks) Scholastic, Inc.
Strand, Jeff. Elrod McBugle on the Loose. 2006. (ENG.). 136p. (YA). per. 9.25 *(978-0-7599-4325-4(7))* Hard Shell Word Factory.
Tamanini, Kara T. I Promised Not to Tell. 2009. 44p. pap. 18.50 *(978-1-60860-470-8(5),* Eloquent Bks.) Strategic Book Publishing & Rights Agency (SBPRA).
Taylor, Shane. The Magic of Mortals. 2006. (YA). pap. 11.95 *(978-1-58736-542-3(1),* Starbound Bks.) Wheatmark, Inc.
Thaler, Mike. The Art Teacher from the Black Lagoon, 1 vol. Lee, Jared, illus. 2012. (Black Lagoon Ser.: No. 2). (ENG.). 32p. (J). (gr. k-4). lib. bdg. 31.36 *(978-1-59961-952-1(0),* 3627, Picture Bk.) Spotlight.
—The Class from the Black Lagoon. Lee, Jared, illus. 2009. (Black Lagoon Adventures Ser.). (ENG.). 32p. (J). (gr. -1-3). pap. 3.99 *(978-0-545-08544-1(6),* Cartwheel Bks.) Scholastic, Inc.
—The Class Picture Day from the Black Lagoon. Lee, Jared, illus. 2016. (Black Lagoon Adventures Set 4 Ser.). (ENG.). 64p. (J). (gr. 2-6). lib. bdg. 31.36 *(978-1-61479-602-2(5),* 24335, Chapter Bks.) Spotlight.
—The Computer Teacher from the Black Lagoon. Lee, Jared, illus. 2007. (J). *(978-0-439-87133-4(6))* Scholastic, Inc.
—The Computer Teacher from the Black Lagoon, 1 vol. Lee, Jared, illus. 2012. (Black Lagoon Ser.: No. 2). (ENG.). 32p. (J). (gr. k-4). lib. bdg. 31.36 *(978-1-59961-955-2(5),* 3630, Picture Bk.) Spotlight.
—The Music Teacher from the Black Lagoon, 1 vol. Lee, Jared, illus. 2011. (Black Lagoon Ser.: No. 1). (ENG.). 32p. (J). (gr. k-4). lib. bdg. 31.36 *(978-1-59961-796-1(X),* 3622, Picture Bk.) Spotlight.
—School Play from the Black Lagoon, 1 vol. Lee, Jared, illus. 2014. (Black Lagoon Adventures Ser.). (ENG.). 64p. (J). (gr. 2-6). lib. bdg. 31.36 *(978-1-61479-205-5(4),* 3614, Chapter Bks.) Spotlight.
—The Substitute Teacher from the Black Lagoon. Lee, Jared, illus. 2014. (Black Lagoon Ser.). (ENG.). 32p. (J). (gr. -1-4). 31.36 *(978-1-61479-199-7(6),* 3639, Picture Bk.) Spotlight.
—The Teacher from the Black Lagoon. Lee, Jared, illus. 2008. (From the Black Lagoon Ser.). (gr. -1-3). 14.00 *(978-0-7569-8779-4(2))* Perfection Learning Corp.
—The Teacher from the Black Lagoon. Lee, Jared, illus. 2008. (Black Lagoon Adventures Ser.). (ENG.). 32p. (J). (gr. -1-3). pap. 5.99 *(978-0-545-06522-1(4),* Cartwheel Bks.) Scholastic, Inc.
—The Teacher from the Black Lagoon, 1 vol. Lee, Jared, illus. 2011. (Black Lagoon Ser.: No. 1). (ENG.). 32p. (J). (gr. k-4). lib. bdg. 31.36 *(978-1-59961-799-2(4),* 3625, Picture Bk.) Spotlight.
—The Teacher from the Black Lagoon. Lee, Jared, illus. 2004. (J). (gr. k-3). 18.95 *(978-1-55592-495-9(6))* Weston Woods Studios, Inc.
Thomas, Carroll, creator. Under the Open Sky: A Matty Trescott Novel. 2005. (Illus.). 184p. (J). per. 12.95 *(978-0-9762091-2-6(8))* Antrim Hse.
Thompson, Kay. Eloise Has a Lesson: Ready-To-Read Level 1. 2018. (Eloise Ser.). (ENG., Illus.). 32p. (J). (gr. -1-1). 17.99 *(978-1-5344-1509-6(2),* Simon Spotlight) Simon Spotlight.
Thompson, Tate. Senioritis. 2nd ed. 2003. (YA). per. 13.50 *(978-0-943864-47-1(X))* Davenport, May Pubs.
Tidwell, Deborah Swayne. Magic Eraser: And the Substitute Teacher. 2008. 24p. pap. 12.99 *(978-1-4343-8107-1(2))* AuthorHouse.
Townsend, Lois Ritter. Our Journey Through Breast Cancer: -a story based on a teacher's journey through breast cancer with her kindergarten Class. 2005. (Illus.). 20p. (J). pap. 6.99 *(978-1-933570-93-8(8))* Aardvark Global Publishing.
Trapped by a Teacher: Individual Title Six-Packs. (Action Packs Ser.). 128p. (gr. 3-5). 44.00 *(978-0-7635-3309-0(2))* Rigby Education.
Underwood, Deborah. Here Comes Teacher Cat. Rueda, Claudia, illus. 2017. 88p. (J). (-k). 17.99 *(978-0-399-53905-3(0),* Dial Bks) Penguin Young Readers Group.
Van Draanen, Wendelin. Sammy Keyes & the Wedding Crasher. 2011. (Sammy Keyes Ser.: 13). (ENG.). 320p. (J). (gr. 5). 8.99 *(978-0-375-85456-9(8),* Yearling) Random Hse. Children's Bks.
Volk, Gretchen. The Amazing Adventures of Tristy Ruth, Raisin Girl. 2012. 258p. pap. *(978-1-105-51531-6(1))* Lulu.com.
Volponi, Paul. The Hand You're Dealt. 2010. (ENG.). 192p. (YA). (gr. 7). pap. 12.99 *(978-1-4169-3990-0(3),* Atheneum Bks. for Young Readers) Simon & Schuster Children's Publishing.
—The Hand You're Dealt. 2008. (ENG.). 168p. (YA). (gr. 7-12). 24.94 *(978-1-4169-3989-4(X))* Simon & Schuster, Inc.
Waddell, Martin. Class Six & the Very Big Rabbit: Band 10/White (Collins Big Cat) Ross, Tony, illus. 2005. (Collins Big Cat Ser.). (ENG.). 80p. (J). (gr. 1-3). pap. 10.99 *(978-0-00-718629-7(0))* HarperCollins Pubs. Ltd. GBR. Dist: Independent Pubs. Group.
Wagstaff, Janiel. Stella & Class: Information Experts. 2015. (ENG.). pap. 7.95 *(978-1-63133-024-7(1))* Staff Development for Educators.
—Stella Writes an Opinion. 2015. (ENG.). (J). (gr. -1-3). pap. 7.95 *(978-1-63133-022-3(5))* Staff Development for Educators.
Wagstaff, Janiel M. Stella & Class: Information Experts. 2018. (ENG.). 32p. (gr. k-3). pap. 7.99 *(978-1-338-26477-7(X))* Scholastic, Inc.
—Stella Tells Her Story. 2018. (ENG.). 32p. (gr. k-3). pap. 7.99 *(978-1-338-26475-3(3))* Scholastic, Inc.
Walker-Renner, Christa. Santa's Magic. 2009. 20p. pap. 11.00 *(978-1-4389-8206-9(2))* AuthorHouse.
Warner, Sally. EllRay Jakes Is Magic. Biggs, Brian, illus. 2014. (EllRay Jakes Ser.: 6). (ENG.). 176p. (J). (gr. 1-3). pap. 6.99 *(978-0-14-242360-8(2),* Puffin Books) Penguin Young Readers Group.
—Ellray Jakes Is Magic. 2014. (EllRay Jakes Ser.: 6). lib. bdg. 16.00 *(978-0-606-34215-5(X))* Turtleback.
—EllRay Jakes Stands Tall. Biggs, Brian, illus. 2016. (EllRay Jakes Ser.: 9). (ENG.). 176p. (J). (gr. 1-3). 6.99 *(978-0-14-751253-6(0),* Puffin Books) Penguin Young Readers Group.
—Ellray Jakes Stands Tall. 2016. (EllRay Jakes Ser.: 9). lib. bdg. 16.00 *(978-0-606-38420-9(0))* Turtleback.
Wasserman, Sand. The Sun's Special Blessing: Happens Only Once in 28 Years - French Flap. Koffsky, Ann, illus. 2009. 36p. 12.95 *(978-1-934440-76-6(0),* Pitspopany Pr.) Simcha Media Group.
—The Sun's Special Blessing: Happens Only Once in 28 Years - HC. Koffsky, Ann, illus. 2009. 36p. 17.95 *(978-1-934440-92-6(2),* Pitspopany Pr.) Simcha Media Group.
Waters, Daniel. Break My Heart 1,000 Times. 2013. (ENG., Illus.). 352p. (J). (gr. 7-17). pap. 9.99 *(978-1-4231-2228-9(3))* Hyperion Pr.
Watts, Jeri. Kizzy Ann Stamps. 2013. (ENG., Illus.). 192p. (J). (gr. 4-7). pap. 8.99 *(978-0-7636-6976-8(8))* Candlewick Pr.
Weil, Zoe. Claude & Medea: The Hellburn Dogs. 2007. (ENG., Illus.). 112p. (J). (gr. 2-7). per. 12.00 *(978-1-59056-105-8(8))* Lantern Publishing & Media.
Wesson, André. Mrs. Applebee & the Sunshine Band, Book 1: Meet the Class! 2007. 48p. pap. 18.50 *(978-0-615-14849-6(2))* Se7enth Swan Publishing Group, LLC.
Weston, Greg. Ocean View Terrace & the Blue Pirate Eater. 2008. 232p. pap. 14.95 *(978-1-4092-0278-3(X))* Lulu Pr., Inc.
Weston Woods Staff, creator. The Gym Teacher from the Black Lagoon. 2011. 38.75 *(978-0-545-19711-3(2))* Weston Woods Studios, Inc.
Whisler, Barbara. Shag Finds a Home. Jackson, Kay, illus. 2008. 24p. pap. 24.95 *(978-1-60703-730-9(0))* America Star Bks.
White, Michelle A. Anthony with an A. 2011. 16p. pap. 9.50 *(978-1-4634-1641-6(5))* AuthorHouse.
White, Russ. Cat Got Your Tongue? A Book of Idioms. Cornelison, Reuel, illus. l.t. ed. 2004. 44p. (J). per. *(978-0-9742885-0-5(0),* 00) White, Russ.
Wiggin, Kate Douglas. Polly Oliver's Problem. 2007. 108p. per. 9.95 *(978-1-60312-369-3(5));* 22.95 *(978-1-60312-707-3(0))* Aegypan.
—Polly Oliver's Problem. 2016. (ENG., Illus.). (J). 24.95 *(978-1-357-78791-2(X))* Creative Media Partners, LLC.
Wiggin, Kate Douglas Smith. Polly Oliver's Problem. 2017. (ENG., Illus.). (J). 22.95 *(978-1-374-96499-0(9))* Capital Communications, Inc.
Wiggins, Rosie. Adventures at a Ray of Hope Preschool. 2007. 32p. per. 12.95 *(978-1-4327-1657-8(3))* Outskirts Pr., Inc.
Wilder, Laura Ingalls. These Happy Golden Years. 2007. (Little House Ser.). (ENG.). 304p. (J). (gr. 3-7). pap., pap. 6.99 *(978-0-06-088544-1(0),* Harper Trophy) HarperCollins Pubs.
Williams, Stanley R. Not Me. 2008. 47p. pap. 24.95 *(978-1-4241-9577-0(2))* America Star Bks.
Wimberly, Nikisha. Hair Like That. Drewes, Dan, illus. 2010. 24p. 13.00 *(978-1-4520-0177-7(4))* AuthorHouse.
Winfrey, Michelle Whitaker. It's My Birthday. . . Finally! A Leap Year Story. Turley, Joyce M., illus. 2003. 88p. (J). (gr. 3-7). per. 11.95 *(978-0-9727179-0-8(0))* Hobby Hse. Publishing Group.
Winters, Ben H. The Secret Life of Ms. Finkleman. 2011. (ENG.). 272p. (J). (gr. 3-7). pap. 5.99 *(978-0-06-196543-2(X),* HarperCollins) HarperCollins Pubs.
Winters, Kay. My Teacher for President. Brunkus, Denise, illus. 2008. (ENG.). 32p. (J). (gr. k-3). pap. 7.99 *(978-0-14-241170-4(1),* Puffin Books) Penguin Young Readers Group.
—My Teacher for President. Brunkus, Denise, illus. 2008. (gr. -1-k). 17.00 *(978-0-7569-8925-5(6))* Perfection Learning Corp.
Wood, Maryrose. The Incorrigible Children of Ashton Place: The Mysterious Howling Howlin G, Bk. I. Klassen, Jon, illus. 2010. (Incorrigible Children of Ashton Place Ser.: 1). (ENG.). 272p. (J). (gr. 3-7). 16.99 *(978-0-06-179105-5(9),* Balzer & Bray) HarperCollins Pubs.
Woodard, Amy. The Day the Teacher Rode a Horse to School. 2008. 24p. pap. 24.95 *(978-1-60441-736-4(6))* America Star Bks.
Woodrow, Allan. Class Dismissed. 2017. (ENG.). 272p. (J). (gr. 3-7). pap. 6.99 *(978-0-545-80072-3(2),* Scholastic Paperbacks) Scholastic, Inc.
Woods, Linda J. The Gift of the Jumping Goldfish (A True Story) 2011. 48p. (gr. 1-2). pap. 19.46 *(978-1-4567-5796-0(2))* AuthorHouse.
Wright, Pauline. Why Did My Dad Go to War? 2008. 48p. pap. 19.49 *(978-1-4343-4677-3(3))* AuthorHouse.
Yankovic, Al, pseud. My New Teacher & Me! Hargis, Wes, illus. 2013. (ENG.). 40p. (J). (gr. -1-3). 18.99 *(978-0-06-219203-5(5),* HarperCollins) HarperCollins Pubs.
Zemach, Kaethe. Ms. McCaw Learns to Draw. 2006. (J). *(978-0-439-82915-1(1),* Levine, Arthur A. Bks.) Scholastic, Inc.
Zepeda, Frank. A Wad of Gum. 2012. (ENG.). 39p. pap. 19.99 *(978-1-105-73944-6(9))* Lulu Pr., Inc.

TEACHERS—TRAINING OF

Here are entered works dealing with the history and methods of training teachers, including the educational functions of teachers colleges. Works on the study of education as a science are entered under Education—Study and teaching.

Calhoun, Florence. Choosing a Career in Teaching. 2009. (World of Work Ser.). 64p. (gr. 5-5). 58.50 *(978-1-60854-336-6(6))* Rosen Publishing Group, Inc., The.
Nesbitt, Shawntelle. The Kids' Power Series Teacher Resource, 1 vol. 2011. (Kids' Power Ser.). (ENG.). 125p. (J). spiral bd. 29.95 *(978-1-926920-35-1(X))* Second Story Pr. CAN. Dist: Orca Bk. Pubs. USA.

TEACHERS AND PARENTS

see Home and School

TEACHING

see also Education; Educational Psychology; Kindergarten; Project Method in Teaching; Study Skills; Teachers—Training of
also subjects with the subdivision Study and Teaching, e.g. Science—Study and Teaching

Bigelow, Bill, et al, eds. Rethinking Our Classrooms Vol. 2: Teaching for Equity & Justice, 2 vols., Volume 2. 2004. (ENG., Illus.). 240p. pap. 16.95 *(978-0-942961-27-0(7))* Rethinking Schls., Ltd.
Crane, Natalie. I Go to Work as a Teacher. 2003. (I Go to Work As Ser.). (Illus.). (J). lib. bdg. *(978-1-58417-044-0(1))* Lake Street Pubs.
Culham, Ruth. The Trait Crate Grade 6, 1 vol. 2011. (Trait Crate(r) Ser.). (ENG.). (gr. 6-6). pap. 125.00 *(978-0-545-31862-4(9),* Teaching Resources) Scholastic, Inc.
—The Trait Crate Grade 7, 1 vol. 2011. (Trait Crate(r) Ser.). (ENG.). (gr. 7-7). pap., pap. 125.00 *(978-0-545-31863-1(7),* Teaching Resources) Scholastic, Inc.
—The Trait Crate Grade 8, 1 vol. 2011. (Trait Crate(r) Ser.). (ENG.). (gr. 8-8). pap., pap. 125.00 *(978-0-545-31864-8(5),* Teaching Resources) Scholastic, Inc.
Early Macken, JoAnn. Teachers, 1 vol. 2010. (People in My Community (Second Edition) Ser.). (ENG., Illus.). 24p. (J). (gr. k-2). 25.27 *(978-1-4339-3347-9(0),* 67197f32-ddc4-4201-934c-84344cf39571) Stevens, Gareth Publishing LLLP.
Given-Wilson, Rachel & Silivanch, Annalise. Your Future As a Teacher, 1 vol. 2019. (High-Demand Careers Ser.). (ENG., Illus.). 80p. (J). (gr. 7-7). 37.47 *(978-1-5081-8795-0(9),* bec46db0-40a0-4d9f-a3f4-0e2989fcdb02, Rosen Young Adult) Rosen Publishing Group, Inc., The.

T U V

Hart, Melissa. A Guide for Using Walk Two Moons in the Classroom. 2003. (ENG.). 48p. (gr. 5-8). pap. 9.99 *(978-0-7439-3160-1(2))* Teacher Created Resources, Inc.

La Bella, Laura. Getting a Job in Education, 1 vol. 2016. (Job Basics: Getting the Job You Need Ser.). (ENG.). 80p. (J). (gr. 8-8). 38.41 *(978-1-4777-8566-9(3),* 0fd901db-8e67-4a55-b441-8217eeed931e) Rosen Publishing Group, Inc., The.

Liebman, Dan & Liebman, Dan. I Want to Be a Teacher. 2nd rev. ed. 2018. (I Want to Be Ser.). (ENG., Illus.). 24p. (J). (gr. -1-2). pap. 3.99 *(978-0-2281-0102-4(6),* 62e6d9b6-000a-4c19-8ac8-13f5a65bdbab) Firefly Bks., Ltd.

Matthews, John. Interactive Whiteboards. 2008. (21st Century Skills Library: Global Products Ser.). (ENG., Illus.). 32p. (gr. 4-8). 32.07 *(978-1-60279-254-8(2),* 200121) Cherry Lake Publishing.

Miller, Connie Colwell. I'll Be a Teacher. Baroncelli, Silvia, illus. 2018. (When I Grow Up Ser.). (ENG.). 24p. (J). (gr. 1-4). pap. 8.99 *(978-1-68152-319-4(1),* 15060); lib. bdg. *(978-1-68151-399-7(4),* 15054) Amicus.

Nardo, Don. Great Jobs in Education. 2019. (Great Jobs Ser.). (ENG.). 80p. (YA). (gr. 6-12). *(978-1-68282-519-8(1))* ReferencePoint Pr., Inc.

Waxman, Laura Hamilton. Teacher Tools. 2019. (Bumba Books (r) — Community Helpers Tools of the Trade Ser.). (ENG., Illus.). 24p. (J). (gr. -1-1). pap. 8.99 *(978-1-5415-7355-0(2),* 12551f52-2e23-49f9-840a-f3e017eed616); lib. bdg. 26.65 *(978-1-5415-5559-4(7),* 414e7a90-0e9a-4e98-a1bd-b1b2c81fcdbe) Lerner Publishing Group. (Lerner Pubns.).

TEACHING—VOCATIONAL GUIDANCE

Anthony, David. Teachers on the Job, 1 vol. 2016. (Jobs in Our Community Ser.). (ENG.). 24p. (J). (gr. 1-1). lib. bdg. 26.23 *(978-1-5345-2147-6(X),* d6f20b27-8e02-459f-bb33-a70dfa6b7012, KidHaven Publishing) Greenhaven Publishing LLC.

Calhoun, Florence. Choosing a Career in Teaching. 2009. (World of Work Ser.). 64p. (gr. 5-5). 58.50 *(978-1-60854-336-6(6))* Rosen Publishing Group, Inc., The.

Crane, Natalie. I Go to Work as a Teacher. 2003. (I Go to Work As Ser.). (Illus.). (J). pap. *(978-1-58417-106-5(5));* lib. bdg. *(978-1-58417-043-3(3))* Lake Street Pubs.

Early Macken, JoAnn. Teachers, 1 vol. 2010. (People in My Community (Second Edition) Ser.). (ENG., Illus.). 24p. (gr. k-2). pap. 9.15 *(978-1-4339-3348-6(9),* e00cd7cc-f89d-4484-9310-c7e273b27d86) Stevens, Gareth Publishing LLLP.

—Teachers / Maestros, 1 vol. 2010. (People in My Community / Mi Comunidad Ser.). (SPA & ENG., Illus.). 24p. (gr. k-2). pap. 9.15 *(978-1-4339-3766-8(2),* 96dde7f4-8a3e-4bdf-a3b9-7bd2ea7a44b6) Stevens, Gareth Publishing LLLP.

Ferguson, creator. Teaching. 2nd rev. ed. 2008. (Discovering Careers for Your Future Ser.). (ENG.). 92p. (gr. 4-9). 21.95 *(978-0-8160-7292-7(2),* P179095, Ferguson Publishing Company) Infobase Holdings, Inc.

Ferguson Publishing Staff, contrib. by. Education. 2010. (What Can I Do Now? Ser.). 224p. (J). (gr. 6-12). 32.95 *(978-0-8160-8079-3(8),* Ferguson Publishing Company) Infobase Holdings, Inc.

Heaton, J. Barrett. Careers in Teaching. 2009. (Careers in the New Economy Ser.). 144p. (gr. 7-7). 63.90 *(978-1-61511-821-2(7))* Rosen Publishing Group, Inc., The.

Kampff, Joseph. What Degree Do I Need to Pursue a Career in Education?, 1 vol. 2014. (Right Degree for Me Ser.). (ENG., Illus.). 80p. (J). (gr. 7-7). 37.80 *(978-1-4777-7873-9(X),* edaa1ca7-3f11-4784-9088-3c93d40b5207, Rosen Young Adult) Rosen Publishing Group, Inc., The.

Kidde, Rita. What Do Teachers Do?, 1 vol. 2014. (Jobs in My School Ser.). (ENG.). 24p. (J). (gr. 1-2). lib. bdg. 25.27 *(978-1-4777-6556-2(5),* 3032e037-150b-4488-a9db-551266933cd7, PowerKids Pr.) Rosen Publishing Group, Inc., The.

Kirk, Amanda. Education. 2009. (Field Guides to Finding a New Career (Hardcover) Ser.). (ENG., Illus.). 134p. (gr. 9-18). 39.95 *(978-0-8160-7597-3(2),* P179105, Ferguson Publishing Company) Infobase Holdings, Inc.

Lesinski, Jeanne M. Bill Gates. 2005. (First Step Nonfiction Ser.). (Illus.). 112p. (J). (gr. 3-7). lib. bdg. 27.93 *(978-0-8225-2642-1(5),* Lerner Pubns.) Lerner Publishing Group.

McAlpine, Margaret. Working with Children, 1 vol. 2005. (My Future Career Ser.). (ENG., Illus.). 64p. (gr. 4-6). lib. bdg. 29.67 *(978-0-8368-4241-8(3),* e9721b2f-8cea-47ec-be17-0891d59599d2, Gareth Stevens Learning Library) Stevens, Gareth Publishing LLLP.

Miller, Malinda. Tomorrow's Teachers: Urban Leadership, Empowering Students & Improving Lives. 2010. (New Careers for the 21st Century Ser.). 64p. (YA). (gr. 7-18). pap. 9.95 *(978-1-4222-2044-3(3))* Mason Crest.

—Tomorrow's Teachers: Urban Leadership, Empowering Students, & Improving Lives. 2010. (New Careers for the 21st Century Ser.). 64p. (YA). (gr. 7-18). lib. bdg. 22.95 *(978-1-4222-1823-5(6))* Mason Crest.

Mitchell, Melanie. Teachers. 2005. (Pull Ahead Bks.). (Illus.). 32p. (J). lib. bdg. 22.60 *(978-0-8225-1696-5(9))* Lerner Publishing Group.

Reeves, Diane Lindsey. Education & Training. 2017. (Bright Futures Press: World of Work Ser.). (ENG., Illus.). 32p. (J). (gr. 4-7). lib. bdg. 32.07 *(978-1-5341-0172-2(1),* 210158) Cherry Lake Publishing.

Reeves, Diane Lindsey & Karlitz, Gail. Career Ideas for Teens in Education & Training. 2005. (Career Ideas for Teens Ser.). (Illus.). 192p. (gr. 6-12). 40.00 *(978-0-8160-5295-0(6),* Ferguson Publishing Company) Infobase Holdings, Inc.

Rivera, Sheila. Teacher. 2005. (First Step Nonfiction — Work People Do Ser.). (ENG., Illus.). 8p. (J). (gr. k-2). pap. 5.99 *(978-0-8225-5361-8(9),* d875a484-662c-4500-9c59-69c98406ac2f) Lerner Publishing Group.

Sheen, Barbara. Careers in Education. 2015. (ENG., Illus.). 80p. (J). lib. bdg. *(978-1-60152-808-7(6))* ReferencePoint Pr., Inc.

Silivanch, Annalise. A Career as a Teacher, 1 vol. 2010. (Essential Careers Ser.). (ENG.). 80p. (YA). (gr. 6-6). lib. bdg. 37.47 *(978-1-4358-9468-6(5),* a3a6ce81-b08f-4e58-a8aa-2e492aa57c19) Rosen Publishing Group, Inc., The.

TEACHINGS OF JESUS

see Jesus Christ—Teachings

TEAROOMS

see Restaurants

TECHNICAL ASSISTANCE

Morkes, Andrew. Heating & Cooling Technician, Vol. 10. 2018. (Careers in the Building Trades: a Growing Demand Ser.). 80p. (J). (gr. 7). lib. bdg. 33.27 *(978-1-4222-4116-5(5))* Mason Crest.

TECHNICAL EDUCATION

see also Apprentices; Employees—Training of
also technical subjects with the subdivision Study and Teaching, e.g. Mathematics—Study and Teaching

Bily, Cynthia A., ed. Career & Technical Education, 1 vol. 2013. (Issues That Concern You Ser.). (ENG., Illus.). 136p. (gr. 7-10). lib. bdg. 43.63 *(978-0-7377-6285-3(3),* d919820f-2233-4b87-8cea-8629d65ce01e, Greenhaven Publishing) Greenhaven Publishing LLC.

Kallen, Stuart A. Careers If You Like the Creative Arts. 2019. (Career Exploration Ser.). (ENG.). 80p. (J). (gr. 6-12). 41.27 *(978-1-68282-595-2(7))* ReferencePoint Pr., Inc.

Makerspaces. 2014. (Makerspaces Ser.). 64p. (YA). (gr. 6-12). pap. 77.70 *(978-1-4777-8112-8(9))* Rosen Publishing Group, Inc., The.

Tech3000. 2003. (J). cd-rom 99.00 *(978-1-932166-06-4(8))* Achieve3000.

TECHNICAL SCHOOLS

see Technical Education

TECHNICAL TERMS

see Technology—Dictionaries

TECHNOLOGY

see also Building; Chemistry, Technical; Engineering; Inventions; Machinery; Manufactures; Measurement; Technical Education

Alkire, Jessie. Technology You Can Taste. 2018. (Super Simple Science You Can Snack On Ser.). (ENG., Illus.). 32p. (J). (gr. k-4). lib. bdg. 34.21 *(978-1-5321-1727-5(2),* 30742, Super SandCastle) ABDO Publishing Co.

Allen, John. What Is the Future of Artificial Intelligence? 2016. (ENG.). 80p. (J). (gr. 5-12). *(978-1-68282-060-5(2))* ReferencePoint Pr., Inc.

—What Is the Future of Nanotechnology? 2016. (ENG.). 80p. (YA). (gr. 5-12). *(978-1-60152-962-6(7))* ReferencePoint Pr., Inc.

Allen, Roger MacBride & Allen, Thomas B. Mr. Lincoln's High-Tech War: How the North Used the Telegraph, Railroads, Surveillance Balloons, Ironclads, High-Powered Weapons, & More to Win the Civil War. 2009. (Illus.). 144p. (J). (gr. 5-9). 18.95 *(978-1-4263-0379-1(3),* National Geographic Kids) Disney Publishing Worldwide.

Amstutz, Lisa J. Discover Nanotechnology. 2016. (Searchlight Books (tm) — What's Cool about Science? Ser.). (ENG., Illus.). 40p. (J). (gr. 3-5). 30.65 *(978-1-5124-0806-5(9),* 63c5e11c-44f6-495b-8b8f-3d472bf3f2f7, Lerner Pubns.) Lerner Publishing Group.

Anderson, Jenna. How It Happens at the ATV Plant. Wolfe, Bob & Wolfe, Diane, photos by. 2004. (How It Happens Ser.). (Illus.). 32p. (J). (gr. 2-5). lib. bdg. 19.95 *(978-1-881508-94-6(3))* Oliver Pr., Inc.

Anniss, Matthew. The Impact of Technology in Music. 2015. (Impact of Technology Ser.). (ENG., Illus.). 56p. (J). (gr. 6-9). 37.32 *(978-1-4846-2638-2(9),* 130097, Heinemann) Capstone.

Bailey, Gerry. Technology, 1 vol. 2009. (Simply Science Ser.). (ENG., Illus.). 32p. (YA). (gr. 3-5). lib. bdg. 28.67 *(978-1-4339-0034-1(3),* 41fecaf2-f9dd-41d3-b0d6-0cb4a013b4fd) Stevens, Gareth Publishing LLLP.

Ball, Jacqueline A. All about Systems. Bowser, Ken, illus. 2017. (Space Cat Explores STEM Ser.). (ENG.). 24p. (J). (gr. 1-3). lib. bdg. 19.99 *(978-1-63440-195-1(6),* 50adb897-bff5-4d5d-a052-e4488534900b) Red Chair Pr.

—We Use Tools All Day. Bowser, Ken, illus. 2017. (Space Cat Explores STEM Ser.). (ENG.). 24p. (J). (gr. 1-3). lib. bdg. 19.99 *(978-1-63440-196-8(4),* 042ec7c9-4308-4f37-a7c4-45c8b7d8421d) Red Chair Pr.

—What Makes a Building Strong? Bowser, Ken, illus. 2017. (Space Cat Explores STEM Ser.). (ENG.). 24p. (J). (gr. 1-3). pap. 4.99 *(978-1-63440-201-9(4),* e3126715-6870-44e7-b8d3-88bf6b093a2a); lib. bdg. 19.99 *(978-1-63440-197-5(2),* 93c1ac9f-bba1-45ef-8076-4255691cf83f) Red Chair Pr.

—The World Humans Made. Bowser, Ken, illus. 2017. (Space Cat Explores STEM Ser.). (ENG.). 24p. (J). (gr. 1-3). pap. 4.99 *(978-1-63440-198-2(0),* ffc91773-1c86-4e57-a2c7-dbe2345f02b7); lib. bdg. 19.99 *(978-1-63440-194-4(8),* f8232bc3-ca8d-459d-aecd-4fcfaa8efd89) Red Chair Pr.

Barnes, John, et al. Science. Maths & Technology. 2003. (ENG., Illus.). 184p. pap. *(978-0-7487-7121-9(2))* Nelson Thornes Ltd.

Barnham, Kay. Could a Robot Make My Dinner? And Other Questions about Technology, 1 vol. 2013. (Questions You Never Thought You'd Ask Ser.). (ENG.). 32p. (J). (gr. 3-5). 32.65 *(978-1-4109-5200-4(2),* 122401); pap. 8.95 *(978-1-4109-5206-6(1),* 122406) Capstone. (Raintree).

Bartos, Judeen, ed. What Is the Role of Technology in Education?, 1 vol. 2012. (At Issue Ser.). (ENG.). 120p. (gr. 10-12). pap. 28.80 *(978-0-7377-6218-1(7),* 0c8db295-fc50-4e91-940b-0493de57a5da); lib. bdg. 41.03 *(978-0-7377-6217-4(9),* b05f5a32-4dc1-4f15-90f5-e05a9a9a70e5) Greenhaven Publishing LLC. (Greenhaven Publishing).

Basher, Simon & Green, Dan. Basher Science: Technology: A Byte-Sized World! Basher, Simon, illus. 2012. (Basher Science Ser.). (ENG., Illus.). 128p. (J). (gr. 5-9). pap. 8.99 *(978-0-7534-6820-3(4),* 900081818, Kingfisher) Roaring Brook Pr.

Benchmark Education Co., LLC Staff, et al. Technology at Home & School: Past & Present: Big Book Edition. 2015. (Content Connections Ser.). (J). (gr. k). *(978-1-4900-0475-4(0))* Benchmark Education Co.

—Using Technology at Work: Big Book Edition. 2015. (Content Connections Ser.). (J). (gr. 1). *(978-1-4900-0477-8(7))* Benchmark Education Co.

Benchmark Education Company, LLC Staff. Disasters of Technology Teacher's Guide. 2004. *(978-1-4108-2591-9(4))* Benchmark Education Co.

Benchmark Education Company, LLC Staff, compiled by. Invention & Technology: Theme Set. 2006. (J). 158.00 *(978-1-4108-7100-8(2))* Benchmark Education Co.

—Science & Technology. 2006. spiral bd. 105.00 *(978-1-4108-6935-7(0))* 2006. spiral bd. 115.00 *(978-1-4108-6923-4(7))* 2005. spiral bd. 115.00 *(978-1-4108-3854-4(4))* 2005. spiral bd. 130.00 *(978-1-4108-5856-6(1))* 2005. spiral bd. 170.00 *(978-1-4108-5855-9(3))* 2005. spiral bd. 145.00 *(978-1-4108-5445-2(0))* 2005. spiral bd. 255.00 *(978-1-4108-5444-5(2))* 2005. spiral bd. 235.00 *(978-1-4108-4520-7(6))* 2005. spiral bd. 42.00 *(978-1-4108-3880-3(3))* 2005. spiral bd. 110.00 *(978-1-4108-3866-7(8))* 2005. spiral bd. 55.00 *(978-1-4108-3855-1(2))* 2005. spiral bd. 60.00 *(978-1-4108-3843-8(9))* 2005. spiral bd. 125.00 *(978-1-4108-3842-1(0))* Benchmark Education Co.

—Science, Technology & Society. 2005. spiral bd. 185.00 *(978-1-4108-3753-0(X))* Benchmark Education Co.

—Science, Technology, & Society. 2005. spiral bd. 110.00 *(978-1-4108-5425-4(6));* spiral bd. 74.00 *(978-1-4108-5842-9(1));* spiral bd. 115.00 *(978-1-4108-5841-2(3));* spiral bd. 145.00 *(978-1-4108-4499-6(4));* spiral bd. 80.00 *(978-1-4108-3962-6(1));* spiral bd. 70.00 *(978-1-4108-3954-1(0));* spiral bd. 80.00 *(978-1-4108-3961-9(3))* Benchmark Education Co.

—Tools & Technology. 2006. (J). 148.00 *(978-1-4108-7034-6(0))* Benchmark Education Co.

Bensinger, Henry. Ancient Greek Technology, 1 vol. 2013. (Spotlight on Ancient Civilizations: Greece Ser.). (ENG.). 24p. (J). (gr. 3-4). 26.27 *(978-1-4777-0774-6(3),* 2265e58a-03cd-4a8b-9b10-49cd79d06643, PowerKids Pr.) Rosen Publishing Group, Inc., The.

Berger, Melvin & Berger, Gilda. The Byte-Sized World of Technology (Fact Attack #2) Rocco, Frank & Watanabe-Rocco, Sarah, illus. 2017. (ENG.). 96p. (J). (gr. 1-3). pap. 7.99 *(978-1-338-04186-6(X))* Scholastic, Inc.

Biskup, Agnieszka. The Science Behind Batman's Tools. Vecchio, Luciano, illus. 2016. (Science Behind Batman Ser.). (ENG.). 24p. (J). (gr. 1-3). lib. bdg. 27.99 *(978-1-5157-2038-6(1),* 132668, Stone Arch Bks.) Capstone.

Bjerklie, David. Technology for All: Wi-Fi Around the World (Level 3) rev. ed. 2017. (TIME for KIDS(r): Informational Text Ser.). (ENG., Illus.). 32p. (J). (gr. 3-4). pap. 12.99 *(978-1-4258-4974-0(1))* Teacher Created Materials, Inc.

Blaxland, Wendy. How Are They Made?, 12 vols., Set. Incl. Knives & Forks. lib. bdg. 21.27 *(978-0-7614-3805-2(X),* 846fcbe0-3b94-4c8f-877b-013ae40ec621); Paper. lib. bdg. 21.27 *(978-0-7614-3806-9(8),* 81fcc268-4d2b-47c1-825a-c7bbdc65e4e5); Pencils. lib. bdg. 21.27 *(978-0-7614-3807-6(6),* 99891504-99f3-4677-9886-cd40671dde6d); Plates & Mugs. lib. bdg. 21.27 *(978-0-7614-3809-0(2),* fe26eb45-3422-48ed-a72d-9123447563b1); Sneakers. lib. bdg. 21.27 *(978-0-7614-3810-6(6),* 4865c803-4127-4111-82e3-e488b914e616); T-Shirts. (Illus.). lib. bdg. 21.27 *(978-0-7614-3812-0(2),* c452146b-43b0-4a87-8f90-e2753faf8caa); 32p. (gr. 4-4). (How Are They Made? Ser.). (ENG.). 2009. Set lib. bdg. 127.62 *(978-0-7614-3803-8(3),* aebb5950-1ca4-4787-878c-9554bcaf93ae, Cavendish Square) Cavendish Square Publishing LLC.

Bodden, Valerie. Wearable Technology. 2017. (Modern Engineering Marvels Ser.). (ENG., Illus.). 32p. (J). (gr. 3-6). lib. bdg. 32.79 *(978-1-5321-1092-4(8),* 25760, Checkerboard Library) ABDO Publishing Co.

Book Steps, 6 Pack. (Bookweb Ser.). 32p. (gr. 5-18). 34.00 *(978-0-7635-3800-2(0))* Rigby Education.

Bow, James. Industry Entrepreneurs. 2018. (Science & Technology Start-Up Stars Ser.). (ENG., Illus.). 32p. (J). (gr. 5-5). *(978-0-7787-4420-7(5))* Crabtree Publishing Co.

Brandt, Allison & Benchmark Education Co. Staff. Careers on the Cutting Edge. 2014. (Text Connections Ser.). (J). (gr. 5). *(978-1-4900-1369-5(5))* Benchmark Education Co.

Brezina, Corona. Careers in Nanotechnology. 2009. (Cutting-Edge Careers Ser.). 64p. (gr. 7-7). 55.90 *(978-1-61512-100-7(5))* Rosen Publishing Group, Inc., The.

Britannica, Learning Library. Technology & Inventions. 2003. (Illus.). 64p. 14.95 *(978-1-59339-034-1(3))* Encyclopaedia Britannica, Inc.

Brookes, Olivia. Uncover Technology, 1 vol. Kent, Peter, illus. 2009. (Hide-And-Seek Visual Adventures Ser.). (ENG.). 24p. (J). (gr. 2-2). lib. bdg. 27.27 *(978-1-60754-658-0(2),* 7dc4d624-cde6-447c-af8b-64499fa2e011, Windmill Bks.) Rosen Publishing Group, Inc., The.

Brown Bear Books. The Ages of Steam & Electricity. 2010. (Technology Through the Ages Ser.). (ENG.). 112p. (J). (gr. 9-12). 39.95 *(978-1-933834-86-3(2),* 16805) Brown Bear Bks.

—The Early 20th Century. 2010. (Technology Through the Ages Ser.). (ENG.). 112p. (J). (gr. 9-12). 42.80 *(978-1-933834-87-0(0),* 16806) Brown Bear Bks.

—The Modern World. 2010. (Technology Through the Ages Ser.). (ENG.). 112p. (J). (gr. 9-12). 42.80 *(978-1-933834-88-7(9),* 16807) Brown Bear Bks.

—Prehistory & the Classical Period. 2010. (Technology Through the Ages Ser.). (ENG.). 112p. (J). (gr. 9-12). 42.80 *(978-1-933834-83-2(8),* 16804) Brown Bear Bks.

Bryan, Dale-Marie. Smartphone Safety & Privacy, 1 vol. 2013. (21st Century Safety & Privacy Ser.). (ENG.). 64p. (J). (gr. 6-6). 37.12 *(978-1-4488-9573-1(1),* 815ef943-1a6d-4487-b220-1defe482c06c) Rosen Publishing Group, Inc., The.

Bryant, Jill. Technology Mysteries Revealed. 2010. (ENG., Illus.). 32p. (J). pap. *(978-0-7787-7432-7(5));* (gr. 4-7). lib. bdg. *(978-0-7787-7417-4(1))* Crabtree Publishing Co.

Burling, Alexis. Netflix. 2018. (Tech Titans Ser.). (ENG., Illus.). 112p. (J). (gr. 6-12). lib. bdg. 41.36 *(978-1-5321-1690-2(X),* 30632, Essential Library) ABDO Publishing Co.

Burns Chong, Susan. Step-By-Step Guide to Innovating at School & Work, 1 vol. 2014. (Winning at Work Readiness Ser.). (ENG.). 64p. (J). (gr. 6-6). 36.13 *(978-1-4777-7786-2(5),* a9b6d8cd-1b3a-4ef0-8bc3-c4b1e42ca353) Rosen Publishing Group, Inc., The.

Burton, Margie, et al. Technology Today. 2011. (Early Connections Ser.). (J). *(978-1-61672-540-2(0))* Benchmark Education Co.

Butterfield, Moira & Jacobs, Pat. Technology, 1 vol. 2015. (Know It All! Ser.). (ENG., Illus.). 32p. (gr. 5-5). pap. 11.58 *(978-1-5026-0902-1(9),* b7644d0a-7c36-4d90-a567-825c04c24032) Cavendish Square Publishing LLC.

Byers, Ann. Strategic Inventions of the Civil War, 1 vol. 2015. (Tech in the Trenches Ser.). (ENG., Illus.). 112p. (YA). (gr. 9-9). lib. bdg. 44.50 *(978-1-5026-1030-0(2),* 4e1aa84d-c159-48a7-979f-475635875d0d) Cavendish Square Publishing LLC.

Cain, Marie Mowery. Then & Now. 2013. (Big Books, Blue Ser.). (ENG & SPA., Illus.). 16p. pap. 33.00 *(978-1-59246-007-6(0))* Big Books, by George!

Canfield, Michael. Freaky Stories about Inventions, 1 vol. 2016. (Freaky True Science Ser.). (ENG., Illus.). 32p. (J). (gr. 4-5). pap. 11.50 *(978-1-4824-4819-1(X),* 5935f06e-e2a7-464c-adb3-827bc3936e55) Stevens, Gareth Publishing LLLP.

Carey, Bjorn. Answers to the World's Greatest Questions, 1 vol. 2017. (Popular Science Fact Book for Inquiring Minds Ser.). (ENG.). 224p. (YA). (gr. 8-8). lib. bdg. 49.50 *(978-1-5026-3290-6(X),* e4165398-d00f-41f0-bd2a-5ad106fa14ae) Cavendish Square Publishing LLC.

Chambers, Jo. High Tech. 2007. (Trackers-Math Ser.). (gr. 2-5). pap. 5.00 *(978-1-59055-934-5(7))* Pacific Learning, Inc.

Chase, Alex. Technology in the 20th Century. 2007. (20th Century Ser.). (Illus.). 100p. (gr. 7-18). pap. 9.95 *(978-0-912517-25-4(5))* Bluewood Bks.

Colson, Mary. Get Inventing!, 1 vol. 2014. (Dream It, Do It! Ser.). (ENG., Illus.). 32p. (gr. 3-5). pap. 8.95 *(978-1-4109-6269-0(5),* 124863, Raintree) Capstone.

Cooper, Bob. Little Leonardo's Fascinating World of Technology, 1 vol. Paprocki, Greg, illus. 2018. 24p. (J). (gr. -1-3). 12.99 *(978-1-4236-4956-4(7))* Gibbs Smith, Publisher.

Crozier, A. J. Technology & the Civil War: Text Pairs. 2008. (Bridges/Navigators Ser.). (J). (gr. 5). 89.00 *(978-1-4108-8423-7(6))* Benchmark Education Co.

Culp, Jennifer. Ancient Chinese Technology, 1 vol. 2016. (Spotlight on the Rise & Fall of Ancient Civilizations Ser.). (ENG., Illus.). 48p. (J). (gr. 6-6). pap. 12.75 *(978-1-4777-8897-4(2),* dd3b59dd-ac62-494b-8cd3-d0bafe1e9aa7) Rosen Publishing Group, Inc., The.

Cunningham, Anne, VII & Cunningham, Anne, eds. Populism in the Digital Age, 1 vol. 2017. (At Issue Ser.). (ENG.). 120p. (YA). (gr. 10-12). pap. 28.80 *(978-1-5345-0214-7(9),* 321c7033-62bf-46c0-9426-23cc245d74f0); lib. bdg. 41.03 *(978-1-5345-0207-9(6),* a5f305ed-ffed-49ec-ba66-9bd1fa3ec5cb) Greenhaven Publishing LLC.

Curious Jane, Curious. Curious Jane: Science + Design + Engineering for Inquisitive Girls. 2017. (Illus.). 128p. (J). (gr. 1-6). pap. 16.95 *(978-1-4549-2235-3(4))* Sterling Publishing Co., Inc.

Cutting-Edge Science & Technology, 8 vols. 2015. (Cutting-Edge Science & Technology Ser.: 8). (ENG.). 112p. (J). (gr. 6-12). lib. bdg. 330.88 *(978-1-62403-911-9(1),* 19112, Essential Library) ABDO Publishing Co.

Cutting-Edge Technology, 12 vols. 2016. (Cutting-Edge Technology Ser.). 48p. (ENG.). (gr. 6-8). lib. bdg. 201.60 *(978-1-4824-5118-4(2),* ffe9a32a-5bf3-4011-a48b-ac53fb6ad103); (gr. 8-6). pap. 84.30 *(978-1-4824-5317-1(7))* Stevens, Gareth Publishing LLLP.

Daynes, Katie. Toilets, Telephones & Other Useful Inventions. 2005. (Young Reading Series 1 Ser.). 48p. (J). (gr. 2-18). pap. 5.95 *(978-0-7945-0888-3(X),* Usborne) EDC Publishing.

Diehn, Andi. Technology: Cool Women Who Code. 2015. (Girls in Science Ser.). (ENG., Illus.). 112p. (J). (gr. 3-7). 19.95 *(978-1-61930-321-8(3),* 6659d6ae-7818-4ecf-9b8b-459fe76748db) Nomad Pr.

Digital & Information Literacy: Set 6, 10 vols. 2013. (Digital & Information Literacy Ser.). (ENG.). 48p. (J). (gr. 5-5). 167.35 *(978-1-4488-9522-9(7),* b2444750-e390-4d31-864f-7e9e06ee53be) Rosen Publishing Group, Inc., The.

Digital & Information Literacy: Set 7, 12 vols. 2014. (Digital & Information Literacy Ser.). (ENG.). 48p. (YA). (gr. 6-6). 200.82 *(978-1-4777-7663-6(X),* fe9f261c-b9ad-4c9e-b319-a20f8cfd0b40, Rosen Reference) Rosen Publishing Group, Inc., The.

Digital & Information Literacy: Sets 1 - 6. 2013. (Digital & Information Literacy Ser.). 48p. (J). (gr. 5-8). 1023.75 *(978-1-4777-0617-6(8))* Rosen Publishing Group, Inc., The.

Digital & Information Literacy: Sets 1 - 7. 2014. (Digital & Information Literacy Ser.). 48p. (YA). (gr. 5-8). 1240.25 *(978-1-4777-8099-2(8),* Rosen Reference) Rosen Publishing Group, Inc., The.

Digital & Information Literacy: Sets 1-8. 2014. (Digital & Information Literacy Ser.). 48p. (YA). (gr. 5-8). pap. 376.00 *(978-1-4777-8118-0(8),* Rosen Reference) Rosen Publishing Group, Inc., The.

DK. Big Book of Knowledge. 2019. (ENG., Illus.). 480p. (J). (gr. 4-7). pap. 17.99 *(978-1-4654-8041-5(2),* DK Children) Dorling Kindersley Publishing, Inc.

—How to Be Good at Science, Technology, & Engineering. 2018. (DK How to Be Good At Ser.). (ENG., Illus.). 320p. (J). (gr. 4-7). pap. 19.99 *(978-1-4654-7359-2(9),* DK Children) Dorling Kindersley Publishing, Inc.

Doyle, Eamon, ed. The Role of Science in Public Policy, 1 vol. 2018. (At Issue Ser.). (ENG.). 128p. (gr. 10-12). 41.03 *(978-1-5345-0334-2(X),* 76285a4b-fb66-45d0-8f2a-8383105de819) Greenhaven Publishing LLC.

Dramer, Kim. The Chinese, 1 vol. 2012. (Technology of the Ancients Ser.). (ENG.). 64p. (gr. 6-6). 35.50

(978-1-60870-766-9(0), c2e1ad44-6328-4fa2-be1f-1ee382c68d19) Cavendish Square Publishing LLC.

Duke, Shirley. Enterprise Stem. 2011. (Let's Explore Science Ser.). (ENG., Illus.). 48p. (gr. 4-6). pap. 10.95 (978-1-61741-983-6(4), 9781617419836) Rourke Educational Media.

Dunn, Karen Lewit. Saturday Night Pizza. 2008. (Discovering & Exploring Science Ser.). (Illus.). 16p. (J). (gr. -1-3). lib. bdg. 12.95 (978-0-7569-8419-9(X)) Perfection Learning Corp.

—Technology & Natural Disasters. 2008. (Discovering & Exploring Science Ser.). (Illus.). 16p. (J). (gr. -1-3). lib. bdg. 12.95 (978-0-7569-8435-9(1)) Perfection Learning Corp.

—What's the Solution? 2008. (Discovering & Exploring Science Ser.). (Illus.). 16p. (J). (gr. -1-3). lib. bdg. 12.95 (978-0-7569-8433-5(5)) Perfection Learning Corp.

Encyclopaedia Britannica, Inc. Staff. Britannica Illustrated Science Library Series (18 Title Series), 18 vols. 2010. 599.00 (978-1-61535-423-8(9)) Encyclopaedia Britannica, Inc.

Encyclopaedia Britannica, Inc. Staff, compiled by. Britannica Illustrated Science Library: Technology. 2009. 29.95 (978-1-59339-854-5(9)) Encyclopaedia Britannica, Inc.

Esbaum, Jill. National Geographic Little Kids First Big Book of How. 2016. (National Geographic Little Kids First Big Bks.). (Illus.). 128p. (J). (gr. -1-k). 14.99 (978-1-4263-2329-4(8), National Geographic Kids) Disney Publishing Worldwide.

Espejo, Roman, ed. Has Technology Increased Learning?, 1 vol. 2008. (At Issue Ser.). (ENG., Illus.). 136p. (gr. 10-12). pap. 28.80 (978-0-7377-4103-2(1), 4b1dd571-35fb-4652-bb75-e961fbdd9229); lib. bdg. 41.03 (978-0-7377-4102-5(3), 52019bb1-8dc7-4197-9239-0ea96188d143) Greenhaven Publishing LLC. (Greenhaven Publishing).

Essential Library of the Information Age, 6 vols. 2016. (Essential Library of the Information Age Ser.). (ENG.). 112p. (J). (gr. 8-12). lib. bdg. 248.16 (978-1-68078-281-3(9), 21717, Essential Library) ABDO Publishing Co.

Faiella, Graham. The Technology of Mesopotamia. (Technology of the Ancient World Ser.). 48p. (gr. 6-6). 2009. 61.20 (978-1-60854-243-7(2), Rosen Reference) 2006. (ENG., Illus.). (J). lib. bdg. 34.47 (978-1-4042-0560-4(8), 92fd3ae6-c7e9-4e8c-a519-f2a5817a3b27) Rosen Publishing Group, Inc., The.

Fales, et al. Technology: Today & Tomorrow, Student Edition. 5th ed. 2003. (TECHNOLOGY: TODAY & TOMORROW Ser.). (ENG., Illus.). 624p. (gr. 9-10). stu. ed. 83.96 (978-0-07-830829-1(1), 0078308291) McGraw-Hill Education.

Farndon, John. Science & Technology: The Greatest Innovations in Human History. 2016. (Illus.). 64p. (J). (gr. -1-12). 12.99 (978-1-86147-780-4(5), Armadillo) Anness Publishing GBR. Dist: National Bk. Network.

—Stickmen's Guide to Aircraft. Paul de Quay, John, illus. 2016. (Stickmen's Guides to How Everything Works). (ENG.). 32p. (J). (gr. 3-6). lib. bdg. 27.99 (978-1-4677-9359-9(0), b5c3675a-f96c-421f-96dc-6ea8600b1e77); E-Book 42.65 (978-1-5124-0690-0(2), 9781512406900); E-Book 42.65 (978-1-4677-9592-0(5)) Lerner Publishing Group. (Hungry Tomato (r)).

—Stickmen's Guide to Gigantic Machines. Paul de Quay, John, illus. 2016. (Stickmen's Guides to How Everything Works). (ENG.). 32p. (J). (gr. 3-6). lib. bdg. 27.99 (978-1-4677-9361-2(2), ef86552b-68cc-48fb-8652-4d2895fcd8e6); E-Book 42.65 (978-1-4677-9596-8(8)) Lerner Publishing Group. (Hungry Tomato (r)).

—The Story of Science & Technology, 1 vol. 2010. (Journey Through History Ser.). (ENG.). 64p. (YA). (gr. 5-6). lib. bdg. 37.13 (978-1-4488-0621-8(6), 2918e756-bad8-430b-aae8-83c5e631b0a2, Rosen Reference) Rosen Publishing Group, Inc., The.

Farndon, John & Beattie, Rob. Stuff You Need to Know! 2015. (ENG., Illus.). 80p. (J). (gr. 4-7). 19.95 (978-1-77085-656-1(0), 05bc71b6-bf30-49a9-af58-ab078a3845f2) Firefly Bks., Ltd.

Farndon, John, et al. Stuff You Need to Know! 2015. (ENG., Illus.). 80p. (J). (gr. 4-7). pap. 12.95 (978-1-77085-494-9(0), b1c76cec-77bd-4fcd-9fcd-fd677c74e60a) Firefly Bks., Ltd.

Faulkner, Nicholas. A Visual History of Science & Technology, 1 vol. 2016. (Visual History of the World Ser.). (ENG., Illus.). 96p. (J). (gr. 8-8). 38.80 (978-1-4994-6596-9(3), 90bec01a-ee04-4a60-9d4b-d75d5abe2c40) Rosen Publishing Group, Inc., The.

Faulkner, Nicholas, ed. 101 Women of STEM, 1 vol. 2016. (People You Should Know Ser.). (ENG., Illus.). 184p. (J). (gr. 8-8). lib. bdg. 38.84 (978-1-68048-511-0(3), 315dc040-0784-49a3-80dd-a86ebb329319) Rosen Publishing Group, Inc., The.

Fontichiaro, Kristin. Creating Data Visualizations. 2017. (21st Century Skills Library: Data Geek Ser.). (ENG., Illus.). 32p. (J). (gr. 4-7). lib. bdg. 32.07 (978-1-63472-709-9(6), 210094) Cherry Lake Publishing.

Fourth Grade Technology: 32-Lesson Comprehensive Curriculum, 6 vols. 2016. (ENG., Illus.). 249p. 32.99 net. (978-0-9787800-4-3(3)) Structured Learning LLC.

Freedman, Jeri. Strategic Inventions of the Napoleonic Wars, 1 vol. 2016. (Tech in the Trenches Ser.). (ENG., Illus.). 112p. (J). (gr. 9-9). 44.50 (978-1-5026-2351-5(X), 5374cf10-2ca1-427a-a1ee-cf76bcf4c4d8) Cavendish Square Publishing LLC.

—Strategic Inventions of World War II, 1 vol. 2015. (Tech in the Trenches Ser.). (ENG., Illus.). 112p. (YA). (gr. 9-9). lib. bdg. 44.50 (978-1-5026-1026-3(4), 56d8e5a6-deb5-44f5-bfc5-9c75c0877db1) Cavendish Square Publishing LLC.

—What Is a Technical Text?, 1 vol. 2014. (Britannica Common Core Library). (ENG., Illus.). 32p. (J). (gr. 2-3). 27.04 (978-1-62275-672-8(X), 94461080-154a-4cef-817f-c7f913185d6e, Britannica Educational Publishing) Rosen Publishing Group, Inc., The.

Fridell, Ron. Earth-Friendly Energy. 2009. pap. 58.95 (978-0-7613-4692-0(9)) Lerner Publishing Group.

—Military Techonology. 2008. pap. 52.95 (978-0-8225-9328-7(9)) Lerner Publishing Group.

Friesen, Helen Lepp. Who Lives Here? 2008. (Discovering & Exploring Science Ser.). (Illus.). 16p. (J). (gr. -1-3). lib. bdg. 12.95 (978-0-7569-8425-0(4)) Perfection Learning Corp.

Gagne, Tammy. American Revolution Technology. 2017. (War Technology Ser.). (ENG., Illus.). 48p. (J). (gr. 4-8). lib. bdg. 35.64 (978-1-5321-1188-4(6), 25952) ABDO Publishing Co.

—World War I Technology. 2017. (War Technology Ser.). (ENG., Illus.). 48p. (J). (gr. 4-8). lib. bdg. 35.64 (978-1-5321-1192-1(4), 25960) ABDO Publishing Co.

Garassino, Alessandro. La Vida. (SPA.). 40p. (YA). (gr. 5-8). (978-84-207-5697-4(0)) Grupo Anaya, S.A. ESP. Dist: Lectorum Pubns., Inc.

Gedacht, Daniel C. Technology of Ancient Rome. 2009. (Primary Sources of Ancient Civilizations Ser.). 24p. (gr. 3-3). 42.50 (978-1-60851-564-6(8), PowerKids Pr.) Rosen Publishing Group, Inc., The.

Gerdes, Louise I., ed. Robotic Technology, 1 vol. 2014. (Opposing Viewpoints Ser.). (ENG.). 200p. (gr. 10-12). pap. 34.80 (978-0-7377-6339-3(6), a8a25a81-bf19-42cc-96ca-42f82a34d8e3); lib. bdg. 50.43 (978-0-7377-6338-6(8), 3fe70e9b-2710-42f3-af35-3b4bccae2caf) Greenhaven Publishing LLC. (Greenhaven Publishing).

Gifford, Clive. Computing & Coding in the Real World. 2017. (Get Connected to Digital Literacy Ser.). (Illus.). 32p. (J). (gr. 4-5). (978-0-7787-3621-9(0)) Crabtree Publishing Co.

—Technology. 2012. (J). lib. bdg. (978-0-531-22960-6(2)) Scholastic, Inc.

Gitlin, Martin. Smartphones. 2019. (21st Century Skills Innovation Library: Disruptors in Tech Ser.). (ENG., Illus.). 32p. (J). (gr. 4-8). pap. 14.21 (978-1-5341-5046-1(3), 213491); lib. bdg. 32.07 (978-1-5341-4760-7(6), 213490) Cherry Lake Publishing.

Glencoe McGraw-Hill Staff, creator. Technology Student Workbook: Today & Tomorrow. 5th ed. 2003. (TECHNOLOGY: TODAY & TOMORROW Ser.). (ENG., Illus.). 238p. (gr. 9-10). stu. ed., per., wbk. ed. 32.84 (978-0-07-830831-4(3), 0078308313) McGraw-Hill Education.

Green, Dan. Technology: A Byte-Sized World! 2012. (Basher Science Ser.). (J). lib. bdg. 19.65 (978-0-606-26712-0(3)) Turtleback.

Greenberger, Robert. The Technology of Ancient China. (Technology of the Ancient World Ser.). 48p. (gr. 6-6). 2009. 61.20 (978-1-60854-238-3(6), Rosen Reference) 2006. (ENG., Illus.). (J). lib. bdg. 34.47 (978-1-4042-0558-1(6), 09c651f6-006e-41c6-a90e-375cc55f84b9) Rosen Publishing Group, Inc., The.

Greene, Meg. The Technology of Ancient Japan. 2009. (Technology of the Ancient World Ser.). 48p. (gr. 6-6). 61.20 (978-1-60854-241-3(6), Rosen Reference) Rosen Publishing Group, Inc., The.

Greenling, Jason. The Technology of Ancient China, 1 vol. 2016. (Ancient Innovations Ser.). (ENG., Illus.). 64p. (gr. 6-6). 35.93 (978-1-5026-2235-8(1), c72737ab-45b0-4f71-aee0-91b356953737) Cavendish Square Publishing LLC.

—The Technology of the Vikings, 1 vol. 2016. (Ancient Innovations Ser.). (ENG., Illus.). 64p. (gr. 6-6). 35.93 (978-1-5026-2241-9(6), 43cd570e-0050-4300-81fa-2dd9c5ee8ed5) Cavendish Square Publishing LLC.

Group/McGraw-Hill, Wright. On the Move: Level H, 6 vols. (First Explorers Ser.). 24p. (gr. 1-2). 29.95 (978-0-7699-1449-7(7)) Shortland Pubns. (U. S. A.) Inc.

Groves, Marcia, et al. Science & Technology in the Middle Ages, 1 vol. 2004. (Medieval World Ser.). (ENG., Illus.). 32p. (J). pap. (978-0-7787-1386-9(5)) Crabtree Publishing Co.

Gunston, Bill Tudor & Guy, John. Battle Machines. 2009. (ENG.). 112p. (J). (gr. 4-7). pap. 12.95 (978-1-84696-201-1(3), TickTock Books) Octopus Publishing Group GBR. Dist: Independent Pubs. Group.

Hagler, Gina. The Technology of Ancient India, 1 vol. 2016. (Spotlight on the Rise & Fall of Ancient Civilizations Ser.). (ENG.). 48p. (YA). (gr. 6-6). pap. 12.75 (978-1-4777-8942-1(1), 570bb2ec-28dd-4ef7-9e72-bb28cd2f9b45) Rosen Publishing Group, Inc., The.

Hakala, John. How Nanotechnology Will Impact Society. 2018. (Technology's Impact Ser.). (ENG.). 80p. (YA). (gr. 6-12). 39.93 (978-1-68282-495-5(0)) ReferencePoint Pr., Inc.

Harding, Sandra & Figueroa, Robert, eds. Science & Other Cultures: Issues in Philosophies of Science & Technology. 2003. (ENG.). 284p. (C). (gr. 13-18). 51.95 (978-0-415-93992-8(5), RT3570) Routledge.

Harris, Nic. The Greatest Invention of All Time Low Intermediate Book with Online Access, 1 vol. 2014. (ENG., Illus.). 24p. (J). pap., E-Book 9.50 (978-1-107-62161-9(5)) Cambridge Univ. Pr.

Harris, Patricia. Understanding Coding Through Simulations, 1 vol. 2016. (Spotlight on Kids Can Code Ser.). (ENG.). 24p. (J). (gr. 4-5). pap. 12.75 (978-1-4994-2794-3(8), d32eae9b-832b-4d82-9f9a-39fe745eaa24, PowerKids Pr.) Rosen Publishing Group, Inc., The.

Haugen, David M. & Musser, Susan, eds. Technology & the Cloud, 1 vol. 2012. (At Issue Ser.). (ENG.). 128p. (gr. 10-12). pap. 28.80 (978-0-7377-6208-2(X), 30e27b75-8861-4dd5-80fb-da80fd141369); lib. bdg. 41.03 (978-0-7377-6207-5(1), 34efd1a0-ab00-4677-94d5-af3b902160db) Greenhaven Publishing LLC. (Greenhaven Publishing).

Havelka, Jacqueline. STEM in Auto Racing. 2019. (Connecting STEM & Sports Ser.). (Illus.). 80p. (J). (gr. 12). lib. bdg. 34.60 (978-1-4222-4330-5(3)) Mason Crest.

—STEM in Extreme Sports. 2019. (Connecting STEM & Sports Ser.). (Illus.). 80p. (J). (gr. 12). lib. bdg. 34.60 (978-1-4222-4333-6(8)) Mason Crest.

—STEM in Football. 2019. (Connecting STEM & Sports Ser.). (Illus.). 80p. (J). (gr. 12). lib. bdg. 34.60 (978-1-4222-4334-3(6)) Mason Crest.

—STEM in Gymnastics. 2019. (Connecting STEM & Sports Ser.). (Illus.). 80p. (J). (gr. 12). lib. bdg. 34.60 (978-1-4222-4335-0(4)) Mason Crest.

Hayes, Vicki C. The 12 Biggest Breakthroughs in Communication Technology. 2019. (Technology Breakthroughs Ser.). (ENG., Illus.). 32p. (J). (gr. 3-6). 9.95 (978-1-63235-635-2(X), 14034); lib. bdg. 32.80 (978-1-63235-581-2(7), 14026) Bookstaves, LLC. (12-Story Library).

Heinrichs, Ann. Nanotechnologist. 2009. (21st Century Skills Library: Cool Science Careers Ser.). (ENG., Illus.). 32p. (gr. 4-8). lib. bdg. 32.07 (978-1-60279-307-1(7), 200203) Cherry Lake Publishing.

Heinz, Brian J. Nathan of Yesteryear & Michael of Today. Friar, Joanne, illus. 2006. (Exceptional Social Studies Titles for Intermediate Grades). (ENG.). 32p. (J). (gr. 3-6). lib. bdg. 22.60 (978-0-7613-2893-3(9), Millbrook Pr.) Lerner Publishing Group.

Heitkamp, Kristina Lyn. Fab Lab Creating with Digital Sewing Machines, 1 vol. 2016. (Getting Creative with Fab Lab Ser.). (ENG., Illus.). 64p. (J). (gr. 6-6). 36.13 (978-1-4994-6508-2(4), 9278c82f-b150-4f25-97bf-8320b4e68f37) Rosen Publishing Group, Inc., The.

Henderson, Harry. How Mobile Devices Are Changing Society. 2015. (ENG., Illus.). 80p. (J). lib. bdg. (978-1-60152-902-2(3)) ReferencePoint Pr., Inc.

Hessel-Mial, Michael. How STEM Built the Chinese Dynasties, 1 vol. 2019. (How STEM Built Empires Ser.). (ENG.). 80p. (gr. 7-7). pap. 16.30 (978-1-7253-4137-1(9), 52c40482-3afd-4b12-b46b-eb95bffaa821) Rosen Publishing Group, Inc., The.

—How STEM Built the Incan Empire, 1 vol. 2019. (How STEM Built Empires Ser.). (ENG.). 80p. (gr. 7-7). pap. 16.30 (978-1-7253-4146-3(8), 8e00ab78-4c0f-4950-9a94-e3ae4af76b2e) Rosen Publishing Group, Inc., The.

Hibbert, Clare. The World of Technology, 1 vol. 2018. (Science Explorers Ser.). (ENG.). 32p. (gr. 3-3). lib. bdg. 26.93 (978-1-9785-0647-3(3), af7c31e1-2f21-4961-951a-4a0581699f32) Enslow Publishing, LLC.

Higginson, Sheila Sweeny. Disasters of Technology: Set Of 6. 2011. (Navigators Ser.). (J). pap. 50.00 net. (978-1-4108-2576-6(0)) Benchmark Education Co.

High-Tech DIY Projects with 3D Printing. 2014. (Maker Kids Ser.). (Illus.). 32p. (J). (gr. 3-6). pap. 70.50 (978-1-4777-6657-6(X)); (ENG., (gr. 4-5). pap. 12.75 (978-1-4777-6676-7(6), 4724aab7-62c9-4c84-919a-344a202cd89d); (ENG., (gr. 4-5). lib. bdg. 29.27 (978-1-4777-6670-5(7), 0a61c080-633c-4699-90af-a0abd4515633) Rosen Publishing Group, Inc., The. (PowerKids Pr.).

Hinton, Kerry. Becoming a User Interface & User Experience Engineer, 1 vol. 2017. (Tech Track: Building Your Career in IT Ser.). (ENG., Illus.). 80p. (J). (gr. 7-7). 37.47 (978-1-5081-7564-3(0), 03d97a6c-541e-472e-92da-b73bc1ff25d2, Rosen Young Adult) Rosen Publishing Group, Inc., The.

—Fab Lab Creating with 3D Scanners, 1 vol. 2016. (Getting Creative with Fab Lab Ser.). (ENG., Illus.). 64p. (J). (gr. 6-6). 36.13 (978-1-4994-6502-0(5), 7c074c98-bbf2-4a4b-bfb7-d48dcab2bb5a) Rosen Publishing Group, Inc., The.

Hogan, Christa C. How Artificial Intelligence Will Impact Society. 2018. (Technology's Impact Ser.). (ENG.). 80p. (YA). (gr. 6-12). 39.93 (978-1-68282-491-7(8)) ReferencePoint Pr., Inc.

Holl, Kristi. Ancient Mesopotamian Technology, 1 vol. 2016. (Spotlight on the Rise & Fall of Ancient Civilizations Ser.). (ENG.). 48p. (YA). (gr. 6-6). pap. 12.75 (978-1-4777-8953-7(7), 6157a27f-8c99-4fb0-8157-fabca824370f) Rosen Publishing Group, Inc., The.

Holper, Paul & Torok, Simon. Imagining the Future: Invisibility, Immortality & 40 Other Incredible Ideas. 2017. (Illus.). 146p. (gr. 4-10). pap. 17.95 (978-1-4863-0272-7(6)) CSIRO Publishing AUS. Dist: Stylus Publishing, LLC.

Holt, Rinehart and Winston Staff. Harcourt Science & Technology: Strategies & Practice Answer Key. 4th ed. 2004. (Illus.). pap. 6.00 (978-0-03-019863-2(1)) Holt McDougal.

—Holt Science & Technology. 4th annot. ed. 2004. tchr. ed. 128.80 (978-0-03-073174-7(7)) Holt McDougal.

—Holt Science & Technology: Chapter Resources. 5th ed. 2005. pap. 87.36 (978-0-03-030632-7(9)) Holt McDougal.

Hosein, Ann. Technology of the Ancient World, 1 vol., 1. 2015. (History of Technology Ser.). (ENG., Illus.). 112p. (J). (gr. 8-8). 35.47 (978-1-68048-273-7(4), 5dbb4a9a-907d-4331-931b-5226e51a1e12, Britannica Educational Publishing) Rosen Publishing Group, Inc., The.

Howell, Izzi. The Genius of the Ancient Greeks. 2019. (Genius of the Ancients Ser.). (ENG.). 32p. (J). (gr. 4-5). pap. (978-0-7787-6592-9(X), 001becc9-e8d5-4a52-878b-7ca35bd83c02); lib. bdg. (978-0-7787-6572-1(5), 373ad2a8-51a7-4ddc-9f0d-76618a43da20) Crabtree Publishing Co.

—The Genius of the Anglo-Saxons. 2019. (Genius of the Ancients Ser.). (ENG.). 32p. (J). (gr. 4-5). pap. (978-0-7787-6593-6(8), fe311313-8d0a-4651-b079-ec5ddb271ac0); lib. bdg. (978-0-7787-6573-8(3), 1936b976-75e3-4f65-84c3-d04b72d5a21f) Crabtree Publishing Co.

—The Genius of the Maya. 2019. (Genius of the Ancients Ser.). (ENG.). 32p. (J). (gr. 4-5). pap. (978-0-7787-6595-0(4), 563991fb-e6b8-4fb1-af89-fc664dc20c05); lib. bdg. (978-0-7787-6575-2(X), dce158c4-eb30-4443-907b-901a14c1f198) Crabtree Publishing Co.

—The Genius of the Romans. 2019. (Genius of the Ancients Ser.). (ENG., Illus.). 32p. (J). (gr. 4-5). pap. (978-0-7787-6596-7(2), 948b0c95-b8b5-42df-978f-c19bed21c491); lib. bdg. (978-0-7787-6576-9(8), 013e1d5a-0403-48c8-b5a3-53b33a6aaba5) Crabtree Publishing Co.

—The Genius of the Stone, Bronze, & Iron Ages. 2019. (Genius of the Ancients Ser.). (ENG.). 32p. (J). (gr. 4-5). pap. (978-0-7787-6597-4(0), eacecb69-7a4f-49fb-9595-76c5efced2a9); lib. bdg. (978-0-7787-6577-6(6), de4e945d-a2a1-4548-8257-d5cb3c914ce4) Crabtree Publishing Co.

Hubbard, Rita L. Getting the Most Out of MOOC: Massive Open Online Courses, 1 vol. 2014. (Digital & Information Literacy Ser.). (ENG.). 48p. (YA). (gr. 5-5). 33.47 (978-1-4777-7950-7(7), cdd33d0b-68a6-4571-b336-a889419a311b, Rosen Reference) Rosen Publishing Group, Inc., The.

Hunter, Charlotte. Cotton Candy Machines. 2016. (How It Works). (ENG.). 24p. (gr. 1-3). 28.50 (978-1-68191-687-3(8), 9781681916873) Rourke Educational Media.

Hunter, Dru. How Do We Apply Science? 2015. (Think Like a Scientist Ser.). (ENG., Illus.). 48p. (J). (gr. 4-7). (978-1-60818-592-4(3), 21060, Creative Education) Creative Co., The.

—How Does It Work? (Think Like a Scientist Ser.). (ENG.). 48p. (J). (gr. 4-7). 2016. pap. 12.00 (978-1-62832-198-2(9), 21064, Creative Paperbacks) 2015. (Illus.). (978-1-60818-593-1(1), 21063, Creative Education) Creative Co., The.

Hunter, Nick. Technology in the Battle of Britain: Band 17/Diamond (Collins Big Cat) 2016. (Collins Big Cat Ser.). (ENG.). 56p. (J). (gr. 5-6). pap. 11.99 (978-0-00-816400-3(2)) HarperCollins Pubs. Ltd. GBR. Dist: Independent Pubs. Group.

Hynson, Colin. Dream Jobs in Technology. 2017. (Cutting-Edge Careers in STEM Ser.). (Illus.). 32p. (J). (978-0-7787-2967-9(2)) Crabtree Publishing Co.

Idzikowski, Lisa. Innovation & Entrepreneurship, 1 vol. 2018. (Understanding Economics Ser.). (ENG.). 48p. (gr. 6-7). lib. bdg. 28.41 (978-1-5383-0267-5(5), eab5bdc3-b987-4317-b68b-1529b184233d, Britannica Educational Publishing) Rosen Publishing Group, Inc., The.

Incentive Publications by World Book (Firm) Staff, contrib. by. 3D Printing & Other Industrial Tech. 2019. (Illus.). 48p. (J). (978-0-7166-2432-5(X)) World Bk., Inc.

Iyer, Rani. The Science of Super Strength & Super Speed, 1 vol. 2018. (Science of Superpowers Ser.). (ENG.). 48p. (J). (gr. 4-4). 33.07 (978-1-5026-3793-2(6), 4f749d7c-9328-4125-bd3c-ce66be4d0999) Cavendish Square Publishing LLC.

Johanson, Paula. Tech Industry. 2017. (Techno Planet Ser.). (Illus.). 32p. (J). (gr. 5-5). (978-0-7787-3604-2(0)) Crabtree Publishing Co.

Johnson, Rebecca L. Nanotechnology. 2005. (Cool Science Ser.). (ENG., Illus.). 48p. (J). (gr. 4-8). lib. bdg. 27.93 (978-0-8225-2111-2(3), Lerner Pubns.) Lerner Publishing Group.

Jones, Tammy. I Go! 2009. (Sight Word Readers Set A Ser.). (J). 3.49 net. (978-1-60719-143-8(1)) Newmark Learning LLC.

Kallen, Stuart A. Cutting Edge Energy Technology. 2016. (ENG., Illus.). 80p. (J). (gr. 5-12). (978-1-68282-038-4(6)) ReferencePoint Pr., Inc.

Kamberg, Mary-Lane. Drones & Commerce, 1 vol. 2016. (Inside the World of Drones Ser.). (ENG., Illus.). 64p. (J). (gr. 7-7). 36.13 (978-1-5081-7341-0(9), ce3424a2-8dea-4f13-a865-467a5f1255f6) Rosen Publishing Group, Inc., The.

Kawa, Katie. Does Technology Make People Lazy?, 1 vol. 2018. (Points of View Ser.). (ENG.). 24p. (gr. 3-3). 26.23 (978-1-5345-2563-4(7), c6b4ad82-67b0-4d91-a644-e0bb55f7740b, KidHaven Publishing) Greenhaven Publishing LLC.

Kelly, Tracey. Computer Technology: From Punch Cards to Supercomputers. 2019. (History of Inventions Ser.). (ENG.). 24p. (J). (gr. 2-4). lib. bdg. (978-1-78121-454-1(9), 16731) Brown Bear Bks.

Kindergarten Technology: 32-Lesson Comprehensive Curriculum. 2016. (ENG., Illus.). 214p. 32.99 net. (978-0-9787800-0-5(0)) Structured Learning LLC.

Kobasa, Paul A. Personal & Household Items. 2009. (J). (978-0-7166-0390-0(X)) World Bk., Inc.

Koellhoffer, Tara, ed. Computers & Technology. 2006. (Science News for Kids Ser.). (Illus.). 144p. (gr. 4-6). lib. bdg. 30.00 (978-0-7910-9120-3(1), Chelsea Clubhse.) Infobase Holdings, Inc.

Kopp, Megan. Creating in the Digital World. 2018. (ENG.). (J). (gr. 3-7). (978-0-7787-4271-5(5)); (Illus.). 32p. (gr. 5-5). (978-0-7787-4601-0(1)); (Illus.). 32p. (gr. 5-5). pap. (978-0-7787-4605-8(4)) Crabtree Publishing Co.

Kops, Deborah. Were Early Computers Really the Size of a School Bus? And Other Questions about Inventions. 2011. (Is That a Fact? Ser.). (ENG.). 40p. (gr. 4-6). 26.60 (978-0-7613-6098-8(0)) Lerner Publishing Group.

Kortemeier, Todd. Unsung Heroes of Technology. 2017. (Unsung Heroes Ser.). (ENG., Illus.). 32p. (J). (gr. 3-6). 32.80 (978-1-63235-311-5(3), 11831, 12-Story Library) Bookstaves, LLC.

Kroll, Jennifer. The Cutting Edge: Breakthroughs in Technology, 1 vol. 2nd rev. ed. 2013. (TIME for KIDS(r): Informational Text Ser.). (ENG., Illus.). 64p. (J). (gr. 4-8). pap. 14.99 (978-1-4333-4947-8(7)) Teacher Created Materials, Inc.

Kuhtz, Russell. Physical Science, 1 vol. 2016. (Study of Science Ser.). (ENG., Illus.). 156p. (YA). (gr. 8-8). lib. bdg. 37.82 (978-1-5081-0425-4(5), 8a0bdce8-b0c3-41f8-8ed8-c2a73ededb28) Rosen Publishing Group, Inc., The.

Kulz, George Anthony. Nanotechnology. 2018. (Tech Bytes Ser.). (ENG.). 48p. (J). (gr. 4-6). 26.60 (978-1-59953-936-2(5)) Norwood Hse. Pr.

Leavitt, Amie Jane. Fab Lab Creating with 3D Printers, 1 vol. 2016. (Getting Creative with Fab Lab Ser.). (ENG.). 64p. (J). (gr. 6-6). 36.13 (978-1-4994-6500-6(9), 81808d70-f655-4dfd-9a9b-4c31b6050a5e) Rosen Publishing Group, Inc., The.

—How STEM Built the Aztec Empire, 1 vol. 2019. (How STEM Built Empires Ser.). (ENG.). 80p. (gr. 7-7). pap. 16.30 (978-1-7253-4134-0(4), 4018fd21-706c-4ecc-975f-0a94efc7e4c3) Rosen Publishing Group, Inc., The.

—How STEM Built the Mayan Empire, 1 vol. 2019. (How STEM Built Empires Ser.). (ENG.). 80p. (gr. 7-7). pap. 16.30 (978-1-7253-4149-4(2), ccee7b83-7ab1-4a52-8605-764ba3b58500) Rosen Publishing Group, Inc., The.

Lee, Dora. Biomimicry: Inventions Inspired by Nature. Thompson, Margot, illus. 2011. (ENG.). 40p. (J). (gr. 3-7).

TUV

18.95 (978-1-55453-467-8(4)) Kids Can Pr., Ltd. CAN. Dist: Hachette Bk. Group.

Lew, Kristi. Powering up a Career in Nanotechnology, 1 vol. 2015. (Preparing for Tomorrow's Careers Ser.). (ENG., Illus.). 80p. (J). (gr. 7-8). 37.47 (978-1-4994-6087-2(2), 0a8c577e-2a35-46b2-babf-4949f94f06ae, Rosen Young Adult) Rosen Publishing Group, Inc., The.

Lindeen, Mary. Then & Now, 1 vol. 2011. (Wonder Readers Fluent Level Ser.). (ENG.). 16p. (gr. -1-2). (J). pap. 6.25 (978-1-4296-7972-5(7), 118304); pap. 35.94 (978-1-4296-8177-3(2)) Capstone. (Capstone Pr.).

Loh-Hagan, Virginia. Girl Innovators. 2019. (History's Yearbook Ser.). (ENG., Illus.). 32p. (J). (gr. 4-8). pap. 14.21 (978-1-5341-5076-8(5), 213611); lib. bdg. 32.07 (978-1-5341-4790-4(X), 213610) Cherry Lake Publishing. (45th Parallel Press).

Lowery, Zoe. Technology of the Modern World, 1 vol., 1. 2015. (History of Technology Ser.). (ENG., Illus.). 112p. (J). (gr. 8-8). 35.47 (978-1-68048-276-8(9), fbe97c58-d409-4dd7-9189-00a47b32d9ab, Britannica Educational Publishing) Rosen Publishing Group, Inc., The.

Luke, Andrew. STEM in Ice Hockey. 2019. (Connecting STEM & Sports Ser.). (Illus.). 80p. (J). (gr. 12). lib. bdg. 34.60 (978-1-4222-4336-7(2)) Mason Crest.

Macaulay, David. The Way Things Work: Newly Revised Edition. 2023. (ENG., Illus.). 408p. (J). (gr. 5). 35.00 (978-0-544-82438-6(5), 1643334, Clarion Bks.) HarperCollins Pubs.

MacKay, Jennifer. Online Schools, 1 vol. 2013. (Technology 360 Ser.). (ENG., Illus.). 112p. (gr. 7-10). lib. bdg. 41.53 (978-1-4205-0942-7(X), 63229946-dc11-4e86-95a5-682d7c4e4d0b, Lucent Pr.) Greenhaven Publishing LLC.

—Roller Coasters, 1 vol. 2012. (Technology 360 Ser.). (ENG., Illus.). 112p. (gr. 7-10). lib. bdg. 41.53 (978-1-4205-0825-3(3), fb0ed3f1-e4f5-4e2e-9e3c-18fe301bf17a, Lucent Pr.) Greenhaven Publishing LLC.

Mahoney, Emily. The Industrial Revolution: The Birth of Modern America, 1 vol. 2017. (American History Ser.). (ENG.). 104p. (gr. 7-7). lib. bdg. 41.03 (978-1-5345-6133-5(1), 614f7d58-9e93-4a2e-bcbd-6b880ed31008, Lucent Pr.) Greenhaven Publishing LLC.

Mahoney, Emily Jankowski. Ancient Aztec Technology, 1 vol. 2016. (Spotlight on the Maya, Aztec, & Inca Civilizations Ser.). (ENG., Illus.). 32p. (J). (gr. 4-6). pap. 12.75 (978-1-4994-1923-8(6), 64c7714e-3c60-4376-b40f-1c89ed65e7c2, PowerKids Pr.) Rosen Publishing Group, Inc., The.

Mara, Wil. The Mesopotamians, 1 vol. 2012. (Technology of the Ancients Ser.). (ENG., Illus.). 64p. (gr. 6-6). 35.50 (978-1-60870-767-6(9), 00958fae-07f7-4813-87b7-d738e5fb4a87) Cavendish Square Publishing LLC.

—The Romans, 1 vol. 2012. (Technology of the Ancients Ser.). (ENG.). 64p. (gr. 6-6). 35.50 (978-1-60870-768-3(7), b291559d-ec79-4731-9cb9-7c154b88abe3) Cavendish Square Publishing LLC.

Marcovitz, Hal. Technology. 2008. (Gallup Major Trends & Events Ser.). (Illus.). 128p. (J). (gr. 7-18). lib. bdg. 22.95 (978-1-59084-969-9(8)) Mason Crest.

—What Is the Future of 3D Printing? 2016. (ENG., Illus.). 80p. (J). (gr. 5-12). (978-1-68282-066-7(1)) ReferencePoint Pr., Inc.

—3-D Printing. 2016. (Tech Bytes Ser.). (ENG., Illus.). 48p. (J). (gr. 4-6). pap. 14.60 (978-1-60357-867-7(6)); lib. bdg. 26.60 (978-1-59953-759-7(1)) Norwood Hse. Pr.

Marquardt, Meg. Incredible Technology. 2018. (Unbelievable Ser.). (ENG., Illus.). 32p. (J). (gr. 3-6). 32.80 (978-1-63235-422-8(5), 13770, 12-Story Library) Bookstaves, LLC.

Martin, Brett S. Inside Wearable Technology. 2018. (Inside Technology Ser.). (ENG., Illus.). 48p. (J). (gr. 4-8). lib. bdg. 35.64 (978-1-5321-1795-4(7), 30878) ABDO Publishing Co.

Mason, Conrad. See Inside How Things Work. 2010. (See Inside Board Bks). 16p. (J). bds. 12.99 (978-0-7945-2406-7(0), Usborne) EDC Publishing.

Maxim, Bailey. The 100 Most Influential Technology Leaders, 1 vol., 1. 2016. (Britannica Guide to the World's Most Influential People Ser.). (ENG., Illus.). 336p. (J). (gr. 10-10). lib. bdg. 56.59 (978-1-68048-280-5(7), 50b95650-416b-4aaf-bf8e-a95266a3d92f, Britannica Educational Publishing) Rosen Publishing Group, Inc., The.

Maynard, Charles W. The Technology of Ancient Greece. 2009. (Technology of the Ancient World Ser.). 48p. (gr. 6-6). 61.20 (978-1-60854-240-6(8), Rosen Reference) Rosen Publishing Group, Inc., The.

—The Technology of Ancient Rome. (Technology of the Ancient World Ser.). 48p. (gr. 6-6). 2009. 61.20 (978-1-60854-242-0(4), Rosen Reference) 2006. (ENG., Illus.). (J). lib. bdg. 34.47 (978-1-4042-0556-7(X), 567ff699-46a1-40b3-9ffd-e7793b6b7c4f) Rosen Publishing Group, Inc., The.

McArdle, Matthew. 19th Century Innovations: Paving the Way. rev. ed. 2017. (Social Studies: Informational Text Ser.). (ENG., Illus.). 32p. (gr. 4-8). pap. 11.99 (978-1-4938-3796-0(6)) Teacher Created Materials, Inc.

McCullough, Naomi V. The Technology of the Aztecs, 1 vol. 2016. (Ancient Innovations Ser.). (ENG., Illus.). 64p. (J). (gr. 6-6). 35.93 (978-1-5026-2239-6(4), 39cf373b-1888-49fa-8286-ebf8416c517a) Cavendish Square Publishing LLC.

McKinney, Donna Bowen. How STEM Built the Greek Empire, 1 vol. 2019. (How STEM Built Empires Ser.). (ENG.). 80p. (gr. 7-7). pap. 16.30 (978-1-7253-4143-2(3), 4b7c4e01-adb4-4aa2-9f8e-2ada50a64347) Rosen Publishing Group, Inc., The.

Miller, John & Scott, Chris Fornell. Unofficial Minecraft STEM Lab for Kids: Family-Friendly Projects for Exploring Concepts in Science, Technology, Engineering, & Math, Volume 16. 2018. (Lab for Kids Ser.: 16). (ENG., Illus.). 144p. (J). (gr. 2-5). pap. 24.99 (978-1-63159-483-0(4), 301354, Quarry Bks.) Quarto Publishing Group USA.

Mitchell, Melanie. From Cloth to American Flag. 2004. (Start to Finish Ser.). (J). pap. 5.95 (978-0-8225-2142-6(3)) Lerner Publishing Group.

Mooney, Carla. What Is the Future of Virtual Reality? 2016. (ENG., Illus.). 80p. (J). (gr. 5-12). lib. bdg. (978-1-68282-094-0(7)) ReferencePoint Pr., Inc.

Murray, Jacqui. Fifth Grade Technology: 32-Lesson Comprehensive Curriculum, 6 vols. 2016. (ENG., Illus.). 250p. 32.99 net. (978-0-9787800-5-0(1)) Structured Learning LLC.

Murray, Laura K. World War II Technology. 2017. (War Technology Ser.). (ENG.). 48p. (J). (gr. 4-8). lib. bdg. 35.64 (978-1-5321-1193-8(2), 25962) ABDO Publishing Co.

Nagelhout, Ryan. Ancient Inca Technology, 1 vol. 2016. (Spotlight on the Maya, Aztec, & Inca Civilizations Ser.). (ENG., Illus.). 32p. (J). (gr. 4-6). pap. 12.75 (978-1-4994-1953-5(8), 2614cf0c-21f8-46a4-8e76-675d0d814904, PowerKids Pr.) Rosen Publishing Group, Inc., The.

—Freaky Stories about Technology, 1 vol. 2016. (Freaky True Science Ser.). (ENG., Illus.). 32p. (J). (gr. 4-5). pap. 11.50 (978-1-4824-4838-2(6), edc8cf75-3ae2-469d-bd9c-fad157133892) Stevens, Gareth Publishing LLLP.

National Geographic Learning. Reading Expeditions (Science: Everyday Science): Science at the Mall. 2007. (ENG., Illus.). 24p. (J). pap. 15.95 (978-0-7922-4569-8(5)) CENGAGE Learning.

—Reading Expeditions (Social Studies: Seeds of Change in American History): the Industrial Revolution. 2006. (Nonfiction Reading & Writing Workshops Ser.). (ENG., Illus.). 40p. (J). pap. 21.95 (978-0-7922-8685-1(5)) CENGAGE Learning.

NETS Project Staff, et al. NETS*S Curriculum Series: Multidisciplinary Units for Prekindergarten Through Grade 2. 2003. (National Educational Technology Standards for Students Curriculum Ser.). 306p. (J). pap. 34.95 (978-1-56484-200-8(2)) International Society for Technology in Education.

Nichols, Susan. For People Who Love Tech, 1 vol. 2016. (Cool Careers Without College Ser.). (ENG., Illus.). 104p. (J). (gr. 7-7). 41.12 (978-1-5081-7280-2(3), 468ada9d-1209-4c32-ba67-a2f7e2ab074b) Rosen Publishing Group, Inc., The.

Nsrc. Science & Technology for Children Books: Technology of Paper. 2004. (Illus.). 64p. (J). (978-1-933008-11-0(3)) Smithsonian Science Education Ctr. (SSEC).

Oakes, Quenton. Looking Inside a 3D Printer. 2017. (21st Century Skills Innovation Library: Makers As Innovators Junior Ser.). (ENG., Illus.). 24p. (J). (gr. 2-5). pap. 12.79 (978-1-63472-321-3(X), 209329); lib. bdg. 30.64 (978-1-63472-189-9(6), 209328) Cherry Lake Publishing.

O'Brien, Cynthia. Parts Work Together. 2019. (Full STEAM Ahead! - Technology Time Ser.). (Illus.). 24p. (J). (gr. 1-1). (978-0-7787-6201-0(7)); pap. (978-0-7787-6238-6(6)) Crabtree Publishing Co.

—Technology & You! 2019. (Full STEAM Ahead! - Technology Time Ser.). (Illus.). 24p. (J). (gr. 1-1). (978-0-7787-6202-7(5)); pap. (978-0-7787-6239-3(4)) Crabtree Publishing Co.

—Technology Then & Now. 2019. (Full STEAM Ahead! - Technology Time Ser.). (Illus.). 24p. (J). (gr. 1-1). (978-0-7787-6203-4(3)); pap. (978-0-7787-6240-9(8)) Crabtree Publishing Co.

—What Is Technology? 2019. (Full STEAM Ahead! - Technology Time Ser.). (Illus.). 24p. (J). (gr. 1-1). (978-0-7787-6204-1(1)); pap. (978-0-7787-6249-2(1)) Crabtree Publishing Co.

O'Hara, Susan & McMahon, Maureen. NETS*S Curriculum Series: Multidisciplinary Units for Grades 6-8. 2003. (National Educational Technology Standards for Students Curriculum Ser.). (Illus.). 241p. (J). pap. 34.95 (978-1-56484-206-0(1)) International Society for Technology in Education.

O'Neill, Terence & Williams, Josh. 3D Printing. 2013. (21st Century Skills Innovation Library: Makers As Innovators Ser.). (ENG.). 32p. (J). (gr. 4-8). pap. 14.21 (978-1-62431-270-0(5), 202874); (Illus.). 32.07 (978-1-62431-138-3(5), 202872) Cherry Lake Publishing.

Otfinoski, Steven. 3D Printing: Science, Technology, & Engineering (Calling All Innovators: a Career for You) 2016. (Calling All Innovators: a Career for You Ser.). (ENG., Illus.). 64p. (J). (gr. 5-8). pap. 8.95 (978-0-531-21988-1(7), Children's Pr.) Scholastic Library Publishing.

Out & About: Level Q, 6 vols., Vol. 2. (Explorers Ser.). 32p. (gr. 3-6). 44.95 (978-0-7699-0608-9(7)) Shortland Pubns. (U. S. A.) Inc.

Oxlade, Chris. How Things Work. 2004. (Knowledge Masters Plus Ser.). (Illus.). 32p. (YA). pap. incl. cd-rom (978-1-903954-43-0(6), Pavilion Children's Books) Pavilion Bks.

Paisley, Erinne. Can Your Smartphone Change the World?, 1 vol. 2017. (PopActivism Ser.: 1). (ENG., Illus.). 144p. (YA). (gr. 8-12). pap. 14.95 (978-1-4598-1303-8(0)) Orca Bk. Pubs. USA.

Paley, Caitlyn. Strategic Inventions of the Revolutionary War, 1 vol. 2015. (Tech in the Trenches Ser.). (ENG., Illus.). 112p. (YA). (gr. 9-9). lib. bdg. 44.50 (978-1-5026-1028-7(0), dfdfd520-1a3e-48aa-af45-9ceba531f4f7) Cavendish Square Publishing LLC.

Pamplona, Alberto Hernández. A Visual Guide to Technology, 1 vol. 2017. (Visual Exploration of Science Ser.). (ENG., Illus.). 104p. (J). (gr. 8-8). 38.80 (978-1-5081-7584-1(5), 5f67c385-83d8-444f-ad67-a4a94cf2011a, Rosen Young Adult) Rosen Publishing Group, Inc., The.

Paris, Stephanie. Technology Feats & Failures. 2nd rev. ed. 2012. (TIME for KIDS(r): Informational Text Ser.). (ENG.). 48p. (gr. 4-5). pap. 13.99 (978-1-4333-4869-3(1)) Teacher Created Materials, Inc.

Parker, Steve. How It Works, 10 vols., Set. Incl. Aircraft. lib. bdg. 19.95 (978-1-4222-1791-7(4)); Cars Trucks & Bikes. (Illus.). lib. bdg. 19.95 (978-1-4222-1792-4(2), 1317905); Emergency Vehicles. (Illus.). lib. bdg. 19.95 (978-1-4222-1793-1(0), 1317906); Energy & Power. lib. bdg. 19.95 (978-1-4222-1794-8(9)); Gadgets. lib. bdg. 19.95 (978-1-4222-1795-5(7)); Giant Machines. lib. bdg. 19.95 (978-1-4222-1796-2(5)); Military Machines. lib. bdg. 19.95 (978-1-4222-1797-9(3)); Ships & Submarines. lib. bdg. 19.95 (978-1-4222-1798-6(1)); Space Exploration. lib. bdg. 19.95 (978-1-4222-1799-3(X)); Speed Machines. Pang, Alex, illus. lib. bdg. 19.95 (978-1-4222-1800-6(7), 1317938); (J). (gr. 3-18). 40p. 2010. Set lib. bdg. 199.50 (978-1-4222-1790-0(6)) Mason Crest.

Payne, Jan & Wilder, Steven. Penicillin Was Discovered by Accident: And Other Facts about Inventions & Discoveries, 1 vol. 2016. (True or False? Ser.). (ENG., Illus.). 48p. (gr. 3-3). pap. 12.70 (978-0-7660-7739-3(X), e293e4c7-83a7-498f-bc0e-99664c84ae15) Enslow Publishing, LLC.

Pedal Power: Individual Title Six-Packs. (Bookweb Ser.). 32p. (gr. 6-18). 34.00 (978-0-7578-0913-2(8)) Rigby Education.

Perdew, Laura. Information Literacy in the Digital Age, 1 vol. 2016. (Essential Library of the Information Age Ser.). (ENG., Illus.). 112p. (J). (gr. 8-12). lib. bdg. 41.36 (978-1-68078-285-1(1), 21725, Essential Library) ABDO Publishing Co.

Perritano, John. Science & Technology, Vol. 9. van Dijk, Ruud, ed. 2016. (Making of the Modern World: 1945 to the Present Ser.). (Illus.). 64p. (J). (gr. 7). 23.95 (978-1-4222-3641-3(2)) Mason Crest.

Pierce, Franklin. Fiberglass Ding Repair: The Art of Polyester Resin/Fiberglas & Polyurathane Foam Surfboard Repairwork. 2004. (Illus.). 64p. (gr. 7-18). per. 19.95 (978-0-9744247-0-5(6)) Impulse Surf.

Platt, Richard. The Egyptians. Lawrence, David, illus. 2011. (How They Made Things Work! Ser.). 32p. (J). (gr. 2-5). lib. bdg. 28.50 (978-1-59771-287-3(6)) Sea-To-Sea Pubns.

—The Greeks. Lawrence, David, illus. 2011. (How They Made Things Work! Ser.). 32p. (J). (gr. 2-5). lib. bdg. 28.50 (978-1-59771-288-0(4)) Sea-To-Sea Pubns.

—How They Made Things Work: in the Age of Industry. Lawrence, David, illus. 2022. (How They Made Things Work Ser.). (ENG.). 32p. (J). (gr. 4-6). pap. 13.99 (978-1-4451-6431-1(0), Franklin Watts) Hachette Children's Group GBR. Dist: Hachette Bk. Group.

—In the Renaissance. Lawrence, David, illus. 2011. (How They Made Things Work! Ser.). 32p. (YA). (gr. 2-5). lib. bdg. 28.50 (978-1-59771-289-7(2)) Sea-To-Sea Pubns.

Platt, Richard & Biesty, Stephen. Stephen Biesty's Incredible Cross-Sections Book. (Illus.). (J). pap. 24.95 (978-0-590-73870-5(4)) Scholastic, Inc.

Porterfield, Jason. Fab Lab Creating with Milling Machines, 1 vol. 2016. (Getting Creative with Fab Lab Ser.). (ENG., Illus.). 64p. (J). (gr. 6-6). 36.13 (978-1-4994-6506-8(8), f2dfca2b-df76-4290-afb7-e8b8f62e1045) Rosen Publishing Group, Inc., The.

Publishers, Chelsea House, creator. Scientific American Set. 2007. (Scientific American Ser.). (ENG.). (gr. 5-8). 240.00 (978-0-7910-9811-0(7), P179192, Facts On File) Infobase Holdings, Inc.

Radley, Gail. Facebook. 2018. (Tech Titans Ser.). (ENG., Illus.). 112p. (J). (gr. 6-12). lib. bdg. 41.36 (978-1-5321-1687-2(X), 30626, Essential Library) ABDO Publishing Co.

Reher, Matt. Apples Make Juice. 2005. (1B Our Natural World Ser.). (ENG., Illus.). 28p. (J). pap. 8.00 (978-1-63437-038-7(4)) American Reading Co.

Resler, T. J. How Things Work: Inside Out: Discover Secrets & Science Behind Trick Candles, 3D Printers, Penguin Propulsions, & Everything in Between. 2017. (ENG., Illus.). 208p. (J). (gr. 3-7). 29.90 (978-1-4263-2878-7(8), National Geographic Kids) Disney Publishing Worldwide.

—How Things Work Inside Out: Discover Secrets & Science Behind Trick Candles, 3D Printers, Penguin Propulsions, & Everything in Between. 2017. (Illus.). 208p. (J). (gr. 3-7). 19.99 (978-1-4263-2877-0(X), National Geographic Kids) Disney Publishing Worldwide.

—How Things Work: Then & Now. 2018. (Illus.). 208p. (J). (gr. 3-7). 19.99 (978-1-4263-3166-4(5)); (ENG., lib. bdg. 29.90 (978-1-4263-3167-1(3)) Disney Publishing Worldwide. (National Geographic Kids).

Rhatigan, Joe. Inventions That Could Have Changed the World... but Didn't! Owsley, Anthony, illus. 2018. 80p. (J). (gr. 3-7). pap. 9.99 (978-1-62354-101-9(8)) Charlesbridge Publishing, Inc.

Rhatigan, Joe & Owsley, Anthony. Inventions That Could Have Changed the World... But Didn't! 2015. (Illus.). 80p. (J). (gr. 3-7). 14.95 (978-1-62354-024-1(0)) Charlesbridge Publishing, Inc.

Rich, Mari. Technology, Vol. 10. Gilmore, Malinda & Pouson, Mel, eds. 2016. (Black Achievement in Science Ser.). (Illus.). 64p. (J). (gr. 7). 23.95 (978-1-4222-3564-5(5)) Mason Crest.

Richards, Jon & Simkins, Ed. The Human-Made World. 2016. (Mapographica Ser.). (ENG., Illus.). 32p. (J). (gr. 3-6). (978-0-7787-2657-9(6)) Crabtree Publishing Co.

—Today's Technology, 1 vol. 2017. (Infographics: How It Works). (ENG.). 32p. (J). (gr. 4-5). pap. 11.50 (978-1-5382-1428-2(8), 61ecdf5a-8e28-41e6-a268-4383316b44b6); lib. bdg. 28.27 (978-1-5382-1364-3(8), 91145ad5-b610-4fee-8af7-ac5c120d6018) Stevens, Gareth Publishing LLLP.

RIGBY. Technology Matters! Fifth Grade Class Collection Books. 2003. (Rigby on Our Way to English Ser.). (ENG.). 32p. (gr. 5-5). pap. 50.70 (978-0-7578-4472-0(3)) Rigby Education.

Ring, Susan. What Is Technology? Date not set. (Early Science Big Bks.). (Illus.). 16p. (J). (gr. -1-2). pap. 16.95 (978-1-58273-119-3(5)) Sundance/Newbridge Educational Publishing.

Roby, Cynthia A. Strategic Inventions of World War I, 1 vol. 2015. (Tech in the Trenches Ser.). (ENG., Illus.). 112p. (YA). (gr. 9-9). lib. bdg. 44.50 (978-1-5026-1024-9(8), 1b749332-332f-49b6-ba53-8d49e7f27ffa) Cavendish Square Publishing LLC.

Rockwood, Leigh. Ancient Egyptian Technology, 1 vol. 2013. (Spotlight on Ancient Civilizations: Egypt Ser.). (ENG.). 24p. (J). (gr. 3-4). 26.27 (978-1-4777-0768-5(9), 2fb43418-54c3-4902-980b-06e084cb1daa); pap. 11.00 (978-1-4777-0869-9(3), f5d9a7bc-aec5-4c27-90a2-23098d95a2c0) Rosen Publishing Group, Inc., The. (PowerKids Pr.).

Rose, Simon. Evaluating Arguments about Technology. 2018. (State Your Case Ser.). (Illus.). 48p. (J). (gr. 5-6). (978-0-7787-5079-6(5)) Crabtree Publishing Co.

Ryles, Briony & Hall, Derek. Medieval Period & the Renaissance. 2010. (CC: Technology Through the Ages Ser.). 112p. (gr. 6-12). 42.80 (978-1-933834-84-9(6)) Brown Bear Bks.

—The Scientific Revolution. 2010. (Curriculum Connections: Technology Through the Ages Ser.). 112p. 39.95 (978-1-933834-85-6(4)) Brown Bear Bks.

Samuels, Charlie. Medieval Science (500 - 1500), 1 vol. 2010. (Science Highlights: a Gareth Stevens Timeline Ser.). (ENG.). 48p. (J). (gr. 6-8). pap. 15.05 (978-1-4339-4140-5(6), 7f53e548-3ae3-4089-9292-abd78c196f41); lib. bdg. 34.60 (978-1-4339-4139-9(2), ead83189-db33-4574-80b5-01ad0f58cb57) Stevens, Gareth Publishing LLLP. (Gareth Stevens Secondary Library).

Santos, Penelope. Old & New, 1 vol. 2015. (Rosen REAL Readers: STEM & STEAM Collection). (ENG.). 8p. (gr. k-1). pap. 5.46 (978-1-4994-9715-1(6), 69fde47a-0890-41f1-8e27-645b09775020, Rosen Classroom) Rosen Publishing Group, Inc., The.

Saunders-Smith, Gail. Tiny Robots, 1 vol. 2014. (Cool Robots Ser.). (ENG.). 24p. (J). (gr. -1-2). 27.32 (978-1-4914-0587-1(2), 125925, Capstone Pr.) Capstone.

Schmermund, Elizabeth. Women in Technology, 1 vol. 2016. (Defying Convention: Women Who Changed the Rules Ser.). (ENG., Illus.). 128p. (gr. 6-6). 38.93 (978-0-7660-8149-9(4), e827fb9f-7ca6-4d1a-86ff-4492be4630c5) Enslow Publishing, LLC.

Schwartz, Heather, et al. Tech Safety Smarts Classroom Collection. 2013. (Tech Safety Smarts Ser.). (ENG.). 32p. (J). (gr. 3-4). pap., pap., pap. 190.80 (978-1-62065-805-5(4), 19386, Capstone Pr.) Capstone.

Schwartz, Heather E. Incredible Tech Trivia: Fun Facts & Quizzes. 2018. (Trivia Time! (Alternator Books (r)) Ser.). (ENG., Illus.). 32p. (J). (gr. 3-6). lib. bdg. 29.32 (978-1-5124-8332-1(X), b604beb4-0a2a-4a42-82d4-26b3ef2e1d05, Lerner Pubns.) Lerner Publishing Group.

Science & Technology for Children Books, Physical Sciences & Technology Library Set, 6 vols. 2004. (Illus.). 64p. (J). (978-1-933008-26-4(1)) Smithsonian Science Education Ctr. (SSEC).

Science & Technology for Children Books, Technology of Paper Set, 8 vols. 2004. (Illus.). 64p. (J). (978-1-933008-23-3(7)) Smithsonian Science Education Ctr. (SSEC).

Scientific American Staff. Extreme Engineering. 2009. (Scientific American Cutting-Edge Science Ser.). 120p. (gr. 9-9). 63.90 (978-1-60853-075-5(2)) Rosen Publishing Group, Inc., The.

—The Nanotech Revolution. 2009. (Scientific American Cutting-Edge Science Ser.). 136p. (gr. 9-9). 63.90 (978-1-60853-082-3(5)) Rosen Publishing Group, Inc., The.

Scott Foresman Reading: Technology. 2004. (Scott Foresman Reading Ser.). (gr. 1-18). cd-rom (978-0-328-04995-0(6)); (gr. 2-18). cd-rom (978-0-328-09379-3(3)); (gr. 2-18). cd-rom (978-0-328-08691-7(6)); (gr. 2-18). cd-rom (978-0-328-04996-7(4)); (gr. 2-18). cd-rom (978-0-328-09374-8(2)); (gr. 2-18). cd-rom (978-0-328-08681-8(9)); (gr. 2-6). cd-rom (978-0-328-09384-7(X)); (gr. 2-6). cd-rom (978-0-328-08680-1(0)); (gr. 3-18). cd-rom (978-0-328-09380-9(7)); (gr. 3-18). cd-rom (978-0-328-08692-4(4)); (gr. 3-18). cd-rom (978-0-328-04997-4(2)); (gr. 3-18). cd-rom (978-0-328-09375-5(0)); (gr. 3-18). cd-rom (978-0-328-08682-5(7)); (gr. 4-18). cd-rom (978-0-328-08693-1(2)); (gr. 4-18). cd-rom (978-0-328-08683-2(5)); (gr. 4-18). cd-rom (978-0-328-04998-1(0)); (gr. 4-18). cd-rom (978-0-328-09381-6(5)); (gr. 5-18). cd-rom (978-0-328-08694-8(0)); (gr. 5-18). cd-rom (978-0-328-08684-9(3)); (gr. 5-18). cd-rom (978-0-328-04999-8(9)); (gr. 5-18). cd-rom (978-0-328-09377-9(7)); (gr. 5-18). cd-rom (978-0-328-09382-3(3)); (gr. 6-18). cd-rom (978-0-328-08695-5(9)); (gr. 6-18). cd-rom (978-0-328-08685-6(1)); (gr. 6-18). cd-rom (978-0-328-05000-0(8)); (gr. 6-18). cd-rom (978-0-328-09378-6(5)); (gr. 6-18). cd-rom (978-0-328-09383-0(1)) Addison-Wesley Educational Pubs., Inc. (Scott Foresman).

Sebastian, Emily. Technology of the Medieval & Early Modern Worlds, 1 vol., 1. 2015. (History of Technology Ser.). (ENG.). 112p. (J). (gr. 8-8). 35.47 (978-1-68048-274-4(2), 876e5df8-9fb4-42b2-9374-280c159a27ee, Britannica Educational Publishing) Rosen Publishing Group, Inc., The.

Second Grade Technology: 32-Lesson Comprehensive Curriculum, 6 vols. 2016. (ENG., Illus.). 225p. 32.99 net. (978-0-9787800-2-9(7)) Structured Learning LLC.

Shand, Jennifer. Why Do Computers Know So Much? 2015. (Why Do... ? Ser.). lib. bdg. 19.65 (978-1-4867-0622-8(3)) Turtleback.

Shoup, Kate. The Technology of Ancient Greece, 1 vol. 2016. (Ancient Innovations Ser.). (ENG.). 64p. (gr. 6-6). 35.93 (978-1-5026-2231-0(9), b89700dd-0c36-4559-8cc3-9d8c4d20dffd) Cavendish Square Publishing LLC.

Sirota, Lyn A. Science Lab: Technological Design. 2011. (Explorer Library: Language Arts Explorer Ser.). (ENG.). 32p. (gr. 4-8). pap. 14.21 (978-1-61080-297-0(7), 201219) Cherry Lake Publishing.

—Science Lab: Technological Design. 2011. (Explorer Library: Language Arts Explorer Ser.). (ENG., Illus.). 32p. (gr. 4-8). lib. bdg. 32.07 (978-1-61080-208-6(X), 201192) Cherry Lake Publishing.

Slingerland, Janet. Wi-Fi. 2017. (How It Works). (ENG., Illus.). 32p. (J). (gr. 3-5). pap. 9.95 (978-1-63517-305-5(1), 1635173051); lib. bdg. 31.35 (978-1-63517-240-9(3), 1635172403) North Star Editions. (Focus Readers).

Small, Cathleen. Fab Lab Creating with Vinyl Cutters, 1 vol. 2016. (Getting Creative with Fab Lab Ser.). (ENG.). 64p. (J). (gr. 6-6). 36.13 (978-1-5081-7350-2(8), e849f08c-76ad-4558-a5ef-9a99fbad08d7) Rosen Publishing Group, Inc., The.

Smibert, Angie. Technology Myths, Busted! 2017. (Science Myths, Busted! Ser.). (ENG., Illus.). 32p. (J). (gr. 3-6). 32.80 (978-1-63235-306-1(7), 11811, 12-Story Library) Bookstaves, LLC.

Smith, Jonathan. Struggling with Social Media. 2017. (J). *(978-1-939881-17-5(X))* TRISTAN Publishing, Inc.
Snedden, Robert. Ancient China. 2009. (Technology in Times Past Ser.). 32.80 *(978-1-59920-298-3(0))* Black Rabbit Bks.
—Ancient China. 2009. (Technology in Times Past Ser.). (ENG., Illus.). 48p. (J). (gr. 4-7). pap. *(978-1-897563-60-1(4))* Saunders Bk. Co.
—Ancient Greece. 2009. (Technology in Times Past Ser.). 32.80 *(978-1-59920-296-9(4))* Black Rabbit Bks.
—Aztec, Inca & Maya. 2009. (Technology in Times Past Ser.). (J). 32.80 *(978-1-59920-299-0(9))* Black Rabbit Bks.
—Aztec, Inca, & Maya. 2009. (Technology in Times Past Ser.). (ENG., Illus.). 48p. (J). (gr. 4-7). pap. *(978-1-897563-64-9(7))* Saunders Bk. Co.
—The Medieval World. 2009. (Technology in Times Past Ser.). (ENG., Illus.). 48p. (J). (gr. 4-7). pap. *(978-1-897563-65-6(5))* Saunders Bk. Co.
Solodky, M. The Technology of Ancient Egypt. (Technology of the Ancient World Ser.). 48p. (gr. 6-6). 2009. 61.20 *(978-1-60854-239-0(4)*, Rosen Reference) 2006. (ENG., Illus.). (J). lib. bdg. 34.47 *(978-1-4042-0557-4(8)*, fdcfa82d-1557-4dd1-ae2f-4c42b04f1bf9) Rosen Publishing Group, Inc., The.
Spence, Kelly. Tech Living. 2017. (Techno Planet Ser.). (Illus.). 32p. (J). (gr. 5-5). *(978-0-7787-3605-9(9))* Crabtree Publishing Co.
Spilsbury, Louise. Wheels & Axles, 1 vol. 2018. (Technology in Action Ser.). (ENG.). 32p. (gr. 3-3). 27.93 *(978-1-5383-3769-1(X)*, 5eb2218d-4d7f-409c-85e1-811b930210fa, PowerKids Pr.) Rosen Publishing Group, Inc., The.
Step-By-Step Transformations, 12 vols. 2014. (Step-By-Step Transformations Ser.). (ENG.). 24p. (J). (gr. 1-1). 155.58 *(978-1-62713-142-1(6)*, 6f042ede-4cdb-43c9-b88a-abd3839fd380, Cavendish Square) Cavendish Square Publishing LLC.
Steve, Parker. What about Science & Technology. 2008. 40p. pap. *(978-1-84810-074-9(4))* Miles Kelly Publishing, Ltd.
Strain Trueit, Trudi. The Vikings, 1 vol. 2012. (Technology of the Ancients Ser.). (ENG.). 64p. (gr. 6-6). 35.50 *(978-1-60870-769-0(5)*, bfde65a9-f39b-43d0-98ff-f355d9f71ac8) Cavendish Square Publishing LLC.
Sundance/Newbridge LLC Staff. For Your Information. 2007. (Early Science Ser.). (gr. k-3). 18.95 *(978-1-4007-6567-6(6))*; pap. 6.10 *(978-1-4007-6563-8(3))* Sundance/Newbridge Educational Publishing.
—How Life Changed. 2004. (Reading PowerWorks Ser.). (gr. 1-3). 37.50 *(978-0-7608-7815-6(3))*; pap. 6.10 *(978-0-7608-7816-3(1))* Sundance/Newbridge Educational Publishing.
—People & Technology. 2004. (Reading PowerWorks Ser.). (gr. 1-3). 37.50 *(978-0-7608-9771-3(9))*; pap. 6.10 *(978-0-7608-9772-0(7))* Sundance/Newbridge Educational Publishing.
—What Is Technology? 2007. (Early Science Ser.). (gr. k-3). 18.95 *(978-1-4007-6585-0(4))*; pap. 6.10 *(978-1-4007-6581-2(1))* Sundance/Newbridge Educational Publishing.
Tech Girls: Set 2, 14 vols. 2018. (Tech Girls Ser.). (ENG.). 80p. (gr. 7-7). lib. bdg. 262.29 *(978-1-5081-8089-0(X)*, 0d9f7abd-9e0e-40c2-b675-94611be11a61) Rosen Publishing Group, Inc., The.
Technology Takes on Nature. 2016. (Technology Takes on Nature Ser.). 00032p. (J). pap. 63.00 *(978-1-4824-5846-6(2))* Stevens, Gareth Publishing LLLP.
Technology Through Time, 3 bks., Set. Incl. Communication Through Time. Oxlade, Chris. lib. bdg. 18.98 *(978-0-8172-4141-4(8))*; Ships Through Time. Richards, Roy. lib. bdg. 18.98 *(978-0-8172-4138-4(8))*; Toys Through Time. Oxlade, Chris. lib. bdg. 18.98 *(978-0-8172-4139-1(6))*; 48p. (J). (gr. 4-8). 1996. (Illus.). Set lib. bdg. 56.94 *(978-0-7398-3299-8(9))* Heinemann-Raintree.
Technosports: Individual Title, 6 packs. (Bookweb Ser.). 32p. (gr. 4-18). 34.00 *(978-0-7635-3746-3(2))* Rigby Education.
Third Grade Technology: 32-Lesson Comprehensive Curriculum, 6 vols. 2016. (ENG., Illus.). 242p. 32.99 net. *(978-0-9787800-3-6(5))* Structured Learning LLC.
Thomas, Mark. Maracana: El Estadio de Futbol Mas Grande del Mundo, 1 vol. 2003. (Estructuras Extraordinarias (Record-Breaking Structures) Ser.). (SPA., Illus.). 24p. (J). (gr. 2-2). lib. bdg. 26.27 *(978-0-8239-6863-3(4)*, 08dba28b-cd8a-4778-a0e1-b5dcb10377ac, Editorial Buenas Letras) Rosen Publishing Group, Inc., The.
—La Represa de Itaipu: La Represa Mas Grande Del Mundo, 1 vol. 2003. (Estructuras Extraordinarias (Record-Breaking Structures) Ser.). (SPA., Illus.). 24p. (J). (gr. 2-2). lib. bdg. 26.27 *(978-0-8239-6865-7(0)*, 20a9ed26-3a13-4f41-ad09-56f9b54f55f8, Editorial Buenas Letras) Rosen Publishing Group, Inc., The.
Thompson, Veronica. Earth-Friendly Tech Crafts. Thompson, Veronica, photos by. 2018. (Green STEAM Ser.). (ENG., Illus.). 32p. (J). (gr. 3-5). pap. 9.99 *(978-1-5415-2783-6(6)*, e8358290-a14a-4efa-9b60-4f947388db68); lib. bdg. 29.32 *(978-1-5415-2417-0(9)*, cd62244f-4bf2-4e99-9101-65cbf48ef5de, Lerner Pubns.) Lerner Publishing Group.
Time for Kids Editors. Stellar Space. 2014. (Time for Kids Book of Why Ser.). (ENG., Illus.). 48p. (J). (gr. 3-17). pap. 4.99 *(978-1-60320-985-4(9)*, Time For Kids) Time Inc. Bks.
Top That Publishing Staff. Today's Technology. 2006. (Illus.). 48p. *(978-1-84510-013-1(1))* Top That! Publishing PLC.
Transforming Power of Technology, 6 vols. 2005. (Transforming Power of Technology Ser.). (Illus.). 100p. (C). (gr. 9-13). 180.00 *(978-0-7910-7447-3(1)*, Facts On File) Infobase Holdings, Inc.
Trowbridge, J. T. Lawrence's Adventures among the Ice-Cutters, Glass-Makers, Coal-Miners, Iron-Men, & Ship-Builders by J T Trowbridge. 2006. 256p. per. 23.99 *(978-1-4255-2277-3(7))* Michigan Publishing.
Turney, Jon. Technology - Ethical Debates about the Application of Science. 2008. (Dilemmas in Modern Science Ser.). (ENG., Illus.). 48p. (J). 23.99 *(978-0-237-53370-0(7))* Evans Brothers, Ltd. GBR. Dist: Independent Pubs. Group.
Uhl, Xina M. How STEM Built the Roman Empire, 1 vol. 2019. (How STEM Built Empires Ser.). (ENG.). 80p. (gr. 7-7). pap. 16.30 *(978-1-7253-4152-4(2)*, aea2ce53-1be1-444e-b122-08dbb30985d4) Rosen Publishing Group, Inc., The.
—The Railroad, the Telegraph, & Other Technologies. 2017. (Westward Expansion: America's Push to the Pacific Ser.). (Illus.). 48p. (J). (gr. 10-14). 84.30 *(978-1-5383-0016-9(8)*, Britannica Educational Publishing) Rosen Publishing Group, Inc., The.
Vallencourt, Margaret. Technology of the Industrial Revolution, 1 vol., 1. 2015. (History of Technology Ser.). (ENG., Illus.). 112p. (J). (gr. 8-8). lib. bdg. 35.47 *(978-1-68048-275-1(0)*, 4344a53d-aa08-4fe4-9c37-a58a82148c7e, Britannica Educational Publishing) Rosen Publishing Group, Inc., The.
Vance, Ashlee. Elon Musk & the Quest for a Fantastic Future Young Readers' Edition. 2017. (ENG.). 288p. (J). (gr. 3). pap. 7.99 *(978-0-06-246327-2(6))*; (Illus.). 16.99 *(978-0-06-246328-9(4))* HarperCollins Pubs. (HarperCollins).
—Elon Musk & the Quest for a Fantastic Future Young Reader's Edition. 2018. (ENG.). 288p. (J). (gr. 3). pap. 6.99 *(978-0-06-286243-3(X)*, HarperCollins) HarperCollins Pubs.
Verstraete, Larry. Innovations in Everyday Technologies. 2016. (Problem Solved! Your Turn to Think Big Ser.). (ENG., Illus.). 32p. (J). (gr. 3-6). *(978-0-7787-2678-4(9))* Crabtree Publishing Co.
Wainewright, Max. I'm an App Developer. 2017. (Generation Code Ser.). (Illus.). 32p. (J). (gr. 5-5). *(978-0-7787-3514-4(1))* Crabtree Publishing Co.
Ward, Lesley. Tech World: Cell Phone Pros & Cons (Level 4) 2017. (TIME for KIDS(r): Informational Text Ser.). (ENG., Illus.). 32p. (J). (gr. 3-5). pap. 12.99 *(978-1-4258-4977-1(6))* Teacher Created Materials, Inc.
Weaver, Janice. The a to Z of Everyday Things. Blake, Francis, illus. 2004. 128p. (J). (gr. 5). pap. 8.95 *(978-0-88776-671-8(4)*, Tundra Bks.) Tundra Bks. CAN. Dist: Penguin Random Hse. LLC.
Welsbacher, Anne. Earth-Friendly Design. 2009. pap. 58.95 *(978-0-7613-4693-7(7))* Lerner Publishing Group.
What About..., 10 vols., Set. Incl. Dinosaurs. Matthews, Rupert. lib. bdg. 19.95 *(978-1-4222-1558-6(X))*; History. Williams, Brian. lib. bdg. 19.95 *(978-1-4222-1559-3(8))*; How We Live. Williams, Brian. lib. bdg. 19.95 *(978-1-4222-1560-9(1))*; Human Body. Parker, Steve. lib. bdg. 19.95 *(978-1-4222-1561-6(X))*; Natural World. Williams, Brian. lib. bdg. 19.95 *(978-1-4222-1562-3(8))*; People & Places. Williams, Brian. lib. bdg. 19.95 *(978-1-4222-1563-0(6))*; Planet Earth. Williams, Brian. lib. bdg. 19.95 *(978-1-4222-1564-7(4))*; Science & Technology. Parker, Steve. lib. bdg. 19.95 *(978-1-4222-1565-4(2))*; Universe. Williams, Brian. lib. bdg. 19.95 *(978-1-4222-1566-1(0))*; World Wonders. Williams, Brian. lib. bdg. 19.95 *(978-1-4222-1567-8(9))*; (J). (gr. 6-8). 2010. (Question & Answer Book Ser.). (Illus.). 40p. 2009. Set lib. bdg. 199.50 *(978-1-4222-1557-9(1))* Mason Crest.
Wilcox, Dominic & Mengardon, Katherine. The Little Inventors Handbook. 2019. (Little Inventors Ser.). (ENG.). 152p. (J). (gr. k-3). pap. 16.95 *(978-0-00-830615-1(X))* HarperCollins Pubs. Ltd. GBR. Dist: Independent Pubs. Group.
Willis, Laurie, ed. Electronic Devices in Schools, 1 vol. 2012. (Issues That Concern You Ser.). (ENG., Illus.). 104p. (gr. 7-10). lib. bdg. 43.63 *(978-0-7377-6292-1(6)*, c8431956-6cac-43ae-9218-e0b5e4388802, Greenhaven Publishing) Greenhaven Publishing LLC.
Wirkner, Linda. Learning about the American Revolution with Graphic Organizers. 2009. (Graphic Organizers in Social Studies). 24p. (gr. 3-4). 42.50 *(978-1-61513-083-2(7)*, PowerKids Pr.) Rosen Publishing Group, Inc., The.
Wood, John. Gaming Technology: Streaming, VR, & More, 1 vol. 2018. (STEM in Our World Ser.). (ENG.). 32p. (gr. 4-5). lib. bdg. 28.27 *(978-1-5382-2638-4(3)*, 83e47978-d96c-4323-a9d4-827b44408167) Stevens, Gareth Publishing LLLP.
—Space Technology: Landers, Space Tourism, & More, 1 vol. 2018. (STEM in Our World Ser.). (ENG.). 32p. (gr. 4-5). lib. bdg. 28.27 *(978-1-5382-2642-1(1)*, ee6b06a6-170b-4ebc-a2ba-bc16006dcac6) Stevens, Gareth Publishing LLLP.
—Sports Technology: Cryotherapy, LED Courts, & More, 1 vol. 2018. (STEM in Our World Ser.). (ENG.). 32p. (gr. 4-5). lib. bdg. 28.27 *(978-1-5382-2634-6(0)*, d3b5857c-3ce7-4d27-adaa-0cd8da1c2185) Stevens, Gareth Publishing LLLP.
Woods, Michael & Woods, Mary B. Technology in Ancient Cultures, 8 vols., Set. Incl. Ancient Agricultural Technology: From Sickles to Plows. lib. bdg. 31.93 *(978-0-7613-6526-6(5))*; Ancient Communication Technology: From Hieroglyphics to Scrolls. lib. bdg. 31.93 *(978-0-7613-6529-7(X))*; Ancient Computing Technology: From Abacuses to Water Clocks. lib. bdg. 31.93 *(978-0-7613-6528-0(1))*; Ancient Construction Technology: From Pyramids to Fortresses. (Illus.). (J). lib. bdg. 31.93 *(978-0-7613-6527-3(3))*; Ancient Machine Technology: From Wheels to Forges. lib. bdg. 31.93 *(978-0-7613-6523-5(0))*; Ancient Medical Technology: From Herbs to Scalpels. lib. bdg. 31.93 *(978-0-7613-6522-8(2))*; Ancient Transportation Technology: From Oars to Elephants. (Illus.). (J). lib. bdg. 31.93 *(978-0-7613-6524-2(9))*; Ancient Warfare Technology: From Javelins to Chariots. (Illus.). (J). lib. bdg. 31.93 *(978-0-7613-6525-9(7))*; 96p. (gr. 6-12). 2011. (Technology in Ancient Cultures Ser.). (ENG.). 2011. Set lib. bdg. 255.44 *(978-0-7613-6521-1(4)*, Twenty-First Century Bks.) Lerner Publishing Group.
Woolf, Alex. The Impact of Technology in Art. 2015. (Impact of Technology Ser.). (ENG., Illus.). 56p. (J). (gr. 6-9). 37.32 *(978-1-4846-2635-1(4)*, 130094, Heinemann) Capstone.
World Book, Inc. Staff, contrib. by. Architecture & Engineering. 2009. (J). *(978-0-7166-0386-3(1))* World Bk., Inc.
—Earth & Space. 2008. (J). *(978-0-7166-3016-6(8))* World Bk., Inc.
—Science & Technology. 2008. (J). *(978-0-7166-3018-0(4))* World Bk., Inc.
—Smoke Signals to Smartphones: A Timeline of Long-Distance Communication. 2016. (Illus.). 40p. (J). *(978-0-7166-3543-7(7))*; *(978-0-7166-3539-0(9))* World Bk., Inc.
Yomtov, Nel. War on Terror Technology. 2017. (War Technology Ser.). (ENG., Illus.). 48p. (J). (gr. 4-8). lib. bdg. 35.64 *(978-1-5321-1191-4(6)*, 25958) ABDO Publishing Co.
Zuckerman, Amy & Daly, James. 2030: A Day in the Life of Tomorrow's Kids. Manders, John, illus. 2009. 32p. (J). (gr. 1-3). 17.99 *(978-0-525-47860-7(4)*, Dutton Books for Young Readers) Penguin Young Readers Group.
Zumbusch, Amelie von. Ancient Roman Technology, 1 vol. 2013. (Spotlight on Ancient Civilizations: Rome Ser.). (ENG., Illus.). 24p. (J). (gr. 3-4). pap. 11.00 *(978-1-4777-0893-4(6)*, d6c2dd67-6877-4ff3-b870-972522b18165, PowerKids Pr.) Rosen Publishing Group, Inc., The.
Zumbusch, Amelie Von & Von Zumbusch, Amelie. Ancient Roman Technology, 1 vol. 2013. (Spotlight on Ancient Civilizations: Rome Ser.). (ENG.). 24p. (J). (gr. 3-4). 26.27 *(978-1-4777-0780-7(8)*, 0f5fd559-8cfd-4234-8f30-9e29e8780433, PowerKids Pr.) Rosen Publishing Group, Inc., The.

TECHNOLOGY—DICTIONARIES

Hackney Blackwell, Amy & Manar, Elizabeth P. UXL Encyclopedia of Science. 2015. (Illus.). 10p. (YA). *(978-1-4144-3085-0(X))* Cengage Gale.
Holt, Rinehart and Winston Staff. Earth Science. 5th ed. 2003. (Holt Science & Technology Ser.). (ENG., Illus.). 880p. (gr. 7-7). 103.35 *(978-0-03-066478-6(0))* Houghton Mifflin Harcourt Publishing Co.
—Holt Science & Technology: Online Edition Upgrade. 2nd ed. 2003. Level A. 2.60 *(978-0-03-037236-0(4))*Level K. 2.60 *(978-0-03-037248-3(8))* Holt McDougal.
—Life Science. 5th ed. 2003. (Holt Science & Technology Ser.). (ENG., Illus.). 912p. (gr. 6-6). 103.35 *(978-0-03-066476-2(4))* Houghton Mifflin Harcourt Publishing Co.
—Physical Science. 5th ed. 2003. (Holt Science & Technology Ser.). (ENG., Illus.). 848p. (gr. 8-8). 103.35 *(978-0-03-066481-6(0))* Houghton Mifflin Harcourt Publishing Co.
U X L, ed. UXL Encyclopedia of Science, 10 vols. 3rd ed. 2015. (U-X-L Encyclopedia of Science Ser.). (ENG., Illus.). 10p. 995.00 *(978-1-4144-3075-1(2)*, UXL) Cengage Gale.
World Book, Inc. Staff, contrib. by. Technology. 2014. (Illus.). 352p. (J). *(978-0-7166-7517-4(X))* World Bk., Inc.

TECHNOLOGY—FICTION

Anderson, Taylor. Storm Surge. 2014. (Destroyermen Ser.: 8). 512p. (gr. 12). mass mkt. 9.99 *(978-0-451-41909-5(X)*, Ace) Penguin Publishing Group.
Anne, Paula. Sultry Smith. 2009. 80p. pap. 9.99 *(978-1-60860-970-3(7)*, Eloquent Bks.) Strategic Book Publishing & Rights Agency (SBPRA).
Appleton, Victor. Tom Swift & His Wireless Message. 2007. 220p. 24.95 *(978-1-4344-9231-9(1))*; per. 14.95 *(978-1-4344-9137-4(4))* Wildside Pr., LLC.
Bacon, Lee. The Last Human. 2019. (Last Human Ser.). (ENG., Illus.). 288p. (YA). (gr. 3-7). 16.99 *(978-1-4197-3691-9(4)*, 1266301, Amulet Bks.) Abrams, Inc.
Burton, Virginia Lee. Mike Mulligan & His Steam Shovel Lap Board Book. 2010. (ENG., Illus.). 40p. (J). (gr. -1-k). bds. 11.99 *(978-0-547-38566-2(8)*, 1425919, Clarion Bks.) HarperCollins Pubs.
Cannon, Deborah. The Pirate Vortex: Elizabeth Latimer, Pirate Hunter. 2009. 260p. pap. 20.00 *(978-1-4269-0532-2(7))* Trafford Publishing.
Carman, Patrick. Pulse. 2013. (Pulse Ser.: 1). (ENG.). 384p. (YA). (gr. 8). 17.99 *(978-0-06-208576-4(X)*, Tegen, Katherine Bks) HarperCollins Pubs.
—Quake. 2016. (Pulse Ser.: 3). (ENG.). 288p. (YA). (gr. 8). pap. 10.99 *(978-0-06-208597-9(2)*, Tegen, Katherine Bks) HarperCollins Pubs.
Chwast, Seymour. Arno & the MiniMachine. Chwast, Seymour, illus. 2019. (Illus.). 32p. (J). (gr. -1-3). 17.95 *(978-1-60980-879-2(7)*, Triangle Square) Seven Stories Pr.
Darke, J. A. Tech Fury. Evergreen, Nelson, illus. 2015. (Spine Shivers Ser.). (ENG.). 128p. (J). (gr. 4-6). lib. bdg. 27.32 *(978-1-4965-0218-6(3)*, 128032, Stone Arch Bks.) Capstone.
Fine, Sarah. Beneath the Shine. 2017. (ENG.). 304p. (YA). (gr. 10-13). pap. 9.99 *(978-1-4778-2327-9(1)*, 9781477823279, Skyscape) Amazon Publishing.
Flores, Valeria R. ¿Como Se Metieron Ahi?/How'd They Get In There? Flores, Valeria R., illus. 2012. (ENG.). 28p. pap. 21.99 *(978-1-4653-0884-9(9))* Xlibris Corp.
Golden Books. Combine It & Design It! (Rusty Rivets) Golden Books, illus. 2018. (ENG., Illus.). 64p. (J). (gr. -1-2). pap. 5.99 *(978-1-5247-6793-8(X)*, Golden Bks.) Random Hse. Children's Bks.
Grant, Michael. Bzrk. (Bzrk Ser.). (ENG.). 400p. (YA). (gr. 9-12). 2013. pap. 9.99 *(978-1-60684-418-2(0)*, be48eae0-186e-42f3-9a8f-7a9a80661ce8) 2012. 17.99 *(978-1-60684-312-3(5)*, ba9d46d5-5aa2-4bc4-bb35-da33ac28de6c) Lerner Publishing Group. (Carolrhoda Lab™).
—BZRK Reloaded. 2013. (Bzrk Ser.). (ENG.). 432p. (YA). (gr. 9-12). 18.99 *(978-1-60684-394-9(X)*, 20fe8bbb-63fa-40af-8c0e-54890e077fe3, Carolrhoda Lab™) Lerner Publishing Group.
Harmer, Wendy. I Lost My Mobile at the Mall. 2011. (ENG.). 272p. (YA). (gr. 7-18). 10.99 *(978-1-935279-97-6(1))* Kane Miller.
Hautman, Pete. The Flinkwater Factor. 2015. (Flinkwater Chronicles Ser.: 1). (ENG.). 256p. (J). (gr. 4-8). 19.99 *(978-1-4814-3251-1(6)*, Simon & Schuster Bks. For Young Readers) Simon & Schuster Bks. For Young Readers.
Hawking, Lucy. George & the Ship of Time. Parsons, Garry, illus. 2019. (George's Secret Key Ser.). (ENG.). 416p. (J). (gr. 3-7). 18.99 *(978-1-5344-3730-2(4)*, Simon & Schuster Bks. For Young Readers) Simon & Schuster Bks. For Young Readers.
Holden, Pam. Simple Technology & Other Stories. 2018. (ENG., Illus.). 136p. (J). lib. bdg. *(978-1-77654-204-8(5)*, Red Rocket Readers) Flying Start Bks.
Hord, Colleen. Everyone Uses Technology. 2015. (Little World Everyone Everywhere Ser.). (ENG.). 24p. (gr. k-3). 28.50 *(978-1-63430-361-3(X)*, 9781634303613) Rourke Educational Media.
Kesselring, Mari. Digital Reveal. Epelbaum, Mariano, illus. 2015. (Bridget Gadget Ser.). (ENG.). 64p. (J). (gr. 3-6). *(978-1-63235-040-4(8)*, 11635, 12-Story Library) Bookstaves, LLC.
—Techie Cheater. Epelbaum, Mariano, illus. 2015. (Bridget Gadget Ser.). (ENG.). 64p. (J). (gr. 3-6). *(978-1-63235-038-1(6)*, 11633, 12-Story Library) Bookstaves, LLC.
Klise, Kate. The Phantom of the Post Office. Klise, M. Sarah, illus. 2013. (43 Old Cemetery Road Ser.: 4). (ENG.). 160p. (J). (gr. 3-7). pap. 7.99 *(978-0-544-02281-2(5)*, 1528502, Clarion Bks.) HarperCollins Pubs.
—The Phantom of the Post Office. 2013. (43 Old Cemetery Road Ser.: 4). lib. bdg. 17.20 *(978-0-606-31668-2(X))* Turtleback.
Lancaster, Mike A. Dotwav. (ENG.). 2017. 456p. (YA). (gr. 7-7). pap. 9.99 *(978-1-5107-2659-8(4))* 2016. 448p. (J). (gr. 6-6). 17.99 *(978-1-5107-0404-6(3))* Skyhorse Publishing Co., Inc. (Sky Pony Pr.).
Leiber, Fritz. The Creature from Cleveland Depths. 2009. 76p. pap. 7.95 *(978-1-60664-286-3(3))* Rodgers, Alan Bks.
Lynch, Chris. In a Wired Future, Animals Need Our Help. 2010. (Cyberia Ser.: 1). (ENG.). 160p. (J). (gr. 4-6). 18.69 *(978-0-545-02796-0(9))* Scholastic, Inc.
—Monkey See, Monkey Don't. 2011. (Cyberia Ser.: 2). (ENG.). 144p. (J). (gr. 4-7). pap. 5.99 *(978-0-545-02797-7(7))* Scholastic, Inc.
Mbuyazi, Phiwayinkosi G. The Wiby Kids - How It All Began. 2011. 204p. pap. 12.99 *(978-1-61667-337-6(0))* Raider Publishing International.
McCloskey, Shanda. Doll-E 1. 0. 2018. (ENG., Illus.). 40p. (J). (gr. -1-3). 18.99 *(978-0-316-51031-8(9))* Little, Brown Bks. for Young Readers.
Melbourne, Lois. The STEM Club Goes Exploring. 2016. (ENG., Illus.). 48p. 15.95 *(978-1-62634-303-0(9))* Greenleaf Book Group.
Nanatsuki, Kyoichi. Project Arms, Vol. 13. Nanatsuki, Kyoichi, illus. 2006. (Project Arms Ser.). (ENG., Illus.). 208p. pap. 9.99 *(978-1-4215-0502-2(9))* Viz Media.
Nye, Barry. Hannah & the Magic Blanket - Land of the Robots. 2009. (ENG.). 40p. pap. 18.50 *(978-0-557-06602-5(6))* Lulu Pr., Inc.
Perry, Fred & Dlin, Doug. Gold Digger Tech Manual. 2011. (ENG.). 352p. (YA). pap., pap. 19.99 *(978-0-9844879-7-4(2)*, d4b0f957-8fe9-4c47-bc07-786055531e90) Antarctic Pr., Inc.
Reeve, Philip. Fever Crumb (the Fever Crumb Trilogy, Book 1), Bk. 1. 2011. (Fever Crumb Ser.: 1). (ENG.). 336p. (YA). (gr. 7-7). pap. 12.99 *(978-0-545-22215-0(X))* Scholastic, Inc.
—A Web of Air (the Fever Crumb Trilogy, Book 2), 2. Seife, Emily, ed. 2013. (Fever Crumb Ser.: 2). (ENG.). 304p. (YA). (gr. 7-12). pap. 9.99 *(978-0-545-22217-4(6))* Scholastic, Inc.
Savage, J. Scott. Fires of Invention. 2015. (Mysteries of Cove Ser.: 1). (ENG., Illus.). 320p. (J). (gr. 5). 17.99 *(978-1-62972-092-0(5)*, 5139121, Shadow Mountain) Shadow Mountain Publishing.
—Gears of Revolution. 2016. (Mysteries of Cove Ser.: 2). (ENG., Illus.). 352p. (J). (gr. 3-6). 17.99 *(978-1-62972-223-8(5)*, 5155663, Shadow Mountain) Shadow Mountain Publishing.
Serwacki, Kevin & Pallace, Chris. Joey & Johnny, the Ninjas: Get Mooned. Serwacki, Kevin & Pallace, Chris, illus. 2015. (Joey & Johnny, the Ninjas Ser.: 1). (ENG., Illus.). 320p. (J). (gr. 3-7). 12.99 *(978-0-06-229933-8(6)*, Balzer & Bray) HarperCollins Pubs.
Snell, Roy J. Curlie Carson Listens In. 2009. 108p. 22.95 *(978-1-60664-674-8(5))*; 100p. pap. 8.95 *(978-1-60664-303-7(7))* Rodgers, Alan Bks.
Stepp, Shirley. Santa Lost His Cell Phone. 2012. 24p. 24.95 *(978-1-4626-5479-6(7))* America Star Bks.
Wallach, Tommy. Slow Burn. 2018. (Anchor & Sophia Ser.: 2). (ENG., Illus.). 416p. (YA). (gr. 9). 18.99 *(978-1-4814-6841-1(3)*, Simon & Schuster Bks. For Young Readers) Simon & Schuster Bks. For Young Readers.
—Strange Fire. 2017. (Anchor & Sophia Ser.: 1). (ENG., Illus.). 400p. (YA). (gr. 9). 17.99 *(978-1-4814-6838-1(3)*, Simon & Schuster Bks. For Young Readers) Simon & Schuster Bks. For Young Readers.
Zuckerberg, Randi. Dot. Berger, Joe, illus. 2013. (ENG.). 32p. (J). (gr. -1-3). 18.99 *(978-0-06-228751-9(6)*, HarperCollins) HarperCollins Pubs.

TECHNOLOGY—VOCATIONAL GUIDANCE

Ching, Jacqueline. Jobs in Green Travel & Tourism. 2010. (Green Careers Ser.). 80p. (YA). (gr. 7-12). E-Book 61.20 *(978-1-4488-0134-3(6))* Rosen Publishing Group, Inc., The.
Colby, Jennifer. Computer Store. 2016. (21st Century Junior Library: Explore a Workplace Ser.). (ENG., Illus.). 24p. (J). (gr. 2-5). 29.21 *(978-1-63471-078-7(9)*, 208391) Cherry Lake Publishing.
Digital Career Building. 2013. (Digital Career Building Ser.). 64p. (YA). (gr. 7-12). pap. 466.20 *(978-1-4777-7806-7(3))*; pap. 77.70 *(978-1-4777-7807-4(1))* Rosen Publishing Group, Inc., The.
Digital Career Building: Set 3, 12 vols. 2013. (Digital Career Building Ser.). (ENG.). 64p. (YA). (gr. 6-6). 222.78 *(978-1-4777-1734-9(X)*, 6a3f2a57-6020-46e5-801e-a828f1338395) Rosen Publishing Group, Inc., The.
Hagler, Gina. Top STEM Careers in Engineering, 1 vol. 2014. (Cutting-Edge STEM Careers Ser.). (ENG.). 128p. (YA). (gr. 9-9). 38.80 *(978-1-4777-7672-8(9)*, 0da9fd1b-3bd5-479e-b127-d90e614c1ab3); pap. 19.85 *(978-1-4777-7674-2(5)*, 46f9ee79-18ed-498b-915a-13b307dc437f) Rosen Publishing Group, Inc., The.
Hand, Carol. Careers for Tech Girls in Technology, 1 vol. 2015. (Tech Girls Ser.). (ENG., Illus.). 80p. (J). (gr. 7-8). 37.47 *(978-1-4994-6099-5(6)*, 0501d6cf-8b6a-4972-bf7b-1aef5339af1e, Rosen Young Adult) Rosen Publishing Group, Inc., The.
La Bella, Laura. Top STEM Careers in Technology, 1 vol. 2014. (Cutting-Edge STEM Careers Ser.). (ENG., Illus.). 128p. (J). (gr. 9-9). 38.80 *(978-1-4777-7668-1(0)*, 22e22df9-16f7-4ce9-bffd-bfcb0882084d) Rosen Publishing Group, Inc., The.
LeBoutillier, Linda. Unusual & Awesome Jobs Using Technology: Roller Coaster Designer, Space Robotics Engineer, & More. 2015. (You Get Paid for THAT? Ser.). (ENG., Illus.). 32p. (J). (gr. 3-9). 28.65 *(978-1-4914-2029-4(4)*, 127507, Capstone Pr.) Capstone.
Marsico, Katie. Working at a Computer Store. 2009. (21st Century Junior Library: Careers Ser.). (ENG., Illus.). 24p. (gr. 2-5). lib. bdg. 29.21 *(978-1-60279-513-6(4)*, 200277) Cherry Lake Publishing.

TUV

Reeves, Diane Lindsey. Stem. 2017. (Bright Futures Press: World of Work Ser.). (ENG., Illus.). 32p. (J). (gr. 4-7). lib. bdg. 32.07 *(978-1-63472-628-3(6),* 209546) Cherry Lake Publishing.

Suen, Anastasia. Top STEM Careers in Science, 1 vol. 2014. (Cutting-Edge STEM Careers Ser.). (ENG., Illus.). 128p. (J). (gr. 9-9). 38.80 *(978-1-4777-7664-3(8),* 37125832-da8b-4594-8b87-788b3b896c8c) Rosen Publishing Group, Inc., The.

Turning Your Tech Hobbies into a Career, 14 vols. 2016. (Turning Your Tech Hobbies into a Career Ser.). (ENG.). 00080p. (J). (gr. 7-7). 262.29 *(978-1-5081-7362-5(1),* f2bc769b-b3f7-4401-b094-b38711d3c0b8, Rosen Young Adult) Rosen Publishing Group, Inc., The.

TECHNOLOGY AND CIVILIZATION

see also Machinery in the Workplace

Apel, Melanie Ann. Technology of Ancient Greece, 1 vol. 2003. (Primary Sources of Ancient Civilizations: Egypt, Greece, & Rome Ser.). (ENG., Illus.). 24p. (gr. 3-4). pap. 8.25 *(978-0-8239-8941-6(0),* 817d62fc-27bb-4223-b77f-70d342061276, PowerKids Pr.) Rosen Publishing Group, Inc., The.

Gedacht, Daniel C. Technology of Ancient Rome, 1 vol. 2003. (Primary Sources of Ancient Civilizations: Egypt, Greece, & Rome Ser.). (ENG., Illus.). 24p. (gr. 3-4). pap. 8.25 *(978-0-8239-8947-8(X),* 8dcd30b7-f2ef-4143-af99-9d0c2a688aab); (J). lib. bdg. 26.27 *(978-0-8239-6779-7(4),* 070ba49b-afa9-41b3-b831-63f186a9a8cc) Rosen Publishing Group, Inc., The. (PowerKids Pr.).

Maxim, Bailey. The 100 Most Influential Technology Leaders, 1 vol., 1. 2016. (Britannica Guide to the World's Most Influential People Ser.). (ENG., Illus.). 336p. (J). (gr. 10-10). lib. bdg. 56.59 *(978-1-68048-280-5(7),* 50b95650-416b-4aaf-bf8e-a95266a3d92f, Britannica Educational Publishing) Rosen Publishing Group, Inc., The.

Miller, Reagan & Richardson, Hazel. Technology in the Ancient World. 2011. (ENG., Illus.). 32p. (J). *(978-0-7787-1736-2(4))* Crabtree Publishing Co.

Miller, Reagan, et al. Technology in the Ancient World, 1 vol. Crabtree Publishing Co. Staff, ed. 2011. (Life in the Ancient World Ser.: No. 5). (ENG., Illus.). 32p. (J). (gr. 5-8). pap. *(978-0-7787-1743-0(7))* Crabtree Publishing Co.

Snedden, Robert. Ancient Egypt. 2009. (Technology in Times Past Ser.). (ENG., Illus.). 48p. (J). (gr. 4-7). pap. *(978-1-897563-61-8(2))* Saunders Bk. Co.

—Ancient Rome. 2009. (Technology in Times Past Ser.). (ENG., Illus.). 48p. (J). (gr. 4-7). pap. *(978-1-897563-63-2(9))* Saunders Bk. Co.

TECUMSEH, SHAWNEE CHIEF, 1768-1813

Aller, Susan Bivin. Tecumseh. 2004. (History Maker Bios Ser.). (J). pap. 6.95 *(978-0-8225-2073-3(7));* (ENG., Illus.). 48p. (gr. 3-6). 27.93 *(978-0-8225-0699-7(8),* Carolrhoda Bks.) Lerner Publishing Group.

Collier, James Lincoln. The Tecumseh You Never Knew. 2004. (You Never Knew Ser.). (ENG., Illus.). 80p. (J). 25.50 *(978-0-516-24426-6(4),* Children's Pr.) Scholastic Library Publishing.

Gordon, Irene. Tecumseh: Diplomat & Warrior in the War Of 1812. 2009. (Amazing Stories Ser.). (ENG., Illus.). 128p. (J). (gr. 6-12). pap. 9.95 *(978-1-55277-430-4(9),* 430) James Lorimer & Co. Ltd., Pubs. CAN. Dist: Formac Lorimer Bks. Ltd.

LaPlante, Walter. Tecumseh, 1 vol. 2015. (Native American Heroes Ser.). (ENG., Illus.). 24p. (J). (gr. 1-2). 24.27 *(978-1-4824-2706-6(0),* efb57d85-b12e-45a6-b2b3-2d384566022b) Stevens, Gareth Publishing LLLP.

Sjonger, Rebecca. Tecumseh: Speech at Vincennes. 2019. (Deconstructing Powerful Speeches Ser.). 48p. (J). (gr. 6-6). *(978-0-7787-5242-4(9));* pap. *(978-0-7787-5256-1(9))* Crabtree Publishing Co.

Zimmerman, Dwight Jon. Tecumseh: Shooting Star of the Shawnee. 2010. (Sterling Biographies Ser.). (ENG., Illus.). 128p. (J). (gr. 6-8). 18.69 *(978-1-4027-6847-7(8))* Sterling Publishing Co., Inc.

TEDDY BEARS

Bart, Kathleen. A Tale of Two Teddies. 2005. (ENG.). 32p. (J). *(978-1-932485-23-3(6))* Reverie Publishing Co.

Beck, Isabel L., et al. Trophies Kindergarten: Where's My Teddy? 2003. (Trophies Ser.). (gr. k-6). 13.80 *(978-0-15-329517-1(1))* Harcourt Schl. Pubs.

Hudson, Amanda. This Is My Bear / Éste Es Mi Oso, 1 vol. 2008. (Our Toys / Nuestros Juguetes Ser.). (SPA & ENG.). 16p. (gr. k-k). pap. 6.30 *(978-0-8368-9356-4(5),* c0f08e9a-97e6-4d05-a8ab-c3e7ee4c5936); (Illus.). (J). lib. bdg. 21.67 *(978-0-8368-9257-4(7),* f77425f0-d46b-4c49-bca2-e13c85e883ff) Stevens, Gareth Publishing LLLP. (Weekly Reader Leveled Readers).

Innes, Stephanie & Endrulat, Harry. A Bear in War. Deines, Brian, illus. 2019. (ENG.). 40p. (J). (gr. k-4). pap. 14.95 *(978-1-77278-086-4(3))* Pajama Pr. CAN. Dist: Publishers Group West (PGW).

Kay, Helen. The First Teddy Bear. Detwiler, Susan, illus. 2nd enl. ed. 2005. (ENG.). 38p. (J). (gr. -1-3). 18.95 *(978-0-88045-154-3(8))* Stemmer Hse. Pubs.

—First Teddy Bear, 2nd Edition: Enlarged Edition. 2nd rev. enl. ed. 2005. (ENG., Illus.). 38p. (J). (gr. -1-3). per. 11.95 *(978-0-88045-153-6(X))* Stemmer Hse. Pubs.

Watt, Fiona. Este No Es Mi Osito. rev. ed. 2008. (Touchy-Feely Board Bks).Tr. of That's Not My Teddy. 10p. (J). bds. 7.99 *(978-0-7460-9208-8(3),* Usborne) EDC Publishing.

TEDDY BEARS—FICTION

A Mother's Pen, A. Mother's. The Adventures of Backwards Bear & Baby Curl. 2011. (ENG.). 30p. pap. 16.19 *(978-1-4634-4412-9(5))* AuthorHouse.

Abshier, Stan. Teddy's Journal: Cruise to Japan, China, & Singapore. 2012. 96p. pap. 31.99 *(978-1-4685-2319-5(8))* AuthorHouse.

Adeney, Anne. Five Teddy Bears. Shimmen, Cathy, illus. 2008. (Tadpoles Ser.). (ENG.). 24p. (J). (gr. -1-k). pap. *(978-0-7787-3884-8(1));* lib. bdg. *(978-0-7787-3853-4(1))* Crabtree Publishing Co.

Alborough, Jez. Where's My Teddy? Alborough, Jez, illus. 2017. (ENG., Illus.). 32p. (J). (gr. -1-2). 8.99 *(978-0-7636-9871-3(7));* 25th ed. 17.99 *(978-0-7636-9816-4(4))* Candlewick Pr.

Arcynski, Charlene. The Adventures of Little Sugarbear Boy: The Beginning. 2010. 28p. 15.49 *(978-1-4520-5430-8(4))* AuthorHouse.

Ashby, Gaylene. STORY TIME A Collection of Three Children's Stories. 2008. 28p. 14.95 *(978-1-4357-1929-3(8))* Lulu Pr., Inc.

Austin, Rikey. Chunky & the Bone: Alice's Bear Shop. 2012. 28p. pap. *(978-1-78092-152-5(7))* MX Publishing, Ltd.

Bauman, Amy. Everyone Is Special! 2010. 12p. (J). (gr. -1). 9.95 *(978-1-60747-719-8(X),* Pickwick Pr.) Phoenix Bks., Inc.

Baxter, Nicola. Stories for Little Ones. Shuttleworth, Cathie, illus. 2018. (ENG.). 256p. (J). (gr. -1-12). 9.99 *(978-0-85723-894-8(9),* Armadillo) Anness Publishing GBR. Dist: National Bk. Network.

—The Teddy Bears' Picnic. Howarth, Daniel, illus. 2015. 24p. (J). (gr. -1-12). pap. 6.99 *(978-1-86147-654-8(X),* Armadillo) Anness Publishing GBR. Dist: National Bk. Network.

Beal, T. J. Wash Day: A Teddy Doonamen Adventure. 2012. 24p. pap. 11.95 *(978-1-60693-609-2(3),* Strategic Bk. Publishing) Strategic Book Publishing & Rights Agency (SBPRA).

The Bear Who Had No Name. 2006. (J). 10.00 *(978-0-9760076-1-6(4))* Juniper Berry Pr.

Beavington, Ruth. Edward Bear. 2012. (Illus.). 112p. (gr. 1-2). 19.95 *(978-1-84624-721-7(7))* Book Guild, Ltd. GBR. Dist: Trans-Atlantic Pubns., Inc.

Beecroft, Susan. Teddy Goes to Buckingham Palace. 2013. (ENG., Illus.). 24p. pap. 9.50 *(978-1-78035-606-8(4),* Fastprint Publishing) Upfront Publishing Ltd. GBR. Dist: Printondemand-worldwide.com.

Believe It Or Not!, Ripleys, compiled by. Sharkee & the Teddy Bear. 2018. (Story Book Ser.: 1). (ENG., Illus.). 40p. (J). 16.99 *(978-1-60991-208-6(X))* Ripley Entertainment, Inc.

Bernal, Sandra Marie. I Want a Pand. 2011. 32p. pap. 24.95 *(978-1-4626-2897-1(4))* America Star Bks.

Blackman, Malorie. Sinclair, Wonder Bear. Allwright, Deborah, illus. 2005. (Blue Go Bananas Ser.). (ENG.). 48p. (J). (gr. 1-2). lib. bdg. *(978-0-7787-2631-9(2))* Crabtree Publishing Co.

Bolton, Violet. Heidi & Huber the Adventures Begin. 2011. (Illus.). 60p. pap. *(978-1-908447-90-6(7))* Grosvenor Hse. Publishing Ltd.

Bond, Michael. Paddington & the Christmas Surprise. Alley, R. W., illus. 2008. (Paddington Ser.). (ENG.). 32p. (J). (gr. -1-3). 16.99 *(978-0-06-168740-2(5),* HarperCollins) HarperCollins Pubs.

Booking, Walt. Teddy's Tale, 1 vol. 2006. (Neighborhood Readers Ser.). (ENG.). 12p. (gr. 1-2). pap. 5.90 *(978-1-4042-7054-1(X),* b9bd6f15-8022-48bd-ae11-5544e85a5587, Rosen Classroom) Rosen Publishing Group, Inc., The.

Bradley, Timothy J. Teddy Bear, Teddy Bear, Say Good Night. Medina, Conni & Stark, Kristy, eds. 2009. (Early Literacy Ser.). (ENG., Illus.). 16p. (gr. -1-1). 19.99 *(978-1-4333-1472-8(X))* Teacher Created Materials, Inc.

—Teddy Bear, Teddy Bear, Say Good Night, 1 vol. rev. ed. 2009. (Early Literacy Ser.). (ENG., Illus.). 16p. (gr. -1-1). 6.99 *(978-1-4333-1471-1(1))* Teacher Created Materials, Inc.

Bragg, Jane. Teddy Bears Christmas Miracle. 2009. (ENG.). 49p. pap. 18.70 *(978-0-557-22087-8(4))* Lulu Pr., Inc.

Branchaud, R. Gary. Toasty Town! 2011. 64p. pap. 19.50 *(978-1-60976-039-7(5),* Eloquent Bks.) Strategic Book Publishing & Rights Agency (SBPRA).

Brannock, Martha Lee. Teddy Bear Too-Too. 2007. 28p. per. 18.65 *(978-1-4257-4143-3(6))* Xlibris Corp.

Brooks, Felicity. Dress the Teddy Bears for Christmas. 2015. (Dress the Teddy Bears Sticker Bks.). (ENG.). 16+8p. (J). pap. 6.99 *(978-0-7945-3585-8(2),* Usborne) EDC Publishing.

—Dress the Teddy Bears Going Shopping. 2015. (Dress the Teddy Bears Sticker Bks.). (ENG.). 16+8p. (J). pap. 6.99 *(978-0-7945-3530-8(5),* Usborne) EDC Publishing.

Brown, Gwen. Clifford & His Bear. 2006. (Illus.). 48p. pap. *(978-1-84401-650-1(1))* Athena Pr.

Brown, Margaret Wise. Buenas Noches Oso. 2006. (Illus.). 24p. (J). (gr. -1-k). 12.95 *(978-1-882077-61-8(X))* Sweetwater Pr.

Brown, Ruth. Night-Time Tale. Brown, Ruth, illus. 2007. (ENG., Illus.). 32p. (J). (gr. -1-k). pap. 10.99 *(978-1-84270-475-2(3))* Andersen Pr. GBR. Dist: Independent Pubs. Group.

Buckley, Charlie. How to Wash Your Hands. 2007. (Show Jo Language Development Ser.). (Illus.). 16p. (J). (gr. -1-1). per., bds. 14.95 *(978-1-933669-09-0(8))* Literary Architects, LLC.

—Show Jo How to Make a Sandwich. 2007. (Show Jo Language Development Ser.). (Illus.). 16p. (J). (gr. -1-1). per., bds. 14.95 *(978-1-933669-08-3(X))* Literary Architects, LLC.

Burfoot, Ella, illus. Bear & Me. 2013. (J). *(978-1-4351-4753-9(7))* Barnes & Noble, Inc.

Burke, Ellinor Rozecki. Susana Worrywart & the Magical Teddy Bear Balloon: With CD for Relaxation. Perciopelo, illus. 2003. 32p. (J). 27.00 incl. audio compact disk *(978-0-9741586-0-0(7))* Comfort Tales, LLC.

Butterworth, Nick. Albert the Bear to the Rescue. 2008. (J). 16.99 *(978-0-06-147406-2(5))* HarperCollins Pubs.

Calder, Catherine. A Teddy Tale. 2012. 24p. pap. 15.99 *(978-1-4771-0339-5(2))* Xlibris Corp.

Capucilli, Alyssa Satin. Biscuit & the Lost Teddy Bear. 2011. (My First I Can Read Ser.). (ENG., Illus.). 32p. (J). (gr. -1 — 1). pap. 5.99 *(978-0-06-117753-8(9),* HarperCollins) HarperCollins Pubs.

—Biscuit & the Lost Teddy Bear. Schories, Pat, illus. 2011. (My First I Can Read Ser.). (ENG.). 32p. (J). (gr. -1 — 1). 17.99 *(978-0-06-117751-4(2),* HarperCollins) HarperCollins Pubs.

Carey, Cassandra L. The Adventures of Uncle Joe: Uncle Joe & His Bear. 2012. 30p. 24.95 *(978-1-4626-5563-2(7))* America Star Bks.

Children of Appalachia. Teddy Bear Helps on the Farm. Children of Appalachia, illus. 2007. (Illus.). 64p. (J). per. 14.95 *(978-0-929915-73-9(9))* Headline Bks., Inc.

Coleman, Tamala J. Donovan's Shoes. 2010. 28p. pap. 9.95 *(978-1-4327-5801-1(2))* Outskirts Pr., Inc.

Copes, Liz Pecchi. Whompoo: The First Night. 2011. 24p. pap. 14.95 *(978-1-4634-3585-1(1))* AuthorHouse.

Cox, Phil Roxbee. Ted in a Red Bed. Tyler, Jenny, ed. Cartwright, Stephen, illus. rev. ed. 2006. (Phonics Reader, A: Easy Words to Read Ser.). 16p. (J). (gr. -1-3). 6.99 *(978-0-7945-1510-2(X),* Usborne) EDC Publishing.

—Ted's Shed. Tyler, Jenny, ed. Cartwright, Stephen, illus. rev. ed. 2006. (Phonics Readers Ser.). 16p. (J). (gr. -1-3). pap. 6.99 *(978-0-7945-1511-9(8),* Usborne) EDC Publishing.

Cox, Phil Roxbee & Cartwright, S. Ted's Shed, Toad Makes a Road, Fat Cat on a Mat & Sam Sheep Can't Sleep. 2004. (Easy Words to Read Ser.). (Illus.). 16p. (J). (gr. 1-18). pap. 9.95 *(978-0-7945-0245-4(8),* Usborne) EDC Publishing.

Cox, Phil Roxbee & Cartwright, Stephen. Ted's Shed. 2004. (Phonics Board Bks.). (Illus.). 10p. (J). 4.95 *(978-0-7945-0304-8(7),* Usborne) EDC Publishing.

Curtiss, A. B. & Lucarelli, Sue. T Bear's Tale. 2005. (ENG.). 40p. (J). (gr. -1-3). 18.95 *(978-0-932529-80-0(1))* Oldcastle Publishing.

Dale, Jay. Where Is Molly's Teddy? Jackson, Katy, illus. 2012. (Wonder Words Ser.). (ENG.). 16p. (J). (gr. k-2). pap. 36.94 *(978-1-4296-8915-1(3),* 18353, Capstone Pr.) Capstone.

Dale, Jay & Scott, Kay. Where Is Molly's Teddy?, 1 vol. Jackson, Katy, illus. 2012. (Wonder Words Ser.). (ENG.). 16p. (J). (gr. k-2). pap. 6.99 *(978-1-4296-8914-4(5),* 119960, Capstone Pr.) Capstone.

Davies, Benji, illus. Bizzy Bear: Christmas Helper. 2016. (Bizzy Bear Ser.). (ENG.). 8p. (J). (— 1). bds. 7.99 *(978-0-7636-8004-6(4))* Candlewick Pr.

De Bear, Tedrick & Rizzi, Trefoni Michael. Teddy's Travels: America's National Parks. 2006. (ENG., Illus.). 128p. (J). spiral bd. 19.95 *(978-0-9740494-0-3(9))* TdB Pr. LLC.

De Castro, Ines E. The Teddy Bear Faeries. De Castro, Ines E., illus. 2011. (Illus.). 24p. (J). (gr. -1-3). 16.95 *(978-1-935359-72-2(X))* Bk. Pubs. Network.

De Marco, Clare. Freddy's Teddy. 2011. (Tadpoles Ser.). (ENG., Illus.). 24p. (J). (gr. k-2). lib. bdg. *(978-0-7787-0577-2(3));* pap. *(978-0-7787-0588-8(9))* Crabtree Publishing Co.

deVet, L. J. Teddy's Christmas Wish. Zabarylo-Duma, Ewa, illus. 2013. (J). (ENG.). 48p. *(978-0-9873686-0-7(5));* 46p. pap. *(978-0-9873686-5-2(6));* (ENG.). 48p. pap. *(978-0-9873686-1-4(3))* Print-Rite Publishers.

Dietrich, Sean, creator. Industriacide. 2004. (Illus.). 120p. (YA). per. 11.99 *(978-0-9748654-0-9(0))* Rorschach Entertainment.

Disney Press Staff, ed. Mickey's New Friend. 2011. (Illus.). 32p. (J). *(978-1-4231-4585-1(2))* Disney Pr.

Disney Staff. Winnie the Pooh. (FRE.). 96p. (J). (gr. k-5). pap. 9.95 *(978-0-7859-8848-9(3))* French & European Pubns., Inc.

d'Lacey, Chris. Frankin's Bear. Taylor, Thomas, illus. 2005. (Red Go Bananas Ser.). (ENG.). 48p. (J). (gr. 2-3). lib. bdg. *(978-0-7787-2674-6(6))* Crabtree Publishing Co.

Don, Freeman. Corduroy. 2014. (Corduroy Ser.). (ENG.). 32p. (J). (gr. k-12). 11.24 *(978-1-63245-291-7(X))* Lectorum Pubns., Inc.

Douglas, Babette. Blue Wise. Johnson, John, illus. 2006. (Kiss a Me Teacher Creature Stories Ser.). 62p. (J). (gr. -1-3). *(978-1-890343-07-1(2))* Kiss A Me Productions, Inc.

—Larkspur: And His Wooden Nose. Johnson, John, illus. 2006. (Kiss a Me Teacher Creature Stories Ser.). (J). (gr. -1-3). 9.99 *(978-1-890343-23-1(4))* Kiss A Me Productions, Inc.

Dracker, Pune. Doll & Teddy Bear Activity Book. Bart, Kathleen & Hofmann, Ginnie, illus. 2005. (ENG.). 96p. (J). pap. *(978-1-932485-24-0(4))* Reverie Publishing Co.

Dray, Matt. Dougal, the Garbage Dump Bear. Dray, Matt, illus. 2005. (Illus.). 32p. (J). pap. *(978-0-14-350097-1(X))* Penguin Publishing Group.

Dunn, Jancee. I'm Afraid Your Teddy Is in Trouble Today. Nash, Scott, illus. 2017. (ENG.). 40p. (J). (gr. -1-2). 15.99 *(978-0-7636-7537-0(7))* Candlewick Pr.

Dyan, Penelope. Don't Wake up the Bear! Dyan, Penelope, illus. 2013. (Illus.). 34p. pap. 11.95 *(978-1-61477-094-7(8))* Bellissima Publishing, LLC.

—Ted E Bearaes Most Unfortunate Experience to Date. Dyan, Penelope, illus. 2009. (Illus.). 44p. pap. 11.95 *(978-1-935118-44-2(7))* Bellissima Publishing, LLC.

—There's a Teddy Bear in My Heart! Dyan, Penelope, illus. 2012. (Illus.). 34p. pap. 11.95 *(978-1-61477-048-0(4))* Bellissima Publishing, LLC.

Earp-Bridgmon, Krista D. The Adventures of Jim-Bob: A Bearography. 2013. 24p. pap. 10.99 *(978-1-4582-1005-0(7),* Abbott Pr.) Author Solutions, LLC.

Elliot, Rachel. Teddy Bear Tales & Rhymes! 2016. (ENG., Illus.). 48p. (J). (gr. -1-12). bds. 9.99 *(978-1-86147-741-5(4),* Armadillo) Anness Publishing GBR. Dist: National Bk. Network.

Elliott, David. What the Grizzly Knows. Grafe, Max, illus. 2008. (ENG.). 32p. (J). (gr. -1-2). 16.99 *(978-0-7636-2778-2(X))* Candlewick Pr.

Ellwand, David. Twinkle Twinkle Little Star: David Ellwand's Bears. Ellwand, David, illus. 2018. (ENG., Illus.). 14p. (J). (— 1). bds. 6.99 *(978-1-5362-0220-5(7))* Candlewick Pr.

Faundez, Anne. Teddy's Birthday. 2004. (QEB Start Talking Ser.). (Illus.). 24p. (J). lib. bdg. 15.95 *(978-1-59566-004-6(6))* QEB Publishing Inc.

Feinman, Myke. The Teddy Bear Conspiracies. 2004. (ENG.). 386p. 32.99 *(978-1-4134-4070-6(3));* pap. 22.99 *(978-1-4134-4069-0(X))* Xlibris Corp.

Fischel, Emma. Land of the lost Teddies. Howarth, Daniel, illus. rev. ed. 2003. 32p. (J). (gr. 2-18). pap. 4.95 *(978-0-7945-0402-1(7),* Usborne) EDC Publishing.

Fox, Nita. Captain Benjamin Dale. Wallace, Andrea, illus. 2008. 32p. (J). (gr. -1-3). pap. 5.99 *(978-0-9816107-0-2(6))* Fox's Den Publishing.

Freedman, Claire. Cuddle Bear. Scott, Gavin, illus. (J). 2018. *(978-1-61067-730-1(7))* 2013. 28p. 12.99 *(978-1-61067-081-4(7))* Kane Miller.

—Night-Night, Emily! Massey, Jane, illus. 2005. 32p. (J). 6.95 *(978-1-58925-390-2(6))* Tiger Tales.

—Night-Night, Emily! Massey, Jane, tr. Massey, Jane, illus. 2003. 32p. (J). (gr. -1-1). tchr. ed. 15.95 *(978-1-58925-032-1(X))* Tiger Tales.

Freedman, Claire & Scott, Gavin. Cuddle Bear. 2013. (ENG.). (J). 26.99 *(978-1-61067-193-4(7))* Kane Miller.

Freeman, Don. Christmas Is Here, Corduroy! 2007. (Corduroy Ser.). (Illus.). 16p. (J). (gr. -1-k). 7.99 *(978-0-448-44650-9(2),* Grosset & Dunlap) Penguin Young Readers Group.

—Corduroy: Giant Board Book. 2011. (Corduroy Ser.). 34p. (J). (gr. -1 — 1). bds. 11.99 *(978-0-670-01311-1(0),* Viking Books for Young Readers) Penguin Young Readers Group.

—Corduroy Book & Bear. 2008. (Corduroy Ser.). 32p. (J). (gr. -1-k). 22.99 *(978-0-670-06342-0(8),* Viking Books for Young Readers) Penguin Young Readers Group.

—Corduroy's Tiny Treasury, 5 vols., Set. McCue, Lisa, illus. 2010. (Corduroy Ser.). 30p. (J). (gr. -1 — 1). bds. 10.99 *(978-0-670-01230-5(0),* Viking Books for Young Readers) Penguin Young Readers Group.

—A Pocket for Corduroy. 2015. (Corduroy Ser.). (Illus.). 34p. (J). (— 1). bds. 8.99 *(978-0-451-47113-0(X),* Viking Books for Young Readers) Penguin Young Readers Group.

French, Mary B. Bear-Ly There with Compass. Coffey, Kevin, illus. 2012. 122p. pap. 6.00 *(978-0-9852821-0-3(X))* Mary B./French.

Garton, Sam. I Am Otter. Garton, Sam, illus. 2014. (ENG., Illus.). 32p. (J). (gr. -1-3). 16.99 *(978-0-06-224775-9(1),* Balzer & Bray) HarperCollins Pubs.

—Otter: Hello, Sea Friends! 2016. (My First I Can Read Ser.). (ENG., Illus.). 32p. (J). (gr. -1-3). pap. 4.99 *(978-0-06-236660-3(2),* Balzer & Bray) HarperCollins Pubs.

—Otter Goes to School. Garton, Sam, illus. 2016. (ENG., Illus.). 32p. (J). (gr. -1-3). 17.99 *(978-0-06-235225-5(3),* Balzer & Bray) HarperCollins Pubs.

—Otter in Space. Garton, Sam, illus. 2015. (ENG., Illus.). 32p. (J). (gr. -1-3). 16.99 *(978-0-06-224776-6(X),* Balzer & Bray) HarperCollins Pubs.

—Otter: Oh No, Bath Time! Garton, Sam, illus. 2016. (My First I Can Read Ser.). (ENG., Illus.). 32p. (J). (gr. -1-3). pap. 4.99 *(978-0-06-236657-3(2),* Balzer & Bray) HarperCollins Pubs.

—Otter: the Best Job Ever! Garton, Sam, illus. 2016. (My First I Can Read Ser.). (ENG., Illus.). 32p. (J). (gr. -1-3). pap. 5.99 *(978-0-06-236654-2(8),* Balzer & Bray) HarperCollins Pubs.

Gilpin, Esther. How the Bear Got Its Hair. 2008. 24p. pap. 12.99 *(978-1-4389-1584-5(5))* AuthorHouse.

Goldman, Marcia. Lola's Teddy Bear. 2019. (Lola Ser.). (ENG., Illus.). 32p. (J). (gr. -1-k). 16.95 *(978-1-939547-50-7(4),* 4972b2cd-cd6c-4cfa-bc83-ea19dede52d9) Creston Bks.

Goss, Matt. Bear Crimbo. 2010. (ENG., Illus.). 72p. (J). 17.95 *(978-0-9815381-3-6(4))* Hilton Publishing Co.

Graham, Crystal L. My Little Teddy Bear: Has Anybody Seen... . . 2010. 16p. 8.49 *(978-1-4520-0425-9(0))* AuthorHouse.

Grams, Kimberly. Smedley & the Sprinkle Machine. 2005. 59p. pap. 16.95 *(978-1-4241-0184-9(0))* PublishAmerica, Inc.

Granger, Trudi. Always There Bear. Llewhellin, Gareth, illus. (ENG.). (J). (-k). 2015. 32p. 16.99 *(978-1-63220-434-9(7))* 2018. 24p. bds. 8.99 *(978-1-5107-3561-3(5))* Skyhorse Publishing Co., Inc. (Sky Pony Pr.).

Greening, Rosie. Ten Little Teddy Bears Splashing in the Bath. Machell, Dawn, illus. 2016. (ENG.). 24p. (J). (gr. -1 — 1). bds. 10.99 *(978-1-78598-469-3(1))* Make Believe Ideas GBR. Dist: Scholastic, Inc.

Group/McGraw-Hill, Wright. The Humpback Tedy: Level E, 6 vols. (Take Twostm Ser.). 16p. 29.95 *(978-0-322-08952-5(2))* Wright Group/McGraw-Hill.

Guy, Ginger Foglesong. Siesta: Bilingual English-Spanish. Moreno, Rene King, illus. 2005. (ENG.). 32p. (J). (gr. -1-k). 17.99 *(978-0-06-056061-4(4),* Greenwillow Bks.) HarperCollins Pubs.

Hall, Caroline V. Rhett & Abby: Abby's New Home. 2011. 40p. pap. 15.95 *(978-1-4497-1887-9(6),* WestBow Pr.) Author Solutions, LLC.

Hall, Christina. Can Checkers Come Too? Hall, Lowell, illus. 2011. 36p. pap. 24.95 *(978-1-4560-7753-2(8))* America Star Bks.

Hankins, Jim. Teddy Scares Volume 3. 2008. (Illus.). 52p. (YA). pap. 6.95 *(978-0-9791050-2-9(1))* Ape Entertainment.

Hannigan, Paula. Hugs for You. Brown, Heather, illus. 2012. (ENG.). 10p. (J). (-k). bds. 7.99 *(978-1-4494-2192-2(X))* Andrews McMeel Publishing.

Hardwell, Gary D. A Boo Bears' Story: Stormy Night. 2007. (Illus.). 36p. per. 10.00 *(978-0-9792016-9-1(1))* Professional Publishing Hse. LLC.

Hay, Sam. Do Not Wash This Bear. East, Nick, illus. 2016. (J). *(978-1-4351-6399-7(0))* Barnes & Noble, Inc.

Hayes, Geoffrey. Patrick Eats His Peas & Other Stories: Toon Books Level 2. Hayes, Geoffrey, illus. 2013. (ENG., Illus.). 32p. (J). (gr. -1-3). 12.95 *(978-1-935179-34-4(9),* TOON Books) Astra Publishing Hse.

—Patrick in a Teddy Bear's Picnic & Other Stories: Toon Books Level 2. 2011. (ENG., Illus.). 32p. (J). (gr. -1-3). 12.95 *(978-1-935179-09-2(8),* Toon Books) Astra Publishing Hse.

Hayward, Jason. Teddy Bear Adventures. 2011. 40p. pap. 24.95 *(978-1-4560-4068-0(5))* America Star Bks.

Hegg, Tom & Hanson, Warren. Peef & the Baby Sister. Hegg, Tom & Hanson, Warren, illus. 2006. (ENG., Illus.). 36p. (J). (gr. -1-3). 16.95 *(978-0-931674-67-9(0),* Waldman House Pr.) TRISTAN Publishing, Inc.

Henisz, Jerzy E. SOPHIE in PARIS & other Stories. 2009. (ENG.). 99p. pap. 9.46 *(978-0-557-09520-9(4))* Lulu Pr., Inc.

Henisz, Jerzy E. & Henisz, Sophie, illustrator. TEDDY BEAR who went on a Trip around the World & other Stories. 2006. (ENG.). 88p. (J). pap. *(978-0-615-13851-0(9))* Henisz, Jerzy E.

Hennessy, B. G. A Christmas Wish for Corduroy. Wheeler, Jody, illus. 2017. (Corduroy Ser.). 34p. (J). (— 1). bds. 8.99 *(978-0-425-28875-7(7),* Viking Books for Young Readers) Penguin Young Readers Group.

—Corduroy Lost & Found. Wheeler, Jody, illus. 2006. (Corduroy Ser.). 32p. (J). (gr. -1-k). 17.99 *(978-0-670-06100-6(X),* Viking Books for Young Readers) Penguin Young Readers Group.

Henry, Rose. Teddy Finds His Way: A Teddy Tale. Henny, Rose, illus. I.t. ed. 2005. (Illus.). 22p. (J). per. 17.95 *(978-0-9705458-7-9(8))* Royalty Bks. International, Inc.

Herrington, Chris. Harry & Hannah: The American Adventure. Pacheco, Jorge M., illus. 2003. (Adventures of Harry & Hannah Ser.). (ENG.). 72p. (J). (gr. 1-5). 15.00 *(978-0-9722343-0-6(6))* Herrington Teddy Bears.

Hesse, Karen. Brooklyn Bridge: A Novel. Sheban, Chris, illus. 2011. (ENG.). 256p. (J). (gr. 6-8). pap. 11.99 *(978-0-312-67428-1(7),* 900072843) Square Fish.

Hill, Eric. Spot's Easter Surprise. Hill, Eric, illus. 2007. (Spot Ser.). (ENG., Illus.). 10p. (J). (gr. -1 — 1). bds. 6.99 *(978-0-399-24743-9(2),* Warne) Penguin Young Readers Group.

Ho, Jannie, illus. Bunny Boo Has Lost Her Teddy: A Tiny Tab Book. 2014. (Tiny Tab Ser.). (ENG.). 8p. (J). (— 1). bds. 7.99 *(978-0-7636-7274-4(2))* Candlewick Pr.

Holl, Robert. Apúrate, Teddy: Fiction-to-Fact Big Book. Forss, Ian, illus. enl. ed. 2004. (SPA.). (J). pap. 26.00 *(978-1-4108-2362-5(8)*, 23628) Benchmark Education Co.

—Teddy on the Move. 2004. (Shared Connections Ser.). (J). pap. *(978-1-4108-1629-0(X))*; instr.'s gde. ed. 27.00 *(978-1-4108-1605-4(2))* Benchmark Education Co.

Hope, Laura. The Story of a Plush Bear. 2005. pap. 9.95 *(978-1-55742-463-1(2))* Wildside Pr., LLC.

Hughes, Meredith A. My Sissy & Me. Simon, Anna, illus. 2005. (ENG.). 52p. pap. 22.50 *(978-1-4208-5463-3(1))* AuthorHouse.

Hulst, W. G. van de & Hulst, Willem G. van de, illus. Bruno the Bear. 2014. 48p. (J). *(978-1-928136-03-3(6))* Inheritance Pubns.

Huser, Glen. The Snuggly, 1 vol. Pavlović, Milan, illus. 2018. (ENG.). 32p. (J). (gr. k-2). 16.95 *(978-1-55498-901-0(9))* Groundwood Bks. CAN. Dist: Publishers Group West (PGW).

Ira Sleeps Over. 2005. (J). *(978-1-59564-973-7(5))* Steps To Literacy, LLC.

Joyce, Melanie. A New House, 1 vol. 2008. (Fred Bear & Friends Ser.). (ENG., Illus.). 24p. (gr. k-1). pap. 9.15 *(978-0-8368-8974-1(6)*, 729ef204-73a0-4460-ae95-d8361712127e, Gareth Stevens Learning Library) Stevens, Gareth Publishing LLLP.

Judd, Christopher M. Bearable Moments. 2005. (Illus.). (J). 16.95 *(978-0-9766666-1-5(8))* Arcadian Hse.

Kantorovitz, Sylvie. The Very Tiny Baby. Kantorovitz, Sylvie, illus. 2014. (Illus.). 240p. (J). (gr. -1-2). lib. bdg. 14.95 *(978-1-58089-445-6(3))* Charlesbridge Publishing, Inc.

—The Very Tiny Baby. 2014. (J). pap. *(978-1-58089-446-3(1))* Charlesbridge Publishing, Inc.

Karpinski, David. Sarah's Christmas Presence. 2006. 58p. pap. 8.95 *(978-0-7414-3411-1(3))* Infinity Publishing.

Kats, Jewel. Teddy Bear Princess: A Story about Sharing & Caring. Arts, Richa Kinra, illus. 2012. 24p. (-18). pap. 13.95 *(978-1-61599-163-1(8)*, Marvelous Spirit Pr.) Loving Healing Pr., Inc.

Kelly, Katherine, text. Albert Bear & the Big Celebration. 2005. (J). 12.95 *(978-0-9773481-0-7(5))* Kelly, Katherine.

Kimball, Michael D. Alligator Bay: A Beary Tale. 2009. 132p. pap. 11.95 *(978-1-4401-1804-3(3))* iUniverse, Inc.

Kleback, Amanda. Hoo Hoo's Song. Kleback, Amanda & Kleback, Brian, illus. 2009. 24p. pap. 12.00 *(978-1-4389-1322-3(2))* AuthorHouse.

Kreloff, Elliot, illus. Where's Your Nose. 2010. 24p. (J). bds. *(978-1-60906-004-6(0))* Begin Smart LLC.

Landsberry, Belinda. Anzac Ted. 2016. (ENG., Illus.). 32p. (J). (gr. -1-5). 17.99 *(978-1-921966-56-9(4)*, EK Bks.) Exisle Publishing Pty Ltd. AUS. Dist: Two Rivers Distribution.

Legrand, Martine & Delvaux, Nancy. ¡una nalgada por Favor! 2006. (SPA.). 28p. (J). *(978-958-30-1886-2(4))* Panamericana Editorial.

Lesley, Sharon. The Red Scarf & Other Stories. 2010. 165p. pap. 14.95 *(978-1-4457-6720-8(1))* Lulu Pr., Inc.

Little Teddy. (Bedtime Babies Ser.). (J). 6.99 *(978-1-57755-500-1(7))* Flying Frog Publishing, Inc.

Ludde & His Naughty Teddy Bear. 2003. Orig. Title: Ludde Och Busiga Nalle. (NOR, FIN, GER, FLE & DAN.). lib. bdg. 7.95 *(978-0-9740419-0-2(4))* words4u.

Mahadeo Rdh, Elizabeth. Teddy Visits the Dentist. Barth, Alexandra, illus. 2012. 40p. pap. *(978-0-9569438-0-4(2))* Mahadeo Movement, The.

—Teddy Visits the Dentist: Teddy Gets a Filling. Barth, Alexandra, illus. 2012. 42p. (-18). pap. *(978-0-9569438-2-8(9))* Mahadeo Movement, The.

Mason, Bonita. T-Bear the Most Special Bear. Hendricks, Sandy, illus. 2008. 26p. (J). 19.95 *(978-0-9798718-0-1(8))* Encore Pubns.

Matsutani, Miyoko. Peek-A-Boo. Segawa, Yasuo, illus. 2006. 20p. (J). (gr. -1). 10.95 *(978-1-74126-047-2(7))* R.I.C. Pubns. AUS. Dist: SCB Distributors.

Mauldin, Mary. What a Carrot-Astrophy! 2011. 32p. pap. 14.99 *(978-1-4634-3366-6(2))* AuthorHouse.

McCue, Lisa, illus. Corduroy's Thanksgiving. 2006. (Corduroy Ser.). 16p. (J). (gr. -1 — 1). bds. 6.99 *(978-0-670-06108-2(5)*, Viking Books for Young Readers) Penguin Young Readers Group.

McGrath, Barbara Barbieri. Teddy Bear Counting. Nihoff, Tim, illus. 2010. (McGrath Math Ser.: 1). (ENG.). 32p. (J). (gr. -1-2). pap. 7.95 *(978-1-58089-216-2(7))* Charlesbridge Publishing, Inc.

McKee, David. Elmer & the Lost Teddy. McKee, David, illus. 2004. (Elmer Bks.). (Illus.). 32p. (J). 9.99 *(978-0-06-075243-9(2))* HarperCollins Pubs.

—El Principe Pedro y el oso de Peluche. (SPA.). (J). 7.95 *(978-958-04-6258-3(5))* Norma S.A. COL. Dist: Distribuidora Norma, Inc.

McKennon, Tony. You're Moving Where?! 2008. 40p. pap. 18.55 *(978-1-4389-1397-1(4))* AuthorHouse.

McLean, P. J. The Bears & the Baby. Jenkins, C. S., illus. 2012. 44p. pap. 17.44 *(978-1-4669-1335-6(5))* Trafford Publishing.

McMahon, Susan. Sean O'Grady. 2009. 12p. pap. 9.50 *(978-1-4389-5149-2(3))* AuthorHouse.

McPhail, David. The Teddy Bear. McPhail, David, illus. 2005. (ENG., Illus.). 32p. (J). (gr. -1-1). reprint ed. pap. 8.99 *(978-0-8050-7882-4(7)*, 900030909) Square Fish.

McRitchie, Mike. Best Friends. 2009. 25p. 13.95 *(978-0-578-03644-1(4))* McRitchie, Mike.

Meserve, Jessica. Bedtime Without Arthur. Meserve, Jessica, illus. 2010. (ENG., Illus.). 32p. (J). (gr. -1-3). 16.95 *(978-0-7613-5497-0(2)*, 8255c966-c581-4056-a251-c10096e0b470) Lerner Publishing Group.

Milne, Alan Alexander. Winnie Ille Pu. Lenardo, Alexandro, tr. from ENG. 2015.Tr. of Winnie-the-Pooh. (LAT., Illus.). 170p. (J). pap. 19.95 *(978-4-87187-394-9(3))* Ishi Pr. International.

Minarik, Else Holmelund. Un Beso para Osito. 2006. (Osito / Little Bear Ser.).Tr. of Kiss for Little Bear. (SPA.). 34p. (gr. k-3). pap. 9.95 *(978-84-204-0202-4(8))* Santillana USA Publishing Co., Inc.

Mooney, Bel. Mr. Tubs Is Lost. 2006. (Blue Bananas Ser.). (ENG., Illus.). 48p. (J). (gr. -1-3). lib. bdg. *(978-0-7787-0858-2(6))* Crabtree Publishing Co.

Moore, Mel. Mr P's Tale or Two. 2006. (Illus.). 21p. (J). per. *(978-0-9775919-1-6(3))* Carpe Diem Publishing.

Myers, Robin. Pinky Rabbit Learns to Share. 2008. 20p. pap. 24.95 *(978-1-60703-937-2(0))* America Star Bks.

Nash, Sarah. Scaredy Bear, 1 vol. Everitt-Stewart, Andy, illus. 2009. (Stories to Grow With Ser.). (ENG.). 24p. (J). (gr. 1-2). 27.27 *(978-1-60754-472-2(5)*, bf59d50c-0e89-4065-97dd-9028097bd68a, Windmill Bks.) Rosen Publishing Group, Inc., The.

Nield, Joan. Children's Story Book. 2008. (Illus.). 24p. 11.04 *(978-1-4251-2449-6(6))* Trafford Publishing.

Niland, Kilmeny. Two Tough Teddies Boxed Set. 2008. (ENG., Illus.). *(978-1-921272-63-9(5))* Little Hare Bks. AUS. Dist: HarperCollins Pubs. Australia.

Outram, Evelyn. Sav & Josh O Lucky's Christmas Adventure & Magic Street. 2010. 56p. pap. 17.95 *(978-1-60911-876-1(6)*, Eloquent Bks.) Strategic Book Publishing & Rights Agency (SBPRA).

Paragon Staff. Celebrate the Year with Winnie the Pooh. 2010. (Disney Diecut Classics). (Illus.). 72p. (J). (gr. -1-1). *(978-1-4075-8902-2(4))* Parragon, Inc.

Payne-Sylvester, Linda. Here Comes Christmas & the Teddy Bears Get Ready. 2012. (ENG.). pap. 12.95 *(978-1-4675-5249-3(6))* Independent Pub.

Peck, James E. Meet Mr. Chair Bear. 2008. 52p. pap. 16.95 *(978-1-4241-7959-6(9))* America Star Bks.

Petrovic, Svetlana. Brown Bear, White Bear. Hardy, Vincent, illus. 2009. 28p. (J). (gr. -1-3). 17.00 *(978-0-8028-5353-0(6)*, Eerdmans Bks For Young Readers) Eerdmans, William B. Publishing Co.

Publications International Ltd. Staff, ed. Dora Says Good Night. 2011. 12p. (J). bds. 11.98 *(978-1-4508-0764-7(X))* Phoenix International Publications, Inc.

—Winnie the Pooh. 2005. (J). 14.98 *(978-1-4127-3470-7(3))* Publications International, Ltd.

Rack, Charlene. The Adventures of Delaware Bear & Young George Washington. 2011. 24p. (gr. 1-2). pap. 12.79 *(978-1-4567-5681-9(8))* AuthorHouse.

Randall, Chuck. Curley's Wish Comes True. 2013. 28p. pap. 24.95 *(978-1-4626-9795-3(X))* America Star Bks.

Richards, J. Danielle Jennson, Life Lessons of a Little Clown. 2006. 72p. per. 8.95 *(978-1-59824-187-7(7))* E-BookTime LLC.

Robinson, Marquita E. Teddy's Bear, 1 vol. Roscoe Robinson, illus. 2009. 15p. pap. 24.95 *(978-1-60749-249-8(0))* America Star Bks.

Roman, Javier. Adventures of Tinturu & Kurnachan the M. 2007. (Illus.). 48p. pap. 16.95 *(978-1-4241-1626-3(0))* PublishAmerica, Inc.

Rose, Alea. There's a Bear in my House. Witt, Rici, illus. 2009. (ENG.). 24p. (J). reprint ed. 10.59 *(978-0-9803367-1-9(6))* Buttermoth Pr. AUS. Dist: Lulu Pr., Inc.

Rose, Eya. The Magic Blanket. 2011. 24p. pap. 15.99 *(978-1-4653-4617-9(1))* Xlibris Corp.

Sarah Taylor. The Teddy That Went to Iraq. Baker, David, illus. 2011. 28p. pap. 24.95 *(978-1-4560-8382-3(1))* America Star Bks.

Saunders, Kate. The Land of Neverendings. 2017. (ENG.). 336p. (J). 14.50 *(978-0-571-31084-5(2)*, Faber & Faber Children's Bks.) Faber & Faber, Inc.

Schaffer, Jacqueline. Porsha & the Great Snowmen Adventure. 2009. 36p. pap. 15.99 *(978-1-4490-5421-2(8))* AuthorHouse.

Schauer, Tosca M. J. J. Bear. 2013. 28p. pap. 16.99 *(978-1-4582-0783-8(8)*, Abbott Pr.) Author Solutions, LLC.

Schertle, Alice. The Adventures of Old Bo Bear. Parkins, David, illus. 2005. (J). 16.95 *(978-978-081-183-9(4))* Chronicle Bks. LLC.

Schliewen, Richard. Paulina's Teddy Bear Journey. Visaya, Artemio, illus. 2012. 104p. 24.95 *(978-1-62709-055-1(X))*; pap. 19.95 *(978-1-4626-9597-3(3))* America Star Bks.

Scott, MaryJo. Corduroy's Seasons. McCue, Lisa, illus. 2016. (Corduroy Ser.). 14p. (J). (— 1). bds. 6.99 *(978-0-451-47249-6(7)*, Viking Books for Young Readers) Penguin Young Readers Group.

Shanks, Ronnie. Oh Where, Oh Where Is My Teddy Bear? 2004. 22p. pap. 24.95 *(978-1-4137-2693-0(3))* PublishAmerica, Inc.

Sharp, Kevin. The Amazing Adventures of Ted Shuttle: Book One. 2012. (Illus.). 24p. pap. 19.82 *(978-1-4772-4286-5(4))* AuthorHouse.

Sovago-Royal, Sandra. Magimus. 2009. 33p. (J). pap. 19.95 *(978-1-4327-4375-8(9))* Outskirts Pr., Inc.

Stein, Peter. The Boy & the Bear. 2019. (Illus.). 40p. (J). (gr. -1-2). 17.99 *(978-0-8234-4095-5(8))* Holiday Hse., Inc.

Stephens, Edna Cucksey, et al. You & Me Make Three. Drescher, Heather, illus. 2008. (Build-A-Bear Workshop Ser.). 32p. (J). (gr. -1-3). 0.00 *(978-0-9798088-0-7(4))* EDCO Publishing, Inc.

—You & Me Make Three & Accompanying Plush B. B. the Bear. Drescher, Heather, illus. 2008. 32p. (J). 35.00 *(978-0-9798088-2-1(0))* EDCO Publishing, Inc.

Stoddard, Jutta. Miss Elli. 2004. 28p. per. 18.65 *(978-1-4134-3423-1(1))* Xlibris Corp.

Sullivan, Silvia. Hip Hip Hurray We Found Teddy: A Book Series to Teach Children Practical Life Skills & Eco-Friendly Skills. 2008. 32p. pap. 15.48 *(978-1-4343-5897-4(6))* AuthorHouse.

Sutherland, Keith. Two Tubby Teddies Have a Very Busy Week. 2013. 40p. pap. *(978-0-9545288-7-4(5))* D S Press.

Teddy Bear-Duck. 2003. (J). per. *(978-1-57657-160-6(2))* Paradise Pr., Inc.

Teddy Bear Frog. 2003. (J). per. *(978-1-57657-161-3(0))* Paradise Pr., Inc.

Teddy Bear-House. 2003. (J). per. *(978-1-57657-162-0(9))* Paradise Pr., Inc.

Teddy Bear-Sheep. 2003. (J). per. *(978-1-57657-163-7(7))* Paradise Pr., Inc.

Teddy in the Toyshop. Date not set. (Illus.). (J). bds. 1.98 *(978-0-7525-9841-3(4))* Parragon, Inc.

Toews, Sheena. Beary Fun! 2004. 48p. pap. 10.95 *(978-1-57377-189-4(9)*, 0-1988-4-02506-1) Eas'l Pubns.

—Beary Snowy. 2004. 56p. pap. 10.95 *(978-1-57377-196-2(1)*, 0-1988-4-02512-2) Eas'l Pubns.

Vaughan, Richard & Crews, Marcia. Three Bears of the Pacific Northwest. Trammell, Jeremiah, illus. 2016. (Pacific Northwest Fairy Tales Ser.). 20p. (J). (— 1). bds. 10.99 *(978-1-63217-076-7(0)*, Little Bigfoot) Sasquatch Bks.

Vaughan, Richard Lee & Vaughn, Marcia. Three Bears of the Pacific Northwest. Trammell, Jeremiah, illus. 2011. (Pacific Northwest Fairy Tales Ser.). (ENG.). 32p. (J). (gr. -1-2). 17.99 *(978-1-57061-684-6(1)*, Little Bigfoot) Sasquatch Bks.

Verrett, Michael. Cozmo the Elf. 2010. 86p. pap. 32.00 *(978-0-557-25717-1(4))* Lulu Pr., Inc.

Voigt, Cynthia. Teddy & Co. Zakimi, Paola, illus. 2018. (ENG.). 192p. (J). (gr. 2-5). 7.99 *(978-0-553-51163-5(7)*, Yearling) Random Hse. Children's Bks.

Voremberg, Linda. Robbie: A Journey of Hope, 1 vol. 2009. 52p. pap. 16.95 *(978-1-60703-486-5(7))* America Star Bks.

Waber, Bernard. Quique Duerme Fuera de Casa. Mlawer, Teresa, tr. 2003. (SPA., Illus.). (J). (gr. k-2). pap. *(978-968-6579-15-4(X)*, SI6510) Sistemas Tecnicos de Edicion, S.A. de C.V. MEX. Dist: Lectorum Pubns., Inc.

Wach, Martin. The Great West Virginia Snow Adventure: Teddy Bear Guardians of the Rain Forest. 2006. (Illus.). 32p. (J). 16.95 *(978-0-929915-42-5(9))* Headline Bks., Inc.

Walling, Lani. Clyde-Fred & the Color of Friendship. 2005. 23p. (J). 9.98 *(978-1-4116-6091-5(9))* Lulu Pr., Inc.

Walton, Jessica. Introducing Teddy: A Gentle Story about Gender & Friendship. MacPherson, Dougal, illus. 2016. (ENG.). 32p. (J). 17.99 *(978-1-68119-210-9(1)*, 900164037); E-Book 12.59 *(978-1-68119-211-6(X))* Bloomsbury Publishing USA. (Bloomsbury USA Childrens).

Watt, Fiona. That's Not My Teddy... Wells, Rachel, illus. 2008. (Usborne Touchy-Feely Board Bks.). 8p. (J). (gr. -1). bds. 7.99 *(978-0-7945-2026-7(X)*, Usborne) EDC Publishing.

Watt, Fiona & Wells, Rachel, eds. That's Not My Teddy: Its Paws Are Too Woolly. 2004. (Touchy-Feely Board Bks.). (SPA & ENG., Illus.). 1p. (J). (gr. -1-18). 7.95 *(978-0-7460-3782-9(1))* EDC Publishing.

Webber, Barbara. Feeling Loved: A Ted E. Bear Story. 2013. 40p. pap. 15.95 *(978-1-4525-7162-1(7)*, Balboa Pr.) Author Solutions, LLC.

Wells-Dunn, Mildred. Tid Bit the Teddy Bear. 2011. 36p. pap. 21.99 *(978-1-4500-5729-5(2))* Xlibris Corp.

Weston Woods Staff, creator. Corduroy. 2011. 29.95 *(978-0-545-14916-7(9))*; 38.75 *(978-0-545-14080-5(3))*; 18.95 *(978-0-545-14078-2(1))* Weston Woods Studios, Inc.

Wickstrom, Sylvie K. I Love You, Mister Bear. 2004. (Illus.). 40p. (J). (gr. -1-1). pap. 14.99 *(978-0-06-029331-4(4))* HarperCollins Pubs.

Wolfe, Frances. The Little Toy Shop. Wolfe, Frances, illus. 2008. (Illus.). 32p. (J). (gr. -1-2). 19.95 *(978-0-88776-865-1(2)*, Tundra Bks.) Tundra Bks. CAN. Dist: Penguin Random Hse. LLC.

Young, Billy. Teddy the Bear. 2007. 27p. 19.95 *(978-1-84799-068-6(1))* Lulu Pr., Inc.

TEENAGE

see Adolescence; Youth

TEENAGE MUTANT NINJA TURTLES (FICTITIOUS CHARACTERS)—FICTION

Belle, Magnolia. Teen Titans: Hot Garbage. 2016. (J). lib. bdg. 13.55 *(978-0-606-38325-7(5))* Turtleback.

Chanda, J-P. Four's a Crowd. Let's Draw Studio Staff, illus. 2005. (Teenage Mutant Ninja Turtles Ser.: No. 7). 24p. lib. bdg. 15.00 *(978-1-59054-832-5(9))* Fitzgerald Bks.

DiCicco, Peter & Flynn, Ian. Teenage Mutant Ninja Turtles Amazing Adventures, Volume 2. 2016. (Teenage Mutant Ninja Turtles Amazing Adventures Ser.: 2). lib. bdg. 30.60 *(978-0-606-38731-6(5))* Turtleback.

Farago, Andrew. Teenage Mutant Ninja Turtles: The Ultimate Visual History. 2014. (ENG., Illus.). 192p. 50.00 *(978-1-60887-185-8(1)*, 5ebd2cc6-cf97-460f-b0b8-9807fa78f20e) Pocket Books.

Golden Books. Follow the Ninja! (Teenage Mutant Ninja Turtles) Lambe, Steve, illus. 2015. (Little Golden Book Ser.). (ENG.). 24p. (J). (-k). 5.99 *(978-0-553-51204-5(8)*, Golden Bks.) Random Hse. Children's Bks.

Lewman, David. Out of the Shadows Junior Novelization. 2016. lib. bdg. 17.20 *(978-0-606-38886-3(9))* Turtleback.

—The Rise of Tiger Claw. 2016. lib. bdg. 16.00 *(978-0-606-38489-6(8))* Turtleback.

Manning, Matthew K. Batman / Teenage Mutant Ninja Turtles Adventures. Sommariva, Jon, illus. 2018. (Batman / Teenage Mutant Ninja Turtles Adventures Ser.). (ENG.). 32p. (J). (gr. 2-6). 143.94 *(978-1-4965-7388-9(9)*, 28659, Stone Arch Bks.) Capstone.

—Batman/Teenage Mutant Ninja Turtles Adventures. Sommariva, Jon, illus. 2017. 144p. (J). (gr. 4-7). pap. 19.99 *(978-1-63140-909-7(3))* Idea & Design Works, LLC.

P. I. Kids. Teenage Mutant Ninja Turtles Look- O/P. 2013. (ENG.). 24p. (J). (gr. 1-3). 7.98 *(978-1-4508-1972-5(9)*, ceaa0b59-853d-401a-91e5-5d3db3d7adab) Phoenix International Publications, Inc.

Peter, David. Teenage Mutant Ninja Turtles: Out of the Shadows. Thomas, LeSean, illus. 2007. (ENG.). 96p. pap. 12.95 *(978-1-84576-146-2(4)*, Titan Bks.) Titan Bks. Ltd. GBR. Dist: Penguin Random Hse. LLC.

Publications International Ltd. Staff, ed. Teenage Mutant Ninja Turtles(tm) Dojo: A Flashlight Adventure Sound Book. 2013. 12p. (J). bds. *(978-1-4508-7438-0(X)*, 145087438X) Publications International, Ltd.

Random House. Monkey Business (Teenage Mutant Ninja Turtles) Spaziante, Patrick, illus. 2013. (Pictureback(R) Ser.). (ENG.). 16p. (J). (gr. -1-2). 3.99 *(978-0-449-81852-7(7)*, Random Hse. Bks. for Young Readers) Random Hse. Children's Bks.

Random House Editors. Mean Team. Spaziante, Patrick, illus. 2016. (Step into Reading Level 2 Ser.). (ENG.). 24p. (J). (gr. -1-1). 14.75 *(978-0-606-39354-6(4))* Turtleback.

—Ninja Dad! 2016. (Step into Reading - Level 1 Ser.). lib. bdg. 14.75 *(978-0-606-38484-1(7))* Turtleback.

—Pizza Party! 2017. (Step into Reading Level 2 Ser.). lib. bdg. 14.75 *(978-0-606-40253-8(5))* Turtleback.

Random House Staff. Saved by the Shell! 2012. lib. bdg. 13.55 *(978-0-606-26800-4(6))* Turtleback.

Spaziante, Patrick, illus. Meet Casey Jones. 2005. (Teenage Mutant Ninja Turtles Ser.: No. 1). 24p. (J). lib. bdg. 15.00 *(978-1-59054-836-3(1))* Fitzgerald Bks.

Teenage Mutant Ninja Turtles: New Animated Adventures, 4 vols. 2015. (Teenage Mutant Ninja Turtles: New Animated Adventures Ser.: 4). (ENG.). 24p. (J). (gr. 1-5). lib. bdg. 125.44 *(978-1-61479-458-5(8)*, 19555, Graphic Novels) Spotlight.

Teenage Mutant Ninja Turtles Sticker Activity Books. 2004. (J). act. bk. ed. 3.49 *(978-0-7666-1299-0(6)*, 69645) Modern Publishing.

Thomas, Jim. Super Slam Turtles! Spaziante, Patrick, illus. 2005. 22p. (J). lib. bdg. 15.00 *(978-1-4242-0971-2(4))* Fitzgerald Bks.

Tillworth, Mary. Skate Like a Ninja! (Teenage Mutant Ninja Turtles) Lambe, Steve, illus. 2017. (Little Golden Book Ser.). (ENG.). 24p. (J). (-k). 5.99 *(978-0-399-55796-5(2)*, Golden Bks.) Random Hse. Children's Bks.

Walker, Landry. Teenage Mutant Ninja Turtles Amazing Adventures, Vol. 1. 2016. (Teenage Mutant Ninja Turtles Amazing Adventures Ser.: 1). lib. bdg. 30.60 *(978-0-606-37809-3(X))* Turtleback.

Waltz, Tom & Eastman, Kevin. Teenage Mutant Ninja Turtles Volume 3: Shadows of the Past, Vol. 3. Duncan, Dan, illus. 2016. (Teenage Mutant Ninja Turtles Ser.: 3). (ENG.). 104p. pap. 17.99 *(978-1-61377-405-2(2)*, 9781613774052) Idea & Design Works, LLC.

—Teenage Mutant Ninja Turtles Volume 4: Sins of the Fathers, Vol. 4. Kuhn, Andy, illus. 2013. (Teenage Mutant Ninja Turtles Ser.: 4). (ENG.). 104p. pap. 17.99 *(978-1-61377-568-4(7)*, 9781613775684) Idea & Design Works, LLC.

Waltz, Tom & Eastman, Kevin B. Teenage Mutant Ninja Turtles Volume 5: Krang War, Vol. 5. Bates, Ben, illus. 2013. (Teenage Mutant Ninja Turtles Ser.: 5). (ENG.). 104p. pap. 17.99 *(978-1-61377-640-7(3)*, 9781613776407) Idea & Design Works, LLC.

Webster, Christy. Green Team! 2012. (Step into Reading Level 4 Ser.). lib. bdg. 13.55 *(978-0-606-26801-1(4))* Turtleback.

—Green Team! (Teenage Mutant Ninja Turtles) Spaziante, Patrick, illus. 2012. (Step into Reading Ser.). (ENG.). 48p. (J). (gr. k-3). pap. 5.99 *(978-0-307-98070-0(7)*, Random Hse. Bks. for Young Readers) Random Hse. Children's Bks.

—Robot Rampage! 2013. (Step into Reading Level 4 Ser.). lib. bdg. 13.55 *(978-0-606-26985-8(1))* Turtleback.

—Robot Rampage! (Teenage Mutant Ninja Turtles) Spaziante, Patrick, illus. 2013. (Step into Reading Ser.). (ENG.). 48p. (J). (gr. k-3). pap. 5.99 *(978-0-307-98212-4(2)*, Random Hse. Bks. for Young Readers) Random Hse. Children's Bks.

TEETH

see also Dentistry

Allsop, Marcus. Nos Gustan Nuestros Dientes We Like Our Teeth. 2nd ed. 2012. (We Like Toi Ser.). (ENG.). 32p. (J). pap. 10.95 *(978-1-935826-09-5(3))* Kalindi Pr.

—We Like Our Teeth. 2nd alt. ed. 2012. (We Like To Ser.). (ENG.). 32p. (J). pap. 9.95 *(978-1-935826-06-4(9))* Kalindi Pr.

Anderson, Michelle. Animal Teeth. 2018. (Plants, Animals, & People Ser.). (ENG., Illus.). 16p. (gr. -1-2). pap. 9.95 *(978-1-64156-246-1(3)*, 9781641562461) Rourke Educational Media.

Andrus, Aubre. Gloss, Floss, & Wash: DIY Crafts & Recipes for a Fresh Face & Teeth. 2017. (DIY Day Spa Ser.). (ENG., Illus.). 48p. (J). (gr. 4-8). lib. bdg. 31.99 *(978-1-5157-3447-5(1)*, 133425, Capstone Pr.) Capstone.

Arnold, Quinn M. Dentists. 2017. (Seedlings Ser.). (ENG., Illus.). 24p. (J). (gr. -1-k). pap. 8.99 *(978-1-62832-487-7(2)*, 20352, Creative Paperbacks); *(978-1-60818-872-7(8)*, 20351, Creative Education) Creative Co., The.

Barr, Brady. Chomp! Fierce Facts about the BITE FORCE, CRUSHING JAWS, & MIGHTY TEETH of Earth's Champion Chewers. 2017. (ENG., Illus.). 96p. (J). (gr. 3-7). lib. bdg. 22.90 *(978-1-4263-2840-4(0)*, National Geographic Kids) Disney Publishing Worldwide.

Bozzo, Linda. Amazing Animal Teeth. (Creature Features Ser.). 24p. (gr. 2-3). 2009. 42.50 *(978-1-61512-069-7(6))* 2008. (ENG., Illus.). (J). lib. bdg. 26.27 *(978-1-4042-4170-1(1)*, aa212505-3c79-45e0-b9e0-cd0ee23dd0bb) Rosen Publishing Group, Inc., The. (PowerKids Pr.).

Capici, Gaetano. What Do They Do? Dentists. 2010. (Community Connections: What Do They Do? Ser.). (ENG., Illus.). 24p. (gr. 2-5). lib. bdg. 29.21 *(978-1-60279-806-9(0)*, 200502) Cherry Lake Publishing.

Casado, Dami & Casado, Alicia. Los Dientes. 2005. (Sentidos y Algo Más). (SPA & ESP.). 16p. 8.99 *(978-84-272-6418-2(6))* Molino, Editorial ESP. Dist: Santillana USA Publishing Co., Inc.

Chambers, Catherine. The Tooth Fairy. Billiau, Loic, illus. 2015. (Autobiographies You Never Thought You'd Read! Ser.). (ENG.). 32p. (J). (gr. 3-5). pap. 7.99 *(978-1-4109-7969-8(5)*, 129645, Raintree) Capstone.

Chandra, Deborah & Comora, Madeleine. George Washington's Teeth. Cole, Brock, illus. 2007. (ENG.). 40p. (J). (gr. -1-3). pap. 8.99 *(978-0-312-37604-8(9)*, 900048324) Square Fish.

Cherrington, Janelle. Who Needs Teeth?, 6 vols., Set. 2003. (Phonics Readers 1-36 Ser.). (ENG.). 8p. (gr. k-1). pap. 29.70 *(978-0-7368-3211-3(4))* Capstone.

Cobb, Vicki. Your Body Battles A Cavity. 2009. pap. 40.95 *(978-0-7613-4623-4(6))* Lerner Publishing Group.

—Your Body Battles a Cavity. Harris, Andrew, illus. Kunkel, Dennis, photos by. 2009. (Body Battles Ser.). (ENG.). 32p. (gr. 2-5). 25.26 *(978-0-8225-7469-9(1))* Lerner Publishing Group.

Collard, Sneed B., III. Teeth. Saroff, Phyllis V., illus. 2008. 32p. (J). (gr. k-3). per. 7.95 *(978-1-58089-121-9(7))*; (ENG.). 21.19 *(978-1-58089-120-2(9))* Charlesbridge Publishing, Inc.

Curry, Don L. Rookie Read-About Health: Take Care of Your Teeth. 2005. (Rookie Read-About Health Ser.). (ENG., Illus.). 32p. (J). (gr. k-2). 20.50 *(978-0-516-25875-1(3)*, Children's Pr.) Scholastic Library Publishing.

Dakota, Heather. Fangs! 2007. (Illus.). 96p. (J). *(978-0-545-02564-5(8)*, Scholastic) Scholastic, Inc.

Dakota, Heather & Salzano, Tammi. Fangs! 2015. (Illus.). 94p. (J). spiral bd. *(978-0-545-92617-1(3)*, Tangerine Pr.) Scholastic, Inc.

de Nijs, Erika. A Dentist's Job, 1 vol. 2015. (Community Workers Ser.). (ENG., Illus.). 16p. (gr. 1-1). pap. 9.23 *(978-1-5026-0424-8(8)*, 9d40944d-74c2-42f6-90b4-801feb65496a) Cavendish Square Publishing LLC.

TUV

Dyan, Penelope. Teeth! Dyan, Penelope, illus. 2012. (Illus.). 34p. pap. 11.95 *(978-1-61477-060-2(3))* Bellissima Publishing, LLC.

Encyclopaedia Britannica, Inc. Staff, compiled by. How Many Teeth? 2008. 49.95 *(978-1-59339-661-9(9))* Encyclopaedia Britannica, Inc.

Ferguson, Beth. Teeth, 1 vol. 2005. (Kaleidoscope: Human Body Ser.). (ENG., Illus.). 48p. (gr. 4-4). lib. bdg. 32.64 *(978-0-7614-1589-3(0),* b09e0a08-f4ad-437d-b922-85583fde3ec2) Cavendish Square Publishing LLC.

Gogerly, Liz. Teeth. Gordon, Mike, illus. 2008. (Looking after Me Ser.). (ENG.). 32p. (J). (gr. -1-3). pap. *(978-0-7787-4122-0(2));* lib. bdg. *(978-0-7787-4115-2(X))* Crabtree Publishing Co.

Gray, Susan H. Dinosaur Teeth. 2007. (Scholastic News Nonfiction Readers Ser.). (ENG., Illus.). 24p. (J). (gr. 1-2). 22.00 *(978-0-531-17484-5(0))* Scholastic Library Publishing.

Greenwood, Nancy. I Can Be a Dentist, 1 vol. 2020. (I Can Be Anything! Ser.). (ENG.). 24p. (J). (gr. k-k). pap. 9.15 *(978-1-5382-5546-9(4),* ec3cd076-03ec-4005-a271-546b4bf8ed16) Stevens, Gareth Publishing LLLP.

Harrison, Emma. From Head to Toe: The Girls' Life Guide to Taking Care of You. Montagna, Frank, illus. 2004. 124p. (J). *(978-0-439-44983-0(9))* Scholastic, Inc.

Herrington, Lisa M. I Have a Cavity (Rookie Read-About Health) (Library Edition) 2015. (Rookie Read-About Health Ser.). (ENG., Illus.). 32p. (J). (gr. 1-2). lib. bdg. 25.00 *(978-0-531-21038-3(3),* Children's Pr.) Scholastic Library Publishing.

Hoffman, Stephanie. Sharp Teeth, Flat Teeth, 1 vol. 2008. (Real Life Readers Ser.). (ENG.). 12p. (gr. 1-2). pap. 5.90 *(978-1-4042-7917-9(2),* 51ce5e7b-2dca-4d4b-9f63-b2f9c5d24ed5, Rosen Classroom) Rosen Publishing Group, Inc., The.

Honders, Christine. Why Should I Listen to My Dentist?, 1 vol. 2019. (Listening to Leaders Ser.). (ENG.). 24p. (gr. 2-2). pap. 9.25 *(978-1-5383-4156-8(5),* 263641b2-09d6-4fc3-8f17-bb68cbe9bf67, PowerKids Pr.) Rosen Publishing Group, Inc., The.

Jenkins, Pete. Brush Your Teeth! 2018. (Let's Learn Ser.). (ENG., Illus.). 16p. (gr. -1-2). lib. bdg. 28.50 *(978-1-64156-202-7(1),* 9781641562027) Rourke Educational Media.

Johanson, Sarah Margaret. Caillou: I Can Brush My Teeth: Healthy Toddler. Brignaud, Pierre, illus. 2017. (Caillou's Essentials Ser.). (ENG.). 24p. (J). (gr. -1-k). bds. 7.99 *(978-2-89718-356-1(X))* Caillouet, Gerry.

Kenan, Tessa. ¡Que Vivan Los Dentistas! (Hooray for Dentists!) 2018. (Bumba Books (r) en Español — ¡Que Vivan Los Ayudantes Comunitarios! (Hooray for Community Helpers!) Ser.). (SPA., Illus.). 24p. (J). (gr. -1-1). 26.65 *(978-1-5124-9760-1(6),* e39e1adf-4b0c-41a5-8f4f-332c9a49fe89, Ediciones Lerner) Lerner Publishing Group.

Kimmelman, Leslie. Ben Lost a Tooth. 2004. (ENG., Illus.). 8p. (J). (gr. k-k). pap. 7.56 *(978-0-7652-5132-9(9),* Celebration Pr.) Savvas Learning Co.

Kirk, Bill. My Tooth Is Loose: The Sum of Our Parts. Ruble, Eugene, illus. 2012. 20p. pap. 10.95 *(978-1-61633-258-7(1))* Guardian Angel Publishing, Inc.

Klug, Kirsten. Healthy Smiles! 2011. (Illus.). 12p. (J). pap. 6.50 *(978-0-9798173-6-6(6))* Bamboo River Pr.

Landau, Elaine. Cavities & Toothaches, 1 vol. 2009. (Head-To-Toe Health Ser.). (ENG.). 32p. (J). (gr. 2-2). lib. bdg. 31.21 *(978-0-7614-2848-0(8),* b2e9fdd3-1584-4b0d-8d85-545fbb25b871) Cavendish Square Publishing LLC.

Lee, David. My Visit to the Dentist, 1 vol. 2016. (Community Helpers Ser.). (ENG., Illus.). 24p. (J). (gr. 1-1). pap. 9.25 *(978-1-4994-2704-2(2),* 8484dfe8-2330-4df0-b88d-56b571e40fb9, PowerKids Pr.) Rosen Publishing Group, Inc., The.

Leed, Percy. The Mouth (a Nauseating Augmented Reality Experience) 2020. (Gross Human Body in Action: Augmented Reality Ser.). (ENG., Illus.). 32p. (J). (gr. 3-5). 31.99 *(978-1-5415-9809-6(1),* 4dd6bf0d-d3f5-4bc9-9f91-612838958380, Lerner Pubns.) Lerner Publishing Group.

Less, Emma. Dentists. 2018. (Real-Life Superheroes Ser.). (ENG.). 16p. (J). (gr. k-2). pap. 7.99 *(978-1-68152-274-6(8),* 14913) Amicus.

Levine, Sara. Tooth by Tooth: Comparing Fangs, Tusks, & Chompers. Spookytooth, T. S., illus. 2016. (Animal by Animal Ser.). (ENG.). 32p. (J). (gr. k-4). 26.65 *(978-1-4677-5215-2(0),* 7acaba15-e659-40a5-8cd9-127da28c5c4a); E-Book 39.99 *(978-1-5124-0732-7(1),* 9781512407327); E-Book 39.99 *(978-1-4677-9727-6(8))* Lerner Publishing Group. (Millbrook Pr.).

Libal, Autumn. Dental Care. Noyes, Nancy & Forman, Sara, eds. 2013. (Young Adult's Guide to the Science of Health Ser.). 128p. (J). (gr. 7-18). pap. 14.95 *(978-1-4222-3006-0(6));* 24.95 *(978-1-4222-2807-4(X))* Mason Crest.

Libal, Autumn & Hovius, Christopher. Taking Care of Your Smile: A Teen's Guide to Dental Care. 2006. (Science of Health Ser.). (Illus.). 128p. (YA). lib. bdg. 24.95 *(978-1-59084-846-3(2))* Mason Crest.

Lindeen, Mary. A Visit to the Dentist. 2018. (BeginningtoRead Ser.). (ENG.). 32p. (J). (gr. -1-2). 22.60 *(978-1-59953-912-6(8));* (gr. k-2). pap. 13.26 *(978-1-68404-168-8(6))* Norwood Hse. Pr.

Llewellyn, Claire. Your Teeth. 2008. (Look after Yourself Ser.). (Illus.). 30p. (J). (gr. 1-4). lib. bdg. 28.50 *(978-1-59771-099-2(7))* Sea-To-Sea Pubns.

Machajewski, Sarah. What If I Break a Tooth?, 1 vol. 2016. (Benched: Dealing with Sports Injuries Ser.). (ENG., Illus.). 24p. (J). (gr. 2-3). 24.27 *(978-1-4824-4886-3(6),* 21693496-6b37-4964-9ea3-6fd562869354) Stevens, Gareth Publishing LLLP.

Markle, Sandra. What If You Had Animal Teeth? McWilliam, Howard, illus. 2013. (What If You Had... ? Ser.). (ENG.). 32p. (J). (gr. -1-3). pap. 4.99 *(978-0-545-48438-1(3),* Scholastic Paperbacks) Scholastic, Inc.

—What If You Had Animal Teeth!? McWilliam, Howard, illus. 2013. 32p. (J). *(978-0-545-56727-5(0))* Scholastic, Inc.

—What If You Had Animal Teeth? 2013. (What If You Had... ? Ser.). (Illus.). 32p. (J). lib. bdg. 14.75 *(978-0-606-31504-3(7))* Turtleback.

Marsico, Katie. Brush Your Teeth! Bane, Jeff, illus. 2019. (My Early Library: My Healthy Habits Ser.). (ENG.). 24p. (J). (gr. k-1). pap. 12.79 *(978-1-5341-3930-5(3),* 212549); lib. bdg. 30.64 *(978-1-5341-4274-9(6),* 212548) Cherry Lake Publishing.

—Floss Your Teeth! Bane, Jeff, illus. 2019. (My Early Library: My Healthy Habits Ser.). (ENG.). 24p. (J). (gr. k-1). pap. 12.79 *(978-1-5341-3933-6(8),* 212561); lib. bdg. 30.64 *(978-1-5341-4277-0(0),* 212560) Cherry Lake Publishing.

Miller, Edward. The Tooth Book: A Guide to Healthy Teeth & Gums. 2009. (ENG., Illus.). 32p. (J). (gr. k-3). pap. 7.99 *(978-0-8234-2206-7(2))* Holiday Hse., Inc.

O'hehir, Trisha. The Toothpaste Secret. O'hehir, Trisha, illus. 2003. (Illus.). 56p. (J). (gr. 2-6). 9.95 *(978-0-9659236-1-3(4))* Perio Reports.

Olberg, Henry. The Magical Tooth Fairies: The Secret of the Magic Dust. 2012. (J). pap. *(978-0-86715-567-9(1))* Quintessence Publishing Co., Inc.

Padron, Alicia, illus. Brush, Brush, Brush! (Rookie Toddler) 2010. (Rookie Toddler Ser.). (ENG.). 14p. (J). (gr. -1 — 1). bds. 6.95 *(978-0-531-25236-9(1),* Children's Pr.) Scholastic Library Publishing.

The Perfect Prescription for Your Teeth. 2003. 29.95 *(978-0-9747253-0-7(7))* Health & Beauty Ctr., LLC.

Pirotta, Saviour. Teeth. 2003. (Starters Ser.). 24p. (J). lib. bdg. 21.35 *(978-1-58340-259-7(4))* Black Rabbit Bks.

QEB Start Reading Together National Book Stores Edition: First Experiences: Going to the Dentist. 2006. (J). per. *(978-1-59566-260-6(X))* QEB Publishing Inc.

Randolph, Joanne. Whose Teeth Are These? (Animal Clues Ser.). 24p. (gr. 1-1). 2009. 42.50 *(978-1-61511-434-4(3))* 2008. (ENG., Illus.). (J). lib. bdg. 26.27 *(978-1-4042-4456-6(5),* 12fb4268-202f-4bc0-9e8a-068ab3e7364c) Rosen Publishing Group, Inc., The. (PowerKids Pr.).

—Whose Teeth Are These? De Quién Son Estos Dientes?, 1 vol. 2008. (Animal Clues / ¿Adivina de Quién Es? Ser.). (SPA & ENG., Illus.). 24p. (J). (gr. 1-1). lib. bdg. 26.27 *(978-1-4358-2533-8(0),* 3cea0107-57b9-49a1-91d5-b20dad973abb, PowerKids Pr.) Rosen Publishing Group, Inc., The.

—Whose Teeth Are These? / ¿de quién son estos Dientes? 2009. (Animal Clues / ¿Adivina de Quién Es? Ser.). (ENG & SPA.). 24p. (gr. 1-1). 42.50 *(978-1-61511-440-5(8),* Editorial Buenas Letras) Rosen Publishing Group, Inc., The.

Riehecky, Janet. Teeth, Claws, & Jaws: Animal Weapons & Defenses. 2012. (Animal Weapons & Defenses Ser.). (ENG.). 32p. (gr. 1-2). pap. 47.70 *(978-1-4296-8504-7(2),* Capstone Pr.); (J). (gr. 3-9). pap. 8.10 *(978-1-4296-8012-7(1),* 118344) Capstone.

Rissman, Rebecca. Teeth, 1 vol. 2011. (Animal Spikes & Spines Ser.). (ENG.). 24p. (J). (gr. -1-1). pap. 6.29 *(978-1-4329-5049-1(5),* 115101, Heinemann) Capstone.

Rissman, Rebecca & Smith, Sian. Caring for Your Teeth, 1 vol. 2012. (Take Care of Yourself! Ser.). (ENG.). 24p. (gr. -1-1). 23.32 *(978-1-4329-6708-6(8),* Heinemann) Capstone.

Royston, Angela. Tooth Decay. 2009. (How's Your Health? Ser.). (J). (gr. 1-4). 28.50 *(978-1-59920-221-1(2))* Black Rabbit Bks.

—Why Do I Brush My Teeth? 2012. (My Body Ser.). (ENG., Illus.). 24p. (gr. k-4). pap. 7.95 *(978-1-926853-99-4(7))* Saunders Bk. Co. CAN. Dist: RiverStream Publishing.

Rustad, Martha E. H. I Care for My Teeth. 2017. (Healthy Me Ser.). (ENG., Illus.). 24p. (J). (gr. -1-2). lib. bdg. 22.65 *(978-1-5157-3985-2(6),* 133884, Pebble) Capstone.

Salzmann, Mary Elizabeth. Taking Care of Your Teeth. 2004. (Healthy Habits Ser.). (ENG., Illus.). 24p. (J). (gr. k-3). lib. bdg. 24.21 *(978-1-59197-554-0(9),* SandCastle) ABDO Publishing Co.

Santillo, LuAnn. The Dentist. Santillo, LuAnn, ed. 2003. (Half-Pint Kids Readers Ser.). (Illus.). 7p. (J). (gr. -1-1). pap. 1.00 *(978-1-59256-120-9(9))* Half-Pint Kids, Inc.

Schuh, Mari. All about Teeth, 1 vol. 2008. (Healthy Teeth Ser.). (ENG., Illus.). 24p. (J). (gr. -1-2). pap. 7.29 *(978-1-4296-1784-0(5),* 94831, Capstone Pr.) Capstone.

—At the Dentist, 1 vol. 2008. (Healthy Teeth Ser.). (ENG., Illus.). 24p. (J). (gr. -1-2). pap. 7.29 *(978-1-4296-1788-8(8),* 94835, Capstone Pr.) Capstone.

—Brushing Teeth, 1 vol. 2008. (Healthy Teeth Ser.). (ENG., Illus.). 24p. (J). (gr. -1-2). pap. 7.29 *(978-1-4296-1786-4(1),* 94833, Capstone Pr.) Capstone.

—Dentists. 2018. (Community Helpers Ser.). (ENG., Illus.). 24p. (J). (gr. k-3). pap. 7.99 *(978-1-61891-305-0(0),* 12091, Blastoff! Readers) Bellwether Media.

—Un Diente Está Flojo/Loose Tooth. 2010. (Dientes Sanos/Healthy Teeth Ser.).Tr. of Loose Tooth. (MUL.). 24p. (J). (gr. -1-2). lib. bdg. 29.32 *(978-1-4296-4598-0(9),* 103075) Capstone.

—Snacks for Healthy Teeth, 1 vol. 2008. (Healthy Teeth Ser.). (ENG., Illus.). 24p. (J). (gr. -1-2). pap. 7.29 *(978-1-4296-1785-7(3),* 94832, Capstone Pr.) Capstone.

Shaw, Jessica. The Gross Science of Bad Breath & Cavities, 1 vol. 2018. (Way Gross Science Ser.). (ENG.). 48p. (gr. 5-5). 33.47 *(978-1-5081-8162-0(4),* 1cce1909-e9ca-4540-8fb0-dc1aa5d59e1f, Rosen Reference) Rosen Publishing Group, Inc., The.

Siemens, Jared. Dentists. 2017. 24p. *(978-1-4896-4221-9(8),* AV2 by Weigl) Weigl Pubs., Inc.

Silverstein, Alvin, et al. Handy Health Guide to Your Teeth, 1 vol. 2013. (Handy Health Guides). (ENG.). 48p. (gr. 5-6). lib. bdg. 27.93 *(978-0-7660-4280-3(4),* 6505828a-67b2-4f80-b441-4a2a44f69ac3) Enslow Publishing, LLC.

Silverstein, Virginia & Silverstein Nunn, Laura. Handy Health Guide to Your Teeth, 1 vol. 2013. (Handy Health Guides). (ENG.). 48p. (gr. 5-6). pap. 11.53 *(978-1-4644-0503-7(4),* 23e5a9fe-302c-4ecc-b810-f3d7e31c8acb) Enslow Publishing, LLC.

Smith, Michael & Aguiler, Manny. A Smile: B una Sonrisa. Aguiler, Manny, illus. 2015. (SPA & ENG., Illus.). 36p. (J). *(978-0-9913454-5-8(2))* East West Discovery Pr.

Smith, Penny. DK Readers L1: a Trip to the Dentist. 2006. (DK Readers Level 1 Ser.). (ENG., Illus.). 32p. (J). (gr. k-2). pap. 4.99 *(978-0-7566-1914-5(9),* DK Children) Dorling Kindersley Publishing, Inc.

Smith, Sian. Caring for Your Teeth, 1 vol. 2012. (Take Care of Yourself! Ser.). (ENG.). 24p. (gr. -1-1). pap. 6.29 *(978-1-4329-6715-4(0),* 119344, Heinemann) Capstone.

Somervill, Barbara A. Dental Hygienist. 2010. (21st Century Skills Library: Cool Careers Ser.). (ENG., Illus.). 32p. (gr. 4-8). lib. bdg. 32.07 *(978-1-60279-938-7(5),* 200621) Cherry Lake Publishing.

Squires, Susanne. When I Lose My Tooth. 2011. 12p. (gr. 10-12). pap. 8.32 *(978-1-4567-6724-2(0))* AuthorHouse.

Stein, Lori. Shark-Tastic! 2011. (Science with Stuff Ser.: 1). (ENG.). 64p. (J). (gr. 1). lib. bdg. 12.99 *(978-1-935703-29-7(3))* Downtown Bookworks.

Swanson, Diane. Teeth That Stab & Grind. 2003. (Up Close Ser.). (Illus.). 32p. (J). (gr. 2-4). 5.95 *(978-1-55054-770-2(4),* Da Capo Pr. Inc.) Hachette Bks.

Teeth Sets: 1 Each of 3 Big Books. (Sunshinetm Science Ser.). (gr. 1-2). 111.50 *(978-0-7802-1449-1(8))* Wright Group/McGraw-Hill.

Telgemeier, Raina. Smile. 2010. 21.00 *(978-1-60686-896-6(9))* Perfection Learning Corp.

—Smile. Telgemeier, Raina, illus. 2010. (ENG., Illus.). 224p. (J). (gr. 3-7). pap. 10.99 *(978-0-545-13206-0(1),* Graphix) Scholastic, Inc.

—Smile. 2010. lib. bdg. 22.10 *(978-0-606-14082-9(4))* Turtleback.

—Smile: a Graphic Novel. Telgemeier, Raina, illus. 2010. (ENG.). 224p. (J). (gr. 3-7). 24.99 *(978-0-545-13205-3(3),* Graphix) Scholastic, Inc.

Verdick, Elizabeth. Teeth Are Not for Biting. Heinlen, Marieka, illus. 2003. (Best Behavior(r) Board Book Ser.). (ENG.). 26p. (J). bds. 9.99 *(978-1-57542-128-5(3),* 794) Free Spirit Publishing Inc.

—Teeth Are Not for Biting / Los Dientes No Son para Morder. Heinlen, Marieka, illus. 2017. (Best Behavior(r) Board Book Ser.). (ENG.). 26p. (J). (— 1). bds. 9.99 *(978-1-63198-157-9(9),* 81579) Free Spirit Publishing Inc.

Vogel, Elizabeth. ¡A lavarse los dientes! (Brushing My Teeth) 2009. (Limpieza y salud todo el día (Clean & Healthy All Day Long) Ser.). (SPA.). 24p. (gr. 1-1). 37.50 *(978-1-61514-293-4(2),* Editorial Buenas Letras) Rosen Publishing Group, Inc., The.

Waxman, Laura Hamilton. Dentist Tools. 2019. (Bumba Books (r) — Community Helpers Tools of the Trade Ser.). (ENG., Illus.). 24p. (J). (gr. -1-1). 26.65 *(978-1-5415-5560-0(0),* 27aac04e-bb15-43f4-ad91-7a85c65a88cb); pap. 8.99 *(978-1-5415-7349-9(8),* 62c74d62-b135-47f4-bbbe-d9439523d6bf) Lerner Publishing Group. (Lerner Pubns.).

Weston Woods Staff, creator. Open Wide- Tooth School Inside. 2011. 38.75 *(978-0-439-84913-5(6))* Weston Woods Studios, Inc.

Willebrandt, Isabella. Why Do My Teeth Fall Out?, 1 vol., Vol. 1. 2013. (My Body Does Strange Stuff! Ser.). (ENG.). 24p. (J). (gr. 1-2). 25.27 *(978-1-4824-0296-4(3),* a9e00d5b-c6e1-4089-86a5-93e36969fbb0) Stevens, Gareth Publishing LLLP.

Williams, Rozanne. Where's Your Tooth. 2017. (Learn-To-Read Ser.). (ENG., Illus.). (J). pap. 3.49 *(978-1-68310-190-1(1))* Pacific Learning, Inc.

TEETH—FICTION

Andersdatter, Karla Margaret. Marissa the Tooth Fairy. Koff, Deborah, illus. 2nd ed. 2005. (J). *(978-0-9717611-2-4(4))* Depot Bks.

Arnoff, Rebecca D. The Trouble with Tooth Fairies: The Adventures of Sam & Angela. 2013. 24p. 22.99 *(978-1-4582-1028-9(6));* pap. 12.99 *(978-1-4582-1026-5(X))* Author Solutions, LLC. (Abbott Pr.).

Balzola, Asun. Munia y el Cocolilo Naranja. (SPA.). 32p. (J). *(978-84-233-1335-8(2))* Ediciones Destino ESP. Dist: Lectorum Pubns., Inc.

Baxter, Nicola. A Visit from the Tooth Fairy: Magical Stories & a Special Message from the Little Friend Who Collects Your Baby Teeth. Manson, Beverlie, illus. 2013. (ENG.). 40p. (J). (gr. k-4). 14.99 *(978-1-84322-987-2(0),* Armadillo) Anness Publishing GBR. Dist: National Bk. Network.

Bb. Matt's 1st Tooth. 2012. 28p. pap. 24.95 *(978-1-4626-6134-3(3))* America Star Bks.

Beckford, Avril. The Tooth Fairy. 2010. 28p. (J). pap. 12.49 *(978-1-4490-9060-9(5))* AuthorHouse.

Beeler, Selby B. Throw Your Tooth on the Roof. Karas, G. Brian, illus. 2015. 32p. pap. 7.00 *(978-1-61003-501-9(1))* Center for the Collaborative Classroom.

Bell-Rehwoldt, Sheri. You Think It's Easy Being the Tooth Fairy? Slonim, David, illus. 2007. (ENG.). 32p. (J). (gr. -1-3). 15.99 *(978-0-8118-5460-3(4))* Chronicle Bks. LLC.

Bernadine, Joyce. The Teeth Keepers. 2008. 73p. pap. 19.95 *(978-1-60563-848-5(X))* America Star Bks.

Bloomfield, Denise. Toby Gets the Brush Off. 2007. 28p. (J). pap. 5.95 *(978-0-9778113-3-5(6))* HeartFelt Stories LLC.

Bond, Juliana. Pixie Tales the Wobbly Tooth. 2005. 30p. spiral bd. 12.08 *(978-1-4116-6046-5(3))* Lulu Pr., Inc.

Borden, Louise. The Lost-And-Found Tooth. Gustavson, Adam, illus. 2008. (ENG.). 40p. (J). (gr. 2-5). 16.99 *(978-1-4169-1814-1(0),* McElderry, Margaret K. Bks.) McElderry, Margaret K. Bks.

Brooks, Felicity. Brush Your Teeth, Max & Millie. 2011. (Toddler Bks). 24p. (J). ring bd. 7.99 *(978-0-7945-2998-7(4),* Usborne) EDC Publishing.

Brown, Marc. Arthur's Tooth. Brown, Marc, illus. 2005. (ENG., Illus.). 32p. (J). (gr. -1-3). pap. 10.99 *(978-0-316-05960-2(9))* Little, Brown Bks. for Young Readers.

Burkert, Rand. Mouse & Lion. Burkert, Nancy Ekholm, illus. 2011. (ENG.). 32p. (J). (gr. -1-3). 18.99 *(978-0-545-10147-9(6),* Di Capua, Michael) Scholastic, Inc.

Butler, Dori Hillestad. King & Kayla & the Case of the Lost Tooth, 1 vol. Meyers, Nancy, illus. 2018. (King & Kayla Ser.: 4). 48p. (J). (gr. 2-4). pap. 6.99 *(978-1-68263-018-1(8));* 14.99 *(978-1-56145-880-6(5))* Peachtree Publishing Co. Inc.

Caldwell, J. Lynn. The Tooth Fairy's Guide to Lost Teeth: A Fortune for Every Day a Tooth Is Lost. Jepson, Beth, illus. 2005. (J). per. 11.95 *(978-0-9774463-0-8(1))* Caldwell, Judy.

Callahan, Charlie. Samantha Loses Her Sweet Tooth. Callahan, Charlie, illus. 2004. (Illus.). (J). *(978-0-9754019-0-3(4))* Periscope Pr.

Callen, Sharon. Safari Camp, 1 vol. rev. ed. 2013. (Literary Text Ser.). (ENG., Illus.). 20p. (gr. 1-2). (J). lib. bdg. 15.96 *(978-1-4807-1150-1(0));* 7.99 *(978-1-4333-5494-6(2))* Teacher Created Materials, Inc.

Capone, Deb. Tooth Fairy Tales. 2005. (J). 14.95 *(978-0-9728666-7-5(1))* As Simple As That Publishing.

Capone, Deb & compiled by. Tooth Fairy Tales Learning & Activity Guide. Capone, Deb, compiled by. 2007. (Illus.). 20p. (J). 9.95 *(978-0-9728666-8-2(X))* As Simple As That Publishing.

Chatman, Dudley D. I Brush My Teeth & I Smile, 1 vol. 2009. 48p. pap. 16.95 *(978-1-4489-2179-9(1))* America Star Bks.

Child, Lauren. My Wobbly Tooth Must Not Ever Never Fall Out. 2006. (Charlie & Lola Ser.). (ENG., Illus.). 32p. (J). (gr. -1-2). mass mkt. 6.99 *(978-0-448-44255-6(8),* Grosset & Dunlap) Penguin Young Readers Group.

Civardi, Anne. Going to the Dentist. 2009. (First Experiences Sticker Bks). 18p. (J). pap. 6.99 *(978-0-7945-2429-6(X),* Usborne) EDC Publishing.

Clark, CoraMarie. Emily's Magical Journey with Toothena the Tooth Fairy. Lawton, Val, illus. 2007. (ENG.). 32p. (J). *(978-0-9783779-0-8(7))* Strategix Ltd.

Clarke, Jacqueline A. Moose's Loose Tooth. McNally, Bruce, illus. 2003. (J). *(978-0-439-41183-7(1))* Scholastic, Inc.

Clarke, Jane. How to Brush Your Teeth with Snappy Crocodile. Birkett, Georgie, illus. 2017. 16p. (J). bds. 8.99 *(978-1-61067-494-2(4))* Kane Miller.

Clifford, Patricia. Fox Loses a Tooth. 2012. 24p. (-18). pap. 14.93 *(978-1-4669-6790-8(0))* Trafford Publishing.

Cook, E. Diann. The Andersuns: Jarrell's Sweet Tooth. 2010. 36p. pap. 16.99 *(978-1-4490-4997-3(4))* AuthorHouse.

Cook, Julia & Jana, Laura A. Melvin the Magnificent Molar. Valentine, Allison, illus. 2010. (ENG.). 32p. (J). (gr. -1-3). pap. 10.95 *(978-1-931636-74-2(5),* A752) National Ctr. For Youth Issues.

Coombs, Kate. The Tooth Fairy Wars. Parker, Jake, illus. 2014. (ENG.). 40p. (J). (gr. -1-3). 17.99 *(978-1-4169-7915-9(8))* Simon & Schuster Children's Publishing.

Cooper, Mimi. Me Versus the Tooth. 2006. 17p. (J). 9.99 *(978-1-4116-6933-8(9))* Lulu Pr., Inc.

Costamagna, Beatrice, illus. Crocodile Snap! 2016. (Crunchy Board Bks.). (ENG.). 12p. (J). (gr. -1-1). bds. 7.99 *(978-1-4998-0201-6(3))* Little Bee Books Inc.

Coven, Wanda. Heidi Heckelbeck Says "Cheese!" Burris, Priscilla, illus. 2015. (Heidi Heckelbeck Ser.: 14). (ENG.). 128p. (J). (gr. k-4). pap. 6.99 *(978-1-4814-2327-4(4),* Little Simon) Little Simon.

Cruise, Robin. Lunette, the True Story of the Tooth Fairy. Docampo, Valeria, illus. 2015. (J). *(978-1-938298-89-9(6))* Compendium, Inc., Publishing & Communications.

Dahl, Michael. Pony Brushes His Teeth, 1 vol. Vidal, Oriol, illus. 2010. (Hello Genius Ser.). (ENG.). 20p. (J). (gr. -1 — 1). bds. 7.99 *(978-1-4048-5727-8(3),* 102304, Picture Window Bks.) Capstone.

Dale, Jay. Jo & Jess Go to the Dentist. Chapman, Katriona, illus. 2012. (Wonder Words Ser.). (ENG.). 16p. (J). (gr. k-2). pap. 36.94 *(978-1-4296-8913-7(7),* 18352, Capstone Pr.) Capstone.

Dale, Jay & Scott, Kay. Jo & Jess Go to the Dentist, 1 vol. Chapman, Katriona, illus. 2012. (Wonder Words Ser.). (ENG.). 16p. (J). (gr. k-2). pap. 6.99 *(978-1-4296-8912-0(9),* 119959, Capstone Pr.) Capstone.

deGroat, Diane. Gilbert & the Lost Tooth. deGroat, Diane, illus. 2012. (I Can Read Level 2 Ser.). (ENG., Illus.). 32p. (J). (gr. k-3). pap. 4.99 *(978-0-06-125216-7(6),* HarperCollins) HarperCollins Pubs.

Degroat, Diane. Gilbert & the Lost Tooth. 2012. (I Can Read Level 2 Ser.). (ENG., Illus.). 32p. (J). (gr. k-3). 16.99 *(978-0-06-125214-3(X),* HarperCollins) HarperCollins Pubs.

Dewdney, Anna. Llama Llama Loses a Tooth. 2018. (Penguin Young Readers Level 2 Ser.). (Illus.). 32p. (J). lib. bdg. 13.55 *(978-0-606-40882-0(7))* Turtleback.

Dyan, Penelope. The Story of Snagatooth — -Who Is Commonly Known As the Tooth Fairy. Dyan, Penelope, illus. 2008. (Illus.). 44p. pap. 11.95 *(978-1-935118-42-8(0))* Bellissima Publishing, LLC.

—Teeth! Dyan, Penelope, illus. 2012. (Illus.). 34p. pap. 11.95 *(978-1-61477-060-2(3))* Bellissima Publishing, LLC.

Erickson, Melissa. When the Tooth Fairy Comes... Erickson, Melissa, illus. 2007. (Illus.). 15p. (J). (gr. -1-3). 10.99 *(978-1-59879-369-7(1))* Lifevest Publishing, Inc.

Friden, Chris. Toothtime with Chomper. 2008. (Illus.). 27p. (J). bds. 14.99 *(978-0-9758785-7-6(3))* Haydenburri Lane.

—Toothtime with Chomper. Rodriguez Braojos, Alberto et al, illus. 2008. (J). *(978-0-9801849-3-8(2))* Haydenburri Lane.

Ginsburg, Herbert P., et al. Two-Two the Tooth Fairy. 2003. (Illus.). 9.95 *(978-0-7690-3039-5(4))* Seymour, Dale Pubns.

Gossett, Dean L. The Hair Angel. Jorgensen, Jessica W., illus. 2006. (ENG.). 32p. per. 15.99 *(978-1-4259-7677-4(8))* AuthorHouse.

Groshek, Jodie. Brush, Brush, Brush. 2011. 28p. pap. 15.99 *(978-1-4568-5871-1(8))* Xlibris Corp.

Groves, Odessa M. Playful Teeth: Login. 2008. (Illus.). 68p. pap. 21.95 *(978-0-9820002-1-2(9))* G Publishing LLC.

Gutierrez-Haley, Lisa. The Wiggly Tooth: Adventures of Hayden & Jace. 2011. 16p. pap. 24.95 *(978-1-4626-1874-3(X))* America Star Bks.

Hall, Kirsten. The Tooth Fairy. Apperley, Dawn, illus. 2003. (My First Reader Ser.). (ENG.). 32p. (J). 18.50 *(978-0-516-22938-6(9),* Children's Pr.) Scholastic Library Publishing.

Haris, Martha & Haris, Kimberli. The Adventures of Fairyella the Tooth Fairy & Dragonfly Floyd. 2012. 24p. pap. 14.95 *(978-1-4575-1039-7(1))* Dog Ear Publishing, LLC.

Hawley, Bill. El Diente Suelto de Carlitos, Level 2. 2003. (Dejame Leer Ser.). (SPA., Illus.). (gr. 1-4). 6.50 *(978-0-673-36330-5(9),* Good Year Bks.) Celebration Pr.

Hay, Sam. Stella & the Night Sprites: Tooth Bandits, Vol. 2. Manuzak, Lisa, illus. 2016. (Stella & the Night Sprites Ser.: 2). (ENG.). 96p. (J). (gr. 1-3). 15.99 *(978-0-545-82001-1(4))* Scholastic, Inc.

Hill, Amanda. A Brush with the Super Dentists. 2007. (Illus.). 22p. (J). 14.99 *(978-0-9798506-0-8(6))* Super Dentists, The.

Hillert, Margaret. Dear Dragon Goes to the Dentist. Schimmell, David, illus. rev. ed. 2014. (BeginningtoRead Ser.). (ENG.). 32p. (J). (gr. k-2). lib. bdg. 22.60 *(978-1-59953-577-7(7))* Norwood Hse. Pr.

Hodgson, Sandra. The Toof Fairies. 2011. (Illus.). 44p. (gr. -1). pap. 16.76 *(978-1-4567-7978-8(8))* AuthorHouse.

Holloway, Jamie. Beaver Works On His Dam, 1 vol. 2015. (Rosen REAL Readers: STEM & STEAM Collection). (ENG.). 8p. (gr. k-1). pap. 5.46 *(978-1-4994-9489-1(0)*, f8b16438-3c26-4f05-8d28-5fa677cce9e8, Rosen Classroom) Rosen Publishing Group, Inc., The.

Holt, Jessica. A Night in the Life of a Tooth Fairy. 2008. 16p. pap. 10.00 *(978-1-60693-396-1(5)*, Strategic Bk. Publishing) Strategic Book Publishing & Rights Agency (SBPRA).

Hood, Karen Jean Matsko. Adventures of My Dentist & the Tooth Fairy: Activity & Coloring Book, bk. 2. Whispering Pine Press International, Inc. Staff, ed. Artistic Book and Web Design, illus. 2013. (ENG & JPN.). 174p. (J). pap. 19.95 *(978-1-59649-535-7(9))* Whispering Pine Pr. International, Inc.

—My Dentist & the Tooth Fairy: Activity & Coloring Book, bk. 10. Whispering Pine Press International, Inc. Staff, ed. 2013. (Hood Activity & Coloring Book Ser.). (ENG., Illus.). 160p. (J). pap. 19.95 *(978-1-59210-596-0(3))* Whispering Pine Pr. International, Inc.

Howell, Julie Ann. The Tooth Be Told. Cotton, Sue Lynn, illus. 2011. 24p. 18.95 *(978-1-61493-061-7(9))* Peppertree Pr., The.

Hutchinson, Carol Bates. Tooth Fairy Castles. 2008. (ENG.). 26p. pap. 20.99 *(978-1-4343-4678-0(1))* AuthorHouse.

Jacobs, Sherry. Grampa's Teeth. 2012. (ENG.). 42p. (J). pap. 16.95 *(978-1-4327-8104-0(9))* Outskirts Pr., Inc.

Jarvis. Alan's Big, Scary Teeth. Jarvis, illus. 2016. (ENG., Illus.). 32p. (J). (-k). 17.99 *(978-0-7636-8120-3(2))* Candlewick Pr.

Kann, Victoria. Silverlicious. Kann, Victoria, illus. 2011. (ENG., Illus.). 40p. (J). (gr. k-3). 17.99 *(978-0-06-178123-0(1))*; lib. bdg. 18.89 *(978-0-06-178124-7(X))* HarperCollins Pubs. (HarperCollins).

Kauffman, Christopher G. Faith's Star. Jenkins, Jacqueline, illus. 2011. 32p. pap. 24.95 *(978-1-4560-9584-0(6))* America Star Bks.

Klein, Abby. Ready, Freddy! #9: Shark Tooth Tale. McKinley, John, illus. 2006. (Ready, Freddy! Ser.: 9). (ENG.). 96p. (J). (gr. -1-3). 5.99 *(978-0-439-78458-0(1)*, Blue Sky Pr., The) Scholastic, Inc.

—Tooth Trouble. 2011. (Ready, Freddy Ser.: Bk. 1). 8.32 *(978-0-7848-3613-2(2)*, Everbind) Marco Bk. Co.

—Tooth Trouble (Ready, Freddy! #1) McKinley, John, illus. 2004. (Ready, Freddy! Ser.: 1). (ENG.). 96p. (J). (gr. -1-3). 5.99 *(978-0-439-55596-8(5)*, Blue Sky Pr., The) Scholastic, Inc.

Kredensor, Diane. Buck's Tooth. Kredensor, Diane, illus. 2015. (Pix Ser.). (ENG., Illus.). 64p. (J). (gr. 1-4). 12.99 *(978-1-4814-2382-3(7)*, Aladdin) Simon & Schuster Children's Publishing.

Ledger, Kate. Twin Magic: School Bully, Beware! 2013. (Scholastic Reader Level 2 Ser.). (Illus.). 32p. (J). lib. bdg. 13.55 *(978-0-606-31972-0(7))* Turtleback.

Lemke, Donald. Book-O-Teeth: a Wearable Book. Lentz, Bob, illus. 2015. (Wearable Bks.). (ENG.). 12p. (J). (gr. -1-1). bds. 7.99 *(978-1-62370-186-4(4)*, 127005, Capstone Young Readers) Capstone.

Loveridge, Pamela. The Tooth Fairy Who Lost a Tooth. 2012. 24p. pap. 28.03 *(978-1-4797-4928-7(1))* Xlibris Corp.

Luppens, Michel & Béha, Philippe. What Do the Fairies Do with All Those Teeth? (Illus.). (J). pap. 15.95 *(978-0-590-74050-0(4))* Scholastic, Inc.

MacHado, Cj & Jones, Gareth P. Even Cowgirls Brush Their Teeth. 2012. 26p. pap. 13.99 *(978-1-4624-0463-6(4)*, Inspiring Voices) Author Solutions, LLC.

Maconie, Robin. Alice & Her Fabulous Teeth! Fruisen, Catherine Myler, illus. 2004. 32p. (J). per. *(978-1-893974-21-0(9)*, Design Pr. Bks.) Savannah College of Art & Design Exhibitions.

Mahadeo Rdh, Elizabeth. Teddy Visits the Dentist: Teddy Gets a Filling. Barth, Alexandra, illus. 2012. 42p. (-18). pap. *(978-0-9569438-2-8(9))* Mahadeo Movement, The.

Maloney, Peter & Zekauskas, Felicia. Lose That Tooth! 2005. (Illus.). 32p. (J). *(978-0-439-67639-7(8))* Scholastic, Inc.

Manci, Arlene. The Grumpy Troll, 1 vol. Rawcliffe, Lee, illus. 2009. 25p. pap. 19.95 *(978-1-4489-2456-1(1))* PublishAmerica, Inc.

Mann, Jennifer K. Josie's Lost Tooth. Mann, Jennifer K., illus. 2018. (ENG., Illus.). 40p. (J). (gr. k-3). 16.99 *(978-0-7636-9694-8(3))* Candlewick Pr.

Manushkin, Fran. The Tricky Tooth, 1 vol. Lyon, Tammie, illus. 2011. (Katie Woo Ser.). (ENG.). 32p. (J). (gr. k-2). pap. 5.95 *(978-1-4048-6611-9(6)*, 114669, Picture Window Bks.) Capstone.

Maya Z And Nadajia R. Hall. The New-Fangled Adventures of Alexia & Z: The Case of Grams' Missing Teeth. 2009. 36p. pap. 15.95 *(978-1-4389-4508-8(6))* AuthorHouse.

Mcghee, Alison. Mrs. Watson Wants Your Teeth. Bliss, Harry, illus. 2007. 32p. (J). reprint ed. 16.00 *(978-1-4223-6777-3(0))* DIANE Publishing Co.

—Mrs. Watson Wants Your Teeth. Bliss, Harry, illus. unabr. ed. 2007. (Picture Book Readalong Ser.). (J). (gr. -1-2). 28.95 incl. audio compact disk *(978-1-59519-902-7(0))* Live Oak Media.

McRae, G. c. The Tooth. Anderson, David, illus. 2012. 36p. pap. *(978-0-9876845-2-3(3))* Warne, MacDonald Media.

Meadows, Daisy. Brianna the Tooth Fairy. 2013. (Rainbow Magic — Special Edition Ser.). lib. bdg. 17.20 *(978-0-606-31990-4(5))* Turtleback.

Medders, James. The Tooth Fairy's Quest. Hardin, Teresa, illus. 2008. 32p. pap. 24.95 *(978-1-60672-549-8(1))* America Star Bks.

Miller, Jules, illus. Ellie & the Truth about the Tooth Fairy. 2014. (ENG.). 36p. (J). (gr. -1-k). 16.95 *(978-1-62873-590-1(2)*, Sky Pony Pr.) Skyhorse Publishing Co., Inc.

Mills, David. Wibble Wobble. Crouth, Julia, illus. 2004. (ENG & GER.). 32p. (J). pap. *(978-1-85269-961-1(2))*; pap. *(978-1-85269-951-2(5))*; pap. *(978-1-85269-946-8(9))*; pap. *(978-1-85269-932-1(9))*; pap. *(978-1-85269-927-7(2))*; pap. *(978-1-85269-922-2(1))*; pap. *(978-1-85269-917-8(5))*; pap. *(978-1-85269-912-3(4))*; pap. *(978-1-85269-907-9(8))*; pap. *(978-1-85269-902-4(7))*; pap. *(978-1-85269-926-0(4))*; pap. *(978-1-85269-966-6(3))*; pap. *(978-1-85269-971-0(X))*; pap. *(978-1-85269-976-5(0))*; pap. *(978-1-85269-981-9(7))*; pap. *(978-1-85269-986-4(8))*; pap. *(978-1-85269-991-8(4))*; pap. *(978-1-85269-996-3(5))*; pap. *(978-1-85269-937-6(X))* Mantra Lingua.

—Wibbly Wobbly Tooth. Crouth, Julia, illus. 2004. (ENG & CHI.). 32p. (J). pap. *(978-1-85269-941-3(8))*; pap. *(978-1-85269-936-9(1))*; pap. *(978-1-85269-931-4(0))*; pap. *(978-1-85269-956-7(6))* Mantra Lingua.

Milton, Cathlene. The Wonders of Billy Sniggles. 2013. 18p. pap. 9.99 *(978-1-62697-179-0(X))* Salem Author Services.

Munsch, Robert. Andrew's Loose Tooth. 2004. (Illus.). (J). (gr. k-3). spiral bd. *(978-0-616-01732-6(4))*; spiral bd. *(978-0-616-00403-6(6))* Canadian National Institute for the Blind/Institut National Canadien pour les Aveugles.

—Andrew's Loose Tooth. Martchenko, Michael, illus. 2019. (ENG.). 32p. (J). pap. 8.99 *(978-0-590-12435-5(8))* Scholastic Canada, Ltd. CAN. Dist: Publishers Group West (PGW).

Nelson, James Gary. Dientecito y la Placa Peligros. Bumstead, Debbie, illus. 2011. 16p. pap. 9.95 *(978-1-61633-132-0(1))* Guardian Angel Publishing, Inc.

—Smileytooth & the Castle Hassle. Bumstead, Debbie, illus. 2008. 24p. pap. 10.95 *(978-1-933090-95-5(2))* Guardian Angel Publishing, Inc.

—Smileytooth & the Plaque Attack. Bumstead, Debbie, illus. 2008. 20p. pap. 10.95 *(978-1-935137-48-1(4))* Guardian Angel Publishing, Inc.

Nichols, Jon & Nichols, Tucker, illus. Crabtree. 2013. 32p. (J). (gr. -1-3). 17.95 *(978-1-936365-82-1(0)*, 5e73c97e-5c97-47e8-b80b-e011b4933e27) McSweeney's Publishing.

O'Connor, Jane. Fancy Nancy & the Too-Loose Tooth. Glasser, Robin Preiss, illus. 2012. (I Can Read Level 1 Ser.). (ENG.). 32p. (J). (gr. -1-3). 17.99 *(978-0-06-208301-2(5))*; pap. 4.99 *(978-0-06-208302-9(3))* HarperCollins Pubs. (HarperCollins).

—Fancy Nancy & the Too-Loose Tooth. 2012. (Fancy Nancy - I Can Read! Ser.). (J). lib. bdg. 13.55 *(978-0-606-23551-8(5))* Turtleback.

Olberg, Henry, illus. The Magical Tooth Fairies: A Surprise in Mexico. 2012. (J). *(978-0-86715-568-6(X))* Edition Q, Inc.

Palatini, Margie. No Biting, Louise. Reinhart, Matthew, illus. 2007. 32p. (J). (gr. -1-3). 16.99 *(978-0-06-052627-6(0))*; (ENG.). lib. bdg. 17.89 *(978-0-06-052628-3(9))* HarperCollins Pubs. (Tegen, Katherine Bks).

—Sweet Tooth. Davis, Jack E., illus. 2004. (ENG.). 40p. (J). (gr. -1-3). 19.99 *(978-0-689-85159-9(6)*, Simon & Schuster Bks. For Young Readers) Simon & Schuster Bks. For Young Readers.

Pammer, Victoria. Katelyn & the Crooked Tooth. 2011. 28p. pap. 24.95 *(978-1-4560-0996-0(6))* America Star Bks.

Park, Barbara. Junie B. Jones #20: Toothless Wonder. Brunkus, Denise, illus. 2003. (Junie B. Jones Ser.: 20). (ENG.). 96p. (J). (gr. 1-4). pap. 4.99 *(978-0-375-82223-0(2)*, Random Hse. Bks. for Young Readers) Random Hse. Children's Bks.

—Toothless Wonder. Brunkus, Denise, illus. 2003. (Junie B. Jones Ser.: Bk. 3). 80p. (gr. 1-4). 15.00 *(978-0-7569-1621-3(6))* Perfection Learning Corp.

—Toothless Wonder. 2003. (Junie B. Jones Ser.: 20). (gr. k-3). lib. bdg. 14.75 *(978-0-613-71014-5(2))* Turtleback.

PI Kids. Disney Doc Mcstuffins: I Can Brush My Teeth! Sound Book. 2013. (ENG.). 12p. (J). bds. 14.99 *(978-1-4508-8991-9(3)*, 1677, PI Kids) Phoenix International Publications, Inc.

Pidgeon, Jean, illus. Brush Your Teeth, Please: A Pop-Up Book. 2013. (Pop-Up Book Ser.: 2). (ENG.). 12p. (J). (gr. -1-k). 14.99 *(978-0-7944-3040-5(6)*, Studio Fun International) Printers Row Publishing Group.

Rankine-Van Wassenhoven, Jacqueline. Who Stole Grandpa's Teeth? 2008. 20p. 10.94 *(978-1-4357-0522-7(X))* Lulu Pr., Inc.

Ransom, Candice. Tooth Fairy's Night. 2017. (Step into Reading Ser.). (Illus.). 32p. (J). (gr. -1-1). 5.99 *(978-0-399-55364-6(9)*, Random Hse. Bks. for Young Readers) Random Hse. Children's Bks.

Remkiewicz, Frank. Gus Loses a Tooth. 2013. (Illus.). (J). *(978-0-545-46911-1(2))* Scholastic, Inc.

Rissi, Anica Mrose. Anna, Banana, & the Big-Mouth Bet. Park, Meg, illus. 2016. (Anna, Banana Ser.: 3). (ENG.). 128p. (J). (gr. 1-5). pap. 6.99 *(978-1-4814-1612-2(X)*, Simon & Schuster Bks. For Young Readers) Simon & Schuster Bks. For Young Readers.

Roberts, Tony. Turquie the Turkey. 2011. 28p. pap. 15.99 *(978-1-4568-5969-5(2))* Xlibris Corp.

Ross, Tony. I Want My Tooth! 2018. (Little Princess Ser.). (ENG., Illus.). 32p. (J). (gr. k-2). pap. 9.99 *(978-1-78344-601-8(3))* Andersen Pr. GBR. Dist: Independent Pubs. Group.

Russell, Erin Danielle. How to Trick the Tooth Fairy. Hansen Rolli, Jennifer, illus. 2018. (ENG.). 40p. (J). (gr. -1-3). 17.99 *(978-1-4814-6732-2(8)*, Aladdin) Simon & Schuster Children's Publishing.

Rutledge, Mary. The Toothless Tooth Fairy. 2011. 24p. pap. 12.74 *(978-1-4634-6005-1(8))* AuthorHouse.

Santa Goes to the Dentist. 2005. (J). 5.95 net. *(978-0-9769321-5-4(6))* Steingart, Nathan Publishing.

Saunders, Helen. So, Where do all the teeth Go? Bolick, Brian, illus. 2006. (J). *(978-0-9763143-3-2(9))* Happy Heart Kids Publishing.

Schaefer, Lola M. Loose Tooth. Wickstrom, Sylvie K., tr. Wickstrom, Sylvie K., illus. 2004. (My First I Can Read Bks.). 32p. (J). (gr. -1-18). 14.99 *(978-0-06-052776-1(5))* HarperCollins Pubs.

Scotto, Michael. Sweet Tooth Bun. Gabriel, Evette, illus. 2009. (J). *(978-1-935193-48-7(1))* Lincoln Learning Solutions.

Seuss. The Tooth Book. Mathieu, Joe, illus. (Big Bright & Early Board Book Ser.). (ENG.). 24p. (J). (— 1). 2017. bds. 6.99 *(978-0-553-53864-9(0))* 2003. bds. 4.99 *(978-0-375-82492-0(8))* Random Hse. Children's Bks. (Random Hse. Bks. for Young Readers).

Shehane, Kristen. Chomp! 2012. 20p. pap. 24.95 *(978-1-4626-7745-0(2))* America Star Bks.

Smileytooth & the Plaque Attack: The Adventures of Smileytooth. 2006. (J). 6.95 *(978-0-9778456-0-6(5))* Pontrelli, Jeany.

Speakes, Leslie. The Hygiene Mystery. 2004. 31p. pap. 24.95 *(978-1-4137-1860-7(4))* PublishAmerica, Inc.

Spinelle, Nancy Louise. Moose's Loose Tooth. Gedeon, Gloria, illus. l.t. ed. 2005. (ENG.). 16p. (gr. k-2). pap. 7.95 *(978-1-57874-032-1(0)*, Kaeden Bks.) Kaeden Corp.

Star the Tooth Fairy from Treasure Cloud Shares Secrets with You! 2006. (J). per. 9.99 *(978-0-9792992-0-9(9))* Twinkle Bks.

Star the Tooth Fairy Is Checking on You! 2004. (J). per. 9.99 *(978-0-9792992-2-3(5))* Twinkle Bks.

Star the Tooth Fairy Wants to Know If You Need Braces? 2006. (J). per. 9.99 *(978-0-9792992-1-6(7))* Twinkle Bks.

Steinberg, Harriet. A Tooth with a Hole. 2012. 24p. pap. 15.99 *(978-1-4797-0711-9(2))* Xlibris Corp.

Stockham, Jess, illus. Dentist. 2011. (First Time Ser.). 24p. (J). (gr. 2-2). pap. *(978-1-84643-335-1(5))* Child's Play International Ltd.

Suen, Anastasia. Loose Tooth. Eitzen, Allan, illus. 2004. 28p. (gr. -1-3). 14.00 *(978-0-7569-1955-9(X))* Perfection Learning Corp.

—The Tooth Fairy. Myer, Ed, illus. 2012. (Little Birdie Bks.). (ENG.). 24p. (gr. k-1). pap. 9.95 *(978-1-61810-307-9(5)*, 9781618103079) Rourke Educational Media.

Swanson Sateren, Shelley. Max & Zoe at the Dentist, 1 vol. Sullivan, Mary, illus. 2013. (Max & Zoe Ser.). (ENG.). 32p. (J). (gr. k-2). pap. 5.19 *(978-1-4048-8057-3(7)*, 121733, Picture Window Bks.) Capstone.

Tagliaferri, Saria & Spada, Alberto. My Baby Teeth, 1 vol. 2011. (ENG.). 20p. pap. 9.95 *(978-90-79761-20-3(6))* Tectum B.V.B.A. BEL. Dist: Innovative Logistics.

Taylor, Tracy Carol. Tale of Two Teeth. 2012. 48p. pap. 25.00 *(978-1-300-17956-6(2))* Lulu Pr., Inc.

Thompson, Deanna. 100 Years Old with Baby Teeth: Will Caroline Ever Lose Her Tooth? Wolf, Claudia, illus. 2006. 24p. (J). per. 2.99 *(978-1-59958-000-5(4))* Journey Stone Creations, LLC.

Thorpe, Linda W. Teeny-Weeny's Two Front Teeth. 2007. (Illus.). 16p. (J). 6.95 *(978-0-9799671-0-8(4))* ThunderBolt Publishing.

Tillman, Gloria J. Teeth for Thanksgiving. Tillman, Gloria J., ed. 2023. (ENG., Illus.). 32p. (J). lib. bdg. 18.82 *(978-0-9841260-7-1(4))* Tamaja Pr. L.L.C.

Tobias, Anne B. Harry's Problem First Loose Tooth. Tobias, Tom, illus. 2008. 16p. pap. 9.95 *(978-0-9818683-9-4(8))* Peppertree Pr., The.

Tooth, Lucy. Star the Tooth Fairy from Treasure Cloud Shares Secrets with You! 2010. (ENG.). 36p. 16.95 *(978-0-557-37985-9(7))* Lulu Pr., Inc.

—Star the Tooth Fairy Haunted by Mr. Jack-O-Lantern in Pumpkinland! 2009. (ENG.). 36p. 16.95 *(978-0-557-10300-3(2))* Lulu Pr., Inc.

—Star the Tooth Fairy Is Checking on You! 36p. 2010. (ENG.). 16.95 *(978-0-557-49450-7(8))* 2009. 16.95 *(978-0-557-07500-3(9))* Lulu Pr., Inc.

—Star the Tooth Fairy Takes A Holiday to Visit Santa at the North Pole! 2010. (ENG.). 40p. 17.95 *(978-0-557-41623-3(X))* Lulu Pr., Inc.

—Star the Tooth Fairy Wants to Know If You Need Braces? 36p. 2010. (ENG.). 16.95 *(978-0-557-49455-2(9))* 2009. 16.95 *(978-0-557-07542-3(4))* Lulu Pr., Inc.

—Tooth Fairy Loose & Lost Baby Tooth Coloring Log. 2010. (ENG.). 32p. pap. 15.95 *(978-0-557-56268-8(6))* Lulu Pr., Inc.

—Tooth Fairy Loose & Lost Tooth Coloring Log. 2010. (ENG.). 32p. pap. 15.95 *(978-0-557-33177-2(3))* Lulu Pr., Inc.

Trumbauer, Lisa. Un Diente esta Flojo: A Tooth Is Loose. Gray, Steve, illus. 2005. (Rookie Reader Español Ser.). (SPA & ENG.). 24p. (gr. k-2). 19.50 *(978-0-516-24449-5(3)*, Children's Pr.) Scholastic Library Publishing.

—Rookie Ready to Learn en Español: un Diente Está Flojo. Gray, Steve, illus. 2011. (Rookie Ready to Learn Español Ser.). Orig. Title: Rookie Ready to Learn: a Tooth Is Loose. (SPA.). 32p. (J). pap. 5.95 *(978-0-531-26785-1(7)*, Children's Pr.) Scholastic Library Publishing.

—A Tooth Is Loose. Gray, Steve, illus. (Rookie Ready to Learn Ser.). (J). 2011. 32p. pap. 5.95 *(978-0-531-26735-6(0))* 2005. (ENG.). 24p. pap. 4.95 *(978-0-516-25841-6(9))* Scholastic Library Publishing. (Children's Pr.).

Tsitoukis, Kristen L. The Tooth Song. 2008. 16p. pap. 8.50 *(978-1-4343-9539-9(1))* AuthorHouse.

Twinkle the Tooth Fairy. 2008. (Deluxe Charm Book Ser.). 12p. *(978-1-4075-3332-2(0))* Parragon, Inc.

Van Leeuwen, Jean. Amanda Pig & the Wiggly Tooth. Schweninger, Ann, illus. 2009. (Oliver & Amanda Ser.). (ENG.). 48p. (J). (gr. 1-3). mass mkt. 4.99 *(978-0-14-241290-9(2)*, Penguin Young Readers) Penguin Young Readers Group.

Vanek, Karen & Schmidt, Sharon Vanek. Santa Claus Meets the Tooth Fairy. 2012. 44p. pap. 21.99 *(978-1-4772-4535-4(9))* AuthorHouse.

Victoria's Tooth Fairy Adventure. 2007. (Illus.). 40p. (J). 19.95 *(978-0-615-17773-1(5))* Created For You.

Vries, Lizzette de & Vries, Cecile de. How the Tooth Mouse Met the Tooth Fairy. Suwannakit, Tul, illus. 2010. (J). 19.95 *(978-0-86715-507-5(8))* Quintessence Publishing Co., Inc.

Wallace, Jazey. Smile Bright. Fraser, Sigmund, illus. 2012. 24p. pap. 11.50 *(978-1-61897-755-7(5)*, Strategic Bk. Publishing) Strategic Book Publishing & Rights Agency (SBPRA).

Walsh, Alice. Uncle Farley's False Teeth. 2004. (Illus.). (J). (gr. k-3). spiral bd. *(978-0-616-01807-1(X))* Canadian National Institute for the Blind/Institut National Canadien pour les Aveugles.

—Uncle Farley's False Teeth, 1 vol. Martchenko, Michael, illus. 2019. (ENG.). 32p. (J). pap. 10.95 *(978-1-77108-719-3(6)*, 54ec217a-9510-4cf5-a907-ddcf8cbf0b11) Nimbus Publishing, Ltd. CAN. Dist: Baker & Taylor Publisher Services (BTPS).

Webb, Carla. The Magic in Believing: The Tooth Fairies. Lee, Kim, illus. (Magic in Believing Ser.). 36p. (J). (gr. k-5). *(978-0-9705726-0-8(3))* Ageless Treasures.

Weinbrenner, Darlene. My Silly Willy Loose Tooth. Weinbrenner, Jacquelyn, illus. 2012. 24p. 24.95 *(978-1-4626-5180-1(1))* America Star Bks.

Wells, Mark & Wells, Meagan. Tommy's Lost Tooth. Wells, Mark, illus. 2011. (Illus.). 28p. pap. 11.99 *(978-1-61170-020-6(5))* Robertson Publishing.

Westen, Leah. Jack the Tooth Rat. 2009. (Illus.). 28p. pap. 12.50 *(978-1-60693-558-3(5)*, Eloquent Bks.) Strategic Book Publishing & Rights Agency (SBPRA).

Weston Woods Staff, creator. Ready, Freddy! #1: Tooth Trouble. 2011. 20.95 *(978-0-545-05008-1(1))* Weston Woods Studios, Inc.

Willems, Mo. I Lost My Tooth!-An Unlimited Squirrels Book. 2018. (Unlimited Squirrels Ser.: 1). (ENG.). 96p. (J). (gr. -1-3). 12.99 *(978-1-368-02457-0(2)*, Hyperion Books for Children) Disney Publishing Worldwide.

Williamson, Melanie. El magnífico plan de Lobo/ Wolf's Magnificent Plan. Williamson, Melanie, illus. 2008. (SPA., Illus.). 29p. 20.95 *(978-84-263-6837-9(9))* Vives, Luis Editorial (Edelvives) ESP. Dist: Baker & Taylor Bks.

Wilson, Karma. Bear's Loose Tooth. Chapman, Jane, illus. 2014. (Bear Bks.). (ENG.). 34p. (J). (gr. -1-k). bds. 8.99 *(978-1-4424-8936-3(7)*, Little Simon) Little Simon.

—Bear's Loose Tooth. Chapman, Jane, illus. 2011. (Bear Bks.). (ENG.). 40p. (J). (gr. -1-3). 18.99 *(978-1-4169-5855-0(X)*, McElderry, Margaret K. Bks.) McElderry, Margaret K. Bks.

Wing, Natasha. The Night Before the Tooth Fairy. Johansen Newman, Barbara, illus. 2003. (Night Before Ser.). 32p. (J). (gr. -1-3). pap. 5.99 *(978-0-448-43252-6(8)*, Grosset & Dunlap) Penguin Young Readers Group.

The Wobbly Tooth: Individual Title Six-Packs. (Literatura 2000 Ser.). (gr. 1-2). 28.00 *(978-0-7635-0158-7(1))* Rigby Education.

Wood, Audrey. Tooth Fairy. 2005. (Audrey Wood Bks.). (Illus.). 32p. (J). (gr. -1-1). pap. 24.94 *(978-0-85953-293-8(3))* Child's Play International Ltd. GBR. Dist: Children's Plus, Inc.

—Tooth Fairy. 2003. (ENG.). (J). (gr. -1-2). lib. bdg. 18.60 *(978-0-7569-6492-4(X))* Perfection Learning Corp.

—Tooth Fairy. 2003. (gr. -1-2). 18.40 *(978-0-613-76960-0(0))* Turtleback.

Xavier, Imbeus & Sanders, Martin B. Super Dentist Guy: Attack of the Yukkies. Sanders, Martin B., illus. 2003. (Illus.). 64p. lib. bdg. 11.99 *(978-0-9708523-2-8(0))* DeMosi Publishing.

—Super Dentist Guy: Attack of the Yukkies. Sanders, Martin B. et al, illus. 2003. 52p. 7.99 *(978-0-9708523-0-4(4))* DeMosi Publishing.

TELECOMMUNICATION

see also Artificial Satellites in Telecommunication; Interstellar Communication; Radio; Telegraph; Telephone; Television

Aaseng, Nathan. Business Builders in Broadcasting. 2005. (Business Builders Ser.: Vol. 8). (Illus.). 160p. (J). (gr. 5-18). lib. bdg. 24.95 *(978-1-881508-83-0(8))* Oliver Pr., Inc.

Ball, Jacqueline A., et al. Communication Inventions: From Hieroglyphics to DVDs. 2006. (Which Came First? Ser.). (Illus.). 32p. (YA). (gr. 3-6). lib. bdg. 28.50 *(978-1-59716-129-9(2))* Bearport Publishing Co., Inc.

Bell, Samantha S. Before Cell Phones. 2020. (What Did We Do? Ser.). (ENG.). 32p. (J). (gr. 2-3). pap. 9.95 *(978-1-64493-120-2(6)*, 1644931206); lib. bdg. 31.35 *(978-1-64493-041-0(2)*, 1644930412) North Star Editions. (Focus Readers).

Bozzo, Linda. Staying in Touch in the Past, Present, & Future, 1 vol. 2010. (Imagining the Future Ser.). (ENG., Illus.). 24p. (gr. k-2). lib. bdg. 25.27 *(978-0-7660-3438-9(0)*, e955973c-d2ad-4139-a7b3-ce0d3774d7a5, Enslow Elementary) Enslow Publishing, LLC.

Christensen, Laurel. LYFSGUD: If God Sent You a Text Message. 2009. xi, 115p. (J). *(978-1-60641-108-7(X))* Deseret Bk. Co.

Cleveland, Donald. Seven Wonders of Communication. 2010. (Seven Wonders Ser.). (Illus.). 80p. (J). (gr. 5-9). lib. bdg. 33.26 *(978-0-7613-4240-3(0))* Twenty First Century Bks.

Colson, Rob. Trailblazers of Technology. 2018. (STEM-Gineers Ser.). (Illus.). 32p. (J). (gr. 5-5). pap. *(978-0-7787-5825-9(7))* Crabtree Publishing Co.

Currie-McGhee, Leanne K. Brittany & Robbie Bergquist: Cell Phones for Soldiers, 1 vol. 2007. (Young Heroes Ser.). (ENG., Illus.). 48p. (gr. 4-8). lib. bdg. 37.33 *(978-0-7377-3866-7(9)*, 6a000c1f-f55d-48b8-9560-0fc4e8f8e37d, KidHaven Publishing) Greenhaven Publishing LLC.

Einspruch, Andrew. Wired World, 1 vol. 2012. (Discovery Education: Technology Ser.). (ENG., Illus.). 32p. (J). (gr. 4-5). pap. 11.00 *(978-1-4488-7970-0(1)*, dd8382ce-4e95-4921-979e-dcd6be6d1861); lib. bdg. 28.93 *(978-1-4488-7888-8(8)*, ee32e81c-4f5d-48c2-a6bf-ba71c0ec6fbe) Rosen Publishing Group, Inc., The. (PowerKids Pr.).

Engdahl, Sylvia, ed. Mobile Apps, 1 vol. 2014. (Current Controversies Ser.). (ENG., Illus.). 160p. (gr. 10-12). pap. 33.00 *(978-0-7377-6891-6(6)*, 5c2274bc-774d-426f-af83-96e299334150); lib. bdg. 48.03 *(978-0-7377-6890-9(8)*, 2b228e13-a004-486d-bc2e-54369fc82c47) Greenhaven Publishing LLC. (Greenhaven Publishing).

Espejo, Roman, ed. Cell Phones in Schools, 1 vol. 2014. (At Issue Ser.). (ENG.). 88p. (gr. 10-12). pap. 28.80 *(978-0-7377-6156-6(3)*, 9a639cc9-50f4-4107-a343-69173d58fc6f); lib. bdg. 41.03 *(978-0-7377-6155-9(5)*, 76a56225-8a3f-4a5a-9d7d-c67f7a6f69f3) Greenhaven Publishing LLC. (Greenhaven Publishing).

Farris Naff, Clay, ed. Do Cell Phones Cause Cancer?, 1 vol. 2013. (At Issue Ser.). (ENG.). 104p. (gr. 10-12). pap. 28.80 *(978-0-7377-6168-9(7)*, f2a11996-37ff-44b5-a03b-093130f1b2b5); lib. bdg. 41.03 *(978-0-7377-6167-2(9)*, d6e63562-cf8a-4e5d-88c7-bbf6817e636b) Greenhaven Publishing LLC. (Greenhaven Publishing).

Ferguson. Careers in Focus: Internet. 3rd rev. ed. 2006. (Careers in Focus Ser.). (ENG., Illus.). 224p. (gr. 6-12). 32.95 *(978-0-8160-6564-6(0)*, P179063, Ferguson Publishing Company) Infobase Holdings, Inc.

Firestone, Mary. Wireless Technology. 2009. pap. 52.95 *(978-0-7613-4786-6(0))* 2008. (ENG., Illus.). 48p. (J). (gr. 4-8). 27.93 *(978-0-8225-7590-0(6))* Lerner Publishing Group.

Fontichiaro, Kristin. Podcasting 101. 2010. (Explorer Library: Information Explorer Ser.). (ENG., Illus.). 32p. (gr. 4-8). lib.

TUV

bdg. 32.07 *(978-1-60279-953-0(9)*, 200631) Cherry Lake Publishing.
—Speak Out! Creating Podcasts & Other Audio Recordings. 2013. (Explorer Junior Library: Information Explorer Junior Ser.). (ENG.). 24p. (gr. 1-4). pap. 12.79 *(978-1-62431-046-1(X)*, 202541); (Illus.). 32.07 *(978-1-62431-022-5(2)*, 202539) Cherry Lake Publishing.
Gagne, Tammy. Smartphones. 2018. (21st Century Inventions Ser.). (ENG.). 24p. (J). (gr. 1-1). pap. 8.95 *(978-1-63517-794-7(4)*, 1635177944) North Star Editions.
—Smartphones. 2018. (21st Century Inventions Ser.). (ENG., Illus.). 24p. (J). (gr. k-3). lib. bdg. 31.36 *(978-1-5321-6043-1(7)*, 28718, Pop! Cody Koala) Pop!
Gintzler, A. S. How Wi-Fi Works, 1 vol. 2018. (Everyday STEM Ser.). (ENG.). 32p. (J). (gr. 3-3). 30.21 *(978-1-5026-3760-4(X)*, d692a2b6-df7b-4ca3-8d6f-8c77fe29c6aa) Cavendish Square Publishing LLC.
Graham, Ian. Great Electronic Gadget Designs 1900 - Today. 2015. (Iconic Designs Ser.). (ENG., Illus.). 48p. (J). (gr. 4-6). pap. 8.99 *(978-1-4846-2623-8(0)*, 130092, Heinemann) Capstone.
Green, Sara. Netflix. 2017. (Brands We Know Ser.). (ENG., Illus.). 24p. (J). (gr. 3-8). 27.95 *(978-1-62617-653-9(1)*, Pilot Bks.) Bellwether Media.
Grinapol, Corinne. Reed Hastings & Netflix, 1 vol. 2013. (Internet Biographies Ser.). (ENG., Illus.). 128p. (YA). (gr. 7-7). lib. bdg. 39.80 *(978-1-4488-9525-0(1)*, 8f830ea5-dbe1-4b69-b465-0af2daa0bacd, Rosen Classroom) Rosen Publishing Group, Inc., The.
Hayes, Vicki C. The 12 Biggest Breakthroughs in Communication Technology. 2019. (Technology Breakthroughs Ser.). (ENG., Illus.). 32p. (J). (gr. 3-6). 9.95 *(978-1-63235-635-2(X)*, 14034); lib. bdg. 32.80 *(978-1-63235-581-2(7)*, 14026) Bookstaves, LLC. (12-Story Library).
Higgins, Nadia. Making a Podcast. 2018. (Sequence Entertainment Ser.). (ENG.). 32p. (J). (gr. 2-5). lib. bdg. *(978-1-68151-442-0(7)*, 15196) Amicus.
Hurt, Avery Elizabeth. How Bluetooth Works, 1 vol. 2018. (Everyday STEM Ser.). (ENG.). 32p. (J). (gr. 3-3). 30.21 *(978-1-5026-3736-9(7)*, c859d081-9da8-47d6-93a1-c9d2ba6eae94) Cavendish Square Publishing LLC.
Hyde, Natalie. Net Neutrality. 2018. (Get Informed — Stay Informed Ser.). (Illus.). 48p. (J). (gr. 5-6). *(978-0-7787-4968-4(1))* Crabtree Publishing Co.
Jackson, Aurelia. Netflix: How Reed Hastings Changed the Way We Watch Movies & TV. 2014. (Wizards of Technology Ser.: 10). 64p. (J). (gr. 7-18). 23.95 *(978-1-4222-3184-5(4))* Mason Crest.
Kallen, Stuart A., ed. The Wireless Society, 1 vol. 2006. (At Issue Ser.). (ENG.). 120p. (gr. 10-12). pap. 28.80 *(978-0-7377-2750-0(0)*, 65d1ef88-cf85-4a06-abb1-681f04d5d07e); lib. bdg. 41.03 *(978-0-7377-2749-4(7)*, 3847d56e-fce1-4991-8ffb-3fb619c83439) Greenhaven Publishing LLC. (Greenhaven Publishing).
Kamberg, Mary-Lane. Cybersecurity: Protecting Your Identity & Data, 1 vol. 2017. (Digital & Information Literacy Ser.). (ENG., Illus.). 48p. (J). (gr. 6-6). pap. 12.75 *(978-1-4994-3907-6(5)*, c599788e-4eea-4fb3-9f97-80a001dbc3b1, Rosen Reference) Rosen Publishing Group, Inc., The.
Klein, Rebecca T. Frequently Asked Questions about Texting, Sexting, & Flaming, 1 vol. 2012. (FAQ: Teen Life Ser.). (ENG., Illus.). 64p. (J). (gr. 5-6). lib. bdg. 37.13 *(978-1-4488-8331-8(8)*, e0421e7d-c848-4acf-bbee-f05ac056aa87) Rosen Publishing Group, Inc., The.
Klepeis, Alicia Z. How Smartphones Work, 1 vol. 2018. (Everyday STEM Ser.). (ENG.). 32p. (J). (gr. 3-3). 30.21 *(978-1-5026-3752-9(9)*, b9d8f6d6-0765-47e0-9e32-a3afc862d7b8) Cavendish Square Publishing LLC.
Kopp, Megan. Communicating in the Digital World. 2018. (Your Positive Digital Footprint Ser.). (ENG.). 32p. (J). (gr. 5-5). *(978-0-7787-4600-3(3))*; pap. *(978-0-7787-4604-1(6))* Crabtree Publishing Co.
Kraus, Stephanie. The Information Revolution. rev. ed. 2019. (Social Studies: Informational Text Ser.). (ENG., Illus.). 32p. (J). (gr. 4-8). pap. 11.99 *(978-1-4258-5077-7(4))* Teacher Created Materials, Inc.
Lewis, Daniel. Computers, Communications & the Arts, Vol. 10. 2018. (Careers in Demand for High School Graduates Ser.). 112p. (J). (gr. 7). 34.60 *(978-1-4222-4134-9(3))* Mason Crest.
Lyons, Heather. Coding to Create & Communicate. Westgate, Alex, illus. 2017. (Kids Get Coding Ser.). (ENG.). 24p. (J). (gr. 1-4). 26.65 *(978-1-5124-3944-1(4)*, c20a25b4-b4ef-4c7f-a81a-33804fa76ee9, Lerner Pubns.); pap. 10.99 *(978-1-5124-5584-7(9)*, 400d604e-d71b-4e63-bd03-15bf622ed604) Lerner Publishing Group.
Maddison, Simon. Telecoms. 2003. 48p. (J). lib. bdg. 27.10 *(978-1-58340-352-5(3))* Black Rabbit Bks.
Mapua, Jeff. Net Neutrality & What It Means to You, 1 vol. 2016. (Digital & Information Literacy Ser.). (ENG.). 48p. (J). (gr. 6-6). pap. 12.75 *(978-1-4994-6511-2(4)*, 0a8d6b73-ee0b-41f6-a0a2-53ccc1beb27b, Rosen Reference) Rosen Publishing Group, Inc., The.
Mara, Wil. Streaming TV. 2018. (21st Century Skills Library: Global Citizens: Modern Media Ser.). (ENG., Illus.). 32p. (J). (gr. 4-7). lib. bdg. 32.07 *(978-1-5341-2932-0(4)*, 211772) Cherry Lake Publishing.
Mooney, Carla. Music & Video Streaming, 1 vol., 1. 2015. (Digital & Information Literacy Ser.). (ENG.). 48p. (J). (gr. 6-6). pap. 12.75 *(978-1-4994-3769-0(2)*, 654bfdcd-2539-4a4a-988f-20c6b303e45a, Rosen Central) Rosen Publishing Group, Inc., The.
Murray, Laura K. ATandT. 2015. (Built for Success Ser.). (ENG., Illus.). 48p. (J). (gr. 4-7). *(978-1-60818-556-6(7)*, 20852, Creative Education) Creative Co., The.
—The Story of At&T. 2016. (Built for Success Ser.). (ENG.). 48p. (J). (gr. 4-7). pap. 12.00 *(978-1-62832-157-9(1)*, 20853, Creative Paperbacks) Creative Co., The.
Nakaya, Andrea C. Cell Phones. 2016. (Matters of Opinion Ser.). (ENG., Illus.). 64p. (J). (gr. 4-6). pap. 14.60 *(978-1-60357-858-5(7))* Norwood Hse. Pr.
Newman, Heather. A Better App. 2019. (21st Century Skills Innovation Library: Design a Better World Ser.). (ENG., Illus.). 32p. (J). (gr. 4-7). pap. 14.21 *(978-1-5341-3979-4(6)*, 212745); lib. bdg. 32.07 *(978-1-5341-4323-4(8)*, 212744) Cherry Lake Publishing.
O'Brien, Cynthia. Innovations in Communication. 2016. (Problem Solved! Your Turn to Think Big Ser.). (ENG., Illus.). 32p. (J). (gr. 3-6). *(978-0-7787-2672-2(X))* Crabtree Publishing Co.
Oxlade, Chris. The History of Telecommunications. 2017. (History of Technology Ser.). (ENG., Illus.). 32p. (J). (gr. 2-5). pap. 8.29 *(978-1-4846-4039-5(X)*, 135140, Heinemann) Capstone.
Parker, Janice. Communication. 2009. (Science Q & A Ser.). (Illus.). 48p. (YA). (gr. 5-8). pap. 10.95 *(978-1-60596-067-8(5))*; lib. bdg. 29.05 *(978-1-60596-066-1(7))* Weigl Pubs., Inc.
Perritano, John. Revolution in Communications, 1 vol. 2010. (It Works! Ser.). (ENG.). 32p. (J). (gr. 3-3). 31.21 *(978-0-7614-4373-5(8)*, 99c0b297-f62b-46eb-8b58-4b1665880ce3) Cavendish Square Publishing LLC.
Prentzas, G. S. Gps. 2009. (21st Century Skills Library: Global Products Ser.). (ENG., Illus.). 32p. (gr. 4-8). lib. bdg. 32.07 *(978-1-60279-506-8(1)*, 200321) Cherry Lake Publishing.
Radios, Phones & Telecommunications. 2005. (Inventions Ser.). (Illus.). 30p. (J). pap. 15.95 incl. audio *(978-0-9724983-4-0(6))* Jazwares Distribution, Inc.
Robinson, Peg. How Streaming Works, 1 vol. 2018. (Everyday STEM Ser.). (ENG.). 32p. (J). (gr. 3-3). 30.21 *(978-1-5026-3756-7(1)*, f2701ea2-00d5-49ff-8cb2-029953227421) Cavendish Square Publishing LLC.
Sawyer, Sarah. Career Building Through Podcasting. (Digital Career Building Ser.). 64p. (gr. 6-6). 2009. 58.50 *(978-1-61512-170-0(6))* 2007. (ENG., Illus.). (YA). lib. bdg. 37.13 *(978-1-4042-1944-1(7)*, fc1ec406-774f-467d-8206-e4d805db1b39) Rosen Publishing Group, Inc., The.
Scott, Celicia. YouTube: How Steve Chen Changed the Way We Watch Videos. 2014. (Wizards of Technology Ser.: 10). (Illus.). 64p. (J). (gr. 7-18). 23.95 *(978-1-4222-3188-3(7))* Mason Crest.
Small, Cathleen. American Life & Communication from the Telephone to Twitter, 1 vol. 2016. (Pop Culture Ser.). (ENG.). 112p. (J). (gr. 7-7). 41.64 *(978-1-5026-1977-8(6)*, facc0764-e0e2-4c74-99cc-64a9d2834f15) Cavendish Square Publishing LLC.
Solwey, Andrew. Communication: The Impact of Science & Technology, 1 vol. 2009. (Pros & Cons Ser.). (ENG.). 64p. (YA). (gr. 5-8). lib. bdg. 37.67 *(978-1-4339-1986-2(9)*, 13014760-e0e1-4a82-9d26-416749db013f) Stevens, Gareth Publishing LLLP.
Steffens, Bradley. Cell Phone Addiction. 2019. (Emerging Issues in Public Health Ser.). (ENG.). 80p. (YA). (gr. 6-12). 41.27 *(978-1-68282-665-2(1))* ReferencePoint Pr., Inc.
—Thinking Critically: Cell Phones. 2018. (ENG.). 80p. (YA). (gr. 5-12). *(978-1-68282-335-4(0))* ReferencePoint Pr., Inc.
Way, Steve & Bailey, Gerry. Communication, 1 vol. 2008. (Simply Science Ser.). (ENG., Illus.). 32p. (YA). (gr. 3-5). lib. bdg. 28.67 *(978-0-8368-9226-0(7)*, 3fefc888-023f-4f35-af08-4fba711bb4aa) Stevens, Gareth Publishing LLLP.
Whiting, Jim. John R. Pierce: Pioneer in Satellite Communication. 2003. (Unlocking the Secrets of Science Ser.). (Illus.). 56p. (J). (gr. 4-10). lib. bdg. 25.70 *(978-1-58415-205-7(2))* Mitchell Lane Pubs.
Wooster, Patricia. YouTube Founders Steve Chen, Chad Hurley, & Jawed Karim. 2014. (STEM Trailblazer Bios Ser.). (ENG., Illus.). 32p. (J). (gr. 2-5). lib. bdg. 26.65 *(978-1-4677-2457-9(2)*, a24aeadc-969a-4609-b1a8-9493e2094c3c, Lerner Pubns.) Lerner Publishing Group.

TELEGRAPH

Davis, Lynn. Samuel Morse, 1 vol. 2015. (Amazing Inventors & Innovators Ser.). (ENG., Illus.). 24p. (J). (gr. k-3). 32.79 *(978-1-62403-725-2(9)*, 17956, Super SandCastle) ABDO Publishing Co.
Figley, Marty Rhodes. President Lincoln, Willie Kettles, & the Telegraph Machine. 2010. pap. 56.72 *(978-0-7613-6929-5(5))* Lerner Publishing Group.
Jarrow, Jesse. Telegraph & Telephone Networks: Groundbreaking Developments in American Communications, 1 vol. 2003. (Primary Sources of America's Industrial Society in the 19th Century Ser.). (ENG., Illus.). 32p. (gr. 4-5). pap. 10.00 *(978-0-8239-4279-4(1)*, 77e1a824-50d8-4605-bba2-8a65c23c3365); lib. bdg. 29.13 *(978-0-8239-4025-7(X)*, 7792e725-74c8-4fd8-9677-6d3999293b44, Rosen Reference) Rosen Publishing Group, Inc., The.
—Telegraph & Telephone Networks: Groundbreaking Developments in American Communications. 2009. (America's Industrial Society in the 19th Century Ser.). 32p. (gr. 4-4). 47.90 *(978-1-61511-341-5(X))* Rosen Publishing Group, Inc., The.
Kulling, Monica. Making Contact! Marconi Goes Wireless. Rudnicki, Richard, illus. (Great Idea Ser.: 5). 32p. (J). (gr. k-3). 2016. pap. 6.99 *(978-1-101-91842-5(X))* 2013. 17.95 *(978-1-77049-378-0(6))* Tundra Bks. CAN. (Tundra Bks.). Dist: Penguin Random Hse. LLC.
Maurer, Tracy Nelson. Samuel Morse, That's Who! The Story of the Telegraph & Morse Code. Ramón, El Primo, illus. 2019. (ENG.). 40p. (J). 19.99 *(978-1-62779-130-4(2)*, 900136046, Holt, Henry & Co. Bks. For Young Readers) Holt, Henry & Co.
Worth, Richard. The Telegraph & Telephone, 1 vol. 2005. (Great Inventions Ser.). (ENG., Illus.). 48p. (gr. 5-8). lib. bdg. 33.67 *(978-0-8368-5879-2(4)*, 306e7b3e-d923-4ce1-ba37-c78ddabddd24, Gareth Stevens Secondary Library) Stevens, Gareth Publishing LLLP.
Zannos, Susan. Samuel Morse & the Telegraph. 2004. (Uncharted, Unexplored, & Unexplained Ser.). (Illus.). 48p. (J). (gr. 4-8). lib. bdg. 29.95 *(978-1-58415-269-9(9))* Mitchell Lane Pubs.

TELEGRAPH—FICTION

Appleton, Victor. Tom Swift & his Wireless Message. 2005. 26.95 *(978-1-4218-1506-0(0))*; 196p. pap. 11.95 *(978-1-4218-1606-7(7))* 1st World Publishing, Inc. (1st World Library - Literary Society).
Rozier, Lucy Margaret. Jackrabbit Mccabe & the Electric Telegraph. Espinosa, Leo, illus. 2015. 40p. (J). (gr. -1-3). 18.99 *(978-0-385-37843-7(2)*, Schwartz & Wade Bks.) Random Hse. Children's Bks.
Stockton, Frank Richard. What Might Have Been Expected. 2009. 128p. 23.95 *(978-1-60664-676-2(1))*; pap. 10.95 *(978-1-60664-305-1(3))* Rodgers, Alan Bks.

TELEPATHY

see Thought Transference

TELEPHONE

Allen, Kathy. Cell Phone Safety, 6 vols. 2013. (Tech Safety Smarts Ser.). (ENG.). 32p. (J). (gr. 3-4). pap. 48.60 *(978-1-62065-797-3(X)*, 19381); pap. 8.10 *(978-1-62065-796-6(1)*, 121758) Capstone. (Capstone Pr.).
Ashley, Susan. I Can Use the Telephone, 1 vol. 2004. (I Can Do It! Ser.). (ENG., Illus.). 24p. (gr. k-2). pap. 9.15 *(978-0-8368-4334-7(7)*, 6c88c319-2b1a-4729-994d-65337f5f9154, Weekly Reader Leveled Readers) Stevens, Gareth Publishing LLLP.
Bader, Bonnie. Who Was Alexander Graham Bell? 2013. (Who Was... ? Ser.). lib. bdg. 16.00 *(978-0-606-32132-7(2))* Turtleback.
Bader, Bonnie & Who HQ. Who Was Alexander Graham Bell? Groff, David, illus. 2013. (Who Was? Ser.). 112p. (J). (gr. 3-7). 5.99 *(978-0-448-46460-2(8)*, Penguin Workshop) Penguin Young Readers Group.
Bankston, John. Alexander Graham Bell & the Story of the Telephone. 2004. (Uncharted, Unexplored, & Unexplained Ser.). (Illus.). 48p. (J). (gr. 4-8). lib. bdg. 29.95 *(978-1-58415-243-9(5))* Mitchell Lane Pubs.
Banting, Erinn. Inventing the Telephone, 1 vol. 2006. (Breakthrough Inventions Ser.). (ENG., Illus.). 32p. (J). (gr. 4-7). pap. *(978-0-7787-2837-5(4))*; lib. bdg. *(978-0-7787-2815-3(3))* Crabtree Publishing Co.
Berger, Melvin. Telephones, Televisions, & Toilets. (Discovery Readers Ser.). (ENG.). 48p. (J). pap. 3.95 *(978-0-8249-5311-9(8)*, Ideals Pubns.) Worthy Publishing.
Brown, Natalie. Who Was Alexander Graham Bell?, 1 vol. 2012. (InfoMax Readers Ser.). (ENG., Illus.). 24p. (J). (gr. 1-1). pap. 8.25 *(978-1-4488-9085-9(3)*, 2e86d69c-bef5-4692-b5e1-27664b4bd962, Rosen Classroom) Rosen Publishing Group, Inc., The.
Bryan, Dale-Marie. Smartphone Safety & Privacy. 2013. (21st Century Safety & Privacy Ser.). 64p. (J). (gr. 5-8). pap. 77.70 *(978-1-4488-9587-8(1))*; (ENG.). (gr. 6-6). 37.12 *(978-1-4488-9573-1(1)*, 815ef943-1a6d-4487-b220-1defe482c06c); (ENG.). (gr. 6-6). pap. 13.95 *(978-1-4488-9586-1(3)*, b28fda74-e025-451e-aecb-5b6f40255f93) Rosen Publishing Group, Inc., The.
Career Building Through Creating Mobile Apps. 2013. (Digital Career Building Ser.). 64p. (YA). (gr. 7-12). pap. 77.70 *(978-1-4777-1738-7(2))* Rosen Publishing Group, Inc., The.
Carson, Mary Kay. Alexander Graham Bell for Kids: His Life & Inventions, with 21 Activities. 2018. (For Kids Ser.: 70). (Illus.). 144p. (J). (gr. 4). pap. 18.99 *(978-0-912777-13-9(3))* Chicago Review Pr., Inc.
Chambers, Catherine. Alexander Graham Bell, 1 vol. 2014. (Science Biographies Ser.). (ENG.). 32p. (J). (gr. 2-4). lib. bdg. 33.32 *(978-1-4109-6238-6(5)*, 124848, Raintree) Capstone.
Coates, Eileen S. Alexander Graham Bell's Telephone, 1 vol. 2018. (STEM Milestones: Historic Inventions & Discoveries Ser.). (ENG.). 24p. (gr. 3-3). 25.27 *(978-1-5383-4354-8(1)*, 4399785d-9a23-4454-8af0-3cbcc608d4da, PowerKids Pr.) Rosen Publishing Group, Inc., The.
Colby, Jennifer. Telephone to Smartphones. 2019. (21st Century Junior Library: Then to Now Tech Ser.). (ENG.). 24p. (J). (gr. 2-5). pap. 12.79 *(978-1-5341-5011-9(0)*, 213351); (Illus.). lib. bdg. 30.64 *(978-1-5341-4725-6(X)*, 213350) Cherry Lake Publishing.
Cunningham, Kevin. Cell Phones. 2007. (21st Century Skills Library: Global Products Ser.). (ENG., Illus.). 32p. (gr. 4-8). lib. bdg. 32.07 *(978-1-60279-022-3(1)*, 200023) Cherry Lake Publishing.
Davis, Lynn. Alexander Graham Bell, 1 vol. 2015. (Amazing Inventors & Innovators Ser.). (ENG.). 24p. (J). (gr. k-3). lib. bdg. 32.79 *(978-1-62403-721-4(6)*, 17948, Super SandCastle) ABDO Publishing Co.
Delafosse, Claude. El teléfono: Y los medios de comunicación. (Coleccion Mundo Maravilloso). (SPA., Illus.). 40p. (J). (gr. 2-4). *(978-84-348-5484-0(8)*, SM8407) SM Ediciones.
Einhorn, Kama. The 4-1-1 on Phones! Ready-To-Read Level 3. Borgions, Mark, illus. 2015. (History of Fun Stuff Ser.). (ENG.). 48p. (J). (gr. 1-3). pap. 4.99 *(978-1-4814-4404-0(2)*, Simon Spotlight) Simon Spotlight.
Enz, Tammy. Amazing Story of Cell Phone Technology. Pop Art Properties Staff, illus. 2013. (STEM Adventures Ser.). (ENG.). 32p. (J). (gr. 3-9). 31.32 *(978-1-4765-0137-6(8)*, 122214); pap. 8.95 *(978-1-4765-3457-2(8)*, 123556) Capstone. (Capstone Pr.).
Espejo, Roman, ed. Smartphones, 1 vol. 2013. (Opposing Viewpoints Ser.). (ENG., Illus.). 208p. (gr. 10-12). pap. 34.80 *(978-0-7377-6343-0(4)*, b4476d5a-802b-43a0-8ee8-ade29d7d6a7e); lib. bdg. 50.43 *(978-0-7377-6342-3(6)*, 59a65d8f-bb3f-4b95-9589-56244aa168ed) Greenhaven Publishing LLC. (Greenhaven Publishing).
Fraser, Mary Ann. Alexander Graham Bell Answers the Call. Fraser, Mary Ann, illus. 2017. (Illus.). 32p. (J). (gr. 1-4). lib. bdg. 16.99 *(978-1-58089-721-1(5))* Charlesbridge Publishing, Inc.
Hamen, Susan E. Who Invented the Telephone? Bell vs. Meucci. 2018. (STEM Smackdown (Alternator Books (r)) Ser.). (ENG., Illus.). 32p. (J). (gr. 3-6). 29.32 *(978-1-5124-8322-2(2)*, 9395c877-1f4e-477d-a9a1-4dd157b99843, Lerner Pubns.) Lerner Publishing Group.
Hantula, Richard & Voege, Debra. How Do Cell Phones Work? 2009. (Science in the Real World Ser.). (ENG., Illus.). 32p. (gr. 4-6). 28.00 *(978-1-60413-475-9(5)*, P173444, Chelsea Clubhse.) Infobase Holdings, Inc.
Henneberg, Susan. Are Mobile Devices Harmful. 2016. (ENG.). 80p. (J). (gr. 5-12). lib. bdg. *(978-1-68282-096-4(3))* ReferencePoint Pr., Inc.
Higgins, Nadia. Making an App. 2018. (Sequence Entertainment Ser.). (ENG.). 32p. (J). (gr. 2-5). pap. 9.99 *(978-1-68152-365-1(5)*, 15205) Amicus.
Jackman, Vernon. Bunnies & Butterflies in the Backyard & the Pirates Who Know Where They Live: Stories That Help Children Learn & Remember Their Address & Telephone Number. Theagene, Jeannisse, illus. l.t. ed. 2010. (ENG.). 32p. (J). pap. 6.99 *(978-0-9829371-1-2(3))* New Kid Safety.
Jackson, Tom. Telephones & Cell Phones. 2015. (Technology Timelines Ser.). (ENG., Illus.). 32p. (J). (gr. 2-4). 31.35 *(978-1-78121-239-4(2)*, 16813) Brown Bear Bks.
James, Emily. Alexander Graham Bell. 2017. (Great Scientists & Inventors Ser.). (ENG., Illus.). 24p. (J). (gr. -1-2). lib. bdg. 27.32 *(978-1-5157-3883-1(3)*, 133786, Capstone Pr.) Capstone.
Jarrow, Jesse. Telegraph & Telephone Networks: Groundbreaking Developments in American Communications, 1 vol. 2003. (Primary Sources of America's Industrial Society in the 19th Century Ser.). (ENG., Illus.). 32p. (gr. 4-5). pap. 10.00 *(978-0-8239-4279-4(1)*, 77e1a824-50d8-4605-bba2-8a65c23c3365); lib. bdg. 29.13 *(978-0-8239-4025-7(X)*, 7792e725-74c8-4fd8-9677-6d3999293b44, Rosen Reference) Rosen Publishing Group, Inc., The.
—Telegraph & Telephone Networks: Groundbreaking Developments in American Communications. 2009. (America's Industrial Society in the 19th Century Ser.). 32p. (gr. 4-4). 47.90 *(978-1-61511-341-5(X))* Rosen Publishing Group, Inc., The.
Kaul, Jennifer. Inside Smartphones. 2018. (Inside Technology Ser.). (ENG., Illus.). 48p. (J). (gr. 4-8). lib. bdg. 35.64 *(978-1-5321-1793-0(0)*, 30874) ABDO Publishing Co.
Kramer, Barbara. National Geographic Readers: Alexander Graham Bell. 2015. (Readers Bios Ser.). 32p. (J). (gr. 1-3). pap. 4.99 *(978-1-4263-1935-8(5)*, National Geographic Kids) Disney Publishing Worldwide.
Kulling, Monica. Listen Up! Alexander Graham Bell's Talking Machine. Walz, Richard, illus. 2007. (Step into Reading Ser.). 48p. (J). (gr. k-3). per. 5.99 *(978-0-375-83115-7(0)*, Random Hse. Bks. for Young Readers) Random Hse. Children's Bks.
Lassieur, Allison. Phones 100 Years Ago. 2011. (Amicus Readers. 100 Years Ago (Level 2) Ser.). (ENG.). 24p. (J). (gr. 1-4). lib. bdg. 25.65 *(978-1-60753-165-4(8)*, 17053) Amicus.
Lin, Yoming S. Alexander Graham Bell & the Telephone, 1 vol. 2011. (Eureka! Ser.). (ENG., Illus.). 24p. (J). (gr. 2-3). lib. bdg. 26.27 *(978-1-4488-5034-1(7)*, 5ee009ad-0937-49e7-9508-53277f496c6d) Rosen Publishing Group, Inc., The.
Lyons, Heather. Programming Awesome Apps. Westgate, Alex, illus. 2017. (Kids Get Coding Ser.). (ENG.). 24p. (J). (gr. 1-4). 26.65 *(978-1-5124-3942-7(8)*, c8d27d27-e864-4737-b212-ed6ff05dbf8a, Lerner Pubns.) Lerner Publishing Group.
Masters, Nancy Robinson. How Did That Get to My House? Telephone. 2009. (Community Connections: How Did That Get to My House? Ser.). (ENG.). 24p. (gr. 2-5). lib. bdg. 29.21 *(978-1-60279-480-1(4)*, 200251) Cherry Lake Publishing.
McLeese, Don. Cell Phones. 2008. (Let's Explore Science Ser.). (ENG., Illus.). 48p. (gr. 4-8). pap. 10.95 *(978-1-60694-908-5(X)*, 9781606949085) Rourke Educational Media.
Meucci, Sandra. Antonio & the Electric Scream: The Man Who Invented the Telephone. 2010. (ENG.). 138p. (J). pap. *(978-0-8283-2197-6(3))* Branden Bks.
Nakaya, Andrea C. Cell Phones. 2016. (Matters of Opinion Ser.). (ENG., Illus.). 64p. (J). (gr. 4-6). lib. bdg. 27.93 *(978-1-59953-755-9(9))* Norwood Hse. Pr.
Netzley, Patricia. Cell Phones: Threats to Privacy & Security. 2014. (Cell Phones & Society). (ENG., Illus.). 80p. (J). lib. bdg. *(978-1-60152-668-7(7))* ReferencePoint Pr., Inc.
Netzley, Patricia D. How Do Cell Phones Affect Health? 2014. (Cell Phones & Society). (ENG., Illus.). 80p. (J). lib. bdg. *(978-1-60152-670-0(9))* ReferencePoint Pr., Inc.
Nobleman, Marc Tyler & Beevor, Lucy. The Invention of the Telephone. 2018. (World-Changing Inventions Ser.). (ENG., Illus.). 32p. (J). (gr. 3-6). lib. bdg. 27.99 *(978-1-5157-9843-9(7)*, 136898, Capstone Pr.) Capstone.
Oxlade, Chris. The Mobile Continent White Band. 2016. (Cambridge Reading Adventures Ser.). (ENG., Illus.). 32p. pap. 9.50 *(978-1-316-60067-2(X))* Cambridge Univ. Pr.
Pipe, Jim. You Wouldn't Want to Live Without Cell Phones! Walker, Rory, illus. 2014. (You Wouldn't Want to Live Without... Ser.). (ENG.). 32p. (J). lib. bdg. 29.00 *(978-0-531-21217-2(3)*, Watts, Franklin) Scholastic Library Publishing.
Radios, Phones & Telecommunications. 2005. (Inventions Ser.). (Illus.). 30p. (J). pap. 15.95 incl. audio *(978-0-9724983-4-0(6))* Jazwares Distribution, Inc.
Rivera, Sheila. Alexander Graham Bell: A Life of Helpfulness. 2007. (Pull Ahead Bks.). (Illus.). 32p. (J). (gr. 3-7). lib. bdg. 22.60 *(978-0-8225-6463-8(7)*, Lerner Pubns.) Lerner Publishing Group.
Rowe, Brooke. Making a Telephone. Bane, Jeff, illus. 2016. (My Early Library: My Science Fun Ser.). (ENG.). 24p. (J). (gr. k-1). 30.64 *(978-1-63471-029-9(0)*, 208196) Cherry Lake Publishing.
Schuman, Michael A. Alexander Graham Bell: Scientist & Inventor, 1 vol. 2014. (Legendary American Biographies Ser.). (ENG.). 96p. (gr. 6-6). 29.60 *(978-0-7660-6430-0(1)*, 4c8c7c5b-ed21-4769-bacf-69d5abfb0a27); pap. 13.88 *(978-0-7660-6431-7(X)*, 484d9737-03f4-4149-a848-2aebf8668a48) Enslow Publishing, LLC.
Spilsbury, Louise. Alexander Graham Bell & the Telephone, 1 vol., 1. 2015. (Inventions That Changed the World Ser.). (ENG.). 32p. (J). (gr. 4-5). pap. 11.00 *(978-1-5081-4623-0(3)*, 5bd36094-57d1-4748-aa05-a2f02088271b, PowerKids Pr.) Rosen Publishing Group, Inc., The.
Staley, Erin. Career Building Through Creating Mobile Apps, 1 vol. 2013. (Digital Career Building Ser.). (ENG.). 64p. (YA). (gr. 6-6). 37.13 *(978-1-4777-1727-1(7)*,

eb8044f7-c027-4a55-981a-27460347973b) Rosen Publishing Group, Inc., The.
Stark, Kristy. The History of Telephones: Fractions (Grade 4) 2017. (Mathematics in the Real World Ser.). (ENG., Illus.). 32p. (J). (gr. 4-5). pap. 11.99 *(978-1-4258-5556-7(3))* Teacher Created Materials, Inc.
Stefoff, Rebecca. The Telephone, 1 vol. 2007. (Great Inventions Ser.). (ENG., Illus.). 144p. (YA). (gr. 8-8). lib. bdg. 45.50 *(978-0-7614-1879-5(2),* 564380bd-c0be-4780-bc33-6d17eb506d95) Cavendish Square Publishing LLC.
Wilcox, Christine. Cell Phones & Teens. 2014. (Cell Phones & Society). (ENG., Illus.). 80p. (J). lib. bdg. *(978-1-60152-666-3(0))* ReferencePoint Pr., Inc.
Worth, Richard. The Telegraph & Telephone, 1 vol. 2005. (Great Inventions Ser.). (ENG., Illus.). 48p. (gr. 5-8). lib. bdg. 33.67 *(978-0-8368-5879-2(4),* 306e7b3e-d923-4ce1-ba37-c78ddabddd24, Gareth Stevens Secondary Library) Stevens, Gareth Publishing LLLP.
Zoehfeld, Kathleen Weidner. Phones Keep Us Connected. Nowowiejska, Kasia, illus. 2017. (Let's-Read-And-Find-Out Science 2 Ser.). (ENG.). 40p. (J). (gr. -1-3). pap. 6.99 *(978-0-06-238667-0(0),* HarperCollins) HarperCollins Pubs.

TELEPHONE—FICTION

Ackerman, Peter. The Lonely Phone Booth. Dalton, Max, illus. 2010. (ENG.). 32p. (J). (gr. k-2). 16.95 *(978-1-56792-414-5(X))* Godine, David R. Pub.
Appleton, Victor. Tom Swift & His Photo Telephone. 2007. 100p. per. *(978-1-4068-1621-1(3))* Echo Library.
—Tom Swift & his Photo Telephone. 2005. 27.95 *(978-1-4218-1503-9(6));* 204p. pap. 12.95 *(978-1-4218-1603-6(2))* 1st World Publishing, Inc. (1st World Library - Literary Society).
—Tom Swift & His Photo Telephone or the. 2006. pap. *(978-1-4065-0906-9(X))* Dodo Pr.
Arnold, Janet. The Special Number. 2011. 28p. pap. 15.99 *(978-1-4568-8982-1(6))* Xlibris Corp.
Bour, Daniele. Petit ours brun repond au Teleph. pap. 12.95 *(978-2-227-74805-7(2))* Bayard Editions FRA. Dist: Distribooks, Inc.
Deutsch, Stacia & Cohon, Rhody. Bell's Breakthrough. Wenzel, David, illus. 2013. (Blast to the Past Ser.: 3). (ENG.). 128p. (J). (gr. 2-5). pap. 6.99 *(978-1-4424-9536-4(7),* Simon & Schuster/Paula Wiseman Bks.) Simon & Schuster/Paula Wiseman Bks.
Esbensen, Barbara Juster. Who Is Calling? Date not set. 15.95 *(978-0-8050-4899-5(5))* Holt, Henry & Co.
Hinton, Nigel. 2 Die 4. 2012. (Stoke Books Titles Ser.). (ENG.). 88p. (YA). (gr. 8-12). pap. 6.95 *(978-1-78112-109-2(5));* lib. bdg. 22.60 *(978-1-78112-110-8(9))* Lerner Publishing Group.
Hope, Laura Lee. Outdoor Girls in the Saddle. 2006. 26.95 *(978-1-4218-2983-8(5));* pap. 11.95 *(978-1-4218-3083-4(3))* 1st World Publishing, Inc.
Kesselring, Mari. Tuned Out. Epelbaum, Mariano, illus. 2015. (Bridget Gadget Ser.). (ENG.). 64p. (J). (gr. 3-6). pap. 8.95 *(978-1-63235-099-2(8),* 11642, 12-Story Library) Bookstaves, LLC.
Kulling, Monica. The Tweedles Go Online, 1 vol. Lafrance, Marie, illus. 2015. (ENG.). 32p. (J). (gr. -1-2). 16.95 *(978-1-55498-353-7(3))* Groundwood Bks. CAN. Dist: Publishers Group West (PGW).
Mlynowski, Sarah. Gimme a Call. 2011. (ENG.). 320p. (YA). (gr. 7). pap. 9.99 *(978-0-385-73589-6(8),* Ember) Random Hse. Children's Bks.
Publications International Ltd. Staff. Dora PNO BK Follow Music. 2008. 10p. (J). 16.98 *(978-1-4127-8996-7(6),* PIL Kids) Publications International, Ltd.
Reynolds, Wendy. Moby for Justice. 2006. 17.00 *(978-0-8059-8861-1(0))* Dorrance Publishing Co., Inc.
School Zone Staff, ed. Talking Telephone. 2007. (J). 7.99 *(978-1-58947-873-2(8))* School Zone Publishing Co.
Slater, Teddy. Emergency, Call 911. Lewis, Anthony, illus. 2010. 16p. (J). *(978-0-545-24601-9(6))* Scholastic, Inc.
Witherow, Wendy. Miranda's Makeover. Pulley, Kelly, illus. 2007. 93p. (J). *(978-1-934306-11-6(8))* Mission City Pr., Inc.

TELESCOPES

Bortz, Fred. Beyond Jupiter: The Story of Planetary Astronomer Heidi Hammel. 2006. (ENG., Illus.). 128p. (gr. 7-9). per. 19.95 *(978-0-309-09552-5(2),* Joseph Henry Pr.) National Academies Pr.
Building Blocks of Science: Sky Watchers Teacher's Guide. 2007. (Illus.). ring bd. *(978-0-89278-325-0(7))* Carolina Biological Supply Co.
Coates, Eileen S. Galileo, Jupiter's Moons, & the Telescope, 1 vol. 2018. (STEM Milestones: Historic Inventions & Discoveries Ser.). (ENG.). 24p. (gr. 3-3). 25.27 *(978-1-5383-4357-9(6),* db41cac0-ded3-470c-9ed4-ffe42e79d84a, PowerKids Pr.) Rosen Publishing Group, Inc., The.
Dinmont, Kerry. Tom's Telescope: A Book about the Moon & the Sun. 2017. (My Day Readers Ser.). (ENG.). 24p. (J). (gr. -1-2). lib. bdg. 32.79 *(978-1-5038-2017-3(3),* 211868) Child's World, Inc, The.
Gibson, Brylee. The World Beyond Earth. 2007. (Connectors Ser.). (gr. 2-5). pap. *(978-1-877453-11-3(0))* Global Education Systems Ltd.
Hamilton, John. Hubble Space Telescope: Photographing the Universe. 2017. (Xtreme Spacecraft Ser.). (ENG., Illus.). 32p. (J). (gr. 3-9). lib. bdg. 32.79 *(978-1-5321-1012-2(X),* 25600, Abdo & Daughters) ABDO Publishing Co.
Jefferis, David. Star Spotters: Telescopes & Observatories. 2008. (Exploring Our Solar System Ser.). (ENG., Illus.). 32p. (J). (gr. 3-8). lib. bdg. *(978-0-7787-3725-4(X));* (gr. 4-9). pap. *(978-0-7787-3742-1(X))* Crabtree Publishing Co.
Kain, Kathleen. Telescopes & Space Probes. 2006. (World Book's Solar System & Space Exploration Library). (Illus.). 63p. (J). *(978-0-7166-9510-3(3))* World Bk., Inc.
Langley, Andrew. Space Telescopes: Instagram of the Stars. 2019. (Future Space Ser.). (ENG., Illus.). 32p. (J). (gr. 3-9). pap. 7.95 *(978-1-5435-7519-4(6),* 141050); lib. bdg. 28.65 *(978-1-5435-7271-1(5),* 140602) Capstone.
Lin, Yoming S. Galileo & the Telescope, 1 vol. 2011. (Eureka! Ser.). (ENG., Illus.). 24p. (J). (gr. 2-3). lib. bdg. 26.27 *(978-1-4488-5030-3(4),* 1522b684-5908-4216-9cea-c9972661ecc8) Rosen Publishing Group, Inc., The.
Mattern, Joanne. The Telescope: Looking into Space. 2009. (Technology That Changed the World Ser.). 24p. (gr. 2-3). 42.50 *(978-1-60853-279-7(8),* PowerKids Pr.) Rosen Publishing Group, Inc., The.
Orr, Tamra. The Telescope. 2004. (Inventions That Shaped the World Ser.). (ENG., Illus.). 80p. (J). 30.50 *(978-0-531-12344-7(6),* Watts, Franklin) Scholastic Library Publishing.
Orr, Tamra B. The Telescope. 2006. (Inventions That Shaped the World Ser.). (Illus.). 80p. (gr. 5-8). 19.95 *(978-0-7569-6863-2(1))* Perfection Learning Corp.
Phoenix International Staff, illus. Thomas & the Telescope. 2014. 12p. (J). bds. 17.98 *(978-1-4508-7993-4(4),* 1450879934) Phoenix International Publications, Inc.
Rau, Heather. Through My Telescope, 1 vol. 2013. (Rosen Readers Ser.). (ENG.). 24p. (J). (gr. 3-3). pap. 8.25 *(978-1-4777-2617-4(9),* def4fb98-67f0-42b0-a001-f1395f600d82); pap. 49.50 *(978-1-4777-2618-1(7))* Rosen Publishing Group, Inc., The. (Rosen Classroom).
Read, John A. 50 Things to See with a Telescope: A Young Stargazer's Guide. 2018. (Beginner's Guide to Space Ser.). (ENG., Illus.). 72p. (J). (gr. 2-5). 26.65 *(978-1-4595-0536-0(0),* 56f56cba-0d4f-41d6-998e-83f7c8bbb70f) Formac Publishing Co., Ltd. CAN. Dist: Lerner Publishing Group.
Rosewald, Mary. Tara's Telescope, 1 vol. 2013. (InfoMax Readers Ser.). (ENG.). 24p. (J). (gr. 3-3). pap. 8.25 *(978-1-4777-2655-6(1),* df47d286-1b2a-43af-b226-973a89e00b8a); pap. 49.50 *(978-1-4777-2656-3(X))* Rosen Publishing Group, Inc., The. (Rosen Classroom).
Roza, Greg. The Hubble Space Telescope: Understanding & Representing Numbers in the Billions. (PowerMath: Proficiency Plus Ser.). 32p. 2009. (gr. 4-5). 47.90 *(978-1-60851-422-9(6))* 2004. (ENG., Illus.). (J). (gr. 5-6). lib. bdg. 28.93 *(978-1-4042-2931-0(0),* 7af2f6d7-2234-4b48-ae6e-bc071138672d) Rosen Publishing Group, Inc., The. (PowerKids Pr.).
—The Hubble Space Telescope: Understanding & Representing Numbers up to 1 Billion, 1 vol. 2010. (Math for the REAL World Ser.). (ENG., Illus.). 32p. (gr. 5-6). pap. 10.00 *(978-1-4042-5129-8(4),* 881be7c6-f2f5-4e5e-bf41-3aab27d0b7a2) Rosen Publishing Group, Inc., The.
Schwartz, Heather E. NASA Astronomer Nancy Grace Roman. 2018. (STEM Trailblazer Bios Ser.). (ENG., Illus.). 32p. (J). (gr. 2-5). 26.65 *(978-1-5124-9979-7(X),* f9d26d58-4169-4b0f-8e65-837456b8c53a, Lerner Pubns.) Lerner Publishing Group.
Simon, Seymour. Destination: Space. 2004. (ENG.). 32p. (J). pap. 6.99 *(978-0-06-059681-1(3),* Harper Trophy) HarperCollins Pubs.
Sparrow, Giles. Observing the Universe, 1 vol. 2006. (Secrets of the Universe Ser.). (ENG., Illus.). 48p. (gr. 6-8). pap. 15.05 *(978-0-8368-7284-2(3),* 81eb04fd-ae19-41d7-aec6-30d9e2bffc3d); lib. bdg. 33.67 *(978-0-8368-7277-4(0),* 2aa34e1b-2839-4bf0-b51d-5e7fe7793a8d) Stevens, Gareth Publishing LLLP. (Gareth Stevens Secondary Library).
Stefoff, Rebecca. Microscopes & Telescopes, 1 vol. 2007. (Great Inventions Ser.). (ENG., Illus.). 144p. (YA). (gr. 8-8). lib. bdg. 45.50 *(978-0-7614-2230-3(7),* 11dc8094-4cd3-42ab-964c-4d6b85996783) Cavendish Square Publishing LLC.
Villard, Ray. Supertelescopios: Por dentro y por fuera (Large Telescopes: Inside & Out) 2009. (Tecnología: Mapas para el Futuro Ser.). (SPA.). 48p. (gr. 4-4). 53.00 *(978-1-60853-290-2(9),* Editorial Buenas Letras) Rosen Publishing Group, Inc., The.
Villard, Raymond. Large Telescopes: Inside & Out. 2009. (Technology: Blueprints of the Future Ser.). 48p. (gr. 4-4). 53.00 *(978-1-60853-283-4(6))* Rosen Publishing Group, Inc., The.
World Book, Inc. Staff, contrib. by. Observatories on Earth. 2010. (Illus.). 64p. (J). *(978-0-7166-9553-0(7))* World Bk., Inc.
—Telescopes & Space Probes. (J). 2010. *(978-0-7166-9541-7(3))* 2nd ed. 2006. (Illus.). 64p. *(978-0-7166-9520-2(0))* World Bk., Inc.

TELETUBBIES (FICTITIOUS CHARACTERS)—FICTION

Davenport, Andrew. Here Come the Teletubbies. 2004. (Illus.). (J). (gr. -1-2). spiral bd. *(978-0-616-04551-0(4));* spiral bd. *(978-0-616-03029-5(0))* Canadian National Institute for the Blind/Institut National Canadien pour les Aveugles.
—Teletubbies (Ce p'Tit Agneau) 2004. (J). (gr. -1-2). spiral bd. *(978-0-616-03071-4(1))* Canadian National Institute for the Blind/Institut National Canadien pour les Aveugles.
Follow The Leader. 2003. (J). per. *(978-1-57657-861-2(5))* Paradise Pr., Inc.

TELEVISION

Berger, Melvin. Telephones, Televisions, & Toilets. (Discovery Readers Ser.). (ENG.). 48p. (J). pap. 3.95 *(978-0-8249-5311-9(8),* Ideals Pubns.) Worthy Publishing.
Bodden, Valerie. Television. 2008. (Media Sources Ser.). (Illus.). 24p. (J). lib. bdg. 24.25 *(978-1-58341-559-7(9),* Creative Education) Creative Co., The.
Cantor, Joanne. Teddy's TV Troubles. Lowes, Tom, illus. 2004. 36p. (J). mass mkt. 16.95 *(978-0-9647663-7-2(X))* HenschelHAUS Publishing, Inc.
Carlson Berne, Emma, ed. Television, 1 vol. 2007. (Introducing Issues with Opposing Viewpoints Ser.). (ENG., Illus.). 120p. (gr. 7-10). lib. bdg. 43.63 *(978-0-7377-3853-7(7),* af477f23-93af-45fc-a0cf-eaa7ce985834, Greenhaven Publishing) Greenhaven Publishing LLC.
Chmielewski, Gary T. How Did That Get to My House? Television. 2009. (Community Connections: How Did That Get to My House? Ser.). (ENG.). 24p. (gr. 2-5). lib. bdg. 29.21 *(978-1-60279-476-4(6),* 200247) Cherry Lake Publishing.
Clark, Katie. Animal Actors. 2013. (We Work! Animals with Jobs Ser.). (Illus.). 24p. (J). (gr. -1-3). lib. bdg. 25.65 *(978-1-61772-897-6(7))* Bearport Publishing Co., Inc.
Enz, Tammy. Terrific Tale of Television Technology. Pop Art Properties Staff, illus. 2013. (STEM Adventures Ser.). (ENG.). 32p. (J). (gr. 3-9). pap. 8.95 *(978-1-4765-3458-9(6),* 123557, Capstone Pr.) Capstone.
Gibson, Karen. What It's Like to Be George Lopez. de la Vega, Eida, tr. from ENG. 2011. (What It's Like to Be... = Que Se Sienta Al Ser... Ser.). (SPA., Illus.). 32p. (J). (gr. -1-2). lib. bdg. 25.70 *(978-1-58415-991-9(X))* Mitchell Lane Pubs.
Grayson, Robert. Performers, 1 vol. 2011. (Working Animals Ser.). (ENG.). 64p. (gr. 5-5). 31.21 *(978-1-60870-165-0(4),* 060ee4d6-1293-4c2d-ad41-fc5792bd7360) Cavendish Square Publishing LLC.
Haerens, Margaret, ed. Television, 1 vol. 2011. (Opposing Viewpoints Ser.). (ENG.). 216p. (gr. 10-12). pap. 34.80 *(978-0-7377-5244-1(0),* 0edae5d5-29e6-47a9-a187-0910c37a351b); lib. bdg. 50.43 *(978-0-7377-5243-4(2),* d3684a40-d307-4a2b-b767-2722a0d8505f) Greenhaven Publishing LLC. (Greenhaven Publishing).
Hirschmann, Kris. HDTV - High Definition Television. 2010. (Great Idea Ser.). 48p. (J). (gr. 4-6). lib. bdg. 26.60 *(978-1-59953-379-7(0))* Norwood Hse. Pr.
Kawa, Katie. Is Television Bad for Kids?, 1 vol. 2019. (Points of View Ser.). (ENG.). 24p. (gr. 3-3). 26.23 *(978-1-5345-3192-5(0),* 9a843c89-2ae3-4ea0-995c-547878f8c6af, KidHaven Publishing) Greenhaven Publishing LLC.
La Bella, Laura. Hulu & Jason Kilar, 1 vol. 2014. (Internet Biographies Ser.). (ENG.). 128p. (YA). (gr. 7-7). 39.80 *(978-1-4777-7921-7(3),* 2f1b85cc-395a-4dd0-a180-b59f4a72a78b, Rosen Young Adult) Rosen Publishing Group, Inc., The.
Mattern, Joanne. The Television: Window to the World. 2009. (Technology That Changed the World Ser.). 24p. (gr. 2-3). 42.50 *(978-1-60853-280-3(1),* PowerKids Pr.) Rosen Publishing Group, Inc., The.
Mullins, Matt. Scriptwriter. 2011. (21st Century Skills Library: Cool Arts Careers Ser.). (ENG., Illus.). 32p. (gr. 4-8). lib. bdg. 32.07 *(978-1-61080-135-5(0),* 201148) Cherry Lake Publishing.
Nagle, Jeanne M. Careers in Television. 2009. (Career Resource Library). 192p. (gr. 7-12). 63.90 *(978-1-60853-404-3(9))* Rosen Publishing Group, Inc., The.
Reid, Aimee. You Are My Friend: The Story of Mister Rogers & His Neighborhood. Phelan, Matt, illus. 2019. (ENG.). 40p. (J). (gr. k-3). 17.99 *(978-1-4197-3617-9(5),* 1270901, Abrams Bks. for Young Readers) Abrams, Inc.
Richter, Joanne. Inventing the Television. 2006. (Breakthrough Inventions Ser.). (ENG., Illus.). 32p. (J). (gr. 4-7). pap. *(978-0-7787-2835-1(8));* lib. bdg. *(978-0-7787-2813-9(7))* Crabtree Publishing Co.
Somervill, Barbara A. Actor. 2011. (21st Century Skills Library: Cool Arts Careers Ser.). (ENG., Illus.). 32p. (gr. 4-8). lib. bdg. 32.07 *(978-1-61080-129-4(6),* 201136) Cherry Lake Publishing.
Teitelbaum, Michael. Television. 2008. (21st Century Skills Innovation Library: Innovation in Entertainment Ser.). (ENG., Illus.). 32p. (gr. 4-8). lib. bdg. 32.07 *(978-1-60279-263-0(1),* 200146) Cherry Lake Publishing.

TELEVISION—BROADCASTING

see Television Broadcasting

TELEVISION—FICTION

Adams, Karin. No TV? No Fair!, 1 vol. 2010. (Lorimer Streetlights Ser.). (ENG.). 120p. (J). (gr. 2-4). 8.95 *(978-1-55277-471-7(6),* 471) James Lorimer & Co. Ltd., Pubs. CAN. Dist: Formac Lorimer Bks. Ltd.
Ainslie, Claire. The One. 2019. (Reality Show Ser.). (ENG.). 120p. (YA). (gr. 6-12). 26.65 *(978-1-5415-4026-2(3),* 1847e354-5b92-4df8-b635-ebd681ac8ae3, Darby Creek) Lerner Publishing Group.
Aldredge, Betsy & DuBois-Shaw, Carrie. Sasquatch, Love, & Other Imaginary Things. 2017. (ENG., Illus.). 272p. (YA). (gr. 9). 19.99 *(978-1-5072-0280-7(6),* Simon Pulse) Simon Pulse.
Atinsky, Steve. Tyler on Prime Time. 2004. 176p. (J). (gr. 5-9). pap. 29.00 incl. audio *(978-0-8072-2279-9(8),* Listening Library) Random Hse. Audio Publishing Group.
Atwood, Megan. Olive Becomes Famous (and Hopes She Can Become Un-Famous) Llewhellin, Gareth, illus. 2018. (Dear Molly, Dear Olive Ser.). (ENG.). 96p. (J). (gr. 1-3). lib. bdg. 21.99 *(978-1-5158-2922-5(7),* 138458, Picture Window Bks.) Capstone.
Auerbach, Annie. Spongebob Superstar, Vol. 5. 2004. 64p. (J). (gr. 2-5). pap. 17.00 incl. audio *(978-1-4000-8628-3(0),* Listening Library) Random Hse. Audio Publishing Group.
Bell, Christine. Oh No! the Television Won't Work! 2005. (Illus.). 52p. pap. *(978-1-84401-340-1(5))* Athena Pr.
Biedrzycki, David. Breaking News: Alien Alert. Biedrzycki, David, illus. 2018. (Breaking News Ser.: 3). (Illus.). 32p. (J). (gr. -1-3). lib. bdg. 17.99 *(978-1-58089-804-1(1))* Charlesbridge Publishing, Inc.
—Breaking News: Bear Alert. Biedrzycki, David, illus. 2018. (Breaking News Ser.: 1). (Illus.). 32p. (J). (gr. -1-3). 8.99 *(978-1-58089-664-1(2))* Charlesbridge Publishing, Inc.
Bonin, Liane. Pretty on the Outside: Fame Unlimited. 2007. 288p. (YA). pap. 9.99 *(978-0-451-22122-3(2),* NAL) Penguin Publishing Group.
Calonita, Jen. Reality Check. 2011. (ENG.). 288p. (YA). (gr. 7-17). pap. 15.99 *(978-0-316-04553-7(5),* Poppy) Little, Brown Bks. for Young Readers.
—There's No Place Like Home. 2011. (Secrets of My Hollywood Life Ser.: 6). (ENG.). 400p. (YA). (gr. 7-17). pap. 19.99 *(978-0-316-04555-1(1),* Poppy) Little, Brown Bks. for Young Readers.
Carlson, Melody. Premiere, 1 vol. 2014. (On the Runway Ser.: 1). (ENG.). 224p. (YA). pap. 9.99 *(978-0-310-74728-4(7))* Zondervan.
—Spotlight, 1 vol. 2014. (On the Runway Ser.: 4). (ENG.). 224p. (YA). pap. 9.99 *(978-0-310-74821-2(6))* Zondervan.
Christensen-Jowers, Rae. A Day I Spent Without Tv. 2011. 24p. pap. 12.79 *(978-1-4634-2202-8(4))* AuthorHouse.
Collins, Suzanne. Catching Fire. 2009. (Hunger Games Trilogy: Bk. 2). (YA). 74.99 *(978-1-61574-572-2(6))* Findaway World, LLC.
—Catching Fire. 2009. 12.04 *(978-0-7848-3842-6(9),* Everbind) Marco Bk. Co.
—Catching Fire. 2011. (ENG.). 448p. pap. *(978-1-4071-3209-9(1))* Scholastic.
—Catching Fire. l.t. ed. (Hunger Games Trilogy: 2). (ENG.). (YA). 2012. 498p. (gr. 7-12). pap. 14.99 *(978-1-59413-585-9(1),* Large Print Pr.) 2009. 499p. 23.95 *(978-1-4104-2044-2(2))* Thorndike Pr.
—Catching Fire. 2013. (Hunger Games Trilogy Ser.: 2). lib. bdg. 24.50 *(978-0-606-32025-2(3))* Turtleback.
—Catching Fire. 2011. (Hunger Games Trilogy: Bk. 2). (CHI.). 344p. (YA). (gr. 7-12). pap. *(978-7-5063-5566-7(3))* Writers' Publishing Hse.
—Catching Fire (Hunger Games, Book Two), 1 vol. (Hunger Games Ser.: 2). (ENG.). 400p. (gr. 7). 2013. (YA). pap. 14.99 *(978-0-545-58617-7(8))* 2009. (J). pap. 22.99 *(978-0-439-02349-8(1))* Scholastic, Inc. (Scholastic Pr.).
—En llamas (los Juegos del Hambre 2), Bk. 2. 2010. (Hunger Games Trilogy: Bk. 2). (SPA.). 416p. (J). (gr. 8-12). pap. 19.99 *(978-84-272-0000-5(5))* Lectorum Pubns., Inc.
—En llamas (los Juegos del Hambre 2) 2012. (Hunger Games Trilogy: Bk. 2). (SPA.). 416p. (gr. 8-12). pap. 21.99 *(978-84-272-0213-9(X))* Molino, Editorial ESP. Dist: Lectorum Pubns., Inc.
—The Hunger Games. 2009. (Hunger Games Trilogy: Bk. 1). 10.85 *(978-0-7848-3801-3(1),* Everbind) Marco Bk. Co.
—The Hunger Games. 2010. (Hunger Games Trilogy: Bk. 1). (ENG.). 374p. (gr. 7-12). 21.00 *(978-1-60686-581-1(1))* Perfection Learning Corp.
—The Hunger Games. Fournier, Guillaume, tr. 2011. (Hunger Games Trilogy: Bk. 1). (FRE.). 398p. (YA). (gr. 7-12). pap. *(978-2-266-18269-0(2))* Presses Pocket.
—The Hunger Games. 2011. (Hunger Games Trilogy: 1). (YA). 69.75 *(978-1-4561-3196-8(6))* Recorded Bks., Inc.
—The Hunger Games. 2009. (Hunger Games Trilogy: Bk. 1). (ENG., Illus.). 448p. pap. *(978-1-4071-0908-4(1),* Scholastic) Scholastic, Inc.
—The Hunger Games. l.t. ed. (Hunger Games Trilogy: Bk. 1). (ENG.). (YA). 2012. 484p. (gr. 7-12). pap. 14.99 *(978-1-59413-587-3(8),* Large Print Pr.) 2009. 485p. 23.95 *(978-1-4104-1986-6(X))* Thorndike Pr.
—The Hunger Games. 2010. (Hunger Games Trilogy Ser.: 1). (SWE.). lib. bdg. 22.10 *(978-1-4178-3173-9(1))* Turtleback.
—The Hunger Games. 2010. (Hunger Games Trilogy: Bk. 1). (CHI.). 324p. (YA). (gr. 7-12). pap. *(978-7-5063-5153-9(6))* Writers' Publishing Hse.
—The Hunger Games (Hunger Games, Book One), 1 vol. (Hunger Games Ser.: 1). (ENG.). 384p. (J). (gr. 7-18). 2010. pap. 14.99 *(978-0-439-02352-8(1))* 2008. 22.99 *(978-0-439-02348-1(3))* Scholastic, Inc. (Scholastic Pr.).
—The Hunger Games (Hunger Games, Book One) (Unabridged Edition), 9 vols., Vol. 1. unabr. ed. 2018. (Hunger Games Ser.: 1). (ENG.). 2p. (YA). (gr. 7). audio compact disk 44.99 *(978-1-338-33492-0(1))* Scholastic, Inc.
—The Hunger Games Trilogy Boxed Set Set. 2010. (Hunger Games Ser.: 1). (ENG.). (J). (gr. 7-7). 53.97 *(978-0-545-26535-5(5),* Scholastic Pr.) Scholastic, Inc.
—Los Juegos del Hambre (los Juegos del Hambre 1) 2012. (Hunger Games Trilogy: Bk. 1). (SPA.). 400p. (gr. 8-12). pap. 21.99 *(978-84-272-0212-2(1))* Molino, Editorial ESP. Dist: Lectorum Pubns., Inc.
—Mockingjay. 2011. (Hunger Games Trilogy: Bk. 3). (CHI.). 435p. (YA). (gr. 7-12). pap. *(978-986-213-216-6(7))* Locus Publishing Co.
—Mockingjay. (Hunger Games Trilogy: 3). (YA). 2011. 77.75 *(978-1-4561-3203-3(2))* 2010. 75.75 *(978-1-4561-3205-7(9))* 2010. 1.25 *(978-1-4640-2636-2(X))* Recorded Bks., Inc.
—Mockingjay. 2011. (Hunger Games Ser.: Vol. 3). (ENG.). 448p. (YA). (gr. 8-12). pap. *(978-1-4071-3210-5(5))* Scholastic Canada, Ltd.
—Mockingjay. 2010. pap. *(978-0-439-02354-2(8),* Scholastic Pr.) Scholastic, Inc.
—Mockingjay. l.t. ed. (Hunger Games Trilogy: Bk. 3). (ENG.). (YA). 2012. 502p. (gr. 7-12). pap. 14.99 *(978-1-59413-586-6(X),* Large Print Pr.) 2010. 503p. 23.99 *(978-1-4104-2841-7(9))* Thorndike Pr.
—Mockingjay. 2014. (Hunger Games Trilogy Ser.: 3). lib. bdg. 24.50 *(978-0-606-36328-0(9));* lib. bdg. 24.50 *(978-0-606-35133-1(7))* Turtleback.
—Mockingjay (Hunger Games, Book Three), 1 vol. (Hunger Games Ser.: 3). (ENG.). 400p. (J). (gr. 7). 2014. pap. 14.99 *(978-0-545-66326-7(1))* 2010. 19.99 *(978-0-439-02351-1(3))* Scholastic, Inc. (Scholastic Pr.).
Collins, Yvonne & Rideout, Sandy. The Black Sheep. 2007. 348p. (J). *(978-1-4287-4665-7(X))* Hyperion Pr.
Conrad, Lauren. The Fame Game. 2012. (YA). (Fame Game Ser.: 1). (ENG.). 336p. (gr. 9). pap. 10.99 *(978-0-06-207519-2(5),* HarperCollins); 313p. 12.99 *(978-0-06-209271-7(5))* HarperCollins Pubs.
—L. A. Candy. (L. A. Candy Ser.: 1). (ENG.). (YA). (gr. 9-18). 2010. 352p. pap. 9.99 *(978-0-06-176759-3(X))* 2009. 336p. 17.99 *(978-0-06-176758-6(1))* HarperCollins Pubs. (HarperCollins).
—Starstruck. (YA). 2013. (Fame Game Ser.: 2). (ENG.). 320p. (gr. 9). pap. 10.99 *(978-0-06-207982-4(4),* HarperCollins) 2012. 304p. pap. *(978-0-06-220964-1(7))* HarperCollins Pubs.
—Sugar & Spice. (YA). 2011. (L. A. Candy Ser.: 3). (ENG.). 288p. (gr. 9). pap. 9.99 *(978-0-06-176763-0(8),* HarperCollins) 2010. (L. A. Candy Ser.: 3). (ENG.). 288p. (gr. 9-18). 17.99 *(978-0-06-176762-3(X),* HarperCollins) 2010. 279p. 9.99 *(978-0-06-201148-0(0))* HarperCollins Pubs.
—Sweet Little Lies. 2010. (L. A. Candy Ser.: 2). (YA). (ENG.). 336p. (gr. 9). pap. 9.99 *(978-0-06-176761-6(1),* HarperCollins); 309p. 9.99 *(978-0-06-198572-0(4))* HarperCollins Pubs.
Cooney, Caroline B. If the Witness Lied. 2010. (ENG.). 224p. (YA). (gr. 7). pap. 8.99 *(978-0-385-73449-3(2),* Ember) Random Hse. Children's Bks.
Damico, Gina. Waste of Space. 2017. (ENG.). 400p. (YA). (gr. 9). 17.99 *(978-0-544-63316-2(4),* 1619759, Clarion Bks.) HarperCollins Pubs.
Darke, J. A. Fade to Black. Evans, Neil, illus. 2016. (Spine Shivers Ser.). (ENG.). 128p. (J). (gr. 4-6). lib. bdg. 27.32 *(978-1-4965-3070-7(5),* 131945, Stone Arch Bks.) Capstone.
DeVillers, Julia & Roy, Jennifer. Double Feature. 2012. (Mix Ser.). (ENG.). (J). (gr. 4-8). 288p. pap. 7.99 *(978-1-4424-3403-5(1));* 272p. 16.99 *(978-1-4424-3402-8(3))* Simon & Schuster Children's Publishing. (Aladdin).

TUV

Donaldson, Julia. The Quick Brown Fox Cub. 2006. (Red Bananas Ser.). (ENG., Illus.). 48p. (J). (gr. -1-3). lib. bdg. *(978-0-7787-1080-6(7))* Crabtree Publishing Co.

Faris, Stephanie. Piper Morgan Makes a Splash. Fleming, Lucy, illus. 2017. (Piper Morgan Ser.: 4). (ENG.). 96p. (J). (gr. 1-4). pap. 5.99 *(978-1-4814-5717-0(9)*, Simon & Schuster/Paula Wiseman Bks.) Simon & Schuster/Paula Wiseman Bks.

Friedman, Robin. The Importance of Wings. 2017. 176p. (J). (gr. 5). pap. 7.99 *(978-1-58089-331-2(7))* Charlesbridge Publishing, Inc.

Graham, D. A. The Right Note. 2019. (Reality Show Ser.). (ENG.). 112p. (YA). (gr. 6-12). 26.65 *(978-1-5415-4025-5(5)*, 8be9b624-d5a9-4a1f-916d-efd82d827d4e, Darby Creek) Lerner Publishing Group.

Green, D. L. Zeke Meeks vs the Horrifying TV-Turnoff Week, 1 vol. Alves, Josh, illus. 2012. (Zeke Meeks Ser.). (ENG.). 128p. (J). (gr. 2-4). pap. 5.95 *(978-1-4048-7220-2(5)*, 118072, Picture Window Bks.) Capstone.

Greene, Janice. The Plot, 1 vol. unabr. ed. 2010. (Q Reads Ser.). (ENG.). 32p. (YA). (gr. 9-12). pap. 8.50 *(978-1-61651-204-0(0))* Saddleback Educational Publishing, Inc.

Greene, Kimberly. My Life on TV. 2011. (My Sister's a Pop Star Ser.). (ENG.). 320p. (J). (gr. 6-8). 18.69 *(978-0-7945-2901-7(1))* EDC Publishing.

—My Sister's a Pop Star. 2011. (My Sister's a Pop Star Ser.). (ENG.). 277p. (J). (gr. 4-6). 18.69 *(978-0-7945-2899-7(6))* EDC Publishing.

Gurevich, Margaret. Chloe by Design: Making the Cut, 1 vol. Hagel, Brooke, illus. 2014. (Chloe by Design Ser.). (ENG.). 384p. (J). (gr. 4-8). 14.95 *(978-1-62370-112-3(0)*, 125655, Capstone Young Readers) Capstone.

—Design Destiny, 1 vol. Hagel, Brooke, illus. 2014. (Chloe by Design Ser.). (ENG.). 96p. (J). (gr. 5-8). 25.32 *(978-1-4342-9180-6(4)*, 125654, Stone Arch Bks.) Capstone.

Harper, Charise Mericle. The Heat Is On. Blard-Quintard, Aurélie, illus. 2018. (Next Best Junior Chef Ser.: 2). (ENG.). 192p. (J). (gr. 3-7). 12.99 *(978-0-544-98028-0(X)*, 1664276, Clarion Bks.) HarperCollins Pubs.

—Lights, Camera, Cook! Blard-Quintard, Aurélie, illus. (Next Best Junior Chef Ser.: 1). (ENG.). 192p. (J). (gr. 3-7). 2018. pap. 7.99 *(978-1-328-50701-3(7)*, 1719056) 2017. 12.99 *(978-0-544-91260-1(8)*, 1655497) HarperCollins Pubs. (Clarion Bks.).

—The Winner Is ... Blard-Quintard, Aurélie, illus. 2019. (Next Best Junior Chef Ser.: 3). (ENG.). 192p. (J). (gr. 3-7). pap. 7.99 *(978-1-328-55902-9(5)*, 1725609, Clarion Bks.) HarperCollins Pubs.

Harrison, John. Fergal Onions. 2005. (Illus.). 32p. pap. *(978-0-7022-3481-1(8))* Univ. of Queensland Pr.

Hiaasen, Carl. Chomp. (ENG.). 320p. (J). (gr. 5). 2020. 8.99 *(978-0-593-17766-2(5)*, Yearling) 2013. pap. 9.99 *(978-0-375-86827-6(5)*, Ember) Random Hse. Children's Bks.

Hiassen, Carl. Chomp. l.t. ed. 2012. (ENG.). 364p. 23.99 *(978-1-4104-5101-9(1))* Thorndike Pr.

—Chomp. 2013. lib. bdg. 19.65 *(978-0-606-27006-9(X))* Turtleback.

John, Jory. The Couch Potato. Oswald, Pete, illus. 2020. (Food Group Ser.). (ENG.). 40p. (J). (gr. -1-3). 18.99 *(978-0-06-295453-4(9)*, HarperCollins) HarperCollins Pubs.

John, Jory & Arthur, Jeremy. The Couch Potato. Oswald, Pete, illus. 2020. (ENG.). (J). 41.95 *(978-1-952183-55-3(3))* Library Ideas, LLC.

Johnson, Gabriel. Heroes of Dreams: A Heroic Dream Begins. 2011. 33p. (J). pap. 18.95 *(978-1-4327-7413-4(1))* Outskirts Pr., Inc.

Kain, P. G. Famous for Thirty Seconds. 2012. (Commercial Breaks Ser.: 1). (ENG.). 320p. (J). (gr. 4-8). pap. 6.99 *(978-1-4169-9786-3(5)*, Aladdin) Simon & Schuster Children's Publishing.

Kimpton, Diana. Princess Ellie's Royal Jamboree No. 11. Finlay, Lizzie, illus. 11th ed. 2008. (ENG.). 96p. (gr. 1-4). pap. 3.99 *(978-1-4231-1531-1(7))* Hyperion Pr.

—Princess Ellie's Snowy Ride. Finlay, Lizzie, illus. 2007. (Pony-Crazed Princess Ser.). 90p. (J). 11.65 *(978-0-7569-8352-9(5))* Perfection Learning Corp.

Leblanc, Louise. Maddie on TV. Cummins, Sarah, tr. Gay, Marie-Louise, illus. 2003. (Formac First Novels Ser.: 48). (ENG.). 64p. (J). (gr. 2-5). 14.95 *(978-0-88780-613-1(9)*, 613) Formac Publishing Co., Ltd. CAN. Dist: Formac Lorimer Bks. Ltd.

Lee, G. I Want My Kitty Cat Tv! Scott, E., illus. 2012. 24p. pap. 24.95 *(978-1-4626-6610-2(8))* America Star Bks.

Levine, Deborah A. & Riley, JillEllyn. Kitchen Chaos. 2015. (Saturday Cooking Club Ser.: 1). (ENG., Illus.). 336p. (J). (gr. 4-9). 17.99 *(978-1-4424-9939-3(7)*, Aladdin) Simon & Schuster Children's Publishing.

London, C. Alexander. We Are Not Eaten by Yaks. 2013. (Accidental Adventure Ser.: 1). 384p. (J). (gr. 3-7). pap. 8.99 *(978-0-14-242056-0(5)*, Puffin Books) Penguin Young Readers Group.

—We Dine with Cannibals. 2013. (Accidental Adventure Ser.: 2). 384p. (J). (gr. 3-7). pap. 7.99 *(978-0-14-242474-2(9)*, Puffin Books) Penguin Young Readers Group.

Lundin, Britta. Ship It. 2018. *(978-1-368-01698-8(7))* Disney Publishing Worldwide.

McCarty, Peter. Chloe. McCarty, Peter, illus. 2012. (ENG., Illus.). 40p. (J). (gr. -1-1). 16.99 *(978-0-06-114291-8(3)*, Balzer & Bray) HarperCollins Pubs.

McOmber, Rachel B., ed. McOmber Phonics Storybooks: On TV. rev. ed. (Illus.). (J). *(978-0-944991-17-6(3))* Swift Learning Resources.

—McOmber Phonics Storybooks: The TV Box. rev. ed. (Illus.). (J). *(978-0-944991-18-3(1))* Swift Learning Resources.

—McOmber Phonics Storybooks: The Video Show. rev. ed. (Illus.). (J). *(978-0-944991-63-3(7))* Swift Learning Resources.

Oelke, Lianne. Nice Try, Jane Sinner. (ENG.). 432p. (YA). (gr. 9). 2019. pap. 9.99 *(978-0-358-09756-3(8)*, 1747620) 2018. 17.99 *(978-0-544-86785-7(8)*, 1648799) HarperCollins Pubs. (Clarion Bks.).

Oliver, Lin & Winkler, Henry. Alien Superstar (Book #1) 2019. (Alien Superstar Ser.). (ENG., Illus.). 264p. (YA). (gr. 3-7). 14.99 *(978-1-4197-3369-7(9)*, 1259301, Amulet Bks.) Abrams, Inc.

O'Toole, Detra. Ty-Ty Quackers & the Hidden Treasure: Biblical Lessons with Barnyard Fun. 2009. 32p. pap. 13.99 *(978-1-4343-6799-0(1))* AuthorHouse.

Papademetriou, Lisa & Minsky, Terri. A Very Lizzie Summer. 2005. (Lizzie Mcguire Super Special Ser.). (Illus.). 265p. (J). *(978-1-4155-9625-8(5))* Disney Pr.

Patterson, James. Pottymouth & Stoopid. Gilpin, Stephen, illus. (ENG.). 336p. (J). (gr. 3-7). 2019. pap. 7.99 *(978-0-316-51498-9(5))* 2017. 13.99 *(978-0-316-34963-5(1))* Little Brown & Co. (Jimmy Patterson).

Proimos, James. Todd's TV. Proimos, James, illus. 2010. (ENG., Illus.). 40p. (J). (gr. -1-3). 15.99 *(978-0-06-170985-2(9)*, HarperCollins) HarperCollins Pubs.

Russell, Rachel Renée. Tales from a Not-So-Glam TV Star. 2014. (Dork Diaries: 7). lib. bdg. 25.75 *(978-0-606-36240-5(1))* Turtleback.

Ryan, Tom. Pop Quiz, 1 vol. 2017. (Orca Limelights Ser.). (ENG.). 128p. (J). (gr. 4-7). pap. 9.95 *(978-1-4598-1222-2(0))* Orca Bk. Pubs. USA.

SaBerre, Kristen. Warrior Zone. 2019. (Reality Show Ser.). (ENG.). 104p. (YA). (gr. 6-12). pap. 7.99 *(978-1-5415-4546-5(X)*, 37733c24-ae7b-4b32-8d1d-75d1576367eb); 26.65 *(978-1-5415-4023-1(9)*, 5eaeeec3-9c6d-47b1-97f2-4e0edfff3f6a) Lerner Publishing Group. (Darby Creek).

Schwab, Victoria & Schwab, V. E. City of Ghosts. (City of Ghosts Ser.: 1). (ENG.). (J). (gr. 4-7). 2019. 320p. pap. 8.99 *(978-1-338-11102-6(7))* 2018. (Illus.). 304p. 17.99 *(978-1-338-11100-2(0)*, Scholastic Pr.) Scholastic, Inc.

Smith, Nikki Shannon. Treasure Hunt. 2019. (Reality Show Ser.). (ENG.). 120p. (YA). (gr. 6-12). pap. 7.99 *(978-1-5415-4545-8(1)*, 86b165aa-f559-440e-812c-5e2c39f1c19f); 26.65 *(978-1-5415-4024-8(7)*, 71b1d250-8fbb-4bba-9b12-abaf5757d2e6) Lerner Publishing Group. (Darby Creek).

Stine, R. L. Rotten School #16: Dumb Clucks. Park, Trip, illus. 4.99 *(978-0-06-123280-0(7))* HarperCollins Pubs.

Suzanne, Collins. Los juegos del hambre. 2009. (Hunger Games Trilogy: Bk. 1). (SPA.). pap. 19.99 *(978-84-9867-539-9(1))* RBA Libros, S.A. ESP. Dist: Lectorum Pubns., Inc.

Tait, Anne. Li Jun & the Iron Road. 2015. (ENG., Illus.). 184p. (YA). pap. 10.99 *(978-1-4597-3142-4(5))* Dundurn Pr. CAN. Dist: Publishers Group West (PGW).

Tayleur, Karen. Famous (Scholastic) The Awesome Life of David Mortimore Baxter. Garvey, Brann, illus. 2009. (David Mortimore Baxter Ser.). 88p. pap. 0.80 *(978-1-4342-2503-0(8)*, Stone Arch Bks.) Capstone.

Thaler, Mike. Groundhog Day from Black Lagoon. Lee, Jared, illus. 2015. 64p. (J). *(978-0-545-78520-4(0))* Scholastic, Inc.

Waters, Summer. High Tide (Silver Dolphins, Book 9), Book 9. 2010. (Silver Dolphins Ser.: 9). (ENG.). 176p. (J). (gr. 2-4). pap. 7.99 *(978-0-00-736749-8(X)*, HarperCollins Children's Bks.) HarperCollins Pubs. Ltd. GBR. Dist: HarperCollins Pubs.

White, Andrea. Surviving Antarctica: Reality TV 2083. 2005. 336p. (J). (gr. 7-18). 16.99 *(978-0-06-055454-5(1)*, HarperCollins) HarperCollins Pubs.

Williams, Kathryn. Pizza, Love, & Other Stuff That Made Me Famous: A Novel. 2013. (ENG.). 256p. (YA). (gr. 7-12). pap. 14.99 *(978-1-250-02745-0(4)*, 900098318) Square Fish.

Winkler, Henry & Oliver, Lin. Lights, Camera, Danger! (Alien Superstar #2) 2020. (Alien Superstar Ser.). (ENG., Illus.). 256p. (YA). (gr. 3-7). 14.99 *(978-1-4197-4099-2(7)*, 1260901, Amulet Bks.) Abrams, Inc.

Young, Judy. Danger at the Dinosaur Stomping Grounds. 2017. (Wild World of Buck Bray Ser.). (ENG., Illus.). 240p. (J). (gr. 3-6). 16.99 *(978-1-58536-368-1(5)*, 204321); pap. 9.99 *(978-1-58536-369-8(3)*, 204334) Sleeping Bear Pr.

—The Missing Grizzly Cubs. 2016. (Wild World of Buck Bray Ser.). (ENG.). 240p. (J). (gr. 3-6). 16.99 *(978-1-58536-970-6(5)*, 204107) Sleeping Bear Pr.

—The Wolves of Slough Creek. 2019. (Wild World of Buck Bray Ser.). (ENG., Illus.). 240p. (J). (gr. 3-6). pap. 9.99 *(978-1-5341-1021-2(6)*, 204662);Bk. 3. 16.99 *(978-1-5341-1020-5(8)*, 204651) Sleeping Bear Pr.

Zentner, Jeff. Rayne & Delilah's Midnite Matinee. 2019. (ENG.). 400p. (YA). (gr. 9). 17.99 *(978-1-5247-2020-9(8)*, Crown Books For Young Readers) Random Hse. Children's Bks.

Zink, Rui. The Boy Who Did Not Like Television. Dreher, Patrick, tr. from POR. Ramos, Manuel Joao, illus. 2004. (ENG.). 24p. (J). *(978-1-931561-96-9(6))* MacAdam/Cage Publishing, Inc.

TELEVISION—HISTORY

Amstutz, Lisa J. Before Television. 2020. (What Did We Do? Ser.). (ENG., Illus.). 32p. (J). (gr. 2-3). pap. 9.95 *(978-1-64493-125-7(7)*, 1644931257); lib. bdg. 31.35 *(978-1-64493-046-5(3)*, 1644930463) North Star Editions. (Focus Readers).

Carson, Mary Kay. Who Invented Television? Philo Farnsworth, 1 vol. 2012. (I Like Inventors! Ser.). (ENG.). 24p. (gr. k-2). 25.27 *(978-0-7660-3974-2(9)*, 39a14224-889a-4a53-a99a-869610cca7bb); (Illus.). pap. 10.35 *(978-1-4644-0134-3(9)*, 2349dddf-1799-4206-98dc-6a3ea15350a8) Enslow Publishing, LLC. (Enslow Elementary).

Collins, Phoebe. Megyn Kelly: From Lawyer to Prime-Time Anchor, 1 vol. 2017. (Leading Women Ser.). (ENG.). 112p. (YA). (gr. 7-7). pap. 20.99 *(978-1-5026-3409-2(0)*, 4cb49a55-daaa-465c-b155-7d79cd804e0d) Cavendish Square Publishing LLC.

Kenney, Karen Latchana. Who Invented the Television? Sarnoff vs. Farnsworth. 2018. (STEM Smackdown (Alternator Books (r)) Ser.). (ENG., Illus.). 32p. (J). (gr. 3-6). 29.32 *(978-1-5124-8319-2(2)*, 40e75331-9576-4d30-815e-905b2a4c2ef3, Lerner Pubns.) Lerner Publishing Group.

Krull, Kathleen. The Boy Who Invented TV: The Story of Philo Farnsworth. Couch, Greg, illus. 2014. 40p. (J). (gr. 1-4). 8.99 *(978-0-385-75557-3(0)*, Dragonfly Bks.) Random Hse. Children's Bks.

Meucci, Sandra. Antonio & the Electric Scream: The Man Who Invented the Telephone. 2010. (ENG.). 138p. (J). pap. *(978-0-8283-2197-6(3))* Branden Bks.

Nardo, Don. The History of Television, 1 vol. 2009. (World History Ser.). (ENG., Illus.). 104p. (gr. 7-7). 41.53 *(978-1-4205-0162-9(3)*, 523ea591-c926-42cf-b42f-75f164b068d8, Lucent Pr.) Greenhaven Publishing LLC.

Nobleman, Marc Tyler & Beevor, Lucy. The Invention of the Television. 2018. (World-Changing Inventions Ser.). (ENG., Illus.). 32p. (J). (gr. 3-6). lib. bdg. 27.99 *(978-1-5157-9844-6(5)*, 136899, Capstone Pr.) Capstone.

Otfinoski, Steven. Television, 1 vol. 2007. (Great Inventions Ser.). (ENG., Illus.). 144p. (YA). (gr. 8-8). lib. bdg. 45.50 *(978-0-7614-2228-0(5)*, 057969d9-3182-4a2c-9c4d-af1466a5a3d8) Cavendish Square Publishing LLC.

Wyckoff, Edwin Brit. The Man Who Invented Television: The Genius of Philo T. Farnsworth, 1 vol. 2013. (Genius Inventors & Their Great Ideas Ser.). (ENG.). 48p. (gr. 3-3). pap. 11.53 *(978-1-4644-0209-8(4)*, b44aa1d4-ae93-4c15-8837-6cb7dadfe562); (Illus.). 27.93 *(978-0-7660-4139-4(5)*, 7cd4f4da-c2dd-4295-ae8d-f5aff61b059c) Enslow Publishing, LLC. (Enslow Elementary).

TELEVISION—PRODUCTION AND DIRECTION

Blount, Diana. TV Production Student Activity Book. Matthews, Douglas L., ed. 2003. (Illus.). stu. ed., per., wbk. ed. *(978-1-931680-51-6(5)*, Expert Systems for Teachers) Teaching Point, Inc.

Duling, Kaitlyn. Lena Dunham: Feminist Writer, Actor, Producer, & Director, 1 vol. 2017. (Leading Women Ser.). (ENG.). 112p. (YA). (gr. 7-7). 41.64 *(978-1-5026-3176-3(8)*, e1f36df2-1a2e-4a52-942f-edc614f96e37); pap. 20.99 *(978-1-5026-3414-6(7)*, 8a080bc5-574d-4941-b279-336189890f09) Cavendish Square Publishing LLC.

Graham, P. J. Directing in TV & Film, 1 vol. 2018. (Exploring Careers in TV & Film Ser.). (ENG.). 96p. (gr. 7-7). pap. 20.99 *(978-1-5026-4053-6(8)*, 366134e2-23e8-4c53-92aa-86ef5f63c1c9) Cavendish Square Publishing LLC.

Heidelberger, David. Sound Mixing in TV & Film, 1 vol. 2018. (Exploring Careers in TV & Film Ser.). (ENG.). 96p. (gr. 7-7). pap. 20.99 *(978-1-5026-4155-7(0)*, 31966f32-10ff-4661-9120-1131c205e3dd) Cavendish Square Publishing LLC.

Holub, Joan & Who HQ. Who Was Jim Henson? Harrison, Nancy, illus. 2010. (Who Was? Ser.). 112p. (J). (gr. 3-7). pap. 6.99 *(978-0-448-45406-1(8)*, Penguin Workshop) Penguin Young Readers Group.

Mattern, Joanne. Tyler Perry. 2012. (J). lib. bdg. 25.70 *(978-1-61228-334-0(9))* Mitchell Lane Pubs.

Sheen, Barbara. J. J. Abrams, 1 vol. 2015. (People in the News Ser.). (ENG., Illus.). 104p. (gr. 7-7). 41.03 *(978-1-4205-1249-6(8)*, 0ec43891-8e0f-4c2f-af93-f5400570308a, Lucent Pr.) Greenhaven Publishing LLC.

Stoltman, Joan. Jim Henson, 1 vol. 2018. (Little Biographies of Big People Ser.). (ENG.). 24p. (gr. 1-2). 24.27 *(978-1-5382-1847-1(X)*, 3412525d-97de-46bb-b0d1-9b225d6ecf97) Stevens, Gareth Publishing LLLP.

Uschan, Michael V. Tyler Perry, 1 vol. 2010. (People in the News Ser.). (ENG.). 96p. (gr. 7-7). 41.03 *(978-1-4205-0309-8(X)*, 8f0a4aa0-35ed-4241-9d42-57b3b698e2d5, Lucent Pr.) Greenhaven Publishing LLC.

TELEVISION—VOCATIONAL GUIDANCE

Colby, Jennifer. TV Station. 2016. (21st Century Junior Library: Explore a Workplace Ser.). (ENG., Illus.). 24p. (J). (gr. 2-5). 29.21 *(978-1-63471-079-4(7)*, 208395) Cherry Lake Publishing.

Horn, Geoffrey M. Camera Operator, 1 vol. 2009. (Cool Careers: on the Go Ser.). (ENG.). 32p. (gr. 3-3). pap. 11.50 *(978-1-4339-0165-2(X)*, fbae595d-3321-480a-95ad-d0bdbaa7491e); (YA). lib. bdg. 28.67 *(978-1-4339-0001-3(7)*, 49af9276-9a7b-4d38-a456-1ded60ea920d) Stevens, Gareth Publishing LLLP.

McAlpine, Margaret. Working in Film & Television, 1 vol. 2005. (My Future Career Ser.). (ENG., Illus.). 64p. (gr. 4-6). lib. bdg. 29.67 *(978-0-8368-4237-1(5)*, a8151ada-0e90-4192-a2bd-1a6bc6a0f619, Gareth Stevens Learning Library) Stevens, Gareth Publishing LLLP.

Nardo, Don. Careers in Film, TV, & Theater. 2019. (Careers for Creative People Ser.). (ENG.). 80p. (J). (gr. 6-12). 41.27 *(978-1-68282-681-2(3))* ReferencePoint Pr., Inc.

Otfinoski, Steven. Television: From Concept to Consumer. 2014. (Calling All Innovators: a Career for You Ser.). (ENG.). 64p. (J). pap. 8.95 *(978-0-531-21071-0(5))* Scholastic Library Publishing.

Publishing, Ferguson, creator. Broadcasting. 2nd rev. ed. 2003. (Ferguson's Careers in Focus Ser.). (ENG.). 192p. (gr. 6-12). 29.95 *(978-0-89434-440-4(4)*, P053176, Ferguson Publishing Company) Infobase Holdings, Inc.

Raatma, Lucia. Working at a TV Station. 2011. (21st Century Junior Library: Careers Ser.). (ENG., Illus.). 24p. (gr. 2-5). lib. bdg. 29.21 *(978-1-60279-980-6(6)*, 200950) Cherry Lake Publishing.

Rauf, Don. Choose a Career Adventure in Hollywood. 2016. (Bright Futures Press: Choose a Career Adventure Ser.). (ENG., Illus.). 32p. (J). (gr. 4-6). 32.07 *(978-1-63471-911-7(5)*, 208965) Cherry Lake Publishing.

TELEVISION BROADCASTING

see also Television in Politics

Apel, Melanie. Cool Careers Without College for Film & Television Buffs, 1 vol. 2nd ed. 2007. (Cool Careers Without College (2002-2006) Ser.). (ENG., Illus.). 144p. (YA). (gr. 7-7). lib. bdg. 41.13 *(978-1-4042-1429-3(1)*, 4e780e00-46b4-4ac3-a97b-870aa31075ec) Rosen Publishing Group, Inc., The.

Bernay, Emma & Berne, Emma Carlson. TV Captures Terrorism on September 11: 4D an Augmented Reading Experience. 2018. (Captured Television History 4D Ser.). (ENG., Illus.). 64p. (J). (gr. 5-9). lib. bdg. 39.99 *(978-0-7565-5824-6(7)*, 138349, Compass Point Bks.) Capstone.

Burgan, Michael. TV Launches 24-Hour News with CNN: 4D an Augmented Reading Experience. 2019. (Captured Television History 4D Ser.). (ENG., Illus.). 64p. (J). (gr. 5-9). 39.99 *(978-0-7565-6000-3(4)*, 139131, Compass Point Bks.) Capstone.

—TV Shapes Presidential Politics in the Kennedy-Nixon Debates: 4D an Augmented Reading Experience. 2018. (Captured Television History 4D Ser.). (ENG., Illus.). 64p. (J). (gr. 5-9). lib. bdg. 39.99 *(978-0-7565-5823-9(9)*, 138348, Compass Point Bks.) Capstone.

Centore, Michael. Entertainment Industry, Vol. 10. 2016. (Stem in Current Events Ser.). (Illus.). 64p. (J). (gr. 7). 23.95 *(978-1-4222-3590-4(4))* Mason Crest.

Connolly, Sean. Television & Radio. 2009. (Getting the Message Ser.). (ENG.). 48p. (J). (gr. 6-10). 34.25 *(978-1-59920-350-8(2)*, 19272, Smart Apple Media) Black Rabbit Bks.

Crabtree, Marc. Meet My Neighbor, the News Camera Operator. 2012. (ENG., Illus.). 24p. (J). *(978-0-7787-4560-0(0))*; pap. *(978-0-7787-4565-5(1))* Crabtree Publishing Co.

Gilbert, Sara. The Story of CNN. (Built for Success Ser.). (ENG.). 48p. (J). (gr. 5-9). 2013. pap. 12.00 *(978-0-89812-760-7(2)*, 21876, Creative Paperbacks) 2012. 23.95 *(978-1-60818-175-9(8)*, 21872, Creative Education) Creative Co., The.

—The Story of MTV. 2014. (Built for Success Ser.). (ENG.). 48p. (J). (gr. 5-8). *(978-1-60818-395-1(5)*, 21284, Creative Education); pap. 12.00 *(978-0-89812-982-3(6)*, 21285, Creative Paperbacks) Creative Co., The.

Green, Sara. Espn. 2017. (Brands We Know Ser.). (ENG.). 24p. (J). (gr. 3-8). lib. bdg. 27.95 *(978-1-62617-651-5(5)*, Pilot Bks.) Bellwether Media.

—Nickelodeon. 2016. (Brands We Know Ser.). (ENG., Illus.). 24p. (J). (gr. 3-8). 27.95 *(978-1-62617-411-5(3)*, Pilot Bks.) Bellwether Media.

Hulick, Kathryn. Fake News (Thinking Critically) 2019. (Thinking Critically Ser.). (ENG.). 80p. (J). (gr. 6-12). 41.27 *(978-1-68282-659-1(7))* ReferencePoint Pr., Inc.

Hutchings, Amy. What Happens at a TV Station?, 1 vol. 2009. (Where People Work Ser.). (ENG.). 24p. (gr. 1-1). (J). lib. bdg. 24.67 *(978-1-4339-0070-9(X)*, 043c3fcf-7f70-4529-8427-2174b41f1e2c); pap. 9.15 *(978-1-4339-0134-8(X)*, 8b56769b-1a89-4754-ad59-3bbc8472e663) Stevens, Gareth Publishing LLLP. (Weekly Reader Leveled Readers).

—What Happens at a TV Station? / ¿Qué Pasa en una Emisora de Televisión?, 1 vol. 2009. (Where People Work / ¿dónde Trabaja la Gente? Ser.). (SPA & ENG.). 24p. (gr. 1-1). (J). lib. bdg. 24.67 *(978-1-4339-0078-5(5)*, 3edb2ff1-9ca7-435b-b328-4e171eeb56d1); pap. 9.15 *(978-1-4339-0142-3(0)*, 7c150961-d4a2-412f-85e2-1deeb522e315) Stevens, Gareth Publishing LLLP. (Weekly Reader Leveled Readers).

Kenney, Karen Latchana. TV Brings Battle into the Home with the Vietnam War: 4D an Augmented Reading Experience. 2018. (Captured Television History 4D Ser.). (ENG., Illus.). 64p. (J). (gr. 5-9). lib. bdg. 39.99 *(978-0-7565-5825-3(5)*, 138350, Compass Point Bks.) Capstone.

McAlpine, Margaret. Working in Film & Television, 1 vol. 2005. (My Future Career Ser.). (ENG., Illus.). 64p. (gr. 4-6). lib. bdg. 29.67 *(978-0-8368-4237-1(5)*, a8151ada-0e90-4192-a2bd-1a6bc6a0f619, Gareth Stevens Learning Library) Stevens, Gareth Publishing LLLP.

Mooney, Carla. Asking Questions about How the News Is Created. 2015. (21st Century Skills Library: Asking Questions about Media Ser.). (ENG., Illus.). 32p. (J). (gr. 4-8). 32.07 *(978-1-63362-489-4(7)*, 206864) Cherry Lake Publishing.

Otfinoski, Steven. Television: From Concept to Consumer. 2014. (Calling All Innovators: a Career for You Ser.). (ENG.). 64p. (J). pap. 8.95 *(978-0-531-21071-0(5))* Scholastic Library Publishing.

Paddington, Whit. Behind the Scenes at a Newscast, 1 vol. 2014. (VIP Tours Ser.). (ENG.). 48p. (gr. 4-4). 33.07 *(978-1-62713-031-8(4)*, c67014ea-e0a1-4a61-a017-0c8aba4c0855) Cavendish Square Publishing LLC.

Pelusey, Michael & Pelusey, Jane. Film & Television. 2005. (Media Ser.). (ENG., Illus.). 32p. (gr. 5-8). lib. bdg. 21.95 *(978-0-7910-8802-9(2)*, P114423, Facts On File) Infobase Holdings, Inc.

Peppas, Lynn. Miley Cyrus. 2010. (Superstars! Ser.). (ENG.). 32p. (J). (gr. 3-6). lib. bdg. *(978-0-7787-7250-7(0))* Crabtree Publishing Co.

Raatma, Lucia. Working at a TV Station. 2011. (21st Century Junior Library: Careers Ser.). (ENG., Illus.). 24p. (gr. 2-5). lib. bdg. 29.21 *(978-1-60279-980-6(6)*, 200950) Cherry Lake Publishing.

Riggs, Thomas, ed. Reality T. V., 1 vol. 2013. (At Issue Ser.). (ENG.). 112p. (gr. 10-12). pap. 28.80 *(978-0-7377-6196-2(2)*, 08c57d01-f8bc-4159-8034-005ef6216b05); lib. bdg. 41.03 *(978-0-7377-6195-5(4)*, 3a26b8f8-294f-4e8b-8257-9d0921ad7cb2) Greenhaven Publishing LLC. (Greenhaven Publishing).

Rissman, Rebecca. TV Displays Disaster As the Challenger Explodes: 4D an Augmented Reading Experience. 2019. (Captured Television History 4D Ser.). (ENG., Illus.). 64p. (J). (gr. 5-9). pap. 8.99 *(978-0-7565-6002-7(0)*, 139133, Compass Point Bks.) Capstone.

Shofner, Shawndra. How it Happens: At the T. V. Station. 2008. (How It Happens Ser.). (YA). (gr. 2-5). lib. bdg. 21.95 *(978-1-934545-07-2(4))* Oliver Pr., Inc.

Smith-Llera, Danielle. TV Shows the World Freedom As the Berlin Wall Falls: 4D an Augmented Reading Experience. 2018. (Captured Television History 4D Ser.). (ENG., Illus.). 64p. (J). (gr. 5-9). lib. bdg. 39.99 *(978-0-7565-5826-0(3)*, 138351, Compass Point Bks.) Capstone.

Teitelbaum, Michael. Sports Broadcasting. 2008. (21st Century Skills Innovation Library: Innovation in Entertainment Ser.). (ENG., Illus.). 32p. (gr. 4-8). lib. bdg. 32.07 *(978-1-60279-216-6(X)*, 200147) Cherry Lake Publishing.

—Television. 2008. (21st Century Skills Innovation Library: Innovation in Entertainment Ser.). (ENG., Illus.). 32p. (gr.

4-8). lib. bdg. 32.07 *(978-1-60279-263-0(1)*, 200146) Cherry Lake Publishing.

Thiel, Kristin. Television News & the 24-Hour News Cycle, 1 vol. 2018. (Fourth Estate: Journalism in North America Ser.). (ENG.). 112p. (gr. 8-8). lib. bdg. 44.50 *(978-1-5026-3491-7(0)*, a935e42a-e346-42e1-a331-422cacdae25e) Cavendish Square Publishing LLC.

Uhl, Xina M. Using Computer Science in Film & Television Careers, 1 vol. 2018. (Coding Your Passion Ser.). (ENG.). 80p. (gr. 7-7). pap. 16.30 *(978-1-5081-8393-8(7)*, 0c9a4817-caed-44cd-b1f2-8b94f6d5ae48, Rosen Young Adult) Rosen Publishing Group, Inc., The.

Walters, John. Sports Broadcasting, Vol. 10. Ferrer, Al, ed. 2015. (Careers off the Field Ser.). (Illus.). 64p. (J). (gr. 7). 23.95 *(978-1-4222-3271-2(9))* Mason Crest.

Weil, Jamie. Asking Questions about What's on Television. 2015. (21st Century Skills Library: Asking Questions about Media Ser.). (ENG., Illus.). 32p. (J). (gr. 4-8). pap. 14.21 *(978-1-63362-509-9(5)*, 206881) Cherry Lake Publishing.

TELEVISION BROADCASTING—BIOGRAPHY

Abrams, Dennis. Barbara Walters. 2010. (ENG., Illus.). 128p. (J). (gr. 6-12). 35.00 *(978-1-60413-686-9(3)*, P179328, Facts On File) Infobase Holdings, Inc.

Bailey, Diane. Who Was Mister Rogers? 2019. (Who HQ Ser.). (ENG.). 107p. (J). (gr. 2-3). 16.96 *(978-0-87617-914-7(6))* Penworthy Co., LLC, The.

Bailey, Diane & Who HQ. Who Was Mister Rogers? Putra, Dede, illus. 2019. (Who Was? Ser.). 112p. (J). (gr. 3-7). 5.99 *(978-1-5247-9219-0(5)*, Penguin Workshop) Penguin Young Readers Group.

Banting, Erinn. Katie Couric. 2007. (Remarkable People Ser.). (Illus.). 24p. (J). (gr. 4-6). pap. 8.95 *(978-1-59036-644-8(1))*; lib. bdg. 24.45 *(978-1-59036-643-1(3))* Weigl Pubs., Inc.

Blashfield, Jean F. Oprah Winfrey, 1 vol. 2004. (Trailblazers of the Modern World Ser.). (ENG., Illus.). 48p. (gr. 5-8). pap. 15.05 *(978-0-8368-5247-9(8)*, a22221d7-89d8-49af-83a7-22a6b0cab35d, Gareth Stevens Secondary Library) Stevens, Gareth Publishing LLLP.

Boone, Mary. Jennette McCurdy. 2010. (Robbie Reader Ser.). (Illus.). 32p. (J). (gr. 2-5). lib. bdg. 25.70 *(978-1-58415-900-1(6))* Mitchell Lane Pubs.

Brown, Jonatha A. Oprah Winfrey, 1 vol. 2004. (Gente Que Hay Que Conocer (People We Should Know) Ser.). (Illus.). 24p. (gr. 2-4). (SPA.). pap. 9.15 *(978-0-8368-4361-3(4)*, 599563fd-105d-49cc-a311-743e8790647b); (ENG., pap. 9.15 *(978-0-8368-4319-4(3)*, fbcee122-e549-46da-95ea-bb42649ddf91); (ENG., lib. bdg. 24.67 *(978-0-8368-4312-5(6)*, 43b47061-bca8-4d08-a25f-dbffe54c2a5c); (SPA., lib. bdg. 24.67 *(978-0-8368-4354-5(1)*, 9f142926-aec3-4ed2-bbdb-a5384aa293d2) Stevens, Gareth Publishing LLLP. (Weekly Reader Leveled Readers).

Collins, Phoebe. Megyn Kelly: From Lawyer to Prime-Time Anchor, 1 vol. 2017. (Leading Women Ser.). (ENG.). 112p. (YA). (gr. 7-7). pap. 20.99 *(978-1-5026-3409-2(0)*, 4cb49a55-daaa-465c-b155-7d79cd804e0d) Cavendish Square Publishing LLC.

Davidson, Avelyn. Elle Fanning, 1 vol. 2012. (Rising Stars Ser.). (ENG., Illus.). 32p. (J). (gr. 1-1). 27.93 *(978-1-4339-7280-5(8)*, ec5971a8-0b58-4991-a0fe-56e884c3d313); pap. 11.50 *(978-1-4339-7281-2(6)*, b503aa61-1717-4f05-9e35-cece1ce99aea) Stevens, Gareth Publishing LLLP.

—Kendall Jenner, 1 vol. 2012. (Rising Stars Ser.). (ENG., Illus.). 32p. (J). (gr. 1-1). 27.93 *(978-1-4339-7288-1(3)*, 95aa59c2-e838-4614-aff3-e23bb1e1020c); pap. 11.50 *(978-1-4339-7289-8(1)*, 536846d5-bee8-4195-a84d-c5e6574eedbd) Stevens, Gareth Publishing LLLP.

Dougherty, Terri. Tyra Banks, 1 vol. 2009. (People in the News Ser.). (ENG., Illus.). 112p. (gr. 7-7). 41.03 *(978-1-4205-0161-2(5)*, 3b763cdd-2fa0-4afd-af21-641b03845535, Lucent Pr.) Greenhaven Publishing LLC.

Edgers, Geoff & Hempel, Carlene. Who Was Julia Child? Putra, Dede & Harrison, Nancy, illus. 2015. (Who Was? Ser.). 112p. (J). (gr. 3-7). 6.99 *(978-0-448-48297-2(5)*, Penguin Workshop) Penguin Young Readers Group.

Fischer, David. Jimmy Kimmel: Late-Night Talk Show Host, 1 vol. 2018. (Influential Lives Ser.). (ENG.). 128p. (gr. 7-7). 40.27 *(978-1-9785-0342-7(3)*, 1b3e9b01-b665-414d-a5c9-73bf083ac3dc) Enslow Publishing, LLC.

Gagne, Tammy. Day by Day with Bindi Sue Irwin. 2012. 32p. (J). (gr. -1-2). lib. bdg. 25.70 *(978-1-61228-326-5(8))* Mitchell Lane Pubs.

Klein, Rebecca. Jimmy Fallon, 1 vol., 1. 2015. (Giants of Comedy Ser.). (ENG., Illus.). 112p. (J). (gr. 7-7). 38.80 *(978-1-4994-6254-8(9)*, ff06626e-23da-484e-b431-f674e910bf1b, Rosen Young Adult) Rosen Publishing Group, Inc., The.

Krohn, Katherine E. Oprah Winfrey. (Just the Facts Biographies Ser.). (Illus.). 112p. 2004. (ENG.). (gr. 5-12). lib. bdg. 27.93 *(978-0-8225-2472-4(4))* 2003. (J). (gr. 6-18). pap. 7.95 *(978-0-8225-5000-6(8))* Lerner Publishing Group.

Lee, T. S. The Oprah Winfrey Story: The First Oprah Winfrey Comic Biography. 2010. 190p. (J). pap. 14.95 *(978-0-9819542-6-4(X))* DASANBOOKS.

Meltzer, Brad. I Am Jim Henson. Eliopoulos, Christopher, illus. 2017. (Ordinary People Change the World Ser.). 40p. (J). (gr. k-4). 15.99 *(978-0-525-42850-3(X)*, Dial Bks) Penguin Young Readers Group.

Noah, Trevor. It's Trevor Noah: Born a Crime: Stories from a South African Childhood (Adapted for Young Readers) 2019. (ENG.). 304p. (J). (gr. 5). 17.99 *(978-0-525-58216-8(9)*, Delacorte Bks. for Young Readers) Random House Publishing Group.

—It's Trevor Noah: Born a Crime: Stories from a South African Childhood (Adapted for Young Readers) 2019. (ENG.). 304p. (J). (gr. 5). lib. bdg. 20.99 *(978-0-525-58217-5(7)*, Delacorte Bks. for Young Readers) Random Hse. Children's Bks.

Payment, Simone. Michael J. Fox: Parkinson's Disease Research Advocate. 2009. (Celebrity Activists Ser.). 112p. (gr. 8-8). 66.50 *(978-1-61511-831-1(4))* Rosen Publishing Group, Inc., The.

Renauld, Laura. Fred's Big Feelings: The Life & Legacy of Mister Rogers. Barrager, Brigette, illus. 2020. (ENG.). 40p. (J). (gr. -1-3). 17.99 *(978-1-5344-4122-4(0)*, Atheneum Bks. for Young Readers) Simon & Schuster Children's Publishing.

Schuman, Michael A. Tina Fey: TV Comedy Superstar, 1 vol. 2011. (People to Know Today Ser.). (ENG., Illus.). 112p. (gr. 6-7). lib. bdg. 35.93 *(978-0-7660-3557-7(3)*, f10baa8a-662b-432c-8977-33c02cf0829f) Enslow Publishing, LLC.

Seba, Jaime. Ellen DeGeneres: From Comedy Club to Talk Show. 2012. (Illus.). 64p. (J). pap. *(978-1-4222-2308-6(6))*; (gr. 7-8). 22.95 *(978-1-4222-2297-3(7))* Mason Crest.

Snyder, Gail. Brooke Knows Best. 2010. (Major Reality Shows Ser.). 48p. (YA). (gr. 7-18). lib. bdg. 19.95 *(978-1-4222-1680-4(2))* Mason Crest.

Tometich, Annabelle. Today's 12 Hottest TV Superstars. 2015. (Today's Superstars Ser.). (ENG., Illus.). 32p. (J). (gr. 3-6). 32.80 *(978-1-63235-023-7(8)*, 11580, 12-Story Library) Bookstaves, LLC.

Wheeler, Jill C. Ellen Degeneres: Groundbreaking Entertainer. 2017. (Newsmakers Set 2 Ser.). (ENG.). 48p. (J). (gr. 4-8). 55.65 *(978-1-68078-967-6(8)*, 26368) ABDO Publishing Co.

TELEVISION IN POLITICS

Burgan, Michael. TV Shapes Presidential Politics in the Kennedy-Nixon Debates: 4D an Augmented Reading Experience. 2018. (Captured Television History 4D Ser.). (ENG., Illus.). 64p. (J). (gr. 5-9). pap. 8.99 *(978-0-7565-5827-7(1)*, 138352, Compass Point Bks.) Capstone.

Ruschmann, Paul. The FCC & Regulating Indecency. 2004. (Point/Counterpoint Ser.). (ENG., Illus.). 112p. (gr. 9-13). 35.00 *(978-0-7910-8363-5(2)*, P114254, Facts On File) Infobase Holdings, Inc.

TELEVISION PLAYS

Crompton, Richmal. Just William As Seen on TV. 2003. (ENG., Illus.). 176p. (J). pap. 6.95 *(978-0-333-62802-7(0))* Macmillan Pubs., Ltd. GBR. Dist: Trafalgar Square Publishing.

Jozsa, Orsolya. Meaning & Perspective in Tom Stoppard's Three Plays - Rosencrantz & Guildenstern Are Dead, Jumpers, Dogg's Hamlet Cahoot's MacBeth. 2008. 52p. pap. *(978-3-639-02075-5(8))* AV Akademikerverlag GmbH & Co. KG.

TELEVISION PROGRAMS

Anniss, Matthew. Create Your Own Movie or TV Show. 2016. (Media Genius Ser.). (ENG., Illus.). 48p. (J). (gr. 5-8). lib. bdg. 35.99 *(978-1-4109-8110-3(X)*, 131004, Raintree) Capstone.

Baby Boomers, 5 cass.; set. 2004. (People's Century Ser.). (gr. 7-18). 59.95 incl. VHS *(978-1-57807-186-9(0)*, WG590) WGBH Boston Video.

Bailey, Diane. America's Best Dance Crew. 2010. (Major Competitive Reality Shows Ser.). 48p. (YA). (gr. 7-18). pap. 7.95 *(978-1-4222-1932-4(1))*; lib. bdg. 19.95 *(978-1-4222-1669-9(1))* Mason Crest.

BBC. Doctor Who: Official Annual 2018. 2017. (ENG.). 64p. (J). 12.99 *(978-1-4059-3000-0(4)*, 5d884926-c0bc-4b81-9533-f2811b255a9f) Penguin Bks., Ltd. GBR. Dist: Diamond Comic Distributors, Inc.

—Doctor Who: the Companion's Companion. 2017. (ENG., Illus.). 176p. (J). 14.99 *(978-1-4059-2969-1(3)*, 5a59e550-4d20-424f-b6e7-178b42b16406) Penguin Bks., Ltd. GBR. Dist: Diamond Comic Distributors, Inc.

Bbc. The Official Doctionary. 2012. (ENG., Illus.). 176p. (J). 15.99 *(978-1-4059-0896-2(3)*, 39676d7a-5da0-4f25-a564-2d10e5fa4315) Penguin Bks., Ltd. GBR. Dist: Diamond Comic Distributors, Inc.

Bednar, Chuck. American Idol Profiles Index: Top Finalists from Each Season (82 Contestants) 2009. (Dream Big: American Idol Superstars Ser.). 64p. (YA). (gr. 5-18). pap. 9.95 *(978-1-4222-1593-7(8))* Mason Crest.

—Insights into American Idol. 2009. (Dream Big: American Idol Superstars Ser.). 64p. (YA). (gr. 5-18). pap. 9.95 *(978-1-4222-1600-2(4))*; lib. bdg. 22.95 *(978-1-4222-1514-2(8))* Mason Crest.

Beecroft, Simon. Join the Rebels. 2010. (DK Readers Level 2 Ser.). (ENG.). 32p. (J). (gr. k-2). 16.19 *(978-0-7566-6312-4(1))* Dorling Kindersley Publishing, Inc.

Bennett, Adelaide. Global Legends & Lore: Vampires & Werewolves Around the World. 2010. (Making of a Monster Ser.). 64p. (YA). (gr. 7-18). lib. bdg. 22.95 *(978-1-4222-1810-5(4))* Mason Crest.

Blohm, Craig E. & Marcovitz, Hal. The Art of Animation. 2019. (Art Scene Ser.). (ENG.). 80p. (YA). (gr. 6-12). 41.27 *(978-1-68282-577-8(9))* ReferencePoint Pr., Inc.

Boehme, Gerry. Producing in TV & Film, 1 vol. 2018. (Exploring Careers in TV & Film Ser.). (ENG.). 96p. (J). (gr. 7-7). pap. 20.99 *(978-1-5026-4140-3(2)*, 86886987-1bc6-4beb-9273-569b1d160c18) Cavendish Square Publishing LLC.

Books, Triumph, ed. Glee Totally Unofficial: The Ultimate Guide to the Smash-Hit High School Musical. 2010. (ENG., Illus.). 128p. (J). (gr. 7). pap. 14.95 *(978-1-60078-498-9(4))* Triumph Bks.

Brennan, Kristine. The City. 2010. (Major Reality Shows Ser.). 48p. (YA). (gr. 7-18). pap. 7.95 *(978-1-4222-1944-7(5))*; lib. bdg. 19.95 *(978-1-4222-1681-1(0))* Mason Crest.

British Broadcasting Corporation Staff. When's the Doctor? 2012. (ENG., Illus.). 40p. (YA). 14.99 *(978-1-4059-0849-8(1)*, bbfdd1c2-f674-4a70-a218-c1efb8adcc02) Penguin Bks., Ltd. GBR. Dist: Diamond Comic Distributors, Inc.

Burling, Alexis. Netflix. 2018. (Tech Titans Ser.). (ENG., Illus.). 112p. (J). (gr. 6-12). lib. bdg. 41.36 *(978-1-5321-1690-2(X)*, 30632, Essential Library) ABDO Publishing Co.

Cane, David A. Nitro Circus. 2010. (Major Reality Shows Ser.). 48p. (YA). (gr. 7-18). lib. bdg. 19.95 *(978-1-4222-1687-3(X))* Mason Crest.

Capek, Michael. Zorro. 2017. 25.70 *(978-1-61228-972-4(X))* Mitchell Lane Pubs.

Cashin, John. Keeping up with the Kardashians. 2010. (Major Reality Shows Ser.). (Illus.). 48p. (J). (gr. 7-18). pap. 7.95 *(978-1-4222-1948-5(8)*, 1318043); lib. bdg. 19.95 *(978-1-4222-1685-9(3)*, 1318043) Mason Crest.

Clark, Travis. Punk'd. 2010. (Major Reality Shows Ser.). 48p. (YA). (gr. 7-18). pap. 7.95 *(978-1-4222-1951-5(8))*; lib. bdg. 19.95 *(978-1-4222-1688-0(8))* Mason Crest.

—Survivor. 2010. (Major Competitive Reality Shows Ser.). 48p. (YA). (gr. 7-18). lib. bdg. 19.95 *(978-1-4222-1678-1(0))* Mason Crest.

The Dangerous Book of Monsters. 2015. (ENG., Illus.). 176p. (J). 16.99 *(978-1-4059-2003-2(3)*, 831f00b4-5e7d-4d4d-8604-56d796214fc8) Penguin Bks., Ltd. GBR. Dist: Diamond Comic Distributors, Inc.

DK. DK Readers L0: Star Wars: Blast Off! 2010. (DK Readers Pre-Level 1 Ser.). (ENG., Illus.). 32p. (J). (gr. -1-k). pap. 4.99 *(978-0-7566-6692-7(9)*, DK Children) Dorling Kindersley Publishing, Inc.

—DK Readers L1: Star Wars: the Clone Wars: Don't Wake the Zillo Beast! Beware the Galaxy's Baddest Beasts! 2011. (DK Readers Level 1 Ser.). (ENG.). 32p. (J). (gr. -1-1). 4.99 *(978-0-7566-8279-8(7)*, DK Children) Dorling Kindersley Publishing, Inc.

—Thomas & Friends Character Encyclopedia. 2018. (ENG., Illus.). 184p. (J). (gr. -1-k). 19.99 *(978-1-4654-6662-4(2)*, DK Children) Dorling Kindersley Publishing, Inc.

Dorling Kindersley Publishing Staff & East Dubowski, Cathy. Masters of the Force. 2013. (DK Readers Pre-Level 1: Star Wars Ser.). (ENG.). 32p. (J). (gr. -1-1). 16.19 *(978-1-4654-0586-9(0))* Dorling Kindersley Publishing, Inc.

Dougherty, Terry. Rob Dyrdek's Fantasy Factory. 2010. (Major Reality Shows Ser.). 48p. (YA). (gr. 7-18). pap. 7.95 *(978-1-4222-1952-2(6))*; (Illus.). lib. bdg. 19.95 *(978-1-4222-1689-7(6))* Mason Crest.

Downey, Glen R. The 10 Most Memorable TV Moments. 2008. 14.99 *(978-1-55448-544-4(4))* Scholastic Library Publishing.

Englart, Mindi. Televison Show. 2003. (Made in the USA Ser.). 32p. (YA). 24.94 *(978-1-56711-413-3(X)*, Blackbirch Pr., Inc.) Cengage Gale.

ESCAPE! Because Accidents Happen: Abandon Ship. 2004. (NOVA Ser.). (gr. 7-18). 19.95 incl. VHS *(978-1-57807-158-6(5)*, WG2607) WGBH Boston Video.

Fisher, Diana, illus. Watch Me Draw Disney's Little Einsteins Amazing Missions. 2012. (J). *(978-1-936309-43-6(2))* Quarto Publishing Group USA.

Gilbert, Elizabeth T., illus. Watch Me Draw Tiggerific Tales. 2013. (Watch Me Draw Ser.). 24p. (gr. -1-2). 25.65 *(978-1-936309-87-0(4))* Quarto Publishing Group USA.

Gilbert, Matthew J. How to Survive in a Stranger Things World (Stranger Things) Random House, illus. 2018. (ENG.). 96p. (YA). (gr. 7). 13.99 *(978-1-9848-5195-6(0)*, Random Hse. Bks. for Young Readers) Random Hse. Children's Bks.

Gitlin, Martin. The Hills. 2010. (Major Reality Shows Ser.). 48p. (YA). (gr. 7-18). pap. 7.95 *(978-1-4222-1946-1(1))*; lib. bdg. 19.95 *(978-1-4222-1683-5(7))* Mason Crest.

—My Super Sweet 16. 2010. (Major Reality Shows Ser.). 48p. (YA). (gr. 7-18). lib. bdg. 19.95 *(978-1-4222-1686-6(1))* Mason Crest.

Grayson, Robert. The Biggest Loser. 2010. (Major Competitive Reality Shows Ser.). 48p. (YA). (gr. 7-18). pap. 7.95 *(978-1-4222-1935-5(6))*; lib. bdg. 19.95 *(978-1-4222-1672-9(1))* Mason Crest.

—Dancing with the Stars. 2010. (Major Competitive Reality Shows Ser.). 48p. (YA). (gr. 7-18). pap. 7.95 *(978-1-4222-1936-2(4))*; lib. bdg. 19.95 *(978-1-4222-1673-6(X))* Mason Crest.

Green, Sara. Nickelodeon. 2016. (Brands We Know Ser.). (ENG., Illus.). 24p. (J). (gr. 3-8). 27.95 *(978-1-62617-411-5(3)*, Pilot Bks.) Bellwether Media.

—Power Rangers. 2018. (Brands We Know Ser.). (ENG., Illus.). 24p. (J). (gr. 3-8). lib. bdg. 27.95 *(978-1-62617-776-5(7)*, Pilot Bks.) Bellwether Media.

Hasday, Judy. So You Think You Can Dance. 2010. (Major Competitive Reality Shows Ser.). 48p. (YA). (gr. 7-18). lib. bdg. 19.95 *(978-1-4222-1677-4(2))* Mason Crest.

Hermansson, Casie. Parental Guidance Ratings. 2013. (Hot Topics in Media Ser.). (ENG.). 48p. (J). (gr. 4-8). pap. 18.50 *(978-1-61783-784-5(9)*, 10758) ABDO Publishing Co.

Higgins, Nadia. Making a TV Show. 2018. (Sequence Entertainment Ser.). (ENG.). 32p. (J). (gr. 2-5). pap. 9.99 *(978-1-68152-363-7(9)*, 15203); lib. bdg. *(978-1-68151-443-7(5)*, 15197) Amicus.

Holub, Joan & Who HQ. Who Was Jim Henson? Harrison, Nancy, illus. 2010. (Who Was? Ser.). 112p. (J). (gr. 3-7). pap. 6.99 *(978-0-448-45406-1(8)*, Penguin Workshop) Penguin Young Readers Group.

Indovino, Shaina C. Simon Cowell: From the Mailroom to Idol Fame. 2012. (Extraordinary Success with a High School Diploma or Less Ser.). 64p. (J). (gr. 7-8). 22.95 *(978-1-4222-2296-6(9))* Mason Crest.

Indovino, Shaina Carmel. Simon Cowell: From the Mailroom to Idol Fame. 2012. pap. *(978-1-4222-2307-9(8))* Mason Crest.

Isbell, Hannah. Jim Henson: Puppeteer & Producer, 1 vol. 2017. (Junior Biographies Ser.). (ENG.). 24p. (gr. 3-4). pap. 10.35 *(978-0-7660-9053-8(1)*, dec1e1b1-a3d9-4057-96d4-29112bf6ffd9) Enslow Publishing, LLC.

Kopp, Megan. Reality Television. 2013. (Hot Topics in Media Ser.). (ENG., Illus.). 48p. (J). (gr. 4-8). pap. 18.50 *(978-1-61783-785-2(7)*, 10759) ABDO Publishing Co.

Korté, Steve & Who HQ. What Is the Story of Looney Tunes? Hinderliter, John, illus. 2020. (What Is the Story Of? Ser.). (ENG.). 112p. (J). (gr. 3-7). 6.99 *(978-1-5247-8836-0(8))*; 15.99 *(978-1-5247-8837-7(6))* Penguin Young Readers Group. (Penguin Workshop).

Kowalski, Emma. American Idol. 2010. (Major Competitive Reality Shows Ser.). 48p. (YA). (gr. 7-18). pap. 7.95 *(978-1-4222-1931-7(3))*; lib. bdg. 19.95 *(978-1-4222-1668-2(3))* Mason Crest.

—America's Next Top Model. 2010. (Major Competitive Reality Shows Ser.). 48p. (YA). (gr. 7-18). pap. 7.95 *(978-1-4222-1934-8(8))*; lib. bdg. 19.95 *(978-1-4222-1671-2(3))* Mason Crest.

—Project Runway. 2010. (Major Competitive Reality Shows Ser.). 48p. (YA). (gr. 7-18). pap. 7.95 *(978-1-4222-1938-6(0))*; lib. bdg. 19.95 *(978-1-4222-1675-0(6))* Mason Crest.

—Run's House. 2010. (Major Reality Shows Ser.). 48p. (YA). (gr. 7-18). pap. 7.95 *(978-1-4222-1953-9(4))*; lib. bdg. 19.95 *(978-1-4222-1690-3(X))* Mason Crest.

Lindeen, Mary. Trash That Trash, Elmo & Abby! 2020. (Go Green with Sesame Street (r) Ser.). (ENG., Illus.). 32p. (J). (gr. -1-2). lib. bdg. 27.99 *(978-1-5415-7258-4(0)*, c6ffef89-480d-4da4-89db-9356691679f9, Lerner Pubns.) Lerner Publishing Group.

MacKinnon, J. Beyblade: Official Handbook. 2003. (Illus.). 69p. (J). *(978-0-439-62860-0(1))* Scholastic, Inc.

Magid, Jennifer. Miley Cyrus / Hannah Montana, 1 vol. 2008. (Today's Superstars Ser.). (ENG.). 32p. (YA). (gr. 3-3). lib. bdg. 34.60 *(978-0-8368-9236-9(4)*, ee620958-9e98-4d58-b213-7dbbb2e40c30) Stevens, Gareth Publishing LLLP.

Major Competitive Reality Shows, 11 vols., Set. Incl. American Idol. Kowalski, Emma. pap. 7.95 *(978-1-4222-1931-7(3))*; America's Best Dance Crew. Bailey, Diane. pap. 7.95 *(978-1-4222-1932-4(1))*; America's Got Talent. Whiting, Jim. pap. 7.95 *(978-1-4222-1933-1(X))*; America's Next Top Model. Kowalski, Emma. pap. 7.95 *(978-1-4222-1934-8(8))*; Biggest Loser. Grayson, Robert. pap. 7.95 *(978-1-4222-1935-5(6))*; Dancing with the Stars. Grayson, Robert. pap. 7.95 *(978-1-4222-1936-2(4))*; Making the Band. Schweitzer, Karen. pap. 7.95 *(978-1-4222-1937-9(2))*; Project Runway. Kowalski, Emma. pap. 7.95 *(978-1-4222-1938-6(0))*; Real World. Schweitzer, Karen. pap. 7.95 *(978-1-4222-1939-3(9))*; So You Think You Can Dance. Hasday, Judy. pap. 7.95 *(978-1-4222-1940-9(2))*; Survivor. Clark, Travis. pap. 7.95 *(978-1-4222-1941-6(0))*; 48p. (YA). (gr. 7-18). 2010. 2011. Set pap. 87.45 *(978-1-4222-1930-0(5))*; Set lib. bdg. 219.45 *(978-1-4222-1667-5(5))* Mason Crest.

Major Reality Shows, 11 vols., Set. Incl. Brooke Knows Best. Snyder, Gail. (YA). pap. 7.95 *(978-1-4222-1943-0(7))*; City. Brennan, Kristine. (YA). pap. 7.95 *(978-1-4222-1944-7(5))*; Guys from Jackass Go Out on Their Own. Marcovitz, Hal. (YA). pap. 7.95 *(978-1-4222-1945-4(3))*; Hills. Gitlin, Martin. (YA). pap. 7.95 *(978-1-4222-1946-1(1))*; Jackass. Marcovitz, Hal. (Illus.). (YA). pap. 7.95 *(978-1-4222-1947-8(X))*; Keeping up with the Kardashians. Cashin, John. (Illus.). (J). pap. 7.95 *(978-1-4222-1948-5(8)*, 1318043); My Super Sweet 16. Gitlin, Martin. (YA). pap. 7.95 *(978-1-4222-1949-2(6))*; Nitro Circus. Cane, David A. (YA). pap. 7.95 *(978-1-4222-1950-8(X))*; Punk'd. Clark, Travis. (YA). pap. 7.95 *(978-1-4222-1951-5(8))*; Rob Dyrdek's Fantasy Factory. Dougherty, Terry. (YA). pap. 7.95 *(978-1-4222-1952-2(6))*; Run's House. Kowalski, Emma. (YA). pap. 7.95 *(978-1-4222-1953-9(4))*; 48p. (gr. 7-18). 2010. 2011. Set pap. 87.45 *(978-1-4222-1942-3(9))*; Set lib. bdg. 219.45 *(978-1-4222-1679-8(9))* Mason Crest.

Mara, Wil. Oprah Winfrey. 2005. (Rookie Biographies Ser.). (ENG., Illus.). 32p. (J). (gr. 1-2). per. 4.95 *(978-0-516-25819-5(2)*, Children's Pr.) Scholastic Library Publishing.

Marcovitz, Hal. The Guys from Jackass Go Out on Their Own. 2010. (Major Reality Shows Ser.). 48p. (YA). (gr. 7-18). pap. 7.95 *(978-1-4222-1945-4(3))*; lib. bdg. 19.95 *(978-1-4222-1682-8(9))* Mason Crest.

—Jackass. 2010. (Major Reality Shows Ser.). 48p. (YA). (gr. 7-18). lib. bdg. 19.95 *(978-1-4222-1684-2(5))*; (Illus.). pap. 7.95 *(978-1-4222-1947-8(X))* Mason Crest.

Meltzer, Brad. I Am Jim Henson. Eliopoulos, Christopher, illus. 2017. (Ordinary People Change the World Ser.). 40p. (J). (gr. k-4). 15.99 *(978-0-525-42850-3(X)*, Dial Bks) Penguin Young Readers Group.

Mooney, Carla. The Creators & Cast of Glee, 1 vol. 2012. (People in the News Ser.). (ENG., Illus.). 104p. (gr. 7-7). lib. bdg. 41.03 *(978-1-4205-0789-8(3)*, ef329bac-52de-493c-858d-109534c159cb, Lucent Pr.) Greenhaven Publishing LLC.

Mystery of the Senses, 5 cass.; set. 2004. (NOVA Ser.). (gr. 7-18). 69.95 incl. VHS *(978-1-884738-57-9(5)*, WG2214) WGBH Boston Video.

Ninety in The 90's. 2004. (Wgbh Specials Ser.). (gr. 7-18). 19.95 *(978-1-57807-458-7(4)*, WG080) WGBH Boston Video.

Ooten, Tara Broeckel & Cooke, C. W. Fame: Justin Bieber. 2010. (Illus.). 32p. pap. 3.99 *(978-1-4507-0888-3(9))* Bluewater Productions, Inc.

Paddington, Whit. Behind the Scenes at an Animated TV Show, 1 vol. 2014. (VIP Tours Ser.). (ENG.). 48p. (gr. 4-4). lib. bdg. 33.07 *(978-1-62713-022-6(5)*, e44b5822-9d24-418d-9676-cd52f4ee2b71) Cavendish Square Publishing LLC.

Payne, M. D. What Is the Story of Scooby-Doo? 2019. (What Is Ser.). (ENG.). 106p. (J). (gr. 2-3). 16.96 *(978-0-87617-639-9(2))* Penworthy Co., LLC, The.

Payne, M. D. & Who HQ. What Is the Story of Scooby-Doo? Thomson, Andrew, illus. 2019. (What Is the Story Of? Ser.). 112p. (J). (gr. 3-7). 6.99 *(978-1-5247-8824-7(4))*; lib. bdg. 15.99 *(978-1-5247-8825-4(2))* Penguin Young Readers Group. (Penguin Workshop).

Penguin UK & British Broadcasting Company Staff. Doctor Who - The Essential Guide. 12th rev. ed. 2016. (ENG., Illus.). 224p. (YA). 20.00 *(978-1-4059-2677-5(5)*, 2b6f2b71-c8ae-4815-86f6-a0cd6ace7826) Penguin Bks., Ltd. GBR. Dist: Diamond Comic Distributors, Inc.

Perry, S. D., et al. The Walking Dead: the Pop-Up Book. 2015. (ENG., Illus.). 5p. 65.00 *(978-1-60887-444-6(3))* Insight Editions.

Publications International Ltd. Staff, ed. Busy Day - Baby's First Look & Find Sesame. 2011. 14p. (J). bds. 3.75 net. *(978-1-4508-1674-8(6))* Publications International, Ltd.

Quan-D'Eramo, Sandra. The 10 Best TV Game Shows. 2008. 14.99 *(978-1-55448-494-2(4))* Scholastic Library Publishing.

Rowe, Brooke. What TV Show Should You Be On? 2016. (Best Quiz Ever Ser.). (ENG., Illus.). 32p. (J). (gr. 4-8). 32.07 *(978-1-63470-509-7(2)*, 207767) Cherry Lake Publishing.

Sanna, Emily. Pop Monsters: The Modern-Day Craze for Vampires & Werewolves. 2010. (Making of a Monster Ser.). 64p. (YA). (gr. 7-18). lib. bdg. 22.95 *(978-1-4222-1806-8(6))* Mason Crest.

Sarandon, Susan, narrated by. Dying to Be Thin. 2004. (NOVA Ser.). (gr. 4-18). 19.95 *(978-1-57807-232-3(8)*, WG2707) WGBH Boston Video.

Schwartz, Heather E. Science Educator & Advocate Bill Nye. 2018. (STEM Trailblazer Bios Ser.). (ENG., Illus.). 32p. (J). (gr. 2-5). pap. 8.99 *(978-1-5415-1214-6(6)*,

TUV

bf86ac08-f2f5-4989-907d-2e6422d700d7) Lerner Publishing Group.

Schweitzer, Karen. Making the Band. 2010. (Major Competitive Reality Shows Ser.). 48p. (YA). (gr. 7-18). pap. 7.95 *(978-1-4222-1937-9(2));* lib. bdg. 19.95 *(978-1-4222-1674-3(8))* Mason Crest.

—The Real World. 2010. (Major Competitive Reality Shows Ser.). 48p. (YA). (gr. 7-18). pap. 7.95 *(978-1-4222-1939-3(9));* lib. bdg. 19.95 *(978-1-4222-1676-7(4))* Mason Crest.

Sesame Street Workshop Staff. Shalom Sesame DVD Set, 5 DVDs. 2011. (J). 59.95 *(978-1-56086-706-7(X))* Sisu Home Entertainment, Inc.

Sesame Workshop Staff. Shalom Sesame Set. 2011. 59.95 *(978-1-56086-707-4(8))* Sisu Home Entertainment, Inc.

Simon, Jenne. Riverdale Student Handbook (Official) 2018. (Riverdale Ser.). (ENG., Illus.). 112p. (YA). (gr. 7-7). pap. 9.99 *(978-1-338-29895-6(X))* Scholastic, Inc.

Smith, Jordan. Deception: Reality TV. 2018. (TIME(r): Informational Text Ser.). (ENG., Illus.). 48p. (gr. 6-8). pap. 13.99 *(978-1-4258-5002-9(2))* Teacher Created Materials, Inc.

Snyder, Gail. Brooke Knows Best. 2010. (Major Reality Shows Ser.). 48p. (YA). (gr. 7-18). pap. 7.95 *(978-1-4222-1943-0(7))* Mason Crest.

Spencer, Liv. The Miranda Cosgrove & iCarly Spectacular! Unofficial & Unstoppable. 2010. (ENG., Illus.). 142p. (J). (gr. 4-7). pap. 14.95 *(978-1-55022-929-5(X),* a320d589-d63c-4e2d-af5b-ec96858d718a) ECW Pr. CAN. Dist: Baker & Taylor Publisher Services (BTPS).

Stewart, Mark. Television Moments, 1 vol. 2009. (Ultimate 10: Entertainment Ser.). (ENG.). 48p. (gr. 3-3). (J). pap. 11.50 *(978-1-4339-2214-5(2),* b72ec60f-d3a0-4b46-adaf-893fa0d98fec); (YA). lib. bdg. 33.67 *(978-0-8368-9166-9(X),* 62a76745-1158-41f3-973a-809eafdfb97e) Stevens, Gareth Publishing LLLP.

Stock, Lisa. What Is a Droid? 2018. (Star Wars DK Readers Level 1 Ser.). lib. bdg. 14.75 *(978-0-606-41168-4(2))* Turtleback.

Streissguth, Tom. The Art of Anime & Manga. 2019. (Art Scene Ser.). (ENG.). 80p. (YA). (gr. 6-12). 41.27 *(978-1-68282-579-2(5))* ReferencePoint Pr., Inc.

Sublette, Guen. Here's Lookin' at Lizzie. *(978-0-312-32669-2(6))* St. Martin's Pr.

Twin Talk: Advice from a TV Talk Show. 2005. (Illus.). 37p. *(978-0-439-12406-5(9))* Scholastic, Inc.

Unknown. Doctor Who: the Illustrated Adventures. 2018. (Illus.). 208p. (J). 24.99 *(978-1-4059-2722-2(4),* 9e24d6ee-13a7-488a-9b01-fde0026bb671) Penguin Bks., Ltd. GBR. Dist: Diamond Comic Distributors, Inc.

Various. Doctor Who: The Official Annual 2017. 2016. (ENG., Illus.). 64p. (YA). 12.99 *(978-1-4059-2649-2(X),* cf98f33f-721c-450d-b724-673f52c16f8b) Penguin Bks., Ltd. GBR. Dist: Diamond Comic Distributors, Inc.

Whiting, Jim. American Idol Judges. (Modern Role Models Ser.). (YA). 2010. (Illus.). 64p. (gr. 7-12). lib. bdg. 22.95 *(978-1-4222-0496-2(0))* 2007. pap. 9.95 *(978-1-4222-0783-3(8))* Mason Crest.

—America's Got Talent. 2010. (Major Competitive Reality Shows Ser.). 48p. (YA). (gr. 7-18). pap. 7.95 *(978-1-4222-1933-1(X));* lib. bdg. 19.95 *(978-1-4222-1670-5(5))* Mason Crest.

Winick, Judd. Pedro & Me: Friendship, Loss, & What I Learned. 2009. (ENG., Illus.). 192p. (YA). (gr. 9-13). pap. 19.99 *(978-0-8050-8964-6(0),* 900056130) Square Fish.

Winnick, Judd. Pedro & Me. 2011. 14.10 *(978-0-7848-3537-1(3),* Everbind) Marco Bk. Co.

Woog, Adam. Reality TV. 2007. (Ripped from the Headlines Ser.). 64p. (YA). (gr. 7-12). 23.95 *(978-1-60217-005-6(3))* Erickson Pr.

TEMPERANCE

Berry, Joy Wilt. A Book about Overdoing It. 2005. (Illus.). (J). *(978-0-7172-8575-4(8))* Scholastic, Inc.

Beyer, Mark. Temperance & Prohibition: The Movement to Pass Anti-Liquor Laws in America, 1 vol. 2005. (Primary Sources of the Progressive Movement Ser.). (ENG., Illus.). 32p. (gr. 3-4). pap. 10.00 *(978-1-4042-0861-2(5),* 4aaa1a18-e46a-48ec-95e1-aff662d7c87c) Rosen Publishing Group, Inc., The.

—Temperance & Prohibition: The Movement to Pass Anti-liquor Laws in America. 2009. (Progressive Movement 1900-1920: Efforts to Reform America's New Industrial Society Ser.). 32p. (gr. 3-4). 47.90 *(978-1-60854-171-3(1))* Rosen Publishing Group, Inc., The.

Blumenthal, Karen. Bootleg: Murder, Moonshine, & the Lawless Years of Prohibition. 2013. (ENG., Illus.). 176p. (YA). (gr. 7-12). pap. 14.99 *(978-1-250-03427-4(2),* 900120600) Square Fish.

Dunn, John M. Prohibition, 1 vol. 2010. (American History Ser.). (ENG., Illus.). 112p. (gr. 7-7). 41.03 *(978-1-4205-0134-6(8),* 0fae9234-0eb9-402e-b015-58ffac3f9dc9, Lucent Pr.) Greenhaven Publishing LLC.

Stoltman, Joan. Prohibition: Social Movement & Controversial Amendment, 1 vol. 2018. (American History Ser.). (ENG.). 104p. (gr. 7-7). 41.03 *(978-1-5345-6412-1(8),* 08226442-c5cc-4803-8338-0f5416d388d5, Lucent Pr.) Greenhaven Publishing LLC.

Worth, Richard. Prohibition: The Rise & Fall of the Temperance Movement. 2019. (J). pap. *(978-1-9785-1539-0(1))* Enslow Publishing, LLC.

—Teetotalers & Saloon Smashers: The Temperance Movement & Prohibition, 1 vol. 2008. (America's Living History Ser.). (ENG., Illus.). 128p. (gr. 5-6). lib. bdg. 35.93 *(978-0-7660-2908-8(5),* d0e73a04-bdfd-491e-ac05-4eb1c8ec5e17) Enslow Publishing, LLC.

TEMPERATURE

see also Heat; Low Temperatures; Thermometers

Bailer, Darice. Measuring Temperature. Petelinsek, Kathleen, illus. 2014. (Explorer Junior Library: Math Explorer Junior Ser.). (ENG.). 24p. (J). (gr. 1-4). 32.07 *(978-1-62431-648-7(4),* 203104) Cherry Lake Publishing.

Bernhardt, Carolyn. Temperature. 2018. (Science Starters Ser.). (ENG., Illus.). 24p. (J). (gr. k-3). pap. 7.99 *(978-1-61891-468-2(5),* 12121); lib. bdg. 26.95 *(978-1-62617-812-0(7))* Bellwether Media. (Blastoff! Readers).

Blaine, Dalton. We Study Temperature: Organizing Data, 1 vol. 2017. (Computer Kids: Powered by Computational Thinking Ser.). (ENG.). 24p. (J). (gr. 3-4). 25.27 *(978-1-5383-2441-7(5),* 4d0893ed-b2a1-4de8-988b-1d04e282bfa5, PowerKids Pr.); pap. *(978-1-5081-3781-8(1),* d8273f9d-7e08-4729-9f72-fd3c0830f326, Rosen Classroom) Rosen Publishing Group, Inc., The.

Boothroyd, Jennifer. What Is Today's Weather? 2014. (First Step Nonfiction — Let's Watch the Weather Ser.). (ENG., Illus.). 24p. (J). (gr. k-2). pap. 6.99 *(978-1-4677-4500-0(6),* 1ef483d3-0a2a-4e3b-96e1-f387e3950e74); lib. bdg. 23.99 *(978-1-4677-3916-0(2),* 61026b9e-bfff-4bfe-8ceb-6f28ef7ac492, Lerner Pubns.) Lerner Publishing Group.

Burslem, Tobe. Bermendani. 2011. 28p. pap. 21.99 *(978-1-4628-5490-5(7))* Xlibris Corp.

Crane, Cody. Heating & Cooling (Rookie Read-About Science: Physical Science) (Library Edition) 2019. (Rookie Read-About Science Ser.). (ENG., Illus.). 32p. (J). (gr. 1-2). lib. bdg. 25.00 *(978-0-531-13407-8(5),* Children's Pr.) Scholastic Library Publishing.

Doudna, Kelly. If You Prefer, I'll Use a Thermometer!, 1 vol. 2007. (Science Made Simple Ser.). (Illus.). 24p. (J). (gr. k-3). lib. bdg. 24.21 *(978-1-59928-594-8(0),* SandCastle) ABDO Publishing Co.

Fiedler, Julie. Learning about Heat & Temperature with Graphic Organizers. (Graphic Organizers in Science Ser.). 24p. (gr. 3-4). 2009. 42.50 *(978-1-61513-039-9(X),* PowerKids Pr.) 2006. (ENG., Illus.). (YA). lib. bdg. 26.27 *(978-1-4042-3408-6(X),* be8f2add-5935-4caa-9473-f15dd005f256) Rosen Publishing Group, Inc., The.

Frisch-Schmoll, Joy. Temperature. 2008. (Simple Science Ser.). (ENG., Illus.). 24p. (J). (gr. 1-4). lib. bdg. 16.95 *(978-1-58341-579-5(3),* 22291, Creative Education) Creative Co., The.

Gardner, Robert. How Hot Is Hot? Science Projects with Temperature, 1 vol. 2014. (Hot Science Experiments Ser.). (ENG.). 48p. (gr. 3-4). 26.93 *(978-0-7660-6605-2(3),* 2e3c465c-b479-444d-8478-b27294a9e448); pap. 11.53 *(978-0-7660-6606-9(1),* 0b01b06e-aeb3-48ac-b846-ec3cc2fa07dc, Enslow Elementary) Enslow Publishing, LLC.

Gardner, Robert & Kemer, Eric. Easy Genius Science Projects with Temperature & Heat: Great Experiments & Ideas, 1 vol. 2008. (Easy Genius Science Projects Ser.). (ENG., Illus.). 128p. (gr. 5-6). lib. bdg. 35.93 *(978-0-7660-2939-2(5),* d70be169-fe0d-4539-b5b2-7db03444ca01) Enslow Publishing, LLC.

—Experiments with Temperature & Heat, 1 vol. 2017. (Science Whiz Experiments Ser.). (ENG.). 128p. (gr. 5-5). lib. bdg. 38.93 *(978-0-7660-8682-1(8),* c94bb21f-4f54-4783-bf7a-0af1e2e9a5c9) Enslow Publishing, LLC.

Gish, Melissa. Temperature. 2005. (My First Look at Science Ser.). (Illus.). 24p. (J). (gr. k-3). lib. bdg. 15.95 *(978-1-58341-375-3(8),* Creative Education) Creative Co., The.

Gosman, Gillian. What Do You Know about Earth's Atmosphere?, 1 vol. 2013. (20 Questions: Earth Science Ser.). 24p. (J). (ENG.). (gr. 2-3). pap. 9.25 *(978-1-4488-9856-5(0),* 1f65b808-2a20-4f78-b141-c59ea5038f4c); (ENG.). (gr. 2-3). lib. bdg. 26.27 *(978-1-4488-9699-8(1),* 0540c873-a86d-4d23-835c-cae6cd899c6d); (gr. 3-6). pap. 49.50 *(978-1-4488-9857-2(9))* Rosen Publishing Group, Inc., The. (PowerKids Pr.).

Hidalgo, Maria. Heat. 2006. (My First Look at Weather Ser.). (Illus.). 24p. (J). (gr. -1-3). lib. bdg. 15.95 *(978-1-58341-449-1(5),* Creative Education) Creative Co., The.

Hughes, Susan. Is It Hot or Cold? 2012. (ENG., Illus.). 24p. (J). *(978-0-7787-2049-2(7));* pap. *(978-0-7787-2056-0(X))* Crabtree Publishing Co.

Jennings, Terry. Hot & Cold. 2009. (Science Alive Ser.). (ENG., Illus.). 32p. (J). (gr. -1-2). pap. *(978-1-897563-55-7(8))* Saunders Bk. Co.

Jennings, Terry J. Hot & Cold. 2009. (J). 28.50 *(978-1-59920-274-7(3))* Black Rabbit Bks.

Johnson, Robin. What Is Temperature? 2012. (ENG.). 24p. (J). *(978-0-7787-0755-4(5));* (Illus.). pap. *(978-0-7787-0762-2(8))* Crabtree Publishing Co.

Jordan, Apple. Hot / Cold, 1 vol. 2nd rev. ed. 2012. (Opposites Ser.). (ENG., Illus.). 16p. (J). (gr. k-1). 24.07 *(978-1-60870-409-5(2),* 1f87f308-e1e4-428f-9019-bd0162e0dec4) Cavendish Square Publishing LLC.

Lilly, Melinda. Hot & Cold. 2005. (Read & Do Science Ser.). (ENG.). 24p. (gr. 1-4). pap. 8.95 *(978-1-62717-259-2(9),* 9781627172592) Rourke Educational Media.

Manolis, Kay. Temperature. (Illus.). 24p. (J). 2009. pap. *(978-1-60014-432-5(2),* Blastoff! Readers) 2007. (ENG., (gr. 2-5). lib. bdg. 26.95 *(978-1-60014-100-3(5))* Bellwether Media.

—Temperature. 2007. (Blastoff! Readers Ser.). (ENG.). 24p. (J). (gr. k-2). 20.00 *(978-0-531-14729-0(0),* Children's Pr.) Scholastic Library Publishing.

Mattern, Joanne. The Sun & Animals. 2019. (Power of the Sun Ser.). (ENG.). 32p. (gr. 3-3). 63.48 *(978-1-5026-4663-7(3))* Cavendish Square Publishing LLC.

Minden, Cecilia. Hot & Cold. 2016. (21st Century Basic Skills Library: Animal Opposites Ser.). (ENG., Illus.). 24p. (J). (gr. k-3). 26.35 *(978-1-63470-473-1(8),* 207623) Cherry Lake Publishing.

Moore, Rob. Why Does Water Evaporate?, 1 vol. 2010. (Solving Science Mysteries Ser.). (ENG., Illus.). 24p. (gr. 4-5). (J). pap. 9.25 *(978-1-61531-915-2(8),* 37bce3e2-1a32-434a-8d3a-ac813df3bde7, PowerKids Pr.); (YA). lib. bdg. 26.27 *(978-1-61531-892-6(5),* a61ea7af-15fc-4977-80d6-6c83a0a62c8d) Rosen Publishing Group, Inc., The.

Rowe, Brooke. Melting Ice. Bane, Jeff, illus. 2017. (My Early Library: My Science Fun Ser.). (ENG.). 24p. (J). (gr. k-1). lib. bdg. 30.64 *(978-1-63472-823-2(8),* 209718) Cherry Lake Publishing.

Rustad, Martha E. H. Today Is a Hot Day. 2017. (What Is the Weather Today? Ser.). (ENG., Illus.). 24p. (J). (gr. -1-2). lib. bdg. 24.65 *(978-1-5157-4923-3(1),* 134539, Pebble) Capstone.

Schmauss, Judy Kentor. Too, Too Hot! 2006. (Illus.). 24p. (J). lib. bdg. 11.00 *(978-1-4242-1587-4(0))* Dingles & Co.

Schuetz, Kristin. Temperature. 2015. (Understanding Weather Ser.). (ENG., Illus.). 24p. (J). (gr. k-3). lib. bdg. 26.95 *(978-1-62617-255-5(2),* Blastoff! Readers) Bellwether Media.

Sheehan, Thomas F. Para Calentarse, para Refrescarse (Keeping Warm, Keeping Cool) Sarfatti, Esther, tr. 2005. (Ciencia Citadina Ser.). (ENG & SPA., Illus.). 24p. (J). (gr. 3-7). lib. bdg. 21.36 *(978-1-59515-666-2(6))* Rourke Educational Media.

Smith, Sian. Hot & Cold, 1 vol. 2014. (Opposites Ser.). (ENG.). 24p. (J). (gr. -1-1). pap. 5.99 *(978-1-4846-0334-5(6),* 126422, Heinemann) Capstone.

Solway, Andrew. Secrets of Heat & Cold, 1 vol. 2011. (Science Secrets Ser.). (ENG.). 32p. (gr. 4-4). 31.21 *(978-1-60870-138-4(7),* 32cbf5aa-7bd5-406a-beda-a9a0948f5cb1) Cavendish Square Publishing LLC.

Stille, Darlene R. Temperature: Heating up & Cooling Down, 1 vol. Boyd, Sheree, illus. 2004. (Amazing Science Ser.). (ENG.). 24p. (J). (gr. k-4). per. 8.95 *(978-1-4048-0345-9(9),* 92666, Picture Window Bks.) Capstone.

Sullivan, Navin. Temperature, 1 vol. 2007. (Measure Up! Ser.). (ENG., Illus.). 48p. (gr. 4-4). lib. bdg. 34.07 *(978-0-7614-2322-5(2),* f5d8ab18-4ea4-486e-8a2c-d6e996d4c6bc) Cavendish Square Publishing LLC.

Sundance/Newbridge LLC Staff. Time & Temperature. 2004. (Reading PowerWorks Ser.). (gr. 1-3). 37.50 *(978-0-7608-8976-3(7));* pap. 6.10 *(978-0-7608-8977-0(5))* Sundance/Newbridge Educational Publishing.

Woodford, Chris. Temperature, 1 vol. 2012. (Measure up Math Ser.). (ENG., Illus.). 32p. (J). (gr. 4-4). 29.27 *(978-1-4339-7449-6(5),* b05e90f9-db26-43e3-9d85-9cbdd23e5d01); pap. 11.50 *(978-1-4339-7450-2(9),* 790d839a-eecb-417c-87bf-9a7a1046506f) Stevens, Gareth Publishing LLLP. (Gareth Stevens Learning Library).

TEMPERATURE MEASUREMENTS

Amstutz, Lisa J. Thermometers. 2019. (Science Tools Ser.). (ENG., Illus.). 24p. (J). (gr. k-2). pap. 6.95 *(978-1-9771-0063-4(5),* 138214); lib. bdg. 27.32 *(978-1-9771-0059-7(7),* 138210) Capstone. (Pebble).

Bailer, Darice. Measuring Temperature. Petelinsek, Kathleen, illus. 2014. (Explorer Junior Library: Math Explorer Junior Ser.). (ENG.). 24p. (J). (gr. 1-4). 32.07 *(978-1-62431-648-7(4),* 203104) Cherry Lake Publishing.

Bernhardt, Carolyn. Temperature. 2018. (Science Starters Ser.). (ENG., Illus.). 24p. (J). (gr. k-3). lib. bdg. 26.95 *(978-1-62617-812-0(7),* Blastoff! Readers) Bellwether Media.

Hinton, John. Hot or Cold? Describe & Compare Measurable Attributes. 2013. (Rosen Math Readers Ser.). (ENG.). 16p. (J). (gr. k-1). pap. 42.00 *(978-1-4777-1627-4(0));* (Illus.). pap. 7.00 *(978-1-4777-1626-7(2),* c6de2be7-9017-4b59-97c6-7e012ef85fea) Rosen Publishing Group, Inc., The. (Rosen Classroom).

Lin, Yoming S. Fahrenheit, Celsius, & Their Temperature Scales, 1 vol. 2011. (Eureka! Ser.). (ENG., Illus.). 24p. (YA). (gr. 2-3). lib. bdg. 26.27 *(978-1-4488-5035-8(5),* 81827d65-afba-4a2b-ac0a-6c010a6999e9) Rosen Publishing Group, Inc., The.

Lipschultz, Wes. Is It Hot or Cold? Learning to Use a Thermometer, 1 vol. 2010. (Math for the REAL World Ser.). (ENG.). 12p. (gr. 1-2). pap. 5.90 *(978-0-8239-8848-8(1),* 6ad9e6e8-75d6-4385-9f90-178944487318, Rosen Classroom) Rosen Publishing Group, Inc., The.

Manolis, Kay. Temperature. (Illus.). 24p. (J). 2009. pap. *(978-1-60014-432-5(2),* Blastoff! Readers) 2007. (ENG., (gr. 2-5). lib. bdg. 26.95 *(978-1-60014-100-3(5))* Bellwether Media.

—Temperature. 2007. (Blastoff! Readers Ser.). (ENG.). 24p. (J). (gr. k-2). 20.00 *(978-0-531-14729-0(0),* Children's Pr.) Scholastic Library Publishing.

Moore, Rob. Why Does Water Evaporate?, 1 vol. 2010. (Solving Science Mysteries Ser.). (ENG., Illus.). 24p. (gr. 4-5). (J). pap. 9.25 *(978-1-61531-915-2(8),* 37bce3e2-1a32-434a-8d3a-ac813df3bde7, PowerKids Pr.); (YA). lib. bdg. 26.27 *(978-1-61531-892-6(5),* a61ea7af-15fc-4977-80d6-6c83a0a62c8d) Rosen Publishing Group, Inc., The.

—Why Does Water Evaporate? All about Heat & Temperature. 2010. (Illus.). 24p. (J). 49.50 *(978-1-61531-916-9(6),* 1307166, PowerKids Pr.) Rosen Publishing Group, Inc., The.

O'Mara, John. How Does a Thermometer Work?, 1 vol. 2020. (Everyday Mysteries Ser.). (ENG.). 24p. (J). (gr. 1-2). pap. 9.15 *(978-1-5382-5663-3(0),* b79f45ef-abbc-4e32-84ac-23c2ed1373c3) Stevens, Gareth Publishing LLLP.

Roberts, Abigail B. Using a Thermometer. 2017. (Super Science Tools Ser.). 24p. (gr. 1-2). pap. 48.90 *(978-1-4824-6410-8(1))* Stevens, Gareth Publishing LLLP.

Rustad, Martha E. H. Measuring Temperature. 2019. (Measuring Masters Ser.). (ENG., Illus.). 24p. (J). (gr. -1-2). lib. bdg. 27.32 *(978-1-9771-0369-7(3),* 139343, Capstone Pr.) Capstone.

Stille, Darlene R. & Picture Window Books Staff. La Temperatura: Caliente y Frío. Robledo, Sol, tr. Boyd, Sheree, illus. 2007. (Ciencia Asombrosa Ser.). (SPA.). 24p. (J). (gr. k-4). 27.32 *(978-1-4048-3234-3(3),* 93776, Picture Window Bks.) Capstone.

Woodford, Chris. Temperature, 1 vol. 2012. (Measure up Math Ser.). (ENG., Illus.). 32p. (J). (gr. 4-4). 29.27 *(978-1-4339-7449-6(5),* b05e90f9-db26-43e3-9d85-9cbdd23e5d01); pap. 11.50 *(978-1-4339-7450-2(9),* 790d839a-eecb-417c-87bf-9a7a1046506f) Stevens, Gareth Publishing LLLP. (Gareth Stevens Learning Library).

TEMPERATURES, LOW

see Low Temperatures

TEMPLES

Barnes, Kathleen. I Love to See the Temple Reprint. 2009. 32p. pap. 8.95 *(978-1-60641-112-4(8))* Deseret Bk. Co.

Bodden, Valerie. Temples. 2007. (Built to Last Ser.). (Illus.). 24p. (J). (gr. 3-7). lib. bdg. 24.25 *(978-1-58341-560-3(2),* Creative Education) Creative Co., The.

D'Ecsery, Claire. Temples Dot the Earth. 2016. (ENG.). (J). bds. 9.99 *(978-1-4621-1842-7(9))* Cedar Fort, Inc./CFI Distribution.

Jani, Mehendra & Jani, Vandana. What You Will See Inside a Hindu Temple. Bhargava, Neirah & Dave, Vijay, photos by. 2005. (What You Will See Inside ... Ser.). (ENG., Illus.). 32p. (J). (gr. 3-7). 17.99 *(978-1-59473-116-7(0),* 08eb9a41-a019-4d4a-a3a6-430015c2e2c1, Skylight Paths Publishing) LongHill Partners, Inc.

Levy, Leah. The Waiting Wall. Rosenfeld, D. L. & Leverton, Yossi, eds. 2009. (ENG., Illus.). 26p. (J). (gr. -1-1). 13.99 *(978-1-929628-49-0(8))* Hachai Publishing.

Rose, Simon. Sri Harmandir Sahib. 2014. (J). *(978-1-4896-2609-7(3))* Weigl Pubs., Inc.

TEN COMMANDMENTS

Allen, Jan. Now I Know the 10 Commandments. Allen, Russ, illus. 2005. 32p. (J). (gr. k-5). *(978-0-9765514-0-9(3))* Light Bugs Publishing.

Alsbrooks, Stephanie. The Ten Commandments: The Second Commandment. 2004. (J). bds. 9.99 *(978-1-4183-0000-5(4))* Christ Inspired, Inc.

Bianchi, Andrew. 10 Rulz. 2005. (Illus.). 128p. pap. *(978-1-84427-053-8(X))* Scripture Union.

Cameron, William J. You & the Ten Commandments. Bacon, Irving R., illus. 2011. 210p. 44.95 *(978-1-258-08112-6(1))* Literary Licensing, LLC.

CrossStaff Publishing, creator. The Ten Commandments Movie Coloring Book: Part 1. 2007. (Epic Stories of the Bible Ser.). (Illus.). 32p. (J). (gr. -1-3). 5.99 *(978-0-9743876-1-1(4))* CrossStaff Publishing.

David C. Cook Publishing Company Staff. The Ten Commandments. 2003. (My Jesus Pocket Bks.). (Illus.). 32p. (J). (gr. -1-3). pap., pap. 8.90 *(978-1-55513-859-2(4),* 1555138594) Cook, David C.

Dobson, Shirley, contrib. by. God's Ten Best: The Ten Commandments Comic & Activity Book. 2004. 16p. act. bk. ed. 1.49 *(978-0-8307-3060-5(5),* Gospel Light) Gospel Light Pubns.

Escalera, Manuel Silva. Cassandrita y Los Sabios: De Los 10 Mandamientos y Filosofía. 2012. (SPA.). 108p. (gr. -1). pap. 14.95 *(978-1-4772-0516-7(0))* AuthorHouse.

Forster, Pamela R. Honor Your Father & Mother: The Fifth Commandment for Little Ones. 2006. (J). spiral bd. 10.00 *(978-1-891206-23-8(0))* Doorposts.

Glickman, Jeff. Have You Heard? A Child's Introduction to the Ten Commandments, 1 vol. Krackow, Eric, illus. 2017. (ENG.). 32p. (J). (gr. -1-3). 14.99 *(978-0-7643-5395-6(0),* 7767) Schiffer Publishing, Ltd.

Jenkins, Sharon I. Remember the Ten Commandments with Jam & Jean Jellybean. Jenkins, Sharon I., illus. l.t. ed. 2006. (Illus.). 32p. (J). (gr. -1-3). per. 10.99 *(978-1-59879-240-9(7))* Lifevest Publishing, Inc.

Killian, Rick & Yaxley, Trevor. The Making of the Ten Commandments. 2008. (Illus.). 120p. 16.99 *(978-0-9743876-8-0(1))* CrossStaff Publishing.

Long, V. Philips. 1 & 2 Samuel. 2016. (Zondervan Illustrated Bible Backgrounds Commentary Ser.). (ENG., Illus.). 227p. E-Book 9.43 *(978-0-310-52760-2(0),* 9780310527602) Zondervan.

MacKenzie, Carine. God, the Ten Commandments & Jesus. rev. ed. 2003. (ENG.). 48p. (J). 12.99 *(978-1-85792-850-1(4),* f3a73706-7f26-4bdb-b50d-80d41637f069) Christian Focus Pubns. GBR. Dist: Baker & Taylor Publisher Services (BTPS).

Manhardt, Laurie Watson. Friends of God: Catholic Bible Study for Children. Co, Aileen & Dayton, Melissa, illus. 2006. (Come & See Kids Ser.). 124p. (J). (gr. -1-2). per. 9.95 *(978-1-931018-41-8(3))* Emmaus Road Publishing.

Mathews, Janice. Jack & the 10 Rules. 2012. 32p. (J). 7.99 *(978-0-8280-2690-1(4))* Review & Herald Publishing Assn.

McDonough, Yona Zeldis & Who HQ. What Are the Ten Commandments? Foley, Tim, illus. 2017. (What Was? Ser.). 112p. (J). (gr. 3-7). 5.99 *(978-0-515-15723-9(6),* Penguin Workshop) Penguin Young Readers Group.

McGinnis, Mary Lane. The Ten Commandments for Children. 2012. 24p. pap. 10.99 *(978-1-4624-0084-3(1),* Inspiring Voices) Author Solutions, LLC.

McNeil, Niki, et al. HOCPP 1134 10 Commandments. 2006. spiral bd. 16.00 *(978-1-60308-134-4(8))* In the Hands of a Child.

Murphy, W. Ten Commandments for Children. Date not set. (J). (gr. -1-3). pap. 1.95 *(978-0-88271-159-1(8))* Regina Pr., Malhame & Co.

Naha, Ed. The Ten Commandments Movie Storybook. 2007. (Epic Stories of the Bible Ser.). (Illus.). 77p. (J). (gr. -1-3). 14.99 *(978-0-9743876-4-2(9))* CrossStaff Publishing.

Nolan, Allia Zobel. The Ten Commandments for Little Ones. Samuel, Janet, illus. 2009. (ENG.). 32p. (J). 14.99 *(978-0-7369-2545-7(7))* Harvest Hse. Pubs.

Notto, E. T. Light of God Bible Books: Book 1 (Creation, God's Commandments, Faith) 2008. 52p. pap. 22.49 *(978-1-4389-1702-3(3))* AuthorHouse.

Ostrowski, Thaddeus & Smith, Robert J. Primary Source Readings in Christian Morality. 2008. (ENG.). 242p. (J). pap. 14.50 *(978-0-88489-989-1(6))* Saint Mary's Press of Minnesota.

Piscitelli, Donna & Gortler, Rosemarie. Living the 10 Commandments for Children. Sternhagen, Mimi, illus. 2006. 48p. (J). pap. 6.95 *(978-1-59276-231-6(X))* Our Sunday Visitor, Publishing Div.

Richards, Virginia Helen. The Ten Commandments. Richards, Virginia Helen & Halpin, D. Thomas, illus. 2007. (J). 1.95 *(978-0-8198-7420-7(5))* Pauline Bks. & Media.

Rosenfeld, Dina. It's Called Kibud Av Va'Eim: A Story about Honoring Parents. Ebert, Len, illus. 2014. (ENG.). 20p. (J). 11.99 *(978-1-929628-78-0(1))* Hachai Publishing.

Topek, Susan R. Ten Good Rules. Schanzer, Rosalyn, illus. 2004. (General Jewish Interest Ser.). 24p. (J). (gr. -1-1). pap. 6.95 *(978-0-929371-30-6(5),* Kar-Ben Publishing) Lerner Publishing Group.

Topek, Susan Remick. Ten Good Rules: A Counting Book. Cohen, Tod, photos by. 2007. (ENG., Illus.). 24p. (J). (gr. -1-1). lib. bdg. 15.95 (978-0-8225-7293-0(1), Kar-Ben Publishing) Lerner Publishing Group.

Trahan, Kendra Swain. Following Jesus: Obeying His Commandments (Children's Version) 2006. (Illus.). 35p. (J). (gr. -1-3). per. 14.99 (978-1-59879-201-0(6)) Lifevest Publishing, Inc.

Van Leeuwen, Wendy. The Ten Commandments Activity Book. 2007. (Illus.). 16p. (J). pap. 1.89 (978-1-59317-210-7(9)) Warner Pr., Inc.

Vecchini, Silvia. The 10 Commandments Explained. Vincenti, Antonio, illus. 2015. (J). 6.95 (978-0-8198-7523-5(6)) Pauline Bks. & Media.

VonSeggen, Liz. The King's Commandments: Teaching Unit. rev. ed. 2003. (Illus.). 228p. (J). spiral bd. 45.00 (978-1-58302-247-4(3)) Creative Ministry Solutions.

Walker, Joni. Gods Ten Commandments. 2004. (Follow & Do Ser.). (Illus.). 32p. (J). 7.49 (978-0-7586-0227-5(8)) Concordia Publishing Hse.

Warner Press, creator. The Ten Commandments Coloring Book. 2009. (Illus.). 16p. (J). (gr. -1-2). pap. 11.34 (978-1-59317-340-1(7)) Warner Pr., Inc.

The 10 Commandments. (Illus.). 16p. (J). pap. 1.50 (978-0-87162-872-5(4), E6037) Warner Pr., Inc.

TENNESSEE

Barrett, Tracy. Tennessee, 1 vol. 2nd rev. ed. 2007. (Celebrate the States (Second Edition) Ser.). (ENG., Illus.). 144p. (gr. 6-6). lib. bdg. 39.79 (978-0-7614-2151-1(3), d1e4aa04-d839-47c6-b608-025245be4d52) Cavendish Square Publishing LLC.

Brown, Vanessa. Tennessee, 1 vol. Brusca, Maria Cristina, tr. 2005. (Bilingual Library of the United States of America Ser.: Set 2). (ENG & SPA., Illus.). 32p. (J). (gr. 2-2). lib. bdg. 28.93 (978-1-4042-3108-5(0), f071b366-4490-4554-8fa7-c24403149322) Rosen Publishing Group, Inc., The.

Davidson, Tish. East South-Central States: Kentucky & Tennessee, Vol. 19. 2015. (Let's Explore the States Ser.). (Illus.). 64p. (J). (gr. 5). 23.95 (978-1-4222-3322-1(7)) Mason Crest.

Downey, Tika. Tennessee: The Volunteer State, 1 vol. 2010. (Our Amazing States Ser.). (ENG.). 24p. (J). (gr. 3-3). lib. bdg. 26.27 (978-1-4358-9352-8(2), 95c6b4f2-c2b8-4e1f-86c7-cbd3d56813d4, PowerKids Pr.) Rosen Publishing Group, Inc., The.

Fretland VanVoorst, Jenny. What's Great about Tennessee? 2014. (Our Great States Ser.). (ENG., Illus.). 32p. (J). (gr. 2-5). lib. bdg. 26.65 (978-1-4677-3392-2(X), 4f93985c-1bd8-4d2a-9d0a-c2d26ab26c2e, Lerner Pubns.) Lerner Publishing Group.

Furstinger, Nancy. Davy Crockett. 2018. (Illus.). 24p. (J). pap. (978-1-4896-9548-2(6), AV2 by Weigl) Weigl Pubs., Inc.

Herman, Gail & Who HQ. Who Was Davy Crockett? Squier, Robert, illus. 2013. (Who Was? Ser.). (ENG.). 112p. (J). (gr. 3-7). 5.99 (978-0-448-46704-7(6), Penguin Workshop) Penguin Young Readers Group.

Jarnow, Jesse. Davy Crockett: Defensor de la frontera (Davy Crockett: Frontier Hero) 2009. (Grandes personajes en la historia de los Estados Unidos (Famous People in American History) Ser.). (SPA.). 32p. (gr. 2-3). 47.90 (978-1-61512-797-9(6), Editorial Buenas Letras) Rosen Publishing Group, Inc., The.

—Davy Crockett: Frontier Hero / Defensor de la Frontera. 2009. (Famous People in American History/Grandes personajes en la historia de los Estados Unidos Ser.). (ENG & SPA.). 32p. (gr. 2-3). 47.90 (978-1-61512-543-2(4), Editorial Buenas Letras) Rosen Publishing Group, Inc., The.

Johnston, Marianne. Davy Crockett. 2009. (American Legends Ser.). 24p. (gr. 3-3). 42.50 (978-1-61511-381-1(9), PowerKids Pr.) Rosen Publishing Group, Inc., The.

Marsh, Carole. The Big Tennessee Reproducible Activity Book! 2004. (Carole Marsh Tennessee Bks.). (Illus.). 96p. (gr. 2-6). per. 9.95 (978-0-7933-9957-4(2)) Gallopade International.

—My First Book about Tennessee. 2004. (Carole Marsh Tennessee Bks.). 32p. (J). (gr. k-4). pap. 7.95 (978-0-7933-9899-7(1)) Gallopade International.

—Tennessee Current Events Projects: 30 Cool, Activities, Crafts, Experiments & More for Kids to Do to Learn about Your State! 2003. (Tennessee Experience Ser.). 32p. (gr. k-5). pap. 5.95 (978-0-635-02061-1(0), Marsh, Carole Bks.) Gallopade International.

—The Tennessee Experience Pocket Guide. 2004. (Carole Marsh Tennessee Bks.). (Illus.). 96p. (J). (gr. 3-8). pap. 6.95 (978-0-7933-9928-4(9)) Gallopade International.

—Tennessee Geography Projects: 30 Cool, Activities, Crafts, Experiments & More for Kids to Do to Learn about Your State! 2003. (Tennessee Experience Ser.). 32p. (gr. k-5). pap. 5.95 (978-0-635-01860-1(8), Marsh, Carole Bks.) Gallopade International.

—Tennessee Government Projects: 30 Cool, Activities, Crafts, Experiments & More for Kids to Do to Learn about Your State! 2003. (Tennessee Experience Ser.). 32p. (gr. k-5). pap. 5.95 (978-0-635-01961-5(2), Marsh, Carole Bks.) Gallopade International.

—Tennessee Jeopardy! Answers & Questions about Our State! Line Art Staff, illus. 2004. 32p. (J). (gr. 3-8). pap. 7.95 (978-0-7933-9812-6(6)) Gallopade International.

—Tennessee People Projects: 30 Cool, Activities, Crafts, Experiments & More for Kids to Do to Learn about Your State! 2003. (Tennessee Experience Ser.). 32p. (gr. k-5). pap. 5.95 (978-0-635-02011-6(4), Marsh, Carole Bks.) Gallopade International.

—Tennessee Symbols & Facts Projects: 30 Cool, Activities, Crafts, Experiments & More for Kids to Do to Learn about Your State! 2003. (Tennessee Experience Ser.). 32p. (gr. k-5). pap. 5.95 (978-0-635-01911-0(6), Marsh, Carole Bks.) Gallopade International.

—The Terrific Tennessee Coloring Book! 2004. (Carole Marsh Tennessee Bks.). (Illus.). 32p. (J). (gr. k-2). 3.95 (978-0-7933-9870-6(3)) Gallopade International.

McDaniel, Melissa. Tennessee (a True Book: My United States) (Library Edition) 2018. (True Book (Relaunch) Ser.). (ENG., Illus.). 48p. (J). (gr. 3-5). 31.00 (978-0-531-23581-2(5), Children's Pr.) Scholastic Library Publishing.

McNamara, Connie. My First University of Tennessee Words. 2004. (J). bds. 11.95 (978-0-9759703-3-1(X)) Shamrock Publishing, Inc.

Mis, M. S. How to Draw Tennessee's Sights & Symbols. 2009. (Kid's Guide to Drawing America Ser.). 32p. (gr. k-k). 50.50 (978-1-61511-096-4(8), PowerKids Pr.) Rosen Publishing Group, Inc., The.

Moriarty, J. T. Davy Crockett: Frontier Hero. 2009. (Primary Sources of Famous People in American History Ser.). 32p. (gr. 2-3). 47.90 (978-1-60851-670-4(9)) Rosen Publishing Group, Inc., The.

—Davy Crockett: Frontier Hero = Defensor de la Frontera, 1 vol. 2003. (Famous People in American History / Grandes Personajes en la Historia de Los Estados Unidos Ser.). (ENG & SPA., Illus.). 32p. (J). (gr. 2-3). lib. bdg. 29.13 (978-0-8239-4156-8(6), 053f4de4-9a56-4d3b-81e2-66f81220ca56) Rosen Publishing Group, Inc., The.

Murray, Julie. Tennessee, 1 vol. 2006. (United States Ser.). (ENG., Illus.). 32p. (gr. 2-4). 27.07 (978-1-59197-701-8(0), Buddy Bks.) ABDO Publishing Co.

Parker, Bridget. Tennessee. 2016. (States Ser.). (ENG., Illus.). 32p. (J). (gr. 3-6). lib. bdg. 27.99 (978-1-5157-0430-0(0), 132041, Capstone Pr.) Capstone.

Petreycik, Rick. Tennessee, 1 vol. Santoro, Christopher, illus. 2006. (It's My State! (First Edition)(r) Ser.). (ENG.). 80p. (gr. 4-4). lib. bdg. 34.07 (978-0-7614-1909-9(8), 57cd2820-c99a-4fa5-bf94-929a66dbd534) Cavendish Square Publishing LLC.

—Tennessee, 1 vol. 2nd rev. ed. 2013. (It's My State! (Second Edition)(r) Ser.). (ENG.). 80p. (gr. 4-4). pap. 18.64 (978-1-62712-104-0(8), d584bb07-981d-410c-b194-9437e1e01b56) Cavendish Square Publishing LLC.

Shoulders, Michael. Count on Us: A Tennessee Number Book. Langton, Bruce, illus. 2003. (America by the Numbers Ser.). (ENG.). 40p. (J). (gr. 1-3). 16.95 (978-1-58536-131-1(3), 201993) Sleeping Bear Pr.

Sirvaitis, Karen. Tennessee. 2012. (J). lib. bdg. 25.26 (978-0-7613-4558-9(2), Lerner Pubns.) Lerner Publishing Group.

Skogen, J. M. On the Hardwood: Memphis Grizzlies. 2014. (On the Hardwood Ser.). (ENG.). 48p. (gr. 3-8). pap. 8.95 (978-1-61570-917-5(7)) Scobre Pr. Corp.

Skogen, J. m. & Skogen, J. M. Memphis Grizzlies. 2014. (On the Hardwood Ser.). (gr. 3-8). 27.93 (978-1-61570-918-2(5)) Scobre Pr. Corp.

Sparkman, Winette. Tennessee Trailblazers. Laughbaum, Steve & Crutchfield, Jim, illus. 56p. (J). pap., wbk. ed., act. bk. ed. 6.95 (978-0-9634824-1-9(6)) March Media, Inc.

Sullivan, E. J. T Is for Tennessee. Cross, Neal, illus. 2007. (State Alphabet Bks.). 24p. (J). (gr. -1-3). (978-1-58173-527-7(8)) Sweetwater Pr.

Valzania, Kimberly. Tennessee. 2003. (Rookie Read-About Geography Ser.). (ENG., Illus.). 32p. (J). (gr. 1-2). 20.50 (978-0-516-22699-6(1), Children's Pr.) Scholastic Library Publishing.

Wagner, Heather Lehr. Benjamin Hooks. 2003. (African American Leaders Ser.). (ENG., Illus.). 112p. (gr. 6-12). 30.00 (978-0-7910-7685-9(7), P113974, Facts On File) Infobase Holdings, Inc.

Weatherly, Myra S. From Sea to Shining Sea: Tennessee. 2008. (ENG.). 80p. (J). pap. 7.95 (978-0-531-20814-4(1), Children's Pr.) Scholastic Library Publishing.

Winders, Richard Bruce. Davy Crockett: The Legend of the Wild Frontier. 2009. (Library of American Lives & Times Ser.). 112p. (gr. 5-5). 69.20 (978-1-60853-476-0(6)) Rosen Publishing Group, Inc., The.

TENNESSEE—FICTION

Altsheler, Joseph A. The Guns of Shiloh. 2006. (Civil War Ser.: Vol. 2). 292p. (J). reprint ed. 28.95 (978-1-4218-1774-3(8)); pap. 13.95 (978-1-4218-1874-0(4)) 1st World Publishing, Inc. (1st World Library - Literary Society).

—The Guns of Shiloh. 2010. (Civil War Ser.: Vol. 2). (ENG.). 356p. (J). (gr. 4-7). reprint ed. pap. 32.75 (978-1-177-56053-5(4)) Creative Media Partners, LLC.

—The Guns of Shiloh. 2006. (Civil War Ser.: Vol. 2). (J). reprint ed. pap. (978-1-4065-0813-0(6)) Dodo Pr.

—The Guns of Shiloh. 2006. (Civil War Ser.: Vol. 2). (J). reprint ed. pap. (978-1-4068-0745-5(1)) Echo Library.

—The Guns of Shiloh. 2010. 156p. pap. 24.39 (978-1-152-46676-0(3)); (Civil War Ser.: Vol. 2). (Illus.). (J). (gr. 4-7). reprint ed. pap. 19.99 (978-1-153-70505-9(2)) General Bks. LLC.

—The Guns of Shiloh. (Civil War Ser.: Vol. 2). (J). 2010. 216p. pap. (978-1-4076-3068-7(7)) 2012. 362p. reprint ed. pap. (978-1-290-02433-4(2)) HardPr.

—The Guns of Shiloh. 2003. (Civil War Ser.: Vol. 2). 232p. (J). reprint ed. pap. 36.99 (978-1-4043-5087-8(X)) IndyPublish.com.

—The Guns of Shiloh. (Civil War Ser.: Vol. 2). (J). reprint ed. 2010. 226p. (gr. 4-7). 31.96 (978-1-169-29437-0(5)) 2010. 226p. (gr. 4-7). pap. 19.96 (978-1-162-69671-3(0)) 2010. 39.95 (978-1-161-46536-5(7)) 2004. pap. 1.99 (978-1-4192-6520-4(2)) 2004. pap. 24.95 (978-1-4191-6520-7(8)) Kessinger Publishing, LLC.

—The Guns of Shiloh. (Civil War Ser.: Vol. 2). reprint ed. 2008. 228p. (J). pap. 14.45 (978-1-60597-269-5(X)) 2007. 232p. per. 12.45 (978-1-60424-259-1(0)) Standard Publications, Inc. (Bk. Jungle).

—The Guns of Shiloh. 2009. (Civil War Ser.: Vol. 2). 278p. (J). (gr. 4-7). reprint ed. pap. 16.95 (978-1-933573-83-0(X)) Zeezok Publishing, LLC.

—The Guns of Shiloh. 2011. (Civil War Ser.: Vol. 2). 260p. (J). (gr. 4-7). reprint ed. pap. (978-3-8424-2812-6(X)) tredition Verlag.

—The Sword of Antietam: A Story of the Nation's Crisis. 2006. (Civil War Ser.: Vol. 4). 296p. (J). reprint ed. 28.95 (978-1-4218-1776-7(4)); pap. 13.95 (978-1-4218-1876-4(0)) 1st World Publishing, Inc. (1st World Library - Literary Society).

—The Sword of Antietam: A Story of the Nation's Crisis. l.t. ed. (Civil War Ser.: Vol. 4). (J). reprint ed. 2006. 262p. pap. 23.99 (978-1-4264-2714-5(X)) 2011. 358p. (gr. 4-7). pap. 32.75 (978-1-245-13385-2(3)) 2008. 264p. 28.99 (978-0-554-22582-1(4)) 2008. 264p. 25.99 (978-0-554-31885-1(7)) 2007. (ENG.). 242p. pap. 20.99 (978-1-4264-2657-5(7)) Creative Media Partners, LLC.

—The Sword of Antietam: A Story of the Nation's Crisis. 2006. (Civil War Ser.: Vol. 4). (J). reprint ed. pap. (978-1-4065-0825-3(X)) Dodo Pr.

—The Sword of Antietam: A Story of the Nation's Crisis. 2007. (Civil War Ser.: Vol. 4). 176p. (J). reprint ed. per. (978-1-4068-1690-7(6)) Echo Library.

—The Sword of Antietam: A Story of the Nation's Crisis. 2010. (Civil War Ser.: Vol. 4). (Illus.). 160p. (J). (gr. 4-7). reprint ed. pap. 19.99 (978-1-153-72276-6(3)) General Bks. LLC.

—The Sword of Antietam: A Story of the Nation's Crisis. 2010. (Civil War Ser.: Vol. 4). 224p. (J). reprint ed. pap. (978-1-4076-4642-8(7)) HardPr.

—The Sword of Antietam: A Story of the Nation's Crisis. (Civil War Ser.: Vol. 4). (J). reprint ed. 2010. 352p. (gr. 4-7). 37.56 (978-1-163-20537-2(0)) 2010. 352p. (gr. 4-7). pap. 25.56 (978-1-162-77564-7(5)) 2005. 352p. 46.95 (978-1-4326-1485-0(1)) 2004. pap. 1.99 (978-1-4192-8469-4(X)) Kessinger Publishing, LLC.

—The Sword of Antietam: A Story of the Nation's Crisis. 2009. (Civil War Ser.: Vol. 4). (J). reprint ed. pap. 16.95 (978-1-933573-85-4(6)) Zeezok Publishing, LLC.

Bare, Bart. Girl. 2010. 188p. (YA). pap. 11.95 (978-0-9825396-4-4(9)) Canterbury Hse. Publishing, Ltd.

Benton, Justin. Moonshine. 2019. 192p. (J). (gr. 3-7). 17.99 (978-1-62979-811-0(8), Calkins Creek) Highlights Pr., c/o Highlights for Children, Inc.

Bougie, Matt. The Bell Witch: Ghost of Tennessee, 1 vol. Garvey, Brian, illus. 2016. (American Legends & Folktales Ser.). (ENG.). 32p. (J). (gr. 3-3). pap. 11.58 (978-1-5026-2220-4(3), 6fc28983-60aa-4735-8f04-7f6462d914b4) Cavendish Square Publishing LLC.

Brouwer, Sigmund. Rock the Boat, 1 vol. 2015. (Orca Limelights Ser.). (ENG.). 128p. (J). (gr. 4-7). pap. 9.95 (978-1-4598-0455-5(4)) Orca Bk. Pubs. USA.

Brouwer, Sigmund & Morgan, Cindy. True Blue, 1 vol. 2018. (Orca Limelights Ser.). (ENG.). 128p. (J). (gr. 4-7). pap. 9.95 (978-1-4598-1580-3(7), 1459815807) Orca Bk. Pubs. USA.

Bryant, Jen. Ringside 1925. 2009. 240p. (J). (gr. 5). 7.99 (978-0-440-42189-4(6), Yearling) Random Hse. Children's Bks.

Carr, Patrick W. The Legend's Granddaughter: Not Quite Super, Book 1. Dabbs, Douglas, illus. 2007. 281p. (J). pap. (978-0-9793168-0-7(4)) NQSBks.

Crist-Evans, Craig. Moon over Tennessee: A Boy's Civil War Journal. Christensen, Bonnie, illus. 2003. (ENG.). 64p. (J). (gr. 5-7). pap. 8.95 (978-0-618-31107-1(6), 460020, Clarion Bks.) HarperCollins Pubs.

Donaldson, Joan. On Viney's Mountain. 2009. (ENG.). 192p. (YA). (gr. 5-18). 16.95 (978-0-8234-2129-9(5)) Holiday Hse., Inc.

Dorr, Shay. Khloe Dutch! 2011. 48p. pap. 8.95 (978-1-4502-8332-8(2)) iUniverse, Inc.

Dowell, Frances O'Roark. Where I'd Like to Be. 2004. (Aladdin Fiction Ser.). 232p. (gr. 5-9). 17.00 (978-0-7569-4357-8(4)) Perfection Learning Corp.

—Where I'd Like to Be. (ENG., (J). (gr. 5-9). 2003. Illus.). 240p. 17.99 (978-0-689-84420-1(4)) 2004. 256p. reprint ed. pap. 7.99 (978-0-689-87067-5(1)) Simon & Schuster Children's Publishing. (Atheneum Bks. for Young Readers).

—Where I'd Like to Be. l.t. ed. 2003. 162p. (J). 22.95 (978-0-7862-5741-6(5)) Thorndike Pr.

Dudley, Marie Luther. Tennessee Ocean Frogs. Primm, Patricia, illus. 2008. 24p. pap. 24.95 (978-1-60474-261-9(5)) America Star Bks.

Duncan, Alice Faye. Memphis, Martin, & the Mountaintop: The Sanitation Strike Of 1968. Christie, R. Gregory, illus. 2018. (ENG.). 40p. (J). (gr. 2-5). 17.99 (978-1-62979-718-2(9), Calkins Creek) Highlights Pr., c/o Highlights for Children, Inc.

Duncan Gurley, Ann. Esbe's Halo. 2009. 108p. (J). pap. 15.95 (978-1-4327-3453-4(9)) Outskirts Pr., Inc.

Faulkerson, Jeffery A. It's Good to Be Golden: The Stranger in the Shadows. 2008. 26p. pap. 24.95 (978-1-60441-863-7(X)) America Star Bks.

Frillman, K. Country Stars: The Road Less Traveled. 2007. 348p. per. 21.95 (978-1-4303-1234-5(3)) Lulu Pr., Inc.

Gamble, Adam. Good Night Tennessee. Veno, Joe, illus. 2007. (Good Night Our World Ser.). (ENG.). 20p. (J). (gr. -1 — 1). bds. 9.95 (978-1-60219-019-1(4)) Good Night Bks.

Godfrey, John. The Green Enamel Kid. 2008. 64p. per. 9.95 (978-1-4357-0508-1(4)) Lulu Pr., Inc.

Grant, Natalie. Miracle in Music City, 1 vol. 2016. (Faithgirlz / Glimmer Girls Ser.: 3). (ENG.). 208p. (J). pap. 8.99 (978-0-310-75250-9(7)) Zonderkidz.

Gratz, Alan. Something Rotten, 1. 2007. (Horatio Wilkes Mystery Ser.). (ENG.). 208p. (J). (gr. 7-12). 21.19 (978-0-8037-3216-2(3)) Penguin Young Readers Group.

—Something Wicked, 2. 2008. (Horatio Wilkes Mystery Ser.). (ENG.). 272p. (YA). (gr. 7-12). 22.44 (978-0-8037-3666-5(5), Dial) Penguin Publishing Group.

Gratz, Alan M. Something Rotten. 2009. 224p. (YA). (gr. 7-18). 8.99 (978-0-14-241297-8(X), Speak) Penguin Young Readers Group.

—Something Wicked. 2009. 288p. (YA). (gr. 7-18). 10.99 (978-0-14-241496-5(4), Speak) Penguin Young Readers Group.

Green, Connie Jordan. The War at Home. 2nd ed. 2003. 144p. (J). pap. 15.00 (978-0-916078-75-1(2)) Iris Publishing Group, Inc., The.

Guiffre, William A. Eddie, the Elf Who Would Be Elvis. Fannon, Chris, illus. 2011. (ENG.). 40p. (J). 17.95 (978-0-9830172-0-2(4)); pap. 9.95 (978-0-9830172-1-9(2)) Guiffre Bk. Publishing.

Harrison, Emma. Escaping Perfect. 2016. (ENG., Illus.). 336p. (YA). (gr. 9). 17.99 (978-1-4814-4212-1(0), Simon Pulse) Simon Pulse.

Hembree, G. Wil. The Willisby Orphans: In the Keys to the Bottomless Pit. 2011. 552p. (gr. -1 — 1). 44.95 (978-1-4497-2366-8(7)); pap. 34.95 (978-1-4497-2365-1(9)) Author Solutions, LLC. (WestBow Pr.).

Higginbotham, Mary. Only Feature. 2012. 56p. pap. 16.95 (978-1-4626-7953-9(6)) America Star Bks.

Holley, Marietta. Samantha at the World's Fair. 2007. (ENG.). 428p. pap. 26.99 (978-1-4264-5101-0(6)) Creative Media Partners, LLC.

Huggins, Peter. In the Company of Owls. Koz, Paula Goodman, illus. 2008. (ENG.). 96p. (J). 15.95 (978-1-58838-036-4(X), 8845, NewSouth Bks.) NewSouth, Inc.

Isbell, Rebecca & Buchanan, Marilyn. Everyone Has a Story to Tell. Bledsoe, William B., illus. 2004. (J). 14.95 (978-0-9755906-0-7(X)) Olde Town Publishing.

Ivy, Maggie, illus. Beware the Bell Witch. 2018. (Haunted States of America Ser.). (ENG.). 136p. (J). (gr. 3-4). lib. bdg. 27.13 (978-1-63163-203-7(5), 1631632035, Jolly Fish Pr.) North Star Editions.

Jacobs, Lily. The Littlest Bunny in Nashville. Dunn, Robert, illus. 2016. (Littlest Bunny Ser.). (ENG.). 32p. (J). (gr. -1-3). 9.99 (978-1-4926-3351-8(8), 9781492633518, Hometown World) Sourcebooks, Inc.

—The Littlest Bunny in Tennessee: An Easter Adventure. Dunn, Robert, illus. 2015. (Littlest Bunny Ser.). (ENG.). 32p. (J). (gr. -1-3). 9.99 (978-1-4926-1207-0(3), Hometown World) Sourcebooks, Inc.

James, Eric. Santa's Sleigh Is on Its Way to Tennessee: A Christmas Adventure. Dunn, Robert, illus. 2015. (Santa's Sleigh Is on Its Way Ser.). (ENG.). 32p. (J). (gr. k-2). 12.99 (978-1-4926-2752-4(6), Hometown World) Sourcebooks, Inc.

—The Spooky Express Tennessee. Piwowarski, Marcin, illus. 2017. (Spooky Express Ser.). (ENG.). 32p. (J). (gr. k-6). 9.99 (978-1-4926-5402-5(7), Hometown World) Sourcebooks, Inc.

—Tiny the Tennessee Easter Bunny. 2018. (Tiny the Easter Bunny Ser.). (ENG.). 40p. (J). (gr. k-3). 9.99 (978-1-4926-5967-9(3), Hometown World) Sourcebooks, Inc.

Jamison, Jo Lynn & Elliott, Lela Mae. Siren's Call of the Caves, 1 vol. 2009. 55p. pap. 16.95 (978-1-4489-8627-9(3)) PublishAmerica, Inc.

John Philip Duck. 2004. (J). 27.95 incl. audio (978-0-8045-6932-3(0)); 29.95 incl. audio compact disk (978-0-8045-4127-5(2)) Spoken Arts, Inc.

Johnson, Allen, Jr. My Brother's Story. McMorris, Kelley, illus. 2014. (Blackwater Novels Ser.: Vol. 1). (ENG.). 191p. (J). (gr. 4-7). 14.99 (978-1-933725-37-6(0)) Premium Pr. America.

Johnston, Tony. Bone by Bone by Bone. 2007. (ENG.). 192p. (YA). (gr. 7-12). 30.99 (978-1-59643-113-3(X), 900031670) Roaring Brook Pr.

Keith, Patty J. Will You Be My Friend? Even If I Am Different from You. Keith, Patty J., photos by. 2013. (Illus.). 36p. pap. 12.95 (978-0-615-78050-4(4)) Patty's Blooming Words.

Kenneally, Miranda. Racing Savannah, 1 vol. unabr. ed. 2015. (Hundred Oaks Ser.: Bk. 4). (ENG.). (YA). (gr. 7-9). 14.99 (978-1-5012-1560-5(4), 9781501215605, Audible Studios on Brilliance Audio) Brilliance Publishing, Inc.

—Racing Savannah. 2013. (Hundred Oaks Ser.: 4). 304p. (YA). (gr. 7-12). pap. 14.99 (978-1-4022-8476-2(4), 9781402284762) Sourcebooks, Inc.

—Things I Can't Forget. 2013. (Hundred Oaks Ser.: 3). 320p. (YA). (gr. 7-12). pap. 14.99 (978-1-4022-7190-8(5), 9781402271908) Sourcebooks, Inc.

Kidd, Ronald. Lord of the Mountain. 2018. (ENG.). 296p. (J). (gr. 3-7). 16.99 (978-0-8075-4751-9(4), 807547514) Whitman, Albert & Co.

—Monkey Town: The Summer of the Scopes Trial. 2006. (ENG., Illus.). 250p. (YA). (gr. 7-12). 18.69 (978-1-4169-0572-1(3)) Simon & Schuster, Inc.

Lee, Dakota. Flash of Freedom. 2009. 128p. pap. 11.95 (978-0-595-52557-7(1)) iUniverse, Inc.

Lloyd, Natalie. The Key to Extraordinary. 2017. (ENG.). 240p. (J). (gr. 3-7). pap. 8.99 (978-0-545-55276-9(1), Scholastic Pr.) Scholastic, Inc.

—A Snicker of Magic. 2015. lib. bdg. 17.20 (978-0-606-37089-9(7)) Turtleback.

—A Snicker of Magic (Scholastic Gold) 2015. (ENG.). 336p. (J). (gr. 3-7). pap. 7.99 (978-0-545-55273-8(7), Scholastic Pr.) Scholastic, Inc.

—A Snicker of Magic (Scholastic Gold) (Unabridged Edition), 2 vols. unabr. ed. 2014. (ENG.). 2p. (J). (gr. 3-7). audio compact disk 34.99 (978-0-545-70679-7(3)) Scholastic, Inc.

Lloyd, Natalie, et al. A Snicker of Magic. 2014. (ENG.). mass mkt. (978-0-545-68447-7(1)) Scholastic, Inc.

MacKay, Lisa. Nick Finds a Home. 2009. 32p. pap. 12.99 (978-1-4490-3245-6(1)) AuthorHouse.

Marshall, Catherine. The Angry Intruder, 1 vol. 2018. (Christy of Cutter Gap Ser.: 3). 112p. (J). pap. 7.99 (978-1-68370-161-3(5)) Evergreen Farm.

—The Bridge to Cutter Gap, 1 vol. 2018. (Christy of Cutter Gap Ser.: 1). 112p. (J). pap. 7.99 (978-1-68370-157-6(7)) Evergreen Farm.

—Silent Superstitions, 1 vol. 2018. (Christy of Cutter Gap Ser.: 2). 112p. (J). pap. 7.99 (978-1-68370-159-0(3)) Evergreen Farm.

Martone, Ginny. Trouble at Big Bear Falls. 2011. 90p. pap. 19.95 (978-1-4626-2558-1(4)) America Star Bks.

Mary E. Gale. Mountain Boy in the City. 2009. 136p. 21.95 (978-1-4401-6771-3(0)); pap. 11.95 (978-1-4401-6773-7(7)) iUniverse, Inc.

McDaniel, Lurlene. The Year of Chasing Dreams. 2015. (Luminous Love Ser.). (ENG.). 336p. (YA). (gr. 7). pap. 9.99 (978-0-385-74174-3(X), Ember) Random Hse. Children's Bks.

—The Year of Luminous Love. 2014. (Luminous Love Ser.). (ENG.). 384p. (YA). (gr. 7). pap. 13.99 (978-0-385-74172-9(3), Ember) Random Hse. Children's Bks.

McKissack, Patricia. Abby Takes a Stand. James, Gordon C., illus. 2006. (Scraps of Time Ser.). (ENG.). 128p. (J). (gr. 3-7). 7.99 (978-0-14-240687-8(2), Puffin Books) Penguin Young Readers Group.

—The Home-Run King. 2009. (Scraps of Time Ser.). (ENG.). 112p. (J). (gr. 3-7). 7.99 (978-0-14-241459-0(X), Puffin Books) Penguin Young Readers Group.

McKissack, Patricia C. Abby Takes a Stand. James, Gordon C., illus. 2007. 104p. (J). (978-0-439-02797-7(7)) Scholastic, Inc.

—Goin' Someplace Special. Pinkney, Jerry, illus. 2008. (ENG.). 40p. (J). (gr. -1-3). 8.99 (978-1-4169-2735-8(2), Aladdin) Simon & Schuster Children's Publishing.

—Tippy Lemmey. Keeter, Susan, illus. 2003. (Ready-for-Chapters Ser.). 59p. (gr. 2-5). lib. bdg. 15.00 *(978-0-7569-1432-5(9))* Perfection Learning Corp.

Miller, Pat Zietlow. The Quickest Kid in Clarksville. Morrison, Frank, illus. 2016. (ENG.). 40p. (J). (gr. k-3). 16.99 *(978-1-4521-2936-5(3))* Chronicle Bks. LLC.

Moonshower, Candie. The Legend of Zoey. 2007. (ENG.). 224p. (J). (gr. 3-7). 6.99 *(978-0-440-23924-6(9)*, Yearling) Random Hse. Children's Bks.

Murdoch, Emily. If You Find Me: A Novel. 2014. (ENG.). 288p. (YA). (gr. 7). pap. 12.99 *(978-1-250-03327-7(6)*, 900096076, St. Martin's Griffin) St. Martin's Pr.

Nilsson, Al. The Tennessee Tater. Nilsson, Al, illus. 2003. (Illus.). (YA). per. *(978-0-9741294-9-5(6)*, MSP) Yetto Publishing Co.

O'Neill, Elizabeth. Alfred Visits Tennessee. 2006. (Illus.). 24p. 12.00 *(978-0-9771836-5-4(3))* Funny Bone Bks.

Payne, C. C. Lula Bell on Geekdom, Freakdom, & the Challenges of Bad Hair, 0 vols. 2012. (ENG.). 276p. (J). (gr. 4-6). 16.99 *(978-0-7614-6225-5(2)*, 9780761462255, Two Lions) Amazon Publishing.

Pfeffer, Susan Beth. The Shade of the Moon. 2014. (Life As We Knew It Ser.: 4). (ENG.). 304p. (YA). (gr. 7). pap. 9.99 *(978-0-544-33615-5(1)*, 1584161, Clarion Bks.) HarperCollins Pubs.

Polacco, Patricia. John Philip Duck. Polacco, Patricia, illus. 2004. (Illus.). 48p. (J). (gr. k-4). 18.99 *(978-0-399-24262-5(7)*, Philomel Bks.) Penguin Young Readers Group.

Ray, Christie Jones & Ray, Christie Jones. Fox Family of Franklin. 2012. (Illus.). 16p. pap. 10.00 *(978-0-9853223-3-5(0))* Rose Water Cottage Pr.

Reed, Vernon. Children of the Hollow. 2006. (ENG.). 188p. per. 24.95 *(978-1-4241-3668-1(7))* PublishAmerica, Inc.

Reinhardt, Dana. How to Build a House. 2009. (ENG.). 240p. (YA). (gr. 9-11). pap. 8.99 *(978-0-375-84454-6(6)*, Ember) Random Hse. Children's Bks.

Rennison, Louise. Then He Ate My Boy Entrancers: More Mad, Marvy Confessions of Georgia Nicolson. (Confessions of Georgia Nicolson Ser.: 6). 2006. (ENG.). 336p. (YA). (gr. 8-12). pap. 10.99 *(978-0-06-058939-4(6))* 2005. 320p. (J). lib. bdg. 16.89 *(978-0-06-058938-7(8))* HarperCollins Pubs. (HarperTeen).

Saveley, Barb. Dusky II: Journey of Tears. 2010. 40p. 18.95 *(978-1-4389-8243-4(7))* AuthorHouse.

Schwabach, Karen. The Hope Chest. 2010. 288p. (J). (gr. 3-7). 8.99 *(978-0-375-84096-8(6)*, Yearling) Random Hse. Children's Bks.

Singer, Sarah Jane. Two Bullets for Sergeant Franks. 2003. (Illus.). 112p. (YA). pap. 7.99 *(978-0-9721216-9-9(2)*, 0972121692) Computer Classics (R).

Smith, Robert F. Bitten: A Romantic Comedy. 2008. 510p. (YA). pap. *(978-1-59038-904-1(2))* Deseret Bk. Co.

Snyder, Laurel. Penny Dreadful. Halpin, Abigail, illus. 320p. (J). 2012. (ENG.). (gr. 4-6). lib. bdg. 22.44 *(978-0-375-96199-1(2))* 2011. (gr. 3-7). 8.99 *(978-0-375-86169-7(6))* Random Hse. Children's Bks. (Yearling).

Spencer, Octavia. The Case of the Time-Capsule Bandit. To, Vivienne, illus. 2013. (Randi Rhodes, Ninja Detective Ser.: 1). (ENG.). 224p. (J). (gr. 3-7). 16.99 *(978-1-4424-7681-3(8)*, Simon & Schuster Bks. For Young Readers) Simon & Schuster Bks. For Young Readers.

Spruill, Beverle. The Dream Box. 2009. 24p. pap. 13.50 *(978-1-4490-3783-3(6))* AuthorHouse.

Steele, William O. Flaming Arrows. 2004. (ENG., Illus.). 160p. (J). (gr. 3-7). pap. 11.95 *(978-0-15-205213-3(5)*, 1195721, Clarion Bks.) HarperCollins Pubs.

Sully, Katherine. Night-Night Tennessee. Poole, Helen, illus. 2017. (Night-Night Ser.). (ENG.). 20p. (J). (gr. -1-1). bds. 9.99 *(978-1-4926-4777-5(2)*, 9781492647775, Hometown World) Sourcebooks, Inc.

Supplee, Suzanne. Artichoke's Heart. 2009. 288p. (YA). (gr. 7-18). 8.99 *(978-0-14-241427-9(1)*, Speak) Penguin Young Readers Group.

—Somebody Everybody Listens To. 2011. 288p. (YA). (gr. 7-12). 8.99 *(978-0-14-241886-4(2)*, Speak) Penguin Young Readers Group.

Taylor, Pearl Fleming. Snowbird Weenie, 1 vol. 2009. 59p. pap. 16.95 *(978-1-60836-745-0(2))* America Star Bks.

Tubb, Kristin O'Donnell & O'Donnell Tubb, Kristin. Autumn Winifred Oliver Does Things Different. 2008. (ENG.). 224p. (J). (gr. 4-6). lib. bdg. 21.19 *(978-0-385-90558-9(0)*, Delacorte Pr.) Random Hse. Children's Bks.

Tugman, Etta. Smokey Mountain Bears. 2006. 9.00 *(978-0-8059-8189-6(6))* Dorrance Publishing Co., Inc.

Turner, Thomas N. Country Music Night Before Christmas, 1 vol. Rice, James, illus. 2003. (Night Before Christmas Ser.). (ENG.). 32p. (J). (gr. k-3). 16.99 *(978-1-58980-148-6(2)*, Pelican Publishing) Arcadia Publishing.

Tyler-Vaughn, Savanna. Flour Sack Wear. 2006. (ENG.). 48p. per. 16.95 *(978-1-4241-2501-2(4))* America Star Bks.

Vawter, Vince. Copyboy. Trunfio, Alessia, illus. 2018. (ENG.). 240p. (YA). (gr. 6-9). 15.95 *(978-1-63079-105-6(9)*, 138669, Capstone Editions) Capstone.

—Paperboy. 2014. 240p. (J). (gr. 5). pap. 7.99 *(978-0-307-93151-1(X)*, Yearling) Random Hse. Children's Bks.

Watts, Julia. Secret City. 2013. (ENG.). 264p. (gr. 7). pap. 13.95 *(978-1-59493-390-5(1))* Bella Bks., Inc.

White-Adams, Beverly. The Adventures of Rusty: Rusty Goes to Tennessee the Adventures Continue Vol. 4. 2013. 32p. pap. 17.25 *(978-1-4669-8583-4(6))* Trafford Publishing.

TENNESSEE—HISTORY

Bailey, Diane. Tennessee: Past & Present, 1 vol. 2010. (United States: Past & Present Ser.). (ENG., Illus.). 48p. (J). (gr. 5-5). pap. 12.75 *(978-1-4358-8494-6(9)*, d192451a-fbee-43f9-a014-8f5d1ca0197d); lib. bdg. 34.47 *(978-1-4358-3522-1(0)*, 7a5261f6-a0da-4cb5-ac28-3df8853660ff) Rosen Publishing Group, Inc., The. (Rosen Reference).

Brown, Vanessa. Tennessee. 2009. (Bilingual Library of the United States of America Ser.). (ENG & SPA.). 32p. (gr. 2-2). 47.90 *(978-1-60853-386-2(7)*, Editorial Buenas Letras) Rosen Publishing Group, Inc., The.

Chemerka, William. Davy Crockett from a to Z, 1 vol. 2013. (ABC Ser.). (ENG., Illus.). 32p. (J). (gr. k-3). 16.99 *(978-1-4556-1835-4(7)*, Pelican Publishing) Arcadia Publishing.

Dean, Arlan. The Wilderness Trail: From the Shenandoah Valley to the Ohio River. 2009. (Famous American Trails Ser.). 24p. (gr. 3-3). 42.50 *(978-1-61512-493-0(4)*, PowerKids Pr.) Rosen Publishing Group, Inc., The.

Downey, Tika. Tennessee: The Volunteer State, 1 vol. 2010. (Our Amazing States Ser.). (ENG.). 24p. (J). (gr. 3-3). pap. 9.25 *(978-1-4358-9800-4(1)*, 8a2d4ee6-790b-46e7-9f20-9861edfeb680, PowerKids Pr.) Rosen Publishing Group, Inc., The.

English, D. N. Downtown Wanderings & Memories. 2nd ed. 2003. (Illus.). 190p. (YA). pap. *(978-0-9741294-8-8(8)*, MSP) Yetto Publishing Co.

Erlic, Lily. Nashville. 2020. (J). *(978-1-7911-1594-4(2)*, AV2 by Weigl) Weigl Pubs., Inc.

Fretland VanVoorst, Jenny. What's Great about Tennessee? 2014. (Our Great States Ser.). (ENG., Illus.). 32p. (J). (gr. 2-5). pap. 7.95 *(978-1-4677-4542-0(1)*, 8e1aa70b-ef41-43c8-a4a6-8a94084c52df) Lerner Publishing Group.

Furstinger, Nancy. Davy Crockett. 2003. (Folk Heroes Ser.). (Illus.). 24p. (J). lib. bdg. 24.45 *(978-1-59036-073-6(7))* Weigl Pubs., Inc.

Gish, Melissa. Tennessee. 2009. (This Land Called America Ser.). (Illus.). 32p. (YA). (gr. 3-6). 19.95 *(978-1-58341-795-9(8))* Creative Co., The.

Hama, Larry. The Battle of Shiloh: Surprise Attack!, 1 vol. Moore, Scott, illus. 2006. (Graphic Battles of the Civil War Ser.). (ENG.). 48p. (J). (gr. 4-5). lib. bdg. 37.13 *(978-1-4042-0779-0(1)*, 99017b0f-4ba7-42b3-9eb0-3d582b4f973e) Rosen Publishing Group, Inc., The.

Hamilton, John. Tennessee, 1 vol. 2016. (United States of America Ser.). (ENG., Illus.). 48p. (J). (gr. 5-9). 34.21 *(978-1-68078-345-2(9)*, 21675, Abdo & Daughters) ABDO Publishing Co.

Harmon, Leesa, et al. Bullets & Bayonets: A Battle of Frankin Primer. 2014. (ENG.). 117p. 25.00 *(978-0-9911915-2-9(8)*, Academy Park Pr.) Williamson County Public Library.

Herman, Gail. Who Was Davy Crockett? 2013. (Who Was... ? Ser.). lib. bdg. 16.00 *(978-0-606-32133-4(0))* Turtleback.

Hicks, Kyra E. Martha Ann's Quilt for Queen Victoria. Födi, Lee Edward, illus. 2012. 32p. (J). pap. 12.95 *(978-0-9824796-8-1(9))* Black Threads Pr.

Hubbard, Rita Lorraine. Hammering for Freedom, 1 vol. Holyfield, John, illus. 2018. (New Voices Ser.). (ENG.). 32p. (J). (gr. 2-7). 19.95 *(978-1-60060-969-5(4)*, leelowbooks) Lee & Low Bks., Inc.

Jerome, Kate B. Lucky to Live in Tennessee. 2017. (Arcadia Kids Ser.). (ENG., Illus.). 32p. (J). 16.99 *(978-0-7385-2790-1(4))* Arcadia Publishing.

—The Wise Animal Handbook Tennessee. 2017. (Arcadia Kids Ser.). (ENG., Illus.). 32p. (J). 16.99 *(978-0-7385-2844-1(7))* Arcadia Publishing.

Lantier, Pat. Tennessee, 1 vol. 2005. (Portraits of the States Ser.). (ENG., Illus.). 32p. (gr. 3-5). pap. 11.50 *(978-0-8368-4653-9(2)*, 55d9908f-b891-4e77-becb-0c8992748615); lib. bdg. 28.67 *(978-0-8368-4634-8(6)*, 5fe32edc-d370-4ef1-81a4-219ee98c3c9a) Stevens, Gareth Publishing LLLP. (Gareth Stevens Learning Library).

Marsh, Carole. Exploring Tennessee Through Project-Based Learning: Geography, History, Government, Economics & More. 2016. (Tennessee Experience Ser.). (ENG.). (J). pap. 9.99 *(978-0-635-12366-4(5))* Gallopade International.

—Tennessee History Projects: 30 Cool, Activities, Crafts, Experiments & More for Kids to Do to Learn about Your State! 2003. (Tennessee Experience Ser.). 32p. (gr. k-5). pap. 5.95 *(978-0-635-01811-3(X)*, Marsh, Carole Bks.) Gallopade International.

Marthal, Barbara G. Fighting for Freedom: A Documented Story. 2012. (ENG.). 28p. pap. 19.99 *(978-1-4772-2922-4(1))* AuthorHouse.

McDowell, Pamela. Tennessee: The Volunteer State. 2012. (J). *(978-1-61913-405-8(5))*; pap. *(978-1-61913-406-5(3))* Weigl Pubs., Inc.

McMillan, Jenna. East Tennessee from a to Z. Patients from East Tennessee Children's Hospital, illus. 2013. (ENG.). 26p. 20.00 *(978-0-9830954-2-2(6))* Books by Kids LLC.

Petreycik, Rick. Tennessee, 1 vol. 2nd rev. ed. 2013. (It's My State! (Second Edition)(r) Ser.). (ENG., Illus.). 80p. (gr. 4-4). 35.93 *(978-0-7614-8003-7(X)*, 2a5efb5b-bdfe-4b1e-bcc8-7afd5f9b61be) Cavendish Square Publishing LLC.

Petreycik, Rick, et al. Tennessee, 1 vol. 3rd rev. ed. 2015. (It's My State! (Third Edition)(r) Ser.). (ENG., Illus.). 80p. (gr. 4-4). 35.93 *(978-1-62713-225-1(2)*, 3ffdd202-d2d5-4cdd-a33d-f9f9a8291647) Cavendish Square Publishing LLC.

Publications International Ltd. Staff, et al. Yesterday & Today Nashville. 2010. (Illus.). 192p. 24.95 *(978-1-4127-6199-4(9))* Publications International, Ltd.

Semchuk, Rosann. Tennessee. 2011. (Guide to American States Ser.). (Illus.). 48p. (YA). (gr. 3-6). 29.99 *(978-1-61690-815-7(7))*; (J). *(978-1-61690-491-3(7))* Weigl Pubs., Inc.

—Tennessee: The Volunteer State. 2016. (J). *(978-1-4896-4944-7(1))* Weigl Pubs., Inc.

Shoulders, Michael. Little Tennessee. Urban, Helle, illus. 2012. (Little State Ser.). (ENG.). 20p. (J). (gr. -1-1). bds. 9.95 *(978-1-58536-201-1(8)*, 202272) Sleeping Bear Pr.

Somervill, Barbara A. America the Beautiful: Tennessee (Revised Edition) rev. ed. 2014. (ENG.). 144p. (J). lib. bdg. 40.00 *(978-0-531-28294-6(5))* Scholastic Library Publishing.

TENNIS

see also Squash (Game)

Armentrout, David & Armentrout, Patricia. Annika Sorenstam. 2004. (Discover the Life of a Sports Star Ser.). (Illus.). 24p. (gr. 1-4). lib. bdg. *(978-1-59515-130-8(3))* Rourke Educational Media.

Bow, Patricia. Tennis Science. 2008. (Sports Science Ser.). (ENG., Illus.). 32p. (J). (gr. 4-6). pap. *(978-0-7787-4556-3(2))*; lib. bdg. *(978-0-7787-4539-6(2))* Crabtree Publishing Co.

Bratton, Deboral B. & Bratton, Ashley D. Record-a-Sport Tennis Organizer. Bratton, Deboral B. & Bratton, Ashley D., eds. 2003. (Illus.). (gr. 1-18). 18.95 *(978-1-931746-06-9(0))* Sport Your Stuff Corp.

Brown, Jonatha A. Tennis, 1 vol. 2004. (My Favorite Sport Ser.). (ENG., Illus.). 24p. (gr. 2-4). pap. 9.15 *(978-0-8368-4349-1(5)*, ed99a8f1-552e-446d-bed8-2448b5d4c7ee); lib. bdg. 24.67 *(978-0-8368-4342-2(8)*, 1e645605-5042-48ba-9a7d-c6b522a7a3f2) Stevens, Gareth Publishing LLLP. (Weekly Reader Leveled Readers).

Bussiere, Desireé. Tennis by the Numbers, 1 vol. 2013. (Sports by the Numbers Ser.). (ENG.). 24p. (J). (gr. k-3). lib. bdg. 29.93 *(978-1-61783-847-7(0)*, 13708, SandCastle) ABDO Publishing Co.

Challen, Paul. Smash It Tennis, 1 vol. 2010. (ENG., Illus.). 32p. (J). pap. *(978-0-7787-3177-1(4))*; lib. bdg. *(978-0-7787-3145-0(6))* Crabtree Publishing Co.

Consistent Tennis Wins. 2004. per. 14.95 *(978-0-9727444-1-6(X))* Avery's, Tom Totally Tennis.

Crossingham, John & Kalman, Bobbie. Le Tennis. 2008. (FRE.). 32p. (J). pap. 9.95 *(978-2-89579-184-3(8))* Bayard Canada Livres CAN. Dist: Crabtree Publishing Co.

Derr, Aaron. Tennis: An Introduction to Being a Good Sport. Angle, Scott, illus. 2017. (Start Smart (tm) — Sports Ser.). (ENG.). 32p. (J). (gr. k-3). E-Book 39.99 *(978-1-63440-145-6(X))* Red Chair Pr.

Donohue, Moira Rose & Scott, Clarke C. Arthur R. Ashe, Jr. 2012. (Illus.). 32p. (J). *(978-1-935884-58-3(1))*; pap. *(978-1-935884-64-4(6))* State Standards Publishing, LLC.

Drewett, Jim. How to Improve at Tennis. 2007. (How to Improve At- Ser.). (ENG., Illus.). 48p. (J). (gr. 3-7). pap. *(978-0-7787-3593-9(1))*; lib. bdg. *(978-0-7787-3571-7(0))* Crabtree Publishing Co.

Ganeri, Anita. Super Active Tennis. (ENG., Illus.). 126p. pap. *(978-0-340-76446-6(5))* Hodder & Stoughton.

Gifford, Clive. Tennis, 1 vol. 2010. (Tell Me about Sports Ser.). (ENG.). 32p. (gr. 4-4). 31.21 *(978-0-7614-4463-3(7)*, 4daa638d-adec-4d4f-a9ac-41559367ee8c) Cavendish Square Publishing LLC.

Gitlin, Marty. Tennis, 1 vol. 2012. (Best Sport Ever Ser.). (ENG.). 64p. (J). (gr. 4-6). 35.64 *(978-1-61783-147-8(6)*, 3507, SportsZone) ABDO Publishing Co.

Goldsworthy, Steve. Tennis. 2013. (J). *(978-1-62127-504-6(3))*; pap. *(978-1-62127-507-7(8))* Weigl Pubs., Inc.

Guillermo-Newton, Judy. Competitive Tennis for Girls. 2009. (SportsGirl Ser.). 64p. (gr. 5-8). 58.50 *(978-1-60853-194-3(5)*, Rosen Reference) Rosen Publishing Group, Inc., The.

Hellebuyck, Adam & Deimel, Laura. Tennis Grand Slam. 2019. (21st Century Skills Library: Global Citizens: Sports Ser.). (ENG., Illus.). 32p. (J). (gr. 4-7). pap. 14.21 *(978-1-5341-5036-2(6)*, 213451); lib. bdg. 32.07 *(978-1-5341-4750-8(0)*, 213450) Cherry Lake Publishing.

Hoena, Blake. Tennis. 2015. (J). lib. bdg. 25.65 *(978-1-62031-183-7(6)*, Bullfrog Bks.) Jump! Inc.

Horn, Geoffrey M. & Stewart, Mark. Rafael Nadal, 1 vol. 2009. (Today's Superstars Ser.). (ENG.). 32p. (J). (gr. 3-3). pap. 15.05 *(978-1-4339-2158-2(8)*, dd4bfcc2-9044-40c3-bdd4-68b6f8a72e95); lib. bdg. 34.60 *(978-1-4339-1965-7(6)*, 485a588f-296a-4bd2-aa45-69a314348e2d) Stevens, Gareth Publishing LLLP.

Kubik, Jeff. Wimbledon. (J). 2013. 28.55 *(978-1-62127-370-7(9))* 2013. pap. 13.95 *(978-1-62127-375-2(X))* 2007. (Illus.). 32p. (gr. 4-7). lib. bdg. 26.00 *(978-1-59036-697-4(2))* 2007. (Illus.). 32p. (gr. 4-7). per. 9.95 *(978-1-59036-698-1(0))* Weigl Pubs., Inc.

Lagunilla, Cheryl, told to. The ABC's of Tennis. 2003. (Illus.). (J). lib. bdg. 24.95 *(978-0-9726419-0-6(4))* GHL Publishing LLC.

Luke, Andrew. Tennis, Vol. 13. 2016. (Inside the World of Sports Ser.). (ENG.). 80p. (J). (gr. 7-12). 24.95 *(978-1-4222-3466-2(5))* Mason Crest.

Mallick, Nita & Guillermo-Newton, Judith. Tennis: Girls Rocking It, 1 vol., 1. 2015. (Title IX Rocks! Ser.). (ENG., Illus.). 64p. (J). (gr. 6-6). 36.13 *(978-1-5081-7041-9(X)*, 0f9a6cf8-8cec-485d-9905-c23ec1d7d632, Rosen Young Adult) Rosen Publishing Group, Inc., The.

Marsico, Katie. Tennis. 2008. (21st Century Skills Library: Real World Math Ser.). (ENG., Illus.). 32p. (gr. 4-8). lib. bdg. 32.07 *(978-1-60279-248-7(8)*, 200127) Cherry Lake Publishing.

Meltzer, Brad. I Am Billie Jean King. Eliopoulos, Christopher, illus. 2019. (Ordinary People Change the World Ser.). 40p. (J). (gr. k-4). 16.99 *(978-0-7352-2874-0(4)*, Dial Bks) Penguin Young Readers Group.

Mooney, Carla. Tennis, 1 vol. 2013. (Science Behind Sports Ser.). (ENG., Illus.). 128p. (gr. 7-7). lib. bdg. 41.03 *(978-1-4205-0928-1(4)*, fe065b53-e0c9-40aa-b18e-2aa145f7235f, Lucent Pr.) Greenhaven Publishing LLC.

Otten, Jack. Tenis, 1 vol. 2003. (Entrenamiento Deportivo (Sports Training) Ser.). (SPA., Illus.). 24p. (J). (gr. 1-2). lib. bdg. 26.27 *(978-0-8239-6848-0(0)*, 3b29b282-91ce-4b5b-986b-baf294427461) Rosen Publishing Group, Inc., The.

—Tenis (Tennis) 2009. (Entrenamiento deportivo (Sports Training) Ser.). (SPA.). 24p. (gr. 1-2). 42.50 *(978-1-61512-271-4(0)*, Editorial Buenas Letras) Rosen Publishing Group, Inc., The.

—Tennis. 2009. (Sports Training Ser.). 24p. (gr. 1-2). 42.50 *(978-1-60853-189-9(9)*, PowerKids Pr.) Rosen Publishing Group, Inc., The.

Porterfield, Jason. Maria Sharapova: Tennis Grand Slam Champion, 1 vol. 2018. (Living Legends of Sports Ser.). (ENG.). 48p. (gr. 5-6). pap. 15.05 *(978-1-5081-0636-4(3)*, e2cfda1b-ec09-44f0-94a1-5b6fc0bf973f, Britannica Educational Publishing) Rosen Publishing Group, Inc., The.

Rausch, David. United States Tennis Association. 2014. (Major League Sports Ser.). (ENG.). 24p. (J). (gr. 3-7). 26.95 *(978-1-62617-138-1(6)*, Epic Bks.) Bellwether Media.

Sanchez Vicario, Arantxa. Jovenes Tenistas. (SPA.). 46p. (YA). (gr. 2-18). 16.76 *(978-84-272-4967-7(5))* Molino, Editorial ESP. Dist: Lectorum Pubns., Inc.

Stauffacher, Sue. Nothing but Trouble: the Story of Althea Gibson. Couch, Greg, illus. 2011. 40p. (J). (gr. -1-2). pap. 7.99 *(978-0-375-86544-2(6)*, Dragonfly Bks.) Random Hse. Children's Bks.

Venus & Serena Williams. 2015. (Quotes from the Greatest Athletes Ser.). (ENG., Illus.). 24p. (J). lib. bdg. 12.95 *(978-1-4896-3385-9(5)*, AV2 by Weigl) Weigl Pubs., Inc.

Wells, Don. For the Love of Tennis. 2005. (For the Love of Sports Ser.). (Illus.). 24p. (J). (gr. 4-6). lib. bdg. 24.45 *(978-1-59036-298-3(5))* Weigl Pubs., Inc.

—Tennis. (For the Love of Sports Ser.). 24p. (J). (gr. 3-6). 2019. (ENG.). pap. 12.95 *(978-1-7911-0574-7(2))* 2019. (ENG., Illus.). lib. bdg. 28.55 *(978-1-7911-0011-7(2))* 2005. (Illus.). per. 8.95 *(978-1-59036-302-7(7))* Weigl Pubs., Inc.

Wells, Donald. Tennis. 2010. (In the Zone Ser.). (Illus.). 32p. (J). (gr. 3-5). pap. 11.95 *(978-1-60596-905-3(2))*; lib. bdg. 25.70 *(978-1-60596-904-6(4))* Weigl Pubs., Inc.

Wendorff, Anne. Tennis. 2009. (My First Sports Ser.). (ENG., Illus.). 24p. (J). (gr. 2-5). lib. bdg. 26.95 *(978-1-60014-328-1(8)*, Blastoff! Readers) Bellwether Media.

Wheeler, Jill C. Andy Roddick. 2007. (Awesome Athletes Set 4 Ser.). (Illus.). 32p. (gr. 3-7). 27.07 *(978-1-59928-307-4(7)*, Checkerboard Library) ABDO Publishing Co.

Woods, Mark & Owen, Ruth. Ace! 2010. (Top Score Maths Ser.). (Illus.). 32p. pap. *(978-0-237-54280-1(3))* Evans Brothers, Ltd.

—Ace! Tennis Facts & Stats, 1 vol. 2011. (Top Score Math Ser.). (ENG., Illus.). 32p. (J). (gr. 4-5). lib. bdg. 29.27 *(978-1-4339-4986-9(5)*, 50bda16d-ab8c-4787-b50f-1e0fc32ca3ab) Stevens, Gareth Publishing LLLP.

TENNIS—BIOGRAPHY

Anniss, Matt. Venus & Serena Williams in the Community, 1 vol., 1. 2013. (Making a Difference: Athletes Who Are Changing the World Ser.). (ENG.). 48p. (J). (gr. 5-5). 29.44 *(978-1-62275-170-9(1)*, 4be2f4ca-7b11-4468-8ea7-cefe4c598471) Rosen Publishing Group, Inc., The.

Bailey, Diane. Venus & Serena Williams: Tennis Champions, 1 vol. 2010. (Sports Families Ser.). 48p. (gr. 5-5). (ENG.). (J). pap. 12.75 *(978-1-4358-8520-2(1)*, d6c0759c-676f-4178-b999-6834ea6d1c26, Rosen Reference); (YA). lib. bdg., E-Book 53.00 *(978-1-4488-0124-4(9))*; (ENG., Illus.). (YA). lib. bdg. 34.47 *(978-1-4358-3552-8(2)*, 241aae56-ad15-4a0f-97ba-c0b7fd676cf3) Rosen Publishing Group, Inc., The.

Boehme, Gerry. Serena Williams: Setting New Standards, 1 vol. 2017. (At the Top of Their Game Ser.). (ENG.). 128p. (YA). (gr. 9-9). 44.50 *(978-1-5026-2762-9(0)*, 78dcc698-6dda-4e4e-b2be-ab32c963e2d9) Cavendish Square Publishing LLC.

Bradley, Michael. Venus Williams, 1 vol. 2005. (All-Stars Ser.). (ENG., Illus.). 48p. (gr. 4-4). lib. bdg. 34.07 *(978-0-7614-1630-2(7)*, aae35196-fb4a-4f79-9337-bc954d02fea4) Cavendish Square Publishing LLC.

Brown, Anne K. Roger Federer, 1 vol. 2011. (People in the News Ser.). (ENG., Illus.). 112p. (gr. 7-7). lib. bdg. 41.03 *(978-1-4205-0611-2(0)*, 1e627f53-c132-4e1c-a187-ede777f85aa1, Lucent Pr.) Greenhaven Publishing LLC.

Brown, Jonatha A. Venus & Serena Williams, 1 vol. 2004. (People We Should Know Ser.). (ENG., Illus.). 24p. (gr. 2-4). pap. 9.15 *(978-0-8368-4477-1(7)*, 8255fb18-05b5-4f15-b369-e441cf7f355e); lib. bdg. 24.67 *(978-0-8368-4470-2(X)*, 91512202-a7bb-4e33-a448-ac0fa1d73d33) Stevens, Gareth Publishing LLLP. (Weekly Reader Leveled Readers).

Bryant, Howard. Sisters & Champions: the True Story of Venus & Serena Williams. Cooper, Floyd, illus. 2018. 32p. (J). (gr. -1-3). 17.99 *(978-0-399-16906-9(7)*, Philomel Bks.) Penguin Young Readers Group.

Buckley, James, Jr. & Who HQ. Who Are Venus & Serena Williams? Thomson, Andrew, illus. 2017. (Who Was? Ser.). 112p. (J). (gr. 3-7). 6.99 *(978-0-515-15803-8(8)*, Penguin Workshop) Penguin Young Readers Group.

Christopher, Matt. Serena Williams: Legends in Sports. 2017. (ENG., Illus.). 144p. (J). (gr. 3-7). pap. 7.99 *(978-0-316-47180-0(1))* Little, Brown Bks. for Young Readers.

Cline-Ransome, Lesa. Game Changers: The Story of Venus & Serena Williams. Ransome, James E., illus. 2018. (ENG.). 48p. (J). (gr. -1-3). 17.99 *(978-1-4814-7684-3(X)*, Simon & Schuster/Paula Wiseman Bks.) Simon & Schuster/Paula Wiseman Bks.

Donaldson, Madeline. Venus & Serena Williams. (Amazing Athletes Ser.). 32p. 2005. (Illus.). (gr. 3-4). lib. bdg. 22.60 *(978-0-8225-3316-0(2))* 2nd rev. ed. 2011. (J). pap. 45.32 *(978-0-7613-7654-5(2))* Lerner Publishing Group.

—Venus & Serena Williams. rev. ed. 2007. (Amazing Athletes Ser.). (ENG., Illus.). 32p. (gr. 2-5). lib. bdg. 25.26 *(978-0-8225-7595-5(7))* Lerner Publishing Group.

Dorrie, Roxanne. Venus & Serena Williams: The Smashing Sisters. 2003. (High Five Reading - Red Ser.). (ENG., Illus.). 48p. (gr. 3-4). per. 9.00 *(978-0-7368-2827-7(3))* Capstone.

Engsberg Cunningham, Meghan. Serena Williams: International Tennis Superstar, 1 vol. 2016. (Leading Women Ser.). (ENG.). 112p. (YA). (gr. 7-7). 41.64 *(978-1-5026-2014-9(6)*, dcc24e1d-7677-4af8-8d0e-efec16cc05bd) Cavendish Square Publishing LLC.

Fishman, Jon M. Sloane Stephens. 2020. (Sports All-Stars (Lerner (tm) Sports) Ser.). (ENG., Illus.). 32p. (J). (gr. 2-5). pap. 9.99 *(978-1-5415-8958-2(0)*, 5089db2c-4a39-4e4d-af4e-f67629a74600); lib. bdg. 29.32 *(978-1-5415-7728-2(0)*, e4bb1035-e696-4880-9223-7baf944cea1c) Lerner Publishing Group. (Lerner Pubns.).

Franzen, Lenore. Venus Williams. 2003. (Ovations Ser.). (Illus.). 32p. (J). *(978-1-58341-249-7(2)*, Creative Education) Creative Co., The.

Gitlin, Marty. Best Tennis Players of All Time, 1 vol. 2015. (Sports' Best Ever Ser.). (ENG., Illus.). 64p. (J). (gr. 3-6). lib. bdg. 35.64 *(978-1-62403-622-4(8)*, 17321, SportsZone) ABDO Publishing Co.

Glaser, Jason. Maria Sharapova. (Sports Idols Ser.). 24p. (gr. 2-3). 2009. 42.50 *(978-1-60853-142-4(2)*, PowerKids Pr.) 2007. (ENG., Illus.). (J). lib. bdg. 26.27 *(978-1-4042-4181-7(7)*,

156bb605-656e-463c-9237-31009e5b6526) Rosen Publishing Group, Inc., The.
—Roger Federer, 1 vol. 2011. (Today's Sports Greats Ser.). (ENG., Illus.). 32p. (gr. 4-5). (J). pap. 11.50 *(978-1-4339-5872-4(4),* 094ca5e8-3481-4fd8-b0c3-9f94c219d40d, Gareth Stevens Learning Library); (YA). lib. bdg. 29.27 *(978-1-4339-5870-0(8),* fdc15776-68f4-4e78-a0f9-5f4b56b8f379) Stevens, Gareth Publishing LLLP.
Goddu, Krystyna Poray. Serena Williams. 2019. (Player Profiles Ser.). (ENG., Illus.). 32p. (J). (gr. 4-6). lib. bdg. *(978-1-68072-877-4(6),* 12788, Bolt) Black Rabbit Bks.
Gray, Karlin. Serena: the Littlest Sister. Ahanonu, Monica, illus. 2019. (ENG.). 40p. (J). 18.99 *(978-1-62414-694-7(5),* 900197962) Page Street Publishing Co.
Hoena, Blake. Serena Williams: Athletes Who Made a Difference. LeDoyen, Sam, illus. 2020. (Athletes Who Made a Difference Ser.). (ENG.). 32p. (J). (gr. 3-6). 27.99 *(978-1-5415-7818-0(X),* 004897ce-e80b-449f-bed7-0f55f0c5eaa1); pap. 8.99 *(978-1-7284-0296-3(4),* e27a1a4d-c61a-46c5-b659-5555d51aab7f) Lerner Publishing Group. (Graphic Universe™).
Hubbard, Crystal. Game, Set Match, 1 vol. Belford, Kevin, illus. 2010. (ENG.). 48p. (J). (gr. 2-6). pap. 13.95 *(978-1-62014-316-2(X),* leelowbooks) Lee & Low Bks., Inc.
—Game, Set, Match: Champion Arthur Ashe. 2010. (ENG., Illus.). 48p. (J). (gr. 2-6). 19.95 *(978-1-60060-366-2(1))* Lee & Low Bks., Inc.
—The Story of Tennis Champion Arthur Ashe, 1 vol. Belford, Kevin, illus. 2018. (Story Of Ser.). (ENG.). 56p. (J). (gr. 4-8). pap. 10.95 *(978-1-62014-789-4(0),* leelowbooks) Lee & Low Bks., Inc.
Kortemeier, Todd. Superstars of Pro Tennis. 2016. (Pro Sports Superstars Ser.). (ENG., Illus.). 24p. (J). (gr. 1-4). lib. bdg. 20.95 *(978-1-60753-941-4(1),* 15671) Amicus.
Mantell, Paul. Arthur Ashe: Young Tennis Champion. Henderson, Meryl, illus. 2006. (Childhood of Famous Americans Ser.). 213p. (J). 13.65 *(978-0-7569-6387-3(7))* Perfection Learning Corp.
Marcovitz, Hal. Venus & Serena Williams. 2012. (Role Model Athletes Ser.). 64p. (J). (gr. 7). 22.95 *(978-1-4222-2714-5(6))* Mason Crest.
Moening, Kate. Serena Williams: Tennis Star. 2019. (Women Leading the Way Ser.). (ENG., Illus.). 24p. (J). (gr. k-3). pap. 7.99 *(978-1-61891-725-6(0),* 12306); lib. bdg. 26.95 *(978-1-64487-102-7(5))* Bellwether Media. (Blastoff! Readers).
Monnig, Alex. Serena Williams: Tennis Legend. 2017. (Playmakers Set 6 Ser.). (ENG., Illus.). 32p. (J). (gr. 2-6). lib. bdg. 32.79 *(978-1-5321-1152-5(5),* 25880, SportsZone) ABDO Publishing Co.
—Serena Williams vs. Billie Jean King. 2017. (Versus Ser.). (ENG., Illus.). 32p. (J). (gr. 3-6). lib. bdg. 32.79 *(978-1-5321-1357-4(9),* 27655, SportsZone) ABDO Publishing Co.
Morgan, Terri. Venus & Serena Williams: Grand Slam Sisters. (Sports Achievers Biographies Ser.). (Illus.). 2005. 80p. (gr. 7-12). lib. bdg. 22.60 *(978-0-8225-3684-0(6))* 2003. 64p. (J). (gr. 4-9). pap. 5.95 *(978-0-8225-9866-4(3),* Carolrhoda Bks.) Lerner Publishing Group.
Morganelli, Adrianna. Serena Williams. 2018. (Superstars! Ser.). (ENG.). 32p. (J). (gr. 4-4). *(978-0-7787-4842-7(1));* pap. *(978-0-7787-4871-7(5))* Crabtree Publishing Co.
Murray, John. Murray - The Golden Boy of Centre Court. 2018. (Ultimate Sports Heroes Ser.). (ENG.). 176p. (J). (gr. 4-8). pap. 10.99 *(978-1-78606-468-4(5))* Blake, John Publishing, Ltd. GBR. Dist: Independent Pubs. Group.
Nagelhout, Ryan. Serena Williams, 1 vol. 2016. (Sports MVPs Ser.). (ENG., Illus.). 24p. (J). (gr. 1-2). 24.27 *(978-1-4824-4642-5(1),* 3df0797d-66d6-4999-a80c-7c344c256a31) Stevens, Gareth Publishing LLLP.
Pina, Andrew & Uschan, Michael V. Serena Williams: Tennis Ace, 1 vol. 2016. (People in the News Ser.). (ENG.). 104p. (YA). (gr. 7-7). lib. bdg. 41.03 *(978-1-5345-6027-7(0),* cf1324ab-ac03-4396-81b9-5344f7bfee7a, Lucent Pr.) Greenhaven Publishing LLC.
Porter, Esther. Serena Williams. 2016. (Women in Sports Ser.). (ENG., Illus.). 24p. (J). (gr. -1-2). pap. 6.95 *(978-1-4914-8569-9(8),* 131188, Capstone Pr.) Capstone.
Rajczak Nelson, Kristen. Serena Williams: Tennis Star, 1 vol. 2016. (Junior Biographies Ser.). (ENG., Illus.). 24p. (gr. 3-4). pap. 10.35 *(978-0-7660-8181-9(8),* 4f19a894-4607-4463-a256-637865324581) Enslow Publishing, LLC.
Raum, Elizabeth. Pro Sports Biographies: Serena Williams. 2017. (Pro Sports Biographies Ser.). (ENG., Illus.). 24p. (J). (gr. 1-3). pap. 10.99 *(978-1-68152-170-1(9),* 14801) Amicus.
Rockliff, Mara. Billie Jean! How Tennis Star Billie Jean King Changed Women's Sports. Baddeley, Elizabeth, illus. 2019. 40p. (J). (gr. -1-3). 17.99 *(978-0-525-51779-5(0),* G.P. Putnam's Sons Books for Young Readers) Penguin Young Readers Group.
Sapet, Kerrily. Maria Sharapova. 2007. (Role Model Athletes Ser.). (Illus.). 64p. (YA). pap. 9.95 *(978-1-4222-0777-2(3))* Mason Crest.
Savage, Jeff. Annika Sorenstam. 2005. (Amazing Athletes Ser.). (Illus.). 32p. (J). (gr. 2-5). lib. bdg. 23.93 *(978-0-8225-2428-1(7));* pap. 7.95 *(978-0-8225-3107-4(0))* Lerner Publishing Group.
—Maria Sharapova. 2008. (Amazing Athletes Ser.). (Illus.). 32p. (J). (gr. -1). per. 6.95 *(978-0-8225-8977-8(X),* First Avenue Editions); pap. 40.95 *(978-0-8225-9489-5(7));* (ENG., Illus.). 32p. (gr. 2-5). lib. bdg. 25.26 *(978-0-8225-8836-8(6))* Lerner Publishing Group.
—Roger Federer. 2009. pap. 40.95 *(978-0-7613-4778-1(X));* (ENG., Illus.). 32p. (J). (gr. 2-5). 26.65 *(978-0-8225-9995-1(3),* dc9c0f57-46d6-4bad-b147-248d0f2abdfc, Lerner Pubns.) Lerner Publishing Group.
Scheff, Matt. Naomi Osaka: Tennis Star. 2020. (Biggest Names in Sports Set 5 Ser.). (ENG., Illus.). 32p. (J). (gr. 3-5). 31.35 *(978-1-64493-054-0(4),* 1644930544, Focus Readers) North Star Editions.
Shepherd, Jodie. Serena Williams: A Champion on & off the Court. 2016. (Rookie Biographies(tm) Ser.). (ENG., Illus.). 32p. (J). lib. bdg. 25.00 *(978-0-531-21684-2(5),* Children's Pr.) Scholastic Library Publishing.
Shoup, Kate. Billie Jean King: The Battle of the Sexes & Title IX, 1 vol. 2015. (Game-Changing Athletes Ser.). (ENG.). 112p. (YA). (gr. 9-9). 44.50 *(978-1-5026-1053-9(1),* 963d373d-a678-4e72-85fc-ccac94b5538b) Cavendish Square Publishing LLC.
Skinner, J. E. Billie Jean King vs. Bobby Riggs. 2018. (21st Century Skills Library: Sports Unite Us Ser.). (ENG., Illus.). 32p. (J). (gr. 3-6). lib. bdg. 32.07 *(978-1-5341-2962-7(6),* 211892) Cherry Lake Publishing.
Stanmyre, Jackie F. Althea Gibson & Arthur Ashe: Breaking down Tennis's Color Barrier, 1 vol. 2015. (Game-Changing Athletes Ser.). (ENG., Illus.). 112p. (YA). (gr. 9-9). 44.50 *(978-1-5026-1037-9(X),* 75cc0362-a1ab-42ec-8167-9c1bbb1542ce) Cavendish Square Publishing LLC.
Stewart, Mark. Maria Sharapova, 1 vol. 2009. (Today's Superstars Ser.). (ENG.). 48p. (J). (gr. 3-3). pap. 15.05 *(978-1-4339-2160-5(X),* 24baefdc-301b-4986-bba8-d9089f3150cb); lib. bdg. 34.60 *(978-1-4339-1967-1(2),* 51b4d2c6-8be2-4fd4-961d-13284c76cb8e) Stevens, Gareth Publishing LLLP.
Strand, Jennifer. Arthur Ashe. 2016. (Trailblazing Athletes Ser.). (ENG.). 24p. (J). (gr. -1-2). 49.94 *(978-1-68079-416-8(7),* 23037, Abdo Zoom-Launch) ABDO Publishing Co.
—Billie Jean King. 2016. (Trailblazing Athletes Ser.). (ENG.). 24p. (J). (gr. -1-2). 49.94 *(978-1-68079-418-2(3),* 23039, Abdo Zoom-Launch) ABDO Publishing Co.
Swanson, June. Venus & Serena Williams. Burke, Susan S., illus. 2003. (You Must Be Joking! Riddle Bks.). 32p. (J). (gr. 2-5). pap. 5.95 *(978-0-8225-9842-8(6))* Lerner Publishing Group.
Todd, Anne M. Venus & Serena Williams. 2009. (Women of Achievement Ser.). (ENG., Illus.). 144p. (gr. 6-12). 35.00 *(978-1-60413-461-2(5),* P167315, Facts On File) Infobase Holdings, Inc.
Wetzel, Dan. Epic Athletes: Serena Williams. Leong, Sloane, illus. 2019. (Epic Athletes Ser.: 3). (ENG.). 176p. (J). 16.99 *(978-1-250-29578-1(5),* 900195301, Holt, Henry & Co. Bks. For Young Readers) Holt, Henry & Co.
—Epic Athletes: Serena Williams. Leong, Sloane, illus. 2020. (Epic Athletes Ser.: 3). (ENG.). 192p. (J). pap. 7.99 *(978-1-250-25072-8(2),* 900198023) Square Fish.
Wiener, Gary. Serena vs. Venus vs. Sharapova vs. Navratilova, 1 vol. 2019. (Who's the GOAT? Using Math to Crown the Champion Ser.). (ENG.). 64p. (gr. 5-5). pap. 13.95 *(978-1-7253-4852-3(7),* c8f75790-1401-4543-b648-5f866c2f00d9) Rosen Publishing Group, Inc., The.
Williams, Serena & Williams, Venus. Venus & Serena: Serving from the Hip: 10 Rules for Living, Loving, & Winning. 2005. (ENG., Illus.). 144p. (YA). (gr. 7). pap. 14.00 *(978-0-618-57653-1(3),* 498418, Clarion Bks.) HarperCollins Pubs.
Wilson, Mike. The Williams Sisters: Venus & Serena. 2005. (ENG., Illus.). 32p. pap. 8.50 *(978-0-340-84876-0(6))* Cambridge Univ. Pr.
Winter, Jeanette. Sisters: Venus & Serena Williams. Winter, Jeanette, illus. 2019. (ENG., Illus.). 48p. (J). (gr. -1-3). 17.99 *(978-1-5344-3121-8(7),* Beach Lane Bks.) Beach Lane Bks.
Wright, David K. The Life of Arthur Ashe: Smashing the Color Barrier in Tennis, 1 vol. 2014. (Legendary African Americans Ser.). (ENG.). 96p. (gr. 6-6). 31.61 *(978-0-7660-6260-3(0),* 08942673-c749-474f-9fa5-9181cdef5afd); pap. 13.88 *(978-0-7660-6261-0(9),* 25c03496-3d15-43ad-9bbc-80471efeb955) Enslow Publishing, LLC.

TENNIS—FICTION

Adler, David A. Cam Jansen & the Tennis Trophy Mystery #23. Natti, Susanna, illus. 2005. (Cam Jansen Ser.: 23). (ENG.). 64p. (J). (gr. 2-5). 5.99 *(978-0-14-240290-0(7),* Puffin Books) Penguin Young Readers Group.
Arena, Felice & Kettle, Phil. Tennis Ace. Boyer, Susy, illus. 2004. (J). pap. *(978-1-59336-360-4(5))* Mondo Publishing.
Bashford, Taryn. The Harper Effect. 2018. (ENG.). 408p. (YA). (gr. 8-8). 17.99 *(978-1-5107-2665-9(9),* Sky Pony Pr.) Skyhorse Publishing Co., Inc.
Bates, Sonya Spreen. Topspin. 2013. 147p. (J). *(978-1-4598-0647-4(6))* Orca Bk. Pubs.
—Topspin, 1 vol. 2013. (Orca Sports Ser.). (ENG.). 160p. (J). (gr. 4-7). pap. 9.95 *(978-1-4598-0385-5(X))* Orca Bk. Pubs. USA.
Berman, Ron. The Kid from Courage. 2005. (Dream Ser.). (Illus.). 150p. (gr. 3-8). pap. 9.95 *(978-0-9708992-2-4(X))* Scobre Pr. Corp.
Crouch, Cheryl Lynne. Tennis Shoes Trouble. 2006. 48p. 6.50 *(978-0-8341-2227-7(8))* Beacon Hill Pr. of Kansas City.
Dzidrums, Christine. Princess Dessabelle: Tennis Star. Muths, Tohn Fayette, illus. 2013. 50p. pap. 10.99 *(978-1-938438-34-9(5))* Creative Media Publishing.
Egart, Patricia. Alley Learns Something New. 2012. (ENG., Illus.). 32p. pap. 8.95 *(978-0-9831839-3-8(7))* Amber Skye Publishing LLC.
Feinstein, John. Vanishing Act: Mystery at the U. S. Open (the Sports Beat, 2) 2008. (Sports Beat Ser.: 2). (ENG.). 304p. (J). (gr. 3-7). 9.99 *(978-0-440-42125-2(X),* Yearling) Random Hse. Children's Bks.
Flint, Shamini. Diary of a Tennis Prodigy. Heinrich, Sally, illus. 2016. (Diary of A... Ser.). (ENG.). 112p. (J). (gr. 2-6). 8.99 *(978-1-76029-088-7(2))* Allen & Unwin AUS. Dist: Independent Pubs. Group.
Hellman, Charles. Adventures in SportsLand - the Tennis Bully (with accompanying CD) Tiritili, Robert, illus. 2008. (Adventures in SportsLand: the Bully Ser.). 32p. (J). (gr. -1-3). 19.95 *(978-0-935938-32-6(X))* Stogo, Malcolm Assocs.
Hellman, Charles S. & Tiritili, Robert A. The Tennis Bully. 2013. 34p. pap. 9.25 *(978-0-935938-24-1(9))* LuckySports.
Horowitz, Anthony. Skeleton Key. 2006. (Alex Rider Ser.: 3). (ENG.). 368p. (J). (gr. 5-18). 8.99 *(978-0-14-240614-4(7),* Puffin Books) Penguin Young Readers Group.
—Skeleton Key: the Graphic Novel. Kanako & Yuzuru, illus. 2009. (Alex Rider Ser.: Bk. 3). (ENG.). 176p. (J). (gr. 5-18). pap. 16.99 *(978-0-399-25418-5(8),* Philomel Bks.) Penguin Young Readers Group.
Hutton, Sam. Final Shot (Special Agents, Book 2). Book 2. 2010. (Special Agents Ser.: 2). (ENG.). 224p. (J). (gr. 5-7). pap. 9.99 *(978-0-00-714844-8(5),* HarperCollins Children's Bks.) HarperCollins Pubs. Ltd. GBR. Dist: HarperCollins Pubs.
Jackson, Kyle. Racket Rumors. Rumble, Simon, illus. 2018. (Mac's Sports Report). (ENG.). 128p. (J). (gr. 3-4). pap. 7.99 *(978-1-63163-232-7(9),* 1631632329); lib. bdg. 27.13 *(978-1-63163-231-0(0),* 1631632310) North Star Editions. (Jolly Fish Pr.).
Klein, Glasko. The Lie. 2019. (Do-Over Ser.). (ENG.). 104p. (YA). (gr. 6-12). pap. 7.99 *(978-1-5415-4551-9(6),* f87bd7c0-6122-44e1-bfa1-d95fa8232e26); 26.65 *(978-1-5415-4032-3(8),* 8ccda28b-d533-4941-9e47-a18f7789bd8a) Lerner Publishing Group. (Darby Creek).
Maddox, Jake. Doubles Trouble. Tiffany, Sean, illus. 2017. (Jake Maddox Sports Stories Ser.). (ENG.). 72p. (J). (gr. 3-6). lib. bdg. 25.99 *(978-1-4965-4957-0(0),* 135852, Stone Arch Bks.) Capstone.
—Tennis Trouble. Mourning, Tuesday, illus. 2008. (Jake Maddox Girl Sports Stories Ser.). (ENG.). 72p. (J). (gr. 3-6). 25.32 *(978-1-4342-0781-4(1),* 95186, Stone Arch Bks.) Capstone.
Matthew, Annie. Legacy & the Queen. 2019. (Legacy & the Queen Ser.: 1). 208p. (J). (gr. 4-12). 16.99 *(978-1-949520-03-3(X))* Granity Studios.
McG, Shane. Tennis, Anyone? 2007. (Illus.). 40p. (J). (gr. k-3). 16.95 *(978-0-8225-6901-5(9),* Carolrhoda Bks.) Lerner Publishing Group.
Rizzuto, Katherine. Poodles Don't Play Tennis. Murphy, Liz, illus. 2013. (ENG.). 32p. (J). 19.99 *(978-1-938501-06-7(3))* Turn the Page Publishing.
Seles, Monica. The Academy: Love Match. 2014. (Academy Ser.). (ENG.). 224p. (YA). (gr. 7). pap. 9.99 *(978-1-59990-902-8(2),* 900084375, Bloomsbury USA Childrens) Bloomsbury Publishing USA.
Shull, Megan. Amazing Grace. 2006. (ENG.). 256p. (gr. 6-9). pap. 6.99 *(978-0-7868-5691-6(2))* Hyperion Pr.

TENPINS

see Bowling

TENTS

Smith, Sian. Homes That Move, 1 vol. 2013. (Where We Live Ser.). (ENG.). 24p. (J). (gr. -1-1). pap. 6.95 *(978-1-4329-8072-6(6),* 123259, Heinemann) Capstone.
Zayauskas, Victoria. The Tent. 2011. 20p. pap. 10.50 *(978-1-4634-2480-0(9))* AuthorHouse.

TERESA, MOTHER, 1910-1997

Fitzpatrick, Anne. Mother Teresa. 2005. (Genius Ser.). (Illus.). 48p. (J). (gr. 5-9). lib. bdg. 21.95 *(978-1-58341-330-2(8),* Creative Education) Creative Co., The.
Ganeri, Anita. Mother Teresa's Alms Bowl. Radford, Karen & Noyes, Leighton, illus. 2008. (Stories of Great People Ser.). (ENG.). 40p. (J). (gr. 3-8). pap. *(978-0-7787-3712-4(8))* Crabtree Publishing Co.
Ganeri, Anita & Bailey, Gerry. Mother Teresa's Alms Bowl. 2008. (Stories of Great People Ser.). (ENG., Illus.). 40p. (J). (gr. 3-8). lib. bdg. *(978-0-7787-3690-5(3))* Crabtree Publishing Co.
Gigliotti, Jim & Who HQ. Who Was Mother Teresa? Groff, David, illus. 2015. (Who Was? Ser.). 112p. (J). (gr. 3-7). 5.99 *(978-0-448-48299-6(1),* Penguin Workshop) Penguin Young Readers Group.
Glavich, Mary Kathleen. Blessed Teresa of Calcutta: Missionary of Charity. Kiwak, Barbara, tr. Kiwak, Barbara, illus. 2003. (Encounter the Saints Ser.: Vol. 17). 136p. (J). pap. 7.95 *(978-0-8198-1160-8(2),* 332-024) Pauline Bks. & Media.
Gold, Maya & DK. DK Biography: Mother Teresa: A Photographic Story of a Life. 2008. (DK Biography Ser.). (ENG., Illus.). 128p. (J). (gr. 5-12). pap. 6.99 *(978-0-7566-3880-1(1),* DK Children) Dorling Kindersley Publishing, Inc.
Haldy, Emma E. Mother Teresa. Bane, Jeff, illus. 2017. (My Early Library: My Itty-Bitty Bio Ser.). (ENG.). 24p. (J). (gr. k-1). lib. bdg. 30.64 *(978-1-63472-154-7(3),* 209188) Cherry Lake Publishing.
Jones, Brenn. Learning about Love from the Life of Mother Teresa. 2009. (Character Building Book Ser.). 24p. (gr. 2-3). 42.50 *(978-1-61511-001-8(1),* PowerKids Pr.) Rosen Publishing Group, Inc., The.
Kramer, Barbara. National Geographic Readers: Mother Teresa (L1) 2019. (Readers Bios Ser.). (Illus.). 32p. (J). (gr. -1-k). pap. 4.99 *(978-1-4263-3347-7(1));* (ENG.). lib. bdg. 14.90 *(978-1-4263-3348-4(X))* Disney Publishing Worldwide. (National Geographic Kids).
Kudlinski, Kathleen. Mother Teresa: Friend to the Poor. 2006. 171p. (J). lib. bdg. 18.46 *(978-1-4242-1731-1(8))* Fitzgerald Bks.
Miller, Jennifer A. Mother Teresa. 2009. (History Maker Biographies Ser.). (Illus.). 48p. (J). (gr. 3-6). 26.60 *(978-1-58013-702-7(4),* Lerner Pubns.) Lerner Publishing Group.
Nelson, Robin. Mother Teresa: A Life of Caring. (Pull Ahead Books — Biographies Ser.). (Illus.). 32p. (J). 2007. (ENG.). (gr. k-3). pap. 7.99 *(978-0-8225-6433-1(5),* d3ca9c7a-8cce-4f0e-ba3c-b256c4dc2ba9) 2006. (gr. 3-7). lib. bdg. 22.60 *(978-0-8225-6384-6(3),* Lerner Pubns.) Lerner Publishing Group.
Rustad, Martha E. H. & Weiss, Ellen. Mother Teresa: A Life of Kindness. 2007. (People of Character Ser.). (ENG., Illus.). 24p. (J). (gr. 2-5). lib. bdg. 26.95 *(978-1-60014-092-1(0))* Bellwether Media.
Slavicek, Louise Chipley. Mother Teresa. 2007. (Modern Peacemakers Ser.). (ENG., Illus.). 113p. (gr. 9-12). lib. bdg. 30.00 *(978-0-7910-9433-4(2),* P124650, Facts On File) Infobase Holdings, Inc.
Strand, Jennifer. Mother Teresa. 2016. (Great Women Ser.). (ENG.). 24p. (J). (gr. -1-2). 49.94 *(978-1-68079-391-8(8),* 23012, Abdo Zoom-Launch) ABDO Publishing Co.
Sullivan, Anne Marie. Mother Teresa: Religious Humanitarian. 2013. (People of Importance Ser.: 21). (Illus.). 32p. (J). (gr. 4-18). 19.95 *(978-1-4222-2853-1(3))* Mason Crest.
—Mother Theresa: Religious Humanitarian. 2004. (Great Names Ser.). (Illus.). 32p. (J). (gr. 3-18). lib. bdg. 19.95 *(978-1-59084-142-6(5))* Mason Crest.
Trussell-Cullen, Alan. Mother Teresa. 2009. pap. 13.25 *(978-1-60559-066-0(5))* Hameray Publishing Group, Inc.
Valentine, Emily. Mother Teresa: With a Discussion of Compassion. 2004. (Values in Action Ser.). (J). *(978-1-59203-070-5(X))* Learning Challenge, Inc.

TERESA, OF AVILA, SAINT, 1515-1582

Wallace, Susan Helen. Saint Teresa of Avila: Joyful in the Lord. Kiwak, Barbara, illus. 2008. (Encounter the Saints Ser.: No. 24). 106p. (J). (gr. 4-7). pap. 7.95 *(978-0-8198-7116-9(8))* Pauline Bks. & Media.

TERMITES

Best, Arthur. A Termite's Colony, 1 vol. 2018. (Animal Homes Ser.). (ENG.). 24p. (gr. 1-1). lib. bdg. 27.36 *(978-1-5026-3674-4(3),* 29c22d94-294a-4964-a2bb-77e8a8991222) Cavendish Square Publishing LLC.
Bodden, Valerie. Creepy Creatures: Termites. 2013. (Creepy Creatures Ser.). (ENG., Illus.). 24p. (J). (gr. 1-3). pap. 7.99 *(978-0-89812-798-0(X),* 21745, Creative Paperbacks) Creative Co., The.
—Termites. 2013. (Creepy Creatures Ser.). (ENG., Illus.). 24p. (J). (gr. 1-4). 25.65 *(978-1-60818-235-0(5),* 21744, Creative Education) Creative Co., The.
Chung, Liz. Termites, 1 vol. 2016. (Dig Deep! Bugs That Live Underground Ser.). (ENG., Illus.). 24p. (J). (gr. 3-3). pap. 9.25 *(978-1-4994-2062-3(5),* aaa557f3-ae5a-499e-9246-4276abce8c1d, PowerKids Pr.) Rosen Publishing Group, Inc., The.
George, Lynn. Termites: Mound Builders, 1 vol. 2010. (Animal Architects Ser.). (ENG.). 24p. (J). (gr. 2-3). pap. 9.25 *(978-1-4488-1353-7(0),* 71174a22-8323-4014-8e71-e2ab99db6033); lib. bdg. 26.27 *(978-1-4488-0696-6(8),* 86a3a724-3de4-49ed-b94d-04671b0c18eb) Rosen Publishing Group, Inc., The. (PowerKids Pr.).
Gray, Susan H. Termite. 2009. (21st Century Skills Library: Animal Invaders Ser.). (ENG., Illus.). 32p. (gr. 4-8). lib. bdg. 32.07 *(978-1-60279-330-9(1),* 200226) Cherry Lake Publishing.
Harasymiw, Mark J. Termites, 1 vol. 2014. (Animals of Mass Destruction Ser.). 32p. (J). (gr. 2-3). (ENG.). pap. 11.50 *(978-1-4824-1042-6(7),* 89226177-f620-4f93-9f89-abf344f84fd9); pap. 63.00 *(978-1-4824-1041-9(9))* Stevens, Gareth Publishing LLLP.
Markle, Sandra. Termites. 2008. pap. 52.95 *(978-1-58013-287-9(1))* Lerner Publishing Group.
—Termites: Hardworking Insect Families. 2008. (Insect World Ser.). (ENG., Illus.). 48p. (gr. 4-8). lib. bdg. 27.93 *(978-0-8225-7301-2(6),* Lerner Pubns.) Lerner Publishing Group.
Patterson, Jack K. Termites, 1 vol. 2018. (Creepy Crawlers Ser.). (ENG.). 24p. (gr. 1-1). lib. bdg. 25.93 *(978-1-5026-4270-7(0),* ba6a452f-3d03-4bfe-8524-6cc29522680a) Cavendish Square Publishing LLC.
Perish, Patrick. Termites. 2018. (Insects up Close Ser.). (ENG., Illus.). 24p. (J). (gr. k-3). lib. bdg. 26.95 *(978-1-62617-719-2(8),* Blastoff! Readers) Bellwether Media.
Rodger, Marguerite. Termites & Other Home Wreckers. 2010. (Creepy Crawlies Ser.). (ENG.). 32p. (J). (gr. 3-6). *(978-0-7787-2503-9(0));* pap. *(978-0-7787-2510-7(3))* Crabtree Publishing Co.
Rustad, Martha E. H. Termites. 2007. (World of Insects Ser.). (ENG., Illus.). 24p. (J). (gr. k-3). lib. bdg. 26.95 *(978-1-60014-108-9(0))* Bellwether Media.
Schuetz, Kari. Termites. 2015. (Creepy Crawlies Ser.). (ENG., Illus.). 24p. (J). (gr. k-3). lib. bdg. 26.95 *(978-1-62617-228-9(5),* Blastoff! Readers) Bellwether Media.
Schuh, Mari. Termites. 2014. (Illus.). 24p. (J). lib. bdg. 25.65 *(978-1-62031-087-8(2),* Bullfrog Bks.) Jump! Inc.
Sirota, Lyn. Las Termitas. 2019. (Criaturas Rastreras Ser.). (SPA., Illus.). 32p. (J). (gr. 4-6). lib. bdg. *(978-1-62310-203-6(0),* 12855, Bolt) Black Rabbit Bks.
—Termites. 2019. (Crawly Creatures Ser.). (ENG.). 32p. (J). (gr. 4-6). pap. 9.99 *(978-1-64466-025-6(3),* 12689); (Illus.). lib. bdg. *(978-1-68072-814-9(8),* 12688) Black Rabbit Bks. (Bolt).
Squire, Ann O. Termites. 2003. (True Bks.). (ENG., Illus.). 48p. (J). 25.00 *(978-0-516-22660-6(6),* Children's Pr.) Scholastic Library Publishing.
Stefoff, Rebecca. Termites: Secrets of Their Cozy Colonies. 2019. (Amazing Animal Colonies Ser.). (ENG., Illus.). 32p. (J). (gr. 3-6). lib. bdg. 27.99 *(978-1-5435-5555-4(1),* 139396, Capstone Pr.) Capstone.
Yomtov, Nel. From Termite Den to Office Building. 2014. (21st Century Skills Innovation Library: Innovations from Nature Ser.). (ENG., Illus.). 32p. (J). (gr. 4-8). 32.07 *(978-1-62431-755-2(3),* 203288) Cherry Lake Publishing.

TERMITES—FICTION

Caple, Kathy. Termite Tales: Brand New Readers. Caple, Kathy, illus. 2009. (Brand New Readers Ser.). (ENG., Illus.). 48p. (J). (gr. -1-3). pap. 6.99 *(978-0-7636-3901-3(X))* Candlewick Pr.
Laden, Nina. Roberto: the Insect Architect. 2016. (ENG., Illus.). 40p. (J). (gr. k-3). pap. 7.99 *(978-1-4521-5646-0(8))* Chronicle Bks. LLC.
Provenzale, Joseph C. The Teeny, Tiny Termite. 2012. 32p. pap. 21.99 *(978-1-4691-9075-4(3))* Xlibris Corp.
Rouss, Sylvia. The Littlest Pair. Hannon, Holly, illus. 2005. 32p. (J). pap. 9.95 *(978-1-930143-18-0(4),* Devora Publishing) Simcha Media Group.
Weston Woods Staff, creator. Roberto the Insect Architect. 2005. (J). 29.95 *(978-0-439-80455-4(8))* Weston Woods Studios, Inc.

TERRARIUMS

see also Gardens, Miniature

Barger, Jeff. How to Make a Terrarium. 2018. (Step-By-Step Projects Ser.). (ENG., Illus.). 24p. (gr. k-2). lib. bdg. 28.50 *(978-1-64156-428-1(8),* 9781641564281) Rourke Educational Media.

TUV

Bearce, Stephanie. A Kid's Guide to Making a Terrarium. 2009. (Gardening for Kids Ser.). (Illus.). 48p. (J). (gr. 3-6). lib. bdg. 29.95 *(978-1-58415-813-4(1))* Mitchell Lane Pubs.

Janning, Scarlett. Therese's Terrarium, 1 vol. 2013. (Rosen Readers Ser.). (ENG.). 24p. (J). (gr. 3-3). pap. 8.25 *(978-1-4777-2536-8(9),* 3bd61714-2a46-4c0a-85f4-de1f5c39e93e); pap. 49.50 *(978-1-4777-2537-5(7))* Rosen Publishing Group, Inc., The. (Rosen Classroom).

Lunis, Natalie. Making a Terrarium. 2011. (Early Connections Ser.). (J). *(978-1-61672-612-6(1))* Benchmark Education Co.

Stark, Kristy. Terrarium Pets: Volume (Grade 6) 2019. (Mathematics in the Real World Ser.). (ENG., Illus.). 32p. (gr. 5-8). pap. 11.99 *(978-1-4258-5891-9(0))* Teacher Created Materials, Inc.

TERRESTRIAL PHYSICS

see Geophysics

TERROR, REIGN OF

see France—History—Revolution, 1789-1799

TERRORISM

see also Bombings; Sabotage

Allen, John. Thinking Critically: Terrorism. 2018. (Thinking Critically Ser.). (ENG.). 80p. (J). (gr. 6-12). 39.93 *(978-1-68282-445-0(4))* ReferencePoint Pr., Inc.

Amer, Joseph. The War on Terror. 2005. (Behind the News Ser.). (Illus.). 112p. (J). (gr. 5-18). lib. bdg. 24.95 *(978-1-881508-68-7(4))* Oliver Pr., Inc.

Anderson, Dale. The Terrorist Attacks of September 11 2001, 1 vol. 2003. (Landmark Events in American History Ser.). (ENG., Illus.). 48p. (gr. 5-8). pap. 15.05 *(978-0-8368-5408-4(X),* 09da09bc-b75b-4b60-97eb-c06300161720); lib. bdg. 33.67 *(978-0-8368-5380-3(6),* 731c0e2e-4f9b-4b9e-be7c-4c7faabe1171) Stevens, Gareth Publishing LLLP. (Gareth Stevens Secondary Library).

Anderson, Wayne. The ETA: Spain's Basque Terrorists. 2009. (Inside the World's Most Infamous Terrorist Organizations Ser.). 64p. (gr. 5-5). 58.50 *(978-1-61513-578-3(2))* Rosen Publishing Group, Inc., The.

Andryszewski, Tricia. Terrorism in America. 2003. (Headliners Ser.). (Illus.). 64p. (J). (gr. 5-8). lib. bdg. 25.90 *(978-0-7613-2803-2(3),* Millbrook Pr.) Lerner Publishing Group.

Anniss, Matt. Terrorism, 1 vol. 2013. (Crime Science Ser.). (Illus.). 48p. (J). (gr. 4-5). (ENG.). pap. 15.05 *(978-1-4339-9497-5(6),* a1736f35-711c-4662-9483-07da0b33802c); (ENG., lib. bdg. 34.61 *(978-1-4339-9496-8(8),* dd9cc54d-cd1f-4545-9075-85e4141387e9); pap. 84.30 *(978-1-4339-9498-2(4))* Stevens, Gareth Publishing LLLP.

Bailey, Diane. Rescue from an ISIS Prison! Delta Force in Iraq During the War on Terror, Vol. 8. 2018. (Special Forces Stories Ser.). 64p. (J). (gr. 7). lib. bdg. 31.93 *(978-1-4222-4080-9(0))* Mason Crest.

Baldino, Greg. Investigating the Boston Marathon Bombings, 1 vol. 2017. (Terrorism in the 21st Century: Causes & Effects Ser.). (ENG., Illus.). 64p. (J). (gr. 6-6). 36.13 *(978-1-5081-7457-8(1),* d5e5c7f3-657d-47e1-8986-4f39d05d2147, Rosen Young Adult) Rosen Publishing Group, Inc., The.

Barton, Chris. All of a Sudden & Forever: Help & Healing after the Oklahoma City Bombing. Xu, Nicole, illus. 2020. (ENG.). 40p. (J). (gr. 2-5). 19.99 *(978-1-5415-2669-3(4),* bd2374a3-ebaf-42d1-b8e3-1ed4ca3f32da, Carolrhoda Bks.) Lerner Publishing Group.

Benoit, Peter. September 11, 2001: The 10th Anniversary. 2011. (Cornerstones of Freedom, Third Ser.). (Illus.). 64p. (J). (gr. 4-6). lib. bdg. 30.00 *(978-0-531-25040-2(7),* Children's Pr.) Scholastic Library Publishing.

—September 11 Then & Now. 2011. (True Book-Disasters Ser.). (ENG., Illus.). 48p. (J). (gr. 3-5). lib. bdg. 29.00 *(978-0-531-25424-0(0),* Children's Pr.) Scholastic Library Publishing.

Berlatsky, Noah, ed. The War on Terror, 1 vol. 2012. (Global Viewpoints Ser.). (ENG., Illus.). 200p. (gr. 10-12). pap. 32.70 *(978-0-7377-6447-5(3),* 78713cbe-c2e4-42d3-8128-6fac7f57a200); lib. bdg. 47.83 *(978-0-7377-6271-6(3),* 3b3d0464-708e-42c3-82f0-547ec5d1fe17) Greenhaven Publishing LLC. (Greenhaven Publishing).

Bernay, Emma & Berne, Emma Carlson. TV Captures Terrorism on September 11: 4D an Augmented Reading Experience. 2018. (Captured Television History 4D Ser.). (ENG., Illus.). 64p. (J). (gr. 5-9). lib. bdg. 39.99 *(978-0-7565-5824-6(7),* 138349, Compass Point Bks.) Capstone.

Beyer, Mark. Homeland Security & Weapons of Mass Destruction: How Prepared Are We? 2009. (Library of Weapons of Mass Destruction Ser.). 64p. (gr. 5-5). 58.50 *(978-1-60853-952-9(0))* Rosen Publishing Group, Inc., The.

Bledsoe, Karen E., et al. Fighter Planes: Masters of the Sky, 1 vol. 2015. (Military Engineering in Action Ser.). (ENG.). 48p. (gr. 6-6). 29.60 *(978-0-7660-6910-7(9),* 5d25206a-63b8-4064-81c6-be65a4699abf) Enslow Publishing, LLC.

Blohm, Craig E. Catastrophic Events of The 2000s. 2013. (YA). lib. bdg. *(978-1-60152-522-2(2))* ReferencePoint Pr., Inc.

—The 9/11 Investigation, 1 vol. 2009. (Crime Scene Investigations Ser.). (ENG., Illus.). 104p. (gr. 7-7). 37.08 *(978-1-4205-0136-0(4),* 1bc469f1-91f6-4283-937f-8665435465ea, Lucent Pr.) Greenhaven Publishing LLC.

Bodden, Valerie. The 9/11 Terror Attacks: Days of Change. 2015. (Illus.). 80p. (J). *(978-1-60818-529-0(X),* Creative Education) Creative Co., The.

Boutland, Craig. New Generation Vehicles: Drones, Mine Clearance, & Bomb Disposal. 2019. (Military Machines in the War on Terrorism Ser.). (ENG., Illus.). 32p. (J). (gr. 3-9). lib. bdg. 28.65 *(978-1-5435-7385-5(1),* 140673) Capstone.

Brewer, Paul. The Lima Embassy Siege & Latin American Terrorists, 1 vol. 2005. (Terrorism in Today's World Ser.). (ENG., Illus.). 48p. (gr. 5-8). pap. 15.05 *(978-0-8368-6564-6(2),* 55ff82aa-c50c-43fd-b75a-54f3ff449287); lib. bdg. 33.67 *(978-0-8368-6557-8(X),* 225651b4-88d9-4146-9786-36c6f8c709ab) Stevens, Gareth Publishing LLLP. (Gareth Stevens Secondary Library).

Brown Bear Books. War on Terror. 2010. (Modern Military History Ser.). (ENG.). 64p. (J). (gr. 8-11). 39.95 *(978-1-933834-53-5(6),* 16528) Brown Bear Bks.

Brown, Don. America Is under Attack: September 11, 2001: the Day the Towers Fell. 2014. (Actual Times Ser.: 4). (ENG., Illus.). 64p. (J). (gr. 1-5). pap. 10.99 *(978-1-250-04415-0(4),* 900128302) Square Fish.

Brownell, Richard. The Oklahoma City Bombing, 1 vol. 2007. (Crime Scene Investigations Ser.). (ENG., Illus.). 104p. (gr. 7-7). lib. bdg. 42.03 *(978-1-59018-843-9(8),* dcc533b6-e6ce-4b0d-a16c-86ba5c4170a2, Lucent Pr.) Greenhaven Publishing LLC.

Broyles, Janell. Chemical & Biological Weapons in a Post-9/11 World. (Library of Weapons of Mass Destruction Ser.). 64p. (gr. 5-5). 2009. 58.50 *(978-1-60853-951-2(2))* 2004. (ENG., Illus.). (J). lib. bdg. 37.13 *(978-1-4042-0288-7(9),* 2235164b-20b1-4b62-95b0-b2930d696a30) Rosen Publishing Group, Inc., The.

Buell, Tonya. The Crash of United Flight 93 on September 11 2001. 2009. (Terrorist Attacks Ser.). 64p. (gr. 5-5). 58.50 *(978-1-60853-316-9(6))* Rosen Publishing Group, Inc., The.

Burgan, Michael. Captured! Bringing in 9/11 Planner Khalid Sheik Mohammed, Vol. 8. 2018. (Special Forces Stories Ser.). 64p. (J). (gr. 7). 31.93 *(978-1-4222-4078-6(9))* Mason Crest.

Burnett, Betty. The Attack on the USS Cole in Yemen on October 12 2000. 2009. (Terrorist Attacks Ser.). 64p. (gr. 5-5). 58.50 *(978-1-60853-311-4(5))* Rosen Publishing Group, Inc., The.

Byers, Ann. Lebanon's Hezbollah. 2009. (Inside the World's Most Infamous Terrorist Organizations Ser.). 64p. (gr. 5-5). 58.50 *(978-1-61513-576-9(6))* Rosen Publishing Group, Inc., The.

Campbell, Geoffrey A. A Vulnerable America: An Overview of National Security. 2007. (Lucent Library of Homeland Security). (ENG., Illus.). 112p. (J). 30.85 *(978-1-59018-383-0(5),* Lucent Bks.) Cengage Gale.

Challen, Paul C. Surviving 9/11, 1 vol. 2015. (Surviving Disaster Ser.). (ENG., Illus.). 48p. (J). (gr. 5-6). 33.47 *(978-1-4994-3657-0(2),* a6e838c6-ff2e-44cc-8721-69dc469493ed, Rosen Central) Rosen Publishing Group, Inc., The.

Childhood Psychological Disorders: Current Controversies, 1 vol. 2011. (ENG.). 232p. (C). 55.00 *(978-0-313-33696-6(2),* 900305357, Praeger) ABC-CLIO, LLC.

Ching, Jacqueline. Cyberterrorism. 2010. (Doomsday Scenarios: Separating Fact from Fiction Ser.). 64p. (YA). (gr. 5-8). E-Book 58.50 *(978-1-4488-1205-9(4))* Rosen Publishing Group, Inc., The.

Connolly, Kieron. America's Bloody History from Vietnam to the War on Terror, 1 vol. 2017. (Bloody History of America Ser.). (ENG.). 88p. (gr. 8-8). 37.60 *(978-0-7660-9180-1(5),* a92bb720-3a4b-4034-aa1a-44302d2dd1cb); pap. 20.95 *(978-0-7660-9556-4(8),* 2aaa20cd-f1a2-4bce-a811-26f2f83462ab) Enslow Publishing, LLC.

Corrigan, Jim. Causes of the War on Terrorism. 2009. (J). lib. bdg. *(978-1-59556-035-3(1))* OTTN Publishing.

Croce, Nicholas, ed. Anarchism, Revolution, & Terrorism, 1 vol. 2014. (Political & Economic Systems Ser.). (ENG.). 232p. (J). (gr. 10-10). 47.59 *(978-1-62275-353-6(4),* 6e5e3737-bb64-4dc9-aa7a-16283c62c67f) Rosen Publishing Group, Inc., The.

Davenport, John C., ed. Global Extremism & Terrorism. 2007. (World in Focus Ser.). (ENG., Illus.). 222p. (gr. 9-12). lib. bdg. 35.00 *(978-0-7910-9279-8(8),* P124706, Facts On File) Infobase Holdings, Inc.

Decker, Janet & Hecht, Alan. Anthrax. 2nd rev. ed. 2009. (ENG., Illus.). 144p. (gr. 9-18). 34.95 *(978-1-60413-233-5(7),* P159441, Facts On File) Infobase Holdings, Inc.

Derkins, Susie. The Irish Republican Army. 2009. (Inside the World's Most Infamous Terrorist Organizations Ser.). 64p. (gr. 5-5). 58.50 *(978-1-61513-579-0(0))* Rosen Publishing Group, Inc., The.

Doak, Robin S. Homeland Security. 2011. (Cornerstones of Freedom, Third Ser.). (Illus.). 64p. (J). lib. bdg. 30.00 *(978-0-531-25036-5(9),* Children's Pr.) Scholastic Library Publishing.

Docalavich, Heather. Antiterrorism Policy & Fighting Fear, Vol. 10. Russett, Bruce, ed. 2015. (United Nations: Leadership & Challenges in a Global World Ser.). (Illus.). 88p. (J). (gr. 7). lib. bdg. 24.95 *(978-1-4222-3428-0(2))* Mason Crest.

Doeden, Matt. Impact: The Story of the September 11 Terrorist Attacks. 2015. (Tangled History Ser.). (ENG., Illus.). 112p. (J). (gr. 3-9). lib. bdg. 32.65 *(978-1-4914-7079-4(8),* 129461, Capstone Pr.) Capstone.

Donovan, Sandy. Protecting America: A Look at the People Who Keep Our Country Safe. 2003. (How Government Works). (ENG., Illus.). 56p. (gr. 4-8). lib. bdg. 25.26 *(978-0-8225-1345-2(5))* Lerner Publishing Group.

Downing, David. The Debate about Terrorist Tactics, 1 vol. 2007. (Ethical Debates Ser.). (ENG., Illus.). 48p. (YA). (gr. 6-6). lib. bdg. 34.47 *(978-1-4042-3757-5(7),* 8e13c60a-424a-4c12-9643-e082913a0ab0) Rosen Publishing Group, Inc., The.

Ehrman, Ashley M. True Teen Stories from Iraq: Surviving ISIS, 1 vol. 2018. (Surviving Terror: True Teen Stories from Around the World Ser.). (ENG.). 112p. (YA). (gr. 8-8). 45.93 *(978-1-5026-3544-0(5),* 7db7cdff-816e-4490-b269-d3c4f175bc1b) Cavendish Square Publishing LLC.

Elish, Dan. Inside the Situation Room: How a Photograph Showed America Defeating Osama Bin Laden. 2018. (Captured History Ser.). (ENG., Illus.). 64p. (J). (gr. 5-9). pap. 8.95 *(978-0-7565-5881-9(6),* 138649, Compass Point Bks.) Capstone.

Emergency Response to Terrorism. 2nd ed. 2003. cd-rom 89.95 *(978-0-9746186-0-9(8))* RESPONDER911, Inc.

Espejo, Roman. Civil Liberties. 2009. (Opposing Viewpoints Ser.). (ENG., Illus.). 240p. (YA). (gr. 10-12). pap. 29.45 *(978-0-7377-4355-5(7),* LML02109-245310);No. 9. pap. 42.95 *(978-0-7377-4356-2(5),* LML02109-245369) Cengage Gale. (Greenhaven Pr., Inc.).

Espejo, Roman, ed. Bioterrorism, 1 vol. 2012. (Opposing Viewpoints Ser.). (ENG., Illus.). 232p. (gr. 10-12). pap. 34.80 *(978-0-7377-6475-8(9),* 0d925df3-609b-43a9-a6e2-ed48d98ceedb); lib. bdg. 50.43 *(978-0-7377-6474-1(0),* ef0ac6f0-250d-4f60-965c-4e7d6eef4d29) Greenhaven Publishing LLC. (Greenhaven Publishing).

Ferguson, Amanda. The Attack Against the U. S. Embassies in Kenya & Tanzania. 2009. (Terrorist Attacks Ser.). 64p. (gr. 5-5). 58.50 *(978-1-60853-309-1(3))* Rosen Publishing Group, Inc., The.

Fiscus, James W. America's War in Afghanistan, 1 vol. 2003. (War & Conflict in the Middle East Ser.). (ENG., Illus.). 64p. (J). (gr. 5-5). lib. bdg. 37.13 *(978-0-8239-4552-8(9),* 82fb41d7-2f24-4a5c-9598-a4845291d8a7) Rosen Publishing Group, Inc., The.

Freedman, Jeri. America Debates Civil Liberties & Terrorism. 2009. (America Debates Ser.). 64p. (gr. 5-6). 58.50 *(978-1-61511-331-6(2),* Rosen Reference) Rosen Publishing Group, Inc., The.

Friedman, Lauri S., ed. Terrorism, 1 vol. 2010. (Introducing Issues with Opposing Viewpoints Ser.). (ENG.). 168p. (gr. 7-10). 43.63 *(978-0-7377-4944-1(X),* a33b2213-6ec0-44a4-bd0f-fb2a97ded2e0, Greenhaven Publishing) Greenhaven Publishing LLC.

Friedman, Mark. America's Struggle with Terrorism. 2011. (Cornerstones of Freedom, Third Ser.). 64p. (J). lib. bdg. 30.00 *(978-0-531-25026-6(1),* Children's Pr.) Scholastic Library Publishing.

Gard, Carolyn. The Attack on the Pentagon on September 11 2001. 2009. (Terrorist Attacks Ser.). 64p. (gr. 5-5). 58.50 *(978-1-60853-310-7(7))* Rosen Publishing Group, Inc., The.

Giordano, Geraldine. The Oklahoma City Bombing. 2009. (Terrorist Attacks Ser.). 64p. (gr. 5-5). 58.50 *(978-1-60853-318-3(2))* Rosen Publishing Group, Inc., The.

Goodman, Michael E. Modern Spies. (Wartime Spies Ser.). (ENG., Illus.). 48p. (J). (gr. 4-7). 2016. pap. 12.00 *(978-1-62832-205-7(5),* 21085, Creative Paperbacks) 2015. *(978-1-60818-600-6(8),* 21084, Creative Education) Creative Co., The.

Green, Robert. Debates on the 9/11 Attacks. 2018. (Debating History Ser.). (ENG.). 80p. (YA). (gr. 6-12). 39.93 *(978-1-68282-377-4(6))* ReferencePoint Pr., Inc.

—Terrorism. 2008. (21st Century Skills Library: Global Perspectives Ser.). (ENG., Illus.). 32p. (gr. 4-8). lib. bdg. 32.07 *(978-1-60279-125-1(2),* 200110) Cherry Lake Publishing.

Greenberger, Robert. Suicide Bombers. (In the News Ser.). 64p. (gr. 6-6). 2009. 58.50 *(978-1-61513-490-8(5))* 2007. (ENG., Illus.). (YA). lib. bdg. 37.13 *(978-1-4042-0977-0(8),* ae73cb14-a922-4a8c-975a-95283f6f5115) Rosen Publishing Group, Inc., The.

Gregory, Josh. The Hunt for Bin Laden: Operation Neptune Spear. 2013. (ENG.). 64p. (J). pap. 8.95 *(978-0-531-27674-7(0))* Scholastic Library Publishing.

Gunderson, Cory Gideon. Islamic Fundamentalism. 2003. (World in Conflict-the Middle East Ser.). 32p. (gr. 4-8). 27.07 *(978-1-59197-411-6(9),* Abdo & Daughters) ABDO Publishing Co.

—Terrorist Groups. 2003. (World in Conflict-the Middle East Ser.). 32p. (gr. 4-8). 27.07 *(978-1-59197-413-0(5),* Abdo & Daughters) ABDO Publishing Co.

Gunderson, Jessica. Methods of Warfare. 2011. (War on Terror Ser.). (ENG.). 48p. (J). (gr. 5-8). 34.25 *(978-1-60818-101-8(4),* 22304) Creative Co., The.

—Pivotal Moments. 2011. (War on Terror Ser.). (ENG.). 48p. (J). (gr. 5-8). 34.25 *(978-1-60818-102-5(2),* 22305) Creative Co., The.

Halberstam, David. Firehouse. 2003. (ENG., Illus.). 208p. (gr. 8-17). pap. 19.99 *(978-0-7868-8851-1(2),* Hachette Bks.) Hachette Bks.

Hampton, Wilborn. September 11 2001: Attack on New York City. 2011. (ENG., Illus.). 160p. (J). (gr. 5). pap. 14.99 *(978-0-7636-5767-3(0))* Candlewick Pr.

Harris, Nathaniel. Terrorism, 1 vol. 2004. (21st Century Issues Ser.). (ENG., Illus.). 48p. (gr. 5-8). lib. bdg. 33.67 *(978-0-8368-5645-3(7),* 8cf555da-e705-44b9-ba3a-31f80df9f1a6, Gareth Stevens Secondary Library) Stevens, Gareth Publishing LLLP.

Haugen, David M., et al, eds. Iraq, 1 vol. 2009. (Opposing Viewpoints Ser.). (ENG., Illus.). 192p. (gr. 10-12). pap. 34.80 *(978-0-7377-4525-2(8),* 722b2966-c9c2-49cb-b811-f845bdbe4269);No. 9. lib. bdg. 50.43 *(978-0-7377-4524-5(X),* c2c737cd-a425-40a8-8f6f-150e90beb9e4) Greenhaven Publishing LLC. (Greenhaven Publishing).

Haugen, David M. & Musser, Susan, eds. Can the War on Terrorism Be Won?, 1 vol. 2007. (At Issue Ser.). (ENG., Illus.). 112p. (gr. 10-12). 41.03 *(978-0-7377-1973-4(7),* 102c3b1b-646a-4045-8e27-ca5f9d534f9e); pap. 28.80 *(978-0-7377-1974-1(5),* 216aade8-e4c8-4460-a7f8-c2eb412ac5c5) Greenhaven Publishing LLC. (Greenhaven Publishing).

—Terrorism, 1 vol. 2008. (Issues on Trial Ser.). (ENG., Illus.). 224p. (gr. 10-12). 49.93 *(978-0-7377-3982-4(7),* 2a648d8b-1398-4938-863e-c44f171ad5d0, Greenhaven Publishing) Greenhaven Publishing LLC.

Haulley, Fletcher. Critical Perspectives on 9/11, 1 vol. 2004. (Critical Anthologies of Nonfiction Writing Ser.). (ENG.). 176p. (J). (gr. 8-8). lib. bdg. 42.47 *(978-1-4042-0060-9(6),* 3b3fe485-b729-4454-b7a5-4c5a477535d8) Rosen Publishing Group, Inc., The.

—The Deparment of Homeland Security, 1 vol. 2005. (This Is Your Government Ser.). (ENG., Illus.). 64p. (J). (gr. 4-6). lib. bdg. 37.13 *(978-1-4042-0209-2(9),* cb6cd31a-5bf6-494c-8fe0-965b27083d84) Rosen Publishing Group, Inc., The.

—The Department of Homeland Security. (This Is Your Government Ser.). 64p. 2009. (gr. 5-6). 58.50 *(978-1-60854-371-7(4),* Rosen Reference) 2005. (ENG., Illus.). (gr. 4-6). per. 12.95 *(978-1-4042-0662-5(0),* c66a2c7f-a844-416e-b0cc-f92dbb0022f6) Rosen Publishing Group, Inc., The.

Heing, Bridey. The Children Soldiers of ISIS, 1 vol. 2017. (Crimes of ISIS Ser.). (ENG.). 104p. (gr. 8-8). 38.93 *(978-0-7660-9211-2(9),* b02bce7e-1f6e-4774-a4f3-8c9d65714a04) Enslow Publishing, LLC.

—ISIS Brides, 1 vol. 2017. (Crimes of ISIS Ser.). (ENG.). 104p. (gr. 8-8). 38.93 *(978-0-7660-9213-6(5),* 45dd4a6e-487c-4514-b402-10bf802ec914); pap. 20.95 *(978-0-7660-9582-3(7),* 47b8c129-0f0c-469b-a38f-7a6fe1852fdf) Enslow Publishing, LLC.

—The Persecution of Christians & Religious Minorities by ISIS, 1 vol. 2017. (Crimes of ISIS Ser.). (ENG.). 104p. (gr. 8-8). 38.93 *(978-0-7660-9216-7(X),* 9b809955-9b80-4aec-8640-44247674f520); pap. 20.95 *(978-0-7660-9584-7(3),* 32c73849-47b1-46fc-b5c4-d73d8257cc86) Enslow Publishing, LLC.

Hibbert, Adam. Terrorism. 2003. (In the News Ser.). (J). lib. bdg. 24.25 *(978-1-58340-395-2(7))* Black Rabbit Bks.

Hiber, Amanda, ed. Islamic Militancy, 1 vol. 2009. (Opposing Viewpoints Ser.). (ENG., Illus.). 256p. (gr. 10-12). pap. 34.80 *(978-0-7377-4217-6(8),* 19dd12ed-f3b4-45b5-bab2-7f2aa51c0d7f); lib. bdg. 50.43 *(978-0-7377-4216-9(X),* 225b0c87-e454-424c-aa2e-09e0b2110c86) Greenhaven Publishing LLC. (Greenhaven Publishing).

—Should Governments Negotiate with Terrorists?, 1 vol. 2008. (At Issue Ser.). (ENG., Illus.). 128p. (J). (gr. 10-12). lib. bdg. 41.03 *(978-0-7377-3932-9(0),* ada12ba7-2d6a-400a-b051-712fd7c04f5b); pap. 28.80 *(978-0-7377-3933-6(9),* ca4a01f1-b2dc-4d34-95e1-229833261930) Greenhaven Publishing LLC. (Greenhaven Publishing).

Hinton, Kerry. Terrorist Attack: A Practical Survival Guide. 2009. (Library of Emergency Preparedness Ser.). 64p. (gr. 6-6). 58.50 *(978-1-60853-597-2(5),* Rosen Reference) Rosen Publishing Group, Inc., The.

Hoena, Blake. The Boston Marathon Bombing: Running for Their Lives. 2019. (Tangled History Ser.). (ENG., Illus.). 112p. (J). (gr. 3-9). lib. bdg. 32.65 *(978-1-5435-4196-0(8),* 139110) Capstone.

Hunt, Jilly. The Fight Against War & Terrorism. 2017. (Beyond the Headlines! Ser.). (ENG., Illus.). 48p. (J). (gr. 4-8). lib. bdg. 35.99 *(978-1-4846-4142-2(6),* 136196, Heinemann) Capstone.

Immell, Myra, ed. Homeland Security, 1 vol. 2009. (At Issue Ser.). (ENG., Illus.). 136p. (gr. 10-12). 41.03 *(978-0-7377-4420-0(0),* ee6f02cd-66cc-4b74-b372-f168db95e26b); pap. 28.80 *(978-0-7377-4421-7(9),* 23b6bdf6-26f2-4222-a4a0-7c82f2b1e1ed) Greenhaven Publishing LLC. (Greenhaven Publishing).

Innes, Brian. Global Terrorism, Vol. 20. Gomez, Manny, ed. 2016. (Crime & Detection Ser.). 96p. (J). (gr. 7). 24.95 *(978-1-4222-3481-5(9))* Mason Crest.

—International Terrorism. 2004. (Crime & Detection Ser.). (Illus.). 96p. (YA). (gr. 7-18). lib. bdg. 22.95 *(978-1-59084-371-0(1))* Mason Crest.

Isaacs, April, ed. Critical Perspectives on Al Qaeda. 2009. (Critical Anthologies of Nonfiction Writing Ser.). 184p. (gr. 8-8). 63.90 *(978-1-61512-073-4(4))* Rosen Publishing Group, Inc., The.

January, Brendan. Isis: The Global Face of Terrorism. 2017. (ENG., Illus.). 104p. (YA). (gr. 8-12). 37.32 *(978-1-5124-2998-5(8),* 42e58d57-c5ab-47ce-b577-346d107e9285, Twenty-First Century Bks.) Lerner Publishing Group.

Jones, Grace. Terrorism & Extremism. 2018. (Our Values - Level 3 Ser.). (Illus.). 32p. (J). (gr. 5-6). *(978-0-7787-5199-1(6))* Crabtree Publishing Co.

Kaspar, Anna. A Look at Pluto & Other Dwarf Planets, 1 vol. 2007. (Astronomy Now! Ser.). (ENG., Illus.). 24p. (YA). (gr. 2-3). lib. bdg. 26.27 *(978-1-4042-3824-4(7),* 1cf8028f-d4c3-4751-9b44-778c3cd11f24) Rosen Publishing Group, Inc., The.

Katz, Samuel M. At Any Cost: National Liberation Terrorism. 2003. (Terrorists Ser.). (Illus.). 72p. (J). (gr. 6-12). 26.60 *(978-0-8225-0949-3(0))* Lerner Publishing Group.

—Global Counterstrike: International Counterterrorism. 2005. (Terrorist Dossiers Ser.). (Illus.). 72p. (J). (gr. 6-12). 26.60 *(978-0-8225-1566-1(0))* Lerner Publishing Group.

—Jerusalem or Death: Palestinian Terrorism. 72p. (YA). (gr. 9-18). 19.95 *(978-1-58013-208-4(1),* Kar-Ben Publishing); 2003. (Illus.). (J). (gr. 6-12). 26.60 *(978-0-8225-4033-5(9))* Lerner Publishing Group.

—Raging Within: Ideological Terrorism. 2003. (Terrorist Dossiers Ser.). (Illus.). 72p. (J). (gr. 6-12). 26.60 *(978-0-8225-4032-8(0))* Lerner Publishing Group.

—U. S. Counterstrike: American Counterterrorism. 2005. (Terrorist Dossiers Ser.). (Illus.). 72p. (J). (gr. 6-12). 26.60 *(978-0-8225-1569-2(5))* Lerner Publishing Group.

Keeter, Hunter. The U. S. Homeland Security Forces, 1 vol. 2004. (America's Armed Forces Ser.). (ENG., Illus.). 48p. (gr. 5-8). lib. bdg. 33.67 *(978-0-8368-5682-8(1),* b7c9a2ce-1c39-4fd3-8173-a658ff1f4996, Gareth Stevens Secondary Library) Stevens, Gareth Publishing LLLP.

Kenney, Karen Latchana. The Department of Homeland Security: A Look Behind the Scenes. 2019. (U. S. Government Behind the Scenes Ser.). (ENG., Illus.). 64p. (J). (gr. 7-12). pap. 8.95 *(978-0-7565-5910-6(3),* 138704); lib. bdg. 35.32 *(978-0-7565-5901-4(4),* 138700) Capstone. (Compass Point Bks.).

Kennon, Caroline. Battling Terrorism in the United States, 1 vol. 2017. (American History Ser.). (ENG.). 104p. (gr. 7-7). lib. bdg. 41.03 *(978-1-5345-6141-0(2),* c5c41274-cf46-4769-9de2-9c472e50c79c, Lucent Pr.) Greenhaven Publishing LLC.

—The Rise of ISIS: The Modern Age of Terrorism, 1 vol. 2016. (World History Ser.). (ENG.). 104p. (YA). (gr. 7-7). lib. bdg. 41.53 *(978-1-5345-6056-7(4),* a2340241-cfee-4872-ae61-41b82480afc5, Lucent Pr.) Greenhaven Publishing LLC.

Kerrigan, Michael. The Department of Homeland Security. 2004. (Rescue & Prevention Ser.). (Illus.). 96p. (J). (gr. 7-18). lib. bdg. 22.95 *(978-1-59084-409-0(2))* Mason Crest.

—Homeland Security. 2017. (Illus.). 80p. (J). *(978-1-4222-3767-0(2))* Mason Crest.

Koestler-Grack, Rachel A. The Department of Homeland Security. 2007. (U. Government: How It Works). (ENG., Illus.). 104p. (gr. 5-9). lib. bdg. 30.00 *(978-0-7910-9286-6(0),* P125636, Facts On File) Infobase Holdings, Inc.

Koya, Lena & Buell, Tonya. Investigating the Crash of Flight 93, 1 vol. 2017. (Terrorism in the 21st Century: Causes & Effects Ser.). (ENG., Illus.). 64p. (gr. 6-6). 36.13 *(978-1-5081-7459-2(8),* 6c0a7b54-6ade-4ce1-81cb-ae527e8a843a, Rosen Young Adult) Rosen Publishing Group, Inc., The.

Koya, Lena & Gard, Carolyn. Investigating the Attack on the Pentagon, 1 vol. 2017. (Terrorism in the 21st Century: Causes & Effects Ser.). (ENG., Illus.). 64p. (J). (gr. 6-6). 36.13 *(978-1-5081-7453-0(9),* bc1e9ec9-7801-4ace-bd71-16cffa37ffa8, Rosen Young Adult) Rosen Publishing Group, Inc., The.

—Investigating the Attacks on the World Trade Center, 1 vol. 2017. (Terrorism in the 21st Century: Causes & Effects Ser.). (ENG.). 64p. (J). (gr. 6-6). 36.13 *(978-1-5081-7455-4(5),* d0bd35c2-5fcc-4264-bbc2-d1fdae8e1bd0, Rosen Young Adult) Rosen Publishing Group, Inc., The.

La Bella, Laura. The People Behind Deadly Terrorist Attacks, 1 vol. 2016. (Psychology of Mass Murderers Ser.). (ENG., Illus.). 144p. (gr. 8-8). 38.93 *(978-0-7660-7775-1(6),* f819a708-6a50-4528-b3b3-f14874a535bd) Enslow Publishing, LLC.

Langwith, Jacqueline, ed. Bioterrorism. 2008. (Opposing Viewpoints Ser.). (ENG., Illus.). 258p. (YA). (gr. 7-12). 29.45 *(978-0-7377-3991-6(6));* lib. bdg. 42.95 *(978-0-7377-3990-9(8))* Cengage Gale. (Greenhaven Pr., Inc.).

Lawrence, Blythe. War & Terrorism in the Twenty-First Century. 2019. (Defining Events of the Twenty-First Century Ser.). (ENG.). 80p. (J). (gr. 6-12). 41.27 *(978-1-68282-609-6(0))* ReferencePoint Pr., Inc.

Levin, Jack. Domestic Terrorism. 2006. (Roots of Terrorism Ser.). (ENG., Illus.). 93p. (gr. 6-12). lib. bdg. 35.00 *(978-0-7910-8683-4(6),* P114387, Facts On File) Infobase Holdings, Inc.

Lunis, Natalie & Pushies, Fred J. The Takedown of Osama Bin Laden. 2012. (Special Ops Ser.). 32p. (J). (gr. 2-7). lib. bdg. 28.50 *(978-1-61772-459-6(9))* Bearport Publishing Co., Inc.

Luxenberg, Alan H. Radical Islam. 2010. (World of Islam Ser.). (Illus.). 64p. (YA). (gr. 4-7). lib. bdg. 22.95 *(978-1-4222-0536-5(3))* Mason Crest.

Manzano, Megan, ed. Cyberwarfare, 1 vol. 2017. (At Issue Ser.). (ENG.). 120p. (YA). (gr. 10-12). 41.03 *(978-1-5345-0204-8(1),* eb8affdc-6c43-48fe-b16f-c6c4b79be501) Greenhaven Publishing LLC.

Margulies, Phillip. Al Qaeda: Osama bin Laden's Army of Terrorists. 2009. (Inside the World's Most Infamous Terrorist Organizations Ser.). 64p. (gr. 5-5). 58.50 *(978-1-61513-573-8(1))* Rosen Publishing Group, Inc., The.

Maybury, Richard J. World War II: The Rest of the Story & How It Affects You Today, 1930 to September 11 2001. Williams, Jane A., ed. rev. ed. 2003. ("Uncle Eric" Bk.: 11). (ENG., Illus.). 349p. pap. 19.95 *(978-0-942617-43-6(6))* Bluestocking Pr.

McCabe, Matthew. 12 Things to Know about Terrorism. 2015. (Today's News Ser.). (ENG., Illus.). 32p. (J). (gr. 3-6). 32.80 *(978-1-63235-033-6(5),* 11611, 12-Story Library) Bookstaves, LLC.

McNiven, Lauren. The War Against ISIS, 1 vol. 2017. (I Witness War Ser.). (ENG.). 48p. (gr. 5-6). pap. 13.93 *(978-1-5026-3433-7(3),* 49a76dee-1224-44c3-8d83-a26ee4ebb9ea); lib. bdg. 33.07 *(978-1-5026-3256-2(X),* 996dc5ca-3cac-464d-a98e-39342e13d127) Cavendish Square Publishing LLC.

Merino, Noël, ed. Civil Liberties, 1 vol. 2013. (Opposing Viewpoints Ser.). (ENG., Illus.). 256p. (gr. 10-12). lib. bdg. 50.43 *(978-0-7377-6304-1(3),* bbf6ae9a-5bd1-46ca-947c-da270ae431a2, Greenhaven Publishing) Greenhaven Publishing LLC.

—Civil Liberties, 1 vol. 2013. (Opposing Viewpoints Ser.). (ENG., Illus.). 256p. (gr. 10-12). pap. 34.80 *(978-0-7377-6305-8(1),* 4b990e98-ad05-4e4b-9051-0a3359690ba5, Greenhaven Publishing) Greenhaven Publishing LLC.

Miller, Debra A. The Patriot Act, 1 vol. 2007. (Hot Topics Ser.). (ENG., Illus.). 112p. (gr. 7-7). lib. bdg. 41.03 *(978-1-59018-981-8(7),* bbc5ead7-8fa1-4ddf-b860-f44969a6dd51, Lucent Pr.) Greenhaven Publishing LLC.

—Terrorism, 1 vol. 2008. (Hot Topics Ser.). (ENG., Illus.). 112p. (J). (gr. 7-7). lib. bdg. 41.03 *(978-1-4205-0051-6(1),* 462defab-e025-45c2-b812-dd5829b9a4bc, Lucent Pr.) Greenhaven Publishing LLC.

Miller, Debra A., ed. The Middle East, 1 vol. 2007. (Current Controversies Ser.). (ENG., Illus.). 224p. (gr. 10-12). 48.03 *(978-0-7377-3960-2(6),* 13f34d39-21af-498c-ab31-6d7fc422b132); pap. 33.00 *(978-0-7377-3961-9(4),* 3b9a55d8-44f1-4244-89b8-6efbffc75fd8) Greenhaven Publishing LLC. (Greenhaven Publishing).

Miller, Mara. Remembering September 11 2001: What We Know Now, 1 vol. 2011. (Issues in Focus Today Ser.). (ENG.). 112p. (gr. 6-7). 35.93 *(978-0-7660-2931-6(X),* ef1bb047-74cb-4c5f-a4f2-b80a04b76535) Enslow Publishing, LLC.

Miller, Raymond H. The War in Afghanistan. 2003. (American War Library). (ENG., Illus.). 112p. (J). 30.85 *(978-1-59018-331-1(2),* Lucent Bks.) Cengage Gale.

Mooney, Carla. Terrorism: Violence, Intimidation, & Solutions for Peace. Casteel, Tom, illus. 2017. (Inquire & Investigate Ser.). (ENG.). 128p. (J). (gr. 7-9). 22.95 *(978-1-61930-592-2(5),* b851c0e4-60bd-44d3-a9e2-c7f0f326df0e) Nomad Pr.

—Terrorism: Violence, Intimidation, Terrorization, & Solutions for Peace. Casteel, Tom, illus. 2017. (Inquire & Investigate Ser.). (ENG.). 128p. (J). (gr. 7-9). pap. 17.95 *(978-1-61930-596-0(8),* fe08e935-16ca-4bbd-9d12-d57571145839) Nomad Pr.

Mullins, Matt. Homeland Security. 2010. (21st Century Skills Library: Citizens & Their Governments Ser.). (ENG., Illus.). 32p. (gr. 4-8). lib. bdg. 32.07 *(978-1-60279-633-1(5),* 200338) Cherry Lake Publishing.

Murdico, Suzanne J. Osama Bin Laden, 1 vol. 2006. (Middle East Leaders Ser.). (ENG., Illus.). 112p. (J). (gr. 5-8). lib. bdg. 39.80 *(978-1-4042-0875-9(5),* 9faeacea-bc57-4b4f-b1eb-e8ac34879793, Rosen Reference) Rosen Publishing Group, Inc., The.

—Osama bin Laden. 2009. (Middle East Leaders Ser.). 112p. (gr. 5-8). 66.50 *(978-1-61514-647-5(4),* Rosen Reference) Rosen Publishing Group, Inc., The.

Nardo, Don. Cause & Effect: The War on Terror. 2017. (ENG.). 80p. (YA). (gr. 5-12). *(978-1-68282-170-1(6))* ReferencePoint Pr., Inc.

—Massacre in Munich: How Terrorists Changed the Olympics & the World. 2016. (Captured History Sports Ser.). (ENG., Illus.). 64p. (J). (gr. 5-9). lib. bdg. 35.32 *(978-0-7565-5292-3(3),* 130887, Compass Point Bks.) Capstone.

Natural Disasters. 2014. 48p. (J). *(978-1-4222-3044-2(9))* Mason Crest.

Orr, Tamra. Egyptian Islamic Jihad. 2009. (Inside the World's Most Infamous Terrorist Organizations Ser.). 64p. (gr. 5-5). 58.50 *(978-1-61513-574-5(X))* Rosen Publishing Group, Inc., The.

parks, peggy j. Cyberterrorism. 2012. (Illus.). 96p. (J). lib. bdg. *(978-1-60152-264-1(9))* ReferencePoint Pr., Inc.

Paul, Michael. Oklahoma City & Anti-Government Terrorism, 1 vol. 2005. (Terrorism in Today's World Ser.). (ENG., Illus.). 48p. (gr. 5-8). pap. 15.05 *(978-0-8368-6565-3(0),* 7990c4ff-3f07-439c-b53a-4704ddb1d829); lib. bdg. 33.67 *(978-0-8368-6558-5(8),* 12f01c40-96b4-488e-ba9d-a0b1ae68b75a) Stevens, Gareth Publishing LLLP. (Gareth Stevens Secondary Library).

—Pan Am 103 & State-Sponsored Terrorism, 1 vol. 2005. (Terrorism in Today's World Ser.). (ENG., Illus.). 48p. (gr. 5-8). pap. 15.05 *(978-0-8368-6566-0(9),* dbf6dc52-c493-4616-9877-ccf92dae8487); lib. bdg. 33.67 *(978-0-8368-6559-2(6),* 24dd1667-ab69-4cf6-8d84-688dc94847d3) Stevens, Gareth Publishing LLLP. (Gareth Stevens Secondary Library).

Peppas, Lynn & Newton, Sydney. Terrorism Alert! 2005. (Disaster Alert! Ser.). (ENG., Illus.). 32p. (J). (gr. 4-7). pap. *(978-0-7787-1617-4(1));* lib. bdg. *(978-0-7787-1585-6(X))* Crabtree Publishing Co.

Perl, Lila. Terrorism, 1 vol. 2005. (Open for Debate Ser.). (ENG., Illus.). 144p. (YA). (gr. 8-8). lib. bdg. 45.50 *(978-0-7614-1583-1(1),* ec6008e0-9da3-40d2-8a2e-7cbda7cde1bb) Cavendish Square Publishing LLC.

Peters, Jennifer. Inside the Department of Homeland Security, 1 vol. 2018. (Understanding the Executive Branch Ser.). (ENG.). 48p. (gr. 5-5). 29.60 *(978-0-7660-9893-0(1),* c64646e4-c10f-49cb-8e4b-3f1a23675300) Enslow Publishing, LLC.

Poole, Hilary W. Crime & Terrorism. 2017. (Childhood Fears & Anxieties Ser.: Vol. 11). (ENG., Illus.). 48p. (J). (gr. 5-8). 20.95 *(978-1-4222-3724-3(9))* Mason Crest.

Porterfield, Jason. Terrorism, Dirty Bombs, & Weapons of Mass Destruction. (Library of Weapons of Mass Destruction Ser.). 64p. (gr. 5-5). 2009. 58.50 *(978-1-60853-954-3(7))* 2004. (ENG., Illus.). (J). lib. bdg. 37.13 *(978-1-4042-0291-7(9),* 5b2daf98-0603-4a82-87fc-9a8508e1c74c) Rosen Publishing Group, Inc., The.

Rice Jr., Earle. Al Qaeda. 2017. (J). lib. bdg. 29.95 *(978-1-68020-047-8(X))* Mitchell Lane Pubs.

—Islamic State. 2017. (J). lib. bdg. 29.95 *(978-1-68020-055-3(0))* Mitchell Lane Pubs.

Roleff, Tamara L., ed. The World Trade Center Attack. 2003. (History Firsthand Ser.). (Illus.). 202p. (YA). (gr. 7-10). pap. 21.20 *(978-0-7377-1469-2(7),* Greenhaven Pr., Inc.) Cengage Gale.

Romano, Amy. Germ Warfare. (Germs: the Library of Disease-Causing Organisms Ser.). 48p. (gr. 5-5). 2009. 53.00 *(978-1-61512-716-0(X))* 2003. (ENG., Illus.). lib. bdg. 34.47 *(978-0-8239-4493-4(X),* 2a1bc2b5-4059-4f96-acf8-41849963d8a7) Rosen Publishing Group, Inc., The.

Rosaler, Maxine. Hamas: (Rev) Palestinian Terrorists, 1 vol. 2005. (Inside the World's Most Infamous Terrorist Organizations Ser.). (ENG., Illus.). 64p. (J). (gr. 7-7). lib. bdg. 37.13 *(978-1-4042-0634-2(5),* ddf37af9-f019-4844-a295-bd941cb2637f) Rosen Publishing Group, Inc., The.

Rudolph, Jessica. CIA Paramilitary Operatives in Action. 2013. (Special Ops II Ser.). 32p. (J). (gr. 2-7). lib. bdg. 28.50 *(978-1-61772-892-1(6))* Bearport Publishing Co., Inc.

Rudy, Lisa Jo. Bioterror: Deadly Invisible Weapons. 2008. (24/7 Science Behind the Scenes: Spy Files Ser.). (ENG., Illus.). 64p. (J). (gr. 7-12). 22.44 *(978-0-531-12080-4(5),* Watts, Franklin) Scholastic Library Publishing.

Ruffin, David C. The Duties & Responsibilities of the Secretary of Homeland Security. (Your Government in Action Ser.). 32p. (gr. 3-3). 2009. 43.90 *(978-1-60854-918-4(6))* 2004. (ENG., Illus.). (J). lib. bdg. 27.60 *(978-1-4042-2693-7(1),* 97d96ea1-5d59-451f-b7a8-fb9372cf17c6) Rosen Publishing Group, Inc., The. (PowerKids Pr.).

Samuels, Charlie. Timeline of the War on Terror, 1 vol. 2011. (Americans at War: a Gareth Stevens Timeline Ser.). (ENG., Illus.). 48p. (J). (gr. 6-8). pap. 15.05 *(978-1-4339-5924-0(0),* 1131f4ba-9a18-4fd4-a999-6d497b1934f2); lib. bdg. 34.60 *(978-1-4339-5922-6(4),* d74dca4d-47b1-4c63-83c2-74875a65c579) Stevens, Gareth Publishing LLLP. (Gareth Stevens Secondary Library).

Santora, Maureen Crethan. The Day the Towers Fell: The Story of September 11 2001. Cardona, Patricia Santora, illus. 2008. (ENG.). 34p. 31.99 *(978-1-4257-7872-9(0))* Xlibris Corp.

—My Son Christopher: A 9/11 Mother's Tale of Remembrance. 2008. 36p. 31.99 *(978-1-4363-3044-2(0))* Xlibris Corp.

Scheppler, Bill. Guantánamo Bay & Military Tribunals: The Detention & Trial of Suspected Terrorists. 2009. (Frontline Coverage of Current Events Ser.). 48p. (gr. 5-5). 53.00 *(978-1-61512-655-2(4))* Rosen Publishing Group, Inc., The.

—The USA Patriot Act: Antiterror Legislation in Response To 9/11. (Library of American Laws & Legal Principles Ser.). 48p. (gr. 5-8). 2009. 53.00 *(978-1-60853-466-1(9),* Rosen Reference) 2005. (ENG., Illus.). (YA). lib. bdg. 34.47 *(978-1-4042-0457-7(1),* 790e2f71-e5f1-44ee-b9c9-ef137356d001) Rosen Publishing Group, Inc., The.

Schmermund, Elizabeth. Code Breakers & Spies of the War on Terror, 1 vol. 2018. (Code Breakers & Spies Ser.). (ENG.). 80p. (J). (gr. 8-8). lib. bdg. 38.79 *(978-1-5026-3862-5(2),* 6483d1c1-ac0e-4315-9d12-e4d091dd329c) Cavendish Square Publishing LLC.

Schmermund, Elizabeth, ed. Domestic Terrorism, 1 vol. 2016. (At Issue Ser.). (ENG.). 176p. (J). (gr. 10-12). pap. 28.80 *(978-1-5345-0039-6(1),* 7c3016d2-7617-42ea-8d6a-d6734a4bcffe); lib. bdg. 41.03 *(978-1-5345-0015-0(4),* 4111b9a1-273e-46c7-8c2b-39f321c31aa7) Greenhaven Publishing LLC. (Greenhaven Publishing).

Schmermund, Elizabeth & Feinstein, Stephen. Critical Perspectives on Terrorism, 1 vol. 2016. (Analyzing the Issues Ser.). (ENG.). 208p. (gr. 8-8). lib. bdg. 50.93 *(978-0-7660-8127-7(3),* b8d53657-94a1-447f-90e0-366588e3fe40) Enslow Publishing, LLC.

Schorr, Loretta. Attacked, 1 vol. unabr. ed. 2019. (Astonishing Headlines Ser.). (ENG.). 92p. (gr. 5-12). 8.95 *(978-1-61651-918-6(5))* Perfection Learning Corp.

Shahak, Bat-Chen. The Bat-Chen Diaries. Rubanenko, Diana, tr. from HEB. 2008. (Israel Ser.). (ENG., Illus.). 112p. (J). (gr. 5-7). lib. bdg. 16.95 *(978-0-8225-8807-8(2),* Kar-Ben Publishing) Lerner Publishing Group.

Sheen, Barbara. Nuclear Weapons. 2007. (Ripped from the Headlines Ser.). 64p. (YA). (gr. 7-12). 23.95 *(978-1-60217-004-9(5))* Erickson Pr.

Sherrow, Victoria. Homegrown Terror: The Oklahoma City Bombing, 1 vol. 2013. (Disasters: People in Peril Ser.). (ENG., Illus.). 48p. (gr. 5-7). lib. bdg. 27.93 *(978-0-7660-4016-8(X),* 481257c2-e874-4746-b057-51dddb1611a5) Enslow Publishing, LLC.

Shostak, Arthur B., ed. Defeating Terrorism/Developing Dreams: Beyond 9/11 & the Iraq War. 2005. (Defeating Terrorism / Developing Dreams - Beyond 9/11 & the Iraq War Ser.). (Illus.). 185p. (gr. 6-12). 159.75 *(978-0-7910-8421-2(3),* Facts On File) Infobase Holdings, Inc.

—Trade Towers / War Clouds V. 2, 4 vols. 2004. (Defeating Terrorism / Developing Dreams - Beyond 9/11 & the Iraq War Ser.). (ENG., Illus.). 176p. (gr. 6-12). 31.95 *(978-0-7910-7956-0(2),* P114079, Facts On File) Infobase Holdings, Inc.

Silate, Jennifer. Terrorist Attack: True Stories of Survival. (Survivor Stories Ser.). 48p. (gr. 5-5). 2009. 53.00 *(978-1-60853-257-5(7),* Rosen Reference) 2007. (ENG., Illus.). (YA). lib. bdg. 34.47 *(978-1-4042-1001-1(6),* 10abcb01-a7bb-44cd-a028-7ac765cb60ee) Rosen Publishing Group, Inc., The.

Silverstein Gray, Judy & Kiland, Taylor Baldwin. Cyber Technology: Using Computers to Fight Terrorism, 1 vol. 2016. (Military Engineering in Action Ser.). (ENG.). 48p. (gr. 5-6). pap. 12.70 *(978-0-7660-7535-1(4),* bd37435d-2be7-4cb1-bc14-20a58822c23c) Enslow Publishing, LLC.

Sonneborn, Liz. Murder at the 1972 Olympics in Munich. 2009. (Terrorist Attacks Ser.). 64p. (gr. 5-5). 58.50 *(978-1-60853-308-4(5))* Rosen Publishing Group, Inc., The.

Steele, Philip. Hostage Takers. 2016. (Behind the News Ser.). (Illus.). 48p. (J). (gr. 6-9). *(978-0-7787-2587-9(1))* Crabtree Publishing Co.

Stefoff, Rebecca. The Patriot Act, 1 vol. 2011. (Landmark Legislation Ser.). (ENG.). 128p. (YA). (gr. 8-8). 42.64 *(978-1-60870-042-4(9),* ad1dad2b-db9f-4c76-8495-a090e25d0621) Cavendish Square Publishing LLC.

—Security V. Privacy, 1 vol. 2008. (Open for Debate Ser.). (ENG., Illus.). 144p. (YA). (gr. 8-8). lib. bdg. 45.50 *(978-0-7614-2578-6(0),* 03769338-a097-45e0-8d15-575f505a8f98) Cavendish Square Publishing LLC.

Stein, R. Conrad. The Oklahoma City National Memorial. 2003. (Cornerstones of Freedom Ser.). (ENG., Illus.). 48p. (YA). (gr. 4-7). 26.00 *(978-0-516-24205-7(9))* Scholastic Library Publishing.

Stephens, Ronald, ed. Terrorism & Perceived Terrorism Threats. 2014. (Safety First Ser.: 11). 48p. (J). (gr. 5-18). 20.95 *(978-1-4222-3055-8(4))* Mason Crest.

Sterngass, Jon. Terrorism, 1 vol. 2012. (Debating the Issues Ser.). (ENG.). 64p. (gr. 6-6). 35.50 *(978-0-7614-4977-5(9),* 62fc16db-2b19-4d15-9657-fe7d4f9da193) Cavendish Square Publishing LLC.

Stewart, Gail B. Defending the Borders: The Role of Border & Immigration Control. 2003. (Lucent Library of Homeland Security). (Illus.). 112p. (J). 29.95 *(978-1-59018-376-2(2),* Lucent Bks.) Cengage Gale.

Stinson, Doug. Protecting the Nation's Borders. 2005. (At Issue Ser.). (ENG.). 80-128p. (gr. 10-12). pap. 24.45 *(978-0-7377-2740-1(3),* Greenhaven Pr., Inc.) Cengage Gale.

Stinson, Douglass, ed. Protecting America's Borders. 2005. (At Issue Ser.). 94p. (YA). (gr. 10-13). lib. bdg. 29.95 *(978-0-7377-2739-5(X),* Greenhaven Pr., Inc.) Cengage Gale.

Terrorism. 2006. (Understanding Global Issues Ser.). (Illus.). 56p. per. 11.95 *(978-1-59036-508-3(9))* Weigl Pubs., Inc.

Terrorism in the 21st Century: Causes & Effects, 12 vols. 2017. (Terrorism in the 21st Century: Causes & Effects Ser.). (ENG.). 64p. (gr. 6-6). 216.78 *(978-1-4994-6638-6(2),* d42eeff7-b1f2-4403-a087-71fe60890631, Rosen Young Adult) Rosen Publishing Group, Inc., The.

Terrorism in Today's World, 12 vols., Set. 2005. (Terrorism in Today's World Ser.). (ENG.). 48p. (gr. 5-8). lib. bdg. 202.02 *(978-0-8368-6555-4(3),* 6cf346ce-d52e-4aa7-afdd-9931b0452281, Gareth Stevens Secondary Library) Stevens, Gareth Publishing LLLP.

Thiel, Kristin. True Stories of Teen Terrorist Hostages, 1 vol. 2017. (True Teen Stories Ser.). (ENG.). 112p. (YA). (gr. 9-9). pap. 20.99 *(978-1-5026-3405-4(8),* 46fcbc21-6e4a-4c01-95dc-31f2ec5da466) Cavendish Square Publishing LLC.

Tomkies, Kelly Kagamas. The National Counterterrorism Center. 2017. (Illus.). 80p. (J). *(978-1-4222-3766-3(4))* Mason Crest.

Torr, James D. Responding to Attack: Firefighters & Police. 2003. (Lucent Library of Homeland Security). (Illus.). 112p. (J). 30.85 *(978-1-59018-375-5(4),* Lucent Bks.) Cengage Gale.

Torres, John A. How Barack Obama Fought the War on Terrorism, 1 vol. 2017. (Presidents at War Ser.). (ENG.). 128p. (gr. 8-8). lib. bdg. 38.93 *(978-0-7660-8535-0(X),* 6808ab9c-609c-4f7e-b33b-789b6476f7fb) Enslow Publishing, LLC.

Townsend, Chris. Global Recruitment by ISIS, 1 vol. 2017. (Crimes of ISIS Ser.). (ENG.). 104p. (gr. 8-8). 38.93 *(978-0-7660-9212-9(7),* 5f0c7814-9092-4aa7-960b-54a9a9afef36); pap. 20.95 *(978-0-7660-9581-6(9),* fb96fb14-1baf-49f4-90d0-9fafd5e2abb9) Enslow Publishing, LLC.

—ISIS Hostages, 1 vol. 2017. (Crimes of ISIS Ser.). (ENG.). 104p. (gr. 8-8). 38.93 *(978-0-7660-9217-4(8),* 1636f9e9-8124-405f-ab42-d347c1af4dca); pap. 20.95 *(978-0-7660-9585-4(1),* c7ac1790-ab33-4e8e-9c40-1ae65bc8d081) Enslow Publishing, LLC.

—Life under the Caliphate, 1 vol. 2017. (Crimes of ISIS Ser.). (ENG.). 104p. (gr. 8-8). 38.93 *(978-0-7660-9218-1(6),* 132aecf2-4a63-450f-b360-8e63b2bf8acc); pap. 20.95 *(978-0-7660-9586-1(X),* 09a84c9a-dad3-48ca-a54c-da0bc3d479ad) Enslow Publishing, LLC.

—The Violent Rise of ISIS, 1 vol. 2017. (Crimes of ISIS Ser.). (ENG.). 104p. (gr. 8-8). 38.93 *(978-0-7660-9210-5(0),* f22ec1a9-c044-419a-a5a2-d36f7f546231); pap. 20.95 *(978-0-7660-9579-3(7),* 51df27e7-92f3-42cf-a90e-8d18e0e3bce0) Enslow Publishing, LLC.

True Teen Stories, 12 vols. 2017. (True Teen Stories Ser.). (ENG.). (J). (gr. 9-9). lib. bdg. 267.00 *(978-1-5026-3231-9(4),* c63f4b7d-cf72-44ba-9744-4fcc0e7437bb) Cavendish Square Publishing LLC.

Uschan, Michael V. The Beslan School Siege & Separatist Terrorism, 1 vol. 2005. (Terrorism in Today's World Ser.). (ENG., Illus.). 48p. (gr. 5-8). pap. 15.05 *(978-0-8368-6563-9(4),* f3ecb2ae-6887-4fba-b5c8-9490712dbe22); lib. bdg. 33.67 *(978-0-8368-6556-1(1),* d43b647f-6332-44bc-9476-d84fa50b17e8) Stevens, Gareth Publishing LLLP. (Gareth Stevens Secondary Library).

—Suicide Bombings in Israel & Palestinian Terrorism, 1 vol. 2005. (Terrorism in Today's World Ser.). (ENG., Illus.). 48p. (gr. 5-8). pap. 15.05 *(978-0-8368-6568-4(5),* 025530c3-45d4-4b1d-829c-f3b5bb6db437); lib. bdg. 33.67 *(978-0-8368-6561-5(8),* 548d13b1-7b5f-4a62-9295-88bbba5a9e51) Stevens, Gareth Publishing LLLP. (Gareth Stevens Secondary Library).

Webb, Glenn. Critical World Issues: Terrorism, Vol. 16. 2016. (Critical World Issues Ser.: Vol. 16). (ENG., Illus.). 112p. (J). (gr. 7-12). 25.95 *(978-1-4222-3661-1(7))* Mason Crest.

Weitzman, Stanley. Terrorism, 1 vol. 2006. (Global Issues Ser.: 0). (ENG., Illus.). 64p. (YA). (gr. 6-10). pap. 12.95 *(978-1-55285-746-5(8),* 917b4bf8-f6f6-461e-a7cb-4cbe7cce7231) Whitecap Bks., Ltd. CAN. Dist: Firefly Bks., Ltd.

Wells, Donald, ed. Terrorism. 2006. (Understanding Global Issues Ser.). (Illus.). 56p. (J). (gr. 3-7). lib. bdg. 28.50 *(978-1-59036-234-1(9))* Weigl Pubs., Inc.

Wicker, R. Doug. The Bombing of Pan Am Flight 103. 2009. (Terrorist Attacks Ser.). 64p. (gr. 5-5). 58.50 *(978-1-60853-315-2(8))* Rosen Publishing Group, Inc., The.

Williams, Brian. America under Attack. 2003. (Dates with History Ser.). 45p. (J). lib. bdg. 28.50 *(978-1-58340-406-5(6))* Black Rabbit Bks.

Wilson, Mike, ed. Terrorism, 1 vol. 2008. (Opposing Viewpoints Ser.). (ENG., Illus.). 216p. (gr. 10-12). 50.43 *(978-0-7377-4234-3(8),* 7065b2b9-e6f5-4ade-bf21-53e26e70644c); pap. 34.80 *(978-0-7377-4235-0(6),* c68db386-9478-4b36-a1de-14be4b4e6ace) Greenhaven Publishing LLC. (Greenhaven Publishing).

Wimmer, Teresa. Causes. 2011. (War on Terror Ser.). (ENG., Illus.). 48p. (J). (gr. 5-8). 34.25 *(978-1-60818-097-4(2),* 22302) Creative Co., The.

—Controversies. 2011. (War on Terror Ser.). (Illus.). 48p. (J). (gr. 5-9). 34.25 *(978-1-60818-098-1(0))* Creative Co., The.

—Ideology & Information. 2011. (War on Terror Ser.). (Illus.). 48p. (J). (gr. 5-9). 34.25 *(978-1-60818-099-8(9))* Creative Co., The.

—Important Figures. 2011. (War on Terror Ser.). (ENG., Illus.). 48p. (J). (gr. 5-8). 34.25 *(978-1-60818-100-1(6),* 22303) Creative Co., The.

Woolf, Alex. Osama Bin Laden. 2004. (A&E Biography Ser.). (Illus.). 112p. (J). 29.27 *(978-0-8225-5003-7(2),* Lerner Pubns.) Lerner Publishing Group.

—Terrorism, 1 vol. 2011. (Global Issues Ser.). (ENG., Illus.). 48p. (YA). (gr. 6-6). lib. bdg. 34.47 *(978-1-4488-1881-5(8),* 29556e09-c143-42ff-bc5c-36a5ad6f99fa, Rosen Reference) Rosen Publishing Group, Inc., The.

Wright, John D. Counterterrorist Forces with the CIA. 2004. (Rescue & Prevention Ser.). (Illus.). 96p. (YA). (gr. 7-18). lib. bdg. 22.95 *(978-1-59084-407-6(6))* Mason Crest.

Yomtov, Nel. Counterterrorism. 2016. (Military Missions Ser.). (ENG., Illus.). 24p. (J). (gr. 3-7). 26.95 *(978-1-62617-434-4(2),* Epic Bks.) Bellwether Media.

Zelinger, Laurie E. Please Explain Terrorism to Me: A Story for Children, PEARLS of Wisdom for Their Parents. Israeli, Ann, illus. 2016. 73p. (J). pap. *(978-1-61599-291-1(X))* Loving Healing Pr., Inc.

Zullo, Allan. Heroes of 9/11. 2011. (Illus.). 181p. (J). pap. *(978-0-545-25506-6(6))* Scholastic, Inc.

TERRORISM—FICTION

Ahmed, Samira. Love, Hate & Other Filters. (ENG.). (YA). (gr. 9). 2019. 312p. pap. 10.99 *(978-1-61695-999-9(1))* 2018. 288p. 18.99 *(978-1-61695-847-3(2))* Soho Pr., Inc. (Soho Teen).

Anthony, Horowitz. Ark Angel. 2007. (Alex Rider Ser.: Bk. 6). 326p. (gr. 5-9). 19.00 *(978-0-7569-8134-1(4))* Perfection Learning Corp.

—Ark Angel. 2007. (Alex Rider Ser.: 6). 326p. lib. bdg. 19.65 *(978-1-4177-7664-1(1))* Turtleback.

TUV

—Scorpia Rising. (J). 2012. 1.25 *(978-1-4640-0577-0(X))* 2012. 256.75 *(978-1-4561-3362-7(4))* 2012. 90.75 *(978-1-4561-3363-4(2))* 2011. 122.75 *(978-1-4561-3365-8(9))* 2011. 120.75 *(978-1-4561-3367-2(5))* Recorded Bks., Inc.
—Scorpia Rising. 2012. (Alex Rider Ser.: 9). lib. bdg. 19.65 *(978-0-606-23638-6(4))* Turtleback.
—Stormbreaker. 2004. (Alex Rider Ser.: Bk. 1). 208p. (J). (gr. 4-7). pap. 38.00 incl. audio *(978-0-8072-2277-5(1),* Listening Library) Random Hse. Audio Publishing Group.
Appleton, Victor. The Robot Olympics. 2007. (Tom Swift, Young Inventor Ser.). (ENG.). 160p. (gr. 4-7). 27.07 *(978-1-59961-351-2(4))* Spotlight.
Arcos, Carrie. We Are All That's Left. 2018. 400p. (YA). (gr. 7). 17.99 *(978-0-399-17554-1(7),* Philomel Bks.) Penguin Young Readers Group.
Barry, Dave. The Worst Class Trip Ever. 2015. (Class Trip Ser.). (ENG.). 224p. (J). (gr. 3-7). 13.99 *(978-1-4847-0849-1(0))* Disney Pr.
—The Worst Class Trip Ever. 2020. (Penworthy Picks YA Fiction Ser.). (ENG.). 214p. (J). (gr. 6-8). 17.49 *(978-1-64697-236-4(8))* Penworthy Co., LLC, The.
Barry, Dave & Barry, Dave. The Worst Class Trip Ever. 2019. (Class Trip Ser.). (ENG.). 240p. (J). (gr. 3-7). pap. 9.99 *(978-1-368-04059-4(4))* Little, Brown Bks. for Young Readers.
Baskin, Nora Raleigh. Nine, Ten: a September 11 Story. 2016. (ENG., Illus.). 208p. (J). (gr. 3-7). 17.99 *(978-1-4424-8506-8(X))* Simon & Schuster Children's Publishing.
Blackman, Malorie. Black & White. 2007. (ENG.). 512p. (YA). (gr. 9-12). pap. 13.99 *(978-1-4169-0017-7(9),* Simon & Schuster Bks. For Young Readers) Simon & Schuster Bks. For Young Readers.
Bowen, Carl. Dragon Teeth. Tortosa, Wilson, illus. 2015. (Shadow Squadron Ser.). (ENG.). 112p. (J). (gr. 4-8). lib. bdg. 27.32 *(978-1-4965-0383-1(X),* 128362, Stone Arch Bks.) Capstone.
Bradford, Chris. Bodyguard: Recruit (Book 1), Bk. 1. 2017. (Bodyguard Ser.: 1). (ENG.). 272p. (J). (gr. 5). pap. 8.99 *(978-1-5247-3697-2(X),* Philomel Bks.) Penguin Young Readers Group.
Bradley, F. T. Double Vision: the Alias Men. 2015. (Double Vision Ser.: 3). (ENG.). 256p. (J). (gr. 3-7). pap. 7.99 *(978-0-06-210444-1(6),* HarperCollins) HarperCollins Pubs.
Brayden, Elyse. Shadow State. 2018. (ENG.). 288p. (YA). 27.99 *(978-1-250-12423-4(9),* 900174368) Imprint IND. Dist: Macmillan.
Bunting, Eve. The Man with the Red Bag. 2007. 230p. (J). (gr. 5-9). 15.99 *(978-0-06-081828-9(X),* Cotler, Joanna Books) HarperCollins Pubs.
Burns, Joanne. What Is Heaven Like? 2005. 35p. (J). 10.99 *(978-1-4116-3360-5(1))* Lulu Pr., Inc.
Burrows, Jennifer S. Most Beautiful. 2012. (ENG.). 50p. (J). (gr. 4-7). pap. 9.99 *(978-0-89824-376-5(9))* Royal Fireworks Publishing Co.
Butcher, Andrew & Butcher, Andrew J. Factoria Frankestein. Morales, Andrea, tr. 2004. (SPA., Illus.). 240p. *(978-84-95618-57-3(5),* Umbriel) Ediciones Urano S. A.
Buxbaum, Julie. Hope & Other Punch Lines. 2019. (ENG.). 320p. (YA). (gr. 7). 18.99 *(978-1-5247-6677-1(1),* Delacorte Pr.) Random Hse. Children's Bks.
Carter, Ally. United We Spy. 2016. (Gallagher Girls Ser.: 6). (ENG.). 320p. (YA). (gr. 7-17). pap. 10.99 *(978-1-4847-8508-9(8))* Hyperion Bks. for Children.
Cerra, Kerry O'Malley. Just a Drop of Water. 2014. (ENG.). 320p. (J). (gr. 2-7). 14.95 *(978-1-62914-613-3(7),* Sky Pony Pr.) Skyhorse Publishing Co., Inc.
Chima, Cinda Williams. The Enchanter Heir. 2013. (Heir Chronicles Ser.: 4). (ENG.). 464p. (YA). (gr. 7-12). E-Book 45.00 *(978-1-4231-8789-9(X))* Little, Brown Bks. for Young Readers.
Clancy, Tom. Patriot Games. 2013. (gr. 7-12). 20.85 *(978-0-8335-1643-5(4))* Turtleback.
Cooney, Caroline B. The Terrorist. 2012. (ENG.). 144p. (YA). (gr. 7-12). pap. 6.99 *(978-1-4532-7467-5(7))* Open Road Integrated Media, Inc.
Cray, Jordan. Firestorm. 2009. (Danger. com Ser.: 2). (ENG.). 208p. (YA). (gr. 7). pap. 9.99 *(978-1-4169-9846-4(2),* Simon Pulse) Simon Pulse.
Dashner, James. The Eye of Minds. 2013. 310p. (YA). *(978-0-385-38370-7(3),* Delacorte Pr) Random House Publishing Group.
—The Eye of Minds (the Mortality Doctrine, Book One) 2014. (Mortality Doctrine Ser.: 1). (ENG.). 352p. (YA). (gr. 7). pap. 13.99 *(978-0-385-74140-8(5),* Ember) Random Hse. Children's Bks.
—The Game of Lives (the Mortality Doctrine, Book Three) 2017. (Mortality Doctrine Ser.: 3). (ENG.). 384p. (YA). (gr. 7). pap. 11.99 *(978-0-385-74144-6(8).* Ember) Random Hse. Children's Bks.
—The Rule of Thoughts (the Mortality Doctrine, Book Two), Bk. 2. 2016. (Mortality Doctrine Ser.: 2). (ENG.). 352p. (YA). (gr. 7). pap. 11.99 *(978-0-385-74142-2(1),* Ember) Random Hse. Children's Bks.
David, Christopher. Denholme & the Skeleton Mystery. 2006. 274p. pap. 22.52 *(978-1-4120-8014-9(2))* Trafford Publishing.
Davidson, Jenny. The Explosionist. 2008. 464p. (YA). (gr. 7-18). lib. bdg. 18.89 *(978-0-06-123976-2(3),* HarperTeen) HarperCollins Pubs.
Davies, Stephen. Outlaw. 2011. (ENG.). 304p. (YA). (gr. 7). 16.99 *(978-0-547-39017-8(3))* Houghton Mifflin Harcourt Publishing Co.
Deuker, Carl. Runner. 2007. (ENG.). 224p. (YA). (gr. 7-12). pap. 15.99 *(978-0-618-73505-1(4),* 410112, Clarion Bks.) HarperCollins Pubs.
Doctorow, Cory. Little Brother. (Little Brother Ser.: 1). (ENG.). (YA). (gr. 8-13). 2010. 432p. pap. 12.99 *(978-0-7653-2311-8(7),* 900057453) 2008. 384p. 19.99 *(978-0-7653-1985-2(3),* 900049020) Doherty, Tom Assocs., LLC. (Tor Teen).
—Little Brother. 2010. (YA). lib. bdg. 24.50 *(978-0-606-14347-9(5))* Turtleback.
Dowd, Siobhan. Bog Child. 2010. (ENG.). 336p. (YA). (gr. 7). pap. 10.99 *(978-0-375-84135-4(0))* Fickling, David Bks. GBR. Dist: Penguin Random Hse. LLC.
Dunlop, Ed. Sherlock Jones: The Assassination Plot. 2004. 116p. (J). 8.99 *(978-1-59166-315-7(6))* BJU Pr.
Ellis, Deborah. The Breadwinner Trilogy, 1 vol. 2009. (Breadwinner Ser.: 1 - 3). (ENG.). 440p. (J). (gr. 5-9). pap. 19.99 *(978-0-88899-959-7(3))* Groundwood Bks. CAN. Dist: Publishers Group West (PGW).
Everheart, Chris. Demolition Day, 1 vol. Arcana Studio, Arcana, illus. 2010. (Recon Academy Ser.). (ENG.). 64p. (J). (gr. 4-8). 27.32 *(978-1-4342-1917-6(8),* 102376, Stone Arch Bks.) Capstone.
—Mixed Signals, 1 vol. Arcana Studio, Arcana, illus. 2010. (Recon Academy Ser.). (ENG.). 64p. (J). (gr. 4-8). 27.32 *(978-1-4342-1915-2(1),* 102374, Stone Arch Bks.) Capstone.
—Prep Squadron, 1 vol. Arcana Studio, Arcana, illus. 2009. (Recon Academy Ser.). (ENG.). 64p. (J). (gr. 4-8). lib. bdg. 27.32 *(978-1-4342-1168-2(1),* 95382, Stone Arch Bks.) Capstone.
—Storm Surge, 1 vol. Arcana Studio, Arcana, illus. 2010. (Recon Academy Ser.). (ENG.). 64p. (J). (gr. 4-8). 27.32 *(978-1-4342-1918-3(6),* 102377, Stone Arch Bks.) Capstone.
Floreen, Tim. Willful Machines. 2016. (ENG., Illus.). 384p. (YA). (gr. 9). pap. 12.99 *(978-1-4814-3278-8(8),* Simon Pulse) Simon Pulse.
Girard, Geoffrey. Truthers. 2017. (ENG.). 360p. (YA). (gr. 7-12). 17.99 *(978-1-5124-2779-0(9),* 0d09002c-e9fc-4b30-baed-e1251cfe8f3e, Carolrhoda Lab™) Lerner Publishing Group.
Grainger, A. J. Captive. 2016. (ENG.). 272p. (YA). (gr. 7). pap. 11.99 *(978-1-4814-2904-7(3))* Simon & Schuster Children's Publishing.
Gratz, Alan. Code of Honor. 2015. (ENG.). 288p. (J). (gr. 7). 18.99 *(978-0-545-69519-0(8),* Scholastic Pr.) Scholastic, Inc.
—Ground Zero, 1 vol. 2021. (ENG., Illus.). 336p. (J). (gr. 4-7). 17.99 *(978-1-338-24575-2(9),* Scholastic Pr.) Scholastic, Inc.
Higgins, Jack & Richards, Justin. First Strike. 2011. (Chance Twins Ser.: Bk. 4). (ENG.). 240p. (YA). (gr. 7-12). 24.94 *(978-0-399-25240-2(1))* Penguin Young Readers Group.
—Sharp Shot. 2010. (ENG.). 240p. (YA). (gr. 7-18). 8.99 *(978-0-14-241730-0(0),* Speak) Penguin Young Readers Group.
Hirsch, Jeff. Unnatural Disasters. 2019. (ENG.). 352p. (YA). (gr. 7). 17.99 *(978-0-544-99916-9(9),* 1666807, Clarion Bks.) HarperCollins Pubs.
Horowitz, Anthony. Ark Angel. 2007. (Alex Rider Ser.: 6). (ENG.). 352p. (J). (gr. 5-18). 8.99 *(978-0-14-240738-7(0),* Puffin Books) Penguin Young Readers Group.
—Never Say Die. (Alex Rider Ser.: 11). (ENG.). 368p. (J). (gr. 5). 2018. 9.99 *(978-1-5247-3932-4(4),* Puffin Books) 2017. 17.99 *(978-1-5247-3930-0(8),* Philomel Bks.) Penguin Young Readers Group.
—Scorpia. 2006. (Alex Rider Ser.: 5). (ENG.). 416p. (J). (gr. 5-18). pap. 8.99 *(978-0-14-240578-9(7),* Puffin Books) Penguin Young Readers Group.
—Scorpia Rising. 2012. (Alex Rider Ser.: 9). (ENG.). 432p. (J). (gr. 5-18). 9.99 *(978-0-14-241985-4(0),* Puffin Books) Penguin Young Readers Group.
—Skeleton Key. 2006. (Alex Rider Ser.: 3). (ENG.). 368p. (J). (gr. 5-18). 8.99 *(978-0-14-240614-4(7),* Puffin Books) Penguin Young Readers Group.
—Skeleton Key: the Graphic Novel. Kanako & Yuzuru, illus. 2009. (Alex Rider Ser.: Bk. 3). (ENG.). 176p. (J). (gr. 5-18). pap. 16.99 *(978-0-399-25418-5(8),* Philomel Bks.) Penguin Young Readers Group.
—Stormbreaker. 2006. (Alex Rider Ser.: 1). (ENG.). 304p. (J). (gr. 5-18). 9.99 *(978-0-14-240611-3(2),* Puffin Books) Penguin Young Readers Group.
—Stormbreaker: the Graphic Novel. Kanako & Yuzuru, illus. 2006. (Alex Rider Ser.). (ENG.). 144p. (J). (gr. 5-18). pap. 14.99 *(978-0-399-24633-3(9),* Philomel Bks.) Penguin Young Readers Group.
Jones, Don. When the Firewood Comes. 2009. 86p. pap. 19.95 *(978-1-4489-9667-4(8))* America Star Bks.
Kalkowski, John. Red Cell. 2010. 164p. 21.95 *(978-1-4502-1209-0(3))* iUniverse, Inc.
Kass, Pnina Moed. Real Time. 2006. (ENG.). 192p. (YA). (gr. 7-12). reprint ed. pap. 9.99 *(978-0-618-69174-6(X),* 418618, Clarion Bks.) HarperCollins Pubs.
Klavan, Andrew. Hostage Run, 1 vol. 2016. (MindWar Trilogy Ser.: 2). (ENG.). 352p. (YA). pap. 12.99 *(978-1-4016-8897-4(7))* Nelson, Thomas Inc.
—The Last Thing I Remember, 1 vol. 2010. (Homelanders Ser.: 1). (ENG.). 352p. (YA). pap. 9.99 *(978-1-59554-586-2(7))* Nelson, Thomas Inc.
Klein. Operation Firestorm. (Bloomfield 3-in-1 Mini Ser.). (J). 17.99 *(978-1-56871-309-0(6))* Targum Pr., Inc.
Langston, Laura. In Plain Sight, 1 vol. 2017. (Orca Soundings Ser.). (ENG.). 160p. (YA). (gr. 8-12). pap. 9.95 *(978-1-4598-1416-5(9))* Orca Bk. Pubs. USA.
—In Plain Sight. 2017. (Orca Soundings Ser.). lib. bdg. 20.80 *(978-0-606-40455-6(4))* Turtleback.
Lee, Fonda. Cross Fire: an Exo Novel. (ENG.). 384p. (YA). (gr. 7-7). 2019. pap. 9.99 *(978-1-338-13911-2(8),* Scholastic Paperbacks) 2018. 17.99 *(978-1-338-13909-9(6),* Scholastic Pr.) Scholastic, Inc.
—Exo (a Novel) 2017. (ENG.). 384p. (YA). (gr. 7). 17.99 *(978-0-545-93343-8(9),* Scholastic Pr.) Scholastic, Inc.
Levithan, David. Love Is the Higher Law. 2010. 176p. (YA). (gr. 7). pap. 9.99 *(978-0-375-83469-1(9),* Knopf Bks. for Young Readers) Random Hse. Children's Bks.
Levy, Marilyn. Checkpoints. 2009. (ENG.). 256p. (gr. 7). pap. 14.95 *(978-0-8276-0870-2(5))* Jewish Pubn. Society.
Logie, Mark. Storm Troopers Tz9. 2011. 108p. pap. *(978-0-7552-1333-7(5))* Authors OnLine, Ltd.
McAndrew, Matthew. Headshot: A Thriller. 2017. (ENG., Illus.). 178p. (YA). pap. 10.99 *(978-0-692-97450-6(4))* Dark Mantle Publishing.
McKay, Sharon E. Thunder over Kandahar. Kinnaird, Ross, illus. 3rd ed. 2010. 264p. (YA). (gr. 7-12). pap. 12.95 *(978-1-55451-266-9(2),* 9781554512669) Annick Pr., Ltd. CAN. Dist: Publishers Group West (PGW).
McKenzie, Sophie. Every Second Counts. 2016. 405p. (YA). pap. *(978-1-4814-3927-5(8))* Simon & Schuster Children's Publishing.
—In a Split Second. 2015. (ENG., Illus.). 368p. (YA). (gr. 7). 17.99 *(978-1-4814-1394-7(5))* Simon & Schuster Children's Publishing.
Meminger, Neesha. Shine, Coconut Moon. 2010. (ENG.). 256p. (YA). (gr. 9). pap. 11.99 *(978-1-4424-0305-5(5),* McElderry, Margaret K. Bks.) McElderry, Margaret K. Bks.
Mohsenian, Javad. 9/11 Children. 2006. (ENG.). 128p. per. 10.95 *(978-0-7414-3218-6(8))* Infinity Publishing.
Monaghan, Annabel. A Girl Named Digit. 2013. (ENG.). 192p. (YA). (gr. 7). pap. 8.99 *(978-0-544-02248-5(3),* 1528483, Clarion Bks.) HarperCollins Pubs.
Morris, Robert. Grandma Ursu, Think Blue. 2003. (Illus.). 32p. (J). 15.95 *(978-0-9741634-0-6(6))* Ursu Pubns.
Muchamore, Robert. The Recruit. 2010. (Cherub Ser.: 1). (ENG.). 352p. (YA). (gr. 7). pap. 12.99 *(978-1-4424-1360-3(3));* 21.99 *(978-1-4169-9940-9(X))* Simon Pulse. (Simon Pulse).
—The Sleepwalker. 2015. (Cherub Ser.: 9). (ENG., Illus.). 336p. (YA). (gr. 7). 17.99 *(978-1-4814-5663-0(6),* Simon Pulse) Simon Pulse.
Muchamore, Robert & Edginton, Ian. CHERUB: the Recruit Graphic Novel: Book 1. Aggs, John, illus. 2012. (Cherub Ser.). (ENG.). 176p. (YA). (gr. 7-17). pap. 11.99 *(978-1-4449-0318-8(7))* Hachette Children's Group GBR. Dist: Hachette Bk. Group.
Mullin, Mike. Surface Tension. 2018. (ENG.). 424p. (YA). (gr. 8-12). 17.99 *(978-1-939100-16-0(X))* Tanglewood Pr.
Norris, Elizabeth. Unraveling. 2013. (Unraveling Ser.: 1). (ENG.). 480p. (YA). (gr. 8). pap. 9.99 *(978-0-06-210374-1(1),* Balzer & Bray) HarperCollins Pubs.
Nwaubani, Adaobi Tricia & Mazza, Viviana. Buried Beneath the Baobab Tree. 2018. (ENG.). 336p. (YA). (gr. 8). 17.99 *(978-0-06-269672-4(6),* Tegen, Katherine Bks) HarperCollins Pubs.
Payne, Mary Jennifer. Darkness Rising: Daughters of Light. 2019. (Daughters of Light Ser.: 3). (ENG.). 312p. (YA). (gr. 7-10). pap. 12.99 *(978-1-4597-4103-4(X))* Dundurn Pr. CAN. Dist: Publishers Group West (PGW).
Peretti, Frank E. Trapped at the Bottom of the Sea. 2004. 144p. (Cooper Kids Adventure Ser.: No. 4). (gr. 4-7). 5.99 *(978-0-89107-594-3(1));* Vol. 4. (Cooper Kids Adventure Ser.: 4). (ENG.). (J). (gr. 3-6). pap. 6.99 *(978-1-58134-621-3(2))* Crossway.
Plum-Ucci, Carol. Fire Will Fall. 2011. (ENG.). 492p. (YA). (gr. 9). pap. 25.99 *(978-0-547-55007-7(3),* 1450217, Clarion Bks.) HarperCollins Pubs.
—Fire Will Fall. 2011. (ENG.). 496p. (YA). (gr. 9-12). 24.94 *(978-0-15-216562-8(2))* Houghton Mifflin Harcourt Publishing Co.
Prose, Francine. Bullyville. 2007. 260p. (YA). (gr. 7-12). 16.99 *(978-0-06-057497-0(6));* lib. bdg. 17.89 *(978-0-06-057498-7(4))* HarperCollins Pubs. (HarperTeen).
Readler, Blaine C. Under the Radar: The Spy Drone Adventure. 2006. (ENG.). 248p. (J). (gr. 7-12). per. *(978-1-933255-18-7(8))* DNA Pr.
Rhodes, Jewell Parker. Towers Falling. (ENG., Illus.). (J). (gr. 3-7). 2018. 256p. pap. 8.99 *(978-0-316-26221-7(8))* 2016. 240p. 16.99 *(978-0-316-26222-4(6))* Little, Brown Bks. for Young Readers.
Saddleback Educational Publishing Staff, ed. Neptune, 1 vol. unabr. ed. 2010. (Heights Ser.). (ENG.). 50p. (gr. 4-8). pap. 9.75 *(978-1-61651-285-9(7))* Saddleback Educational Publishing, Inc.
Seabrooke, Brenda. Stonewolf. 2004. (ENG.). 240p. (J). (gr. 7-18). tchr. ed. 16.95 *(978-0-8234-1848-0(0))* Holiday Hse., Inc.
Smibert, Angie. Memento Nora, 0 vols. 2013. (Memento Nora Ser.: 1). (ENG.). 192p. (YA). (gr. 7-12). pap. 9.99 *(978-1-4778-1624-0(0),* 9781477816240, Skyscape) Amazon Publishing.
Smith, Dan. Boy X. 2017. 274p. (J). *(978-1-338-17150-1(X))* Scholastic, Inc.
Smith, Roland. Independence Hall. (I, Q Ser.: Bk. 1). (ENG., 312p. (YA). (gr. 6-8). 2009. Illus.). 15.95 *(978-1-58536-468-8(1),* 202188) 2008. pap. 12.99 *(978-1-58536-325-4(1),* 202289) Sleeping Bear Pr.
—The White House. 2010. (I, Q Ser.: Bk. 2). (ENG.). 256p. (YA). (gr. 6-8). pap. 9.99 *(978-1-58536-456-5(8),* 202378);Bk. 2. 16.99 *(978-1-58536-478-7(9),* 202191) Sleeping Bear Pr.
Smith, Roland & Spradlin, Michael P. The Alamo. 2013. (I, Q Ser.). (ENG.). 288p. (YA). (gr. 5-8). 16.99 *(978-1-58536-822-8(9),* 202356); pap. 9.99 *(978-1-58536-821-1(0),* 202369) Sleeping Bear Pr.
—Alcatraz. 2014. (I, Q Ser.). (ENG.). 272p. (J). (gr. 5-7). 16.99 *(978-1-58536-826-6(1),* 203667);Bk. 6. pap. 9.99 *(978-1-58536-825-9(3),* 203727) Sleeping Bear Pr.
—I, Q the Windy City, Bk.5. 2014. (I, Q Ser.). (ENG.). 240p. (YA). (gr. 5-7). 9.99 *(978-1-58536-823-5(7),* 202902) Sleeping Bear Pr.
Stanley, Diane. Saving Sky. 2012. (ENG.). 208p. (J). (gr. 3-7). pap. 6.99 *(978-0-06-123907-6(0),* HarperCollins) HarperCollins Pubs.
Strasser, Todd. American Terrorist. 2017. (YA). pap. *(978-1-4814-6134-4(6),* Simon & Schuster Bks. For Young Readers) Simon & Schuster Bks. For Young Readers.
Stratton, Allan. Borderline. 2012. (ENG.). 320p. (YA). (gr. 8). pap. 10.99 *(978-0-06-145113-3(4),* HarperTeen) HarperCollins Pubs.
Tarshis, Lauren. I Survived the Attacks of September 11, 2001. 2012. (I Survived Ser.: No. 6). lib. bdg. 14.75 *(978-0-606-26205-7(9))* Turtleback.
—I Survived the Attacks of September 11th, 2001 (I Survived #6) Dawson, Scott, illus. 2012. (I Survived Ser.: 6). (ENG.). 112p. (J). (gr. 3-7). pap. 5.99 *(978-0-545-20700-3(2),* Scholastic Paperbacks) Scholastic, Inc.
Taylor, Ed. The Dirty Bombers: Terrorism with a Twist. 2013. (ENG.). 192p. pap. *(978-1-78306-044-3(1))* Troubador Publishing Ltd.
Terry, Teri. Fractured: Book Two in the Slated Trilogy. 2014. (Slated Ser.: 2). (ENG.). 352p. (YA). (gr. 7). pap. 10.99 *(978-0-14-242504-6(4),* Speak) Penguin Young Readers Group.
Tzvieli, Neta. The Private Eyes & the Mysterious Submarine. 2009. 149p. 17.99 *(978-1-59826-286-5(6))* Feldheim Pubs.
Walsh, Alice. A Long Way from Home, 1 vol. 2012. (ENG.). 188p. (J). (gr. 4-8). 11.95 *(978-1-926920-79-5(1))* Second Story Pr. CAN. Dist: Orca Bk. Pubs. USA.
Walters, Eric. We All Fall Down. 2006. (We All Fall Down Ser.: 1). (ENG.). 192p. (J). (gr. 5). pap. 9.99 *(978-0-385-66192-8(4))* Doubleday Canada, Ltd. CAN. Dist: Penguin Random Hse. LLC.
Wells, Robison. Blackout. 2014. (Blackout Ser.: 1). (ENG.). 448p. (YA). (gr. 8). pap. 9.99 *(978-0-06-202613-2(5),* HarperTeen) HarperCollins Pubs.
—Dead Zone. 2014. (Blackout Ser.: 2). (ENG.). 384p. (YA). (gr. 8). 17.99 *(978-0-06-227502-8(X),* HarperTeen) HarperCollins Pubs.
Willis, Meredith Sue. Meli's Way. 2015. 178p. (YA). *(978-1-932727-15-9(9))* Montemayor Pr.
Zucker, Jonny. Stunt Girl. 2009. pap. 1.00 *(978-1-4074-4531-1(6))* Recorded Bks., Inc.

TESLA, NIKOLA, 1856-1943

Aldrich, Lisa J. Nikola Tesla & the Taming of Electricity. 2005. (Profiles in Science Ser.). (Illus.). 160p. (J). (gr. 3-7). lib. bdg. 26.95 *(978-1-931798-46-4(X))* Reynolds, Morgan Inc.
Diggory, Nikki. Inventor Nikola Tesla, 1 vol. 2013. (Rosen Readers Ser.). (ENG.). 24p. (J). (gr. 3-3). pap. 8.25 *(978-1-4777-2506-1(7),* 85207d8a-98f4-4d6a-85e2-4f9409be4bf3); pap. 49.50 *(978-1-4777-2507-8(5))* Rosen Publishing Group, Inc., The. (Rosen Classroom).
Gigliotti, Jim & Who HQ. Who Was Nikola Tesla? Hinderliter, John, illus. 2018. (Who Was? Ser.). 112p. (J). (gr. 3-7). 5.99 *(978-0-448-48859-2(0),* Penguin Workshop) Penguin Young Readers Group.
Green, Samantha. Thomas Alva Edison & Nikola Tesla, 1 vol. 2018. (Joined by Fate: Intertwined Biographies Ser.). (ENG.). 128p. (gr. 7-7). 40.27 *(978-0-7660-9821-3(4),* e2c92c1b-90f7-4626-a631-799d25e47646) Enslow Publishing, LLC.
Hardyman, Robyn. Nikola Tesla & Thomas Edison. 2014. (Dynamic Duos of Science Ser.). 48p. (YA). (gr. 5-8). pap. 84.30 *(978-1-4824-1285-7(3))* Stevens, Gareth Publishing LLLP.
Jacobson, Fiona. Nikola Tesla Lights the World, 1 vol. 2013. (InfoMax Readers Ser.). (ENG.). 24p. (J). (gr. 3-3). pap. 8.25 *(978-1-4777-2510-8(5),* 264754b0-a12c-4686-b942-1ebfca7de237); pap. 49.50 *(978-1-4777-2511-5(3))* Rosen Publishing Group, Inc., The. (Rosen Classroom).
Kulling, Monica. Zap! Nikola Tesla Takes Charge. Slavin, Bill, illus. (Great Idea Ser.: 8). 32p. (J). (gr. k-3). 2019. pap. 6.99 *(978-0-7352-6481-6(3))* 2016. 17.99 *(978-1-77049-522-7(3))* Tundra Bks. CAN. (Tundra Bks.). Dist: Penguin Random Hse. LLC.
Marsico, Katie. Inventor, Engineer, & Physicist Nikola Tesla. 2017. (STEM Trailblazer Bios Ser.). (ENG., Illus.). 32p. (J). (gr. 2-5). 26.65 *(978-1-5124-3448-4(5),* aa8b091d-2c4f-440b-8c18-e8195320b211, Lerner Pubns.) Lerner Publishing Group.
O'Quinn, Amy M. Nikola Tesla for Kids: His Life, Ideas, & Inventions, with 21 Activities. 2019. (For Kids Ser.: 72). (Illus.). 144p. (J). (gr. 4). pap. 18.99 *(978-0-912777-21-4(4))* Chicago Review Pr., Inc.
Rusch, Elizabeth. Electrical Wizard. 2015. (Candlewick Biographies Ser.). lib. bdg. 14.75 *(978-0-606-36873-5(6))* Turtleback.
—Electrical Wizard: How Nikola Tesla Lit up the World. Dominguez, Oliver, illus. 2013. (ENG.). 40p. (J). (gr. 2-5). 17.99 *(978-0-7636-5855-7(3))* Candlewick Pr.
Winchell, Mike. The Electric War: Edison, Tesla, Westinghouse, & the Race to Light the World. 2019. (ENG., Illus.). 272p. (YA). 19.99 *(978-1-250-12016-8(0),* 900172928, Holt, Henry & Co. Bks. For Young Readers) Holt, Henry & Co.
Yount, Lisa. Nikola Tesla: Harnessing Electricity. 2011. (Trailblazers in Science & Technology Ser.). (ENG.). 146p. (gr. 6-12). 35.00 *(978-1-60413-670-8(7),* P466236, Facts On File) Infobase Holdings, Inc.

TEST PILOTS

see Air Pilots; Airplanes—Testing

TESTS

see Educational Tests and Measurements

TEXAS

Barenblat, Rachel. Texas, 1 vol. 2003. (World Almanac(r) Biblioteca de Los Estados (World Almanac(r) Library of the States) Ser.). (SPA., Illus.). 48p. (gr. 4-6). lib. bdg. 33.67 *(978-0-8368-5547-0(7),* ea36956f-e4aa-49a2-8434-bff315a1336c, Gareth Stevens Learning Library) Stevens, Gareth Publishing LLLP.
Bodden, Valerie. Texas. 2010. (Let's Explore America Ser.). 24p. (J). (gr. k-2). 19.95 *(978-1-58341-837-6(7))* Creative Co., The.
Boehm Jerome, Kate. Austin & the State of Texas: Cool Stuff Every Kid Should Know. 2011. (Arcadia Kids Ser.). (ENG., Illus.). 48p. (J). (gr. 3-6). pap. 11.99 *(978-1-4396-0088-7(0))* Arcadia Publishing.
Bredeson, Carmen. Rookie Español: Geografía: Estados: Texas. 2005. (Rookie Espanol: Geografia Ser.). (SPA., Illus.). 32p. (J). (gr. k-2). pap. 5.95 *(978-0-516-25516-3(9),* Children's Pr.) Scholastic Library Publishing.
—Texas. 2004. (Rookie Readers Spanish Ser.). (J). 19.50 *(978-0-516-25110-3(4),* Watts, Franklin) Scholastic Library Publishing.
Caravantes, Peggy. O. Henry: William Sidney Porter: Texas Cowboy Writer. 2003. (J). *(978-1-57168-768-5(8),* Eakin Pr.) Eakin Pr.
Craft, Jerry & Sullivan, Kathleen. Pitching for the Stars: My Seasons Across the Color Line. 2013. (ENG., Illus.). 136p. (J). (gr. 4-6). 18.95 *(978-0-89672-787-8(4),* P219178) Texas Tech Univ. Pr.
Davis, Lucile. The Caddo of Texas. 2009. (Library of Native Americans Ser.). 64p. (gr. 4-4). 58.50 *(978-1-60853-743-3(9),* PowerKids Pr.) Rosen Publishing Group, Inc., The.
Doeden, Matt. Yao Ming. 2009. (Sports Heroes & Legends Ser.). (ENG.). 120p. (gr. 5-12). 30.60 *(978-0-7613-4227-4(3))* Lerner Publishing Group.
Dorling Kindersley Publishing Staff. Eyewitness Books - Texas. 2003. (DK Guias Visuales / DK Eyewitness Bks.). (Illus.).

64p. (J). (gr. 5-8). 28.69 *(978-0-7894-9744-4(1))* Dorling Kindersley Publishing, Inc.

Downey, Tika. Texas: The Lone Star State, 1 vol. 2009. (Our Amazing States Ser.). (ENG., Illus.). 24p. (J). (gr. 3-3). pap. 9.25 *(978-1-4358-3344-9(9),* e8d04608-af8d-45ea-a5cc-24e32c6243be); lib. bdg. 26.27 *(978-1-4042-8112-7(6),* f5f87f4f-008a-41ca-8ce8-29d4b3a93fcc) Rosen Publishing Group, Inc., The. (PowerKids Pr.).

Flatt, Lizann. Life in an Industrial City, 1 vol. 2010. (Learn about Urban Life Ser.). (ENG., Illus.). 32p. (J). (gr. 4-9). pap. *(978-0-7787-7402-0(3));* lib. bdg. *(978-0-7787-7392-4(2))* Crabtree Publishing Co.

Flynn, Jean. Texas Women Who Dared to Be First. 2004. (Illus.). 144p. (gr. 4-7). 18.95 *(978-1-57168-232-1(5))* Eakin Pr.

Gamble, Adam & Jasper, Mark. Count to Sleep Texas. Veno, Joe, illus. 2014. (Count to Sleep Ser.). (ENG.). 20p. (J). (— 1). bds. 9.95 *(978-1-60219-326-0(6))* Good Night Bks.

—Good Night Austin. Veno, Joe, illus. 2015. (Good Night Our World Ser.). (ENG.). 20p. (J). (— 1). bds. 9.95 *(978-1-60219-233-1(2))* Good Night Bks.

Golden, Nancy. Life with the Comanches: The Kidnapping of Cynthia Ann Parker. 2009. (Great Moments in American History Ser.). 32p. (gr. 3-3). 47.90 *(978-1-61513-146-4(9))* Rosen Publishing Group, Inc., The.

Hanson-Harding, Alexandra. From Sea to Shining Sea: Texas. 2008. (From Sea to Shining Sea, Second Ser.). (ENG., Illus.). 80p. (J). (gr. 3-5). pap. 7.95 *(978-0-531-18809-5(4),* Children's Pr.) Scholastic Library Publishing.

Heinrichs, Ann. Texas. Kania, Matt, illus. 2017. (U. S. A. Travel Guides). (ENG.). 40p. (J). (gr. 2-5). lib. bdg. 38.50 *(978-1-5038-1983-2(3),* 211620) Child's World, Inc, The.

Herold, Vickey. A Cattle Town: Forth Worth. 2006. (J). pap. *(978-1-4108-6427-7(8))* Benchmark Education Co.

Jacobs Altman, Linda. Texas, 1 vol. Santoro, Christopher, illus. 2003. (It's My State! (First Edition)(r) Ser.). (ENG.). 80p. (gr. 4-4). 34.07 *(978-0-7614-1423-0(1),* bf828cfe-4380-4337-9326-b86f65846c6b) Cavendish Square Publishing LLC.

Levy, Janey. Juneteenth: Celebrating the End of Slavery. 2009. (Reading Room Collection 2 Ser.). 24p. (gr. 3-4). 42.50 *(978-1-60851-976-7(7),* PowerKids Pr.) Rosen Publishing Group, Inc., The.

Madson, Trish. Let's Count Texas: Numbers & Colors in the Lone Star State. Miles, David W., illus. 2017. (ENG.). 20p. (J). (gr. -1 — 1). bds. 12.99 *(978-1-942934-79-0(3),* 553479) Familius LLC.

Marsh, Carole. Texas Current Events Projects: 30 Cool, Activities, Crafts, Experiments & More for Kids to Do to Learn about Your State! 2003. (Texas Experience Ser.). 32p. (gr. k-5). pap. 5.95 *(978-0-635-02062-8(9),* Marsh, Carole Bks.) Gallopade International.

—Texas Geography Projects: 30 Cool, Activities, Crafts, Experiments & More for Kids to Do to Learn about Your State! 2003. (Texas Experience Ser.). 32p. (gr. k-5). pap. 5.95 *(978-0-635-01861-8(6),* Marsh, Carole Bks.) Gallopade International.

—Texas Government Projects: 30 Cool, Activities, Crafts, Experiments & More for Kids to Do to Learn about Your State! 2003. (Texas Experience Ser.). 32p. (gr. k-5). pap. 5.95 *(978-0-635-01962-2(0),* Marsh, Carole Bks.) Gallopade International.

—Texas People Projects: 30 Cool, Activities, Crafts, Experiments & More for Kids to Do to Learn about Your State! 2003. (Texas Experience Ser.). 32p. (gr. k-5). pap. 5.95 *(978-0-635-02012-3(2),* Marsh, Carole Bks.) Gallopade International.

—Texas Symbols & Facts Projects: 30 Cool, Activities, Crafts, Experiments & More for Kids to Do to Learn about Your State! 2003. (Texas Experience Ser.). 32p. (gr. k-5). pap. 5.95 *(978-0-635-01912-7(4),* Marsh, Carole Bks.) Gallopade International.

McAdam, Claudia Cangilla. Do You See What I See? Texas. 2007. (Illus.). (J). (gr. 3-7). 14.95 *(978-1-56579-589-1(X),* Westcliffe Pubs.) Bower Hse.

McNeil, Niki, et al. HOCPP 1120 Texas. 2006. spiral bd. 24.00 *(978-1-60308-120-7(8))* In the Hands of a Child.

Murray, Julie. Texas, 1 vol. 2006. (United States Ser.). (ENG., Illus.). 32p. (gr. 2-4). 27.07 *(978-1-59197-702-5(9),* Buddy Bks.) ABDO Publishing Co.

Obregon, Jose Maria. Texas, 1 vol. De Leon, Mauricio Velzaquez, tr. 2005. (Bilingual Library of the United States of America Ser.: Set 1). (ENG & SPA., Illus.). 32p. (J). (gr. 2-2). lib. bdg. 28.93 *(978-1-4042-3109-2(9),* 8f7de7c6-5274-46aa-9dda-568d1e9903ae) Rosen Publishing Group, Inc., The.

Obregón, José María. Texas. 2009. (Bilingual Library of the United States of America Ser.). 32p. (gr. 2-2). 47.90 *(978-1-60853-387-9(5),* Editorial Buenas Letras) Rosen Publishing Group, Inc., The.

Parker, Bridget. Texas. 2016. (States Ser.). (ENG., Illus.). 32p. (J). (gr. 3-6). lib. bdg. 27.99 *(978-1-5157-0431-7(9),* 132042, Capstone Pr.) Capstone.

Parker, Janice. Texas: The Lone Star State. 2016. (Illus.). 48p. (J). *(978-1-5105-2095-0(3))* SmartBook Media, Inc.

Pelta, Kathy. Texas. (J). 2012. lib. bdg. 25.26 *(978-0-7613-4559-6(0),* Lerner Pubns.) 2nd rev. exp. ed. 2003. (Illus.). 84p. (gr. 3-6). pap. 6.95 *(978-0-8225-4142-4(4))* Lerner Publishing Group.

Peppas, Lynn. Why Charles Goodnight Matters to Texas, 1 vol. 2013. (Texas Perspectives Ser.). (ENG., Illus.). 32p. (J). (gr. 4-4). lib. bdg. 28.93 *(978-1-4777-0907-8(X),* 275a14bc-e2cc-4ff3-88dc-bff250ac8e56) Rosen Publishing Group, Inc., The.

—Why Martín de Léon Matters to Texas, 1 vol. 2013. (Texas Perspectives Ser.). (ENG., Illus.). 32p. (J). (gr. 4-4). lib. bdg. 28.93 *(978-1-4777-0916-0(9),* 137bd19a-875c-40dd-9aa4-4267a46f79a9) Rosen Publishing Group, Inc., The.

Perry, Lucinda. The Ninth Child: Third Edition. 2008. 256p. pap. 19.95 *(978-0-595-52455-6(9))* iUniverse, Inc.

Salch, Megan. 100+ Activities for Houston Kids 2006. 2005. (Illus.). 40p. pap. 19.95 *(978-0-9776154-0-7(5))* Salch, Megan F.

Sanford, William R. & Green, Carl R. Richard King: Courageous Texas Cattleman, 1 vol. 2013. (Courageous Heroes of the American West Ser.). (ENG., Illus.). 48p. (J). (gr. 5-7). pap. 11.53 *(978-1-4644-0088-9(1),* 96233e19-4fed-4d10-bc24-7ca0d56b1d0e) Enslow Publishing, LLC.

Sasek, Miroslav. This Is Texas: A Children's Classic. 2006. (This Is ... Ser.). (ENG., Illus.). 64p. (J). (gr. 2-12). 17.95 *(978-0-7893-1389-8(8))* Universe Publishing.

Smith, Karla. All Around Texas: Regions & Resources. 2003. (Heinemann State Studies). (Illus.). 48p. (J). lib. bdg. 27.07 *(978-1-4034-0686-6(3))* Heinemann-Raintree.

Somervill, Barbara A. America the Beautiful, Third Series: Texas (Revised Edition) 2014. (America the Beautiful Ser.; 3). (ENG., Illus.). 144p. (J). lib. bdg. 40.00 *(978-0-531-24898-0(4))* Scholastic Library Publishing.

—Texas. 2011. (America the Beautiful, Third Ser.). (Illus.). 144p. (J). pap. 12.95 *(978-0-531-22918-7(1),* Children's Pr.) Scholastic Library Publishing.

Stumpff, April D. & Messersmith, Patrick. Ann Richards: A Woman's Place Is in the Dome. 2006. (Stars of Texas Ser.: 6). (ENG., Illus.). 80p. (J). (gr. 4-7). 14.95 *(978-1-933337-12-8(5),* P148096) State Hse. Pr.

Wade, Mary Dodson. Uniquely Texas. 2003. (Heinemann State Studies). (Illus.). 48p. (J). lib. bdg. 27.07 *(978-1-4034-0691-0(X))* Heinemann-Raintree.

Weintraub, A. How to Draw Texas's Sights & Symbols. 2009. (Kid's Guide to Drawing America Ser.). 32p. (gr. k-k). 50.50 *(978-1-61511-097-1(6),* PowerKids Pr.) Rosen Publishing Group, Inc., The.

White, Andrea & Mimi, Vance. Tummies on the Run. Shepperson, Rob, illus. 2012. 32p. pap. 11.95 *(978-1-60898-134-2(7))* namelos llc.

TEXAS—FICTION

Alegria, Malin. Border Town #2: Quince Clash. 2012. (Border Town Ser.). (ENG.). 192p. (J). (gr. 7). pap. 5.99 *(978-0-545-40241-5(7),* Scholastic Paperbacks) Scholastic, Inc.

Allen, George L. Thelma's Boy. 2010. (ENG.). 60p. 24.99 *(978-1-4415-8326-0(2));* pap. 15.99 *(978-1-4415-8325-3(4))* Xlibris Corp.

Altsheler, Joseph A. The Texan Scouts. 2007. (Texan Ser.: Vol. 2). 272p. reprint ed. per. 10.45 *(978-1-60424-305-5(8),* Bk. Jungle) Standard Publications, Inc.

—The Texan Scouts: A Story of the Alamo & Goliad. 2006. (Texan Ser.). 352p. (J). reprint ed. pap. 15.95 *(978-1-4218-1881-8(7),* 1st World Library - Literary Society) 1st World Publishing, Inc.

—The Texan Scouts: A Story of the Alamo & Goliad. 2010. (Texan Ser.: Vol. 2). 376p. (J). (gr. 4-7). reprint ed. pap. 33.75 *(978-1-177-24805-1(0))* Creative Media Partners, LLC.

—The Texan Scouts: A Story of the Alamo & Goliad. 2006. (Texan Ser.: Vol. 2). (J). reprint ed. pap. *(978-1-4065-0826-0(8))* Dodo Pr.

—The Texan Scouts: A Story of the Alamo & Goliad. 2007. (Texan Ser.: Vol. 2). 208p. (J). reprint ed. per. *(978-1-4068-1691-4(4))* Echo Library.

—The Texan Scouts: A Story of the Alamo & Goliad. 2010. (Texan Ser.: Vol. 2). (Illus.). 184p. (J). (gr. 4-7). reprint ed. pap. 19.99 *(978-1-4432-3075-9(8))* General Bks. LLC.

—The Texan Scouts: A Story of the Alamo & Goliad. (Texan Ser.: Vol. 2). (J). reprint ed. 2012. 380p. (gr. 4-7). pap. *(978-1-290-32714-5(9))* 2010. 258p. pap. *(978-1-4076-1525-7(4))* HardPr.

—The Texan Scouts: A Story of the Alamo & Goliad. (Texan Ser.: Vol. 2). (J). reprint ed. 2011. 362p. (gr. 4-7). 46.95 *(978-1-169-83723-2(9))* 2010. 362p. (gr. 4-7). 37.56 *(978-1-163-21368-1(3))* 2010. 362p. (gr. 4-7). pap. 25.56 *(978-1-162-64067-9(7))* 2004. 360p. 46.95 *(978-1-4326-1538-3(6))* 2004. pap. 31.95 *(978-1-4179-1479-1(3))* Kessinger Publishing, LLC.

—The Texan Scouts: A Story of the Alamo & Goliad. 2008. (Texan Ser.: Vol. 2). 364p. (J). reprint ed. per. *(978-1-4086-5013-4(4))* Read Bks.

—The Texan Scouts: A Story of the Alamo & Goliad. 2011. (Texan Ser.: Vol. 2). 290p. (J). (gr. 4-7). reprint ed. pap. *(978-3-8424-7933-3(6))* tredition Verlag.

—The Texan Star: The Story of a Great Fight for Liberty. 2006. (Texan Ser.: Vol. 1). 364p. (J). reprint ed. 31.95 *(978-1-4218-1782-8(9));* pap. 15.95 *(978-1-4218-1882-5(5))* 1st World Publishing, Inc. (1st World Library - Literary Society).

—The Texan Star: The Story of a Great Fight for Liberty. (Texan Ser.: Vol. 1). (J). reprint ed. 26.95 *(978-0-8488-0729-0(4))* Amereon Ltd.

—The Texan Star: The Story of a Great Fight for Liberty. 2010. (Texan Ser.: Vol. 1). 398p. (J). pap. 33.75 *(978-1-145-48797-0(1))* Creative Media Partners, LLC.

—The Texan Star: The Story of a Great Fight for Liberty. 2006. (Texan Ser.: Vol. 1). (J). reprint ed. pap. *(978-1-4065-0827-7(6))* Dodo Pr.

—The Texan Star: The Story of a Great Fight for Liberty. 2007. (Texan Ser.: Vol. 1). 216p. (J). reprint ed. per. *(978-1-4068-1692-1(2))* Echo Library.

—The Texan Star: The Story of a Great Fight for Liberty. (Texan Ser.: Vol. 1). (J). reprint ed. 2010. 192p. (gr. 4-7). pap. 19.99 *(978-1-4432-0955-7(4))* 2009. 228p. pap. 12.02 *(978-1-150-78580-1(2))* General Bks. LLC.

—The Texan Star: The Story of a Great Fight for Liberty. 2010. (Texan Ser.: Vol. 1). 268p. (J). reprint ed. pap. *(978-1-4076-1570-7(X))* HardPr.

—The Texan Star: The Story of a Great Fight for Liberty. 2011. (Texan Ser.: Vol. 1). 304p. (J). (gr. 4-7). reprint ed. pap. *(978-3-8424-7958-6(1))* tredition Verlag.

—The Texan Triumph: A Romance of the San Jacinto Campaign. (Texan Ser.: Vol. 3). (J). reprint ed. 24.95 *(978-0-8488-0731-3(6))* Amereon Ltd.

Ames, Joseph B. Pete Cow Puncher a Story of the Texas Plains. Perard, Victor, illus. 2005. reprint ed. pap. 31.95 *(978-0-7661-9421-2(3))* Kessinger Publishing, LLC.

Anderson, T. Neill. City of the Dead: Galveston Hurricane 1900. 2013. (J). pap. 16.95 *(978-1-58089-515-6(8))* Charlesbridge Publishing, Inc.

—Horrors of History: City of the Dead: Galveston Hurricane 1900. 2013. (Horrors of History Ser.). (Illus.). 144p. (J). (gr. 5). 16.95 *(978-1-58089-514-9(X))* Charlesbridge Publishing, Inc.

Appelt, Kathi. Angel Thieves. (ENG.). 336p. (YA). (gr. 9). 2020. pap. 11.99 *(978-1-4423-3966-8(7),* Atheneum Bks. for Young Readers) 2019. 18.99 *(978-1-4424-2109-7(6),* Atheneum/Caitlyn Dlouhy Books) Simon & Schuster Children's Publishing.

Aryal, Aimee. How 'Bout Them Cowboys! De Angel, Miguel, illus. 2007. 24p. (J). 17.95 *(978-1-932888-90-4(X))* Amplify Publishing Group.

—How 'Bout Them Cowboys! Coloring Book. 2007. (YA). pap. 4.95 *(978-1-932888-77-5(2))* Amplify Publishing Group.

Ashford, Rachel. My First Santa's Coming to Texas. Dunn, Robert, illus. 2015. (Santa Claus Is on His Way Ser.). (ENG.). 18p. (J). (gr. -1-k). bds. 9.99 *(978-1-4926-2870-5(0),* Hometown World) Sourcebooks, Inc.

Aunt Julie. Paddleduck! #2: Julie, Living in Texas. 2011. 56p. pap. *(978-1-4269-6656-9(3))* Trafford Publishing (UK) Ltd.

Badeaux, Dewey. Sam & Skully. Ball, Lauren, illus. 2013. 126p. pap. 12.99 *(978-0-9884057-4-5(1))* Alligator Pr.

Balcarcel, Rebecca. The Other Half of Happy: (Middle Grade Novel for Ages 9-12, Bilingual Tween Book) 2019. (ENG., Illus.). 332p. (J). (gr. 5-9). 16.99 *(978-1-4521-6998-9(5))* Chronicle Bks. LLC.

Bass, William E. Santa Revisits His Secret Little Helper. Salazar, Vivian, illus. 2012. 26p. 24.95 *(978-1-4626-5396-6(0))* America Star Bks.

Bauer, Joan. Rules of the Road. 2005. (ENG.). 208p. (YA). (gr. 7-7). pap. 9.99 *(978-0-14-240425-6(X),* Speak) Penguin Young Readers Group.

Bauld, Jane Scoggins. Hector Visits His Country Cousin, Vol. 3. Laronde, Gary, illus. 2003. (Hector's Escapades Ser.). 25p. (J). (gr. -1). per. 7.95 *(978-1-57168-676-3(2))* Eakin Pr.

Bedford, David A. Angela. 2009. 190p. 25.50 *(978-1-60860-755-6(0),* Eloquent Bks.) Strategic Book Publishing & Rights Agency (SBPRA).

Bertrand, Diane Gonzales. The F Factor. 2010. 256p. (J). (gr. 6-18). pap. 12.95 *(978-1-55885-598-4(X),* Piñata Books) Arte Publico Pr.

Bhakta, Sanjini. My Life as a Dollar Bill. 2010. 28p. pap. 12.95 *(978-1-4520-6152-8(1))* AuthorHouse.

Blair, Eric. Pecos Bill, 1 vol. Chambers-Goldberg, Micah, illus. 2013. (My First Classic Story Ser.).Tr. of Pecos Bill. (ENG.). 32p. (J). (gr. k-3). pap. 7.10 *(978-1-4795-1860-9(3),* 123450, Picture Window Bks.) Capstone.

Blue, Parker. Catch Me. 2015. (ENG., Illus.). 222p. (J). pap. 14.95 *(978-1-61194-623-9(9))* BelleBks., Inc.

Borgia, Mary. Tales of the Texas Mermaid: The Boot. 2006. (Illus.). 47p. (J). 17.95 *(978-0-9778451-0-1(9))* Goretti Publishing.

—Tales of the Texas Mermaid: The Charro. 2007. (J). 17.95 *(978-0-9778451-1-8(7))* Goretti Publishing.

Borntrager, Mary Christner. Polly. 2015. (ENG.). 176p. (YA). (gr. 4-7). pap. 9.99 *(978-0-8361-3670-8(5))* Herald Pr.

Bradley, Sharon. Walking Away from Texas. 2004. 112p. (YA). pap. 10.95 *(978-0-595-32672-3(2))* iUniverse, Inc.

Brehm, David L. Willy Nilly Volume 1. Claerhout, Paul, illus. 2013. 94p. (J). pap. 19.95 *(978-0-9860669-0-0(7))* Blue Logic Publishing.

Brett, Jan. Armadillo Rodeo. Brett, Jan, illus. 2004. (Illus.). 32p. (J). (gr. -1-3). pap. 8.99 *(978-0-14-240125-5(0),* Puffin Books) Penguin Young Readers Group.

A Brother's Sin. 2008. 84p. pap. 9.95 *(978-1-934335-21-5(5))* WordWright.biz, Inc.

Burns, A. M. & Ricci, Caitlin. Running with the Pack. 2017. (ENG., Illus.). (YA). 25.99 *(978-1-64080-359-6(9),* Harmony Ink Pr.) Dreamspinner Pr.

Cagan, Kayla. Piper Perish. 2017. (ENG., Illus.). 416p. (YA). 17.99 *(978-1-4521-5583-8(6))* Chronicle Bks. LLC.

Caine, Rachel, pseud. Bite Club: The Morganville Vampires, 10 vols. 2011. (Morganville Vampires Ser.: 10). (ENG.). 368p. (YA). (gr. 9). pap. 9.99 *(978-0-451-23468-1(5),* Berkley) Penguin Publishing Group.

—Bitter Blood: The Morganville Vampires. 2013. (Morganville Vampires Ser.: 13). (ENG.). 432p. (YA). (gr. 9). pap. 9.99 *(978-0-451-41424-3(1),* Berkley) Penguin Publishing Group.

—Black Dawn: The Morganville Vampires. 2012. (Morganville Vampires Ser.: 12). (ENG.). 400p. (YA). (gr. 9). pap. 9.99 *(978-0-451-23793-4(5),* Berkley) Penguin Publishing Group.

—Carpe Corpus: The Morganville Vampires, Book 6. 2009. (Morganville Vampires Ser.: 6). (ENG.). 256p. (YA). (gr. 9-18). mass mkt. 7.99 *(978-0-451-22719-5(0),* Berkley) Penguin Publishing Group.

—Feast of Fools. 2008. (Morganville Vampires Ser.: Bk. 4). 256p. (YA). lib. bdg. 20.00 *(978-1-4242-4702-8(0))* Fitzgerald Bks.

—Feast of Fools: The Morganville Vampires, Book 4. 2008. (Morganville Vampires Ser.: 4). (ENG.). 256p. (YA). (gr. 9-18). mass mkt. 7.99 *(978-0-451-22463-7(9),* Berkley) Penguin Publishing Group.

—Ghost Town: The Morganville Vampires, 9 vols. 2011. (Morganville Vampires Ser.: 9). (ENG.). 368p. (YA). (gr. 9-18). 9.99 *(978-0-451-23291-5(7),* Berkley) Penguin Publishing Group.

—Kiss of Death: The Morganville Vampires, 8 vols. 2010. (Morganville Vampires Ser.: 8). (ENG.). 256p. (YA). (gr. 9-18). 6.99 *(978-0-451-22973-1(8),* Berkley) Penguin Publishing Group.

—Last Breath: The Morganville Vampires, 11 vols. 2012. (Morganville Vampires Ser.: 11). (ENG.). 368p. (YA). (gr. 9). 9.99 *(978-0-451-23580-0(0),* Berkley) Penguin Publishing Group.

—Lord of Misrule. 2009. (Morganville Vampires Ser.: Bk. 5). 352p. (YA). lib. bdg. 20.00 *(978-1-4242-4704-2(7))* Fitzgerald Bks.

—Lord of Misrule: The Morganville Vampires, Book 5. 2009. (Morganville Vampires Ser.: 5). (ENG.). 256p. (YA). (gr. 9-18). mass mkt. 7.99 *(978-0-451-22572-6(4),* Berkley) Penguin Publishing Group.

—Midnight Alley. 2007. (Morganville Vampires Ser.: Bk. 3). 256p. (YA). lib. bdg. 20.00 *(978-1-4242-4705-9(5))* Fitzgerald Bks.

—Midnight Alley: The Morganville Vampires, Book III. 2007. (Morganville Vampires Ser.: 3). (ENG.). 256p. (YA). (gr. 9-18). mass mkt. 7.99 *(978-0-451-22238-1(5),* Berkley) Penguin Publishing Group.

—The Morganville Vampires, Volume 2, 2. 2010. (Morganville Vampires Ser.: Bks. 3-4). (ENG.). 464p. (YA). (gr. 9-12). pap. 9.99 *(978-0-451-23289-2(5),* Berkley) Penguin Publishing Group.

—The Morganville Vampires, Volume 3, Vol. 3. 2011. (Morganville Vampires Ser.: Bks. 5-6). (ENG.). 464p. (YA). (gr. 9-18). 9.99 *(978-0-451-23355-4(7),* Berkley) Penguin Publishing Group.

—The Morganville Vampires, Volume 4, Vol. 4. 2011. (Morganville Vampires Ser.: Bks. 7-8). (ENG.). 464p. (YA). (gr. 9-18). 12.99 *(978-0-451-23426-1(X),* Berkley) Penguin Publishing Group.

Campbell, Isaiah. AbrakaPOW. Perillo, Dave, illus. 2016. (ENG.). 400p. (J). (gr. 3-7). 16.99 *(978-1-4814-2634-3(6),* Simon & Schuster Bks. For Young Readers) Simon & Schuster Bks. For Young Readers.

Canales, Viola. The Tequila Worm. 2007. (ENG., Illus.). 208p. (YA). (gr. 7-11). pap. 7.99 *(978-0-375-84089-0(3),* Lamb, Wendy Bks.) Random Hse. Children's Bks.

Castilla, Julia Mercedes. Strange Parents. 2009. 144p. (J). (gr. 6-18). pap. 9.95 *(978-1-55885-590-8(4),* Piñata Books) Arte Publico Pr.

Chrismer, Melanie. Phoebe Clappsaddle for Sheriff, 1 vol. Roeder, Virginia M., illus. 2003. (Phoebe Clappsaddle Ser.). (ENG.). 32p. (J). (gr. k-3). 16.99 *(978-1-58980-127-1(X),* Pelican Publishing) Arcadia Publishing.

Christian, Diana. The Lucky Seven. 2005. 71p. pap. 19.95 *(978-1-4137-5471-1(6))* America Star Bks.

Clement-Moore, Rosemary. Texas Gothic. 2012. (ENG.). 416p. (YA). (gr. 9). pap. 10.99 *(978-0-385-73694-7(0),* Ember) Random Hse. Children's Bks.

Clifton, Lutricia. Seeking Cassandra. 2016. (ENG.). 192p. (J). (gr. 3-7). 16.95 *(978-0-8234-3560-9(1))* Holiday Hse., Inc.

Clifton Wisler, G. All for Texas. 2004. 140p. (J). lib. bdg. 16.92 *(978-1-4242-0767-1(3))* Fitzgerald Bks.

Coleman, Jennifer. The Texas Nutcracker, 1 vol. 2018. (ENG., Illus.). 32p. (gr. k-3). 16.99 *(978-1-4556-2331-0(8),* Pelican Publishing) Arcadia Publishing.

Cooner, Donna. Worthy. 2017. (ENG.). 288p. (YA). (gr. 7). 17.99 *(978-0-545-90393-6(9))* Scholastic, Inc.

Cooper, Floyd. Juneteenth for Mazie. Cooper, Floyd, illus. 2015. (ENG., Illus.). 40p. (J). (gr. 1-4). lib. bdg. 25.32 *(978-1-4795-5819-3(2),* 126912, Picture Window Bks.) Capstone.

Corgliano, K. L. Millie & Me, 1 vol. 2009. 29p. pap. 24.95 *(978-1-60813-935-4(2))* America Star Bks.

Cousins Camp. 2010. 32p. pap. 12.99 *(978-1-4490-8387-8(0))* AuthorHouse.

Crawford, Ann Fears. Keechee: The Witch of the Woods. 2005. (J). *(978-1-931823-21-0(9))* Halcyon Pr.

Crosby, Jeff, illus. Ten Texas Babies, 1 vol. 2014. (ENG.). 32p. (gr. k-3). 16.99 *(978-1-4556-1874-3(8),* Pelican Publishing) Arcadia Publishing.

Crowley, Suzanne. The Very Ordered Existence of Merilee Marvelous. 2007. 380p. (J). (gr. 5-9). 16.99 *(978-0-06-123197-1(5),* Greenwillow Bks.) HarperCollins Pubs.

Crownover, Rebecca. Texas Farm Girl. Daigle, Brian, illus. 2013. (ENG.). (J). (gr. -1-3). 14.95 *(978-1-62086-265-0(4))* Amplify Publishing Group.

Cuate, Melodie A. Journey to Galveston. 2014. (Mr. Barrington's Mysterious Trunk Ser.). (ENG., Illus.). 192p. (J). 18.95 *(978-0-89672-852-3(8))* Texas Tech Univ. Pr.

—Journey to Goliad. 2009. (Mr. Barrington's Mysterious Trunk Ser.). (ENG., Illus.). 176p. (J). (gr. 4-6). 18.95 *(978-0-89672-649-9(5),* P171404) Texas Tech Univ. Pr.

—Journey to Gonzales. 2008. (Mr. Barrington's Mysterious Trunk Ser.). (ENG., Illus.). 174p. (J). (gr. 4-6). 18.95 *(978-0-89672-624-6(X),* P171712) Texas Tech Univ. Pr.

—Journey to la Salle's Settlement. 2010. (Mr. Barrington's Mysterious Trunk Ser.). (ENG., Illus.). 184p. (J). (gr. 4-6). lib. bdg. 18.95 *(978-0-89672-704-5(1),* P176357) Texas Tech Univ. Pr.

—Journey to San Jacinto. 2007. (Mr. Barrington's Mysterious Trunk Ser.). (ENG., Illus.). 160p. (J). (gr. 4-6). 18.95 *(978-0-89672-602-4(9),* P171713) Texas Tech Univ. Pr.

Cummings, W. L. A Far West Texas Christmas, 1 vol. 2009. 25p. pap. 19.95 *(978-1-4489-9402-1(0))* PublishAmerica, Inc.

Czerw, Nancy Carpenter. Itty & Bitty - On the Road. Berlin, Rose Mary, illus. 2008. (Itty & Bitty Ser.: 3). (ENG.). 32p. (J). (gr. -1-3). 16.95 *(978-0-9755618-4-3(7))* McWitty Pr., Inc.

Dahlstrom, S. J. Texas Grit: the Adventures of Wilder Good #2. 2014. (Adventures of Wilder Good Ser.: 2). (ENG.). 141p. (J). (gr. 3). pap. 9.95 *(978-1-58988-094-8(3))* Dry, Paul Bks., Inc.

Davis, David. Texas Zeke & the Longhorn, 1 vol. Stacy, Alan, illus. 2018. (ENG.). 36p. (gr. -1-3). 11.95 *(978-1-4556-2421-8(7),* Pelican Publishing) Arcadia Publishing.

Davis, Peg. After the Storm: A Napoleon & Marigold Adventure. 2009. 40p. pap. 16.50 *(978-1-60860-222-3(2),* Eloquent Bks.) Strategic Book Publishing & Rights Agency (SBPRA).

—Napoleon & Marigold. 2008. 24p. pap. 13.50 *(978-1-60693-114-1(8),* Eloquent Bks.) Strategic Book Publishing & Rights Agency (SBPRA).

Dean, Carolee. Comfort. 2004. (ENG.). 256p. (YA). (gr. 7-18). pap. 14.95 *(978-0-618-43912-6(9),* 410118, Clarion Bks.) HarperCollins Pubs.

—Take Me There. 2010. (ENG.). 336p. (YA). (gr. 9-18). pap. 8.99 *(978-1-4169-8950-9(1),* Simon Pulse) Simon Pulse.

Decter, Ed. VIP Lounge. 2009. (Chloe Gamble Ser.). (ENG.). 352p. (YA). (gr. 9-18). pap. 9.99 *(978-1-4169-5436-1(8),* Simon Pulse) Simon Pulse.

Delp, Randy. The Ugly Bug & the Beautiful Butterfly. 2011. 76p. pap. *(978-1-4269-5354-5(2))* Trafford Publishing (UK) Ltd.

Dillon, Kimberly M. The Ghosts of Wolf Creek. 2008. 73p. pap. 19.95 *(978-1-60563-996-3(6))* America Star Bks.

Edgell, Ernest. The Cowbears of Texas: The Hero. Haycraft, Marilynn J., illus. 2004. 25p. pap. 24.95 *(978-1-4137-3507-9(X))* PublishAmerica, Inc.

Elliott, Alan. Willy the Texas Longhorn, 1 vol. Ford, Stephanie, illus. 2013. (ENG.). 32p. (J). (gr. k-3). 16.99 *(978-1-4556-1870-5(5),* Pelican Publishing) Arcadia Publishing.

Ellsberry, Sharon. The Spaniel Family Goes to the State Fair. Espinosa, Chris, illus. 2004. 24p. (J). 9.00 *(978-0-9724637-2-0(0))* Sky Rocket Pr.

Enderle, Dotti. The Cotton Candy Catastrophe at the Texas State Fair, 1 vol. Galey, Chuck, illus. 2004. (ENG.). 32p. (J).

TUV

(gr. k-3). 19.99 (978-1-58980-189-9(X), Pelican Publishing) Arcadia Publishing.
Epner, Paul. Herbert Hilligan's Lone Star Adventure. Kuon, Vuthy & Nguyen, Duke, illus. 2003. 32p. (J). 15.95 (978-0-9743335-3-3(0)) Imaginative Publishing, Ltd.
Erdman, Loula Grace. The Good Land. 2008. (ENG.). 185p. (J). (gr. 3-4). pap. 12.95 (978-1-932350-13-5(6)) Ignatius Pr.
—The Wind Blows Free. 2006. (Tales of the Texas Panhandle Ser.). (ENG.). 271p. (J). (gr. 7-9). pap. 13.95 (978-1-932350-09-8(8)) Ignatius Pr.
Erickson, John. The Big Question. Holmes, Gerald L., illus. 2012. 128p. (J). pap. (978-1-59188-160-5(9)) Maverick Bks.
—The Big Question. Holmes, Gerald L., illus. 2012. (Hank the Cowdog Ser.: Vol. 60). (ENG.). 128p. (J). (gr. 3-6). 15.99 (978-1-59188-260-2(5)) Maverick Bks., Inc.
—The Case of the Blazing Sky. Holmes, Gerald L., illus. 2011. (Hank the Cowdog Ser.). (ENG.). 129p. (J). (gr. 3-6). pap. 5.99 (978-1-59188-151-3(X)) Maverick Bks., Inc.
—The Case of the Booby-Trapped Pickup. Holmes, Gerald L., illus. 2011. (Hank the Cowdog Ser.). (ENG.). 129p. (J). (gr. 3-6). pap. 5.99 (978-1-59188-149-0(8)) Maverick Bks., Inc.
—The Case of the Coyote Invasion. Holmes, Gerald L., illus. 2011. (Hank the Cowdog Ser.: No. 56). (ENG.). 132p. (J). (gr. 3-6). pap. 5.99 (978-1-59188-156-8(0)) Maverick Bks., Inc.
—The Case of the Dinosaur Birds. Holmes, Gerald L., illus. 2011. (Hank the Cowdog Ser.). (ENG.). 125p. (J). (gr. 3-6). pap. 5.99 (978-1-59188-154-4(4)) Maverick Bks., Inc.
—The Case of the Mysterious Voice. Holmes, Gerald L., illus. 2012. (Hank the Cowdog (Quality) Ser.: Vol. 58). (ENG.). 123p. (J). (gr. 3-6). pap. 5.99 (978-1-59188-158-2(7)) Maverick Bks., Inc.
—The Case of the Perfect Dog. Holmes, Gerald L., illus. 2012. 127p. (J). (978-1-59188-259-6(1)) Maverick Bks.
—The Case of the Perfect Dog. Holmes, Gerald L., illus. 2012. (Hank the Cowdog (Quality) Ser.). (ENG.). 127p. (J). (gr. 3-6). pap. 5.99 (978-1-59188-159-9(5)) Maverick Bks., Inc.
—The Case of the Secret Weapon. Holmes, Gerald L., illus. 2011. (Hank the Cowdog Ser.). (ENG.). 125p. (J). (gr. 3-6). pap. 5.99 (978-1-59188-155-1(2)) Maverick Bks., Inc.
—The Disappearance of Drover. Holmes, Gerald L., illus. 2011. (Hank the Cowdog Ser.). (ENG.). 122p. (J). (gr. 3-6). pap. 5.99 (978-1-59188-157-5(9)) Maverick Bks., Inc.
—Drover's Secret Life. Holmes, Gerald L., illus. 2011. (Hank the Cowdog Ser.). (ENG.). 118p. (J). (gr. 3-6). pap. 5.99 (978-1-59188-153-7(6)) Maverick Bks., Inc.
Erickson, John & Holmes, Gerald L., illus. The Case of the Prowling Bear. 2013. 126p. (J). (978-1-59188-261-9(3)) Maverick Bks.
Estevis, Anne. Chicken Foot Farm. 2008. 154p. (J). (gr. 6-18). pap. 10.95 (978-1-55885-505-2(X), Piñata Books) Arte Publico Pr.
—Down Garrapata Road. 2003. 128p. (J). pap. 12.95 (978-1-55885-397-3(9)) Arte Publico Pr.
Fehlbaum, Beth. Big Fat Disaster. (ENG.). (YA). 2015. 286p. pap. 9.99 (978-1-4405-9267-6(5)) 2014. 288p. 17.99 (978-1-4405-7048-3(5)) Simon Pulse. (Simon Pulse).
—Hope in Patience. 2010. 312p. (YA). (gr. 8-18). 16.95 (978-1-934813-41-6(9)) Westside Bks.
Fields, Jan. Chase the Chupacabra, 1 vol. Brundage, Scott, illus. 2014. (Monster Hunters Ser.). (ENG.). 80p. (J). (gr. 2-5). 35.64 (978-1-62402-044-5(5), 1523, Calico Chapter Bks.) ABDO Publishing Co.
Fisher, Karianne M. A Pup Named Moose. 2011. 20p. pap. 24.95 (978-1-4512-3373-5(6)) America Star Bks.
Fisher, Karianne Marie. In a Land Called Hogeye, 1 vol. 2010. 24p. pap. 24.95 (978-1-4489-8798-6(9)) PublishAmerica, Inc.
Fitzgibbon, Diana. Somewhere in Texas. Gonzales, Diana, ed. Del Toro, Mark, illus. 2004. 32p. (J). (978-0-9747587-0-1(1)) Mike-Auri Bks.
Flemmer, Chip. Out of Texas, 1 vol. 2010. 183p. pap. 24.95 (978-1-4489-2918-4(0)) America Star Bks.
Flores, Carlos Nicolas. Our House on Hueco. 2006. (ENG.). 234p. (gr. 8-12). per. 17.95 (978-0-89672-573-7(1), P171748) Texas Tech Univ. Pr.
Freeman, Shannon. Traumatized. 2014. (Port City High Ser.: 7). (YA). lib. bdg. 20.80 (978-0-606-36619-9(9)) Turtleback.
G & G Wilcox. Tex, the Little Caterpillar from Texas. 2009. 68p. pap. 41.99 (978-1-4363-6494-2(9)) Xlibris Corp.
Gaard, Betty. Jericho Ride. 2003. (Illus.). 165p. (J). pap. 8.99 (978-1-57924-968-7(X)) BJU Pr.
Galbraith, Julie. Stable Ground: The Riding Series #1. 2013. 136p. pap. (978-1-927794-05-0(6)) Lechner Syndications.
Gamble, Adam. Good Night Texas. Veno, Joe & Kelly, Cooper, illus. 2nd ed. 2011. (Good Night Our World Ser.). (ENG.). 20p. (J). (gr. k — 1). bds. 9.95 (978-1-60219-053-5(4)) Good Night Bks.
Gamble, Adam & Jasper, Mark. Buenas Noches, Texas. 2013. (Buenas Noches Ser.). (SPA., Illus.). 20p. (J). (— 1). bds. 9.95 (978-1-60219-093-1(3)) Good Night Bks.
Garcia McCall, Guadalupe. All the Stars Denied, 1 vol. 2018. (ENG.). 336p. (YA). (gr. 6-12). 19.95 (978-1-62014-281-3(3), leelowtu, Tu Bks.) Lee & Low Bks., Inc.
—Shame the Stars, 1 vol., 1. 2016. (Shame the Stars Ser.: 1). (ENG.). 320p. (YA). (gr. 7-12). 21.95 (978-1-62014-278-3(3), leelowtu) Lee & Low Bks., Inc.
—Summer of the Mariposas. 2012. (ENG.). 352p. (YA). 19.95 (978-1-60060-900-8(7), Tu Bks.) Lee & Low Bks., Inc.
Garza, Xavier. Creepy Creatures & Other Cucuys. 2004. (Illus.). 144p. pap. 9.95 (978-1-55885-410-9(X), Piñata Books) Arte Publico Pr.
—Maximilian & the Mystery of the Guardian Angel, 1 vol. Garza, Xavier, illus. 2011. (Max's Lucha Libre Adventures Ser.: 1). (ENG., Illus.). 208p. (J). (gr. 3-7). pap. 18.95 (978-1-933693-98-9(3), 23353382, Cinco Puntos Press) Lee & Low Bks., Inc.
Gentry, Jennifer Mills. Maria's 4th of July. 2011. 32p. pap. 24.95 (978-1-4560-7300-8(1)) America Star Bks.
Gibbs, Stuart. Poached. (FunJungle Ser.). (ENG., Illus.). 352p. (J). (gr. 3-7). 2015. pap. 8.99 (978-1-4424-6778-1(9)) 2014. 18.99 (978-1-4424-6777-4(0)) Simon & Schuster Bks. For Young Readers. (Simon & Schuster Bks. For Young Readers).
Gipson, Fred. Old Yeller. Date not set. 192p. (J). 20.95 (978-0-8488-2273-6(0)) Amereon Ltd.
—Old Yeller. 2009. (Perennial Classics Ser.). 132p. (gr. 4-7). 20.85 (978-0-613-85744-4(5)) Turtleback.
Gipson, Fred & Polson, Steven. Old Yeller. 2009. (ENG., Illus.). 144p. (gr. 4-7). pap. 13.99 (978-0-06-093547-4(2), Harper Perennial Modern Classics) HarperCollins Pubs.
Goode, John. 151 Days. 2016. (ENG., Illus.). (J). 32.99 (978-1-63477-925-8(8), Harmony Ink Pr.) Dreamspinner Pr.
Green, Tim. The Big Game. (ENG.). (J). (gr. 3-7). 2019. 336p. pap. 9.99 (978-0-06-248561-8(X)) 2018. 320p. 16.99 (978-0-06-248504-5(0)) HarperCollins Pubs. (HarperCollins).
Griffin, Kitty & Combs, Kathy. Stinker & the Onion Princess. Manders, John, illus. 2005. (J). (978-0-8037-2976-6(6), Dial) Penguin Publishing Group.
Gunderson, Jessica. Carrie & the Great Storm: A Galveston Hurricane Survival Story. Forsyth, Matt, illus. 2019. (Girls Survive Ser.). (ENG.). 112p. (J). (gr. 3-7). pap. 7.95 (978-1-4965-8447-2(3), 140972); lib. bdg. 26.65 (978-1-4965-8385-7(X), 140681) Capstone. (Stone Arch Bks.).
Gurevich, Margaret. Gina's Balance. 2016. (What's Your Dream? Ser.). (ENG., Illus.). 96p. (J). (gr. 4-6). lib. bdg. 25.99 (978-1-4965-3443-9(3), 132565) Capstone.
Haden, Robbie. Run Girl Run. 2013. 116p. 28.95 (978-1-4525-6779-2(4)); pap. 11.99 (978-1-4525-6777-8(8)) Author Solutions, LLC. (Balboa Pr.).
Hale, Marian. Dark Water Rising. 2010. (ENG.). 256p. (J). (gr. 6-8). pap. 8.99 (978-0-312-62908-3(7), 900066872) Square Fish.
—The Truth about Sparrows. 2007. (ENG.). 288p. (YA). (gr. 6-8). pap. 11.99 (978-0-312-37133-3(0), 900044661) Square Fish.
Harper, Jo. Mayor Jalapeno Hal from Presidio, Texas. 2003. (Illus.). (J). (978-1-57168-767-8(X), Eakin Pr.) Eakin Pr.
—Teresa's Journey. 2006. (ENG., Illus.). 162p. (J). (gr. 4-6). per. 17.95 (978-0-89672-591-1(X), P171799) Texas Tech Univ. Pr.
Harper, Suzanne. The Unseen World of Poppy Malone: A Gaggle of Goblins. 2012. (Unseen World of Poppy Malone Ser.: 1). (ENG.). 320p. (J). (gr. 3-7). pap. 6.99 (978-0-06-199609-2(2), Greenwillow Bks.) HarperCollins Pubs.
Harrington, Karen. Sure Signs of Crazy. 2014. (ENG.). 304p. (J). (gr. 5-17). pap. 7.00 (978-0-316-21049-2(8)) Little, Brown Bks. for Young Readers.
Heasley, Gwendolyn. Where I Belong. 2011. (Where I Belong Ser.: 1). (ENG.). 304p. (YA). (gr. 8-18). pap. 9.99 (978-0-06-197884-5(1), HarperTeen) HarperCollins Pubs.
Hees, Miriam. The Adventures of Jilly & Brad: Noises in the Attic. Kinneman, D. Michael, illus. 2003. 128p. (J). pap. 5.95 (978-0-9718348-4-2(9)) Blooming Tree Pr.
Heflin, Ronald. Caddo Lake. 2011. 156p. pap. 24.95 (978-1-4626-0093-9(X)) America Star Bks.
Herbert Hilligan & His Magical Adventure Curriculum Guide. 2004. ring bd. 24.95 (978-0-9743335-4-0(9)) Imaginative Publishing, Ltd.
Herbert Hilligan's Lone Star Adventure Curriculum Guide. 2004. ring bd. 24.95 (978-0-9743335-7-1(3)) Imaginative Publishing, Ltd.
Hesse, Monica. The War Outside. (ENG.). (YA). (gr. 7-17). 2019. 352p. pap. 10.99 (978-0-316-31671-2(7)) 2018. (Illus.). 336p. 34.99 (978-0-316-31669-9(5)) Little, Brown Bks. for Young Readers.
Higman, Anita. The Living Darkness: Texas Caves. 2nd ed. 2003. (Illus.). xiii, 93p. (J). (978-1-57168-783-8(1), Eakin Pr.) Eakin Pr.
Hobbs, Will. Take Me to the River. (ENG.). (J). (gr. 5). 2012. 208p. pap. 6.99 (978-0-06-074146-4(5)) 2011. 192p. 15.99 (978-0-06-074144-0(9)) HarperCollins Pubs. (HarperCollins).
Holt, Kimberly Willis. Dancing in Cadillac Light. 2003. 176p. (J). (gr. 5-9). 5.99 (978-0-698-11970-3(3), Puffin Books) Penguin Young Readers Group.
—Dancing in Cadillac Light. 2004. 176p. (J). (gr. 4-7). pap. 36.00 incl. audio (978-0-8072-2095-5(7), Listening Library) Random Hse. Audio Publishing Group.
—When Zachary Beaver Came to Town. unabr. ed. 2004. 227p. (J). (gr. 5-9). pap. 36.00 incl. audio (978-0-8072-8394-3(0), Listening Library) Random Hse. Audio Publishing Group.
—When Zachary Beaver Came to Town. 2011. (ENG.). 256p. (J). (gr. 5-9). pap. 8.99 (978-0-312-63212-0(6), 900077470) Square Fish.
Inagaki, Riichiro. Eyeshield 21, Vol. 12. 2007. (Eyeshield 21 Ser.: 12). (ENG., Illus.). 208p. pap. 9.99 (978-1-4215-1061-3(8)) Viz Media.
—Eyeshield 21, Vol. 13. 2007. (Eyeshield 21 Ser.: 13). (ENG., Illus.). 216p. pap. 9.99 (978-1-4215-1062-0(6)) Viz Media.
Ivy, Maggie, illus. Spirits of the Storm. 2018. (Haunted States of America Ser.). (ENG.). 136p. (J). (gr. 3-4). lib. bdg. 27.13 (978-1-63163-211-2(6), 1631632116, Jolly Fish Pr.) North Star Editions.
—Spirits of the Storm. 2018. (Haunted States of America Ser.). (ENG.). 136p. (J). (gr. 3-4). pap. 7.99 (978-1-63163-212-9(4), 1631632124, Jolly Fish Pr.) North Star Editions.
Jackson, Laura Gower. The Snowman & the Magic Eyeglasses. 2010. 24p. 11.99 (978-1-4520-3544-4(X)) AuthorHouse.
Jackson, Sarah. Preep of Old Washington Square: A Collection of East Texas Tales. Jenkins, Delores, illus. Lt. ed. 2005. 48p. (J). 16.95 (978-1-931823-25-8(1)) Halcyon Pr., Ltd.
Jacobs, Lily. The Littlest Bunny in Austin. Dunn, Robert, illus. 2016. (Littlest Bunny Ser.). (ENG.). 32p. (J). (gr. -1-3). 9.99 (978-1-4926-3347-1(X), 9781492633471, Hometown World) Sourcebooks, Inc.
—The Littlest Bunny in Texas: An Easter Adventure. Dunn, Robert, illus. 2015. (Littlest Bunny Ser.). (ENG.). 32p. (J). (gr. -1-3). 9.99 (978-1-4926-1210-0(3), Hometown World) Sourcebooks, Inc.
James, Eric. Santa's Sleigh Is on Its Way to Texas: A Christmas Adventure. Dunn, Robert, illus. 2015. (Santa's Sleigh Is on Its Way Ser.). (ENG.). 32p. (J). (gr. k-2). 12.99 (978-1-4926-2739-5(9), Hometown World) Sourcebooks, Inc.
—The Spooky Express Texas. Piwowarski, Marcin, illus. 2017. (Spooky Express Ser.). (ENG.). 32p. (J). (gr. k-6). 9.99 (978-1-4926-5314-1(4), Hometown World) Sourcebooks, Inc.
—Tiny the Texas Easter Bunny. 2018. (Tiny the Easter Bunny Ser.). (ENG.). 40p. (J). (gr. k-3). 9.99 (978-1-4926-5968-6(1), Hometown World) Sourcebooks, Inc.
(Jerry) Deal, Gerald R. Famous Dog Chowski. 2013. 44p. pap. 20.72 (978-1-4669-9707-3(9)) Trafford Publishing.
Jones, Patrick. Raising Heaven. 2015. (Locked Out Ser.). (ENG.). 96p. (YA). (gr. 6-12). E-Book 6.99 (978-1-4677-7697-4(1), 9781467776974, Darby Creek) Lerner Publishing Group.
Jones, Ralph E. The Adventures of Kele: Boy of the Rock Shelter. 2012. 156p. pap. 41.99 (978-1-4772-9405-5(8)); 56p. pap. 24.99 (978-1-4685-7696-2(8)) AuthorHouse.
Julie, Aunt. State Symbols of Texas - Paddleduck #8. 2012. (ENG.). 50p. pap. 5.95 (978-1-105-91163-7(2)) Lulu Pr., Inc.
Karr, Kathleen. Exiled: Memoirs of a Camel, 0 vols. 2012. (ENG.). 242p. (J). (gr. 4-6). pap. 9.99 (978-0-7614-5291-1(5), 9780761452911, Two Lions) Amazon Publishing.
Kelly, David A. The Astro Outlaw. 2012. (Ballpark Mysteries Ser.: Bk. 4). lib. bdg. 14.75 (978-0-606-23861-8(1)) Turtleback.
—Ballpark Mysteries #12: the Rangers Rustlers. Meyers, Mark, illus. 2016. (Ballpark Mysteries Ser.: 12). (ENG.). 112p. (J). (gr. 1-4). pap. 5.99 (978-0-385-37881-9(5), Random Hse. Bks. for Young Readers) Random Hse. Children's Bks.
Kelly, Jacqueline. Counting Sheep: Calpurnia Tate, Girl Vet. White, Teagan & Meyer, Jennifer L., illus. 2017. (Calpurnia Tate, Girl Vet Ser.: 2). (ENG.). 128p. (J). pap. 6.99 (978-1-250-12945-1(1), 900161283) Square Fish.
—The Curious World of Calpurnia Tate. 2017. (Calpurnia Tate Ser.: 2). (J). lib. bdg. 18.40 (978-0-606-39939-5(9)) Turtleback.
—La Evolución de Calpurnia Tate. 2010.Tr. of Evolution of Calpurnia Tate. (SPA.). 272p. (YA). pap. 20.95 (978-84-9918-103-5(1)) Roca Editorial ESP. Dist: Spanish Pubs., LLC.
—La evolución de Calpurnia Tate, Vol. 2. 2011. (SPA.). 272p. pap. 12.95 (978-84-92833-15-3(7)) Roca Editorial ESP. Dist: Spanish Pubs., LLC.
—The Evolution of Calpurnia Tate. 2010. (CHI.). 344p. (J). (gr. 5-9). pap. (978-986-216-538-6(3)) Commonwealth Publishing Co., Ltd.
—The Evolution of Calpurnia Tate. 2018. (CHI.). (J). (gr. 5-9). pap. (978-7-221-14182-8(7)) Guizhou People's Publishing Hse.
—The Evolution of Calpurnia Tate. 2011. (JPN.). 412p. (J). (gr. 5-9). (978-4-593-53474-6(7)) Holp Shuppan, Publishing.
—The Evolution of Calpurnia Tate. 2009. (Calpurnia Tate Ser.: 1). (ENG.). 352p. (J). (gr. 4-7). 19.99 (978-0-8050-8841-0(5), 900051792, Holt, Henry & Co. Bks. For Young Readers) Holt, Henry & Co.
—The Evolution of Calpurnia Tate. 2010. 340p. 18.00 (978-1-60686-849-2(7)) Perfection Learning Corp.
—The Evolution of Calpurnia Tate. 2011. (Calpurnia Tate Ser.: 1). (ENG.). 368p. (J). (gr. 4-7). pap. 8.99 (978-0-312-65930-1(X), 900070517) Square Fish.
—The Evolution of Calpurnia Tate. 2011. (Calpurnia Tate Ser.: 1). (J). lib. bdg. 18.40 (978-0-606-20974-8(3)) Turtleback.
—A Prickly Problem: Calpurnia Tate, Girl Vet. 2018. (Calpurnia Tate, Girl Vet Ser.: 4). (ENG., Illus.). 112p. (J). pap. 6.99 (978-1-250-17719-3(7), 900161295) Square Fish.
—Skunked!: Calpurnia Tate, Girl Vet. White, Teagan & Meyer, Jennifer L., illus. 2016. (Calpurnia Tate, Girl Vet Ser.: 1). (ENG.). 112p. (J). 15.99 (978-1-62779-868-6(4), 900161279, Holt, Henry & Co. Bks. For Young Readers) Holt, Henry & Co.
—Skunked!: Calpurnia Tate, Girl Vet. White, Teagan & Meyer, Jennifer L., illus. 2017. (Calpurnia Tate, Girl Vet Ser.: 1). (ENG.). 128p. (J). pap. 6.99 (978-1-250-12944-4(3), 900161280) Square Fish.
—A Squirrelly Situation: Calpurnia Tate, Girl Vet. Meyer, Jennifer L., illus. 2021. (Calpurnia Tate, Girl Vet Ser.: 5). (ENG.). 112p. (J). pap. 6.99 (978-1-250-21115-6(8), 900161298) Square Fish.
—Who Gives a Hoot?: Calpurnia Tate, Girl Vet. Meyer, Jennifer L., illus. 2018. (Calpurnia Tate, Girl Vet Ser.: 3). (ENG.). 128p. (J). pap. 6.99 (978-1-250-14339-6(X), 900161290) Square Fish.
Kerr, P. B., pseud. One Small Step. 2009. (ENG.). 320p. (J). (gr. 3-9). pap. 8.99 (978-1-4169-4214-6(9), McElderry, Margaret K. Bks.) McElderry, Margaret K. Bks.
Ketteman, Helen. The Three Little Gators. Terry, Will, illus. 2009. (ENG.). 32p. (J). (gr. -1-3). 16.99 (978-0-8075-7824-7(X), 080757824X) Whitman, Albert & Co.
Kimmel, Eric A. Jack & the Giant Barbecue, 0 vols. Manders, John, illus. 2012. (ENG.). 32p. (J). (gr. -1-3). 17.99 (978-0-7614-6128-9(0), 9780761461289, Two Lions) Amazon Publishing.
Komechak, Marilyn Gilbert. Paisano Pete: Snake-Killer Bird. Eckhardt, Jason C., illus. 2003. 100p. (J). (gr. 3-7). per. 11.95 (978-1-57168-770-8(X), Eakin Pr.) Eakin Pr.
Kralovansky, Susan. Twelve Cowboys Ropin', 1 vol. Kralovansky, Susan, illus. 2015. (ENG., Illus.). 32p. (J). (gr. k-3). 16.99 (978-1-4556-2081-4(5), Pelican Publishing) Arcadia Publishing.
Krueger, Kathryn L. Road to Grandma's House. 2005. 128p. pap. 13.95 (978-1-59800-366-6(6)) Outskirts Pr., Inc.
Krulik, Nancy. Rootin' Tootin' Cow Dog #8. Braun, Sebastien, illus. 2015. (Magic Bone Ser.: 8). 128p. (J). (gr. 1-3). bds. 5.99 (978-0-448-48097-8(2), Grosset & Dunlap) Penguin Young Readers Group.
—She's Got the Beat. 2010. (Romantic Comedies Ser.). (ENG.). 320p. (YA). (gr. 9). pap. 14.99 (978-1-4424-1419-8(7), Simon Pulse) Simon Pulse.
Lai, Thanhhà. Butterfly Yellow. 2019. (ENG.). 304p. (YA). (gr. 8). 17.99 (978-0-06-222921-2(4), HarperCollins) HarperCollins Pubs.
Lansdale, Joe R. All the Earth, Thrown to the Sky. 2012. (ENG.). 256p. (YA). (gr. 7). pap. 8.99 (978-0-385-73932-0(X), Ember) Random Hse. Children's Bks.
Lasher, Olga Rivera. La Historieta (the Storyteller) 2008. 88p. per. 7.95 (978-1-4327-0914-3(3)) Outskirts Pr., Inc.
Ledford, Mary"Aunt Sissy"Ledlowtranette. Cowboy Will & the Magic Rope. 2012. 32p. pap. 19.99 (978-1-4772-5167-6(7)) AuthorHouse.
Leitich Smith, Greg. Chronal Engine. Henry, Blake, illus. 2013. (ENG.). 192p. (J). (gr. 5-7). pap. 6.99 (978-0-544-02277-5(7), 1528498, Clarion Bks.) HarperCollins Pubs.
Lindsey, Julie Anne. Reinventing Chloe. 2013. 278p. pap. 13.99 (978-1-62237-152-5(6)) Turquoise Morning Pr.
Literature Connections English: ... & the Earth Did Not Devour Him. 2004. (gr. 6-12). (978-0-395-77139-6(0), 2-70217) Holt McDougal.
Lupica, Mike. Lone Stars. (ENG.). (J). (gr. 5). 2018. 256p. pap. 8.99 (978-0-14-751492-9(4), Puffin Books) 2017. 240p. 17.99 (978-0-399-17280-9(7), Philomel Bks.) Penguin Young Readers Group.
—Qb 1. 2014. (ENG.). 288p. (J). (gr. 5). pap. 8.99 (978-0-14-751152-2(6), Puffin Books) Penguin Young Readers Group.
MacHalek, Bj. The Adventures of a Noble Duchess: Duchess on Yard Patrol. 2012. 32p. pap. 17.37 (978-1-4389-6886-5(8)) AuthorHouse.
Mackey, Weezie Kerr. Throwing Like a Girl, 0 vols. 2013. (ENG.). 272p. (YA). (gr. 7-12). pap. 9.99 (978-0-7614-5606-3(6), 9780761456063, Skyscape) Amazon Publishing.
Madson, Trish. 10 Little Monsters Visit Texas, Volume 5. Hardyman, Nathan, illus. 2017. (10 Little Monsters Ser.: 5). (ENG.). 32p. (J). (gr. k-3). 14.99 (978-1-945547-08-9(1), 554708) Familius LLC.
Maliszewski, Julia. Grandmas Got the Goodies. 2013. 28p. pap. 14.93 (978-1-4669-8718-0(9)) Trafford Publishing.
Mangum, James A. & Spires, Sidney. The Fairy the Chupacabra & Those Marfa Lights: A West Texas Fable. Mangum, James A., illus. 2008. (Illus.). 32p. (J). 17.95 (978-0-9798391-5-3(7)) Texas Bk. Pubs. Assn.
Manley, Candance. Skeeter's Dream. 2010. (ENG.). 192p. (J). (gr. 7-18). pap. 14.95 (978-0-9785634-8-6(4)) La Frontera Publishing.
Mantell, Paul & Christopher, Matt. Snowboard Champ. 2005. (Matt Christopher Sports Ser.). 146p. (gr. 3-7). 16.00 (978-0-7569-5198-6(4)) Perfection Learning Corp.
Marie, Charity. Jason, Lizzy & the Snowman Village: Jason & Lizzy's Legendary Adventures Book 1. 2013. (ENG., Illus.). 132p. (J). 19.99 (978-0-9859601-1-7(6)) Texas Pride Publishing.
Marquith, M. Delmore. Flying Buddies of Texas. 2012. 250p. 46.95 (978-1-258-22955-9(2)); pap. 31.95 (978-1-258-24387-6(3)) Literary Licensing, LLC.
Marsh, Carole. The Mystery at Rattlesnake Ridge. 2014. (Wildlife Mysteries Ser.). (ENG., Illus.). 158p. (J). (gr. 2-9). pap. 7.99 (978-0-635-11188-3(8), Marsh, Carole Bks.) Gallopade International.
Martin, Bridgitt. Bunny & the Amazing Gift: God Cares for All His Creation. 2013. 28p. pap. 13.99 (978-1-4908-0952-6(X), WestBow Pr.) Author Solutions, LLC.
Martin, Joan Watson. Inventing Chloe. 2008. 140p. 19.95 (978-1-934335-25-3(8)); pap. 9.95 (978-1-934335-24-6(X)) WordWright.biz, Inc. (One Night Bks.).
Martin, LaJoyce. The Silver Ghost. 2004. (Illus.). 161p. (J). pap. 9.99 (978-1-56722-643-0(4)) Word Aflame Pr.
Martínez, Arturo O. & Martínez, Arturo O. Pedrito's World. 2007. (ENG., Illus.). 160p. (J). (gr. 4-6). pap. 16.95 (978-0-89672-600-0(2), P171756) Texas Tech Univ. Pr.
Marusak, Elaine. Truly Tales & Girl Fish Stories. 2006. 93p. pap. 16.95 (978-1-4241-3244-7(4)) PublishAmerica, Inc.
Marusak, Elaine Truly. Truly Tales: Aunt Gertie & Uncle George's Haunted House. 2007. (ENG.). 84p. per. 19.95 (978-1-4241-5959-8(8)) America Star Bks.
Mastrud, Karen. Fucious. 2012. 34p. 24.95 (978-1-61863-419-1(4)) Bookstand Publishing.
—Fucious: The True Story of the Ugly Duckling. Margolis, Al, illus. 2012. 32p. (J). 24.95 (978-1-61863-414-6(3)) Bookstand Publishing.
Mathieu, Jennifer. Moxie: A Novel. 2018. (ENG.). 352p. (YA). pap. 10.99 (978-1-250-10426-7(2), 900163699) Square Fish.
Mayhall, Robin. He Loves Me, He Loves Me Not: Book 7, No. 7. Irwin, Jane Elizabeth et al, illus. 2013. (My Boyfriend Is a Monster Ser.: 7). (ENG.). 128p. (YA). (gr. 7-12). lib. bdg. 29.32 (978-0-7613-6005-6(0), ae79c15f-787b-43fa-9d0a-94255bbea1be, Graphic Universe™) Lerner Publishing Group.
McBride-Smith, Barbara. Greek Myths, Western Style: Toga Tales with an Attitude. 2005. (ENG.). 128p. (J). (gr. 5-17). pap. 8.95 (978-0-87483-617-2(4)) August Hse. Pubs., Inc.
McBride, Susan. The Debs: Gloves Off. 2010. (YA). (978-0-385-73796-8(3)); (978-0-385-90703-3(6)) Random House Publishing Group. (Delacorte Pr).
McCall, Guadalupe Garcia. Under the Mesquite, 1 vol. 2013. (ENG., Illus.). 240p. (J). (gr. 6-12). 21.95 (978-1-60060-429-4(3), leelowbooks) Lee & Low Bks., Inc.
McCall, Guadalupe Garcia. El Verano de Las Mariposas, 1 vol. Bowles, David, tr. 2018. Orig. Title: Summer of the Mariposas. (SPA.). 384p. (YA). (gr. 6-12). pap. 16.95 (978-1-62014-786-3(6), leelowtu, Tu Bks.) Lee & Low Bks., Inc.
McLellan, Sean. The Red Booted Chicken. 2009. 48p. (J). pap. 17.49 (978-1-4389-5610-7(X)) AuthorHouse.
McMahon, P. J. Case of the Psychic Hamster. Manders, John, illus. 2005. 153p. (J). lib. bdg. 15.38 (978-1-4242-0404-5(6)) Fitzgerald Bks.
—Case of the Singing Sea Dragons. Manders, John, illus. 2005. 153p. (J). lib. bdg. 15.38 (978-1-4242-0406-9(2)) Fitzgerald Bks.
McManis, Margaret. The Wild Texas Stampede!, 1 vol. Dupree, Bruce, illus. 2008. (ENG.). 32p. (J). (gr. 1-3). 16.99 (978-1-58980-568-2(2), Pelican Publishing) Arcadia Publishing.
Mendez, Matt. Barely Missing Everything. (ENG.). 320p. (YA). (gr. 9). 2020. pap. 11.99 (978-1-5344-0446-5(5)) 2019. (Illus.). 18.99 (978-1-5344-0445-8(7)) Simon & Schuster Children's Publishing.
Meyer, Carolyn. Jubilee Journey. 2007. (ENG., Illus.). 288p. (J). (gr. 5-7). pap. 17.95 (978-0-15-205845-6(1), 253003, Clarion Bks.) HarperCollins Pubs.

—Jubilee Journey. 2007. 271p. (J). (gr. 5-9). 14.60 *(978-0-7569-6682-9(5))* Perfection Learning Corp.
—White Lilacs. 2007. (ENG., Illus.). 256p. (J). (gr. 3-7). pap. 8.99 *(978-0-15-205851-7(6),* 1197572, Clarion Bks.) HarperCollins Pubs.
—White Lilacs. 2006. (Illus.). 242p. (gr. 4-7). 16.95 *(978-0-7569-6683-6(3))* Perfection Learning Corp.
Michael, Todd. Texas State Bird Pageant. Randall, Lee Brandt, illus. 2005. 32p. (J). (gr. -1-3). 16.95 *(978-1-893062-75-7(9))* Quail Ridge Pr., Inc.
Minton, Ross. Baseball, from the Street to the Diamond, 1 vol. 2010. 94p. pap. 19.95 *(978-1-4489-4918-2(1))* America Star Bks.
Mitchell, Carolann. The Song of the Snow. 2011. 68p. (gr. 4-6). pap. 8.95 *(978-0-595-46609-2(5))* iUniverse, Inc.
Moberg, Julia. Skies over Sweetwater. 2007. (ENG.). 152p. (gr. 7-18). per. 15.00 *(978-0-9792371-2-6(2))* Keene Publishing.
Moss, Patricia Crocker. Dillie's Encounter with the Bucket Man. 2010. 36p. pap. 21.99 *(978-1-4535-4460-0(7))* Xlibris Corp.
Moulder, Holly. Crystal City Lights. 2013. (ENG.). 190p. (J). pap. 8.99 *(978-0-9885295-0-2(5))* Blue Marlin Pubns.
Moussavi, Sam. Austin. 2016. (Texas Fridays Ser.). (ENG.). 208p. (YA). (gr. 6-12). 32.84 *(978-1-68076-491-8(8),* 24671, Epic Escape) EPIC Pr.
—Dallas. 2016. (Texas Fridays Ser.). (ENG.). 208p. (YA). (gr. 6-12). 32.84 *(978-1-68076-492-5(6),* 24673, Epic Escape) EPIC Pr.
—Odessa. 2016. (Texas Fridays Ser.). (ENG.). 208p. (YA). (gr. 6-12). 32.84 *(978-1-68076-495-6(0),* 24679, Epic Escape) EPIC Pr.
Mowry, Tia & Mowry, Tamera. Twintuition: Double Cross. 2018. (Twintuition Ser.: 4). (ENG.). 208p. (J). (gr. 3-7). 16.99 *(978-0-06-237295-6(5),* HarperCollins) HarperCollins Pubs.
—Twintuition: Double Vision. 2015. (Twintuition Ser.: 1). (ENG.). 208p. (J). (gr. 3-7). 16.99 *(978-0-06-237286-4(6),* HarperCollins) HarperCollins Pubs.
Murphy, Julie. Dumplin' (Dumplin' Ser.: 1). (ENG.). (YA). (gr. 8). 2017. 400p. pap. 10.99 *(978-0-06-232719-2(4))* 2015. 384p. 17.99 *(978-0-06-232718-5(6))* HarperCollins Pubs. (Balzer & Bray).
—Dumplin' 2017. (YA). lib. bdg. 20.85 *(978-0-606-39647-9(0))* Turtleback.
—Dumplin' Movie Tie-In Edition. movie tie-in ed. 2018. (Dumplin' Ser.: 1). (ENG.). 400p. (YA). (gr. 8). pap. 9.99 *(978-0-06-293467-3(8),* Balzer & Bray) HarperCollins Pubs.
—Puddin' (Dumplin' Ser.: 2). (ENG.). (YA). (gr. 8). 2019. 464p. pap. 9.99 *(978-0-06-241839-5(4))* 2018. 448p. 17.99 *(978-0-06-241838-8(6))* HarperCollins Pubs. (Balzer & Bray).
Murray, Pamela. Pirates of Texas. 2012. 28p. (-18). pap. 24.95 *(978-1-4626-9996-4(0))* America Star Bks.
Neighbors, Jared. Rivals, 1 vol. 2009. 73p. pap. 19.95 *(978-1-61582-021-4(3))* America Star Bks.
Neugeboren, Jay. Poli: A Mexican Boy in Early Texas. 25th ed. 2014. (ENG., Illus.). 144p. (J). pap. 21.95 *(978-0-89672-905-6(2))* Texas Tech Univ. Pr.
Nichols, Travis. Matthew Meets the Man. 2012. (ENG., Illus.). 176p. (YA). (gr. 6-9). 24.99 *(978-1-59643-545-2(3),* 900061886) Roaring Brook Pr.
Nielson, Ane O. The Lone Star G Brand on My Behind. 2004. (Illus.). 96p. (J). per. 9.95 *(978-1-930580-56-5(8),* Luminary Media Group) Pine Orchard, Inc.
Noble, Diana J. Evangelina Takes Flight. 2017. (ENG.). 152p. (J). (gr. 5-8). pap. 10.95 *(978-1-55885-848-0(2),* Piñata Books) Arte Publico Pr.
Norton, Tamra. Comfortable in My Own Genes: A Novel. 2004. 175p. (J). pap. 15.95 *(978-1-55517-772-0(7))* Cedar Fort, Inc./CFI Distribution.
Novel Units. Old Yeller Novel Units Teacher Guide. 2019. (ENG.). (J). pap. 12.99 *(978-1-56137-081-8(9),* Novel Units, Inc.) Classroom Library Co.
—Tex Novel Units Teacher Guide. 2019. (ENG.). (YA). (gr. 7-12). pap. 12.99 *(978-1-56137-146-4(7),* BK8619, Novel Units, Inc.) Classroom Library Co.
—When Zachary Beaver Came to Town Novel Units Student Packet. 2019. (ENG.). (YA). pap., stu. ed. 13.99 *(978-1-58130-675-0(X),* Novel Units, Inc.) Classroom Library Co.
—When Zachary Beaver Came to Town Novel Units Teacher Guide. 2019. (ENG.). (J). pap., tchr. ed. 12.99 *(978-1-58130-674-3(1),* Novel Units, Inc.) Classroom Library Co.
O Flatharta, Antoine. Hurry & the Monarch. So, Meilo, illus. 2009. (ENG.). 40p. (J). (gr. k-3). pap. 8.99 *(978-0-385-73719-7(X),* Dragonfly Bks.) Random Hse. Children's Bks.
Oakes, Colleen. The Black Coats. 2020. (ENG.). 416p. (YA). (gr. 9). pap. 10.99 *(978-0-06-267964-2(3),* HarperTeen) HarperCollins Pubs.
O'Kane, George & McEntee, Bill, illus. Hook Em's Colorful Campus Tour - University of Texas A-Z: Forty Acres (A-Z) 2004. (J). 9.99 *(978-1-933069-01-2(5))* Odd Duck Ink, Inc.
O'Neill, Elizabeth. Alfred Visits Texas. 2007. 24p. (J). pap. 12.00 *(978-0-9790240-9-2(9))* Funny Bone Bks.
Osborne, Mary Pope. Hurricane Heroes in Texas. Ford, A. G., illus. 2018. (Magic Tree House (R) Ser.: 30). 112p. (J). (gr. 1-4). 13.99 *(978-1-5247-1312-6(0),* Random Hse. Bks. for Young Readers) Random Hse. Children's Bks.
Papademetriou, Lisa. Chasing Normal. 2008. (ENG.). 193p. (J). (gr. 4-6). 18.69 *(978-1-4231-0341-7(6))* Hyperion Bks. for Children.
Pascal, Francine. The Ruling Class. 2010. (ENG.). 208p. (YA). (gr. 9). pap. 10.99 *(978-1-4424-1423-5(5),* Simon Pulse) Simon Pulse.
Paulsen, Gary. Canyons. 2011. (ENG.). 192p. (YA). (gr. 7). pap. 7.99 *(978-0-385-74234-4(7),* Ember) Random Hse. Children's Bks.
—Canyons. 2011. 184p. (gr. 4-7). lib. bdg. 18.40 *(978-0-8335-6467-2(6))* Turtleback.
—The Legend of Bass Reeves. 2008. (ENG., Illus.). 160p. (YA). (gr. 7-9). mass mkt. 7.99 *(978-0-553-49429-7(5),* Laurel Leaf) Random Hse. Children's Bks.
Payton, Belle. Two Cool for School. 2014. (It Takes Two Ser.: 2). (ENG., Illus.). 160p. (J). (gr. 3-7). 16.99 *(978-1-4814-0645-1(0),* Simon Spotlight) Simon Spotlight.
—A Whole New Ball Game. 2014. (It Takes Two Ser.: 1). (ENG., Illus.). 160p. (J). (gr. 3-7). 16.99 *(978-1-4814-0642-0(6));* pap. 7.99 *(978-1-4814-0641-3(8))* Simon Spotlight. (Simon Spotlight).
Pearl, Paige. ARTLANTICA: the Secret Kingdom Beneath Galveston Island. 2008. 38p. 18.95 *(978-1-4357-0389-6(8))* Lulu Pr., Inc.
Pearson, Mary E. A Room on Lorelei Street. 2008. (ENG.). 288p. (YA). (gr. 9-13). pap. 19.99 *(978-0-312-38019-9(4),* 900050545) Square Fish.
Pérez, Ashley Hope. Out of Darkness. 2019. 400p. (YA). (gr. 9). pap. 12.99 *(978-0-8234-4503-5(8))* Holiday Hse., Inc.
—Out of Darkness. 2015. (ENG., Illus.). 408p. (YA). (gr. 8-12). 20.99 *(978-1-4677-4202-3(3),* ba661708-6e62-4586-8cfb-a9177c8dc6e3, Carolrhoda Lab™) Lerner Publishing Group.
Peschke, Marci. Art Queen. Mourning, Tuesday, illus. 2018. (Kylie Jean Ser.). (ENG.). 112p. (J). (gr. 1-3). lib. bdg. 22.65 *(978-1-5158-2927-0(8),* 138470, Picture Window Bks.) Capstone.
—Blueberry Queen, 1 vol. Mourning, Tuesday & Mourning, Tuesday, illus. 2011. (Kylie Jean Ser.). (ENG.). 112p. (J). (gr. 1-3). pap. 4.95 *(978-1-4048-6615-7(9),* 114676, Picture Window Bks.) Capstone.
—Cooking Queen. Mourning, Tuesday, illus. 2017. (Kylie Jean Ser.). (ENG.). 112p. (J). (gr. 1-3). lib. bdg. 22.65 *(978-1-4795-9899-1(2),* 135431, Picture Window Bks.) Capstone.
—Dancing Queen, 1 vol. Mourning, Tuesday, illus. 2012. (Kylie Jean Ser.). (ENG.). 112p. (J). (gr. 1-3). lib. bdg. 22.65 *(978-1-4048-6798-7(8),* 116240, Picture Window Bks.) Capstone.
—Fishing Queen. Mourning, Tuesday, illus. 2017. (Kylie Jean Ser.). (ENG.). 112p. (J). (gr. 1-3). lib. bdg. 22.65 *(978-1-4795-9900-4(X),* 135433, Picture Window Bks.) Capstone.
—Gymnastics Queen. Mourning, Tuesday, illus. 2016. (Kylie Jean Ser.). (ENG.). 112p. (J). (gr. 1-3). lib. bdg. 22.65 *(978-1-5158-0052-1(0),* 131862, Picture Window Bks.) Capstone.
—Hoop Queen, 1 vol. Mourning, Tuesday & Mourning, Tuesday, illus. 2011. (Kylie Jean Ser.). (ENG.). 112p. (J). (gr. 1-3). pap. 4.95 *(978-1-4048-6617-1(5),* 114679, Picture Window Bks.) Capstone.
—Robot Queen. Mourning, Tuesday, illus. 2018. (Kylie Jean Ser.). (ENG.). 112p. (J). (gr. 1-3). 8.95 *(978-1-5158-2934-8(0),* 138473); lib. bdg. 22.65 *(978-1-5158-2926-3(X),* 138469) Capstone. (Picture Window Bks.).
—Rodeo Queen, 1 vol. Mourning, Tuesday & Mourning, Tuesday, illus. 2011. (Kylie Jean Ser.). (ENG.). 112p. (J). (gr. 1-3). pap. 4.95 *(978-1-4048-6618-8(3),* 114680, Picture Window Bks.) Capstone.
—Singing Queen, 1 vol. Mourning, Tuesday, illus. 2012. (Kylie Jean Ser.). (ENG.). 112p. (J). (gr. 1-3). lib. bdg. 22.65 *(978-1-4048-6800-7(3),* 116242, Picture Window Bks.) Capstone.
—Soccer Queen. Mourning, Tuesday, illus. 2015. (Kylie Jean Ser.). (ENG.). 112p. (J). (gr. 1-3). 22.65 *(978-1-4795-5882-7(6),* 126953, Picture Window Bks.) Capstone.
—Vacation Queen. Mourning, Tuesday, illus. 2016. (Kylie Jean Ser.). (ENG.). 112p. (J). (gr. 1-3). lib. bdg. 22.65 *(978-1-5158-0058-3(X),* 131864, Picture Window Bks.) Capstone.
Philippe, Ben. The Field Guide to the North American Teenager. (ENG.). 384p. (YA). (gr. 8). 2020. pap. 11.99 *(978-0-06-282412-7(0))* 2019. 18.99 *(978-0-06-282411-0(2))* HarperCollins Pubs. (Balzer & Bray).
Pierotti, Jr. Toward the Setting Sun. 2007. 268p. per. 17.95 *(978-0-595-45469-3(0))* iUniverse, Inc.
Pittman, Seth. Raggy's Island. 2010. 124p. pap. 9.95 *(978-0-557-59557-0(6))* Lulu Pr., Inc.
Platt, Randall. Liberty's Christmas. 2012. (ENG.). 200p. (YA). (gr. 7-12). 19.95 *(978-0-89672-766-3(1),* P208775) Texas Tech Univ. Pr.
Powell, Lenora Y. Ardo: The Mysterious New House. 2008. 105p. pap. 19.95 *(978-1-60672-133-9(X))* America Star Bks.
Rand, Johnathan. Freddie Fernortner #11: Tadpole Trouble. 2010. 95p. (J). pap. 4.99 *(978-1-893699-29-8(3))* AudioCraft Publishing, Inc.
Ransom, Candice. The Night of the Hurricane's Fury. Tong, Paul, illus. 2011. (On My Own History Ser.). 48p. (J). pap. 39.62 *(978-0-7613-7621-7(6));* (ENG.). (gr. 2-4). pap. 7.99 *(978-0-7613-3940-3(X),* afb90020-dc2c-40e6-aeef-321654eb8791) Lerner Publishing Group. (First Avenue Editions).
Reeves, Dia. Bleeding Violet. 2010. (ENG.). 480p. (YA). (gr. 9). pap. 20.99 *(978-1-4169-8619-5(7),* Simon Pulse) Simon Pulse.
—Slice of Cherry. 2011. (ENG.). (YA). (gr. 9). 528p. pap. 14.99 *(978-1-4169-8621-8(9));* 512p. 16.99 *(978-1-4169-8620-1(0))* Simon Pulse. (Simon Pulse).
Restrepo, Bettina. Illegal. (ENG.). (YA). (gr. 8). 2019. 288p. pap. 15.99 *(978-0-06-195343-9(1))* 2011. 272p. 17.99 *(978-0-06-195342-2(3))* HarperCollins Pubs. (Tegen, Katherine Bks).
Rice, David. Crazy Loco. 2008. 135p. 16.00 *(978-0-7569-8951-4(5))* Perfection Learning Corp.
Rice, David & Garcia, Mike D. Heart-Shaped Cookies. 2011. (YA). pap. *(978-1-931010-79-5(X))* Bilingual Pr./Editorial Bilingue.
Rinaldi, Ann. Come Juneteenth. 2007. (Great Episodes Ser.). (ENG., Illus.). 256p. (J). (gr. 6-8). 21.19 *(978-0-15-205947-7(4))* Harcourt Children's Bks.
—Come Juneteenth. 2009. (Great Episodes Ser.). (ENG., Illus.). 256p. (YA). (gr. 7). pap. 7.99 *(978-0-15-206392-4(7),* 1099019, Clarion Bks.) HarperCollins Pubs.
Rizzo, Cynthia Marie. Julie & the Unicorn. 2003. 49p. pap. 16.95 *(978-1-4137-0785-4(8))* PublishAmerica, Inc.
Roach, Joyce Gibson, tr. Cowgirl of the Rocking R. 2003. (J). *(978-0-9726573-0-3(4))* Crosswinds Bks.
Roberts, Tina. Dream Watchman: Quest for the Missing Talisman Book I. 2011. 244p. pap. 15.95 *(978-1-60976-636-8(9),* Eloquent Bks.) Strategic Book Publishing & Rights Agency (SBPRA).
Sachar, Louis. Hoyos. 2003. (SPA.). (gr. 5-8). lib. bdg. 25.75 *(978-0-613-64523-2(5))* Turtleback.
Safi, Aminah Mae. Not the Girls You're Looking For. 2019. (ENG.). 352p. pap. 14.99 *(978-1-250-30886-3(0),* 900183488) Square Fish.
Saldaña, Jr. A Good Long Way. 2010. 128p. (J). (gr. 6-18). pap. 10.95 *(978-1-55885-607-3(2),* Piñata Books) Arte Publico Pr.
Saldana, Rene, Jr. The Jumping Tree. 2008. 181p. (gr. 5-7). 16.50 *(978-0-7569-8950-7(7))* Perfection Learning Corp.
Sally Spencer. Juanita's Flowers. Phil Brannan & Sunni Brannan, illus. 2009. 32p. pap. 14.49 *(978-1-4389-4841-6(7))* AuthorHouse.
Sanders, Russell J. All You Need Is Love. 2017. (ENG., (YA). Illus.). 25.99 *(978-1-64080-344-2(0));* 220p. pap. 14.99 *(978-1-63533-321-3(0))* Dreamspinner Pr. (Harmony Ink Pr.).
Sargent, Dave & Sargent, Pat. Grady: (Dappled Grey) Proud to Be an American, 30 vols., Vol. 30. Lenoir, Jane, illus. 2003. (Saddle up Ser.: Vol. 30). 42p. (J). lib. bdg. 23.60 *(978-1-56763-813-4(9))* Ozark Publishing.
—Grady: Proud to Be an American, 30 vols. Lenoir, Jane, illus. 2003. (Saddle up Ser.: Vol. 30). 42p. (J). pap. 10.95 *(978-1-56763-814-1(7))* Ozark Publishing.
Schult, Sherry. There's a Horse in My Closet..., 1 vol. 2010. 48p. pap. 16.95 *(978-1-4489-5412-4(6))* PublishAmerica, Inc.
Scott, Victoria. Violet Grenade. 2017. (ENG.). 300p. (J). 17.99 *(978-1-63375-687-8(4),* 9781633756878) Entangled Publishing, LLC.
Seals, Hollie. When You Can't Find the Words. 2007. 144p. per. 11.95 *(978-0-595-45023-7(7))* iUniverse, Inc.
Shafer, Patty. Annie the Texas Ranch Dog - Danger at Lost Maples. Retzlaff, Shay, illus. 2012. (ENG.). 96p. (J). pap. 9.95 *(978-1-61899-009-9(8),* Tadpole Pr. 4 Kids) Mystic Harbor Pr., LLC.
—Annie the Texas Ranch Dog - Injured Hero. Retzlaff, Shay, illus. 2012. 96p. (J). pap. 9.95 *(978-1-61899-008-2(X),* Tadpole Pr. 4 Kids) Mystic Harbor Pr., LLC.
—Annie the Texas Ranch Dog - New Life in Utopia. Retzlaff, Shay, illus. 2012. 96p. (J). pap. 9.95 *(978-1-61899-007-5(1),* Tadpole Pr. 4 Kids) Mystic Harbor Pr., LLC.
Smallman, Steve. Santa Is Coming to Texas. Dunn, Robert, illus. (ENG.). (J). 2012. 32p. (-3). 9.99 *(978-1-4022-7512-8(9),* Sourcebooks Jabberwocky) 2nd ed. 2019. 40p. (gr. -1-3). 12.99 *(978-1-7282-0104-7(7),* Hometown World) Sourcebooks, Inc.
Smart, Kimberly. A New Home for Gabril. 2008. 32p. 15.95 *(978-1-4357-0762-7(1))* Lulu Pr., Inc.
Smith, Andrew. The Size of the Truth. 2019. (Sam Abernathy Bks.). (ENG., Illus.). 272p. (J). (gr. 3-7). 17.99 *(978-1-5344-1955-1(1),* Simon & Schuster Bks. For Young Readers) Simon & Schuster Bks. For Young Readers.
Smith, Cynthia Leitich. Blessed. 2011. (Tantalize Ser.: 3). (ENG., Illus.). 480p. (YA). (gr. 9-18). 17.99 *(978-0-7636-4326-3(2))* Candlewick Pr.
—Tantalize. 2008. (Tantalize Ser.: 1). (ENG., Illus.). 336p. (YA). (gr. 9). pap. 9.99 *(978-0-7636-4059-0(X))* Candlewick Pr.
Spradlin, Joe. Sugar. 2007. 48p. per. 14.95 *(978-1-4327-0200-7(9))* Outskirts Pr., Inc.
Stamper, Phil. The Gravity of Us. 2020. (ENG.). 320p. (YA). 17.99 *(978-1-5476-0014-4(4),* 900195006, Bloomsbury Young Adult) Bloomsbury Publishing USA.
Stauffer, Sharon. Cornfield Baby: And Other Nature Surprises. 2003. (Illus.). 179p. 8.40 *(978-0-7399-2314-6(5),* 2344) Rod & Staff Pubs., Inc.
Stem, Jacqueline. The Ghosts of Goliad. 2003. iii, 165p. (J). 17.95 *(978-1-57168-785-2(8),* Eakin Pr.) Eakin Pr.
—The Haunted Tunnel. 96p. 8.95 *(978-1-57168-310-6(0))* Eakin Pr.
Stephenson, Lynda. Dancing with Elvis. (YA). (gr. 7). 2006. (ENG.). 331p. per. 8.00 *(978-0-8028-5300-4(5))* 2005. 323p. 17.00 *(978-0-8028-5293-9(9))* Eerdmans, William B. Publishing Co. (Eerdmans Bks For Young Readers).
Stone, B. J. Girl on the Bluff. (Illus.). 160p. 8.95 *(978-1-57168-297-0(X))* Eakin Pr.
Strauss, Kevin. Pecos Bill Invents the Ten-Gallon Hat, 1 vol. Harrington, David, illus. 2012. (ENG.). 32p. (J). (gr. k-3). 17.99 *(978-1-4556-1502-5(1),* Pelican Publishing) Arcadia Publishing.
Stripland, Rubye Weldon. Lucy Bell, Queen of the Pasture. 2008. 92p. pap. 10.95 *(978-1-4357-1472-4(5))* Lulu Pr., Inc.
—Lucy Bell, Queen of the Pasture Book Four. 2009. 94p. pap. 10.96 *(978-1-4357-4742-5(9))* Lulu Pr., Inc.
—Lucy Bell, Queen of the Pasture, Book Three. 2008. 90p. pap. 10.95 *(978-1-4357-3418-0(1))* Lulu Pr., Inc.
—Lucy Bell, Queen of the Pasture Book Two. 2008. 100p. pap. 10.95 *(978-1-4357-1895-1(X))* Lulu Pr., Inc.
Sully, Katherine. Night-Night Texas. Poole, Helen, illus. 2016. (Night-Night Ser.). (ENG.). 20p. (J). (gr. -1-1). bds. 9.99 *(978-1-4926-3936-7(2),* 9781492639367, Hometown World) Sourcebooks, Inc.
Tata, Cb. Ernie the Eagle Goes to Texas. Hanley, Zachary, illus. 2012. 44p. 24.95 *(978-1-4626-5374-4(X))* America Star Bks.
Temblador, Alex. Secrets of the Casa Rosada. 2018. (ENG.). 160p. (YA). (gr. 6-10). pap. 12.95 *(978-1-55885-870-1(9),* Piñata Books) Arte Publico Pr.
Tingle, Tim. Danny Blackgoat, Navajo Prisoner. 2013. (Danny Blackgoat Ser.: 1). (ENG.). 160p. (YA). (gr. 8-12). pap. 9.95 *(978-1-939053-03-9(X),* 193905303X, 7th Generation) BPC.
—Danny Blackgoat, Rugged Road to Freedom. 2014. (Danny Blackgoat Ser.: 2). (ENG.). 144p. (YA). (gr. 8-12). pap. 9.95 *(978-1-939053-05-3(6),* 7th Generation) BPC.
Tingle, Tim & Moore, Doc. More Spooky Texas Tales. Benas, Jeanne, illus. 2010. (ENG.). 104p. (gr. 4-6). lib. bdg. 18.95 *(978-0-89672-700-7(9),* P200878) Texas Tech Univ. Pr.
Tingle, Tim & Moore, James W. Spooky Texas Tales. Miller, Gina, illus. 2005. x, 85p. (J). pap. *(978-0-89672-566-9(9))* Texas Tech Univ. Pr.
Townsend, Tom. Powderhorn Passage. 112p. 9.95 *(978-1-57168-433-2(6))* Eakin Pr.
Trenchard, Robert. The Famous Frog Fiasco. 2008. 265p. (J). pap. 13.99 *(978-0-615-20974-6(2))* Soxwings Publishing.
Treviño, Hilda L. Ladybugs on a Mission. 2013. 70p. (gr. 4-6). pap. 8.95 *(978-1-4759-7762-2(X))* iUniverse, Inc.
Tribolet, Leslie L. Danny's Tale: Adventures of an Arabian Horse in his Own Words. 2010. (Illus.). 112p. 24.95 *(978-1-4490-6065-7(X));* pap. 14.95 *(978-1-4490-6064-0(1))* AuthorHouse.
Turner, Juliette. That's Not Hay in My Hair, 1 vol. 2016. (ENG.). 240p. (J). pap. 8.99 *(978-0-310-73244-0(1))* Zonderkidz.
Villareal, Ray. Alamo Wars. 2008. 187p. (J). (gr. 6-18). pap. 10.95 *(978-1-55885-513-7(0),* Piñata Books) Arte Publico Pr.
—Who's Buried in the Garden? 2009. 160p. (YA). (gr. 6-18). pap. 10.95 *(978-1-55885-546-5(7),* Piñata Books) Arte Publico Pr.
Walthers, Joanie. The Fish Smuggler. Walthers, Don, illus. 2013. (ENG.). 24p. (J). 19.95 *(978-1-4787-1167-4(1))* Outskirts Pr., Inc.
Watson, J. A. Monarch Mystery: A Butterfly Researcher's Journal. 2018. (Science Squad Ser.). (ENG., Illus.). 192p. (J). (gr. 3-4). lib. bdg. 28.50 *(978-1-63163-183-2(7),* 1631631837, Jolly Fish Pr.) North Star Editions.
—Monarch Mystery: A Butterfly Researcher's Journal. Olbey, Arpad, illus. 2018. (Science Squad Ser.). (ENG.). 192p. (J). (gr. 3-4). pap. 9.99 *(978-1-63163-184-9(5),* 1631631845, Jolly Fish Pr.) North Star Editions.
Webb, Susan. A Tale of Two Brothers. 2012. 24p. pap. 12.95 *(978-1-4497-6053-3(8),* WestBow Pr.) Author Solutions, LLC.
Webster-Tyson, Paulette L. I Gotta Get a Nickname! 2011. (ENG.). 32p. (gr. -1-2). pap. 17.25 *(978-1-4269-5625-6(8))* Trafford Publishing.
Weihrich, Carroll. On Jim Street. 2003. 144p. 24.50 *(978-1-932621-19-8(9));* per. 15.00 *(978-1-932621-18-1(0))* Open Bk. Publishing.
Weisenberg, Marit. Select. (Select Ser.: 1). (YA). (gr. 9). 2018. 384p. pap. 10.99 *(978-1-58089-895-9(5))* 2017. 352p. lib. bdg. 17.99 *(978-1-58089-806-5(8))* Charlesbridge Publishing, Inc. (Charlesbridge Teen).
Weldon, Stayton. Whitey on the Ranch. Anderson-Shorter, Susan, illus. 2010. 52p. pap. 12.95 *(978-1-4490-5474-8(9))* AuthorHouse.
Wells, Tom. Strange Seasons: Summer. 2008. 212p. 24.95 *(978-0-595-50888-4(X));* pap. 14.95 *(978-0-595-52016-9(2))* iUniverse, Inc.
White, Tom. Lost in the Texas Desert. 2004. (Illus.). 132p. per. 7.95 *(978-0-9753611-0-8(4))* Arlington Pubns.
Williams, Lori Aurelia. When Kambia Elaine Flew in from Neptune. unabr. ed. 2004. 246p. (J). (gr. 7-18). pap. 50.00 incl. audio *(978-0-8072-8851-1(9),* Listening Library) Random Hse. Audio Publishing Group.
Wilsdon, Christina. A Wild Ride in Texas. Jaekel, Susan, illus. 2006. 26p. (J). 7.99 *(978-1-59939-011-6(6))* Cornerstone Pr.
Woolley, Bryan. Mr. Green's Magnificent Machine. Arbuckle, Scott, illus. 2003. 32p. 15.95 *(978-1-57168-606-0(1))* Eakin Pr.
Worcester, Daryl D. Traves Travislot's Going South for the Winter. 2011. 46p. pap. 16.95 *(978-1-4626-1091-4(9))* America Star Bks.
Wright, Lynda. Flowers for Addison. 2012. 24p. pap. 24.95 *(978-1-4626-5787-2(7))* America Star Bks.
Zeleny, Sylvia. The Everything I Have Lost, 1 vol. 2020. (ENG.). 256p. (YA). (gr. 9-12). 15.95 *(978-1-947627-17-8(1),* 23353382, Cinco Puntos Press) Lee & Low Bks., Inc.
Ziegler, Jennifer. How Not to Be Popular. 2010. 352p. (YA). (gr. 7). mass mkt. 8.99 *(978-0-440-24024-2(7),* Delacorte Bks. for Young Readers) Random Hse. Children's Bks.
—Revenge of the Angels. 2015. (Brewster Triplets Ser.). (ENG.). 256p. (J). (gr. 3-7). 16.99 *(978-0-545-83899-3(1),* Scholastic Pr.) Scholastic, Inc.
—Revenge of the Angels: a Wish Novel (the Brewster Triplets) 2017. (Brewster Triplets Ser.). (ENG.). 256p. (J). (gr. 3-7). pap. 6.99 *(978-0-545-83902-0(5),* Scholastic Pr.) Scholastic, Inc.
—Revenge of the Teacher's Pets. 2018. (ENG.). 256p. (J). (gr. 3-7). 16.99 *(978-1-338-09123-6(9),* Scholastic Pr.) Scholastic, Inc.

TEXAS—HISTORY

Alter, Judy. Martin de Leon: Tejano Empresario. 2007. (Stars of Texas Ser.: 4). (ENG., Illus.). 72p. (J). (gr. 4-7). 14.95 *(978-1-933337-08-1(7),* P121287) State Hse. Pr.
Alter, Judy & Messersmith, Patrick. Mirabeau B. Lamar: Second President of Texas. 2005. (Stars of Texas Ser.: 2). (ENG., Illus.). 72p. (J). (gr. 4-7). 17.95 *(978-1-880510-97-1(9),* P067769) State Hse. Pr.
—Miriam Ma Ferguson: First Woman Governor of Texas. 2006. (Stars of Texas Ser.: 3). (ENG., Illus.). 72p. (J). (gr. 4-7). 17.95 *(978-1-933337-01-2(X),* P109862) State Hse. Pr.
Amberson, Mary. A Brave Boy & a Good Soldier: John C. C. Hill & the Texas Expedition to Mier. 2006. (ENG., Illus.). 100p. (J). (gr. 3-7). 24.95 *(978-0-87611-214-4(9),* 27FF) Texas State Historical Assn.
AMBROZIAK, Ambroziak. Texas in 3D. 2018. (Illus.). 40p. (J). (gr. k-1). pap. 12.95 *(978-1-63076-320-6(9))* Lone Star Bks.
Antonio Lopez de Santa Anna. 2010. (ENG., Illus.). 104p. (gr. 6-12). 35.00 *(978-1-60413-734-7(7),* P179359, Facts On File) Infobase Holdings, Inc.
Baker, Karle Wilson. Texas Flag Primer. 2005. reprint ed. pap. 20.95 *(978-0-7661-9572-1(4))* Kessinger Publishing, LLC.
Barenblat, Rachel. Texas, 1 vol. 2003. (World Almanac(r) Biblioteca de Los Estados (World Almanac(r) Library of the States) Ser.). (SPA., Illus.). 48p. (gr. 4-6). pap. 15.05 *(978-0-8368-5554-8(X),* 48b95754-aabd-45bc-94ff-ad64ec8ef8ab, Gareth Stevens Learning Library) Stevens, Gareth Publishing LLLP.
Barton, Chris. What Do You Do with a Voice Like That? The Story of Extraordinary Congresswoman Barbara Jordan. Holmes, Ekua, illus. 2018. (ENG.). 48p. (J). (gr. -1-3). 18.99 *(978-1-4814-6561-8(9),* Beach Lane Bks.) Beach Lane Bks.
Bauer, Marion Dane. Celebrating Texas: 50 States to Celebrate. Canga, C. B., illus. 2013. (ENG.). 40p. (J). (gr. 1-4). pap. 3.99 *(978-0-547-89786-8(3),* 1509708, Clarion Bks.) HarperCollins Pubs.
Belviso, Meg & Pollack, Pamela. What Was the Alamo? 2013. (What Was... Ser.). lib. bdg. 16.00 *(978-0-606-32129-7(2))* Turtleback.
Benduhn, Tea, et al. Texas, 1 vol. 3rd rev. ed. 2014. (It's My State! (Third Edition)(r) Ser.). (ENG., Illus.). 80p. (gr. 4-4). 35.93 *(978-1-5026-0017-2(X),* 76cc5ce4-e802-4278-a72b-addb643b3a26) Cavendish Square Publishing LLC.
Berman, Ron. On the Hardwood: Houston Rockets. 2013. (On the Hardwood Ser.). (ENG., Illus.). 48p. (gr. 3-8). pap. 8.95 *(978-1-61570-837-6(5))* Scobre Pr. Corp.

TUV

Blake, Kevin. Houston's Hurricane Harvey Floods. 2018. (Code Red Ser.). (ENG., Illus.). 32p. (J). (gr. 2-7). lib. bdg. 18.95 (978-1-68402-661-6(X)) Bearport Publishing Co., Inc.

Boehm Jerome, Kate. Houston, TX: Cool Stuff Every Kid Should Know. 2010. (Arcadia Kids Ser.). (ENG., Illus.). 48p. (J). (gr. 3-6). pap. 11.99 (978-1-4396-0066-5(X)) Arcadia Publishing.

Bredeson, Carmen & Dodson Wade, Mary. Texas, 1 vol. 2nd rev. ed. 2007. (Celebrate the States (Second Edition) Ser.). (ENG., Illus.). 144p. (gr. 6-6). lib. bdg. 39.79 (978-0-7614-1736-1(2), a3bcc616-75c8-4757-bb26-68da992129cc) Cavendish Square Publishing LLC.

Brindell Fradin, Dennis. The Alamo, 1 vol. 2007. (Turning Points in U. S. History Ser.). (ENG., Illus.). 48p. (gr. 4-4). lib. bdg. 34.07 (978-0-7614-2127-6(0), a890134e-b43a-4bc9-b810-370f9e8fdba1) Cavendish Square Publishing LLC.

Brown, Jonatha A. Texas, 1 vol. 2005. (Portraits of the States Ser.). (ENG., Illus.). 32p. (gr. 3-5). pap. 11.50 (978-0-8368-4654-6(0), 97477f9b-3ead-42c1-964e-67f368e27848, Gareth Stevens Learning Library) Stevens, Gareth Publishing LLLP.

Burke, Johanna. The American Civil War in Texas, 1 vol. 2010. (Spotlight on Texas Ser.). (ENG., Illus.). 32p. (J). (gr. 3-4). pap. 11.75 (978-1-61532-472-9(0), 7693461c-9c2f-4d02-8750-5dadc40866a9); lib. bdg. 28.93 (978-1-61532-474-3(7), c997ea17-cc53-4c08-9613-944de605c0f6) Rosen Publishing Group, Inc., The.

Cameron, Charles. Why Lizzie Johnson Matters to Texas, 1 vol. 2013. (Texas Perspectives Ser.). (ENG., Illus.). 32p. (J). (gr. 4-4). lib. bdg. 28.93 (978-1-4777-0908-5(8), 3dbc605b-a618-4499-8ca8-04f4bd9c2864) Rosen Publishing Group, Inc., The.

—Why Richard King Matters to Texas, 1 vol. 2013. (Texas Perspectives Ser.). (ENG., Illus.). 32p. (J). (gr. 4-4). lib. bdg. 28.93 (978-1-4777-0910-8(X), 93194c6d-ef92-4bb2-a6e0-4a3d11620cd5) Rosen Publishing Group, Inc., The.

Cane, Sutter. Governing Texas: Local, State, & National Governments, 1 vol. 2010. (Spotlight on Texas Ser.). (ENG., Illus.). 32p. (J). (gr. 3-4). pap. 11.75 (978-1-61532-481-1(X), 8a1c0c82-0884-48a0-9ce2-c0e984bb7442); lib. bdg. 28.93 (978-1-61532-483-5(6), d171b66b-cfbe-47d3-b5dd-c088a154a4a8) Rosen Publishing Group, Inc., The.

Caravantes, Peggy. American in Texas: The Story of Sam Houston. 2004. (Notable Americans Ser.). (Illus.). 144p. (YA). (gr. 6-12). 23.95 (978-1-931798-19-8(2)) Reynolds, Morgan Inc.

Chrismer, Melanie. Lone Star Legacy: The Texas Rangers Then & Now, 1 vol. 2016. (ENG., Illus.). 144p. (J). (gr. 4-7). pap. 10.95 (978-1-4556-2104-0(8), Pelican Publishing) Arcadia Publishing.

Clemens Warrick, Karen. Alamo: Victory or Death on the Texas Frontier, 1 vol. 2008. (America's Living History Ser.). (ENG., Illus.). 128p. (gr. 5-6). lib. bdg. 35.93 (978-0-7660-2937-8(9), f72968bc-602a-4098-b535-64afe9266d91) Enslow Publishing, LLC.

Clinton, Greg. Life in Contemporary Texas, 1 vol. 2014. (Spotlight on Texas Ser.). (ENG.). 32p. (J). (gr. 3-4). 28.93 (978-1-4777-4506-9(8), d400a87f-651b-4b65-a9f5-ce2c89f58a52, Rosen Classroom) Rosen Publishing Group, Inc., The.

—Texas During Reconstruction, 1 vol. 2014. (Spotlight on Texas Ser.). (ENG.). 32p. (J). (gr. 3-4). 28.93 (978-1-4777-4517-5(3), 818c37cf-9db2-41b6-9d22-cb67a7a29230, Rosen Classroom) Rosen Publishing Group, Inc., The.

Colmenares, Sandra. Gastronomy of Texas, 1 vol. 2018. (Explore Texas Ser.). (ENG.). 24p. (gr. 9-12). 26.27 (978-1-5081-8659-5(6), 86b92c04-bf8e-4105-86d6-30d8a16b2b3f, Rosen Young Adult) Rosen Publishing Group, Inc., The.

Connors, Kathleen. Let's Explore the Southwest, 1 vol. 2013. (Road Trip: Exploring America's Regions Ser.). (ENG.). 24p. (J). (gr. 2-3). pap. 9.15 (978-1-4339-9150-9(0), 4ee82a8d-5ce9-4343-8469-83c76dfb91f2); (Illus.). lib. bdg. 25.27 (978-1-4339-9149-3(7), c4111111-1d5e-4dd0-8a2f-834a0f08659a) Stevens, Gareth Publishing LLLP.

Corporate Contributor. Drew Brees. 2012. (ENG.). 32p. (J). (978-0-7787-7616-1(6)); pap. (978-0-7787-7629-1(8)) Crabtree Publishing Co.

Crane, Carol. Little Texas. Monroe, Michael Glenn, illus. 2010. (Little State Ser.). (ENG.). 20p. (J). (gr. -1-1). bds. 9.95 (978-1-58536-488-6(6), 202250) Sleeping Bear Pr.

Curry, Jane Louise. Hold up the Sky: And Other Native American Tales from Texas & The. Watts, James, illus. 2010. (ENG.). 176p. (J). (gr. 3-7). pap. 9.99 (978-1-4424-2155-4(X), McElderry, Margaret K. Bks.) McElderry, Margaret K. Bks.

Dorling Kindersley Publishing Staff. Eyewitness Books - Texas. 2003. (DK Guias Visuales / DK Eyewitness Bks.). (Illus.). 64p. (J). (gr. 5-8). 28.69 (978-0-7894-9744-4(1)) Dorling Kindersley Publishing, Inc.

Drez, Jennifer & Bumstead, Robin. Goodnight Cowtown. Voight, Lisa, illus. 2012. 40p. (J). 17.95 (978-0-615-54492-2(4)) Petit Chou Chou, LLC.

Durden-Nelson, Mae. I Just Called Her Momma. 2003. (Illus.). xii, 162p. (J). 18.95 (978-1-57168-714-2(9)) Eakin Pr.

Early American Wars, 8 vols., Set. Incl. American Revolutionary War. Marston, Daniel & O'Neill, Robert John. lib. bdg. 38.47 (978-1-4488-1331-5(X), 97fdd7f5-b6c0-4a56-9c61-1c0f72d38d88); Texas War of Independence. Huffines, Alan C. & O'Neill, Robert. lib. bdg. 38.47 (978-1-4488-1332-2(8), 36cb7ba9-dc13-4896-8a71-3cada86c271c); War of 1812: The Fight for American Trade Rights. Benn, Carl & O'Neill, Robert. lib. bdg. 38.47 (978-1-4488-1333-9(6), d72506c9-ca2b-4440-b2de-85ad9710d12d); (YA). (gr. 10-10). 2011. (Early American Wars Ser.). (ENG., Illus.). 96p. 2010. Set lib. bdg. 153.88 (978-1-4488-1387-2(5), 2707729f-2e44-4276-a727-6c417d4c68f7) Rosen Publishing Group, Inc., The.

Edmondson, J. R. Jim Bowie: Frontier Legend, Alamo Hero. 2009. (Library of American Lives & Times Ser.). 112p. (gr. 5-5). 69.20 (978-1-60853-488-3(X)) Rosen Publishing Group, Inc., The.

Egan, Tracie. Cynthia Ann Parker: Comanche Captive = Cautiva de los Comanches, 1 vol. Gonzalez, Tomas, tr. 2003. (Famous People in American History / Grandes Personajes en la Historia de Los Estados Unidos Ser.). (SPA & ENG., Illus.). 32p. (J). (gr. 2-3). lib. bdg. 29.13 (978-0-8239-4155-1(8), 6e20de72-4518-4a36-8fe1-d1bde81121d9) Rosen Publishing Group, Inc., The.

—Francisca Alavez, the Angel of Goliad, 1 vol. 2003. (Primary Sources of Famous People in American History Ser.). (ENG., Illus.). 32p. (gr. 3-4). pap. 10.00 (978-0-8239-4181-0(7), 613c87ab-8793-466f-b2ba-e27df8520e76); (J). lib. bdg. 29.13 (978-0-8239-4109-4(4), 09802509-6753-48f4-b7e8-0bcf07c4aa8b, Rosen Reference) Rosen Publishing Group, Inc., The.

—Francisca Alvarez: El angel de Goliad, 1 vol. 2003. (Grandes Personajes en la Historia de Los Estados Unidos (Famous People in American History) Ser.). (SPA.). 32p. (gr. 3-4). pap. 10.00 (978-0-8239-4227-5(9), 9281ea04-af45-4d44-b992-87e389c837f6, Rosen Classroom) Rosen Publishing Group, Inc., The.

—Francisca Alvarez: El ángel de Goliad (Francisca Alvarez: the Angel of Goliad) 2009. (Grandes personajes en la historia de los Estados Unidos (Famous People in American History) Ser.). (SPA.). 32p. (gr. 2-3). 47.90 (978-1-61512-798-6(4), Editorial Buenas Letras) Rosen Publishing Group, Inc., The.

—Francisca Alvarez: The Angel of Goliad. (Primary Sources of Famous People in American History Ser.). 32p. (gr. 2-3). 2009. 47.90 (978-1-60851-675-9(X)) 2003. (ENG & SPA., Illus.). lib. bdg. 29.13 (978-0-8239-4157-5(4), 8d646879-3215-45e0-97ba-5af78ef58304, Editorial Buenas Letras) Rosen Publishing Group, Inc., The.

—Francisca Alvarez: The Angel of Goliad / el ángel de Goliad. 2009. (Famous People in American History/Grandes personajes en la historia de los Estados Unidos Ser.). (ENG & SPA.). 32p. (gr. 2-3). 47.90 (978-1-61512-544-9(2), Editorial Buenas Letras) Rosen Publishing Group, Inc., The.

Ellis, Paula. Texas Activity Book, 1 vol. Nitzsche, Shane, illus. 2012. (Color & Learn Ser.). (ENG.). 64p. (J). (gr. k-5). pap. 6.95 (978-1-59193-376-2(5), Adventure Pubns.) AdventureKEEN.

Espinosa, Chris & Rawlett, Robert. Rocket Megabyte's Texas Adventure. Espinosa, Chris, illus. 2004. (Illus.). 68p. (J). 14.00 (978-0-9724637-1-3(2)) Sky Rocket Pr.

Fehrenbach, T. R. Lone Star: The Story of Texas. 2003. (Illus.). xxxii, 600p. (J). 60.00 (978-0-13-058625-4(0)) Prentice Hall PTR.

Fein, Eric. Outnumbered: Davy Crockett's Final Battle at the Alamo. 2009. (Great Moments in American History Ser.). 32p. (gr. 3-3). 47.90 (978-1-61513-148-8(5)) Rosen Publishing Group, Inc., The.

Felix, Rebecca. Hurricane Harvey: Disaster in Texas & Beyond. 2018. (ENG., Illus.). 32p. (J). (gr. 3-6). 27.99 (978-1-5415-2888-8(3), bfee6b3a-17e1-4db5-ad02-543e4274f1e9, Millbrook Pr.) Lerner Publishing Group.

Flynn, Jean. Henry B. Gonzalez: Rebel with a Cause. 2003. (Illus.). v, 140p. (J). 16.95 (978-1-57168-780-7(7), Eakin Pr.) Eakin Pr.

Gamble, Adam & Jasper, Mark. Good Night Houston. Veno, Joe, illus. 2016. (Good Night Our World Ser.). (ENG.). 20p. (J). (— 1). bds. 9.95 (978-1-60219-504-2(8)) Good Night Bks.

Garland, Sherry. Voices of the Alamo, 1 vol. Himler, Ronald, illus. 2017. (Voices of History Ser.). (ENG.). 40p. (J). (gr. k-5). 19.99 (978-1-58980-222-3(5), Pelican Publishing) Arcadia Publishing.

Gendell, Megan. A True Book: Spanish Missions of Texas. 2010. (True Book Ser.). (ENG., Illus.). 48p. (J). pap. 6.95 (978-0-531-21243-1(2)) Scholastic Library Publishing.

—True Books: the Spanish Missions of Texas. 2010. (True Book(tm), a — Spanish Missions Ser.). (ENG.). 48p. (J). (gr. 2-5). 31.00 (978-0-531-20580-8(0)) Scholastic Library Publishing.

Gibson, Karen Bush. Texas History for Kids: Lone Star Lives & Legends, with 21 Activities. 2015. (For Kids Ser.: 57). (ENG., Illus.). 144p. (J). (gr. 4). pap. 19.99 (978-1-61374-989-0(9)) Chicago Review Pr., Inc.

Goldsworthy, Steve. El Alamo. 2013. (Iconos Americanos Ser.). (SPA., Illus.). 24p. (J). (gr. k-2). lib. bdg. 27.13 (978-1-62127-615-9(5), AV2 by Weigl) Weigl Pubs., Inc.

González, Blanca. Distinguished Texans, 1 vol. 2018. (Explore Texas Ser.). (ENG.). 24p. (gr. 9-12). 26.27 (978-1-5081-8664-9(2), b8da3e9b-7b8b-4da2-9185-4a3bbf947216, Rosen Young Adult) Rosen Publishing Group, Inc., The.

Haley, James. Stephen Austin & the Founding of Texas. 2009. (Library of American Lives & Times Ser.). 112p. (gr. 5-5). 69.20 (978-1-60853-506-4(1)) Rosen Publishing Group, Inc., The.

Haley, James L. The Handy Texas Answer Book. 2018. (Handy Answer Book Ser.). (ENG., Illus.). 416p. pap. 44.95 (978-1-57859-634-8(3)) Visible Ink Pr.

Hamilton, John. Texas, 1 vol. 2016. (United States of America Ser.). (ENG., Illus.). 48p. (J). (gr. 5-9). 34.21 (978-1-68078-346-9(7), 21677, Abdo & Daughters) ABDO Publishing Co.

Harasymiw, Therese. Causes & Effects of the Texas Revolution, 1 vol. 2010. (Spotlight on Texas Ser.). (ENG., Illus.). 32p. (J). (gr. 3-4). pap. 11.75 (978-1-61532-466-8(6), 8dac42be-0ef3-4815-814a-e105b5f4892a); lib. bdg. 28.93 (978-1-61532-468-2(2), 085d3faa-a2ee-4962-88b0-c3e2af291930) Rosen Publishing Group, Inc., The.

Herold, Vickey. Discover a Cattle Town: Forth Worth. 2006. (J). pap. (978-1-4108-6430-7(8)) Benchmark Education Co.

Hicks, Dwayne. Questions & Answers about the Alamo, 1 vol. 2018. (Eye on Historical Sources Ser.). (ENG.). 32p. (gr. 4-4). 27.93 (978-1-5383-4107-0(7), aad9cb16-e9a3-4da8-b816-82c29ab6df3b, PowerKids Pr.) Rosen Publishing Group, Inc., The.

Hoffman, Mary Ann. The Alamo, 1 vol. 2010. (Spotlight on Texas Ser.). (ENG., Illus.). 32p. (J). (gr. 3-4). lib. bdg. 28.93 (978-1-61532-461-3(5), f8c42bff-17a8-45c5-a18f-6d679d62fc37) Rosen Publishing Group, Inc., The.

Hollmann, Robert E. William Barret Travis. 2012. (ENG.). 130p. pap. 9.95 (978-0-9779863-9-2(X)) Fireside Pr., Inc.

Holt, Rinehart and Winston Staff. Holt Texas! 3rd ed. 2003. (SPA., Illus.). 83.00 (978-0-03-073767-1(2)) Holt McDougal.

Hopkins, Jackie Mims. Our Texas. Spearing, Craig J., illus. 2010. 44p. (J). (gr. 1-4). pap. 8.95 (978-1-57091-726-4(4)) Charlesbridge Publishing, Inc.

Hughes, Bill. Texas History Coloring Book & Punch Out Playset. 2004. (Illus.). 16p. (J). 4.95 (978-0-9746784-0-5(6)) Great Big Comics, Big Tex Films.

Isecke, Harriet. Finding Texas: Exploration in New Lands, 1 vol. rev. ed. 2012. (Social Studies: Informational Text Ser.). (ENG.). 32p. (gr. 3-5). pap. 11.99 (978-1-4333-5042-9(4)) Teacher Created Materials, Inc.

—Stephen F. Austin: The Father of Texas, 1 vol. rev. ed. 2012. (Social Studies: Informational Text Ser.). (ENG.). 32p. (gr. 3-5). pap. 11.99 (978-1-4333-5045-0(9)) Teacher Created Materials, Inc.

—Texas en el Siglo XX (Texas in the 20th Century) 2013. (Primary Source Readers Ser.). (SPA.). lib. bdg. 19.65 (978-0-606-31872-3(0)) Turtleback.

—Texas Hoy: Guiando a los Estados Unidos Hacia el Futuro. 2013. (Primary Source Readers (Spanish) Ser.). (SPA.). lib. bdg. 19.65 (978-0-606-31874-7(7)) Turtleback.

—Texas in the 20th Century: Building Industry & Community, 1 vol. rev. ed. 2012. (Social Studies: Informational Text Ser.). (ENG.). 32p. (gr. 3-5). pap. 11.99 (978-1-4333-5209-6(5)) Teacher Created Materials, Inc.

—Texas Today: Leading America into the Future, 1 vol. rev. ed. 2012. (Social Studies: Informational Text Ser.). (ENG.). 32p. (gr. 3-5). pap. 11.99 (978-1-4333-5053-5(X)) Teacher Created Materials, Inc.

Isecke, Harriet & Kuligowski, Stephanie. Descubriendo Texas. 2013. (Primary Source Readers Ser.). (SPA.). lib. bdg. 19.65 (978-0-606-31862-4(3)) Turtleback.

—Stephen F. Austin: El Padre de Texas / Stephen F. Austin - The Father of Texas. 2013. (Primary Source Readers Ser.). (SPA.). lib. bdg. 19.65 (978-0-606-31865-5(8)) Turtleback.

Jackson, Jack. New Texas History Movies. 2007. (ENG., Illus.). 50p. pap. 9.95 (978-0-87611-223-6(8), 27FO) Texas State Historical Assn.

Jackson, Jack & Magruder, Jana. New Texas History Movies. Jackson, Jack, illus. 2007. (ENG., Illus.). 66p. pap. 19.95 (978-0-87611-231-1(9)) Texas State Historical Assn.

Jackson, Sarah. Preep II: More Tales of Early Texas. Jenkins, Delores, illus. 2007. 48p. (J). 19.95 (978-1-931823-52-4(9)) Halcyon Pr., Ltd.

Jacobs Altman, Linda & Benduhn, Tea. Texas, 1 vol. 2nd rev. ed. 2011. (It's My State! (Second Edition)(r) Ser.). (ENG.). 80p. (gr. 4-4). lib. bdg. 34.07 (978-1-60870-059-2(3), 4e440bc3-cef2-49ef-b843-c744ceb3790c) Cavendish Square Publishing LLC.

James, Trisha. Cattle & Oil: The Growth of Texas Industries, 1 vol. 2010. (Spotlight on Texas Ser.). (ENG., Illus.). 32p. (J). (gr. 3-4). pap. 11.75 (978-1-61532-475-0(5), 53376bc9-f598-46bc-bb9f-9b9d794aec51); lib. bdg. 28.93 (978-1-61532-477-4(1), 4a615f41-ad49-4537-87c6-c9ab4bc9bd62) Rosen Publishing Group, Inc., The.

—Celebrating Texas: Patriotic Symbols & Landmarks, 1 vol. 2010. (Spotlight on Texas Ser.). (ENG., Illus.). 32p. (J). (gr. 3-4). pap. 11.75 (978-1-61532-484-2(4), 61edd9b1-91e6-4364-ad92-9834cf6a495e); lib. bdg. 28.93 (978-1-61532-486-6(0), 2f1ac580-4512-48ee-91b5-f030e002c736) Rosen Publishing Group, Inc., The.

Jari's Year: Inside the U. S. A. 2009. (Inside the USA Ser.). (Illus.). 16p. (C). pap. 14.95 (978-0-7362-7065-6(5)) CENGAGE Learning.

Jerome, Kate B. Lucky to Live in Texas. 2017. (Arcadia Kids Ser.). (ENG., Illus.). 32p. (J). 16.99 (978-0-7385-2769-7(6)) Arcadia Publishing.

—The Wise Animal Handbook Texas. 2017. (Arcadia Kids Ser.). (ENG., Illus.). 32p. (J). 16.99 (978-0-7385-2845-8(5)) Arcadia Publishing.

Johnson, Robin. Why Mirabeau Lamar Matters to Texas, 1 vol. 2013. (Texas Perspectives Ser.). (ENG., Illus.). 32p. (J). (gr. 4-4). lib. bdg. 28.93 (978-1-4777-0915-3(0), 9a524f75-7fb1-4734-83db-fd638a6e26be) Rosen Publishing Group, Inc., The.

Johnston, Marianne. Texas, 1 vol. 2007. (Conflict Resolution Library). (ENG.). (J). E-Book 25.27 (978-1-4042-3136-8(6), e1653f23-d2c8-4c04-8bbd-fd95a3465dee, PowerKids Pr.) Rosen Publishing Group, Inc., The.

Kiely Miller, Barbara. Sam Houston, 1 vol. 2007. (Grandes Personajes (Great Americans) Ser.). 24p. (gr. 2-4). (SPA.). pap. 9.15 (978-0-8368-8336-7(5), c6ff82ce-7527-4a48-acc7-8db99cbe62ff); (ENG.). pap. 9.15 (978-0-8368-8323-7(3), 181dab52-3918-43bb-b2a9-666f98196091); (ENG.). lib. bdg. 24.67 (978-0-8368-8316-9(0), c0d85d45-374f-44a0-82b7-fe4611ee39a8); (SPA., Illus.). lib. bdg. 24.67 (978-0-8368-8329-9(2), 468581b2-c389-4f19-87a2-91fb6d86c83c) Stevens, Gareth Publishing LLLP. (Weekly Reader Leveled Readers).

Kleinmartin, Hex, et al. Texas. 2015. (J). lib. bdg. (978-1-62712-769-1(0)) Cavendish Square Publishing LLC.

Kuligowski, Stephanie. La Colonizacion de Texas / the Colonization of Texas. 2013. (Primary Source Readers Ser.). (SPA.). lib. bdg. 19.65 (978-0-606-31864-8(X)) Turtleback.

—The Colonization of Texas: Missions & Settlers, 1 vol. rev. ed. 2012. (Social Studies: Informational Text Ser.). (ENG.). 32p. (gr. 3-5). pap. 11.99 (978-1-4333-5044-3(0)) Teacher Created Materials, Inc.

—La Salle: Early Texas Explorer, 1 vol. rev. ed. 2012. (Social Studies: Informational Text Ser.). (ENG.). 32p. (gr. 3-5). pap. 11.99 (978-1-4333-5043-6(2)) Teacher Created Materials, Inc.

—La Salle: Uno de los Primeros Exploradores de Texas. 2013. (Primary Source Readers Ser.). (SPA.). lib. bdg. 19.65 (978-0-606-31863-1(1)) Turtleback.

Laird, Johnna M. Southwest: New Mexico, Oklahoma, Texas, Vol. 19. 2015. (Let's Explore the States Ser.). (Illus.). 64p. (J). (gr. 5). 23.95 (978-1-4222-3334-4(0)) Mason Crest.

Lanier, Wendy Hinote. The Kickapoo. 2016. (Illus.). 32p. (978-1-938813-44-3(8)) State Standards Publishing, LLC.

Lanser, Amanda. What's Great about Texas? 2014. (Our Great States Ser.). (ENG., Illus.). 32p. (J). (gr. 2-5). lib. bdg. 26.65 (978-1-4677-3348-9(2), be551795-ebea-4623-a243-aca927e6006e, Lerner Pubns.) Lerner Publishing Group.

Let's Explore the Southwest. 2013. (Road Trip: Exploring America's Regions Ser.). 24p. (J). (gr. 2-5). pap. 48.90 (978-1-4339-9151-6(9)) Stevens, Gareth Publishing LLLP.

Levy, Janey. The Battle of the Alamo. (American History Flashpoints! Ser.). 32p. (gr. 4-4). 2009. 47.90 (978-1-61511-369-9(X), PowerKids Pr.) 2009. (ENG.). (J). lib. bdg. 28.93 (978-1-4358-2991-6(3), 8be7db00-99bc-423d-9fff-680274e8149e, PowerKids Pr.) 2008. (ENG.). pap. 10.00 (978-1-4358-0167-7(9), 92794efd-7ddf-4f34-9dcb-d7c99ab32b7c, Rosen Classroom) Rosen Publishing Group, Inc., The.

Levy, Janey & Donnell, Kerri. The Missions of Texas, 1 vol. 2010. (Spotlight on Texas Ser.). (ENG., Illus.). 32p. (J). (gr. 3-4). 28.93 (978-1-61532-465-1(8), b23f0d8c-7a08-49f5-8f3a-3845c5db8516); pap. 11.75 (978-1-61532-456-9(9), 8b6ad879-d8ef-47e4-859a-c90d4f4d4e5a) Rosen Publishing Group, Inc., The.

Magruder, Jana & Amberson, Mary. A Brave Boy & a Good Soldier Educator Guide: John C. C. Hill & the Texas Expedition to Mier. 2006. (ENG., Illus.). 100p. pap., tchr.'s training gde. ed. 19.95 (978-0-87611-229-8(7)) Texas State Historical Assn.

Marfa, Isabelle. The Land & Resources of Texas: Shaping the Growth of the State, 1 vol. 2010. (Spotlight on Texas Ser.). (ENG., Illus.). 32p. (J). (gr. 3-4). pap. 11.75 (978-1-61532-478-1(X), 37cfdc00-8cea-43d9-ab4c-31e32f0e88bc); lib. bdg. 28.93 (978-1-61532-480-4(1), ccfc673c-de8c-4cc5-a9a7-c32e75942b0e) Rosen Publishing Group, Inc., The.

Marsh, Carole. Exploring Texas Through Project-Based Learning: Geography, History, Government, Economics & More. 2016. (Texas Experience Ser.). (ENG.). (J). pap. 9.99 (978-0-635-12367-1(3)) Gallopade International.

—Texas History Projects: 30 Cool, Activities, Crafts, Experiments & More for Kids to Do to Learn about Your State! 2003. (Texas Experience Ser.). 32p. (gr. k-5). pap. 5.95 (978-0-635-01812-0(8), Marsh, Carole Bks.) Gallopade International.

Marsico, Katie. The Rio Grande. 2013. (Explorer Library: Social Studies Explorer Ser.). (ENG.). 32p. (gr. 4-8). (J). pap. 14.21 (978-1-62431-036-2(2), 202501); (Illus.). 32.07 (978-1-62431-012-6(5), 202499) Cherry Lake Publishing.

Mattern, Joanne. La Anexion de Texas /The Annexation of Texas. 2013. (Primary Source Readers Ser.). (SPA.). lib. bdg. 19.65 (978-0-606-31868-6(2)) Turtleback.

—The Annexation of Texas: From Republic to Statehood, 1 vol. rev. ed. 2012. (Social Studies: Informational Text Ser.). (ENG.). 32p. (gr. 3-5). pap. 11.99 (978-1-4333-5048-1(3)) Teacher Created Materials, Inc.

—Sam Houston: A Fearless Statesman, 1 vol. rev. ed. 2012. (Social Studies: Informational Text Ser.). (ENG.). 32p. (gr. 3-5). pap. 11.99 (978-1-4333-5049-8(1)) Teacher Created Materials, Inc.

McAneney, Caitlin. Becoming Texas: Early Statehood, 1 vol. 2014. (Spotlight on Texas Ser.). (ENG.). 32p. (J). (gr. 3-4). 28.93 (978-1-4777-4527-4(0), 8af17fdc-ebda-450d-b90e-c368708f823c, Rosen Classroom) Rosen Publishing Group, Inc., The.

McGowen, Tom. The Alamo. 2017. (J). (978-0-531-22617-9(4), Orchard Bks.) Scholastic, Inc.

McKinley, Fred B. Chinqua Where? The Spirit of Rural America, 1947-1955. Blassingame, Calvin, illus. 2003. 319p. 24.95 (978-0-9729655-0-7(5)) Willow Creel Publishing Co.

Mitchell, Mark. Raising la Belle. Mitchell, Mark, illus. (Professor Wigglestix & the Weather Ser.). (Illus.). 112p. 10.95 (978-1-57168-703-6(3)) Eakin Pr.

Moore, Jess. The Economy of Texas, 1 vol. 2014. (Spotlight on Texas Ser.). (ENG.). 32p. (J). (gr. 3-4). pap. 11.75 (978-1-4777-4512-0(2), 2ce2ff7d-1ce1-4a98-8d62-581b25d19b07, Rosen Classroom) Rosen Publishing Group, Inc., The.

—Texas During the Great Depression, 1 vol. 2013. (Spotlight on Texas Ser.). (ENG.). 32p. (J). (gr. 3-4). 28.93 (978-1-4777-4511-3(4), 5b5641dc-30d6-4589-acde-2994bf10a926, Rosen Classroom) Rosen Publishing Group, Inc., The.

Nagle, Jeanne M. Texas: Past & Present. 2009. (Illus.). 48p. (J). 70.50 (978-1-4358-5573-1(6)); (ENG., (gr. 5-5). pap. 12.75 (978-1-4358-5572-4(8), e8f0acbc-2b97-49ab-bd79-00fe20e87636); (ENG., (gr. 5-5). lib. bdg. 34.47 (978-1-4358-5287-7(7), 7796f8a9-30f8-4763-ba02-e002c6c8dc85) Rosen Publishing Group, Inc., The. (Rosen Reference).

Nelson, Kristin L. The Alamo. 2003. (Pull Ahead Books — American Symbols Ser.). (ENG., Illus.). 32p. (J). (gr. k-3). pap. 7.99 (978-0-8225-3760-1(5), 6c5f5ef4-5435-4505-8d25-7a9486b8aa3c, First Avenue Editions) Lerner Publishing Group.

Osborne, Mary Pope & Boyce, Natalie Pope. Texas: A Nonfiction Companion to Magic Tree House #30: Hurricane Heroes in Texas. Mones, Isidre, illus. 2018. (Magic Tree House (R) Fact Tracker Ser.: 39). 128p. (J). (gr. 2-5). 6.99 (978-1-101-93648-1(7), Random Hse. Bks. for Young Readers) Random Hse. Children's Bks.

Otfinoski, Steven. The Battle of the Alamo: Texans under Siege. 2019. (Tangled History Ser.). (ENG., Illus.). 112p. (J). (gr. 3-9). pap. 6.95 (978-1-5435-4202-8(6), 139116) Capstone.

—The Story of Juneteenth: An Interactive History Adventure. 2015. (You Choose: History Ser.). (ENG., Illus.). 112p. (J). (gr. 3-7). lib. bdg. 32.65 (978-1-4914-1802-4(8), 127246, Capstone Pr.) Capstone.

Owens, Sharon. Immigration & Migration in Texas, 1 vol. 2014. (Spotlight on Texas Ser.). (ENG.). 32p. (J). (gr. 3-4). 28.93 (978-1-4777-4522-9(X),

8a7d3620-b3cd-4345-838d-d10fdcbf6d5a, Rosen Classroom) Rosen Publishing Group, Inc., The.

Paradis, Anne. Texas Monsters. Legdani, Sanaa, illus. 2017. (ENG.). 22p. (gr. -1). bds. 9.99 *(978-2-924734-07-0(X))* City Monsters Bks. CAN. Dist: Publishers Group West (PGW).

Parker, Janice. Texas. 2011. (Guide to American States Ser.). (Illus.). 48p. (YA). (gr. 3-6). 29.99 *(978-1-61690-816-4(5))*; (J). *(978-1-61690-492-0(5))* Weigl Pubs., Inc.

—Texas: The Lone Star State. 2016. (J). *(978-1-4896-4947-8(6))* Weigl Pubs., Inc.

Peppas, Lynn. The Battle of the Alamo. 2017. (Uncovering the Past: Analyzing Primary Sources Ser.). (Illus.). 48p. (J). (gr. 5-6). *(978-0-7787-3940-1(6))* Crabtree Publishing Co.

—Why Anson Jones Matters to Texas, 1 vol. 2013. (Texas Perspectives Ser.). (ENG., Illus.). 32p. (J). (gr. 4-4). lib. bdg. 28.93 *(978-1-4777-0911-5(8)*, 92d13227-1293-4a6c-9ba9-4e668df35827) Rosen Publishing Group, Inc., The.

—Why Cabeza de Vaca Matters to Texas, 1 vol. 2013. (Texas Perspectives Ser.). (ENG., Illus.). 32p. (J). (gr. 4-4). lib. bdg. 28.93 *(978-1-4777-0913-9(4)*, 99187d06-5c9b-4171-8e2d-abd99916f04f) Rosen Publishing Group, Inc., The.

—Why Francisco Coronado Matters to Texas, 1 vol. 2013. (Texas Perspectives Ser.). (ENG., Illus.). 32p. (J). (gr. 4-4). lib. bdg. 28.93 *(978-1-4777-0909-2(6)*, ea11e18a-2750-4bf4-ad7a-d5d0300c739e) Rosen Publishing Group, Inc., The.

—Why José Antonio Navarro Matters to Texas, 1 vol. 2013. (Texas Perspectives Ser.). (ENG., Illus.). 32p. (J). (gr. 4-4). lib. bdg. 28.93 *(978-1-4777-0936-8(3)*, 0143289d-1cb7-4f6e-8c3b-f4449a309e61) Rosen Publishing Group, Inc., The.

—Why Sam Houston Matters to Texas, 1 vol. 2013. (Texas Perspectives Ser.). (ENG., Illus.). 32p. (J). (gr. 4-4). lib. bdg. 28.93 *(978-1-4777-0912-2(6)*, 60e60101-a7ab-4741-8c21-e08fda6394f0) Rosen Publishing Group, Inc., The.

—Why Sieur de La Salle Matters to Texas, 1 vol. 2013. (Texas Perspectives Ser.). (ENG., Illus.). 32p. (J). (gr. 4-4). lib. bdg. 28.93 *(978-1-4777-0917-7(7)*, 0b3a3eaf-af71-420f-acc9-7bcff56efa29) Rosen Publishing Group, Inc., The.

—Why Stephen F. Austin Matters to Texas, 1 vol. 2013. (Texas Perspectives Ser.). (ENG., Illus.). 32p. (J). (gr. 4-4). lib. bdg. 28.93 *(978-1-4777-0914-6(2)*, b0ede1c3-3d3c-4048-8910-51b139ab69d1) Rosen Publishing Group, Inc., The.

Peterson, Sheryl. Texas. Kania, Matt, illus. 2009. (This Land Called America Ser.). 32p. (YA). (gr. 3-6). 19.95 *(978-1-58341-796-6(6))* Creative Co., The.

Petrick, Neila Skinner. Jane Wilkinson Long: Texas Pioneer, 1 vol. Haynes, Joyce, illus. 2004. (ENG.). 32p. (J). (gr. k-3). 16.99 *(978-1-58980-147-9(4)*, Pelican Publishing) Arcadia Publishing.

Phan, Sandy. American Indians in Texas: Conflict & Survival, 1 vol. rev. ed. 2012. (Social Studies: Informational Text Ser.). (ENG., Illus.). 32p. (J). (gr. 3-5). pap. 11.99 *(978-1-4333-5040-5(8))* Teacher Created Materials, Inc.

—The Caddo & Comanche: American Indians Tribes in Texas, 1 vol. rev. ed. 2012. (Social Studies: Informational Text Ser.). (ENG.). 32p. (gr. 3-5). pap. 11.99 *(978-1-4333-5041-2(6))* Teacher Created Materials, Inc.

—Los Caddo y los Comanche. 2013. (Primary Source Readers Ser.). (SPA.). lib. bdg. 19.65 *(978-0-606-31861-7(5))* Turtleback.

—Los Indígenas Americanos de Texas (American Indians in Texas) 2013. (Primary Source Readers Ser.). (SPA.). lib. bdg. 19.65 *(978-0-606-31860-0(7))* Turtleback.

Pickman, Richard. Anglo-American Colonization of Texas, 1 vol. 2010. (Spotlight on Texas Ser.). (ENG.). 32p. (J). (gr. 3-4). pap. 11.75 *(978-1-61532-462-0(3)*, 50a3af17-958b-42c8-aff4-c58f776a825a); (Illus.). lib. bdg. 28.93 *(978-1-61532-464-4(X)*, bc876178-4f44-4a2a-b4f5-14388abf3a04) Rosen Publishing Group, Inc., The.

Pratt, Laura. Texas: The Lone Star State. 2012. (J). *(978-1-61913-407-2(1))*; pap. *(978-1-61913-408-9(X))* Weigl Pubs., Inc.

Quezada, José Luis. Geography of Texas, 1 vol. 2018. (Explore Texas Ser.). (ENG.). 24p. (gr. 9-12). 26.27 *(978-1-5081-8660-1(X)*, 2ff30a94-33e1-46a9-b9c1-c926c205bf5b, Rosen Young Adult) Rosen Publishing Group, Inc., The.

Raatma, Lucia. Barbara Jordan, 1 vol. 2013. (Leading Women Ser.). (ENG.). 96p. (YA). (gr. 7-7). pap. 20.99 *(978-1-62712-114-9(5)*, c1f7fc2d-5916-43ad-b6a4-acdad06e7612) Cavendish Square Publishing LLC.

Rajczak, Kristin. The Civil Rights Movement in Texas, 1 vol. 2014. (Spotlight on Texas Ser.). (ENG., Illus.). 32p. (J). (gr. 3-4). 28.93 *(978-1-4777-4562-5(9)*, 80cdebeb-b6eb-43a6-b251-a68ed2039f2a, Rosen Classroom) Rosen Publishing Group, Inc., The.

Rajczak, Michael. Texas Geography, 1 vol. 2014. (Spotlight on Texas Ser.). (ENG.). 32p. (J). (gr. 3-4). 28.93 *(978-1-4777-4532-8(7)*, 9d1ddfed-a253-41d4-9500-9a65e626c0ec, Rosen Classroom) Rosen Publishing Group, Inc., The.

Randolph, Joanne. The Angel of Goliad: Francisca Alvarez & the Texas War for Independence. (Great Moments in American History Ser.). 32p. (gr. 3-3). 2009. 47.90 *(978-1-61513-151-8(5))* 2003. (ENG., Illus.). (YA). lib. bdg. 29.13 *(978-0-8239-4350-0(X)*, 13ceef35-38a5-4af7-a18e-3412d36df256) Rosen Publishing Group, Inc., The.

Rea, Amy C. The Battle of the Alamo Ignites Independence. 2018. (Events That Changed America Ser.). (ENG.). 32p. (J). (gr. 3-6). lib. bdg. 35.64 *(978-1-5038-2519-2(1)*, 212327, MOMENTUM) Child's World, Inc, The.

Riehecky, Janet & O'Hern, Kerri. La Batalla de el Álamo (the Battle of the Alamo), 1 vol. 2007. (Historias Gráficas (Graphic Histories) Ser.). (SPA., Illus.). 32p. (gr. 3-3). pap. 11.50 *(978-0-8368-7900-1(7)*, 4b965390-9b12-4920-84f7-170f9007db3d); lib. bdg. 29.67 *(978-0-8368-7893-6(0)*, 6e6d81a2-3bed-40f8-ae41-f557ba50781c) Stevens, Gareth Publishing LLLP.

—The Battle of the Alamo, 1 vol. 2005. (Graphic Histories Ser.). (ENG., Illus.). 32p. (gr. 3-3). pap. 11.50 *(978-0-8368-6253-9(8)*, 4f0bf604-8278-4d83-9b24-445ded5259ca); lib. bdg. 29.67 *(978-0-8368-6201-0(5)*, eeeda695-f91c-4d37-888d-50b3a29fa9ec) Stevens, Gareth Publishing LLLP.

RJF Publishing Staff & Burgan, Michael. The Alamo. 2009. (Symbols of American Freedom Ser.). 48p. (gr. 4-6). 30.00 *(978-1-60413-512-1(3)*, Chelsea Clubhse.) Infobase Holdings, Inc.

Roberts, Russell. The Life & Times of Stephen F. Austin. 2007. (Profiles in American History Ser.). (Illus.). 48p. (J). (gr. 4-7). lib. bdg. 29.95 *(978-1-58415-531-7(0))* Mitchell Lane Pubs.

—Texas Joins the United States. 2007. (Building America Ser.). (Illus.). 48p. (J). (gr. 4-8). lib. bdg. 29.95 *(978-1-58415-550-8(7))* Mitchell Lane Pubs.

Rodgers, Kelly. Leaders in the Texas Revolution: United for a Cause, 1 vol. rev. ed. 2012. (Social Studies: Informational Text Ser.). (ENG.). 32p. (gr. 3-5). pap. 11.99 *(978-1-4333-5047-4(5))* Teacher Created Materials, Inc.

—Líderes de la Revolución de Texas (Leaders in the Texas Revolution) 2013. (Primary Source Readers Ser.). (SPA.). lib. bdg. 19.65 *(978-0-606-31867-9(4))* Turtleback.

—La Revolución de Texas. 2013. (Primary Source Readers Ser.). (SPA.). lib. bdg. 19.65 *(978-0-606-31866-2(6))* Turtleback.

—The Texas Revolution: Fighting for Independence, 1 vol. rev. ed. 2012. (Social Studies: Informational Text Ser.). (ENG.). 32p. (gr. 3-5). pap. 11.99 *(978-1-4333-5046-7(7))* Teacher Created Materials, Inc.

Roza, Greg. Early Explorers of Texas, 1 vol. 2010. (Spotlight on Texas Ser.). (ENG., Illus.). 32p. (J). (gr. 3-4). pap. 11.75 *(978-1-61532-454-5(2)*, 7050558f-a298-4ff0-9da2-01cc42f50718); lib. bdg. 28.93 *(978-1-61532-489-7(5)*, de361511-24e5-429e-ab90-546e2a6a9bae) Rosen Publishing Group, Inc., The.

—The Karankawa of Texas. 2009. (Library of Native Americans Ser.). 64p. (gr. 4-4). 58.50 *(978-1-60853-748-8(X)*, PowerKids Pr.) Rosen Publishing Group, Inc., The.

—Texas Cities: Then & Now, 1 vol. 2014. (Spotlight on Texas Ser.). (ENG.). 32p. (J). (gr. 3-4). 28.93 *(978-1-4777-4551-9(3)*, b3032ba4-c388-4248-829a-6323bf1fd936, Rosen Classroom) Rosen Publishing Group, Inc., The.

Ruffin, Frances E. The Alamo, 1 vol. 2005. (Places in American History Ser.). (ENG., Illus.). 24p. (gr. 2-4). pap. 9.15 *(978-0-8368-6414-4(X)*, badf965a-9986-4d6f-b1b0-448864fa948b); lib. bdg. 24.67 *(978-0-8368-6407-6(7)*, 05c51642-aaca-436a-91a5-9e2b789ef7a0) Stevens, Gareth Publishing LLLP. (Weekly Reader Leveled Readers).

Ryckman, Tatiana, et al. Texas: The Lone Star State, 1 vol. 2019. (It's My State! (Fourth Edition)(r) Ser.). (ENG.). 80p. (gr. 4-4). lib. bdg. 35.93 *(978-1-5026-4289-9(1)*, 74f8ee87-5227-4e99-a078-66db809a4aae) Cavendish Square Publishing LLC.

Sanford, William R. & Green, Carl R. Richard King: Courageous Texas Cattleman, 1 vol. 2013. (Courageous Heroes of the American West Ser.). (ENG., Illus.). 48p. (J). (gr. 5-7). 25.27 *(978-0-7660-4003-8(8)*, 61d735bd-1176-4a8c-85c5-7ad480486444) Enslow Publishing, LLC.

Sarantou, Katlin. James Bowie. Bane, Jeff, illus. 2019. (My Early Library: My Itty-Bitty Bio Ser.). (ENG.). 24p. (J). (gr. k-1). pap. 12.79 *(978-1-5341-4991-5(0)*, 213271); lib. bdg. 30.64 *(978-1-5341-4705-8(5)*, 213270) Cherry Lake Publishing.

Scher, Linda. The Texas City Disaster. 2007. (Code Red Ser.). (Illus.). 32p. (YA). (gr. 2-5). lib. bdg. 28.50 *(978-1-59716-363-7(5))* Bearport Publishing Co., Inc.

Schwartz, Heather. Lizzie Johnson: Texan Cowgirl, 1 vol. rev. ed. 2012. (Social Studies: Informational Text Ser.). (ENG.). 32p. (gr. 3-5). pap. 11.99 *(978-1-4333-5051-1(3))* Teacher Created Materials, Inc.

—War, Cattle, & Cowboys: Texas as a Young State, 1 vol. rev. ed. 2012. (Social Studies: Informational Text Ser.). (ENG.). 32p. (gr. 3-5). pap. 11.99 *(978-1-4333-5050-4(5))* Teacher Created Materials, Inc.

Shoup, Kate. Texas & the Mexican War, 1 vol. 2015. (Expanding America Ser.). (ENG., Illus.). 96p. (YA). (gr. 8-8). 44.50 *(978-1-5026-0964-9(9)*, 13856eb5-390f-40da-8db6-c8e09c49ab01) Cavendish Square Publishing LLC.

Sirota, Lyn A. Houston. 2017. (Illus.). 24p. (J). *(978-1-4896-7297-1(4)*, AV2 by Weigl) Weigl Pubs., Inc.

Skewes, John & Mullin, Michael. Larry Gets Lost in Texas. Skewes, John, illus. 2010. (Larry Gets Lost Ser.). (ENG., Illus.). 32p. (J). (gr. -1-2). 17.99 *(978-1-57061-680-8(9)*, Little Bigfoot) Sasquatch Bks.

Smith, Andrea P. Jim Bowie. (Illus.). 24p. (J). 2012. 63.60 *(978-1-4488-5231-4(5))* 2011. (ENG., (gr. 2-3). pap. 11.60 *(978-1-4488-5230-7(7)*, 350e3856-77a0-4675-80e7-d692a70b936b) 2011. (ENG., (gr. 2-3). lib. bdg. 28.93 *(978-1-4488-5196-6(3)*, 1d58db0c-2356-4f99-8a9c-b1fa3cc8f0f6) Rosen Publishing Group, Inc., The. (PowerKids Pr.).

Sorrels, Roy. The Legend of the Alamo: Stories in American History, 1 vol. 2012. (Stories in American History Ser.). (ENG., Illus.). 128p. (gr. 5-6). 35.93 *(978-0-7660-3952-0(8)*, a5f11f65-06b9-486e-baeb-cba5de6774d0) Enslow Publishing, LLC.

South, Victor. Remember the Alamo: Americans Fight for Texas, 1820-1845. 2012. (Illus.). 48p. (J). pap. *(978-1-4222-2416-8(3))* Mason Crest.

—Remember the Alamo: Americans Fight for Texas, 1820-1845. Rakove, Jack N., ed. 2012. (How America Became America Ser.). (Illus.). 48p. (J). (gr. 3-4). 19.95 *(978-1-4222-2402-1(3))* Mason Crest.

—Remember the Alamo (1820-1845) 2018. (J). *(978-1-5105-3598-5(5))* SmartBook Media, Inc.

Spotlight on Texas: Sets 1 - 2, 48 vols. 2014. (Spotlight on Texas Ser.). (ENG.). 32p. (J). (gr. 3-4). 694.32 *(978-1-4777-4567-0(X)*, dff28c31-7ae5-42b0-a71d-3a885a6815da, Rosen Classroom) Rosen Publishing Group, Inc., The.

Spotlight on Texas: The Growth & Development of the Lone Star State, 24 vols. Set. Incl. Alamo. Hoffman, Mary Ann. lib. bdg. 28.93 *(978-1-61532-461-3(5)*, f8c42bff-17a8-45c5-a18f-6d679d62fc37); American Civil War in Texas. Burke, Johanna. lib. bdg. 28.93 *(978-1-61532-474-3(7)*, c997ea17-cc53-4c08-9613-944de605c0f6); Anglo-American Colonization of Texas. Pickman, Richard. lib. bdg. 28.93 *(978-1-61532-464-4(X)*, bc876178-4f44-4a2a-b4f5-14388abf3a04); Cattle & Oil: The Growth of Texas Industries. James, Trisha. lib. bdg. 28.93 *(978-1-61532-477-4(1)*, 4a615f41-ad49-4537-87c6-c9ab4bc9bd62); Causes & Effects of the Texas Revolution. Harasymiw, Therese. lib. bdg. 28.93 *(978-1-61532-468-2(2)*, 085d3faa-a2ee-4962-88b0-c3e2af291930); Celebrating Texas: Patriotic Symbols & Landmarks. James, Trisha. lib. bdg. 28.93 *(978-1-61532-486-6(0)*, 2f1ac580-4512-48ee-91b5-f030e002c736); Early Explorers of Texas. Roza, Greg. lib. bdg. 28.93 *(978-1-61532-489-7(5)*, de361511-24e5-429e-ab90-546e2a6a9bae); Governing Texas: Local, State, & National Governments. Cane, Sutter. lib. bdg. 28.93 *(978-1-61532-483-5(6)*, d171b66b-cfbe-47d3-b5dd-c088a154a4a8); Land & Resources of Texas: Shaping the Growth of the State. Marfa, Isabelle. lib. bdg. 28.93 *(978-1-61532-480-4(1)*, ccfc673c-de8c-4cc5-a9a7-c32e75942b0e); (J). (gr. 3-4). (Spotlight on Texas Ser.). (ENG., Illus.). 32p. 2010. Set lib. bdg. 347.16 *(978-1-61532-856-7(4)*, 2c7bc668-367c-4990-b61c-fb512826f360, PowerKids Pr.) Rosen Publishing Group, Inc., The.

Spotlight on Texas: The Growth & Development of The Lone Star State: Set 2, 24 vols. 2014. (Spotlight on Texas Ser.). (ENG.). 32p. (J). (gr. 3-4). 347.16 *(978-1-4777-4561-8(0)*, b81c9ae7-0a74-43bf-89f0-1cb9b66a9f1b, Rosen Classroom) Rosen Publishing Group, Inc., The.

The State of Texas 8-Book Set. 2014. (Book Collection). (ENG., Illus.). 32p. (gr. 4-5). 79.92 *(978-1-4938-0876-2(1))* Teacher Created Materials, Inc.

Steele, Christy. Texas Joins the United States, 1 vol. 2004. (America's Westward Expansion Ser.). (ENG., Illus.). 48p. (gr. 5-8). lib. bdg. 33.67 *(978-0-8368-5791-7(7)*, 5bbe3e00-4e06-4bfe-b879-5ee9087bba68, Gareth Stevens Secondary Library) Stevens, Gareth Publishing LLLP.

Steinagle, Jason. Citizenship: What It Means to Be from Texas, 1 vol. 2014. (Spotlight on Texas Ser.). (ENG., Illus.). 32p. (J). (gr. 3-4). 28.93 *(978-1-4777-4546-5(7)*, 1ffb5267-4a8c-4867-ab88-442b5d149b7c, Rosen Classroom) Rosen Publishing Group, Inc., The.

Temple, Teri & Temple, Bob. Remember the Alamo. 2006. (Events in American History Ser.). (Illus.). 48p. (YA). (gr. 3-6). lib. bdg. 31.36 *(978-1-60044-125-7(4))* Rourke Educational Media.

Thomas, Deborah. I Spy in the Texas Sky, 1 vol. Thomas, Deborah, illus. 2018. (I Spy Ser.). (ENG., Illus.). 32p. (J). (gr. -1-3). 8.99 *(978-1-4556-2420-1(9)*, Pelican Publishing) Arcadia Publishing.

Turner, Carolyn. Sam Houston. 2010. pap. 9.95 *(978-1-61690-066-3(0))*; 24p. (J). (gr. 2-4). lib. bdg. 25.70 *(978-1-61690-065-6(2))* Weigl Pubs., Inc.

Uhl, Xina M. The Texas Revolution. 2018. (Expansion of Our Nation Ser.). (ENG.). 32p. (J). (gr. 3-5). pap. 9.95 *(978-1-63517-988-0(2)*, 1635179882); lib. bdg. 31.35 *(978-1-63517-887-6(8)*, 1635178878) North Star Editions. (Focus Readers).

Wade, Mary Dodson. Texas History. 2003. (Heinemann State Studies). (Illus.). 48p. (J). lib. bdg. 27.07 *(978-1-4034-0687-3(1))* Heinemann-Raintree.

—Texas Plants & Animals. 2003. (Heinemann State Studies). (Illus.). 48p. (J). lib. bdg. 27.07 *(978-1-4034-0690-3(1))* Heinemann-Raintree.

Walker, Paul & Walker, Paul Robert. Remember the Alamo: Texians, Tejanos, & Mexicans Tell Their Stories. 2015. (Illus.). 64p. (J). (gr. 5-9). pap. 7.99 *(978-1-4263-2249-5(6)*, National Geographic Kids) Disney Publishing Worldwide.

Warrick, Karen Clemens. Remember the Alamo! The Battle for Texas Independence. 2019. (J). pap. *(978-1-9785-1533-8(2))* Enslow Publishing, LLC.

Wimberley, John. Life in the Republic of Texas, 1 vol. 2010. (Spotlight on Texas Ser.). (ENG., Illus.). 32p. (J). (gr. 3-4). 28.93 *(978-1-61532-471-2(2)*, 4b72cb7f-c591-4282-882c-0fe60e318846); pap. 11.75 *(978-1-61532-469-9(0)*, 9fee09ff-4c6a-4417-b05f-1c856d9a5fe7) Rosen Publishing Group, Inc., The.

Woodward, Mac. Sam Houston: For Texas & the Union. 2009. (Library of American Lives & Times Ser.). 112p. (gr. 5-5). 69.20 *(978-1-60853-504-0(5))* Rosen Publishing Group, Inc., The.

Worth, Richard. The Texas War of Independence: The 1800s, 1 vol. 2009. (Hispanic America Ser.). (ENG.). 80p. (gr. 5-5). lib. bdg. 36.93 *(978-0-7614-2934-0(4)*, 15e26fa2-4c55-418b-9cdd-d43ad323078b) Cavendish Square Publishing LLC.

TEXAS RANGERS

Newton, Michael. The Texas Rangers. 2010. (Law Enforcement Agencies Ser.). (Illus.). 128p. (gr. 6-12). 35.00 *(978-1-60413-626-5(X)*, Facts On File) Infobase Holdings, Inc.

TEXAS RANGERS (BASEBALL TEAM)

Gilbert, Sara. The Story of the Texas Rangers. 2011. (Baseball: the Great American Game Ser.). (Illus.). 48p. (J). (gr. 5-8). lib. bdg. 34.25 *(978-1-60818-058-5(1)*, Creative Education) Creative Co., The.

Lace, William W. Nolan Ryan: Hall of Fame Baseball Superstar, 1 vol. 2013. (Hall of Fame Sports Greats Ser.). (ENG.). 64p. (gr. 4-6). pap. 12.71 *(978-1-62285-026-6(2)*, 7b79d045-1d7c-4192-b92f-ddc195a4f1fb) Enslow Publishing, LLC.

Lajiness, Katie. Texas Rangers. 2018. (MLB's Greatest Teams Ser.). (ENG., Illus.). 32p. (J). (gr. 2-5). lib. bdg. 34.21 *(978-1-5321-1521-9(0)*, 28878, Big Buddy Bks.) ABDO Publishing Co.

Richardson, Adele. The Story of the Texas Rangers. 2007. (Baseball, the Great American Game Ser.). (Illus.). 48p. (YA). (gr. 4-7). lib. bdg. 32.80 *(978-1-58341-502-3(5))* Creative Co., The.

Stewart, Mark. The Texas Rangers. 2012. (Team Spirit Ser.). 48p. (J). (gr. 3-6). lib. bdg. 29.27 *(978-1-59953-499-2(1))* Norwood Hse. Pr.

TEXTILE FABRICS

see Textile Industry

TEXTILE INDUSTRY

see also Cotton Manufacture; Dyes and Dyeing; Tapestry; Weaving

also names of special textile fabrics, (e.g. Silk); and names of articles manufactured, e.g. Carpets

American History Arts & Crafts, 12 vols. 2014. (American History Arts & Crafts Ser.). (ENG.). 32p. (J). (gr. 4-5). lib. bdg. 175.62 *(978-1-4777-5727-7(9)*, e23f7171-2d17-4074-81a9-92d08969d17b, PowerKids Pr.) Rosen Publishing Group, Inc., The.

Carlson, Laurie. Knit, Hook, & Spin: A Kid's Activity Guide to Fiber Arts & Crafts. 2016. (ENG., Illus.). 144p. (J). (gr. 4-7). pap. 16.99 *(978-1-61373-400-1(X))* Chicago Review Pr., Inc.

Delta Education. Sci Res Bk Foss Grade K Next Gen Ea. 2015. (Illus.). 231p. (J). lib. bdg. *(978-1-62571-444-2(0))* Delta Education, LLC.

Grack, Rachel. Cotton to T-Shirt. 2020. (Beginning to End Ser.). (ENG.). 24p. (J). (gr. k-3). 26.95 *(978-1-64487-139-3(4)*, Blastoff! Readers) Bellwether Media.

Kinsner, Kathy. Fabric Around the World. 2004. (Shared Connections Ser.). (J). instr.'s gde. ed. 27.00 *(978-1-4108-1622-1(2))* Benchmark Education Co.

—Fabric Around the World: Small Book. 2004. (Shared Connections Ser.). (J). pap. *(978-1-4108-1646-7(X))* Benchmark Education Co.

Mara, Wil. From Sharks to... Swimsuits. 2012. (21st Century Skills Innovation Library: Innovations from Nature Ser.). (ENG.). 32p. (gr. 4-8). pap. 14.21 *(978-1-61080-673-2(5)*, 202283); (Illus.). 32.07 *(978-1-61080-499-8(6)*, 202109) Cherry Lake Publishing.

Mitchell, Melanie S. Cloth. 2003. (First Step Nonfiction - Materials Ser.). (ENG., Illus.). 24p. (gr. k-2). lib. bdg. 23.93 *(978-0-8225-4616-0(7))* Lerner Publishing Group.

Morris, Neil. Textiles. 2010. (Materials That Matter Ser.). (ENG.). 32p. (J). (gr. 4-6). lib. bdg. 28.50 *(978-1-60753-069-5(4)*, 14868) Amicus.

Nelson, Robin. From Cotton to T-Shirt. 2013. (Start to Finish, Second Ser.). (ENG., Illus.). 24p. (J). (gr. k-3). pap. 7.99 *(978-0-7613-8572-1(X)*, 321b05d5-f88a-481b-b2d8-1b93eeba025a) Lerner Publishing Group.

—From Sheep to Sweater. 2013. (Start to Finish, Second Ser.). (ENG., Illus.). 24p. (J). (gr. k-3). pap. 7.99 *(978-0-7613-8575-2(4)*, 6b960d33-c81c-4352-89bb-9b9e4a47e33d) Lerner Publishing Group.

Poratto, Maria Laura. Costura para Ninos. 2004. (SPA., Illus.). 48p. (J). pap. 7.95 *(978-987-550-297-0(9))* Longseller S.A. ARG. Dist: Libros Sin Fronteras.

Rivera, Andrea. Cloth. 2017. (Materials Ser.). (ENG., Illus.). 24p. (J). (gr. -1-2). lib. bdg. 31.36 *(978-1-5321-2029-9(X)*, 25294, Abdo Zoom-Launch) ABDO Publishing Co.

Senker, Cath. Immigrants & Refugees. 2012. (Mapping Global Issues Ser.). 48p. (J). (gr. 7-9). lib. bdg. 34.25 *(978-1-59920-509-0(2))* Black Rabbit Bks.

Sohn, Emily. Fabric. 2019. (iScience Ser.). (ENG., Illus.). 24p. (J). (gr. k-2). pap. 13.26 *(978-1-68404-359-0(X))* Norwood Hse. Pr.

Spilsbury, Louise. Tapestries & Textiles, 1 vol. 2008. (Stories in Art Ser.). (ENG., Illus.). 32p. (J). (gr. 4-4). lib. bdg. 30.27 *(978-1-4042-4436-8(0)*, 25a63e00-4efd-4b42-ae94-0c1b086c617e) Rosen Publishing Group, Inc., The.

Storey, Rita. Wool & Cotton. 2007. (How We Use Materials/Watts Ser.). (Illus.). 30p. (J). (gr. 4-7). lib. bdg. 28.50 *(978-1-59920-001-9(5))* Black Rabbit Bks.

Thomson, Ruth. What Are Textiles? 2005. (Art's Alive! Ser.). (Illus.). 30p. (J). (gr. 3-7). lib. bdg. 27.10 *(978-1-932889-90-1(6))* Sea-To-Sea Pubns.

Tiner, John Hudson. Cloth. 2003. (Matter & Materials Ser.). (J). *(978-1-58417-168-3(5))*; *(978-1-58417-162-1(6))* Lake Street Pubs.

Top That Publishing Staff, ed. Funky Fabrics. 2004. (Creative Studios Ser.). (Illus.). 48p. (J). *(978-1-84510-249-4(5))* Top That! Publishing PLC.

Toth-Chernin, Jan. E-Textiles. 2013. (21st Century Skills Innovation Library: Makers As Innovators Ser.). (ENG., Illus.). 32p. (J). (gr. 4-8). pap. 14.21 *(978-1-62431-272-4(1)*, 202882); lib. bdg. 32.07 *(978-1-62431-140-6(7)*, 202880) Cherry Lake Publishing.

Warwick, Ellen. Injeanuity. Lum, Bernice, illus. 2006. (Planet Girl Ser.). 80p. (J). (gr. 7-12). 12.95 *(978-1-55337-681-1(1))* Kids Can Pr., Ltd. CAN. Dist: Hachette Bk. Group.

Wilman, Lisa. Art & Culture: Patterns of the Past: Partitioning Shapes (Grade 2) 2018. (Mathematics in the Real World Ser.). (ENG., Illus.). 32p. (J). (gr. 2-3). pap. 10.99 *(978-1-4258-5759-2(0))* Teacher Created Materials, Inc.

Wilman, Lisa A. Diseños Del Pasado: Partición de Figuras. rev. ed. 2018. (Mathematics in the Real World Ser.). (SPA., Illus.). 32p. (J). (gr. 2-3). pap. 10.99 *(978-1-4258-2876-9(0))* Teacher Created Materials, Inc.

Wyckoff, Edwin Brit. The Woman Who Invented the Thread That Stops Bullets: The Genius of Stephanie Kwolek, 1 vol. 2013. (Genius Inventors & Their Great Ideas Ser.). (ENG.). 48p. (gr. 3-3). pap. 11.53 *(978-1-4644-0211-1(6)*, f841a11a-d92b-4e4e-a7de-2bfd3590872b, Enslow Elementary); (Illus.). 27.93 *(978-0-7660-4141-7(7)*, 24c27399-4f45-4030-9d60-c3f00e51f0fa) Enslow Publishing, LLC.

TEXTILE PAINTING

Books, Applewood. Textiles (Pictorial America) Vintage Images of America's Living Past. 2009. (Pictorial America Ser.). (ENG.). 56p. (J). pap. 9.95 *(978-1-60889-013-2(9))* Applewood Bks.

TUV

THACKERAY, WILLIAM MAKEPEACE, 1811-1863

Salmon, Richard. William Makepeace Thackeray. 2005. (Writers & Their Work Ser.). (ENG.). 128p. 99.00 *(978-0-7463-1030-4(7),* 9780746310304); pap. 32.95 *(978-0-7463-0996-4(1),* 9780746309964) Liverpool Univ. Pr. GBR. Dist: Oxford Univ. Pr., Inc.

THAILAND

Aloian, Molly. Cultural Traditions in Thailand. 2012. (ENG.). 32p. (J). *(978-0-7787-7519-5(4));* (Illus.). pap. *(978-0-7787-7524-9(0))* Crabtree Publishing Co.

Daniels-Cowart, Catrina. Thailand. 2019. (Asian Countries Today Ser.). (Illus.). 96p. (J). (gr. 12). lib. bdg. 34.60 *(978-1-4222-4271-1(4))* Mason Crest.

Donaldson, Madeline. Thailand. 2011. (Country Explorers Ser.). (ENG., Illus.). 48p. (J). (gr. 2-4). lib. bdg. 29.32 *(978-0-7613-6414-6(5),* c998d94f-7157-4bc2-b566-cefbbac0cfd0, Lerner Pubns.) Lerner Publishing Group.

Furstinger, Nancy. Bangkok, 1 vol. 2005. (Cities Set 1 Ser.). (Illus.). 32p. (gr. k-6). 27.07 *(978-1-59197-852-7(1),* Checkerboard Library) ABDO Publishing Co.

Glaser, Chaya. Thailand. 2018. (Countries We Come From Ser.). (ENG., Illus.). 32p. (J). (gr. k-3). 19.95 *(978-1-68402-687-6(3))* Bearport Publishing Co., Inc.

Goodman, Jim. Thailand, 1 vol. 2nd ed. 2003. (Cultures of the World (First Edition)(r) Ser.). (ENG., Illus.). 144p. (gr. 5-5). lib. bdg. 49.79 *(978-0-7614-1478-0(9),* 728c6d9f-393a-4d51-bf31-da29a423c3dc) Cavendish Square Publishing LLC.

Goodman, Jim & Spilling, Michael. Thailand, 1 vol. 3rd rev. ed. 2012. (Cultures of the World (Third Edition)(r) Ser.). (ENG.). 144p. (gr. 5-5). lib. bdg. 48.79 *(978-1-60870-995-3(7),* 2b419f65-b0e7-450c-aee2-d1949d9a8b8f) Cavendish Square Publishing LLC.

Hill, Valerie. Thailand. 2004. (Ask about Asia Ser.). (Illus.). 48p. (J). (gr. 4-18). lib. bdg. 19.95 *(978-1-59084-205-8(7))* Mason Crest.

Mattern, Joanne. Thailand. 2019. (Exploring World Cultures Ser.). (ENG.). 32p. (gr. 3-3). 66.96 *(978-1-5026-4723-8(0))* Cavendish Square Publishing LLC.

Meachen Rau, Dana. Thailand, 1 vol. 2007. (Discovering Cultures Ser.). (ENG., Illus.). 48p. (gr. 3-4). lib. bdg. 31.21 *(978-0-7614-1989-1(6),* cae376d1-2a07-4372-a85f-dc412c842884) Cavendish Square Publishing LLC.

Oachs, Emily Rose. Thailand. 2018. (Country Profiles Ser.). (ENG., Illus.). 32p. (J). (gr. 3-8). lib. bdg. 27.95 *(978-1-62617-736-9(8),* Blastoff! Discovery) Bellwether Media.

Orr, Tamra. Thailand. 2018. (Illus.). 32p. (J). *(978-1-4896-7508-6(6),* AV2 by Weigl) Weigl Pubs., Inc.

Poole, H. W. The Thai Family Table, Vol. 11. 2018. (Connecting Cultures Through Family & Food Ser.). (Illus.). 64p. (J). (gr. 7). lib. bdg. 31.93 *(978-1-4222-4052-6(5))* Mason Crest.

Poole, Hilary W. & Rich, Mari. The Thai Family Table, Vol. 11. 2018. (Connecting Cultures Through Family & Food Ser.). (Illus.). 64p. (J). (gr. 7). 31.93 *(978-1-4222-4047-2(9))* Mason Crest.

Raatma, Lucia. It's Cool to Learn about Countries: Thailand. 2012. (Explorer Library: Social Studies Explorer Ser.). (ENG.). 48p. (gr. 4-8). pap. 15.64 *(978-1-61080-615-2(8),* 202225) Cherry Lake Publishing.

—It's Cool to Learn about Countries: Thailand. 2012. (Explorer Library: Social Studies Explorer Ser.). (ENG., Illus.). 48p. (gr. 4-8). 34.93 *(978-1-61080-441-7(4),* 202051) Cherry Lake Publishing.

Russell, Elaine. All about Thailand: Stories, Songs, Crafts & Games for Kids. Meesukhon, Patcharee & Yeesman, Vinit, illus. 2016. 64p. (J). (gr. 3-6). 14.95 *(978-0-8048-4427-7(5))* Tuttle Publishing.

Sheen, Barbara. Foods of Thailand, 1 vol. 2006. (Taste of Culture Ser.). (ENG., Illus.). 64p. (gr. 3-6). lib. bdg. 30.38 *(978-0-7377-3037-1(4),* c3c7b77c-66d8-4482-8180-de97d6c8f33d, KidHaven Publishing) Greenhaven Publishing LLC.

Sobol, Richard, photos by. An Elephant in the Backyard. 2004. (Illus.). (J). *(978-0-525-46970-4(2),* Dutton Juvenile) Penguin Publishing Group.

Taus-Bolstad, Stacy. Thailand in Pictures. 2nd ed. 2003. (Visual Geography Series, Second Ser.). (ENG., Illus.). 80p. (gr. 5-12). 31.93 *(978-0-8225-0939-4(3))* Lerner Publishing Group.

Tecco, Betsy Dru. How to Draw Thailand's Sights & Symbols. 2009. (Kid's Guide to Drawing the Countries of the World Ser.). 48p. (gr. 4-4). 53.00 *(978-1-61511-127-5(1),* PowerKids Pr.) Rosen Publishing Group, Inc., The.

THAILAND—FICTION

Ayer, Jacqueline, creator. Nu Dang & His Kite. 2017. (Illus.). 40p. (J). (gr. -1-3). 16.95 *(978-1-59270-231-2(7))* Enchanted Lion Bks., LLC.

—The Paper-Flower Tree. 2017. (Illus.). 40p. (J). (gr. -1-3). 16.95 *(978-1-59270-224-4(4))* Enchanted Lion Bks., LLC.

Bridges, Shirin Yim. The Umbrella Queen. 2008. (ENG., Illus.). 40p. (J). (gr. k-3). 17.99 *(978-0-06-075040-4(5),* Greenwillow Bks.) HarperCollins Pubs.

Fleischman, Sid. The White Elephant. McGuire, Robert, illus. 2006. 112p. (J). (gr. 3-7). 15.99 *(978-0-06-113136-3(9),* Greenwillow Bks.) HarperCollins Pubs.

Gilligan, Shannon. The Case of the Silk King. Pornkerd, Vorrarit et al, illus. 2006. (ENG.). 144p. (J). (gr. 4-8). per. 7.99 *(978-1-933390-14-7(X),* CHCL14) Chooseco LLC.

—The Case of the Silk King. 2005. 116p. (J). pap. *(978-0-7608-9702-7(6))* Sundance/Newbridge Educational Publishing.

Joo, Mi-hwa. I Am a Little Monk: Thailand. Cowley, Joy, ed. Gahng, Hwa-kyeong, illus. 2015. (Global Kids Storybooks Ser.). (ENG.). 32p. (gr. 1-4). 26.65 *(978-1-925246-06-3(X));* 7.99 *(978-1-925246-58-2(2));* 26.65 *(978-1-925246-32-2(9))* ChoiceMaker Pty. Ltd., The AUS. (Big and SMALL). Dist: Lerner Publishing Group.

—I Am a Little Monk: Thailand. Gahng, Hwa-kyeong, illus. 2015. (Global Kids Storybooks Ser.). (ENG.). 32p. (J). (gr. 1-4). pap. 8.99 *(978-1-925233-47-6(2),* d02968dc-c93f-4e77-957c-627f3c234e51, Big and SMALL) ChoiceMaker Pty. Ltd., The AUS. Dist: Lerner Publishing Group.

Jordan, Lana. The Sleepytime Ponies Trick a Trickster. Allen, Kd & Giraud, Teresa, illus. 2004. 32p. (J). 12.95 *(978-0-9710696-1-9(1))* Jordan Publishing, Inc.

Martin, Tamra. My Wish, Our Little Oat. Tinker, Jason, illus. 2007. 36p. (J). 21.99 *(978-1-59879-522-6(8),* Lifevest) Lifevest Publishing, Inc.

Oliviero, Jamie. Som See & the Magic Elephant. Kelly, Joanne, illus. 2005. 27p. (J). (gr. -1-2). reprint ed. 17.00 *(978-0-7567-8929-9(X))* DIANE Publishing Co.

Pedigo, Kim Tran. Having Fun with Kandai the Elephant. 2nd ed. 2013. (Illus.). 34p. pap. 11.95 *(978-0-9885603-1-4(3))* Outrival Publishing.

—Kandai the Elephant Goes Bananas. 2013. 32p. pap. 11.95 *(978-0-9885603-0-7(5));* 2nd ed. 17.95 *(978-0-9885603-2-1(1))* Outrival Publishing.

Phumiruk, Dow. Mela & the Elephant. Chen, Ziyue, illus. 2018. (ENG.). 32p. (J). (gr. k-3). 18.99 *(978-1-58536-998-0(5),* 204407) Sleeping Bear Pr.

Towe, H.P. Mr. Monkey Sees & Mr. Monkey Do. 2013. 24p. pap. 14.93 *(978-1-4669-8760-9(X))* Trafford Publishing.

VanArsdale, Anthony, illus. The Detour of the Elephants. 2017. (Boxcar Children Great Adventure Ser.: 3). (ENG.). 144p. (J). (gr. 2-5). 6.99 *(978-0-8075-0685-1(0),* 807506850, Random Hse. Bks. for Young Readers) Random Hse. Children's Bks.

THAMES RIVER AND VALLEY

Manning, Paul. The Thames. (River Adventures Ser.). 2014. (J). lib. bdg. 31.35 *(978-1-59920-918-0(7))* 2013. 48p. (gr. 5-11). lib. bdg. 37.10 *(978-1-59920-924-1(1))* Black Rabbit Bks.

THANKSGIVING DAY

Adams, Colleen. The True Story of the First Thanksgiving. (What Really Happened? Ser.). 24p. (gr. 2-3). 2009. 42.50 *(978-1-60854-769-2(8),* PowerKids Pr.) 2008. (ENG., Illus.). (YA). lib. bdg. 26.27 *(978-1-4042-4476-4(X),* 75e4ee5b-1790-44d7-9f9b-f53612dfdaf3) Rosen Publishing Group, Inc., The.

Adams, Michelle Medlock. What Is Thanksgiving? 2014. (ENG., Illus.). 22p. (J). (gr. -1-1). bds. 7.99 *(978-0-8249-1938-2(6),* Ideals Pubns.) Worthy Publishing.

Anderson, Laurie Halse. Thank You, Sarah: The Woman Who Saved Thanksgiving. Faulkner, Matt, illus. 2005. (ENG.). 40p. (J). (gr. 1-3). 7.99 *(978-0-689-85143-8(X),* Simon & Schuster Bks. For Young Readers) Simon & Schuster Bks. For Young Readers.

Appleby, Alex. ¡Feliz día de Acción de Gracias! / Happy Thanksgiving!, 1 vol., Vol. 1. 2013. (¡Felices Fiestas! / Happy Holidays! Ser.). (SPA & ENG.). 24p. (J). (gr. k-k). 25.27 *(978-1-4339-9968-0(4),* 31a1bda4-52b2-47fc-8f72-bd2c48a3ad17) Stevens, Gareth Publishing LLLP.

—Happy Thanksgiving!, 1 vol., Vol. 1. 2013. (Happy Holidays! Ser.). (ENG., Illus.). 24p. (J). (gr. k-k). 25.27 *(978-1-4339-9947-5(1),* 42ab3a5c-fc15-4750-9f87-49460499ea91) Stevens, Gareth Publishing LLLP.

Balfour, Barbara. Thanksgiving Day. 2006. (American Holidays Ser.). (Illus.). 24p. (J). (gr. 3-7). lib. bdg. 24.45 *(978-1-59036-405-5(8));* per. 8.95 *(978-1-59036-408-6(2))* Weigl Pubs., Inc.

Bartlett, Robert Merrill. The Story of Thanksgiving. Comport, Sally Wern, illus. rev. ed. 2004. 30p. (J). (gr. k-4). reprint ed. *(978-0-7567-7757-9(7))* DIANE Publishing Co.

—The Story of Thanksgiving. Comport, Sally Wern, illus. Date not set. 40p. (J). (gr. 2-5). 5.99 *(978-0-06-446238-9(2))* HarperCollins Pubs.

Bodden, Valerie. Thanksgiving. 2005. (My First Look at Holidays Ser.). (Illus.). 24p. (J). (gr. k-3). lib. bdg. 15.95 *(978-1-58341-370-8(7),* Creative Education) Creative Co., The.

Borgert-Spaniol, Megan. Super Simple Thanksgiving Activities: Fun & Easy Holiday Projects for Kids. 2017. (Super Simple Holidays Ser.). (ENG., Illus.). 32p. (J). (gr. k-4). lib. bdg. 34.21 *(978-1-5321-1247-8(5),* 27634, Super SandCastle) ABDO Publishing Co.

Bullard, Lisa. My Family Celebrates Thanksgiving. Saunders, Katie, illus. 2018. (Holiday Time (Early Bird Stories (tm)) Ser.). (ENG.). 24p. (J). (gr. k-2). pap. 9.99 *(978-1-5415-2743-0(7),* 9756b948-53c6-48cd-a028-79d5d2001fc8); lib. bdg. 29.32 *(978-1-5415-2009-7(2),* 0db1bbf3-fad7-4375-b807-8d45c6b8bf61, Lerner Pubns.) Lerner Publishing Group.

Carr, Aaron & Gillespie, Katie. Thanksgiving. 2016. (Illus.). 24p. (J). *(978-1-5105-1014-2(1))* SmartBook Media, Inc.

Coffelt, Soraya Diase. It's Not about You, Mrs. Turkey: A Love Letter about the True Meaning of Thanksgiving. 2015. (Love Letters Book Ser.). (ENG., Illus.). 32p. (J). pap. 8.99 *(978-1-63047-636-6(6))* Morgan James Publishing.

Colman, Penny. Thanksgiving: The True Story. 2008. (ENG., Illus.). 160p. (YA). (gr. 5-11). 30.99 *(978-0-8050-8229-6(8),* 900041217, Holt, Henry & Co. Bks. For Young Readers) Holt, Henry & Co.

Connors, Kathleen. The First Thanksgiving, 1 vol., Vol. 1. 2013. (What You Didn't Know about History Ser.). (ENG., Illus.). 24p. (J). (gr. 2-3). 25.27 *(978-1-4824-0581-1(4),* a32acce5-2977-40eb-a4fe-4662b029fe08); pap. 9.15 *(978-1-4824-0582-8(2),* 2da75e09-1664-42bc-8b67-0924117edce0) Stevens, Gareth Publishing LLLP.

Crane, Carol. P Is for Pilgrim: A Thanksgiving Alphabet. Urban, Helle, illus. rev. ed. 2007. (ENG.). 40p. (J). (gr. 1-4). 7.95 *(978-1-58536-353-7(7),* 202306) Sleeping Bear Pr.

Dash, Meredith. Thanksgiving, 1 vol. 2014. (National Holidays Ser.). (ENG., Illus.). 24p. (J). (gr. -1-2). lib. bdg. 32.79 *(978-1-62970-047-2(9),* 1536, Abdo Kids) ABDO Publishing Co.

Dayton, Connor. Thanksgiving, 1 vol. 2012. (American Holidays Ser.). (ENG., Illus.). 24p. (J). (gr. 1-1). pap. 9.25 *(978-1-4488-6240-5(X),* c7cf34b3-c16e-4de9-9a4d-ca02591fc5e5); lib. bdg. 26.27 *(978-1-4488-6141-5(1),* 6b0074e0-33fa-4017-8970-48ad7427b17f) Rosen Publishing Group, Inc., The. (PowerKids Pr.).

—Thanksgiving: Día de Accion de Gracias, 1 vol. Alamán, Eduardo, tr. 2012. (American Holidays / Celebraciones en Los Estados Unidos Ser.). (ENG & SPA.). 24p. (gr. 1-1). lib. bdg. 26.27 *(978-1-4488-6707-3(X),* f77ead92-da2e-4d4a-96c4-80c142e48ec7, PowerKids Pr.) Rosen Publishing Group, Inc., The.

Dean, Sheri. Thanksgiving, 1 vol. (Our Country's Holidays (Second Edition) Ser.). (ENG.). 24p. (gr. k-2). 2010. (J). pap. 9.15 *(978-1-4339-3927-3(4),* 949c175a-2ad8-404f-b009-87f5c589d5d2) 2010. (J). lib. bdg. 25.27 *(978-1-4339-3926-6(6),* 3874f962-05f4-47e9-887e-31413ee54cee) 2005. (Illus.). pap. 9.15 *(978-0-8368-6516-5(2),* 4b5ba5fe-3376-4f9b-92a1-ff9370f6f72d, Weekly Reader Leveled Readers) 2005. (Illus.). lib. bdg. 24.67 *(978-0-8368-6509-7(X),* b9a88dc3-6dd1-4810-bce2-05d4e01d06ed) Stevens, Gareth Publishing LLLP.

—Thanksgiving / día de Acción de Gracias, 1 vol. 2005. (Our Country's Holidays / Las Fiestas de Nuestra Nación Ser.). (SPA & ENG., Illus.). 24p. (gr. k-2). pap. 9.15 *(978-0-8368-6530-1(8),* c4b97b4e-cbd7-4a98-8099-2fab5261274a, Weekly Reader Leveled Readers) Stevens, Gareth Publishing LLLP.

Dear Santa: Individual Title Six-Packs. (Literatura 2000 Ser.). (gr. k-1). 28.00 *(978-0-7635-0048-1(8))* Rigby Education.

Douglas, Punchye. Safari Oklahoma Presents: Thanksgiving History Coloring Book. (Illus.). 16p. (J). (gr. k-6). 5.00 *(978-0-9703183-3-6(2))* Douglas, Bettye Forum, Inc., The.

Englar, Mary. The Pilgrims & the First Thanksgiving, 1 vol. McDonnell, Peter, illus. 2006. (Graphic History Ser.). (ENG.). 32p. (J). (gr. 3-9). 8.10 *(978-0-7368-9656-6(2),* 93441); 31.32 *(978-0-7368-5492-4(4),* 90729) Capstone. (Capstone Pr.).

Erlbach, Arlene & Erlbach, Herbert. Fun Thanksgiving Day Crafts, 1 vol. Ponte, June, illus. 2014. (Kid Fun Holiday Crafts! Ser.). (ENG.). 32p. (gr. 3-4). pap. 10.35 *(978-0-7660-6251-1(1),* c409b0bc-c9fe-47df-bc89-397f9d9a1d7d, Enslow Elementary) Enslow Publishing, LLC.

Felix, Rebecca. We Celebrate Thanksgiving in Fall. 2013. (21st Century Basic Skills Library: Let's Look at Fall Ser.). (ENG.). 24p. (gr. k-3). pap. 12.79 *(978-1-61080-929-0(7),* 202597); (Illus.). 26.35 *(978-1-61080-904-7(1),* 202595); (Illus.). E-Book 43.50 *(978-1-61080-979-5(3),* 202598) Cherry Lake Publishing.

Fields, Terri. The First Thanksgiving. 2018. (Time to Discover Ser.). (ENG.). 16p. (gr. -1-2). lib. bdg. 28.50 *(978-1-64156-206-5(4),* 9781641562065) Rourke Educational Media.

Gibbons, Gail. Thanksgiving Is ... 2005. (ENG., Illus.). 32p. (J). (gr. -1-3). pap. 7.99 *(978-0-8234-1979-1(7))* Holiday Hse., Inc.

Gleisner, Jenna Lee. Celebrating Thanksgiving. 2017. (Welcoming the Seasons Ser.). (ENG.). 24p. (J). (gr. -1-2). lib. bdg. 32.79 *(978-1-5038-1662-6(1),* 211498) Child's World, Inc, The.

Goeller, Dorothy. Thanksgiving Day, 1 vol. 2010. (All about Holidays Ser.). (ENG., Illus.). 24p. (-1). pap. 10.35 *(978-1-59845-178-8(2),* 18bc301a-674a-46e9-b59a-0abe16352832); (gr. -1-1). 25.27 *(978-0-7660-3809-7(2),* e9e9de4d-8a3b-47ba-8690-cd58f54db902) Enslow Publishing, LLC. (Enslow Publishing).

Grace, Catherine O'Neill. 1621: A New Look at Thanksgiving. 2004. (Illus.). 48p. (J). (gr. 3-7). pap. 7.95 *(978-0-7922-6139-1(9),* National Geographic Kids) Disney Publishing Worldwide.

Grack, Rachel. Thanksgiving. 2017. (Celebrating Holidays Ser.). (ENG., Illus.). 24p. (J). (gr. k-3). pap. 7.99 *(978-1-61891-277-0(1),* 12066); lib. bdg. 26.95 *(978-1-62617-598-3(5))* Bellwether Media. (Blastoff! Readers).

Gunderson, Jessica. The Pilgrims' First Thanksgiving, 1 vol. Lucke, Deb, illus. 2010. (Thanksgiving Ser.). (ENG.). 24p. (J). (gr. k-3). pap. 8.95 *(978-1-4048-6720-8(1),* 115519, Picture Window Bks.) Capstone.

Haley, Charly. Thanksgiving. 2019. (Holidays Ser.). (ENG., Illus.). 24p. (J). (gr. 1-1). pap. 8.95 *(978-1-64185-571-6(1),* 1641855711) North Star Editions.

—Thanksgiving. 2018. (Holidays (Cody Koala) Ser.). (ENG., Illus.). 24p. (J). (gr. k-3). lib. bdg. 31.36 *(978-1-5321-6200-8(6),* 30183, Pop! Cody Koala) Pop!

Happy Thanksgiving. 32p. (J). 2.69 *(978-0-7847-1128-6(3))* Standard Publishing.

Happy Thanksgiving Coloring Book. 2006. 16p. (J). pap. 1.99 *(978-0-7847-1744-8(3),* 04370) Standard Publishing.

Harte, May. Thanksgiving. (My Library of Holidays Ser.). 24p. (gr. 1-1). 2009. 37.50 *(978-1-61514-697-0(0))* 2003. (ENG., Illus.). (J). lib. bdg. 22.27 *(978-1-4042-2527-5(7),* 2fe3e988-2fa2-4cde-a679-e5eacf48e71e) Rosen Publishing Group, Inc., The. (PowerKids Pr.).

Hayes, Dan, illus. The Thanksgiving. 24p. (J). pap., act. bk. ed. 7.95 *(978-0-8249-5324-9(X),* Ideals Pubns.) Worthy Publishing.

Heiligman, Deborah. Holidays Around the World - Celebrate Thanksgiving. 2017. (Holidays Around the World Ser.). (Illus.). 32p. (J). (gr. 1-3). pap. 7.99 *(978-1-4263-2847-3(8),* National Geographic Kids) Disney Publishing Worldwide.

—Holidays Around the World: Celebrate Thanksgiving: With Turkey, Family, & Counting Blessings. 2006. (Holidays Around the World Ser.). (ENG., Illus.). 32p. (J). (gr. 1-4). 15.95 *(978-0-7922-5928-2(9),* National Geographic Children's Bks.) National Geographic Society.

Herrington, Lisa M. Thanksgiving. 2013. (ENG.). 32p. (J). 23.00 *(978-0-531-27206-0(0));* pap. 5.95 *(978-0-531-27356-2(3))* Scholastic Library Publishing.

Hinkler Books, ed. Baby's First Thanksgiving. 2012. (Baby's First Ser.). 24p. (J). bds. 5.99 *(978-1-74308-537-0(0))* Hinkler Bks. Pty. Ltd. AUS. Dist: Ideals Pubns.

Holub, Joan. What Was the First Thanksgiving? 2013. (What Was... Ser.). lib. bdg. 16.00 *(978-0-606-31687-3(6))* Turtleback.

Jennings, Dorothy. Why Do We Celebrate Thanksgiving?, 1 vol. 2018. (Celebrating U. S. Holidays Ser.). (ENG.). 24p. (gr. 1-1). 25.27 *(978-1-5081-6667-2(6),* cddbb7c4-e68b-4b1c-8057-09a813f91899, PowerKids Pr.) Rosen Publishing Group, Inc., The.

Keogh, Josie. Thanksgiving, 1 vol. 2013. (PowerKids Readers: Happy Holidays! Ser.). (ENG., Illus.). 24p. (J). (gr. k-k). pap. 9.25 *(978-1-4488-9704-9(1),* e02261c3-d3c7-4d5e-9dc4-071402ed207b); lib. bdg. 26.27 *(978-1-4488-9624-0(X),* f8c14282-2de5-44ce-925d-7301e1263cf8) Rosen Publishing Group, Inc., The. (PowerKids Pr.).

—Thanksgiving: Día de Acción de Gracias, 1 vol. Alamán, Eduardo, tr. 2013. (PowerKids Readers: !Felices Fiestas! / Happy Holidays! Ser.). (ENG & SPA., Illus.). 24p. (gr. k-k). lib. bdg. 26.27 *(978-1-4488-9967-8(2),* 3fafcc84-80ad-4703-8657-07f7c1435572, PowerKids Pr.) Rosen Publishing Group, Inc., The.

Kessel, Joyce K. Squanto & the First Thanksgiving. Donze, Lisa, illus. rev. ed. 2003. (On My Own Holidays Ser.). (ENG.). 48p. (gr. 2-4). lib. bdg. 25.26 *(978-0-87614-941-6(7))* Lerner Publishing Group.

—Squanto & the First Thanksgiving, 2nd Edition. Donze, Lisa, illus. 2nd rev. ed. 2003. (On My Own Holidays Ser.). (ENG.). 48p. (J). (gr. 2-4). pap. 8.99 *(978-1-57505-585-5(6),* 7a820627-e0ae-495a-9499-accc5d2a0944, First Avenue Editions) Lerner Publishing Group.

—Squanto y el Primer Dia de Accion de Gracias. Donze, Lisa, illus. 2007. (Yo Solo - Festividades (on My Own - Holidays) Ser.). 48p. (J). (gr. 4-7). per. 6.95 *(978-0-8225-7795-9(X))* Lerner Publishing Group.

—Squanto y el Primer Día de Acción de Gracias. Translations.com Staff, tr. from ENG. Donze, Lisa, illus. 2007. (Yo Solo - Festividades (on My Own - Holidays) Ser.). (SPA.). 48p. (gr. 2-4). lib. bdg. 25.26 *(978-0-8225-7792-8(5))* Lerner Publishing Group.

—Squanto Y el Primer Dia de Accion de Gracias; Squanto & the First Thanksgiving. 2008. pap. 40.95 *(978-0-8225-9678-3(4))* Lerner Publishing Group.

Landau, Elaine. What Is Thanksgiving?, 1 vol. 2012. (I Like Holidays! Ser.). (ENG., Illus.). 24p. (gr. k-2). pap. 10.35 *(978-1-59845-294-5(0),* f55cd531-6aba-4cbf-b1fa-9f5cafd36233, Enslow Elementary); lib. bdg. 25.27 *(978-0-7660-3701-4(0),* 5f4606f7-0ae6-44ec-b44c-6ee8862c8c41) Enslow Publishing, LLC.

Lawrence, Elizabeth K. Celebrate Thanksgiving, 1 vol. 2015. (Our Holidays Ser.). (ENG., Illus.). 24p. (J). (gr. 1-1). pap. 9.23 *(978-1-5026-0412-5(4),* 242d3809-141d-405a-9afc-1d696a6566b7) Cavendish Square Publishing LLC.

Loewen, James W. Lies My Teacher Told Me: Young Readers' Edition: Everything American History Textbooks Get Wrong. adapted ed. 2019. (ENG., Illus.). 256p. (J). (gr. 7-12). 19.99 *(978-1-62097-469-8(X))* New Pr., The.

Ludgate, Kevin. Pilgrim Village: A Thanksgiving Diorama, 1 vol. 2010. (ENG., Illus.). 32p. (J). (gr. -1-3). pap. 9.99 *(978-0-7643-3563-1(4),* 3970, Schiffer Craft) Schiffer Publishing, Ltd.

Lynette, Rachel. Let's Throw a Thanksgiving Party!, 1 vol. 2011. (Holiday Parties Ser.). (J). (ENG.). 24p. (gr. 2-3). pap. 9.25 *(978-1-4488-2735-0(3),* cd8b6597-f679-4b9c-9aaf-d12746554878); (ENG.). 24p. (gr. 2-3). lib. bdg. 26.27 *(978-1-4488-2573-8(3),* 50891f89-6bd7-4324-ab4a-b3310f076733); 49.50 *(978-1-4488-2736-7(1))* Rosen Publishing Group, Inc., The. (PowerKids Pr.).

Markovics, Pearl. Thanksgiving. 2018. (Happy Holidays! Ser.). (ENG., Illus.). 16p. (J). (gr. -1-1). 6.99 *(978-1-64280-150-7(X))* Bearport Publishing Co., Inc.

McGee, Randel. Paper Crafts for Thanksgiving, 1 vol. 2012. (Paper Craft Fun for Holidays Ser.). (ENG., Illus.). 48p. (gr. 3-3). pap. 11.53 *(978-1-59845-336-2(X),* 11211fe1-2dc7-4ff6-a816-9f295964b23b, Enslow Elementary); lib. bdg. 27.93 *(978-0-7660-3722-9(3),* 96c2149d-5087-4dab-b253-976b82a1bf80) Enslow Publishing, LLC.

McGill, Jordan, ed. Thanksgiving. 2011. (J). (gr. 3-5). pap. 12.95 *(978-1-61690-686-3(3),* AV2 by Weigl); (Illus.). 24p. (gr. 2-5). 27.13 *(978-1-61690-680-1(4))* Weigl Pubs., Inc.

Mercer, Abbie. Happy Thanksgiving. (Holiday Fun Ser.). 24p. (gr. 2-3). 2009. 42.50 *(978-1-61513-378-9(X),* PowerKids Pr.) 2007. (ENG., Illus.). (J). lib. bdg. 26.27 *(978-1-4042-3807-7(7),* 9fad18ff-fc35-4cbe-b673-447c1100d876) Rosen Publishing Group, Inc., The.

Metaxas, Eric. Squanto & the First Thanksgiving: The Legendary American Tale. Donato, Michael A., illus. 2004. 36p. (J). (gr. 3-8). reprint ed. 19.00 *(978-0-7567-7123-2(4))* DIANE Publishing Co.

Morey, Allan. Thanksgiving Day. Hartley, Brian, illus. 2017. (Holidays in Rhythm & Rhyme Ser.). (ENG.). 24p. (J). (gr. -1-3). 33.99 *(978-1-68410-055-2(0),* 31521) Cantata Learning.

Morrison, Jessica. Thanksgiving. 2010. (Illus.). 24p. *(978-1-55388-613-6(5));* pap. *(978-1-55388-614-3(3))* Weigl Educational Pubs. Ltd.

Muehlenhardt, Amy Bailey. Thanksgiving Crafts, 1 vol. Takvorian, Nadine, illus. 2010. (Thanksgiving Ser.). (ENG.). 24p. (J). (gr. k-3). lib. bdg. 27.99 *(978-1-4048-6282-1(X),* 113751, Picture Window Bks.) Capstone.

Owen, Ruth. Thanksgiving Origami, 1 vol. 2012. (Holiday Origami Ser.). (ENG., Illus.). 32p. (J). (gr. 2-3). pap. 12.75 *(978-1-4488-7923-6(X),* 6bafb57d-e2fd-47de-95b1-031628624b51, PowerKids Pr.) Rosen Publishing Group, Inc., The.

Peppas, Lynn. Thanksgiving. 2009. (Celebrations in My World Ser.). (ENG., Illus.). 32p. (J). (gr. -1-3). pap. *(978-0-7787-4309-5(8))* Crabtree Publishing Co.

Perry, Rex, illus. Over the River & Through the Woods. 2004. 24p. (J). lib. bdg. 8.00 *(978-1-4242-0640-7(5))* Fitzgerald Bks.

Pettiford, Rebecca. Día de Acción de Gracias. 2015.Tr. of Thanksgiving Day. (SPA., Illus.). 24p. (J). lib. bdg. *(978-1-62031-240-7(9),* Bullfrog Bks.) Jump! Inc.

—Thanksgiving. 2015. (Illus.). 24p. (J). lib. bdg. *(978-1-62031-186-8(0),* Bullfrog Bks.) Jump! Inc.

Ponto, Joanna. Thanksgiving, 1 vol. 2016. (Story of Our Holidays Ser.). (ENG., Illus.). 32p. (gr. 3-3). pap. 11.52 *(978-0-7660-7631-0(8),* c1698f29-9d01-431c-aac7-f7f8c7759333) Enslow Publishing, LLC.

Rader, Laura & Utt, Mary Ann, illus. A Child's Story of Thanksgiving. 24p. (J). 7.95 *(978-0-8249-5327-0(4),* Ideals Pubns.) Worthy Publishing.

Randall, Ronne. Thanksgiving Sweets & Treats. 1 vol. 2012. (Holiday Cooking for Kids! Ser.). (ENG., Illus.). 32p. (J). (gr. 2-3). 31.27 *(978-1-4488-8082-9(3),* 5e8a308c-6304-48b7-a403-bb90a4f8f400); pap. 12.75 *(978-1-4488-8129-1(3),* f16c352c-513b-4767-8746-3f336dade663) Rosen Publishing Group, Inc., The. (Windmill Bks.).

Richardson, Betsy. Ringing in the Western & Chinese New Year. 2018. (J). *(978-1-4222-4143-1(2))* Mason Crest.

Robertson, Brynn, compiled by. Standard Christmas Program Book: Poems & Programs for Christmas & Thanksgiving. 2006. (Illus.). 48p. pap. 6.99 *(978-0-7847-1647-2(1))* Standard Publishing.

Rooney, Ronnie. Thanksgiving Recipes. 1 vol. Rooney, Ronnie, illus. 2010. (Thanksgiving Ser.). (ENG., Illus.). 24p. (J). (gr. k-3). lib. bdg. 27.99 *(978-1-4048-6283-8(8),* 113752, Picture Window Bks.) Capstone.

Ross, Kathy. All New Crafts for Thanksgiving. Holm, Sharon Lane, illus. 2005. 48p. (J). (gr. k-2). per. 7.95 *(978-0-7613-2394-5(5),* First Avenue Editions); (ENG.). lib. bdg. 25.26 *(978-0-7613-2922-0(6),* Millbrook Pr.) Lerner Publishing Group.

Santella, Andrew. Cornerstones of Freedom: the First Thanksgiving. 2003. (Cornerstones of Freedom Ser.). (ENG., Illus.). 48p. (YA). (gr. 4-7). 26.00 *(978-0-516-24204-0(0))* Scholastic Library Publishing.

Skaermas, Nancy J. The Story of Thanksgiving. 2011. (ENG., Illus.). 22p. (J). (gr. -1-1). bds. 7.99 *(978-0-8249-1883-5(5),* Ideals Pubns.) Worthy Publishing.

Smith, Andrea P. The First Thanksgiving. (Illus.). 24p. (J). 2012. 63.60 *(978-1-4488-5213-0(7))* 2011. (ENG., (gr. 2-3). pap. 11.60 *(978-1-4488-5212-3(9),* 29193eb1-58fc-449e-8ffd-c34f8ba58a56) 2011. (ENG., (gr. 2-3). lib. bdg. 28.93 *(978-1-4488-5187-4(4),* 558ed541-f06a-434a-870b-4905820ff6a9) Rosen Publishing Group, Inc., The. (PowerKids Pr.).

Stiegemeyer, Julie. Thanksgiving: A Harvest Celebration. Benoit, Renne, illus. 2003. 32p. (J). 13.49 *(978-0-7586-0530-6(7))* Concordia Publishing Hse.

Stilwell, Norma Minturn. A Thought for Thanksgiving. Bingham, Pamela E., illus. 2011. 24p. pap. 14.95 *(978-1-936343-93-5(2))* Peppertree Pr., The.

Strain Trueit, Trudi. Thanksgiving. 1 vol. 2011. (Holiday Fun Ser.). (ENG.). 24p. (gr. k-1). 25.50 *(978-0-7614-4888-4(8),* 0cdaa2d1-798b-4130-bf43-a46ac5e030dd) Cavendish Square Publishing LLC.

Sweet, Melissa. Balloons over Broadway: The True Story of the Puppeteer of Macy's Parade. Sweet, Melissa, illus. 2011. (ENG., Illus.). 40p. (J). (gr. -1-3). 17.99 *(978-0-547-19945-0(7),* 1058458, Clarion Bks.) HarperCollins Pubs.

Tani, Branca. Art for Thanksgiving. 1 vol. 2015. (Rosen REAL Readers: STEM & STEAM Collection). (ENG.). 8p. (gr. k-1). pap. 5.46 *(978-1-4994-9698-7(2),* b5a625c6-49af-4e78-a70a-76fda873db87, Rosen Classroom) Rosen Publishing Group, Inc., The.

Thomas, Mario & Cerf, Christopher, eds. Thanks & Giving: All Year Long. 2004. (ENG., Illus.). 96p. (J). (gr. 1-7). 21.99 *(978-0-689-87732-2(3))* Simon & Schuster Children's Publishing.

Vidrine, Beverly Barras. Thanksgiving Day Alphabet. 1 vol. Lyne, Alison D., illus. 2006. (ABC Ser.). (ENG.). 32p. (J). (gr. k-3). 8.95 *(978-1-58980-338-1(8),* Pelican Publishing) Arcadia Publishing.

Walker, Nan. Thanksgiving Then & Now. 2011. (Early Connections Ser.). (J). *(978-1-61672-378-1(5))* Benchmark Education Co.

Webster, Christine. How to Draw Thanksgiving Symbols. 2009. (Kid's Guide to Drawing Ser.). 24p. (gr. 3-3). 47.90 *(978-1-61511-041-4(0),* PowerKids Pr.) Rosen Publishing Group, Inc., The.

Wesemann, Tim. Tassel-Free Living for Grads: God's Grace for Grads. 2003. (Illus.). 64p. (YA). 9.99 *(978-0-9718985-8-5(8))* C T A, Inc.

Williams, Colleen Madonna Flood. My Adventure on Thanksgiving Day. 2006. 44p. (J). 8.99 *(978-1-59092-557-7(2))* Blue Forge Pr.

Yero, Judith Lloyd & Yero, Judith. American Documents: the Mayflower Compact (Direct Mail Edition) 2006. (American Documents Ser.). (ENG., Illus.). 40p. (J). (gr. 5-9). 15.95 *(978-0-7922-5891-9(6))* National Geographic Society.

Zocchi, Judy. On Thanksgiving Day. Wallis, Rebbeca, illus. 2005. (Holiday Happenings Ser.). 32p. (J). pap. 10.95 *(978-1-59646-212-0(4))* Dingles & Co.

—On Thanksgiving Day. Wallis, Rebecca, illus. 2005. (Holiday Happenings Ser.). 32p. (J). per. 10.95 *(978-1-59646-213-7(2))* Dingles & Co.

—On Thanksgiving Day/el Día de Acción de Gracias. Wallis, Rebecca, illus. 2005. (Holiday Happenings Ser.).Tr. of Día de Acción de Gracias. (ENG & SPA.). 32p. (J). pap. 10.95 *(978-1-59646-214-4(0));* lib. bdg. 21.65 *(978-1-891997-75-4(0));* per. 10.95 *(978-1-59646-215-1(9))* Dingles & Co.

THANKSGIVING DAY—FICTION

Alcott, Louisa. An Old-Fashioned Thanksgiving. Wheeler, Jody, illus. 2010. 40p. (J). (gr. -1-3). 14.99 *(978-0-8249-5620-2(6),* Ideals Pubns.) Worthy Publishing.

Alsdurf, Phyllis. Thanksgiving in the Woods. Lovlie, Jenny, illus. 2017. (Countryside Holidays Ser.). 40p. (J). 16.99 *(978-1-5064-2508-5(9),* Sparkhouse Family) 1517 Media.

Anastos, Ernie. Ernie & the Big Newz. 2007. 32p. pap. 15.95 *(978-0-9705100-5-1(5))* NK Pubns.

Balaban, Mariah. Scooby-Doo & the Thanksgiving Terror. 1 vol. Duendes Del Sur Staff, illus. 2011. (Scooby-Doo! Ser.: No. 2). (ENG.). 24p. (J). (gr. k-4). lib. bdg. 31.36 *(978-1-59961-870-8(2),* 13248, Picture Bk.) Spotlight.

Balian, Lorna. Sometimes It's Turkey, Sometimes It's Feathers. 1 vol. Balian, Lecia, illus. 2003. (ENG.). 32p. (J). 14.95 *(978-1-932065-33-6(4));* pap. 5.95 *(978-1-932065-41-1(5))* Star Bright Bks., Inc.

Balsley, Tilda. Ten Hungry Turkeys. 1 vol. Stott, Dorothy & Richard, Ilene, illus. 2018. (ENG.). 32p. (J). (gr. -1-3). 16.99 *(978-1-4556-2235-1(4),* Pelican Publishing) Arcadia Publishing.

Banks, Steven. Thanks a Lot, Robo-Turkey! LaPadula, Tom, illus. 2005. (Adventures of Jimmy Neutron Ser.: 10). 24p. (J). lib. bdg. 15.00 *(978-1-59054-787-8(X))* Fitzgerald Bks.

Barbara, Cohen. Molly's Pilgrim. 97th rev. ed. 2014. (ENG.). 32p. (J). (gr. 1-5). 8.24 *(978-1-63245-244-3(8))* Lectorum Pubns., Inc.

Barbo, Maria S. & Bridwell, Norman. Thanksgiving Parade. Artful Doodlers, illus. 2010. (J). *(978-0-545-25332-1(2))* Scholastic, Inc.

Berenstain, Mike, et al. The Berenstain Bears Give Thanks. 1 vol. Berenstain, Stan, illus. 2009. (Berenstain Bears/Living Lights: a Faith Story Ser.). (ENG.). 32p. (J). (gr. -1-2). pap. 4.99 *(978-0-310-71251-0(3))* Zonderkidz.

Bildner, Phil. Turkey Bowl. 2008. (ENG., Illus.). 32p. (J). (gr. k-3). 19.99 *(978-0-689-87896-1(6),* Simon & Schuster Bks. For Young Readers) Simon & Schuster Bks. For Young Readers.

Bourgeois, Paulette. Franklin y el Dia de Accion de Gracias. Varela, Alejandra López, tr. Clark, Brenda, illus.Tr. of Franklin's Thanksgiving. (SPA.). (J). (gr. k-2). 10.95 *(978-1-930332-07-2(6),* LC30184) Lectorum Pubns., Inc.

Brown, L. McDougal's Feast. 2013. (ENG.). 24p. (J). pap. 11.95 *(978-1-4787-0596-3(5))* Outskirts Pr., Inc.

Bunting, Eve. Frog & Friends Celebrate Thanksgiving, Christmas, & New Year's Eve. Masse, Josée, illus. 2015. (I AM a READER!: Frog & Friends Ser.). (ENG.). 40p. (J). (gr. 1-2). 9.99 *(978-1-58536-897-6(0),* 203949) Sleeping Bear Pr.

Burton, Jeffrey. The Itsy Bitsy Pilgrim. Rescek, Sanja, illus. 2016. (Itsy Bitsy Ser.). (ENG.). 16p. (J). (gr. -1 — 1). bds. 5.99 *(978-1-4814-6852-7(9),* Little Simon) Little Simon.

Bush, Leanne. Sarah's Happy Harvest Time. 1 vol. Briggs, Charlotte, illus. 2009. 32p. pap. 24.95 *(978-1-60813-818-0(6))* America Star Bks.

Capozzi, Suzy. I Am Thankful: A Positive Power Story. Unten, Eren & Unten, Eren, illus. 2017. (Rodale Kids Curious Readers/Level 2 Ser.: 1). 32p. (J). (gr. -1-1). pap. 4.99 *(978-1-62336-876-0(6),* 9781623368760, Rodale Kids) Random Hse. Children's Bks.

Capucilli, Alyssa Satin. Happy Thanksgiving, Biscuit! Schories, Pat, illus. 2019. (Biscuit Ser.). (ENG.). 20p. (J). (gr. -1-3). pap. 6.99 *(978-0-694-01221-3(1),* HarperFestival) HarperCollins Pubs.

Cazet, Denys. Minnie & Moo & the Thanksgiving Tree. 2003. (Minnie & Moo Ser.). 48p. (J). (gr. -1-2). pap. 31.95 incl. audio compact disk *(978-1-59112-586-0(3))* Live Oak Media.

Cohen, Barbara. Molly's Pilgrim. Bricking, Jennifer, illus. 2018. (ENG.). 48p. (J). (gr. 1-5). pap. 5.99 *(978-0-06-287094-0(7),* HarperCollins) HarperCollins Pubs.

—Molly's Pilgrim. 97th rev. ed. 2005. (ENG., Illus.). 32p. (J). (gr. 1-5). pap. 3.99 *(978-0-688-16280-1(0),* HarperCollins) HarperCollins Pubs. Ltd. GBR. Dist: HarperCollins Pubs.

—Molly's Pilgrim. (Literature to Go Ser.). pap., tchr. ed. incl. VHS *(978-0-7919-2685-7(0))* Phoenix Films & Video.

Cole, Joanna. The Magic School Bus at the First Thanksgiving. Bracken, Carolyn, illus. 2006. (J). pap. *(978-0-439-89935-2(4))* Scholastic, Inc.

Cox, Judy. One Is a Feast for Mouse: A Thanksgiving Tale. Ebbeler, Jeffrey, illus. 2009. (Adventures of Mouse Ser.: 1). (ENG.). 32p. (J). (gr. -1-3). pap. 7.99 *(978-0-8234-2231-9(3))* Holiday Hse., Inc.

Davis, Kathryn Lynn. The First Thanksgiving: A Lift-The-Flap Book. Davis, Kathryn Lynn, illus. 2010. (ENG., Illus.). 14p. (J). (gr. -1 — 1). bds. 6.99 *(978-1-4424-0807-4(3),* Little Simon) Little Simon.

Dean, James & Dean, Kimberly. Pete the Cat: the First Thanksgiving. Dean, James, illus. 2013. (Pete the Cat Ser.). (ENG., Illus.). 16p. (J). (gr. -1-3). 6.99 *(978-0-06-219869-3(6),* HarperFestival) HarperCollins Pubs.

Dellinger, Hampton. Thanks for Nothing: How Willie & Abe Saved Thanksgiving. 2008. 24p. 12.99 *(978-0-615-24971-1(X))* Dellinger, Hampton.

dePaola, Tomie. My First Thanksgiving. 2008. 14p. (J). (gr. -1 — 1). bds. 6.99 *(978-0-448-44857-2(2),* Grosset & Dunlap) Penguin Young Readers Group.

Devlin, Wende. Cranberry Thanksgiving. Devlin, Harry, illus. 2012. (ENG.). 32p. (J). (gr. -1-3). 18.95 *(978-1-930900-63-9(5))* Purple Hse. Pr.

Dewdney, Anna. Llama Llama Gives Thanks. 2017. (Llama Llama Ser.). (Illus.). 14p. (J). (— 1). bds. 7.99 *(978-1-101-99715-4(X),* Viking Books for Young Readers) Penguin Young Readers Group.

Dickinson, Asa Don. Good Cheer Stories Every Child Should Know. 2017. (ENG., Illus.). (J). 25.95 *(978-1-374-84726-2(7));* pap. 15.95 *(978-1-374-84725-5(9))* Capital Communications, Inc.

Elliott, Laura Malone. Thanksgiving Day Thanks. Munsinger, Lynn, illus. 2013. (ENG.). 32p. (J). (gr. -1-3). 17.99 *(978-0-06-000236-7(0),* Tegen, Katherine Bks) HarperCollins Pubs.

Evans, Karen & Urmston, Kathleen. Thanksgiving. Kaeden Corp. Staff, ed. Graves, Dennis, illus. 2006. (ENG.). 12p. (gr. k-2). pap. 7.95 *(978-1-879835-57-3(6),* Kaeden Bks.) Kaeden Corp.

Evans, Rhonda Boone. Thanksgiving with the Lumpkins. 2009. 40p. pap. 16.50 *(978-1-60860-783-9(6),* Eloquent Bks.) Strategic Book Publishing & Rights Agency (SBPRA).

Fearing, Mark. The Great Thanksgiving Escape. Fearing, Mark, illus. 2017. (ENG., Illus.). 32p. (J). (gr. -1-3). 6.99 *(978-0-7636-9511-8(4))* Candlewick Pr.

Flor Ada, Alma. Celebrate Thanksgiving Day with Beto & Gaby. Hayes, Joe & Franco, Sharon, trs. from SPA. Rueda, Claudia, illus. 2006. (Cuentos para Celebrar / Stories to Celebrate Ser.). 30p. (J). (gr. k-6). per. 11.95 *(978-1-59820-133-8(6))* Santillana USA Publishing Co., Inc.

Friedman, Laurie. Mallory Makes a Difference. Kalis, Jennifer, illus. 2018. (Mallory Ser.). (ENG.). 152p. (J). (gr. 2-5). pap. 6.99 *(978-1-5415-2816-1(6),* a33b0439-34ff-42da-8e72-ae42a5d91648, Darby Creek) Lerner Publishing Group.

Fronis, Aly. This Little Turkey. Blanco, Migy, illus. 2016. (ENG.). 16p. (J). (gr. -1-k). bds. 5.99 *(978-1-4998-0302-0(8))* Little Bee Books Inc.

Gibson, Sherri L. In the Mind of a Child: Children's Stories. 2013. 36p. pap. 24.95 *(978-1-62709-750-5(3))* America Star Bks.

Goodspeed, Judy. Perky Turkey's Perfect Plan. (Illus.). 22p. (J). 2007. per. 11.99 *(978-0-9797574-3-3(6))* 2006. lib. bdg. 24.95 *(978-0-9778651-1-6(8))* Dragonfly Publishing, Inc.

—Perky Turkey's Perfect Plan. Taylor, Chet, illus. 2005. 22p. (J). 18.99 *(978-0-9765786-0-4(3))* Dragonfly Publishing, Inc.

Greene, Rhonda Gowler. The Very First Thanksgiving Day. Gaber, Susan, illus. 2006. (ENG.). 32p. (J). (gr. -1-1). 7.99 *(978-1-4169-1916-2(3),* Atheneum Bks. for Young Readers) Simon & Schuster Children's Publishing.

Gutman, Dan. Dr. Carbles Is Losing His Marbles! Paillot, Jim, illus. 2007. (My Weird School Ser.: No. 19). 112p. (J). (gr. 2-5). lib. bdg. 15.89 *(978-0-06-123478-1(8))* HarperCollins Pubs.

—Dr. Carbles Is Losing His Marbles! Paillot, Jim, illus. 2007. (My Weird School Ser.: No. 19). 99p. (J). (gr. 2-5). 11.65 *(978-0-7569-8810-4(1))* Perfection Learning Corp.

—My Weird School #19: Dr. Carbles Is Losing His Marbles! Paillot, Jim, illus. 2007. (My Weird School Ser.: 19). (ENG.). 112p. (J). (gr. 1-5). pap. 5.99 *(978-0-06-123477-4(X),* HarperCollins) HarperCollins Pubs.

Hallinan, P. K. How to Celebrate Thanksgiving! Holiday Traditions, Rituals, & Rules in a Delightful Story. 2019. (ENG.). 24p. (J). (gr. 1-4). 12.99 *(978-1-5107-4541-4(6),* Sky Pony Pr.) Skyhorse Publishing Co., Inc.

Hapka, Cathy, pseud. Giving Thanks. Byrne, Mike, illus. 2014. 32p. (J). pap. *(978-0-545-75841-3(6))* Scholastic, Inc.

Hargreaves, Adam. Mr. Men: a Very Thankful Thanksgiving. 2018. (Mr. Men & Little Miss Ser.). (ENG., Illus.). 32p. (J). (gr. -1-2). pap. 4.99 *(978-1-5247-8763-9(9),* Grosset & Dunlap) Penguin Young Readers Group.

Harley, Bill. Charlie Bumpers vs. the Perfect Little Turkey. 1 vol. Gustavson, Adam, illus. 2016. (Charlie Bumpers Ser.: 4). 176p. (J). (gr. 2-5). pap. 6.95 *(978-1-56145-963-6(1))* Peachtree Publishing Co. Inc.

—Charlie Bumpers vs. the Puny Pirates. 1 vol. Gustavson, Adam, illus. 2017. (Charlie Bumpers Ser.: 5). 176p. (J). (gr. 2-5). pap. 6.95 *(978-1-68263-001-3(3))* Peachtree Publishing Co. Inc.

Hawley, Mabel C. Four Little Blossoms Through the Holidays. 2005. pap. 22.95 *(978-1-4179-9003-0(1))* Kessinger Publishing, LLC.

Higgins, M. G. Party of Nine. Taylor, Jo, illus. 2016. (Sibling Split Ser.). (ENG.). 112p. (J). (gr. 3-6). lib. bdg. 25.32 *(978-1-4965-2592-5(2),* 130721, Stone Arch Bks.) Capstone.

Hill, Eric. Spot's Thanksgiving. Hill, Eric, illus. 2016. (Spot Ser.). (ENG., Illus.). 10p. (J). (gr. -1-k). bds. 6.99 *(978-0-399-24186-4(8),* Warne) Penguin Young Readers Group.

Hillert, Margaret. Why We Have Thanksgiving. Marchesi, Stephen, illus. 2016. (BeginningtoRead Ser.). (ENG.). 32p. (J). (gr. 1-2). 22.60 *(978-1-59953-809-9(1))* Norwood Hse. Pr.

Holub, Joan. More Snacks! A Thanksgiving Play. Terry, Will, illus. 2006. (Ant Hill Ser.: 1). (ENG.). 24p. (J). (gr. -1-k). lib. bdg. 11.89 *(978-1-4169-2559-0(7),* Simon Spotlight) Simon Spotlight.

—More Snacks! A Thanksgiving Play (Ready-To-Read Pre-Level 1) Terry, Will, illus. 2006. (Ant Hill Ser.: 1). (ENG.). 24p. (J). (gr. -1-k). pap. 4.99 *(978-1-4169-0954-5(0),* Simon Spotlight) Simon Spotlight.

Honeycutt, Scarlet. Turkeys in Disguise. Aarvig, Cindy, illus. 2007. 48p. per. 24.95 *(978-1-4137-4035-6(9))* America Star Bks.

Horowitz, Dave. The Ugly Pumpkin. Horowitz, Dave, illus. (ENG., Illus.). (J). 2017. 32p. (— 1). bds. 7.99 *(978-1-5247-4084-9(5),* Nancy Paulsen Books) 2008. 40p. (gr. -1-k). pap. 8.99 *(978-0-14-241145-2(0),* Puffin Books) Penguin Young Readers Group.

Hurley, Wes. How the Winter Frog Came to Was: Or, How to Get a Nice Surprise on Thanksgiving! Lee, Susan, illus. 2007. 36p. per. 24.95 *(978-1-4241-8395-1(2))* America Star Bks.

James, Cheryl D. Leah's Treasure Book. 2012. 36p. pap. 16.99 *(978-1-4624-0422-3(7),* Inspiring Voices) Author Solutions, LLC.

Jones, Kia. The Adventures of Shamya & Friends: The Thanksgiving Day Wish. 2009. 28p. pap. 12.49 *(978-1-4389-5127-0(2))* AuthorHouse.

Jones, Marcia & Dadey, Debbie. Wizards Do Roast Turkeys. Dreidemy, Joëlle, illus. 2007. 64p. (J). pap. *(978-0-545-00235-6(4))* Scholastic, Inc.

Jules, Jacqueline. Duck for Turkey Day. 2018. (ENG.). 32p. (J). (gr. -1-1). 19.49 *(978-1-64310-547-5(7))* Penworthy Co., LLC, The.

—Duck for Turkey Day. 2018. (2019 Av2 Fiction Ser.). (ENG.). 32p. (J). (gr. 1-3). lib. bdg. 34.28 *(978-1-4896-8259-8(7),* AV2 by Weigl) Weigl Pubs., Inc.

—Duck for Turkey Day. Mitter, Kathryn, illus. 2017. (ENG.). 32p. (J). (gr. -1-3). pap. 8.99 *(978-0-8075-1735-2(6),* 807517356) Whitman, Albert & Co.

Kann, Victoria. Pinkalicious: Thanksgiving Helper. Kann, Victoria, illus. 2014. (Pinkalicious Ser.). (ENG., Illus.). 24p. (J). (gr. -1-3). pap. 6.99 *(978-0-06-218774-1(0),* HarperFestival) HarperCollins Pubs.

Katschke, Judy. First Grade Feast!/By Judy Katschke; Illustrated by Clare Elsom. Elsom, Clare, illus. 2014. 32p. (J). pap. *(978-0-545-75844-4(0))* Scholastic, Inc.

Katz, Karen. Where Is Baby's Turkey? A Karen Katz Lift-The-Flap Book. Katz, Karen, illus. 2017. (ENG., Illus.). 14p. (J). (gr. -1 — 1). bds. 7.99 *(978-1-5344-0089-4(3),* Little Simon) Little Simon.

Kennedy, Anne Vittur. One Big Turkey. 1 vol. 2016. (ENG., Illus.). 20p. (J). bds. 8.99 *(978-0-7180-8711-1(9),* Tommy Nelson) Nelson, Thomas Inc.

Kimmelman, Leslie. Round the Turkey: A Grateful Thanksgiving. Cote, Nancy, illus. 2012. (J). 34.28 *(978-1-61913-130-9(7))* Weigl Pubs., Inc.

Klein, Abby. Thanks for Giving. McKinley, John, illus. 2009. (Ready, Freddy! Reader List: No. 4). 32p. (J). pap. *(978-0-545-14176-5(1))* Scholastic, Inc.

—Thanksgiving Turkey Trouble. McKinley, John, illus. 2008. (Ready, Freddy! Ser.: Bk. 15). 95p. (gr. -1-3). 16.00 *(978-0-7569-8838-8(1))* Perfection Learning Corp.

Klimo, Kate. Dash. 2014. (Dog Diaries: 5). lib. bdg. 18.40 *(978-0-606-36021-0(2))* Turtleback.

—Dog Diaries #5: Dash. Bk. 5. Jessell, Tim, illus. 2014. (Dog Diaries: 5). 160p. (J). (gr. 2-5). pap. 7.99 *(978-0-385-37338-8(4),* Random Hse. Bks. for Young Readers) Random Hse. Children's Bks.

Kroll, Virginia. The Thanksgiving Bowl. 1 vol. O'Neill, Philomena, illus. 2007. (ENG.). 32p. (J). (gr. k-3). 16.99 *(978-1-58980-365-7(5),* Pelican Publishing) Arcadia Publishing.

Krulik, Nancy. Don't Be Such a Turkey! John and Wendy, illus. 2010. (Katie Kazoo, Switcheroo Ser.). 160p. (J). (gr. 2-4). pap. 6.99 *(978-0-448-45448-1(3),* Grosset & Dunlap) Penguin Young Readers Group.

Lewis, Michael. The Great Thanksgiving Food Fight. 1 vol. Jaskiel, Stan, illus. 2017. (ENG.). 32p. (J). (gr. -1-3). 16.99 *(978-1-4556-2285-6(0),* Pelican Publishing) Arcadia Publishing.

Long, Ethan. Fangsgiving. 2018. (ENG., Illus.). 32p. (J). 18.99 *(978-1-68119-825-5(8),* 900188260, Bloomsbury Children's Bks.) Bloomsbury Publishing USA.

Longstreet, Barbara, et al. Woodsey School Kids Thanksgiving Feast. 2004. 28p. pap. 24.95 *(978-1-4137-1992-5(9))* PublishAmerica, Inc.

Lowry, Lois. Gooney Bird & the Room Mother. 2006. (Gooney Bird Ser.: No. 2). (ENG., Illus.). 80p. (J). (gr. 3-7). 5.99 *(978-0-440-42133-7(0),* Yearling) Random Hse. Children's Bks.

Mackall, Dandi Daley. Thank You for Thanksgiving. Walker, John, illus. 2008. 32p. (J). (gr. -1). 13.49 *(978-0-7586-1500-8(0))* Concordia Publishing Hse.

Madden, Colleen. The Kiddie Table. 2018. (ENG., Illus.). 32p. (J). (gr. -1-2). 15.95 *(978-1-68446-002-1(6),* 138585, Capstone Editions) Capstone.

Maloney, Peter & Zekauskas, Felicia. Thanks for Nothing! 2003. (Illus.). 31p. (J). *(978-0-439-55360-5(1))* Scholastic, Inc.

Manushkin, Fran. Katie Saves Thanksgiving. 1 vol. Lyon, Tammie, illus. 2010. (Katie Woo Ser.). (ENG.). 32p. (J). (gr. k-2). pap. 5.95 *(978-1-4048-6367-5(2),* 114019); lib. bdg. 21.32 *(978-1-4048-5988-3(8),* 102856) Capstone. (Picture Window Bks.).

Markes, Julie. Thanks for Thanksgiving. Barrette, Doris, illus. (ENG.). 32p. (J). (gr. -1-3). 2008. pap. 7.99 *(978-0-06-051098-5(6))* 2004. 14.99 *(978-0-06-051096-1(X))* HarperCollins Pubs. (HarperCollins).

—Thanks for Thanksgiving Board Book. Barrette, Doris, illus. 2017. (ENG.). 32p. (J). (gr. -1 — 1). bds. 7.99 *(978-0-06-264331-5(2),* HarperFestival) HarperCollins Pubs.

Martin, Ann M. Needle & Thread. 2007. (Main Street Ser.). (Illus.). 205p. (J). (gr. 4-7). 14.65 *(978-0-7569-8328-4(2))* Perfection Learning Corp.

—Needle & Thread. Andreasen, Dan, illus. 2007. 205p. (J). pap. *(978-0-545-03660-3(7))* Scholastic, Inc.

—Needle & Thread. 2. 2007. (Main Street Ser.: 2). (ENG., Illus.). 205p. (J). (gr. 4-6). 21.19 *(978-0-439-86880-8(7))* Scholastic, Inc.

Mayer, Mercer. Just a Special Thanksgiving. 2015. (Little Critter Ser.). (J). lib. bdg. 14.75 *(978-0-606-37605-1(4))* Turtleback.

—Little Critter: Just a Special Thanksgiving. Mayer, Mercer, illus. 2015. (Little Critter Ser.). (ENG., Illus.). 24p. (J). (gr. -1-3). pap. 4.99 *(978-0-06-147811-6(3),* HarperFestival) HarperCollins Pubs.

Mayr, Diane. Run, Turkey, Run! Rader, Laura, illus. 2009. (ENG.). 32p. (J). (gr. -1-2). pap. 7.99 *(978-0-8027-8481-0(X),* 900062746, Bloomsbury USA Childrens) Bloomsbury Publishing USA.

McCourt, Lisa. Thank You, Stinky Face. Moore, Cyd, illus. 2018. (ENG.). 20p. (J). (gr. -1 — 1). bds. 7.99 *(978-1-338-27020-4(6),* Cartwheel Bks.) Scholastic, Inc.

McCue, Lisa, illus. Corduroy's Thanksgiving. 2006. (Corduroy Ser.). 16p. (J). (gr. -1 — 1). bds. 6.99 *(978-0-670-06108-2(5),* Viking Books for Young Readers) Penguin Young Readers Group.

McDonald, Megan. Judy Moody & Stink: the Wishbone Wish. Reynolds, Peter H., illus. 2015. (Judy Moody & Stink Ser.: 4). (ENG.). 128p. (J). (gr. 1-4). 14.99 *(978-0-7636-7206-5(8))* Candlewick Pr.

Mcdonald, Megan. The Wishbone Wish. Reynolds, Peter H., illus. 2016. (Judy Moody & Stink Ser.: 4). (ENG.). 116p. (J). (gr. 1-4). lib. bdg. 18.40 *(978-0-606-39093-4(6))* Turtleback.

McGrath, Barbara Barbieri. Thanksgiving Counting. Tagel, Peggy, illus. 2016. (First Celebrations Ser.: 2). 12p. (J). (— 1). bds. 6.95 *(978-1-58089-534-7(4))* Charlesbridge Publishing, Inc.

Meddaugh, Susan. Martha Speaks: Thanksgiving Reunion (Chapter Book) 2013. (Martha Speaks Ser.). (ENG., Illus.). 96p. (J). (gr. 1-4). 14.99 *(978-0-547-86580-5(5))* Houghton Mifflin Harcourt Publishing Co.

—Thanksgiving Reunion. 2013. (Martha Speaks Ser.). (ENG., Illus.). 96p. (J). (gr. 1-4). pap. 5.99 *(978-0-547-86581-2(3))* Houghton Mifflin Harcourt Publishing Co.

Meister, Cari. Happy Thanksgiving, Tiny! 2018. (Penguin Young Readers: Level 1 Ser.). lib. bdg. 13.55 *(978-0-606-41333-6(2))* Turtleback.

Melmed, Laura Krauss. This First Thanksgiving Day: A Counting Story. Buehner, Mark, illus. 2003. (ENG.). 32p. (J). (gr. -1-3). pap. 7.99 *(978-0-06-054184-2(9),* HarperCollins) HarperCollins Pubs.

Menard, Michele R. The Thanksgiving Ring. 2013. 56p. 24.95 *(978-0-9891734-8-3(8))* Four Menards, The.

Metzger, Steve. The Amazing Turkey Rescue. Paillot, Jim, illus. 2007. (J). *(978-0-545-01420-5(4))* Scholastic, Inc.

—The Great Turkey Race. Paillot, Jim, illus. 2006. (J). *(978-0-439-85930-1(1))* Scholastic, Inc.

Miller, Pat Zietlow. Sharing the Bread: An Old-Fashioned Thanksgiving Story. McElmurry, Jill, illus. 2015. (ENG.). 32p. (J). (gr. -1-3). 18.99 *(978-0-307-98182-0(7),* Schwartz & Wade Bks.) Random Hse. Children's Bks.

Moon, Alice. Lucky's Special Thanksgiving. 2007. (Illus.). (J). pap. 9.95 *(978-0-9795831-2-4(8))* PeachMoon Publishing.

Morrison, Jessica. Le Jour de L'Action de Grâce: Les Célébrations Canadiennes. Karvonen, Tanjah, tr. from ENG. 2011. (FRE.). 24p. (gr. k-3). *(978-1-77071-400-7(6))* Weigl Educational Pubs. Ltd.

Morse, William A. and & Morse, William A. And Dana Jo. Kurkle Kids: Spirit of America. 2009. 44p. pap. 16.99 *(978-1-4490-1009-6(1))* AuthorHouse.

Neely, Kirk H. Santa Almost Got Caught: Stories for Thanksgiving, Christmas, & the New Year. Cash, Emory, illus. 2011. 152p. pap. 14.99 *(978-1-4575-0477-8(4))* Dog Ear Publishing, LLC.

TUV

Oceanak, Karla. Finicky. Spanjer, Kendra, illus. 2012. (Aldo Zelnick Comic Novel Ser.: 6). (ENG.). 160p. (J). (gr. 3-7). 12.95 *(978-1-934649-24-4(4))* Bailiwick Pr.

O'Connor, Jane. Fancy Nancy: Our Thanksgiving Banquet: With More Than 30 Fabulous Stickers! Glasser, Robin Preiss, illus. 2011. (Fancy Nancy Ser.). (ENG.). 24p. (J). (gr. -1-3). pap. 4.99 *(978-0-06-123598-6(9)*, HarperFestival) HarperCollins Pubs.

Olson, Nancy. Thanksgiving at Grandma's. Marino, Michael F., illus. 2009. 24p. pap. 10.95 *(978-1-4251-8909-9(1))* Trafford Publishing.

Osborne, Mary Pope, et al. Jueves de Acción de Gracias. Murdocca, Sal, illus. 2014. (SPA.). 88p. (J). (gr. 2-4). pap. 6.99 *(978-1-933032-94-8(4))* Lectorum Pubns., Inc.

Parish, Herman. Amelia Bedelia Talks Turkey. 2009. (I Can Read Level 2 Ser.). (ENG., Illus.). 64p. (J). (gr. k-3). pap. 4.99 *(978-0-06-084354-0(3)*, Greenwillow Bks.) HarperCollins Pubs.

—Amelia Bedelia Talks Turkey. Sweat, Lynn, illus. 2008. (Amelia Bedelia Ser.). (ENG.). 64p. (J). (gr. k-4). 16.99 *(978-0-06-084352-6(7)*, Greenwillow Bks.) HarperCollins Pubs.

Park, Barbara. Turkeys We Have Loved & Eaten (and Other Thankful Stuff) 2014. (Junie B. Jones Ser.: 28). lib. bdg. 14.75 *(978-0-606-36015-9(8))* Turtleback.

Peacock, L. A. The Truth (and Myths) about Thanksgiving. Wigsby, Nick, illus. 2013. 89p. (J). pap. *(978-0-545-56846-3(3))* Scholastic, Inc.

Peterson, Joel & Rogers, Jacqueline, illus. The Littles & the Surprise Thanksgiving Guests. 2004. (Littles First Readers Ser.). 105p. (J). *(978-0-439-68704-1(7))* Scholastic, Inc.

Priddy, Roger. Alphaprints: Gobble Gobble: Touch & Feel. 2016. (Alphaprints Ser.). (ENG.). 10p. (J). bds. 7.99 *(978-0-312-52057-1(3)*, 900160015) St. Martin's Pr.

—Bright Baby: Happy Thanksgiving. 2015. (Bright Baby Ser.). (ENG.). 16p. (J). (gr. -1 — 1). bds. 5.99 *(978-0-312-51871-4(4)*, 900146441) St. Martin's Pr.

—Shiny Shapes: Hooray for Thanksgiving! 2018. (Shiny Shapes Ser.). (ENG., Illus.). 10p. (J). bds. 7.99 *(978-0-312-52724-2(1)*, 900189781) St. Martin's Pr.

Rains, Deborah Jane. Cuddles & Snuggles. 2011. 24p. pap. 24.95 *(978-1-4489-3917-6(8))* America Star Bks.

—St Patrick's Day with Cuddles & Snuggles. 2011. 16p. pap. 24.95 *(978-1-4489-4926-7(2))* America Star Bks.

—Thanksgiving with Cuddles & Snuggles, 1 vol. 2010. 20p. 24.95 *(978-1-4489-4924-3(6))* PublishAmerica, Inc.

Randall, Emma, illus. Over the River & Through the Wood. 2018. 32p. (J). (gr. -1-2). 17.99 *(978-0-515-15765-9(1)*, Penguin Workshop) Penguin Young Readers Group.

Rey, H. A. Happy Thanksgiving, Curious George Tabbed Board Book. 2010. (Curious George Ser.). (ENG., Illus.). 14p. (J). (gr. -1 — 1). bds. 8.99 *(978-0-547-13106-1(2)*, 1048360, Clarion Bks.) HarperCollins Pubs.

Roberts, Bethany. Thanksgiving Mice! Cushman, Doug, illus. 2005. (ENG.). 32p. (J). (gr. -1 — 1). 5.95 *(978-0-618-60486-9(3))* Houghton Mifflin Harcourt Publishing Co.

Roe, E. P. Three Thanksgiving Kisses. 2004. reprint ed. pap. 15.95 *(978-1-4191-8991-3(3))* Kessinger Publishing, LLC.

Roy, Ron. Calendar Mysteries #11: November Night. Gurney, John Steven, illus. 2014. (Calendar Mysteries Ser.: 11). 80p. (J). (gr. 1-4). 7.99 *(978-0-385-37165-0(9)*, Random Hse. Bks. for Young Readers) Random Hse. Children's Bks.

—Capital Mysteries #14: Turkey Trouble on the National Mall. Bush, Timothy, illus. 2012. (Capital Mysteries Ser.: 14). 96p. (J). (gr. 1-4). 6.99 *(978-0-307-93220-4(6)*, Random Hse. Bks. for Young Readers) Random Hse. Children's Bks.

Roy, Ronald. Capital Mysteries #14: Turkey Trouble on the National Mall, 14. Bush, Timothy, illus. 2012. (Capital Mysteries Ser.). (ENG.). 96p. (J). (gr. 1-4). lib. bdg. 17.44 *(978-0-375-87004-0(0))* Random House Publishing Group.

Rusu, Meredith. Peppa Gives Thanks (Peppa Pig) EOne, illus. 2018. (ENG.). 24p. (J). (gr. -1-k). pap. 6.99 *(978-1-338-22876-2(5))* Scholastic, Inc.

Rylant, Cynthia. Annie & Snowball & the Thankful Friends. 2012. (Annie & Snowball Ready-To-Read Ser.). lib. bdg. 13.55 *(978-0-606-26917-9(7))* Turtleback.

—Annie & Snowball & the Thankful Friends: Ready-To-Read Level 2. Stevenson, Suçie & Stevenson, Suçie, illus. (Annie & Snowball Ser.: 10). (ENG.). 40p. (J). (gr. k-2). 2012. pap. 4.99 *(978-1-4169-7202-0(1))* 2011. 15.99 *(978-1-4169-7200-6(5))* Simon Spotlight. (Simon Spotlight).

Santa's Thanksgiving. 2005. (J). 5.95 *(978-0-9769321-0-9(5))* Steingart, Nathan Publishing.

Schulz, Charles M. A Charlie Brown Thanksgiving. Jeralds, Scott, illus. 2016. (Peanuts Ser.). (ENG.). 32p. (J). (gr. -1). 7.99 *(978-1-4814-6805-3(7)*, Simon Spotlight) Simon Spotlight.

—Snoopy's Thanksgiving. 2014. (Peanuts Seasonal Collection: 0). (ENG., Illus.). 64p. (J). (gr. 1-12). 9.99 *(978-1-60699-778-9(5)*, 699778) Fantagraphics Bks.

Scieszka, Jon. Trucksgiving: Ready-To-Read Level 1. Shannon, David et al, illus. 2010. (Jon Scieszka's Trucktown Ser.). (ENG.). 24p. (J). (gr. -1-1). 16.99 *(978-1-4169-4157-6(6))*; pap. 4.99 *(978-1-4169-4146-0(0))* Simon Spotlight. (Simon Spotlight).

Shore, Diane Z. This Is the Feast. Lloyd, Megan, illus. 2011. (ENG.). 32p. (J). (gr. -1-3). pap. 8.99 *(978-0-06-443850-6(3)*, HarperCollins) HarperCollins Pubs.

Silvano, Wendi. Turkey Trouble, 0 vols. Harper, Lee, illus. 2012. (Turkey Trouble Ser.: 1). (ENG.). 40p. (J). (gr. -1-2). 15.99 *(978-0-7614-5529-5(9)*, 9780761455295, Two Lions) Amazon Publishing.

Smith, Jane. It's Thanksgiving, Chloe Zoe! Smith, Jane, illus. 2017. (Chloe Zoe Ser.). (ENG., Illus.). 32p. (J). (gr. -1-3). 12.99 *(978-0-8075-1212-8(5)*, 807512125) Whitman, Albert & Co.

Spinelli, Eileen. Thanksgiving at the Tappletons' 2015. (ENG., Illus.). 32p. (J). (gr. -1-3). pap. 8.99 *(978-0-06-236397-8(2)*, HarperCollins) HarperCollins Pubs.

—Thanksgiving at the Tappletons' Lloyd, Megan, illus. 2005. (gr. -1-3). 17.00 *(978-0-7569-5762-9(1))* Perfection Learning Corp.

Stanley, Diane. Thanksgiving on Plymouth Plantation. Berry, Holly, illus. 2004. (ENG.). 48p. (J). (gr. k-5). 17.99 *(978-0-06-027069-8(1)*, HarperCollins) HarperCollins Pubs.

Star, Nancy. The Case of the Thanksgiving Thief. Bernardin, James, illus. 2004. 79p. (J). *(978-0-439-67261-0(9))* Scholastic, Inc.

Steinberg, Jessica. Not This Turkey! 2018. (2019 Av2 Fiction Ser.). (ENG.). 32p. (J). (gr. k-3). lib. bdg. 34.28 *(978-1-4896-8273-4(2)*, AV2 by Weigl) Weigl Pubs., Inc.

—Not This Turkey! Pike, Amanda, illus. 2016. (ENG.). 32p. (J). (gr. -1-3). 16.99 *(978-0-8075-7908-4(4)*, 807579084) Whitman, Albert & Co.

Stern, Ricki. Mission Impossible. Date not set. (Beryl E. Bean Ser.: Vol. 3). (Illus.). (J). lib. bdg. 15.89 *(978-0-06-028773-3(X)*, Harper Trophy) HarperCollins Pubs.

Stone, Tanya Lee. T Is for Turkey. Kelley, Gerald, illus. 2009. 24p. (J). (gr. -1-k). mass mkt. 6.99 *(978-0-8431-2570-2(5)*, Price Stern Sloan) Penguin Young Readers Group.

Suhay, Lisa. Pardon Me, It's Ham, Not Turkey. Barcita, Pamela, illus. 2007. (J). (gr. -1-3). 17.95 *(978-1-933982-01-4(2))* Bumble Bee Publishing.

Sullivan, Maureen & Josephs, Alison. Ankle Soup: A Thanksgiving Story. Josephs, Alison, illus. 2008. (Illus.). 32p. 17.95 *(978-0-9820381-0-9(0))* MoJo InkWorks.

Thaler, Mike. The Thanksgiving Day from the Black Lagoon. Lee, Jared, illus. 2009. 64p. (J). *(978-0-545-16812-0(0))* Scholastic, Inc.

Tillman, Gloria J. Teeth for Thanksgiving. Tillman, Gloria J., ed. 2023. (ENG., Illus.). 32p. (J). lib. bdg. 18.82 *(978-0-9841260-7-1(4))* Tamaja Pr. L.L.C.

Wallace, Adam. How to Catch a Turkey. Elkerton, Andy, illus. 2018. (How to Catch Ser.: 0). 40p. (J). (gr. k-6). 10.99 *(978-1-4926-6435-2(9))* Sourcebooks, Inc.

Wheeler, Lisa. Dino-Thanksgiving. Gott, Barry, illus. 2020. (Dino-Holidays Ser.). (ENG.). 32p. (J). (gr. k-3). 18.99 *(978-1-5124-0318-3(0)*, 967cec8a-0a13-4116-a015-3be1da5e4709, Carolrhoda Bks.) Lerner Publishing Group.

—Turk & Runt: A Thanksgiving Comedy. Ansley, Frank, illus. 2005. (ENG.). 32p. (J). (gr. -1-2). 7.99 *(978-1-4169-0714-5(9)*, Atheneum Bks. for Young Readers) Simon & Schuster Children's Publishing.

Wilce, Colin. The Youngsters' Adventure & Thanksgiving (Rabbit Brook Tales Volume 4) 2007. (ENG.). 80p. pap. 17.95 *(978-1-84753-202-2(0))* Lulu Pr., Inc.

Wood, Francis Eugene. Autumn's Reunion: A Story of Thanksgiving. Dean, Tina & Marken, Jon, eds. McDermott, Robert W., illus. 2006. 47p. pap. 8.00 *(978-0-9746372-2-8(X))* Tip-Of-The-Moon Publishing Co.

Yundt, Katherine. Thankful Tonight. 2018. (ENG., Illus.). 22p. (J). bds. 12.99 *(978-1-4621-2239-4(6))* Cedar Fort, Inc./CFI Distribution.

THEATER

see also Acting; Actors and Actresses; Ballet; Bible Plays; Opera; Puppets; Shadow Shows; Theaters

Alexander, Martha, et al. Teatro para Niños. Tenorio, Miguel A., ed. 2005. (SPA.). 246p. (J). (gr. 4-7). pap. 14.95 *(978-968-860-739-8(8))* Editorial Pax MEX. Dist: Independent Pubs. Group.

Bell, Samantha S. You Can Work on Broadway. 2018. (You Can Work in the Arts Ser.). (ENG., Illus.). 32p. (J). (gr. 4-6). lib. bdg. 28.65 *(978-1-5435-4144-1(5)*, 139098, Capstone Pr.) Capstone.

Berne, Emma Carlson. William Shakespeare: Playwright & Poet, 1 vol. 2008. (Essential Lives Set 2 Ser.). (ENG., Illus.). 112p. (YA). (gr. 6-12). lib. bdg. 41.36 *(978-1-60453-042-1(1)*, 6665, Essential Library) ABDO Publishing Co.

Bjorklund, Ruth. Singing in Theater, 1 vol. 2017. (Exploring Theater Ser.). (ENG.). 96p. (YA). (gr. 7-7). pap. 20.99 *(978-1-5026-3429-0(5)*, 92d2bea8-9531-4161-a4f9-6b00d804840c); lib. bdg. 44.50 *(978-1-5026-3007-0(9)*, 02682f68-8a8b-4b56-a2e5-53ff8ff828a1) Cavendish Square Publishing LLC.

Blackwell, Su, et al. The Sleeping Beauty Theatre: Put on Your Own Show. 2015. (Illus.). 28p. (J). (gr. 1-5). 29.95 *(978-0-500-65054-7(3)*, 565054) Thames & Hudson.

Brita, Granström. Mi primer libro de teatro. 2006. (Mi Primer Libro Ser.). (SPA., Illus.). 48p. (J). (gr. 2-3). 17.99 *(978-84-241-1311-7(X))* Everest Editora ESP. Dist: Lectorum Pubns., Inc.

Capaccio, George. Advertising & Marketing in Theater, 1 vol. 2017. (Exploring Theater Ser.). (ENG.). 96p. (YA). (gr. 7-7). pap. 20.99 *(978-1-5026-3430-6(9)*, ac3bb200-766c-43cb-bb86-efa25b4f99f6); lib. bdg. 44.50 *(978-1-5026-2999-9(2)*, e0024756-f406-4e49-93e5-d9e59cc2c8c4) Cavendish Square Publishing LLC.

Clements, Gillian. Tudor Theatre. 2009. (Building History Ser.). (Illus.). 32p. (J). (gr. 3-5). 27.10 *(978-1-59771-147-0(0))* Sea-To-Sea Pubns.

Cobb, Lisa K. Literary Ideas & Scripts for Young Playwrights, 1 vol. 2004. (ENG., Illus.). 192p. pap. 37.00 *(978-1-59158-071-3(4)*, 900318663, Libraries Unlimited) ABC-CLIO, LLC.

Cohan, George M. & Schwaeber, Barbie. Give My Regards to Broadway. Newsom, Carol, illus. 2008. (American Favorites Ser.). (ENG.). 32p. (J). (gr. -1-3). 14.95 *(978-1-59249-726-3(8))*; 8.95 *(978-1-59249-727-0(6))* Soundprints.

Culp, Jennifer. What Is a Play?, 1 vol. 2014. (Britannica Common Core Library). (ENG., Illus.). 32p. (J). (gr. 2-3). 27.04 *(978-1-62275-668-1(1)*, af4c22b4-5697-4d47-ae37-9d72e97b1bef, Britannica Educational Publishing) Rosen Publishing Group, Inc., The.

Draper, Penny. Breaking Big, 1 vol. 2016. (Orca Limelights Ser.). (ENG.). 144p. (J). (gr. 4-7). pap. 9.95 *(978-1-4598-0923-9(8))* Orca Bk. Pubs. USA.

Dunleavy, Deborah. The Jumbo Book of Drama. Kurisu, Jane, tr. Kurisu, Jane, illus. 2004. (Jumbo Bks.). (ENG.). 208p. (J). (gr. 4-6). 14.95 *(978-1-55337-008-6(2))* Kids Can Pr., Ltd. CAN. Dist: Hachette Bk. Group.

Emmer, Rae. Drama Club. 2009. (School Activities Ser.). 24p. (gr. 1-1). 42.50 *(978-1-60852-998-8(3)*, PowerKids Pr.) Rosen Publishing Group, Inc., The.

—Drama Club / Club de Teatro. 2009. (School Activities / Actividades escolares Ser.). (ENG & SPA.). 24p. (gr. 1-2). 42.50 *(978-1-60853-004-5(3)*, Editorial Buenas Letras) Rosen Publishing Group, Inc., The.

Evans, Cheryl & Smith, Lucy. Acting & Theatre. Evans, Cheryl, ed. Jude, Conny, illus. Putsman, Helen, photos by. 2008. (Acting & Theatre Ser.). 64p. (J). pap. 8.99 *(978-0-7945-2216-2(5)*, Usborne) EDC Publishing.

Exploring Theater (Group 2), 12 vols. 2017. (Exploring Theater Ser.). (ENG.). (J). (gr. 7-7). lib. bdg. 267.00 *(978-1-5026-3215-9(2)*, 8a2fa90c-4e9b-41c5-91ff-c7fb3ff7fb75) Cavendish Square Publishing LLC.

Firth, Melissa. Behind the Scenes at a Play, 1 vol. 2014. (VIP Tours Ser.). (ENG.). 48p. (gr. 4-4). 33.07 *(978-1-62713-019-6(5)*, 3f977be8-3be9-4032-9ed0-893a52c3efe9) Cavendish Square Publishing LLC.

Gallegos, Manuel. Mi Primer Teatro. 2003. (J). *(978-956-240-371-9(8))* Arrayán Editores S.A.

Hilliam, David. William Shakespeare: England's Greatest Playwright & Poet. 2009. (Rulers, Scholars, & Artists of the Renaissance Ser.). 112p. (gr. 5-8). 66.50 *(978-1-60852-945-2(2)*, Rosen Reference) Rosen Publishing Group, Inc., The.

In the Movies, 6 vols. (Book2WebTM Ser.). (gr. 4-8). 36.50 *(978-0-322-02982-8(1))* Wright Group/McGraw-Hill.

Lewis, Jan, illus. Performance. 2012. (First Time Ser.). 24p. (J). *(978-1-84643-487-7(4))* Child's Play International Ltd.

Madl-Palfi, L. & Tujner-Marko, B. Kaspertheater Rund ums Jahr. (Illus.). 144p. pap. *(978-3-12-675640-2(9))* Klett Lerntraining bei PONS DEU. Dist: International Bk. Import Service, Inc.

Malam, John. Theater: From First Rehearsal to Opening Night! a Building Works Book. Malam, John, illus. 2006. (Illus.). 32p. (J). (gr. k-4). 17.00 *(978-1-4223-5179-6(3))* DIANE Publishing Co.

Matthews, Sheelagh. The Sydney Opera House. 2008. (Structural Wonders Ser.). (Illus.). 32p. (J). (gr. 4-6). pap. 9.95 *(978-1-59036-937-1(8))* Weigl Pubs., Inc.

McGraw Hill. The Stage & the School, Student Edition. 9th ed. 2004. (STAGE & SCHOOL Ser.). (ENG., Illus.). 672p. (gr. 9-12). stu. ed. 111.52 *(978-0-07-861627-3(1)*, 0078616271) McGraw-Hill Education.

Meister, Cari. El Teatro. 2016. (Los Primeros Viajes Escolares (First Field Trips)).Tr. of Theater. 24p. (J). (gr. k-2). lib. bdg. 25.65 *(978-1-62031-332-9(4)*, Bullfrog Bks.) Jump! Inc.

—Theater. Fretland VanVoorst, Jenny, ed. 2016. (First Field Trips). (Illus.). 24p. (J). (gr. k-2). lib. bdg. 25.65 *(978-1-62031-298-8(0)*, Bullfrog Bks.) Jump! Inc.

Moore Niver, Heather. Plays, 1 vol. 2018. (Let's Learn about Literature Ser.). (ENG.). 24p. (gr. 1-2). lib. bdg. 24.27 *(978-0-7660-9751-3(X)*, 4fd35bec-96dc-40f6-b940-c425690ca7c8) Enslow Publishing, LLC.

Nardo, Don. Careers in Film, TV, & Theater. 2019. (Careers for Creative People Ser.). (ENG.). 80p. (J). (gr. 6-12). 41.27 *(978-1-68282-681-2(3))* ReferencePoint Pr., Inc.

Owings, Lisa. What Are Plays? 2014. (Name That Text Type! Ser.). (ENG., Illus.). 32p. (J). (gr. 2-4). lib. bdg. 26.65 *(978-1-4677-4060-9(8)*, 8cc890a7-f932-409e-83b7-6d7d04374479, Lerner Pubns.) Lerner Publishing Group.

Rauf, Don. Choreography & Dance in Theater, 1 vol. 2017. (Exploring Theater Ser.). (ENG.). 96p. (YA). (gr. 7-7). lib. bdg. 44.50 *(978-1-5026-3001-8(X)*, f25c6ded-2050-456b-862b-8d351edcb56f) Cavendish Square Publishing LLC.

—Music in Theater, 1 vol. 2016. (Exploring Theater Ser.). (ENG., Illus.). 96p. (YA). (gr. 7-7). lib. bdg. 44.50 *(978-1-5026-2271-6(8)*, 089380b8-c3fa-4cfe-8a95-b9eceda90d3b) Cavendish Square Publishing LLC.

Regan, Lisa. Broadway Star, 1 vol. 2012. (Stage School Ser.). (ENG., Illus.). 32p. (J). (gr. 2-3). 29.93 *(978-1-4488-8092-8(0)*, 9df4b6dd-cedd-48fa-be1e-7b61fc5eb5f0); pap. 11.00 *(978-1-4488-8151-2(X)*, 584ddf15-0ccf-49eb-83b4-e0023dfeee41) Rosen Publishing Group, Inc., The. (Windmill Bks.).

Rice, Dona Herweck. Fantastic Kids: Theater Kids (Level 1) 2018. (TIME for KIDS(r): Informational Text Ser.). (ENG., Illus.). 24p. (gr. 1-2). pap. 8.99 *(978-1-4258-4960-3(1))* Teacher Created Materials, Inc.

Vescia, Monique. Choose a Career Adventure on Broadway. 2016. (Bright Futures Press: Choose a Career Adventure Ser.). (ENG., Illus.). 32p. (J). (gr. 4-6). 32.07 *(978-1-63471-909-4(3)*, 208957) Cherry Lake Publishing.

Yacka, Douglas, et al. Where Is Broadway? Hinderliter, John, illus. 2019. (Where Is? Ser.). 112p. (J). (gr. 3-7). 7.99 *(978-1-5247-8650-2(0))*; 15.99 *(978-1-5247-8651-9(9))* Penguin Young Readers Group. (Penguin Workshop).

Zimmerman, Suzi. Introduction to Theatre Arts 2: Student Handbook. 2007. (ENG., Illus.). 255p. stu. ed., per. 24.95 *(978-1-56608-148-1(3))* Meriwether Publishing, Ltd.

THEATER—FICTION

Aliki. Play's the Thing. Aliki, illus. 2005. (ENG., Illus.). 32p. (J). 16.99 *(978-0-06-074355-0(7))* HarperCollins Pubs.

Alsenas, Linas. Beyond Clueless. 2015. (ENG., Illus.). 256p. (YA). (gr. 7-11). 16.95 *(978-1-4197-1496-2(1)*, 681301, Amulet Bks.) Abrams, Inc.

Andrews, Julie & Hamilton, Emma Walton. The Great American Mousical. Walton, Tony, illus. 2006. (Julie Andrews Collection). (J). (gr. k-4). 160p. 15.99 *(978-0-06-057918-0(8)*, Julie Andrews Collection); 147p. lib. bdg. 16.89 *(978-0-06-057919-7(6))* HarperCollins Pubs.

Anthony, Horowitz. The Devil & His Boy. 2007. (ENG.). 192p. (YA). (gr. 6-8). 18.69 *(978-0-399-23432-3(2))* Penguin Young Readers Group.

Appelt, Kathi. Bat Jamboree. Sweet, Melissa, illus. 2004. 17.00 *(978-0-7569-4074-4(5))* Perfection Learning Corp.

Barkley, Callie. All about Ellie. Riti, Marsha, illus. 2013. (Critter Club Ser.: 2). (ENG.). 128p. (J). (gr. k-2). 17.99 *(978-1-4424-5789-8(9))*; pap. 6.99 *(978-1-4424-5788-1(0))* Little Simon. (Little Simon).

—All about Ellie. 2013. (Critter Club Ser.: 2). lib. bdg. 16.00 *(978-0-606-27024-3(8))* Turtleback.

Barshaw, Ruth McNally. The Ellie Mcdoodle Diaries: the Show Must Go On. 2013. (Ellie Mcdoodle Diaries). (ENG., Illus.). 176p. (YA). (gr. 3-6). 13.99 *(978-1-61963-059-8(1)*, 900118518, Bloomsbury USA Childrens) Bloomsbury Publishing USA.

Berenstain, Mike. The Berenstain Bears Blessed Are the Peacemakers, 1 vol. 2014. (Berenstain Bears/Living Lights: a Faith Story Ser.). (ENG.). 24p. (J). pap. 5.99 *(978-0-310-73481-9(9))* Zonderkidz.

Berenstain, Mike, et al. The Berenstain Bears Give Thanks, 1 vol. Berenstain, Stan, illus. 2009. (Berenstain Bears/Living Lights: a Faith Story Ser.). (ENG.). 32p. (J). (gr. -1-2). pap. 4.99 *(978-0-310-71251-0(3))* Zonderkidz.

Bergen, Lara. Drama Queen. 2007. 164p. (J). pap. *(978-0-545-03702-0(6))* Scholastic, Inc.

Blount, Patty. The Way It Hurts. 2017. (ENG., Illus.). 400p. (YA). (gr. 8-12). pap. 10.99 *(978-1-4926-3278-8(3))* Sourcebooks, Inc.

Blume, Judy. The One in the Middle Is the Green Kangaroo. Ohi, Debbie Ridpath, illus. 2014. (ENG.). 48p. (J). (gr. 1-5). pap. 5.99 *(978-1-4814-1131-8(4)*, Atheneum Bks. for Young Readers) Simon & Schuster Children's Publishing.

Bond, Felicia. The Halloween Play. Bond, Felicia, illus. 2008. Orig. Title: The Halloween Performance. (ENG., Illus.). 32p. (J). (gr. -1-1). pap. 7.99 *(978-0-06-135796-1(0)*, HarperCollins) HarperCollins Pubs.

Bowe, Julie. So Much Drama. 2016. (Victoria Torres, Unfortunately Average Ser.). (ENG., Illus.). 160p. (J). (gr. 4-8). pap. 5.95 *(978-1-4965-3807-9(2)*, 133115); lib. bdg. 27.99 *(978-1-4965-3799-7(8)*, 133112) Capstone. (Stone Arch Bks.).

Brown, Monica. Drama Queen. 2016. (Lola Levine Ser.: 2). (J). lib. bdg. 16.00 *(978-0-606-38329-5(8))* Turtleback.

—Lola Levine: Drama Queen. 2016. (Lola Levine Ser.: 2). (ENG., Illus.). (J). (gr. 1-5). 112p. pap. 5.99 *(978-0-316-25842-5(3))*; 96p. 15.99 *(978-0-316-25843-2(1))* Little, Brown Bks. for Young Readers.

Bryant, Megan E. Set the Stage! (Tiny Geniuses #2) 2018. (Tiny Geniuses Ser.: 2). (ENG.). 128p. (J). (gr. 2-5). pap. 5.99 *(978-0-545-90957-0(0)*, Scholastic Paperbacks) Scholastic, Inc.

Capetta, A. R. Echo after Echo. 2017. (ENG.). 432p. (YA). (gr. 9). 17.99 *(978-0-7636-9164-6(X))* Candlewick Pr.

Carretero, Mónica & Carretero, Mónica. Roly-Polies. Brokenbrow, Jon, tr. Carretero, Mónica & Carretero, Mónica, illus. 2011. (Mini-Animalist Ser.). (ENG., Illus.). 32p. (J). (gr. k-3). 14.95 *(978-84-938240-1-3(1))* Cuento de Luz SL ESP. Dist: Publishers Group West (PGW).

Chen, Bill. The Musical. Sun, Jun, illus. 2013. (J). *(978-0-9845523-1-3(6))* Heryin Publishing Corp.

Cocks, Heather & Morgan, Jessica. Spoiled. 2012. (ENG.). 384p. (YA). (gr. 10-17). pap. 19.99 *(978-0-316-09827-4(2)*, Poppy) Little, Brown Bks. for Young Readers.

Condie, Ally. Summerlost. 2017. (ENG.). 272p. (J). (gr. 5). 8.99 *(978-0-399-18721-6(9)*, Puffin Books) Penguin Young Readers Group.

—Summerlost. 2017. lib. bdg. 19.65 *(978-0-606-40105-0(9))* Turtleback.

Conford, Ellen. Annabel the Actress Starring in the Hound of the Barkervilles. Andriani, Renee W., illus. 2004. (Annabel the Actress Ser.). 83p. (gr. 2-5). 14.00 *(978-0-7569-2180-4(5))* Perfection Learning Corp.

Creech, Sharon. Replay. (J). (gr. 3-7). 2013. (ENG.). 224p. pap. 9.99 *(978-0-06-054021-0(4)*, HarperCollins) 2005. 240p. lib. bdg. 16.89 *(978-0-06-054020-3(6)*, Cotler, Joanna Books) HarperCollins Pubs.

Culbertson, Kim. Instructions for a Broken Heart. 2011. (ENG.). 304p. (YA). (gr. 7-12). pap. 14.99 *(978-1-4022-4302-8(2))* Sourcebooks, Inc.

Dadey, Debbie. Wish upon a Starfish. Avakyan, Tatevik, illus. 2015. (Mermaid Tales Ser.: 12). (ENG.). 128p. (J). (gr. 1-4). pap. 6.99 *(978-1-4814-0263-7(3)*, Aladdin) Simon & Schuster Children's Publishing.

Dahl, Michael. Curtains! A High School Musical Mystery. Prothero, Tiffany, illus. 2008. (Vortex Bks.). (ENG.). 112p. (J). (gr. 5-9). 26.65 *(978-1-4342-0801-9(X)*, 95206, Stone Arch Bks.) Capstone.

De Baun, Hillary Hall. The Last Stop Before Heaven. Cooper, Floyd, illus. 2012. (ENG.). 236p. (J). pap. 9.00 *(978-0-8028-5398-1(6)*, Eerdmans Bks For Young Readers) Eerdmans, William B. Publishing Co.

Dee, Barbara. Star-Crossed. 2017. (ENG., Illus.). 288p. (J). (gr. 4-8). 18.99 *(978-1-4814-7848-9(6)*, Simon & Schuster/Paula Wiseman Bks.) Simon & Schuster/Paula Wiseman Bks.

—Trauma Queen. 2011. (Mix Ser.). (ENG.). 272p. (J). (gr. 4-8). pap. 8.99 *(978-1-4424-0923-1(1)*, Aladdin) Simon & Schuster Children's Publishing.

Deen, Natasha. Lark Takes a Bow, 1 vol. Cutler, Marcus, illus. 2018. (Orca Echoes Ser.: 3). (ENG.). 96p. (J). (gr. 1-3). pap. 7.95 *(978-1-4598-1715-9(X))* Orca Bk. Pubs. USA.

dePaola, Tomie. Stagestruck. 2007. (Illus.). 32p. (J). (gr. -1-3). pap. 6.99 *(978-0-14-240899-5(9)*, Puffin Books) Penguin Young Readers Group.

—Stagestruck. dePaola, Tomie, illus. 2005. (ENG., Illus.). 32p. (J). (gr. -1-1). 21.19 *(978-0-399-24338-7(0))* Penguin Young Readers Group.

—Stagestruck. dePaola, Tomie, illus. 2007. (Illus.). (gr. -1-3). 17.00 *(978-0-7569-8159-4(X))* Perfection Learning Corp.

Destiny, A. & Helms, Rhonda. Never Too Late. 2015. (Flirt Ser.). (ENG., Illus.). 224p. (YA). (gr. 7). pap. 9.99 *(978-1-4814-5188-8(X)*, Simon Pulse) Simon Pulse.

DiTerlizzi, Tony. Kenny & the Dragon. 2008. (Playaway Children Ser.). (J). (gr. 3-7). 39.99 *(978-1-60640-958-9(1))* Findaway World, LLC.

—Kenny & the Dragon. DiTerlizzi, Tony, illus. 2012. (Kenny & the Dragon Ser.). (ENG., Illus.). 176p. (J). (gr. 3-7). pap. 8.99 *(978-1-4424-3651-0(4)*, Simon & Schuster Bks. For Young Readers) Simon & Schuster Bks. For Young Readers.

—Kenny & the Dragon. DiTerlizzi, Tony, illus. 2008. (Illus.). 160p. (J). (gr. 3-7). 15.99 Simon & Schuster Children's Publishing.

—Kenny & the Dragon. DiTerlizzi, Tony, illus. 2008. (Kenny & the Dragon Ser.). (ENG., Illus.). 160p. (J). (gr. 3-7). 17.99 *(978-1-4169-3977-1(6))* Simon & Schuster, Inc.

Dixon, Franklin W. Talent Show Tricks. David, Matt, illus. 2016. (Hardy Boys Clue Book Ser.: 4). (ENG.). 96p. (J). (gr. 1-4). pap. 5.99 *(978-1-4814-5180-2(4)*, Aladdin) Simon & Schuster Children's Publishing.

Donnelly, Rebecca. How to Stage a Catastrophe. 2017. (ENG., Illus.). 256p. (J). (gr. 4-7). 12.95

(978-1-62370-807-8(9), 133357, Capstone Young Readers) Capstone.
Elliott, Rebecca. Eva in the Spotlight: a Branches Book (Owl Diaries #13) Elliott, Rebecca, illus. 2020. (Owl Diaries: 13). (ENG., Illus.). 80p. (J). (gr. k-2). pap. 4.99 (978-1-338-29875-8(5)) Scholastic, Inc.
—Eva in the Spotlight: a Branches Book (Owl Diaries #13) (Library Edition) Elliott, Rebecca, illus. 2020. (Owl Diaries: 13). (ENG., Illus.). 80p. (J). (gr. k-2). lib. bdg. 24.99 (978-1-338-29876-5(3)) Scholastic, Inc.
Federle, Tim. Better Nate Than Ever. 2013. (Nate Ser.). (ENG., Illus.). 288p. (J). (gr. 4-8). 18.99 (978-1-4424-4689-2(7), Simon & Schuster Bks. For Young Readers) Simon & Schuster Bks. For Young Readers.
—Five, Six, Seven, Nate! (Nate Ser.). (ENG.). (J). (gr. 5). 2018. 336p. pap. 7.99 (978-1-5344-2914-7(X)) 2014. (Illus.). 298p. 19.99 (978-1-4424-4693-9(5)) Simon & Schuster Bks. For Young Readers. (Simon & Schuster Bks. For Young Readers).
—Nate Expectations. (Nate Ser.). (ENG.). (J). (gr. 5). 2019. 272p. pap. 8.99 (978-1-4814-0413-6(X)) 2018. (Illus.). 256p. 17.99 (978-1-4814-0412-9(1)) Simon & Schuster Bks. For Young Readers. (Simon & Schuster Bks. For Young Readers).
Feldman, Thea, et al. Harry Cat & Tucker Mouse: Harry to the Rescue! 2011. (My Readers: Level 2 Ser.). (ENG., Illus.). 48p. (J). (gr. k-2). 16.19 (978-0-312-62507-8(3)) Square Fish.
Fiedler, Lisa & Wallach, Anya. Curtain Up. 2015. (Stagestruck Ser.). (ENG.). 256p. (J). (gr. 4-7). 11.99 (978-1-58536-923-2(3), 203816) Sleeping Bear Pr.
—Showstopper. 2015. (Stagestruck Ser.). (ENG.). 280p. (J). (gr. 4-6). 11.99 (978-1-58536-925-6(X), 203948) Sleeping Bear Pr.
Fields, Jan. Ghost Light Burning: An Up2U Mystery Adventure, 1 vol. Fabbretti, Valerio, illus. 2015. (Up2U Adventures Ser.). (ENG.). 80p. (J). (gr. 2-5). 35.64 (978-1-62402-092-6(5), 17353, Calico Chapter Bks.) ABDO Publishing Co.
Friedman, Laurie. Mallory in the Spotlight. Kalis, Jennifer, illus. (Mallory Ser.). 2011. pap. 33.92 (978-0-7613-8359-8(X)) 2011. (ENG.). 160p. (J). (gr. 2-5). pap. 6.99 (978-0-7613-3948-9(5), b60d9d35-7f73-4915-b0b6-80f3cbac5d25) 2010. (ENG.). 160p. (J). (gr. 2-5). 15.95 (978-0-8225-8884-9(6), d124d3d1-c47a-4c88-a381-c43b43796758) Lerner Publishing Group. (Darby Creek).
Gibaldi, Lauren. This Tiny Perfect World. 2019. (ENG.). 320p. (YA). (gr. 8). pap. 10.99 (978-0-06-249008-7(7), HarperTeen) HarperCollins Pubs.
Giff, Patricia Reilly. Star Time. Bright, Alasdair, illus. 2011. (Zigzag Kids Ser.: 4). (ENG.). 80p. (J). (gr. 1-4). 4.99 (978-0-375-85912-0(8), Yearling) Random Hse. Children's Bks.
Gilman, Grace. Dixie. McConnell, Sarah, illus. 2011. (I Can Read Level 1 Ser.). (ENG.). 32p. (J). (gr. -1-3). 16.99 (978-0-06-171914-1(5)); pap. 4.99 (978-0-06-171913-4(7)) HarperCollins Pubs. (HarperCollins).
Giulieri, Anne. In the Playhouse, 1 vol. Aranda, Omar, illus. 2012. (Engage Literacy Magenta Ser.). (ENG.). 16p. (J). (gr. k-2). pap. 6.99 (978-1-4296-8852-9(1), 119929, Capstone Pr.) Capstone.
Grabenstein, Chris. The Demons' Door. 2017. (Haunted Mystery Ser.: 2). 352p. (J). (gr. 3-7). 8.99 (978-1-5247-6520-0(1), Yearling) Random Hse. Children's Bks.
Green, John. Will Grayson, Will Grayson. 2011. lib. bdg. 22.10 (978-0-606-15358-4(6)) Turtleback.
Green, John & Levithan, David. Will Grayson, Will Grayson. (ENG., (YA). (gr. 9-18). 2011. Illus.). 326p. 12.99 (978-0-14-241847-5(1), Speak) 2010. 320p. 19.99 (978-0-525-42158-0(0), Dutton Books for Young Readers) Penguin Young Readers Group.
—Will Grayson, Will Grayson (Spanish Edition) 2019. (SPA.). 336p. (YA). (gr. 7). pap. 12.95 (978-607-31-3340-1(5), Nube De Tinta) Penguin Random House Grupo Editorial ESP. Dist: Penguin Random Hse. LLC.
Greenwald, Tommy. Charlie Joe Jackson's Guide to Extra Credit. Coovert, J. P., illus. 2013. (Charlie Joe Jackson Ser.: 2). (ENG.). 288p. (J). (gr. 4-7). pap. 10.99 (978-1-250-01670-6(3), 900087084) Square Fish.
—Charlie Joe Jackson's Guide to Extra Credit. 2013. (Charlie Joe Jackson's Guide Ser.: 2). (J). lib. bdg. 18.40 (978-0-606-28461-5(3)) Turtleback.
Guest, Elissa Haden. Iris & Walter - The School Play. Davenier, Christine, illus. 2006. (Iris & Walter Ser.). 44p. (gr. 1-4). 15.95 (978-0-7569-6679-9(5)) Perfection Learning Corp.
Gutman, Dan. Miss Laney Is Zany! 2010. (My Weird School Daze Ser.: 8). (J). lib. bdg. 14.75 (978-0-606-10112-7(8)) Turtleback.
Hale, Bruce. Give My Regrets to Broadway. 2005. (Chet Gecko Mystery Ser.). (Illus.). 115p. (gr. 3-7). 16.00 (978-0-7569-5247-1(6)) Perfection Learning Corp.
Hale, Nathan. Apocalypse Taco. 2019. (ENG., Illus.). 128p. (YA). (gr. 3-7). 14.99 (978-1-4197-3373-4(7), 1256501, Amulet Bks.) Abrams, Inc.
Harley, Bill. Charlie Bumpers vs. the Really Nice Gnome, 1 vol. Gustavson, Adam, illus. (Charlie Bumpers Ser.: 2). 160p. (J). (gr. 2-5). 2015. pap. 7.99 (978-1-56145-831-8(7)) 2014. 13.95 (978-1-56145-740-3(X)) Peachtree Publishing Co. Inc.
Harris, Fiona. Super Moopers: Dramatic Dom. Edgar, Scott, illus. 2017. (Super Moopers Ser.). (ENG.). 48p. (J). pap. 11.99 (978-1-76040-648-6(1)) Bonnier Publishing GBR. Dist: Independent Pubs. Group.
Hayes, John C. Splurge & the Theatre of Magic. 2008. 348p. pap. 22.00 (978-1-84426-500-8(5)) Upfront Publishing Ltd. GBR. Dist: Printondemand-worldwide.com.
Heilig, Heidi. For a Muse of Fire. (ENG.). (YA). (gr. 8). 2019. 528p. pap. 10.99 (978-0-06-238082-1(6)) 2018. (Illus.). 512p. 17.99 (978-0-06-238081-4(8)) HarperCollins Pubs. (Greenwillow Bks.).
Henson, Heather. Here's How I See It - Here's How It Is. 2009. (ENG.). 224p. (J). (gr. 6-8). 18.69 (978-1-4169-4901-5(1)) Simon & Schuster, Inc.
—Here's How I See It— Here's How It Is. 2010. (ENG., Illus.). 304p. (J). (gr. 5-9). pap. 6.99 (978-1-4169-9773-3(3), Atheneum Bks. for Young Readers) Simon & Schuster Children's Publishing.
Hill, Grace Brooks. The Corner House Girls in a Play. 2011. (Illus.). 154p. pap. 9.99 (978-1-61203-171-2(4)) Bottom of the Hill Publishing.
Hoffman, Mary. Amazing Grace. (Illus.). 32p. (J). (ARA & ENG.). (978-1-85430-334-9(1), 93433); (ENG & VIE., (978-1-85430-340-0(6), 93435) Little Tiger Pr. Group.
—Encore, Grace! 2011. (ENG.). 112p. (J). (gr. 3-7). 5.99 (978-0-14-241854-3(4), Puffin Books) Penguin Young Readers Group.
Holden, Pam. Our Puppet Show, 1 vol. 2015. (ENG., Illus.). 16p. (-1). pap. (978-1-77654-072-3(7), Red Rocket Readers) Flying Start Bks.
Holm, Jennifer L. & Holm, Matthew. Babymouse #10: the Musical. Holm, Jennifer L. & Holm, Matthew, illus. 2009. (Babymouse Ser.: 10). (ENG., Illus.). 96p. (J). (gr. 2-5). pap. 6.99 (978-0-375-84388-4(4)); lib. bdg. 12.99 (978-0-375-93791-0(9)) Penguin Random Hse. LLC.
Hopkins, Cathy. The Princess of Pop. 2012. (Truth or Dare Ser.). (ENG.). 224p. (YA). (gr. 7). pap. 10.99 (978-1-4424-6057-7(1), Simon Pulse) Simon Pulse.
Hughes, Virginia. Peggy Finds the Theater. Leone, Sergio, illus. 2011. 186p. 42.95 (978-1-258-10513-6(6)) Literary Licensing, LLC.
Hyman, Fracaswell. Mango Delight. Morrison, Frank, illus. 2018. (Mango Delight Ser.: 1). (ENG.). 224p. (J). (gr. 4-8). pap. 8.99 (978-1-4549-2962-8(6)) Sterling Publishing Co., Inc.
Jakubowski, Michele. Dodgeball, Drama, & Other Dilemmas. Montalto, Luisa, illus. 2013. (Sidney & Sydney Ser.). (ENG.). 128p. (J). (gr. 1-3). 8.95 (978-1-4795-2116-6(7), 123811); lib. bdg. 25.32 (978-1-4048-8061-0(5), 121784) Capstone. (Picture Window Bks.).
Kear, Nicole C. The Fix-It Friends: the Show Must Go On. Dockray, Tracy, illus. 2017. (Fix-It Friends Ser.: 3). (ENG.). 160p. (J). pap. 7.99 (978-1-250-08668-6(X), 900157576) Imprint IND. Dist: Macmillan.
Keenan-Bolger, Andrew & Wetherhead, Kate. Act 3. 2018. (Jack & Louisa Ser.: 3). (Illus.). 256p. (J). (gr. 3-7). 8.99 (978-1-5247-8497-3(4), Penguin Workshop) Penguin Young Readers Group.
Kehret, Peg. Backstage Fright. 2008. (ENG.). 128p. (J). (gr. 3-7). pap. 7.99 (978-1-4169-9107-6(7), Simon & Schuster/Paula Wiseman Bks.) Simon & Schuster/Paula Wiseman Bks.
Kirby, Stan. Captain Awesome Saves the Winter Wonderland. O'Connor, George, illus. 2012. (Captain Awesome Ser.: 6). (ENG.). 128p. (J). (gr. k-4). 17.99 (978-1-4424-4335-8(9)); pap. 6.99 (978-1-4424-4334-1(0)) Little Simon. (Little Simon).
—Captain Awesome Saves the Winter Wonderland. 2012. (Captain Awesome Ser.: 6). lib. bdg. 16.00 (978-0-606-26894-3(4)) Turtleback.
—Captain Awesome Saves the Winter Wonderland: #6. O'Connor, George, illus. 2018. (Captain Awesome Ser.). (ENG.). 128p. (J). (gr. k-4). lib. bdg. 31.36 (978-1-5321-4204-8(8), 28548, Chapter Bks.) Spotlight.
Klein, Abby. Thanksgiving Turkey Trouble. McKinley, John, illus. 2008. (Ready, Freddy! Ser.: Bk. 15). 95p. (gr. -1-3). 16.00 (978-0-7569-8838-8(1)) Perfection Learning Corp.
Klein, Jen. Summer Unscripted. 2017. 320p. (YA). (gr. 7). 17.99 (978-1-5247-0004-1(5), Random Hse. Bks. for Young Readers) Random Hse. Children's Bks.
Kline, Suzy. Horrible Harry Bugs the Three Bears. Remkiewicz, Frank, illus. 2009. (Horrible Harry Ser.: 22). 80p. (J). (gr. 2-4). 4.99 (978-0-14-241295-4(3), Puffin Books) Penguin Young Readers Group.
Kluck, Ted. The Outstanding Life of an Awkward Theater Kid: God, I'll Do Anything — Just Don't Let Me Fail. 2020. (Adventures with Flex Ser.). (ENG., Illus.). 192p. (J). (gr. 2-7). 12.99 (978-0-7369-7886-6(0), 6978866) Harvest Hse. Pubs.
Koja, Kathe. Talk. 2008. (ENG.). 144p. (YA). (gr. 7-12). per. 16.99 (978-0-312-37605-5(7), 900048334) Square Fish.
Korman, Gordon. No More Dead Dogs. 2017. Orig. Title: Touchdown Stage Left. (J). lib. bdg. 17.20 (978-0-606-40570-6(4)) Turtleback.
Krishnaswami, Uma. El árbol más feliz: un cuento sobre Yoga, 1 vol. Jeyaveeran, Ruth, illus. 2008. (SPA.). 32p. (J). (gr. k-5). pap. 12.95 (978-1-62014-149-6(3), leelowbooks) Lee & Low Bks., Inc.
Krulik, Nancy. The Twelve Burps of Christmas. 2012. (George Brown, Class Clown Ser.: No. 1). lib. bdg. 16.00 (978-0-606-26652-9(6)) Turtleback.
Krulik, Nancy & Burwasser, Amanda. Phone-Y Friends. Moran, Mike, illus. 2017. (Project Droid Ser.). (ENG.). 104p. (J). (gr. 1-3). pap. 9.99 (978-1-5107-2654-3(3), Sky Pony Pr.) Skyhorse Publishing Co., Inc.
Landon, Kristen. Life in the Pit. 2008. (ENG., Illus.). 248p. (YA). (gr. 5-13). pap. 8.95 (978-1-933831-08-4(1)) Blooming Tree Pr.
LaZebnik, Claire. The Trouble with Flirting. 2013. (ENG.). 336p. (YA). (gr. 8). pap. 9.99 (978-0-06-192127-8(0), HarperTeen) HarperCollins Pubs.
Levy, Janice. Showtime for Flip-Flop, 1 vol. Madden, Colleen M., illus. 2011. (Flip-Flop Adventure Ser.). (ENG.). 32p. (J). (gr. -1-4). 32.79 (978-1-61641-654-6(8), 7774, Looking Glass Library) Magic Wagon.
Lin, Grace. The Year of the Dog. 2007. (Pacy Lin Novel Ser.: 1). (ENG., Illus.). 160p. (J). (gr. 3-7). per. 8.99 (978-0-316-06002-8(X)) Little, Brown Bks. for Young Readers.
—The Year of the Dog. 2007. (Illus.). 134p. (gr. 3-7). 16.00 (978-0-7569-8143-3(3)) Perfection Learning Corp.
Lithgow, John. Marsupial Sue Presents "the Runaway Pancake" Davis, Jack E., illus. 2008. (ENG.). 40p. (J). (gr. -1-3). 8.99 (978-0-689-87848-0(6), Simon & Schuster Bks. For Young Readers) Simon & Schuster Bks. For Young Readers.
—Marsupial Sue Presents "the Runaway Pancake" Marsupial Sue Presents "the Runaway Pancake" 2005. (ENG., Illus.). 40p. (J). (gr. -1-3). 19.99 (978-0-689-87847-3(8), Simon & Schuster Bks. For Young Readers) Simon & Schuster Bks. For Young Readers.
Lorimer, Janet. The Bad Luck Play, 1 vol. unabr. ed. 2010. (Q Reads Ser.). (ENG.). 32p. (YA). (gr. 9-12). pap. 8.50 (978-1-61651-198-2(2)) Saddleback Educational Publishing, Inc.
MacDonald, Bailey. Wicked Will: A Mystery of Young William Shakespeare. 2010. (ENG.). 224p. (J). (gr. 4-7). pap. 5.99 (978-1-4169-8661-4(8), Aladdin) Simon & Schuster Children's Publishing.
MacDonald, Maryann. Starring Francie O'Leary. Richards, Virginia Helen, illus. 2010. 64p. (J). (gr. 1-3). pap. 6.95 (978-0-8198-7132-9(X)) Pauline Bks. & Media.
Mackall, Dandi Daley. Natalie Really Very Much Wants to Be a Star, 1 vol. Blakeslee, Lys, illus. 2009. (That's Nat! Ser.: 2). (ENG.). 96p. (J). (gr. 1-4). pap. 4.99 (978-0-310-71567-2(9)) Zonderkidz.
Mantchev, Lisa. Eyes Like Stars: Theatre Illuminata, Act I. 2010. (Theatre Illuminata Ser.: 1). (ENG.). 384p. (YA). (gr. 7-12). pap. 17.99 (978-0-312-60866-8(7), 900065167) Square Fish.
—Perchance to Dream: Theatre Illuminata #2, 2. 2011. (Theatre Illuminata Ser.: 2). (ENG.). 368p. (YA). (gr. 7-12). pap. 17.99 (978-0-312-67510-3(0), 900072953) Square Fish.
Manushkin, Fran. Star of the Show, 1 vol. Lyon, Tammie, illus. 2011. (Katie Woo Ser.). (ENG.). 32p. (J). (gr. k-2). pap. 5.95 (978-1-4048-6613-3(2), 114674); lib. bdg. 21.32 (978-1-4048-6515-0(2), 114211) Capstone. (Picture Window Bks.).
Marie, Lynne. The Star in the Christmas Play. Hussey, Lorna, illus. 2018. 32p. (J). 16.99 (978-1-5064-3813-9(X), Beaming Books) 1517 Media.
Marsh, Robert. Monster & Me, Set. Percival, Tom, illus. Incl. Monster Moneymaker. (ENG., Illus.). 40p. (J). (gr. 2-5). 2010. lib. bdg. 23.99 (978-1-4342-1891-9(0), 102350, Stone Arch Bks.); (Monster & Me Ser.). (ENG., Illus.). 40p. 2010. 71.97 o.p. (978-1-4342-2671-6(9), 15368, Stone Arch Bks.) Capstone.
Martin, Ann M. Needle & Thread. 2007. (Main Street Ser.). (Illus.). 205p. (J). (gr. 4-7). 14.65 (978-0-7569-8328-4(2)) Perfection Learning Corp.
—Needle & Thread. Andreasen, Dan, illus. 2007. 205p. (J). pap. (978-0-545-03660-3(7)) Scholastic, Inc.
Martin, C. K. Kelly. The Lighter Side of Life & Death. 2010. (YA). pap. (978-0-375-84590-1(9)) Random Hse. Children's Bks.
Martin, R. T. Mind over Matter. 2018. (Superhuman Ser.). (ENG.). 112p. (YA). (gr. 6-12). pap. 7.99 (978-1-5415-1048-7(8), 331f58f1-f78d-4f1c-a9b5-5e35e012222a); lib. bdg. 25.32 (978-1-5124-9832-5(7), ea451f11-ccb2-4291-8564-1427489277a9) Lerner Publishing Group. (Darby Creek).
McCowan, Patricia. Upstaged, 1 vol. 2016. (Orca Limelights Ser.). (ENG.). 160p. (J). (gr. 4-7). pap. 9.95 (978-1-4598-1004-4(X)) Orca Bk. Pubs. USA.
McDaniel, Lurlene. The End of Forever. 2013. (Erin Bennett Ser.). (ENG.). 320p. (YA). (gr. 7). pap. 8.99 (978-0-385-74380-8(7), Ember) Random Hse. Children's Bks.
Mcdonald, Megan. Hamlet & Cheese, 11. 2019. (Judy Moody & Stink Ser.). (ENG.). 124p. (J). (gr. 2-3). 15.49 (978-0-87617-953-6(7)) Penworthy Co., LLC, The.
McDonald, Megan. The Sisters Club: Rule of Three. (Sisters Club Ser.: 2). (ENG., Illus.). 240p. (J). (gr. 3-7). 2010. pap. 7.99 (978-0-7636-4830-5(2)) 2009. 15.99 (978-0-7636-4153-5(7)) Candlewick Pr.
Mcgaffey, Kenneth. The Sorrows of a Show Girl. 2005. 144p. pap. 10.95 (978-1-4218-1579-4(6), 1st World Library - Literary Society) 1st World Publishing, Inc.
McGaffey, Kenneth. The Sorrows of a Show Girl. 2017. (ENG., Illus.). (J). pap. 12.95 (978-1-374-82885-8(8)) Capital Communications, Inc.
Mcgaffey, Kenneth. The Sorrows of a Show Girl. 2004. reprint ed. pap. 15.95 (978-1-4191-8297-6(8)) Kessinger Publishing, LLC.
McGaffey, Kenneth. The Sorrows of A Show Girl. 2004. reprint ed. pap. 1.99 (978-1-4192-8297-3(2)) Kessinger Publishing, LLC.
Meister, Cari. Happy Thanksgiving, Tiny! Davis, Rich, illus. 2018. (Tiny Ser.). 32p. (J). (gr. k-1). pap. 4.99 (978-1-5247-8388-4(9), Penguin Young Readers) Penguin Young Readers Group.
Messner, Kate. Marty Mcguire, 1. Floca, Brian, illus. 2011. (ENG.). 144p. (J). (gr. 1-4). pap. 6.99 (978-0-545-14246-5(6), Scholastic Paperbacks) Scholastic, Inc.
Mientus, Andy. The Backstagers & the Ghost Light (Backstagers #1) Sygh, Rian, illus. 2018. (Backstagers Ser.). (ENG.). 208p. (J). (gr. 5-9). 14.99 (978-1-4197-3120-4(3), 1220801, Amulet Bks.) Abrams, Inc.
—The Backstagers & the Theater of the Ancients (Backstagers #2) Sygh, Rian & BOOM! Studios, illus. 2019. (Backstagers Ser.). (ENG.). 192p. (YA). (gr. 5-9). 14.99 (978-1-4197-3365-9(6), 1262501, Amulet Bks.) Abrams, Inc.
Morgan, Melissa J. Freaky Tuesday #17, 17 vols. 2007. (Camp Confidential Ser.: 17). 160p. (J). (gr. 3-7). pap. 4.99 (978-0-448-44651-6(0), Grosset & Dunlap) Penguin Young Readers Group.
Moulton, Erin E. Tracing Stars. 2013. (ENG.). 256p. (J). (gr. 3-7). pap. 6.99 (978-0-14-242653-1(9), Puffin Books) Penguin Young Readers Group.
Mullins, Julie. School Play Stars. Maddock, Monika, illus. 2005. (Girlz Rock! Ser.). (J). pap. (978-1-59336-706-0(6)) Mondo Publishing.
Nees, Susan. School Play. 2013. (Missy's Super Duper Royal Deluxe Ser.: 3). (ENG., Illus.). 80p. (J). (gr. k-2). pap. 4.99 (978-0-545-43853-7(5)) Scholastic, Inc.
Night, P. J. The Show Must Go On! (You're Invited to a Creepover Ser.: 4). (ENG.). 160p. (J). (gr. 3-7). 2018. 17.99 (978-1-5344-2108-0(4)) 2011. pap. 6.99 (978-1-4424-2905-5(4)) Simon Spotlight. (Simon Spotlight).
—The Show Must Go On! 2011. (Creepover Ser.: 4). lib. bdg. 16.00 (978-0-606-23748-2(8)) Turtleback.
—You're Invited to a Creep over: The Show Must Go On!, 1 vol. 2013. (You're Invited to a Creepover Ser.). (ENG.). 160p. (J). (gr. 3-6). lib. bdg. 31.36 (978-1-61479-063-1(9), 15851, Chapter Bks.) Spotlight.
Osborne, Mary Pope, et al. Miedo Escénico en una Noche de Verano. Murdocca, Sal, illus. 2014. (SPA.). 86p. (J). (gr. 2-4). pap. 6.99 (978-1-933032-92-4(8)) Lectorum Pubns., Inc.
—A Time to Dance: Virginia's Civil War Diary. 2003. (My America Ser.). (ENG.). 112p. (J). 12.95 (978-0-439-44341-8(5)) Scholastic, Inc.
Paratore, Coleen Murtagh. Willa by Heart. 2008. (Wedding Planner's Daughter Ser.). (ENG.). 240p. (J). (gr. 3-7). 15.99 (978-1-4169-4076-0(6), Simon & Schuster Bks. For Young Readers) Simon & Schuster Bks. For Young Readers.
—Willa by Heart. 2009. (Wedding Planner's Daughter Ser.). (ENG.). 240p. (J). (gr. 4-8). pap. 6.99 (978-1-4169-7470-3(9), Aladdin) Simon & Schuster Children's Publishing.
Parish, Herman. Amelia Bedelia Talks Turkey. Sweat, Lynn, illus. 2008. (Amelia Bedelia Ser.). (ENG.). 64p. (J). (gr. k-4). 16.99 (978-0-06-084352-6(7), Greenwillow Bks.) HarperCollins Pubs.
Park, Barbara. Junie B. Jones #23: Shipwrecked, No. 23. Brunkus, Denise, illus. 2005. (Junie B. Jones Ser.: 23). (ENG.). 96p. (J). (gr. 1-4). mass mkt. 5.99 (978-0-375-82805-8(2), Random Hse. Bks. for Young Readers) Random Hse. Children's Bks.
Patterson, James & Grabenstein, Chris. Jacky Ha-Ha. Kerascoët, illus. (Jacky Ha-Ha Ser.: 1). (ENG.). 384p. (J). (gr. 3-7). 2017. pap. 7.99 (978-0-316-43253-5(9)) 2016. 36.99 (978-0-316-26249-1(8)) Little Brown & Co. (Jimmy Patterson).
—Jacky Ha-Ha. Kerascoët, illus. 2023. (Jacky Ha-Ha Ser.: 1). (ENG.). 384p. (J). (gr. 3-7). pap. 7.99 (978-0-316-50834-6(9), Jimmy Patterson) Little Brown & Co.
—Jacky Ha-Ha. 2017. (Jacky Ha-Ha Ser.: 1). (J). lib. bdg. 18.40 (978-0-606-40732-8(4)) Turtleback.
—Jacky Ha-Ha: My Life Is a Joke. Kerascoët, illus. 2017. (Jacky Ha-Ha Ser.: 2). (ENG.). 352p. (J). (gr. 3-7). 13.99 (978-0-316-43376-1(4), Jimmy Patterson) Little Brown & Co.
—Jacky Ha-Ha: My Life Is a Joke. Kerascoët, illus. 2023. (Jacky Ha-Ha Ser.: 2). (ENG.). 368p. (J). (gr. 3-7). pap. 8.99 (978-0-316-50837-7(3), Jimmy Patterson) Little Brown & Co.
Patterson, Nancy Ruth. A Simple Gift. 2009. 128p. (gr. 3-7). pap. 10.95 (978-1-4401-1206-5(1)) iUniverse, Inc.
Perez, Marlene. The Comeback. 2009. (ENG.). 208p. (J). (gr. 7). pap. 8.99 (978-0-545-08807-7(0)) Scholastic, Inc.
Perlov, Rebecca Rosenberg. Rifka Takes a Bow. Kawa, Cosei, illus. 2013. (ENG.). 32p. (J). (gr. k-3). 9.99 (978-0-7613-8128-0(7), d57777e5-7e97-46e6-9ab1-3e429f027bc8, Kar-Ben Publishing) Lerner Publishing Group.
Polacco, Patricia. Mr. Wayne's Masterpiece. Polacco, Patricia, illus. 2014. (Illus.). 40p. (J). (gr. k-3). 18.99 (978-0-399-16095-0(7), G.P. Putnam's Sons Books for Young Readers) Penguin Young Readers Group.
Poydar, Nancy. Bunny Business. 2003. (ENG., Illus.). 32p. (J). (gr. k-3). tchr. ed. 16.95 (978-0-8234-1771-1(9)) Holiday Hse., Inc.
Primavera, Elise. Louise the Big Cheese: Divine Diva. Goode, Diane, illus. (ENG.). 40p. (J). (gr. k-3). 2011. 8.99 (978-1-4424-2066-3(9)) 2009. 16.99 (978-1-4169-7180-1(7)) Simon & Schuster/Paula Wiseman Bks. (Simon & Schuster/Paula Wiseman Bks.).
Rasheed, Leila. Doughnuts, Dreams & Drama Queens. 2013. (Fantastic Diary of Bathsheba Claric de Trop Ser.). 299p. (J). pap. 5.99 (978-0-7945-3030-3(3), Usborne) EDC Publishing.
Reich, Susanna. Penelope Bailey Takes the Stage, 1 vol. 2006. (ENG.). 32p. (J). (gr. 3-7). 16.95 (978-0-7614-5287-4(7)) Marshall Cavendish Corp.
Rennison, Louise. Are These My Basoomas I See Before Me? 2010. (Confessions of Georgia Nicolson Ser.: 10). (ENG.). 336p. (YA). (gr. 8-12). pap. 9.99 (978-0-06-145937-5(2), HarperTeen) HarperCollins Pubs.
Reynolds Naylor, Phyllis. I Like Him, He Likes Her: Alice Alone; Simply Alice; Patiently Alice. 2010. (Alice Ser.). (ENG.). 640p. (J). (gr. 7). pap. 12.99 (978-1-4424-0978-1(9), Atheneum Bks. for Young Readers) Simon & Schuster Children's Publishing.
—Incredibly Alice. (Alice Ser.: 23). (ENG., (YA). (gr. 9). 2012. Illus.). 304p. pap. 8.99 (978-1-4169-7556-4(X)) 2011. 288p. 16.99 (978-1-4169-7553-3(5)) Simon & Schuster Children's Publishing. (Atheneum Bks. for Young Readers).
Roberts, Bethany. Thanksgiving Mice! Cushman, Doug, illus. 2005. (ENG.). 32p. (J). (gr. -1 — 1). 5.95 (978-0-618-60486-9(3)) Houghton Mifflin Harcourt Publishing Co.
Ruditis, Paul. Entrances & Exits. 2008. (Drama! Ser.). (ENG.). 256p. (YA). (gr. 9). pap. 12.99 (978-1-4169-5906-9(8), Simon Pulse) Simon Pulse.
Rylant, Cynthia. Annie & Snowball & the Shining Star: Ready-To-Read Level 2. Stevenson, Suçie & Stevenson, Suçie, illus. (Annie & Snowball Ser.: 6). (ENG.). 40p. (J). (gr. k-2). 2010. pap. 4.99 (978-1-4169-3950-4(4)) 2009. 17.99 (978-1-4169-3946-7(6)) Simon Spotlight. (Simon Spotlight).
Saunders, Kate. The Land of Neverendings. 2017. (ENG.). 336p. (J). 14.50 (978-0-571-31084-5(2), Faber & Faber Children's Bks.) Faber & Faber, Inc.
Schotter, Roni. Purim Play, 0 vols. Hafner, Marylin, illus. 2012. (ENG.). 34p. (J). (gr. -1-3). pap. 6.99 (978-0-7614-5800-5(X), 9780761458005, Two Lions) Amazon Publishing.
Schreiber, Elisheva. The Miniature Puppet Theater Book. Pollack, Gadi & Markovitch, Evegeny, illus. (J). 14.95 (978-1-58330-617-8(X)) Feldheim Pubs.
Schreiber, Joe. Lenny Cyrus, School Virus. Smith, Matt, illus. 2014. (ENG.). 288p. (J). (gr. 5-7). pap. 16.99 (978-0-544-33628-5(3), 1584174, Clarion Bks.) HarperCollins Pubs.
Scieszka, Jon. SPHDZ Book #2! Prigmore, Shane, illus. 2011. (Spaceheadz Ser.: 2). (ENG.). 256p. (J). (gr. 2-5). pap. 7.99 (978-1-4169-7954-8(9), Simon & Schuster Bks. For Young Readers) Simon & Schuster Bks. For Young Readers.
Selznick, Brian. The Marvels. 2016. (CHI.). (J). (978-986-479-039-5(0)) Commonwealth Publishing Co., Ltd.
—The Marvels. Selznick, Brian, illus. 2015. (ENG., Illus.). 672p. (J). (gr. 5-7). 32.99 (978-0-545-44868-0(9), Scholastic Pr.) Scholastic, Inc.
Sinclair, Gardine. Mystery at Stageschool. 2013. 190p. (J). pap. (978-1-78299-388-9(6)) FeedARead.com.
Sloan, Brian. Tale of Two Summers. 2014. (ENG., Illus.). 256p. (YA). (gr. 7). pap. 12.99 (978-1-4169-5794-2(4), Simon & Schuster Bks. For Young Readers) Simon & Schuster Bks. For Young Readers.

T U V

Sloan, Holly Goldberg. Short. (ENG.). (J). (gr. 3-7). 2018. 320p. 9.99 *(978-0-399-18622-6(0)*, Puffin Books) 2017. 304p. 17.99 *(978-0-399-18621-9(2)*, Dial Bks) Penguin Young Readers Group.

—Short. 2018. lib. bdg. 19.65 *(978-0-606-40875-2(4))* Turtleback.

Smith, Emma Bland. Pop-Up Movie Theater. Marlin, Lissy, illus. 2018. (Maddy Mcguire, CEO Ser.). (ENG.). 112p. (J). (gr. 2-5). lib. bdg. 38.50 *(978-1-5321-3186-8(0)*, 28467, Calico Chapter Bks.) ABDO Publishing Co.

Snyder, Zilpha Keatley. William's Midsummer Dreams. (ENG., (J). (gr. 3-7). 2012. illus.). 240p. pap. 6.99 *(978-1-4424-1998-8(9))* 2011. 224p. 16.99 *(978-1-4424-1997-1(0))* Simon & Schuster Children's Publishing. (Atheneum Bks. for Young Readers).

Spirn, Michele Sobel. I Am the Turkey. Allen, Joy, illus. 2006. (I Can Read Level 2 Ser.). (ENG.). 48p. (J). (gr. k-3). pap. 4.99 *(978-0-06-053232-1(7)*, HarperCollins) HarperCollins Pubs.

—I Am the Turkey. Allen, Joy, illus. 2007. (I Can Read Bks.). 48p. (gr. -1-3). 14.00 *(978-0-7569-8055-9(0))* Perfection Learning Corp.

Spirn, Michele Sobel & Spirn, Michele S. I Am the Turkey. Allen, Joy, illus. 2004. (I Can Read Bks.). 48p. (J). (gr. k-3). 15.99 *(978-0-06-053230-7(0))* HarperCollins Pubs.

Stahler, David, Jr. Spinning Out. 2011. (ENG.). 288p. (YA). (gr. 7-17). 16.99 *(978-0-8118-7780-0(9))* Chronicle Bks. LLC.

Stewart, Shawn. Donny & the Doorman's Nightmare. 2004. 54p. pap. 8.11 *(978-1-4116-2188-6(3))* Lulu Pr., Inc.

Stilton, Thea & Schaffer, Andrea. The Royal Ball. Pellizzari, Barbara et al, illus. 2017. 108p. (J). *(978-1-338-18275-0(7))* Scholastic, Inc.

Stine, R. L. The 12 Screams of Christmas. 2014. (Goosebumps Most Wanted Ser.). lib. bdg. 18.40 *(978-0-606-36066-1(2))* Turtleback.

Strohm, Stephanie Kate. The Taming of the Drew. (ENG.). 304p. 2017. (YA). (gr. 7-12). pap. 9.99 *(978-1-5107-2636-9(5))* 2016. (J). (gr. 6-6). 17.99 *(978-1-5107-0215-8(6))* Skyhorse Publishing Co., Inc. (Sky Pony Pr.).

Surviving the Applewhites. (J). tchr. ed. *(978-0-06-058369-9(X))* HarperCollins Pubs.

Sutherland, Tui T. This Must Be Love. 256p. (J). 2005. pap. 7.99 *(978-0-06-056477-3(6)*, Harper Trophy) 2004. (gr. 7-18). lib. bdg. 16.89 *(978-0-06-056476-6(8))* HarperCollins Pubs.

Telgemeier, Raina. Drama. 2012. lib. bdg. 22.10 *(978-0-606-26738-0(7))* Turtleback.

—Drama: a Graphic Novel. Telgemeier, Raina, illus. 2012. (ENG., Illus.). 240p. (J). (gr. 5-9). pap. 10.99 *(978-0-545-32699-5(0)*, Graphix) Scholastic, Inc.

—Drama: a Graphic Novel. Telgemeier, Raina, illus. 2012. (ENG., Illus.). 240p. (J). (gr. 5-9). 24.99 *(978-0-545-32698-8(2)*, Graphix) Scholastic, Inc.

—Drama (Spanish Edition) Telgemeier, Raina, illus. 2018. (SPA., Illus.). 240p. (J). (gr. 4-7). pap. 12.99 *(978-1-338-26916-1(X)*, Scholastic en Espanol) Scholastic, Inc.

Terrell, Brandon. High Drama. 2015. (Suspended Ser.). (ENG.). 112p. (YA). (gr. 6-12). 27.99 *(978-1-4677-5710-2(1)*, 69b6a1cf-f764-4c60-ab45-5f974b73e897, Darby Creek) Lerner Publishing Group.

Thompson, Jan & Sharpe, Jaime. Amara's Magical Playhouse: The Adventure Begins. 2010. 108p. pap. 37.99 *(978-1-4520-8284-4(7))* AuthorHouse.

Tillworth, Mary. King for a Day! (PAW Patrol) Jackson, Mike, illus. 2016. (Step into Reading Ser.). (ENG.). 24p. (J). (gr. -1-1). 4.99 *(978-1-101-93684-9(3)*, Random Hse. Bks. for Young Readers) Random Hse. Children's Bks.

Tirabassi, Maren C. Footlights & Fairy Dust: Matt & Maria Go to the Theatre. Kramer, Brandie, illus. 2007. (ENG.). 48p. (J). (gr. 2-7). pap. 14.95 *(978-1-933002-26-2(3))* PublishingWorks.

Trigiani, Adriana. Viola in the Spotlight. 2012. (Viola Ser.: 2). (ENG.). 288p. (YA). (gr. 8). pap. 9.99 *(978-0-06-145107-2(X)*, HarperTeen) HarperCollins Pubs.

Understudies: Individual Title Six-Packs. (Bookweb Ser.). 32p. (gr. 4-18). 34.00 *(978-0-7635-3724-1(1))* Rigby Education.

Van Vleet, Carmella. Eliza Bing Is (Not) a Star. (Eliza Bing Ser.). (ENG.). 256p. (J). (gr. 3-7). 2019. pap. 7.99 *(978-0-8234-4430-4(9))* 2018. 16.99 *(978-0-8234-4024-5(9))* Holiday Hse., Inc.

Verdi, Jessica. My Life after Now. 2013. (ENG.). 304p. (YA). (gr. 7-12). pap. 9.99 *(978-1-4022-7785-6(7)*, 9781402277856) Sourcebooks, Inc.

Villareal, Ray. Alamo Wars. 2008. 187p. (J). (gr. 6-18). pap. 10.95 *(978-1-55885-513-7(0)*, Piñata Books) Arte Publico Pr.

Vinopol, Corinne & Bednarczyk, Angela. ASL Tales & Games for Kids - Biscuit Blvd: Computer Software in American Sign Language. 2004. (J). cd-rom 34.95 *(978-0-9667589-9-3(4))* Institute for Disabilities Research & Training, Inc.

Wallis, Quvenzhané. Shai & Emmie Star in Break an Egg! Miller, Sharee, illus. 2017. (Shai & Emmie Story Ser.: 1). (ENG.). 128p. (J). (gr. 1-5). 17.99 *(978-1-4814-5882-5(5)*, Simon & Schuster Bks. For Young Readers) Simon & Schuster Bks. For Young Readers.

Warner, Gertrude Chandler, creator. The Ghost at the Drive-In Movie. 2008. (Boxcar Children Mysteries Ser.: 116). (ENG., Illus.). 128p. (J). (gr. 2-5). pap. 5.99 *(978-0-8075-5578-1(9)*, 807555789, Random Hse. Bks. for Young Readers) Random Hse. Children's Bks.

Weatherly, Lee. Child X. 2004. 211p. 16.00 *(978-0-7569-3211-4(4))* Perfection Learning Corp.

Webb, Holly. The Case of the Vanishing Emerald: The Mysteries of Maisie Hitchins Book 2. Lindsay, Marion, illus. 2016. (Mysteries of Maisie Hitchins Ser.: 2). (ENG.). 176p. (J). (gr. 3-7). pap. 6.99 *(978-0-544-66851-5(0)*, 1625474, Clarion Bks.) HarperCollins Pubs.

Wesley, Valerie Wilson. How to Almost Ruin Your School Play. 2005. (Illus.). 105p. (J). lib. bdg. 15.00 *(978-1-4242-0645-2(6))* Fitzgerald Bks.

Whitten, A. J. The Cellar. 2011. (ENG.). 288p. (YA). (gr. 7-18). pap. 16.99 *(978-0-547-23253-9(5)*, 1082798, Clarion Bks.) HarperCollins Pubs.

Wibberley, Emily & Siegemund-Broka, Austin. Always Never Yours. 2019. 384p. (YA). (gr. 7). pap. 12.99 *(978-0-451-47864-1(9)*, Penguin Books) Penguin Young Readers Group.

Wilkinson, Lili. Pink. 2012. (ENG.). 320p. (YA). (gr. 8). pap. 9.99 *(978-0-06-192654-9(X)*, HarperTeen) HarperCollins Pubs.

Winkler, Henry & Oliver, Lin. The Curtain Went up, My Pants Fell Down #11. 2007. (Hank Zipzer Ser.: 11). (ENG., Illus.). 160p. (J). (gr. 3-7). pap. 6.99 *(978-0-448-44267-9(1)*, Grosset & Dunlap) Penguin Young Readers Group.

Wunsch, Emma. Banana Pants! (Miranda & Maude #2) von Innerebner, Jessika, illus. 2019. (ENG.). 144p. (J). (gr. 2-5). 12.99 *(978-1-4197-3180-8(7)*, 1247401, Amulet Bks.) Abrams, Inc.

Yee, Lisa. Bobby the Brave (Sometimes) Santat, Dan, illus. 2012. (ENG.). 160p. (J). (gr. 2-5). pap. 5.99 *(978-0-545-05595-6(4)*, Scholastic Paperbacks) Scholastic, Inc.

—Warp Speed. 2011. (ENG.). 320p. (J). (gr. 4-7). 16.99 *(978-0-545-12276-4(7)*, Levine, Arthur A. Bks.) Scholastic, Inc.

Young, Judy. Star in a Play. Sullivan, Dana, illus. 2015. (Digger & Daisy Ser.). (ENG.). 32p. (J). (gr. k-2). 9.99 *(978-1-58536-929-4(2)*, 203950) Sleeping Bear Pr.

Ziegler, Maddie. The Callback. (Maddie Ziegler Ser.: 2). (ENG.). (J). (gr. 4-8). 2019. 272p. pap. 8.99 *(978-1-4814-8640-8(3))* 2018. (Illus.). 256p. 17.99 *(978-1-4814-8639-2(X))* Simon & Schuster Children's Publishing. (Aladdin).

THEATER—HISTORY

Carew-Miller, Anna. William Shakespeare: Great English Playwright & Poet. 2013. (People of Importance Ser.: 21). (Illus.). 32p. (J). (gr. 4-18). 19.95 *(978-1-4222-2859-3(2))* Mason Crest.

Hosein, Ann. The History of Theatre, 1 vol. 2015. (Britannica Guide to the Visual & Performing Arts Ser.). (ENG., Illus.). 224p. (J). (gr. 9-10). 47.59 *(978-1-68048-082-5(0)*, cd76fc15-aa0a-41d5-9607-d245fc7184cf, Britannica Educational Publishing) Rosen Publishing Group, Inc., The.

McDonnell, Kathleen. Putting on a Show: Theater for Young People. 1 vol. 2004. (ENG., Illus.). 200p. (J). (gr. 4-9). pap. 14.95 *(978-1-896764-89-4(4))* Second Story Pr. CAN. Dist: Orca Bk. Pubs. USA.

Morley, Jacqueline. You Wouldn't Want to Be a Shakespearean Actor! Antram, David, illus. 2010. (You Wouldn't Want to Ser.). (ENG.). 32p. (J). 29.00 *(978-0-531-20471-9(5))* Scholastic Library Publishing.

—You Wouldn't Want to Be a Shakespearean Actor! Some Roles You Might Not Want to Play. Antram, David, illus. 2010. (You Wouldn't Want to Ser.). (ENG.). 32p. (J). (gr. 3-18). pap. 9.95 *(978-0-531-22826-5(6))* Scholastic Library Publishing.

Sitarz, Paula Gaj. The Curtain Rises Vol. 1: A History of Theatre from Its Origins in Greek & Roman Times Through the English Restoration. Landes, William-Alan, ed. 2003. (Illus.). 144p. (YA). (gr. 5-12). pap. 28.00 *(978-0-88734-685-9(5))* Players Pr., Inc.

Woollard, Mary. An Illustrated Guide to Staging History. unabr. ed. 2003. (Illus.). 302p. (YA). (gr. 4-12). pap. 30.00 *(978-0-85343-624-9(X))* Miller, J. Garnet Ltd. GBR. Dist: Empire Publishing Service.

THEATER—PRODUCTION AND DIRECTION

Bryan, Bethany. Hair & Makeup in Theater, 1 vol. 2017. (Exploring Theater Ser.). (ENG.). 96p. (YA). (gr. 7-7). 44.50 *(978-1-5026-3003-2(6)*, 8724cfc9-93b3-444d-9874-fcfb01def823); pap. 20.99 *(978-1-5026-3427-6(9)*, 7ba0fa06-9d6d-437a-8d21-29eabf9d88e1) Cavendish Square Publishing LLC.

Freedman, Jeri. Directing in Theater, 1 vol. 2016. (Exploring Theater Ser.). (ENG., Illus.). 96p. (YA). (gr. 7-7). lib. bdg. 44.50 *(978-1-5026-2283-9(1)*, 097c5589-fae0-44db-ab1d-877b2e723726) Cavendish Square Publishing LLC.

—Stage Management in Theater, 1 vol. 2017. (Exploring Theater Ser.). (ENG.). 96p. (YA). (gr. 7-7). pap. 20.99 *(978-1-5026-3462-7(7)*, 93aa2a6c-35a3-45e3-9607-853e16b4d211); lib. bdg. 44.50 *(978-1-5026-3009-4(5)*, c6881503-7143-463d-a6cd-6caa5057e43d) Cavendish Square Publishing LLC.

Garrett, Dan, ed. Masks & Faces. 11th ed. 2003. (Drama Workshop Plays Ser.). (Illus.). 96p. (Orig.). (YA). (gr. 6-12). pap. 15.00 *(978-0-333-36056-9(7))* Macmillan Education, Ltd. GBR. Dist: Players Pr., Inc.

—Scapegoats. 11th ed. 2003. (Drama Workshop Plays Ser.). (Illus.). 96p. (Orig.). (YA). (gr. 6-12). pap. 15.00 *(978-0-333-36055-2(9))* Macmillan Education, Ltd. GBR. Dist: Players Pr., Inc.

Guillain, Charlotte. Writing & Staging Adventure Plays. 2016. (Writing & Staging Plays Ser.). (ENG., Illus.). 48p. (J). (gr. 4-6). lib. bdg. 35.99 *(978-1-4846-2770-9(9)*, 131329, Heinemann) Capstone.

—Writing & Staging Funny Plays. 2016. (Writing & Staging Plays Ser.). (ENG., Illus.). 48p. (J). (gr. 4-6). lib. bdg. 35.99 *(978-1-4846-2769-3(5)*, 131328, Heinemann) Capstone.

—Writing & Staging Myths & Legends. 2016. (Writing & Staging Plays Ser.). (ENG., Illus.). 48p. (J). (gr. 4-6). lib. bdg. 35.99 *(978-1-4846-2772-3(5)*, 131331, Heinemann) Capstone.

—Writing & Staging Real-Life Plays. 2016. (Writing & Staging Plays Ser.). (ENG., Illus.). 48p. (J). (gr. 4-6). lib. bdg. 35.99 *(978-1-4846-2771-6(7)*, 131330, Heinemann) Capstone.

Harmon, Don. Producing in Theater, 1 vol. 2016. (Exploring Theater Ser.). (ENG., Illus.). 96p. (YA). (gr. 7-7). lib. bdg. 44.50 *(978-1-5026-2281-5(5)*, d5e16beb-093c-4ab3-9deb-ea79f7061a93) Cavendish Square Publishing LLC.

Poulsson, Emilie. Finger Plays for Nursery & Kindergarten. Bridgman, L. T., illus. 70th ed. 2011. (Dover Children's Activity Bks.). (ENG.). 80p. (J). (gr. 4-7). reprint ed. pap. 8.95 *(978-0-486-22588-3(7))* Dover Pubns., Inc.

THEATERS

Camisa, Kathryn. Teatros Espectrales. 2018. (De Puntillas en Lugares Escalofriantes/Tiptoe into Scary Places Ser.). (SPA.). 24p. (J). (gr. k-3). 18.95 *(978-1-68402-610-4(5))* Bearport Publishing Co., Inc.

Capaccio, George. Lighting & Sound in Theater, 1 vol. 2016. (Exploring Theater Ser.). (ENG., Illus.). 96p. (YA). (gr. 7-7). lib. bdg. 44.50 *(978-1-5026-2275-4(0)*, b5797643-28d0-4d75-8aed-87bdced83554) Cavendish Square Publishing LLC.

Clements, Gillian. Tudor Theatre. 2009. (Building History Ser.). (Illus.). 32p. (J). (gr. 3-5). 27.10 *(978-1-59771-147-0(0))* Sea-To-Sea Pubns.

Cohn, Jessica. On the Job in the Theatre. Scheuer, Lauren, illus. 2016. (Core Content Social Studies — on the Job Ser.). (ENG.). 32p. (J). (gr. 2-5). lib. bdg. 26.65 *(978-1-63440-113-5(1)*, b0afd95a-d25a-421b-9e7a-867039762333) Red Chair Pr.

Hansen, Grace. Colosseum. 2017. (World Wonders Ser.). (ENG., Illus.). 24p. (J). (gr. -1-2). lib. bdg. 32.79 *(978-1-5321-0439-8(1)*, 26565, Abdo Kids) ABDO Publishing Co.

Harman, Paul, ed. A Guide to UK Theatre for Young Audiences. 2010. (ENG.). 104p. (J). pap. 18.95 *(978-1-906582-09-8(2))* Aurora Metro Pubns. Ltd. GBR. Dist: Publishers Group West (PGW).

Kreisman, Rachelle. Things We Do: A Kids' Guide to Community Activity. Haggerty, Tim, illus. 2015. (Start Smart (tm) — Community Ser.). (ENG.). 32p. (J). (gr. 1-3). E-Book 39.99 *(978-1-937529-51-2(7))* Red Chair Pr.

Matthews, Sheelagh. The Sydney Opera House. 2008. (Structural Wonders Ser.). (Illus.). 32p. (J). (gr. 4-6). lib. bdg. 26.00 *(978-1-59036-936-4(X))* Weigl Pubs., Inc.

Rose, Simon. Colosseum. (Structural Wonders of the World Ser.). (J). 2018. (ENG.). 24p. (gr. 2-5). lib. bdg. 28.55 *(978-1-4896-8163-8(9)*, AV2 by Weigl) 2012. 27.13 *(978-1-61913-249-8(4))* 2012. pap. 12.95 *(978-1-61913-255-9(9))* Weigl Pubs., Inc.

Shofner, Shawndra. Sydney Opera House. 2006. (Modern Wonders of the World Ser.). (Illus.). 32p. (J). (gr. 4-7). lib. bdg. 18.95 *(978-1-58341-442-2(8)*, Creative Education) Creative Co., The.

THEATERS—STAGE SETTING AND SCENERY

Bryan, Bethany. Set Design & Prop Making in Theater, 1 vol. 2016. (Exploring Theater Ser.). (ENG., Illus.). 96p. (YA). (gr. 7-7). lib. bdg. 44.50 *(978-1-5026-2279-2(3)*, 5507a915-26e9-498f-9980-c8f54008970a) Cavendish Square Publishing LLC.

Cobb, Vicki. On Stage. 2008. pap. 52.95 *(978-0-8225-9450-5(1))* Lerner Publishing Group.

—On Stage. Gold, Michael, photos by. 2005. (Where's the Science Here? Ser.). (ENG., Illus.). 48p. (gr. 3-5). lib. bdg. 23.93 *(978-0-7613-2774-5(6)*, Millbrook Pr.) Lerner Publishing Group.

Larson, Jeff. FX! Lighting & Sound (Grade 7) 2nd rev. ed. 2017. (TIME(r): Informational Text Ser.). (ENG., Illus.). 64p. (gr. 6-8). pap. 13.99 *(978-1-4938-3612-3(9))* Teacher Created Materials, Inc.

Woollard, Mary. An Illustrated Guide to Staging History. unabr. ed. 2003. (Illus.). 302p. (YA). (gr. 4-12). pap. 30.00 *(978-0-85343-624-9(X))* Miller, J. Garnet Ltd. GBR. Dist: Empire Publishing Service.

THEATRICAL COSTUME

see Costume

THEATRICAL MAKEUP

Craig, Jonathan & Light, Bridget. Special Effects Make-Up Artist: The Coolest Jobs on the Planet, 1 vol. 2013. (Coolest Jobs on the Planet Ser.). (ENG.). 48p. (J). (gr. 5-8). pap. 8.99 *(978-1-4109-5491-6(9)*, 123419, Raintree) Capstone.

Garstecki, Julia. Make Your Own Fake Skin. 24p. (J). 2019. (Illus.). pap. *(978-1-68072-758-6(3))* 2018. (ENG.). (gr. 1-3). pap. 8.99 *(978-1-64466-311-0(2)*, 12539, Hi Jinx) 2018. (ENG., Illus.). (gr. 4-6). lib. bdg. 28.50 *(978-1-68072-622-0(6)*, 12538, Hi Jinx) Black Rabbit Bks.

Hammelef, Danielle S. Mind-Blowing Makeup in Special Effects. 2015. (Awesome Special Effects Ser.). (ENG., Illus.). 32p. (J). (gr. 3-9). lib. bdg. 27.32 *(978-1-4914-2002-7(2)*, 127476, Capstone Pr.) Capstone.

Larson, Jessica. FX! Makeup & Costumes. 2nd rev. ed. 2017. (TIME(r): Informational Text Ser.). (ENG., Illus.). 64p. (gr. 6-8). pap. 13.99 *(978-1-4938-3613-0(7))* Teacher Created Materials, Inc.

Mason, Helen. Makeup Artist. 2014. (Creative Careers Ser.). 48p. (J). (gr. 4-8). pap. 84.30 *(978-1-4824-1303-8(5))* Stevens, Gareth Publishing LLLP.

THEATRICAL SCENERY

see Theaters—Stage Setting and Scenery

THEFT

Berry, Joy. Help Me Be Good about Stealing. 2009. (Help Me Be Good Ser.). 32p. pap. 7.95 *(978-1-60577-124-3(4))* Berry, Joy Enterprises.

Berry, Joy Wilt. A Book about Stealing. 2005. (Illus.). (J). *(978-0-7172-8585-3(5))* Scholastic, Inc.

Booth, Jack. The 10 Most Daring Heists. 2007. (J). 14.99 *(978-1-55448-486-7(3))* Scholastic Library Publishing.

Dodge Cummings, Judy. TOMB RAIDERS: REAL TALES OF GRAVE ROBBERIES. 2018. (Mystery & Mayhem Ser.). (ENG., Illus.). 128p. (J). (gr. 5-8). pap. 9.95 *(978-1-61930-622-6(0)*, 59875f68-62bc-42e6-8d32-f2e662e155eb) Nomad Pr.

Guillain, Charlotte. Great Art Thefts, 1 vol. 2013. (Treasure Hunters Ser.). (ENG.). 48p. (J). (gr. 5-8). lib. bdg. 32.65 *(978-1-4109-4951-6(6)*, 120943); (Illus.). pap. 9.25 *(978-1-4109-4958-5(3)*, 120949) Capstone. (Raintree).

Hanel, Rachael. Identity Theft, 1 vol. 2011. (Controversy! Ser.). (ENG.). 112p. (YA). (gr. 8-8). 39.79 *(978-0-7614-4901-0(9)*, 4efa2b63-c62e-4707-a3a9-1c404e6e1163) Cavendish Square Publishing LLC.

Kiesbye, Stefan, ed. Identity Theft, 1 vol. 2011. (At Issue Ser.). (ENG.). 112p. (gr. 10-12). 41.03 *(978-0-7377-5582-4(2)*, ccc10931-143b-47fa-9058-a6c8cca12a00); pap. 28.80 *(978-0-7377-5583-1(0)*, c0e67521-ae4f-4fc6-8246-5db0d726ec99) Greenhaven Publishing LLC. (Greenhaven Publishing).

Maule, David. Stealing High Beginning Book with Online Access, 1 vol. 2014. (ENG., Illus.). 24p. (J). pap., E-Book, E-Book 9.50 *(978-1-107-67774-6(2))* Cambridge Univ. Pr.

McCoy, Erin L. & Hanel, Rachael. Identity Theft: Private Battle or Public Crisis?, 1 vol. 2018. (Today's Debates Ser.). (ENG.). 144p. (gr. 7-7). pap. 22.16 *(978-1-5026-4322-3(7)*, 71320fd7-3502-4315-baba-af81c1e7761e) Cavendish Square Publishing LLC.

Naish, Sarah & Jefferies, Rosie. Charley Chatty & the Disappearing Pennies: A Story about Lying & Stealing. Evans, Megan, illus. 2017. (Therapeutic Parenting Bks.). (ENG.). 32p. (C). pap. 17.95 *(978-1-78592-303-6(X)*, 696533) Kingsley, Jessica Pubs. GBR. Dist: Hachette UK Distribution.

Sheinkin, Steve. Lincoln's Grave Robbers (Scholastic Focus) 2013. (ENG.). 224p. (J). (gr. 5-8). 16.99 *(978-0-545-40572-0(6)*, Scholastic Pr.) Scholastic, Inc.

whiting, jim. Identity Theft. 2012. (Illus.). 96p. (J). lib. bdg. *(978-1-60152-454-6(4))* ReferencePoint Pr., Inc.

Wood, Alix. Body Snatching, 1 vol. Wood, Alix, illus. 2013. (Why'd They Do That? Strange Customs of the Past Ser.). (ENG., Illus.). 32p. (J). (gr. 4-5). pap. 11.50 *(978-1-4339-9573-6(5)*, 84830fc8-bcdf-4385-bbc6-bc4409731d6f); lib. bdg. 29.27 *(978-1-4339-9572-9(7)*, 0fc06c87-40da-4c89-a24d-1b29879837bc) Stevens, Gareth Publishing LLLP.

Wood, Alix, illus. Body Snatching. 2013. (Why'd They Do That? Strange Customs of the Past Ser.). 32p. (J). (gr. 4-6). pap. 63.00 *(978-1-4339-9574-3(3))* Stevens, Gareth Publishing LLLP.

THEFT—FICTION

Adler, David A. Bones & the Big Yellow Mystery, No. 1. Johansen Newman, Barbara, illus. 2008. (Bones Ser.: 1). (ENG.). 32p. (J). (gr. 1-3). mass mkt. 4.99 *(978-0-14-241042-4(X)*, Penguin Young Readers) Penguin Young Readers Group.

—Cam Jansen & the Millionaire Mystery. Allen, Joy, illus. 2013. (Cam Jansen Ser.: 32). (ENG.). 64p. (J). (gr. 2-5). pap. 4.99 *(978-0-14-242747-7(0)*, Puffin Books) Penguin Young Readers Group.

—Cam Jansen: Cam Jansen & the Valentine Baby Mystery #25. Natti, Susanna, illus. 25th ed. 2006. (Cam Jansen Ser.: 25). (ENG.). 80p. (J). (gr. 2-5). 4.99 *(978-0-14-240694-6(5)*, Puffin Books) Penguin Young Readers Group.

Aldridge, Janet. The Meadow-Brook Girls by the Sea, or Th. 2006. pap. *(978-1-4065-0693-8(1))* Dodo Pr.

Alexander, Carol. The Book Thief. Friedland, Joyce & Kessler, Rikki, eds. 2009. (Novel-Ties Ser.). (Illus.). 40p. pap. 16.95 *(978-0-7675-4277-7(0))* Learning Links Inc.

Alexander, Heather. Wallace & Grace & the Cupcake Caper. Zarrin, Laura, illus. 2018. (Wallace & Grace Ser.). (ENG.). 80p. (J). pap. 7.99 *(978-1-68119-011-2(7)*, 900154812, Bloomsbury Children's Bks.) Bloomsbury Publishing USA.

Angleberger, Tom. Didi Dodo, Future Spy: Recipe for Disaster (Didi Dodo, Future Spy #1) Chapman, Jared, illus. 2019. (Flytrap Files Ser.). (ENG.). (J). (gr. 1-4). 128p. pap. 5.99 *(978-1-4197-3706-0(6)*, 1259503); 112p. 12.99 *(978-1-4197-3370-3(2)*, 1259501) Abrams, Inc. (Amulet Bks.).

Archer, Dosh. The Case of Piggy's Bank (Detective Paw of the Law: Time to Read, Level 3) Archer, Dosh, illus. 2018. (Time to Read Ser.: 1). (ENG., Illus.). 48p. (J). (gr. k-2). 12.99 *(978-0-8075-1557-0(4)*, 807515574) Whitman, Albert & Co.

Aretha, David. A Hall Lot of Trouble at Cooperstown: The Baseball Geeks Adventures Book 1, 1 vol. 2014. (Baseball Geeks Adventures Ser.). (ENG., Illus.). 96p. (J). (gr. 4-6). 21.61 *(978-1-62285-118-8(8)*, d5d575ab-0a1f-4417-872f-daaad22d518f) Enslow Publishing, LLC.

Ashby, Freya Katrina. Summer at the Dunes: A Deirdre Carlisle Mystery. 2007. 108p. per. 9.95 *(978-0-595-43663-7(3))* iUniverse, Inc.

Ashworth, Sherry. Something Wicked. 2004. (ENG.). 224p. (gr. 7). pap. 9.99 *(978-0-00-712335-3(3)*, HarperCollins Children's Bks.) HarperCollins Pubs. Ltd. GBR. Dist: HarperCollins Pubs.

Asselin, Kristine & Malone, Jen. The Art of the Swap. (ENG., Illus.). 352p. (J). (gr. 3-7). 2019. pap. 8.99 *(978-1-4814-7872-4(9))* 2018. 17.99 *(978-1-4814-7871-7(0))* Simon & Schuster Children's Publishing. (Aladdin).

Atkins, Ron. Abby & the Bicycle Caper. 2004. 48p. pap. 8.95 *(978-0-595-30565-0(2))* iUniverse, Inc.

Balliett, Blue. Pieces & Players. 2015. (ENG., Illus.). 320p. (J). (gr. 3-7). 17.99 *(978-0-545-29990-9(X)*, Scholastic Pr.) Scholastic, Inc.

Barnett, Mac. Danger Goes Berserk. Myers, Matt, illus. 2013. (Brixton Brothers Ser.: 4). (ENG.). 256p. (J). (gr. 3-7). pap. 8.99 *(978-1-4424-3978-8(5)*, Simon & Schuster Bks. For Young Readers) Simon & Schuster Bks. For Young Readers.

—The Impossible Crime (Mac B., Kid Spy #2) Lowery, Mike, illus. 2018. (Mac B., Kid Spy Ser.: 2). (ENG.). 160p. (J). (gr. 2-5). 12.99 *(978-1-338-14368-3(9)*, Orchard Bks.) Scholastic, Inc.

—Mac Undercover (Mac B., Kid Spy #1) Lowery, Mike, illus. 2018. (Mac B., Kid Spy Ser.: 1). (ENG.). 160p. (J). (gr. 2-5). 12.99 *(978-1-338-14359-1(X)*, Orchard Bks.) Scholastic, Inc.

Barwin, Steven. Cold Grab. 2019. (Lorimer SideStreets Ser.). (ENG.). 192p. (YA). (gr. 9-12). lib. bdg. 27.99 *(978-1-4594-1381-8(4)*, 326efc22-52e3-4935-87c5-6a2bff67785d) James Lorimer & Co. Ltd., Pubs. CAN. Dist: Lerner Publishing Group.

Bellingham, Brenda. Lilly's Special Gift. 2005. (Illus.). 59p. (J). lib. bdg. 12.00 *(978-1-4242-1204-0(9))* Fitzgerald Bks.

Berne, Emma Carlson. The Lady's Slipper: A Melody Mystery. 2017. 183p. (J). *(978-1-5182-4313-4(4)*, American Girl) American Girl Publishing, Inc.

Braffet, Holly, illus. Kekoa & the Egg Mystery. 2010. (ENG.). 32p. (J). (gr. -1-2). 14.95 *(978-1-933067-35-3(7))* Beachhouse Publishing, LLC.

Brezenoff, Steve. The Carnival Caper: An Interactive Mystery Adventure. Calo, Marcos, illus. 2017. (You Choose Stories: Field Trip Mysteries Ser.). (ENG.). 112p. (J). (gr. 3-7). lib. bdg. 32.65 *(978-1-4965-2645-8(7)*, 131209, Stone Arch Bks.) Capstone.

—The Case of the Counterfeit Painting. Weber, Lisa K., illus. 2016. (Museum Mysteries Ser.). (ENG.). 128p. (J). pap. 42.70 *(978-1-4965-2530-7(2)*, 23936); (gr. 3-6). pap. 6.95 *(978-1-4965-2522-2(1)*, 130495); (gr. 3-6). lib. bdg. 26.65 *(978-1-4965-2518-5(3)*, 130491) Capstone. (Stone Arch Bks.).

—The Disappearing Fruit: An Interactive Mystery Adventure. Calo, Marcos, illus. 2017. (You Choose Stories: Field Trip Mysteries Ser.). (ENG.). 112p. (J). (gr. 3-7). lib. bdg. 32.65

(978-1-4965-2643-4(0), 131206, Stone Arch Bks.) Capstone.

—Field Trip Mysteries: the Ballgame with No One at Bat. Calo, Marcos, illus. 2013. (Field Trip Mysteries Ser.). (ENG.). 88p. (J). (gr. 2-3). pap. 35.70 *(978-1-4342-6230-1(8)*, 20035); (gr. 3-6). pap. 5.95 *(978-1-4342-6211-0(1)*, 123509); (gr. 3-6). lib. bdg. 25.32 *(978-1-4342-5978-3(1)*, 122935) Capstone. (Stone Arch Bks.).

—Field Trip Mysteries: the Dinosaur That Disappeared. Calo, Marcos, illus. 2013. (Field Trip Mysteries Ser.). (ENG.). 88p. (J). (gr. 2-3). pap. 35.70 *(978-1-4342-6233-2(2)*, 20037); (gr. 3-6). pap. 5.95 *(978-1-4342-6213-4(8)*, 123512); (gr. 3-6). lib. bdg. 25.32 *(978-1-4342-5980-6(3)*, 122937) Capstone. (Stone Arch Bks.).

Bright, J. E. Batman vs. Catwoman, 1 vol. Levins, Tim, illus. 2013. (DC Super Heroes Ser.). (ENG.). 56p. (J). (gr. 3-6). lib. bdg. 26.65 *(978-1-4342-6013-0(5)*, 123073, Stone Arch Bks.) Capstone.

Bright, Philip & Ramos, Sarah. Jimmy Rat. 2008. (Illus.). 32p. pap. 17.95 *(978-0-9556105-9-2(1))* Picnic Publishing Ltd. GBR. Dist: Trans-Atlantic Pubns., Inc.

Broad, Michael. Ghost Diamond!, No. 1. Broad, Michael, illus. 2011. (Agent Amelia Ser.: 1). (ENG., Illus.). 144p. (J). (gr. 2-5). lib. bdg. 22.60 *(978-0-7613-8056-6(6))* Lerner Publishing Group.

—#1 Ghost Diamond! 2011. (Agent Amelia Ser.). pap. 33.92 *(978-0-7613-8341-3(7)*, Darby Creek) Lerner Publishing Group.

Brown, Jeff. Flat Stanley's Worldwide Adventures #11: Framed in France. Pamintuan, Macky, illus. 2014. (Flat Stanley's Worldwide Adventures Ser.: 11). (ENG.). 128p. (J). (gr. 1-5). 15.99 *(978-0-06-218985-1(9))*; pap. 4.99 *(978-0-06-218984-4(0))* HarperCollins Pubs. (HarperCollins).

—Flat Stanley's Worldwide Adventures #14: on a Mission for Her Majesty. Pamintuan, Macky, illus. 2017. (Flat Stanley's Worldwide Adventures Ser.: 14). (ENG.). 128p. (J). (gr. 1-5). 15.99 *(978-0-06-236607-8(6))*; pap. 4.99 *(978-0-06-236606-1(8))* HarperCollins Pubs. (HarperCollins).

—Flat Stanley's Worldwide Adventures #2: the Great Egyptian Grave Robbery. Pamintuan, Macky, illus. 2009. (Flat Stanley's Worldwide Adventures Ser.: 2). (ENG.). 96p. (J). (gr. 2-5). pap. 6.99 *(978-0-06-142992-7(9)*, HarperCollins) HarperCollins Pubs.

—Flat Stanley's Worldwide Adventures #2: the Great Egyptian Grave Robbery No. 2. Pamintuan, Macky, illus. 2009. (Flat Stanley's Worldwide Adventures Ser.: 2). (ENG.). 96p. (J). (gr. 2-5). 15.99 *(978-0-06-142993-4(7)*, HarperCollins) HarperCollins Pubs.

Brown, Marc. Arthur & the Mystery of the Stolen Bike. 2012. (ENG., Illus.). 64p. (J). (gr. 1-4). pap. 5.99 *(978-0-316-13363-0(9))* Little, Brown Bks. for Young Readers.

Carter, Ally. Heist Society. 2011. (Heist Society Novel Ser.: 1). (ENG.). 304p. (YA). (gr. 7-17). pap. 10.99 *(978-1-4231-1661-5(5))* Hyperion Pr.

Cazet, Denys. Minnie & Moo: The Case of the Missing Jelly Donut. Cazet, Denys, illus. 2007. (Minnie & Moo Ser.). (Illus.). 45p. (J). (gr. -1-3). pap. 29.95 incl. audio *(978-1-4301-0088-1(5))* Live Oak Media.

Chandra, Rohini S. The Dragon in the Candle Jar. 2013. 52p. pap. 16.95 *(978-1-4626-9842-4(5))* America Star Bks.

Cheshire, Simon. The Treasure of Dead Man's Lane & Other Case Files: Saxby Smart, Private Detective: Book 2. Alley, R. W., illus. 2011. (Saxby Smart, Private Detective Ser.: 2). (ENG.). 224p. (J). (gr. 3-7). pap. 14.99 *(978-0-312-67434-2(1)*, 900072849) Square Fish.

Choksi, Sean. The Theft of Time. 2010. 67p. pap. 14.95 *(978-1-4327-6598-9(1))* Outskirts Pr., Inc.

Clark, Lillian. Immoral Code. 2019. 320p. (YA). (gr. 7). 17.99 *(978-0-525-58046-1(8)*, Knopf Bks. for Young Readers) Random Hse. Children's Bks.

Clement, Emily. Thea Stilton & the Hollywood Hoax. Pellizzari, Barbara & Balleello, Chiara, illus. 2015. 159p. (J). *(978-1-5182-1175-1(5))* Scholastic, Inc.

Clements, Andrew. The Map Trap. Andreasen, Dan, illus. 2016. (ENG.). 160p. (J). (gr. 3-7). pap. 7.99 *(978-1-4169-9728-3(8))* Simon & Schuster Children's Publishing.

—The Map Trap. 2016. lib. bdg. 18.40 *(978-0-606-38977-8(6))* Turtleback.

Collins, A. L. Raiders: Water Thieves of Mars. Tikulin, Tomislav, illus. 2017. (Redworld Ser.). (ENG.). 128p. (J). (gr. 3-8). lib. bdg. 25.99 *(978-1-4965-4820-7(5)*, 135342, Stone Arch Bks.) Capstone.

Coxe, Molly. Rat Attack. 2018. (Bright Owl Bks.). (Illus.). 40p. (J). (gr. -1-2). pap. 6.99 *(978-1-57565-973-2(5)*, 34bdb775-fddd-4009-b783-5c0e1b6665d2); lib. bdg. 17.99 *(978-1-57565-972-5(7)*, b1838b00-5a75-4e2b-b0f5-3c67b44a1465) Astra Publishing Hse. (Kane Press).

Cushman, Doug. Dirk Bones & the Mystery of the Missing Books. Cushman, Doug, illus. 2009. (I Can Read Level 1 Ser.). (ENG., Illus.). 32p. (J). (gr. -1-3). 16.99 *(978-0-06-073768-9(9)*, HarperCollins) HarperCollins Pubs.

Dahl, Michael. Blood Shark! Sinkovec, Igor, illus. 2015. (Igor's Lab of Fear Ser.). (ENG.). 40p. (J). (gr. 4-8). lib. bdg. 23.99 *(978-1-4965-0456-2(9)*, 128481, Stone Arch Bks.) Capstone.

—The Clown Prince of Cards. Vecchio, Luciano, illus. 2016. (Batman Tales of the Batcave Ser.). (ENG.). 40p. (J). (gr. 4-8). lib. bdg. 24.65 *(978-1-4965-4013-3(1)*, 133212, Stone Arch Bks.) Capstone.

—The Frozen Zone Freeze Ray. Vecchio, Luciano, illus. 2018. (Batman Tales of the Batcave Ser.). (ENG.). 40p. (J). (gr. 4-8). lib. bdg. 24.65 *(978-1-4965-5977-7(0)*, 137326, Stone Arch Bks.) Capstone.

—The Jaguar's Jewel. Vecchio, Luciano, illus. 2018. (Batman Tales of the Batcave Ser.). (ENG.). 40p. (J). (gr. 4-8). lib. bdg. 24.65 *(978-1-4965-5984-5(3)*, 137333, Stone Arch Bks.) Capstone.

—The Thirteenth Mystery. Weber, Lisa K., illus. 2016. (Hocus Pocus Hotel Ser.). (ENG.). 224p. (J). (gr. 3-6). pap., pap. 7.95 *(978-1-4965-0755-6(X)*, 128800, Stone Arch Bks.) Capstone.

Dakers, Diane. Bad Business, 1 vol. 2015. (Orca Currents Ser.). (ENG.). 128p. (J). (gr. 4-7). pap. 9.95 *(978-1-4598-0969-7(6))* Orca Bk. Pubs. USA.

Davies, Nicola. The Promise. Carlin, Laura, illus. 2014. (ENG.). 40p. (J). (gr. k-4). 18.99 *(978-0-7636-6633-0(5))* Candlewick Pr.

Deutsch, Stacia. A Picture's Worth a Thousand Clues. Boyden, Robin, illus. 2017. (Mysterious Makers of Shaker Street Ser.). (ENG.). 112p. (J). (gr. 2-4). pap. 6.95 *(978-1-4965-4681-4(4)*, 135210); lib. bdg. 22.65 *(978-1-4965-4677-7(6)*, 135202) Capstone. (Stone Arch Bks.).

—Sounds Like Trouble. Boyden, Robin, illus. 2017. (Mysterious Makers of Shaker Street Ser.). (ENG.). 112p. (J). (gr. 2-4). pap. 6.95 *(978-1-4965-4680-7(6)*, 135211); lib. bdg. 22.65 *(978-1-4965-4676-0(8)*, 135201) Capstone. (Stone Arch Bks.).

Devargas, Casey Anthony. The Kindergarten Treasure. 2012. 44p. pap. 7.00 *(978-0-9859042-0-3(8))* CD Publishing.

Dhami, Narinder. Samosa Thief. Blundell, Tony, illus. 2005. (ENG.). 24p. (J). lib. bdg. 23.65 *(978-1-59646-708-8(8))* Dingles & Co.

DiCamillo, Kate. Mercy Watson Fights Crime. Van Dusen, Chris, illus. (Mercy Watson Ser.: 3). (ENG.). 80p. (J). (gr. k-3). 2010. pap. 6.99 *(978-0-7636-4952-4(X))* 2006. 15.99 *(978-0-7636-2590-0(6))* Candlewick Pr.

Dicamillo, Kate. Mercy Watson Fights Crime. 2010. (Mercy Watson Ser.: Bk. 3). lib. bdg. 16.00 *(978-0-606-14927-3(9))* Turtleback.

Dickson, Louise. The Disappearing Magician. Cupples, Pat, illus. 2007. (Kids Can Read Ser.). 32p. (J). (gr. 1-2). 3.95 *(978-1-55453-034-2(2))* Kids Can Pr., Ltd. CAN. Dist: Hachette Bk. Group.

Dixon, Franklin. A con Artist in Paris. 2017. 122p. (J). *(978-1-5379-7447-7(5)*, Simon & Schuster/Paula Wiseman Bks.) Simon & Schuster/Paula Wiseman Bks.

—Ship of Secrets. 2014. (Hardy Boys: Secret Files Ser.: 15). lib. bdg. 14.75 *(978-0-606-35781-4(5))* Turtleback.

Dixon, Franklin W. The Bicycle Thief. Burroughs, Scott, illus. 2011. (Hardy Boys: the Secret Files Ser.: 6). (ENG.). 96p. (J). (gr. 1-4). pap. 5.99 *(978-1-4169-9396-4(7)*, Aladdin) Simon & Schuster Children's Publishing.

—The Curse of the Ancient Emerald. 2015. (Hardy Boys Adventures Ser.: 9). (ENG., Illus.). 128p. (J). (gr. 3-7). pap. 6.99 *(978-1-4814-2475-2(0)*, Aladdin) Simon & Schuster Children's Publishing.

—Showdown at Widow Creek. 2016. (Hardy Boys Adventures Ser.: 11). (ENG., Illus.). 128p. (J). (gr. 3-7). 17.99 *(978-1-4814-3878-0(6)*, Aladdin) Simon & Schuster Children's Publishing.

Douglas, Erin. Get That Pest! Yee, Wong Herbert, illus. 2003. (ENG.). 24p. (J). (gr. -1-3). pap. 5.99 *(978-0-15-204833-4(2)*, 1194595, Clarion Bks.) HarperCollins Pubs.

Duk, Lor. The Firestorm Heart: A Dragon Friend Story. 2010. 236p. pap. 15.95 *(978-1-4401-9474-0(2))* iUniverse, Inc.

Eason, Sarah. Hand it over, Harry, 1 vol. 2013. (You Choose Ser.). (ENG.). 32p. (gr. 2-2). pap. 11.52 *(978-1-4644-0561-7(1)*, f9ff427b-cb23-4889-a42f-475dd8f0d607, Enslow Elementary) Enslow Publishing, LLC.

Eggleton, Jill. Mickey Maloney's Missing Bag. Pye, Trevor, illus. 2004. (Rigby Sails Early Ser.). (ENG.). 16p. (gr. 1-2). pap. 6.95 *(978-0-7578-9299-8(X))* Houghton Mifflin Harcourt Publishing Co.

Elliott, Rebecca. A Woodland Wedding. 2016. (Owl Diaries: 3). (ENG.). 80p. (J). (gr. k-2). lib. bdg. 14.75 *(978-0-606-38068-3(X))* Turtleback.

—A Woodland Wedding: a Branches Book (Owl Diaries #3) (Library Edition), Vol. 3. Elliott, Rebecca, illus. 2016. (Owl Diaries: 3). (ENG., Illus.). 80p. (J). (gr. k-2). 24.99 *(978-0-545-82558-0(X))* Scholastic, Inc.

Elliott, Zetta. The Dragon Thief. Geneva B, Geneva, illus. 2019. (Dragons in a Bag Ser.: 2). 176p. (J). (gr. 3-7). 16.99 *(978-1-5247-7049-5(3)*, Random Hse. Bks. for Young Readers) Random Hse. Children's Bks.

Everett, George W. G. W. Frog & the Pumpkin Patch Bandit. 2010. 40p. 16.95 *(978-1-4497-0759-0(9)*, WestBow Pr.) Author Solutions, LLC.

Fanning, Kieran. Code Crackers: Trapdoor to Treachery. 2010. (Dover Children's Classics Ser.). (ENG., Illus.). 128p. (J). (gr. 3-5). pap. 5.99 *(978-0-486-47880-7(7))* Dover Pubns., Inc.

Fenn, Jennifer. Flight Risk: A Novel. 2017. (ENG.). 384p. (YA). 21.99 *(978-1-62672-760-1(0)*, 900172860) Roaring Brook Pr.

Fertig, Dennis. Something Rotten at Village Market. McMahon, Bob, tr. McMahon, Bob, illus. 2003. 60p. 11.60 net. *(978-0-7398-5170-8(5))* Steck-Vaughn.

Fisch, Sholly & Hagan, Merrill. Food Fright & Par for the Course. Bates, Ben & Corona, Jorge, illus. 2019. (DC Teen Titans Go! Ser.). (ENG.). 32p. (J). (gr. 2-6). lib. bdg. 21.93 *(978-1-4965-7993-5(3)*, 139824, Stone Arch Bks.) Capstone.

Fisher, Justin. The Gold Thief (Ned's Circus of Marvels, Book 2) 2018. (Ned's Circus of Marvels Ser.: 2). (ENG.). 432p. (J). 6.99 *(978-0-00-826221-1(7)*, HarperCollins Children's Bks.) HarperCollins Pubs. Ltd. GBR. Dist: HarperCollins Pubs.

Foster, Martha S. Ginger Box. Geer, Charles, illus. 2011. 126p. 40.95 *(978-1-258-06588-1(6))* Literary Licensing, LLC.

Gibbes, Lesley. Fizz & the Show Dog Jewel Thief. King, Stephen Michael, illus. 2017. (J). (ENG.). 80p. pap. 4.99 *(978-1-61067-614-4(9))*; 67p. *(978-1-61067-641-0(6))* Kane Miller.

Gosling, Sharon. The Diamond Thief. 2014. (Diamond Thief Ser.). (ENG.). 336p. (J). (gr. 9-12). 16.95 *(978-1-63079-002-8(8)*, 126763, Switch Pr.) Capstone.

Gottesfeld, Jeff. The Bank of Badness, 1 vol. 2012. (Robinson's Hood Ser.). (ENG.). 128p. (gr. 5-8). pap. 10.75 *(978-1-62250-001-7(6))* Saddleback Educational Publishing, Inc.

—The Bank of Badness. 2013. (Robinson's Hood Ser.: 2). lib. bdg. 19.60 *(978-0-606-27019-9(1))* Turtleback.

—Chopped!, 1 vol. 2012. (Robinson's Hood Ser.). (ENG.). 124p. (gr. 5-8). pap. 10.75 *(978-1-62250-002-4(4))* Saddleback Educational Publishing, Inc.

—Chopped! 2013. (Robinson's Hood Ser.: 3). lib. bdg. 19.60 *(978-0-606-27020-5(5))* Turtleback.

Grant, Vicki. Identificación, 1 vol. 2009. (Spanish Soundings Ser.). (SPA.). 112p. (YA). (gr. 8-12). pap. 9.95 *(978-1-55469-134-0(6))* Orca Bk. Pubs. USA.

Graves, Judith. Exposed, 1 vol. 2015. (Orca Soundings Ser.: 2). (ENG.). 144p. (YA). (gr. 8-12). pap. 9.95 *(978-1-4598-0722-8(7))* Orca Bk. Pubs. USA.

—Infiltrate, 1 vol. 2017. (Orca Soundings Ser.: 5). (ENG.). 160p. (YA). (gr. 8-12). pap. 9.95 *(978-1-4598-0723-5(5))* Orca Bk. Pubs. USA.

Greenfield, A. B. Ra the Mighty: Cat Detective. Horne, Sarah, illus. (Ra the Mighty Ser.: 1). (ENG.). (J). (gr. 2-5). 2019. 240p. pap. 7.99 *(978-0-8234-4438-0(4))* 2018. 224p. 16.99 *(978-0-8234-4027-6(3))* Holiday Hse., Inc.

Griffin, N. Smashie Mcperter & the Mystery of Room 11. Hindley, Kate, illus. 2015. (Smashie Mcperter Investigates Ser.: 1). (ENG.). 256p. (J). (gr. 2-5). 15.99 *(978-0-7636-6145-8(7))* Candlewick Pr.

Grisham, John. The Accused. 2013. (Theodore Boone Ser.: 3). lib. bdg. 18.40 *(978-0-606-31696-5(5))* Turtleback.

—Theodore Boone: the Accused. 2013. (Theodore Boone Ser.: 3). (ENG.). 304p. (J). (gr. 3-7). pap. 8.99 *(978-0-14-242613-5(X)*, Puffin Books) Penguin Young Readers Group.

Gutman, Dan. Babe Ruth & the Ice Cream Mess: Ready-To-Read Level 2. Garvin, Elaine, illus. 2004. (Ready-To-Read Childhood of Famous Americans Ser.). (ENG.). 32p. (J). (gr. k-2). pap. 4.99 *(978-0-689-85529-0(X)*, Simon Spotlight) Simon Spotlight.

Hale, Bruce. Hiss Me Deadly: A Chet Gecko Mystery. Hale, Bruce, illus. 2009. (Chet Gecko Ser.: 13). (ENG., Illus.). 128p. (J). (gr. 3-7). pap. 6.99 *(978-0-15-206424-2(9)*, 1063327, Clarion Bks.) HarperCollins Pubs.

Hannibal, James R. The Fourth Ruby. 2017. (Section 13 Ser.: 2). (ENG., Illus.). 416p. (J). (gr. 3-7). 16.99 *(978-1-4814-6712-4(3)*, Simon & Schuster Bks. For Young Readers) Simon & Schuster Bks. For Young Readers.

Herz, Henry. How the Squid Got Two Long Arms, 1 vol. Graber, Luke, illus. 2018. (ENG.). 32p. (J). (gr. -1-3). 16.99 *(978-1-4556-2388-4(1)*, Pelican Publishing) Arcadia Publishing.

Hope, Lee Laura. Six Little Bunkers at Aunt Jo's. 2007. (ENG.). 144p. pap. 18.99 *(978-1-4346-3234-0(2))* Creative Media Partners, LLC.

Hughes, Shirley. Digby o'Day & the Great Diamond Robbery. Vulliamy, Clara, illus. 2015. (ENG.). 136p. (J). (gr. k-3). 12.99 *(978-0-7636-7445-8(1))* Candlewick Pr.

Hunt, Elizabeth Singer. Secret Agent Jack Stalwart: Book 11: the Theft of the Samurai Sword: Japan. 2009. (Secret Agent Jack Stalwart Ser.: 11). (ENG., Illus.). 128p. (J). (gr. 1-4). pap. 5.99 *(978-1-60286-098-8(X))* Hachette Bk. Group.

—Secret Agent Jack Stalwart: Book 3: the Mystery of the Mona Lisa: France, Bk. 3. 2007. (Secret Agent Jack Stalwart Ser.: 3). (ENG., Illus.). 128p. (J). (gr. 1-4). per. 5.99 *(978-1-60286-001-8(7)*, Running Pr. Kids) Running Pr.

—Secret Agent Jack Stalwart: Book 4: the Caper of the Crown Jewels: England, Bk. 4. 2008. (Secret Agent Jack Stalwart Ser.: 4). (ENG., Illus.). 144p. (J). (gr. 1-4). per. 5.99 *(978-1-60286-013-1(0))* Hachette Bk. Group.

—Secret Agents Jack & Max Stalwart: Book 3: the Fate of the Irish Treasure: Ireland. Williamson, Brian, illus. 2019. (Secret Agents Jack & Max Stalwart Ser.: 3). (ENG.). 140p. (J). (gr. 1-4). pap. 5.99 *(978-1-60286-578-5(7)*, Running Pr. Kids) Running Pr.

—Theft of the Samurai Sword: Japan #11. 2009. (ENG., Illus.). 128p. (J). lib. bdg. 15.38 *(978-1-4242-4452-2(8))* Fitzgerald Bks.

Hutchins, Hazel. The Great Bike Rescue, 1 vol. 2013. (Orca Young Readers Ser.). (ENG.). 112p. (J). (gr. 4-7). pap. 7.95 *(978-1-4598-0478-4(3))* Orca Bk. Pubs. USA.

Hyder, M. A. Donia: Stolen Raindrops or Honour among Thieves. 2011. (Illus.). 364p. pap. 20.53 *(978-1-4567-7428-8(X))* AuthorHouse.

Hymas, Allison K. Arts & Thefts. 2018. (Max Ser.). (ENG., Illus.). 352p. (J). (gr. 4-8). pap. 7.99 *(978-1-4814-6345-4(4)*, Aladdin) Simon & Schuster Children's Publishing.

—Under Locker & Key. 2017. (Max Ser.). (ENG., Illus.). 256p. (J). (gr. 4-8). pap. 7.99 *(978-1-4814-6342-3(X)*, Simon & Schuster/Paula Wiseman Bks.) Simon & Schuster/Paula Wiseman Bks.

Inches, Alison. Súper Bebés! Miller, Victoria, illus. 2006. (Dora la Exploradora Ser.). (SPA.). 24p. (J). (gr. -1-3). pap. 3.99 *(978-1-4169-2461-6(2)*, Libros Para Ninos) Libros Para Ninos.

Ish-Kishor, Sulamith. A Boy of Old Prague. Shahn, Ben, illus. 2008. (Dover Children's Classics Ser.). (ENG.). 96p. (J). (gr. 4-6). pap. 3.99 *(978-0-486-46766-5(X)*, 46766X) Dover Pubns., Inc.

Ius, Dawn. Overdrive. (ENG.). (YA). (gr. 9). 2017. 368p. pap. 10.99 *(978-1-4814-3945-9(6))* 2016. (Illus.). 352p. 17.99 *(978-1-4814-3944-2(8))* Simon Pulse. (Simon Pulse).

Jackson, Ellen. The Cupcake Thief. 2008. pap. 34.95 *(978-1-58013-765-2(2))* Astra Publishing Hse.

—The Cupcake Thief. Sims, Blanche, illus. 2007. (Social Studies Connects Ser.). 32p. (J). (gr. 1-3). pap. 5.95 *(978-1-57565-247-4(1)*, 081b7736-fccb-4c97-afb0-316316c1edd1, Kane Press) Astra Publishing Hse.

Jackson, Melanie. Tick Tock Terror, 1 vol. 2019. (Orca Currents Ser.). (ENG.). 144p. (J). (gr. 4-7). pap. 9.95 *(978-1-4598-1955-9(1))* Orca Bk. Pubs. USA.

Jacobson, Rick. The Mona Lisa Caper. Jacobson, Rick & Fernandez, Laura, illus. 2005. 24p. (J). (gr. k-3). 17.99 *(978-0-88776-726-5(5)*, Tundra Bks.) Tundra Bks. CAN. Dist: Penguin Random Hse. LLC.

Jakubowski, Michele. The Professor's Discovery. Pinelli, Amerigo, illus. 2016. (Sleuths of Somerville Ser.). (ENG.). 144p. (J). (gr. 4-6). lib. bdg. 25.99 *(978-1-4965-3177-3(9)*, 132216, Stone Arch Bks.) Capstone.

—The Professor's Discovery. Pinelli, Amerigo, illus. 2017. (Sleuths of Somerville Ser.). (ENG.). 144p. (J). (gr. 4-6). pap. 6.95 *(978-1-4965-3181-0(7)*, Stone Arch Bks.) Capstone.

James, Dalton. The Sneakiest Pirates. 2008. 20p. pap. 10.95 *(978-1-4327-2477-1(0))* Outskirts Pr., Inc.

Jennings, Sharon. Jingle Bats. Malloy, Kalle, illus. 72p. pap. *(978-1-897039-22-9(0))* High Interest Publishing (HIP).

Jones, Allan Frewin. Blood Stone, Vol. 6. 6th ed. 2003. (ENG.). 176p. (J). mass mkt. *(978-0-330-37476-7(1)*, Pan) Pan Macmillan.

Judge, Chris. The Snow Beast. Judge, Chris, illus. 2015. (ENG., Illus.). 32p. (J). (gr. -1-3). 17.99 *(978-1-4677-9313-1(2)*, a711d3a5-9c18-4a5e-a4f5-dd8ef98bb756) Lerner Publishing Group.

Juslin, Lee. Nurse Frosty Saves the Day. 2009. 35p. pap. 22.00 *(978-0-557-09486-8(0))* Lulu Pr., Inc.

Keene, Carolyn. The Apple Bandit. Jones, Jan Naimo, illus. 2005. (Nancy Drew Notebooks). 74p. (J). (gr. 1-4). 11.65 *(978-0-7569-6505-1(5))* Perfection Learning Corp.

—The Nancy Drew & the Clue Crew Collection (Boxed Set) Sleepover Sleuths; Scream for Ice Cream; Pony Problems; the Cinderella Ballet Mystery; Case of the Sneaky Snowman. Pamintuan, Macky, illus. 2014. (Nancy Drew & the Clue Crew Ser.). (ENG.). 480p. (J). (gr. 1-4). pap. 29.99 *(978-1-4814-1472-2(0)*, Aladdin) Simon & Schuster Children's Publishing.

—The Orchid Thief. 19th ed. 2006. (Nancy Drew (All New) Girl Detective Ser.: 19). (ENG.). 144p. (J). (gr. 3-7). pap. 6.99 *(978-1-4169-0980-4(X)*, Aladdin) Simon & Schuster Children's Publishing.

—Time Thief. Pamintuan, Macky, illus. 2011. (Nancy Drew & the Clue Crew Ser.: 28). (ENG.). 96p. (J). (gr. 1-4). pap. 5.99 *(978-1-4169-9458-9(0)*, Aladdin) Simon & Schuster Children's Publishing.

Kehret, Peg & the Cat, Pete. Spy Cat. 2008. (Pete the Cat Ser.: 2). (ENG.). 192p. (J). (gr. 3-7). 5.99 *(978-0-14-241219-0(8)*, Puffin Books) Penguin Young Readers Group.

Kelley, J. Patrick. The Stolen Smile. Kelley, Gary, illus. 2nd ed. 2015. (ENG.). 40p. (J). (gr. 2-4). 16.99 *(978-1-56846-281-3(6)*, 21102, Creative Editions) Creative Co., The.

Kelly, David A. Ballpark Mysteries #1: the Fenway Foul-Up. Meyers, Mark, illus. 2011. (Ballpark Mysteries Ser.: 1). (ENG.). 112p. (J). (gr. 1-4). pap. 6.99 *(978-0-375-86703-3(1)*, Random Hse. Bks. for Young Readers) Random Hse. Children's Bks.

—Ballpark Mysteries #15: the Baltimore Bandit. Meyers, Mark, illus. 2019. (Ballpark Mysteries Ser.: 15). (ENG.). 112p. (J). (gr. 1-4). 12.99 *(978-1-5247-6755-6(7))*; pap. 6.99 *(978-1-5247-6754-9(9))* Random Hse. Children's Bks. (Random Hse. Bks. for Young Readers).

—Ballpark Mysteries Super Special #2: Christmas in Cooperstown. Meyers, Mark, illus. 2017. (Ballpark Mysteries Ser.: 2). (ENG.). 144p. (J). (gr. 1-4). 5.99 *(978-0-399-55192-5(1)*, Random Hse. Bks. for Young Readers) Random Hse. Children's Bks.

Kline, Suzy. Horrible Harry Takes the Cake. Remkiewicz, Frank, illus. 2007. (Horrible Harry Ser.: 19). 64p. (J). (gr. 2-4). 4.99 *(978-0-14-240939-8(1)*, Puffin Books) Penguin Young Readers Group.

Korman, Gordon. Framed. (J). 2010. *(978-0-545-27081-6(2)*, Scholastic Pr.)Bk. 3. 2011. (Swindle Ser.: 3). (ENG.). 240p. (gr. 3-7). pap. 7.99 *(978-0-545-19763-2(5)*, Scholastic Paperbacks) Scholastic, Inc.

—Zoobreak. 2009. 230p. (J). *(978-0-545-20027-1(X)*, Scholastic Pr.) Scholastic, Inc.

Kropp, Alex. Hacker! (Illus.). 93p. *(978-1-897039-09-0(3))* High Interest Publishing (HIP).

Kulper, Kendall. Drift & Dagger. 2015. (ENG.). 368p. (YA). (gr. 7-17). 18.00 *(978-0-316-40453-2(5))* Little, Brown Bks. for Young Readers.

Kysiak, Penelope Ann. You Can't Steal One's Wishes, 1 vol. 2009. 35p. pap. 24.95 *(978-1-60749-149-1(4))* America Star Bks.

La Rose, Melinda. Surfin' Turf. 2019. (Illus.). 31p. (J). *(978-1-4242-5739-3(5))* Disney Publishing Worldwide.

Lagonegro, Melissa. Super Agents (Barbie Spy Squad) 2016. (Step into Reading Ser.). (ENG., Illus.). 24p. (J). (gr. -1-1). pap. 5.99 *(978-1-101-93140-0(X)*, Random Hse. Bks. for Young Readers) Random Hse. Children's Bks.

Lawson, JonArno. Uncle Holland, 1 vol. Nelson, Natalie, illus. 2017. (ENG.). 32p. (J). (gr. k-2). 17.95 *(978-1-55498-929-4(9))* Groundwood Bks. CAN. Dist: Publishers Group West (PGW).

Lee, HaeDa. Ida's Present. Kim, ihHyeon, illus. 2014. (MySELF Bookshelf Ser.). (ENG.). 32p. (J). (gr. k-2). pap. 11.94 *(978-1-60357-694-9(0))*; lib. bdg. 25.27 *(978-1-59953-659-0(5))* Norwood Hse. Pr.

Levins, Sandra. Bumblebee Bike. Keay, Claire, illus. 2014. 32p. (J). *(978-1-4338-1645-1(8))*; pap. *(978-1-4338-1646-8(6))* American Psychological Assn. (Magination Pr.).

Lockwood, Vicki. The Magnificent Lizzie Brown & the Ghost Ship. Hans, Stephanie, illus. 2015. (Magnificent Lizzie Brown Ser.). (ENG.). 200p. (J). (gr. 5-9). lib. bdg. 26.65 *(978-1-4342-9806-5(X)*, 127184, Stone Arch Bks.) Capstone.

London, Jack. The Call of the Wild. Moser, Barry, illus. 2011. (ENG.). 144p. (J). (gr. 4-9). pap. 8.99 *(978-1-4424-3411-0(2)*, Simon & Schuster Bks. For Young Readers) Simon & Schuster Bks. For Young Readers.

—La Llamada de la Naturaleza. 2003. (Historias de Siempre Ser.).Tr. of Call of the Wild. (SPA., Illus.). 92p. (J). (gr. 5-8). pap. 10.95 *(978-84-204-5731-4(0))* Santillana USA Publishing Co., Inc.

Lorimer, Janet. The Tiger Lily Code, 1 vol. unabr. ed. 2010. (Q Reads Ser.). (ENG.). 32p. (YA). (gr. 9-12). pap. 8.50 *(978-1-61651-195-1(8))* Saddleback Educational Publishing, Inc.

Lowery, Rae. The Case of the Pack-Rat Park. 2008. 57p. pap. 19.95 *(978-1-60610-426-2(8))* America Star Bks.

Lucky, A. E. Kyle the Detective, 1 vol. 2010. 70p. pap. 19.95 *(978-1-4512-2042-1(1))* America Star Bks.

Lynn, Jenna. Rivals: Book 2. Cruz, Abigail Dela, illus. 2018. (Robyn Hood Ser.). (ENG.). 48p. (J). (gr. 3-7). lib. bdg. 34.21 *(978-1-5321-3377-0(4)*, 31177, Spellbound) Magic Wagon.

Lysiak, Hilde & Lysiak, Matthew. Hero Dog!: a Branches Book (Hilde Cracks the Case #1) Lew-Vriethoff, Joanne, illus. 2017. (Hilde Cracks the Case Ser.: 1). (ENG.). 112p. (J). (gr. 1-3). pap. 5.99 *(978-1-338-14155-9(4))* Scholastic, Inc.

—Thief Strikes!: a Branches Book (Hilde Cracks the Case #6) Lew-Vriethoff, Joanne, illus. 2019. (Hilde Cracks the Case Ser.: 6). (ENG.). 96p. (J). (gr. 1-3). pap. 5.99 *(978-1-338-28391-4(X))* Scholastic, Inc.

Maddox, Jake. Caught Stealing. Aburto, Jesus, illus. 2015. (Jake Maddox Sports Stories Ser.). (ENG.). 72p. (J). (gr.

T
U
V

3-6). lib. bdg. 25.99 *(978-1-4965-0493-7(3)*, 128565, Stone Arch Bks.) Capstone.

Malaspina, Ann. Guinea Fowl & Rabbit Get Justice: An African Folktale. Wendland, Paula, illus. 2013. (Folktales from Around the World Ser.). (ENG.). 24p. (J). (gr. k-3). 32.79 *(978-1-62323-614-4(2)*, 206381) Child's World, Inc, The.

Manning, Matthew K. Revenge of the One-Trick Pony. Ellis, Joey, illus. 2018. (Xander & the Rainbow-Barfing Unicorns Ser.). (ENG.). 128p. (J). (gr. 3-5). pap. 7.95 *(978-1-4965-5716-2(6)*, 136705, Stone Arch Bks.) Capstone.

Marciano, John Bemelmans. Madeline & the Old House in Paris. 2013. (Madeline Ser.). (ENG., Illus.). 48p. (J). (gr. -1-2). 18.99 *(978-0-670-78485-1(0)*, Viking Books for Young Readers) Penguin Young Readers Group.

Martin, Gary. The Witch of Endor, 1 vol. Cariello, Sergio, illus. 2008. (Z Graphic Novels / Son of Samson Ser.). (ENG.). 160p. (J). pap. 6.99 *(978-0-310-71283-1(1))* Zonderkidz.

Matheson, Shirlee Smith. Fastback Beach, 1 vol. 2003. (Orca Soundings Ser.). (ENG.). 97p. (YA). (gr. 9-12). 22.44 *(978-1-55143-580-0(2))* Orca Bk. Pubs. USA.

Maxwell, Lisa. The Devil's Thief. 2018. (Last Magician Ser.: 2). (ENG., Illus.). 704p. (YA). (gr. 9). 18.99 *(978-1-4814-9445-8(7)*, Simon Pulse) Simon Pulse.

Maynard, Adam G. The Adventures of Dynamo Dog & the Case of the Missing Jewelery. 2010. 24p. 15.49 *(978-1-4490-9186-6(5))* AuthorHouse.

Mazer, Anne. Now You See It, Now You Don't. 2005. (Amazing Days of Abby Hayes Ser.: Bk. 15). (Illus.). 126p. (J). (gr. 4-7). 12.65 *(978-0-7569-5932-6(2))* Perfection Learning Corp.

McClintock, Norah. Marked, 1 vol. 2008. (Orca Currents Ser.). (ENG.). 128p. (J). (gr. 4-7). pap. 9.95 *(978-1-55143-992-1(1))* Orca Bk. Pubs. USA.

—Marqué, 1 vol. 2011. (Orca Currents en Français Ser.).Tr. of Marked. (FRE.). 128p. (J). (gr. 4-7). pap. 9.95 *(978-1-55469-855-4(3))* Orca Bk. Pubs. USA.

—Watch Me, 1 vol. 2008. (Orca Currents Ser.). (ENG.). 128p. (J). (gr. 4-7). pap. 9.95 *(978-1-55469-039-8(0))* Orca Bk. Pubs. USA.

McLean, Hope. Catch Us If You Can, 1. 2013. (Jewel Society Ser.: 1). (ENG.). 144p. (J). (gr. 4-6). 18.69 *(978-0-545-60762-9(0))* Scholastic, Inc.

Meadows, Daisy. Emily, the Emerald Fairy. Ripper, Georgie, illus. 2005. 65p. (J). pap. *(978-0-545-01190-7(6))* Scholastic, Inc.

Meddaugh, Susan. Martha Speaks: Secret Agent Dog (Chapter Book) 2012. (Martha Speaks Ser.). (ENG., Illus.). 96p. (J). (gr. 1-4). pap. 5.99 *(978-0-547-57660-2(9))* Houghton Mifflin Harcourt Publishing Co.

Meyerhoff, Jenny. Pumpkin Spice. Chatelain, Éva & Chatelain, Éva, illus. 2015. (Friendship Garden Ser.: 2). (ENG.). 144p. (J). (gr. 2-5). pap. 5.99 *(978-1-4814-3909-1(X)*, Aladdin) Simon & Schuster Children's Publishing.

—Pumpkin Spice. 2015. (Friendship Garden Ser.: 2). lib. bdg. 16.00 *(978-0-606-37833-8(2))* Turtleback.

Montgomery-Higham, Amanda. Max & the Doglins. 2007. (Child's Play Library). (Illus.). 32p. (J). (gr. 2-3). pap. *(978-1-84643-043-5(7))* Child's Play International Ltd.

Montgomery, Lewis B. The Case of the Locked Box. Wummer, Amy, illus. 2013. (Milo & Jazz Mysteries Ser.: Vol. 11). (ENG.). 106p. (J). (gr. 2-4). lib. bdg. 22.60 *(978-1-57565-625-0(6))* Astra Publishing Hse.

—The Case of the Locked Box (Book 11), No. 11. Wummer, Amy, illus. 2013. (Milo & Jazz Mysteries Ser.: 11). 112p. (J). (gr. 2-6). pap. 6.99 *(978-1-57565-626-7(4)*, 4eb267cb-73d0-4237-8cdc-45a0c519fde1, Kane Press) Astra Publishing Hse.

Murphy, Bonnie S. The Puzzle Piece Thief. 2010. 28p. pap. 15.99 *(978-1-4500-2649-9(4))* Xlibris Corp.

Ofelia, Dumas Lachtman. Big Enough Bastante Grande. Enrique, Sanchez, illus. 2008. 32p. (J). pap. 7.95 *(978-1-55885-239-6(5))* Arte Publico Pr.

Oldfield, Jenny. Crazy Horse. 2009. (Horses of Half Moon Ranch Ser.: 3). (ENG.). 160p. (J). (gr. 4-7). pap. 9.99 *(978-1-4022-1702-9(1))* Sourcebooks, Inc.

Oliver, Andrew. Scrambled. 2007. 288p. (J). per. 12.95 *(978-0-9661009-8-3(0))* Adams-Pomeroy Pr.

Ondaatje, Griffin. Muddy: The Raccoon Who Stole Dishes. Wolfsgruber, Linda, illus. 2019. (ENG.). 32p. (J). (gr. -1-2). 17.95 *(978-0-7358-4337-0(6))* North-South Bks., Inc.

O'Neill, S. Rocket Robinson & the Secret of the Saint. 2018. (Illus.). 248p. (J). (gr. 5-9). pap. 14.99 *(978-1-5067-0679-5(7)*, Dark Horse Books) Dark Horse Comics.

O'Reilly, Sean. The Monster Crooks, 1 vol. Arcana Studio Staff, illus. 2012. (Mighty Mighty Monsters Ser.). (ENG.). 48p. (J). (gr. 2-4). pap. 6.10 *(978-1-4342-4610-3(8)*, 120598, Stone Arch Bks.) Capstone.

Ott, Alexandra. Rules for Thieves. 2017. (Rules for Thieves Ser.: 1). (ENG., Illus.). 320p. (J). (gr. 3-7). 17.99 *(978-1-4814-7274-6(7)*, Aladdin) Simon & Schuster Children's Publishing.

—Rules for Thieves. 2018. (Rules for Thieves Ser.: 1). (ENG.). 336p. (J). (gr. 3-7). pap. 8.99 *(978-1-4814-7275-3(5)*, Simon & Schuster/Paula Wiseman Bks.) Simon & Schuster/Paula Wiseman Bks.

—The Shadow Thieves. 2018. (Rules for Thieves Ser.: 2). (ENG., Illus.). 400p. (J). (gr. 3-7). 17.99 *(978-1-4814-7277-7(1)*, Aladdin) Simon & Schuster Children's Publishing.

Padma, T. V. The Cleverest Thief. 2008. (Story Cove Ser.). (ENG., Illus.). 32p. (J). (gr. -1-3). pap. 4.95 *(978-0-87483-882-4(7))* August Hse. Pubs., Inc.

Papp, Robert, illus. Monkey Trouble. 2011. (Boxcar Children Mysteries Ser.: 127). (ENG.). 128p. (J). (gr. 2-5). pap. 7.99 *(978-0-8075-5240-7(2)*, 807552402, Random Hse. Bks. for Young Readers) Random Hse. Children's Bks.

Park, Barbara. Junie B. Jones Is Not a Crook. unabr. ed. 2004. (Junie B. Jones Ser.: No. 9). 67p. (J). (gr. k-3). pap. 17.00 incl. audio *(978-0-8072-0530-3(3)*, Listening Library) Random Hse. Audio Publishing Group.

Pearce, Margaret. Jumping into Trouble Book 3: Missing! a Horse. 2013. 66p. pap. *(978-1-922066-61-9(3))* Writers Exchange E-Publishing.

Pearson, Carol Lynn. A Christmas Thief. 2008. 80p. 12.99 *(978-1-59955-184-5(5))* Cedar Fort, Inc./CFI Distribution.

Peck, Robert Newton. Horse Thief. 2003. 277p. (YA). (gr. 7). 13.65 *(978-0-7569-1461-5(2))* Perfection Learning Corp.

Penn, Tony. The Misadventures of Michael McMichaels: The Borrowed Bracelet, Volume 2. Martin, Brian, illus. 2016. (Misadventures of Michael Mcmichaels Ser.). (ENG.). 91p. (J). (gr. 1-6). pap. 7.95 *(978-1-944882-03-7(0))* Boys Town Pr.

Perelman, Helen. Taffy Trouble. Waters, Erica-Jane, illus. 2015. (Candy Fairies Ser.: 16). (ENG.). 128p. (J). (gr. -1-5). pap. 6.99 *(978-1-4814-0613-0(2)*, Aladdin) Simon & Schuster Children's Publishing.

Phillips, Dee. Joyride, 1 vol. unabr. ed. 2010. (Right Now! Ser.). (ENG., Illus.). 45p. (YA). (gr. 9-12). pap. 10.75 *(978-1-61651-251-4(2))* Saddleback Educational Publishing, Inc.

Pick, Alice. Jamey's Promise, 1 vol. 2009. 61p. pap. 19.95 *(978-1-61582-547-9(9))* America Star Bks.

Polak, Monique. Home Invasion. 2006. (Orca Soundings Ser.). 105p. (gr. 7-11). 19.95 *(978-0-7569-6871-7(2))* Perfection Learning Corp.

Ponti, James. Framed! 2016. (Framed! Ser.: 1). (ENG., Illus.). 304p. (J). (gr. 3-7). 19.99 *(978-1-4814-3630-4(9)*, Aladdin) Simon & Schuster Children's Publishing.

Pratcher, Roger & Pratcher, Birgit. June Bear Adventures: The Missing Pies. 2007. 236p. per. 11.95 *(978-1-4327-0352-3(8))* Outskirts Pr., Inc.

Preller, James. Jigsaw Jones: the Case of the Hat Burglar. Alley, R. W., illus. 2019. (Jigsaw Jones Mysteries Ser.). (ENG.). 96p. (J). pap. 6.99 *(978-1-250-20768-5(1)*, 900201639) Feiwel & Friends.

—Jigsaw Jones: the Case of the Smelly Sneaker. 2017. (Jigsaw Jones Mysteries Ser.). (ENG., Illus.). 96p. (J). pap. 6.99 *(978-1-250-11080-0(7)*, 900169768) Feiwel & Friends.

Press, Judy. The Case of the Missing Kiddush Cup. 2018. (J). *(978-1-5415-0015-0(6)*, Kar-Ben Publishing) Lerner Publishing Group.

Prineas, Sarah. The Magic Thief. Caparo, Antonio Javier, illus. 2008. (Magic Thief Ser.: 1). (ENG.). 432p. (J). (gr. 5-9). 16.99 *(978-0-06-137587-3(X)*, HarperCollins) HarperCollins Pubs.

Quinn, Spencer, pseud. Woof. 2016. lib. bdg. 18.40 *(978-0-606-39011-8(1))* Turtleback.

—Woof: a Bowser & Birdie Novel. 2016. (ENG.). 304p. (J). (gr. 3-7). pap. 7.99 *(978-0-545-64332-0(5))* Scholastic, Inc.

Rabley, Stephen. Easystart: Marcel & the Mona Lisa Book & MP3 Pack: Industrial Ecology, Pack. 2nd ed. 2008. (ENG., Illus.). 99999p. pap., pap. 14.65 incl. cd-rom *(978-1-4058-8064-0(3))* Pearson Education.

Rankine-Van Wassenhoven, Jacqueline. Who Stole Grandpa's Teeth? 2008. 20p. 10.94 *(978-1-4357-0522-7(X))* Lulu Pr., Inc.

Richardson, E. E. The Curse Box. 2013. (ENG.). 64p. (YA). (gr. 6-12). pap. 6.95 *(978-1-78112-176-4(1))*; lib. bdg. 22.60 *(978-1-78112-175-7(3))* Lerner Publishing Group.

Rinaldi, Ann. An Acquaintance with Darkness. 2005. (Great Episodes Ser.). 374p. (gr. 7-12). 18.00 *(978-0-7569-5040-8(6))* Perfection Learning Corp.

Robins, Eleanor. Aztec Ring Mystery, 1 vol. unabr. ed. 2011. (Carter High Mysteries Ser.). (ENG.). 48p. (YA). (gr. 9-12). 9.75 *(978-1-61651-561-4(9))* Saddleback Educational Publishing, Inc.

—Drama Club Mystery, 1 vol. unabr. ed. 2011. (Carter High Mysteries Ser.). (ENG.). 48p. (YA). (gr. 9-12). 9.75 *(978-1-61651-562-1(7))* Saddleback Educational Publishing, Inc.

Rowley, M'lin. Knights of Right, BK 4: The Fiery Gloves. 2010. 80p. (J). pap. 6.99 *(978-1-60641-241-1(8)*, Shadow Mountain) Shadow Mountain Publishing.

Roy, Ron. Capital Mysteries #7: Trouble at the Treasury. Bush, Timothy, illus. 2006. (Capital Mysteries Ser.: 7). 96p. (J). (gr. 1-4). per. 6.99 *(978-0-375-83969-6(0)*, Random Hse. Bks. for Young Readers) Random Hse. Children's Bks.

—Capital Mysteries #9: a Thief at the National Zoo. Bush, Timothy, illus. 2007. (Capital Mysteries Ser.: 9). 96p. (J). (gr. 1-4). per. 5.99 *(978-0-375-84804-9(5)*, Random Hse. Bks. for Young Readers) Random Hse. Children's Bks.

—The Missing Mummy. (A to Z Mystery Ser.: Vol. 13). (J). 11.32 *(978-0-7383-3465-3(0))* Booksource, The.

—Mystery at the Washington Monument. Bush, Timothy, illus. 2007. (Capital Mysteries Ser.: No. 8). 87p. (gr. 1-4). 15.00 *(978-0-7569-7845-7(9))* Perfection Learning Corp.

—September Sneakers. 2013. (Calendar Mysteries Ser.: 9). lib. bdg. 14.75 *(978-0-606-32231-7(0))* Turtleback.

—A Thief at the National Zoo. Bush, Timothy, illus. 2008. (Capital Mysteries Ser.: No. 9). 87p. (gr. k-3). 15.00 *(978-0-7569-8329-1(0))* Perfection Learning Corp.

—A Thief at the National Zoo, 9. Bush, Timothy, illus. 2007. (Capital Mysteries Ser.: No. 9). (ENG.). 87p. (J). (gr. 2-4). lib. bdg. 17.44 *(978-0-375-94804-6(X))* Random House Publishing Group.

Russell, Rachel Renée. The Misadventures of Max Crumbly 2: Middle School Mayhem. Russell, Rachel Renée, illus. 2017. (Misadventures of Max Crumbly Ser.: 2). (ENG., Illus.). 240p. (J). (gr. 4-8). 13.99 *(978-1-4814-6003-3(X)*, Aladdin) Simon & Schuster Children's Publishing.

Santopolo, Jill. Nina, the Pinta, & the Vanishing Treasure (an Alec Flint Mystery #1), 1. 2009. (ENG.). 192p. (J). (gr. 2-5). mass mkt. 6.99 *(978-0-439-90353-0(X)*, Scholastic Paperbacks) Scholastic, Inc.

Schraff, Anne. Like a Broken Doll. 2011. (Urban Underground — Harriet Tubman High School Ser.). (YA). lib. bdg. 20.80 *(978-0-606-14799-6(3))* Turtleback.

—Stolen Treasure. 2014. (Red Rhino Ser.). (J). lib. bdg. 18.40 *(978-0-606-36203-0(7))* Turtleback.

Shaskan, Trisha Speed. Foul Play at Elm Tree Park: Case 3. Shaskan, Stephen, illus. 2018. (Q & Ray Ser.). (ENG.). 48p. (J). (gr. 2-5). 26.65 *(978-1-5124-1149-2(3)*, 4ca0215d-12ac-4838-90b8-6d7c4d9f7cbc, Graphic Universe™) Lerner Publishing Group.

Shepard, Sara. Pretty Little Liars #13: Crushed. 2014. (Pretty Little Liars Ser.: 13). (ENG.). 368p. (YA). (gr. 9). pap. 10.99 *(978-0-06-219972-0(2)*, HarperTeen) HarperCollins Pubs.

Skead, Robert. Elves Can't Kick. 2005. 84p. per. 7.99 *(978-1-929478-66-8(6))* Cross Training Publishing.

Snicket, Lemony, pseud. "Who Could That Be at This Hour?" Seth, illus. I.t. ed. 2012. (All the Wrong Questions Ser.: 1). (ENG.). 304p. (J). (gr. 3-17). 25.99 *(978-0-316-22425-3(1))* Little, Brown Bks. for Young Readers.

—"Who Could That Be at This Hour?" Also Published As "All the Wrong Questions: Question 1" Seth, illus. (All the Wrong Questions Ser.: 1). (ENG.). (J). (gr. 3-17). 2014. 288p. pap. 9.99 *(978-0-316-33547-8(9))* 2012. 272p. 15.99 *(978-0-316-12308-2(0))* Little, Brown Bks. for Young Readers.

Snicket, Lemony, pseud & Seth. Who Could That Be at This Hour? 2012. *(978-0-316-24771-9(5))* Little Brown & Co.

Song, Amira. Horse Lovers Forever. 2012. 64p. pap. *(978-1-4602-0144-2(2))* FriesenPress.

Sonnebom, Scott. The Computer Meltdown. Lozano, Omar, illus. 2015. (North Police Ser.). (ENG.). 32p. (J). (gr. k-2). lib. bdg. 21.32 *(978-1-4795-6485-9(0)*, 128338, Picture Window Bks.) Capstone.

Spector, Baron. Tracking Your Nightmare, 1 vol. Kneupper, Setch, illus. 2012. (Graveyard Diaries). (ENG.). 128p. (J). (gr. 2-5). lib. bdg. 38.50 *(978-1-61641-898-4(2)*, 9174, Calico Chapter Bks.) ABDO Publishing Co.

Spencer, Katherine. More Than Friends: A Saving Grace Novel. 2008. (Saving Grace Ser.). (ENG., Illus.). 224p. (YA). (gr. 7-12). pap. 14.95 *(978-0-15-205746-6(3)*, 1197270, Clarion Bks.) HarperCollins Pubs.

Sridhar, Priya. Stolen. Owenson, Meg, illus. 2019. (Powered Ser.). (ENG.). 112p. (J). (gr. 3-6). lib. bdg. 26.65 *(978-1-4965-7885-3(6)*, 139561, Stone Arch Bks.) Capstone.

Steele, Michael Anthony. Battle of the Pirate Bands: A 4D Book. Reeves, Pauline, illus. 2018. (Nearly Fearless Monkey Pirates Ser.). (ENG.). 48p. (J). (gr. k-2). pap. 7.95 *(978-1-5158-2687-3(2)*, 137838, Picture Window Bks.) Capstone.

Stephens, Sarah Hines. Catwoman's Purrfect Plot. Vecchio, Luciano, illus. 2017. (Batman & Robin Adventures Ser.). (ENG.). 88p. (J). (gr. 2-6). lib. bdg. 26.65 *(978-1-4965-5349-2(7)*, 136291, Stone Arch Bks.) Capstone.

Stevenson, Steve. The Crown of Venice. 2014. (Agatha Girl of Mystery Ser.: 7). lib. bdg. 16.00 *(978-0-606-36164-4(2))* Turtleback.

Stilton, Gerónimo. Don't Wake the Dinosaur! 2014. (Geronimo Stilton Cavemice Ser.: 6). lib. bdg. 18.40 *(978-0-606-36057-9(3))* Turtleback.

Stilton, Geronimo. The Helmet Holdup (Geronimo Stilton Micekings #6) 2017. (Geronimo Stilton Micekings Ser.: 6). (ENG., Illus.). 128p. (J). (gr. 2-5). pap. 7.99 *(978-1-338-15921-9(6)*, Scholastic Paperbacks) Scholastic, Inc.

Stilton, Gerónimo & Heim, Julia. Operation: Secret Recipe. Loizedda, Danilo et al, illus. 2017. 107p. (J). *(978-1-5379-1881-5(8))* Scholastic, Inc.

Stilton, Gerónimo & Schaffer, Andrea. The Helmet Holdup. Facciotto, Giuseppe & Costa, Alessandro, illus. 2017. 112p. (J). *(978-1-5379-5611-4(6))* Scholastic, Inc.

Stilton, Thea. Thea Stilton & the Blue Scarab Hunt. 2012. (Thea Stilton Ser.: 11). lib. bdg. 19.65 *(978-0-606-26183-8(4))* Turtleback.

—Thea Stilton & the Hollywood Hoax. 2016. (Thea Stilton Ser.: 23). lib. bdg. 18.40 *(978-0-606-38799-6(4))* Turtleback.

—Thea Stilton & the Prince's Emerald. 2012. (Thea Stilton Ser.: 12). lib. bdg. 19.65 *(978-0-606-26534-8(1))* Turtleback.

Styles, Walker. The Very First Case. Whitehouse, Ben, illus. 2018. (Rider Woofson Ser.: 10). (ENG.). 128p. (J). (gr. k-4). 16.99 *(978-1-5344-1272-9(7))*; pap. 5.99 *(978-1-5344-1271-2(9))* Little Simon. (Little Simon).

Summy, Barrie. I So Don't Do Famous. 2012. (I So Don't Do... Ser.). (ENG.). 304p. (J). (gr. 5). 7.99 *(978-0-385-73791-3(2)*, Yearling) Random Hse. Children's Bks.

Taylor, Joseph. Allison Investigates. 2009. 202p. pap. 12.95 *(978-0-9815894-1-1(3))* Four Star Publishing.

Terrell, Brandon. The Vanishing Treasure. Epelbaum, Mariano, illus. 2017. (Snoops, Inc Ser.). (ENG.). 112p. (J). (gr. 4-8). lib. bdg. 27.32 *(978-1-4965-4345-5(9)*, 134262, Stone Arch Bks.) Capstone.

Titus, Eve. Basil in Mexico. Galdone, Paul, illus. 2016. (Great Mouse Detective Ser.: 3). (ENG.). 112p. (J). (gr. 1-4). pap. 6.99 *(978-1-4814-6407-9(8)*, Aladdin) Simon & Schuster Children's Publishing.

—Basil in Mexico. Galdone, Paul, illus. 2016. (Great Mouse Detective Ser.: 3). (ENG.). 112p. (J). (gr. 1-4). 16.99 *(978-1-4814-6408-6(6)*, Simon & Schuster/Paula Wiseman Bks.) Simon & Schuster/Paula Wiseman Bks.

Toliver, Wendy. Lifted. 2010. (ENG.). 352p. (YA). (gr. 9-18). pap. 9.99 *(978-1-4169-9048-2(8)*, Simon Pulse) Simon Pulse.

Top Ten Clues You're Clueless. 2014. (ENG.). 304p. (YA). (gr. 8). pap. 9.99 *(978-0-06-227242-3(X)*, HarperTeen) HarperCollins Pubs.

Tosten, S. Kennedy. Troy's Amazing Universe Bk. 2: T for Toy. 2004. (Illus.). 149p. (YA). (gr. 2-18). pap. 13.95 *(978-0-9743185-1-6(5))* Brite Pr.

Twintig, Gus. The Clock Without a Face: A Gus Twintig Mystery. 2010. (Illus.). 30p. (J). (gr. 2-18). bds. 19.95 *(978-1-934781-71-5(1)*, 57ce4b2f-3c83-44ed-891c-1ae966831e7a) McSweeney's Publishing.

Umansky, Kaye. Solomon Snow & the Stolen Jewel. Nash, Scott, illus. 2007. (ENG.). 256p. (J). (gr. 2-5). 12.99 *(978-0-7636-2793-5(3))* Candlewick Pr.

Van der Merwe, Avril. Once upon a Rhinoceros. Greeff, Heidi-Kate, illus. 2018. (ENG.). 16p. pap. 7.50 *(978-1-4859-0037-5(9))* Penguin Random House South Africa ZAF. Dist: Casemate Pubs. & Bk. Distributors, LLC.

Vernon, Ursula. Dragonbreath #9: The Case of the Toxic Mutants. 2013. (Dragonbreath Ser.: 9). (ENG., Illus.). 208p. (J). (gr. 3-7). 14.99 *(978-0-8037-3847-8(1)*, Dial Bks) Penguin Young Readers Group.

Vicente, Alidis. The Missing Chancleta & Other Top-Secret Cases / la Chancleta Perdida y Otros Casos Secretos. 2013. (SPA & ENG., Illus.). 64p. (J). pap. 9.95 *(978-1-55885-779-7(6)*, Piñata Books) Arte Publico Pr.

Vulliamy, Clara. The Vacation Mystery (Dotty Detective, Book 6) 2019. (Dotty Detective Ser.: 6). (ENG.). 176p. (J). 4.99 *(978-0-00-830091-3(7)*, HarperCollins Children's Bks.) HarperCollins Pubs. Ltd. GBR. Dist: HarperCollins Pubs.

Wallace, Karen. Diamond Takers. 2007. (Lady Violet Mysteries Ser.: 3). (ENG.). 240p. (J). (gr. 4-7). pap. 9.95 *(978-1-4169-0100-6(0)*, Simon & Schuster Children's) Simon & Schuster, Ltd. GBR. Dist: Simon & Schuster, Inc.

Wells, Marcia. Doom at Grant's Tomb. Calo, Marcos, illus. 2017. (Eddie Red Undercover Ser.: 3). (ENG.). (J). (gr. 5-7). lib. bdg. 17.20 *(978-0-606-39813-8(9))* Turtleback.

—Eddie Red Undercover: Mystery in Mayan Mexico. Calo, Marcos, illus. 2016. (Eddie Red Undercover Ser.: 2). (ENG.). 224p. (J). (gr. 5-7). pap. 7.99 *(978-0-544-66850-8(2)*, 1625472, Clarion Bks.) HarperCollins Pubs.

West, Tracey. Secret of the Water Dragon. 2015. (Dragon Masters Ser.: 3). lib. bdg. 14.75 *(978-0-606-39886-2(4))* Turtleback.

—Secret of the Water Dragon: a Branches Book (Dragon Masters #3) Jones, Damien, illus. 2015. (Dragon Masters Ser.: 3). (ENG.). 96p. (J). (gr. 1-3). pap. 5.99 *(978-0-545-64628-4(6))* Scholastic, Inc.

White, Paul. Jungle Doctor in Slippery Places. 2011. (Flamingo Fiction 9-13s Ser.). (ENG., Illus.). 160p. (J). (gr. 4-7). pap. 8.99 *(978-1-84550-298-0(1)*, 2d5341c8-b7a7-41d9-9f98-f018ae7cd7c8) Christian Focus Pubns. GBR. Dist: Baker & Taylor Publisher Services (BTPS).

Widmark, Martin. The Diamond Mystery #1, No. 1. Willis, Helena, illus. 2014. (Whodunit Detective Agency Ser.: 1). (ENG.). 80p. (J). (gr. 2-4). 5.99 *(978-0-448-48066-4(2)*, Grosset & Dunlap) Penguin Young Readers Group.

Windsor, Justine. Goodly & Grave in a Deadly Case of Murder (Goodly & Grave, Book 2) 2019. (Goodly & Grave Ser.: 2). (ENG.). 320p. (J). 6.99 *(978-0-00-829426-7(7)*, HarperCollins Children's Bks.) HarperCollins Pubs. Ltd. GBR. Dist: HarperCollins Pubs.

Woodfine, Katherine. The Mystery of the Jeweled Moth. 2017. (Illus.). 352p. (J). pap. 6.99 *(978-1-61067-438-6(3))* Kane Miller.

—The Mystery of the Painted Dragon. 2017. (Illus.). 332p. (J). *(978-1-61067-695-3(5))* Kane Miller.

Woodson, Marion. Dinosaur Fever. 2008. (ENG.). 160p. (J). (gr. 4). pap. 11.99 *(978-1-55002-690-0(9))* Dundurn Pr. CAN. Dist: Publishers Group West (PGW).

Yee, Paul. Shu-Li & Tamara, 1 vol. Wang, Shaoli, illus. 2008. (Shu-Li Ser.: 1). (ENG.). 72p. (J). (gr. 1-3). per. 7.95 *(978-1-896580-93-7(9))* Tradewind Bks. CAN. Dist: Orca Bk. Pubs. USA.

THEOLOGY

see also Baptism; Christianity; Church; Ethics; Faith; God; Jesus Christ; Religion; Religion and Science; Spiritual Life; Worship

Arbo, Barbara. Scriptures for Kids. Ross, Melissa, illus. 2013. 24p. 19.95 *(978-1-61633-402-4(9))*; pap. 10.95 *(978-1-61633-403-1(7))* Guardian Angel Publishing, Inc.

Berlatsky, Noah, ed. The Catholic Church, 1 vol. 2010. (Opposing Viewpoints Ser.). (ENG.). 232p. (gr. 10-12). 50.43 *(978-0-7377-5104-8(5)*, af6ba42b-8d43-4bcf-a59a-aff18d500b61); pap. 34.80 *(978-0-7377-5105-5(3)*, e53a786a-56a1-4125-bde6-7e58b74a95a7) Greenhaven Publishing LLC. (Greenhaven Publishing).

Colkmire, Lance. Know It, Live It: Helping Kids Embrace Pentecostal Teachings. 2004. (Illus.). (J). per. 9.99 *(978-0-87148-468-0(4))* Pathway Pr.

Dant, Jennifer. Everybody Is Important: A Kids' Guide to Our Seven Principles. 2010. (J). pap. 6.00 *(978-1-55896-564-5(5)*, Skinner Hse. Bks.) Unitarian Universalist Assn.

Davenport, Jeff. God Is Really, Really Real: 30 Easily Taught Bible Doctrines. Looney, Bill, illus. 2015. (ENG.). 96p. (J). 16.99 *(978-0-89221-738-0(3)*, New Leaf Pr.) New Leaf Publishing Group.

Derrick, Tara. Theocracy: Religious Government, Vol. 8. 2018. (Systems of Government Ser.). (Illus.). 96p. (J). (gr. 7). 34.60 *(978-1-4222-4022-9(3))* Mason Crest.

Discover 1 John. (Discover Your Bible Ser.). (KOR.). (J). pap., stu. ed. 2.75 *(978-1-55883-240-4(8)*, 600220) C R C World Literature Ministries/Libros Desafio.

Una Historia Que no Cesa, 2 vols. 2003. (SPA., Illus.). 240p. (YA). 24.95 *(978-0-915741-18-2(0))* Stampley, C. D. Enterprises, Inc.

Is There Really a God? 2003. (BUL.). (YA). 0.75 *(978-1-893345-14-0(9))* Answers In Genesis.

Melilli, Julie. Special God. Stevens, Matt, illus. 2018. 64p. (J). 16.99 *(978-1-4335-6251-8(0))* Crossway.

Mudge, Michael. Spiritual Warfare Basic Training. 2012. 44p. pap. 21.99 *(978-1-4772-8539-8(3))* AuthorHouse.

Peckham, Lori, ed. Guide's Greatest Grace Stories. 2008. 160p. (J). pap. 11.99 *(978-0-8280-2390-0(5))* Review & Herald Publishing Assn.

Pierce, Seth J. What We Believe for Teens. 2007. (J). pap. 11.99 *(978-0-8163-2213-8(9))* Pacific Pr. Publishing Assn.

Reynolds, Ralph V. Dividing the Word of Truth. 193p. (YA). (gr. 9). pap. 14.95 *(978-1-877917-08-0(7))* Alpha Bible Pubns.

—Usando Bien la Palabra de Verdad. Geissler, Darry & Geissler, Kimberly, eds. Crossley, Darry, tr. (SPA.). 220p. (Orig.). (YA). pap. 14.95 *(978-1-877917-12-7(5))* Alpha Bible Pubns.

Shewan, Edward. Manual of Christian Doctrine, Answer Key. 2004. pap. 3.95 *(978-1-930367-99-9(6)*, CLP10091) Christian Liberty Pr.

Strobel, Lee. Case for Grace for Kids, 1 vol. 2015. (Case for... Series for Kids Ser.). (ENG., Illus.). 176p. (J). pap. 7.99 *(978-0-310-73656-1(0))* Zonderkidz.

Thomas, Jerry D. & Thomas, Kitty. Step by Step: Helping Children Understand the Principles of Steps to Christ. 2008. (Illus.). 80p. (J). pap. 11.99 *(978-0-8163-2277-0(5))* Pacific Pr. Publishing Assn.

Through Christ Our Lord. (YA). (gr. 9-12). 19.00 *(978-1-931555-42-5(7))* Our Lady of Victory Schl.

Tyner, Stuart. The Meanest Man in the Army: And Other Stories of Grace. 2014. (ENG.). (J). pap. 12.99 *(978-0-8280-2729-8(3))* Review & Herald Publishing Assn.

THEOLOGY, DEVOTIONAL

see Prayers

THEORETICAL CHEMISTRY

see Chemistry, Physical and Theoretical

THEORY OF NUMBERS
see Number Theory

THEORY OF SETS
see Set Theory

THEOTOCOPULI, DOMINICO, CALLED EL GRECO, 1541?-1614
see Greco, 1541?-1614

THERESE, DE LISIEUX, SAINT, 1873-1897

Glavich, Mary Kathleen. Saint Therese of Lisieux: The Way of Love. Esquinaldo, Virginia, tr. Esquinaldo, Virginia, illus. 2003. (Encounter the Saints Ser.). 132p. (J). pap. 5.95 *(978-0-8198-7074-2(9)*, 332-370) Pauline Bks. & Media.

Monahan, Joan. St. Therese of Lisieux: Missionary of Love. 2003. (ENG., Illus.). 144p. (J). pap. 9.95 *(978-0-8091-6710-4(7)*, 6710-7) Paulist Pr.

THERMODYNAMICS
see also Heat; Quantum Theory

Berne, Emma Carlson. Hot! Heat Energy, 1 vol. 2013. (Energy Everywhere Ser.). (ENG., Illus.). 24p. (J). (gr. 2-3). pap. 9.25 *(978-1-4488-9752-0(1)*, b2f8e980-d884-450a-838f-d190fe539726); lib. bdg. 26.27 *(978-1-4488-9647-9(9)*, 1c9000b7-f353-4455-aee6-4006dbdaeb31) Rosen Publishing Group, Inc., The. (PowerKids Pr.)

Connors, Kathleen. Heat, 1 vol. 2018. (Look at Physical Science Ser.). (ENG.). 32p. (gr. 2-2). 28.27 *(978-1-5382-2147-1(0)*, 0f62c6aa-d308-48c1-8fb1-14fd3bd50d02) Stevens, Gareth Publishing LLLP.

Jennings, Terry J. Hot & Cold. 2009. (J). 28.50 *(978-1-59920-274-7(3))* Black Rabbit Bks.

Klepeis, Alicia Z. How Does Heat Move?, 1 vol. 2018. (How Does It Move? Forces & Motion Ser.). (ENG.). 32p. (gr. 3-3). 30.21 *(978-1-5026-3775-8(8)*, 002a92a7-7180-4326-b1c3-29375f2aeb52) Cavendish Square Publishing LLC.

Lawrence, Ellen. Heat. 2016. (FUN-Damental Experiments Ser.). (ENG., Illus.). 24p. (J). (gr. -1-3). 26.99 *(978-1-943553-19-8(X))* Bearport Publishing Co., Inc.

Lindeen, Mary. Hot & Cold. 2017. (Beginning-To-Read Ser.). (ENG.). 32p. (J). (gr. k-2). pap. 13.26 *(978-1-68404-102-2(3))*; (Illus.). 22.60 *(978-1-59953-883-9(0))* Norwood Hse. Pr.

Magloff, Lisa. Experiments with Heat & Energy, 1 vol. 2010. (Cool Science Ser.). (ENG.). 32p. (J). (gr. 4-5). lib. bdg. 30.67 *(978-1-4339-3450-6(7)*, efd098e5-7e3e-477d-98d8-95e1eb17e64f); (Illus.). pap. 11.50 *(978-1-4339-3451-3(5)*, 7d0f8294-a8b8-4ef5-93a0-ad1dadef3748) Stevens, Gareth Publishing LLLP. (Gareth Stevens Learning Library).

Rivera, Sheila. Heating. 2007. (First Step Nonfiction — Changing Matter Ser.). (ENG., Illus.). 8p. (J). (gr. k-2). pap. 5.99 *(978-0-8225-6415-7(7)*, f6e755d5-997c-47bd-8a5e-b591f3d38ddb) Lerner Publishing Group.

Spilsbury, Richard. Investigating Heat. 2018. (Investigating Science Challenges Ser.). (ENG., Illus.). 32p. (J). (gr. 4-4). *(978-0-7787-4206-7(7))*; pap. *(978-0-7787-4265-4(2))* Crabtree Publishing Co.

Steinberg, Lynnae D. What Is Heat Energy?, 1 vol. 2017. (Let's Find Out! Forms of Energy Ser.). (ENG., Illus.). 32p. (J). (gr. 2-3). pap. 13.90 *(978-1-68048-701-5(9)*, 43000ab3-6c64-492b-8492-2017a7074a29, Britannica Educational Publishing) Rosen Publishing Group, Inc., The.

Thomas, Isabel. Experiments with Heating & Cooling. 2015. (Read & Experiment Ser.). (ENG., Illus.). 32p. (J). (gr. 2-4). 33.32 *(978-1-4109-6839-5(1)*, 128049, Raintree) Capstone.

THERMOMETERS
see also Temperature

Amstutz, Lisa J. Thermometers. 2019. (Science Tools Ser.). (ENG., Illus.). 24p. (J). (gr. k-2). pap. 6.95 *(978-1-9771-0063-4(5)*, 138214); lib. bdg. 27.32 *(978-1-9771-0059-7(7)*, 138210) Capstone. (Pebble).

Doudna, Kelly. If You Prefer, I'll Use a Thermometer!, 1 vol. 2007. (Science Made Simple Ser.). (Illus.). 24p. (J). (gr. k-3). lib. bdg. 24.21 *(978-1-59928-594-8(0)*, SandCastle) ABDO Publishing Co.

Johnson, Robin. What Is Temperature? 2012. (ENG.). 24p. (J). *(978-0-7787-0755-4(5))*; (Illus.). pap. *(978-0-7787-0762-2(8))* Crabtree Publishing Co.

Lin, Yoming S. Fahrenheit, Celsius, & Their Temperature Scales, 1 vol. 2011. (Eureka! Ser.). (ENG., Illus.). 24p. (YA). (gr. 2-3). lib. bdg. 26.27 *(978-1-4488-5035-8(5)*, 81827d65-afba-4a2b-ac0a-6c010a6999e9) Rosen Publishing Group, Inc., The.

Lipschultz, Wes. Is It Hot or Cold? Learning to Use a Thermometer, 1 vol. 2010. (Math for the REAL World Ser.). (ENG.). 12p. (gr. 1-2). pap. 5.90 *(978-0-8239-8848-8(1)*, 6ad9e6e8-75d6-4385-9f90-178944487318, Rosen Classroom) Rosen Publishing Group, Inc., The.

Metz, Lorijo. Using Thermometers, 1 vol. 2013. (Science Tools Ser.). (ENG., Illus.). 24p. (J). (gr. 2-3). 26.27 *(978-1-4488-9684-4(3)*, e1673e75-bc28-4d89-844f-a59aa846ed4e); pap. 9.25 *(978-1-4488-9826-8(9)*, 97041806-9183-43f6-9f4c-1f0d6141dd76) Rosen Publishing Group, Inc., The. (PowerKids Pr.).

O'Mara, John. How Does a Thermometer Work?, 1 vol. 2020. (Everyday Mysteries Ser.). (ENG.). 24p. (J). (gr. 1-2). pap. 9.15 *(978-1-5382-5663-3(0)*, b79f45ef-abbc-4e32-84ac-23c2ed1373c3) Stevens, Gareth Publishing LLLP.

Roberts, Abigail B. Using a Thermometer. 2017. (Super Science Tools Ser.). 24p. (gr. 1-2). pap. 48.90 *(978-1-4824-6410-8(1))* Stevens, Gareth Publishing LLLP.

Rustad, Martha E. H. Measuring Temperature. 2019. (Measuring Masters Ser.). (ENG., Illus.). 24p. (J). (gr. -1-2). lib. bdg. 27.32 *(978-1-9771-0369-7(3)*, 139343, Capstone Pr.) Capstone.

Sullivan, Navin. Temperature, 1 vol. 2007. (Measure Up! Ser.). (ENG., Illus.). 48p. (gr. 4-4). lib. bdg. 34.07 *(978-0-7614-2322-5(2)*, f5d8ab18-4ea4-486e-8a2c-d6e996d4c6bc) Cavendish Square Publishing LLC.

THERMOMETERS AND THERMOMETRY
see Temperature Measurements; Thermometers

THERMOPOLIS, MIA (FICTITIOUS CHARACTER)—FICTION

Cabot, Meg. The Princess Diaries. 2008. (Princess Diaries: 1). (ENG.). 256p. (YA). (gr. 8). pap. 10.99 *(978-0-06-147993-9(4))*Vols. 1-3, Set. 2006. (Princess Diaries: Vol. I). (J). pap., pap. 19.99 *(978-0-06-115389-1(3))* HarperCollins Pubs. (HarperTeen).

—The Princess Diaries. 2008. 20.00 *(978-0-7569-8793-0(8))* Perfection Learning Corp.

—The Princess Diaries. unabr. ed. 2004. (Princess Diaries: Vol. I). 240p. (J). (gr. 7-18). pap. 38.00 incl. audio *(978-0-8072-0669-0(5)*, Listening Library) Random Hse. Audio Publishing Group.

—The Princess Diaries. 2008. (Princess Diaries: 1). (YA). lib. bdg. 20.85 *(978-1-4178-2328-4(3))* Turtleback.

—The Princess Diaries Box Set: The Princess Diaries; Princess in the Spotlight; Princess in Love. 2003. (Princess Diaries). 304p. (gr. 7-18). pap. 19.99 *(978-0-06-058745-1(8))* HarperCollins Pubs.

—The Princess Diaries, Volume IV: Princess in Waiting. 2008. (Princess Diaries: 4). (ENG.). 256p. (YA). (gr. 8). pap. 10.99 *(978-0-06-154364-7(0)*, HarperTeen) HarperCollins Pubs.

THESEUS (GREEK MYTHOLOGY)

Davis, Graeme. Theseus & the Maze of the Minotaur, 1 vol. 2015. (Heroes & Legends Ser.). (ENG., Illus.). 88p. (J). (gr. 8-8). 38.80 *(978-1-4994-6178-7(X)*, 12ba68ef-46df-47c2-bea3-62fd8c6cb6bb, Rosen Young Adult) Rosen Publishing Group, Inc., The.

Ehrmann, Johanna. Theseus & the Minotaur, 1 vol., 1. 2013. (Jr. Graphic Myths: Greek Heroes Ser.). (ENG., Illus.). 24p. (J). (gr. 2-3). 28.93 *(978-1-4777-6236-3(1)*, 8fd6fee2-e179-42e6-a39f-3aa79126a15b, PowerKids Pr.) Rosen Publishing Group, Inc., The.

Haus, Estudio, illus. Theseus & the Minotaur: A Graphic Retelling. 2015. (Ancient Myths Ser.). (ENG.). 32p. (J). (gr. 3-9). lib. bdg. 31.32 *(978-1-4914-2075-1(8)*, 127553, Capstone Pr.) Capstone.

Hoena, Blake. The Quest of Theseus: An Interactive Mythological Adventure. Arcabascio, Carolyn, illus. 2017. (You Choose: Ancient Greek Myths Ser.). (ENG.). 112p. (J). (gr. 3-7). pap. 6.95 *(978-1-5157-4826-7(X)*, 134441, Capstone Pr.) Capstone.

—The Quest of Theseus: An Interactive Mytholoical Adventure. Arcabascio, Carolyn, illus. 2017. (You Choose: Ancient Greek Myths Ser.). (ENG.). 112p. (J). (gr. 3-7). lib. bdg. 32.65 *(978-1-5157-4821-2(9)*, 134437, Capstone Pr.) Capstone.

Jeffrey, Gary. Theseus Battles the Minotaur, 1 vol. 2012. (Graphic Mythical Heroes Ser.). (ENG., Illus.). 24p. (J). (gr. 3-3). pap. 9.15 *(978-1-4339-7528-8(9)*, 35a68f89-baca-4fa5-9a5e-25ec8c12fcbe); lib. bdg. 26.60 *(978-1-4339-7527-1(0)*, 94383b1b-7d20-48d0-8a69-0a5b89429254) Stevens, Gareth Publishing LLLP.

Limke, Jeff. Theseus: Battling the Minotaur. 2009. pap. 52.95 *(978-0-7613-4761-3(5))* Lerner Publishing Group.

—Theseus: Battling the Minotaur [a Greek Myth]. McCrea, John, illus. 2008. (Graphic Myths & Legends Ser.). (ENG.). 48p. (J). (gr. 4-8). pap. 9.99 *(978-0-8225-8517-6(0)*, bdb17585-82db-4390-8512-a245de69425a, Graphic Universe™) Lerner Publishing Group.

McCaughrean, Geraldine, retold by. Theseus. 2005. (Heroes Ser.). (ENG., Illus.). 120p. (J). (gr. 4-10). 17.95 *(978-0-8126-2739-8(3))* Cricket Bks.

Nagle, Frances. The Minotaur, 1 vol. 2016. (Monsters! Ser.). (ENG., Illus.). 32p. (J). (gr. 1-2). pap. 11.50 *(978-1-4824-4871-9(8)*, ebfbbc24-ece1-4113-bff2-cd07e87e3c3e) Stevens, Gareth Publishing LLLP.

Tracy, Kathleen. Theseus. 2007. (Profiles in Greek & Roman Mythology Ser.). (Illus.). 48p. (YA). (gr. 4-7). lib. bdg. 29.95 *(978-1-58415-554-6(X))* Mitchell Lane Pubs.

THIEVES
see Robbers and Outlaws

THINKING
see Thought and Thinking

THIRTY YEARS' WAR, 1618-1648

Roscoe, Kelly, ed. The Emergence of Modern Europe, 1 vol. 2017. (Power & Religion in Medieval & Renaissance Times Ser.). (ENG., Illus.). 112p. (gr. 10-10). 37.82 *(978-1-68048-621-6(7)*, 7a7149ed-cb3a-4624-949f-b3d634fbd13b, Britannica Educational Publishing) Rosen Publishing Group, Inc., The.

THOMAS, A BECKET, SAINT, 1118?-1170

Hilliam, David. Thomas Becket: English Saint & Martyr. 2009. (Leaders of the Middle Ages Ser.). 112p. (gr. 5-8). 66.50 *(978-1-61513-902-6(8)*, Rosen Reference) Rosen Publishing Group, Inc., The.

THOMAS, AQUINAS, SAINT, 1225?-1274

Trouvé, Marianne Lorraine. Saint Thomas Aquinas: Missionary of Truth. Morrison, Cathy, illus. 2015. 137p. (J). pap. 8.95 *(978-0-8198-9026-9(X))* Pauline Bks. & Media.

THOMAS MORE, SAINT, 1478-1535
see More, Thomas, Sir, Saint, 1478-1535

THOMAS, THE TANK ENGINE (FICTITIOUS CHARACTER)—FICTION

Allcroft, Britt, et al. Thomas & the Buzzy Bees. 2017. (Illus.). 23p. (J). *(978-1-5182-3651-8(0))* Random Hse., Inc.

Awdry, W. A Crack in the Track (Thomas & Friends) 2004. (Bright & Early Board Books(TM) Ser.). (ENG., Illus.). 24p. (J). (— 1). bds. 4.99 *(978-0-375-82755-6(2)*, Random Hse. Bks. for Young Readers) Random Hse. Children's Bks.

—Fast Train, Slow Train (Thomas & Friends) 2014. (Big Bright & Early Board Book Ser.). (ENG., Illus.). 24p. (J). (— 1). bds. 6.99 *(978-0-385-37408-8(9)*, Random Hse. Bks. for Young Readers) Random Hse. Children's Bks.

—Go, Go, Thomas! 2013. (Thomas & Friends 8X8 Ser.). lib. bdg. 14.75 *(978-0-606-26992-6(4))* Turtleback.

—The Good Sport. Courtney, Richard, illus. 2016. 24p. (J). *(978-1-5182-1481-3(9))* Random Hse., Inc.

—Hero of the Rails (Thomas & Friends) 2010. (Little Golden Book Ser.). (ENG., Illus.). 24p. (J). (gr. -1-k). 5.99 *(978-0-375-85950-2(0)*, Golden Bks.) Random Hse. Children's Bks.

—The Lost Crown of Sodor. 2013. (Thomas & Friends 8X8 Ser.). lib. bdg. 13.55 *(978-0-606-32227-0(2))* Turtleback.

—The Lost Ship (Thomas & Friends) Courtney, Richard, illus. 2015. (Step into Reading Ser.). (ENG.). 32p. (J). (gr. -1-1). 5.99 *(978-0-553-52171-9(3)*, Random Hse. Bks. for Young Readers) Random Hse. Children's Bks.

—Not So Fast, Bash & Dash! 2013. (Thomas & Friends Step into Reading Ser.). lib. bdg. 13.55 *(978-0-606-32228-7(0))* Turtleback.

—The Rocket Returns. 2014. (Thomas & Friends Step into Reading Ser.). lib. bdg. 13.55 *(978-0-606-35207-9(4))* Turtleback.

—Santa's Little Engine. 2014. (Thomas & Friends Step into Reading Ser.). lib. bdg. 13.55 *(978-0-606-36014-2(X))* Turtleback.

—Search & Rescue! (Thomas & Friends) Random House, illus. 2012. (Pictureback(R) Ser.). (ENG.). 16p. (J). (gr. -1-2). pap. 4.99 *(978-0-307-93029-3(7)*, Random Hse. Bks. for Young Readers) Random Hse. Children's Bks.

—Secret of the Green Engine. 2012. (Thomas & Friends Step into Reading Ser.). lib. bdg. 13.55 *(978-0-606-26804-2(9))* Turtleback.

—Thomas' 123 Book. 2013. (Thomas & Friends 8X8 Ser.). lib. bdg. 13.55 *(978-0-606-26991-9(6))* Turtleback.

—Thomas & Friends: Blue Train, Green Train (Thomas & Friends) Stubbs, Tommy, illus. 2007. (Bright & Early Board Books(TM) Ser.). (ENG.). 24p. (J). (— 1). bds. 4.99 *(978-0-375-83984-9(4)*, Random Hse. Bks. for Young Readers) Random Hse. Children's Bks.

—Thomas & Friends Little Golden Book Library (Thomas & Friends) Thomas & the Great Discovery; Hero of the Rails; Misty Island Rescue; Day of the Diesels; Blue Mountain Mystery, 5 vols. Stubbs, Tommy, illus. 2013. (Little Golden Book Ser.). (ENG.). 120p. (J). (-k). 29.95 *(978-0-449-81482-6(3)*, Golden Bks.) Random Hse. Children's Bks.

—Thomas & Friends: My Red Railway Book Box (Thomas & Friends) Go, Train, GO!; Stop, Train, Stop!; a Crack in the Track!; & Blue Train, Green Train, 4 vols. Stubbs, Tommy, illus. 2008. (Bright & Early Board Books(TM) Ser.). (ENG.). 96p. (J). (— 1). bds. 16.99 *(978-0-375-84322-8(1)*, Random Hse. Bks. for Young Readers) Random Hse. Children's Bks.

—Thomas & Friends Story Time Collection (Thomas & Friends) Courtney, Richard & Stubbs, Tommy, illus. 2014. (ENG.). 320p. (J). (gr. -1-2). 19.99 *(978-0-553-49678-9(6)*, Random Hse. Bks. for Young Readers) Random Hse. Children's Bks.

—Thomas & the Great Discovery (Thomas & Friends) Stubbs, Tommy, illus. 2009. (Little Golden Book Ser.). (ENG.). 24p. (J). (gr. -1-2). 5.99 *(978-0-375-85153-7(4)*, Golden Bks.) Random Hse. Children's Bks.

—Thomas & the Shark (Thomas & Friends) Courtney, Richard, illus. 2013. (Step into Reading Ser.). (ENG.). 32p. (J). (gr. -1-1). pap. 5.99 *(978-0-307-98200-1(9)*, Random Hse. Bks. for Young Readers) Random Hse. Children's Bks.

—Thomas Comes to Breakfast (Thomas & Friends) Courtney, Richard, illus. 2004. (Step into Reading Ser.). (ENG.). 32p. (J). (gr. -1-1). pap. 4.99 *(978-0-375-82892-8(3)*, Random Hse. Bks. for Young Readers) Random Hse. Children's Bks.

—Treasure on the Tracks. 2013. (Thomas & Friends Step into Reading Ser.). lib. bdg. 13.55 *(978-0-606-32229-4(9))* Turtleback.

—A Valentine for Percy. Courtney, Richard, illus. 2015. 24p. (J). *(978-1-4806-9757-7(5))* Random Hse., Inc.

Awdry, Wilbert V. Risky Rails! 2012. (Thomas & Friends 8X8 Ser.). lib. bdg. 13.55 *(978-0-606-26803-5(0))* Turtleback.

—Thomas & the Shark. 2013. (Thomas & Friends Step into Reading Ser.). lib. bdg. 13.55 *(978-0-606-26996-4(7))* Turtleback.

From Self to God. 2010. (ENG.). 140p. 21.95 *(978-1-4502-2116-0(5))* iUniverse, Inc.

Golden Books. Thomas & the Dinosaur (Thomas & Friends) Lapadula, Thomas, illus. 2015. (Little Golden Book Ser.). (ENG.). 24p. (J). (-k). 5.99 *(978-0-553-49681-9(6)*, Golden Bks.) Random Hse. Children's Bks.

—Thomas & the Easter Eggs (Thomas & Friends) 2016. (Little Golden Book Ser.). (ENG., Illus.). 24p. (J). (gr. -1-k). 4.99 *(978-1-101-93252-0(X)*, Golden Bks.) Random Hse. Children's Bks.

PI Kids. Thomas & Friends: On Time with Thomas. 2016. (ENG., Illus.). 12p. 21.99 ***(978-1-5037-1436-6(5)***, 2294, PI Kids) Phoenix International Publications, Inc.

PI Kids. Thomas & Friends: 12 Board Books. Artful Doodlers et al, illus. 2015. (ENG.). 120p. (J). bds., bds., bds. 16.99 *(978-1-4508-9373-2(2)*, 4213, PI Kids) Phoenix International Publications, Inc.

PI, Kids. Thomas Little Steering Wheel. 2015. (ENG., Illus.). 12p. (J). *(978-1-4508-8632-1(9)*, 1450886329) Publications International, Ltd.

Publications International Ltd. Staff, creator. Thomas & Friends Musical Pop-up Treasury. 2007. (Thomas & Friends Ser.). (Illus.). 24p. (gr. -1). 15.98 *(978-1-4127-9293-6(2))* Publications International, Ltd.

Publications International Ltd. Staff, ed. Right on Time Rescues. 2010. 14p. (J). bds. 16.98 *(978-1-4127-1872-1(4))* Phoenix International Publications, Inc.

—Thomas & Friends: A Busy Day on Sodor. 2009. (Illus.). 18p. (J). bds. 10.98 *(978-1-4127-1735-9(3)*, PIL Kids) Publications International, Ltd.

—Thomas & Friends: Engine Roll Call. 2011. 8p. (J). bds. 7.98 *(978-1-4508-1435-5(2))* Publications International, Ltd.

—Thomas & Friends: Let's Go, Thomas! 2010. 14p. (J). 17.98 *(978-1-4508-0212-3(5))* Phoenix International Publications, Inc.

—Thomas & Friends: Lights, Music & Me! 2011. 14p. (J). bds. 10.98 *(978-1-4508-1562-8(6))* Publications International, Ltd.

—Thomas & Friends: Play-a-Tune Puzzle Book. 2010. 10p. (J). bds. 13.98 *(978-1-60553-756-6(X))* Publications International, Ltd.

—Thomas & Friends: Super Look & Find Activity Pad with Stickers. 2011. 64p. (J). 10.98 *(978-1-4508-1563-5(4))* Publications International, Ltd.

—Thomas & Friends Super Look & Find Activity Pad. 2011. 64p. (J). 10.98 *(978-1-4508-1863-6(3))*; 13.98 *(978-1-4508-1199-6(X))* Publications International, Ltd.

—Thomas Songs Play & Learn. 2010. 24p. (J). 12.98 *(978-1-4508-0115-7(3))* Phoenix International Publications, Inc.

—Thomas the Tank Good Morning Engines. 2012. (ENG.). 12p. (J). bds. 14.99 *(978-0-7853-8282-9(8)*, 1340) Phoenix International Publications, Inc.

—Trains. 2011. 12p. (J). bds. 13.98 *(978-1-4508-1138-5(8))* Publications International, Ltd.

Random House. Five Tank Engine Tales (Thomas & Friends) Courtney, Richard, illus. 2015. (Step into Reading Ser.). (ENG.). 160p. (J). (gr. -1-1). pap. 8.99 *(978-0-385-38496-4(3)*, Random Hse. Bks. for Young Readers) Random Hse. Children's Bks.

—My Thomas Potty Book (Thomas & Friends) 2016. (ENG., Illus.). 14p. (J). (gr. -1 — 1). bds. 9.99 *(978-1-101-93427-2(1)*, Random Hse. Bks. for Young Readers) Random Hse. Children's Bks.

—The Runaway Kite. 2018. (Thomas & Friends Step into Reading Ser.). lib. bdg. 14.75 *(978-0-606-40931-5(9))* Turtleback.

—The Runaway Kite (Thomas & Friends) 2018. (Step into Reading Ser.). (ENG., Illus.). 24p. (J). (gr. -1-2). pap. 4.99 *(978-0-399-55768-2(7))*; lib. bdg. 12.99 *(978-1-5247-6903-1(7))* Random Hse. Children's Bks. (Random Hse. Bks. for Young Readers).

—Thomas & Friends 5-Minute Stories: the Sleepytime Collection (Thomas & Friends) 2016. (ENG., Illus.). 160p. (J). (gr. -1-2). 12.99 *(978-0-399-55207-6(3)*, Random Hse. Bks. for Young Readers) Random Hse. Children's Bks.

Rev. Awdry, W. Thomas Saves Easter! (Thomas & Friends) Stubbs, Tommy, illus. 2013. (ENG.). 12p. (J). (-k). bds. 6.99 *(978-0-307-98158-5(4)*, Golden Bks.) Random Hse. Children's Bks.

Thomas The Tank Engine & Egmont Staff. Thomas & Friends. 2008. (Illus.). 140p. *(978-0-603-56338-6(4))* Farshore.

Thomas the Tank Engine. 2012. *(978-0-7948-3764-8(6))* Farshore.

Webster, Christy. Get Rolling with Phonics (Thomas & Friends) 12 Step into Reading Books, 12 vols. 2016. (Step into Reading Ser.). (ENG., Illus.). 144p. (J). (gr. -1-2). pap. 12.99 *(978-1-101-93726-6(2)*, Random Hse. Bks. for Young Readers) Random Hse. Children's Bks.

THOMSON, J. J. (JOSEPH JOHN), SIR, 1856-1940

Sherman, Josepha. J. J. Thomson & the Discovery of Electrons. 2005. (Uncharted, Unexplored, & Unexplained Ser.). (Illus.). 48p. (J). (gr. 4-8). lib. bdg. 29.95 *(978-1-58415-370-2(9))* Mitchell Lane Pubs.

THOREAU, HENRY DAVID, 1817-1862

Coddington, Andrew. Henry David Thoreau: Writer of the Transcendentalist Movement, 1 vol. 2016. (Great American Thinkers Ser.). (ENG.). 128p. (YA). (gr. 9-9). 47.36 *(978-1-5026-1928-0(8)*, c7412a25-5d57-4984-96fe-10de8f021b02) Cavendish Square Publishing LLC.

Johnson, D. B. Henry Builds a Cabin. 2019. (Henry Book Ser.). (ENG., Illus.). 32p. (J). (gr. -1-3). pap. 7.99 *(978-0-358-11202-0(8)*, 1749849, Clarion Bks.) HarperCollins Pubs.

Locker, Thomas. Walking with Henry: The Life & Works of Henry David Thoreau. 2011. (ENG., Illus.). 32p. (J). (gr. -1-5). pap. 21.95 *(978-1-55591-016-7(5))* Fulcrum Publishing.

McCurdy, Michael. Walden Then & Now: An Alphabetical Tour of Henry Thoreau's Pond. McCurdy, Michael, illus. 2010. (ENG., Illus.). 32p. (J). (gr. 2-12). 16.95 *(978-1-58089-253-7(1))* Charlesbridge Publishing, Inc.

Meltzer, Milton. Henry David Thoreau: A Biography. 2007. (Literary Greats Ser.). (ENG., Illus.). 160p. (gr. 7-12). lib. bdg. 33.26 *(978-0-8225-5893-4(9)*, Twenty-First Century Bks.) Lerner Publishing Group.

Miller, Derek. Henry David Thoreau: Civil Disobedience, 1 vol. 2017. (Peaceful Protesters Ser.). (ENG.). 112p. (YA). (gr. 9-9). 44.50 *(978-1-5026-3112-1(1)*, 4b717c79-3772-4863-b139-314149e81f94); pap. 20.99 *(978-1-5026-3394-1(9)*, 76a179c1-ef69-4873-9b81-1b0d2136d836) Cavendish Square Publishing LLC.

Niver, Heather Moore. Henry David Thoreau: Author of Civil Disobedience. 2017. (Spotlight on Civic Courage: Heroes of Conscience Ser.). 48p. (J). (gr. 10-15). 70.50 *(978-1-5383-8113-7(3))*; (ENG.). (gr. 6-6). pap. 12.75 *(978-1-5383-8112-0(5)*, 7c10f464-f9db-4f25-8dab-18c09483a071) Rosen Publishing Group, Inc., The. (Rosen Young Adult).

Olson, Steven P. Henry David Thoreau: American Naturalist, Writer, & Transcendentalist. 2009. (Library of American Thinkers Ser.). 112p. (gr. 6-6). 66.50 *(978-1-60853-513-2(4)*, Rosen Reference) Rosen Publishing Group, Inc., The.

Porcellino, John. Thoreau at Walden. Porcellino, John, illus. 2009. (ENG., Illus.). 112p. (J). (gr. 5-18). pap. 9.99 *(978-1-4231-0039-3(5))* Hyperion Pr.

—Thoreau at Walden. Porcellino, John, illus. 2018. (Center for Cartoon Studies Presents Ser.). (ENG., Illus.). 112p. (J). (gr. 5-9). 17.99 *(978-1-368-02233-0(2))*; pap. 12.99 *(978-1-368-02710-6(5))* Little, Brown Bks. for Young Readers.

Smith, Corinne Hosfeld. Henry David Thoreau for Kids: His Life & Ideas, with 21 Activities. 2016. (For Kids Ser.: 64). (ENG., Illus.). 128p. (J). (gr. 4). pap. 16.95 *(978-1-61373-146-8(9))* Chicago Review Pr., Inc.

Thoreau, Henry D. Walking. Clifton Johnson, illus. 2010. 100p. pap. 3.49 *(978-1-60386-305-6(2)*, Watchmaker Publishing) Wexford College Pr.

THOROUGHFARES
see Roads; Streets

THORPE, JIM, 1888-1953

Bruchac, Joseph. Jim Thorpe, Original All-American. 2008. 288p. (YA). (gr. 7-18). 10.99 *(978-0-14-241233-6(3)*, Speak) Penguin Young Readers Group.

Cain, Marie Mowery. Who Was Jim Thorpe? 2013. (Big Books, Red Ser.). (ENG & SPA., Illus.). 16p. pap. 33.00 *(978-1-59246-226-1(X))* Big Books, by George!

Fandel, Jennifer. Jim Thorpe: Greatest Athlete in the World, 1 vol. Whigham, Rod, illus. 2008. (Graphic Biographies Ser.). (ENG.). 32p. (J). (gr. 3-9). per. 8.10 *(978-1-4296-1773-4(X)*, 94820) Capstone.

T U V

Golus, Carrie. Jim Thorpe. 2008. pap. 58.95 *(978-0-8225-9399-7(8))* Lerner Publishing Group.

Jim Thorpe, Mejor Atleta del Mundo. 2003. (Notas Biograficas Ser.). (SPA., Illus.). pap. 48.95 *(978-0-8136-5916-9(7))* Modern Curriculum Pr.

Schuman, Michael A. Jim Thorpe: There's No Such Thing As 'Can't', 1 vol. 2008. (Americans: the Spirit of a Nation Ser.). (ENG., Illus.). 128p. (gr. 5-6). lib. bdg. 35.93 *(978-0-7660-3021-3(0)*, 6e11a4a1-2ad5-4fa7-bc8c-6182bd6e3be3) Enslow Publishing, LLC.

Sheinkin, Steve. Undefeated: Jim Thorpe & the Carlisle Indian School Football Team. 2017. (ENG., Illus.). 288p. (J). 21.99 *(978-1-59643-954-2(8)*, 900125600) Roaring Brook Pr.

—Undefeated: Jim Thorpe & the Carlisle Indian School Football Team. 2019. (ENG., Illus.). 288p. (J). pap. 14.99 *(978-1-250-29447-0(9)*, 900195080) Square Fish.

THOUGHT AND THINKING

see also Intellect; Logic; Perception; Reasoning

Athans, Sandra K. & Parente, Robin W. Tips & Tricks for Determining Point of View & Purpose, 1 vol. 2014. (Common Core Readiness Guide to Reading Ser.). (ENG.). 64p. (J). (gr. 6-6). 36.13 *(978-1-4777-7555-4(2)*, d947b5da-ca60-4d30-8084-35038bcf3a8f, Rosen Reference) Rosen Publishing Group, Inc., The.

—Tips & Tricks for Evaluating an Argument & Its Claims, 1 vol. 2014. (Common Core Readiness Guide to Reading Ser.). (ENG.). 64p. (YA). (gr. 6-6). 36.13 *(978-1-4777-7559-2(5)*, 438b0b58-4c39-45ea-9115-7c51509714d1) Rosen Publishing Group, Inc., The.

Baker, Michael. Mind Benders Level 1: Deductive Thinking Skills. 2013. (Mind Benders Ser.). 56p. (gr. -1-k). pap. 9.99 *(978-0-89455-872-6(2))* Critical Thinking Co., The.

—Mind Benders Level 2: Deductive Thinking Skills. 2013. (Mind Benders Ser.). 64p. (gr. 1-2). pap. 9.99 *(978-0-89455-873-3(0))* Critical Thinking Co., The.

Black, Howard & Parks, Sandra. Building Thinking Skills Level 1. 2013. (Building Thinking Skills Ser.). (ENG.). 376p. (gr. 2-3). pap. 29.99 *(978-1-60144-149-2(5))* Critical Thinking Co., The.

—Building Thinking Skills Level 2. 2013. (Building Thinking Skills Ser.). (ENG.). 408p. (gr. 4-6). pap. 29.99 *(978-1-60144-150-8(9))* Critical Thinking Co., The.

Bluedorn, Nathaniel & Bluedorn, Hans. The Thinking Toolbox: Thirty-Five Lessons That Will Build Your Reasoning Skills. LaPierre, Richard, illus. 2005. 234p. per. 25.00 *(978-0-9745315-1-9(0)*, 4000) Christian Logic.

Bow, James. Evaluating Arguments about Education. 2018. (State Your Case Ser.). 48p. (J). (gr. 5-6). *(978-0-7787-5076-5(0))* Crabtree Publishing Co.

—Evaluating Arguments about Sports & Entertainment. 2018. (State Your Case Ser.). (Illus.). 48p. (J). (gr. 5-6). *(978-0-7787-5078-9(7))* Crabtree Publishing Co.

Bright & Beyond - Thinking. 2004. (J). *(978-0-9763648-1-8(6))* Pal Toys, LLC.

Buzan, Tony. Mind Maps for Kids: an Introduction. 2005. (ENG., Illus.). 128p. pap. 19.95 *(978-0-00-715133-2(0)*, HarperThorsons) HarperCollins Pubs. Ltd. GBR. Dist: HarperCollins Pubs.

Carr, Mary. Great Chocolate Caper: Mystery That Teaches Logic Skills. 2005. (ENG.). 64p. pap. 11.95 *(978-1-59363-035-5(2))* Prufrock Pr.

Critical Thinking Publishing Staff, et al. Can You Find Me? K-1: Reading, Math, Science, Social Studies. 2010. (Can You Find Me? Ser.). (ENG., Illus.). 112p. (gr. k-1). pap. 14.99 *(978-0-89455-794-1(7))* Critical Thinking Co., The.

—Can You Find Me? PreK: Reading, Math, Science, Social Studies. 2011. (Can You Find Me? Ser.). (ENG.). 112p. (gr. -1 — 1). pap. 14.99 *(978-0-89455-793-4(9))* Critical Thinking Co., The.

Critical Thinking-What's Wrong with This Picture? (Gr. 1-3) 2003. (J). *(978-1-58232-066-3(7))* ECS Learning Systems, Inc.

Dale, Andrew. Graphic Novels. 2016. (Essential Literary Genres Ser.). (ENG.). 112p. (J). (gr. 6-12). lib. bdg. 41.36 *(978-1-68078-379-7(3)*, 23523, Essential Library) ABDO Publishing Co.

Friedman, Lauri S., ed. Nuclear Power, 1 vol. 2009. (Introducing Issues with Opposing Viewpoints Ser.). (ENG., Illus.). 144p. (gr. 7-10). 43.63 *(978-0-7377-4482-8(0)*, 882707e8-089a-4c94-bcb6-df1312a9a5f6, Greenhaven Publishing) Greenhaven Publishing LLC.

Gilbert, Ian. Little Owl's Book of Thinking: An Introduction to Thinking Skills, 1 vol. 2004. (Little Bks.). (ENG., Illus.). 96p. (C). 12.95 *(978-1-904424-35-2(X))* Crown Hse. Publishing LLC.

Gordon, Carol. Super Smart Information Strategies: Make the Grade. 2010. (Explorer Library: Information Explorer Ser.). (ENG.). 32p. (gr. 4-8). pap. 14.21 *(978-1-61080-259-8(4)*, 200907) Cherry Lake Publishing.

Gordon, Carol A. Make the Grade. 2010. (Explorer Library: Information Explorer Ser.). (ENG., Illus.). 32p. (gr. 4-8). lib. bdg. 32.07 *(978-1-60279-642-3(4)*, 200345) Cherry Lake Publishing.

Imagine That! Celebrating God's Gift of Creative Thinking. (Imagine That! Activity Bks.). (Illus.). 48p. (J). (gr. k-3). pap. 5.95 *(978-0-87162-832-9(5)*, E2300); (gr. 3-7). pap. 5.95 *(978-0-87162-834-3(1)*, E2301) Warner Pr., Inc.

Johnson, Robin. Above & Beyond with Creativity & Innovation. 2016. (Fueling Your Future! Going above & Beyond in the 21st Century Ser.). (ENG., Illus.). 48p. (J). (gr. 5-9). *(978-0-7787-2831-3(5))* Crabtree Publishing Co.

Kopp, Megan. Above & Beyond with Critical Thinking & Problem Solving. 2016. (Fueling Your Future! Going above & Beyond in the 21st Century Ser.). (ENG., Illus.). 48p. (J). (gr. 5-9). *(978-0-7787-2842-9(0))* Crabtree Publishing Co.

Lanza, Janet & Flahive, Lynn. Blooming Category Activities. 2006. (ACO., Illus.). 190p. (J). per. 37.95 *(978-0-7606-0654-4(4))* LinguiSystems, Inc.

Levin, Daniel, et al. Becoming a Responsive Science Teacher: Focusing on Student Thinking in Secondary Science. 2013. (ENG.). 270p. pap. 29.95 *(978-1-936959-05-1(4)*, P218225) National Science Teachers Assn.

Levine, Melvin D., contrib. by. Developing Minds Library, 22 cass.; set. 2004. (gr. -1-18). stu. ed. 499.95 incl. VHS *(978-1-57807-643-7(9)*, WG1166) WGBH Boston Video.

Meister, Cari. Totally Wacky Facts about the Mind. 2016. (Mind Benders Ser.). (ENG., Illus.). 112p. (J). (gr. 3-6). lib. bdg. 23.99 *(978-1-4914-8361-9(X)*, 130827, Capstone Pr.) Capstone.

Metzroth, Rupert A. Think for Yourself. 2004. (Illus.). 170p. per. 18.95 *(978-1-931934-30-5(4))* Back Yard Pub.

Morrison, Matthew. Big Questions: Incredible Adventures in Thinking. 2011. (ENG., Illus.). 204p. (J). (gr. 4-8). pap. 7.95 *(978-1-84046-670-6(7))* Icon Bks., Ltd. GBR. Dist: Publishers Group West (PGW).

Murrie, Matt & McHugh, Andrew R. The Book of What If... ? Questions & Activities for Curious Minds. (ENG., Illus.). 240p. (J). (gr. 3-7). 2017. pap. 15.99 *(978-1-58270-528-6(3))* 2016. 17.99 *(978-1-58270-529-3(1))* Aladdin/Beyond Words.

National Geographic Learning. Reading Expeditions (Science: Math Behind the Science): Thinking It Through. 2007. (ENG., Illus.). 24p. (J). pap. 15.95 *(978-0-7922-4593-3(8))* CENGAGE Learning.

Pizza, Andy J. & Miller, Sophie. Invisible Things. 2023. (ENG., Illus.). 52p. (J). (gr. k-3). 17.99 *(978-1-7972-1520-4(5))* Chronicle Bks. LLC.

Price, Joan A. Ancient & Hellenistic Thought. 2008. (ENG., Illus.). 118p. (gr. 9). lib. bdg. 35.00 *(978-0-7910-8739-8(5)*, P145708, Facts On File) Infobase Holdings, Inc.

—Contemporary Thought. 2008. (ENG., Illus.). 160p. (gr. 9-12). lib. bdg. 35.00 *(978-0-7910-8792-3(1)*, P145670, Facts On File) Infobase Holdings, Inc.

Rando, Caterina. You Can Think Differently, 1 vol. 2017. (Be Your Best Self Ser.). (ENG., Illus.). 158p. (J). (gr. 9-9). 46.27 *(978-1-4994-6666-9(8)*, aef88636-94c6-44fa-9afb-7da96093c389, Rosen Young Adult) Rosen Publishing Group, Inc., The.

Risby, Bonnie. Logic Safari: Book 2, Grades 3-4, Bk. 2. Palouda, Annelise, illus. 2005. (ENG.). 36p. (gr. 3-4). pap. 12.95 *(978-1-59363-090-4(5)*, Routledge) Taylor & Francis Group.

Rodriguez, Ana Maria. A Day in the Life of the Brain. 2006. (Gray Matter for Juniors Ser.). (ENG., Illus.). 112p. (gr. 5-9). 32.95 *(978-0-7910-8947-7(9)*, P159775, Facts On File) Infobase Holdings, Inc.

Rose, Simon. Evaluating Arguments about Food. 2018. (State Your Case Ser.). (Illus.). 48p. (J). (gr. 5-6). *(978-0-7787-5077-2(9))* Crabtree Publishing Co.

—Evaluating Arguments about Technology. 2018. (State Your Case Ser.). (Illus.). 48p. (J). (gr. 5-6). *(978-0-7787-5079-6(5))* Crabtree Publishing Co.

Rozines Roy, Jennifer & Roy, Gregory. Graphing in the Desert, 1 vol. (Math All Around Ser.). (ENG., Illus.). 32p. (gr. 2-2). 2008. pap. 9.23 *(978-0-7614-3382-8(1)*, 03dc25a8-d072-47a9-92e2-6b415471c6e6) 2007. lib. bdg. 32.64 *(978-0-7614-2262-4(5)*, 3b38981c-e014-4cff-8abe-33f993f138b1) Cavendish Square Publishing LLC.

—Multiplication on the Farm, 1 vol. (Math All Around Ser.). (ENG., Illus.). 32p. (gr. 2-2). 2008. pap. 9.23 *(978-0-7614-3386-6(4)*, 7ad54927-7c76-4350-8119-d3e508569105) 2007. lib. bdg. 32.64 *(978-0-7614-2268-6(4)*, 189febc4-621f-4f52-a61b-e181f071180a) Cavendish Square Publishing LLC.

—Subtraction at School, 1 vol. 2008. (Math All Around Ser.). (ENG.). 32p. (gr. 2-2). pap. 9.23 *(978-0-7614-3409-2(7)*, a919fade-8d01-4085-9d98-260e95dca964) Cavendish Square Publishing LLC.

School Zone Publishing Company Staff. Thinking Skills Bilingual. 2007. (ENG.). 64p. (J). pap. 2.69 *(978-1-58947-975-3(0))* School Zone Publishing Co.

Sleeping Bear Press. Diary of an American Kid. Moore, Cyd, illus. 2011. (Country Journal Ser.). (ENG.). 128p. (J). (gr. 4-8). pap. 9.95 *(978-1-58536-171-7(2)*, 202262) Sleeping Bear Pr.

Spalding, Maddie. 12 Tips to Maintain Brain Health. 2017. (Healthy Living Ser.). (ENG., Illus.). 32p. (J). (gr. 3-6). 32.80 *(978-1-63235-368-9(7)*, 11846); pap. 9.95 *(978-1-63235-386-3(5)*, 11854) Bookstaves, LLC. (12-Story Library).

Spiegel, Al. Ideas. Mortimer, Mitch, illus. 2003. 32p. (J). lib. bdg. 13.99 *(978-0-9743553-0-6(5))* Crazy Man Press, LLC.

The Guide for Curious Minds: Set 2, 10 vols. 2014. (Guide for Curious Minds Ser.). (ENG.). 136p. (YA). (gr. 8-8). lib. bdg. 212.05 *(978-1-4777-8131-9(5)*, 563bfd07-177d-4276-90f4-68c384f87316, Rosen Young Adult) Rosen Publishing Group, Inc., The.

The Library of Higher Order of Thinking Skills, 12 vols. 2005. (Library of Higher Order Thinking Skills Ser.). (ENG.). (YA). (gr. 5-8). 206.82 *(978-1-4042-0624-3(8)*, 50df289f-b44c-44d2-a570-105857745945, Rosen Reference) Rosen Publishing Group, Inc., The.

Thornton, Geoffrey. What's Wrong? Visual Adventures in Critical Thinking. 2007. 32p. per. 19.95 *(978-1-59858-296-3(8))* Dog Ear Publishing, LLC.

Zimmer, Gretchen. Stinkin' Thinkin' 2012. (ENG.). (J). pap. 10.95 *(978-1-4675-2929-7(X))* Independent Pub.

THOUGHT TRANSFERENCE

see also Clairvoyance; Extrasensory Perception; Hypnotism

Bristol, Claude M. The Magic of Believing for Young People. 2008. 148p. pap. *(978-1-60796-063-8(X))* Editorial Benei Noaj.

Brunke, Dawn Baumann. Animal Voices, Animal Guides: Discover Your Deeper Self Through Communication with Animals. 2nd ed. 2009. (ENG.). 256p. pap. 16.00 *(978-1-59143-098-8(4))* Bear & Co.

Fullman, Joe. Mind Tricks. 2009. (Magic Handbook Ser.). (ENG., Illus.). 32p. (J). (gr. 3-12). pap. 6.95 *(978-1-55407-571-3(8)*, 36b851b7-4af2-4efe-8370-a31d1caa813e) Firefly Bks., Ltd.

Heos, Bridget. Do You Really Want to Visit Uranus? Fabbri, Daniele, illus. 2013. (Do You Really Want to Visit the Solar System? Ser.). (ENG.). 24p. (J). (gr. 1-4). 27.10 *(978-1-60753-202-6(6)*, 16270) Amicus.

Lane, Mike. Mind Magic, 1 vol. Mostyn, David, illus. 2012. (Miraculous Magic Tricks Ser.). (ENG.). 32p. (J). (gr. 3-3). pap. 12.75 *(978-1-4488-6735-6(5)*, 51fc2dda-48d5-4ad0-9a6a-540289d07415); lib. bdg. 31.27 *(978-1-61533-514-5(5)*, 1fb99e60-c039-4e8b-b558-f3207f9d9f83) Rosen Publishing Group, Inc., The. (Windmill Bks.).

Tilden, Thomasine E. Lewis. Mind Games! Can a Psychic Tell What You're Thinking? 2011. (J). pap. *(978-0-545-32943-9(4))* Scholastic, Inc.

Turnbull, Stephanie. Do You Really Want to Visit Uranus? 2011. (Secrets of Magic Ser.). 32p. (gr. 4-7). lib. bdg. 31.35 *(978-1-59920-498-7(3))* Black Rabbit Bks.

—Mind-Reading Tricks. 2011. (ENG., Illus.). 32p. (J). pap. 10.95 *(978-1-77092-044-6(7))* Saunders Bk. Co. CAN. Dist: RiverStream Publishing.

THREATENED PLANTS

see Endangered Plants

THREATENED SPECIES

see Endangered Species

THREE MUSKETEERS (FICTITIOUS CHARACTERS)—FICTION

Dumas, Alexandre. Los Tres Mosqueteros.Tr. of Trois Mousquetaires. (SPA.). (J). 2.49 *(978-968-890-125-0(3))* Edivision Compania Editorial, S.A. de C.V. MEX. Dist: Continental Bk. Co., Inc.

Golden Books Staff. Barbie & the Three Musketeers. 2009. (Little Golden Book Ser.). (ENG., Illus.). 24p. (J). (gr. -1-2). 3.99 *(978-0-375-85448-4(7)*, Golden Bks.) Random Hse. Children's Bks.

THUNDERSTORMS

see also Lightning

Adams, Renee. Can Thunder Hurt Me? Adams, Renee, illus. 2012. (Illus.). 24p. pap. 17.99 *(978-1-4685-5852-4(8))* AuthorHouse.

Bailer, Darice. Why Does It Thunder & Lightning?, 1 vol. 2011. (Tell Me Why, Tell Me How Ser.). (ENG.). 32p. (gr. 3-3). 32.64 *(978-0-7614-4825-9(X)*, cb67043a-050a-40c9-9906-aa8cdfb227e7) Cavendish Square Publishing LLC.

Bodden, Valerie. Our Wonderful Weather: Thunderstorms. 2014. (Our Wonderful Weather Ser.). (ENG., Illus.). 24p. (J). (gr. 1-3). pap. 9.99 *(978-0-89812-724-9(6)*, 22269, Creative Paperbacks) Creative Co., The.

—Thunderstorms. 2012. (Our Wonderful Weather Ser.). (ENG., Illus.). 24p. (J). (gr. 1-4). 25.65 *(978-1-60818-149-0(9)*, 22264, Creative Education) Creative Co., The.

Boothroyd, Jennifer. What is Severe Weather? 2014. (First Step Nonfiction — Let's Watch the Weather Ser.). (ENG., Illus.). 24p. (J). (gr. k-2). pap. 6.99 *(978-1-4677-4499-7(9)*, 0cf19a8f-2424-4a12-aa52-f32b05403a57) Lerner Publishing Group.

Broeders, Rebecca. How to Survive a Thunderstorm. 2012. 20p. pap. 17.99 *(978-1-4685-7672-6(0))* AuthorHouse.

Cox Cannons, Helen. Thunder & Lightning, 1 vol. 2014. (Weather Wise Ser.). (ENG., Illus.). 24p. (J). (gr. -1-1). 25.32 *(978-1-4846-0548-6(9)*, 126643, Heinemann) Capstone.

Doeden, Matt. Thunderstorms. 2008. pap. 40.95 *(978-0-8225-9444-4(7))* Lerner Publishing Group.

Galiano, Dean. Thunderstorms & Lightning. (Weather Watcher's Library). 48p. (gr. 5-8). 2009. 53.00 *(978-1-60854-275-8(0))* 2003. (Illus.). (YA). lib. bdg. 23.95 *(978-0-8239-3093-7(9)*, WETHLI) Rosen Publishing Group, Inc., The. (Rosen Reference).

Gonzales, Doreen. Thunderstorms, 1 vol. 2012. (Killer Disasters Ser.). (ENG., Illus.). 24p. (J). (gr. 2-3). 26.27 *(978-1-4488-7443-9(2)*, f6be8711-e735-4d38-b2bb-61f50dea6c0d); pap. 9.25 *(978-1-4488-7516-0(1)*, 3a3160c4-ff41-4d8b-a0f9-5a154ccd9f27) Rosen Publishing Group, Inc., The. (PowerKids Pr.).

Gustaitis, Joseph Alan. Storm Chaser, 1 vol. 2011. (Dirty & Dangerous Jobs Ser.). (ENG.). 32p. (gr. 3-3). 31.21 *(978-1-60870-179-7(4)*, 4572b2b2-1437-424b-9bff-d73fb68fd3d1) Cavendish Square Publishing LLC.

Jensen, Belinda. A Party for Clouds: Thunderstorms. Kurilla, Renée, illus. 2016. (Bel the Weather Girl Ser.). (ENG.). 24p. (J). (gr. -1-3). 25.32 *(978-1-4677-7959-3(8)*, 05c13d56-d481-47e8-a443-c771705f753f, Millbrook Pr.) Lerner Publishing Group.

Johanson, Paula. Lightning & Thunder, 1 vol. 2018. (Nature's Mysteries Ser.). (ENG.). 32p. (gr. 2-3). pap. 13.90 *(978-1-5081-0651-7(7)*, e3f46e0d-fd22-4519-8fc7-5aa5aa23bb0a, Britannica Educational Publishing) Rosen Publishing Group, Inc., The.

Johnson, Robin. What Is a Thunderstorm? 2016. (ENG., Illus.). 24p. (J). *(978-0-7787-2400-1(X))* Crabtree Publishing Co.

Lawrence, Ellen. What Is Lightning? 2015. (Weather Wise Ser.). (ENG., Illus.). 24p. (J). (gr. -1-3). lib. bdg. 26.99 *(978-1-62724-863-1(3))* Bearport Publishing Co., Inc.

McAuliffe, Bill. Thunderstorms. (X-Books: Weather Ser.). (ENG., (J). 2017. Illus.). 32p. (gr. 3-6). pap. 9.99 *(978-1-62832-430-3(9)*, 20415, Creative Paperbacks) 2017. (Illus.). 32p. (gr. 3-6). *(978-1-60818-827-7(2)*, 20414, Creative Education) 2010. 48p. (gr. 5-8). lib. bdg. 23.95 *(978-1-58341-930-4(6)*, 22286) Creative Co., The.

Mezzanotte, Jim. Thunderstorms, 1 vol. (Wild Weather Ser.). (ENG.). 24p. 2009. (J). (gr. 1-1). pap. 9.15 *(978-1-4339-2364-7(5)*, f3fe6943-1335-4f5f-9d58-ddf1d0922d54) 2009. (J). (gr. 1-1). lib. bdg. 24.67 *(978-1-4339-2350-0(5)*, 9f7bd39f-59b1-4d24-b555-c0474fdfd97b) 2007. (Illus.). (gr. 2-4). pap. 9.15 *(978-0-8368-7922-3(8)*, c71706b1-661e-4a88-98ca-da74f6bffade) 2007. (Illus.). (gr. 2-4). lib. bdg. 24.67 *(978-0-8368-7915-5(5)*, a7b22811-ccc2-420b-ae06-329ce872c44c) Stevens, Gareth Publishing LLLP. (Weekly Reader Leveled Readers).

—Tormentas Eléctricas (Thunderstorms), 1 vol. (Tiempo Extremo (Wild Weather) Ser.). (SPA.). 24p. 2009. (J). (gr. 1-1). pap. 9.15 *(978-1-4339-2371-5(8)*, 3638dfb4-1d2c-465c-be13-028907a2767a) 2009. (J). (gr. 1-1). lib. bdg. 24.67 *(978-1-4339-2357-9(2)*, 25f41b00-5873-43f0-9c11-a8404ac8c668) 2007. (Illus.). (gr. 2-4). pap. 9.15 *(978-0-8368-8081-6(1)*, 4af09454-13c8-4999-a6dd-ca10dcaec18d) 2007. (Illus.). (gr. 2-4). lib. bdg. 24.67 *(978-0-8368-8074-8(9)*, 70e5b0b8-b930-46d6-a5aa-77112d1b6be2) Stevens, Gareth Publishing LLLP. (Weekly Reader Leveled Readers).

Murray, Julie. Thunderstorms. 2017. (Wild Weather Ser.). (ENG., Illus.). 24p. (J). (gr. k-4). lib. bdg. 31.36 *(978-1-5321-2089-3(3)*, 26772, Abdo Zoom-Dash) ABDO Publishing Co.

Rehberg, Emily. Thunder Is Not Scary. Craig, Branden Chapin & Chapin, Jimmy, illus. 2013. 26p. pap. 12.00 *(978-0-9800108-3-1(7))* Bilbo Bks.

Rossiter, Brienna. Thunderstorms. 2019. (Weather Ser.). (ENG., Illus.). 16p. (J). (gr. k-1). pap. 7.95 *(978-1-64185-862-5(1)*, 1641858621); lib. bdg. 25.64 *(978-1-64185-793-2(5)*, 1641857935) North Star Editions. (Focus Readers).

Schuh, Mari. What Are Thunderstorms? 2019. (Wicked Weather Ser.). (ENG., Illus.). 24p. (J). (gr. -1-2). lib. bdg. 22.65 *(978-1-9771-0330-7(8)*, 139321, Pebble) Capstone.

Stiefel, Chana. Thunderstorms. 2009. (True Book(tm), a — Earth Science Ser.). (ENG., Illus.). 48p. (J). (gr. 2-5). 31.00 *(978-0-531-16884-4(0))* Scholastic Library Publishing.

Thomas, Rick & Picture Window Books Staff. ¡Rambum! ¡Pum! Un Libro Sobre Tormentas. Robledo, Sol, tr. Shea, Denise, illus. 2007. (Ciencia Asombrosa: el Tiempo Ser.). (SPA.). 24p. (J). (gr. -1-3). 27.32 *(978-1-4048-3227-5(0)*, 93784, Picture Window Bks.) Capstone.

World Book, Inc. Staff, contrib. by. Thunderstorms. (J). 2007. *(978-0-7166-9812-8(9))* 2nd ed. 2009. (Illus.). 47p. *(978-0-7166-9828-9(5))* World Bk., Inc.

THUNDERSTORMS—FICTION

Adams, William J. Hate that Thunder. Stiglich, Tom, illus. 2005. 24p. (J). pap. 8.95 *(978-0-9772757-0-0(1))* Mandy & Andy Bks., Inc.

—Hate That Thunder/Odio Ese Trueno, 1 vol. Stiglich, Tom, illus. 2007. (Mandy & Andy Bks.). (ENG & SPA.). 49p. (J). (gr. k-2). per. 10.95 *(978-0-9772757-1-7(X))* Mandy & Andy Bks., Inc.

Arnold, Marsha Diane. May I Come In? Poh, Jennie, illus. 2018. (ENG.). 32p. (J). (gr. k-3). 16.99 *(978-1-58536-394-0(4)*, 204396) Sleeping Bear Pr.

Batson, Susann. Scaredy: A Cloud Afraid of Thunder. 2010. 16p. pap. 9.95 *(978-1-61633-053-8(8))* Guardian Angel Publishing, Inc.

Blackman, Christy. Mr. Thunder Is Here, but There's No Reason to Fear. 2008. 36p. pap. 24.95 *(978-1-60441-695-4(5))* America Star Bks.

Bluemle, Elizabeth. Tap Tap Boom Boom. Karas, G. Brian, illus. 2014. (ENG.). 32p. (J). (gr. -1-2). 17.99 *(978-0-7636-5696-6(8))* Candlewick Pr.

Brewer, Janey. Mist & Moonlight. 2007. 76p. per. 19.95 *(978-1-4241-9525-1(X))* America Star Bks.

Bright, Belle. Crash, Bang, Boom, Zing. Bright, Michael, illus. 2009. 12p. pap. 24.95 *(978-1-60749-383-9(7))* America Star Bks.

Brown, Peter. Flight of the Dodo. 2010. (ENG., Illus.). 32p. (J). (gr. -1-3). pap. 7.99 *(978-0-316-08339-3(9))* Little, Brown Bks. for Young Readers.

Carol Henson Keesee. The Angry Thunderstorm. Rachel Henson, illus. 2009. 40p. pap. 20.00 *(978-1-4389-4334-3(2))* AuthorHouse.

Cazet, Denys. Minnie & Moo Meet Frankenswine. Cazet, Denys, illus. 2004. (Readalongs for Beginning Readers Ser.). (Illus.). 28.95 incl. audio compact disk *(978-1-59112-876-2(5))*; (J). 25.95 incl. audio *(978-1-59112-262-3(7))*; (J). pap. 29.95 incl. audio *(978-1-59112-263-0(5))* Live Oak Media.

—Minnie & Moo Meet Frankenswine, 4 bks. 2004. (Readalongs for Beginning Readers Ser.). (Illus.). 48p. (J). (gr. -1-2). pap. 31.95 incl. audio compact disk *(978-1-59112-877-9(3))* Live Oak Media.

Crum, Shutta. Thunder-Boomer! Thompson, Carol, illus. 2009. (ENG.). 40p. (J). (gr. -1-3). 18.99 *(978-0-618-61865-1(1)*, 100451, Clarion Bks.) HarperCollins Pubs.

D'Agata, Tabatha Jean. Storm Tunes: Yes, I Can Read! Nature Series, Book 2. Lineberger, Judy, illus. 2006. (Yes, I Can Read! Ser.: Bk. 2). 30p. (J). pap. 6.95 *(978-1-934138-02-1(9))* Bouncing Ball Bks., Inc.

Derting, Kimberly & Johannes, Shelli R. Cece Loves Science & Adventure. Harrison, Vashti, illus. 2019. (Loves Science Ser.: 2). (ENG.). 40p. (J). (gr. -1-3). 17.99 *(978-0-06-249962-2(9)*, Greenwillow Bks.) HarperCollins Pubs.

Graber, Lois, illus. A Song in the Storm. 2012. 32p. (J). *(978-0-7399-2445-7(1))* Rod & Staff Pubs., Inc.

High, Gracia. I am not going to sleep Now. 2004. 21p. pap. 24.95 *(978-1-4137-3000-5(0))* PublishAmerica, Inc.

Hileman, Jane & Pitt, Marilyn. The Storm. Bianchi, John, illus. 2011. (Power 50 - Potato Chip Bks). 12p. pap. 33.92 *(978-1-61541-233-4(6))* American Reading Co.

Hobbie, Holly. Toot & Puddle: You Are My Sunshine. 2010. (Toot & Puddle Ser.: 3). (ENG., Illus.). 32p. (J). (gr. -1-3). pap. 8.99 *(978-0-316-16703-1(7))* Little, Brown Bks. for Young Readers.

Hulst, W. G. van de & Hulst, Willem G. van de, illus. Through the Thunderstorm. 2014. 48p. (J). *(978-1-928136-02-6(8))* Inheritance Pubns.

Kleyn, Diana & Beeke, Joel R. How God Used a Thunderstorm. rev. ed. 2007. (Building on the Rock Ser.). (ENG., Illus.). 176p. (J). pap. 8.99 *(978-1-85792-815-0(6)*, 80cd94a8-760f-4d9e-a1b6-ca963981156f, CF4Kids) Christian Focus Pubns. GBR. Dist: Baker & Taylor Publisher Services (BTPS).

Leslie, Lashawn. Thundermonsters. 2012. 16p. pap. 15.99 *(978-1-4772-5422-6(6))* AuthorHouse.

Lignell, Kirk. Listen to the Raindrops: Featuring the Storm Song. Lignell, Brent, illus. 2007. 32p. (J). (gr. -1-3). 17.95 *(978-1-932399-15-8(1))* Huron River Pr.

McNaughton, Karen. What Makes the Thunder? 2011. 24p. pap. 11.50 *(978-1-60976-224-7(X)*, Eloquent Bks.) Strategic Book Publishing & Rights Agency (SBPRA).

Merkel, Tara & Monahan, Ryan. The Thunderstorm. 2007. 20p. per. 11.00 *(978-1-4343-0585-5(6))* AuthorHouse.

Moss, Miriam. Wiley & Jasper. Bucker, Jutta, tr. Bucker, Jutta, illus. 2003. (J). 25p. pap. *(978-1-59336-061-0(4))*; 32p. 15.95 *(978-1-59336-060-3(6))* Mondo Publishing.

Mullarkey, Lisa. Gaston the Goat. Franco, Paula, illus. 2017. (Farmyard Friends Ser.). (ENG.). 32p. (J). (gr. -1-3). lib. bdg. 32.79 *(978-1-5321-4045-7(2)*, 25518, Calico Chapter Bks) Magic Wagon.

Norton, Jack, Jr., as told by. Brave from Thunders. 2003. pap. 15.00 *(978-0-9740071-3-7(7))* Ctr. for the Affirmation of Responsible Education.

Novick, Rona Milch. Mommy, Can You Stop the Rain? Kubaszewska, Anna, illus. 2020. (ENG.). 32p. (J). 17.95 *(978-1-68115-555-5(9),* 0af463f0-a462-4701-8221-bd14af153516, Apples & Honey Pr.) Behrman Hse., Inc.

Pitt, Marilyn & Sanchez, Lucia M. La Tormenta: The Storm. Bianchi, John, illus. 2011. (poder de 50 - Libros papas fritas Ser.). (SPA.). 12p. pap. 33.92 *(978-1-61541-441-3(X))* American Reading Co.

Polacco, Patricia. Thunder Cake. 2015. 32p. pap. 8.00 *(978-1-61003-536-1(4))* Center for the Collaborative Classroom.

Rivera-Ashford, Roni Capin & Johnson, Richard. Hip Hip Hooray, It's Monsoon Day! 2007. (ENG & SPA.). (YA). pap. 15.95 *(978-1-886679-36-8(3))* Arizona Sonora Desert Museum Pr.

Spear, Lisa D. Thunderburps. Baker, David, illus. 2012. 26p. 24.95 *(978-1-4626-0793-8(4))* America Star Bks.

Testa, Maggie. Daniel Gets Scared. 2015. (Daniel Tiger's Neighborhood Ready-To-Read Ser.). lib. bdg. 13.55 *(978-0-606-38243-4(7))* Turtleback.

Torres, J. The Sound of Thunder. Hicks, Faith Erin, illus. 2014. (Bigfoot Boy Ser.). (ENG.). 100p. (J). (gr. 2-5). pap. 9.95 *(978-1-894786-59-1(9))* Kids Can Pr., Ltd. CAN. Dist: Hachette Bk. Group.

TIBET AUTONOMOUS REGION (CHINA)

Deasy, H. H. P. In Tibet & Chinese Turkestan: Being the Record of Three Years' Exploration. 2008. 95.00 *(978-1-57898-702-3(4));* pap. *(978-1-57898-703-0(2))* Martino Fine Bks.

Dolphin, Laurie. Our Journey from Tibet. Johnson, Nancy Jo, photos by. 2006. (Illus.). 40p. (J). (gr. k-4). 16.00 *(978-0-7567-9812-3(4))* DIANE Publishing Co.

Gray, Nick. Escape from Tibet: A True Story. 2014. (ENG., Illus.). 164p. (YA). (gr. 6-12). pap. 12.95 *(978-1-55451-662-9(5),* 9781554516629) Annick Pr., Ltd. CAN. Dist: Publishers Group West (PGW).

Haerens, Margaret, ed. Tibet, 1 vol. 2014. (Opposing Viewpoints Ser.). (ENG.). 224p. (gr. 10-12). pap. 34.80 *(978-0-7377-7363-7(4),* 241274d1-d637-4014-b7d4-160b3eb96481, Greenhaven Publishing) Greenhaven Publishing LLC.

Harris, Joseph. Tibet, 1 vol. 2010. (Global Hotspots Ser.). (ENG.). 32p. (gr. 5-5). lib. bdg. 21.27 *(978-0-7614-4762-7(8),* a39a0e73-9e12-4b41-8a0b-43f909c93214) Cavendish Square Publishing LLC.

Hay, Jeff, ed. Tibet, 1 vol. 2014. (Genocide & Persecution Ser.). (ENG., Illus.). 208p. (gr. 10-12). lib. bdg. 43.63 *(978-0-7377-6901-2(7),* 881d7f9a-a41b-4ea2-b978-362f043b4691, Greenhaven Publishing) Greenhaven Publishing LLC.

Hellstrom, Travis. My Day with the Dalai Lama: A Coloring Book for All Ages. Hoyle, Leighanna, illus. 2017. 64p. (J). (gr. -1-2). pap. 5.99 *(978-1-57826-639-5(4),* Hatherleigh Pr.) Hatherleigh Co., Ltd., The.

Kummer, Patricia K. Enchantment of the World: Tibet. 2003. (Enchantment of the World Ser.). (ENG., Illus.). 144p. (YA). (gr. 5-9). 39.00 *(978-0-516-22693-4(2))* Scholastic Library Publishing.

Levy, Patricia & Bosco, Don. Tibet, 1 vol. 2nd rev. ed. 2007. (Cultures of the World (Second Edition)(r) Ser.). (ENG., Illus.). 144p. (gr. 5-5). lib. bdg. 49.79 *(978-0-7614-2076-7(2),* 51f93797-12fa-4845-acc7-43f8e465ee0a) Cavendish Square Publishing LLC.

Nagle, Jeanne. The 14th Dalai Lama: Spiritual Leader of Tibetan Buddhists. 2017. (Spotlight on Civic Courage: Heroes of Conscience Ser.). (Illus.). 48p. (J). (gr. 10-15). 70.50 *(978-1-5081-7745-6(7));* (ENG., (gr. 6-6). pap. 12.75 *(978-1-5383-8079-6(X),* 3575c6d0-a60c-4ea9-b28a-45445ac1ad52) Rosen Publishing Group, Inc., The.

Nevins, Debbie, et al. Tibet, 1 vol. 3rd enl. rev. ed. 2016. (Cultures of the World (Third Edition)(r) Ser.). (ENG., Illus.). 144p. (J). (gr. 5-5). 48.79 *(978-1-5026-2213-6(0),* eb2caec1-a8b0-4329-9b90-5130de2de823) Cavendish Square Publishing LLC.

TIBET AUTONOMOUS REGION (CHINA)—FICTION

Carlson, Dale Bick. The Mountain of Truth. Nicklaus, Carol, illus. 2nd ed. 2005. (ENG.). 169p. (gr. 8-12). reprint ed. pap. 14.95 *(978-1-884158-30-8(7))* Bick Publishing Hse.

Giancamilli, Vanessa. Gecko Gathering. Kest, Kristin, illus. 2005. (Soundprints' Amazing Animal Adventures! Ser.). (ENG.). (J). (gr. -1-2). 32p. 9.95 *(978-1-59249-323-4(8),* PS7157); 36p. 2.95 *(978-1-59249-289-3(4),* S7157); 36p. 15.95 *(978-1-59249-288-6(6),* B7107); 36p. pap. 6.95 *(978-1-59249-290-9(8),* S7107); 32p. 19.95 *(978-1-59249-321-0(1),* BC7107) Soundprints.

Hergé. Tintin au Tibet.Tr. of Tintin in Tibet. (J). (gr. 7-9). ring bd. 24.95 *(978-0-8288-5092-6(5))* French & European Pubns., Inc.

—Tintin en Tibet. (SPA., Illus.). 62p. (J). 24.95 *(978-0-8288-4996-8(X))* French & European Pubns., Inc.

—Tintin in Tibet. Orig. Title: Tintin au Tibet. (Illus.). 62p. (J). 24.95 *(978-0-8288-5001-8(1))* French & European Pubns., Inc.

—Tintin in Tibet (the Adventures of Tintin) 2003. Orig. Title: Tintin au Tibet. (ENG., Illus.). 64p. *(978-1-4052-0819-2(8))* Farshore.

Moffett, Rodney. The Eighth Crest. 2006. (ENG.). 228p. per. 24.95 *(978-1-4241-3907-1(4))* PublishAmerica, Inc.

Rose, Naomi. Tibetan Tales for Little Buddhas. 2003. (TIB & ENG., Illus.). 64p. (J). pap. 16.95 *(978-1-57416-081-9(8))* Clear Light Pubs.

Soros, Barbara. Tenzin's Deer. Mayer, Danuta, illus. (ENG.). 32p. (J). (gr. 2-4). 2007. pap. 7.99 *(978-1-84686-130-7(6))* 2005. 16.99 *(978-1-905236-57-2(3))* Barefoot Bks., Inc.

Thomey, Zedar. Red Star Red Tar. 2010. 66p. pap. 20.00 *(978-1-60860-360-2(1),* Eloquent Bks.) Strategic Book Publishing & Rights Agency (SBPRA).

Trottier, Maxine. Little Dog Moon, 1 vol. Fernandez, Laura & Jacobson, Rick, illus. 2006. (ENG.). 24p. (J). (gr. 1-4). 7.95 *(978-1-55005-160-5(1),* 4e40b252-6693-4dac-bd01-e48fb557632e) Fitzhenry & Whiteside, Ltd. CAN. Dist: Firefly Bks., Ltd.

TIDAL WAVES

see Ocean Waves

TIDES

Brasch, Nicolas. Times, Tides, & Revolutions. 2010. (Science Behind Ser.). 32p. lib. bdg. 28.50 *(978-1-59920-563-2(7))* Black Rabbit Bks.

Bullard, Lisa. Tides. 2018. (Natural Phenomena Ser.). (ENG., Illus.). 32p. (J). (gr. 3-5). pap. 9.95 *(978-1-64185-015-5(9),* 1641850159); lib. bdg. 31.35 *(978-1-63517-913-2(0),* 1635179130) North Star Editions. (Focus Readers).

Declus, Jennifer. What Might I Find in a Tidepool. Kalasea, illus. 2004. (J). *(978-0-9743690-4-4(7))* Britt Allcroft Productions.

Dickmann, Nancy. Harnessing Wave & Tidal Energy, 1 vol. 2016. (Future of Power Ser.). (ENG.). 32p. (J). (gr. 4-5). pap. 11.00 *(978-1-4994-3213-8(5),* c12dcabf-35bb-471d-a583-2ffae4844273, PowerKids Pr.) Rosen Publishing Group, Inc., The.

Jacobs, Marian B. Why Does the Ocean Have Tides?, 1 vol. 2003. (Library of Why Ser.). (ENG., Illus.). 24p. (J). (gr. 3-4). lib. bdg. 26.27 *(978-0-8239-5272-4(X),* 286efcbf-5637-4962-bd6e-1430da88ffd6, PowerKids Pr.) Rosen Publishing Group, Inc., The.

Richter, Al. Ocean Tides. (Reading Room Collection 1 Ser.). 16p. (gr. 2-3). 2009. 37.50 *(978-1-60851-947-7(3))* 2005. (ENG., Illus.). (J). lib. bdg. 22.27 *(978-1-4042-3343-0(1),* e3d4b6ba-70ff-4175-83ed-702b7290670c) Rosen Publishing Group, Inc., The. (PowerKids Pr.).

TIDES—FICTION

Curious George Chasing Waves. 2014. (Curious George Ser.). (ENG., Illus.). 24p. (J). (gr. -1-3). pap. 4.99 *(978-0-544-24004-9(9),* 1565434, Clarion Bks.) HarperCollins Pubs.

Herman, Gail. The Creeping Tide. Nez, John, illus. 2003. (Science Solves It! Ser.). (ENG.). 32p. (J). (gr. k-2). pap. 5.95 *(978-1-57565-128-6(9),* 0df45891-2536-4413-b0c3-a1f81d7cb5ea, Kane Press) Astra Publishing Hse.

McClure, Nikki. Waiting for High Tide. 2016. (ENG., Illus.). 48p. (J). (gr. k-2). 19.95 *(978-1-4197-1656-0(5),* 1090101, Abrams Bks. for Young Readers) Abrams, Inc.

TIGER

Amstutz, Lisa J. Tigers on the Hunt. 2017. (Searchlight Books (tm) — Predators Ser.). (ENG., Illus.). 32p. (J). (gr. 3-5). pap. 9.99 *(978-1-5124-5613-4(6),* f1265b4c-b460-4d8b-86ec-76d33ecee9ce); lib. bdg. 30.65 *(978-1-5124-3400-2(0),* 0319abef-e9a2-48c4-9f5f-98ff6c4f24b1, Lerner Pubns.) Lerner Publishing Group.

Archer, Claire. Tigers, 1 vol. 2014. (Big Cats Ser.). (ENG., Illus.). 24p. (J). (gr. -1-2). lib. bdg. 32.79 *(978-1-62970-006-9(1),* 1229, Abdo Kids) ABDO Publishing Co.

AZ Books, creator. Hello, I'm Tiger! 2012. (Who Lives in the Book? Ser.). (ENG., Illus.). 10p. (J). (gr. -1-k). bds. 11.95 *(978-1-61889-211-9(8))* AZ Bks. LLC.

Baker, David G. & Stewart, Margaret Taylor. Tales of Mike the Tiger: Facts & Fun for Everyone. Lockwood, C. C., photos by. 2006. (ENG., Illus.). 144p. (gr. 4-7). 19.95 *(978-0-8071-3118-3(0),* 1181) Louisiana State Univ. Pr.

Barnes, J. Lou. The Secret Lives of Tigers, 1 vol. 2007. (Secret Lives of Animals Ser.). (ENG., Illus.). 32p. (gr. 3-5). lib. bdg. 28.67 *(978-0-8368-7659-8(8),* 649fe6cb-9e49-4a51-940e-f50e7592168a, Gareth Stevens Learning Library) Stevens, Gareth Publishing LLLP.

—101 Facts about Tigers, 1 vol. 2004. (101 Facts about Predators Ser.). (ENG., Illus.). 32p. (gr. 2-4). lib. bdg. 28.67 *(978-0-8368-4041-4(0),* 637834bb-e55c-42c9-a2d2-c99b69a19534, Gareth Stevens Learning Library) Stevens, Gareth Publishing LLLP.

Beer, Amy-Jane. Tigers. 2009. (Illus.). 52p. (J). *(978-0-7172-8035-3(7))* Grolier, Ltd.

Bergeron, Alain M., et al. Les Tigres. 2010. (FRE., Illus.). 64p. (J). pap. 8.95 *(978-2-89435-465-0(7))* Quintin Pubs./Editions Michel Quintin CAN. Dist: Crabtree Publishing Co.

Besel, Jen. Tiger Cubs. 2020. (Baby Animals Ser.). 24p. (J). (gr. k-3). pap. 8.99 *(978-1-64466-099-7(7),* 14391, Bolt Jr.) Black Rabbit Bks.

Big Cats, 1 vol. 2014. (Animal Q & A Ser.). (ENG., Illus.). 24p. (J). (gr. 2-2). lib. bdg. 26.27 *(978-1-4777-9182-0(5),* ef15a050-1d4a-480e-be87-af3038b278d1, Windmill Bks.) Rosen Publishing Group, Inc., The.

Bodden, Valerie. Amazing Animals - Tigers. 2012. (Amazing Animals Ser.). (ENG.). 24p. (J). (gr. 1-4). 24.25 *(978-1-58341-720-1(6),* 22094, Creative Education) Creative Co., The.

Books Are Fun 8 Title Animal Lives Set: Tigers. 2006. (J). *(978-1-59566-312-2(6))* QEB Publishing Inc.

Bortolotti, Dan. Tiger Rescue: Changing the Future for Endangered Wildlife. 2003. (Firefly Animal Rescue Ser.). (ENG., Illus.). 64p. (J). (gr. 5-18). 19.95 *(978-1-55297-599-2(1),* cce46ce9-2a43-47e9-b60d-2178196781ac); pap. 9.95 *(978-1-55297-558-9(4),* 85cb0295-d0a5-400b-8d22-8de9bb5d4a79) Firefly Bks., Ltd.

Bowman, Donna H. Big Cats. Wald, Christina, illus. 2008. (ENG.). 24p. (J). (gr. 3-18). 19.95 *(978-1-58117-781-7(X),* Intervisual/Piggy Toes) Bendon, Inc.

Bozzo, Linda. How Tigers Grow Up, 1 vol. 2019. (Animals Growing Up Ser.). (ENG.). 24p. (gr. 1-2). pap. 10.35 *(978-1-9785-1249-8(X),* 55d8e2f2-d0f0-45a4-9e94-3089f32e2378) Enslow Publishing, LLC.

Brayley, Genevieve. Noah Saves the Tigers. 2010. 28p. pap. 28.03 *(978-1-4500-3077-9(7))* Xlibris Corp.

Butterworth, Nick. Tiger in the Snow! 2008. (ENG., Illus.). 32p. 9.95 *(978-0-00-725774-4(0))* HarperCollins Pubs. Ltd. GBR. Dist: Independent Pubs. Group.

Clark, Willow. Bengal Tigers, 1 vol. 2012. (Animals of Asia Ser.). (ENG., Illus.). 24p. (J). (gr. 2-3). 26.27 *(978-1-4488-7417-0(3),* cd1f54f6-217d-47ee-b6fb-65d45dbc3635); pap. 9.25 *(978-1-4488-7490-3(4),* 641f8f2b-ef2d-4bc2-8906-4933bfdbfdb1) Rosen Publishing Group, Inc., The. (PowerKids Pr.).

Clay, Kathryn. Saber-Toothed Cat. 2018. (Little Paleontologist Ser.). (ENG., Illus.). 32p. (J). (gr. k-3). lib. bdg. 28.65 *(978-1-5435-0538-2(4),* 137353, Capstone Pr.) Capstone.

—Tigers: A 4D Book. 2018. (Mammals in the Wild Ser.). (ENG., Illus.). 24p. (J). (gr. -1-2). lib. bdg. 24.65 *(978-1-9771-0076-4(7),* 138282, Pebble) Capstone.

Crossley, Laura C. Three Little Tiger Cubs: A Journey Through the Seasons with a Mom & Her Cubs. 2005. (ENG., Illus.). 29p. (J). (gr. -1-3). per. 19.99 *(978-1-59926-853-8(1))* Xlibris Corp.

Davies, Ann & Davies, Gill. The One Tiger. 2008. (Illus.). 32p. (J). pap. 7.99 *(978-1-905470-23-5(1))* SeaSquirt Pubns. GBR. Dist: Basic Distribution, Inc.

Dickmann, Nancy. Bengal Tigers. 2019. (Animals in Danger Ser.). (ENG.). 24p. (J). (gr. 2-4). lib. bdg. *(978-1-78121-440-4(9),* 16558) Brown Bear Bks.

Early Macken, JoAnn. Tigers / Los Tigres, 1 vol. 2004. (Animals I See at the Zoo / Animales Que Veo en el Zoológico Ser.). (SPA & ENG., Illus.). 24p. (gr. k-2). pap. 9.15 *(978-0-8368-4391-0(6),* 7e285342-064a-4664-95e2-28e79bfb8a76, Weekly Reader Leveled Readers); lib. bdg. 24.67 *(978-0-8368-4386-6(X),* 60046507-adbc-4440-a11a-9eb95c43178f) Stevens, Gareth Publishing LLLP.

Eason, Sarah. Save the Tiger, 1 vol. Geeson, Andrew & Veldhoven, Marijke, illus. 2009. (Save The... Ser.). (ENG.). 32p. (J). (gr. 2-3). lib. bdg. 28.93 *(978-1-4358-2813-1(5),* dc7b9abf-a85d-4449-87e6-28b03105f1d0) Rosen Publishing Group, Inc., The.

Einhorn, Kama. Tiger Time. 2019. (True Tales of Rescue Ser.). (ENG., Illus.). 144p. (J). (gr. 3-7). 14.99 *(978-1-328-76707-3(8),* 1680380, Clarion Bks.) HarperCollins Pubs.

Emminizer, Theresa. What If Tigers Disappeared?, 1 vol. 2019. (Life Without Animals Ser.). (ENG.). 24p. (gr. 1-2). pap. 9.15 *(978-1-5382-3830-1(6),* 275b0e6e-060a-42cb-aeea-bee936e18220) Stevens, Gareth Publishing LLLP.

Esbaum, Jill. Explore My World Tigers. 2016. (Explore My World Ser.). (Illus.). 32p. (J). (gr. -1-k). pap. 4.99 *(978-1-4263-2426-0(X),* National Geographic Kids) Disney Publishing Worldwide.

Feldman, Thea. Katya's Busy Morning. 2006. (Illus.). (J). *(978-0-696-23292-3(8))* Meredith Bks.

Firestone, Mary. Top 50 Reasons to Care about Tigers: Animals in Peril, 1 vol. 2010. (Top 50 Reasons to Care about Endangered Animals Ser.). (ENG., Illus.). 104p. (gr. 5-6). 35.93 *(978-0-7660-3452-5(6),* 48eee25c-3a00-4794-a818-0f107a504d93) Enslow Publishing, LLC.

Franchino, Vicky. Tigers. 2012. (Nature's Children Ser.). (ENG.). 48p. (J). pap. 6.95 *(978-0-531-25484-4(4))* Scholastic Library Publishing.

—Tigers - Nature's Children. 2012. (ENG.). 48p. (J). lib. bdg. 28.00 *(978-0-531-26839-1(X))* Scholastic Library Publishing.

Frost, Helen. Sabertooth Cat [Scholastic]. Hughes, Jon, illus. 2009. (Dinosaurs & Prehistoric Animals Ser.). 24p. (gr. k-1). pap. 1.00 *(978-1-4296-4249-1(1),* Capstone Pr.) Capstone.

—Tigers [Scholastic]. 2011. (Rain Forest Animals Ser.). 24p. pap. 0.50 *(978-1-4296-6311-3(1),* Pebble) Capstone.

Galvin, Laura Gates. Tiger Cub See-and-Do. Cohen, Jessie, illus. 2005. (Let's Go to the Zoo! Ser.). (ENG.). 16p. (J). (gr. -1-k). 5.95 *(978-1-56899-856-5(2),* B9006) Soundprints.

Gilbert, Sara. Saber-Toothed Cats. 2017. (Ice Age Mega Beasts Ser.). (ENG., Illus.). 24p. (J). (gr. 1-4). pap. 8.99 *(978-1-62832-377-1(9),* 20081, Creative Paperbacks); *(978-1-60818-769-0(1),* 20083, Creative Education) Creative Co., The.

Gish, Melissa. Tiger. 2019. (Spotlight on Nature Ser.). (ENG.). 32p. (J). (gr. 4-7). pap. 9.99 *(978-1-62832-749-6(9),* 19197, Creative Paperbacks) Creative Co., The.

Goecke, Michael P. Saber-Toothed Cat, 1 vol. 2003. (Prehistoric Animals Ser.). (ENG.). 24p. (gr. k-4). 25.65 *(978-1-57765-970-9(8),* Buddy Bks.) ABDO Publishing Co.

Goldish, Meish. Siberian Tiger: The World's Biggest Cat. 2010. (More SuperSized! Ser.). (Illus.). 24p. (J). (gr. k-3). lib. bdg. 26.99 *(978-1-936087-28-0(6))* Bearport Publishing Co., Inc.

Goodman, Susan E. Saber-Toothed Cats. Maguire, Kerry, illus. 2005. (On My Own Science Ser.). 48p. (J). (gr. 3-7). lib. bdg. 25.26 *(978-1-57505-759-0(X))* Lerner Publishing Group.

Green, Carl R. & Katirgis, Jane. Endangered Tigers, 1 vol. 2015. (Wildlife at Risk Ser.). (ENG.). 48p. (gr. 6-6). pap. 12.70 *(978-0-7660-6904-6(4),* 658fd740-d8fe-4596-b45d-54243628a925); (Illus.). 29.60 *(978-0-7660-6906-0(0),* 4adb7449-adbe-4a60-a5b8-2035b98a95e5) Enslow Publishing, LLC.

Gregoire, Maryellen. Un Cachorro de Tigre. 2012. (Wonder Readers Spanish Emergent Ser.). (SPA.). 8p. (J). (gr. -1-1). pap. 37.50 *(978-1-62065-573-3(X),* 19238) Capstone.

—A Tiger Cub, 1 vol. 2012. (Wonder Readers Emergent Level Ser.). (ENG.). 8p. (J). (gr. -1-1). pap. 6.25 *(978-1-4296-7788-2(0),* 117962, Capstone Pr.) Capstone.

Guarnotta, Lucia, illus. We Are Tigers. 2006. (We Are... Ser.). 40p. (J). (gr. -1-k). bds. *(978-2-7641-1456-8(7))* Tormont Pubns.

Hall, Margaret. Tigers & Their Cubs. 2007. (Animal Offspring Ser.). (ENG.). 24p. (J). (gr. k-1). pap. 41.70 *(978-1-4296-0565-6(0),* Capstone Pr.) Capstone.

—Tigers & Their Cubs: A 4D Book. rev. ed. 2018. (Animal Offspring Ser.). (ENG., Illus.). 24p. (J). (gr. -1-2). pap. 6.95 *(978-1-5435-0838-3(3),* 137601); lib. bdg. 29.32 *(978-1-5435-0826-0(X),* 137589) Capstone. (Capstone Pr.).

Hanel, Rachael. Tigers. 2008. (Living Wild Ser.). (Illus.). 46p. (J). (gr. 4-6). lib. bdg. 22.95 *(978-1-58341-660-0(9),* Creative Education) Creative Co., The.

Hansen, Grace. Siberian Tigers. 2018. (Super Species Ser.). (ENG., Illus.). 24p. (J). (gr. -1-2). lib. bdg. 32.79 *(978-1-5321-0826-6(5),* 28213, Abdo Kids) ABDO Publishing Co.

—Tigres Siberianos. 2018. (Especies Extraordinarias (Super Species) Ser.).Tr. of Siberian Tigers. (SPA.). 24p. (J). (gr. -1-2). lib. bdg. 32.79 *(978-1-5321-8411-6(5),* 30015, Abdo Kids) ABDO Publishing Co.

Hendrix, Emilia. Tigers & Cubs, 1 vol. 2015. (Animal Family Ser.). (ENG.). 24p. (J). (gr. k-k). pap. 9.15 *(978-1-4824-3791-1(0),* 6756743e-b02c-495e-b8ab-98f18cc63c5b) Stevens, Gareth Publishing LLLP.

Hoff, Mary King. Tigers. 2005. (Wild World of Animals (Creative Education) Ser.). (Illus.). 32p. (J). (gr. 2-5). lib. bdg. 18.95 *(978-1-58341-355-5(3),* Creative Education) Creative Co., The.

Jazynka, Kitson. National Geographic Kids Mission: Tiger Rescue: All about Tigers & How to Save Them. 2015. (NG Kids Mission: Animal Rescue Ser.). (Illus.). 112p. (J). (gr. 5-9). pap. 12.99 *(978-1-4263-1895-5(2),* National Geographic Kids) Disney Publishing Worldwide.

Jeffrey, Gary. Sabertooth Tiger. 2017. (Graphic Prehistoric Animals Ser.). (ENG., Illus.). 32p. (J). (gr. 5-8). lib. bdg. 31.35 *(978-1-62588-411-4(7),* 19280, Smart Apple Media) Black Rabbit Bks.

Jenkins, Martin. Can We Save the Tiger? White, Vicky, illus. 2014. (ENG.). 56p. (J). (gr. k-3). 9.99 *(978-0-7636-7378-9(1))* Candlewick Pr.

Kalman, Bobbie. Endangered Tigers. 2008. (FRE.). 32p. (J). pap. 9.95 *(978-2-89579-204-8(6))* Bayard Canada Livres CAN. Dist: Crabtree Publishing Co.

—Endangered Tigers, 1 vol. 2004. (Earth's Endangered Animals Ser.). (ENG., Illus.). 32p. (J). pap. *(978-0-7787-1896-3(4))* Crabtree Publishing Co.

Kelley, K. C. Baby Hippos. 2018. (Spot Baby Animals Ser.). (ENG.). 16p. (J). (gr. -1-2). pap. 7.99 *(978-1-68152-256-2(X),* 14845) Amicus.

Latta, Jan. Timba el Tigre (Timba the Tiger), 1 vol. 2007. (Familias de Animales Salvajes (Wild Animal Families) Ser.). (SPA., Illus.). 24p. (gr. 2-4). lib. bdg. 26.67 *(978-0-8368-7971-1(6),* 56203303-5562-4393-b304-8d47aa759e0b, Gareth Stevens Learning Library) Stevens, Gareth Publishing LLLP.

—Timba the Tiger, 1 vol. 2007. (Wild Animal Families Ser.). (ENG., Illus.). 24p. (gr. 2-4). pap. 9.15 *(978-0-8368-7779-3(9),* 85b81615-79e3-40fc-9eac-ad5c82b050cb); lib. bdg. 26.67 *(978-0-8368-7772-4(1),* 786a6cfb-2a52-452d-8a6b-fd67049672ca) Stevens, Gareth Publishing LLLP. (Gareth Stevens Learning Library).

Leaf, Christina. Baby Tigers. 2015. (Super Cute! Ser.). (ENG., Illus.). 24p. (J). (gr. k-3). lib. bdg. 26.95 *(978-1-62617-173-2(4),* Blastoff! Readers) Bellwether Media.

Ledu-Frattini, Stéphanie. The Tiger. Uhlig, Elizabeth, tr. from FRE. Sah, Anup, photos by. 2004. (Animal Close-Ups Ser.). (Illus.). 28p. (J). pap. 6.95 *(978-1-57091-373-0(0))* Charlesbridge Publishing, Inc.

Lynch, Seth. Tigers at the Zoo, 1 vol. 2019. (Zoo Animals Ser.). (ENG.). 24p. (gr. k-k). pap. 9.15 *(978-1-5382-3950-6(7),* b5de3383-c42c-4d07-b0bb-0ecf82daf56a) Stevens, Gareth Publishing LLLP.

Macheske, Felicia. Striped Stalkers: Tiger. 2017. (Guess What Ser.). (ENG., Illus.). 24p. (J). (gr. k-2). lib. bdg. 30.64 *(978-1-63472-172-1(1),* 209260) Cherry Lake Publishing.

Maclaine, James. Tigers IR. 2012. (Beginner's Nature Ser.). 32p. (J). bds. 4.99 *(978-0-7945-3286-4(1),* Usborne) EDC Publishing.

Macleod, Steve. Soy el Tigre. 2012. (SPA.). (J). *(978-1-61913-179-8(X))* Weigl Pubs., Inc.

—Tiger. 2011. (J). 27.13 *(978-1-61690-853-9(X));* pap. 12.95 *(978-1-61690-854-6(8))* Weigl Pubs., Inc.

Marsh, Laura. National Geographic Readers: Tigers. 2012. (Readers Ser.). (Illus.). 32p. (J). (gr. 1-3). pap. 4.99 *(978-1-4263-0911-3(2));* (ENG., lib. bdg. 14.90 *(978-1-4263-0912-0(0))* Disney Publishing Worldwide. (National Geographic Kids).

McRae, Anne & Morris, Neil. Celia the Tiger. De Luca, Daniela, illus. 2017. 31p. (J). *(978-0-7166-3524-6(0))* World Bk., Inc.

Meister, Cari. Do You Really Want to Meet a Tiger? Fabbri, Daniele, illus. 2014. (Do You Really Want to Meet ... ? Ser.). (ENG.). 24p. (J). (gr. 1-4). 27.10 *(978-1-60753-459-4(2),* 15901) Amicus.

—Tigers. 2015. (J). lib. bdg. 25.65 *(978-1-62031-169-1(0),* Bullfrog Bks.) Jump! Inc.

Montgomery, Sy. The Man-Eating Tigers of Sundarbans. Briggs, Eleanor, photos by. 2004. (Illus.). 57p. (J). 14.60 *(978-0-7569-5180-1(1))* Perfection Learning Corp.

Moore, S. Tiger Talk: Learning the T Sound. 2009. (PowerPhonics Ser.). 24p. (gr. 1-1). 39.90 *(978-1-60851-475-5(7),* PowerKids Pr.) Rosen Publishing Group, Inc., The.

Morgan, Sally. Amazing Animals - Tigers. 2004. (QEB Animal Lives Ser.). (Illus.). 32p. (J). lib. bdg. 18.95 *(978-1-59566-035-0(6))* QEB Publishing Inc.

—Amazing Animals - Tigers. 2012. (ENG., Illus.). 32p. (gr. 3-5). pap. 8.95 *(978-1-926722-53-5(1))* Saunders Bk. Co. CAN. Dist: RiverStream Publishing.

—Tigers. 2010. (Amazing Animal Hunters Ser.). (ENG.). 32p. (J). (gr. 3-5). lib. bdg. 28.50 *(978-1-60753-049-7(X),* 17204) Amicus.

Murray, Julie. Tiger Cubs. 2018. (Baby Animals (Abdo Kids Junior) Ser.). (ENG., Illus.). 24p. (J). (gr. -1-2). lib. bdg. 31.36 *(978-1-5321-8168-9(X),* 29893, Abdo Kids) ABDO Publishing Co.

—Tigers. 2019. (Animal Kingdom Ser.). (ENG., Illus.). 32p. (J). (gr. 2-5). lib. bdg. 34.21 *(978-1-5321-1654-4(3),* 32419, Big Buddy Bks.) ABDO Publishing Co.

National Wildlife Federation Staff & Tomio, Stacy. Wild Cats. 2017. (Ranger Rick: Amazing Animals Ser.). (Illus.). 40p. (J). (gr. 2-5). pap. 7.95 *(978-1-63076-220-9(2))* Muddy Boots Pr.

Nobleman, Marc Tyler. Tigers, 1 vol. 2009. (Endangered! Ser.). (ENG.). 48p. (gr. 3-3). lib. bdg. 32.64 *(978-0-7614-2986-9(7),* 09541cd4-e7a3-4f5b-854a-2076a965ba40) Cavendish Square Publishing LLC.

O'Neal, Claire. Threat to the Bengal Tiger. 2008. (On the Verge of Extinction Ser.). (Illus.). 32p. (J). (gr. 1-5). lib. bdg. 25.70 *(978-1-58415-688-8(0))* Mitchell Lane Pubs.

Owen, Ruth. Tiger Cubs. (Wild Baby Animals Ser.). 24p. (J). (gr. k-3). 2016. (ENG.). pap. 7.99 *(978-1-944998-39-4(X))* 2011. lib. bdg. 25.65 *(978-1-61772-158-8(1))* 2011. lib. bdg., E-Book 39.93 *(978-1-61772-245-5(6))* Bearport Publishing Co., Inc.

Owings, Lisa. Tiger Attack. 2012. (Animal Attacks Ser.). (ENG., Illus.). 24p. (J). (gr. 3-7). lib. bdg. 26.95 *(978-1-60014-792-0(5),* Torque Bks.) Bellwether Media.

Pallotta, Jerry. Lion vs. Tiger (Who Would Win?) Bolster, Rob, illus. 2015. (Who Would Win? Ser.). (ENG.). 32p. (J). (gr. 1-3). pap. 3.99 (978-0-545-17571-5(2)) Scholastic, Inc.

Pearl, Norman. Tigers: Hunters of Asia. (Powerful Predators Ser.). 24p. (gr. 2-3). 2009. 42.50 (978-1-60851-350-5(5)) 2008. (ENG., Illus.). (J). lib. bdg. 26.27 (978-1-4042-4507-5(3), 5adedb68-3798-42a6-a938-00906c23ddbd) Rosen Publishing Group, Inc., The. (PowerKids Pr.).

Pelusey, Michael & Pelusey, Jane. Lions & Tigers, 1 vol. 2009. (Zoo Animals Ser.). (ENG.). 32p. (gr. 2-2). lib. bdg. 21.27 (978-0-7614-3151-0(9), 0b10e42f-c952-460e-8738-7ecf87a74c11) Cavendish Square Publishing LLC.

Peterson, Megan Cooley & Rustad, Martha E. H. Bengal Tigers Are Awesome! 2015. (Awesome Asian Animals Ser.). (ENG., Illus.). 32p. (J). (gr. -1-2). lib. bdg. 27.99 (978-1-4914-3903-6(3), 128620, Capstone Pr.) Capstone.

Poitier, Anton. Once I Was a Comic... But Now I'm a Book about Tigers. Evans, Melvyn, illus. 2010. 24p. (J). (gr. k-3). 7.99 (978-0-8416-7201-7(6)) Hammond World Atlas Corp.

Portman, Michael. Tigers in Danger, 1 vol. 2011. (Animals at Risk Ser.). (ENG., Illus.). 24p. (J). (gr. 2-3). pap. 9.15 (978-1-4339-5812-0(0), 5bcdedb8-da37-476a-8a73-a6cf308052bb); lib. bdg. 25.27 (978-1-4339-5810-6(4), 23824c98-9d79-4cc5-b96e-52b2572eaf25) Stevens, Gareth Publishing LLLP. (Gareth Stevens Learning Library).

Quality Productions Staff. Tigres. Rountree, Monica, tr. 2003. (Zoobooks Ser.). Orig. Title: Tigers. (SPA., Illus.). 24p. (J). (gr. k-6). lib. bdg. 15.95 (978-1-888153-75-0(X)) National Wildlife Federation.

Quintin, Michel & Bergeron, Alain M. Do You Know Tigers?, 1 vol. Messier, Solange, tr. Sampar, illus. 2015. (Do You Know? Ser.). (ENG.). 64p. (J). (gr. 2-4). pap. 9.95 (978-1-55455-355-6(5), 0f2029f9-3641-401e-ae9e-eff825f2f572) Trifolium Bks., Inc. CAN. Dist: Firefly Bks., Ltd.

Reher, Matt. Could a Tiger Be My Pet? 2015. (1B Animal Behaviors Ser.). (ENG., Illus.). 24p. (J). pap. 8.00 (978-1-63437-448-4(7)) American Reading Co.

Riddolls, Tom. Tigers. 2014. (J). pap. (978-1-4896-0931-1(8)) Weigl Pubs., Inc.

Riggs, Kate. Seedlings: Tigers. 2014. (Seedlings Ser.). (ENG.). 24p. (J). (gr. -1-k). pap. 9.99 (978-0-89812-889-5(7), 21687, Creative Paperbacks) Creative Co., The.

—Tigers. 2013. (Seedlings Ser.). (ENG.). 24p. (J). (gr. -1-k). 25.65 (978-1-60818-344-9(0), 21686, Creative Education) Creative Co., The.

Ring, Susan. Project Tiger. Marshall, Diana & Nault, Jennifer, eds. 2003. (Zoo Life Ser.). (Illus.). 24p. (J). pap. 8.95 (978-1-59036-061-3(3)) Weigl Pubs., Inc.

Ringstad, Arnold. Tigers. 2014. (Wild Cats Ser.). (ENG., Illus.). 24p. (J). (gr. 1-4). lib. bdg. 27.10 (978-1-60753-605-5(6), 16068) Amicus.

Ritchey, Kate. Lion, Tiger, & Bear. 2015. (Penguin Young Readers, Level 4 Ser.). (ENG., Illus.). 48p. (J). (gr. 3-4). pap. 4.99 (978-0-448-48336-8(X), Penguin Young Readers) Penguin Young Readers Group.

Rober, Harold. Saber-Toothed Cat. 2017. (Bumba Books (r) — Dinosaurs & Prehistoric Beasts Ser.). (ENG., Illus.). 24p. (J). (gr. -1-1). 26.65 (978-1-5124-2645-9(8), 76e4daaf-5c3b-4b77-8405-9bb89df219c8); E-Book 39.99 (978-1-5124-2739-4(X)); E-Book 39.99 (978-1-5124-3716-4(6), 9781512437164); E-Book 4.99 (978-1-5124-3717-1(4), 9781512437171) Lerner Publishing Group. (Lerner Pubns.).

Royston, Angela. Save the Tiger, 1 vol., 1. 2013. (Animal SOS! Ser.). (ENG.). 32p. (J). (gr. 2-3). 29.92 (978-1-4777-6029-1(6), 0c924356-32ca-4a7a-9c4d-2b1e1cd1c7ca, Windmill Bks.) Rosen Publishing Group, Inc., The.

Schafer, Susan & Robinson, Fay. Tigers, 1 vol. 2010. (Animals Ser.). (ENG.). 24p. (gr. 3-3). 26.93 (978-0-7614-4345-2(2), 0971603a-524b-4f71-a101-1964d8a8b5ea) Cavendish Square Publishing LLC.

Server, Lee. Tigers, Vol. 12. 2018. (Animals in the Wild Ser.). (Illus.). 72p. (J). (gr. 7). 33.27 (978-1-4222-4174-5(2)) Mason Crest.

—Tigers - Pb: A Portrait of the Animal World. 2013. (Portrait of the Animal World Ser.). (Illus.). 72p. pap. 9.95 (978-1-59764-319-1(X)) New Line Bks.

Sexton, Colleen. The Bengal Tiger. 2011. (Nature's Deadliest Ser.). (ENG., Illus.). 24p. (J). (gr. 3-8). lib. bdg. 27.95 (978-1-60014-663-3(5), Pilot Bks.) Bellwether Media.

Shafer, Barbara. Baby Tigers. 2018. (Adorable Animals Ser.). (ENG.). 32p. (J). (gr. 4-6). pap. 9.99 (978-1-64466-247-2(7), 12243); (Illus.). lib. bdg. (978-1-68072-400-4(2), 12242) Black Rabbit Bks. (Bolt).

Sirota, Lyn A. Bengal Tigers, 1 vol. 2010. (Asian Animals Ser.). (ENG.). 24p. (J). (gr. -1-2). pap. 7.29 (978-1-4296-4843-1(0), 112824); (gr. k-1). pap. 43.74 (978-1-4296-5093-9(1), 15144) Capstone. (Capstone Pr.).

Smith, Lucy Sackett. Tigers: Prowling Predators, 1 vol. 2009. (Mighty Mammals Ser.). (ENG.). 24p. (J). (gr. 2-3). pap. 9.25 (978-1-4358-3285-5(X), 18b1c29d-aaad-432d-854a-14384b328eb7, PowerKids Pr.); (Illus.). lib. bdg. 26.27 (978-1-4042-8107-3(X), fd8d64b8-98cd-42ce-a405-266baaf584ec) Rosen Publishing Group, Inc., The.

Soundprints, creator. Tiger Cub See-and-Do. 2011. (Let's Go to the Zoo! Ser.). (ENG., Illus.). 16p. (gr. -1). 5.95 (978-1-60727-460-5(4)) Soundprints.

Staff, Gareth Editorial Staff. Tigers, 1 vol. 2004. (All about Wild Animals Ser.). (ENG., Illus.). 32p. (gr. 2-4). lib. bdg. 28.67 (978-0-8368-4189-3(1), 4808804b-a781-4ff2-bd09-bf611c5e8796, Gareth Stevens Learning Library) Stevens, Gareth Publishing LLLP.

Statts, Leo. Tigers. 2016. (Savanna Animals Ser.). (ENG.). 24p. (J). (gr. -1-2). 49.94 (978-1-68079-371-0(3), 22992, Abdo Zoom-Launch) ABDO Publishing Co.

Steffora, Tracey. Animal Math: Adding, Taking Away, & Skip Counting, 1 vol. 2014. (Animal Math Ser.). (ENG.). 32p. (J). (gr. -1-1). 29.99 (978-1-4846-0061-0(4), Heinemann) Capstone.

—Taking Away with Tigers, 1 vol. 2013. (Animal Math Ser.). (ENG.). 24p. (J). (gr. -1-1). pap. 6.95 (978-1-4329-7570-8(6), 122529, Heinemann) Capstone.

Stefoff, Rebecca. Tigers, 1 vol. 2003. (Animal Ways Ser.). (ENG.). 112p. (gr. 6-6). 38.36 (978-0-7614-1391-2(X), 9bd4c5bf-d564-42d6-8b93-e910fdda1fcf) Cavendish Square Publishing LLC.

Stone, Lynn M. Tigers. 2004. (Nature Watch Ser.). (ENG.). 48p. (gr. 4-8). 27.93 (978-1-57505-578-7(3), Carolrhoda Bks.) Lerner Publishing Group.

Stone, Tanya Lee. Tigers. 2003. (Wild Wild World Ser.). 24p. (YA). 24.94 (978-1-56711-826-1(7), Blackbirch Pr., Inc.) Cengage Gale.

Taylor, Trace. Tigers of Asia. 2016. (1-3Y Mammals Ser.). (ENG.). 24p. (J). (gr. k-2). pap. 8.00 (978-1-59301-425-4(2)) American Reading Co.

Thomson, Sarah L. Amazing Tigers! 2005. (I Can Read Level 2 Ser.). (ENG., Illus.). 32p. (J). (gr. k-3). pap. 4.99 (978-0-06-054452-2(X), HarperCollins) HarperCollins Pubs.

Ticktock Media, Ltd. Staff. What Do Tigers Do? 2008. (What Do Animals Do? Ser.). (ENG.). 10p. (J). (gr. k — 1). bds. 4.95 (978-1-84696-794-8(5), TickTock Books) Octopus Publishing Group GBR. Dist: Independent Pubs. Group.

Tigers. 2003. (J). per. (978-1-57657-946-6(8)) Paradise Pr., Inc.

Tigers: Level R, 6 vols. (Wonder Worldtm Ser.). 48p. 44.95 (978-0-7802-7068-8(1)) Wright Group/McGraw-Hill.

Tiger's Tail. Date not set. (Touch & Feel Ser.). (J). 4.98 (978-0-7525-9570-2(9)) Parragon, Inc.

Turnbull, Stephanie. Tiger. 2013. (Big Beasts Ser.). (ENG., Illus.). 24p. (J). (gr. 1-4). 28.50 (978-1-59920-837-4(7), 17288) Black Rabbit Bks.

Unwin, Mike. Why Do Tigers Have Stripes? Morton, Robert et al, illus. 2006. (Usborne Starting Point Science Ser.). 22p. (J). (gr. 1-4). pap. 4.99 (978-0-7945-1408-2(1), Usborne) EDC Publishing.

Vogel, Elizabeth. Tigers. 2009. (Big Cats (Powerkids Readers) Ser.). 24p. (gr. 1-1). 37.50 (978-1-61511-572-3(2), PowerKids Pr.) Rosen Publishing Group, Inc., The.

Von Zumbusch, Amelie. Tigers: World's Largest Cats, 1 vol. 2007. (Dangerous Cats Ser.). (ENG., Illus.). 24p. (J). (gr. 2-3). lib. bdg. 26.27 (978-1-4042-3632-5(5), 213592a1-d40e-426f-82d3-dac0c0ccae8d) Rosen Publishing Group, Inc., The.

von Zumbusch, Amelie. Tigers: World's Largest Cats. 2009. (Dangerous Cats Ser.). 24p. (gr. 2-3). 42.50 (978-1-61512-131-1(5), PowerKids Pr.) Rosen Publishing Group, Inc., The.

Watson, Galadriel Findlay. Tigers. 2008. (Amazing Animals Ser.). (Illus.). 24p. (J). (gr. 2-4). pap. 8.95 (978-1-59036-963-0(7)); lib. bdg. 24.45 (978-1-59036-962-3(9)) Weigl Pubs., Inc.

Watt, E. Melanie. Tigers. 2012. (Animals on the Brink Ser.). (ENG., Illus.). 48p. (J). (gr. 4-7). pap. 14.95 (978-1-61913-432-4(2)); lib. bdg. 29.99 (978-1-61913-431-7(4)) Weigl Pubs., Inc. (AV2 by Weigl).

Wechterowicz, Przemyslaw. Secret Life of a Tiger. Dziubak, Emilia, illus. 2017. (ENG.). 32p. (J). (gr. -1-2). 18.99 (978-1-68297-154-3(6), Words & Pictures) Quarto Publishing Group UK GBR. Dist: Hachette Bk. Group.

Wells, Robert E. Can We Share the World with Tigers? Wells, Robert E., illus. 2012. (Wells of Knowledge Science Ser.). (ENG., Illus.). 32p. (J). (gr. -1-3). 16.99 (978-0-8075-1055-1(6), 807510556) Whitman, Albert & Co.

Whyte, Elizabeth. Tigers, 1 vol. 2012. (Killer Cats Ser.). (ENG., Illus.). 24p. (J). (gr. 2-3). pap. 9.15 (978-1-4339-7016-0(3), ac25f9e0-3607-4abc-9abb-72917d2c2baa); lib. bdg. 25.27 (978-1-4339-7015-3(5), ae782372-ca49-4e8e-92a5-0cb642f38cde) Stevens, Gareth Publishing LLLP.

Wildlife Education. Tigers. 2007. (Illus.). (J). 5.99 (978-1-932396-35-5(7), Critters Up Close) National Wildlife Federation.

Wildlife Education, contrib. by. Tigers. 2005. (Zootles Ser.). (Illus.). 23p. (J). (gr. -1-k). lib. bdg. 10.95 (978-1-932396-10-2(1)) National Wildlife Federation.

Wilsdon, Christina. Tigers, 1 vol. (Amazing Animals Ser.). (ENG.). 48p. (gr. 3-5). 2009. pap. 11.50 (978-1-4339-2020-2(4), e0eef10d-738d-474e-83a4-f3ead2b516b0, Gareth Stevens Learning Library) 2008. (J). lib. bdg. 30.67 (978-0-8368-9103-4(1), 199e1f5d-d39a-4f38-8ca8-d7b4ad802e8e) Stevens, Gareth Publishing LLLP.

—Tigers. 2007. (J). (978-1-59939-117-5(1), Reader's Digest Young Families, Inc.) Studio Fun International.

Yoyo Books Staff. We are Tigers. 2005. 40p. bds. (978-90-5843-818-8(X)) YoYo Bks.

Zeiger, Jennifer. Saber-Toothed Cat. 2015. (21st Century Junior Library: Dinosaurs & Prehistoric Creatures Ser.). (ENG., Illus.). 24p. (J). (gr. 2-5). lib. bdg. 29.21 (978-1-63362-386-6(6), 206964) Cherry Lake Publishing.

Zobel, Derek. Tigers. 2011. (Animal Safari Ser.). (ENG., Illus.). 24p. (J). (gr. k-3). lib. bdg. 26.95 (978-1-60014-610-7(4), Blastoff! Readers) Bellwether Media.

TIGER—FICTION

Abery, Julie. Little Tiger. 2019. (Illus.). 20p. (J). (gr. -1-k). bds. 9.99 (978-1-68152-413-9(9), 17590) Amicus.

Abraham, Rayna M. Just Imagine: Rayna Abraham's Creative Collection for Kids. 2011. 44p. pap. 16.59 (978-1-4634-1529-7(X)) AuthorHouse.

Adams, Pam. Tiger. 2005. (ENG., Illus.). 12p. (J). (gr. -1-k). bds. (978-1-904550-28-0(2)) Child's Play International Ltd.

Alzial, Sylvain. Panthera Tigris. Rajcak, Hélène, illus. 2019. (ENG.). 32p. (J). (978-0-8028-5529-9(6), Eerdmans Bks For Young Readers) Eerdmans, William B. Publishing Co.

Amazing Mallika - Evaluation Guide: Evaluation Guide. 2006. (J). (978-1-55942-398-4(6)) Witcher Productions.

Angel, Ido. Vipo in Moscow: The Siberian Tiger Is Hungry! 2015. (AV2 Animated Storytime Ser.). (ENG.). (J). lib. bdg. 29.99 (978-1-4896-3914-1(4), AV2 by Weigl) Weigl Pubs., Inc.

Aryal, Aimee. Hello Tiger! Graybill, Joni, illus. 2004. 24p. (J). 19.95 (978-1-932888-25-6(X)) Amplify Publishing Group.

Aubuchon, Hope L. Tiger, Ruler of the Universe. 2009. 48p. pap. 24.95 (978-1-60749-896-4(0)) America Star Bks.

Ayers, Linda. Tiger Does the Write Thing. Hunt, Jane, illus. l.t. ed. 2005. 35p. (J). per. 7.95 (978-0-9760505-4-4(4)) Blue Thistle Pr.

—Tiger Goes Collecting. Hunt, Jane, illus. l.t. ed. 2004. 55p. (J). per. 7.95 (978-0-9760505-2-0(8)) Blue Thistle Pr.

AZ Books. Tiger & His Stripes. 2013. (Amusing Stories Ser.). (ENG.). 10p. (J). (-k). bds. 7.95 (978-1-61889-307-9(6)) AZ Bks. LLC.

AZ Books Staff. Who Is the Tiger Looking For? Gridina, Anna, ed. 2012. (Who Is There Ser.). (ENG.). 10p. (J). (-k). bds. 11.95 (978-1-61889-037-5(9)) AZ Bks. LLC.

Banks, Lynne Reid. Tiger, Tiger. 2007. (ENG.). 208p. (YA). (gr. 7-11). mass mkt. 6.99 (978-0-440-42044-6(X), Laurel Leaf) Random Hse. Children's Bks.

Bannerman, Helen. Little Black Sambo. 2007. (Illus.). 72p. per. 11.45 (978-1-59462-581-7(6), Bk. Jungle) Standard Publications, Inc.

—Short Works of Helen Bannerman. l.t. ed. 2007. (ENG.). 54p. pap. 18.99 (978-1-4346-4066-6(3)) Creative Media Partners, LLC.

—The Story of Little Babaji. 2004. (Illus.). (J). (gr. -1-18). spiral bd. (978-0-616-14615-6(9)) Canadian National Institute for the Blind/Institut National Canadien pour les Aveugles.

—The Story of Little Black Sambo. 2007. pap. 7.99 (978-1-59986-912-4(8), FQ Classics) Filiquarian Publishing, LLC.

Barkow, Henriette. Buri & the Marrow. Finlay, Lizzie, illus. 2004. (ENG & FRE.). 24p. (J). pap. (978-1-85269-583-5(8)) Mantra Lingua.

Beck, Lynn G. & Sesa. Powercat, the Pacific Tiger. 2012. (J). 14.95 (978-1-937406-00-4(8)) Amplify Publishing Group.

Berkeley, Jon. The Palace of Laughter. Dorman, Brandon, illus. 2006. (Wednesday Tales Ser.: No. 1). 427p. (J). (gr. 3-7). 16.99 (978-0-06-075507-2(5), Julie Andrews Collection) HarperCollins Pubs.

—The Tiger's Egg. Dorman, Brandon, illus. (Wednesday Tales Ser.: No. 2). (J). 2009. (ENG.). 432p. pap. 7.99 (978-0-06-075512-6(1), Harper Trophy) 2007. 416p. (gr. 3-7). 16.99 (978-0-06-075510-2(5), Julie Andrews Collection) HarperCollins Pubs.

Bonnell, Kris. What Tigers Do. 2006. (J). pap. 5.95 (978-1-933727-41-7(1)) Reading Reading Bks., LLC.

Brennan, Sarah. The Tale of Temujin. Harrison, Harry, illus. 2012. (ENG.). 32p. (J). (978-1-937160-23-4(8)) Auspicious Times.

Brett, Jan. The Tale of the Tiger Slippers. Brett, Jan, illus. 2019. (Illus.). 32p. (J). (gr. -1-3). 18.99 (978-0-399-17074-4(X), G.P. Putnam's Sons Books for Young Readers) Penguin Young Readers Group.

Bright, J. E. The Fastest Pet on Earth, 1 vol. Baltazar, Art, illus. 2011. (DC Super-Pets Ser.). (ENG.). 56p. (J). (gr. 1-3). lib. bdg. 25.32 (978-1-4048-6264-7(1), 113677, Stone Arch Bks.) Capstone.

Brönner, Nele. The Tiger's Egg. 2018. (ENG., Illus.). 32p. (J). (gr. -1-2). 17.95 (978-0-7358-4319-6(8)) North-South Bks., Inc.

Brooks, John. The Sundarbans Tiger. 2006. 115p. (J). pap. 13.58 (978-0-9661789-4-4(7)) Canis Lupus Productions.

Brown, Peter. Mr. Tiger Goes Wild. 2014. (CHI & ENG.). 52p. (J). (gr. -1-2). (978-986-320-369-8(6)) Commonwealth Publishing Co., Ltd.

—Mr. Tiger Goes Wild. 2013. (ENG., Illus.). 48p. (J). (gr. -1-3). 18.99 (978-0-316-20063-9(8)) Little, Brown Bks. for Young Readers.

Butler, M. Christina & Pedler, Caroline. Don't Be Afraid Little Ones. 2018. (ENG.). 32p. (J). (gr. -1-1). bds. 9.99 (978-1-68099-425-4(5), Good Bks.) Skyhorse Publishing Co., Inc.

—Don't Be Afraid Little Ones - Choice Edition. 2018. (ENG.). 32p. (J). (gr. -1-1). bds. 9.99 (978-1-68099-428-5(X), Good Bks.) Skyhorse Publishing Co., Inc.

Cadet, John. The Kangaroo's Adventure. 2012. 24p. pap. 24.95 (978-1-4560-2861-9(8)) America Star Bks.

Cha, Hanna. Tiny Feet Between the Mountains. Cha, Hanna, illus. 2019. (ENG., Illus.). 40p. (J). (gr. -1-3). 17.99 (978-1-5344-2992-5(1), Simon & Schuster Bks. For Young Readers) Simon & Schuster Bks. For Young Readers.

Chan, Janette Shipston. The Tiny Tiger. 2010. 24p. (J). 13.50 (978-1-4520-4106-3(7)) AuthorHouse.

Child, Lauren. Maude the Not-So-Noticeable Shrimpton. Krauss, Trisha, illus. 2013. (ENG.). 32p. (J). (gr. k-3). 16.99 (978-0-7636-6515-9(0)) Candlewick Pr.

Choi, Susan. Camp Tiger. Rocco, John, illus. 2019. 40p. (J). (gr. -1-1). 17.99 (978-0-399-17329-5(3), G.P. Putnam's Sons Books for Young Readers) Penguin Young Readers Group.

Christie, Jacky. Roger's Big Adventure. 2005. (J). pap. 8.00 (978-0-8059-6889-7(X)) Dorrance Publishing Co., Inc.

Chronicle Books. Baby Tiger: Finger Puppet Book: (Finger Puppet Book for Toddlers & Babies, Baby Books for First Year, Animal Finger Puppets) Huang, Yu-Hsuan, illus. 2016. (Baby Animal Finger Puppets Ser.: 2). (ENG.). 12p. (J). (gr. -1 — 1). 7.99 (978-1-4521-4236-4(X)) Chronicle Bks. LLC.

Clarke, E. J. A Fairy's Courage. (Oakwing Ser.: 2). (ENG.). 208p. (J). (gr. 2-6). 2019. pap. 7.99 (978-1-4814-8193-9(2)) 2018. (Illus.). 16.99 (978-1-4814-8194-6(0)) Simon & Schuster Children's Publishing. (Aladdin).

Cline, Renee. Kawndra the Tiger. 2009. 28p. pap. 15.49 (978-1-4389-6484-3(6)) AuthorHouse.

Cook, Sherry & Johnson, Terri. Timothy Tornado, 26. Kuhn, Jesse, illus. l.t. ed. 2006. (Quirkles — Exploring Phonics through Science Ser.: 20). 32p. 7.99 (978-1-933815-19-0(1), Quirkles, The) Creative 3, LLC.

Corris, Charles R. Donald Ditz & the Red Tiger, 1 vol. 2010. 64p. pap. 19.95 (978-1-4512-2193-0(2)) America Star Bks.

Counts, Monika, illus. LSU Countdown to Touchdown. 2010. (Countdown to Touchdown Ser.). 20p. 14.95 (978-1-61524-081-4(0), Intervisual/Piggy Toes) Bendon, Inc.

Daniel Visits the Doctor. 2014. (Daniel Tiger's Neighborhood Ser.). (ENG., Illus.). 24p. (J). (gr. -1-1). pap. 4.99 (978-1-4814-1734-1(7), Simon Spotlight) Simon Spotlight.

De Luca, Daniela. Celia the Tiger. 2008. (It's a Wildlife, Buddy! Ser.). (ENG., Illus.). 30p. (J). (gr. -1-1). 12.95 (978-88-6098-089-2(5)) McRae Bks. Srl ITA. Dist: Independent Pubs. Group.

Derrick, David G., Jr. I'm the Scariest Thing in the Jungle! 2013. (ENG., Illus.). 36p. (J). (gr. -1-3). 15.95 (978-1-59702-087-9(7)) Immedium.

Derubertis, Barbara. Tessa Tiger's Temper Tantrums. Alley, R. W., illus. 2011. (Animal Antics A to Z Set III Ser.). pap. 45.32 (978-0-7613-8429-8(4)) Astra Publishing Hse.

deRubertis, Barbara. Tessa Tiger's Temper Tantrums. Alley, R. W., illus. 2011. (Animal Antics a to Z Ser.). 32p. (J). (gr. -1-3). pap. 7.95 (978-1-57565-345-7(1), d57fd885-dfc5-4308-b709-6bbbf0fff54e, Kane Press) Astra Publishing Hse.

deRubertis, Barbara & DeRubertis, Barbara. Tessa Tiger's Temper Tantrums. Alley, R. W., illus. 2012. (Animal Antics A to Z Ser.). 32p. (J). (gr. 2 — 1). cd-rom 7.95 (978-1-57565-413-3(X)) Astra Publishing Hse.

Dicamillo, Kate. The Tiger Rising. Sheban, Chris, illus. 2006. 144p. (J). (gr. 5). pap. 5.99 (978-0-7636-2916-8(2)) Candlewick Pr.

DiCamillo, Kate. The Tiger Rising. 2015. (ENG.). 144p. (J). (gr. 5). pap. 7.99 (978-0-7636-8087-9(7)) Candlewick Pr.

Dicamillo, Kate. The Tiger Rising. unabr. ed. 2004. (Middle Grade Cassette Librariestm Ser.). 128p. (J). (gr. 5-9). pap. 29.00 incl. audio (978-0-8072-0998-1(8), S YA 285 SP, Listening Library) Random Hse. Audio Publishing Group.

Dietl, Erhard. A Veces Quisiera Ser un Tigre. (Torre de Papel Ser.). (SPA., Illus.). (J). 7.95 (978-958-04-5040-5(4)) Norma S.A. COL. Dist: Distribuidora Norma, Inc.

Dowson, Nick. Tigress: Read & Wonder. Chapman, Jane, illus. 2007. (Read & Wonder Ser.). (ENG.). 32p. (J). (gr. -1-3). pap. 8.99 (978-0-7636-3314-1(3)) Candlewick Pr.

—Tigress with Audio: Read, Listen, & Wonder. Chapman, Jane, illus. 2008. (Read, Listen, & Wonder Ser.). (ENG.). 32p. (J). (gr. -1-3). pap. 8.99 (978-0-7636-3872-6(2)) Candlewick Pr.

—Tigress with Audio, Peggable: Read, Listen, & Wonder. Pack. Chapman, Jane, illus. 2008. (Read, Listen, & Wonder Ser.). (ENG.). 32p. (J). (gr. -1-3). pap. 9.99 (978-0-7636-4189-4(8)) Candlewick Pr.

Dufresne, Michèle. Baby Tiger's Blanket. 2005. (Georgie Giraffe Chapter Ser.). (J). pap. 7.67 (978-1-932570-44-1(6)) Pioneer Valley Bks.

Durant, Alan. If You Go Walking in Tiger Wood. Boon, Debbie, illus. 2005. (ENG.). 24p. (J). (gr. -1-k). pap. 9.99 (978-0-00-710390-4(5), HarperSport) HarperCollins Pubs. Ltd. GBR. Dist: Independent Pubs. Group.

Eliot, Margaret. Cat & Tiger Go to the Seaside. 2012. 24p. pap. 28.03 (978-1-4691-7674-1(2)) Xlibris Corp.

Ellie. Bengal & Sengal. 2006. (J). pap. 8.00 (978-0-8059-7273-3(0)) Dorrance Publishing Co., Inc.

Ellison, James W., et al. Two Brothers: The Story of Kumal & Sangha. novel ed. 2005. (ENG., Illus.). 192p. pap. 12.99 (978-1-55704-632-1(8), William Morrow Paperbacks) HarperCollins Pubs.

Flood, Pansie Hart. Tiger Turcotte Takes on the Know-It-All. Wummer, Amy, illus. 2005. 72p. (J). (gr. 1-4). pap. 6.95 (978-1-57505-900-6(2)) Lerner Publishing Group.

Forsythe, Amanda J. The Contabulous Adventures of M E. 2012. 28p. 24.95 (978-1-4626-6531-0(4)) America Star Bks.

Friedman, Becky. Daniel Goes to School. 2014. (Daniel Tiger's Neighborhood 8X8 Ser.). lib. bdg. 13.55 (978-0-606-35756-2(4)) Turtleback.

—Daniel Learns to Share. 2016. (Simon & Schuster Ready-To-Read Level 1 Ser.). lib. bdg. 13.55 (978-0-606-39754-4(X)) Turtleback.

—Daniel Tries a New Food. 2015. (Daniel Tiger's Neighborhood 8X8 Ser.). lib. bdg. 13.55 (978-0-606-37874-1(X)) Turtleback.

—Daniel Visits the Doctor. 2014. (Daniel Tiger's Neighborhood 8X8 Ser.). lib. bdg. 13.55 (978-0-606-36112-5(X)) Turtleback.

—Daniel's First Fireworks. 2016. (Daniel Tiger's Neighborhood 8X8 Ser.). lib. bdg. 13.55 (978-0-606-38990-7(3)) Turtleback.

—Daniel's Winter Adventure. Fruchter, Jason, illus. 2016. (Daniel Tiger's Neighborhood 8X8 Ser.). (ENG.). 24p. (gr. -1-2). 13.55 (978-0-606-39247-1(5)) Turtleback.

—Munch Your Lunch! 2018. (Daniel Tiger's Neighborhood 8X8 Ser.). (Illus.). (J). lib. bdg. 16.00 (978-0-606-41413-5(4)) Turtleback.

—What Is Daniel Wearing? Fruchter, Jason, illus. 2015. (Daniel Tiger's Neighborhood Ser.). (ENG.). 14p. (J). (gr. -1 — 1). 8.99 (978-1-4814-2899-6(3), Simon Spotlight) Simon Spotlight.

Fruchter, Jason, illus. The Baby Is Here! 2015. (Daniel Tiger's Neighborhood Ser.). (ENG.). 24p. (J). (gr. -1-2). pap. 4.99 (978-1-4814-3013-5(0), Simon Spotlight) Simon Spotlight.

—Big Enough to Help. 2015. (Daniel Tiger's Neighborhood Ser.). (ENG.). 24p. (J). (gr. -1-1). pap. 5.99 (978-1-4814-2942-9(6), Simon Spotlight) Simon Spotlight.

—Daniel & the Nutcracker. 2018. (Daniel Tiger's Neighborhood Ser.). (ENG.). 20p. (J). (gr. -1 — 1). bds. 6.99 (978-1-5344-2206-3(4), Simon Spotlight) Simon Spotlight.

—Daniel Feels Left Out: Ready-To-Read Pre-Level 1. 2015. (Daniel Tiger's Neighborhood Ser.). (ENG.). 32p. (J). (gr. -1-k). 17.99 (978-1-4814-3836-0(0), Simon Spotlight) Simon Spotlight.

—Daniel Goes to School. 2014. (Daniel Tiger's Neighborhood Ser.). (ENG.). 24p. (J). (gr. -1-2). pap. 4.99 (978-1-4814-0318-4(4), Simon Spotlight) Simon Spotlight.

—Daniel Goes to the Playground. 2015. (Daniel Tiger's Neighborhood Ser.). (ENG.). 24p. (J). (gr. -1-2). pap. 3.99 (978-1-4814-5198-7(7), Simon Spotlight) Simon Spotlight.

—Daniel Learns to Share: Ready-To-Read Pre-Level 1. 2016. (Daniel Tiger's Neighborhood Ser.). (ENG.). 32p. (J). (gr. -1-k). pap. 4.99 (978-1-4814-6751-3(4), Simon Spotlight) Simon Spotlight.

—Daniel Plays at School: Ready-To-Read Pre-Level 1. 2016. (Daniel Tiger's Neighborhood Ser.). (ENG.). 32p. (J). (gr. -1-k). pap. 4.99 (978-1-4814-6102-3(8), Simon Spotlight) Simon Spotlight.

—Daniel Tries a New Food. 2015. (Daniel Tiger's Neighborhood Ser.). (ENG.). 24p. (J). (gr. -1-2). pap. 4.99 (978-1-4814-4170-4(1), Simon Spotlight) Simon Spotlight.

—Daniel's First Fireworks. 2016. (Daniel Tiger's Neighborhood Ser.). (ENG.). 24p. (J). (gr. -1-2). pap. 4.99 (978-1-4814-6053-8(6), Simon Spotlight) Simon Spotlight.

—Daniel's First Sleepover. 2015. (Daniel Tiger's Neighborhood Ser.). (ENG.). 24p. (J). (gr. -1-2). pap. 4.99 (978-1-4814-2893-4(4), Simon Spotlight) Simon Spotlight.

—Daniel's New Friend. 2015. (Daniel Tiger's Neighborhood Ser.). (ENG.). 24p. (J). (gr. -1-2). pap. 4.99 (978-1-4814-3543-7(4), Simon Spotlight) Simon Spotlight.

—Friends Help Each Other: Ready-To-Read Pre-Level 1. 2014. (Daniel Tiger's Neighborhood Ser.). (ENG.). 32p. (J). (gr. -1-k). pap. 4.99 *(978-1-4814-0366-5(4)*, Simon Spotlight) Simon Spotlight.

—Happy Love Day, Daniel Tiger! A Lift-The-Flap Book. 2015. (Daniel Tiger's Neighborhood Ser.). (ENG.). 14p. (J). (gr. -1-2). bds. 6.99 *(978-1-4814-4855-0(2)*, Simon Spotlight) Simon Spotlight.

—How Is Daniel Feeling? 2015. (Daniel Tiger's Neighborhood Ser.). (ENG.). 14p. (J). (gr. -1-k). bds. 12.99 *(978-1-4814-3856-8(5)*, Simon Spotlight) Simon Spotlight.

—I Love You, Dad. 2015. (Daniel Tiger's Neighborhood Ser.). (ENG.). 26p. (J). (gr. -1-k). bds. 8.99 *(978-1-4814-5736-1(5)*, Simon Spotlight) Simon Spotlight.

—Munch Your Lunch! 2018. (Daniel Tiger's Neighborhood Ser.). (ENG.). 16p. (J). (gr. -1-2). pap. 5.99 *(978-1-5344-1778-6(8)*, Simon Spotlight) Simon Spotlight.

—What Time Is It, Daniel Tiger? 2016. (Daniel Tiger's Neighborhood Ser.). (ENG.). 14p. (J). (gr. -1-k). bds. 10.99 *(978-1-4814-6934-0(7)*, Simon Spotlight) Simon Spotlight.

—You're Still You! 2016. (Daniel Tiger's Neighborhood Ser.). (ENG.). 12p. (J). (gr. -1-k). bds. 5.99 *(978-1-4814-6743-8(3)*, Simon Spotlight) Simon Spotlight.

Fusek Peters, Andrew. The Tiger & the Wise Man. Mayo, Diana, illus. (Traditional Tales with a Twist Ser.). 32p. (J). 2010. (gr. -1-2). *(978-1-84643-346-7(0))* 2004. (gr. 2-3). *(978-1-904550-07-5(X))* Child's Play International Ltd.

Gaiman, Neil. Cinnamon. Srinivasan, Divya, illus. 2017. (ENG.). 40p. (J). (gr. -1-3). 19.99 *(978-0-06-239961-8(6)*, HarperCollins) HarperCollins Pubs.

Gallo, Tina. Daniel Will Pack a Snack. 2018. (Ready-To-Read Ser.). (ENG.). 32p. (J). (gr. -1-1). 13.89 *(978-1-64310-720-2(8))* Penworthy Co., LLC, The.

—Daniel Will Pack a Snack. 2018. (Daniel Tiger's Neighborhood Ready-To-Read Ser.). (Illus.). 31p. (J). lib. bdg. 14.75 *(978-0-606-40860-8(6))* Turtleback.

—Daniel Will Pack a Snack: Ready-To-Read Ready-to-Go! Fruchter, Jason, illus. 2017. (Daniel Tiger's Neighborhood Ser.). (ENG.). 32p. (J). (gr. -1-k). 16.99 *(978-1-5344-1118-0(6))*; pap. 4.99 *(978-1-5344-1117-3(8))* Simon Spotlight. (Simon Spotlight).

Garwood, Gord, illus. Thank You Day: Ready-To-Read Pre-Level 1. 2014. (Daniel Tiger's Neighborhood Ser.). (ENG.). 24p. (J). (gr. -1-k). pap. 4.99 *(978-1-4424-9833-4(1)*, Simon Spotlight) Simon Spotlight.

Gorbachev, Valeri. Cats Are Cats. 2019. (I Like to Read Ser.). (Illus.). 32p. (J). (gr. -1-3). pap. 7.99 *(978-0-8234-4524-0(0))* Holiday Hse., Inc.

Grambling, Lois G. Can I Bring Saber to New York, Ms. Mayor? Love, Judy, illus. 2014. (Prehistoric Pets Ser.: 3). 32p. (J). (gr. k-3). 17.95 *(978-1-58089-570-5(0))* Charlesbridge Publishing, Inc.

Grant, Neil. The Honeyman & the Hunter. 2020. (ENG., Illus.). 288p. (YA). (gr. 9). pap. 14.99 *(978-1-76063-187-1(6)*, A&U Children's) Allen & Unwin AUS. Dist: Independent Pubs. Group.

Hale, Bruce. Danny & the Dinosaur & the New Puppy. 2015. (I Can Read! Level 1 Ser.). (J). lib. bdg. 13.55 *(978-0-606-37608-2(9))* Turtleback.

Hamburg, Jennifer. Daniel Goes to the Playground. 2015. (Daniel Tiger's Neighborhood 8X8 Ser.). lib. bdg. 13.55 *(978-0-606-38256-4(9))* Turtleback.

Hamilton, Linda. Smile & Say Cheetah! Brown, Kevin, illus. 2005. *(978-1-933248-00-4(9))* World Quest Learning.

Harris, Wendy. Daniel Visits the Library. 2015. (Daniel Tiger's Neighborhood Ready-To-Read Ser.). lib. bdg. 13.55 *(978-0-606-37875-8(8))* Turtleback.

Harrison, David L. & Yolen, Jane. Rum Pum Pum. Sarkar, Anjan, illus. 2020. 40p. (J). (gr. -1-2). 18.99 *(978-0-8234-4100-6(8))* Holiday Hse., Inc.

Harvey, Charlene A. The Adventures of the Tiger Club. 2011. 14p. pap. 10.99 *(978-1-61215-027-7(6))* Salem Author Services.

Hoffmire, Baird, illus. How Tiger Got His Stripes: A Folktale from Vietnam. 2006. (Story Cove Ser.). (ENG.). 32p. (J). (gr. -1-3). pap. 4.95 *(978-0-87483-799-5(5))* August Hse. Pubs., Inc.

Hong, Chen Jiang. The Tiger Prince. Waters, Alyson, tr. 2018. (ENG., Illus.). 40p. (J). (gr. -1-3). 18.95 *(978-1-68137-294-5(0)*, NYR Children's Collection) New York Review of Bks., Inc., The.

Houck, Colleen. Tiger's Curse, Bk. 1. 2012. (Tiger's Curse Ser.: 1). (ENG.). 456p. (J). (gr. 7). pap. 12.99 *(978-1-4549-0249-2(3))* Sterling Publishing Co., Inc.

—Tiger's Curse. 2012. (Tiger's Curse Ser.: Bk. 1). lib. bdg. 20.80 *(978-0-606-23822-9(0))* Turtleback.

—Tiger's Destiny. 2015. (Tiger's Curse Ser.: 4). (ENG.). 464p. (J). (gr. 7). pap. 12.99 *(978-1-4549-0356-7(2))* Sterling Publishing Co., Inc.

—Tiger's Quest. 2013. (Tiger's Curse Ser.: 2). (ENG.). 512p. (J). (gr. 7). pap. 11.95 *(978-1-4549-0358-1(9))* Sterling Publishing Co., Inc.

—Tiger's Voyage. 2014. (Tiger's Curse Ser.: 3). (ENG.). 568p. (J). (gr. 7). pap. 12.99 *(978-1-4549-0357-4(0))* Sterling Publishing Co., Inc.

Irwin, Bindi & Black, Jess. Roar!, 6. 2011. (Bindi's Wildlife Adventures Ser.: 6). (ENG.). 112p. (J). (gr. 3-6). pap. 8.99 *(978-1-4022-5931-9(X)*, Sourcebooks Jabberwocky) Sourcebooks, Inc.

Izquierdo, Ana, tr. Caritas Felices: Winnie-the-Pooh. 2007. (Disney Winnie the Pooh (SilverDolphin) Ser.). (SPA., Illus.). 10p. (J). (gr. -1). bds. *(978-970-718-393-3(4)*, Silver Dolphin en Español) Advanced Marketing, S. de R. L. de C. V.

Jones, Thomas Rumsey. Boris: The Bengal Tiger. Eguiguren, India J. & Eguiguren, A. R., illus. 2013. 46p. pap. 5.99 *(978-1-883378-81-3(8))* Sun on Earth Bks.

Kasza, Keiko. The Rat & the Tiger. 2007. (Illus.). 32p. (J). (gr. -1-2). pap. 7.99 *(978-0-14-240900-8(6)*, Puffin Books) Penguin Young Readers Group.

Katz, Karen. Roar, Roar, Baby! A Karen Katz Lift-The-Flap Book. Katz, Karen, illus. 2015. (ENG., Illus.). 14p. (J). (gr. -1 — 1). bds. 6.99 *(978-1-4814-1788-4(6)*, Little Simon) Little Simon.

Keller, Tae. When You Trap a Tiger. 2020. 304p. (J). *(978-0-593-17534-7(4))* Random Hse., Inc.

—When You Trap a Tiger: (Newbery Medal Winner) (J). (gr. 3-7). 2023. 320p. pap. 8.99 *(978-1-5247-1573-1(5)*, Yearling) 2020. (ENG.). 304p. 17.99 *(978-1-5247-1570-0(0)*, Random Hse. Bks. for Young Readers) 2020. (ENG.). 304p. lib. bdg. 19.99 *(978-1-5247-1571-7(9)*, Random Hse. Bks. for Young Readers) Random Hse. Children's Bks.

Kerr, Judith. The Judith Kerr Treasury. 2014. (ENG., Illus.). 176p. (J). 29.99 *(978-0-00-758653-0(1)*, HarperCollins Children's Bks.) HarperCollins Pubs. Ltd. GBR. Dist: HarperCollins Pubs.

—The Tiger Who Came to Tea. 2006. pap. *(978-0-06-052468-5(5))* HarperCollins Canada, Ltd.

Khan, Nicholai. Nicho the Tiger - Create Your World. 2011. (Illus.). 28p. (J). 14.95 *(978-0-9820801-2-2(3))* Nicho The Tiger LLC.

Khanna, Balraj. Rajah: King of the Jungle. 2011. (ENG.). 112p. 16.95 *(978-1-935677-03-1(9))* Mapin Publishing Pvt. Ltd IND. Dist: National Bk. Network.

Kinney, Kendall. Tiger Tails. 2004. 68p. (J). per. 10.95 *(978-1-932196-21-4(8))* WordWright.biz, Inc.

Kite, Justin. Even Tigers Need to Sleep. 2012. 24p. pap. 28.03 *(978-1-4691-8880-5(5))* Xlibris Corp.

Kleinman, Estelle. Tears of a Tiger. Friedland, Joyce & Kessler, Rikki, eds. 2008. (Novel-Ties Ser.). (Illus.). 31p. pap. 16.95 *(978-0-7675-4259-3(2))* Learning Links Inc.

Kung, Annie, tr. Auntie Tigress & Other Favorite Chinese Folk Tales. Wang, Eva, illus. 2006. (ENG.). 48p. (J). (gr. -1). lib. bdg. 16.50 *(978-1-933327-29-7(4))* Purple Bear Bks., Inc.

Lambert, Jonny. Tiger Tiger. Lambert, Jonny, illus. 2017. (ENG., Illus.). 32p. (J). (gr. -1-2). 16.99 *(978-1-68010-044-0(0))* Tiger Tales.

LaRochelle, David. It's a Tiger! Tankard, Jeremy, illus. 2012. (ENG.). 36p. (J). (gr. -1-k). 17.99 *(978-0-8118-6925-6(3))* Chronicle Bks. LLC.

Leathers, Philippa. The Tiptoeing Tiger. Leathers, Philippa, illus. 2018. (ENG., Illus.). 32p. (J). (gr. -1-2). 17.99 *(978-0-7636-8843-1(6))* Candlewick Pr.

Lee, Lucas Taekwon. The Legend of Baeoh: How Baeoh Got His Stripes. Forward, Max, illus. 2007. (ENG.). 36p. (J). (gr. 1-7). 17.95 *(978-1-931741-88-0(3))* Reed, Robert D. Pubs.

Lindgren, Barbro. Soda Pop. Adbage, Lisen, illus. 2017. (ENG.). 112p. (J). (gr. 3-5). 16.99 *(978-1-77657-010-2(3)*, c3b73484-9b40-4328-9c96-dc4ccb4d06ea) Gecko Pr. NZL. Dist: Lerner Publishing Group.

Litton, Jonathan. Planet Pop-Up: Tiger Takes Off. Anderson, Nicola, illus. 2015. (Planet Pop-Up Ser.). (ENG.). 12p. (J). (gr. -1). 12.95 *(978-1-62686-373-6(3)*, Silver Dolphin Bks.) Readerlink Distribution Services, LLC.

London, Jonathan. Little Lost Tiger, 0 vols. Spirin, Ilya, illus. 2012. (ENG.). 32p. (J). (gr. -1-3). 17.99 *(978-0-7614-6130-2(2)*, 9780761461302, Two Lions) Amazon Publishing.

Lorenz, Jinye. Ryong's Story: Extended Version of Grandfather, the Tiger & Ryong. Lorenz, Virginia O., ed. 2006. (Illus.). 135p. (YA). per. 14.95 *(978-1-888350-11-1(3))* Lighted Lamp Pr.

Lumry, Amanda & Hurwitz, Laura. Tigers in Terai. McIntyre, Sarah, illus. 2nd rev. ed. 2007. (Adventures of Riley (Unnumbered) Ser.). 36p. (J). (gr. -1-3). 15.95 *(978-1-60040-003-2(5))* Centro Bks., LLC.

—Tigers in Terai. McIntyre, Sarah, illus. (Adventures of Riley Ser.). 36p. 2003. 15.95 *(978-0-9662257-7-8(5))* 2nd ed. 2007. *(978-0-9748411-6-8(1))* Eaglemont Pr.

Marinaro, Stacy. Carter Finds a Tiger. 2009. 19p. 12.50 *(978-0-578-02365-6(2))* Marinaro, Stacy.

Marlow, Herb. The Tiger's Den. Head, Pat, illus. 2003. 22p. (J). 19.95 *(978-1-893595-37-8(4))* Four Seasons Bks., Inc.

Marsh, Carole. The Mystery in Las Vegas. 2009. (Real Kids, Real Places Ser.). (Illus.). 145p. (J). lib. bdg. 18.99 *(978-0-635-07045-6(6)*, Marsh, Carole Mysteries) Gallopade International.

Mathis, Tabitha. The Princess & the Tyger. 2012. 28p. pap. 24.95 *(978-1-4626-8265-2(0))* America Star Bks.

Mcdoogle, Farrah. Thank You Day. 2014. (Daniel Tiger's Neighborhood Ready-To-Read Ser.). lib. bdg. 13.55 *(978-0-606-35449-3(2))* Turtleback.

McGonagle, Joanne L. The Tiniest Tiger. 2008. (ENG.). 52p. pap. 15.00 *(978-1-4196-8467-8(1))* CreateSpace Independent Publishing Platform.

Millhouse, Jackie. The Tiger & the General. Girouard, Patrick, illus. 2007. 21p. (J). *(978-1-932911-32-9(4))* World Tribune Pr.

Milne, Alan Alexander. In Which It Is Shown That Tiggers Don't Climb Trees. Shepard, Ernest H., illus. unabr. ed. (Classic Pooh Treasury Ser.). (J). incl. audio *(978-1-57375-529-0(X)*, 71414) Audioscope.

—Pu Baut ein Haus.Tr. of Pooh Builds a House. (GER.). (J). pap. 12.95 *(978-3-423-07395-0(0))* Deutscher Taschenbuch Verlag GmbH & Co KG DEU. Dist: Distribooks, Inc.

—Tigger Tales. Shepard, Ernest H., illus. 2006. 36p. (J). (gr. k-4). reprint ed. 15.00 *(978-1-4223-5453-7(9))* DIANE Publishing Co.

Minz-Kammer, Koda. Pinpot Tiger & the Lost Monkey. 2008. (ENG.). 54p. pap. 20.00 *(978-0-557-01646-4(0))* Lulu Pr., Inc.

Morris, Richard T. Fear the Bunny. Burris, Priscilla, illus. 2019. (ENG.). 40p. (J). (gr. -1-3). 17.99 *(978-1-4814-7800-7(1))* Simon & Schuster Children's Publishing.

Moynahan, Jamie. Tiger Bunnies. 2009. (Illus.). 16p. pap. 9.49 *(978-1-4389-7000-4(5))* AuthorHouse.

Murakami, Jon & Yeh, Phil. The Winged Tiger & the Dragons of Hawaii. 2005. 48p. pap. 11.95 *(978-0-9755635-0-2(5))* Eastwind Studios.

Nagda, Ann Whitehead. A Tiger Tale. Kratter, Paul, illus. (Soundprints' Amazing Animal Adventures! Ser.). (ENG.). 36p. (J). 2005. (gr. -1-2). 2.95 *(978-1-59249-044-8(1)*, S7151) 2005. (gr. -1-2). 15.95 *(978-1-59249-042-4(5)*, B7101) 2005. (gr. -1-2). pap. 6.95 *(978-1-59249-043-1(3)*, S7101) 2005. (gr. -1-2). 19.95 *(978-1-59249-388-3(2)*, BC7101) 2005. (gr. 2-2). 8.95 *(978-1-59249-389-0(0)*, SC7101) 2003. (gr. -1-3). 9.95 *(978-1-59249-057-8(3)*, PS7151) Soundprints.

Naughton, Patrick. Colonel Tiger on the Raft. 2010. 76p. pap. 12.95 *(978-1-4452-6095-2(6))* Lulu Pr., Inc.

Nesquens, Daniel. A Good Day. Lora, Miren Asiain, illus. 2019. (ENG.). 32p. (J). *(978-0-8028-5530-5(X)*, Eerdmans Bks For Young Readers) Eerdmans, William B. Publishing Co.

Newton-Kowalsky, Jacqueline. Itsy Bitsy Stories for Itsy Bitsy Tigers. 2012. 32p. pap. *(978-1-77097-138-7(6))* FriesenPress.

Nowra, Louis. Into That Forest, 0 vols. 2013. (ENG.). 160p. (YA). (gr. 7-9). 16.99 *(978-1-4778-1725-4(5)*, 9781477817254, Skyscape); 162p. 16.99 *(978-1-4778-6725-9(2))* Amazon Publishing.

O'Campo, Allicia. Tinky Goes to North Americ. 2009. 28p. pap. 15.50 *(978-1-60860-412-8(8)*, Eloquent Bks.) Strategic Book Publishing & Rights Agency (SBPRA).

Olien, Jessica. When a Tiger Comes to Dinner. Olien, Jessica, illus. 2019. (ENG., Illus.). 32p. (J). (gr. -1-3). 17.99 *(978-0-06-256829-8(9)*, Balzer & Bray) HarperCollins Pubs.

Osborne, Mary Pope. Tigers at Twilight. unabr. ed. 2004. (Magic Tree House Ser.: No. 19). 72p. (J). (gr. k-3). pap. 17.00 incl. audio *(978-0-8072-0928-8(7)*, S FTR 251 SP, Listening Library) Random Hse. Audio Publishing Group.

Osborne, Mary Pope, et al. Tigres Al Anochecer. Murdocca, Sal, illus. 2008. (Casa del Arbol Ser.: 19).Tr. of Tigers at Twilight. (SPA.). (J). (gr. 2-4). pap. 8.99 *(978-1-933032-49-8(9))* Lectorum Pubns., Inc.

Ostermeyer, Tim, photos by. Titus & Tiana: Lesson for Baby Tigers. 2011. (Illus.). 18.95 *(978-0-9794228-6-7(8))* Ostermeyer Photography.

PaleoJoe & Caszatt-Allen, Wendy. Secret Sabertooth. 2007. (PaleoJoe's Dinosaur Detective Club Ser.: 3). (Illus.). 168p. (J). (gr. 2-5). pap. 8.95 *(978-1-934133-10-1(8)*, Mackinac Island Press, Inc.) Charlesbridge Publishing, Inc.

Parish, Scott. Tigre a la Mesa. 2005. 14p. (J). 10.00 *(978-1-4116-6003-8(X))* Lulu Pr., Inc.

Parragon Staff. Tigger's Adventure. 2010. (Disney Diecut Classics). (Illus.). 72p. (J). (gr. -1-1). *(978-1-4075-8903-9(2))* Parragon, Inc.

Partis, Joanne. Stripe. Partis, Joanne, illus. (Carolrhoda Picture Books Ser.). (Illus.). 32p. (J). 2004. pap. 6.95 *(978-1-57505-667-8(4))* 2003. (gr. -1-3). 14.95 *(978-1-57505-450-6(7))* Lerner Publishing Group.

—Stripe's Naughty Sister. 2003. (Picture Bks.). (Illus.). 32p. (J). (gr. -1-3). 15.95 *(978-0-87614-466-4(0)*, Carolrhoda Bks.) Lerner Publishing Group.

Pelley, Kathleen T. Raj the Bookstore Tiger. Keiser, Paige, illus. 2011. 32p. (J). (gr. -1-3). 15.95 *(978-1-58089-230-8(2))* Charlesbridge Publishing, Inc.

Pendergrass, Daphne. Daniel Plays at School. 2016. (Daniel Tiger's Neighborhood Ready-To-Read Ser.). lib. bdg. 13.55 *(978-0-606-38991-4(1))* Turtleback.

Perkins, Mitali. Tiger Boy. 2017. 144p. (J). (gr. 2-5). pap. 7.99 *(978-1-58089-661-0(8))* Charlesbridge Publishing, Inc.

—Tiger Boy. Hogan, Jamie, illus. 2015. (ENG.). 144p. (J). (gr. 2-5). lib. bdg. 15.99 *(978-1-58089-660-3(X))* Charlesbridge Publishing, Inc.

Peter Pauper Press, Inc., creator. Stripes the Cat Tiger. 2016. (ENG., Illus.). 32p. (J). 15.99 *(978-1-4413-2184-8(5)*, ed47cdf2-0b8b-4364-9814-fa9eb1b09fd7) Peter Pauper Pr. Inc.

Pogo the Clown. The Littlest Tiger: Harley's Great Adventures. Miller, Richard, illus. 2004. (J). 12.95 *(978-0-9755253-2-6(8))* Chilinic Pubns.

Powell, Richard. Timmy Tiger. Rhodes, Katie, illus. 2004. (Fuzzy Friends Ser.). 10p. (J). 7.95 *(978-1-58925-722-1(7))* Tiger Tales.

Prebeg, Rick. You've Got Cheetah Mail. Prebeg, Rick, photos by. 2005. (Illus.). (J). *(978-1-933248-11-0(4))* World Quest Learning.

Priddy, Roger. Little Friends: All You Need Is Love: A Lift the Flaps Book. 2017. (Little Friends Ser.). (ENG., Illus.). 10p. (J). bds. 8.99 *(978-0-312-52147-9(2)*, 900178605) St. Martin's Pr.

Proimos III, James, Jr. Knuckle & Potty Destroy Happy World. Proimos III, James, Jr., illus. 2012. (ENG., Illus.). 80p. (J). (gr. 2-5). 12.99 *(978-0-8050-9155-7(6)*, 900064073, Holt, Henry & Co. Bks. For Young Readers) Holt, Henry & Co.

Publications International Ltd. Staff, ed. Potty Time with Tiger: Boy. 2010. (J). bds. 5.98 *(978-1-4127-6915-0(9))* Publications International, Ltd.

—Potty Time with Tiger: Girl. 2010. (SPA.). (J). bds. 5.98 *(978-1-4127-6916-7(7))* Publications International, Ltd.

—A Ring-A-Ling Day! 2009. 12p. (J). bds. 11.98 *(978-1-4127-9614-9(8)*, PIL Kids) Publications International, Ltd.

Rance, Alex. Tiger's Roar. McG, Shane, illus. 2019. (ENG.). 32p. (J). (gr. k-3). 16.99 *(978-1-76052-391-6(7))* Allen & Unwin AUS. Dist: Independent Pubs. Group.

Rigo, Laura, illus. Little Tiger. 2017. (Mini Look at Me Bks.). 10p. (J). (gr. -1 — 1). bds. 4.99 *(978-0-7641-6881-9(9))* Sourcebooks, Inc.

Robert, Kraus. Leo the Late Bloomer. 2014. (Trophy Picture Bks). (ENG.). 32p. (J). (gr. k-3). 11.24 *(978-1-63245-278-8(2))* Lectorum Pubns., Inc.

Ross, Dev. We Both Read Bilingual Edition-Frank & the Tiger/Sapi y el Tigre. Canetti, Yanitzia, tr. from ENG. Reinhart, Larry, illus. 2014. (We Both Read - Level K-1 (Quality) Ser.). (ENG & SPA.). 44p. (J). (gr. k-1). pap. 5.99 *(978-1-60115-058-5(X))* Treasure Bay, Inc.

Ross, Patrick. Oliver: The Great Escape. Burcham, David, illus. 2009. 34p. pap. 24.95 *(978-1-60749-151-4(6))* America Star Bks.

Roth, Carol. Hold Your Temper, Tiger. Kheiriyeh, Rashin, illus. 2017. (ENG.). 32p. (J). (gr. -1-3). 17.95 *(978-0-7358-4274-8(4))* North-South Bks., Inc.

Rouncville, Bibi. Bog Nymphs & Tiger Stones. 2008. 52p. pap. 15.50 *(978-1-4357-3966-6(3))* Lulu Pr., Inc.

Roy, Ron. Capital Mysteries #9: a Thief at the National Zoo. Bush, Timothy, illus. 2007. (Capital Mysteries Ser.: 9). 96p. (J). (gr. 1-4). per. 5.99 *(978-0-375-84804-9(5)*, Random Hse. Bks. for Young Readers) Random Hse. Children's Bks.

—A Thief at the National Zoo. Bush, Timothy, illus. 2008. (Capital Mysteries Ser.: No. 9). 87p. (gr. k-3). 15.00 *(978-0-7569-8329-1(0))* Perfection Learning Corp.

—A Thief at the National Zoo, 9. Bush, Timothy, illus. 2007. (Capital Mysteries Ser.: No. 9). (ENG.). 87p. (J). (gr. 2-4). lib. bdg. 17.44 *(978-0-375-94804-6(X))* Random House Publishing Group.

Rubio, Gabriela. Terrible/Terrible. 2006. (Jardin de los Ninos (Ediciones Ekare) Ser.). (SPA., Illus.). 22p. (J). (gr. 3-5). *(978-84-933060-7-6(X))* Ekare, Ediciones.

Rubio, Gabriela & Rubio Márquez, Gabriela. Se Acabo! 2004. (SPA., Illus.). 30p. (J). 6.50 *(978-84-348-7875-4(5))* SM Ediciones ESP. Dist: Lectorum Pubns., Inc.

Ruddra, Anshumani. Dorje's Stripes. 2011. (ENG., Illus.). 40p. (J). (gr. k-4). 9.99 *(978-1-935279-98-3(X))* Kane Miller.

Safari Press Staff, ed. Book Buddy - Tiger with Story Book. (Illus.). 10p. (J). (gr. -1-3). reprint ed. pap. *(978-1-881469-85-8(9))* Safari, Ltd.

Samson, Lucretia. Hungry Tiger & Clever Rabbit: A Tale from Korea, 1 vol. Bijloo, Adrian, illus. 2016. (ENG.). 24p. (J). pap. 9.95 *(978-1-927244-58-6(7))* Clean Slate Pr. Ltd. NZL. Dist: Flying Start Bks.

—Hungry Tiger & Clever Rabbit (Big Book Edition) A Tale from Korea. Bijloo, Adrian, illus. 2016. 24p. (J). pap. *(978-1-927244-68-5(4))* Flying Start Bks.

Sanner, Jennifer Jackson, ed. The Three Little Jayhawks. Pearson, Larry Leroy, illus. 2006. 40p. (J). per. 20.00 *(978-0-9742918-1-9(1))* Kansas Alumni Assoc.

Santomero, Angela C. Big Brother Daniel. Fruchter, Jason, illus. 2015. (Daniel Tiger's Neighborhood Ser.). (ENG.). 14p. (J). (gr. -1-k). bds. 6.99 *(978-1-4814-3172-9(2)*, Simon Spotlight) Simon Spotlight.

—Daniel's First Sleepover. 2015. (Daniel Tiger's Neighborhood 8X8 Ser.). lib. bdg. 13.55 *(978-0-606-36315-0(7))* Turtleback.

—Goodnight, Daniel Tiger. Style Guide, illus. 2014. (Daniel Tiger's Neighborhood Ser.). (ENG.). 26p. (J). (gr. -1-2). 12.99 *(978-1-4814-0048-0(7)*, Simon Spotlight) Simon Spotlight.

—Goodnight, Daniel Tiger. 2014. (Daniel Tiger's Neighborhood 8X8 Ser.). lib. bdg. 13.55 *(978-0-606-36113-2(8))* Turtleback.

—Merry Christmas, Daniel Tiger! A Lift-The-Flap Book. Fruchter, Jason, illus. 2015. (Daniel Tiger's Neighborhood Ser.). (ENG.). 14p. (J). (gr. -1-2). bds. 6.99 *(978-1-4814-4660-0(6)*, Simon Spotlight) Simon Spotlight.

Scelsa, Greg. Rhyme Time. Faulkner, Stacey, ed. Hanke, Karen, illus. 2006. (J). pap. 2.99 *(978-1-59198-323-1(1))* Creative Teaching Pr., Inc.

Schulz, Charles. Alle Achtung. Herbst, Gabriele & Rolle, Ekkehard, trs. from ENG. (Snoopy & die Peanuts Ser.: Vol. 5). (GER., Illus.). 128p. (J). pap. *(978-3-8105-1818-7(2))* Kruger, Wolfgang Verlag, GmbH DEU. Dist: International Bk. Import Service, Inc.

Seidon, Bonnie Bale. The Adventures of Trevor & the Tiger. 2012. 104p. 21.79 *(978-1-4669-4389-6(0))*; pap. 11.79 *(978-1-4669-4391-9(2))* Trafford Publishing.

Shaw, Natalie. I'm Feeling Happy. Fruchter, Jason, illus. 2016. (Daniel Tiger's Neighborhood Ser.). (ENG.). 14p. (J). (gr. -1 — 1). bds. 6.99 *(978-1-4814-6178-8(8)*, Simon Spotlight) Simon Spotlight.

—I'm Feeling Silly. Fruchter, Jason, illus. 2016. (Daniel Tiger's Neighborhood Ser.). (ENG.). 14p. (J). (gr. -1 — 1). bds. 6.99 *(978-1-4814-6815-2(4)*, Simon Spotlight) Simon Spotlight.

—Meet the Neighbors! Style Guide, illus. 2014. (Daniel Tiger's Neighborhood Ser.). (ENG.). 16p. (J). (gr. -1-k). bds. 7.99 *(978-1-4424-9837-2(4)*, Simon Spotlight) Simon Spotlight.

Simon, Mary Manz. Tiger Forgives. Clearwater, Linda & Couri, Kathy, illus. 2006. (First Virtues for Toddlers Ser.). 20p. (J). 5.99 *(978-0-7847-1413-3(4)*, 04065) Standard Publishing.

Smith, Sherri. Counting with Mike the Tiger. Walsh, D. T., illus. 2013. (ENG.). (J). (gr. -1-k). 14.95 *(978-1-62086-349-7(9))* Amplify Publishing Group.

—Mike the Tiger Teaches the Alphabet. Walsh, D. T., illus. 2013. (ENG.). (J). (gr. -1-k). 14.95 *(978-1-62086-348-0(0))* Amplify Publishing Group.

Snowflake Day! 2014. (Daniel Tiger's Neighborhood Ser.). (ENG., Illus.). 14p. (J). (gr. -1-k). bds. 5.99 *(978-1-4814-1771-6(1)*, Simon Spotlight) Simon Spotlight.

So-Un, Kim. The Tigers of the Kumgang Mountains: A Korean Folktale. Kyoung-Sim, Jeong, illus. 2005. (ENG.). 1p. (J). (gr. 4-11). 16.95 *(978-0-8048-3653-1(1))* Tuttle Publishing.

Spagnoli, Cathy. Nine-In-One.Grr! Grr! Hom, Nancy, illus. 2013. (ENG.). 32p. (J). (gr. -1-5). pap. 9.95 *(978-0-89239-048-9(4))* Lee & Low Bks., Inc.

Sparrow, Steve. The Wooden Tiger. 2009. 52p. pap. *(978-1-84923-773-4(5))* YouWriteOn.

Spinner, Cala. A Busy Day in the Neighborhood. Fruchter, Jason, illus. 2017. (Daniel Tiger's Neighborhood Ser.). (ENG.). 12p. (J). (gr. -1-k). bds. 14.99 *(978-1-4814-8583-8(0)*, Simon Spotlight) Simon Spotlight.

—Trolley Ride! 2018. (Daniel Tiger's Neighborhood Ready-To-Read Ser.). lib. bdg. 14.75 *(978-0-606-41418-0(5))* Turtleback.

—Trolley Ride! Ready-To-Read Ready-to-Go! Fruchter, Jason, illus. 2018. (Daniel Tiger's Neighborhood Ser.). (ENG.). 32p. (J). (gr. -1-k). 17.99 *(978-1-5344-1627-7(7))*; pap. 4.99 *(978-1-5344-1626-0(9))* Simon Spotlight. (Simon Spotlight).

Spreng, Robert C. The Tahoe Tiger & the Lahontan Lion. 2008. 38p. pap. 14.50 *(978-0-557-02370-7(X))* Lulu Pr., Inc.

Stewart, Lizzy. There's a Tiger in the Garden. Stewart, Lizzy, illus. 2018. (ENG., Illus.). 40p. (J). (gr. -1-3). 17.99 *(978-1-328-79183-2(1)*, 1685033, Clarion Bks.) HarperCollins Pubs.

—There's a Tiger in the Garden. 2016. (ENG., Illus.). (J). 40p. pap. 9.99 *(978-1-84780-807-3(7))*; 32p. 18.99 *(978-1-84780-806-6(9))* Quarto Publishing Group UK GBR. (Frances Lincoln Children's Bks.). Dist: Littlehampton Bk Services, Ltd.

Studio Mouse Staff. Pooh & Eeyore, Pooh & Tigger. rev. ed. 2004. (Friends Collection). (ENG., Illus.). 36p. (J). (gr. -1-3). 15.99 *(978-1-59069-390-2(6)*, 1A302) Studio Mouse LLC.

—Pooh & Tigger. 2008. (ENG., Illus.). 36p. (J). (gr. -1). 7.99 *(978-1-59069-417-6(1))* Studio Mouse LLC.

Tabor, Corey R. Fox the Tiger. Tabor, Corey R., illus. 2018. (My First I Can Read Ser.). (ENG., Illus.). 32p. (J). (gr. -1-3). 16.99 *(978-0-06-239869-7(5))*; pap. 4.99 *(978-0-06-239867-3(9))* HarperCollins Pubs. (Balzer & Bray).

Taylor, Thomas. The Loudest Roar. 2003. (Illus.). (J). pap. *(978-0-439-50131-6(8)*, Levine, Arthur A. Bks.) Scholastic, Inc.

Teckentrup, Britta. Don't Wake up the Tiger. Teckentrup, Britta, illus. 2016. (ENG., Illus.). 30p. (J). (-k). 18.99 *(978-0-7636-8996-4(3))* Candlewick Pr.

Tenbeth, Kate. Burly & Grum & the Tiger's Tale. Jones, Rob, illus. 2013. 36p. pap. *(978-0-9572119-7-1(X))* Magic Toy Bks.

Testa, Maggie. Daniel Plays Ball. 2014. (Daniel Tiger's Neighborhood Ready-To-Read Ser.). lib. bdg. 13.55 *(978-0-606-36114-9(6))* Turtleback.

—Friends Are the Best! Fruchter, Jason, illus. 2014. (Daniel Tiger's Neighborhood Ser.). (ENG.). 12p. (J). (gr. -1-k). bds. 6.99 *(978-1-4424-9547-0(2)*, Simon Spotlight) Simon Spotlight.

—A Ride Through the Neighborhood. Style Guide, illus. 2014. (Daniel Tiger's Neighborhood Ser.). (ENG.). 12p. (J). (gr. -1-1). bds. 8.99 *(978-1-4424-9839-6(0)*, Simon Spotlight) Simon Spotlight.

—Who Can? Daniel Can! Ready-To-Read Ready-to-Go! Fruchter, Jason, illus. 2017. (Daniel Tiger's Neighborhood Ser.). (ENG.). 32p. (J). (gr. -1-k). pap. 4.99 *(978-1-4814-9518-9(6)*, Simon Spotlight) Simon Spotlight.

Thurber, James. The Tiger Who Would Be King. Yoon, JooHee, illus. 2015. 40p. (J). (gr. k-4). 18.95 *(978-1-59270-182-7(5))* Enchanted Lion Bks., LLC.

The Tiger's Stripes & the Water Buffalo's Teeth. 2010. 40p. 19.57 *(978-1-4269-3110-9(7))* Trafford Publishing.

Tommy's Tummy Ache: Individual Title Six-Packs. (Literatura 2000 Ser.). (gr. -1-1). 28.00 *(978-0-7635-0015-3(1))* Rigby Education.

Turnbull, Victoria. The Sea Tiger. Turnbull, Victoria, illus. 2015. (ENG., Illus.). 40p. (J). (gr. -1-2). 16.99 *(978-0-7636-7986-6(0)*, Templar) Candlewick Pr.

Van der Merwe, Avril. How Cheetah Got His Tears. Greeff, Heidi-Kate, illus. 2017. (ENG.). 16p. pap. 7.00 *(978-1-4859-0034-4(4))* Penguin Random House South Africa ZAF. Dist: Casemate Pubs. & Bk. Distributors, LLC.

Wallace Hunchak, Lisa. It Could Happen. 2013. 32p. pap. 17.25 *(978-1-4669-7130-1(4))* Trafford Publishing.

Walsh, Joanna. I Love Mom. Abbot, Judi, illus. 2019. (Classic Board Bks.). (ENG.). 28p. (J). (gr. -1 — 1). bds. 7.99 *(978-1-5344-3900-9(5)*, Little Simon) Little Simon.

—I Love Mom. Abbot, Judi, illus. 2014. (ENG.). 32p. (J). (gr. -1-3). 16.99 *(978-1-4814-2808-8(X)*, Simon & Schuster/Paula Wiseman Bks.) Simon & Schuster/Paula Wiseman Bks.

Walters, Eric. Tiger by the Tail. 2009. (ENG.). 176p. (J). (gr. 6). pap. *(978-1-55488-175-8(7))* Beach Holme Pubs., Ltd.

Wang, Eva, illus. Auntie Tigress & Other Favorite Chinese Folk Tales. 2006. (ENG.). 48p. (J). 15.95 *(978-1-933327-28-0(6))* Purple Bear Bks., Inc.

Warnes, Tim & Sykes, Julie. Bathtime, Little Tiger! Warnes, Tim, illus. 2003. (Little Tiger Lift-the-Flap Ser.). (Illus.). 12p. (J). 5.95 *(978-1-58925-693-4(X))* Tiger Tales.

—Hide & Seek, Little Tiger. Warnes, Tim, illus. 2003. (Little Tiger Lift-the-Flap Ser.). (Illus.). 14p. (J). 5.95 *(978-1-58925-694-1(8))* Tiger Tales.

Warren, Vince H. The Adventures of Meka & Her Two Cubs. 2013. (ENG.). 28p. (J). pap. 7.95 *(978-1-4787-0308-2(3))* Outskirts Pr., Inc.

Watt, Fiona. That's Not My Tiger. Wells, Rachel, illus. 2010. (Touchy-Feely Board Bks.). 10p. (J). bds. 8.99 *(978-0-7945-2820-1(1))* EDC Publishing.

Watterson, William. Achtung, Fertig, Los! Goetting, Waltraud, tr. from ENG. (Calvin & Hobbes Ser.: Vol. 8). (GER., Illus.). 64p. (J). pap. *(978-3-8105-0336-7(3))* Kruger, Wolfgang Verlag, GmbH DEU. Dist: International Bk. Import Service, Inc.

—Alles unter Kontrolle. Goetting, Waltraud, tr. from ENG. (Calvin & Hobbes Ser.: Vol. 3). (GER., Illus.). 64p. (J). pap. *(978-3-8105-0330-5(4))* Kruger, Wolfgang Verlag, GmbH DEU. Dist: International Bk. Import Service, Inc.

—Auf dem Sprung. Goetting, Waltraud, tr. from ENG. (Calvin & Hobbes Ser.: Bk. 1). (GER., Illus.). 96p. (J). pap. *(978-3-8105-0320-6(7))* Kruger, Wolfgang Verlag, GmbH DEU. Dist: International Bk. Import Service, Inc.

—Bloss nicht Aergern. Goetting, Waltraud, tr. from ENG. (Calvin & Hobbes Ser.: Bk. 3). (GER., Illus.). 96p. (J). pap. *(978-3-8105-0322-0(3))* Kruger, Wolfgang Verlag, GmbH DEU. Dist: International Bk. Import Service, Inc.

—Calvin & Hobbes: Das Jubilaumsalbum, 10 vols. Bartoszko, Alexandra, tr. from ENG. (Calvin & Hobbes Ser.). (GER., Illus.). 208p. (J). *(978-3-8105-0370-1(3))* Kruger, Wolfgang Verlag, GmbH DEU. Dist: International Bk. Import Service, Inc.

—Einfach Umwerfend. Goetting, Waltraud, tr. from ENG. (Calvin & Hobbes Ser.: Vol. 13). (GER., Illus.). 48p. (J). pap. *(978-3-8105-0350-3(9))* Kruger, Wolfgang Verlag, GmbH DEU. Dist: International Bk. Import Service, Inc.

—Enorm in Form. Goetting, Waltraud, tr. from ENG. (Calvin & Hobbes Ser.: Vol. 9). (GER., Illus.). 64p. (J). pap. *(978-3-8105-0340-4(1))* Kruger, Wolfgang Verlag, GmbH DEU. Dist: International Bk. Import Service, Inc.

—Feine Freunde. Goetting, Waltraud, tr. from ENG. (Calvin & Hobbes Ser.: Vol. 15). (GER., Illus.). 80p. (J). pap. *(978-3-8105-0353-4(3))* Kruger, Wolfgang Verlag, GmbH DEU. Dist: International Bk. Import Service, Inc.

—Fix & Fertig. Goetting, Waltraud, tr. from ENG. (Calvin & Hobbes Ser.: Bk. 2). (GER., Illus.). 96p. (J). pap. *(978-3-8105-0321-3(5))* Kruger, Wolfgang Verlag, GmbH DEU. Dist: International Bk. Import Service, Inc.

—Ganz schoen Daneben. Goetting, Waltraud, tr. from ENG. (Calvin & Hobbes Ser.: Vol. 7). (GER., Illus.). 64p. (J). pap. *(978-3-8105-0335-0(5))* Kruger, Wolfgang Verlag, GmbH DEU. Dist: International Bk. Import Service, Inc.

—Immer mit der Ruhe. Goetting, Waltraud, tr. from ENG. (Calvin & Hobbes Ser.: Vol. 4). (GER., Illus.). 64p. (J). pap. *(978-3-8105-0331-2(2))* Kruger, Wolfgang Verlag, GmbH DEU. Dist: International Bk. Import Service, Inc.

—Immer Voll Drauf. Goetting, Waltraud, tr. from ENG. (Calvin & Hobbes Ser.: Vol. 5). (GER., Illus.). 64p. (J). pap. *(978-3-8105-0332-9(0))* Kruger, Wolfgang Verlag, GmbH DEU. Dist: International Bk. Import Service, Inc.

—Jetzt Erst Recht. Goetting, Waltraud, tr. from ENG. (Calvin & Hobbes Ser.: Vol. 10). (GER., Illus.). 64p. (J). pap. *(978-3-8105-0339-8(8))* Kruger, Wolfgang Verlag, GmbH DEU. Dist: International Bk. Import Service, Inc.

—Jetzt geht's Rund. Goetting, Waltraud, tr. from ENG. (Calvin & Hobbes Ser.: Vol. 1). (GER., Illus.). 64p. (J). pap. *(978-3-8105-0328-2(2))* Kruger, Wolfgang Verlag, GmbH DEU. Dist: International Bk. Import Service, Inc.

—Mach mir den Tiger. Goetting, Waltraud, tr. from ENG. (Calvin & Hobbes Ser.: Vol. 11). (GER., Illus.). 64p. (J). pap. *(978-3-8105-0341-1(X))* Kruger, Wolfgang Verlag, GmbH DEU. Dist: International Bk. Import Service, Inc.

—Die Phantastischen Zwei. Goetting, Waltraud, tr. from ENG. (Calvin & Hobbes Ser.: Vol. 14). (GER., Illus.). 80p. (J). pap. *(978-3-8105-0351-0(7))* Kruger, Wolfgang Verlag, GmbH DEU. Dist: International Bk. Import Service, Inc.

—Steil nach Oben. Goetting, Waltraud, tr. from ENG. (Calvin & Hobbes Ser.: Vol. 6). (GER., Illus.). 64p. (J). pap. *(978-3-8105-0333-6(9))* Kruger, Wolfgang Verlag, GmbH DEU. Dist: International Bk. Import Service, Inc.

—Tierisch Lyrisch. Goetting, Waltraud, tr. from ENG. (Calvin & Hobbes Ser.: Vol. 12). (GER., Illus.). 64p. (J). pap. *(978-3-8105-0349-7(5))* Kruger, Wolfgang Verlag, GmbH DEU. Dist: International Bk. Import Service, Inc.

Watts, Katherine. Tiger Tails. 2008. 76p. pap. 35.95 *(978-0-9556878-0-8(2))* Watts, Katherine GBR. Dist: Lulu Pr., Inc.

Weaver, Jo. Little Tigers, 1 vol. 2019. (ENG., Illus.). 32p. (J). (gr. -1-2). 17.95 *(978-1-68263-110-2(9))* Peachtree Publishing Co. Inc.

Weintroub, Alex. Tilly the Tiger. 2016. (ENG., Illus.). 29p. (J). 13.95 *(978-1-78612-173-8(5)*, d0732cd7-c12c-423d-b74a-8a7dd35bb1d6) Austin Macauley Pubs. Ltd. GBR. Dist: Baker & Taylor Publisher Services (BTPS).

Willis, Jeanne. Supercat vs the Pesky Pirate (Supercat, Book 3) 2015. (Supercat Ser.: 3). (ENG., Illus.). 224p. (J). pap. 5.99 *(978-0-00-812470-0(1)*, HarperCollins Children's Bks.) HarperCollins Pubs. Ltd. GBR. Dist: HarperCollins Pubs.

Wilson, Essdale. Horses, Tigers & Neighbors. 2007. 160p. per. 24.95 *(978-1-4241-5811-9(7))* America Star Bks.

Zahradka, Miroslav. The Un-Terrible Tiger. Zahradka, Miroslav, illus. (Illus.). 32p. (J). (gr. -1-3). 12.95 *(978-0-87592-056-6(X))* Scroll Pr., Inc.

TIGERS

see Tiger

TIGRIS RIVER VALLEY

Miller, Gary G. & Miller, Gary. The Tigris & Euphrates: Rivers of the Fertile Crescent, 1 vol. 2010. (Rivers Around the World Ser.). (ENG., Illus.). 32p. (J). (gr. 5-8). pap. *(978-0-7787-7471-6(6))*; lib. bdg. *(978-0-7787-7448-8(1))* Crabtree Publishing Co.

Rice Jr., Earle. The Tigris/Euphrates River. 2012. (Illus.). 47p. (J). lib. bdg. 29.95 *(978-1-61228-298-5(9))* Mitchell Lane Pubs.

TIMBER

see Forests and Forestry; Lumber and Lumbering; Trees; Wood

TIME

see also Calendars; Clocks and Watches

Adams, Colleen. A Weekend in the City: Adding & Subtracting Times to the Nearest Minute, 1 vol. 2010. (Math for the REAL World Ser.). (ENG., Illus.). 24p. (gr. 3-4). pap. 8.25 *(978-0-8239-8897-6(X)*, d4d07135-80d5-4917-8481-1d7a7f0bb134, PowerKids Pr.) Rosen Publishing Group, Inc., The.

Adamson, Heather & Adamson, Thomas K. How Do You Measure Time? 2010. (Measure It! Ser.). (ENG.). 32p. (J). (gr. 1-2). pap. 48.60 *(978-1-4296-6459-2(2)*, 16214, Capstone Pr.) Capstone.

Adamson, Thomas K. & Adamson, Heather. How Do You Measure Time?, 1 vol. 2010. (Measure It! Ser.). (ENG.). 32p. (J). (gr. -1-2). pap. 8.10 *(978-1-4296-6332-8(4)*, 115533, Capstone Pr.) Capstone.

Adler, David A. Telling Time. Miller, Edward, illus. 2019. 32p. (J). (gr. 1-4). 18.99 *(978-0-8234-4092-4(3))* Holiday Hse., Inc.

Amery, H. Telling the Time. 2004. (Treasury of Farmyard Tales Ser.). (SPA.). 24p. (J). (gr. -1-18). 8.95 *(978-0-7945-0146-4(X)*, Usborne) EDC Publishing.

Amery, Heather. Telling the Time. Tyler, Jenny & Lacey, Minna, eds. Cartwright, Stephen, illus. 2007. (Usborne Farmyard Tales Ser.). 24p. (J). (gr. -1-2). bds. 12.99 *(978-0-7945-1519-5(3)*, Usborne) EDC Publishing.

Andrus, Aubre & Bluth, Karen. Me Time: How to Manage a Busy Life. Collignon, Veronica, illus. 2017. (Stress-Busting Survival Guides). (ENG.). 48p. (J). (gr. 4-8). lib. bdg. 31.99 *(978-1-5157-6821-0(X)*, 135350, Capstone Pr.) Capstone.

Bailer, Darice. Measuring Time with a Calendar. Petelinsek, Kathleen, illus. 2014. (Explorer Junior Library: Math Explorer Junior Ser.). (ENG.). 24p. (J). (gr. 1-4). 32.07 *(978-1-62431-649-4(2)*, 203108) Cherry Lake Publishing.

Baxter, Nicola. Learn to Tell Time: With Magnets to Use Again & Again! Elliott, Rebecca, illus. 2013. (ENG.). 16p. (J). (gr. -1-12). bds. 17.99 *(978-1-84322-638-3(3)*, Armadillo) Anness Publishing GBR. Dist: National Bk. Network.

Benchmark Education Company, LLC Staff, compiled by. Measuring Time: Theme Set. 2006. (J). 274.00 *(978-1-4108-7074-2(X))* Benchmark Education Co.

—Telling Time. 2006. (J). 235.00 *(978-1-4108-7050-6(2))* Benchmark Education Co.

Bernardi, Philip & Havens, Diane. Twice upon a Time. 2003. (Theater for Young Audiences Ser.). (Illus.). 24p. (J). (gr. k-6). pap. 6.00 *(978-0-88734-425-1(9))* Players Pr., Inc.

Bernay, Emma & Berne, Emma Carlson. Telling Time. Palin, Tim, illus. 2019. (Patterns of Time Ser.). (ENG.). 24p. (J). (gr. -1-2). pap. 7.95 *(978-1-68410-438-3(6)*, 141233) Cantata Learning.

Bernhard, Durga. While You Are Sleeping. 2011. (J). pap. 14.95 *(978-1-57091-474-4(5))* Charlesbridge Publishing, Inc.

Boswell, Kelly. Timelines, Timelines, Timelines!, 1 vol. 2013. (Displaying Information Ser.). (ENG.). 32p. (J). (gr. -1-2). 27.99 *(978-1-4765-0261-8(7)*, 122455); pap. 8.95 *(978-1-4765-3338-4(5)*, 123454) Capstone. (Capstone Pr.).

Branley, Franklyn M. What Makes Day & Night. Dorros, Arthur, illus. 2015. (Let's-Read-And-Find-Out Science 2 Ser.). (ENG.). 32p. (J). (gr. -1-3). pap. 8.99 *(978-0-06-238197-2(0)*, HarperCollins) HarperCollins Pubs.

Brasch, Nicolas. Times, Tides, & Revolutions. 2010. (Science Behind Ser.). 32p. lib. bdg. 28.50 *(978-1-59920-563-2(7))* Black Rabbit Bks.

Brezina, Corona. Time Travel, 1 vol. 2018. (Sci-Fi or STEM? Ser.). (ENG.). 64p. (gr. 7-7). 36.13 *(978-1-5081-8046-3(6)*, 7d15399e-6b4e-4497-aa8e-89dbebbdcae3) Rosen Publishing Group, Inc., The.

Brighter Child, compiled by. Time & Money. 2006. (ENG., Illus.). 54p. (gr. k-3). 2.99 *(978-0-7696-6480-4(6)*, 0769664806, Brighter Child) Carson-Dellosa Publishing, LLC.

Brooks, Marigold. It's Time for Summer Camp, 1 vol. 2017. (Let's Tell Time Ser.). (ENG., Illus.). 24p. (J). (gr. 1-1). 25.27 *(978-1-5081-5726-7(X)*, 62e8be9a-2c86-4d23-b470-92b111935f91, PowerKids Pr.) Rosen Publishing Group, Inc., The.

Brunner- Jass, Renata. Field of Play: Measuring Distance, Rate, & Time. 2013. (iMath Ser.). (ENG., Illus.). 48p. (J). (gr. 5-6). pap. 13.26 *(978-1-60357-510-2(3))* Norwood Hse. Pr.

Bryan, Lara. Telling the Time Activity Book. 2018. (Math Sticker Activity Bks.). (ENG.). 64p. pap. 9.99 *(978-0-7945-4130-9(5)*, Usborne) EDC Publishing.

Burstein, John. Keeping Track of Time: Go Fly a Kite!, 1 vol. 2003. (Math Monsters(tm) Ser.). (ENG., Illus.). 24p. (J). (gr. k-3). pap. 9.15 *(978-0-8368-3825-1(4)*, 2169b0b5-9f2f-46fa-b9ff-f242b5a115e6, Weekly Reader Leveled Readers) Stevens, Gareth Publishing LLLP.

Burton, Margie, et al. Keeping Time. 2011. (Early Connections Ser.). (J). *(978-1-61672-524-2(9))* Benchmark Education Co.

Bussiere, Desirée. What in the World Is a Leap Year? & Other Time Measurements, 1 vol. 2013. (Let's Measure Ser.). (ENG.). 24p. (J). (gr. -1-3). lib. bdg. 29.93 *(978-1-61783-597-1(8)*, 11111, SandCastle) ABDO Publishing Co.

Cernek, Kim. Build-a-Skill Instant Books Time & Money. Faulkner, Stacey, ed. Campbell, Jenny & Tom, Darcy, illus. 2007. (J). 4.99 *(978-1-59198-417-7(3))* Creative Teaching Pr., Inc.

Clark, Claire. The Calendar. 2012. (Calendar Ser.). (ENG.). 24p. (gr. k-1). pap. 166.80 *(978-1-4296-8339-5(2)*, Capstone Pr.) Capstone.

—How Long Is a Day? 2012. (Calendar Ser.). (ENG.). 24p. (gr. k-1). pap. 41.70 *(978-1-4296-8334-0(1)*, Capstone Pr.) Capstone.

—How Long Is a Month? 2012. (Calendar Ser.). (ENG.). 24p. (gr. k-1). pap. 41.70 *(978-1-4296-8335-7(X)*, Capstone Pr.) Capstone.

—How Long Is a Week? 2012. (Calendar Ser.). (ENG.). 24p. (gr. k-1). pap. 41.70 *(978-1-4296-8336-4(8)*, Capstone Pr.) Capstone.

—How Long Is a Year? 2012. (Calendar Ser.). (ENG.). 24p. (gr. k-1). pap. 41.70 *(978-1-4296-8337-1(6)*, Capstone Pr.) Capstone.

Cleary, Brian P. A Second, a Minute, a Week with Days in It: A Book about Time. Gable, Brian, illus. 2015. (Math Is CATegorical (r) Ser.). (ENG.). 32p. (J). (gr. k-3). pap. 8.99 *(978-1-4677-2050-2(X)*, bc397046-11e2-4b51-bfc2-5055e12c8cf8, Millbrook Pr.) Lerner Publishing Group.

Collins Easy Learning. Telling the Time Ages 5-7: Ideal for Home Learning (Collins Easy Learning KS1) 2015. (Collins Easy Learning Ser.). (ENG.). 32p. (J). (gr. -1-2). pap. 6.95 *(978-0-00-813437-2(5))* HarperCollins Pubs. Ltd. GBR. Dist: Independent Pubs. Group.

—Telling the Time Ages 7-9: Ideal for Home Learning (Collins Easy Learning KS2) 2015. (Collins Easy Learning Ser.). (ENG.). 32p. (J). (gr. 2-4). pap. 6.95 *(978-0-00-813425-9(1))* HarperCollins Pubs. Ltd. GBR. Dist: Independent Pubs. Group.

—Telling the Time Wipe Clean Activity Book: Ideal for Home Learning (Collins Easy Learning KS1) 2018. (Collins Easy Learning KS1 Ser.). (ENG.). 24p. (J). (gr. -1-k). 7.95 *(978-0-00-827538-9(6))* HarperCollins Pubs. Ltd. GBR. Dist: Independent Pubs. Group.

—Times Tables Flashcards: Ideal for Home Learning (Collins Easy Learning KS2) 2018. (Collins Easy Learning KS2 Ser.). (ENG.). 134p. (J). (gr. 3-5). 15.99 *(978-0-00-828150-2(5))* HarperCollins Pubs. Ltd. GBR. Dist: Independent Pubs. Group.

Conklin, Wendy. Fun & Games: Clockwork Carnival: Measuring Time (Grade 3) rev. ed. 2017. (Mathematics in the Real World Ser.). (ENG., Illus.). 32p. (J). (gr. 3-4). pap. 11.99 *(978-1-4807-5805-6(1))* Teacher Created Materials, Inc.

Conley, Kate. How to Read Calendars & Clocks. 2018. (Understanding the Basics Ser.). (ENG.). 24p. (J). (gr. 1-4). lib. bdg. 32.79 *(978-1-5038-2335-8(0)*, 212210) Child's World, Inc, The.

Dapice, Carmine. Lets Rhyme with Time. 2013. 38p. pap. 13.95 *(978-1-4497-8822-3(X)*, WestBow Pr.) Author Solutions, LLC.

Davies, Ann & Ne, Harriet. What Time Is It? Asks Elephant. (Illus.). 10p. (J). pap. 15.95 *(978-1-85479-262-4(8))* O'Mara, Michael Bks., Ltd. GBR. Dist: Trans-Atlantic Pubns., Inc.

de Klerk, Roger, illus. Foxy Learns to Tell Time, 1 vol. 2009. (Foxy Learns Ser.). (ENG.). 16p. (J). pap. 4.95 *(978-1-59496-180-9(8))* Teora USA LLC.

Donovan, Sandra. Teen Wise Guide to Time Management. 2012. (USA TODAY Teen Wise Guides: Time, Money, & Relationships Ser.). (ENG.). 64p. (gr. 8-12). lib. bdg. 31.93 *(978-0-7613-7019-2(6))* Lerner Publishing Group.

Dowdy, Penny. Time, 1 vol. 2008. (My Path to Math Ser.). (ENG., Illus.). 24p. (J). (gr. k-3). pap. *(978-0-7787-4362-0(4))*; lib. bdg. *(978-0-7787-4344-6(6))* Crabtree Publishing Co.

Estellon, Pascale. It's about Time: Untangling Everything You Need to Know about Time. 2018. (ENG., Illus.). 48p. (J). (gr. k-4). pap. 9.95 *(978-1-77147-342-2(8))* Owlkids Bks. Inc. CAN. Dist: Publishers Group West (PGW).

Falligant, Erin. A Smart Girl's Guide: Getting It Together: How to Organize Your Space, Your Stuff, Your Time — And Your Life. Vaughan, Brenna, illus. 2017. (American Girl(r) Wellbeing Ser.). (ENG.). 96p. (J). pap. 12.99 *(978-1-60958-888-5(6))* American Girl Publishing, Inc.

Farndon, John. Time, 1 vol. 2003. (Science Experiments Ser.). (ENG., Illus.). 32p. (gr. 4-4). 32.64 *(978-0-7614-1470-4(3)*, 0fcbc1a8-6de3-46a9-a447-b12b26762ab4) Cavendish Square Publishing LLC.

Faulkner, Keith & Tyger, Rory. Time's Up! Faulkner, Keith & Tyger, Rory, illus. Lambert, Jonathan, illus. 2003. (J). *(978-0-439-56155-6(8))* Scholastic, Inc.

Fischer, James. Keeping Your Business Organized: Time Management & Workflow. Madrian, Brigitte, ed. 2013. (Young Adult Library of Small Business & Finance Ser.). (Illus.). 64p. (J). (gr. 7-18). pap. 12.95 *(978-1-4222-2982-8(3))* Mason Crest.

—Time Math. 2013. (Math 24/7 Ser.: 10). 48p. (J). (gr. 5-18). 19.95 *(978-1-4222-2910-1(6))* Mason Crest.

Flash Kids Editors, ed. Time & Money: Grade 1 (Flash Skills) 2010. (Flash Skills Ser.). (ENG.). 64p. (J). pap. 4.95 *(978-1-4114-3450-9(1)*, Spark Publishing Group) Sterling Publishing Co., Inc.

Formichelli, Linda & Anderson, Maxine. Timekeeping: Explore the History & Science of Telling Time with 15 Projects. Carbaugh, Samuel, illus. 2012. (Build It Yourself Ser.). (ENG.). 128p. (J). (gr. 3-7). pap. 15.95 *(978-1-61930-033-0(8)*, 9fd535cf-9dd7-435a-a4e2-9e877aa0daba) Nomad Pr.

Formichelli, Linda & Martin, W. Eric. Timekeeping: Explore the History & Science of Telling Time with 15 Projects. Carbaugh, Sam, illus. 2012. (Build It Yourself Ser.). (ENG.). 128p. (J). (gr. 3-7). 21.95 *(978-1-61930-136-8(9)*, 2d8d6ee7-09f3-4739-b919-5da28346264c) Nomad Pr.

Fortuna, Lois. Getting Ready for School, 1 vol. 2015. (We Can Do It! Ser.). (ENG.). 24p. (J). (gr. k-k). pap. 9.15 *(978-1-4824-3799-7(6)*, 2c500370-0ac3-4bcd-a8df-7efdbb2f2398) Stevens, Gareth Publishing LLLP.

Gaddi, Rosalie. Austin's Airplane Adventure: Solve Problems Involving Measurement, 1 vol. 2014. (Rosen Math Readers Ser.). (ENG., Illus.). 24p. (J). (gr. 3-3). pap. 8.25 *(978-1-4777-4915-9(2)*, 5eedc106-eb9b-453a-b7ef-ea635b8ab016, PowerKids Pr.) Rosen Publishing Group, Inc., The.

Gardner, Robert & Conklin, Joshua. A Kid's Book of Experiments with Time, 1 vol. 2015. (Surprising Science Experiments Ser.). (ENG., Illus.). 48p. (gr. 4-4). pap. 12.70 *(978-0-7660-7272-5(X)*, d010024d-392a-4903-8712-782dabf00dfd) Enslow Publishing, LLC.

Gerard, Franck J. Time Waits for No One! Prioritize to Change Your Life! 2005. (Illus.). 90p. per., training bk. ed. 14.99 net. *(978-0-9772685-0-4(0))* ABC Pubs.

Greathouse, Perlman Lisa. Life in Numbers: Managing Time (Level 3) 2017. (TIME for KIDS(r): Informational Text Ser.). (ENG., Illus.). 32p. (J). (gr. 3-4). pap. 12.99 *(978-1-4258-4969-6(5))* Teacher Created Materials, Inc.

Green, Jen. Day & Night, 1 vol. 2007. (Our Earth Ser.). (ENG., Illus.). 24p. (J). (gr. 2-3). lib. bdg. 26.27 *(978-1-4042-4275-3(9)*, f2032ba1-e9d0-4d33-acd8-a1f74f1c4c7d) Rosen Publishing Group, Inc., The.

Greenes, Carol, et al. Time & Money. 2003. (Illus.). 60p. (J). (gr. -1-3). 16.95 *(978-0-7690-0004-6(5))* Seymour, Dale Pubns.

Greenwell, Jessica. Wipe-Clean Telling the Time. Scott, Kimberley, illus. 2013. (Usborne Wipe-Clean Ser.). (ENG.). 20p. (J). (gr. -1-3). pap. 7.99 *(978-0-7945-3403-5(1)*, Usborne) EDC Publishing.

Haslam, Andrew, et al. Time. (Make It Work! Ser.). (Illus.). 48p. (J). pap. 7.99 *(978-0-590-24915-7(0))*; pap. 16.99 *(978-0-590-24914-0(2))* Scholastic, Inc.

Havener, Katherine. Nurses When the Sun Shines: A Little Book on Night Weaning. Burrier, Sara, illus. 2nd ed. 2013. 20p. (J). pap. 9.99 *(978-0-615-75642-4(5))* Elea Pr.

Heddle, Becca. What's up with Time? Band 14/Ruby. Rowe, Alan, illus. 2017. (Collins Big Cat Ser.). (ENG.). 48p. (J). pap. 11.99 *(978-0-00-820884-4(0))* HarperCollins Pubs. Ltd. GBR. Dist: Independent Pubs. Group.

Heos, Bridget. Telling Time. Longhi, Katya, illus. 2014. (Math World Ser.). (ENG.). 24p. (J). (gr. 1-4). lib. bdg. 27.10 *(978-1-60753-461-7(4)*, 15916) Amicus.

Hibbert, Clare. My Busy Day. Raga, Silvia, illus. 2011. (Busy Times Ser.). 24p. (J). (gr. -1-k). lib. bdg. 25.65 *(978-1-60753-101-2(1))* Amicus Learning.

—My Busy Week. Raga, Silvia, illus. 2011. (Busy Times Ser.). 24p. (J). (gr. -1-k). lib. bdg. 25.65 *(978-1-60753-102-9(X))* Amicus Learning.

—My Busy Year. Raga, Silvia, illus. 2011. (Busy Times Ser.). 24p. (J). (gr. -1-k). lib. bdg. 25.65 *(978-1-60753-103-6(8))* Amicus Learning.

—Our Busy Lives. Raga, Silvia, illus. 2011. (Busy Times Ser.). 24p. (J). (gr. -1-k). lib. bdg. 25.65 *(978-1-60753-104-3(6))* Amicus Learning.

Hoffman, Juliet. 24 Hours: From Day to Night, 1 vol. 2008. (Real Life Readers Ser.). (ENG.). 12p. (gr. 1-2). pap. 5.90 *(978-1-4042-7925-4(3)*, e70bdd1b-038f-4692-baaa-f1a1dc70fe2d, Rosen Classroom) Rosen Publishing Group, Inc., The.

Holt, Rinehart and Winston Staff. Horizons: Time for Kids Collection, 18 vols. 2003. (Harcourt Horizons Ser.). (Illus.). (gr. k-18). 63.70 *(978-0-15-333097-1(X))* Harcourt Schl. Pubs.

House, Behrman. Building Jewish Identity 2: Sacred Time. 2012. (ENG.). 1p. (J). pap. 9.95 *(978-0-87441-863-7(1)*, 61c2102b-1738-4f7c-b394-0b3b702558f5) Behrman Hse., Inc.

Houser, Grace. Why Do We Have to Be on Time?, 1 vol. 2018. (Common Good Ser.). (ENG.). 24p. (gr. 2-2). 25.27 *(978-1-5383-3075-3(X)*, ad5fac88-68d6-413f-9399-44088d5e075b, PowerKids Pr.) Rosen Publishing Group, Inc., The.

Hubbard, Ben. Top 10 Longest. 2010. (ENG., Illus.). 32p. (J). pap. *(978-0-7787-7510-2(0))*; lib. bdg. *(978-0-7787-7489-1(9))* Crabtree Publishing Co.

Hutchins, Hazel. A Second Is a Hiccup: A Child's Book of Time. Denton, Kady MacDonald, illus. 2008. (J). 16.99 *(978-0-439-83110-9(5)*, Levine, Arthur A. Bks.) Scholastic, Inc.

Hutmacher, Kimberly M. Hours, 1 vol. 2012. (It's about Time Ser.). (ENG., Illus.). 24p. (J). (gr. -1-2). lib. bdg. 24.65 *(978-1-4296-8577-1(8)*, 118558) Capstone.

—Minutes. 2012. (It's about Time Ser.). (ENG.). 24p. (J). (gr. k-1). pap. 37.74 *(978-1-4296-9353-0(3)*, 18570, Pebble); (Illus.). (gr. -1-2). pap. 6.29 *(978-1-4296-9352-3(5)*, 120382) Capstone.

—Seconds, 1 vol. 2012. (It's about Time Ser.). (ENG.). 24p. (J). (gr. -1-2). lib. bdg. 24.65 *(978-1-4296-8575-7(1)*, 118555) Capstone.

Jackson, Dona. Let's Get Moving! Tell & Write Time. 2013. (InfoMax Math Readers Ser.). (ENG.). 24p. (J). (gr. 1-2). pap. 49.50 *(978-1-4777-2176-6(2))*; (Illus.). pap. 8.25 *(978-1-4777-2175-9(4)*, ab890231-5cda-40e4-8274-c2c4dc7a97c5) Rosen Publishing Group, Inc., The. (Rosen Classroom).

Jackson, Lora Z. Around the Clock: A Story about Telling Time. Martin, Miles J., illus. 2011. 58p. 36.95 *(978-1-258-06483-9(9))* Literary Licensing, LLC.

Jenkins, Steve. Just a Second. Jenkins, Steve, illus. 2011. (ENG., Illus.). 40p. (J). (gr. -1-3). 18.99 *(978-0-618-70896-3(0)*, 518919, Clarion Bks.) HarperCollins Pubs.

—Just a Second. Jenkins, Steve, illus. 2017. (ENG., Illus.). 32p. (J). (gr. -1-3). pap. 7.99 *(978-1-328-74086-1(2)*, 1677123, Clarion Bks.) HarperCollins Pubs.

Jones, Tammy. What Is the Time? 2009. (Sight Word Readers Set A Ser.). (J). 3.49 net. *(978-1-60719-150-6(4))* Newmark Learning LLC.

Kalman, Bobbie. ¿Qué Es el Tiempo? 2009. (SPA.). 24p. (J). *(978-0-7787-8703-7(6))*; pap. *(978-0-7787-8742-6(7))* Crabtree Publishing Co.

—What Time Is It? 2008. (Looking at Nature Ser.). (ENG., Illus.). 24p. (J). (gr. -1-2). pap. *(978-0-7787-3345-4(9))*; lib. bdg. *(978-0-7787-3325-6(4))* Crabtree Publishing Co.

Karapetkova, Holly. Seconds, Minutes, & Hours. 2009. (Illus.). 24p. (J). lib. bdg. 22.79 *(978-1-60694-379-3(0))* Rourke Educational Media.

Katirgis, Jane. Day & Night, 1 vol. 2011. (All about Opposites Ser.). (ENG., Illus.). 24p. (gr. -1-1). (J). lib. bdg. 25.27 *(978-0-7660-3915-5(3)*, 485378d7-4d0d-477e-9ae7-f50d300be7c8); pap. 10.35 *(978-1-59845-262-4(2)*, 41142589-e229-47b1-8f2d-4e5d40470dad) Enslow Publishing, LLC. (Enslow Publishing).

Kawa, Katie. Are Students Given Too Much Homework?, 1 vol. 2018. (Points of View Ser.). (ENG.). 24p. (gr. 3-3). pap. 9.25 *(978-1-5345-2777-5(X)*, 7d701a44-e2d0-454c-85c4-d5412657f081, KidHaven Publishing) Greenhaven Publishing LLC.

Kay, Jill. Fernando Exercises!, 1 vol. 2013. (Core Math Skills: Measurement & Geometry Ser.). (ENG.). 24p. (J). (gr. 1-1). 26.27 *(978-1-4777-2228-2(9)*, 44c9baf4-0a7a-4e58-802d-9a241830bd35); pap. 8.25 *(978-1-4777-2106-3(1)*, c0a1c61d-9aa0-48dd-bc88-a5f68eef956b) Rosen Publishing Group, Inc., The. (Rosen Classroom).

—Fernando Exercises! Tell & Write Time. 2013. (Rosen Math Readers Ser.). (ENG.). 24p. (J). (gr. 1-2). pap. 49.50 *(978-1-4777-2107-0(X)*, Rosen Classroom) Rosen Publishing Group, Inc., The.

Kompelien, Tracy. I Can Tell Time with a Rhyme!, 1 vol. 2007. (Math Made Fun Ser.). (Illus.). 24p. (J). (gr. k-3). lib. bdg. 24.21 *(978-1-59928-525-2(8)*, SandCastle) ABDO Publishing Co.

Koscielniak, Bruce. About Time: A First Look at Time & Clocks. 2013. (ENG., Illus.). 32p. (J). (gr. -1-3). pap. 7.99 *(978-0-544-10512-6(5)*, 1540811, Clarion Bks.) HarperCollins Pubs.

—About Time: A First Look at Time & Clocks. 2013. lib. bdg. 18.40 *(978-0-606-33538-6(2))* Turtleback.

Krieg, Katherine. How Many Days? 2015. (Measuring Time Ser.). (ENG., Illus.). 16p. (J). (gr. k-2). lib. bdg. 17.95 *(978-1-60753-723-6(0)*, 15250) Amicus.

—How Many Hours? 2015. (Measuring Time Ser.). (ENG., Illus.). 16p. (J). (gr. k-2). lib. bdg. 17.95 *(978-1-60753-722-9(2)*, 15251) Amicus.

—How Many Minutes? 2015. (Measuring Time Ser.). (ENG., Illus.). 16p. (J). (gr. k-2). lib. bdg. 17.95 *(978-1-60753-721-2(4)*, 15252) Amicus.

—How Many Months? 2015. (Measuring Time Ser.). (ENG., Illus.). 16p. (J). (gr. k-2). lib. bdg. 17.95 *(978-1-60753-725-0(7)*, 15253) Amicus.

—How Many Seconds? 2015. (Measuring Time Ser.). (ENG., Illus.). 16p. (J). (gr. k-2). lib. bdg. 17.95 *(978-1-60753-720-5(6)*, 15254) Amicus.

—How Many Weeks? 2015. (Measuring Time Ser.). (ENG., Illus.). 16p. (J). (gr. k-2). lib. bdg. 17.95 *(978-1-60753-724-3(9)*, 15255) Amicus.

—How Many Years? 2015. (Measuring Time Ser.). (ENG., Illus.). 16p. (J). (gr. k-2). lib. bdg. 17.95 *(978-1-60753-726-7(5)*, 15256) Amicus.

Kumon Publishing North America, creator. Easy Telling Time Write & Wipe! Kumon Publishing North America, . 2007. (Kumon Flash Cards Ser.). (ENG., Illus.). 32p. (J). pap. 9.95 *(978-1-933241-45-6(4))* Kumon Publishing North America, Inc.

—My Book of Easy Telling Time: Learning about Hours & Half-Hours. Kumon Publishing North America, . 2006. (Kumon Workbooks Ser.). (ENG., Illus.). 80p. (J). (gr. -1-1). per. 7.95 *(978-1-933241-26-5(8))* Kumon Publishing North America, Inc.

—My Book of Telling Time: Learning about Minutes. Kumon Publishing North America, . 2006. (Kumon Workbooks Ser.). (ENG., Illus.). 80p. (J). (gr. k-2). per. 7.95 *(978-1-933241-27-2(6))* Kumon Publishing North America, Inc.

Learn to Tell the Time. 2003. (Illus.). (J). bds. 4.98 *(978-1-4054-1145-5(7))* Parragon, Inc.

Let's Tell Time, 8 vols. 2017. (Let's Tell Time Ser.). 24p. (ENG.). (gr. 1-1). 101.08 *(978-1-5081-5782-3(0)*, cfa864ac-29c7-4369-953e-272cda13167e); (gr. 4-6). pap. 33.00 *(978-1-5081-5801-1(0))* Rosen Publishing Group, Inc., The. (PowerKids Pr.).

Let's Tell Time. 2003. 16p. (J). 3.79 *(978-1-58792-052-3(2))* Trend Enterprises, Inc.

Levy, Janey. Keeping Time Through the Ages: The History of Tools Used to Measure Time, 1 vol. (Math for the REAL World Ser.). (ENG., Illus.). 32p. (gr. 4-5). 2010. pap. 10.00 *(978-0-8239-8917-1(8)*, 91ca6d54-9373-42c8-9232-1c43e0d31ee7) 2003. (J). lib. bdg. 28.93 *(978-0-8239-8993-5(3)*, 2d8a5c33-c311-43fe-84ec-11529d94ed1f) Rosen Publishing Group, Inc., The. (PowerKids Pr.).

Lift-The-Flap Telling the Time. 2017. (Advanced Lift-The-Flap BDs* Ser.). (ENG.). (J). bds. 14.99 *(978-0-7945-3865-1(7)*, Usborne) EDC Publishing.

Little, Richard. I Know about Telling Time, 1 vol. 2018. (What I Know Ser.). (ENG.). 24p. (gr. k-k). 24.27 *(978-1-5382-1726-9(0)*, e83de44e-d535-4c8e-9a03-caae0231708b) Stevens, Gareth Publishing LLLP.

Llewellyn, Claire. Day & Night. 2006. (I Know That, Cycles of Nature Set Ser.). (Illus.). 24p. (J). (gr. -1-3). lib. bdg. 22.80 *(978-1-59771-018-3(0))* Sea-To-Sea Pubns.

Loughran, Donna. Time Ticks By: How Do You Read a Clock? 2013. (iMath Ser.). (ENG., Illus.). 24p. (J). (gr. k-2). pap. 13.26 *(978-1-60357-490-7(5))* Norwood Hse. Pr.

Loughran, Donna & Brunner-Jass, Renata. Field of Play: Measuring Distance, Rate, & Time. 2013. (iMath Ser.). (Illus.). 48p. (J). (gr. 5-6). lib. bdg. 23.94 *(978-1-59953-571-5(8))* Norwood Hse. Pr.

Macdonald, Fiona. You Wouldn't Want to Live Without Clocks & Calendars! 2015. (You Wouldn't Want to Live Without Ser.). lib. bdg. 20.80 *(978-0-606-37469-9(8))* Turtleback.

MacDonald, Lucy. You Can Manage Your Time, 1 vol. 2017. (Be Your Best Self Ser.). (ENG.). 158p. (gr. 9-9). lib. bdg. 46.27 *(978-1-5383-8002-4(1)*, 7838eb5a-1e9c-4a4c-b2b0-87ef7c548fc5, Rosen Young Adult) Rosen Publishing Group, Inc., The.

Martins, Isabel Minhos. The World in a Second. Carvalho, Bernardo, illus. 2015. 56p. (J). (gr. -1-3). 18.95 *(978-1-59270-157-5(4))* Enchanted Lion Bks., LLC.

Meachen Rau, Dana. El día y la Noche / Day & Night, 1 vol. 2010. (Los Ciclos de la Naturaleza / Nature's Cycles Ser.). (ENG & SPA.). 32p. (gr. 1-2). lib. bdg. 25.50 *(978-0-7614-4788-7(1)*, 58939adc-79dd-4faf-8102-a671170e34f9) Cavendish Square Publishing LLC.

—Space & Time, 1 vol. 2009. (Earth Matters Ser.). (ENG.). 32p. (gr. 1-2). pap. 9.23 *(978-0-7614-3573-0(5)*, e4668759-d4ab-49ff-a79f-c0f71b32a844); lib. bdg. 25.50 *(978-0-7614-3049-0(0)*, 91797fe1-a50e-4ea7-b87b-7e4d7caab1a8) Cavendish Square Publishing LLC.

—El Tiempo y el Espacio / Space & Time, 1 vol. 2010. (Nuestro Planeta Es Importante / Earth Matters Ser.). (ENG & SPA.). 32p. (gr. 1-2). lib. bdg. 25.50 *(978-0-7614-3496-2(8)*, 363b2c2d-4381-40c1-8cc1-c313d066b158) Cavendish Square Publishing LLC.

—El Tiempo y el Espacio (Space & Time), 1 vol. 2010. (Nuestro Planeta Es Importante (Earth Matters) Ser.). (SPA.). 32p. (gr. 1-2). lib. bdg. 25.50 *(978-0-7614-3470-2(4)*, 2f501a84-2a44-4e71-b2bd-84314a5f4c7d) Cavendish Square Publishing LLC.

Meyers, Nancy. Doodles Time. Meyers, Nancy, illus. 2012. (Doodles Ser.). (ENG., Illus.). 64p. (J). (gr. k-5). pap. 7.95 *(978-1-61608-670-1(X)*, 608670, Sky Pony Pr.) Skyhorse Publishing Co., Inc.

Miglis, Jenny. My Talking Clock: Hannah's Busy Day. 2005. 12p. bds. 9.95 *(978-1-932915-06-8(0))* Sandvik Publishing.

Minden, Cecilia. It Is about Time! 2010. (21st Century Basic Skills Library: Measurements Ser.). (ENG., Illus.). 24p. (gr. k-3). lib. bdg. 26.35 *(978-1-60279-847-2(8)*, 200560) Cherry Lake Publishing.

Moffatt, Judith, illus. Slide & Discover: It's Time! 2005. (Slide & Discover Ser.). 8p. (J). bds. 7.95 *(978-1-58117-247-8(8)*, Intervisual/Piggy Toes) Bendon, Inc.

Moran, Lisa. Making a Difference SB1 the Gift of Time. 2010. (Connect to Literacy Ser.). 8p. pap. *(978-1-4334-0503-7(2))* Millmark Education.

Murphy, Patricia J. Learning to Tell Time with Puppies & Kittens, 1 vol. 2017. (Math Fun with Puppies & Kittens Ser.). (ENG.). 32p. (gr. 1-2). pap. 11.52 *(978-0-7660-9075-0(2)*, caa0939d-afd5-4356-83eb-c02c54cd9f93) Enslow Publishing, LLC.

—Telling Time with Puppies & Kittens, 1 vol. 2007. (Puppy & Kitten Math Ser.). (ENG., Illus.). 32p. (gr. k-2). lib. bdg. 26.60 *(978-0-7660-2728-2(7)*, b42fda31-fcf2-41aa-93d5-dc62f0fdf135, Enslow Elementary) Enslow Publishing, LLC.

Murphy, Stuart J. It's about Time! Speirs, John, illus. 2005. (MathStart Ser.). 40p. (J). 16.99 *(978-0-06-055768-3(0))*; (ENG.). (gr. -1). pap. 6.99 *(978-0-06-055769-0(9)*, HarperCollins) HarperCollins Pubs.

—It's about Time! Speirs, John, illus. 2005. (Mathstart Ser.). 33p. (gr. -1-3). 16.00 *(978-0-7569-5224-2(7))* Perfection Learning Corp.

—Rodeo Time. Wenzel, David T., illus. 2006. (MathStart 3 Ser.). (ENG.). 40p. (J). (gr. 2-5). pap. 6.99 *(978-0-06-055779-9(6)*, HarperCollins) HarperCollins Pubs.

Nadeau, Isaac. Learning about Earth's Cycles with Graphic Organizers. (Graphic Organizers in Science Ser.). 24p. 2009. (gr. 3-4). 42.50 *(978-1-61513-029-0(2))* 2005. (ENG., Illus.). (J). (gr. 4-5). lib. bdg. 26.27 *(978-1-4042-2807-8(1)*, ada0811a-5be4-4a76-9321-4e8ca97250a0) 2005. (ENG., Illus.). (gr. 4-5). pap. 8.25 *(978-1-4042-5044-4(1)*, 57687033-db1f-42ec-8e67-7ab5242f6329) Rosen Publishing Group, Inc., The. (PowerKids Pr.).

Nagelhout, Ryan. Time Zones, 1 vol. 2014. (Map Basics Ser.). (ENG.). 24p. (J). (gr. 2-3). 24.27 *(978-1-4824-1068-6(0)*, 93017597-b293-4118-be23-0b9d239ae433) Stevens, Gareth Publishing LLLP.

Pezzimenti, Grace. Busy Families: Learning to Tell Time by the Hour, 1 vol. (Math for the REAL World Ser.). (ENG., Illus.). 8p. (gr. k-1). 2010. pap. 5.15 *(978-0-8239-8912-6(7)*, 4b93df85-4e2d-4e44-939f-9796e4a6b43a) 2004. 29.95 *(978-0-8239-7627-0(0))* Rosen Publishing Group, Inc., The.

Picthall, Chez & Award, Anna. Tell The Time Sticker Book. 2017. (ENG.). 12p. (J). pap. 8.00 *(978-1-907604-70-6(7))* Award Pubns. Ltd. GBR. Dist: Parkwest Pubns., Inc.

Pistoia, Sara. Time. 2016. (J). *(978-1-4896-5122-8(5))* Weigl Pubs., Inc.

Pluckrose, Henry. Time (Math Counts: Updated Editions) (Library Edition) 2018. (Math Counts, New & Updated Ser.). (ENG., Illus.). 32p. (J). (gr. k-3). 25.00 *(978-0-531-17514-9(6)*, Children's Pr.) Scholastic Library Publishing.

Race Against Time: Individual Title Six-Packs. (Bookweb Ser.). 32p. (gr. 4-18). 34.00 *(978-0-7635-3745-6(4))* Rigby Education.

Rajczak Nelson, Kristen. How Do You Gain Time When You Fly West? And Other FAQs about Time & Travel, 1 vol. 2016. (Q & a: Life's Mysteries Solved! Ser.). (ENG.). 32p. (J). (gr. 3-4). pap. 11.50 *(978-1-4824-4752-1(5)*, 18714e9f-a182-43c2-9e01-b78b38d9288d) Stevens, Gareth Publishing LLLP.

Randolph, Joanne. All about a Day. 2009. (It's about Time Ser.). 24p. (gr. 1-1). 42.50 *(978-1-61513-630-8(4)*, PowerKids Pr.) Rosen Publishing Group, Inc., The.

—All about a Day/Los Días. 2009. (It's about Time/Los libros del tiempo Ser.). (SPA.). 24p. (gr. 1-1). 42.50 *(978-1-61513-626-1(6)*, Editorial Buenas Letras) Rosen Publishing Group, Inc., The.

—All about A Day/Los Dias, 1 vol. Brusca, Maria Cristina, tr. 2007. (It's about Time / Los Libros Del Tiempo Ser.). (ENG & SPA., Illus.). 24p. (J). (gr. 1-1). lib. bdg. 26.27 *(978-1-4042-7627-7(0)*, 0a0c5223-d7fe-4ae6-9e6e-c06f60784f64) Rosen Publishing Group, Inc., The.

—All about an Hour. (It's about Time Ser.). 24p. (gr. 1-1). 2009. 42.50 *(978-1-61513-631-5(2)*, PowerKids Pr.) 2007. (ENG., Illus.). (J). lib. bdg. 26.27 *(978-1-4042-3766-7(6)*, 3802511b-595d-4e58-8753-0325b9623898) Rosen Publishing Group, Inc., The.

—All about an Hour/Las Horas. 2009. (It's about Time/Los libros del tiempo Ser.). (SPA.). 24p. (gr. 1-1). 42.50 *(978-1-61513-627-8(4)*, Editorial Buenas Letras) Rosen Publishing Group, Inc., The.

—All about an Hour/Las Horas, 1 vol. Brusca, Maria Cristina, tr. 2007. (It's about Time / Los Libros Del Tiempo Ser.). (ENG & SPA., Illus.). 24p. (J). (gr. 1-1). lib. bdg. 26.27 *(978-1-4042-7626-0(2)*, 41521b04-4e51-4993-a6a5-bd89eff43ff0) Rosen Publishing Group, Inc., The.

Reid, Stephanie. Time. 2012. (Early Literacy Ser.). (ENG.). 16p. (gr. k-1). 19.99 *(978-1-4333-3490-0(9))*; 6.99 *(978-1-4333-3489-4(5))* Teacher Created Materials, Inc.

Rice, Dona Herweck. Day & Night. 2012. (Early Literacy Ser.). (ENG.). 16p. (gr. k-1). 19.99 *(978-1-4333-3492-4(5))* Teacher Created Materials, Inc.

—Day & Night: Time, 1 vol. rev. ed. 2012. (Early Literacy Ser.). (ENG.). 16p. (gr. k-1). 6.99 *(978-1-4333-3491-7(7))* Teacher Created Materials, Inc.

Robinson, Fay. It's 6 P. M. 2016. (Spring Forward Ser.). (J). (gr. 1). *(978-1-4900-9370-3(2))* Benchmark Education Co.

Roegiers, Maud. Take the Time: Mindfulness for Kids. Roegiers, Maud, illus. 2010. (ENG., Illus.). 32p. (J). (gr. -1-3). 14.95 *(978-1-4338-0794-7(7)*, Magination Pr.) American Psychological Assn.

—Take the Time: Mindfulness for Kids. 2010. (Illus.). 32p. (J). (gr. -1-3). pap. 9.95 *(978-1-4338-0796-1(3)*, Magination Pr.) American Psychological Assn.

Roper, Dawn. 30 Fun Ways to Learn about Time & Money. 2011. (30 Fun Ways to Learn Ser.). (ENG.). 80p. (gr. -1-k). pap. 12.95 *(978-0-87659-370-7(8)*, Gryphon House Inc) Gryphon Hse., Inc.

Rosa-Mendoza, Gladys. My Week/Mi Semana. Wesley, Milliana, ed. Grosshauser, Peter, illus. 2007. (English Spanish Foundations Ser.). (gr. -1-k). bds. 6.95 *(978-1-931398-25-1(9))* Me+Mi Publishing.

—What Time Is It? Cifuentes, Carolina, ed. 2004. (English-Spanish Foundations Ser.: Vol. 7).Tr. of Que Hora Es? (ENG & SPA., Illus.). 20p. (J). (gr. -1-4). bds. 6.95 *(978-0-9679748-9-7(5))* Me+Mi Publishing.

—What Time Is It?, 1 vol. Chapman Calitri, Susan, illus. 2010. (My World Ser.).Tr. of Que Hora Es? (ENG.). 24p. (J). (gr. k-1). pap. 9.15 *(978-1-61533-041-6(0)*, e458144b-641d-4263-8743-bdd775acf47f); lib. bdg. 27.27 *(978-1-60754-954-3(9)*, 5f73bd39-7dab-44c5-8964-59fe6b33f6c1) Rosen Publishing Group, Inc., The. (Windmill Bks.).

School Zone Interactive Staff. Time, Money & Fractions. rev. ed. 2004. (ENG.). 64p. (J). (gr. k-2). 15.99 *(978-1-58947-832-9(0))* School Zone Publishing Co.

School Zone Staff. Time & Money. 2004. (ENG.). 56p. (J). 2.79 *(978-1-58947-990-6(4))* School Zone Publishing Co.

School Zone Staff, ed. Time & Money. 2005. (ENG.). 26p. (J). (gr. 1-2). pap. 3.79 *(978-1-58947-788-9(X))* School Zone Publishing Co.

—Time, Money & Fractions. 2003. (ENG.). (J). (gr. 1-2). cd-rom 19.99 *(978-1-58947-930-2(0))* School Zone Publishing Co.

The Science of Time. 2016. (Illus.). 48p. (J). *(978-1-4222-3516-4(5))* Mason Crest.

Sharp, Jean. TELLING TIME All the Time, 1 vol. 2008. (Math in Our World - Level 2 Ser.). (ENG.). 24p. (gr. 2-2). pap. 9.15 *(978-0-8368-9010-5(8)*, cb741721-a448-49ea-84a2-6046d0edb62c); (Illus.). lib. bdg. 24.67 *(978-0-8368-9001-3(9)*, c9609b20-6b2a-4e85-b9e4-f6d30554debc) Stevens, Gareth Publishing LLLP. (Weekly Reader Leveled Readers).

—Vamos a DECIR la HORA Todo el Tiempo (TELLING TIME All the Time), 1 vol. 2008. (Las Matemáticas en Nuestro Mundo - Nivel 2 (Math in Our World - Level 2) Ser.). (SPA.). 24p. (gr. 2-2). pap. 9.15 *(978-0-8368-9028-0(0)*, 5fb0bb33-7bf6-4df9-81c7-c40fc4862f34); (Illus.). lib. bdg. 24.67 *(978-0-8368-9019-8(1)*, 9f3e2b85-8de9-4b5d-9c03-6f88d72e5880) Stevens, Gareth Publishing LLLP. (Weekly Reader Leveled Readers).

Shaskan, Trisha Speed. If You Were a Minute, 1 vol. Carabelli, Francesca, illus. 2009. (Math Fun Ser.). (ENG.). 24p. (J). (gr. 2-4). pap. 7.95 *(978-1-4048-5202-0(6)*, 95509, Picture Window Bks.) Capstone.

Sherman, Josepha. How Do We Know the Nature of Time. (Great Scientific Questions & the Scientists Who Answered Them Ser.). 112p. (gr. 7-12). 2009. 63.90 *(978-1-61513-205-8(8))* 2004. (ENG., Illus.). (J). lib. bdg. 39.80 *(978-1-4042-0073-9(8)*, a2292393-15ab-42f2-bfac-5ee9989dab8d) Rosen Publishing Group, Inc., The.

Steck-Vaughn Staff. At-Home Workbooks: Time. 2004. (Illus.). pap., wbk. ed. *(978-0-7398-8538-3(3))* Steck-Vaughn.

—Early Math: Time I. 2005. pap. 2.99 *(978-1-4190-0327-1(5))* Steck-Vaughn.

—Early Math: Time II. 2005. pap. 2.99 *(978-1-4190-0337-0(2))* Steck-Vaughn.

Steffora, Tracey. Measuring Time, 6 vols., Set. Incl. Seasons of the Year. (ENG.). 24p. (J). (gr. -1-1). 2011. pap. 6.29 *(978-1-4329-4909-9(8)*, 114810, Heinemann); (Measuring Time Ser.). (ENG.). 24p. 2011. pap., pap., pap. 18.87 o.p. *(978-1-4329-4913-6(6)*, 15872, Heinemann) Capstone.

—Seasons of the Year, 1 vol. 2011. (Measuring Time Ser.). (ENG.). 24p. (J). (gr. -1-1). pap. 6.29 *(978-1-4329-4909-9(8)*, 114810, Heinemann) Capstone.

—What Is Time?, 1 vol. 2011. (ENG.). 24p. (J). (gr. -1-1). 26.65 *(978-1-4329-5357-7(5)*, 116069, Heinemann) Capstone.

Studio Mouse Staff. Time to Learn!, 4 vols. rev. ed. 2007. (ENG., Illus.). 4x20p. (J). (gr. -1-k). 14.99 *(978-1-59069-564-7(X))* Studio Mouse LLC.

Sullivan, Navin. Time, 1 vol. 2007. (Measure Up! Ser.). (ENG., Illus.). 48p. (gr. 4-4). lib. bdg. 34.07 *(978-0-7614-2321-8(4)*, d4c49b00-fe7c-49f2-9885-6585e0edeb0a) Cavendish Square Publishing LLC.

Sundance/Newbridge LLC Staff. Time & Temperature. 2004. (Reading PowerWorks Ser.). (gr. 1-3). 37.50 *(978-0-7608-8976-3(7))*; pap. 6.10 *(978-0-7608-8977-0(5))* Sundance/Newbridge Educational Publishing.

Sweeney, Joan. Me Counting Time. Willmore, Alex, illus. 2019. (ENG.). 32p. (J). (gr. -1-2). 12.99 *(978-0-525-64684-6(1)*, Knopf Bks. for Young Readers) Random Hse. Children's Bks.

Tell Me the Time. (First Bks.: No. S808-3). (Illus.). (J). (gr. -1). pap. 3.95 *(978-0-7214-5054-4(7)*, Dutton Juvenile) Penguin Publishing Group.

Tell the Time. 2004. (Wall Charts Ser.). (J). 4.99 *(978-1-904586-22-7(8))*; 32p. wbk. ed. 3.99 *(978-1-904586-16-6(3))* Byeway Bks.

Thomas, Mary Ann. Our Train Trip: Learning to Add Times by the Half Hour, 1 vol. 2010. (Math for the REAL World Ser.). (ENG.). 12p. (gr. 1-2). pap. 5.90 *(978-0-8239-8849-5(X)*, f80b45b5-a444-45e0-b417-6675e2a6d2a8, Rosen Classroom) Rosen Publishing Group, Inc., The.

Time. (Make it Work Ser.). 42p. (J). (gr. 4-8). pap. *(978-1-882210-40-4(9))* Action Publishing, Inc.

Time - Set 1: What Time Is It. 2005. (J). spiral bd. 23.40 *(978-0-9770248-6-5(5))* Sidedoor Publishing LLC.

Time for a Party, 6, Pack. (Discovery World Ser.). 16p. (gr. 1-2). 28.00 *(978-0-7635-8457-3(6))* Rigby Education.

Time, Inc. Library Bound Titles [Capstone Sole Source]. 2010. (Time, Inc. Library-Bound Titles Ser.). 139.96 *(978-1-4296-5885-0(1))* Capstone.

Top That Publishing Staff, ed. Lets Explore Time. 2004. (Fun Kits Ser.). (Illus.). 48p. (J). *(978-1-84510-246-3(0))* Top That! Publishing PLC.

Tyler, Jenny & Gee, R. Time. Bryant-Mole, K., ed. rev. ed. 2004. (First Learning Ser.). (ENG., Illus.). 1p. (J). (gr. -1-3). pap., act. bk. ed. 4.95 *(978-0-7460-3806-2(2))* EDC Publishing.

Wadsworth, Pamela. Golwg Gyntaf Ar Amser a Gofod. 2005. (WEL., Illus.). 24p. pap. *(978-1-85596-248-4(9))* Dref Wen.

Walker, Nan. Day Camp. 2011. (Early Connections Ser.). (J). *(978-1-61672-347-7(5))* Benchmark Education Co.

Wallace, Elise. Fun & Games: World Records: Time (Grade 4) 2017. (Mathematics in the Real World Ser.). (ENG., Illus.). 32p. (gr. 4-5). pap. 11.99 *(978-1-4258-5558-1(X))* Teacher Created Materials, Inc.

Walpole, Brenda. I Wonder Why the Sun Rises: And Other Questions about Time & Seasons. Tremblay, Marie-Ave, illus. 2011. (I Wonder Why Ser.). (ENG.). 32p. (J). (gr. k-3). pap. 6.99 *(978-0-7534-6529-5(9)*, 900070356, Kingfisher) Roaring Brook Pr.

—I Wonder Why the Sun Rises & Other Questions about Time & Seasons. 2008. (I Wonder Why Ser.). (Illus.). 32p. (gr. k-3). 17.00 *(978-0-7569-9054-1(8))* Perfection Learning Corp.

Williams, Rozanne. The Time Song. 2017. (Learn-To-Read Ser.). (ENG., Illus.). (J). pap. 3.49 *(978-1-68310-231-1(2))* Pacific Learning, Inc.

—What Time Is It? 2017. (Learn-To-Read Ser.). (ENG., Illus.). (J). pap. 3.49 *(978-1-68310-219-9(3))* Pacific Learning, Inc.

Wilmes, Liz, et al. Circle Time Book: For Holiday & Seasons. Dane, Donna, illus. 2004. 128p. (J). pap. 12.95 *(978-0-943452-00-5(7)*, 20002) Building Blocks, LLC.

Woodford, Chris. Time, 1 vol. 2012. (Measure up Math Ser.). (ENG., Illus.). 32p. (J). (gr. 4-4). 29.27 *(978-1-4339-7453-3(3)*, c5ea847f-6b71-427e-96d1-719486650dfe); pap. 11.50 *(978-1-4339-7454-0(1)*, 078086b0-5a72-4df0-a249-6359eb318ed4) Stevens, Gareth Publishing LLLP. (Gareth Stevens Learning Library).

Woods, Sadie. It's Time for the Soccer Game, 1 vol. 2017. (Let's Tell Time Ser.). (ENG., Illus.). 24p. (J). (gr. 1-1). 25.27 *(978-1-5081-5727-4(8)*, 5055753c-f6e5-48fe-8669-c681efe6d2fa, PowerKids Pr.) Rosen Publishing Group, Inc., The.

TIME—FICTION

Adams, Colleen. The Big Day!, 1 vol. 2006. (Neighborhood Readers Ser.). (ENG.). 8p. (gr. k-1). pap. 5.15 *(978-1-4042-5708-5(X)*, 62499b9f-40ab-4c55-a0b2-d9cf2dd19ed8, Rosen Classroom) Rosen Publishing Group, Inc., The.

Baldwin, J. R. Ashley & Mr. Sunshine. 2009. 24p. pap. 24.95 *(978-1-60836-180-9(2))* America Star Bks.

Barchers, Suzanne I. Late Kate, 1 vol. rev. ed. 2011. (Phonics Ser.). (ENG.). 16p. (gr. k-2). 6.99 *(978-1-4333-2906-7(9))* Teacher Created Materials, Inc.

Bondor-Stone, Annabeth & White, Connor. Time Tracers: the Stolen Summers. 2018. (ENG.). 256p. (J). (gr. 3-7). 16.99 *(978-0-06-267142-4(1)*, HarperCollins) HarperCollins Pubs.

Britt, Paige. The Lost Track of Time. White, Lee, illus. 2015. (ENG.). 320p. (J). (gr. 3-7). 17.99 *(978-0-545-53812-1(2)*, Scholastic Pr.) Scholastic, Inc.

Bryson, Theresa. Farm Alarm. 2011. (Early Connections Ser.). (J). *(978-1-61672-350-7(5))* Benchmark Education Co.

Butler, Dori. Late Again! 2005. (J). pap. *(978-1-4108-4209-1(6))* Benchmark Education Co.

Carey, Kelly. How Long Is Forever? Zhuang, Qing, illus. 2020. 32p. (J). (gr. -1-2). lib. bdg. 16.99 *(978-1-58089-578-1(6))* Charlesbridge Publishing, Inc.

Charlesworth, Kate & Gribbin, John. The Cartoon History of Time. 2013. (ENG., Illus.). 64p. pap. 19.95 *(978-0-486-49097-7(1)*, 490971) Dover Pubns., Inc.

Cirrone, Dorian. The First Last Day. (ENG., Illus.). 240p. (J). (gr. 3-7). 2017. pap. 8.99 *(978-1-4814-5814-6(0))* 2016. 17.99 *(978-1-4814-5813-9(2))* Simon & Schuster Children's Publishing. (Aladdin).

Coates, Kimberly & Coates, Ashley. If I Only Knew How to Tell Time. 2013. 32p. pap. 19.99 *(978-1-4772-9963-0(7))* AuthorHouse.

T
U
V

Cole, Bob. Power Reading: Chapter/Sci-Fi/Time Warp. Ford, David, illus. 2004. 25p. (J). (gr. 4-18). vinyl bd. 39.95 *(978-1-883186-60-9(9),* PPSF3) National Reading Styles Institute, Inc.

Cousins, Lucy. Maisy's First Clock: A Maisy Fun-To-Learn Book. Cousins, Lucy, illus. 2011. (Maisy Ser.). (ENG., Illus.). 16p. (J). (gr. k-k). bds. 14.99 *(978-0-7636-5095-7(1))* Candlewick Pr.

Cuyler, Margery. Tick Tock Clock. Neubecker, Robert, illus. 2012. (My First I Can Read Ser.). (ENG.). 32p. (J). (gr. -1 — 1). pap. 4.99 *(978-0-06-136311-5(1),* HarperCollins) HarperCollins Pubs.

Cuyler, Margery & Neubecker, Robert. Tick Tock Clock. 2012. (My First I Can Read Ser.). (ENG., Illus.). 32p. (J). (gr. -1 — 1). 16.99 *(978-0-06-136309-2(X),* HarperCollins) HarperCollins Pubs.

Dahl, Michael. The Lost Page. Evergreen, Nelson, illus. 2015. (Library of Doom: the Final Chapters Ser.). (ENG.). 40p. (J). (gr. 4-8). 23.99 *(978-1-4342-9679-5(2),* 126988, Stone Arch Bks.) Capstone.

Danziger, Paula. It's Justin Time, Amber Brown. Ross, Tony, illus. (Amber Brown Ser.). 9.95 *(978-1-59112-294-4(5))* Live Oak Media.

—Justo a Tiempo, Ambar Dorado. Ross, Tony, illus. 2007. (Amber Brown Ser.). (SPA.). 48p. (gr. k-3). per. 8.95 *(978-1-59820-595-4(1),* Alfaguara) Santillana USA Publishing Co., Inc.

Darlison, Aleesah. Keep It Real No. 2. 2016. (Netball Gems Ser.: 6). (Illus.). 160p. (J). (gr. 3-6). pap. 8.99 *(978-0-14-378115-8(4))* Random Hse. Australia AUS. Dist: Independent Pubs. Group.

Derrick, Patricia. Mr. Walrus & the Old School Bus. Martinez, J-P Loppo, illus. 2007. 32p. 18.95 incl. audio compact disk *(978-1-933818-13-9(1))* Animalations.

Dodd, Emma, illus. Tick Tock Dog: A Tell the Time Book - with a Special Movable Clock! 2016. (ENG.). 12p. (J). (gr. -1-k). bds. 14.99 *(978-1-86147-718-7(X),* Armadillo) Anness Publishing GBR. Dist: National Bk. Network.

Ficocelli, Elizabeth. Kid Tea. Dibley, Glin, illus. 2009. 32p. (J). (gr. -1). bds. 7.99 *(978-0-7614-5533-2(7))* Marshall Cavendish Corp.

Freeman, Tor. Benji Bear's Busy Day. Freeman, Tor, illus. 2015. (ENG., Illus.). 18p. (J). (-k). bds. 17.99 *(978-1-5098-0111-4(1))* Pan Macmillan GBR. Dist: Independent Pubs. Group.

Fruchter, Jason, illus. What Time Is It, Daniel Tiger? 2016. (Daniel Tiger's Neighborhood Ser.). (ENG.). 14p. (J). (gr. -1-k). bds. 10.99 *(978-1-4814-6934-0(7),* Simon Spotlight) Simon Spotlight.

Garrity, Jennifer Johnson. Calendar Quest: A 5,000 Year Trek Through Western History with Father Time. 2004. (ENG., Illus.). 160p. (J). per. 14.00 *(978-0-9770704-0-4(9),* CQ-001, Tools For Young Historians) BrimWood Pr.

Giles, Lamar. The Last Last-Day-Of-Summer. Adeola, Dapo, illus. 2019. (Legendary Alston Boys Adventure Ser.). (ENG.). 304p. (J). (gr. 3-7). 17.99 *(978-1-328-46083-7(5),* 1712835, Versify) HarperCollins Pubs.

Gilmore, Rachna. Catching Time, 1 vol. Wakelin, Kristy Anne, illus. 2010. (ENG.). 32p. (J). (gr. -1-1). 17.95 *(978-1-55455-162-0(5),* 89389062-aa0b-42b9-85e1-859cf56892ba) Trifolium Bks., Inc. CAN. Dist: Firefly Bks., Ltd.

Hall, Michael. Monkey Time. Hall, Michael, illus. 2019. (ENG., Illus.). 48p. (J). (gr. -1-3). 17.99 *(978-0-06-238302-0(7),* Greenwillow Bks.) HarperCollins Pubs.

Harris, Trudy. The Clock Struck One: A Time-Telling Tale. Hartman, Carrie, illus. 2009. (Math Is Fun! Ser.). (ENG.). 32p. (J). (gr. k-2). 19.99 *(978-0-8225-9067-5(0),* 96912699-1d73-456d-b3c2-39ed189e8f7a, Millbrook Pr.) Lerner Publishing Group.

Havercroft, Elizabeth. A Year in the World of Dinosaurs. 2009. (Time Goes By Ser.). (ENG., Illus.). 24p. (J). (gr. k-3). pap. 7.99 *(978-1-58013-802-4(0),* 563d6a5d-da87-4ce5-8196-74314fb87c36, First Avenue Editions) Lerner Publishing Group.

Hennessy, B. G. Mr. Ouchy's First Day. Meisel, Paul, illus. 2007. (J). (gr. k-3). 27.95 incl. audio *(978-0-8045-6946-0(0));* 29.95 incl. audio compact disk *(978-0-8045-4160-2(4))* Spoken Arts, Inc.

Holland, Sara. Everless. 2018. (SPA.). 352p. (YA). (gr. 8). 15.95 *(978-84-96886-88-9(3))* Ediciones Urano S. A. ESP. Dist: Spanish Pubs., LLC.

—Everless. 2018. (ENG.). (YA). (gr. 8). 384p. pap. 11.99 *(978-0-06-265367-3(9));* 368p. 17.99 *(978-0-06-265365-9(2))* HarperCollins Pubs. (HarperTeen).

Howard, Cheryl L. Duster Dustbunny's Seven Days of the Week & Twelve Months in a Year. 2009. (Illus.). 48p. pap. 17.50 *(978-1-60860-787-7(9),* Eloquent Bks.) Strategic Book Publishing & Rights Agency (SBPRA).

Hueller, P. W. The Wish. 2015. (Tartan House Ser.). (ENG.). 96p. (J). (gr. 3-6). *(978-1-63235-059-6(9),* 11686, 12-Story Library) Bookstaves, LLC.

It's Time. 2016. (It's Time Ser.). 24p. (gr. 1-1). pap. 33.00 *(978-1-4994-2488-1(4),* PowerKids Pr.) Rosen Publishing Group, Inc., The.

It's Time: Set 1, 8 vols. 2016. (It's Time Ser.). (ENG.). 24p. (gr. 1-1). 101.08 *(978-1-4994-2431-7(0),* 612c4aec-d156-42dd-bd72-ec1622f23936, PowerKids Pr.) Rosen Publishing Group, Inc., The.

Jacoby, Sarah. Forever or a Day: (Children's Picture Book for Babies & Toddlers, Preschool Book) 2018. (ENG., Illus.). 40p. (J). (gr. -1-k). 17.99 *(978-1-4521-6463-2(0))* Chronicle Bks. LLC.

Jakubowski, Kristan E. Paint the Town. 2008. 24p. pap. 11.85 *(978-1-4343-6912-3(9))* AuthorHouse.

James, Lincoln. Sal Sleeps In, 1 vol. 2006. (Neighborhood Readers Ser.). (ENG.). 8p. (gr. k-1). pap. 5.15 *(978-1-4042-5780-1(2),* 3ccfab18-4749-4780-93d3-fc4b7a34c502, Rosen Classroom) Rosen Publishing Group, Inc., The.

Jocelyn, Marthe, ed. First Times: Stories Selected by Marthe Jocelyn. 2007. 200p. (J). (gr. 5-8). pap. 9.95 *(978-0-88776-777-7(X),* Tundra Bks.) Tundra Bks. CAN. Dist: Penguin Random Hse. LLC.

Jones, Christianne C. Morning Mystery, 1 vol. Simard, Rémy, illus. 2010. (My First Graphic Novel Ser.). (ENG.). 32p. (J). (gr. k-2). lib. bdg. 24.65 *(978-1-4342-1890-2(2),* 102349, Stone Arch Bks.) Capstone.

Kondrchek, Jamie. My Favorite Time of Day (Mi Hora Preferida del Dia) Vega, Eida de la, tr. from ENG. Rasemas, Joe, illus. 2009. (Day in the Life Ser.). (SPA & ENG.). 32p. (J). (gr. -1-1). lib. bdg. 25.70 *(978-1-58415-837-0(9))* Mitchell Lane Pubs.

Krivitzky, Nathan & Nathan, Krivitzky. Always Late Nate. O'Connell, Dave, illus. 2009. (ENG.). 32p. (J). pap. 10.95 *(978-1-933916-41-5(9))* Nelson Publishing & Marketing.

Kubler, Annie, illus. What's the Time, Mr Wolf? 2003. (Finger Puppet Bks.). 24p. (J). (gr. 1-1). *(978-0-85953-944-9(X))* Child's Play International Ltd.

Lowery, Mark A. Magic Time, Time Is Magical. 2012. 154p. pap. 19.95 *(978-1-62709-345-3(1))* America Star Bks.

Marshall, Wendy. The O'Clocks: Mr. O'Clock Goes to A Party. 2008. 40p. pap. 18.49 *(978-1-4389-2403-8(8))* AuthorHouse.

Mass, Wendy. 11 Birthdays. 2010. (Willow Falls Ser.: 1). lib. bdg. 17.20 *(978-0-606-13990-8(7))* Turtleback.

—11 Birthdays: a Wish Novel. 2010. (ENG.). 272p. (J). (gr. 4-7). pap. 8.99 *(978-0-545-05240-5(8),* Scholastic Paperbacks) Scholastic, Inc.

McKay, C. R. The Secret of the Five Bugs, 1 vol. Gennari, Joel, illus. 2018. (Power Coders Ser.). (ENG.). 32p. (gr. 5-5). 27.93 *(978-1-5383-4013-4(5),* 03034c73-6233-4b40-9a47-85e4e761e0da); pap. 11.60 *(978-1-5383-4014-1(3),* f34a0878-0c39-428d-bbce-90e134778f82) Rosen Publishing Group, Inc., The. (PowerKids Pr.).

McKee, Brett & McKee, David. George's Invisible Watch. McKee, David, illus. 2013. (Illus.). 32p. (J). (gr. -1-k). pap. 8.99 *(978-1-84270-864-4(3))* Andersen Pr. GBR. Dist: Independent Pubs. Group.

Millman, M. C. Time Will Tell. 2004. 272p. (YA). 19.95 *(978-1-932443-25-7(8),* TWTH) Judaica Pr., Inc., The.

Molesworth, Mary Louisa S. The Cuckoo Clock. 2008. 112p. 23.95 *(978-1-60664-856-8(X));* pap. 9.95 *(978-1-60664-103-3(4))* Aegypan.

MUSS, Anon E. Time Portal. 2010. (ENG.). 221p. pap. 11.84 *(978-0-557-46606-1(7))* Lulu Pr., Inc.

My Time on Nantucket. 2005. (J). cd-rom 11.95 *(978-0-9755078-2-7(6))* Sweet Punkin Pr.

Myers, Bill. Baseball for Breakfast: The Story of a Boy Who Hated to Wait. Riccio, Frank, illus. 2005. 29p. (J). (gr. 4-8). reprint ed. 15.00 *(978-0-7567-9248-0(7))* DIANE Publishing Co.

O'Mara, Blanche. A Year with Carmen, 1 vol. 2006. (Neighborhood Readers Ser.). (ENG.). 12p. (gr. 1-2). pap. 5.90 *(978-1-4042-6835-7(9),* 11fe4f7a-ad96-4325-a4e8-112ecc614d48, Rosen Classroom) Rosen Publishing Group, Inc., The.

Omololu, Cynthia Jaynes. When It's Six o'clock in San Francisco: A Trip Through Time Zones. DuBurke, Randy, illus. 2009. (ENG.). 32p. (J). (gr. -1-3). 16.99 *(978-0-618-76827-1(0),* 100541, Clarion Bks.) HarperCollins Pubs.

Pace, Anne Marie. Sunny's Tow Truck Saves the Day! Lee, Christopher, illus. 2019. (ENG.). 24p. (J). (gr. -1-1). 14.99 *(978-1-4197-3191-4(2),* 1247701) Abrams, Inc.

Pilegard, Virginia Walton. The Warlord's Alarm, 1 vol. Debon, Nicolas, illus. 2006. (Warlord's Ser.). (ENG.). 32p. (J). (gr. k-3). 16.99 *(978-1-58980-378-7(7),* Pelican Publishing) Arcadia Publishing.

Poulin, Andrée. The Best Time, 1 vol. Beha, Philippe, illus. 2009. (My First Stories Ser.). (ENG.). 24p. (J). (gr. -1-3). 27.27 *(978-1-60754-350-3(8),* 7a523864-0e0f-4b71-aaba-079cabc8dfb3, Windmill Bks.) Rosen Publishing Group, Inc., The.

Poulin, Andrée & Poulin, Andrée. The Worst Time, 1 vol. Beha, Philippe, illus. 2009. (My First Stories Ser.). (ENG.). 24p. (J). (gr. -1-3). 27.27 *(978-1-60754-367-1(2),* 3fc1c4e2-ea78-4657-b9c9-b05430417d3c); pap. 9.15 *(978-1-60754-368-8(0),* 6e466059-eec3-47c6-a6c2-d8cec3ec6749) Rosen Publishing Group, Inc., The. (Windmill Bks.).

Publications International Ltd. Staff, ed. Exploring Time with Dora Clock. 2004. 10p. (J). bds. 16.98 *(978-1-4127-3050-1(3),* 7228800) Publications International, Ltd.

—Spongebob Clock It's Time Sound Book. 2004. 10p. (J). bds. 16.98 *(978-1-4127-3030-3(9),* 7226500) Publications International, Ltd.

Regier, Demar. What Time Is It? Woodruff, Liza, illus. 2005. (My First Reader Ser.). (ENG.). 32p. (J). (gr. k-1). 18.50 *(978-0-516-25180-6(5),* Children's Pr.) Scholastic Library Publishing.

Ruffenach, Jessie, ed. Baby Learns about Time. Thomas, Peter, tr. from ENG. Blacksheep, Beverly, illus. 2005. (NAV & ENG.). 16p. (J). (gr. 4-7). 7.95 *(978-1-893354-64-7(4))* Salina Bookshelf Inc.

Rupp, Rebecca. Journey to the Blue Moon: In Which Time Is Lost & Then Found Again. 2006. (ENG., Illus.). 272p. (J). (gr. 5-7). 15.99 *(978-0-7636-2544-3(2))* Candlewick Pr.

Salerni, Dianne K. The Eighth Day. McClellan, David, illus. 2015. (Eighth Day Ser.: 1). (ENG.). 336p. (J). (gr. 3-7). pap. 6.99 *(978-0-06-227216-4(0),* HarperCollins) HarperCollins Pubs.

—The Eighth Day. 2014. (Eighth Day Ser.: 1). (ENG., Illus.). 320p. (J). (gr. 3-7). 16.99 *(978-0-06-227215-7(2),* HarperCollins) HarperCollins Pubs.

—The Inquisitor's Mark. 2015. (Eighth Day Ser.: 2). (ENG.). 368p. (J). (gr. 3-7). pap. 6.99 *(978-0-06-227219-5(5),* HarperCollins) HarperCollins Pubs.

Schuepbach, Lynnette. Cat Time. 2006. 28p. pap. 12.95 *(978-0-9759613-2-2(2))* Creative Sources.

Shaw, Natalie. It's Time to Save the Day! 2017. (PJ Masks Ser.). (ENG., Illus.). 14p. (J). (gr. -1-k). bds. 10.99 *(978-1-5344-0423-6(6),* Simon Spotlight) Simon Spotlight.

Simon, Jenne. Tell the Time! Hino, Sachiho, illus. 2015. (J). *(978-0-545-74720-2(1))* Scholastic, Inc.

Smith, C. Michelle. Skeeter Sneeter Doodlebop. Foreman, A., illus. 2009. 24p. pap. 15.63 *(978-1-934840-54-2(8))* Nimble Bks. LLC.

Stilton, Geronimo. The Hour of Magic (Geronimo Stilton & the Kingdom of Fantasy #8) 2016. (Geronimo Stilton & the Kingdom of Fantasy Ser.: 8). (ENG., Illus.). 320p. (J). (gr. 2-5). 16.99 *(978-0-545-82336-4(6))* Scholastic, Inc.

Teague, David. How Oscar Indigo Broke the Universe (and Put It Back Together Again) 2017. (ENG.). 256p. (J). (gr. 3-7). 16.99 *(978-0-06-237749-4(3),* HarperCollins) HarperCollins Pubs.

Time Goes By, 8 vols., Set. Incl. Day at a Zoo. Harrison, Sarah. (J). lib. bdg. 22.60 *(978-1-58013-554-2(4),* 1c1a6444-1558-46fb-a710-1875244d8dbe, Millbrook Pr.); Day in a City. Harris, Nicholas. (J). lib. bdg. 22.60 *(978-1-58013-552-8(8));* Year at a Construction Site. Harris, Nicholas. (J). lib. bdg. 22.60 *(978-1-58013-549-8(8));* Year at a Farm. Harris, Nicholas. lib. bdg. 22.60 *(978-1-58013-553-5(6));* Year in a Castle. Coombs, Rachel. (J). lib. bdg. 22.60 *(978-1-58013-550-4(1));* Year on a Pirate Ship. Havercroft, Elizabeth. lib. bdg. 22.60 *(978-1-58013-547-4(1));* (Illus.). 24p. (gr. k-3). 2008. (Time Goes By Ser.). (ENG.). 2008. Set lib. bdg. 113.00 *(978-1-58013-546-7(3))* Lerner Publishing Group.

Time Slime. 2003. 156p. (YA). (gr. 5-12). pap. 7.95 *(978-0-9702176-3-9(3),* 0004) Night Howl Productions.

Tulien, Sean. Clock King's Time Bomb, 1 vol. Schoening, Dan & Doescher, Erik, illus. 2011. (Flash Ser.). (ENG.). 56p. (J). (gr. 3-6). lib. bdg. 26.65 *(978-1-4342-2626-6(3),* 113671, Stone Arch Bks.) Capstone.

Turley, Sandy. The Clock & the Mouse: A Teaching Rhyme about Time. Peterson, Sara & Lindstrom, Brita, illus. 2006. 32p. (J). lib. bdg. 26.95 *(978-0-9778548-0-6(9))* Helps4Teachers.

Vernick, Audrey & Scanlon, Liz Garton. Five Minutes: (That's a Lot of Time) (No, It's Not) (Yes, It Is) Tallec, Olivier, illus. 2019. 32p. (J). (gr. -1-2). 16.99 *(978-0-525-51631-6(X),* G.P. Putnam's Sons Books for Young Readers) Penguin Young Readers Group.

Vink, Amanda. A Peculiar Sequence of Events, 1 vol. Gennari, Joel, illus. 2018. (Power Coders Ser.). (ENG.). 32p. (J). (gr. 5-5). 27.93 *(978-1-5383-4029-5(1),* 848571c6-1450-4e66-a534-fe4f102f2a94, PowerKids Pr.) Rosen Publishing Group, Inc., The.

Vitale, Samantha. Wasted Time. 2007. 56p. per. 16.95 *(978-1-4241-7436-2(8))* America Star Bks.

West, Hannah. Realm of Ruins: A Nissera Novel. 2018. (Nissera Chronicles Ser.: 2). (Illus.). 464p. (YA). (gr. 7). 18.99 *(978-0-8234-3986-7(0))* Holiday Hse., Inc.

What Time Is It Jeanne-Marie. 2005. (Illus.). 34p. (J). mass mkt. 9.99 *(978-0-9740599-7-6(8))* Omnibus Publishing.

Whybrow, Ian, et al. Owain A'r Cloc. 2005. (WEL., Illus.). 20.0p. 6.99 *(978-1-84323-366-4(5))* Gomer Pr. GBR. Dist: Gomer Pr.

Williams, David K. Tick Tock. Ovresat, Laura, illus. 2006. (Green Light Readers Level 1 Ser.). (ENG.). 24p. (J). (gr. -1-3). pap. 5.99 *(978-0-15-205605-6(X),* 1196859, Clarion Bks.) HarperCollins Pubs.

Winfrey, Michelle/w. It's My Birthday... Finally! A Leap Year Story. 2007. (Illus.). 96p. (J). per. 11.95 *(978-0-9727179-5-3(1))* Hobby Hse. Publishing Group.

Woodruff, Liza, illus. What Time Is It? 2005. (My First Reader Ser.). (ENG.). 32p. (J). (gr. k-4). per. 3.95 *(978-0-516-25279-7(8),* Children's Pr.) Scholastic Library Publishing.

TIME—POETRY

Low, Elizabeth Cothen. Big Book of Seasons, Holidays, & Weather: Rhymes, Fingerplays, & Songs for Children. 2011. (ENG., Illus.). 168p. E-Book 45.00 *(978-1-59884-624-9(8),* A3162E, Libraries Unlimited) ABC-CLIO, LLC.

Smith, Roland & Smith, Marie. T Is for Time. Graef, Renée, illus. 2015. (ENG.). 40p. (J). (gr. 2-5). 16.99 *(978-1-58536-512-8(2),* 203809) Sleeping Bear Pr.

Wright, Blanche Fisher, illus. Real Mother Goose Clock Book. 22p. (J). (gr. -1-2). 6.95 *(978-1-56288-095-8(0))* Checkerboard Pr., Inc.

TIME TRAVEL

Borgert-Spaniol, Megan. Time Travel: Is Visiting the Past & Future Possible? 2018. (Science Fact or Science Fiction? Ser.). (ENG., Illus.). 32p. (J). (gr. 3-6). lib. bdg. 32.79 *(978-1-5321-1541-7(5),* 28936, Checkerboard Library) ABDO Publishing Co.

Brezina, Corona. Time Travel, 1 vol. 2018. (Sci-Fi or STEM? Ser.). (ENG.). 64p. (gr. 7-7). 36.13 *(978-1-5081-8046-3(6),* 7d15399e-6b4e-4497-aa8e-89dbebbdcae3) Rosen Publishing Group, Inc., The.

Fast Forward, 12 vols., Set. Incl. Castles Through Time. Harris, Nicolas. lib. bdg. 28.93 *(978-1-4358-2798-1(8),* e8c355df-22d6-451f-b3e0-f1076229359e); Dinosaurs Through Time. Harris, Nicolas. Dennis, Peter, illus. lib. bdg. 28.93 *(978-1-4358-2802-5(X),* 14724128-75e6-4a65-bfa0-1db117d374cc); Earthquakes Through Time. Harris, Nicolas. lib. bdg. 28.93 *(978-1-4358-2803-2(8),* bd3db881-2ede-415f-b3a7-fe7a6909d4d8); Pyramids Through Time. Harris, Nicolas. lib. bdg. 28.93 *(978-1-4358-2801-8(1),* 954c210c-e9f6-406c-97ab-1f5a5c11f3ca); Volcanoes Through Time. Harris, Nicolas. lib. bdg. 28.93 *(978-1-4358-2800-1(3),* 379f6c00-8d18-4dbf-9342-8597147e2ae1); Wild West Through Time. Aston, Claire. lib. bdg. 28.93 *(978-1-4358-2799-8(6),* 63cfa34f-bfc7-44f5-9f23-d75072ffbf04); 32p. (YA). (gr. 4-4). 2009. (Fast Forward Ser.). (ENG.). 2008. Set lib. bdg. 173.58 *(978-1-4358-2819-3(4),* ee990d27-8e88-43c6-91f0-c7c7349bdf2b, PowerKids Pr.) Rosen Publishing Group, Inc., The.

Jackson, Tom. Is Time Travel Possible? Theories about Time, 1 vol. 2018. (Beyond the Theory: Science of the Future Ser.). (ENG.). 48p. (gr. 5-6). lib. bdg. 33.60 *(978-1-5382-2661-2(8),* 3f937698-edc1-493a-b4cd-edd3f25da02c) Stevens, Gareth Publishing LLLP.

Kallen, Stuart A. Time Travel, 1 vol. 2009. (Mysterious Encounters Ser.). (ENG.). 48p. (gr. 4-8). 30.63 *(978-0-7377-4573-3(8),* a9c34d8b-80a1-4df2-bbef-5701246a86ac, KidHaven Publishing) Greenhaven Publishing LLC.

Robinson, Peg. The Science of Time Travel, 1 vol. 2018. (Science of Superpowers Ser.). (ENG.). 48p. (gr. 4-4). pap. 13.93 *(978-1-5026-3802-1(9),* 8bdff7fc-b48e-441d-88a3-cd70d80445d7) Cavendish Square Publishing LLC.

TIME TRAVEL—FICTION

Abbott, Tony. The Hawk Bandits of Tarkoom (the Secrets of Droon #11) Jessell, Tim, illus. 2018. (True Book (Relaunch) Ser.: 11). (ENG.). 128p. (J). (gr. 3-5). E-Book 31.00 *(978-0-545-41824-9(0),* Scholastic Paperbacks) Scholastic, Inc.

—The Moon Scroll. Jessell, Tim, illus. 2004. (Secrets of Droon Ser.: No. 15). 129p. (gr. 2-5). 15.00 *(978-0-7569-3946-5(1))* Perfection Learning Corp.

—Voyagers of the Silver Sand (the Secrets of Droon: Special Edition #3) Merrell, David, illus. 2022. (Five Nights at Freddy's Ser.: 3). (ENG.). 192p. (YA). (gr. 7-5). E-Book 12.99 *(978-0-545-41860-7(7),* Scholastic Paperbacks) Scholastic, Inc.

Alexander, Lloyd. Time Cat: The Remarkable Journeys of Jason & Gareth. 2012. (ENG., Illus.). 240p. (J). (gr. 3-7). pap. 9.99 *(978-0-312-63213-7(4),* 900077471) Square Fish.

Alfred Oscar Valentine: Tales from Spoon Creek. 2005. (J). *(978-0-9766894-4-7(8))* Stanley, Donna Lacy.

Alt, Jeff. The Adventures of Bubba Jones: Time Traveling Through the Great Smoky Mountains. Tuohy, Hannah, illus. 2015. (National Park Ser.: 1). (ENG.). 179p. (J). (gr. 3-7). pap. 9.99 *(978-0-8253-0786-7(4))* Beaufort Bks., Inc.

Amara, Phil & Chin, Oliver. The Discovery of Anime & Manga: The Asian Hall of Fame. Calle, Juan, illus. 2019. (Asian Hall of Fame Ser.). (ENG.). 36p. (J). 16.95 *(978-1-59702-146-3(6))* Immedium.

—The Discovery of Fireworks & Gunpowder: The Asian Hall of Fame. Calle, Juan, illus. 2018. (Asian Hall of Fame Ser.). (ENG.). 40p. (J). (gr. -1-3). 16.95 *(978-1-59702-142-5(3))* Immedium.

—The Discovery of Ramen: The Asian Hall of Fame. 2017. (Asian Hall of Fame Ser.). (ENG., Illus.). 40p. (J). (gr. -1-3). 16.95 *(978-1-59702-134-0(2))* Immedium.

Andrews, Jane. Ten Boys Who Lived on the Road from Long Ago to Now (Yesterday's Classics) 2006. (J). 9.95 *(978-1-59915-064-2(6))* Yesterday's Classics.

Angleberger, Tom & Hemphill, Michael. Stonewall Hinkleman & the Battle of Bull Run. 2014. 192p. (J). (gr. 3-7). pap. 7.99 *(978-0-14-751182-9(8),* Puffin Books) Penguin Young Readers Group.

Anzalone, Karen. Time in a Bottle. 2003. 100p. (YA). pap. 9.00 *(978-0-7599-3840-3(7))* Hard Shell Word Factory.

Asselin, Kristine & Malone, Jen. The Art of the Swap. (ENG., Illus.). 352p. (J). (gr. 3-7). 2019. pap. 8.99 *(978-1-4814-7872-4(9))* 2018. 17.99 *(978-1-4814-7871-7(0))* Simon & Schuster Children's Publishing. (Aladdin).

Aureliani, Franco. Dino-Mike & the Living Fossils. Aureliani, Franco, illus. 2016. (Dino-Mike! Ser.). (ENG., Illus.). 128p. (J). (gr. 2-3). lib. bdg. 25.32 *(978-1-4965-2489-8(6),* 130421, Stone Arch Bks.) Capstone.

Aureliani, Franco, illus. Dino-Mike & the Museum Mayhem. 2015. (J). lib. bdg. *(978-1-4062-9391-3(1),* Stone Arch Bks.) Capstone.

Avi. Something Upstairs. 2010. (ENG.). 144p. (J). (gr. 4-7). 9.99 *(978-0-545-21491-9(2),* Scholastic Pr.) Scholastic, Inc.

—Something Upstairs. 2010. lib. bdg. 16.00 *(978-0-606-14682-1(2))* Turtleback.

Ayasta, Ayasta. Star. 2007. 117p. 34.95 *(978-1-4303-1520-9(2))* Lulu Pr., Inc.

Ayers, Linda. The Time Bridge Travelers, 3 bks., Bk. 1. Ayers, Ryan, illus. 56p. (J). 2006. 13.95 *(978-0-9760505-8-2(7))* 2004. per. 7.95 *(978-0-9760505-0-6(1))* Blue Thistle Pr.

—The Time Bridge Travelers & the Mysterious Map, 3 bks., Bk. 2. Ayers, Ryan, illus. l.t. ed. (Time Bridge Travelers Ser.: 2). 80p. (J). 2006. 13.95 *(978-0-9760505-6-8(0))* 2005. per. 7.95 *(978-0-9760505-3-7(6))* Blue Thistle Pr.

—The Time Bridge Travelers & the Time Travel Station, 3 bks., Bk. 3. Ayers, Ryan, illus. l.t. ed. 2007. (Time Bridge Travelers Ser.: 3). 140p. (J). lib. bdg. 16.95 *(978-0-9786302-8-7(9));* per. 7.95 *(978-0-9786302-7-0(0))* Blue Thistle Pr.

Bagdanov, Patricia. The Adventures of Charlie & a Dragon Named Trevor. 2013. 26p. pap. 16.95 *(978-1-63004-985-0(9))* PublishAmerica, Inc.

Bailer, Darice. The Last Rail. 2011. (ENG.). 32p. (J). 9.95 *(978-1-60727-173-4(7))* Soundprints.

—The Pony Express. Antonishak, Tom, illus. 3rd ed. 2003. (Soundprints' Read-and-Discover Ser.). (ENG.). 48p. (J). (gr. -1-3). pap. 3.95 *(978-1-59249-019-6(0),* S2008) Soundprints.

Bailey, Linda. Hot on the Trail in Ancient Egypt. Slavin, Bill, illus. 2018. (Time Travel Guides). (ENG.). 56p. (J). (gr. 3-7). pap. 11.99 *(978-1-77138-985-3(0))* Kids Can Pr., Ltd. CAN. Dist: Hachette Bk. Group.

Baldwin, Quinn. Crossover. 2010. (ENG.). 166p. pap. *(978-0-557-74844-0(5))* Lulu Pr., Inc.

Baltazar, Armand. Timeless: Diego & the Rangers of the Vastlantic. Baltazar, Armand, illus. 2019. (Timeless Ser.: 1). (ENG., Illus.). 624p. (J). (gr. 3-7). pap. 12.99 *(978-0-06-240237-0(4),* Tegen, Katherine Bks) HarperCollins Pubs.

Banks, Steven. Lost in Time. The Artifact Group, illus. 2006. 22p. (J). lib. bdg. 15.00 *(978-1-4242-0977-4(3))* Fitzgerald Bks.

Baraitser, Marion & Evans, Anna. Home Number One. 2006. (ENG., Illus.). 63p. (YA). pap. *(978-0-9529426-7-2(4))* Loki Books Ltd.

Barnett, Mac. Oh No! Not Again! (or How I Built a Time Machine to Save History) (or at Least My History Grade) Santat, Dan, illus. 2012. (Oh No! Picture Book Ser.). (ENG.). 40p. (J). (gr. -1-3). 17.99 *(978-1-4231-4912-5(2))* Little, Brown Bks. for Young Readers.

Barron, T. A. The Ancient One. 2016. (Adventures of Kate Ser.: 2). (ENG.). 320p. (J). (gr. 5). 8.99 *(978-1-101-99702-4(8),* Puffin Books) Penguin Young Readers Group.

—The Ancient One. 2003. (Illus.). 304p. 14.65 *(978-0-7569-6642-3(6))* Perfection Learning Corp.

Barrowman, John & Barrowman, Carole. Conjuror. 2016. (Orion Chronicles Ser.). (ENG.). 320p. (YA). (gr. 7). 16.99 *(978-1-78185-637-6(0))* Head of Zeus GBR. Dist: Independent Pubs. Group.

Barrows, Annie. Magic in the Mix. 2015. (ENG.). 288p. (YA). (gr. 3-6). pap. 8.99 *(978-1-61963-798-6(7),* 900148899, Bloomsbury USA Childrens) Bloomsbury Publishing USA.

Basic, Zdenko, illus. Steampunk: H. G. Wells. 2013. (ENG.). 408p. (YA). (gr. 7-17). 18.95 *(978-0-7624-4444-1(4),* Running Pr. Kids) Running Pr.
Baskin, Nora Raleigh. Subway Love. 2014. (ENG.). 224p. (YA). (gr. 9). 16.99 *(978-0-7636-6845-7(1))* Candlewick Pr.
Bateman, Jordan. Dunamis Heroes: Issue #1: the Lost Kingdom. Save, Ken, illus. 2007. 120p. (J). per. *(978-0-9781953-0-4(2))* Dunamis Media.
Bauer, Christina. The Pirate Queen: A Timewalker Journey. 2005. 280p. (YA). 14.99 *(978-1-59092-224-8(7))* Blue Forge Pr.
Bauer, Marion Dane. The Blue Ghost. 2006. (Stepping Stone Book(TM) Ser.). (Illus.). 96p. (J). (gr. 1-4). 6.99 *(978-0-375-83339-7(0),* Random Hse. Bks. for Young Readers) Random Hse. Children's Bks.
Bellairs, John. The Ghost in the Mirror - the House with a Clock in Its Walls 4. 2019. (House with a Clock in Its Walls Ser.: 4). (ENG., Illus.). 256p. (J). (gr. 4-7). pap. 11.99 *(978-1-84812-816-3(9))* Bonnier Publishing GBR. Dist: Independent Pubs. Group.
—The House with a Clock in Its Walls. Gorey, Edward, illus. 2004. (Lewis Barnavelt Ser.: Bk. 1). (ENG.). 192p. (J). (gr. 3-7). pap. 7.99 *(978-0-14-240257-3(5),* Puffin Books) Penguin Young Readers Group.
—The House with a Clock in Its Walls. Gorey, Edward, illus. 2004. (John Bellairs Mysteries Ser.). 179p. (J). (gr. 3-7). 13.65 *(978-0-7569-5257-0(3))* Perfection Learning Corp.
—The House with a Clock in Its Walls. (Lewis Barnavelt Ser.: Bk. 1). 179p. (J). (gr. 4-6). pap. 4.50 *(978-0-8072-1423-7(X),* Listening Library) Random Hse. Audio Publishing Group.
—The House with a Clock in Its Walls. 2004. 17.20 *(978-1-4176-3513-9(4))* Turtleback.
Benderly, Beryl Lieff. Jason's Miracle: A Hanukkah Story. 2004. 114p. (J). (gr. 4-8). reprint ed. *(978-0-7567-7792-0(5))* DIANE Publishing Co.
Benton, Jim. The Fran That Time Forgot. Benton, Jim, illus. 4th ed. 2005. (Franny K. Stein, Mad Scientist Ser.: 4). (ENG., Illus.). 112p. (J). (gr. 2-5). mass mkt. 6.99 *(978-0-689-86298-4(9));* 17.99 *(978-0-689-86294-6(6))* Simon & Schuster Bks. For Young Readers. (Simon & Schuster Bks. For Young Readers).
—The Fran with Four Brains. Benton, Jim, illus. 2011. (Franny K. Stein, Mad Scientist Ser.). (ENG., Illus.). 112p. (J). (gr. 2-6). 31.36 *(978-1-59961-822-7(2),* 7832, Chapter Bks.) Spotlight.
Berard, Robin M. King Tut & the Girl Who Loved Him: The Strange Adventures of Johanna Wilson. 2007. 212p. per. 12.95 *(978-1-58348-477-7(9),* iUniverse Star) iUniverse, Inc.
Berenstain, Mike. Long, Long Ago. 2018. (Berenstain Bears Ser.). (Illus.). (J). lib. bdg. 13.55 *(978-0-606-41044-1(9))* Turtleback.
Bernard, Romily. Never Apart. 2017. (ENG.). 400p. (J). 17.99 *(978-1-63375-822-3(2),* 9781633758223) Entangled Publishing, LLC.
Berneger, Marcia. A Dreidel in Time: A New Spin on an Old Tale. Castro, Beatriz, illus. 2019. (ENG.). 88p. (J). (gr. 3-7). 17.99 *(978-1-5415-4672-1(5),* 192e3233-0d85-465d-9d2d-d3070039f409, Kar-Ben Publishing) Lerner Publishing Group.
Bessey, Siân Ann. Escape from Germany. 2004. 183p. (J). *(978-1-59156-436-2(0))* Covenant Communications.
—Uprising in Samoa: A Novel. 2004. 178p. (J). *(978-1-59156-890-2(0))* Covenant Communications.
Bethany: Adventures of the Mighty Mustard Seed. 2004. Orig. Title: Bethany in Beulah Land. (J). mass mkt. 12.95 *(978-0-9745440-0-7(0))* McKatlib Pr.
Beveridge, Cathy. Stormstruck. 2006. (ENG., Illus.). 214p. (J). pap. *(978-1-55380-041-5(9))* Ronsdale Pr.
Biggs, Stephen. The Time Barrel. 2009. 152p. pap. *(978-1-84923-434-4(5))* YouWriteOn.
Bilgrey, Marc. And Don't Forget to Rescue the Other Princess. 2009. 252p. 25.95 *(978-1-59414-744-9(2),* Five Star) Cengage Gale.
Blair, Margaret Whitman. The Sand Castle: Blockade Running & the Battle of Fort Fisher. 2005. (White Mane Kids Ser.: 17). (Illus.). 187p. (J). (gr. 4-7). per. 8.95 *(978-1-57249-346-9(1),* White Mane Kids) White Mane Publishing Co., Inc.
Bloor, Edward. London Calling. 2008. (Illus.). 304p. (YA). (gr. 7-9). per. 8.99 *(978-0-375-84363-1(9),* Ember) Random Hse. Children's Bks.
Bobulski, Chelsea. The Wood. 2017. (ENG.). 320p. (YA). 27.99 *(978-1-250-09426-1(7),* 900160379) Feiwel & Friends.
Boeve, Eunice. Echoes of Kansas Past. Peterson-Shea, Julie, illus. 2012. 176p. pap. 10.99 *(978-0-9851196-9-0(1))* Rowe Publishing.
Bold, Emily. Breath of Yesterday, 0 vols. Bell, Katja, tr. 2014. (Curse Ser.: 2). (ENG.). 376p. (YA). (gr. 9-12). pap. 9.99 *(978-1-4778-4714-5(6),* 9781477847145, Skyscape) Amazon Publishing.
Bond, Nancy. A String in the Harp. 2006. (ENG.). 384p. (J). (gr. 5-9). pap. 8.99 *(978-1-4169-2771-6(9),* Aladdin) Simon & Schuster Children's Publishing.
Boniface, William. The Extraordinary Adventures of Ordinary Boy: Book 2: the Return of Mete or Boy. 2008. (Extraordinary Adventures of Ordinary Boy Ser.: 2). (ENG., Illus.). 368p. (J). (gr. 3-7). pap. 9.99 *(978-0-06-077469-1(X),* HarperCollins) HarperCollins Pubs.
Bosch, Pseudonymous. This Isn't What It Looks Like. 2011. (Secret Ser.: 4). (ENG.). 448p. (J). (gr. 3-7). pap. 9.99 *(978-0-316-07624-1(4))* Little, Brown Bks. for Young Readers.
Boston, L. M. The Stones of Green Knowe. Boston, Peter, illus. 2006. (Green Knowe Ser.: 6). (ENG.). 144p. (J). (gr. 3-7). 17.00 *(978-0-15-205560-8(6),* 1196721); pap. 10.95 *(978-0-15-205566-0(5),* 1196740) HarperCollins Pubs. (Clarion Bks.).
Bow, James. The Young City: The Unwritten Books. 2008. (Unwritten Bks.: 3). (ENG.). 264p. (YA). (gr. 7). pap. 12.99 *(978-1-55002-846-1(4))* Dundurn Pr. CAN. Dist: Publishers Group West (PGW).
Bower, Eric. The Tremendous Baron Time Machine. (Bizarre Baron Inventions Ser.: 4). (ENG.). (J). (gr. 4-7). 2020. 240p. pap. 8.99 *(978-1-948705-68-4(0))* 2019. 229p. 15.99 *(978-1-944995-78-2(1))* Amberjack Publishing Co.
Boyce, Frank Cottrell. Chitty Chitty Bang Bang & the Race Against Time. Berger, Joe, illus. (Chitty Chitty Bang Bang Ser.: 3). (ENG.). 240p. (J). (gr. 4-7). 2014. pap. 6.99 *(978-0-7636-6931-7(8))* 2013. 15.99 *(978-0-7636-5982-0(7))* Candlewick Pr.
—Chitty Chitty Bang Bang Flies Again. Berger, Joe, illus. 2013. (Chitty Chitty Bang Bang Ser.: 2). (ENG.). 224p. (J). (gr. 4-7). pap. 6.99 *(978-0-7636-6353-7(0))* Candlewick Pr.
Bracken, Alexandra. Passenger-Passenger, Series Book 2. 2016. (Passenger Ser.: 2). (ENG.). 512p. (YA). (gr. 9-12). pap. 9.99 *(978-1-4847-3279-3(0),* Disney-Hyperion) Disney Publishing Worldwide.
Bradbury, Ray. The Halloween Tree. (J). 20.95 *(978-0-8488-0432-9(5))* Amereon Ltd.
—The Halloween Tree. Eller, Jon, ed. Bradbury, Ray & Mugnaini, Joe, illus. 2005. 494p. (J). (gr. 4-12). per. 75.00 *(978-1-887368-80-3(9))* Gauntlet, Inc.
Brashares, Ann. The Here & Now. 2014. 242p. (YA). *(978-0-385-39008-8(4),* Delacorte Pr) Random House Publishing Group.
—The Here & Now. 2015. (ENG.). 256p. (YA). (gr. 7). pap. 10.99 *(978-0-385-73683-1(5),* Ember) Random Hse. Children's Bks.
Brezenoff, Steve. Time Voyage, 1 vol. Murphy, Scott, illus. 2012. (Return to Titanic Ser.). (ENG.). 112p. (J). (gr. 3-6). pap. 6.95 *(978-1-4342-3909-9(8),* 118094, Stone Arch Bks.) Capstone.
Briggs, Elizabeth. Future Lost. 2018. (Future Shock Ser.: 3). (ENG.). 256p. (YA). (gr. 8-12). 16.99 *(978-0-8075-2687-3(8),* 807526878); pap. 9.99 *(978-0-8075-2689-7(4),* 807526894) Whitman, Albert & Co.
—Future Shock. 2016. (YA). (Future Shock Ser.: 1). (ENG.). 288p. (gr. 8-12). pap. 9.99 *(978-0-8075-2680-4(0),* 807526800); *(978-0-8075-2683-5(5));* (Future Shock Ser.: 1). (ENG.). 272p. (gr. 8-12). 16.99 *(978-0-8075-2682-8(7),* 807526827) Whitman, Albert & Co.
—Future Threat. 2017. (Future Shock Ser.: 2). (ENG.). 272p. (YA). (gr. 8-12). 16.99 *(978-0-8075-2684-2(3),* 807526843); pap. 9.99 *(978-0-8075-2686-6(X),* 080752686X) Whitman, Albert & Co.
Brodien-Jones, Chris. The Glass Puzzle. 2013. (Illus.). 319p. (J). *(978-0-385-74298-6(3),* Delacorte Pr) Random House Publishing Group.
Buckley-Archer, Linda. The Time Quake. 2010. (Gideon Trilogy Ser.: 3). (ENG.). 464p. (J). (gr. 5-9). pap. 10.99 *(978-1-4169-1530-0(3),* Simon & Schuster Bks. For Young Readers) Simon & Schuster Bks. For Young Readers.
—The Time Quake, 3. 2009. (Gideon Trilogy Ser.: 3). (ENG.). 464p. (J). (gr. 5-9). 17.99 *(978-1-4169-1529-4(X))* Simon & Schuster, Inc.
—The Time Travelers. (Gideon Trilogy Ser.: 1). (ENG.). 416p. (J). (gr. 5-9). 2012. 17.99 *(978-1-4424-6551-0(4))* 2007. pap. 9.99 *(978-1-4169-1526-3(5))* Simon & Schuster Bks. For Young Readers. (Simon & Schuster Bks. For Young Readers).
Buckley, Michael. Nerds 5: Attack of the Bullies. 2013. (Nerds Ser.). (ENG.). 336p. (YA). (gr. 3-7). pap. 7.95 *(978-1-4197-1046-9(X))* Abrams, Inc.
Buehrlen, M. G. The Fifty-Seven Lives of Alex Wayfare. 2015. (ENG., Illus.). 324p. (YA). pap. 15.99 *(978-1-62681-872-9(X),* Diversion Bks.) Diversion Publishing Corp.
—The Untimely Deaths of Alex Wayfare. 2016. (ENG.). 232p. (YA). pap. 15.99 *(978-1-68230-058-9(7),* Diversion Bks.) Diversion Publishing Corp.
Burbidge, Clark Rich. Honor & Mercy, Bk. 3. 2018. (StarPassage Ser.: 3). (ENG.). 320p. (YA). 15.99 *(978-1-63269-478-2(6),* 1225f4f1-4d3c-4110-b1b2-39c2eb1cf1df) Deep River Bks.
Burgess, Barbara. The Magic Manuscript: The Nine Companions. 2013. 234p. pap. 12.99 *(978-0-9918574-3-2(7))* Sulby Hall Publishing.
—The Magic Manuscript: Voyage to Eve Ilion. 2013. 202p. pap. 9.99 *(978-0-9918574-4-9(5))* Sulby Hall Publishing.
Burnell, Pamela H. The Light Keeper: An Epps Kids Mystery. 2008. 76p. pap. 19.95 *(978-1-60474-847-5(8))* America Star Bks.
Butler, Dori. The Time Capsule. 2005. (J). pap. *(978-1-4108-4198-8(7))* Benchmark Education Co.
Byng, Georgia. Molly Moon, Micky Minus, & the Mind Machine. (Molly Moon Ser.). (ENG.). (J). (gr. 3-7). 2007. 384p. 16.99 *(978-0-06-075036-7(7))* 4. 2008. 416p. pap. 7.99 *(978-0-06-075038-1(3),* HarperCollins) HarperCollins Pubs.
—Molly Moon Viaja a Traes del Tiempo. Crispin, Maria Dolores, tr. 2005. (SPA.). 350p. *(978-84-675-0570-2(2))* SM Ediciones.
—Molly Moon's Hypnotic Time Travel Adventure. (ENG.). 400p. (J). 2006. (Molly Moon Ser.: 3). (gr. 3-7). pap. 8.99 *(978-0-06-075034-3(0),* HarperCollins) 2005. (Illus.). 16.99 *(978-0-06-075032-9(4))* HarperCollins Pubs.
—Molly Moon's Hypnotic Time Travel Adventure. 2007. (Molly Moon Ser.). (Illus.). 392p. (gr. 3-7). 18.00 *(978-0-7569-7761-0(4))* Perfection Learning Corp.
—Molly Moon's Hypnotic Time-Travel Adventure. 2005. (Illus.). 400p. (J). lib. bdg. 18.89 *(978-0-06-075033-6(2))* HarperCollins Pubs.
Cabot, Meg. The Mediator: Shadowland & Ninth Key. 2010. (Mediator Ser.). (ENG.). 544p. (YA). (gr. 8). pap. 9.99 *(978-0-06-204020-6(0),* HarperTeen) HarperCollins Pubs.
—Twilight. 2005. (Mediator Ser.: No. 6). (ENG.). 256p. (J). 15.99 *(978-0-06-072467-2(6))* HarperCollins Pubs.
Cameron, Ian. Stirling Bridge. (Illus.). 32p. pap. 6.95 *(978-1-899827-07-7(2))* Scottish Children's Pr. GBR. Dist: Gatewood Pr.
Card, Orson Scott. Pathfinder. (Pathfinder Trilogy Ser.). (ENG.). 672p. (YA). (gr. 7). 2011. pap. 13.99 *(978-1-4169-9179-3(4))* 2010. 21.99 *(978-1-4169-9176-2(X))* Simon Pulse. (Simon Pulse).
—Pathfinder. Lt. ed. 2011. (Pathfinder Ser.). (ENG.). 802p. 23.99 *(978-1-4104-3681-8(0))* Thorndike Pr.
—Ruins. 2013. (Pathfinder Trilogy Ser.). (ENG.). 544p. (YA). (gr. 7). pap. 14.99 *(978-1-4169-9180-9(8),* Simon Pulse) Simon Pulse.
—Visitors. 2015. (Pathfinder Trilogy Ser.). (ENG., Illus.). 608p. (YA). (gr. 7). pap. 13.99 *(978-1-4169-9181-6(6),* Simon Pulse) Simon Pulse.
Carpenter, Chad. Morry Moose's Time-Traveling Outhouse Adventure. 2013. (ENG.). 48p. (J). pap. 12.95 *(978-1-62343-163-1(8))* Willow Creek Pr., Inc.
Carter, Rachel. Find Me Where the Water Ends. 2014. (ENG.). 352p. (YA). (gr. 9). 17.99 *(978-0-06-208111-7(X),* HarperTeen) HarperCollins Pubs.
—This Strange & Familiar Place. 2013. (ENG.). 272p. (YA). (gr. 9). 17.99 *(978-0-06-208108-7(X),* HarperTeen) HarperCollins Pubs.
Castellan, Andrea. Mickey Mouse & the Orbiting Nightmare. 2011. (ENG., Illus.). 128p. (J). pap. *(978-1-60886-630-4(0))* BOOM! Studios.
Chan, Aletheia. Kody Chan: the Time Vortex. 2018. (ENG., Illus.). 126p. (J). pap. 13.77 *(978-1-5437-4639-6(X))* Partridge Pub.
Chapman, Bob. Visitors. 2006. 304p. pap. *(978-1-84401-693-8(5))* Athena Pr.
Chapman, Jared, illus. T. Rex Time Machine: (Funny Books for Kids, Dinosaur Book, Time Travel Adventure Book) 2018. (T. Rex Time Machine Ser.). (ENG.). 44p. (J). (gr. -1-k). 16.99 *(978-1-4521-6154-9(2))* Chronicle Bks. LLC.
—T. Rex Time Machine: Dinos in De-Nile. 2019. (T. Rex Time Machine Ser.). (ENG.). 44p. (J). (gr. -1-k). 16.99 *(978-1-4521-6155-6(0))* Chronicle Bks. LLC.
Cheasebro, Margaret. The Healing Tree. 2015. (ENG.). 304p. (YA). 15.95 *(978-1-937240-60-8(6))* Casa de Snapdragon LLC.
Childress, Jamie. Galactic Treasure Hunt #4: Lost in Time. Braun, Chris, illus. 2008. (Galactic Treasure Hunt Ser.). (ENG.). 176p. (J). pap. 5.99 *(978-1-931882-89-7(4))* Adventures Unlimited Pr.
Christopher, John. Fireball. 2015. (Fireball Trilogy Ser.: 1). (ENG., Illus.). 256p. (J). (gr. 4-8). pap. 7.99 *(978-1-4814-2009-9(7),* Aladdin) Simon & Schuster Children's Publishing.
Citra, Becky. Jeremy & the Enchanted Theater. Milne, Jessica, illus. 2004. 64p. (J). lib. bdg. 20.00 *(978-1-4242-1258-3(8))* Fitzgerald Bks.
—Jeremy & the Fantastic Flying Machine, 1 vol. Milne, Jessica, illus. 2008. (Orca Echoes Ser.). (ENG.). 64p. (J). (gr. 1-3). pap. 6.95 *(978-1-55143-950-1(6))* Orca Bk. Pubs. USA.
Claire, Bethany. Morna's Magic: A Sweet Scottish Time Travel Romance. 2017. 258p. pap. 12.99 *(978-1-947731-08-0(4))* Bethany Claire Bks.
Clarizio, Laura. Traveling Through Time: If I Had a Magic Carpet IV. 2012. 100p. 21.95 *(978-1-4489-3229-0(7))* America Star Bks.
Clark, Hattie Mae. It Happened at a Hanging. 2003. (Single Titles Ser.: up). (ENG.). 160p. (YA). (gr. 7-12). lib. bdg. 18.95 *(978-0-7613-2521-5(2),* Millbrook Pr.) Lerner Publishing Group.
Clark, Henry. The Book That Proves Time Travel Happens. 2015. (ENG., Illus.). 416p. (J). (gr. 3-7). 17.00 *(978-0-316-40617-8(1))* Little, Brown Bks. for Young Readers.
Cockcroft, Jason. Counter Clockwise. 2009. 208p. (J). lib. bdg. 16.89 *(978-0-06-125555-7(6),* Tegen, Katherine Bks) HarperCollins Pubs.
Cohagan, Carolyn. The Lost Children. 2011. (ENG.). 320p. (J). (gr. 3-7). pap. 8.99 *(978-1-4169-8617-1(0),* Aladdin) Simon & Schuster Children's Publishing.
Cohen, Rich. Alex & the Amazing Time Machine. Murphy, Kelly, illus. 2013. (ENG.). 176p. (J). (gr. 3-7). pap. 14.99 *(978-1-250-02729-0(2),* 900098301) Square Fish.
Colfer, Eoin. The Time Paradox. 2009. (Artemis Fowl Ser.: 6). (J). lib. bdg. 19.65 *(978-0-606-10579-8(4))* Turtleback.
Collard, Sneed B., III. Dog 4491. 2013. (Illus.). 256p. (J). 13.99 *(978-0-9844460-4-9(4))* Bucking Horse Bks.
Collard, Sneed B., 3rd. Dog 4491. 2013. (ENG., Illus.). 256p. (J). pap. 8.00 *(978-0-9844460-5-6(2))* Mountain Pr. Publishing Co., Inc.
The Complete Gideon Trilogy (Boxed Set) The Time Travelers; the Time Thief; the Time Quake. 2014. (Gideon Trilogy Ser.). (ENG., Illus.). 1424p. (J). (gr. 5-9). pap. 29.99 *(978-1-4814-2613-8(3),* Simon & Schuster Bks. For Young Readers) Simon & Schuster Bks. For Young Readers.
Considine-Johnson, Joan. Olivia Makes Memories. Spaziante, Patrick, illus. 2015. (J). *(978-1-4806-9185-8(2),* Simon Spotlight) Simon Spotlight.
Cooper, Clare. Time Ball. 2003. (ENG.). 72p. pap. 11.95 *(978-1-84323-255-1(3))* Beekman Bks., Inc.
Coughlin, Shirley. Toby & the Pirates. 2012. 58p. pap. 13.00 *(978-1-61204-745-4(9),* Strategic Bk. Publishing) Strategic Book Publishing & Rights Agency (SBPRA).
Cowden, Matt. Emma Mcdougal & the Quest for Father Time. Black, Ilene, illus. 2008. 190p. (J). 24.95 *(978-0-9799189-0-2(1))* His Work Christian Publishing.
Crawford, Charlene E. Adventures with Granny in the Garden. 2006. (J). pap. 7.95 *(978-1-882185-69-6(2))* Cornerstone Publishing, Inc.
Crawford, Quinton Douglass. Moochie the Soochie Visits the Peace People. 2007. (ENG.). 29p. 12.50 *(978-0-615-14879-3(4))* Crawford, Quinton Douglass.
Crewe, Megan. The Clouded Sky, 0 vols. 2015. (Earth & Sky Trilogy Ser.: 2). (ENG.). 354p. (YA). (gr. 7-12). pap. 9.99 *(978-1-4778-2912-7(1),* 9781477829127, Skyscape) Amazon Publishing.
Cross, Julie. Tempest: A Novel. 2012. (Tempest Trilogy Ser.: 1). (ENG.). 368p. (YA). (gr. 9-12). pap. 14.99 *(978-1-250-01120-6(5),* 900098879, St. Martin's Griffin) St. Martin's Pr.
—Vortex: A Tempest Novel. 2013. (Tempest Trilogy Ser.: 2). (ENG.). 384p. (YA). (gr. 9-12). pap. 14.99 *(978-1-250-04478-5(2),* 900127471, St. Martin's Griffin) St. Martin's Pr.
Cuate, Melodie A. Journey to Galveston. 2014. (Mr. Barrington's Mysterious Trunk Ser.). (ENG., Illus.). 192p. (J). 18.95 *(978-0-89672-852-3(8))* Texas Tech Univ. Pr.
—Journey to Goliad. 2009. (Mr. Barrington's Mysterious Trunk Ser.). (ENG., Illus.). 176p. (J). (gr. 4-6). 18.95 *(978-0-89672-649-9(5),* P171404) Texas Tech Univ. Pr.
—Journey to Gonzales. 2008. (Mr. Barrington's Mysterious Trunk Ser.). (ENG., Illus.). 174p. (J). (gr. 4-6). 18.95 *(978-0-89672-624-6(X),* P171712) Texas Tech Univ. Pr.
—Journey to la Salle's Settlement. 2010. (Mr. Barrington's Mysterious Trunk Ser.). (ENG., Illus.). 184p. (J). (gr. 4-6). lib. bdg. 18.95 *(978-0-89672-704-5(1),* P176357) Texas Tech Univ. Pr.
—Journey to Plum Creek. 2012. (Mr. Barrington's Mysterious Trunk Ser.). (ENG., Illus.). 192p. (J). (gr. 4-6). 18.95 *(978-0-89672-741-0(6),* P208774) Texas Tech Univ. Pr.
—Journey to San Jacinto. 2007. (Mr. Barrington's Mysterious Trunk Ser.). (ENG., Illus.). 160p. (J). (gr. 4-6). 18.95 *(978-0-89672-602-4(9),* P171713) Texas Tech Univ. Pr.
—Journey to the Alamo. 2006. (Mr. Barrington's Mysterious Trunk Ser.). (ENG., Illus.). 144p. (J). (gr. 4-6). 18.95 *(978-0-89672-592-8(8),* P171714) Texas Tech Univ. Pr.
Cunningham, Mary. The Magic Medallion. 2006. (Cynthia's Attic Ser.). 158p. (J). (gr. 4-7). per. 9.99 *(978-1-59080-460-5(0))* Echelon Press Publishing.
Dalton, Annie. Budding Star, Book 8. 2008. (Mel Beeby Agent Angel Ser.). (ENG.). 208p. (J). (gr. 4-7). pap. 6.95 *(978-0-00-720478-6(7))* HarperCollins Pubs. Ltd. GBR. Dist: Independent Pubs. Group.
—The Divine Collection: Three Amazing Missions in One Book! 2008. (Mel Beeby Agent Angel Ser.). (ENG., Illus.). 608p. (J). (gr. 4-7). pap. 19.95 *(978-0-00-719074-4(3))* HarperCollins Pubs. Ltd. GBR. Dist: Independent Pubs. Group.
—Fighting Fit (Mel Beeby, Agent Angel, Book 6), Book 6. 2009. (Mel Beeby, Agent Angel Ser.: 6). (ENG.). 192p. (gr. 4-7). pap. 7.99 *(978-0-00-720476-2(0),* HarperCollins Children's Bks.) HarperCollins Pubs. Ltd. GBR. Dist: HarperCollins Pubs.
—Flying High, No. 3. 2003. (Angels Unlimited Ser.). (ENG., Illus.). 144p. (J). pap. 4.99 *(978-0-06-008817-0(6))* HarperCollins Pubs.
—Flying High (Mel Beeby, Agent Angel, Book 3), Book 3. 2010. (Mel Beeby, Agent Angel Ser.: 3). (ENG.). 144p. (gr. 4-7). pap. 7.99 *(978-0-00-720473-1(6),* HarperCollins Children's Bks.) HarperCollins Pubs. Ltd. GBR. Dist: HarperCollins Pubs.
—Fogging over (Mel Beeby, Agent Angel, Book 5), Book 5. 2010. (Mel Beeby, Agent Angel Ser.: 5). (ENG.). 160p. (gr. 4-7). pap. 7.99 *(978-0-00-720475-5(2),* HarperCollins Children's Bks.) HarperCollins Pubs. Ltd. GBR. Dist: HarperCollins Pubs.
—Losing the Plot: Mission: Rescue a Teenage Trio! 2008. (Mel Beeby Agent Angel Ser.). (ENG.). 160p. (J). (gr. 4-7). pap. 6.95 *(978-0-00-720472-4(8))* HarperCollins Pubs. Ltd. GBR. Dist: Independent Pubs. Group.
—Making Waves (Mel Beeby, Agent Angel, Book 7), Book 7. 2010. (Mel Beeby, Agent Angel Ser.: 7). (ENG.). 208p. (gr. 4-7). pap. 9.99 *(978-0-00-720477-9(9),* HarperCollins Children's Bks.) HarperCollins Pubs. Ltd. GBR. Dist: HarperCollins Pubs.
—Winging It: Mission: Enrol at Angel School! 2008. (Mel Beeby Agent Angel Ser.). (ENG.). 144p. (J). (gr. 4-7). pap. 6.95 *(978-0-00-720471-7(X))* HarperCollins Pubs. Ltd. GBR. Dist: Independent Pubs. Group.
Dateno, Maria Grace. Courageous Quest. Cunningham, Paul, illus. 2014. 81p. (J). pap. 5.95 *(978-0-8198-1628-3(0))* Pauline Bks. & Media.
—Danger at Sea. Cunningham, Paul, illus. 2013. 80p. (J). pap. 5.95 *(978-0-8198-1891-1(7))* Pauline Bks. & Media.
—Discovery at Dawn. Cunningham, Paul, illus. 2014. (ENG.). 79p. (J). pap. 5.95 *(978-0-8198-1895-9(X))* Pauline Bks. & Media.
—Mystery of the Missing Jars. Cunningham, Paul, illus. 2014. 77p. (J). 5.95 *(978-0-8198-4922-9(7))* Pauline Bks. & Media.
Davie, Jan. Apollo Cafe. 2005. 76p. pap. *(978-1-84401-565-8(3))* Athena Pr.
Davies, Linda. Longbow Girl. 2016. (ENG.). 336p. (YA). (gr. 7). 17.99 *(978-0-545-85345-3(1),* Chicken Hse., The) Scholastic, Inc.
de los Santos, Marisa. Saving Lucas Biggs. 2015. (ENG.). 320p. (J). (gr. 3-7). pap. 7.99 *(978-0-06-227463-2(5),* HarperCollins) HarperCollins Pubs.
Deborah Strandberg, Rebecca Reynolds and. Trammler Triplet Tales #2 - HIDDEN in TIME. 2007. 116p. pap. 8.94 *(978-1-4303-2097-5(4))* Lulu Pr., Inc.
—Trammler Triplet Tales-Adventure #3 SEEKING the SOURCE. 2007. 175p. pap. 11.38 *(978-1-4303-1197-3(5))* Lulu Pr., Inc.
Deering, Leta. Patriotic Samáand the Mendez Twins at the Alamo. 2008. 112p. pap. 19.95 *(978-1-60610-689-1(9))* America Star Bks.
Deutsch, Stacia & Cohon, Rhody. Bell's Breakthrough. Wenzel, David, illus. 2013. (Blast to the Past Ser.: 3). (ENG.). 128p. (J). (gr. 2-5). pap. 6.99 *(978-1-4424-9536-4(7),* Simon & Schuster/Paula Wiseman Bks.) Simon & Schuster/Paula Wiseman Bks.
—Disney's Dream. Wenzel, David, illus. 2013. (Blast to the Past Ser.: 2). (ENG.). 128p. (J). (gr. 2-5). pap. 6.99 *(978-1-4424-9535-7(9),* Simon & Schuster/Paula Wiseman Bks.) Simon & Schuster/Paula Wiseman Bks.
—Lincoln's Legacy. Wenzel, David, illus. 2005. (Blast to the Past Ser.: 1). (ENG.). 112p. (J). (gr. 2-5). pap. 6.99 *(978-0-689-87024-8(8),* Simon & Schuster/Paula Wiseman Bks.) Simon & Schuster/Paula Wiseman Bks.
—Washington's War. Francis, Guy, illus. 2015. (Blast to the Past Ser.: 7). (ENG.). 128p. (J). (gr. 2-5). pap. 6.99 *(978-1-4424-9540-1(5),* Simon & Schuster/Paula Wiseman Bks.) Simon & Schuster/Paula Wiseman Bks.
Deutsch/Cohon. Disney's Dream. Wenzel, David, illus. 2005. 108p. (J). lib. bdg. 16.92 *(978-1-4242-1714-4(8))* Fitzgerald Bks.
Dinsdale, Christopher. Broken Circle. 2004. (ENG.). 104p. (J). pap. 7.95 *(978-1-894917-15-5(4),* Napoleon & Co.) Dundurn Pr. CAN. Dist: Publishers Group West (PGW).
Disney Books. Gravity Falls: Once upon a Swine. 2014. (Gravity Falls Chapter Book Ser.: 2). (ENG., Illus.). 112p. (J). (gr. 1-3). pap. 4.99 *(978-1-4847-1140-8(8),* Disney Press Books) Disney Publishing Worldwide.
Disney Press Staff. Once upon a Swine. 2014. (Gravity Falls Ser.: 2). (J). lib. bdg. 14.75 *(978-0-606-35916-0(8))* Turtleback.
Divakaruni, Chitra Banerjee. The Mirror of Fire & Dreaming. 2007. (ENG.). 336p. (J). (gr. 3-7). pap. 14.99 *(978-1-4169-1768-7(3),* Aladdin) Simon & Schuster Children's Publishing.
Dorfman, Joaquin. The Long Wait for Tomorrow. 2009. (YA). *(978-0-375-84696-0(4))* Random Hse., Inc.
Doty, Jean Slaughter. Can I Get There by Candlelight? 2012. (ENG.). 128p. (YA). (gr. 7). pap. 7.99 *(978-1-4424-8608-9(2),*

TUV

Simon & Schuster Bks. For Young Readers) Simon & Schuster Bks. For Young Readers.

Douglas, Helen. Chasing Stars. 2016. (ENG.). 352p. (YA). 17.99 *(978-1-61963-410-7(4)*, 900135715, Bloomsbury USA Childrens) Bloomsbury Publishing USA.

Dowding, Philippa. Carter & the Curious Maze: Weird Stories Gone Wrong. 2016. (Weird Stories Gone Wrong Ser.: 3). (ENG., Illus.). 136p. (J). pap. 9.99 *(978-1-4597-3249-0(9))* Dundurn Pr. CAN. Dist: Publishers Group West (PGW).

Downer, Ann. Hatching Magic. Rayyan, Omar, illus. 2004. 242p. 16.00 *(978-0-7569-3481-1(8))* Perfection Learning Corp.

Downie, Mary Alice & Downie, John. Alison's Ghosts, 1 vol. 2008. (Lorimer Streetlights Ser.). (ENG.). 104p. (J). (gr. 2-4). 8.95 *(978-1-55277-013-9(3)*, 013) James Lorimer & Co. Ltd., Pubs. CAN. Dist: Formac Lorimer Bks. Ltd.

Drexler, Sam & Shelby, Fay. Murder in Bozeman. 2005. (Erika & Oz Adventures in American History Ser.: Vol. 2). 152p. (YA). (gr. 9-12). pap. 9.99 *(978-0-9669988-2-5(0))* Aunt Strawberry Bks.

Duey, Kathleen. Leonardo. Epstein, Eugene, illus. 2009. (Time Soldiers Ser.). (ENG.). (J). (gr. k-2). 95p. 9.95 *(978-1-929945-89-4(2))*;Bk. 8. 48p. 15.95 *(978-1-929945-88-7(4))* Big Guy Bks., Inc.

—Rex. Epstein, Eugene, illus. Gould, Robert, photos by. 2003. (Time Soldiers Ser.: Bk. 1). (ENG.). 43p. (J). (gr. k-2). pap. 7.95 *(978-1-929945-20-7(5))* Big Guy Bks., Inc.

—Rex. Epstein, Eugene, illus. 2006. (Time Soldiers Ser.: Bk. 1). 96p. (J). (gr. -1-7). lib. bdg. 24.21 *(978-1-59961-227-0(5))* Spotlight.

—Rex 2. Epstein, Eugene, illus. Gould, Robert, photos by. 2003. (Time Soldiers Ser.: Bk. 2). (ENG.). 48p. (J). (gr. k-2). pap. 8.95 *(978-1-929945-27-6(2))* Big Guy Bks., Inc.

Duey, Kathleen & Gould, Robert. Rex 2. Epstein, Eugene, illus. Gould, Robert, photos by. 2003. (Soldados de Tiempo Libro: Vol. 2). (SPA & ENG.). 48p. (J). (gr. k-4). pap. 8.95 *(978-1-929945-36-8(1))* Big Guy Bks., Inc.

—Rex2. Epstein, Eugene, illus. Gould, Robert, photos by. 2003. (Time Soldiers Ser.). 48p. (J). (gr. 4-7). 17.10 *(978-0-7569-3472-9(9))* Perfection Learning Corp.

Durkin, Frances. An Egyptian Adventure. Cooke, Grace, illus. 2019. (Histronauts Ser.). (ENG.). (J). (gr. 3-4). 88p. pap. 10.99 *(978-1-63163-240-2(X)*, 163163240X); 81p. lib. bdg. 29.99 *(978-1-63163-239-6(6)*, 1631632396) North Star Editions. (Jolly Fish Pr.).

—A Roman Adventure. Cooke, Grace, illus. 2019. (Histronauts Ser.). (ENG.). (J). (gr. 3-4). 88p. pap. 10.99 *(978-1-63163-244-0(2)*, 1631632442); 81p. lib. bdg. 29.99 *(978-1-63163-243-3(4)*, 1631632434) North Star Editions. (Jolly Fish Pr.).

dyer, kc. Shades of Red: An Eagle Glen Trilogy Book. 2005. (Eagle Glen Trilogy Ser.: 3). (ENG.). 272p. (YA). (gr. 7). pap. 8.99 *(978-1-55002-545-3(7))* Dundurn Pr. CAN. Dist: Publishers Group West (PGW).

Eade, Oliver. The Terminus. 2013. 264p. pap. *(978-1-909411-26-5(4))* Mauve Square Publishing.

Earl, Cheri Pray & Williams, Carol Lynch. Secret in Pennsylvania. 2009. (J). *(978-1-56145-477-8(X)*, Peachtree Junior) Peachtree Publishing Co. Inc.

Ernst, Kathleen. Gunpowder & Tea Cakes: My Journey with Felicity. 2017. 185p. (J). *(978-1-5182-4407-0(6)*, American Girl) American Girl Publishing, Inc.

Falcone, L. M. Walking with the Dead. 2005. (Illus.). 200p. (J). (gr. 4-7). 7.95 *(978-1-55337-709-2(5))* Kids Can Pr., Ltd. CAN. Dist: Hachette Bk. Group.

Falkner, Brian. The Project. 2012. (ENG.). 288p. (J). (gr. 7-12). lib. bdg. 24.94 *(978-0-375-96945-4(4))* Random Hse. Bks. for Young Readers.

—The Project. 2012. (ENG.). 288p. (YA). (gr. 7). pap. 8.99 *(978-0-375-87188-7(8)*, Ember) Random Hse. Children's Bks.

Falligant, Erin. Prints in the Sand. 2017. 183p. (J). *(978-1-5182-5318-8(0)*, American Girl) American Girl Publishing, Inc.

Fanning, Kieran. Code Crackers: Voyage to Victory. 2010. (Dover Kids Activity Books: Fantasy Ser.). (ENG., Illus.). 128p. (J). (gr. 3-5). pap. 5.99 *(978-0-486-47861-4(5)*, 478815) Dover Pubns., Inc.

Farmer, Penelope. Charlotte Sometimes. 2017. (ENG., Illus.). 208p. (J). (gr. 7-9). pap. 11.99 *(978-1-68137-104-7(9)*, NYRB Kids) New York Review of Bks., Inc., The.

Feldman, Ruth Tenzer. The Ninth Day. 2013. (Blue Thread Saga Ser.). (ENG., Illus.). 288p. (YA). pap. 13.95 *(978-1-932010-65-7(3)*, 9781932010657) Ooligan Pr.

Finn, Perdita. Crashing the Party. Dorman, Brandon, illus. 2007. 109p. (J). *(978-0-439-74436-2(9))* Scholastic, Inc.

—Going for the Gold. 2007. 118p. (J). *(978-0-439-89208-7(2))* Scholastic, Inc.

—Stealing the Show. Moran, Mike, illus. 2006. (Time Flyers Ser.: Vol. 1). 109p. (J). pap. *(978-0-439-74433-1(4))* Scholastic, Inc.

Fleischman, Sid. The 13th Floor: A Ghost Story. Sis, Peter, illus. 2007. (ENG.). 240p. (J). (gr. 3-7). per. 7.99 *(978-0-06-134503-6(2)*, Greenwillow Bks.) HarperCollins Pubs.

Fleming, Candace. Ben Franklin's in My Bathroom! Fearing, Mark, illus. 2017. (History Pals Ser.). 272p. (J). (gr. 2-5). 13.99 *(978-1-101-93406-7(9)*, Schwartz & Wade Bks.) Random Hse. Children's Bks.

Fleming, Ian. Chitty Chitty Bang Bang: the Magical Car. Berger, Joe, illus. 2013. (Chitty Chitty Bang Bang Ser.: 1). (ENG.). 160p. (J). (gr. 4-7). pap. 8.99 *(978-0-7636-6666-8(1))* Candlewick Pr.

Focus on the Family Staff & Hering, Marianne. Light in the Lions' Den. 2017. (AIO Imagination Station Bks.: 19). (ENG., Illus.). 144p. (J). pap. 5.99 *(978-1-58997-878-2(1)*, 20_28513) Focus on the Family Publishing.

Fogarty, Paula. Slave of the Lamp. l.t. ed. 2013. 354p. pap. *(978-1-4596-6705-1(0))* ReadHowYouWant.com, Ltd.

Fontes, Justine & Fontes, Ron. Casebook: The Bermuda Triangle, 1 vol. 2009. (Top Secret Graphica Mysteries Ser.). (ENG., Illus.). 48p. (YA). (gr. 4-4). 33.93 *(978-1-60754-591-0(8)*, ce4dd6aa-44d7-47ea-affe-dfbfb2c434ae); pap. 12.75 *(978-1-60754-592-7(6)*, 6f4cc6c9-b1ce-4460-aa2c-bd98329ba34e) Rosen Publishing Group, Inc., The. (Windmill Bks.).

Foreman, Colin. A Moment Comes. Colin Foreman. 2007. (Keepers & Seekers Ser.). (ENG., Illus.). 320p. pap. *(978-0-9548949-2-4(8))* Myroy Bks. Ltd.

Fox Mazer, Norma. Saturday, the Twelfth of October. 2015. (ENG.). 274p. (J). (gr. 3). pap. 13.95 *(978-1-939601-31-5(2))* Ig Publishing, Inc.

French, Gillian. The Door to January, 1 vol. 2nd ed. 2019. (ENG.). 212p. (YA). pap. 14.95 *(978-1-944762-61-2(2)*, bfd61ab4-190b-41be-a973-f62e0568c1f7) Islandport Pr., Inc.

Fridolfs, Derek. Black Adam & the Eternity War. Levins, Tim, illus. 2018. (Justice League Ser.). (ENG.). 88p. (J). (gr. 2-6). lib. bdg. 27.32 *(978-1-4965-5981-4(9)*, 137330, Stone Arch Bks.) Capstone.

Friedman, Stanley. Quantum Outlaws. 2010. 210p. pap. 11.95 *(978-1-935630-09-8(1))* Bellissima Publishing, LLC.

Funk, Rachel. Christabelle in the Museum of Time. 2007. 217p. pap. 14.95 *(978-1-4303-2572-7(0))* Lulu Pr., Inc.

Garfinkle, D. L. Stuck in the 70's. 2007. 182p. (YA). *(978-1-4287-4661-9(7))* Penguin Publishing Group.

Gaston County Museum of Art & History, ed. The Secret Adventures of Hamster Sam: Attack of the Evil Boll Weevils! 2008. (Illus.). 32p. (J). 15.95 *(978-0-9798445-0-8(9))* DM Creative.

Gayle, Sharon Shavers. Emma's Escape: A Story of America's Underground Railroad. Velasquez, Eric, illus. 3rd ed. 2003. (Soundprints' Read-and-Discover Ser.). (ENG.). 48p. (J). (gr. -1-3). pap. 3.95 *(978-1-59249-021-9(2)*, S2009) Soundprints.

Gewirtz, Adina Rishe. Blue Window. 2018. (ENG.). 576p. (J). (gr. 7). 18.99 *(978-0-7636-6036-9(1))* Candlewick Pr.

Gibbs, Stuart. The Last Musketeer. (ENG.). 272p. (J). (gr. 3-7). 2018. pap. 7.99 *(978-0-06-285215-1(9)*, HarperCollins) 2012. (Last Musketeer Ser.: 1). pap. 6.99 *(978-0-06-204839-4(2))* HarperCollins Pubs.

—The Last Musketeer #2: The Traitor's Chase. 2nd ed. 2012. (Last Musketeer Ser.: 2). (ENG.). 256p. (J). (gr. 3-7). 16.99 *(978-0-06-204841-7(4)*, HarperCollins) HarperCollins Pubs.

—The Last Musketeer #2: Traitor's Chase. 2019. (ENG.). 272p. (J). (gr. 3-7). pap. 7.99 *(978-0-06-204842-4(2)*, HarperCollins) HarperCollins Pubs.

—The Last Musketeer #3: Double Cross. (ENG.). 256p. (J). (gr. 3-7). 2019. pap. 7.99 *(978-0-06-204845-5(7))* 2013. (Last Musketeer Ser.: 3). 16.99 *(978-0-06-204844-8(9))* HarperCollins Pubs. (HarperCollins).

Gier, Kerstin. Ruby Red. Bell, Anthea, tr. 2012. (Ruby Red Trilogy Ser.: 1). (ENG.). 352p. (YA). (gr. 7-12). pap. 11.99 *(978-0-312-55151-3(7)*, 900074429) Square Fish.

—Sapphire Blue, 2. Bell, Anthea, tr. 2013. (Ruby Red Trilogy Ser.: 2). (ENG.). 384p. (YA). (gr. 6-8). pap. 11.99 *(978-1-250-03416-8(7)*, 900120588) Square Fish.

Giles, Katharine. The Princess of Skye, an Archer Adventure. 2013. (ENG.). 280p. (YA). pap. 12.99 *(978-1-939927-79-8(X))* Telemachus Pr., LLC.

Goodman, Alison. Singing the Dogstar Blues. 2008. (ENG.). 240p. (YA). *(978-0-7322-8863-1(0))* HarperCollins Pubs. Australia.

Gould, Robert & Duey, Kathleen. Time Soldiers. 2005. 384p. pap. 16.95 *(978-1-929945-60-3(4))* Big Guy Bks., Inc.

—Time Soldiers - Rex. Epstein, Eugene, illus. Gould, Robert, photos by. 2005. (Time Soldiers Ser.: Bk. 1). (ENG.). 96p. (J). (gr. k-2). per. 5.95 *(978-1-929945-53-5(1))*; per. 5.95 *(978-1-929945-54-2(X))* Big Guy Bks., Inc.

Graham, J. Lee. In the Nick of Time. 2008. 108p. pap. 10.95 *(978-0-595-52621-5(7))* iUniverse, Inc.

Graudin, Ryan. Invictus. 2018. (ENG.). 480p. (YA). (gr. 9-17). pap. 10.99 *(978-0-316-50308-2(8))* Little, Brown Bks. for Young Readers.

—Invictus. l.t. ed. 2019. (ENG.). 660p. (YA). (gr. 9-17). pap. 12.99 *(978-1-4328-6451-4(3)*, Large Print Pr.) Thorndike Pr.

Green, John. Sparta! Warriors of the Ancient World. 2013. (Dover Ancient History Coloring Bks.). (ENG.). 32p. (gr. 3-12). pap. 3.99 *(978-0-486-49813-3(1)*, 498131) Dover Pubns., Inc.

Greenburg, Dan. It's Itchcraft! Davis, Jack E., illus. 2004. (Zack Files Ser.). 118p. lib. bdg. 15.00 *(978-0-7569-2238-2(0))* Perfection Learning Corp.

—Zack Files 30: It's Itchcraft! SuperSpecial, 30 vols. Davis, Jack E., illus. 2003. (Zack Files Ser.: 30). (ENG.). 128p. (J). (gr. 2-5). pap. 4.99 *(978-0-448-42888-8(1)*, Grosset & Dunlap) Penguin Young Readers Group.

Greenburg, J. C. Andrew Lost #10: on Earth. Gerardi, Jan, illus. 10th ed. 2005. (Andrew Lost Ser.: 10). 96p. (J). (gr. 1-4). 6.99 *(978-0-375-82950-5(4)*, Random Hse. Bks. for Young Readers) Random Hse. Children's Bks.

—Andrew Lost #11: with the Dinosaurs. Gerardi, Jan, illus. 2005. (Andrew Lost Ser.: 11). (ENG.). 96p. (J). (gr. 1-4). 4.99 *(978-0-375-82951-2(2)*, Random Hse. Bks. for Young Readers) Random Hse. Children's Bks.

—Andrew Lost #12: in the Ice Age. Gerardi, Jan, illus. 2005. (Andrew Lost Ser.: 12). 96p. (J). (gr. 1-4). 4.99 *(978-0-375-82952-9(0)*, Random Hse. Bks. for Young Readers) Random Hse. Children's Bks.

—Andrew Lost #9: in Time. Gerardi, Jan, illus. 2004. (Andrew Lost Ser.: 9). 96p. (J). (gr. 1-4). 6.99 *(978-0-375-82949-9(0)*, Random Hse. Bks. for Young Readers) Random Hse. Children's Bks.

—On Earth, 10. Gerardi, Jan, illus. 2005. (Andrew Lost Ser.: Bk. 10). (ENG.). 90p. (J). (gr. 3-6). lib. bdg. 16.19 *(978-0-375-92950-2(9))* Random House Publishing Group.

Greenspan, Paul. Crystal of Dreams. 2006. (ENG.). 192p. pap. 12.96 *(978-0-615-13477-2(7))* Flying Cloud Bks.

Gutman, Dan. Abner & Me. 2007. (Baseball Card Adventures Ser.). (ENG., Illus.). 176p. (J). (gr. 5-9). pap. 7.99 *(978-0-06-053445-5(1)*, HarperCollins) HarperCollins Pubs.

—Abner & Me. 2007. (Baseball Card Adventures Ser.). (Illus.). 166p. (gr. 5-9). 16.00 *(978-0-7569-7920-1(X))* Perfection Learning Corp.

—Flashback Four #1: the Lincoln Project. 2016. (Flashback Four Ser.: 1). (ENG.). 240p. (J). (gr. 3-7). 16.99 *(978-0-06-237441-7(9)*, HarperCollins) HarperCollins Pubs.

—Flashback Four #3: the Pompeii Disaster. (Flashback Four Ser.: 3). (ENG.). (J). (gr. 3-7). 2019. 272p. pap. 7.99 *(978-0-06-237445-5(1))* 2018. 256p. 16.99 *(978-0-06-237444-8(3))* HarperCollins Pubs. (HarperCollins).

—Flashback Four #4: the Hamilton-Burr Duel. 2019. (Flashback Four Ser.: 4). (ENG., Illus.). 240p. (J). (gr. 3-7). 16.99 *(978-0-06-237447-9(8)*, HarperCollins) HarperCollins Pubs.

—Honus & Me. 2003. (Baseball Card Adventures Ser.). (J). (gr. 3-6). lib. bdg. 16.00 *(978-0-613-07982-2(5))* Turtleback.

—Honus & Me: A Baseball Card Adventure. 2003. (Baseball Card Adventures Ser.). (ENG., Illus.). 144p. (J). (gr. 5-9). pap. 9.99 *(978-0-380-78878-1(0)*, HarperCollins) HarperCollins Pubs.

—Jackie & Me. 2005. (Baseball Card Adventures Ser.). (Illus.). 145p. (YA). (gr. 4-8). reprint ed. 20.00 *(978-0-7567-9569-6(9))* DIANE Publishing Co.

—Jim & Me. 2010. (Baseball Card Adventures Ser.). (ENG.). 224p. (J). (gr. 5-9). pap. 7.99 *(978-0-06-059496-1(9)*, HarperCollins) HarperCollins Pubs.

—Jim & Me. 2010. (Baseball Card Adventures Ser.). (J). lib. bdg. 17.20 *(978-0-606-09536-5(5))* Turtleback.

—Mickey & Me. 2004. (Baseball Card Adventures Ser.). (ENG., Illus.). 160p. (J). (gr. 5-9). pap. 7.99 *(978-0-06-447258-6(2)*, HarperCollins) HarperCollins Pubs.

—Mickey & Me. 2004. (Baseball Card Adventures Ser.). (J). lib. bdg. 16.00 *(978-0-613-99233-6(4))* Turtleback.

—Ray & Me. 2011. (Baseball Card Adventures Ser.). (ENG.). 192p. (J). (gr. 5-9). pap. 7.99 *(978-0-06-123483-5(4)*, HarperCollins) HarperCollins Pubs.

—Roberto & Me. 2012. (Baseball Card Adventures Ser.). (ENG.). 192p. (J). (gr. 5-9). pap. 7.99 *(978-0-06-123486-6(9)*, HarperCollins) HarperCollins Pubs.

—Roberto & Me. 2012. (Baseball Card Adventures Ser.). (J). lib. bdg. 16.00 *(978-0-606-23591-4(4))* Turtleback.

—Satch & Me. 2009. (Baseball Card Adventures Ser.). (ENG.). 192p. (J). (gr. 5-9). pap. 9.99 *(978-0-06-059493-0(4)*, HarperCollins) HarperCollins Pubs.

—Satch & Me. 2009. (Baseball Card Adventures Ser.). (J). lib. bdg. 16.00 *(978-0-606-00023-9(2))* Turtleback.

—Shoeless Joe & Me. 2003. (Baseball Card Adventures Ser.). (ENG., Illus.). 176p. (J). (gr. 5-9). pap. 9.99 *(978-0-06-447259-3(0)*, HarperCollins) HarperCollins Pubs.

—Shoeless Joe & Me. 2003. (Baseball Card Adventures Ser.). (Illus.). 163p. (gr. 3-7). 16.00 *(978-0-7569-1438-7(8))* Perfection Learning Corp.

—Shoeless Joe & Me. 2003. (Baseball Card Adventures Ser.). (J). (gr. 3-6). lib. bdg. 16.00 *(978-0-613-61816-8(5))* Turtleback.

—Ted & Me. 2012. (Baseball Card Adventures Ser.). (ENG., Illus.). 208p. (J). (gr. 5-9). 15.99 *(978-0-06-123487-3(7)*, HarperCollins) HarperCollins Pubs.

—Willie & Me. 2015. (Baseball Card Adventures Ser.: 12). (ENG.). 176p. (J). (gr. 3-7). 16.99 *(978-0-06-170404-8(0)*, HarperCollins) HarperCollins Pubs.

Haddix, Margaret Peterson. Caught. 2013. (Missing Ser.: 5). (ENG., Illus.). 368p. (J). (gr. 3-7). pap. 8.99 *(978-1-4169-8983-7(8)*, Simon & Schuster Bks. For Young Readers) Simon & Schuster Bks. For Young Readers.

—Caught. 2013. (Missing Ser.: 5). lib. bdg. 18.40 *(978-0-606-27045-8(0))* Turtleback.

—Found. (Missing Ser.: 1). (ENG.). (J). (gr. 3-7). 2009. 336p. pap. 8.99 *(978-1-4169-5421-7(X))* 2008. 320p. 19.99 *(978-1-4169-5417-0(1))* Simon & Schuster Bks. For Young Readers. (Simon & Schuster Bks. For Young Readers).

—Redeemed. 2015. (Missing Ser.: 8). (ENG.). 416p. (J). (gr. 3-7). 19.99 *(978-1-4424-9756-6(4)*, Simon & Schuster Bks. For Young Readers) Simon & Schuster Bks. For Young Readers.

—Redeemed. 2016. (Missing Ser.: 8). lib. bdg. 18.40 *(978-0-606-39234-1(3))* Turtleback.

—Revealed. 2015. (Missing Ser.: 7). lib. bdg. 19.65 *(978-0-606-37847-5(2))* Turtleback.

—Risked. 2013. (Missing Ser.: 6). (ENG., Illus.). 320p. (J). (gr. 3-7). 18.99 *(978-1-4169-8984-4(6)*, Simon & Schuster Bks. For Young Readers) Simon & Schuster Bks. For Young Readers.

—Risked. 2014. (Missing Ser.: 6). lib. bdg. 19.65 *(978-0-606-36096-8(4))* Turtleback.

—Torn. (Missing Ser.: 4). (ENG.). (J). (gr. 3-7). 2012. 368p. pap. 8.99 *(978-1-4169-8981-3(1))* 2011. 352p. 19.99 *(978-1-4169-8980-6(3))* Simon & Schuster Bks. For Young Readers. (Simon & Schuster Bks. For Young Readers).

—Torn. l.t. ed. 2011. (Missing Ser.: Bk. 4). (ENG.). 566p. 23.99 *(978-1-4104-4078-5(8))* Thorndike Pr.

—Torn. 2012. (Missing Ser.: 4). lib. bdg. 18.40 *(978-0-606-26333-7(0))* Turtleback.

Hahn, Mary Downing. The Doll in the Garden; The Old Willis Place. 2009. pap. 11.90 *(978-0-547-37542-7(5))* Houghton Mifflin Harcourt Trade & Reference Pubs.

Handford, Martin. Where's Waldo? 2007. (Where's Waldo? Ser.). (Illus.). 24p. (gr. 4-7). lib. bdg. 18.40 *(978-1-4178-2424-3(7))* Turtleback.

—Where's Waldo Now? Handford, Martin, illus. 2019. (Where's Waldo? Ser.). (ENG., Illus.). 32p. (J). (gr. k-4). 8.99 *(978-1-5362-1066-8(8))* Candlewick Pr.

—Where's Waldo Now? Deluxe Edition. Handford, Martin, illus. 25th anniv. deluxe ed. 2012. (Where's Waldo? Ser.). (ENG., Illus.). 32p. (J). (gr. k-4). 17.99 *(978-0-7636-4526-7(5))* Candlewick Pr.

Hansen, Lynne. Reckless Revolution. 2007. (YA). *(978-1-4114-9672-9(8)*, Spark Publishing Group) Sterling Publishing Co., Inc.

—Shades of Blue & Gray. 2007. (YA). pap. *(978-1-4114-9674-3(4)*, Spark Publishing Group) Sterling Publishing Co., Inc.

—A Time for Witches. 2007. (YA). *(978-1-4114-9671-2(X)*, Spark Publishing Group) Sterling Publishing Co., Inc.

Hardie, Richard. Leap of Faith. 2013. (Illus.). 272p. pap. *(978-1-909841-26-0(9))* Crooked Cat Publishing.

Hardman, Ron & Hardman, Jessica. Shadow Fox: Sons of Liberty. Barnecut, Suzanne, ed. Harrigan, Mike, illus. 2010. (Shadow Fox Ser.). 186p. (J). (gr. 4-8). 22.99 *(978-0-9819607-1-5(5))* Fox Run Pr., LLC.

—Shadow Fox: Sons of Liberty. Barnecut, Suzanne, ed. Harrigan, Mike, illus. 2010. (Shadow Fox Ser.). 186p. (J). (gr. 4-8). pap. 11.99 *(978-0-9819607-0-8(7))* Fox Run Pr., LLC.

—Shadow Fox: Sons of Liberty Teacher's Edition. Barnecut, Suzanne, ed. Harrigan, Mike, illus. 2010. (Shadow Fox Ser.: 1). 186p. (J). 34.99 *(978-0-9819607-2-2(3))* Fox Run Pr., LLC.

Harness, Cheryl. Ghosts of the Civil War. Harness, Cheryl, illus. 2004. (ENG., Illus.). 48p. (J). (gr. 2-5). 8.99 *(978-0-689-86992-1(4)*, Simon & Schuster Bks. For Young Readers) Simon & Schuster Bks. For Young Readers.

Harris, Rachel. A Tale of Two Centuries. 2017. (ENG., Illus.). (YA). pap. 14.99 *(978-1-68281-442-0(4))* Entangled Publishing, LLC.

Harris, Stanley. The First Shot: A Tale of a Boy's Trip Through Time to the Battle of Lexington. 2007. per. *(978-1-59872-958-0(6))* Instant Pub.

Heilig, Heidi. The Girl from Everywhere. 2016. (ENG.). 464p. (YA). (gr. 8). 17.99 *(978-0-06-238075-3(3)*, Greenwillow Bks.) HarperCollins Pubs.

Heimerdinger, Chris. Drums of Desolation: A Novel. 2014. 419p. (YA). *(978-1-62108-821-9(9))* Covenant Communications.

—Escape from Zarahemla. 2011. 263p. (YA). pap. *(978-1-60861-539-1(1))* Covenant Communications.

—Kingdoms & Conquerors: A Novel. 2005. 434p. (YA). *(978-1-59156-740-0(8))* Covenant Communications.

—Tower of Thunder Vol. 9: A Novel. 2004. (Tennis Shoes Adventure Ser.). 406p. pap. 14.95 *(978-1-59156-177-4(9))* Covenant Communications, Inc.

—The Warriors of Cumorah, Vol. 8. 2004. (Tennis Shoes Adventure Ser.). xi, 394p. pap. 14.95 *(978-1-57734-922-8(9))* Covenant Communications, Inc.

Helliar, Peter. Frankie Fish & the Great Wall of Chaos, Volume 2. Vamos, Lesley, illus. 2018. (Frankie Fish Ser.: 2). (ENG.). 288p. (J). (gr. 2-4). pap. 14.99 *(978-1-76050-082-5(8))* Hardie Grant Children?s Publishing AUS. Dist: Independent Pubs. Group.

Helliar, Peter & Vamos, Lesley. Frankie Fish & the Sonic Suitcase, Volume 1. 2017. (Frankie Fish Ser.: 1). (ENG., Illus.). 280p. (J). (gr. 2-4). pap. 14.99 *(978-1-76012-849-4(X))* Hardie Grant Children?s Publishing AUS. Dist: Independent Pubs. Group.

Helwani, Najiyah Diana. Sophia's Journal: Time Warp 1857. 2008. (YA). per. *(978-0-9793577-2-5(1))* Muslim Writers Publishing.

Henn, Pamela. Nick & Slim: The Legend of the Falcon Mine. 2006. (Illus.). 472p. (YA). 19.95 *(978-0-9760654-0-1(1))* White Wolf Studio, Inc.

Hering, Marianne. In Fear of the Spear. 2016. (AIO Imagination Station Bks.: 17). (ENG., Illus.). 144p. (J). pap. 5.99 *(978-1-58997-804-1(8)*, 4622356) Focus on the Family Publishing.

—Trouble on the Orphan Train. 2016. (AIO Imagination Station Bks.: 18). (ENG.). 144p. (J). pap. 5.99 *(978-1-58997-805-8(6)*, 20_27692) Focus on the Family Publishing.

Hernandez, David. Land of the Pharaohs, 1 vol., 1. 2003. (Adventures of Toby Digz Ser.: 1). (ENG., Illus.). 96p. (J). pap. 5.99 *(978-1-4003-0195-9(5)*, Tommy Nelson) Nelson, Thomas Inc.

—The Mighty Armor, 1 vol., 2. 2003. (Adventures of Toby Digz Ser.: 2). (ENG., Illus.). 96p. (YA). pap. 5.99 *(978-1-4003-0196-6(3)*, Tommy Nelson) Nelson, Thomas Inc.

Higgins, Lawrence. Demons & Dragons: Time, Space & Magic. 2010. (ENG., Illus.). 93p. pap. 20.99 *(978-1-906791-68-1(6))* Arena Bks. GBR. Dist: Lightning Source UK, Ltd.

Hill, C. J. Echo in Time. 2014. 387p. (YA). *(978-0-06-212395-4(5))* HarperCollins Pubs.

Hillyer, Lexa. Proof of Forever. 2016. (ENG.). 352p. (YA). (gr. 8). pap. 9.99 *(978-0-06-233038-3(1)*, HarperTeen) HarperCollins Pubs.

Hoffman, Mary. Special Powers. (ENG.). 200p. pap. *(978-0-340-62670-2(4))* Hodder & Stoughton.

Holliday, Susan. The Time Street Gang & the Rag & Bone Boy. l.t. ed. 2007. 132p. pap. *(978-1-905665-64-8(4))* Pollinger In Print.

Hood, Ann. Crazy Horse: Brave Warrior, 5. Altmann, Scott, illus. 2013. (Treasure Chest: the Time-Traveling Adventures of the Robbins Twins Ser.: 5). (ENG.). 192p. (J). (gr. 4-6). 18.69 *(978-0-448-45738-3(5))* Penguin Young Readers Group.

—Prince of Air, 4. Altmann, Scott & Zilber, Denis, illus. 2012. (Treasure Chest: the Time-Traveling Adventures of the Robbins Twins Ser.: 4). 208p. (J). (gr. 4-6). 21.19 *(978-0-448-45474-0(2))* Penguin Young Readers Group.

Hopper, Ada. Don't Disturb the Dinosaurs. Ricks, Sam, illus. 2016. (DATA Set Ser.: 2). (ENG.). 128p. (J). (gr. k-4). pap. 5.99 *(978-1-4814-5731-6(4)*, Little Simon) Little Simon.

—Don't Disturb the Dinosaurs. Ricks, Sam, illus. 2018. 125p. (J). (gr. 1-4). 15.96 *(978-1-64310-198-9(6))* Penworthy Co., LLC, The.

—Out of Remote Control. Ross, Graham, illus. 2017. (DATA Set Ser.: 7). (ENG.). 128p. (J). (gr. k-4). 17.99 *(978-1-4814-9192-1(X))*; pap. 5.99 *(978-1-4814-9191-4(1))* Little Simon. (Little Simon).

Hosie, Donna. The 48. 2018. 360p. (YA). (gr. 9). 17.99 *(978-0-8234-3856-3(2))* Holiday Hse., Inc.

Howard, Abby. Dinosaur Empire! (Earth Before Us #1): Journey Through the Mesozoic Era. 2017. (Earth Before Us Ser.). (ENG., Illus.). 128p. (J). (gr. 3-7). 15.99 *(978-1-4197-2306-3(5)*, 1144901, Amulet Bks.) Abrams, Inc.

—Mammal Takeover! (Earth Before Us #3) Journey Through the Cenozoic Era. 2019. (Earth Before Us Ser.). (ENG., Illus.). 128p. (J). (gr. 3-7). 15.99 *(978-1-4197-3624-7(8)*, 1145101, Amulet Bks.) Abrams, Inc.

—Ocean Renegades! (Earth Before Us #2) Journey Through the Paleozoic Era. 2018. (Earth Before Us Ser.). (ENG., Illus.). 128p. (J). (gr. 3-7). 15.99 *(978-1-4197-3136-5(X)*, 1145001, Amulet Bks.) Abrams, Inc.

Howard, Martin. Blast to the Past, 6. Janes, Andy, illus. 2017. (Shaun the Sheep: Tales from Mossy Bottom Farm Ser.). (ENG.). 112p. (J). (gr. 1-3). 17.44 *(978-1-5364-1044-0(6))* Candlewick Pr.

Hubbell, Mary A. The Miracle of Annie's Ring. 2010. 138p. pap. 11.50 *(978-1-60911-530-2(9)*, Eloquent Bks.) Strategic Book Publishing & Rights Agency (SBPRA).

Hulme-Cross, Benjamin. The Egyptian Warrior. 2016. (Warrior Heroes Ser.). (ENG., Illus.). 160p. (J). (gr. 5-9). *(978-0-7787-2864-1(1))* Crabtree Publishing Co.

—The Gladiator's Victory. Rinaldi, Angelo, illus. 2015. (Warrior Heroes Ser.). (ENG.). 160p. (J). (gr. 6-6). *(978-0-7787-1764-5(X))* Crabtree Publishing Co.

—The Knight's Enemies. Rinaldi, Angelo, illus. 2015. (Warrior Heroes Ser.). (ENG.). 160p. (J). (gr. 6-6). *(978-0-7787-1765-2(8))* Crabtree Publishing Co.

—The Samurai's Assassin. Rinaldi, Angelo, illus. 2015. (Warrior Heroes Ser.). (ENG.). 160p. (J). (gr. 6-6). *(978-0-7787-1766-9(6))* Crabtree Publishing Co.

—The Spartan's March. 2016. (Warrior Heroes Ser.). (ENG., Illus.). 160p. (J). (gr. 5-9). *(978-0-7787-2865-8(X))* Crabtree Publishing Co.

—The Viking's Revenge. Rinaldi, Angelo, illus. 2015. (Warrior Heroes Ser.). (ENG.). 160p. (J). (gr. 6-6). *(978-0-7787-1767-6(4))* Crabtree Publishing Co.

Hurmence, Belinda. A Girl Called Boy. 2006. (ENG.). 176p. (J). (gr. 5-7). pap. 12.95 *(978-0-618-68925-5(7),* 100474, Clarion Bks.) HarperCollins Pubs.

Hurst, Melissa E. The Edge of Forever. 2015. (ENG.). 272p. (J). (gr. 6-6). pap. 14.99 *(978-1-63220-424-0(X),* Sky Pony Pr.) Skyhorse Publishing Co., Inc.

—On Through the Never. 2017. (ENG.). 272p. (J). (gr. 6-6). pap. 14.99 *(978-1-5107-0761-0(1),* Sky Pony Pr.) Skyhorse Publishing Co., Inc.

Jakobsen, Lars. The Mysterious Manuscript. Jakobsen, Lars, illus. 2012. (Mortensen's Escapades Ser.: 1). (Illus.). 48p. (gr. 6-12). pap. 6.95 *(978-0-8225-9409-3(9),* Graphic Universe™) Lerner Publishing Group.

—The Santa Fe Jail. Jakobsen, Lars, illus. 2012. (Mortensen's Escapades Ser.: 2). (Illus.). 48p. (gr. 6-12). pap. 6.95 *(978-0-8225-9421-5(8),* Graphic Universe™) Lerner Publishing Group.

James, Lauren. The Next Together. 2017. (ENG., Illus.). 368p. (J). (gr. 8-8). 17.99 *(978-1-5107-1021-4(3),* Sky Pony Pr.) Skyhorse Publishing Co., Inc.

Jane, Yolen. The Devil's Arithmetic. 2014. (ENG.). 176p. (J). 11.24 *(978-1-63245-218-4(9))* Lectorum Pubns., Inc.

Jarman, Julia. The Magic Scooter. 2015. (Race Further with Reading Ser.). (ENG., Illus.). 48p. (J). (gr. 3-3). *(978-0-7787-2086-7(1))* Crabtree Publishing Co.

—The Time-Travelling Cat & the Aztec Sacrifice. 2018. (Time-Travelling Cat Ser.: 4). (ENG., Illus.). 160p. (J). (gr. 4-6). pap. 11.99 *(978-1-78344-688-9(9))* Andersen Pr. GBR. Dist: Independent Pubs. Group.

—The Time-Travelling Cat & the Egyptian Goddess. 2018. (Time-Travelling Cat Ser.). (ENG.). 128p. (J). (gr. 4-6). pap. 9.99 *(978-1-78344-573-8(4))* Andersen Pr. GBR. Dist: Independent Pubs. Group.

—Time-Travelling Cat & the Great Victorian Stink. 2011. (Time-Travelling Cat Ser.: 6). (ENG.). 160p. (J). (gr. 4-7). pap. 12.99 *(978-1-84939-019-4(3))* Andersen Pr. GBR. Dist: Independent Pubs. Group.

—The Time-Travelling Cat & the Great Victorian Stink. 2018. (Time-Travelling Cat Ser.). (ENG.). 160p. (J). (gr. 4-6). pap. 9.99 *(978-1-78344-618-6(8))* Andersen Pr. GBR. Dist: Independent Pubs. Group.

—The Time-Travelling Cat & the Roman Eagle. (ENG., Illus.). (J). 128p. 16.95 *(978-0-86264-861-9(0));* 2018. (Time-Travelling Cat Ser.: 3). 160p. (gr. 4-6). 11.99 *(978-1-78344-619-3(6))* Andersen Pr. GBR. Dist: Trafalgar Square Publishing, Independent Pubs. Group.

—The Time-Travelling Cat & the Tudor Treasure. 2018. (Time-Travelling Cat Ser.). (ENG.). 144p. (J). (gr. 4-6). pap. 9.99 *(978-1-78344-574-5(2))* Andersen Pr. GBR. Dist: Independent Pubs. Group.

—The Time-Travelling Cat & the Viking Terror. 2018. (Time-Travelling Cat Ser.: 5). (ENG., Illus.). 176p. (J). (gr. 4-6). pap. 12.99 *(978-1-78344-625-4(0))* Andersen Pr. GBR. Dist: Independent Pubs. Group.

Jeb. Destinations in Time. 2008. 101p. pap. 19.95 *(978-1-60672-653-2(6))* America Star Bks.

Johnson, Cara. Looking Forward Back: The Dream Travelers Book Three. 2008. 162p. (J). per. 9.99 *(978-0-9768870-3-4(7))* Whirling Dirvish Publishing.

Johnson, Charles & Johnson, Elisheba. The Adventures of Emery Jones, Boy Science Wonder: Bending Time. Johnson, Charles, illus. 2013. (Illus.). 110p. pap. 9.99 *(978-1-62015-181-5(2),* Booktrope Editions) Booktrope.

Jones, Cath. The Magic Helmet. Gray, Dean, illus. 2021. (Early Bird Readers — Gold (Early Bird Stories (tm)) Ser.). (ENG.). 32p. (J). (gr. k-3). 30.65 *(978-1-5415-9009-0(0),* 2cb67c0e-c1b9-458b-ab34-b7f29347e3a4, Lerner Pubns.) Lerner Publishing Group.

Jones, Chris. Cameron Jack & the Ghosts of World War 2. 2010. 120p. pap. 12.49 *(978-1-4520-2839-2(7))* AuthorHouse.

Jones, Diana Wynne. A Tale of Time City. 2012. (ENG.). 384p. (YA). (gr. 7-18). 10.99 *(978-0-14-242015-7(8),* Firebird) Penguin Young Readers Group.

The Journal: Dear Future II: Individual Title Six-Packs. (Action Packs Ser.). 104p. (gr. 3-5). 44.00 *(978-0-7635-8417-7(7))* Rigby Education.

Kassirer, Sue. Thar She Blows! Whaling in The 1860s. Fridell, Pat, illus. 2007. 32p. (J). 15.00 *(978-1-4223-6721-6(5))* DIANE Publishing Co.

Kehret, Peg. The Flood Disaster. 2008. (ENG.). 160p. (J). (gr. 3-7). pap. 8.99 *(978-1-4169-9109-0(3),* Simon & Schuster/Paula Wiseman Bks.) Simon & Schuster/Paula Wiseman Bks.

Kennedy Center, The. Unleashed: The Lives of White House Pets. Hoyt, Ard, illus. 2011. (ENG.). 112p. (J). (gr. 2-5). pap. 5.99 *(978-1-4169-4862-9(7),* Simon & Schuster Bks. For Young Readers) Simon & Schuster Bks. For Young Readers.

Kessler, Jackie Morse. Loss. 2012. (Riders of the Apocalypse Ser.: 3). (ENG.). 272p. (YA). (gr. 7-12). pap. 8.99 *(978-0-547-71215-4(4),* 1480762, Clarion Bks.) HarperCollins Pubs.

—Loss. 2012. (Riders of the Apocalypse Ser.: 3). lib. bdg. 19.65 *(978-0-606-24742-9(4))* Turtleback.

Kessler, Liz. A Year Without Autumn. 2012. (ENG.). 304p. (J). (gr. 4-7). pap. 9.99 *(978-0-7636-6060-4(4))* Candlewick Pr.

Kientz, Chris & Hockensmith, Steve. It's Treason, by George! Nielsen, Lee, illus. 2017. (Secret Smithsonian Adventures Ser.: 3). 64p. (gr. 3-7). pap. 10.95 *(978-1-58834-586-8(6),* Smithsonian Bks.) Smithsonian Institution Scholarly Pr.

Kimmel, Eric A. Escape from Egypt. Stevanovic, Ivica, illus. 2015. (Scarlett & Sam Ser.). (ENG.). 168p. (J). (gr. 1-3). E-Book 23.99 *(978-1-4677-6207-6(5),* Kar-Ben Publishing) Lerner Publishing Group.

—Search for the Shamir. Stevanovic, Ivica, illus. 2018. (Scarlett & Sam Ser.). (ENG.). 152p. (J). (gr. 1-3). pap. 6.99 *(978-1-5124-2938-1(4),* fa05c70d-97fc-4c41-af59-93be9cd9769f, Kar-Ben Publishing) Lerner Publishing Group.

Klass, David. Timelock: The Caretaker Trilogy: Book 3. 2010. (Caretaker Trilogy Ser.: 3). (ENG.). 272p. (YA). (gr. 9-12). pap. 15.99 *(978-0-312-60863-7(2),* 900065165) Square Fish.

Kramer, Alan & Kramer, Candice. The Star-Spangled Banner Story. 2005. (J). pap. *(978-1-4108-4203-9(7))* Benchmark Education Co.

Kriyananda, Swami. The Time Tunnel: A Tale for All Ages & for the Child in You. 2013. (ENG., Illus.). 180p. (J). (gr. 3-7). 14.95 *(978-1-56589-270-5(4))* Crystal Clarity Pubs.

Laperla, Artur. Super Potato's Mega Time-Travel Adventure: Book 3. Laperla, Artur, illus. 2019. (Super Potato Ser.). (ENG., Illus.). 56p. (J). (gr. 2-5). 27.99 *(978-1-5124-4023-2(X),* 6c817cd3-67aa-4b6b-8347-1abf104ca1ef); pap. 9.99 *(978-1-5415-7287-4(4),* 70dcd150-ec2c-44bd-967d-f4a30b62574d) Lerner Publishing Group. (Graphic Universe™).

Larkin, Angela & Haverlock, Catina. Before. 2018. (ENG.). 256p. (YA). pap. 17.99 *(978-1-4621-2205-9(1),* Sweetwater Bks.) Cedar Fort, Inc./CFI Distribution.

Larsen, Angela Sage. Keeping Secrets, Bk. 2. 2012. (Fifties Chix Ser.: 2). (ENG.). 220p. (YA). pap. 9.95 *(978-1-60746-367-2(9),* Premiere) FastPrncil, Inc.

—Third Time's a Charm, Bk. 3. 2013. (Fifties Chix Ser.: 3). (ENG.). 200p. (YA). pap. 9.95 *(978-1-60746-155-5(2),* Premiere) FastPrncil, Inc.

—Till the End of Time. 2013. (Fifties Chix Ser.: 5). (ENG.). 200p. (YA). pap. 9.95 *(978-1-60746-468-6(3),* Premiere) FastPrncil, Inc.

Lasky, Kathryn. Tangled in Time: the Portal. 2019. (ENG.). (J). (gr. 3-7). 400p. pap. 6.99 *(978-0-06-269326-6(3));* (Illus.). 384p. 16.99 *(978-0-06-269325-9(5))* HarperCollins Pubs. (HarperCollins).

Leighton-Porter, Wendy. The Shadow of Camelot. 2013. 262p. pap. *(978-1-909411-06-7(X))* Mauve Square Publishing.

Leitch Smith, Greg. Borrowed Time. 2015. (ENG., Illus.). 192p. (J). (gr. 5-7). 16.99 *(978-0-544-23711-7(0),* 1564706, Clarion Bks.) HarperCollins Pubs.

—Chronal Engine. Henry, Blake, illus. 2013. (ENG.). 192p. (J). (gr. 5-7). pap. 6.99 *(978-0-544-02277-5(7),* 1528498, Clarion Bks.) HarperCollins Pubs.

Lem, Stanislaw. The Seventh Voyage: a Graphic Novel. Kandel, Michael, tr. Muth, Jon J., illus. 2019.Tr. of Star Diaries. (ENG.). 80p. (YA). (gr. 3-7). 19.99 *(978-0-545-00462-6(4),* Graphix) Scholastic, Inc.

L'Engle, Madeleine. An Acceptable Time. 2007. (Wrinkle in Time Quintet Ser.: 5). (ENG.). 384p. (J). (gr. 5-9). per. 7.99 *(978-0-312-36858-6(5),* 900042675) Square Fish.

—Many Waters. 2007. (Wrinkle in Time Quintet Ser.: 3). (ENG.). 368p. (J). (gr. 5-9). per. 7.99 *(978-0-312-36857-9(7),* 900042674) Square Fish.

Limbaugh, Rush. Rush Revere & the Brave Pilgrims: Time-Travel Adventures with Exceptional Americans. 2013. (Rush Revere Ser.: 1). (ENG., Illus.). 224p. 21.00 *(978-1-4767-5586-1(8),* Threshold Editions) Threshold Editions.

—Rush Revere & the First Patriots: Time-Travel Adventures with Exceptional Americans. 2014. (Rush Revere Ser.: 2). (ENG., Illus.). 256p. 21.00 *(978-1-4767-5588-5(4),* Threshold Editions) Threshold Editions.

Limbaugh, Rush & Adams Limbaugh, Kathryn. Rush Revere & the American Revolution: Time-Travel Adventures with Exceptional Americans. 2014. (Rush Revere Ser.: 3). (ENG.). 256p. 21.00 *(978-1-4767-8987-3(8),* Threshold Editions) Threshold Editions.

—Rush Revere & the Presidency. 2016. (Rush Revere Ser.: 5). (ENG., Illus.). 272p. (gr. 4-7). 21.00 *(978-1-5011-5689-2(6),* Threshold Editions) Threshold Editions.

Liparulo, Robert. Gatekeepers, 1 vol. 2009. (Dreamhouse Kings Ser.: 3). (ENG.). 320p. (YA). pap. 14.99 *(978-1-59554-729-3(0))* Nelson, Thomas Inc.

—Watcher in the Woods, 1 vol. 2009. (Dreamhouse Kings Ser.: 2). (ENG.). 304p. (YA). pap. 14.99 *(978-1-59554-728-6(2))* Nelson, Thomas Inc.

—Whirlwind, 1 vol. 2010. (Dreamhouse Kings Ser.: 5). (ENG.). 320p. (YA). pap. 14.99 *(978-1-59554-892-4(0))* Nelson, Thomas Inc.

Litrel, Suzanne M. Jackie Tempo & the Emperor's Seal. 2007. 172p. (YA). per. 13.95 *(978-0-595-46822-5(5))* iUniverse, Inc.

Little, Kimberley Griffiths. The Last Snake Runner. 2006. 201p. (YA). (gr. 7-10). reprint ed. 16.00 *(978-1-4223-5838-2(0))* DIANE Publishing Co.

Locke, Katherine. The Girl with the Red Balloon. 2017. (Balloonmakers Ser.: 1). (ENG.). 288p. (YA). (gr. 8-12). pap. 9.99 *(978-0-8075-2937-9(0),* 807529370) Whitman, Albert & Co.

Lopez, David Mark. Maddie's Magic Markers: Ride Like an Indian. 2006. (J). (gr. 3-7). *(978-0-9744097-1-9(5))* Lopez, David.

—Run Like a Fugitive. 2006. (J). (gr. 4-8). *(978-0-9744097-2-6(3))* Lopez, David.

—Walk Like an Egyptian. 2006. (J). (gr. 3-7). *(978-0-9744097-0-2(7))* Lopez, David.

Lovett, Vienna. Mission from God. 2013. 256p. *(978-1-77069-833-8(7))* Word Alive Pr.

Lowell, Susan. The Great Grand Canyon Time Train. Shroades, John / W., illus. 2011. 32p. (J). 15.95 *(978-1-933855-63-9(0))* Rio Nuevo Pubs.

MacCullough, Carolyn. Once a Witch. 2010. (ENG.). 320p. (YA). (gr. 7). pap. 17.99 *(978-0-547-41730-1(6),* 1430229, Clarion Bks.) HarperCollins Pubs.

—Once a Witch. 2009. (ENG.). 304p. (YA). (gr. 7-12). 24.94 *(978-0-547-22399-5(4))* Houghton Mifflin Harcourt Publishing Co.

MacHale, D. J. The Never War. 2003. (Pendragon Ser.: 3). (ENG., Illus.). 352p. (J). (gr. 5-9). pap. 10.99 *(978-0-7434-3733-2(0),* Aladdin) Simon & Schuster Children's Publishing.

Mackay, Janis. The Reluctant Time Traveller, 30 vols. 2014. (Time Traveller Ser.). 240p. (J). 9.95 *(978-1-78250-111-4(8),* Kelpies) Floris Bks. GBR. Dist: Consortium Bk. Sales & Distribution.

—The Unlikely Time Traveller, 30 vols. 2016. (Time Traveller Ser.). 240p. (J). 9.95 *(978-1-78250-266-1(1),* Kelpies) Floris Bks. GBR. Dist: Consortium Bk. Sales & Distribution.

Madonia, Kristen-Paige. Invisible Fault Lines. 2016. (ENG.). 320p. (YA). (gr. 7). 17.99 *(978-1-4814-3071-5(8),* Simon & Schuster Bks. For Young Readers) Simon & Schuster Bks. For Young Readers.

Maes, Nicholas. Laughing Wolf. 2009. (Felix Taylor Adventure Ser.: 1). (ENG.). 248p. (J). (gr. 7-18). pap. 10.99 *(978-1-55488-385-1(7))* Dundurn Pr. CAN. Dist: Publishers Group West (PGW).

Magnason, Andri Sner. The Casket of Time. Arnadottir, Bjorg & Cauthery, Andrew, trs. 2019. (ENG.). 240p. (YA). (gr. 5). 17.99 *(978-1-63206-205-5(4))* Restless Bks.

Mahy, Margaret. Maddigan's Fantasia. 2012. (ENG.). 512p. (J). (gr. 5-9). pap. 22.99 *(978-1-4424-6053-9(9),* McElderry, Margaret K. Bks.) McElderry, Margaret K. Bks.

Maihack, Mike. Secret of the Time Tablets: a Graphic Novel (Cleopatra in Space #3) 2016. (Cleopatra in Space Ser.: 3). (ENG., Illus.). 192p. (J). (gr. 3-7). pap. 14.99 *(978-0-545-83867-2(3),* Graphix) Scholastic, Inc.

Malcolm, Jahnna N. Pirate's Revenge. Comport, Sally Wern, illus. 2003. 77p. (J). *(978-1-931020-09-1(4))* HOP, LLC.

Malone, Marianne. The Pirate's Coin: a Sixty-Eight Rooms Adventure. Call, Greg, illus. 2014. (Sixty-Eight Rooms Adventures Ser.: 3). (ENG.). 240p. (J). (gr. 3-7). 7.99 *(978-0-307-97720-5(X),* Yearling) Random Hse. Children's Bks.

—The Secret of the Key: a Sixty-Eight Rooms Adventure. 2015. (Sixty-Eight Rooms Adventures Ser.: 4). (ENG., Illus.). 256p. (J). (gr. 3-7). 8.99 *(978-0-307-97724-3(2),* Yearling) Random Hse. Children's Bks.

—Stealing Magic. 2. Call, Greg, illus. 2013. (Sixty-Eight Rooms Adventures Ser.). (ENG.). 272p. (J). (gr. 4-6). lib. bdg. 21.19 *(978-0-375-96819-8(9),* Yearling) Random Hse. Children's Bks.

—Stealing Magic: a Sixty-Eight Rooms Adventure. Call, Greg, illus. 2013. (Sixty-Eight Rooms Adventures Ser.: 2). (ENG.). 272p. (J). (gr. 3-7). pap. 9.99 *(978-0-375-86790-3(2),* Yearling) Random Hse. Children's Bks.

Mangum, Lisa. The Hourglass Door. (Hourglass Door Trilogy: Bk. 1). (YA). 2010. 408p. mass mkt. 7.99 *(978-1-60641-679-2(0))* 2009. 432p. (gr. 9-18). 18.95 *(978-1-60641-093-6(8))* Shadow Mountain Publishing. (Shadow Mountain).

Mansbach, Adam & Zweibel, Alan. Benjamin Franklin: You've Got Mail. 2017. (Benjamin Franklin Ser.: 2). (ENG.). 224p. (J). (gr. 5-9). 12.99 *(978-1-4847-1305-1(2))* Hyperion Bks. for Children.

Masciola, Carol. The Yearbook. 2015. (ENG.). 224p. (YA). 17.99 *(978-1-4405-8897-6(X),* Simon Pulse) Simon Pulse.

Mass, Wendy. Escape from Egypt: a Branches Book (Time Jumpers #2) Vidal, Oriol, illus. 2018. (Time Jumpers Ser.: 2). (ENG.). 96p. (J). (gr. 1-3). pap. 5.99 *(978-1-338-21739-1(9))* Scholastic, Inc.

—Fast-Forward to the Future!: a Branches Book (Time Jumpers #3). Vol. 3. Vidal, Oriol, illus. 2019. (Time Jumpers Ser.: 3). (ENG.). 96p. (J). (gr. 1-3). pap. 5.99 *(978-1-338-21742-1(9))* Scholastic, Inc.

—The Last Present: a Wish Novel. 2015. (ENG.). 256p. (J). (gr. 3-7). pap. 7.99 *(978-0-545-31017-8(2))* Scholastic, Inc.

—Stealing the Sword: a Branches Book (Time Jumpers #1) Vidal, Oriol, illus. 2018. (Time Jumpers Ser.: 1). (ENG.). 96p. (J). (gr. 1-3). pap. 5.99 *(978-1-338-21736-0(4))* Scholastic, Inc.

Mawhinney, Art, illus. Dora & Diego Help the Dinosaur. 2011. (Dora & Diego Ser.). (ENG.). 24p. (J). pap. 3.99 *(978-1-4424-1400-6(6),* Simon Spotlight/Nickelodeon) Simon Spotlight/Nickelodeon.

Maxwell, Lisa. The Devil's Thief. 2018. (Last Magician Ser.: 2). (ENG., Illus.). 704p. (YA). (gr. 9). 18.99 *(978-1-4814-9445-8(7),* Simon Pulse) Simon Pulse.

—The Last Magician. (Last Magician Ser.: 1). (ENG., Illus.). (YA). (gr. 9). 2018. 528p. pap. 13.99 *(978-1-4814-3208-5(7))* 2017. 512p. 21.99 *(978-1-4814-3207-8(9))* Simon Pulse. (Simon Pulse).

McBrier, Page. Abracadabra Tut. 2014. (ENG.). (J). pap. 9.99 *(978-0-9960794-0-2(8))* Palm Canyon Pr.

McCardle, Meredith. Blackout, 0 vols. 2015. (Annum Guard Ser.: 2). (ENG.). 351p. (YA). (gr. 7-12). pap. 9.99 *(978-1-4778-2711-6(0),* 9781477827116, Skyscape) Amazon Publishing.

—The Eighth Guardian, 0 vols. 2014. (Annum Guard Ser.: 1). (ENG.). 384p. (YA). (gr. 7-12). pap. 9.99 *(978-1-4778-4766-4(9),* 9781477847664, Skyscape) Amazon Publishing.

McCranie, Stephen. Mal & Chad: the Biggest, Bestest Time Ever! McCranie, Stephen, illus. 2011. (Mal & Chad Ser.: 1). (Illus.). 224p. (J). (gr. 3-7). 12.99 *(978-0-399-25221-1(5),* Philomel Bks.) Penguin Young Readers Group.

McCusker, Paul. Strange Journey Back. 2006. (Adventures in Odyssey Bks.: No. 1). (ENG., Illus.). 304p. (J). (gr. 3-7). per. 16.99 *(978-1-58997-325-1(9),* 2673259) Focus on the Family Publishing.

McDonnell, Kathleen. The Shining World, 1 vol. 2003. (Notherland Journeys Ser.: 2). (ENG.). 236p. (J). (gr. 7-9). pap. 6.95 *(978-1-896764-79-5(7))* Second Story Pr. CAN. Dist: Orca Bk. Pubs. USA.

Mcgowan, Michael. Newton & the Time Machine. 2008. (ENG., Illus.). 216p. (J). pap. 11.99 *(978-0-00-639550-8(3),* Harper Trophy) HarperCollins Pubs.

McGrath, Robin. Livyers World. 2007. (ENG.). 150p. (J). (gr. 4-7). per. *(978-1-897174-15-9(2))* Breakwater Bks., Ltd.

McMann, Lisa. The Trap Door. 2015. (Infinity Ring Ser.: 3). lib. bdg. 17.20 *(978-0-606-37788-1(3))* Turtleback.

McMasters, Gretchen. Aesock's Travels & Los Viajes de Aesock: Lights, Camera, Edison! & Luz, Cámara, Edison. 2004. (Aesock's Travels & Los Viajes de Aesock Ser.: 1). (ENG & SPA., Illus.). 160p. (J). pap. 5.99 *(978-0-9713756-9-7(0))* Stargazer Publishing Co.

McMullen, Sean. Before the Storm. 2009. 262p. (Orig.). pap. *(978-1-879462-50-2(8))* Ford Street Publishing Pty, Limited.

McSkimming, Geoffrey. Phyllis Wong & the Waking of the Wizard. 2016. (Phyllis Wong Ser.). (ENG.). 400p. (J). (gr. 3-7). pap. 12.99 *(978-1-76011-338-4(7))* Allen & Unwin AUS. Dist: Independent Pubs. Group.

Meehl, Brian. Blowback '07: When the Only Way Forward Is Back. 2016. (Illus.). 346p. (J). pap. 12.95 *(978-1-63505-185-8(1))* Salem Author Services.

Messner, Kate. D-Day: Battle on the Beach (Ranger in Time #7) McMorris, Kelley, illus. 2018. (Ranger in Time Ser.: 7). (ENG.). 160p. (J). (gr. 2-5). pap. 6.99 *(978-1-338-13390-5(X),* Scholastic Pr.) Scholastic, Inc.

—Danger in Ancient Rome (Ranger in Time #2) McMorris, Kelley, illus. 2015. (Ranger in Time Ser.: 2). (ENG.). 160p. (J). (gr. 2-5). pap. 5.99 *(978-0-545-63917-0(4),* Scholastic Pr.) Scholastic, Inc.

—Disaster on the Titanic (Ranger in Time #9) McMorris, Kelley, illus. 2019. (Ranger in Time Ser.: 9). (ENG.). 144p. (J). (gr. 2-5). pap. 5.99 *(978-1-338-13398-1(5),* Scholastic Pr.) Scholastic, Inc.

—Escape from the Great Earthquake (Ranger in Time #6) McMorris, Kelley, illus. 2017. (Ranger in Time Ser.: 6). (ENG.). 160p. (J). (gr. 2-5). pap. 5.99 *(978-0-545-90983-9(X),* Scholastic Pr.) Scholastic, Inc.

—Escape from the Twin Towers (Ranger in Time #11) McMorris, Kelley, illus. 2020. (Ranger in Time Ser.: 11). (ENG.). 144p. (J). (gr. 2-5). pap. 5.99 *(978-1-338-53794-9(6),* Scholastic Pr.) Scholastic, Inc.

—Hurricane Katrina Rescue (Ranger in Time #8) McMorris, Kelley, illus. 2018. (Ranger in Time Ser.: 8). (ENG.). 160p. (J). (gr. 2-5). pap. 5.99 *(978-1-338-13395-0(0),* Scholastic Pr.) Scholastic, Inc.

—Journey Through Ash & Smoke (Ranger in Time #5) McMorris, Kelley, illus. 2017. (Ranger in Time Ser.: 5). (ENG.). 160p. (J). (gr. 2-5). pap. 5.99 *(978-0-545-90978-5(3),* Scholastic Pr.) Scholastic, Inc.

—Long Road to Freedom (Ranger in Time #3) McMorris, Kelley, illus. 2015. (Ranger in Time Ser.: 3). (ENG.). 160p. (J). (gr. 2-5). pap. 5.99 *(978-0-545-63920-0(4),* Scholastic Pr.) Scholastic, Inc.

—Night of Soldiers & Spies (Ranger in Time #10) (Library Edition) McMorris, Kelley, illus. 2019. (Ranger in Time Ser.: 10). (ENG.). 160p. (J). (gr. 2-5). lib. bdg. 17.99 *(978-1-338-13402-5(7),* Scholastic Pr.) Scholastic, Inc.

—Race to the South Pole (Ranger in Time #4) McMorris, Kelley, illus. 2016. (Ranger in Time Ser.: 4). (ENG.). 160p. (J). (gr. 2-5). pap. 5.99 *(978-0-545-63925-5(5),* Scholastic Pr.) Scholastic, Inc.

—Rescue on the Oregon Trail (Ranger in Time #1) McMorris, Kelley, illus. 2015. (Ranger in Time Ser.: 1). (ENG.). 144p. (J). (gr. 2-5). pap. 5.99 *(978-0-545-63914-9(X),* Scholastic Pr.) Scholastic, Inc.

Metz, Melinda. Raven's Point. 2005. pap. *(978-0-06-052373-2(5))* HarperCollins Canada, Ltd.

Meyer, William. Horace: Secret of Scarab Beetle. 2016. (Horace J. Edwards & the Time Keepers Ser.). (ENG., Illus.). 230p. (J). (gr. 4-6). pap. 9.99 *(978-1-58536-939-3(X),* 204089); 16.99 *(978-1-58536-938-6(1),* 204031) Sleeping Bear Pr.

—The Search for the Lost Prophecy. (Horace J. Edwards & the Time Keepers Ser.). (ENG.). 240p. (J). (gr. 3-6). 2018. pap. 9.99 *(978-1-58536-983-6(7),* 204332) 2017. (Illus.). 16.99 *(978-1-58536-982-9(9),* 204317) Sleeping Bear Pr.

Milway, Alex. Pigsticks & Harold Lost in Time! Milway, Alex, illus. 2017. (Pigsticks & Harold Ser.). (ENG., Illus.). 64p. (J). (gr. k-4). 12.99 *(978-0-7636-8186-9(5))* Candlewick Pr.

Mlynowski, Sarah. Gimme a Call. 2011. (ENG.). 320p. (YA). (gr. 7). pap. 9.99 *(978-0-385-73589-6(8),* Ember) Random Hse. Children's Bks.

Monir, Alexandra. Timekeeper. 2014. (Timeless Ser.). (ENG.). 304p. (YA). (gr. 7). pap. 9.99 *(978-0-385-73841-5(2),* Ember) Random Hse. Children's Bks.

Monson, Marianne. Escape from Egypt. 2010. (Illus.). 85p. (J). *(978-1-60641-670-9(7))* Deseret Bk. Co.

—Pioneer Puzzle. 2010. (Illus.). 84p. (J). *(978-1-60641-669-3(3))* Deseret Bk. Co.

Montgomery, R. A. House of Danger. 2005. (Choose Your Own Adventure Ser.). (Illus.). 108p. (gr. 4-8). pap. 5.50 *(978-0-7608-9694-5(1))* Sundance/Newbridge Educational Publishing.

—House of Danger. Sundaravej, Sittisan, illus. 2006. (ENG.). 144p. (J). (gr. 4-8). per. 7.99 *(978-1-933390-06-2(9),* CHCL06) Chooseco LLC.

—Island of Time. Louie, Wes & Cannella, Marco, illus. 2009. (ENG.). 144p. (J). (gr. 4-8). pap. 6.99 *(978-1-933390-28-4(X))* Chooseco LLC.

—The Trail of Lost Time. Semionov, Vladimir, illus. 2011. (ENG.). 144p. (J). (gr. 4-8). mass mkt. 7.99 *(978-1-937133-03-0(6))* Chooseco LLC.

Moonshower, Candie. The Legend of Zoey. 2007. (ENG.). 224p. (J). (gr. 3-7). 6.99 *(978-0-440-23924-6(9),* Yearling) Random Hse. Children's Bks.

Morrison, Michele. The Comet's Tale. 2007. (ENG.). 136p. pap. 16.95 *(978-1-84753-634-1(4))* Lulu Pr., Inc.

Moss, Helen. Time Dogs: Balto & the Race Against Time. Saburi, Misa, illus. 2020. (Time Dogs Ser.: 1). (ENG.). 160p. (J). pap. 9.99 *(978-1-250-25022-3(6),* 900191580) Square Fish.

—Time Dogs: Seaman & the Great Northern Adventure. Saburi, Misa, illus. 2020. (Time Dogs Ser.: 2). (ENG.). 160p. (J). pap. 20.99 *(978-1-250-25023-0(4),* 900191583) Square Fish.

Moss, Marissa. Bombs over London. 2014. (Mira's Diary Ser.). (ENG., Illus.). 190p. (J). (gr. 2-8). 12.99 *(978-1-939547-12-5(1),* 5ad055a5-1363-4f46-accf-d31871e40e1f) Creston Bks.

—California Dreaming. 2016. (Mira's Diary Ser.). (ENG., Illus.). 190p. (J). (gr. 2-8). 12.99 *(978-1-939547-22-4(9),* 81279f26-461a-4e86-982f-55d09a0047cd) Creston Bks.

Mould, Paul, ed. The Magnificent Six. 2007. (Illus.). 52p. pap. *(978-1-58690-048-9(X))* Mould, Paul Publishing.

Muir, Sabine. Meeting Wolfie: A Story about Mozart. 2006. 129p. pap. 19.95 *(978-1-4241-3968-2(6))* PublishAmerica, Inc.

Murdock, Catherine Gilbert. Da Vinci's Cat. 2021. (ENG., Illus.). 288p. (J). (gr. 3-7). 17.99 *(978-0-06-301525-8(0),* Greenwillow Bks.) HarperCollins Pubs.

T
U
V

Murrell, Belinda. The Locket of Dreams. 288p. (J). (gr. 4-7). 2015. pap. 12.99 *(978-0-85798-695-5(3))* 2nd ed. 2013. 17.99 *(978-0-85798-021-2(1))* Random Hse. Australia AUS. Dist: Independent Pubs. Group.

—The Lost Sapphire. 2016. 320p. (YA). (gr. 4-7). pap. 12.99 *(978-1-925324-11-2(7))* Random Hse. Australia AUS. Dist: Independent Pubs. Group.

Nagatsuki, Tappei. Re:ZERO -Starting Life in Another World-, Chapter 2: a Week at the Mansion, Vol. 5 (manga), Vol. 5. Bourque, Jeremiah, tr. 2018. (Re:ZERO -Starting Life in Another World-, Chapter 2: a Week at the Mansion Manga Ser.: 5). (ENG., Illus.). 194p. (gr. 8-17). pap. 13.00 *(978-1-9753-0179-8(X)*, 9781975301798) Yen Pr. LLC.

—Re:ZERO -Starting Life in Another World- Ex, Vol. 1 (light Novel) The Dream of the Lion King. 2017. (Re:ZERO Ex (light Novel) Ser.: 1). (ENG., Illus.). 224p. (YA). (gr. 8-17). pap. 14.00 *(978-0-316-41290-2(2)*, Yen Pr.) Yen Pr. LLC.

Narine, Vidya D. Kari. 2011. 66p. 24.99 *(978-1-4568-5348-8(1))*; pap. 15.99 *(978-1-4568-5347-1(3))* Xlibris Corp.

Nelson, Peter. Herbert's Wormhole. 1. Rao, Rohitash, illus. 2010. (Herbert's Wormhole Ser.: 1). (ENG.). 304p. (J). (gr. 3-7). pap. 6.99 *(978-0-06-168870-6(3)*, HarperCollins) HarperCollins Pubs.

—Herbert's Wormhole: the Rise & Fall of el Solo Libre. Rao, Rohitash, illus. 2014. (Herbert's Wormhole Ser.: 2). (ENG.). 336p. (J). (gr. 3-7). pap. 6.99 *(978-0-06-201219-7(3)*, HarperCollins) HarperCollins Pubs.

Nesbit, E. The House of Arden. 2006. 184p. (gr. 3-7). per. 14.95 *(978-1-59818-967-4(0))*; 26.95 *(978-1-59818-181-4(5))* Aegypan.

—The Story of the Amulet. 2010. (CHI.). 270p. (YA). pap. *(978-986-146-634-7(7))* Storm & Stress Publishing Co, Ltd.

—The Story of the Amulet. 2009. 176p. (gr. -1-7). pap. 4.95 *(978-1-60459-694-6(5))* Wilder Pubns., Corp.

Nesbo, Jo. Bubble in the Bathtub. Chace, Tara F., tr. Lowery, Mike, illus. 2011. (Doctor Proctor's Fart Powder Ser.). (ENG.). (J). (gr. 3-7). 448p. pap. 8.99 *(978-1-4169-7975-3(1))*; 432p. 17.99 *(978-1-4169-7974-6(3))* Simon & Schuster Children's Publishing. (Aladdin).

Nickel, Scott. Back to the Ice Age. Corts, Enrique, illus. 2008. (Graphic Sparks Ser.). (ENG.). 40p. (J). (gr. 2-5). pap. 5.95 *(978-1-4342-0500-1(2)*, 1278595, Stone Arch Bks.) Capstone.

—Blast to the Past. Harpster, Steve, illus. 2006. (Graphic Sparks Ser.). (ENG.). 40p. (J). (gr. 2-5). 5.95 *(978-1-59889-167-6(7)*, 86491, Stone Arch Bks.) Capstone.

—T. Rex vs Robo-Dog 3000. Corts, Enrique, illus. 2008. (Graphic Sparks Ser.). (ENG.). 40p. (J). (gr. 2-5). pap. 5.95 *(978-1-4342-0857-6(5)*, 95218, Stone Arch Bks.) Capstone.

Nielsen, Jennifer A. Behind Enemy Lines. 2016. (Infinity Ring Ser.: 6). lib. bdg. 17.20 *(978-0-606-38623-4(8))* Turtleback.

—Behind Enemy Lines (Infinity Ring, Book 6) 6th ed. 2016. (Infinity Ring Ser.: 6). (ENG.). 192p. (J). (gr. 3-7). pap. 6.99 *(978-0-545-90121-5(9)*, Scholastic Pr.) Scholastic, Inc.

Norris, Christine. The Ankh of Isis. 2017. (Library of Athena Ser.: bk.2). (J). pap. *(978-1-61271-332-8(7))* Zumaya Pubns. LLC.

—The Crown of Zeus. 2017. (Library of Athena Ser.: bk.1). 241p. (J). pap. *(978-1-61271-335-9(1))* Zumaya Pubns. LLC.

North, Ryan. Adventure Time, Vol. 3. 2013. (Adventure Time Graphic Novels Ser.: 3). lib. bdg. 26.95 *(978-0-606-35462-2(X))* Turtleback.

—Adventure Time Volume 2. 2013. (Adventure Time Graphic Novels Ser.: 2). lib. bdg. 26.95 *(978-0-606-35461-5(1))* Turtleback.

Norton, Andre. Key Out of Time. 2007. 140p. per. 11.95 *(978-1-60312-081-4(5))* Aegypan.

—The Time Traders. 2007. 236p. per. 12.95 *(978-1-4218-2734-6(4))*; 27.95 *(978-1-4218-2634-9(8))* 1st World Publishing, Inc. (1st World Library - Literary Society).

—The Time Traders. 2006. pap. *(978-1-4068-3561-8(7))* Echo Library.

Noyes, Deborah. Plague in the Mirror. 2013. (ENG.). 272p. (YA). (gr. 9). 16.99 *(978-0-7636-5980-6(0))* Candlewick Pr.

O'Brien, Johnny. Day of the Assassins: A Jack Christie Adventure. Hardcastle, Nick, illus. 2010. (Jack Christie Adventure Ser.: 1). (ENG.). 224p. (J). (gr. 4-7). pap. 6.99 *(978-0-7636-4995-1(3)*, Templar) Candlewick Pr.

—Day of the Assassins: A Jack Christie Adventure, 1. Hardcastle, Nick, illus. 2009. (Jack Christie Adventure Ser.: 1). (ENG.). 224p. (J). (gr. 4-7). 15.99 *(978-0-7636-4595-3(8)*, Templar) Candlewick Pr.

Oda, Matthew K. The Time MacHine: Mario's Box A Journey into Creativity. 2011. 36p. pap. 24.95 *(978-1-4626-3892-5(9))* America Star Bks.

O'Doherty, Carolyn. Rewind. (Rewind Ser.: 1). (ENG.). (YA). (gr. 7). 2019. 272p. pap. 8.99 *(978-1-68437-372-7(7))* 2018. 256p. 17.95 *(978-1-62979-814-1(2))* Astra Publishing Hse. (Astra Young Readers).

Osborne, Mary Pope. Abe Lincoln at Last! Murdocca, Sal, illus. 2013. (Magic Tree House (R) Merlin Mission Ser.: 19). 144p. (J). (gr. 2-5). 6.99 *(978-0-375-86797-2(X)*, Random Hse. Bks. for Young Readers) Random Hse. Children's Bks.

—Abe Lincoln at Last! 2013. (Magic Tree House Merlin Missions Ser.: 19). lib. bdg. 16.00 *(978-0-606-35563-6(4))* Turtleback.

—Barcos Vikingos Al Amanecer. Brovelli, Marcela, tr. from ENG. Murdocca, Sal, illus. 2007. (Casa del Arbol Ser.: 15). (SPA.). 73p. (J). per. 6.99 *(978-1-933032-21-4(9))* Lectorum Pubns., Inc.

—A Big Day for Baseball. Ford, A. G., illus. 2017. (Magic Tree House (R) Ser.: 29). (J). (gr. 1-4). 80p. 13.99 *(978-1-5247-1308-9(2))*; (ENG.). 96p. lib. bdg. 16.99 *(978-1-5247-1309-6(0))* Random Hse. Children's Bks. (Random Hse. Bks. for Young Readers).

—Blizzard of the Blue Moon. Murdocca, Sal, illus. 2007. (Magic Tree House (R) Merlin Mission Ser.: 8). 144p. (J). (gr. 2-5). 5.99 *(978-0-375-83038-9(3)*, Random Hse. Bks. for Young Readers) Random Hse. Children's Bks.

—Buffalo Before Breakfast. 2004. (Magic Tree House Ser.: No. 18). 72p. (J). (gr. k-3). pap. 17.00 incl. audio *(978-0-8072-0927-1(9)*, Listening Library) Random Hse. Audio Publishing Group.

—El Caballero Del Alba. 2004. (Casa del Arbol Ser.: 2). (SPA.). (J). pap. 6.99 *(978-1-930332-50-8(5))* Lectorum Pubns., Inc.

—Carnival at Candlelight, Vol. 5. Murdocca, Sal, illus. 2006. (Magic Tree House (R) Merlin Mission Ser.: 5). 144p. (J). (gr. 2-5). 6.99 *(978-0-375-83034-1(0)*, Random Hse. Bks. for Young Readers) Random Hse. Children's Bks.

—Un Castillo Embrujado en la Noche de Halloween. 2015. (Casa De árbol Ser.: 30). (SPA., Illus.). 144p. (J). (gr. 2-4). pap. 6.99 *(978-1-63245-533-8(1))* Lectorum Pubns., Inc.

—Christmas in Camelot. Murdocca, Sal, illus. 2009. (Magic Tree House (R) Merlin Mission Ser.: 1). 144p. (J). (gr. 2-5). 6.99 *(978-0-375-85812-3(1)*, Random Hse. Bks. for Young Readers) Random Hse. Children's Bks.

—Christmas in Camelot. 2009. (Magic Tree House Merlin Missions Ser.: 1). lib. bdg. 16.00 *(978-0-606-06386-9(2))* Turtleback.

—Civil War on Sunday. unabr. ed. 2004. (Magic Tree House Ser.: No. 21). 76p. (J). (gr. k-3). pap. 17.00 incl. audio *(978-0-8072-0930-1(9)*, S FTR 253 SP, Listening Library) Random Hse. Audio Publishing Group.

—A Crazy Day with Cobras. Murdocca, Sal, illus. 2012. (Magic Tree House (R) Merlin Mission Ser.: 17). 144p. (J). (gr. 2-5). 5.99 *(978-0-375-86795-8(3)*, Random Hse. Bks. for Young Readers) Random Hse. Children's Bks.

—A Crazy Day with Cobras. 2012. (Magic Tree House Merlin Missions Ser.: 17). lib. bdg. 16.00 *(978-0-606-26997-1(5))* Turtleback.

—Dark Day in the Deep Sea. Murdocca, Sal, illus. 2009. (Magic Tree House (R) Merlin Mission Ser.: 11). 144p. (J). (gr. 2-5). 6.99 *(978-0-375-83732-6(9)*, Random Hse. Bks. for Young Readers) Random Hse. Children's Bks.

—Dark Day in the Deep Sea. 2009. (Magic Tree House Merlin Missions Ser.: 11). lib. bdg. 16.00 *(978-0-606-01778-7(X))* Turtleback.

—Day of the Dragon King. unabr. ed. 2004. (Magic Tree House Ser.: No. 14). 68p. (J). (gr. k-3). pap. 17.00 incl. audio *(978-0-8072-0783-3(7)*, S FTR 242 SP, Listening Library) Random Hse. Audio Publishing Group.

—Dinosaurios Al Atardecer. 2004. (Casa del Arbol Ser.: 1). (SPA.). (J). pap. 6.99 *(978-1-930332-49-2(1))* Lectorum Pubns., Inc.

—Dinosaurios al Atardecer. 2003. (Magic Tree House Ser.: 1). (SPA.). (gr. 3-6). lib. bdg. 16.00 *(978-0-613-64486-0(7))* Turtleback.

—Dinosaurs Before Dark. unabr. ed. 2004. (Magic Tree House Ser.: No. 1). 68p. (J). (gr. k-5). pap. 17.00 incl. audio *(978-0-8072-0330-9(0)*, FTR208SP, Listening Library) Random Hse. Audio Publishing Group.

—Dogs in the Dead of Night, Bk. 18. Murdocca, Sal, illus. 2013. (Magic Tree House (R) Merlin Mission Ser.: 18). 144p. (J). (gr. 2-5). 6.99 *(978-0-375-86796-5(1)*, Random Hse. Bks. for Young Readers) Random Hse. Children's Bks.

—Dogs in the Dead of Night. 2013. (Magic Tree House Merlin Missions Ser.: 18). lib. bdg. 16.00 *(978-0-606-31939-3(5))* Turtleback.

—Dragon of the Red Dawn. Murdocca, Sal, illus. 2008. (Magic Tree House (R) Merlin Mission Ser.: 9). 144p. (J). (gr. 2-5). 6.99 *(978-0-375-83728-9(0)*, Random Hse. Bks. for Young Readers) Random Hse. Children's Bks.

—Earthquake in the Early Morning. unabr. ed. 2004. (Magic Tree House Ser.: No. 24). 71p. (J). (gr. k-3). pap. 17.00 incl. audio *(978-0-8072-0933-2(3)*, S FTR 256 SP, Listening Library) Random Hse. Audio Publishing Group.

—A Ghost Tale for Christmas Time. Murdocca, Sal, illus. 2012. (Magic Tree House (R) Merlin Mission Ser.: 16). 144p. (J). (gr. 2-5). pap. 6.99 *(978-0-375-85653-2(6)*, Random Hse. Bks. for Young Readers) Random Hse. Children's Bks.

—A Ghost Tale for Christmas Time. 2012. (Magic Tree House Merlin Missions Ser.: 16). lib. bdg. 16.00 *(978-0-606-26808-0(1))* Turtleback.

—Ghost Town at Sundown. unabr. ed. 2004. (Magic Tree House Ser.: No. 10). 73p. (J). (gr. k-3). pap. 17.00 incl. audio *(978-0-8072-0535-8(4)*, Listening Library) Random Hse. Audio Publishing Group.

—A Good Night for Ghosts. 2010. (Magic Tree House Merlin Missions Ser.: No. 14). (Illus.). 157p. (J). pap. *(978-4-8401-3411-8(1))* Fukuinkan Shoten.

—A Good Night for Ghosts. Murdocca, Sal, illus. 2011. (Magic Tree House (R) Merlin Mission Ser.: 14). 144p. (J). (gr. 2-5). 5.99 *(978-0-375-85649-5(8)*, Random Hse. Bks. for Young Readers) Random Hse. Children's Bks.

—Haunted Castle on Hallows Eve. Murdocca, Sal, illus. 2010. (Magic Tree House (R) Merlin Mission Ser.: 2). 144p. (J). (gr. 2-5). pap. 5.99 *(978-0-375-86090-4(8)*, Random Hse. Bks. for Young Readers) Random Hse. Children's Bks.

—Haunted Castle on Hallows Eve. 2010. (Magic Tree House Merlin Missions Ser.: 2). lib. bdg. 16.00 *(978-0-606-13992-2(3))* Turtleback.

—High Tide in Hawaii. Murdocca, Sal, illus. 2003. (Magic Tree House (R) Ser.: 28). 96p. (J). (gr. 1-4). pap. 6.99 *(978-0-375-80616-2(4)*, Random Hse. Bks. for Young Readers) Random Hse. Children's Bks.

—High Tide in Hawaii. 2003. (Magic Tree House Ser.: 28). (gr. k-3). lib. bdg. 16.00 *(978-0-613-62386-5(X))* Turtleback.

—High Time for Heroes. Murdocca, Sal, illus. 2016. (Magic Tree House (R) Merlin Mission Ser.: 23). 144p. (J). (gr. 2-5). 6.99 *(978-0-307-98052-6(9)*, Random Hse. Bks. for Young Readers) Random Hse. Children's Bks.

—La Hora de Los Juegos Olimpicos. Brovelli, Marcela, tr. Murdocca, Sal, illus. 2007. (Casa del Arbol Ser.: 16).Tr. of Hour of the Olympics Games. (ENG & SPA.). 68p. (J). per. 6.99 *(978-1-933032-22-1(7))* Lectorum Pubns., Inc.

—Hour of the Olympics. unabr. ed. 2004. (Magic Tree House Ser.: No. 16). 70p. (J). (gr. k-3). pap. 17.00 incl. audio *(978-0-8072-0785-7(3)*, LFTR 244 SP, Listening Library) Random Hse. Audio Publishing Group.

—Hurricane Heroes in Texas. Ford, A. G., illus. 2018. (Magic Tree House (R) Ser.: 30). 112p. (J). (gr. 1-4). 13.99 *(978-1-5247-1312-6(0)*, Random Hse. Bks. for Young Readers) Random Hse. Children's Bks.

—Hurry up, Houdini! 2015. (Magic Tree House Merlin Missions Ser.: 22). lib. bdg. 16.00 *(978-0-606-37718-8(2))* Turtleback.

—The Knight at Dawn. unabr. ed. 2004. (Magic Tree House Ser.: No. 2). 66p. (J). (gr. k-3). pap. 17.00 incl. audio *(978-0-8072-0331-6(9)*, Listening Library) Random Hse. Audio Publishing Group.

—Leprechaun in Late Winter. Murdocca, Sal, illus. 2012. (Magic Tree House (R) Merlin Mission Ser.: 15). 144p. (J). (gr. 2-5). 6.99 *(978-0-375-85651-8(X)*, Random Hse. Bks. for Young Readers) Random Hse. Children's Bks.

—Leprechaun in Late Winter. 2012. (Magic Tree House Merlin Missions Ser.: 15). lib. bdg. 16.00 *(978-0-606-23860-1(3))* Turtleback.

—Una Momia Al Amanecer. 2004. (Casa del Arbol Ser.: 3). (SPA.). (J). pap. 6.99 *(978-1-930332-51-5(3))* Lectorum Pubns., Inc.

—Una Momia en la Manana. 2003. (Magic Tree House Ser.: 3). (SPA.). (gr. 3-6). lib. bdg. 16.00 *(978-0-613-64609-3(6))* Turtleback.

—Monday with a Mad Genius. Murdocca, Sal, illus. 2009. (Magic Tree House (R) Merlin Mission Ser.: 10). 144p. (J). (gr. 2-5). 5.99 *(978-0-375-83730-2(2)*, Random Hse. Bks. for Young Readers) Random Hse. Children's Bks.

—Monday with a Mad Genius. 2009. (Magic Tree House Merlin Missions Ser.: 10). lib. bdg. 16.00 *(978-0-606-01777-0(1))* Turtleback.

—Moonlight on the Magic Flute, Bk. 13. Murdocca, Sal, illus. 2010. (Magic Tree House (R) Merlin Mission Ser.: 13). 144p. (J). (gr. 2-5). pap. 5.99 *(978-0-375-85647-1(1)*, Random Hse. Bks. for Young Readers) Random Hse. Children's Bks.

—Navidad en Camelot. 2015. (Casa De árbol Ser.: 29). (SPA., Illus.). 144p. (J). (gr. 2-4). pap. 6.99 *(978-1-63245-532-1(3))* Lectorum Pubns., Inc.

—Night of the New Magicians. Murdocca, Sal, illus. 2007. (Magic Tree House (R) Merlin Mission Ser.: 7). 144p. (J). (gr. 2-5). 6.99 *(978-0-375-83036-5(7)*, Random Hse. Bks. for Young Readers) Random Hse. Children's Bks.

—Night of the New Magicians. 2007. (Magic Tree House Merlin Missions Ser.: 7). lib. bdg. 16.00 *(978-1-4177-9108-8(X))* Turtleback.

—Night of the Ninth Dragon. Murdocca, Sal, illus. (Magic Tree House (R) Merlin Mission Ser.: 27). 144p. (J). (gr. 2-5). 2018. 6.99 *(978-0-553-51092-8(4))* 2016. 13.99 *(978-0-553-51089-8(4))* Random Hse. Children's Bks. (Random Hse. Bks. for Young Readers).

—La Noche de Los Ninjas. 2004. (Casa del Arbol Ser.: 5).Tr. of Night of the Ninjas. (SPA., Illus.). (J). pap. 6.99 *(978-1-930332-66-9(1))* Lectorum Pubns., Inc.

—Piratas Despues Del Mediodia. 2004. (Casa del Arbol Ser.: 4). (SPA.). (J). pap. 6.99 *(978-1-930332-52-2(1))* Lectorum Pubns., Inc.

—Piratas Despues del Mediodia. 2003. (Magic Tree House Ser.: 4). (SPA.). (gr. 3-6). lib. bdg. 16.00 *(978-0-613-64578-2(2))* Turtleback.

—Revolutionary War on Wednesday. unabr. ed. 2004. (Magic Tree House Ser.: No. 22). 69p. (J). (gr. k-3). pap. 17.00 incl. audio *(978-0-8072-0931-8(7)*, S FTR 254 SP, Listening Library) Random Hse. Audio Publishing Group.

—Season of the Sandstorms. 2014. (Magic Tree House Merlin Missions Ser.: No. 6). 15.00 *(978-1-63419-681-9(3))* Perfection Learning Corp.

—Season of the Sandstorms, Bk. 6. Murdocca, Sal, illus. 2006. (Magic Tree House (R) Merlin Mission Ser.: 6). 144p. (J). (gr. 2-5). 6.99 *(978-0-375-83032-7(4)*, Random Hse. Bks. for Young Readers) Random Hse. Children's Bks.

—Shadow of the Shark. Murdocca, Sal, illus. 2017. (Magic Tree House (R) Merlin Mission Ser.: 25). 144p. (J). (gr. 2-5). 5.99 *(978-0-553-51084-3(3)*, Random Hse. Bks. for Young Readers) Random Hse. Children's Bks.

—Soccer on Sunday. Murdocca, Sal, illus. 2016. (Magic Tree House (R) Merlin Mission Ser.: 24). 144p. (J). (gr. 2-5). 6.99 *(978-0-307-98056-4(1)*, Random Hse. Bks. for Young Readers) Random Hse. Children's Bks.

—Stallion by Starlight. Murdocca, Sal, illus. 2014. (Magic Tree House (R) Merlin Mission Ser.: 21). 144p. (J). (gr. 2-5). pap. 5.99 *(978-0-307-98044-1(8)*, Random Hse. Bks. for Young Readers) Random Hse. Children's Bks.

—Stallion by Starlight. 2014. (Magic Tree House Merlin Missions Ser.: 21). lib. bdg. 16.00 *(978-0-606-36411-9(0))* Turtleback.

—Summer of the Sea Serpent, Bk. 3. Murdocca, Sal, illus. 2011. (Magic Tree House (R) Merlin Mission Ser.: 3). 144p. (J). (gr. 2-5). 6.99 *(978-0-375-86491-9(1)*, Random Hse. Bks. for Young Readers) Random Hse. Children's Bks.

—Una Tarde en el Amazonas. 2004. (Casa del Arbol Ser.: 6).Tr. of Afternoon on the Amazon. (SPA., Illus.). 66p. (J). pap. 6.99 *(978-1-930332-67-6(X))* Lectorum Pubns., Inc.

—Un Tigre Dientes de Sable en el Ocaso. 2004. (Casa del Arbol Ser.: 7).Tr. of Sunset of the Sabretooth. (SPA., Illus.). (J). pap. 6.99 *(978-1-930332-68-3(8))* Lectorum Pubns., Inc.

—Tonight on the Titanic. unabr. ed. 2004. (Magic Tree House Ser.: No. 17). 71p. (J). (gr. k-3). pap. 17.00 incl. audio *(978-0-8072-0926-4(0)*, S FTR 249 SP, Listening Library) Random Hse. Audio Publishing Group.

—Twister on Tuesday. 2004. (Magic Tree House Ser.: No. 23). 70p. (J). (gr. k-3). pap. 17.00 incl. audio *(978-0-8072-9932-6(4)*, Listening Library) Random Hse. Audio Publishing Group.

—Vacaciones Al Pie de un Volcan. Brovelli, Marcela, tr. from ENG. Murdocca, Sal, illus. 2007. (Casa del Arbol Ser.: 13).Tr. of Vacation under the Volcano. (SPA.). 74p. (J). per. 6.99 *(978-1-933032-19-1(7))* Lectorum Pubns., Inc.

—Vacation under the Volcano. unabr. ed. 2004. (Magic Tree House Ser.: No. 13). 74p. (J). (gr. k-3). pap. 17.00 incl. audio *(978-0-8072-0782-6(9)*, LFTR 241 SP, Listening Library) Random Hse. Audio Publishing Group.

—El Verano de la Serpiente Marina. 2015. (Casa De árbol Ser.: 31). (SPA., Illus.). 144p. (J). (gr. 2-4). pap. 6.99 *(978-1-63245-534-5(X))* Lectorum Pubns., Inc.

—Viking Ships at Sunrise. unabr. ed. 2004. (Magic Tree House Ser.: No. 15). 71p. (J). (gr. k-3). pap. 17.00 incl. audio *(978-0-8072-0784-0(5)*, LFTR 243 SP, Listening Library) Random Hse. Audio Publishing Group.

Osborne, Mary Pope & Murdocca, Sal. Esta Noche en el Titanic. Murdocca, Sal, illus. 2008. (Casa del Arbol Ser.: 17).Tr. of Tonight on the Titanic. (SPA., Illus.). (J). (gr. 2-4). pap. 6.99 *(978-1-933032-47-4(2))* Lectorum Pubns., Inc.

Osborne, Mary Pope & PLC Editors Staff. Carnival at Candlelight. Murdocca, Sal, illus. 2006. (Magic Tree House Merlin Missions Ser.: No. 5). 105p. (gr. 2-6). 15.00 *(978-0-7569-6690-4(6))* Perfection Learning Corp.

Osborne, Mary Pope, et al. Buenos Días, Gorilas. Murdocca, Sal, illus. 2014. (SPA.). 88p. (J). (gr. 2-4). pap. 6.99 *(978-1-933032-93-1(6))* Lectorum Pubns., Inc.

—Búfalos Antes Del Desayuno. Murdocca, Sal, illus. 2008. (Casa del Arbol Ser.: 18).Tr. of Buffalo Before Breakfast. (SPA.). (J). (gr. 2-4). pap. 6.99 *(978-1-933032-48-1(0))* Lectorum Pubns., Inc.

—Carnaval a Media Luz. Murdocca, Sal, illus. 2016. (SPA.). 113p. (J). (gr. 2-4). pap. 6.99 *(978-1-63245-643-4(5))* Lectorum Pubns., Inc.

—Día Negro en el Fondo Del Mar. Murdocca, Sal, illus. 2018. (SPA.). 118p. (J). (gr. 2-4). pap. 6.99 *(978-1-63245-682-3(6))* Lectorum Pubns., Inc.

—El Dragon Del Amanecer Rojo. Murdocca, Sal, illus. 2018. (SPA.). 132p. (J). (gr. 2-4). pap. 6.99 *(978-1-63245-680-9(X))* Lectorum Pubns., Inc.

—La Estación de Las Tormentas de Arena. Murdocca, Sal, illus. 2016. (SPA.). 107p. (J). (gr. 2-4). pap. 5.99 *(978-1-63245-644-1(3))* Lectorum Pubns., Inc.

—The Fun Starts Here! Four Favorite Chapter Books in One: Junie B. Jones, Magic Tree House, Purrmaids, & a to Z Mysteries. Murdocca, Sal, illus. 2018. (ENG.). 336p. (J). (gr. 1-4). 9.99 *(978-1-9848-3059-3(7)*, Random Hse. Bks. for Young Readers) Random Hse. Children's Bks.

—Jueves de Acción de Gracias. Murdocca, Sal, illus. 2014. (SPA.). 88p. (J). (gr. 2-4). pap. 6.99 *(978-1-933032-94-8(4))* Lectorum Pubns., Inc.

—Un Lunes con un Genio Loco. Murdocca, Sal, illus. 2018. (SPA.). 132p. (J). (gr. 2-4). pap. 6.99 *(978-1-63245-681-6(8))* Lectorum Pubns., Inc.

—Maremoto en Hawái. Murdocca, Sal, illus. 2014. (SPA.). 88p. (J). (gr. 2-4). pap. 6.99 *(978-1-933032-95-5(2))* Lectorum Pubns., Inc.

—Miedo Escénico en una Noche de Verano. Murdocca, Sal, illus. 2014. (SPA.). 86p. (J). (gr. 2-4). pap. 6.99 *(978-1-933032-92-4(8))* Lectorum Pubns., Inc.

—La Noche de Los Nuevos Magos. Murdocca, Sal, illus. 2016. (SPA.). 111p. (J). (gr. 2-4). pap. 6.99 *(978-1-63245-645-8(1))* Lectorum Pubns., Inc.

—El Regalo Del Pingüino Emperador. Murdocca, Sal, illus. 2018. (SPA.). 118p. (J). (gr. 2-4). pap. 6.99 *(978-1-63245-683-0(4))* Lectorum Pubns., Inc.

—Tormenta de Nieve en Luna Azul. Murdocca, Sal, illus. 2016. (SPA.). (J). (gr. 2-4). pap. 6.99 *(978-1-63245-646-5(X))* Lectorum Pubns., Inc.

Owen, James A. The Dragon's Apprentice. Owen, James A., illus. (Chronicles of the Imaginarium Geographica Ser.: 5). (ENG., Illus.). (YA). (gr. 7). 2012. 400p. pap. 12.99 *(978-1-4169-5898-7(3))* 2010. 384p. 17.99 *(978-1-4169-5897-0(5))* Simon & Schuster Bks. For Young Readers. (Simon & Schuster Bks. For Young Readers).

—The Dragons of Winter. Owen, James A., illus. (Chronicles of the Imaginarium Geographica Ser.: 6). (ENG., Illus.). (YA). (gr. 7). 2013. 416p. pap. 12.99 *(978-1-4424-1224-8(0))* 2012. 400p. 17.99 *(978-1-4424-1223-1(2))* Simon & Schuster Bks. For Young Readers. (Simon & Schuster Bks. For Young Readers).

—Fall of the Dragons: The Dragon's Apprentice; the Dragons of Winter; the First Dragon. 2016. (Age of Dragons Ser.: 3). (ENG., Illus.). 1056p. pap. 21.99 *(978-1-4814-2998-6(1)*, SAGA Press) Simon & Schuster Bks. For Young Readers.

—The First Dragon. Owen, James A., illus. (Chronicles of the Imaginarium Geographica Ser.: 7). (ENG., Illus.). 304p. (YA). (gr. 7). 2014. pap. 13.99 *(978-1-4424-1227-9(5))* 2013. 17.99 *(978-1-4424-1226-2(7))* Simon & Schuster Bks. For Young Readers. (Simon & Schuster Bks. For Young Readers).

—Here, There Be Dragons. 2008. (Playaway Children Ser.). (YA). (gr. 7-12). 59.99 *(978-1-60640-959-6(X))* Findaway World, LLC.

—Here, There Be Dragons. Owen, James A., illus. (Chronicles of the Imaginarium Geographica Ser.: 1). (ENG., Illus.). (YA). (gr. 7-12). 2007. 352p. pap. 13.99 *(978-1-4169-1228-6(2))* 2006. 336p. 24.99 *(978-1-4169-1227-9(4))* Simon & Schuster Bks. For Young Readers. (Simon & Schuster Bks. For Young Readers).

—The Indigo King. Owen, James A., illus. 2010. (Chronicles of the Imaginarium Geographica Ser.: 3). (ENG., Illus.). 400p. (YA). (gr. 7). pap. 13.99 *(978-1-4169-5108-7(3)*, Simon & Schuster Bks. For Young Readers) Simon & Schuster Bks. For Young Readers.

—The Indigo King, 3. Owen, James A., illus. 2008. (Chronicles of the Imaginarium Geographica Ser.: 3). (ENG., Illus.). 384p. (YA). (gr. 7-12). 17.99 *(978-1-4169-5107-0(5))* Simon & Schuster, Inc.

—The Search for the Red Dragon. Owen, James A., illus. 2008. (Chronicles of the Imaginarium Geographica Ser.: 2). (ENG., Illus.). (YA). (gr. 7). 400p. pap. 13.99 *(978-1-4169-4851-3(1))*; 384p. 17.99 *(978-1-4169-4850-6(3))* Simon & Schuster Bks. For Young Readers. (Simon & Schuster Bks. For Young Readers).

—The Shadow Dragons. Owen, James A., illus. 2009. (Chronicles of the Imaginarium Geographica Ser.: 4). (ENG., Illus.). 432p. (YA). (gr. 7-18). 21.99 *(978-1-4169-5879-6(7)*, Simon & Schuster Bks. For Young Readers) Simon & Schuster Bks. For Young Readers.

Oxridge, Panama. Justin Thyme. 2012. (Tartan of Thyme Ser.). (Illus.). 368p. (YA). (gr. 5-12). pap. 9.99 *(978-0-9567122-8-8(2))* Lerner Publishing Group.

—Justin Thyme. Poxmage, Adrian, illus. 2011. (Tartan of Thyme Ser.). 368p. (YA). 18.99 *(978-0-9562315-9-8(4))* Lerner Publishing Group.

Packard, Edward. Return to the Cave of Time. Willis, Drew, illus. 2012. (U-Ventures Ser.). (ENG.). 160p. (Orig.). (J). (gr. 3-7). pap. 5.99 *(978-1-4424-3427-1(9))* Simon & Schuster, Inc.

Panckridge, Michael & Lee, Brett. Toby Jones & the Clash with Father Time. 5th ed. 2007. (ENG.). 210p. *(978-0-207-20047-2(5))* HarperCollins Pubs. Australia.

Park, Linda Sue. Archer's Quest. 2018. (ENG., Illus.). 176p. (J). (gr. 5-7). pap. 7.99 *(978-1-328-89575-2(0)*, 1699653, Clarion Bks.) HarperCollins Pubs.

Parton, Paula. Room 17 'Where History Comes Alive!' Book Ii, Explorers. 2008. 120p. pap. 8.95 *(978-0-9794815-3-6(8))* Bellissima Publishing, LLC.

Pascoe, Sara. Being a Witch, & Other Things I Didn't Ask For. Lindsey, Alexander, ed. 2nd ed. 2017. (Historicalnovelsociety. Org/Reviews/Ratchet-The-Rel Ser.). (ENG., Illus.). 369p. (YA). (gr. 7-12). pap. *(978-0-9935747-3-3(4))* Trindles & Green, Ltd.

Pati, Geeta. Finny's Voyage Through the Universe: Nebula, Supernova, Open Star Cluster. 2007. 100p. per. 11.95 *(978-1-59526-422-0(1)*, Llumina Pr.) Aeon Publishing Inc.
Patterson, James. Daniel X: Demons & Druids. (Daniel X Ser.: 3). (ENG.). (J). (gr. 3-7). 2011. 304p. pap., pap. 8.99 *(978-0-316-03830-0(X))* 2010. 320p. 33.99 *(978-0-316-08731-5(9))* Little Brown & Co. (Jimmy Patterson).
Patterson, James & Sadler, Adam. Daniel X: Demons & Druids. 2010. (Daniel X Ser.: 3). (ENG.). 256p. (J). (gr. 3-7). 31.99 *(978-0-316-03698-6(6)*, Jimmy Patterson) Little Brown & Co.
Paulsen, Gary & Roberts, Esyllt Nest. Plygu Amser. 2005. (WEL.). 80p. pap. *(978-0-86381-683-3(5))* Gwasg Carreg Gwalch.
Paz, Diana. Timespell. 2013. 312p. pap. 14.99 *(978-1-936850-21-1(4))* Rhemalda Publishing.
Peacock, L. A. Panic in Pompeii. Hale, Nathan, illus. 2011. 92p. (J). pap. *(978-0-545-34062-5(4))* Scholastic, Inc.
—Terror at Troy. Hale, Nathan, illus. 2012. 90p. (J). *(978-0-545-34063-2(2))* Scholastic, Inc.
Pearce, Philippa. Tom's Midnight Garden. Zollars, Jaime, illus. 2018. (ENG.). 320p. (J). (gr. 3-7). pap. 9.99 *(978-0-06-269658-8(0)*, Greenwillow Bks.) HarperCollins Pubs.
Pease, D. Robert. Noah Zarc: Cataclysm. 2nd I.t. ed. 2013. (ENG.). 234p. (gr. 3-8). pap. 11.95 *(978-1-62253-406-7(9))* Evolved Publishing.
—Noah Zarc: Cataclysm. Diamond, Lane, ed. 3rd ed. 2017. (Noah Zarc Ser.: Vol. 2). (ENG., Illus.). (YA). (gr. 7-12). pap. 16.95 *(978-1-62253-419-7(0))* Evolved Publishing.
—Noah Zarc: Omnibus. I.t. ed. 2013. (ENG.). 630p. (gr. 3-8). 36.95 *(978-1-62253-410-4(7))* Evolved Publishing.
—Noah Zarc: Omnibus. Diamond, Lane, ed. 2nd ed. 2017. (Noah Zarc Ser.: Vol. 4). (ENG., Illus.). (YA). (gr. 7-12). 39.95 *(978-1-62253-421-0(2))* Evolved Publishing.
Penner, Stephen. Professor Barrister's Dinosaur Mysteries #2: The Case of the Armored Allosaurus. 2010. 54p. pap. 19.60 *(978-1-60888-018-8(4))* Nimble Bks. LLC.
Perrin, Randy, et al. Time Like a River. 2004. 144p. (gr. 5-18). 14.95 *(978-1-57143-061-8(X))* RDR Bks.
Phelan, Matt. Knights vs. Dinosaurs. Phelan, Matt, illus. (ENG., Illus.). (J). (gr. 3-7). 2019. 176p. pap. 7.99 *(978-0-06-268624-4(0))* 2018. 160p. 16.99 *(978-0-06-268623-7(2))* HarperCollins Pubs. (Greenwillow Bks.).
Phelps, Donna & Phelps, Cameron. Cameron & the Dinosaur Heroes. 2011. (ENG.). 128p. 21.23 *(978-1-4567-2476-4(2))*; pap. 10.68 *(978-1-4389-6353-2(X))* AuthorHouse.
Pilkey, Dav. Captain Underpants & the Revolting Revenge of the Radioactive Robo-Boxers. 2013. (Captain Underpants Ser.: 10). lib. bdg. 20.85 *(978-0-606-31563-0(2))* Turtleback.
Plante, Raymond. Le Monde de Xéros. Delezenne, Christine, illus. 2004. (Roman Jeunesse Ser.). (FRE.). 96p. (J). (gr. 4-7). pap. *(978-2-89021-615-0(2))* Diffusion du livre Mirabel (DLM).
Poore, Michael. Two Girls, a Clock, & a Crooked House. 2019. (Illus.). 304p. (J). (gr. 3-7). 16.99 *(978-0-525-64416-3(4)*, Random Hse. Bks. for Young Readers) Random Hse. Children's Bks.
Post, Bobby. The Adventures of Jimmy. 2007. 48p. per. 16.95 *(978-1-4137-8704-7(5))* America Star Bks.
Poteat, Bruce S. Evil Deception. 2013. 192p. (gr. 10-12). 30.95 *(978-1-4497-9565-8(X))*; pap. 13.95 *(978-1-4497-9570-2(6))* Author Solutions, LLC. (WestBow Pr.).
Potter, David. The Left Behinds: the IPhone That Saved George Washington. 2016. (Left Behinds Ser.: 1). (ENG.). 368p. (J). (gr. 3-7). 8.99 *(978-0-385-39059-0(9)*, Yearling) Random Hse. Children's Bks.
Prevost, Guillaume. The Gate of Days, 2. 2009. (Book of Time Ser.: 2). (ENG.). 272p. (J). (gr. 6-8). 18.69 *(978-0-439-88380-1(6))* Scholastic, Inc.
Prévost, Guillaume & Rodarmor, William. The Circle of Gold: The Book of Time III. 2009. (J). pap. *(978-0-439-88382-5(2)*, Levine, Arthur A. Bks.) Scholastic, Inc.
Price, Susan. A Sterkarm Kiss. 2004. (ENG.). 288p. (J). (gr. 7-18). 16.99 *(978-0-06-072197-8(9))* HarperCollins Pubs.
Prior, Natalie. Lily Quench & the Treasure of Mote Ely, 3. 2004. (Lily Quench Ser.). (ENG., Illus.). 160p. (J). (gr. 3-7). 6.99 *(978-0-14-240022-7(X)*, Puffin) Penguin Young Readers Group.
Pullman, Philip. The Adventures of John Blake: Mystery of the Ghost Ship. Fordham, Fred, illus. 2017. lib. bdg. 33.05 *(978-0-606-40195-1(4))* Turtleback.
Questlove & Cosby, S. A. The Rhythm of Time. 2023. 240p. (J). (gr. 5). 18.99 *(978-0-593-35406-3(0)*, G.P. Putnam's Sons Books for Young Readers) Penguin Young Readers Group.
Quinn, K. A. S. The Queen Alone. 2015. (Chronicles of the Tempus Ser.). (ENG.). 328p. (J). (gr. 4-7). pap. 10.99 *(978-1-84887-056-7(6))* Atlantic Bks., Ltd. GBR. Dist: Independent Pubs. Group.
Quintana, Adrienne. Eruption. 2015. 282p. (YA). pap. 16.99 *(978-1-4621-1536-5(5))* Cedar Fort, Inc./CFI Distribution.
Rabin, Staton. Black Powder. 2005. (ENG.). 256p. (YA). (gr. 7-9). 16.95 *(978-0-689-86876-4(6)*, McElderry, Margaret K. Bks.) McElderry, Margaret K. Bks.
Rallison, Janette. My Unfair Godmother. 2012. (ENG.). 352p. (YA). (gr. 7-12). 26.19 *(978-0-8027-2236-2(9)*, 9780802722362) Bloomsbury Publishing USA.
Ramsay, Elizabeth. The Burning Light. Katz, Avi, illus. 2005. 144p. (J). (gr. 4-9). 14.95 *(978-1-930143-43-2(5))*; pap. 9.95 *(978-1-930143-44-9(3))* Simcha Media Group. (Devora Publishing).
Rapkin, Mickey. It's Not a Bed, It's a Time Machine. Martinez, Teresa, illus. 2019. (It's Not a Book Series, It's an Adventure Ser.). (ENG.). 32p. (J). 17.99 *(978-1-250-16762-0(0)*, 900187570) Imprint IND. Dist: Macmillan.
Rau, Dana Meachen. Moon Walk. Buchs, Thomas, illus. 2004. (Soundprints' Read-and-Discover Ser.). 48p. (gr. -1-3). 13.95 *(978-0-7569-3370-8(6))* Perfection Learning Corp.
Rechlin, Ted. ComicQuest TIME TRAVEL TROUBLE. 2013. (Dover Children's Activity Bks.). (ENG.). 48p. (J). (gr. 3-8). pap. 4.99 *(978-0-486-49949-9(9))* Dover Pubns., Inc.
Reed, Wilfred. Andy & Mark & the Time Machine: Custer's Last Stand. 2003. 240p. (YA). pap. 15.95 *(978-0-595-26496-4(4)*, Writers Club Pr.) iUniverse, Inc.
Reger, Rob & Gruner, Jessica. Emily the Strange: Dark Times. Reger, Rob & Parker, Buzz, illus. 2011. (Emily the Strange Ser.: 3). (ENG.). 248p. (YA). (gr. 8). pap. 10.99 *(978-0-06-145237-6(8)*, HarperCollins) HarperCollins Pubs.
Reid, John. The People & Josh Wilson. 2009. (ENG.). 104p. (gr. 7-10). pap. 12.95 *(978-1-55266-274-8(8)*, 25030) Fernwood Publishing Co., Ltd. CAN. Dist: Columbia Univ. Pr.
Reid, Kate. Operation Timewarp. 2003. (ENG.). 195p. pap. *(978-1-84255-203-2(1)*, Orion Children's Bks.) Hachette Children's Group.
Reiss, Kathryn. Paint by Magic. 2003. (ENG.). 288p. (J). (gr. 5-7). pap. 17.95 *(978-0-15-204925-6(8)*, 1194872, Clarion Bks.) HarperCollins Pubs.
—Paint by Magic. 2003. (Time Travel Mysteries Ser.). 271p. (J). (gr. 5). 14.60 *(978-0-7569-4210-6(1))* Perfection Learning Corp.
—Pale Phoenix. 2003. (ENG., Illus.). 336p. (J). (gr. 5-7). pap. 15.95 *(978-0-15-204927-0(4)*, 1194878, Clarion Bks.) HarperCollins Pubs.
Revealed. 2014. (Missing Ser.: 7). (ENG., Illus.). 448p. (J). (gr. 3-7). 19.99 *(978-1-4169-8986-8(2)*, Simon & Schuster Bks. For Young Readers) Simon & Schuster Bks. For Young Readers.
Reynolds, Justin A. Opposite of Always. (ENG.). (YA). (gr. 9). 2020. 480p. pap. 11.99 *(978-0-06-274838-6(6))* 2019. 464p. 17.99 *(978-0-06-274837-9(8))* HarperCollins Pubs. (Tegen, Katherine Bks).
Richards, Justin. Rewind Assassin. 2007. (Time Runners Ser.: 2). (ENG.). 208p. (J). (gr. 4-7). pap. 8.99 *(978-1-4169-2643-6(7))* Simon & Schuster, Ltd. GBR. Dist: Simon & Schuster, Inc.
Richardson, J. J. It's about Time. 2008. (ENG.). 92p. pap. 12.99 *(978-1-4196-5707-8(0))* CreateSpace Independent Publishing Platform.
Riggs, Ransom. Library of Souls. 2017. (Miss Peregrine's Peculiar Children Ser.: 3). (ENG.). (YA). (gr. 9). lib. bdg. 23.30 *(978-0-606-39808-4(2))* Turtleback.
—Library of Souls: The Third Novel of Miss Peregrine's Peculiar Children. 2015. (Miss Peregrine's Peculiar Children Ser.: 3). (Illus.). 400p. (YA). (gr. 9). 18.99 *(978-1-59474-758-8(X))* Quirk Bks.
Riley, James. Pick the Plot. (Story Thieves Ser.: 4). (ENG.). (J). (gr. 3-7). 2018. 400p. pap. 9.99 *(978-1-4814-6129-0(X))* 2017. (Illus.). 384p. 17.99 *(978-1-4814-6128-3(1))* Simon & Schuster Children's Publishing. (Aladdin).
Riley, Lehman & Austin, Megan. The Life of Babe Didrikson: "Greatness Is Never Forgotten" Wallace, Joshua, illus. 2005. 47p. (J). pap. *(978-0-9760523-2-6(6))* Matter of Africa America Time.
Riley, Lehman C. Meeting Dr. Martin Luther King. 2004. (Adventures of Papa Lemon's Little Wanderers Ser.: Bk. 1). 35p. *(978-0-9760523-0-2(X))* Matter of Africa America Time.
Rits, Susan Katherine. The Pirates of Bair Island. 2013. 234p. pap. 12.99 *(978-0-9894891-1-9(6))* Imprint.ll.
Rocan, Susan. Withershins. 2008. (Spirit Quest Ser.: 1). (ENG.). 225p. (YA). (gr. 12-14). pap. 14.95 *(978-1-894283-75-5(9))* Great Plains Pubns. CAN. Dist: Publishers Group Canada.
Rodda, Emily. The Best-Kept Secret. 2020. 128p. 7.99 *(978-1-4607-5372-9(0)*, HarperCollins) HarperCollins Pubs.
Rollins, Danielle. Stolen Time. (Dark Stars Ser.: 1). (ENG.). (YA). (gr. 9). 2020. 432p. pap. 10.99 *(978-0-06-267995-6(3))* 2019. 416p. 17.99 *(978-0-06-267994-9(5))* HarperCollins Pubs. (HarperTeen).
Rose, John. Wikker. 2007. 248p. pap. 17.95 *(978-1-4303-1523-0(7))* Lulu Pr., Inc.
Rose, Simon. The Sorcerer's Letterbox, 1 vol. 2004. (ENG., Illus.). 116p. (J). (gr. 4-7). per. 7.95 *(978-1-896580-52-4(1))* Tradewind Bks. CAN. Dist: Orca Bk. Pubs. USA.
—Time Camera, 1 vol. 2012. (ENG., Illus.). 96p. (J). (gr. 4-7). pap. 9.95 *(978-1-896580-09-8(2))* Tradewind Bks. CAN. Dist: Orca Bk. Pubs. USA.
Rosenow, Ty. The Historical Adventures of Thomas Balfour. 2012. (ENG.). 184p. pap. 17.95 *(978-1-105-94011-8(X))* Lulu Pr., Inc.
Rowley, M'lin. The Silver Coat. 2009. (Knights of Right Ser.: Bk. 2). 71p. (J). (gr. 1-5). pap. 6.99 *(978-1-60641-104-9(7)*, Shadow Mountain) Shadow Mountain Publishing.
Rowleym'Lin. Knights of Right, BK 3: The Warrior's Guard. 2010. 80p. (J). pap. 6.99 *(978-1-60641-240-4(X)*, Shadow Mountain) Shadow Mountain Publishing.
Ruby, Anne. Children of the Sea. Meier, Ty, illus. 2007. (YA). per. *(978-0-9787881-0-0(9))* Seachild.
Rue, Ginger. Aleca Zamm Fools Them All. 2018. (Aleca Zamm Ser.: 3). (ENG.). 160p. (J). (gr. 2-5). 16.99 *(978-1-4814-7067-4(1))*; (Illus.). pap. 6.99 *(978-1-4814-7066-7(3))* Simon & Schuster Children's Publishing. (Aladdin).
Sage, Angie. Physik. 11 vols. 2007. (Septimus Heap Ser.: 3). (J). (SPA.). 131.75 *(978-1-4281-4582-5(6))*; 113.75 *(978-1-4281-4576-4(1))*; 133.75 *(978-1-4281-4580-1(X))*; 111.75 *(978-1-4281-4578-8(8))*; 277.75 *(978-1-4281-4577-1(X))*; 1.25 *(978-1-4281-4573-3(7))* Recorded Bks., Inc.
—Physik. 2008. (Septimus Heap Ser.: 3). (J). lib. bdg. 18.40 *(978-1-4178-1565-4(5))* Turtleback.
—Queste. Zug, Mark, illus. 2009. (Septimus Heap Ser.: 4). 596p. (J). lib. bdg. 18.40 *(978-0-606-02607-9(X))* Turtleback.
—Septimus Heap, Book Four: Queste. Zug, Mark, illus. (Septimus Heap Ser.: 4). (ENG.). (J). (gr. 4). 2009. 624p. pap. 10.99 *(978-0-06-088209-9(3))* 2008. 608p. 18.99 *(978-0-06-088207-5(7))* HarperCollins Pubs. (Tegen, Katherine Bks).
—Septimus Heap, Book Three: Physik. Zug, Mark, illus. (Septimus Heap Ser.: 3). (ENG.). (J). (gr. 4-7). 2007. 560p. 18.99 *(978-0-06-057737-7(1))*Bk. 3. 2008. 576p. pap. 9.99 *(978-0-06-057739-1(8))* HarperCollins Pubs. (Tegen, Katherine Bks).
Sales, Leila. Once Was a Time. 2016. (ENG., Illus.). 272p. (J). (gr. 5-17). 16.99 *(978-1-4521-4009-4(X))* Chronicle Bks. LLC.
—Once Was a Time: (Middle Grade Fiction Books, Friendship Stories for Young Adults, Middle Grade Novels in Verse) 2017. (ENG.). 340p. (J). (gr. 5-9). pap. 7.99 *(978-1-4521-6139-6(9))* Chronicle Bks. LLC.
Sargent, Alan E. Fortitude: The Adventures of the Esteem Team. Wade, Jerry, illus. 2013. 84p. pap. 10.95 *(978-1-62516-984-6(1)*, Strategic Bk. Publishing) Strategic Book Publishing & Rights Agency (SBPRA).
Saunders, Kate. Beswitched. 2012. (ENG.). 272p. (J). (gr. 4-7). 7.99 *(978-0-375-87329-4(5)*, Yearling) Random Hse. Children's Bks.
Scarrow, Alex & Bale, Tim. TimeRiders, 1. 2011. (TimeRiders Ser.). (ENG.). 416p. (YA). (gr. 7-12). 26.19 *(978-0-8027-2172-3(9)*, 9780802721723) Walker & Co.
Scieszka, Jon. Da Wild, Da Crazy, Da Vinci. McCauley, Adam, illus. 2006. (Time Warp Trio Ser.: No. 14). 72p. (gr. 4-7). 15.00 *(978-0-7569-6677-5(9))* Perfection Learning Corp.
—The Good, the Bad, & the Goofy. Smith, Lane, illus. 2005. (Time Warp Trio Ser.: No. 3). 70p. (gr. 4-7). 15.00 *(978-0-7569-5876-3(8))* Perfection Learning Corp.
—Hey Kid, Want to Buy a Bridge? McCauley, Adam, illus. 2005. (Time Warp Trio Ser.: No. 11). 74p. (gr. 4-7). 15.00 *(978-0-7569-5988-3(8))* Perfection Learning Corp.
—It's All Greek to Me. Smith, Lane, illus. 2006. (Time Warp Trio Ser.: No. 8). 71p. (gr. 4-7). 15.00 *(978-0-7569-6780-2(5))* Perfection Learning Corp.
—Marco? Polo! McCauley, Adam, illus. 2008. (Time Warp Trio Ser.: No. 16). 90p. (J). (gr. 4-6). 12.65 *(978-0-7569-8923-1(X))* Perfection Learning Corp.
—Marco? Polo! #16, No. 16. McCauley, Adam, illus. 2008. (Time Warp Trio Ser.: 16). 96p. (J). (gr. 2-4). 5.99 *(978-0-14-241177-3(9)*, Puffin Books) Penguin Young Readers Group.
—Me Oh Maya. McCauley, Adam, illus. 2005. (Time Warp Trio Ser.: No. 13). 69p. (gr. 2-6). 15.00 *(978-0-7569-5060-6(0))* Perfection Learning Corp.
—Me Oh Maya #13. McCauley, Adam, illus. 2005. (Time Warp Trio Ser.: 13). 96p. (J). (gr. 2-4). 5.99 *(978-0-14-240300-6(8)*, Puffin Books) Penguin Young Readers Group.
—Oh Say, I Can't See #15, No. 15. McCauley, Adam, illus. 2007. (Time Warp Trio Ser.: 15). 80p. (J). (gr. 2-4). 5.99 *(978-0-14-240808-7(5)*, Puffin Books) Penguin Young Readers Group.
—El Pirata Barbanegra. Smith, Lane, illus. (SPA.). (J). (gr. 5-8). 7.95 *(978-958-04-3401-6(8)*, NR8584) Norma S.A. COL. Dist: Lectorum Pubns., Inc., Distribuidora Norma, Inc.
—Sam Samurai. McCauley, Adam, illus. 2006. (Time Warp Trio Ser.: No. 10). 85p. (gr. 4-7). 15.00 *(978-0-7569-6779-6(1))* Perfection Learning Corp.
—Sam Samurai #10. McCauley, Adam, illus. 2004. (Time Warp Trio Ser.: 10). 96p. (J). (gr. 2-4). pap. 5.99 *(978-0-14-240088-3(2)*, Puffin Books) Penguin Young Readers Group.
—See You Later, Gladiator. McCauley, Adam, illus. 2004. (Time Warp Trio Ser.: No. 9). 87p. (J). (gr. 4-7). 12.65 *(978-0-7569-5986-9(1))* Perfection Learning Corp.
—See You Later, Gladiator #9. McCauley, Adam, illus. 2004. (Time Warp Trio Ser.: 9). 96p. (J). (gr. 2-4). pap. 5.99 *(978-0-14-240117-0(X)*, Puffin Books) Penguin Young Readers Group.
—Tut, Tut. Smith, Lane, illus. 2004. (Time Warp Trio Ser.: No. 6). 74p. (gr. 4-7). 15.00 *(978-0-7569-4050-8(8))* Perfection Learning Corp.
—Viking It & Liking It. McCauley, Adam, illus. 2004. (Time Warp Trio Ser.: No. 12). 73p. (gr. 2-6). 15.00 *(978-0-7569-2589-5(4))* Perfection Learning Corp.
—Viking It & Liking It. 2004. (Time Warp Trio Ser.: 12). 16.00 *(978-1-4176-3613-6(0))* Turtleback.
—Viking It & Liking It #12. McCauley, Adam, illus. 2004. (Time Warp Trio Ser.: 12). 96p. (J). (gr. 2-4). pap. 5.99 *(978-0-14-240002-9(5)*, Puffin Books) Penguin Young Readers Group.
—Your Mother Was a Neanderthal. Smith, Lane, illus. 2006. (Time Warp Trio Ser.: No. 4). 78p. (gr. 4-7). 15.00 *(978-0-7569-6782-6(1))* Perfection Learning Corp.
—Your Mother Was a Neanderthal. Smith, Lane, illus. 2004. (Time Warp Trio Ser.: 4). 78p. (J). 16.00 *(978-1-4176-3603-7(3))* Turtleback.
—Your Mother Was a Neanderthal #4. Smith, Lane, illus. 2004. (Time Warp Trio Ser.: 4). 80p. (J). (gr. 2-4). pap. 5.99 *(978-0-14-240048-7(3)*, Puffin Books) Penguin Young Readers Group.
—2095. Smith, Lane, illus. 2005. (Time Warp Trio Ser.: No. 5). 72p. (gr. 4-7). 15.00 *(978-0-7569-5989-0(6))* Perfection Learning Corp.
—2095 #5. Smith, Lane, illus. 2004. (Time Warp Trio Ser.: 5). 80p. (J). (gr. 2-4). pap. 6.99 *(978-0-14-240044-9(0)*, Puffin Books) Penguin Young Readers Group.
Seven, John. The Alchemist War, 1 vol. Phillips, Craig, illus. 2013. (Time-Tripping Faradays Ser.). (ENG.). 160p. (J). (gr. 4-8). 9.95 *(978-1-62370-011-9(6)*, 123720, Capstone Young Readers); pap. 5.95 *(978-1-4342-6438-1(6)*, 124129, Stone Arch Bks.) Capstone.
—The Dragon of Rome, 1 vol. Phillips, Craig, illus. 2013. (Time-Tripping Faradays Ser.). (ENG.). 160p. (J). (gr. 4-8). pap. 5.95 *(978-1-4342-6439-8(4)*, 124130, Stone Arch Bks.) Capstone.
—The Outlaw of Sherwood Forest, 1 vol. Hans, Stephanie, illus. 2014. (Time-Tripping Faradays Ser.). (ENG.). 192p. (J). (gr. 4-8). lib. bdg. 26.65 *(978-1-4342-9174-5(X)*, 125644, Stone Arch Bks.) Capstone.
—The Terror of the Tengu, 1 vol. Hans, Stephanie, illus. 2014. (Time-Tripping Faradays Ser.). (ENG.). 192p. (J). (gr. 4-8). 26.65 *(978-1-4342-9173-8(1)*, 125643, Stone Arch Bks.) Capstone.
Shaw, Alexander William. The Adventures of A Teenage Time Traveller. 2009. (ENG.). 84p. pap., pap. 12.95 *(978-0-9561592-2-9(2))* Hetman Publishing GBR. Dist: Lulu Pr., Inc.
Shay, Michael K. A Flash in Time: A Novel. 2016. 131p. (J). pap. *(978-1-63293-141-2(9))* Sunstone Pr.
Sheinkin, Steve. Abigail Adams, Pirate of the Caribbean. Swaab, Neil, illus. 2019. (Time Twisters Ser.). (ENG.). 176p. (J). pap. 6.99 *(978-1-250-20788-3(6)*, 900201776) Roaring Brook Pr.
Sheley, Kristen. Partners in Time #4: Family Matters. 2008. 216p. pap. 15.95 *(978-0-595-51850-0(8))* iUniverse, Inc.
—Partners in Time #5: A Change of Course. 2010. 236p. 25.95 *(978-1-4502-6658-1(4))*; pap. 15.95 *(978-1-4502-6657-4(6))* iUniverse, Inc.
Sherry, Kevin. Monsters on the Run (the Yeti Files #2) Sherry, Kevin, illus. 2015. (Yeti Files Ser.: 2). (ENG., Illus.). 128p. (J). (gr. 2-5). 8.99 *(978-0-545-55619-4(8)*, Scholastic Pr.) Scholastic, Inc.
Shurtliff, Liesl. Time Castaways #1: the Mona Lisa Key. (Time Castaways Ser.: 1). (ENG.). (J). (gr. 3-7). 2019. 416p. pap. 6.99 *(978-0-06-256816-8(7))* 2018. 400p. 16.99 *(978-0-06-256813-7(2))* HarperCollins Pubs. (Tegen, Katherine Bks).
Silverthorne, Judith. The Secret of Sentinel Rock. 2007. (From Many Peoples Ser.). (Illus.). 159p. (J). (gr. 3-5). per. *(978-1-55050-386-9(3))* Coteau Bks.
Simonds, Kevin. The Tomb of Father Time. 2011. 178p. pap. 24.95 *(978-1-4626-2739-4(0))* America Star Bks.
Smith, Jim. Future Ratboy & the Quest for the Missing Thingy (Future Ratboy) 2017. (Future Ratboy Ser.: 3). (ENG., Illus.). 256p. (J). (gr. 2-4). pap. 5.99 *(978-1-4052-8398-4(X))* Farshore GBR. Dist: HarperCollins Pubs.
Smith, Lindsay. A Darkly Beating Heart. 2016. (ENG.). 272p. (YA). 34.99 *(978-1-62672-044-2(4)*, 900132964) Roaring Brook Pr.
Smith, Molly. Border Breakdown: The Fall of the Berlin Wall. 2011. (ENG.). (J). 9.95 *(978-1-60727-113-0(3))* Soundprints.
Snider, Cindy Gay. Finding Anna Bee. Chambers, Mary, illus. 2007. 163p. (J). (gr. 3-7). per. 9.99 *(978-0-8361-9392-3(X))* Herald Pr.
Solice, Deborah. The Eye of the Undead: The Hidden Channel: an Adventure Series in Time. I.t. ed. 2005. (ENG., Illus.). 100p. (J). per. 7.59 *(978-1-933300-01-6(9))* Wandering Sage Pubns., LLC.
Sommer, Carl. Fast Forward. Budwine, Greg, illus. 2009. (Quest for Success Ser.). (ENG.). 56p. (YA). pap. 4.95 *(978-1-57537-277-8(0))*; lib. bdg. 12.95 *(978-1-57537-252-5(5))* Advance Publishing, Inc.
—Fast Forward(Avance Acelarado) Budwine, Greg, illus. 2009. (Quest for Success Bilingual Ser.). (SPA & ENG.). 104p. (YA). lib. bdg. 14.95 *(978-1-57537-227-3(4))* Advance Publishing, Inc.
—Time Remote! Budwine, Greg, illus. 2014. (J). pap. *(978-1-57537-970-8(8))* Advance Publishing, Inc.
—Time Remote! 2003. (Another Sommer-Time Story Ser.). (Illus.). 48p. (J). (gr. 1-4). 16.95 incl. audio *(978-1-57537-561-8(3))* Advance Publishing, Inc.
—Time Remote! Budwine, Greg, illus. 2003. (Another Sommer-Time Story Ser.). (ENG.). 48p. (J). (gr. 1-4). 16.95 incl. audio compact disk *(978-1-57537-512-0(5))* Advance Publishing, Inc.
—Time Remote!(El Control Del Tiempo!) Budwine, Greg, illus. 2009. (Another Sommer-Time Story Bilingual Ser.). (SPA & ENG.). 48p. (J). lib. bdg. 16.95 *(978-1-57537-170-2(7))* Advance Publishing, Inc.
Stanchfield, Justin. Timewalker. 2011. (Fiction Ser.). 330p. (J). pap. 5.99 *(978-0-7945-3032-7(X)*, Usborne) EDC Publishing.
Stanley, Diane. Thanksgiving on Plymouth Plantation. Berry, Holly, illus. 2004. (ENG.). 48p. (J). (gr. k-5). 17.99 *(978-0-06-027069-8(1)*, HarperCollins) HarperCollins Pubs.
Starobinets, Anna. Catlantis. Bugaeva, Jane, tr. Klimowski, Andrzej, illus. 2016. (ENG.). 136p. (J). (gr. 3-7). 16.95 *(978-1-68137-000-2(X)*, NYR Children's Collection) New York Review of Bks., Inc., The.
Steinkraus, Kyla. Pastries with Pocahontas. Wood, Katie, illus. 2017. (Time Hop Sweets Shop Ser.). (ENG.). 32p. (gr. 1-3). 24.22 *(978-1-68342-330-0(5)*, 9781683423300) Rourke Educational Media.
Stewart, Dianne C. Quimbaya. 2008. (ENG.). 200p. (gr. 1-18). pap. 8.95 *(978-0-9667359-8-7(6)*, BeanPole Bks.) OH Industries.
Stewart, Yale. Escape from Future World!, 1 vol. Stewart, Yale, illus. 2014. (Amazing Adventures of Superman! Ser.). (ENG., Illus.). 32p. (J). (gr. k-2). lib. bdg. 25.32 *(978-1-4795-5732-5(3)*, 126752, Stone Arch Bks.) Capstone.
Stilton, Geronimo. The Journey Through Time (Geronimo Stilton Special Edition) 2014. (Geronimo Stilton Journey Through Time Ser.). (ENG., Illus.). 320p. (J). (gr. 2-5). 16.99 *(978-0-545-55623-1(6)*, Scholastic Paperbacks) Scholastic, Inc.
—The Race Against Time (Geronimo Stilton Journey Through Time #3) 2018. (ENG.). 320p. (J). (gr. -1-3). E-Book 4.99 *(978-0-545-87298-0(7)*, Scholastic Paperbacks) Scholastic, Inc.
Stilton, Gerónimo. Time Machine Trouble. 2016. (Illus.). 128p. (J). pap. *(978-1-338-05290-9(X))* Scholastic, Inc.
Stilton, Gerónimo, et al. The Journey Through Time. 2014. (Illus.). 94p. (J). *(978-0-545-61129-9(6))* Scholastic, Inc.
Stokes, Jordan & Belinkie, Matt. Gilded Delirium. 2007. (YA). pap. *(978-1-4114-9670-5(1)*, Spark Publishing Group) Sterling Publishing Co., Inc.
Strasser, Todd. Abe Lincoln for Class President. 2010. 144p. pap. 10.95 *(978-1-4502-1244-1(1))* iUniverse, Inc.
Stuart, Raff. A Roman Odyssey: Book One of the chronicles of Adam Black the Teenage Time Traveller. 2009. 228p. pap. 14.49 *(978-1-4389-7407-1(8))* AuthorHouse.
Sullivan, Michael John & Petrone, Susan. The Sockkids Meet Lincoln. 2013. 42p. pap. 10.99 *(978-0-9727077-7-0(8))* Scribe Publishing.
Suphandagi, Lale. The Dream Bird. 2013. (ENG., Illus.). 54p. (J). (gr. k-1). pap. 9.95 *(978-1-59784-282-2(6)*, Tughra Bks.) Blue Dome, Inc.
Sutherland, Tui T. So This Is How It Ends. 2006. (Avatars Ser.: Bk. 1). 353p. (YA). (gr. 7-12). 16.99 *(978-0-06-075024-4(3)*, Eos) HarperCollins Pubs.
Sutton, Laurie S. The Crystal Quest. Lozano, Omar, illus. 2019. (You Choose Stories: Wonder Woman Ser.). (ENG.). 112p. (J). (gr. 2-6). pap. 6.95 *(978-1-4965-8441-0(4)*, 140966); lib. bdg. 32.65 *(978-1-4965-8351-2(5)*, 140645) Capstone. (Stone Arch Bks.).
—The Time Vortex. Clarey, Patricio, illus. 2018. (Bug Team Alpha Ser.). (ENG.). 112p. (J). (gr. 3-6). lib. bdg. 26.65 *(978-1-4965-5957-9(6)*, 137177, Stone Arch Bks.) Capstone.
Swindells, Robert. Timesnatch. Riley, Jon, illus. 2008. 176p. (YA). (gr. 7). pap. 12.99 *(978-0-552-55592-0(4)*, Corgi) Transworld Publishers Ltd. GBR. Dist: Independent Pubs. Group.
Taylor, Janet B. Sparks of Light. 2018. (ENG.). 448p. (YA). (gr. 9). pap. 9.99 *(978-1-328-91526-9(3)*, 1701811, Clarion Bks.) HarperCollins Pubs.

TUV

Taylor, Thomas. Haunters. 2013. 327p. (J). *(978-0-545-50253-5(5))* Scholastic, Inc.
Terrell, Brandon. Grit & Gold. Garcia, Eduardo, illus. 2016. (Time Machine Magazine Ser.). (ENG.). 128p. (J). (gr. 3-6). lib. bdg. 23.99 *(978-1-4965-2597-0(3)*, 130726) Capstone.
—Pluck & Perfection. Max, Iman, illus. 2016. (Time Machine Magazine Ser.). (ENG.). 128p. (J). (gr. 3-6). lib. bdg. 23.99 *(978-1-4965-2595-6(7)*, 130724, Stone Arch Bks.) Capstone.
—Time Machine Magazine. 2016. (Time Machine Magazine Ser.). (ENG., Illus.). 128p. (J). (gr. 3-6). 95.96 *(978-1-4965-2742-4(9)*, 24413) Capstone.
—Valor & Victory. Max, Iman, illus. 2016. (Time Machine Magazine Ser.). (ENG.). 128p. (J). (gr. 3-6). lib. bdg. 23.99 *(978-1-4965-2594-9(9)*, 130723, Stone Arch Bks.) Capstone.
A Theft in Time: Timedetectors II, 6 Pack. (Action Packs Ser.). 120p. (gr. 3-5). 44.00 *(978-0-7635-8425-2(8))* Rigby Education.
There's No Room for You, Maddie Morrison. 2006. (J). per. 6.99 *(978-0-9786117-0-5(5))* Neal Morgan Publishing.
Thomas, M. J. The Secret of the Hidden Scrolls: the Shepherd's Stone, Book 5. 2018. (Secret of the Hidden Scrolls Ser.: 5). (ENG., Illus.). 128p. (J). (gr. 1-4). pap. 6.99 *(978-0-8249-5691-2(5)*, Worthy Kids/Ideals) Worthy Publishing.
Thorne, Bella. Autumn's Wish. 2017. (Autumn Falls Ser.: 3). (ENG.). 320p. (YA). (gr. 7). pap. 10.99 *(978-0-385-74438-6(2)*, Ember) Random Hse. Children's Bks.
Thorne MBE, Tony. The junior philosophical Society. 2007. 114p. pap. 12.95 *(978-1-4116-9623-5(9))* Lulu Pr., Inc.
Time, Nicholas O. Going, Going, Gone. 2016. (In Due Time Ser.: 1). (ENG., Illus.). 160p. (J). (gr. 3-7). pap. 6.99 *(978-1-4814-6729-2(8)*, Simon Spotlight) Simon Spotlight.
—Going, Going, Gone. 2016. (In Due Time Ser.: 1). lib. bdg. 17.20 *(978-0-606-38985-3(7))* Turtleback.
—Hang Ten for Dear Life! 2017. (In Due Time Ser.: 6). (ENG., Illus.). 160p. (J). (gr. 3-7). pap. 6.99 *(978-1-4814-9654-4(9)*, Simon Spotlight) Simon Spotlight.
—Stay a Spell. 2016. (In Due Time Ser.: 2). (ENG., Illus.). 160p. (J). (gr. 3-7). pap. 6.99 *(978-1-4814-6726-1(3)*, Simon Spotlight) Simon Spotlight.
—Wrong Place, (Really) Wrong Time. 2016. (In Due Time Ser.: 3). (ENG., Illus.). 160p. (J). (gr. 3-7). pap. 6.99 *(978-1-4814-7233-3(X)*, Simon Spotlight) Simon Spotlight.
Time Slime. 2003. 156p. (YA). (gr. 5-12). pap. 7.95 *(978-0-9702176-3-9(3)*, 0004) Night Howl Productions.
Tomasi-Dubois, Mary. Danger in the Jeweled City: A Matt & Heather Thriller. 2007. 188p. (YA). per. 15.95 *(978-0-9798633-5-6(X))* Robertson Publishing.
Torres, J. Charge of the Army Eternal, 1 vol. Davis, Dan & Suriano, Andy, illus. 2013. (Batman: the Brave & the Bold Ser.). (ENG.). 32p. (J). (gr. 2-5). 22.60 *(978-1-4342-4706-3(6)*, 120837, Stone Arch Bks.) Capstone.
Triana, Gaby. Summer of Yesterday. 2014. (ENG., Illus.). 272p. (YA). (gr. 9). pap. 9.99 *(978-1-4814-0130-2(0)*, Simon Pulse) Simon Pulse.
Trine, Greg. The Brotherhood of the Traveling Underpants. 2009. (Melvin Beederman Superhero Ser.: 7). (J). lib. bdg. 19.65 *(978-0-606-01751-0(8))* Turtleback.
—Pinkbeard's Revenge. Dormer, Frank W., illus. 2015. (Adventures of Jo Schmo Ser.: 4). (ENG.). 128p. (J). (gr. 1-4). pap. 7.99 *(978-0-544-45601-3(7)*, 1599386, Clarion Bks.) HarperCollins Pubs.
—Wyatt Burp Rides Again. Dormer, Frank W., illus. 2014. (Adventures of Jo Schmo Ser.: 2). (ENG.). 112p. (J). (gr. 1-4). pap. 6.99 *(978-0-544-01899-0(0)*, 1528127, Clarion Bks.) HarperCollins Pubs.
Tripp, Valerie. Chances & Changes: My Journey with Molly. 2018. 177p. (J). *(978-1-5444-0749-4(1)*, American Girl) American Girl Publishing, Inc.
Valentine, James. The Future Is Unknown. 2007. (TimeJumpers Ser.: 3). (ENG.). 288p. (J). (gr. 3-7). pap. 13.99 *(978-0-689-87354-6(9)*, Aladdin) Simon & Schuster Children's Publishing.
—The Present Never Happens. 2007. (TimeJumpers Ser.: 2). (ENG.). 304p. (J). (gr. 3-7). pap. 13.99 *(978-1-4169-3956-6(3)*, Simon & Schuster/Paula Wiseman Bks.) Simon & Schuster/Paula Wiseman Bks.
Valentine, Nicole. A Time Traveler's Theory of Relativity. 2019. (ENG., Illus.). 352p. (J). (gr. 4-8). 17.99 *(978-1-5415-5538-9(4)*, 2b60b16e-6e91-4b27-b7dd-76c86cce49dc, Carolrhoda Bks.) Lerner Publishing Group.
Vande Velde, Vivian. A Well-Timed Enchantment. 2006. (ENG., Illus.). 240p. (J). (gr. 5-7). pap. 13.95 *(978-0-15-204919-5(3)*, 1194854, Clarion Bks.) HarperCollins Pubs.
Velde, Vivian Vande. 23 Minutes. 2016. (ENG.). 176p. (J). (gr. 7-9). 17.99 *(978-1-62979-441-9(4)*, Astra Young Readers) Astra Publishing Hse.
Walker, Rysa. Timebound, 0 vols. 2014. (Chronos Files Ser.: 1). (ENG.). 374p. (YA). (gr. 7-12). pap. 14.95 *(978-1-4778-4815-9(0)*, 9781477848159, Skyscape) Amazon Publishing.
—Time's Divide, 0 vols. 2015. (Chronos Files Ser.: 3). (ENG.). 543p. (YA). (gr. 7-12). pap. 12.95 *(978-1-5039-4658-3(4)*, 9781503946583, Skyscape) Amazon Publishing.
—Time's Edge, 0 vols. 2014. (Chronos Files Ser.: 2). (ENG.). 450p. (J). (gr. 7-12). pap. 9.99 *(978-1-4778-2582-2(7)*, 9781477825822, Skyscape) Amazon Publishing.
Ward, David. Archipelago, 1 vol. 2008. (ENG.). 176p. (YA). (gr. 7-12). pap. 6.95 *(978-0-88995-400-7(3)*, cc069aac-4386-4e25-8415-a5f97ad33438) Trifolium Bks., Inc. CAN. Dist: Firefly Bks., Ltd.
Waring, Scott C. West's Time MacHine. 2007. 200p. 24.95 *(978-0-595-88775-0(9))*; per. 14.95 *(978-0-595-41887-9(2))* iUniverse, Inc.
Wartik, David J. The VonNesta Project: Camp Fingerlake. 2007. 148p. per. 13.95 *(978-1-60145-394-5(9))* Booklocker.com, Inc.
Wayne, Matt. Menace of the Time Thief, 1 vol. Suriano, Andy & Davis, Dan W., illus. 2012. (Batman: the Brave & the Bold Ser.). (ENG.). 32p. (J). (gr. 2-5). lib. bdg. 22.60 *(978-1-4342-4548-9(9)*, 120506, Stone Arch Bks.) Capstone.
Welford, Ross. The Dog Who Saved the World. 2020. (ENG.). 400p. (J). (gr. 3-7). lib. bdg. 19.99 *(978-0-525-70749-3(2)*, Schwartz & Wade Bks.) Random Hse. Children's Bks.
—Time Traveling with a Hamster. 2018. (ENG.). 448p. (J). (gr. 3-7). 9.99 *(978-1-5247-1436-9(4)*, Yearling) Random Hse. Children's Bks.
Wells, H. G. The Time Machine. 2008. (Bring the Classics to Life Ser.). (Illus.). 72p. (gr. 4-12). pap., act. bk. ed. 10.95 *(978-0-931334-43-6(8)*, EDCTR-403B) EDCON Publishing Group.
—The Time Machine. 2004. (Fast Track Classics Ser.). (Illus.). 48p. (J). pap. *(978-0-237-52406-7(6))* Evans Brothers, Ltd.
—The Time Machine Graphic Novel. 2010. (Illustrated Classics Ser.). (ENG., Illus.). 64p. (YA). (gr. 4-12). per. 11.95 *(978-1-56254-944-2(8))* Saddleback Educational Publishing, Inc.
Wesley, Mary. Haphazard House. Date not set. (Sky Bks.). 200p. pap. 54.75 *(978-0-582-08108-6(4))* Addison-Wesley Longman, Ltd. GBR. Dist: Trans-Atlantic Pubns., Inc.
West, Tracey. Future of the Time Dragon, 15. 2020. (Branches: Dragon Masters Ser.). (ENG.). 96p. (gr. 1-4). 18.69 *(978-1-5364-6188-6(1))* Scholastic, Inc.
—Future of the Time Dragon: a Branches Book (Dragon Masters #15) Griffo, Daniel, illus. 2020. (Dragon Masters Ser.: 15). (ENG.). 96p. (J). (gr. 1-3). pap. 5.99 *(978-1-338-54025-3(4))* Scholastic, Inc.
—Future of the Time Dragon: a Branches Book (Dragon Masters #15) (Library Edition) Griffo, Daniel, illus. 2020. (Dragon Masters Ser.: 15). (ENG.). 96p. (J). (gr. 1-3). 24.99 *(978-1-338-54026-0(2))* Scholastic, Inc.
Weston, Greg. Charlie Cornwall & the Historymakers. 2011. (ENG.). 459p. pap. 25.50 *(978-1-4467-8713-7(3))* Lulu Pr., Inc.
White, Andrea. Windows on the World. 2011. 238p. (J). 18.95 *(978-1-60898-105-2(3))*; pap. 9.95 *(978-1-60898-106-9(1))* namelos llc.
Whitler, Larry. Oreo & Braun XOB the Full Circle Quest. 2007. 207p. pap. 14.95 *(978-1-4116-6080-9(3))* Lulu Pr., Inc.
Wickham, Martha. Mysterious Journey. 2011. (ENG.). 32p. (J). 9.95 *(978-1-60727-179-6(6))* Soundprints.
Wilson, N. D. Outlaws of Time #3: the Last of the Lost Boys. 2018. (Outlaws of Time Ser.: 3). (ENG., Illus.). 256p. (J). (gr. 3-7). 16.99 *(978-0-06-232732-1(1)*, Tegen, Katherine Bks) HarperCollins Pubs.
—Outlaws of Time: the Legend of Sam Miracle. 2017. (Outlaws of Time Ser.: 1). (ENG.). 352p. (J). (gr. 3-7). pap. 6.99 *(978-0-06-232727-7(5)*, Tegen, Katherine Bks) HarperCollins Pubs.
Wincik, Stephanie. The Journey: A Northern Lights Adventure. 2007. 111p. (J). per. 9.99 *(978-0-9725650-4-2(3))* One Horse Pr.
Wingard, Lucinda. The Turn-Around Bird. 2012. 296p. pap. 16.00 *(978-0-9848400-1-4(X))* Plicata Pr. LLC.
Wiseman, David. Jeremy Visick. 2005. 176p. (YA). (gr. 5-18). 21.25 *(978-0-8446-7271-7(8)*, 3594) Smith, Peter Pub., Inc.
Woodfield, Gary. The Time Thief. 2004. (J). per. 19.95 *(978-0-9761289-2-2(6))* Nightengale Pr.
Woodruff, Elvira. George Washington's Spy. 2012. lib. bdg. 17.20 *(978-0-606-26216-3(4))* Turtleback.
Wrecks, Billy. Time-Travel Trouble! 2014. (Step into Reading Level 2 Ser.). lib. bdg. 13.55 *(978-0-606-36281-8(9))* Turtleback.
Yamada, Debbie Leung. Striking It Rich: Treasures from Gold Mountain. Tang, You-shan, illus. I.t. ed. 2004. 128p. (J). (gr. 4-8). pap. 13.95 *(978-1-879965-21-8(6))* Polychrome Publishing Corp.
Yolen, Jane. The Devil's Arithmetic (Puffin Modern Classics) 2004. (Puffin Modern Classics Ser.). (ENG.). 208p. (J). (gr. 5-5). pap. 8.99 *(978-0-14-240109-5(9)*, Puffin Books) Penguin Young Readers Group.
Yomtov, Nel. Titanic Disaster! Nickolas Flux & the Sinking of the Great Ship. Simmons, Mark, illus. 2015. (Nickolas Flux History Chronicles Ser.). (ENG.). 40p. (J). (gr. 3-9). lib. bdg. 33.32 *(978-1-4914-2070-6(7)*, 127548, Capstone Pr.) Capstone.
Yusagi, Aneko. The Reprise of the Spear Hero Volume 01. 2018. (Reprise of the Spear Hero Series: Light Novel Ser.: 1). (ENG., Illus.). 400p. pap. 13.95 *(978-1-64273-003-6(3))* One Peace Bks., Inc.
Zub, Jim. Figment 2: the Legacy of Imagination: Volume 1. Bachs, Ramon & Beaulieu, Jean-François, illus. 2016. (Disney Kingdoms: Figment Set 2 Ser.). (ENG.). 24p. (J). (gr. k-5). lib. bdg. 31.36 *(978-1-61479-581-0(9)*, 24362, Graphic Novels) Spotlight.
—Figment 2: the Legacy of Imagination: Volume 2. Bachs, Ramon & Beaulieu, Jean-François, illus. 2016. (Disney Kingdoms: Figment Set 2 Ser.). (ENG.). 24p. (J). (gr. k-5). lib. bdg. 31.36 *(978-1-61479-582-7(7)*, 24363, Graphic Novels) Spotlight.
—Figment 2: the Legacy of Imagination: Volume 3. Bachs, Ramon & Beaulieu, Jean-François, illus. 2016. (Disney Kingdoms: Figment Set 2 Ser.). (ENG.). 24p. (J). (gr. k-5). lib. bdg. 31.36 *(978-1-61479-583-4(5)*, 24364, Graphic Novels) Spotlight.
—Figment 2: the Legacy of Imagination: Volume 4. Bachs, Ramon & Beaulieu, Jean-François, illus. 2016. (Disney Kingdoms: Figment Set 2 Ser.). (ENG.). 24p. (J). (gr. k-5). lib. bdg. 31.36 *(978-1-61479-584-1(3)*, 24365, Graphic Novels) Spotlight.
—Figment 2: the Legacy of Imagination: Volume 5. Bachs, Ramon & Beaulieu, Jean-François, illus. 2016. (Disney Kingdoms: Figment Set 2 Ser.). (ENG.). 24p. (J). (gr. k-5). lib. bdg. 31.36 *(978-1-61479-585-8(1)*, 24366, Graphic Novels) Spotlight.

TIMOTHY (BIBLICAL FIGURE)

Rottmann, Erik. Timothy Joins Paul. Snyder, Joel, illus. 2005. (ENG.). 16p. (J). 1.99 *(978-0-7586-0506-1(4))* Concordia Publishing Hse.

TINTIN (FICTITIOUS CHARACTER)—FICTION

Gilchrist, Ellen. Adventures of TinTin. 2009. Vol. 6. pap. 18.99 *(978-0-316-18990-3(1))* Vol. 7. pap. 18.99 *(978-0-316-18992-7(8))* Little, Brown Bks. for Young Readers.
Hergé. The Adventures of Tintin. 2009. 192p. Vol. 1. 18.99 *(978-0-316-18979-8(0))* Vol. 2. 18.99 *(978-0-316-18983-5(9))* Vol. 3. 18.99 *(978-0-316-18986-6(3))* Vol. 4. 18.99 *(978-0-316-18987-3(1))* Little, Brown Bks. for Young Readers.
—America. Orig. Title: Tintin en Amerique. (Illus.). 62p. (J). 24.95 *(978-0-8288-5000-1(3))* French & European Pubns., Inc.
—The Black Island. (Illus.). 62p. (J). 19.95 *(978-0-8288-5012-4(7))* French & European Pubns., Inc.
—The Blue Lotus. (Illus.). (J). 19.95 *(978-0-8288-5480-1(7))* French & European Pubns., Inc.
—The Broken Ear. (Illus.). 62p. (J). 24.95 *(978-0-8288-5086-5(0))* French & European Pubns., Inc.
—The Calculus Affair. (Illus.). 62p. (J). 19.95 *(978-0-8288-5014-8(3))* French & European Pubns., Inc.
—The Castafiore Emerald. (Illus.). 62p. (J). 19.95 *(978-0-8288-5016-2(X))* French & European Pubns., Inc.
—El Cetro de Ottokar. 2007. (Aventuras de Tintin Ser.). (SPA., Illus.). 62p. reprint ed. 22.95 *(978-1-59497-345-1(8))* Public Square Bks.
—Cigars of the Pharaoh.Tr. of Cigares du Pharoan. (Illus.). 62p. (J). 19.95 *(978-0-8288-5021-6(6))* French & European Pubns., Inc.
—The Crab with the Golden Claws. (Illus.). 62p. (J). (gr. 3-8). 19.95 *(978-0-8288-5023-0(2))* French & European Pubns., Inc.
—Le Crabe aux Pinces d'Or.Tr. of Crab with the Golden Claws. (FRE., Illus.). (J). (gr. 7-9). ring bd. 19.95 *(978-0-8288-5025-4(9))* French & European Pubns., Inc.
—Destination Moon.Tr. of Objectif Lune. (J). (gr. 3-8). ring bd. 19.95 *(978-0-8288-5026-1(7))*; (Illus.). 62p. 19.95 *(978-0-8288-5027-8(5))* French & European Pubns., Inc.
—Flight 714. (Illus.). 62p. (J). 19.95 *(978-0-8288-5034-6(8))* French & European Pubns., Inc.
—L' Ile Noire.Tr. of Black Island. (FRE., Illus.). (J). (gr. 7-9). ring bd. 19.95 *(978-0-8288-5039-1(9))* French & European Pubns., Inc.
—La Isla Negra. 2007. (Aventuras de Tintin Ser.). (SPA., Illus.). 62p. reprint ed. 22.95 *(978-1-59497-344-4(X))* Public Square Bks.
—King Ottokar's Sceptre. (Illus.). 62p. (J). 19.95 *(978-0-8288-5044-5(5))* French & European Pubns., Inc.
—Land of Black Gold. Orig. Title: Tintin au Pays de l'Or Noir. (Illus.). 62p. (J). 19.95 *(978-0-8288-5048-3(8))* French & European Pubns., Inc.
—El Loto Azul.Tr. of Blue Lotus. (SPA., Illus.). 62p. (J). 19.95 *(978-0-8288-5049-0(6))* French & European Pubns., Inc.
—Le Lotus Bleu.Tr. of Blue Lotus. (FRE.). (J). (gr. 2-9). 19.95 *(978-0-8288-5050-6(X))* French & European Pubns., Inc.
—Objectif Lune.Tr. of Destination Moon. (FRE., Illus.). (J). (gr. 7-9). ring bd. 19.95 *(978-0-8288-5051-3(8))* French & European Pubns., Inc.
—On a Marche sur la Lune. (Tintin Ser.).Tr. of Explorers on the Moon. (FRE., Illus.). 62p. (J). pap. 21.95 *(978-2-203-00116-9(X))* Casterman, Editions FRA. Dist: Distribooks, Inc.
—On a Marche sur la Lune.Tr. of Explorers on the Moon. (FRE., Illus.). (J). (gr. 7-9). ring bd. 19.95 *(978-0-8288-5053-7(4))* French & European Pubns., Inc.
—L' Oreille Cassee.Tr. of Broken Ear. (FRE., Illus.). 62p. (J). 19.95 *(978-0-8288-5054-4(2))* French & European Pubns., Inc.
—Prisoners of the Sun. (Illus.). 62p. (J). 24.95 *(978-0-8288-5056-8(9))* French & European Pubns., Inc.
—Red Rackham's Treasure. Orig. Title: Tresor de Rackham le Rouge. (Illus.). 62p. (J). 24.95 *(978-0-8288-5057-5(7))* French & European Pubns., Inc.
—The Red Sea Sharks. (Illus.). (J). (gr. 3-8). 24.95 *(978-0-8288-5058-2(5))* French & European Pubns., Inc.
—Secret de la Licorne.Tr. of Secret of the Unicorn. (FRE., Illus.). (J). (gr. 7-9). 24.95 *(978-0-8288-5065-0(8))* French & European Pubns., Inc.
—The Secret of the Unicorn. Orig. Title: Secret de la Licorne. (Illus.). 62p. (J). 24.95 *(978-0-8288-5066-7(6))* French & European Pubns., Inc.
—Sept Boules de Cristal. (FRE., Illus.). (J). (gr. 7-9). 24.95 *(978-0-8288-5069-8(0))* French & European Pubns., Inc.
—The Seven Crystal Balls. (Illus.). 62p. (J). (gr. 3-8). 24.95 *(978-0-8288-5071-1(2))* French & European Pubns., Inc.
—The Shooting Star. (Illus.). (J). (gr. 3-8). ring bd. 24.95 *(978-0-8288-5073-5(9))* French & European Pubns., Inc.
—Tintín: Descubro Las Letras. 2004. (SPA.). 24p. 19.95 *(978-1-59497-066-5(1))* Public Square Bks.
—Tintín: El cangrejo de las pinzas de Oro. 2007. (SPA., Illus.). 64p. reprint ed. 22.95 *(978-1-59497-346-8(6))* Public Square Bks.
—Tintin & the Golden Fleece. (J). (gr. 3-8). 24.95 *(978-0-8288-5087-2(9))* French & European Pubns., Inc.
—Tintin & the Lake of Sharks. (Illus.). 62p. (J). 24.95 *(978-0-416-78950-8(1))* French & European Pubns., Inc.
—Tintin & the Picaros. Orig. Title: Tintin et les Picaros. (Illus.). 62p. (J). 24.95 *(978-0-8288-5089-6(5))* French & European Pubns., Inc.
Herge. Tintin & the Picaros. 2003. (ENG.). 64p. *(978-1-4052-0823-9(6))* Farshore.
Hergé. Tintin au Congo. (FRE., Illus.). (J). (gr. 7-9). 24.95 *(978-0-8288-5090-2(9))* French & European Pubns., Inc.
—Tintin au Pays de l'Or Noir.Tr. of Land of Black Gold. (FRE.). (J). (gr. 7-9). 24.95 *(978-0-8288-5091-9(7))* French & European Pubns., Inc.
—Tintin au Tibet.Tr. of Tintin in Tibet. (J). (gr. 7-9). ring bd. 24.95 *(978-0-8288-5092-6(5))* French & European Pubns., Inc.
—Tintin en Amerique. Orig. Title: Tintin in America. (Illus.). 62p. (J). (FRE.). 24.95 *(978-0-8288-5093-3(3))*; (SPA., 24.95 *(978-0-8288-5094-0(1))* French & European Pubns., Inc.
—Tintin en el Congo. (SPA., Illus.). 62p. (J). 24.95 *(978-0-8288-5095-7(X))* French & European Pubns., Inc.
—Tintin en el Pais del Oro Negro.Tr. of Land of Black Gold. (SPA., Illus.). 62p. (J). 24.95 *(978-0-8288-4995-1(1))* French & European Pubns., Inc.
—Tintin en Tibet. (SPA., Illus.). 62p. (J). 24.95 *(978-0-8288-4996-8(X))* French & European Pubns., Inc.
—Tintin et les Picaros.Tr. of Tintin & the Picaros. (FRE., Illus.). 62p. (J). 24.95 *(978-0-8288-4997-5(8))* French & European Pubns., Inc.
—Tintin im Amerika.Tr. of Tintin in America. (GER., Illus.). 62p. (J). pap. 24.95 *(978-0-8288-4999-9(4))* French & European Pubns., Inc.
—Tintin im Kongo. (GER., Illus.). 62p. (J). pap. 24.95 *(978-0-8288-4998-2(6))* French & European Pubns., Inc.
—Tintin in Tibet. Orig. Title: Tintin au Tibet. (Illus.). 62p. (J). 24.95 *(978-0-8288-5001-8(1))* French & European Pubns., Inc.
—Tintin in Tibet (the Adventures of Tintin) 2003. Orig. Title: Tintin au Tibet. (ENG., Illus.). 64p. *(978-1-4052-0819-2(8))* Farshore.
—Tintin y los Picaros. (SPA., Illus.). 62p. (J). 24.95 *(978-0-8288-5002-5(X))* French & European Pubns., Inc.
—Tresor de Rackham le Rouge.Tr. of Red Rackham's Treasure. (FRE., Illus.). 62p. (J). (gr. 7-9). 24.95 *(978-0-8288-5003-2(8))* French & European Pubns., Inc.
—Le Tresor de Rackham le Rouge. (Tintin Ser.). (FRE., Illus.). (J). pap. 21.95 *(978-2-203-00111-4(9))* Casterman, Editions FRA. Dist: Distribooks, Inc.
—Vol 714 Pour Sydney Vol. 714: Flight 714 for Sydney. (FRE., Illus.). 62p. 21.95 *(978-2-203-00121-3(6))* Casterman, Editions FRA. Dist: Distribooks, Inc.
Hergé & Hergé. The Blue Lotus. 2011. (Adventures of Tintin: Young Readers Edition Ser.). (ENG., Illus.). 96p. (J). (gr. 3-17). pap. 11.99 *(978-0-316-13382-1(5))* Little, Brown Bks. for Young Readers.
—The Crab with the Golden Claws. 2012. (Adventures of Tintin: Young Readers Edition Ser.). (ENG., Illus.). 96p. (J). (gr. 3-17). pap. 11.99 *(978-0-316-19876-9(5))* Little, Brown Bks. for Young Readers.
—King Ottokar's Sceptre. 2012. (Adventures of Tintin: Young Readers Edition Ser.). (ENG., Illus.). 96p. (J). (gr. 3-17). pap. 11.99 *(978-0-316-13383-8(3))* Little, Brown Bks. for Young Readers.
—The Secret of the Unicorn: Collector's Giant Facsimile Edition. fac. ed. 2012. (Adventures of Tintin: Original Classic Ser.). Orig. Title: Secret de la Licorne. (ENG., Illus.). 64p. (J). (gr. 3-17). 60.00 *(978-0-316-23055-1(3))* Little, Brown Bks. for Young Readers.
—Tintin & Alph-Art. 2007. (Adventures of Tintin: Original Classic Ser.). (ENG., Illus.). 64p. (J). (gr. 3-17). pap. 13.99 *(978-0-316-00375-9(1))* Little, Brown Bks. for Young Readers.
—Tintin in the Land of the Soviets. 2007. (Adventures of Tintin: Original Classic Ser.). (ENG., Illus.). 144p. (J). (gr. 3-17). pap. 14.99 *(978-0-316-00374-2(3))* Little, Brown Bks. for Young Readers.
Peters, Stephanie. The Adventures of Tintin: The Chapter Book. 2011. (J). lib. bdg. 14.75 *(978-0-606-23444-3(6))* Turtleback.
Remi, Georges. Aterrizaje en la Luna (rústica) (Tintin Ser.). (SPA.). 64p. (J). 14.95 *(978-84-261-1412-9(1))* Juventud, Editorial ESP. Dist: Distribooks, Inc.
—El Loto Azul (rústica) (Tintin Ser.). (SPA.). 64p. (J). 14.95 *(978-84-261-1418-1(0))* Juventud, Editorial ESP. Dist: Distribooks, Inc.
—Tintín en América (rústica) (Tintin Ser.). (SPA.). 64p. (J). 14.95 *(978-84-261-1400-6(8))* Juventud, Editorial ESP. Dist: Distribooks, Inc.
—Tintín en el Congo (rústica) (Tintin Ser.). (SPA.). 64p. (J). 14.95 *(978-84-261-1401-3(6))* Juventud, Editorial ESP. Dist: Distribooks, Inc.
—Tintín en el país del oro Negro (rústica) (Tintin Ser.). (SPA., Illus.). 64p. (J). 14.95 *(978-84-261-1402-0(4))* Juventud, Editorial ESP. Dist: Distribooks, Inc.
—Tintín y los Pícaros (rústica) (Tintin Ser.). (SPA.). 64p. (J). 14.95 *(978-84-261-1389-4(3))* Juventud, Editorial ESP. Dist: Distribooks, Inc.
Surhone, Lambert M., et al, eds. The Adventures of Tintin: Secret of the Unicorn. 2010. 124p. pap. *(978-613-0-99918-6(6))* AV Akademikerverlag GmbH & Co. KG.

TIRES, RUBBER

Allman, Toney. Recycled Tires. 2009. (Great Idea Ser.). (ENG., Illus.). 48p. (J). (gr. 4-6). lib. bdg. 26.60 *(978-1-59953-197-7(6))* Norwood Hse. Pr.
Ridley, Sarah. A Rubber Tire, 1 vol. 2005. (How It's Made Ser.). (ENG., Illus.). 32p. (gr. 2-4). lib. bdg. 28.67 *(978-0-8368-6295-9(3)*, 6576236a-e513-4022-b372-556cc9420e64, Gareth Stevens Learning Library) Stevens, Gareth Publishing LLLP.

TITANIC (STEAMSHIP)

Amstutz, Lisa J. Titanic, 1 vol. 2014. (Digging up the Past Ser.). (ENG., Illus.). 112p. (YA). (gr. 6-12). lib. bdg. 41.36 *(978-1-62403-238-7(9)*, 1308, Essential Library) ABDO Publishing Co.
Benoit, Peter. The Titanic. 2013. (Cornerstones of Freedom™, Third Ser.). (ENG., Illus.). 64p. (J). pap. 8.95 *(978-0-531-21965-2(8))* Scholastic Library Publishing.
—The Titanic Disaster. 2011. (J). pap. *(978-0-531-29026-2(3))* Children's Pr., Ltd.
—The Titanic Disaster. 2011. (True Bks.). 48p. (J). (gr. 3-5). 29.00 *(978-0-531-20627-0(0)*, Children's Pr.) Scholastic Library Publishing.
Blake, Kevin. Creating Titanic: The Ship of Dreams. 2018. (Titanica Ser.). (ENG.). 32p. (J). (gr. 2-7). 19.95 *(978-1-68402-430-8(7))* Bearport Publishing Co., Inc.
—Titanic's Fatal Voyage. 2018. (Titanica Ser.). (ENG.). 32p. (J). (gr. 2-7). 19.95 *(978-1-68402-432-2(3))* Bearport Publishing Co., Inc.
Blohm, Craig E. The Sinking of the Titanic. 2019. (Historic Disasters & Mysteries Ser.). (ENG.). 64p. (J). (gr. 6-12). 41.27 *(978-1-68282-635-5(X))* ReferencePoint Pr., Inc.
Bodden, Valerie. The Sinking of Titanic. 2018. (Disasters for All Time Ser.). (ENG.). 48p. (J). (gr. 4-7). *(978-1-64026-004-7(8)*, 19722, Creative Education) Creative Co., The.
Brewster, Hugh & Coulter, Laurie. 882 1/2 Amazing Answers to Your Questions about Th. 2018. (ENG., Illus.). 96p. (J). (gr. 3-9). 16.95 *(978-0-2281-0151-2(4)*, de581247-3276-42fe-bf81-3a24486e2a97) Firefly Bks., Ltd.
Brown, Don. All Stations! Distress! April 15, 1912: the Day the Titanic Sank. Brown, Don, illus. 2010. (Actual Times Ser.: 2). (ENG., Illus.). 64p. (J). (gr. 1-5). pap. 10.99 *(978-1-59643-644-2(1)*, 900068840) Square Fish.
Burgan, Michael. Finding the Titanic: How Images from the Ocean Depths Fueled Interest in the Doomed Ship. 2017.

(Captured Science History Ser.). (ENG., Illus.). 64p. (J). (gr. 5-9). lib. bdg. 35.32 *(978-0-7565-5640-2(6)*, 136079, Compass Point Bks.) Capstone.

Burlingame, Jeff. The Titanic Tragedy: The Price of Prosperity in a Gilded Age, 1 vol. 2012. (Perspectives On Ser.). (ENG.). 112p. (YA). (gr. 8-8). 42.64 *(978-1-60870-450-7(5)*, a919bc2c-906f-4261-970b-44a50982ee01) Cavendish Square Publishing LLC.

Callery, Sean. Titanic. 2014. (Scholastic Discover More Ser.). (ENG.). 112p. (J). (gr. 5-9). pap. 15.99 *(978-0-545-50512-3(7)*, Scholastic Reference) Scholastic, Inc.

Caper, William. Nightmare on the Titanic. (Code Red Ser.). 32p. (gr. 2-7). 2018. (ENG.). (J). 7.99 *(978-1-64280-066-1(X))* 2007. (Illus.). (YA). lib. bdg. 28.50 *(978-1-59716-362-0(7))* Bearport Publishing Co., Inc.

Claybourne, Anna & Daynes, Katie. Titanic. McNee, Ian, illus. 2006. (Usborne Young Reading Ser.). 64p. (J). (gr. 3-7). 8.99 *(978-0-7945-1269-9(0)*, Usborne) EDC Publishing.

DK. Story of the Titanic. Noon, Steve, illus. 2012. (DK a History Of Ser.). (ENG.). 48p. (J). (gr. 3-7). 18.99 *(978-0-7566-9171-4(0)*, DK Children) Dorling Kindersley Publishing, Inc.

Doeden, Matt. The Sinking of the Titanic, 1 vol. Barnett, Charles, III & Miller, Phil, illus. 2005. (Graphic History Ser.). (ENG.). 32p. (J). (gr. 3-9). per. 8.10 *(978-0-7368-5247-0(6)*, 86993, Capstone Pr.) Capstone.

Dougherty, Terri, et al. Eyewitness to Titanic: From Building the Great Ship to the Search for Its Watery Grave. 2015. (ENG., Illus.). 160p. (J). (gr. 5-9). pap., pap., pap. 9.95 *(978-1-62370-131-4(7)*, 125876, Capstone Young Readers) Capstone.

Driscoll, Laura. Titanic: The Story Lives On! Kayganich, Bob, illus. 2012. (Penguin Young Readers: Level 4 Ser.). 48p. (J). (ENG.). (gr. 2-4). 17.44 *(978-0-448-45902-8(7))*; (gr. 3-4). mass mkt. 4.99 *(978-0-448-45757-4(1)*, Penguin Young Readers) Penguin Young Readers Group.

Dubowski, Mark. DK Readers L3: Titanic: The Disaster That Shocked the World! 2015. (DK Readers Level 3 Ser.). (ENG., Illus.). 64p. (J). (gr. 2-4). pap. 4.99 *(978-1-4654-2840-0(2)*, DK Children) Dorling Kindersley Publishing, Inc.

Dunn, Joe & Dunn, Ben. The Titanic, 1 vol. 2007. (Graphic History Ser.). (ENG., Illus.). 32p. (J). (gr. 3-8). 32.79 *(978-1-60270-079-6(6)*, 9044, Graphic Planet - Fiction) Magic Wagon.

Fedyszyn, Kirra. Molly Brown, 1 vol. 2014. (Jr. Graphic American Legends Ser.). (ENG., Illus.). 24p. (J). (gr. 2-3). pap. 11.60 *(978-1-4777-7201-0(4)*, 388b9f70-8124-4905-b7df-40c49d57ed37, PowerKids Pr.) Rosen Publishing Group, Inc., The.

Fitzgerald, Dawn. Robert Ballard: Discovering the Titanic & Beyond. 2004. (Gateway Biography Ser.). 48p. (J). lib. bdg. 26.65 *(978-0-7613-2836-0(X)*, Millbrook Pr.) Lerner Publishing Group.

Fullman, Joe. The Story of Titanic for Children: Astonishing Little-Known Facts & Details about the Most Famous Ship in the World. 2018. (Y Ser.). (ENG., Illus.). 48p. (J). (gr. 3-7). pap. 12.95 *(978-1-78312-335-3(4))* Carlton Kids GBR. Dist: Two Rivers Distribution.

Gaetán-Beltrán, Daniel, ed. The Titanic, 1 vol. 2015. (Perspectives on Modern World History Ser.). (ENG., Illus.). 200p. (J). (gr. 10-12). 49.43 *(978-0-7377-7310-1(3)*, 9f14e413-e3c9-44a0-9212-6fe18e5ed2bc, Greenhaven Publishing) Greenhaven Publishing LLC.

Ganeri, Anita & West, David. The Sinking of the Titanic & Other Shipwrecks, 1 vol. 2011. (Incredible True Adventures Ser.). (ENG.). 48p. (YA). (gr. 5-5). pap. 12.75 *(978-1-4488-6663-2(4)*, c075d297-3b57-4a61-8423-9a4230f8e669); lib. bdg. 34.47 *(978-1-4488-6659-5(6)*, ca753712-ff23-45c0-846d-1d9707f33019) Rosen Publishing Group, Inc., The. (Rosen Reference).

Giannini, Alex. Titanic's Passengers & Crew. 2018. (Titanica Ser.). (ENG.). 32p. (J). (gr. 2-7). 19.95 *(978-1-68402-431-5(5))* Bearport Publishing Co., Inc.

Goldish, Meish. Discovering Titanic's Remains. 2018. (Titanica Ser.). (ENG.). 32p. (J). (gr. 2-7). lib. bdg. 28.50 *(978-1-68402-434-6(X))*; E-Book 19.95 *(978-1-68402-492-6(7))* Bearport Publishing Co., Inc.

—Titanic's Last Hours: The Facts. 2018. (Titanica Ser.). (ENG.). 32p. (J). (gr. 2-7). 19.95 *(978-1-68402-429-2(3))* Bearport Publishing Co., Inc.

Hanel, Rachael, et al. You Choose: Can You Survive Collection. 2017. (You Choose: Survival Ser.). (ENG., Illus.). 328p. (J). (gr. 3-7). pap., pap., pap. 9.99 *(978-1-5157-9081-5(9)*, 136490, Capstone Pr.) Capstone.

Hopkinson, Deborah. Titanic: Voices from the Disaster. 2012. (Illus.). 289p. (J). pap. 8.95 *(978-0-545-43677-9(X)*, Scholastic Pr.) Scholastic, Inc.

—Titanic: Voices from the Disaster (Scholastic Focus) 2014. (ENG.). 304p. (J). (gr. 3-7). pap. 8.99 *(978-0-545-11675-6(9))* Scholastic, Inc.

Jenkins, Martin. Titanic. Sanders, Brian, illus. 2012. (ENG.). 32p. (J). (gr. 3-7). pap. 6.99 *(978-0-7636-6034-5(5))* Candlewick Pr.

—Titanic: Disaster at Sea. 2012. (Illus.). 31p. lib. bdg. 17.20 *(978-0-606-23811-3(5))* Turtleback.

Johnson, Robin. Titanic. 2012. (ENG., Illus.). 48p. (J). *(978-0-7787-7929-2(7))*; (gr. 2-6). pap. *(978-0-7787-7938-4(6))* Crabtree Publishing Co.

Krajnik, Elizabeth. Aboard the Titanic, 1 vol. 2019. (History on the High Seas Ser.). (ENG.). 24p. (gr. 2-3). pap. 9.15 *(978-1-5382-3802-8(0)*, 16808908-47a4-45f0-876d-5db172d6af20) Stevens, Gareth Publishing LLLP.

Kupperberg, Paul. The Tragedy of the Titanic. 2009. (When Disaster Strikes! Ser.). 48p. (gr. 5-8). 53.00 *(978-1-60854-782-1(5)*, Rosen Reference) Rosen Publishing Group, Inc., The.

Lassieur, Allison. Can You Survive the Titanic? An Interactive Survival Adventure, 1 vol. 2011. (You Choose: Survival Ser.). (ENG., 112p. (J). (gr. 3-7). Illus.). lib. bdg. 32.65 *(978-1-4296-6586-5(6)*, 115708); pap. 41.70 *(978-1-4296-7352-5(4)*, 16842); pap. 6.95 *(978-1-4296-7351-8(6)*, 116887) Capstone. (Capstone Pr.).

Loh-Hagan, Virginia. The Real Violet Jessop. 2019. (History Uncut Ser.). (ENG., Illus.). 32p. (J). (gr. 4-8). pap. 14.21 *(978-1-5341-3992-3(3)*, 212797); lib. bdg. 32.07 *(978-1-5341-4336-4(X)*, 212796) Cherry Lake Publishing. (45th Parallel Press).

Lohse, Joyce B. Unsinkable: The Molly Brown Story. 2006. (Now You Know Bio Ser.). (Illus.). 76p. (J). pap. 8.95 *(978-0-86541-081-7(X))* Filter Pr., LLC.

Lorbiecki, Marybeth. Escaping Titanic: A Young Girl's True Story of Survival, 1 vol. Lorbiecki, Marybeth & Heinzen, Kory S., illus. 2012. (Na Ser.). (ENG.). 32p. (J). (gr. k-5). pap. 8.95 *(978-1-4048-7235-6(3)*, 118125, Picture Window Bks.) Capstone.

Lusted, Marcia Amidon. The Sinking of the Titanic: A History Perspectives Book. 2013. (Perspectives Library). (ENG., Illus.). 32p. (J). (gr. 4-8). 32.07 *(978-1-62431-421-6(X)*, 202804); pap. 14.21 *(978-1-62431-497-1(X)*, 202806) Cherry Lake Publishing.

McDonnell, Vincent. Titanic Tragedy. 2007. (ENG.). 160p. (J). (gr. -1-3). per. 12.95 *(978-1-905172-41-2(9)*, Collins Pr., The) M.H. Gill & Co. U. C. IRL. Dist: Dufour Editions, Inc.

McPherson, Stephanie Sammartino. Iceberg, Right Ahead! The Tragedy of the Titanic. (Single Titles Ser.). (ENG., Illus.). 112p. (gr. 6-12). 2011. lib. bdg. 33.26 *(978-0-7613-6756-7(X))* 2015. (YA). E-Book 53.32 *(978-1-4677-5932-8(5)*, 9781467759328, Lerner Digital) Lerner Publishing Group.

Merwin, E. A Haunted Titanic. 2018. (Titanica Ser.). (ENG.). 32p. (J). (gr. 2-7). 19.95 *(978-1-68402-433-9(1))* Bearport Publishing Co., Inc.

Navratil, Elisabeth. Survivors: A True-Life Titanic Story. de Sola Pinto, Joan, tr. 2018. (ENG.). 224p. 15.00 *(978-1-78849-057-3(6))* O'Brien Pr., Ltd., The IRL. Dist: Casemate Pubs. & Bk. Distributors, LLC.

Oachs, Emily Rose. The Titanic. 2019. (Digging up the Past Ser.). (ENG., Illus.). 24p. (J). (gr. 3-7). lib. bdg. 26.95 *(978-1-64487-071-6(1)*, Torque Bks.) Bellwether Media.

Ohlin, Nancy. The Titanic. Larkum, Adam, illus. 2016. (Blast Back! Ser.). (ENG.). 112p. (J). (gr. 2-5). pap. 5.99 *(978-1-4998-0273-3(0))* Little Bee Books Inc.

Otfinoski, Steven. Smooth Sea & a Fighting Chance: The Story of the Sinking of Titanic. 2016. (Tangled History Ser.). (ENG., Illus.). 112p. (J). (gr. 3-9). lib. bdg. 32.65 *(978-1-4914-8453-1(5)*, 130900, Capstone Pr.) Capstone.

Park, Louise. The Sinking of the Titanic, 1 vol. 2013. (Discovery Education: Sensational True Stories Ser.). (ENG., Illus.). 32p. (J). (gr. 4-5). pap. 11.00 *(978-1-4777-0099-0(4)*, 395291a0-7c6d-4e04-a217-88b3819fbdc3); lib. bdg. 28.93 *(978-1-4777-0057-0(9)*, 595f2e90-803e-4f97-9b07-5777c37e2880) Rosen Publishing Group, Inc., The. (PowerKids Pr.).

Poehlmann, Tristan. The Titanic Story. 2017. (Famous Ships Ser.). (ENG., Illus.). 112p. (J). (gr. 6-12). lib. bdg. 41.36 *(978-1-5321-1321-5(8)*, 27529, Essential Library) ABDO Publishing Co.

Ruffin, Frances E. Unsinkable Molly Brown. 2009. (American Legends Ser.). 24p. (gr. 3-3). 42.50 *(978-1-61511-377-4(0)*, PowerKids Pr.) Rosen Publishing Group, Inc., The.

Russo, Kristin J. Viewpoints on the Sinking of the Titanic. 2018. (Perspectives Library: Viewpoints & Perspectives Ser.). (ENG., Illus.). 48p. (J). (gr. 5-8). lib. bdg. 39.21 *(978-1-5341-2968-9(5)*, 211916) Cherry Lake Publishing.

Sabol, Stephanie. What Was the Titanic? 2018. (What Was... Ser.). lib. bdg. 16.00 *(978-0-606-40891-2(6))* Turtleback.

Sabol, Stephanie & Who HQ. What Was the Titanic? Copeland, Gregory, illus. 2018. (What Was? Ser.). 112p. (J). (gr. 3-7). 5.99 *(978-0-515-15726-0(0))*; lib. bdg. 15.99 *(978-0-515-15728-4(7))* Penguin Young Readers Group. (Penguin Workshop).

Shea, Therese M. The Sinking of the Titanic, 1 vol. 2015. (Doomed! Ser.). (ENG.). 32p. (J). (gr. 4-5). pap. 11.50 *(978-1-4824-2944-2(6)*, 8973557f-77b2-4330-973a-b5ffe77c3dfd) Stevens, Gareth Publishing LLLP.

Shoulders, Michael & Shoulders, Debbie. T Is for Titanic: A Titanic Alphabet. Frankenhuyzen, Gijsbert van, illus. 2011. (ENG.). 32p. (J). (gr. 1-4). 17.95 *(978-1-58536-176-2(3)*, 202264) Sleeping Bear Pr.

Shoup, Kate. Life As a Passenger on the Titanic, 1 vol. 2017. (Life As... Ser.). (ENG.). 32p. (gr. 3-3). pap. 11.58 *(978-1-5026-3043-8(5)*, 4c85f115-5377-4a78-978e-48067446bb7c) Cavendish Square Publishing LLC.

Silverman, Buffy. Surviving a Shipwreck: The Titanic. 2019. (They Survived (Alternator Books (r)) Ser.). (ENG., Illus.). 32p. (J). (gr. 3-6). 29.32 *(978-1-5415-2352-4(0)*, 29d250a4-cadd-4a1c-a9b6-6d16cb32a121, Lerner Pubns.) Lerner Publishing Group.

Stewart, David. You Wouldn't Want to Sail on the Titanic! 2013. (You Wouldn't Want To Ser.). lib. bdg. 20.80 *(978-0-606-31630-9(2))* Turtleback.

—You Wouldn't Want to Sail on the Titanic! (Revised Edition) (You Wouldn't Want to...: History of the World) Antram, David, illus. rev. ed. 2013. (You Wouldn't Want To — Ser.). (ENG.). 32p. (J). (gr. 3). pap. 9.95 *(978-0-531-24505-7(5)*, Watts, Franklin) Scholastic Library Publishing.

Stewart, Melissa. National Geographic Readers: Titanic. 2012. (Readers Ser.). 48p. (J). (gr. 1-3). (ENG.). lib. bdg. 14.90 *(978-1-4263-1060-7(9)*, National Geographic Children's Bks.); (Illus.). pap. 4.99 *(978-1-4263-1059-1(5)*, National Geographic Kids) Disney Publishing Worldwide.

Stone, Adam. The Titanic Disaster. 2014. (Disaster Stories Ser.). (ENG., Illus.). 24p. (J). (gr. 3-8). 29.95 *(978-1-62617-154-1(8)*, Black Sheep) Bellwether Media.

Temple, Bob. The Titanic: An Interactive History Adventure. rev. ed. 2016. (You Choose: History Ser.). (ENG., Illus.). 112p. (J). (gr. 3-7). pap. 6.95 *(978-1-5157-3388-1(2)*, 133375, Capstone Pr.) Capstone.

—The Titanic [Scholastic]: An Interactive History Adventure. 2010. (You Choose: History Ser.). 112p. pap. 0.86 *(978-1-4296-5119-6(9)*, Capstone Pr.) Capstone.

Troupe, Thomas Kingsley. Titanic's Tragic Journey: A Fly on the Wall History. Tejido, Jomike, illus. 2018. (Fly on the Wall History Ser.). (ENG.). 32p. (J). (gr. 1-3). lib. bdg. 27.99 *(978-1-5158-1599-0(4)*, 136252, Picture Window Bks.) Capstone.

Welldon, Christine. Children of the Titanic, 1 vol. 2012. (Compass: True Stories for Kids Ser.). (ENG., Illus.). 96p. (J). (gr. 4-7). pap. 14.95 *(978-1-55109-892-0(X)*, 79691984-0924-40d3-8b21-486265a7823d) Nimbus Publishing, Ltd. CAN. Dist: Baker & Taylor Publisher Services (BTPS).

Whiting, Jim. The Sinking of the Titanic. 2006. (Monumental Milestones Ser.). (Illus.). 48p. (J). (gr. 3-7). lib. bdg. 29.95 *(978-1-58415-472-3(1))* Mitchell Lane Pubs.

Wishinsky, Frieda. Remembering the Titanic. 2012. (Scholastic Reader Level 3 Ser.). (ENG.). 32p. (J). (gr. 1-3). pap. 3.99 *(978-0-545-35844-6(2)*, Scholastic Paperbacks) Scholastic, Inc.

Yasuda, Anita. Sinking of the Titanic, 1 vol. 2013. (History's Greatest Disasters Ser.). (ENG., Illus.). 48p. (J). (gr. 4-8). lib. bdg. 35.64 *(978-1-61783-960-3(4)*, 9491) ABDO Publishing Co.

—Sinking of the Titanic Paperback. 2013. (History's Greatest Disasters Ser.). (ENG.). (J). (gr. 4-8). pap. 18.50 *(978-1-62403-025-3(4)*, 10774) ABDO Publishing Co.

Zullo, Allan. Titanic: Young Survivors (10 True Tales) 2015. (10 True Tales Ser.). (ENG.). 192p. (J). (gr. 3-7). pap. 5.99 *(978-0-545-81839-1(7)*, Scholastic Nonfiction) Scholastic, Inc.

TITANIC (STEAMSHIP)—FICTION

Brezenoff, Steve. Time Voyage, 1 vol. Murphy, Scott, illus. 2012. (Return to Titanic Ser.). (ENG.). 112p. (J). (gr. 3-6). pap. 6.95 *(978-1-4342-3909-9(8)*, 118094, Stone Arch Bks.) Capstone.

Bunting, Eve. S. O. S. Titanic. 2012. (ENG.). 256p. (YA). (gr. 7-12). pap. 7.99 *(978-0-15-201305-9(9)*, 1189458, Clarion Bks.) HarperCollins Pubs.

Charman, Katrina. The Survival Tails: the Titanic. 2018. (Survival Tails Ser.: 1). (ENG., Illus.). 224p. (J). (gr. 3-7). pap. 7.99 *(978-0-316-47783-3(4))* Little, Brown Bks. for Young Readers.

—Titanic. 2018. (Survival Tails Ser.: 1). (J). lib. bdg. 18.40 *(978-0-606-40981-0(5))* Turtleback.

Crew, Gary. Pig on the Titanic: A True Story. Whatley, Bruce, illus. 2005. 32p. (J). 15.99 *(978-0-06-052305-3(0))* HarperCollins Pubs.

Crisp, Marty. Titanicat. Papp, Robert, illus. 2008. (ENG.). 40p. (J). (gr. 1-4). 17.95 *(978-1-58536-355-1(3)*, 202141) Sleeping Bear Pr.

Duey, K. & Bale, K. A. Salvados! Titanic. 2003. (Survival Ser.).Tr. of Survival! Titanic. (SPA.). (J). pap. 9.95 *(978-0-9715256-4-1(1))* Planeta Publishing Corp.

Duey, Kathleen & Bale, Karen A. Titanic: April 1912. 2014. (Survivors Ser.). (ENG., Illus.). 192p. (J). (gr. 3-7). pap. 7.99 *(978-1-4424-9051-2(9)*, Aladdin) Simon & Schuster Children's Publishing.

—Titanic: April 1912. 2014. (Survivors Ser.). (ENG., Illus.). 192p. (J). (gr. 3-7). 15.99 *(978-1-4424-9052-9(7)*, Simon & Schuster/Paula Wiseman Bks.) Simon & Schuster/Paula Wiseman Bks.

Gray, Claudia. Fateful. 2012. (ENG.). 352p. (YA). (gr. 9). pap. 9.99 *(978-0-06-200621-9(5)*, HarperTeen) HarperCollins Pubs.

Harrison, Cora. Titanic Voyage from Drumshee. 2nd ed. 2003. (Drumshee Timeline Ser.). 134p. (J). (gr. 4-7). per. *(978-0-86327-905-8(8))* Wolfhound Pr.

Jane, Sarah. Maiden Voyage: a Titanic Story. 2018. (ENG.). 256p. (J). (gr. 7-7). pap. 9.99 *(978-1-338-22665-2(7)*, Scholastic Pr.) Scholastic, Inc.

Klimo, Kate. Dog Diaries #14: Sunny. Jessell, Tim, illus. 2019. (Dog Diaries: 14). 160p. (J). (gr. 2-5). pap. 7.99 *(978-0-525-64823-9(2)*, Random Hse. Bks. for Young Readers) Random Hse. Children's Bks.

Korman, Gordon. Unsinkable (Titanic, Book 1), Bk. 1. 2011. (Titanic Ser.: 1). (ENG.). 176p. (J). (gr. 4-7). pap. 6.99 *(978-0-545-12331-0(3)*, Scholastic Paperbacks) Scholastic, Inc.

Messner, Kate. Disaster on the Titanic (Ranger in Time #9) McMorris, Kelley, illus. 2019. (Ranger in Time Ser.: 9). (ENG.). 144p. (J). (gr. 2-5). pap. 5.99 *(978-1-338-13398-1(5)*, Scholastic Pr.) Scholastic, Inc.

Methods, Bryan. Lessons from Underground. 2018. (Master Diplexito & Mr. Scant Ser.). (ENG., Illus.). 272p. (J). (gr. 5-8). 17.99 *(978-1-5124-0581-1(7)*, 199f9813-c1d3-4053-bc16-93f1f1c16c72, Carolrhoda Bks.) Lerner Publishing Group.

Mone, Gregory. Dangerous Waters: An Adventure on the Titanic. 2013. (ENG.). 256p. (J). (gr. 4-6). pap. 11.99 *(978-1-250-01671-3(1)*, 900087085) Square Fish.

Morpurgo, Michael. Kaspar the Titanic Cat. Foreman, Michael, illus. 2012. (ENG.). 208p. (J). (gr. 3-7). 16.99 *(978-0-06-200618-9(5)*, Balzer & Bray) HarperCollins Pubs.

Nielsen, Jennifer A. Iceberg. 2023. (ENG.). 352p. (J). (gr. 3-7). 17.99 *(978-1-338-79502-8(3)*, Scholastic Pr.) Scholastic, Inc.

Osborne, Mary Pope. Tonight on the Titanic. unabr. ed. 2004. (Magic Tree House Ser.: No. 17). 71p. (J). (gr. k-3). pap. 17.00 incl. audio *(978-0-8072-0926-4(0)*, S FTR 249 SP, Listening Library) Random Hse. Audio Publishing Group.

Osborne, Mary Pope & Murdocca, Sal. Esta Noche en el Titanic. Murdocca, Sal, illus. 2008. (Casa del Arbol Ser.: 17).Tr. of Tonight on the Titanic. (SPA., Illus.). (J). (gr. 2-4). pap. 6.99 *(978-1-933032-47-4(2))* Lectorum Pubns., Inc.

Peck, Richard. Amanda/Miranda. 2012. (ENG.). 176p. (YA). (gr. 7-12). 22.44 *(978-0-14-242068-3(9))* Penguin Young Readers Group.

Peters, Stephanie True. The First & Final Voyage: The Sinking of the Titanic, 1 vol. Proctor, Jon, illus. 2008. (Historical Fiction Ser.). (ENG.). 56p. (J). (gr. 3-6). pap. 6.25 *(978-1-4342-0494-3(4)*, 94442, Stone Arch Bks.) Capstone.

Phillips, Dee. Titanic. 2014. (Yesterday's Voices Ser.). (YA). lib. bdg. 19.60 *(978-0-606-35583-4(9))* Turtleback.

Polacco, Patricia. The Bravest Man in the World. Polacco, Patricia, illus. 2019. (ENG., Illus.). 56p. (J). (gr. -1-3). 17.99 *(978-1-4814-9461-8(9)*, Simon & Schuster Bks. For Young Readers) Simon & Schuster Bks. For Young Readers.

Schillow, Ned W. and Schillow. Titanic Hearts. 2007. 100p. per. 10.00 *(978-1-4257-3842-6(7))* Xlibris Corp.

Smith, Nikki Shannon. Noelle at Sea: A Titanic Survival Story. Forsyth, Matt, illus. 2019. (Girls Survive Ser.). (ENG.). 112p. (J). (gr. 3-7). lib. bdg. 25.99 *(978-1-4965-7850-1(3)*, 139368, Stone Arch Bks.) Capstone.

Smyth, Jimmy. Titanic the Untold Story. 2013. 34p. pap. *(978-0-9569314-4-3(8))* Smith, Jimmy.

Tarshis, Lauren. I Survived the Sinking of the Titanic 1912. 2010. (I Survived Ser.: No. 1). lib. bdg. 14.75 *(978-0-606-23741-3(0))* Turtleback.

—I Survived the Sinking of the Titanic, 1912 (I Survived #1) Dawson, Scott, illus. 2010. (I Survived Ser.: 1). (ENG.). 112p. (J). (gr. 2-5). 4.99 *(978-0-545-20694-5(4)*, Scholastic Paperbacks) Scholastic, Inc.

Wallace, Jim. Terror on the Titanic. Sundaravej, Sittisan, illus. 2007. (ENG.). 144p. (J). (gr. 4-8). pap. 7.99 *(978-1-933390-24-6(7))* Chooseco LLC.

Warner, Michael N. The Titanic Game. Ordaz, Frank, illus. 2018. (ENG.). 208p. (J). pap. 11.95 *(978-0-9744446-2-8(6))* All About Kids Publishing.

Watts, Irene N. No Moon. 2010. 240p. (YA). (gr. 7). pap. 12.95 *(978-0-88776-971-9(3)*, Tundra Bks.) Tundra Bks. CAN. Dist: Penguin Random Hse. LLC.

White, Ellen Emerson. Voyage on the Great Titanic. 2010. (Dear America Ser.). (ENG., Illus.). 208p. (J). (gr. 3-9). 12.99 *(978-0-545-23834-2(X)*, Scholastic Pr.) Scholastic, Inc.

Yomtov, Nel. Titanic Disaster! Nickolas Flux & the Sinking of the Great Ship. Simmons, Mark, illus. 2015. (Nickolas Flux History Chronicles Ser.). (ENG.). 40p. (J). (gr. 3-9). lib. bdg. 33.32 *(978-1-4914-2070-6(7)*, 127548, Capstone Pr.) Capstone.

Zullo, Allan. Titanic Young Survivors. 2012. 181p. (J). *(978-0-545-33315-3(6))* Scholastic, Inc.

TITHES

MacKenzie, Catherine. George Müller: Does Money Grow on Trees? rev. ed. 2012. (Little Lights Ser.). (ENG., Illus.). 24p. (J). (gr. -1-3). 7.99 *(978-1-84550-110-5(1)*, 4f6bdd8c-ae41-46d0-96d7-e6168c003a6b) Christian Focus Pubns. GBR. Dist: Baker & Taylor Publisher Services (BTPS).

Mathews, Janice. Jack Gives Back. 2012. (J). 7.99 *(978-0-8280-2667-3(X))* Review & Herald Publishing Assn.

TITIAN, APPROXIMATELY 1488-1576

Venezia, Mike. Getting to Know the World's Greatest Artists - Titian. Venezia, Mike, illus. 2003. (Getting to Know the World's Greatest Artists Ser.). (ENG., Illus.). 32p. (J). (gr. 3-4). pap. 6.95 *(978-0-516-26975-7(5)*, Children's Pr.) Scholastic Library Publishing.

—Titian. Venezia, Mike, illus. 2003. (Getting to Know World Artists Ser.). (ENG., Illus.). 32p. (J). 28.00 *(978-0-516-22575-3(8)*, Children's Pr.) Scholastic Library Publishing.

TIZIANO, APPROXIMATELY 1488-1576

see Titian, approximately 1488-1576

TOADS

see Frogs

TOADSTOOLS

see Mushrooms

TOBACCO HABIT

Allen, John. Teens & Vaping. 2019. (ENG.). 80p. (YA). (gr. 6-12). 41.27 *(978-1-68282-755-0(0))* ReferencePoint Pr., Inc.

Connolly, Sean. Tobacco. 2006. (Straight Talking Ser.). (Illus.). 46p. (YA). (gr. 4-7). lib. bdg. 32.80 *(978-1-58340-649-6(2))* Black Rabbit Bks.

—Tobacco. 2009. (Straight Talking Ser.). (ENG., Illus.). 48p. (YA). (gr. 8-12). pap. *(978-1-895058-55-0(4))* Saunders Bk. Co.

Davani, Keyvan. SmokeReality. 2007. 160p. pap. 13.95 *(978-1-84753-552-8(6))* Lulu Pr., Inc.

Hand, Carol. Tobacco. 2018. (Drugs in Real Life Ser.). (ENG., Illus.). 112p. (J). (gr. 6-12). lib. bdg. 41.36 *(978-1-5321-1421-2(4)*, 28824, Essential Library) ABDO Publishing Co.

Hasan, Heather. Caffeine & Nicotine, 1 vol. 2009. (Drug Abuse & Society Ser.). (ENG.). 64p. (YA). (gr. 6-6). lib. bdg. 37.13 *(978-1-4358-5015-6(7)*, 74f1affd-7b04-4c2f-8511-6434b17bcf13) Rosen Publishing Group, Inc., The.

Holt, Rinehart and Winston Staff. A Lifetime of Health Chptr. 11: Tobacco. 4th ed. Date not set. pap. 11.20 *(978-0-03-068103-5(0))* Holt McDougal.

Horsfield, Alan & Horsfield, Elaine. Talking about the Dangers of Alcohol, Tobacco, & Caffeine, 1 vol. 2010. (Healthy Living Ser.). (ENG., Illus.). 32p. (YA). (gr. 3-4). lib. bdg. 28.67 *(978-1-4339-3661-6(5)*, f8455b09-d20b-4c35-aa6a-b16fab7556f5) Stevens, Gareth Publishing LLLP.

Hunter, David. Born to Smoke: Nicotine & Genetics. 2009. (Illus.). 112p. (J). 26.95 *(978-1-4222-0230-2(5)*, 1291227) Mason Crest.

—But Smoking Makes Me Happy: The Link Between Nicotine & Depression. 2009. (Illus.). 112p. (J). pap. 26.95 *(978-1-4222-1335-3(8))* Mason Crest.

—Thousands of Deadly Chemicals: Smoking & Health. 2007. (Tobacco: the Deadly Drug Ser.). (Illus.). 112p. (YA). pap. 12.95 *(978-1-4222-0817-5(6))* Mason Crest.

Jones, David C. One Person to Another: Smoking, Chewing Tobacco & Young Peopole. I.t. ed. 2003. 20p. (YA). 4.00 *(978-1-878400-17-8(7))* Dolphin Publishing.

Keyishian, Elizabeth. Smoking, 1 vol. rev. ed. 2003. (Need to Know Library (1994-2004) Ser.). (ENG., Illus.). 64p. (J). (gr. 5-5). lib. bdg. 37.13 *(978-0-8239-4092-9(6)*, 99252132-b6f2-4c6d-bf79-63a05e89f907) Rosen Publishing Group, Inc., The.

Malaspina, Ann. False Images, Deadly Promises: Smoking & the Media. 2007. (Tobacco: the Deadly Drug Ser.). (Illus.). 112p. (YA). pap. 12.95 *(978-1-4222-0812-0(5))* Mason Crest.

Mason, Paul. Know the Facts about Drinking & Smoking. 2009. (J). 70.50 *(978-1-4358-5463-5(2))*; (ENG.). 48p. (YA). (gr. 5-6). pap. 12.75 *(978-1-4358-5462-8(4)*, 9f74385e-5423-4c2a-ad5b-60043b320a85) Rosen Publishing Group, Inc., The. (Rosen Reference).

Miller, Heather. Smoking. 2008. (21st Century Skills Library: Health at Risk Ser.). (ENG., Illus.). 32p. (gr. 4-8). lib. bdg. 32.07 *(978-1-60279-286-9(0)*, 200135) Cherry Lake Publishing.

Sharp, Katie John. Smokeless Tobacco: Not a Safe Alternative. 2009. (Illus.). 112p. (J). pap. 26.95 *(978-1-4222-1332-2(3)*, 1291227) Mason Crest.

TUV

—Teenagers & Tobacco: Nicotine & the Adolescent Brain. 2007. (Tobacco: the Deadly Drug Ser.). (Illus.). 112p. (YA). (gr. 3-7). pap. 12.95 *(978-1-4222-0816-8(8))* Mason Crest.
Smoking. 2008. (Current Controversies Ser.). (Illus.). 176-240p. (gr. 10-12). 36.20 *(978-0-7377-3293-1(8))*; pap. 24.95 *(978-0-7377-3294-8(6))* Cengage Gale. (Greenhaven Pr., Inc.).
Wagner, Heather Lehr. Nicotine. 2003. (Drugs: the Straight Facts Ser.). (ENG., Illus.). 112p. (gr. 9-13). 30.00 *(978-0-7910-7264-6(9))*, P113780, Facts On File) Infobase Holdings, Inc.
Walker, Ida. Addiction in America: Society, Psychology & Heredity. 2012. (Illus.). 128p. (J). *(978-1-4222-2443-4(0))*; *(978-1-4222-2424-3(4))* Mason Crest.

TOES

see Foot

TOILET

see Beauty, Personal

TOILET PREPARATIONS

see Cosmetics

TOILET TRAINING

Aaron-Barrada, Tammie, creator. PottieStickers 3-Pack Fireflies, Kites & Fish Tank: How to Toilet Train in 7 Days with Success with the #1 Portable Toilet Training Reward System for Today's Family-on-the-Go-Lifestyle... Because Consistency Counts!, 3 vols. 2004. (Illus.). 6p. (J). 9.99 *(978-0-9768671-2-8(5))* Aaron-Barrada, Inc.
—PottieStickers 3-Pack Tools, Sea Horses & Flowers: How to Toilet Train in 7 Days with Success! #1 Portable Toilet Training Reward System for today's family-on-the-go-lifestyle... because consistency Counts! 2004. Orig. Title: #1 Portable Toilet Training Reward System for today's family-on-the-go-lifestyle... because consistency Counts! (Illus.). 6p. (J). 9.99 *(978-0-615-12767-5(3))* Aaron-Barrada, Inc.
Aaron-Barrada, Tammie, prod. PottieStickers 3-pack Sports Equipment, Seashells & Butterflies: How to Toilet Train in 7 Days with Success with the #1 Portable Toilet Training Reward System for today's family-on-the-go-lifestyle... because consistency Counts!, 3 vols. 2004. (Illus.). 6p. (J). 9.99 *(978-0-9768671-1-1(7))* Aaron-Barrada, Inc.
Berry, Joy. Teach Me about Potty Training. 2009. (ENG.). 40p. (J). (gr. k — 1). bds. 7.95 *(978-1-60577-011-6(6))* Berry, Joy Enterprises.
—Teach Me about Potty Training (Boys) 2009. (Teach Me About Ser.). 40p. 7.95 incl. lp *(978-1-60577-033-8(7))* Berry, Joy Enterprises.
Brooks, Felicity & Allen, Francesca. Baby's Potty. Wells, Rachel, illus. 2006. (Baby's Day Board Book Ser.). 10p. (J). (gr. -1). bds. 8.99 *(978-0-7945-1362-7(X)*, Usborne) EDC Publishing.
Chapman, Jared. Vegetables in Underwear. 2017. (ENG., Illus.). 22p. (J). (gr. -1-k). bds. 7.95 *(978-1-4197-2377-3(4)*, 1098710, Abrams Appleseed) Abrams, Inc.
DK. Big Boys Use the Potty! 2005. (ENG., Illus.). 12p. (J). (gr. -1-k). bds. 7.99 *(978-0-7566-1451-5(1)*, DK Children) Dorling Kindersley Publishing, Inc.
—Boys' Potty Time. 2010. (ENG., Illus.). 14p. (J). (gr. -1-k). bds. 9.99 *(978-0-7566-5884-7(5)*, DK Children) Dorling Kindersley Publishing, Inc.
—Girls' Potty Time: Includes Special Reward Stickers! 2010. (ENG., Illus.). 14p. (J). (gr. -1-k). bds. 9.99 *(978-0-7566-5885-4(3)*, DK Children) Dorling Kindersley Publishing, Inc.
Foote, Tracy. My Potty Reward Stickers for Boys: 126 Boy Potty Training Stickers & Chart to Motivate Toilet Training. 4th ed. 2006. (J). per. 7.95 *(978-0-9708226-8-0(5))* TracyTrends.
—My Potty Reward Stickers for Boys: 126 Boy Stickers & Chart to Motivate Toilet Training. 2003. (J). 7.95 *(978-0-9708226-6-6(9))* TracyTrends.
—My Potty Reward Stickers for Girls: 126 Girl Potty Training Stickers & Chart to Motivate Toilet Training. 4th ed. 2006. (Illus.). (J). 7.95 *(978-0-9708226-7-3(7))* TracyTrends.
—My Potty Reward Stickers for Girls: 126 Girl Stickers & Chart to Motivate Toilet Training. 3rd rev. ed. 2003. (J). 7.95 *(978-0-9708226-5-9(0))* TracyTrends.
Frankel, Alona. Mi Bacinica y Yo (para El) 2013. (SPA., Illus.). 44p. (J). (gr. -1 — 1). 7.95 *(978-1-77085-402-4(9)*, 905179be-95b9-4a5e-90c1-19461ed0f700) Firefly Bks., Ltd.
—Mi Bacinica y Yo (para Ella) 2013. (SPA., Illus.). 44p. (J). (gr. -1 — 1). 7.95 *(978-1-77085-403-1(7)*, a0e51081-6f18-4e85-b9f9-075f94a72d65) Firefly Bks., Ltd.
—Once upon a Potty — Boy. 2014. (Once upon a Potty Ser.). (ENG., Illus.). 24p. (J). (gr. -1 — 1). bds. 9.95 *(978-1-77085-404-8(5)*, 329daeaa-2601-41fe-a71e-109a228d1103) Firefly Bks., Ltd.
—Once upon a Potty — Boy. Frankel, Alona, illus. 2007. (Once upon a Potty Ser.). (ENG., Illus.). 40p. (J). (gr. -1 — 1). 7.95 *(978-1-55407-283-5(2)*, 2a808d56-e84c-457a-baf9-57efbe97d3a8) Firefly Bks., Ltd.
—Once upon a Potty — Boy — Sound Book. Frankel, Alona, illus. 2021. (Once upon a Potty Ser.). (ENG., Illus.). 8p. (J). (gr. -1 — 1). bds. 16.95 *(978-0-2281-0237-3(5)*, f94c8421-a78c-460f-8ea6-d7a256dec65a) Firefly Bks., Ltd.
—Once upon a Potty — Girl. 2014. (Once upon a Potty Ser.). (ENG., Illus.). 24p. (J). (gr. -1 — 1). bds. 9.95 *(978-1-77085-405-5(3)*, 9a244594-1b0a-4c88-b6d8-c4bfc0b03181) Firefly Bks., Ltd.
—Once upon a Potty — Girl. Frankel, Alona, illus. 2007. (Once upon a Potty Ser.). (ENG., Illus.). 40p. (J). (gr. -1 — 1). 7.95 *(978-1-55407-284-2(0)*, 0c038727-2063-4d10-a118-e4fe810124fc) Firefly Bks., Ltd.
—Once upon a Potty — Girl — Sound Book. Frankel, Alona, illus. 2021. (Once upon a Potty Ser.). (ENG., Illus.). 8p. (J). (gr. -1 — 1). bds. 16.95 *(978-0-2281-0238-0(3)*, 0b1dfbe6-309d-466d-ba43-e2a8td5e3ca8) Firefly Bks., Ltd.
Gordon, Rachel & Gold, Claudia M. Potty Palooza: A Step-By-Step Guide to Using a Potty. Bergmann, Sarah, illus. 2013. (ENG.). 32p. (J). (gr. -1 — 1). bds. 9.95 *(978-0-7611-7485-1(0)*, 17485) Workman Publishing Co., Inc.
Hochman, David & Kennison, Ruth. The Potty Train. Anderson, Derek, illus. 2008. (ENG.). 32p. (J). (gr. -1-k). 9.99 *(978-1-4169-2833-1(2)*, Simon & Schuster Bks. For Young Readers) Simon & Schuster Bks. For Young Readers.
Knickerbocker-Silva, Heather. Tinkle, Tinkle When I Go to the Potty. 2009. 40p. pap. 13.95 *(978-1-59858-826-2(5))* Dog Ear Publishing, LLC.
Kroha, Kristin V. Sophie's Magic Underwear. 2012. (ENG., Illus.). 32p. (J). (gr. -1-2). 7.95 *(978-0-9848657-0-3(5))* Lesson Ladder.
Lansky, Bruce & Pottle, Robert. Tinkle, Tinkle, Little Tot: Songs & Rhymes for Toilet Training. Blake, Anne Catharine, illus. 2005. 32p. (J). 8.95 *(978-0-88166-492-8(8)*, 1182) Meadowbrook Pr.
Lewis, Bisa. Let's Potty! Floyd, John, Jr., illus. 2006. (J). bds. 6.99 *(978-1-934214-12-1(4))* OurRainbow Pr., LLC.
L'Heureux, Christine. Caillou, No More Diapers: STEP 2: Potty Training Series. Brignaud, Pierre, illus. 2016. (Hand in Hand Ser.: 2). 24p. (J). (gr. -1-k). bds. 7.99 *(978-2-89718-296-0(2))* Caillouet, Gerry.
Mandell, Sabain. Www.AdorableDiapers.Com Presents How to Create Personalized Diapers for Kids! 2011. 32p. (gr. -1). pap. 19.99 *(978-1-4520-9987-3(1))* AuthorHouse.
Mastel, Julie. Jesus Was with Me All Along: A Book about Bedwetting. 2013. 36p. pap. 15.95 *(978-1-4497-8321-1(X)*, WestBow Pr.) Author Solutions, LLC.
Mcaleer, Sarah & McAleer, Kathleen. Don't Tee Tee in Your Tutu: A Potty Training Book for Young Ballerinas. 2009. 28p. pap. 13.99 *(978-1-4389-4029-8(7))* AuthorHouse.
Morgan, Richard. Zoo Poo: A First Toilet Training Book. 2004. (Barron's Educational Ser.). (ENG., Illus.). 24p. (J). (gr. -1). pap. 6.99 *(978-0-7641-2767-0(5))* Sourcebooks, Inc.
—Zoo Poo: A First Toilet Training Book. 2004. (gr. -1-2). lib. bdg. 15.95 *(978-0-613-81357-0(X))* Turtleback.
Piggy Toes Press, creator. Let's Go Potty! 2008. (ENG., Illus.). 14p. (gr. -1-k). 8.95 *(978-1-58117-688-9(0)*, Intervisual/Piggy Toes) Bendon, Inc.
—Let's Go Potty for Boys. 2008. (ENG., Illus.). 14p. (gr. -1-k). bds. 8.95 *(978-1-58117-689-6(9)*, Intervisual/Piggy Toes) Bendon, Inc.
Publications International Ltd. Staff. Once upon a Potty. 2010. 8p. (J). bds. 7.98 *(978-1-60553-416-9(1))* Phoenix International Publications, Inc.
Publications International Ltd. Staff & Frankel, Alana. Once upon a Potty Girl. 2010. 8p. (J). bds. 7.98 *(978-1-60553-417-6(X))* Phoenix International Publications, Inc.
Sanschagrin, Joceline. Caillou. Brignaud, Pierre, illus. 2016. (Hand in Hand Ser.). (ENG.). 24p. (J). (gr. -1-k). bds. 12.99 *(978-2-89718-344-8(6))* Caillouet, Gerry.
—Caillou: Potty Time: Potty Training Series, STEP 1. Brignaud, Pierre, illus. 2016. (Hand in Hand Ser.: 1). (ENG.). 24p. (J). (gr. -1-k). bds. 7.99 *(978-2-89718-295-3(4))* Caillouet, Gerry.
Tucker, Jason. Ferdinand Uses the Potty. West, D. E., illus. 2009. (J). pap. 13.95 *(978-1-932690-82-8(4))* Loving Healing Pr., Inc.
Verdick, Elizabeth. Diapers Are Not Forever. Heinlen, Marieka, illus. 2008. (Best Behavior(r) Board Book Ser.). (ENG.). 26p. (J). (gr. k — 1). bds. 9.99 *(978-1-57542-296-1(4)*, 22961) Free Spirit Publishing Inc.
—Diapers Are Not Forever / Los Panales No Son para Siempre. Heinlen, Marieka, illus. 2014. (Best Behavior(r) Board Book Ser.). (ENG.). 26p. (J). (— 1). bds. 9.99 *(978-1-57542-429-3(0))* Free Spirit Publishing Inc.
Willems, Mo. Time to Pee! 2003. (ENG., Illus.). 40p. (J). (gr. -1-k). 16.99 *(978-0-7868-1868-6(9)*, Hyperion Books for Children) Disney Publishing Worldwide.
Young, Caroline. Guide to Potty Training Internet-Referenced. 2010. (Parent's Guides). 64p. (J). pap. 9.99 *(978-0-7945-2107-3(X)*, Usborne) EDC Publishing.
Zeavin, Carol & Silverbush, Rhona. Potty! Davis, Jon, illus. 2020. 16p. (J). *(978-1-4338-3251-2(8)*, Magination Pr.) American Psychological Assn.

TOILET TRAINING—FICTION

Ann. We Call Him Puddles. 2007. 24p. per. 24.95 *(978-1-4241-8738-6(9))* America Star Bks.
Apple, Sam. The Saddest Toilet in the World. Ricks, Sam, illus. 2016. (ENG.). 32p. (J). (gr. -1-2). 18.99 *(978-1-4814-5122-2(7)*, Aladdin) Simon & Schuster Children's Publishing.
Barksdale, Miechel & Dunn, Richard. Mommy, Its Time to Go Pee. 2010. 32p. pap. 12.99 *(978-1-4490-6860-8(X))* AuthorHouse.
Berenstain, Jan & Berenstain, Mike. The Berenstain Bears' Valentine Party. Berenstain, Jan & Mike, illus. 2008. (Berenstain Bears Ser.). (ENG.). 16p. (J). (gr. -1-3). pap. 6.99 *(978-0-06-057425-3(9)*, HarperFestival) HarperCollins Pubs.
Berger, Samantha. Pirate Potty. Cartwright, Amy, illus. 2010. (ENG.). 24p. (J). (gr. -1 — 1). pap. 6.99 *(978-0-545-17295-0(0)*, Cartwheel Bks.) Scholastic, Inc.
—Princess Potty. Cartwright, Amy, illus. 2010. (ENG.). 24p. (J). (gr. -1 — 1). pap. 6.99 *(978-0-545-17296-7(9)*, Cartwheel Bks.) Scholastic, Inc.
Chou, Yih-fen. Mimi Goes Potty. Chen, Zhiyuan, illus. 2011. (J). *(978-0-9845523-9-9(1))* Heryin Publishing Corp.
—The Potty Story. Chen, Zhiyuan, illus. 2011. (J). *(978-0-9845523-8-2(3))* Heryin Publishing Corp.
Church, Caroline Jayne. Potty Time! Church, Caroline Jayne, illus. 2012. (ENG., Illus.). 10p. (J). (gr. -1 — 1). bds. 7.99 *(978-0-545-35080-8(8)*, Cartwheel Bks.) Scholastic, Inc.
Cocklico, Marion, illus. No More Diapers. 2018. (Big Steps Ser.). (ENG.). 12p. (J). (— 1). bds. 8.95 *(978-1-4549-2951-2(0))* Sterling Publishing Co., Inc.
Cole, Joanna. My Big Boy Potty. Chambliss, Maxie, illus. 2004. (ENG.). 32p. (J). (gr. -1-3). 6.99 *(978-0-688-17042-4(0)*, Quill Tree Bks.) HarperCollins Pubs.
—My Big Girl Potty. Chambliss, Maxie, illus. 2004. (ENG.). 32p. (J). (gr. -1 — 1). 7.99 *(978-0-688-17041-7(2)*, Quill Tree Bks.) HarperCollins Pubs.
Comtesse, Gavin. Hamish & the Terrible Poo. 2013. 50p. 19.89 *(978-1-4669-9760-8(5))*; pap. 9.89 *(978-1-4669-9761-5(3))* Trafford Publishing.
Corderoy, Tracey. It's Potty Time! Pedler, Caroline, illus. 2014. (ENG.). 22p. (J). (gr. -1-k). bds. 8.99 *(978-1-58925-574-6(7))* Tiger Tales.
Creese, Sarah. Even Pirates Poop. Lynch, Stuart, illus. 2014. (ENG.). 12p. (J). (— 1). bds. 9.99 *(978-1-78393-113-2(2))* Make Believe Ideas GBR. Dist: Scholastic, Inc.
Crikelair, Wendy. Poopie Party. 2011. 28p. pap. 15.99 *(978-1-4628-8093-5(2))* Xlibris Corp.
Crow, Sara. Even Superheroes Use the Potty. Record, Adam, illus. (J). (— 1). 2019. 26p. bds. 6.99 *(978-1-5247-6599-6(6))* 2018. 32p. 16.99 *(978-0-399-55934-1(5))* Random Hse. Children's Bks. (Doubleday Bks. for Young Readers).
Dahl, Michael. Duck Goes Potty, 1 vol. Vidal, Oriol, illus. 2010. (Hello Genius Ser.). (ENG.). 20p. (J). (gr. -1 — 1). bds. 7.99 *(978-1-4048-5726-1(5)*, 102303, Picture Window Bks.) Capstone.
Daniel Goes to the Potty. 2014. (Daniel Tiger's Neighborhood Ser.). (ENG., Illus.). 14p. (J). (gr. -1 — 1). 8.99 *(978-1-4814-2048-8(8)*, Simon Spotlight) Simon Spotlight.
De Smet, Marian & Meijer, Marja. Encerrada: Anna's Tight Squeeze. Pacheco, Laura Emilia, tr. Uitgeverij, Clavis, illus. 2004. 28p. (J). 14.95 *(978-970-29-0665-0(2))* Santillana USA Publishing Co., Inc.
DePrisco, Dorothea & McKendry, Sam. I'm a Big Kid Now. 2006. (ENG.). 36p. bds. 12.95 *(978-1-58117-523-3(X)*, Intervisual/Piggy Toes) Bendon, Inc.
DK. Big Girls Use the Potty! (ENG.). (J). (gr. -1-k). 2008. 20p. 4.99 *(978-0-7566-3928-0(X))* 2005. (Illus.). 12p. bds. 7.99 *(978-0-7566-1452-2(X))* Dorling Kindersley Publishing, Inc. (DK Children).
Edwards, W M, illus. Island Potty Party. 2007. (Playdate Kids Musical Ser.). 27p. (J). (gr. -1-3). 14.95 incl. audio compact disk *(978-1-933721-15-6(4))* Playdate Kids Publishing.
Ford, Bernette. No More Diapers for Ducky! Williams, Sam, illus. 2007. (Ducky & Piggy Ser.). (ENG.). 26p. (J). (gr. -1 — 1). bds. 7.95 *(978-1-905417-38-4(1))* Boxer Bks., Ltd. GBR. Dist: Sterling Publishing Co., Inc.
Fortson, Sarah Glenn. This Cowgirl Ain't Kiddin' about the Potty. Cox, Russ, illus. 2019. (ENG.). 40p. (J). 16.99 *(978-1-4413-3165-6(4)*, 2a1167a3-f124-440f-ad6c-6d68081d6fc8) Peter Pauper Pr. Inc.
Frankel, Alona. Once upon a Potty Sound Book for Girls. Publications International Ltd. Staff, ed. 2010. 8p. (J). bds. 7.98 *(978-1-4508-0828-6(X))* Publications International, Ltd.
Gaydos, Nora. Now I'm Growing! Prince of the Potty - Little Steps for Big Kids! Gutierrez, Akemi, illus. 2011. (ENG.). 30p. (J). (gr. -1-17). 8.99 *(978-1-60169-077-7(0))* Innovative Kids.
—Princess of the Potty - Little Steps for Big Kids! Gutierrez, Akemi, illus. 2011. (ENG.). 30p. (J). (gr. -1-17). 8.99 *(978-1-60169-076-0(2))* Innovative Kids.
Geis, Patricia. Good-bye Diaper! Folch, Sergio, illus. 2009. (Good Habits with Coco & Tula Ser.). 16p. (J). (gr. -1-k). bds. 11.40 *(978-1-60754-404-3(0))* Windmill Bks.
Gramma Debbie. The Poop Book. 2012. 32p. pap. 19.99 *(978-1-4772-5287-1(8))* AuthorHouse.
Hager, Kendra M. Alexander. Potty Praise for Boys & Girls. 2013. 56p. pap. 17.95 *(978-1-60911-459-6(0)*, Strategic Bk. Publishing) Strategic Book Publishing & Rights Agency (SBPRA).
Hayes, Kate. All about Poop. Garnsworthy, Mario, ed. Vaughan, Brenna, illus. 2012. (ENG.). 38p. (J). pap. 14.95 *(978-0-9854248-0-0(X))* Pinwheel Bks.
Hello!Lucky. Super Pooper & Whizz Kid: Potty Power! 2018. (Hello!Lucky Book Ser.). (ENG., Illus.). 24p. (J). (gr. -1 — 1). bds. 9.99 *(978-1-4197-3157-0(2)*, 1212201) Abrams, Inc.
Hodgkinson, Leigh. Goldilocks & the Just Right Potty. Hodgkinson, Leigh, illus. 2017. (ENG., Illus.). 32p. (J). (-k). 16.99 *(978-0-7636-9799-0(0))* Candlewick Pr.
Hodson, Sarah E. Early Social Skills Stories: Going Potty. Platt, Jason, illus. 2013. (J). *(978-0-7606-1408-2(3))* LinguiSystems, Inc.
Jackson, Nikki. Georgia & Reed's: My Potty & Me. 2012. 16p. pap. 15.99 *(978-1-4772-4516-3(2))* AuthorHouse.
Jadoul, Emile. All by Myself! 2012. (ENG.). 26p. (J). 14.00 *(978-0-8028-5411-7(7)*, Eerdmans Bks For Young Readers) Eerdmans, William B. Publishing Co.
Kleinberg, Naomi. P Is for Potty! (Sesame Street) Moroney, Christopher, illus. 2014. (Lift-The-Flap Ser.). (ENG.). 12p. (J). (— 1). bds. 5.99 *(978-0-385-38369-1(X)*, Random Hse. Bks. for Young Readers) Random Hse. Children's Bks.
Kramer, Paul. Do Not Dread Wetting the Bed. 2012. (ENG & ACO.). 32p. (J). (gr. -1-3). 15.95 *(978-0-9819745-0-7(3))* Aloha Wellness Pubs.
Lemke, Donald. Basic Training: Call of Doodie. Lentz, Bob, illus. 2018. (Basic Training Ser.). (ENG.). 30p. (J). (gr. -1 — 1). bds. 7.99 *(978-1-68446-006-3(5)*, 138937, Picture Window Bks.) Capstone.
Lewison, Wendy Cheyette. The Prince & the Potty. Motoyama, Keiko, illus. 2006. (ENG.). 40p. (J). (gr. -1-3). 16.99 *(978-0-689-87808-4(7)*, Simon & Schuster Bks. For Young Readers) Simon & Schuster Bks. For Young Readers.
Lloyd-Jones, Sally. Skip to the Loo! a Potty Book. Jeram, Anita, illus. 2018. (ENG.). 30p. (J). (-k). bds. 8.99 *(978-0-7636-9977-2(2))* Candlewick Pr.
—Skip to the Loo, My Darling! a Potty Book. Jeram, Anita, illus. 2016. (ENG.). 32p. (J). (-k). 11.99 *(978-0-7636-7234-8(3))* Candlewick Pr.
Manushkin, Fran. Big Boy Underpants. Petrone, Valeria, illus. 2016. 24p. (J). (— 1). bds. 7.99 *(978-0-553-53861-8(6)*, Random Hse. Bks. for Young Readers) Random Hse. Children's Bks.
—Big Girl Panties. Petrone, Valeria, illus. 2012. 24p. (J). (gr. k — 1). bds. 7.99 *(978-0-307-93152-8(8)*, Robin Corey Bks.) Random Hse. Children's Bks.
Massey, Jane, illus. Potty Hero. 2016. (J). *(978-0-545-92773-4(0))* Scholastic, Inc.
—Potty Star. 2015. (J). *(978-0-545-92772-7(2))* Scholastic, Inc.
Mayer, Mercer & Mayer, Gina. The New Potty (Little Critter) 2003. (Look-Look Ser.). (Illus.). 24p. (J). (-k). pap. 5.99 *(978-0-375-82631-3(9)*, Random Hse. Bks. for Young Readers) Random Hse. Children's Bks.
McMahon, Kara & Jordan, Apple. My Growing-Up Library (Sesame Street) 2010. (ENG., Illus.). 12p. (J). (gr. k — 1). bds. 10.99 *(978-0-375-85984-7(5)*, Random Hse. Bks. for Young Readers) Random Hse. Children's Bks.
Munsch, Robert. I Have to Go! Martchenko, Michael, illus. 2019. (Classic Munsch Ser.). 24p. (J). 19.95 *(978-1-77321-107-7(2))*; (ENG.). pap. 7.95 *(978-1-77321-106-0(4))* Annick Pr., Ltd. CAN. Dist: Publishers Group West (PGW).
—I Have to Go! 2007. (J). 15.10 *(978-0-7569-7622-4(7))* Perfection Learning Corp.
Munsch, Robert & Martchenko, Michael. I Have to Go! Martchenko, Michael, illus. 8th ed. 2010. (ENG., Illus.). 24p. (J). (gr. -1-k). bds. 7.99 *(978-1-55451-253-9(0)*, 9781554512539) Annick Pr., Ltd. CAN. Dist: Publishers Group West (PGW).
Neis, Izzy. I Want to Potty. Shakir, Susie, illus. 2005. 10p. (J). 9.95 *(978-1-58117-422-9(5)*, Intervisual/Piggy Toes) Bendon, Inc.
Nussbaum, Dori. The Hungry Potty. 2004. 28p. per. 8.95 *(978-1-932344-67-7(5))* Thornton Publishing, Inc.
O'Brien, Melanie. No More Diapers. 2009. 18p. 10.95 *(978-1-58117-920-0(0)*, Intervisual/Piggy Toes) Bendon, Inc.
Patricelli, Leslie. Potty. Patricelli, Leslie, illus. 2010. (Leslie Patricelli Board Bks.). (ENG., Illus.). 28p. (J). (gr. k — 1). bds. 8.99 *(978-0-7636-4476-5(5))* Candlewick Pr.
—Potty/Bacinica. Patricelli, Leslie, illus. 2016. (Leslie Patricelli Board Bks.). (Illus.). 28p. (J). (— 1). bds. 8.99 *(978-0-7636-8777-9(4))* Candlewick Pr.
PI Kids. Sesame Street: Elmo's Potty Book First Look & Find. Brannon, Tom, illus. 2010. (ENG.). 16p. (J). bds. 12.99 *(978-1-60553-840-2(X)*, 3962, PI Kids) Phoenix International Publications, Inc.
—Sesame Street: Potty Time Songs. Berry, Bob et al, illus. 2010. (ENG.). 12p. (J). bds. 15.99 *(978-1-4508-0365-6(2)*, 1401, PI Kids) Phoenix International Publications, Inc.
Publications International Ltd. Staff, ed. Once upon a Potty Sound Book for Boys. 2010. 8p. (J). bds. 7.98 *(978-1-4508-0829-3(8))* Phoenix International Publications, Inc.
—Potty Time with Tiger: Boy. 2010. (J). bds. 5.98 *(978-1-4127-6915-0(9))* Publications International, Ltd.
—Potty Time with Tiger: Girl. 2010. (SPA.). (J). bds. 5.98 *(978-1-4127-6916-7(7))* Publications International, Ltd.
—Sesame Street: Potty Time with Elmo (Look & Find) 2010. 20p. (J). pap. 5.98 *(978-1-4508-1471-3(9))* Publications International, Ltd.
Random House. My Thomas Potty Book (Thomas & Friends) 2016. (ENG., Illus.). 14p. (J). (gr. -1 — 1). bds. 9.99 *(978-1-101-93427-2(1)*, Random Hse. Bks. for Young Readers) Random Hse. Children's Bks.
Richmond, Marianne. Big Boys Go Potty. 2012. (Illus.). 32p. (J). (— 1). 9.99 *(978-1-4022-6659-1(6)*, Sourcebooks Jabberwocky) Sourcebooks, Inc.
—Big Girls Go Potty. 2012. (Illus.). 32p. (J). (gr. -1 — 1). 9.99 *(978-1-4022-6662-1(6)*, Sourcebooks Jabberwocky) Sourcebooks, Inc.
Ross, Tony. I Want My Potty! (ENG., Illus.). (J). (-k). 2018. (Little Princess Ser.: 1). 32p. pap. 11.99 *(978-1-78344-632-2(3))* 2017. 20p. bds. 13.99 *(978-1-78344-544-8(0))* Andersen Pr. GBR. Dist: Independent Pubs. Group.
Slattery, Karen. Piper's Diapers. 2003. (J). pap. 9.00 *(978-0-8059-5765-5(0))* Dorrance Publishing Co., Inc.
Smart Kidz, creator. It's Potty Time for Boys. 2013. (ENG., Illus.). 12p. (J). bds. 12.99 *(978-1-891100-05-5(X)*, Smart Kids) Penton Overseas, Inc.
Snedegar, Eugenia. Ellie Goes Potty, 1 vol. 2009. 24p. pap. 24.95 *(978-1-61546-658-0(4))* America Star Bks.
Snyder, Betsy E., illus. Lily's Potty. 2010. 16p. (J). bds. *(978-1-60906-001-5(6))* Begin Smart LLC.
Trasler, Janee. Pottytime for Chickies. 2014. (Chickies Ser.). (ENG., Illus.). 24p. (J). (gr. -1 — 1). pap. 8.99 *(978-0-06-227469-4(4)*, HarperFestival) HarperCollins Pubs.
Van Genechten, Guido. The Big Potty Book. 2009. (ENG., Illus.). 20p. (J). (gr. k — 1). bds. 12.95 *(978-1-60537-031-6(2))* Clavis Publishing.
van Lieshout, Maria. I Use the Potty: Big Kid Power. 2016. (Big Kid Power Ser.). (ENG., Illus.). 28p. (J). (gr. -1 — 1). 9.99 *(978-1-4521-3535-9(5))* Chronicle Bks. LLC.
Watt, Fiona & Wells, Rachel, eds. Potty Time. 2004. (Baby's World Ser.). (ENG., Illus.). 1p. (J). (gr. -1-18). pap. 4.95 *(978-0-7460-3839-0(9))* EDC Publishing.
Wax, Wendy & Wax, Naomi. Even Firefighters Go to the Potty: A Potty Training Lift-The-Flap Story. Gilpin, Stephen, illus. 2008. (ENG.). 22p. (J). (gr. -1-k). 8.99 *(978-1-4169-2720-4(4)*, Little Simon) Little Simon.
—Even Princesses Go to the Potty: A Potty Training Lift-The-Flap Story. Carabelli, Francesca, illus. 2014. (ENG.). 22p. (J). (gr. -1 — 1). 8.99 *(978-1-4424-8886-1(7)*, Little Simon) Little Simon.
Whelen-Banks, Jane. Liam Goes Poo in the Toilet: A Story about Trouble with Toilet Training. 2008. (Illus.). 32p. 13.95 *(978-1-84310-900-6(X)*, 695773) Kingsley, Jessica Pubs. GBR. Dist: Hachette UK Distribution.
Willis, Jeanne. Don't Go There! Bragadottir, Hrefna, illus. 2019. (ENG.). 32p. (J). (gr. -1-k). 17.99 *(978-1-5415-5508-2(2)*, 89fc0478-8b00-4f74-9ce9-c2c90363b4b8) Lerner Publishing Group.

TOKYO (JAPAN)

Barber, Nicola. Tokyo. 2006. (ENG., Illus.). 61p. (gr. 5-8). 30.00 *(978-0-7910-8855-5(3)*, P114466, Facts On File) Infobase Holdings, Inc.
—Tokyo, 1 vol. 2004. (Great Cities of the World Ser.). (ENG., Illus.). 48p. (gr. 5-8). lib. bdg. 33.67 *(978-0-8368-5033-8(5)*, 2536704b-ae26-4e38-903e-a5b3f87e8e3f, Gareth Stevens Secondary Library) Stevens, Gareth Publishing LLLP.
Claybourne, Anna. Lonely Planet Kids City Trails - Tokyo 1. Bruff, Alex & Taylor, Matt, illus. 2017. (Lonely Planet Kids Ser.). (ENG.). 104p. (J). (gr. 4-7). pap. 12.99 *(978-1-78657-726-9(7)*, 5656) Lonely Planet Global Ltd. IRL. Dist: Hachette Bk. Group.
Smith, Jacquelyn. Pitty the City Kitty; Tokyo. Smith, Jacquelyn & Kalafatis, John, illus. 2009. 32p. (J). 15.99 *(978-1-935479-01-7(6))* A.M. Green Publishing.
Takabayashi, Mari. I Live in Tokyo. 2004. (ENG., Illus.). 32p. (J). (gr. -1-3). reprint ed. pap. 7.99 *(978-0-618-49484-2(7)*, 490015, Clarion Bks.) HarperCollins Pubs.
Verzov, Ella & Oirechman, Chana. Moshe of Japan. 2013. (Illus.). 50p. (J). *(978-1-61465-171-0(X))* Menucha Pubs. Inc.

TOLERATION

see also Discrimination; Freedom of Religion

Alexander, richard. What's Intolerance?, 1 vol. 2017. (What's the Issue? Ser.). (ENG.). 24p. (J). (gr. 3-3). pap. 9.25 *(978-1-5345-2507-8(6)*, 847291d6-6c22-46a9-9f4e-7dcea304599b); lib. bdg. 26.23 *(978-1-5345-2439-2(8)*,

ea892a96-e404-47b3-af97-b2d0db18af5c) Greenhaven Publishing LLC.
All about Us Interactive Packages: Here I Am. (Pebble Soup Explorations Ser.). (gr. -1-18). 52.00 *(978-0-7578-5227-5(0))* Rigby Education.
Burstein, John. Can We Get Along? Dealing with Differences, 1 vol. 2009. (Slim Goodbody's Life Skills 101 Ser.). (ENG., Illus.). 32p. (J). (gr. 3-6). pap. *(978-0-7787-4804-5(9))*; lib. bdg. *(978-0-7787-4788-8(3))* Crabtree Publishing Co.
Cassius, Sonya. My Beautiful World. 2009. (Illus.). 32p. pap. 12.99 *(978-1-4343-0061-4(7))* AuthorHouse.
Chambers, Catherine. How to Handle Discrimination & Prejudice. 2014. (Under Pressure Ser.). 48p. (gr. 4-7). 37.10 *(978-1-59920-827-5(X))* Black Rabbit Bks.
Chang, Kirsten. I Am Tolerant. 2020. (Character Education Ser.). (ENG., Illus.). 24p. (J). (gr. k-3). pap. 7.99 *(978-1-61891-794-2(3)*, 12579, Blastoff! Readers) Bellwether Media.
Charles, Randy. Communication Skills. 2018. (J). *(978-1-4222-3994-0(2))* Mason Crest.
Currie, Stephen. Religious Oppression. 2003. (Great Escapes Ser.). (ENG., Illus.). 112p. (J). 30.85 *(978-1-59018-280-2(4)*, Lucent Bks.) Cengage Gale.
Dawson, Eric David. Putting Peace First: 7 Commitments to Change the World. 2018. (Illus.). 160p. (J). (gr. 5). pap. 9.99 *(978-1-101-99733-8(8)*, Viking Books for Young Readers) Penguin Young Readers Group.
Ford, Jeanne Marie. Respecting Opposing Viewpoints, 1 vol. 2017. (Civic Values Ser.). (ENG.). 32p. (gr. 3-3). pap. 11.58 *(978-1-5026-2936-4(4)*, 2d51c185-7d2b-41d9-a1fb-1fbb0c26baa7) Cavendish Square Publishing LLC.
Gay, Kathlyn. Bigotry & Intolerance: The Ultimate Teen Guide, Vol. 35. 2015. (It Happened to Me Ser.: 35). (Illus.). 182p. pap. 40.00 *(978-1-4422-5659-0(1))* Rowman & Littlefield Publishers, Inc.
—Bigotry & Intolerance: The Ultimate Teen Guide. 2013. (It Happened to Me Ser.: 35). (ENG., Illus.). 182p. 69.00 *(978-0-8108-8360-4(0))* Scarecrow Pr., Inc.
—Cultural Diversity: Conflicts & Challenges. 2003. (It Happened to Me Ser.: 6). (ENG., Illus.). 144p. pap. 55.00 *(978-0-8108-4805-4(8))* Scarecrow Pr., Inc.
Geisen, Cynthia. You Are You, I Am Me: Understanding Diversity. Alley, R. W., illus. 2016. 32p. (J). pap. 7.95 *(978-0-87029-699-4(X))* Abbey Pr.
Hanes, Richard Clay, et al. Prejudice in the Modern World. 2007. (J). *(978-1-4144-0205-5(8))*; *(978-1-4144-0206-2(6))* Cengage Gale.
Hanson, Anders. Everyone Is Equal: The Kids' Book of Tolerance. 2014. (What We Stand For Ser.). (ENG.). 24p. (J). (gr. k-4). lib. bdg. 32.79 *(978-1-62403-293-6(1)*, 1726, Super SandCastle) ABDO Publishing Co.
Hindley, Anna Forgerson & Nat'l Mus Afr Am Hist Culture, Nat'l Mus. A Is for All the Things You Are: A Joyful ABC Book. Bobo, Keturah A., illus. 2019. 26p. (J). (— 1). bds. 9.95 *(978-1-58834-650-6(1)*, Smithsonian Bks.) Smithsonian Institution Scholarly Pr.
Holmes, Kirsty Louise. My Beliefs. 2018. (Our Values - Level 1 Ser.). (Illus.). 24p. (J). (gr. 1-1). *(978-0-7787-4727-7(1))* Crabtree Publishing Co.
James, Emily. How to Be Tolerant: A Question & Answer Book about Tolerance. 2017. (Character Matters Ser.). (ENG., Illus.). 32p. (J). (gr. -1-2). lib. bdg. 27.99 *(978-1-5157-7202-6(0)*, 135559, Capstone Pr.) Capstone.
LaMachia, John. So What Is Tolerance Anyway? 2009. (Student's Guide to American Civics Ser.). 48p. (gr. 5-8). 53.00 *(978-1-61511-241-8(3)*, Rosen Reference) Rosen Publishing Group, Inc., The.
Lindeen, Mary. Working Together at School. 2019. (BeginningtoRead Ser.). (ENG., Illus.). 32p. (J). (gr. -1-2). 22.60 *(978-1-68450-938-6(6))* Norwood Hse. Pr.
Mason, Paul. Religious Extremism. 2010. (Voices Ser.). (Illus.). 48p. pap. *(978-0-237-54219-1(6))* Evans Brothers, Ltd.
McAneney, Caitie. Different but Equal: Appreciating Diversity. 2019. (Spotlight on Social & Emotional Learning Ser.). (ENG.). 24p. (gr. 4-6). 60.00 *(978-1-7253-0670-7(0)*, PowerKids Pr.) Rosen Publishing Group, Inc., The.
Meiners, Cheri J. Accept & Value Each Person. Johnson, Meredith, illus. 2006. (Learning to Get Along(r) Ser.). (ENG.). 40p. (J). (gr. 3-7). pap. 11.99 *(978-1-57542-203-9(4)*, 1087) Free Spirit Publishing Inc.
Miller, Connie Colwell. You Can Respect Differences: Assume or Find Out? Assanelli, Victoria, illus. 2019. (Making Good Choices Ser.). (ENG.). 24p. (J). (gr. 1-3). pap. 9.99 *(978-1-68152-478-8(3)*, 11064) Amicus.
Munson, Derek. Pastel para Enemigos. King, Tara Calahan, illus. 2004.Tr. of Enemy Pie. (SPA.). 40p. (J). (gr. k-2). pap. 9.99 *(978-84-261-3378-6(9))* Juventud, Editorial ESP. Dist: Lectorum Pubns., Inc.
Palmer, Bill. Gallup Guides for Youth Facing Persistent Prejudice. 2012. (Gallup Guides for Youth Facing Persistent Prejudice Ser.). 64p. (J). (gr. 7-8). 22.95 *(978-1-4222-2466-3(X))* Mason Crest.
Pederson, Charles E. Racism & Intolerance. 2008. (Man's Inhumanities Ser.). (YA). (gr. 7-12). 23.95 *(978-1-60217-976-9(X))* Erickson Pr.
Petrikowski, Nicki Peter. Working for Tolerance & Social Change Through Service Learning, 1 vol. 2014. (Service Learning for Teens Ser.). (ENG.). 80p. (J). (gr. 7-7). 37.80 *(978-1-4777-7967-5(1)*, 627a9b71-1638-4068-81f9-ae1220cb52fa, Rosen Young Adult) Rosen Publishing Group, Inc., The.
Pryor, Kimberley Jane. Tolerance, 1 vol. 2009. (Values Ser.). (ENG.). 32p. (gr. 1-1). lib. bdg. 31.21 *(978-0-7614-3129-9(2)*, b0ae1e8f-51ca-446a-ae07-f89640842daf) Cavendish Square Publishing LLC.
Sanna, Ellyn. Gallup Guides for Youth Facing Persistent Prejudice Muslims. 2012. (Gallup Guides for Youth Facing Persistent Prejudice Ser.). 64p. (J). (gr. 7-8). 22.95 *(978-1-4222-2468-7(6))* Mason Crest.
—People with Mental & Physical Challenges. 2012. (Gallup Guides for Youth Facing Persistent Prejudice Ser.). (Illus.). 64p. (J). (gr. 7-8). 22.95 *(978-1-4222-2470-0(8))* Mason Crest.
Santos, Rita. Appreciating Diversity. 2019. (Working for Social Justice Ser.). (ENG.). 32p. (gr. 3-4). 63.18 *(978-1-9785-0796-8(8))* Enslow Publishing, LLC.
Scheunemann, Pam. Tolerance. 2003. (United We Stand Ser.). (Illus.). 24p. (J). (gr. k-3). lib. bdg. 24.21 *(978-1-57765-881-8(7)*, SandCastle) ABDO Publishing Co.
Smith, Sarah. Tolerance & Cooperation, Vol. 7. 2018. (Leadership Skills & Character Building Ser.). 64p. (J). (gr. 7). lib. bdg. 31.93 *(978-1-4222-4001-4(0))* Mason Crest.
Spilsbury, Louise. Racism & Intolerance. Kai, Hanane, illus. 2018. (ENG.). 32p. (J). (gr. 1-2). 9.99 *(978-1-4380-5022-5(4))* Sourcebooks, Inc.
Thomson Gale Staff. Prejudice in the Modern World. Hanes, Sharon M., ed. rev. ed. 2007. (Prejudice in the Modern World Reference Library). (ENG., Illus.). 256p. (J). 129.00 *(978-1-4144-0208-6(2)*, UXL) Cengage Gale.
—Prejudice in the Modern World - Almanac, 2 vols. Hanes, Richard C. et al, eds. rev. ed. 2007. (Prejudice in the Modern World Reference Library). (ENG.). 462p. (YA). 233.00 *(978-1-4144-0204-8(X)*, UXL) Cengage Gale.
Thomson Gale Staff & Hermsen, Sarah. Prejudice in the Modern World: Biographies. Hanes, Richard C. & Rudd, Kelly, eds. rev. ed. 2007. (Prejudice in the Modern World Reference Library). (ENG., Illus.). 288p. (J). 129.00 *(978-1-4144-0207-9(4)*, UXL) Cengage Gale.
—Prejudice in the Modern World: Cumulative Index. rev. ed. 2007. (Prejudice in the Modern World Reference Library). (ENG.). 34p. (YA). 5.00 *(978-1-4144-0209-3(0)*, UXL) Cengage Gale.

TOLERATION—FICTION

Agee, Jon. The Wall in the Middle of the Book. Agee, Jon, illus. 2018. (ENG., Illus.). 48p. (J). (gr. -1-3). 18.99 *(978-0-525-55545-2(5)*, Dial Bks) Penguin Young Readers Group.
Akerson, Julie Chicos. The Life of Riley the Cat. Taylor, Jennifer, illus. 2005. 28p. (J). 15.50 *(978-1-4120-5858-2(9))* Trafford Publishing.
Alary, Laura. Mira & the Big Story. Todd, Sue, illus. 2012. (ENG.). 36p. (J). 12.00 *(978-1-55896-693-2(5)*, Skinner Hse. Bks.) Unitarian Universalist Assn.
Aldrich, Jodi. Bee Mumble & Wug. 2011. 36p. (J). pap. 20.95 *(978-1-4327-6808-9(5))* Outskirts Pr., Inc.
Applegate, Katherine. Wishtree. I.t. ed. 2018. (ENG.). 226p. 22.99 *(978-1-4328-4821-7(6))* Cengage Gale.
—Wishtree. (ENG., Illus.). 224p. 2019. pap. 15.99 *(978-1-250-30686-9(8)*, 900197882) 2017. (J). 16.99 *(978-1-250-04322-1(0)*, 900127764) Feiwel & Friends.
—Wishtree. 2023. (ENG.). 240p. (gr. 3-6). 24.94 *(978-1-5364-7846-4(6))* Square Fish.
Baker, Ed. The Story of Kitten Cuckoo. Baker, Ed, illus. 2007. (ENG., Illus.). 32p. (J). (gr. -1-17). 15.95 *(978-1-933572-04-8(3))* Centro Bks., LLC.
Barry, Debra R. Brady Pickles. 2011. 32p. pap. 24.95 *(978-1-4626-3716-4(7))* America Star Bks.
Bates, Amy June & Bates, Juniper. The Big Umbrella. Bates, Amy June, illus. 2018. (ENG., Illus.). 40p. (J). (gr. -1-3). 18.99 *(978-1-5344-0658-2(1)*, Simon & Schuster/Paula Wiseman Bks.) Simon & Schuster/Paula Wiseman Bks.
Baynes, Jenean Atwood & Atwood, John H. Blue Spots! Yellow Spots! 2012. 28p. (-18). pap. 13.54 *(978-1-4669-4969-0(4))* Trafford Publishing.
Beck, Rachel. Bella & the Little Gray Kitten. 2011. 40p. (gr. -1). pap. 18.50 *(978-1-4567-3365-0(6))* AuthorHouse.
Bembry, Chental-Song. The Honey Bunch Kids. 2010. (ENG.). 64p. pap. 24.99 *(978-1-4500-2519-5(6))* Xlibris Corp.
Bradbury, Jennifer. A Moment Comes. (ENG.). 288p. (YA). (gr. 7). 2019. pap. 11.99 *(978-1-5344-3949-8(8)*, Atheneum/Caitlyn Dlouhy Books) 2013. (Illus.). 18.99 *(978-1-4169-7876-3(3))* Simon & Schuster Children's Publishing.
Carr, Elias. Jo & the Slow Soup: A Book about Patience. Rimmington, Natasha, illus. 2016. (Frolic First Faith Ser.). 32p. (J). (gr. -1-k). 12.99 *(978-1-5064-1048-7(0)*, Sparkhouse Family) 1517 Media.
—Jo y la Sopa Lenta. Garton, Michael, illus. 2016. (SPA.). (J). *(978-1-5064-2097-4(4)*, Sparkhouse Pr.) Spark Hse.
Castonguay, Leo. Piper Peter. 2012. 44p. pap. 24.95 *(978-1-4626-8078-8(X))* America Star Bks.
Cocca-Leffler, Maryann. The Belonging Tree. Lombardi, Kristine A., illus. 2020. (ENG.). 40p. (J). 18.99 *(978-1-250-30513-8(6)*, 900197497, Holt, Henry & Co. Bks. For Young Readers) Holt, Henry & Co.
Cochran, Robert. The Sword & the Dagger: A Novel. 2020. (ENG.). 400p. (YA). pap. 19.99 *(978-0-7653-8384-6(5)*, 900155635, Tor Teen) Doherty, Tom Assocs., LLC.
Collins, A. L. Redworld: Year One. Tikulin, Tomislav, illus. 2018. (Redworld Ser.). (ENG.). 320p. (J). (gr. 3-8). pap., pap., pap. 8.95 *(978-1-62370-986-0(5)*, 137317, Capstone Young Readers) Capstone.
Cook, Julia. I Want to Be the Only Dog!, Volume 6. DuFalla, Anita, illus. 2015. (Building Relationships Ser.). (ENG.). 31p. (J). (gr. k-6). pap. 11.95 *(978-1-934490-86-0(5))* Boys Town Pr.
Cutler, Jane. Susie Q Fights Back. 2018. (ENG.). 112p. (J). (gr. 3-7). pap. 6.99 *(978-0-8234-3993-5(3))* Holiday Hse., Inc.
Defosse, Rosana Curiel. Santiago en el Pantano. Barradas, Leticia, illus. (Santiago Y Los Valores Ser.). (SPA.). 32p. (J). (gr. 3-5). pap. 7.95 *(978-970-29-0133-4(2))* Santillana USA Publishing Co., Inc.
Dickens, Frances. The Giant from Nowhere. Hudspith, Peter, illus. 2018. 56p. 21.95 *(978-1-78592-535-1(0)*, 696800) Kingsley, Jessica Pubs. GBR. Dist: Hachette UK Distribution.
DiPucchio, Kelly. The Sandwich Swap. Tusa, Tricia, illus. 2010. (ENG.). 32p. (J). (gr. -1-2). 18.99 *(978-1-4231-2484-9(7))* Little, Brown Bks. for Young Readers.
Elliott, David. Nobody's Perfect. Zuppardi, Sam, illus. 2015. (ENG.). 32p. (J). (gr. -1-3). 17.99 *(978-0-7636-6699-6(8))* Candlewick Pr.
Ellison, Laura. Hard Rock, Hard Times: Coming of Age in Butte Montana, 1911-1917. 2005. 195p. (YA). per. *(978-0-9722217-7-1(8))* Horse Creek Pubns.
Erskine, Kathryn. Quaking. 2007. (ENG.). 240p. (YA). (gr. 7-12). 22.44 *(978-0-399-24774-3(2))* Penguin Young Readers Group.
Flinn, Alex. Fade to Black. 2006. (ENG.). 208p. (YA). (gr. 9-12). pap. 9.99 *(978-0-06-056842-9(9)*, HarperTeen) HarperCollins Pubs.
Frost, Daniel, tr. from SPA. You, Them, & the Others. 2006. Orig. Title: Tú, ellos y los Otros. (Illus.). 111p. (J). per. 12.95 net. *(978-0-9785270-8-2(9))* Pasiteles Publishing Co.
Frye, Timea Csonka. Wishing Star: Lost in the Woods. 2013. 32p. pap. 24.95 *(978-1-63000-931-1(8))* America Star Bks.
Gilks, Tina M. My Dog Mo. 2011. 32p. pap. 17.25 *(978-1-4269-4931-9(6))* Trafford Publishing.
Greenwald, Lisa. TBH #1: TBH, This Is So Awkward. 2018. (Tbh Ser.: 1). (ENG., Illus.). 224p. (J). (gr. 3-7). 12.99 *(978-0-06-268990-0(8)*, Tegen, Katherine Bks) HarperCollins Pubs.
Hallinan, P. K. A Rainbow of Friends. 2018. (ENG., Illus.). 22p. (J). (gr. -1-k). bds. 7.99 *(978-0-8249-1672-5(7))* Worthy Publishing.
Harris, Robie H. Who We Are! All about Being the Same & Being Different. Westcott, Nadine Bernard, illus. 2016. (Let's Talk about You & Me Ser.). (ENG.). 40p. (J). (-k). 17.99 *(978-0-7636-6903-4(2))* Candlewick Pr.
Henderson, Barbara. Down in Mr Brown's Garden. 2009. 40p. pap. 14.75 *(978-1-60860-703-7(8)*, Strategic Bk. Publishing) Strategic Book Publishing & Rights Agency (SBPRA).
Hess, Mary Rand & Greig, Steve. The One & Only Wolfgang: From Pet Rescue to One Big Happy Family, 1 vol. Sarell, Nadja, illus. 2019. (ENG.). 32p. (J). 17.99 *(978-0-310-76823-4(3))* Zonderkidz.
Hockerman, Dennis, illus. The Country Mouse & the City Mouse: A Tale of Tolerance. 2006. (J). 6.99 *(978-1-59939-003-1(5))* Cornerstone Pr.
Hooray for Boys & Girls! 2006. (J). 15.95 *(978-0-9776837-0-3(2))* West Woods Pr.
Howard, Greg. Social Intercourse. 2018. (ENG., Illus.). 320p. (YA). (gr. 9). 18.99 *(978-1-4814-9781-7(2)*, Simon & Schuster Bks. For Young Readers) Simon & Schuster Bks. For Young Readers.
Hueller, Patrick. Archenemy. 2013. (Counterattack Ser.). (ENG.). 112p. (YA). (gr. 6-12). lib. bdg. 27.99 *(978-1-4677-0306-2(0)*, 216dd675-0b23-439f-a7a1-9e1be6e375cf, Darby Creek) Lerner Publishing Group.
Humphrey, Eleanor Cairns. Building Santa's Work Shop from Tales of the Crystal Cave. 2012. 268p. pap. 27.95 *(978-1-4626-7820-4(3))* America Star Bks.
Ish-Kishor, Sulamith. A Boy of Old Prague. Shahn, Ben, illus. 2008. (Dover Children's Classics Ser.). (ENG.). 96p. (J). (gr. 4-6). pap. 3.99 *(978-0-486-46766-5(X)*, 46766X) Dover Pubns., Inc.
Jay, Stacey. Of Beast & Beauty. 2014. (ENG.). 400p. (YA). (gr. 9). pap. 9.99 *(978-0-385-74321-1(1)*, Ember) Random Hse. Children's Bks.
Jeffers, Oliver. Here We Are: Notes for Living on Planet Earth. Jeffers, Oliver, illus. 2017. (ENG., Illus.). 48p. (J). (gr. -1-2). 19.99 *(978-0-399-16789-8(7)*, Philomel Bks.) Penguin Young Readers Group.
Job, et al. Yakari & the Beavers, Vol. 3. 2007. (Yakari Ser.: 3). (Illus.). 48p. (J). (gr. 4-7). per. 11.95 *(978-1-905460-09-0(0))* CineBook GBR. Dist: National Bk. Network.
Karre, Elizabeth. The Fight. 2013. (Surviving Southside Ser.). (ENG.). 128p. (YA). (gr. 6-12). pap. 7.95 *(978-1-4677-0709-1(0)*, 554aa69c-e617-40b7-bf91-a64fd0acb6c7, Darby Creek) Lerner Publishing Group.
Katz, Karin Jill. There's a Fly in My Soup. 2012. 16p. pap. 15.99 *(978-1-4772-6331-0(4))* AuthorHouse.
Kim, YoeongAh. The Shooting Stars Soccer Team. Lee, Hyeongjin, illus. rev. ed. 2014. (MySELF Bookshelf Ser.). (ENG.). 32p. (J). (gr. k-2). lib. bdg. 25.27 *(978-1-59953-648-4(X))* Norwood Hse. Pr.
Lash, Batton, et al. The Scrapyard Detectives: Collected Cases. 2007. (Illus.). 102p. (J). (gr. 3-5). per. *(978-0-9797193-0-1(5))* Diversity Foundation, The.
Lennon, John. Imagine. Jullien, Jean, illus. 2017. (ENG.). 32p. (J). (gr. -1-3). 18.99 *(978-1-328-80865-3(3)*, 1688259, Clarion Bks.) HarperCollins Pubs.
Luchsinger, Dena. Sometimes Smart Is Good/A Veces Es Bueno Ser Listo. Jerome, Karen A., illus. 2007. (SPA & ENG.). 32p. (J). (gr. -1). 16.00 *(978-0-8028-5215-1(7)*, Eerdmans Bks For Young Readers) Eerdmans, William B. Publishing Co.
Luciani, Brigitte. A Hubbub: Book 2, No. 2. Tharlet, Eve, illus. 2010. (Mr. Badger & Mrs. Fox Ser.: 2). (ENG.). 32p. (J). (gr. k-3). pap. 7.99 *(978-0-7613-5632-5(0)*, 16271d6f-0029-4813-9c24-d51cd664aca3, Graphic Universe™) Lerner Publishing Group.
—The Meeting: Book 1, No. 1. Tharlet, Eve, illus. 2010. (Mr. Badger & Mrs. Fox Ser.: 1). (ENG.). 32p. (J). (gr. k-3). pap. 7.99 *(978-0-7613-5631-8(2)*, 071a498b-43a0-413d-9653-5f39dd220232, Graphic Universe™) Lerner Publishing Group.
M. Alvarado. We Are Different, but the Same. 2012. 16p. pap. 15.99 *(978-1-4685-4425-1(X))* AuthorHouse.
Mantchev, Lisa. Strictly No Elephants. Yoo, Taeeun, illus. 2015. (ENG.). 32p. (J). (gr. -1-3). 18.99 *(978-1-4814-1647-4(2)*, Simon & Schuster Bks. For Young Readers) Simon & Schuster Bks. For Young Readers.
Marin, Cheech. Cheech y el Autobus Fantasma. Fabiancic, Miriam, tr. Ramirez, Orlando L., illus. 2009. (SPA.). 32p. (J). (gr. -1-3). 17.99 *(978-0-06-113214-8(4)*, Rayo) HarperCollins Pubs.
McGoran, Jon. Spiked. 2020. (Spliced Ser.: 3). 352p. (YA). (gr. 9). 18.99 *(978-0-8234-4091-7(5))* Holiday Hse., Inc.
—Spliced. (Spliced Ser.: 1). (YA). 2019. 416p. (gr. 7). pap. 9.99 *(978-0-8234-4234-8(9))* 2017. (ENG.). 400p. (gr. 9). 18.95 *(978-0-8234-3855-6(4))* Holiday Hse., Inc.
—Splintered. 2019. (Spliced Ser.: 2). 352p. (YA). (gr. 9). 18.99 *(978-0-8234-4090-0(7))* Holiday Hse., Inc.
Moulton, Mark K. A Royal Wedding. Good, Karen H., illus. 2007. (ENG.). 32p. (J). (gr. k-3). 14.99 *(978-0-8249-8677-3(6)*, Ideals Pubns.) Worthy Publishing.
Moulton, Mark Kimball. One Enchanted Evening. Crouch, Karen Hillard, illus. 2003. 32p. (J). 14.95 *(978-0-8249-5480-2(7)*, Ideals Pubns.) Worthy Publishing.
Mullinax, Jerry. Enoree. 2009. (YA). pap. *(978-0-88092-646-1(5))* Royal Fireworks Publishing Co.
Muschla, Gary Robert. The Sword & the Cross. 2009. (YA). pap. *(978-0-88092-472-6(1))* Royal Fireworks Publishing Co.
Owens, Robert. Butterfly Love. 2008. (ENG.). 34p. pap. 16.70 *(978-0-557-01168-1(X))* Lulu Pr., Inc.
Pelley, Kathleen T. & Manning, Maurie J. The Giant King. 2003. (ENG., Illus.). 32p. (gr. -1-4). 14.95 *(978-0-87868-880-7(3)*, P544300, Child & Family Pr.) Child Welfare League of America, Inc.
Peterson, Lois. Meeting Miss 405, 1 vol. 2008. (Orca Young Readers Ser.). (ENG.). 112p. (J). (gr. 4-7). pap. 7.95 *(978-1-55469-015-2(3))* Orca Bk. Pubs. USA.
Pitman, Gayle E. A Church for All. Fournier, Laure, illus. 2018. (ENG.). 32p. (J). (gr. -1-3). 16.99 *(978-0-8075-1179-4(X)*, 080751179X) Whitman, Albert & Co.
Regan, Lisa. Wait Your Turn, Tilly: Be Patient, 1 vol. 2017. (You Choose Ser.). (ENG.). 32p. (gr. 2-2). lib. bdg. 26.93 *(978-0-7660-8704-0(2)*, f8941a1a-1c41-44d7-9cb3-033e2885200f) Enslow Publishing, LLC.
Reynolds Naylor, Phyllis. Faith, Hope, & Ivy June. 2011. 288p. (J). (ENG.). (gr. 4-6). 21.19 *(978-0-385-73615-2(0)*, Delacorte Pr.); (gr. 3-7). 8.99 *(978-0-375-84491-1(0)*, Yearling) Random Hse. Children's Bks.
Robertson, Claire & Shirvington, Jessica. Just the Way We Are. 2020. 24p. pap. 6.99 *(978-0-7333-3164-0(5))* ABC Bks. AUS. Dist: HarperCollins Pubs.
Scott, Kevin John. Frederik Sandwich & the Earthquake That Couldn't Possibly Be. (Frederik Sandwich Ser.: 1). (ENG.). (J). (gr. 3-7). 2019. 336p. pap. 12.99 *(978-1-4926-6799-5(4))* 2018. (Illus.). 320p. 16.99 *(978-1-4926-4853-6(1))* Sourcebooks, Inc.
Shelley, Mary. Frankenstein: With a Discussion of Tolerance. Clift, Eva, tr. Clift, Eva, illus. 2003. (Values in Action Illustrated Classics Ser.). (J). *(978-1-59203-048-4(3))* Learning Challenge, Inc.
Simmons, Jane. Beryl: a Pig's Tale. 2011. (ENG.). 224p. (J). (gr. 3-7). pap. 13.99 *(978-0-316-04413-4(X))* Little, Brown Bks. for Young Readers.
Smithem, Beth. Cocoa Bean & Squirt. 2010. 68p. pap. 10.49 *(978-1-4520-1929-1(0))* AuthorHouse.
Storm, Hannah, frwd. Buddy Booby's Birthmark. 2006. (Illus.). 36p. (J). 21.99 *(978-0-9794413-0-1(7))*; pap. 15.99 *(978-0-9794413-1-8(5))* E & D Bks., Ltd.
Swift, Jonathan. Gulliver's Travels: And A Discussion of Tolerance. Clift, Eva, illus. 2003. (Values in Action Illustrated Classics Ser.). 191p. (J). *(978-1-59203-029-3(7))* Learning Challenge, Inc.
Taylor, Chloë. Clothes Minded. Zhang, Nancy, illus. 2015. (Sew Zoey Ser.: 11). (ENG.). 160p. (J). (gr. 3-7). pap. 7.99 *(978-1-4814-2927-6(2)*, Simon Spotlight) Simon Spotlight.
Thompson, Michael. Los Otros Osos/ the Other Bears (Spanish Edition) (Spanish & English Edition) 2013. (ENG., Illus.). 40p. (J). 16.99 *(978-1-59572-644-5(6))* Star Bright Bks., Inc.
—The Other Bears: English, 1 vol. Thompson, Michael, illus. 2013.Tr. of Os Outros Ursos. (ENG., Illus.). 32p. (J). 16.99 *(978-1-59572-638-4(1))*; pap. 6.99 *(978-1-59572-639-1(X))* Star Bright Bks., Inc.
Troupe, Thomas Kingsley. Carma Comes Home. Tayal, Amit, illus. 2017. (Star Belchers Ser.). (ENG.). 128p. (J). (gr. 3-6). pap. 7.95 *(978-1-4965-4877-1(9)*, 135642); lib. bdg. 25.99 *(978-1-4965-4873-3(6)*, 135638) Capstone. (Stone Arch Bks.).
Uhlberg, Myron. Dad, Jackie, & Me, 1 vol. Bootman, Colin, illus. 32p. (J). (gr. -1-3). 2010. pap. 8.99 *(978-1-56145-531-7(8))* 2007. 16.95 *(978-1-56145-329-0(3))* Peachtree Publishing Co. Inc.
Vanoosting, James. Walking Mary. 2005. 144p. (J). (gr. 7-18). lib. bdg. 16.89 *(978-0-06-028472-5(2))* HarperCollins Pubs.
Vaughn, Royce, illus. Seymour Bluffs & Robert Wadlow, the Tallest Man in the World: A Story about Diversity & Tolerance. 2007. 28p. (J). 12.95 *(978-0-9728538-4-2(7))* Amica Publishing.
Wahl, Jan. Candy Shop. Wong, Nicole, illus. 2005. (ENG.). 32p. (J). (gr. -1-3). pap. 7.95 *(978-1-57091-668-7(3))* Charlesbridge Publishing, Inc.
Wood, Douglas. Old Turtle & the Broken Truth. Muth, Jon J., illus. 2003. (ENG.). 64p. (J). (gr. -1-3). 21.99 *(978-0-439-32109-9(3)*, Scholastic Pr.) Scholastic, Inc.

TOLKIEN, J. R. R. (JOHN RONALD RUEL), 1892-1973

Clinton, Greg. Reading & Interpreting the Works of J. R. R. Tolkien, 1 vol. 2016. (Lit Crit Guides). (ENG., Illus.). 176p. (gr. 6-6). 41.60 *(978-0-7660-8362-2(4)*, 353c7314-d0af-4cf4-9ded-1b606737b584) Enslow Publishing, LLC.
Collins, David R. J. R. R. Tolkien. 2004. (Just the Facts Biographies Ser.). (ENG., Illus.). 112p. (gr. 5-12). lib. bdg. 27.93 *(978-0-8225-2470-0(8))* Lerner Publishing Group.
Coren, Michael. J. R. R. Tolkien: The Man Who Created the Lord of the Rings, 1 vol. 2004. (ENG., Illus.). 135p. pap. 12.95 *(978-1-55005-087-5(7)*, 6cacb34b-c4c4-493d-b130-edbad0fef62f) Trifolium Bks., Inc. CAN. Dist: Firefly Bks., Ltd.
Hamen, Susan E. Quest, 1 vol. 2015. (Essential Literary Themes Ser.). (ENG., Illus.). 112p. (YA). (gr. 6-12). 41.36 *(978-1-62403-807-5(7)*, 17812, Essential Library) ABDO Publishing Co.
McAlister, Caroline. John Ronald's Dragons. 2017. (ENG., Illus.). 48p. (J). 21.99 *(978-1-62672-092-3(4)*, 900135560) Roaring Brook Pr.
Neimark, Anne E. Mythmaker: The Life of J. R. R. Tolkien, Creator of the Hobbit & the Lord of the Rings. Weinman, Brad, illus. 2014. (ENG.). 144p. (J). (gr. 5-7). pap. 7.99 *(978-0-544-02324-6(2)*, 1528648, Clarion Bks.) HarperCollins Pubs.
Pollack, Pam & Belviso, Meg. Who Was J. R. R. Tolkien? Moore, Jonathan & Harrison, Nancy, illus. 2015. 105p. (J). *(978-1-4806-8935-0(1))* Baker & Taylor, CATS.
Pollack, Pam, et al. Who Was J. R. R. Tolkien? Moore, Jonathan, illus. 2015. (Who Was? Ser.). 112p. (J). (gr. 3-7). 6.99 *(978-0-448-48302-3(5)*, Penguin Workshop) Penguin Young Readers Group.

TONGUE

Bozzo, Linda. Amazing Animal Tongues. (Creature Features Ser.). 24p. (gr. 2-3). 2009. 42.50 *(978-1-61512-070-3(X)*, PowerKids Pr.) 2008. (ENG., Illus.). (J). lib. bdg. 26.27 *(978-1-4042-4172-5(8)*, cc74744b-4153-47d3-8b7c-8be4cf7f2fc8) Rosen Publishing Group, Inc., The.
Canetti, Yanitzia. La adaptación, ¡qué Sensación! Lenguas. 2010. (SPA.). 24p. (J). pap. *(978-1-59835-188-0(5)*, BrickHouse Education) Cambridge BrickHouse, Inc.

TUV

—Amazing Adaptations! Tongues. 2010. 24p. (J). pap. (978-1-59835-213-9(X), BrickHouse Education) Cambridge BrickHouse, Inc.
Fernandez, A. & Fernandez, Q. Hooray for My Taste. (Hooray for My Senses Ser.). (Illus.). (J). 19.27 (978-1-58952-376-0(8)) Rourke Educational Media.
Gianferrari, Maria. Terrific Tongues! Liu, Jia, illus. 2018. 32p. (J). (gr. -1-3). 17.99 (978-1-62091-784-8(X), Astra Young Readers) Astra Publishing Hse.
Hopper, Karina. Mouth & Tongue Let's Have Some Fun! 2010. (Illus.). 48p. (J). pap. 10.95 (978-1-84905-161-3(5), 692635) Kingsley, Jessica Pubs. GBR. Dist: Hachette UK Distribution.
Kubler, Annie, illus. What Can I Taste? 2011. (Small Senses Ser.). 12p. (J). spiral bd. (978-1-84643-375-7(4)) Child's Play International Ltd.
Libra, Anna. Why Does That Taste Bad? An Inside Look at the Tongue. 2003. (J). pap. (978-1-58417-069-3(7)); lib. bdg. (978-1-58417-006-8(9)) Lake Street Pubs.
Lynch, Wayne. Whose Tongue Is This? 2011. (Whose? Animal Ser.: 9). (ENG., Illus.). 32p. (J). (gr. k-2). pap. 5.95 (978-1-77050-035-8(9), 7a653ce0-7333-44ce-b06a-fc2b55e9b5d7) Whitecap Bks., Ltd. CAN. Dist: Firefly Bks., Ltd.
Meachen Rau, Dana. Yum! [Scholastic]: A Book about Taste. Peterson, Rick, illus. 2010. (Amazing Body: the Five Senses Ser.). 24p. pap. 0.56 (978-1-4048-6543-3(8), Picture Window Bks.) Capstone.
Owings, Lisa. Tasting. 2018. (Five Senses Ser.). (ENG., Illus.). 24p. (J). (gr. k-3). pap. 7.99 (978-1-61891-299-2(2), 12104, Blastoff! Readers) Bellwether Media.
Randolph, Joanne. Whose Tongue Is This? (Animal Clues Ser.). 24p. (gr. 1-1). 2009. 42.50 (978-1-61511-436-8(X)) 2008. (ENG., Illus.). (J). lib. bdg. 26.27 (978-1-4042-4455-9(7), 1b60ef6a-81a2-4375-ba0d-581c1c22ba28) Rosen Publishing Group, Inc., The. (PowerKids Pr.).
—Whose Tongue Is This? De Quién Es Esta Lengua?, 1 vol. 2008. (Animal Clues / ¿Adivina de Cuién Es? Ser.). (SPA & ENG., Illus.). 24p. (J). (gr. 1-1). lib. bdg. 26.27 (978-1-4358-2532-1(2), 3a308802-7b9f-4223-af97-057cb63472dd, PowerKids Pr.) Rosen Publishing Group, Inc., The.
—Whose Tongue Is This? / ¿de quién es esta Lengua? 2009. (Animal Clues / ¿Adivina de Quién Es? Ser.). (ENG & SPA.). 24p. (gr. 1-1). 42.50 (978-1-61511-442-9(4), Editorial Buenas Letras) Rosen Publishing Group, Inc., The.
Rustad, Martha E. H. Tasting. 2014. (Illus.). 24p. (J). lib. bdg. 25.65 (978-1-62031-118-9(6), Bullfrog Bks.) Jump! Inc.
Stewart, Melissa. Terrific Tongues up Close, 1 vol. 2012. (Animal Bodies up Close Ser.). (ENG.). 24p. (gr. k-2). 25.27 (978-0-7660-3894-3(7), d0b01ac5-8bab-48de-8bed-a54b3eda7393); (Illus.). pap. 10.35 (978-1-4644-0083-4(0), 19b0f8db-1520-4a49-b996-619c440bb8ad) Enslow Publishing, LLC. (Enslow Elementary).
Wearing, Judy. Taste. 2009. (World of Wonder Ser.). (Illus.). 24p. (J). (gr. 2-4). pap. 8.95 (978-1-60596-057-9(8)); lib. bdg. 24.45 (978-1-60596-056-2(X)) Weigl Pubs., Inc.

TOOLS

see also Agricultural Machinery; Machinery

Adams, Barbara. A World of Tools. Date not set. (Early Science Big Bks.). (Illus.). 16p. (J). (gr. -1-2). pap. 16.95 (978-1-58273-115-5(2)) Sundance/Newbridge Educational Publishing.
Ball, Jacqueline A. We Use Tools All Day. Bowser, Ken, illus. 2017. (Space Cat Explores STEM Ser.). (ENG.). 24p. (J). (gr. 1-3). lib. bdg. 19.99 (978-1-63440-196-8(4), 042ec7c9-4308-4f37-a7c4-45c8b7d8421d) Red Chair Pr.
Benchmark Education Company, LLC Staff, compiled by. Tools & Technology. 2006. (J). 148.00 (978-1-4108-7034-6(0)) Benchmark Education Co.
Blevins, Wiley. Tools Scientists Use, 6 vols., Set. 2004. (Phonics Readers Books 37-72 Ser.). (ENG.). 8p. (gr. k-1). pap. 35.70 (978-0-7368-4080-4(X)) Capstone.
Braun, Eric. Curious Pearl Tinkers with Simple Machines: 4D an Augmented Reading Science Experience. Lewis, Anthony, illus. 2018. (Curious Pearl, Science Girl 4D Ser.). (ENG.). 24p. (J). (gr. k-2). lib. bdg. 25.99 (978-1-5158-2973-7(1), 138575, Picture Window Bks.) Capstone.
Buzzeo, Toni. Whose Tools? (a Guess-The-Job Book) Datz, Jim, illus. 2015. (Guess-The-Job Book Ser.). (ENG.). 16p. (J). (gr. -1 — 1). bds. 10.99 (978-1-4197-1431-3(7), 1098510) Abrams, Inc.
Cain, Marie Mowery. Tools Rule. 2013. (Big Books, Red Ser.). (ENG & SPA., Illus.). 16p. pap. 33.00 (978-1-59246-212-4(X)) Big Books, by George!
Carrino, Anthony & Colaneri, John. What Can You Do with a Toolbox? Lam, Maple, illus. 2018. (ENG.). 32p. (J). (gr. -1-3). 17.99 (978-1-5344-0296-6(9), Simon & Schuster/Paula Wiseman Bks.) Simon & Schuster/Paula Wiseman Bks.
Gibbons, Gail. Tool Book. 2017. (ENG.). 18p. (J). (gr. -1 — 1). bds. 7.99 (978-0-8234-3872-3(4)) Holiday Hse., Inc.
Gosman, Gillian. Simple Machines at School. 2014. (Simple Machines Everywhere Ser.). (Illus.). 24p. (J). (gr. k-3). pap. 49.50 (978-1-4777-6645-3(6), PowerKids Pr.) Rosen Publishing Group, Inc., The.
Gregory, Josh. Drills. 2013. (21st Century Junior Library: Basic Tools Ser.). (ENG.). 24p. (J). (gr. 2-5). pap. 12.79 (978-1-62431-302-8(7), 203002); (Illus.). 29.21 (978-1-62431-170-3(9), 203000) Cherry Lake Publishing.
—Hammers. 2013. (21st Century Junior Library: Basic Tools Ser.). (ENG.). 24p. (J). (gr. 2-5). pap. 12.79 (978-1-62431-300-4(0), 202994); (Illus.). 29.21 (978-1-62431-168-0(7), 202992) Cherry Lake Publishing.
—Screwdrivers. 2013. (21st Century Junior Library: Basic Tools Ser.). (ENG.). 24p. (J). (gr. 2-5). pap. 12.79 (978-1-62431-301-1(9), 202998); (Illus.). 29.21 (978-1-62431-169-7(5), 202996) Cherry Lake Publishing.
—Wrenches. 2013. (21st Century Junior Library: Basic Tools Ser.). (ENG.). 24p. (J). (gr. 2-5). pap. 12.79 (978-1-62431-307-3(8), 203022); (Illus.). 29.21 (978-1-62431-175-8(X), 203020) Cherry Lake Publishing.
Keppeler, Jill. Weird Food Inventions, 1 vol. 2018. (Wild & Wacky Inventions Ser.). (ENG.). 32p. (J). (gr. 4-5). 28.27 (978-1-5382-2071-9(7), bd756b29-258e-49db-ac4c-9236a064bd07) Stevens, Gareth Publishing LLLP.
King, Aven. A Doctor's Tools, 1 vol. 2015. (Community Helpers & Their Tools Ser.). (ENG., Illus.). 24p. (J). (gr. 2-3). pap. 9.25 (978-1-4994-0838-6(2), 0d1de156-fa5b-4681-a017-74289ecacbe6, PowerKids Pr.) Rosen Publishing Group, Inc., The.
Machut, Ronald. Working with Screws: Ronald Machut, 1 vol. 2019. (Doing Work with Simple Machines Ser.). (ENG.). 24p. (gr. 3-3). 25.27 (978-1-5383-4363-0(0), 50bddf26-a095-4506-81cd-a8dab63cc7a5, PowerKids Pr.) Rosen Publishing Group, Inc., The.
Mangieri, Catherine. Using Measuring Tools, 1 vol. 2008. (Real Life Readers Ser.). (ENG.). 12p. (gr. 1-2). pap. 5.90 (978-1-4042-7921-6(0), cf38961a-2edd-450d-b5b3-f6d70ab74063, Rosen Classroom) Rosen Publishing Group, Inc., The.
Manolis, Kay. Ramps. 2009. (Simple Machines Ser.). (ENG., Illus.). 24p. (J). (gr. 2-5). lib. bdg. 26.95 (978-1-60014-346-5(6), Blastoff! Readers) Bellwether Media.
—Screws. 2009. (Simple Machines Ser.). (ENG., Illus.). 24p. (J). (gr. 2-5). lib. bdg. 26.95 (978-1-60014-322-9(9), Blastoff! Readers) Bellwether Media.
—Wedges. 2009. (Simple Machines Ser.). (ENG., Illus.). 24p. (J). (gr. 2-5). lib. bdg. 26.95 (978-1-60014-323-6(7), Blastoff! Readers) Bellwether Media.
Markovics, Pearl. In the Tool Shed. 2019. (Farm Charm Ser.). (ENG.). 16p. (J). (gr. -1-1). 6.99 (978-1-64280-380-8(4)) Bearport Publishing Co., Inc.
Marsico, Katie. Pliers. 2013. (21st Century Junior Library: Basic Tools Ser.). (ENG., Illus.). 24p. (J). (gr. 2-5). 29.21 (978-1-62431-174-1(1), 203016); pap. 12.79 (978-1-62431-306-6(X), 203018) Cherry Lake Publishing.
—Saws. 2013. (21st Century Junior Library: Basic Tools Ser.). (ENG.). 24p. (J). (gr. 2-5). pap. 12.79 (978-1-62431-303-5(5), 203006); (Illus.). 29.21 (978-1-62431-171-0(7), 203004) Cherry Lake Publishing.
Masterson, Josephine. My Grandfather's Workshop, 1 vol. 2015. (Rosen REAL Readers: STEM & STEAM Collection). (ENG.). 8p. (gr. k-1). pap. 5.46 (978-1-4994-9708-3(3), 23598cdf-2d8c-4248-aa5e-beef2a226655, Rosen Classroom) Rosen Publishing Group, Inc., The.
McFadden, Jesse. A Construction Worker's Tools, 1 vol. 2015. (Community Helpers & Their Tools Ser.). (ENG., Illus.). 24p. (J). (gr. 2-3). pap. 9.25 (978-1-4994-0836-2(6), 736f3297-5114-4f29-8401-8b2c81317a8f, PowerKids Pr.) Rosen Publishing Group, Inc., The.
McKinney, Devon. A Firefighter's Tools, 1 vol. 2015. (Community Helpers & Their Tools Ser.). (ENG.). 24p. (J). (gr. 2-3). 25.27 (978-1-4994-0897-3(8), fdc614a5-dcbe-48c8-a7f8-64b5c2482815, PowerKids Pr.) Rosen Publishing Group, Inc., The.
Meachen Rau, Dana. Builders, 1 vol. 2008. (Tools We Use Ser.). (ENG.). 32p. (gr. k-1). pap. 9.23 (978-0-7614-3289-0(2), 9a74bc42-2a53-4d58-8347-97b1343fd1dc) Cavendish Square Publishing LLC.
—Los Constructores / Builders, 1 vol. 2009. (Instrumentos de Trabajo / Tools We Use Ser.). (ENG & SPA., Illus.). 32p. (gr. k-2). lib. bdg. 25.50 (978-0-7614-2821-3(6), 574410b8-03bc-47a1-9082-2210698ec54a) Cavendish Square Publishing LLC.
—Los Constructores (Builders), 1 vol. 2009. (Instrumentos de Trabajo (Tools We Use) Ser.). (SPA., Illus.). 32p. (gr. k-2). lib. bdg. 25.50 (978-0-7614-2797-1(X), aa288231-d51e-491c-adc2-85f236cf8417) Cavendish Square Publishing LLC.
Milet Publishing Staff. My First Bilingual Book - Tools, 1 vol. 2014. (My First Bilingual Book Ser.). (ENG & SPA., Illus.). 20p. (J). (— 1). bds. 7.99 (978-1-84059-918-3(9)); bds. 7.99 (978-1-84059-919-0(7)); bds. 7.99 (978-1-84059-916-9(2)); bds. 7.99 (978-1-84059-906-0(5)); bds. 7.99 (978-1-84059-907-7(3)); bds. 7.99 (978-1-84059-920-6(0)); bds. 7.99 (978-1-84059-914-5(6)); bds. 7.99 (978-1-84059-911-4(1)) Milet Publishing.
—My First Bilingual Book - Tools - English, 1 vol. 2014. (My First Bilingual Book Ser.). (ENG., Illus.). 20p. (J). (— 1). bds. 7.99 (978-1-84059-921-3(9)) Milet Publishing.
—My First Bilingual Book - Tools - Ferramentas, 1 vol. 2014. (My First Bilingual Book Ser.). (ENG & POR., Illus.). 20p. (J). (— 1). bds. 7.99 (978-1-84059-915-2(4)) Milet Publishing.
—My First Bilingual Book - Tools (English-Somali), 1 vol. 2014. (My First Bilingual Book Ser.). (ENG., Illus.). 20p. (J). (— 1). bds. 7.99 (978-1-84059-917-6(0)) Milet Publishing.
—Tools, 1 vol. 2014. (My First Bilingual Book Ser.). (ENG & ITA., Illus.). 20p. (J). (— 1). bds. 7.99 (978-1-84059-912-1(X)) Milet Publishing.
—Tools - My First Bilingual Book, 1 vol. 2014. (My First Bilingual Book Ser.). (ENG., Illus.). 20p. (J). (— 1). bds. 7.99 (978-1-84059-908-4(1)); bds. 7.99 (978-1-84059-913-8(8)); bds. 7.99 (978-1-84059-909-1(X)) Milet Publishing.
—Tools (English-French), 1 vol. 2014. (My First Bilingual Book Ser.). (ENG & FRE., Illus.). 20p. (J). (— 1). bds. 7.99 (978-1-84059-910-7(3)) Milet Publishing.
Monroe, Andrea. The Science of Tools. 2003. (Living Science Ser.). (Illus.). 32p. (J). (gr. 1-3). pap. 9.95 (978-1-930954-31-1(X)) Weigl Pubs., Inc.
Morris, Ann. Tools. Heyman, Ken, photos by. 2015. (Illus.). 32p. pap. 7.00 (978-1-61003-622-1(0)) Center for the Collaborative Classroom.
Nelson, Robin. What Does a Hammer Do? 2012. (First Step Nonfiction — Tools at Work Ser.). (ENG., Illus.). 24p. (J). (gr. k-2). pap. 6.99 (978-1-58013-947-2(7), 09360237-05e0-4539-a735-e6e5e7ec9a1b) Lerner Publishing Group.
—What Does a Screwdriver Do? 2012. (First Step Nonfiction — Tools at Work Ser.). (ENG., Illus.). 24p. (J). (gr. k-2). pap. 6.99 (978-1-58013-951-9(5), 11bb80de-a872-4dc2-8fc4-d0ef88b84f24) Lerner Publishing Group.
Orme, David. Amazing Gadgets. 2010. (Fact to Fiction Grafx Ser.). (Illus.). 36p. (J). lib. bdg. 16.95 (978-1-60686-471-5(8)) Perfection Learning Corp.
Oxlade, Chris. Levers. 2009. (Simple Machines (Smart Apple Media Paperback) Ser.). (Illus.). 32p. (J). (gr. k-2). pap. 7.95 (978-1-59920-200-6(X)) Black Rabbit Bks.
—Screws. 2009. (Simple Machines (Smart Apple Media Paperback) Ser.). (Illus.). 32p. (J). (gr. k-2). pap. 7.95 (978-1-59920-202-0(6)) Black Rabbit Bks.
—Wedges & Ramps. 2009. (Simple Machines (Smart Apple Media Paperback) Ser.). (Illus.). 32p. (J). (gr. 4-7). pap. 7.95 (978-1-59920-203-7(4)) Black Rabbit Bks.
Puri, Devi. Making Tools in the Wild, 1 vol., 1. 2015. (Wilderness Survival Skills Ser.). (ENG., Illus.). 24p. (J). (gr. 3-4). pap. 9.25 (978-1-5081-4327-7(7), 02893825-db41-49fe-a002-f056d4748ba1, PowerKids Pr.) Rosen Publishing Group, Inc., The.
Research Tools You Can Use, 12 vols. 2014. (Research Tools You Can Use Ser.). (ENG.). 32p. (J). (gr. 2-3). 156.36 (978-1-62275-389-5(5), 92ae1fa0-6156-4c38-846b-9a512e18e68b) Rosen Publishing Group, Inc., The.
Rice, Dona Herweck. Good Work. 2nd rev. ed. 2015. (TIME for KIDS(r): Informational Text Ser.). (ENG., Illus.). 12p. (gr. -1-k). 7.99 (978-1-4938-2141-9(5)) Teacher Created Materials, Inc.
—Hit It! - History of Tools, 1 vol. 2nd rev. ed. 2012. (TIME for KIDS(r): Informational Text Ser.). (ENG.). 32p. (gr. 3-5). pap. 12.99 (978-1-4333-3680-5(4)) Teacher Created Materials, Inc.
Schuh, Mari. Tools for the Garden, 1 vol. 2010. (Gardens Ser.). (ENG.). 24p. (J). (gr. -1-2). lib. bdg. 24.65 (978-1-4296-3983-5(0), 102593, Pebble) Capstone.
Schwartz, Ella. Make This! Building Thinking, & Tinkering Projects for the Amazing Maker in You. 2019. (Illus.). 160p. (J). (gr. 3-7). pap. 16.99 (978-1-4263-3324-8(2)); (ENG., lib. bdg. 26.90 (978-1-4263-3325-5(0)) Disney Publishing Worldwide. (National Geographic Kids).
Spilsbury, Louise. Screws, 1 vol. 2018. (Technology in Action Ser.). (ENG.). 32p. (gr. 3-3). 27.93 (978-1-5383-3761-5(4), 0e0f947f-cb1d-4e48-8f93-f6d1547e724c, PowerKids Pr.) Rosen Publishing Group, Inc., The.
Sundance/Newbridge LLC Staff. A World of Tools. 2007. (Early Science Ser.). (gr. k-3). 18.95 (978-1-4007-6504-1(8)); pap. 6.10 (978-1-4007-6500-3(5)) Sundance/Newbridge Educational Publishing.
Tieck, Sarah. Screws, 1 vol. 2006. (Simple Machines Ser.). (ENG., Illus.). 24p. (gr. -1-3). 25.65 (978-1-59679-817-5(3), Buddy Bks.) ABDO Publishing Co.
TOOLS & MACHINES. 2010. (ENG., Illus.). 184p. (gr. 6-12). 35.00 (978-1-60413-171-0(3), P179241, Facts On File) Infobase Holdings, Inc.
Truran, Stacy. Troy's Tree Fort: Measure Lengths in Standard Units, 1 vol. 2014. (Rosen Math Readers Ser.). (ENG.). 24p. (J). (gr. 2-2). pap. 8.25 (978-1-4777-4784-1(2), 878e16d7-01e5-446a-8ce2-b894c3b66284, Rosen Classroom) Rosen Publishing Group, Inc., The.
A Worker's Tools: Individual Title Six-Packs. (Discovery World Ser.). 16p. (gr. 1-2). 28.00 (978-0-7635-8459-7(2)) Rigby Education.

TOOLS—FICTION

Barchers, Suzanne I. Fix It!, 1 vol. rev. ed. 2011. (Phonics Ser.). (ENG., Illus.). 16p. (gr. k-1). 6.99 (978-1-4333-2423-9(7)) Teacher Created Materials, Inc.
Briggs, Korwin. The Invention Hunters Discover How Machines Work. 2019. (Invention Hunters Ser.: 1). (ENG., Illus.). 48p. (J). (gr. -1-3). 18.99 (978-0-316-43679-3(8)) Little, Brown Bks. for Young Readers.
Cerato, Mattia. Drew the Screw. 2016. (I Like to Read Ser.). (ENG., Illus.). 24p. (J). (gr. -1-3). pap. 7.99 (978-0-8234-3541-8(5)) Holiday Hse., Inc.
Connor, Leslie. Miss Bridie Chose a Shovel. Azarian, Mary, illus. unabr. ed. 2005. (J). (gr. k-3). 29.95 incl. audio compact disk (978-0-8045-4135-0(3), SACD4135); 27.95 incl. audio (978-0-8045-6936-1(3), SAC6936) Spoken Arts, Inc.
Fliess, Sue. Let's Build, 0 vols. Sakamoto, Miki, illus. 2014. (ENG.). 24p. (J). (gr. -1-3). 14.99 (978-1-4778-4724-4(3), 9781477847244, Two Lions) Amazon Publishing.
Fox, Will. Bertie Bolt. Fox, Will, illus. 2013. (ENG., Illus.). 20p. (J). pap. 6.04 (978-1-908865-20-5(2)) Beecroft Publishing GBR. Dist: Ingram Content Group.
—Billy Brush. Fox, Will, illus. 2013. (ENG., Illus.). 20p. (J). pap. 6.04 (978-1-908865-25-0(3)) Beecroft Publishing GBR. Dist: Ingram Content Group.
—Hector Hacksaw. Fox, Will, illus. 2013. (ENG., Illus.). 20p. (J). pap. 6.04 (978-1-908865-28-1(8)) Beecroft Publishing GBR. Dist: Ingram Content Group.
—Molly Mallet. Fox, Will, illus. 2013. (ENG., Illus.). 20p. (J). pap. 6.04 (978-1-908865-27-4(X)) Beecroft Publishing GBR. Dist: Ingram Content Group.
—Peggy Peg. Fox, Will, illus. 2013. (ENG., Illus.). 20p. (J). pap. 6.04 (978-1-908865-22-9(9)) Beecroft Publishing GBR. Dist: Ingram Content Group.
—Rusty Nail. Fox, Will, illus. 2013. (ENG., Illus.). 20p. (J). pap. 6.04 (978-1-908865-21-2(0)) Beecroft Publishing GBR. Dist: Ingram Content Group.
—Sally Screw. Fox, Will, illus. 2013. (ENG., Illus.). 20p. (J). pap. 6.04 (978-1-908865-23-6(7)) Beecroft Publishing GBR. Dist: Ingram Content Group.
—Spiky Saw. Fox, Will, illus. 2013. (ENG., Illus.). 16p. (J). pap. 6.04 (978-1-908865-26-7(1)) Beecroft Publishing GBR. Dist: Ingram Content Group.
—Suzy Scissors. Fox, Will, illus. 2013. (ENG., Illus.). 20p. (J). pap. 6.04 (978-1-908865-29-8(6)) Beecroft Publishing GBR. Dist: Ingram Content Group.
—Twisty Drill. Fox, Will, illus. 2013. (ENG., Illus.). 16p. (J). pap. 6.04 (978-1-908865-24-3(5)) Beecroft Publishing GBR. Dist: Ingram Content Group.
Fritz, Betty. Bang Bang Bang, Hammers in the Morning. 2009. (J). 16.95 (978-1-61623-624-3(8)) Independent Pub.
Garcia, Emma. Tap Tap Bang Bang. 2013. (All about Sounds Ser.). (ENG., Illus.). 26p. (J). (— 1). bds. 7.99 (978-1-907967-67-2(2)) Boxer Bks., Ltd. GBR. Dist: Sterling Publishing Co., Inc.
Handy Manny Pop-up Tool Book. 2009. 6p. 12.99 (978-1-4231-2114-5(7)) Disney Pr.
Klein, Adria F. Hank Hammer, 1 vol. Rowland, Andrew, illus. 2011. (Tool School Ser.). (ENG.). 32p. (J). (gr. 1-2). lib. bdg. 22.65 (978-1-4342-3043-0(0), 114621, Stone Arch Bks.) Capstone.
—Hank Hammer & the Puppy, 1 vol. Rowland, Andrew, illus. 2012. (Tool School Ser.). (ENG.). 32p. (J). (gr. 1-3). lib. bdg. 22.65 (978-1-4342-4020-0(7), 118401, Stone Arch Bks.) Capstone.
—Sammy Saw, 1 vol. Rowland, Andrew, illus. 2011. (Tool School Ser.). (ENG.). 32p. (J). (gr. 1-2). lib. bdg. 22.65 (978-1-4342-3045-4(7), 114623, Stone Arch Bks.) Capstone.
—Sophie Screwdriver, 1 vol. Rowland, Andrew, illus. 2011. (Tool School Ser.). (ENG.). 32p. (J). (gr. 1-2). pap. 6.25 (978-1-4342-3386-8(3), 116393); lib. bdg. 22.65 (978-1-4342-3044-7(9), 114622) Capstone. (Stone Arch Bks.).
—Sophie Screwdriver & the Classroom, 1 vol. Rowland, Andrew, illus. 2012. (Tool School Ser.). (ENG.). 32p. (J). (gr. 1-3). pap. 6.25 (978-1-4342-4235-8(8), 120292, Stone Arch Bks.) Capstone.
—Tia Tape Measure, 1 vol. Rowland, Andrew, illus. 2011. (Tool School Ser.). (ENG.). 32p. (J). (gr. 1-2). pap. 6.25 (978-1-4342-3388-2(X), 116395); lib. bdg. 22.65 (978-1-4342-3046-1(5), 114624) Capstone. (Stone Arch Bks.).
—Tia Tape Measure & the Move, 1 vol. Rowland, Andrew, illus. 2012. (Tool School Ser.). (ENG.). 32p. (J). (gr. 1-3). lib. bdg. 22.65 (978-1-4342-4023-1(1), 118404, Stone Arch Bks.) Capstone.
—Tia Tape Measure & the Move, 1 vol. Rowland, Andrew, illus. 2012. (Tool School Ser.). (ENG.). 32p. (J). (gr. 1-3). pap. 6.25 (978-1-4342-4236-5(6), 120293, Stone Arch Bks.) Capstone.
McNeil, Niki, et al. HOCPP 1070 Mike & Mary Anne the Steam Shovel. 2006. spiral bd. (978-1-60308-070-5(8)) In the Hands of a Child.
Meshon, Aaron. Tools Rule! Meshon, Aaron, illus. 2014. (ENG., Illus.). 40p. (J). (gr. -1-3). 19.99 (978-1-4424-9601-9(0), Atheneum Bks. for Young Readers) Simon & Schuster Children's Publishing.
Monroe, Chris. Monkey with a Tool Belt. Monroe, Chris, illus. 2008. (Monkey with a Tool Belt Ser.). (ENG., Illus.). 32p. (J). (gr. -1-2). lib. bdg. 17.99 (978-0-8225-7631-0(7), 1a4939c4-35a1-48ef-bfc0-2a63bac96957, Carolrhoda Bks.) Lerner Publishing Group.
—Monkey with a Tool Belt & the Maniac Muffins. Monroe, Chris, illus. 2016. (Monkey with a Tool Belt Ser.). (ENG., Illus.). 32p. (J). (gr. -1-2). 17.99 (978-1-4677-2155-4(7), 72e58124-43b0-441a-ba6a-44699c291b1a); E-Book 35.99 (978-1-4677-9562-3(3)) Lerner Publishing Group. (Carolrhoda Bks.).
—Monkey with a Tool Belt & the Noisy Problem. Monroe, Chris, illus. 2009. (Monkey with a Tool Belt Ser.). (ENG., Illus.). 32p. (J). (gr. -1-2). 17.99 (978-0-8225-9247-1(9), 9324df12-db0d-4e72-a01a-673555bee853, Carolrhoda Bks.) Lerner Publishing Group.
Pflugfelder, Bob & Hockensmith, Steve. Nick & Tesla's Secret Agent Gadget Battle: A Mystery with Spy Cameras, Code Wheels, & Other Gadgets You Can Build Yourself. 2014. (Nick & Tesla Ser.: 3). (Illus.). 256p. (J). (gr. 4-7). 12.95 (978-1-59474-676-5(1)) Quirk Bks.
Pommier, Maurice. Grandpa's Workshop. Anderson, Brian, tr. from FRE. Pommier, Maurice, illus. 2012.Tr. of Grandpa's Workshop. (ENG., Illus.). 48p. (J). 22.00 (978-0-9850777-2-3(7)) Lost Art Pr. LLC.
Publications International Ltd. Staff, ed. Handy Manny. 2008. 16p. (J). bds. 9.98 (978-1-4127-9373-5(4), PIL Kids) Publications International, Ltd.
—Handy Manny: Fiesta Fun. 2008. (J). bds. 10.98 (978-1-4127-8867-0(6)) Publications International, Ltd.
Rockwell, Anne & Rockwell, Harlow. The Toolbox. Rockwell, Anne, illus. 2006. (ENG., Illus.). 20p. (J). (gr. -1-k). bds. 7.99 (978-0-8027-9609-7(5), 900040903, Bloomsbury USA Childrens) Bloomsbury Publishing USA.
Shulman, Lisa. Old MacDonald Had a Woodshop. Wolff, Ashley, illus. 2004. 32p. (J). (gr. -1-k). reprint ed. pap. 7.99 (978-0-14-240186-6(2), Puffin Books) Penguin Young Readers Group.
Smith, Kourtney. The Adventures of Stanley the Staple. 2013. 28p. pap. 24.95 (978-1-63004-276-9(5)) America Star Bks.
Sturges, Philemon. I Love Tools! Halpern, Shari, illus. 2006. 24p. (J). (gr. -1-1). 14.89 (978-0-06-009288-7(2)) HarperCollins Pubs.

TOPOLOGY

Piddock, Claire. Position & Direction. 2010. (ENG., Illus.). 24p. (J). (978-0-7787-5248-6(8)); pap. (978-0-7787-5295-0(X)) Crabtree Publishing Co.
Rapoport, Rebecca & Yoder, J. A. Geometry & Topology: Fun, Hands-On Activities for Learning Math. 2018. (Math Lab for Kids Ser.). (ENG., Illus.). 32p. (J). (gr. 3-6). lib. bdg. 27.99 (978-1-63159-454-0(0), 279f0793-3b04-43de-96a3-9e0e2ceb7f41, Quarry Bks.) Quarto Publishing Group USA.

TORNADOES

see also Storms

Abdo, Kenny. How to Survive a Tornado. 2018. (How to Survive Ser.). (ENG., Illus.). 24p. (J). (gr. 2-8). lib. bdg. 31.36 (978-1-5321-2327-6(2), 28421, Abdo Zoom-Fly) ABDO Publishing Co.
Aboff, Marcie. Tornadoes!, 1 vol. Sotirovski, Aleksandar, illus. 2012. (First Graphics: Wild Earth Ser.). (ENG.). 24p. (J). (gr. k-3). pap. 6.29 (978-1-4296-7952-7(2), 118284); (gr. 1-2). pap. 35.70 (978-1-4296-8372-2(4)) Capstone.
Armentrout, David. Tornadoes. 2009. (ENG.). 32p. pap. 3.99 (978-0-8249-1413-4(9), Ideals Pubns.) Worthy Publishing.
Armour, Cy. Tornadoes & Hurricanes!, 1 vol. 2nd rev. ed. 2011. (TIME for KIDS(r): Informational Text Ser.). (ENG.). 24p. (gr. 2-3). pap. 9.99 (978-1-4333-3614-0(6)) Teacher Created Materials, Inc.
Aronin, Miriam. Oklahoma's Devastating May 2013 Tornado. 2014. (Code Red Ser.). 32p. (J). (gr. 2-7). lib. bdg. 28.50 (978-1-62724-131-1(0)) Bearport Publishing Co., Inc.
Baker, John R. The World's Worst Tornadoes. 2016. (World's Worst Natural Disasters Ser.). (ENG., Illus.). 32p. (J). (gr. 3-9). pap. 7.95 (978-1-5157-1792-8(5), 132534); lib. bdg. 27.32 (978-1-5157-1788-1(7), 132532) Capstone. (Capstone Pr.).
Ball, Jacqueline A. Tornado! The 1974 Super Outbreak. 2005. (X-Treme Disasters That Changed America Ser.). 32p. (J). lib. bdg. 25.27 (978-1-59716-009-4(1)) Bearport Publishing Co., Inc.
Barrett, Tracy. How Do Tornadoes Form?, 1 vol. 2011. (Tell Me Why, Tell Me How Ser.). (ENG.). 32p. (gr. 3-3). 32.64

(978-0-7614-4828-0(4), 5ba9abc6-e5cf-4bec-96db-3a87aa21880a) Cavendish Square Publishing LLC.

Berger, Melvin & Berger, Gilda. Hurricanes Have Eyes but Can't See: And Other Amazing Facts about Wild Weather. 2003. (Illus.). 48p. (J). (978-0-439-54980-6(9)) Scholastic, Inc.

Bodden, Valerie. Our Wonderful Weather: Tornadoes. 2014. (Our Wonderful Weather Ser.). (ENG., Illus.). 24p. (J). (gr. 1-3). pap. 9.99 (978-0-89812-923-6(0), 22270, Creative Paperbacks) Creative Co., The.

—Tornadoes. 2012. (Our Wonderful Weather Ser.). (ENG., Illus.). 24p. (J). (gr. 1-4). 25.65 (978-1-60818-150-6(2), 22265, Creative Education) Creative Co., The.

Boothroyd, Jennifer. What Is Severe Weather? 2014. (First Step Nonfiction — Let's Watch the Weather Ser.). (ENG., Illus.). 24p. (J). (gr. k-2). pap. 6.99 (978-1-4677-4499-7(9), 0cf19a8f-2424-4a12-aa52-f32b05403a57) Lerner Publishing Group.

Bowman, Chris. Survive a Tornado. 2016. (Survival Zone Ser.). (ENG., Illus.). 24p. (J). (gr. 3-7). 26.95 (978-1-62617-444-3(X), Torque Bks.) Bellwether Media.

Brennan, Linda Crotta. We Have Tornadoes. 2014. (Tell Me Why Library). (ENG., Illus.). 24p. (J). (gr. 2-5). 29.21 (978-1-63188-012-4(8), 205455) Cherry Lake Publishing.

Carson, Mary Kay. Inside Tornadoes. 2010. (Inside Ser.). (ENG., Illus.). 48p. (J). (gr. 3-6). pap. 12.95 (978-1-4027-7781-3(7)) Sterling Publishing Co., Inc.

—The Tornado Scientist: Seeing Inside Severe Storms. Uhlman, Tom, illus. 2019. (Scientists in the Field Ser.). (ENG.). 80p. (J). (gr. 5-7). 18.99 (978-0-544-96582-9(5), 1662355, Clarion Bks.) HarperCollins Pubs.

Cassie, Brian. Tornadoes. (Science Readers Ser.). (Illus.). 32p. (J). pap. 3.99 (978-0-439-42505-6(0)) Scholastic, Inc.

Cernak, Linda. The Science of a Tornado. 2015. (21st Century Skills Library: Disaster Science Ser.). (ENG., Illus.). 32p. (J). (gr. 4-8). 32.07 (978-1-63362-482-5(X), 206836) Cherry Lake Publishing.

Chambers, Catherine. Tornado. 2nd rev. ed. 2016. (Wild Weather Ser.). (ENG.). 32p. (J). (gr. 1-3). pap. 7.99 (978-1-4846-3586-5(8), 133460, Heinemann) Capstone.

Close, Edward. Extreme Weather, 1 vol., 1. 2014. (Discovery Education: Earth & Space Science Ser.). (ENG.). 32p. (gr. 4-5). 28.93 (978-1-4777-6194-6(2), 1b048c95-feb0-48ca-8404-bf5d9bbd0dd1, PowerKids Pr.) Rosen Publishing Group, Inc., The.

Cox Cannons, Helen. Wind, 1 vol. 2014. (Weather Wise Ser.). (ENG., Illus.). 24p. (J). (gr. -1-1). pap. 5.99 (978-1-4846-0559-2(4), 126650, Heinemann) Capstone.

Davies, Jon. Storm Chasers! on the Trail of Twisters. Rath, Robert, illus. Davies, Jon & Reed, Jim, photos by. 2007. 48p. (J). (gr. 3-7). pap. 12.95 (978-1-56037-407-7(1)) Farcountry Pr.

Davies, Monika. Tornadoes, 1 vol. 2020. (Force of Nature Ser.). (ENG.). 48p. (J). (gr. 4-5). pap. 12.71 (978-1-9785-1848-3(X), 3daa47c9-94f0-4fe1-9c5d-b8eca35a0ae3) Enslow Publishing, LLC.

Doeden, Matt. Tornadoes. 2008. pap. 40.95 (978-0-8225-9445-1(5)); (ENG., Illus.). 32p. lib. bdg. 22.60 (978-0-8225-7910-6(3), Lerner Pubns.) Lerner Publishing Group.

Donnelly, Karen. Storms of the Past & the Future. 2009. (Earth's Changing Weather & Climate Ser.). 24p. (gr. 4-4). 42.50 (978-1-61512-250-9(8), PowerKids Pr.) Rosen Publishing Group, Inc., The.

Dougherty, Terri. The Worst Tornadoes of All Time. 2012. (Epic Disasters Ser.). (ENG.). 32p. (gr. 3-4). pap. 47.70 (978-1-4296-8509-2(3), Capstone Pr.) Capstone.

Drummond, Allan. Green City: How One Community Survived a Tornado & Rebuilt for a Sustainable Future. 2016. (Green Power Ser.). (ENG., Illus.). 40p. (J). 18.99 (978-0-374-37999-5(8), 900065068, Farrar, Straus & Giroux (BYR)) Farrar, Straus & Giroux.

Elkins, Elizabeth. Investigating Tornadoes. 2017. (Investigating Natural Disasters Ser.). (ENG., Illus.). 32p. (J). (gr. 3-9). lib. bdg. 28.65 (978-1-5157-4037-7(4), 133918, Capstone Pr.) Capstone.

Fradin, Judy. Tornado! The Story Behind These Twisting, Turning, Spinning, & Spiraling Storms. 2011. (ENG., Illus.). 64p. (J). (gr. 5-9). 16.95 (978-1-4263-0779-9(9), National Geographic Kids) Disney Publishing Worldwide.

Friesen, Helen Lepp. Tornadoes. 2016. (Illus.). 32p. (J). (978-1-5105-2077-6(5)) SmartBook Media, Inc.

Gibbons, Gail. Tornadoes! (New & Updated Edition) 2019. (Illus.). 32p. (J). (gr. -1-3). 18.99 (978-0-8234-4168-6(7)); pap. 8.99 (978-0-8234-4187-7(3)) Holiday Hse., Inc.

Gifford, Clive. Chasing the World's Most Dangerous Storms. 2010. (Extreme! Ser.). (ENG.). 32p. (gr. 3-4). pap. 47.70 (978-1-4296-5123-3(7), Capstone Pr.) Capstone.

Gonzales, Doreen. Tornadoes, 1 vol. 2012. (Killer Disasters Ser.). (ENG., Illus.). 24p. (J). (gr. 2-3). pap. 9.25 (978-1-4488-7512-2(9), b99eb366-a603-4d4d-a05a-ddb2b5da0d8a); lib. bdg. 26.27 (978-1-4488-7439-2(4), 0a5a6d94-a90e-4981-9d1f-163be86023a1) Rosen Publishing Group, Inc., The. (PowerKids Pr.).

Group/McGraw-Hill, Wright. Savage Storms: Tornadoes & Hurricanes, 6 vols. (Book2WebTM Ser.). (gr. 4-8). 36.50 (978-0-322-04424-1(3)) Wright Group/McGraw-Hill.

Gullo, Arthur. Tornadoes. 2015. (J). lib. bdg. (978-1-62713-517-7(0)) Cavendish Square Publishing LLC.

Hand, Carol. The Science of Tornadoes, 1 vol. 2019. (Science of Natural Disasters Ser.). (ENG.). 32p. (J). (gr. 3-3). pap. 11.58 (978-1-5026-4654-5(4), db5bb952-80d9-4261-a69a-31126cb32b54) Cavendish Square Publishing LLC.

Hansen, Grace. Tornadoes, 1 vol. 2015. (Weather Ser.). (ENG., Illus.). 24p. (J). (gr. -1-2). 32.79 (978-1-62970-935-2(2), 18328, Abdo Kids) ABDO Publishing Co.

—Tornados. 2016. (Clima Ser.). (SPA.). 24p. (J). (gr. -1-2). pap. 7.95 (978-1-4966-0696-9(5), 131740, Capstone Classroom) Capstone.

Harasymiw, Mark J. Chasing a Tornado, 1 vol. 2013. (Thrill Seekers Ser.). (ENG., Illus.). 32p. (J). (gr. 3-4). 29.27 (978-1-4824-0138-7(X), 9226fba7-05db-4bd7-9198-8afbe53fbe70) Stevens, Gareth Publishing LLLP.

Hayden, Kate. Twisters! 2010. (DK Reader Level 2 Ser.). (gr. k-3). lib. bdg. 13.55 (978-0-613-33171-5(0)) Turtleback.

Heinrichs, Ann. Storm Chaser. 2009. (21st Century Skills Library: Cool Science Careers Ser.). (ENG., Illus.). 32p. (gr. 4-8). lib. bdg. 32.07 (978-1-60279-308-8(5), 200204) Cherry Lake Publishing.

Honders, Christine. A Trip Inside a Tornado, 1 vol. 2014. (Fantastic Science Journeys Ser.). (ENG.). 32p. (J). (gr. 2-3). pap. 11.50 (978-1-4824-1998-6(X), 9d3d1184-7b96-48f3-b0cc-f4f30d6af084) Stevens, Gareth Publishing LLLP.

Hubbard, Ben. Tornado: Perspectives on Tornado Disasters, 1 vol. 2014. (Disaster Dossiers Ser.). (ENG., Illus.). 56p. (J). (gr. 6-10). pap. 9.49 (978-1-4846-0189-1(0), 126170, Heinemann) Capstone.

Jeffrey, Gary. Tornadoes & Superstorms. 2007. (Graphic Natural Disasters Ser.). (ENG.). 48p. (YA). 58.50 (978-1-4488-1667-5(X), Rosen Reference) Rosen Publishing Group, Inc., The.

—Tornadoes & Superstorms, 1 vol. Riley, Terry, illus. 2007. (Graphic Natural Disasters Ser.). (ENG.). 48p. (gr. 5-5). (J). lib. bdg. 37.13 (978-1-4042-1993-9(5), 341abb57-9639-4eda-b52c-cd55d0121d81); pap. 14.05 (978-1-4042-1985-4(4), 47b4b752-3b70-4880-a791-75d17e2d453d) Rosen Publishing Group, Inc., The.

Jensen, Belinda. The Sky Stirs up Trouble: Tornadoes. Kurilla, Renée, illus. 2016. (Bel the Weather Girl Ser.). (ENG.). 24p. (J). (gr. -1-3). 25.32 (978-1-4677-7960-9(1), 2efb9266-e56d-483f-9f6f-2ae5eb715581, Millbrook Pr.) Lerner Publishing Group.

Johnson, Robin. What Is a Tornado? 2016. (ENG., Illus.). 24p. (J). (978-0-7787-2423-0(9)) Crabtree Publishing Co.

Kallio, Jamie. 12 Things to Know about Wild Weather. 2015. (Today's News Ser.). (ENG., Illus.). 32p. (J). (gr. 3-6). 32.80 (978-1-63235-035-0(1), 11613, 12-Story Library) Bookstaves, LLC.

Krajnik, Elizabeth. Twisted by Tornadoes, 1 vol. 2017. (Natural Disasters: How People Survive Ser.). (ENG.). 32p. (J). (gr. 4-5). 27.93 (978-1-5383-2567-4(5), 5a1de1f3-739d-4e2b-b896-146c9a1e418e, PowerKids Pr.) Rosen Publishing Group, Inc., The.

Leathers, Daniel. Tornado Outbreak 1985. 2007. (Natural Disasters Ser.). (Illus.). 32p. (J). (gr. 1-4). lib. bdg. 25.70 (978-1-58415-571-3(X)) Mitchell Lane Pubs.

Lindop, Laurie. Chasing Tornadoes. 2003. (Science on the Edge Ser.). (Illus.). 80p. (gr. 5-18). lib. bdg. 26.90 (978-0-7613-2703-5(7), Twenty-First Century Bks.) Lerner Publishing Group.

Lusted, Marcia Amidon. The 12 Worst Tornadoes of All Time. 2019. (All-Time Worst Disasters Ser.). (ENG., Illus.). 32p. (J). (gr. 3-6). 32.80 (978-1-63235-541-6(8), 13915, 12-Story Library) Bookstaves, LLC.

McAuliffe, Bill. Tornadoes. (X-Books: Weather Ser.). 2017. (ENG., Illus.). 32p. (J). (gr. 3-6). pap. 9.99 (978-1-62832-431-0(7), 20418, Creative Paperbacks) 2017. (ENG., Illus.). 32p. (J). (gr. 3-6). (978-1-60818-828-4(0), 20417, Creative Education) 2010. 47p. (YA). (gr. 4-7). lib. bdg. 23.95 (978-1-58341-931-1(4)) Creative Co., The.

Meister, Cari. Tornadoes. 2015. (Illus.). 24p. (J). lib. bdg. (978-1-62031-225-4(5)) Jump! Inc.

Mezzanotte, Jim. Tornadoes, 1 vol. (Wild Weather Ser.). (ENG.). 24p. 2009. (J). (gr. 1-1). pap. 9.15 (978-1-4339-2365-4(3), e2c598e2-24f9-43ce-9eb7-38702d843e67) 2009. (J). (gr. 1-1). lib. bdg. 24.67 (978-1-4339-2351-7(3), 9b771209-6c04-4078-bb68-30220c24717c) 2007. (Illus.). (gr. 2-4). pap. 9.15 (978-0-8368-7923-0(6), 2203c8d2-a5f8-4e61-9f29-ec2245e98edb) 2007. (Illus.). (gr. 2-4). lib. bdg. 24.67 (978-0-8368-7916-2(3), f5eb5e94-2852-467b-b75c-9e1d14f82014) Stevens, Gareth Publishing LLLP. (Weekly Reader Leveled Readers).

—Tornados (Tornadoes), 1 vol. (Tiempo Extremo (Wild Weather) Ser.). (SPA.). 24p. 2009. (J). (gr. 1-1). pap. 9.15 (978-1-4339-2372-2(6), 0c9f12b3-1bdc-4a0f-981a-5dcb5cfa98f5) 2009. (J). (gr. 1-1). lib. bdg. 24.67 (978-1-4339-2358-6(0), 7e3a973a-f5c9-477d-ad99-cc6f39cc4d74) 2007. (Illus.). (gr. 2-4). pap. 9.15 (978-0-8368-8082-3(X), 6f4f46d3-d47f-436d-ae4b-be7a42325b5c) 2007. (Illus.). (gr. 2-4). lib. bdg. 24.67 (978-0-8368-8075-5(7), 124e472b-0f51-4690-bafe-fd2f8a4d00b0) Stevens, Gareth Publishing LLLP. (Weekly Reader Leveled Readers).

Minden, Cecilia. Tornadoes! 2010. (21st Century Basic Skills Library: Natural Disasters Ser.). (ENG., Illus.). 24p. (gr. k-3). lib. bdg. 26.35 (978-1-60279-863-2(X), 200592) Cherry Lake Publishing.

Murray, Julie. Tornadoes. 2017. (Wild Weather Ser.). (ENG., Illus.). 24p. (J). (gr. k-4). lib. bdg. 31.36 (978-1-5321-2090-9(7), 26773, Abdo Zoom-Dash) ABDO Publishing Co.

National Geographic Learning. Reading Expeditions (Science: Earth Science): Extreme Weather. 2007. (ENG., Illus.). 32p. (J). pap. 18.95 (978-0-7922-4575-9(X)) CENGAGE Learning.

Orr, Tamra B. Tornadoes. 2012. (21st Century Skills Library: Real World Math Ser.). (ENG., Illus.). 32p. (gr. 4-8). (J). pap. 14.21 (978-1-61080-413-4(9), 201345); lib. bdg. 32.07 (978-1-61080-326-7(4), 201312) Cherry Lake Publishing.

Otfinoski, Steven. Tornadoes (a True Book: Extreme Earth) (Library Edition) 2016. (True Book (Relaunch) Ser.). (ENG., Illus.). 48p. (J). (gr. 3-5). lib. bdg. 31.00 (978-0-531-22297-3(7), Children's Pr.) Scholastic Library Publishing.

Oxlade, Chris. Why Why Why Do Tornadoes Spin. 2008. 32p. pap. (978-1-84810-004-6(3)) Miles Kelly Publishing, Ltd.

—Why Why Why... Do Tornadoes Spin? 2010. (Why Why Why Ser.). 32p. (J). (gr. 1-3). lib. bdg. 18.95 (978-1-4222-1586-9(5)) Mason Crest.

Patty, Kate. The Awesome Book of Tornadoes & Other Storms: Awesome. Roberts, Peter, illus. 2014. (ENG.). 32p. (J). (gr. 3-7). 7.99 (978-1-4867-0261-9(9)) Flowerpot Children's Pr. Inc. CAN. Dist: Cardinal Pubs. Group.

Penner, Lucille Recht. Twisters! Garns, Allen, illus. 2009. (Step into Reading Ser.). 48p. (J). (gr. k-3). pap. 4.99 (978-0-375-86224-3(2), Random Hse. Bks. for Young Readers) Random Hse. Children's Bks.

Person, Stephen. Saving Animals after Tornadoes. 2012. (Rescuing Animals from Disasters Ser.). 32p. (J). (gr. 2-7). lib. bdg. 28.50 (978-1-61772-458-9(0)) Bearport Publishing Co., Inc.

Peterson, Judy Monroe. Tornadoes, 1 vol. 2018. (Nature's Mysteries Ser.). (ENG.). 32p. (gr. 2-3). pap. 13.90 (978-1-5081-0652-4(5), 74941d9b-e682-464d-bf7e-81496af14044, Britannica Educational Publishing) Rosen Publishing Group, Inc., The.

Plattner, Josh & Craig, Diane. Tornado or Dust Devil?, 1 vol. 2015. (This or That? Weather Ser.). (ENG., Illus.). 24p. (J). (gr. k-4). 32.79 (978-1-62403-957-7(X), 19570, Super SandCastle) ABDO Publishing Co.

Prokos, Anna. Tornadoes, 1 vol. 2008. (Ultimate 10: Natural Disasters Ser.). (ENG.). 48p. (YA). (gr. 3-3). lib. bdg. 33.67 (978-0-8368-9153-9(8), 2731cf19-97f4-44c7-a2ef-bd538de9519f) Stevens, Gareth Publishing LLLP.

Rajczak Nelson, Kristen. Terrifying Tornadoes, 1 vol. 2012. (Angry Earth Ser.). (ENG., Illus.). 32p. (J). (gr. 3-4). pap. 11.50 (978-1-4339-6543-2(7), 100a42fb-9914-493d-afa3-193ea51c7886, Gareth Stevens Learning Library); lib. bdg. 29.27 (978-1-4339-6541-8(0), 92e035b1-307b-42cd-acf5-191fcf1b6184) Stevens, Gareth Publishing LLLP.

Randolph, Joanne, ed. Tornado Alert!, 1 vol. 2017. (Weather Report). (ENG.). 32p. (gr. 3-3). pap. 11.52 (978-0-7660-9025-5(6), 5d7dd9f4-d240-43f3-a372-9effc285941a) Enslow Publishing, LLC.

Rathburn, Betsy. Tornadoes. 2019. (Natural Disasters Ser.). (ENG., Illus.). 24p. (J). (gr. k-3). pap. 7.99 (978-1-61891-748-5(X), 12317, Blastoff! Readers) Bellwether Media.

Raum, Elizabeth. Surviving Tornadoes, 1 vol. 2011. (Children's True Stories: Natural Disasters Ser.). (ENG.). 32p. (J). (gr. 3-5). pap. 8.29 (978-1-4109-4099-5(3), 114633, Raintree) Capstone.

—Tornado! 2016. (Natural Disasters Ser.). (ENG., Illus.). 32p. (J). (gr. 2-5). lib. bdg. 20.95 (978-1-60753-992-6(6), 15790) Amicus.

Rice, William B. Tornadoes, 1 vol. rev. ed. 2009. (Science: Informational Text Ser.). (ENG.). 32p. (J). (gr. 3-5). pap. 11.99 (978-1-4333-0311-1(6)) Teacher Created Materials, Inc.

Rivera, Andrea. Tornadoes. 2017. (Natural Disasters (Launch!) Ser.). (ENG., Illus.). 24p. (J). (gr. -1-2). lib. bdg. 31.36 (978-1-5321-2039-8(7), 25328, Abdo Zoom-Launch) ABDO Publishing Co.

Roberts, Becca. Tornadoes. 2016. (Illus.). 32p. (J). pap. (978-0-545-86282-0(5)) Scholastic, Inc.

Rudolph, Jessica. Erased by a Tornado! 2010. (Disaster Survivors Ser.). (Illus.). 32p. (YA). (gr. 4-7). lib. bdg. 28.50 (978-1-936087-52-5(9)) Bearport Publishing Co., Inc.

—Tornado. 2014. (It's a Disaster! Ser.). 24p. (J). (gr. -1-3). lib. bdg. 26.99 (978-1-62724-126-7(4)) Bearport Publishing Co., Inc.

Rustad, Martha E. H. & Kalz, Jill. Tornadoes: Be Aware & Prepare, 1 vol. 2014. (Weather Aware Ser.). (ENG.). 32p. (J). (gr. -1-2). lib. bdg. 27.99 (978-1-4765-9906-9(8), 125744, Capstone Pr.) Capstone.

Scavuzzo, Wendy. Tornado Alert! 3rd rev. ed. 2011. (ENG., Illus.). 32p. (J). (978-0-7787-1594-8(9)); (Disaster Alert! Ser.: No. 18). (gr. 3-6). pap. (978-0-7787-1627-3(9)) Crabtree Publishing Co.

Schreiber, Ann. Twister Trouble. Speirs, John, illus. 2010. (Magic School Bus Science Chapter Bks.). (KOR.). 82p. (J). (978-89-491-5320-9(3)) Biryongso Publishing Co.

Schuh, Mari. Tornadoes. rev. ed. 2016. (Earth in Action Ser.). (ENG.). 24p. (J). (gr. -1-2). pap. 6.95 (978-1-5157-6215-7(7), 135056, Capstone Pr.) Capstone.

—What Are Tornadoes? 2019. (Wicked Weather Ser.). (ENG., Illus.). 24p. (J). (gr. -1-2). lib. bdg. 22.65 (978-1-9771-0328-4(6), 139319, Pebble) Capstone.

Schuh, Mari C. Tornadoes [Scholastic]. 2010. (Earth in Action Ser.). (ENG.). 24p. pap. 0.49 (978-1-4296-5801-0(0), Capstone Pr.) Capstone.

Shea, Therese M. When Tornadoes Touch Down, 1 vol. 2015. (Eye on the Sky Ser.). (ENG., Illus.). 32p. (J). (gr. 3-4). pap. 11.50 (978-1-4824-2896-4(2), 7133cdd0-daf9-468a-a176-db9ef68945aa) Stevens, Gareth Publishing LLLP.

Shores, Lori. How to Build a Tornado in a Bottle: A 4D Book. rev. ed. 2018. (Hands-On Science Fun Ser.). (ENG., Illus.). 24p. (J). (gr. -1-2). lib. bdg. 29.32 (978-1-5435-0944-1(4), 137651, Capstone Pr.) Capstone.

Silverstein, Alvin & Silverstein, Virginia. Tornadoes: The Science Behind Terrible Twisters, 1 vol. 2009. (Science Behind Natural Disasters Ser.). (ENG., Illus.). 48p. (gr. 5-7). lib. bdg. 27.93 (978-0-7660-2976-7(X), 5adf3fbe-1f70-4de6-9273-077ccd1c0961) Enslow Publishing, LLC.

Simon, Seymour. Tornadoes: Revised Edition. rev. ed. 2017. (ENG., Illus.). 32p. (J). (gr. 1-5). pap. 7.99 (978-0-06-247032-4(9), HarperCollins) HarperCollins Pubs.

Sood, Malini. Hurricanes & Tornadoes. (Wild Nature Ser.). 48p. (gr. 4-5). 2009. 53.00 (978-1-60854-794-4(9), PowerKids Pr.) 2007. (ENG., Illus.). (YA). lib. bdg. 32.93 (978-1-4042-3900-5(6), 59124b6b-649a-4885-ad4b-d2ea08212148) Rosen Publishing Group, Inc., The.

Spilsbury, Louise & Spilsbury, Richard. Hurricanes & Tornadoes in Action, 1 vol. 2008. (Natural Disasters in Action Ser.). (ENG., Illus.). 48p. (J). (gr. 5-5). pap. 11.75 (978-1-4358-5133-7(1), de1f4ca8-5fef-4ec8-be8a-62b8e11bb2b8, Rosen Reference) Rosen Publishing Group, Inc., The.

—Tornado Rips up City, 1 vol. 2017. (Earth under Attack! Ser.). (ENG.). 48p. (J). (gr. 5-5). pap. 15.05 (978-1-5382-1311-7(7), 44dfc9ab-447c-4fe6-bcec-75885c31f53e) Stevens, Gareth Publishing LLLP.

—Tornado Rips up City, 1 vol. 2017. (Earth under Attack! Ser.). (ENG.). 48p. (J). (gr. 5-5). lib. bdg. 33.60 (978-1-5382-1313-1(3), 0066bb5f-707f-47fb-99db-22bb2acac235) Stevens, Gareth Publishing LLLP.

Steele, Philip & Morris, Neil. Inside Hurricanes & Tornadoes, 1 vol. 2006. (Inside Nature's Disasters Ser.). (ENG., Illus.). 36p. (gr. 4-6). lib. bdg. 28.67 (978-0-8368-7249-1(5), ed4e4ac3-8aa8-4a67-a288-eea3e56c40b7, Gareth Stevens Learning Library) Stevens, Gareth Publishing LLLP.

Steele, Philip, et al. Extreme Planet. 2014. (Illus.). 128p. (J). (978-1-4351-5523-7(8)) Barnes & Noble, Inc.

Stoltman, Joan. Following Extreme Weather with a Storm Chaser, 1 vol. 2018. (Get to Work! Ser.). (ENG.). 24p. (gr. 2-3). pap. 9.15 (978-1-5382-1229-5(3), e250c222-bef2-4ad9-9560-6d0a39b47719) Stevens, Gareth Publishing LLLP.

Tarshis, Lauren. Tornado Terror (I Survived True Stories #3) True Tornado Survival Stories & Amazing Facts from History & Today. 2017. (I Survived True Stories Ser.: 3). (ENG.). 176p. (J). (gr. 2-5). 12.99 (978-0-545-91943-2(6), Scholastic Pr.) Scholastic, Inc.

Thoron, Joe. Tornadoes, 1 vol. 2007. (Kaleidoscope: Earth Science Ser.). (ENG., Illus.). 48p. (gr. 4-4). lib. bdg. 32.64 (978-0-7614-2104-7(1), 4e144da4-5aa7-4d0f-b6b3-7f0abdc14d79) Cavendish Square Publishing LLC.

Tornadoes. 3rd ed. 2018. (J). (978-0-7166-9940-8(0)) World Bk., Inc.

Ventura, Marne. Detecting Tornadoes. 2017. (Detecting Disasters Ser.). (ENG., Illus.). 32p. (J). (gr. 3-5). lib. bdg. 31.35 (978-1-63517-004-7(4), 1635170044, Focus Readers) North Star Editions.

—How to Survive a Tornado. 2015. (Survival Guides). (ENG.). 24p. (J). (gr. 2-5). 32.79 (978-1-60973-161-8(1), 208792) Child's World, Inc, The.

WalkerTheo. THE CITY EXPERIMENT: REBUILDING GREENSBURG, KANSAS LOW INTERMEDIATE BOOK WITH ONLINE ACCESS, 1 vol. 2014. (ENG., Illus.). 24p. (J). pap., E-Book 9.50 (978-1-107-62256-2(5)) Cambridge Univ. Pr.

Wendorff, Anne. Tornadoes. 2008. (Extreme Weather Ser.). (ENG., Illus.). 24p. (J). (gr. 2-5). lib. bdg. 26.95 (978-1-60014-187-4(0)) Bellwether Media.

Woods, Michael & Woods, Mary B. Tornadoes. 2006. (Disasters up Close Ser.). (Illus.). 64p. (J). (gr. 3-7). lib. bdg. 27.93 (978-0-8225-4714-3(7), Lerner Pubns.) Lerner Publishing Group.

World Book, Inc. Staff, contrib. by. Library of Natural Disasters, 15 vols., Set. 2007. (J). wbk. ed. 329.00 (978-0-7166-9801-2(3)) World Bk., Inc.

—Tornadoes. (J). 2007. (978-0-7166-9813-5(7)) 2nd ed. 2009. (Illus.). 47p. (978-0-7166-9829-6(3)) World Bk., Inc.

—Zac Newton Investigates Wild Weather. 2018. (J). (978-0-7166-4059-2(7)) World Bk., Inc.

TORNADOES—FICTION

Acton, Vanessa. Vortex. 2017. (Day of Disaster Ser.). (ENG.). 104p. (YA). (gr. 6-12). E-Book 6.99 (978-1-5124-3513-9(9), 9781512435139); E-Book 39.99 (978-1-5124-2780-6(2)); E-Book 39.99 (978-1-5124-3512-2(0), 9781512435122) Lerner Publishing Group. (Darby Creek).

Beard, Darleen Bailey. Twister. Carpenter, Nancy, illus. 2003. (ENG.). 32p. (J). (gr. -1-3). pap. 10.99 (978-0-374-48014-1(1), 900020242) Square Fish.

Bishop, Jenn. 14 Hollow Road. 2017. (ENG.). 288p. (J). (gr. 3-7). lib. bdg. 19.99 (978-1-101-93876-8(5), Knopf Bks. for Young Readers) Random Hse. Children's Bks.

Blake, Ashley Herring. Ivy Aberdeen's Letter to the World. 2018. (ENG.). 320p. (J). (gr. 3-7). 16.99 (978-0-316-51546-7(9)) Little, Brown Bks. for Young Readers.

Byars, Betsy. Tornado. Ben-Ami, Doron, illus. 2020. (ENG.). 64p. (J). (gr. 1-5). pap. 6.99 (978-0-06-442063-1(9), HarperCollins) HarperCollins Pubs.

—Tornado. 2004. (J). (gr. 3-6). lib. bdg. 14.75 (978-0-613-01485-4(5)) Turtleback.

Christopher, Matt. Slam Dunk. 2004. (Matt Christopher Sports Ser.). 118p. (gr. 3-7). 15.00 (978-0-7569-3046-2(4)) Perfection Learning Corp.

—Slam Dunk. 2018. (Matt Christopher: the #1 Sports Series for Kids Ser.). (ENG.). 128p. (J). (gr. 3-7). lib. bdg. 31.36 (978-1-5321-4270-3(6), 31080, Chapter Bks.) Spotlight.

Clay, Shenise Tiana. The Kids Who Were Left Alone When There Was A Tornado. 2004. (J). 6.00 (978-0-9701482-6-1(7)) Changing Lives Publishing.

Clements, Andrew. About Average. Elliott, Mark, illus. (ENG.). (J). (gr. 3-7). 2014. 144p. pap. 7.99 (978-1-4169-9725-2(3)) 2012. 128p. 18.99 (978-1-4169-9724-5(5)) Simon & Schuster Children's Publishing. (Atheneum Bks. for Young Readers).

Cook, Sherry & Johnson, Terri. Timothy Tornado, 26. Kuhn, Jesse, illus. l.t. ed. 2006. (Quirkles — Exploring Phonics through Science Ser.: 20). 32p. 7.99 (978-1-933815-19-0(1), Quirkles, The) Creative 3, LLC.

Duff, Jc. Tornado Watch. 2012. 32p. pap. 21.99 (978-1-4771-1866-5(7)) Xlibris Corp.

Ellis, Melody A. An Unexpected Hero. 2009. 48p. pap. 16.95 (978-1-60749-834-6(0)) America Star Bks.

Fields, Terri. Tornado Tamer, 1 vol. Jacques, Laura, illus. 2016. (J). (gr. k-1). (SPA.). 39p. pap. 11.95 (978-1-62855-747-3(8), d75f3130-0b73-46e8-9921-a9c0195f71ef); (ENG.). 39p. 17.95 (978-1-62855-733-6(8)); (ENG.). 32p. pap. 9.95 (978-1-62855-740-4(0)) Arbordale Publishing.

Fisher, Carolyn. A Twisted Tale. 2004. (Illus.). 33p. (J). (gr. k-4). reprint ed. 16.00 (978-0-7567-8412-6(3)) DIANE Publishing Co.

Garretson, Jerri. Kansas Tall Tales: Tenth Anniversary Anthology. Garretson, Jerri & Dollar, Diane A., illus. 2008. 106p. (J). pap. 19.95 (978-0-9659712-7-0(9)) Ravenstone Pr.

Garrett, Lyn. Horatio & the Sea Tornado. 2012. 28p. (-18). pap. 12.50 (978-1-62212-615-6(7), Strategic Bk. Publishing) Strategic Book Publishing & Rights Agency (SBPRA).

Geisert, Arthur, creator. Thunderstorm. (ENG., Illus.). (J). 2015. 34p. (gr. k). 60.00 (978-1-59270-170-4(1)) 2013. 32p. (gr. -1). 17.95 (978-1-59270-133-9(7)) Enchanted Lion Bks., LLC.

Ghigna, Charles & Ghigna, Debra. Barn Storm. Greenseid, Diane, illus. 2010. (Step into Reading Ser.). 32p. (J). (gr.

TUV

-1-1). pap. 4.99 *(978-0-375-86114-7(9)*, Random Hse. Bks. for Young Readers) Random Hse. Children's Bks.

Gutman, Dan. The Talent Show. 2010. (ENG.). 224p. (J). (gr. 3-7). 18.99 *(978-1-4169-9003-1(8)*, Simon & Schuster Bks. For Young Readers) Simon & Schuster Bks. For Young Readers.

Hansen, Susan. The Flying Quilt. 2011. pap. 9.95 *(978-0-7414-6469-9(1))* Infinity Publishing.

Hoyt, Kathleen. Kerloon & Cooley. 2012. 24p. pap. *(978-1-77097-833-1(X))* FriesenPress.

Jenkins, Amanda. Tornado! 2005. (J). pap. *(978-1-4108-4212-1(6))* Benchmark Education Co.

Kennedy, Marlane. Tornado Alley. 2014. (Disaster Strikes Ser.: 2). lib. bdg. 14.75 *(978-0-606-35828-6(5))* Turtleback.

Lester, Helen. Batter up Wombat. Munsinger, Lynn, illus. 2006. (ENG.). 32p. (J). (gr. k-3). 24.80 *(978-1-4287-0160-1(5)*, Follettbound) Follett School Solutions.

Long, Loren. Otis & the Tornado. Long, Loren, illus. 2011. (Otis Ser.: 2). (Illus.). 40p. (J). (gr. -1-2). 18.99 *(978-0-399-25477-2(3)*, Philomel Bks.) Penguin Young Readers Group.

Lysiak, Hilde & Lysiak, Matthew. Tornado Hits!: a Branches Book (Hilde Cracks the Case #5) Lew-Vriethoff, Joanne, illus. 2018. (Hilde Cracks the Case Ser.: 5). (ENG.). 96p. (J). (gr. 1-3). pap. 5.99 *(978-1-338-26677-1(2))* Scholastic, Inc.

Marsh, Carole. The Ferocious Forest Fire Mystery. 2008. (Masters of Disasters Ser.). (Illus.). 118p. (J). (gr. 3-5). 14.95 *(978-0-635-06468-4(5))*;6. (ENG., (gr. 2-4). 18.69 *(978-0-635-06465-3(0))* Gallopade International.

—The Treacherous Tornado Mystery. 2007. (Masters of Disasters Ser.). (Illus.). 118p. (J). (gr. 2-9). 14.95 *(978-0-635-06394-6(8))*; per. 5.99 *(978-0-635-06338-0(7))* Gallopade International.

McMullan, Kate. A Fine Start Bk. 3: Meg's Prairie Diary. 2003. (My America Ser.). (ENG.). 112p. (J). 12.95 *(978-0-439-37061-5(2))* Scholastic, Inc.

Messenger, Shannon. Let the Sky Fall. 2013. (Sky Fall Ser.: 1). (ENG., (YA). (gr. 7). Illus.). 432p. pap. 12.99 *(978-1-4424-5042-4(8))*; 416p. 17.99 *(978-1-4424-5041-7(X))* Simon Pulse. (Simon Pulse).

Mikkelsen, Jon. Storm Shelter. Lueth, Nathan, illus. 2008. (We Are Heroes Ser.). (ENG.). 40p. (J). (gr. 5-9). lib. bdg. 24.65 *(978-1-4342-0787-6(0)*, 95192, Stone Arch Bks.) Capstone.

Osborne, Mary Pope. Twister on Tuesday. 2004. (Magic Tree House Ser.: No. 23). 70p. (J). (gr. k-3). pap. 17.00 incl. audio *(978-0-8072-9932-6(4)*, Listening Library) Random Hse. Audio Publishing Group.

Saddleback Educational Publishing Staff, ed. Twister, 1 vol. unabr. ed. 2011. (Heights Ser.). (ENG.). 50p. (gr. 4-8). 9.75 *(978-1-61651-626-0(7))* Saddleback Educational Publishing, Inc.

Scott, Leah. Tincup & the Tornado. 2012. (ENG.). 34p. (J). pap. 12.95 *(978-1-4327-8695-3(4))*; pap. 18.95 *(978-1-4327-8826-1(4))* Outskirts Pr., Inc.

Scrimger, Richard. Into the Ravine. 2007. 264p. (J). (gr. 5-12). per. 9.95 *(978-0-88776-822-4(9)*, Tundra Bks.) Tundra Bks. CAN. Dist: Penguin Random Hse. LLC.

Tarshis, Lauren. I Survived the Joplin Tornado, 2011 (I Survived #12) Dawson, Scott, illus. 2015. (I Survived Ser.: 12). (ENG.). 112p. (J). (gr. 2-5). pap. 5.99 *(978-0-545-65848-5(9)*, Scholastic Paperbacks) Scholastic, Inc.

Tougas, Chris. Mechanimals, 1 vol. 2012. (ENG., Illus.). 32p. (J). (gr. -1-k). 14.95 *(978-1-4598-0273-5(X))* Orca Bk. Pubs. USA.

Ward, Pat Mays. Big Mama's Storm Cellar. 2010. 24p. 14.99 *(978-1-4490-8236-9(X))* AuthorHouse.

Watkins, Elaine. Tornado Nine. 2016. (ENG.). 56p. (J). (gr. 4-6). 10.95 *(978-1-78554-532-0(9)*, 4348bbd3-dda9-423c-bd3d-e4a267fcdc46) Austin Macauley Pubs. Ltd. GBR. Dist: Baker & Taylor Publisher Services (BTPS).

TORONTO (ONT.)

Boudreau, Hélène, et al. Life in a Residential City, 1 vol. 2010. (Learn about Urban Life Ser.). (ENG., Illus.). 32p. (J). (gr. 3-6). pap. *(978-0-7787-7403-7(1))*; lib. bdg. *(978-0-7787-7393-1(0))* Crabtree Publishing Co.

Covello, Paul. Toronto ABC. 2014. (ENG., Illus.). 15p. (J). bds. 10.50 *(978-1-4434-3144-6(3)*, Harper Trophy) HarperCollins Pubs.

Moak, Allan. A Big City Alphabet. 2009. (ABC Our Country Ser.). (Illus.). 32p. (J). (gr. -1-3). pap. 7.95 *(978-0-88776-939-9(X)*, Tundra Bks.) Tundra Bks. CAN. Dist: Penguin Random Hse. LLC.

Rowe, Percy. Toronto, 1 vol. 2003. (Great Cities of the World Ser.). (ENG., Illus.). 48p. (gr. 5-8). lib. bdg. 33.67 *(978-0-8368-5026-0(2)*, c51c875a-24d3-41b4-b68d-5dd387a7894c, Gareth Stevens Secondary Library) Stevens, Gareth Publishing LLLP.

TORONTO BLUE JAYS (BASEBALL TEAM)

Frisch, Aaron. Toronto Blue Jays. 2009. (World Series Champions Ser.). 23p. (J). (gr. 2-3). 24.25 *(978-1-58341-686-0(2)*, Creative Education) Creative Co., The.

Gerstner, Joanne. Toronto Blue Jays, 1 vol. 2015. (Inside MLB Ser.). (ENG.). 48p. (J). (gr. 3-6). lib. bdg. 34.21 *(978-1-62403-488-6(8)*, 17139, SportsZone) ABDO Publishing Co.

Gilbert, Sara. Toronto Blue Jays. 2013. (World Series Champions Ser.). (ENG.). 24p. (J). (gr. 1-4). pap. 7.99 *(978-0-89812-824-6(2)*, 21867, Creative Paperbacks); (Illus.). 25.65 *(978-1-60818-273-2(8)*, 21866, Creative Education) Creative Co., The.

LeBoutillier, Nate. The Story of the Toronto Blue Jays. 2011. (Illus.). 48p. (J). 35.65 *(978-1-60818-059-2(X)*, Creative Education) Creative Co., The.

Shofner, Shawndra. The Story of the Toronto Blue Jays. 2007. (Baseball, the Great American Game Ser.). (Illus.). 48p. (YA). (gr. 4-7). lib. bdg. 32.80 *(978-1-58341-503-0(3))* Creative Co., The.

Stewart, Mark. The Toronto Blue Jays. 2012. (Team Spirit Ser.). 48p. (J). (gr. 3-6). lib. bdg. 29.27 *(978-1-59953-500-5(9))* Norwood Hse. Pr.

TORTOISES

see Turtles

TOTALITARIANISM

see also Communism; Dictators; National Socialism

Bailey, Diane. Dictatorship. Colton, Timothy J., ed. 2012. (Major Forms of World Government Ser.). 64p. (J). (gr. 5). 22.95 *(978-1-4222-2138-9(5))* Mason Crest.

Butler, Denice. Dictatorship: Authoritarian Rule, Vol. 8. 2018. (Systems of Government Ser.). (Illus.). 96p. (J). (gr. 7). 34.60 *(978-1-4222-4017-5(7))* Mason Crest.

Connolly, Sean. Dictatorship. 2012. (Systems of Government Ser.). (ENG., Illus.). 48p. (J). (gr. 6-9). lib. bdg. 37.10 *(978-1-59920-804-6(0)*, 17436, Smart Apple Media) Black Rabbit Bks.

McCarthy, Rose. Dictatorship: A Primary Source Analysis. 2009. (Primary Sources of Political Systems Ser.). 64p. (gr. 5-8). 58.50 *(978-1-60851-837-1(X))* Rosen Publishing Group, Inc., The.

Portus, Sam. Fascism: Radical Nationalism, Vol. 8. 2018. (Systems of Government Ser.). (Illus.). 96p. (J). (gr. 7). 34.60 *(978-1-4222-4019-9(3))* Mason Crest.

TOTALITARIANISM—FICTION

Brody, Jennifer. The 13th Continuum: The Continuum Trilogy, Book 1. 2016. (Continuum Trilogy Ser.: 1). (ENG., Illus.). 416p. (YA). pap. 20.95 *(978-1-68162-254-5(8))* Turner Publishing Co.

Fukui, Isamu. Truancy: A Novel. 2010. (Truancy Ser.: 1). (ENG.). 432p. (YA). (gr. 8-12). pap. 20.99 *(978-0-7653-2258-6(7)*, 900055488, Tor Teen) Doherty, Tom Assocs., LLC.

—Truancy Origins: A Novel. 2011. (Truancy Ser.: 2). (ENG.). 384p. (YA). (gr. 8-12). pap. 19.99 *(978-0-7653-2264-7(1)*, 900055685, Tor Teen) Doherty, Tom Assocs., LLC.

Mafi, Tahereh. Shatter Me. 2013. (Shatter Me Ser.: 1). (ENG.). (YA). (gr. 9). 448p. 21.99 *(978-0-06-274173-8(X))*; 368p. pap. 15.99 *(978-0-06-208550-4(6))* HarperCollins Pubs. (HarperCollins).

—Shatter Me. 2012. (Shatter Me Ser.: 1). (YA). lib. bdg. 20.85 *(978-0-606-26868-4(5))* Turtleback.

—Unravel Me. 2013. (Shatter Me Ser.: 2). (ENG.). (YA). (gr. 9). 496p. pap. 15.99 *(978-0-06-208554-2(9))*; 480p. 19.99 *(978-0-06-208553-5(0))* HarperCollins Pubs. (HarperCollins).

—Unravel Me. 2013. (Shatter Me Ser.: 2). (YA). lib. bdg. 20.85 *(978-0-606-35049-5(7))* Turtleback.

Maynard, Case. The Surrendered. 2016. (ENG.). 266p. (YA). (gr. 9). pap. 9.95 *(978-0-9970104-7-3(9))* Blaze Publishing, LLC.

Mourlevat, Jean-Claude. Winter's End. Bell, Anthea, tr. 2009. (ENG., Illus.). 432p. (YA). (gr. 9-18). 17.99 *(978-0-7636-4450-5(1))* Candlewick Pr.

Patterson, James. The Fire. 2011. (Playaway Children Ser.). (ENG.). (YA). (gr. 8-12). 59.99 *(978-1-61113-385-1(8))* Hachette Audio.

Patterson, James & Dembowski, Jill. The Fire. (Witch & Wizard Ser.: 3). (ENG.). (YA). (gr. 5-17). 2013. 352p. mass mkt. 8.00 *(978-1-4555-2152-4(3))* 2011. 352p. 35.99 *(978-0-316-10190-5(7))* 2011. 448p. 30.99 *(978-0-316-19620-8(7))* Little Brown & Co. (Jimmy Patterson).

—The Fire. 2012. (Witch & Wizard Ser.: 3). (YA). lib. bdg. 20.85 *(978-0-606-26698-7(4))* Turtleback.

TOTEMS AND TOTEMISM

Batdorf, Carol. Totem Poles Coloring Book: An Ancient Art. 2005. (Act Ser.). (ENG., Illus.). 24p. (J). (gr. 1-6). pap. 4.95 *(978-0-88839-248-0(6))* Hancock Hse. Pubs.

Howse, Jennifer. Totem Poles: Canadian Icons. 2010. (Illus.). 24p. *(978-1-77071-574-5(6))*; pap. *(978-1-77071-581-3(9))* Weigl Educational Pubs. Ltd.

Kramer, Pat. Totem Poles for Kids: A Kids Own SuperGuide. Kramer, Pat, photos by. (Illus.). 48p. (J). pap. *(978-1-55153-626-2(9))* Altitude Publishing Canada Ltd.

TOTEMS AND TOTEMISM—FICTION

Powell, Jim S. The Mystery of the Totem Trees: A Plumroy Pack Adventure. 2009. 124p. pap. 10.95 *(978-1-4401-3921-5(0))* iUniverse, Inc.

Sargent, Dave, et al. Once upon a Totem Pole Vol. 14: (Haida) Be Creative, 20 vols. Lenoir, Jane, illus. l.t. ed. 2003. (Story Keeper Ser.: 14). 42p. (J). pap. 10.95 *(978-1-56763-930-8(5))*; Vol. 14. lib. bdg. 23.60 *(978-1-56763-929-2(1))* Ozark Publishing.

TOUCANS

Borgert-Spaniol, Megan. Toucans. 2014. (Animal Safari Ser.). (ENG., Illus.). 24p. (J). (gr. k-3). lib. bdg. 26.95 *(978-1-62617-065-0(7)*, Blastoff! Readers) Bellwether Media.

Golkar, Golriz. Toucans. 2018. (Rain Forest Animals Ser.). (ENG., Illus.). 24p. (J). (gr. 1-1). pap. 8.95 *(978-1-63517-824-1(X)*, 163517824X) North Star Editions.

—Toucans. 2018. (Rain Forest Animals (Cody Koala) Ser.). (ENG., Illus.). 24p. (J). (gr. k-3). lib. bdg. 31.36 *(978-1-5321-6029-5(1)*, 28690, Pop! Cody Koala) Pop!

Grack, Rachel. Toucans. 2019. (Animals of the Rain Forest Ser.). (ENG., Illus.). 24p. (J). (gr. k-3). lib. bdg. 26.95 *(978-1-62617-952-3(2)*, Blastoff! Readers) Bellwether Media.

Lynch, Seth. Toucans at the Zoo, 1 vol. 2019. (Zoo Animals Ser.). (ENG.). 24p. (gr. k-k). pap. 9.15 *(978-1-5382-3954-4(X)*, e302b288-bd3a-4249-9fcd-971502a6e929) Stevens, Gareth Publishing LLLP.

Ponka, Katherine. Being a Toucan, 1 vol. 2013. (Can You Imagine? Ser.). (ENG., Illus.). 32p. (J). (gr. 2-3). 27.92 *(978-1-4824-0130-1(4)*, bdb87259-d6b9-4383-9d11-184840db0d52) Stevens, Gareth Publishing LLLP.

Ryndak, Rob. Toucans, 1 vol. 2014. (Jungle Animals Ser.). (ENG., Illus.). 24p. (J). (gr. k-k). 24.27 *(978-1-4824-1764-7(2)*, 56ede88f-6eb7-42e6-a3a9-6c388f4c997c) Stevens, Gareth Publishing LLLP.

Schuh, Mari. Toucans. 2014. (Illus.). 24p. (J). lib. bdg. 25.65 *(978-1-62031-113-4(5)*, Bullfrog Bks.) Jump! Inc.

Statts, Leo. Toucans. 2016. (Rain Forest Animals Ser.). (ENG.). 24p. (J). (gr. -1-2). 49.94 *(978-1-68079-365-9(9)*, 22986, Abdo Zoom-Launch) ABDO Publishing Co.

Suen, Anastasia. Toco Toucans: Bright Enough to Disappear. 2010. (Disappearing Acts Ser.). (Illus.). 24p. (J). (gr. k-3). lib. bdg. 26.99 *(978-1-936087-45-7(6))* Bearport Publishing Co., Inc.

TOUCANS—FICTION

Achrafi, Sherihan. Over the Rainbow. 2017. (ENG., Illus.). 30p. (J). pap. 28.22 *(978-1-5245-2215-5(5))* Xlibris Corp.

Keefer, Mikal. Never Fear, God Is Near. Perez, Nomar, illus. 2018. (Best of Li'l Buddies Ser.). (ENG.). 16p. bds. 6.99 *(978-1-4707-5036-7(8))* Group Publishing, Inc.

Lehrhaupt, Adam. Warning: Do Not Open This Book! Forsythe, Matthew, illus. 2013. (ENG.). 40p. (J). (gr. -1-3). 18.99 *(978-1-4424-3582-7(8)*, Simon & Schuster Bks. For Young Readers) Simon & Schuster Bks. For Young Readers.

Mayfield, Sue. I Can, You Can, Toucan! 2006. (Green Bananas Ser.). (ENG., Illus.). 48p. (J). (gr. -1-3). lib. bdg. *(978-0-7787-1032-5(7))* Crabtree Publishing Co.

McBrayer, Cassidy. You Can, Toucan! You Can. 2008. 20p. pap. 15.95 *(978-1-4327-1132-0(0))* Outskirts Pr., Inc.

TOUCH

Aloian, Molly. What Is Touch? 2013. (ENG., Illus.). 24p. (J). *(978-0-7787-0968-8(X))*; (gr. 1-2). pap. *(978-0-7787-0991-6(4))* Crabtree Publishing Co.

Appleby, Alex. Lo Que Toco / What I Touch, 1 vol. 2014. (Mis Cinco Sentidos / My Five Senses Ser.). (SPA & ENG.). 24p. (J). (gr. k-k). 24.27 *(978-1-4824-0877-5(5)*, eaa24db5-9dd7-476d-9819-f4ffbe35e3c5) Stevens, Gareth Publishing LLLP.

—What I Touch, 1 vol. 2014. (My Five Senses Ser.). 24p. (J). (gr. k-k). (ENG.). pap. 9.15 *(978-1-4824-0823-2(6)*, 9ea243d7-cfb0-4a26-9b01-8849cfa8176d); pap. 48.90 *(978-1-4824-0824-9(4))* Stevens, Gareth Publishing LLLP.

Baggott, Stella. Baby's Very First Touchy-Feely Book. 2010. (Baby's Very First Board Bks). 10p. (J). bds. 9.99 *(978-0-7945-2647-4(0)*, Usborne) EDC Publishing.

Ballard, Carol. Your Sense of Touch, 1 vol. 2010. (Your Body at Work Ser.). (ENG.). 32p. (YA). (gr. 2-4). lib. bdg. 29.27 *(978-1-4339-4115-3(5)*, 3585c295-56ff-43c0-a6ca-8170da28a2fc) Stevens, Gareth Publishing LLLP.

Barraclough, Sue. What Can I Feel? 2005. (J). *(978-1-4034-7077-5(4))*; (ENG.). 32p. pap. *(978-1-4034-7083-6(9))* Steck-Vaughn.

Beaumont, Susanna. Baby Senses Touch. 2005. (Baby Senses Ser.). (Illus.). 12p. (gr. -1-k). per., bds. *(978-1-905051-47-2(6))* Make Believe Ideas.

Bellamy, Adam. What's That I Feel?, 1 vol. 2017. (All about My Senses Ser.). (ENG.). 24p. (gr. k-1). lib. bdg. 24.27 *(978-0-7660-8720-0(4)*, 59c87403-bf41-483f-9854-3f01352a5e30) Enslow Publishing, LLC.

Best, Arthur. Texture, 1 vol. 2018. (Properties of Matter Ser.). (ENG.). 24p. (J). (gr. 1-1). 25.93 *(978-1-5026-4275-2(1)*, 619644d5-28ea-4c88-8fed-6a40cddeea5b) Cavendish Square Publishing LLC.

Braun, Eric. Awesome, Disgusting, Unusual Facts about Everything Stinky, Squishy, & Slimy. 24p. (J). 2019. (Illus.). pap. *(978-1-68072-752-4(4))* 2018. (ENG.). (gr. 4-6). pap. 8.99 *(978-1-64466-305-9(8)*, 12515, Hi Jinx) 2018. (ENG., Illus.). (gr. 4-6). lib. bdg. 28.50 *(978-1-68072-610-7(2)*, 12514, Hi Jinx) Black Rabbit Bks.

—Beurk! le Livre Différent et Fascinant Sur Tout Ce Qui Pue, Qui Est Mou et Gluant. 2018. (Notre Monde: dégoûtant Mais Génial! Ser.). (FRE.). 24p. (J). (gr. 4-6). *(978-1-77092-454-3(X)*, 12583, Hi Jinx) Black Rabbit Bks.

Carr, Aaron. Tacto. 2014. (SPA., Illus.). 24p. (J). *(978-1-62127-583-1(3))* Weigl Pubs., Inc.

Clarke, Asiya, illus. Allah Gave Me Two Hands & Feet. 2015. (ENG.). 32p. (J). 8.95 *(978-0-86037-348-3(7))* Kube Publishing Ltd. GBR. Dist: Consortium Bk. Sales & Distribution.

Cotta, Susan. I Can Show You I Care: Compassionate Touch for Children. Crawford, Gregory, illus. 2003. 32p. (J). (gr. k-4). 21.95 *(978-1-55643-433-4(2))* North Atlantic Bks.

Cottin, Menena. The Black Book of Colors. Faria, Rosana, illus. 2008. (ENG.). 24p. (J). (gr. k-5). 19.99 *(978-0-88899-873-6(2))* Groundwood Bks. CAN. Dist: Publishers Group West (PGW).

Dayton, Connor. Touch, 1 vol. 2014. (Your Five Senses & Your Sixth Sense Ser.). (ENG., Illus.). 24p. (J). (gr. 1-2). 26.27 *(978-1-4777-2855-0(4)*, cf5f7694-8455-49c1-af49-88bda533633a, PowerKids Pr.) Rosen Publishing Group, Inc., The.

DeMedeiros, James. Touch. 2009. (World of Wonder Ser.). (Illus.). 24p. (J). (gr. 2-4). lib. bdg. 24.45 *(978-1-60596-058-6(6))* Weigl Pubs., Inc.

Durrie, Karen. Touch. 2012. (J). 27.13 *(978-1-61913-313-6(X))*; pap. 12.95 *(978-1-61913-318-1(0))* Weigl Pubs., Inc.

Ganeri, Anita. Touch. 2013. (Senses Ser.). (ENG., Illus.). 24p. (J). (gr. k-3). 28.50 *(978-1-59920-855-8(5)*, 17389) Black Rabbit Bks.

Gillespie, Katie. My Senses: Touch. 2017. (Eyediscover Ser.). (ENG., Illus.). 24p. (J). (gr. k-2). 28.55 *(978-1-4896-5707-7(X)*, AV2 by Weigl) Weigl Pubs., Inc.

Gordon, Sharon. Duro, Blando / Hard, Soft, 1 vol. 2008. (Exactamente lo Opuesto / Just the Opposite Ser.). (ENG & SPA., Illus.). 24p. (gr. k-1). lib. bdg. 25.50 *(978-0-7614-2448-2(2)*, e7a0b9fe-3b20-4d53-8a86-dbe4029fea9e) Cavendish Square Publishing LLC.

—Duro, Blando (Hard, Soft), 1 vol. 2008. (Exactamente lo Opuesto (Just the Opposite) Ser.). (SPA., Illus.). 24p. (gr. k-1). lib. bdg. 25.50 *(978-0-7614-2368-3(0)*, ee981e10-202d-411b-bd7e-97638fc06451) Cavendish Square Publishing LLC.

—Hard, Soft, 1 vol. 2008. (Just the Opposite Ser.). (ENG.). 24p. (gr. k-1). pap. 9.23 *(978-0-7614-3282-1(5)*, 95986292-9ea2-4c60-bb28-0e5fb90be301) Cavendish Square Publishing LLC.

Hall, Kirsten. Animal Touch, 1 vol. 2005. (Animals & Their Senses Ser.). (ENG., Illus.). 24p. (gr. k-2). pap. 9.15 *(978-0-8368-4812-0(8)*, f40b1f22-e631-429f-a0e9-e387cc2a8c98); lib. bdg. 24.67 *(978-0-8368-4806-9(3)*, 6038d430-473c-437f-9be4-e3af38b2489d) Stevens, Gareth Publishing LLLP. (Weekly Reader Leveled Readers).

—Animal Touch / el Tacto en Los Animales, 1 vol. 2005. (Animals & Their Senses / Los Sentidos de Los Animales Ser.). (ENG & SPA., Illus.). 24p. (gr. k-2). pap. 9.15 *(978-0-8368-4824-3(1)*, d9f3564f-2522-41ac-935f-144b3c11e3bf); lib. bdg. 24.67 *(978-0-8368-4818-2(7)*, 01529c73-9d4f-4068-9a32-3d700ac7962d) Stevens, Gareth Publishing LLLP. (Weekly Reader Leveled Readers).

Hewitt, Sally. Touch That! 2008. (Let's Start Science Ser.). (ENG., Illus.). 24p. (J). (gr. 3-7). pap. *(978-0-7787-4062-9(5))* Crabtree Publishing Co.

Hidalgo, Maria. Touch. 2003. 24p. (J). lib. bdg. 21.35 *(978-1-58340-307-5(8))* Black Rabbit Bks.

Issa, Joanna. What Can I Feel?, 1 vol. 2014. (These Are My Senses Ser.). (ENG., Illus.). 24p. (J). (gr. -1-1). pap. 5.99 *(978-1-4846-0432-8(6)*, 126588, Heinemann) Capstone.

Jordan, Apple. Smooth / Rough, 1 vol. 2nd rev. ed. 2012. (Opposites Ser.). (ENG.). 16p. (gr. k-1). 24.07 *(978-1-60870-422-4(X)*, f8c31c69-3b96-42c9-b28c-dbc2cdaa9598) Cavendish Square Publishing LLC.

Kalman, Bobbie. ¿Cómo se siente al Tocarlo? 2008. (SPA.). 24p. (J). lib. bdg. *(978-0-7787-8722-8(2))* Crabtree Publishing Co.

—¿Como Se Siente Al Tocarlo? 2008.Tr. of How Does It Feel? (SPA.). 24p. (J). pap. *(978-0-7787-8731-0(1))* Crabtree Publishing Co.

Kubler, Annie, illus. What Can I Feel? 2011. (Small Senses Ser.). 12p. (J). spiral bd. *(978-1-84643-374-0(6))* Child's Play International Ltd.

Llewellyn, Claire. Touching. 2005. (I Know That! Ser.). (Illus.). 24p. (J). (gr. 1-3). lib. bdg. 22.80 *(978-1-932889-50-5(7))* Sea-To-Sea Pubns.

Manasco, Mckinley Hunter. An Exceptional Children's Guide to Touch: Teaching Social & Physical Boundaries to Kids. Manasco, Katharine, illus. 2012. 72p. 20.95 *(978-1-84905-871-1(7)*, 694463) Kingsley, Jessica Pubs. GBR. Dist: Hachette UK Distribution.

Martin, Emmett. What Is Bumpy?, 1 vol. 2019. (Let's Learn Textures! Ser.). (ENG.). 24p. (gr. k-k). pap. 9.15 *(978-1-5382-4429-6(2)*, 7bfe9387-d511-4a1c-b596-1a1e9d2ceed3) Stevens, Gareth Publishing LLLP.

—What Is Dry?, 1 vol. 2019. (Let's Learn Textures! Ser.). (ENG.). 24p. (gr. k-k). pap. 9.15 *(978-1-5382-4433-3(0)*, 55251ddf-43b9-478f-af69-3fc0f662c89d) Stevens, Gareth Publishing LLLP.

—What Is Hard?, 1 vol. 2019. (Let's Learn Textures! Ser.). (ENG.). 24p. (gr. k-k). pap. 9.15 *(978-1-5382-4437-1(3)*, 911d9051-2268-4529-ae5e-2c9b1c9dab93) Stevens, Gareth Publishing LLLP.

—What Is Smooth?, 1 vol. 2019. (Let's Learn Textures! Ser.). (ENG.). 24p. (gr. k-k). pap. 9.15 *(978-1-5382-4441-8(1)*, fe49cbf7-5b44-4db5-aa60-f7653e3cdaf0) Stevens, Gareth Publishing LLLP.

—What Is Soft?, 1 vol. 2019. (Let's Learn Textures! Ser.). (ENG.). 24p. (gr. k-k). pap. 9.15 *(978-1-5382-4445-6(4)*, 26b88374-d01c-4977-b64b-83e64604873a) Stevens, Gareth Publishing LLLP.

—What Is Wet?, 1 vol. 2019. (Let's Learn Textures! Ser.). (ENG.). 24p. (gr. k-k). pap. 9.15 *(978-1-5382-4449-4(7)*, 3a394020-31ee-4211-b648-265a2e4bffa0) Stevens, Gareth Publishing LLLP.

McKendry, Sam. Bless Everyone. 2006. (ENG., Illus.). 12p. (J). (gr. -1-k). 8.95 *(978-1-58117-445-8(4)*, Intervisual/Piggy Toes) Bendon, Inc.

Meachen Rau, Dana. Soft & Smooth, Rough & Bumpy [Scholastic]: A Book about Touch. Peterson, Rick, illus. 2010. (Amazing Body: the Five Senses Ser.). 24p. pap. 0.56 *(978-1-4048-6544-0(6)*, Picture Window Bks.) Capstone.

Medeiros, J. de. Touch. 2009. (World of Wonder Ser.). (Illus.). 24p. (J). (gr. 2-4). pap. *(978-1-60596-059-3(4))* Weigl Pubs., Inc.

Milet Publishing Staff. My Bilingual Book-Touch, 1 vol. 2014. (My Bilingual Book Ser.). (ENG., Illus.). 24p. (J). (gr. -1-k). 9.95 *(978-1-84059-843-8(3))* Milet Publishing.

—My Bilingual Book-Touch (English-Arabic), 1 vol. 2014. (My Bilingual Book Ser.). (ENG & ARA., Illus.). 24p. (J). (gr. -1-k). 9.95 *(978-1-84059-836-0(0))* Milet Publishing.

—My Bilingual Book-Touch (English-Bengali), 1 vol. 2014. (My Bilingual Book Ser.). (ENG & BEN., Illus.). 24p. (J). (gr. -1-k). 9.95 *(978-1-84059-837-7(9))* Milet Publishing.

—My Bilingual Book-Touch (English-Chinese), 1 vol. 2014. (My Bilingual Book Ser.). (ENG & CHI., Illus.). 24p. (J). (gr. -1-k). 9.95 *(978-1-84059-838-4(7))* Milet Publishing.

—My Bilingual Book-Touch (English-Farsi), 1 vol. 2014. (My Bilingual Book Ser.). (ENG., Illus.). 24p. (J). (gr. -1-k). 9.95 *(978-1-84059-839-1(5))* Milet Publishing.

—My Bilingual Book-Touch (English-German), 1 vol. 2014. (My Bilingual Book Ser.). (ENG & GER., Illus.). 24p. (J). (gr. -1-k). 9.95 *(978-1-84059-841-4(7))* Milet Publishing.

—My Bilingual Book-Touch (English-Italian), 1 vol. 2014. (My Bilingual Book Ser.). (ENG & ITA., Illus.). 24p. (J). (gr. -1-k). 9.95 *(978-1-84059-842-1(5))* Milet Publishing.

—My Bilingual Book-Touch (English-Portuguese), 1 vol. 2014. (My Bilingual Book Ser.). (ENG & POR., Illus.). 24p. (J). (gr. -1-k). 9.95 *(978-1-84059-845-2(X))* Milet Publishing.

—My Bilingual Book-Touch (English-Russian), 1 vol. 2014. (My Bilingual Book Ser.). (ENG & RUS., Illus.). 24p. (J). (gr. -1-k). 9.95 *(978-1-84059-846-9(8))* Milet Publishing.

—My Bilingual Book-Touch (English-Somali), 1 vol. 2014. (My Bilingual Book Ser.). (ENG., Illus.). 24p. (J). (gr. -1-k). 9.95 *(978-1-84059-847-6(6))* Milet Publishing.

—My Bilingual Book-Touch (English-Turkish), 1 vol. 2014. (My Bilingual Book Ser.). (ENG., Illus.). 24p. (J). (gr. -1-k). 9.95 *(978-1-84059-849-0(2))* Milet Publishing.

—My Bilingual Book-Touch (English-Urdu), 1 vol. 2014. (My Bilingual Book Ser.). (ENG., Illus.). 24p. (J). (gr. -1-k). 9.95 *(978-1-84059-850-6(6))* Milet Publishing.

—My Bilingual Book-Touch (English-Vietnamese), 1 vol. 2014. (My Bilingual Book Ser.). (ENG., Illus.). 24p. (J). (gr. -1-k). 9.95 *(978-1-84059-851-3(4))* Milet Publishing.

—Touch - My Bilingual Book, 1 vol. 2014. (My Bilingual Book Ser.). (ENG & FRE., Illus.). 24p. (J). (gr. -1-k). 9.95 *(978-1-84059-840-7(9))* Milet Publishing.

Mlawer, Teresa, tr. What Do I Feel? / ¿Qué Siento? Kubler, Annie, illus. 2015. (Small Senses Bilingual Ser.: 5). (ENG.). 12p. (J). bds. *(978-1-84643-721-2(0))* Child's Play International Ltd.

Morgan, Sally. How Touch Works. 2010. (Our Senses Ser.). 24p. (J). (gr. k-2). pap. 8.25 *(978-1-61532-565-8(4)*, PowerKids Pr.) Rosen Publishing Group, Inc., The.

Murphy, Patricia J. True Books: Touch. 2003. (True Bks.). (ENG.). 48p. (gr. 3-5). pap. 6.95 *(978-0-516-26972-6(0),* Children's Pr.) Scholastic Library Publishing.

Murray, Julie. I Can Touch, 1 vol. 2015. (Senses Ser.). (ENG., Illus.). 24p. (J). (gr. -1-2). 31.36 *(978-1-62970-929-1(8),* 18316, Abdo Kids) ABDO Publishing Co.

Nelson, Robin. El Tacto. Translations.com Staff, tr. from ENG. 2006. (Mi Primer Paso Al Mundo Real - Los Sentidos (First Step Nonfiction - Senses) Ser.). (SPA., Illus.). 24p. (gr. k-2). lib. bdg. 23.93 *(978-0-8225-6225-2(1),* Ediciones Lerner) Lerner Publishing Group.

—El Tacto (Touching) 2006. (Mi Primer Paso al Mundo Real Ser.). (Illus.). 23p. (J). (gr. -1-3). per. 4.25 *(978-0-8225-6544-4(7),* Ediciones Lerner) Lerner Publishing Group.

—Touching. 2005. (First Step Nonfiction Ser.). (Illus.). 24p. (gr. k-2). lib. bdg. 17.27 *(978-0-8225-1266-0(1))* Lerner Publishing Group.

Owings, Lisa. Touching. 2018. (Five Senses Ser.). (ENG., Illus.). 24p. (J). (gr. k-3). pap. 7.99 *(978-1-61891-300-5(X),* 12105, Blastoff! Readers) Bellwether Media.

Ransom, Candice. Let's Explore the Sense of Touch. 2020. (Bumba Books (r) — Discover Your Senses Ser.). (ENG., Illus.). 24p. (J). (gr. -1-1). 26.65 *(978-1-5415-7685-8(3),* 3582d21b-a277-4170-962e-a4914e922dec, Lerner Pubns.) Lerner Publishing Group.

Rector, Rebecca Kraft. Texture, 1 vol. 2019. (Let's Learn about Matter Ser.). (ENG.). 24p. (gr. 1-2). 24.27 *(978-1-9785-0755-5(0),* c809329e-e139-4114-9784-60b47756f5b2) Enslow Publishing, LLC.

Rivera, Sheila. How Does It Feel? (First Step Nonfiction — Properties of Matter Ser.). (J). (gr. k-2). 2005. (ENG., Illus.). 8p. pap. 5.99 *(978-0-8225-5405-9(4),* a79cc4f6-a319-4fc8-bd7c-ab320b171dbb) 2004. lib. bdg. 23.99 *(978-0-8225-2863-0(0),* Lerner Pubns.) Lerner Publishing Group.

Rustad, Martha E. H. Touching. 2014. (Illus.). 24p. (J). lib. bdg. 25.65 *(978-1-62031-119-6(4),* Bullfrog Bks.) Jump! Inc.

Schuh, Mari. The Sense of Touch. 2007. (Senses Ser.). (ENG., Illus.). 24p. (J). (gr. 2-5). lib. bdg. 26.95 *(978-1-60014-074-7(2),* 11283) Bellwether Media.

Tsiang, Sarah Yi-Mei. Toesy Toes, 1 vol. 2018. (ENG., Illus.). 26p. (J). (gr. -1 — 1). bds. 9.95 *(978-1-4598-1342-7(1))* Orca Bk. Pubs. USA.

Verdick, Elizabeth & Lisovskis, Marjorie. Reach: A Board Book about Curiosity. 2013. (Happy Healthy Baby(r) Ser.). (ENG., Illus.). 24p. (J). (— 1). bds. 7.99 *(978-1-57542-424-8(X))* Free Spirit Publishing Inc.

Woodward, Kay. Touch, 1 vol. 2004. (Our Senses Ser.). (ENG., Illus.). 24p. (gr. 1-3). lib. bdg. 25.67 *(978-0-8368-4410-8(6),* f3b1f68d-54ec-4447-a773-faa477de58f0, Gareth Stevens Learning Library) Stevens, Gareth Publishing LLLP.

Wright, Frankie. Touch. 2016. (Illus.). 16p. (J). pap. *(978-1-338-03049-5(3))* Scholastic, Inc.

TOUCH—FICTION

Beth, Robinson. God Made Me: The Safe Touch Coloring Book. Noel, Green, illus. 2007. 20p. (J). pap. 3.99 *(978-0-9799092-0-7(1))* Robinson, Beth.

Cole, Kathryn. That Uh-Oh Feeling: A Story about Touch, 1 vol. Leng, Qin, illus. 2016. (I'm a Great Little Kid Ser.: 11). (ENG.). 24p. (J). (gr. 1-3). 15.95 *(978-1-927583-91-3(8))* Second Story Pr. CAN. Dist: Orca Bk. Pubs. USA.

Isadora, Rachel. I Hear a Pickle: And Smell, See, Touch, & Taste It, Too! Isadora, Rachel, illus. (Illus.). (J). (— 1). 2017. 30p. bds. 8.99 *(978-1-5247-3958-4(8))* 2016. 32p. 17.99 *(978-0-399-16049-3(3))* Penguin Young Readers Group. (Nancy Paulsen Books).

Jackson, Richard. Have a Look, Says Book. Hawkes, Kevin, illus. 2016. (ENG.). 48p. (J). (gr. -1-2). 17.99 *(978-1-4814-2105-8(0))* Simon & Schuster Children's Publishing.

Katz, Karen. Mommy Hugs: Lap Edition. Katz, Karen, illus. 2010. (ENG., Illus.). 26p. (J). (gr. -1 — 1). bds. 12.99 *(978-1-4424-0791-6(3),* Little Simon) Little Simon.

Verdick, Elizabeth & Lisovskis, Marjorie. Cuddle: A Board Book about Snuggling. 2013. (Happy Healthy Baby(r) Ser.). (ENG., Illus.). 24p. (J). (— 1). bds. 7.99 *(978-1-57542-423-1(1))* Free Spirit Publishing Inc.

—Cuddle / Abrazos y Mimos: A Board Book about Snuggling/un Libro de Carton Sobre Afectos y Sentimientos. 2019. (Happy Healthy Baby(r) Ser.). (ENG., Illus.). 24p. (J). (— 1). bds. 7.99 *(978-1-63198-448-8(9),* 84488) Free Spirit Publishing Inc.

Watt, Fiona. That's Not My Kitten. Wells, Rachel, illus. rev. ed. 2006. (Touchy-Feely Board Bks.). 10p. (J). (gr. -1-k). bds. 7.99 *(978-0-7945-1266-8(6),* Usborne) EDC Publishing.

Weston Woods Staff, creator. A Kiss for Little Bear. 2011. 38.75 *(978-0-439-72739-6(1));* 29.95 *(978-0-439-73481-3(9));* 18.95 *(978-0-439-72735-8(9))* Weston Woods Studios, Inc.

TOULOUSE-LAUTREC, HENRI DE, 1864-1901

Burleigh, Robert. Toulouse-Lautrec: The Moulin Rouge & the City of Light. 2006. (Illus.). 32p. (J). (gr. 4-8). 18.00 *(978-1-4223-5493-3(8))* DIANE Publishing Co.

Cook, Diane. Henri Toulouse-Lautrec: 19th Century French Painter. 2004. (Great Names Ser.). (Illus.). 32p. (J). (gr. 3-18). lib. bdg. 19.95 *(978-1-59084-155-6(7))* Mason Crest.

TOURISM

see also Travel

Bellamy, Rufus. Tourism. 2010. (Sustaining Our Environment Ser.). 48p. (J). 35.65 *(978-1-60753-138-8(0))* Amicus Learning.

Bianchi, Sebastian & Sebastian Bianchi. A AS Spanish: Tourism & Leisure. 2010. (ENG., Illus.). 64p. pap., wbk. ed. 13.95 *(978-0-340-99098-8(8))* Hodder Education Group GBR. Dist: Trans-Atlantic Pubns., Inc.

Burton, Margie, et al. Travel Money, U. S. A. 2011. (Early Connections Ser.). (J). *(978-1-61672-508-2(7))* Benchmark Education Co.

Ching, Jacqueline. Jobs in Green Travel & Tourism. 2010. (Green Careers Ser.). 80p. (YA). (gr. 7-12). E-Book 61.20 *(978-1-4488-0134-3(6))* Rosen Publishing Group, Inc., The.

Espejo, Roman, ed. What Is the Impact of Tourism?, 1 vol. 2008. (At Issue Ser.). (ENG., Illus.). 112p. (gr. 10-12). 41.03 *(978-0-7377-4120-9(1),* a5f51335-36cb-4ca7-ac49-14247e5c3868); pap. 28.80 *(978-0-7377-4121-6(X),* 37e83346-4a48-4bb7-bea8-3c203e1da6b5) Greenhaven Publishing LLC. (Greenhaven Publishing).

Feldman, Heather. Dennis Tito: The First Space Tourist. 2009. (Space Firsts Ser.). 24p. (gr. 3-4). 42.50 *(978-1-60853-112-7(0),* PowerKids Pr.) Rosen Publishing Group, Inc., The.

Goldstein, Margaret J. Private Space Travel: A Space Discovery Guide. 2017. (Space Discovery Guides). (ENG., Illus.). 48p. (J). (gr. 4-6). 31.99 *(978-1-5124-2589-5(3),* 2d08579d-21f9-4260-89cd-5ffef4d2d88d); E-Book 4.99 *(978-1-5124-3816-1(2),* 9781512438161); E-Book 47.99 *(978-1-5124-3815-4(4),* 9781512438154); E-Book 47.99 *(978-1-5124-2797-4(7))* Lerner Publishing Group. (Lerner Pubns.).

Goldsworthy, Steve. Travel Green. 2010. (Being Green Ser.). (Illus.). 32p. (YA). (gr. 3-6). lib. bdg. 27.13 *(978-1-61690-085-4(7));* (J). (gr. 4-6). pap. 12.95 *(978-1-61690-086-1(5))* Weigl Pubs., Inc.

—Travelling Green. 2016. (Illus.). 32p. (J). *(978-1-5105-2223-7(9))* SmartBook Media, Inc.

Goodman, Susan E. How Do You Burp in Space? And Other Tips Every Space Tourist Needs to Know. Slack, Michael, illus. 2013. (ENG.). 80p. (J). (gr. 3-6). 17.99 *(978-1-59990-068-1(8),* 900042509, Bloomsbury USA Childrens) Bloomsbury Publishing USA.

Hauser, Mindy Moser. The Vo-Tech Track to Success in Hospitality & Tourism, 1 vol. 2014. (Learning a Trade, Preparing for a Career Ser.). (ENG., Illus.). 80p. (J). (gr. 6-6). 37.47 *(978-1-4777-7728-2(8),* 5301c226-20d6-4a7e-bc20-349fb22e4d66) Rosen Publishing Group, Inc., The.

Inskipp, Carol. Travel & Tourism. 2009. (J). 32.80 *(978-1-59920-100-9(3))* Black Rabbit Bks.

Jefferis, David. Space Tourists. 2017. (Our Future in Space Ser.). (Illus.). 32p. (J). (gr. 5-5). *(978-0-7787-3536-6(2));* pap. *(978-0-7787-3548-9(6))* Crabtree Publishing Co.

Kallen, Stuart A. Careers in Travel & Hospitality. 2018. (Exploring Careers Ser.). (ENG.). 80p. (YA). (gr. 5-12). 39.93 *(978-1-68282-317-0(2))* ReferencePoint Pr., Inc.

Mason, Paul. Extreme Storms. 2012. (Disaster Watch! Ser.). 32p. (gr. 4-6). 28.50 *(978-1-59920-424-6(X))* Black Rabbit Bks.

McAlpine, Margaret. Working in Travel & Tourism, 1 vol. 2005. (My Future Career Ser.). (ENG., Illus.). 64p. (gr. 4-6). lib. bdg. 29.67 *(978-0-8368-4239-5(1),* e85217fa-4ae8-43bd-aba8-d975478999ba, Gareth Stevens Learning Library) Stevens, Gareth Publishing LLLP.

McMahon, Peter. The Space Adventurer's Guide: Your Passport to the Coolest Things to See & Do in the Universe. Holinaty, Josh, illus. 2018. (ENG.). 100p. (J). (gr. 3-7). pap. 17.99 *(978-1-77138-032-4(2))* Kids Can Pr., Ltd. CAN. Dist: Hachette Bk. Group.

Owings, Lisa. Salton Riviera: The Deserted Resort Community. 2020. (Abandoned Places Ser.). (ENG.). 24p. (J). (gr. 3-7). lib. bdg. 26.95 *(978-1-64487-163-8(7),* Torque Bks.) Bellwether Media.

Parks, Peggy J. Careers If You Like to Travel. 2019. (Career Exploration Ser.). (ENG.). 80p. (J). (gr. 6-12). 41.27 *(978-1-68282-597-6(3))* ReferencePoint Pr., Inc.

Pasternak, Ceel. Cool Careers for Girls in Travel & Hospitality. 2003. (ENG., Illus.). 144p. (YA). (gr. 8-17). pap. 13.95 *(978-1-57023-192-6(3))* Impact Pubns.

Payment, Simone. Cool Careers Without College for People Who Love to Travel. 2009. (Cool Careers Without College Ser.). 144p. (gr. 6-6). 66.50 *(978-1-61511-980-6(9))* Rosen Publishing Group, Inc., The.

Penta, Mark. Cape Cod Invasion! 2007. (ENG., Illus.). 32p. 17.95 *(978-1-933212-49-4(7),* Commonwealth Editions) Applewood Bks.

Randolph, Joanne. Dennis Tito: First Space Tourist. 2009. (Reading Room Collection 2 Ser.). 24p. (gr. 3-4). 42.50 *(978-1-60851-962-0(7),* PowerKids Pr.) Rosen Publishing Group, Inc., The.

Reeves, Diane Lindsey. Hospitality & Tourism. 2017. (Bright Futures Press: World of Work Ser.). (ENG., Illus.). 32p. (J). (gr. 4-7). lib. bdg. 32.07 *(978-1-5341-0175-3(6),* 210170) Cherry Lake Publishing.

Riley, Rowan. Great Careers with a High School Diploma: Hospitality, Human Services, & Tourism. 2008. (Great Careers with a High School Diploma Ser.). 93p. (C). (gr. 9). 32.95 *(978-0-8160-7048-0(2),* Ferguson Publishing Company) Infobase Holdings, Inc.

Roza, Greg. Reducing Your Carbon Footprint on Vacation. 2009. (Your Carbon Footprint Ser.). 48p. (gr. 5-5). 53.00 *(978-1-60854-913-9(5),* Rosen Reference) Rosen Publishing Group, Inc., The.

Smith, Jr. Cambridge Igcse(r) Travel & Tourism. Per le Scuole Superiori. 2012. (Cambridge International IGCSE Ser.). (ENG., Illus.). 265p. pap. 40.80 *(978-0-521-14922-8(3))* Cambridge Univ. Pr.

Sparrow, Giles. Space Travel, 1 vol. 2017. (Space Explorers Ser.). (ENG.). 32p. (gr. 2-2). 26.93 *(978-0-7660-9268-6(2),* 971af130-d004-4de1-aa0a-aea03a7e081a) Enslow Publishing, LLC.

Stearman, Kaye. Travel & Tourism Careers. 2010. (In the Workplace Ser.). 48p. (J). 35.65 *(978-1-60753-096-1(1))* Amicus Learning.

Stearman, Kaye & Savery, Annabel. Travel & Tourism. 2011. (Been There! Ser.). 32p. (gr. 3-6). lib. bdg. 31.35 *(978-1-59920-476-5(2))* Black Rabbit Bks.

Truesdale, Lisa. Tourism. 2018. *(978-1-5105-3554-1(3))* SmartBook Media, Inc.

Turner, Cherie. Adventure Tour Guides: Life on Extreme Outdoor Adventures. 2009. (Extreme Careers Ser.). 64p. (gr. 5-5). 58.50 *(978-1-61512-383-4(0),* Rosen Reference) Rosen Publishing Group, Inc., The.

Walker, Robin & Harding, Keith. Oxford English for Careers: Tourism 2: Student's Book. 2009. (ENG., Illus.). 144p. stu. ed. 37.40 *(978-0-19-455103-8(2))* Oxford Univ. Pr., Inc.

TOURISM—FICTION

Bean, Raymond. The Curse of Mars. Vimislik, Matthew, illus. 2016. (Out of This World Ser.). (ENG.). 112p. (J). (gr. 2-5). lib. bdg. 32.65 *(978-1-4965-3615-0(0),* 132831, Stone Arch Bks.) Capstone.

Class Trip, 6 vols., Set. 2009. (J). (gr. 2-5). lib. bdg. 179.70 *(978-1-58415-812-7(3))* Mitchell Lane Pubs.

Friedman, Laurie. Red, White & True Blue Mallory. Kalis, Jennifer, illus. (Mallory Ser.: 11). (ENG.). 184p. (J). (gr. 2-5). 2010. pap. 7.99 *(978-0-7613-3946-5(9),* 126fea1d-13ec-4070-9e5e-70227e5a6a73) 2009. 15.95 *(978-0-8225-8882-5(X),* 25f4d989-183f-4ef3-89d8-84c63c627d23) Lerner Publishing Group. (Darby Creek).

Keyes, Diane. Spirit of the Snowpeople. Stevens, Helen, illus. 2008. (ENG.). 32p. (J). (gr. -1-3). 15.95 *(978-0-89272-710-0(1))* Down East Bks.

Spalding, Andrea. An Island of My Own. 2008. (ENG., Illus.). 112p. (YA). (gr. 8-12). pap. 11.99 *(978-1-55002-635-1(6))* Dundurn Pr. CAN. Dist: Publishers Group West (PGW).

TOURIST TRADE

see Tourism

TOUSSAINT LOUVERTURE, 1743?-1803

Worth, Richard. Toussaint L'Ouverture: Fighting for Haitian Independence, 1 vol. 2017. (Rebels with a Cause Ser.). (ENG.). 128p. (gr. 8-8). lib. bdg. 38.93 *(978-0-7660-8521-3(X),* 26e85755-1c85-4f8f-8f94-785b8d5da7a0) Enslow Publishing, LLC.

TOWER OF LONDON (LONDON, ENGLAND)

Hoena, Blake. The Tower of London: A Chilling Interactive Adventure. 2016. (You Choose: Haunted Places Ser.). (ENG., Illus.). 112p. (J). (gr. 3-7). lib. bdg. 32.65 *(978-1-5157-2579-4(0),* 132922, Capstone Pr.) Capstone.

Hynson, Colin. The Tower of London, 1 vol. 2004. (Places in History Ser.). (ENG., Illus.). 48p. (gr. 5-8). lib. bdg. 33.67 *(978-0-8368-5813-6(1),* d323d772-34da-4e90-bf37-a381ea9691d7, Gareth Stevens Secondary Library) Stevens, Gareth Publishing LLLP.

Nelson, Drew. Haunted! the Tower of London. 2013. (History's Most Haunted Ser.). 32p. (J). (gr. 3-6). pap. 63.00 *(978-1-4339-9265-0(5));* (ENG., Illus.). 29.27 *(978-1-4339-9263-6(9),* 3ced6df9-0dcf-4682-a924-3512158bd930); (ENG., Illus.). pap. 11.50 *(978-1-4339-9264-3(7),* b56257db-e379-4918-98c0-5a10998df1f1) Stevens, Gareth Publishing LLLP.

Pascal, Janet B. & Who HQ. Where Is the Tower of London? Malan, David, illus. 2018. (Where Is? Ser.). 112p. (J). (gr. 3-7). 7.99 *(978-1-5247-8606-9(3));* lib. bdg. 15.99 *(978-1-5247-8608-3(X))* Penguin Young Readers Group. (Penguin Workshop).

Riley, Gail Blasser. Tower of London: England's Ghostly Castle. 2006. (Castles, Palaces, & Tombs Ser.). (Illus.). 32p. (YA). (gr. 2-5). lib. bdg. 28.50 *(978-1-59716-249-4(3))* Bearport Publishing Co., Inc.

TOWN OFFICERS

see Local Government

TOWN PLANNING

see City Planning

TOWNS

see Cities and Towns

TOXIC WASTES

see Hazardous Wastes

TOXICOLOGY

see Poisons

TOY AND MOVABLE BOOKS

Aardman Animation Ltd. Early Man Sticker & Activity Book. 2018. (ENG., Illus.). 72p. (J). (gr. 2-5). 6.99 *(978-1-5107-3539-2(9),* Sky Pony Pr.) Skyhorse Publishing Co., Inc.

Abbot, Judi. Hugs & Kisses. Abbot, Judi, illus. 2016. (ENG., Illus.). 20p. (J). (gr. -1 — 1). bds. 7.99 *(978-1-4814-9168-6(7),* Little Simon) Little Simon.

Abbott Orloff, Chrissy. Lady Humming Fly's Lesson on Staying Safe. 2009. 80p. pap. 28.99 *(978-1-4389-9938-8(0))* AuthorHouse.

Abel, Simone, illus. Where Is Caterpillar Look & Play. (Lamaze Ser.). bds. 8.99 *(978-1-58663-731-6(2))* Friedman, Michael Publishing Group, Inc.

Abery, Julie. Little Panda. Mason, Suzie, illus. 2019. (ENG.). 20p. (J). (gr. -1-k). bds. 9.99 *(978-1-68152-414-6(7),* 17591) Amicus.

Abrams Appleseed. Making Faces: A First Book of Emotions. 2017. (ENG., Illus.). 14p. (J). (gr. -1 — 1). bds. 7.99 *(978-1-4197-2383-4(9),* 1165410) Abrams, Inc.

Abrams, Pam. Can I Push the Button. 2009. 14p. 10.95 *(978-1-58117-903-3(0),* Intervisual/Piggy Toes) Bendon, Inc.

Accord Publishing, Accord. Colors: A Silly Slider Book. 2011. (ENG., Illus.). 10p. (J). bds. 10.99 *(978-1-4494-0831-2(1))* Andrews McMeel Publishing.

—Hop, Pop, & Play: A Mini Animotion Book. 2011. (ENG.). 12p. (J). 9.99 *(978-1-4494-0177-1(5))* Andrews McMeel Publishing.

—Numbers: A Caterpillar-Shaped Book. 2012. (ENG.). 24p. (J). 11.99 *(978-1-4494-1736-9(1))* Andrews McMeel Publishing.

—What Do You See? A Lift-The-Flap Book. 2014. (ENG.). 12p. (J). (-k). bds. 6.99 *(978-1-4494-4385-6(0))* Andrews McMeel Publishing.

—Where Does Love Come From? Kirkova, Milena, illus. 2012. (ENG.). 18p. (J). bds. 5.99 *(978-1-4494-2884-6(3))* Andrews McMeel Publishing.

Accord Publishing Staff. Dinosaurs: A Mini Animotion Book. 2011. (ENG.). 12p. (J). 9.99 *(978-1-4494-0172-6(4))* Andrews McMeel Publishing.

—Oliver's First Christmas. Valiant, Kristi, illus. 2012. (ENG.). 14p. (J). (-k). bds. 5.99 *(978-1-4494-2245-5(4))* Andrews McMeel Publishing.

Ackerman, Jill. Old MacDonald: a Hand-Puppet Board Book. Berg, Michelle, illus. 2007. (Little Scholastic Ser.). (ENG.). 6p. (J). (gr. -1 — 1). bds. 12.99 *(978-0-545-02603-1(2))* Scholastic, Inc.

—This Little Piggy: a Hand-Puppet Board Book. Berg, Michelle, illus. 2007. (Little Scholastic Ser.). (ENG.). 6p. (J). (gr. -1 — 1). bds. 12.99 *(978-0-545-03038-0(2))* Scholastic, Inc.

Ackland, Nick. Colors. 2015. (Bright Beginnings Ser.). (ENG.). 20p. (J). (gr. -1 — 1). bds. 7.99 *(978-0-7641-6742-3(1))* Sourcebooks, Inc.

Acosta, Jamey & Reid, Stephanie. Health & Safety. 2010. (Early Literacy Ser.). (ENG., Illus.). 16p. (gr. k-1). 19.99 *(978-1-4333-1809-2(1))* Teacher Created Materials, Inc.

Acredolo, Linda & Goodwyn, Susan. I Can Sign! Playtime. 2007. (Baby Signs (Ideals) Ser.). (ENG., Illus.). 12p. (gr. -1). 9.99 *(978-0-8249-6708-6(9),* Ideals Pubns.) Worthy Publishing.

Active Minds, 6 bks. (Illus.). (J). (gr. -1-3). lib. bdg. 71.70 *(978-1-56674-926-8(3))* Forest Hse. Publishing Co., Inc.

Adair, Amy. Jay Jay's Special Delivery. 2003. (Illus.). (J). 15.98 *(978-0-7853-8625-4(4))* Publications International, Ltd.

Adams, Ben. The Pig with the Curliest Tail. Cameron, Craig, illus. 2013. (Googly Eyes Ser.). 12p. (J). (gr. -1-k). bds. 6.99 *(978-1-84322-618-5(9),* Armadillo) Anness Publishing GBR. Dist: National Bk. Network.

—Polly the Farm Puppy. Cameron, Craig, illus. 2013. (Googly Eyes Ser.). 12p. (J). (gr. -1-k). bds. 6.99 *(978-1-84322-319-1(8),* Armadillo) Anness Publishing GBR. Dist: National Bk. Network.

Adams, David J. Good Night Vancouver. Rosen, Anne, illus. 2010. (Good Night Our World Ser.). (ENG.). 20p. (J). (gr. -1 — 1). bds. 9.95 *(978-1-60219-039-9(9))* Good Night Bks.

Adams, Jennifer. Alice in Wonderland: A BabyLit(TM) Colors Primer, 1 vol. Oliver, Alison, illus. 2012. (BabyLit Ser.). 22p. (J). (gr. k-1). bds. 11.99 *(978-1-4236-2477-6(7))* Gibbs Smith, Publisher.

—Anna Karenina: A BabyLit(TM) Fashion Primer, 1 vol. Oliver, Alison, illus. 2013. (ENG.). 22p. (J). (gr. k-1). bds. 9.99 *(978-1-4236-3483-6(7))* Gibbs Smith, Publisher.

—Around the World in 80 Days: A BabyLit(TM) Transportation Primer, 1 vol. Oliver, Alison, illus. 2018. (BabyLit Ser.). 22p. (J). (— 1). bds. 9.99 *(978-1-4236-4746-1(7))* Gibbs Smith, Publisher.

—A Christmas Carol: A BabyLit(TM) Colors Primer, 1 vol. Oliver, Alison, illus. 2012. (BabyLit Ser.). 22p. (J). (gr. k-1). bds. 11.99 *(978-1-4236-2575-9(7))* Gibbs Smith, Publisher.

—Dracula: A BabyLit(TM) Counting Primer, 1 vol. Oliver, Alison, illus. 2012. (BabyLit Ser.). 22p. (J). (gr. k-1). bds. 11.99 *(978-1-4236-2480-6(7))* Gibbs Smith, Publisher.

—Edgar Gets Ready for Bed: Inspired by Edgar Allan Poe's the Raven, 1 vol. Stucki, Ron, illus. 2015. (Edgar the Raven Ser.). 22p. (J). (— 1). 11.99 *(978-1-4236-4175-9(2))* Gibbs Smith, Publisher.

—Edgar Gets Ready for Bed: a BabyLit(TM) Book: Inspired by Edgar Allan Poe's the Raven, 1 vol. Stucki, Ron, illus. 2014. (ENG.). 32p. (J). 16.99 *(978-1-4236-3528-4(0))* Gibbs Smith, Publisher.

—Frankenstein: A BabyLit(TM) Anatomy Primer, 1 vol. Oliver, Alison, illus. 2014. 22p. (J). (gr. k-1). bds. 9.99 *(978-1-4236-3741-7(0))* Gibbs Smith, Publisher.

—Jabberwocky: A BabyLit(TM) Nonsense Primer, 1 vol. Oliver, Alison, illus. 2013. 22p. (J). (gr. k-1). bds. 9.99 *(978-1-4236-3408-9(X))* Gibbs Smith, Publisher.

—Jane Eyre: A BabyLit(TM) Counting Primer, 1 vol. Oliver, Alison, illus. 2012. 22p. (J). (gr. k-1). bds. 9.99 *(978-1-4236-2474-5(2))* Gibbs Smith, Publisher.

—A Midsummer Night's Dream: A BabyLit(TM) Fairies Primer, 1 vol. Oliver, Alison, illus. 2016. (BabyLit Ser.). 22p. (J). (— 1). bds. 11.99 *(978-1-4236-4181-0(7))* Gibbs Smith, Publisher.

—Moby Dick: A BabyLit(TM) Ocean Primer, 1 vol. Oliver, Alison, illus. 2013. (BabyLit Ser.). 22p. (J). (gr. k-1). bds. 9.99 *(978-1-4236-3204-7(4))* Gibbs Smith, Publisher.

—My Little Cities: Paris: (Board Books for Toddlers, Travel Books for Kids, City Children's Books) Pizzoli, Greg, illus. 2017. (My Little Cities Ser.). (ENG.). 22p. (J). (gr. -1 — 1). bds. 9.99 *(978-1-4521-5390-2(6))* Chronicle Bks. LLC.

—My Little Cities: San Francisco: (Board Books for Toddlers, Travel Books for Kids, City Children's Books) Pizzoli, Greg, illus. 2017. (My Little Cities Ser.). (ENG.). 22p. (J). (gr. -1 — 1). bds. 9.99 *(978-1-4521-5391-9(4))* Chronicle Bks. LLC.

—Romeo & Juliet: A BabyLit(TM) Counting Primer, 1 vol. Oliver, Alison, illus. 2011. (ENG.). 22p. (J). (gr. k-1). bds. 9.99 *(978-1-4236-2205-5(7))* Gibbs Smith, Publisher.

—Sense & Sensibility: A BabyLit(TM) Opposites Primer, 1 vol. Oliver, Alison, illus. 2013. 22p. (J). (gr. k-1). bds. 9.99 *(978-1-4236-3170-5(6))* Gibbs Smith, Publisher.

—Sherlock Holmes: A BabyLit(TM) Sounds Primer, 1 vol. Oliver, Alison, illus. 2013. 22p. (J). (gr. k-1). bds. 9.99 *(978-1-4236-3411-9(X))* Gibbs Smith, Publisher.

—Wuthering Heights: A BabyLit(TM) Weather Primer, 1 vol. Oliver, Alison, illus. 2013. 22p. (J). (gr. k-1). bds. 9.99 *(978-1-4236-3173-6(0))* Gibbs Smith, Publisher.

Adams, Michelle Medlock. Why I Thank You, God. Koeller, Carol, illus. 2006. 20p. (J). (gr. -1). bds. 5.49 *(978-0-7586-0911-3(6))* Concordia Publishing Hse.

Adams, Pam, illus. The Farmer in the Dell. 2013. (Classic Books with Holes 8x8 with CD Ser.). (ENG.). 16p. (J). (gr. -1). *(978-1-84643-624-6(9))* Child's Play International Ltd.

—The First Day. 2009. 10p. (J). bds. *(978-0-85953-149-8(X))* Child's Play International Ltd.

—Old Macdonald Had a Farm. (Classic Books with Holes 8x8 with CD Ser.). (ENG.). 16p. (J). 2007. (gr. -1-1). *(978-1-904550-64-8(9))* 2003. pap. *(978-0-85953-135-1(X))* Child's Play International Ltd.

—There Was an Old Lady Who Swallowed a Fly. (Classic Books with Holes 8x8 with CD Ser.). (ENG.). 16p. (J). 2007. (gr. -1-1). *(978-1-904550-62-4(2))* 2003. pap. *(978-0-85953-134-4(1))* Child's Play International Ltd.

Adler, Victoria. All of Baby, Nose to Toes. Nakata, Hiroe, illus. 2011. 30p. (J). (gr. k — 1). bds. 7.99 *(978-0-8037-3531-6(6),* Dial Bks) Penguin Young Readers Group.

Ageledis, Ida. First Foil Poetry Seasons, 2 vols. Berg, Michelle, illus. 2005. (First Foil Poetry Haikus Ser.). 10p. (J). 6.95 *(978-1-58117-188-4(9),* Intervisual/Piggy Toes) Bendon, Inc.

Agell, Charlotte. Mud, Sand, & Snow, 1 vol. 2019. (ENG., Illus.). 24p. (J). bds. 10.95 *(978-1-944762-63-6(9),* d78dec78-9cf2-4564-827f-b22713342f84) Islandport Pr., Inc.

Agliardi, Allegra. All the Colors I See. 2018. (ENG., Illus.). 64p. (J). (gr. -1-k). 19.95 *(978-1-84976-577-0(4))* Tate Publishing, Ltd. GBR. Dist: Hachette Bk. Group.

Aigner-Clark, Julie. Baby Einstein Poemas Preciosos: Pretty Poems & Wonderful Words. Zaidi, Nadeem, illus. 2004. (SPA.). 10p. (J). 9.95 *(978-970-718-210-3(5),* Silver Dolphin Bks.) Readerlink Distribution Services, LLC.

T U V

—Master Pieces. Zaidi, Nadeem, illus. 2004. (SPA.). 10p. (J). 9.95 *(978-970-718-211-0(3)*, Silver Dolphin Bks.) Readerlink Distribution Services, LLC.

Ainsworth, Kimberly. Moustache Up! A Playful Game of Opposites. Roode, Daniel, illus. 2013. (ENG.). 18p. (J). (gr. -1-k). bds. 7.99 *(978-1-4424-7526-7(9)*, Little Simon) Little Simon.

Aki. The Nature Girls. Aki, illus. 2019. (ENG., Illus.). 32p. (J). 16.99 *(978-1-62779-621-7(5)*, 900156982, Holt, Henry & Co. Bks. For Young Readers) Holt, Henry & Co.

Albee, Sarah. Andy Alligator. Brown, Jo, illus. 2009. (Snappy Fun Bks.). (ENG.). 10p. (J). (gr. -1 — 1). bds. 7.99 *(978-0-7944-1908-0(9)*, Studio Fun International) Printers Row Publishing Group.

—Elmo Says... (Sesame Street) Leigh, Tom, illus. 2009. (Big Bird's Favorites Board Bks.). (ENG.). 24p. (J). (gr. -1 — 1). bds. 4.99 *(978-0-375-84540-6(2)*, Random Hse. Bks. for Young Readers) Random Hse. Children's Bks.

Albee, Sarah & Hood, Susan. Snappy Heads Tommy T Rex. Brown, Jo, illus. 2009. (New Snappy Fun Ser.). (ENG.). 10p. (J). (gr. -1-k). bds. 7.99 *(978-0-7944-1907-3(0))* Reader's Digest Assn., Inc., The.

Albers, Josef. Squares & Other Shapes: With Josef Albers. 2016. (ENG., Illus.). 30p. (gr. -1 — 1). bds. 12.95 *(978-0-7148-7256-8(3))* Phaidon Pr., Inc.

Albout, Corrine & Mabire, Grégoire. All Aboard. 2011. (One by One Ser.). (Illus.). 14p. bds. *(978-1-84089-687-9(6))* Zero to Ten, Ltd.

Aldrin, Buzz. To the Moon & Back: My Apollo 11 Adventure. 2018. (Illus.). 16p. (J). (gr. 3-7). 32.00 *(978-1-4263-3249-4(1)*, National Geographic Kids) Disney Publishing Worldwide.

Alexander, Rilla, illus. TouchWords: Clothes. 2019. (Touch Think Learn Ser.). (ENG.). 16p. (J). (gr. -1 — 1). 16.99 *(978-1-4521-7561-4(6))* Chronicle Bks. LLC.

Aliens Sticker Book. (Weird & Wacky Ser.). 16p. (J). *(978-2-89393-870-7(1))* Phidal Publishing, Inc./Editions Phidal, Inc.

All Things Bright And Beautiful. 2006. 16p. (J). pap. 1.99 *(978-0-7847-1588-8(2)*, 22135) Standard Publishing.

Allen, Constance. Peekaboo, Elmo! (Sesame Street) Prebenna, David, illus. 2014. (Big Bird's Favorites Board Bks.). (ENG.). 24p. (J). (— 1). bds. 4.99 *(978-0-449-81483-3(1)*, Random Hse. Bks. for Young Readers) Random Hse. Children's Bks.

Allen, Elise. Barbie: A Fashion Fairytale. 2010. (Illus.). (J). *(978-0-7944-2167-0(9)*, Reader's Digest Children's Bks.) Studio Fun International.

Allen-Fletcher, Carly. Goodnight, Seahorse. 2018. (Illus.). 22p. (J). (gr. -1-1). bds. 11.95 *(978-1-63076-333-6(0))* Muddy Boots Pr.

Allen, Francesca, illus. Vacation. 2006. (Usborne Look & Say Ser.). 10p. (J). (gr. -1-k). bds. 7.99 *(978-0-7945-1315-3(8)*, Usborne) EDC Publishing.

Allen, J. J. Hello Kitty's Fun Friend Day! 2003. (Illus.). 32p. (J). pap. *(978-0-439-44917-5(0))* Scholastic, Inc.

Allen, Kathryn Madeline. This Book. Doyle, Lizzy, illus. 2018. (ENG.). 24p. (J). (gr. -1 — 1). bds. 9.99 *(978-0-8075-7881-0(9)*, 807578819) Whitman, Albert & Co.

Allen, Keith. What a Mess! A Pop-Up Misadventure. Allen, Keith, illus. 2017. (Illus.). 7p. (J). (gr. 1-3). 35.00 *(978-0-692-81057-6(9))* 5am Pr., LLC.

Allum, Margaret & Watson, Judy. How Many Peas in a Pod? 2006. (Illus.). 16p. pap. *(978-1-921049-43-9(X))* Little Hare Bks. AUS. Dist: HarperCollins Pubs. Australia.

Alyce, Kathie. Flip Flop Block Quilts. 1 vol. 2010. (ENG., Illus.). 64p. 22.95 *(978-1-57432-675-8(9)*, 1574326759, American Quilter's Society) Collector Bks.

American Museum of Natural History, American Museum. ABC Oceans. 2014. (AMNH ABC Board Bks.). (Illus.). 18p. (J). (gr. -1-k). bds. 9.95 *(978-1-4549-1195-1(6))* Sterling Publishing Co., Inc.

—Camouflage. 2016. (Science for Toddlers Ser.). (Illus.). 18p. (J). (gr. -1). bds. 7.95 *(978-1-4549-2079-3(3))* Sterling Publishing Co., Inc.

American Museum of Natural History Staff. Spot the Animals: A Lift-the-Flap Book of Colors. 2012. (ENG., Illus.). 16p. (J). (gr. -1-2). bds. 6.95 *(978-1-4027-7723-3(X))* Sterling Publishing Co., Inc.

America's 50 States. 2014. (Illus.). (J). *(978-1-4351-5773-6(7))* Barnes & Noble, Inc.

America's Test Kitchen Kids & Frost, Maddie. A Is for Artichoke: A Foodie Alphabet from Artichoke to Zest. 2018. (ENG., Illus.). 26p. (J). (gr. -1-k). bds. 9.99 *(978-1-4926-7003-2(0))* Sourcebooks, Inc.

—1 2 3 the Farm & Me. 2018. (ENG., Illus.). 24p. (J). (gr. -1-k). bds. 9.99 *(978-1-4926-7004-9(9))* Sourcebooks, Inc.

Amery, H. Where's Curly? Cartwright, Stephen, illus. 2004. (Treasury of Farmyard Tales Ser.). 16p. (J). (gr. 1-18). pap. 7.95 *(978-0-7945-0514-1(7))* EDC Publishing.

Amery, H. & Cartwright, S. Where's Rusty? 2004. (Treasury of Farmyard Tales Ser.). 10p. (J). 7.95 *(978-0-7945-0545-5(7))* EDC Publishing.

Amery, Heather. The Farm. Cartwright, Stephen, illus. 2008. (Usborne Talkabout Bks.). 12p. (J). (gr. -1-3). bds. 8.99 *(978-0-7945-1795-3(1)*, Usborne) EDC Publishing.

—Farmyard Tales Christmas Flap Bk And. 2006. 24p. 12.99 *(978-0-7945-0556-1(2)*, Usborne) EDC Publishing.

—Red Tractor Board Book. Cartwright, Stephen, illus. 2004. (Young Farmyard Tales Board Books Ser.). 10p. (J). bds. 3.95 *(978-0-7945-0469-4(8)*, Usborne) EDC Publishing.

—The Seaside. Cartwright, Stephen, illus. 2008. (Usborne Talkabout Bks.). 12p. (J). bds. 8.99 *(978-0-7945-1794-6(3)*, Usborne) EDC Publishing.

—Wind-up Plane. 2009. (Wind-up Bks). 14p. (J). bds. 29.99 *(978-0-7945-2534-7(2)*, Usborne) EDC Publishing.

—Zoo Talkabout Board Book. Cartwright, Stephen, illus. 2008. (Talkabout Board Bks). 12p. (J). bds. 8.99 *(978-0-7945-1793-9(5)*, Usborne) EDC Publishing.

Amery, Heather & Doherty, Gillian. Wind-Up Tractor Book. 2007. (Wind-up Tractor Book Ser.). 14p. (J). bds. 25.99 *(978-0-7945-1861-5(3)*, Usborne) EDC Publishing.

—Wind-up Train Book. 2008. (Wind-up Bks). 14p. (J). bds. 29.99 *(978-0-7945-2192-9(4)*, Usborne) EDC Publishing.

Anastas, Margaret. Mommy's Best Kisses Board Book. Winter, Susan, illus. 2008. (ENG.). 34p. (J). (gr. -1-k). bds. 8.99 *(978-0-06-124130-7(X)*, HarperFestival) HarperCollins Pubs.

Anderson, Airlie. A Very Furry Flap Book. 2004. (Illus.). 10p. (J). bds. 5.95 *(978-1-58925-701-6(4))* Tiger Tales.

Anderson, Airlie, illus. A Very Patchy Flap Book. 2004. 10p. (J). bds. 5.95 *(978-1-58925-702-3(2))* Tiger Tales.

—A Very Spotty Flap Book. 2004. 10p. (J). bds. 5.95 *(978-1-58925-703-0(0))* Tiger Tales.

—A Very Stripy Flap Book. 2004. 10p. (J). bds. 5.95 *(978-1-58925-704-7(9))* Tiger Tales.

Anderson, Debby. Jesus Is Alive. 2017. (Cuddle & Sing Ser.). (ENG., Illus.). 18p. (J). bds. 6.99 *(978-1-4347-1115-1(3)*, 139847) Cook, David C.

Anderson, Hans Christian. The Little Christmas Tree: With an Advent Calendar Just for You! Downer, Maggie, illus. 2015. (ENG.). 10p. (J). (gr. k-3). bds. 7.99 *(978-1-86147-291-5(9)*, Armadillo) Anness Publishing GBR. Dist: National Bk. Network.

—The Snow Queen. Sumberac, Manuel, illus. 2014. (J). *(978-1-4351-5587-9(4))* Barnes & Noble, Inc.

Anderson, Sara. Noisy City Day (2015 Board Book) Anderson, Sara, illus. 2015. (ENG., Illus.). 12p. (J). (gr. -1-1). bds. 10.95 *(978-1-943459-00-1(2))* Sara Anderson Children's Bks.

—Noisy City Night (2015 Board Book) Anderson, Sara, illus. 2015. (ENG., Illus.). 12p. (J). (gr. -1-1). bds. 10.95 *(978-1-943459-01-8(0))* Sara Anderson Children's Bks.

Andreae, Giles. Giraffes Can't Dance (Board Book) Parker-Rees, Guy, illus. 2012. (ENG.). 32p. (J). (gr. -1 — 1). bds. 6.99 *(978-0-545-39255-6(1)*, Cartwheel Bks.) Scholastic, Inc.

—I Love My Grandma. Dodd, Emma, illus. 2018. (ENG.). 24p. (J). (gr. -1 — 1). bds. 7.99 *(978-1-4847-3409-4(2))* Hyperion Bks. for Children.

—I Love You, Baby. Dodd, Emma, illus. 2016. (ENG.). 26p. (J). (gr. -1 — 1). bds. 6.99 *(978-1-4847-2261-9(2))* Hyperion Bks. for Children.

—My Little World of Happy, 9 vols. 2013. (World of Happy Ser.). (ENG., Illus.). 90p. (J). (— 1). bds. 15.99 *(978-1-4052-6082-4(3))* Farshore GBR. Dist: Independent Pubs. Group.

—Rumble in the Jungle. Wojtowycz, David, illus. 2011. (ENG.). 26p. (J). (-k). bds. 9.99 *(978-1-58925-864-8(9))* Tiger Tales.

Andrew, Carol B. Animal Alphabet: An Interactive Book to Learn about Letters. 2005. (Illus.). (J). *(978-1-933577-00-5(2))* Learning Wood, LLC.

—The Colorful Secret: An Interactive Book to Learn about Colors. 2005. (Illus.). (J). *(978-1-933577-01-2(0))* Learning Wood, LLC.

—Counting Dinosaurs: An Interactive Book to Learn about Numbers. 2005. (Illus.). (J). *(978-1-933577-02-9(9))* Learning Wood, LLC.

—Little Farm Puppy. 2006. (Illus.). (J). *(978-1-933577-05-0(3))* Learning Wood, LLC.

—My Beautiful Ballets. 2006. (Illus.). (J). *(978-1-933577-04-3(5))* Learning Wood, LLC.

—Where's My Mommy? 2006. (Illus.). (J). *(978-1-933577-06-7(1))* Learning Wood, LLC.

Andrews McMeel Publishing, Andrews McMeel. Bugs. 2014. (ENG., Illus.). 12p. (J). bds. 5.99 *(978-1-4494-6055-6(0))* Andrews McMeel Publishing.

—Colors. Stone, Kate, illus. 2015. (ENG.). 12p. (J). bds. 10.99 *(978-1-4494-5587-3(5))* Andrews McMeel Publishing.

Andrews McMeel Publishing, LLC Staff. Zoo Babies. 2015. (ENG.). 12p. (J). bds. 5.99 *(978-1-4494-6058-7(5))* Andrews McMeel Publishing.

Andrews McMeel Publishing Staff. Dinosaurs. 2014. (ENG., Illus.). 12p. (J). bds. 5.99 *(978-1-4494-6056-3(9))* Andrews McMeel Publishing.

Angleberger, Tom. Art2-D2's Guide to Folding & Doodling (an Origami Yoda Activity Book) 2013. (Origami Yoda Ser.). (ENG., Illus.). 176p. (J). (gr. 3-7). 12.95 *(978-1-4197-0534-2(2)*, 1042401, Amulet Bks.) Abrams, Inc.

Anholt, Catherine & Anholt, Laurence. Can You Guess? A Lift-the-Flap Birthday Party Book. 2003. (ENG., Illus.). 16p. pap. 7.95 *(978-0-7112-2214-4(2))* Fleming, Randall.

Anne Paradis, Anne. Caillou, My House: Includes 4 Chunky Board Books. Pierre Brignaud, Pierre, illus. 2015. (ENG.). 40p. (J). (gr. -1-k). bds. 16.99 *(978-2-89718-224-3(5))* Caillouet, Gerry.

Anness Publishing Ltd. Let's Look & See: Canadian Animals. 2014. (ENG., Illus.). 24p. (J). (gr. -1-k). bds. 6.99 *(978-1-86147-377-6(X)*, Armadillo) Anness Publishing GBR. Dist: National Bk. Network.

Anness Punlishing. Busy Little People: Fun Pictures & Games for Babies & Toddlers! 2015. (Illus.). 48p. (J). (gr. k-1). bds. 9.99 *(978-1-86147-629-6(9)*, Armadillo) Anness Publishing GBR. Dist: National Bk. Network.

—My First Book of the 50 States of America: With Maps, Dates & Fun Facts! 2015. (ENG., Illus.). 54p. (J). (gr. -1-4). bds. 9.99 *(978-1-86147-628-9(0)*, Armadillo) Anness Publishing GBR. Dist: National Bk. Network.

Anthony, Michelle & Lindert, Reyna. Signing Smart: My First Signs. 2009. (Signing Smart Ser.). (ENG.). 14p. (J). (gr. -1 — 1). 7.99 *(978-0-545-10924-6(8)*, Cartwheel Bks.) Scholastic, Inc.

Antle, Bhagavan "Doc". The Safari Circle: Animal Pals: Lift the Flap. 2018. (ENG., Illus.). 10p. (J). bds. 9.99 *(978-1-68383-194-5(2))* Insight Editions.

—The Safari Circle: Big Cats: Touch & Feel. 2018. (ENG., Illus.). 10p. (J). bds. 9.99 *(978-1-68383-193-8(4)*, Earth Aware Editions) Insight Editions.

Antón, Josef. Deep in the Forest: A Seek-And-Find Adventure. Brunellière, Lucie, illus. 2017. (ENG.). 14p. (J). (gr. -1-k). bds. 17.95 *(978-1-4197-2351-3(0)*, 1161010, Abrams Appleseed) Abrams, Inc.

Antonia, Miller, illus. Baby's Very First Little Book of Bunnies. 2011. (Baby's Very First Board Bks). 10p. (J). ring bd. 6.99 *(978-0-7945-2955-0(0)*, Usborne) EDC Publishing.

—Baby's Very First Little Book of Kittens. 2011. (Baby's Very First Board Bks). 10p. (J). ring bd. 6.99 *(978-0-7945-2956-7(9)*, Usborne) EDC Publishing.

Apel, Peter. Fred Pinsocket Loves Bananas. Apel, Peter, illus. 2015. (ENG., Illus.). (J). (gr. -1). bds. 9.99 *(978-0-9907941-0-3(5))* Fred Pinsocket Productions.

Archer, Charlotte, illus. Playtime for Fox. 2017. (J). *(978-1-62885-270-7(4))* Kidsbooks, LLC.

Ariel & the Lost Whirlpool. 2013. (Illus.). (J). *(978-1-4351-4946-5(7))* Disney Pr.

Arita, Vera. Animals Sing Aloha. Louie, Ron, illus. 2009. (ENG.). 20p. (J). (gr. -1-1). bds. 7.95 *(978-1-933067-29-2(2))* Beachhouse Publishing, LLC.

Armadillo. Kittens. 2015. (Illus.). 24p. (J). (gr. -1-k). bds. 6.99 *(978-1-86147-645-6(0)*, Armadillo) Anness Publishing GBR. Dist: National Bk. Network.

—Let's Count 123: A Very First Number Book. 2015. (Illus.). 48p. (J). (gr. -1-12). bds. 9.99 *(978-1-86147-659-3(0)*, Armadillo) Anness Publishing GBR. Dist: National Bk. Network.

—Let's Learn 250 Words: A Very First Reading Book. 2016. (Illus.). 48p. (J). (gr. -1-12). bds. 9.99 *(978-1-86147-706-4(6)*, Armadillo) Anness Publishing GBR. Dist: National Bk. Network.

—Let's Look & See: Animals. 2014. (ENG., Illus.). 24p. (J). (gr. k-2). bds. 6.99 *(978-1-86147-376-9(1)*, Armadillo) Anness Publishing GBR. Dist: National Bk. Network.

—Let's Look & See: Pets. 2014. (ENG., Illus.). 24p. (J). (gr. k-2). bds. 6.99 *(978-1-86147-378-3(8)*, Armadillo) Anness Publishing GBR. Dist: National Bk. Network.

—Things That Go! Tractors Trucks Trains Planes Helicopters Balloons Ships Ferries Boats Bicycles Motorcycles Cars. 2016. (Illus.). 48p. (J). (gr. -1-12). bds. 9.99 *(978-1-86147-693-7(0)*, Armadillo) Anness Publishing GBR. Dist: National Bk. Network.

Armadillo, Jeffrey. My First Animals: Over 200 Animals to Name & Learn About. Lewis, Jan, illus. 2015. 48p. (J). (gr. -1-12). bds. 9.99 *(978-1-86147-652-4(3)*, Armadillo) Anness Publishing GBR. Dist: National Bk. Network.

Armadillo Press. Dog & Friends! A Box of Exciting Picture Books, 6 vols. 2017. (ENG., Illus.). 54p. (J). (gr. -1-12). bds. 14.99 *(978-1-86147-640-1(X)*, Armadillo) Anness Publishing GBR. Dist: National Bk. Network.

Armadillo Press Staff. Alphabet. 2018. (Illus.). 24p. (J). (gr. -1-12). bds. 6.99 *(978-1-86147-664-7(7)*, Armadillo) Anness Publishing GBR. Dist: National Bk. Network.

—A Little Box of Baby Animals: Six Cute Boardbooks Packed with Pictures!, 6 vols. 2018. (Illus.). 72p. (J). (gr. -1-12). bds. 14.99 *(978-1-86147-639-5(6)*, Armadillo) Anness Publishing GBR. Dist: National Bk. Network.

—My Book of Baby Animals: A Fun-Packed Picture & Puzzle Book for Little Ones. 2016. (Illus.). 48p. (J). (gr. -1-12). bds. 9.99 *(978-1-86147-662-3(0)*, Armadillo) Anness Publishing GBR. Dist: National Bk. Network.

—My Very First Box of Books: A Set of Six Exciting Picture Books, 6 vols. 2018. (Illus.). 72p. (J). (gr. -1-12). bds. 14.99 *(978-1-86147-739-2(2)*, Armadillo) Anness Publishing GBR. Dist: National Bk. Network.

Armadillo Publishing. Australian Animals. 2018. (Illus.). 24p. (J). (gr. -1-12). bds. 6.99 *(978-1-86147-703-3(1)*, Armadillo) Anness Publishing GBR. Dist: National Bk. Network.

Armadillo Publishing Staff. Baby's Bible Stories: The Birth of Jesus. Lewis, Jan, illus. 2015. 24p. (J). (gr. -1 — 1). pap. 6.99 *(978-1-86147-484-1(9)*, Armadillo) Anness Publishing GBR. Dist: National Bk. Network.

—This Little Pig. Lewis, Jan, illus. 2015. 24p. (J). (gr. -1-12). bds. 6.99 *(978-1-86147-486-5(5)*, Armadillo) Anness Publishing GBR. Dist: National Bk. Network.

—Words - Let's Look & See. 2015. (ENG., Illus.). 24p. (J). (gr. -1-12). bds. 6.99 *(978-1-86147-485-8(7)*, Armadillo) Anness Publishing GBR. Dist: National Bk. Network.

Arnold, Damon. I Am / Mirror Mirror. 2009. 50p. pap. 12.95 *(978-1-58909-587-8(1))* Bookstand Publishing.

Arnold, Marsha Diane. Baby Animals Take a Bath. Tildes, Phyllis Limbacher, illus. 2017. 10p. (J). (— 1). bds. 6.99 *(978-1-58089-538-5(7))* Charlesbridge Publishing, Inc.

—Baby Animals Take a Nap. Tildes, Phyllis Limbacher, illus. 2017. 10p. (J). (— 1). bds. 6.99 *(978-1-58089-539-2(5))* Charlesbridge Publishing, Inc.

Arps, Melissa. Shapes. 2006. (Illus.). (J). *(978-0-7364-2383-0(4))* Random Hse., Inc.

Arrhenius, Ingela P., illus. Bookscape Board Books: a Forest's Seasons: (Colorful Children?s Shaped Board Book, Forest Landscape Toddler Book) 2019. (Bookscape Board Bks.). (ENG.). 10p. (J). (gr. -1 — 1). bds. 8.99 *(978-1-4521-7494-5(6))* Chronicle Bks. LLC.

—Bookscape Board Books: a Marvelous Museum: (Artist Board Book, Colorful Art Museum Toddler Book) 2019. (Bookscape Board Bks.). (ENG.). 10p. (J). (gr. -1 — 1). bds. 8.99 *(978-1-4521-7492-1(X))* Chronicle Bks. LLC.

—Bookscape Board Books: Christmas Cheer. 2020. (Bookscape Board Bks.). (ENG.). 10p. (J). (gr. -1 — 1). bds. 8.99 *(978-1-4521-7491-4(1))* Chronicle Bks. LLC.

—Bookscape Board Books: Fun at the Fair: (Lift the Flap Book, Block Books for Preschool) 2020. (Bookscape Board Bks.). (ENG.). 10p. (J). (gr. -1 — 1). bds. 8.99 *(978-1-4521-7493-8(8))* Chronicle Bks. LLC.

—Where's Santa Claus? 2018. (Where's The Ser.). (ENG.). 10p. (J). (— 1). bds. 9.99 *(978-1-5362-0697-5(0))* Candlewick Pr.

—Where's the Bear? 2018. (Where's The Ser.). (ENG.). 10p. (J). (— 1). bds. 9.99 *(978-1-5362-0251-9(7))* Candlewick Pr.

—Where's the Hen? 2017. (Where's The Ser.). (ENG.). 10p. (J). (— 1). bds. 8.99 *(978-0-7636-9640-5(4))* Candlewick Pr.

—Where's the Owl? 2017. (Where's The Ser.). (ENG.). 10p. (J). (— 1). bds. 8.99 *(978-0-7636-9639-9(0))* Candlewick Pr.

—Where's the Penguin? 2018. (Where's The Ser.). (ENG.). 10p. (J). (— 1). bds. 8.99 *(978-1-5362-0250-2(9))* Candlewick Pr.

—Where's the Unicorn? 2018. (Where's The Ser.). (ENG.). 10p. (J). (— 1). bds. 9.99 *(978-1-5362-0696-8(2))* Candlewick Pr.

Arrowsmith, Vicky. Sticker Dolly Dressing Costumes & Parties. 2012. (Sticker Dolly Dressing Ser.). 24p. (J). pap. 8.99 *(978-0-7945-3134-8(2)*, Usborne) EDC Publishing.

Ashdown, Rebecca. Bob & Flo Play Hide-And-Seek Board Book. 2017. (ENG., Illus.). 26p. (J). (— 1). bds. 7.99 *(978-0-544-85959-3(6)*, 1648584, Clarion Bks.) HarperCollins Pubs.

Ashford, Rachel. My First Santa's Coming to My House. Dunn, Robert, illus. 2015. (Santa Claus Is on His Way Ser.). (ENG.). 18p. (J). (gr. -1-k). bds. 9.99 *(978-1-4926-2885-9(9)*, Hometown World) Sourcebooks, Inc.

Assell, Emily. Tonight: A Book of God's Bedtime Promises. Copple, Lauren, illus. 2019. (Generation Claimed Ser.). (ENG.). 20p. (J). bds. 7.99 *(978-1-4964-3624-5(5)*, 20_32346, Tyndale Kids) Tyndale Hse. Pubs.

Atkinson, Cale. Where Oliver Fits. 2019. (Illus.). 38p. (J). (gr. -1-2). bds. 9.99 *(978-0-7352-6511-0(9)*, Tundra Bks.) Tundra Bks. CAN. Dist: Penguin Random Hse. LLC.

Atteberry, Kevan. Bunnies!!! Board Book: An Easter & Springtime Book for Kids. Atteberry, Kevan, illus. 2018. (ENG., Illus.). 34p. (J). (gr. -1 — 1). bds. 7.99 *(978-0-06-274141-7(1)*, HarperFestival) HarperCollins Pubs.

Au, May Parker. Princess Huilua & Kamapuaa. 2007.Tr. of Ke Kamalii Wahine o Huilua a me Kamapuaa. (ENG & HAW.). (J). lib. bdg. *(978-0-9773495-4-8(3))* Na Kamalei Koolauloa Early Education Program.

Auerbach, Annie. Cindy Big Hair: A Twisted (and Teased & Braided) Cinderella Story. Maxey, David, illus. 2005. 16p. (J). 12.95 *(978-1-58117-387-1(3)*, Intervisual/Piggy Toes) Bendon, Inc.

—Furry Bunny. Rigo, Laura, illus. 2018. (ENG.). 10p. (J). (gr. -1-k). bds. 7.99 *(978-1-4380-5011-9(9))* Sourcebooks, Inc.

—Furry Lamb. Rigo, Laura, illus. 2018. (ENG.). 10p. (J). (gr. -1-k). bds. 5.99 *(978-1-4380-5013-3(5))* Sourcebooks, Inc.

—I Can Be Anything! (Peppa Pig) EOne, illus. 2018. (ENG.). 16p. (J). (gr. -1-k). bds. 7.99 *(978-1-338-22883-0(8))* Scholastic, Inc.

Augarde, Steve. Garage: A Pop-up Book. Augarde, Steve, illus. 2005. (Illus.). 10p. (J). (gr. k-4). reprint ed. 15.00 *(978-0-7567-9299-2(1))* DIANE Publishing Co.

Ault, Kelly. Let's Sign, Baby! A Fun & Easy Way to Talk with Baby. Landry, Leo, illus. abr. ed. 2010. (ENG.). 40p. (J). (gr. k — 1). bds. 9.99 *(978-0-547-31596-6(1)*, 1415353, Clarion Bks.) HarperCollins Pubs.

Austin, Richard, photos by. Pocket Piggies Colors! Featuring the Teacup Pigs of Pennywell Farm. 2014. (ENG., Illus.). 22p. (J). (gr. -1 — 1). bds. 5.95 *(978-0-7611-7980-1(1)*, 17980) Workman Publishing Co., Inc.

—Pocket Piggies Numbers! Featuring the Teacup Pigs of Pennywell Farm. 2014. (ENG., Illus.). 22p. (J). (gr. -1 — 1). bds. 5.95 *(978-0-7611-7979-5(8)*, 17979) Workman Publishing Co., Inc.

Austin, Ruth. Hide Seek Stinky Sweet: a Little Book of Opposites: Board Book. 2018. (ENG., Illus.). (gr. -1-k). bds. 12.95 *(978-1-946873-08-8(X))* Compendium, Inc., Publishing & Communications.

Award, Anna. Bathtime: A Teach Your Toddler Tab Book. 2017. (ENG., Illus.). 8p. (J). bds. 8.00 *(978-1-909763-25-8(X))* Award Pubns. Ltd. GBR. Dist: Parkwest Pubns., Inc.

Awdry, W. Go, Go, Thomas! 2013. (Thomas & Friends 8X8 Ser.). lib. bdg. 14.75 *(978-0-606-26992-6(4))* Turtleback.

—Thomas & Friends: My Red Railway Book Box (Thomas & Friends) Go, Train, GO!; Stop, Train, Stop!; a Crack in the Track!; & Blue Train, Green Train, 4 vols. Stubbs, Tommy, illus. 2008. (Bright & Early Board Books(TM) Ser.). (ENG.). 96p. (J). (— 1). bds. 16.99 *(978-0-375-84322-8(1)*, Random Hse. Bks. for Young Readers) Random Hse. Children's Bks.

Awdry, Wilbert V. Good Night, Thomas (Thomas & Friends) Random House Staff, illus. 2012. (ENG.). 12p. (J). (gr. k-k). bds. 7.99 *(978-0-307-97697-0(1)*, Random Hse. Bks. for Young Readers) Random Hse. Children's Bks.

AZ Books. Babies. 2013. (Guess What? Ser.). (ENG.). 10p. (J). (gr. -1 — 1). 5.95 *(978-1-61889-316-1(5))* AZ Bks. LLC.

—Big Knowledge Book. 2013. (Smart Pad Ser.). (ENG.). 14p. (J). (gr. -1-k). bds. 19.95 *(978-1-61889-444-1(7))* AZ Bks. LLC.

—Big Zoo Book. 2013. (Smart Pad Ser.). (ENG.). 14p. (J). (gr. -1-k). bds. 19.95 *(978-1-61889-418-2(8))* AZ Bks. LLC.

—Forest Animals. 2012. (Touch & Feel Ser.). (ENG.). 10p. (J). (— 1). bds. 12.95 *(978-1-61889-222-5(3))* AZ Bks. LLC.

—Forest Life. 2013. (Matching Pictures Ser.). (ENG.). 20p. (J). (gr. -1-k). spiral bd. 5.95 *(978-1-61889-308-6(4))* AZ Bks. LLC.

—Fruits. 2013. (Guess What? Ser.). (ENG.). 10p. (J). (— 1). bds. 5.95 *(978-1-61889-318-5(1))* AZ Bks. LLC.

—Prints. 2013. (Guess What? Ser.). (ENG.). 10p. (J). (— 1). bds. 5.95 *(978-1-61889-315-4(7))* AZ Bks. LLC.

—Tiger & His Stripes. 2013. (Amusing Stories Ser.). (ENG.). 10p. (J). (-k). bds. 7.95 *(978-1-61889-307-9(6))* AZ Bks. LLC.

AZ Books, creator. Brave & Smart. 2013. (Look at Me! Ser.). (ENG., Illus.). 10p. (J). (gr. -1-k). bds. 10.95 *(978-1-61889-393-2(9))* AZ Bks. LLC.

—Farm Animals. 2012. (Touch & Feel Ser.). (ENG., Illus.). 10p. (J). (gr. -1 — 1). bds. 12.95 *(978-1-61889-223-2(1))* AZ Bks. LLC.

—Kitten Searches for a Friend. 2012. (Plush Baby Ser.). (ENG., Illus.). 10p. (J). (gr. -1 — 1). bds. 11.95 *(978-1-61889-219-5(3))* AZ Bks. LLC.

—Lake Animals Moving & Talking. 2012. (Funny Trails Ser.). (ENG., Illus.). 10p. (J). (gr. -1-k). bds. 9.95 *(978-1-61889-216-4(9))* AZ Bks. LLC.

—Lamb Searches for Her Mom. 2012. (Plush Baby Ser.). (ENG., Illus.). 10p. (J). (gr. -1 — 1). 11.95 *(978-1-61889-218-8(5))* AZ Bks. LLC.

—Magic Machines. 2012. (Baby Book Ser.). (ENG., Illus.). 10p. (J). (gr. -1 — 1). bds. 4.95 *(978-1-61889-286-7(X))* AZ Bks. LLC.

—Pond Animals. 2013. (Touch & Feel Ser.). (ENG., Illus.). 10p. (J). (gr. -1-k). bds. 12.95 *(978-1-61889-224-9(X))* AZ Bks. LLC.

—Talking Train. 2012. (Lively Machines Ser.). (ENG., Illus.). 10p. (J). (gr. -1-k). bds. 10.95 *(978-1-61889-325-3(4))* AZ Bks. LLC.

—Tyler Turtle Travels to Australia. 2013. (Pop-Up: Play & Listen Ser.). (ENG., Illus.). 10p. (J). (gr. -1-k). bds. 16.95 *(978-1-61889-036-8(0))* AZ Bks. LLC.

—Walk Around a Farm. 2012. (Put Together Ser.). (ENG., Illus.). 16p. (J). (gr. -1-k). spiral bd. 6.95 *(978-1-61889-189-1(8))* AZ Bks. LLC.

—Water Animals. 2013. (Sounds Around Us Ser.). (ENG., Illus.). 16p. (J). (gr. 1-3). bds. 17.95 *(978-1-61889-283-6(5))* AZ Bks. LLC.

—What Color? 2012. (Smarty Ser.). (ENG., Illus.). 10p. (J). (gr. -1 — 1). 9.95 *(978-1-61889-249-2(5))* AZ Bks. LLC.

—What Number? 2012. (Smarty Ser.). (ENG., Illus.). 10p. (J). (gr. -1 — 1). 9.95 *(978-1-61889-248-5(7))* AZ Bks. LLC.

AZ Books Staff. About the Human Body. Petrovskaya, Olga, ed. 2012. (Million Whys Ser.). (ENG.). 12p. (J). (gr. -1-4). bds. 18.95 *(978-1-61889-058-0(1))* AZ Bks. LLC.

—Amazing Space. Ivinskaya, Snezhana, ed. 2012. (Encyclopedia with Flaps Ser.). (ENG.). 22p. (J). (gr. 1-3). bds. 13.95 *(978-1-61889-150-1(2))* AZ Bks. LLC.

—Animals. Slusar, Julia, ed. 2012. (Pull It Out Ser.). (ENG.). 10p. (J). (gr. -1 — 1). 7.95 *(978-1-61889-195-2(2))* AZ Bks. LLC.
—Babbling Pond. Tulup, Natalia, ed. 2012. (How We Speak Ser.). (ENG.). 12p. (J). (gr. -1-k). bds. 10.95 *(978-1-61889-097-9(2))* AZ Bks. LLC.
—Bear's Forest. Potapenko, Olga, ed. 2012. (Talking Plush Animals Ser.). (ENG.). 10p. (J). (gr. -1-k). bds. 10.95 *(978-1-61889-111-2(1))* AZ Bks. LLC.
—Busy Insects Moving & Talking. Dubovik, Ludmila, ed. 2012. (Funny Trails Ser.). (ENG.). 10p. (J). (gr. -1-k). bds. 9.95 *(978-1-61889-175-4(8))* AZ Bks. LLC.
—Buzzing Meadow. Tulup, Natalia, ed. 2012. (How We Speak Ser.). (ENG.). 12p. (J). (gr. -1-k). bds. 10.95 *(978-1-61889-095-5(6))* AZ Bks. LLC.
—Cinderella. Zyl, Olga, ed. 2012. (Classic Fairy Tales Ser.). (ENG.). 10p. (J). (gr. -1-k). bds. 9.95 *(978-1-61889-007-8(7))* AZ Bks. LLC.
—Colores - Colorful Animals: Colorful Animals. Gorbachenok, Ekaterina, ed. 2012. (Spanish for Kids Ser.). (ENG & SPA.). 10p. (J). (gr. -1-k). bds. 11.95 *(978-1-61889-136-5(7))* AZ Bks. LLC.
—Colors. Slusar, Julia, ed. 2012. (Pull It Out Ser.). (ENG.). 10p. (J). (gr. -1 — 1). 7.95 *(978-1-61889-193-8(6))* AZ Bks. LLC.
—Colors & Shapes. Petrovskaya, Olga, ed. 2012. (Matching Game Ser.). (ENG.). 18p. (J). (gr. -1-k). spiral bd. 4.95 *(978-1-61889-201-0(0))* AZ Bks. LLC.
—Countries & People. Borovik, Alija et al, eds. 2013. (Little Genius Ser.). (ENG.). 150p. (J). (gr. 1-3). bds. 19.95 *(978-1-61889-139-6(1))* AZ Bks. LLC.
—Discoveries & Inventions. Kazimirova, Karina, ed. 2012. (Encyclopedia with Flaps Ser.). (ENG.). 22p. (J). (gr. 1-3). bds. 13.95 *(978-1-61889-152-5(9))* AZ Bks. LLC.
—Discovering the Savanna. Gorojan, Elena, ed. 2012. (Wild Theater Ser.). (ENG.). 8p. (J). (gr. -1-3). bds. 17.95 *(978-1-61889-017-7(4))* AZ Bks. LLC.
—Exploring the Ocean. Vasilkova, Elena, ed. 2012. (Wild Theater Ser.). (ENG.). 8p. (J). (gr. -1-3). bds. 17.95 *(978-1-61889-020-7(4))* AZ Bks. LLC.
—Farm Animals. Gorojan, Elena, ed. 2012. (My First Library). (ENG.). 12p. (J). (gr. -1-k). bds. 8.95 *(978-1-61889-123-5(5))* AZ Bks. LLC.
—Farm Animals Moving & Talking. Harko, Lubov, ed. 2012. (Funny Trails Ser.). (ENG.). 10p. (J). (gr. -1-k). bds. 9.95 *(978-1-61889-174-7(X))* AZ Bks. LLC.
—Fashion Ideas. Batan, Natalia, ed. 2012. (Fashion Ideas Ser.). (ENG.). 60p. (J). bds. 15.95 *(978-1-61889-075-7(1))* AZ Bks. LLC.
—Fast Cars. Tulup, Natasha, ed. 2012. (Workshop Ser.). (ENG.). 10p. (J). (gr. -1-k). bds. 10.95 *(978-1-61889-161-7(8))* AZ Bks. LLC.
—Fast Vehicles Moving & Talking. Harko, Lubov, ed. 2012. (Funny Trails Ser.). (ENG.). 10p. (J). (gr. -1-k). bds. 9.95 *(978-1-61889-177-8(4))* AZ Bks. LLC.
—Feathered Singers. Tulup, Natalia, ed. 2012. (How We Speak Ser.). (ENG.). 12p. (J). (gr. -1-k). bds. 10.95 *(978-1-61889-096-2(4))* AZ Bks. LLC.
—Find a Pair. Petrovskaya, Olga, ed. 2012. (Matching Game Ser.). (ENG.). 18p. (J). (gr. -1-k). spiral bd. 4.95 *(978-1-61889-009-2(3))* AZ Bks. LLC.
—Find My Food & Home. Petrovskaya, Olga, ed. 2012. (Matching Game Ser.). (ENG.). 18p. (J). (gr. -1-k). spiral bd. 4.95 *(978-1-61889-010-8(7))* AZ Bks. LLC.
—Flying Planes. Tulup, Natasha, ed. 2012. (Workshop Ser.). (ENG.). 10p. (J). (gr. -1-k). 10.95 *(978-1-61889-159-4(6))* AZ Bks. LLC.
—Forest Animals. Gorojan, Elena, ed. 2012. (My First Library). (ENG.). 12p. (J). (gr. -1-k). bds. 8.95 *(978-1-61889-120-4(0))* AZ Bks. LLC.
—Forest Animals Moving & Talking. Dubovik, Ludmila, ed. 2012. (Funny Trails Ser.). (ENG.). 10p. (J). (gr. -1-k). bds. 9.95 *(978-1-61889-176-1(6))* AZ Bks. LLC.
—Frog's Pond. Potapenko, Olga, ed. 2012. (Talking Plush Animals Ser.). (ENG.). 10p. (J). (gr. -1-k). bds. 10.95 *(978-1-61889-113-6(8))* AZ Bks. LLC.
—Fruits & Vegetables. Slusar, Julia, ed. 2012. (Pull It Out Ser.). (ENG.). 10p. (J). (— 1). 7.95 *(978-1-61889-192-1(8))* AZ Bks. LLC.
—Great Warriors. Aksinovich, Natalia & Yaroshevich, Angelica, eds. 2012. (Sounds Around Us Ser.). (ENG.). 16p. (J). (gr. 1-3). bds. 17.95 *(978-1-61889-033-7(6))* AZ Bks. LLC.
—Hello, I'm Bear! Gorbachenok, Ekaterina, ed. 2012. (Who Lives in the Book? Ser.). (ENG.). 10p. (J). (-k). bds. 11.95 *(978-1-61889-070-2(0))* AZ Bks. LLC.
—Hello, I'm Horse! Gorbachenok, Ekaterina, ed. 2012. (Who Lives in the Book? Ser.). (ENG.). 10p. (J). (-k). bds. 11.95 *(978-1-61889-069-6(7))* AZ Bks. LLC.
—History & Discoveries. Shumovich, Nadegda et al, eds. 2013. (Little Genius Ser.). (ENG.). 150p. (J). (gr. 1-3). bds. 19.95 *(978-1-61889-138-9(3))* AZ Bks. LLC.
—Horse's Farm. Potapenko, Olga, ed. 2012. (Talking Plush Animals Ser.). (ENG.). 10p. (J). (gr. -1-k). bds. 10.95 *(978-1-61889-112-9(X))* AZ Bks. LLC.
—In the Forest. Ulasevich, Olga & Goncharik, Irina, eds. 2012. (Animal Sounds Ser.). (ENG.). 14p. (J). (gr. -1-k). bds. 7.95 *(978-1-61889-126-6(X))* AZ Bks. LLC.
—In the Jungle. Efimova, Tatiana, ed. 2012. (Animal Sounds Ser.). (ENG.). 14p. (J). (gr. -1-k). bds. 7.95 *(978-1-61889-125-9(1))* AZ Bks. LLC.
—In the Prairie & Desert. Efimova, Tatiana & Goncharik, Irina, eds. 2012. (Animal Sounds Ser.). (ENG.). 14p. (J). (gr. -1-k). bds. 7.95 *(978-1-61889-128-0(6))* AZ Bks. LLC.
—In the Savanna. Ulasevich, Olga & Migits, Anna, eds. 2012. (Animal Sounds Ser.). (ENG.). 14p. (J). (-k). bds. 7.95 *(978-1-61889-124-2(3))* AZ Bks. LLC.
—In the Sea & Ocean. Efimova, Tatiana, ed. 2012. (Animal Sounds Ser.). (ENG.). 14p. (J). (-k). bds. 7.95 *(978-1-61889-127-3(8))* AZ Bks. LLC.
—Jungle Animals. Gorojan, Elena, ed. 2012. (My First Library). (ENG.). 12p. (J). (-k). bds. 8.95 *(978-1-61889-121-1(9))* AZ Bks. LLC.
—Little Thumb. Zyl, Olga, ed. 2012. (Classic Fairy Tales Ser.). (ENG.). 10p. (J). (gr. -1-k). bds. 9.95 *(978-1-61889-008-5(5))* AZ Bks. LLC.
—Living Book of Dinosaurs. Latushko, Julia, ed. 2012. (Our Amazing World Ser.). (ENG.). 12p. (J). (gr. 1-3). bds. 19.95 *(978-1-61889-025-2(5))* AZ Bks. LLC.
—Living Book of the Forest. Vasilkova, Elena, ed. 2012. (Our Amazing World Ser.). (ENG.). 12p. (J). (gr. 1-3). bds. 19.95 *(978-1-61889-022-1(0))* AZ Bks. LLC.
—Living Book of the Jungle. Gasteva, Julia, ed. 2012. (Our Amazing World Ser.). (ENG.). 12p. (J). (gr. 1-3). bds. 19.95 *(978-1-61889-024-5(7))* AZ Bks. LLC.
—Living Book of the Ocean. Aksinovich, Natalia, ed. 2012. (Our Amazing World Ser.). (ENG.). 12p. (J). (gr. 1-3). bds. 19.95 *(978-1-61889-021-4(2))* AZ Bks. LLC.
—Loud Farm. Tulup, Natalia, ed. 2012. (How We Speak Ser.). (ENG.). 12p. (J). (-k). bds. 10.95 *(978-1-61889-093-1(X))* AZ Bks. LLC.
—Making Machines. Sisoj, Natalja, ed. 2012. (Modeling Clay Bks.). (ENG.). 12p. (J). (gr. -1-2). bds. 10.95 *(978-1-61889-198-3(7))* AZ Bks. LLC.
—Making the Farm. Sisoj, Natalja, ed. 2012. (Modeling Clay Bks.). (ENG.). 12p. (J). (gr. -1-2). bds. 10.95 *(978-1-61889-197-6(9))* AZ Bks. LLC.
—Making the Forest. Sisoj, Natalja, ed. 2012. (Modeling Clay Bks.). (ENG.). 12p. (J). (gr. -1-2). bds. 10.95 *(978-1-61889-199-0(5))* AZ Bks. LLC.
—Meeting Dinosaurs. Vasilkova, Elena, ed. 2012. (Wild Theater Ser.). (ENG.). 8p. (J). (gr. -1-3). bds. 17.95 *(978-1-61889-019-1(0))* AZ Bks. LLC.
—Merry Orchestra. Tulup, Natalia, ed. 2012. (Tra-La-la Ser.). (ENG.). 14p. (J). (-k). bds. 10.95 *(978-1-61889-056-6(5))* AZ Bks. LLC.
—Movie Star. Puzik, Ulijana, ed. 2012. (Lovely Charmie Ser.). (ENG.). 16p. (J). (gr. 1-3). pap. 6.95 *(978-1-61889-184-6(7))* AZ Bks. LLC.
—Musical Animals. Tulup, Natalia, ed. 2012. (Tra-La-la Ser.). (ENG.). 14p. (J). (-k). bds. 10.95 *(978-1-61889-057-3(3))* AZ Bks. LLC.
—Musical Machines. Tulup, Natalia, ed. 2012. (Tra-La-la Ser.). (ENG.). 14p. (J). (-k). bds. 10.95 *(978-1-61889-055-9(7))* AZ Bks. LLC.
—My Farm. Yaroshevich, Angelica, ed. 2012. (Open the Book-I Am Alive Ser.). (ENG.). 8p. (J). (— 1). bds. 5.95 *(978-1-61889-043-6(3))* AZ Bks. LLC.
—My Forest. Yaroshevich, Angelica, ed. 2012. (Open the Book-I Am Alive Ser.). (ENG.). 8p. (J). (— 1). bds. 5.95 *(978-1-61889-042-9(5))* AZ Bks. LLC.
—My Pets. Yaroshevich, Angelica, ed. 2012. (Open the Book-I Am Alive Ser.). (ENG.). 8p. (J). (— 1). bds. 5.95 *(978-1-61889-045-0(X))* AZ Bks. LLC.
—My Pond. Yaroshevich, Angelica, ed. 2012. (Open the Book-I Am Alive Ser.). (ENG.). 8p. (J). (— 1). bds. 5.95 *(978-1-61889-046-7(8))* AZ Bks. LLC.
—My Zoo. Yaroshevich, Angelica, ed. 2012. (Open the Book-I Am Alive Ser.). (ENG.). 8p. (J). (— 1). bds. 5.95 *(978-1-61889-044-3(1))* AZ Bks. LLC.
—Ocean Animals. Gorojan, Elena, ed. 2012. (My First Library). (ENG.). 12p. (J). (gr. -1-k). bds. 8.95 *(978-1-61889-119-8(7))* AZ Bks. LLC.
—On the Farm. Ulasevich, Olga, ed. 2012. (Animal Sounds Ser.). (ENG.). 14p. (J). (-k). bds. 7.95 *(978-1-61889-129-7(4))* AZ Bks. LLC.
—Our Cozy Forest. Zayceva, Irina, ed. 2012. (Hook-And-Loop-Pictures Ser.). (ENG.). 8p. (J). (-k). bds. 11.95 *(978-1-61889-157-0(X))* AZ Bks. LLC.
—Our Faraway Jungle. Zayceva, Irina, ed. 2012. (Hook-And-Loop-Pictures Ser.). (ENG.). 12p. (J). (-k). bds. 11.95 *(978-1-61889-158-7(8))* AZ Bks. LLC.
—Our Friendly Farm. Zayceva, Irina, ed. 2012. (Hook-And-Loop-Pictures Ser.). (ENG.). 8p. (J). (-k). bds. 11.95 *(978-1-61889-156-3(1))* AZ Bks. LLC.
—Polar Animals. Gorojan, Elena, ed. 2012. (My First Library). (ENG.). 12p. (J). (-k). bds. 8.95 *(978-1-61889-122-8(7))* AZ Bks. LLC.
—Sailing Ships. Tulup, Natasha, ed. 2012. (Workshop Ser.). (ENG.). 10p. (J). (gr. -1-k). bds. 10.95 *(978-1-61889-162-4(6))* AZ Bks. LLC.
—Sam the Auto Mechanic. Boroda, Janna, ed. 2012. (Little Master Ser.). (ENG.). 10p. (J). (gr. -1-k). bds. 10.95 *(978-1-61889-148-8(0))* AZ Bks. LLC.
—Sam the Builder. Boroda, Janna, ed. 2012. (Little Master Ser.). (ENG.). 10p. (J). (gr. -1-k). bds. 10.95 *(978-1-61889-147-1(2))* AZ Bks. LLC.
—Sam the Constructor. Boroda, Janna, ed. 2012. (Little Master Ser.). (ENG.). 10p. (J). (gr. -1-k). bds. 10.95 *(978-1-61889-149-5(9))* AZ Bks. LLC.
—Savanna Animals. Gorojan, Elena, ed. 2012. (My First Library). (ENG.). 12p. (J). (-k). bds. 8.95 *(978-1-61889-118-1(9))* AZ Bks. LLC.
—Scouting the Forest. Vasilkova, Elena, ed. 2012. (Wild Theater Ser.). (ENG.). 8p. (J). (gr. -1-3). bds. 17.95 *(978-1-61889-018-4(2))* AZ Bks. LLC.
—Secrets of Pirates. Naumovets, Elena, ed. 2012. (Mysteries of History Ser.). (ENG.). 18p. (J). (gr. 1-3). bds. 17.95 *(978-1-61889-089-4(1))* AZ Bks. LLC.
—Shapes. Slusar, Julia, ed. 2012. (Pull It Out Ser.). (ENG.). 10p. (J). (— 1). 7.95 *(978-1-61889-194-5(4))* AZ Bks. LLC.
—Sleeping Beauty. Zyl, Olga, ed. 2012. (Classic Fairy Tales Ser.). (ENG.). 10p. (J). (gr. -1-k). bds. 9.95 *(978-1-61889-006-1(9))* AZ Bks. LLC.
—Sounds of Dinosaurs. Yaroshevich, Angelica, ed. 2012. (Sounds Around Us Ser.). (ENG.). 16p. (J). (gr. 1-3). bds. 17.95 *(978-1-61889-027-6(1))* AZ Bks. LLC.
—Sounds of the Farm. Sheljagovich, Yana, ed. 2012. (Sounds Around Us Ser.). (ENG.). 16p. (J). (gr. 1-3). bds. 17.95 *(978-1-61889-029-0(8))* AZ Bks. LLC.
—Sounds of the Forest. Sheljagovich, Yana, ed. 2012. (Sounds Around Us Ser.). (ENG.). 16p. (J). (gr. 1-3). bds. 17.95 *(978-1-61889-028-3(X))* AZ Bks. LLC.
—Sounds of the Jungle. Migiz, Anna, ed. 2012. (Sounds Around Us Ser.). (ENG.). 16p. (J). (gr. 1-3). bds. 17.95 *(978-1-61889-030-6(1))* AZ Bks. LLC.
—Sounds of the Savanna & Desert. Migiz, Anna, ed. 2012. (Sounds Around Us Ser.). (ENG.). 16p. (J). (gr. 1-3). bds. 17.95 *(978-1-61889-031-3(X))* AZ Bks. LLC.
—Sounds of Wild Nature. Naumovets, Elena, ed. 2012. (Sounds Around Us Ser.). (ENG.). 16p. (J). (gr. 1-3). bds. 17.95 *(978-1-61889-026-9(3))* AZ Bks. LLC.
—Sparrow's Yard. Potapenko, Olga, ed. 2012. (Talking Plush Animals Ser.). (ENG.). 10p. (J). (gr. -1-k). bds. 10.95 *(978-1-61889-114-3(6))* AZ Bks. LLC.
—Terribly Funny Monsters. Shumovich, Nadezhda, ed. 2012. (Terribly Funny Monsters Ser.). (ENG.). 10p. (J). (gr. -1-1). bds. 15.95 *(978-1-61889-133-4(2))* AZ Bks. LLC.
—Visiting Africa. Zuk, Valentina, ed. 2012. (Lively Pictures Ser.). (ENG.). 10p. (J). (gr. -1-k). bds. 9.95 *(978-1-61889-179-2(0))* AZ Bks. LLC.
—Visiting Dinosaurs. Vol, Vera, ed. 2012. (Lively Pictures Ser.). (ENG.). 10p. (J). (gr. -1-k). bds. 9.95 *(978-1-61889-181-5(2))* AZ Bks. LLC.
—Visiting the Farm. Zuk, Valentina, ed. 2012. (Lively Pictures Ser.). (ENG.). 10p. (J). (gr. -1-k). bds. 9.95 *(978-1-61889-182-2(0))* AZ Bks. LLC.
—Visiting the Forest. Zuk, Valentina, ed. 2012. (Lively Pictures Ser.). (ENG.). 10p. (J). (gr. -1-k). bds. 9.95 *(978-1-61889-178-5(2))* AZ Bks. LLC.
—Visiting the Ocean. Lukjanenko, Anna, ed. 2012. (Lively Pictures Ser.). (ENG.). 10p. (J). (gr. -1-1). bds. 9.95 *(978-1-61889-180-8(4))* AZ Bks. LLC.
—What Do I Eat? Sisoj, Natalja, ed. 2012. (Peek-A-Boo Ser.). (ENG.). 10p. (J). (— 1). bds. 10.95 *(978-1-61889-115-0(4))* AZ Bks. LLC.
—Where's My Baby? Sisoj, Natalja, ed. 2012. (Peek-A-Boo Ser.). (ENG.). 10p. (J). (— 1). bds. 10.95 *(978-1-61889-117-4(0))* AZ Bks. LLC.
—Where's My Toy? Sisoj, Natalja, ed. 2012. (Peek-A-Boo Ser.). (ENG.). 10p. (J). (— 1). bds. 10.95 *(978-1-61889-116-7(2))* AZ Bks. LLC.
—Who Is the Bear Looking For? Sharipovas, Alesja, ed. 2012. (Who Is There Ser.). (ENG.). 10p. (J). (-k). bds. 11.95 *(978-1-61889-039-9(5))* AZ Bks. LLC.
—Who Is the Hare Looking For? Zajceva, Ira, ed. 2012. (Who Is There Ser.). (ENG.). 10p. (J). (-k). bds. 11.95 *(978-1-61889-040-5(9))* AZ Bks. LLC.
—Who Is the Lion Looking For? Shestakova, Anna, ed. 2012. (Who Is There Ser.). (ENG.). 10p. (J). (-k). bds. 11.95 *(978-1-61889-041-2(7))* AZ Bks. LLC.
—Who Is the Puppy Looking For? Gridina, Anna, ed. 2012. (Who Is There Ser.). (ENG.). 10p. (J). (-k). bds. 11.95 *(978-1-61889-038-2(7))* AZ Bks. LLC.
—Who Is the Tiger Looking For? Gridina, Anna, ed. 2012. (Who Is There Ser.). (ENG.). 10p. (J). (-k). bds. 11.95 *(978-1-61889-037-5(9))* AZ Bks. LLC.
—Who Lives in the Jungle? Gridina, Anna, ed. 2012. (Funny Animals Ser.). (ENG.). 10p. (J). (-k). bds. 8.95 *(978-1-61889-048-1(4))* AZ Bks. LLC.
—Who Lives in the Pond? Gridina, Anna, ed. 2012. (Funny Animals Ser.). (ENG.). 10p. (J). (-k). bds. 8.95 *(978-1-61889-049-8(2))* AZ Bks. LLC.
—Who Lives in the Savanna? Gridina, Anna, ed. 2012. (Funny Animals Ser.). (ENG.). 10p. (J). (-k). bds. 8.95 *(978-1-61889-050-4(6))* AZ Bks. LLC.
—Who Lives on a Farm? Gridina, Anna, ed. 2012. (Funny Animals Ser.). (ENG.). 10p. (J). (-k). bds. 8.95 *(978-1-61889-047-4(6))* AZ Bks. LLC.
—Wild Nature. Kokash, Elena et al, eds. 2013. (Little Genius Ser.). (ENG.). 150p. (J). (gr. 1-3). bds. 19.95 *(978-1-61889-140-2(5))* AZ Bks. LLC.

AZ Books Staff & Evans, Olivia. Haunted Castle. Shumovich, Nadezhda, ed. 2012. (Terribly Funny Monsters Ser.). (ENG., Illus.). 10p. (J). bds. 15.95 *(978-1-61889-134-1(0))* AZ Bks. LLC.
—Making the Zoo. Sisoj, Natalja, ed. 2012. (Modeling Clay Bk Ser.). (ENG., Illus.). 12p. (J). (gr. -1-2). bds. 10.95 *(978-1-61889-196-9(0))* AZ Bks. LLC.

B&H Kids Editorial Staff. Braving the Big Battle with the Baroness / Repelling the Ronin of Wrong, Flip-Over Book. 2016. (Bibleman Ser.). (ENG., Illus.). 32p. (J). (gr. -1-2). pap. 3.99 *(978-1-4336-4573-0(4)*, 005788236, B&H Kids) B&H Publishing Group.
—Easter, Board Book. Conger, Holli, illus. 2017. (Little Words Matter(tm) Ser.). (ENG.). 24p. (J). (gr. -1 — 1). bds. 8.99 *(978-1-4336-4453-5(3)*, 005787711, B&H Kids) B&H Publishing Group.
—1, 2, 3 God Made Me. Conger, Holli, illus. 2018. (Little Words Matter(tm) Ser.). (ENG.). 22p. (J). (— 1). bds. 7.99 *(978-1-4627-7407-4(5)*, 005797599, B&H Kids) B&H Publishing Group.
—100+ Little Bible Words (padded Board Book) 2017. (Little Words Matter(tm) Ser.). (ENG., Illus.). 38p. (J). (gr. -1 — 1). bds. 12.99 *(978-1-4336-4923-3(3)*, 005791039, B&H Kids) B&H Publishing Group.

Babbott-Klein, Libby. Baby Feminists Too. 2019. (Illus.). 26p. (J). (— 1). bds. 9.99 *(978-0-451-48013-2(9)*, Viking Books for Young Readers) Penguin Young Readers Group.

Baby's Very First Touchy-Feely Christmas. 2015. (Baby's Very First Touchy-Feely Board Bks.). (ENG.). (J). 7.99 *(978-0-7945-3629-9(8)*, Usborne) EDC Publishing.

Bach, Annie. Night-Night, Forest Friends. 2018. (Illus.). 24p. (J). (-k). bds. 8.99 *(978-1-5247-8792-9(2)*, Grosset & Dunlap) Penguin Young Readers Group.
—Night-Night, Forest Friends. Bach, Annie, illus. 2013. (Illus.). 24p. (J). (gr. -1-k). bds. 9.99 *(978-0-8431-7278-2(9)*, Grosset & Dunlap) Penguin Young Readers Group.

Backpack Books (Firm) Staff, contrib. by. My Big Animal Book: Includes Touch-And-Feel, Flaps, Pull-Out Tabs, & a Puzzle! 2005. (Illus.). (J). *(978-0-7607-6966-9(4))* backpackbook.

Baggott, Stella. Baby's Very First Touchy-Feely Animals Book. 2011. (Baby's Very First Ser.). 10p. (J). ring bd. 7.99 *(978-0-7945-2895-9(3)*, Usborne) EDC Publishing.
—Baby's Very First Touchy-Feely Book. 2010. (Baby's Very First Board Bks). 10p. (J). bds. 9.99 *(978-0-7945-2647-4(0)*, Usborne) EDC Publishing.
—Baby's Very First Touchy-Feely Christmas Book. Baggott, Stella, illus. 2010. (Baby's Very First Board Bks). (Illus.). 10p. (J). bds. 6.99 *(978-0-7945-2852-2(X)*, Usborne) EDC Publishing.
—Baby's Very First Touchy-Feely Lift the Flap Play Book. 2013. (Baby's Very First Board Bks). 10p. (J). ring bd. 12.99 *(978-0-7945-3386-1(8)*, Usborne) EDC Publishing.

Baggott, Stella, illus. Baby's Very First Noisy Book Farm. 2013. (Baby's Very First Noisy Book Ser.). (ENG.). 10p. (gr. -1). 15.99 *(978-0-7945-2703-7(5)*, Usborne) EDC Publishing.

Bagley, Val. Gospel Truths from the Book of Mormon. 2004. (Seek & Ye Shall Find Flap Book Ser.). (Illus.). (J). bds. 13.95 *(978-1-59156-279-5(1))* Covenant Communications, Inc.

Bagley, Val Chadwick & Mullins, Amy. My Favorite Stories from the Bible. 2006. (Illus.). 28p. (J). *(978-1-59811-173-6(6))* Covenant Communications.
—My Favorite Stories from the Book of Mormon. 2007. (Carry-Along Lift-The-Flap Book Ser.). (Illus.). (J). *(978-1-59811-385-3(2))* Covenant Communications.

Bailey, Linda. When Santa Was a Baby. Godbout, Geneviève, illus. 2017. 30p. (J). (— 1). bds. 9.99 *(978-1-101-91916-3(7)*, Tundra Bks.) Tundra Bks. CAN. Dist: Penguin Random Hse. LLC.

Baker, Kate. Walk This Wild World. Brewster, Sam, illus. 2018. (ENG.). 24p. (J). (gr. k-3). 19.99 *(978-0-7636-9899-7(7)*, Big Picture Press) Candlewick Pr.

Baker, Keith. Little Green Peas. Baker, Keith, illus. 2016. (Peas Ser.). (ENG., Illus.). 36p. (J). (gr. -1 — 1). bds. 8.99 *(978-1-4814-6248-8(2)*, Little Simon) Little Simon.
—Quack & Count. Baker, Keith, illus. 2004. (ENG., Illus.). 24p. (J). (gr. -1 — 1). pap. 8.99 *(978-0-15-205025-2(6)*, 1195176, Clarion Bks.) HarperCollins Pubs.
—Quack & Count Baord Book. Baker, Keith, illus. 2003. (ENG., Illus.). 22p. (J). (gr. -1-k). bds. 6.95 *(978-0-15-204751-1(4)*, 1194328, Clarion Bks.) HarperCollins Pubs.

Baker, Sue. Oh Baby! Stockham, Jess, illus. 2006. (Blanket Babies Ser.). (ENG.). 12p. (J). (gr. -1-k). bds. *(978-1-904550-87-7(8))* Child's Play International Ltd.

Baker, Sue & Stockham, Jessica. Sleep Tight! Stockham, Jess, illus. 2006. (Blanket Babies Ser.). (ENG.). 12p. (J). (gr. -1-k). bds. *(978-1-904550-90-7(8))* Child's Play International Ltd.

Balas, Vincent. Where Is Your Mama? Slide & See Board Book. Durbiano, Lucie, illus. 2011. (ENG.). 8p. (J). (gr. -1-3). bds. 5.99 *(978-0-547-54807-4(9)*, 1449290, Clarion Bks.) HarperCollins Pubs.

Balas, Vincent & Durbiano, Lucie. Where Is Your Home? Slide & See Board Book. Balas, Vincent & Durbiano, Lucie, illus. 2011. (ENG., Illus.). 8p. (J). (gr. -1-3). bds. 5.99 *(978-0-547-54808-1(7)*, 1449291, Clarion Bks.) HarperCollins Pubs.

Bannister, Emily, illus. Itsy Bitsy Spider. 2016. (Touch & Trace Nursery Rhymes Ser.). (ENG.). 10p. (J). (gr. -1 — 1). bds. 7.99 *(978-1-62686-764-2(X)*, Silver Dolphin Bks.) Printers Row Publishing Group.

Barad, Alexis. Puppy Love. East, Jacqueline, illus. 2013. (J). *(978-0-545-47733-8(6))* Scholastic, Inc.

Barash, Chris. One Fine Shabbat. Mai-Wyss, Tatjana, illus. 2016. (ENG.). 12p. (J). (gr. -1 — 1). E-Book 23.99 *(978-1-4677-9614-9(X)*, Kar-Ben Publishing) Lerner Publishing Group.

Barbas, Keri, des. Travel Scratch & Sketch. 2005. (Activity Journal Ser.). (J). 12.99 *(978-0-88088-486-0(X))* Peter Pauper Pr. Inc.

Bardaus, Anna W. Bounce, Bounce, Baby! Grove, Christine, illus. 2013. (J). *(978-0-545-61897-7(5))* Scholastic, Inc.
—Dance, Dance, Baby! Grove, Christine, illus. 2013. (J). *(978-0-545-61899-1(1))* Scholastic, Inc.
—Reach, Reach, Baby! Grove, Christine, illus. 2013. (J). *(978-0-545-61900-4(9))* Scholastic, Inc.
—Read, Read, Baby! Grove, Christine, illus. 2013. (J). *(978-0-545-61898-4(3))* Scholastic, Inc.

Bardhan-Quallen, Sudipta. Tyrannosaurus Wrecks! A Preschool Story. OHora, Zachariah, illus. 2018. (ENG.). 32p. (J). (gr. -1 — 1). pap. 7.99 *(978-1-4197-3322-2(2)*, 1051110, Abrams Appleseed) Abrams, Inc.

Barefoot Books. Big & Small. Teckentrup, Britta, illus. 2013. (ENG.). 16p. (J). (gr. -1-k). bds. 7.99 *(978-1-84686-951-8(X))* Barefoot Bks., Inc.
—Fast & Slow. Teckentrup, Britta, illus. 2013. (ENG.). 16p. (J). (gr. -1-k). bds. 7.99 *(978-1-84686-952-5(8))* Barefoot Bks., Inc.

Barella, Laura, illus. The Brave Little Tailor. 2014. (Flip-Up Fairy Tales Ser.). 24p. (J). *(978-1-84643-654-3(0))* Child's Play International Ltd.
—Donkey Skin. 2011. (Flip-Up Fairy Tales Ser.). 24p. (J). *(978-1-84643-410-5(6))*; (gr. 2-2). *(978-1-84643-371-9(1))* Child's Play International Ltd.
—Sleeping Beauty. 2009. (Flip-Up Fairy Tales Ser.). 24p. (J). (gr. -1-2). *(978-1-84643-295-8(2))*; pap. *(978-1-84643-252-1(9))* Child's Play International Ltd.
—The Stonecutter. 2012. (Flip-Up Fairy Tales Ser.). 24p. (J). *(978-1-84643-478-5(5))* Child's Play International Ltd.

Bari, Ellen. Does Your Dog Speak Hebrew? A Book of Animal Sounds. Clifton-Brown, Holly, illus. 2020. (ENG.). 14p. (J). (gr. -1 — 1). bds. 7.99 *(978-1-5415-6089-5(2)*, 36d82c5a-b2dd-43bf-af99-463931d0c2cb, Kar-Ben Publishing) Lerner Publishing Group.

Barrance, Reuben & Whatmore, Candice, illus. Birthday. 2008. (Usborne Look & Say Ser.). 12p. (J). (gr. -1-3). bds. 7.99 *(978-0-7945-1988-9(1)*, Usborne) EDC Publishing.

Barton, Byron. My House Board Book. Barton, Byron, illus. 2017. (ENG., Illus.). 44p. (J). (gr. -1-3). bds. 8.99 *(978-0-06-233705-4(X)*, Greenwillow Bks.) HarperCollins Pubs.

Bateson, Margaret. Acorn Farm. Slater, Nicola, illus. 2016. (J). *(978-1-4351-6320-1(6))* Barnes & Noble, Inc.

Bauer, Marion Dane. Toes, Ears, & Nose! A Lift-The-Flap Book. Katz, Karen, illus. 2003. (ENG.). 16p. (J). (gr. -1 — 1). bds. 7.99 *(978-0-689-84712-7(2)*, Little Simon) Little Simon.

Bauman, Amy. Everyone Is Special! 2010. 12p. (J). (gr. -1). 9.95 *(978-1-60747-719-8(X)*, Pickwick Pr.) Phoenix Bks., Inc.

Baur, Laura, illus. The Riverbank. 2012. (ENG.). 24p. (J). (gr. -1-k). spiral bd. 19.99 *(978-1-85103-393-5(9))* Moonlight Publishing, Ltd. GBR. Dist: Independent Pubs. Group.

Baxter, Nicola. Bedtime Lullabies: Fall Asleep to Your Free Cd. Finn, Rebecca, illus. 2014. 12p. (J). (gr. -1-12). bds. 14.99 *(978-1-86147-360-8(5)*, Armadillo) Anness Publishing GBR. Dist: National Bk. Network.
—The Great Pirate Adventure: Peek Inside the 3D Windows. Goulding, June, illus. 2012. 12p. (J). (gr. -1-12). 16.99 *(978-1-84322-966-7(8))* Anness Publishing GBR. Dist: National Bk. Network.
—Head, Shoulders, Knees & Toes & Other Action Rhymes. Buckingham, Gabriella, illus. 2013. 16p. (J). (gr. -1-6). bds.

7.99 (978-1-84322-829-5(7), Armadillo) Anness Publishing GBR. Dist: National Bk. Network.
—I Can Learn Times Tables: With Magnetic Numbers to Use Again & Again! Elliott, Rebecca, illus. 2013. (ENG.). 16p. (J). (gr. -1-7). bds. 17.99 (978-1-84322-986-5(2), Armadillo) Anness Publishing GBR. Dist: National Bk. Network.
—Jewels for a Princess. Chaffey, Samantha, illus. 2012. 12p. (J). (gr. 1-6). 16.99 (978-1-84322-926-1(9)) Anness Publishing GBR. Dist: National Bk. Network.
—Kaleidoscope Book: My First Book of Learning. Elliott, Rebecca, illus. 2013. (ENG.). 16p. (J). (gr. -1-12). bds. 16.99 (978-1-84322-930-8(7), Armadillo) Anness Publishing GBR. Dist: National Bk. Network.
—Learn about Our World. Elliott, Rebecca, illus. 2013. (ENG.). 16p. (J). (gr. k-2). bds. 17.99 (978-1-84322-985-8(4), Armadillo) Anness Publishing GBR. Dist: National Bk. Network.
—Learn to Count. Elliott, Rebecca, illus. 2013. (ENG.). 16p. (J). (gr. -1-2). bds. 17.99 (978-1-84322-984-1(6), Armadillo) Anness Publishing GBR. Dist: National Bk. Network.
—Learn to Tell Time: With Magnets to Use Again & Again! Elliott, Rebecca, illus. 2013. (ENG.). 16p. (J). (gr. -1-12). bds. 17.99 (978-1-84322-638-3(3), Armadillo) Anness Publishing GBR. Dist: National Bk. Network.
—The Mermaid & the Star. Rigby, Deborah, illus. 2025. 14p. (J). bds. (978-1-84322-907-0(2), Armadillo) Anness Publishing.
—My Ballet Theatre: Peek Inside the 3-D Windows. Chaffey, Samantha, illus. 2014. (ENG.). 24p. (J). (gr. -1-12). 16.99 (978-1-84322-949-0(8), Armadillo) Anness Publishing GBR. Dist: National Bk. Network.
—The Mystery of the Haunted House: Dare You Peek Through the 3-D Windows? Goulding, June, illus. 2013. 12p. (J). (gr. -1-12). 16.99 (978-1-84322-754-0(1)) Anness Publishing GBR. Dist: National Bk. Network.
—Party at the Fairy Palace: Peek Inside the 3D Windows. Chaffey, Samantha, illus. 2013. 12p. (J). (gr. -1-4). 16.99 (978-1-84322-725-0(8)) Anness Publishing GBR. Dist: National Bk. Network.
—Pull the Lever: Who's at Nursery? Lawson, Peter, illus. 2014. (ENG.). 8p. (J). (gr. -1-1). bds. 6.99 (978-1-86147-393-6(1), Armadillo) Anness Publishing GBR. Dist: National Bk. Network.
—Shapes. Siewert, Pauline, illus. 2021. 5p. (J). (gr. -1-12). bds. 2.99 (978-1-84322-782-3(7), Armadillo) Anness Publishing GBR. Dist: National Bk. Network.
—The Starlight Ballerina. Jones, Deborah, illus. 2025. 14p. (J). bds. (978-1-84322-885-1(8)) Anness Publishing.
—A Visit from the Tooth Fairy: Magical Stories & a Special Message from the Little Friend Who Collects Your Baby Teeth. Manson, Beverlie, illus. 2013. (ENG.). 40p. (J). (gr. k-4). 14.99 (978-1-84322-987-2(0), Armadillo) Anness Publishing GBR. Dist: National Bk. Network.
Baxter, Nicola, ed. Christmas Lullabies for Children. Finn, Rebecca, illus. 2014. (ENG.). 12p. (J). (gr. k-5). bds. 14.99 incl. audio compact disk (978-1-84322-931-5(5), Armadillo) Anness Publishing GBR. Dist: National Bk. Network.
Baxter, Nicola & Adams, Ben. Freddie the Fish, Star of the Show. Cameron, Craig, illus. 2013. (Googly Eyes Ser.). 12p. (J). (gr. -1-k). bds. 6.99 (978-1-84322-621-5(9), Armadillo) Anness Publishing GBR. Dist: National Bk. Network.
Baxter, Nicola & Francis, Jan. Traditional Fairy Tales: Eight Exciting Picture Stories for Little Ones. Parry, Jo, illus. 2013. 16p. (J). (gr. -1-2). 13.99 (978-1-84322-992-6(7), Armadillo) Anness Publishing GBR. Dist: National Bk. Network.
Beach, Kathleen H. & Weeber, Stephanie B. Madison's Mixed-up Flower Girl Magic & Aiden's Amazing Ring Bearer Act Aiden's Amazing Ring Bearer Act. Baisley, Maryann Leake, illus. 2009. 32p. pap. 19.95 (978-1-4251-7059-2(5)) Trafford Publishing.
BeachHouse Publishing. Geckos Go to Bed. Murakami, Jon, illus. 2008. (ENG.). 24p. (J). (gr. -1-k). bds. 8.95 (978-1-933067-26-1(8)) Beachhouse Publishing, LLC.
Beardshaw, Rosalind, illus. Walk & See: 123. 2018. (Walk & See Ser.). (ENG.). 26p. (J). (— 1). bds. 7.99 (978-0-7636-9338-1(3)) Candlewick Pr.
—Walk & See: Colors. 2018. (Walk & See Ser.). (ENG.). 26p. (J). (— 1). bds. 7.99 (978-0-7636-9917-8(9)) Candlewick Pr.
Beaton, Clare. Clare Beaton's Animal Rhymes. Beaton, Clare, illus. 2014. (ENG., Illus.). 16p. (J). (gr. -1-k). bds. 7.99 (978-1-78285-080-9(5)) Barefoot Bks., Inc.
—Clare Beaton's Bedtime Rhymes. Beaton, Clare, illus. 2012. (ENG., Illus.). 16p. (J). (gr. -1-k). bds. 7.99 (978-1-84686-737-8(1)) Barefoot Bks., Inc.
—Clare Beaton's Garden Rhymes. Beaton, Clare, illus. 2014. (ENG., Illus.). 16p. (J). (gr. -1-k). bds. 7.99 (978-1-78285-081-6(3)) Barefoot Bks., Inc.
Beaumont, Karen. I Like Myself! Lap Board Book. Catrow, David, illus. 2010. (ENG.). 32p. (J). (gr. -1 — 1). bds. 14.99 (978-0-547-40163-8(9), 1427978, Clarion Bks.) HarperCollins Pubs.
Beauvisage, Alice. My Blankie. 2013. (ENG., Illus.). 12p. (J). (gr. -1-k). bds. 6.95 (978-1-927018-08-8(0)) Simply Read Bks. CAN. Dist: Ingram Publisher Services.
Beckett-Bowman, Lucy. Sticker Dolly Dressing Bridesmaids. 2009. (Sticker Dolly Dressing Ser.). 24p. (J). pap. 8.99 (978-0-7945-2519-4(9), Usborne) EDC Publishing.
—Sticker Dolly Dressing on Vacation. 2009. (Sticker Dolly Dressing Ser.). 24p. (J). pap. 8.99 (978-0-7945-2369-5(2), Usborne) EDC Publishing.
—Sticker Dolly Dressing Popstars. 2009. (Sticker Dolly Dressing Ser.). 26p. (J). pap. 8.99 (978-0-7945-2360-2(9), Usborne) EDC Publishing.
Bedford, David & Worthington, Leonie. Big. 2006. (Illus.). 16p. pap. (978-1-921049-22-4(7)) Little Hare Bks. AUS. Dist: HarperCollins Pubs. Australia.
—Mums. 2007. (Illus.). 16p. (978-1-921049-78-1(2)) Little Hare Bks. AUS. Dist: HarperCollins Pubs. Australia.
—Who's Laughing? 2007. (Illus.). 16p. pap. (978-1-921272-11-0(2)) Little Hare Bks. AUS. Dist: HarperCollins Pubs. Australia.
Believe It Or Not, Ripley's, compiled by. Ripley's Believe It or Not! ODDphabet. 2017. (Little Bks.: 2). (ENG., Illus.). 26p. (J). bds. 6.99 (978-1-60991-170-6(9)) Ripley Entertainment, Inc.
Believe It Or Not!, Ripleys, compiled by. Ripley's Believe It or Not! It's a Circle: But Not Just a Circle! 2018. (Little Bks.: 3). (ENG., Illus.). 20p. (J). bds. 6.99 (978-1-60991-211-6(X)) Ripley Entertainment, Inc.
—Ripley's Believe It or Not! Lobsters Are Red: But Sometimes They're Not! 2018. (Little Bks.: 4). (ENG., Illus.). 20p. (J). bds. 6.99 (978-1-60991-210-9(1)) Ripley Entertainment, Inc.
—Ripley's Believe It or Not! Wacky 1-2-3. 2017. (Little Bks.: 1). (ENG., Illus.). 26p. (J). bds. 6.99 (978-1-60991-181-2(4)) Ripley Entertainment, Inc.
—Ripley's Fun Facts & Silly Stories: PLAY IT LOUD! 2018. (Fun Facts Ser.: 5). (ENG., Illus.). 94p. (J). 16.95 (978-1-60991-221-5(7)) Ripley Entertainment, Inc.
Bell-Martin, Janelle. Head & Shoulders. 2011. (Early Literacy Ser.). (ENG.). 16p. (gr. -1-1). 19.99 (978-1-4333-2372-0(9)) Teacher Created Materials, Inc.
—Mary Had a Little Lamb. 2011. (Early Literacy Ser.). (ENG.). 16p. (gr. k-1). 19.99 (978-1-4333-2358-4(3)) Teacher Created Materials, Inc.
Bellón, Teresa, illus. Speak up, Mouse! 2018. (J). bds. 7.99 (978-1-61067-779-0(X)) Kane Miller.
—Splish Splash, Seahorse! 2018. (J). bds. 7.99 (978-1-61067-780-6(3)) Kane Miller.
—Time for Bed, Hippo! 2018. (J). bds. 7.99 (978-1-61067-781-3(1)) Kane Miller.
BELTEI, Nadia. Emily's BOOKS: Coloring & Activity book, age Level: 2-3 (B&W) 2010. 39p. pap. 7.47 (978-0-557-32886-4(1)) Lulu Pr., Inc.
Bennett, Elizabeth. I Love You to the Moon. Poh, Jennie, illus. 2014. (ENG.). 22p. (J). (gr. -1). bds. 8.95 (978-1-58925-642-5(5)) Tiger Tales.
—It's Spring Time! Baccala, Gladys, illus. 2013. (ENG.). 16p. (J). (gr. -1). bds. 8.95 (978-1-58925-639-5(5)) Tiger Tales.
Bentley, Dawn. Goodnight Bear: A Book & Night Light. Couri, Kathryn A., illus. 2005. (Stories to Share Ser.). 12p. (J). 12.95 (978-1-58117-034-4(3), Intervisual/Piggy Toes) Bendon, Inc.
—Three Hungry Spiders & One Fat Fly! Twinem, Neecy, illus. 2010. (Stretchies Book Ser.). 16p. (J). (gr. -1-k). 8.99 (978-0-8249-1460-8(0), Ideals Pubns.) Worthy Publishing.
—Three Stretchy Frogs. Wallis, Becky, illus. 2010. (Stretchies Book Ser.). 16p. (J). 8.99 (978-0-8249-1459-2(7)) Hinkler Bks. Pty, Ltd. AUS. Dist: Ideals Pubns.
Bentley, Dawn & Studio Mouse Staff. Triceratops. Carr, Karen, illus. 2008. (ENG.). 24p. (J). (gr. 3-7). 4.99 (978-1-59069-622-4(0)) Studio Mouse LLC.
—Tyrannosaurus Rex. Carr, Karen, illus. 2008. (ENG.). 24p. (J). (gr. 3-7). 4.99 (978-1-59069-621-7(2)) Studio Mouse LLC.
Bentley, Tadgh. Little Penguin Gets the Hiccups Board Book. Bentley, Tadgh, illus. 2016. (ENG., Illus.). 34p. (J). (gr. -1 — 1). bds. 8.99 (978-0-06-265224-9(9), Balzer & Bray) HarperCollins Pubs.
Benton, Jim. Where's My Fnurgle? Benton, Jim, illus. 2015. (ENG.). 16p. (J). (— 1). bds. 5.99 (978-0-545-64787-8(8), Cartwheel Bks.) Scholastic, Inc.
Berenstain, Jan & Berenstain, Stan. The Berenstain Bears' New Pup. Berenstain, Jan, illus. 2017. (I Can Read Level 1 Ser.). (ENG., Illus.). 40p. (J). (gr. -1-3). 9.99 (978-0-06-257272-1(5), HarperCollins) HarperCollins Pubs.
Berenstain, Mike. The Berenstain Bears All God's Creatures. 2016. (Berenstain Bears Ser.). (ENG., Illus.). 20p. (J). bds. 7.99 (978-0-8249-1968-9(8), Ideals Pubns.) Worthy Publishing.
—The Berenstain Bears Easter Blessings. 2016. (Berenstain Bears Ser.). (ENG., Illus.). 20p. (J). bds. 7.99 (978-0-8249-1967-2(X), Ideals Pubns.) Worthy Publishing.
—The Berenstain Bears Get Ready for School. Berenstain, Mike, illus. 2015. (Berenstain Bears Ser.). (ENG., Illus.). 16p. (J). (gr. -1-1). pap. 6.99 (978-0-06-207552-9(7), HarperFestival) HarperCollins Pubs.
—The Berenstain Bears Love One Another. 2016. (Berenstain Bears Ser.). (ENG., Illus.). 20p. (J). bds. 7.99 (978-0-8249-1983-2(1), Ideals Pubns.) Worthy Publishing.
Bergen, Lara. Don't Throw That Away! A Lift-The-Flap Book about Recycling & Reusing. Snyder, Betsy, illus. 2009. (Little Green Bks.). (ENG.). 14p. (J). (gr. -1-1). bds. 8.99 (978-1-4169-7517-5(9), Little Simon) Little Simon.
—Enchanted Library, 6 vols. 2005. (Illus.). (J). (978-0-7868-3550-8(8)); (978-0-7868-3551-5(6)); (978-0-7868-3546-1(X)); (978-0-7868-3548-5(6)); (978-0-7868-3549-2(4)); (978-0-7868-3547-8(8)) Disney Pr.
—Let's Dig It! Shannon, David et al, illus. 2010. (Jon Scieszka's Trucktown Ser.). (ENG.). 12p. (J). (gr. -1-k). bds. 5.99 (978-1-4169-4190-3(8), Little Simon) Little Simon.
Bernd & Richter, Susan. I See You Through My Heart. 2008. bds. 8.95 (978-1-931353-44-1(1)) Saddle Pal Creations, Inc.
Berrios, Frank. Let's Cruise!, 4 vols. 2006. (Illus.). (J). (978-0-7364-2435-6(0)); (978-0-7364-2434-9(2)); (978-0-7364-2433-2(4)); (978-0-7364-2436-3(9)) Random Hse. Children's Bks.
—A Very Mater Christmas (Disney/Pixar Cars) RH Disney, illus. 2011. (ENG.). 12p. (J). (— 1). bds. 7.99 (978-0-7364-2793-7(7), RH/Disney) Random Hse. Children's Bks.
Berry Byrd, Holly. Babies Love Christmas. Cottage Door Press, ed. Peterson, Stacy, illus. 2016. (Babies Love Ser.). (ENG.). 12p. (J). (gr. -1 — 1). bds. 7.99 (978-1-68052-116-0(0), 1001091) Cottage Door Pr.
—Babies Love Valentines. Cottage Door Press, ed. Hogan, Martina, illus. 2016. (Babies Love Ser.). (ENG.). 12p. (J). (gr. -1 — 1). bds. 7.99 (978-1-68052-149-8(7), 1001430) Cottage Door Pr.
—Jingle & Joy. 2019. (ENG., Illus.). 10p. (J). (gr. -1-k). bds. 10.99 (978-1-68052-128-3(4), 1001211) Cottage Door Pr.
—Jingle Bells. Cottage Door Press, ed. Bos, Miriam, illus. 2017. (ENG.). 12p. (J). (gr. -1-k). bds. 10.99 (978-1-68052-230-3(2), 1002160) Cottage Door Pr.
Berry, Joy. I Love Mealtime. Regan, Dana, illus. 2010. (Teach Me About Ser.). (ENG.). 20p. (J). (gr. k — 1). pap. 5.99 (978-1-60577-006-2(X)) Berry, Joy Enterprises.
—I Love Mommies & Daddies. Regan, Dana, illus. 2010. (Teach Me About Ser.). (ENG.). 20p. (J). (gr. k — 1). pap. 5.99 (978-1-60577-001-7(9)) Berry, Joy Enterprises.
—I Love Preschool. Regan, Dana, illus. 2010. (Teach Me About Ser.). (ENG.). 20p. (J). (gr. k — 1). bds. 5.99 (978-1-60577-015-4(9)) Berry, Joy Enterprises.
—Let's Talk about Being Patient. Smith, Maggie, illus. 2010. (Let's Talk About Ser.). (ENG.). 32p. (J). (gr. -1-k). pap. 4.99 (978-1-60577-209-7(7)) Berry, Joy Enterprises.
Berry, Ron. Charlie the Can-Do Choo-Choo! Sharp, Chris, illus. 2006. (ENG.). 7p. (J). (gr. -1). bds. 12.95 (978-0-8249-6678-2(3), Ideals Pubns.) Worthy Publishing.
—The Easter Bunny's Colorful Day! 2008. (Slide-N-Color Bks.). (Illus.). 10p. (J). (gr. -1). bds. 6.99 (978-0-8249-6698-0(8), Ideals Pubns.) Worthy Publishing.
—Jingle Bells. Smart Kidz, ed. Sharp, Chris, illus. 2019. (Christmas Carol Book Ser.). (ENG.). 12p. (J). (gr. -1-2). bds. 14.99 (978-1-64123-246-3(3)) Smart Kidz Media, Inc.
—Let Your Light Shine. 2007. (ENG., Illus.). 16p. (J). (gr. -1-k). bds. 12.99 (978-0-8249-6723-9(2), Ideals Pubns.) Worthy Publishing.
—Rise & Shine! Sharp, Chris, illus. 2008. 14p. (J). bds. 12.99 (978-0-8249-6735-2(6), Ideals Pubns.) Worthy Publishing.
—The Silly Safari Bus! Sharp, Chris, illus. 2008. (ENG.). 12p. (J). bds. 12.99 (978-0-8249-6736-9(4), Ideals Pubns.) Worthy Publishing.
—Where Is Daddy? Smart Kids Publishing Staff, ed. 2009. (ENG.). 20p. (J). bds. 7.99 (978-0-8249-1405-9(8), Ideals Pubns.) Worthy Publishing.
—Where Is Mommy? Smart Kids Publishing Staff, ed. 2009. (ENG.). 20p. (J). bds. 7.99 (978-0-8249-1404-2(X), Ideals Pubns.) Worthy Publishing.
Berry, Ron & Mead, David. All Aboard! Charlie the Can-Do Choo Choo. Sharp, Chris, illus. 2009. (ENG.). 8p. 12.99 (978-0-8249-1420-2(1), Ideals Pubns.) Worthy Publishing.
—The Little Drummer Boy. Sharp, Chris, illus. 2009. (ENG.). 16p. 12.99 (978-0-8249-1429-5(5), Ideals Pubns.) Worthy Publishing.
Bevan, Clare. Comet the Fairy Unicorn. 2015. (Mimi's Magical Fairy Friends Ser.: 3). (ENG., Illus.). 32p. (J). (gr. -1-2). pap. 10.99 (978-1-4472-9424-5(6)) Pan Macmillan GBR. Dist: Independent Pubs. Group.
Bewley, Elizabeth. Choose to Recycle. Latimer, Miriam, illus. 2009. 10p. 7.95 (978-1-58117-904-0(9), Intervisual/Piggy Toes) Bendon, Inc.
Bicknell, J. Buby Baby 123_Padded. 2010. 12p. (978-1-84879-163-3(1)) Make Believe Ideas.
—Buby Baby Colors_Padded. 2010. 12p. pap. (978-1-84879-164-0(X)) Make Believe Ideas.
—Buby Baby Words_Padded. 2010. (Illus.). 12p. pap. (978-1-84879-161-9(5)) Make Believe Ideas.
Big Dog & Little Dog Getting in Trouble Glr L1. 2015. (Green Light Readers Ser.). (ENG., Illus.). 24p. (J). (gr. -1-3). pap. 4.99 (978-0-544-53095-9(0), 1607572, Clarion Bks.) HarperCollins Pubs.
Biggs, Brian. At the Firehouse (a Tinyville Town Book) 2019. (ENG., Illus.). 22p. (J). (gr. -1 — 1). bds. 9.99 (978-1-4197-3151-8(3), 1119901, Abrams Appleseed) Abrams, Inc.
—Everything Goes: Blue Bus, Red Balloon: a Book of Colors. Biggs, Brian, illus. 2013. (ENG., Illus.). 24p. (J). (gr. -1 — 1). bds. 7.99 (978-0-06-195814-4(X), Balzer & Bray) HarperCollins Pubs.
—Everything Goes: Good Night, Trucks: a Bedtime Book. Biggs, Brian, illus. 2013. (ENG., Illus.). 24p. (J). (gr. -1 — 1). bds. 7.99 (978-0-06-195815-1(8), Balzer & Bray) HarperCollins Pubs.
—I'm a Mail Carrier (a Tinyville Town Book) 2018. (Tinyville Town Ser.). (ENG., Illus.). 22p. (J). (gr. -1 — 1). bds. 7.99 (978-1-4197-2833-4(4), 1119801, Abrams Appleseed) Abrams, Inc.
Billet, Marion, illus. Noisy Farm: My First Sound Book. 2017. (ENG.). 16p. (J). (gr. -1 — 1). 9.99 (978-1-338-13220-5(2), Cartwheel Bks.) Scholastic, Inc.
Bingo. 2017. (Illus.). (J). (978-1-62885-390-2(5)) Kidsbooks, LLC.
The Birthday Ball. 2013. (Illus.). (J). (978-1-4351-4947-2(5)) Disney Pr.
Bixley, Donovan. My First Board Book: Shapes. 2022. (My First Board Book Ser.). (ENG., Illus.). 24p. (J). (gr. -1-k). bds. 13.99 (978-1-86971-347-8(8)) Hachette New Zealand NZL. Dist: Hachette Bk. Group.
—My First Board Book: Things That Go! 2022. (My First Board Book Ser.). (ENG., Illus.). 24p. (J). (gr. -1-k). bds. 13.99 (978-1-86971-348-5(6)) Hachette New Zealand NZL. Dist: Hachette Bk. Group.
Black, Robyn Hood. Wolves. Howard, Colin, illus. 2008. (ENG.). 24p. (J). (gr. 3-18). 19.95 (978-1-58117-817-3(4), Intervisual/Piggy Toes) Bendon, Inc.
Blackburn, Ken & Lammers, Jeff. Pocket Flyers Paper Airplane Book: 69 Mini Planes to Fold & Fly. 2017. (Paper Airplanes Ser.). (ENG., Illus.). 160p. pap. 9.95 (978-1-5235-0204-2(5), 100204) Workman Publishing Co., Inc.
Blackstone, Stella. Baby Talk. 2015. (ENG., Illus.). 16p. (J). (gr. -1-k). bds. 7.99 (978-1-78285-222-3(0)) Barefoot Bks., Inc.
—Baby Talk / Hablando con Bebé. 2017. (ENG.). 16p. (J). (gr. -1-k). bds. 7.99 (978-1-78285-350-3(2)) Barefoot Bks., Inc.
—Cleo on the Move. Mockford, Caroline, illus. 2013. 24p. (J). bds. 6.99 (978-1-78285-056-4(2)) Barefoot Bks., Inc.
Blackstone, Stella & Harter, Debbie. Oso en un Cuadrado. 2013. (Illus.). 24p. (J). bds. 7.99 (978-1-78285-030-4(9)) Barefoot Bks., Inc.
Blackstone, Stella & Scribens, Sunny. Baby's First Words. Engel, Christiane, illus. 2017. (ENG.). 30p. (J). (gr. -1-k). bds. 14.99 (978-1-78285-321-3(9)) Barefoot Bks., Inc.
—Mis Primeras Palabras. 2017. (SPA.). 30p. (J). (gr. -1-k). bds. 14.99 (978-1-78285-325-1(1)) Barefoot Bks., Inc.
Bledsoe, Michele. Kitty Treats Cookbook. Rupert, Chris & Schaefer, Kelly, illus. 2010. (ENG.). 15p. (gr. 6). bds. 10.95 (978-0-9753883-8-9(X)) Come & Get It Publishing.
Blevins, Wiley. Ten Missing Princesses. Cox, Steve, illus. 2017. (Scary Tales Retold Ser.). (ENG.). 24p. (J). (gr. k-3). pap. 6.99 (978-1-63440-172-2(7), 97967ed0-13a8-4453-839f-022d2bc5b970) Red Chair Pr.
Bloom, Jan, et al. You Track it Weather Lab. Free Jenna Staff, ed. 2012. (ENG.). 12p. 14.99 (978-1-60380-087-7(5)) becker&mayer! books.
Bloomsbury. Carry & Play: Snowman. 2016. (ENG.). 10p. (J). bds. 6.99 (978-1-68119-096-9(6), 900158418, Bloomsbury Activity Bks.) Bloomsbury Publishing USA.
—Lift-The-Flap Friends: Fairy. 2016. (ENG.). 14p. (J). bds. 9.99 (978-1-68119-098-3(2), 900158429, Bloomsbury Activity Bks.) Bloomsbury Publishing USA.
Bloomsbury USA. Baby's First Words: Animals. 2016. (ENG., Illus.). 10p. (J). bds. 5.99 (978-1-61963-994-2(7), 9781619639942, Bloomsbury Activity Bks.) Bloomsbury Publishing USA.
—Carry & Play: Pumpkin. 2016. (ENG., Illus.). 10p. (J). bds. 6.99 (978-1-61963-982-9(3), 900154186, Bloomsbury Activity Bks.) Bloomsbury Publishing USA.
—Carry & Play: Spring Friends. 2016. (ENG., Illus.). 10p. (J). (— 1). bds. 6.99 (978-1-61963-828-0(2), 900150128, Bloomsbury Activity Bks.) Bloomsbury Publishing USA.
—Lift & Look: at the Park. 2016. (ENG., Illus.). 12p. (J). (— 1). bds. 8.99 (978-1-61963-940-9(8), 9781619639409, Bloomsbury Activity Bks.) Bloomsbury Publishing USA.
—Lift & Look: in Space. 2016. (ENG., Illus.). 12p. (J). (— 1). bds. 8.99 (978-1-61963-826-6(6), 9781619638266, Bloomsbury Activity Bks.) Bloomsbury Publishing USA.
—Lift-The-Flap Friends: Pirates. 2017. (ENG.). 14p. (J). bds. 9.99 (978-1-68119-241-3(1), 900164373, Bloomsbury Activity Bks.) Bloomsbury Publishing USA.
—Lift-The-Flap Friends: Princess. 2017. (ENG.). 14p. (J). bds. 9.99 (978-1-68119-240-6(3), 900164377, Bloomsbury Activity Bks.) Bloomsbury Publishing USA.
Blyton, Enid, et al. My First 123 & Nursery Rhymes. 2013. (ENG., Illus.). 20p. (J). bds. 11.50 (978-1-84135-759-1(6)) Award Pubns. Ltd. GBR. Dist: Parkwest Pubns., Inc.
—My First Abc. 2013. (ENG., Illus.). 20p. (J). bds. 11.50 (978-1-84135-757-7(X)) Award Pubns. Ltd. GBR. Dist: Parkwest Pubns., Inc.
—My First Animals. 2013. (ENG., Illus.). 20p. (J). bds. 11.50 (978-1-84135-758-4(8)) Award Pubns. Ltd. GBR. Dist: Parkwest Pubns., Inc.
—My First Colours & Shapes. 2013. (ENG., Illus.). 20p. (J). bds. 11.50 (978-1-84135-760-7(X)) Award Pubns. Ltd. GBR. Dist: Parkwest Pubns., Inc.
—Things That Go. 2013. 10p. (J). bds. 9.95 (978-1-84135-724-9(3)) Award Pubns. Ltd. GBR. Dist: Parkwest Pubns., Inc.
—Under the Sea. 2013. 10p. (J). bds. 9.95 (978-1-84135-723-2(5)) Parkwest Pubns., Inc.
Boardworks Learning Centers: Across the U. S. A. 2006. (J). bds. (978-0-9755252-5-8(5)) Evergreen Pr. of Brainerd, LLC.
Boardworks Learning Centers: Figure It Out. 2006. (J). bds. (978-0-9755252-4-1(7)) Evergreen Pr. of Brainerd, LLC.
Boardworks Learning Centers: I've Got It! 2006. (J). bds. (978-0-9755252-8-9(X)) Evergreen Pr. of Brainerd, LLC.
Boardworks Learning Centers: Sentence Fixer-Uppers. 2006. (J). bds. (978-0-9755252-7-2(1)) Evergreen Pr. of Brainerd, LLC.
Boardworks Learning Centers: Where in the World? 2006. (J). bds. (978-0-9755252-6-5(3)) Evergreen Pr. of Brainerd, LLC.
Boisrobert, Anouck. That's My Hat! 2016. (Illus.). 24p. (J). (gr. -1-1). pap. 24.95 (978-0-500-65057-8(8), 565057) Thames & Hudson.
Bolivar, Lisa & Martinez, Matthew. Good Night Miami. 2011. (Good Night Our World Ser.). (ENG.). 20p. (J). (gr. k — 1). bds. 9.95 (978-1-60219-051-1(8)) Good Night Bks.
Bond, Elaine Miller. Running Wild. 2011. (ENG., Illus.). 28p. (J). bds. 8.99 (978-1-59714-364-6(2)) Heyday.
Bond, Michael. Paddington Bear All Day Board Book. Alley, R. W., illus. 2014. (Paddington Ser.). (ENG.). 14p. (J). (gr. -1-3). bds. 7.99 (978-0-06-231721-6(0), HarperFestival) HarperCollins Pubs.
—Paddington Bear Goes to Market Board Book. Alley, R. W., illus. 2014. (Paddington Ser.). (ENG.). 14p. (J). (gr. -1-3). bds. 7.99 (978-0-06-231722-3(9), HarperFestival) HarperCollins Pubs.
—Paddington Plays On. Alley, R. W., illus. 2016. (I Can Read Level 1 Ser.). (ENG.). 32p. (J). (gr. -1-3). pap. 4.99 (978-0-06-243070-0(X), HarperCollins) HarperCollins Pubs.
Bone, Emily. Lift-The-Flap First Questions & Answers Why Do We Need Bees? 2017. (Lift-The-Flap First Questions & Answers Ser.). (ENG.). 12p. 14.99 (978-0-7945-4030-2(9), Usborne) EDC Publishing.
—See Inside Where Food Comes from IR. 2017. (See Inside Board Bks.). (ENG.). 16p. 14.99 (978-0-7945-4015-9(5), Usborne) EDC Publishing.
—Sticker Dolly Dressing Around the World. 2011. (Sticker Dolly Dressing Ser.). 24p. (J). pap. 8.99 (978-0-7945-2968-0(2), Usborne) EDC Publishing.
—Sticker Dolly Dressing Dream Jobs. 2012. (Sticker Dolly Dressing Ser.). 24p. (J). pap. 8.99 (978-0-7945-3253-6(5), Usborne) EDC Publishing.
Bone, Emily & King, Colin. See Inside Trains. 2013. (Usborne Flap Book Ser.). (ENG., Illus.). 16p. (J). 13.99 (978-0-7945-3377-9(9), Usborne) EDC Publishing.
Boniface, William. Lights Out, Night's Out. Kirkova, Milena, illus. 2011. (ENG.). 24p. (J). pap. 6.99 (978-1-4494-0236-5(4)) Andrews McMeel Publishing.
—There's a Dinosaur in My Soup! Poling, Kyle, illus. 2012. (ENG.). 12p. (J). (gr. -1-1). bds. 9.99 (978-1-4424-4610-6(2), Little Simon) Little Simon.
Boniface, William & Sullivan, Don. The Adventures of Max the Minnow. 2015. (ENG., Illus.). 26p. (J). bds. 9.99 (978-1-4494-6490-5(4)) Andrews McMeel Publishing.
Bonnet, Rosalind. Animals. rev. ed. 2013. (First Words Board Bks). 12p. (J). ring bd. 6.99 (978-0-7945-3389-2(2), Usborne) EDC Publishing.
Bonnet, Rosalinde. Very First Christmas Carols. 2011. (Very First Words Board Book Ser.). 12p. (J). ring bd. 6.99 (978-0-7945-3117-1(2), Usborne) EDC Publishing.
Bonnett-Rampersaud, Louise. How Do You Sleep?, 1 vol. Kest, Kristin, illus. 2008. (ENG.). 34p. (J). (gr. -1). 6.99 (978-0-7614-5449-6(7)) Marshall Cavendish Corp.
Book Company Staff. Animal World. 2003. (Novelty Bks.). (Illus.). (J). bds. 9.95 (978-1-74047-366-8(3)) Book Co. Publishing Pty, Ltd., The AUS. Dist: Penton Overseas, Inc.
A Book of Babies. 2015. (ENG.). 24p. (J). (— 1). bds. 7.99 (978-0-553-50779-9(6), Knopf Bks. for Young Readers) Random Hse. Children's Bks.
A Book of Sleep. 2011. (ENG.). 24p. (J). (gr. k — 1). bds. 6.99 (978-0-375-86618-0(3), Knopf Bks. for Young Readers) Random Hse. Children's Bks.
Boon, Fiona. The Story of Jesus. Ede, Lara, illus. 2014. (ENG.). 22p. (J). (— 1). bds. 6.99 (978-1-78235-883-1(8)) Make Believe Ideas GBR. Dist: Scholastic, Inc.

Borando, Silvia & Clerici, Lorenzo. Open up, Please! A Minibombo Book. 2016. (Minibombo Ser.). (ENG., Illus.). 24p. (J). (-k). 14.00 *(978-0-7636-9037-3(6))* Candlewick Pr.
Border, Terry. Ready or Not, Here Comes Peanut Butter! A Scratch-And-Sniff Book. 2018. (Illus.). 12p. (J). (— 1). bds. 12.99 *(978-1-5247-8483-6(4),* Grosset & Dunlap) Penguin Young Readers Group.
Bortins, Robert. My CC ABCs, Cycle 3. Neverov, Leah, illus. 2017. 26p. (J). bds. 10.99 *(978-0-9972442-5-0(9))* Classical Conversations, Inc.
Bostrom, Kathleen Long. Count Your Blessings. Reed, Lisa, illus. 2017. (VeggieTales Ser.). (ENG.). 20p. (J). (gr. -1-k). bds. 7.99 *(978-0-8249-1664-0(6))* Worthy Publishing.
Botman, Loes, illus. Hello Animals, Where Do You Live?, 65 vols. 2015. (Hello Animals Ser.). 12p. (J). 9.95 *(978-1-78250-219-7(X))* Floris Bks. GBR. Dist: Consortium Bk. Sales & Distribution.
—Hello Birds, What Do You Say?, 30 vols. 2018. (Hello Animals Ser.). Orig. Title: Klein Vogelboek. 12p. (J). 9.95 *(978-1-78250-488-7(5))* Floris Bks. GBR. Dist: Consortium Bk. Sales & Distribution.
—Hello Bugs, What Do You Do?, 30 vols. 2017. (Hello Animals Ser.). Orig. Title: Klein Insectenboek. 12p. (J). 9.95 *(978-1-78250-383-5(8))* Floris Bks. GBR. Dist: Consortium Bk. Sales & Distribution.
Boultwood, Ellie, et al. Build Your Own Play Train. Bradley, Jennie, illus. 2019. (J). *(978-0-312-52957-4(0))* St. Martin's Pr.
Bourgeois, Paulette. Franklin's Christmas: A Sticker Activity Book. Clark, Brenda, illus. 2003. 16p. (J). (ENG.). 6.95 *(978-1-55337-561-6(0));* 6.95 *(978-1-55337-506-7(8))* Kids Can Pr., Ltd. CAN. Dist: Hachette Bk. Group.
Bowen, Anne. I Loved You Before You Were Born Board Book. Shed, Greg, illus. 2017. (ENG.). 30p. (J). (gr. -1 — 1). bds. 8.99 *(978-0-06-269094-4(9),* HarperFestival) HarperCollins Pubs.
Bower, Gary. Mommy Love. Bower, Jan, illus. 2012. (Little Lovable Board Bks.). (ENG.). 16p. (J). bds. 8.50 *(978-0-9845236-0-3(X))* Storybook Meadow Publishing.
Bowman, Crystal. My Christmas Stocking: Filled with God's Love, 1 vol. Gevry, Claudine, illus. 2015. (ENG.). 14p. (J). bds. 6.99 *(978-0-310-73823-7(7))* Zonderkidz.
—My Happy Pumpkin: God's Love Shining Through Me, 1 vol. 2014. (ENG.). 14p. (J). bds. 6.99 *(978-0-310-73828-2(8))* Zonderkidz.
Bowman, Donna H. Big Cats. Wald, Christina, illus. 2008. (ENG.). 24p. (J). (gr. 3-18). 19.95 *(978-1-58117-781-7(X),* Intervisual/Piggy Toes) Bendon, Inc.
Bowman, Lucy. Sticker Dolly Dressing Fashion Long Ago. Baggott, Stella, illus. 2010. (Sticker Dolly Dressing Ser.). 24p. (J). pap. 8.99 *(978-0-7945-2547-7(4),* Usborne) EDC Publishing.
Box, Su. My Rainbow Book of Everyday Prayers, 1 vol. Brown, Jo, illus. 2009. 16p. (J). bds. 9.99 *(978-0-8254-7918-2(5),* Lion Children's) Lion Hudson PLC GBR. Dist: Kregel Pubns.
Boyd, Lizi. Hide-And-Sleep: A Flip-Flap Book (Lift the Flap Books, Interactive Board Books, Board Books for Toddlers) 2019. (ENG., Illus.). 20p. (J). (gr. -1 — 1). bds. 12.99 *(978-1-4521-7096-1(7))* Chronicle Bks. LLC.
—Night Play: (Kids Books for Nighttime, Kids Imagination Books) 2018. (ENG., Illus.). 44p. (J). (gr. -1-k). 17.99 *(978-1-4521-5529-6(1))* Chronicle Bks. LLC.
Boyer, Cecile. Run, Dog! 2014. (ENG., Illus.). 48p. (J). (gr. -1-k). 16.99 *(978-1-4521-2708-8(5))* Chronicle Bks. LLC.
Boynton, Sandra. Happy Birthday, Little Pookie. Boynton, Sandra, illus. 2017. (Little Pookie Ser.). (ENG., Illus.). 18p. (J). (gr. -1-k). bds. 6.99 *(978-1-4814-9770-1(7))* Simon & Schuster, Inc.
—Happy Hippo, Angry Duck. Boynton, Sandra, illus. 2011. (ENG., Illus.). 16p. (J). (gr. -1-k). bds. 6.99 *(978-1-4424-1731-1(5))* Simon & Schuster, Inc.
—Let's Dance, Little Pookie. Boynton, Sandra, illus. 2017. (Little Pookie Ser.). (ENG., Illus.). 18p. (J). (gr. -1-k). bds. 5.99 *(978-1-4814-9772-5(3))* Simon & Schuster, Inc.
—What's Wrong, Little Pookie? Boynton, Sandra, illus. 2017. (Little Pookie Ser.). (ENG., Illus.). 18p. (J). (gr. -1-k). bds. 6.99 *(978-1-4814-9769-5(3))* Simon & Schuster, Inc.
Brainy Baby Animals. 2004. *(978-1-59394-234-2(6))* Bendon, Inc.
Brainy Baby Quad Book. 2005. (Brainy Baby Ser.). 40p. (J). bds. 10.39 *(978-1-59394-240-3(0))* Bendon, Inc.
Brandon, Wendy. Cinderbear: Board Book & Puppet Theater. Winter, Janet, illus. 2004. (J). *(978-1-883043-47-6(6))* Straight Edge Pr., The.
—The Frog Prince: Board Book & Puppet Theater. Beckes, Shirley V., illus. 2004. (J). *(978-1-883043-46-9(8))* Straight Edge Pr., The.
Brannon, Tom, illus. I Love You Valentine Songs. 2012. (J). *(978-1-4508-3303-5(9))* Phoenix International Publications, Inc.
Braun, Sebastian. Peek-A-Boo Baby. Braun, Sebastian, illus. 2012. (ENG., Illus.). 16p. (J). (gr. -1 — 1). bds. 7.99 *(978-0-7636-5933-2(9))* Candlewick Pr.
Braun, Sebastian, illus. I'm a Clown! 2012. (Look at Me Ser.). 12p. (J). spiral bd. *(978-1-84643-472-3(6))* Child's Play International Ltd.
—I'm a Monster! 2012. (Look at Me Ser.). 12p. (J). spiral bd. *(978-1-84643-470-9(X))* Child's Play International Ltd.
—I'm an Alien! 2012. (Look at Me Ser.). 12p. (J). spiral bd. *(978-1-84643-471-6(8))* Child's Play International Ltd.
Braun, Sebastien. I Love My Daddy Board Book. Braun, Sebastien, illus. 2017. (ENG., Illus.). 26p. (J). (gr. -1 — 1). bds. 8.99 *(978-0-06-256425-2(0),* Tegen, Katherine Bks) HarperCollins Pubs.
—I Love My Mommy Board Book. Braun, Sebastien, illus. 2017. (ENG., Illus.). 26p. (J). (gr. -1 — 1). bds. 8.99 *(978-0-06-256424-5(2),* Tegen, Katherine Bks) HarperCollins Pubs.
Braun, Sebastien, illus. Can You Say It, Too? Growl! Growl! 2014. (Can You Say It, Too? Ser.). (ENG.). 10p. (J). (— 1). bds. 8.99 *(978-0-7636-7396-3(X))* Candlewick Pr.
—Can You Say It, Too? Hoot! Hoot! 2015. (Can You Say It, Too? Ser.). (ENG.). 10p. (J). (— 1). bds. 8.99 *(978-0-7636-7588-2(1))* Candlewick Pr.
—Can You Say It, Too? Moo! Moo! 2014. (Can You Say It, Too? Ser.). (ENG.). 10p. (J). (— 1). bds. 9.99 *(978-0-7636-7066-5(9))* Candlewick Pr.
—Can You Say It, Too? Quack! Quack! 2015. (Can You Say It, Too? Ser.). (ENG.). 10p. (J). (— 1). bds. 8.99 *(978-0-7636-7589-9(X))* Candlewick Pr.
—Can You Say It, Too? Stomp! Stomp! 2018. (Can You Say It, Too? Ser.). (ENG.). 10p. (J). (— 1). bds. 8.99 *(978-0-7636-9934-5(9))* Candlewick Pr.
—Can You Say It, Too? Woof! Woof! 2014. (Can You Say It, Too? Ser.). (ENG.). 10p. (J). (— 1). bds. 9.99 *(978-0-7636-6605-7(X))* Candlewick Pr.
—I'm a Robot! 2012. (Look at Me Ser.). 12p. (J). spiral bd. *(978-1-84643-469-3(6))* Child's Play International Ltd.
Braun, Sébastien, illus. Shapes & Colors. 2012. (J). *(978-1-58865-852-4(X))* Kidsbooks, LLC.
—The Tiger Prowls: A Pop-Up Book of Wild Animals. 2016. (ENG.). 12p. (J). 16.99 *(978-1-4711-2215-6(8),* Simon & Schuster Children's) Simon & Schuster, Ltd. GBR. Dist: Simon & Schuster, Inc.
Brett, Jan. Gingerbread Baby. Brett, Jan, illus. 2003. (Illus.). 32p. (J). (gr. -1 — 1). bds. 9.99 *(978-0-399-24166-6(3),* G.P. Putnam's Sons Books for Young Readers) Penguin Young Readers Group.
—Gingerbread Friends. Brett, Jan, illus. (Illus.). 32p. (J). 2017. (-k). bds. 8.99 *(978-1-5247-3942-3(1))* 2008. (gr. -1-k). 19.99 *(978-0-399-25161-0(8))* Penguin Young Readers Group. (G.P. Putnam's Sons Books for Young Readers).
—The Mitten: Oversized Board Book. Brett, Jan, illus. 2014. (ENG., Illus.). 32p. (J). (gr. -1 — 1). bds. 15.99 *(978-0-399-16981-6(4),* G.P. Putnam's Sons Books for Young Readers) Penguin Young Readers Group.
Brett, Jeannie. Little Maine. Brett, Jeannie, illus. 2010. (Little State Ser.). (ENG., Illus.). 20p. (J). (gr. -1-1). bds. 9.95 *(978-1-58536-497-8(5),* 202242) Sleeping Bear Pr.
Brett, Tyler & Romano, Tony, illus. False Creek. 2010. (ENG.). 22p. bds. 9.95 *(978-1-897476-66-6(3))* Simply Read Bks. CAN. Dist: Ingram Publisher Services.
Bridwell, Norman. Clifford at the Circus. Bridwell, Norman, illus. 2010. (ENG., Illus.). 32p. (J). (gr. -1-2). pap. 3.99 *(978-0-545-21584-8(6),* Cartwheel Bks.) Scholastic, Inc.
—Clifford's Family (Classic Storybook), 1 vol. Bridwell, Norman, illus. 2010. (ENG., Illus.). 32p. (J). (gr. -1-2). pap. 4.99 *(978-0-545-21585-5(4),* Cartwheel Bks.) Scholastic, Inc.
—Clifford's First Christmas. Bridwell, Norman, illus. 2010. (ENG., Illus.). 20p. (J). (gr. -1 — 1). bds. 6.99 *(978-0-545-21773-6(3),* Cartwheel Bks.) Scholastic, Inc.
—Clifford's First Easter. Bridwell, Norman, illus. 2010. (ENG., Illus.). 14p. (J). (gr. -1 — 1). bds. 6.99 *(978-0-545-20010-3(5),* Cartwheel Bks.) Scholastic, Inc.
Bridwell, Norman & Scholastic, Inc. Staff. The Big Red Dog. 2010. (Clifford Ser.). (ENG.). (J). (gr. -1-3). pap. 12.99 incl. audio compact disk *(978-0-545-25415-1(9))* Scholastic, Inc.
Bright & Beyond - Age 1. 2004. (J). *(978-0-9726170-5-5(1))* Pal Toys, LLC.
Bright & Beyond - Age 2. 2004. (J). *(978-0-9726170-6-2(X))* Pal Toys, LLC.
Bright & Beyond - Baby. 2004. (J). *(978-0-9726170-4-8(3))* Pal Toys, LLC.
Bright & Beyond - Math. 2004. (J). *(978-0-9763648-0-1(8))* Pal Toys, LLC.
Bright & Beyond - Preschool. 2004. (J). *(978-0-9726170-7-9(8))* Pal Toys, LLC.
Bright & Beyond - Reading. 2004. (J). *(978-0-9726170-8-6(6))* Pal Toys, LLC.
Bright & Beyond - Thinking. 2004. (J). *(978-0-9763648-1-8(6))* Pal Toys, LLC.
Bright & Beyond - Writing. 2004. (J). *(978-0-9726170-9-3(4))* Pal Toys, LLC.
Brighter Minds, creator. Fact Book. 2008. (DreamWorks Kung Fu Panda Ser.). (Illus.). 10p. (J). (gr. -1-3). 9.95 *(978-1-57791-420-4(1))* Brighter Minds Children's Publishing.
—Kung Fu Panda: Create-A-Story. 2008. (Illus.). 8p. (J). (gr. k-2). 9.95 *(978-1-57791-419-8(8))* Brighter Minds Children's Publishing.
—Kung Fu Panda Magnetic Storybook. 2008. (DreamWorks Kung Fu Panda Ser.). (Illus.). 10p. (J). (gr. 1-3). bds. 12.95 *(978-1-57791-421-1(X))* Brighter Minds Children's Publishing.
Brignaud, Pierre, illus. Caillou: What Should I Wear? 2010. (Interactive Bks.). (ENG.). 10p. (J). (gr. -1-1). bds. 12.95 *(978-2-89450-767-4(4))* Caillouet, Gerry.
Broach, Elise. Barnyard Baby. Doerrfeld, Cori, illus. 2013. (Baby Seasons Ser.). (ENG.). 14p. (J). (gr. -1 — 1). bds. 7.99 *(978-0-316-21203-8(2))* Little, Brown Bks. for Young Readers.
Broderick, Kathy. Disney Princess: Belle (Giant First Play -a-Sound) 2010. 10p. (J). bds. 17.98 *(978-1-60553-543-2(5))* Publications International, Ltd.
Brooke, Jasmine. Goldilocks & the Three Bears: Take the Temperature Test & Solve the Porridge Puzzle! 2017. (Fairy Tale Fixers: Fixing Fairy Tale Problems with STEM Ser.). 32p. (gr. 3-4). pap. 63.00 *(978-1-5382-0665-2(X))* Stevens, Gareth Publishing LLLP.
Brooke, Susan Rich. World of Eric Carle: Sing Sound Book. 2018. (ENG., Illus.). 12p. (J). bds. 15.99 *(978-1-5037-2205-7(8),* 2509, PI Kids) Phoenix International Publications, Inc.
—World of Eric Carle: Where Do You Live? Lift-A-Flap Sound Book. 2018. (ENG., Illus.). 10p. (J). bds. 14.99 *(978-1-5037-2206-4(6),* 2510, PI Kids) Phoenix International Publications, Inc.
Brooke, Susan Rich, adapted by. The Lion King. 2003. (Illus.). (J). *(978-0-7853-9380-1(3))* Publications International, Ltd.
Brooke, Susan Rich & Seuss, Dr. The Cat in the Hat Flips His Lid. Enik, Ted, illus. 2003. (J). *(978-0-7853-8446-5(4))* Publications International, Ltd.
Brooks, F. & Litchfield, J. Nativity Lift-the-Flap. 2004. (First Stories Ser.). 24p. (J). 10.95 *(978-0-7945-0529-5(5))* EDC Publishing.
Brooks, Felicity. Cars. Newell, Keith, illus. 2008. (Usborne Lift & Look Ser.). 12p. (J). (gr. -1-3). bds. 9.99 *(978-0-7945-1958-2(X),* Usborne) EDC Publishing.
—Construction Sites. Newell, Keith, illus. 2010. (Lift & Look Board Bks.). 12p. (J). bds. 9.99 *(978-0-7945-2728-0(0),* Usborne) EDC Publishing.
—Farms lift & Look. Litchfield, Jo, illus. 2005. 12p. (J). 9.95 *(978-0-7945-0932-3(0),* Usborne) EDC Publishing.
—Lift-out Colors Book. 2008. (Shapes & Colors Jigsaw Bks). 12p. (J). bds. 12.99 *(978-0-7945-2136-3(3),* Usborne) EDC Publishing.
—Lift-the-Flap Counting Book. 2011. (Lift-the-Flap Bks). 14p. (J). ring bd. 11.99 *(978-0-7945-2916-1(X),* Usborne) EDC Publishing.
—Lift-The-Flap First Math. 2017. (Lift-The-Flap Board Bks.). (ENG.). 16p. (J). 13.99 *(978-0-7945-3926-9(2),* Usborne) EDC Publishing.
—Lift-the-Flap Word Book. 2011. (Lift-the-Flap Word Book Ser.). 14p. (J). pap. 11.99 *(978-0-7945-2562-0(8),* Usborne) EDC Publishing.
—This Is My Duck. 2008. (NoisyTouchy-Feely Board Bks). 10p. (J). (gr. -1). bds. 16.99 *(978-0-7945-2187-5(8),* Usborne) EDC Publishing.
—This Is My Tractor. Dimitri, Simona, illus. 2009. (Noisy Touchy-Feely Board Bks). 10p. (J). bds. 16.99 *(978-0-7945-2473-9(7),* Usborne) EDC Publishing.
—Tractors Chunky Jigsaw Book. 2005. (Chunky Jigsaw Books Ser.). 14p. (J). 7.95 *(978-0-7945-0861-6(8),* Usborne) EDC Publishing.
—Trains Chunky Jigsaw Book. 2005. (Chunky Jigsaw Books Ser.). 14p. (J). 7.95 *(978-0-7945-0859-3(6),* Usborne) EDC Publishing.
—Trucks Lift-and-Look. 2005. (Illus.). 12p. (J). (gr. -1-k). per., bds. 9.95 *(978-0-7945-1068-8(X),* Usborne) EDC Publishing.
—Under the Sea Lift & Look. 2010. (Lift & Look Board Bks). 12p. (J). bds. 9.99 *(978-0-7945-2576-7(8),* Usborne) EDC Publishing.
—Very First Animals Board Book. 2010. (Very First Words Board Bks). 10p. (J). bds. 6.99 *(978-0-7945-2479-1(6),* Usborne) EDC Publishing.
—Very First Colors Board Book. 2010. (Very First Words Board Bks). 10p. (J). bds. 6.99 *(978-0-7945-2763-1(9),* Usborne) EDC Publishing.
Brooks, Felicity, des. Build a Picture Trains Sticker Book. 2012. (Build a Picture Sticker Bks). 24p. (J). pap. 6.99 *(978-0-7945-3261-1(6),* Usborne) EDC Publishing.
—Build a Picture Trucks Sticker Book. 2012. (Build a Picture Sticker Bks). 24p. (J). pap. 6.99 *(978-0-7945-3248-2(9),* Usborne) EDC Publishing.
Brooks, Felicity & Litchfield, Jo. First Picture Animals. Van Wyk, Hanri, illus. 2008. (First Picture Board Bks.). 12p. (J). (gr. -1). bds. 11.99 *(978-0-7945-1831-8(1),* Usborne) EDC Publishing.
Brooks, Felicity & Mackinnon, Mairi. Spanish Words & Phrases - Internet Referenced. 2008. (First Picture Spanish Ser.). (Illus.). 50p. (J). 9.99 *(978-0-7945-2229-2(7),* Usborne) EDC Publishing.
Brooks, Felicity, et al. The Counting Train. Cartwright, Stephen, illus. 2006. (J). *(978-0-439-89922-2(2))* Scholastic, Inc.
Brooks, Susie. 5 Cheeky Monkeys. Tarbett, Debbie, illus. 2016. (J). *(978-1-84857-539-4(4))* Little Tiger Pr. Group.
—5 Chirpy Birds. Tarbett, Debbie, illus. 2016. (J). *(978-1-84857-540-0(8))* Little Tiger Pr.
Brown, Carron. En la Estación Espacial: Shine-A-light. Johnson, Bee, illus. 2019.Tr. of On the Space Station. (SPA.). (J). 12.99 *(978-1-61067-913-8(X))* Kane Miller.
—Maravillas de EE. UU: Shine-A-light. Robbins, Wesley, illus. 2019.Tr. of Wonders of the USA. (SPA.). (J). 12.99 *(978-1-61067-916-9(4))* Kane Miller.
—Secretos de la Costa: Shine-A-light. Nassner, Alyssa, illus. 2019.Tr. of Secrets of the Seashore. (SPA.). (J). 12.99 *(978-1-61067-912-1(1))* Kane Miller.
—Secretos Del Planeta Tierra: Shine-A-light. Robbins, Wesley, illus. 2019.Tr. of Secrets of Our Earth. (SPA.). (J). 12.99 *(978-1-61067-911-4(3))* Kane Miller.
—Secrets of Our Earth. Robins, Wesley, illus. 2017. (ENG.). 36p. (J). 12.99 *(978-1-61067-536-9(3))* Kane Miller.
—Secrets of the Seashore. 2014. (ENG., Illus.). 36p. (J). 12.99 *(978-1-61067-309-9(3))* Kane Miller.
—Wonders of the USA: Shine-A-light. 2017. (ENG., Illus.). 36p. (J). 12.99 *(978-1-61067-543-7(6))* Kane Miller.
Brown, Heather. Chomp! Zoo: A Pull-Tab Book. 2012. (ENG.). 12p. (J). (gr. -1-k). bds. 7.99 *(978-1-4494-2312-4(4))* Andrews McMeel Publishing.
—The Robot Book. (ENG.). 12p. (J). 2013. bds. 9.99 *(978-1-4494-3250-8(6))* 2010. (Illus.). bds. 16.99 *(978-0-7407-9725-5(5))* Andrews McMeel Publishing.
Brown, James. Farm. Brown, James, illus. 2013. (ENG., Illus.). 16p. (J). (gr. -1 — 1). bds. 8.99 *(978-0-7636-5931-8(2))* Candlewick Pr.
Brown, Janet. Goldilocks & the Three Bears (Floor Book) My First Reading Book. Morton, Ken, illus. 2013. (ENG.). 24p. (J). (gr. -1-2). pap. 6.99 *(978-1-84322-901-8(3),* Armadillo) Anness Publishing GBR. Dist: National Bk. Network.
Brown, Margaret Wise. A Child's Good Morning Book. Katz, Karen, illus. 2016. (ENG.). 32p. (J). (gr. -1 — 1). bds. 7.99 *(978-0-06-233792-4(0),* HarperFestival) HarperCollins Pubs.
—Goodnight Moon 123 Padded Board Book: A Counting Book. Hurd, Clement, illus. 2013. (ENG.). 30p. (J). (gr. -1-k). bds. 9.99 *(978-0-06-224405-5(1),* HarperFestival) HarperCollins Pubs.
—Goodnight Moon ABC Padded Board Book: An Alphabet Book. Hurd, Clement, illus. 2013. (ENG.). 30p. (J). (gr. -1-k). bds. 9.99 *(978-0-06-224404-8(3),* HarperFestival) HarperCollins Pubs.
—Goodnight Moon Padded Board Book. Hurd, Clement, illus. 2017. (ENG.). 34p. (J). (gr. -1 — 1). bds. 10.99 *(978-0-06-257309-4(8),* HarperFestival) HarperCollins Pubs.
—Goodnight Moon/Buenas Noches, Luna: Bilingual English-Spanish. Hurd, Clement, illus. 2014. (ENG.). 34p. (J). (gr. -1-3). bds. 9.99 *(978-0-06-236791-4(9),* HarperFestival) HarperCollins Pubs.
—The Noisy Book Board Book. Weisgard, Leonard, illus. 2017. (ENG.). 36p. (J). (gr. -1 — 1). bds. 7.99 *(978-0-06-248465-9(6),* HarperFestival) HarperCollins Pubs.
—The Quiet Noisy Book Board Book. Weisgard, Leonard, illus. 2017. (ENG.). 34p. (J). (gr. -1 — 1). bds. 7.99 *(978-0-06-248466-6(4),* HarperFestival) HarperCollins Pubs.
—The Runaway Bunny Padded Board Book: An Easter & Springtime Book for Kids. Hurd, Clement. 2017. (ENG.). 36p. (J). (gr. -1 — 1). bds. 10.99 *(978-0-06-245959-6(7),* HarperFestival) HarperCollins Pubs.
Brown, Petra, illus. Itsy Bitsy Spider. 2015. (Grandma's Nursery Rhymes Ser.). (ENG.). 18p. (J). (gr. -1-k). bds. 6.99 *(978-1-58536-607-1(2),* 203946) Sleeping Bear Pr.
—Old MacDonald. 2015. (Grandma's Nursery Rhymes Ser.). (ENG.). 18p. (J). (gr. -1-k). bds. 8.99 *(978-1-58536-609-5(9),* 203945) Sleeping Bear Pr.
Brownjohn, Emma. All Kinds of Feelings: A Lift-The-Flap Book. 2003. (All Kinds Of Ser.). (ENG., Illus.). 16p. (J). (gr. -1-k). 12.99 *(978-1-85707-596-0(X))* Tango Bks. GBR. Dist: Independent Pubs. Group.
Broyles, Beverly Ashley, illus. Grandmother's Alligator/Burukenge Wa Nyanya Activity Guide. 2005. (ENG & SWA.). (J). 12.95 *(978-0-9703632-7-5(3))* Wakefield Connection, The.
Bruin, Jessica. Cube Book. 2011. (ENG., Illus.). 48p. (J). (gr. -1-1). bds. 16.95 *(978-1-77049-325-4(5),* Tundra Bks.) Tundra Bks. CAN. Dist: Penguin Random Hse. LLC.
Brunellière, Lucie. Deep in the Ocean. 2019. (ENG., Illus.). 14p. (J). (gr. -1-k). bds. 15.99 *(978-1-4197-3356-7(7),* 1254910, Abrams Appleseed) Abrams, Inc.
Buck, Deanna. My First Story of the First Easter. 2008. (Illus.). 32p. (J). 13.95 *(978-1-59038-871-6(2))* Deseret Bk. Co.
Budnick, Madeleine. Animal Amigos! Artsy Creatures in English y Espanol. 2013. (ArteKids Ser.). (ENG., Illus.). 16p. (J). (-k). bds. 7.95 *(978-1-59534-152-5(8))* Trinity Univ. Pr.
—Black & Blanco! Engaging Art in English y Español. 2013. (ArteKids Ser.). (ENG., Illus.). 16p. (J). (-k). bds. 7.95 *(978-1-59534-154-9(4))* Trinity Univ. Pr.
—Colores Everywhere! Colors in English & Spanish. 2013. (ArteKids Ser.). (ENG., Illus.). 16p. (J). (gr. k-k). bds. 7.95 *(978-1-59534-139-6(0))* Trinity Univ. Pr.
Buehner, Caralyn & Buehner, Mark. The Escape of Marvin the Ape. 2010. (Illus.). 16.10 *(978-0-7569-9295-8(8))* Penguin Publishing Group.
Bug Mania. (Flip Flap Fun Book Ser.). 10p. (J). bds. *(978-2-7643-0183-8(9))* Phidal Publishing, Inc./Editions Phidal, Inc.
Bunting, Eve. Flower Garden. Hewitt, Kathryn, illus. 2004. 28p. (gr. -1-2). 17.00 *(978-0-7569-4113-0(X))* Perfection Learning Corp.
—Scary, Scary Halloween Gift Edition. Brett, Jan, illus. 2017. (ENG.). 40p. (J). (gr. -1-3). 8.99 *(978-0-544-88034-4(X),* 1651183, Clarion Bks.) HarperCollins Pubs.
Burach, Ross. I Love My Tutu Too! (a Never Bored Book!) Burach, Ross, illus. 2020. (ENG., Illus.). 30p. (J). (gr. -1 — 1). bds. 7.99 *(978-1-338-50427-9(4),* Scholastic Pr.) Scholastic, Inc.
Burke, Zoe. CatBook. 2016. (ENG., Illus.). 24p. (J). bds. 10.95 *(978-0-7649-7371-0(1),* POMEGRANATE KIDS) Pomegranate Communications, Inc.
—Charley Harper's Count the Birds. Harper, Charley, illus. 2015. (ENG.). 24p. (J). bds. 10.95 *(978-0-7649-7246-1(4),* POMEGRANATE KIDS) Pomegranate Communications, Inc.
—Molly Hashimoto's Birds! Season by Season. Hashimoto, Molly, illus. 2018. 24p. (J). bds. 10.95 *(978-0-7649-8217-0(6),* POMEGRANATE KIDS) Pomegranate Communications, Inc.
—Owls & Loons. Inuit artists and printmakers of Kinngait Studios, illus. 2016. 24p. (J). bds. 10.95 *(978-0-7649-7542-4(0),* POMEGRANATE KIDS) Pomegranate Communications, Inc.
Burns, Helen Marie. Ryleigh's Little Bug Book, 1 vol. Vareberg, Gladys, illus. 2009. 24p. pap. 24.95 *(978-1-60813-701-5(5))* America Star Bks.
Burrill, Jenny. Yoga. Kushnir, Hilli, illus. 2020. (Baby's Big World Ser.). 18p. (J). bds. 8.99 *(978-1-946000-03-5(5),* Starry Forest Bks.) Starry Forest Bks., Inc.
Burroughs, Caleb. Cars. 2006. (Look & Find Ser.). (Illus.). 18p. (J). (gr. -1-3). pap. 24.98 *(978-1-4127-3775-3(3),* 7269900) Phoenix International Publications, Inc.
—Dora the Explorer to the Moon. Miller, Victoria, illus. 2007. (Play a Tune Tale Ser.). 16p. (J). (gr. -1-3). 12.98 *(978-1-4127-8830-4(7))* Publications International, Ltd.
—Transformers. Mawhinney, Art, illus. 2007. (Look & Find (Publications International) Ser.). 16p. (J). (gr. -1-3). 7.98 *(978-1-4127-8673-7(8))* Publications International, Ltd.
Burton, Jeffrey. Delivery Trucks! Cooper, Jay, illus. 2017. (ENG.). 12p. (J). (gr. -1). bds. 7.99 *(978-1-4814-9219-5(5),* Little Simon) Little Simon.
—Food Trucks! A Lift-The-Flap Meal on Wheels! Cooper, Jay, illus. 2016. (ENG.). 12p. (J). (gr. -1). bds. 8.99 *(978-1-4814-6521-2(X),* Little Simon) Little Simon.
—The Itsy Bitsy Bunny. Rescek, Sanja, illus. 2016. (Itsy Bitsy Ser.). (ENG.). 16p. (J). (gr. -1 — 1). bds. 5.99 *(978-1-4814-5621-0(0),* Little Simon) Little Simon.
—The Itsy Bitsy Pilgrim. Rescek, Sanja, illus. 2016. (Itsy Bitsy Ser.). (ENG.). 16p. (J). (gr. -1 — 1). bds. 5.99 *(978-1-4814-6852-7(9),* Little Simon) Little Simon.
—Jingle Bells at the Zoo. Trithart, Emma, illus. 2018. (ENG.). 14p. (J). (gr. -1 — 1). bds. 8.99 *(978-1-5344-2034-2(7),* Little Simon) Little Simon.
—My Sweet Little Megabyte. Roode, Laura, illus. 2016. (ENG.). 16p. (J). (gr. -1 — 1). bds. 5.99 *(978-1-4814-6809-1(X),* Little Simon) Little Simon.
Burton, Virginia Lee. Katy & the Big Snow Board Book: A Winter & Holiday Book for Kids. 2010. (ENG., Illus.). 38p. (J). (gr. -1-k). bds. 7.99 *(978-0-547-37145-0(4),* 1423786, Clarion Bks.) HarperCollins Pubs.
—Katy & the Big Snow Lap Board Book: A Christmas Holiday Book for Kids. 2014. (ENG., Illus.). 38p. (J). (— 1). bds. 11.99 *(978-0-544-31717-8(3),* 1582016, Clarion Bks.) HarperCollins Pubs.
—Mike Mulligan & His Steam Shovel 75th Anniversary. 75th anniv. ed. 2014. (ENG., Illus.). 56p. (J). (gr. -1-3). 17.99 *(978-0-544-27992-6(1),* 1570274, Clarion Bks.) HarperCollins Pubs.
Bush, Zack. Made for Me. De Lauretis, Gregorio, illus. 2019. (ENG.). 20p. (J). (gr. -1-k). bds. 12.99 *(978-1-64170-200-3(1),* 550200) Familius LLC.
Busy Builders. (Flip Flap Fun Book Ser.). 10p. (J). bds. *(978-2-7643-0138-8(3))* Phidal Publishing, Inc./Editions Phidal, Inc.
Busy City. (Flip Flap Fun Book Ser.). 10p. (J). bds. *(978-2-89393-820-2(5))* Phidal Publishing, Inc./Editions Phidal, Inc.
Butler Seder, Rufus. Waddle! A Scanimation Picture Book. 2009. (Scanimation Ser.). (ENG., Illus.). 12p. (gr. -1-2). 16.95 *(978-0-7611-5112-8(5),* 15112) Workman Publishing Co., Inc.

TUV

Butterfield, Moira. Found You, Magic Fish! Child, Jeremy, illus. 2010. (Magic Bath Bks.). (ENG.). 8p. (J). (gr. -1 — 1). 5.99 *(978-0-7641-9791-8(6))* Sourcebooks, Inc.
—Wake up, Magic Duck! Child, Jeremy, illus. 2010. (Magic Bath Bks.). (ENG.). 8p. (J). (gr. -1 — 1). 5.99 *(978-0-7641-9792-5(4))* Sourcebooks, Inc.
Butterworth, Nick. The Secret Path (a Percy the Park Keeper Story) Butterworth, Nick, illus. 2011. (Tales from Percy's Park Ser.). (ENG., Illus.). 32p. (J). pap. 11.95 *(978-0-00-715518-7(2)*, HarperCollins Children's Bks.) HarperCollins Pubs. Ltd. GBR. Dist: HarperCollins Pubs.
Buzzeo, Toni. Whose Boat? (a Guess-The-Job Book) Froese, Tom, illus. 2018. (Guess-The-Job Book Ser.). (ENG.). 16p. (J). (gr. -1 — 1). bds. 9.99 *(978-1-4197-2835-8(0)*, 1195910, Abrams Appleseed) Abrams, Inc.
—Whose Truck? (a Guess-The-Job Book) Datz, Jim, illus. 2015. (Guess-The-Job Book Ser.). (ENG.). 16p. (J). (gr. -1 — 1). bds. 10.99 *(978-1-4197-1612-6(3)*, 1098610) Abrams, Inc.
Cabral, Jeane. Bad Dog Ben. 2009. (Jeane Cabral Bks.). (Illus.). (J). bds. 12.99 *(978-1-934650-05-9(6))* Just For Kids Pr., LLC.
—Good Night Little Moo. Howarth, Daniel, illus. 2007. (Night Light Book Ser.). 10p. (gr. -1-k). *(978-1-84666-128-0(5)*, Tide Mill Pr.) Top That! Publishing PLC.
Cabrera, Jane. Animal Opposites. 2017. (ENG.). 18p. (J). (gr. -1-k). bds. 8.99 *(978-1-4998-0630-4(2))* Little Bee Books Inc.
—If You're Happy & You Know It. 2019. (Jane Cabrera's Story Time Ser.). (Illus.). 24p. (J). (-k). 18.99 *(978-0-8234-4465-6(1))*; (gr. -1 — 1). bds. 7.99 *(978-0-8234-4464-9(3))* Holiday Hse., Inc.
—Row, Row, Row Your Boat. 2016. (Jane Cabrera's Story Time Ser.). (ENG., Illus.). 24p. (J). (-k). bds. 7.99 *(978-0-8234-3632-3(2))* Holiday Hse., Inc.
Cabrol, Marta, illus. When Do I Love You?, 1 vol. 2018. (ENG.). 20p. (J). bds. 8.99 *(978-1-4002-0990-3(0)*, Tommy Nelson) Nelson, Thomas Inc.
Calabazza, Della & Monckeberg, Paulina. Ludovico & Ooops 2006. 2005. (Pascualina Family of Products Ser.). (ENG., Illus.). 240p. (J). (gr. 3-7). spiral bd. 11.99 *(978-956-8222-23-9(5))* Pascualina Producciones S.A.
Calder, Alexander. One & Other Numbers: With Alexander Calder. 2017. (ENG., Illus.). 30p. (gr. -1 — 1). bds. 9.95 *(978-0-7148-7510-1(4))* Phaidon Pr., Inc.
Calmenson, Stephanie. Look! Birds! Pinillos, Puy, illus. 2016. (Look! Ser.). (ENG.). 24p. (J). (gr. -1-1). 7.99 *(978-1-4998-0114-9(9))* Little Bee Books Inc.
—Look! Bugs! Newland, Jane, illus. 2018. (Look! Ser.). (ENG.). 24p. (J). (gr. -1-1). 8.99 *(978-1-4998-0543-7(8))* Little Bee Books Inc.
—Look! Flowers! Pinillos, Puy, illus. 2016. (Look! Ser.). (ENG.). 24p. (J). (gr. -1-1). 8.99 *(978-1-4998-0115-6(7))* Little Bee Books Inc.
Campbell, Rod. Dear Zoo. 2005. (Dear Zoo & Friends Ser.). (ENG., Illus.). 20p. (J). (gr. -1-k). 15.99 *(978-0-689-87751-3(X)*, Little Simon) Little Simon.
—Dear Zoo. Campbell, Rod, illus. 2004. (Illus.). 16p. (J). (RUS & ENG.). bds. *(978-1-84444-178-5(4))*; (CHI & ENG., bds. *(978-1-84444-171-6(7))* Mantra Lingua.
—Dear Zoo. 2004. (BEN & ENG., Illus.). 16p. (J). bds. *(978-1-84444-169-3(5))* Mantra Lingua.
—Dear Zoo. Campbell, Rod, illus. 2004. (Illus.). 16p. (J). (VIE & ENG.). bds. *(978-1-84444-183-9(0))*; (ENG & FRE., bds. *(978-1-84444-173-0(3))*; (ENG & PER., bds. *(978-1-84444-172-3(5))*; (CHI & ENG., bds. *(978-1-84444-170-9(9))*; (ENG & SOM., bds. *(978-1-84444-180-8(6))*; (ENG & ALB., bds. *(978-1-84444-167-9(9))*; (URD & ENG., bds. *(978-1-84444-182-2(2))*; (ENG & TUR., bds. *(978-1-84444-181-5(4))*; (ENG & GUJ., bds. *(978-1-84444-174-7(1))*; (ENG & HIN., bds. *(978-1-84444-175-4(X))*; (ENG & PAN., bds. *(978-1-84444-176-1(8))*; (ENG & POR., bds. *(978-1-84444-177-8(6))*; (ENG & SPA., bds. *(978-1-84444-179-2(2))*; (ENG & ARA., bds. *(978-1-84444-168-6(7))* Mantra Lingua.
—Dear Zoo. Campbell, Rod, illus. 2019. (Dear Zoo & Friends Ser.). (ENG., Illus.). 24p. (J). (— 1). 17.99 *(978-1-5344-6012-6(8)*, Little Simon) Little Simon.
—Dear Zoo: A Lift-The-Flap Book. Campbell, Rod, illus. 25th ed. 2007. (Dear Zoo & Friends Ser.). (ENG., Illus.). 18p. (J). (gr. -1 — 1). bds. 7.99 *(978-1-4169-4737-0(X)*, Little Simon) Little Simon.
—Dinosaurs. Campbell, Rod, illus. 2015. (Dear Zoo & Friends Ser.). (ENG., Illus.). 14p. (J). (gr. -1 — 1). bds. 7.99 *(978-1-4814-4985-4(0)*, Little Simon) Little Simon.
—Farm Animals. Campbell, Rod, illus. 2015. (Dear Zoo & Friends Ser.). (ENG., Illus.). 14p. (J). (gr. -1 — 1). bds. 6.99 *(978-1-4814-4984-7(2)*, Little Simon) Little Simon.
Campbell, S Q. Animals. 2006. (Picture Me Ser.). (Illus.). (J). *(978-1-57151-769-2(3))* Playhouse Publishing.
—Shapes. 2006. (Picture Me Ser.). (Illus.). (J). *(978-1-57151-771-5(5))* Playhouse Publishing.
Campling, Hannah. Muddle & Match Fairy Tales. Hinton, Stephanie, illus. 2018. (ENG.). 16p. (J). 8.99 *(978-1-61067-631-1(9))* Kane Miller.
Candlewick Press. Japan: Panorama Pops. Smith, Anne, illus. 2015. (Panorama Pops Ser.). (ENG.). 30p. (J). (gr. k-4). 8.99 *(978-0-7636-7504-2(0))* Candlewick Pr.
Candlewick Press Staff. Creepy-Crawlies: a 3D Pocket Guide. KJA Artists Staff, illus. 2013. (Panorama Pops Ser.). (ENG.). 30p. (J). (gr. -1-2). 8.99 *(978-0-7636-6662-0(9))* Candlewick Pr.
—The Story of Flight: Panorama Pops. Holcroft, John, illus. 2015. (Panorama Pops Ser.). (ENG.). 30p. (J). (gr. k-4). 8.99 *(978-0-7636-7700-8(0))* Candlewick Pr.
Candy Cane Press, creator. Safe at Home! Indoor Safety. 2005. (ENG., Illus.). 14p. (J). (gr. -1-k). bds. 12.95 *(978-0-8249-6592-1(2)*, Ideals Pubns.) Worthy Publishing.
—Safe at Play: Outdoor Safety. 2005. (ENG., Illus.). 14p. (J). (gr. -1-k). bds. 12.95 *(978-0-8249-6593-8(0)*, Ideals Pubns.) Worthy Publishing.
Cannon, Janell. Stellaluna Board Book. 2007. (ENG., Illus.). 42p. (J). (gr. -1 — 1). bds. 8.99 *(978-0-15-206287-3(4)*, 1198845, Clarion Bks.) HarperCollins Pubs.
Capucilli, Alyssa Satin. Biscuit's 123. Schories, Pat & Berlin, Rose Mary, illus. 2012. (Biscuit Ser.). (ENG.). 16p. (J). (gr. -1-1). bds. 6.99 *(978-0-06-162523-7(X)*, HarperFestival) HarperCollins Pubs.
—Biscuit's Pet & Play Bedtime: A Touch & Feel Book. Schories, Pat, illus. 2017. (Biscuit Ser.). (ENG.). 12p. (J). (gr. -1 — 1). bds. 7.99 *(978-0-06-249039-1(7)*, HarperFestival) HarperCollins Pubs.
—Biscuit's Pet & Play Farm Animals: A Touch & Feel Book: an Easter & Springtime Book for Kids. Schories, Pat, illus. 2018. (Biscuit Ser.). (ENG.). 12p. (J). (gr. -1 — 1). bds. 8.99 *(978-0-06-249052-0(4)*, HarperFestival) HarperCollins Pubs.
—Blanket of Love. Boynton-Hughes, Brooke, illus. 2017. (New Books for Newborns Ser.). (ENG.). 16p. (J). (gr. -1 — 1). bds. 7.99 *(978-1-4814-8972-0(0)*, Little Simon) Little Simon.
—Good Night, My Darling Baby. Bach, Annie, illus. 2017. (New Books for Newborns Ser.). (ENG.). 16p. (J). (gr. -1 — 1). bds. 7.99 *(978-1-4814-8119-9(3)*, Little Simon) Little Simon.
—Happy Easter, Biscuit! A Lift-The-Flap Book: an Easter & Springtime Book for Kids. Schories, Pat, illus. 2020. (Biscuit Ser.). (ENG.). 20p. (J). (gr. -1-3). pap. 6.99 *(978-0-694-01223-7(8)*, HarperFestival) HarperCollins Pubs.
—Happy Halloween, Biscuit! Schories, Pat, illus. 2019. (Biscuit Ser.). (ENG.). 20p. (J). (gr. -1-3). pap. 6.99 *(978-0-694-01220-6(3)*, HarperFestival) HarperCollins Pubs.
—Happy Thanksgiving, Biscuit! Schories, Pat, illus. 2019. (Biscuit Ser.). (ENG.). 20p. (J). (gr. -1-3). pap. 6.99 *(978-0-694-01221-3(1)*, HarperFestival) HarperCollins Pubs.
—Katy Duck. Cole, Henry, illus. 2007. (Katy Duck Ser.). (ENG.). 16p. (J). (gr. -1-k). bds. 8.99 *(978-1-4169-1901-8(5)*, Little Simon) Little Simon.
—My First Ballet Class: A Book with Foldout Pages. Jensen, Leyah, illus. Jensen, Leyah, photos by. 2011. (My First Ser.). (ENG.). 14p. (J). (gr. -1-k). 9.99 *(978-1-4424-0895-1(2)*, Little Simon) Little Simon.
—My Mom & Me. Mitchell, Susan, illus. 2009. (ENG.). 16p. (J). (gr. -1-1). 7.99 *(978-1-4169-5829-1(0)*, Little Simon) Little Simon.
Cara, Anwar. 5 Pillars of Islam. Zulkifli, Azhari, illus. 2015. 16p. (J). bds. 9.95 *(978-0-86037-574-6(9))* Kube Publishing Ltd. GBR. Dist: Consortium Bk. Sales & Distribution.
Carle, Eric. Dream Snow. Carle, Eric, illus. 2015. (Illus.). 22p. (J). (gr. -1 — 1). bds. 9.99 *(978-0-399-17314-1(5))* Penguin Young Readers Group.
—From Head to Toe Padded Board Book. Carle, Eric, illus. 2018. (ENG., Illus.). 28p. (J). (gr. -1 — 1). bds. 9.99 *(978-0-06-274766-2(5)*, HarperFestival) HarperCollins Pubs.
—Have You Seen My Cat? A Slide-And-Peek Board Book. Carle, Eric, illus. 2009. (World of Eric Carle Ser.). (ENG., Illus.). 16p. (J). bds. 8.99 *(978-1-4169-8514-3(X)*, Little Simon) Little Simon.
—My First Busy Book. Carle, Eric, illus. 2015. (World of Eric Carle Ser.). (ENG., Illus.). 12p. (J). (gr. -1). bds. 16.99 *(978-1-4814-5791-0(8)*, Little Simon) Little Simon.
—My First Peek-A-Boo Animals. Carle, Eric, illus. 2017. (World of Eric Carle Ser.). (ENG., Illus.). 18p. (J). (gr. -1 — 1). bds. 7.99 *(978-1-5344-0105-1(9)*, Little Simon) Little Simon.
—My Very First Book of Animal Homes. Carle, Eric, illus. 2007. (Illus.). 20p. (J). (gr. -1 — 1). bds. 6.99 *(978-0-399-24647-0(9))* Penguin Young Readers Group.
—My Very First Book of Motion. Carle, Eric, illus. 2007. (Illus.). 18p. (J). (gr. -1 — 1). bds. 6.99 *(978-0-399-24748-4(3))* Penguin Young Readers Group.
—My Very First Book of Shapes / Mi Primer Libro de Formas: Bilingual Edition. Carle, Eric, illus. 2013. (Illus.). 20p. (J). (gr. -1 — 1). bds. 6.99 *(978-0-399-16142-1(2))* Penguin Young Readers Group.
—La Oruga Muy Hambrienta/the Very Hungry Caterpillar: Bilingual Board Book. Carle, Eric, illus. 2011. (Illus.). 24p. (J). (gr. -1 — 1). bds. 10.99 *(978-0-399-25605-9(9))* Penguin Young Readers Group.
—The Very Busy Spider. Carle, Eric, illus. 2011. (ENG., Illus.). 24p. (J). (gr. -1 — 1). bds. 16.99 *(978-0-399-25601-1(6)*, Philomel Bks.) Penguin Young Readers Group.
—The Very Busy Spider: A Lift-The-Flap Book. 2006. (World of Eric Carle Ser.). (Illus.). 24p. (J). (gr. -1-k). 9.99 *(978-0-448-44421-5(6))* Penguin Young Readers Group.
—The Very Busy Spider's Favorite Words. 2007. (ENG., Illus.). 20p. (J). (gr. -1-k). bds. 5.99 *(978-0-448-44703-2(7))* Penguin Young Readers Group.
—The Very Hungry Caterpillar. 2004. (J). (gr. -1-2). spiral bd. *(978-0-616-01611-4(5))*; spiral bd. *(978-0-616-01610-7(7))* Canadian National Institute for the Blind/Institut National Canadien pour les Aveugles.
—The Very Hungry Caterpillar. 2004. (Illus.). (J). (GUJ.). 23p. *(978-1-85269-127-1(1))*; (ENG & SOM., 19p. pap. *(978-1-85269-128-8(X))* Mantra Lingua.
—The Very Hungry Caterpillar. Carle, Eric, illus. 2004. (Illus.). 20p. (J). (ENG & URD.). pap. *(978-1-85269-129-5(8))*; (ENG & BEN., pap. *(978-1-85269-125-7(5))*; (ENG & CHI., (gr. -1-2). pap. *(978-1-85269-126-4(3))*; (ARA & ENG., (gr. -1-5). pap. *(978-1-85269-124-0(7))* Mantra Lingua.
—The Very Hungry Caterpillar. 2008. (CHI., Illus.). 32p. *(978-7-5332-5673-9(5))* Mingtian Chubanshe.
—The Very Hungry Caterpillar: Board Book & CD. Carle, Eric, illus. 2007. (ENG., Illus.). 24p. (J). (gr. -1 — 1). bds., bds. 16.99 *(978-0-399-24745-3(9))* Penguin Young Readers Group.
—The Very Hungry Caterpillar/la Oruga Muy Hambrienta. Carle, Eric, illus. 2011. (Illus.). 32p. (J). (gr. -1-k). 21.99 *(978-0-399-25604-2(0))* Penguin Young Readers Group.
—The Very Hungry Caterpillar's Favorite Words. 2007. (World of Eric Carle Ser.). (ENG., Illus.). 20p. (J). (gr. -1-k). bds. 5.99 *(978-0-448-44704-9(5))* Penguin Young Readers Group.
—The Very Hungry Caterpillar's Finger Puppet Book. 2011. (World of Eric Carle Ser.). (ENG.). 7p. (J). (gr. -1-k). bds. 12.99 *(978-0-448-45597-6(8))* Penguin Young Readers Group.
—The Very Lonely Firefly. 2012. (Penguin Young Readers Level 2 Ser.). lib. bdg. 13.55 *(978-0-606-26069-5(2))* Turtleback.
—1, 2, 3 with the 10 Little Rubber Ducks: A Spring Counting Book. Carle, Eric, illus. 2019. (ENG., Illus.). 22p. (J). (gr. -1 — 1). bds. 8.99 *(978-0-06-288256-1(2)*, HarperFestival) HarperCollins Pubs.
Carpenter, Dan & Kennelly, Sean. Amazing America: an Adventure into American History: American Collection. Gilman, Thomas W., ed. 2014. (ENG., Illus.). 48p. (J). (gr. 4). 8.99 *(978-1-4867-0255-8(4))* Flowerpot Children's Pr. Inc. CAN. Dist: Cardinal Pubs. Group.
Carpenter, Tad. When I Grow Up. 2015. (Who's That? Ser.). (Illus.). 16p. (J). (— 1). bds. 7.95 *(978-1-4549-1228-6(6))* Sterling Publishing Co., Inc.
Carroll, Claudia. Shmadiggle & the Imagination Asteroid. 2008. (ENG.). 68p. pap. 9.95 *(978-0-557-01566-5(9))* Lulu Pr., Inc.
Carroll, Lewis, pseud. Lit for Little Hands: Alice's Adventures in Wonderland, Volume 2. Miles, David W., illus. 2018. (Lit for Little Hands Ser.: 2). (ENG.). 16p. (J). (gr. -1-1). bds. 12.99 *(978-1-945547-68-3(5)*, 554768) Familius LLC.
Carter, David A. Alpha Bugs: A Pop-Up Alphabet. Carter, David A., illus. 2006. (David Carter's Bugs Ser.). (ENG., Illus.). 28p. (J). (gr. -1-2). 13.99 *(978-1-4169-0973-6(7)*, Little Simon) Little Simon.
—B Is for Box — the Happy Little Yellow Box: A Pop-Up Book. Carter, David A., illus. 2014. (ENG., Illus.). 18p. (J). (gr. -1). 14.99 *(978-1-4814-0295-8(1)*, Little Simon) Little Simon.
—Beach Bugs: A Sunny Pop-Up Book by David A. Carter. Carter, David A., illus. 2008. (David Carter's Bugs Ser.). (ENG., Illus.). 16p. (J). (gr. -1-2). 12.99 *(978-1-4169-5055-4(9)*, Little Simon) Little Simon.
—Bedtime Bugs: A Pop-Up Good Night Book by David A. Carter. Carter, David A., illus. 2010. (David Carter's Bugs Ser.). (ENG., Illus.). 16p. (J). (gr. -1-2). 12.99 *(978-1-4169-9960-7(4)*, Little Simon) Little Simon.
—The Big Bug Book: A Pop-Up Celebration by David A. Carter. Carter, David A., illus. 2008. (David Carter's Bugs Ser.). (ENG., Illus.). 16p. (J). (gr. -1-2). 29.99 *(978-1-4169-4095-1(2)*, Little Simon) Little Simon.
—Birthday Bugs: A Pop-Up Party by David A. Carter. 2004. (David Carter's Bugs Ser.). (ENG., Illus.). 16p. (J). (gr. -1-3). 12.99 *(978-0-689-81858-5(0)*, Little Simon) Little Simon.
—Bitsy Bee Goes to School: Ready-To-Read Level 1. Carter, David A., illus. 2014. (David Carter's Bugs Ser.). (ENG., Illus.). 24p. (J). (gr. -1-1). pap. 3.99 *(978-1-4424-9503-6(0)*, Simon Spotlight) Simon Spotlight.
—A Box of Bugs (Boxed Set) 4 Pop-Up Concept Books. Carter, David A., illus. 2011. (David Carter's Bugs Ser.). (ENG., Illus.). 64p. (J). (gr. -1-3). 19.99 *(978-1-4424-2989-5(5)*, Little Simon) Little Simon.
—Bugs That Go! A Bustling Pop-Up Book. Carter, David A., illus. 2011. (David Carter's Bugs Ser.). (ENG., Illus.). 18p. (J). (gr. -1-1). 12.99 *(978-1-4169-4097-5(9)*, Little Simon) Little Simon.
—Builder Bugs: A Busy Pop-Up Book. Carter, David A., illus. 2012. (David Carter's Bugs Ser.). (ENG., Illus.). 16p. (J). (gr. -1-2). 14.99 *(978-1-4424-2648-1(9)*, Little Simon) Little Simon.
—Colors: A Bugs Pop-Up Concept Book. Carter, David A., illus. 2010. (David Carter's Bugs Ser.). (ENG., Illus.). 16p. (J). (gr. -1-1). 10.99 *(978-1-4424-0830-2(8)*, Little Simon) Little Simon.
—Feely Bugs (Mini Edition) To Touch & Feel. Carter, David A., illus. 2005. (David Carter's Bugs Ser.). (ENG., Illus.). 14p. (J). (gr. -1-2). 12.99 *(978-1-4169-0326-0(7)*, Little Simon) Little Simon.
—Five Cars Stuck & One Big Truck: A Pop-Up Road Trip. Carter, David A., illus. 2017. (ENG., Illus.). 18p. (J). (gr. -1 — 1). bds. 15.99 *(978-1-4814-7119-0(8)*, Little Simon) Little Simon.
—Halloween Bugs: Halloween Bugs, Vol. 16. Carter, David A., illus. 2003. (David Carter's Bugs Ser.). (ENG., Illus.). 14p. (J). (gr. -1-3). 12.99 *(978-0-689-85916-8(3)*, Little Simon) Little Simon.
—The Happy Little Yellow Box: A Pop-Up Book of Opposites. Carter, David A., illus. 2012. (ENG., Illus.). 18p. (J). (gr. -1). 14.99 *(978-1-4169-4096-8(0)*, Little Simon) Little Simon.
—Jingle Bugs. 2004. (David Carter's Bugs Ser.). (ENG., Illus.). 22p. (J). (gr. -1-2). 14.99 *(978-0-689-87416-1(2)*, Little Simon) Little Simon.
—Merry Christmas, Bugs! Ready-To-Read Level 1. Carter, David A., illus. 2014. (David Carter's Bugs Ser.). (ENG., Illus.). 24p. (J). (gr. -1-1). pap. 4.99 *(978-1-4424-9506-7(5)*, Simon Spotlight) Simon Spotlight.
—One Red Dot: One Red Dot. 2005. (ENG., Illus.). 18p. (J). (gr. -1-3). 32.99 *(978-0-689-87769-8(2)*, Little Simon) Little Simon.
—School Bugs: An Elementary Pop-Up Book by David A. Carter. Carter, David A., illus. 2009. (David Carter's Bugs Ser.). (ENG., Illus.). 20p. (J). (gr. -1-2). 14.99 *(978-1-4169-5056-1(7)*, Little Simon) Little Simon.
—Welcome to Bugland! A Fun Foldout World from David A. Carter. Carter, David A., illus. 2011. (David Carter's Bugs Ser.). (ENG., Illus.). 24p. (J). (gr. -1-3). 12.99 *(978-1-4424-1962-9(8)*, Little Simon) Little Simon.
—White Noise: A Pop-Up Book for Children of All Ages. Carter, David A., illus. 2009. (ENG., Illus.). 20p. (J). (gr. -1-3). 39.99 *(978-1-4169-4094-4(4)*, Little Simon) Little Simon.
—Yellow Square: A Pop-Up Book for Children of All Ages. Carter, David A., illus. 2008. (ENG., Illus.). 20p. (J). (gr. -1-3). 39.99 *(978-1-4169-4093-7(6)*, Little Simon) Little Simon.
—The 12 Bugs of Christmas: A Pop-Up Christmas Counting Book. Carter, David A., illus. 2011. (David Carter's Bugs Ser.). (ENG., Illus.). 24p. (J). (gr. -1-1). 12.99 *(978-1-4424-2649-8(7)*, Little Simon) Little Simon.
—600 Black Spots: A Pop-Up Book for Children of All Ages. Carter, David A., illus. 2007. (ENG., Illus.). 20p. (J). (gr. -1-2). 29.99 *(978-1-4169-4092-0(8)*, Little Simon) Little Simon.
Cartlidge, Michelle. The Mouse Christmas House: A Press-Out Model Book. (Illus.). 32p. (J). *(978-1-904613-67-1(5)*, Buster Bks.) O'Mara, Michael Bks., Ltd.
Cartogna, Eileen. Jobs Around Town: Learning to Sort & Classify, 1 vol. (Math for the REAL World Ser.). (ENG., Illus.). 8p. (gr. k-1). 2009. pap. 5.15 *(978-0-8239-8910-2(0)*, 46186454-1f29-4ea0-a646-f19141e6c3cc) 2004. 29.95 *(978-0-8239-7629-4(7))* Rosen Publishing Group, Inc., The.
Cartwright, Amy, illus. Jack & the Beanstalk. 2011. (J). pap. *(978-0-545-27434-0(6)*, Cartwheel Bks.) Scholastic, Inc.
Cartwright, Mary, told to. Little Book of Little Puppies. 2011. (Baby's Very First Ser.). 10p. (J). ring bd. 6.99 *(978-0-7945-2957-4(7)*, Usborne) EDC Publishing.
Cartwright, Shannon. Alaska 1 2 3: Colors & Numbers. 2005. (Illus.). (J). *(978-0-9772297-0-3(X))* Taku Graphics.
Casebolt, Christian. Zoey & Bel, 1 vol. Bentley, Anita, illus. 2009. 14p. pap. 24.95 *(978-1-60813-220-1(X))* America Star Bks.
Castella, Krystina & Boyl, Brian. Discovering Nature's Alphabet. 2017. (ENG., Illus.). 28p. (J). bds. 8.99 *(978-1-59714-353-0(7))* Heyday.
A Castle Mystery. 2013. (Illus.). (J). *(978-1-4351-4945-8(9))* Disney Pr.
Catholic Book Publishing Corp. Merry Christmas! 2015. (ENG., Illus.). 10p. 12.95 *(978-0-88271-393-9(0)*, rg10325) Regina Pr., Malhame & Co.
—Saints Teach Us (Rattle Book) 2008. (ENG., Illus.). 14p. (gr. -1 — 1). bds. 7.95 *(978-0-89942-723-2(5)*, 982/22) Catholic Bk. Publishing Corp.
—Thank You Prayers (Rattle Book) 2008. (ENG., Illus.). 14p. (gr. -1-k). bds. 7.95 *(978-0-89942-722-5(7)*, 981/22) Catholic Bk. Publishing Corp.
Caviezel, Giovanni. It's Easter Time. Pagnoni, Roberta, illus. 2010. 10p. (J). (gr. -1-k). bds. 6.99 *(978-0-7641-6334-0(5))* Sourcebooks, Inc.
—Little Bunny. Rigo, Laura, illus. (Mini Look at Me Bks.). 10p. (J). (gr. -1). 2012. bds. 5.99 *(978-0-7641-6509-2(7))* 2010. bds. 8.99 *(978-0-7641-6322-7(1))* Sourcebooks, Inc.
—Little Elf. Mesturini, C., illus. 2012. (Mini People Shape Bks.). 10p. (J). (gr. -1-2). bds. 4.99 *(978-0-7641-6577-1(1))* Sourcebooks, Inc.
—Little Penguin. Rigo, Laura, illus. (Mini Look at Me Bks.). 10p. (J). (gr. -1 — 1). 2014. bds. 4.99 *(978-0-7641-6731-7(6))* 2010. bds. 8.99 *(978-0-7641-6353-1(1))* Sourcebooks, Inc.
—Little Pig. Rigo, Laura, illus. 2010. (Mini Look at Me Bks.). 10p. (J). (gr. -1 — 1). bds. 8.99 *(978-0-7641-6355-5(8))* Sourcebooks, Inc.
—Little Puppy. Rigo, Laura, illus. (Mini Look at Me Bks.). 10p. (J). (gr. -1 — 1). 2012. bds. 5.99 *(978-0-7641-6512-2(7))* 2010. bds. 8.99 *(978-0-7641-6324-1(8))* Sourcebooks, Inc.
—My Own Human Body. Mesturini, C., illus. 2012. (Little People Shape Bks.). 10p. (J). (gr. k-1). bds. 8.99 *(978-0-7641-6570-2(4))* Sourcebooks, Inc.
—Pirates! Mesturini, C., illus. 2011. (Mini People Shape Bks.). 10p. (J). (gr. -1-1). bds. 5.99 *(978-0-7641-6441-5(4))* Sourcebooks, Inc.
Cerasini, Marc. Godzilla Saves America: A Monster Showdown In 3-D! Morgan, Tom & Mounts, Paul, illus. 2006. 20p. (J). (gr. k-4). reprint ed. 12.00 *(978-1-4223-5409-4(1))* DIANE Publishing Co.
Chabbert, Ingrid & Beal, Marjorie. In Shape. 2017. (ENG., Illus.). 18p. (J). bds. 14.95 *(978-1-58423-656-6(6)*, 09094aad-6275-4fc3-a2e0-63b4c11cd321) Gingko Pr., Inc.
Chanko, Pamela. Wash, Wash, Wash! (Rookie Toddler) Padron, Alicia, illus. 2018. (Rookie Toddler Ser.). (ENG.). 14p. (J). (gr. -1 — 1). bds. 6.95 *(978-0-531-22893-7(2)*, Children's Pr.) Scholastic Library Publishing.
Channing, Margot. Around Town. Claude, Jean, illus. 2018. (First Words & Pictures Ser.). (ENG.). 14p. (J). (gr. -1 — 1). bds. 9.99 *(978-1-68152-410-8(4)*, 14942) Amicus.
—At Home. Claude, Jean, illus. 2018. (First Words & Pictures Ser.). (ENG.). 14p. (J). (gr. -1 — 1). bds. 9.99 *(978-1-68152-411-5(2)*, 14943) Amicus.
Chanukah Treats: For Kids, by Kids. 2009. (Illus.). 16p. (J). spiral bd. *(978-0-9772560-2-0(2))* Rite Lite Limited.
Chapman, Jane. Is It Christmas Yet? Chapman, Jane, illus. 2015. (ENG., Illus.). 22p. (J). (gr. -1-k). bds. 8.99 *(978-1-58925-553-1(4))* Tiger Tales.
Chapman, Jason. Who's That Singing? A Pull-The-Tab Book. Chapman, Jason, illus. 2010. (ENG., Illus.). 12p. (J). (gr. -1-1). bds. 9.99 *(978-1-4169-8736-9(3)*, Little Simon) Little Simon.
—Who's That Snoring? A Pull-The-Tab Bedtime Book. Chapman, Jason, illus. 2010. (ENG., Illus.). 12p. (J). (gr. -1-1). bds. 9.99 *(978-1-4169-8937-0(4)*, Little Simon) Little Simon.
Chapman, Simon. Discovering Dinosaurs. 2016. (ENG., Illus.). 32p. (J). *(978-1-4081-9461-4(9)*, 228958, Bloomsbury Children's Bks.) Bloomsbury Publishing Plc.
Charbonnel-Bojman, Severine. My Picture Book of Animals. 2012. (ENG., Illus.). 256p. (J). (gr. -1-k). 9.95 *(978-1-77085-112-2(7)*, 6f78d0e0-ec51-4c33-abd9-7a6d665b51d3) Firefly Bks., Ltd.
Charles, Faustin. The Selfish Crocodile Counting Book. Terry, Michael, illus. Lt. ed. 2008. 12p. (J). (gr. k-k). bds. 8.95 *(978-0-7475-9238-9(1))* Bloomsbury Publishing Plc GBR. Dist: Independent Pubs. Group.
Chatterton, Martin. Can Dogs Fly? Fido's Book of Pop-up Transportation Surprises. 2005. (Illus.). 12p. (J). (gr. k-4). reprint ed. 10.00 *(978-0-7567-8838-4(2))* DIANE Publishing Co.
Chedru, Delphine. What Happens When... 2013. (ENG., Illus.). 32p. (J). (gr. k-2). 15.95 *(978-1-84976-103-1(5))* Tate Publishing, Ltd. GBR. Dist: Hachette Bk. Group.
Chedru, Delphine & Duisit, Bernard. This or That? Industrial Inspiration for Twenty-First-Century Living. 2017. (Flip Flap Pop-Up Ser.: 0). (Illus.). 16p. (J). (gr. -1-1). 14.95 *(978-0-500-65093-6(4)*, 565093) Thames & Hudson.
Cheerios Counting Songs. 2004. (Illus.). (J). *(978-0-7853-9953-7(4))* Publications International, Ltd.
Cheetham, Stephen, illus. Off to the Park! 2014. (Tactile Bks.). 12p. (J). spiral bd. *(978-1-84643-502-7(1))* Child's Play International Ltd.
Cherry, Alison. She's the Liar. 2019. (ENG.). 208p. (J). (gr. 3-7). 17.99 *(978-1-338-30614-9(6)*, Scholastic Pr.) Scholastic, Inc.
Child, Lydia Maria. Bitty Bear's Sleigh Ride. Ackley, Peggy Jo, illus. 2006. (J). *(978-1-59369-157-8(2))* American Girl Publishing, Inc.
Child's Play. City. Cocoretto, illus. 2017. (Wheels at Work (US Edition) Ser.: 4). (ENG.). 12p. (J). bds. *(978-1-78628-081-7(7))* Child's Play International Ltd.
—Construction. Cocoretto, illus. 2017. (Wheels at Work (US Edition) Ser.: 4). (ENG.). 12p. (J). bds. *(978-1-78628-083-1(3))* Child's Play International Ltd.
—Emergency. Cocoretto, illus. alt. ed. 2017. (Wheels at Work (US Edition) Ser.: 4). (ENG.). 12p. (J). bds. *(978-1-78628-080-0(9))* Child's Play International Ltd.
—Spring. Busby, Ailie, illus. 2015. (Seasons Ser.: 4). 12p. (J). (gr. 1-1). spiral bd. *(978-1-84643-741-0(5))* Child's Play International Ltd.
—Summer. Busby, Ailie, illus. 2015. (Seasons Ser.: 4). 12p. (J). (gr. 1-1). spiral bd. *(978-1-84643-742-7(3))* Child's Play International Ltd.

—What's That Noise? CHOO! CHOO! Guess the Vehicle! Cocoretto, illus. 2015. (What's That Noise? Ser.: 4). 12p. (J). spiral bd. *(978-1-84643-746-5(6))* Child's Play International Ltd.

—What's That Noise? SNAP! SNAP! Guess the Animal! Cocoretto, illus. 2015. (What's That Noise? Ser.: 4). 12p. (J). spiral bd. *(978-1-84643-748-9(2))* Child's Play International Ltd.

—What's That Noise? TAP! TAP! Guess the Toy! Cocoretto, illus. 2015. (What's That Noise? Ser.: 4). 12p. (J). spiral bd. *(978-1-84643-747-2(4))* Child's Play International Ltd.

—What's That Noise? TOOT! TOOT! Guess the Instrument! Cocoretto, illus. 2015. (What's That Noise? Ser.: 4). 12p. (J). spiral bd. *(978-1-84643-749-6(0))* Child's Play International Ltd.

—What's up Crocodile? Sport. Cocoretto, illus. 2018. (What's Up? Ser.: 4). 12p. (J). spiral bd. *(978-1-78628-051-0(5))* Child's Play International Ltd.

—What's up Fox? Dressing Up. Cocoretto, illus. 2018. (What's Up? Ser.: 4). 12p. (J). bds. *(978-1-78628-156-2(2))* Child's Play International Ltd.

—What's up Penguin? Art. Cocoretto, illus. 2018. (What's Up? Ser.: 4). 12p. (J). bds. *(978-1-78628-154-8(6))* Child's Play International Ltd.

—What's up Tiger? Food. Cocoretto, illus. 2018. (What's Up? Ser.: 4). 12p. (J). bds. *(978-1-78628-157-9(0))* Child's Play International Ltd.

—Winter. Busby, Ailie, illus. 2015. (Seasons Ser.: 4). 12p. (J). (gr. 1-1). spiral bd. *(978-1-84643-745-8(8))* Child's Play International Ltd.

Chilek, Laurie. Counting at the Zoo: Learning to Add 1 to One-Digit Numbers, 1 vol. (Math for the REAL World Ser.). (ENG., Illus.). 8p. (gr. k-1). 2010. pap. 5.15 *(978-0-8239-8909-6(7),* 22b91f7d-d712-4e42-b958-eb07d568866a) 2004. 29.95 *(978-0-8239-7628-7(9))* Rosen Publishing Group, Inc., The.

Chlebowski, Rachel. Ash & Pikachu: Alola Region/Team Rocket: Alola Region (Pokémon) Random House, illus. 2017. (Pictureback(R) Ser.). (ENG.). 32p. (J). (gr. -1-2). pap. 5.99 *(978-1-5247-7008-2(6),* Random Hse. Bks. for Young Readers) Random Hse. Children's Bks.

Christelow, Eileen. Five Little Monkeys Jumping on the Bed Board Book. Christelow, Eileen, illus. 2017. (Five Little Monkeys Story Ser.). (ENG., Illus.). 30p. (J). (— 1). bds. 7.99 *(978-1-328-88456-5(2),* 1698446, Clarion Bks.) HarperCollins Pubs.

—Five Little Monkeys Jumping on the Bed Lap Board Book. Christelow, Eileen, illus. 2008. (Five Little Monkeys Story Ser.). (ENG., Illus.). 30p. (J). (gr. -1 — 1). bds. 12.99 *(978-0-547-13176-4(3),* 1048452, Clarion Bks.) HarperCollins Pubs.

—Five Little Monkeys Jumping on the Bed Padded Board Book. Christelow, Eileen, illus. 2017. (Five Little Monkeys Story Ser.). (ENG., Illus.). 30p. (J). (gr. -1 — 1). bds. 11.99 *(978-0-547-51075-0(6),* 1443772, Clarion Bks.) HarperCollins Pubs.

—Five Little Monkeys Reading in Bed Board Book. Christelow, Eileen, illus. 2014. (Five Little Monkeys Story Ser.). (ENG., Illus.). 34p. (J). (— 1). bds. 8.99 *(978-0-544-17330-9(9),* 1552170, Clarion Bks.) HarperCollins Pubs.

—Five Little Monkeys Trick-Or-Treat. Christelow, Eileen, illus. 2018. (Five Little Monkeys Story Ser.). (ENG., Illus.). 40p. (J). (gr. -1-3). pap. 7.99 *(978-1-328-86927-2(X),* 1696687, Clarion Bks.) HarperCollins Pubs.

—Five Little Monkeys Trick-Or-Treat Board Book. Christelow, Eileen, illus. 2015. (Five Little Monkeys Story Ser.). (ENG., Illus.). 36p. (J). (— 1). bds. 7.99 *(978-0-544-43062-4(X),* 1595737, Clarion Bks.) HarperCollins Pubs.

—5 Little Monkeys Bake Birthday Cake/Cinco Monitos Hacen un Pastel de Cumpleanos: Bilingual English-Spanish. Christelow, Eileen, illus. 2014. (Five Little Monkeys Story Ser.).Tr. of Five Little Monkeys Bake a Birthday Cake. (ENG., Illus.). 30p. (J). (— 1). bds. 7.99 *(978-0-544-08899-3(9),* 1537637, Clarion Bks.) HarperCollins Pubs.

Christensen, Catherine, told to. Blessing the Nephite Children. 2016. (ENG.). (J). bds. 10.99 *(978-1-4621-1875-5(5))* Cedar Fort, Inc./CFI Distribution.

Christian, Cheryl. How Many? Portugese/English, 1 vol. 2009. (ENG., Illus.). 12p. (J). 5.95 *(978-1-59572-190-7(8))* Star Bright Bks., Inc.

—What Happens Next? Haitian Creole/English, 1 vol. Dwight, Laura, photos by. 2005. (ENG., Illus.). 12p. (J). (gr. -1). 5.95 *(978-1-59572-025-2(1))* Star Bright Bks., Inc.

—What Happens Next? (Traditional Cantonese) Dwight, Laura, photos by. 2004. (CHI., Illus.). 12p. (J). bds. 5.95 *(978-1-932065-63-3(6))* Star Bright Bks., Inc.

—What's in My Toybox? Spanish/English, 1 vol. Ericsson, Annie Beth, illus. 2009. (ENG.). 32p. (J). bds. 6.25 *(978-1-59572-179-2(7))* Star Bright Bks., Inc.

—Where Does It Go? Haitian Creole/English, 1 vol. Dwight, Laura, photos by. 2005. (ENG., Illus.). 12p. (J). 5.95 *(978-1-59572-026-9(X))* Star Bright Bks., Inc.

—Where Does It Go? Spanish/English, 1 vol. Dwight, Laura, photos by. 2004. (Photoflaps Ser.). (ENG., Illus.). 32p. (J). bds. 5.50 *(978-1-932065-59-6(8),* 787849112) Star Bright Bks., Inc.

—Where's the Baby? Haitian Creole/English, 1 vol. Dwight, Laura, illus. 2005. (Photoflaps Ser.). (ENG.). 12p. (J). (gr. -1). 5.95 *(978-1-59572-027-6(8))* Star Bright Bks., Inc.

—Where's the Baby? (Traditional Cantonese) Dwight, Laura, photos by. 2004. (CHI., Illus.). 12p. (J). bds. 5.95 *(978-1-932065-62-6(8))* Star Bright Bks., Inc.

—Where's the Kitten? Chinese (Simp/Trad), 1 vol. Dwight, Laura, photos by. 2004. (ENG., Illus.). 12p. (J). 5.95 *(978-1-932065-60-2(1))* Star Bright Bks., Inc.

—Where's the Kitten? Haitian Creole/English, 1 vol. Dwight, Laura, photos by. 2005. (Photoflaps Ser.). (ENG., Illus.). 12p. (J). (gr. -1). 5.95 *(978-1-59572-028-3(6))* Star Bright Bks., Inc.

—Where's the Kitten? Russian/English, 1 vol. Dwight, Laura, photos by. 2004. (ENG., Illus.). 12p. (J). 5.95 *(978-1-932065-84-8(9))* Star Bright Bks., Inc.

—Where's the Puppy? Haitian Creole/English, 1 vol. Dwight, Laura, photos by. 2005. (Photoflaps Ser.). (ENG., Illus.). 12p. (J). (gr. -1). 5.95 *(978-1-59572-029-0(4))* Star Bright Bks., Inc.

—Where's the Puppy? Russian/English, 1 vol. Dwight, Laura, photos by. 2005. (Photo Flap Bks.). (ENG., Illus.). 12p. (J). 5.95 *(978-1-932065-85-5(7))* Star Bright Bks., Inc.

—Where's the Puppy? (Traditional Cantonese) Dwight, Laura, photos by. 2004. (CHI., Illus.). 12p. (J). bds. 5.95 *(978-1-932065-61-9(X))* Star Bright Bks., Inc.

Christine Battuz, Christine, illus. Goodnight, Sleepy Animals: A Nightlight Book. 2016. (Nightlight Book Ser.). 14p. (J). (gr. -1-k). 12.99 *(978-2-89718-338-7(1),* CrackBoom! Bks.) Chouette Publishing CAN. Dist: Publishers Group West (PGW).

Christmas (Illus.). (gr. 1-4). 3.00 *(978-0-570-05521-1(0),* 54-1031) Concordia Publishing Hse.

The Christmas Carol Book. (Illus.). 10p. (J). bds. *(978-2-89393-929-2(5))* Phidal Publishing, Inc./Editions Phidal, Inc.

Christmas Chunky Set/Made by Emma Jennings, Natalie Munday, & Kate Ward. 2015. (Illus.). (J). *(978-0-312-51995-7(8)); (978-0-312-51996-4(6)); (978-0-312-51997-1(4))* St. Martin's Pr. (Priddy Bks.).

Christmas Stable, 1 vol. 2014. (Candle Tiny Tots Ser.). (ENG., Illus.). 16p. (J). 11.99 *(978-1-78128-122-2(X),* adbd8aec-c73d-44fe-b60a-cb8587021262, Candle Bks.) Lion Hudson PLC GBR. Dist: Baker & Taylor Publisher Services (BTPS).

Chronicle Books. Baby Bear: Finger Puppet Book: (Finger Puppet Book for Toddlers & Babies, Baby Books for First Year, Animal Finger Puppets) Huang, Yu-Hsuan, illus. 2016. (Baby Animal Finger Puppets Ser.: 1). (ENG.). 12p. (J). (gr. -1 — 1). 7.99 *(978-1-4521-4235-7(1))* Chronicle Bks. LLC.

—Baby Bunny: Finger Puppet Book. Huang, Yu-Hsuan, illus. 2017. (Baby Animal Finger Puppets Ser.: 5). (ENG.). 12p. (J). 7.99 *(978-1-4521-5609-5(3))* Chronicle Bks. LLC.

—Baby Chipmunk: Finger Puppet Book. Huang, Yu-Hsuan, illus. 2017. (Baby Animal Finger Puppets Ser.: 8). (ENG.). 12p. (J). (gr. -1 — 1). bds. 7.99 *(978-1-4521-5612-5(3))* Chronicle Bks. LLC.

—Baby Dragon: Finger Puppet Book: (Finger Puppet Book for Toddlers & Babies, Baby Books for First Year, Animal Finger Puppets) Ying, Victoria, illus. 2018. (Baby Animal Finger Puppets Ser.: 14). (ENG.). 12p. (J). (gr. -1 — 1). 7.99 *(978-1-4521-7077-0(0))* Chronicle Bks. LLC.

—Baby Duck: Finger Puppet Book. Huang, Yu-Hsuan, illus. 2018. (Baby Animal Finger Puppets Ser.: 9). (ENG.). 12p. (J). (gr. -1 — 1). 7.99 *(978-1-4521-6373-4(1))* Chronicle Bks. LLC.

—Baby Elephant: Finger Puppet Book: (Finger Puppet Book for Toddlers & Babies, Baby Books for First Year, Animal Finger Puppets) Huang, Yu-Hsuan, illus. 2016. (Baby Animal Finger Puppets Ser.: 3). (ENG.). 12p. (J). (gr. -1 — 1). 7.99 *(978-1-4521-4237-1(8))* Chronicle Bks. LLC.

—Baby Fish: Finger Puppet Book. Huang, Yu-Hsuan, illus. 2017. (Baby Animal Finger Puppets Ser.: 6). (ENG.). 12p. (J). 7.99 *(978-1-4521-5610-1(7))* Chronicle Bks. LLC.

—Baby Giraffe: Finger Puppet Book. Huang, Yu-Hsuan, illus. 2017. (Baby Animal Finger Puppets Ser.: 7). (ENG.). 12p. (J). (gr. -1 — 1). 7.99 *(978-1-4521-5611-8(5))* Chronicle Bks. LLC.

—Baby Hedgehog: Finger Puppet Book. Huang, Yu-Hsuan, illus. 2018. (Baby Animal Finger Puppets Ser.: 12). (ENG.). 12p. (J). (gr. -1 — 1). 7.99 *(978-1-4521-6376-5(6))* Chronicle Bks. LLC.

—Baby Koala: Finger Puppet Book. Huang, Yu-Hsuan, illus. 2018. (Baby Animal Finger Puppets Ser.: 10). (ENG.). 12p. (J). (gr. -1 — 1). bds. 7.99 *(978-1-4521-6374-1(X))* Chronicle Bks. LLC.

—Baby Orca: Finger Puppet Book (Puppet Book for Babies, Baby Play Book, Interactive Baby Book) Huang, Yu-Hsuan, illus. 2019. (Baby Animal Finger Puppets Ser.: 16). (ENG.). 12p. (J). (gr. -1 — 1). 7.99 *(978-1-4521-7079-4(7))* Chronicle Bks. LLC.

—Baby Penguin: Finger Puppet Book. Huang, Yu-Hsuan, illus. 2018. (Baby Animal Finger Puppets Ser.: 11). (ENG.). 12p. (J). (gr. -1 — 1). 7.99 *(978-1-4521-6375-8(8))* Chronicle Bks. LLC.

—Baby Piglet: Finger Puppet Book (Pig Puppet Book, Piggy Book for Babies, Tiny Finger Puppet Books) Huang, Yu-Hsuan, illus. 2019. (Baby Animal Finger Puppets Ser.: 15). (ENG.). 12p. (J). (gr. -1 — 1). 7.99 *(978-1-4521-7078-7(9))* Chronicle Bks. LLC.

—Baby Reindeer: Finger Puppet Book: (Finger Puppet Book for Toddlers & Babies, Baby Books for First Year, Animal Finger Puppets) Huang, Yu-Hsuan, illus. 2016. (Baby Animal Finger Puppets Ser.: 4). (ENG.). 12p. (J). (gr. -1 — 1). 7.99 *(978-1-4521-4661-4(6))* Chronicle Bks. LLC.

—Baby Tiger: Finger Puppet Book: (Finger Puppet Book for Toddlers & Babies, Baby Books for First Year, Animal Finger Puppets) Huang, Yu-Hsuan, illus. 2016. (Baby Animal Finger Puppets Ser.: 2). (ENG.). 12p. (J). (gr. -1 — 1). 7.99 *(978-1-4521-4236-4(X))* Chronicle Bks. LLC.

—Baby Unicorn: Finger Puppet Book: (Unicorn Puppet Book, Unicorn Book for Babies, Tiny Finger Puppet Books) Ying, Victoria, illus. 2018. (Baby Animal Finger Puppets Ser.: 13). (ENG.). 12p. (J). (gr. -1 — 1). 7.99 *(978-1-4521-7076-3(2))* Chronicle Bks. LLC.

—Eggs Are Everywhere: (Baby's First Easter Board Book, Easter Egg Hunt Book, Lift the Flap Book for Easter Basket) Kirwan, Wednesday, illus. 2020. (ENG.). 10p. (J). (gr. -1 — 1). bds. 10.99 *(978-1-4521-7457-0(1))* Chronicle Bks. LLC.

—My Big Evil Brother Packed My Lunch: 20+ Gross Lift-The-flaps (Kids Novelty Book, Children's Lift the Flaps Book, Sibling Rivalry Book) Watson, Laura, illus. 2019. (ENG.). 12p. (J). (gr. -1-3). 16.99 *(978-1-4521-7089-3(4))* Chronicle Bks. LLC.

—Read & Ride: Magical Horses: 4 Board Books Inside! (Toddler Board Books, Unicorn Books, Kids Horse Books) Mytinger, Liz, illus. 2019. (Read & Ride Ser.). (ENG.). 5p. (J). (gr. -1 — 1). 15.99 *(978-1-4521-6547-9(5))* Chronicle Bks. LLC.

—TouchWords: Animals. Alexander, Rilla, illus. 2019. (Touch Think Learn Ser.). (ENG.). 16p. (J). (gr. -1 — 1). 16.99 *(978-1-4521-7392-4(3))* Chronicle Bks. LLC.

—The World of Eric Carle(TM) the Very Hungry Caterpillar(TM) String-Alongs. 2012. (World of Eric Carle by Chronicle Bks.). (ENG., Illus.). 10p. (J). (gr. -1-17). 18.99 *(978-1-4521-0515-4(4))* Chronicle Bks. LLC.

Chronicle Books & ImageBooks. Little Bee: Finger Puppet Book: (Finger Puppet Book for Toddlers & Babies, Baby Books for First Year, Animal Finger Puppets) 2006. (Little Finger Puppet Board Bks.: FING). (ENG., Illus.). 12p. (J). (gr. -1-7). bds. 7.99 *(978-0-8118-5236-4(9))* Chronicle Bks. LLC.

—Little Bunny: Finger Puppet Book: (Finger Puppet Book for Toddlers & Babies, Baby Books for First Year, Animal Finger Puppets) 2006. (Little Finger Puppet Board Bks.: FING). (ENG., Illus.). 12p. (J). (gr. -1 — 1). bds. 7.99 *(978-0-8118-5644-7(5))* Chronicle Bks. LLC.

—Little Butterfly: Finger Puppet Book: (Finger Puppet Book for Toddlers & Babies, Baby Books for First Year, Animal Finger Puppets) Van Der Put, Klaatje, illus. 2006. (Little Finger Puppet Board Bks.: FING). (ENG.). 12p. (J). (gr. -1 — 1). 7.99 *(978-0-8118-5645-4(3))* Chronicle Bks. LLC.

—Little Cat: Finger Puppet Book: (Finger Puppet Book for Toddlers & Babies, Baby Books for First Year, Animal Finger Puppets) 2014. (Little Finger Puppet Board Bks.). (ENG., Illus.). 12p. (J). (gr. -1 — 1). 7.99 *(978-1-4521-2916-7(9))* Chronicle Bks. LLC.

—Little Chick: Finger Puppet Book: (Puppet Book for Baby, Little Easter Board Book) 2015. (Little Finger Puppet Board Bks.). (ENG., Illus.). 12p. (J). (gr. -1 — 1). bds. 7.99 *(978-1-4521-2917-4(7))* Chronicle Bks. LLC.

—Little Crab: Finger Puppet Book: (Finger Puppet Book for Toddlers & Babies, Baby Books for First Year, Animal Finger Puppets) 2010. (Little Finger Puppet Board Bks.). (ENG., Illus.). 12p. (J). (gr. -1 — 1). 7.99 *(978-0-8118-7340-6(4))* Chronicle Bks. LLC.

—Little Dog: Finger Puppet Book: (Finger Puppet Book for Toddlers & Babies, Baby Books for First Year, Animal Finger Puppets) 2014. (Little Finger Puppet Board Bks.). (ENG., Illus.). 12p. (J). (gr. -1 — 1). 7.99 *(978-1-4521-2915-0(0))* Chronicle Bks. LLC.

—Little Dolphin: Finger Puppet Book: (Finger Puppet Book for Toddlers & Babies, Baby Books for First Year, Animal Finger Puppets) 2012. (Little Finger Puppet Board Bks.: FING). (ENG., Illus.). 12p. (J). (gr. -1 — 1). bds. 7.99 *(978-1-4521-0816-2(1))* Chronicle Bks. LLC.

—Little Duck: Finger Puppet Book: (Finger Puppet Book for Toddlers & Babies, Baby Books for First Year, Animal Finger Puppets) 2005. (Little Finger Puppet Board Bks.: FING). (ENG., Illus.). 12p. (J). (gr. -1 — 1). bds. 7.99 *(978-0-8118-4847-3(7))* Chronicle Bks. LLC.

—Little Fish: Finger Puppet Book: (Finger Puppet Book for Toddlers & Babies, Baby Books for First Year, Animal Finger Puppets) 2010. (Little Finger Puppet Board Bks.). (ENG., Illus.). 12p. (J). (gr. -1 — 1). 7.99 *(978-0-8118-7344-4(7))* Chronicle Bks. LLC.

—Little Fox: Finger Puppet Book: (Finger Puppet Book for Toddlers & Babies, Baby Books for First Year, Animal Finger Puppets) 2015. (ENG., Illus.). 12p. (J). (gr. -1 — 1). 7.99 *(978-1-4521-4230-2(0))* Chronicle Bks. LLC.

—Little Horse: Finger Puppet Book: (Finger Puppet Book for Toddlers & Babies, Baby Books for First Year, Animal Finger Puppets) 2013. (Little Finger Puppet Board Bks.). (ENG., Illus.). 12p. (J). (gr. -1 — 1). 7.99 *(978-1-4521-1249-7(5))* Chronicle Bks. LLC.

—Little Ladybug: Finger Puppet Book: (Finger Puppet Book for Toddlers & Babies, Baby Books for First Year, Animal Finger Puppets) 2005. (Little Finger Puppet Board Bks.: FING). (ENG., Illus.). 12p. (J). (gr. -1 — 1). bds. 7.99 *(978-0-8118-4848-0(5))* Chronicle Bks. LLC.

—Little Monkey: Finger Puppet Book: (Finger Puppet Book for Toddlers & Babies, Baby Books for First Year, Animal Finger Puppets) 2013. (Little Finger Puppet Board Bks.). (ENG., Illus.). 12p. (J). (gr. -1 — 1). 7.99 *(978-1-4521-1250-3(9))* Chronicle Bks. LLC.

—Little Moose: Finger Puppet Book: (Finger Puppet Book for Toddlers & Babies, Baby Books for First Year, Animal Finger Puppets) 2015. (ENG., Illus.). 12p. (J). (gr. -1 — 1). 7.99 *(978-1-4521-4231-9(9))* Chronicle Bks. LLC.

—Little Owl: Finger Puppet Book: (Finger Puppet Book for Toddlers & Babies, Baby Books for First Year, Animal Finger Puppets) 2011. (Little Finger Puppet Board Bks.). (ENG.). 12p. (J). (gr. -1 — 1). 7.99 *(978-1-4521-0221-4(X))* Chronicle Bks. LLC.

—Little Penguin: Finger Puppet Book: (Finger Puppet Book for Toddlers & Babies, Baby Books for First Year, Animal Finger Puppets) 2008. (Little Finger Puppet Board Bks.: FING). (ENG., Illus.). 12p. (J). (gr. -1 — 1). bds. 7.99 *(978-0-8118-6355-1(7))* Chronicle Bks. LLC.

—Little Sea Turtle: Finger Puppet Book: (Finger Puppet Book for Toddlers & Babies, Baby Books for First Year, Animal Finger Puppets) 2014. (Little Finger Puppet Board Bks.). (ENG., Illus.). 12p. (J). (gr. -1 — 1). 7.99 *(978-1-4521-2913-6(4))* Chronicle Bks. LLC.

—Little Seal: Finger Puppet Book: (Finger Puppet Book for Toddlers & Babies, Baby Books for First Year, Animal Finger Puppets) 2012. (Little Finger Puppet Board Bks.: FING). (ENG., Illus.). 12p. (J). (gr. -1 — 1). 7.99 *(978-1-4521-0812-4(9))* Chronicle Bks. LLC.

—Little Shark: Finger Puppet Book: (Puppet Book for Baby, Little Toy Board Book, Baby Shark) 2013. (Little Finger Puppet Board Bks.). (ENG., Illus.). 12p. (J). (gr. -1 — 1). 7.99 *(978-1-4521-1251-0(7))* Chronicle Bks. LLC.

—Little Zebra: Finger Puppet Book: (Finger Puppet Book for Toddlers & Babies, Baby Books for First Year, Animal Finger Puppets) 2013. (Little Finger Puppet Board Bks.). (ENG., Illus.). 12p. (J). (gr. -1 — 1). bds. 6.99 *(978-1-4521-1252-7(5))* Chronicle Bks. LLC.

—Snow Baby: Finger Puppet Book. 2011. (Little Finger Puppet Board Bks.). (ENG.). 12p. (J). (gr. -1 — 1). 6.99 *(978-1-4521-0220-7(1))* Chronicle Bks. LLC.

Chronicle Books, et al. Little Giraffe: Finger Puppet Book: (Finger Puppet Book for Toddlers & Babies, Baby Books for First Year, Animal Finger Puppets) 2009. (Little Finger Puppet Board Bks.). (ENG., Illus.). 12p. (J). (gr. -1 — 1). bds. 7.99 *(978-0-8118-6787-0(0))* Chronicle Bks. LLC.

—Little Lion: Finger Puppet Book. 2009. (Little Finger Puppet Board Bks.). (ENG., Illus.). 12p. (J). (gr. -1 — 1). 7.99 *(978-0-8118-6788-7(9))* Chronicle Bks. LLC.

Chronicle Books, Chronicle & ImageBooks. Little Dino: Finger Puppet Book: (Puppet Book for Baby, Little Dinosaur Board Book) 2008. (Little Finger Puppet Board Bks.: FING). (ENG., Illus.). 12p. (J). (gr. -1 — 1). bds. 7.99 *(978-0-8118-6353-7(0))* Chronicle Bks. LLC.

—Little Lamb: Finger Puppet Book: (Finger Puppet Book for Toddlers & Babies, Baby Books for First Year, Animal Finger Puppets) 2006. (Little Finger Puppet Board Bks.: FING). (ENG., Illus.). 12p. (J). (gr. -1-7). bds. 7.99 *(978-0-8118-5235-7(0))* Chronicle Bks. LLC.

—Little Mouse: Finger Puppet Book: (Finger Puppet Book for Toddlers & Babies, Baby Books for First Year, Animal Finger Puppets) 2007. (Little Finger Puppet Board Bks.: FING). (ENG., Illus.). 12p. (J). (gr. -1 — 1). bds. 6.99 *(978-0-8118-6110-6(4))* Chronicle Bks. LLC.

—Little Panda: Finger Puppet Book: (Finger Puppet Book for Toddlers & Babies, Baby Books for First Year, Animal Finger Puppets) 2009. (Little Finger Puppet Board Bks.: FING). (ENG., Illus.). 12p. (J). (gr. -1 — 1). bds. 6.99 *(978-0-8118-6999-7(7))* Chronicle Bks. LLC.

—Little Snowman: Finger Puppet Book: (Finger Puppet Book for Toddlers & Babies, Baby Books for First Year, Animal Finger Puppets) 2008. (Little Finger Puppet Board Bks.). (ENG., Illus.). 12p. (J). (gr. -1 — 1). bds. 7.99 *(978-0-8118-6356-8(5))* Chronicle Bks. LLC.

—Little Spider: Finger Puppet Book: (Finger Puppet Book for Toddlers & Babies, Baby Books for Halloween, Animal Finger Puppets) 2007. (Little Finger Puppet Board Bks.: FING). (ENG., Illus.). 12p. (J). (gr. -1 — 1). bds. 7.99 *(978-0-8118-6104-5(X))* Chronicle Bks. LLC.

Chronicle Books Staff. Nick Jr. Nursery Rhyme Time: A Touch-and-See Activity Book. (J). 15.95 *(978-0-8118-4726-1(8))* Chronicle Bks. LLC.

Church, Caroline Jayne. Giggle!, 1 vol. Church, Caroline Jayne, illus. 2013. (ENG., Illus.). 10p. (J). (— 1). bds. 7.99 *(978-0-545-35082-2(4),* Cartwheel Bks.) Scholastic, Inc.

—I Am a Big Brother. Church, Caroline Jayne, illus. 2015. (ENG., Illus.). 24p. (J). (gr. -1 — 1). 6.99 *(978-0-545-68886-4(8),* Cartwheel Bks.) Scholastic, Inc.

—I Am a Big Brother! / ¡Soy un Hermano Mayor! (Bilingual) (Bilingual Edition) Church, Caroline Jayne, illus. 2015. (SPA., Illus.). 24p. (J). (gr. -1 — 1). 6.99 *(978-0-545-84717-9(6),* Scholastic en Espanol) Scholastic, Inc.

—I Am a Big Sister. Church, Caroline Jayne, illus. 2015. (ENG., Illus.). 24p. (J). (gr. -1 — 1). 6.99 *(978-0-545-68898-7(1),* Cartwheel Bks.) Scholastic, Inc.

—I Am a Big Sister! / ¡Soy una Hermana Mayor! (Bilingual) (Bilingual Edition) Church, Caroline Jayne, illus. 2015.Tr. of ¡Soy una Hermana Mayor! (SPA., Illus.). 24p. (J). (gr. -1 — 1). 6.99 *(978-0-545-84718-6(4),* Scholastic en Espanol) Scholastic, Inc.

—I Love My Puppy (Love Meez) Church, Caroline Jayne, illus. 2015. (Love Meez Ser.). (ENG., Illus.). 10p. (J). (gr. -1 — 1). bds. 7.99 *(978-0-545-83594-7(1),* Cartwheel Bks.) Scholastic, Inc.

—I Will Love You Forever. Church, Caroline Jayne, illus. 2016. (ENG.). 22p. (J). (gr. -1-k). bds. 8.99 *(978-0-545-94200-3(4),* Cartwheel Bks.) Scholastic, Inc.

—Ten Tiny Toes. Church, Caroline Jayne, illus. 2014. (ENG., Illus.). 22p. (J). (— 1). bds. 8.99 *(978-0-545-53601-1(4),* Cartwheel Bks.) Scholastic, Inc.

Chwast, Seymour. Tall City, Wide Country. Chwast, Seymour, illus. 2013. (ENG., Illus.). 32p. (J). (gr. -1-k). 15.99 *(978-1-56846-228-8(X),* 21762, Creative Editions) Creative Co., The.

Ciminera, Siobhan & Rao, Lisa. Hello, Friends! Yoe! Studio Staff, illus. 2009. (Yo Gabba Gabba! Ser.). (ENG.). 64p. (J). 4.99 *(978-1-4169-7460-4(1),* Simon Scribbles) Simon Scribbles.

Cinderella. 2009. (Disney Glitter Board Book Ser.). 5p. *(978-1-4054-9824-1(2))* Parragon, Inc.

Civardi, Anna. New Puppy Sticker Book. 2009. (First Experiences Sticker Book Ser.). 16p. (J). pap. 6.99 *(978-0-7945-2573-6(3),* Usborne) EDC Publishing.

Civardi, Anne. Going to the Dentist. 2010. (First Experiences Ser.). 16p. (J). pap. 4.99 *(978-0-7945-2592-7(X),* Usborne) EDC Publishing.

CLAIRE, Phillip. Convertible Playbook - Farm: Read the Story, Press Out the Characters, Fold Out the Building. 2017. 24p. (J). bds. 19.95 *(978-1-78209-976-5(X))* Miles Kelly Publishing, Ltd. GBR. Dist: Parkwest Pubns., Inc.

Clairmont, Patsy. Sleep Sweet My Little One, 1 vol. 2014. (ENG., Illus.). 24p. (J). bds. 12.99 *(978-1-4003-2401-9(7),* Tommy Nelson) Nelson, Thomas Inc.

Clarion Books, Clarion. Five Silly Ghosts Board Book. Kushnir, Hilli, illus. 2018. (ENG.). 12p. (J). (— 1). bds. 6.99 *(978-1-328-86659-2(9),* 1696027, Clarion Bks.) HarperCollins Pubs.

Clark, M. H. I Am... 2011. (Growth Chart Bks.). (Illus.). (gr. -1-5). bds. 8.95 *(978-1-935414-06-3(2))* Compendium, Inc., Publishing & Communications.

—I Can... 2011. (Growth Chart Bks.). (Illus.). (gr. -1-5). bds. 8.95 *(978-1-932319-81-1(6))* Compendium, Inc., Publishing & Communications.

Clarke, Jane. Creaky Castle. Fox, Christyan, illus. 2013. *(978-1-4351-4951-9(3))* Barnes & Noble, Inc.

—How to Bathe Your Little Dino. Birkett, Georgie, illus. 2017. 16p. (J). bds. 8.99 *(978-1-61067-495-9(2))* Kane Miller.

—How to Brush Your Teeth with Snappy Crocodile. Birkett, Georgie, illus. 2017. 16p. (J). bds. 8.99 *(978-1-61067-494-2(4))* Kane Miller.

—How to Feed Your Cheeky Monkey. Birkett, Georgie, illus. 2017. 16p. (J). bds. 8.99 *(978-1-61067-497-3(9))* Kane Miller.

—How to Tuck in Your Sleepy Lion. Birkett, Georgie, illus. 2017. 16p. (J). bds. 8.99 *(978-1-61067-496-6(0))* Kane Miller.

Clarke, Phil. Sharks. 2005. (Usborne Lift the Flap Bks.). (Illus.). 16p. (J). (gr. -1-3). 11.99 *(978-0-7945-1109-8(0),* Usborne) EDC Publishing.

Clarke, Phillip & Furnival, Keith. Sharks. Scott, Peter David, illus. 2005. (J). *(978-0-439-86358-2(9))* Scholastic, Inc.

Clarkson, Sally & Clarkson, Nathan. Only You Can Be You: What Makes You Different Makes You Great, 1 vol. Warnes, Tim, illus. 2019. (ENG.). 32p. (J). 16.99 *(978-1-4002-1143-2(3),* Tommy Nelson) Nelson, Thomas Inc.

—Only You Can Be You for Little Ones: What Makes You Different Makes You Great, 1 vol. Warnes, Tim, illus. 2020. (ENG.). 20p. (J). bds. 12.99 *(978-1-4002-1144-9(1),* Tommy Nelson) Nelson, Thomas Inc.

Clifford the Best Helper. (Illus.). 10p. (J). bds. 9.98 (978-0-7853-9948-3(8), 7208900) Publications International, Ltd.

Coat, Janik. Hippopposites. 2012. (Grammar Zoo Book Ser.). (ENG., Illus.). 36p. (J). (gr. -1 — 1). bds. 15.95 (978-1-4197-0151-1(7), 1007901, Abrams Appleseed) Abrams, Inc.

—Llamaphones (a Grammar Zoo Book) 2018. (Grammar Zoo Book Ser.). (ENG., Illus.). 36p. (J). (gr. -1 — 1). bds. 16.99 (978-1-4197-2827-3(X), 1189010, Abrams Appleseed) Abrams, Inc.

Coat, Janik & Duisit, Bernard. What Are You Wearing Today? 2018. (Flip Flap Pop-Up Ser.: 0). (ENG., Illus.). 16p. (J). (gr. -1-3). 14.95 (978-0-500-65143-8(4), 565143) Thames & Hudson.

Coates, J. C. Puppy Talk: Opposites. Coates, J. C., illus. 2019. (ENG., Illus.). 20p. (J). (— 1). bds. 7.99 (978-1-58089-847-8(5)) Charlesbridge Publishing, Inc.

Cocklico, Marion, illus. No More Diapers. 2018. (Big Steps Ser.). (ENG.). 12p. (J). (— 1). bds. 8.95 (978-1-4549-2951-2(0)) Sterling Publishing Co., Inc.

Cocoretto, illus. Peekaboo! in the Jungle! 2016. (Peekaboo! Ser.: 4). 12p. (J). spiral bd. (978-1-84643-866-0(7)) Child's Play International Ltd.

—Peekaboo! on the Farm! 2016. (Peekaboo! Ser.: 4). 12p. (J). spiral bd. (978-1-84643-864-6(0)) Child's Play International Ltd.

Cohen, Alana. Heroes! (LEGO City: Lift-The-Flap Board Book) White, David & White, Dave, illus. 2011. (LEGO City Ser.). (ENG.). 16p. (J). (gr. -1-k). bds. 9.99 (978-0-545-27439-5(7)) Scholastic, Inc.

Cohen, Miriam. Daddy's Busy Day. 1 vol. Hu, Ying-Hwa, illus. 2014. (ENG.). 32p. (J). bds. (978-1-59572-668-1(3)) Star Bright Bks., Inc.

Cohn, Arlen. Firsts (Eyeball Animation) Board Book Edition. Vasconcellos, Daniel, illus. gif. ed. 2004. (ENG.). 28p. (J). bds. 9.99 (978-1-57939-168-3(0)) Andrews McMeel Publishing.

Coirault, Christine, illus. My First Book of Learning. 2009. (J). (978-1-74089-930-7(X)) Fog City Pr.

Colby, Rebecca. Captain Bling's Christmas Plunder. 2018. (2019 Av2 Fiction Ser.). (ENG.). 32p. (J). (gr. k-2). lib. bdg. 34.28 (978-1-4896-8253-6(8), AV2 by Weigl) Weigl Pubs., Inc.

—Captain Bling's Christmas Plunder. McClurkan, Rob, illus. 2017. (ENG.). 32p. (J). (gr. -1-3). 16.99 (978-0-8075-1063-6(7), 807510637) Whitman, Albert & Co.

Cole, Jeff, illus. Numbers: A Silly Slider Book. 2011. (ENG.). 12p. (J). (gr. -1-k). bds. 10.99 (978-1-4494-0174-0(0)) Andrews McMeel Publishing.

Coleman, Michelle, compiled by. My Pets. 2012. (Touch & Feel Ser.). (ENG., Illus.). 10p. (J). (— 1). bds. 12.95 (978-1-61889-221-8(5)) AZ Bks. LLC.

—Wild Animals. 2013. (Touch & Feel Ser.). (ENG., Illus.). 10p. (J). (— 1). bds. 12.95 (978-1-61889-209-6(6)) AZ Bks. LLC.

Collins, Elaine Banks. I Like Dressing Up. Floyd, John, Jr., illus. 2005. (J). bds. 5.95 (978-0-9752860-5-0(6)) OurRainbow Pr., LLC.

—See What I Can Do. Floyd, John, Jr., illus. 2006. 10p. (J). (gr. -1). bds. 5.95 (978-0-9752860-4-3(8)) OurRainbow Pr., LLC.

Collins, Sarah Jean. God Made the Rain Forest. Collins, Sarah Jean, illus. 2020. (God Made Ser.). (ENG., Illus.). 20p. (J). bds. 7.99 (978-1-4964-3632-0(6), 20_32354, Tyndale Kids) Tyndale Hse. Pubs.

Collison, Shauna. Heavenites Angels to Zebras Board Book with Audio CD. Nelson, Christine, illus. 2007. 26p. (J). 15.95 (978-0-9792510-0-9(1)) Revelation Products LLC.

Contraire, Bastien. Food: Hide & Sneak. 2018. (ENG., Illus.). 26p. (gr. -1 — 1). bds. 9.95 (978-0-7148-7723-5(9)) Phaidon Pr., Inc.

—Vehicles: Hide & Sneak. 2017. (ENG., Illus.). 26p. (gr. -1 — 1). bds. 9.95 (978-0-7148-7516-3(3)) Phaidon Pr., Inc.

Cooke, Brandy. Where Is Owl's Scarf? A Lift-The-Flap Book. Belloni, Valentina, illus. 2016. (ENG.). 10p. (J). (gr. -1-1). bds. 6.99 (978-1-4998-0176-7(9)) Little Bee Books Inc.

—You Poked My Heart! Logan, Laura, illus. 2016. (ENG.). 16p. (J). (gr. -1-1). bds. 5.99 (978-1-4998-0310-5(9)) Little Bee Books Inc.

Coombs, Kate. Goodnight Mr. Darcy: A BabyLit(TM) Parody Board Book, 1 vol. 2015. (ENG., Illus.). 22p. (J). bds. 9.99 (978-1-4236-4177-3(9)) Gibbs Smith, Publisher.

—Goodnight Mr. Darcy: A BabyLit(TM) Parody Picture Book, 1 vol. 2014. (ENG., Illus.). 32p. (J). 16.99 (978-1-4236-3670-0(8)) Gibbs Smith, Publisher.

Cooney, Caroline B. I'm Going to Give You a Bear Hug!, 1 vol. Warnes, Tim, illus. 2017. (ENG.). 32p. (J). bds. 7.99 (978-0-310-76440-3(8)) Zonderkidz.

Coppage, J. L. Trick or Treat on My Street. Matthews, Melanie, illus. 2017. 18p. (J). (-k). bds. 6.99 (978-0-515-15975-2(1), Grosset & Dunlap) Penguin Young Readers Group.

Corderoy, Tracey. It's Potty Time! Pedler, Caroline, illus. 2014. (ENG.). 22p. (J). (gr. -1-k). bds. 8.99 (978-1-58925-574-6(7)) Tiger Tales.

Corke, Estelle, illus. The Gingerbread Man. 2007. (Flip-Up Fairy Tales Ser.). 24p. (J). (978-1-84643-144-9(1)); (gr. -1-2). (978-1-84643-078-7(X)) Child's Play International Ltd.

Corrigan, Kathleen. ABC, 1 vol. 2014. (Canadian Board Bks.). (ENG & FRE.). 20p. bds. 7.99 (978-1-62370-223-6(2), Capstone Young Readers) Capstone.

Cosgrove, Stephen. Good Night, Wheedle. James, Robin, illus. 2016. 20p. (J). (— 1). bds. 9.99 (978-1-63217-075-0(2), Little Bigfoot) Sasquatch Bks.

Cosneau, Geraldine. Make It Now!: Animals: Press Out & Play. Cosneau, Geraldine, illus. 2018. (Make It Now! Ser.). (ENG., Illus.). 12p. (J). (gr. -1-3). pap. 8.99 (978-1-328-71497-8(7), 1674063, Clarion Bks.) HarperCollins Pubs.

Cosneau, Olivia. Birds of the World: My Nature Sticker Activity Book (Science Activity & Learning Book for Kids, Coloring, Stickers & Quiz) 2017. (ENG., Illus.). 24p. (J). (gr. k-3). 9.99 (978-1-61689-566-2(7)) Princeton Architectural Pr.

—In the Age of Dinosaurs: My Nature Sticker Activity Book. 2016. (ENG., Illus.). 24p. (J). (gr. k-3). 7.99 (978-1-61689-469-6(5)) Princeton Architectural Pr.

—In the Vegetable Garden: My Nature Sticker Activity Book (Ages 5 & up, with 102 Stickers, 24 Activities, & 1 Quiz) 2017. (ENG.). 24p. (J). (gr. k-3). pap. 7.99 (978-1-61689-571-6(3)) Princeton Architectural Pr.

Cosneau, Olivia & Duisit, Bernard. How Do You Sleep? 2018. (Flip Flap Pop-Up Ser.: 0). (ENG., Illus.). 14p. (J). (gr. -1-2). 14.95 (978-0-500-65144-5(2), 565144) Thames & Hudson.

—What's Up? 2017. (Flip Flap Pop-Up Ser.: 0). (ENG., Illus.). 16p. (J). (gr. -1-1). 14.95 (978-0-500-65092-9(6), 565092) Thames & Hudson.

Cossins, Jennifer. The Baby Animal Book. 2019. (ENG.). 64p. (J). (gr. -1-1). 16.99 (978-0-7344-1815-9(9), Lothian Children's Bks.) Hachette Australia AUS. Dist: Hachette Bk. Group.

Costain, Meredith. Daddies Are Awesome. Lovsin, Polona, illus. 2017. (ENG.). 28p. (J). bds. 8.99 (978-1-250-10720-6(2), 900164822, Holt, Henry & Co. Bks. For Young Readers) Holt, Henry & Co.

Costamagna, Beatrice, illus. Crocodile Snap! 2016. (Crunchy Board Bks.). (ENG.). 12p. (J). (gr. -1-1). bds. 7.99 (978-1-4998-0201-6(3)) Little Bee Books Inc.

—Polar Bear Romp! 2016. (Crunchy Board Bks.). (ENG.). 12p. (J). (gr. -1-1). bds. 7.99 (978-1-4998-0345-7(1)) Little Bee Books Inc.

Côté, Patricia. Where Are You Little Red Ball?, 1 vol. Yayo, illus. 2016. (ENG.). 12p. (J). (gr. -1 — 1). bds. 8.95 (978-1-926890-12-8(4)) Tradewind Bks. CAN. Dist: Orca Bk. Pubs. USA.

Cotter, Bill. Don't Push the Button! 2015. (Illus.). 24p. (J). (gr. -1-k). bds. 8.99 (978-1-4926-0763-2(0), Sourcebooks Jabberwocky) Sourcebooks, Inc.

Cotton, Katie. Counting Lions: Portraits from the Wild. Walton, Stephen, illus. 2015. (ENG.). 40p. (J). (gr. k-4). 22.00 (978-0-7636-8207-1(1)) Candlewick Pr.

Count to Ten. (J). 26.20 (978-0-8136-8410-9(2)); 26.20 (978-0-8136-8411-6(0)); (gr. -1-3). 59.50 (978-0-8136-7942-6(7)) Modern Curriculum Pr.

Counting Cards Staff. LP-Counting: Level 1 Math. 2004. (ENG.). (J). 9.99 (978-1-59204-013-1(6)) Learning Wrap-Ups, Inc.

Coupe, Robert. Antiguo Egipto/Acient Egypt. 2011. 16p. pap. (978-607-404-320-4(5), Silver Dolphin en Español) Advanced Marketing, S. de R. L. de C. V.

Courtney-Tickle, Jessica. Little Christmas Tree. Courtney-Tickle, Jessica, illus. 2018. (ENG., Illus.). 12p. (J). (-k). bds. 15.99 (978-1-5362-0311-0(4), Big Picture Press) Candlewick Pr.

Courtney-Tickle, Jessica, illus. The Story Orchestra: Four Seasons in One Day: Press the Note to Hear Vivaldi's Music, Volume 1. 2016. (Story Orchestra Ser.: 1). (ENG.). 24p. (J). (gr. 1-4). 24.99 (978-1-84780-877-6(8), 314669, Frances Lincoln Children's Bks.) Quarto Publishing Group UK GBR. Dist: Hachette UK Distribution.

Courtney, Todd & Courtney, Jackie. Daydream with Max & Molly. 2018. (Max Rhymes Ser.). (ENG., Illus.). 32p. (J). (gr. 1-2). (978-1-945200-26-7(X)) Inspired Imaginations, LLC.

Cousins, Lucy. I Am Little Fish! a Finger Puppet Book. Cousins, Lucy, illus. 2018. (Little Fish Ser.). (ENG., Illus.). 16p. (J). (— 1). bds. 12.99 (978-1-5362-0023-2(9)) Candlewick Pr.

—Maisy Goes to Preschool: A Maisy First Experiences Book. Cousins, Lucy, illus. 2010. (Maisy Ser.). (ENG., Illus.). 32p. (J). (gr. k-k). pap. 7.99 (978-0-7636-5086-5(2)) Candlewick Pr.

—Maisy's Bus. Cousins, Lucy, illus. 2017. (Maisy Ser.). (ENG., Illus.). 18p. (J). (— 1). bds. 7.99 (978-0-7636-9406-7(1)) Candlewick Pr.

—Maisy's Digger: A Go with Maisy Board Book. Cousins, Lucy, illus. 2015. (Maisy Ser.). (ENG., Illus.). 18p. (J). (— 1). bds. 7.99 (978-0-7636-8010-7(9)) Candlewick Pr.

—Maisy's First Clock: A Maisy Fun-To-Learn Book. Cousins, Lucy, illus. 2011. (Maisy Ser.). (ENG., Illus.). 16p. (J). (gr. k-k). bds. 14.99 (978-0-7636-5095-7(1)) Candlewick Pr.

—Maisy's First Colors: A Maisy Concept Book. Cousins, Lucy, illus. 2013. (Maisy Ser.). (ENG., Illus.). 14p. (J). (-k). bds. 7.99 (978-0-7636-6804-4(4)) Candlewick Pr.

—Maisy's Race Car: A Go with Maisy Board Book. Cousins, Lucy, illus. 2015. (Maisy Ser.). (ENG., Illus.). 18p. (J). (— 1). bds. 6.99 (978-0-7636-8011-4(7)) Candlewick Pr.

—Maisy's Tractor. Cousins, Lucy, illus. 2015. (Maisy Ser.). (ENG., Illus.). 18p. (J). (— 1). bds. 7.99 (978-0-7636-7305-5(6)) Candlewick Pr.

—Maisy's Wonderful Weather Book: A Maisy First Science Book. 2011. (Maisy Ser.). (ENG., Illus.). 16p. (J). (gr. -1-2). 16.99 (978-0-7636-5096-4(X)) Candlewick Pr.

—Sweet Dreams, Maisy. Cousins, Lucy, illus. 2009. (Maisy Ser.). (ENG., Illus.). 32p. (J). (gr. -1-2). bds. 6.99 (978-0-7636-4532-8(X)) Candlewick Pr.

—Where Are Maisy's Friends? A Maisy Lift-The-Flap Book. Cousins, Lucy, illus. 2010. (Maisy Ser.). (ENG., Illus.). 12p. (J). (-k). bds. 6.99 (978-0-7636-4669-1(5)) Candlewick Pr.

—Where Does Maisy Live? 2010. 12p. bds. 4.99 (978-976-3-64668-7(5)) Candlewick Pr.

—Where Does Maisy Live? A Maisy Lift-The-Flap Book. Cousins, Lucy, illus. 2010. (Maisy Ser.). (ENG., Illus.). 12p. (J). (-k). bds. 6.99 (978-0-7636-4668-4(7)) Candlewick Pr.

—Where Is Maisy? A Maisy Lift-The-Flap Book. Cousins, Lucy, illus. 2010. (Maisy Ser.). (ENG., Illus.). 14p. (J). (gr. k-k). bds. 6.99 (978-0-7636-4673-8(3)) Candlewick Pr.

Covello, Paul. Canada 123. 2017. (ENG.). 30p. (J). (gr. -1-k). bds. 10.50 (978-1-4434-5381-3(1), Harper Trophy) HarperCollins Pubs.

Cowley, Joy. Freddy Bear & the Big Bed. Webb, Philip, illus. 2017. (Freddy Bear Ser.). 20p. (J). (— 1). bds. 7.99 (978-1-927262-96-2(8)) Upstart Pr. NZL. Dist: Independent Pubs. Group.

—Mrs. WishyWashy & the Big Tub. 2009. pap. 8.25 (978-1-60559-233-6(1)) Hameray Publishing Group, Inc.

Cox, Phil Roxbee. Big Pig on a Dig. Tyler, Jenny, ed. Cartwright, Stephen, illus. rev. ed. 2006. (Phonics Readers Ser.). 16p. (J). (gr. -1-3). pap. 6.99 (978-0-7945-1501-0(0), Usborne) EDC Publishing.

—Curly's Friends. Cartwright, Stephen, illus. rev. ed. 2005. (Usborne Farmyard Tales Touchy-Feely Ser.). 10p. (J). (gr. -1-k). bds. 7.95 (978-0-7945-1180-7(5), Usborne) EDC Publishing.

—Frog on a Log. Tyler, Jenny, ed. Cartwright, Stephen, illus. rev. ed. 2006. (Phonics Readers Ser.). 16p. (J). (gr. -1). pap. 6.99 (978-0-7945-1504-1(5), Usborne) EDC Publishing.

—Hen's Pens. Tyler, Jenny, ed. Cartwright, Stephen, illus. rev. ed. 2006. (Phonics Readers Ser.). 16p. (J). (gr. -1-3). pap. 6.99 (978-0-7945-1506-5(1), Usborne) EDC Publishing.

Cox, Phil Roxbee & Cartwright, S. Rusty's Bone. 2004. (Farmyard Tales Touchy Feely Board Bks.). (ENG., Illus.). 1p. (J). bds. 7.95 (978-0-7945-0012-2(9), Usborne) EDC Publishing.

—Wolly's Walk. 2004. (Farmyard Tales Touchy Feely Board Bks.). (ENG., Illus.). 1p. (J). bds. 7.95 (978-0-7945-0039-9(0), Usborne) EDC Publishing.

Cox, Phil Roxbee & Cartwright, Stephen. Frog on a Log. 2004. (Easy Words to Read Ser.). (Illus.). 16p. (J). (gr. 1-18). pap. 6.95 (978-0-7945-0114-3(1), Usborne) EDC Publishing.

—Hen's Pens. 2004. (Easy Words to Read Ser.). (Illus.). 16p. (J). (gr. 1-18). pap. 6.95 (978-0-7945-0113-6(3), Usborne) EDC Publishing.

—Shark in the Park. 2004. (Easy Words to Read Ser.). (Illus.). 16p. (J). (gr. 1-18). pap. 6.95 (978-0-7945-0171-6(0), Usborne) EDC Publishing.

Coxon, Michele. Where's My Kitten? (Illus.). 16p. (J). pap. 5.95 (978-1-903285-02-2(X)) Happy Cat Bks. GBR. Dist: Star Bright Bks., Inc.

Craig, Lindsey. Dancing Feet! Brown, Marc, illus. 2012. 32p. (J). (gr. k-k). 6.99 (978-0-307-93081-1(5), Knopf Bks. for Young Readers) Random Hse. Children's Bks.

Crane, Carol. Little Georgia. Knorr, Laura, illus. 2013. (Little State Ser.). (ENG.). 20p. (J). (gr. -1-k). bds. 9.95 (978-1-58536-203-5(4), 202355) Sleeping Bear Pr.

Crazy Animals Sticker Book. (Weird & Wacky Ser.). 16p. (J). (978-2-89393-869-1(8)) Phidal Publishing, Inc./Editions Phidal, Inc.

Creepy Crawlers Sticker Book. (Weird & Wacky Ser.). 16p. (J). (978-2-89393-872-1(8)) Phidal Publishing, Inc./Editions Phidal, Inc.

Creese, Sarah. Even Pirates Poop. Lynch, Stuart, illus. 2014. (ENG.). 12p. (J). (— 1). bds. 9.99 (978-1-78393-113-2(2)) Make Believe Ideas GBR. Dist: Scholastic, Inc.

Cregg, R. J. Meet Catboy! 2016. (PJ Masks Ser.). (ENG., Illus.). 14p. (J). (gr. -1-k). bds. 5.99 (978-1-4814-8897-6(X), Simon Spotlight) Simon Spotlight.

Cregg, R. J., adapted by. Meet Owlette! 2017. (PJ Masks Ser.). (ENG., Illus.). 14p. (J). (gr. -1-k). bds. 5.99 (978-1-5344-0179-2(2), Simon Spotlight) Simon Spotlight.

Crisp, Dan. Trabajo/ Work. 2007. 14p. 10.95 (978-84-263-6452-4(7)) Vives, Luis Editorial (Edelvives) ESP. Dist: Baker & Taylor Bks.

Crisp, Dan, illus. Five Little Men in a Flying Saucer. 2005. (Classic Books with Holes Board Book Ser.). 14p. (J). spiral bd. (978-1-904550-58-7(4)) Child's Play International Ltd.

Croll, Carolyn. The Story of Christmas Story Book Set & Advent Calendar. 2008. (ENG., Illus.). 96p. (J). (gr. -1-12). 19.99 (978-0-7611-5250-7(4), 15250) Workman Publishing Co., Inc.

Crowe, Carmen. Brave Little Camper. Cottage Door Press, ed. Taylor, Jen, illus. 2016. (ENG.). 10p. (J). (gr. -1-k). bds. 12.99 (978-1-68052-074-3(1), 1000770) Cottage Door Pr.

Crowe, Ellie. Go to Sleep, Hide & Seek. Wu, Julie, illus. 2009. 10p. (J). bds. 11.95 (978-1-59700-759-7(5)) Island Heritage Publishing.

Crowson, Andrew. Flip Flap Christmas. Crowson, Andrew, illus. 2003. (ENG., Illus.). 12p. (J). bds. (978-1-85602-476-1(8), Pavilion Children's Books) Pavilion Bks.

—Flip Flap Fairytale. 2003. (Illus.). 12p. bds. (978-1-85602-444-0(X), Pavilion Children's Books) Pavilion Bks.

—Flip Flap People. 2003. (Illus.). 12p. bds. (978-1-85602-443-3(1), Pavilion Children's Books) Pavilion Bks.

—Flip Flap Prehistoric. Crowson, Andrew, illus. 2003. (Illus.). 12p. (J). pap. (978-1-85602-474-7(1), Pavilion Children's Books) Pavilion Bks.

—Flip Flap Safari. Crowson, Andrew, illus. 2003. (ENG., Illus.). 12p. (J). bds. (978-1-85602-473-0(3), Pavilion Children's Books) Pavilion Bks.

—Flip Flap Spooky. Crowson, Andrew, illus. 2003. (Illus.). 12p. (J). bds. (978-1-85602-475-4(X), Pavilion Children's Books) Pavilion Bks.

Crowther, Robert. Deep down under Ground: A Pop-up Book of Amazing Facts & Feats. Crowther, Robert, illus. 2004. (Illus.). 18p. (J). (gr. 3-8). reprint ed. pap. 22.00 (978-0-7567-7179-9(X)) DIANE Publishing Co.

—Robert Crowther's Pop-Up Dinosaur ABC. Crowther, Robert, illus. 2015. (ENG., Illus.). 10p. (J). (gr. -1-3). 19.99 (978-0-7636-7296-6(3)) Candlewick Pr.

Croyle, Paula. Today I'll Be a Princess. Brown, Heather, illus. 2015. (ENG.). 12p. (J). bds. 5.99 (978-1-4494-6057-0(7)) Andrews McMeel Publishing.

Crozier, Lorna. More Than Balloons, 1 vol. Miller, Rachelle Anne, illus. 2017. (ENG.). 26p. (J). (gr. -1 — 1). bds. 9.95 (978-1-4598-1028-0(7)) Orca Bk. Pubs. USA.

Crozon, Alain. All Shook Up! 2015. (All Shook Up! Ser.). (ENG., Illus.). 12p. (J). (gr. -1 — 1). bds. 10.99 (978-1-4521-4013-1(8)) Chronicle Bks. LLC.

—Who's There? 2015. (All Shook Up! Ser.). (ENG., Illus.). 10p. (J). (gr. -1 — 1). bds. 10.99 (978-1-4521-4014-8(6)) Chronicle Bks. LLC.

Crystal, Billy. I Already Know I Love You Board Book. Sayles, Elizabeth, illus. 2008. (ENG.). 32p. (J). (gr. -1-3). bds. 7.99 (978-0-06-145057-0(X), HarperFestival) HarperCollins Pubs.

Cullis, Megan. Big Book of Big Trains. 2013. (Big Bks). 16p. (J). ring bd. 14.99 (978-0-7945-3378-6(7), Usborne) EDC Publishing.

—Sticker Dressing Heroes. 2012. (Sticker Dressing Ser.). 24p. (J). pap. 8.99 (978-0-7945-3267-3(5), Usborne) EDC Publishing.

Cummings, Priscilla. Chadwick & Friends: A Lift-The-Flap Board Book, 1 vol. Cohen, A. R., illus. 2018. (ENG.). 22p. (J). bds. 12.99 (978-0-7643-5579-0(1), 16206) Schiffer Publishing, Ltd.

Cummings, Troy, illus. Read & Ride: Cars & Trucks: 4 Board Books Inside! (Toy Book for Children, Kids Book about Trucks & Cars. 2018. (ENG.). 5p. (J). (gr. -1 — 1). 15.99 (978-1-4521-6546-2(7)) Chronicle Bks. LLC.

Curato, Mike. Little Elliot, Big City. Curato, Mike, illus. 2016. (Little Elliot Ser.: 1). (ENG., Illus.). 34p. (J). bds. 8.99 (978-1-62779-698-9(3), 900158360, Holt, Henry & Co. Bks. For Young Readers) Holt, Henry & Co.

Curious George Before & after (Lift-The-Flap Board Book) 2007. (Curious George Ser.). (ENG., Illus.). 12p. (J). (gr. -1 — 1). bds. 6.99 (978-0-618-72399-7(4), 562611, Clarion Bks.) HarperCollins Pubs.

Curious George Discovery Day. 2007. (Curious George Ser.). (ENG., Illus.). 14p. (J). (gr. k — 1). bds. 13.95 (978-0-618-73761-1(8), 529819, Clarion Bks.) HarperCollins Pubs.

Curious George Makes Pancakes. 2018. (Curious George Ser.). (ENG., Illus.). 24p. (J). (— 1). bds. 12.99 (978-1-328-76461-4(3), 1681069, Clarion Bks.) HarperCollins Pubs.

Curious George Ready for School. 2017. (Curious George Ser.). (ENG., Illus.). 14p. (J). (— 1). bds. 7.99 (978-0-544-93120-6(3), 1657523, Clarion Bks.) HarperCollins Pubs.

Curious George the Movie: Touch & Feel Book. movie tie-in ed. 2006. (Curious George Ser.). (ENG., Illus.). 10p. (J). (gr. -1 — 1). bds. 6.99 (978-0-618-60587-3(8), 521621, Clarion Bks.) HarperCollins Pubs.

Curious George's Day at the Farm (Tabbed Lift-The-Flap) 2017. (Curious George Ser.). (ENG., Illus.). 16p. (J). (— 1). bds. 10.99 (978-0-544-98874-3(4), 1665846, Clarion Bks.) HarperCollins Pubs.

Curley, Paola. Ben's New Hat! 2017. (ENG., Illus.). (J). 12.95 (978-1-68401-309-8(7)) Amplify Publishing Group.

Curry, Don, ed. Esape Africa. 2008. 22p. (J). 15.95 (978-0-696-23488-0(2)) Meredith Bks.

Cusimano Love, Maryann. You Are My I Love You. Ichikawa, Satomi, illus. 2012. 30p. (J). (gr. -1 — 1). bds. 7.99 (978-0-399-24396-7(8), Philomel Bks.) Penguin Young Readers Group.

—You Are My I Love You: Board Book. Ichikawa, Satomi, illus. 2010. 30p. (J). (gr. -1 — 1). bds. 6.99 (978-0-399-24395-0(X), Philomel Bks.) Penguin Young Readers Group.

Dahl, Michael. Be a Star, Wonder Woman! Lozano, Omar, illus. 2018. (DC Super Heroes Ser.). (ENG.). 30p. (J). (gr. -1-2). bds. 7.99 (978-1-68436-222-6(9), 138938, Stone Arch Bks.) Capstone.

—Bear Says Thank You. Vidal, Oriol, illus. 2012. (Hello Genius Ser.). (ENG.). 20p. (J). (gr. -1 — 1). bds. 7.99 (978-1-4048-6786-4(4), 116224, Picture Window Bks.) Capstone.

—Big Bed for Giraffe. Vidal, Oriol, illus. 2015. (Hello Genius Ser.). (ENG.). 20p. (J). (gr. -1 — 1). bds. 7.99 (978-1-4795-5791-2(9), 126821, Picture Window Bks.) Capstone.

—Bye-Bye Bottles, Zebra. Vidal, Oriol, illus. 2015. (Hello Genius Ser.). (ENG.). 20p. (J). (gr. -1 — 1). bds. 7.99 (978-1-4795-5792-9(7), 126822, Picture Window Bks.) Capstone.

—Hello Genius. Vidal, Oriol, illus. 2016. (Hello Genius Ser.). (ENG.). 20p. (J). (gr. -1 — 1). bds., bds., bds. 199.75 (978-1-4795-8747-6(8), 24197, Picture Window Bks.) Capstone.

—Hello Genius, 4 vols., Set. Vidal, Oriol, illus. Incl. Bunny Eats Lunch. bds. 7.99 (978-1-4048-5728-5(1), 102305); Duck Goes Potty. bds. 7.99 (978-1-4048-5726-1(5), 102303); Pig Takes a Bath. bds. 7.99 (978-1-4048-5729-2(X), 102306); Pony Brushes His Teeth. bds. 7.99 (978-1-4048-5727-8(3), 102304); (J). (gr. -1 — 1). 2010. (Hello Genius Ser.). (ENG., Illus.). 20p. 2009. bds., bds., bds. 31.96 o.p. (978-1-4048-6198-5(X), 158432, Picture Window Bks.) Capstone.

—Hippo Says Excuse Me. Vidal, Oriol, illus. 2012. (Hello Genius Ser.). (ENG.). 20p. (J). (gr. -1 — 1). bds. 7.99 (978-1-4048-6787-1(2), 116225, Picture Window Bks.) Capstone.

—Little Dinos Don't Bite, 1 vol. Record, Adam, illus. 2013. (Little Dinos Ser.). (ENG.). 20p. (J). (gr. -1-k). bds. 7.99 (978-1-4048-7536-4(0), 119833, Picture Window Bks.) Capstone.

—Little Dinos Don't Hit, 1 vol. Record, Adam, illus. 2013. (Little Dinos Ser.). (ENG.). 20p. (J). (gr. -1-k). bds. 7.99 (978-1-4048-7533-3(6), 119830, Picture Window Bks.) Capstone.

—Little Dinos Don't Push, 1 vol. Record, Adam, illus. 2013. (Little Dinos Ser.). (ENG.). 20p. (J). (gr. -1-k). bds. 7.99 (978-1-4048-7534-0(4), 119831, Picture Window Bks.) Capstone.

—Little Dinos Don't Yell, 1 vol. Record, Adam, illus. 2013. (Little Dinos Ser.). (ENG.). 20p. (J). (gr. -1-k). bds. 7.99 (978-1-4048-7912-6(9), 120611, Picture Window Bks.) Capstone.

—Little Elephant Listens, 1 vol. Vidal, Oriol, illus. 2014. (Hello Genius Ser.). (ENG.). 20p. (J). (gr. -1 — 1). bds. 7.99 (978-1-4795-2289-7(9), 124332, Picture Window Bks.) Capstone.

—Little Lion Shares, 1 vol. Vidal, Oriol, illus. 2014. (Hello Genius Ser.). (ENG.). 20p. (J). (gr. -1 — 1). bds. 7.99 (978-1-4795-2287-3(2), 124330, Picture Window Bks.) Capstone.

—Little Monkey Calms Down, 1 vol. Vidal, Oriol, illus. 2014. (Hello Genius Ser.). (ENG.). 20p. (J). (gr. -1 — 1). bds. 7.99 (978-1-4795-2286-6(4), 124329, Picture Window Bks.) Capstone.

—Little Tiger Picks Up, 1 vol. Vidal, Oriol, illus. 2014. (Hello Genius Ser.). (ENG.). 20p. (J). (gr. -1 — 1). bds. 7.99 (978-1-4795-2288-0(0), 124331, Picture Window Bks.) Capstone.

—Mouse Says Sorry, 1 vol. Vidal, Oriol, illus. 2012. (Hello Genius Ser.). (ENG.). 20p. (J). (gr. -1 — 1). bds. 7.99 (978-1-4048-6789-5(9), 116227, Picture Window Bks.) Capstone.

—No More Pacifier, Duck. Vidal, Oriol, illus. 2015. (Hello Genius Ser.). (ENG.). 20p. (J). (gr. -1 — 1). bds. 7.99 (978-1-4795-5793-6(5), 126823, Picture Window Bks.) Capstone.

—Penguin Misses Mom. Vidal, Oriol, illus. 2016. (Hello Genius Ser.). (ENG.). 20p. (J). (gr. -1 — 1). bds. 7.99 (978-1-4795-8739-1(7), 131128, Picture Window Bks.) Capstone.

—Penguin Says Please, 1 vol. Vidal, Oriol, illus. 2012. (Hello Genius Ser.). (ENG.). 20p. (J). (gr. -1 — 1). bds. 7.99

(978-1-4048-6788-8(0), 116226, Picture Window Bks.) Capstone.
—Thumbs up, Brown Bear. Vidal, Oriol, illus. 2015. (Hello Genius Ser.) (ENG.). 20p. (J). (gr. -1 — 1). bds. 7.99 *(978-1-4795-5794-3(3)*, 126824, Picture Window Bks.) Capstone.
Dahlen, Noelle & Stickers. Glitter Candy Stickers. 2011. (Dover Little Activity Books Stickers Ser.). (ENG.). 2p. (J). (gr. 1-4). pap. 2.99 *(978-0-486-48282-8(0)*, 482820) Dover Pubns., Inc.
Daisy Dinosaur's Opposites. 2015. (Illus.). (J). *(978-1-58865-881-4(3))* Kidsbooks, LLC.
Dakota, Heather. Shark Bites. Jankowski, Daniel, illus. 2016. 48p. (J). pap. *(978-1-338-13718-7(2))* Scholastic, Inc.
Dale, Kim. What Am I? (Illus.). 32p. pap. *(978-0-7344-0125-0(6)*, Lothian Children's Bks.) Hachette Australia.
Dale, Penny. Dinosaurs on the Go!, 3 vols. Dale, Penny, illus. 2016. (Dinosaurs on the Go Ser.). (ENG., Illus.). 74p. (J). (-k). bds. 19.99 *(978-0-7636-8936-0(X))* Candlewick Pr.
Daley, Michael J. Babies on the Go, 1 vol. 2013. (ENG., Illus.). 32p. (J). bds. 5.99 *(978-1-59572-173-0(8))* Star Bright Bks., Inc.
—Beach Socks, 1 vol. Corke, Estelle, illus. 2013. (ENG.). 10p. (J). bds. 6.99 *(978-1-59572-637-7(3))* Star Bright Bks., Inc.
Daley, Robert. What Color Are You? 2007. (Illus.). 34p. (J). pap. 8.75 *(978-0-9800839-1-0(5))* Daley, Robert.
Dalmatian Press Staff. Fuzzy Ducky's Birthday! 2008. (ENG.). 5p. bds. 4.95 *(978-1-58117-725-1(9)*, Intervisual/Piggy Toes) Bendon, Inc.
—The Icky Sticky Anteater. 2008. (ENG.). 8p. bds. 4.95 *(978-1-58117-711-4(9)*, Intervisual/Piggy Toes) Bendon, Inc.
—The Icky Sticky Frog. 2008. (ENG.). 8p. (J). bds. 4.95 *(978-1-58117-712-1(7)*, Intervisual/Piggy Toes) Bendon, Inc.
—Maggie Can Count. 2008. (ENG.). 5p. (J). bds. 4.95 *(978-1-58117-728-2(3)*, Intervisual/Piggy Toes) Bendon, Inc.
—On Top of Spaghetti. 2008. (ENG.). 6p. (J). bds. 4.95 *(978-1-58117-720-6(8)*, Intervisual/Piggy Toes) Bendon, Inc.
—Pizza! Pizza! Pizza! 2008. (ENG.). 6p. (J). bds. 4.95 *(978-1-58117-721-3(6)*, Intervisual/Piggy Toes) Bendon, Inc.
—Pop & Shine Colors. 2008. (ENG.). 12p. (J). bds. 10.95 *(978-1-58117-673-5(2)*, Intervisual/Piggy Toes) Bendon, Inc.
—Pop & Shine Trucks. 2008. (ENG.). 12p. (J). 10.95 *(978-1-58117-672-8(4)*, Intervisual/Piggy Toes) Bendon, Inc.
—Pop & Sniff Fruit. 2008. (ENG.). 12p. (J). 10.95 *(978-1-58117-676-6(7)*, Intervisual/Piggy Toes) Bendon, Inc.
—Pop & Touch Baby Animals. 2008. (ENG.). 12p. (J). 10.95 *(978-1-58117-674-2(0)*, Intervisual/Piggy Toes) Bendon, Inc.
—Say Moo! 2008. (ENG.). 5p. (J). bds. 4.95 *(978-1-58117-722-0(4)*, Intervisual/Piggy Toes) Bendon, Inc.
—Thanks You, God: Board Book with Plush Toy. rev. ed. 2007. (ENG.). 7p. 12.99 *(978-1-4037-3074-9(1)*, Spirit Pr.) Bendon, Inc.
Daly, Kathleen N. Richard Scarry's Colors. Scarry, Richard, illus. 2017. (Little Golden Book Ser.). 20p. (J). (gr. -1-2). 5.99 *(978-0-399-55367-7(3)*, Golden Bks.) Random Hse. Children's Bks.
Daly, Niki. Little Artists. Daly, Niki, illus. 2016. (ENG., Illus.). 5p. (J). bds. 10.99 *(978-1-61067-436-2(7))* Kane Miller.
D'Andrea, Deborah, creator. Words. 2006. (Picture Me Ser.). (Illus.). (J). *(978-1-57151-768-5(5))* Playhouse Publishing.
D'Andrea, Deborah & Borlasca, Hector. Pretend & Play Superhero. 2005. (Illus.). (J). *(978-1-57151-751-7(0))* Playhouse Publishing.
Daniel Goes to the Potty. 2014. (Daniel Tiger's Neighborhood Ser.). (ENG., Illus.). 14p. (J). (gr. -1 — 1). 8.99 *(978-1-4814-2048-8(8)*, Simon Spotlight) Simon Spotlight.
Danson, Lesley, illus. Snow White. (Flip-Up Fairy Tales Ser.). 24p. (J). 2007. (gr. -1-2). *(978-1-84643-096-1(8))* 2006. (gr. 1-2). *(978-1-84643-023-7(2))* Child's Play International Ltd.
Dapre, Alan & Rooney, Ronnie. Brum Big Town Songs. 2004. (Illus.). 10p. (J). bds. *(978-0-7853-9898-1(8))* Publications International, Ltd.
David & Goliath Bible Sticker Book. 2003. (Illus.). 16p. (J). 2.98 *(978-1-4054-1554-5(1))* Parragon, Inc.
David, Juliet. Amazing Bible Stories. Parry, Jo, illus. 2019. (ENG.). 16p. (J). (gr. -1-k). 18.99 *(978-1-78128-288-5(9)*, 91cabf54-a0a5-46d7-afd5-bd3db0410222, Candle Bks.) Lion Hudson PLC GBR. Dist: Baker & Taylor Publisher Services (BTPS).
—Busy Christmas Stable, 1 vol. Pitt, Sarah, illus. 2010. (Candle Peek-A-boo Ser.). (ENG.). 8p. (J). (gr. -1 — 1). bds. 11.99 *(978-1-85985-803-5(1)*, Candle Bks.) Lion Hudson PLC GBR. Dist: Kregel Pubns.
—Candle Bible for Kids, 1 vol. Parry, Jo, illus. 2018. 400p. (J). 16.99 *(978-0-8254-5557-5(X))* Kregel Pubns.
—The Christmas Story, 1 vol. Ellis, Elina, illus. 2016. (99 Stories from the Bible Ser.). (ENG.). 24p. (J). (gr. k-3). 7.99 *(978-1-78128-282-3(X)*, 6c214623-2042-49ba-85fc-363e557d832b, Candle Bks.) Lion Hudson PLC GBR. Dist: Baker & Taylor Publisher Services (BTPS).
—Daniel & the Lions' Den, 1 vol. Denham, Gemma, illus. 2009. (Candle Playbook Ser.). 18p. (J). bds. 7.99 *(978-0-8254-7385-2(3)*, Candle Bks.) Lion Hudson PLC GBR. Dist: Kregel Pubns.
—God Loves Me, 1 vol. Byrne, Mike, illus. 2014. (ENG.). 10p. (J). 7.99 *(978-1-78128-114-7(9)*, Candle Bks.) Lion Hudson PLC GBR. Dist: Kregel Pubns.
—The Great Flood, 1 vol. Parry, Jo, illus. 2014. 12p. (J). bds. 3.99 *(978-1-85985-991-9(7)*, Candle Bks.) Lion Hudson PLC GBR. Dist: Kregel Pubns.
—My Very First Bible, 1 vol. Prole, Helen, illus. 2019. (Candle Bible for Toddlers Ser.). 40p. (J). pap. 4.99 *(978-0-8254-5559-9(6))* Kregel Pubns.
—Noah & His Boat, 1 vol. Denham, Gemma, illus. 2008. (Candle Playbook Ser.). 18p. (J). bds. 7.99 *(978-0-8254-7378-4(0)*, Candle Bks.) Lion Hudson PLC GBR. Dist: Kregel Pubns.
—Puddle Pen Bible Stories, 1 vol. Martin, Stuart, illus. 2010. (Candle Puddle Pen Ser.). 10p. (J). (gr. -1). bds. 12.99 *(978-0-8254-7394-4(2)*, Candle Bks.) Lion Hudson PLC GBR. Dist: Kregel Pubns.
—Puddle Pen Christmas, 1 vol. Poole, Helen, illus. 2010. (Candle Puddle Pen Ser.). 10p. (J). (gr. -1-k). bds. 12.99 *(978-1-85985-868-4(6)*, Candle Bks.) Lion Hudson PLC GBR. Dist: Kregel Pubns.
Davidson, Alice Joyce. Baby Blessings Christmas. 2009. (Baby Blessings Ser.). (ENG.). 18p. (J). (gr. -1-k). bds. 12.99 *(978-0-7847-2374-6(5)*, B&H Kids) B&H Publishing Group.
Davidson, Carli, photos by. Heads & Tails: (Dog Books, Books about Dogs, Dog Gifts for Dog Lovers) 2017. (ENG., Illus.). 20p. (J). bds. 8.99 *(978-1-4521-5137-3(7))* Chronicle Bks. LLC.
—Shake, Wiggle & Roll. 2017. (ENG., Illus.). 20p. (J). bds. 8.99 *(978-1-4521-5136-6(9))* Chronicle Bks. LLC.
Davidson, S. & Daynes, K. Princess Jewelry Kid Kit (Bag) 2008. (Kid Kits Ser.). 96p. (J). 15.99 *(978-1-60130-104-8(9)*, Usborne) EDC Publishing.
—Princess Jewelry Kid Kit (Box) 2008. (Kid Kits Ser.). 96p. (J). 15.99 *(978-1-60130-115-4(4)*, Usborne) EDC Publishing.
Davidson, Susanna. See Inside Fairyland. Ligi, Raffaella, illus. 2007. (See Inside Board Bks). 14p. (J). (gr. -1-k). bds. 12.99 *(978-0-7945-1570-6(3)*, Usborne) EDC Publishing.
—That's Not My Puppy. 2009. (Touchy-Feely Board Bks). 10p. (J). bds. 8.99 *(978-0-7945-2511-8(3)*, Usborne) EDC Publishing.
Davies, Benji, illus. Bizzy Bear: Ambulance Rescue. 2018. (Bizzy Bear Ser.). (ENG.). 8p. (J). (— 1). bds. 7.99 *(978-1-5362-0256-4(8))* Candlewick Pr.
—Bizzy Bear: Deep-Sea Diver. 2016. (Bizzy Bear Ser.). (ENG.). 8p. (J). (— 1). bds. 7.99 *(978-0-7636-8647-5(6))* Candlewick Pr.
—Bizzy Bear: Fun on the Farm. 2011. (Bizzy Bear Ser.). (ENG.). 8p. (J). (gr. k — 1). bds. 8.99 *(978-0-7636-5879-3(0))* Candlewick Pr.
—Bizzy Bear: Knights' Castle. 2015. (Bizzy Bear Ser.). (ENG.). 8p. (J). (— 1). bds. 7.99 *(978-0-7636-7602-5(0))* Candlewick Pr.
—Bizzy Bear: off We Go! 2012. (Bizzy Bear Ser.). (ENG.). 8p. (J). (gr. k — 1). bds. 7.99 *(978-0-7636-5900-4(2))* Candlewick Pr.
—Bizzy Bear: Zookeeper. 2015. (Bizzy Bear Ser.). (ENG.). 8p. (J). (— 1). bds. 7.99 *(978-0-7636-7603-2(9))* Candlewick Pr.
Davies, Gill. A Letter to Santa. Taylor, Ned, illus. 2015. (J). *(978-1-4351-6225-9(0))* Barnes & Noble, Inc.
Davies, Kate. See under the Sea. 2008. (See Inside Board Bks). 16p. (J). (gr. 2). bds. 12.99 *(978-0-7945-2238-4(6)*, Usborne) EDC Publishing.
Davies, Kate, illus. Little Squeak School. 2014. (J). *(978-1-4351-5582-4(3))* Barnes & Noble, Inc.
—Welcome to the Mouse House. 2014. (J). *(978-1-4351-5583-1(1))* Barnes & Noble, Inc.
Davis, Caroline. First Abc. 2012. (ENG., Illus.). 10p. (J). (gr. k-1). pap. 7.99 *(978-1-84322-772-4(X))* Anness Publishing GBR. Dist: National Bk. Network.
—First Opposites. 2012. (Illus.). 10p. (J). (gr. -1-1). bds. 7.99 *(978-1-84322-844-8(0)*, Armadillo) Anness Publishing GBR. Dist: National Bk. Network.
—First Pictures. 2012. (Illus.). 196p. (J). (gr. -1-12). bds. 7.99 *(978-1-84322-774-8(6)*, Armadillo) Anness Publishing GBR. Dist: National Bk. Network.
—Sparkly Farm. Davis, Caroline, illus. 2008. (Tiger Tales Ser.). (Illus.). 8p. (J). (gr. -1). bds. 6.95 *(978-1-58925-831-0(2))* Tiger Tales.
—Sparkly Ocean. Davis, Caroline, illus. 2008. (Tiger Tales Ser.). (Illus.). 8p. (J). (gr. -1). bds. 6.95 *(978-1-58925-832-7(0))* Tiger Tales.
Davis, Jacky. Ladybug Girl & Her Mama. Soman, David, illus. 2013. (Ladybug Girl Ser.). 12p. (J). (gr. -1 — 1). bds. 8.99 *(978-0-8037-3891-1(9)*, Dial Bks) Penguin Young Readers Group.
—Ladybug Girl & Her Papa. Soman, David, illus. 2017. (Ladybug Girl Ser.). 14p. (J). (— 1). bds. 6.99 *(978-0-8037-4035-8(2)*, Dial Bks) Penguin Young Readers Group.
—Ladybug Girl Feels Happy. Soman, David, illus. 2012. (Ladybug Girl Ser.). 12p. (J). (gr. -1 — 1). bds. 5.99 *(978-0-8037-3890-4(0)*, Dial Bks) Penguin Young Readers Group.
—Ladybug Girl Plays. Soman, David, illus. 2013. (Ladybug Girl Ser.). (ENG.). 14p. (J). (gr. -1 — 1). bds. 5.99 *(978-0-8037-3892-8(7)*, Dial Bks) Penguin Young Readers Group.
—Ladybug Girl Ready for Snow. Soman, David, illus. 2014. (Ladybug Girl Ser.). 14p. (J). (gr. -1 — 1). bds. 7.99 *(978-0-8037-4137-9(5)*, Dial Bks) Penguin Young Readers Group.
Davis, Kathryn Lynn. The First Thanksgiving: A Lift-The-Flap Book. Davis, Kathryn Lynn, illus. 2010. (ENG., Illus.). 14p. (J). (gr. -1 — 1). bds. 6.99 *(978-1-4424-0807-4(3)*, Little Simon) Little Simon.
Day, Anna. Scotland 123: A Counting Book for Cool Kids. Gentry, Lauren, illus. 2015. (ENG.). 20p. (J). pap. 10.95 *(978-0-9575456-2-5(2))* Playroom Pr.
Daynes, Katie. Flip Flap Airport. 2009. (Flip Flap Board Bks). 13p. (J). (gr. -1). bds. 14.99 *(978-0-7945-2401-2(X)*, Usborne) EDC Publishing.
—Lift-The-Flap Questions & Answers about Nature IR. 2018. (Lift-The Flap Questions & Answers Ser.). (ENG.). 14p. (J). 14.99 *(978-0-7945-4121-7(6)*, Usborne) EDC Publishing.
—Lift-The-Flap Very First Questions & Answers What Are Germs? 2017. (Lift-The-Flap Very First Questions & Answers Ser.). (ENG.). 12p. 12.99 *(978-0-7945-4093-7(7)*, Usborne) EDC Publishing.
—Lift-The-Flap Very First Questions & Answers What Are Stars. 2018. (Lift-The-Flap Very First Questions & Answers Ser.). (ENG.). 12p. (J). 12.99 *(978-0-7945-4211-5(5)*, Usborne) EDC Publishing.
—Look Inside a Farm. rev. ed. 2012. (Look Inside Board Bks). 13p. (J). ring bd. 15.99 *(978-0-7945-3249-9(7)*, Usborne) EDC Publishing.
—Questions & Answers. 2013. (Usborne Lift the Flap Bks.). (ENG., Illus.). 14p. (J). 14.99 *(978-0-7945-3207-9(1)*, Usborne) EDC Publishing.
—See Inside Space. Allen, Peter, illus. 2009. (See Inside Board Bks). 16p. (J). (gr. 2). bds. 12.99 *(978-0-7945-2088-5(X)*, Usborne) EDC Publishing.
—See Inside Your Body. King, Colin, illus. 2006. 15p. (J). (gr. -1-3). bds. 12.99 *(978-0-7945-1233-0(X)*, Usborne) EDC Publishing.
Daynes, Katie & Allen, Peter. See Inside Planet Earth - Internet Referenced. 2008. (See Inside Board Bks). 16p. (J). bds. 12.99 *(978-0-7945-2070-0(7)*, Usborne) EDC Publishing.
Daynes, Katie & Watt, Fiona, eds. Baby Scrapbook. 2008. (Baby Scrapbook Ser.). (Illus.). 32p. (J). bds. 19.99 *(978-0-7945-1957-5(1)*, Usborne) EDC Publishing.
DaySpring Greeting Card Staff & Jensen, Bonnie Rickner. Really Woolly Nighttime Lullabies, 1 vol. 2015. (Really Woolly Ser.). (ENG., Illus.). 40p. (J). bds. 9.99 *(978-0-7180-2295-2(5)*, Tommy Nelson) Nelson, Thomas Inc.
Daywalt, Drew. The Crayons' Book of Numbers. Jeffers, Oliver, illus. 2016. (ENG.). 18p. (J). (-k). bds. 8.99 *(978-0-451-53405-7(0)*, Grosset & Dunlap) Penguin Young Readers Group.
—The Crayons' Christmas. Jeffers, Oliver, illus. 2019. (ENG.). 52p. (J). (gr. -1-2). 19.99 *(978-0-525-51574-6(7)*, Penguin Workshop) Penguin Young Readers Group.
de Beer, Hans. Little Polar Bear Board Book. 2018. (Little Polar Bear Ser.: 13). (ENG., Illus.). 24p. (J). (— 1). bds. 7.95 *(978-0-7358-4316-5(3))* North-South Bks., Inc.
de Brunhoff, Laurent. Babar & His Family. 2012. (ENG., Illus.). 24p. (J). (gr. -1 — 1). bds. 8.99 *(978-1-4197-0263-1(7)*, 1019801, Abrams Appleseed) Abrams, Inc.
de La Cour, Gary, et al, illus. Wheels on the Bus. rev. ed. 2007. (ENG.). 24p. (J). (gr. -1-3). 4.99 *(978-1-59069-562-3(3))* Studio Mouse LLC.
de la Mare, Walter. Snow. Rabei, Carolina, illus. 2018. (Four Seasons of Walter de la Mare Ser.). (ENG.). 16p. bds. 7.95 *(978-0-571-33713-2(9)*, Faber & Faber Children's Bks.) Faber & Faber, Inc.
De Saint-Exupéry, Antoine. Le Petit Prince: Avec les dessins de l'auteur. (FRE., Illus.). 64p. (J). (gr. 1-7). audio, audio compact disk 12.95 *(978-2-921997-41-6(X))* Coffragants CAN. Dist: Penton Overseas, Inc.
de Saint-Exupéry, Antoine. The Little Prince 70th Anniversary Gift Set Book & CD. de Saint-Exupéry, Antoine, illus. 70th ed. 2013. (Little Prince Ser.). (ENG., Illus.). 96p. (J). (gr. 7). audio compact disk 24.99 *(978-0-547-97048-6(X)*, 1522017, Clarion Bks.) HarperCollins Pubs.
Dean, James & Dean, Kimberly. Pete the Kitty: I Love Pete the Kitty. Dean, James, illus. 2017. (Pete the Cat Ser.). (ENG., Illus.). 24p. (J). (gr. -1 — 1). bds. 7.99 *(978-0-06-243581-1(7)*, HarperFestival) HarperCollins Pubs.
D'Ecsery, Claire. Temples Dot the Earth. 2016. (ENG.). (J). bds. 9.99 *(978-1-4621-1842-7(9))* Cedar Fort, Inc./CFI Distribution.
Dee, Noor H. I Say Alhamdulillah. Iput, illus. 2019. (I Say Board Bks.). (ENG.). 20p. (J). bds. 9.95 *(978-0-86037-638-5(9))* Kube Publishing Ltd. GBR. Dist: Consortium Bk. Sales & Distribution.
Degen, Bruce. Jamberry Padded Board Book. Degen, Bruce, illus. 2017. (ENG., Illus.). 34p. (J). (gr. -1 — 1). bds. 10.99 *(978-0-06-264379-7(7)*, HarperFestival) HarperCollins Pubs.
DeGregorio, Chieri & DeGregorio, Steve. Vehicles. 2019. (Kids' Picture Show Ser.). (Illus.). 16p. (J). (-k). bds. 7.99 *(978-1-5247-9076-9(1)*, Penguin Workshop) Penguin Young Readers Group.
Del Moral, Susana. Como Me Siento. Zaidi, Nadeem, illus. 2005. (Baby Einstein: Libros de Carton Ser.). (SPA.). 14p. (J). (gr. -1). bds. *(978-970-718-308-7(X)*, Silver Dolphin en Español) Advanced Marketing, S. de R. L. de C. V.
—El Juego de las Formas. Zaidi, Nadeem, illus. 2005. (Baby Einstein: Libros de Carton Ser.). (SPA.). 6p. (J). (gr. -1). bds. *(978-970-718-303-2(9)*, Silver Dolphin en Español) Advanced Marketing, S. de R. L. de C. V.
—Las Rimas de Bard: Un Libro con Ventanas. Zaidi, Nadeem, illus. 2005. (Baby Einstein: Libros de Carton Ser.). (SPA.). 16p. (J). (gr. -1). bds. *(978-970-718-304-9(7)*, Silver Dolphin en Español) Advanced Marketing, S. de R. L. de C. V.
Demarest, Chris. Bus/el Autobús Board Book: Bilingual English-Spanish. 2017. (ENG., Illus.). 16p. (J). (— 1). bds. 4.99 *(978-0-544-99114-9(1)*, 1665902, Clarion Bks.) HarperCollins Pubs.
—Plane Board Book. 2017. (ENG., Illus.). 16p. (J). (— 1). bds. 6.99 *(978-0-544-97703-7(3)*, 1663472, Clarion Bks.) HarperCollins Pubs.
—Ship Board Book. 2017. (ENG., Illus.). 16p. (J). (— 1). bds. 6.99 *(978-0-544-97702-0(5)*, 1663470, Clarion Bks.) HarperCollins Pubs.
—Train. 2017. (ENG., Illus.). 16p. (J). (— 1). bds. 6.99 *(978-0-544-87608-8(3)*, 1651101, Clarion Bks.) HarperCollins Pubs.
Denchfield, Nick & Denchdfield, Nick. Charlie Chick Finds an Egg. Parker, Ant, illus. 2017. (Charlie Chick Ser.: 5). (ENG.). 16p. (J). (gr. -1-k). 11.99 *(978-1-5098-2883-8(4)*, Campbell Bks.) Pan Macmillan GBR. Dist: Independent Pubs. Group.
Deneux, Xavier. TouchThinkLearn: 123. 2018. (Touch Think Learn Ser.). (ENG., Illus.). 40p. (J). (gr. -1 — 1). bds. 24.99 *(978-1-4521-7390-0(7))* Chronicle Bks. LLC.
—TouchThinkLearn: ABC (Baby Board Books, Baby Touch & Feel Books, Sensory Books for Toddlers) 2016. (Touch Think Learn Ser.). (ENG., Illus.). 32p. (J). (gr. -1 — 1). bds. 24.99 *(978-1-4521-4503-7(2))* Chronicle Bks. LLC.
—TouchThinkLearn: Colors: (Early Learners Book, New Baby or Baby Shower Gift) 2013. (Touch Think Learn Ser.). (ENG.). 20p. (J). (gr. -1 — 1). bds. 16.99 *(978-1-4521-1726-3(8))* Chronicle Bks. LLC.
—TouchThinkLearn: Farm: (Childrens Books Ages 1-3, Interactive Books for Toddlers, Board Books for Toddlers) 2015. (Touch Think Learn Ser.). (ENG., Illus.). 22p. (J). (gr. -1 — 1). bds. 16.99 *(978-1-4521-4517-4(2))* Chronicle Bks. LLC.
—TouchThinkLearn: Fly! 2017. (Touch Think Learn Ser.). (ENG., Illus.). 14p. (J). bds. 17.99 *(978-1-4521-5922-5(X))* Chronicle Bks. LLC.
—TouchThinkLearn: Homes. 2016. (Touch Think Learn Ser.). (ENG., Illus.). 16p. (J). (gr. -1 — 1). bds. 14.99 *(978-1-4521-4518-1(0))* Chronicle Bks. LLC.
—TouchThinkLearn: Little Critters: (Early Elementary Board Book, Interactive Children's Books) 2017. (Touch Think Learn Ser.). (ENG., Illus.). 16p. (J). (gr. -1 — 1). bds. 14.99 *(978-1-4521-6594-3(7))* Chronicle Bks. LLC.
—TouchThinkLearn: Numbers: (Board Books for Baby Learners, Touch Feel Books for Children) 2014. (Touch Think Learn Ser.). (ENG., Illus.). 22p. (J). (gr. -1 — 1). bds. 15.99 *(978-1-4521-1724-9(1))* Chronicle Bks. LLC.
—TouchThinkLearn: Shapes. 2014. (Touch Think Learn Ser.). (ENG., Illus.). 20p. (J). (gr. -1 — 1). bds. 15.99 *(978-1-4521-1727-0(6))* Chronicle Bks. LLC.
—TouchThinkLearn: Vehicles: (Board Books for Baby Learners, Touch Feel Books for Children) 2015. (Touch Think Learn Ser.). (ENG., Illus.). 22p. (J). (gr. -1 — 1). bds. 16.99 *(978-1-4521-4516-7(4))* Chronicle Bks. LLC.
—TouchThinkLearn: Wild Animals: (Childrens Books Ages 1-3, Interactive Books for Toddlers, Board Books for Toddlers) 2017. (Touch Think Learn Ser.). (ENG., Illus.). 22p. (J). (gr. -1 — 1). bds. 15.99 *(978-1-4521-6288-1(3))* Chronicle Bks. LLC.
Denise, Anika. Monster Trucks Board Book. Wragg, Nate, illus. 2018. (ENG.). 32p. (J). (gr. -1 — 1). bds. 7.99 *(978-0-06-274162-2(4)*, HarperFestival) HarperCollins Pubs.
dePaola, Tomie. Strega Nona. dePaola, Tomie, illus. 2017. (Strega Nona Book Ser.). (ENG., Illus.). 36p. (J). (gr. -1-k). bds. 8.99 *(978-1-4814-8724-5(8)*, Little Simon) Little Simon.
Depken, Kristen L. Where's Woody? (Disney/Pixar Toy Story) RH Disney, illus. 2012. (Pictureback(R) Ser.). (ENG.). 16p. (J). (gr. -1-2). pap. 5.99 *(978-0-7364-2850-7(X)*, RH/Disney) Random Hse. Children's Bks.
DePrisco, Dorothea. Apple. Taxali, Gary, illus. 2005. (Plush Learning Books Ser.). 10p. (J). bds. 6.95 *(978-1-58117-191-4(9)*, Intervisual/Piggy Toes) Bendon, Inc.
—Lemon. Taxali, Gary, illus. 2005. (Plush Learning Books Ser.). 10p. (J). bds. 6.95 *(978-1-58117-194-5(3)*, Intervisual/Piggy Toes) Bendon, Inc.
—Meet Gator: A Picture Clues Touch & Feel Book. Croft, James Lee, illus. 2005. (Learn to Read Ser.). 10p. (J). (gr. -1-18). 10.95 *(978-1-58117-123-5(4)*, Intervisual/Piggy Toes) Bendon, Inc.
—Pear. Taxali, Gary, illus. 2005. (Plush Learning Books Ser.). 10p. (J). bds. 6.95 *(978-1-58117-193-8(5)*, Intervisual/Piggy Toes) Bendon, Inc.
—Peek-A-Boooo Who? A Lift-the-Flap & Sound Book. Hedgecock, Lucie, illus. 2009. 12p. 8.95 *(978-1-58117-952-1(9)*, Intervisual/Piggy Toes) Bendon, Inc.
—Pig-A-Boo! A Farmyard Peekaboo Book. Runnells, Treesha, illus. 2009. (ENG.). 14p. (J). (gr. -1-k). 9.99 *(978-1-4169-7226-6(9)*, Little Simon) Little Simon.
—Tub-A-Tub. 2006. (Illus.). 10p. (J). (gr. -1-k). 9.95 *(978-1-58117-463-2(2)*, Intervisual/Piggy Toes) Bendon, Inc.
—Who's in the Jungle? Gilvan-Cartwright, Chris, illus. 2006. (ENG.). 10p. (J). bds. 4.95 *(978-1-58117-507-3(8)*, Intervisual/Piggy Toes) Bendon, Inc.
—Who's in the Ocean? Gilvan-Cartwright, Chris, illus. 2006. (ENG.). 10p. (gr. -1-k). bds. 4.95 *(978-1-58117-509-7(4)*, Intervisual/Piggy Toes) Bendon, Inc.
—Who's on the Farm? Gilvan-Cartwright, Chris, illus. 2006. (ENG.). 10p. (gr. -1-k). bds. 4.95 *(978-1-58117-508-0(6)*, Intervisual/Piggy Toes) Bendon, Inc.
Design Eye Publishing Staff, et al. Amazing Automata — Dinosaurs! 2013. (Dover Origami Papercraft Ser.). (ENG.). 24p. (J). (gr. 5). 14.99 *(978-0-486-49981-9(2)*, 499812) Dover Pubns., Inc.
—Amazing Automata — Pirates! 2013. (Dover Origami Papercraft Ser.). (ENG.). 24p. (J). (gr. 5). 14.99 *(978-0-486-49980-2(4)*, 499804) Dover Pubns., Inc.
Dewdney, Anna. Llama Llama Easter Egg. 2015. (Llama Llama Ser.). (Illus.). 14p. (J). (— 1). bds. 7.99 *(978-0-451-46982-3(8)*, Viking Books for Young Readers) Penguin Young Readers Group.
—Llama Llama Gives Thanks. 2017. (Llama Llama Ser.). (Illus.). 14p. (J). (— 1). bds. 7.99 *(978-1-101-99715-4(X)*, Viking Books for Young Readers) Penguin Young Readers Group.
—Llama Llama I Love You. 2014. (Llama Llama Ser.). (Illus.). 14p. (J). (gr. -1 — 1). bds. 6.99 *(978-0-451-46981-6(X)*, Viking Books for Young Readers) Penguin Young Readers Group.
—Llama Llama Jingle Bells. Dewdney, Anna, illus. 2014. (Llama Llama Ser.). (Illus.). 14p. (J). (— 1). bds. 6.99 *(978-0-451-46980-9(1)*, Viking Books for Young Readers) Penguin Young Readers Group.
—Llama Llama Yum Yum Yum! A Scratch-And-Sniff Book. 2016. (Llama Llama Ser.). (Illus.). 14p. (J). (— 1). bds. 12.99 *(978-0-448-49638-2(0)*, Grosset & Dunlap) Penguin Young Readers Group.
—Llama Llama's Little Library, 4 vols. 2013. (Llama Llama Ser.). (ENG., Illus.). 56p. (J). (— 1). bds. 27.96 *(978-0-670-01648-8(9)*, Viking Books for Young Readers) Penguin Young Readers Group.
—Nobunny's Perfect. 2012. (ENG.). 32p. (J). (gr. -1-k). bds. 7.99 *(978-0-670-01408-8(7)*, Viking Books for Young Readers) Penguin Young Readers Group.
Dewin, Howard & Barba, M. J. Scooby-Doo! A to Z Ultimate Joke Book. 2011. (Illus.). 63p. (J). pap. *(978-0-545-37944-1(X))* Scholastic, Inc.
DeYoung, Andrew J. & Krueger, Naomi Joy. Lift-The-Flap Bible Stories for Young Children. 2018. (Lift-The-Flap Bible Stories Ser.). (Illus.). 16p. (J). 12.99 *(978-1-5064-4684-4(1)*, Beaming Books) 1517 Media.
Diaz, James & Gerth, Melanie, illus. Numbers: Learning Fun for Little Ones! 2007. 10p. (J). reprint ed. *(978-1-4223-6683-7(9))* DIANE Publishing Co.
DiCicco, Sue. 1, 2 at the Zoo. DiCicco, Sue, illus. 2012. (ENG., Illus.). 12p. (J). (— 1). bds. 6.99 *(978-0-545-43239-9(1))* Scholastic, Inc.
Dickens, Rosie. My Very First Art Coloring Book with Stickers. 2012. (Art Ser.). 24p. (J). pap. 5.99 *(978-0-7945-3273-4(X)*, Usborne) EDC Publishing.
Dickins, Rosie. See Inside a Space Station & Other Spacecraft. 2017. (See Inside Board Bks.). (ENG.). 16p. 14.99 *(978-0-7945-4020-3(1)*, Usborne) EDC Publishing.
Dicmas, Courtney. Bathtime. Dicmas, Courtney, illus. 2014. (Wild! Ser.: 4). (Illus.). 14p. (J). (gr. k-k). spiral bd. *(978-1-84643-686-4(9))* Child's Play International Ltd.
—Bedtime. Dicmas, Courtney, illus. 2014. (Wild! Ser.: 4). (Illus.). 14p. (J). (gr. k-k). spiral bd. *(978-1-84643-687-1(7))* Child's Play International Ltd.
—Colors. Dicmas, Courtney, illus. 2017. (Wild! Concepts Ser.: 4). (ENG., Illus.). 14p. (J). bds. *(978-1-84643-996-4(5))* Child's Play International Ltd.
—Colours. Dicmas, Courtney, illus. 2017. (Wild! Concepts Ser.: 4). (Illus.). 14p. (J). spiral bd. *(978-1-84643-995-7(7))* Child's Play International Ltd.
—Mealtime. Dicmas, Courtney, illus. 2014. (Wild! Ser.: 4). (Illus.). 14p. (J). (gr. k-k). spiral bd. *(978-1-84643-684-0(2))* Child's Play International Ltd.

TUV

—Numbers. Dicmas, Courtney, illus. 2017. (Wild! Concepts Ser.: 4). (Illus.). 14p. (J). spiral bd. *(978-1-84643-993-3(0))* Child's Play International Ltd.

—Opposites. Dicmas, Courtney, illus. 2017. (Wild! Concepts Ser.: 4). (Illus.). 14p. (J). spiral bd. *(978-1-84643-997-1(3))* Child's Play International Ltd.

—Playtime. Dicmas, Courtney, illus. 2014. (Wild! Ser.: 4). (Illus.). 14p. (J). (gr. k-k). spiral bd. *(978-1-84643-685-7(0))* Child's Play International Ltd.

—Shapes. Dicmas, Courtney, illus. 2017. (Wild! Concepts Ser.: 4). (Illus.). 14p. (J). spiral bd. *(978-1-84643-994-0(9))* Child's Play International Ltd.

—WILD! Mealtime/¡QUÉ LOCURA! a la Hora de Comer. Dicmas, Courtney, illus. 2016. (Wild!/¡quÉ Locura! Ser.: 4). (ENG., Illus.). 14p. (J). bds. *(978-1-84643-905-6(1))* Child's Play International Ltd.

Diesen, Deborah. Happy Easter, Pout-Pout Fish. Hanna, Dan, illus. 2017. (Pout-Pout Fish Mini Adventure Ser.: 8). (ENG.). 12p. (J). bds. 5.99 *(978-0-374-30400-3(9))*, 900158630, Farrar, Straus & Giroux (BYR)) Farrar, Straus & Giroux.

—Lift-The-Flap Tab: Hide-and-Seek, Pout-Pout Fish. Hanna, Dan, illus. 2015. (Pout-Pout Fish Novelty Ser.). (ENG.). 18p. (J). (gr. -1 — 1). bds. 12.99 *(978-1-250-06011-2(7))*, 900140949) Square Fish.

—The Pout-Pout Fish Halloween Faces. 2018. (Pout-Pout Fish Novelty Ser.). (ENG., Illus.). 10p. (J). bds. 9.99 *(978-0-374-30450-8(5))*, 900159861, Farrar, Straus & Giroux (BYR)) Farrar, Straus & Giroux.

—The Pout-Pout Fish Undersea Alphabet: Touch & Feel. Hanna, Dan, illus. 2016. (Pout-Pout Fish Novelty Ser.). (ENG.). 20p. (J). bds. 16.99 *(978-1-250-06392-2(2))*, 900143400, Farrar, Straus & Giroux (BYR)) Farrar, Straus & Giroux.

—Smile, Pout-Pout Fish. Hanna, Dan, illus. 2014. (Pout-Pout Fish Mini Adventure Ser.: 1). (ENG.). 12p. (J). (gr. -1 — 1). bds. 5.99 *(978-0-374-37084-8(2))*, 900122559, Farrar, Straus & Giroux (BYR)) Farrar, Straus & Giroux.

Dietrich, Christopher & Character Building Studio (Firm) Staff. Doc on Call. 2015. (Illus.). (J). *(978-1-4847-2292-3(2))* Disney Publishing Worldwide.

—Pirate Tales. 2015. (Illus.). (J). *(978-1-4847-2335-7(X))* Disney Publishing Worldwide.

Dingeldein, Noelle. Walter's Wheels. 2015. (ENG., Illus.). 14p. (J). (gr. -1 — 1). bds. 7.99 *(978-1-936669-36-3(6))*, 1395558) Blue Manatee Press.

Discovering Dinos. (Flip Flap Fun Book Ser.). 10p. (J). bds. *(978-2-7643-0137-1(5))* Phidal Publishing, Inc./Editions Phidal, Inc.

Disney Books. Disney Baby: 100 First Words LifttheFlap. 2018. (ENG., Illus.). 12p. (J). (gr. -1 — 1). bds. 10.99 *(978-1-4847-1801-8(1))*, Disney Press Books) Disney Publishing Worldwide.

—Disney Baby: My ABCs. 2018. (ENG., Illus.). 14p. (J). (gr. -1 — 1). bds. 9.99 *(978-1-368-01397-0(X))*, Disney Press Books) Disney Publishing Worldwide.

—Disney Baby: My First Colors. 2016. (ENG., Illus.). 10p. (J). (gr. -1 — 1). bds. 6.99 *(978-1-4847-2943-4(9))*, Disney Press Books) Disney Publishing Worldwide.

—Disney Baby: My First Easter. 2018. (ENG., Illus.). 12p. (J). (gr. -1 — 1). bds. 8.99 *(978-1-368-01116-7(0))*, Disney Press Books) Disney Publishing Worldwide.

—Disney Baby: My First Halloween. 2017. (ENG., Illus.). 12p. (J). (gr. -1 — 1). bds. 8.99 *(978-1-4847-9936-9(4))*, Disney Press Books) Disney Publishing Worldwide.

—Disney Baby: My First Words. 2016. (ENG., Illus.). 24p. (J). (gr. -1 — 1). bds. 7.99 *(978-1-4847-5261-6(9))*, Disney Press Books) Disney Publishing Worldwide.

—Disney Baby: One, Two, Winnie the Pooh. 2018. (ENG., Illus.). 10p. (J). (gr. -1 — 1). bds. 8.99 *(978-1-368-02372-6(X))*, Disney Press Books) Disney Publishing Worldwide.

—Disney Bunnies: Thumper's Hoppy Home: A Lift-The-Flap Board Book. 2018. (ENG., Illus.). 10p. (J). (gr. -1-k). bds. 8.99 *(978-1-4847-7371-0(3))*, Disney Press Books) Disney Publishing Worldwide.

—Disney It's a Small World: Guess Who! 2012. (ENG., Illus.). 14p. (J). (gr. -1-k). bds. 6.99 *(978-1-4231-6008-3(8))*, Disney Press Books) Disney Publishing Worldwide.

—Disney It's a Small World: Hello, World! 2011. (ENG., Illus.). 14p. (J). (gr. -1-k). bds. 6.99 *(978-1-4231-4140-2(7))*, Disney Press Books) Disney Publishing Worldwide.

—Disney Nursery Rhymes ReadAlong Storybook & CD. 2011. (Read-Along Storybook & CD Ser.). (ENG., Illus.). 32p. (J). (gr. -1-k). 10.99 *(978-1-4231-3743-6(4))*, Disney Press Books) Disney Publishing Worldwide.

—Haunted Clubhouse. 2010. (ENG., Illus.). 12p. (J). (gr. -1-k). bds. 6.99 *(978-1-4231-2832-8(X))*, Disney Press Books) Disney Publishing Worldwide.

—Mickey Mouse Clubhouse: Whose Birthday Is It? 2007. (ENG., Illus.). 16p. (J). (gr. -1-k). 4.99 *(978-1-4231-0652-4(0))*, Disney Press Books) Disney Publishing Worldwide.

—Minnie Saves Christmas ReadAlong Storybook & CD. 2018. (Read-Along Storybook & CD Ser.). (ENG., Illus.). 14p. (J). (gr. -1-k). bds. 8.99 *(978-1-368-02234-7(0))*, Disney Press Books) Disney Publishing Worldwide.

—Olaf's Frozen Adventure: Olaf's Journey: A Light-Up Board Book. 2017. (Light-Up Board Book Ser.). (ENG., Illus.). 10p. (J). (gr. -1-k). bds. 12.99 *(978-1-368-00674-3(4))*, Disney Press Books) Disney Publishing Worldwide.

Disney, Princesses, ed. Snow White, My Best Friends Audio Tales: Disney. 2009. (ENG.). 32p. 8.99 *(978-1-59069-772-6(3))* Studio Mouse LLC.

Disney Publishing Staff & Studiomouse Staff. Panda Cub Explores. 2011. (ENG., Illus.). 20p. (J). *(978-1-59069-944-7(0))* Studio Mouse LLC.

Disney Staff, contrib. by. Write, Slide & Learn Disney Mickey Mouse Clubhouse: Colors & Shapes. 2011. (Disney Write, Slide & Learn Ser.). 12p. (J). 9.99 *(978-1-74183-850-3(9))* Hinkler Bks. Pty, Ltd. AUS. Dist: Ideals Pubns.

—Write, Slide & Learn Disney Pixar Cars: Numbers. 2011. (Disney Write, Slide & Learn Ser.). 12p. (J). 9.99 *(978-1-74183-851-0(7))* Hinkler Bks. Pty, Ltd. AUS. Dist: Ideals Pubns.

—Write, Slide & Learn Disney Princess: Spelling. 2011. (Disney Write, Slide & Learn Ser.). 12p. (J). 9.99 *(978-1-74183-852-7(5))* Hinkler Bks. Pty, Ltd. AUS. Dist: Ideals Pubns.

—Write, Slide & Learn Disney Winnie the Pooh: ABC. 2011. (Disney Write, Slide & Learn Ser.). 12p. (J). bds. 9.99 *(978-1-74183-853-4(3))* Hinkler Bks. Pty, Ltd. AUS. Dist: Ideals Pubns.

Disney Storybook Artists Staff, contrib. by. Princess Songs. 2011. (Illus.). 12p. (J). bds. *(978-1-4508-2074-5(3))*, 1450820743) Publications International, Ltd.

Disney Storybook Artists Staff, et al, illus. Disney's the Lion King. 2007. (Play-A-Sound Ser.). 16p. (J). (gr. -1-3). 16.98 *(978-1-4127-8776-5(9))* Publications International, Ltd.

Disney Storybook Artists Staff, illus. Finding Nemo. 2007. (Play-A-Sound Ser.). 15p. (J). (gr. -1-3). 15.98 *(978-1-4127-8754-3(8))* Publications International, Ltd.

DiTerlizzi, Angela. Seeking a Bunny. Smith, Allie, illus. 2017. (ENG.). 30p. (J). (gr. -1 — 1). bds. 7.99 *(978-1-4814-7672-0(6))*, Little Simon) Little Simon.

—Seeking a Santa. Smith, Allie, illus. 2016. (ENG.). 30p. (J). (gr. -1 — 1). bds. 7.99 *(978-1-4814-7674-4(2))*, Little Simon) Little Simon.

Division Mastery w/Audio CD: Kit with Book, Wrap-up & CD. 2004. (ENG.). (J). 19.99 *(978-0-943343-98-3(4))* Learning Wrap-Ups, Inc.

DK. Baby Faces. 2016. (Baby Sparkle Ser.). (ENG., Illus.). 14p. (J). (— 1). bds. 5.99 *(978-1-4654-4466-0(1))*, 1403588, DK Children) Dorling Kindersley Publishing, Inc.

—Baby: First Words! 2013. (Chunky Baby Ser.). (ENG.). 16p. (J). (gr. -1 — 1). bds. 7.99 *(978-1-4654-0168-7(7))*, DK Children) Dorling Kindersley Publishing, Inc.

—Baby Touch & Feel: Animals. 2008. (Baby Touch & Feel Ser.). (ENG., Illus.). 14p. (J). (gr. -1 — 1). bds. 7.99 *(978-0-7566-3468-1(7))*, DK Children) Dorling Kindersley Publishing, Inc.

—Baby Touch & Feel: Baby Animals. 2009. (Baby Touch & Feel Ser.). (ENG.). 14p. (J). (gr. -1 — 1). bds. 7.99 *(978-0-7566-4301-0(5))*, DK Children) Dorling Kindersley Publishing, Inc.

—Baby Touch & Feel: Baby Dinosaur. 2018. (Baby Touch & Feel Ser.). (ENG., Illus.). 14p. (J). (— 1). bds. 5.99 *(978-1-4654-6841-3(2))*, DK Children) Dorling Kindersley Publishing, Inc.

—Baby Touch & Feel: Bedtime. 2008. (Baby Touch & Feel Ser.). (ENG., Illus.). 14p. (J). (gr. -1 — 1). bds. 7.99 *(978-0-7566-4511-3(5))*, DK Children) Dorling Kindersley Publishing, Inc.

—Baby Touch & Feel: Bible Animals. 2018. (Baby Touch & Feel Ser.). (ENG., Illus.). 14p. (J). (— 1). bds. 5.99 *(978-1-4654-8015-6(3))*, DK Children) Dorling Kindersley Publishing, Inc.

—Baby Touch & Feel: Bunny. 2011. (Baby Touch & Feel Ser.). (ENG.). 14p. (J). (gr. -1 — 1). bds. 7.99 *(978-0-7566-8987-2(2))*, DK Children) Dorling Kindersley Publishing, Inc.

—Baby Touch & Feel: Cuddly Animals. 2011. (Baby Touch & Feel Ser.). (ENG.). 14p. (J). (gr. -1 — 1). bds. 7.99 *(978-0-7566-8688-8(1))*, DK Children) Dorling Kindersley Publishing, Inc.

—Baby Touch & Feel: Farm Friends. 2013. (Baby Touch & Feel Ser.). (ENG., Illus.). 14p. (J). (gr. -1 — 1). bds. 7.99 *(978-1-4654-1672-8(2))*, DK Children) Dorling Kindersley Publishing, Inc.

—Baby Touch & Feel: Fluffy Animals. 2012. (Baby Touch & Feel Ser.). (ENG.). 14p. (J). (gr. -1 — 1). bds. 7.99 *(978-0-7566-9786-0(7))*, DK Children) Dorling Kindersley Publishing, Inc.

—Baby Touch & Feel: Halloween. 2017. (Baby Touch & Feel Ser.). (ENG., Illus.). 14p. (J). (— 1). bds. 7.99 *(978-1-4654-6235-0(X))*, DK Children) Dorling Kindersley Publishing, Inc.

—Baby Touch & Feel: Kittens. 2017. (Baby Touch & Feel Ser.). (ENG., Illus.). 14p. (J). (— 1). bds. 7.99 *(978-1-4654-5622-9(8))*, DK Children) Dorling Kindersley Publishing, Inc.

—Baby Touch & Feel Merry Christmas. 2018. (Baby Touch & Feel Ser.). (ENG., Illus.). 14p. (J). (— 1). bds. 7.99 *(978-1-4654-7282-3(7))*, DK Children) Dorling Kindersley Publishing, Inc.

—Baby Touch & Feel: Puppies & Kittens. 2008. (Baby Touch & Feel Ser.). (ENG., Illus.). 14p. (J). (gr. -1 — 1). bds. 7.99 *(978-0-7566-3835-1(6))*, DK Children) Dorling Kindersley Publishing, Inc.

—Baby Touch & Feel: Sophie la Girafe: Sophie's Busy Day. 2013. (Sophie la Girafe Ser.). (ENG., Illus.). 14p. (J). (gr. -1 — 1). bds. 5.99 *(978-1-4654-0967-6(X))*, DK Children) Dorling Kindersley Publishing, Inc.

—Baby Touch & Feel: Tractor. 2010. (Baby Touch & Feel Ser.). (ENG.). 14p. (J). (gr. -1 — 1). bds. 7.99 *(978-0-7566-7132-7(9))*, DK Children) Dorling Kindersley Publishing, Inc.

—Baby Touch & Feel: Wild Animals. 2009. (Baby Touch & Feel Ser.). (ENG., Illus.). 14p. (J). (gr. -1 — 1). bds. 7.99 *(978-0-7566-5150-3(6))*, DK Children) Dorling Kindersley Publishing, Inc.

—Baby's First 123. 2018. (Baby's First Board Bks.). (ENG., Illus.). 14p. (J). (— 1). bds. 6.99 *(978-1-4654-6645-7(2))*, DK Children) Dorling Kindersley Publishing, Inc.

—Baby's First Chinese New Year. 2018. (Baby's First Holidays Ser.). (Illus.). 14p. (J). (— 1). bds. 6.99 *(978-1-4654-8401-7(9))*, DK Children) Dorling Kindersley Publishing, Inc.

—Baby's First Christmas. 2018. (Baby's First Holidays Ser.). (ENG., Illus.). 14p. (J). (— 1). bds. 6.99 *(978-1-4654-6867-3(6))*, DK Children) Dorling Kindersley Publishing, Inc.

—Baby's First Colors. 2018. (Baby's First Board Bks.). (ENG., Illus.). 14p. (J). (— 1). bds. 6.99 *(978-1-4654-6366-1(6))*, DK Children) Dorling Kindersley Publishing, Inc.

—Baby's First Thanksgiving. 2017. (Baby's First Holidays Ser.). (ENG., Illus.). 14p. (J). (— 1). bds. 6.99 *(978-1-4654-6349-4(6))*, DK Children) Dorling Kindersley Publishing, Inc.

—Bedtime Peekaboo! Touch-And-Feel & Lift-the-Flap. 2006. (Peekaboo! Ser.). (ENG., Illus.). 12p. (J). (gr. -1-k). bds. 7.99 *(978-0-7566-1622-9(0))*, DK Children) Dorling Kindersley Publishing, Inc.

—Big Dump Truck. 2003. (Wheelie Bks.). (ENG., Illus.). 12p. (J). (gr. -1-k). bds. 8.99 *(978-0-7894-9714-7(X))*, DK Children) Dorling Kindersley Publishing, Inc.

—Boys' Potty Time. 2010. (ENG., Illus.). 14p. (J). (gr. -1-k). bds. 9.99 *(978-0-7566-5884-7(5))*, DK Children) Dorling Kindersley Publishing, Inc.

—Crunch! Munch! Bunny. 2019. (Super Noisy Bks.). (ENG.). 12p. (J). (— 1). bds. 14.99 *(978-1-4654-7853-5(1))*, DK Children) Dorling Kindersley Publishing, Inc.

—Diggers. 2009. (ENG.). 10p. (J). (gr. -1-k). bds. 8.99 *(978-0-7566-5229-6(4))*, DK Children) Dorling Kindersley Publishing, Inc.

—Eyes, Nose, Toes Peekaboo! Touch-And-Feel & Lift-the-Flap. 2008. (Peekaboo! Ser.). (ENG.). 12p. (J). (gr. -1-k). bds. 7.99 *(978-0-7566-3759-0(7))*, DK Children) Dorling Kindersley Publishing, Inc.

—Farm Tractor. 2003. (Wheelie Bks.). (ENG., Illus.). 12p. (J). (gr. -1-k). bds. 8.99 *(978-0-7894-9713-0(1))*, DK Children) Dorling Kindersley Publishing, Inc.

—Follow the Trail: Trucks. 2016. (Follow the Trail Ser.). (ENG., Illus.). 14p. (J). (-k). bds. 9.99 *(978-1-4654-5126-2(9))*, DK Children) Dorling Kindersley Publishing, Inc.

—FUN FLAPS: All about Me! 2008. (Fun Flaps Ser.). (ENG., Illus.). 14p. (J). (gr. -1-k). bds. 6.99 *(978-0-7566-3438-4(5))*, DK Children) Dorling Kindersley Publishing, Inc.

—How Does a Butterfly Grow? 2019. (Life Cycle Board Bks.). (ENG., Illus.). 18p. (J). (-k). bds. 13.99 *(978-1-4654-7867-2(1))*, DK Children) Dorling Kindersley Publishing, Inc.

—I Can Grow a Flower. 2018. (Life Cycle Board Bks.). (ENG., Illus.). 18p. (J). (-k). bds. 12.99 *(978-1-4654-6570-2(7))*, DK Children) Dorling Kindersley Publishing, Inc.

—Is It Warm Enough for Ice Cream? 2018. (ENG., Illus.). 18p. (J). (-k). bds. 9.99 *(978-1-4654-6786-7(6))*, DK Children) Dorling Kindersley Publishing, Inc.

—LEGO CITY: Busy Word Book. 2018. (ENG., Illus.). 64p. (J). (gr. -1-k). 15.99 *(978-1-4654-6627-3(4))*, DK Children) Dorling Kindersley Publishing, Inc.

—LEGO(r) NINJAGO: Build Your Own Adventure: With Lloyd Minifigure & Exclusive Ninja Merch, Book Includes More Than 50 Buil. 2015. (LEGO Build Your Own Adventure Ser.). (ENG.). 80p. (J). (gr. 2-5). 24.99 *(978-1-4654-3590-3(5))*, DK Children) Dorling Kindersley Publishing, Inc.

—LEGO NINJAGO Build Your Own Adventure Greatest Ninja Battles: With Nya Minifigure & Exclusive Hover-Bike Model. 2018. (LEGO Build Your Own Adventure Ser.). (ENG.). 80p. (J). (gr. 1-3). 24.99 *(978-1-4654-7335-6(1))*, DK Children) Dorling Kindersley Publishing, Inc.

—LEGO Star Wars: Choose Your Path. 2018. (ENG., Illus.). 128p. (J). (gr. 1-4). 19.99 *(978-1-4654-6756-0(4))*, DK Children) Dorling Kindersley Publishing, Inc.

—My Best Pop-Up Noisy Train Book. 2017. (Noisy Pop-Up Bks.). (ENG., Illus.). 18p. (J). (-k). bds. 15.99 *(978-1-4654-6173-5(6))*, DK Children) Dorling Kindersley Publishing, Inc.

—My Best Pop-Up Space Book. 2015. (Noisy Pop-Up Bks.). (ENG., Illus.). 18p. (J). (-k). bds. 15.99 *(978-1-4654-3914-7(5))*, DK Children) Dorling Kindersley Publishing, Inc.

—My First 123. 2015. (My First Board Bks.). (ENG.). 36p. (J). (gr. -1 — 1). bds. 6.99 *(978-1-4654-2903-2(4))*, DK Children) Dorling Kindersley Publishing, Inc.

—My First Animals. 2015. (My First Board Bks.). (ENG.). 36p. (J). (gr. -1 — 1). bds. 6.99 *(978-1-4654-2901-8(8))*, DK Children) Dorling Kindersley Publishing, Inc.

—My First Body. 2016. (My First Board Bks.). (ENG., Illus.). 36p. (J). (— 1). bds. 6.99 *(978-1-4654-4492-9(0))*, DK Children) Dorling Kindersley Publishing, Inc.

—My First Farm. 2016. (My First Board Bks.). (ENG., Illus.). 36p. (J). (— 1). bds. 6.99 *(978-1-4654-4487-5(4))*, DK Children) Dorling Kindersley Publishing, Inc.

—My First Shapes. 2017. (My First Board Bks.). (ENG., Illus.). 36p. (J). (— 1). bds. 6.99 *(978-1-4654-6082-0(9))*, DK Children) Dorling Kindersley Publishing, Inc.

—My First Sophie la Girafe: Let's Get Counting! 2013. (Sophie la Girafe Ser.). (ENG., Illus.). 36p. (J). (gr. -1 — 1). bds. 5.99 *(978-1-4654-0958-4(0))*, DK Children) Dorling Kindersley Publishing, Inc.

—My First Touch & Feel Picture Cards: Animals. 2018. (My First Board Bks.). (ENG.). 17p. (J). (— 1). 9.99 *(978-1-4654-6571-9(5))*, DK Children) Dorling Kindersley Publishing, Inc.

—My First Touch & Feel Picture Cards: Farm. 2018. (My First Board Bks.). (ENG.). 17p. (J). (— 1). 9.99 *(978-1-4654-6814-7(5))*, DK Children) Dorling Kindersley Publishing, Inc.

—My First Touch & Feel Picture Cards: First Words. 2018. (My First Board Bks.). (ENG.). 17p. (J). (— 1). 12.99 *(978-1-4654-6813-0(7))*, DK Children) Dorling Kindersley Publishing, Inc.

—Peek & Seek. Milner, Charlotte, illus. 2018. (ENG.). 18p. (J). (gr. -1-1). bds. 12.99 *(978-1-4654-6865-9(X))*, DK Children) Dorling Kindersley Publishing, Inc.

—Pop-Up Peekaboo! Baby Dinosaur. 2018. (Pop-Up Peekaboo! Ser.). (ENG., Illus.). 12p. (J). (— 1). bds. 12.99 *(978-1-4654-7455-1(2))*, DK Children) Dorling Kindersley Publishing, Inc.

—Pop-Up Peekaboo! Farm: Pop-Up Surprise under Every Flap! 2011. (Pop-Up Peekaboo! Ser.). (ENG., Illus.). 12p. (J). (gr. -1 — 1). bds. 12.99 *(978-0-7566-7172-3(8))*, DK Children) Dorling Kindersley Publishing, Inc.

—Pop-Up Peekaboo: First Words. 2018. (Pop-Up Peekaboo! Ser.). (ENG., Illus.). 12p. (J). (— 1). bds. 12.99 *(978-1-4654-6839-0(0))*, DK Children) Dorling Kindersley Publishing, Inc.

—Pop-Up Peekaboo! I Love You. 2018. (Pop-Up Peekaboo! Ser.). (ENG., Illus.). 12p. (J). (— 1). bds. 12.99 *(978-1-4654-6526-9(X))*, DK Children) Dorling Kindersley Publishing, Inc.

—Pop-Up Peekaboo! Kitten: Pop-Up Surprise under Every Flap! 2012. (Pop-Up Peekaboo! Ser.). (ENG., Illus.). 12p. (J). (gr. -1 — 1). bds. 12.99 *(978-0-7566-9309-1(8))*, DK Children) Dorling Kindersley Publishing, Inc.

—Pop-Up Peekaboo! Numbers. 2018. (Pop-Up Peekaboo! Ser.). (ENG., Illus.). 12p. (J). (— 1). bds. 12.99 *(978-1-4654-6840-6(4))*, DK Children) Dorling Kindersley Publishing, Inc.

—Pop-Up Peekaboo! Pumpkin: Pop-Up Surprise under Every Flap! 2016. (Pop-Up Peekaboo! Ser.). (ENG.). 12p. (J). (— 1). bds. 12.99 *(978-1-4654-5276-4(1))*, DK Children) Dorling Kindersley Publishing, Inc.

—Pop-Up Peekaboo! Puppies: Pop-Up Surprise under Every Flap! 2013. (Pop-Up Peekaboo! Ser.). (ENG., Illus.). 12p. (J). (gr. -1 — 1). bds. 12.99 *(978-1-4654-0929-4(7))*, DK Children) Dorling Kindersley Publishing, Inc.

—Pop-Up Peekaboo! Things That Go: Pop-Up Surprise under Every Flap! 2012. (Pop-Up Peekaboo! Ser.). (ENG., Illus.). 12p. (J). (gr. -1 — 1). bds. 12.99 *(978-0-7566-9009-0(9))*, DK Children) Dorling Kindersley Publishing, Inc.

—Pop-Up Peekaboo! Unicorn. 2019. (Pop-Up Peekaboo! Ser.). (ENG., Illus.). 12p. (J). (— 1). bds. 12.99 *(978-1-4654-8331-7(4))*, DK Children) Dorling Kindersley Publishing, Inc.

—Really Feely Trucks. 2017. (Really Feely Board Bks.). (ENG., Illus.). 12p. (J). (— 1). bds. 7.99 *(978-1-4654-6204-6(X))*, DK Children) Dorling Kindersley Publishing, Inc.

—Sophie la Girafe: ABC Flashcards. 2017. (Sophie la Girafe Ser.). (ENG.). 26p. (J). (— 1). 12.99 *(978-1-4654-5702-8(X))*, DK Children) Dorling Kindersley Publishing, Inc.

—Sophie la Girafe: Good Night, Sophie: A Touch & Feel Book. 2017. (Sophie la Girafe Ser.). (ENG., Illus.). 12p. (J). (— 1). bds. 7.99 *(978-1-4654-5625-0(2))*, DK Children) Dorling Kindersley Publishing, Inc.

—Sophie la Girafe: Playtime with Sophie: A Touch & Feel Book. 2014. (Sophie la Girafe Ser.). (ENG., Illus.). 14p. (J). (gr. -1 — 1). bds. 7.99 *(978-1-4654-2042-8(8))*, DK Children) Dorling Kindersley Publishing, Inc.

—Sophie la Girafe: Sophie's Big First Word Book. 2016. (Sophie la Girafe Ser.). (ENG., Illus.). 18p. (J). (gr. -1 — 1). bds. 9.99 *(978-1-4654-4494-3(7))*, DK Children) Dorling Kindersley Publishing, Inc.

—Sports Car. 2003. (Wheelie Bks.). (ENG., Illus.). 12p. (J). (gr. -1-k). bds. 8.99 *(978-0-7894-9711-6(5))*, DK Children) Dorling Kindersley Publishing, Inc.

—Tabbed Board Books: My First Trucks & Diggers: Let's Get Driving! 2013. (My First Tabbed Board Book Ser.). (ENG.). 28p. (J). (gr. -1 — 1). bds. 12.99 *(978-1-4654-1673-5(0))*, DK Children) Dorling Kindersley Publishing, Inc.

—Tabbed Board Books: My First Zoo: Let's Meet the Animals! 2016. (My First Tabbed Board Book Ser.). (ENG., Illus.). 28p. (J). (— 1). bds. 12.99 *(978-1-4654-4883-5(7))*, DK Children) Dorling Kindersley Publishing, Inc.

—The Three Little Pigs. Di Lernia, Giuseppe, illus. 2019. (Storytime Lap Bks.). (ENG.). 30p. (J). (-k). bds. 14.99 *(978-1-4654-7848-1(5))*, DK Children) Dorling Kindersley Publishing, Inc.

—Touch & Feel: 123. 2013. (Touch & Feel Ser.). (ENG.). 12p. (J). (gr. -1-k). bds. 6.99 *(978-1-4654-0917-1(3))*, DK Children) Dorling Kindersley Publishing, Inc.

—Touch & Feel: Animal Library: Includes Baby Animals, Wild Animals, & Jungle Animals, 3 vols. 2014. (Touch & Feel Ser.). (ENG., Illus.). 36p. (J). (gr. -1-k). bds. 19.99 *(978-1-4654-2766-3(X))*, DK Children) Dorling Kindersley Publishing, Inc.

—Touch & Feel Baby Animals. 2011. (Touch & Feel Ser.). (ENG.). 12p. (J). (gr. -1 — 1). bds. 6.99 *(978-0-7566-8991-9(0))*, DK Children) Dorling Kindersley Publishing, Inc.

—Touch & Feel: Dinosaur. 2012. (Touch & Feel Ser.). (ENG.). 12p. (J). (gr. -1-k). bds. 6.99 *(978-0-7566-9288-9(1))*, DK Children) Dorling Kindersley Publishing, Inc.

—Touch & Feel: Farm. 2011. (Touch & Feel Ser.). (ENG.). 12p. (J). (gr. -1-k). bds. 6.99 *(978-0-7566-8989-6(9))*, DK Children) Dorling Kindersley Publishing, Inc.

—Touch & Feel: Fire Engine. 2011. (Touch & Feel Ser.). (ENG.). 12p. (J). (gr. -1-k). bds. 6.99 *(978-0-7566-8992-6(9))*, DK Children) Dorling Kindersley Publishing, Inc.

—Touch & Feel: Jungle Animals. 2012. (Touch & Feel Ser.). (ENG.). 12p. (J). (gr. -1-k). bds. 6.99 *(978-0-7566-9289-6(X))*, DK Children) Dorling Kindersley Publishing, Inc.

—Touch & Feel: Kitten. 2011. (Touch & Feel Ser.). (ENG.). 12p. (J). (gr. -1-k). bds. 6.99 *(978-0-7566-9165-3(6))*, DK Children) Dorling Kindersley Publishing, Inc.

—Touch & Feel: Ponies. 2013. (Touch & Feel Ser.). (ENG.). 12p. (J). (gr. -1 — 1). bds. 6.99 *(978-1-4654-0919-5(X))*, DK Children) Dorling Kindersley Publishing, Inc.

—Touch & Feel: Puppy. 2011. (Touch & Feel Ser.). (ENG.). 12p. (J). (gr. -1-k). bds. 6.99 *(978-0-7566-9166-0(4))*, DK Children) Dorling Kindersley Publishing, Inc.

—Tractor. 2010. (ENG., Illus.). 10p. (J). (gr. -1-k). bds. 8.99 *(978-0-7566-6302-5(4))*, DK Children) Dorling Kindersley Publishing, Inc.

—Ultimate Sticker Book: Dog: More Than 60 Reusable Full-Color Stickers. 2005. (Ultimate Sticker Book Ser.). (ENG., Illus.). 16p. (J). (gr. k-3). pap. 6.99 *(978-0-7566-1457-7(0))*, DK Children) Dorling Kindersley Publishing, Inc.

—Ultimate Sticker Book: Tangled: More Than 60 Reusable Full-Color Stickers. 2010. (Ultimate Sticker Book Ser.). (ENG.). 16p. (J). (gr. k-3). pap. 6.99 *(978-0-7566-6687-3(2))*, DK Children) Dorling Kindersley Publishing, Inc.

—Ultimate Sticker Collection: Marvel: Heroes Unite! More Than 1,000 Reusable Full-Color Stickers. 2014. (Ultimate Sticker Collection). (ENG.). 96p. (J). (gr. k-2). pap. 12.99 *(978-1-4654-1684-1(6))*, DK Children) Dorling Kindersley Publishing, Inc.

DK, et al. LEGO Star Wars Ideas Book: More Than 200 Games, Activities, & Building Ideas. 2018. (Lego Ideas Ser.). (ENG., Illus.). 200p. (J). (gr. 2-5). 24.99 *(978-1-4654-6705-8(X))*, DK Children) Dorling Kindersley Publishing, Inc.

Dodd, Emma. Counting. 2017. (Illus.). 12p. (J). (gr. -1-12). bds. 9.99 *(978-1-86147-839-9(9))*, Armadillo) Anness Publishing GBR. Dist: National Bk. Network.

—Dog & Friends: Shapes. 2017. (Illus.). 12p. (J). (gr. -1-12). bds. 9.99 *(978-1-86147-844-3(5))*, Armadillo) Anness Publishing GBR. Dist: National Bk. Network.

—Dog & Friends: Sounds. 2017. (Illus.). 12p. (J). (gr. -1-12). bds. 9.99 *(978-1-86147-841-2(0))*, Armadillo) Anness Publishing GBR. Dist: National Bk. Network.

—On the Farm. 2017. (Illus.). 12p. (J). (gr. -1-12). bds. 9.99 *(978-1-86147-838-2(0))*, Armadillo) Anness Publishing GBR. Dist: National Bk. Network.

—Opposites. 2017. (Illus.). 12p. (J). (gr. -1-12). bds. 9.99 (978-1-86147-843-6(7), Armadillo) Anness Publishing GBR. Dist: National Bk. Network.
—Playtime. 2017. (Illus.). 12p. (J). (gr. -1-1). bds. 9.99 (978-1-86147-842-9(9), Armadillo) Anness Publishing GBR. Dist: National Bk. Network.
—Rainbow Fun. 2017. (Illus.). 12p. (J). (gr. -1-12). bds. 9.99 (978-1-86147-840-5(2), Armadillo) Anness Publishing GBR. Dist: National Bk. Network.
Dodd, Emma, illus. Dog & Friends: Birthday. 2017. 12p. (J). (gr. -1-12). bds. 9.99 (978-1-86147-836-8(4), Armadillo) Anness Publishing GBR. Dist: National Bk. Network.
—Dog & Friends: Busy Day. 2017. 12p. (J). (gr. -1-12). bds. 9.99 (978-1-86147-835-1(6), Armadillo) Anness Publishing GBR. Dist: National Bk. Network.
—Dog's 123: A Canine Counting Adventure! 2016. (ENG.). 14p. (J). (gr. -1-12). bds. 14.99 (978-1-86147-698-2(1), Armadillo) Anness Publishing GBR. Dist: National Bk. Network.
—Dog's ABC: An Alphabet Adventure! 2016. 14p. (J). (gr. -1-12). bds. 14.99 (978-1-86147-699-9(X), Armadillo) Anness Publishing GBR. Dist: National Bk. Network.
—Tick Tock Dog: A Tell the Time Book - with a Special Movable Clock! 2016. (ENG.). 12p. (J). (gr. -1-k). bds. 14.99 (978-1-86147-718-7(X), Armadillo) Anness Publishing GBR. Dist: National Bk. Network.
Doerrfeld, Cori. Wild Baby Board Book. Doerrfeld, Cori, illus. 2019. (ENG., Illus.). 36p. (J). (gr. -1 — 1). bds. 7.99 (978-0-06-269893-3(1), HarperFestival) HarperCollins Pubs.
Donaghy, Thomas J. Angels All Around Us. 2004. (Illus.). (J). (978-0-89942-717-1(0)) Catholic Bk. Publishing Corp.
—Celebrating Mass (St. Joseph Tab Book) 2009. (ENG., Illus.). 12p. (J). bds. 7.95 (978-0-89942-662-4(X), 855/22) Catholic Bk. Publishing Corp.
—Joyful Prayers (St. Joseph Tab Book) 2009. (ENG., Illus.). 12p. (J). bds. 7.95 (978-0-89942-663-1(8), 856/22) Catholic Bk. Publishing Corp.
Donaher, D F. & Bibleco. Daniel & the Lions. 2004. (Illus.). (J). bds. (978-0-9746058-2-1(4), Biblemania) Bibleco, Inc.
Donahue, Peter & Whelon, Chuck. 3-D Mazes — Robots. 2012. (Dover 3-D Mazes Ser.). (ENG.). 32p. (J). (gr. 1-6). 5.99 (978-0-486-49017-5(3)) Dover Pubns., Inc.
Donaldson, Julia. Chocolate Mousse for Greedy Goose. Sharratt, Nick, illus. 2015. (ENG.). 18p. (J). (-k). bds. 12.99 (978-1-4472-8788-9(6), 900326058, Macmillan Children's Bks.) Pan Macmillan GBR. Dist: Macmillan.
—The Detective Dog. Ogilvie, Sara, illus. 2018. (ENG.). 32p. (J). 19.99 (978-1-250-15676-1(9), 900185100, Holt, Henry & Co. Bks. For Young Readers) Holt, Henry & Co.
—Goat Goes to Playgroup. Sharratt, Nick, illus. 2015. (ENG.). 24p. (J). (-k). bds. 12.99 (978-1-4472-8791-9(6), 900326061, Macmillan Children's Bks.) Pan Macmillan GBR. Dist: Macmillan.
—One Mole Digging a Hole. Sharratt, Nick, illus. 2015. (ENG.). 22p. (J). (-k). bds. 12.99 (978-1-4472-8790-2(8), 900326060, Macmillan Children's Bks.) Pan Macmillan GBR. Dist: Macmillan.
—One Ted Falls Out of Bed. Currey, Anna, illus. 2012. (ENG.). 26p. (J). (gr. -1 — 1). bds. 12.99 (978-1-4472-0995-9(8), 900326069, Macmillan Children's Bks.) Pan Macmillan GBR. Dist: Macmillan.
—Room on the Broom. Scheffler, Axel, illus. 2012. (ENG.). 24p. (J). (— 1). bds. 7.99 (978-0-8037-3841-6(2), Dial Bks) Penguin Young Readers Group.
—Toddle Waddle. Sharratt, Nick, illus. 2015. (ENG.). 24p. (J). (-k). bds. 12.99 (978-1-4472-8792-6(4), 900326062, Macmillan Children's Bks.) Pan Macmillan GBR. Dist: Macmillan.
Donna, Gelsinger, ed. In My Father's Garden. 2007. (ENG.). 10p. (J). bds. 6.99 (978-1-4037-3625-3(1), Spirit Pr.) Bendon, Inc.
Don't Stick Sticks up Your Nose! Don't Stuff Stuff in Your Ears! 2013. (Don't Stick Sticks up Your Nose! Don't Stuff Stuff in Your Ears! Ser.). (ENG.). 22p. bds. 5.99 (978-0-9888861-0-0(3), 9780988886100) Dontstickdontstuff.
Doodler, Todd H. Peas on Earth. 2012. (Illus.). 20p. (J). (gr. -1 — 1). 6.99 (978-0-307-93088-0(2), Robin Corey Bks.) Random Hse. Children's Bks.
—Veggies with Wedgies Present Doin' the Wedgie. Doodler, Todd H., illus. 2015. (ENG., Illus.). 26p. (J). (gr. -1-k). bds. 7.99 (978-1-4424-9351-3(8), Little Simon) Little Simon.
Dorling Kindersley Publishing Staff. Baby's First 123. 2018. (ENG., Illus.). 14p. (J). bds. (978-0-241-30180-7(7)) Dorling Kindersley Publishing, Inc.
—Baby's First Baby Animals. 2018. (Illus.). 14p. (J). bds. (978-0-241-30179-1(3)) Dorling Kindersley Publishing, Inc.
—Baby's First Words. 2018. (Illus.). 14p. (J). bds. (978-0-241-30177-7(7)) Dorling Kindersley Publishing, Inc.
—Christmas Peekaboo! 2008. (Peekaboo! Ser.). (ENG.). 12p. (J). (gr. -1-k). bds. 9.99 (978-0-7566-4022-4(9), DK Children) Dorling Kindersley Publishing, Inc.
—Dinosaur. 2016. (ENG., Illus.). 36p. (J). bds. (978-0-241-23758-8(0)) Dorling Kindersley Publishing, Inc.
—Is It Warm Enough for Ice Cream? 2018. (ENG., Illus.). 18p. (J). bds. (978-0-241-31305-3(8)) Dorling Kindersley Publishing, Inc.
—LEGO(r) Star Wars Minifigures Ultimate Sticker Collection. 2012. (ENG.). 96p. pap. (978-1-4053-9826-8(4)) Dorling Kindersley.
—RHS How Does a Butterfly Grow? 2019. (Illus.). 18p. (J). bds. (978-0-241-35546-6(X)) Dorling Kindersley Publishing, Inc.
Dotlich, Rebecca Kai. You & Me. Reagan, Susan, illus. 2018. (ENG.). 14p. (J). (gr. -1-1). bds. 9.99 (978-1-56846-321-6(9), 19711, Creative Editions) Creative Co., The.
Douglas, Lisa Jo. Active Animals A Thru Z. 2008. (ENG., Illus.). 30p. (J). per. 12.99 (978-1-59879-311-6(X), Lifevest) Lifevest Publishing, Inc.
Dowley, Tim. Bible Animal Stencil Book, 1 vol. 2008. 6p. (J). bds. 11.99 (978-0-8254-7365-4(9), Candle Bks.) Lion Hudson PLC GBR. Dist: Kregel Pubns.
Down, Hayley. Reindeer's Snowy Adventure. Machell, Dawn, illus. 2016. (ENG.). 12p. (J). (gr. -1 — 1). bds. 6.99 (978-1-78598-437-2(3)) Make Believe Ideas GBR. Dist: Scholastic, Inc.
Downing, Julie, illus. All the Ways I Love You (bilingual Edition) 2005. (SPA & ENG.). 10p. (J). 8.95 (978-1-58117-335-2(0), Intervisual/Piggy Toes) Bendon, Inc.
Downing, Sue. Lost in the City: Daytime. 2020. (Lost in the City Ser.). (ENG.). 12p. (J). (— 1). bds. 15.99 (978-1-76040-935-7(9)) Little Hare Bks. AUS. Dist: Independent Pubs. Group.
Dowswell, P. Secret Agent Spy. 2009. (Kid Kits Ser.). 144p. (J). 16.99 (978-1-60130-152-9(9)); 16.99 (978-1-60130-153-6(7)) EDC Publishing. (Usborne).
Doxey, Heidi. Jesus Was Just Like Me. Talbot, Josh, illus. 2017. (ENG.). (J). (gr. -1-k). bds. 12.99 (978-1-4621-2120-5(9)) Cedar Fort, Inc./CFI Distribution.
—Jesus Was Just Like Me. 2017. (ENG.). (J). bds. 10.99 (978-1-4621-1925-7(5)) Cedar Fort, Inc./CFI Distribution.
The Dragon & the Knight: A Pop-Up Misadventure. 2014. (ENG., Illus.). 22p. (J). (gr. k). 29.99 (978-1-4169-6081-2(3), Little Simon) Little Simon.
Dragonwagon, Crescent. All the Awake Animals Are Almost Asleep. McPhail, David, illus. 2016. (ENG.). 30p. (J). (gr. -1 — 1). bds. 7.99 (978-0-316-33627-7(0)) Little, Brown Bks. for Young Readers.
Drake, Ernest. Dragonology: The Complete Book of Dragons. Steer, Dugald A., ed. 2003. (Ologies Ser.). (ENG., Illus.). 32p. (J). (gr. 3-7). 29.99 (978-0-7636-2329-6(6)) Candlewick Pr.
Drescher, Daniela. Pippa & Pelle in the Spring Garden, 30 vols. 2018. (Pippa & Pelle Ser.). Orig. Title: Pippa & Pelle Im Garten. (Illus.). 12p. (J). 9.95 (978-1-78250-471-9(0)) Floris Bks. GBR. Dist: Consortium Bk. Sales & Distribution.
—Pippa & Pelle in the Summer Sun, 30 vols. 2017. (Pippa & Pelle Ser.). Orig. Title: Pippa und Pelle Auf Reisen. (Illus.). 12p. (J). 9.95 (978-1-78250-379-8(X)) Floris Bks. GBR. Dist: Consortium Bk. Sales & Distribution.
—What's Hiding in There?, 24 vols. 2008. Orig. Title: Was Raschelt Denn Da? (ENG., Illus.). 16p. (J). (978-0-86315-634-2(7)) Floris Bks.
Driscoll, Laura. Disney Bunnies: Thumper Goes AThumpin' 2015. (ENG., Illus.). 12p. (J). (gr. -1 — 1). bds. 6.99 (978-1-4847-0960-3(8), Disney Press Books) Disney Publishing Worldwide.
Ducatteau, Florence. A Day at the Museum. Peten, Chantal, illus. 2013. (Want to Know Ser.: 3). (ENG.). 32p. (J). (gr. k-2). 16.95 (978-1-60537-142-9(4)) Clavis Publishing.
Duksta, Laura. I Love You More. Keesler, Karen, illus. 24p. (J). 2013. (gr. -1-k). bds. 8.99 (978-1-4022-9250-7(3)) 2009. bds. 6.99 (978-1-4022-2460-7(5)) Sourcebooks, Inc. (Sourcebooks Jabberwocky).
—Te Quiero Más. Keesler, Karen, illus. 2013. 24p. (J). bds. 7.99 (978-1-4022-8177-8(3), Sourcebooks Jabberwocky) Sourcebooks, Inc.
Dunrea, Olivier. Jasper & Joop Board Book. Dunrea, Olivier, illus. 2014. (Gossie & Friends Ser.). (ENG., Illus.). 32p. (J). (— 1). bds. 7.99 (978-0-544-17320-0(1), 1552169, Clarion Bks.) HarperCollins Pubs.
—Ollie's Halloween Board Book. Dunrea, Olivier, illus. 2013. (Gossie & Friends Ser.). (ENG., Illus.). 30p. (J). (gr. -1 — 1). bds. 9.99 (978-0-544-05720-3(1), 1533611, Clarion Bks.) HarperCollins Pubs.
duopress labs. Do You Know a Superhero? Escudero, Jesus, illus. 2018. 22p. (J). (— 1). bds. 7.95 (978-1-947458-24-6(8), 805824) Duo Pr. LLC.
—Go, New York, Go! Cleland, Josh, illus. 2018. (ENG.). 22p. (J). (gr. -1-k). bds. 9.99 (978-1-946064-97-4(1), 806497) Duo Pr. LLC.
—My Feminist ABC: Skyline. Pizzolante, Irene, illus. 2018. 20p. (J). (gr. -1-k). bds. 7.95 (978-1-946064-98-1(X), 806498) Duo Pr. LLC.
—My First Lift-The-Flap Animal Book. Mullen, Amy, illus. 2018. (Natural World Ser.). 20p. (J). (gr. -1-1). bds. 9.95 (978-1-946064-95-0(5), 806495) Duo Pr. LLC.
—Zoom! Beep! Vroom! Busy Cities. Cleland, Josh, illus. 2018. 22p. (J). (gr. -1 — 1). bds. 9.95 (978-1-947458-27-7(2), 805827) Duo Pr. LLC.
duopress labs & Margie & Jimbo. My Fridge: My First Book of Food. 2017. (Illus.). 20p. (J). (gr. -1-k). bds. 7.95 (978-1-946064-00-4(9), 806400) Duo Pr. LLC.
Durant, Alan. If You Go Walking in Tiger Wood. Boon, Debbie, illus. 2005. (ENG.). 24p. (J). (gr. -1-k). pap. 9.99 (978-0-00-710390-4(5), HarperSport) HarperCollins Pubs. Ltd. GBR. Dist: Independent Pubs. Group.
Dyckman, Ame. Huggy the Python Hugs Too Hard. Griffiths, Alex G., illus. 2018. (Wee Beasties Ser.). (ENG.). 22p. (J). (gr. -1-k). bds. 8.99 (978-1-5344-1080-0(5), Little Simon) Little Simon.
—Roary the Lion Roars Too Loud. Griffiths, Alex G., illus. 2018. (Wee Beasties Ser.). (ENG.). 22p. (J). (gr. -1-k). bds. 8.99 (978-1-5344-1078-7(3), Little Simon) Little Simon.
Dynamo. Googly Eyes: Flipper the Seal Makes a Discovery! 2014. (ENG., Illus.). 12p. (J). (gr. -1-2). bds. 6.99 (978-1-84322-905-6(6), Armadillo) Anness Publishing GBR. Dist: National Bk. Network.
—Googly Eyes: Fluffy Kitten Goes Exploring! 2014. (ENG., Illus.). 12p. (J). (gr. 3-2). bds. 6.99 (978-1-84322-880-6(7), Armadillo) Anness Publishing GBR. Dist: National Bk. Network.
—Googly Eyes: Goodnight, Benjy Bunny! 2014. (ENG., Illus.). 12p. (J). (gr. -1-12). bds. 6.99 (978-1-84322-879-0(3), Armadillo) Anness Publishing GBR. Dist: National Bk. Network.
—Googly Eyes: Leo Lion's Noisy Roar! 2014. (ENG., Illus.). 12p. (J). (gr. -1-2). bds. 6.99 (978-1-84322-906-3(4), Armadillo) Anness Publishing GBR. Dist: National Bk. Network.
Dyson, Nikki, illus. Flip Flap Dogs. 2018. (Flip Flap Bks.). (ENG.). 28p. (J). (gr. -1-2). 12.99 (978-1-5362-0258-8(4)) Candlewick Pr.
East, Jacqueline. Lots of Love, 1 vol. 2016. (ENG., Illus.). 18p. (J). bds. 8.99 (978-0-310-75861-7(0)) Zonderkidz.
East, Jacqueline, illus. Princess Palace: A Three-Demensional Playset. 2006. 8p. (J). (gr. -1-3). 22.95 (978-1-58117-492-2(6), Intervisual/Piggy Toes) Bendon, Inc.
Eastman, P. D. Are You My Mother? 2015. (Big Bright & Early Board Book Ser.). (ENG., Illus.). 24p. (J). (— 1). bds. 7.99 (978-0-553-49680-2(8), Random Hse. Bks. for Young Readers) Random Hse. Children's Bks.
—Go, Dog. Go! 2015. (Big Bright & Early Board Book Ser.). (ENG., Illus.). 24p. (J). (gr. -1-2). bds. 7.99 (978-0-553-52109-2(8), Random Hse. Bks. for Young Readers) Random Hse. Children's Bks.
Eastman, P. D. & Frith, Michael. The Little Red Box of Bright & Early Board Books: Go, Dog. Go!; Big Dog ... Little Dog; the Alphabet Book; I'll Teach My Dog a Lot of Words, 4 vols. 2014. (Bright & Early Board Books(TM) Ser.). (ENG., Illus.). 24p. (J). (— 1). bds. 19.96 (978-0-385-39207-5(9), Random Hse. Bks. for Young Readers) Random Hse. Children's Bks.
Eastman, Peter. Fred & Ted Like to Fly. 2011. (Bright & Early Board Books(TM) Ser.). (Illus.). 24p. (J). (— 1). 4.99 (978-0-375-86802-3(X), Random Hse. Bks. for Young Readers) Random Hse. Children's Bks.
Eaton, Kait. I Want to Be A... Fairy. Enright, Amanda, illus. 2014. (J). (978-1-4351-5499-5(1)) Barnes & Noble, Inc.
Echeverria, Jessica. Dora y el Día lluvioso. Savitsky, Steven, illus. 2009. (Dora la Exploradora Ser.). Orig. Title: Dora & the Rainy Day. (SPA.). 26p. (J). (gr. -1). bds. 5.99 (978-1-4169-7186-3(6), Libros Para Ninos) Libros Para Ninos.
Edgson, Alison, illus. The Emperor's New Clothes. (Flip-Up Fairy Tales Ser.). 24p. (J). 2007. (gr. -1-2). (978-1-84643-093-0(3)) 2006. (gr. 2-2). (978-1-84643-020-6(8)) Child's Play International Ltd.
—Three Billy Goats Gruff. (Flip-Up Fairy Tales Ser.). 24p. (J). 2007. (gr. -1-2). (978-1-84643-089-3(5)) 2006. (gr. 1-2). (978-1-904550-72-3(X)) Child's Play International Ltd.
Editions Phidal Staff. Radical Rides Super Sticker Book. (Illus.). 64p. (J). pap. (978-2-7643-0024-4(7)) Phidal Publishing, Inc./Editions Phidal, Inc.
Editors of Klutz. Lettering in Crazy, Cool, Quirky Style: In Crazy Cool Quirky Style. Editors of Klutz, ed. 2006. (ENG., Illus.). 56p. (J). (gr. 3-7). 18.95 (978-1-57054-428-6(X)) Klutz.
—The World According to Klutz. 2013. (ENG.). 300p. (J). (gr. 3). 14.99 (978-0-545-61213-5(6)) Klutz.
Editors of Klutz & Pilkey, Dav. The Captain Underpants Super-Silly Sticker Studio: An EPIC Color & Stick Activity Book. 2013. (ENG.). 42p. (J). (gr. 1). act. bk. ed. 16.99 (978-0-545-61522-8(4)) Klutz.
Educational Insights. The Sneaky, Snacky Squirrel. Gaggiotti, Lucia, illus. 2017. (ENG.). 12p. (J). (— 1). bds. 11.99 (978-0-7636-9465-4(7), Candlewick Entertainment) Candlewick Pr.
Edwards, Josh. Pull-Out Christmas, 1 vol. Embleton-Hall, Chris, illus. 2014. (Candle Pull-Out Ser.). (ENG.). 10p. (J). (gr. -1-k). bds. 9.99 (978-1-85985-999-5(2), 8e2d1272-478c-46e6-853b-8a5970c418b6, Lion Children's) Lion Hudson PLC GBR. Dist: Baker & Taylor Publisher Services (BTPS).
—Pull-Out David & Goliath, 1 vol. Embleton-Hall, Chris, illus. 2014. (Candle Pull-Out Ser.). (ENG.). 10p. (J). (gr. -1-k). bds. 9.99 (978-1-85985-997-1(6), be674cf2-0724-4737-bc32-49e069ff7c54, Candle Bks.) Lion Hudson PLC GBR. Dist: Baker & Taylor Publisher Services (BTPS).
Edwards, Nicola. Night Night, Dino-Snores. Elliott, Thomas, illus. 2018. (ENG.). 22p. (J). (gr. -1-k). bds. 12.99 (978-1-68010-548-3(5)) Tiger Tales.
—You're My Little Cuddle Bug. Marshall, Natalie, illus. 2018. (You're My Little Ser.). (ENG.). 18p. (J). (gr. -1 — 1). bds. 8.99 (978-1-68412-258-5(9), Silver Dolphin Bks.) Printers Row Publishing Group.
Egielski, Richard. Itsy Bitsy Spider. Egielski, Richard, illus. 2012. (ENG., Illus.). 12p. (J). (gr. -1-1). 19.99 (978-1-4169-9895-2(0), Atheneum Bks. for Young Readers) Simon & Schuster Children's Publishing.
Ehlert, Lois. Hands: Growing up to Be an Artist. Ehlert, Lois, illus. 2004. (ENG., Illus.). 48p. (J). (gr. -1-3). 16.99 (978-0-15-205107-5(4), 1195421, Clarion Bks.) HarperCollins Pubs.
—Leaf Man Big Book. Ehlert, Lois, illus. 2014. (ENG., Illus.). 40p. (J). (gr. -1-3). pap. 26.99 (978-0-544-33916-3(9), 1584487, Clarion Bks.) HarperCollins Pubs.
—Planting a Rainbow Lap Board Book. Ehlert, Lois, illus. 2008. (ENG., Illus.). 32p. (J). (gr. -1 — 1). bds. 12.99 (978-0-15-206304-7(8), 1198887, Clarion Bks.) HarperCollins Pubs.
Eight Jolly Reindeer. 2014. (ENG., Illus.). 16p. (J). (gr. -1 — 1). bds. 6.99 (978-0-545-65145-5(X), Cartwheel Bks.) Scholastic, Inc.
Electric Confetti. Neon Baby: Numbers. 2017. (Neon Baby Ser.). (ENG., Illus.). 20p. (J). (— 1). bds. 12.99 (978-1-76012-931-6(3)) Little Hare Bks. AUS. Dist: Independent Pubs. Group.
Elgar, Rebecca. Where's My Dinner? 2003. (ENG., Illus.). 12p. (J). bds. 9.99 (978-1-4052-0451-4(6)) Farshore GBR. Dist: Trafalgar Square Publishing.
Eliot, Hannah. If Everything Were Blue. Lalalimola, illus. 2015. (ENG.). 16p. (J). (gr. -1-k). bds. 8.99 (978-1-4814-3539-0(6), Little Simon) Little Simon.
—If Everything Were Pink. Lalalimola, illus. 2015. (ENG.). 16p. (J). (gr. -1-k). bds. 8.99 (978-1-4814-3538-3(8), Little Simon) Little Simon.
Eliot, T. S. Macavity's Not There! A Lift-The-Flap Book. Robins, Arthur, illus. (Old Possum Picture Bks.). (ENG.). 16p. 2018. (J). bds. 8.00 (978-0-571-33528-2(4)) 2017. 14.95 (978-0-571-32863-5(6)) Faber & Faber, Inc.
Elliott, Rebecca. God Loves Little Me, 1 vol. 2016. (ENG., Illus.). 10p. (J). (— 1). bds. 7.99 (978-0-7459-6559-8(8), 7a465e75-ae75-483c-92cb-092189bdda57, Lion Children's) Lion Hudson PLC GBR. Dist: Baker & Taylor Publisher Services (BTPS).
—Noah's Noisy Animals, 1 vol. 2016. (ENG., Illus.). 5p. (J). (— 1). bds. 7.99 (978-0-7459-6561-1(X), 88bbce0e-3f1c-4a69-90bd-47734452d124, Lion Children's) Lion Hudson PLC GBR. Dist: Baker & Taylor Publisher Services (BTPS).
Ellis, Belinda. Tractor. 2007. (Pull-Alongs Ser.). (Illus.). 12p. (gr. -1). per. (978-1-84610-443-5(2)) Make Believe Ideas.
Ellis, Greg & BeachHouse Publishing. Baby's First 1-2-3 in Hawaii. 2008. (ENG.). 20p. (J). (gr. -1-1). bds. 7.95 (978-1-933067-24-7(1)) Beachhouse Publishing, LLC.
Ellis, Gwen. The First Christmas, 1 vol. Pichon, Liz, illus. 2007. 10p. (J). bds. 15.99 (978-0-8254-5538-4(3)) Kregel Pubns.
Ellis, Paula. Yellowstone & Grand Teton Activity Book. Nitzsche, Shane, illus. 2011. (Color & Learn Ser.). (ENG.). 64p. (J). (gr. 3-7). pap. 6.95 (978-1-59193-356-4(0), Adventure Pubns.) AdventureKEEN.
Ellwand, David. Twinkle Twinkle Little Star: David Ellwand's Bears. Ellwand, David, illus. 2018. (ENG., Illus.). 14p. (J). (— 1). bds. 6.99 (978-1-5362-0220-5(7)) Candlewick Pr.
Elmquist, Laurie. Beach Baby, 1 vol. MacKay, Elly, illus. 2016. (ENG.). 24p. (J). (gr. -1 — 1). bds. 10.95 (978-1-4598-0954-3(8)) Orca Bk. Pubs. USA.
—Forest Baby, 1 vol. Robinson, Shantala, illus. 2018. (ENG.). 24p. (J). (gr. -1 — 1). bds. 10.95 (978-1-4598-1333-5(2)) Orca Bk. Pubs. USA.
Emberley, Ed. Bye-Bye, Big Bad Bullybug! Emberley, Ed, illus. 2007. (ENG., Illus.). 32p. (J). (gr. -1-3). 16.99 (978-0-316-01762-6(0)) Little, Brown Bks. for Young Readers.
Embleton, Christopher, illus. Is This My Tail? 2017. (J). (978-1-62885-286-8(0)) Kidsbooks, LLC.
Emma Treehouse Ltd. My Babies. Davis, Caroline, illus. 2007. (Easy Flaps Ser.). 10p. (J). (gr. -1). bds. 6.95 (978-1-58925-822-8(3)) Tiger Tales.
—My Friends. Davis, Caroline, illus. 2007. (Easy Flaps Ser.). 10p. (J). (gr. -1). bds. 6.95 (978-1-58925-823-5(1)) Tiger Tales.
—My Pets. Davis, Caroline, illus. 2007. (Easy Flaps Ser.). 10p. (J). (gr. -1). bds. 6.95 (978-1-58925-824-2(X)) Tiger Tales.
—My Toys. Davis, Caroline, illus. 2007. (Easy Flaps Ser.). 10p. (J). (gr. -1). bds. 6.95 (978-1-58925-825-9(8)) Tiger Tales.
Emmett, Jonathan. Alphabet Street. Arrhenius, Ingela P., illus. 2019. (ENG.). 26p. (J). (-k). bds. 18.99 (978-1-5362-0827-6(2)) Candlewick Pr.
Endle, Kate. Who Hoo Are You? An Animals Book by Kate Endle. 2010. (ENG., Illus.). 18p. (J). (gr. k-k). bds. 9.99 (978-1-57061-647-1(7), Little Bigfoot) Sasquatch Bks.
Engel, Christiane. ABC for Me: ABC Mindful Me, Volume 4. 2018. (ABC for Me Ser.: 4). (ENG., Illus.). 36p. (J). (gr. -1-1). bds. 16.95 (978-1-63322-510-7(0), 301672, Walter Foster Jr) Quarto Publishing Group USA.
Engel, Christiane, illus. Astronauts. 2018. (First Explorers Ser.). (ENG.). 10p. (J). (— 1). bds. 9.95 (978-1-4549-2940-6(5)) Sterling Publishing Co., Inc.
Engelbreit, Mary. Mary Engelbreit's Mother Goose Board Book. Engelbreit, Mary, illus. 2018. (ENG., Illus.). 36p. (J). (gr. -1-3). bds. 8.99 (978-0-06-274223-0(X), HarperFestival) HarperCollins Pubs.
English Heritage Staff. My Life as a Knight. 2005. (Illus.). 32p. pap. 19.95 (978-1-85074-985-1(X)) Historic England Publishing GBR. Dist: Casemate Academic.
—My Life as a Princess. 2005. (Illus.). 32p. pap. 19.95 (978-1-85074-984-4(1)) Historic England Publishing GBR. Dist: Casemate Academic.
Enos, Randall. Jibber-Jabber. Enos, Randall, illus. 2018. (Illus.). 14p. (J). (gr. -1-k). bds. 8.99 (978-1-56846-315-5(4), 19576, Creative Editions) Creative Co., The.
Epstein, Brad M. Army 101: My First Text-Board-Book. l.t. ed. 2007. (101 — My First Text-Board Books). (Illus.). 20p. (J). bds. (978-1-932530-42-1(8), 101 Bk.) Michaelson Entertainment.
—Atlanta Braves 101: My First Team-Board-Book. l.t. ed. 2007. (Illus.). 22p. (J). bds. (978-1-932530-74-2(6), 101 Bk.) Michaelson Entertainment.
—Boston 101. l.t. ed. 2009. (My First City Ser.). (Illus.). 24p. (J). (gr. -1-k). bds. (978-1-60730-000-7(1), 101 Bk.) Michaelson Entertainment.
—Chicago 101: My First City-Board-book. l.t. ed. 2009. (101 — My First Text-Board Books). (Illus.). 24p. (J). (978-1-60730-001-4(X), 101 Bk.) Michaelson Entertainment.
—Kansas State Univ 101: My First Text-Board-Book. l.t. ed. 2007. (101 — My First Text-Board Books). (Illus.). 20p. (J). bds. (978-1-932530-57-5(6), 101 Bk.) Michaelson Entertainment.
—Los Angeles 101: My First City-Board-book. l.t. ed. 2009. (Illus.). 24p. (J). (978-1-60730-002-1(8), 101 Bk.) Michaelson Entertainment.
—Milwaukee Brewers 101: My First Team-Board-Book. l.t. ed. 2007. (101 — My First Text-Board Books). (Illus.). 22p. (J). (978-1-932530-75-9(4), 101 Bk.) Michaelson Entertainment.
—New York 101. l.t. ed. 2009. (My First City Ser.). (Illus.). 24p. (J). (gr. -1-k). bds. (978-1-60730-003-8(6), 101 Bk.) Michaelson Entertainment.
—Stanford 101. 2013. (My First Text-Board-Book Ser.). (ENG., Illus.). 20p. (J). (gr. -1). bds. (978-1-60730-066-3(4), 101 Bk.) Michaelson Entertainment.
—University of Kansas 101: My First Text-Board-Book. 2006. (101 — My First Text-Board Books). (ENG., Illus.). 20p. (J). bds. (978-1-932530-40-7(1), 101 Bk.) Michaelson Entertainment.
—University of Nebraska 101: My First Text-Board-book. 2013. (My First Text-Board-Book Ser.). (ENG., Illus.). 20p. (J). bds. (978-1-60730-063-2(X)) Michaelson Entertainment.
—University of Washington 101. 2013. (My First Text-Board-Book Ser.). (ENG., Illus.). 20p. (J). (gr. -1). bds. (978-1-60730-068-7(0), 101 Bk.) Michaelson Entertainment.
—Washington D. C. 101: My First City-Board-book. l.t. ed. 2009. (ENG., Illus.). 24p. (J). 9.95 (978-1-60730-004-5(4), 101 Bk.) Michaelson Entertainment.
epstein, brad M. & lee-Epstein, michael. Pittsburgh Steelers Doodle Playbook: For Kids & Fans. 2012. (ENG., Illus.). 200p. (J). pap. (978-1-60730-324-4(8)) Michaelson Entertainment.
Ericsson, Annie Beth & Christian, Cheryl. ¿Que hay en mi Jardin? (Spanish/English) Un libro de colores/A Book of Colors. del Risco, Eida, tr. 2009. (ENG & SPA., Illus.). 16p. (J). bds. 6.25 (978-1-59572-181-5(9)) Star Bright Bks., Inc.
Ernst, Lisa Campbell. Turn-Around, Upside-Down Alphabet Book. 2004. (ENG., Illus.). 32p. (J). (gr. -1-3). 19.99 (978-0-689-85685-3(7), Simon & Schuster Bks. For Young Readers) Simon & Schuster Bks. For Young Readers.
Esquinaldo, Virginia. What Did Baby Jesus Do? Esquinaldo, Virginia, illus. 2006. (Illus.). 12p. (J). bds. 6.95 (978-0-8198-8310-0(7)) Pauline Bks. & Media.
Eubank, Patricia Reeder. Countdown to Christmas. 2003. (ENG., Illus.). 14p. (J). (gr. -1-k). bds. 9.95 (978-0-8249-6505-1(1), Ideals Pubns.) Worthy Publishing.
—Halloween 123. 2012. (ENG., Illus.). 22p. (J). (gr. -1 — 1). bds. 6.99 (978-0-8249-1868-2(1), Ideals Pubns.) Worthy Publishing.

Eubank, Patti Reeder. Count Your Blessings! 2004. (ENG., Illus.). 14p. (J). bds. 9.95 (978-0-8249-6544-0(2), Ideals Pubns.) Worthy Publishing.
Evans, Lynette. Whose Egg? Troughton, Guy, illus. 2013. (ENG.). 36p. (J). (gr. -1). 16.99 (978-1-60887-203-9(3)) Insight Editions.
Evanson, Ashley. London: A Book of Opposites. Evanson, Ashley, illus. 2015. (Hello, World Ser.). (Illus.). 16p. (J). (— 1). bds. 7.99 (978-0-448-48916-2(3), Penguin Workshop) Penguin Young Readers Group.
—Paris: A Book of Shapes. Evanson, Ashley, illus. 2015. (Hello, World Ser.). (Illus.). 16p. (J). (— 1). bds. 7.99 (978-0-448-48915-5(5), Penguin Workshop) Penguin Young Readers Group.
—San Francisco: A Book of Numbers. Evanson, Ashley, illus. 2015. (Hello, World Ser.). (Illus.). 16p. (J). (— 1). bds. 7.99 (978-0-448-48914-8(7), Penguin Workshop) Penguin Young Readers Group.
Everett, Forrest. Dear Santa, Love, Washington: An Evergreen State Christmas Celebration - with Real Letters! Quang Phuc, Pham, illus. 2018. (ENG.). 32p. (J). (gr. 1-4). 16.99 (978-1-64170-039-9(4), 550039) Familius LLC.
—Old MacDonald Had a Farm in Oregon. Sergeeva, Mary, illus. 2018. (Old MacDonald Had a Farm Regional Board Ser.). (ENG.). 16p. (J). (gr. k-3). bds. 12.99 (978-1-64170-014-6(9), 550014) Familius LLC.
—Row, Row, Row Your Boat in Oregon. Sergeeva, Mary, illus. 2018. (Row, Row, Row Your Boat Regional Board B Ser.). (ENG.). 16p. (J). (gr. k-3). bds. 12.99 (978-1-64170-015-3(7), 550015) Familius LLC.
Everett, Melissa. Do Your Ears Hang Low? Doss, Andrea, illus. 2014. (ENG.). 20p. (J). (gr. -1-2). bds. 8.99 (978-1-4867-0358-6(5)) Flowerpot Children's Pr. Inc. CAN. Dist: Cardinal Pubs. Group.
—I Wish I Was a Little. Paiva, Johannah Gilman, ed. Manning, Mary, illus. 2014. (ENG.). 20p. (J). 8.99 (978-1-77093-844-1(3)) Flowerpot Children's Pr. Inc. CAN. Dist: Cardinal Pubs. Group.
—Jack & Jill. Imodraj, illus. 2014. (ENG.). 20p. (J). (gr. -1-1). 8.99 (978-1-77093-843-4(5)) Flowerpot Children's Pr. Inc. CAN. Dist: Cardinal Pubs. Group.
—Pat-A-Cake. Kummer, Mark, illus. 2013. (ENG.). 20p. (J). (gr. -1-1). 8.99 (978-1-77093-521-1(5)) Flowerpot Children's Pr. Inc. CAN. Dist: Cardinal Pubs. Group.
Evert, Lori. The Brave Little Puppy. Breiehagen, Per, illus. 2016. (Wish Book Ser.). 28p. (J). (-k). bds. 8.99 (978-0-399-54945-8(5), Random Hse. Bks. for Young Readers) Random Hse. Children's Bks.
Eyre, Richard & Eyre, Linda. The Creation. 2016. (ENG., Illus.). 10p. (J). bds. 9.95 (978-1-939629-55-5(1)) Familius LLC.
Faces. Date not set. (Illus.). 40p. (J). 3.98 (978-1-4054-0174-6(5)) Parragon, Inc.
Fact Families Staff. LP-Fact Families: Level 1 Math. 2004. (ENG.). (J). 9.99 (978-1-59204-016-2(0)) Learning Wrap-Ups, Inc.
Fairley, Melissa. Ding! Dong! Harland, Jackie, illus. 2011. (ENG.). 12p. (J). (gr. -1-k). 15.95 (978-1-84898-362-5(X), TickTock Books) Octopus Publishing Group GBR. Dist: Independent Pubs. Group.
Fairy Tale- Cinderella. 2005. (J). bds. (978-1-4194-0039-1(8)) Paradise Pr., Inc.
Falconer, Ian. Olivia Cuenta. 2006. (Olivia Ser.).Tr. of Olivia Counts. (SPA.). (J). (gr. -1-k). bds. 6.99 (978-1-930332-89-8(0), LC33420) Lectorum Pubns., Inc.
—Olivia Helps with Christmas. Falconer, Ian, illus. 2013. (Classic Board Bks.). (ENG., Illus.). 40p. (J). (gr. -1-2). bds. 7.99 (978-1-4424-9446-6(8), Atheneum Bks. for Young Readers) Simon & Schuster Children's Publishing.
Faliere, Amélie. 123 in a Tree. 2017. (ENG., Illus.). 24p. (J). (gr. -1 — 1). 9.99 (978-1-4998-0628-1(0)) Little Bee Books Inc.
Faria, Kimberley, et al. Booo! 2015. (Illus.). (J). (978-0-312-51993-3(1)) St. Martin's Pr.
—Ha-Ha-Ha! 2015. (Illus.). (J). (978-0-312-51992-6(3)) St. Martin's Pr.
—Meow! 2015. (Illus.). (J). (978-0-312-51994-0(X)) St. Martin's Pr.
Farley, Christin & Miles, Stephanie. F Is for Florida. 2018. (ENG., Illus.). 20p. (J). (gr. -1-k). bds. 12.99 (978-1-64170-021-4(1), 550021) Familius LLC.
—Let's Count Colorado: Numbers & Colors in the Centennial State. Kaliaha, Volha, illus. 2018. (Let's Count Regional Board Bks.). (ENG.). 20p. (J). (gr. -1 — 1). bds. 12.99 (978-1-945547-85-0(5), 554785) Familius LLC.
—Let's Count Florida. 2018. (ENG., Illus.). 20p. (J). (gr. -1-1). bds. 12.99 (978-1-64170-020-7(3), 550020) Familius LLC.
Farnsworth, Lauren. Clever Babies Love Art: Wild Animals. 2016. (Clever Babies Love Art Ser.). (ENG., Illus.). 14p. (J). (— 1). bds. 7.99 (978-1-78055-397-9(8), Buster Bks.) O'Mara, Michael Bks., Ltd. GBR. Dist: Independent Pubs. Group.
Farshtey, Greg. Way of the Ninja. 2012. (LEGO Ninjago Ser.). (ENG.). 32p. (J). (gr. 1-3). pap. 3.99 (978-0-545-40113-5(5)) Scholastic, Inc.
Fascinating Firefly. 2004. (Illus.). 10p. (J). (978-1-59340-144-3(2)) Grandreams Bks., Inc.
Fashion Fun Sticker Book. (Girlfriend Gang Ser.). 16p. (J). (978-2-7643-0018-3(2)) Phidal Publishing, Inc./Editions Phidal, Inc.
Faulkner, Keith. Charlie Chimp's Christmas: A Pop-up Extravaganza of Festive Friends. Lambert, Jonathan, illus. 2006. 12p. (J). (gr. -1-3). reprint ed. 10.00 (978-1-4223-5446-9(6)) DIANE Publishing Co.
—Flip-Flap Math: Flip the Flpas to Check Your Answers! Irish, Martin, illus. 2005. 12 p.p. (J). (978-0-439-78578-5(2)) Scholastic, Inc.
—Maths Machine: A Fun New Way to Do Maths! Tyger, Rory, illus. 2004. (J). (978-0-439-72174-5(1)) Scholastic, Inc.
Faulkner, Keith & Holmes, Stephen. Animal ? Math. Faulkner, Keith & Holmes, Stephen, illus. 2003. (Illus.). (J). (978-0-439-62755-9(9)) Scholastic, Inc.
Faulkner, Keith & Tyger, Rory. Time's Up! Faulkner, Keith & Tyger, Rory, illus. Lambert, Jonathan, illus. 2003. (J). (978-0-439-56155-6(8)) Scholastic, Inc.
Fernandes, Eugenie. Kitten's Summer. Fernandes, Eugenie, illus. 2013. (ENG., Illus.). 24p. (J). (gr. -1 — 1). bds. 7.95 (978-1-55453-721-1(5)) Kids Can Pr., Ltd. CAN. Dist: Hachette Bk. Group.
Fernandez, Rajiv. Baby to Big. 2017. (ENG., Illus.). 32p. (J). (— 1). 6.99 (978-1-57687-826-2(0), powerHouse Bks.) powerHse. Bks.
—Baby to Brooklyn. 2017. (ENG., Illus.). 32p. (J). (— 1). bds. 6.99 (978-1-57687-785-2(X), powerHouse Bks.) powerHse. Bks.
Ferreri, Della Ross. Precious Baby. Dong, Monique, illus. 2019. 20p. (J). (gr. -1 — 1). 7.99 (978-1-5064-4773-5(2), Beaming Books) 1517 Media.
Ferri, Francesca, illus. Elephant & Friends: A Soft & Fuzzy Book for Baby. 2014. (Friends Cloth Bks.). (ENG.). 8p. (J). (gr. -1-k). 12.99 (978-1-4380-0527-0(X)) Sourcebooks, Inc.
—Giraffe & Friends: A Soft & Fuzzy Book for Baby. 2014. (Friends Cloth Bks.). (ENG.). 8p. (J). (gr. -1-k). 12.99 (978-1-4380-0528-7(8)) Sourcebooks, Inc.
Ferrie, Chris. General Relativity for Babies. 2017. (Baby University Ser.: 0). (Illus.). 24p. (J). (gr. -1-k). bds. 9.99 (978-1-4926-5626-5(7)) Sourcebooks, Inc.
—Quantum Information for Babies. 2018. (Baby University Ser.: 0). (Illus.). 24p. (J). (gr. -1-k). bds. 9.99 (978-1-4926-5630-2(5)) Sourcebooks, Inc.
—Quantum Physics for Babies. 2017. (Baby University Ser.: 0). (Illus.). 24p. (J). (gr. -1-k). bds. 9.99 (978-1-4926-5622-7(4)) Sourcebooks, Inc.
—Statistical Physics for Babies. 2018. (Baby University Ser.: 0). (Illus.). 24p. (J). (gr. -1-k). bds. 9.99 (978-1-4926-5627-2(5)) Sourcebooks, Inc.
Ferrie, Chris & Florance, Cara. ABCs of Biology. 2018. (Baby University Ser.: 0). (Illus.). 26p. (J). (gr. -1-k). bds. 9.99 (978-1-4926-7114-5(2)) Sourcebooks, Inc.
—Nuclear Physics for Babies. 2018. (Baby University Ser.: 0). (Illus.). 24p. (J). (gr. -1-k). bds. 9.99 (978-1-4926-7117-6(7)) Sourcebooks, Inc.
Ferrie, Chris & Kregenow, Julia. Astrophysics for Babies. 2018. (Baby University Ser.: 0). (Illus.). 24p. (J). (gr. -1-k). bds. 9.99 (978-1-4926-7113-8(4)) Sourcebooks, Inc.
Ferrie, Chris & whurley. Quantum Computing for Babies. 2018. (Baby University Ser.: 0). (ENG., Illus.). 24p. (J). (gr. -1-k). bds. 9.99 (978-1-4926-7118-3(5)) Sourcebooks, Inc.
Filigenzi, Courtney & Bersani, Shennen. Let My Colors Out. Bersani, Shennen, illus. 2009. (ENG., Illus.). 16p. (J). (gr. -1-k). 11.95 (978-1-60443-011-0(7), 1604430117) American Cancer Society, Inc.
Filipek, Nina. Colors. O'Toole, Jeanette, illus. 2009. (Bright Basics Ser.). 12p. (J). (gr. -1-k). bds. 11.40 (978-1-60754-687-0(6)) Windmill Bks.
—Counting. O'Toole, Jeanette, illus. 2009. (Bright Basics Ser.). 12p. (J). (gr. -1-k). bds. 11.40 (978-1-60754-686-3(8)) Windmill Bks.
Filipek, Nina & Award, Anna. Farm Animals. 2017. (ENG., Illus.). 10p. (J). bds. 9.00 (978-1-909763-38-8(1)) Award Pubns. Ltd. GBR. Dist: Parkwest Pubns., Inc.
—Wild Animals. 2017. (ENG., Illus.). 10p. (J). bds. 9.00 (978-1-909763-37-1(3)) Award Pubns. Ltd. GBR. Dist: Parkwest Pubns., Inc.
Fincher, Kathy, illus. Baby's First Christmas. 2006. 8p. (gr. -1-k). bds. 7.95 (978-0-88271-705-0(7)) Regina Pr., Malhame & Co.
Finn, Rebecca, illus. Little Bunny. (Cuddly Cuffstm Ser.). 6p. (J). 6.95 (978-1-58925-767-2(7)) Tiger Tales.
—Little Ducky. (Cuddly Cuffstm Ser.). 6p. (J). 6.95 (978-1-58925-766-5(9)) Tiger Tales.
The First Christmas. (Illus.). 12p. (J). 4.95 (978-1-58989-102-9(3)) Thurman Hse., LLC.
Fischer, Jean. Little Book of Easter Blessings, 1 vol. 2018. (Precious Moments Ser.). (ENG., Illus.). 32p. (J). bds. 9.99 (978-0-7180-9866-7(8), Tommy Nelson) Nelson, Thomas Inc.
—Little Book of Thanks, 1 vol. 2018. (Precious Moments Ser.). (ENG., Illus.). 32p. (J). bds. 9.99 (978-0-7180-9864-3(1), Tommy Nelson) Nelson, Thomas Inc.
Fisher-Golton, Karin. My Amazing Day: A Celebration of Wonder & Gratitude. Cheung, Lori A., photos by. 2013. (ENG., Illus.). 26p. (J). bds. 8.99 (978-0-9896145-1-1(4)) Pacific Dogwood Pr.
Fisher-Price Little People Lift the Flap Library 2. 2014. (ENG.). 50p. bds. 49.95 (978-0-7944-2979-9(3)) Studio Fun International.
Fitch, Sheree. Kisses Kisses Baby-O!, 1 vol. Rose, Hilda, illus. 2008. (ENG.). 12p. (J). (gr. -1 — 1). bds. 6.50 (978-1-55109-646-9(3), 1f8e14b6-0f34-475e-b22d-a2f8f5c217d1) Nimbus Publishing, Ltd. CAN. Dist: Baker & Taylor Publisher Services (BTPS).
Flintham, Thomas. Animal Noises. Flintham, Thomas, illus. 2016. (ENG., Illus.). 24p. (J). (gr. -1 — 1). bds. 7.99 (978-1-4814-6935-7(5), Little Simon) Little Simon.
—Animal Numbers. Flintham, Thomas, illus. 2016. (ENG., Illus.). 24p. (J). (gr. -1 — 1). bds. 7.99 (978-1-4814-6937-1(1), Little Simon) Little Simon.
Flip Flaps Colours. 2014. (ENG., Illus.). 36p. 10.00 (978-1-906572-79-2(8)) Award Pubns. Ltd. GBR. Dist: Parkwest Pubns., Inc.
Flowerpot Children's Press Staff, contrib. by. My Animal Buddies: With Duck, Pig, & Frog. 2015. (Illus.). (J). (978-1-4351-6023-1(1)) Barnes & Noble, Inc.
Flowerpot Press. Good Morning, Dear God. 2013. (ENG., Illus.). 20p. (J). 8.99 (978-1-77093-635-5(1)) Flowerpot Children's Pr. Inc. CAN. Dist: Cardinal Pubs. Group.
Flowerpot Press, contrib. by. Sockheadz: 5 Little Sockheadz. 2013. (ENG., Illus.). 20p. (J). (gr. -1-k). 8.99 (978-1-77093-618-8(1)) Flowerpot Children's Pr. Inc. CAN. Dist: Cardinal Pubs. Group.
—Sockheadz: Hide & Seek. 2013. (Illus.). 20p. (J). (gr. -1-k). 8.99 (978-1-77093-619-5(X)) Flowerpot Children's Pr. Inc. CAN. Dist: Cardinal Pubs. Group.
Flowerpot Press Staff. A Child's Book of Prayers: Good Night, Dear God. 2013. (ENG., Illus.). 20p. (J). 8.99 (978-1-77093-636-2(X)) Flowerpot Children's Pr. Inc. CAN. Dist: Cardinal Pubs. Group.
Flowerpot Press Staff, contrib. by. Sockheadz: Counting. 2013. (ENG., Illus.). 20p. (J). (gr. -1-k). 6.99 (978-1-77093-594-5(0)) Flowerpot Children's Pr. Inc. CAN. Dist: Cardinal Pubs. Group.
—Sockheadz: First Words. 2013. (ENG., Illus.). 20p. (J). (gr. -1-k). 6.99 (978-1-77093-595-2(9)) Flowerpot Children's Pr. Inc. CAN. Dist: Cardinal Pubs. Group.
—Sockheadz: Shapes. 2013. (ENG., Illus.). 20p. (J). (gr. -1-k). 6.99 (978-1-77093-596-9(7)) Flowerpot Children's Pr. Inc. CAN. Dist: Cardinal Pubs. Group.
Flying Frog Pub, creator. ABC Fun with Elmo & Friends. 2011. (Sesame Street (Publications International) Ser.). (ENG., Illus.). 14p. (J). (gr. -1). bds. 3.99 (978-1-60745-030-6(5)) Flying Frog Publishing.
—Big & Small Fun with Elmo & Friends. 2011. (ENG., Illus.). 14p. (gr. -1-k). bds. 3.99 (978-1-60745-033-7(X)) Flying Frog Publishing.
—Color Fun with Elmo & Friends. 2011. (ENG., Illus.). 14p. (gr. -1-k). bds. 3.99 (978-1-60745-031-3(3)) Flying Frog Publishing.
—Counting Fun with Elmo & Friends. 2011. (Sesame Street (Publications International) Ser.). (ENG., Illus.). 14p. (J). (gr. -1). bds. 3.99 (978-1-60745-032-0(1)) Flying Frog Publishing.
Flyte, Min. Would You Dare... ? A Lift-The-flap Adventure. Hunt, Matt, illus. 2017. (ENG.). 24p. (J). (gr. -1-2). 14.99 (978-0-7636-9619-1(6)) Candlewick Pr.
Foley, Tim. American Presidents Sticker Book. 2011. (Dover Sticker Bks.). (ENG., Illus.). 4p. (J). (gr. 1-5). 6.99 (978-0-486-47879-1(3), 478793) Dover Pubns., Inc.
Fordham, Kate. Me & My Kitten. 2006. (Illus.). 80p. (J). (978-0-439-89293-3(7)) Scholastic, Inc.
Forshaw, Louise, illus. Dinosaur Safari. 2014. (ENG.). 10p. (J). 14.99 (978-1-4711-2121-0(6), Simon & Schuster Children's) Simon & Schuster, Ltd. GBR. Dist: Simon & Schuster, Inc.
Foster, Kate, ed. Nice & Pretty. 2013. (Look at Me! Ser.). (ENG., Illus.). 10p. (J). (-k). bds. 10.95 (978-1-61889-392-5(0)) AZ Bks. LLC.
Fox, Mem. Time for Bed Padded Board Book. Dyer, Jane, illus. 2010. (ENG.). 28p. (J). (gr. -1 — 1). bds. 10.99 (978-0-547-40856-9(0), 1428814, Clarion Bks.) HarperCollins Pubs.
—Time for Bed/Es Hora de Dormir: Bilingual English-Spanish. Dyer, Jane, illus. 2012. (ENG.). 28p. (J). (gr. -1 — 1). bds. 6.99 (978-0-547-71907-8(8), 1481834, Clarion Bks.) HarperCollins Pubs.
Fractions Cards Staff. LP-Fractions: Level 2 Math. 2004. (ENG.). (J). 9.99 (978-1-59204-020-9(9)) Learning Wrap-Ups, Inc.
Franceschelli, Christopher. Alphablock (an Abrams Block Book) 2013. (Abrams Block Book Ser.). (ENG., Illus.). 104p. (J). (gr. -1 — 1). bds. 17.99 (978-1-4197-0936-4(4), 1063210) Abrams, Inc.
—A Box of Blocks. Peski Studio, illus. 2017. (ENG.). 290p. (J). (gr. -1 — 1). bds. 50.00 (978-1-4197-2818-1(0)) Abrams, Inc.
—Buildablock (an Abrams Block Book) 2017. (Abrams Block Book Ser.). (ENG., Illus.). 90p. (J). (gr. -1 — 1). bds. 17.99 (978-1-4197-2569-2(6), 1146310) Abrams, Inc.
—Hello, New York! Cosneau, Géraldine, illus. 2018. (Hello, Big City! Ser.). (ENG.). 46p. (J). (gr. -1 — 1). bds. 12.99 (978-1-4197-2829-7(6), 1184410) Abrams, Inc.
Francia, Giada. Alex & Penny's Italy Jigsaw Book. Colombo, Angelo, illus. 2007. (ENG.). 14p. (gr. 1-3). pap. 14.95 (978-88-544-0242-3(7), White Star) Rizzoli International Pubns., Inc.
Francis, Pope. Pope Francis Says... Boyd, Sheree, illus. 2019. (ENG.). 32p. (J). bds. 14.99 (978-0-8294-4653-1(2)) Loyola Pr.
Frankel, Alona. Once upon a Potty Sound Book for Girls. Publications International Ltd. Staff, ed. 2010. 8p. (J). bds. 7.98 (978-1-4508-0828-6(X)) Publications International, Ltd.
Frantz, Jennifer. Color & Iron-Ons Book. Middleton, Gayle, illus. 2005. (My Little Pony Ser.). 32p. (J). (gr. -1-1). 3.99 (978-0-06-074441-0(3), HarperFestival) HarperCollins Pubs.
Frazier, Craig. Sitting Board Book. Frazier, Craig, illus. 2019. (ENG., Illus.). 32p. (J). (gr. -1 — 1). bds. 7.99 (978-0-06-279630-1(5), HarperFestival) HarperCollins Pubs.
Freedman, Claire. Cuddle Bear. Scott, Gavin, illus. 2018. (J). (978-1-61067-730-1(7)) Kane Miller.
Freeman, Don. Corduroy. 2014. (Corduroy Ser.). (Illus.). 34p. (J). (gr. -1 — 1). bds. 7.99 (978-0-451-47079-9(6), Viking Books for Young Readers) Penguin Young Readers Group.
—Corduroy: Giant Board Book. 2011. (Corduroy Ser.). 34p. (J). (gr. -1 — 1). bds. 11.99 (978-0-670-01311-1(0), Viking Books for Young Readers) Penguin Young Readers Group.
—A Pocket for Corduroy. 2015. (Corduroy Ser.). (Illus.). 34p. (J). (— 1). bds. 8.99 (978-0-451-47113-0(X), Viking Books for Young Readers) Penguin Young Readers Group.
Freeman, Tina, illus. Ten Little Monkeys Jumping on the Bed. 2007. (Classic Books with Holes 8x8 with CD Ser.). (ENG.). 16p. (J). (gr. -1-1). (978-1-904550-67-9(3)) Child's Play International Ltd.
Freeman, Tor. Benji Bear's Busy Day. Freeman, Tor, illus. 2015. (ENG., Illus.). 18p. (J). (-k). bds. 17.99 (978-1-5098-0111-4(1)) Pan Macmillan GBR. Dist: Independent Pubs. Group.
French, Jackie. Pete the Sheep. Whatley, Bruce, illus. 2008. 30p. (J). bds. (978-0-7322-8794-8(4)) HarperCollins Pubs. Australia.
Friden, Chris. Bathtime with Bubbles. Zapater Oliva, Carlos & Depew, Robert, illus. 2008. (J). (978-0-9801849-2-1(4)) Haydenburri Lane.
—Bedtime Safari. 2008. (Illus.). 27p. (J). bds. 14.99 (978-0-9758785-4-5(9)) Haydenburri Lane.
—Bedtime Safari. Otoshi, Kathryn & Ciccarelli, Gary, illus. 2007. (J). (978-0-9758785-3-8(0)) Haydenburri Lane.
—Pajamatime with P.J. Zapater Oliva, Carlos & Glazier, Garth, illus. 2008. (J). (978-0-9801849-5-2(9)); (978-0-9758785-9-0(X)) Haydenburri Lane.
—Sleepytime with Rory. Zapater Oliva, Carlos & Glazier, Garth, illus. 2008. (J). (978-0-9801849-1-4(6)) Haydenburri Lane.
—Toothtime with Chomper. Rodríguez Braojos, Alberto et al, illus. 2008. (J). (978-0-9801849-3-8(2)) Haydenburri Lane.
Friden, Chris & Rodríguez Braojos, Alberto. Storytime with Paige. Jaraiz, David, illus. 2008. (J). (978-0-9758785-8-3(1)); (978-0-9801849-4-5(0)) Haydenburri Lane.
Friedman, Becky. What Is Daniel Wearing? Fruchter, Jason, illus. 2015. (Daniel Tiger's Neighborhood Ser.). (ENG.). 14p. (J). (gr. -1 — 1). 8.99 (978-1-4814-2899-6(3), Simon Spotlight) Simon Spotlight.
Friester, Paul. Owl Howl Board Book. Goossens, Philippe, illus. 2nd rev. ed. 2016. (ENG.). 26p. (J). (gr. -1-1). bds. 8.95 (978-0-7358-4234-2(5)) North-South Bks., Inc.
Frith, Alex. Lift the Flap Picture Atlas. 2010. (Atlases Ser.). (Illus.). 16p. (J). bds. 15.99 (978-0-7945-2402-9(8), Usborne) EDC Publishing.
—See Inside Science. 2007. 16p. (J). bds. 12.99 (978-0-7945-1549-2(5), Usborne) EDC Publishing.
—See Inside the World of Dinosaurs. Scott, Peter, illus. 2007. 16p. (J). bds. 13.99 (978-0-7945-1436-5(7), Usborne) EDC Publishing.
Frith, Alex & King, Colin. See Inside Inventions IR. 2012. (See Inside Board Bks). 16p. (J). ring bd. 13.99 (978-0-7945-3239-0(X), Usborne) EDC Publishing.
—See Inside Your Head. 2008. (Usborne Lift the Flap Bks.). 15p. (J). (gr. 4-7). bds. 12.99 (978-0-7945-1948-3(2), Usborne) EDC Publishing.
—See under the Ground. 2007. (See Inside Science Ser.). (Illus.). 15p. (J). bds. 12.99 (978-0-7945-1600-0(9), Usborne) EDC Publishing.
Frith, Alex & Lacey, Minna. See Inside Math - Internet Referenced. 2008. (See Inside Board Bks). 16p. (J). bds. 12.99 (978-0-7945-2093-9(6), Usborne) EDC Publishing.
Fritz, Greg. God Made You Special! 2015. (VeggieTales Ser.). (ENG., Illus.). 20p. (J). bds. 7.99 (978-0-8249-1947-4(5), Ideals Pubns.) Worthy Publishing.
Froeb, Lori C. Noah's Ark, 1 vol. Rinaldo, Luana, illus. 2008. 12p. (J). bds. 7.99 (978-0-8254-5546-9(4)) Kregel Pubns.
Fronis, Aly. If You're Spooky & You Know It. Ho, Jannie, illus. 2016. (ENG.). 16p. (J). (gr. -1-k). bds. 5.99 (978-1-4998-0165-1(3)) Little Bee Books Inc.
—This Little Pumpkin. Flowers, Luke, illus. 2018. (ENG.). 16p. (J). (gr. -1-k). bds. 5.99 (978-1-4998-0645-8(0)) Little Bee Books Inc.
—This Little Turkey. Blanco, Migy, illus. 2016. (ENG.). 16p. (J). (gr. -1-k). bds. 5.99 (978-1-4998-0302-0(8)) Little Bee Books Inc.
Frost, Maddie, illus. Alfie & Bet's ABC. 2018. (J). 12.99 (978-1-61067-647-2(5)) Kane Miller.
—Candy Apple Blessings, 1 vol. 2018. (Sweet Blessings Ser.). (ENG.). 20p. (J). bds. 8.99 (978-1-4003-1779-0(7), Tommy Nelson) Nelson, Thomas Inc.
Fruchter, Jason, illus. A Duckling for Daniel. 2016. (Daniel Tiger's Neighborhood Ser.). (ENG.). 14p. (J). (gr. -1-k). bds. 5.99 (978-1-4814-5781-1(0), Simon Spotlight) Simon Spotlight.
—How Is Daniel Feeling? 2015. (Daniel Tiger's Neighborhood Ser.). (ENG.). 14p. (J). (gr. -1-k). bds. 12.99 (978-1-4814-3856-8(5), Simon Spotlight) Simon Spotlight.
—What Time Is It, Daniel Tiger? 2016. (Daniel Tiger's Neighborhood Ser.). (ENG.). 14p. (J). (gr. -1-k). bds. 10.99 (978-1-4814-6934-0(7), Simon Spotlight) Simon Spotlight.
—You're Still You! 2016. (Daniel Tiger's Neighborhood Ser.). (ENG.). 12p. (J). (gr. -1-k). bds. 5.99 (978-1-4814-6743-8(3), Simon Spotlight) Simon Spotlight.
Fruits & Vegetables. 2019. (Illus.). (J). (978-1-4351-6977-7(8)) Barnes & Noble, Inc.
Fry, Sonali. I'm a Little Vampire. Rescek, Sanja, illus. 2014. (ENG.). 16p. (J). (gr. -1 — 1). bds. 5.99 (978-1-4814-0504-1(7), Little Simon) Little Simon.
—The Itsy Bitsy Pumpkin. Rescek, Sanja, illus. 2014. (Itsy Bitsy Ser.). (ENG.). 16p. (J). (gr. -1 — 1). bds. 5.99 (978-1-4814-0505-8(5), Little Simon) Little Simon.
—Where Are You, Blue? Clifton-Brown, Holly, illus. 2015. (Dot Town Ser.). (ENG.). 32p. (J). (gr. -1 — 1). bds. 8.99 (978-1-4814-3589-5(2), Little Simon) Little Simon.
Fujikawa, Gyo, illus. Sleepy Time. 2011. 20p. (J). (gr. k-k). bds. 8.99 (978-1-4027-6820-0(6)) Sterling Publishing Co., Inc.
Fuller, Rachel. All Kinds of Festivals. 2012. (All Kinds Of Ser.). (ENG., Illus.). 16p. (J). (gr. -1-k). 12.99 (978-1-85707-801-5(2)) Tango Bks. GBR. Dist: Independent Pubs. Group.
Fuller, Rachel, illus. Look at Me! 2009. (New Baby Ser.). 12p. (J). (gr. -1). spiral bd. (978-1-84643-278-1(2)) Child's Play International Ltd.
Furlong, Frank, illus. Pop Pop's Magic Chair. 2010. 24p. pap. 12.95 (978-1-60844-658-2(1)) Dog Ear Publishing, LLC.
Furman, Eric. Sesame Street: Elmo (Giant First Play-a-Sound) 2010. 10p. (J). bds. 17.98 (978-1-60553-546-3(X)) Publications International, Ltd.
Furukawa, Masumi, illus. The Ugly Duckling. (Flip-Up Fairy Tales Ser.). 24p. (J). 2007. (gr. -1-2). (978-1-84643-095-4(X)) 2006. (gr. 2-2). pap. (978-1-84643-022-0(4)) Child's Play International Ltd.
Fy Llyfr Geiriau Croes Cyntaf. 2005.Tr. of My First Opposites. (WEL., Illus.). 34p. (978-1-85596-671-0(9)) Dref Wen.
G., Ashley. Critter Colors. G., Ashley, illus. 2015. (ENG., Illus.). 28p. (J). (gr. -1-k). bds. 7.99 (978-1-4814-4218-3(X), Little Simon) Little Simon.
Gaffney, Michael. Time-Life Programa de Aprendizaje Infantil (Time-Life Early Learning Program), 10 bks. Incl. Cuantos Hipopotamos Hay? 1963. 16.95 (978-0-7835-3512-8(0)); Cuentos para un Dia de Tormenta (Takes for a Stormy Day) 1996. 16.95 (978-0-7835-3533-3(3)); Dia en la Vida del Sr. Atolondron. 1996. 16.95 (978-0-7835-3525-8(2)); Relojes Magicos del Abuelo Roberto (Roberto's Magical Clocks) 1996. 16.95 (978-0-7835-3504-3(X)); Secretos del Bosque (The Secret Forest) 1996. 16.95 (978-0-7835-3500-5(7)); Tania y Sus Amigos (Tanya Thinker & the Gummy Gang) 1996. 16.95 (978-0-7835-3516-6(3)); Tomasol, el Mago del Color (Balderdash the Brilliant) 1996. 16.95 (978-0-7835-3529-6(5)); Viaje de los "Micronautas" (Voyage of the Micronauts) 1996. 16.95 (978-0-7835-3537-1(6)); (Illus.). 64p. (J). (gr. k-2). 144.08 (978-0-7835-3541-8(4)) Time-Life, Inc.
Gaiman, Neil. Chu's Day Board Book. Rex, Adam, illus. 2014. (ENG.). 36p. (J). (gr. -1 — 1). bds. 7.99 (978-0-06-234746-6(2), HarperFestival) HarperCollins Pubs.
Gaines, Isabel & Milne, Alan Alexander. Pooh's Halloween Parade. Wenzel, Paul & Enik, Ted, illus. 2012. (J). (978-1-4351-4175-9(X)) Disney Publishing Worldwide.
—Pooh's Leaf Pile. Rigol, Francesc, illus. 2012. (J). (978-1-4351-4190-2(3)) Disney Pr.
Galbraith, Kathryn O. Boo, Bunny! Board Book. Mack, Jeff, illus. 2012. (ENG.). 32p. (J). (gr. -1 — 1). bds. 5.99 (978-0-547-81850-4(5), 1496581, Clarion Bks.) HarperCollins Pubs.

Gall, Chris. Revenge of the Dinotrux. 2015. (Dinotrux Ser.: 2). (ENG., Illus.). 28p. (J). (gr. -1 — 1). bds. 6.99 *(978-0-316-40635-2(X))* Little, Brown Bks. for Young Readers.

Gallo, Tina. Cinderella: A Wheel-Y Silly Fairy Tale. Scott, Kimberley, illus. 2011. (Little Simon Sillies Ser.). (ENG.). 14p. (J). (gr. -1-1). lib. bdg. 5.99 *(978-1-4424-2106-6(1)*, Little Simon) Little Simon.

—Lettuce In! And Other Knock-Knock Jokes. Chollat, Emilie, illus. 2011. (Little Simon Sillies Ser.). (ENG.). 20p. (J). (gr. -1-1). 5.99 *(978-1-4424-1404-4(9)*, Little Simon) Little Simon.

—The Three Little Pigs: A Wheel-Y Silly Fairy Tale. Bryne, Kelly, illus. 2011. (Little Simon Sillies Ser.). (ENG.). 14p. (J). (gr. -1-1). 6.99 *(978-1-4424-2107-3(X)*, Little Simon) Little Simon.

Galloway, Fhiona, illus. Fall Is Here! 2015. (ENG.). 16p. (J). (gr. -1 — 1). bds. 5.99 *(978-1-4998-0110-1(6))* Little Bee Books Inc.

—Fire Engine. 2016. (J). *(978-1-62885-168-7(6))* Kidsbooks, LLC.

—Follow Me: Animal Faces. 2016. (ENG.). 10p. (J). (gr. -1 — 1). bds. 7.99 *(978-1-4998-0268-9(4))* Little Bee Books Inc.

—Where's the Pumpkin? 2015. (ENG.). 16p. (J). (gr. -1 — 1). bds. 5.99 *(978-1-4998-0097-5(5))* Little Bee Books Inc.

Galloway, Ruth, illus. Ten Busy, Whizzy Bugs. 2017. (J). *(978-1-84857-561-5(0))* Little Tiger Pr. Group.

Galvin, Laura G. & Galvin, Laura. I Love My Mommy (with Download) 2011. (ENG.). 16p. (J). *(978-1-60727-345-5(4))* Soundprints.

Galvin, Laura Gates. Baby Dolphins Busy Day. 2011. (Baby Animals (Soundprints) Ser.). (ENG., Illus.). 16p. (gr. -1-k). 15.95 *(978-1-60727-329-5(2))* Soundprints.

—Fawn & Her Family. 2011. (Baby Animals (Soundprints) Ser.). (ENG., Illus.). 16p. (J). (gr. -1-k). 6.95 *(978-1-60727-283-0(0))* Soundprints.

—First Look at Aircraft. Eaddy, Susan, illus. 2008. (ENG.). 16p. (J). (gr. -1-k). bds. 6.95 *(978-1-59249-862-8(0))* Soundprints.

—First Look at Dinosaurs. Pindroh, Paula, illus. 2011. (First Look At... (Soundprints) Ser.). (ENG.). 16p. 6.95 *(978-1-60727-285-4(7))* Soundprints.

—First Look at Rescue Vehicles. Eaddy, Susan, illus. 2009. (ENG.). 16p. (J). (gr. -1-k). 6.95 *(978-1-60727-106-2(0))*; bds. 6.95 *(978-1-60727-093-5(5))* Soundprints.

—First Look at Trucks. Eaddy, Susan, illus. 2008. (ENG.). 16p. (J). (gr. -1-k). 6.95 *(978-1-59249-861-1(2))* Soundprints.

—I Love My Family. 2011. (ENG.). 16p. (J). *(978-1-60727-621-0(6))* Soundprints.

—I Love My Sister. Oughton, Taylor et al, illus. 2011. (I Love My... Ser.). (ENG.). 16p. (gr. -1-k). 6.95 *(978-1-60727-311-0(X))* Soundprints.

—If I Were a Bird. 2014. (Illus.). (J). *(978-1-58865-787-9(6))* Kidsbooks, LLC.

Galvin, Laura Gates & Odierno, Lisa. Puppy Explores. 2008. (ENG.). 16p. (J). (gr. -1-k). 13.95 *(978-1-59249-864-2(7))* Soundprints.

Galvin, Laura Gates & Studio Mouse Editorial. Cinderella: Dreams Do Come True. 2008. (ENG., Illus.). 36p. (J). (gr. -1). 7.99 *(978-1-59069-436-7(8))* Studio Mouse LLC.

Galvin, Laura Gates & Studio Mouse Staff. Write-with-Me Alphabet. Giblin, Brian E., ed. (Write-with-Me Ser.). (ENG., Illus.). 28p. (J). 2011. 15.99 *(978-1-59069-921-8(1))* 2008. 14.99 *(978-1-59069-618-7(2))* Studio Mouse LLC.

Gamble, Adam. Buenas Noches, California. Stevenson, Harvey, illus. 2012. (Buenas Noches Ser.). (SPA.). 24p. (J). (gr. k — 1). bds. 9.95 *(978-1-60219-070-2(4))* Good Night Bks.

—Buenas Noches, Estados Unidos. Chan, Suwin, illus. 2012. (Buenas Noches Ser.). (SPA & ENG.). 28p. (J). (gr. k — 1). bds. 9.95 *(978-1-60219-069-6(0))* Good Night Bks.

—Buenas Noches, Nueva York. Veno, Joe, illus. 2013. (Buenas Noches Ser.). (SPA.). 24p. (J). (— 1). bds. 9.95 *(978-1-60219-091-7(7))* Good Night Bks.

—Good Night Baby Jesus. 2010. (Good Night Our World Ser.). (ENG.). 20p. (J). (gr. -1 — 1). bds. 9.95 *(978-1-60219-049-8(6))* Good Night Bks.

—Good Night Country Store. Jasper, Mark, illus. 2010. (Good Night Our World Ser.). (ENG.). 20p. (J). (gr. k — 1). bds. 9.95 *(978-1-60219-044-3(5))* Good Night Bks.

—Good Night Families. Cooper, Kelly, illus. 2017. (Good Night Our World Ser.). 20p. (J). (— 1). bds. 9.95 *(978-1-60219-465-6(3))* Good Night Bks.

—Good Night Michigan. Rosen, Anne, illus. 2011. (Good Night Our World Ser.). (ENG.). 20p. (J). (gr. k — 1). bds. 9.95 *(978-1-60219-054-2(2))* Good Night Bks.

—Good Night Montana. 2013. (Good Night Our World Ser.). (ENG., Illus.). 20p. (J). (— 1). bds. 9.95 *(978-1-60219-080-1(1))* Good Night Bks.

—Good Night North Pole. Jasper, Mark, illus. 2012. (Good Night Our World Ser.). (ENG.). 20p. (J). (gr. k — 1). bds. 9.95 *(978-1-60219-071-9(2)*, 1350772) Good Night Bks.

—Good Night Ohio. Jasper, Mark, illus. 2013. (Good Night Our World Ser.). (ENG.). 20p. (J). (— 1). bds. 9.95 *(978-1-60219-076-4(3))* Good Night Bks.

—Good Night Texas. Veno, Joe & Kelly, Cooper, illus. 2nd ed. 2011. (Good Night Our World Ser.). (ENG.). 20p. (J). (gr. k — 1). bds. 9.95 *(978-1-60219-053-5(4))* Good Night Bks.

—Good Night World. Kelly, Cooper, illus. 2009. (Good Night Our World Ser.). (ENG.). 28p. (J). (gr. -1-k). bds. 9.95 *(978-1-60219-030-6(5))* Good Night Bks.

Gamble, Adam & Adams, Dave. Good Night Canada. Kelly, Cooper, illus. 2010. (Good Night Our World Ser.). (ENG.). 26p. (J). (gr. k — 1). bds. 9.95 *(978-1-60219-038-2(0))* Good Night Bks.

Gamble, Adam & Jasper, Mark. Buenas Noches, Florida. 2013. (Buenas Noches Ser.). (SPA., Illus.). 20p. (J). (— 1). bds. 9.95 *(978-1-60219-092-4(5))* Good Night Bks.

—Buenas Noches, Texas. 2013. (Buenas Noches Ser.). (SPA., Illus.). 20p. (J). (— 1). bds. 9.95 *(978-1-60219-093-1(3))* Good Night Bks.

—Count to Sleep America. Veno, Joe, illus. 2015. (Count to Sleep Ser.). (ENG.). 20p. (J). (— 1). bds. 9.95 *(978-1-60219-231-7(6))* Good Night Bks.

—Count to Sleep California. Veno, Joe, illus. 2014. (Count to Sleep Ser.). (ENG.). 20p. (J). (— 1). bds. 9.95 *(978-1-60219-200-3(6))* Good Night Bks.

—Count to Sleep Florida. Veno, Joe, illus. 2014. (Count to Sleep Ser.). (ENG.). 20p. (J). (— 1). bds. 9.95 *(978-1-60219-202-7(2))* Good Night Bks.

—Count to Sleep Michigan. Veno, Joe, illus. 2014. (Count to Sleep Ser.). (ENG.). 20p. (J). (— 1). bds. 9.95 *(978-1-60219-327-7(4))* Good Night Bks.

—Count to Sleep Minnesota. Veno, Joe, illus. 2014. (Count to Sleep Ser.). (ENG.). 20p. (J). (— 1). bds. 9.95 *(978-1-60219-205-8(7))* Good Night Bks.

—Count to Sleep Texas. Veno, Joe, illus. 2014. (Count to Sleep Ser.). (ENG.). 20p. (J). (— 1). bds. 9.95 *(978-1-60219-326-0(6))* Good Night Bks.

—Count to Sleep Wisconsin. Veno, Joe, illus. 2014. (Count to Sleep Ser.). (ENG.). 20p. (J). (— 1). bds. 9.95 *(978-1-60219-328-4(2))* Good Night Bks.

—Good Night Aerospace Museum. Leonard, David, illus. 2018. (Good Night Our World Ser.). 20p. (J). (— 1). bds. 9.95 *(978-1-60219-679-7(6))* Good Night Bks.

—Good Night Aruba. Kelly, Cooper & Calo, Marcos, illus. 2017. (Good Night Our World Ser.). 20p. (J). (— 1). bds. 9.95 *(978-1-60219-516-5(1))* Good Night Bks.

—Good Night Baby Animals. Chan, Suwin, illus. 2016. (Good Night Our World Ser.). (ENG.). 20p. (J). (— 1). bds. 9.95 *(978-1-60219-499-1(8))* Good Night Bks.

—Good Night Baby Dragons. Chan, Suwin, illus. 2018. (Good Night Our World Ser.). 20p. (J). (— 1). bds. 9.95 *(978-1-60219-511-0(0))* Good Night Bks.

—Good Night Bears. Blackmore, Katherine, illus. 2018. (Good Night Our World Ser.). 20p. (J). (— 1). bds. 9.95 *(978-1-60219-515-8(3))* Good Night Bks.

—Good Night Boats. Veno, Joe, illus. 2016. (Good Night Our World Ser.). (ENG.). 20p. (J). (— 1). bds. 9.95 *(978-1-60219-500-4(5))* Good Night Bks.

—Good Night Broadway. Veno, Joe, illus. 2017. (Good Night Our World Ser.). 20p. (J). (gr. -1 — 1). bds. 9.95 *(978-1-60219-436-6(X))* Good Night Bks.

—Good Night Brooklyn. 2013. (Good Night Our World Ser.). (ENG., Illus.). 20p. (J). (— 1). bds. 9.95 *(978-1-60219-094-8(1))* Good Night Bks.

—Good Night Campsite. Stevenson, Harvey, illus. 2018. (Good Night Our World Ser.). 20p. (J). (— 1). bds. 9.95 *(978-1-60219-514-1(5))* Good Night Bks.

—Good Night Central Park. Palmer, Ruth, illus. 2013. (Good Night Our World Ser.). (ENG.). 20p. (J). (— 1). bds. 9.95 *(978-1-60219-082-5(8))* Good Night Bks.

—Good Night Children's Museum. Veno, Joe, illus. 2018. (Good Night Our World Ser.). 20p. (J). (— 1). bds. 9.95 *(978-1-60219-578-3(1))* Good Night Bks.

—Good Night Christmas. 2015. (Good Night Our World Ser.). (ENG., Illus.). 20p. (J). (— 1). bds. 9.95 *(978-1-60219-197-6(2))* Good Night Bks.

—Good Night Christmas Tree. Kelly, Cooper, illus. 2017. (Good Night Our World Ser.). 20p. (J). (— 1). bds. 9.95 *(978-1-60219-469-4(6))* Good Night Bks.

—Good Night Daddy. Kelly, Cooper, illus. 2015. (Good Night Our World Ser.). (ENG.). 20p. (J). (— 1). bds. 9.95 *(978-1-60219-229-4(4))* Good Night Bks.

—Good Night Delaware. 2012. (Good Night Our World Ser.). (ENG., Illus.). 20p. (J). (gr. k — 1). bds. 9.95 *(978-1-60219-066-5(6))* Good Night Bks.

—Good Night Dump Truck. Stevenson, Harvey, illus. 2014. (Good Night Our World Ser.). (ENG.). 26p. (J). (— 1). bds. 9.95 *(978-1-60219-189-1(1))* Good Night Bks.

—Good Night Fairies. Holder, Jimmy, illus. 2018. (Good Night Our World Ser.). 20p. (J). (— 1). bds. 9.95 *(978-1-60219-433-5(5))* Good Night Bks.

—Good Night Fire Engines. Veno, Joe, illus. 2015. (Good Night Our World Ser.). (ENG.). 20p. (J). (— 1). bds. 9.95 *(978-1-60219-501-1(3))* Good Night Bks.

—Good Night Fish. Veno, Joe, illus. 2016. (Good Night Our World Ser.). (ENG.). 20p. (J). (— 1). bds. 9.95 *(978-1-60219-502-8(1))* Good Night Bks.

—Good Night Florida. Veno, Joe, illus. 2nd ed. 2010. (Good Night Our World Ser.). (ENG.). 20p. (J). (gr. k — 1). bds. 9.95 *(978-1-60219-045-0(3))* Good Night Bks.

—Good Night Galaxy. Kelly, Cooper, illus. 2012. (Good Night Our World Ser.). (ENG.). 20p. (J). (gr. k — 1). bds. 9.95 *(978-1-60219-065-8(8))* Good Night Bks.

—Good Night Grandma. Stevenson, Harvey, illus. 2016. (ENG.). 20p. (J). (— 1). bds. 9.95 *(978-1-60219-409-0(2))* Good Night Bks.

—Good Night Idaho. Veno, Joe, illus. 2018. (Good Night Our World Ser.). 20p. (J). (— 1). bds. 9.95 *(978-1-60219-410-6(6))* Good Night Bks.

—Good Night Illinois. 2013. (Good Night Our World Ser.). (ENG., Illus.). 20p. (J). (— 1). bds. 9.95 *(978-1-60219-086-3(0))* Good Night Bks.

—Good Night Indiana. 2013. (Good Night Our World Ser.). (ENG., Illus.). 20p. (J). (— 1). bds. 9.95 *(978-1-60219-075-7(5))* Good Night Bks.

—Good Night Iowa. 2013. (Good Night Our World Ser.). (ENG., Illus.). 20p. (J). (— 1). bds. 9.95 *(978-1-60219-085-6(2))* Good Night Bks.

—Good Night Kansas. Veno, Joe, illus. 2017. (Good Night Our World Ser.). 20p. (J). (— 1). bds. 9.95 *(978-1-60219-223-2(5))* Good Night Bks.

—Good Night Little Brother. Kelly, Cooper, illus. 2016. (Good Night Our World Ser.). (ENG.). 20p. (J). (— 1). bds. 9.95 *(978-1-60219-505-9(6))* Good Night Bks.

—Good Night Little Monsters. Kelly, Cooper, illus. 2017. (Good Night Our World Ser.). 20p. (J). (gr. -1 — 1). bds. 9.95 *(978-1-60219-489-2(0))* Good Night Bks.

—Good Night Little Sister. Stevenson, Harvey, illus. 2016. (Good Night Our World Ser.). (ENG.). 20p. (J). (— 1). bds. 9.95 *(978-1-60219-506-6(4))* Good Night Bks.

—Good Night Maryland. Rosen, Anne, illus. 2011. (Good Night Our World Ser.). (ENG.). 20p. (J). (gr. k — 1). bds. 9.95 *(978-1-60219-046-7(1))* Good Night Bks.

—Good Night Massachusetts. 2013. (Good Night Our World Ser.). (ENG., Illus.). 20p. (J). (— 1). bds. 9.95 *(978-1-60219-084-9(4))* Good Night Bks.

—Good Night Mermaids. Chan, Suwin, illus. 2015. (Good Night Our World Ser.). (ENG.). 20p. (J). (— 1). bds. 9.95 *(978-1-60219-226-3(X))* Good Night Bks.

—Good Night Mississippi. Veno, Joe, illus. 2015. (Good Night Our World Ser.). (ENG.). 20p. (J). (— 1). bds. 9.95 *(978-1-60219-221-8(9))* Good Night Bks.

—Good Night Missouri. Veno, Joe, illus. 2013. (Good Night Our World Ser.). (ENG.). 20p. (J). (— 1). bds. 9.95 *(978-1-60219-077-1(1))* Good Night Bks.

—Good Night Mountains. 2013. (Good Night Our World Ser.). (ENG., Illus.). 24p. (J). (— 1). bds. 9.95 *(978-1-60219-090-0(9))* Good Night Bks.

—Good Night Museums. Kelly, Cooper, illus. 2018. (Good Night Our World Ser.). 20p. (J). (— 1). bds. 9.95 *(978-1-60219-576-9(5))* Good Night Bks.

—Good Night Nebraska. 2015. (Good Night Our World Ser.). (ENG., Illus.). 20p. (J). (— 1). bds. 9.95 *(978-1-60219-087-0(9))* Good Night Bks.

—Good Night Nevada. Veno, Joe, illus. 2012. (Good Night Our World Ser.). (ENG.). 20p. (J). (gr. -1 — 1). bds. 9.95 *(978-1-60219-060-3(7))* Good Night Bks.

—Good Night New Mexico. Palmer, Ruth, illus. 2014. (Good Night Our World Ser.). (ENG.). 20p. (J). (— 1). bds. 9.95 *(978-1-60219-088-7(7))* Good Night Bks.

—Good Night New Orleans. Stevenson, Harvey, illus. 2012. (Good Night Our World Ser.). (ENG.). 20p. (J). (gr. k — 1). bds. 9.95 *(978-1-60219-061-0(5))* Good Night Bks.

—Good Night New York State. 2012. (Good Night Our World Ser.). (ENG., Illus.). 20p. (J). (gr. k — 1). bds. 9.95 *(978-1-60219-063-4(1))* Good Night Bks.

—Good Night Outer Banks. Veno, Joe, illus. 2018. (Good Night Our World Ser.). 20p. (J). (— 1). bds. 9.95 *(978-1-60219-604-9(4))* Good Night Bks.

—Good Night Pennsylvania. 2013. (Good Night Our World Ser.). (ENG., Illus.). 20p. (J). (— 1). bds. 9.95 *(978-1-60219-074-0(7))* Good Night Bks.

—Good Night Pirate Ship. Stevenson, Harvey, illus. 2015. (Good Night Our World Ser.). (ENG.). 26p. (J). (— 1). bds. 9.95 *(978-1-60219-217-1(0))* Good Night Bks.

—Good Night Planes. Stevenson, Harvey, illus. 2015. (Good Night Our World Ser.). (ENG.). 26p. (J). (— 1). bds. 9.95 *(978-1-60219-218-8(9))* Good Night Bks.

—Good Night Princesses. Gardner, Louise, illus. 2016. (Good Night Our World Ser.). (ENG.). 20p. (J). (— 1). bds. 9.95 *(978-1-60219-225-6(1))* Good Night Bks.

—Good Night Seashore. Kelly, Cooper, illus. 2019. (Good Night Our World Ser.). 26p. (J). (— 1). bds. 9.95 *(978-1-60219-665-0(6))* Good Night Bks.

—Good Night Snow. 2016. (Good Night Our World Ser.). (ENG., Illus.). 20p. (J). (— 1). bds. 9.95 *(978-1-60219-412-0(2))* Good Night Bks.

—Good Night St Louis. Veno, Joe, illus. 2017. (Good Night Our World Ser.). 20p. (J). (— 1). bds. 9.95 *(978-1-60219-467-0(X))* Good Night Bks.

—Good Night Statue of Liberty. Stevenson, Harvey, illus. 2017. (Good Night Our World Ser.). 20p. (J). (gr. -1 — 1). bds. 9.95 *(978-1-60219-429-8(7))* Good Night Bks.

—Good Night Summer. Blackmore, Katherine, illus. 2017. (Good Night Our World Ser.). 20p. (J). (— 1). bds. 9.95 *(978-1-60219-440-3(8))* Good Night Bks.

—Good Night Toronto. Stevenson, Harvey, illus. 2011. (Good Night Our World Ser.). (ENG.). 20p. (J). (gr. k — 1). bds. 9.95 *(978-1-60219-048-1(8))* Good Night Bks.

—Good Night Washington State. Kelly, Cooper, illus. 2012. (Good Night Our World Ser.). (ENG.). 20p. (J). (gr. -1-k). bds. 9.95 *(978-1-60219-072-6(0))* Good Night Bks.

—Good Night Whales. Stevenson, Harvey, illus. 2016. (Good Night Our World Ser.). (ENG.). 20p. (J). (— 1). bds. 9.95 *(978-1-60219-507-3(2))* Good Night Bks.

—Good Night Wisconsin. Kelly, Cooper, illus. 2012. (Good Night Our World Ser.). (ENG.). 20p. (J). (gr. k — 1). bds. 9.95 *(978-1-60219-064-1(X))* Good Night Bks.

—Good Night Yosemite. Chan, Suwin, illus. 2016. (Good Night Our World Ser.). (ENG.). 20p. (J). (— 1). bds. 9.95 *(978-1-60219-389-5(4))* Good Night Bks.

Gamble, Adam & Mackey, Bill. Good Night Colorado. Rosen, Anne, illus. 2012. (Good Night Our World Ser.). (ENG.). 20p. (J). (gr. k — 1). bds. 9.95 *(978-1-60219-055-9(0))* Good Night Bks.

Gamble, Adam, et al. Good Night Kentucky. 2014. (Good Night Our World Ser.). (ENG., Illus.). 20p. (J). (— 1). bds. 9.95 *(978-1-60219-089-4(5))* Good Night Bks.

—Good Night New Baby. 2014. (Good Night Our World Ser.). (ENG., Illus.). 20p. (J). (— 1). bds. 9.95 *(978-1-60219-188-4(3))* Good Night Bks.

—Good Night South Carolina. 2014. (Good Night Our World Ser.). (ENG.). 20p. (J). (— 1). bds. 9.95 *(978-1-60219-190-7(5))* Good Night Bks.

Ganeri, Anita. My Pop-Up World Atlas. Waterhouse, Stephen, illus. 2012. (ENG.). 16p. (J). (gr. k-3). 24.99 *(978-0-7636-6094-9(9)*, Templar) Candlewick Pr.

—Volcanes y terremotos/Earthquakes & Volcanoes. 2011. 16p. pap. *(978-607-404-319-8(1)*, Silver Dolphin en Español) Advanced Marketing, S. de R. L. de C. V.

Gardiner, Lisa. Things That Work. Flowerpot Press, ed. 2012. (Illus.). 20p. (J). *(978-1-926988-03-0(5))* Flowerpot Children's Pr. Inc.

Gardner, Charlie. Digger. 2009. (Illus.). (J). *(978-1-4654-5513-0(2))* Dorling Kindersley Publishing, Inc.

Gardner, Louise, illus. Five Little Easter Eggs. (ENG.). 10p. (J). 2009. (gr. -1). 5.95 *(978-1-58117-849-4(2))* 2008. 9.95 *(978-1-58117-682-7(1))* Bendon, Inc. (Intervisual/Piggy Toes).

Garland, Michael. Wake up, Tug! 2017. (ENG.). 18p. (J). (gr. -1 — 1). bds. 7.99 *(978-0-8234-3785-6(X))* Holiday Hse., Inc.

Garnett, Jaye. Dig! Cottage Door Press, ed. Cerato, Mattia, illus. 2018. (Peek-A-Flap Ser.). (ENG.). 12p. (J). (gr. -1-1). bds. 9.99 *(978-1-68052-299-0(X)*, 1002770) Cottage Door Pr.

—Zoo. Cottage Door Press, ed. Nowowiejska, Kasia, illus. 2016. (Peek-A-Flap Ser.). (ENG.). 12p. (J). (gr. -1-1). bds. 9.99 *(978-1-68052-126-9(8)*, 1001190) Cottage Door Pr.

Garralon, Claire. Black Cat & White Cat. 2016. (ENG., Illus.). 30p. (J). (gr. -1-k). bds. 7.99 *(978-1-4926-3781-3(5)*, 9781492637813, Sourcebooks Jabberwocky) Sourcebooks, Inc.

Garton, Michael. Countdown by the Sea. 2012. (ENG.). 20p. (J). bds. *(978-1-60727-701-9(8))* Soundprints.

Garton, Sam. I Am Otter Board Book. 2016. (ENG., Illus.). 34p. (J). (gr. -1 — 1). 7.99 *(978-0-06-240908-9(5)*, Balzer & Bray) HarperCollins Pubs.

Gates Galvin, Laura. First Look at Insects. Oh, Charlotte, illus. 2011. (ENG.). 16p. (J). *(978-1-60727-223-6(7))* Soundprints.

Gay, Susana & Gay, Owen. First Christmas. 2018. (ENG., Illus.). 16p. (J). (gr. -1 — 1). bds. 6.99 *(978-0-8249-1679-4(4))* Worthy Publishing.

—First Easter. 2019. (ENG., Illus.). 16p. (J). (gr. -1 — 1). bds. 6.99 *(978-0-8249-1685-5(9)*, Worthy Kids/Ideals) Worthy Publishing.

—In the Beginning. 2017. (ENG., Illus.). 16p. (J). (gr. -1 — 1). bds. 6.99 *(978-0-8249-1992-4(0))* Worthy Publishing.

Géhin, Elisa. One & All. 2016. (ENG., Illus.). 42p. (J). (gr. -1-k). 14.95 *(978-1-4197-1904-2(1)*, 1115403, Abrams Appleseed) Abrams, Inc.

Géhin, Élisa & Duisit, Bernard. Can You Keep a Straight Face? 2017. (Flip Flap Pop-Up Ser.: 0). (ENG., Illus.). 16p. (J). (gr. -1-1). 14.95 *(978-0-500-65091-2(8)*, 565091) Thames & Hudson.

Gehl, Laura. Baby Astronaut. Wiseman, Daniel, illus. 2019. (Baby Scientist Ser.: 2). (ENG.). 22p. (J). (gr. -1 — 1). bds. 8.99 *(978-0-06-284134-6(3)*, HarperFestival) HarperCollins Pubs.

—Baby Oceanographer. Wiseman, Daniel, illus. 2019. (Baby Scientist Ser.: 1). (ENG.). 22p. (J). (gr. -1 — 1). bds. 8.99 *(978-0-06-284133-9(5)*, HarperFestival) HarperCollins Pubs.

Geis, Patricia. Good-bye Pacifier! Folch, Sergio, illus. 2009. (Good Habits with Coco & Tula Ser.). 16p. (J). (gr. -1-k). bds. 11.40 *(978-1-60754-405-0(9))* Windmill Bks.

—Henri Matisse: Meet the Artist. 2014. (Meet the Artist Ser.). (ENG., Illus.). 16p. (J). (gr. 2-7). 24.95 *(978-1-61689-282-1(X))* Princeton Architectural Pr.

—Let's Get Well! Folch, Sergio, illus. 2009. (Good Habits with Coco & Tula Ser.). 16p. (J). (gr. -1-k). bds. 11.40 *(978-1-60754-407-4(5))* Windmill Bks.

—Let's Wash Up! Folch, Sergio, illus. 2009. (Good Habits with Coco & Tula Ser.). 16p. (J). (gr. -1-k). bds. 11.40 *(978-1-60754-410-4(5))* Windmill Bks.

Geller, Amy. My First Words Outside, 1 vol. 2013. (ENG., Illus.). 20p. (J). bds. 6.99 *(978-1-59572-332-1(3))* Star Bright Bks., Inc.

George, Bobby & George, June. Montessori: Number Work. Nassner, Alyssa, illus. 2012. (Montessori Ser.). (ENG.). 24p. (J). (gr. -1-k). bds. 10.99 *(978-1-4197-0412-3(5)*, 1040310) Abrams, Inc.

—Montessori: Shape Work. 2013. (Montessori Ser.). (ENG., Illus.). 18p. (J). (gr. -1-k). bds. 10.99 *(978-1-4197-0935-7(6)*, 1063410, Abrams Appleseed) Abrams, Inc.

George, Joshua. Goodnight Bear. Ovocheva, Zhanna, illus. 2018. (Magic Flashlight Bks.). (ENG.). 10p. (J). bds. 9.99 *(978-1-78700-611-9(5))* Top That! Publishing PLC GBR. Dist: Independent Pubs. Group.

—Goodnight Lion. Ovocheva, Zhanna, illus. 2018. (Magic Flashlight Bks.). (ENG.). 10p. (J). bds. 9.99 *(978-1-78700-612-6(3))* Top That! Publishing PLC GBR. Dist: Independent Pubs. Group.

—I'm Just a Little Ghost. Green, Barry, illus. 2017. (Googley-Eye Bks.). (ENG.). 12p. (J). (gr. -1-k). bds. 7.99 *(978-1-78700-077-3(X))* Top That! Publishing PLC GBR. Dist: Independent Pubs. Group.

—I'm Just a Little Snowman. Green, Barry, illus. 2017. (Googley-Eye Bks.). (ENG.). 12p. (J). (gr. -1-k). bds. 7.99 *(978-1-78700-079-7(6))* Top That! Publishing PLC GBR. Dist: Independent Pubs. Group.

—I'm Santa Claus. Green, Barry, illus. 2017. (Googley-Eye Bks.). (ENG.). 12p. (J). (gr. -1-k). bds. 7.99 *(978-1-78700-078-0(8))* Top That! Publishing PLC GBR. Dist: Independent Pubs. Group.

—In My Little Snowman Bed. Gulliver, Amanda, illus. 2017. (In My Bed Bks.). (ENG.). 24p. (J). (gr. -1-k). bds. 9.99 *(978-1-78700-080-3(X))* Top That! Publishing PLC GBR. Dist: Independent Pubs. Group.

—Magnetic Play Fairies. Ellis, Lauren, illus. 2018. (Magnetic Play Ser.). (ENG.). 12p. (J). (gr. -1-1). 12.99 *(978-1-78700-261-6(6))* Top That! Publishing PLC GBR. Dist: Independent Pubs. Group.

—Tiny Town Hide & Seek Counting. Ribbon, Lemon, illus. 2018. (Tiny Town Hide & Seek Board Bks.). (ENG.). 12p. (J). (-k). bds. 6.99 *(978-1-78700-379-8(5))* Top That! Publishing PLC GBR. Dist: Independent Pubs. Group.

—Tiny Town Hide & Seek Words. Ribbon, Lemon, illus. 2018. (Tiny Town Hide & Seek Board Bks.). (ENG.). 12p. (J). (-k). bds. 6.99 *(978-1-78700-380-4(9))* Top That! Publishing PLC GBR. Dist: Independent Pubs. Group.

—Tiny Town Picnic Fun. Ribbon, Lemon, illus. 2018. (Soft Felt Play Bks.). (ENG.). 10p. (J). (gr. -1-k). bds. 9.99 *(978-1-78700-386-6(8))* Top That! Publishing PLC GBR. Dist: Independent Pubs. Group.

Gershator, Phillis. Who's in the Farmyard? McDonald, Jill, illus. 2012. (ENG.). 13p. (J). (gr. -1-k). bds. 14.99 *(978-1-84686-574-9(3))* Barefoot Bks., Inc.

—Who's in the Garden? McDonald, Jill, illus. 2010. (ENG.). 13p. (J). (gr. -1-k). bds. 14.99 *(978-1-84686-403-2(8))* Barefoot Bks., Inc.

Gershator, Phillis & Green, Mim. Time for a Hug. Walker, David, illus. 2013. (Snuggle Time Stories Ser.: 1). 22p. (J). (gr. -1-k). bds. 7.99 *(978-1-4549-0856-2(4))* Sterling Publishing Co., Inc.

Gerstein, Sherry. Imagination Vacation: A Color-Foil Shapes Book. Bennett, Andy, illus. 2006. 14p. (J). (gr. -1-3). bds. 6.95 *(978-1-57791-261-3(6))* Brighter Minds Children's Publishing.

—Moo, Moo Who Are You? Bennett, Andy, illus. 2006. 14p. (J). (gr. -1-k). bds. 7.95 *(978-1-57791-258-3(6))* Brighter Minds Children's Publishing.

Gerver, Jane E. Who's at Home? A Lift-The-Flap Book. Davis, Kathryn Lynn, illus. 2010. (ENG.). 14p. (J). (gr. -1 — 1). bds. 6.99 *(978-1-4169-9758-0(X)*, Little Simon) Little Simon.

Gevry, Claudine, illus. One Little Penguin & His Friends: A Pushing, Turning, Counting Book. 2012. (ENG.). 10p. (J). bds. *(978-1-84956-027-6(7))* Top That! Publishing PLC.

Gibbons, Gail. Planes. 2019. (Illus.). 24p. (J). (— 1). bds. 7.99 *(978-0-8234-4154-9(7))* Holiday Hse., Inc.

Gibbs Smith. La Catrina: Emotions/Emociones, 1 vol. 2018. (SPA., Illus.). 22p. (J). (gr. -1-k). bds. 9.99 *(978-0-9861099-6-6(7))* Little Libros, LLC.

Gibby, Shauna. Jesus Is Born! A Flashlight Discovery Book. 2018. (Illus.). (J). 16.99 *(978-1-62972-469-0(6))* Deseret Bk. Co.

Gifford, Clive. Robots. 2011. 48p. 11.99 *(978-84-96252-41-7(8))* Edilupa Ediciones, S.L. ESP. Dist: Lectorum Pubns., Inc.

Gifford, Kathie Lee. The Gift That I Can Give for Little Ones, 1 vol. Seal, Julia, illus. 2018. (ENG.). 26p. (J). bds. 9.99 *(978-1-4002-0925-5(0),* Tommy Nelson) Nelson, Thomas Inc.

Giles, Angela & Award, Anna. Patterns. 2017. (Illus.). 10p. (J). bds. 9.00 *(978-1-909763-45-6(4))* Award Pubns. Ltd. GBR. Dist: Parkwest Pubns., Inc.

Gili, Phillida. Cinderella: A Pop-up Book. Gili, Phillida, illus. 2007. (Illus.). 12p. (J). 25.00 *(978-1-4223-9031-3(4))* DIANE Publishing Co.

Gill, Shelley. If I Were a Bird. Brooks, Erik, illus. 2019. (If I Were Ser.). 22p. (J). (— 1). bds. 9.99 *(978-1-63217-211-2(9),* Little Bigfoot) Sasquatch Bks.

Gillingham, Sara. Snuggle the Baby. 2014. (ENG., Illus.). 12p. (J). (gr. -1-17). bds. 12.99 *(978-1-4197-1124-4(5),* 1074401, Abrams Appleseed) Abrams, Inc.

Girard, Alexander. Alexander Girard Color. 2011. (ENG., Illus.). 58p. (J). bds. 14.95 *(978-1-934429-77-8(5))* AMMO Bks., LLC.

Girard, Alexander, illus. Alexander Girard Coloring Book. 2014. (ENG.). 30p. pap. 9.95 *(978-1-934429-86-0(4))* AMMO Bks., LLC.

Girl Friends Super Sticker Book. (Illus.). 64p. (J). pap. *(978-2-7643-0026-8(3))* Phidal Publishing, Inc./Editions Phidal, Inc.

Glaser, Rebecca. Boats Float. 2018. (Amicus Ink Board Bks.). 14p. (J). (gr. -1 — 1). bds. 7.99 *(978-1-68152-243-2(8),* 14941) Amicus.

—Bunnies Hop. 2017. (Amicus Ink Board Bks.). (Illus.). 14p. (J). (gr. -1 — 1). bds. 7.99 *(978-1-68152-199-2(7),* 14730) Amicus.

—Cars Zoom. 2016. (Illus.). 14p. (J). (gr. -1 — 1). bds. 7.99 *(978-1-68152-121-3(0),* 15810) Amicus.

—Dolphins Play. 2016. (ENG., Illus.). 16p. (J). (gr. -1 — 1). bds. 7.99 *(978-1-68152-067-4(2),* 15812) Amicus.

—Ducks Quack. 2016. (Illus.). 14p. (J). (gr. -1 — 1). bds. 7.99 *(978-1-68152-127-5(X),* 15813) Amicus.

—Fire Trucks Rescue. 2018. (Amicus Ink Board Bks.). (ENG.). 14p. (J). (gr. -1 — 1). bds. 7.99 *(978-1-68152-240-1(3),* 14939) Amicus.

—Fish Swim. 2017. (Amicus Ink Board Bks.). (Illus.). 14p. (J). (gr. -1 — 1). bds. 7.99 *(978-1-68152-198-5(9),* 14729) Amicus.

—Giraffes Stretch. 2016. (ENG., Illus.). 16p. (J). (gr. -1 — 1). bds. 7.99 *(978-1-68152-069-8(9),* 15815) Amicus.

—Horses Neigh. 2016. (Amicus Ink Board Bks.). (ENG., Illus.). 14p. (J). (gr. -1-k). bds. 7.99 *(978-1-68152-126-8(1),* 15816) Amicus.

—Kittens Pounce. 2017. (Amicus Ink Board Bks.). (Illus.). 14p. (J). (gr. -1 — 1). bds. 7.99 *(978-1-68152-197-8(0),* 14728) Amicus.

—Lions Roar. 2016. (ENG., Illus.). 16p. (J). (gr. -1 — 1). bds. 7.99 *(978-1-68152-071-1(0),* 15817) Amicus.

—Penguins Waddle. 2016. (ENG., Illus.). 16p. (J). (gr. -1 — 1). bds. 7.99 *(978-1-68152-070-4(2),* 15819) Amicus.

—Pigs Oink. 2016. (Illus.). 14p. (J). (gr. -1 — 1). bds. 7.99 *(978-1-68152-128-2(8),* 15820) Amicus.

—Planes Soar. 2016. (ENG., Illus.). 14p. (J). (gr. -1 — 1). bds. 7.99 *(978-1-68152-122-0(9),* 15821) Amicus.

—Puppies Chase. 2017. (Amicus Ink Board Bks.). (Illus.). 14p. (J). (gr. -1 — 1). bds. 7.99 *(978-1-68152-196-1(2),* 14727) Amicus.

—Tractors Pull. 2016. (ENG., Illus.). 14p. (J). (gr. -1 — 1). bds. 7.99 *(978-1-68152-123-7(7),* 15822) Amicus.

—Trucks Haul. 2016. (ENG., Illus.). 14p. (J). (gr. -1 — 1). bds. 7.99 *(978-1-68152-124-4(5),* 15823) Amicus.

Gliori, Debi. No Matter What Lap Board Book. Gliori, Debi, illus. 2012. (ENG., Illus.). 24p. (J). (gr. -1 — 1). bds. 12.99 *(978-0-547-71905-4(1),* 1481812, Clarion Bks.) HarperCollins Pubs.

Glow in the Dark Advent Sticker Book. (Illus.). 16p. (J). (gr. -1-5). 6.99 *(978-0-8254-7233-6(4))* Kregel Pubns.

Godwin, Laura. This First Christmas Night. Szabla, Liz, ed. Low, William, illus. 2017. (ENG.). 22p. (J). bds. 7.99 *(978-1-250-12793-8(9),* 900175582) Feiwel & Friends.

Going Shopping! Sticker Book. (Girlfriend Gang Ser.). 16p. (J). *(978-2-7643-0020-6(4))* Phidal Publishing, Inc./Editions Phidal, Inc.

Goldberg, Ella, ed. Farm Life. 2013. (Matching Pictures Ser.). (ENG.). 20p. (J). (gr. -1-k). bds. 5.95 *(978-1-61889-309-3(2))* AZ Bks. LLC.

—Simple Shapes. 2013. (Matching Pictures Ser.). (ENG.). 20p. (J). (gr. -1-k). bds. 5.95 *(978-1-61889-311-6(4))* AZ Bks. LLC.

Goldberg, Malky. What Else Do I Say? A Lift the Flap Book. Argoff, Patti, illus. 2007. (ENG.). (J). (gr. -1-k). bds. 11.99 *(978-1-929628-34-6(X))* Hachai Publishing.

Golden Books. The Little Red Hen. Miller, J. P., illus. 2015. 26p. (J). (-k). bds. 7.99 *(978-0-385-39094-1(7),* Golden Bks.) Random Hse. Children's Bks.

—Pat the Zoo (Pat the Bunny) LV Studio, illus. 2012. (Touch-And-Feel Ser.). 16p. (J). (gr. k — 1). spiral bd. 14.99 *(978-0-307-97797-7(8),* Golden Bks.) Random Hse. Children's Bks.

—Trains, Cranes & Troublesome Trucks (Thomas & Friends) 2015. (Big Bright & Early Board Book Ser.). (ENG., Illus.). 24p. (J). (— 1). bds. 7.99 *(978-0-385-37393-7(7),* Random Hse. Bks. for Young Readers) Random Hse. Children's Bks.

The Golden Key. 2013. (Illus.). (J). *(978-1-4351-4948-9(3))* Disney Pr.

Golding, Elizabeth. Moonlight Animals. Lodge, Ali, illus. 2011. (ENG.). 12p. (J). (gr. -1-3). 14.99 *(978-0-7624-4316-1(2),* Running Pr. Kids) Running Pr.

—Moonlight Ocean. Lodge, Ali, illus. 2012. (ENG.). 12p. (J). (gr. -1-3). 14.99 *(978-0-7624-4486-1(X),* Running Pr. Kids) Running Pr.

Goldsack, Gaby. Fairies Die Cut. (Die-Cut Kids Ser.). 10p. bds. *(978-1-4054-6966-1(8))* Parragon, Inc.

—Fishing Boat. Lawson, Peter, illus. 2009. (Turn the Wheel Ser.). (ENG.). 10p. (J). (gr. -1-k). bds. 5.95 *(978-0-7892-1025-8(8),* Abbeville Kids) Abbeville Pr., Inc.

Goldsmith, Mike. Dinosaurs. Abbott, Simon, illus. 2011. (Flip Flap Science Ser.). (ENG.). 10p. (J). (gr. -1-k). 9.95 *(978-1-84898-365-6(4),* TickTock Books) Octopus Publishing Group GBR. Dist: Independent Pubs. Group.

—Space Adventure. Abbott, Simon, illus. 2011. (Flip Flap Science Ser.). (ENG.). 10p. (J). (gr. -1-k). 9.95 *(978-1-84898-364-9(6),* TickTock Books) Octopus Publishing Group GBR. Dist: Independent Pubs. Group.

Gomi, Taro. Little Truck: (Transportation Books for Toddlers, Board Book for Toddlers) 2018. (Taro Gomi by Chronicle Bks.). (ENG., Illus.). 22p. (J). (gr. -1 — 1). bds. 6.99 *(978-1-4521-6300-0(6))* Chronicle Bks. LLC.

—Peekaboo! 2013. (ENG., Illus.). 16p. (J). (gr. -1 — 1). bds. 7.99 *(978-1-4521-0835-3(8))* Chronicle Bks. LLC.

—Wiggle! 2013. (ENG., Illus.). 16p. (J). (gr. -1 — 1). bds. 6.99 *(978-1-4521-0836-0(6))* Chronicle Bks. LLC.

Gompper, Gail. Every Day by the Bay. Gompper, Gail, illus. 2011. (ENG., Illus.). 24p. (J). bds. 9.95 *(978-0-9726487-7-6(1))* Puddle Jump Pr., Ltd.

Gondek, Heather. Who's in the Jungle? Lift-the-Flap 'n' Learn. Gilvan-Cartwright, Chris, illus. 2005. (Fun with Animals Ser.). 10p. (J). 9.95 *(978-1-58117-075-7(0),* Intervisual/Piggy Toes) Bendon, Inc.

Gondek, Heather J. Who's on the Farm? Lift-the-Flap 'n' Learn Book. Gilvan-Cartwright, Chris, illus. 2005. (Fun with Animals Ser.). 10p. (J). (gr. -1-k). act. bk. ed. 9.95 *(978-1-58117-143-3(9),* Intervisual/Piggy Toes) Bendon, Inc.

Good Night, Little Love, 1 vol. 2015. (ENG., Illus.). 24p. (J). bds. 8.99 *(978-0-7180-3467-2(8),* Tommy Nelson) Nelson, Thomas Inc.

Goodreau, Sarah. The World-Famous Book of Counting. Goodreau, Sarah, illus. 2018. (ENG., Illus.). 16p. (J). (gr. -1-2). bds. 18.99 *(978-0-7636-9894-2(6),* Big Picture Press) Candlewick Pr.

Gordon, Gordon Coyle. Do Princesses Wear Hiking Boots? 2016. (Do Princesses Ser.). (Illus.). 32p. (J). (gr. -1-1). bds. 7.95 *(978-1-63076-164-6(8))* Taylor Trade Publishing.

Gore, Leonid. Mommy, Where Are You? Gore, Leonid, illus. 2009. (ENG., Illus.). 32p. (J). (gr. -1-2). 18.99 *(978-1-4169-5505-4(4),* Atheneum Bks. for Young Readers) Simon & Schuster Children's Publishing.

Gormley, Greg. Daddy's Day at Work. 2007. (Fantastic Phones Ser.). (Illus.). 12p. (J). (gr. k-k). bds. 9.99 *(978-0-7475-8378-3(1))* Bloomsbury Publishing Plc GBR. Dist: Independent Pubs. Group.

Gosling, Cherie & Disney Storybook Artists Staff. Mulan Is Loyal: Merida Is Brave. 2017. (Illus.). 24p. (J). *(978-1-5379-5745-6(7))* Random Hse., Inc.

Gowan, Barbara. Little Arizona. Urban, Helle, illus. 2012. (Little State Ser.). (ENG.). 20p. (J). (gr. -1-1). bds. 9.95 *(978-1-58536-208-0(5),* 202274) Sleeping Bear Pr.

Gozansky, Shana. My Art Book of Sleep. 2019. (ENG., Illus.). 48p. (gr. -1 — 1). bds. 18.95 *(978-0-7148-7865-2(0))* Phaidon Pr., Inc.

Graham, Oakley. Tiny Town What Did Busy Bunny Hear? Ribbon, Lemon, illus. 2018. (Tiny Town Touch & Trace Ser.). (ENG.). 10p. (J). (— 1). bds. 7.99 *(978-1-78700-378-1(7))* Top That! Publishing PLC GBR. Dist: Independent Pubs. Group.

—A Visit from Santa. Gulliver, Amanda, illus. 2017. (In My Bed Bks.). (ENG.). 24p. (J). (gr. -1-k). bds. 9.99 *(978-1-78700-081-0(8))* Top That! Publishing PLC GBR. Dist: Independent Pubs. Group.

Grandgirard, Mélanie. Mary's Story. 2017. (ENG., Illus.). 20p. (J). (gr. -1 — 1). bds. 14.99 *(978-1-61261-916-3(9))* Paraclete Pr., Inc.

Grange, Emma. DK Braille: LEGO DUPLO: Farm. 2018. (DK Braille Bks.). (ENG.). 18p. (J). (-k). bds. 15.99 *(978-1-4654-6855-0(2),* DK Children) Dorling Kindersley Publishing, Inc.

Grant, Callie. Jesus Shows Me: Knowing My God Series. Jay, Missi, illus. 2013. (Knowing My God Ser.). (ENG.). 18p. (J). bds. 8.99 *(978-0-9854090-3-6(7))* Blanchard, Graham.

—Mud Puddle Hunting Day. Magee, Melanie, illus. 2013. (ENG.). 20p. (J). bds. 8.99 *(978-0-9854090-0-5(2))* Blanchard, Graham.

Graper, Helen, illus. Bingo. 2016. (J). *(978-1-62885-144-1(9))* Kidsbooks, LLC.

Graux, Amélie. I Love to Eat: Deluxe Touch-And-Feel. Graux, Amélie, illus. deluxe ed. 2012. (ENG., Illus.). 12p. (J). (gr. k — 1). bds. 9.99 *(978-0-547-84842-6(0),* 1500671, Clarion Bks.) HarperCollins Pubs.

—I Love to Sleep: Deluxe Touch-And-Feel. Graux, Amélie, illus. deluxe ed. 2012. (ENG., Illus.). 12p. (J). (gr. k — 1). bds. 9.99 *(978-0-547-84843-3(9),* 1500672, Clarion Bks.) HarperCollins Pubs.

Gravett, Emily. Little Mouse's Big Book of Fears. Gravett, Emily, illus. 2008. (ENG., Illus.). 32p. (J). (gr. -1-3). 24.99 *(978-1-4169-5930-4(0),* Simon & Schuster Bks. For Young Readers) Simon & Schuster Bks. For Young Readers.

—Meerkat Mail. Gravett, Emily, illus. 2007. (ENG., Illus.). 32p. (J). (gr. -1-3). 19.99 *(978-1-4169-3473-8(1),* Simon & Schuster Bks. For Young Readers) Simon & Schuster Bks. For Young Readers.

—The Rabbit Problem. Gravett, Emily, illus. 2010. (ENG., Illus.). 32p. (J). (gr. -1-3). 24.99 *(978-1-4424-1255-2(0),* Simon & Schuster Bks. For Young Readers) Simon & Schuster Bks. For Young Readers.

Gray, Amy & Holland, Lucy E. Myths, Angels, & Masquerades: Exploring European Art. 2017. (ENG., Illus.). 104p. (J). (gr. -1-12). 18.95 *(978-0-692-39101-3(0))* Marquand Bks., Inc.

Gray Smith, Monique. My Heart Fills with Happiness, 1 vol. Flett, Julie, illus. 2016. (ENG.). 24p. (J). (gr. -1 — 1). bds. 12.95 *(978-1-4598-0957-4(2))* Orca Bk. Pubs. USA.

Green, John. Horses Tattoos. 2003. (Dover Tattoos Ser.). (ENG., Illus.). 2p. (J). (gr. 1-4). pap. 2.50 *(978-0-486-43029-4(4),* 430294) Dover Pubns., Inc.

Green, John, illus. Who Lives on the Farm? 2004. (Who Lives... Ser.). 12p. (J). bds. 4.99 *(978-1-85854-647-6(8))* Brimax Books Ltd. GBR. Dist: Byeway Bks.

Greene, Melanie W., et al. Goodnight, Boone. Marlowe, Susan B., illus. 2012. (J). *(978-1-933251-80-6(8))* Parkway Pubs., Inc.

Greene, Rhonda Gowler. Push! Dig! Scoop! A Construction Counting Rhyme. Kirk, Daniel, illus. 2017. (ENG.). 26p. (J). bds. 7.99 *(978-1-68119-085-3(0),* 900158430, Bloomsbury USA Childrens) Bloomsbury Publishing USA.

Greene, Sefton. Space Painters. 2003. 18p. bds. *(978-1-904502-30-2(X))* MediaWorld/BestBooks.

Greening, Rosie. Touch & Sparkle: Farm Animals. 2016. (ENG.). 12p. (J). (gr. -1 — 1). bds. 6.99 *(978-1-78598-133-3(1))* Make Believe Ideas GBR. Dist: Scholastic, Inc.

—Touch & Sparkle: Pets. 2016. (ENG.). 12p. (J). (gr. -1 — 1). bds. 6.99 *(978-1-78598-131-9(5))* Make Believe Ideas GBR. Dist: Scholastic, Inc.

Greenway, Bethany. Waikiki Lullaby. America, illus. 2009. (ENG.). 20p. (J). (gr. -1-1). bds. 7.95 *(978-1-933067-30-8(6))* Beachhouse Publishing, LLC.

Greenwell, Jessica. First Colors Sticker Book. 2015. (Get Ready for School Sticker Bks.). (ENG.). 24+8p. (J). pap. 7.99 *(978-0-7945-3600-8(X),* Usborne) EDC Publishing.

—First Sticker Book Easter. 2012. (First Sticker Bks). 16p. (J). pap. 8.99 *(978-0-7945-3266-6(7),* Usborne) EDC Publishing.

—Noisy Body Book. 2012. (Noisy Bks). 10p. (J). ring bd. 18.99 *(978-0-7945-3133-1(4),* Usborne) EDC Publishing.

—This Is My Car. 2009. (Touchy-Feely Board Bks). 10p. (J). bds. 16.99 *(978-0-7945-2545-3(8),* Usborne) EDC Publishing.

—This Is My Digger. 2009. (Noisy Touchy-Feely Board Bks). 10p. (J). bds. 16.99 *(978-0-7945-2520-0(2),* Usborne) EDC Publishing.

Greenwell, Jessical. Farm Animals Lift & Look. 2010. (Lift & Look Board Bks). 12p. (J). bds. 9.99 *(978-0-7945-2612-2(8),* Usborne) EDC Publishing.

Gregory, Lorraine NAR NEEDED. One, Two, Tie Your Shoes! Carlson, Nancy Gayle, illus. 2010. (J). *(978-0-545-26482-2(0))* Scholastic, Inc.

Gresham, Jennifer. Backyard Animals. 2013. (Illus.). (J). *(978-1-58865-838-8(4))* Kidsbooks, LLC.

—Jungle Animals. 2013. (Illus.). (J). *(978-1-58865-832-6(5))* Kidsbooks, LLC.

—Sea Creatures. 2013. (Illus.). (J). *(978-1-58865-831-9(7))* Kidsbooks, LLC.

Griffiths, Neil. Who'd Be a Fly? Nash, Doug, illus. 2015. (ENG.). 24p. (J). pap. 9.99 *(978-0-9545353-5-3(9),* Red Robin Bks.) Corner To Learn Ltd. GBR. Dist: Parkwest Pubns., Inc.

Grimes, Nikki. Welcome, Precious. Collier, Bryan, illus. 2008. (ENG.). 28p. (J). (gr. -1 — 1). bds. 6.99 *(978-0-545-04635-0(1))* Scholastic, Inc.

Grimm, Jacob & Grimm, Wilhelm. Little Red Riding Hood. 2014. (ENG., Illus.). 28p. (J). (gr. -1-3). 16.95 *(978-3-89955-723-7(9))* Die Gestalten Verlag DEU. Dist: Ingram Publisher Services.

Grindley, Sally. Shhh! 2008. (ENG.). 32p. (J). (gr. -1-3). 16.95 *(978-1-933718-19-4(6))* Tanglewood Pr.

Grobarek, Erin Rose. Old MacDonald's Farm Me Reader Jr Electronic Reader & 8-Book Library Sound Book Set: Me Reader Jr: Electronic Reader & 8-Book Library. Seatter, Pamela & Hodges, Angie, illus. 2015. (ENG.). 80p. (J). bds., bds., bds. 34.99 *(978-1-4508-9401-2(1),* 1718, PI Kids) Phoenix International Publications, Inc.

Grogan, John. Marley Looks for Love. Cowdrey, Richard, illus. 2010. (Marley Ser.). (ENG.). 16p. (J). (gr. -1-1). 6.99 *(978-0-06-185590-0(1),* HarperFestival) HarperCollins Pubs.

Gross, Sandra & Busch, Leah. Toast to Counting: Toast to Baby. Hutton, John, ed. 2012. (Toast to Baby Ser.). (ENG., Illus.). 14p. (J). (— 1). bds. 7.99 *(978-1-936669-09-7(9))* Blue Manatee Press.

Grossblatt, Ben. Keep Out! Door Alarm: Build Your Own Key-Card Security System! 2004. (Illus.). 24p. (J). *(978-0-439-66835-4(2))* Scholastic, Inc.

Grosset and Dunlap Staff & Penguin Young Readers Group Staff. Ruby Scores a Goal. 2009. (All Aboard Reading: Station Stop 1 Ser.). (ENG.). 32p. (J). (gr. -1-1). 16.19 *(978-0-448-45235-7(9))* Penguin Young Readers Group.

Grover, Lorie Ann. Bright Night, 1 vol. Parry, Jo, illus. 2017. (ENG.). 16p. (J). bds. 8.99 *(978-0-310-75736-8(3))* Zonderkidz.

Gruelle, Deb. Ten Little Night Stars, 1 vol. Murphy, Gabi, illus. 2018. (ENG.). 22p. (J). bds. 9.99 *(978-0-310-76212-6(X))* Zonderkidz.

Gruelle, Johnny. Raggedy Ann & Andy & the Camel with the Wrinkled Knees. collector's ed. 2003. (Raggedy Ann Ser.). (ENG., Illus.). 14p. (J). (gr. -1-2). 34.99 *(978-0-689-85775-1(6),* Little Simon) Little Simon.

Guess Who? Christmas: A Flip-The-Flap Book. 2014. (ENG., Illus.). 6p. (J). (— 1). bds. 9.99 *(978-0-7459-6408-9(7),* 6d672ab0-8922-4179-915d-ddd3f66f0cfd, Lion Children's) Lion Hudson PLC GBR. Dist: Baker & Taylor Publisher Services (BTPS).

Guest, Elissa Haden. Who's My Cupcake? Fedotova, Marina, illus. 2011. (ENG.). 16p. (J). (gr. -1 — 1). bds. 6.99 *(978-1-4424-2051-9(0),* Little Simon) Little Simon.

Guettier, Bénédicte. At the Circus. 2011. (Funny Faces Ser.). (Illus.). 14p. bds. *(978-1-84089-678-7(7))* Zero to Ten, Ltd.

—Dinosaur Dinners. 2011. (Funny Faces Ser.). (Illus.). 14p. bds. *(978-1-84089-677-0(9))* Zero to Ten, Ltd.

—In the Jungle. 2010. (Funny Faces Ser.). (Illus.). 14p. bds. *(978-1-84089-645-9(0))* Zero to Ten, Ltd.

—On the Farm. 2010. (Funny Faces Ser.). (Illus.). 14p. bds. *(978-1-84089-646-6(9))* Zero to Ten, Ltd.

Guicciardini, Desideria & McNicholas, Shelagh, illus. Hop, Skip & Jump. 2008. (Usborne Baby Board Bks.). 8p. (J). (gr. -1). bds. 15.99 incl. audio compact disk *(978-0-7945-1914-8(8),* Usborne) EDC Publishing.

Guile, Gill, illus. Bear Picks a Pumpkin, 1 vol. 2018. (ENG.). 24p. (J). bds. 8.99 *(978-0-310-76621-6(4))* Zonderkidz.

Gulbis, Stephen, illus. Old MacDonald Had a Barn. 2003. 22p. (YA). *(978-1-85602-453-2(9),* Pavilion Children's Books) Pavilion Bks.

Gunzi, Christane. My Favourite Things. 2013. (Illus.). 6p. (J). bds. 7.95 *(978-1-907604-37-9(5))* Award Pubns. Ltd. GBR. Dist: Parkwest Pubns., Inc.

—My Lovely Day. 2013. (Illus.). 6p. (J). bds. 7.95 *(978-1-907604-36-2(7))* Award Pubns. Ltd. GBR. Dist: Parkwest Pubns., Inc.

Gunzi, Christiane. Colours. 2015. (Illus.). 6p. (J). bds. 7.99 *(978-1-907604-95-9(2))* Award Pubns. Ltd. GBR. Dist: Parkwest Pubns., Inc.

—Little Ponies: A Feels Real Book to Touch & Share. 2015. (ENG., Illus.). 8p. (J). bds. 9.99 *(978-1-909763-10-4(1))* Award Pubns. Ltd. GBR. Dist: Parkwest Pubns., Inc.

—Numbers. 2015. (Illus.). 6p. (J). bds. 7.99 *(978-1-907604-94-2(4))* Award Pubns. Ltd. GBR. Dist: Parkwest Pubns., Inc.

—On the Farm. 2015. (ENG., Illus.). 8p. (J). bds. 9.99 *(978-1-909763-09-8(8))* Award Pubns. Ltd. GBR. Dist: Parkwest Pubns., Inc.

Gunzi, Christiane & Award, Anna. Cuddly Puppies. 2017. (ENG., Illus.). 8p. (J). bds. 9.00 *(978-1-909763-07-4(1))* Award Pubns. Ltd. GBR. Dist: Parkwest Pubns., Inc.

—Farm Babies: A Teach Your Toddler Tab Book. 2017. (Illus.). 8p. (J). bds. 8.00 *(978-1-907604-96-6(0))* Award Pubns. Ltd. GBR. Dist: Parkwest Pubns., Inc.

—Furry Kittens. 2017. (ENG., Illus.). 8p. (J). bds. 9.00 *(978-1-909763-08-1(X))* Award Pubns. Ltd. GBR. Dist: Parkwest Pubns., Inc.

Guttiere, Benedicte. When Christmas Comes. 2011. (Funny Faces Ser.). (Illus.). 14p. bds. *(978-1-84089-710-4(4))* Zero to Ten, Ltd.

Guy, Ginger Foglesong. Siesta Board Book: Bilingual English-Spanish. Moreno, Rene King, illus. 2009. (ENG.). 34p. (J). (gr. -1 — 1). bds. 7.99 *(978-0-06-168884-3(3))* HarperCollins Español.

Gynux. Jesus Loves Me, 1 vol. 2017. (Sing-Along Book Ser.). (ENG., Illus.). 20p. (J). bds. 8.99 *(978-0-310-75894-5(7))* Zonderkidz.

H & T Imaginations Unlimited, Inc. Kid's Sand Box Fun with Professor Woodpecker: Good Old Fashion Wholesome Fun Children's Story. 2008. 12p. pap. 8.49 *(978-1-4389-1116-8(5))* AuthorHouse.

Hächler, Bruno. I Am Who I Am. Wolfermann, Iris, illus. 2010. (ENG.). 16p. (J). (gr. -1-k). bds. 8.95 *(978-0-7358-2299-3(9))* North-South Bks., Inc.

Hacohen, Dean. Tuck Me In! Scharschmidt, Sherry, illus. 2010. (ENG.). 40p. (J). (gr. -1 — 1). 14.99 *(978-0-7636-4728-5(4))* Candlewick Pr.

Hacohen, Dean & Scharschmidt, Sherry. Tuck Me In! 2010. (Illus.). (J). *(978-0-7636-5363-7(2))* Candlewick Pr.

Hahn, Blair. My Purple Kisses. Nation, Tate, illus. 2011. (My Purple Toes Ser.). 26p. (J). bds. 10.99 *(978-0-9844556-7-6(1))* My Purple Toes, LLC.

Haji, Hanifa. Get a Grip on Life: What Every Teen Must Know to Have a Great Life. 2004. 240p. (YA). per. 14.00 *(978-0-9748994-0-4(2))* Youth Quest Institute.

Hale, Kate. Little Massachusetts. Brett, Jeannie, illus. 2016. (Little State Ser.). (ENG.). 20p. (J). (gr. -1-k). bds. 9.95 *(978-1-58536-949-2(7),* 204035) Sleeping Bear Pr.

Hale, Ohara. Who Did It? Boxed Set Containing Who Sneezed? Who Burped? Who Farted? Who Peed? Who Pooped?, 5 vols. 2014. (ENG., Illus.). 50p. (J). (-k). bds. 14.95 *(978-1-57687-681-7(0),* powerHouse Bks.) powerHse. Bks.

Hall, Hannah. God Bless My Boo Boo, 1 vol. 2015. (God Bless Book Ser.). (ENG., Illus.). 20p. (J). bds. 9.99 *(978-0-7180-3051-3(6),* Tommy Nelson) Nelson, Thomas Inc.

—God Bless Our Bedtime Prayers, 1 vol. Whitlow, Steve, illus. 2018. (God Bless Book Ser.). (ENG.). 20p. (J). bds. 9.99 *(978-0-7180-9639-7(8),* Tommy Nelson) Nelson, Thomas Inc.

—God Bless You & Good Night Touch & Feel, 1 vol. Whitlow, Steve, illus. 2018. (God Bless Book Ser.). (ENG.). 18p. (J). bds. 12.99 *(978-1-4002-0923-1(4),* Tommy Nelson) Nelson, Thomas Inc.

Hall, Hannah C. Daddy Snuggles. Szmidt, Aleksandra, illus. 2019. (ENG.). 20p. (J). (gr. -1-k). bds. 7.99 *(978-0-8249-5696-7(6))* Worthy Publishing.

—God Bless Our Fall, 1 vol. Whitlow, Steve, illus. 2015. (God Bless Book Ser.). (ENG.). 20p. (J). bds. 9.99 *(978-0-529-12333-6(9),* Tommy Nelson) Nelson, Thomas Inc.

—God Made the World. 2019. (Buck Denver Asks... What's in the Bible? Ser.). (ENG., Illus.). 24p. (J). (gr. -1 — 1). bds. 8.99 *(978-1-5460-1197-2(8),* Jelly Telly Pr.) FaithWords.

—Mommy Cuddles. Szmidt, Aleksandra, illus. 2019. (ENG.). 20p. (J). (gr. -1-k). bds. 7.99 *(978-0-8249-5695-0(8))* Worthy Publishing.

—Star Bright, Christmas Night. Jatkowska, Ag, illus. 2017. (ENG.). 20p. (J). (gr. -1-k). bds. 7.99 *(978-0-8249-1658-9(1))* Worthy Publishing.

Hall, Michael. It's an Orange Aardvark! Hall, Michael, illus. 2014. (ENG., Illus.). 40p. (J). (gr. -1-3). 17.99 *(978-0-06-225206-7(2),* Greenwillow Bks.) HarperCollins Pubs.

Hall, Nancy. Let's Play Basketball. 2018. (Let's Play Ser.). (ENG., Illus.). 16p. (J). (gr. -1). bds. 9.99 *(978-1-5344-3137-9(3),* Little Simon) Little Simon.

Hall, Pamela. ELEMENOPEE, the Day I, M, N, O & P Left the Abc's. Williamson, James, illus. 2005. 16p. (J). 12.95 *(978-1-58117-209-6(5),* Intervisual/Piggy Toes) Bendon, Inc.

Hallinan, P. K. How Do I Love You? 2018. (ENG., Illus.). 22p. (J). (gr. -1-k). bds. 7.99 *(978-0-8249-1682-4(4))* Worthy Publishing.

—A Rainbow of Friends. 2018. (ENG., Illus.). 22p. (J). (gr. -1-k). bds. 7.99 *(978-0-8249-1672-5(7))* Worthy Publishing.

—Sisters Forever. 2014. (ENG., Illus.). 22p. (J). bds. 7.99 *(978-0-8249-1921-4(1),* Ideals Pubns.) Worthy Publishing.

—That's What a Friend Is! 2016. (ENG., Illus.). 22p. (J). bds. 7.99 *(978-0-8249-1969-6(6),* Ideals Pubns.) Worthy Publishing.

Hamilton, Kersten. Blue Boat. Petrone, Valeria, illus. 2016. (Red Truck & Friends Ser.). (ENG.). 30p. (J). (— 1). bds. 8.99 *(978-1-101-99853-3(9),* Viking Books for Young Readers) Penguin Young Readers Group.

Hanna, Virginie. The Secret Life of Princesses. Delanssay, Cathy, illus. 2009. 26p. (J). (gr. -1-3). 17.99 *(978-0-8437-1476-0(X))* Hammond World Atlas Corp.

Hannigan, Paula. Hugs for You. Brown, Heather, illus. 2012. (J). (-k). (ENG.). 10p. bds. 7.99 *(978-1-4494-2192-2(X));* *(978-1-4351-5022-5(8))* Andrews McMeel Publishing.

—Music Star. Slade, Christian, illus. 2011. (ENG.). 16p. (J). (gr. -1-3). 14.99 *(978-1-4494-0173-3(2))* Andrews McMeel Publishing.

—Under Construction. Brown, Heather, illus. 2013. (ENG.). 18p. (J). bds. 5.99 *(978-1-4494-3556-1(4))* Andrews McMeel Publishing.

Hannigan, Paula & Kirkova, Milena. When I'm Big: A Silly Slider Book. 2010. (ENG.). 12p. (J). (gr. -1-1). bds. 14.99 *(978-0-7407-9727-9(1))* Andrews McMeel Publishing.

Hansel, Karen & Ham, Ken. Charlie & Trike in the Grand Canyon Adventure. 2010. (ENG., Illus.). 23p. (J). 15.99 *(978-0-89051-569-3(7)*, Master Books) New Leaf Publishing Group.

Hanson, P. H. My Mommy's Tote. 2013. (ENG.). 16p. (J). (gr. -1-1). 19.99 *(978-0-7611-7740-1(X)*, 17740) Workman Publishing Co., Inc.

Hanton, Sophie. Colors by the Sea. 2009. (Mag-NUT-Tics! Ser.). (Illus.). (J). bds. 9.99 *(978-1-934650-73-8(0))* Just For Kids Pr., LLC.

Hapka, Catherine, pseud. Clue by Clue. 2019. (Carmen Sandiego Ser.). (ENG., Illus.). 144p. (J). (gr. 5-7). 12.99 *(978-1-328-55308-9(6)*, 1725090, Clarion Bks.) HarperCollins Pubs.

Hapka, Cathy, pseud. Dancing. 2006. (Illus.). (J). *(978-1-57151-775-3(8))* Playhouse Publishing.

—Pretend & Play Kitty: With Real Crown You Can Wear! Borlasca, Hector, illus. 2004. (Role Play Ser.). 10p. (J). (gr. -1-18). bds. 6.99 *(978-1-57151-742-5(1))* Playhouse Publishing.

Happy Halloween, Curious George Tabbed Board Book. 2008. (Curious George Ser.). (ENG., Illus.). 14p. (J). (gr. -1 — 1). bds. 7.99 *(978-0-618-91952-9(X)*, 1015625, Clarion Bks.) HarperCollins Pubs.

Happy St. Patrick's Day, Curious George: Tabbed Board Book. 2014. (Curious George Ser.). (ENG., Illus.). 14p. (J). (— 1). bds. 7.99 *(978-0-544-08888-7(3)*, 1537662, Clarion Bks.) HarperCollins Pubs.

Happy Valentine's Day Curious George. 2011. (Curious George Ser.). (ENG., Illus.). 14p. (J). (gr. -1-3). 8.99 *(978-0-547-13107-8(0)*, 1048361, Clarion Bks.) HarperCollins Pubs.

Harbo, Christopher. Humpty Dumpty Flip-Side Rhymes. Chatzikonstantinou, Danny, illus. 2015. (Flip-Side Nursery Rhymes Ser.). (ENG.). 24p. (J). (gr. -1-2). lib. bdg. 27.99 *(978-1-4795-5986-2(5)*, 127227, Picture Window Bks.) Capstone.

Hargreaves, Roger. Little Miss Giggles. 2011. (Mr. Men & Little Miss Ser.). (ENG.). 32p. (J). (gr. -1-2). mass mkt. 5.99 *(978-0-8431-9890-4(7)*, Price Stern Sloan) Penguin Young Readers Group.

Harper, Charise Mericle. Go! Go! Go! Stop! 2015. (ENG.). 32p. (J). (-k). bds. 7.99 *(978-0-553-53391-0(6)*, Knopf Bks. for Young Readers) Random Hse. Children's Bks.

Harper, Charley. Charley Harper ABCs: Chunky Edition. 2008. (ENG., Illus.). 62p. (J). (gr. -1-3). bds. 14.95 *(978-1-934429-07-5(4))* AMMO Bks., LLC.

—123's. Harper, Charley, illus. 2008. (ENG., Illus.). 20p. (J). (gr. -1-3). bds. 9.95 *(978-1-934429-22-8(8))* AMMO Bks., LLC.

Harrast, Tracy. My Giant Fold-Out Book: Christmas. Doherty, Paula, illus. 2008. 10p. (J). (gr. -1). bds. 13.49 *(978-0-7586-1425-4(X))* Concordia Publishing Hse.

Harris, Jim & Harris, Marian. Ten Little Kittens Board Book: An Eyeball Animation Book. 2011. (ENG., Illus.). 26p. (J). (gr. -1-k). bds. 9.99 *(978-1-4494-0175-7(9))* Andrews McMeel Publishing.

Harris, Robie H. Who?: a Celebration of Babies: A Celebration of Babies. Rosenberg, Natascha, illus. 2018. (ENG.). 20p. (J). (gr. -1 — 1). bds. 8.99 *(978-1-4197-2834-1(2)*, 1206110, Abrams Appleseed) Abrams, Inc.

Harrison, Kenny. Hide & Seek Harry on the Farm. Harrison, Kenny, illus. 2015. (ENG., Illus.). 20p. (J). (-k). bds. 6.99 *(978-0-7636-7370-3(6))* Candlewick Pr.

Harter, Debbie. Cha-Cha-Cha en la Selva. Canetti, Yanitzia, tr. Harter, Debbie, illus. 2003.Tr. of Animal Boogie. (SPA., Illus.). 32p. (J). pap. 6.99 *(978-1-84148-265-1(X))* Barefoot Bks., Inc.

Haskamp, Steven, illus. Five Silly Monkeys. 2006. (ENG.). 12p. (J). (gr. -1-k). 12.95 *(978-1-58117-460-1(8)*, Intervisual/Piggy Toes) Bendon, Inc.

Haughom, Lisa, illus. People, Places & Things. 2010. (J). *(978-1-58865-541-7(5))* Kidsbooks, LLC.

—Things That Go! 2010. 16p. (J). *(978-1-58865-542-4(3))* Kidsbooks, LLC.

Haughton, Chris. Goodnight Everyone. Haughton, Chris, illus. 2016. (ENG., Illus.). 32p. (J). (-k). 18.99 *(978-0-7636-9079-3(1))* Candlewick Pr.

—Oh No, George! Haughton, Chris, illus. 2015. (ENG., Illus.). 32p. (J). (-k). bds. 10.99 *(978-0-7636-7652-0(7))* Candlewick Pr.

Hawcock, David. Leonardo Da Vinci: Incredible Machines. 2019. (Dover Science for Kids Ser.). (ENG., Illus.). 24p. 24.95 *(978-0-486-83236-4(8)*, 832368) Dover Pubns., Inc.

Hawk, Benjamin. Meadow Mystery. 2008. (Illus.). (J). *(978-1-4127-8875-5(7))* Publications International, Ltd.

Hawkins, Colin. Mr. Wolf's Week. 2005. (ENG., Illus.). 12p. (J). pap. 8.99 *(978-1-4052-0708-9(6))* Farshore GBR. Dist: Trafalgar Square Publishing.

—Pirate Ship: A Pop-up Adventure. Hawkins, Colin et al, illus. 2006. 28p. (J). (gr. 4-8). reprint ed. 20.00 *(978-0-7567-9827-7(2))* DIANE Publishing Co.

—What's the Time,Mr. Wolf? Mini Pop-Up. 2005. (ENG., Illus.). 14p. (J). bds. 8.99 *(978-1-4052-0707-2(8))* Farshore GBR. Dist: Trafalgar Square Publishing.

Hawksley, Gerald, illus. Danny Dog's Car: Press Out Parts Make a Car Carrying Danny Dog!, 1 vol. 2009. (Toddler Make & Play Ser.). (ENG.). 10p. (J). 6.95 *(978-1-59496-184-7(0))* Teora USA LLC.

—Patty Cow's Tractor: Press Out Parts Make a Tractor Carrying Patty Cow, 1 vol. 2009. (Toddler Make & Play Ser.). (ENG.). 10p. 6.95 *(978-1-59496-182-3(4))* Teora USA LLC.

—Quacky Duck's Plane: Press Out Parts Make an Airplane Carrying Quacky Duck!, 1 vol. 2009. (Toddler Make & Play Ser.). (ENG.). 10p. 6.95 *(978-1-59496-185-4(9))* Teora USA LLC.

—Splashy Dolphin's Boat: Press Out Parts Make a Boat Carrying Splashy Dolphin, 1 vol. 2009. (Toddler Make & Play Ser.). (ENG.). 10p. 6.95 *(978-1-59496-183-0(2))* Teora USA LLC.

Hawthorn, Philip & Tyler, Jenny. Who's Making That Mess? Cartwright, Stephen, illus. 2008. (Luxury Flap Bks). (gr. -1-k). 9.99 *(978-0-7945-1694-9(7))* EDC Publishing.

Hawthorn, Phillip & Tyler, Jenny. There's A Monster in My House. 2007. 16p. (J). 9.99 *(978-0-7945-1567-6(3)*, Usborne) EDC Publishing.

Hawthorne, Philip & Tyler, Jenny. Who's Making That Noise? Cartwright, Stephen, illus. 2005. (Flap Books Ser.). 16p. (J). (gr. 1-18). pap. 7.95 *(978-0-7945-0432-8(9)*, Usborne) EDC Publishing.

Hay DeSimone, Corkey. Mammal Animal Board Book 2nd Edition. Hay DeSimone, Corkey, illus. 2007. (Illus.). 24p. (J). 7.95 *(978-0-9777394-2-4(2))* Gentle Giraffe Pr.

Head, Vivian. Times Tables. 2013. (Illus.). 14p. (J). (gr. 1-5). 9.99 *(978-1-84322-936-0(6)*, Armadillo) Anness Publishing GBR. Dist: National Bk. Network.

Heath, Beverly C. A Bedtime Lullaby. Floyd, John, Jr., illus. 2006. 9p. (J). (gr. -1). bds. 5.95 *(978-0-9752860-1-2(3))* OurRainbow Pr., LLC.

—Counting with Colors. Floyd, John, Jr., illus. 2005. 8p. (J). (gr. -1). bds. 5.95 *(978-0-9752860-0-5(5))* OurRainbow Pr., LLC.

—My Parts Equal Me! Floyd, John, Jr., illus. 2005. 15p. (J). (gr. -1). bds. 5.95 *(978-0-9752860-2-9(1))* OurRainbow Pr., LLC.

—Opposites. Floyd, John, Jr., illus. 2006. 8p. (J). (gr. -1). bds. 5.95 *(978-0-9752860-3-6(X))* OurRainbow Pr., LLC.

Hegarty, Pat. If I Were a... Ballerina. Pope, Liz & Pope, Kate, illus. 2008. (If I Were A Ser.). 10p. (J). (gr. -1-k). bds. 6.95 *(978-1-58925-834-1(7))* Tiger Tales.

—If I Were a... Soccer Star. Pope, Liz & Pope, Kate, illus. 2008. (If I Were A Ser.). 10p. (J). (gr. -1-k). bds. 6.95 *(978-1-58925-835-8(5))* Tiger Tales.

Hegarty, Patricia. Five Black Cats. Woolf, Julia, illus. 2016. (ENG.). 22p. (J). (gr. -1-k). bds. 6.99 *(978-1-58925-239-4(X))* Tiger Tales.

Heinz, Brian J. Adirondack Lullaby. Henry, Maggie, illus. 2016. (ENG.). (J). bds. *(978-1-59531-053-8(3))* North Country Bks., Inc.

Heinze, Monica Bacon. A Day with Shapes. Dow, S. B., illus. 2004. (J). *(978-0-9761710-0-3(7))* Paisley Publishing.

Hellen, Nancy. My Magic House. 2003. (Illus.). 11p. (J). 9.99 *(978-0-333-66000-3(5))* Macmillan Pubs., Ltd. GBR. Dist: Trafalgar Square Publishing.

Heller, Sarah. Tinker Bell My Music MP3 Player: Storybook & Personal Music Player. 2008. (RD Innovative Book & Player Format Ser.). (ENG.). 36p. (YA). bds. 24.99 *(978-0-7944-1673-7(X))* Reader's Digest Assn., Inc., The.

Heller, Sarah & Reader's Digest Staff. Disney Fairies Music Player. 2008. (RD Innovative Book & Player Format Ser.). (ENG.). 36p. (J). 24.99 *(978-0-7944-1300-2(5))* Reader's Digest Assn., Inc., The.

Hello!Lucky. Kindness Rules! (a Hello!Lucky Book) 2019. (Hello!Lucky Book Ser.). (ENG., Illus.). 24p. (J). (gr. -1 — 1). bds. 8.99 *(978-1-4197-3426-7(1)*, 1265510) Abrams, Inc.

—My Dad Is Amazing! (a Hello!Lucky Book) 2018. (Hello!Lucky Book Ser.). (ENG., Illus.). 24p. (J). (gr. -1 — 1). bds. 8.99 *(978-1-4197-2961-4(6)*, 1212010) Abrams, Inc.

—Super Pooper & Whizz Kid: Potty Power! 2018. (Hello!Lucky Book Ser.). (ENG., Illus.). 24p. (J). (gr. -1 — 1). bds. 9.99 *(978-1-4197-3157-0(2)*, 1212201) Abrams, Inc.

Hello!Lucky & Moyle, Sabrina. My Mom Is Magical! (a Hello!Lucky Book) Moyle, Eunice, illus. 2018. (Hello!Lucky Book Ser.). (ENG.). 24p. (J). (gr. -1 — 1). bds. 7.99 *(978-1-4197-2962-1(4)*, 1212110) Abrams, Inc.

Helman, Andrea. 1, 2, 3 Moose: An Animal Counting Book. Wolfe, Art, photos by. 2016. (Illus.). 20p. (J). (— 1). bds. 10.99 *(978-1-63217-032-3(9)*, Little Bigfoot) Sasquatch Bks.

Helmer, Grace. Kahlo's Koalas: 1, 2, 3, Count Art with Me. 2019. (ENG.). 24p. (J). bds. 8.99 *(978-1-4494-9728-6(4))* Andrews McMeel Publishing.

Henderson, Robert. I See, I See. 2019. (ENG., Illus.). 48p. (J). (gr. -1-k). 17.99 *(978-1-4521-8334-3(1))* Chronicle Bks. LLC.

Hendra, Sue & Linnet, Paul. Keith the Cat with the Magic Hat. Hendra, Sue, illus. 2018. (ENG., Illus.). 32p. (J). (gr. -1-3). 14.99 *(978-1-4814-9035-1(4)*, Aladdin) Simon & Schuster Children's Publishing.

Hendry, Diana. The Very Snowy Christmas. Chapman, Jane, illus. 2013. (ENG.). 16p. (J). (gr. -1-k). bds. 8.95 *(978-1-58925-617-0(4))* Tiger Tales.

Henkes, Kevin. A Good Day Board Book. Henkes, Kevin, illus. 2010. (ENG., Illus.). 28p. (J). (gr. -1 — 1). bds. 7.99 *(978-0-06-185778-2(5)*, Greenwillow Bks.) HarperCollins Pubs.

—In the Middle of Fall Board Book. Dronzek, Laura, illus. 2018. (ENG.). 36p. (J). (gr. -1 — 1). bds. 8.99 *(978-0-06-274726-6(6)*, Greenwillow Bks.) HarperCollins Pubs.

—Kitten's First Full Moon Board Book: A Caldecott Award Winner. Henkes, Kevin, illus. 2015. (ENG., Illus.). 34p. (J). (gr. -1 — 1). bds. 9.99 *(978-0-06-241710-7(X)*, Greenwillow Bks.) HarperCollins Pubs.

Henley, Claire. Lost Sheep & the Scary Day, 1 vol. 2009. (All Join In Ser.). 18p. (J). bds. 6.99 *(978-0-8254-7882-6(0)*, Lion Children's) Lion Hudson PLC GBR. Dist: Kregel Pubns.

—Noah & the Flood, 1 vol. 2009. (All Join In Ser.). 18p. (J). bds. 6.99 *(978-0-8254-7880-2(4)*, Lion Children's) Lion Hudson PLC GBR. Dist: Kregel Pubns.

Henning, Heather. Christmas. Bull, Nicola, ed. Chapman, Gillian, illus. 2007. (Touch & Feel Ser.). 14p. (J). (gr. -1-3). bds. 10.49 *(978-0-7586-1383-7(0))* Concordia Publishing Hse.

—Creation. Bull, Nicola, ed. Chapman, Gillian, illus. 2007. (Touch & Feel Ser.). 14p. (J). (gr. -1-3). bds. 10.49 *(978-0-7586-1384-4(9))* Concordia Publishing Hse.

Hepworth, Amelia. I Love You to the Moon & Back. Warnes, Tim, illus. 2017. (ENG.). 24p. (J). (gr. -1-k). bds. 9.99 *(978-1-68010-522-3(1))* Tiger Tales.

Herbauts, Anne, creator. What Color Is the Wind? 2016. (Illus.). 48p. (J). (gr. k). pap. 21.95 *(978-1-59270-221-3(X))* Enchanted Lion Bks., LLC.

Hergé. On a Marche sur la Lune. (Tintin Ser.).Tr. of Explorers on the Moon. (FRE., Illus.). 62p. (J). pap. 21.95 *(978-2-203-00116-9(X))* Casterman, Editions FRA. Dist: Distribooks, Inc.

—On a Marche sur la Lune.Tr. of Explorers on the Moon. (FRE., Illus.). (J). (gr. 7-9). ring bd. 19.95 *(978-0-8288-5053-7(4))* French & European Pubns., Inc.

Heuninck, Ronald. Rain or Shine, 40 vols. 2nd rev. ed. 2014. Orig. Title: Buiten Spelen. (Illus.). 14p. (J). 9.95 *(978-1-78250-044-5(8))* Floris Bks. GBR. Dist: Consortium Bk. Sales & Distribution.

Hewitt, Angie. First Numbers: Touch-And-Trace Early Learning Fun! 2017. (Little Groovers Ser.). (ENG., Illus.). 12p. (J). (— 1). bds. 7.99 *(978-1-5107-0838-9(3)*, Sky Pony Pr.) Skyhorse Publishing Co., Inc.

Hewitt, Sally. Happy Dresser. Cameron, Craig, illus. 2003. 14p. (J). pap. 10.95 *(978-1-57145-733-2(X)*, Silver Dolphin Bks.) Readerlink Distribution Services, LLC.

Heyer, Carol. Humphrey's First Christmas. 2018. (ENG., Illus.). 26p. (J). (gr. -1-k). bds. 7.99 *(978-0-8249-1681-7(6))* Worthy Publishing.

Hickman, Jessica. Alligator Seder. Elissambura, illus. 2020. (ENG.). 12p. (J). (gr. -1 — 1). bds. 6.99 *(978-1-5415-6041-3(8)*, 328acd50-3eca-4a22-a925-629f27e06cde, Kar-Ben Publishing) Lerner Publishing Group.

Higginson, Sheila Sweeny. You're Getting a Baby Brother! Williams, Sam, illus. 2012. (ENG.). 24p. (J). (gr. -1-k). bds. 8.99 *(978-1-4424-2021-2(9)*, Little Simon) Little Simon.

—You're Getting a Baby Sister! Williams, Sam, illus. 2012. (ENG.). 24p. (J). (gr. -1-k). bds. 8.99 *(978-1-4424-2050-2(2)*, Little Simon) Little Simon.

Highlights, creator. Find It Animals: Baby's First Puzzle Book. 2019. (Highlights Find It Board Bks.). (Illus.). 14p. (J). (— 1). bds. 7.99 *(978-1-68437-251-5(8)*, Highlights) Highlights Pr., c/o Highlights for Children, Inc.

—That's Silly!(TM) at the Zoo: A Very Silly Lift-The-Flap Book. 2019. (Highlights Lift-The-Flap Bks.). (Illus.). 10p. (J). (-k). bds. 9.99 *(978-1-68437-255-3(0)*, Highlights) Highlights Pr., c/o Highlights for Children, Inc.

—Who Says Boo? Baby's First Halloween Book. 2018. (Highlights Baby Mirror Board Bks.). (Illus.). 14p. (J). (— 1). bds. 7.99 *(978-1-68437-155-6(4)*, Highlights) Highlights Pr., c/o Highlights for Children, Inc.

Hill, Eric. Get Well Soon, Spot. 2017. (Spot Ser.). (ENG., Illus.). 12p. (J). (-k). bds. 6.99 *(978-0-14-137242-6(7)*, Warne) Penguin Young Readers Group.

—Happy New Year, Spot! 2016. (Spot Ser.). (ENG., Illus.). 10p. (J). (-k). bds. 6.99 *(978-0-14-137009-5(2)*, Warne) Penguin Young Readers Group.

—I Love You, Spot. 2016. (Spot Ser.). (ENG., Illus.). 10p. (J). (— 1). bds. 7.99 *(978-0-14-136613-5(3)*, Warne) Penguin Young Readers Group.

—Spot Bakes a Cake. Hill, Eric, illus. 2005. (Spot Ser.). (ENG., Illus.). 20p. (J). (gr. k — 1). 7.99 *(978-0-14-240329-7(6)*, Warne) Penguin Young Readers Group.

—Spot Can Count. 2009. (Spot (Chinese) Ser.). (CHI., Illus.). 22p. *(978-957-762-468-0(5))* Hsin Yi Pubns.

—Spot Can Count. Hill, Eric, illus. 2005. (ENG., Illus.). 22p. (J). (gr. -1-1). bds. 7.99 *(978-0-399-24361-5(5))* Penguin Publishing Group.

—Spot Goes to School (color) Hill, Eric, illus. 2004. (Spot Ser.). (ENG., Illus.). 24p. (J). (gr. -1-k). 7.99 *(978-0-14-240167-5(6)*, Warne) Penguin Young Readers Group.

—Spot Goes to the Beach. Hill, Eric, illus. 2019. (Spot Ser.). (ENG., Illus.). 12p. (J). (-k). bds. 6.99 *(978-0-241-35182-6(0)*, Warne) Penguin Young Readers Group.

—Spot Goes to the Farm. 2003. (Spot Ser.). (gr. -1-2). lib. bdg. 18.40 *(978-0-613-86708-5(4))* Turtleback.

—Spot Goes to the Farm (color) Hill, Eric, illus. 2003. (Spot Ser.). (ENG., Illus.). 24p. (J). (gr. -1-k). 7.99 *(978-0-14-250123-8(9)*, Warne) Penguin Young Readers Group.

—Spot Goes to the Park. Hill, Eric, illus. 2005. (Spot Ser.). (ENG., Illus.). 24p. (J). (gr. -1 — 1). bds. 9.99 *(978-0-399-24363-9(1)*, Warne) Penguin Young Readers Group.

—Spot Goes to the Swimming Pool. 2018. (Spot Ser.). (ENG., Illus.). 14p. (J). (-k). bds. 6.99 *(978-0-241-32708-1(3)*, Warne) Penguin Young Readers Group.

—Spot Loves Bedtime. 2016. (Spot Ser.). (ENG., Illus.). 14p. (J). (— 1). bds. 6.99 *(978-0-241-23502-7(2)*, Warne) Penguin Young Readers Group.

—Spot Loves His Daddy. Hill, Eric, illus. 2005. (Spot Ser.). (ENG., Illus.). 14p. (J). (gr. -1 — 1). bds. 6.99 *(978-0-399-24351-6(8)*, Warne) Penguin Young Readers Group.

—Spot Loves School. Hill, Eric, illus. 2015. (Spot Ser.). (ENG., Illus.). 12p. (J). (gr. -1 — 1). bds. 6.99 *(978-0-14-135654-9(5)*, Warne) Penguin Young Readers Group.

—Spot Says Please. Hill, Eric, illus. 2013. (Spot Ser.). (ENG., Illus.). 14p. (J). (gr. -1-k). bds. 6.99 *(978-0-7232-7832-0(6)*, Warne) Penguin Young Readers Group.

—Spot's First Walk. Hill, Eric, illus. 2005. (Spot Ser.). (ENG., Illus.). 24p. (J). (gr. -1 — 1). bds. 9.99 *(978-0-399-24482-7(4)*, Warne) Penguin Young Readers Group.

—Spot's Peekaboo. Hill, Eric, illus. 2015. (Spot Ser.). (ENG., Illus.). 12p. (J). (-k). bds. 9.99 *(978-0-14-136170-3(0)*, Warne) Penguin Young Readers Group.

—Where's Spot? Hill, Eric, illus. 2003. (Spot Ser.). (ENG., Illus.). 22p. (J). (gr. -1 — 1). bds. 7.99 *(978-0-399-24046-1(2)*, 53517281, Warne) Penguin Young Readers Group.

—Where's Spot? Hill, Eric, illus. 2007. (Spot Ser.). (ENG., Illus.). 18.00 *(978-0-7569-7965-2(X))* Perfection Learning Corp.

—Where's Spot? 2003. (Spot Ser.). 18.40 *(978-1-4176-3889-5(3))* Turtleback.

—Where's Spot (color) Hill, Eric, illus. 2003. (Spot Ser.). (ENG., Illus.). 24p. (J). (gr. -1-k). 8.99 *(978-0-14-250126-9(3)*, Warne) Penguin Young Readers Group.

Hill, Kelly, illus. Anne's Colors: Inspired by Anne of Green Gables. 2018. (Anne of Green Gables Ser.). 20p. (J). (— 1). bds. 7.99 *(978-0-7352-6284-3(5)*, Tundra Bks.) Tundra Bks. CAN. Dist: Penguin Random Hse. LLC.

—Anne's Numbers: Inspired by Anne of Green Gables. 2018. (Anne of Green Gables Ser.). 22p. (J). (— 1). bds. 8.99 *(978-0-7352-6285-0(3)*, Tundra Bks.) Tundra Bks. CAN. Dist: Penguin Random Hse. LLC.

Hill, Susanna Leonard. Airplane Flight! A Lift-The-Flap Adventure. Larrañaga, Ana Martín & Larrañaga, Ana Martín, illus. 2009. (ENG.). 12p. (J). (gr. -1-k). bds. 7.99 *(978-1-4169-7832-9(1)*, Little Simon) Little Simon.

—When Your Elephant Has the Sniffles. Wiseman, Daniel, illus. 2017. (When Your... Ser.). (ENG.). 26p. (J). (gr. -1 — 1). bds. 7.99 *(978-1-4814-9504-2(6)*, Little Simon) Little Simon.

—When Your Lion Needs a Bath. Wiseman, Daniel, illus. 2017. (When Your... Ser.). (ENG.). 26p. (J). (gr. -1 — 1). bds. 7.99 *(978-1-4814-9502-8(X)*, Little Simon) Little Simon.

Hills, Tad. Duck & Goose, Find a Pumpkin (Oversized Board Book) Hills, Tad, illus. 2012. (Duck & Goose Ser.). (ENG., Illus.). 22p. (J). (gr. k-k). bds. 10.99 *(978-0-307-98155-4(X))* Random Hse. Children's Bks.

—Duck & Goose, Goose Needs a Hug. Hills, Tad, illus. 2012. (Duck & Goose Ser.). (ENG., Illus.). 22p. (J). (-k). bds. 8.99 *(978-0-307-98293-3(9))* Random Hse. Children's Bks.

—Duck & Goose, Here Comes the Easter Bunny! An Easter Book for Kids & Toddlers. Hills, Tad, illus. 2012. (Duck & Goose Ser.). (ENG., Illus.). 22p. (J). (gr. k-k). bds. 7.99 *(978-0-375-87280-8(9)*, Schwartz & Wade Bks.) Random Hse. Children's Bks.

—Duck & Goose, How Are You Feeling? Hills, Tad, illus. 2009. (Duck & Goose Ser.). (ENG., Illus.). 22p. (J). (gr. -1 — 1). bds. 7.99 *(978-0-375-84629-8(8))* Random Hse. Children's Bks.

—Duck & Goose, It's Time for Christmas! Hills, Tad, illus. 2010. (Duck & Goose Ser.). (Illus.). 22p. (J). (gr. -1 — 1). 7.99 *(978-0-375-86484-1(9))* Random Hse. Children's Bks.

—Duck & Goose, It's Time for Christmas! (Oversized Board Book) Hills, Tad, illus. 2011. (Duck & Goose Ser.). (ENG., Illus.). 22p. (J). (gr. -1 — 1). bds. 10.99 *(978-0-375-87112-2(8)*, Schwartz & Wade Bks.) Random Hse. Children's Bks.

Hilton, Dave, et al. Star Wars. Rood, Brian, illus. 2015. 8p. (J). *(978-1-5037-0033-8(X))* Phoenix International Publications, Inc.

Hilton, Jennifer & McCurry, Kristen. Clap, Sing, Dance! A Book about Praising God. Rimmington, Natasha, illus. 2017. (Frolic First Faith Ser.). 22p. (J). 6.99 *(978-1-5064-1783-7(3)*, Sparkhouse Family) 1517 Media.

—Everyone Gets Upset: A Book about Frustration. Rimmington, Natasha, illus. 2018. (Frolic First Faith Ser.). 22p. (J). (gr. -1 — 1). bds. 6.99 *(978-1-5064-2501-6(1)*, Sparkhouse Family) 1517 Media.

—God Finds Us: A Book about Being Found. 2016. (Frolic First Faith Ser.). (Illus.). 28p. (J). (gr. -1 — 1). bds. 6.99 *(978-1-5064-1045-6(6)*, Sparkhouse Family) 1517 Media.

—God Made Us All: A Book about Big & Little. 2016. (Frolic First Faith Ser.). (Illus.). 22p. (J). (gr. -1 — 1). bds. 6.99 *(978-1-5064-1044-9(8)*, Sparkhouse Family) 1517 Media.

—God's Wonderful World: A Book about the Five Senses. 2016. (Frolic First Faith Ser.). (Illus.). 22p. (J). (gr. -1 — 1). bds. 6.99 *(978-1-5064-1047-0(2)*, Sparkhouse Family) 1517 Media.

—Good Morning, World! A Book about Morning Routines. Rimmington, Natasha, illus. 2017. (Frolic First Faith Ser.). 22p. (J). 6.99 *(978-1-5064-1785-1(X)*, Sparkhouse Family) 1517 Media.

—I Can Help: A Book about Helping Others. Rimmington, Natasha, illus. 2017. (Frolic First Faith Ser.). 22p. (J). 6.99 *(978-1-5064-1784-4(1)*, Sparkhouse Family) 1517 Media.

—Pray to God: A Book about Prayer. 2016. (Frolic First Faith Ser.). (Illus.). 22p. (J). (gr. -1 — 1). bds. 6.99 *(978-1-5064-1046-3(4)*, Sparkhouse Family) 1517 Media.

Hilton, Jennifer Sue & McCurry, Kristen. El Mundo Maravilloso de Dios. Rimmington, Natasha, illus. 2016. (SPA.). (J). *(978-1-5064-2094-3(X))* 1517 Media.

—Ora a Dios. Garton, Michael, illus. 2016. (SPA.). (J). *(978-1-5064-2093-6(1))* 1517 Media.

Hinckley, Peter. Little Lacers: 123: Lace & Learn Your First Numbers! Kaliaha, Volha, illus. 2019. (Little Lacers Ser.). (ENG.). 14p. (J). (gr. -1-k). bds. 16.99 *(978-1-64170-008-5(4)*, 550008) Familius LLC.

Hinder, Sarah Jane. Yoga Bear: Simple Animal Poses for Little Ones. 2018. (Yoga Kids & Animal Friends Board Bks.: 2). (ENG., Illus.). 24p. (J). bds. 9.99 *(978-1-68364-075-2(6)*, 900220862) Sounds True, Inc.

—Yoga Bug: Simple Poses for Little Ones. 2017. (Yoga Kids & Animal Friends Board Bks.: 1). (ENG., Illus.). 24p. (J). bds. 9.99 *(978-1-62203-979-1(3)*, 900220837) Sounds True, Inc.

Hindley, Anna Forgerson & Nat'l Mus Afr Am Hist Culture, Nat'l Mus. A Is for All the Things You Are: A Joyful ABC Book. Bobo, Keturah A., illus. 2019. 26p. (J). (— 1). bds. 9.95 *(978-1-58834-650-6(1)*, Smithsonian Bks.) Smithsonian Institution Scholarly Pr.

Hinkler Books, creator. 101 First Words. 2011. (101 First Words Ser.). (Illus.). 16p. (J). (gr. -1). bds. 7.99 *(978-1-74184-816-8(4))* Hinkler Bks. Pty, Ltd. AUS. Dist: Ideals Pubns.

—101 First Words: Animals. 2011. (101 First Words Ser.). (Illus.). 16p. (J). (gr. -1). bds. 7.99 *(978-1-74184-817-5(2))* Hinkler Bks. Pty, Ltd. AUS. Dist: Ideals Pubns.

—101 First Words: At Home. 2011. (101 First Words Ser.). (Illus.). 16p. (J). (gr. -1). bds. 7.99 *(978-1-74184-819-9(9))* Hinkler Bks. Pty, Ltd. AUS. Dist: Ideals Pubns.

—101 First Words: Things That Go. 2011. (101 First Words Ser.). (Illus.). 16p. (J). (gr. -1). bds. 7.99 *(978-1-74184-818-2(0))* Hinkler Bks. Pty, Ltd. AUS. Dist: Ideals Pubns.

Hinkler Books Staff. My Cool Box of Dress-up Dolls. 2012. 16p. (J). 9.99 *(978-1-74184-277-7(8))* Hinkler Bks. Pty, Ltd. AUS. Dist: Ideals Pubns.

Hinkler Books Staff, ed. Spelling. 2009. (ENG.). 24p. (J). 9.99 *(978-0-8249-1402-8(3)*, Ideals Pubns.) Worthy Publishing.

Hinkler Studios Staff., ed. Baby's First Christmas. 2011. (Baby's First Ser.). 12p. (J). bds. 5.99 *(978-1-74184-699-7(4))* Hinkler Bks. Pty, Ltd. AUS. Dist: Ideals Pubns.

—Baby's First Halloween. 2011. (Baby's First Ser.). 12p. (J). bds. 5.99 *(978-1-74184-700-0(1))* Hinkler Bks. Pty, Ltd. AUS. Dist: Ideals Pubns.

—Little Red Riding Hood. 2011. (Fairytale Pop-Ups Ser.). 12p. (J). 12.99 *(978-1-74185-088-8(6))* Hinkler Bks. Pty, Ltd. AUS. Dist: Ideals Pubns.

Hinkler Studios Staff, ed. Snow White. 2011. (Fairytale Pop-Ups Ser.). 12p. (J). 12.99 *(978-1-74185-089-5(4))* Hinkler Bks. Pty, Ltd. AUS. Dist: Ideals Pubns.

Hinkler Studios Staff., ed. Three Little Pigs. 2011. (Fairytale Pop-Ups Ser.). 12p. (J). 12.99 *(978-1-74185-086-4(X))* Hinkler Bks. Pty, Ltd. AUS. Dist: Ideals Pubns.

Hinton, Steph. Let's Learn First Words with Stickers. 2015. (Illus.). (J). *(978-1-4351-5921-1(7))* Barnes & Noble, Inc.

T
U
V

Hinton, Stephanie, illus. Busy Book for Boys: 550 Things to Find. 2014. (J). *(978-1-4351-5358-5(8))* Barnes & Noble, Inc.

—Muddle & Match: Adventure. 2014. 16p. (J). bds. 8.99 *(978-1-61067-288-7(7))* Kane Miller.

—Muddle & Match: Imagine. 2014. 16p. (J). bds. 8.99 *(978-1-61067-289-4(5))* Kane Miller.

—Muddle & Match Farm Animals. 2018. (ENG.). 16p. (J). bds. 8.99 *(978-1-61067-687-8(4))* Kane Miller.

—Muddle & Match Jungle Animals. 2015. (ENG.). 16p. (J). bds. 8.00 *(978-1-61067-401-0(4))* Kane Miller.

—Muddle & Match Monsters. 2015. (ENG.). 16p. (J). bds. *(978-1-61067-423-2(5))* Kane Miller.

Hirschi, Ron. Winter Is for Whales: A Book of Hawaiian Seasons. Green, Yuko, illus. 2007. (ENG.). 36p. (J). (gr. -1-3). *(978-1-59700-504-3(5))* Island Heritage Publishing.

Hirschmann, Kris. Blast Off. 2006. (Illus.). 63p. (J). *(978-0-439-55092-5(0))* Scholastic, Inc.

Hitchen, Danielle. Holy Week: An Emotions Primer. 2019. (Baby Believer Ser.). (ENG., Illus.). 20p. (J). (— 1). bds. 12.99 *(978-0-7369-7696-1(5)*, 6976961) Harvest Hse. Pubs.

—Jesus Heals: An Anatomy Primer. 2020. (Baby Believer Ser.). (ENG., Illus.). 20p. (J). (— 1). bds. 12.99 *(978-0-7369-7944-3(1)*, 6979443) Harvest Hse. Pubs.

—Psalms of Praise: A Movement Primer. 2018. (Baby Believer Ser.). (ENG., Illus.). 20p. (J). (— 1). bds. 12.99 *(978-0-7369-7234-5(X)*, 6972345) Harvest Hse. Pubs.

Hnatov, Catherine. Up & Down. 1 vol. Hnatov, Catherine, illus. 2014. (ENG., Illus.). 32p. (J). bds. 5.99 *(978-1-59572-340-6(4))* Star Bright Bks., Inc.

—Up & Down: Spanish/English. 1 vol. Hnatov, Catherine, illus. 2014. (ENG., Illus.). 32p. (J). bds. 5.99 *(978-1-59572-341-3(2))* Star Bright Bks., Inc.

—Yum, Yum. 1 vol. Hnatov, Catherine, illus. 2011. (ENG., Illus.). 32p. (J). bds. 5.95 *(978-1-59572-276-8(9))* Star Bright Bks., Inc.

Ho, Jannie, illus. Bunny Boo Has Lost Her Teddy: A Tiny Tab Book. 2014. (Tiny Tab Ser.). (ENG.). 8p. (J). (— 1). bds. 7.99 *(978-0-7636-7274-4(2))* Candlewick Pr.

—Cutie Pie Looks for the Easter Bunny: A Tiny Tab Book. 2015. (Tiny Tab Ser.). (ENG.). 8p. (J). (— 1). bds. 7.99 *(978-0-7636-7599-8(7))* Candlewick Pr.

—The Great Matzoh Hunt. 2010. 12p. (J). (gr. -1 — 1). bds. 7.99 *(978-0-8431-8969-8(X)*, Price Stern Sloan) Penguin Young Readers Group.

Hoban, Tana. Black & White. 2007. (ENG., Illus.). 16p. (J). (gr. -1 — 1). pap. 7.99 *(978-0-06-117211-3(1)*, Greenwillow Bks.) HarperCollins Pubs.

—Black White: A High Contrast Book for Newborns. Hoban, Tana, illus. 2017. (ENG., Illus.). 36p. (J). (gr. -1 — 1). bds. 9.99 *(978-0-06-265690-2(2)*, Greenwillow Bks.) HarperCollins Pubs.

Hodge, Bodie & Welch, Laura, eds. Dragons: Legends & Lore of Dinosaurs. Looney, Bill, illus. 2009. 24p. (J). 19.99 *(978-0-89051-558-7(1)*, Master Books) New Leaf Publishing Group.

Hodgman, Ann. Do Touch! Don't Touch! Barnard, Lucy, illus. 2012. (ENG.). 18p. (J). bds. *(978-1-58925-867-9(3))* Tiger Tales.

—Monsters Dance. Wood, Hannah, illus. 2013. (ENG.). 16p. (J). (gr. -1). bds. 8.95 *(978-1-58925-627-9(1))* Tiger Tales.

—That's My Mommy! Logan, Laura, illus. 2013. (ENG.). 22p. bds. *(978-1-58925-645-3(X))* Tiger Tales.

Hodson, Sarah E. Wh- Questions. 2012. (Illus.). 7p. (J). *(978-0-7606-1382-5(6))* LinguiSystems, Inc.

Hoffmann, E. T. A. & Ventura, Paola Fratalocchi. The Nutcracker. 2010. (ENG., Illus.). 32p. (J). 14.99 *(978-0-7944-2044-4(3))* Reader's Digest Assn., Inc., The.

Holcroft, John & Candlewick Press Staff. Space Exploration: Panorama Pops. Holcroft, John, illus. 2015. (Panorama Pops Ser.). (ENG., Illus.). 30p. (J). (gr. k-4). 8.99 *(978-0-7636-7699-5(3))* Candlewick Pr.

Holtfreter, Nastja. Colorful World: Farm. Holtfreter, Nastja, illus. 2017. (ENG., Illus.). 14p. (J). bds. 5.99 *(978-1-61067-578-9(9))* Kane Miller.

—Colorful World: Forest. Holtfreter, Nastja, illus. 2017. (ENG., Illus.). 14p. (J). bds. 5.99 *(978-1-61067-577-2(0))* Kane Miller.

—Colorful World: Mountain. Holtfreter, Nastja, illus. 2017. (ENG., Illus.). 14p. (J). bds. 5.99 *(978-1-61067-579-6(7))* Kane Miller.

—Colorful World: Sea. Holtfreter, Nastja, illus. 2017. (ENG., Illus.). 14p. (J). bds. 5.99 *(978-1-61067-576-5(2))* Kane Miller.

Holtfreter, Nastja, illus. Push Puzzles: in the Woods. 2016. (ENG.). 10p. (J). (gr. -1 — 1). bds. 7.99 *(978-1-4998-0349-5(4))* Little Bee Books Inc.

Holub, Joan. Dragon Dance: A Chinese New Year Lift-The-Flap Book. Huang, Benrei, illus. 2003. (Puffin Lift-The-Flap Ser.). 16p. (J). (gr. -1-k). 8.99 *(978-0-14-240000-5(9)*, Puffin Books) Penguin Young Readers Group.

—This Little Explorer: A Pioneer Primer. Roode, Daniel, illus. 2016. (This Little Ser.). (ENG.). 26p. (J). (gr. -1-k). bds. 7.99 *(978-1-4814-7175-6(9)*, Little Simon) Little Simon.

—This Little President: A Presidential Primer. Roode, Daniel, illus. 2016. (This Little Ser.). (ENG.). 26p. (J). (gr. -1-k). bds. 7.99 *(978-1-4814-5850-4(7)*, Little Simon) Little Simon.

—This Little Scientist: A Discovery Primer. Roode, Daniel, illus. 2018. (This Little Ser.). (ENG.). 26p. (J). (gr. -1-k). bds. 7.99 *(978-1-5344-0108-2(3)*, Little Simon) Little Simon.

Hommedieu, Arthur John. Egg, Tadpole, Frog. 2006. (Metamorphoses Ser.). (Illus.). 16p. (J). (gr. 1-5). spiral bd. *(978-1-84643-012-1(7))* Child's Play International Ltd.

Honda, Liana. Kou Lima. Kukahiko, Puni, illus. 2010. 22p. 8.00 *(978-0-87336-236-8(5))* Kamehameha Publishing.

—Kou Wawae. Kukahiko, Puni, illus. 2010. 22p. 8.00 *(978-0-87336-237-5(3))* Kamehameha Publishing.

Honey, Alison. My Ashmolean Discovery Book. 2010. (ENG., Illus.). 24p. (J). (gr. -1-3). pap. 9.95 *(978-1-85444-242-0(2))* Ashmolean Museum GBR. Dist: National Bk. Network.

Honsek, Larissa. Opposites. 2019. (ENG., Illus.). 20p. (J). (gr. -1-k). bds. 9.99 *(978-1-64170-143-3(9)*, 550143) Familius LLC.

Hood, Susan. Tickly Toes. Barroux, illus. 2014. (ENG.). 24p. (J). (gr. -1 — 1). bds. 9.95 *(978-1-894786-52-2(1))* Kids Can Pr., Ltd. CAN. Dist: Hachette Bk. Group.

hooks, bell. Happy to Be Nappy. Raschka, Chris, illus. 2017. (ENG.). 32p. (J). (gr. -1-1). bds. 8.99 *(978-1-4847-8841-7(9))* Little, Brown Bks. for Young Readers.

Hooper, Ruth. Santa's Factory. Charbonnel, Olivier & Mostyn, David, illus. 2004. 6p. (J). (gr. k-4). reprint ed. 16.00 *(978-0-7567-7585-8(X))* DIANE Publishing Co.

Hopgood, Sally. A Day on the Farm: A Pull-The-Tab Book. Hinton, Stephanie, illus. 2014. (J). *(978-1-4351-5688-3(9))* Barnes & Noble, Inc.

—In the Forest: A Pull-The-Tab Book. Hinton, Stephanie, illus. 2014. (J). *(978-1-4351-5689-0(7))* Barnes & Noble, Inc.

—Let's Find Things That Go. Hinton, Steph, illus. 2017. (Let's Find Pull-The-Tab Bks.). (ENG.). 12p. (J). (gr. -1-k). bds. 9.99 *(978-1-78700-083-4(4))* Top That! Publishing PLC GBR. Dist: Independent Pubs. Group.

—A Trip to Busy Town: A Pull-The-Tab Book. Hinton, Stephanie, illus. 2014. (J). *(978-1-4351-5690-6(0))* Barnes & Noble, Inc.

Horácek, Petr. A Surprise for Tiny Mouse. Horácek, Petr, illus. 2015. (ENG., Illus.). 16p. (J). (— 1). bds. 8.99 *(978-0-7636-7967-5(4))* Candlewick Pr.

—Time for Bed. Horácek, Petr, illus. 2014. (ENG., Illus.). 16p. (J). (— 1). bds. 7.99 *(978-0-7636-6779-5(X))* Candlewick Pr.

Horacek, Petr. Who Is Sleeping? Horacek, Petr, illus. 2019. (ENG., Illus.). 16p. (J). (— 1). bds. 8.99 *(978-1-5362-0172-7(3))* Candlewick Pr.

—Who Is the Biggest? Horacek, Petr, illus. 2019. (ENG., Illus.). 16p. (J). (— 1). bds. 8.99 *(978-1-5362-0171-0(5))* Candlewick Pr.

Horacek, Petr & Horacek, Petr. The Mouse Who Wasn't Scared. Horacek, Petr & Horacek, Petr, illus. 2018. (ENG., Illus.). 32p. (J). (-k). 15.99 *(978-0-7636-9881-2(4))* Candlewick Pr.

Hore, Rosie. Lift-The-Flap Adding & Subtracting. 2018. (Advanced Lift-The-Flap Board Bks.). (ENG.). 16p. 14.99 *(978-0-7945-4233-7(6)*, Usborne) EDC Publishing.

—Lift-The-Flap Measuring Things. 2017. (Advanced Lift-The-Flap Board Bks.). (ENG.). 16p. 14.99 *(978-0-7945-4022-7(8)*, Usborne) EDC Publishing.

Horne, Jane. Busy Baby Noisy Book. 2007. (Busy Baby Ser.). (Illus.). 12p. (gr. -1). per., bds. *(978-1-84610-434-3(3))* Make Believe Ideas.

—Flip & Find 123. 2008. (Illus.). 12p. (J). (gr. -1-3). bds. *(978-1-84610-731-3(8))* Make Believe Ideas.

—Flip & Find Abc. 2008. (Illus.). 12p. (J). (gr. -1-3). bds. *(978-1-84610-730-6(X))* Make Believe Ideas.

—Sparklies Colors. 2008. (Illus.). 12p. (gr. -1-k). bds. *(978-1-84610-608-8(7))* Make Believe Ideas.

Horne, Jane, et al. Five Noisy Ducks: An Action-Packed Counting Book. 2014. (Illus.). (J). *(978-1-4351-6034-7(7))* Barnes & Noble, Inc.

Horning, Sandra. Baby Code! Crowton, Melissa, illus. 2018. (Girls Who Code Ser.). 14p. (J). (— 1). bds. 7.99 *(978-0-399-54257-2(4)*, Penguin Workshop) Penguin Young Readers Group.

Horstschafer, Felicitas. X-Ray Me! Look Inside Your Body. Vogt, Johannes, illus. 2019. (ENG.). 22p. (J). (gr. 1-5). bds. 12.99 *(978-0-06-288996-6(6)*, Greenwillow Bks.) HarperCollins Pubs.

Hostetler, Bob. Don't Close Your Eyes: A Silly Bedtime Story. 1 vol. Chambers, Mark, illus. 2019. (ENG.). 20p. (J). bds. 9.99 *(978-1-4002-0951-4(X)*, Tommy Nelson) Nelson, Thomas Inc.

Houbre, Gilbert. Vegetables. Houbre, Gilbert, illus. 2012. (ENG., Illus.). 36p. (J). (gr. -1-k). spiral bd. 19.99 *(978-1-85103-402-4(1))* Moonlight Publishing, Ltd. GBR. Dist: Independent Pubs. Group.

Houck, Lisa. Flowers Grow All in a Row. 2016. (ENG., Illus.). 24p. (J). bds. 10.95 *(978-0-7649-7446-5(7)*, POMEGRANATE KIDS) Pomegranate Communications, Inc.

Houle, Kelly. Gracie's Gallery: A Magic Mirror Book. 2008. (ENG., Illus.). 28p. (J). (gr. -1). 14.95 *(978-1-58117-784-8(4)*, Intervisual/Piggy Toes) Bendon, Inc.

Howarth, Jill. 1-2-3, You Love Me. 2017. (ENG., Illus.). 14p. (J). (gr. -1 — 1). bds. 7.99 *(978-0-7624-6269-8(8)*, Running Pr. Kids) Running Pr.

Howarth, Jill, illus. The 12 Days of Christmas. 2018. (ENG.). 26p. (J). (gr. -1 — 1). bds. 7.99 *(978-0-7624-9142-1(6)*, Running Pr. Kids) Running Pr.

Howell, Gail L. Sarah & the Blue Sled: Sarah's World (Series) 2010. 32p. pap. 12.99 *(978-1-4389-7597-9(X))* AuthorHouse.

Howie, Vickie & MacLean, Moira. Easter Surprise: A Lift-the-Flap Board Book. 2006. (Illus.). 32p. (J). (gr. -1-k). bds. 9.49 *(978-0-7586-1148-2(X))* Concordia Publishing Hse.

Hruby, Patrick. ABC Is for Circus: Hardcover Popular Edition. 2017. (ENG., Illus.). 56p. 9.95 *(978-1-62326-107-8(4))* AMMO Bks., LLC.

Hubbard, Ben. My Very Own Kitten. Guile, Gill, illus. 2014. (ENG.). 12p. (J). (gr. -1). *(978-1-78244-602-6(8))* Top That! Publishing PLC.

—My Very Own Puppy. Guile, Gill, illus. 2014. (ENG.). 12p. (gr. -1). *(978-1-78244-603-3(6))* Top That! Publishing PLC.

Hughes, John Ceiriog. All Through the Night. Boulton, Harold, tr. Alizadeh, Kate, illus. 2013. (ENG.). 24p. (J). (gr. -1-2). bds. 12.95 *(978-1-927018-09-5(9))* Simply Read Bks. CAN. Dist: Ingram Publisher Services.

Hughes, Shirley. Alfie Gets in First. 2018. (Alfie Ser.). (Illus.). 30p. (J). (gr. -1-k). bds. 12.99 *(978-1-78295-658-7(1)*, Red Fox) Random House Children's Books GBR. Dist: Independent Pubs. Group.

Hulme, Joy N. Eerie Feary Feeling: A Hairy Scary Pop-up Book. Ely, Paul & Dudley, Dick, illus. 2006. 12p. (J). (gr. k-4). reprint ed. 14.00 *(978-1-4223-5171-0(8))* DIANE Publishing Co.

Hurry, Helen, illus. Peepo! Boo! Who Are You? 2014. (ENG.). 12p. (J). 17.00 *(978-0-85707-679-3(5)*, Simon & Schuster Children's) Simon & Schuster, Ltd. GBR. Dist: Simon & Schuster, Inc.

Hurt-Newton, Tania. Yee-Ha Harvey. 2007. (ENG., Illus.). 14p. (J). (gr. k — 1). 14.95 *(978-0-00-724414-0(2))* HarperCollins Pubs. Ltd. GBR. Dist: Independent Pubs. Group.

Husar, Lisa & Husar, Mike. Grand Canyon Babies. 2011. 26p. 8.95 *(978-1-56037-507-4(8))* Farcountry Pr.

HuskMitNavn, illus. The Wrong Book. 2018. (ENG.). 14p. (J). bds. 14.95 *(978-1-58423-673-3(6)*, 2a00f5cc-f841-4c71-bc2d-b1df524a6413) Gingko Pr., Inc.

Hutchings, Tony, illus. A Day on the Farm. 2016. (J). *(978-1-4351-6337-9(0))* Barnes & Noble, Inc.

—A Week at the Seaside. 2014. (J). *(978-1-4351-5464-3(9))* Barnes & Noble, Inc.

Hutchins, Pat. Good-Night, Owl! Hutchins, Pat, illus. 2015. (Classic Board Bks.). (ENG., Illus.). 34p. (J). (gr. -1 — 1). bds. 8.99 *(978-1-4814-4424-8(7)*, Little Simon) Little Simon.

Hutchinson McMullen, Angela. I Like Me. 2013. 24p. pap. *(978-1-926831-01-5(2))* Navarone Bks.

Hutton, John. Blocks: Baby Unplugged. Hutton, John, ed. Kang, Andrea, illus. 2013. (Baby Unplugged Ser.). (ENG.). 14p. (J). (— 1). bds. 7.99 *(978-1-936669-13-4(7))* Blue Manatee Press.

—Box: Baby Unplugged. Kang, Andrea, illus. 2012. (Baby Unplugged Ser.). (ENG.). 14p. (J). (— 1). bds. 7.99 *(978-1-936669-08-0(0))* Blue Manatee Press.

—Fiona's Feelings. Cincinnati Zoo and Botanical Garden Staff, photos by. 2018. (ENG., Illus.). 14p. (J). (— 1). bds. 7.99 *(978-1-936669-65-3(0))* Blue Manatee Press.

—Pets: Baby Unplugged. Kang, Andrea, illus. 2011. (Baby Unplugged Ser.). (ENG.). 14p. (J). (— 1). bds. 7.99 *(978-1-936669-02-8(1))* Blue Manatee Press.

—SHARE This Book. Brown, Christina, illus. 2018. (ENG.). 14p. (J). (— 1). bds. 7.99 *(978-1-936669-67-7(6))* Blue Manatee Press.

Huven, Kim. The Birthday Bears. Padron, Alicia, illus. 2010. 10p. bds. 10.95 *(978-1-60747-774-7(2)*, Pickwick Pr.) Phoenix Bks., Inc.

Huws, Emily & Gomer, Gwasg. CAE Berllan. 2005. (WEL.). 28.0p. 5.99 *(978-1-85902-998-5(1))* Gomer Pr. GBR. Dist: Gomer Pr.

Ideals Publications Inc. Staff. Thomas & Friends Write, Slide & Learn: Numbers. 2011. (Write, Slide & Learn Ser.). 14p. (J). pap. *(978-1-74184-161-9(5))* Hinkler Bks. Pty. Ltd.

Idle, Molly. Flora & the Chicks: A Counting Book by Molly Idle (Flora & Flamingo Board Books, Baby Counting Books for Easter, Baby Farm Picture Book) 2017. (Flora & Friends Ser.). (ENG., Illus.). 20p. (J). bds. 9.99 *(978-1-4521-4657-7(8))* Chronicle Bks. LLC.

—Flora & the Ostrich: An Opposites Book by Molly Idle (Flora & Flamingo Board Books, Picture Books for Toddlers, Baby Books with Animals) 2017. (Flora & Friends Ser.). (ENG., Illus.). 20p. (J). (gr. -1 — 1). bds. 9.99 *(978-1-4521-4658-4(6))* Chronicle Bks. LLC.

—Flora & the Peacocks. 2016. (Flora & Friends Ser.). (ENG., Illus.). 40p. (J). (gr. -1-k). 17.99 *(978-1-4521-3816-9(8))* Chronicle Bks. LLC.

—Flora & the Penguin. 2014. (Flora & Friends Ser.). (ENG., Illus.). 40p. (J). (gr. -1-k). 16.99 *(978-1-4521-2891-7(X))* Chronicle Bks. LLC.

IglooBooks. Colors: Explore First Colors with Peep-Through Learning Fun. 2017. (Foiled Board Bks.: 1). (ENG., Illus.). 12p. (J). 7.99 *(978-1-78810-727-3(6))* Igloo Bks. GBR. Dist: Simon & Schuster, Inc.

Ikids Staff. Animals Everywhere. Phillips, Jillian, illus. 2010. (ENG.). 20p. (J). (gr. -1-17). 6.99 *(978-1-60169-006-7(1))* Innovative Kids.

—Little Turtles. Larranaga, Ana, illus. 2008. (iBaby Float-Alongs Ser.). (ENG.). 6p. (J). (gr. -1). 12.99 *(978-1-58476-808-1(8))* Innovative Kids.

Ikids Staff & Francis, Guy. Pets. 2009. (ENG., Illus.). 10p. (J). (gr. -1-1). 15.99 *(978-1-58476-940-8(8))* Innovative Kids.

Imodraj, illus. The Brave Little Tailor. 2014. (ENG.). 16p. (J). (gr. -1-3). 7.99 *(978-1-4867-0016-5(0))* Flowerpot Children's Pr. Inc. CAN. Dist: Cardinal Pubs. Group.

Imperato, Teresa. Colors All Around: A Turn & Pop Book. Petrone, Valeria, illus. 2005. (Turn & Pop Book Ser.). 10p. (J). bds. 5.95 *(978-1-58117-277-5(X)*, Intervisual/Piggy Toes) Bendon, Inc.

—Fiona's Fairy Magic. Huang, Benrei, illus. 2005. 14p. (J). 10.95 *(978-1-58117-322-2(9)*, Intervisual/Piggy Toes) Bendon, Inc.

—Good Morning, Good Night! Mitchell, Melanie, illus. 2006. (ENG.). 12p. (J). (gr. -1-18). 9.95 *(978-1-58117-279-9(6)*, Intervisual/Piggy Toes) Bendon, Inc.

—How Many Ducks in a Row? A Turn & Pop Book. Petrone, Valeria, illus. 2005. 10p. (J). bds. 5.95 *(978-1-58117-278-2(8)*, Intervisual/Piggy Toes) Bendon, Inc.

—On the Farm: A Barnyard Book. Rayner, Olivia, illus. 2005. 10p. (J). 7.95 *(978-1-58117-270-6(2)*, Intervisual/Piggy Toes) Bendon, Inc.

—On the Go! A Transportation Book. Rayner, Olivia, illus. 2005. 10p. (J). 7.95 *(978-1-58117-271-3(0)*, Intervisual/Piggy Toes) Bendon, Inc.

—Ten Christmas Lights: Count the Lights from One to Ten! Parry, Jo, illus. 2005. (ENG.). 20p. (J). 10.95 *(978-1-58117-321-5(0)*, Intervisual/Piggy Toes) Bendon, Inc.

—This Little Piggy. Haskamp, Steve, illus. 2006. (ENG.). 22p. (J). 9.95 *(978-1-58117-281-2(8)*, Intervisual/Piggy Toes) Bendon, Inc.

Impey, Rose. Dumper Truck Danger. Chatterton, Chris, illus. 2018. (Dino Diggers Ser.). (ENG.). 24p. (J). pap. *(978-1-4088-7248-2(X)*, 296272, Bloomsbury Children's Bks.) Bloomsbury Publishing Plc.

Ingram, Zoë, illus. Press Out & Color: Butterflies. 2017. (ENG.). 20p. (J). (gr. 5). 15.99 *(978-0-7636-9506-4(8))* Candlewick Pr.

Intrater, Roberta Grobel. Peek-a-Boo, You! Intrater, Roberta Grobel, photos by. 2nd rev. l.t. ed. 2005. (Illus.). 14p. (J). 14.99 *(978-0-9764985-0-6(2))* 1212 Pr.

Ipcar, Dahlov. Dahlov Ipcar's Farmyard Alphabet. 1 vol. 2010. (ENG., Illus.). 18p. (J). bds. 10.95 *(978-1-934031-43-8(7)*, 04192e00-20e8-4017-aca0-76d0db93c26b) Islandport Pr., Inc.

Iriyama, Satoshi. Good Night, Chirp. 2015. (Chirp the Chick Ser.). (ENG., Illus.). 36p. (J). (— 1). 8.99 *(978-0-544-35994-9(1)*, 1587557, Clarion Bks.) HarperCollins Pubs.

Ishida, Jui, illus. Who Says Moo? A Touch & Feel Board Book. 2005. 16p. (J). bds. 6.95 *(978-1-58117-178-5(1)*, Intervisual/Piggy Toes) Bendon, Inc.

Ismail, Yasmeen, illus. Inside, Outside, Upside Down: Draw & Discover. 2017. (ENG.). 56p. (J). (gr. -1-2). pap. 9.99 *(978-1-78067-929-7(7)*, King, Laurence Publishing) Orion Publishing Group, Ltd. GBR. Dist: Hachette Bk. Group.

—Push, Pull, Empty, Full: Draw & Discover. 2017. (ENG.). 56p. (J). (gr. -1-2). pap. 9.99 *(978-1-78067-931-0(9)*, King, Laurence Publishing) Orion Publishing Group, Ltd. GBR. Dist: Hachette Bk. Group.

Jackson, Mike, illus. Nickelodeon PAW Patrol: Super Star Pups. 2018. (Magnetic Hardcover Ser.). (ENG.). 10p. (J). (gr. -1-k). 12.99 *(978-0-7944-4045-9(2)*, Studio Fun International) Printers Row Publishing Group.

Jackson, Richard. Have a Look, Says Book. Hawkes, Kevin, illus. 2016. (ENG.). 48p. (J). (gr. -1-2). 17.99 *(978-1-4814-2105-8(0))* Simon & Schuster Children's Publishing.

Jam, Teddy. This New Baby. 1 vol. Johnson, Virginia, illus. 2011. (ENG.). 22p. (J). (gr. -1 — 1). bds. 8.95 *(978-1-55498-088-8(7))* Groundwood Bks. CAN. Dist: Publishers Group West (PGW).

James, Alice. See Inside Energy IR. 2018. (See Inside Board Bks.). (ENG.). 16p. 14.99 *(978-0-7945-4131-6(3)*, Usborne) EDC Publishing.

James, Annabelle. Jack & the Beanstalk Story in a Box. Ackerman, Michele L., illus. 2003. (Story in a Box Ser.). 12p. (J). bds. 8.99 *(978-1-883043-42-1(5))* Straight Edge Pr., The.

James, Helen Foster. Little America. Brett, Jeannie et al, illus. 2011. (Little Country Ser.). (ENG.). 20p. (J). (gr. -1-1). bds. 8.99 *(978-1-58536-179-3(8)*, 202235) Sleeping Bear Pr.

Jansson, Tove. Moomin's Lift-The-Flap Hide & Seek: With Big Flaps for Little Hands. 2011. (Moomins Ser.). (ENG., Illus.). 24p. (J). (gr. -1 — 1). 10.99 *(978-0-374-35051-2(5)*, 900070721, Farrar, Straus & Giroux (BYR)) Farrar, Straus & Giroux.

—Moomin's Little Book of Words. 2011. (Moomins Ser.). (ENG., Illus.). 16p. (J). (gr. -1 — 1). bds. 9.99 *(978-0-374-35048-2(5)*, 900070718, Farrar, Straus & Giroux (BYR)) Farrar, Straus & Giroux.

Jason Fulford, Tamara Shopsin. Find Colors: Published in Association with the Whitney Museum of American Art. 2018. (ENG., Illus.). 28p. (gr. -1 — 1). bds. 14.95 *(978-0-7148-7659-7(3))* Phaidon Pr., Inc.

—A Pile of Leaves: Published in Collaboration with the Whitney Museum of American Art. 2018. (ENG., Illus.). 24p. (gr. -1 — 1). bds. 18.95 *(978-0-7148-7720-4(4))* Phaidon Pr., Inc.

Jasper, Mark. Good Night Israel. Rosen, Anne, illus. 2010. (Good Night Our World Ser.). (ENG.). 22p. (J). (gr. k — 1). bds. 9.95 *(978-1-60219-043-6(7))* Good Night Bks.

—Good Night Pittsburgh. Palmer, Ruth, illus. 2012. (Good Night Our World Ser.). (ENG.). 20p. (J). (gr. k — 1). bds. 9.95 *(978-1-60219-073-3(9))* Good Night Bks.

—Good Night Utah. Hart, Jason, illus. 2012. (Good Night Our World Ser.). (ENG.). 20p. (J). (gr. -1 — 1). bds. 9.95 *(978-1-60219-059-7(3))* Good Night Bks.

Jay, Alison. Song of the Stars. 1 vol. 2015. (ENG., Illus.). 32p. (J). bds. 7.99 *(978-0-310-73630-1(7))* Zonderkidz.

Jenkins, Steve. The Animal Book: A Collection of the Fastest, Fiercest, Toughest, Cleverest, Shyest — And Most Surprising — Animals on Earth. Jenkins, Steve, illus. 2013. (ENG., Illus.). 208p. (J). (gr. -1-3). 24.99 *(978-0-547-55799-1(X)*, 1453456, Clarion Bks.) HarperCollins Pubs.

Jenkins, Ward, illus. New York, Baby! 2012. (ENG.). 24p. (J). (gr. -1 — 1). 12.99 *(978-1-4521-0619-9(3))* Chronicle Bks. LLC.

—San Francisco, Baby! 2012. (ENG.). 24p. (J). (gr. -1 — 1). 12.99 *(978-1-4521-0620-5(7))* Chronicle Bks. LLC.

Jennings, Sarah, illus. Feelings. 2017. (ENG.). 14p. (J). bds. 9.99 *(978-1-68119-539-1(9)*, 900176716, Bloomsbury Activity Bks.) Bloomsbury Publishing USA.

Jensen, Bonnie Rickner. I Love You, Little One. 1 vol. Chapman, Donna, illus. 2018. (Really Woolly Ser.). (ENG.). 40p. (J). bds. 9.99 *(978-1-4003-1015-9(6)*, Tommy Nelson) Nelson, Thomas Inc.

—A Very Happy Easter Prayer. 1 vol. 2018. (Time to Pray Ser.). (ENG., Illus.). 24p. (J). bds. 8.99 *(978-0-7180-7523-1(4)*, Tommy Nelson) Nelson, Thomas Inc.

Jin, Cindy. Catch Me If You Can. Lomp, Stephan, illus. 2017. (ENG.). 16p. (J). (gr. -1 — 1). bds. 6.99 *(978-1-4814-9218-8(7)*, Little Simon) Little Simon.

Jin, Susie Lee. It's Bedtime for Little Monkeys. 2010. (ENG., Illus.). 10p. (J). (-k). bds. 5.99 *(978-0-7369-2832-8(4)*, 6928328) Harvest Hse. Pubs.

Johnson, Crockett. Harold & the Purple Crayon Board Book. Johnson, Crockett, illus. 60th ed. 2015. (ENG., Illus.). 34p. (J). (gr. -1-3). bds. 7.99 *(978-0-06-208652-5(9)*, HarperFestival) HarperCollins Pubs.

—Harold & the Purple Crayon Lap Edition. Johnson, Crockett, illus. 2016. (ENG., Illus.). 34p. (J). (gr. -1 — 1). pap. 12.99 *(978-0-06-242730-4(X)*, HarperFestival) HarperCollins Pubs.

Johnson, Penny, illus. Here Comes Santa! 2016. (J). *(978-1-4351-6387-4(7))* Barnes & Noble, Inc.

Johnson, Richard, illus. Three Little Pigs. (Flip-Up Fairy Tales Ser.). 24p. (J). 2007. (gr. -1-2). *(978-1-84643-087-9(9))* 2005. pap. *(978-1-904550-21-1(5))* Child's Play International Ltd.

Johnson, Tim, et al. LEGO Disney Princess: Build Your Own Adventure. 2018. (LEGO Build Your Own Adventure Ser.). (ENG.). 80p. (J). (gr. 1-3). 24.99 *(978-1-4654-7368-4(8)*, DK Children) Dorling Kindersley Publishing, Inc.

Jolivet, Joëlle, illus. Moby-Dick: A Pop-Up Book from the Novel by Herman Melville (Pop up Books for Adults & Kids, Classic Books for Kids, Interactive Books for Adults & Children) 2019. (ENG.). 16p. 40.00 *(978-1-4521-7384-9(2))* Chronicle Bks. LLC.

Jonah Bible Sticker Book. 2003. (Illus.). 16p. (J). 2.98 *(978-1-4054-1555-2(X))* Parragon, Inc.

Jonath, Leslie & Christy, Jana. In Your Dreams. 2013. (ENG.). 14p. (J). bds. 5.99 *(978-1-4494-2858-7(4))* Andrews McMeel Publishing.

—In Your Dreams: A Mini Animation Book. 2011. (ENG., Illus.). 12p. (J). 9.99 *(978-1-4494-0332-4(8))* Andrews McMeel Publishing.

Jones, Frankie. Muddle & Match Jobs. Hinton, Stephanie, illus. 2016. 16p. (J). bds. 8.99 *(978-1-61067-491-1(X))* Kane Miller.

Jones, Lara, illus. Poppy Cat's Garden. 2008. (ENG.). 8p. (J). (gr. 3-6). bds. 16.95 *(978-0-230-01715-3(0),* Macmillan) Pan Macmillan GBR. Dist: Trans-Atlantic Pubns., Inc.

Jones, Rebecca, illus. My Body. 2018. (First Explorers Ser.) (ENG.). 10p. (J). (— 1). bds. 8.95 *(978-1-4549-2942-0(1))* Sterling Publishing Co., Inc.

Jones, Rob Lloyd. Flip Flap Cars. 2010. (Flip Flap Board Bks). 14p. (J). (gr. 1). bds. 14.99 *(978-0-7945-2554-5(7),* Usborne) EDC Publishing.

—Look Inside a Construction Sites IR. 2017. (Look Inside Board Bks.). (ENG.). 14p. 14.99 *(978-0-7945-3955-9(6),* Usborne) EDC Publishing.

—Look Inside an Airport. rev. ed. 2012. (Look Inside Board Bks). 14p. (J). ring bd. 15.99 *(978-0-7945-3234-5(9),* Usborne) EDC Publishing.

—Look Inside Space. 2012. (Look Inside Board Bks). 14p. (J). bds. 14.99 *(978-0-7945-3282-6(9),* Usborne) EDC Publishing.

—See Inside Famous Buildings. Ablett, Barry, illus. 2009. (See Inside Board Bks). 16p. (J). (gr. 2). bds. 13.99 *(978-0-7945-2350-3(1),* Usborne) EDC Publishing.

—See Inside the Second World War. Pritelli, Maria Cristina, illus. 2012. (See Inside Board Bks). 16p. (J). ring bd. 13.99 *(978-0-7945-3085-3(0),* Usborne) EDC Publishing.

Jones, Sally Lloyd. Lift the Flap Bible. Moroney, Trace, illus. 2011. (Lift-The-Flap Ser.). (ENG.). 20p. (J). (gr. -1-k). bds. 10.99 *(978-0-7944-2278-3(0),* Studio Fun International) Printers Row Publishing Group.

Jones, Sarah. Ears, Nose, Eyes... Surprise! 2018. (ROYGBaby Ser.). (ENG., Illus.). 14p. (J). (— 1). bds. 7.99 *(978-1-936669-62-2(5))* Blue Manatee Press.

Jorden, Brooke. I Dig Bathtime. Ladatko, Ekaterina, illus. 2018. (ENG.). 16p. (J). (gr. -1-k). bds. 8.99 *(978-1-64170-030-6(0),* 550030) Familius LLC.

—Lit for Little Hands: the Secret Garden, Volume 4. Miles, David, illus. 2019. (Lit for Little Hands Ser.: 4). (ENG.). 16p. (J). (gr. -1-1). bds. 12.99 *(978-1-64170-105-1(6),* 550105) Familius LLC.

—100 First Words for Little Geeks. Kershner, Kyle, illus. 2018. (100 First Words Ser.). (ENG.). 20p. (J). (gr. -1 — 1). bds. 9.99 *(978-1-945547-95-9(2),* 554795) Familius LLC.

Jorden, Tyler. Physics Animated! Martins, Elsa, illus. 2019. (ENG.). 14p. (J). (gr. k-2). bds. 14.99 *(978-1-64170-132-7(3),* 550132) Familius LLC.

—100 First Words for Little Geniuses, Volume 2. Kershner, Kyle, illus. 2018. (100 First Words Ser.: 2). (ENG.). 20p. (J). (gr. -1-3). bds. 9.99 *(978-1-64170-034-4(3),* 550034) Familius LLC.

Josephs, Mary. All Aboard Noah's Ark! Bratun, Katy, illus. 2007. (Chunky Book(R) Ser.). 22p. (J). (— 1). 3.99 *(978-0-679-86054-9(1),* Golden Inspirational) Random Hse. Children's Bks.

Joyce, Bridget & Furman, Eric. Tonka Rescue Trucks! Dean Kleven Studios & Finley, Shawn, illus. 2007. (Fold & Go Vehicles Ser.). 15.98 *(978-1-4127-2981-9(5))* Publications International, Ltd.

Jugran, Jan. Baby Dolphins. Larranaga, Ana Martin, illus. 2006. (ENG.). 6p. (J). (gr. -1 — 1). 14.99 *(978-1-58476-490-8(2),* IKIDS) Innovative Kids.

—Goodnight Faces: A Book of Masks. Larranaga, Ana Martin, illus. 2007. (ENG.). 12p. (J). (gr. -1 — 1). bds. 6.99 *(978-1-58476-672-8(7),* IKIDS) Innovative Kids.

—Hugs. Larranaga, Ana Martin, illus. 2007. (ENG.). 12p. (J). (gr. -1 — 1). 9.99 *(978-1-58476-620-9(4),* IKIDS) Innovative Kids.

—Three Little Duckies. Parsons, Jackie & Larranaga, Ana Martin, illus. 2006. (ENG.). 6p. (J). (gr. -1 — 1). 14.99 *(978-1-58476-352-9(3),* IKIDS) Innovative Kids.

Julian, Russell. Busy Dog. 2005. (Farm Board Book Ser.). (ENG., Illus.). 12p. (J). bds. 9.99 *(978-1-4052-1031-7(1))* Farshore GBR. Dist: Trafalgar Square Publishing.

—Happy Cockerel. 2005. (Farm Board Book Ser.). (ENG., Illus.). 12p. (J). bds. 9.99 *(978-1-4052-1030-0(3))* Farshore GBR. Dist: Trafalgar Square Publishing.

Julian, Russell, illus. Ten Twinkly Stars. 2017. (J). *(978-1-84857-579-0(3))* Little Tiger Pr. Group.

Jullien, Jean. Before & After. 2017. (ENG., Illus.). 40p. (gr. -1 — 1). bds. 16.95 *(978-0-7148-7408-1(6))* Phaidon Pr., Inc.

Jumbo's Jungle: Colors. 2011. (Illus.). (J). *(978-1-58865-893-7(7))* Kidsbooks, LLC.

Kalban, Rachel. I Like to Be with My Family. Fruchter, Jason, illus. 2016. (Daniel Tiger's Neighborhood Ser.). (ENG.). 26p. (J). (gr. -1-k). bds. 8.99 *(978-1-4814-6100-9(1),* Simon Spotlight) Simon Spotlight.

Kantor, Susan. What Is Soft? Barker, Erin, illus. 2018. (ENG.). 14p. (J). (— 1). bds. 7.99 *(978-1-936669-63-9(3))* Blue Manatee Press.

Kanzler, John. Rock-a -Bye Baby. Tiger Tales Staff, ed. Kanzler, John, illus. 2011. (ENG., Illus.). 24p. (J). (gr. -1-k). bds. 8.95 *(978-1-58925-853-2(3))* Tiger Tales.

Karr, Lily. Five Bouncing Bunnies. Rogers, Jacqueline, illus. 2013. (ENG.). 10p. (J). (gr. -1 — 1). bds. 6.99 *(978-0-545-45825-2(0),* Cartwheel Bks.) Scholastic, Inc.

—Noah's Ark. Berg, Michelle, illus. 2007. (ENG.). 6p. (J). (gr. -1). bds. 12.99 *(978-0-439-86396-4(1))* Scholastic, Inc.

Kasso, Martin. Sharks. Jeffirs, Matt, illus. 2008. (ENG.). 24p. (J). (gr. 3-18). 19.95 *(978-1-58117-797-6(6),* Intervisual/Piggy Toes) Bendon, Inc.

Kate, Maggie, ed. Glitter Roses Stickers. 2004. (Dover Stickers Ser.). (ENG., Illus.). 2p. (J). (gr. -1-5). 1.99 *(978-0-486-43534-3(2),* 435342) Dover Pubns., Inc.

Katschke, Judy. Shrek the Third. 2007. (Illus.). (J). *(978-0-696-23949-6(3))* Meredith Bks.

Katz, David Bar. DC Super Heroes Colors, Shapes & More! 2012. (DC Super Heroes Ser.). (ENG.). 20p. (J). (gr. -1 — 1). bds. 9.99 *(978-1-935703-73-0(0))* Downtown Bookworks.

—My First Wonder Woman Book: Touch & Feel. 2011. (DC Super Heroes Ser.). (ENG.). 12p. (J). (— 1). bds. 11.99 *(978-1-935703-13-6(7))* Downtown Bookworks.

Katz, Karen. Baby at the Farm: A Touch-And-Feel Book. Katz, Karen, illus. 2009. (ENG., Illus.). 12p. (J). (gr. -1 — 1). bds. 7.99 *(978-1-4169-8568-6(9),* Little Simon) Little Simon.

—Baby Loves Fall! A Karen Katz Lift-The-Flap Book. Katz, Karen, illus. 2013. (ENG., Illus.). 14p. (J). (gr. -1 — 1). bds. 7.99 *(978-1-4424-5209-1(9),* Little Simon) Little Simon.

—Baby Loves Spring! A Karen Katz Lift-The-Flap Book. Katz, Karen, illus. 2012. (ENG., Illus.). 14p. (J). (gr. -1 — 1). bds. 7.99 *(978-1-4424-2745-7(0),* Little Simon) Little Simon.

—Baby Loves Summer! A Karen Katz Lift-The-Flap Book. Katz, Karen, illus. 2012. (ENG., Illus.). 14p. (J). (gr. -1 — 1). bds. 7.99 *(978-1-4424-2746-4(9),* Little Simon) Little Simon.

—Baby Loves Winter! A Karen Katz Lift-The-Flap Book. Katz, Karen, illus. 2013. (ENG., Illus.). 14p. (J). (gr. -1 — 1). bds. 6.99 *(978-1-4424-5213-8(7),* Little Simon) Little Simon.

—Baby's Big Busy Book. Katz, Karen, illus. 2017. (ENG., Illus.). 12p. (J). (gr. -1 — 1). bds. 14.99 *(978-1-4814-8830-3(9),* Little Simon) Little Simon.

—Baby's Colors. Katz, Karen, illus. 2010. (ENG., Illus.). 14p. (J). (gr. -1 — 1). bds. 7.99 *(978-1-4169-9821-1(7),* Little Simon) Little Simon.

—Baby's Numbers. Katz, Karen, illus. 2010. (ENG., Illus.). 14p. (J). (gr. -1 — 1). bds. 7.99 *(978-1-4424-0827-2(8),* Little Simon) Little Simon.

—Baby's Shapes. Katz, Karen, illus. 2010. (ENG., Illus.). 14p. (J). (gr. -1 — 1). bds. 7.99 *(978-1-4169-9824-2(1),* Little Simon) Little Simon.

—Beddy-Bye, Baby: A Touch-And-Feel Book. Katz, Karen, illus. 2009. (ENG., Illus.). 12p. (J). (gr. -1 — 1). bds. 7.99 *(978-1-4169-8048-3(2),* Little Simon) Little Simon.

—Buzz, Buzz, Baby! A Karen Katz Lift-The-Flap Book. Katz, Karen, illus. 2014. (ENG., Illus.). 14p. (J). (gr. -1 — 1). bds. 7.99 *(978-1-4424-9313-1(5),* Little Simon) Little Simon.

—¡Cu-Cú, Bebé! (Peek-A-Baby) Katz, Karen, illus. 2009. (SPA., Illus.). 14p. (J). (gr. -1 — 1). bds. 7.99 *(978-1-4169-7938-8(7),* Libros Para Ninos) Libros Para Ninos.

—¿dónde Está el Ombliguito? (Where Is Baby's Belly Button?) Un Libro para Levantar Ta Tapita Por Karen Katz (a Lift-The-Flap Story) Ziegler, Argentina Palacios, tr. Katz, Karen, illus. 2004. (SPA., Illus.). 14p. (J). (gr. -1-1). bds. 7.99 *(978-0-689-86977-8(0),* Libros Para Ninos) Libros Para Ninos.

—Grandpa & Me: Grandpa & Me. Katz, Karen, illus. 2004. (ENG., Illus.). 14p. (J). bds. 7.99 *(978-0-689-86644-9(5),* Little Simon) Little Simon.

—How Does Baby Feel? A Karen Katz Lift-The-Flap Book. Katz, Karen, illus. 2013. (ENG., Illus.). 14p. (J). (gr. -1 — 1). bds. 7.99 *(978-1-4424-5204-6(8),* Little Simon) Little Simon.

—I Can Share! 2011. 24p. (J). (gr. -1-k). mass mkt. 5.99 *(978-0-448-45592-1(7),* Grosset & Dunlap) Penguin Young Readers Group.

—Kiss Baby's Boo-Boo: A Karen Katz Lift-The-Flap Book. Katz, Karen, illus. 2016. (ENG., Illus.). 14p. (J). (gr. -1 — 1). bds. 6.99 *(978-1-4814-4208-4(2),* Little Simon) Little Simon.

—Mommy Hugs: Lap Edition. Katz, Karen, illus. 2010. (ENG., Illus.). 26p. (J). (gr. -1 — 1). bds. 12.99 *(978-1-4424-0791-6(3),* Little Simon) Little Simon.

—My Big Boy Undies. 2012. 14p. (J). (gr. -1-k). bds. 7.99 *(978-0-448-45705-5(9),* Grosset & Dunlap) Penguin Young Readers Group.

—My Big Girl Undies. 2012. 14p. (J). (gr. -1-k). bds. 7.99 *(978-0-448-45703-1(2),* Grosset & Dunlap) Penguin Young Readers Group.

—No Biting! 2011. (ENG.). 24p. (J). (gr. -1-k). mass mkt. 6.99 *(978-0-448-45581-5(1),* Grosset & Dunlap) Penguin Young Readers Group.

—No Hitting! 2011. 24p. (J). (gr. -1-k). mass mkt. 5.99 *(978-0-448-45596-9(X),* Grosset & Dunlap) Penguin Young Readers Group.

—No Hitting! A Lift-The-Flap Book. 2004. (ENG., Illus.). 14p. (J). (gr. -1-k). 7.99 *(978-0-448-43612-8(4),* Grosset & Dunlap) Penguin Young Readers Group.

—Peek-A-Baby: A Lift-The-Flap Book. Katz, Karen, illus. 2007. (ENG., Illus.). 14p. (J). (gr. -1 — 1). bds. 7.99 *(978-1-4169-3622-0(X),* Little Simon) Little Simon.

—Peek-A-Baby: A Lift-The-Flap Book/Lap Edition. Katz, Karen, illus. 2010. (ENG., Illus.). 14p. (J). (gr. -1 — 1). 11.99 *(978-1-4424-0790-9(5),* Little Simon) Little Simon.

—Princess Baby. Katz, Karen, illus. 2012. (Princess Baby Ser.). (Illus.). 30p. (J). (gr. k-k). 7.99 *(978-0-307-93146-7(3),* Schwartz & Wade Bks.) Random Hse. Children's Bks.

—Princess Baby, Night-Night. Katz, Karen, illus. 2014. (Princess Baby Ser.). (ENG., Illus.). 28p. (J). (— 1). bds. 7.99 *(978-0-385-37848-2(3),* Schwartz & Wade Bks.) Random Hse. Children's Bks.

—Roar, Roar, Baby! A Karen Katz Lift-The-Flap Book. Katz, Karen, illus. 2015. (ENG., Illus.). 14p. (J). (gr. -1 — 1). bds. 6.99 *(978-1-4814-1788-4(6),* Little Simon) Little Simon.

—Shake It up, Baby! Katz, Karen, illus. 2009. (ENG., Illus.). 14p. (J). (gr. -1 — 1). bds. 7.99 *(978-1-4169-6737-8(0),* Little Simon) Little Simon.

—Splish, Splash, Baby! Katz, Karen, illus. 2015. (ENG., Illus.). 14p. (J). (gr. -1 — 1). bds. 7.99 *(978-1-4814-1789-1(4),* Little Simon) Little Simon.

—Ten Tiny Babies. Katz, Karen, illus. 2011. (Classic Board Bks.). (ENG., Illus.). 32p. (J). (gr. -1-k). bds. 8.99 *(978-1-4424-1394-8(8),* Little Simon) Little Simon.

—Ten Tiny Tickles. Katz, Karen, illus. 2008. (Classic Board Bks.). (ENG., Illus.). 32p. (J). (gr. -1-k). bds. 8.99 *(978-1-4169-5101-8(6),* Little Simon) Little Simon.

—Vroom, Vroom, Trucks! Katz, Karen, illus. 2016. (ENG., Illus.). 14p. (J). (gr. -1 — 1). bds. 6.99 *(978-1-4814-4209-1(0),* Little Simon) Little Simon.

—Where Is Baby's Beach Ball? A Lift-The-Flap Book. Katz, Karen, illus. 2009. (ENG., Illus.). 14p. (J). (gr. -1 — 1). bds. 7.99 *(978-1-4169-4962-6(3),* Little Simon) Little Simon.

—Where Is Baby's Belly Button? 2005. (CHI.). 12p. (J). 6.95 *(978-986-7517-72-2(5))* Shan Jen Publishing Co., Ltd. TWN. Dist: Chinasprout, Inc.

—Where Is Baby's Belly Button? Anniversary Edition/Lap Edition. Katz, Karen, illus. anniv. ed. 2009. (ENG., Illus.). 14p. (J). (gr. -1 — 1). bds. 12.99 *(978-1-4169-8733-8(9),* Little Simon) Little Simon.

—Where Is Baby's Birthday Cake? A Lift-The-Flap Book. Katz, Karen, illus. 2008. (ENG., Illus.). 14p. (J). (gr. -1 — 1). bds. 7.99 *(978-1-4169-5817-8(7),* Little Simon) Little Simon.

—Where Is Baby's Christmas Present? A Lift-The-Flap Book. Katz, Karen, illus. 2009. (ENG., Illus.). 14p. (J). (gr. -1 — 1). bds. 7.99 *(978-1-4169-7145-0(9),* Little Simon) Little Simon.

—Where Is Baby's Home? A Karen Katz Lift-The-Flap Book. Katz, Karen, illus. 2017. (ENG., Illus.). 14p. (J). (gr. -1 — 1). bds. 6.99 *(978-1-5344-0088-7(5),* Little Simon) Little Simon.

—Where Is Baby's Puppy? A Lift-The-Flap Book. Katz, Karen, illus. 2011. (ENG., Illus.). 14p. (J). (gr. -1 — 1). bds. 7.99 *(978-1-4169-8684-3(7),* Little Simon) Little Simon.

—Where Is Baby's Turkey? A Karen Katz Lift-The-Flap Book. Katz, Karen, illus. 2017. (ENG., Illus.). 14p. (J). (gr. -1 — 1). bds. 7.99 *(978-1-5344-0089-4(3),* Little Simon) Little Simon.

—Where Is Baby's Valentine? A Lift-The-Flap Book. Katz, Karen, illus. 2006. (ENG., Illus.). 14p. (J). (gr. -1 — 1). bds. 7.99 *(978-1-4169-0971-2(0),* Little Simon) Little Simon.

—Where Is Baby's Yummy Tummy? A Karen Katz Lift-The-Flap Book. Katz, Karen, illus. 2011. (ENG., Illus.). 14p. (J). (gr. -1 — 1). bds. 7.99 *(978-1-4424-2165-3(7),* Little Simon) Little Simon.

—Wiggle Your Toes. Katz, Karen, illus. 2006. (ENG., Illus.). 14p. (J). (gr. -1-k). bds. 11.99 *(978-1-4169-0365-9(8),* Little Simon) Little Simon.

—Zoom, Zoom, Baby! A Karen Katz Lift-The-Flap Book. Katz, Karen, illus. 2014. (ENG., Illus.). 14p. (J). (gr. -1 — 1). bds. 7.99 *(978-1-4424-9314-8(3),* Little Simon) Little Simon.

Katz, Karen & Bauer, Marion Dane. Baby's Box of Fun (Boxed Set) A Karen Katz Lift-The-Flap Gift Set: Where Is Baby's Bellybutton?; Where Is Baby's Mommy?; Toes, Ears, & Nose! Katz, Karen, illus. gif. ed. 2004. (ENG., Illus.). 44p. (J). (gr. -1 — 1). bds. 19.99 *(978-0-689-03862-4(3),* Little Simon) Little Simon.

Kavanaugh, Missy & Gurman, Sarah, texts. Fish. 2009. (Illus.). 9p. (J). *(978-1-4351-1780-8(8))* Barnes & Noble, Inc.

—Kittens. 2009. (Illus.). 18p. (J). *(978-1-4351-1782-2(4))* Barnes & Noble, Inc.

—Puppies. 2009. (Illus.). 8p. (J). *(978-1-4351-1783-9(2))* Barnes & Noble, Inc.

—Sea Creatures. 2009. (Illus.). (J). *(978-1-4351-1785-3(9))* Barnes & Noble, Inc.

Keast, Jennifer H. Dora the Explorer (Giant First Play-a-Sound) 2010. 10p. (J). bds. 17.98 *(978-1-60553-544-9(3))* Publications International, Ltd.

—Mickey Mouse Clubhouse (Giant First Play-a-Sound) 2010. 10p. (J). bds. 17.98 *(978-1-60553-545-6(1))* Phoenix International Publications, Inc.

Keith, Donna. I Love You Even When. 1 vol. 2015. (ENG., Illus.). 20p. (J). bds. 9.99 *(978-0-7180-3644-7(1),* Tommy Nelson) Nelson, Thomas Inc.

Kelly, Richard, ed. Convertible Playbook - Castle: Read the Story, Press Out the Characters, Fold Out the Building. 2017. (ENG.). 24p. (J). 19.95 *(978-1-78209-975-8(1))* Miles Kelly Publishing, Ltd. GBR. Dist: Parkwest Pubns., Inc.

—Convertible Playbook - Fire Station: Read the Story, Press Out the Characters, Fold Out the Building. 2017. 24p. (J). 19.95 *(978-1-78209-974-1(3))* Miles Kelly Publishing, Ltd. GBR. Dist: Parkwest Pubns., Inc.

—Read & Play - Princess: Read, Play, Puzzlw & Color for Hours! 2017. (ENG.). 40p. (J). pap. 19.95 *(978-1-78209-980-2(8))* Miles Kelly Publishing, Ltd. GBR. Dist: Parkwest Pubns., Inc.

Kenison, Misti. The Lost Race Car: A Fox & Goat Mystery, 1 vol. 2018. (Fox & Goat Mysteries Ser.: 2). (ENG., Illus.). 28p. (J). bds. 12.99 *(978-0-7643-5599-8(6),* 16098) Schiffer Publishing, Ltd.

—The Missing Bouncy Ball: A Fox & Goat Mystery, 1 vol. 2018. (Fox & Goat Mysteries Ser.: 1). (ENG., Illus.). 28p. (J). bds. 12.99 *(978-0-7643-5600-1(3),* 16097) Schiffer Publishing, Ltd.

Kenison, Misti, illus. The Tiny Traveler: Egypt: A Book of Shapes. 2015. (ENG.). 24p. (J). (— 1). bds. 5.95 *(978-1-62914-607-2(2),* Sky Pony Pr.) Skyhorse Publishing Co., Inc.

—The Tiny Traveler: France: A Book of Colors. 2015. (ENG.). 24p. (J). (— 1). bds. 5.95 *(978-1-62914-609-6(9),* Sky Pony Pr.) Skyhorse Publishing Co., Inc.

Kennedy, Anne Vittur. Go Baby! Go Dog! Kennedy, Anne Vittur, illus. 2018. (ENG., Illus.). 20p. (J). (gr. -1 — 1). bds. 7.99 *(978-0-8075-2971-3(0),* 807529710) Whitman, Albert & Co.

Kennedy, Jimmy. The Teddy Bears' Picnic. Day, Alexandra, illus. 2015. (Classic Board Bks.). (ENG.). 34p. (J). (gr. -1-k). bds. 8.99 *(978-1-4814-2274-1(X),* Little Simon) Little Simon.

Kennedy, Pamela. Night-Night, Bunny. Keay, Claire, illus. 2017. (ENG.). 16p. (J). (gr. -1-k). bds. 7.99 *(978-0-8249-1660-2(3))* Worthy Publishing.

—We Wish You a Merry Christmas! Reed, Lisa, illus. 2017. (VeggieTales Ser.). (ENG.). 16p. (J). (gr. -1-k). bds. 12.99 *(978-0-8249-1663-3(8))* Worthy Publishing.

Kent, Lorna, illus. Baby's First Board Books: On the Move; Animals; My Home; Playtime. 2004. (Baby's First Board Books Gift Set Ser.). 12p. (J). bds. 12.99 *(978-1-85854-694-0(X))* Brimax Books Ltd. GBR. Dist: Byeway Bks.

Kerley, Barbara. Portland Baby. Cleland, Josh, illus. 2017. (Local Baby Bks.). (ENG.). 22p. (J). (gr. -1 — 1). bds. 8.95 *(978-1-946064-05-9(X),* 806405) Duo Pr. LLC.

Kernahan, Maria. R Is for Rocky Mountains. Schafbuch, Michael, illus. 2017. (ENG.). 56p. (J). (gr. -1-k). bds. 9.95 *(978-1-942402-46-6(5),* b4b42ae7-d425-495c-a90b-11ddf96d8ba3) Dry Climate Studios.

Kerr, Judith. Mog's Christmas. Kerr, Judith, illus. 2019. (ENG., Illus.). 30p. (J). bds. 7.99 *(978-0-00-834764-2(6),* HarperCollins Children's Bks.) HarperCollins Pubs. Ltd. GBR. Dist: HarperCollins Pubs.

—My First Mog Books. Kerr, Judith, illus. 2019. (ENG., Illus.). 40p. (J). bds. 8.99 *(978-0-00-834765-9(4),* HarperCollins Children's Bks.) HarperCollins Pubs. Ltd. GBR. Dist: HarperCollins Pubs.

Kershner, Kyle. 100 First Words for Little Artists, Volume 3. 2019. (100 First Words Ser.: 3). (ENG., Illus.). 20p. (J). (gr. -1-3). bds. 9.99 *(978-1-64170-128-0(5),* 550128) Familius LLC.

Kertell, Lynn Maslen. My First Bob Books - Alphabet Box Set | Phonics, Letter Sounds, Ages 3 & up, Pre-K (Reading Readiness), 1 vol. Maslen, John R. & Hendra, Sue, illus. 2008. (Bob Bks.). (ENG.). 120p. (J). (gr. -1-k). pap., pap., pap. 17.99 *(978-0-545-01921-7(4),* Cartwheel Bks.) Scholastic, Inc.

Khan, Sarah. Pets Lift-the-Flap. 2005. (Luxury Lift-the-Flap Learners Ser.). 16p. (J). (gr. 1-18). 11.95 *(978-0-7945-0914-9(2),* Usborne) EDC Publishing.

Khemka, Nitya. Good Night Delhi. Kale, Kavita Singh, illus. 2017. (Good Night Our World Ser.). 20p. (J). (— 1). bds. 9.95 *(978-1-60219-481-6(5))* Good Night Bks.

—Good Night India. Kale, Kavita Singh, illus. 2017. (Good Night Our World Ser.). 20p. (J). (— 1). bds. 9.95 *(978-1-60219-477-9(7))* Good Night Bks.

—Good Night Mumbai. Kale, Kavita Singh, illus. 2017. (Good Night Our World Ser.). 20p. (J). (— 1). bds. 9.95 *(978-1-60219-483-0(1))* Good Night Bks.

Kids, National Geographic. National Geographic Kids Little Kids First Board Book: Wild Animal Sounds. 2019. (First Board Bks.). (Illus.). 26p. (J). (gr. -1 — 1). bds. 7.99 *(978-1-4263-3466-5(4),* National Geographic Kids) Disney Publishing Worldwide.

—Weird but True Animals. 2018. (Weird but True Ser.). (Illus.). 208p. (J). (gr. 3-7). pap. 8.99 *(978-1-4263-2981-4(4),* National Geographic Kids) Disney Publishing Worldwide.

Kiely, Orla. Numbers. Kiely, Orla, illus. 2012. (ENG., Illus.). 20p. (J). (gr. -1 — 1). bds. 12.99 *(978-0-8050-9492-3(X),* 900080253, Holt, Henry & Co. Bks. For Young Readers) Holt, Henry & Co.

Kiffel-Alcheh, Jamie. A Hoopoe Says Oop! Animals of Israel. Kuman, Ivana, illus. 2019. (ENG.). 12p. (J). (gr. -1 — 1). bds. 5.99 *(978-1-5415-0049-5(0),* 0715077e-df5d-44b8-b9eb-42d0f4777f59, Kar-Ben Publishing) Lerner Publishing Group.

Killen, Nicola. Bobo & Co. Colours. Killen, Nicola, illus. 2017. (ENG., Illus.). 10p. (J). bds. *(978-1-4088-8001-2(6),* 298891, Bloomsbury Children's Bks.) Bloomsbury Publishing Plc.

—Bobo & Co. Numbers. Killen, Nicola, illus. 2017. (ENG., Illus.). 10p. (J). bds. *(978-1-4088-8002-9(4),* 298892, Bloomsbury Children's Bks.) Bloomsbury Publishing Plc.

Kim, Melissa. A Little Brown Bat Story, 1 vol. Fitch, Jada, illus. 2015. (ENG.). 24p. (J). bds. 10.95 *(978-1-939017-70-3(X),* 586f104f-245a-45a2-b62a-5ccd0f40d0dc) Islandport Pr., Inc.

Kimmelman, Leslie. Belly Breathe. Dale-Scott, Lindsey, illus. 2018. (ENG.). 22p. (J). (gr. -1 — 1). bds. 8.99 *(978-0-8075-2167-0(1),* 807521671) Whitman, Albert & Co.

—You're the Cheese in My Blintz. Kaulitzki, Ramona, illus. 2020. (ENG.). 12p. (J). (gr. -1 — 1). bds. 6.99 *(978-1-5415-3467-4(0),* 3d66852f-012f-48cc-ab8b-c39cc70b188a, Kar-Ben Publishing) Lerner Publishing Group.

Kimmelman, Leslie & Shepherd, Jodie. Do You Know Noses? (Rookie Toddler) 2016. (Rookie Toddler Ser.). (ENG., Illus.). 14p. (J). (gr. -1 — 1). bds. 6.95 *(978-0-531-22618-6(2),* Children's Pr.) Scholastic Library Publishing.

Kingfisher Editors, ed. Puzzling Puzzles: What Shape Is This? Book + 2004. (J). pap. 7.95 *(978-0-7534-5644-6(3))* Kingfisher Bks.

Kirk, Daniel. Honk Honk! Beep Beep! Kirk, Daniel, illus. 2014. (ENG., Illus.). 32p. (J). (gr. -1-k). bds. 6.99 *(978-1-4231-8041-8(0))* Hyperion Bks. for Children.

Kirwan, Wednesday. Baby Loves to Boogie! Kirwan, Wednesday, illus. 2014. (ENG., Illus.). 30p. (J). (gr. -1 — 1). bds. 5.99 *(978-1-4814-0383-2(4),* Little Simon) Little Simon.

—Baby Loves to Party! Kirwan, Wednesday, illus. 2015. (ENG., Illus.). 30p. (J). (gr. -1 — 1). bds. 6.99 *(978-1-4814-2994-8(9),* Little Simon) Little Simon.

—Baby Loves to Rock! Kirwan, Wednesday, illus. 2013. (ENG., Illus.). 28p. (J). (gr. -1 — 1). bds. 7.99 *(978-1-4424-5989-2(1),* Little Simon) Little Simon.

Kitten & Friends. 2008. (Illus.). (J). *(978-0-312-50638-4(4))* St. Martin's Pr.

Klaassen, Sandra. Peg & Uan: Making Friends, 52 vols. 2017. (Illus.). 14p. (J). 9.95 *(978-1-78250-441-2(9),* Kelpies) Floris Bks. GBR. Dist: Consortium Bk. Sales & Distribution.

Kleinberg, Naomi. Elmo's Book of Friends (Sesame Street) 2016. (ENG., Illus.). 16p. (J). (-k). bds. 7.99 *(978-0-399-55211-3(1),* Random Hse. Bks. for Young Readers) Random Hse. Children's Bks.

—Elmo's Christmas Snowman (Sesame Street) Brannon, Tom, illus. 2013. (ENG.). 12p. (J). (— 1). bds. 6.99 *(978-0-449-81257-0(X),* Random Hse. Bks. for Young Readers) Random Hse. Children's Bks.

Koeppel, Ruth. In the Wild. McBee, Scott, illus. 2009. (ENG.). 10p. (J). (gr. -1-1). 15.99 *(978-1-58476-816-6(9))* Innovative Kids.

Korman, Justine. The Poky Little Puppy's First Christmas. Korman, Justine, illus. 2014. (Illus.). 26p. (J). (-k). bds. 7.99 *(978-0-385-38473-5(4),* Golden Bks.) Random Hse. Children's Bks.

Korngold, Jamie S. Mazel Tov! It's a Boy: Mazel Tov! It's a Girl. Finkelstein, Jeff, illus. Finkelstein, Jeff, photos by. 2015. (J). 6.99 *(978-1-4677-6206-9(7),* Kar-Ben Publishing) Lerner Publishing Group.

Kovacs, Victoria. Elijah/John the Baptist Flip-Over Book. Ryley, David, illus. 2016. (Little Bible Heroes(tm) Ser.). (ENG.). 32p. (J). (gr. k-2). pap. 3.99 *(978-1-4336-4324-8(3),* 005786142, B&H Kids) B&H Publishing Group.

—The Little Giver/Zacchaeus Flip-Over Book. Ryley, David, illus. 2016. (Little Bible Heroes(tm) Ser.). (ENG.). 32p. (J). (gr. k-2). pap. 5.99 *(978-1-4336-4326-2(X),* 005786144, B&H Kids) B&H Publishing Group.

Kralovansky, Susan. Counting Colors in Texas, 1 vol. Crane, Robert, photos by. 2018. (SPA & ENG., Illus.). 10p. bds. 9.95 *(978-1-4556-2383-9(0),* Pelican Publishing) Arcadia Publishing.

Krensky, Stephen. Now I Am Big! Gillingham, Sara, illus. 2012. (Empowerment Ser.). (ENG.). 12p. (J). (gr. -1 — 1). bds. 7.99 *(978-1-4197-0416-1(8),* 1033101, Abrams Appleseed) Abrams, Inc.

Krinsky, Rivkah. Touch of Shabbat: A Touch & Feel Book. Becker, Boruch, illus. 2011. (J). bds. 9.95 *(978-0-8266-0019-6(0))* Kehot Pubn. Society.

Kroll, Steven. The Biggest Pumpkin Surprise Ever. Bassett, Jeni, illus. 2012. (ENG.). 10p. (J). (gr. -1-k). bds. 6.99 *(978-0-545-40285-9(9),* Cartwheel Bks.) Scholastic, Inc.

Krutop, Lee, creator. Go Out to Play. 2008. (Illus.). 10p. (J). (gr. -1-1). bds. *(978-1-74178-572-2(3))* Brimax Books Ltd.

Kubler, Annie. Dinosaur Diner. 2008. (Finger Puppet Bks.). (Illus.). 24p. (J). (gr. -1-1). *(978-1-84643-183-8(2))* Child's Play International Ltd.

—See You Later, Alligator! 2004. (Finger Puppet Bks.). (Illus.). 24p. (J). (gr. 1-2). *(978-1-904550-05-1(3))* Child's Play International Ltd.

TUV

Kubler, Annie, illus. Dress Up! 2012. (Mix & Match Babies Ser.). (ENG.). 12p. (J). bds. *(978-1-84643-485-3(8))* Child's Play International Ltd.
—Ride On! 2012. (Mix & Match Babies Ser.). (ENG.). 12p. (J). bds. *(978-1-84643-483-9(1))* Child's Play International Ltd.
—What Can I Feel? 2011. (Small Senses Ser.). 12p. (J). spiral bd. *(978-1-84643-374-0(6))* Child's Play International Ltd.
—What Can I Hear? 2011. (Small Senses Ser.). 12p. (J). spiral bd. *(978-1-84643-377-1(0))* Child's Play International Ltd.
—What Can I See? 2011. (Small Senses Ser.). 12p. (J). spiral bd. *(978-1-84643-378-8(9))* Child's Play International Ltd.
—What Can I Smell? 2011. (Small Senses Ser.). 12p. (J). spiral bd. *(978-1-84643-376-4(2))* Child's Play International Ltd.
—What Can I Taste? 2011. (Small Senses Ser.). 12p. (J). spiral bd. *(978-1-84643-375-7(4))* Child's Play International Ltd.
—Work Out! 2012. (Mix & Match Babies Ser.). (ENG.). 12p. (J). bds. *(978-1-84643-484-6(X))* Child's Play International Ltd.
Kumon. What Does Baby See? 2008. (Illus.). 12p. (J). bds. *(978-1-934618-27-1(6))* Begin Smart LLC.
Kunhardt, Dorothy. Pat the Bunny: First Books for Baby (Pat the Bunny; Pat the Puppy; Pat the Cat, 3 vols. 2015. (Touch-And-Feel Ser.). (Illus.). 20p. (J). (— 1). 29.99 *(978-0-553-50838-3(5)*, Golden Bks.) Random Hse. Children's Bks.
Kurtz, John, illus. Disney Princess: Look & Find. 2004. (Disney Princess Ser.). 24p. (J). 7.98 *(978-0-7853-7918-8(5)*, 7179200) Phoenix International Publications, Inc.
Kwant, Admar. Pip the Gnome's Bedtime, 72 vols. 2017. (Illus.). 12p. (J). 9.95 *(978-1-78250-413-9(3))* Floris Bks. GBR. Dist: Consortium Bk. Sales & Distribution.
L' Hommedieu, Arthur John. Butterfly. 2006. (Metamorphoses Ser.). (Illus.). 16p. (J). (gr. 1-5). spiral bd. *(978-1-84643-013-8(5))* Child's Play International Ltd.
La Coccinella. Look & See: Mommy, Where Are You? 2014. (Look & See! Ser.). (ENG., Illus.). 24p. (J). (gr. -1 — 1). bds. 8.95 *(978-1-4549-0615-5(4))* Sterling Publishing Co., Inc.
Lacey, Minna. Look Inside Science. 2011. (Look Inside Board Bks). 13p. (J). ring bd. 15.99 *(978-0-7945-2946-8(1)*, Usborne) EDC Publishing.
Laden, Nina. Peek-A Moo! 2017. (Peek-A-Who? Ser.). (ENG., Illus.). 22p. (J). (gr. -1 — 1). bds. 7.99 *(978-1-4521-5474-9(0))* Chronicle Bks. LLC.
Ladwig, Tim & Norris, Jeannine Q. Tonight You Are My Baby Board Book. 2010. (ENG., Illus.). 30p. (J). (gr. -1-k). bds. 7.99 *(978-0-06-147999-1(3)*, HarperFestival) HarperCollins Pubs.
Ladybird. On the Farm - Read It Yourself with Ladybird Level 2. 2016. (Read It Yourself with Ladybird Ser.). (ENG., Illus.). 32p. (J). (gr. 2-4). 5.99 *(978-0-241-23731-1(9))* Penguin Bks., Ltd. GBR. Dist: Independent Pubs. Group.
Laidlaw, Sarah. Through the Seasons, 30 vols. 2018. (Illus.). 12p. (J). 9.95 *(978-1-78250-469-6(9))* Floris Bks. GBR. Dist: Consortium Bk. Sales & Distribution.
Lajiness, Katie. Cars & Trucks. 2016. (First Drawings (Big Buddy Books) Ser.). (ENG., Illus.). 32p. (J). (gr. 2-5). lib. bdg. 34.21 *(978-1-68078-520-3(6)*, 23603, Big Buddy Bks.) ABDO Publishing Co.
Lamb, Stacey, illus. Wipe-Clean Doodles. 2013. (Wipe-Clean Bks). 20p. (J). pap. 7.99 *(978-0-7945-3312-0(4)*, Usborne) EDC Publishing.
—123 Sticker Book. 2009. (Sticker Bks). 24p. (J). pap. 6.99 *(978-0-7945-2361-9(7)*, Usborne) EDC Publishing.
Lambert, Jonny. Jonny Lambert's Animal 123. Lambert, Jonny, illus. 2018. (Jonny Lambert Illustrated Ser.). (ENG., Illus.). 24p. (J). (— 1). bds. 12.99 *(978-1-4654-7845-0(0)*, DK Children) Dorling Kindersley Publishing, Inc.
—Jonny Lambert's Animal ABC. Lambert, Jonny, illus. 2018. (Jonny Lambert Illustrated Ser.). (ENG., Illus.). 24p. (J). (— 1). bds. 12.99 *(978-1-4654-7571-8(0)*, DK Children) Dorling Kindersley Publishing, Inc.
Lambert, Nat. Beep-Beep! Magnetic First Words. 2018. (Play & Learn Ser.). (ENG.). 10p. (J). (gr. -1-1). bds. 7.99 *(978-1-78700-385-9(X))* Top That! Publishing PLC GBR. Dist: Independent Pubs. Group.
Lamere, Jill. Upside Down. Lamere, Jill, illus. 2005. (Illus.). (J). bds. 12.95 *(978-0-9772320-0-0(X))* Minikin Pr.
Land of Milk & Honey, 2 vols. 2008. (LMH Ser.). (Illus.). (J). Bk. 5. bds. 6.99 *(978-0-7814-4529-0(9))*Bk. 6. bds. 6.99 *(978-0-7814-4530-6(2))* Cook, David C.
Landers, Ace. I Am a Garbage Truck. Migliari, Paola, illus. 2008. (ENG.). 8p. (J). (gr. -1 — 1). bds. 4.99 *(978-0-545-07963-1(2)*, Cartwheel Bks.) Scholastic, Inc.
—I Am a Train. Migliari, Paola, illus. 2008. (ENG.). 8p. (J). (gr. -1 — 1). bds. 4.99 *(978-0-545-07962-4(4)*, Cartwheel Bks.) Scholastic, Inc.
—Lego Star Wars: The Yoda Chronicles Trilogy. 2014. (LEGO Star Wars Chapter Bks.). lib. bdg. 18.40 *(978-0-606-35414-1(X))* Turtleback.
Landwehr, Neil. Listen & Learn with Love. 2016. (ENG., Illus.). 26p. (J). pap. 7.99 *(978-1-61984-465-0(6)*, BlogIntoBook.com) Gatekeeper Pr.
Langen, Annette. Letters from Felix: A Little Rabbit on a World Tour. Droop, Constanza, illus. 2003. 47p. (J). 14.99 *(978-1-59384-034-1(9))* Parklane Publishing.
Langlois, Florence. The Extraordinary Gift. Goodman, John, tr. from FRE. Langlois, Florence, illus. 2005. (Illus.). 48p. (J). (gr. -1-2). reprint ed. 15.00 *(978-0-7567-8942-8(7))* DIANE Publishing Co.
Larkin, Susan. All the Ways I Love You. East, Jacqueline, illus. 2014. (J). *(978-1-4351-5821-4(0))* Barnes & Noble, Inc.
—All the Ways I Love You. Trotter, Stuart, illus. 2012. 16p. (J). *(978-1-4351-3857-5(0))* Barnes & Noble, Inc.
Larrañaga, Martin & Innovative Kids Staff. I Love You, Little One. 2009. (ENG., Illus.). 12p. (J). (gr. -1 — 1). bds. 9.99 *(978-1-58476-791-6(X))* Innovative Kids.
Larsen, Carolyn. My 123 Bible Storybook. Turk, Caron, illus. 2008. (My Bible Storybooks Ser.). 30p. (J). (gr. -1-3). bds. *(978-1-86920-925-4(7))* Christian Art Pubs.
—My ABC Bible Storybook. Turk, Caron, illus. 2008. (My Bible Storybooks Ser.). 30p. (J). (gr. -1-3). bds. *(978-1-86920-926-1(5))* Christian Art Pubs.
Larson, Beverly. Toca y Siente las Historias de la Biblia. Pineda, Nancy, tr. Dillard, Sarah, illus. 2003. (Touch & Feel Ser.). (SPA.). (J). (gr. -1-k). bds. 8.99 *(978-0-7899-1088-2(8))* Editorial Unilit.
Latimer, Mariam. Choose to Reuse. 2009. (Touch & Feel Ser.). (ENG.). 10p. (J). (gr. -1). 7.95 *(978-1-58117-869-2(7)*, Intervisual/Piggy Toes) Bendon, Inc.
Latyk, Olivier. Follow the Little Fish. 2015. (Illus.). (J). *(978-1-4351-5985-3(3))* Barnes & Noble, Inc.
Latyk, Olivier, illus. Follow the Red Balloon. 2015. (J). *(978-1-4351-5986-0(1))* Barnes & Noble, Inc.
Lawler, Janet. If Kisses Were Colors Board Book. Jay, Alison, illus. 2010. (ENG.). 22p. (J). (gr. -1 — 1). bds. 7.99 *(978-0-8037-3530-9(8)*, Dial Bks) Penguin Young Readers Group.
Lawrence, Carol. Leaves. Zito, Francesco, illus. 2018. (Baby Explorer Ser.). (ENG.). 24p. (J). (gr. -1 — 1). bds. 6.99 *(978-0-8075-0516-8(1)*, 807505161) Whitman, Albert & Co.
Lawrence, Trisha. A Princess's Crown: A Magnetic Storybook. Barnard, Lucy, illus. 2008. 6p. (J). (gr. -1-1). bds. 10.99 *(978-2-7641-2186-3(5))* Gardner Pubns.
Lawson-Miller, Barb. I Love Daddy Because... 2004. (Illus.). 14p. bds. *(978-0-9688553-0-0(X))* Barbamel Bks., Inc.
—I Love Mommy Because... 2004. (Illus.). 14p. bds. *(978-0-9688553-1-7(8))* Barbamel Bks., Inc.
Lawson, Peter. Tractor. 2009. (Turn the Wheel Ser.). (ENG., Illus.). 10p. (J). (gr. -1-k). bds. 5.95 *(978-0-7892-1023-4(1)*, Abbeville Kids) Abbeville Pr., Inc.
Layton, Neal. The Story of Stars: From the Stars, Solar Systems & Galaxies to Beyond. 2013. (Illus.). 19p. (J). *(978-1-4351-5110-9(0))* Barnes & Noble, Inc.
—The Story of Things: From the Stone Age to the Modern Age in 10 Pop-Up Spreads. 2013. (Illus.). 19p. (J). *(978-1-4351-5111-6(9))* Barnes & Noble, Inc.
Leapfrog Learners - Pirates. (Awesome Adventures Ser.). 16p. (J). *(978-2-7643-0117-3(0))* Phidal Publishing, Inc./Editions Phidal, Inc.
Learn As You Grow. God Loves You So Much... Reuben, Borgen & Jenny, Lindley, photos by. 2010. (ENG., Illus.). 24p. (J). 12.95 *(978-0-9824652-3-3(8))* Learn As You Grow, L.L.C.
Learn Your Numbers. 2003. (Illus.). 10p. (J). bds. *(978-1-74047-003-2(6))* Book Co. Publishing Pty, Ltd., The.
Learning Wrap Ups Palette Base. 2004. (ENG.). (J). 14.99 *(978-1-59204-000-1(4))* Learning Wrap-Ups, Inc.
Leblond, Michaël. Pajamarama - Carnival: Make it Move with Magic Stripes! Bertrand, Frédérique, illus. 2017. 22p. (J). (gr. k-4). pap. 16.95 *(978-0-500-65125-4(6)*, 565125) Thames & Hudson.
Leblond, Michaël & Bertrand, Frédérique. Pajamarama - Fever: Make It Move with Magic Stripes! 2017. (Illus.). 22p. (J). (gr. k-5). pap. 16.95 *(978-0-500-65115-5(9)*, 565115) Thames & Hudson.
Lee, Brian, illus. A Construction Site. 2005. (What's Inside Ser.). (J). *(978-0-7607-6570-8(7))* backpackbook.
—A Pirate Ship. 2005. (What's Inside? Ser.). *(978-0-7607-6809-9(9))* backpackbook.
—The World of Dinosaurs. 2005. (J). *(978-0-7607-6569-2(3))* backpackbook.
Lee, Dennis. Zoomberry Board Book. Petricic, Dusan, illus. 2016. (ENG.). 26p. (J). bds. 10.50 *(978-1-4434-1166-0(3)*, HarperCollins) HarperCollins Pubs.
Lee, Howard. A Day at the Zoo. Reasoner, Charles, illus. 2009. (Inside Outside Board Bks.). 10p. (J). bds. 10.99 *(978-1-934650-55-4(2))* Just For Kids Pr., LLC.
Lee, Vickie. 12 Lucky Animals: a Bilingual Baby Book. Chou, Joey, illus. 2018. (ENG.). 24p. (J). bds. 7.99 *(978-1-250-18424-5(X)*, 900191035, Holt, Henry & Co. Bks. For Young Readers) Holt, Henry & Co.
Leeson, Tom and Pat, et al, photos by. Cascade Babies. 2013. (Illus.). 26p. (J). 8.95 *(978-1-56037-330-8(X))* Farcountry Pr.
LeFalle, Deborah. Bitty Brown Babe. Morris, Keisha, illus. 2019. 24p. (J). (gr. -1 — 1). 7.99 *(978-1-5064-4853-4(4)*, Beaming Books) 1517 Media.
LeLeu, Lisa. Diggity the Dog Puppet Show Play Set. 2004. (Lisa Leleu Puppet Show Books Ser.). (J). 19.95 *(978-0-9710537-2-4(3)*, LeLeu, Lisa Puppet Show Bks.) LeLeu, Lisa Studios! Inc.
—Percilla the Gorilla Gift Set: Puppet Book Gift Set with 2 Books. 2004. (J). bds. 19.99 *(978-0-9710537-3-1(1))* LeLeu, Lisa Studios! Inc.
Lemay, Violet, illus. The Obamas: A Lift-The-Flap Book. 2019. 22p. (J). (gr. -1-k). bds. 9.95 *(978-1-947458-82-6(5)*, 805882) Duo Pr. LLC.
Lemke, Donald. Book-O-Beards: a Wearable Book. Lentz, Bob, illus. 2015. (Wearable Bks.). (ENG.). 12p. (J). (gr. -1-1). bds. 7.99 *(978-1-62370-183-3(X)*, 127003, Capstone Young Readers) Capstone.
—Book-O-Hats: a Wearable Book. Lentz, Bob, illus. 2015. (Wearable Bks.). (ENG.). 12p. (J). (gr. -1-1). bds. 7.99 *(978-1-62370-184-0(8)*, 127002, Capstone Young Readers) Capstone.
—Book-O-Masks: a Wearable Book. Lentz, Bob, illus. 2015. (Wearable Bks.). (ENG.). 12p. (J). (gr. -1-1). bds. 7.99 *(978-1-62370-185-7(6)*, 127004, Capstone Young Readers) Capstone.
—Book-O-Teeth: a Wearable Book. Lentz, Bob, illus. 2015. (Wearable Bks.). (ENG.). 12p. (J). (gr. -1-1). bds. 7.99 *(978-1-62370-186-4(4)*, 127005, Capstone Young Readers) Capstone.
Lemmens, Riske. A Box Full of Monsters. 2004. (Illus.). 26p. (J). *(978-1-85269-837-9(3))*; (ARA.). *(978-1-85269-827-0(6))*; *(978-1-85269-842-3(X))*; *(978-1-85269-847-8(0))*; *(978-1-85269-852-2(7))* Mantra Lingua.
Lemmens, Riske & Dutta, Kunal, texts. A Box Full of Monsters: Kutia Plot Me Monstra. 2004. (ALB., Illus.). 25p. (J). *(978-1-85269-822-5(5))* Mantra Lingua.
Lendroth, Susan. Old Manhattan Has Some Farms. Endle, Kate, illus. 2017. 28p. (J). (— 1). bds. 7.99 *(978-1-58089-573-6(5))* Charlesbridge Publishing, Inc.
Leonard, Dion. Gobi for Little Ones: The Race for Home, 1 vol. Manuzak, Lisa, illus. 2018. (ENG.). 24p. (J). bds. 9.99 *(978-0-7180-7530-9(7)*, Tommy Nelson) Nelson, Thomas Inc.
Leroy, Jean. Where Is Santa's Beard? A Novelty Lift-The-flap Book. Chetaud, Helene, illus. 2017. (ENG.). 12p. (J). 16.00 *(978-1-4711-6126-1(9)*, Simon & Schuster Children's) Simon & Schuster, Ltd. GBR. Dist: Simon & Schuster, Inc.
Lester, Anna. Stories of Fairies. Gower, Teri, illus. 2006. (Young Reading Series 1 Gift Bks.). 47p. (J). (gr. 2-5). 8.99 *(978-0-7945-1326-9(3)*, Usborne) EDC Publishing.
Let's Learn Animals. 2013. (Illus.). 10p. (J). *(978-1-4351-4938-0(6))* Barnes & Noble, Inc.
Let's Look at Boats. 2009. (Let's Go! Ser.). (Illus.). 18p. (J). (gr. -1-k). bds. 12.75 *(978-1-60754-417-3(2))* Windmill Bks.
Let's Look at Planes. 2009. (Let's Go! Ser.). (Illus.). 18p. (J). (gr. -1-k). bds. 12.75 *(978-1-60754-416-6(4))* Windmill Bks.
Let's Say Our Numbers. 2007. (Simple First Words Ser.). (Illus.). 14p. (J). *(978-1-84332-520-8(9))* Priddy Bks.
Leung, Hilary. Will Sheep Sleep? 2018. (ENG., Illus.). 38p. (J). (gr. -1 — 1). bds. 7.99 *(978-1-338-21562-5(0)*, Cartwheel Bks.) Scholastic, Inc.
Levine, Julia Pimsleur. Little Pim: Animals. 2012. (ENG.). 10p. (J). (gr. -1 — 1). bds. 8.95 *(978-1-4197-0174-0(6)*, 687501) Abrams, Inc.
Levison, Jesse. U Is for Underwear. 2014. (ENG., Illus.). 28p. (J). (-k). bds. 9.95 *(978-1-57687-690-9(X)*, powerHouse Bks.) powerHse. Bks.
Lewis, Anthony. Teddy or Train? 2008. (Pick & Choose Ser.). (Illus.). 12p. (J). (gr. -1). spiral bd. *(978-1-84643-241-5(3))* Child's Play International Ltd.
Lewis, Anthony, illus. Carrots or Peas? 2008. (Pick & Choose Ser.). 12p. (J). (gr. -1). spiral bd. *(978-1-84643-242-2(1))* Child's Play International Ltd.
—Wind or Rain? 2008. (Pick & Choose Ser.). 12p. (J). (gr. -1). spiral bd. *(978-1-84643-240-8(5))* Child's Play International Ltd.
Lewis, Edwina. Who Jumps? Parker, Ant, illus. 2003. (Who... Ser.). 16p. (YA). *(978-1-85602-447-1(4)*, Pavilion Children's Books) Pavilion Bks.
—Who Plays? Parker, Ant, illus. 2003. (Who... Ser.). 16p. (J). *(978-1-85602-469-3(5)*, Pavilion Children's Books) Pavilion Bks.
—Who Swims? Parker, Ant, illus. 2003. (Who... Ser.). 16p. (YA). *(978-1-85602-448-8(2)*, Pavilion Children's Books) Pavilion Bks.
Lewis, J. Patrick & Lewis, Leigh. It's Not the Baby. Frost, Maddie, illus. 2017. 14p. (J). (gr. -1 — 1). bds. 9.99 *(978-1-68152-194-7(6)*, 14725) Amicus.
Lewis, Jan. Baby's First Book of Prayers. 2013. (Illus.). 24p. (J). (gr. -1-12). bds. 6.99 *(978-1-86147-340-0(0)*, Armadillo) Anness Publishing GBR. Dist: National Bk. Network.
—Baby's First Stories of Jesus. 2015. (Illus.). 24p. (J). (gr. -1-2). bds. 6.99 *(978-1-86147-415-5(6)*, Armadillo) Anness Publishing GBR. Dist: National Bk. Network.
—Best-Ever Rhymes. 2015. (Illus.). 24p. (J). (gr. -1-12). bds. 6.99 *(978-1-86147-499-5(7)*, Armadillo) Anness Publishing GBR. Dist: National Bk. Network.
—Farm. 2015. (Illus.). 24p. (J). (gr. -1-k). bds. 6.99 *(978-1-86147-635-7(3)*, Armadillo) Anness Publishing GBR. Dist: National Bk. Network.
—First Fairy Tales: Puss in Boots. 2015. (ENG., Illus.). 24p. (J). (gr. -1-12). bds. 6.99 *(978-1-86147-626-5(4)*, Armadillo) Anness Publishing GBR. Dist: National Bk. Network.
—First Fairy Tales Aladdin & the Lamp. 2013. (Illus.). 24p. (J). (gr. -1-12). bds. 6.99 *(978-1-86147-337-0(0)*, Armadillo) Anness Publishing GBR. Dist: National Bk. Network.
—First Fairy Tales Goldilocks & the Three Bears. 2013. (Illus.). 24p. (J). (gr. -1-12). bds. 6.99 *(978-1-86147-332-5(X)*, Armadillo) Anness Publishing GBR. Dist: National Bk. Network.
—First Fairy Tales Little Red Riding Hood. 2013. (Illus.). 24p. (J). (gr. -1-12). bds. 6.99 *(978-1-86147-336-3(2)*, Armadillo) Anness Publishing GBR. Dist: National Bk. Network.
—First Fairy Tales Snow White. 2013. (Illus.). 24p. (J). (gr. -1-12). bds. 6.99 *(978-1-86147-335-6(4)*, Armadillo) Anness Publishing GBR. Dist: National Bk. Network.
—Look & Learn with Little Dino: Colour Fun. Lewis, Jan, illus. 2014. (ENG., Illus.). 24p. (J). (gr. -1-2). bds. 6.99 *(978-1-86147-380-6(X)*, Armadillo) Anness Publishing GBR. Dist: National Bk. Network.
—Mother Goose Nursery Rhymes. 2015. (Illus.). 48p. (J). (gr. -1-12). bds. 9.99 *(978-1-86147-649-4(3)*, Armadillo) Anness Publishing GBR. Dist: National Bk. Network.
—My First Box of Bible Stories: Tales from the Old & New Testament Retold in Six Charming Boardbooks, 6 vols. 2018. (Illus.). 72p. (J). (gr. -1-12). bds. 14.99 *(978-1-86147-854-2(2)*, Armadillo) Anness Publishing GBR. Dist: National Bk. Network.
—My First Words. 2015. (ENG., Illus.). 24p. (J). (gr. -1 — 1). bds. 6.99 *(978-1-86147-498-8(9)*, Armadillo) Anness Publishing GBR. Dist: National Bk. Network.
—My Treasure Box of Fairy Tales: Classic Stories Retold in Six Charming Boardbooks, 6 vols. 2018. (Illus.). 72p. (J). (gr. -1-12). bds. 14.99 *(978-1-86147-845-0(3)*, Armadillo) Anness Publishing GBR. Dist: National Bk. Network.
—Princess Fairy Tales: Cinderella, the Princess & the Pea, Sleeping Beauty, the Little Mermaid. Lewis, Jan, illus. 2015. (Illus.). 48p. (J). (gr. -1-k). bds. 9.99 *(978-1-86147-423-0(7)*, Armadillo) Anness Publishing GBR. Dist: National Bk. Network.
Lewis, Jan, illus. ABC: Turn the Wheels; Find the Words. 2016. 10p. (J). (gr. -1-12). bds. 14.99 *(978-1-86147-712-5(0)*, Armadillo) Anness Publishing GBR. Dist: National Bk. Network.
—Animals. 2017. 14p. (J). (gr. -1-12). 11.99 *(978-1-86147-727-9(9)*, Armadillo) Anness Publishing GBR. Dist: National Bk. Network.
—Animals: Turn the Wheels Find the Pictures. 2016. 10p. (J). (gr. -1-12). bds. 14.99 *(978-1-86147-713-2(9)*, Armadillo) Anness Publishing GBR. Dist: National Bk. Network.
—At School. 2017. 14p. (J). (gr. -1-12). 11.99 *(978-1-86147-726-2(0)*, Armadillo) Anness Publishing GBR. Dist: National Bk. Network.
—The Emperor's New Clothes. 2015. 24p. (J). (gr. -1-2). bds. 6.99 *(978-1-86147-413-1(X)*, Armadillo) Anness Publishing GBR. Dist: National Bk. Network.
—Fairy Palace: You Are Invited to a Party in the Fairy Palace! 2015. 10p. (J). (gr. k-3). bds. 7.99 *(978-1-86147-315-8(X)*, Armadillo) Anness Publishing GBR. Dist: National Bk. Network.
—First Fairy Tales: Cinderella. 2013. (ENG.). 24p. (J). (gr. -1-k). bds. 6.99 *(978-1-86147-334-9(6)*, Armadillo) Anness Publishing GBR. Dist: National Bk. Network.
—First Fairy Tales: Sleeping Beauty. 2013. (ENG.). 24p. (J). (gr. -1-k). bds. 6.99 *(978-1-86147-338-7(9)*, Armadillo) Anness Publishing GBR. Dist: National Bk. Network.
—First Fairy Tales: The Ugly Duckling. 2013. (ENG.). 24p. (J). (gr. -1-k). bds. 6.99 *(978-1-86147-333-2(8)*, Armadillo) Anness Publishing GBR. Dist: National Bk. Network.
—First Fairy Tales: Three Little Pigs. 2013. (ENG.). 24p. (J). (gr. -1-k). bds. 6.99 *(978-1-86147-331-8(1)*, Armadillo) Anness Publishing GBR. Dist: National Bk. Network.
—First Prayers for Little Ones: Prayers for Every Day, Special Occasions & the Family. 2016. 48p. (J). (gr. -1-12). 9.99 *(978-1-86147-716-3(3)*, Armadillo) Anness Publishing GBR. Dist: National Bk. Network.
—Lift-The-Flap Word House: 200 Things to Find, See & Say. 2016. (ENG.). 10p. (J). (gr. -1-12). bds. 7.99 *(978-1-86147-778-1(3)*, Armadillo) Anness Publishing GBR. Dist: National Bk. Network.
—Look & Learn with Little Dino: Action Words. 2014. (ENG.). 24p. (J). (gr. k-2). bds. 6.99 *(978-1-86147-382-0(6)*, Armadillo) Anness Publishing GBR. Dist: National Bk. Network.
—Look & Learn with Little Dino: Busy Day. 2014. (ENG.). 24p. (J). (gr. k-2). bds. 6.99 *(978-1-86147-379-0(6)*, Armadillo) Anness Publishing GBR. Dist: National Bk. Network.
—Look & Learn with Little Dino: Count 123. 2014. (ENG.). 24p. (J). (gr. -1-1). bds. 6.99 *(978-1-86147-381-3(8)*, Armadillo) Anness Publishing GBR. Dist: National Bk. Network.
—Love from Santa, 6 vols. 2013. (ENG.). 60p. (J). (gr. -1-2). bds. 7.99 *(978-1-86147-313-4(3)*, Armadillo) Anness Publishing GBR. Dist: National Bk. Network.
—Magical Fairy Tales: Aladdin & the Lamp; the Ugly Duckling; the Emperor's New Clothes; Puss in Boots. 2016. 48p. (J). (gr. -1-12). bds. 9.99 *(978-1-86147-700-2(7)*, Armadillo) Anness Publishing GBR. Dist: National Bk. Network.
—Mother Goose Rhymes: One, Two, Buckle My Shoe. 2015. 24p. (J). (gr. -1-12). bds. 6.99 *(978-1-86147-637-1(X)*, Armadillo) Anness Publishing GBR. Dist: National Bk. Network.
—My First 123. 2014. (ENG.). 24p. (J). (gr. -1-k). bds. 6.99 *(978-1-86147-371-4(0)*, Armadillo) Anness Publishing GBR. Dist: National Bk. Network.
—My First 123: Learn to Count from 1 To 100! 2015. 48p. (J). (gr. -1-12). pap. 9.99 *(978-1-86147-425-4(3)*, Armadillo) Anness Publishing GBR. Dist: National Bk. Network.
—My First ABC. 2014. (ENG.). 24p. (J). (gr. -1-k). bds. 6.99 *(978-1-86147-372-1(9)*, Armadillo) Anness Publishing GBR. Dist: National Bk. Network.
—My First Animals. 2014. (ENG.). 24p. (J). (gr. -1-k). bds. 6.99 *(978-1-86147-373-8(7)*, Armadillo) Anness Publishing GBR. Dist: National Bk. Network.
—My First Colours. 2014. (ENG.). 24p. (J). (gr. -1-k). bds. 6.99 *(978-1-86147-374-5(5)*, Armadillo) Anness Publishing GBR. Dist: National Bk. Network.
—My First Learning Library: 3 Great Books: First Abc First 123 First Words, 3 vols. 2014. (ENG.). 72p. (J). (gr. -1-1). bds. 9.99 *(978-1-86147-387-5(7)*, Armadillo) Anness Publishing GBR. Dist: National Bk. Network.
—My First Words: Over 300 Everyday Words & Pictures. 2015. 48p. (J). (gr. -1-12). bds. 9.99 *(978-1-86147-627-2(2)*, Armadillo) Anness Publishing GBR. Dist: National Bk. Network.
—Old MacDonald Had a Farm. 2015. 24p. (J). (gr. -1-12). bds. 6.99 *(978-1-86147-468-1(7)*, Armadillo) Anness Publishing GBR. Dist: National Bk. Network.
—On the Farm: A Friendly Story with Flaps to Lift. 2016. (ENG.). 10p. (J). (gr. -1-12). bds. 7.99 *(978-1-86147-779-8(1)*, Armadillo) Anness Publishing GBR. Dist: National Bk. Network.
—Pirate Ship: Lift the Flaps to Follow the Clues & Discover the Fabulous Treasure. 2016. 10p. (J). (gr. -1-12). 7.99 *(978-1-86147-767-5(8)*, Armadillo) Anness Publishing GBR. Dist: National Bk. Network.
—Playtime Rhymes: My Mother Goose Collection. 2018. 24p. (J). (gr. -1-12). bds. 6.99 *(978-1-86147-694-4(9)*, Armadillo) Anness Publishing GBR. Dist: National Bk. Network.
—The Princess & the Pea. 2015. 24p. (J). (gr. -1-12). bds. 6.99 *(978-1-86147-467-4(9)*, Armadillo) Anness Publishing GBR. Dist: National Bk. Network.
—Round & Round the Garden. 2015. 24p. (J). (gr. -1-12). bds. 6.99 *(978-1-86147-636-4(1)*, Armadillo) Anness Publishing GBR. Dist: National Bk. Network.
—Santa's Workshop: The Inside Story! 2015. 10p. (J). (gr. k-4). bds. 7.99 *(978-1-86147-314-1(1)*, Armadillo) Anness Publishing GBR. Dist: National Bk. Network.
—Words: Turn the Wheels, Find the Pictures. 2015. 10p. (J). (gr. -1-12). bds. 14.99 *(978-1-86147-660-9(4)*, Armadillo) Anness Publishing GBR. Dist: National Bk. Network.
—123: Turn the Wheels - Learn to Count! 2015. 10p. (J). (gr. -1-12). bds. 14.99 *(978-1-86147-661-6(2)*, Armadillo) Anness Publishing GBR. Dist: National Bk. Network.
Lift-The-Flap Fractions & Decimals IR. 2017. (Advanced Lift-The-Flap BDs* Ser.). (ENG.). (J). bds. 14.99 *(978-0-7945-3727-2(8)*, Usborne) EDC Publishing.
Lift-The-Flap Questions & Answers about Food IR. 2017. (Lift-The-Flap Questions & Answers Ser.). (ENG.). (J). bds. 14.99 *(978-0-7945-3927-6(0)*, Usborne) EDC Publishing.
Lift-The-Flap Questions & Answers about Science IR. 2017. (Lift-The-Flap Questions & Answers Ser.). (ENG.). (J). bds. 14.99 *(978-0-7945-3940-5(8)*, Usborne) EDC Publishing.
Lift-The-Flap Telling the Time. 2017. (Advanced Lift-The-Flap BDs* Ser.). (ENG.). (J). bds. 14.99 *(978-0-7945-3865-1(7)*, Usborne) EDC Publishing.
Light, Steve. Planes Go: (Airplane Books for Kids 2-4, Transporation Books for Kids) 2014. (ENG., Illus.). 16p. (J). (gr. -1 — 1). bds. 9.99 *(978-1-4521-2899-3(5))* Chronicle Bks. LLC.
—Trains Go. 2012. (Vehicles Go! Ser.). (ENG., Illus.). 16p. (J). (gr. -1 — 1). bds. 9.99 *(978-0-8118-7942-2(9))* Chronicle Bks. LLC.
Lightfoot, Martha, illus. The Lion's Share. 2009. (Finger Puppet Bks.). 24p. (J). (gr. -1-1). *(978-1-84643-248-4(0))* Child's Play International Ltd.
Lindman, Flicka, Ricka, Dicka & the New Dotted Dresses. Lindman, illus. 2012. (Flicka, Ricka, Dicka Ser.). (ENG., Illus.). 32p. (J). (gr. -1-3). 9.99 *(978-0-8075-2484-8(0)*, 807524840) Whitman, Albert & Co.

Linenthal, Peter. Look Look Outside. 2012. 16p. (J). (gr. -1 — 1). bds. 7.99 *(978-0-8037-3729-7(7),* Dial Bks) Penguin Young Readers Group.

Linn, Susie. Copying: Early Learning Through Art. Stanley, Mandy, illus. 2017. (Arty Mouse Creativity Bks.). (ENG.). 48p. (J). (gr. -1-k). pap. 6.99 *(978-1-78445-626-9(8))* Top That! Publishing PLC GBR. Dist: Independent Pubs. Group.

—Old MacDonald Had a Farm. Crisp, Dan, illus. 2019. (Counting to Ten Bks.). (ENG.). 22p. (J). 9.99 *(978-1-78700-978-3(5))* Top That! Publishing PLC GBR. Dist: Independent Pubs. Group.

—Ten Little Unicorns. Hunt, Brad, illus. 2018. (Counting to Ten Bks.). (ENG.). 20p. (J). (gr. -1-1). bds. 10.99 *(978-1-78700-376-7(0))* Top That! Publishing PLC GBR. Dist: Independent Pubs. Group.

Lionni, Leo. Inch by Inch. 2018. lib. bdg. 18.40 *(978-0-606-40949-0(1))* Turtleback.

—What? 2014. (ENG., Illus.). 16p. (J). (— 1). bds. 6.99 *(978-0-385-75406-4(X),* Knopf Bks. for Young Readers) Random Hse. Children's Bks.

—Where? 2014. (ENG., Illus.). 16p. (J). (— 1). bds. 5.99 *(978-0-385-75407-1(8),* Knopf Bks. for Young Readers) Random Hse. Children's Bks.

—Who? 2014. (ENG., Illus.). 16p. (J). (— 1). bds. 6.99 *(978-0-385-75405-7(1),* Knopf Bks. for Young Readers) Random Hse. Children's Bks.

Lippman, Peter. Mini Express. (J). 119.40 *(978-0-7611-2876-2(X),* 22876) Workman Publishing Co., Inc.

—Mini Wheels: the Mini-Express 8-Copy Counter Display. (ENG.). (J). bds. 79.60 *(978-0-7611-2883-0(2),* 22883) Workman Publishing Co., Inc.

Litchfield, Jo. At Home. rev. ed. 2013. (First Words Board Bks). 12p. (J). ring bd. 6.99 *(978-0-7945-2617-7(9),* Usborne) EDC Publishing.

—Usborne Lift-The-Flap Nitivity. Allman, Howard, photos by. 2004. (Illus.). (J). *(978-0-439-68683-9(0))* Scholastic, Inc.

—Very First ABC. 2010. (Very First Words Board Bks). 10p. (J). bds. 6.99 *(978-0-7945-2709-9(4),* Usborne) EDC Publishing.

—Weather. Maynard, Marc, illus. 2008. (Usborne Look & Say Ser.). 12p. (J). (gr. -1-3). bds. 7.99 *(978-0-7945-1989-6(X),* Usborne) EDC Publishing.

Litchfield, Jo, illus. Baby Brother Look & Say. 2008. (Look & Say Board Bks). 12p. (J). bds. 7.99 *(978-0-7945-2101-1(0),* Usborne) EDC Publishing.

Litten, Kristyna. Rome: a 3D Keepsake Cityscape. Litten, Kristyna, illus. 2013. (Panorama Pops Ser.). (ENG., Illus.). 15p. (J). (gr. k-4). 8.99 *(978-0-7636-6415-2(4))* Candlewick Pr.

Little Bee Books. Animal Patterns. 2017. (Guess the Animals Ser.). (ENG., Illus.). 16p. (J). (gr. -1 — 1). bds. 5.99 *(978-1-4998-0530-7(6))* Little Bee Books Inc.

—My Book of Blue. 2017. (My Color Bks.). (ENG., Illus.). 16p. (J). (gr. -1 — 1). bds. 5.99 *(978-1-4998-0531-4(4))* Little Bee Books Inc.

—My Book of Green. 2017. (My Color Bks.). (ENG., Illus.). 16p. (J). (gr. -1 — 1). bds. 5.99 *(978-1-4998-0548-2(9))* Little Bee Books Inc.

—My Garden Home. carciofocontento, illus. 2017. (ENG.). 16p. (J). (gr. -1-k). bds. 7.99 *(978-1-4998-0443-0(1))* Little Bee Books Inc.

—My Snowman Book. 2015. (ENG., Illus.). 12p. (J). (gr. -1 — 1). bds. 5.99 *(978-1-4998-0130-9(0))* Little Bee Books Inc.

—Our Christmas Stockings: A Touch-And-Feel Book. 2015. (ENG., Illus.). 12p. (J). (gr. -1 — 1). 6.99 *(978-1-4998-0144-6(0))* Little Bee Books Inc.

Little Letters, Set. 2006. (Chicken Socks Ser.). (Illus.). 24p. (J). (gr. -1-3). spiral bd. 9.95 *(978-1-59174-244-9(7),* Chicken Socks) Klutz.

Little Mermaid. 2009. (Disney Glitter Board Book Ser.). 5p. *(978-1-4054-9825-8(0))* Parragon, Inc.

Litton, Jonathan. Mouse in the Haunted House. Anderson, Nicola, illus. 2015. (Planet Pop-Up Ser.). (ENG.). 12p. (J). (gr. -1). 12.95 *(978-1-62686-485-6(3),* Silver Dolphin Bks.) Readerlink Distribution Services, LLC.

—Planet Pop-Up: Shark Makes a Splash! Anderson, Nicola, illus. 2015. (Planet Pop-Up Ser.). (ENG.). 12p. (J). (gr. -1). 12.95 *(978-1-62686-353-8(9),* Silver Dolphin Bks.) Readerlink Distribution Services, LLC.

—Planet Pop-Up: Tiger Takes Off. Anderson, Nicola, illus. 2015. (Planet Pop-Up Ser.). (ENG.). 12p. (J). (gr. -1). 12.95 *(978-1-62686-373-6(3),* Silver Dolphin Bks.) Readerlink Distribution Services, LLC.

—Roar. Galloway, Fhiona, illus. 2014. (My Little World Ser.). (ENG.). 16p. (J). (-k). bds. 7.99 *(978-1-58925-593-7(3))* Tiger Tales.

—Snap: A Peek-Through Book of Shapes. Galloway, Fhiona, illus. 2014. (My Little World Ser.). (ENG.). 16p. (J). (gr. -1-k). bds. 7.99 *(978-1-58925-566-1(6))* Tiger Tales.

—Surprise: A Book of Christmas Shapes. Galloway, Fhiona, illus. 2014. (ENG.). 16p. (J). (gr. -1-k). bds. 7.99 *(978-1-58925-567-8(4))* Tiger Tales.

—Touch-And-Feel Colors. Galloway, Fhiona, illus. 2017. (My Little World Ser.). (ENG.). 10p. (J). (gr. -1-k). bds. 8.99 *(978-1-68010-510-0(8))* Tiger Tales.

Livanios, Eleni. The Best Grandma in the World! Lütje, Susanne, illus. 2015. (ENG.). 16p. (J). (gr. -1-1). bds. 7.95 *(978-0-7358-4225-0(6))* North-South Bks., Inc.

—The Best Grandpa in the World! Lütje, Susanne, illus. 2015. (ENG.). 16p. (J). (gr. -1-1). bds. 7.95 *(978-0-7358-4237-3(X))* North-South Bks., Inc.

Ljungkvist, Laura. A Line Can Be ... 2015. (ENG., Illus.). 24p. (J). (-k). bds. 12.99 *(978-1-57687-753-1(1),* powerHouse Bks.) powerHse. Bks.

Llenas, Anna. The Color Monster: A Pop-Up Book of Feelings. 2015. (ENG., Illus.). 20p. (J). (gr. -1-2). 24.99 *(978-1-4549-1729-8(6))* Sterling Publishing Co., Inc.

Lloyd-Jones, Sally. My Merry Christmas (padded Board Book) Gianassi, Sara, illus. 2017. (ENG.). 20p. (J). (gr. -1-k). bds. 12.99 *(978-1-4336-4895-3(4),* 005790558, B&H Kids) B&H Publishing Group.

—Tiny Bear's Bible, 1 vol. Oleynikov, Igor, illus. 2009. (Furry Bible Stories Ser.). (ENG.). 22p. (J). (gr. -1-k). pap. 14.99 *(978-0-310-71818-5(X))* Zonderkidz.

—Tiny Bear's Bible (Girls), 1 vol. Oleynikov, Igor, illus. 2015. (ENG.). 22p. (J). bds. 16.99 *(978-0-310-74787-1(2))* Zonderkidz.

Lloyd-Jones, Sally & Jago. Loved: The Lord's Prayer, 1 vol. 2018. (Jesus Storybook Bible Ser.). (ENG., Illus.). 20p. (J). bds. 10.99 *(978-0-310-75761-0(4))* Zonderkidz.

Lloyd, Sam. What's in Your Tummy Mummy? 2007. (ENG., Illus.). 24p. (J). (gr. -1-k). pap. 13.95 *(978-1-84365-091-1(6),* Pavilion Children's Books) Pavilion Bks. GBR. Dist: HarperCollins Pubs.

Lluch, Alex A. Animal Alphabet: Slide & Seek the ABCs. Defenbaugh, David, illus. 2013. 13p. (J). (-k). bds. 12.99 *(978-1-61351-041-4(1))* WS Publishing.

—Animal Numbers: Slide & Seek Counting. 2012. 14p. (J). bds. 7.95 *(978-1-936061-90-7(2))* WS Publishing.

—I Like to Learn Alphabet: Zoo Clues. 2011. 32p. (J). (gr. -1-k). bds. 4.95 *(978-1-934386-00-2(6))* WS Publishing.

—I Like to Learn Colors: Curious Penguin. 2011. 32p. (J). (gr. -1-k). bds. 4.95 *(978-1-934386-02-6(2))* WS Publishing.

—I Like to Learn Numbers: Hungry Chameleon. 2011. 32p. (J). (gr. -1-k). bds. 4.95 *(978-1-934386-01-9(4))* WS Publishing.

—I Like to Learn Opposites: Amazing Bugs. 2011. 32p. (J). (gr. -1-k). bds. 4.95 *(978-1-934386-03-3(0))* WS Publishing.

—Touch the Red Button. 2014. 60p. (J). (gr. -1-k). 9.99 *(978-1-61351-094-0(2))* WS Publishing.

Lo Monaco, Gérard. The Carousel of Animals. 2018. (ENG.). 10p. (J). (gr. k-12). 19.95 *(978-3-89955-801-2(4))* Die Gestalten Verlag DEU. Dist: Ingram Publisher Services.

Lobo, Julia. Eek! That's Creepy! Look & Find. Cavallini, Linda, illus. 2010. 24p. (J). 7.98 *(978-1-60553-898-3(1))* Publications International, Ltd.

—Grandma Wishes. Cottage Door Press, ed. Rowe, Helen, illus. 2015. (ENG.). 18p. (J). (gr. -1-1). bds. 9.99 *(978-1-68052-008-8(3),* 1000090) Cottage Door Pr.

—Grandma Wishes. Rowe, Helen, illus. 2015. (J). *(978-1-68052-135-1(7))* Cottage Door Pr.

—Will You Be My Sunshine. Cottage Door Press, ed. Slater, Nicola, illus. 2015. (ENG.). 18p. (J). (gr. -1-1). bds. 9.99 *(978-1-68052-027-9(X),* 1000280) Cottage Door Pr.

Lodge, Jo. Little Roar's Red Boots. 2013. (Little Roar Ser.). (ENG., Illus.). 20p. (J). (gr. -1-k). 8.99 *(978-1-4449-0482-6(5))* Hachette Children's Group GBR. Dist: Hachette Bk. Group.

—Little Roar's Round Balloon. 2013. (Little Roar Ser.). (ENG., Illus.). 20p. (J). (gr. -1-k). 5.99 *(978-1-4449-0483-3(3))* Hachette Children's Group GBR. Dist: Hachette Bk. Group.

Lodge, Yvette. Noah's Ark: Baby's First Pop-up! Lodge, Ali, illus. gif. ed. 2006. 8p. (J). 19.95 *(978-1-57791-217-0(9))* Brighter Minds Children's Publishing.

Lombardi, Kristine & Disney Storybook Artists Staff. Disney Cars Carry along Treasury. 2010. (Carry along Bks.). (ENG., Illus.). 20p. (J). (gr. -1). bds. 14.99 *(978-0-7944-1947-9(X))* Reader's Digest Assn., Inc., The.

Long, Ethan. Thank You! 2016. (Animal Sounds Ser.). (ENG., Illus.). 20p. (J). (gr. -1 — 1). bds. 7.95 *(978-1-4197-1364-4(7),* 1092810) Abrams, Inc.

López, Oscar J., illus. Sing along with Abuelita Rosa: Hispanic Lullabies = Canciones de Cuna. 2006. (ENG & SPA.). 13p. (J). *(978-0-9788379-0-7(8))* Baby Abuelita Productions, Inc.

The Lost Treasure of Skull Island. 2012. (Illus.). (J). *(978-1-4351-4328-9(0))* Barnes & Noble, Inc.

Lovasik, Lawrence G. A Child's Prayer Treasury (Puzzle Book) St. Joseph Puzzle Book: Book Contains 5 Exciting Jigsaw Puzzles. 2004. (ENG., Illus.). 12p. bds. 9.95 *(978-0-89942-719-5(7),* 973/97) Catholic Bk. Publishing Corp.

Love-Byrd, Cheri. How Many Do I Love You? a Valentine Counting Book. Cottage Door Press, ed. Stoyva, Mei, illus. 2017. (ENG.). 13p. (J). (gr. -1-k). bds. 7.99 *(978-1-68052-274-7(4),* 1002590) Cottage Door Pr.

Low, Susan. Just Draw! 2006. (Illus.). 24p. *(978-2-7643-0295-8(9))* Phidal Publishing, Inc./Editions Phidal, Inc.

LP-Addition: Level 2 Math. 2004. (ENG.). (J). 9.99 *(978-1-59204-018-6(7))* Learning Wrap-Ups, Inc.

LP-Blends & Digraphs: Level 1 Reading. 2004. (ENG.). (J). 9.99 *(978-1-59204-005-6(5))* Learning Wrap-Ups, Inc.

LP-Capitalization & Punctuation: Level 2 Reading. 2004. (ENG.). (J). 9.99 *(978-1-59204-009-4(8))* Learning Wrap-Ups, Inc.

LP-Place Value: Level 2 Math. 2004. (ENG.). (J). 9.99 *(978-1-59204-017-9(9))* Learning Wrap-Ups, Inc.

LP-Reading Comprehension: Level 2 Reading. 2004. (ENG.). (J). 9.99 *(978-1-59204-011-7(X))* Learning Wrap-Ups, Inc.

LP-Subtraction: Level 2 Math. 2004. (ENG.). (J). 9.99 *(978-1-59204-019-3(5))* Learning Wrap-Ups, Inc.

Lubber, William. Pirateology: The Pirate Hunter's Companion. Steer, Dugald A., ed. 2006. (Ologies Ser.). (ENG., Illus.). 32p. (J). (gr. 3-7). 29.99 *(978-0-7636-3143-7(4))* Candlewick Pr.

Ludwig, Ashley. You Tickle My Heart: and other ways you make me laugh. 2008. (Illus.). 18p. (J). (gr. k-1). bds. 11.50 *(978-0-9800630-0-4(0))* Beachcomber Press.com.

Luffman, Alice, et al. Santa Street. Pigott, Louise, illus. 2018. (J). *(978-0-312-52889-8(2))* St. Martin's Pr.

Luiz, Fernando, illus. How to Be a Princess: A Girly Girl Book. 2009. 12p. (J). bds. 6.95 *(978-1-58117-850-0(6),* Intervisual/Piggy Toes) Bendon, Inc.

Lund, Deb. All Aboard the Dinotrain Board Book. Fine, Howard, illus. 2011. (ENG.). 30p. (J). (gr. -1 — 1). bds. 7.99 *(978-0-547-55415-0(X),* 1452006, Clarion Bks.) HarperCollins Pubs.

Lundie, Isobel. The Amicus Book Of 123. 2019. (ENG.). 10p. (J). (gr. -1-1). bds. 8.99 *(978-1-68152-569-3(0),* 10870) Amicus.

—The Amicus Book of ABC. 2019. (ENG.). 26p. (J). (gr. -1-1). bds. 8.99 *(978-1-68152-568-6(2),* 10869) Amicus.

—The Amicus Book of Colors. 2020. (ENG., Illus.). 10p. (J). (gr. -1 — 1). pap. 8.99 *(978-1-68152-571-6(2),* 10721) Amicus.

Lunney, Lizz. Build Your Own Theme Park: A Paper Cut-Out Book. 2019. (ENG., Illus.). 80p. (J). pap. 18.99 *(978-1-4494-9632-6(6))* Andrews McMeel Publishing.

Lyons, P. J. Thank You, Lord, for Everything, 1 vol. Warnes, Tim, illus. 2015. (ENG.). 16p. (J). bds. 9.99 *(978-0-310-74812-0(7))* Zonderkidz.

Macaulay, David. How Machines Work: Zoo Break! 2015. (DK First Reference Ser.). (ENG., Illus.). 32p. (J). (gr. 2-5). 19.99 *(978-1-4654-4012-9(7),* DK Children) Dorling Kindersley Publishing, Inc.

Maccarone, Grace. The Gingerbread Family: A Scratch-And-Sniff Book. Gardner, Louise, illus. 2010. (ENG.). 14p. (J). (gr. -1-k). bds. 8.99 *(978-1-4424-0678-0(X),* Little Simon) Little Simon.

Macdonald, Fiona. The Medieval Chronicles: Vikings, Knights, & Castles. Antram, David, illus. 2013. 92p. (J). *(978-1-4351-5067-6(8))* Barnes & Noble, Inc.

MacKenzie, Catherine. I Can Say to God, Please. rev. ed. 2015. (Board Books Prayer Ser.). (ENG.). 10p. (J). bds. 3.99 *(978-1-85792-691-0(9),* 01cee985-bd56-4f5d-be3b-d0461a3812fd) Christian Focus Pubns. GBR. Dist: Baker & Taylor Publisher Services (BTPS).

MacKenzie, Lachlan. The Duke's Daughter. 2008. (Story Time Ser.). (ENG., Illus.). 24p. (J). (gr. -1-3). 7.99 *(978-1-84550-326-0(0),* 55c39b86-6732-4df2-a209-0be940187130) Christian Focus Pubns. GBR. Dist: Baker & Taylor Publisher Services (BTPS).

MacLaine, James. The Usborne Little Children's Travel Activity Book. Watt, Fiona, ed. Harrison, Erica et al, illus. 2013. (Activity Books for Little Children Ser.). (ENG.). 63p. (J). pap. 9.99 *(978-0-7945-3127-0(X),* Usborne) EDC Publishing.

MacLean, Kerry Lee. Just Me & My Mind. 2014. (ENG., Illus.). 16p. (J). (gr. -1-1). 18.95 *(978-1-61429-124-4(1))* Wisdom Pubns.

MacMillan, Kathy. Nita's First Signs, Volume 1. Brezzi, Sara, illus. 2018. (Little Hands Signing Ser.: 1). (ENG.). 12p. (J). (gr. -1 — 1). bds. 14.99 *(978-1-945547-67-6(7),* 554767) Familius LLC.

Maddox, Jake. Striker Assist, 1 vol. Tiffany, Sean, illus. 2012. (Jake Maddox Sports Stories Ser.). (ENG.). 72p. (J). (gr. 3-6). pap. 5.95 *(978-1-4342-4208-2(0),* 120267, Stone Arch Bks.) Capstone.

Madinabeitia Manso, Susana. In Summer/en Verano. Hanako Momohara, Emily, illus. 2018. (Seasons/Estaciones Ser.). (ENG.). 14p. (J). (— 1). bds. 7.99 *(978-1-936669-64-6(1))* Blue Manatee Press.

Madson, Trish. A Is for Arizona: A Grand Canyon State ABC Primer. W. Miles, David, illus. 2017. (ENG.). 20p. (J). (gr. -1 — 1). bds. 12.99 *(978-1-944822-78-1(X),* 552278) Familius LLC.

—Let's Count Arizona: Numbers & Colors in the Grand Canyon State. 2017. (ENG., Illus.). 20p. (J). (gr. -1 — 1). bds. 12.99 *(978-1-944822-73-6(9),* 552273) Familius LLC.

—O Is for Oregon: A Beaver State ABC Primer. W. Miles, David, illus. 2017. (ENG.). 20p. (J). (gr. -1 — 1). bds. 12.99 *(978-1-944822-72-9(0),* 552272) Familius LLC.

—T Is for Texas: A Lone Star State ABC Primer. 2017. (ENG., Illus.). 20p. (J). (gr. -1 — 1). bds. 12.99 *(978-1-944822-75-0(5),* 552275) Familius LLC.

—W Is for Washington: An Evergreen State ABC Primer. Miles, David W., illus. 2016. (ENG.). 20p. (J). (gr. -1 — 1). bds. 12.95 *(978-1-944822-02-6(X),* 552202) Familius LLC.

Magsamen, Sandra. Baby Love. Magsamen, Sandra, illus. 2019. (ENG., Illus.). 10p. (J). (gr. -1 — 1). bds. 8.99 *(978-1-338-24320-8(9),* Cartwheel Bks.) Scholastic, Inc.

—Beecause I Love You. Magsamen, Sandra, illus. 2017. (Made with Love Ser.). (ENG., Illus.). 14p. (J). (— 1). bds. 7.99 *(978-1-338-11090-6(X),* Cartwheel Bks.) Scholastic, Inc.

—Boo, Boo, I Love You! (Made with Love) Magsamen, Sandra, illus. 2019. (Made with Love Ser.). (ENG., Illus.). 10p. (J). (gr. -1 — 1). bds. 7.99 *(978-1-338-11091-3(8),* Cartwheel Bks.) Scholastic, Inc.

—Everybody Goes Nighty-Night (Heart-Felt Books) Magsamen, Sandra, illus. 2018. (Heart-Felt Bks.). (ENG.). 10p. (J). (gr. -1 — 1). bds. 7.99 *(978-0-545-92799-4(4),* Cartwheel Bks.) Scholastic, Inc.

—I Love Hugs & Kisses (heart-Felt Books) Magsamen, Sandra, illus. 2016. (Heart-Felt Bks.). (ENG.). 10p. (J). (gr. -1-k). 7.99 *(978-0-545-92796-3(X),* Cartwheel Bks.) Scholastic, Inc.

—I Love to Gobble You Up! Magsamen, Sandra, illus. 2018. (Made with Love Ser.). (ENG., Illus.). 10p. (J). (gr. -1 — 1). bds. 7.99 *(978-1-338-11092-0(6),* Cartwheel Bks.) Scholastic, Inc.

—I Love You, Honey Bunny (Made with Love) Magsamen, Sandra, illus. 2016. (Made with Love Ser.). (ENG., Illus.). 14p. (J). (— 1). bds. 7.99 *(978-1-338-11084-5(5),* Cartwheel Bks.) Scholastic, Inc.

—I Love You Snow Much. Magsamen, Sandra, illus. 2017. (Made with Love Ser.). (ENG., Illus.). 10p. (J). (— 1). bds. 7.99 *(978-1-338-11086-9(1),* Cartwheel Bks.) Scholastic, Inc.

—I'm Wild about You! (heart-Felt Books) Heartfelt Stories. Magsamen, Sandra, illus. 2016. (Heart-Felt Bks.). (ENG., Illus.). 10p. (J). (— 1). 8.99 *(978-0-545-46839-8(6),* Cartwheel Bks.) Scholastic, Inc.

—Itsy-Bitsy I Love You! (heart-Felt Books) Heartfelt Stories. Magsamen, Sandra, illus. 2016. (Heart-Felt Bks.). (ENG., Illus.). 10p. (J). (— 1). 7.99 *(978-0-545-46841-1(8),* Cartwheel Bks.) Scholastic, Inc.

—Merry Christmas, Little One! Magsamen, Sandra, illus. 2018. (ENG., Illus.). 10p. (J). (gr. -1 — 1). bds. 8.99 *(978-1-338-24309-3(8),* Cartwheel Bks.) Scholastic, Inc.

—Our Little Deer (Made with Love) Magsamen, Sandra, illus. 2016. (Made with Love Ser.). (ENG., Illus.). 14p. (J). bds. 7.99 *(978-1-338-11081-4(0),* Cartwheel Bks.) Scholastic, Inc.

—Peek-A-Boo, I Love You! Magsamen, Sandra, illus. 2017. (ENG., Illus.). 10p. (J). (gr. -1 — 1). bds. 8.99 *(978-1-338-11088-3(8),* Cartwheel Bks.) Scholastic, Inc.

—Peek-A-Boooo! (Heart-felt Books) Magsamen, Sandra, illus. 2018. (Heart-Felt Bks.). (ENG., Illus.). 10p. (J). (gr. -1 — 1). bds. 7.99 *(978-0-545-92798-7(6),* Cartwheel Bks.) Scholastic, Inc.

—Twinkle, Twinkle, You're My Star. Magsamen, Sandra, illus. 2018. (ENG., Illus.). 10p. (J). (gr. -1 — 1). 7.99 *(978-1-338-24312-3(8),* Cartwheel Bks.) Scholastic, Inc.

—Whooo Loves You? Magsamen, Sandra, illus. 2017. (Made with Love Ser.). (ENG., Illus.). 10p. (J). (gr. -1 — 1). bds. 8.99 *(978-1-338-11087-6(X),* Cartwheel Bks.) Scholastic, Inc.

Mahoney, Daniel J., illus. I See a Monster. 2008. (ENG.). 12p. (J). bds. 5.95 *(978-1-58117-729-9(1),* Intervisual/Piggy Toes) Bendon, Inc.

Mahoney, Jean. Swan Lake Ballet Theatre. Seddon, Viola Anne, illus. 2009. (ENG.). 16p. (J). (gr. 1-4). 24.99 *(978-0-7636-4396-6(3))* Candlewick Pr.

Maizels, Jennie. Pop-Up New York. Maizels, Jennie, illus. 2014. (ENG., Illus.). 12p. (J). (gr. k-4). 19.99 *(978-0-7636-7162-4(2))* Candlewick Pr.

Make Believe Ideas. Baby Animals. 2014. (ENG.). 12p. (J). (— 1). bds. 6.99 *(978-1-78393-153-8(1))* Make Believe Ideas GBR. Dist: Scholastic, Inc.

—Hatch. Make Believe Ideas, illus. 2017. (ENG.). 16p. (J). (gr. -1 — 1). 7.99 *(978-1-78692-081-2(6))* Make Believe Ideas GBR. Dist: Scholastic, Inc.

—Old Macdonald Had a Farm, 1 vol. Ede, Lara, illus. 2018. (ENG.). 12p. (J). (gr. -1 — 1). 8.99 *(978-1-78692-904-4(X))* Make Believe Ideas GBR. Dist: Scholastic, Inc.

—Touch & Feel Animal Babies. Petit, Véronique, illus. 2017. (ENG.). 12p. (J). (gr. -1 — 1). 6.99 *(978-1-78692-129-1(4))* Make Believe Ideas GBR. Dist: Scholastic, Inc.

—Touch & Feel First Words. Petit, Véronique, illus. 2017. (ENG.). 12p. (J). (gr. -1 — 1). 6.99 *(978-1-78692-131-4(6))* Make Believe Ideas GBR. Dist: Scholastic, Inc.

—Touch & Feel Peekaboo! Petit, Véronique, illus. 2017. (ENG.). 12p. (J). (gr. -1 — 1). 6.99 *(978-1-78692-123-9(5))* Make Believe Ideas GBR. Dist: Scholastic, Inc.

—Vroom. Make Believe Ideas, illus. 2015. (ENG.). 12p. (J). (gr. -1 — 1). 9.99 *(978-1-78393-437-9(9))* Make Believe Ideas GBR. Dist: Scholastic, Inc.

Make Believe Ideas, Ltd., creator. Pets & Puppies Pack. 2007. (Touch & Sparkle Ser.). (Illus.). (gr. -1-k). per., bds. *(978-1-84610-692-7(3))* Make Believe Ideas.

Malepart, Celine, illus. When Pigs Fly: A Piggy Pop-up Book! 2008. (ENG.). 12p. 16.95 *(978-1-58117-671-1(6),* Intervisual/Piggy Toes) Bendon, Inc.

Mandy and Ness Staff, et al. George's Garden. 2005. (Senses Ser.). (URD, ENG, VIE, CHI & BEN., Illus.). 16p. (J). pap. 9.95 *(978-1-84059-168-2(4))* Milet Publishing.

—Peter's Party. 2005. (Senses Ser.). (URD, ENG, VIE, CHI & BEN., Illus.). 16p. (J). pap. 9.95 *(978-1-84059-150-7(1))* Milet Publishing.

—Rosie's Room. 2005. (Senses Ser.). (URD, ENG, TUR, VIE & CHI., Illus.). 16p. (J). (gr. -1-1). pap. 9.95 *(978-1-84059-162-0(5))* Milet Publishing.

Manley, Victoria. Lightning & Friends (Disney/Pixar Cars 3) RH Disney, illus. 2017. (ENG.). 16p. (J). (— 1). bds. 7.99 *(978-0-7364-3748-6(7),* RH/Disney) Random Hse. Children's Bks.

Mansfield, Andy. Lonely Planet Kids Pop-Up London 1. Mansfield, Andy, illus. 2016. (Lonely Planet Kids Ser.). (ENG., Illus.). 8p. (J). (gr. -1-k). 9.99 *(978-1-76034-339-2(0),* 5339) Lonely Planet Global Ltd. IRL. Dist: Hachette Bk. Group.

—Lonely Planet Kids Pop-Up Paris 1. Mansfield, Andy, illus. 2016. (Lonely Planet Kids Ser.). (ENG., Illus.). 8p. (J). (gr. -1-k). 9.99 *(978-1-76034-335-4(8),* 5335) Lonely Planet Global Ltd. IRL. Dist: Hachette Bk. Group.

—See the Stripes. Mansfield, Andy, illus. 2018. (ENG., Illus.). 14p. (J). (gr. -1-2). 15.00 *(978-0-7636-9895-9(4))* Candlewick Pr.

Manson, Beverlie, illus. Stories to Share: The Twelve Dancing Princesses. 2017. 24p. (J). (gr. -1-12). pap. 7.99 *(978-1-86147-829-0(1),* Armadillo) Anness Publishing GBR. Dist: National Bk. Network.

Mara, Nichole. All Aboard! (an Abrams Extend-A-Book) Let's Ride a Train. Kolb, Andrew, illus. 2017. (Abrams Extend-A-Book Ser.). (ENG.). 10p. (J). (gr. -1 — 1). bds. 9.95 *(978-1-4197-2567-8(X),* 1180210, Abrams Appleseed) Abrams, Inc.

—So Many Feet. Santillanes, Alexander Vidal, illus. 2017. (ENG.). 34p. (J). (gr. -1 — 1). bds. 12.95 *(978-1-4197-2318-6(9),* 1157910) Abrams, Inc.

Marchesi, Stephen, illus. Glow-In-The-Dark Constellations. 2006. (J). *(978-1-59412-171-5(0))* Mud Puddle, Inc.

Marchon, Benoit. Good Night! A Peek-A-Boo Book. Bravi, Soledad, illus. 2013. (ENG.). 40p. (J). (gr. k — 1). bds. 8.99 *(978-0-547-89314-3(0),* 1508644, Clarion Bks.) HarperCollins Pubs.

Markes, Julie. Thanks for Thanksgiving Board Book. Barrette, Doris, illus. 2017. (ENG.). 32p. (J). (gr. -1 — 1). bds. 7.99 *(978-0-06-264331-5(2),* HarperFestival) HarperCollins Pubs.

Marks, Burton. Tanya Tinker & the Gizmo Gang. Smath, Jerry, illus. 2003. 20p. (J). (gr. -1-3). reprint ed. 22.00 *(978-0-7567-6760-0(1))* DIANE Publishing Co.

Marley, Cedella & Marley, Bob. Every Little Thing: Based on the Song Three Little Birds by Bob Marley. Brantley-Newton, Vanessa, illus. 2015. (Marley Ser.). (ENG.). 24p. (J). (gr. -1-k). bds. 7.99 *(978-1-4521-4290-6(4))* Chronicle Bks. LLC.

Marqina, Mignon. Shapes & Me: A Flip & Learn Book. Lt. ed. 2006. (Illus.). 32p. (J). lib. bdg. *(978-1-934190-05-0(5))* Ocean Front Bk. Publishing, Inc.

Marsh, Carole. Alaska Wheel of Fortune: Game Book. (Orig.). pap. 9.95 *(978-0-7933-9621-4(2))* Gallopade International.

Marshall, Linda Elovitz. Shh ... Shh ... Shabbat. Golubeva, Evgenia, illus. 2016. (ENG.). 12p. (J). (gr. -1 — 1). bds. 5.99 *(978-1-4677-5873-4(6),* 3ba0a891-35f6-4c89-9695-9ac65bea93f1, Kar-Ben Publishing) Lerner Publishing Group.

Marshall, Natalie. Five Little Ducks: a Fingers & Toes Nursery Rhyme Book. Marshall, Natalie, illus. 2017. (Fingers & Toes Nursery Rhymes Ser.). (ENG., Illus.). 12p. (J). (gr. -1 — 1). bds. 6.99 *(978-1-338-09116-8(6),* Cartwheel Bks.) Scholastic, Inc.

—Millie-Mae: In Winter. 2014. (Illus.). (J). *(978-1-4351-5613-5(7))* Barnes & Noble, Inc.

Marshall, Natalie, illus. Millie-Mae: In Autumn. 2014. (J). *(978-1-4351-5612-8(9))* Barnes & Noble, Inc.

—Seaside Sandcastle! 2014. (J). *(978-1-4351-5505-3(X))* Barnes & Noble, Inc.

—Tiny Creatures: Touch & Feel Book. 2015. (J). *(978-1-4351-5935-8(7))* Barnes & Noble, Inc.

—Zoo Fun: A Lift the Flap Guessing Book. 2013. (J). *(978-1-4351-4930-4(0))* Barnes & Noble, Inc.

Marshall, Rita. Taste the Clouds. 2016. (ENG., Illus.). 14p. (J). (gr. -1-k). bds. 8.99 *(978-1-56846-285-1(9),* 20558, Creative Editions) Creative Co., The.

—Wake up, Weather. Felix, Monique, illus. 2016. (ENG.). 14p. (J). (gr. -1-k). bds. 8.99 *(978-1-56846-286-8(7),* 20562, Creative Editions) Creative Co., The.

T
U
V

Marsoli, Lisa Ann. Harold Takes a Trip: Harold & the Purple Crayon. Chiang, Andy, illus. 2005. 10p. (J). 7.95 (978-1-58117-262-1(1), Intervisual/Piggy Toes) Bendon, Inc.

Marti, Meritxell. Grow, Baby, Grow! Watch Baby Grow Month by Month! Salomo, Xavier, illus. 2019. (ENG.). 18p. (J). (gr. k-2). 24.99 (978-1-64170-100-6(5), 550100) Familius LLC.

Martin, Bill, Jr. Baby Bear, Baby Bear, What Do You See? Carle, Eric, illus. 2014. (Brown Bear & Friends Ser.). (ENG.). 28p. (J). (gr. -1-k). bds. 12.99 (978-0-8050-9949-2(2), 900127480, Holt, Henry & Co. Bks. For Young Readers) Holt, Henry & Co.

—Brown Bear, Brown Bear, What Do You See? / Oso Pardo, Oso Pardo, ¿qué Ves Ahí? (Bilingual Board Book - English / Spanish) Carle, Eric, illus. 2017. (ENG.). 28p. (J). bds. 9.99 (978-1-250-15232-9(1), 900183597, Holt, Henry & Co. Bks. For Young Readers) Holt, Henry & Co.

—Brown Bear, Brown Bear, What Do You See? Slide & Find. Carle, Eric, illus. 2010. (Brown Bear & Friends Ser.). (ENG.). 22p. (J). (-1). bds. 12.99 (978-0-312-50926-2(X), 900070116) St. Martin's Pr.

Martin, Bill, Jr. & Archambault, John. Chica Chica Bum Bum ABC (Chicka Chicka ABC) Ehlert, Lois, illus. 2011. (SPA.). 16p. (J). (gr. -1-1). bds. 7.99 (978-1-4424-2292-6(0), Libros Para Ninos) Libros Para Ninos.

—Chicka Chicka ABC: Lap Edition. Ehlert, Lois, illus. 2009. (Chicka Chicka Book Ser.). (ENG.). 16p. (J). (gr. -1-1). bds. 11.99 (978-1-4169-8447-4(X), Little Simon) Little Simon.

Martin, Bill, Jr. & Sampson, Michael. Chicka Chicka 1, 2, 3. Ehlert, Lois, illus. 2014. (Chicka Chicka Book Ser.). (ENG.). 36p. (J). (gr. -1 — 1). bds. 7.99 (978-1-4814-0056-5(8), Little Simon) Little Simon.

Martin, David. Christmas Tree. Sweet, Melissa, illus. 2009. (ENG.). 26p. (J). (— 1). bds. 5.99 (978-0-7636-3030-0(6)) Candlewick Pr.

—Hanukkah Lights. Sweet, Melissa, illus. 2009. (ENG.). 26p. (J). (gr. -1 — 1). bds. 6.99 (978-0-7636-3029-4(2)) Candlewick Pr.

Martin, Emily Winfield. Day Dreamers: A Journey of Imagination. 2016. (ENG., Illus.). 32p. (J). (— 1). bds. 8.99 (978-1-101-93522-4(7), Random Hse. Bks. for Young Readers) Random Hse. Children's Bks.

—Dream Animals: A Bedtime Journey. 2015. (ENG., Illus.). 34p. (J). (— 1). bds. 8.99 (978-0-553-52190-0(X), Random Hse. Bks. for Young Readers) Random Hse. Children's Bks.

Martin, Ruth. Little Explorers: My Amazing Body. Sanders, Allan, illus. 2015. (Little Explorers Ser.). (ENG.). 18p. (J). (gr. -1-3). 10.99 (978-1-4998-0040-1(1)) Little Bee Books Inc.

—Little Explorers: Outer Space. Sanders, Allan, illus. 2016. (Little Explorers Ser.). (ENG.). 18p. (J). (gr. -1-3). 10.99 (978-1-4998-0250-4(1)) Little Bee Books Inc.

—Little Explorers: the Animal World. Sanders, Allan, illus. 2016. (Little Explorers Ser.). (ENG.). 18p. (J). (gr. -1-3). 10.99 (978-1-4998-0249-8(8)) Little Bee Books Inc.

—Noisy Nature: in the Jungle. Pledger, Maurice, illus. 2015. (ENG.). 12p. (J). (gr. -1). 16.95 (978-1-62686-104-6(8), Silver Dolphin Bks.) Readerlink Distribution Services, LLC.

—Noisy Nature: on the Farm. Pledger, Maurice, illus. 2015. (ENG.). 12p. (J). (gr. -1). 16.95 (978-1-62686-103-9(X), Silver Dolphin Bks.) Readerlink Distribution Services, LLC.

Mason, Conrad. See Inside How Things Work. 2010. (See Inside Board Bks). 16p. (J). bds. 12.99 (978-0-7945-2406-7(0), Usborne) EDC Publishing.

—See Inside Ships. King, Colin, illus. 2011. (See Inside Board Books Ser.). 16p. (J). ring bd. 12.99 (978-0-7945-3005-1(2), Usborne) EDC Publishing.

Mason, Tom & Danko, Dan. A Christmas Surprise: A Lift-The-Flap Adventure. Shannon, David et al, illus. 2011. (Jon Scieszka's Trucktown Ser.). (ENG.). 12p. (J). (gr. -1-k). 8.99 (978-1-4169-4193-4(2), Simon & Schuster Bks. For Young Readers) Simon & Schuster Bks. For Young Readers.

Mason, Tom, et al. Who's That Truck? Shannon, David et al, illus. 2008. (Jon Scieszka's Trucktown Ser.). (ENG.). 14p. (J). (gr. -1-1). bds. 7.99 (978-1-4169-4175-0(4), Little Simon) Little Simon.

Massey, Jane, illus. Potty Hero. 2016. (J). (978-0-545-92773-4(0)) Scholastic, Inc.

—Potty Star. 2015. (J). (978-0-545-92772-7(2)) Scholastic, Inc.

Massironi, Daniela, illus. Frankie the Frog. 2014. (J). (978-1-4351-5573-2(4)) Barnes & Noble, Inc.

—Freddie the Fish. 2014. (J). (978-1-4351-5574-9(2)) Barnes & Noble, Inc.

Matheson, Christie. Tap the Magic Tree. Matheson, Christie, illus. 2013. (ENG., Illus.). 40p. (J). (gr. -1-3). 18.99 (978-0-06-227445-8(7), Greenwillow Bks.) HarperCollins Pubs.

—Tap the Magic Tree Board Book. Matheson, Christie, illus. 2016. (ENG., Illus.). 42p. (J). (gr. -1-3). bds. 7.99 (978-0-06-227446-5(5), Greenwillow Bks.) HarperCollins Pubs.

Matisse, Henri. Blue & Other Colors: With Henri Matisse. 2016. (ENG., Illus.). 30p. (gr. -1 — 1). bds. 12.95 (978-0-7148-7142-4(7)) Phaidon Pr., Inc.

Matthews, Derek. Animales de la Granja. 2005. (Escucha y Aprende Ser.). (SPA., Illus.). 10p. (J). (gr. -1-1). (978-970-718-300-1(4), Silver Dolphin en Español) Advanced Marketing, S. de R. L. de C. V.

—Animales de la Selva. 2005. (Escucha y Aprende Ser.). (SPA., Illus.). 10p. (J). (gr. -1-1). (978-970-718-298-1(9), Silver Dolphin en Español) Advanced Marketing, S. de R. L. de C. V.

—Escucha y Aprende - Mascotas. 2005. (Escucha y Aprende Ser.). (SPA., Illus.). 10p. (J). (gr. -1-k). (978-970-718-299-8(7), Silver Dolphin en Español) Advanced Marketing, S. de R. L. de C. V.

—Tráfico: Con Graciosos Sonidos de vehículos. 2005. (Escucha y Aprende Ser.). (SPA., Illus.). 10p. (J). (gr. -1-1). (978-970-718-297-4(0), Silver Dolphin en Español) Advanced Marketing, S. de R. L. de C. V.

Matyjaszek, Kasia, illus. This Bonny Baby: A Mirror Board Book, 96 vols. 2017. 12p. (J). 9.95 (978-1-78250-465-8(6), Kelpies) Floris Bks. GBR. Dist: Consortium Bk. Sales & Distribution.

Mawhinney, Art & Disney Storybook Artists Staff, illus. Fairies. 2007. (Look & Find Ser.). 7.98 (978-1-4127-7423-9(3)) Publications International, Ltd.

Max and Sid, illus. Animal Homes. 2015. (Tiny Touch Ser.). (ENG.). 12p. (J). (gr. -1 — 1). bds. 4.99 (978-1-4998-0023-4(1)) Little Bee Books Inc.

—Counting. 2016. (What Can You Spot? Ser.). (ENG.). 18p. (J). (gr. -1 — 1). bds. 7.99 (978-1-4998-0269-6(2)) Little Bee Books Inc.

—My First Animals. 2016. (My First Ser.). (ENG.). 12p. (J). (gr. -1 — 1). bds. 5.99 (978-1-4998-0185-9(8)) Little Bee Books Inc.

Maxwell-Hyslop, Miranda. Fish Go Woof! 2005. (ENG., Illus.). 36p. (J). (978-0-340-87338-0(8)) Hodder & Stoughton.

May, Darcy. Glitter Fairies Stickers. 2004. (Dover Little Activity Books Stickers Ser.). (ENG., Illus.). 2p. (J). (gr. 1-4). pap. 1.99 (978-0-486-43530-5(X), 43530X) Dover Pubns., Inc.

Mayer, Ellen. Red Socks: English, bks. 7, bk. 2. Hu, Ying-Hwa, illus. 2015. (ENG.). 18p. (J). pap. 6.99 (978-1-59572-706-0(X)) Star Bright Bks., Inc.

Mayer, Helena. The Lost Riolu: Pokémon Academy. 2009. (Pokémon Ser.). (Illus.). 62p. (J). pap. (978-0-545-20050-9(4)) Scholastic, Inc.

Mayer, Mercer. Little Critter: to the Rescue! Mayer, Mercer, illus. 2008. (My First I Can Read Ser.). (ENG., Illus.). 32p. (J). (gr. -1-3). pap. 4.99 (978-0-06-083547-7(8), HarperCollins) HarperCollins Pubs.

—To the Rescue! Mayer, Mercer, illus. 2008. (My First I Can Read Bks.). (ENG., Illus.). 32p. (J). (gr. -1-3). 16.99 (978-0-06-083548-4(6)) HarperCollins Pubs.

Mayfield, Marilee Joy. My First Book of Planes, Trains, & Cars. 2016. (Illus.). 51p. (J). (978-1-4351-6528-1(4)) Barnes & Noble, Inc.

—My First Book of United States Monuments & Parks. 2017. (Illus.). 51p. (J). (978-1-4351-6637-0(X)) Barnes & Noble, Inc.

Mazzenga, Mark. Baby Geek. Briggs, Korwin, illus. 2019. (ENG.). 20p. (J). (gr. -1 — 1). bds. 10.99 (978-1-941367-63-6(1)) Downtown Bookworks.

McBratney, Sam. Guess How Much I Love You Lap-Size Board Book. Jeram, Anita, illus. 2013. (Guess How Much I Love You Ser.). (ENG.). 24p. (J). (— 1). bds. 14.99 (978-0-7636-7006-1(5)) Candlewick Pr.

—Guess How Much I Love You: One More Tickle! A Puppet Book. Jeram, Anita, illus. 2016. (Guess How Much I Love You Ser.). (ENG.). 14p. (J). (gr. k-k). bds. 18.99 (978-0-7636-8819-6(3)) Candlewick Pr.

—Guess How Much I Love You: Pop-Up. Jeram, Anita, illus. 2011. (Guess How Much I Love You Ser.). (ENG.). 16p. (J). (gr. -1-2). 21.99 (978-0-7636-5378-1(0)) Candlewick Pr.

—There, There. Bates, Ivan, illus. 2015. (ENG.). 32p. (J). (-k). bds. 7.99 (978-0-7636-7565-3(2), Templar) Candlewick Pr.

McCarthy, Dan. Good Night Oregon. Veno, Joe, illus. 2010. (Good Night Our World Ser.). (ENG.). 20p. (J). (gr. k — 1). bds. 9.95 (978-1-60219-041-2(0)) Good Night Bks.

McClure, Nikki. Mama, Is It Summer Yet? 2018. (ENG., Illus.). 30p. (J). (gr. -1 — 1). bds. 9.99 (978-1-4197-2828-0(8), 1202510, Abrams Appleseed) Abrams, Inc.

McCombs, Margi. Dios Es Bueno Todo el Tiempo (God Is Good... All the Time) Ivanov, Aleksey & Ivanov, Olga, illus. 2012. Orig. Title: God Is Good... All the Time. (SPA.). 20p. (J). (gr. -1-k). bds. 12.99 (978-0-545-45618-0(5), Scholastic en Espanol) Scholastic, Inc.

McCourt, Lisa. Merry Christmas, Stinky Face. Moore, Cyd, illus. 2008. (ENG.). 32p. (J). (gr. -1-k). bds. 6.99 (978-0-439-73123-2(2), Cartwheel Bks.) Scholastic, Inc.

—You Can Do It, Stinky Face!: a Stinky Face Book. Moore, Cyd, illus. 2016. (ENG.). 32p. (J). (— 1). bds. 7.99 (978-0-545-80648-0(8), Cartwheel Bks.) Scholastic, Inc.

McCue, Lisa, illus. Corduroy's Thanksgiving. 2006. (Corduroy Ser.). 16p. (J). (gr. -1 — 1). bds. 6.99 (978-0-670-06108-2(5), Viking Books for Young Readers) Penguin Young Readers Group.

McCurry, Kristen & Hilton, Jennifer. Dios No Creo Todos. Garton, Michael, illus. 2016. (SPA.). (J). (978-1-5064-2092-9(3)) 1517 Media.

McDonald, Jill. Hello, World! Dinosaurs. 2018. (Hello, World! Ser.). (Illus.). 26p. (J). (— 1). bds. 8.99 (978-1-5247-1934-0(X), Doubleday Bks. for Young Readers) Random Hse. Children's Bks.

—Hello, World! My Body. 2018. (Hello, World! Ser.). (Illus.). 26p. (J). (— 1). bds. 7.99 (978-1-5247-6636-8(4), Doubleday Bks. for Young Readers) Random Hse. Children's Bks.

McDonnell, Patrick. The Little Gift of Nothing. 2016. (ENG., Illus.). 30p. (J). (gr. -1 — 1). bds. 7.99 (978-0-316-39473-4(4)) Little, Brown Bks. for Young Readers.

McDonough, Amanda, illus. Woodland Babies: Fun for Little Fingers. 2018. (ENG.). 8p. (J). (gr. -1-k). bds. 6.99 (978-1-4380-5054-6(2)) Sourcebooks, Inc.

McDougall, Carol & LaRamee-Jones, Shanda. Baby Look, 1 vol. 2012. (Baby Steps Ser.). (ENG., Illus.). 12p. (J). (gr. -1 — 1). bds. 8.95 (978-1-55109-937-8(3), 07551a77-cf7c-46ee-9a51-ad85e9ec62ef) Nimbus Publishing, Ltd. CAN. Dist: Baker & Taylor Publisher Services (BTPS).

McElroy, Jean. Baby's Colorful World. 2011. (ENG.). 14p. (J). (gr. -1 — 1). 4.99 (978-1-4424-1197-5(X), Little Simon) Little Simon.

McFadden, Patricia. Oh No, Wolly Bear!, 1 vol. Coxon, Michele, illus. 2008. (ENG.). 32p. (J). (gr. -1-3). 6.50 (978-1-59572-149-5(5)) Star Bright Bks., Inc.

McGrath, Barbara Barbieri. Birthday Counting. Tagel, Peggy, illus. 2017. (First Celebrations Ser.: 7). 12p. (J). (— 1). bds. 6.99 (978-1-58089-537-8(9)) Charlesbridge Publishing, Inc.

—Easter Counting. Tagel, Peggy, illus. 2017. (First Celebrations Ser.: 5). 12p. (J). (— 1). bds. 6.99 (978-1-58089-535-4(2)) Charlesbridge Publishing, Inc.

—Halloween Colors. Tagel, Peggy, illus. 2016. (First Celebrations Ser.: 1). 12p. (J). (— 1). bds. 6.95 (978-1-58089-533-0(6)) Charlesbridge Publishing, Inc.

—Parade Colors. Tagel, Peggy, illus. 2017. (First Celebrations Ser.: 6). 12p. (J). (— 1). bds. 6.99 (978-1-58089-536-1(0)) Charlesbridge Publishing, Inc.

—Thanksgiving Counting. Tagel, Peggy, illus. 2016. (First Celebrations Ser.: 2). 12p. (J). (— 1). bds. 6.95 (978-1-58089-534-7(4)) Charlesbridge Publishing, Inc.

—Valentine's Shapes. Tagel, Peggy, illus. 2016. (First Celebrations Ser.: 4). 12p. (J). (— 1). bds. 6.95 (978-1-58089-532-3(8)) Charlesbridge Publishing, Inc.

McGuirk, Leslie. Ho, Ho, Ho, Tucker!: Candlewick Storybook Animations. McGuirk, Leslie, illus. 2010. (Candlewick Storybook Animations Ser.). (ENG., Illus.). 32p. (J). (-k). 8.99 (978-0-7636-5043-8(9)) Candlewick Pr.

McKee, David. Elmer & Wilbur. 2018. (Elmer Ser.). (ENG., Illus.). 26p. (J). (-k). bds. 9.99 (978-1-78344-530-1(0)) Andersen Pr. GBR. Dist: Independent Pubs. Group.

Mckee, David. Elmer Board Book. Mckee, David, illus. 2014. (ENG., Illus.). 32p. (J). (gr. -1 — 1). bds. 7.99 (978-0-06-232405-4(5), HarperFestival) HarperCollins Pubs.

—Elmer Padded Board Book. Mckee, David, illus. 2018. (ENG., Illus.). 32p. (J). (gr. -1 — 1). bds. 9.99 (978-0-06-274160-8(8), HarperFestival) HarperCollins Pubs.

McKellar, Danica. Bathtime Mathtime. Padrón, Alicia, illus. 2018. (McKellar Math Ser.). 20p. (J). (-k). bds. 8.99 (978-1-101-93394-7(1), Crown Books For Young Readers) Random Hse. Children's Bks.

McKendry, Sam. Are You Ticklish?/Tienes Cosquillas? Mitchell, Melanie, illus. 2005. (ENG.). 12p. (gr. -1-k). 10.95 (978-1-58117-472-4(1), Intervisual/Piggy Toes) Bendon, Inc.

—Bless Everyone. 2006. (ENG., Illus.). 12p. (J). (gr. -1-k). 8.95 (978-1-58117-445-8(4), Intervisual/Piggy Toes) Bendon, Inc.

—Curious Kitties: A Colors Book. Mitchell, Melanie, illus. 2005. (ENG.). 16p. (J). bds. 9.95 (978-1-58117-417-5(9), Intervisual/Piggy Toes) Bendon, Inc.

McLaughlin, Eoin. The Hug. Dunbar, Polly, illus. 2019. (Hedgehog & Friends Ser.). (ENG.). 56p. (J). 15.95 (978-0-571-34875-6(0), Faber & Faber Children's Bks.) Faber & Faber, Inc.

McLean, Danielle. Good Night, I Love You. Macnaughton, Tina, illus. 2018. (ENG.). 16p. (J). (gr. -1-k). bds. 9.99 (978-1-68010-540-7(X)) Tiger Tales.

—Grandma Loves You! Edgson, Alison, illus. 2018. (ENG.). 28p. (J). (gr. -1-k). bds. 7.99 (978-1-68010-546-9(9)) Tiger Tales.

McMahon, Kara. Dress up Dora! Aikins, Dave, illus. 2009. (Dora the Explorer Ser.). (ENG.). 12p. (J). 8.99 (978-1-4169-6067-6(8), Simon Spotlight/Nickelodeon) Simon Spotlight/Nickelodeon.

McMahon, Kara & Jordan, Apple. My Growing-Up Library (Sesame Street) 2010. (ENG., Illus.). 12p. (J). (gr. k — 1). bds. 10.99 (978-0-375-85984-7(5), Random Hse. Bks. for Young Readers) Random Hse. Children's Bks.

McMullan, Kate. Supercat to the Rescue. Lemaître, Pascal, illus. (ENG.). 1p. (J). bds. 55.60 (978-0-7611-3234-9(1), 23234) Workman Publishing Co., Inc.

McNamara, Connie. My First Wisconsin Words Go Badgers. 2012. (ENG.). 16p. 10.99 (978-0-06-219606-4(5)) HarperCollins Pubs.

McNeil, Kelli. Sleepy Toes (a Padded Board Book) Doerrfeld, Cori, illus. 2017. (ENG.). 26p. (J). (gr. -1 — 1). bds. 8.99 (978-1-338-03072-3(8), Cartwheel Bks.) Scholastic, Inc.

McPhail, David. Baby Pig Pig Talks. McPhail, David, illus. 2014. (ENG., Illus.). 14p. (J). (— 1). bds. 6.95 (978-1-58089-597-2(2)) Charlesbridge Publishing, Inc.

—Baby Pig Pig Walks. McPhail, David, illus. 2014. (ENG., Illus.). 14p. (J). (— 1). bds. 6.95 (978-1-58089-596-5(4)) Charlesbridge Publishing, Inc.

—Brothers/Hermanos: Bilingual English-Spanish. McPhail, David, illus. 2017. (ENG., Illus.). 28p. (J). (— 1). bds. 4.99 (978-0-544-91586-2(0), 1655576, Clarion Bks.) HarperCollins Pubs.

—I Hug You & You. 2018. (ENG., Illus.). 28p. (J). (— 1). bds. 7.99 (978-0-8234-3994-2(1)) Holiday Hse., Inc.

—Olivia Loves Owl. 2016. (ENG., Illus.). 20p. (J). (gr. -1 — 1). bds. 8.95 (978-1-4197-2127-4(5), 1128510, Abrams Appleseed) Abrams, Inc.

McQuinn, Anna. Wanda's Washing Machine. McCafferty, Jan, illus. 2005. 20p. (J). (gr. -1-2). 12.95 (978-1-58925-768-9(5)) Tiger Tales.

Mead, David & Berry, Ron. Who's at the Door? 2010. (Illus.). 12p. (J). (gr. -1-1). 10.99 (978-0-8249-1431-8(7), Ideals Pubns.) Worthy Publishing.

Meaders, Sandra. Lehi, Lehi, What Do You See? 2018. (ENG.). (J). (gr. -1-k). bds. 12.99 (978-1-4621-2242-4(6)) Cedar Fort, Inc./CFI Distribution.

Meet the Little Prince (Padded Board Book) 2015. (Little Prince Ser.). (ENG., Illus.). 10p. (J). (— 1). bds. 7.99 (978-0-544-70902-7(0), 1628913, Clarion Bks.) HarperCollins Pubs.

Melcher, Mary, illus. Puppies Count. 2010. (J). (978-1-58865-596-7(2)) Kidsbooks, LLC.

Mellor, Corinne & Ericksson, Ashe. Snowlies Find a Letter. 2007. 22p. (J). (978-1-84666-410-6(1), Tide Mill Pr.) Top That! Publishing PLC.

Melmoth, Jonathan. See Inside New York. 2017. (See Inside Board Bks.). (ENG.). 16p. 14.99 (978-0-7945-4021-0(X), Usborne) EDC Publishing.

Melvin, Alice. Grandma's House. 2015. (ENG., Illus.). 32p. (J). (gr. -1-3). 19.95 (978-1-84976-222-9(8), 1637101) Tate Publishing, Ltd. GBR. Dist: Hachette Bk. Group.

—The World of Alice Melvin: Me & You: A Book of Opposites. 2018. (ENG., Illus.). 20p. (J). (gr. -1 — 1). 9.99 (978-1-84976-585-5(5), 1325110) Tate Publishing, Ltd. GBR. Dist: Abrams, Inc.

—The World of Alice Melvin: My Day: A Book of Actions. 2018. (ENG., Illus.). 20p. (J). 9.99 (978-1-84976-586-2(3), 1325210) Tate Publishing, Ltd. GBR. Dist: Abrams, Inc.

Membrino, Anna. I Look up to... Michelle Obama. Burke, Fatti, illus. 2018. 22p. (J). (— 1). bds. 7.99 (978-0-525-57954-0(0), Random Hse. Bks. for Young Readers) Random Hse. Children's Bks.

Meng, Cece. Tough Chicks Lap Board Book: An Easter & Springtime Book for Kids. Suber, Melissa, illus. 2018. (ENG.). 28p. (J). (— 1). bds. 12.99 (978-1-328-95985-0(6), 1706952, Clarion Bks.) HarperCollins Pubs.

Merberg, Julie. My Favorite Shoes: A Touch-And-feel Shoe-stravaganza. Rucker, Georgia, illus. 2013. (ENG.). 16p. (J). (gr. -1 — 1). bds. 12.99 (978-1-935703-64-8(1)) Downtown Bookworks.

—Turn the Key: Who Do You See? McQueen, Lucinda, illus. 2011. (ENG.). 12p. (J). (gr. -1). bds. 11.99 (978-1-935703-11-2(0)) Downtown Bookworks.

—Turn the Key: Around Town: Look & See! McQueen, Lucinda, illus. 2012. (ENG.). 12p. (J). (gr. -1 — 1). bds. 11.99 (978-1-935703-44-0(7)) Downtown Bookworks.

Merberg, Julie & Bober, Suzanne. Mini French Masters Boxed Set: 4 Board Books Inside! (Books for Learning Toddler, Language Baby Book), 1 vol. 2018. (Mini Masters Ser.: 11). (ENG., Illus.). 22p. (J). (gr. -1 — 1). 19.99 (978-1-4521-7653-6(1)) Chronicle Bks. LLC.

Merer, Laura, illus. Fuzzy Ducky's Birthday: A Touch-and-Feel Pop-up Book. 2005. 10p. (J). 8.95 (978-1-58117-324-6(5), Intervisual/Piggy Toes) Bendon, Inc.

Mettler, René & Mettler, René. Birds. Mettler, René & Mettler, René, illus. 2012. (My First Discoveries Ser.: 15). (ENG., Illus.). 36p. (J). (gr. -1-k). spiral bd. 13.99 (978-1-85103-397-3(1)) Moonlight Publishing, Ltd. GBR. Dist: Independent Pubs. Group.

Metzger, Steve. I Love You All Year Long. Keay, Claire, illus. 2009. 20p. (J). (gr. -1-k). 8.95 (978-1-58925-847-1(9)) Tiger Tales.

Meyers, Haily & Meyers, Kevin. All Aboard! California: A Landscape Primer, 1 vol. 2015. (Lucy Darling Ser.). (ENG., Illus.). 22p. (J). (— 1). bds. 11.99 (978-1-4236-4080-6(2)) Gibbs Smith, Publisher.

—Gotta Go, Buffalo: A Silly Book of Fun Goodbyes, 1 vol. 2017. (Lucy Darling Ser.). (Illus.). 20p. (J). (-k). bds. 16.99 (978-1-4236-4598-6(7)) Gibbs Smith, Publisher.

—If You Were Spaghetti: A Silly Book of Fun I Love Yous, 1 vol. 2018. (Lucy Darling Ser.). (ENG., Illus.). 20p. (J). (— 1). bds. 16.99 (978-1-4236-5032-4(8)) Gibbs Smith, Publisher.

Meyers, Susan. Everywhere Babies Lap Board Book. Frazee, Marla, illus. 2011. (ENG.). 30p. (J). (gr. -1 — 1). bds. 12.99 (978-0-547-51074-3(8), 1443771, Clarion Bks.) HarperCollins Pubs.

—Everywhere Babies Padded Board Book. Frazee, Marla, illus. 2016. (ENG.). 30p. (J). (— 1). bds. 10.99 (978-0-544-79120-6(7), 1639294, Clarion Bks.) HarperCollins Pubs.

Milbourne, Anna. Peek Inside Animal Homes. Dimitri, Simona, illus. 2014. (Peek Inside Board Bks.). (ENG.). 14p. (gr. -1). bds. 11.99 (978-0-7945-2549-1(0), Usborne) EDC Publishing.

Miles, David. Christmas Train. 2019. (On-Track Learning Ser.). (ENG., Illus.). 14p. (J). (gr. k-1). bds. 12.99 (978-1-64170-165-5(X), 550165) Familius LLC.

—Wild about the Bible Sticker & Activity Book, 1 vol. 2016. (Adventure Bible Ser.). (ENG., Illus.). 32p. (J). pap. 6.99 (978-0-310-75405-3(4)) Zonderkidz.

Miles, David W. Color Train. 2019. (ENG., Illus.). 14p. (J). (gr. -1-k). bds. 12.99 (978-1-64170-106-8(4), 550106) Familius LLC.

Miles, David W., creator. But First, We Nap: A Little Book about Nap Time. 2018. (ENG., Illus.). 16p. (J). (gr. -1-k). bds. 9.99 (978-1-64170-017-7(3), 550017) Familius LLC.

Miles Kelly Staff. Mix-Ups. 2003. (Illus.). 14p. 9.95 (978-1-902947-83-9(5)) Miles Kelly Publishing, Ltd. GBR. Dist: Independent Pubs. Group.

—Noises: Let's Learn. Nilsen, Anna, ed. 2003. (Let's Learn Ser.). (Illus.). 20p. (J). 7.95 (978-1-84236-139-9(2)) Miles Kelly Publishing, Ltd. GBR. Dist: Independent Pubs. Group.

—Opposites: Let's Learn. Nilsen, Anna, ed. 2003. (Let's Learn Ser.). (Illus.). 20p. (J). 7.95 (978-1-84236-138-2(4)) Miles Kelly Publishing, Ltd. GBR. Dist: Independent Pubs. Group.

—Sizes: Let's Learn. Nilsen, Anna, ed. 2003. (Let's Learn Ser.). (Illus.). 20p. (J). 7.95 (978-1-84236-140-5(6)) Miles Kelly Publishing, Ltd. GBR. Dist: Independent Pubs. Group.

Miles Kelly Staff & Nilsen, Anna. Actions: Let's Learn. 2003. (Let's Learn Ser.). (Illus.). 20p. (J). 7.95 (978-1-84236-137-5(6)) Miles Kelly Publishing, Ltd. GBR. Dist: Independent Pubs. Group.

—Numbers: Let's Learn. 2003. (Let's Learn Ser.). (Illus.). 20p. (J). 7.95 (978-1-84236-018-7(3)) Miles Kelly Publishing, Ltd. GBR. Dist: Independent Pubs. Group.

—Shapes: Let's Learn. 2003. (Let's Learn Ser.). (Illus.). 20p. (J). 7.95 (978-1-84236-016-3(7)) Miles Kelly Publishing, Ltd. GBR. Dist: Independent Pubs. Group.

Miles, Stephanie. Mommy Loves Me: The Book That Comes with a Hug! Miles, David W., illus. 2018. (ENG.). 10p. (J). (gr. -1 — 1). bds. 12.99 (978-1-945547-94-2(4), 554794) Familius LLC.

Miles, Stephanie & Farley, Christin. C Is for Colorado. Kaliaha, Volha, illus. 2018. (ABC Regional Board Bks.). (ENG.). 20p. (J). (gr. -1 — 1). bds. 12.99 (978-1-945547-86-7(3), 554786) Familius LLC.

—M Is for Montana. Kaliaha, Volha, illus. 2018. (ABC Regional Board Bks.). (ENG.). 20p. (J). (gr. -1 — 1). bds. 12.99 (978-1-945547-88-1(X), 554788) Familius LLC.

Milet Publishing. My First Bilingual Book-Colors (English-Farsi), 60 vols. 2011. (My First Bilingual Book Ser.). (ENG.). 24p. (J). (gr. k — 1). bds. 8.99 (978-1-84059-599-4(X)) Milet Publishing.

—My First Bilingual Book-Colors (English-Vietnamese) 2011. (My First Bilingual Book Ser.). (ENG.). 24p. (J). (gr. k — 1). bds. 8.99 (978-1-84059-606-9(6)) Milet Publishing.

—My First Bilingual Book-Jobs (English-Spanish), 1 vol. 2012. (My First Bilingual Book Ser.). (ENG & SPA., Illus.). 24p. (J). (gr. k — 1). bds. 7.99 (978-1-84059-712-7(7)) Milet Publishing.

—My First Bilingual Book-Love (English-Russian), 1 vol. 2018. (My First Bilingual Book Ser.). (ENG & RUS., Illus.). 24p. (J). (— 1). bds. 8.99 (978-1-78508-902-2(1)) Milet Publishing.

—My First Bilingual Book-Numbers (English-Arabic), 1 vol. 2011. (My First Bilingual Book Ser.). (ENG & ARA., Illus.). 24p. (J). (gr. k — 1). bds. 8.99 (978-1-84059-570-3(1)) Milet Publishing.

—My First Bilingual Book-Numbers (English-Italian), 1 vol. 2010. (My First Bilingual Book Ser.). (ENG & ITA., Illus.). 24p. (J). (gr. k — 1). bds. 8.99 (978-1-84059-543-7(4)) Milet Publishing.

—My First Bilingual Book-Numbers (English-Japanese), 1 vol. 2011. (My First Bilingual Book Ser.). (ENG., Illus.). 24p. (J). (gr. k — 1). bds. 8.99 (978-1-84059-573-4(6)) Milet Publishing.

—My First Bilingual Book-Numbers (English-Spanish), 1 vol. 2010. (My First Bilingual Book Ser.). (ENG & SPA., Illus.). 24p. (J). (gr. k — 1). bds. 8.99 (978-1-84059-545-1(0)) Milet Publishing.

Milet Publishing Staff. Animals, 1 vol. 2011. (My First Bilingual Book Ser.). (ENG & FRE., Illus.). 24p. (J). (gr. k — 1). bds. 8.99 *(978-1-84059-612-0(0))*; bds. 8.99 *(978-1-84059-615-1(5))*; bds. 8.99 *(978-1-84059-622-9(8))*; bds. 8.99 *(978-1-84059-613-7(9))* Milet Publishing.

—Animals - My First Bilingual Book, 60 vols. 2011. (My First Bilingual Book Ser.). (ENG & ARA., Illus.). 24p. (J). (gr. k — 1). bds. 8.99 *(978-1-84059-608-3(2))*; bds. 8.99 *(978-1-84059-623-6(6))*; bds. 8.99 *(978-1-84059-618-2(X))* Milet Publishing.

—Clothes, 1 vol. 2014. (My First Bilingual Book Ser.). (ENG & SPA., Illus.). 20p. (J). (— 1). bds. 8.99 *(978-1-84059-870-4(0))*; bds. 7.99 *(978-1-84059-865-0(4))* Milet Publishing.

—Clothes - My First Bilingual Book, 1 vol. 2014. (My First Bilingual Book Ser.). (ENG., Illus.). 20p. (J). (— 1). bds. 8.99 *(978-1-84059-860-5(3))*; bds. 8.99 *(978-1-84059-864-3(6))*; bds. 8.99 *(978-1-84059-867-4(0))*; bds. 8.99 *(978-1-84059-873-5(5))* Milet Publishing.

—Colors, 1 vol. (My First Bilingual Book Ser.). (ENG & ARA.). 24p. (J). (gr. k — 1). 2011. bds. 8.99 *(978-1-84059-597-0(3))* 2010. (Illus.). bds. 8.99 *(978-1-84059-539-0(6))* Milet Publishing.

—Colors - My First Bilingual Book, 1 vol. 2011. (My First Bilingual Book Ser.). (ENG.). 24p. (J). (gr. k — 1). bds. 8.99 *(978-1-84059-601-4(5))* Milet Publishing.

—Colours, 1 vol. 2010. (My First Bilingual Book Ser.). (ENG., Illus.). 24p. (J). (gr. k — 1). bds. 7.99 *(978-1-84059-563-5(9))*; bds. 7.99 *(978-1-84059-569-7(8))* Milet Publishing.

—Colours - My First Bilingual Book, 1 vol. 2010. (My First Bilingual Book Ser.). (ENG., Illus.). 24p. (J). (gr. k — 1). bds. 7.99 *(978-1-84059-565-9(5))*; bds. 8.99 *(978-1-84059-537-6(X))*; bds. 8.99 *(978-1-84059-536-9(1))*; bds. 8.99 *(978-1-84059-538-3(8))*; bds. 7.99 *(978-1-84059-568-0(X))*; bds. 7.99 *(978-1-84059-560-4(4))* Milet Publishing.

—Fruit, 1 vol. 2011. (My First Bilingual Book Ser.). (ENG., Illus.). 24p. (J). (gr. k — 1). bds. 7.99 *(978-1-84059-625-0(2))* Milet Publishing.

—Fruit - My First Bilingual Book, 1 vol. 2011. (My First Bilingual Book Ser.). (ENG & ITA., Illus.). 24p. (J). (gr. k — 1). bds. 8.99 *(978-1-84059-630-4(9))*; bds. 8.99 *(978-1-84059-624-3(4))*; bds. 7.99 *(978-1-84059-632-8(5))*; bds. 8.99 *(978-1-84059-634-2(1))*; bds. 8.99 *(978-1-84059-637-3(6))* Milet Publishing.

—Fruit (English-French), 1 vol. 2011. (My First Bilingual Book Ser.). (ENG & FRE., Illus.). 24p. (J). (gr. k — 1). bds. 8.99 *(978-1-84059-628-1(7))* Milet Publishing.

—Home, 1 vol. 2011. (My First Bilingual Book Ser.). (ENG., Illus.). 24p. (J). (gr. k — 1). bds. 7.99 *(978-1-84059-642-7(2))*; bds. 8.99 *(978-1-84059-646-5(5))* Milet Publishing.

—Home - My First Bilingual Book, 1 vol. 2011. (My First Bilingual Book Ser.). (ENG., Illus.). 24p. (J). (gr. k — 1). bds. 8.99 *(978-1-84059-641-0(4))*; bds. 8.99 *(978-1-84059-645-8(7))* Milet Publishing.

—Home (English-Arabic), 60 vols. 2011. (My First Bilingual Book Ser.). (ENG & ARA., Illus.). 24p. (J). (gr. k — 1). bds. 8.99 *(978-1-84059-640-3(6))* Milet Publishing.

—Home (English-French), 60 vols. 2011. (My First Bilingual Book Ser.). (ENG & FRE., Illus.). 24p. (J). (gr. k — 1). bds. 8.99 *(978-1-84059-644-1(9))* Milet Publishing.

—Home (English-Polish), 1 vol. 2011. (My First Bilingual Book Ser.). (ENG & POR., Illus.). 24p. (J). (gr. k — 1). bds. 8.99 *(978-1-84059-648-9(1))* Milet Publishing.

—Home (English-Portuguese), 60 vols. 2011. (My First Bilingual Book Ser.). (ENG., Illus.). 24p. (J). (gr. k — 1). bds. 8.99 *(978-1-84059-649-6(X))* Milet Publishing.

—Music, 1 vol. 2012. (My First Bilingual Book Ser.). (ENG & POR., Illus.). 24p. (J). (gr. k — 1). bds. 8.99 *(978-1-84059-724-0(0))* Milet Publishing.

—Music - My First Bilingual Book, 1 vol. 2012. (My First Bilingual Book Ser.). (ENG., Illus.). 24p. (J). (gr. k — 1). bds. 7.99 *(978-1-84059-725-7(9))* Milet Publishing.

—My First Bilingual Book - Animals, 60 vols. 2011. (My First Bilingual Book Ser.). (ENG., Illus.). 24p. (J). (gr. k — 1). bds. 8.99 *(978-1-84059-611-3(2))*; bds. 8.99 *(978-1-84059-621-2(X))*; bds. 8.99 *(978-1-84059-609-0(0))* Milet Publishing.

—My First Bilingual Book - Animals (English-Somali), 1 vol. 2011. (My First Bilingual Book Ser.). (ENG., Illus.). 24p. (J). (gr. k — 1). bds. 8.99 *(978-1-84059-619-9(8))* Milet Publishing.

—My First Bilingual Book - Clothes, 1 vol. 2014. (My First Bilingual Book Ser.). (ENG., Illus.). 20p. (J). (— 1). bds. 7.99 *(978-1-84059-859-9(X))*; bds. 8.99 *(978-1-84059-866-7(2))*; bds. 7.99 *(978-1-84059-858-2(1))*; bds. 7.99 *(978-1-84059-872-8(7))*; bds. 7.99 *(978-1-84059-861-2(1))*; bds. 7.99 *(978-1-84059-863-6(8))*; bds. 7.99 *(978-1-84059-869-8(7))*; bds. 8.99 *(978-1-84059-862-9(X))*; bds. 7.99 *(978-1-84059-871-1(9))*; bds. 7.99 *(978-1-84059-868-1(9))* Milet Publishing.

—My First Bilingual Book - Colors, 60 vols. 2011. (My First Bilingual Book Ser.). (ENG.). 24p. (J). (gr. k — 1). bds. 8.99 *(978-1-84059-603-8(1))*; bds. 8.99 *(978-1-84059-602-1(3))*; bds. 8.99 *(978-1-84059-598-7(1))*; bds. 8.99 *(978-1-84059-600-7(7))*; bds. 8.99 *(978-1-84059-604-5(X))* Milet Publishing.

—My First Bilingual Book - Colors (English-Urdu) 2011. (My First Bilingual Book Ser.). (ENG.). 24p. (J). (gr. k — 1). bds. 8.99 *(978-1-84059-605-2(8))* Milet Publishing.

—My First Bilingual Book - Colours, 1 vol. 2010. (My First Bilingual Book Ser.). (ENG., Illus.). 24p. (J). (gr. k — 1). bds. 8.99 *(978-1-84059-540-6(X))*; bds. 8.99 *(978-1-84059-535-2(3))* Milet Publishing.

—My First Bilingual Book - Fruit, 1 vol. 2011. (My First Bilingual Book Ser.). (ENG., Illus.). 24p. (J). (gr. k — 1). bds. 8.99 *(978-1-84059-633-5(3))*; bds. 8.99 *(978-1-84059-626-7(0))*; bds. 8.99 *(978-1-84059-627-4(9))*; bds. 8.99 *(978-1-84059-631-1(7))*; bds. 8.99 *(978-1-84059-629-8(5))* Milet Publishing.

—My First Bilingual Book - Home, 60 vols. 2011. (My First Bilingual Book Ser.). (ENG., Illus.). 24p. (J). (gr. k — 1). bds. 8.99 *(978-1-84059-643-4(0))*; bds. 8.99 *(978-1-84059-647-2(3))* Milet Publishing.

—My First Bilingual Book - Numbers, 60 vols. (My First Bilingual Book Ser.). (ENG., Illus.). 24p. (J). (gr. k — 1). 2011. bds. 8.99 *(978-1-84059-579-6(5))* 2011. bds. 8.99 *(978-1-84059-574-1(4))* 2011. bds. 7.99 *(978-1-84059-575-8(2))* 2011. bds. 8.99 *(978-1-84059-578-9(7))* 2011. bds. 8.99 *(978-1-84059-571-0(X))* 2011. bds. 8.99 *(978-1-84059-572-7(8))* 2010. bds. 7.99 *(978-1-84059-546-8(9))* Milet Publishing.

—My First Bilingual Book - Plants, 1 vol. 2014. (My First Bilingual Book Ser.). (ENG & GER., Illus.). 20p. (J). (— 1). bds. 8.99 *(978-1-84059-879-7(4))*; bds. 8.99 *(978-1-84059-876-6(X))*; bds. 7.99 *(978-1-84059-887-2(5))*; bds. 7.99 *(978-1-84059-883-4(2))*; bds. 8.99 *(978-1-84059-874-2(3))*; bds. 7.99 *(978-1-84059-885-8(9))* Milet Publishing.

—My First Bilingual Book - Plants (English-Farsi), 1 vol. 2014. (My First Bilingual Book Ser.). (ENG., Illus.). 20p. (J). (— 1). bds. 7.99 *(978-1-84059-877-3(8))* Milet Publishing.

—My First Bilingual Book - Plants (English-Korean), 1 vol. 2014. (My First Bilingual Book Ser.). (ENG., Illus.). 20p. (J). (— 1). bds. 7.99 *(978-1-84059-881-0(6))* Milet Publishing.

—My First Bilingual Book - School, 1 vol. 2014. (My First Bilingual Book Ser.). (ENG & POR., Illus.). 20p. (J). (— 1). bds. 7.99 *(978-1-84059-899-5(9))*; bds. 7.99 *(978-1-84059-891-9(3))*; bds. 8.99 *(978-1-84059-905-3(7))*; bds. 7.99 *(978-1-84059-895-7(6))*; bds. 7.99 *(978-1-84059-892-6(1))*; bds. 7.99 *(978-1-84059-903-9(0))* Milet Publishing.

—My First Bilingual Book - School (English-Korean), 1 vol. 2014. (My First Bilingual Book Ser.). (ENG., Illus.). 20p. (J). (— 1). bds. 7.99 *(978-1-84059-897-1(2))* Milet Publishing.

—My First Bilingual Book - School (English-Somali), 1 vol. 2014. (My First Bilingual Book Ser.). (ENG., Illus.). 20p. (J). (— 1). bds. 8.99 *(978-1-84059-901-5(4))* Milet Publishing.

—My First Bilingual Book - Tools, 1 vol. 2014. (My First Bilingual Book Ser.). (ENG., Illus.). 20p. (J). (— 1). bds. 7.99 *(978-1-84059-907-7(3))*; bds. 7.99 *(978-1-84059-916-9(2))*; bds. 7.99 *(978-1-84059-914-5(6))*; bds. 7.99 *(978-1-84059-911-4(1))*; bds. 7.99 *(978-1-84059-906-0(5))*; bds. 7.99 *(978-1-84059-920-6(0))*; bds. 7.99 *(978-1-84059-919-0(7))*; bds. 7.99 *(978-1-84059-918-3(9))* Milet Publishing.

—My First Bilingual Book - Tools - English, 1 vol. 2014. (My First Bilingual Book Ser.). (ENG., Illus.). 20p. (J). (— 1). bds. 7.99 *(978-1-84059-921-3(9))* Milet Publishing.

—My First Bilingual Book - Tools - Ferramentas, 1 vol. 2014. (My First Bilingual Book Ser.). (ENG & POR., Illus.). 20p. (J). (— 1). bds. 7.99 *(978-1-84059-915-2(4))* Milet Publishing.

—My First Bilingual Book - Tools (English-Somali), 1 vol. 2014. (My First Bilingual Book Ser.). (ENG., Illus.). 20p. (J). (— 1). bds. 7.99 *(978-1-84059-917-6(0))* Milet Publishing.

—My First Bilingual Book - Vehicles, 1 vol. 2014. (My First Bilingual Book Ser.). (ENG., Illus.). 20p. (J). (— 1). bds. 8.99 *(978-1-84059-937-4(5))*; bds. 7.99 *(978-1-84059-933-6(2))*; bds. 7.99 *(978-1-84059-929-9(4))*; bds. 7.99 *(978-1-84059-925-1(1))*; bds. 7.99 *(978-1-84059-935-0(9))*; bds. 8.99 *(978-1-84059-924-4(3))* Milet Publishing.

—My First Bilingual Book - Vehicles (English-Russian), 1 vol. 2014. (My First Bilingual Book Ser.). (ENG., Illus.). 20p. (J). (— 1). bds. 7.99 *(978-1-84059-932-9(4))* Milet Publishing.

—My First Bilingual Book-Fruit (English-Somali), 1 vol. 2011. (My First Bilingual Book Ser.). (ENG., Illus.). 24p. (J). (gr. k — 1). bds. 7.99 *(978-1-84059-635-9(X))* Milet Publishing.

—My First Bilingual Book-Fruit (English-Spanish), 60 vols. 2011. (My First Bilingual Book Ser.). (ENG & SPA., Illus.). 24p. (J). (gr. k — 1). bds. 8.99 *(978-1-84059-636-6(8))* Milet Publishing.

—My First Bilingual Book-Fruit (English-Urdu), 1 vol. 2011. (My First Bilingual Book Ser.). (ENG., Illus.). 24p. (J). (gr. k — 1). bds. 7.99 *(978-1-84059-638-0(4))* Milet Publishing.

—My First Bilingual Book-Home (English-Russian), 1 vol. 2011. (My First Bilingual Book Ser.). (ENG., Illus.). 24p. (J). (gr. k — 1). bds. 8.99 *(978-1-84059-650-2(3))* Milet Publishing.

—My First Bilingual Book-Jobs, 1 vol. 2012. (My First Bilingual Book Ser.). (ENG & ARA., Illus.). 24p. (J). (gr. k — 1). bds. 7.99 *(978-1-84059-700-4(3))* Milet Publishing.

—My First Bilingual Book-Jobs (English-Korean), 1 vol. 2012. (My First Bilingual Book Ser.). (ENG., Illus.). 24p. (J). (gr. k — 1). bds. 7.99 *(978-1-84059-707-3(0))* Milet Publishing.

—My First Bilingual Book-Music (English-Russian), 1 vol. 2012. (My First Bilingual Book Ser.). (ENG., Illus.). 24p. (J). (gr. k — 1). bds. 7.99 *(978-1-84059-726-4(7))* Milet Publishing.

—My First Bilingual Book-Music (English-Somali), 1 vol. 2012. (My First Bilingual Book Ser.). (ENG., Illus.). 24p. (J). (gr. k — 1). bds. 8.99 *(978-1-84059-727-1(5))* Milet Publishing.

—My First Bilingual Book-Opposites, 1 vol. 2012. (My First Bilingual Book Ser.). (ENG., Illus.). 24p. (J). (gr. k — 1). bds. 8.99 *(978-1-84059-734-9(8))* Milet Publishing.

—Numbers, 1 vol. 2011. (My First Bilingual Book Ser.). (ENG., Illus.). 24p. (J). (gr. k — 1). bds. 8.99 *(978-1-84059-577-2(9))* Milet Publishing.

—Numbers - My First Bilingual Book, 60 vols. (My First Bilingual Book Ser.). (ENG., Illus.). 24p. (J). (gr. k — 1). 2011. bds. 7.99 *(978-1-84059-576-5(0))* 2010. bds. 8.99 *(978-1-84059-541-3(8))* 2010. bds. 8.99 *(978-1-84059-544-4(2))* Milet Publishing.

—Opposites, 1 vol. 2012. (My First Bilingual Book Ser.). (ENG., Illus.). 24p. (J). (gr. k — 1). bds. 8.99 *(978-1-84059-735-6(6))* Milet Publishing.

—Plants - My First Bilingual Book, 1 vol. 2014. (My First Bilingual Book Ser.). (ENG., Illus.). 20p. (J). (— 1). bds. 7.99 *(978-1-84059-875-9(1))*; bds. 7.99 *(978-1-84059-880-3(8))*; bds. 7.99 *(978-1-84059-888-9(3))*; bds. 7.99 *(978-1-84059-886-5(7))*; bds. 8.99 *(978-1-84059-884-1(0))*; bds. 7.99 *(978-1-84059-882-7(4))*; bds. 8.99 *(978-1-84059-878-0(6))*; bds. 7.99 *(978-1-84059-889-6(1))* Milet Publishing.

—School, 1 vol. 2014. (My First Bilingual Book Ser.). (ENG & ITA., Illus.). 20p. (J). (— 1). bds. 7.99 *(978-1-84059-896-4(4))* Milet Publishing.

—School - My First Bilingual Book, 1 vol. 2014. (My First Bilingual Book Ser.). (ENG & SPA., Illus.). 20p. (J). (— 1). bds. 8.99 *(978-1-84059-902-2(2))*; bds. 7.99 *(978-1-84059-904-6(9))*; bds. 7.99 *(978-1-84059-890-2(5))*; bds. 8.99 *(978-1-84059-900-8(6))* Milet Publishing.

—School - My First Bilingual Book (Szkola), 1 vol. 2014. (My First Bilingual Book Ser.). (ENG & POR., Illus.). 20p. (J). (— 1). bds. 7.99 *(978-1-84059-898-8(0))* Milet Publishing.

—Sports, 1 vol. 2012. (My First Bilingual Book Ser.). (ENG., Illus.). 24p. (J). (gr. k — 1). bds. 7.99 *(978-1-84059-757-8(7))* Milet Publishing.

—Sports - My First Bilingual Book, 1 vol. 2012. (My First Bilingual Book Ser.). (ENG., Illus.). 24p. (J). (gr. k — 1). bds. 7.99 *(978-1-84059-759-2(3))* Milet Publishing.

—Tools, 1 vol. 2014. (My First Bilingual Book Ser.). (ENG & ITA., Illus.). 20p. (J). (— 1). bds. 7.99 *(978-1-84059-912-1(X))* Milet Publishing.

—Tools - My First Bilingual Book, 1 vol. 2014. (My First Bilingual Book Ser.). (ENG., Illus.). 20p. (J). (— 1). bds. 7.99 *(978-1-84059-908-4(1))*; bds. 7.99 *(978-1-84059-909-1(X))*; bds. 7.99 *(978-1-84059-913-8(8))* Milet Publishing.

—Tools (English-French), 1 vol. 2014. (My First Bilingual Book Ser.). (ENG & FRE., Illus.). 20p. (J). (— 1). bds. 7.99 *(978-1-84059-910-7(3))* Milet Publishing.

—Vehicles, 1 vol. 2014. (My First Bilingual Book Ser.). (ENG & SPA., Illus.). 20p. (J). (— 1). bds. 7.99 *(978-1-84059-934-3(0))*; bds. 8.99 *(978-1-84059-922-0(7))*; bds. 7.99 *(978-1-84059-928-2(6))* Milet Publishing.

—Vehicles - My First Bilingual Book, 1 vol. 2014. (My First Bilingual Book Ser.). (ENG., Illus.). 20p. (J). (— 1). bds. 7.99 *(978-1-84059-936-7(7))*; bds. 8.99 *(978-1-84059-926-8(X))*; bds. 8.99 *(978-1-84059-931-2(6))*; bds. 7.99 *(978-1-84059-923-7(5))*; bds. 8.99 *(978-1-84059-930-5(8))* Milet Publishing.

—Vehicles (English-German), 1 vol. 2014. (My First Bilingual Book Ser.). (ENG & GER., Illus.). 20p. (J). (— 1). bds. 8.99 *(978-1-84059-927-5(8))* Milet Publishing.

Milich, Zoran. City 123, 0 vols. 2014. (ENG., Illus.). 32p. (J). (gr. -1-k). bds. 12.95 *(978-1-77138-120-8(5))* Kids Can Pr., Ltd. CAN. Dist: Hachette Bk. Group.

Millard, Bart. I Can Only Imagine for Little Ones: A Friendship with Jesus Now & Forever, 1 vol. Collina, Sumiti, illus. 2018. (ENG.). 24p. (J). bds. 9.99 *(978-1-4003-2201-5(4)*, Tommy Nelson) Nelson, Thomas Inc.

Miller, Amanda. Eat Your Colors (Rookie Toddler) 2016. (Rookie Toddler Ser.). (ENG., Illus.). 14p. (J). (gr. -1 — 1). bds. 6.95 *(978-0-531-22619-3(0)*, Children's Pr.) Scholastic Library Publishing.

Miller, Bryan. Dinosaur Fun with Letters: With Letters. 2008. (Illus.). 24p. (J). (gr. -1-k). 12.99 *(978-0-89051-488-7(7)*, Master Books) New Leaf Publishing Group.

Miller, Jonathan, illus. Farm Noises: My Bath Book. 2017. 6p. (J). (gr. -1 — 1). 5.99 *(978-2-924786-15-4(0)*, CrackBoom! Bks.) Chouette Publishing CAN. Dist: Publishers Group West (PGW).

—When I Grow Up. 2011. 16p. (J). *(978-1-58865-637-7(3))* Kidsbooks, LLC.

—Winter, Spring, Summer, Fall. 2010. 16p. (J). *(978-1-58865-578-3(4))* Kidsbooks, LLC.

Milne, A. A. Winnie the Pooh's Giant Lift The-Flap. Shepard, Ernest H., illus. 2009. (Winnie-The-Pooh Ser.). (ENG.). 12p. (J). (gr. -1 — 1). bds. 9.99 *(978-0-525-42088-0(6)*, Dutton Books for Young Readers) Penguin Young Readers Group.

Mischel, Jenny Ann. Animal Alphabet. Bell-Myers, Darcy, illus. 2006. (J). bds. *(978-0-9769239-0-9(4))* Perfect 4 Preschool.

Misslin, Sylvie. Number Circus. Brocoli, Steffie, illus. 2019. (ENG.). 22p. (J). (gr. -1-2). 19.99 *(978-1-78285-765-5(6))* Barefoot Bks., Inc.

Mitchell, Melanie, illus. Good Morning. 2008. (ENG.). 10p. (J). bds. 5.95 *(978-1-58117-708-4(9)*, Intervisual/Piggy Toes) Bendon, Inc.

—Good Morning, Good Night! 2007. (Touch & Feel Ser.). 13p. 15.95 *(978-1-58117-572-1(8)*, Intervisual/Piggy Toes) Bendon, Inc.

—Good Morning, Good Night! A Touch & Feel Bedtime Book. 2006. 12p. (J). (gr. -1-k). 12.95 *(978-1-58117-461-8(6)*, Intervisual/Piggy Toes) Bendon, Inc.

—Good Night. 2008. (ENG.). 6p. (J). bds. 5.95 *(978-1-58117-709-1(7)*, Intervisual/Piggy Toes) Bendon, Inc.

—Three Craws: A Lift-The-Flap Scottish Rhyme, 30 vols. 2018. (Scottish Rhymes Ser.). 12p. (J). 9.95 *(978-1-78250-511-2(3)*, Kelpies) Floris Bks. GBR. Dist: Consortium Bk. Sales & Distribution.

—Wake up Little Ones. 2009. (ENG.). 12p. 10.95 *(978-1-58117-927-9(8)*, Intervisual/Piggy Toes) Bendon, Inc.

—Who Do You Love? 2008. (ENG.). 6p. (J). bds. 5.95 *(978-1-58117-707-7(0)*, Intervisual/Piggy Toes) Bendon, Inc.

Mitton, Tony. Amazing Machines: First Numbers. Parker, Ant, illus. 2018. (Amazing Machines Ser.). (ENG.). 22p. (J). bds. 9.99 *(978-0-7534-7440-2(9)*, 900192346, Kingfisher) Roaring Brook Pr.

—Amazing Machines: First Words. Parker, Ant, illus. 2018. (Amazing Machines Ser.). (ENG.). 22p. (J). bds. 9.99 *(978-0-7534-7439-6(5)*, 900192345, Kingfisher) Roaring Brook Pr.

—Dinosaurumpus! (a StoryPlay Book) Parker-Rees, Guy, illus. 2016. (StoryPlay Ser.). (ENG.). 40p. (J). (gr. -1-k). 5.99 *(978-1-338-11536-9(7)*, Cartwheel Bks.) Scholastic, Inc.

—Terrific Trains. 2017. (Amazing Machines Ser.). (ENG.). 20p. (J). bds. 6.99 *(978-0-7534-7372-6(0)*, 900178406, Kingfisher) Roaring Brook Pr.

Mitton, Tony & Parker, Ant. Flashing Fire Engines. 2017. (Amazing Machines Ser.). (ENG.). 20p. (J). bds. 6.99 *(978-0-7534-7373-3(9)*, 900178407, Kingfisher) Roaring Brook Pr.

—Roaring Rockets. 2017. (Amazing Machines Ser.). (ENG.). 20p. (J). bds. 6.99 *(978-0-7534-7371-9(2)*, 900178401, Kingfisher) Roaring Brook Pr.

Mitzo Thompson, Kim, et al. Good Night, God: Bedtime Prayers for Little Ones. 2018. (ENG.). 8p. (J). bds. 4.99 *(978-1-68322-583-6(X)*, Shiloh Kidz) Barbour Publishing, Inc.

Miura, Taro. There, There. Miura, Taro, illus. 2016. (ENG., Illus.). 22p. (J). (— 1). bds. 8.99 *(978-0-7636-8785-4(5))* Candlewick Pr.

Mizielinska, Aleksandra & Mizielinski, Daniel. Maps Activity Book. 2015. (ENG., Illus.). 72p. (J). (gr. 2-5). 19.99 *(978-0-7636-7771-8(X)*, Big Picture Press) Candlewick Pr.

MMStudios & Allman, Howard, photos by. Big & Little: A Book about Opposites. 2007. (Usborne Look & Say Ser.). (Illus.). 18p. (J). (gr. -1-3). bds. 14.99 *(978-0-7945-1884-4(2)*, Usborne) EDC Publishing.

Modern Publishing Staff. Look at Me! 2007. (Illus.). (J). (gr. -1-3). bds. 4.99 *(978-0-7666-2607-2(5))* Modern Publishing.

—When I Grow Up: Giant Wall Art Flash Cards. 2007. (Illus.). (J). (gr. -1-k). bds. 12.99 *(978-0-7666-2700-0(4))* Modern Publishing.

Moerbeek, Kees. Cinderella. 2006. (Roly Poly Box Bks.). (Illus.). 24p. (J). spiral bd. *(978-1-84643-019-0(4))* Child's Play International Ltd.

Monaco, Gérard Lo. A Sea Voyage: A Pop-Up Story about All Sorts of Boats. 2016. (ENG., Illus.). 8p. (J). (gr. k-2). 29.95 *(978-0-500-65088-2(8)*, 565088) Thames & Hudson.

Monckeberg, Paulina. Pascualina 2006. 2005. (Pascualina Family of Products Ser.). (ENG., Illus.). 272p. (J). spiral bd. 16.99 *(978-956-8222-28-4(6))* Pascualina Producciones S.A.

—Rosamunda Della Calabazza 2006 Agenda & Stationary 2006: The Youngest & Most Dangerous Sister of Pascualina. 2005. (Pascualina Family of Products Ser.). (ENG., Illus.). 228p. (J). spiral bd. 11.99 *(978-956-8222-21-5(9))* Pascualina Producciones S.A.

Monroe-Daley, J. S. A Is for Arizona. 2009. (Illus.). (J). 14.95 *(978-1-934878-65-1(0))* Amplify Publishing Group.

Moon, Jo, illus. A Whale of a Tail! 2017. (J). *(978-1-62885-287-5(9))* Kidsbooks, LLC.

Moore, Clement C. My First Night Before Christmas. Newsom, Tom, illus. 2008. (ENG.). 12p. (J). 9.95 *(978-1-58117-808-1(5)*, Intervisual/Piggy Toes) Bendon, Inc.

—The Night Before Christmas. Newsom, Tom, illus. 2007. (ENG.). 18p. (J). (gr. -1-3). 19.95 *(978-1-4037-2947-7(6)*, Intervisual/Piggy Toes) Bendon, Inc.

Moore, Clement Clarke. The Night Before Christmas. Birmingham, Christian, illus. 2007. (ENG.). 26p. (J). (gr. -1 — 1). bds. 5.95 *(978-0-7624-3014-7(1)*, Running Pr. Kids) Running Pr.

Moore, Jodi. I Love My Dragon. McWilliam, Howard, illus. 2019. (When a Dragon Moves In Ser.). (ENG.). 24p. (J). bds. 7.99 *(978-1-947277-30-4(8))* Flashlight Pr.

Moroney, Trace. Bathtime: Baxter Bear Chubby. Moroney, Trace, illus. 2008. (Baxter Bear Collection). (Illus.). 10p. (J). (gr. -1-1). bds. *(978-1-86463-175-3(9))* Brimax Books Ltd.

—The Things I Love about Pets. 2019. (Things I Love about Ser.). (ENG.). 10p. (J). (— 1). bds. 8.99 *(978-1-76068-127-2(X))* Bonnier Publishing GBR. Dist: Independent Pubs. Group.

Moroney, Trace, creator. Baa, Baa, Black Sheep. 2008. (Illus.). 10p. (gr. -1-1). bds. 4.99 *(978-1-74178-526-5(X))* Gardner Pubns.

—The Owl & the Pussy Cat. 2008. (Illus.). 10p. (gr. -1-1). bds. 4.99 *(978-1-74178-515-9(4))* Gardner Pubns.

Morris, Jennifer E. May I Please Have a Cookie? Morris, Jennifer E., illus. 2015. (Scholastic Reader, Level 1 Ser.). (ENG., Illus.). 30p. (J). (— 1). bds. 6.99 *(978-0-545-81502-4(9)*, Cartwheel Bks.) Scholastic, Inc.

Mottahedeh Bos, Elaheh, illus. Bahá'í Prayers for Children. 2018. (ENG.). 15p. (J). (gr. -1-k). bds. 9.95 *(978-1-61851-123-2(8))* Baha'i Publishing.

—Bahá'í Readings for Children: Selections from the Words of Bahá'u'lláh And 'Abdu'l-Bahá. 2018. (ENG.). 15p. (J). (gr. -1-k). bds. 9.95 *(978-1-61851-124-9(6))* Baha'i Publishing.

—Divine Springtime: Selections from the Hidden Words of Bahá'u'lláh. 2018. (ENG.). 15p. (J). (gr. -1-k). bds. 9.95 *(978-1-61851-125-6(4))* Baha'i Publishing.

Motuelle, Bérengère, illus. Opposites. 2014. *(978-1-4351-5503-9(3))* Barnes & Noble, Inc.

Mroziewicz, Elsa. Peek-A-Who Too? Mroziewicz, Elsa, illus. 2019. (Illus.). 22p. (J). (gr. -1-k). bds. 11.99 *(978-988-8341-81-8(2)*, Minedition) Penguin Young Readers Group.

Mullen, Amy. Colors of New England: Explore the Colors of Nature. Kids Will Love Discovering the Colors of New England with Vivid & Beautiful Art, from the Purple Northern Blazing Star to the Green Mallard Duck. 2017. (Naturally Local Ser.). (ENG., Illus.). 20p. (J). (gr. -1-k). bds. 8.95 *(978-1-938093-99-9(2)*, 809399) Duo Pr. LLC.

—Colors of the Pacific Northwest: Explore the Colors of Nature. Kids Will Love Discovering the Amazing Natural Colors in the Pacific Northwest, from the Red Sapsucker to the Green Douglas Fir. 2017. (Naturally Local Ser.). (ENG., Illus.). 20p. (J). (gr. -1 — 1). bds. 8.99 *(978-1-938093-80-7(1)*, 809380) Duo Pr. LLC.

Mullen, Amy, illus. The Colors of Ancient Egypt. 2016. 24p. (J). bds. 10.95 *(978-0-7649-7541-7(2)*, POMEGRANATE KIDS) Pomegranate Communications, Inc.

Mullins, Amy. I'm Reverent When- Bagley, Val Chadwick, illus. 2005. ("Move-About" Book Ser.). (J). *(978-1-59156-951-0(6))* Covenant Communications.

Multiplication Mastery W/CD: Multiplication Mastery with Audio CD. 2004. (ENG.). (J). 19.99 *(978-0-943343-00-6(3))* Learning Wrap-Ups, Inc.

Mumford, Martha. Hop Little Bunnies. 2020. (Bunny Adventures Ser.). (ENG., Illus.). 24p. (J). 17.99 *(978-1-5476-0268-1(6)*, 900209360, Bloomsbury Children's Bks.) Bloomsbury Publishing USA.

—We're Going on an Egg Hunt: A Lift-The-Flap Adventure. Hughes, Laura, illus. (Bunny Adventures Ser.). (ENG.). (J). 2018. 22p. bds. 7.99 *(978-1-68119-838-5(X)*, 900188675) 2017. 24p. 17.99 *(978-1-68119-314-4(0)*, 900165670) Bloomsbury Publishing USA. (Bloomsbury USA Childrens).

Munsch, Robert. Angela's Airplane. Martchenko, Michael, illus. 2016. (ENG.). 24p. (J). (-k). bds. 7.99 *(978-1-55451-829-6(6))* Annick Pr., Ltd. CAN. Dist: Publishers Group West (PGW).

—The Fire Station. Martchenko, Michael, illus. (Classic Munsch Ser.). (ENG.). 24p. (J). 2018. (gr. k-2). 19.95 *(978-1-77321-081-0(5))* 5th ed. 2012. (gr. -1-k). bds. 7.99 *(978-1-55451-423-6(1)*, 9781554514236) Annick Pr., Ltd. CAN. Dist: Publishers Group West (PGW).

—Love You Forever. McGraw, Sheila, illus. 2018. (ENG.). 32p. (J). (gr. -1-1). bds. 8.95 *(978-0-2281-0104-8(2)*, 93279bc2-9280-4ed0-8e4f-216516529c98) Firefly Bks., Ltd.

—Love You Forever Pop-Up Edition. McGraw, Sheila, illus. 2017. (ENG.). 14p. (J). (gr. -1-1). 29.95 *(978-1-77085-965-4(9)*, a9e2dca8-f177-424e-8b80-a3c02dd73a41) Firefly Bks., Ltd.

—Moose! Martchenko, Michael, illus. 2019. (ENG.). 30p. (J). bds. 9.99 *(978-1-4431-4292-2(1))* Scholastic Canada, Ltd. CAN. Dist: Publishers Group West (PGW).

—Mud Puddle. Suomalainen, Sami, illus. 2012. (ENG.). 26p. (J). (gr. -1 — 1). bds. 7.99 *(978-1-55451-754-1(0),* 9781554517541) Annick Pr., Ltd. CAN. Dist: Publishers Group West (PGW).

—Murmel, Murmel, Murmel. Martchenko, Michael, illus. 2014. (ENG.). 32p. (J). (gr. -1 — 1). bds. 7.99 *(978-1-55451-656-8(0),* 9781554516568) Annick Pr., Ltd. CAN. Dist: Publishers Group West (PGW).

—The Paper Bag Princess. Martchenko, Michael, illus. (Classic Munsch Ser.). (J). (gr. -1-2). 2018. 32p. 19.95 *(978-1-77321-030-8(0))* 2018. 32p. pap. 6.95 *(978-1-77321-029-2(7))* 10th ed. 2009. (ENG.). 28p. bds. 7.99 *(978-1-55451-211-9(5),* 9781554512119) Annick Pr., Ltd. CAN. Dist: Publishers Group West (PGW).

—Pigs. Martchenko, Michael, illus. 2014. (ENG.). 26p. (J). (gr. -1-k). bds. 7.99 *(978-1-55451-628-5(5),* 9781554516285) Annick Pr., Ltd. CAN. Dist: Publishers Group West (PGW).

—Thomas' Snowsuit. Martchenko, Michael, illus. 6th ed. 2011. 22p. (J). (gr. -1 — 1). bds. 7.99 *(978-1-55451-363-5(4),* 9781554513635) Annick Pr., Ltd. CAN. Dist: Publishers Group West (PGW).

—50 below Zero. Martchenko, Michael, illus. 3rd ed. 2013. (Munsch for Kids Ser.). (ENG.). 22p. (J). (gr. -1-k). bds. 7.99 *(978-1-55451-532-5(7),* 9781554515325) Annick Pr., Ltd. CAN. Dist: Publishers Group West (PGW).

Munsch, Robert & Martchenko, Michael. I Have to Go! Martchenko, Michael, illus. 8th ed. 2010. (ENG., Illus.). 24p. (J). (gr. -1-k). bds. 7.99 *(978-1-55451-253-9(0),* 9781554512539) Annick Pr., Ltd. CAN. Dist: Publishers Group West (PGW).

Muntean, Michaela. Elmo Can... Taste! Touch! Smell! See! Hear! (Sesame Street) Swanson, Maggie, illus. 2013. (Big Bird's Favorites Board Bks.). (ENG.). 24p. (J). (— 1). bds. 4.99 *(978-0-307-98078-6(2),* Random Hse. Bks. for Young Readers) Random Hse. Children's Bks.

Munton, Gill. Who Ate All the Lettuce? Top That Publishing Staff, ed. Elliott, Rebecca, illus. 2007. 12p. (gr. -1-k). bds. *(978-1-84666-177-8(3),* Tide Mill Pr.) Top That! Publishing PLC.

Murphy, Harriet. Diego in Action! Follow the Reader Level 2. 2007. (Go, Diego, Go! Ser.). (ENG., Illus.). 24p. (J). (gr. -1-2). 24.99 *(978-1-4169-4993-0(3),* Simon Scribbles) Simon Scribbles.

Murphy, Mary. Good Night Like This. Murphy, Mary, illus. 2016. (ENG., Illus.). 32p. (J). (gr. -1-k). 12.99 *(978-0-7636-7970-5(4))* Candlewick Pr.

—Let's Go! 2005. (ENG., Illus.). 16p. (J). bds. 14.99 *(978-1-4052-1115-4(6))* Farshore GBR. Dist: Trafalgar Square Publishing.

Musgrave, Ruth A. National Geographic Kids Little Kids First Board Book: Space. 2019. (First Board Bks.). (Illus.). 26p. (J). (gr. -1 — 1). bds. 7.99 *(978-1-4263-3314-9(5),* National Geographic Kids) Disney Publishing Worldwide.

—National Geographic Kids Little Kids First Board Book: Animals on the Go. 2019. (First Board Bks.). (Illus.). 26p. (J). (gr. -1 — 1). bds. 7.99 *(978-1-4263-3312-5(9),* National Geographic Kids) Disney Publishing Worldwide.

—National Geographic Kids Look & Learn: Before & After. 2018. (Illus.). 24p. (J). (gr. -1-k). bds. 6.99 *(978-1-4263-3170-1(3),* National Geographic Kids) Disney Publishing Worldwide.

—Things That Go. 2020. (First Board Bks.). (Illus.). 26p. (J). (gr. -1 — 1). bds. 7.99 *(978-1-4263-3698-0(5),* National Geographic Kids) Disney Publishing Worldwide.

Musical Robot. If You're a Robot & You Know It. Carter, David A., illus. 2015. (ENG.). 14p. (J). (gr. -1-k). 16.99 *(978-0-545-81980-0(6),* Cartwheel Bks.) Scholastic, Inc.

My Clothes. 2019.Tr. of Mi Ropa. (Illus.). *(978-1-4351-6979-1(4))* Barnes & Noble, Inc.

My Day. 2011.Tr. of Mi dia. (Illus.). (J). *(978-1-4508-1610-6(X))* Publications International, Ltd.

My Friends Around the World: Sticker Book. (Girlfriend Gang Ser.). 16p. (J). *(978-2-7643-0016-9(6))* Phidal Publishing, Inc./Editions Phidal, Inc.

My Little Library of Baby Animals. 2008. (Pocket Libraries Ser.). 5p. bds. *(978-1-4075-3191-5(3))* Parragon, Inc.

My Little Library of Things That do. 2008. (Pocket Libraries Ser.). 5p. bds. *(978-1-4075-3192-2(1))* Parragon, Inc.

Nagara, Innosanto. Counting on Community. 2015. (Illus.). 24p. (J). (gr. -1-2). bds. 11.95 *(978-1-60980-632-3(8),* Triangle Square) Seven Stories Pr.

—A Is for Activist. 2016. (Illus.). 32p. (J). (gr. -1-2). 17.95 *(978-1-60980-693-4(X),* Triangle Square) Seven Stories Pr.

Napier, Matt. Little Canada. Benoit, Renné, illus. 2012. (Little Country Ser.). (ENG.). 20p. (J). (gr. -1-1). bds. 9.95 *(978-1-58536-178-6(X),* 202265) Sleeping Bear Pr.

National Geographic Kids. National Geographic Kids Look & Learn: Bugs. 2015. (Look & Learn Ser.). (Illus.). 24p. (J). (gr. -1-k). bds. 7.99 *(978-1-4263-1876-4(6),* National Geographic Kids) Disney Publishing Worldwide.

—National Geographic Kids Look & Learn: Colors! 2012. (Illus.). 24p. (J). (gr. -1-k). bds. 6.99 *(978-1-4263-0929-8(5),* National Geographic Kids) Disney Publishing Worldwide.

—National Geographic Kids Look & Learn: Dig. 2015. (Look & Learn Ser.). (Illus.). 24p. (J). (gr. -1-k). bds. 6.99 *(978-1-4263-2062-0(0),* National Geographic Kids) Disney Publishing Worldwide.

—National Geographic Kids Look & Learn: Ocean Creatures. 2015. (Look & Learn Ser.). (Illus.). 24p. (J). (gr. -1-k). bds. 6.99 *(978-1-4263-2063-7(9),* National Geographic Kids) Disney Publishing Worldwide.

—National Geographic Kids Look & Learn: Opposites! 2012. (Look & Learn Ser.). (Illus.). 24p. (J). (gr. -1-k). bds. 6.99 *(978-1-4263-1043-0(9),* National Geographic Kids) Disney Publishing Worldwide.

—National Geographic Kids Look & Learn: Patterns! 2013. (Look & Learn Ser.). 24p. (J). (gr. -1-k). bds. 6.99 *(978-1-4263-1123-9(0),* National Geographic Kids) Disney Publishing Worldwide.

—National Geographic Kids Look & Learn: Same & Different. 2012. (Illus.). 24p. (J). (gr. -1-k). bds. 6.99 *(978-1-4263-0928-1(7),* National Geographic Kids) Disney Publishing Worldwide.

—National Geographic Kids Look & Learn: Shapes! 2012. (Look & Learn Ser.). (Illus.). 24p. (J). (gr. -1-k). bds. 6.99 *(978-1-4263-1042-3(0),* National Geographic Kids) Disney Publishing Worldwide.

—Weird but True Animals. 2018. (Weird but True Ser.). (ENG., Illus.). 208p. (J). (gr. 3-7). lib. bdg. 17.90 *(978-1-4263-2982-1(2),* National Geographic Kids) Disney Publishing Worldwide.

National Geographic Society (U.S.) Staff, contrib. by. Shapes! 2013. (Illus.). (J). *(978-0-545-62212-7(3))* Scholastic, Inc.

National Wildlife Federation. My First Book of Funny Animals (National Wildlife Federation) 2015. (Illus.). 20p. (J). (— 1). bds. 6.95 *(978-1-62354-051-7(8))* Charlesbridge Publishing, Inc.

Neal, Tony, illus. Seek & Peek Jungle: A Lift the Flap Pop-Up Book about Colors! 2018. (ENG.). 10p. (J). (gr. -1 — 1). 9.99 *(978-1-4380-5046-1(1))* Sourcebooks, Inc.

Neis, Izzy. I Want to Potty. Shakir, Susie, illus. 2005. 10p. (J). 9.95 *(978-1-58117-422-9(5),* Intervisual/Piggy Toes) Bendon, Inc.

Nellist, Glenys. Christmas Love Letters from God: Bible Stories, 1 vol. Clowes, Rachel, illus. 2016. (Love Letters from God Ser.). (ENG.). 32p. (J). 17.99 *(978-0-310-74824-3(0))* Zonderkidz.

—God Made Mommy Special, 1 vol. Corke, Estelle, illus. 2018. (ENG.). 20p. (J). bds. 9.99 *(978-0-310-76233-1(2))* Zonderkidz.

Nelson-Schmidt, Michelle. Cats, Cats! 2011. (ENG., Illus.). 32p. (J). pap. 5.99 *(978-1-61067-042-5(6))* Kane Miller.

—Dogs, Dogs! 2011. (ENG., Illus.). 32p. (J). pap. 5.99 *(978-1-61067-041-8(8))* Kane Miller.

Nelson, Thomas. Big Trucks: A Touch-And-Feel Book, 1 vol. 2018. (ENG., Illus.). 12p. (J). bds. 9.99 *(978-1-4003-1058-6(X),* Tommy Nelson) Nelson, Thomas Inc.

—Daddy Loves You So Much, 1 vol. 2015. (ENG., Illus.). 20p. (J). bds. 9.99 *(978-0-529-12335-0(5),* Tommy Nelson) Nelson, Thomas Inc.

—Go to Sleep, Sheep!, 1 vol. 2018. (Bedtime Barn Ser.). (ENG., Illus.). 20p. (J). bds. 8.99 *(978-1-4003-1027-2(X),* Tommy Nelson) Nelson, Thomas Inc.

—Mommy Loves You So Much, 1 vol. 2015. (ENG., Illus.). 20p. (J). bds. 9.99 *(978-0-529-12338-1(X),* Tommy Nelson) Nelson, Thomas Inc.

Nestling, Rose. Babies Love Opposites. Cottage Door Press, ed. Hogan, Martina, illus. 2015. (Babies Love Ser.). (ENG.). 12p. (J). (gr. -1 — 1). bds. 7.99 *(978-1-68052-028-6(8),* 1000291) Cottage Door Pr.

—Bedtime Songs. Rescek, Sanja, illus. 2016. (ENG.). 12p. (J). (gr. -1-2). bds. 19.99 *(978-1-68052-123-8(3),* 1001160) Cottage Door Pr.

Neubecker, Robert. Too Many Monsters! A Halloween Counting Book. Neubecker, Robert, illus. 2010. (ENG., Illus.). 26p. (J). (gr. -1-k). bds. 7.99 *(978-1-4424-0172-3(9),* Little Simon) Little Simon.

Newman, Lesléa. Where Is Bear? Padded Board Book. Gorbachev, Valeri, illus. 2018. (ENG.). 32p. (J). (— 1). bds. 8.99 *(978-1-328-91891-8(2),* 1702525, Clarion Bks.) HarperCollins Pubs.

Newman, Tracy. Havdalah Is Coming! Garofoli, Viviana, illus. 2020. (ENG.). 12p. (J). (gr. -1 — 1). bds. 6.99 *(978-1-5415-2163-6(3),* 701faafe-bdd8-4b76-b195-3290a39c1d77, Kar-Ben Publishing) Lerner Publishing Group.

—Passover Is Coming! Garofoli, Viviana, illus. 2016. (ENG.). 12p. (J). (gr. -1 — 1). bds. 5.99 *(978-1-4677-5242-8(8),* 6a3273e6-8c04-4222-8780-1c92ca1c3660); E-Book 23.99 *(978-1-4677-9610-1(7))* Lerner Publishing Group. (Kar-Ben Publishing).

—Purim Is Coming! Garofoli, Viviana, illus. 2017. (ENG.). 12p. (J). (gr. -1 — 1). bds. 7.99 *(978-1-5124-0827-0(1),* 8ce8b152-c9bb-4654-b45e-04c5bd767de7); E-Book 23.99 *(978-1-5124-2725-7(X),* 9781512427257) Lerner Publishing Group. (Kar-Ben Publishing).

—Rosh Hashanah Is Coming! Garofoli, Viviana, illus. 2016. (ENG.). 12p. (J). (gr. -1 — 1). bds. 8.99 *(978-1-4677-7988-3(1),* d7c7e5b8-b6c1-4b95-8c2c-89fa58a2586e, Kar-Ben Publishing) Lerner Publishing Group.

—Simchat Torah Is Coming! Garofoli, Viviana, illus. 2018. (ENG.). 12p. (J). (gr. -1 — 1). bds. 5.99 *(978-1-5124-2100-2(6),* 388c65f8-ce27-4342-bcf0-20442cb0c9cf, Kar-Ben Publishing) Lerner Publishing Group.

Newsom, Tom, illus. The First Noel. 2006. 14p. (J). (gr. k-4). reprint ed. 8.00 *(978-1-4223-5413-1(X))* DIANE Publishing Co.

Nex, Anthony, photos by. Little Feet Love. 2009. (Illus.). 12p. 7.95 *(978-1-58117-881-4(6),* Intervisual/Piggy Toes) Bendon, Inc.

Nguyen Lay, Ngoc. Together Bears. Ott, Candace, illus. 2017. (ENG.). 10p. (J). bds. 12.95 *(978-0-692-03261-9(4),* 9780692032619) Skybox Event Productions.

Nicely, Adam. Bedtime for Tad. 2009. (ENG., Illus.). 28p. (J). (gr. k — 1). bds. 7.95 *(978-1-894965-84-2(1))* Simply Read Bks. CAN. Dist: Ingram Publisher Services.

Nicholls, Paul, illus. I Want to Be A... Pirate. 2014. (J). *(978-1-4351-5500-8(9))* Barnes & Noble, Inc.

Nicholls, Sally. The Button Book. Woollvin, Bethan, illus. 2020. (ENG.). 32p. (J). (gr. -1-2). 16.99 *(978-0-7352-6715-2(4),* Tundra Bks.) Tundra Bks. CAN. Dist: Penguin Random Hse. LLC.

Nicholson, Sue. All about Me. (All about Me Ser.). *(978-1-4054-6547-2(6))* Parragon, Inc.

Nickelodeon Staff, ed. Words - Dora the Explorer. 2010. (Write, Slide & Learn Ser.). 14p. (J). (gr. -1-1). 9.99 *(978-1-74184-519-8(X),* Ideals Pubns.) Worthy Publishing.

Nieminen, Lotta. Cookies! An Interactive Recipe Book. 2018. (Cook in a Book Ser.). (ENG., Illus.). 16p. (gr. -1 — 1). bds. 19.95 *(978-0-7148-7773-0(5))* Phaidon Pr., Inc.

—Pancakes! An Interactive Recipe Book. 2016. (Cook in a Book Ser.). (ENG., Illus.). 16p. (gr. -1 — 1). bds. 19.95 *(978-0-7148-7283-4(0))* Phaidon Pr., Inc.

Niland, Kilmeny. The Gingerbread Man. 2006. (Illus.). 16p. *(978-1-921049-49-1(9))* Little Hare Bks. AUS. Dist: HarperCollins Pubs. Australia.

Nister, Ernest, illus. Merry Magic-Go-Round: An Antique Book of Changing Pictures. 2005. 14p. (J). (gr. k-4). reprint ed. 19.00 *(978-0-7567-9156-8(1))* DIANE Publishing Co.

Noah's Ark Bible Sticker Book. 2003. (Illus.). 16p. (J). 2.98 *(978-1-4054-1558-3(4))* Parragon, Inc.

Noble, Trinka Hakes. Little New Jersey. Brett, Jeannie, illus. 2012. (Little State Ser.). (ENG.). 20p. (J). (gr. -1-1). bds. 9.95 *(978-1-58536-786-3(9),* 202349) Sleeping Bear Pr.

—Little Pennsylvania. Brett, Jeannie, illus. 2010. (Little State Ser.). (ENG.). 20p. (J). (gr. -1-1). bds. 9.95 *(978-1-58536-506-7(8),* 202247) Sleeping Bear Pr.

Nolan, Allia Zobel. Animal Parade: A Lift-The-Flap Hear-the-Sound Book. Maddocks, Maria, illus. 2011. (ENG.). 10p. (J). (gr. -1 — 1). pap. 12.99 *(978-0-547-55867-7(8),* 1453623, Clarion Bks.) HarperCollins Pubs.

—God's Oak Tree. Chung, Chi, illus. 2007. 16p. (J). (gr. -1). 12.99 *(978-0-8254-5536-0(7))* Kregel Pubns.

—God's Winter Wonderland. Mitchell, Melanie, illus. 2006. 10p. (J). bds. 8.99 *(978-0-8254-5526-1(X))* Kregel Pubns.

Noll, Amanda. Are You My Monster? McWilliam, Howard, illus. 2019. (I Need My Monster Ser.). 26p. (J). bds. 8.99 *(978-1-947277-32-8(4))* Flashlight Pr.

Norman, Kim. If It's Snowy & You Know It, Clap Your Paws! Woodruff, Liza, illus. abr. ed. 2015. (ENG.). 26p. (J). (— 1). bds. 6.95 *(978-1-4549-1692-5(3))* Sterling Publishing Co., Inc.

North, Dawn. Pull-Alongs: Digger. 2007. 12p. (gr. -1). per. *(978-1-84610-446-6(7))* Make Believe Ideas.

North, Merry. My Grandma & Me: A Picture, Play & Tote Book. 2004. 10p. (J). (gr. -1-18). bds. 5.99 *(978-1-57151-724-1(3))* Playhouse Publishing.

—Squeaky Clean. 2005. 9p. *(978-1-57151-752-4(9))* Playhouse Publishing.

Nouvion, Judith. Shapes. 2015. (Picture This Ser.). (ENG., Illus.). 40p. (J). (gr. -1-3). bds. 7.99 *(978-0-544-51830-8(6),* 1606228, Clarion Bks.) HarperCollins Pubs.

Novesky, Amy. Love Is a Truck. Gillingham, Sara, illus. 2016. (ENG.). 24p. (J). (gr. -1-1). bds. 13.99 *(978-1-937359-86-7(7),* 1330001) Abrams, Inc.

—Love Is a Tutu. Gillingham, Sara, illus. 2016. (ENG.). 24p. (J). (gr. -1-k). bds. 13.99 *(978-1-937359-81-2(6),* 1330101, Cameron Kids) Cameron + Co.

Novick, Mary. The Big Book of Animals & Bugs. Hale, Jenny, illus. (Double Delights Ser.). (ENG.). 32p. (J). pap. *(978-1-877003-38-7(7))* Little Hare Bks. AUS. Dist: HarperCollins Pubs. Australia.

—Bugs. Hale, Jenny, illus. 2003. 16p. (Orig.). pap. *(978-1-877003-32-5(8))* Little Hare Bks. AUS. Dist: HarperCollins Pubs. Australia.

—Nursery Songs. Hale, Jenny, illus. 2003. (ENG.). 16p. (Orig.). pap. *(978-1-877003-33-2(6))* Little Hare Bks. AUS. Dist: HarperCollins Pubs. Australia.

Novick, Mary & Hale, Jenny. Farm & Zoo. 2006. (Illus.). 32p. *(978-1-921049-26-2(X))* Little Hare Bks. AUS. Dist: HarperCollins Pubs. Australia.

Numeroff, Laura. The Best Mouse Cookie Padded Board Book. Bond, Felicia, illus. 2018. (If You Give... Ser.). (ENG.). 24p. (J). (gr. -1 — 1). bds. 10.99 *(978-0-06-284483-5(0),* HarperFestival) HarperCollins Pubs.

—Happy Birthday, Mouse! Bond, Felicia, illus. 2020. (If You Give... Ser.). (ENG.). 24p. (J). (gr. -1 — 1). bds. 7.99 *(978-0-694-01425-5(7),* HarperFestival) HarperCollins Pubs.

—Happy Easter, Mouse! An Easter & Springtime Book for Kids. Bond, Felicia, illus. 2019. (If You Give... Ser.). (ENG.). 24p. (J). (gr. -1 — 1). bds. 7.99 *(978-0-694-01422-4(2),* HarperFestival) HarperCollins Pubs.

—Happy Valentine's Day, Mouse! Lap Edition. Bond, Felicia, illus. 2015. (If You Give... Ser.). (ENG.). 24p. (J). (gr. -1-3). bds. 12.99 *(978-0-06-242740-3(7),* HarperFestival) HarperCollins Pubs.

—What Brothers Do Best: (Big Brother Books for Kids, Brotherhood Books for Kids, Sibling Books for Kids) 2012. (What Brothers/Sisters Do Best Ser.). (ENG., Illus.). 20p. (J). (gr. -1 — 1). bds. 8.99 *(978-1-4521-1073-8(5))* Chronicle Bks. LLC.

—What Sisters Do Best: (Big Sister Books for Kids, Sisterhood Books for Kids, Sibling Books for Kids) Munsinger, Lynn, illus. 2012. (What Brothers/Sisters Do Best Ser.). (ENG.). 20p. (J). (gr. -1 — 1). bds. 7.99 *(978-1-4521-1074-5(3))* Chronicle Bks. LLC.

Nussbaum, Ben. Take Me Out to the Ballgame. Studio Mouse Staff, ed. rev. ed. 2007. (ENG.). 24p. 4.99 *(978-1-59069-603-3(4))* Studio Mouse LLC.

O'Brien, Anne Sibley & Gal, Susan. Abracadabra, It's Spring! 2016. (Seasonal Magic Ser.). (ENG., Illus.). 24p. (J). (gr. -1-k). 15.99 *(978-1-4197-1891-5(6),* 1121301, Abrams Appleseed) Abrams, Inc.

O'Brien, Joan. Fashion Accessories Stickers. 2003. (Dover Little Activity Bks.). (ENG., Illus.). 4p. 1.50 *(978-0-486-43071-3(5))* Dover Pubns., Inc.

—Lucky Ladybug Stickers. 2004. (Dover Little Activity Books Stickers Ser.). (ENG., Illus.). 4p. (J). (gr. k-3). pap. 2.50 *(978-0-486-43008-9(1),* 430081) Dover Pubns., Inc.

O'Brien, Kristen. Little Red Riding Hood Story in a Box. Winter, Janet, illus. 2003. (Story in a Box Ser.). 12p. (J). (gr. -1-1). bds. 8.99 *(978-1-883043-41-4(7))* Straight Edge Pr., The.

O'Brien, Melanie. My Belly Button. 2009. 12p. 9.95 *(978-1-58117-917-0(0),* Intervisual/Piggy Toes) Bendon, Inc.

—No More Pacifiers! With Disappearing Pacifiers! Enright, Amanda, illus. 2008. (ENG.). 18p. (J). (gr. -1-k). 10.95 *(978-1-58117-684-1(8),* Intervisual/Piggy Toes) Bendon, Inc.

O'Connell, Rebecca. The Baby Goes Beep. Wilson-Max, Ken, illus. 2010. (ENG.). 16p. (J). (gr. -1 — 1). bds. 7.99 *(978-0-8075-0508-3(0),* 807505080) Whitman, Albert & Co.

O'Connor, Jane. Fancy Nancy: The Marvelous Mother's Day Brunch. 2011. (Fancy Nancy Ser.). (ENG., Illus.). 16p. (J). (gr. -1-3). pap. 6.99 *(978-0-06-170380-5(X),* HarperFestival) HarperCollins Pubs.

O'Dare, Helen. Love. O'Byrne, Nicola, illus. 2016. (ENG.). 26p. (J). (gr. -1 — 1). bds. 6.99 *(978-1-62686-677-5(5),* Silver Dolphin Bks.) Printers Row Publishing Group.

Odierno, Lisa. Bunny Hide-and-Seek. 2009. (Smithsonian Baby Animals Ser.). (ENG., Illus.). 16p. (J). (gr. -1-k). 6.95 *(978-1-60727-092-8(7))* Soundprints.

Odierno, Lisa & Soundprints Staff. Bunny Hide-and-Seek. 2009. (Smithsonian Baby Animals Ser.). (ENG., Illus.). 16p. (J). (gr. -1-k). 6.95 *(978-1-60727-105-5(2))* Soundprints.

Ohrt, Kate. The Rainbow Book. 2011. (ENG.). 18p. (J). (gr. -1-1). pap. 9.99 *(978-1-4494-0171-9(6))* Andrews McMeel Publishing.

O'Leary, Sara. This Is Sadie. Morstad, Julie, illus. 2018. 30p. (J). (— 1). bds. 8.99 *(978-0-7352-6324-6(8),* Tundra Bks.) Tundra Bks. CAN. Dist: Penguin Random Hse. LLC.

Olesen, Cecilie. My First Handy Bible: Timeless Bible Stories for Toddlers. Mazali, Gustavo, illus. 2006. (ENG.). 64p. (gr. -1-k). bds. 12.99 *(978-1-59052-608-8(2),* Multnomah Bks.) Crown Publishing Group, The.

Oliver, Alison. Be Bold, Baby: Oprah. Oliver, Alison, illus. 2018. (Be Bold, Baby Ser.). (ENG., Illus.). 20p. (J). (— 1). bds. 9.99 *(978-1-328-51990-0(2),* 1720771, Clarion Bks.) HarperCollins Pubs.

Opal, Paola, illus. Saffy & Ollie. 2012. (ENG.). 24p. (J). (gr. -1 — 1). bds. 7.95 *(978-1-897476-69-7(8))* Simply Read Bks. CAN. Dist: Ingram Publisher Services.

Orodan, Mike. Peek-A-Baby: Farm: Peekaboo Flaps Inside! 2019. (Peek-A-Baby Ser.). (ENG., Illus.). 14p. (J). (gr. -1 — 1). bds. 9.99 *(978-1-4521-6645-2(5))* Chronicle Bks. LLC.

—Peek-A-Baby: Ocean: Peekaboo Flaps Inside! 2019. (Peek-A-Baby Ser.). (ENG., Illus.). 14p. (J). (gr. -1 — 1). bds. 9.99 *(978-1-4521-6646-9(3))* Chronicle Bks. LLC.

Ortiz, Estrella. A Bailar: Let's Dance. Valdivia, Paloma, illus. 2015. (ENG & SPA.). (J). *(978-0-545-85368-2(0))* Scholastic, Inc.

—De Paseo: Out & About. Valdivia, Paloma, illus. 2015. (SPA & ENG.). (J). *(978-0-545-85369-9(9))* Scholastic, Inc.

Osteen, Victoria. My Happy Heart Books (Boxed Set) A Touch-And-Feel Book Boxed Set. Day, Betsy, illus. 2009. (ENG.). 66p. (J). (gr. -1-k). bds. 19.99 *(978-1-4169-5549-8(6),* Little Simon Inspirations) Little Simon Inspirations.

O'Toole, Janet. On the Farm: Lift the Flaps to Find Out about Farms! Adams, Ben, illus. 2013. 16p. (J). (gr. -1-12). bds. 6.99 *(978-1-84322-794-6(0),* Armadillo) Anness Publishing GBR. Dist: National Bk. Network.

O'Toole, Janet & Anness Publishing Staff. First Words: Lift the Flaps to Find Out about Words! Adams, Ben, illus. 2013. 16p. (J). (gr. -1-12). bds. 6.99 *(978-1-84322-795-3(9),* Armadillo) Anness Publishing GBR. Dist: National Bk. Network.

—Vehicles: Lift the Flaps to Find Out about Vehicles! Adams, Ben, illus. 2013. 16p. (J). (gr. -1-12). bds. 6.99 *(978-1-84322-728-1(2),* Armadillo) Anness Publishing GBR. Dist: National Bk. Network.

Owl's Forest Numbers. 2015. (Illus.). (J). *(978-1-58865-882-1(1))* Kidsbooks, LLC.

Oxenbury, Helen. Baby Love (Boxed Set) Set: A Board Book Gift Set/All Fall down; Clap Hands; Say Goodnight; Tickle, Tickle. Oxenbury, Helen, illus. gif. ed. 2009. (ENG., Illus.). 40p. (J). (gr. -1 — 1). bds. 9.99 *(978-1-4169-9546-3(3),* Little Simon) Little Simon.

P. I. Kids. Dora First Look & Find - O/P. 2006. (ENG.). 18p. (J). 9.98 *(978-1-4127-3909-2(8))* Phoenix International Publications, Inc.

—Little Flashlight Box Jake & Nev- O/P. 2013. (ENG.). 8p. (J). (gr. k-4). pap. 10.99 *(978-1-4508-6836-5(3),* 2baa77ff-d973-4d57-acdb-676cb1d56b2d) Phoenix International Publications, Inc.

—LSD Dora Potty Time with Dora - O/P. 2011. (ENG.). 12p. (J). 11.98 *(978-1-4508-1438-6(7))* Phoenix International Publications, Inc.

—Planes Play a Sound O/P. 2013. (ENG., Illus.). 10p. (J). *(978-1-4508-6284-4(5))* Publications International, Ltd.

Packard, Mary. The Storyteller. Land Eagle, illus. 2009. 196p. (J). *(978-1-4351-1557-6(0))* Metro Bks.

Padgett, JoAnn. Marvel Super Hero Adventures: Captain Marvel & the Epic Clash. 2019. (Magnetic Hardcover Ser.). (ENG., Illus.). 10p. (J). (gr. -1-k). 12.99 *(978-0-7944-4111-1(4),* Studio Fun International) Printers Row Publishing Group.

Paes, Rob, illus. Mighty Machines. 2003. 12p. (J). (gr. k-3). 20.00 *(978-0-7567-6652-8(4))* DIANE Publishing Co.

Page, Claire. Five Noisy Ducks: An Action-Packed Counting Book. 2008. (Illus.). 18p. (J). (gr. -1-k). bds. *(978-1-84610-587-6(0))* Make Believe Ideas.

Page, Nick. Touch & Feel Noisy Dinosaurs. 2007. (Touch & Feel Ser.). (Illus.). 12p. (gr. -1). per., bds. *(978-1-84610-444-2(0))* Make Believe Ideas.

Page, Nick & Page, Claire. Finger Puppet Books Christmas Story. 2008. (Illus.). 12p. (gr. -1-k). bds. *(978-1-84610-821-1(7))* Make Believe Ideas.

—Funny Faces: Baby Animals. 2006. (Funny Faces Ser.). (Illus.). 10p. (gr. -1-k). per., bds. *(978-1-84610-118-2(2))* Make Believe Ideas.

Paiva, Johannah Gilman, ed. A Child's Book of Prayers: Please. 2013. (ENG., Illus.). 20p. (J). 8.99 *(978-1-77093-637-9(8))* Flowerpot Children's Pr. Inc. CAN. Dist: Cardinal Pubs. Group.

—A Child's Book of Prayers: Thank You. 2013. (ENG., Illus.). 20p. (J). 8.99 *(978-1-77093-638-6(6))* Flowerpot Children's Pr. Inc. CAN. Dist: Cardinal Pubs. Group.

—Crazy Critters. Gardiner, Lisa M., illus. 2013. (Big Padded Lift-The-Flap Ser.). (ENG.). 20p. (J). (gr. -1-2). 8.99 *(978-1-77093-630-0(0))* Flowerpot Children's Pr. Inc. CAN. Dist: Cardinal Pubs. Group.

—Farm Find. Gardiner, Lisa M., illus. 2013. 20p. (J). (gr. -1-1). 8.99 *(978-1-77093-688-1(2))* Flowerpot Children's Pr. Inc. CAN. Dist: Cardinal Pubs. Group.

—Zoo Friends. 2013. (Illus.). 20p. (J). bds. 8.99 *(978-1-77093-629-4(7))* Flowerpot Children's Pr. Inc. CAN. Dist: Cardinal Pubs. Group.

Pallotta, Jerry. The Very Berry Counting Book. Newton, Joy, illus. 2017. (Jerry Pallotta's Counting Bks.). 10p. (J). (— 1). bds. 6.99 *(978-1-58089-784-6(3))* Charlesbridge Publishing, Inc.

Pankova, Yuliya, ed. Veggies - Guess What? 2013. (Guess What? Ser.). (ENG.). 10p. (J). (— 1). bds. 5.95 *(978-1-61889-319-2(X))* AZ Bks. LLC.

Paquette, Ammi-Joan. Ghost in the House. Record, Adam, illus. 2019. (ENG.). 32p. (J). (gr. -1-2). 5.99 *(978-0-7636-9892-8(X))* Candlewick Pr.

Paradis, Anne. Caillou: My Little Bed. Sévigny, Eric, illus. 2012. (ENG.). 10p. (J). (gr. -1-k). 9.99 *(978-2-89450-951-7(0))* Caillouet, Gerry.

Parent, Nancy. Disney Junior Fancy Nancy: Meet Fancy Nancy. Imaginism Studios, Imaginism, illus. 2018. (Disney Junior Fancy Nancy Ser.). (ENG.). 18p. (J). (gr. -1 — 1). bds. 8.99 *(978-0-06-284398-2(2)*, HarperCollins) HarperCollins Pubs.

Parisi, Anthony. First Look at Space. Pindroh, Paula, illus. 2011. (ENG.). 16p. (J). *(978-1-60727-225-0(3)*, Blackbirch Pr., Inc.) Soundprints.

Parker, Amy. How Big Is Love? (padded Board Book) Brookshire, Breezy, illus. 2016. (Faith, Hope, Love Ser.). (ENG.). 24p. (J). (gr. -1-k). bds. 9.99 *(978-1-4336-9042-6(X)*, 005778804, B&H Kids) B&H Publishing Group.

—How Far Is Faith? (padded Board Book) Brookshire, Breezy, illus. 2016. (Faith, Hope, Love Ser.). (ENG.). 24p. (J). (gr. -1-k). bds. 9.99 *(978-1-4336-9040-2(3)*, 005778802, B&H Kids) B&H Publishing Group.

—How High Is Hope? (padded Board Book) Brookshire, Breezy, illus. 2016. (Faith, Hope, Love Ser.). (ENG.). 24p. (J). (gr. -1-k). bds. 9.99 *(978-1-4336-9041-9(1)*, 005778803, B&H Kids) B&H Publishing Group.

—Night Night, Farm, 1 vol. Allyn, Virginia, illus. 2016. (Night Night Ser.). (ENG.). 20p. (J). bds. 8.99 *(978-0-7180-8831-6(X)*, Tommy Nelson) Nelson, Thomas Inc.

—Night Night, Farm Touch & Feel, 1 vol. Allyn, Virginia, illus. 2018. (Night Night Ser.). (ENG.). 18p. (J). bds. 12.99 *(978-1-4003-1059-3(8)*, Tommy Nelson) Nelson, Thomas Inc.

—Night Night, Jungle, 1 vol. Allyn, Virginia, illus. 2018. (Night Night Ser.). (ENG.). 20p. (J). bds. 9.99 *(978-0-7180-9086-9(1)*, Tommy Nelson) Nelson, Thomas Inc.

—A Night Night Prayer, 1 vol. 2014. (Night Night Ser.). (ENG., Illus.). 20p. (J). bds. 9.99 *(978-1-4003-2431-6(9)*, Tommy Nelson) Nelson, Thomas Inc.

—Night Night, Sleepytown, 1 vol. Allyn, Virginia, illus. 2018. (Night Night Ser.). (ENG.). 20p. (J). bds. 9.99 *(978-1-4003-1003-6(2)*, Tommy Nelson) Nelson, Thomas Inc.

—Tiny Blessings: for a Merry Christmas. Walsh, Sarah, illus. 2016. (ENG.). 10p. (J). (gr. -1-1). bds. 7.95 *(978-0-7624-6095-3(4)*, Running Pr. Kids) Running Pr.

Parker, Ant, illus. Amazing Machines First Concepts: Colors. 2015. (ENG.). 12p. (J). (gr. -1-1). bds. 5.99 *(978-0-7534-7233-0(3)*, 9780753472330, Kingfisher) Roaring Brook Pr.

Parmley, Dave & Ruffing, Eric. Alternative ABCs (Chunky Edition) 2010. (ENG., Illus.). 58p. bds. 14.95 *(978-1-934429-39-6(2))* AMMO Bks., LLC.

Parr, todd. The Daddy Book. 2015. (ENG., Illus.). 20p. (J). (gr. -1 — 1). bds. 7.99 *(978-0-316-25784-8(2))* Little, Brown Bks. for Young Readers.

—Planet Color by Todd Parr Jumbo Journal Save the Blue. 2009. (Todd Parr by Chronicle Bks.). (ENG.). 160p. (J). (gr. -1-3). 9.99 *(978-0-8118-7153-2(3))* Chronicle Bks. LLC.

Parragon Publishing Staff. Busy Day at the Airport. (Busy Books Large Ser.). *(978-1-4054-7873-1(X))* Parragon, Inc.

Parrish, Emma. Flutterby Butterfly: A Slide-And-Seek Book. 2015. (Slide-And-Seek Ser.). (ENG., Illus.). 10p. (J). (gr. -1-k). bds. 12.99 *(978-1-4998-0029-6(0))* Little Bee Books Inc.

—Hoppity Frog: A Slide-And-Seek Book. 2015. (Slide-And-Seek Ser.). (ENG., Illus.). 10p. (J). (gr. -1-k). 9.99 *(978-1-4998-0030-2(4))* Little Bee Books Inc.

—Little Owl Says Goodnight: A Slide-And-Seek Book. 2016. (Slide-And-Seek Ser.). (ENG., Illus.). 10p. (J). (gr. -1-k). bds. 9.99 *(978-1-4998-0406-5(7))* Little Bee Books Inc.

Parrott, Leslie. God Made You Nose to Toes, 1 vol. Corke, Estelle, illus. 2017. (ENG.). 18p. (J). bds. 9.99 *(978-0-310-75740-5(1))* Zonderkidz.

Parry, Jo. Blast Off! 2009. (Wow! Bks.). (Illus.). (J). bds. 12.99 *(978-1-934650-26-4(9))* Just For Kids Pr., LLC.

Parsons Yazzie, Evangeline. Little Woman Warrior Who Came Home/Dzani Yazhi Naazbaa' (Paperback) Parsons Yazzie, Evangeline & Toddy, Irving, illus. 2005. (CAI, ENG & NAV.). (J). pap. 14.95 *(978-1-893354-65-4(2))* Salina Bookshelf Inc.

Partridge, Rose. Whiskers & Tails. Cottage Door Press, ed. Mack, Steve, illus. 2017. (ENG.). 10p. (J). (gr. -1-k). bds. 9.99 *(978-1-68052-161-0(6)*, 1001590) Cottage Door Pr.

Pascal, Erinn. Marauder's Map Guide to Hogwarts (Harry Potter) Cann, Helen, illus. 2018. (ENG.). 52p. (J). (gr. 2-2). 14.99 *(978-1-338-25280-4(1))* Scholastic, Inc.

Patchett, F. Plane Fun. 2009. (Kid Kits Ser.). 32p. (J). 11.99 *(978-1-60130-162-8(6)*, Usborne) EDC Publishing.

Patel, Shobhna. The Nutcracker: A Papercut Pop-Up Book. 2017. (ENG., Illus.). 32p. (J). (gr. -1-7). 19.95 *(978-0-500-65124-7(8)*, 565124) Thames & Hudson.

Patricelli, Leslie. Big Kid Bed. Patricelli, Leslie, illus. 2018. (Leslie Patricelli Board Bks.). (ENG., Illus.). 26p. (J). (— 1). bds. 8.99 *(978-0-7636-7934-7(8))* Candlewick Pr.

—Big Little. Patricelli, Leslie, illus. 2003. (Leslie Patricelli Board Bks.). (ENG., Illus.). 24p. (J). (— 1). bds. 8.99 *(978-0-7636-1951-0(5))* Candlewick Pr.

—The Birthday Box. Patricelli, Leslie, illus. 2009. (Leslie Patricelli Board Bks.). (ENG., Illus.). 26p. (J). (gr. -1 — 1). bds. 8.99 *(978-0-7636-4449-9(8))* Candlewick Pr.

—Blankie/Mantita. Patricelli, Leslie, illus. 2016. (Leslie Patricelli Board Bks.). (Illus.). 24p. (J). (— 1). bds. 8.99 *(978-0-7636-8897-4(5))* Candlewick Pr.

—Fa la La. Patricelli, Leslie, illus. 2012. (Leslie Patricelli Board Bks.). (ENG., Illus.). 26p. (J). (gr. k — 1). bds. 8.99 *(978-0-7636-3247-2(3))* Candlewick Pr.

—Fa la La/Tra-La-la. Patricelli, Leslie, illus. 2017. (Leslie Patricelli Board Bks.). (Illus.). 26p. (J). (— 1). bds. 8.99 *(978-0-7636-9524-8(6))* Candlewick Pr.

—Higher! Higher! Patricelli, Leslie, illus. 2010. (Leslie Patricelli Board Bks.). (ENG., Illus.). 30p. (J). (-k). bds. 7.99 *(978-0-7636-4433-8(1))* Candlewick Pr.

—Hop! Hop! Patricelli, Leslie, illus. 2015. (Leslie Patricelli Board Bks.). (ENG., Illus.). 26p. (J). (— 1). bds. 8.99 *(978-0-7636-6319-3(0))* Candlewick Pr.

—Huggy Kissy. Patricelli, Leslie, illus. 2012. (Leslie Patricelli Board Bks.). (ENG., Illus.). 26p. (J). (gr. -1 — 1). bds. 7.99 *(978-0-7636-3246-5(5))* Candlewick Pr.

—Huggy Kissy: Padded Board Book. Patricelli, Leslie, illus. 2019. (Leslie Patricelli Board Bks.). (ENG., Illus.). 26p. (J). (— 1). bds. 9.99 *(978-1-5362-1135-1(4))* Candlewick Pr.

—Potty/Bacinica. Patricelli, Leslie, illus. 2016. (Leslie Patricelli Board Bks.). (Illus.). 28p. (J). (— 1). bds. 8.99 *(978-0-7636-8777-9(4))* Candlewick Pr.

—Tickle. Patricelli, Leslie, illus. 2014. (Leslie Patricelli Board Bks.). (ENG., Illus.). 26p. (J). (— 1). bds. 7.99 *(978-0-7636-6322-3(0))* Candlewick Pr.

—Toot. Patricelli, Leslie, illus. 2014. (Leslie Patricelli Board Bks.). (ENG., Illus.). 24p. (J). (— 1). bds. 8.99 *(978-0-7636-6321-6(2))* Candlewick Pr.

—Tooth. Patricelli, Leslie, illus. 2018. (Leslie Patricelli Board Bks.). (ENG., Illus.). 26p. (J). (— 1). bds. 7.99 *(978-0-7636-7933-0(X))* Candlewick Pr.

—Tubby/Bañito. Patricelli, Leslie, illus. 2017. (Leslie Patricelli Board Bks.). (Illus.). 28p. (J). (— 1). bds. 8.99 *(978-0-7636-9316-9(2))* Candlewick Pr.

—Yummy Yucky. Patricelli, Leslie, illus. 2003. (Leslie Patricelli Board Bks.). (ENG., Illus.). 24p. (J). (gr. -1 — 1). bds. 8.99 *(978-0-7636-1950-3(7))* Candlewick Pr.

Patterson, Sandra Jean. Crabby Crab. 2006. bds. 12.95 *(978-1-59700-246-2(1))* Island Heritage Publishing.

Paul, Cinco & Daurio, Ken. Minions: Sleepy Kittens. Guillon, Eric, illus. 2010. (Minions Ser.). (ENG.). 10p. (J). (gr. -1 — 1). bds. 8.99 *(978-0-316-08381-2(X))* Little, Brown Bks. for Young Readers.

Paul, Miranda. 10 Little Ninjas. Wragg, Nate, illus. 2018. 26p. (J). (-k). bds. 7.99 *(978-1-5247-7071-6(X)*, Knopf Bks. for Young Readers) Random Hse. Children's Bks.

Pavlova, Chrisi É. da. Animal Stories from Green Lane Estate: Series Four. 2012. (ENG., Illus.). 290p. pap. 22.00 *(978-1-78035-357-9(X)*, Fastprint Publishing) Upfront Publishing Ltd. GBR. Dist: Printondemand-worldwide.com.

Pavlova, Chrisi É. da. Animal Stories from Green Lane Estate Series 5. 2012. (ENG., Illus.). 290p. pap. 22.00 *(978-1-78035-452-1(5)*, Fastprint Publishing) Upfront Publishing Ltd. GBR. Dist: Printondemand-worldwide.com.

PAW Patrol on the Roll! 2016. (Illus.). (J). *(978-1-5182-2638-0(8))* Random House Children's Books.

Peanuckle. Mrs. Peanuckle's Vegetable Alphabet. Ford, Jessie, illus. 2017. (Mrs. Peanuckle's Alphabet Ser.: 1). 28p. (J). (— 1). bds. 8.99 *(978-1-62336-870-8(7)*, 9781623368708, Rodale Kids) Random Hse. Children's Bks.

Pearlman, Bobby. Passover Is Here! Passover Is Here! Desmoinaux, Christel, illus. 2005. (ENG.). 16p. (J). (gr. k-2). pap. 6.99 *(978-0-689-86587-9(2)*, Little Simon) Little Simon.

Pearse, Asha, illus. Wizard of Oz. 2017. (10 Minute Classics Ser.). (ENG.). 32p. (J). (gr. 1-4). 16.99 *(978-1-4867-1221-2(5)*, 341fccfd-893b-4e64-bc14-77b725bee85d) Flowerpot Pr.

—Wizard of Oz. 2017. (ENG.). 32p. (J). (gr. 1-5). *(978-1-4867-1269-4(X))* Flowerpot Children's Pr. Inc.

—Wizard of Oz. 2014. (ENG.). 16p. (J). (gr. -1-4). 7.99 *(978-1-4867-0009-7(8))* Flowerpot Children's Pr. Inc. CAN. Dist: Cardinal Pubs. Group.

Pedigree Books. Turbo Annual 2014. 2013. 80p. (J). 12.99 *(978-1-907602-93-1(3))* Pedigree Bks., Ltd. GBR. Dist: Diamond Bk. Distributors.

Pelham, David. Sam's Sandwich. Pelham, David, illus. 2015. (ENG., Illus.). 24p. (J). (gr. -1-2). 14.99 *(978-0-7636-7808-1(2))* Candlewick Pr.

Penn, Audrey. A Color Game for Chester Raccoon. Gibson, Barbara, illus. 2012. (Kissing Hand Ser.). (ENG.). 14p. (J). (gr. -1-2). bds. 7.95 *(978-1-933718-58-3(7))* Tanglewood Pr.

#People Date not set. (I Can Draw Ser.). 32p. (J). 4.98 *(978-1-4054-0020-6(X))* Parragon, Inc.

Perez, Jessica. Under Construction: A Moving Track Book. Schneider, Christine, illus. 2005. (ENG.). 12p. (J). 12.95 *(978-1-58117-272-0(9)*, Intervisual/Piggy Toes) Bendon, Inc.

—Who's Hiding Inside? Dinosaurs. Lensch, Chris, illus. 2005. (Who's Hiding Inside Ser.). 12p. (J). bds. 7.95 *(978-1-58117-246-1(X)*, Intervisual/Piggy Toes) Bendon, Inc.

Perkins, Al. The Nose Book. Mathieu, Joe, illus. 2017. (Big Bright & Early Board Book Ser.). 24p. (J). (— 1). bds. 6.99 *(978-0-553-53863-2(2)*, Random Hse. Bks. for Young Readers) Random Hse. Children's Bks.

Perkins, Chloe. Rapunzel. Sreenivasan, Archana, illus. 2017. (Once upon a World Ser.). (ENG.). 24p. (J). (gr. -1 — 1). bds. 8.99 *(978-1-4814-9072-6(9)*, Little Simon) Little Simon.

Perrin, Clotilde. Inside the Villains. Perrin, Clotilde, illus. 2018. (ENG., Illus.). 12p. (J). (gr. k-3). 24.99 *(978-1-77657-198-7(3)*, a3c42c40-9d9a-451e-af85-f14ff9b12ddb) Gecko Pr. NZL. Dist: Lerner Publishing Group.

Perrin, Martine. What Do You See? 2011. (ENG., Illus.). 16p. (J). (gr. -1 — 1). bds. 8.99 *(978-0-8075-6712-8(4)*, 807567124) Whitman, Albert & Co.

Perry, Robert. The Ferryboat Ride. Guzek, Greta, illus. 2017. (ENG.). 20p. (J). bds. 9.95 *(978-0-88971-340-6(5)*, 8cdb6fe9-780a-47da-970b-f97975872ddb) Nightwood Editions CAN. Dist: Harbour Publishing Co., Ltd.

Perry, S. D., et al. The Walking Dead: the Pop-Up Book. 2015. (ENG., Illus.). 5p. 65.00 *(978-1-60887-444-6(3))* Insight Editions.

Pesenti, Antonia. Rhyme Flies. 2018. (ENG., Illus.). 40p. (gr. -1 — 1). bds. 14.95 *(978-0-7148-7639-9(9))* Phaidon Pr., Inc.

Peskimo. Marvel Alphablock (an Abrams Block Book) The Marvel Cinematic Universe from a to Z. 2019. (Abrams Block Book Ser.). (ENG., Illus.). 106p. (J). (gr. -1-17). bds. 17.99 *(978-1-4197-3588-2(8)*, 1269601) Abrams, Inc.

Peter Pauper Press Staff & Zschock, Heather. Princess Bella: An Art Activity Story Book for Princesses of All Ages. Barbas, Kerren, illus. 2005. (Scratch & Sketch Trace-Along Ser.). (ENG.). 64p. (J). (gr. -1-7). spiral bd. 14.99 *(978-1-59359-972-0(2)*, 391a0eb0-45ad-4f59-bbdc-8d1bae189421) Peter Pauper Pr. Inc.

Peters, Elizabeth Anne. Worms Like to Wiggle. Yerbey, Lindsey Blake, illus. 2007. (J). *(978-0-9769737-1-3(5))* Creative Minds Pubns.

Peters, Rob, illus. Kansas City Chiefs ABCs And 1-2-3s. 2015. (ENG.). 26p. (J). bds. 18.95 *(978-0-9961944-0-2(1))* Ascend Bks., LLC.

Petrlik, Andrea, illus. Hansel & Gretel. (Flip-Up Fairy Tales Ser.). 24p. (J). 2007. (gr. -1-2). *(978-1-84643-090-9(9))* 2006. (gr. 1-2). *(978-1-904550-73-0(8))* Child's Play International Ltd.

Petruccio, Steven James. Cowboy Tattoos. 2003. (Dover Tattoos Ser.). (ENG., Illus.). 2p. (J). (gr. 1-4). 2.50 *(978-0-486-43028-7(6)*, 430286) Dover Pubns., Inc.

Pezzimenti, Grace. Busy Families: Learning to Tell Time by the Hour, 1 vol. (Math for the REAL World Ser.). (ENG., Illus.). 8p. (gr. k-1). 2010. pap. 5.15 *(978-0-8239-8912-6(7)*, 4b93df85-4e2d-4e44-939f-9796e4a6b43a) 2004. 29.95 *(978-0-8239-7627-0(0))* Rosen Publishing Group, Inc., The.

Pfeffer, Wendy. Sounds All Around. Chernyshova, Anna, illus. 2016. (Let's-Read-And-Find-Out Science 1 Ser.). (ENG.). 40p. (J). (gr. -1-3). pap. 8.99 *(978-0-06-238669-4(7)*, HarperCollins) HarperCollins Pubs.

Pfister, Marcus. Good Night, Little Rainbow Fish. 2017. (Rainbow Fish Ser.: 1). (ENG., Illus.). 12p. (J). (gr. -1-k). bds. 10.95 *(978-0-7358-4285-4(X))* North-South Bks., Inc.

—Milo & the Magical Stones. 2010. (Milo Ser.). (ENG., Illus.). 32p. (J). (gr. k-2). 17.95 *(978-0-7358-2253-5(0))* North-South Bks., Inc.

—Questions, Questions. 2014. (ENG., Illus.). 32p. (J). (gr. -1 — 1). bds. 8.95 *(978-0-7358-4170-3(5)*, 9780735841703) North-South Bks., Inc.

—The Rainbow Fish Opposites. 2013. (Rainbow Fish Ser.). (ENG., Illus.). 12p. (J). (gr. -1-1). bds. 7.95 *(978-0-7358-4146-8(2))* North-South Bks., Inc.

Phidal Publishing Staff, ed. Totally Girls: Super Sticker Book. (Illus.). 64p. (J). pap. *(978-2-7643-0190-6(1))* Phidal Publishing, Inc./Editions Phidal, Inc.

Phillips, Dee. Baby's Day. 2009. (Flip Flap Fun Bks.). (ENG.). 5p. (J). (gr. -1-k). bds. 5.95 *(978-1-84696-087-1(8)*, TickTock Books) Octopus Publishing Group GBR. Dist: Independent Pubs. Group.

—Big Zoo. 2009. (Flip Flap Fun Bks.). (ENG.). 5p. (J). (gr. -1-k). bds. 5.95 *(978-1-84696-086-4(X)*, TickTock Books) Octopus Publishing Group GBR. Dist: Independent Pubs. Group.

—Colors. 2009. (Christmas Lift the Flap Ser.). (ENG.). 10p. (J). (gr. -1-k). bds. 5.95 *(978-1-84696-966-9(2)*, TickTock Books) Octopus Publishing Group GBR. Dist: Independent Pubs. Group.

—First Addition. 2009. (Christmas Lift the Flap Ser.). (ENG.). 10p. (J). (gr. -1-k). bds. 5.95 *(978-1-84696-967-6(0)*, TickTock Books) Octopus Publishing Group GBR. Dist: Independent Pubs. Group.

—First Words. 2009. (Christmas Lift the Flap Ser.). (ENG.). 10p. (J). (gr. -1-k). bds. 5.95 *(978-1-84696-968-3(9)*, TickTock Books) Octopus Publishing Group GBR. Dist: Independent Pubs. Group.

—Numbers. 2009. (Christmas Lift the Flap Ser.). (ENG.). 10p. (J). (gr. -1-k). bds. 5.95 *(978-1-84696-969-0(7)*, TickTock Books) Octopus Publishing Group GBR. Dist: Independent Pubs. Group.

Phillips, Sara & Running Press Staff. Animals. 2003. (Illus.). 8p. (J). pap. 4.95 *(978-0-7624-1650-9(5))* Running Pr.

Phoenix International Publications. Thomas And Friends: First Look & Find. 2016. (ENG.). 16p. (J). bds. 12.99 *(978-1-4508-1139-2(6)*, 1414) Phoenix International Publications, Inc.

Phoenix International Staff, illus. Doc Mcstuffins the Doc Is in. 2014. 10p. (J). bds. 17.98 *(978-1-4508-8186-9(6)*, 1450881866) Phoenix International Publications, Inc.

PI Kids. Baby Einstein: Let's Look! First Look & Find. Kleven, Dean & Zaidi, Nadeem, illus. 2014. (ENG.). 16p. (J). bds. 12.99 *(978-1-4508-8374-0(5)*, 1642, PI Kids) Phoenix International Publications, Inc.

—Disney: Baby Animal Stories 12 Board Books. The Disney Storybook Art Team, illus. 2011. (ENG.). 120p. (J). bds., bds., bds. 16.99 *(978-1-4508-1571-0(5)*, 4194, PI Kids) Phoenix International Publications, Inc.

—Disney Baby: Head to Toe! Head, Shoulders, Knees & Toes Sound Book. 2017. (ENG., Illus.). 20p. (J). bds. 18.99 *(978-1-5037-2567-6(7)*, 2607, PI Kids) Phoenix International Publications, Inc.

—Disney: Disney Junior Jake & the Neverland Pirates Sound Book. 2014. (ENG.). 6p. (J). bds. 7.99 *(978-1-4508-7763-3(X)*, 1605, PI Kids) Phoenix International Publications, Inc.

—Disney Doc Mcstuffins: I Can Brush My Teeth! Sound Book. 2013. (ENG.). 12p. (J). bds. 14.99 *(978-1-4508-8991-9(3)*, 1677, PI Kids) Phoenix International Publications, Inc.

—Disney Frozen: Sing-Along Songs! Piano Book. 2015. (ENG.). 12p. (J). bds. 21.99 *(978-1-4508-9139-4(X)*, 1688, PI Kids) Phoenix International Publications, Inc.

—Disney Junior Minnie: Minnie's Big Day Sound Book. The Disney Storybook Art Team, illus. 2013. (ENG.). 6p. (J). bds. 7.99 *(978-1-4508-6139-7(3)*, 1519, PI Kids) Phoenix International Publications, Inc.

—Disney: Little First Look & Find: 4 Book Set. 2010. (ENG.). 18p. (J). bds., bds., bds. 21.99 *(978-1-4508-0334-2(2)*, 4181, PI Kids) Phoenix International Publications, Inc.

—Disney Pixar Cars 3: Lightning & Friends Sound Book. 2017. (ENG., Illus.). 12p. (J). bds. 14.99 *(978-1-5037-1521-9(3)*, 2308, PI Kids) Phoenix International Publications, Inc.

—Disney Pixar Finding Dory: Going Home Sound Book. The Disney Storybook Art Team, illus. 2016. (ENG.). 12p. (J). bds. 21.99 *(978-1-5037-0940-9(X)*, 2127, PI Kids) Phoenix International Publications, Inc.

—Disney Pixar Incredibles 2: Elastigirl to the Rescue! Sound Book. 2018. (ENG., Illus.). 12p. (J). bds. 14.99 *(978-1-5037-3047-2(6)*, 2733, PI Kids) Phoenix International Publications, Inc.

—Disney Pixar Incredibles 2: Look & Find. 2018. (ENG., Illus.). 24p. (J). 10.99 *(978-1-5037-3044-1(1)*, 2731, PI Kids) Phoenix International Publications, Inc.

—Disney Princess: Storytime with Belle. 2017. (ENG., Illus.). 12p. (J). bds. 21.99 *(978-1-5037-2198-2(1)*, 2505, PI Kids) Phoenix International Publications, Inc.

—Disney Sofia the First: Princess in Training Sound Book. 2013. (ENG.). 12p. (J). (gr. k-3). bds. 15.99 *(978-1-4508-6278-3(0)*, 1530, PI Kids) Phoenix International Publications, Inc.

PI, Kids. M1LF Book & Puzzle Disney Princes- O/P. 2010. (ENG.). 18p. (J). 22.98 *(978-1-4508-0802-6(6))* Phoenix International Publications, Inc.

—M1LF N Shaped Puzzle Disney Cars - O/P. 2010. (ENG.). (J). pap. *(978-1-4508-0801-9(8)*, d8ddb8bd-fa84-450f-86ae-89ebcbac1871) Phoenix International Publications, Inc.

PI Kids. Marvel Avengers: Assembled We Stand Sound Book. 2018. (ENG., Illus.). 12p. (J). bds. 14.99 *(978-1-5037-3406-7(4)*, 2828, PI Kids) Phoenix International Publications, Inc.

—Marvel: Sound Storybook Treasury. 2017. (ENG., Illus.). 34p. (J). 29.99 *(978-1-5037-1386-4(5)*, 2275, PI Kids) Phoenix International Publications, Inc.

PI, Kids. Mickey Mouse Flashlight Adventure O/P. 2011. (ENG.). 14p. (J). 8.45 net. *(978-1-4508-0564-3(7))* Phoenix International Publications, Inc.

PI Kids. Nickelodeon Blaze & the Monster Machines Monster Machine Music Sound Book. 2017. (ENG., Illus.). 12p. bds. 15.99 ***(978-1-5037-0997-3(3)***, 2145, PI Kids) Phoenix International Publications, Inc.

—Nickelodeon PAW Patrol: Ready, Set, Rescue! Sound Book. 2018. (ENG., Illus.). 12p. (J). bds. 14.99 *(978-1-5037-3118-9(9)*, 2739, PI Kids) Phoenix International Publications, Inc.

—Sesame Street: in Your Neighborhood: Listen & Learn. Kwiat, Ernie & Sesame Workshop, illus. 2014. (ENG.). 20p. (J). bds. 18.99 *(978-1-4508-7519-6(X)*, 1592, PI Kids) Phoenix International Publications, Inc.

—Sesame Street: Potty Time Songs. Berry, Bob et al, illus. 2010. (ENG.). 12p. (J). bds. 15.99 *(978-1-4508-0365-6(2)*, 1401, PI Kids) Phoenix International Publications, Inc.

—Sesame Street: Trick or Treat with Elmo Sound Book. McGee, Warner & Goldberg, Barry, illus. 2009. (ENG.). 12p. (J). bds. 14.99 *(978-1-4127-7896-1(4)*, 12530, PI Kids) Phoenix International Publications, Inc.

PI, Kids. Teenage Mutant Ninja Turtles Flashli O/P. 2013. (ENG.). 14p. (J). (gr. 1-3). 17.98 *(978-1-4127-5339-5(2)*, 0c51eeb7-c20f-4b72-a87f-c492bcc6f86f) Phoenix International Publications, Inc.

PI Kids. Thomas & Friends: On Time with Thomas. 2016. (ENG., Illus.). 12p. 21.99 ***(978-1-5037-1436-6(5)***, 2294, PI Kids) Phoenix International Publications, Inc.

PI Kids. Thomas & Friends: Thomas' Piano Book. 2014. (ENG., Illus.). 12p. (J). bds. 21.99 *(978-1-4127-4552-9(7)*, 1359) Phoenix International Publications, Inc.

—Thomas & Friends: 12 Board Books. Artful Doodlers et al, illus. 2015. (ENG.). 120p. (J). bds., bds., bds. 16.99 *(978-1-4508-9373-2(2)*, 4213, PI Kids) Phoenix International Publications, Inc.

—World of Eric Carle: Baby Animals Lift-A-Flap Sound Book. 2011. (ENG.). 10p. (J). bds. 14.99 *(978-1-4508-0508-7(6)*, 1403, PI Kids) Phoenix International Publications, Inc.

—The World of Eric Carle: Froggie Went Hopping a Pop-Up Songbook. 2014. (ENG., Illus.). 10p. (J). (gr. k-4). bds. 15.99 *(978-1-4508-6821-1(5)*, 1549, PI Kids) Phoenix International Publications, Inc.

—World of Eric Carle: Hear Bear Roar Sound Book. 2014. (ENG.). 24p. (J). 19.99 *(978-1-4508-7477-9(0)*, 1585, PI Kids) Phoenix International Publications, Inc.

Picthall, Chez. Flip Flaps Zoo. 2015. (Illus.). 18p. (J). bds. 9.99 *(978-1-907604-53-9(7))* Award Pubns. Ltd. GBR. Dist: Parkwest Pubns., Inc.

—Puppies. 2015. (Illus.). 10p. (J). bds. 7.99 *(978-1-905503-77-3(6))* Award Pubns. Ltd. GBR. Dist: Parkwest Pubns., Inc.

Picthall, Chez, creator. Flip Flaps Shapes. 2014. (ENG., Illus.). 32p. 10.00 *(978-1-906572-80-8(1))* Award Pubns. Ltd. GBR. Dist: Parkwest Pubns., Inc.

Picthall, Chez, des. Flowers. 2015. (Illus.). 10p. (J). bds. 9.99 *(978-1-907604-76-8(6))* Award Pubns. Ltd. GBR. Dist: Parkwest Pubns., Inc.

—Hearts & Stars. 2015. (Illus.). 10p. (J). bds. 9.99 *(978-1-909763-05-0(5))* Award Pubns. Ltd. GBR. Dist: Parkwest Pubns., Inc.

—Spots & Dots. 2015. (Illus.). 10p. (J). bds. 9.99 *(978-1-909763-02-9(0))* Award Pubns. Ltd. GBR. Dist: Parkwest Pubns., Inc.

Picthall, Chez & Award, Anna. Beach. 2017. (Illus.). 10p. (J). bds. 9.00 *(978-1-907604-75-1(8))* Award Pubns. Ltd. GBR. Dist: Parkwest Pubns., Inc.

Pidgeon, Jean, illus. Brush Your Teeth, Please: A Pop-Up Book. 2013. (Pop-Up Book Ser.: 2). (ENG.). 12p. (J). (gr. -1-k). 14.99 *(978-0-7944-3040-5(6)*, Studio Fun International) Printers Row Publishing Group.

Pienkowski, Jan. The First Noel: A Christmas Carousel. Pienkowski, Jan, illus. 2004. (ENG., Illus.). 5p. (J). (gr. -1-3). 14.99 *(978-0-7636-2190-2(0))* Candlewick Pr.

Pierce, Terry. Mama Loves You So. Shin, Simone, illus. 2017. (New Books for Newborns Ser.). (ENG.). 16p. (J). (gr. -1 — 1). bds. 7.99 *(978-1-4814-8159-5(2)*, Little Simon) Little Simon.

Piercy, Helen. Animation Studio. 2013. (ENG., Illus.). 32p. (J). (gr. 3-7). 22.99 *(978-0-7636-6701-6(3))* Candlewick Pr.

Piggy Toes Press. Our Ballet Recital. Maddocks, Maria, illus. 2005. (ENG.). 12p. (J). (gr. -1-3). 12.95 *(978-1-58117-425-0(X)*, Intervisual/Piggy Toes) Bendon, Inc.

Piggy Toes Press, creator. Crayola Sea Life: Counting Sea Life. 2011. (Crayola (Piggy Toes Press) Ser.). (ENG., Illus.). 6p. (gr. -1). bds. 5.95 *(978-1-61524-289-4(9)*, Intervisual/Piggy Toes) Bendon, Inc.

—Five Little Kisses. 2007. (ENG., Illus.). 10p. (J). (gr. -1-3). 9.95 *(978-1-58117-683-4(X)*, Intervisual/Piggy Toes) Bendon, Inc.

—Pop & Touch Kittens. 2008. (ENG., Illus.). 12p. (J). 10.95 *(978-1-58117-675-9(9)*, Intervisual/Piggy Toes) Bendon, Inc.

Pingry, Patricia A. Noah & His Friends. Cowman, Joseph, illus. 2017. (ENG.). 24p. (J). (gr. -1-k). bds. 9.99 *(978-1-945470-25-7(9))* Worthy Publishing.

—Story of Star Spangled Banner. 2014. (ENG., Illus.). 24p. (J). (gr. -1-1). bds. 6.99 *(978-0-8249-1930-6(0)*, Ideals Pubns.) Worthy Publishing.

Pinky's Farm: Moms & Babies. 2011. (Illus.). (J). *(978-1-58865-894-4(5))* Kidsbooks, LLC.

Piper, Watty. The Little Engine That Could. Hauman, George and Doris, illus. 2015. (Little Engine That Could Ser.). 26p. (J). (gr. -1 — 1). bds. 11.99 *(978-0-448-48731-1(4)*, Grosset & Dunlap) Penguin Young Readers Group.

—The Little Engine That Could: Loren Long Edition. Long, Loren, illus. 2005. (Little Engine That Could Ser.). 48p. (J). (gr. -1-2). 18.99 *(978-0-399-24467-4(0)*, Philomel Bks.) Penguin Young Readers Group.

Pirotta. Baby's First Animals. 2017. (J). bds. 7.98 *(978-1-946000-05-7(1))* Starry Forest Bks., Inc.

TUV

—Baby's First Sea Creatures. 2017. (Illus.). (J). bds. 7.98 *(978-1-946000-07-1(8))* Starry Forest Bks., Inc.

Pitt, Sarah. Peek a Boo! Farm. 2009. (Little Peek a Boo Bks.). (Illus.). (J). bds. 9.99 *(978-1-934650-59-2(5))* Just For Kids Pr., LLC.

Pixton, Kaaren. Indestructibles: Jungle Rumble! Chew Proof · Rip Proof · Nontoxic · 100% Washable (Book for Babies, Newborn Books, Safe to Chew) 2010. (Indestructibles Ser.). (ENG., Illus.). 12p. (J). (gr. -1 — 1). pap. 5.99 *(978-0-7611-5858-5(8),* 15858) Workman Publishing Co., Inc.

—Indestructibles: Mama & Baby! Chew Proof · Rip Proof · Nontoxic · 100% Washable (Book for Babies, Newborn Books, Safe to Chew) 2010. (Indestructibles Ser.). (ENG., Illus.). 12p. (J). (gr. -1 — 1). pap. 5.99 *(978-0-7611-5859-2(6),* 15859) Workman Publishing Co., Inc.

—Indestructibles: Plip-Plop Pond! Chew Proof · Rip Proof · Nontoxic · 100% Washable (Book for Babies, Newborn Books, Safe to Chew) 2010. (Indestructibles Ser.). (ENG., Illus.). 12p. (J). (gr. -1 — 1). pap. 5.99 *(978-0-7611-5857-8(X),* 15857) Workman Publishing Co., Inc.

Play, Laugh, & Learn All Year Long. 2007. (ENG., Illus.). 28p. (J). (gr. -1-1). 16.99 *(978-1-59069-503-6(8),* 1P1000) Studio Mouse LLC.

Poelman, Heidi. Courageous People Who Changed the World, Volume 1. Kershner, Kyle, illus. 2018. (People Who Changed the World Ser.: 1). (ENG.). 16p. (J). (gr. -1-k). bds. 9.99 *(978-1-945547-75-1(8),* 554775) Familius LLC.

—Inventors Who Changed the World. Kershner, Kyle, illus. 2018. (People Who Changed the World Ser.). (ENG.). 20p. (J). (gr. -1-3). bds. 9.99 *(978-1-64170-035-1(1),* 550035) Familius LLC.

Poitier, Anton. Flippy Floppy Farm Animals. Touliatou, Sophia, illus. 2014. 10p. (J). 12.99 *(978-1-61067-310-5(7))* Kane Miller.

—Flippy Floppy Ocean Animals. Touliatou, Sophia, illus. 2015. 10p. (J). 12.99 *(978-1-61067-346-4(8))* Kane Miller.

Pop-Up Dinosaurs. 2017. (Pop-Up Bks.). (ENG.). (J). 14.99 *(978-0-7945-3862-0(2),* Usborne) EDC Publishing.

Porcella, Teresa. Night & Day. Fatus, Sophie, illus. 2020. (ENG.). 16p. (J). (gr. -1-2). bds. 8.99 *(978-1-78285-974-1(8))* Barefoot Bks., Inc.

—Wild Week. Queralt, Carmen, illus. 2020. (ENG.). 16p. (J). (gr. -1). bds. 8.99 *(978-1-78285-975-8(6))* Barefoot Bks., Inc.

Porter, Matthew. Flowers. 2010. (ENG., Illus.). 28p. (J). (gr. -1-k). bds. 8.95 *(978-1-897476-13-0(2))* Simply Read Bks. CAN. Dist: Ingram Publisher Services.

Portis, Antoinette. Not a Box Board Book. 2011. (Not a Box Ser.). (ENG., Illus.). 28p. (J). (gr. -1 — 1). bds. 9.99 *(978-0-06-199442-5(1),* HarperFestival) HarperCollins Pubs.

Posner-Sanchez, Andrea. A Frozen Christmas (Disney Frozen) RH Disney, illus. 2015. (ENG.). 12p. (J). (gr. -1 — 1). bds. 8.99 *(978-0-7364-3479-9(8),* RH/Disney) Random Hse. Children's Bks.

—Good Night, Princess! (Disney Princess) Legramandi, Francesco & Matta, Gabriella, illus. 2012. (Pictureback(R) Ser.). (ENG.). 16p. (J). (gr. -1-2). pap. 5.99 *(978-0-7364-2851-4(8),* RH/Disney) Random Hse. Children's Bks.

—I Am Ariel (Disney Princess) Batson, Alan, illus. 2018. (Little Golden Book Ser.). (ENG.). 24p. (J). (-k). 5.99 *(978-0-7364-3852-0(1),* Golden/Disney) Random Hse. Children's Bks.

Potter, Beatrix. Hello, Peter! 2012. (Peter Rabbit Ser.). (ENG.). 10p. (J). (gr. -1-k). bds. 6.99 *(978-0-7232-6744-7(8),* Warne) Penguin Young Readers Group.

—Peter Rabbit Book & Toy. 2006. (Peter Rabbit Ser.). (ENG., Illus.). 70p. (J). (gr. -1 — 1). 17.99 *(978-0-7232-5356-3(0),* Warne) Penguin Young Readers Group.

—Peter Rabbit Finger Puppet Book. 2011. (Peter Rabbit Ser.). (ENG., Illus.). 14p. (J). (gr. -1 — 1). bds. 12.99 *(978-0-7232-6639-6(5),* Warne) Penguin Young Readers Group.

—Peter Rabbit Large Shaped Board Book. 2008. (Peter Rabbit Ser.). (ENG., Illus.). 12p. (J). (gr. -1 — 1). bds. 8.99 *(978-0-7232-5956-5(9),* Warne) Penguin Young Readers Group.

—Peter Rabbit Lift-the-Flap Words, Colors, & Numbers. 2007. (Potter Ser.). (ENG., Illus.). 12p. (J). (gr. -1-18). 14.99 *(978-0-7232-5828-5(7),* Warne) Penguin Publishing Group.

—Tickle, Tickle, Peter! A First Touch-And-Feel Book. 2012. (Peter Rabbit Ser.). (ENG.). 10p. (J). (gr. -1 — 1). bds. 9.99 *(978-0-7232-6750-8(2),* Warne) Penguin Young Readers Group.

Powell, Richard. Quiet as a Mouse: A Moving Picture Storybook. Hendra, Sue, illus. 2003. 16p. (J). 7.95 *(978-1-58925-678-1(6))* Tiger Tales.

—Whose Hat Is That? Martin Larrañaga, Ana, illus. 2004. (Ana's Mini Movers Ser.). 12p. (J). 5.95 *(978-1-58925-740-5(5))* Tiger Tales.

Powell-Tuck, Maudie. A Very Merry Christmas. Guile, Gill, illus. 2014. (ENG.). 22p. (J). (gr. -1-k). bds. 8.99 *(978-1-58925-560-9(7))* Tiger Tales.

Powers, Mark. I Want to Be a Reader! Montag, Maria, illus. 2017. (ENG.). 14p. (J). (— 1). bds. 7.99 *(978-1-936669-55-4(2))* Blue Manatee Press.

Prasadam, Smriti. Hello, Animals! Bolam, Emily, illus. 2010. (ENG.). 10p. (J). (gr. -1-k). bds. 6.99 *(978-1-58925-861-7(4))* Tiger Tales.

—Hello, Bugs! Bolam, Emily, illus. 2010. (ENG.). 10p. (J). (gr. -1-k). bds. 6.99 *(978-1-58925-862-4(2))* Tiger Tales.

Prasadam, Smriti & Mitchell, Melanie. Peepo Paw Printes. 2008. (Illus.). 14p. (J). bds. 13.95 *(978-0-7475-9535-9(6))* Bloomsbury Publishing Plc GBR. Dist: Independent Pubs. Group.

Pratt, Leonie. Sticker Dolly Dressing Ballerinas. Baggott, Stella & Leyhane, Vici, illus. 2007. (Usborne Activities Ser.). 24p. (J). (gr. -1-3). pap. 8.99 *(978-0-7945-1392-4(1),* Usborne) EDC Publishing.

—Sticker Dolly Dressing Fairies. Baggott, Stella & Leyhane, Vici, illus. 2007. (Usborne Activities Ser.). 24p. (J). (gr. -1-3). pap. 8.99 *(978-0-7945-1391-7(3),* Usborne) EDC Publishing.

Precious Moments: Happy Harvest, 1 vol. 2016. (Precious Moments Ser.). (ENG., Illus.). 32p. (J). bds. 9.99 *(978-0-7180-3241-8(1),* Tommy Nelson) Nelson, Thomas Inc.

Press, Pikachu. Super Pokemon Pop-Up: White Kyurem. 2013. (ENG.). 5p. (J). (gr. 3-6). 9.99 *(978-1-60438-180-1(9))* Pokemon, USA, Inc.

Preston-Gannon, Frann. Deep Deep Sea. 2014. (ENG., Illus.). 14p. (J). (-k). bds. 7.99 *(978-1-84365-268-7(4),* Pavilion Children's Books) Pavilion Bks. GBR. Dist: HarperCollins Pubs.

Price, Dana Lynn. G Is for Gorilla. 2018. (ENG., Illus.). 10p. (J). bds. 14.95 *(978-1-63177-670-0(3))* Amplify Publishing Group.

Price, Denise D. Freedom Trail Pop up Book of Boston. 2015. (ENG., Illus.). 17p. (J). 29.99 *(978-0-9907781-0-3(X))* White Dharma Ltd.

Price, Mathew. Cachorro. Goldman, Judy, tr. Kemp, Moira, illus. 2010. (SPA & ENG.). 10p. bds. 5.99 *(978-1-935021-64-3(8))* Price, Mathew Ltd.

—Gatito. Goldman, Judy, tr. Kemp, Moira, illus. 2010. (SPA & ENG.). 10p. bds. 5.99 *(978-1-935021-99-5(0))* Price, Mathew Ltd.

Price, Olivia. All Aboard Noah's Ark: A Touch & Feel Book. Mitchell, Melanie, illus. 2008. (ENG.). 12p. (J). (gr. -1). 12.95 *(978-1-58117-778-7(X),* Intervisual/Piggy Toes) Bendon, Inc.

—Bible Stories: A Touch & Feel Book. Mitchell, Melanie, illus. 2008. (ENG.). 12p. (J). (gr. -1). 12.95 *(978-1-58117-802-9(6),* Intervisual/Piggy Toes) Bendon, Inc.

Priddy, Roger. Alphaprints: ABC. 2013. (Alphaprints Ser.). (ENG.). 26p. (J). (gr. -1 — 1). bds. 9.99 *(978-0-312-51646-8(0),* 900121769) St. Martin's Pr.

—Alphaprints First Words. 2018. (Alphaprints Ser.). (ENG., Illus.). 14p. (J). bds. 9.99 *(978-0-312-52812-6(4),* 900195209) St. Martin's Pr.

—Alphaprints: Gobble Gobble: Touch & Feel. 2016. (Alphaprints Ser.). (ENG.). 10p. (J). bds. 7.99 *(978-0-312-52057-1(3),* 900160015) St. Martin's Pr.

—Alphaprints: Ho, Ho, Ho! A Touch-And-Feel Book. 2015. (Alphaprints Ser.). (ENG., Illus.). 10p. (J). (gr. -1 — 1). bds. 7.99 *(978-0-312-51896-7(X),* 900149123) St. Martin's Pr.

—Alphaprints: Sweet Heart: A Touch-And-Feel Book. 2015. (Alphaprints Ser.). (ENG., Illus.). 10p. (J). (gr. -1 — 1). bds. 7.99 *(978-0-312-51913-1(3),* 900149109) St. Martin's Pr.

—Alphaprints: Tweet! Tweet! A Touch-And-Feel Book. 2015. (Alphaprints Ser.). (ENG.). 10p. (J). (gr. -1 — 1). bds. 7.99 *(978-0-312-51781-6(5),* 900141262) St. Martin's Pr.

—Animals. 2005. (ENG.). 12p. (J). bds. 0.97 *(978-0-312-49610-4(9),* Priddy Bks.) St. Martin's Pr.

—Baby's First Bible Boxed Set: The Story of Moses, the Story of Jesus, Noah's Ark, & Adam & Eve, Set. 2012. (Bible Stories Ser.). (ENG., Illus.). (J). (gr. -1 — 1). bds., bds., bds. 15.99 *(978-0-312-51458-7(1),* 900084801) St. Martin's Pr.

—Bilingual Bright Baby First Words / Primeras Palabras: Primeras Palabras. 2007. (Bright Baby Ser.). (SPA., Illus.). 26p. (J). (gr. -1 — 1). bds. 5.99 *(978-0-312-50300-0(8),* 900051446) St. Martin's Pr.

—Bilingual Bright Baby Trucks / Camiones: English-Spanish Bilingual. 2007. (Bright Baby Ser.). (SPA., Illus.). 26p. (J). (gr. -1 — 1). bds. 6.99 *(978-0-312-50299-7(0),* 900051445) St. Martin's Pr.

—Bright Baby Touch & Feel at the Zoo. 2006. (Bright Baby Touch & Feel Ser.). (ENG., Illus.). 10p. (J). (gr. -1 — 1). bds. 5.99 *(978-0-312-49857-3(8),* 900041828) St. Martin's Pr.

—Bright Baby Touch & Feel Baby Animals. 2006. (Bright Baby Touch & Feel Ser.). (ENG., Illus.). 10p. (J). (gr. -1 — 1). bds. 5.99 *(978-0-312-49858-0(6),* 900041831) St. Martin's Pr.

—Bright Baby Touch & Feel: Bilingual Numbers / Números: English-Spanish Bilingual. 2008. (Bright Baby Touch & Feel Ser.). (SPA., Illus.). 10p. (J). (gr. -1 — 1). bds. 5.99 *(978-0-312-50215-7(X),* 900051282) St. Martin's Pr.

—Bright Baby Touch & Feel: Bilingual Words / Palabras: English-Spanish Bilingual. 2008. (Bright Baby Touch & Feel Ser.). (SPA., Illus.). 10p. (J). (gr. -1 — 1). bds. 5.99 *(978-0-312-50216-4(8),* 900051283) St. Martin's Pr.

—Bright Baby Touch & Feel Boxed Set: On the Farm, Baby Animals, at the Zoo & Perfect Pets, Set. 2006. (Bright Baby Touch & Feel Ser.). (ENG.). (J). (gr. -1 — 1). 23.96 *(978-0-312-49872-6(1),* 900044229) St. Martin's Pr.

—Bright Baby Touch & Feel Colors. 2008. (Bright Baby Touch & Feel Ser.). (ENG.). 10p. (J). (gr. -1 — 1). bds. 4.99 *(978-0-312-50425-0(X),* 900054692) St. Martin's Pr.

—Bright Baby Touch & Feel Easter. 2012. (Bright Baby Touch & Feel Ser.). (ENG., Illus.). 10p. (J). (gr. -1 — 1). bds. 4.95 *(978-0-312-51375-7(5),* 900082318) St. Martin's Pr.

—Bright Baby Touch & Feel Hanukkah. 2011. (Bright Baby Touch & Feel Ser.). (ENG., Illus.). 10p. (J). (gr. -1 — 1). bds. 5.99 *(978-0-312-51338-2(0),* 900078357) St. Martin's Pr.

—Bright Baby Touch & Feel Merry Christmas. 2009. (Bright Baby Touch & Feel Ser.). (ENG.). 10p. (J). (gr. -1 — 1). bds. 5.99 *(978-0-312-50652-0(X),* 900063066) St. Martin's Pr.

—Bright Baby Touch & Feel Numbers. 2008. (Bright Baby Touch & Feel Ser.). (ENG.). 10p. (J). (gr. -1 — 1). bds. 5.99 *(978-0-312-50423-6(3),* 900054925) St. Martin's Pr.

—Bright Baby Touch & Feel on the Farm. 2006. (Bright Baby Touch & Feel Ser.). (ENG., Illus.). 10p. (J). (gr. -1 — 1). bds. 5.99 *(978-0-312-49859-7(4),* 900041830) St. Martin's Pr.

—Bright Baby Touch & Feel Perfect Pets. 2006. (Bright Baby Touch & Feel Ser.). (ENG., Illus.). 10p. (J). (gr. -1 — 1). bds. 4.95 *(978-0-312-49860-3(8),* 900041829) St. Martin's Pr.

—Bright Baby Touch & Feel Slipcase: Includes Words, Colors, Numbers, & Shapes. 2008. (Bright Baby Touch & Feel Ser.). (ENG.). 12p. (J). (gr. -1 — 1). bds., bds., bds. 19.99 *(978-0-312-50428-1(4),* 900055418) St. Martin's Pr.

—Bright Baby Touch & Feel Spring. 2011. (Bright Baby Touch & Feel Ser.). (ENG., Illus.). 10p. (J). (gr. -1 — 1). bds. 4.95 *(978-0-312-51006-0(3),* 900073555) St. Martin's Pr.

—Bright Baby Touch & Feel Winter. 2011. (Bright Baby Touch & Feel Ser.). (ENG., Illus.). 10p. (J). (gr. -1 — 1). bds. 5.99 *(978-0-312-50976-7(6),* 900078359) St. Martin's Pr.

—Bright Baby Touch & Feel Words. 2008. (Bright Baby Touch & Feel Ser.). (ENG.). 10p. (J). (gr. -1 — 1). bds. 4.99 *(978-0-312-50424-3(1),* 900054924) St. Martin's Pr.

—Bunny & Friends Touch & Feel. 2017. (Baby Touch & Feel Ser.). (ENG., Illus.). 10p. (J). bds. 8.99 *(978-0-312-52200-1(2),* 900171719) St. Martin's Pr.

—Carry-Along Tab Book: My Easter Basket. 2019. (Lift-The-Flap Tab Bks.). (ENG., Illus.). 10p. (J). bds. 8.99 *(978-0-312-52791-4(8),* 900194740) St. Martin's Pr.

—Changing Picture Book: Dinosaur Galore! 2018. (Changing Picture Ser.). (ENG., Illus.). 10p. (J). bds. 9.99 *(978-0-312-52658-0(X),* 900185564) St. Martin's Pr.

—Changing Picture Book: Red Car, Green Car: A Changing Colors Book. 2017. (Changing Picture Ser.). (ENG., Illus.). 10p. (J). bds. 9.99 *(978-0-312-52161-5(8),* 900170060) St. Martin's Pr.

—Duckling & Friends Touch & Feel. 2017. (Baby Touch & Feel Ser.). (ENG., Illus.). 10p. (J). bds. 7.99 *(978-0-312-52201-8(0),* 900171718) St. Martin's Pr.

—Early Learning Fun: Match It! Includes Wipe-Clean Pen. 2015. (Early Learning Fun Ser.). (ENG.). 56p. (J). (gr. k-3). spiral bd. 12.99 *(978-0-312-51802-8(1),* 900141280) St. Martin's Pr.

—Easter Croc: Full of Pop-Up Surprises! 2018. (ENG., Illus.). 10p. (J). bds. 9.99 *(978-0-312-52558-3(3),* 900180422) St. Martin's Pr.

—First 100 Animals. 2011. (First 100 Ser.). (ENG., Illus.). 24p. (J). (gr. -1 — 1). bds. 5.99 *(978-0-312-51079-4(9),* 900075561) St. Martin's Pr.

—First 100 Animals Lift-The-Flap: Over 50 Fun Flaps to Lift & Learn. 2014. (First 100 Ser.). (ENG., Illus.). 14p. (J). (gr. -1 — 1). bds. 9.99 *(978-0-312-51752-6(1),* 900136764) St. Martin's Pr.

—First 100 Christmas Words. 2018. (First 100 Ser.). (ENG., Illus.). 24p. (J). bds. 6.99 *(978-0-312-52768-6(3),* 900191839) St. Martin's Pr.

—First 100 Padded: Numbers, Colors, Shapes. 2011. (First 100 Ser.). (ENG., Illus.). 24p. (J). (gr. -1 — 1). bds. 5.99 *(978-0-312-51081-7(0),* 900075562) St. Martin's Pr.

—First 100 Trucks: And Things That Go. 2011. (First 100 Ser.). (ENG., Illus.). 24p. (J). (gr. -1 — 1). bds. 5.99 *(978-0-312-51080-0(2),* 900075563) St. Martin's Pr.

—First 100 Trucks & Things That Go Lift-The-Flap: Over 50 Fun Flaps to Lift & Learn. 2015. (First 100 Ser.). (ENG., Illus.). 14p. (J). (gr. -1 — 1). bds. 9.99 *(978-0-312-51782-3(3),* 900141264) St. Martin's Pr.

—First 100 Words: A Padded Board Book. 2011. (First 100 Ser.). (ENG., Illus.). 24p. (J). (— 1). bds. 5.99 *(978-0-312-51078-7(0),* 900075564) St. Martin's Pr.

—Funny Faces: Easter Parade: With Googly Eyes. 2015. (Funny Faces Ser.). (ENG.). 10p. (J). (gr. -1-1). bds. 8.99 *(978-0-312-51785-4(8),* 900141263) St. Martin's Pr.

—Funny Faces Halloween Jack. 2012. (Funny Faces Ser.). (ENG., Illus.). 10p. (J). (gr. -1-1). bds. 8.99 *(978-0-312-51554-6(5),* 900097397) St. Martin's Pr.

—Funny Faces Santa Claus: With Lights & Sound. 2012. (Funny Faces Ser.). (ENG., Illus.). 10p. (J). (gr. -1-1). bds. 8.99 *(978-0-312-51558-4(8),* 900097399) St. Martin's Pr.

—Giraffe Is Lost: An Animal Search-And-find Book. 2019. (Search & Find Ser.). (ENG., Illus.). 10p. (J). bds. 9.99 *(978-0-312-52789-1(6),* 900194735) St. Martin's Pr.

—Hello Baby: Baby Grip: A High Contrast Book. 2012. (Hello Baby Ser.). (ENG., Illus.). 6p. (J). (gr. -1 — 1). bds. 7.99 *(978-0-312-51505-8(7),* 900096057) St. Martin's Pr.

—Hello Baby: Words: A High-Contrast Board Book. 2013. (Hello Baby Ser.). (ENG., Illus.). 16p. (J). (gr. -1 — 1). bds. 5.99 *(978-0-312-51598-0(7),* 900118661) St. Martin's Pr.

—Let's Pretend Builders Tool Kit: With Book & Puzzle Pieces. 2009. (Let's Pretend Ser.). (ENG.). 6p. (J). (gr. -1 — 1). bds. 14.99 *(978-0-312-50490-8(X),* 900054715) St. Martin's Pr.

—Lift the Flap: Fairy Tales: Search for Your Favorite Fairytale Characters. 2016. (Can You Find Me? Ser.). (ENG.). 16p. (J). bds. 9.99 *(978-0-312-52059-5(X),* 900160051) St. Martin's Pr.

—Lift-The-Flap Tab: Colors, Numbers, Shapes. 2018. (Lift-The-Flap Tab Bks.). (ENG., Illus.). 16p. (J). bds. 8.99 *(978-0-312-52811-9(6),* 900195208) St. Martin's Pr.

—Lift-The-Flap Tab: on the Go. 2014. (Lift-The-Flap Tab Bks.). (ENG., Illus.). 16p. (J). (gr. -1 — 1). bds. 8.99 *(978-0-312-51731-1(9),* 900132617) St. Martin's Pr.

—Lift-The-Flap Tab: Santa's Workshop. 2015. (Lift-The-Flap Tab Bks.). (ENG., Illus.). 16p. (J). (gr. -1 — 1). bds. 8.99 *(978-0-312-51898-1(6),* 900149125) St. Martin's Pr.

—Little Friends: All You Need Is Love: A Lift the Flaps Book. 2017. (Little Friends Ser.). (ENG., Illus.). 10p. (J). bds. 8.99 *(978-0-312-52147-9(2),* 900178605) St. Martin's Pr.

—Little Friends: Home Sweet Home: A Lift-The-Flap Book. 2014. (Little Friends Ser.). (ENG.). 10p. (J). (gr. -1 — 1). bds. 6.99 *(978-0-312-51679-6(7),* 900126035) St. Martin's Pr.

—Little Friends: Trick or Treat: A Lift-The-flap Book. 2017. (Little Friends Ser.). (ENG., Illus.). 10p. (J). bds. 8.99 *(978-0-312-52205-6(3),* 900171722) St. Martin's Pr.

—Maze Book: Follow Me Halloween. 2018. (Finger Mazes Ser.). (ENG., Illus.). 14p. (J). bds. 7.99 *(978-0-312-52723-5(3),* 900189644) St. Martin's Pr.

—Maze Book: Follow Me Santa. 2018. (Finger Mazes Ser.). (ENG., Illus.). 14p. (J). bds. 8.99 *(978-0-312-52742-6(X),* 900189899) St. Martin's Pr.

—Maze Book: Follow My Heart. 2018. (Follow Me Maze Bks.). (ENG., Illus.). 14p. (J). bds. 7.99 *(978-0-312-52763-1(2),* 900190145) St. Martin's Pr.

—Mini Tab: Easter. 2017. (Mini Tab Ser.). (ENG., Illus.). 16p. (J). bds. 5.99 *(978-0-312-52157-8(X),* 900169993) St. Martin's Pr.

—Mix & Match: Halloween. 2016. (Mix & Match Ser.). (ENG., Illus.). 12p. (J). bds. 5.99 *(978-0-312-52021-2(2),* 900156774) St. Martin's Pr.

—Mo Chéad Foclóir. Ó Murchadha, Niall, tr. 2013. (GLE.). 10p. (J). 20.00 *(978-0-7171-5807-2(1))* M.H. Gill & Co. U. C. IRL. Dist: Dufour Editions, Inc.

—My Big Animal Book. 2011. (My Big Board Bks.). (ENG., Illus.). 10p. (J). (gr. -1 — 1). bds. 8.99 *(978-0-312-51107-4(8),* 900075565) St. Martin's Pr.

—My Big Train Book. 2015. (My Big Board Bks.). (ENG.). 10p. (J). (gr. -1 — 1). bds. 7.99 *(978-0-312-51943-8(5),* 900150606) St. Martin's Pr.

—My Big Truck Book. 2011. (My Big Board Bks.). (ENG., Illus.). 10p. (J). (gr. -1 — 1). bds. 8.99 *(978-0-312-51106-7(X),* 900075566) St. Martin's Pr.

—Picture Fit Board Books: a Caboodle of Cuddles. 2018. (Picture Fit Ser.: 1). (ENG., Illus.). 14p. (J). bds. 8.99 *(978-0-312-52762-4(4),* 900190126) St. Martin's Pr.

—Playtown: A Lift-The-Flap Book. 2014. (Playtown Ser.). (ENG.). 16p. (J). (gr. -1-k). bds. 14.99 *(978-0-312-51737-3(8),* 900132631) St. Martin's Pr.

—Playtown: Airport (revised Edition) A Lift-The-Flap Book. rev. ed. 2016. (Playtown Ser.). (ENG., Illus.). 14p. (J). bds. 12.99 *(978-0-312-52170-7(7),* 900169732) St. Martin's Pr.

—Playtown: Emergency: A Lift-The-Flap Book. 2016. (Playtown Ser.). (ENG., Illus.). 14p. (J). bds. 12.99 *(978-0-312-52009-0(3),* 900156775) St. Martin's Pr.

—Pop-Up Dinosaurs: A Pop-Up Book to Get Your Jaws Into. 2012. (Priddy Pop-Up Ser.). (ENG., Illus.). 10p. (J). (gr. -1-k). 9.99 *(978-0-312-51511-9(1),* 900096092) St. Martin's Pr.

—Pop-Up Surprise Haunted House: A Seriously Spooky Pop-Up Book. 2012. (Priddy Pop-Up Ser.). (ENG., Illus.). 10p. (J). (gr. -1-1). 7.99 *(978-0-312-51471-6(9),* 900085037) St. Martin's Pr.

—See, Touch, Feel: A First Sensory Book. 2018. (See, Touch, Feel Ser.). (ENG., Illus.). 16p. (J). bds. 12.99 *(978-0-312-52759-4(4),* 900189944) St. Martin's Pr.

—Shiny Shapes: Easter Surprise. 2017. (Shiny Shapes Ser.). (ENG., Illus.). 10p. (J). bds. 7.99 *(978-0-312-52159-2(6),* 900169935) St. Martin's Pr.

—Shiny Shapes: Hooray for Thanksgiving! 2018. (Shiny Shapes Ser.). (ENG., Illus.). 10p. (J). bds. 7.99 *(978-0-312-52724-2(1),* 900189781) St. Martin's Pr.

—Shiny Shapes: Love You Always. 2016. (Shiny Shapes Ser.). (ENG.). 10p. (J). bds. 7.99 *(978-0-312-52053-3(0),* 900161214) St. Martin's Pr.

—Simple First Words Let's Talk. 2011. (Simple First Words Ser.). (ENG.). 12p. (J). (gr. -1 — 1). bds. 14.95 *(978-0-312-51421-1(2),* 900081754) St. Martin's Pr.

—Slide & Find Spooky. 2011. (Slide & Find Ser.). (ENG., Illus.). 8p. (J). (— 1). bds. 8.99 *(978-0-312-51095-4(0),* 900076055) St. Martin's Pr.

—Smart Kids Dinosaurs: With More Than 30 Stickers. 2018. (Smart Kids Ser.). (ENG., Illus.). 24p. (J). pap. 5.99 *(978-0-312-50605-6(8),* 900178657) St. Martin's Pr.

—Soft to Touch: First 100 Numbers. 2017. (First 100 Ser.). (ENG., Illus.). 24p. (J). bds. 5.99 *(978-0-312-52282-7(7),* 900175469) St. Martin's Pr.

—What's in My House? A Slide & Find Book. 2018. (What's in My? Ser.). (ENG., Illus.). 10p. (J). bds. 12.99 *(978-0-312-52557-6(5),* 900180421) St. Martin's Pr.

—What's in My Truck? A Slide & Find Book. 2018. (What's in My? Ser.). (ENG., Illus.). 10p. (J). bds. 12.99 *(978-0-312-52556-9(7),* 900180420) St. Martin's Pr.

—Where Does Pig Live? A Barnyard Search-And-find Book. 2018. (Search & Find Ser.). (ENG., Illus.). 10p. (J). bds. 9.99 *(978-0-312-52545-3(1),* 900180399) St. Martin's Pr.

—Wipe Clean: First Words. 2012. (Wipe Clean Ser.). (ENG., Illus.). 26p. (J). (gr. -1-1). bds. 8.95 *(978-0-312-51393-1(3),* 900082333) St. Martin's Pr.

—Wipe Clean: Starting School. 2015. (Wipe Clean Ser.). (ENG.). 26p. (J). (gr. -1-1). bds. 8.99 *(978-0-312-51790-8(4),* 900141279) St. Martin's Pr.

Princess Teatime, 5 vols. 2005. (Illus.). (J). *(978-0-7868-3663-5(6)); (978-0-7868-3668-0(7)); (978-0-7868-3667-3(9)); (978-0-7868-3664-2(4)); (978-0-7868-3665-9(2))* Disney Pr.

Pristash, Nicole. Purple. 2010. (My Colorful World Ser.). (ENG., Illus.). 16p. (J). bds. 11.95 *(978-1-4358-9318-4(2),* PowerKids Pr.) Rosen Publishing Group, Inc., The.

Provencher, Devon. The Gospel. Provencher, Jessica, illus. 2020. (Big Theology for Little Hearts Ser.). (ENG.). 22p. (J). bds. 9.99 *(978-1-4335-6525-0(0))* Crossway.

Pruett, Jason. Seek & Find: Book of Mormon Stories (Board Book) 2017. (ENG., Illus.). (gr. -1). bds. 12.99 *(978-1-4621-2099-4(7))* Cedar Fort, Inc./CFI Distribution.

Pruett, Joshua. DreamWorks Dragons: Adventures with Dragons: A Pop-Up History. 2019. (ENG.). 12p. (J). 65.00 *(978-1-60887-847-5(3))* Insight Editions.

Prunier, James & Matthews, Sarah. Dinosaurs. Prunier, James & Galeron, Henri, illus. 2012. (My First Discoveries Ser.: 3). (ENG.). 36p. (J). (gr. -1-k). 19.99 *(978-1-85103-379-9(3))* Moonlight Publishing, Ltd. GBR. Dist: Independent Pubs. Group.

Publications International Ltd. Staff. Baby's Day. 2010. 8p. (J). bds. 9.98 *(978-1-60553-401-5(3),* PIL Kids) Publications International, Ltd.

—Chuggington Little Lift & Listen. 2011. 12p. (J). bds. 10.98 *(978-1-4508-0504-9(3))* Phoenix International Publications, Inc.

—Disney Adventure Look & Find. 2013. (gr. 1-3). 7.98 *(978-1-4127-7146-7(3),* 1412771463) Phoenix International Publications, Inc.

—Disney Princess PNO BK. 2010. 10p. (J). 16.98 *(978-1-4127-8997-4(4))* Phoenix International Publications, Inc.

—Disney Princess Songs. 2013. 12p. (J). (gr. k-4). bds. 21.99 *(978-1-4127-8016-2(0),* fdc578c6-8169-40c1-acde-e3e9449607c7) Phoenix International Publications, Inc.

—Dora PNO BK Follow Music. 2008. 10p. (J). 16.98 *(978-1-4127-8996-7(6),* PIL Kids) Publications International, Ltd.

—Elmo PNO BK. 2008. 10p. (J). 16.98 *(978-1-4127-8995-0(8))* Phoenix International Publications, Inc.

—First Look & Find Wonder Pets. 2008. 16p. (J). bds. 9.98 *(978-1-4127-9394-0(7),* PIL Kids) Publications International, Ltd.

—For the Love of Hockey BK Brick. 2008. 320p. 12.98 *(978-1-4127-1535-5(0),* PIL Kids) Publications International, Ltd.

—Giant Look & Find Disney Pixar Cars. 2008. 24p. (J). 15.98 *(978-1-4127-8967-7(2),* PIL Kids) Publications International, Ltd.

—Giant Look & Find Elmo. 2008. 24p. (J). 15.98 *(978-1-4127-8975-2(3),* PIL Kids) Publications International, Ltd.

—Interactive Sound Surfs Up. 2007. 24p. (J). 16.98 *(978-1-4127-6829-0(2),* PIL Kids) Publications International, Ltd.

—Interactive Sound Transformers. 2007. 24p. (J). 16.98 *(978-1-4127-6797-2(0),* PIL Kids) Publications International, Ltd.

—Little English Spanish Sound Diego. 2007. 12p. (J). 10.98 *(978-1-4127-6738-5(5))* Publications International, Ltd.

—Little Lift & Listen Sound Dora Go to School. 2007. 12p. (J). 10.98 *(978-1-4127-8575-4(8)*, PIL Kids) Publications International, Ltd.
—Little Sound Barbie Fairytopia. 2007. 12p. (J). 10.98 *(978-1-4127-6770-5(9)*, PIL Kids) Publications International, Ltd.
—Little Sound Mickey Mouse Club. 2007. 10p. (J). 10.98 *(978-1-4127-6711-8(3))* Phoenix International Publications, Inc.
—Look & Find Ratatouille. 2007. 24p. (J). 7.10 *(978-1-4127-6837-5(3)*, PIL Kids) Publications International, Ltd.
—Look & Find Transformers. 2007. 24p. (J). 7.10 *(978-1-4127-6817-7(9)*, PIL Kids) Publications International, Ltd.
—Mickey Mouse Club First Look & Find. 2008. 18p. (J). bds. 9.98 *(978-1-4127-7455-0(1))* Phoenix International Publications, Inc.
—Mickey Mouse Club House Little Pop up Sd. 2008. 8p. (J). 10.50 *(978-1-4127-8869-4(2))* Phoenix International Publications, Inc.
—My 1St Libraries Disney Princess. 2011. 12p. 12.98 *(978-1-4508-1303-7(8))* Publications International, Ltd.
—My 1St Libraries Winnie the Pooh. 2011. 10p. (J). bds. 13.98 *(978-1-4508-0870-5(0))* Phoenix International Publications, Inc.
—My Little Pony Magic Friendship Songs. 2013. 10p. (J). (gr. k-4). bds. 10.99 *(978-1-4508-6352-0(3)*, e11c6844-0b70-40b4-a490-b56ef2e7ed9f) Phoenix International Publications, Inc.
—Nemo First Look & Find. 2007. 18p. (J). 9.98 *(978-1-4127-6838-2(1))* Phoenix International Publications, Inc.
—Open Season Little Sound Bk. 2006. 12p. (J). 10.50 *(978-1-4127-6378-3(9)*, PIL Kids) Publications International, Ltd.
—Sound Pooh Clues. 2007. 14p. (J). 16.98 *(978-1-4127-6201-4(4))* Publications International, Ltd.
—Steering Wheel Sound Cars. 2007. 12p. (J). 17.98 *(978-1-4127-5884-0(X))* Phoenix International Publications, Inc.
—Steering Wheel Sound Elmo Away We Go. 2008. 12p. (J). bds. 17.98 *(978-1-4127-8948-6(6)*, PIL Kids) Publications International, Ltd.
—Wall E Large Sound BK. 2008. 24p. (J). 17.98 *(978-1-4127-8991-2(5)*, PIL Kids) Publications International, Ltd.
Publications International Ltd. Staff, creator. Disney Pixar Cars Tour the Town. 2007. (Steering Wheel Sound Ser.). (Illus.). (gr. -1-k). 16.98 *(978-1-4127-8804-5(8))* Publications International, Ltd.
—Disney Princess: Musical Pop-up Treasury. 2007. (Disney Princess Ser.). (Illus.). (J). (gr. -1-3). 15.98 *(978-1-4127-7431-4(4))* Publications International, Ltd.
—Dora the Explorer Laugh-along Sing-along. 2007. (Play-A-Song Ser.). (Illus.). bds. 15.98 *(978-1-4127-7417-8(9))* Publications International, Ltd.
—Dora the Explorer Learn to Write. 2007. (Play-A-Sound Bks.). (Illus.). (J). (gr. -1-3). 19.98 *(978-1-4127-6659-3(1))* Publications International, Ltd.
—Get Ready for Fun! 2007. (Sesame Street Music Works). (Illus.). 6p. (J). bds. 9.98 *(978-1-4127-8746-8(7))* Publications International, Ltd.
—Hello Elmo! 2007. (Sesame Street Ser.). (Illus.). 10p. (J). (gr. -1-3). bds. 19.98 *(978-1-4127-8724-6(6))* Publications International, Ltd.
—Help along Sing a Song. 2007. (Play-A-Song Ser.). (Illus.). bds. 15.98 *(978-1-4127-7419-2(5))* Publications International, Ltd.
—Magic Songs. 2007. (Play-A-Song Ser.). (Illus.). (gr. -1-k). bds. 15.98 *(978-1-4127-8813-7(7))* Publications International, Ltd.
—Pooh Surprise Sing-along. 2007. (Surprise Mirror Book Ser.). (Illus.). (gr. -1-k). 15.98 *(978-1-4127-7418-5(7))* Publications International, Ltd.
Publications International Ltd. Staff, ed. Baby Animals (Listen & Learn Sound Book) 2011. 19p. (J). bds. 11.98 *(978-1-4508-1440-9(9))* Phoenix International Publications, Inc.
—Baby Einstein. 2007. (J). 5.98 *(978-1-4127-8481-8(6))* Phoenix International Publications, Inc.
—Baby Einstein. 2007. (J). 10.98 *(978-1-4127-7467-3(5))* Publications International, Ltd.
—Baby Faces. 2011. 10p. (J). bds. 12.98 *(978-1-4508-1404-1(2))* Phoenix International Publications, Inc.
—A Baby Is Born. 2011. (ENG.). 22p. (J). bds. *(978-1-4508-1865-0(X)*, 0e517b46-6fbd-4311-a3ab-15d5a6cf31b8) Phoenix International Publications, Inc.
—Baby's 123. 2010. (Illus.). 18p. (J). bds. 7.98 *(978-1-60553-960-7(0))* Publications International, Ltd.
—Baby's ABC. 2010. 18p. (J). bds. 7.98 *(978-1-60553-961-4(9))* Publications International, Ltd.
—Baby's Shapes. 2010. 18p. (J). bds. 7.98 *(978-1-60553-963-8(5))*; (Illus.). bds. 7.98 *(978-1-60553-965-2(1))* Phoenix International Publications, Inc.
—Barney: I Love You Songs. 2011. 14p. (J). bds. 22.98 *(978-1-4508-1249-8(X))* Publications International, Ltd.
—Barney: Let's Play Together. 2011. (Illus.). 10p. (J). bds. 8.98 *(978-1-4508-0859-0(X))* Publications International, Ltd.
—Barney: Music All Around. 2008. (J). bds. 10.98 *(978-1-4127-9990-4(2))* Publications International, Ltd.
—Barney & Friends Book Box & Plush. 2011. 8p. (J). 14.98 *(978-1-4508-0854-5(9))* Publications International, Ltd.
—The Big Fix-It Day. 2010. 14p. (J). 19.98 *(978-1-60553-110-6(3)*, PIL Kids) Publications International, Ltd.
—Busy Little Monster. 2010. 14p. (J). bds. 10.98 *(978-1-60553-125-0(1)*, PIL Kids) Publications International, Ltd.
—Cars: Fun with Friends. 2018. (Play-A-Sound Ser.). (ENG.). 8p. (J). bds. *(978-1-60553-038-3(7)*, 0256ed99-819a-402b-991d-eafaf60c9e6c, PI Kids) Phoenix International Publications, Inc.
—Cars (Musical Treasury) 2011. 40p. (J). bds. 15.98 *(978-1-4508-1085-2(3))* Publications International, Ltd.
—Chuggington Little Music Note Sound: Traintastic Tunes. 2011. 12p. (J). (gr. k-3). bds. 10.99 *(978-1-4508-1141-5(8)*, dd98fbb4-eb4f-47f8-80b4-3d7a907afc5f) Phoenix International Publications, Inc.
—Come along, Sing a Song! 2010. 12p. (J). bds. 12.98 *(978-1-60553-438-1(2)*, PIL Kids) Publications International, Ltd.
—Custom Cool. 2008. (Illus.). 8p. (J). bds. 11.98 *(978-1-4127-7503-8(5))* Phoenix International Publications, Inc.
—Dance Mat Sound Book Dora Lets Dance. 2007. (J). 17.98 *(978-1-4127-8305-7(4))* Publications International, Ltd.
—A Day with Hello Kitty: Play-A-Sound. 2013. 10p. (J). bds. 7.98 *(978-1-4508-6154-0(7)*, 1450861547) Phoenix International Publications, Inc.
—Diego What a Team. 2007. (Illus.). (J). 10.98 *(978-1-4127-6744-6(X))* Publications International, Ltd.
—Dinosaur Train All Aboard! 2011. 10p. (J). bds. 10.98 *(978-1-4508-1140-8(X))* Publications International, Ltd.
—Discover the Day. 2010. 12p. (J). bds. 9.98 *(978-1-4127-6747-7(4))* Phoenix International Publications, Inc.
—Disney Classics Shaped Books. 2011. 8p. (J). bds. 4.98 *(978-1-4508-0909-2(X))* Publications International, Ltd.
—Disney Fairies: Bienvenuda Tinker Bell! 2011. 12p. (J). bds. 10.98 *(978-1-4508-1402-7(6))* Publications International, Ltd.
—Disney Fairies: Wellcome Tinker Bell: (Lenticular Play-a-Sound Book) 2010. 14p. (J). bds. 17.98 *(978-1-60553-606-4(7))* Phoenix International Publications, Inc.
—Disney Mickey Mouse Clubhouse: Mickey's Adventure. 2010. (ENG.). 14p. (J). bds. 21.99 *(978-1-4127-4599-4(3)*, 13903) Phoenix International Publications, Inc.
—Disney Pixar: School Memory Keeper. 2011. 48p. (J). spiral bd. 16.98 *(978-1-4508-1137-8(X))* Phoenix International Publications, Inc.
—Disney Pixar ABC Board Books. 2010. 10p. (J). 23.98 *(978-1-4508-0370-0(9))* Phoenix International Publications, Inc.
—Disney Pixar (book Block) 2010. (J). 10.98 *(978-1-4508-0674-9(0))* Publications International, Ltd.
—Disney Pixar Cars: Cuentos de Miedo (Little English Spanish Sound Book) 2011. 12p. (J). bds. 10.98 *(978-1-4508-1401-0(8))* Phoenix International Publications, Inc.
—Disney Pixar Cars: First Look & Find & Shaped Puzzle Box Set. 2010. (J). 22.98 *(978-1-4508-0136-2(6))* Publications International, Ltd.
—Disney Pixar Cars: Road Trip Adventure. 2010. (J). 10.98 *(978-1-4508-0387-8(3))* Phoenix International Publications, Inc.
—Disney Pixar Cars: (Stereo Play-a-Sound) 2010. 24p. (J). 19.98 *(978-1-60553-857-0(4))* Publications International, Ltd.
—Disney Pixar Cars: Story Reader 2. 0 3 Storybook Library. 2011. (J). 19.98 *(978-1-4508-0606-0(6))* Publications International, Ltd.
—Disney Pixar Cars 2 - World Tour. 2011. 14p. (J). 17.98 *(978-1-4508-1473-7(5))* Phoenix International Publications, Inc.
—Disney Pixar Cars 2 (Look & Find Soft Cover) 2011. 20p. (J). pap. 5.98 *(978-1-4508-1457-7(3))* Publications International, Ltd.
—Disney Pixar Cars (book Block) 2010. (J). 10.98 *(978-1-4508-0671-8(6))* Phoenix International Publications, Inc.
—Disney Pixar Cars; Cruising' Cool. 2011. 12p. (J). bds. 10.98 *(978-1-4508-0915-3(4))* Publications International, Ltd.
—Disney Pixar Cars Ride-along Songs. 2010. 14p. (J). bds. 19.98 *(978-1-4127-5368-5(6))* Phoenix International Publications, Inc.
—Disney Pixar Cars Story Reader 2. 0 Unit. 2011. (J). 30.98 *(978-1-4508-0588-9(4))* Publications International, Ltd.
—Disney Pixar Little First Look & Find 4 pack in carry Case. 2010. 18p. (J). 14.98 *(978-1-4508-0333-5(4))* Phoenix International Publications, Inc.
—Disney Pixar School Memories. 2011. 24p. (J). spiral bd. 10.98 *(978-1-4508-1136-1(1))* Publications International, Ltd.
—Disney Pixar Shaped Books. 2011. (J). bds. 4.98 *(978-1-4508-0826-2(3))* Publications International, Ltd.
—Disney Princess: 26 Stories of Virtue. 2010. 12p. (J). 25.98 *(978-1-60553-692-7(X))* Phoenix International Publications, Inc.
—Disney Princess: Canciones the Princesas. 2011. 24p. (J). 17.98 *(978-1-4508-1615-1(0))* Publications International, Ltd.
—Disney Princess: Dreams Come True (Talking Look & Find) 2010. 16p. (J). bds. 12.98 *(978-1-60553-538-8(9))* Publications International, Ltd.
—Disney Princess: Enchanted Dreams. 2010. 40p. (J). bds. 14.98 *(978-1-60553-685-9(7))* Publications International, Ltd.
—Disney Princess: Enchanted Stables (Look & Find) 2010. 24p. (J). 7.98 *(978-1-60553-633-0(4))* Phoenix International Publications, Inc.
—Disney Princess: Follow Your Dreams. 2010. 24p. (J). 19.98 *(978-1-4127-5357-9(0)*, PIL Kids) Publications International, Ltd.
—Disney Princess: Magical Princess Songs. 2011. 14p. (J). bds. 17.98 *(978-1-4508-1132-3(9))* Publications International, Ltd.
—Disney Princess: Royal Recital. 2011. 14p. (J). bds. 17.98 *(978-1-4508-1006-7(3))* Phoenix International Publications, Inc.
—Disney Princess: Stories of Virtue. 2010. 10p. (J). bds. 12.98 *(978-1-4508-0164-5(1))* Phoenix International Publications, Inc.
—Disney Princess (book Block) 2010. (J). 10.98 *(978-1-4508-0672-5(4))* Phoenix International Publications, Inc.
—Disney Princess First Look & Find & Giant Puzzle. 2010. (J). 22.98 *(978-1-4508-0135-5(8))* Publications International, Ltd.
—Disney Princess (Musical Treasury) 2011. 40p. (J). bds. 15.98 *(978-1-4508-1082-1(9))* Publications International, Ltd.
—Disney Princess Storybook & Magic Bracelet. 2010. 12p. (J). bds. 12.98 *(978-1-4127-9912-6(0))* Phoenix International Publications, Inc.
—Disney Princess under the Starry Sky. 2013. 8p. (J). bds. *(978-1-4508-7130-3(5)*, 1450871305) Phoenix International Publications, Inc.
—Disney(r) Sofia the First the Perfect Party: A Flashlight Adventure Sound Book. 2014. 14p. (J). 16.98 *(978-1-4508-7476-2(2)*, 31bc99fe-fde1-4d89-9e76-09c40bd0ccb5) Phoenix International Publications, Inc.
—Disney Tinkerbell Book Box Plush. 2011. 8p. (J). bds. 7.04 net. *(978-1-4508-0576-6(0)*, 1450805760) Publications International, Ltd.
—Doodles for Kids. 2011. 100p. (J). spiral bd. 13.98 *(978-1-4508-0991-7(X))* Publications International, Ltd.
—Dora Little Stars, Big Adventure. 2013. 14p. (J). bds. 16.98 *(978-1-4127-8950-9(8)*, 1412789508) Phoenix International Publications, Inc.
—Dora Says Good Night. 2011. 12p. (J). bds. 11.98 *(978-1-4508-0764-7(X))* Phoenix International Publications, Inc.
—Dora the Explorer. (J). 2010. 128p. pap. 12.98 *(978-1-60553-793-1(4))* 2007. (Illus.). 4.00 *(978-1-4127-8442-9(5))* Phoenix International Publications, Inc.
—Dora the Explorer: Island Adventure (Talking Look & Find) 2010. 16p. (J). bds. 12.98 *(978-1-60553-471-8(4))* Publications International, Ltd.
—Dora the Explorer: Little Star's Big Adventure. 2010. (J). 10.98 *(978-1-4508-0391-5(1))* Phoenix International Publications, Inc.
—Dora the Explorer: Little Star's Big Adventure (Flashlight Adventure Book & Dora Plush) 2010. (J). 24.98 *(978-1-4508-0129-4(3))* Publications International, Ltd.
—Dora the Explorer: Scavenger Hunt (Little Look & Find) 2010. 24p. (J). 2.98 *(978-1-4127-7113-9(7))* Phoenix International Publications, Inc.
—Dora the Explorer: Sounds All Around! 2011. 24p. (J). 20.98 *(978-1-4508-0011-2(4))* Phoenix International Publications, Inc.
—Dora the Explorer: We Did It! 2010. 10p. (J). bds. 14.98 *(978-1-4508-0384-7(9))* Phoenix International Publications, Inc.
—Dora the Explorer, Ding Dong! It's Dora! 2009. 12p. (J). bds. 11.98 *(978-1-4127-7598-4(1))* Phoenix International Publications, Inc.
—Dragon Boat Festival. 2009. 9p. (J). bds. 10.98 *(978-1-4127-7782-7(8)*, PIL Kids) Publications International, Ltd.
—Electronic Time for Learning: Music. 2011. 120p. (J). *(978-1-4508-0260-4(5))* Publications International, Ltd.
—Electronic Time for Learning: The Human Body. 2010. 120p. 18.98 *(978-1-4127-9854-9(X)*, PIL Kids) Publications International, Ltd.
—Elmo. 2007. (J). 9.98 *(978-1-4127-8301-9(1))* Phoenix International Publications, Inc.
—The Enchanted Forest. 2011. 14p. (J). 17.98 *(978-1-4508-0565-0(5))* Phoenix International Publications, Inc.
—Finding Nemo. 2007. (J). 9.98 *(978-1-4127-6516-9(1))* Publications International, Ltd.
—Finding Nemo: A Party for Nemo. 2009. 9p. (J). bds. 4.50 *(978-1-4127-2926-0(2)*, PIL Kids) Publications International, Ltd.
—Fire Truck: (Play-a-Sound Book) 2010. 12p. (J). bds. 12.98 *(978-1-4508-0110-2(2))* Phoenix International Publications, Inc.
—First Look & Find Hello Kitty. 2013. (gr. -1-1). bds. 7.98 *(978-1-4508-6378-0(7)*, 900f7270-d27c-4dbf-8614-52373c31c3df) Phoenix International Publications, Inc.
—First Look & Find Little Elf. 2013. (Illus.). 18p. (J). bds. *(978-1-4508-7093-1(7)*, 1450870937) Phoenix International Publications, Inc.
—First Words (Listen & Learn Sound Book) 2011. 19p. (J). bds. 11.98 *(978-1-4508-1441-6(7))* Phoenix International Publications, Inc.
—Halloween Is Coming! 2010. 14p. (J). bds. 10.98 *(978-1-60553-691-0(1)*, PIL Kids) Publications International, Ltd.
—Handy Manny: Fiesta Fun. 2008. (J). bds. 10.98 *(978-1-4127-8867-0(6))* Publications International, Ltd.
—Happy Baby. 2011. 8p. (J). bds. 7.98 *(978-1-4508-1243-6(0))* Publications International, Ltd.
—Hello Kitty: My Friend Hello Kitty: Play-A-Sound Book & Cuddly Hello Kitty. 2013. (J). (gr. -1-4). bds. 13.99 *(978-1-4508-1181-1(7)*, 21ea0785-0317-4c86-b812-bf2727f2df16) Phoenix International Publications, Inc.
—Hello Kitty Sweet Songs: Play-A-Sound. 2013. 12p. (J). bds. 9.98 *(978-1-4508-6167-0(9)*, 1450861679) Phoenix International Publications, Inc.
—I Love You. 2010. 14p. (J). bds. 10.98 *(978-1-4127-4504-8(7)*, PIL Kids) Publications International, Ltd.
—Interactive Play a Sound Thomas the Tank. 2009. 24p. (J). 17.98 *(978-0-7853-1360-1(5)*, PIL Kids) Publications International, Ltd.
—It's Riddle Time! 2009. 10p. (J). bds. 11.98 *(978-1-4127-1689-5(6)*, PIL Kids) Publications International, Ltd.
—Jesus Loves Me. 2010. 14p. (J). bds. 10.98 *(978-1-4127-4471-3(7)*, PIL Kids) Publications International, Ltd.
—Let's Have a Race, Surprises, Little Engines. 2010. 14p. (J). 12.98 *(978-1-4127-4716-5(3))* Phoenix International Publications, Inc.
—Lights & Music. 2008. 160p. (J). bds. 17.98 *(978-1-4127-8500-6(6)*, PIL Kids) Publications International, Ltd.
—Lights & Music Treasury. 2010. 160p. (J). bds. 16.98 *(978-1-4127-7911-1(1))* Phoenix International Publications, Inc.
—Lights & Music Treasury 10Led Spa Disney Classics. 2009. 160p. 15.98 *(978-1-4127-5454-5(2))* Phoenix International Publications, Inc.
—Lights, Music, & Me! Love Sparkles. 2010. 14p. (J). bds. 10.98 *(978-1-4127-1884-4(8)*, PIL Kids) Publications International, Ltd.
—Little Carry Case Spa Cars 8 Bks. 2009. 8p. 9.98 *(978-1-4127-6434-6(3)*, PIL Kids) Publications International, Ltd.
—Little Lift & Listen Sound Mickey Mouse Clubhouse. 2007. (J). 10.98 *(978-1-4127-8457-3(3))* Phoenix International Publications, Inc.
—Little Sound the Princess & the Frog. 2009. 24p. (J). bds. 10.98 *(978-1-4127-6446-9(7))* Publications International, Ltd.
—Look & Find - My First Look & Find Barney. 2011. 18p. (J). bds. 3.75 net. *(978-1-4508-1892-6(7)*, 1450818927) Publications International, Ltd.
—Marvel Heroes. 2007. (J). 9.98 *(978-1-4127-8449-8(2))* Phoenix International Publications, Inc.
—Marvel Heroes. 2007. (J). 7.10 *(978-1-4127-6665-4(6))* Publications International, Ltd.
—Mater Saves the Day. 2011. 12p. (J). bds. 10.98 *(978-1-4508-0695-4(3))* Phoenix International Publications, Inc.
—Los Mejores Amigos. 2009.Tr. of Toy Story Best Friends. 12p. (J). bds. 10.98 *(978-1-4127-0269-0(0))* Phoenix International Publications, Inc.
—Mickey Mouse Clubhouse: Doctor Kit Book & Mickey Plush. 2010. (J). 24.98 *(978-1-4508-0124-9(2))* Publications International, Ltd.
—Mickey Mouse Clubhouse: Play Day Songs. 2011. (Illus.). 12p. (J). bds. 15.98 *(978-1-4508-0925-2(1))* Publications International, Ltd.
—Mickey Mouse Clubhouse - Who's Not Sleepy? 2011. 12p. (J). bds. *(978-1-4508-0398-4(9))* Publications International, Ltd.
—Mickey Mouse Clubhouse: Colors: Sing & Learn. 2010. 12p. (J). bds. 10.98 *(978-1-4127-1729-8(9))* Publications International, Ltd.
—Mickey Mouse Clubhouse: Mickey's Surprise! 2013. 14p. (J). (gr. k-3). bds. 16.99 *(978-1-4508-2188-9(X)*, 87b7723a-b11c-4ce1-8b21-522e3e8ff7e2) Phoenix International Publications, Inc.
—Mickey Mouse Clubhouse: Sing-along Christmas Songs: Holiday Play-a-Song Book. 2010. 10p. (J). bds. 12.98 *(978-1-4127-7862-6(X))* Publications International, Ltd.
—Mickey's Clubhouse Drum Song Sound. 2011. 14p. (J). bds. 20.98 *(978-1-4508-1240-5(6))* Phoenix International Publications, Inc.
—Mickey's Piano Songs Play & Learn. 2010. 24p. (J). 12.98 *(978-1-4508-0114-0(5))* Phoenix International Publications, Inc.
—Move to the Music. 2011. 14p. (J). bds. 20.98 *(978-1-4508-1242-9(2))* Phoenix International Publications, Inc.
—Musical Pop up Disney Princess. 2008. (SPA.). (J). 15.98 *(978-1-4127-8980-6(X))* Publications International, Ltd.
—My 1st Libraries Disney Classics. 2011. 10p. (J). bds. 13.98 *(978-1-4508-1029-6(2))* Phoenix International Publications, Inc.
—My First Book Block - First Words. 2011. 12p. (J). bds. 3.75 net. *(978-1-4508-1666-3(5)*, 1450816665) Publications International, Ltd.
—My First Book Block Set Animals. 2011. 12p. (J). bds. 14.98 *(978-1-4508-1244-3(9))* Publications International, Ltd.
—My First Book Block Set Disey Princess. 2011. 5p. (J). bds. 14.98 *(978-1-4508-1630-4(4))* Phoenix International Publications, Inc.
—My First Story Reader Dora the Explorer. 2011. (J). 31.98 *(978-1-4508-0618-3(X))* Phoenix International Publications, Inc.
—My First Story Reader Sesame Street, 3 vols. 2007. (Illus.). (J). 31.98 *(978-1-4127-8989-9(3))* Phoenix International Publications, Inc.
—My Shapes Book. 2011. 32p. (J). bds. *(978-1-4508-1023-4(3))* Publications International, Ltd.
—Nickelodeon Dora the Explorer: Cook with Dora: Abuela's Birthday Fiesta. 2010. 14p. (J). bds. 16.98 *(978-1-4508-0842-2(5))* Phoenix International Publications, Inc.
—Numbers (Listen & Learn Sound Book) 2011. 19p. (J). bds. 11.98 *(978-1-4508-1705-9(X))* Phoenix International Publications, Inc.
—Old MacDonald Had a Farm. 2010. 12p. (J). bds. 3.98 *(978-1-60553-146-5(4))* Publications International, Ltd.
—On Sesame Street. 2010. 10p. (J). bds. 14.98 *(978-1-4127-4610-6(8))* Publications International, Ltd.
—Once upon a Potty Sound Book for Boys. 2010. 8p. (J). bds. 7.98 *(978-1-4508-0829-3(8))* Phoenix International Publications, Inc.
—Out & About. 2010. 18p. (J). bds. 12.98 *(978-1-4127-4466-9(0)*, PIL Kids) Publications International, Ltd.
—Phineas & Ferb Time for Fun Play-A-Sound. 2013. (Illus.). 24p. (J). (gr. 1-3). 12.98 *(978-1-4508-6604-0(2)*, fea3b34e-591a-41e6-a62a-78ca59cb997d) Publications International, Ltd.
—Pirate. 2008. (J). bds. 9.98 *(978-1-4127-9357-5(2))* Publications International, Ltd.
—Play-a-Puzzle Book: Halloween. 2010. 12p. (J). bds. 10.98 *(978-1-60553-736-8(5))* Publications International, Ltd.
—Play-a-Puzzle trade; Book: Alphabet. 2010. 12p. (J). bds. 10.98 *(978-1-60553-799-3(3))* Publications International, Ltd.
—Play & Learn Piano Dora. 2011. 24p. (J). 17.98 *(978-1-4508-1165-1(5))* Phoenix International Publications, Inc.
—Play & Learn Piano Elmo. 2011. 24p. (J). 17.98 *(978-1-4508-0871-2(9))* Phoenix International Publications, Inc.
—Pooh's Pop-up Stories. 2010. (J). 8.98 *(978-1-60553-497-8(8))* Phoenix International Publications, Inc.
—Pooh's Pop-up Stories 2. 2010. (J). 8.98 *(978-1-60553-838-9(8))* Phoenix International Publications, Inc.
—Popping up on Sesame Street. 2010. 14p. (J). 19.98 *(978-1-4127-4512-3(8))* Phoenix International Publications, Inc.
—Potty Time for Monsters. 2011. 14p. (J). bds. 17.98 *(978-1-4508-0572-8(8))* Phoenix International Publications, Inc.

T U V

—Potty Time with Elmo. 2011. 12p. (J). 4.69 net. *(978-1-4508-1353-2(4)*, 1450813534) Phoenix International Publications, Inc.
—Potty Time with Tiger: Boy. 2010. (J). bds. 5.98 *(978-1-4127-6915-0(9))* Publications International, Ltd.
—Potty Time with Tiger: Girl. 2010. (SPA.). (J). bds. 5.98 *(978-1-4127-6916-7(7))* Publications International, Ltd.
—Prince Elmo & the Pea. 2007. (J). 10.98 *(978-1-4127-6745-3(8))* Publications International, Ltd.
—The Princess & the Frog. 2009. 24p. (J). 16.98 *(978-1-4127-6421-6(1))* Publications International, Ltd.
—Princess Magic. 2010. (My First Look & Find Ser.). (Illus.). 12p. (gr. -1). bds. 7.98 *(978-1-4127-3074-7(0)*, 7227000) Phoenix International Publications, Inc.
—Race Car. 2013. 12p. (J). bds. 9.98 *(978-1-4508-0112-6(9)*, 1450801129) Phoenix International Publications, Inc.
—Race Day. 2010. 10p. (J). bds. 11.98 *(978-1-4127-4931-2(X)*, PIL Kids) Publications International, Ltd.
—Really Useful Engines. 2010. 40p. (J). bds. 14.98 *(978-1-60553-744-3(6))* Phoenix International Publications, Inc.
—Record A Story: My Grandma Is Special. 2011. 20p. (J). bds. 19.99 *(978-1-4508-1352-5(6))* Phoenix International Publications, Inc.
—Record a Story: My Grandpa Is Special. 2011. 20p. (J). bds. 25.98 *(978-1-4508-1381-5(X))* Phoenix International Publications, Inc.
—Record a Story: 'Twas the Night Before Christmas. 2010. 20p. (J). (gr. k-3). bds. 19.99 *(978-1-4508-0201-7(X)*, 145080201X) Phoenix International Publications, Inc.
—Ring-a-Ling! A Friend Is Here. 2010. 12p. (J). 9.98 *(978-1-4127-7939-5(1))* Phoenix International Publications, Inc.
—A Ring-A-Ling Day! 2009. 12p. (J). bds. 11.98 *(978-1-4127-9614-9(8)*, PIL Kids) Publications International, Ltd.
—Rock & Roll with Elmo. 2010. 24p. (J). bds. 19.98 *(978-1-4127-4475-1(X)*, PIL Kids) Publications International, Ltd.
—Rockin' on the Railway. 2010. 24p. (J). 17.98 *(978-1-60553-339-1(4)*, PIL Kids) Publications International, Ltd.
—Rudolph the Red-Nosed Reindeer(r): A Flashlight Adventure Sound Book. 2014. 14p. (J). *(978-1-4508-9047-2(4)*, 1450890474) Publications International, Ltd.
—Rudolph the Red-Nosed Reindeer (Book & Plush) 2011. 8p. (J). bds. 11.98 *(978-1-4508-2170-4(7))* Publications International, Ltd.
—Sesame Street: Good Night Stories. 2010. 40p. (J). bds. 14.98 *(978-1-60553-861-7(2))* Phoenix International Publications, Inc.
—Sesame Street: Merry Christmas, Elmo! 2010. 8p. (J). bds. 5.98 *(978-1-60553-980-5(5))* Phoenix International Publications, Inc.
—Sesame Street: Merry Christmas, Elmo! (Book & Plush) 2011. 8p. (J). bds. 11.98 *(978-1-4508-2169-8(3))* Publications International, Ltd.
—Sesame Street: Potty Time Songs. 2011. 12p. (J). bds. *(978-1-4508-0401-1(2))* Phoenix International Publications, Inc.
—Sesame Street: Sing with Elmo, Let's Sing! & Wake up, Elmo! 2011. (J). bds. 14.98 *(978-1-4508-0627-5(9))* Phoenix International Publications, Inc.
—Sesame Street: The Itsy Bitsy Spider. 2011. 10p. (J). bds. 7.98 *(978-1-4508-0858-3(1)*, 6461bf3e-ab03-4ebc-81c6-091daf4fbc8e) Phoenix International Publications, Inc.
—Sesame Street (Musical Treasury) 2011. 40p. (J). bds. 15.98 *(978-1-4508-1081-4(0))* Publications International, Ltd.
—Sesame Street, Ding Dong, Elmo's Here! 2009. 12p. (J). bds. 11.98 *(978-1-4127-9613-2(X))* Phoenix International Publications, Inc.
—Sesame Street: Find a Friend: A Busy Box Book. 2010. 14p. (J). bds. 16.98 *(978-1-60553-622-4(9))* Phoenix International Publications, Inc.
—Sesame Street: Sing & Play Guitar Songs. 2014. 12p. (J). *(978-1-4508-7988-0(8)*, d11d1f4c-d61d-46f5-a30f-cd01ce8a740a) Phoenix International Publications, Inc.
—Sesame Street(r) Where Is Elmo's Friend? Play-A-Sound(r) Lift-a-Flap Sound Book. 2014. 10p. (J). bds. *(978-1-4508-8976-6(X)*, 145088976X) Publications International, Ltd.
—Sesame Write & Erase Board Book. 2014. 28p. (J). bds. 9.98 *(978-1-4508-8130-2(0)*, 1450881300) Phoenix International Publications, Inc.
—Shapes Wipe off Learning Board. 2011. 1p. (J). bds. *(978-1-4508-1432-4(8))* Publications International, Ltd.
—The Smurfs Large Play a Sound. 2011. 24p. (J). 14.98 *(978-1-60553-403-9(X))* Phoenix International Publications, Inc.
—Soft! Furry! Bumpy! A Touch, Hear, & Learn with Elmo Book. 2010. 10p. (J). bds. 11.98 *(978-1-4127-5805-5(X)*, PIL Kids) Publications International, Ltd.
—Spider Sense Spider-Man: Super Villain Showdown. 2010. 12p. (J). bds. 12.98 *(978-1-4127-9911-9(2))* Phoenix International Publications, Inc.
—Spooky Stories. 2008. (J). 12.98 *(978-1-4127-9384-1(X))* Publications International, Ltd.
—Steering Wheel Spa Cars. 2009. 14p. 16.98 *(978-1-4127-9241-7(X))* Phoenix International Publications, Inc.
—Stories to Grow on Spa Disney Classics. 2009. 40p. 9.98 *(978-1-4127-1109-8(6))* Phoenix International Publications, Inc.
—Stories to Grow on Spa Mickey Mouse Clubhous. 2009. 40p. 9.98 *(978-1-4127-1127-2(4)*, PIL Kids) Publications International, Ltd.
—A Surprise for Belle. 2010. 12p. (J). bds. 9.98 *(978-1-4127-4454-6(7))* Phoenix International Publications, Inc.
—Teenage Ninja Turtles: Skateboard Heroes! 2014. 12p. (J). bds. 12.98 *(978-1-4508-8453-2(9)*, 5b3a6351-f0d0-4a36-b0d1-c89677f0352a) Phoenix International Publications, Inc.
—Things That Go Board Book. 2014. (Illus.). 22p. (J). bds. 4.98 *(978-1-4508-8581-2(0)*, 1450885810) Phoenix International Publications, Inc.
—Thomas & Friends: Engine Roll Call. 2011. 8p. (J). bds. 7.98 *(978-1-4508-1435-5(2))* Publications International, Ltd.
—Thomas & Friends: Let's Go, Thomas! 2010. 14p. (J). 17.98 *(978-1-4508-0212-3(5))* Phoenix International Publications, Inc.
—Thomas & Friends: Play-a-Tune Puzzle Book. 2010. 10p. (J). bds. 13.98 *(978-1-60553-756-6(X))* Publications International, Ltd.
—Thomas & Friends: Sodor Snapshots. 2010. 14p. (J). bds. 19.98 *(978-1-4127-1918-6(6))* Publications International, Ltd.
—Thomas & Friends(tm) Super Look & Find(r) Activity Pad: Spot the Find 'ems, Find the Differences! Giant Play Scene! More Than 50 Stickers! 2014. 64p. (J). *(978-1-4508-8559-1(4)*, 1450885594) Publications International, Ltd.
—Thomas Celebration Pop Up Sound. 2010. 14p. 19.98 *(978-1-4127-4513-0(6))* Publications International, Ltd.
—Thomas Songs Play & Learn. 2010. 24p. (J). 12.98 *(978-1-4508-0115-7(3))* Phoenix International Publications, Inc.
—Thomas the Tank Good Morning Engines. 2012. (ENG.). 12p. (J). bds. 14.99 *(978-0-7853-8282-9(8)*, 1340) Phoenix International Publications, Inc.
—Tinker Bell. 2010. 10p. (J). 11.98 *(978-1-4127-4472-0(5)*, PIL Kids) Publications International, Ltd.
—Tinker Bell: Songs from Pixie Hollow. 2010. 12p. (J). bds. 9.98 *(978-1-4508-0366-3(0))* Phoenix International Publications, Inc.
—Tinker Bell -Tink's Magical Day. 2011. 8p. (J). bds. *(978-1-4508-0910-8(3))* Publications International, Ltd.
—Tinker Bell (Book & Plush) 2011. 8p. (J). bds. 11.98 *(978-1-4508-2171-1(5))* Publications International, Ltd.
—Touch & Hear Adventure. 2010. 10p. (J). 11.98 *(978-1-4127-4932-9(8)*, PIL Kids) Publications International, Ltd.
—Toy Story 3: New Friends. 2010. 12p. (J). bds. 10.98 *(978-1-4127-4584-0(5)*, PIL Kids) Publications International, Ltd.
—Toys to the Rescue. 2010. 14p. (J). 16.98 *(978-1-4127-4585-7(3)*, PIL Kids) Publications International, Ltd.
—Trains. 2011. 12p. (J). bds. 13.98 *(978-1-4508-1138-5(8))* Publications International, Ltd.
—Treasure Hunt. 2010. 12p. (J). bds. 9.98 *(978-1-4127-9885-3(X))* Phoenix International Publications, Inc.
—Up & down! Play-a-Sound Book & Huggable Kai-lan. 2010. (J). 14.98 *(978-1-4127-5591-7(3))* Publications International, Ltd.
—Vampires & Other Scary Creatures(Look & Find) 2010. (Illus.). 24p. (J). 7.98 *(978-1-60553-839-6(6))* Publications International, Ltd.
—Video Play a Sound Dora. 2010. 24p. (J). 19.98 *(978-1-4127-9210-3(X)*, PIL Kids) Publications International, Ltd.
—What Do You See? 2012. (Illus.). 14p. (J). (gr. 2-4). 17.98 *(978-1-4508-4545-8(2)*, 23956fd6-2821-435f-aef0-d47191d0621e) Phoenix International Publications, Inc.
—What's Different. 2009. 24p. (J). 7.98 *(978-1-4127-1725-0(6)*, PIL Kids) Publications International, Ltd.
—What's Different Finding Nemo. 2009. 24p. (J). 9.98 *(978-1-4127-7769-8(0)*, PIL Kids) Publications International, Ltd.
—Winnie the Pooh. 2007. (J). 15.98 *(978-1-4127-8351-4(8))* Publications International, Ltd.
—Winnie the Pooh Drum Sound. 2011. 14p. (J). bds. 20.98 *(978-1-4508-0911-5(1))* Phoenix International Publications, Inc.
—Winnie the Pooh (Find-A-Friend Book) 2011. 14p. (J). bds. 17.98 *(978-1-4508-0694-7(5))* Phoenix International Publications, Inc.
—Wonder Pets: Save the Baby Kitten. 2008. (J). bds. 10.98 *(978-1-4127-9198-4(7))* Publications International, Ltd.
—Write-And-Erase Look & Find(r) Disney Minnie: Packed with 'find 'ems & Picture Puzzles! Look, Circle, Wipe Clean, & Play Again! 2014. 28p. (J). bds. 9.98 *(978-1-4508-7918-7(7)*, 1450879187) Phoenix International Publications, Inc.
—Writing Skills Wipe off Leaning Board. 2011. 1p. (J). bds. *(978-1-4508-1433-1(6))* Publications International, Ltd.
—Zoom! 2010. 14p. (J). bds. 17.98 *(978-1-4127-4594-9(2))* Phoenix International Publications, Inc.
Publications International Ltd. Staff & Red Giraffe, Ltd Staff, eds. The Big Race - Stories Come to Life, 3Bks. 2011. (J). *(978-1-4508-0586-5(8))* Phoenix International Publications, Inc.
Publishing, Sterling. Daddy & Me. 2008. (Illus.). 12p. (J). bds. *(978-1-934618-44-8(6))* Begin Smart LLC.
—Hello, Baby! 2008. (Illus.). 10p. (J). bds. *(978-1-934618-26-4(8))* Begin Smart LLC.
—Look at Me! 2008. (Illus.). 10p. (J). bds. *(978-1-934618-41-7(1))* Begin Smart LLC.
—Woof. 2008. (Books for Brainy Babies). (Illus.). 12p. (J). bds. *(978-1-934618-33-2(0))* Begin Smart LLC.
Puck. My Foodie ABC: A Little Gourmet's Guide. 2010. (Foodie Bks.). (Illus.). 22p. (J). (gr. -1-k). bds. 8.95 *(978-0-9825295-2-2(X)*, 802952) Duo Pr. LLC.
—123 Chicago. 2009. (Cool Counting Bks.). (ENG., Illus.). 22p. (J). (gr. -1-k). bds. 8.95 *(978-0-9796213-5-2(6)*, 802135) Duo Pr. LLC.
Puppy. 2004. (J). per. *(978-1-57657-397-6(4))* Paradise Pr., Inc.
Puppy. (Buggy Buddies Ser.) (Illus.). (J). (gr. -1). bds. *(978-1-56021-351-2(5)*, 202) W.J. Fantasy, Inc.
Puppy & Friends. 2008. (Illus.). (J). *(978-0-312-50640-7(6))* St. Martin's Pr.
Putumayo Kids Staff, creator. African Sticker Collection. 2010. (J). 11.95 *(978-1-58759-273-7(8))* Putumayo World Music & Crafts.
Pyle, Gabe. Fourteen Animals (That Are Definitely Not an Octopus) That Are Definitely Not an Octopus. 2018. (ENG., Illus.). 16p. (J). (gr. -1-k). bds. 9.99 *(978-1-64170-009-2(2)*, 550009) Familius LLC.
Quinton, Sasha, text. Ears. 2010. (Illus.). 10p. (J). *(978-1-936199-15-0(7))* Book Shop, Ltd., The.
—Noses. 2010. (Illus.). 10p. (J). *(978-1-936199-17-4(3))* Book Shop, Ltd., The.
—Paws. 2010. (Illus.). 10p. (J). *(978-1-936199-16-7(5))* Book Shop, Ltd., The.
—Tails. 2010. (Illus.). 10p. (J). *(978-1-936199-14-3(9))* Book Shop, Ltd., The.
Rabe, Tish. Love You, Hug You, Read to You! Endersby, Frank, illus. 2015. (ENG.). 32p. (J). (gr. -1 — 1). bds. 8.99 *(978-1-101-93655-9(X)*, Random Hse. Bks. for Young Readers) Random Hse. Children's Bks.
Rader, Mark. Dinosaur. Sanborn, Casey, illus. 2008. (J). *(978-1-4127-9359-9(9))* Publications International, Ltd.
Ramljak, Marijan. Are You My Friend? 2009. (Look for Me Bks.). (Illus.). (J). bds. 9.99 *(978-1-934650-67-7(6))* Just For Kids Pr., LLC.
—Are You My Mommy? 2009. (Look for Me Bks.). (Illus.). (J). bds. 9.99 *(978-1-934650-65-3(X))* Just For Kids Pr., LLC.
Randall, Ronne. Snuggle up, Little Penguin! Church, Caroline Jayne, illus. 2003. (Little Friends Ser.). 14p. (J). 12.95 *(978-1-57145-919-0(7)*, Silver Dolphin Bks.) Readerlink Distribution Services, LLC.
Random House. Big Fish, Little Fish: a Book of Opposites (Bubble Guppies) Random House, illus. 2015. (Board Book Ser.). (ENG., Illus.). 24p. (J). (-k). bds. 4.99 *(978-0-385-38442-1(4)*, Random Hse. Bks. for Young Readers) Random Hse. Children's Bks.
—Colors Everywhere! (Bubble Guppies) Random House, illus. 2013. (Board Book Ser.). (ENG., Illus.). 24p. (J). (-k). bds. 5.99 *(978-0-449-81782-7(2)*, Random Hse. Bks. for Young Readers) Random Hse. Children's Bks.
—Elmo's World: Dancing! (Sesame Street) Random House, illus. 2018. (Lift-The-Flap Ser.). (ENG., Illus.). 12p. (J). (— 1). bds. 7.99 *(978-0-525-57838-3(2)*, Random Hse. Bks. for Young Readers) Random Hse. Children's Bks.
—Here Comes Peter Cottontail Board Book (Peter Cottontail) Random House, illus. 2015. (Board Book Ser.). (Illus.). 24p. (J). (-k). bds. 4.99 *(978-0-553-50975-5(6)*, Random Hse. Bks. for Young Readers) Random Hse. Children's Bks.
—Hide-And-Go-Swim! (Bubble Guppies) MJ Illustrations, illus. 2014. (ENG.). 12p. (J). (— 1). bds. 5.99 *(978-0-385-38515-2(3)*, Random Hse. Bks. for Young Readers) Random Hse. Children's Bks.
—Jingle Pups (PAW Patrol) Random House, illus. 2017. (ENG., Illus.). 12p. (J). (— 1). bds. 8.99 *(978-1-5247-6397-8(7)*, Random Hse. Bks. for Young Readers) Random Hse. Children's Bks.
—Let's Find Adventure! (Paw Patrol) Jackson, Mike, illus. 2015. (ENG.). 12p. (J). (-k). bds. 5.99 *(978-0-553-51027-0(4)*, Random Hse. Bks. for Young Readers) Random Hse. Children's Bks.
—My Blue Railway Book Box (Thomas & Friends) 2017. (Bright & Early Board Books(TM) Ser.). (ENG., Illus.). 96p. (J). (— 1). bds. 14.99 *(978-1-5247-7224-6(0)*, Random Hse. Bks. for Young Readers) Random Hse. Children's Bks.
—Patrol Pals (Paw Patrol) Random House, illus. 2015. (ENG., Illus.). 48p. (J). (— 1). bds. 10.99 *(978-0-553-50796-6(6)*, Random Hse. Bks. for Young Readers) Random Hse. Children's Bks.
—PAW Patrol Big Lift-And-Look Board Book (PAW Patrol) Moore, Harry, illus. 2017. (ENG.). 12p. (J). (— 1). bds. 11.99 *(978-1-5247-1722-3(3)*, Random Hse. Bks. for Young Readers) Random Hse. Children's Bks.
—The Pups Save the Bunnies (Paw Patrol) Jackson, Mike, illus. 2016. (Pictureback(R) Ser.). (ENG.). 16p. (J). (gr. -1-1). 4.99 *(978-1-101-93168-4(X)*, Random Hse. Bks. for Young Readers) Random Hse. Children's Bks.
—Team Colors (Paw Patrol) Random House, illus. 2015. (Board Book Ser.). (ENG., Illus.). 24p. (J). (— 1). bds. 6.99 *(978-0-553-49771-7(5)*, Random Hse. Bks. for Young Readers) Random Hse. Children's Bks.
Random, Melanie, des. The Alphabet Song Book. 2006. (ENG., Illus.). 16p. (J). (gr. -1-3). 12.95 *(978-1-58117-444-1(6)*, Intervisual/Piggy Toes) Bendon, Inc.
Ranson, Erin. A Bright New Star: With Color-Changing Star Light. Crisp, Dan, illus. 2007. (Story Book Ser.). 16p. (J). (gr. -1-3). bds. *(978-1-84666-161-7(7)*, Tide Mill Pr.) Top That! Publishing PLC.
—Ocean Wonders. Wood, Hannah, illus. 2007. (Sparkling Slide Nature Bks.). (ENG.). 12p. (J). (gr. -1). 9.99 *(978-1-84666-167-9(6))* Top That! Publishing PLC GBR. Dist: Independent Pubs. Group.
—One Little Bear & Her Friends. Gévry, Claudine, illus. 2007. 10p. (J). (gr. -1-k). bds. *(978-1-84666-354-3(7)*, Tide Mill Pr.) Top That! Publishing PLC.
—Rainforest Wonders. Wood, Hannah, illus. 2007. (Sparkling Slide Nature Bks.). (ENG.). 12p. (J). (gr. -1-k). 9.99 *(978-1-84666-356-7(3)*, Tide Mill Pr.) Top That! Publishing PLC GBR. Dist: Independent Pubs. Group.
—The Story of Noah's Ark. Petrlik, Andrea, illus. 2007. (Interactive Magnetic Book Ser.). 10p. (J). (gr. -1). *(978-1-84666-359-8(8)*, Tide Mill Pr.) Top That! Publishing PLC.
—Woodland Fairies. Top That Publishing Staff, ed. Richards, Kirsten, illus. 2008. (Magnetic Story & Play Scene Ser.). 9p. (J). (gr. -1). bds. *(978-1-84666-440-3(3)*, Tide Mill Pr.) Top That! Publishing PLC.
Rasmussen, Jason. The House of the Lord: A Pop-Up Book. 2011. (Illus.). 32p. (J). 29.99 *(978-1-60641-939-7(0))* Deseret Bk. Co.
Ratnett, Michael. Dracula Steps Out. Goulding, June & Smyth, Iain, illus. 2005. 12p. (J). (gr. k-4). reprint ed. 16.00 *(978-0-7567-8585-7(5))* DIANE Publishing Co.
Ray, Mary Lyn. Goodnight, Good Dog Padded Board Book. Malone, Rebecca, illus. 2018. (ENG.). 30p. (J). (— 1). bds. 8.99 *(978-1-328-85242-7(3)*, 1694366, Clarion Bks.) HarperCollins Pubs.
Rayner, Catherine. Ernest, the Moose Who Doesn't Fit. Rayner, Catherine, illus. 2010. (ENG., Illus.). 32p. (J). (gr. -1-1). 19.99 *(978-0-374-32217-5(1)*, 900065793, Farrar, Straus & Giroux (BYR)) Farrar, Straus & Giroux.
Rayner, Katy. Trucks. 2014. (ENG., Illus.). 22p. 8.95 *(978-1-906572-11-2(9))* Award Pubns. Ltd. GBR. Dist: Parkwest Pubns., Inc.
Read Together Books Inc Staff & Shoule, Michael. My Daddy Loves Boston College Football. 2010. (ENG.). 20p. (J). bds. 11.95 *(978-0-9822615-0-7(0)*, 9780982261507) Read Together Bks.
Read with Me Bible for Little Ones, 1 vol. 2016. (ENG., Illus.). 32p. (J). bds. 9.99 *(978-0-310-75386-5(4))* Zonderkidz.
Reader's Digest Staff. Tractor Trouble Drive Through Storybook. Pitt, Sarah, illus. 2011. (Drive-Through Storybooks Ser.). (ENG.). 10p. (J). (gr. -1-1). bds. 12.99 *(978-0-7944-2169-4(5))* Reader's Digest Assn., Inc., The.
Reasoner, Charles. Animal Friends on the Farm. Pitt, Sarah, illus. 2009. (3D Board Bks.). 12p. (J). (gr. -1-k). bds. 9.99 *(978-1-934650-35-6(8))* Just For Kids Pr., LLC.
—Animals in the Jungle. Pitt, Sarah, illus. 2009. (3D Board Bks.). 12p. (J). (gr. -1-k). bds. 9.99 *(978-1-934650-38-7(2))* Just For Kids Pr., LLC.
—Brrr! 2009. (Lift & Learn Ser.). (Illus.). 10p. (J). (gr. -1-k). 10.99 *(978-1-934650-09-7(9))* Just For Kids Pr., LLC.
—Bug Babies. Devaney, Adam, illus. 2009. (Baby Animal Board Bks.). 12p. (J). (gr. -1-k). bds. 7.99 *(978-1-934650-51-6(X))* Just For Kids Pr., LLC.
—Color Crunch! 2009. (Bite Bks.). (Illus.). (J). bds. 7.99 *(978-1-934650-15-8(3))* Just For Kids Pr., LLC.
—Colors in the Garden. Pitt, Sarah, illus. 2009. (3D Board Bks.). 12p. (J). (gr. -1-k). bds. 9.99 *(978-1-934650-40-0(4))* Just For Kids Pr., LLC.
—A Day Around Town. 2009. (Inside Outside Board Bks.). (Illus.). (J). bds. 10.99 *(978-1-934650-53-0(6))* Just For Kids Pr., LLC.
—A Day at School. 2009. (Inside Outside Board Bks.). (Illus.). (J). bds. 10.99 *(978-1-934650-56-1(0))* Just For Kids Pr., LLC.
—A Day at the Farm. 2009. (Inside Outside Board Bks.). (Illus.). 10p. (J). bds. 10.99 *(978-1-934650-54-7(4))* Just For Kids Pr., LLC.
—Dinosaur Babies. Devaney, Adam, illus. 2009. (Baby Animal Board Bks.). 12p. (J). (gr. -1-k). bds. 7.99 *(978-1-934650-49-3(8))* Just For Kids Pr., LLC.
—Dinosaurs. Doherty, Paula, illus. 2009. (Little Big Flap Bks.). 10p. (J). (gr. -1-k). 9.99 *(978-1-934650-24-0(2))* Just For Kids Pr., LLC.
—Farm Babies. Devaney, Adam, illus. 2009. (Baby Animal Board Bks.). 12p. (J). (gr. -1-k). bds. 7.99 *(978-1-934650-52-3(8))* Just For Kids Pr., LLC.
—Hey, Diddle, Diddle, 1 vol. Le Ray, Marina, illus. 2014. (Charles Reasoner Nursery Rhymes Ser.). (ENG.). 10p. (J). (gr. -1 — 1). bds. 4.99 *(978-1-4795-3807-2(8)*, 124649, Picture Window Bks.) Capstone.
—Hickory, Dickory, Dock. Le Ray, Marina, illus. 2014. (Charles Reasoner Nursery Rhymes Ser.). (ENG.). 10p. (J). (gr. -1 — 1). bds. 4.99 *(978-1-4795-3805-8(1)*, 124647, Picture Window Bks.) Capstone.
—I'm Just a Bird. 2008. *(978-1-84666-153-2(6))* Top That! Publishing PLC.
—I'm Just a Bird. Reasoner, Charles, illus. 2007. (I'm Just Book Ser.). (Illus.). 12p. (J). (gr. -1). bds. *(978-1-84666-289-8(3)*, Tide Mill Pr.) Top That! Publishing PLC.
—I'M Just a Crab! 2018. (Googley Eye Bks.). (ENG., Illus.). 12p. (J). (gr. -1-k). bds. 8.99 *(978-1-84666-157-0(9))* Top That! Publishing PLC GBR. Dist: Independent Pubs. Group.
—I'm Just a Frog. 2008. *(978-1-84666-159-4(5))* Top That! Publishing PLC.
—Inside Jolly Rodger's Pirate Ship. 2014. (Illus.). (J). *(978-1-4351-5466-7(5))* Barnes & Noble, Inc.
—Inside Old MacDonald's Barn. 2014. (Illus.). (J). *(978-1-4351-5467-4(3))* Barnes & Noble, Inc.
—Inside Old Mcdonald's Barn. Reasoner, Charles, illus. 2007. (Story Book Ser.). (Illus.). 12p. (J). (gr. k). bds. *(978-1-84666-287-4(7)*, Tide Mill Pr.) Top That! Publishing PLC.
—Inside Santa's Toy Shop. Reasoner, Charles, illus. 2007. (Story Book Ser.). (Illus.). 12p. (J). (gr. k-3). bds. *(978-1-84666-151-8(X)*, Tide Mill Pr.) Top That! Publishing PLC.
—Itsy Bitsy Spider, 1 vol. Le Ray, Marina, illus. 2013. (Charles Reasoner Nursery Rhymes Ser.). (ENG.). 10p. (J). (gr. -1 — 1). bds. 4.99 *(978-1-4795-1691-9(0)*, 123217, Picture Window Bks.) Capstone.
—Jungle Animals. Doherty, Paula, illus. 2009. (Little Big Flap Bks.). 10p. (J). (gr. -1-k). 9.99 *(978-1-934650-22-6(6))* Just For Kids Pr., LLC.
—Ooink! 2009. (Lift & Learn Ser.). (Illus.). 10p. (J). (gr. -1-k). 10.99 *(978-1-934650-12-7(9))* Just For Kids Pr., LLC.
—Whooo? 2009. (Lift & Learn Ser.). (Illus.). 10p. (J). (gr. -1-k). 10.99 *(978-1-934650-11-0(0))* Just For Kids Pr., LLC.
—The 3 Blind Mice Inside the Spooky Scary & Creepy Haunted House. Reasoner, Charles, illus. 2007. (Story Book Ser.). (Illus.). 10p. (J). (gr. -1-3). bds. *(978-1-84666-381-9(4)*, Tide Mill Pr.) Top That! Publishing PLC.
Reasoner, Charles, illus. Bear Hugs. 2015. (J). *(978-1-4795-5944-2(X)*, Picture Window Bks.) Capstone.
—Honey Bunny. 2015. (J). *(978-1-4795-5945-9(8)*, Picture Window Bks.) Capstone.
—Peep! Peep! 2015. (J). *(978-1-4795-5943-5(1)*, Picture Window Bks.) Capstone.
—Puppy Love. 2015. (J). *(978-1-4795-5946-6(6)*, Picture Window Bks.) Capstone.
Reasoner, Charles & Borgert-Spaniol, Megan. Twinkle, Twinkle, Little Star, 1 vol. Le Ray, Marina & McNicholas, Shelagh, illus. 2013. (Charles Reasoner Nursery Rhymes Ser.). (ENG.). 10p. (J). (gr. -1 — 1). bds. 4.99 *(978-1-4795-1693-3(7)*, 123219, Picture Window Bks.) Capstone.
Reasoner, Charles E. I'm Just a Fish. Reasoner, Charles E., illus. 2008. (Googley-Eye Bks.). (ENG.). 12p. (J). (gr. -1). 8.99 *(978-1-84666-155-6(2))* Top That! Publishing PLC GBR. Dist: Independent Pubs. Group.
Redd, R. I. Happy & Hoppy. Cottage Door Press, ed. Wu, Yi-Hsuan, illus. 2017. (ENG.). 10p. (J). (gr. -1-k). bds. 10.99 *(978-1-68052-287-7(6)*, 1002720) Cottage Door Pr.
Redenbaugh, Vicki. Skar's Picnic ... A Bear's Tale. Redenbaugh, Vicki, illus. 2005. (Illus.). (J). 14.95 *(978-1-59091-034-4(6))* Eastern National.
Reed, Jonathan & Hale, Jenny. Christmas Surprise. 2007. (Illus.). 16p. *(978-1-921049-59-0(6))* Little Hare Bks. AUS. Dist: HarperCollins Pubs. Australia.
Reeve, Tim. Action Robots: A Pop-up Book Showing How They Work. MacLeod, Gavin, illus. 2004. 14p. (YA). (gr.

4-10). reprint ed. 17.00 (978-0-7567-7284-0(2)) DIANE Publishing Co.

Regan, Patricia, illus. Musical Christmas Tree. 2017. (ENG.). 16p. (J). (gr. -1-1). bds. 14.99 (978-0-7641-6899-4(1)) Sourcebooks, Inc.

Regan, Patrick. The Nutcracker. Kuricheva, Natasha, illus. 2016. (ENG.). 26p. (J). bds. 9.99 (978-1-4494-5586-6(7)) Andrews McMeel Publishing.

Reid, Camilla. Lulu & the Noisy Baby. Busby, Ailie, illus. 2016. (Lulu Ser.). (ENG.). 20p. (J). (gr. -1-k). 12.99 (978-1-4088-2818-2(9), 900146195, Bloomsbury Children's Bks.) Bloomsbury Publishing USA.

—Lulu Loves Colours. Busby, Ailie, illus. 2015. (ENG.). 12p. (J). (gr. -1-k). bds. 8.99 (978-1-4088-4964-4(X), 900146185, Bloomsbury Children's Bks.) Bloomsbury Publishing USA.

—Lulu Loves Noises. Busby, Ailie, illus. 2014. (Lulu Ser.). (ENG.). 12p. (J). (gr. -1-k). bds. (978-1-4088-4963-7(1), 233928, Bloomsbury Children's Bks.) Bloomsbury Publishing Plc.

—Lulu Loves Numbers. Busby, Ailie, illus. 2015. (ENG.). 12p. (J). (gr. -1-1). bds. 8.99 (978-1-4088-4957-6(7), 900143539, Bloomsbury Children's Bks.) Bloomsbury Publishing USA.

—Lulu Loves Shapes. Busby, Ailie, illus. 2015. (Lulu Ser.). (ENG.). 12p. (J). (gr. -1-1). bds. (978-1-4088-4958-3(5), 233927, Bloomsbury Children's Bks.) Bloomsbury Publishing Plc.

Reid, Hunter. At the Carnival! Hinton, Stephanie, illus. 2017. (Fluorescent Pop! Ser.). (ENG.). 14p. (J). (gr. -1-k). bds. 5.99 (978-1-4998-0242-9(0)) Little Bee Books Inc.

—Beach Day! Hinton, Stephanie, illus. 2016. (Fluorescent Pop! Ser.). (ENG.). 14p. (J). (gr. -1-k). bds. 5.99 (978-1-4998-0219-1(6)) Little Bee Books Inc.

—Bright Lights, Bright City. Hinton, Stephanie, illus. 2017. (Fluorescent Pop! Ser.). (ENG.). 14p. (J). (gr. -1-k). bds. 5.99 (978-1-4998-0243-6(9)) Little Bee Books Inc.

—Bright Lights Bright City. 2017. (Illus.). (J). bds. (978-1-76040-545-8(0)) Little Bee Books Inc.

—In the Rainforest. Chiu, Alex, illus. 2017. (Fluorescent Pop! Ser.). (ENG.). 14p. (J). (gr. -1-k). bds. 5.99 (978-1-4998-0420-1(2)) Little Bee Books Inc.

—Let's Have a Picnic! Hinton, Stephanie, illus. 2016. (Fluorescent Pop! Ser.). (ENG.). 14p. (J). (gr. -1-k). bds. 5.99 (978-1-4998-0220-7(X)) Little Bee Books Inc.

—Mighty Dinos. Chiu, Alex, illus. 2017. (Fluorescent Pop! Ser.). (ENG.). 14p. (J). (gr. -1-k). bds. 5.99 (978-1-4998-0524-6(1)) Little Bee Books Inc.

Reid, Stephanie. My Body. 2011. (Early Literacy Ser.). (ENG.). 16p. (gr. k-1). 19.99 (978-1-4333-2368-3(0)) Teacher Created Materials, Inc.

—My Country. rev. ed. 2011. (Early Literacy Ser.). (ENG.). 16p. (gr. -1-1). 19.99 (978-1-4333-2361-4(3)) Teacher Created Materials, Inc.

—School. 2011. (Early Literacy Ser.). (ENG.). 16p. (gr. k-1). 19.99 (978-1-4333-2354-6(0)) Teacher Created Materials, Inc.

Reinhart, Matthew. The Ark: A Pop-up Book. Reinhart, Matthew, illus. 2006. (Illus.). 12p. (J). (gr. k-4). reprint ed. 17.00 (978-1-4223-5673-9(6)) DIANE Publishing Co.

—Cinderella: A Pop-Up Fairy Tale. Reinhart, Matthew, illus. 2005. (ENG., Illus.). 12p. (J). (gr. -1-3). 39.99 (978-1-4169-0501-1(4), Little Simon) Little Simon.

—The Jungle Book: A Pop-Up Adventure. Reinhart, Matthew, illus. 2006. (ENG., Illus.). 12p. (J). 39.99 (978-1-4169-1824-0(8), Little Simon) Little Simon.

—A Pop-Up Book of Nursery Rhymes: A Classic Collectible Pop-Up. Reinhart, Matthew, illus. 2009. (ENG., Illus.). 12p. (J). (gr. -1-3). 34.99 (978-1-4169-1825-7(6), Little Simon) Little Simon.

Reinhart, Matthew & Sabuda, Robert. Encyclopedia Mythologica: Gods & Heroes Pop-Up. Reinhart, Matthew & Sabuda, Robert, illus. 2010. (Encyclopedia Mythologica Ser.: 2). (ENG., Illus.). 12p. (J). (gr. k-4). 29.99 (978-0-7636-3171-0(X)) Candlewick Pr.

Reisch, J. A. Frolic First Bible. Rimmington, Natasha, illus. 2016. (Frolic First Faith Ser.). 40p. (J). (gr. -1 — 1). 14.99 (978-1-5064-1043-2(X), Sparkhouse Family) 1517 Media.

—Mi Primera Biblia. Rimmington, Natasha, illus. 2016. (SPA.). (J). (978-1-5064-2103-2(2)) 1517 Media.

Reiss, John J. Numbers. Reiss, John J., illus. 2016. (ENG., Illus.). 34p. (J). (gr. -1 — 1). bds. 8.99 (978-1-4814-7647-8(5), Little Simon) Little Simon.

—Shapes. Reiss, John J., illus. 2016. (ENG., Illus.). 34p. (J). (gr. -1 — 1). bds. 8.99 (978-1-4814-7645-4(9), Little Simon) Little Simon.

Remond-Dalyac, Emmanuelle. Good Night: A Toddler's Bedtime Prayer. Dieterle, Nathatlie, illus. 2017. (ENG.). (J). bds. 7.99 (978-1-5064-2497-2(X), Sparkhouse Family) 1517 Media.

Rennocks, Sam. Under the Sea ABC. 2018. (Padded Board Bks.). (ENG., Illus.). 28p. (J). (gr. -1-k). bds. 9.99 (978-1-78700-452-8(X)) Top That! Publishing PLC GBR. Dist: Independent Pubs. Group.

Rescue Vehicles. (Illus.). 24p. (J). 1.99 (978-1-59445-057-0(9)) Dogs in Hats Children's Publishing Co.

Rescue Vehicles. (Radical Rides Ser.). 16p. (J). (978-2-7643-0014-5(X)) Phidal Publishing, Inc./Editions Phidal, Inc.

Rettore, Kenny. At the Beach. Ferri, Francesca, illus. 2018. 8p. (J). (gr. -1 — 1). 6.99 (978-1-4380-7862-5(5)) Sourcebooks, Inc.

Reul, Sarah Lynne. Pet the Pets: A Lift-The-Flap Book. Reul, Sarah Lynne, illus. 2018. (ENG., Illus.). 18p. (J). (gr. -1 — 1). bds. 8.99 (978-1-5344-0939-2(4), Little Simon) Little Simon.

Rey, H. A. Curious Baby: Curious about Christmas Touch-And-Feel Board Book: A Christmas Holiday Book for Kids. 2011. (Curious Baby Curious George Ser.). (ENG., Illus.). 12p. (J). (gr. k — 1). bds. 8.99 (978-0-547-58841-4(0), 1461240, Clarion Bks.) HarperCollins Pubs.

—Curious Baby: My Favorite Things Padded Board Book. 2011. (Curious Baby Curious George Ser.). (ENG., Illus.). 14p. (J). (gr. -1 — 1). bds. 8.99 (978-0-547-42893-2(6), 1432083, Clarion Bks.) HarperCollins Pubs.

—Curious Baby: My First Words at the Farm Book & Hat Gift Set, Set. gif. ed. 2010. (Curious Baby Curious George Ser.). (ENG., Illus.). 12p. (J). (gr. k — 1). pap. 14.99 (978-0-547-24306-1(5), 1099429, Clarion Bks.) HarperCollins Pubs.

—Curious Baby: My Little Bath Book & Toy Boat. 2009. (Curious Baby Curious George Ser.). (ENG., Illus.). 8p. (J). (gr. -1 — 1). pap. 12.99 (978-0-547-21541-9(X), 1060649, Clarion Bks.) HarperCollins Pubs.

—Curious George Hide-And-Seek Tabbed Board Book. 2008. (Curious George Ser.). (ENG., Illus.). 10p. (J). (gr. -1 — 1). bds. 6.99 (978-0-618-89199-3(4), 569446, Clarion Bks.) HarperCollins Pubs.

—Curious George Neighborhood Friends (CGTV Pull Tab Board Book) 2010. (Curious George Ser.). (ENG., Illus.). 12p. (J). (gr. -1 — 1). bds. 6.99 (978-0-547-23875-3(4), 1084264, Clarion Bks.) HarperCollins Pubs.

—Curious George Parade Day Tabbed Board Book. 2011. (Curious George Ser.). (ENG., Illus.). 14p. (J). (gr. -1 — 1). bds. 8.99 (978-0-547-47282-9(X), 1438167, Clarion Bks.) HarperCollins Pubs.

—Curious George's Fire Truck (Mini Movers Shaped Board Books) 2014. (Curious George Ser.). (ENG., Illus.). 12p. (J). (— 1). bds. 8.99 (978-0-544-14709-6(X), 1547361, Clarion Bks.) HarperCollins Pubs.

—Curious George's Train (Mini Movers Shaped Board Books) 2014. (Curious George Ser.). (ENG., Illus.). 12p. (J). (— 1). bds. 8.99 (978-0-544-32074-1(3), 1582513, Clarion Bks.) HarperCollins Pubs.

—Happy Thanksgiving, Curious George Tabbed Board Book. 2010. (Curious George Ser.). (ENG., Illus.). 14p. (J). (gr. -1 — 1). bds. 8.99 (978-0-547-13106-1(2), 1048360, Clarion Bks.) HarperCollins Pubs.

Reynolds, Alison. Let's Grow a Garden. Hopgood, Andrew, illus. 2009. (Save Our Planet! Ser.). 12p. (J). (gr. -1-3). bds. 11.40 (978-1-60754-412-8(1)) Windmill Bks.

—Let's Save Water. Hopgood, Andrew, illus. 2009. (Save Our Planet! Ser.). 12p. (J). (gr. -1-3). bds. 11.40 (978-1-60754-413-5(X)) Windmill Bks.

—Let's Turn It Off. Hopgood, Andrew, illus. 2009. (Save Our Planet! Ser.). 12p. (J). (gr. -1-3). bds. 11.40 (978-1-60754-414-2(8)) Windmill Bks.

—Let's Use It Again. Hopgood, Andrew, illus. 2009. (Save Our Planet! Ser.). 12p. (J). (gr. -1-3). bds. 11.40 (978-1-60754-415-9(6)) Windmill Bks.

Reynolds, Luke. If My Love Were a Fire Truck: A Daddy's Love Song. Mack, Jeff, illus. 2018. 26p. (J). (— 1). bds. 7.99 (978-0-525-58066-9(2), Doubleday Bks. for Young Readers) Random Hse. Children's Bks.

RH Disney & RH Disney. Olaf's 1-2-3 (Disney Frozen) RH Disney & RH Disney, illus. 2013. (ENG., Illus.). 12p. (J). (— 1). bds. 6.99 (978-0-7364-3064-7(4), Golden/Disney) Random Hse. Children's Bks.

Rice, Dona. What Kind of Weather? 2009. (Early Literacy Ser.). (ENG., Illus.). 16p. (gr. k-1). 19.99 (978-1-4333-1459-9(2)) Teacher Created Materials, Inc.

Rice, Dona Herweck. American Through & Through Lap Book, 1 vol. 2011. (Early Literacy Ser.). (ENG.). 16p. (gr. k-1). 19.99 (978-1-4333-2363-8(X)) Teacher Created Materials, Inc.

—Big Kid School. 2011. (Early Literacy Ser.). (ENG.). 16p. (gr. k-1). 19.99 (978-1-4333-2356-0(7)) Teacher Created Materials, Inc.

—Delicious & Nutritious. 2011. (Early Literacy Ser.). (ENG.). 16p. (gr. k-1). 19.99 (978-1-4333-2370-6(2)) Teacher Created Materials, Inc.

Richmond, Marianne. The Night Night Book. 2011. (Marianne Richmond Ser.: 0). (Illus.). 24p. (J). (gr. -1-k). bds. 7.95 (978-1-934082-90-4(2), Sourcebooks Jabberwocky) Sourcebooks, Inc.

Richter, Bernd & Richter, Susan. Listen to Alaskas Animals. Richter, Bernd, illus. (Illus.). 12p. 2006. (J). act. bk. ed. 12.95 (978-1-931353-25-0(5)) 2003. bds. 12.95 (978-1-931353-12-0(3)) Saddle Pal Creations, Inc.

Rickards, Lynne. Skye the Puffling: A Wee Puffin Board Book, 30 vols. Mitchell, Jon, illus. 2018. 12p. (J). 9.95 (978-1-78250-487-0(7), Kelpies) Floris Bks. GBR. Dist: Consortium Bk. Sales & Distribution.

Riegelman, Rianna. Safari: A Build & Play Story. Chandler, Shannon, illus. 2012. (ENG.). 10p. (J). (gr. -1-1). bds. 15.99 (978-1-4494-2191-5(1)) Andrews McMeel Publishing.

Riggs, Kate. Colors of Nature. Paolo, Domeniconi, illus. 2017. (ENG.). 14p. (J). (gr. -1 — 1). bds. 8.99 (978-1-56846-299-8(9), 20160, Creative Education) Creative Co., The.

—Counting on Birds. van der Linde, Jori, illus. 2017. (ENG.). 14p. (J). (gr. -1 — 1). bds. 8.99 (978-1-56846-300-1(6), 20162, Creative Education) Creative Co., The.

—Crowds of Creatures. Fiammetta, Dogi, illus. 2017. (ENG.). 14p. (J). (gr. -1 — 1). bds. 7.99 (978-1-56846-301-8(4), 20164, Creative Education) Creative Co., The.

—Let's Go Outside. Felix, Monique, illus. 2018. 14p. (J). (gr. -1-k). bds. 8.99 (978-1-56846-316-2(2), 19590, Creative Editions) Creative Co., The.

—Shapes All Around. Devernay, Laëtitia, illus. 2018. (ENG.). 14p. (J). (gr. -1-k). bds. 8.99 (978-1-56846-317-9(0), 19651, Creative Editions) Creative Co., The.

—Sounds of the Forest. Dogi, Fiammetta, illus. 2019. (ENG.). 14p. (J). (gr. -1-k). bds. 8.99 (978-1-56846-318-6(9), 18680, Creative Editions) Creative Co., The.

Riggs, Kate & Sheban, Chris. Beyond the Stars. 2019. (Illus.). 12p. (J). (gr. -1-k). bds. 8.99 (978-1-56846-336-0(7), 18678, Creative Editions) Creative Co., The.

Rigo, Laura. Little Duckling. 2011. (Mini Look at Me Bks.). (Illus.). 10p. (J). bds. 8.99 (978-0-7641-6425-5(2)) Sourcebooks, Inc.

—Little Pony. 2011. (Look at Me Bks.). (Illus.). 10p. (J). (gr. -1). bds. 8.99 (978-0-7641-6448-4(1)) Sourcebooks, Inc.

—Little Reindeer. 2011. (Mini Look at Me Bks.). (Illus.). 10p. (J). (gr. -1). bds. 7.99 (978-0-7641-6450-7(3)) Sourcebooks, Inc.

Rigo, Laura, illus. Little Chimp. 2011. (Mini Look at Me Bks.). 10p. (J). (gr. -1). bds. 7.99 (978-0-7641-6428-6(7)) Sourcebooks, Inc.

—Little Duckling. 2012. (Mini Look at Me Bks.). 10p. (J). (gr. -1). bds. 5.99 (978-0-7641-6510-8(0)) Sourcebooks, Inc.

—Little Elephant. (Mini Look at Me Bks.). 10p. (J). (gr. -1 — 1). 2017. bds. 5.99 (978-0-7641-6879-6(7)) 2011. bds. 8.99 (978-0-7641-6426-2(0)) Sourcebooks, Inc.

—Little Lamb. 2012. (Mini Look at Me Bks.). 10p. (J). (gr. -1). bds. 4.99 (978-0-7641-6511-5(9)) Sourcebooks, Inc.

—Little Panda Bear. 2014. (Mini Look at Me Bks.). 10p. (J). (gr. -1 — 1). bds. 5.99 (978-0-7641-6739-3(1)) Sourcebooks, Inc.

—Little Polar Bear. 2017. (Mini Look at Me Bks.). 10p. (J). (gr. -1 — 1). bds. 4.99 (978-0-7641-6880-2(0)) Sourcebooks, Inc.

—Little Tiger. 2017. (Mini Look at Me Bks.). 10p. (J). (gr. -1 — 1). bds. 4.99 (978-0-7641-6881-9(9)) Sourcebooks, Inc.

—Off to School. 2010. 10p. (J). (gr. -1-1). bds. 7.99 (978-0-7641-6363-0(9)) Sourcebooks, Inc.

Riley, Cooper. Absolutely Awesome Island Animals. 2009. 24p. pap. 9.95 (978-0-9740582-4-5(6)) Tiki Tales.

Riley, Kellee, illus. Happy Halloween, Kai-lan! A Lift-the-Flap Story. 2010. (Ni Hao, Kai-Lan Ser.). (ENG.). 16p. (J). pap. 6.99 (978-1-4424-0178-5(8), Simon Spotlight/Nickelodeon) Simon Spotlight/Nickelodeon.

Ring, Susan. Body: An Interactive & 3-D Exploration. Graham, Michele, illus. 2008. (ENG.). 20p. (J). (gr. 2). 19.95 (978-1-58117-801-2(8), Intervisual/Piggy Toes) Bendon, Inc.

—On the Farm. Melmon, Deborah, illus. 2008. (ENG.). 10p. (J). (gr. 3-17). 12.99 (978-1-58476-729-9(4)) Innovative Kids.

Rinkel, Ken, illus. Giant Machines. 2003. 12p. (J). (gr. k-3). 20.00 (978-0-7567-6653-5(2)) DIANE Publishing Co.

Rinker, Sherri Duskey. Goodnight, Goodnight, Construction Site: Let's Go! (Construction Vehicle Board Books, Construction Site Books, Children's Books for Toddlers) Lichtenheld, Tom, illus. 2017. (Goodnight, Goodnight Construction Site Ser.). (ENG.). 10p. (J). (gr. -1 — 1). bds. 8.99 (978-1-4521-6476-2(2)) Chronicle Bks. LLC.

Ripley, Robert Leroy. Ripley's Oddphabet. 2016. (ENG., Illus.). 24p. (J). (978-1-78475-822-6(1)) Ripley Entertainment, Inc.

Ristuccia, Christine & Ristuccia, James. The Entire World of WH? Questions. 2004. (J). 39.99 (978-0-9723457-9-8(5)) Say It Right.

—The Entire World of WH? Questions Flip Book. 2004. (Illus.). 9p. (J). spiral bd. 14.99 (978-0-9723457-8-1(7)) Say It Right.

Ritchie, Alison. The Tortoise & the Hare. Noj, Nahta, illus. 2015. (ENG.). 32p. (J). (-k). 15.99 (978-0-7636-7601-8(2), Templar) Candlewick Pr.

Ritchie, Joseph R. Baby Looney Tunes Visit a Haunted House. Halverson, Lydia, illus. 2005. (Baby Looney Tunes Ser.). 14p. (J). (gr. -1-3). bds. 9.95 (978-0-8249-6609-6(0), Ideals Pubns.) Worthy Publishing.

—Peter Cottontail's Easter Surprise. Halverson, Lydia, illus. 2006. (ENG.). 18p. (J). (gr. -1-k). bds. 9.95 (978-0-8249-6627-0(9), Ideals Pubns.) Worthy Publishing.

—Where's Santa? Halverson, Lydia, illus. 2006. (ENG.). 14p. (J). (gr. -1-k). bds. 7.95 (978-0-8249-6673-7(2), Ideals Pubns.) Worthy Publishing.

Rivers-Moore, Debbie. Five Christmas Reindeer: A Slide & Count Book. Everitt-Stewart, Andy, illus. 2015. (ENG.). 10p. (J). (gr. -1 — 1). bds. 8.99 (978-1-4998-0169-9(6)) Little Bee Books Inc.

—God Made the World, 1 vol. Haines, Emma, illus. 2017. 4p. 11.99 (978-0-8254-4520-0(5)) Kregel Pubns.

Rizzi, Kathleen. What's in My Dresser?, 1 vol. Riggs, Jenna, illus. 2013. (ENG.). 32p. (J). bds. 7.99 (978-1-59572-165-5(7)) Star Bright Bks., Inc.

—Who Lives Here? Forest, 1 vol. 2013. (Photoflap Board Books Ser.). (ENG., Illus.). 16p. (J). bds. 5.99 (978-1-59572-354-3(4)) Star Bright Bks., Inc.

Roan, Anna. Farm Friends Novelty Board Book. Stockhill, A. M., illus. 2008. (ENG.). 10p. (J). (gr. -1 — 1). bds. 8.99 (978-0-618-91959-8(7), 1015626, Clarion Bks.) HarperCollins Pubs.

Robaard, Jedda. The Little Bird Who Lost His Song. 2015. (ENG., Illus.). 10p. (J). (gr. -1-k). 7.99 (978-1-4998-0093-7(2)) Little Bee Books Inc.

—The Little Lion Who Lost Her Roar. 2014. (Illus.). 9p. (J). (978-1-4351-5391-2(X)) Barnes & Noble, Inc.

—The Little Mouse Who Lost Her Squeak. 2015. (ENG., Illus.). 12p. (J). (gr. -1-k). 7.99 (978-1-4998-0002-9(9)) Little Bee Books Inc.

—The Little Zebra Who Lost His Stripes. 2013. (Illus.). (J). (978-1-4351-5392-9(8)) Barnes & Noble, Inc.

Robbins, Karen S. Think Circles! A Lift-The-Flap Counting, Color, & Shape Book, 1 vol. 2017. (ENG., Illus.). 24p. (J). bds. 12.99 (978-0-7643-5382-6(9), 9780764353826) Schiffer Publishing, Ltd.

—Think Squares! A Lift-The-Flap Counting, Color, & Shape Book, 1 vol. 2017. (ENG., Illus.). 24p. (J). bds. 12.99 (978-0-7643-5383-3(7), 9780764353833) Schiffer Publishing, Ltd.

—Think Triangles! A Lift-The-Flap Counting, Color, & Shape Book, 1 vol. 2017. (ENG., Illus.). 24p. (J). bds. 12.99 (978-0-7643-5381-9(0), 9780764353819) Schiffer Publishing, Ltd.

—Think Zoo Animals: A Lift-The-Flap Guessing Book, 1 vol. Brunson, Rachael, illus. 2018. (ENG.). 24p. (J). bds. 12.99 (978-0-7643-5583-7(X), 9908) Schiffer Publishing, Ltd.

Roberts, Bethany. Valentine Mice! Cushman, Doug, illus. 2016. (Green Light Readers Level 1 Ser.). (ENG.). 32p. (J). (gr. -1-3). 12.99 (978-0-544-80897-3(5), 1641296, Clarion Bks.) HarperCollins Pubs.

—Valentine Mice! Board Book. Cushman, Doug, illus. 2011. (Green Light Readers Level 1 Ser.). (ENG.). 28p. (J). (gr. k — 1). bds. 5.99 (978-0-547-37144-3(6), 1423785, Clarion Bks.) HarperCollins Pubs.

Roberts, Victoria. Best Pet Ever. Allwright, Deborah, illus. 2011. (ENG.). 32p. pap. 7.95 (978-1-58925-432-9(5)) Tiger Tales.

Robertson, James. Katie's a Tae Z: An Alphabet for Wee Folk. Sutherland, Karen, illus. 2014. 20p. (J). (-k). bds. 12.99 (978-1-84502-754-4(X)) Black and White Publishing Ltd. GBR. Dist: Independent Pubs. Group.

Roche, Maite. My First Pictures of Easter. 2012. (ENG.). 14p. (J). 6.99 (978-1-58617-653-2(6)) Ignatius Pr.

Rock, Lois. Look Inside Bible Times. Lewis, Anthony, illus. 2016. (ENG.). 8p. (J). (gr. k-2). 14.99 (978-0-7459-7614-3(X), 9c28a355-7bd7-4298-8d20-f9b642302fd7, Lion Children's) Lion Hudson PLC GBR. Dist: Baker & Taylor Publisher Services (BTPS).

—Look Inside Nativity, 1 vol. Coloji, Livia, illus. 2016. (ENG.). 12p. (J). (gr. -1 — 1). 11.99 (978-0-7459-7611-2(5), 393911bd-4af2-4e29-b555-344646b2bac9, Lion Books) Lion Hudson PLC GBR. Dist: Baker & Taylor Publisher Services (BTPS).

Rodriguez, Patty & Stein, Ariana. Un Elefante: Numbers / Numeros: Numbers- Numeros, 1 vol. Reyes, Citlali, illus. 2018.Tr. of Spanish. 22p. (J). (gr. -1-k). bds. 9.99 (978-0-9861099-4-2(0)) Little Libros, LLC.

—Life of/la Vida de Celia, 1 vol. Reyes, Citlali, illus. 2018. (SPA.). 22p. (J). (gr. -1-k). bds. 9.99 (978-0-9861099-5-9(9)) Little Libros, LLC.

—The Life of/la Vida de Selena, 1 vol. Reyes, Citlali, illus. 2018. (SPA.). 22p. (J). (gr. -1-k). bds. 9.99 (978-0-9861099-9-7(1), Lil' Libros) Little Libros, LLC.

—La Llorona: Counting down / Contando Hacia Atras: Counting down - Contando Hacia Atras, 1 vol. Reyes, Citlali, illus. 2018. (ENG.). 22p. (J). bds. 9.99 (978-0-9861099-2-8(4)) Little Libros, LLC.

—Lucha Libre: Anatomy / Anatomia: Anatomy - Anatomia, 1 vol. Reyes, Citlali, illus. 2018. (ENG.). 22p. (J). bds. 9.99 (978-0-9861099-1-1(6)) Little Libros, LLC.

—Zapata: Colors / Colores, 1 vol. Reyes, Citlali, illus. 2018. 22p. (J). bds. 9.99 (978-1-4951-2657-4(9)) Little Libros, LLC.

Roe, David & Reader's Digest Editors. Mix & Match. Milne, Alex & Ruffolo, Rob, illus. 2007. (ENG.). 12p. (J). (gr. -1-1). bds. 14.99 (978-0-7944-1286-9(6)) Reader's Digest Assn., Inc., The.

Roger Priddy. My Big Animal Book. 2011. (ENG.). 14p. (J). bds. (978-0-312-51365-8(8), Priddy Bks.) St. Martin's Pr.

Rogers, Alan. En Forme de Bateau. 2003. (Little Giants Ser.). (FRE., Illus.). 16p. (J). (gr. -1-k). 5.95 (978-1-58728-177-8(5), Two-Can Publishing) T&N Children's Publishing.

—Higher & Higher. 2004. (Little Giants Ser.). (ENG., Illus.). 16p. (J). (gr. -1-k). 5.95 (978-1-58728-153-2(8), Two-Can Publishing) T&N Children's Publishing.

Romero, Bernardita. Mummy, What's in Your Tummy? Romero, Bernardita, illus. 2020. (ENG., Illus.). 20p. (J). (gr. -1-k). bds. 8.99 (978-1-78285-976-5(4)) Barefoot Bks., Inc.

Ron, Berry. Daddy Do You Love Me. 2009. (ENG.). 20p. bds. 5.99 (978-0-8249-1423-3(6), Ideals Pubns.) Worthy Publishing.

Rookie Toddler(r) (Fall 2014 Set Of 4) 2014. (Rookie Toddler(r) Ser.). (J). bds. 27.80 (978-0-531-24361-9(3)) Scholastic Library Publishing.

Rooney, Anne. Wallace & Gromit's World of Mysteries. 2004. (Illus.). 30p. (gr. 5-9). reprint ed. 30.00 (978-0-7567-7410-3(1)) DIANE Publishing Co.

Roop, Connie & Roop, Peter. Our Solar System. 2016. (Science for Toddlers Ser.: 1). (Illus.). 26p. (J). (gr. -1 — 1). bds. 8.99 (978-1-4549-1418-1(1), 1404673) Sterling Publishing Co., Inc.

Root, Phyllis. The House That Jill Built: A Pop-up Book. Durand, Delphine, illus. 2007. 18p. (J). reprint ed. 16.00 (978-1-4223-6756-8(8)) DIANE Publishing Co.

Roper, Robert. Dora Goes to the Doctor. 2013. (Dora the Explorer 8X8 Ser.). lib. bdg. 14.75 (978-0-606-32216-4(7)) Turtleback.

Rosa-Mendoza, Gladys. I Live Here!/Yo Vivo Aqui! Gonzalez, Margarita E. & Weber, Amy, eds. Burnett, Lindy, illus. 2007. (# 1 Bilingual Board Book Ser.). (ENG & SPA.). 20p. (J). (gr. -1-k). bds. 6.95 (978-1-931398-19-0(4)) Me+Mi Publishing.

Rosario, Sherwin, illus. Meet the Letters. 2005. 26p. (J). 9.99 (978-0-9767008-0-7(8)) Preschool Prep Co.

—Meet the Numbers Lift the Flap Book. 2005. 12p. (J). bds. 9.99 (978-0-9767008-1-4(6)) Preschool Prep Co.

Rosart, Sharyn. I Spy the 50 States. 2018. (J). lib. bdg. 29.40 (978-0-606-41513-2(0)) Turtleback.

Rose, Alexa. The Prankster Handbook. 2014. (PACKtivities Ser.: 4). (ENG.). 48p. (J). 11.99 (978-1-935703-45-7(5)) Downtown Bookworks.

Rose, Robin. New Little Puppy. Cottage Door Press, ed. Hanson, Sydney, illus. 2017. (ENG.). 10p. (J). (gr. -1-k). bds. 10.99 (978-1-68052-159-7(4), 1001570) Cottage Door Pr.

—Sweet Little Unicorn. Cottage Door Press, ed. Uno, Kat, illus. 2017. (ENG.). 12p. (J). (gr. -1-k). bds. 10.99 (978-1-68052-158-0(6), 1001560) Cottage Door Pr.

Rosen, Michael J. Chanukah Lights. Sabuda, Robert, illus. 2011. (ENG.). 16p. (J). (gr. k-4). 34.99 (978-0-7636-5533-4(3)) Candlewick Pr.

Rosenbaum, Andria Warmflash. A Grandma Like Yours: A Grandpa Like Yours. Björnson, Barbara, illus. 2006. 32p. (J). 16.95 (978-1-58013-167-4(0), Kar-Ben Publishing) Lerner Publishing Group.

Rosenberg, Amye. A Surprise in the Mail! Salanitro, Robert, illus. 2009. (Discovery Ser.). (ENG.). 12p. (J). 7.99 (978-1-60436-018-9(6)) Educational Publishing LLC.

Rosenthal, Amy Krouse. Little Oink: (Animal Books for Toddlers, Board Book for Toddlers) Corace, Jen, illus. 2017. (Little Bks.). (ENG.). 24p. (J). bds. 7.99 (978-1-4521-5319-3(1)) Chronicle Bks. LLC.

Rosenthal, Marc. Big Bot, Small Bot: A Book of Robot Opposites. 2015. (ENG., Illus.). 24p. (J). (-k). 17.95 (978-1-57687-750-0(7), powerHouse Bks.) powerHse. Bks.

—1 Robot Lost His Head: a Robot Counting Book. 2015. (ENG., Illus.). 16p. (J). (-k). 17.95 (978-1-57687-749-4(3), powerHouse Bks.) powerHse. Bks.

Rosewarne, Graham, illus. My First Dinosaur Book. 2015. 48p. (J). (gr. -1-12). bds. 9.99 (978-1-86147-424-7(5), Armadillo) Anness Publishing GBR. Dist: National Bk. Network.

Ross, Anna. Knock, Knock! Who's There? (Sesame Street) A Lift-The-Flap Board Book. Mathieu, Joe, illus. 2018. (ENG.). 22p. (J). (— 1). bds. 6.99 (978-1-5247-7032-7(9), Random Hse. Bks. for Young Readers) Random Hse. Children's Bks.

Ross, Tony. Goldilocks & the Three Bears. 2016. (ENG., Illus.). 10p. (J). (-k). bds. 9.99 (978-1-78344-409-0(6)) Andersen Pr. GBR. Dist: Independent Pubs. Group.

—I Want My Potty! (ENG., Illus.). (J). (-k). 2018. (Little Princess Ser.: 1). 32p. pap. 11.99 (978-1-78344-632-2(3)) 2017. 20p. bds. 13.99 (978-1-78344-544-8(0)) Andersen Pr. GBR. Dist: Independent Pubs. Group.

—Jack & the Beanstalk. 2016. (ENG., Illus.). 10p. (J). (-k). bds. 9.99 (978-1-78344-410-6(X)) Andersen Pr. GBR. Dist: Independent Pubs. Group.

Rossetti-Shustak, Bernadette. I Love You Through & Through / Te Quiero, Yo Te Quiero (Bilingual) (Bilingual Edition) Church, Caroline Jayne, illus. 2013. (SPA.). 24p. (J). (gr. -1 — 1). bds. 8.95 (978-0-545-58416-6(7)) Scholastic, Inc.

—I Love You Through & Through at Christmas, Too! Church, Caroline Jayne, illus. 2018. (ENG.). 26p. (J). (gr. -1 — 1). bds. 8.99 (978-1-338-23010-9(7), Cartwheel Bks.) Scholastic, Inc.

Rouss, Sylvia A. Sammy Spider's Passover Shapes. Kahn, Katherine Janus, illus. 2017. (ENG.). 12p. (J). (gr. -1 — 1).

bds. 5.99 *(978-1-4677-7970-8(9),* ff930d1d-18ff-4e40-ae02-3260511dc5f1, Kar-Ben Publishing) Lerner Publishing Group.

Rousseau, Stephanie. Make It Now!: Princesses: Press Out & Play. 2018. (Make It Now! Ser.) (ENG., Illus.). 12p. (J). (gr. -1-3). pap. 8.99 *(978-1-328-71498-5(5),* 1674064, Clarion Bks.) HarperCollins Pubs.

Roussos, Eleni. The Moviemaking Magic of Marvel Studios: Heroes & Villains. 2019. (ENG., Illus.). 176p. (gr. 5-17). 29.99 *(978-1-4197-3587-5(X),* 1269701, Abrams Bks. for Young Readers) Abrams, Inc.

Rowe, Amanda. If There Never Was a You. Skomorokhova, Olga, illus. 2019. (ENG.). 20p. (J). (gr. -1 — 1). bds. 12.99 *(978-1-64170-111-2(0),* 550111) Familius LLC.

Rowe, Helen, illus. Fun with Pets: A Pop-Up Book. 2016. (ENG.). 12p. (J). (gr. -1-k). bds. 8.99 *(978-1-4998-0300-6(1))* Little Bee Books Inc.

Roxbee-Cox, Phil. Ted's Shed. 2004. (Easy Words to Read Ser.). (ENG., Illus.). 1p. (J). (gr. 1-18). pap. 6.95 *(978-0-7460-4210-6(8))* EDC Publishing.

Rubin, Susan Goldman. Jacob Lawrence in the City. 2009. (Mini Masters Modern Ser.). (ENG., Illus.). 24p. (J). (gr. -1 — 1). bds. 7.99 *(978-0-8118-6582-1(7))* Chronicle Bks. LLC.

Rudi, Julie A. That's How Much I Love You. Beeke, Tiphanie, illus. 2013. (ENG.). 20p. (gr. -1). bds. 8.95 *(978-1-58925-644-6(1))* Tiger Tales.

Rueda, Claudia. Bunny Slopes: (Winter Books for Kids, Snow Children's Books, Skiing Books for Kids) 2016. (Bunny Interactive Picture Bks.). (ENG., Illus.). 60p. (J). (gr. -1-k). 16.99 *(978-1-4521-4197-8(5))* Chronicle Bks. LLC.

Rueda, Claudia, illus. I Know an Old Lady Who Swallowed a Fly. 2005. 14p. (J). 12.95 *(978-1-58117-267-6(2),* Intervisual/Piggy Toes) Bendon, Inc.

Rumbaugh, Melinda. Somebunny Loves You! (ENG., Illus.). (J). 2019. 18p. (gr. -1-k). bds. 9.99 *(978-0-8249-1687-9(5))* 2015. 16p. bds. 13.99 *(978-0-8249-1950-4(5))* Worthy Publishing. (Worthy Kids/Ideals).

Runnells, Treesha. Forest Friends: A Fold-Out Fun Book. Runnells, Treesha, illus. 2005. (Fold-Out Fun Ser.). (Illus.). 10p. (J). 4.95 *(978-1-58117-275-1(3),* Intervisual/Piggy Toes) Bendon, Inc.

Rutherford, Peter, illus. Noah's Ark. 2015. 24p. (J). (gr. -1-k). bds. 6.99 *(978-1-86147-644-9(2),* Armadillo) Anness Publishing GBR. Dist: National Bk. Network.

Sabuda, Robert. Beauty & the Beast: A Pop-Up Book of the Classic Fairy Tale. Sabuda, Robert, illus. 2010. (ENG., Illus.). 12p. (J). (gr. -1-2). 39.99 *(978-1-4169-6079-9(1),* Little Simon) Little Simon.

—Ten Horse Farm. Sabuda, Robert, illus. 2018. (ENG., Illus.). 20p. (J). (gr. -1-2). 29.99 *(978-0-7636-6398-8(0))* Candlewick Pr.

—The 12 Days of Christmas Anniversary Edition: A Pop-Up Celebration. Sabuda, Robert, illus. 10th anniv. ed. 2006. (ENG., Illus.). 14p. (J). (gr. -1-3). 39.99 *(978-1-4169-2792-1(1),* Little Simon) Little Simon.

Sabuda, Robert, illus. America the Beautiful: America the Beautiful. 2004. (ENG.). 16p. (J). (gr. -1-3). 39.99 *(978-0-689-84744-8(0),* Little Simon) Little Simon.

—Winter in White: Winter in White. 2007. (ENG.). 18p. (J). (gr. -1-3). 17.99 *(978-0-689-85365-4(3),* Little Simon) Little Simon.

—Winter's Tale: Winter's Tale. 2005. (ENG.). 12p. (J). (gr. -1-3). 39.99 *(978-0-689-85363-0(7),* Little Simon) Little Simon.

Sabuda, Robert & Reinhart, Matthew. Encyclopedia Prehistorica Dinosaurs Pop-Up. Sabuda, Robert & Reinhart, Matthew, illus. 2005. (Encyclopedia Prehistorica Ser.: 1). (ENG., Illus.). 12p. (J). (gr. k-4). 44.99 *(978-0-7636-2228-2(1))* Candlewick Pr.

Safran, Sheri. All Kinds of Festivals. Fuller, Rachel, illus. 2012. (ENG.). 12p. (J). (gr. -1). 12.99 *(978-1-60887-162-9(2))* Insight Editions.

—All Kinds of People. Damon, Emma, illus. 2012. (ENG.). 12p. (J). (gr. -1). 12.99 *(978-1-60887-160-5(6))* Insight Editions.

—Bully. Tipping, Naomi, illus. 2012. (ENG.). 12p. (J). (gr. -1). 12.99 *(978-1-60887-163-6(0))* Insight Editions.

Salmon, Michael. Dinosaur. 2006. (Illus.). 32p. (J). *(978-1-74178-213-4(9))* Five Mile Australia.

Saltzberg, Barney. Beautiful Oops! 2010. (ENG., Illus.). 28p. (J). (gr. -1-3). 16.95 *(978-0-7611-5728-1(X),* 15728) Workman Publishing Co., Inc.

—My Book of Beautiful Oops! A Scribble It, Smear It, Fold It, Tear It Journal for Young Artists. 2017. (ENG., Illus.). 52p. (J). (gr. -1-7). 16.99 *(978-0-7611-8950-3(5),* 18950) Workman Publishing Co., Inc.

—Redbird: Colors, Colors, Everywhere! 2015. (ENG., Illus.). 22p. (J). bds. *(978-0-7611-8185-9(7),* 18185) Workman Publishing Co., Inc.

—Twinkle, Twinkle, ABC: A Mixed-Up, Mashed-up Melody. 2017. (ENG., Illus.). 32p. (J). (gr. -1 — 1). bds. 12.95 *(978-0-7148-7507-1(4))* Phaidon Pr., Inc.

Salyards, Jeffrey. Dino Thunder. 2004. (Illus.). (J). *(978-1-4127-0493-9(6))* Publications International, Ltd.

Salzano, Tammi. One Sunny Day. 2013. pap. *(978-0-545-53655-4(3))* Scholastic, Inc.

—Truck Party. Wood, Hannah, illus. 2011. (ENG.). 20p. (J). bds. 7.95 *(978-1-58925-865-5(7))* Tiger Tales.

SAMi. Flip-a-Face: Colors. (ENG.). 24p. (J). bds. 8.95 *(978-1-59354-137-8(6))* Blue Apple Bks.

—Let's Learn Colors & Shapes. 2012. (Illus.). (J). *(978-1-60905-243-0(9))* Handprint Bks.

Sams, Carl R., II. Stranger in the Woods. 2004. (ENG.). 14.95 *(978-0-9671748-7-7(2))* Sams, II, Carl R. Photography, Inc.

Sams, Carl R., II & Stoick, Jean. Happy Bird Day! Sams, Carl R., II & Stoick, Jean, photos by. 2012. (ENG., Illus.). 14p. (J). bds. 7.95 *(978-0-9827625-2-3(6))* Sams, II, Carl R. Photography, Inc.

Sams II, Carl R. & Stoick, Jean, photos by. When Snowflakes Fall. 2009. (ENG., Illus.). 14p. bds. 7.95 *(978-0-9770108-9-9(9))* Sams, II, Carl R. Photography, Inc.

Samuel, Anna. Glitter Butterflies Stickers. 2004. (Dover Stickers Ser.). (ENG., Illus.). 2p. (gr. -1). 2.99 *(978-0-486-43537-4(7),* 435377) Dover Pubns., Inc.

Samuel, Janet, illus. One Sneaky Sheep: The Sheep Who Didn't Want to Get Sheared. 2009. (ENG.). 20p. (J). 9.95 *(978-1-58117-841-8(7),* Intervisual/Piggy Toes) Bendon, Inc.

Sands, Emily. Egyptology: Search for the Tomb of Osiris. Steer, Dugald A., ed. 2004. (Ologies Ser.). (ENG., Illus.). 32p. (J). (gr. 3-7). 29.99 *(978-0-7636-2638-9(4))* Candlewick Pr.

Sandviks HOP, Inc. Staff, contrib. by. My Colors Wipe-off Board Book with DVD. DVD 10.99 *(978-1-60143-896-6(6))* HOP, LLC.

Sandy Creek (Firm) Staff, contrib. by. Discover Dinosaurs: Prehistoric Beast, Fossils, & Fun Facts! 2015. (Illus.). 51p. (J). *(978-1-4351-6223-5(4))* Barnes & Noble, Inc.

—Let's Learn Shapes. 2013. (Illus.). *(978-1-4351-4941-0(6))* Barnes & Noble, Inc.

—Medical Chart. 2016. (Illus.). 8p. (J). *(978-1-4351-6397-3(4))* Barnes & Noble, Inc.

—My First Book of Ocean Creatures: Learn about Jellyfish, Sharks, Deep Sea Creatures, & More with Fun Facts! 2016. (Illus.). 51p. (J). *(978-1-4351-6406-2(7))* Barnes & Noble, Inc.

—My First Book of Pets: Learn about Dogs, Cats, Lizards, & More with Fun Facts! 2016. (Illus.). 51p. (J). *(978-1-4351-6527-4(6))* Barnes & Noble, Inc.

—My First Book of Sharks: Learn about Great Whites, Hammerheads, Goblin Sharks, & More with Fun Facts! 2016. (Illus.). 51p. (J). *(978-1-4351-6321-8(4))* Barnes & Noble, Inc.

—My First Book of Wild Animals: Learn about Zebras, Elephants, Pandas, & More with Fun Facts! 2016. (Illus.). 51p. (J). *(978-1-4351-6322-5(2))* Barnes & Noble, Inc.

—Our Solar System & Beyond: Planets, Stars, Space Travel & Fun Facts! 2014. (Illus.). (J). *(978-1-4351-5603-6(X))* Barnes & Noble, Inc.

Sanfilippo, Simona, illus. Rapunzel. 2009. (Flip-Up Fairy Tales Ser.). 24p. (J). (gr. -1-2). *(978-1-84643-292-7(8));* pap. *(978-1-84643-249-1(9))* Child's Play International Ltd.

Sanschagrin, Joceline. Caillou at the Doctor. Brignaud, Pierre, illus. 3rd ed. 2013. (Step by Step Ser.). (ENG.). 24p. (J). (gr. -1-k). bds. 5.99 *(978-2-89718-058-4(7))* Caillouet, Gerry.

Santomero, Angela C. Big Brother Daniel. Fruchter, Jason, illus. 2015. (Daniel Tiger's Neighborhood Ser.). (ENG.). 14p. (J). (gr. -1-k). bds. 6.99 *(978-1-4814-3172-9(2),* Simon Spotlight) Simon Spotlight.

—Happy Halloween, Daniel Tiger! A Lift-The-Flap Book. Fruchter, Jason, illus. 2014. (Daniel Tiger's Neighborhood Ser.). (ENG.). 14p. (J). (gr. -1-2). bds. 6.99 *(978-1-4814-0429-7(6),* Simon Spotlight) Simon Spotlight.

Santore, Charles. Night Before Christmas Board Book: The Classic Edition (the New York Times Bestseller) 2013. (Classic Edition Ser.). (ENG., Illus.). 24p. (J). (gr. -1). bds. 8.95 *(978-1-60433-438-8(X),* Applesauce Pr.) Cider Mill Pr. Bk. Pubs., LLC.

Santoro, Christopher. Open the Barn Door... 2016. (Illus.). 22p. (J). (— 1). bds. 6.99 *(978-0-399-54948-9(X),* Random Hse. Bks. for Young Readers) Random Hse. Children's Bks.

—Open the Garage Door. 2018. (Lift-The-Flap Ser.). (Illus.). 22p. (J). (— 1). bds. 6.99 *(978-1-5247-6778-5(6),* Random Hse. Bks. for Young Readers) Random Hse. Children's Bks.

Santoro, Lucio & Santoro, Meera. Wild Oceans: A Pop-Up Book with Revolutionary Technology. 2010. (ENG.). 12p. (J). (gr. 1-5). 32.99 *(978-1-4169-8467-2(4),* Little Simon) Little Simon.

Sapp, Karen, illus. Ellie's Christmas. 2013. (J). *(978-1-4351-4835-2(5))* Barnes & Noble, Inc.

Sarell, Nadja, illus. Little Dove & the Story of Easter, 1 vol. 2019. (ENG.). 22p. (J). bds. 7.99 *(978-0-310-76668-1(0))* Zonderkidz.

Sassi, Laura. Goodnight, Ark, 1 vol. Chapman, Jane, illus. 2015. (ENG.). 24p. (J). bds. 8.99 *(978-0-310-74938-7(7))* Zonderkidz.

Sattler, Jennifer. Bundle Up. Sattler, Jennifer, illus. 2018. (ENG., Illus.). 22p. (J). (gr. -1-k). bds. 7.99 *(978-1-5341-1002-1(X),* 204582) Sleeping Bear Pr.

—Dirty Birdies. Sattler, Jennifer, illus. 2018. (ENG., Illus.). 22p. (J). (gr. -1-k). bds. 8.99 *(978-1-58536-389-6(8),* 204397) Sleeping Bear Pr.

—Frankie the Blankie. 2016. (ENG., Illus.). 32p. (J). 16.99 *(978-1-61963-675-0(1),* 900145316, Bloomsbury USA Childrens) Bloomsbury Publishing USA.

—Jungle Gym. Sattler, Jennifer, illus. 2018. (ENG., Illus.). 22p. (J). (gr. -1-k). bds. 7.99 *(978-1-58536-390-2(1),* 204398) Sleeping Bear Pr.

—Oink-Oink! Moo! Cock-A-Doodle-Doo! Sattler, Jennifer, illus. 2019. (ENG., Illus.). 22p. (J). (gr. -1-k). bds. 8.99 *(978-1-58536-391-9(X),* 204654) Sleeping Bear Pr.

Sauer, Tammi. Truck, Truck, Goose! Board Book. Waring, Zoe, illus. 2018. (ENG.). 40p. (J). (gr. -1 — 1). bds. 7.99 *(978-0-06-242154-8(9),* HarperFestival) HarperCollins Pubs.

Saunders, Katie, illus. Let's Learn Opposites. 2013. 10p. (J). *(978-1-4351-4940-3(8))* Barnes & Noble, Inc.

—Little Reindeer. 2012. 10p. (J). *(978-1-4351-4314-2(0))* Barnes & Noble, Inc.

Savage, Stephen. Little Tug. Savage, Stephen, illus. 2015. (ENG., Illus.). 34p. (J). (gr. -1-1). bds. 10.99 *(978-1-62672-124-1(6),* 900138367) Roaring Brook Pr.

—Seven Orange Pumpkins Board Book. 2015. (Illus.). 28p. (J). (gr. -1 — 1). bds. 7.99 *(978-0-8037-4138-6(3),* Dial Bks) Penguin Young Readers Group.

Sayre, April Pulley. Rah, Rah, Radishes! A Vegetable Chant. Sayre, April Pulley, photos by. 2014. (Classic Board Bks.). (ENG., Illus.). 34p. (J). (gr. -1 — 1). bds. 8.99 *(978-1-4424-9927-0(3),* Little Simon) Little Simon.

Scarry, Richard. Richard Scarry's Boats. Scarry, Richard, illus. 2015. (Illus.). 24p. (J). (— 1). bds. 4.99 *(978-0-385-39269-3(9),* Golden Bks.) Random Hse. Children's Bks.

—Richard Scarry's Bunnies. Scarry, Richard, illus. 2014. (Illus.). 26p. (J). (-k). 8.99 *(978-0-385-38518-3(8),* Golden Bks.) Random Hse. Children's Bks.

—Richard Scarry's Cars & Trucks. Scarry, Richard, illus. 2017. (Little Golden Book Ser.). (Illus.). 24p. (J). (-k). 5.99 *(978-1-101-93927-7(3),* Golden Bks.) Random Hse. Children's Bks.

—Richard Scarry's Planes. Scarry, Richard, illus. 2015. (Illus.). 24p. (J). (— 1). bds. 4.99 *(978-0-385-39270-9(2),* Golden Bks.) Random Hse. Children's Bks.

—Richard Scarry's the Rooster Struts. 2015. (Illus.). 26p. (J). (— 1). bds. 7.99 *(978-0-553-50852-9(0),* Golden Bks.) Random Hse. Children's Bks.

Schaefer, Lola. Easter Surprises. McCue, Lisa, illus. 2009. (ENG.). 18p. (J). (gr. -1-1). 7.99 *(978-1-4169-6476-6(2),* Little Simon) Little Simon.

Schaefer, Lola M. Boo Who? A Foldout Halloween Adventure. Frost, Michael, photos by. 2009. (ENG., Illus.). 12p. (J). (gr. -1-k). bds. 7.99 *(978-1-4169-5911-3(4),* Little Simon) Little Simon.

Scheffler, Axel. Noisy Farm. 2014. (ENG., Illus.). 10p. (J). (gr. -1-k). 23.95 *(978-0-230-76680-8(3))* Pan Macmillan GBR. Dist: Independent Pubs. Group.

Scheffler, Axel, illus. Cuddly Cow: A Farm Friends Sound Book. 2017. (Farm Friends Sound Book Ser.). (ENG.). 12p. (J). (— 1). bds. 9.99 *(978-0-7636-9325-1(1))* Candlewick Pr.

Schertle, Alice. El Camioncito Azul: Little Blue Truck (Spanish Edition) McElmurry, Jill, illus. 2013.Tr. of Little Blue Truck. (SPA.). 30p. (J). (gr. -1 — 1). bds. 9.99 *(978-0-547-98397-4(2),* 1524121, Clarion Bks.) HarperCollins Pubs.

—Little Blue Truck's Springtime: An Easter & Springtime Book for Kids. McElmurry, Jill, illus. 2018. (ENG.). 16p. (J). (gr. -1 — 1). bds. 13.99 *(978-0-544-93809-0(7),* 1658575, Clarion Bks.) HarperCollins Pubs.

Schiller, Pam. Five Little Ducks. Newsom, Carol, illus. 2014. 19p. (J). *(978-1-60128-879-0(4))* Frog Street Pr.

Schiller, Pamela Byrne. I Like Yellow. Weekly, Debbie, illus. 2014. 15p. (J). *(978-1-60128-861-5(1))* Frog Street Pr.

Schindel, John. Busy Pandas. Husar, Lisa & Husar, Mike, photos by. 2008. (Busy Book Ser.). (Illus.). 20p. (J). (gr. -1 — 1). 6.99 *(978-1-58246-259-2(3),* Knopf Bks. for Young Readers) Random Hse. Children's Bks.

Schindel, John & Woodward, Molly. The Babies & Doggies Book. 2015. (ENG.). 26p. (J). (— 1). bds. 7.99 *(978-0-544-44477-5(9),* 1597681, Clarion Bks.) HarperCollins Pubs.

Schneider, Judy. But Not Quite. Weeks, Mary, illus. 2004. (J). 19.95 *(978-1-59404-005-4(2))* Peanut Butter Publishing.

Scholastic. Animals ABC: Scholastic Early Learners (Slide & Find) 2016. (Scholastic Early Learners Ser.). (ENG.). 10p. (J). (gr. -1 — 1). bds. 9.99 *(978-0-545-90344-8(0))* Scholastic, Inc.

—Dreidel, Dreidel, Dreidel! Kober, Shahar, illus. 2014. (ENG.). 10p. (J). (gr. -1 — 1). bds. 4.99 *(978-0-545-53364-5(3),* Cartwheel Bks.) Scholastic, Inc.

—First 100 Things That Go: Scholastic Early Learners (Touch & Lift) 2016. (Scholastic Early Learners Ser.). (ENG.). 12p. (J). (gr. -1 — 1). bds. 6.99 *(978-0-545-90343-1(2))* Scholastic, Inc.

—Learn to Write: Scholastic Early Learners (Write & Wipe) 2016. (Scholastic Early Learners Ser.). (ENG.). 28p. (J). (gr. -1-k). pap. 8.99 *(978-0-545-90345-5(9))* Scholastic, Inc.

—My First Book of Shapes: Scholastic Early Learners (My First) 2017. (Scholastic Early Learners Ser.). (ENG.). 14p. (J). (gr. -1 — 1). bds. 6.99 *(978-1-338-16151-9(2),* Cartwheel Bks.) Scholastic, Inc.

—My First Learning Library Box Set: Scholastic Early Learners (My First). Set. 2017. (Scholastic Early Learners Ser.). (ENG.). 104p. (J). (gr. -1 — 1). 12.99 *(978-1-338-20243-4(X),* Cartwheel Bks.) Scholastic, Inc.

—Touch & Feel Trucks: Scholastic Early Learners (Touch & Feel) 2016. (Scholastic Early Learners Ser.). (ENG.). 14p. (J). (gr. -1 — 1). bds. 6.99 *(978-1-338-11663-2(0),* Cartwheel Bks.) Scholastic, Inc.

—Touch & Feel Winter: Scholastic Early Learners (Touch & Feel) 2017. (Scholastic Early Learners Ser.). (ENG.). 14p. (J). (gr. -1 — 1). bds. 6.99 *(978-1-338-16145-8(8),* Cartwheel Bks.) Scholastic, Inc.

Scholastic Early Learners Staff. Noisy Touch & Lift Truck. 2018. (Scholastic Early Learners Ser.). (ENG.). 14p. (J). (gr. -1-k). 12.99 *(978-1-338-28398-3(7),* Cartwheel Bks.) Scholastic, Inc.

Scholastic Early Learners Staff & Scholastic. Touch & Feel 123. 2017. (Scholastic Early Learners Ser.). (ENG.). 28p. (J). (gr. -1 — 1). bds. 12.99 *(978-1-338-16146-5(6),* Cartwheel Bks.) Scholastic, Inc.

Scholastic, Inc. Staff. Hidden Hogwarts: Scratch Magic. Warner Bros. & Bull, Carolyn, illus. 2018. (Harry Potter Ser.). (ENG.). 64p. (J). (gr. 2-2). 12.99 *(978-1-338-24610-0(0))* Scholastic, Inc.

—Noisy Touch & Lift Farm. 2018. (Scholastic Early Learners Ser.). (ENG.). 14p. (J). (gr. -1-k). 12.99 *(978-1-338-28397-6(9),* Cartwheel Bks.) Scholastic, Inc.

—Shapes at Home. 2015. (Rookie Toddler(r) Ser.). (ENG.). 12p. (J). bds. 6.95 *(978-0-531-20573-0(8))* Scholastic Library Publishing.

Scholastic, Inc. Staff, contrib. by. ABC. 2013. (Rookie Toddler(r) Ser.). (ENG.). 12p. (J). bds. 6.95 *(978-0-531-21576-0(8),* Children's Pr.) Scholastic Library Publishing.

—Counting 1 to 10. 2012. (Rookie Toddler Ser.). (ENG., Illus.). 12p. (J). bds. 6.95 *(978-0-531-20851-9(6),* Children's Pr.) Scholastic Library Publishing.

Scholastic, Inc. Staff & DreamWorks Animation Staff, contrib. by. Over the Hedge: Animal Antics. 2006. (Illus.). 16p. (J). *(978-1-4156-7542-7(2))* Scholastic, Inc.

School Zone. Animal Alphabet. 2008. (ENG.). 26p. (J). 5.99 *(978-1-58947-932-6(7))* School Zone Publishing Co.

School Zone Publishing Company Staff. Numbers & Shapes. 2008. (ENG.). (J). 5.99 *(978-1-60159-102-9(0))* School Zone Publishing Co.

—3D Think & Blink Alphabet. 2007. (ENG.). (J). 7.99 *(978-1-60159-101-2(2))* School Zone Publishing Co.

School Zone Staff. My First Smart Art Alphabet. 2009. pap. 2.99 *(978-1-60159-250-7(7))* School Zone Publishing Co.

Schories, Pat, illus. Biscuit Visits the Farm. 2012. (J). *(978-1-4351-4383-8(3),* HarperFestival) HarperCollins Pubs.

—Biscuit's Fourth of July. 2005. (J). *(978-1-4156-0311-6(1),* HarperFestival) HarperCollins Pubs.

—Biscuit's Graduation Day. 2005. (J). *(978-1-4155-9660-9(3),* HarperFestival) HarperCollins Pubs.

Schrader, Missy Wolgemuth & Schrader, Missy W. Hooray! I Obeyed!, 1 vol. Nuffer, Bruce, ed. 2008. (ENG., Illus.). 12p. (J). (gr. -1). bds. 3.99 *(978-0-310-71396-8(X))* Zondervan.

Schrey, Sophie. Follow Me: Play for Little Hands. Sheridan, Lucie, illus. 2019. (Play for Little Hands Ser.). (ENG.). 14p. (J). (— 1). bds. 9.99 *(978-1-910552-80-3(1))* O'Mara, Michael Bks., Ltd. GBR. Dist: Independent Pubs. Group.

Schulman, Janet. 10 Easter Egg Hunters. 2015. lib. bdg. 14.75 *(978-0-606-36379-2(3))* Turtleback.

—10 Trim-The-Tree'ers. Davick, Linda, illus. 2011. (ENG.). 32p. (J). (gr. -1 — 1). bds. 6.99 *(978-0-375-87302-7(3),* Knopf Bks. for Young Readers) Random Hse. Children's Bks.

Schulz, Charles M. It's the Great Pumpkin, Charlie Brown: with Sound & Music. 2012. (ENG., Illus.). 48p. (J). (gr. -1-3). 19.95 *(978-0-7624-4606-3(4),* Running Pr. Kids) Running Pr.

Schwartz, Betty & Seresin, Lynn. Puppies, Puppies, Everywhere! A Back-And-Forth Opposites Book. Powell, Luciana Navarro, illus. 2015. (J). *(978-1-62370-236-6(4),* Capstone Young Readers) Capstone.

Schwartz, Betty Ann. One to Ten... & Back Again. Shakir, Susie, illus. 2009. 24p. bds. 12.99 *(978-0-8249-1436-3(8),* Ideals Pubns.) Worthy Publishing.

—What Makes a Rainbow? Turner, Dona, illus. 2006. (Magic Ribbon Books). (ENG.). 14p. (J). 4.95 *(978-1-58117-220-1(6),* Intervisual/Piggy Toes) Bendon, Inc.

Schwartz, Betty Ann & Seresin, Lynn. Run, Run Piglet: A Follow-Along Book. Ng, Neiko, illus. 2015. (Follow-Along Book Ser.). (ENG.). 10p. (J). (gr. -1 — 1). bds. 9.99 *(978-1-4521-2467-4(1))* Chronicle Bks. LLC.

Schwartz, Roslyn. The Mole Sisters & the Blue Egg. 2019. (Mole Sisters Ser.). (Illus.). 32p. (J). bds. 7.99 *(978-1-77321-219-7(2))* Annick Pr., Ltd. CAN. Dist: Publishers Group West (PGW).

—The Mole Sisters & the Question. 2019. (Mole Sisters Ser.). (ENG., Illus.). 32p. (J). (gr. -1-k). bds. 7.99 *(978-1-77321-224-1(9))* Annick Pr., Ltd. CAN. Dist: Publishers Group West (PGW).

—The Mole Sisters & the Rainy Day. 2019. (Mole Sisters Ser.). (ENG., Illus.). 32p. (J). (gr. -1-k). bds. 7.99 *(978-1-77321-229-6(X))* Annick Pr., Ltd. CAN. Dist: Publishers Group West (PGW).

—The Mole Sisters & the Wavy Wheat. 2019. (Mole Sisters Ser.). (ENG., Illus.). 32p. (J). (gr. -1-k). bds. 7.99 *(978-1-77321-214-2(1))* Annick Pr., Ltd. CAN. Dist: Publishers Group West (PGW).

Scoggins, Terry. Electric Ellie & Lightning Lucy: Firefly Friends Forever. 2008. 16p. pap. 8.99 *(978-1-4389-1254-7(4))* AuthorHouse.

Scollon, Bill, et al. Sofia's Princess Adventures. 2015. (Illus.). (J). *(978-1-4847-2563-4(8))* Disney Publishing Worldwide.

Scott, MaryJo. Corduroy's Colors. McCue, Lisa, illus. 2016. (Corduroy Ser.). 14p. (J). (— 1). bds. 5.99 *(978-0-451-47247-2(0),* Viking Books for Young Readers) Penguin Young Readers Group.

—Corduroy's Seasons. McCue, Lisa, illus. 2016. (Corduroy Ser.). 14p. (J). (— 1). bds. 6.99 *(978-0-451-47249-6(7),* Viking Books for Young Readers) Penguin Young Readers Group.

Scotton, Rob. Splat the Cat Board Book. Scotton, Rob, illus. 2016. (Splat the Cat Ser.). (ENG., Illus.). 34p. (J). (gr. -1 — 1). bds. 7.99 *(978-0-06-229436-4(9),* HarperFestival) HarperCollins Pubs.

—Splish, Splash, Splat! Board Book. Scotton, Rob, illus. 2016. (Splat the Cat Ser.). (ENG., Illus.). 36p. (J). (gr. -1 — 1). bds. 7.99 *(978-0-06-229438-8(5),* HarperFestival) HarperCollins Pubs.

Scribens, Sunny. Baby Dream. 2019. (ENG., Illus.). 16p. (J). (gr. -1-k). bds. 7.99 *(978-1-78285-729-7(X))* Barefoot Bks., Inc.

Scudamore, Angelika. Noah's Ark Animal ABCs, 1 vol. 2018. (ENG., Illus.). 28p. (J). bds. 9.99 *(978-0-310-76700-8(8))* Zonderkidz.

Scudamore, Angelika, illus. Little Puppy's Busy Day. 2016. (J). *(978-1-62885-142-7(2))* Kidsbooks, LLC.

Seal, Kerry. Five Silly Pumpkins: A Pop-up Halloween Book. Smith, Jane, illus. 2009. 10p. (J). 5.95 *(978-1-58117-908-8(1),* Intervisual/Piggy Toes) Bendon, Inc.

Seder, Rufus Butler. AL Galope! 2009. (Scanimation Ser.). (SPA., Illus.). 12p. (J). (gr. -1-3). 12.95 *(978-0-7611-5415-0(9),* 15415) Workman Publishing Co., Inc.

Segal, Nechamy. The Torah Book of Opposites. Lumer, Marc, illus. 2012. (ENG.). 12p. (J). pap. 8.99 *(978-1-929628-67-4(6))* Hachai Publishing.

Seiss, Ellie. Best Friends: A Chock-a-Block Book. Scanlon, Michael, illus. 2010. (Yo Gabba Gabba! Ser.). (ENG.). 12p. (J). 5.99 *(978-1-4424-0970-5(3),* Simon Spotlight) Simon Spotlight.

Selbert, Kathryn, illus. Ally Bally Bee: A Lift-The-flap Book, 30 vols. 2022. (Scottish Rhymes Ser.). 12p. (J). 9.95 *(978-1-78250-439-7(7),* Kelpies) Floris Bks. GBR. Dist: Consortium Bk. Sales & Distribution.

Sellier, Marie. Renoir's Colors. 2010. (ENG., Illus.). 40p. (gr. -1-k). 16.95 *(978-1-60606-003-2(1))* Getty Pubns.

Seltzer, Eric. Arf! Buzz! Cluck! A Rather Noisy Alphabet. Creighton-Pester, David, illus. 2018. (ENG.). 24p. (J). (gr. -1 — 1). bds. 7.99 *(978-1-5344-1297-2(2),* Little Simon) Little Simon.

Sendak, Maurice. Alligators All Around Board Book: An Alphabet. Sendak, Maurice, illus. 2017. (ENG., Illus.). 32p. (J). (gr. -1-3). bds. 8.95 *(978-0-06-266807-3(2),* HarperCollins) HarperCollins Pubs.

—Chicken Soup with Rice Board Book: A Book of Months. Sendak, Maurice, illus. 2017. (ENG., Illus.). 32p. (J). (gr. -1 — 1). bds. 7.95 *(978-0-06-266808-0(0),* HarperCollins) HarperCollins Pubs.

—One Was Johnny Board Book: A Counting Book. Sendak, Maurice, illus. 2017. (ENG., Illus.). 46p. (J). (gr. -1-3). bds. 7.95 *(978-0-06-266809-7(9),* HarperCollins) HarperCollins Pubs.

—Pierre Board Book: A Cautionary Tale in Five Chapters & a Prologue. Sendak, Maurice, illus. 2017. (ENG., Illus.). 38p. (J). (gr. -1-3). bds. 7.95 *(978-0-06-266810-3(2),* HarperCollins) HarperCollins Pubs.

Senior, Suzy. Teddy Bear Says Good Night. Mitchell, Melanie, illus. 2014. (Teddy Bear Says Ser.). (ENG.). 12p. (J). (— 1). bds. 6.99 *(978-0-7459-6436-2(2),* 9c45181d-511c-4096-98c0-033b661f8d29, Lion Children's) Lion Hudson PLC GBR. Dist: Baker & Taylor Publisher Services (BTPS).

Serrano, Francisco. Our Lady of Guadalupe, 1 vol. Davalos, Felipe, 1st & Davalos, Felipe, illus. 2nd ed. 2010. (ENG.). 12p. (J). (gr. -1 — 1). 22.95 *(978-1-55498-074-1(7))*

Groundwood Bks. CAN. Dist: Publishers Group West (PGW).

Sesame Street Staff. Fairly Furry 2 bk Big Red Riding Hood 3 Little Grouches. 2007. 15.99 *(978-1-59069-625-5(5))* Studio Mouse LLC.

—Fairly Furry 2 bk Rhyming Rapunzel Rosita & Beanstalk. 2007. 15.99 *(978-1-59069-624-8(7))* Studio Mouse LLC.

—Fairly Furry Fairy Tales 3 bk Pack. 2007. 19.99 *(978-1-59069-623-1(9))* Studio Mouse LLC.

Sesame Street Staff, creator. Sesame Street: Early Learning Boxed Set. 2011. 72p. (J). bds. 12.99 *(978-1-60745-237-9(5))* Flying Frog Pubs.

—Sesame Street: Elmo & Me! Boxed Set. 2011. 40p. (J). bds. 12.99 *(978-1-60745-166-2(2))* Flying Frog Pubs.

—Sesame Street: My First Manners Boxed Set. 2011. 72p. (J). bds. 12.99 *(978-1-60745-238-6(3))* Flying Frog Pubs.

Sesame Street Staff & Studio Mouse Staff. Learning Fun. 2008. (ENG.). 60p. (J). 4.99 *(978-1-59069-671-2(9))* Studio Mouse LLC.

Seuss. All Aboard the Circus Mcgurkus. 2004. (Dr. Seuss Nursery Collection). (ENG., Illus.). 10p. (J). (— 1). bds. 8.99 *(978-0-375-83011-2(1),* Random Hse. Bks. for Young Readers) Random Hse. Children's Bks.

—The Big Boxed Set of Bright & Early Board Books about Me: The Foot Book; the Eye Book; the Tooth Book; the Nose Book, 4 vols. 2015. (Big Bright & Early Board Book Ser.). (ENG., Illus.). 24p. (J). (gr. -1-3). bds. 29.95 *(978-0-553-53629-4(X),* Random Hse. Bks. for Young Readers) Random Hse. Children's Bks.

—Dr. Seuss's ABC: An Amazing Alphabet Book! 2014. (Big Bright & Early Board Book Ser.). (ENG., Illus.). 24p. (J). (— 1). bds. 7.99 *(978-0-385-37516-0(6),* Random Hse. Bks. for Young Readers) Random Hse. Children's Bks.

—Fox in Socks. 2015. (Big Bright & Early Board Book Ser.). (ENG., Illus.). 24p. (J). (— 1). bds. 7.99 *(978-0-553-51336-3(2),* Random Hse. Bks. for Young Readers) Random Hse. Children's Bks.

—The Grinch's Great Big Flap Book. 2014. (ENG.). 12p. (J). (-k). bds. 12.99 *(978-0-385-38494-0(7),* Random Hse. Bks. for Young Readers) Random Hse. Children's Bks.

—Happy Birthday to You! Great Big Flap Book. 2017. (ENG., Illus.). 12p. (J). (-k). bds. 12.99 *(978-1-5247-1460-4(7),* Random Hse. Bks. for Young Readers) Random Hse. Children's Bks.

—Hop on Pop. 2015. (Big Bright & Early Board Book Ser.). (ENG., Illus.). 24p. (J). (— 1). bds. 6.99 *(978-0-553-49679-6(4),* Random Hse. Bks. for Young Readers) Random Hse. Children's Bks.

—The Little Blue Boxed Set of Bright & Early Board Books by Dr. Seuss: Hop on Pop; Oh, the Thinks You Can Think!; Ten Apples up on Top!; the Shape of Me & Other Stuff, 4 vols. 2012. (Bright & Early Board Books(TM) Ser.). (ENG., Illus.). 24p. (J). (— 1). bds. 19.96 *(978-0-307-97586-7(X),* Random Hse. Bks. for Young Readers) Random Hse. Children's Bks.

—What Was I Scared Of? 2009. (ENG., Illus.). 32p. (J). (gr. k-4). 12.99 *(978-0-375-85342-5(1),* Random Hse. Bks. for Young Readers) Random Hse. Children's Bks.

—Would You Rather Be a Bullfrog? 2014. (Big Bright & Early Board Book Ser.). (ENG., Illus.). 24p. (J). (— 1). bds. 6.99 *(978-0-385-37515-3(8),* Random Hse. Bks. for Young Readers) Random Hse. Children's Bks.

Seven, John. Happy, Sad, Silly, Mad. Christy, Jana, illus. 2012. (ENG.). 26p. (J). (-k). bds. 6.99 *(978-1-4494-2229-5(2))* Andrews McMeel Publishing.

Seven, John & Christy, Jana. Happy Punks 1 2 3: A Counting Story. 2013. (Wee Rebel Ser.). (ENG., Illus.). 32p. (gr. -1). bds. 15.95 *(978-1-933149-67-7(1))* Manic D Pr.

Sévigny, Eric, illus. Caillou: Family Fun Story Box, 4 vols. 2014. (Boxset Ser.). (ENG.). 40p. (J). (gr. -1-k). bds. 12.99 *(978-2-89718-123-9(0))* Caillouet, Gerry.

Seymour, Arlene. The Moon Book: A Lunar Pop-up Celebration. Seymour, Arlene, illus. 2004. (Illus.). 14p. (YA). (gr. k-4). reprint ed. 22.00 *(978-0-7567-7645-9(7))* DIANE Publishing Co.

Shaffer, Christy. Glitter Unicorns Stickers. 2004. (Dover Little Activity Books Stickers Ser.). (ENG., Illus.). 2p. (J). (gr. 1-4). pap. 2.99 *(978-0-486-43538-1(5),* 435385) Dover Pubns., Inc.

Shand, Jennifer. Why Do Tractors Have Such Big Tires? 2015. (Why Do... ? Ser.). lib. bdg. 19.65 *(978-1-4867-0624-2(X))* Turtleback.

—Why Do Tractors Have Such Big Tires? Stern. Fabbri, Daniele, illus. 2014. (ENG.). 20p. (J). (gr. k-4). 8.99 *(978-1-4867-0382-1(8))* Flowerpot Children's Pr. Inc. CAN. Dist: Cardinal Pubs. Group.

Shand, Jennifer & Fabbri, Daniele. Why Do Rainbows Have So Many Colors? Paiva, Johannah Gilman, ed. 2014. (ENG., Illus.). 20p. (J). (gr. k-4). 8.99 *(978-1-4867-0383-8(6))* Flowerpot Children's Pr. Inc. CAN. Dist: Cardinal Pubs. Group.

Shanklin, Sandra, told to. Tales of Cat Canyon. 2005. (Illus.). 143p. pap. 12.95 *(978-0-9632459-2-2(9))* Great Plains Pr.

Sharp, N. L. The Flower Girl / the Ring Bear. Hantula, Timothy James, illus. 2009. 40p. (J). 19.95 *(978-0-9759829-3-8(1))* Prairieland Pr.

Shaw, Nancy E. Sheep Go to Sleep Lap Board Book. Apple, Margot, illus. 2018. (Sheep in a Jeep Ser.). (ENG.). 30p. (J). (— 1). bds. 12.99 *(978-1-328-91049-3(0),* 1701058, Clarion Bks.) HarperCollins Pubs.

—Sheep in a Jeep. Apple, Margot, illus. 2013. (Sheep in a Jeep Ser.). (ENG.). 32p. (J). (gr. -1-3). pap. 26.99 *(978-0-547-99383-6(8),* 1525236, Clarion Bks.) HarperCollins Pubs.

—Sheep in a Shop Board Book. Apple, Margot, illus. 2017. (Sheep in a Jeep Ser.). (ENG.). 28p. (J). (— 1). bds. 7.99 *(978-1-328-70286-9(3),* 1672394, Clarion Bks.) HarperCollins Pubs.

Shaw, Natalie. I'm Feeling Happy. Fruchter, Jason, illus. 2016. (Daniel Tiger's Neighborhood Ser.). (ENG.). 14p. (J). (gr. -1 — 1). bds. 6.99 *(978-1-4814-6178-8(8),* Simon Spotlight) Simon Spotlight.

—I'm Feeling Mad. Fruchter, Jason, illus. 2016. (Daniel Tiger's Neighborhood Ser.). (ENG.). 14p. (J). (gr. -1 — 1). bds. 6.99 *(978-1-4814-6176-4(1),* Simon Spotlight) Simon Spotlight.

—I'm Feeling Silly. Fruchter, Jason, illus. 2016. (Daniel Tiger's Neighborhood Ser.). (ENG.). 14p. (J). (gr. -1 — 1). bds. 6.99 *(978-1-4814-6815-2(4),* Simon Spotlight) Simon Spotlight.

—It's Time to Save the Day! 2017. (PJ Masks Ser.). (ENG., Illus.). 14p. (J). (gr. -1-k). bds. 10.99 *(978-1-5344-0423-6(6),* Simon Spotlight) Simon Spotlight.

—Meet the Neighbors! Style Guide, illus. 2014. (Daniel Tiger's Neighborhood Ser.). (ENG.). 16p. (J). (gr. -1-k). bds. 7.99 *(978-1-4424-9837-2(4),* Simon Spotlight) Simon Spotlight.

Shaw-Russell, Susan. Animal ABC. 2011. (Dover Sticker Bks.). (ENG., Illus.). 4p. (J). (gr. 1-5). 7.99 *(978-0-486-48396-2(7))* Dover Pubns., Inc.

Shea, Bob. Dinosaur vs. Bedtime. Shea, Bob, illus. 2011. (Dinosaur vs. Book Ser.: 1). (ENG., Illus.). 30p. (J). (gr. -1-k). bds. 6.99 *(978-1-4231-3788-7(4))* Hyperion Pr.

Shea, Kevin. H Is for Hockey. Dewar, Ken, illus. 2013. (ENG.). 28p. (J). (gr. k-2). bds. 8.99 *(978-1-58536-891-4(1),* 203002) Sleeping Bear Pr.

Sheehan, Monica. Be Happy! A Little Book for a Happy You & a Better World. Sheehan, Monica, illus. 2014. (ENG., Illus.). 68p. (J). (gr. -1-3). 14.99 *(978-1-4424-9857-0(9),* Little Simon) Little Simon.

—Love Is You & Me. Sheehan, Monica, illus. 2010. (ENG., Illus.). 38p. (J). (gr. -1-k). bds. 8.99 *(978-1-4424-0765-7(4),* Little Simon) Little Simon.

Sheehy, Shawn. Beyond the Sixth Extinction: A Post-Apocalyptic Pop-Up. Solano, Jordi, illus. 2018. (ENG.). 40p. (J). (gr. 9). 65.00 *(978-0-7636-8788-5(X))* Candlewick Pr.

—Welcome to the Neighborwood. Sheehy, Shawn, illus. 2015. (ENG., Illus.). 18p. (J). (gr. -1-3). 29.99 *(978-0-7636-6594-4(0))* Candlewick Pr.

Sheikh-Miller, Jonathan. Sharks. 2009. (Discovery Nature Ser.). 64p. (YA). (gr. 3-18). 8.99 *(978-0-7945-2241-4(6),* Usborne) EDC Publishing.

Shepherd, Jodie. Guess Who Ocean Friends. Ovresat, Laura, illus. 2007. (Guess Who Ser.). (ENG.). 12p. (J). (gr. -1-k). bds. 8.99 *(978-0-7944-1122-0(3),* Studio Fun International) Printers Row Publishing Group.

—Presidents of the United States of America. 2015. (Illus.). 50p. (J). *(978-1-4351-6156-6(4))* Barnes & Noble, Inc.

Shepherd, Rajean Luebs. Little Nebraska. Urban, Helle, illus. 2015. (Little State Ser.). (ENG.). 22p. (J). (gr. -1-k). bds. 9.95 *(978-1-58536-928-7(4),* 203819) Sleeping Bear Pr.

Sheridan, Lucie. Find Me: Play for Little Hands. Sheridan, Lucie, illus. 2019. (Play for Little Hands Ser.). (ENG., Illus.). 14p. (J). (-k). bds. 10.99 *(978-1-910552-81-0(X))* O'Mara, Michael Bks., Ltd. GBR. Dist: Independent Pubs. Group.

Sherry, Kevin. I'm the Biggest Thing in the Ocean! 2010. 28p. (J). (gr. -1 — 1). bds. 8.99 *(978-0-8037-3529-3(4),* Dial Bks) Penguin Young Readers Group.

Shin, Yujin, illus. My Magical Mermaid. 2019. (My Magical Friends Ser.). (ENG.). 8p. (J). (gr. -1 — 1). bds. 8.99 *(978-1-4197-3730-5(9),* 1278010, Abrams Appleseed) Abrams, Inc.

—My Magical Unicorn. 2019. (My Magical Friends Ser.). (ENG.). 8p. (J). (gr. -1 — 1). bds. 8.99 *(978-1-4197-3729-9(5),* 1277910) Abrams, Inc.

Shoulders, Michael. Little Mississippi. Urban, Helle, illus. 2016. (Little State Ser.). (ENG.). 20p. (J). (gr. -1-k). bds. 9.95 *(978-1-58536-974-4(8),* 204111) Sleeping Bear Pr.

—Say Daddy! Weidner, Teri, illus. 2013. (ENG.). 26p. (J). (gr. 1-4). bds. 9.99 *(978-1-58536-863-1(6),* 202383) Sleeping Bear Pr.

Shubuck, Sheila. I Love You All Year Round. Padron, Alicia, illus. 2008. (ENG.). 16p. (J). (gr. -1). 10.95 *(978-1-58117-786-2(0),* Intervisual/Piggy Toes) Bendon, Inc.

Shulman, Mark. Big Cat. Chambers, Sally, illus. 2004. 8p. (J). bds. 6.95 *(978-1-58925-737-5(5))* Tiger Tales.

—Foxy Fox. Chambers, Sally, illus. 2004. 8p. (J). bds. 6.95 *(978-1-58925-738-2(3))* Tiger Tales.

Siddell, Robert. Sea Life 3D. 2013. (Illus.). 27p. 19.99 *(978-0-9830127-4-0(1))* Digital Tech Frontier, LLC.

Siede Preis Photography (Firm) Staff & Brian Warling Photography (Firm) Staff, contrib. by. First Words. 2003. (Lift-A-Flap Ser.). (Illus.). 12p. (J). bds. 12.98 *(978-0-7853-8624-7(6),* 7188400) Publications International, Ltd.

Sight Words/ESL Intro Kit. 2004. (ENG.). (J). 44.99 *(978-0-943343-75-4(5))* Learning Wrap-Ups, Inc.

Silberg, Francis Barry. The Story of Chanukah. Levy, Pamela R., illus. 2017. (ENG.). 24p. (J). (gr. -1-k). bds. 7.99 *(978-0-8249-1665-7(4))* Worthy Publishing.

Silver Dolphin en Español Editors. Seqorita Cmrculo: Miss Circle, Spanish-Language Edition. 2005. (Mis figuras Geometricas Ser.). (SPA., Illus.). 6p. (J). *(978-970-718-293-6(8),* Silver Dolphin en Español) Advanced Marketing, S. de R. L. de C. V.

Silver Dolphin en Español Editors, creator. Mis Figuras Geometricas, Srita Estrella. 2005. (Mis figuras Geometricas Ser.). (SPA., Illus.). 6p. (J). (gr. -1-k). *(978-970-718-295-0(4),* Silver Dolphin en Español) Advanced Marketing, S. de R. L. de C. V.

Silver Dolphin Staff. Cuerpo humano/Human Body. 2011. 16p. *(978-607-404-318-1(3),* Silver Dolphin en Español) Advanced Marketing, S. de R. L. de C. V.

Silver, Skye. Baby Play. 2019. (ENG., Illus.). 16p. (J). (gr. -1-k). bds. 7.99 *(978-1-78285-728-0(1))* Barefoot Bks., Inc.

Siminovich, Lorena, illus. You Are My Baby: Farm. 2013. (You Are My Baby Ser.). (ENG.). 10p. (J). (gr. -1 — 1). bds. 8.99 *(978-1-4521-0643-4(6))* Chronicle Bks. LLC.

—You Are My Baby: Garden. 2014. (You Are My Baby Ser.). (ENG.). 10p. (J). (gr. -1 — 1). bds. 8.99 *(978-1-4521-2649-4(6))* Chronicle Bks. LLC.

—You Are My Baby: Ocean. 2014. (You Are My Baby Ser.). (ENG.). 10p. (J). (gr. -1 — 1). bds. 8.99 *(978-1-4521-2650-0(X))* Chronicle Bks. LLC.

Simon, Jenne. Tell the Time! Hino, Sachiho, illus. 2015. (J). *(978-0-545-74720-2(1))* Scholastic, Inc.

Simpson, Dana. Today I'll Be a Unicorn. 2018. (Phoebe & Her Unicorn Ser.). (ENG., Illus.). 12p. (J). bds. 7.99 *(978-1-4494-8999-1(0))* Andrews McMeel Publishing.

Sims, Lesley. Illustrated Classics for Girls. Mason, Conrad, illus. 2009. (Illustrated Stories Ser.). 384p. (YA). (gr. 3-18). 19.99 *(978-0-7945-2419-7(2),* Usborne) EDC Publishing.

Singer, Marilyn. Fun with Animals Friendship Box. Zaidi, Nadeem, illus. 2009. (J). *(978-1-4231-2799-4(4)); (978-1-4231-2797-0(8)); (978-1-4231-2798-7(6))* Disney Pr.

Skewes, John. Larry Loves Boston! A Larry Gets Lost Book. 2016. (Larry Gets Lost Ser.). (Illus.). 20p. (J). (— 1). bds. 10.99 *(978-1-63217-047-7(7),* Little Bigfoot) Sasquatch Bks.

—Larry Loves San Francisco! A Larry Gets Lost Book. Skewes, John, illus. 2014. (Larry Gets Lost Ser.). (ENG., Illus.). 20p. (J). (— 1). bds. 10.99 *(978-1-57061-912-0(3),* Little Bigfoot) Sasquatch Bks.

—Larry Loves Washington, DC! A Larry Gets Lost Book. 2016. (Larry Gets Lost Ser.). (Illus.). 20p. (J). (— 1). bds. 10.99 *(978-1-63217-048-4(5),* Little Bigfoot) Sasquatch Bks.

Skewes, John & Ode, Eric. Larry Gets Lost in Seattle: 10th Anniversary Edition. 10th ed. 2017. (Larry Gets Lost Ser.). (Illus.). 32p. (J). (gr. -1-2). 17.99 *(978-1-63217-092-7(2),* Little Bigfoot) Sasquatch Bks.

Slater, Jean M. At the Fire Station: An Interactive Book. 2nd ed. 2003. (Illus.). 13p. (J). bds. *(978-0-9743149-0-7(0))* Slater Software, Inc.

Slater, Nicola. Where Is My Pink Sweater? 2019. (ENG., Illus.). 24p. (J). (gr. -1-k). bds. 8.99 *(978-1-4197-3679-7(5),* 1268110, Abrams Appleseed) Abrams, Inc.

Slater, Nicola, illus. We're Bored. 2005. 12p. (J). 12.95 *(978-1-58117-384-0(9),* Intervisual/Piggy Toes) Bendon, Inc.

Sleeping Bear Press. Little Dance. Benoit, Renné, illus. 2013. (ENG.). 20p. (J). (gr. -1-k). bds. 9.99 *(978-1-58536-884-6(9),* 202899) Sleeping Bear Pr.

—Little Oklahoma. Urban, Helle, illus. 2015. (Little State Ser.). (ENG.). 22p. (J). (gr. -1-k). bds. 9.95 *(978-1-58536-927-0(6),* 203817) Sleeping Bear Pr.

Slegers, Liesbet. Que Veo?/ What Do I See? 2008. 24p. bds. 11.95 *(978-84-263-6705-1(4))* Vives, Luis Editorial (Edelvives) ESP. Dist: Baker & Taylor Bks.

—Surprise! 2012. (ENG.). 12p. (J). (gr. k — 1). bds. 7.95 *(978-1-60537-117-7(3))* Clavis Publishing.

Slier, Debby. Loving Me, 1 vol. 2013. (ENG., Illus.). 32p. (J). bds. 5.99 *(978-1-59572-334-5(X))* Star Bright Bks., Inc.

Slobodkina, Esphyr. Caps for Sale Board Book: A Tale of a Peddler, Some Monkeys & Their Monkey Business. Slobodkina, Esphyr, illus. 75th ed. 2015. (ENG., Illus.). 32p. (J). (gr. -1-3). bds. 8.99 *(978-0-06-147453-8(3),* HarperFestival) HarperCollins Pubs.

Smart Kidz, creator. The ABC's of How I Love You: You're My Alphabet of Love! 2013. (Parent Love Letters Ser.). (ENG., Illus.). 12p. (gr. -1). bds. 12.99 *(978-1-891100-30-7(0),* Smart Kids) Penton Overseas, Inc.

—I'm a Little Teapot. 2013. (Sing N Play Songs Ser.). (ENG., Illus.). 12p. (J). bds. 12.99 *(978-1-891100-07-9(6),* Smart Kids) Penton Overseas, Inc.

—It's Potty Time for Boys. 2013. (ENG., Illus.). 12p. (J). bds. 12.99 *(978-1-891100-05-5(X),* Smart Kids) Penton Overseas, Inc.

—Jingle Bells. 2013. (ENG., Illus.). 12p. (gr. -1). bds. 12.99 *(978-1-939658-03-6(9),* Smart Kids) Penton Overseas, Inc.

—The 123s of How I Love You. 2013. (Parent Love Letters Ser.). (ENG., Illus.). 12p. (gr. -1). bds. 12.99 *(978-1-891100-31-4(9),* Smart Kids) Penton Overseas, Inc.

Smart Kidz Media, creator. O Christmas Tree! 2013. (ENG., Illus.). 12p. (J). bds. 12.99 *(978-1-939658-05-0(5),* Smart Kids) Penton Overseas, Inc.

—Silent Night. 2013. (ENG., Illus.). 12p. (J). bds. 12.99 *(978-1-939658-01-2(2),* Smart Kids) Penton Overseas, Inc.

—Up on the Housetop! 2013. (ENG., Illus.). 12p. (J). bds. 12.99 *(978-1-939658-04-3(7),* Smart Kids) Penton Overseas, Inc.

Smart Kidz Media Studios Staff, ed. It's Bedtime! 2011. 16p. 7.99 *(978-1-891100-78-9(5),* Smart Kids) Penton Overseas, Inc.

Smart Start Pencil Skills: Numbers. 2017. (ENG., Illus.). 64p. (J). pap. 8.00 *(978-1-907604-90-4(1))* Award Pubns. Ltd. GBR. Dist: Parkwest Pubns., Inc.

SMARTLAB Creative Team. Space Exploration. 2010. 10p. mass mkt. 39.99 *(978-1-60380-050-1(6))* becker&mayer! books.

Smith, A. & Tatchell, J. How are Babies Made? How do Your Senses Work? What Happens to Your Food? rev. ed. 2004. (Flip Flaps Ser.). 48p. (J). (gr. 2-18). 14.95 *(978-0-7945-0618-6(6),* Usborne) EDC Publishing.

Smith, Alastair. Baby Animals. 2004. (Lift-the-Flap Learners Ser.). (SPA & ENG., Illus.). 1p. (J). (gr. 1-18). pap. 8.95 *(978-0-7945-0133-4(8),* Usborne) EDC Publishing.

—Nighttime Lift-the-flap. Butler, John, illus. 2005. 16p. (J). (gr. 1-18). 11.95 *(978-0-7945-0967-5(3),* Usborne) EDC Publishing.

—On the Farm Lift-the-Flap. Torode, Justine, illus. 2004. (Luxury Lift-the-Flap Ser.). 16p. (J). (gr. 1-18). 11.95 *(978-0-7945-0508-0(2),* Usborne) EDC Publishing.

Smith, Alastair, ed. Homes & Houses Then & Now. 2004. (Then & Now Flip Flaps Ser.). (SPA & ENG., Illus.). 1p. (J). (gr. 2-18). pap. 7.95 *(978-0-7460-3100-1(9))* EDC Publishing.

—Travel & Transport Then & Now. 2004. (Then & Now Flip Flaps Ser.). (ENG., Illus.). 1p. (J). (gr. 2-18). pap. 7.95 *(978-0-7460-3102-5(5))* EDC Publishing.

Smith, Alastair & Howell, Laura. On the Beach. 2004. (Lift-the-Flap Learners Ser.). (Illus.). 16p. (J). (gr. 1-18). pap. 8.95 *(978-0-7945-0213-3(X),* Usborne) EDC Publishing.

Smith, Alastair & Tachell, Judy. Under the Sea. Scott, Peter David, illus. 2007. (J). *(978-0-545-03305-3(5))* Scholastic, Inc.

Smith, Alastair & Tatchell, Judy. Dinosaurs. 2004. (Jumbo Lift-the-Flap Learners Ser.). (Illus.). 16p. (J). (gr. 1-18). 11.99 *(978-0-7945-0418-2(3),* Usborne) EDC Publishing.

—Dinosaurs. Scott, Peter David, illus. 2005. (J). *(978-0-439-68903-8(1))* Scholastic, Inc.

Smith Bresciani, Cathleen & Eldredge, Richard. Sassafrass Jones & the Search for a Forever Home. 2013. 54p. 24.99 *(978-0-578-12084-3(4))* Misfit Mouse.

Smith, Iain. Angel Fish: A Pull & Lift Book. Smith, Iain, illus. 2005. (Stories to Share Ser.). (Illus.). 12p. (J). 10.95 *(978-1-58117-084-9(X),* Intervisual/Piggy Toes) Bendon, Inc.

Smith, Jodene Lynn & Rice, Dona Herweck. If I Were a Tree. 2010. (Early Literacy Ser.). (ENG., Illus.). 16p. (gr. k-1). 19.99 *(978-1-4333-1488-9(6))* Teacher Created Materials, Inc.

Smith, Jodene Lynn & Thompson, Chad. Baa, Baa, Black Sheep. 2010. (Early Literacy Ser.). (ENG., Illus.). 16p. (gr. k-1). 19.99 *(978-1-4333-1484-1(3))* Teacher Created Materials, Inc.

—Beh, Beh, Borreguito Negro. rev. ed. 2010. (Early Literacy Ser.). (SPA., Illus.). 16p. (gr. k-1). 19.99 *(978-1-4333-2095-8(9))* Teacher Created Materials, Inc.

Smith, Lane. It's a Little Book. 2011. (ENG., Illus.). 24p. (J). (— 1). bds. 7.99 *(978-1-59643-758-6(8),* 900079372) Roaring Brook Pr.

Smith, Miranda. What's Inside? McLelland, Kate, illus. 2019. (ENG.). 12p. (J). (gr. -1-k). 21.99 *(978-1-4052-8863-7(9),* Red Shed) Farshore GBR. Dist: Independent Pubs. Group, HarperCollins Pubs.

Snape, Emily. Motor Mix: Emergency: (Interactive Children's Books, Transportation Books for Kids) Alexander, Rilla, illus. 2017. (Motor Mix Ser.). (ENG.). 16p. (J). (gr. -1 — 1). bds. 9.99 *(978-1-4521-4838-0(4))* Chronicle Bks. LLC.

—Motor Mix: Flight: (Interactive Children's Books, Transportation Books for Kids) Alexander, Rilla, illus. 2017. (Motor Mix Ser.). (ENG.). 16p. (J). (gr. -1 — 1). bds. 9.99 *(978-1-4521-4839-7(2))* Chronicle Bks. LLC.

Snow, Ivy. A Christmas Advent Story. Tolson, Hannah, illus. 2018. (ENG.). 32p. (J). 14.99 *(978-1-68119-851-4(7),* 900189419, Bloomsbury Children's Bks.) Bloomsbury Publishing USA.

Snow, Todd. Feelings to Share. Hartman, Carrie, illus. 2007. (ENG.). 24p. (J). bds. 7.99 *(978-1-934277-01-0(0))* Marn Green Publishing, Inc.

—You Are Beautiful. Strong, Melodee, illus. 2007. (You Are Important Ser.). (ENG.). 24p. (J). (gr. -1-k). bds. 7.99 *(978-1-934277-10-2(X))* Marn Green Publishing, Inc.

—You Are Brave. Strong, Melodee, illus. 2007. (ENG.). 24p. (J). bds. 7.99 *(978-1-934277-08-9(8))* Marn Green Publishing, Inc.

—You Are Creative. Strong, Melodee, illus. 2007. (ENG.). 24p. (J). bds. 7.99 *(978-1-934277-07-2(X))* Marn Green Publishing, Inc.

—You Are Friendly. Strong, Melodee, illus. 2007. (You Are Important Ser.). (ENG.). 24p. (J). (gr. -1-k). bds. 7.99 *(978-1-934277-09-6(6))* Marn Green Publishing, Inc.

—You Are Important. Strong, Melodee, illus. 2007. (You Are Important Ser.). (ENG.). 24p. (J). (gr. -1-k). bds. 7.99 *(978-1-934277-06-5(1))* Marn Green Publishing, Inc.

Snowflake Day! 2014. (Daniel Tiger's Neighborhood Ser.). (ENG., Illus.). 14p. (J). (gr. -1-k). bds. 5.99 *(978-1-4814-1771-6(1),* Simon Spotlight) Simon Spotlight.

Snyder, Betsy, illus. I Can Dream: (Baby Board Book, Book for Learning, Toddler Book. 2018. (I Can Ser.). (ENG.). 14p. (J). (gr. -1 — 1). bds. 8.99 *(978-1-4521-6214-0(X))* Chronicle Bks. LLC.

—I Can Explore: (Baby Board Book, Book for Learning, Toddler Book. 2018. (I Can Ser.). (ENG.). 14p. (J). (gr. -1 — 1). bds. 8.99 *(978-1-4521-6213-3(1))* Chronicle Bks. LLC.

—I Can Play. 2015. (I Can Interactive Board Bks.). (ENG.). 14p. (J). (gr. -1 — 1). bds. 8.99 *(978-1-4521-2905-1(3))* Chronicle Bks. LLC.

Snyder, Betsy E. Bulldozer. 2015. (Illus.). (J). *(978-1-62885-064-2(7))* Kidsbooks, LLC.

—Fire Engine. 2015. (Illus.). (J). *(978-1-62885-065-9(5))* Kidsbooks, LLC.

—Train. 2015. (Illus.). (J). *(978-1-62885-066-6(3))* Kidsbooks, LLC.

Sobel, June. B Is for Bulldozer Lap Board Book: A Construction ABC. Iwai, Melissa, illus. 2018. (ENG.). 32p. (J). (— 1). bds. 12.99 *(978-1-328-77052-3(4),* 1681071, Clarion Bks.) HarperCollins Pubs.

—The Goodnight Train Lap Board Book. Huliska-Beith, Laura, illus. 2017. (Goodnight Train Ser.). (ENG.). 30p. (J). (— 1). bds. 12.99 *(978-1-328-76438-6(9),* 1681068, Clarion Bks.) HarperCollins Pubs.

Sollinger, Emily. This Is Our World: A Story about Taking Care of the Earth. Brown, Jo, illus. 2010. (Little Green Bks.). (ENG.). 12p. (J). (gr. -1-1). bds. 8.99 *(978-1-4169-7821-3(6),* Little Simon) Little Simon.

Soman, David. Little Box of Ladybug Girl, 4 vols. 2013. (Ladybug Girl Ser.). (Illus.). 14p. (J). (gr. -1-k). bds. 23.96 *(978-0-8037-4102-7(2),* Dial Bks) Penguin Young Readers Group.

Sookocheff, Carey. Solutions for Cold Feet & Other Little Problems. 2018. (Illus.). 38p. (J). (— 1). bds. 9.99 *(978-0-7352-6464-9(3),* Tundra Bks.) Tundra Bks. CAN. Dist: Penguin Random Hse. LLC.

Soundprints, creator. Orang Utan's Playtime. 2011. (Let's Go to the Zoo! Ser.). (ENG., Illus.). 16p. (gr. -1). 5.95 *(978-1-60727-456-8(6))* Soundprints.

Soundprints Staff & Galvin, Laura Gates. First Look at Aircraft. 2009. (ENG.). 16p. (J). 6.95 *(978-1-60727-118-5(4))* Soundprints.

Spafford, Suzy. Witzy's Fall Collection. 2010. (Illus.). (J). *(978-1-4037-9599-1(1))* Creative Edge.

Spanish Intro Kit. 2004. (ENG & SPA.). (J). 44.99 *(978-0-943343-76-1(3))* Learning Wrap-Ups, Inc.

Spanyol, Jessica. Clive Is a Librarian. Spanyol, Jessica, illus. 2017. (Clive's Jobs Ser.: 4). (Illus.). 14p. (J). spiral bd. *(978-1-84643-989-6(2))* Child's Play International Ltd.

—Clive Is a Nurse. Spanyol, Jessica, illus. 2017. (Clive's Jobs Ser.: 4). (Illus.). 14p. (J). spiral bd. *(978-1-84643-991-9(4))* Child's Play International Ltd.

—Clive Is a Teacher. Spanyol, Jessica, illus. 2017. (Clive's Jobs Ser.: 4). (Illus.). 14p. (J). spiral bd. *(978-1-84643-990-2(6))* Child's Play International Ltd.

—Clive Is a Waiter. Spanyol, Jessica, illus. 2017. (Clive's Jobs Ser.: 4). (Illus.). 14p. (J). spiral bd. *(978-1-84643-992-6(2))* Child's Play International Ltd.

Spelman, Cornelia Maude. When I Feel Scared. Parkinson, Kathy, illus. 2010. (Way I Feel Bks.). (ENG.). 16p. (J). (gr. -1 — 1). bds. 7.99 *(978-0-8075-8905-2(5),* 0807589055) Whitman, Albert & Co.

Spence, Ann. Elmo's Play Day. 2003. (Play-A-Sound Ser.). (ENG., Illus.). 6p. (J). bds. 6.10 net. *(978-0-7853-8441-0(3),* bf44e002-35f9-4261-a92b-a83ebb9e048b) Phoenix International Publications, Inc.

Sper, Emily. The Kids' Fun Book of Jewish Time. Sper, Emily, illus. 2006. (HEB & ENG., Illus.). 24p. (J). (gr. -1-1). 16.99 *(978-1-58023-311-8(2),* 1260461, Jewish Lights Publishing) LongHill Partners, Inc.

Sperring, Mark. The Shape of My Heart. Paterson, Alys, illus. 2015. (ENG.). 32p. (J). (gr. -1-1). bds. 8.99 *(978-1-68119-017-4(6),* 900155505, Bloomsbury USA Childrens) Bloomsbury Publishing USA.

TUV

Spinelli, Eileen. Love You Always. Flint, Gillian, illus. 2018. (ENG.). 22p. (J). (gr. -1-k). bds. 7.99 *(978-0-8249-1667-1(0))* Worthy Publishing.

—Nora's Ark, 1 vol. Hilb, Nora, illus. 2018. (ENG.). 24p. (J). bds. 8.99 *(978-0-310-76144-0(1))* Zonderkidz.

Spinner, Cala. A Busy Day in the Neighborhood. Fruchter, Jason, illus. 2017. (Daniel Tiger's Neighborhood Ser.). (ENG.). 12p. (J). (gr. -1-k). bds. 14.99 *(978-1-4814-8583-8(0),* Simon Spotlight) Simon Spotlight.

Spiro, Ruth. ¡Al Bebé le Encanta Codificar! / Baby Loves Coding! Chan, Irene, illus. 2019. (Baby Loves Science Ser.). 20p. (J). (— 1). bds. 8.99 *(978-1-62354-114-9(X))* Charlesbridge Publishing, Inc.

—Baby Loves Aerospace Engineering! Chan, Irene, illus. 2016. (Baby Loves Science Ser.: 1). 20p. (J). (— 1). bds. 8.99 *(978-1-58089-541-5(7))* Charlesbridge Publishing, Inc.

—Baby Loves Coding! Chan, Irene, illus. 2018. (Baby Loves Science Ser.: 6). 22p. (J). (— 1). bds. 8.99 *(978-1-58089-884-3(X))* Charlesbridge Publishing, Inc.

Spurr, Elizabeth. Happy Sparkling Hanukkah. Madden, Colleen, illus. 2011. (J). *(978-1-4027-9660-9(9))* Sterling Publishing Co., Inc.

—In the Snow, 1 vol. Oliphant, Manelle, illus. 2017. (In the Weather Ser.). 22p. (J). (gr. -1 — 1). bds. 6.99 *(978-1-56145-855-4(4))* Peachtree Publishing Co. Inc.

—In the Wind, 1 vol. Oliphant, Manelle, illus. 2016. (In the Weather Ser.). 22p. (J). (gr. -1 — 1). bds. 6.99 *(978-1-56145-854-7(6))* Peachtree Publishing Co. Inc.

Squillace, Elisa, illus. Down in the Jungle. 2005. (Classic Books with Holes Board Book Ser.). 14p. (J). (gr. -1-1). spiral bd. *(978-1-904550-61-7(4))* Child's Play International Ltd.

Srinivasan, Divya. Little Owl's Colors. Srinivasan, Divya, illus. 2015. (Little Owl Ser.). (Illus.). 18p. (J). (— 1). bds. 7.99 *(978-0-451-47456-8(2),* Viking Books for Young Readers) Penguin Young Readers Group.

Stahl, Stephanie. The Best Snowman Ever. Vasylenko, Veronica, illus. 2013. (ENG.). 16p. (J). (gr. -1-k). bds. 8.95 *(978-1-58925-605-7(0))* Tiger Tales.

Stanley, Mandy. Arty Mouse Wipe Clean Numbers. Stanley, Mandy, illus. 2017. (Arty Mouse Wipe Clean Board Bks.). (ENG., Illus.). 24p. (J). (gr. -1-1). bds. 8.99 *(978-1-78700-253-1(5))* Top That! Publishing PLC GBR. Dist: Independent Pubs. Group.

—Arty Mouse Wipe Clean Words. Stanley, Mandy, illus. 2017. (Arty Mouse Wipe Clean Board Bks.). (ENG., Illus.). 24p. (J). (gr. -1-1). bds. 8.99 *(978-1-78700-254-8(3))* Top That! Publishing PLC GBR. Dist: Independent Pubs. Group.

Stanley, Mandy, illus. Busy Bear's Counting. 2014. (J). bds. 0.00 *(978-0-9906156-8-2(5))* Bookworks, LLC.

Star Bright Books. Carry Me: Portugese/English, 1 vol. 2009. (Babies Everywhere Ser.). (ENG., Illus.). 20p. (J). (gr. -1). 6.95 *(978-1-59572-200-3(9))* Star Bright Bks., Inc.

—Carry Me: Spanish/English, 1 vol. 2010. (Babies Everywhere Ser.). (ENG., Illus.). 16p. (J). (gr. -1). bds. 6.95 *(978-1-59572-199-0(1))* Star Bright Bks., Inc.

Star Wars Block (an Abrams Block Book) Over 100 Words Every Fan Should Know. 2018. (Abrams Block Book Ser.). (ENG., Illus.). 104p. (gr. -1-17). 17.99 *(978-1-4197-2831-0(8),* 1213610) Abrams, Inc.

Star Wars Villains. 2011. (Illus.). (J). *(978-0-545-28664-0(6))* Scholastic, Inc.

Stauffer, Lisa Lowe. Two by Two, 1 vol. Scudamore, Angelika, illus. 2018. (ENG.). 18p. (J). bds. 8.99 *(978-0-310-76273-7(1))* Zonderkidz.

Steadman, Barbara. Little Flower Girls Sticker Paper Dolls. 2003. (Dover Little Activity Books Paper Dolls Ser.). (ENG., Illus.). 4p. (J). (gr. k-3). pap. 1.99 *(978-0-486-43019-5(7))* Dover Pubns., Inc.

Steer, Dugald A. Snappy Little Halloween. Matthews, Derek, illus. 2004. 20p. (J). (gr. k-4). reprint ed. 13.00 *(978-0-7567-7403-5(9))* DIANE Publishing Co.

Steers, Billy. Tractor Mac Farm Days. 2016. (Tractor Mac Ser.). (ENG., Illus.). 16p. (J). bds. 7.99 *(978-0-374-30117-0(4),* 900138398, Farrar, Straus & Giroux (BYR)) Farrar, Straus & Giroux.

Steigemeyer, Julie. My Little Easter Book. Regan, Dana, illus. 2008. 20p. (J). (gr. -1-k). bds. 6.49 *(978-0-7586-1444-5(6))* Concordia Publishing Hse.

Sterling Children's, Sterling. Clothes/la Ropa. 2016. (Say & Play Ser.). (ENG., Illus.). 28p. (J). (— 1). bds. 4.95 *(978-1-4549-1997-1(3))* Sterling Publishing Co., Inc.

—Food/Los Alimentos. 2016. (Say & Play Ser.). (ENG., Illus.). 28p. (J). (— 1). bds. 4.95 *(978-1-4549-1998-8(1))* Sterling Publishing Co., Inc.

Sterling Publishing Co., Inc. Staff. Garage. Finn, Rebecca, illus. 2015. (Busy Bks.). (ENG.). 10p. (J). (— 1). bds. 8.95 *(978-1-4549-1734-2(2))* Sterling Publishing Co., Inc.

Stern, Ariella. Chanukah Guess Who? A Lift the Flap Book. Argoff, Patti, illus. 2012. (ENG.). 32p. (J). 10.99 *(978-1-929628-68-1(4))* Hachai Publishing.

Stewart, Melissa. Caterpillar to Butterfly. 2016. (Science for Toddlers Ser.). (Illus.). 24p. (J). (gr. -1 — 1). bds. 8.99 *(978-1-4549-1406-8(8))* Sterling Publishing Co., Inc.

Stewart, Whitney. Mindful Tots: Loving Kindness. Alejandro, Rocío, illus. 2019. (Mindful Tots Ser.). (ENG.). 14p. (J). (gr. -1-k). bds. 7.99 *(978-1-78285-749-5(4))* Barefoot Bks., Inc.

—Mindful Tots: Tummy Ride. Alejandro, Rocío, illus. 2019. (Mindful Tots Ser.). (ENG.). 14p. (J). (gr. -1-k). bds. 7.99 *(978-1-78285-748-8(6))* Barefoot Bks., Inc.

Stiegemeyer, Julie. God's Little Lambs: My First Bible, 1 vol. Leng, Qin, illus. 2018. (ENG.). 32p. (J). bds. 9.99 *(978-0-310-76159-4(X))* Zonderkidz.

Stileman, Kali. Roly Poly Egg. 2011. (ENG.). 26p. (J). (gr. -1-k). 12.95 *(978-1-58925-852-5(5))* Tiger Tales.

Stiles, Dan. Put on Your Shoes! 2013. (ENG., Illus.). 16p. (J). (-k). bds. 9.95 *(978-1-57687-646-5(2),* powerHouse Bks.) powerHse. Bks.

—Today I'm Going to Wear ... 2014. (ENG., Illus.). 16p. (J). (gr. -1-2). bds. 9.95 *(978-1-57687-718-0(3),* powerHouse Bks.) powerHse. Bks.

Stinson, Kathy. Red Is Best. Lewis, Robin Baird, illus. 6th ed. 2011. 24p. (J). (gr. -1 — 1). bds. 7.99 *(978-1-55451-364-2(2),* 9781554513642) Annick Pr., Ltd. CAN. Dist: Publishers Group West (PGW).

Stockham, Jess, illus. Cinderella. (Flip-Up Fairy Tales Ser.). 24p. (J). 2007. (gr. -1-2). *(978-1-84643-091-6(7))* 2006. (gr. 2-2). *(978-1-904550-74-7(6))* Child's Play International Ltd.

—The Cockerel, the Mouse & the Little Red Hen. (Flip-Up Fairy Tales Ser.). 24p. (J). 2007. (gr. -1-2). *(978-1-84643-092-3(5))* 2006. (gr. 2-2). *(978-1-904550-75-4(4))* Child's Play International Ltd.

—Down by the Station. (Classic Books with Holes 8x8 with CD Ser.). (ENG.). 16p. (J). 2007. (gr. -1-1). *(978-1-904550-68-6(1))* 2003. *(978-0-85953-132-0(5))* Child's Play International Ltd.

—Little Red Riding Hood. (Flip-Up Fairy Tales Ser.). 24p. (J). 2007. (gr. -1-2). *(978-1-84643-088-6(7))* 2005. pap. *(978-1-904550-22-8(3))* Child's Play International Ltd.

—The Princess & the Pea. 2010. (Flip-Up Fairy Tales Ser.). 24p. (J). (gr. -1-2). *(978-1-84643-332-0(0))* Child's Play International Ltd.

—The Steadfast Tin Soldier. 2012. (Flip-Up Fairy Tales Ser.). 24p. (J). *(978-1-84643-477-8(7))* Child's Play International Ltd.

—Stone Soup. (Flip-Up Fairy Tales Ser.). 24p. (J). 2007. (gr. -1-2). *(978-1-84643-094-7(1))* 2006. (gr. 2-2). pap. *(978-1-84643-021-3(6))* Child's Play International Ltd.

Stone, Jamie, ed. Danny Dino Ventures Out. 2013. (Pop-Up: Play & Listen Ser.). (ENG., Illus.). 10p. (J). (gr. -1-k). bds. 16.95 *(978-1-61889-034-4(4))* AZ Bks. LLC.

Stone, Jon. The Monster at the End of This Book. Smollin, Michael, illus. 2015. (ENG.). 26p. (J). (— 1). bds. 7.99 *(978-0-553-50873-4(3),* Golden Bks.) Random Hse. Children's Bks.

Stone, Judith. Billie the Buffalo Goes to Town. 2008. 20p. pap. 12.95 *(978-1-4389-2877-7(7))* AuthorHouse.

Stone, Kate. Happy Birthday, Mouse! 2014. (ENG.). 16p. (J). bds. 5.99 *(978-1-4494-4387-0(7))* Andrews McMeel Publishing.

Stone, Kate, illus. ABC Train. 2013. (ENG.). 20p. (J). bds. 10.99 *(978-1-4494-3157-0(7))* Andrews McMeel Publishing.

—Heads & Tails. 2013. (ENG.). 20p. (J). bds. 10.99 *(978-1-4494-3246-1(8))* Andrews McMeel Publishing.

Stortz, Diane. I Am: The Names of God for Little Ones, 1 vol. Le Feyer, Diane, illus. 2018. (ENG.). 24p. (J). bds. 9.99 *(978-1-4003-1079-1(2),* Tommy Nelson) Nelson, Thomas Inc.

Stosuy, Brandon. Music Is ... Martin, Amy, illus. 2016. (ENG.). 32p. (J). (gr. -1 — 1). bds. 8.99 *(978-1-4814-7702-4(1),* Little Simon) Little Simon.

Stott, Dorothy, illus. Ten in the Bed. 2010. (Padded Board Book W/CD Ser.). 8p. (J). (gr. k-2). bds. 10.99 incl. audio compact disk *(978-1-59922-578-4(6))* Twin Sisters IP, LLC.

Stowell, Louie. Look Inside Your Body. (Look Inside Board Bks.). (J). 2011. 13p. ring bd. 15.99 *(978-0-7945-2996-3(8))* 2013. 10p. ring bd. 14.99 *(978-0-7945-3311-3(6))* EDC Publishing. (Usborne).

—Wind-Up Pirate Ship. Fox, Christyan, illus. 2010. (Wind-up Bks). 13p. (J). bds. 29.99 *(978-0-7945-2835-5(X),* Usborne) EDC Publishing.

Strasser, Susanne. So Far Up. Strasser, Susanne, illus. 2018. (ENG., Illus.). 22p. (J). (— 1). bds. 7.99 *(978-1-58089-848-5(3))* Charlesbridge Publishing, Inc.

—So Light, So Heavy. Strasser, Susanne, illus. 2018. (ENG., Illus.). 22p. (J). (— 1). bds. 7.99 *(978-1-58089-849-2(1))* Charlesbridge Publishing, Inc.

Strawberry Shortcake Paint n' Play with Sticker Rolls. 2005. (J). spiral bd. *(978-1-59487-146-7(9))* Artist Studios, Ltd.

Strawberry Shortcake Secret Diary with Pendant. 2005. (J). *(978-1-59487-155-9(8))* Artist Studios, Ltd.

Stren, Ariella. Bracha Do You Know? Argoff, Patti, illus. 2015. (ENG.). 28p. (J). 11.95 *(978-1-929628-76-6(5))* Hachai Publishing.

Strong, Belinda. Hold & Touch Bedtime. 2015. (Hold & Touch Ser.). (ENG., Illus.). (J). bds. *(978-1-74363-413-4(7))* Hinkler Bks. Pty, Ltd.

Studio Mouse. Princess Colors & Shapes Pack. 2003. (ENG., Illus.). 36p. (J). (gr. -1-3). 12.99 *(978-1-59069-366-7(3),* 1A501) Studio Mouse LLC.

Studio Mouse, creator. Get Your Grouchies Out! A Vocabulary of Feelings. rev. ed. 2007. (ENG., Illus.). (J). 12.99 *(978-1-59069-610-1(7))* Studio Mouse LLC.

—Kindness Counts. rev. ed. 2008. (Learn-Aloud Bks.). (ENG., Illus.). (J). 12.99 *(978-1-59069-627-9(1))* Studio Mouse LLC.

—Rhymes on the Go! rev. ed. 2008. (ENG., Illus.). 36p. (J). 12.99 *(978-1-59069-614-9(X))* Studio Mouse LLC.

Studio Mouse, ed. Disney Preincess Best Friends: Flat Learn & Carry 4 Board Books & CD. rev. ed. 2008. 80p. (J). 12.99 *(978-1-59069-553-1(4))* Studio Mouse LLC.

—Disney Time to Learn with Pooh: Flat Learn & Carry 4 Board Books & CD. rev. ed. 2007. (ENG.). 12.99 *(978-1-59069-626-2(3))* Studio Mouse LLC.

—Jojo's Circus Get up & Move! Flat Learn & Carry 4 Board Books & CD. rev. ed. 2007. (ENG.). 12.99 *(978-1-59069-548-7(8))* Studio Mouse LLC.

Studio Mouse Editorial. Ariel: The Brave Little Mermaid. 2008. (ENG., Illus.). 36p. (gr. -1-k). 7.99 *(978-1-59069-434-3(1))* Studio Mouse LLC.

—Belle: The Power of Love. 2008. (ENG., Illus.). 36p. (gr. -1-k). 7.99 *(978-1-59069-435-0(X))* Studio Mouse LLC.

Studio Mouse Staff. Cars on the Road to Learning: Flat Learn & Carry 4 Board Books & CD. rev. ed. 2007. (ENG.). 80p. 12.99 *(978-1-59069-549-4(6))* Studio Mouse LLC.

—Five Little Monkeys: And Other Counting Rhymes. Elliott, Rebecca et al, illus. rev. ed. 2007. (ENG.). 24p. (J). (gr. -1-k). 4.99 *(978-1-59069-608-8(5))* Studio Mouse LLC.

—Let's Move: Nursery Rhymes for Moving & Learning. 2008. (ENG., Illus.). 36p. (gr. -1-k). 7.99 *(978-1-59249-796-6(9))* Studio Mouse LLC.

—Mickey Mouse Clubhouse Count Along. rev. ed. 2007. (ENG.). 36p. 12.99 *(978-1-59069-613-2(1))* Studio Mouse LLC.

—Musical Fun: Colors & Patterns. rev. ed. 2008. (ENG., Illus.). 24p. (J). 4.99 *(978-1-59069-605-7(0))* Studio Mouse LLC.

—Pet Friends. rev. ed. 2008. (ENG.). 12p. (J). 12.99 *(978-1-59069-611-8(5))* Studio Mouse LLC.

—Pooh & Friends ABCs & 123s: First Concepts. rev. ed. 2007. (ENG., Illus.). 24p. (J). (gr. -1-3). 4.99 *(978-1-59069-606-4(9))* Studio Mouse LLC.

—Sesame Street Bert & Ernie Work Together. rev. ed. 2008. (ENG.). 24p. 4.99 *(978-1-59069-620-0(4))* Studio Mouse LLC.

—Sesame Street Rosita Reads a Recipe. rev. ed. 2008. (ENG.). 24p. 4.99 *(978-1-59069-619-4(0))* Studio Mouse LLC.

—Space Adventure. rev. ed. 2008. (ENG., Illus.). (J). 12.99 *(978-1-59069-609-5(3))* Studio Mouse LLC.

—Spelling Fun. 2011. (Cars Ser.). (ENG., Illus.). 28p. (J). 15.99 *(978-1-59069-938-6(6))* Studio Mouse LLC.

—Time to Learn!, 4 vols. rev. ed. 2007. (ENG., Illus.). 4x20p. (J). (gr. -1-k). 14.99 *(978-1-59069-564-7(X))* Studio Mouse LLC.

—Walt Disney Bambi Learning Library. rev. ed. 2007. (ENG.). 60p. 12.99 *(978-1-59069-612-5(3))* Studio Mouse LLC.

—Wedding Countdown. 2008. (ENG.). 36p. (J). (gr. -1). 12.99 *(978-1-59069-740-5(5))* Studio Mouse LLC.

—Winnie Pooh y sus amigos Ejercicios: Puffy Book with CD. rev. ed. 2007. (ESP & ENG.). 36p. (J). 14.99 *(978-1-59069-528-9(3))* Studio Mouse LLC.

Style Guide, illus. PJ Masks Save Headquarters! 2017. (PJ Masks Ser.). (ENG.). 12p. (J). (gr. -1-k). bds. 12.99 *(978-1-4814-9552-3(6),* Simon Spotlight) Simon Spotlight.

Style Guide Staff, illus. Patricks Backpack Book. 2003. (SpongeBob SquarePants Ser.). (ENG.). 16p. (J). bds. 6.99 *(978-0-689-85649-5(0),* Simon Spotlight/Nickelodeon) Simon Spotlight/Nickelodeon.

—SpongeBob's Backpack Book. 2003. (SpongeBob SquarePants Ser.). (ENG.). 16p. (J). bds. 6.99 *(978-0-689-85648-8(2),* Simon Spotlight/Nickelodeon) Simon Spotlight/Nickelodeon.

Subtraction Mastery w/Audio CD: Kit with Book, Wrap-up & CD. 2004. (ENG.). (J). 19.99 *(978-0-943343-99-0(2))* Learning Wrap-Ups, Inc.

Suigit, Nicole. Caillou Leads the Parade. Poupart, Jean-Sébastien, illus. 2004. (J). *(978-0-7853-9949-0(6))* Publications International, Ltd.

Sullivan, Kyle. Get Dressed, Sasquatch! Sullivan, Derek, illus. 2018. (Hazy Dell Press Monster Ser.). 30p. (J). (gr. k-1). bds. 13.95 *(978-0-9965787-3-8(0))* Hazy Dell Pr.

—Goodnight Krampus. Sullivan, Derek, illus. 2018. (Hazy Dell Press Monster Ser.). 30p. (J). (gr. k-1). bds. 13.95 *(978-0-9965787-2-1(2))* Hazy Dell Pr.

—Hush Now, Banshee! A Not-So-Quiet Counting Book. Sullivan, Derek, illus. 2018. (Hazy Dell Press Monster Ser.). 30p. (J). (gr. k-1). bds. 13.95 *(978-0-9965787-5-2(7))* Hazy Dell Pr.

—Monster ABC. Sullivan, Derek, illus. 2018. (Hazy Dell Press Monster Ser.). 30p. (J). (gr. k-1). bds. 13.95 *(978-0-9965787-0-7(6))* Hazy Dell Pr.

Sully, Katherine. Night-Night California. Poole, Helen, illus. 2016. (Night-Night Ser.). (ENG.). 20p. (J). (gr. -1-1). bds. 9.99 *(978-1-4926-3939-8(7),* 9781492639398, Hometown World) Sourcebooks, Inc.

—Night-Night Chicago. Poole, Helen, illus. 2016. (Night-Night Ser.). (ENG.). 20p. (J). (gr. -1-1). bds. 9.99 *(978-1-4926-3935-0(4),* 9781492639350, Hometown World) Sourcebooks, Inc.

—Night-Night Colorado. Poole, Helen, illus. 2016. (Night-Night Ser.). (ENG.). 20p. (J). (gr. -1-1). bds. 9.99 *(978-1-4926-3938-1(9),* 9781492639381, Hometown World) Sourcebooks, Inc.

—Night-Night Florida. Poole, Helen, illus. 2016. (Night-Night Ser.). (ENG.). 20p. (J). (gr. -1-1). bds. 9.99 *(978-1-4926-4218-3(5),* 9781492642183, Hometown World) Sourcebooks, Inc.

—Night-Night Georgia. Poole, Helen, illus. 2016. (Night-Night Ser.). (ENG.). 20p. (J). (gr. -1-1). bds. 9.99 *(978-1-4926-4216-9(9),* 9781492642169, Hometown World) Sourcebooks, Inc.

—Night-Night Kansas. Poole, Helen, illus. 2016. (Night-Night Ser.). (ENG.). 20p. (J). (gr. -1-1). bds. 9.99 *(978-1-4926-3941-1(9),* 9781492639411, Hometown World) Sourcebooks, Inc.

—Night-Night Michigan. Poole, Helen, illus. 2016. (Night-Night Ser.). (ENG.). 20p. (J). (gr. -1-1). bds. 9.99 *(978-1-4926-3934-3(6),* 9781492639343, Hometown World) Sourcebooks, Inc.

—Night-Night Minnesota. Poole, Helen, illus. 2016. (Night-Night Ser.). (ENG.). 20p. (J). (gr. -1-1). bds. 9.99 *(978-1-4926-3940-4(0),* 9781492639404, Hometown World) Sourcebooks, Inc.

—Night-Night New Jersey. Poole, Helen, illus. 2016. (Night-Night Ser.). (ENG.). 20p. (J). (gr. -1-1). bds. 9.99 *(978-1-4926-3933-6(8),* 9781492639336, Hometown World) Sourcebooks, Inc.

—Night-Night New York City. Poole, Helen, illus. 2016. (Night-Night Ser.). (ENG.). 20p. (J). (gr. -1-1). bds. 9.99 *(978-1-4926-3932-9(X),* 9781492639329, Hometown World) Sourcebooks, Inc.

—Night-Night Ohio. Poole, Helen, illus. 2016. (Night-Night Ser.). (ENG.). 20p. (J). (gr. -1-1). bds. 9.99 *(978-1-4926-4220-6(7),* 9781492642206, Hometown World) Sourcebooks, Inc.

—Night-Night Pennsylvania. Poole, Helen, illus. 2016. (Night-Night Ser.). (ENG.). 20p. (J). (gr. -1-1). bds. 9.99 *(978-1-4926-4219-0(3),* 9781492642190, Hometown World) Sourcebooks, Inc.

—Night-Night Texas. Poole, Helen, illus. 2016. (Night-Night Ser.). (ENG.). 20p. (J). (gr. -1-1). bds. 9.99 *(978-1-4926-3936-7(2),* 9781492639367, Hometown World) Sourcebooks, Inc.

—Night-Night Wisconsin. Poole, Helen, illus. 2016. (Night-Night Ser.). (ENG.). 20p. (J). (gr. -1-1). bds. 9.99 *(978-1-4926-4217-6(7),* 9781492642176, Hometown World) Sourcebooks, Inc.

Surplice, Holly. I Love You, Little One. Surplice, Holly, illus. 2019. (ENG., Illus.). 24p. (J). (-k). bds. 9.99 *(978-1-5362-0578-7(8))* Candlewick Pr.

Sussman, Joni Kibort. Shanah Tovah, Grover! Leigh, Tom, illus. 2019. (ENG.). 12p. (J). (gr. -1 — 1). bds. 6.99 *(978-1-5415-2922-9(7),* f6a2d4ee-a53f-49a0-8a9c-762d7254701f, Kar-Ben Publishing) Lerner Publishing Group.

Sutton, Sally. Demolicion. Lovelock, Brian, illus. 2014. (Construction Crew Ser.). (SPA.). 22p. (J). (-k). bds. 8.99 *(978-0-7636-7031-3(6))* Candlewick Pr.

—Demolition. Lovelock, Brian, illus. 2014. (Construction Crew Ser.). (ENG.). 22p. (J). (-k). bds. 8.99 *(978-0-7636-6493-0(6))* Candlewick Pr.

Sweeney, Samantha, et al. My First Farm Stories. Harry, Rebecca, illus. 2018. (ENG.). 44p. (J). (gr. -1-k). bds. 9.99 *(978-1-68010-544-5(2))* Tiger Tales.

—My First Night-Night Stories. 2017. (ENG., Illus.). 44p. (J). (gr. -1-k). bds. 9.99 *(978-1-68010-529-2(9))* Tiger Tales.

Sweet Dreams, Pout-Pout Fish. 2015. (Pout-Pout Fish Mini Adventure Ser.: 3). (ENG., Illus.). 12p. (J). (gr. -1 — 1). bds. 6.99 *(978-0-374-38010-6(4),* 900122563, Farrar, Straus & Giroux (BYR)) Farrar, Straus & Giroux.

Swift, Ginger. All God's Creatures (Little Sunbeams) Cottage Door Press, ed. Sosa, Daniela, illus. 2019. (Little Sunbeams Ser.). (ENG.). 12p. (J). (gr. -1 — 1). bds. 7.99 *(978-1-68052-523-6(9),* 1003790) Cottage Door Pr.

—Good Morning, God. Cottage Door Press, ed. Sosa, Daniela, illus. 2018. (Little Sunbeams Ser.). (ENG.). 12p. (J). (gr. -1 — 1). bds. 7.99 *(978-1-68052-377-5(5),* 1003420) Cottage Door Pr.

—Good Night, God. Cottage Door Press, ed. Sosa, Daniela, illus. 2018. (Little Sunbeams Ser.). (ENG.). 12p. (J). (gr. -1 — 1). bds. 7.99 *(978-1-68052-375-1(9),* 1003400) Cottage Door Pr.

—Little Blue Boat. Cottage Door Press, ed. Persico, Zoe, illus. 2016. (ENG.). 12p. (J). (gr. -1 — 1). bds. 7.99 *(978-1-68052-077-4(6),* 1000800) Cottage Door Pr.

—Little Green Frog. Cottage Door Press, ed. Demidova, Olga, illus. 2016. (ENG.). 12p. (J). (gr. -1 — 1). bds. 7.99 *(978-1-68052-082-8(2),* 1000650) Cottage Door Pr.

—Little Red Barn. Cottage Door Press, ed. Pavon, David, illus. 2015. (ENG.). 12p. (J). (gr. -1 — 1). bds. 7.99 *(978-1-68052-055-2(5),* 1000560) Cottage Door Pr.

—Little Yellow Bee. Cottage Door Press, ed. Longhi, Katya, illus. 2016. (ENG.). 12p. (J). (gr. -1 — 1). bds. 7.99 *(978-1-68052-083-5(0),* 1000660) Cottage Door Pr.

Sysewrda, Jean E. My Bedtime Story Bible for Little Ones, 1 vol. Howarth, Daniel, illus. 2016. (ENG.). 32p. (J). bds. 9.99 *(978-0-310-75330-8(9))* Zonderkidz.

Taback, Simms. Joseph Had a Little Overcoat. Taback, Simms, illus. (Illus.). pap. incl. audio compact disk *(978-1-59112-608-9(8))* Live Oak Media.

Tabby, Abigail. Welcome Home, Baby! Williams, Sam, illus. 2017. (New Books for Newborns Ser.). (ENG.). 16p. (J). (— 1). bds. 8.99 *(978-1-5344-0103-7(2),* Little Simon) Little Simon.

Tabby's Pet Pals: Shapes. 2011. (Illus.). (J). *(978-1-58865-895-1(3))* Kidsbooks, LLC.

Tafuri, Nancy. Whose Chick Are You? Board Book: An Easter & Springtime Book for Kids. Tafuri, Nancy, illus. 2019. (ENG., Illus.). 38p. (J). (gr. -1 — 1). bds. 7.99 *(978-0-06-285739-2(8),* Greenwillow Bks.) HarperCollins Pubs.

Tagel, Peggy, illus. On the Go. 2003. (Squishy Shapes Ser.). 10p. (J). 12.95 *(978-1-57145-739-4(9),* Silver Dolphin Bks.) Readerlink Distribution Services, LLC.

Tallec, Olivier, illus. What's Going on Here? A Tell-Your-Own-Tale Book. 2019. (ENG.). 28p. (J). (gr. -1-k). 15.99 *(978-1-4521-7317-7(6))* Chronicle Bks. LLC.

—Who Was That? 2018. (Who Done It? Ser.). (ENG.). 32p. (J). (gr. -1-k). 15.99 *(978-1-4521-6990-3(X))* Chronicle Bks. LLC.

Taplin, Sam. Are You There Little Bunny? 2018. (Little Peek Through Books* Ser.). (ENG.). 12p. (J). 9.99 *(978-0-7945-4269-6(7),* Usborne) EDC Publishing.

—Baby Animals. 2014. (Usborne Flap Book Ser.). (ENG., Illus.). 10p. (gr. -1). bds. 7.99 *(978-0-7945-2105-9(3),* Usborne) EDC Publishing.

—Easter Bunny Flap Book. 2019. (Flap Bks.). (ENG.). 10ppp. (J). 7.99 *(978-0-7945-3256-7(X),* Usborne) EDC Publishing.

—Little Stories for Bedtime. Chiara, Francesca De, illus. 2010. (Bedtime Stories Ser.). 12p. (J). bds. 12.99 *(978-0-7945-2673-3(X),* Usborne) EDC Publishing.

—Noisy Building Site Board Book. 2008. (Busy Sounds Board Bks). 10p. (J). bds. 18.99 *(978-0-7945-2076-2(6),* Usborne) EDC Publishing.

—Noisy Diggers. 2012. (Noisy Bks). 10p. (J). bds. 18.99 *(978-0-7945-3264-2(0),* Usborne) EDC Publishing.

—Pop-Up Haunted House. 2015. (Pop-Up Bks.). (ENG.). 10p. (J). 29.99 *(978-0-7945-2185-1(1),* Usborne) EDC Publishing.

—Santa Flap Book. Bonnett, Rosalind, illus. 2019. (Flap Bks.). (ENG.). 10ppp. (J). 7.99 *(978-0-7945-3316-8(7),* Usborne) EDC Publishing.

—Sleeping Beauty. 2008. (First Fairytales Look & Say Ser.). 12p. (J). (gr. -1). bds. 9.99 *(978-0-7945-2200-1(9),* Usborne) EDC Publishing.

—Sleepytime Stories. Chaira, Francesca di, illus. 2011. (Baby Board Books Ser.). 12p. (J). ring bd. 12.99 *(978-0-7945-3006-8(0),* Usborne) EDC Publishing.

—This Is My Dinosaur. 2009. (Noisy Touchy-Feely Board Bks). (Illus.). 10p. (J). bds. 16.99 *(978-0-7945-2366-4(8),* Usborne) EDC Publishing.

—This Is My Monster. Furukawa, Masumi, illus. 2008. (Noisy Touchy-Feely Board Bks). 10p. (J). bds. 16.99 *(978-0-7945-2353-4(6),* Usborne) EDC Publishing.

Tarbett, Debbie, illus. Ten Cheepy, Chirpy Chicks. 2017. (J). *(978-1-84857-576-9(9))* Little Tiger Pr. Group.

—Ten Splishy, Splashy Fish. 2017. (J). *(978-1-84857-577-6(7))* Little Tiger Pr. Group.

—Ten Wriggly, Wiggly Caterpillars. 2017. (J). *(978-1-84857-562-2(9))* Little Tiger Pr. Group.

—5 Little Ducks. 2016. (J). *(978-1-84857-541-7(6))* Little Tiger Pr.

—5 Stomping Elephants. 2016. (J). *(978-1-84857-542-4(4))* Little Tiger Pr.

Tatchell, Judy. Dragons. Scott, Peter David & Furnival, Keith, illus. 2006. (J). *(978-0-439-82790-4(6))* Scholastic, Inc.

—Dragons Lift-the-flap. Scott, Peter, illus. 2005. 16p. (J). (gr. 1-18). 11.99 *(978-0-7945-0968-2(1),* Usborne) EDC Publishing.

Tatcheva, Eva. Witch Zelda's Birthday Cake: A Wild & Wicked Pop-up, Pull-the-Tab Book. Tatcheva, Eva, illus. 2004. (Illus.). 12p. (J). (gr. k-3). reprint ed. 18.00 *(978-0-7567-7225-3(7))* DIANE Publishing Co.

Tawa, Renee. Tink's Magical Day. 2011. (Illus.). (J). *(978-1-4508-1707-3(6))* Publications International, Ltd.

Taylor, Dereen. Alien Adventure: Peek Inside the Pop-Up Windows! Hutchinson, Tim, illus. 2015. (ENG.). 12p. (J). (gr. 1-3). 16.99 *(978-1-86147-487-2(3),* Armadillo) Anness Publishing GBR. Dist: National Bk. Network.

—The Dragon's Magic Wish. Hutchinson, Tim, illus. 2012. 12p. (J). (gr. 1-6). 16.99 *(978-1-84322-856-1(4))* Anness Publishing GBR. Dist: National Bk. Network.
—The Fairy Midnight Surprise Party. Stone, Lyn, illus. 2012. 12p. (J). (gr. 1-6). 16.99 *(978-1-84322-763-2(0))* Anness Publishing GBR. Dist: National Bk. Network.
—Journey to the World of the Dinosaurs: Peek Inside the Pop-Up Windows! Kavanagh, Peter, illus. 2014. (ENG.). 12p. (J). (gr. 2-7). 16.99 *(978-1-86147-319-6(2),* Armadillo) Anness Publishing GBR. Dist: National Bk. Network.
—The Knight's First Tournament. Kavanagh, Peter, illus. 2012. 12p. (J). (gr. 1-6). 16.99 *(978-1-84322-760-1(6))* Anness Publishing GBR. Dist: National Bk. Network.
—The Lost Treasure of the Jungle Temple: Peek Inside the 3D Windows! Hutchinson, Tim, illus. 2013. (ENG.). 12p. (J). (gr. 1-8). 16.99 *(978-1-84322-822-6(X),* Armadillo) Anness Publishing GBR. Dist: National Bk. Network.
—The Mystery of the Vampire Boy: Dare You Peek Through the Pop-Up Windows? Spoor, Mike, illus. 2014. 12p. (J). (gr. k-5). 16.99 *(978-1-86147-410-0(5),* Armadillo) Anness Publishing GBR. Dist: National Bk. Network.
—Paulo & the Football Thieves: Peek Inside the Pop-Up Windows! Hutchinson, Tim, illus. 2014. 12p. (J). (gr. -1-12). 16.99 *(978-1-86147-409-4(1),* Armadillo) Anness Publishing GBR. Dist: National Bk. Network.
—Robo-Pup to the Rescue! Hutchinson, Tim, illus. 2013. (ENG.). 12p. (J). (gr. 1-8). 16.99 *(978-1-84322-821-9(1),* Armadillo) Anness Publishing GBR. Dist: National Bk. Network.
—Rosie Rides to the Rescue: Peek Inside the Pop-Up Windows! Stone, Lyn, illus. 2015. (ENG.). 12p. (J). (gr. -1-4). 16.99 *(978-1-86147-488-9(1),* Armadillo) Anness Publishing GBR. Dist: National Bk. Network.
—Trapped in the Witch's Lair: Peek Inside the Pop-Up Windows! Catchpole, Diana, illus. 2014. (ENG.). 12p. (J). (gr. 2-7). 16.99 *(978-1-86147-320-2(6),* Armadillo) Anness Publishing GBR. Dist: National Bk. Network.
Taylor, Helen. Kakapo Dance. 2019. 14p. (J). (— 1). bds. 10.99 *(978-0-14-377222-4(8))* Penguin Group New Zealand, Ltd. NZL. Dist: Independent Pubs. Group.
Taylor, Jon, illus. Tower of Babel. 2007. 24p. (J). (gr. 4-7). 14.99 *(978-0-89051-487-0(9),* Master Books) New Leaf Publishing Group.
Taylor, Martin. The Lost Treasure of the Sunken City. Catling, Andy, illus. 2012. (J). *(978-1-4351-4330-2(2))* Barnes & Noble, Inc.
Taylor, W. Y. I'm Not too Little to Help the Earth. 2009. 14p. 9.95 *(978-1-58117-913-2(8),* Intervisual/Piggy Toes) Bendon, Inc.
—This Little Piggy Goes Green. 2009. (ENG.). 12p. bds. 3.95 *(978-1-58117-925-5(1),* Intervisual/Piggy Toes) Bendon, Inc.
Teckentrup, Britta. Moon: a Peek-Through Picture Book. 2018. (ENG., Illus.). 32p. (J). (gr. -1-2). 17.99 *(978-1-5247-6966-6(5),* Doubleday Bks. for Young Readers) Random Hse. Children's Bks.
—Tree: a Peek-Through Picture Book. 2016. (ENG.). 32p. (J). (gr. -1-2). 16.99 *(978-1-101-93242-1(2),* Doubleday Bks. for Young Readers) Random Hse. Children's Bks.
—Up & Down. Teckentrup, Britta, illus. 2014. (ENG., Illus.). 28p. (J). (-k). 17.99 *(978-0-7636-7129-7(0),* Templar) Candlewick Pr.
Teckentrup, Britta, illus. My Book of Opposites. 2014. (J). *(978-1-4351-5678-4(1))* Barnes & Noble, Inc.
Tegen, Katherine. The Story of the Easter Bunny Board Book: An Easter & Springtime Book for Kids. Lambert, Sally Anne, illus. 2017. (ENG.). 32p. (J). (gr. -1-3). bds. 7.99 *(978-0-06-238155-2(5),* HarperFestival) HarperCollins Pubs.
Teitelbaum, Michael. On the Move! Shannon, David et al, illus. 2009. (Jon Scieszka's Trucktown Ser.). (ENG.). 10p. (J). (gr. -1-k). bds. 6.99 *(978-1-4169-4178-1(9),* Little Simon) Little Simon.
—Steer the Wheel! Shannon, David et al, illus. 2011. (Jon Scieszka's Trucktown Ser.). (ENG.). 12p. (J). (gr. -1-1). bds. 7.99 *(978-1-4169-4185-9(1),* Simon & Schuster Bks. For Young Readers) Simon & Schuster Bks. For Young Readers.
Tekiela, Stan. Critter Litter. 2016. (Wildlife Picture Bks.). (ENG., Illus.). 26p. (J). (gr. -1-3). 12.95 *(978-1-59193-590-2(3),* Adventure Pubns.) AdventureKEEN.
—Floppers & Loppers, 1 vol. 2013. (Adventure Boardbook Ser.). (ENG., Illus.). 22p. (J). (gr. -1-k). bds. 8.95 *(978-1-59193-424-0(9),* Adventure Pubns.) AdventureKEEN.
—Paws & Claws, 1 vol. 2013. (Adventure Boardbook Ser.). (ENG., Illus.). 22p. (J). (gr. -1-k). bds. 8.95 *(978-1-59193-425-7(7),* Adventure Pubns.) AdventureKEEN.
—Peepers & Peekers, 1 vol. 2013. (Adventure Boardbook Ser.). (ENG., Illus.). 22p. (J). (gr. -1-k). bds. 8.95 *(978-1-59193-423-3(0),* Adventure Pubns.) AdventureKEEN.
Tempest, Annabel, illus. Moby Dick: a BabyLit(TM) Storybook: A BabyLit(TM) Storybook, 1 vol. 2017. (BabyLit Ser.). 28p. (J). (gr. -1-k). 12.99 *(978-1-4236-4784-3(X))* Gibbs Smith, Publisher.
Terada, Junzo. Animal Friends: Barnyard Jamboree! (Animal Books for Toddlers, Farm Animal Board Book) 2017. (Animal Friends Ser.). (ENG., Illus.). 10p. (J). bds. 9.99 *(978-1-4521-5189-2(X))* Chronicle Bks. LLC.
—Animal Friends: Swimming Hole Party! (Animal Books for Toddlers, Jungle Animal Board Book) 2017. (Animal Friends Ser.). (ENG., Illus.). 10p. (J). bds. 9.99 *(978-1-4521-4983-7(6))* Chronicle Bks. LLC.
Testa, Maggie. Friends Are the Best! Fruchter, Jason, illus. 2014. (Daniel Tiger's Neighborhood Ser.). (ENG.). 12p. (J). (gr. -1-k). bds. 6.99 *(978-1-4424-9547-0(2),* Simon Spotlight) Simon Spotlight.
—Meet the Heroes ... & the Villains, Too! Style Guide, illus. 2016. (PJ Masks Ser.). (ENG.). 14p. (J). (gr. -1-k). bds. 7.99 *(978-1-4814-8650-7(0),* Simon Spotlight) Simon Spotlight.
—A Ride Through the Neighborhood. Style Guide, illus. 2014. (Daniel Tiger's Neighborhood Ser.). (ENG.). 12p. (J). (gr. -1-1). bds. 8.99 *(978-1-4424-9839-6(0),* Simon Spotlight) Simon Spotlight.
Teves, Miles, illus. The Dragon Hunter's Handbook. 2008. (J). *(978-1-4351-0204-0(5))* Metro Bks.
That's Not My Badger. 2017. (Touchy-Feely BDs Ser.). (ENG.). (J). bds. 9.99 *(978-0-7945-3808-8(8),* Usborne) EDC Publishing.
That's Not My... Puppy & Kitten Box Set. 2017. (Touchy-Feely BDs Ser.). (ENG.). (J). bds. 14.99 *(978-0-7945-3978-8(5),* Usborne) EDC Publishing.
The Global Fund for Children. American Babies. 2010. (Global Babies Ser.: 4). (Illus.). 16p. (J). (gr. -1 — 1). bds. 6.95 *(978-1-58089-280-3(9))* Charlesbridge Publishing, Inc.
—Global Baby Bedtimes. 2015. (Global Babies Ser.: 5). (ENG., Illus.). 16p. (J). (— 1). bds. 6.95 *(978-1-58089-708-2(8))* Charlesbridge Publishing, Inc.
—Global Baby Boys. 2014. (Global Babies Ser.: 2). (Illus.). 16p. (J). (— 1). bds. 6.95 *(978-1-58089-440-1(2))* Charlesbridge Publishing, Inc.
The Library Fairy. The Magical Tree & Musical Wind. Faust, Laurie A., illus. 2008. 32p. pap. 16.95 *(978-1-59858-604-6(1))* Dog Ear Publishing, LLC.
The Trustees of the British Museum, illus. Opposites: Early Learning at the Museum. 2018. (Early Learning at the Museum Ser.). (ENG.). 20p. (J). (— 1). bds. 7.99 *(978-1-5362-0270-0(3))* Candlewick Pr.
—123: Early Learning at the Museum. 2018. (Early Learning at the Museum Ser.). (ENG.). 22p. (J). (— 1). bds. 7.99 *(978-1-5362-0267-0(3))* Candlewick Pr.
Things That Go! (Flip Flap Fun Book Ser.). 10p. (J). bds. *(978-2-89393-933-9(3))* Phidal Publishing, Inc./Editions Phidal, Inc.
Thomas: It's Great to Be an Engine. 2004. (Little Music Note Ser.). (Illus.). 10p. (J). bds. *(978-0-7853-9950-6(X),* 7209400) Phoenix International Publications, Inc.
Thomas, Jan. The Doghouse Board Book. Thomas, Jan, illus. 2015. (Giggle Gang Ser.). (ENG., Illus.). 36p. (J). (— 1). bds. 7.99 *(978-0-544-43063-1(8),* 1595738, Clarion Bks.) HarperCollins Pubs.
Thomas, Martin. Dad Can Do Anything. Jatkowska, Ag, illus. 2018. (ENG.). 18p. (gr. -1 — 1). bds. 8.99 *(978-1-5107-3617-7(4),* Sky Pony Pr.) Skyhorse Publishing Co., Inc.
—My Mom Is There. Jatkowska, Ag, illus. 2018. (ENG.). 20p. (gr. -1 — 1). bds. 8.99 *(978-1-5107-3616-0(6),* Sky Pony Pr.) Skyhorse Publishing Co., Inc.
Thomas Nelson Community College Staff. God's Love in My Heart, 1 vol. 2014. (ENG.). 24p. bds. 9.99 *(978-0-529-11141-8(1),* Tommy Nelson) Nelson, Thomas Inc.
Thomas Nelson Publishing Staff. All Things Bright & Beautiful: Make Believe Ideas, 1 vol. 2017. (ENG.). 10p. (J). bds. 6.99 *(978-0-7180-9337-2(2))* Make Believe Ideas GBR. Dist: Nelson, Thomas Inc.
—Grandma Kisses, 1 vol. 2015. (ENG., Illus.). 20p. (J). bds. 9.99 *(978-0-7180-3659-1(X),* Tommy Nelson) Nelson, Thomas Inc.
—Starter Bible, 1 vol. 2016. (ENG., Illus.). 40p. (J). bds. 9.99 *(978-0-7180-9005-0(5),* Tommy Nelson) Nelson, Thomas Inc.
Thompson, Carol. Dance. Thompson, Carol, illus. 2018. (Amazing Me! Ser.: 4). (Illus.). 12p. (J). (gr. k-k). spiral bd. *(978-1-84643-959-9(0))* Child's Play International Ltd.
—Dressing Up. Thompson, Carol, illus. 2018. (Amazing Me! Ser.: 4). (Illus.). 12p. (J). (gr. k-k). spiral bd. *(978-1-84643-960-5(4))* Child's Play International Ltd.
—Music. Thompson, Carol, illus. 2018. (Amazing Me! Ser.: 4). (Illus.). 12p. (J). (gr. k-k). spiral bd. *(978-1-84643-961-2(2))* Child's Play International Ltd.
—Rain. Thompson, Carol, illus. 2014. (Whatever the Weather Ser.: 4). (Illus.). 12p. (J). (gr. k-k). spiral bd. *(978-1-84643-683-3(4))* Child's Play International Ltd.
—Sing. Thompson, Carol, illus. 2018. (Amazing Me! Ser.: 4). (Illus.). 12p. (J). (gr. k-k). spiral bd. *(978-1-84643-962-9(0))* Child's Play International Ltd.
—Snow. Thompson, Carol, illus. 2014. (Whatever the Weather Ser.). (Illus.). 12p. (J). (gr. k-k). spiral bd. *(978-1-84643-681-9(8))* Child's Play International Ltd.
—Sun. Thompson, Carol, illus. 2014. (Whatever the Weather Ser.). (Illus.). 12p. (J). (gr. k-k). spiral bd. *(978-1-84643-680-2(X))* Child's Play International Ltd.
—Wind. Thompson, Carol, illus. 2014. (Whatever the Weather Ser.). (Illus.). 12p. (J). (gr. k-k). spiral bd. *(978-1-84643-682-6(6))* Child's Play International Ltd.
Thompson, Chad. The Itsy Bitsy Spider. 2009. (Early Literacy Ser.). (ENG., Illus.). 16p. (gr. k-1). 19.99 *(978-1-4333-1455-1(X))* Teacher Created Materials, Inc.
—Yankee Doodle. 2011. (Early Literacy Ser.). (ENG.). 16p. (gr. k-1). 19.99 *(978-1-4333-2365-2(6))* Teacher Created Materials, Inc.
Thompson, Kay. Eloise & Friends. Knight, Hilary, illus. 2015. (Eloise Ser.). (ENG.). 26p. (J). (gr. -1-2). bds. 8.99 *(978-1-4814-5158-1(8),* Little Simon) Little Simon.
—Eloise at the Plaza. Knight, Hilary, illus. 2015. (Eloise Ser.). (ENG.). 26p. (J). (gr. -1-2). bds. 8.99 *(978-1-4814-5159-8(6),* Little Simon) Little Simon.
Thompson, Kim Mitzo. Old MacDonald Had a Farm. Girouard, Patrick, illus. 2010. (Padded Board Book W/CD Ser.). 8p. (J). (gr. k-2). bds. 10.99 incl. audio compact disk *(978-1-59922-579-1(4))* Twin Sisters IP, LLC.
Thompson, Lauren. Cuaquito (Little Quack) Anderson, Derek, illus. 2010. (SPA.). 34p. (J). (gr. -1-1). bds. 8.99 *(978-1-4169-9894-5(2),* Libros Para Ninos) Libros Para Ninos.
—Little Quack Counts. Anderson, Derek, illus. 2009. (Super Chubbies Ser.). (ENG.). 26p. (J). (gr. -1 — 1). bds. 5.99 *(978-1-4169-6093-5(7),* Little Simon) Little Simon.
—Little Quack Loves Colors. Anderson, Derek, illus. 2009. (Super Chubbies Ser.). (ENG.). 26p. (J). (gr. -1 — 1). bds. 6.99 *(978-1-4169-6094-2(5),* Little Simon) Little Simon.
—Little Quack's ABC's. Anderson, Derek, illus. 2010. (Super Chubbies Ser.). (ENG.). 26p. (J). (gr. -1 — 1). bds. 5.99 *(978-1-4169-6091-1(0),* Little Simon) Little Simon.
—Little Quack's Bath Book. Anderson, Derek, illus. 2006. (ENG.). 8p. (J). (gr. -1 — 1). 9.99 *(978-1-4169-0803-6(X),* Little Simon) Little Simon.
—Little Quack's Opposites. Anderson, Derek, illus. 2010. (Super Chubbies Ser.). (ENG.). 26p. (J). (gr. -1 — 1). bds. 5.99 *(978-1-4169-6092-8(9),* Little Simon) Little Simon.
—Mouse's First Spring. Erdogan, Buket, illus. 2012. (Classic Board Bks.). (ENG.). 34p. (J). (gr. -1-3). bds. 8.99 *(978-1-4424-3431-8(7),* Little Simon) Little Simon.
—Mouse's First Summer. Erdogan, Buket, illus. 2014. (J). *(978-1-4351-5506-0(8))* Simon & Schuster.
—Mouse's First Valentine. Erdogan, Buket, illus. 2013. (J). *(978-1-4351-5014-0(7))* Barnes & Noble, Inc.
Thornley, Rebecca Gundersen. I Know He Is There: A Lift-A-Flap Book about Faith. Dorman, Brandon, illus. 2006. (J). *(978-1-59038-550-0(0))* Deseret Bk. Co.
Ticktock Media, Ltd. Staff. At the Beach with the Snappy Little Crab. 2009. (Touch & Feel Fun Ser.). (ENG.). 10p. (J). (gr. k — 1). bds. 5.95 *(978-1-84696-809-9(7),* TickTock Books) Octopus Publishing Group GBR. Dist: Independent Pubs. Group.
—Birthday Party. 2009. (Busy Tots Ser.). (ENG.). 10p. (J). (gr. -1-k). bds. 6.95 *(978-1-84696-801-3(1),* TickTock Books) Octopus Publishing Group GBR. Dist: Independent Pubs. Group.
—Dinosaurs. 2009. (Animal Fun Touch & Feel Ser.). (ENG.). 10p. (J). (gr. -1-k). bds. 4.95 *(978-1-84696-829-7(1),* TickTock Books) Octopus Publishing Group GBR. Dist: Independent Pubs. Group.
—Farm. 2009. (Animal Fun Touch & Feel Ser.). (ENG.). 10p. (J). (gr. -1-k). bds. 4.95 *(978-1-84696-827-3(5),* TickTock Books) Octopus Publishing Group GBR. Dist: Independent Pubs. Group.
—Favorite Foods: Colors & Shapes. 2008. (Tab Bks.). (ENG.). 10p. (J). (gr. -1-k). bds. 4.95 *(978-1-84696-821-1(6),* TickTock Books) Octopus Publishing Group GBR. Dist: Independent Pubs. Group.
—Guess What? Everyday Things. 2008. (Mini Flap Ser.). (ENG.). 10p. (J). (gr. k — 1). bds. 5.95 *(978-1-84696-818-1(6),* TickTock Books) Octopus Publishing Group GBR. Dist: Independent Pubs. Group.
—Guess What? Things That Go. 2008. (Mini Flap Ser.). (ENG.). 10p. (J). (gr. k — 1). bds. 5.95 *(978-1-84696-819-8(4),* TickTock Books) Octopus Publishing Group GBR. Dist: Independent Pubs. Group.
—Hungry Dinosaurs. 2009. (Dinosaur Shape Bks.). (ENG.). 10p. (J). (gr. -1-k). bds. 5.95 *(978-1-84696-834-1(8),* TickTock Books) Octopus Publishing Group GBR. Dist: Independent Pubs. Group.
—In the Garden with the Hungry Little Snail. 2009. (Touch & Feel Fun Ser.). (ENG.). 10p. (J). (gr. k — 1). bds. 5.95 *(978-1-84696-810-5(0),* TickTock Books) Octopus Publishing Group GBR. Dist: Independent Pubs. Group.
—Itsy Bitsy Spider. 2011. (Sing-Along Songs Ser.). (ENG.). 10p. (J). (gr. k — 1). bds. 6.95 *(978-1-84898-170-6(8),* TickTock Books) Octopus Publishing Group GBR. Dist: Independent Pubs. Group.
—Jungle. 2009. (Animal Fun Touch & Feel Ser.). (ENG.). 10p. (J). (gr. -1-k). bds. 4.95 *(978-1-84696-828-0(3),* TickTock Books) Octopus Publishing Group GBR. Dist: Independent Pubs. Group.
—Kittens & Puppies: Counting. 2008. (Tab Bks.). (ENG.). 10p. (J). (gr. -1-k). bds. 4.95 *(978-1-84696-822-8(4),* TickTock Books) Octopus Publishing Group GBR. Dist: Independent Pubs. Group.
—Little Helper. 2009. (Busy Tots Ser.). (ENG.). 10p. (J). (gr. -1-k). bds. 6.95 *(978-1-84696-798-6(8),* TickTock Books) Octopus Publishing Group GBR. Dist: Independent Pubs. Group.
—Living Planet: Uncovering the Wonders of the Natural World. 2008. (ENG.). 128p. (J). (gr. 4-7). pap. 12.95 *(978-1-84696-816-7(X),* TickTock Books) Octopus Publishing Group GBR. Dist: Independent Pubs. Group.
—My Fairy Garden. 2008. (Sparkle Bks.). (ENG.). 10p. (J). (gr. -1-k). bds. 6.95 *(978-1-84696-802-0(X),* TickTock Books) Octopus Publishing Group GBR. Dist: Independent Pubs. Group.
—My Night-Time Animals. 2008. (Sparkle Bks.). (ENG.). 10p. (J). (gr. -1-k). bds. 6.95 *(978-1-84696-803-7(8),* TickTock Books) Octopus Publishing Group GBR. Dist: Independent Pubs. Group.
—My Ocean Creatures. 2008. (Sparkle Bks.). (ENG.). 10p. (J). (gr. -1-k). bds. 6.95 *(978-1-84696-804-4(6),* TickTock Books) Octopus Publishing Group GBR. Dist: Independent Pubs. Group.
—My Space Adventure. 2008. (Sparkle Bks.). (ENG.). 10p. (J). (gr. -1-k). bds. 6.95 *(978-1-84696-805-1(4),* TickTock Books) Octopus Publishing Group GBR. Dist: Independent Pubs. Group.
—My World: Opposites. 2008. (Tab Bks.). (ENG.). 10p. (J). (gr. -1-k). bds. 4.95 *(978-1-84696-823-5(2),* TickTock Books) Octopus Publishing Group GBR. Dist: Independent Pubs. Group.
—Ocean. 2009. (Animal Fun Touch & Feel Ser.). (ENG.). 10p. (J). (gr. -1-k). bds. 4.95 *(978-1-84696-830-3(5),* TickTock Books) Octopus Publishing Group GBR. Dist: Independent Pubs. Group.
—Scary Dinosaurs. 2009. (Dinosaur Shape Bks.). (ENG.). 10p. (J). (gr. -1-k). bds. 5.95 *(978-1-84696-835-8(6),* TickTock Books) Octopus Publishing Group GBR. Dist: Independent Pubs. Group.
—Shopping Day. 2009. (Busy Tots Ser.). (ENG.). 10p. (J). (gr. -1-k). bds. 6.95 *(978-1-84696-799-3(6),* TickTock Books) Octopus Publishing Group GBR. Dist: Independent Pubs. Group.
—Summer Vacation. 2009. (Busy Tots Ser.). (ENG.). 10p. (J). (gr. -1-k). bds. 6.95 *(978-1-84696-800-6(3),* TickTock Books) Octopus Publishing Group GBR. Dist: Independent Pubs. Group.
—Under the Ocean with the Little Yellow Submarine. 2009. (Touch & Feel Fun Ser.). (ENG.). 10p. (J). (gr. k — 1). bds. 5.95 *(978-1-84696-811-2(9),* TickTock Books) Octopus Publishing Group GBR. Dist: Independent Pubs. Group.
—What Am I? Animal Moms & Babies. 2008. (Mini Flap Ser.). (ENG.). 10p. (J). (gr. k — 1). bds. 5.95 *(978-1-84696-817-4(8),* TickTock Books) Octopus Publishing Group GBR. Dist: Independent Pubs. Group.
—What Do Cows Do? 2008. (What Do Animals Do? Ser.). (ENG.). 10p. (J). (gr. k — 1). bds. 4.95 *(978-1-84696-796-2(1),* TickTock Books) Octopus Publishing Group GBR. Dist: Independent Pubs. Group.
—What Do Hippos Do? 2008. (What Do Animals Do? Ser.). (ENG.). 10p. (J). (gr. k — 1). bds. 4.95 *(978-1-84696-791-7(0),* TickTock Books) Octopus Publishing Group GBR. Dist: Independent Pubs. Group.
—What Do Penguins Do? 2008. (What Do Animals Do? Ser.). (ENG.). 10p. (J). (gr. k — 1). bds. 4.95 *(978-1-84696-792-4(9),* TickTock Books) Octopus Publishing Group GBR. Dist: Independent Pubs. Group.
—What Do Sheep Do? 2008. (What Do Animals Do? Ser.). (ENG.). 10p. (J). (gr. k — 1). bds. 4.95 *(978-1-84696-793-1(7),* TickTock Books) Octopus Publishing Group GBR. Dist: Independent Pubs. Group.
—What Do Tigers Do? 2008. (What Do Animals Do? Ser.). (ENG.). 10p. (J). (gr. k — 1). bds. 4.95 *(978-1-84696-794-8(5),* TickTock Books) Octopus Publishing Group GBR. Dist: Independent Pubs. Group.
—What Do Zebras Do? 2008. (What Do Animals Do? Ser.). (ENG.). 10p. (J). (gr. k — 1). bds. 4.95 *(978-1-84696-795-5(3),* TickTock Books) Octopus Publishing Group GBR. Dist: Independent Pubs. Group.
—Zoom into Space with the Shiny Red Rocket. 2009. (Touch & Feel Fun Ser.). (ENG.). 10p. (J). (gr. k — 1). bds. 5.95 *(978-1-84696-812-9(7),* TickTock Books) Octopus Publishing Group GBR. Dist: Independent Pubs. Group.
Tidholm, Anna-Clara. Knock! Knock! Bradley, MaryChris, tr. 2009. (Illus.). 32p. (J). (gr. -1). 9.95 *(978-0-9815761-6-9(8))* Mackenzie Smiles, LLC.
Tiger Tales. A Bedtime Prayer. Rescek, Sanja, illus. 2013. (ENG.). 24p. (J). (gr. -1-k). bds. 8.99 *(978-1-58925-606-4(9))* Tiger Tales.
—A Christmas Prayer. Rescek, Sanja, illus. 2014. (ENG.). 22p. (J). (gr. -1-k). bds. 8.95 *(978-1-58925-596-8(8))* Tiger Tales.
—Count 123. 2013. (My First Ser.). (ENG., Illus.). 26p. (J). (gr. -1-k). bds. 7.99 *(978-1-58925-625-5(5))* Tiger Tales.
—Five Little Pumpkins. Mantle, Ben, illus. 2010. (ENG.). 24p. (J). (gr. -1-k). bds. 8.95 *(978-1-58925-856-3(8))* Tiger Tales.
—I Love You, Grandma. Tyger, Rory, illus. 2017. (ENG.). 28p. (J). (gr. -1-k). bds. 7.99 *(978-1-68010-524-7(8))* Tiger Tales.
—A Is for Apple. Birkett, Georgie, illus. 2011. (ENG.). 26p. (J). (-k). bds. 7.95 *(978-1-58925-872-3(X))* Tiger Tales.
—Ten Sparkly Snowflakes: Twinkly Countdown Fun! Julian, Russell, illus. 2017. (ENG.). 26p. (J). (gr. -1-k). mass mkt. 4.99 *(978-1-68010-413-4(6))* Tiger Tales.
—Ten Splishy, Splashy Fish. Tarbett, Debbie, illus. 2017. (ENG.). 26p. (J). (gr. -1-k). mass mkt. 4.99 *(978-1-68010-412-7(8))* Tiger Tales.
—Ten Twinkly Stars. Julian, Russell, illus. 2016. (ENG.). 28p. (J). (gr. -1-k). mass mkt. 3.99 *(978-1-58925-475-6(9))* Tiger Tales.
—100 First Words. 2018. (My First Ser.). (ENG., Illus.). 24p. (J). (gr. -1-k). mass mkt. 4.99 *(978-1-68010-418-9(7))* Tiger Tales.
—123 Count with Me. Birkett, Georgie, illus. 2011. (ENG.). 26p. (J). (-k). bds. 7.95 *(978-1-58925-873-0(8))* Tiger Tales.
Tiger Tales Staff. Lift & See Animals. 2013. (My First Matching Book Ser.). (ENG.). 10p. bds. 7.99 *(978-1-58925-613-2(1))* Tiger Tales Pubns.
—Peek-A-Boo! Mantle, Ben, illus. 2013. (ENG.). 16p. (J). bds. *(978-1-58925-636-1(0))* Tiger Tales.
Tiger Tales Staff, creator. Things That Go. 2014. (My First Jumbo Tab Bks.). (ENG., Illus.). 12p. (J). (gr. -1). bds. 8.99 *(978-1-58925-589-0(5))* Tiger Tales.
—100 First Animals. 2013. (My Big Book of Lift & Learn Ser.). (ENG., Illus.). 12p. (gr. -1). bds. 9.99 *(978-1-58925-608-8(5))* Tiger Tales.
—100 First Words. 2013. (My Big Book of Lift & Learn Ser.). (ENG., Illus.). 12p. (gr. -1). bds. 9.99 *(978-1-58925-607-1(7))* Tiger Tales.
Tiger Tales Staff, ed. Animals Go. Emily, Bolam, illus. 2010. (Touch, Look, & Learn! Ser.). (ENG.). 10p. (J). (gr. -1). bds. 5.95 *(978-1-58925-854-9(1))* Tiger Tales.
—Animals Talk. Emily, Bolam, illus. 2010. (Touch, Look, & Learn! Ser.). (ENG.). 10p. (J). (gr. -1). bds. 5.95 *(978-1-58925-855-6(X))* Tiger Tales.
—Easter Surprise: My First Lift & Learn. 2014. (ENG.). 10p. (J). bds. 7.99 *(978-1-58925-580-7(1))* Tiger Tales.
Tiger Tales Staff, ed. & compiled by. Kittens. Tiger Tales Staff, compiled by. 2014. (My First Touch & Feel Ser.). (ENG.). 10p. (J). (gr. -1 — 1). bds. 8.99 *(978-1-58925-563-0(1))* Tiger Tales.
—Puppies. Tiger Tales Staff, compiled by. 2014. (My First Touch & Feel Ser.). (ENG.). 10p. (J). (gr. -1 — 1). bds. 8.99 *(978-1-58925-564-7(X))* Tiger Tales.
Tiger's Tail. Date not set. (Touch & Feel Ser.). (J). 4.98 *(978-0-7525-9570-2(9))* Parragon, Inc.
Tildes, Phyllis Limbacher. Baby Animals Day & Night. Tildes, Phyllis Limbacher, illus. 2016. (Illus.). 12p. (J). (— 1). bds. 6.95 *(978-1-58089-609-2(X))* Charlesbridge Publishing, Inc.
—Baby's First Book of Birds & Colors. Tildes, Phyllis Limbacher, illus. 2017. (Illus.). 18p. (J). (— 1). bds. 8.99 *(978-1-58089-742-6(8))* Charlesbridge Publishing, Inc.
—Eye Guess: A Forest Animal Guessing Game. Tildes, Phyllis Limbacher, illus. 2005. (ENG., Illus.). 36p. (J). (gr. -1-2). 11.95 *(978-1-57091-650-2(0))* Charlesbridge Publishing, Inc.
Tillman, Nancy. Tumford the Terrible. Tillman, Nancy, illus. 2015. (Tumford Ser.). (ENG., Illus.). 32p. (J). (gr. -1-1). bds. 11.99 *(978-1-250-03364-2(0),* 900120149) Feiwel & Friends.
Tillworth, Mary. I Am Buzz Lightyear (Disney/Pixar Toy Story) RH Disney, illus. 2011. (ENG.). 12p. (J). (— 1). bds. 6.99 *(978-0-7364-2821-7(6),* Golden/Disney) Random Hse. Children's Bks.
—Up in the Air!/under the Waves! (PAW Patrol) Random House, illus. 2018. (Step into Reading Ser.). (ENG.). 48p. (J). (gr. -1-2). pap. 5.99 *(978-1-5247-7279-6(8),* Random Hse. Bks. for Young Readers) Random Hse. Children's Bks.
Time for Toys! (Flip Flap Fun Book Ser.). 10p. (J). bds. *(978-2-7643-0040-4(9))* Phidal Publishing, Inc./Editions Phidal, Inc.
Tolkien, J. R. R. & Tolkien, Baillie. Letters from Father Christmas. 2004. (ENG., Illus.). 128p. pap. 25.00 *(978-0-618-51265-2(9),* 689483, William Morrow Paperbacks) HarperCollins Pubs.
Toms, Kate. The Bear Who Dares Book & Plush. 2008. (Illus.). 26p. (gr. -1-k). bds. *(978-1-84610-855-6(1))* Make Believe Ideas.
—Duckie Duck Boxed Set. 2008. (Illus.). 26p. (gr. -1-k). bds. *(978-1-84610-740-5(7))* Make Believe Ideas.
—I Udderly Love You! 2007. (Illus.). 25p. (gr. -1). *(978-1-84610-680-4(X))* Make Believe Ideas.

Top That. Let's Stencil Things That Go. 2008. *(978-1-84666-584-4(1))* Top That! Publishing PLC.
—Press Out & Play Magic Castle. 2008. *(978-1-84666-600-1(7))* Top That! Publishing PLC.
Top That, ed. Let's Play Magnetic Play Scene Trains. 2008. *(978-1-84666-557-8(4))* Top That! Publishing PLC.
—Sammy the Snake. 2008. (Story Book Ser.). 18p. (J). (gr. -1). *(978-1-84666-541-7(8)*, Tide Mill Pr.) Top That! Publishing PLC.
Top That Publishing. Writing My First Sums. 2007. (Early Days Ser.). (Illus.). 10p. bds. *(978-1-84666-338-3(5))* Top That! Publishing PLC.
Top That Publishing, creator. Writing My First Words: Early Days Magic Writing Book. 2007. (Illus.). 8p. (gr. -1-k). bds. *(978-1-84666-340-6(7))* Top That! Publishing PLC.
Top That Publishing Staff, ed. Alphabet Farm. Parry, Jo, illus. 2007. (Magnetic - Alphabet Ser.). 10p. (J). (gr. -1). bds. *(978-1-84666-272-0(9)*, Tide Mill Pr.) Top That! Publishing PLC.
—Counting on the Farm. Sapp, Karen, illus. 2007. (Magnetic Fun Ser.). 16p. (J). (gr. -1). *(978-1-84666-270-6(2)*, Tide Mill Pr.) Top That! Publishing PLC.
—Jungle Numbers. Parry, Jo, illus. 2007. (Magnetic - Numbers Ser.). 10p. (J). (gr. -1). bds. *(978-1-84666-163-1(3)*, Tide Mill Pr.) Top That! Publishing PLC.
—The Midnight Fairies. Atkins, Alison, illus. 2007. (Sparkling Jigsaw Book Ser.). 10p. (J). (gr. -1). bds. *(978-1-84666-278-2(8)*, Tide Mill Pr.) Top That! Publishing PLC.
—There Were Ten Bears in a Bed: A Count-and-Feel Book. Atkins, Alison, illus. 2007. (Story Book Ser.). 22p. (J). (gr. -1). bds. *(978-1-84666-130-3(7)*, Tide Mill Pr.) Top That! Publishing PLC.
Top That! Jungle Numbers (large Version) Parry, Jo, illus. 2007. 10p. (J). (gr. -1). *(978-1-84666-552-3(3)*, Tide Mill Pr.) Top That! Publishing PLC.
—Playtime Shapes (large Version) Parry, Jo, illus. 2007. 10p. (J). (gr. -1). *(978-1-84666-555-4(8)*, Tide Mill Pr.) Top That! Publishing PLC.
Top That!, creator. ABC Train. 2007. (Jigsaw Book Ser.). (Illus.). 18p. (J). (gr. -1-3). bds. *(978-1-84666-095-5(5))* Top That! Publishing PLC.
—Shapes with Penny the Penguin. 2012. (Learn with Magnets Ser.). (ENG., Illus.). 10p. (J). (gr. -1). *(978-1-84956-671-1(2))* Top That! Publishing PLC.
—123 Train. 2007. (Jigsaw Book Ser.). (Illus.). 18p. (J). (gr. -1-3). bds. *(978-1-84666-097-9(1))* Top That! Publishing PLC.
Top That! Kids, creator. Things That Go. 2008. (Magnetic Play & Learn Ser.). (ENG., Illus.). 12p. (J). (gr. -1-k). *(978-1-84510-726-0(8))* Top That! Publishing PLC.
Torres, J. Checkers & Dot at the Beach. Lum, J., illus. 2013. (Checkers & Dot Ser.: 4). 16p. (J). (— 1). bds. 7.95 *(978-1-77049-444-2(8)*, Tundra Bks.) Tundra Bks. CAN. Dist: Penguin Random Hse. LLC.
—Checkers & Dot at the Zoo. Lum, J., illus. 2012. (Checkers & Dot Ser.: 2). 16p. (J). (gr. k — 1). bds. 7.95 *(978-1-77049-442-8(1)*, Tundra Bks.) Tundra Bks. CAN. Dist: Penguin Random Hse. LLC.
—Checkers & Dot on the Farm. Lum, J., illus. 2013. (Checkers & Dot Ser.: 3). 16p. (J). (— 1). bds. 7.95 *(978-1-77049-443-5(X)*, Tundra Bks.) Tundra Bks. CAN. Dist: Penguin Random Hse. LLC.
Touch & Feel Playtime. braille ed. 2004. (J). (gr. -1-18). bds. *(978-0-616-14614-9(0))* Canadian National Institute for the Blind/Institut National Canadien pour les Aveugles.
Tougas, Chris. Tinkle, Tinkle, Little Star. Tougas, Chris, illus. 2018. (ENG., Illus.). 24p. (J). (gr. -1 — 1). bds. 9.99 *(978-1-77138-839-9(0))* Kids Can Pr., Ltd. CAN. Dist: Hachette Bk. Group.
Tractor. 2010. (Illus.). (J). *(978-1-4654-5514-7(0))* Dorling Kindersley Publishing, Inc.
Traini, Agostino. The Birth of Jesus: A Christmas Pop-Up Book. 2016. (Agostino Traini Pop-Ups Ser.). (Illus.). 14p. (J). 19.99 *(978-1-5064-1769-1(8)*, Sparkhouse Family) 1517 Media.
Traini, Agostino, illus. Jesus Is Risen! An Easter Pop-Up Book. 2018. (Agostino Traini Pop-Ups Ser.). 14p. (J). (gr. -1-3). 19.99 *(978-1-5064-3340-0(5)*, Sparkhouse Family) 1517 Media.
Trasler, Janee. Bedtime for Chickies: An Easter & Springtime Book for Kids. Trasler, Janee, illus. 2014. (Chickies Ser.). (ENG., Illus.). 24p. (J). (gr. -1 — 1). bds. 8.99 *(978-0-06-227468-7(6)*, HarperFestival) HarperCollins Pubs.
—Big Chickie, Little Chickie. 2016. (ENG., Illus.). 24p. (J). (gr. -1 — 1). bds. 8.99 *(978-0-06-234231-7(2)*, HarperFestival) HarperCollins Pubs.
—Dinnertime for Chickies. 2014. (Chickies Ser.). (ENG., Illus.). 24p. (J). (gr. -1 — 1). bds. 8.99 *(978-0-06-227470-0(8)*, HarperFestival) HarperCollins Pubs.
Trivizas, Eugene. The Three Little Wolves & the Big Bad Pig. 2004. (ENG., Illus.). 16p. (J). 24.95 *(978-1-4052-0669-3(1))* Farshore GBR. Dist: Trafalgar Square Publishing.
Trukhan, Ekaterina, illus. Five Little Ducks. 2012. (J). *(978-1-58865-854-8(6))* Kidsbooks, LLC.
Tu Cuerpo: Conoce Por Dentro. 2007. (Titles in Spanish Ser.). (SPA., Illus.). 15p. (J). (gr. -1). bds. 12.99 *(978-0-7460-8386-4(6)*, Usborne) EDC Publishing.
Tuchman, Gail. Eat 'em Ups Apples. Voerg, Kathy, illus. 2019. (ENG.). 12p. (J). (gr. -1-1). pap. 7.99 *(978-0-486-82508-3(6)*, 825086) Dover Pubns., Inc.
—Eat 'em Ups Bananas. Voerg, Kathy, illus. 2019. (ENG.). 12p. (J). (gr. -1-1). pap. 7.99 *(978-0-486-82511-3(6)*, 825116) Dover Pubns., Inc.
Tucker, Stephen. Jack & the Beanstalk, 2 vols. Sharratt, Nick, illus. 2016. (Lift-The-Flap Fairy Tales Ser.). (ENG.). 24p. (J). (gr. -1-k). bds. 12.99 *(978-1-5098-1714-6(X))* Pan Macmillan GBR. Dist: Independent Pubs. Group.
—Little Red Riding Hood, 2 vols. Sharratt, Nick, illus. 2017. (Lift-The-Flap Fairy Tales Ser.). (ENG.). 24p. (J). (gr. -1-1). 10.99 *(978-1-5098-2815-9(X))* Pan Macmillan GBR. Dist: Independent Pubs. Group.
—The Three Little Pigs, 2 vols. Sharratt, Nick, illus. 2016. (Lift-The-Flap Fairy Tales Ser.). (ENG.). 24p. (J). (gr. -1-k). bds. 11.99 *(978-1-5098-1713-9(1))* Pan Macmillan GBR. Dist: Independent Pubs. Group.
Tudor, Tasha. A Tale for Easter. Tudor, Tasha, illus. 2014. (Classic Board Bks.). (ENG., Illus.). 34p. (J). (gr. -1 — 1). bds. 7.99 *(978-1-4424-8857-1(3)*, Little Simon) Little Simon.
Tulip, Jenny, illus. Who's Hiding in the Jungle? A Mystery Touch-and-Feel Flap Book! 2008. 10p. (gr. -1-k). bds. 6.99 *(978-1-57755-784-5(0))* Flying Frog Publishing.
Tullet, Hervé. The Game of Let's Go! Edicare, ed. 2011. (ENG., Illus.). 14p. (gr. -1 — 1). 12.95 *(978-0-7148-6075-6(1))* Phaidon Pr., Inc.
—Presiona Aqui (Press Here Spanish Language Edition) Press Here Spanish Language Edition. 2012. (ENG., Illus.). 56p. (J). (gr. -1-3). 15.99 *(978-1-4521-1287-9(8))* Chronicle Bks. LLC.
—Press Here. 2011. (Herve Tullet Ser.). (ENG., Illus.). 56p. (J). (gr. -1-k). 15.99 *(978-0-8118-7954-5(2))* Chronicle Bks. LLC.
—Press Here: Board Book Edition. 2019. (Herve Tullet Ser.). (ENG., Illus.). 46p. (J). (gr. -1-k). bds. 8.99 *(978-1-4521-7859-2(3))* Chronicle Bks. LLC.
Tullet, Hervé & Tullet, Hervé. The Countryside Game. 2013. (ENG., Illus.). 14p. 12.95 *(978-0-7148-6074-9(3))* Phaidon Pr., Inc.
—The Finger Sports Game. 2015. (ENG., Illus.). 14p. (gr. -1 — 1). 12.95 *(978-0-7148-6979-7(1))* Phaidon Pr., Inc.
—The Game of Lines. 2015. (ENG., Illus.). 14p. (gr. -1-17). 12.95 *(978-0-7148-6873-8(6))* Phaidon Pr., Inc.
—The Game of Patterns. 2011. (ENG., Illus.). 14p. (gr. -1 — 1). bds. 8.95 *(978-0-7148-6187-6(1))* Phaidon Pr., Inc.
—The Game of Tops & Tails. 2015. (ENG., Illus.). 14p. (gr. -1-17). 12.95 *(978-0-7148-6874-5(4))* Phaidon Pr., Inc.
—The Trail Game. 2015. (ENG., Illus.). 14p. (gr. -1-17). 12.95 *(978-0-7148-6876-9(0))* Phaidon Pr., Inc.
Turley, Gerry, illus. Lois Looks for Bob at Home. 2018. (Lois Looks for Bob Ser.). (ENG.). 12p. (J). (— 1). bds. 8.99 *(978-1-5362-0254-0(1))* Candlewick Pr.
—Lois Looks for Bob at the Park. 2018. (Lois Looks for Bob Ser.). (ENG.). 12p. (J). (— 1). bds. 8.99 *(978-1-5362-0255-7(X))* Candlewick Pr.
Turn-the-Wheel, 4 bks., Set. Incl. Fishing Boat. Goldsack, Gaby. Lawson, Peter, illus. bds. 5.95 *(978-0-7892-1025-8(8))*; Tractor. Lawson, Peter. bds. 5.95 *(978-0-7892-1023-4(1))*; 10p. (J). (gr. -1-k). (Turn the Wheel Ser.). (ENG., Illus.). 40p. 2009. Set bds. 22.95 *(978-0-7892-1027-2(4)*, Abbeville Kids) Abbeville Pr., Inc.
Turnbull, Stephanie. Trains. 2009. (Discovery History Ser.). 48p. (YA). (gr. 3-18). 8.99 *(978-0-7945-2246-9(7)*, Usborne) EDC Publishing.
Turner, Marie. God Made the Animals. Romero, Naomi, illus. 2017. 22p. (J). 6.99 *(978-1-5064-2185-8(7)*, Sparkhouse Family) 1517 Media.
Tuttle, Sarah Grace. Spot, Spike, Spiral. Nerlove, Miriam, illus. 2019. (ENG.). 28p. (J). (gr. -1-k). bds. 8.99 *(978-1-56846-333-9(2)*, 18672, Creative Editions) Creative Co., The.
Tuxworth, Nicola. Animals. 2014. (Illus.). 20p. (J). (gr. -1-k). bds. 6.99 *(978-1-84322-859-2(9)*, Armadillo) Anness Publishing GBR. Dist: National Bk. Network.
—Baby Animals. 2015. (Illus.). 20p. (J). (gr. -1-12). bds. 6.99 *(978-1-86147-357-8(5)*, Armadillo) Anness Publishing GBR. Dist: National Bk. Network.
—Bodies. 2014. (Illus.). 20p. (J). (gr. k-2). bds. 6.99 *(978-1-84322-860-8(2)*, Armadillo) Anness Publishing GBR. Dist: National Bk. Network.
—Clothes. 2014. (Illus.). 20p. (J). (gr. -1 — 1). bds. 6.99 *(978-1-84322-861-5(0)*, Armadillo) Anness Publishing GBR. Dist: National Bk. Network.
—Colours. 2014. (Illus.). 20p. (J). (gr. -1-12). bds. 6.99 *(978-1-84322-749-6(5)*, Armadillo) Anness Publishing GBR. Dist: National Bk. Network.
—Farm Animals. 2016. (Illus.). 20p. (J). (gr. -1-12). bds. 6.99 *(978-1-86147-476-6(8)*, Armadillo) Anness Publishing GBR. Dist: National Bk. Network.
—Funny Faces. 2015. (Illus.). 20p. (J). (gr. -1-12). bds. 6.99 *(978-1-86147-358-5(3)*, Armadillo) Anness Publishing GBR. Dist: National Bk. Network.
—Messy. 2016. (Illus.). 20p. (J). (gr. -1-k). bds. 6.99 *(978-1-86147-690-6(6)*, Armadillo) Anness Publishing GBR. Dist: National Bk. Network.
—Pets. 2015. (Illus.). 20p. (J). (gr. -1-12). bds. 6.99 *(978-1-86147-647-0(7)*, Armadillo) Anness Publishing GBR. Dist: National Bk. Network.
—Shapes. 2015. (Illus.). 20p. (J). (gr. -1-12). bds. 6.99 *(978-1-86147-648-7(5)*, Armadillo) Anness Publishing GBR. Dist: National Bk. Network.
—Sizes. 2016. (Illus.). 20p. (J). (gr. -1-12). bds. 6.99 *(978-1-84322-751-9(7)*, Armadillo) Anness Publishing GBR. Dist: National Bk. Network.
—Things That Go. 2016. (Illus.). 20p. (J). (gr. -1-12). bds. 6.99 *(978-1-84322-752-6(5)*, Armadillo) Anness Publishing GBR. Dist: National Bk. Network.
Tuxworth, Nicole. Kittens. 2015. (Illus.). 20p. (J). (gr. -1 — 1). bds. 6.99 *(978-1-86147-384-4(2)*, Armadillo) Anness Publishing GBR. Dist: National Bk. Network.
Twin Sisters(r) Staff. B-i-n-g-o. 2010. (J). (gr. k-1). 14.99 *(978-1-59922-630-9(8))* Twin Sisters IP, LLC.
Twin Sisters(r) Staff, et al, adapted by. B-i-n-g-o. 2010. (J). (gr. k-1). 14.99 *(978-1-59922-422-0(4))* Twin Sisters IP, LLC.
Twin Sisters(r) Staff, et al. Five Little Bunnies. 2010. (J). (gr. k-1). 14.99 *(978-1-59922-421-3(6))*; 14.99 *(978-1-59922-629-3(4))* Twin Sisters IP, LLC.
—I Thank God for You. 2010. (J). (gr. k-2). pap. 4.99 *(978-1-59922-497-8(6))* Twin Sisters IP, LLC.
Two Little Hands Productions, creator. Good Night, Alex & Leah. 2010. (ENG., Illus.). (J). *(978-1-933543-73-4(6))* Two Little Hands Productions LLC.
Two Little Hands Productions, prod. Board Book 5: ABC Signs. 2010. (Illus.). (J). bds. *(978-1-933543-50-5(7))* Two Little Hands Productions LLC.
—Board Book 6: My Favorite Things. 2010. (Illus.). (J). bds. *(978-1-933543-51-2(5))* Two Little Hands Productions LLC.
Tyler, Jenny & Hawthorn, P. There's a Monster in My House. 2004. (Illus.). 16p. (J). (gr. 1-18). pap. 7.95 *(978-0-7945-0624-7(0))* EDC Publishing.
—Who's Making That Mess? rev. ed. 2004. (Illus.). 16p. (J). (gr. 1-18). pap. 7.99 *(978-0-7945-0431-1(0))* EDC Publishing.
—Who's Making That Smell? rev. ed. 2004. (Illus.). 16p. (J). (gr. 1-18). pap. 7.95 *(978-0-7945-0523-3(6))* EDC Publishing.
Tyler, Jenny & Hawthorn, Phillip. Who's Making That Noise? 2008. (Luxury Flap Bks). 16p. (J). 9.99 *(978-0-7945-1695-6(5)*, Usborne) EDC Publishing.
—Who's Making That Smell? Cartwright, Stephen, illus. 2007. (Luxury Flap Bks). 16p. (J). (gr. -1-3). 9.99 *(978-0-7945-1696-3(3)*, Usborne) EDC Publishing.
Ug, Philippe. In the Butterfly Garden. 2015. (ENG., Illus.). 16p. (J). (gr. -1-3). 19.95 *(978-3-7913-7207-5(6))* Prestel Verlag GmbH & Co KG. DEU. Dist: Penguin Random Hse. LLC.
Ultimate Boats Sticker Book. (Radical Rides Ser.). 16p. (J). *(978-2-7643-0012-1(3))* Phidal Publishing, Inc./Editions Phidal, Inc.
Ultimate Cars Sticker Book. (Radical Rides Ser.). 16p. (J). *(978-2-7643-0010-7(7))* Phidal Publishing, Inc./Editions Phidal, Inc.
Ultimate Planes Sticker Book, 4 vols. (Radical Rides Ser.). (Illus.). 16p. (J). *(978-2-7643-0008-4(5))* Phidal Publishing, Inc./Editions Phidal, Inc.
Ultman, Suzy, illus. Masha & Her Sisters: (Russian Doll Board Books, Children's Activity Books, Interactive Kids Books) 2017. (ENG.). 10p. (J). bds. 9.99 *(978-1-4521-5159-5(8))* Chronicle Bks. LLC.
—Tiny Farm: (Board Books for Toddlers, Interactive Children's Books) 2017. (Tiny Places Ser.). (ENG.). 16p. (J). (gr. -1 — 1). bds. 7.99 *(978-1-4521-5158-8(X))* Chronicle Bks. LLC.
—Tiny Town: (Board Books for Toddlers, Interactive Children's Books) 2017. (Tiny Places Ser.). (ENG.). 16p. (J). (gr. -1 — 1). bds. 7.99 *(978-1-4521-5157-1(1))* Chronicle Bks. LLC.
—A to Z Menagerie: (ABC Baby Book, Sensory Alphabet Board Book for Babies & Toddlers, Interactive Book for Babies) 2019. (ENG.). 28p. (J). (gr. -1 — 1). 24.99 *(978-1-4521-7711-3(2))* Chronicle Bks. LLC.
Underwood, Deborah. The Loud Book! Padded Board Book. Liwska, Renata, illus. 2015. (ENG.). 32p. (J). (— 1). bds. 8.99 *(978-0-544-43064-8(6)*, 1595739, Clarion Bks.) HarperCollins Pubs.
University Games Staff. Very Hungrey Caterpillar. 2006. 24p. (J). *(978-1-57528-891-8(5))* Univ. Games.
Urban, Chieu Anh. Color Wonder Hooray for Spring! Urban, Chieu Anh, illus. 2016. (Color Wonder Ser.). (ENG., Illus.). 14p. (J). (gr. -1 — 1). bds. 7.99 *(978-1-4814-8720-7(5)*, Little Simon) Little Simon.
Vagnozzi, Barbara, illus. Jack & the Beanstalk. (Flip-Up Fairy Tales Ser.). 24p. (J). 2007. (gr. -1-2). pap. incl. audio compact disk *(978-1-84643-086-2(0))* 2005. pap. *(978-1-904550-20-4(7))* Child's Play International Ltd.
—The Musicians of Bremen. 2007. (Flip-Up Fairy Tales Ser.). 24p. (J). (gr. 1-2). *(978-1-84643-115-9(8))* Child's Play International Ltd.
Valat, Pierre-Marie. Pirates. 2018. (My First Discoveries Ser.). (ENG., Illus.). 36p. (J). (gr. -1-3). spiral bd. 19.99 *(978-1-85103-469-7(2))* Moonlight Publishing, Ltd. GBR. Dist: Independent Pubs. Group.
—Water. Valat, Pierre-Marie, illus. 2012. (ENG., Illus.). 36p. (J). (gr. -1-k). spiral bd. 19.99 *(978-1-85103-403-1(X))* Moonlight Publishing, Ltd. GBR. Dist: Independent Pubs. Group.
Van Buren, David. I Love You As Big As the World. Warnes, Tim, illus. 2013. (ENG.). 22p. (J). (-k). bds. 8.95 *(978-1-58925-603-3(4))* Tiger Tales.
Van Camp, Richard. Little You, 1 vol. Flett, Julie, illus. 2013. (ENG.). 24p. (J). (gr. -1 — 1). bds. 12.95 *(978-1-4598-0248-3(9))* Orca Bk. Pubs. USA.
Van Fleet, Mara. Little Color Fairies. Van Fleet, Mara, illus. 2012. (ENG., Illus.). 16p. (J). (gr. -1-1). 15.99 *(978-1-4424-3434-9(1)*, Simon & Schuster/Paula Wiseman Bks.) Simon & Schuster/Paula Wiseman Bks.
—Night-Night, Princess. Van Fleet, Mara, illus. 2014. (ENG., Illus.). 16p. (J). (gr. -1-1). 14.99 *(978-1-4424-8646-1(5)*, Simon & Schuster/Paula Wiseman Bks.) Simon & Schuster/Paula Wiseman Bks.
Van Fleet, Matthew. Color Dog. 2015. (ENG., Illus.). 22p. (J). (gr. -1-k). 24.99 *(978-1-4814-4986-1(9)*, Simon & Schuster Bks. For Young Readers) Simon & Schuster Bks. For Young Readers.
—Dance. Van Fleet, Matthew, illus. 2017. (ENG., Illus.). 16p. (J). (gr. -1). 24.99 *(978-1-4814-8707-8(8)*, Simon & Schuster/Paula Wiseman Bks.) Simon & Schuster/Paula Wiseman Bks.
—Lick! Mini Board Book. Van Fleet, Matthew, illus. 2013. (ENG., Illus.). 14p. (J). (gr. -1-1). 12.99 *(978-1-4424-6049-2(0)*, Simon & Schuster/Paula Wiseman Bks.) Simon & Schuster/Paula Wiseman Bks.
—Monday the Bullfrog: A Huggable Puppet Concept Book about the Days of the Week. Van Fleet, Matthew, illus. 2010. (ENG., Illus.). 20p. (J). (gr. -1). 24.99 *(978-1-4424-0958-3(4)*, Simon & Schuster/Paula Wiseman Bks.) Simon & Schuster/Paula Wiseman Bks.
—Moo. 2011. (ENG., Illus.). 18p. (J). (gr. -1-1). 24.99 *(978-1-4424-3503-2(8)*, Simon & Schuster/Paula Wiseman Bks.) Simon & Schuster/Paula Wiseman Bks.
—Tails. 2017. (ENG., Illus.). 20p. (J). (— 1). bds. 14.99 *(978-1-328-88685-9(9)*, 1699384, Clarion Bks.) HarperCollins Pubs.
van Gageldonk, Mack. Mommy, Look What I Can Do! 2013. (ENG., Illus.). 14p. (J). (— 1). bds. 10.95 *(978-1-60537-169-6(6))* Clavis Publishing.
Van Genechten, Guido. The Big Baby Book. 2011. (ENG.). 22p. (J). (gr. k — 1). bds. 12.95 *(978-1-60537-079-8(7))* Clavis Publishing.
—The Big Potty Book. 2009. (ENG., Illus.). 20p. (J). (gr. k — 1). bds. 12.95 *(978-1-60537-031-6(2))* Clavis Publishing.
—Guess Where? 2012. (Guess Along Ser.). (ENG.). 16p. (J). (gr. k — 1). 9.95 *(978-1-60537-115-3(7))* Clavis Publishing.
van Genechten, Guido. Moon Is Sad. 2010. (ENG.). 12p. (J). (gr. k — 1). bds. 8.95 *(978-1-60537-048-4(7))* Clavis Publishing.
Van Zuyen, Gregory. Levi's Book of Barnyard Animals. 2012. (ENG., Illus.). 20p. (J). 14.99 *(978-1-62209-477-6(8))* Primedia eLaunch LLC.
Vanden-Heuvel, John C., Sr. & Ostrovsky, Andrey. ABCs of the Web. Holmes, Tom, illus. 2016. (ENG.). 28p. (J). (gr. -1-3). bds. 8.99 *(978-1-4998-0312-9(5))* Little Bee Books Inc.
Vander Klipp, Michael. God Made Animals, 1 vol. 2008. (God Made... Ser.). 14p. (J). bds. 3.99 *(978-0-8254-3911-7(6))* Kregel Pubns.
—God Made My Body, 1 vol. 2008. (God Made... Ser.). 14p. (J). bds. 3.99 *(978-0-8254-3912-4(4))* Kregel Pubns.
—God Made the World, 1 vol. 2008. (God Made... Ser.). 14p. (J). bds. 3.99 *(978-0-8254-3914-8(0))* Kregel Pubns.
Vasquez, Natalia, illus. The Pied Piper of Hamelin. 2012. (Flip-Up Fairy Tales Ser.). 24p. (J). *(978-1-84643-480-8(7))* Child's Play International Ltd.
Vast, Émilie. From Father to Father. Vast, Émilie, illus. 2018. (ENG., Illus.). 14p. (J). (— 1). bds. 7.99 *(978-1-58089-814-0(9))* Charlesbridge Publishing, Inc.
—From Mother to Mother. Vast, Émilie, illus. 2018. (ENG., Illus.). 14p. (J). (— 1). bds. 7.99 *(978-1-58089-813-3(0))* Charlesbridge Publishing, Inc.
Vasylenko, Veronica. Deck the Halls. Tiger Tales Staff, ed. 2011. (ENG., Illus.). 20p. bds. 8.95 *(978-1-58925-868-6(1))* Tiger Tales.
Vehicles. 2016. (Illus.). (J). *(978-1-62885-155-7(4))* Kidsbooks, LLC.
Veitch, Catherine. Animal Babies Classroom Collections. 2013. (Animal Babies Ser.). (ENG.). 24p. (J). (gr. -1-1). pap., pap., pap. 210.50 *(978-1-4329-8429-8(2)*, 20521, Heinemann) Capstone.
Velthuijs, Max. Where Is Frog? 2017. (ENG., Illus.). 14p. (J). (gr. -1-k). bds. 8.95 *(978-0-2281-0002-7(X)*, f160cafb-5292-4031-b9d3-ebd20c041d70) Firefly Bks., Ltd.
Verde, Susan. I Am Yoga. 2017. (I Am Bks.). (ENG., Illus.). 24p. (J). (gr. -1 — 1). bds. 8.95 *(978-1-4197-2697-2(8)*, 1191610, Abrams Appleseed) Abrams, Inc.
Verdick, Elizabeth. Bye-Bye Time. Heinlen, Marieka, illus. 2008. (Toddler Tools(r) Ser.). (ENG.). 24p. (J). (gr. k — 1). 9.99 *(978-1-57542-299-2(9)*, 22992) Free Spirit Publishing Inc.
—Bye-Bye Time / Momento de la Despedida. Heinlen, Marieka, illus. 2017. (Toddler Tools(r) Ser.). (ENG.). 26p. (J). bds. 9.99 *(978-1-63198-151-7(X)*, 81517) Free Spirit Publishing Inc.
—Clean-Up Time. Heinlen, Marieka, illus. 2008. (Toddler Tools(r) Ser.). (ENG.). 26p. (J). (gr. -1 — 1). bds. 9.99 *(978-1-57542-298-5(0)*, 22985) Free Spirit Publishing Inc.
—Listening Time / Momento para Escuchar. Heinlen, Marieka, illus. 2016. (Toddler Tools(r) Ser.). (ENG.). 26p. (J). (— 1). bds. 9.99 *(978-1-63198-117-3(X))* Free Spirit Publishing Inc.
—Manners Time / Los Buenos Modales. Heinlen, Marieka, illus. 2016. (Toddler Tools(r) Ser.). (ENG.). 26p. (J). (— 1). bds. 9.99 *(978-1-63198-120-3(X))* Free Spirit Publishing Inc.
Verdick, Elizabeth & Lisovskis, Marjorie. Cuddle: A Board Book about Snuggling. 2013. (Happy Healthy Baby(r) Ser.). (ENG., Illus.). 24p. (J). (— 1). bds. 7.99 *(978-1-57542-423-1(1))* Free Spirit Publishing Inc.
—Cuddle / Abrazos y Mimos: A Board Book about Snuggling/un Libro de Carton Sobre Afectos y Sentimientos. 2019. (Happy Healthy Baby(r) Ser.). (ENG., Illus.). 24p. (J). (— 1). bds. 7.99 *(978-1-63198-448-8(9)*, 84488) Free Spirit Publishing Inc.
—Move: A Board Book about Movement. 2013. (Happy Healthy Baby(r) Ser.). (ENG., Illus.). 24p. (J). (— 1). bds. 7.99 *(978-1-57542-422-4(3)*, 24224) Free Spirit Publishing Inc.
Vere, Ed. Everyone's Hungry. 2003. (ENG., Illus.). 12p. (J). 6.95 *(978-0-333-78041-1(8))* Macmillan Pubs., Ltd. GBR. Dist: Trafalgar Square Publishing.
—Everyone's Little. 2003. (ENG., Illus.). 12p. (J). bds. 6.95 *(978-0-333-78039-8(6))* Macmillan Pubs., Ltd. GBR. Dist: Trafalgar Square Publishing.
—Everyone's Noisy. 2003. (ENG., Illus.). 14p. (J). 8.99 *(978-0-333-78040-4(X))* Macmillan Pubs., Ltd. GBR. Dist: Trafalgar Square Publishing.
—Everyone's Sleepy. 2003. (ENG., Illus.). 12p. (J). 8.99 *(978-0-333-78038-1(8))* Macmillan Pubs., Ltd. GBR. Dist: Trafalgar Square Publishing.
Verhille, Alexandre & Tavernier, Sarah. Legendary Routes of the World. 2015. (ENG., Illus.). 18p. (J). (gr. k-4). 29.99 *(978-3-89955-759-6(X))* Die Gestalten Verlag DEU. Dist: Ingram Publisher Services.
Vernick, Shirley. I Love You, Michigan Baby. Bergin, Molly, illus. 2018. (ENG.). 22p. (J). (gr. -1-k). bds. 8.99 *(978-1-946064-96-7(3)*, 806496) Duo Pr. LLC.
Vickers, Roy Henry & Budd, Robert. One Eagle Soaring. 2018. (First West Coast Bks.: 2). (Illus.). 20p. (J). bds. *(978-1-55017-828-9(8)*, 75bb6098-eb13-47f7-b260-09aa207b64e6) Harbour Publishing Co., Ltd.
—Sockeye Silver, Saltchuck Blue. Vickers, Roy Henry, illus. 2019. (First West Coast Bks.: 3). (ENG., Illus.). 20p. (J). bds. *(978-1-55017-870-8(9)*, 520ce3c0-4f6a-4af7-9ce5-9d7f6dd08fa5) Harbour Publishing Co., Ltd.
Vilcoq, Marianne. Espero un Hermanito. (SPA.). 24p. (J). *(978-84-8470-013-5(5))* Corimbo, Editorial S.L. ESP. Dist: Lectorum Pubns., Inc.
Vize, Dania. Lift, Stick & Learn Baby Animals. 2006. (Illus.). 24p. (J). (gr. -1-k). pap. *(978-1-84610-032-1(1))* Make Believe Ideas.
Vocabulary Flip Chart. 2004. (Scott Foresman Reading Ser.). (gr. 1-18). suppl. ed. 109.15 *(978-0-673-62166-5(9))*; (gr. 2-18). suppl. ed. 109.15 *(978-0-673-62167-2(7))* Addison-Wesley Educational Pubs., Inc.
Voce, Karma. Forever Inspired Coloring Book: Tokyo Fashions. 2016. (Forever Inspired Coloring Bks.). (ENG., Illus.). 96p. (J). (gr. 3-7). pap. 7.99 *(978-1-944686-61-1(4)*, Racehorse Publishing) Skyhorse Publishing Co., Inc.
Volker, Kerstin. Suzie Goes to Sleep. 2003. (Funny Friends Lift-and-Learn Bks.). (Illus.). 14p. (J). 5.99 *(978-1-59384-024-2(1))* Parklane Publishing.
Von Feder, Rosa. Babies Love Halloween. Cottage Door Press, ed. Peterson, Stacy, illus. 2016. (Babies Love Ser.). (ENG.). 12p. (J). (gr. -1 — 1). bds. 7.99 *(978-1-68052-115-3(2)*, 1001081) Cottage Door Pr.
von Olfers, Sibylle. My First Snow Children, 30 vols. 2018. (Illus.). 12p. (J). bds. 9.95 *(978-1-78250-523-5(7))* Floris Bks. GBR. Dist: Consortium Bk. Sales & Distribution.
VonFeder, Rosa. Happy Halloween. Cottage Door Press, ed. Barbieri, Pamela, illus. 2018. (ENG.). 10p. (J). (gr. -1-k). bds. 10.99 *(978-1-68052-341-6(4)*, 1003130) Cottage Door Pr.

—Trick or Treat. Cottage Door Press, ed. Dale-Scott, Lindsay, illus. 2017. (ENG.). 12p. (J). (gr. -1-k). bds. 10.99 (978-1-68052-197-9(7), 1001950) Cottage Door Pr.

Waber, Bernard. Courage Lap Board Book. 2018. (ENG., Illus.). 32p. (J). (— 1). bds. 12.99 (978-1-328-88647-7(6), 1698511, Clarion Bks.) HarperCollins Pubs.

Wagner, Veronica. Disney Mickey Mouse Clubhouse: 3 Book Play-A-Sound Set, 3 vols. 2011. (Illus.). (J). bds. (978-1-4508-1724-0(6), 1450817246) Phoenix International Publications, Inc.

—DreamWorks Trolls: Get Back up Again Sound Book. 2016. (ENG., Illus.). 12p. (J). bds. 15.99 (978-1-5037-1242-3(7), 2222, PI Kids) Phoenix International Publications, Inc.

—Sound Storybook Treasury Disney Princess Bedtime. 2017. (ENG., Illus.). 34p. (J). 29.99 (978-1-5037-1889-0(1), 2413, PI Kids) Phoenix International Publications, Inc.

Walden, Libby. Bear Hugs. Riley, Vicky, illus. 2017. (ENG.). 18p. (J). (gr. -1-k). bds. 7.99 (978-1-68010-519-3(1)) Tiger Tales.

—Hidden World: Ocean. Coleman, Stephanie Fizer, illus. 2018. (ENG.). 18p. (J). (gr. -1-2). 14.99 (978-1-944530-15-0(0), 360 Degrees) Tiger Tales.

—Noisy Touch & Feel: Cow Says Moo. Enright, Amanda, illus. 2016. (Noisy Touch & Feel Ser.). (ENG.). 12p. (J). bds. 14.99 (978-1-62686-575-4(2), Silver Dolphin Bks.) Readerlink Distribution Services, LLC.

—Noisy Touch & Feel: Owl Says Hoot. Enright, Amanda, illus. 2016. (Noisy Touch & Feel Ser.). (ENG.). 12p. (J). bds. 14.99 (978-1-62686-576-1(0), Silver Dolphin Bks.) Readerlink Distribution Services, LLC.

Walker, John, illus. The Story of Christmas: The Birth of Jesus. 2008. (ENG.). 24p. (J). (gr. 2). 19.95 (978-1-58117-793-0(3), Intervisual/Piggy Toes) Bendon, Inc.

Walker, Joni, illus. Jesus Hears Me. 2008. 20p. (J). (gr. -1). bds. 6.49 (978-0-7586-1508-4(6)) Concordia Publishing Hse.

Wall, Laura. Goose on the Farm Board Book. Wall, Laura, illus. 2017. (ENG., Illus.). 36p. (J). (gr. -1 — 1). bds. 7.99 (978-0-06-232440-5(3), HarperFestival) HarperCollins Pubs.

Wallace, Karen. I Wonder Why Flip the Flaps Farm Animals. 2009. (978-0-7534-6222-5(2), Kingfisher) Roaring Brook Pr.

Walsh, Ellen Stoll. Mouse Paint/Pintura de Raton Board Book: Bilingual English-Spanish. 2010. (ENG., Illus.). 30p. (J). (gr. -1-k). bds. 5.99 (978-0-547-33332-8(3), 1417608, Clarion Bks.) HarperCollins Pubs.

Walsh, Liza Gardner. Do Fairies Bring the Spring. Mitchell, Hazel, illus. 2019. 22p. (J). (gr. -1-12). 8.95 (978-1-60893-660-1(0)) Down East Bks.

—Fairies 1, 2, 3. Mitchell, Hazel, illus. 2017. 24p. (J). (gr. -1 — 1). 7.95 (978-1-60893-951-0(0)) Down East Bks.

Walsh, Melanie. Living with Mom & Living with Dad. Walsh, Melanie, illus. 2012. (ENG., Illus.). 40p. (J). (gr. -1-2). 17.99 (978-0-7636-5869-4(3)) Candlewick Pr.

—Trick or Treat? Walsh, Melanie, illus. 2009. (ENG., Illus.). 16p. (J). (gr. -1-2). bds. 7.99 (978-0-7636-4295-2(9)) Candlewick Pr.

Walt Disney Company Staff & Phidal Publishing Staff, contrib. by. Cars. 2006. (Illus.). 24p. (978-2-7643-0261-3(4)) Phidal Publishing, Inc./Editions Phidal, Inc.

Walton, Rick. Mini Mysteries 2: 20 More Tricky Tales to Untangle. Scheuer, Lauren, illus. 2006. 87p. (J). (978-1-4156-6869-6(8), American Girl) American Girl Publishing, Inc.

Wan, Joyce. Are You My Mommy? Wan, Joyce, illus. 2014. (ENG.). 18p. (J). (gr. -1 — 1). bds. 6.99 (978-0-545-54047-6(X), Cartwheel Bks.) Scholastic, Inc.

—My Lucky Little Dragon. Wan, Joyce, illus. 2014. (ENG., Illus.). 14p. (J). (— 1). bds. 6.99 (978-0-545-54046-9(1), Cartwheel Bks.) Scholastic, Inc.

—Peek-A-Boo Farm. Wan, Joyce, illus. 2015. (ENG., Illus.). 14p. (J). (— 1). bds. 7.99 (978-0-545-75045-5(8), Cartwheel Bks.) Scholastic, Inc.

—Peek-A-Boo Zoo. Wan, Joyce, illus. 2015. (ENG., Illus.). 14p. (J). (— 1). bds. 6.99 (978-0-545-75042-4(3), Cartwheel Bks.) Scholastic, Inc.

—You Are My Magical Unicorn. Wan, Joyce, illus. 2018. (ENG., Illus.). 14p. (J). (gr. -1-k). bds. 6.99 (978-1-338-33410-4(7), Cartwheel Bks.) Scholastic, Inc.

—You Are My Merry Little Christmas. Wan, Joyce, illus. 2016. (ENG., Illus.). 14p. (J). (— 1). bds. 6.99 (978-0-545-88093-0(9), Cartwheel Bks.) Scholastic, Inc.

—You Are My Sweetheart. Wan, Joyce, illus. 2018. (ENG., Illus.). 14p. (J). (gr. -1 — 1). bds. 6.99 (978-1-338-04536-9(9), Cartwheel Bks.) Scholastic, Inc.

Wang, Dorothea DePrisco & Imperato, Teresa. All the Ways I Love You. Downing, Julie, illus. 2005. (ENG.). 10p. (J). bds. 8.95 (978-1-58117-190-7(0), Intervisual/Piggy Toes) Bendon, Inc.

Wang, Dorthea Deprisco. Five Minutes until Bed. Vaux, Patricia, illus. 2012. (ENG.). 14p. (J). (-k). bds. 5.99 (978-1-4494-2244-8(6)) Andrews McMeel Publishing.

Wang, Margaret. I Love You, Every Little Bit. Butler, John, illus. 2006. (ENG.). 10p. (gr. -1-k). bds. 9.95 (978-1-58117-482-3(9), Intervisual/Piggy Toes) Bendon, Inc.

—Who Do You Love? A Touch & Feel Book. Mitchell, Melanie, illus. 2007. (gr. -1-k). 15.95 (978-1-58117-570-7(1), Intervisual/Piggy Toes) Bendon, Inc.

Wang, Margaret C. When I Grow Up: A Touch & Feel Book. Gévry, Claudine, illus. 2005. (ENG.). 12p. (J). bds. 10.95 (978-1-58117-423-6(3), Intervisual/Piggy Toes) Bendon, Inc.

Ward, Lindsay. Let's Go! A Flip-And-Find-Out Book. Ward, Lindsay, illus. 2019. (Wheels on the Go Ser.). (ENG., Illus.). 30p. (J). (gr. -1-3). bds. 8.99 (978-0-06-286863-3(2), HarperFestival) HarperCollins Pubs.

Ward, Sarah, illus. My Little Storybook: Little Duck Learns to Swim. 2016. (ENG.). 12p. (J). (gr. -1 — 1). bds. 4.99 (978-1-4998-0190-3(4)) Little Bee Books Inc.

Wargin, Kathy-jo. Little Minnesota. Urban, Helle, illus. 2011. (Little State Ser.). (ENG.). 20p. (J). (gr. -1-1). bds. 9.95 (978-1-58536-174-8(7), 202263) Sleeping Bear Pr.

—Little Wisconsin. Monroe, Michael Glenn, illus. 2012. (Little State Ser.). (ENG.). 20p. (J). (gr. -1-1). bds. 9.95 (978-1-58536-209-7(3), 202275) Sleeping Bear Pr.

Warnes, Tim. I'm Going to Give You a Bear Hug!, 1 vol. 2016. (ENG., Illus.). 32p. (J). 16.99 (978-0-310-75473-2(9)) Zonderkidz.

Washburn, Kim. Bunny Blessings, 1 vol. East, Jacqueline, illus. 2018. (ENG.). 18p. (J). bds. 8.99 (978-0-310-76209-6(X)) Zonderkidz.

Watanabe, Kaori. I Love You (My First Taggies Book) Watanabe, Kaori, illus. 2004. (My First Taggies Book Ser.). (ENG., Illus.). 8p. (J). (gr. -1 — 1). 12.99 (978-0-439-64947-6(1), Cartwheel Bks.) Scholastic, Inc.

Watson, Hannah. Lift-The-Flap ABC. 2018. (Lift-The-Flap Board Bks.). (ENG.). 16p. (J). 13.99 (978-0-7945-4112-5(7), Usborne) EDC Publishing.

—Lift-The-Flap Sizes & Measuring. 2017. (Lift-The-Flap Board Bks.). (ENG.). 16p. 13.99 (978-0-7945-4039-5(2), Usborne) EDC Publishing.

—Slide & See Taking Away Subtracting. 2017. (First Math Slide & See* Ser.). (ENG.). 10p. 14.99 (978-0-7945-3962-7(9), Usborne) EDC Publishing.

Watson, Wendy. Bedtime Bunnies Padded Board Book. 2018. (ENG., Illus.). 26p. (J). (— 1). bds. 8.99 (978-0-544-85958-6(8), 1648585, Clarion Bks.) HarperCollins Pubs.

Watt, F. & Wells, R. That's Not My Dinosaur... It's Body Is Too Squashy. 2004. (Touchy-Feely Board Bks.). (SPA & ENG., Illus.). 1p. (J). (gr. -1-18). bds. 7.95 (978-0-7945-0129-7(X), Usborne) EDC Publishing.

—That's Not My Lion. 2004. (Touchy-Feely Board Bks.). (SPA.). 10p. (J). 7.99 (978-0-7945-0047-4(1), Usborne) EDC Publishing.

Watt, Fiona. ABC. Elkerton, Andy, illus. 2009. (Luxury Touchy-Feely Board Bks). 10p. (J). (gr. -1). bds. 15.99 (978-0-7945-2094-6(4), Usborne) EDC Publishing.

—Baby's Very First Book of Little Babies. 2011. (Baby's Very First Board Bks). 10p. (J). ring bd. 6.99 (978-0-7945-3109-6(1), Usborne) EDC Publishing.

—Baby's Very First Noisy Book Jungle. 2017. (Picture Bks.). (ENG.). 10p. (J). 15.99 (978-0-7945-3986-3(6), Usborne) EDC Publishing.

—Baby's Very First Slide & See Animals. 2015. (Baby's Very First Slide & See Board Bks.). (ENG.). 10p. (J). 14.99 (978-0-7945-3479-0(1), Usborne) EDC Publishing.

—Baby's Very First Slide & See under the Sea. 2015. (Baby's Very First Slide & See Board Bks.). (ENG.). 10p. (J). 14.99 (978-0-7945-3482-0(1), Usborne) EDC Publishing.

—Big Doodling Book. 2012. (Activity Bks). 96p. (J). bds. 11.99 (978-0-7945-3269-7(1), Usborne) EDC Publishing.

—Busy Bug Book. Mantle, Ben, illus. 2011. (Pull-Back Books Ser.). 10p. (J). ring bd. 24.99 (978-0-7945-2941-3(0), Usborne) EDC Publishing.

—Busy Helicopter Book. 2012. (Pull-Back Bks). 10p. (J). ring bd. 24.99 (978-0-7945-3203-1(9), Usborne) EDC Publishing.

—Busy Santa Book. 2011. (Pull-Back Bks). 10p. (J). ring bd. 24.99 (978-0-7945-3178-2(4), Usborne) EDC Publishing.

—Cars. 2011. (Luxury Touchy-Feely Board Books Ser.). 10p. (J). ring bd. 15.99 (978-0-7945-2568-2(7), Usborne) EDC Publishing.

—Christmas Eve. Wells, Rachel, illus. 2007. (Luxury Touchy-Feely Board Bks). 10p. (J). (gr. -1-k). bds. 11.99 (978-0-7945-1478-5(2), Usborne) EDC Publishing.

—Este No Es Mi Tren. rev. ed. 2004. (Titles in Spanish Ser.).Tr. of That's Not My Train. 32p. (J). 12.99 (978-1-58086-585-2(2)) EDC Publishing.

—Fairies. Cartwright, Stephen & Bird, Glen, illus. 2004. 10p. (J). (gr. -1 — 1). per. 15.95 (978-0-7945-0811-1(1), Usborne) EDC Publishing.

—Farm. Wells, Rachel, illus. 2008. (Usborne Touchy-Feely Board Bks.). 8p. (J). (gr. -1-k). bds. 15.99 (978-0-7945-1959-9(8), Usborne) EDC Publishing.

—Go to Sleep Little Baby. Watt, Fiona, illus. 2009. (Baby Board Books w/CD Ser.). (Illus.). 12p. (J). (gr. -1). bds. 15.99 (978-0-7945-1936-0(9), Usborne) EDC Publishing.

—Jungle. Elkerton, Andy, illus. 2009. (Luxury Touchy-Feely Board Bks). 10p. (J). (gr. -1). bds. 15.99 (978-0-7945-2433-3(8), Usborne) EDC Publishing.

—The Nativity. Wells, Rachel, illus. 2005. (Usborne Touchy-Feely Board Bks.). 10p. (J). (gr. -1-k). bds. 15.95 (978-0-7945-1172-2(4), Usborne) EDC Publishing.

—Nursery Rhymes Touchy-Feely Board Book. Meyer, Kerry, illus. 2010. (Luxury Touchy-Feely Board Bks). 10p. (J). bds. 15.99 (978-0-7945-2662-7(4), Usborne) EDC Publishing.

—Penguins Luxury Touchy-Feely Board Book. 2010. (Luxury Touchy-Feely Board Bks). 10p. (J). bds. 15.99 (978-0-7945-2586-6(5), Usborne) EDC Publishing.

—Polar Bears. Chiara, Francesca De, illus. 2010. (Luxury Touchy-Feely Board Bks). 10p. (J). bds. 15.99 (978-0-7945-2544-6(X), Usborne) EDC Publishing.

—Pull-Back Busy Train. Field, Jim, illus. 2013. (Pull-Back Bks). 10p. (J). ring bd. 24.99 (978-0-7945-3333-5(7), Usborne) EDC Publishing.

—Quack, Quack, Quack. 2008. (Bath Bks). 8p. (J). 14.99 (978-0-7945-2304-6(8), Usborne) EDC Publishing.

—Sleepy Baby. MacKinnon, Catherine-Anne, illus. 2006. (Snuggletime Board Bks.). 10p. (J). (gr. -1). bds., bds. 8.99 (978-0-7945-1071-8(X), Usborne) EDC Publishing.

—Sticker Dolly Dressing Back to School. 2012. (Sticker Dolly Dressing Ser.). 34p. (J). pap. 8.99 (978-0-7945-3303-8(5), Usborne) EDC Publishing.

—Sticker Dolly Dressing Ballerinas & Dolls (Combined Volume) 2008. (Sticker Dolly Dressing Ser.). (Illus.). 48p. (J). pap. 14.99 (978-0-7945-2382-4(X), Usborne) EDC Publishing.

—Sticker Dolly Dressing Dancers. Baggott, Stella, illus. 2011. (Sticker Dolly Dressing Ser.). 24p. (J). pap. 8.99 (978-0-7945-2931-4(3), Usborne) EDC Publishing.

—Sticker Dolly Dressing Dolls. Leyhane, Vici & Baggott, Stella, illus. 2006. (Usborne Activities Ser.). 23p. (J). pap. 8.99 (978-0-7945-1389-4(1), Usborne) EDC Publishing.

—Sticker Dolly Dressing Princesses. Leyhane, Vici & Baggott, Stella, illus. 2007. (Sticker Dolly Dressing Ser.). 32p. (J). pap. 8.99 (978-0-7945-1390-0(5), Usborne) EDC Publishing.

—Sticker Dolly Dressing Princesses & Fairies (Combined Volume) 2008. (Sticker Dolly Dressing Ser.). (Illus.). 48p. (J). pap. 14.99 (978-0-7945-2418-0(4), Usborne) EDC Publishing.

—Sticker Dolly Dressing Shopping Girls. 2012. (Sticker Dolly Dressing Ser.). 24p. (J). pap. 8.99 (978-0-7945-3254-3(3), Usborne) EDC Publishing.

—Sticker Dolly Dressing Sportsgirls. 2011. (Sticker Dolly Dressing Ser.). 24p. (J). pap. 8.99 (978-0-7945-3003-7(6), Usborne) EDC Publishing.

—Sticker Dolly Dressing Travel. 2012. (Sticker Dolly Dressing Ser.). 34p. (J). pap. 8.99 (978-0-7945-3313-7(2), Usborne) EDC Publishing.

—Sticker Dolly Dressing Weddings. Baggott, Stella, illus. 2011. (Usborne Activities Ser.). 24p. (J). 8.99 (978-0-7945-3105-8(9), Usborne) EDC Publishing.

—That's Not My Angel. 2009. (Touchy-Feely Board Bks). 10p. (J). bds. 9.99 (978-0-7945-2428-9(1), Usborne) EDC Publishing.

—That's Not My Baby (Boy) 2010. (Touchy Feely Board Book Ser.). 43p. (J). bds. 8.99 (978-0-7945-2604-7(7), Usborne) EDC Publishing.

—That's Not My Baby (Girl) 2010. (Touchy Feely Board Book Ser.). 43p. (J). bds. 8.99 (978-0-7945-2603-0(9), Usborne) EDC Publishing.

—That's Not My Cow. 2015. (Touchy-Feely Board Bks.). (ENG.). 10p. (J). 9.99 (978-0-7945-3544-5(5), Usborne) EDC Publishing.

—That's Not My Dolly. rev. ed. 2012. (Touchy-Feely Board Bks). 10p. (J). bds. 8.99 (978-0-7945-3308-3(6), Usborne) EDC Publishing.

—That's Not My Donkey. Wells, Rachel, illus. 2011. (Touchy-Feely Board Books Ser.). 10p. (J). ring bd. 8.99 (978-0-7945-3012-9(5), Usborne) EDC Publishing.

—That's Not My Duck... Wells, Rachel, illus. 2014. (ENG.). (gr. -1). bds. 9.99 (978-0-7945-3193-5(8), Usborne) EDC Publishing.

—That's Not My Elephant. Wells, Rachel, illus. 2012. (Touchy-Feely Board Bks). 10p. (J). ring bd. 8.99 (978-0-7945-3167-6(9), Usborne) EDC Publishing.

—That's Not My Frog. Wells, Rachel, illus. 2009. (Touchy-Feely Board Bks). 10p. (J). bds. 8.99 (978-0-7945-2505-7(9), Usborne) EDC Publishing.

—That's Not My Hamster. 2012. (Touchy-Feely Board Bks). 10p. (J). bds. 8.99 (978-0-7945-3277-2(2), Usborne) EDC Publishing.

—That's Not My Meerkat. 2015. (Touchy-Feely Board Bks.). (ENG.). 10p. (J). 9.99 (978-0-7945-3599-5(2), Usborne) EDC Publishing.

—That's Not My Mermaid. rev. ed. 2012. (Touchy-Feely Board Bks). 10p. (J). bds. 9.99 (978-0-7945-3307-6(8), Usborne) EDC Publishing.

—That's Not My Monkey. 2008. (Touchy-Feely Board Bks). 10p. (J). bds. 7.99 (978-0-7945-2178-3(9), Usborne) EDC Publishing.

—That's Not My Monster. Wells, Rachel, illus. 2004. 10p. (J). 7.99 (978-0-7945-0818-0(9), Usborne) EDC Publishing.

—That's Not My Penguin. Wells, Rachel, illus. 2007. (Usborne Touchy-Feely Board Bks.). 8p. (gr. -1-k). bds. 7.99 (978-0-7945-1810-3(9), Usborne) EDC Publishing.

—That's Not My Pig... Its Nose Is Too Fuzzy. Wells, Rachel, illus. 2014. (Usborne Touchy-Feely Board Bks.). (ENG.). 10p. (gr. -1). bds. 9.99 (978-0-7945-2666-5(7), Usborne) EDC Publishing.

—That's Not My Pirate. Wells, Rachel, illus. 2007. (Touchy-Feely Board Bks). 10p. (J). (gr. -1-k). bds. 8.99 (978-0-7945-1702-1(1), Usborne) EDC Publishing.

—That's Not My Plane. rev. ed. 2012. (Touchy-Feely Board Bks). 10p. (J). bds. 8.99 (978-0-7945-3294-9(2), Usborne) EDC Publishing.

—That's Not My Polar Bear. 2019. (Touch-Feely Board Bks.). (ENG.). 10ppp. (J). 9.99 (978-0-7945-2551-4(2), Usborne) EDC Publishing.

—That's Not My Prince. Wells, Rachel, illus. 2013. (Usborne Touchy-Feely Board Bks.). (ENG.). 10p. (J). 9.99 (978-0-7945-2838-6(4), Usborne) EDC Publishing.

—That's Not My Princess. Wells, Rachel, illus. 2006. (Usborne Touchy-Feely Board Bks.). 10p. (J). (gr. -1). bds. 9.99 (978-0-7945-1325-2(5), Usborne) EDC Publishing.

—That's Not My Reindeer... Wells, Rachel, illus. 2014. (Usborne Touchy-Feely Bks.). (ENG.). 10p. (gr. -1). bds. 9.99 (978-0-7945-3390-8(6), Usborne) EDC Publishing.

—That's Not My Reindeer: Its Body Is Too Furry. Wells, Rachel, illus. 2008. (Usborne Touchy-Feely Board Bks.). 10p. (J). (gr. -1-k). bds. 9.99 (978-0-7945-1890-5(7), Usborne) EDC Publishing.

—That's Not My Santa. rev. ed. 2012. (Touchy-Feely Board Bks). 10p. (J). bds. 8.99 (978-0-7945-3310-6(8), Usborne) EDC Publishing.

—That's Not My Teddy... Wells, Rachel, illus. 2008. (Usborne Touchy-Feely Board Bks.). 8p. (J). (gr. -1). bds. 7.99 (978-0-7945-2026-7(X), Usborne) EDC Publishing.

—That's Not My Truck. 2009. (Touchy-Feely Board Bks). 10p. (J). bds. 8.99 (978-0-7945-2188-2(6), Usborne) EDC Publishing.

—Tie-a-Bow Book. 2008. (Tie-a-Bow Book Ser.). 10p. (J). bds. 9.99 (978-0-7945-1528-7(2), Usborne) EDC Publishing.

—Tractors. King, Sue, illus. 2009. (Luxury Touchy-Feely Board Bks). 10p. (J). bds. 15.99 (978-0-7945-2432-6(X), Usborne) EDC Publishing.

—Under the Sea Baby Jigsaw Book. 2010. (Baby Jigsaw Bks.). (Illus.). 10p. (J). bds. 9.99 (978-0-7945-1314-6(X), Usborne) EDC Publishing.

—Water Baby. 2011. (Snuggletime Board Books Ser.). 10p. (J). ring bd. 8.99 (978-0-7945-2038-0(3), Usborne) EDC Publishing.

Watt, Fiona, des. Sticker Dolly Dressing Princess Kit. 2011. (Acitivity Kit Ser.). 24p. (J). pap. 15.99 (978-1-60130-278-6(9), Usborne) EDC Publishing.

Watt, Fiona & Cartwright, Stephen. Tie-a-Bow Book. 2004. (Treasury of Farmyard Tales Ser.). (Illus.). 10p. (J). 7.95 (978-0-7945-0330-7(6), Usborne) EDC Publishing.

Watt, Fiona & Wells, Rachel. Anifeiliaid y Fferm. 2005. (WEL., Illus.). 10p. (978-1-84512-000-9(0)) Cymdeithas Lyfrau Ceredigion.

—That's Not My Tractor. 2004. (Touchy-Feely Board Bks.). (SPA & ENG., Illus.). 1p. (J). bds. 7.99 (978-0-7945-0011-5(0), Usborne) EDC Publishing.

Watts, Frances. Goodnight, Mice! Watson, Judy, illus. 2017. (ENG.). 24p. bds. 6.99 (978-0-7333-3530-3(6)) ABC Bks. AUS. Dist: HarperCollins Pubs.

Wax, Wendy. Look Who's Buzzing. 2009. 12p. 9.95 (978-1-58117-911-8(1), Intervisual/Piggy Toes) Bendon, Inc.

Wax, Wendy & Wax, Naomi. Even Princesses Go to the Potty: A Potty Training Life-The-Flap Story. Carabelli, Francesca, illus. 2014. (ENG.). 22p. (J). (gr. -1 — 1). 8.99 (978-1-4424-8886-1(7), Little Simon) Little Simon.

Wax, Wendy A. Musica en Casa: Libro de Cuentos. de Alba, Arlette, tr. 2005. (Disney Princess Ser.). (SPA., Illus.). 38p. (J). (gr. -1-7). incl. audio compact disk (978-970-718-289-9(X), Silver Dolphin en Español) Advanced Marketing, S. de R. L. de C. V.

Weakland, Mark. Football ABC, 1 vol. 2013. (SI Kids Rookie Bks.). (ENG., Illus.). 20p. (J). (gr. -1-2). bds. 7.99 (978-1-4296-9965-5(5), 120669, Capstone Pr.) Capstone.

—Football Opposites, 1 vol. 2013. (SI Kids Rookie Bks.). (ENG., Illus.). 20p. (J). (gr. -1-2). bds. 7.99 (978-1-4296-9967-9(1), 120671) Capstone.

Weeks, Sarah. Who's under That Hat? A Lift-the-Flap Pop-up Adventure. Carter, David A., illus. 2006. 14p. (J). (gr. -1-2). 14.00 (978-1-4223-5440-7(7)) DIANE Publishing Co.

Wehr, Paul. The Animated Bunny's Tail. Wehr, Julian, illus. 2005. 20p. (J). 18.95 (978-0-9748093-1-1(4)) Wehr Animations.

Wehrheim, Carol A. Baptism Promises. Fulcher, Roz, illus. 2018. (ENG.). 18p. (J). bds. 10.00 (978-1-947888-03-6(X), Flyaway Bks.) Westminster John Knox Pr.

Wehrmeijer, Annelien. Emma & Bo Finger Puppet Book: My Best Friend & Me Finger Puppet Books. van de Liejgraaf, Deborah, illus. 2013. (My Best Friend & Me Ser.). (ENG.). 10p. (J). (gr. k-1). bds. 7.99 (978-0-7641-6635-8(2)) Sourcebooks, Inc.

—Lily & Dolly Finger Puppet Book: My Best Friend & Me Finger Puppet Books. van de Liejgraaf, Deborah, illus. 2013. (My Best Friend & Me Ser.). (ENG.). 10p. (J). (gr. k-1). bds. 6.99 (978-0-7641-6636-5(0)) Sourcebooks, Inc.

Weimer, Heidi. I Love You More Than... . 2006. (Ideals Interactive Ser.). (ENG., Illus.). 16p. (J). (gr. -1-k). bds. 12.99 (978-0-8249-6679-9(1), Ideals Pubns.) Worthy Publishing.

—You're My Little Love Bug! 2013. (ENG., Illus.). 12p. (gr. -1). bds. 12.99 (978-1-891100-29-1(7), Smart Kids) Penton Overseas, Inc.

Weimer, Heidi R. Happy Birthday to You! 2007. (ENG., Illus.). 14p. (gr. -1-k). bds. 12.99 (978-0-8249-6699-7(6), Ideals Pubns.) Worthy Publishing.

—How Do I Kiss You? Sharp, Chris, illus. 2008. (ENG.). 18p. (J). (gr. -1-k). bds. 12.99 (978-0-8249-1814-9(2), Ideals Pubns.) Worthy Publishing.

Weir, Patricia. My Kitty & Me. 2008. 20p. per. 24.95 (978-1-60441-908-5(3)) America Star Bks.

Weiser, Florence, illus. Twinkle, Twinkle, Little Star: A Light-Up Bedtime Book. 2017. (ENG.). 10p. (J). (gr. -1 — 1). bds. 10.99 (978-0-7624-6182-0(9), Running Pr. Kids) Running Pr.

Weiss, Ellen & Nelson, Marybeth. Dinosaur Rescue. Weiss, Ellen & Nelson, Marybeth, illus. 2009. (Illus.). (J). (978-1-59292-359-5(3)) SoftPlay, Inc.

—Elmo's Beautiful Day. Weiss, Ellen & Nelson, Marybeth, illus. 2009. (Illus.). (J). (978-1-59292-358-8(5)) SoftPlay, Inc.

Weldon Owen Inc. Staff, contrib. by. My First Emoji Words. 2016. (Illus.). (J). (978-1-4351-6435-2(0)) Barnes & Noble, Inc.

Weldon Owen Inc Staff & Weldon Owen Inc Staff, contrib. by. My First Emoji Feelings. 2016. (Illus.). (J). (978-1-4351-6433-8(4)) Barnes & Noble, Inc.

Wellington, Monica. Apple Farmer Annie Board Book. 2012. (Illus.). 26p. (J). (gr. -1 — 1). bds. 7.99 (978-0-8037-3888-1(9), Dial Bks) Penguin Young Readers Group.

—Firefighter Frank Board Book Edition. 2011. (ENG.). 26p. (J). (gr. -1 — 1). bds. 7.99 (978-0-525-42373-7(7), Dutton Books for Young Readers) Penguin Young Readers Group.

Wells, Rosemary. Max & Ruby's Preschool Pranks. 2016. (Max & Ruby Ser.). (Illus.). 40p. (J). (-k). 17.99 (978-0-670-78462-2(1), Viking Books for Young Readers) Penguin Young Readers Group.

Wen, Dref. Traeth Prysur. 2005.Tr. of Busy Beach. (WEL., Illus.). 12p. (978-1-85596-661-1(1)) Dref Wen.

Weston Woods Staff, creator. Joseph Had a Little Overcoat. 2004. 29.95 (978-1-55592-109-5(4)) Weston Woods Studios, Inc.

What Does Baby Love? 2014. (ENG., Illus.). 14p. (J). (gr. -1 — 1). bds. 7.99 (978-1-4814-0521-8(7), Little Simon) Little Simon.

What Will I Be?, 4 vols. (Girlfriend Gang Ser.). (Illus.). 16p. (J). (978-2-7643-0022-0(0)) Phidal Publishing, Inc./Editions Phidal, Inc.

What's the Time Fairy Princess? 2014. (Illus.). (J). (978-1-4351-5497-1(5)) Barnes & Noble, Inc.

Whelon, Chuck. 3-D Mazes — Treasure Hunters. 2012. (Dover Kids Activity Books: Fantasy Ser.). (ENG.). 32p. (J). (gr. 1-6). 5.99 (978-0-486-49018-2(1), 490181) Dover Pubns., Inc.

Where Do I Live? (Peek A Boo Pockets Ser.). 12p. (J). bds. (978-2-7643-0108-1(1)) Phidal Publishing, Inc./Editions Phidal, Inc.

Where Is Baby's Christmas Present? A Karen Katz Lift-The-Flap Book/Lap Edition. 2014. (ENG., Illus.). 14p. (J). (gr. -1 — 1). bds. 12.99 (978-1-4424-0363-5(2), Little Simon) Little Simon.

Where's My Mommy? 2015. (J). (978-1-4351-5982-2(9)) Barnes & Noble, Inc.

White, George. Halloween at the Zoo: A Pop-up Trick of Treat Experience. 2007. (Illus.). 16p. (J). 16.99 (978-0-9795441-0-1(6)) Jumping Jack Pr.

—Kirby the Easter Dog: A Pop-up Easter Egg Hunt. 2008. (Illus.). 14p. (J). 14.99 (978-0-9795441-2-5(2)) Jumping Jack Pr.

Whitehill, Simcha. Now You See It! Watch Pokémon Evolve — Right Before Your Eyes! 2012. (Illus.). 63p. (J). pap. (978-0-545-45356-1(9)) Scholastic, Inc.

Whitehouse, Ben, illus. Dinner for Dinos: Gulp, Guzzle, Chomp, Chew, 1 vol. 2018. (ENG.). 20p. (J). bds. 9.99 (978-1-4003-1214-6(0), Tommy Nelson) Nelson, Thomas Inc.

Whitlow, Steve, illus. Old MacDonald & Other Stories. 2011. (J). (978-1-4508-2628-0(8)) Phoenix International Publications, Inc.

Who Lives in the Garden? 2004. (Who Lives... Ser.). 12p. (J). bds. 4.99 (978-1-85854-643-8(5)) Brimax Books Ltd. GBR. Dist: Byeway Bks.

Who's Coming to Stay?, 1 vol. 2014. 12p. (J). bds. 6.99 *(978-0-8254-4206-3(0))* Kregel Pubns.

Whybrow, Ian. The Bedtime Bear: A Lift-The-Flap Book. Scheffler, Axel, illus. 2016. (ENG.). 12p. (J). (gr. -1 -2). pap. 9.99 *(978-1-5098-0695-9(4))* Pan Macmillan GBR. Dist: Independent Pubs. Group.

—Say Boo to the Animals! Warnes, Tim, illus. 2017. (J). *(978-1-4351-6509-0(8))* Barnes & Noble, Inc.

—Say Goodnight to the Sleepy Animals! Eaves, Edward, illus. 2017. (J). *(978-1-4351-6510-6(1))* Barnes & Noble, Inc.

—Say Hello to the Animals! Warnes, Tim, illus. 2017. 20p. (J). *(978-1-4351-6512-0(8))* Barnes & Noble, Inc.

—Say Hello to the Baby Animals! Eaves, Edward, illus. 2017. (J). *(978-1-4351-6513-7(6))* Barnes & Noble, Inc.

—Say Hello to the Jungle Animals! Eaves, Edward, illus. 2017. (J). *(978-1-4351-6511-3(X))* Barnes & Noble, Inc.

—The Tickle Book. Scheffler, Axel, illus. 2018. (ENG.). 12p. (J). (gr. -1-k). bds. 11.99 *(978-1-5098-0697-3(0),* 900326054, Macmillan Children's Bks.) Pan Macmillan GBR. Dist: Macmillan.

Whybrow, Ian, et al. Owain A'r Cloc. 2005. (WEL., Illus.). 20.0p. 6.99 *(978-1-84323-366-4(5))* Gomer Pr. GBR. Dist: Gomer Pr.

Whyman, Jennifer E., text. Heavenly Blessings: Baby's Book of Bible Blessing/Baby's Book of Bible Promises. 2008. (Land of Milk & Honey Ser.). (Illus.). 32p. (J). (gr. -1-k). bds. 9.99 *(978-1-4347-9945-6(X))* Cook, David C.

Wick, Walter. Christmas Board Book (Can You See What I See?) Wick, Walter, illus. 2015. (Can You See What I See? Ser.). (ENG.). 24p. (J). (gr. -1-k). bds. 6.99 *(978-0-545-83183-3(0),* Cartwheel Bks.) Scholastic, Inc.

Wick, Walter, photos by. I Spy: Interactive Sound Book of Picture Riddles. 2003. (Illus.). 30p. (J). 15.98 *(978-0-7853-8424-3(3))* Publications International, Ltd.

Widdowson, Kay. Please, Mr Crocodile. 2006. (Lift-the-Flap Books (Child's Play) Ser.). (Illus.). 24p. (J). (gr. -1-1). *(978-1-84643-025-1(9))* Child's Play International Ltd.

Wieder, Stefanie Paige. Baby Food. 2019. (ENG., Illus.). 16p. (J). (gr. -1-k). bds. 7.99 *(978-1-78285-730-3(3))* Barefoot Bks., Inc.

—Baby Food / Comiendo con Bebé. 2019. (ENG.). 16p. (J). (gr. -1-k). bds. 7.99 *(978-1-78285-738-9(9))* Barefoot Bks., Inc.

Wight, Karol. Paperweight Pals. 2012. (Illus.). 22p. (J). *(978-0-87290-191-9(2))* Corning Museum of Glass.

Wild Animals. 2017. (Illus.). (J). *(978-1-62885-353-7(0))* Kidsbooks, LLC.

Wildlife Education, compiled by. Frogs. 2007. (ENG., Illus.). 12p. (J). 5.99 *(978-1-932396-37-9(3),* Critters Up Close) National Wildlife Federation.

—Turtles. 2007. (Illus.). 12p. (J). 5.99 *(978-1-932396-40-9(3),* Critters Up Close) National Wildlife Federation.

Wildsmith, Brian. Daisy, 1 vol. Wildsmith, Brian, illus. 2018. (ENG., Illus.). 48p. (J). *(978-1-59572-803-6(1))* Star Bright Bks., Inc.

Wilhelm, Hans. Pigs in a Blanket (Board Books for Toddlers, Bedtime Stories, Goodnight Board Book) Salcedo, Erica, illus. 2019. (Pigs in A Ser.). (ENG.). 14p. (J). (gr. -1 — 1). bds. 9.99 *(978-1-4521-6451-9(7))* Chronicle Bks. LLC.

Willems, Mo. Who Says That, Cat the Cat? Willems, Mo, illus. 2014. (ENG., Illus.). 22p. (J). (gr. -1 — 1). bds. 6.99 *(978-0-06-230654-8(5),* Balzer & Bray) HarperCollins Pubs.

—Who Sleeps, Cat the Cat? Willems, Mo, illus. 2014. (ENG., Illus.). 22p. (J). (gr. -1 — 1). bds. 7.99 *(978-0-06-230655-5(3),* Balzer & Bray) HarperCollins Pubs.

Williams, Becky. Good Night Little Piggy. Howarth, Daniel, illus. 2007. (Night Light Book Ser.). 10p. (gr. -1-k). bds. *(978-1-84666-129-7(3),* Tide Mill Pr.) Top That! Publishing PLC.

—Ten Little Mermaids. East, Jacqueline, illus. 2007. (Story Book Ser.). 22p. (J). (gr. -1). bds. *(978-1-84666-375-8(X),* Tide Mill Pr.) Top That! Publishing PLC.

Williams, Garth. Baby's First Book. Williams, Garth, illus. 2011. (Golden Baby Ser.). (Illus.). 24p. (J). (— 1). 6.99 *(978-0-375-85905-2(5),* Golden Bks.) Random Hse. Children's Bks.

Williams, Sam. Snack Time. Williams, Sam, illus. 2016. (Noah's Park Ser.: 3). (ENG., Illus.). 14p. (J). (gr. -1-k). bds. 7.99 *(978-1-4814-4263-3(5),* Little Simon) Little Simon.

Willis, Jeanne. We're Going to a Party! Ross, Tony, illus. 2015. (ENG.). 16p. (J). (-k). pap. 14.99 *(978-1-84939-456-7(3))* Andersen Pr. GBR. Dist: Independent Pubs. Group.

—Who's in the Loo? Reynolds, Adrian, illus. 10th ed. 2016. (ENG.). 12p. (J). (— 1). bds. 9.99 *(978-1-78344-420-5(7))* Andersen Pr. GBR. Dist: Independent Pubs. Group.

Wilson, Anne, illus. My First Box of Books: 1 2 3 Colours Animals, 3 vols. 2016. 72p. (J). (gr. -1-2). bds. 9.99 *(978-1-86147-416-2(4),* Armadillo) Anness Publishing GBR. Dist: National Bk. Network.

Wilson, Karma. Baby, I Love You. Williams, Sam, illus. 2009. (ENG.). 30p. (J). (gr. -1 — 1). bds., bds. 8.99 *(978-1-4169-1910-0(4),* Little Simon) Little Simon.

—Beautiful Babies: A Touch-And-Feel Book. 2009. (ENG., Illus.). 14p. (J). (gr. -1 — 1). bds. 7.99 *(978-1-4169-1908-7(2),* Little Simon) Little Simon.

—Trick or Treat, Calico! Erdogan, Buket, illus. 2014. (J). *(978-1-4351-5610-4(2),* Little Simon) Little Simon.

Wilson, Kris E. & Maurer, Toby. How Putter Learned His ABC's: An alphabet Book for Your Littlest Golfer. 2010. 17.00 *(978-0-578-05153-6(2))* Sandy Putter Pr.

Wilson, Samuel Troy. America ABC Board Book. Chan, Irene, illus. 2019. (ENG.). 32p. (J). (gr. -1 — 1). bds. 10.99 *(978-0-06-279527-4(9),* HarperCollins) HarperCollins Pubs.

Windmill Books & Windmill Books. Let's Look at Trains. 2009. (Let's Go! Ser.). (Illus.). 18p. (J). (gr. -1-k). bds. 12.75 *(978-1-60754-419-7(9))* Windmill Bks.

Winkler, Jude. Noah & the Flood (Puzzle Book) St. Joseph Puzzle Book: Book Contains 5 Exciting Jigsaw Puzzles. 2004. (ENG., Illus.). 12p. bds. 9.95 *(978-0-89942-718-8(9),* 972/97) Catholic Bk. Publishing Corp.

—We Go to Mass (Puzzle Book) St. Joseph Puzzle Book: Book Contains 5 Exciting Jigsaw Puzzles. 2004. (ENG., Illus.). 12p. bds. 9.95 *(978-0-89942-716-4(2),* 970/97) Catholic Bk. Publishing Corp.

Winnie the Pooh. The Close-up Day. 2010. 16p. 5.99 *(978-1-4231-3096-3(0))* Disney Pr.

—Goodbye, Honeypot! 2010. 12p. 6.99 *(978-1-4231-3098-7(7))* Disney Pr.

Winteringham, Claire, illus. Claire Winteringham's Alphabet Parade. 2017. 24p. (J). bds. 10.95 *(978-0-7649-7659-9(1),* POMEGRANATE KIDS) Pomegranate Communications, Inc.

Winters, Kay. Whooo's That? A Lift-The-Flap Pumpkin Fun Book. Winston, Jeannie, illus. 2009. (ENG.). 14p. (J). (gr. -1 — 1). 9.99 *(978-0-15-206480-8(X),* 1199346, Clarion Bks.) HarperCollins Pubs.

Witek, Jo. All My Treasures: A Book of Joy. 2016. (Growing Hearts Ser.). (ENG., Illus.). 32p. (J). (gr. -1 — 1). bds. 16.95 *(978-1-4197-2204-2(2),* 1150201, Abrams Appleseed) Abrams, Inc.

Witkowski, Teri. Bitty Bear & the Bugs. Ackley, Peggy Jo, illus. 2008. (J). *(978-1-59369-383-1(4),* American Girl) American Girl Publishing, Inc.

—Bitty Bear, Flower Girl. Ackley, Peggy Jo, illus. 2009. (J). *(978-1-59369-564-4(0),* American Girl) American Girl Publishing, Inc.

—Bitty Bear's Birthday Treats. Ackley, Peggy Jo, illus. 2008. (J). *(978-1-59369-384-8(2),* American Girl) American Girl Publishing, Inc.

—Bitty Bear's New Friend. Ackley, Peggy Jo, illus. 2005. (J). *(978-1-59369-021-2(5))* American Girl Publishing, Inc.

—Bitty Bear's Snowflake Dreams. Ackley, Peggy Jo, illus. 2006. (J). *(978-1-59369-166-0(1))* American Girl Publishing, Inc.

—Bitty Bear's Valentines. Ackley, Peggy Jo, illus. 2004. (J). *(978-1-58485-837-9(0))* American Girl Publishing, Inc.

—Bitty Bear's Walk in the Woods. Ackley, Peggy Jo, illus. 2006. (J). *(978-1-59369-156-1(4))* American Girl Publishing, Inc.

—The Bitty Bunch Bath Book. Ackley, Peggy Jo, illus. 2006. (J). *(978-1-59369-080-9(0))* American Girl Publishing, Inc.

—Bitty Bunny's Bedtime. Ackley, Peggy Jo, illus. 2004. (J). *(978-1-58485-921-5(0))* American Girl Publishing, Inc.

—Bitty Bunny's Slipper Search. Ackley, Peggy Jo, illus. 2009. (J). *(978-1-59369-586-6(1),* American Girl) American Girl Publishing, Inc.

—Bunny & Piggy at the Beach. Ackley, Peggy Jo, illus. 2005. (J). *(978-1-58485-961-1(X))* American Girl Publishing, Inc.

—Happy Birthday, Bitty Bear! Ackley, Peggy Jo, illus. 2005. (J). *(978-1-58485-959-8(8))* American Girl Publishing, Inc.

—It's Spring, Bitty Bear! Ackley, Peggy Jo, illus. 2007. (J). *(978-1-59369-242-1(0))* American Girl Publishing, Inc.

—Time for Bed, Bitty Bunch. Ackley, Peggy Jo, illus. 2008. (J). *(978-1-59369-380-0(X))* American Girl Publishing, Inc.

—Wait Your Turn, Bitty Froggy! Ackley, Peggy Jo, illus. 2008. (J). *(978-1-59369-285-8(4))* American Girl Publishing, Inc.

Wolf, Jackie, et al. My Sparkle Egg Book. 2005. (Illus.). (J). *(978-1-57151-750-0(2))* Playhouse Publishing.

Wolf, Sallie. Truck Stuck. Davies, Andy Robert, illus. 2017. 28p. (J). (— 1). bds. 7.99 *(978-1-58089-781-5(9))* Charlesbridge Publishing, Inc.

Wolfe, Jane. Cheeky Frog. Benham, Tors, illus. 2016. 8p. (J). (gr. -1-12). bds. 6.99 *(978-1-84322-718-2(5),* Armadillo) Anness Publishing GBR. Dist: National Bk. Network.

—Crazy Cow. Benham, Tors, illus. 2013. 8p. (J). (gr. -1-k). bds. 6.99 *(978-1-84322-775-5(4),* Armadillo) Anness Publishing GBR. Dist: National Bk. Network.

—Dizzy Duck. Benham, Tors, illus. 2016. 8p. (J). (gr. -1-12). bds. 6.99 *(978-1-84322-719-9(3),* Armadillo) Anness Publishing GBR. Dist: National Bk. Network.

—Happy Cat. Benham, Tors, illus. 2016. 8p. (J). (gr. -1-k). bds. 6.99 *(978-1-84322-720-5(7),* Armadillo) Anness Publishing GBR. Dist: National Bk. Network.

—Hungry Horse. Benham, Tors, illus. 2016. 8p. (J). (gr. -1-12). bds. 6.99 *(978-1-84322-721-2(5),* Armadillo) Anness Publishing GBR. Dist: National Bk. Network.

—Messy Pig. Benham, Tors, illus. 2013. 8p. (J). (gr. -1-k). bds. 6.99 *(978-1-84322-777-9(0),* Armadillo) Anness Publishing GBR. Dist: National Bk. Network.

—Noisy Dog. Benham, Tors, illus. 2013. 8p. (J). (gr. -1-k). bds. 6.99 *(978-1-84322-779-3(7),* Armadillo) Anness Publishing GBR. Dist: National Bk. Network.

—Pull the Lever: Who Are You? The Toy Box, illus. 2014. (ENG.). 8p. (J). (gr. -1-2). bds. 6.99 *(978-1-86147-391-2(5),* Armadillo) Anness Publishing GBR. Dist: National Bk. Network.

—Pull the Lever: Who Does What? Benham, Tors, illus. 2014. (ENG.). 8p. (J). (gr. -1-2). bds. 6.99 *(978-1-86147-392-9(3),* Armadillo) Anness Publishing GBR. Dist: National Bk. Network.

—Pull the Lever: Who's in Here? Benham, Tors, illus. 2014. (ENG.). 8p. (J). (gr. -1-2). bds. 6.99 *(978-1-86147-394-3(X),* Armadillo) Anness Publishing GBR. Dist: National Bk. Network.

—Sleepy Sheep. Benham, Tors, illus. 2013. 8p. (J). (gr. -1-k). bds. 6.99 *(978-1-84322-778-6(9),* Armadillo) Anness Publishing GBR. Dist: National Bk. Network.

Wood, Amanda. Amazing Baby Touch & Play! 2005. (Illus.). 12p. (J). 15.95 *(978-1-59223-529-2(8),* Silver Dolphin Bks.) Readerlink Distribution Services, LLC.

Wood, Audrey. The Napping House Board Book. Wood, Don, illus. 2015. (ENG.). 32p. (J). (— 1). bds. 9.99 *(978-0-544-60225-0(0),* 1616872, Clarion Bks.) HarperCollins Pubs.

—The Napping House Padded Board Book. Wood, Don, illus. 2010. (ENG.). 34p. (J). (gr. -1-k). bds. 8.99 *(978-0-547-48147-0(0),* 1439512, Clarion Bks.) HarperCollins Pubs.

Wood, Hannah, illus. Dino Pop-up Faces: A Let's Pretend Pop-up Book. 2007. (ENG.). 12p. (J). (gr. -1-3). 14.95 *(978-1-58117-596-7(5),* Intervisual/Piggy Toes) Bendon, Inc.

Woodworth, Viki & Whelon, Chuck. 3-D Mazes — Maze Mania. 2012. (Dover Kids Activity Bks.). (ENG.). 32p. (J). (gr. 1-6). 5.99 *(978-0-486-49016-8(5),* 490165) Dover Pubns., Inc.

Woolf, Julia, illus. Gingerbread Joy. 2008. (ENG.). 10p. (J). bds. 4.95 *(978-1-58117-814-2(X),* Intervisual/Piggy Toes) Bendon, Inc.

—Reindeer Run. 2008. (ENG.). 10p. (J). bds. 4.95 *(978-1-58117-813-5(1),* Intervisual/Piggy Toes) Bendon, Inc.

—Snowman Surprise. 2008. (ENG.). 10p. (J). bds. 4.95 *(978-1-58117-812-8(3),* Intervisual/Piggy Toes) Bendon, Inc.

—Special Star. 2008. (ENG.). 10p. (J). bds. 4.95 *(978-1-58117-815-9(8),* Intervisual/Piggy Toes) Bendon, Inc.

Worthington, Leonie & Bedford, David. Bums. 2004. (ENG., Illus.). 16p. (J). (gr. -1-k). 10.95 *(978-1-877003-71-4(9))* Little Hare Bks. AUS. Dist: Independent Pubs. Group.

WorthyKids. My First Book of Prayers. Flint, Gillian, illus. 2018. (ENG.). 20p. (J). (gr. -1-k). bds. 6.99 *(978-0-8249-1683-1(2))* Worthy Publishing.

Wren, Jenny, illus. Night Animals. 2017. (First Explorers Ser.). (ENG.). 10p. (J). (— 1). bds. 8.95 *(978-1-4549-2657-3(0))* Sterling Publishing Co., Inc.

Wright, Claire. A Kiss Goodnight. Vasylenko, Veronica, illus. 2017. (Padded Board Books for Babies Ser.). (ENG.). 20p. (J). (gr. -1 — 1). bds. 6.99 *(978-1-68412-041-3(1),* Silver Dolphin Bks.) Printers Row Publishing Group.

Wright, Dee. The Peanut Butter Finger Mystery. 2013. (Little Ruth Ser.). (ENG., Illus.). 38p. (J). pap. *(978-1-59684-606-7(2))* Penman Publishers.

Yaccarino, Dan. Five Little Pumpkins Came Back Board Book. Yaccarino, Dan, illus. 2018. (ENG., Illus.). 16p. (J). (gr. -1 — 1). bds. 6.99 *(978-0-06-284021-9(5),* HarperFestival) HarperCollins Pubs.

Yang, Belle. A Nest in Springtime: A Mandarin Chinese-English Bilingual Book of Numbers. Yang, Belle, illus. 2012. (ENG., Illus.). 24p. (J). (gr. k — 1). bds. 6.99 *(978-0-7636-5279-1(2))* Candlewick Pr.

Yarlett, Emma, illus. Nibbles: The Book Monster. 2016. (J). *(978-1-61067-467-6(7))* Kane Miller.

Yates, Gene. The Chameleon Colors Book. 2004. (Illus.). (J). *(978-1-58865-182-2(7))* Kidsbooks, LLC.

Yates, Gene, illus. The Chameleon Colors Book. 2006. (J). *(978-1-58865-361-1(7))* Kidsbooks, LLC.

—The Giraffe Numbers Book. 2006. (J). *(978-1-58865-364-2(1))* Kidsbooks, LLC.

Yates, Gene & Frank, Thomas. What Can Simon Be? Yates, Gene, illus. 2006. (Illus.). (J). *(978-1-58865-366-6(8))* Kidsbooks, LLC.

Ying, Jonathan. Lost & Found, What's That Sound? Ying, Victoria, illus. 2017. (ENG.). 32p. (J). (gr. -1-3). 14.99 *(978-0-06-238068-5(0),* HarperCollins) HarperCollins Pubs.

—Lost & Found, What's That Sound? Board Book. Ying, Victoria, illus. 2018. (ENG.). 28p. (J). (gr. -1 — 1). bds. 7.99 *(978-0-06-238069-2(9),* HarperFestival) HarperCollins Pubs.

Yolen, Jane. What to Do with a Box. Sheban, Chris, illus. 2018. (ENG.). 14p. (J). (gr. -1-1). bds. 8.99 *(978-1-56846-320-9(0),* 19702, Creative Editions) Creative Co., The.

Yolen, Jane & Stemple, Heidi E. Y. You Nest Here with Me. Sweet, Melissa, illus. 2019. 28p. (J). (— 1). bds. 7.99 *(978-1-68437-371-0(9),* Astra Young Readers) Astra Publishing Hse.

Yonezu, Yusuke. We Love Each Other: An Interactive Book Full of Animals & Hugs. Yonezu, Yusuke, illus. 2013. (World of Yonezu Ser.). (Illus.). 28p. (J). (— 1). bds. 9.95 *(978-988-8240-56-2(0),* Minedition) Penguin Young Readers Group.

Yoon, Salina. Deep Sea Dive. 2012. (Lift-The-Flap Adventures Ser.). (Illus.). 12p. (J). (gr. -1-2). bds. 9.99 *(978-1-4027-8525-2(9))* Sterling Publishing Co., Inc.

—Five Trick-or-Treaters. 2010. 10p. bds. 5.95 *(978-1-60747-745-7(9),* Pickwick Pr.) Phoenix Bks., Inc.

—My Chanukah Playbook. Yoon, Salina, illus. 2009. (ENG., Illus.). 10p. (J). (gr. -1-k). 12.99 *(978-1-4169-8957-8(9),* Little Simon) Little Simon.

—Opposnakes: A Lift-The-Flap Book about Opposites. Yoon, Salina, illus. 2009. (ENG., Illus.). 16p. (J). (gr. -1-1). 14.99 *(978-1-4169-7875-6(5),* Little Simon) Little Simon.

—Penguin Gets Dressed! Yoon, Salina, illus. 2010. (Illus.). 10p. bds. 7.95 *(978-1-60747-750-1(5),* Pickwick Pr.) Phoenix Bks., Inc.

—Penguin Gets Ready for Bed! Yoon, Salina, illus. 2010. (Illus.). 10p. bds. 7.95 *(978-1-60747-751-8(3),* Pickwick Pr.) Phoenix Bks., Inc.

—Penguin Goes to the Farm! Yoon, Salina, illus. 2010. (Illus.). 10p. bds. 7.95 *(978-1-60747-752-5(1),* Pickwick Pr.) Phoenix Bks., Inc.

—Penguin's Christmas Wish. 2017. (Penguin Ser.). (ENG.). 32p. (J). bds. 7.99 *(978-1-68119-573-5(9),* 900178387, Bloomsbury USA Childrens) Bloomsbury Publishing USA.

—Where's Boo? 2013. (Illus.). 18p. (J). (— 1). bds. 7.99 *(978-0-307-97808-0(7),* Random Hse. Bks. for Young Readers) Random Hse. Children's Bks.

—Where's Ellie? A Hide-And-Seek Book. 2012. (Illus.). 18p. (J). (gr. k — 1). bds. 6.99 *(978-0-307-97806-6(0),* Random Hse. Bks. for Young Readers) Random Hse. Children's Bks.

—Wings: A Book to Touch & Feel. Yoon, Salina, illus. 2010. (ENG., Illus.). 14p. (J). (gr. -1 — 1). bds. 8.99 *(978-1-4169-8958-5(7),* Little Simon) Little Simon.

Yoon, Salina, creator. Sea Creatures: A Sparkling Little Colors Book, 4 vols. 2005. (ENG., Illus.). 12p. (J). bds. 5.95 *(978-1-58117-169-3(2),* Intervisual/Piggy Toes) Bendon, Inc.

Yoon, Salina, illus. Peek-a-Boo Farm Animals. 2005. (Peek-a-Boo Guess Who Book Ser.: Vol. 2). 10p. (J). 7.95 *(978-1-58117-158-7(7),* Intervisual/Piggy Toes) Bendon, Inc.

—Peek-a-Boo Wild Animals. 2005. (Peek-a-Boo Guess Who Book Ser.: Vol. 1). 10p. (J). (gr. -1-k). 7.95 *(978-1-58117-157-0(9),* Intervisual/Piggy Toes) Bendon, Inc.

Young, Cybèle. Out the Window, 1 vol. 2013. (ENG., Illus.). 30p. (J). (gr. -1 — 1). bds. 12.95 *(978-1-55498-370-4(3))* Groundwood Bks. CAN. Dist: Publishers Group West (PGW).

Young, Ed. Seven Blind Mice. Young, Ed, illus. 2012. (ENG., Illus.). 38p. (J). (gr. -1 — 1). bds. 9.99 *(978-0-399-25742-1(X),* Philomel Bks.) Penguin Young Readers Group.

Young, Jay. Magic World of Learning. Tucker, Sian, illus. 2003. 32p. *(978-1-903174-42-5(2),* Pavilion Children's Books) Pavilion Bks.

Young, Judy. Little Missouri. Urban, Helle, illus. 2012. (Little State Ser.). (ENG.). 20p. (J). (gr. -1-1). bds. 9.95 *(978-1-58536-206-6(9),* 202348) Sleeping Bear Pr.

Young, Laurie. I See a Monster! Mahoney, Daniel J., illus. 2007. (Touch & Feel Ser.). 12p. (gr. -1-k). 15.95 *(978-1-58117-574-5(4),* Intervisual/Piggy Toes) Bendon, Inc.

Young, Sarah. Jesus Calling for Little Ones, 1 vol. Woodward, Antonia, illus. 2015. (Jesus Calling(r) Ser.). (ENG.). 26p. (J). bds. 8.99 *(978-0-7180-3384-2(1),* Tommy Nelson) Nelson, Thomas Inc.

—Jesus Calling Little Book of Prayers, 1 vol. Farias, Carolina, illus. 2018. (Jesus Calling(r) Ser.). (ENG.). 26p. (J). bds. 8.99 *(978-0-7180-9753-0(X),* Tommy Nelson) Nelson, Thomas Inc.

You're One! 2014. (Year-By-Year Bks.). (ENG., Illus.). 16p. (J). (— 1). bds. 7.95 *(978-1-934649-46-6(5))* Bailiwick Pr.

Yoyo Books, creator. Vroom. 2011. (Baby's First Library). (ENG., Illus.). 38p. (gr. -1-k). bds. *(978-90-8622-910-9(7))* YoYo Bks.

Yoyo Books Staff. Bedtime: Learning Words Series. 2004. 12p. bds. *(978-90-5843-607-8(1))* YoYo Bks.

—On the Farm: Learning Words Series. 2005. 12p. bds. *(978-90-5843-605-4(5))* YoYo Bks.

Yuly, Toni. Cat Nap. 2017. (ENG., Illus.). 32p. (J). bds. 9.99 *(978-1-250-11261-3(3),* 900170501) Feiwel & Friends.

—Early Bird: A Picture Book. Yuly, Toni, illus. 2015. (ENG., Illus.). 16p. (J). (— 1). bds. 11.99 *(978-1-250-05706-8(X),* 900139116) Feiwel & Friends.

Zadrozny, Alicia & Church, Caroline Jayne. The Wild Little Jungle: A Mix-and-Match Flap Book. 2008. (ENG.). 10p. (J). bds. 12.99 *(978-0-7944-1605-8(5))* Reader's Digest Assn., Inc., The.

Zakarin, Debra Mostow. First Fairytales. Fiore, Rob, illus. 2010. 10p. 9.95 *(978-1-60747-746-4(7),* Pickwick Pr.) Phoenix Bks., Inc.

Zakiyyah & Zakiyyah. Chatterworld My Numbers in Spanish/My Numbers in French: MIS Numeros en Espanol/Mes Nombres en Francais. 2006. (Illus.). 40p. (J). (gr. -1-3). 14.99 *(978-0-9777085-0-5(0))* Little Linguists Press.

Zapp, et al. Baby Bear's Read-Along Goldilocks & the Three Bears. (Illus.). *(978-2-7641-0516-0(9))* Tormont Pubns.

Zebra's Stripes. Date not set. (Touch & Feel Ser.). (Illus.). (J). 4.98 *(978-0-7525-9571-9(7))* Parragon, Inc.

Zebrowska, Emilia. Simon Says Open the Book. Reagan, Susan, illus. 2019. (ENG.). 14p. (J). (gr. -1-1). bds. 8.99 *(978-1-56846-330-8(8),* 18904, Creative Editions) Creative Co., The.

Ziefert, Harriet. The Best Smelling Christmas Book Ever: 9 Scents to Scratch & Sniff! Rader, Laura, illus. 2004. 18p. (J). (gr. k-4). reprint ed. 13.00 *(978-0-7567-7600-8(7))* DIANE Publishing Co.

—Monkey's Noisy Jungle. Newton, Jill, illus. 2007. bds. 7.95 *(978-1-59354-598-7(3))* Blue Apple Bks.

Ziegler-Sullivan, Ursula. The Pups Save the Bunnies. 2016. (Illus.). (J). *(978-1-5182-1575-9(0))* Random Hse., Inc.

Zimmerman, Andrea. Trashy Town Board Book. Yaccarino, Dan, illus. 2018. (ENG.). 26p. (J). (gr. -1 — 1). bds. 7.99 *(978-0-06-249103-9(2),* HarperFestival) HarperCollins Pubs.

Zimmerman, Andrea & Clemesha, David. Train Man. Zimmerman, Andrea, illus. 2017. (Digger Man Ser.: 3). (ENG., Illus.). 32p. (J). bds. 10.99 *(978-1-62779-504-3(9),* 900152958, Holt, Henry & Co. Bks. For Young Readers) Holt, Henry & Co.

Zobel-Nolan, Allia. Animal Parade. Maddocks, Maria, illus. 2008. 10p. (J). (gr. -1). 12.95 *(978-1-932915-63-1(X))* Sandvik Innovations, LLC.

—Hugs for Baby! Mitchell, Susan, illus. 2008. (Lift-the-Flap Hear-the-Sound Ser.). 10p. (J). (gr. -1). 12.95 *(978-1-932915-64-8(8))* Sandvik Innovations, LLC.

—Lift the Flap Nativity. Moroney, Trace, illus. 2015. (Lift-The-Flap Ser.). (ENG.). 20p. (J). (gr. -1-k). 10.99 *(978-0-7944-3527-1(0),* Studio Fun International) Printers Row Publishing Group.

Zobel Nolan, Allia. What I Like about Me! A Book Celebrating Differences. Yamamoto, Miki, illus. 2009. (What I Like About Ser.). (ENG.). 14p. (J). (gr. -1-k). 6.99 *(978-0-7944-1945-5(3),* Studio Fun International) Printers Row Publishing Group.

Zonderkidz. Bedtime Collection: 20 Favorite Bible Stories & Prayers, 1 vol. 2018. (Beginner's Bible Ser.). (ENG., Illus.). 128p. (J). 13.99 *(978-0-310-76328-4(2))* Zonderkidz.

—Go Wild! Bible Stories for Little Ones, 1 vol. 2018. (ENG., Illus.). 32p. (J). bds. 9.99 *(978-0-310-76169-3(7))* Zonderkidz.

—Jonah's Big Fish Adventure, 1 vol. 2018. (Beginner's Bible Ser.). (ENG., Illus.). 18p. (J). bds. 9.99 *(978-0-310-75994-2(3))* Zonderkidz.

Zondervan. The Beginner's Bible Activity Book, 1 vol. 2017. (Beginner's Bible Ser.). (ENG.). 64p. (J). pap. 5.99 *(978-0-310-75979-9(X))* Zonderkidz.

Zondervan Staff. Ready, Set, Find Christmas, 1 vol. 2016. (Ready, Set, Find Ser.). (ENG.). 12p. (J). bds. 8.99 *(978-0-310-75766-5(5))* Zonderkidz.

—Ready, Set, Find Easter, 1 vol. 2017. (Ready, Set, Find Ser.). (ENG.). 12p. (J). bds. 8.99 *(978-0-310-75769-6(X))* Zonderkidz.

Zondervan Staff & Walburg, Lori. The Legend of the Candy Cane, 1 vol. Cowdrey, Richard, illus. 2014. (ENG.). 30p. (J). bds. 9.99 *(978-0-310-74672-0(8))* Zonderkidz.

Zoo-Zológico Bilingual Board Book. 2008. (ENG & SPA., Illus.). (J). pap. 5.99 *(978-0-9727886-8-7(9))* Osmosis, LLC.

Zschock, Martha. Hello, Cape Cod! 2009. (Hello Ser.). (ENG., Illus.). 16p. (gr. -1-k). bds. 9.99 *(978-0-9819430-1-5(2),* Commonwealth Editions) Applewood Bks.

—Hello, New Orleans! 2011. (Hello Ser.). (ENG., Illus.). 16p. (J). (gr. -1-k). bds. 9.99 *(978-1-933212-63-0(2),* Commonwealth Editions) Applewood Bks.

—Hello, Philadelphia! 2011. (Hello Ser.). (ENG., Illus.). 16p. (J). (gr. -1-k). bds. 9.99 *(978-1-933212-64-7(0),* Commonwealth Editions) Applewood Bks.

—Hello, San Francisco! 2012. (Hello Ser.). (ENG., Illus.). 16p. (J). (gr. -1-k). bds. 9.99 *(978-1-933212-65-4(9),* Commonwealth Editions) Applewood Bks.

Zucchelli-Romer, Claire. TouchThinkLearn: Wiggles: (Childrens Books Ages 1-3, Interactive Books for Toddlers, Board Books for Toddlers) 2018. (Touch Think Learn Ser.). (ENG., Illus.). 26p. (J). (gr. -1 — 1). bds. 15.99 *(978-1-4521-6475-5(4))* Chronicle Bks. LLC.

Zuravicky, Orli. C Is for City: An Alphabet Book. Castellano, Giuseppe, illus. 2011. (Mister Doodle Ser.). (ENG.). 40p. (J). (gr. -1-k). bds. 7.99 *(978-1-4424-2049-6(9),* Little Simon) Little Simon.

123. 2004. (Illus.). (J). *(978-1-59060-333-8(8))* Waldman Publishing Corp.

23andMe Inc. You Share Genes with Me. Killoran, Ariana, illus. 2016. (ENG.). 18p. (J). (gr. -1-k). bds. 9.99 (978-0-9891537-0-6(3), 1330810) Abrams, Inc.

TOY MAKING

Aaseng, Nathan. Business Builders in Toys. 2003. (Business Builders Ser.). (Illus.). 160p. (gr. 5-18). lib. bdg. 22.95 (978-1-881508-81-6(1)) Oliver Pr., Inc.

Ajmera, Maya & Ivanko, John D. Come Out & Play: A Global Journey. 2020. 32p. (J). (gr. -1-3). 16.99 (978-1-62354-163-7(8)) Charlesbridge Publishing, Inc.

Balmer, Alden. Doc Fizzix Mousetrap Racers: The Complete Builder's Manual. 2008. (ENG., Illus.). 144p. (gr. 7-18). pap. 14.95 (978-1-56523-359-1(X), 3591D) Fox Chapel Publishing Co., Inc.

Borgert-Spaniol, Megan. Toy & Game Projects: Making Slime, Flipping Bottles, & More. 2019. (Unplug with Science Buddies (r) Ser.). (ENG., Illus.). 32p. (J). (gr. 2-5). pap. 8.99 (978-1-5415-7491-5(5), 1077ae93-fe38-47e7-b12b-90c69807dc9e); lib. bdg. 27.99 (978-1-5415-5497-9(3), ae3f2779-6160-4fea-a469-a6d5bc81e7b0) Lerner Publishing Group. (Lerner Pubns.).

Cunningham, Kevin. Toys. 2008. (21st Century Skills Library: Global Products Ser.). (ENG., Illus.). 32p. (gr. 4-8). 32.07 (978-1-60279-252-4(6), 200119) Cherry Lake Publishing.

Doney, Meryl. Toys, 1 vol. 2004. (Crafts from Many Cultures Ser.). (ENG., Illus.). 32p. (gr. 3-5). lib. bdg. 28.67 (978-0-8368-4048-3(8), 56881680-310d-4f38-b121-918fcece54e9, Gareth Stevens Learning Library) Stevens, Gareth Publishing LLLP.

Editors of Klutz. Felted Friends: Create Your Own Soft, Fuzzy Animals. 2014. (ENG.). 56p. (J). (gr. 5). 19.99 (978-0-545-64796-0(7)) Klutz.

Elton, Richard & Elton, Candice. Every Kid Needs a Rubber Band Launcher. 2007. (ENG.). 48p. (J). (978-1-4236-0268-2(4)) Gibbs Smith, Publisher.

Felix, Rebecca. Cool Action Figures & Dolls: Crafting Creative Toys & Amazing Games. 2015. (Cool Toys & Games Ser.). (ENG., Illus.). 32p. (J). (gr. 3-6). 34.21 (978-1-68078-045-1(X), 19095, Checkerboard Library) ABDO Publishing Co.

Fryer, Jane Eayre. The Mary Frances Sewing Book 100th Anniversary Edition: A Childrens Story-Instruction Sewing Book with Doll Clothes Patterns for American Girl & Other 18-Inch Dolls. 2011. (ENG., Illus.). 284p. (J). pap. 19.95 (978-1-937564-01-8(0), Classic Bookwrights) Lindaloo Enterprises.

Garstecki, Julia & Derkovitz, Stephanie. Make Your Own Water Balloon Launcher. 2020. (J). pap. (978-1-62310-131-2(X)) Black Rabbit Bks.

Giacobello, John. Choosing a Career in the Toy Industry. 2009. (World of Work Ser.). 64p. (gr. 5-5). 58.50 (978-1-60854-341-0(2)) Rosen Publishing Group, Inc., The.

Harbo, Christopher L. Easy Origami Toys, 1 vol. 2010. (Easy Origami Ser.). (ENG.). 24p. (J). (gr. 1-3). lib. bdg. 25.99 (978-1-4296-5386-2(8), 113812, Capstone Pr.) Capstone.

Heller, D. M. Let's Make a Bike with Everyday Materials. (Let's Do Arts & Crafts Ser.). 24p. (gr. 2-2). 2009. 42.50 (978-1-61514-196-8(0), PowerKids Pr.) 2005. (ENG., Illus.). (J). lib. bdg. 26.27 (978-1-4042-3064-4(5), 903e5661-e084-4011-9c4d-5bf2c8d0288d) Rosen Publishing Group, Inc., The.

Hinkler Books Staff. Balloon Animals. 2004. (ENG., Illus.). 48p. (J). 6.95 (978-1-86515-644-6(2)) Hinkler Bks. Pty, Ltd. AUS. Dist: Penton Overseas, Inc.

Hirschmann, Kris. The Secret Science of Toys: A Toy Story Discovery Book. 2019. (Disney Learning Discovery Bks.). (ENG., Illus.). 48p. (J). (gr. 2-5). pap. 8.99 (978-1-5415-7391-8(9), 9781541573918); lib. bdg. 31.99 (978-1-5415-5490-0(6), 9781541554900) Lerner Publishing Group. (Lerner Pubns.).

Irvine, Joan. How to Make Super Pop-Ups. Hendry, Linda, illus. 2008. (Dover Origami Papercraft Ser.). (ENG.). 96p. (gr. 3-7). per. 9.95 (978-0-486-46589-0(6), 465896) Dover Pubns., Inc.

Owen, Ruth. Ready, Aim, Fire!, 1 vol., 1. 2014. (DIY for Boys Ser.). (ENG.). 32p. (J). (gr. 4-4). 30.17 (978-1-4777-6286-8(8), 40f84193-aa13-43a6-add9-84e0b4cea448, PowerKids Pr.) Rosen Publishing Group, Inc., The.

Oxlade, Chris. Toys Through Time: How Toys Were Designed, Developed, & Made. 2004. (Illus.). 45p. (J). (gr. 4-8). reprint ed. (978-0-7567-7848-4(4)) DIANE Publishing Co.

Pohl, Kathleen. What Happens at a Toy Factory? / ¿Qué Pasa en una Fábrica de Juguetes?, 1 vol. 2006. (Where People Work / ¿dónde Trabaja la Gente? Ser.). (Illus.). 24p. (gr. k-2). (SPA & ENG.). (J). lib. bdg. 24.67 (978-0-8368-7390-0(4), b178da0e-471c-41be-8c72-d35596b67506); (ENG & SPA., pap. 9.15 (978-0-8368-7397-9(1), 4c1ce705-fd33-4a93-b5ec-ff7e1d3e020d) Stevens, Gareth Publishing LLLP. (Weekly Reader Leveled Readers).

Roytman, Arkady & Paper Dolls for Grownups Staff. Glow-in-the-Dark Ghouls Paper Action Figures. 2011. (Dover Paper Dolls Ser.). (ENG.). 32p. (J). (gr. 3-5). pap. 9.99 (978-0-486-48364-1(9), 483649) Dover Pubns., Inc.

Scott-Waters, Marilyn, creator. The Toymaker: Paper Toys That You Can Make Yourself, 1. 2004. (Illus.). 20p. (YA). 12.95 (978-0-9759884-0-4(9)) Scott-Waters, Marilyn.

Storey, Rita. Make Your Own Toys, 1 vol. 2010. (Do It Yourself Projects! Ser.). (ENG., Illus.). 24p. (J). (gr. 4-4). lib. bdg. 28.93 (978-1-61532-592-4(1), c88a6407-20cf-450e-8d0d-928864ea7e4c, PowerKids Pr.) Rosen Publishing Group, Inc., The.

Williams, Pam. Remixing Toys. 2018. (21st Century Skills Innovation Library: Makers As Innovators Junior Ser.). (ENG.). 24p. (J). (gr. 2-5). pap. 12.79 (978-1-5341-0883-7(1), 210896); (Illus.). lib. bdg. 30.64 (978-1-5341-0784-7(3), 210895) Cherry Lake Publishing.

TOYS

see also Dollhouses; Dolls

Adams, Linda. Make & Learn Bible Toys. 2004. (Illus.). 96p. (J). (gr. -1-k). pap. 11.95 (978-1-885358-39-4(3), RB36722) Rainbow Pubs. & Legacy Pr.

Aebersold, Carol V. & Bell, Chanda. The Elf on the Shelf: Spanish Boy Dark Elf. Steinwart, Coe, illus. 2012. 32p. (J). lib. bdg. 15.00 net. (978-0-9769907-5-8(X)) CCA & B, LLC.

Animales Bebes. 2005. (Collection Abre Tus Ojos, Collection Eye Openers Ser.).Tr. of Animal Babies. (SPA.). (J). (gr. k-2). 6.95 (978-950-11-0964-1(X)) Sigmar ARG. Dist: Iaconi, Mariuccia Bk. Imports.

Appleton-Smith, Laura & Blackaby, Susan. Margaret Strong, Toy Collector. Neel, Preston, illus. 2014. (Book to Remember Ser.). (ENG.). 22p. (J). pap. 8.95 (978-1-60541-152-1(3), Books To Remember) Flyleaf Publishing.

Arlon, Penelope. Super Sharks. 2018. (LEGO Nonfiction Ser.: 7). (ENG., Illus.). 32p. (J). (gr. -1-3). pap. 4.99 (978-1-338-26193-6(2)) Scholastic, Inc.

Arlon, Penelope & Gordon-Harris, Tory. Dino Safari: A LEGO Adventure in the Real World. 2016. (Illus.). 32p. (J). (978-1-338-04643-4(8)) Scholastic, Inc.

Arlon, Penelope & Lee, Paul. Super Sharks: A LEGO Adventure in the Real World. Arlon, Penelope & Lee, Paul, illus. 2018. (Illus.). 32p. (J). (978-1-5490-3671-2(8)) Scholastic, Inc.

Avery, Logan. Engineering Marvels: Toys: Partitioning Shapes (Grade 1) rev. ed. 2018. (Mathematics in the Real World Ser.). (ENG., Illus.). 24p. (J). (gr. 1-2). pap. 9.99 (978-1-4258-5695-3(0)) Teacher Created Materials, Inc.

—Juguetes: Partición de Figuras. rev. ed. 2019. (Mathematics in the Real World Ser.). (SPA., Illus.). 24p. (J). (gr. 1-2). pap. 9.99 (978-1-4258-2857-8(4)) Teacher Created Materials, Inc.

AZ Books Staff. Where's My Toy? Sisoj, Natalja, ed. 2012. (Peek-A-Boo Ser.). (ENG.). 10p. (J). (— 1). bds. 10.95 (978-1-61889-116-7(2)) AZ Bks. LLC.

Baby's First Toys. 2004. 10p. (J). bds. 4.99 (978-1-85854-922-4(1)) Brimax Books Ltd. GBR. Dist: Byeway Bks.

Baggott, Stella, illus. Baby's Very First Toys Book. 2009. (Baby Board Bks). 10p. (J). bds. 6.99 (978-0-7945-2466-1(4), Usborne) EDC Publishing.

Baier, Harry. Yo-Yo World Trick Book. 2014. (ENG., Illus.). 96p. (J). (gr. 3). pap. 6.99 (978-0-486-49488-3(8), 494888) Dover Pubns., Inc.

Balaban, Mariah. The Ultimate Handbook. 2007. (Littlest Pet Shop Ser.). (Illus.). 64p. (J). pap. (978-0-545-07697-5(8)) Scholastic, Inc.

Beisner, Monika. Fantastic Toys: A Catalog. 2019. (Illus.). 32p. (J). (-k). 17.95 (978-1-68137-311-9(4), NYR Children's Collection) New York Review of Bks., Inc., The.

Beswick, Clare. 30 Fun Ways to Learn about Blocks & Boxes. 2011. (30 Fun Ways to Learn Ser.). (ENG.). 80p. (gr. -1-k). pap. 12.95 (978-0-87659-369-1(4), Gryphon House Inc) Gryphon Hse., Inc.

Bidder, Jane. Inventions We Use for Play, 1 vol. 2006. (Everyday Inventions Ser.). (ENG., Illus.). 32p. (gr. 2-4). lib. bdg. 28.67 (978-0-8368-6900-2(1), b2a5ce2c-f124-406f-a42a-d74d2a0455df, Gareth Stevens Learning Library) Stevens, Gareth Publishing LLLP.

Bolitho, Mark. Fold Your Own Origami Air Force, 1 vol. 2013. (Origami Army Ser.). (ENG.). 32p. (J). (gr. 4-5). 30.17 (978-1-4777-1319-8(0), 7e8cecf2-ebe7-49f0-80d2-eef4f33bfa12); pap. 12.75 (978-1-4777-1469-0(3), d136c147-9f3b-4b8d-9e62-0f1bc836da42) Rosen Publishing Group, Inc., The. (PowerKids Pr.).

—Fold Your Own Origami Army, 1 vol. 2013. (Origami Army Ser.). (ENG.). 32p. (J). (gr. 4-5). 30.17 (978-1-4777-1317-4(4), 79e2de33-f8c5-4926-8d23-a97cb935d271); pap. 12.75 (978-1-4777-1465-2(0), ddcdf6cf-df53-493d-b4c4-feb11e84fd28) Rosen Publishing Group, Inc., The. (PowerKids Pr.).

—Fold Your Own Origami Navy, 1 vol. 2013. (Origami Army Ser.). (ENG.). 32p. (J). (gr. 4-5). 30.17 (978-1-4777-1318-1(2), bf7d4de7-f93a-46c8-91c4-ba2855630374); pap. 12.75 (978-1-4777-1467-6(7), 27357e93-155b-4e06-aea9-a429de38b1ea) Rosen Publishing Group, Inc., The. (PowerKids Pr.).

—Fold Your Own Origami Weapons, 1 vol. 2013. (Origami Army Ser.). (ENG.). 32p. (J). (gr. 4-5). 30.17 (978-1-4777-1320-4(4), d9bcbd15-0319-4281-aa7f-22af4b647f9d); pap. 12.75 (978-1-4777-1471-3(5), abf46ea1-7817-4701-98dd-6a5b4effc1a2) Rosen Publishing Group, Inc., The. (PowerKids Pr.).

Boothroyd, Jennifer. From Marbles to Video Games: How Toys Have Changed. 2011. (Comparing Past & Present Ser.). pap. 45.32 (978-0-7613-8391-8(3)); pap. 7.95 (978-0-7613-7841-9(3)) Lerner Publishing Group.

Brack, Amanda. Amazing Brick Mosaics: Fantastic Projects to Build with Lego Blocks You Already Have. 2018. (ENG., Illus.). 160p. (J). pap. 19.99 (978-1-250-16361-5(7), 900186485) St. Martin's Pr.

—Big Book of Brick Trucks. 2015. (ENG., Illus.). 32p. (J). (-k). 14.99 (978-1-63220-598-8(X), Sky Pony Pr.) Skyhorse Publishing Co., Inc.

Brick by Brick ABC. 2016. (Illus.). (J). (978-1-4351-6408-6(3)) Barnes & Noble, Inc.

Butterfield, Moira. Toys & Games Around the World, 1 vol. 2015. (Children Like Us Ser.). (ENG., Illus.). 32p. (gr. 3-3). pap. 11.58 (978-1-5026-0850-5(2), c8edbb69-923a-4929-9014-b1231dbd9730) Cavendish Square Publishing LLC.

Carle, Eric. 1, 2, 3 with the 10 Little Rubber Ducks: A Spring Counting Book. Carle, Eric, illus. 2019. (ENG., Illus.). 22p. (J). (gr. -1 — 1). bds. 8.99 (978-0-06-288256-1(2), HarperFestival) HarperCollins Pubs.

La Casa. 2005. (Coleccion Primeras Imagenes). (SPA., Illus.). 86p. (J). (gr. -1-18). pap. 7.95 (978-950-11-0990-0(9), SGM9909) Sigmar ARG. Dist: Continental Bk. Co., Inc.

Castleforte, Brian. Papertoy Monsters: Make Your Very Own Amazing Papertoys! 2010. (ENG., Illus.). 124p. (J). pap. 22.95 (978-0-7611-5882-0(0), 15882) Workman Publishing Co., Inc.

Christian, Cheryl. What's in My Toybox? Spanish/English, 1 vol. Ericsson, Annie Beth, illus. 2009. (ENG.). 32p. (J). bds. 6.25 (978-1-59572-179-2(7)) Star Bright Bks., Inc.

—What's in My Toybox? (Pull-Tab), 1 vol. Ericsson, Annie Beth, illus. 2009. (ENG.). 32p. (J). (gr. -1). bds. 6.25 (978-1-59572-164-8(9)) Star Bright Bks., Inc.

Cohn, Jessica. 10 Fascinating Facts about Toys (Rookie Star: Fact Finder) (Library Edition) 2016. (Rookie Star Ser.). (ENG., Illus.). 32p. (J). (gr. 2-3). lib. bdg. 25.00 (978-0-531-22818-0(5), Children's Pr.) Scholastic Library Publishing.

Cole, Jeff & Stone, Kate. Stick to It - Toys: A Magnetic Puzzle Book. 2011. (ENG., Illus.). 14p. (J). bds. 16.99 (978-1-4494-0499-4(5)) Andrews McMeel Publishing.

Cunningham, Kevin. Calling All Innovators: a Career for You: Toys. 2013. (Calling All Innovators). (ENG.). 64p. (J). pap. 8.95 (978-0-531-22010-8(9)) Scholastic Library Publishing.

—Toys: From Concept to Consumer. 2013. (Calling All Innovators). (ENG.). 64p. (J). 30.00 (978-0-531-26522-2(6)) Scholastic Library Publishing.

Dale, Jay. My Little Toys, 1 vol. 2012. (Engage Literacy Magenta Ser.). (ENG.). 16p. (J). (gr. k-2). pap. 6.99 (978-1-4296-8876-5(9), 119941); pap. 36.94 (978-1-4296-8877-2(7), 18334) Capstone. (Capstone Pr.).

—My Toy Box. 2012. (Engage Literacy Magenta Ser.). (ENG.). 16p. (J). (gr. k-2). pap. 36.94 (978-1-4296-8861-1(0), 18326); (Illus.). pap. 6.99 (978-1-4296-8860-4(2), 119933) Capstone. (Capstone Pr.).

De Compreas. 2005. (Coleccion Primeras Imagenes). (SPA., Illus.). 86p. (J). (gr. -1-18). pap. 7.95 (978-950-11-0985-6(2), SGM9852) Sigmar ARG. Dist: Continental Bk. Co., Inc.

Dees, Sarah. Awesome LEGO Creations with Bricks You Already Have. 2016. (ENG., Illus.). 192p. (J). pap. 19.99 (978-1-62414-281-9(8), 900164740) Page Street Publishing Co.

—Epic LEGO Adventures with Bricks You Already Have: Build Crazy Worlds Where Aliens Live on the Moon, Dinosaurs Walk among Us, Scientists Battle Mutant Bugs & You Bring Their Hilarious Tales to Life. 2017. (ENG., Illus.). 192p. (J). pap. 19.99 (978-1-62414-386-1(5), 900177087) Page Street Publishing Co.

Dinmont, Kerry. Toys & Games Past & Present. 2018. (Bumba Books (r) — Past & Present Ser.). (ENG., Illus.). 24p. (J). (gr. -1-1). pap. 8.99 (978-1-5415-2691-4(0), 2d977349-02e7-4519-9825-ec354567c180); lib. bdg. 26.65 (978-1-5415-0333-5(3), 0ad8c44d-6cdf-427a-9877-c85553ef1dc5, Lerner Pubns.) Lerner Publishing Group.

DK. LEGO Star Wars Visual Dictionary, New Edition: With Exclusive Finn Minifigure. 2019. (ENG., Illus.). 160p. (J). (gr. 2-4). 21.99 (978-1-4654-7888-7(4), DK Children) Dorling Kindersley Publishing, Inc.

DK & Lipkowitz, Daniel. LEGO DC Comics Super Heroes Build Your Own Adventure. 2017. (LEGO Build Your Own Adventure Ser.). (ENG., Illus.). 80p. (J). (gr. 1-4). 24.99 (978-1-4654-6089-9(6), DK Children) Dorling Kindersley Publishing, Inc.

Doney, Meryl. Toys, 1 vol. 2004. (Crafts from Many Cultures Ser.). (ENG., Illus.). 32p. (gr. 3-5). lib. bdg. 28.67 (978-0-8368-4048-3(8), 56881680-310d-4f38-b121-918fcece54e9, Gareth Stevens Learning Library) Stevens, Gareth Publishing LLLP.

Dorling Kindersley Publishing Staff. I Love That Minifigure. 2015. (ENG., Illus.). 208p. (J). (978-0-241-19689-2(2)) Dorling Kindersley Publishing, Inc.

—LEGO Ninjago: Character Encyclopedia. 2012. (ENG., Illus.). 176p. (978-1-4093-7597-5(8)) Penguin Bks., Ltd.

Eck, Kristin. Hide-and-Seek Toys. 2004. (Hide-And-Seek Books). (Illus.). (J). lib. bdg. 21.25 (978-1-4042-2704-0(0), PowerKids Pr.) Rosen Publishing Group, Inc., The.

—Hide & Seek Toys. 2009. (Tough Toddler Bks). 16p. (gr. k-k). 42.50 (978-1-60854-573-5(3), PowerKids Pr.) Rosen Publishing Group, Inc., The.

Editorial Staff, Gareth. Things I Play With, 1 vol. 2007. (Things in My World Ser.). (ENG., Illus.). 16p. (gr. k-1). pap. 6.30 (978-0-8368-6818-0(8), f49a7141-e4e2-4f56-bb6e-4968e525115f, Weekly Reader Leveled Readers) Stevens, Gareth Publishing LLLP.

—Things I Play with / Las Cosas con Las Que Juego, 1 vol. 2006. (Things in My World / Las Cosas de Mi Mundo Ser.). (ENG & SPA.). 16p. (gr. k-1). pap. 6.30 (978-0-8368-7230-9(4), cc9d8dce-82a6-4daa-b9ca-40de87dc1d82, Weekly Reader Leveled Readers) Stevens, Gareth Publishing LLLP.

Ehmann, Mary Pat. Toys Around the World, 1 vol. 2018. (Adventures in Culture Ser.). (ENG.). 24p. (gr. 1-2). 24.27 (978-1-5382-1875-4(5), 0da10d63-3355-449f-a9a5-e01ef1de7dca) Stevens, Gareth Publishing LLLP.

Elsmore, Warren. Brick by Brick Dinosaurs: More Than 15 Awesome LEGO Brick Projects. 2018. (ENG., Illus.). 224p. (J). (gr. 3-7). pap. 19.99 (978-0-7624-9147-6(7), Running Pr. Kids) Running Pr.

—Brick by Brick Space: 20+ LEGO Brick Projects That Are Out of This World. 2018. (ENG., Illus.). 224p. (J). (gr. 3-7). pap. 19.99 (978-0-7624-9051-6(9), Running Pr. Kids) Running Pr.

Emergency! A Lego Adventure in the Real World. 2017. (Illus.). 31p. (978-1-338-20717-0(2)) Scholastic, Inc.

Enz, Tammy. Building Projects for Beginners: 4D an Augmented Reading Experience. Brizuela, Dario, illus. 2018. (Junior Makers 4D Ser.). (ENG.). 48p. (J). (gr. 3-9). lib. bdg. 33.99 (978-1-5157-9488-2(1), 136713, Capstone Classroom) Capstone.

Farshtey, Greg. Lego Ninjago Official Guide. 2011. (Illus.). 128p. (J). pap. (978-0-545-38285-4(8)) Scholastic, Inc.

Felix, Rebecca. Cool Construction & Building Blocks: Crafting Creative Toys & Amazing Games. 2015. (Cool Toys & Games Ser.). (ENG., Illus.). 32p. (J). (gr. 3-6). lib. bdg. 34.21 (978-1-68078-047-5(6), 19099, Checkerboard Library) ABDO Publishing Co.

—Cool Doughs, Putties, Slimes, & Goops: Crafting Creative Toys & Amazing Games. 2015. (Cool Toys & Games Ser.). (ENG., Illus.). 32p. (J). (gr. 3-6). lib. bdg. 34.21 (978-1-68078-049-9(2), 19103, Checkerboard Library) ABDO Publishing Co.

Fold Your Own Origami Air Force. 2013. (Origami Army Ser.). 32p. (J). (gr. 3-6). pap. 70.50 (978-1-4777-1470-6(7), PowerKids Pr.) Rosen Publishing Group, Inc., The.

Fold Your Own Origami Army. 2013. (Origami Army Ser.). 32p. (J). (gr. 3-6). pap. 70.50 (978-1-4777-1466-9(9), PowerKids Pr.) Rosen Publishing Group, Inc., The.

Fold Your Own Origami Navy. 2013. (Origami Army Ser.). 32p. (J). (gr. 3-6). pap. 70.50 (978-1-4777-1468-3(5), PowerKids Pr.) Rosen Publishing Group, Inc., The.

Fold Your Own Origami Weapons. 2013. (Origami Army Ser.). 32p. (J). (gr. 3-6). pap. 70.50 (978-1-4777-1472-0(3), PowerKids Pr.) Rosen Publishing Group, Inc., The.

Fontichiaro, Kristin. Taking Toys Apart. 2017. (21st Century Skills Innovation Library: Makers As Innovators Junior Ser.). (ENG., Illus.). 24p. (J). (gr. 2-5). lib. bdg. 30.64 (978-1-63472-691-7(X), 210062) Cherry Lake Publishing.

Fontichiaro, Kristin & Thomas, AnnMarie P. Squishy Circuits. 2014. (21st Century Skills Innovation Library: Makers As Innovators Ser.). (ENG., Illus.). 32p. (J). (gr. 4-8). 32.07 (978-1-63137-775-4(2), 205343) Cherry Lake Publishing.

French, Cathy;Burton. My Models. #N/A, ed. 2011. (Early Connections Ser.). (ENG.). (J). 6.84 net. (978-1-61672-301-9(7)) Benchmark Education Co.

Fuller, Jill. Toy Box Subtraction. 2004. (Rookie Read-About Math Ser.). (J). 20.50 (978-0-516-24423-5(X), Children's Pr.) Scholastic Library Publishing.

Garcia, Karina. Karina Garcia's Next-Level DIY Slime. 2018. (ENG., Illus.). 80p. (J). (gr. 4). pap. 7.99 (978-1-4998-0799-8(6)) Little Bee Books Inc.

—Karina Garcia's Next-Level DIY Slime. 2018. (Illus.). 80p. (J). pap. (978-1-78741-373-3(X)) Templar Publishing.

Gardner, Robert. Ace Your Science Project Using Chemistry Magic & Toys: Great Science Fair Ideas, 1 vol. 2009. (Ace Your Science Project Ser.). (ENG., Illus.). 128p. (gr. 5-6). lib. bdg. 35.93 (978-0-7660-3226-2(4), 2ddcb01b-d092-4687-bdb1-7d70fd78d371) Enslow Publishing, LLC.

—The Physics of Toys & Games Science Projects, 1 vol. 2013. (Exploring Hands-On Science Projects Ser.). (ENG.). 128p. (gr. 5-6). pap. 13.88 (978-1-4644-0219-7(1), 51857e6a-ef0b-453d-91ad-9147775c17ea); lib. bdg. 30.60 (978-0-7660-4143-1(3), 06eb0f09-d618-462e-b5ba-bdb9acad4c7b) Enslow Publishing, LLC.

Garstecki, Julia & Derkovitz, Stephanie. Make Your Own Dancing Slime: By Julia Garstecki & Stephanie Derkovitz. 2020. (J). pap. (978-1-62310-126-8(3)) Black Rabbit Bks.

Glenn, Lexi & Nia. My Invention: How Lexi Glenn, a fourth grader, came up with an idea & got it in toy stores all over the world. A story of how you must first believe in Yourself. 2011. 32p. 12.99 (978-1-4389-3949-0(3)) AuthorHouse.

Greathouse, Lisa. Cómo Funcionan los Juguetes. rev. ed. 2010. (Science: Informational Text Ser.). (SPA., Illus.). 32p. (gr. 3-5). pap. 11.99 (978-1-4333-2148-1(3)) Teacher Created Materials, Inc.

Green, Sara. Hello Kitty. 2018. (Brands We Know Ser.). (ENG., Illus.). 24p. (J). (gr. 3-8). lib. bdg. 27.95 (978-1-62617-774-1(0), Pilot Bks.) Bellwether Media.

—Lego. 2015. (Brands We Know Ser.). (ENG., Illus.). 24p. (J). (gr. 3-8). pap. 8.99 (978-1-61891-249-7(6), 12001); lib. bdg. 27.95 (978-1-62617-208-1(0)) Bellwether Media. (Pilot Bks.).

—My Little Pony. 2018. (Brands We Know Ser.). (ENG., Illus.). 24p. (J). (gr. 3-8). lib. bdg. 27.95 (978-1-62617-775-8(9), Pilot Bks.) Bellwether Media.

—Nerf. 2016. (Brands We Know Ser.). (ENG., Illus.). 24p. (J). (gr. 3-8). lib. bdg. 27.95 (978-1-62617-349-1(4), Pilot Bks.) Bellwether Media.

—Power Rangers. 2018. (Brands We Know Ser.). (ENG., Illus.). 24p. (J). (gr. 3-8). lib. bdg. 27.95 (978-1-62617-776-5(7), Pilot Bks.) Bellwether Media.

Group/McGraw-Hill, Wright. Toys, Then & Now: Level E, 6 vols. (Take Twostm Ser.). 16p. 29.95 (978-0-322-08950-1(6)) Wright Group/McGraw-Hill.

Grupos. 2005. (Coleccion Primeras Imagenes). (SPA., Illus.). 86p. (J). (gr. -1-18). pap. 7.95 (978-950-11-0986-3(0), SGM9860) Sigmar ARG. Dist: Continental Bk. Co., Inc., Lectorum Pubns., Inc.

Hagar, Erin. Awesome Minds: the Inventors of LEGO(R) Toys: An Entertaining History about the Creation of LEGO Toys. Educational & Entertaining. 2016. (Awesome Minds Ser.). (Illus.). 48p. (J). (gr. 1-7). 14.99 (978-1-938093-53-1(4), 809353) Duo Pr. LLC.

Harper, Sandy. Educational Toys for Kids of All Ages. 2013. 56p. pap. 12.55 (978-1-63022-577-3(0)) Speedy Publishing LLC.

Harris, Patricia. Understanding Coding with Lego Wedo(tm), 1 vol., 1. 2015. (Spotlight on Kids Can Code Ser.). (ENG., Illus.). 24p. (J). (gr. 4-5). pap. 12.75 (978-1-5081-4466-3(4), 7c8821f2-b29f-4f57-8f95-6eb7c9b92d48, PowerKids Pr.) Rosen Publishing Group, Inc., The.

Henderson, Meryl, illus. Things to Play With. (Picture Bks.: No. S8817-5). 28p. (J). (gr. -1). pap. 3.95 (978-0-7214-5144-2(6), Dutton Juvenile) Penguin Publishing Group.

Herrold, Karen L. The Ice Cream Truck. 2012. (ENG.). pap. (978-1-4675-3466-6(8)) Independent Pub.

Hirschmann, Kris. LEGO Toys. 2008. (Great Idea Ser.). (Illus.). 48p. (J). (gr. 4-6). lib. bdg. 26.60 (978-1-59953-194-6(1)) Norwood Hse. Pr.

—The Secret Science of Toys: A Toy Story Discovery Book. 2019. (Disney Learning Discovery Bks.). (ENG., Illus.). 48p. (J). (gr. 2-5). pap. 8.99 (978-1-5415-7391-8(9), 9781541573918); lib. bdg. 31.99 (978-1-5415-5490-0(6), 9781541554900) Lerner Publishing Group. (Lerner Pubns.).

Hixon, Rena. Mindstorms: Level 1. 2016. (21st Century Skills Innovation Library: Unofficial Guides). (ENG., Illus.). 32p. (J). (gr. 4-8). 32.07 (978-1-63470-524-0(6), 207827) Cherry Lake Publishing.

—Mindstorms: Level 2. 2016. (21st Century Skills Innovation Library: Unofficial Guides). (ENG., Illus.). 32p. (J). (gr. 4-8). 32.07 (978-1-63470-525-7(4), 207831) Cherry Lake Publishing.

—Mindstorms: Level 3. 2016. (21st Century Skills Innovation Library: Unofficial Guides). (ENG., Illus.). 32p. (J). (gr. 4-8). 32.07 (978-1-63470-526-4(2), 207835) Cherry Lake Publishing.

—Mindstorms: Level 4. 2016. (21st Century Skills Innovation Library: Unofficial Guides). (ENG., Illus.). 32p. (J). (gr. 4-8). 32.07 (978-1-63470-527-1(0), 207839) Cherry Lake Publishing.

Holden, Pam. Toys That Can Go, 1 vol. 2009. (Red Rocket Readers Ser.). (ENG., Illus.). 16p. (gr. -1-1). pap. (978-1-877435-93-5(7)) Flying Start Bks.

La Hora. 2005. (Coleccion Primeras Imagenes). (SPA., Illus.). 86p. (J). (gr. -1-18). pap. 7.95 (978-950-11-0987-0(9), SGM9879) Sigmar ARG. Dist: Continental Bk. Co., Inc.

Hudson, Amanda. Our Toys, 6 vols., Set. Incl. This Is My Ball. lib. bdg. 21.67 *(978-0-8368-9252-9(6),* 12235892-f7fa-4a8b-b94c-e90d57dcc184); This Is My Bear. lib. bdg. 21.67 *(978-0-8368-9253-6(4),* 7491166d-de9d-4985-931d-1ad8668e381f); This Is My Book. lib. bdg. 21.67 *(978-0-8368-9254-3(2),* 474daae6-8958-407a-947b-ffa935e9c87b); This Is My Truck. lib. bdg. 21.67 *(978-0-8368-9255-0(0),* 9a459ed5-b893-4005-941d-f51b843fa30d); (Illus.). (J). (gr. k-1). (Our Toys Ser.). (ENG.). 16p. 2008. Set lib. bdg. 65.01 *(978-0-8368-9316-8(6),* 39c1fb9d-7a56-458d-828b-3f6e6f99a1d9, Weekly Reader Leveled Readers) Stevens, Gareth Publishing LLLP.

—Our Toys/Nuestros Juguetes, 8 vols., Set. Incl. This Is My Ball / Esta Es Mi Pelota. lib. bdg. 21.67 *(978-0-8368-9256-7(9),* 7a578453-083d-411a-aee4-e2afbde908e1); This Is My Bear / Este Es Mi Oso. lib. bdg. 21.67 *(978-0-8368-9257-4(7),* f77425f0-d46b-4c49-bca2-e13c85e883ff); This Is My Book / Este Es Mi Libro. lib. bdg. 21.67 *(978-0-8368-9258-1(5),* 8b827754-3019-4493-b16b-94ac75f2d656); This Is My Truck / Este Es Mi Camión. lib. bdg. 21.67 *(978-0-8368-9259-8(3),* 14899ea7-40e8-49a1-a34b-ab1675379817); (Illus.). (J). (gr. k-k). (Our Toys / Nuestros Juguetes Ser.). (ENG & SPA.). 16p. 2008. Set lib. bdg. 86.01 *(978-0-8368-9317-5(4),* 95f4a7ca-ac55-4455-b6fd-1a4b056aa374, Weekly Reader Leveled Readers) Stevens, Gareth Publishing LLLP.

—This Is My Bear, 1 vol. 2008. (Our Toys Ser.). (ENG., Illus.). 16p. (gr. k-1). (J). lib. bdg. 21.67 *(978-0-8368-9253-6(4),* 7491166d-de9d-4985-931d-1ad8668e381f); pap. 6.30 *(978-0-8368-9352-6(2),* 4b40f611-49a9-46bc-a88d-feb5c8e85292) Stevens, Gareth Publishing LLLP. (Weekly Reader Leveled Readers).

Hugo, Simon. 365 Things to Do with LEGO Bricks: Lego Fun Every Day of the Year. 2016. (ENG., Illus.). 256p. (J). (gr. 2-6). 24.99 *(978-1-4654-5302-0(4),* DK Children) Dorling Kindersley Publishing, Inc.

Kalman, Bobbie. Toys & Games Then & Now. 2013. (ENG., Illus.). 24p. (J). *(978-0-7787-0128-6(X));* pap. *(978-0-7787-0210-8(3))* Crabtree Publishing Co.

Kemmeter, Jennifer. Build It! Make Supercool Models with Your LEGO(r) Classic Set. 3. 2016. (Brick Bks.: 3). (ENG., Illus.). 86p. (J). (gr. k-3). pap. 16.99 *(978-1-943328-82-6(X),* Graphic Arts Bks.) West Margin Pr.

—Build It! Dinosaurs: Make Supercool Models with Your Favorite LEGO(r) Parts. 2018. (Brick Bks.: 10). (ENG., Illus.). 100p. (J). (gr. k). 32.99 *(978-1-5132-6111-9(8));* pap. 17.99 *(978-1-5132-6110-2(X))* West Margin Pr. (Graphic Arts Bks.).

—Build It! Farm Animals: Make Supercool Models with Your Favorite LEGO(r) Parts. 2017. (Brick Bks.: 8). (ENG., Illus.). 86p. (J). (gr. -1-2). 32.99 *(978-1-5132-6085-3(5));* pap. 16.99 *(978-1-5132-6082-2(0))* West Margin Pr. (Graphic Arts Bks.).

—Build It! Robots: Make Supercool Models with Your Favorite LEGO(r) Parts. 2017. (Brick Bks.: 9). (ENG., Illus.). 86p. (J). (gr. -1-2). pap. 16.99 *(978-1-5132-6083-9(9),* Graphic Arts Bks.) West Margin Pr.

Kenney, Sean. Cool Cars & Trucks. Kenney, Sean, illus. 2009. (Sean Kenney's Cool Creations Ser.). (ENG., Illus.). 32p. (J). (gr. -1-3). 14.99 *(978-0-8050-8761-1(3),* 900049948, Holt, Henry & Co. Bks. For Young Readers) Holt, Henry & Co.

—Cool Creations in 101 Pieces. 2014. (Sean Kenney's Cool Creations Ser.). (ENG., Illus.). 32p. (J). (gr. -1-4). 15.99 *(978-1-62779-017-8(9),* 900130257, Holt, Henry & Co. Bks. For Young Readers) Holt, Henry & Co.

Kent, Lorna, illus. Baby's First Toys Book. 2004. 10p. (J). bds. 7.99 *(978-1-85854-882-1(9))* Brimax Books Ltd. GBR. Dist: Byeway Bks.

King, David, et al. Fun with Fidget Spinners: 50 Super Cool Tricks & Activities. 2017. (ENG.). 80p. (J). pap. 6.99 *(978-1-4972-0377-8(5),* DO5913) Fox Chapel Publishing Co., Inc.

Lassieur, Allison. Toys 100 Years Ago. 2011. (Amicus Readers. 100 Years Ago (Level 2) Ser.). (ENG.). 24p. (J). (gr. 1-4). lib. bdg. 25.65 *(978-1-60753-166-1(6),* 17055) Amicus.

Lim, Annalees. Fun with Fabric, 1 vol. 2013. (Clever Crafts Ser.). (ENG., Illus.). 24p. (gr. 2-3). 29.93 *(978-1-4777-0180-5(X),* faf6fbce-9ae8-4493-b9c2-500d1424e00b); pap. 11.60 *(978-1-4777-0188-1(5),* 74ee0afb-2223-4727-8a5b-21115ebae08f) Rosen Publishing Group, Inc., The. (Windmill Bks.).

Lipkowitz, Daniel. The LEGO Book, New Edition: With Exclusive LEGO Brick. 2018. (ENG., Illus.). 280p. 25.00 *(978-1-4654-6714-0(9),* DK) Dorling Kindersley Publishing, Inc.

—The LEGO Book, New Edition (Library Edition) 2018. (ENG., Illus.). 280p. lib. bdg. 25.00 *(978-1-4654-7820-7(5),* DK) Dorling Kindersley Publishing, Inc.

—The LEGO Ideas Book: Unlock Your Imagination. 2011. (Lego Ideas Ser.). (ENG., Illus.). 200p. (J). (gr. 2-5). 24.99 *(978-0-7566-8606-2(7),* DK Children) Dorling Kindersley Publishing, Inc.

—LEGO Play Book: Ideas to Bring Your Bricks to Life. 2013. (ENG., Illus.). 200p. (J). (gr. 2-5). 24.99 *(978-1-4654-1412-0(6),* DK Children) Dorling Kindersley Publishing, Inc.

—LEGO Star Wars: the Yoda Chronicles. 2013. (ENG., Illus.). 64p. (J). (gr. 1-4). 18.99 *(978-1-4654-0868-6(1),* DK Children) Dorling Kindersley Publishing, Inc.

Lipkowitz, Daniel & Dorling Kindersley Publishing Staff. The Lego Ideas Book: You Can Build Anything! 2011. (Illus.). 200p. *(978-1-4053-5067-9(9))* Dorling Kindersley.

Littlewood, Peter. Rain Forest Destruction. 2012. (Mapping Global Issues Ser.). 48p. (J). (gr. 7-9). lib. bdg. 34.25 *(978-1-59920-512-0(2))* Black Rabbit Bks.

Lyles, Brian & Lyles, Jason. The Lego Neighborhood Book: Build Your Own Town! 2014. (Illus.). 204p. (gr. 5). 19.95 *(978-1-59327-571-6(4))* No Starch Pr., Inc.

MacDonald, Margaret. Toys Long Ago. 2011. (Learn-Abouts: Level 10 Ser.). (Illus.). 16p. (J). pap. 7.95 *(978-1-59920-597-7(1))* Black Rabbit Bks.

—What Things Did Your Parents Play With? 2012. (Level E Ser.). (ENG., Illus.). 16p. (J). (gr. k-2). pap. 7.95 *(978-1-927136-41-6(5),* 19427) RiverStream Publishing.

Macken, JoAnn Early. Toys. 2010. (Everyday Science Ser.). (ENG.). 24p. (J). (gr. k-2). lib. bdg. 25.65 *(978-1-60753-017-6(1),* 17138) Amicus.

Markovics, Pearl. My Favorite Toys. 2019. (My Favorite Things Ser.). (ENG.). 16p. (J). (gr. -1-1). 6.99 *(978-1-64280-382-2(0))* Bearport Publishing Co., Inc.

McDonnell, Rory. Matemáticas con Juguetes / Math with Toys, 1 vol. de la Vega, Eida, tr. 2016. (¡Matemáticas en Todas Partes! / Math Is Everywhere! Ser.). (ENG & SPA.). 24p. (gr. k-k). lib. bdg. 24.27 *(978-1-4824-5214-3(6),* 1109dbd5-1304-4cf2-b0e2-5317273a8a78) Stevens, Gareth Publishing LLLP.

Meachen Rau, Dana. Juegos y Diversiones en la Historia de América (Toys, Games, & Fun in American History), 1 vol. 2006. (Cómo Era la Vida en América (How People Lived in America) Ser.). (SPA., Illus.). 24p. (gr. 2-4). lib. bdg. 24.67 *(978-0-8368-7429-7(3),* 26078b12-9436-40fe-8616-500ef880b56a, Weekly Reader Leveled Readers) Stevens, Gareth Publishing LLLP.

—Juegos y Diversiones en la Historia de América (Toys, Games, & Fun in American History), 1 vol. 2006. (Cómo Era la Vida en América (How People Lived in America) Ser.). (SPA.). 24p. (gr. 2-4). pap. 9.15 *(978-0-8368-7436-5(6),* 1d625f58-65e8-4b0f-87e4-ebc13b42671b, Weekly Reader Leveled Readers) Stevens, Gareth Publishing LLLP.

—Toys, Games, & Fun in American History, 1 vol. (How People Lived in America Ser.). (ENG., Illus.). 24p. (gr. 2-4). 2007. lib. bdg. 24.67 *(978-0-8368-7209-5(6),* e0afbc6b-6385-4b6e-85f4-aad5f58b7ac1) 2006. pap. 9.15 *(978-0-8368-7216-3(9),* 5e04904b-e11e-4fb2-86ec-dcb2a3b3c190) Stevens, Gareth Publishing LLLP. (Weekly Reader Leveled Readers).

Mighty Machines: A Lego Adventure in the Real World. 2017. (Illus.). 32p. (J). *(978-1-5182-4494-0(7))* Scholastic, Inc.

Modern Publishing Staff, ed. First to the Finish Line. 2005. 12p. pap. 3.99 *(978-0-7666-1911-1(7))* Modern Publishing.

—Lean Mean Screamin Machines. 2005. 12p. pap. 3.99 *(978-0-7666-1910-4(9))* Modern Publishing.

Moore, Elizabeth. Toys from the Past. 2011. (Wonder Readers Emergent Level Ser.). (ENG.). 8p. (gr. -1-1). pap. 35.94 *(978-1-4296-8236-7(1),* Capstone Pr.) Capstone.

—Toys in the Past, 1 vol. 2011. (Wonder Readers Emergent Level Ser.). (ENG.). 8p. (J). (gr. -1-1). pap. 6.25 *(978-1-4296-7850-6(X),* 118163, Capstone Pr.) Capstone.

Morey, Allan. Miniature Pinschers. 2016. (Tiny Dogs Ser.). (ENG., Illus.). 24p. (J). (gr. -1-2). lib. bdg. 27.32 *(978-1-5157-1968-7(5),* 132641, Capstone Pr.) Capstone.

—Yorkshire Terriers. 2016. (Tiny Dogs Ser.). (ENG., Illus.). 24p. (J). (gr. -1-2). lib. bdg. 27.32 *(978-1-5157-1966-3(9),* 132638, Capstone Pr.) Capstone.

Murphy, Stuart J. Jack the Builder. Rex, Michael, illus. 2006. (MathStart 1 Ser.). (ENG.). 40p. (J). (gr. -1-3). pap. 6.99 *(978-0-06-055775-1(3),* HarperCollins) HarperCollins Pubs.

Murphy, Stuart J. & Rex, Michael. Jack the Builder. 2006. (Mathstart Ser.). (Illus.). 33p. (gr. -1-3). 16.00 *(978-0-7569-6667-6(1))* Perfection Learning Corp.

My Little Firehouse. (Illus.). 12p. (J). (gr. -1-k). bds. *(978-1-56021-354-3(X),* 205) W.J. Fantasy, Inc.

Opuestos. (Coleccion Libritos Acordeon). (SPA., Illus.). (J). 10p. pap. 5.50 *(978-950-11-0826-2(0),* SGM260); 2005. 86p. (gr. -1-18). pap. 7.95 *(978-950-11-0906-1(2),* SGM9062) Sigmar ARG. Dist: Continental Bk. Co., Inc.

Owen, Ruth. Chugs, 1 vol. 2014. (Designer Dogs Ser.). (ENG., Illus.). 32p. (J). (gr. 2-3). lib. bdg. 28.93 *(978-1-4777-7047-4(X),* b0646023-066b-49a6-94c8-d78a0ce94cd2, PowerKids Pr.) Rosen Publishing Group, Inc., The.

—Malshis, 1 vol. 2014. (Designer Dogs Ser.). (ENG., Illus.). 32p. (J). (gr. 2-3). lib. bdg. 28.93 *(978-1-4777-7027-6(5),* 49cff6b5-84f7-43cf-84e0-a5787a227b20, PowerKids Pr.) Rosen Publishing Group, Inc., The.

—Peekapoos, 1 vol. 2014. (Designer Dogs Ser.). (ENG., Illus.). 32p. (J). (gr. 2-3). lib. bdg. 28.93 *(978-1-4777-7031-3(3),* d82ca6d1-d6c6-4c96-86c1-f2d4b3a5a93a, PowerKids Pr.) Rosen Publishing Group, Inc., The.

—Ready, Aim, Fire!, 1 vol., 1. 2014. (DIY for Boys Ser.). (ENG.). 32p. (J). (gr. 4-4). 30.17 *(978-1-4777-6286-8(8),* 40f84193-aa13-43a6-add9-84e0b4cea448, PowerKids Pr.) Rosen Publishing Group, Inc., The.

—Yochons, 1 vol. 2014. (Designer Dogs Ser.). (ENG., Illus.). 32p. (J). (gr. 2-3). lib. bdg. 28.93 *(978-1-4777-7043-6(7),* 723dae03-4452-4967-80be-3a3ae485745c, PowerKids Pr.) Rosen Publishing Group, Inc., The.

—Yorkipoos, 1 vol. 2014. (Designer Dogs Ser.). (ENG., Illus.). 32p. (J). (gr. 2-3). lib. bdg. 28.93 *(978-1-4777-7035-1(6),* f44f05f6-4533-4538-83b3-918841a9c800, PowerKids Pr.) Rosen Publishing Group, Inc., The.

Pack, Linda Hager. Appalachian Toys & Games from a to Z. Banks, Pat, illus. 2013. (ENG.). 56p. 19.95 *(978-0-8131-4104-6(4),* 978-0-8131-4104-6) Univ. Pr. of Kentucky.

Parker, Steve. Robots for Work & Fun. 2010. (Robot World Ser.). 32p. (J). 28.50 *(978-1-60753-071-8(6))* Amicus Learning.

—Robots in Dangerous Places. 2010. (Robot World Ser.). (ENG.). 32p. (J). (gr. 4-6). lib. bdg. 28.50 *(978-1-60753-072-5(4),* 17227) Amicus.

Rice, Dona Herweck. What Toys Can Do. rev. ed. 2019. (Smithsonian: Informational Text Ser.). (ENG., Illus.). 20p. (J). (gr. k-1). 7.99 *(978-1-4938-6638-0(9))* Teacher Created Materials, Inc.

Rigsby, Mike. Amazing Rubber Band Cars: Easy-To-Build Wind-up Racers, Models, & Toys. 2007. (ENG., Illus.). 134p. (J). (gr. 4-18). pap. 16.99 *(978-1-55652-736-4(5))* Chicago Review Pr., Inc.

La Ropa. 2005. (Coleccion Primeras Imagenes). (SPA., Illus.). 86p. (J). (gr. -1-18). pap. 7.95 *(978-950-11-0988-7(7),* SGM9887) Sigmar ARG. Dist: Continental Bk. Co., Inc.

Rosen, Michael J. Balls! Margeson, John, illus. 2006. 72p. (J). (gr. 4-8). 18.95 *(978-1-58196-030-3(1),* Darby Creek) Lerner Publishing Group.

Rosie Raccoon & her Messy Room. 2004. (Play Pals Ser.). (Illus.). 12p. (J). bds. *(978-1-84229-650-9(7))* Top That! Publishing PLC.

Rothrock, Megan H. The LEGO Adventure Book, Vol. 2 Vol. 2: Spaceships, Pirates, Dragons & More! 2013. (Illus.). 196p. (J). (gr. 5). 24.95 *(978-1-59327-512-9(9),* 9781593275129) No Starch Pr., Inc.

—The LEGO Adventure Book, Vol. 3: Robots, Planes, Cities & More!, Vol. 3. 2015. (Illus.). 192p. (J). (gr. 5). 24.95 *(978-1-59327-610-2(9))* No Starch Pr., Inc.

Salzmann, Mary Elizabeth. Know Your Numbers: Toys. 2014. (Numbers 1-20 Ser.). (ENG.). 24p. (J). (gr. -1-3). lib. bdg. 29.93 *(978-1-62403-269-1(9),* 1600, SandCastle) ABDO Publishing Co.

—Money for Toys, 1 vol. 2010. (Your Piggy Bank: a Guide to Spending & Saving for Kids! Ser.). (ENG.). 24p. (J). (gr. k-4). 31.36 *(978-1-61641-032-2(9),* 15846, Looking Glass Library) Magic Wagon.

Sandy Creek (Firm) Staff, contrib. by. Brick by Brick 123. 2016. (Illus.). (J). *(978-1-4351-6407-9(5))* Barnes & Noble, Inc.

Sévigny, Eric, illus. Caillou Puts Away His Toys. 3rd ed. 2012. (Clubhouse Ser.). (ENG.). 24p. (J). (gr. -1-1). pap. 3.99 *(978-2-89450-938-8(3))* Caillouet, Gerry.

Shaughnessy, Mara. LEGO Man in Space: A True Story. 2013. (ENG., Illus.). 32p. (J). (gr. -1-3). 14.95 *(978-1-62087-544-5(6),* 620544, Sky Pony Pr.) Skyhorse Publishing Co., Inc.

Slater, Lee. Lego Manufacturers: The Kristiansen Family. 2015. (Toy Trailblazers Ser.). (ENG., Illus.). 32p. (J). (gr. 3-6). lib. bdg. 32.79 *(978-1-62403-977-5(4),* 19589, Checkerboard Library) ABDO Publishing Co.

—Play-Doh Pioneer: Joseph McVicker. 2015. (Toy Trailblazers Ser.). (ENG., Illus.). 32p. (J). (gr. 3-6). lib. bdg. 32.79 *(978-1-62403-978-2(2),* 19591, Checkerboard Library) ABDO Publishing Co.

—Slinky Innovators: The James Family. 2015. (Toy Trailblazers Ser.). (ENG., Illus.). 32p. (J). (gr. 3-6). lib. bdg. 32.79 *(978-1-62403-979-9(0),* 19593, Checkerboard Library) ABDO Publishing Co.

Smith, Brendan Powell. Assassination! The Brick Chronicle of Attempts on the Lives of Twelve US Presidents. 2013. (ENG., Illus.). 272p. 19.95 *(978-1-62087-998-6(0),* 620998) Skyhorse Publishing Co., Inc.

—The Complete Brick Bible for Kids: Six Classic Bible Stories. 2015. (Illus.). 192p. (J). (gr. -1-k). 15.99 *(978-1-63450-209-2(4),* Sky Pony Pr.) Skyhorse Publishing Co., Inc.

—The Easter Story. 2018. (Illus.). 32p. (J). 14.99 *(978-1-5107-1277-5(1),* Sky Pony Pr.) Skyhorse Publishing Co., Inc.

—Jonah & the Whale: The Brick Bible for Kids. 2014. (Brick Bible for Kids Ser.). (ENG., Illus.). 32p. (J). (gr. -1-k). 12.95 *(978-1-62873-589-5(9),* Sky Pony Pr.) Skyhorse Publishing Co., Inc.

—The Miracles of Jesus: The Brick Bible for Kids. 2017. (ENG.). 32p. (J). 12.99 *(978-1-5107-2697-0(7),* Sky Pony Pr.) Skyhorse Publishing Co., Inc.

—Noah's Ark: The Brick Bible for Kids. 2015. (Brick Bible for Kids Ser.). (ENG., Illus.). 32p. (J). (gr. -1-k). 3.99 *(978-1-63450-054-8(7),* Sky Pony Pr.) Skyhorse Publishing Co., Inc.

Smith, Sian. Levers, 1 vol. 2012. (How Toys Work Ser.). (ENG.). 24p. (gr. -1-1). pap. 6.29 *(978-1-4329-6586-0(7),* 119230, Heinemann) Capstone.

—Pulleys, 1 vol. 2012. (How Toys Work Ser.). (ENG.). 24p. (gr. -1-1). (J). lib. bdg. 25.32 *(978-1-4329-6580-8(8),* 119225); pap. 6.29 *(978-1-4329-6587-7(5),* 119231) Capstone. (Heinemann).

—Ramps & Wedges, 1 vol. 2012. (How Toys Work Ser.). (ENG.). 24p. (gr. -1-1). pap. 6.29 *(978-1-4329-6588-4(3),* 119232, Heinemann) Capstone.

—Screws, Nuts, & Bolts, 1 vol. 2012. (How Toys Work Ser.). (ENG.). 24p. (gr. -1-1). pap. 6.29 *(978-1-4329-6589-1(1),* 119234, Heinemann) Capstone.

—Springs, 1 vol. 2012. (How Toys Work Ser.). (ENG.). 24p. (J). (gr. -1-1). lib. bdg. 25.32 *(978-1-4329-6583-9(2),* 119227, Heinemann) Capstone.

—Wheels & Axles, 1 vol. 2012. (How Toys Work Ser.). (ENG.). 24p. (gr. -1-1). pap. 6.29 *(978-1-4329-6591-4(3),* 119235, Heinemann) Capstone.

Sohn, Emily. Experiments in Forces & Motion with Toys & Everyday Stuff. 2015. (Fun Science Ser.). (ENG., Illus.). 24p. (J). (gr. 1-3). lib. bdg. 27.99 *(978-1-4914-5032-1(0),* 128756, Capstone Pr.) Capstone.

Spinning Top: Level L, 6 vols. (Wonder Worldtm Ser.). 16p. 34.95 *(978-0-7802-2908-2(8))* Wright Group/McGraw-Hill.

Stacia, Ann. Make Your Own Squishies: 15 Slow-Rise & Smooshy Projects for You to Create. 2018. (ENG., Illus.). 96p. (J). (gr. 3-9). pap. 12.99 *(978-1-63158-451-0(0),* Racehorse Publishing) Skyhorse Publishing Co., Inc.

Staff, Gareth Editorial Staff. Things I Play With, 1 vol. 2006. (Things in My World Ser.). (ENG., Illus.). 16p. (gr. k-1). lib. bdg. 21.67 *(978-0-8368-6811-1(0),* 1d12b862-901a-4f65-85bc-83a714901 06d, Weekly Reader Leveled Readers) Stevens, Gareth Publishing LLLP.

—Things I Play with / Las Cosas con Las Que Juego, 1 vol. 2006. (Things in My World / Las Cosas de Mi Mundo Ser.). (ENG & SPA., Illus.). 16p. (gr. k-1). lib. bdg. 21.67 *(978-0-8368-7223-1(1),* 3cf90720-9500-4bef-80ff-dff9e4345b79, Weekly Reader Leveled Readers) Stevens, Gareth Publishing LLLP.

Swank, Samantha. Witches & Wizards Character Handbook (LEGO Harry Potter) 2018. (LEGO Wizarding World of Harry Potter Ser.). (ENG., Illus.). 80p. (J). (gr. 2-5). pap. 7.99 *(978-1-338-26096-0(0))* Scholastic, Inc.

TBD. David & Goliath: the Brick Bible for Kids. 2013. (ENG., Illus.). 32p. (gr. -1-1). 12.95 *(978-1-62087-982-5(4),* 620982, Sky Pony Pr.) Skyhorse Publishing Co., Inc.

Thomas, AnnMarie, et al. Building Squishy Circuits. 2017. (21st Century Skills Innovation Library: Makers As Innovators Junior Ser.). (ENG., Illus.). 24p. (J). (gr. 2-5). lib. bdg. 30.64 *(978-1-63472-690-0(1),* 210058) Cherry Lake Publishing.

Tietjens, Harold. Cybertronian Transformers Index. Tietjens, Harold, photos by. 2003. (ENG., Illus.). 128p. (YA). pap. 29.95 *(978-0-9663588-3-4(X),* 7449ed10-1065-4a68-a5d7-0e409c652f63) Antarctic Pr., Inc.

Time for Toys! (Flip Flap Fun Book Ser.). 10p. (J). bds. *(978-2-7643-0040-4(9))* Phidal Publishing, Inc./Editions Phidal, Inc.

Tocando. (Coleccion Mil Preguntas). (SPA., Illus.). (J). 24p. pap. 5.50 *(978-950-11-0657-2(8),* SGM625); 2005. 86p. (gr. -1-18). pap. 7.95 *(978-950-11-0902-3(X),* SGM902X) Sigmar ARG. Dist: Continental Bk. Co., Inc.

Toy Trailblazers, 6 vols. 2015. (Toy Trailblazers Ser.: 6). (ENG.). 32p. (J). (gr. 3-6). lib. bdg. 196.74 *(978-1-62403-973-7(1),* 19581, Checkerboard Library) ABDO Publishing Co.

Toys with Wheels: Individual Title Six-Packs. (gr. -1-2). 23.00 *(978-0-7635-9006-2(1))* Rigby Education.

The True Cost of Toys. 2014. (Consumer Nation: How to Shop to Change the World Ser.). (ENG., Illus.). 48p. (J). (gr. 6-6). *(978-0-7787-0486-7(6))* Crabtree Publishing Co.

West, Tracey. World of Ninjago Official Guide. 2015. (Illus.). 128p. (J). pap. *(978-0-545-80813-2(8))* Scholastic, Inc.

Which Toys? Individual Title Six-Packs. (gr. -1-2). 23.00 *(978-0-7635-9007-9(X))* Rigby Education.

Wick, Walter. Can You See What I See? Toyland Express: Picture Puzzles to Search & Solve. Wick, Walter, photos by. 2011. (Can You See What I See? Ser.). (ENG., Illus.). 40p. (J). (gr. 1-2). 14.99 *(978-0-545-24483-1(8))* Scholastic, Inc.

Williams, Pam. Remixing Toys. 2018. (21st Century Skills Innovation Library: Makers As Innovators Junior Ser.). (ENG.). 24p. (J). (gr. 2-5). pap. 12.79 *(978-1-5341-0883-7(1),* 210896); (Illus.). lib. bdg. 30.64 *(978-1-5341-0784-7(3),* 210895) Cherry Lake Publishing.

Wolf, Laurie Goldrich. The Lonely Sock Club: One Sock, Tons of Cool Projects! 2011. (Green & Groovy Ser.: 1). (ENG.). 64p. (J). (gr. 3). 16.99 *(978-1-935703-06-8(4))* Downtown Bookworks.

World Book, Inc. Staff, contrib. by. Robots at Play. 2019. (Illus.). 48p. (J). *(978-0-7166-4134-6(8))* World Bk., Inc.

Wulffson, Don. Toys! Amazing Stories Behind Some Great Inventions. Keller, Laurie, illus. 2014. (ENG.). 208p. (J). (gr. 3-7). pap. 10.99 *(978-1-250-03409-0(4),* 900120579) Square Fish.

TOYS—FICTION

Abruzzo, Nancy. Pop Flop's Great Balloon Ride. 2005. (ENG., Illus.). 32p. (J). (gr. k-17). bds. 12.95 *(978-0-89013-475-7(8))* Museum of New Mexico Pr.

Adams, Colleen. At the Toy Store, 1 vol. 2006. (Neighborhood Readers Ser.). (ENG.). 8p. (gr. k-1). pap. 5.15 *(978-1-4042-5732-0(2),* c0b916af-358d-49d9-94dd-62f040e7010c, Rosen Classroom) Rosen Publishing Group, Inc., The.

Adan, Jennifer. I Don't See Heaven. 2013. 24p. pap. 10.99 *(978-1-4808-0307-7(3))* Archway Publishing.

Adderson, Caroline. Jasper John Dooley: Lost & Found. Shiell, Mike, illus. 2015. (Jasper John Dooley Ser.). (ENG.). 128p. (J). (gr. k-3). 15.95 *(978-1-77138-014-0(4))* Kids Can Pr., Ltd. CAN. Dist: Hachette Bk. Group.

Addino, Victoria. Sadie's Wish: Three Little Elves. Garafalo, Beatrice, illus. 2012. 32p. (-18). pap. 24.95 *(978-1-4626-9907-0(3))* America Star Bks.

Ahn, Flora, illus. Two's a Crowd. 2018. 119p. (J). *(978-1-338-27713-5(8),* Scholastic Pr.) Scholastic, Inc.

Akins, David. Tyler's Toys & the Bully. 2010. 28p. 13.99 *(978-1-4520-0304-7(1))* AuthorHouse.

Alfau, Georgette. Alfred & Alex & the Toy Eating Monster. 2009. 16p. 18.95 *(978-0-557-15276-6(3))* Lulu Pr., Inc.

Allison, Teresa J. Bobble Stories: The Bobbleup Pup. Allison, Charles T., illus. 2013. 42p. pap. 12.99 *(978-0-9887612-2-3(X))* Tawnsy Publishing.

Applegate, Katherine. Never Swipe a Bully's Bear. Biggs, Brian, illus. 2008. (Roscoe Riley Rules Ser.: 2). (ENG.). 96p. (J). (gr. 1-5). pap. 4.99 *(978-0-06-114883-5(0))* HarperCollins Pubs.

Arnold, Shauna. Baa. Hines, Irene, illus. 2004. 19p. (J). (gr. -1-3). 12.00 *(978-0-9743669-0-6(0))* Trinity Bks.

Auerbach, Annie. Toy Story 3 (Disney/Pixar Toy Story 3) Molina, Adrian, illus. 2010. (Little Golden Book Ser.). (ENG.). 24p. (J). (gr. -1-2). 5.99 *(978-0-7364-2668-8(X),* Golden/Disney) Random Hse. Children's Bks.

Ballou, Kathy. The Tracks Out Back. l.t. ed. 2005. (Illus.). 24p. (J). per. 10.00 *(978-1-932338-50-8(0))* Lifevest Publishing, Inc.

Banks, Lynne Reid. The Indian in the Cupboard. 2011. 9.14 *(978-0-7848-3449-7(0),* Everbind) Marco Bk. Co.

—The Indian in the Cupboard. 2010. (Indian in the Cupboard Ser.). (ENG.). 240p. (J). (gr. 3-7). 8.99 *(978-0-375-84753-0(7),* Yearling) Random Hse. Children's Bks.

—The Mystery of the Cupboard. Newsom, Tom, illus. 2004. (ENG.). 256p. (J). (gr. 4-18). pap. 7.99 *(978-0-380-72013-2(2),* HarperCollins) HarperCollins Pubs.

—The Return of the Indian. 2010. (Indian in the Cupboard Ser.). (ENG.). 208p. (J). (gr. 3-7). 7.99 *(978-0-375-85523-8(8),* Yearling) Random Hse. Children's Bks.

—The Secret of the Indian. 2010. (Indian in the Cupboard Ser.). (ENG.). 192p. (J). (gr. 3-7). 7.99 *(978-0-375-85524-5(6),* Yearling) Random Hse. Children's Bks.

—Secret of the Indian. 2003. (ENG., Illus.). 160p. pap. *(978-0-00-714900-1(X),* Collins) HarperCollins Pubs. Ltd.

Banks, Lynne Reid & Banks, L. The Return of the Indian. 2010. (Indian in the Cupboard Ser.: 2). (gr. 3-6). lib. bdg. 17.20 *(978-0-8335-0902-4(0))* Turtleback.

Banks, Steven. The Song That Never Ends. DePorter, Vince, illus. 2004. (Spongebob Squarepants Ser.). 32p. (J). (gr. k-2). 11.65 *(978-0-7569-5374-4(X))* Perfection Learning Corp.

—Special Delivery. DePorter, Vince, illus. 2005. (Ready-to-Read Ser.). 32p. (J). lib. bdg. 15.00 *(978-1-59054-986-5(4))* Fitzgerald Bks.

Barchers, Suzanne I. Get to Bed, Ren!, 1 vol. rev. ed. 2011. (Phonics Ser.). (ENG.). 16p. (gr. k-1). 6.99 *(978-1-4333-2416-1(4))* Teacher Created Materials, Inc.

Barradel, Isabel. Toyshop Tales. 2006. 275p. pap. 27.95 *(978-1-4241-2798-6(X))* PublishAmerica, Inc.

Barradell, Isabel. Even More Tales from the Toyshop. 2008. 380p. pap. 29.95 *(978-1-60474-508-5(8))* America Star Bks.

Baxter, Nicola. Tales from the Toy Box. Press, Jenny, illus. 2012. 80p. (J). (gr. k-4). pap. 9.99 *(978-1-84322-951-3(X))* Anness Publishing GBR. Dist: National Bk. Network.

Bell, Cece. Sock Monkey Boogie Woogie: A Friend Is Made. Bell, Cece, illus. 2015. (Cece Bell's Sock Monkey Ser.).

(ENG., Illus.). 32p. (J). (gr. -1-3). 14.00 *(978-0-7636-7758-9(2))* Candlewick Pr.
—Sock Monkey Takes a Bath. Bell, Cece, illus. 2015. (Cece Bell's Sock Monkey Ser.). (ENG., Illus.). 32p. (J). (gr. -1-3). 14.00 *(978-0-7636-7759-6(0))* Candlewick Pr.
Bell, Tom. Where the Lost Things Go. 2012. (Illus.). 48p. (J). 15.00 *(978-1-84135-874-1(6))*; (ENG., pap. 9.95 *(978-1-84135-892-5(4))* Award Pubns. Ltd. GBR. Dist: Parkwest Pubns., Inc.
Bellisario, Gina. Super Fluffy to the Rescue. Von Innerebner, Jessika, illus. 2016. (Ellie Ultra Ser.). (ENG.). 128p. (J). (gr. 1-3). lib. bdg. 25.99 *(978-1-4965-3142-1(6)*, 132196, Stone Arch Bks.) Capstone.
Benedictus, David. Return to the Hundred Acre Wood. Burgess, Mark, illus. 2009. (Winnie-The-Pooh Ser.). (ENG.). 216p. (J). (gr. 3-7). 21.99 *(978-0-525-42160-3(2)*, Dutton Books for Young Readers) Penguin Young Readers Group.
Bernstein, Ariel. Warren & Dragon 100 Friends. Malbrough, Mike, illus. 2018. (Warren & Dragon Ser.: 1). 96p. (J). (gr. k-3). 5.99 *(978-0-425-28846-7(3)*, Puffin Books); 14.99 *(978-0-425-28844-3(7)*, Viking Books for Young Readers) Penguin Young Readers Group.
Bernstein, Susan H. N. E. Pominonous Epstein Minds His Mind. (E. Pominonous Epstein Ser.). 18p. (J). (gr. -1-3). pap. 8.95 *(978-0-9706596-0-6(1))* Bernstein, Susan.
Bianco, Margery Williams. Poor Cecco. Rackham, Arthur, illus. 2013. (ENG.). 160p. (J). (gr. 3-12). pap. 9.99 *(978-0-486-49226-1(5))* Dover Pubns., Inc.
—The Velveteen Rabbit. Felix, Monique, illus. 2013. (ENG.). 40p. (J). (gr. 2-5). pap. 8.99 *(978-0-89812-831-4(5)*, 22070, Creative Paperbacks) Creative Co., The.
—The Velveteen Rabbit, or, How Toys Become Real. Nicholson, William, illus. 2015. iii, 27p. (J). pap. *(978-1-4677-9307-0(8)*, First Avenue Editions) Lerner Publishing Group.
Birchall, Mark. Rabbit's Birthday Surprise. Birchall, Mark, illus. 2003. (Illus.). 32p. (J). (gr. -1-3). 15.95 *(978-0-87614-910-2(7)*, Carolrhoda Bks.) Lerner Publishing Group.
—Rabbit's Wooly Sweater. Birchall, Mark, illus. 2003. (Picture Bks.). (Illus.). 32p. (J). (gr. -1-3). 15.95 *(978-1-57505-465-0(5)*, Carolrhoda Bks.) Lerner Publishing Group.
Birney, Betty G. Humphrey's Really Wheely Racing Day. Burris, Priscilla, illus. 2014. (Humphrey's Tiny Tales Ser.: 1). (ENG.). 96p. (J). (gr. k-3). pap. 6.99 *(978-0-14-751485-1(1)*, Puffin Books) Penguin Young Readers Group.
Blizzard on Moose Mountain. 2007. (J). pap. *(978-0-9794542-0-2(4))* Battat, Inc.
Blyton, Enid. The Little Toy Engine & Other Stories. 2013. (Illus.). 192p. (J). 9.95 *(978-1-84135-460-6(0))* Award Pubns. Ltd. GBR. Dist: Parkwest Pubns., Inc.
Boldt, Mike. Attack of the 50-Foot Fluffy. Boldt, Mike, illus. 2018. (ENG., Illus.). 32p. (J). (gr. -1-3). 18.99 *(978-1-4814-4887-1(0)*, McElderry, Margaret K. Bks.) McElderry, Margaret K. Bks.
Bolger, Kevin. Zombiekins 2. Blecha, Aaron, illus. 2011. (J). 10.99 *(978-1-59514-432-4(3)*, Razorbill) Penguin Publishing Group.
Breece, Beverly. The Curwood Acorns. DeWeese, Susan, illus. 2012. 40p. pap. 24.95 *(978-1-4626-8202-7(2))* America Star Bks.
Brett, Jan. Jan Brett's the Nutcracker. Brett, Jan, illus. 2021. (Illus.). 32p. (J). (gr. -1-3). 18.99 *(978-0-593-10982-3(1)*, G.P. Putnam's Sons Books for Young Readers) Penguin Young Readers Group.
Brezenoff, Steve. Curses for Sale, 1 vol. Percival, Tom, illus. 2012. (Ravens Pass Ser.). (ENG.). 96p. (J). (gr. 3-6). pap. 6.15 *(978-1-4342-4209-9(9)*, 120266, Stone Arch Bks.) Capstone.
Bright, J. E. Attack of the Legion of Doom! 2016. (LEGO DC Super Heroes Ser.). (ENG., Illus.). 64p. (J). (gr. 2-5). pap. 4.99 *(978-0-545-86799-3(1))* Scholastic, Inc.
—Escape from Prison Island. 2016. (LEGO City 8X8 Ser.). lib. bdg. 13.55 *(978-0-606-38828-3(1))* Turtleback.
Brinkley, Lonnie. I Believe: Lost at the North Pole. 2008. (Illus.). 450p. (J). 29.95 *(978-0-9801215-3-7(1))* Big Bear Publishing U.S.
Brody, Jessica. A Dragon in the Castle? 2018. (Illus.). 94p. (J). *(978-1-5444-2142-1(7))* Disney Publishing Worldwide.
—A Dragon in the Castle?, 2. 2019. (Lego Disney Princess Ch Bks). (ENG., Illus.). 96p. (J). (gr. 2-4). 16.79 *(978-1-64310-791-2(7))* Penworthy Co., LLC, The.
Brooke, Samantha. Fire in the Forest! Kiernan, Kenny, illus. 2012. 31p. (J). *(978-1-4242-5340-1(3))* Scholastic, Inc.
—Fire in the Forest! 2012. (LEGO City Scholastic Readers Level 1 Ser.). (Illus.). 31p. (J). lib. bdg. 13.55 *(978-0-606-23730-7(5))* Turtleback.
Brown, Alan James. Love-a-Duck. Chessa, Francesca, illus. 2010. (ENG.). 32p. (J). (gr. -1-1). pap. 16.95 *(978-0-8234-2263-0(1))* Holiday Hse., Inc.
Brown, Gwen. Clifford & His Bear. 2006. (Illus.). 48p. pap. *(978-1-84401-650-1(1))* Athena Pr.
Buell, Janet. Sail Away, Little Boat. Ishida, Jui, illus. 2006. 32p. (J). 15.95 *(978-1-57505-821-4(9)*, Carolrhoda Bks.) Lerner Publishing Group.
Buller, Laura. The Friendship Bridge. 2018. (Illus.). 27p. (J). *(978-1-5490-5626-0(3))* Disney Publishing Worldwide.
—The Friendship Bridge. 2019. (World of Reading Ser.). (ENG., Illus.). 32p. (J). (gr. k-2). 13.89 *(978-1-64310-799-8(2))* Penworthy Co., LLC, The.
—Lost & Found. 2018. (Illus.). 31p. (J). *(978-1-5490-5625-3(5))* Disney Publishing Worldwide.
—Lost & Found. 2019. (World of Reading Ser.). (ENG., Illus.). 32p. (J). (gr. k-2). 13.89 *(978-1-64310-800-1(X))* Penworthy Co., LLC, The.
Bunting, Eve. Ducky. Wisniewski, David, illus. 2004. (ENG.). 32p. (J). (gr. -1-k). 7.99 *(978-0-618-43240-0(X)*, 100352, Clarion Bks.) HarperCollins Pubs.
—Reggie. Burkett, D. Brent, illus. 2006. (ENG.). 112p. (J). (gr. 1-4). 16.95 *(978-0-8126-2746-6(6))* Cricket Bks.
Butterworth, Nick. Albert the Bear to the Rescue. 2008. (J). 16.99 *(978-0-06-147046-2(5))* HarperCollins Pubs.
Byrd, B. N. My Favorite Toy. 2011. 40p. pap. 21.99 *(978-1-4500-5290-0(8))* Xlibris Corp.
Calhoun, Terry. The Muggwapps. 2007. (J). pap. 8.00 *(978-0-8059-7223-8(4))* Dorrance Publishing Co., Inc.
Carle, Eric. 10 Little Rubber Ducks: An Easter & Springtime Book for Kids. Carle, Eric, illus. 2005. (ENG., Illus.). 36p. (J). (gr. -1-1). 22.99 *(978-0-06-074075-7(2)*, HarperCollins) HarperCollins Pubs.
—10 Little Rubber Ducks Board Book: An Easter & Springtime Book for Kids. Carle, Eric, illus. 2010. (ENG., Illus.). 34p. (J). (gr. -1-k). bds. 10.99 *(978-0-06-196428-2(X)*, HarperFestival) HarperCollins Pubs.
Carsey, Alice, illus. Pinocchio. 2005.Tr. of Avventure di Pinocchio. (ENG.). 136p. (J). (gr. 2-5). 19.95 *(978-1-933327-00-6(6))* Purple Bear Bks., Inc.
Casado, Dami. Como Comes Tu? (SPA.). 8p. 9.95 *(978-84-272-8325-1(3))* Molino, Editorial ESP. Dist: Distribooks, Inc.
—Como Te Lavas? (SPA.). 8p. 9.95 *(978-84-272-8326-8(1))* Molino, Editorial ESP. Dist: Distribooks, Inc.
—Como Te Vistes? (SPA.). 8p. 9.95 *(978-84-272-8328-2(8))* Molino, Editorial ESP. Dist: Distribooks, Inc.
Castillo, Lauren. The Troublemaker. 2014. (ENG., Illus.). 48p. (J). (gr. -1-3). 16.99 *(978-0-547-72991-6(X)*, 1483968, Clarion Bks.) HarperCollins Pubs.
Cecil, Lauren. Pooh's Cleanup. Grey, Andrew, illus. 2011. (Disney Classic Pooh Ser.). (ENG.). 24p. (J). (gr. -1-3). 16.19 *(978-0-448-45558-7(7)*, Grosset & Dunlap) Penguin Publishing Group.
Chester, Malcolm. Elysia: The World in Children's Dreams. 2012. (ENG.). 320p. 29.11 *(978-1-4669-4812-9(4))*; pap. 19.11 *(978-1-4669-4810-5(8))* Trafford Publishing.
Chichester Clark, Emma. Merry Christmas, Blue Kangaroo! (Blue Kangaroo) Chichester Clark, Emma, illus. 2017. (Blue Kangaroo Ser.). (ENG., Illus.). 32p. 17.99 *(978-0-00-824219-0(4)*, HarperCollins Children's Bks.) HarperCollins Pubs. Ltd. GBR. Dist: HarperCollins Pubs.
—When I First Met You, Blue Kangaroo! (Blue Kangaroo) Chichester Clark, Emma, illus. 2018. (Blue Kangaroo Ser.). (ENG., Illus.). 32p. (J). pap. 6.99 *(978-0-00-825430-8(3)*, HarperCollins Children's Bks.) HarperCollins Pubs. Ltd. GBR. Dist: HarperCollins Pubs.
—Where Are You, Blue Kangaroo? (Blue Kangaroo) Chichester Clark, Emma, illus. 2019. (Blue Kangaroo Ser.). (ENG., Illus.). 32p. (J). pap. 6.99 *(978-0-00-826628-8(X)*, HarperCollins Children's Bks.) HarperCollins Pubs. Ltd. GBR. Dist: HarperCollins Pubs.
Choldenko, Gennifer. Dad & the Dinosaur. Santat, Dan, illus. 2017. (ENG.). 40p. (J). (gr. k-3). 18.99 *(978-0-399-24353-0(4)*, G.P. Putnam's Sons Books for Young Readers) Penguin Young Readers Group.
Chou, Yih-fen. Mimi Tidies Up. Chen, Zhiyuan, illus. 2011. (J). *(978-0-9845523-6-8(7))* Heryin Publishing Corp.
Clark, Harriet. Davy Asks His Dad. Clark, Tim, photos by. 2012. (Illus.). 32p. pap. *(978-1-77097-977-2(8))* FriesenPress.
CleverKits, creator. Safari Adventure. 2006. (J). (gr. -1-2). audio compact disk 19.95 *(978-0-9778771-1-9(6))* CleverKits,LLC.
—Under the Sea. 2006. (J). (gr. -1-2). audio compact disk 19.95 *(978-0-9778771-0-2(8))* CleverKits,LLC.
Cole, Henry. The Somewhat True Adventures of Sammy Shine, 1 vol. 2018. (Illus.). 272p. (J). (gr. 3-7). pap. 7.95 *(978-1-56145-778-6(7))* Peachtree Publishing Co. Inc.
Collins, Heather, illus. Jack & Jill. 2003. (Traditional Nursery Rhymes Ser.). (ENG.). 12p. (J). (gr. -1 — 1). bds. 3.95 *(978-1-55337-075-8(9))* Kids Can Pr., Ltd. CAN. Dist: Hachette Bk. Group.
—Little Miss Muffet. 2003. (Traditional Nursery Rhymes Ser.). (ENG.). 12p. (J). (gr. -1 — 1). bds. 3.95 *(978-1-55337-076-5(7))* Kids Can Pr., Ltd. CAN. Dist: Hachette Bk. Group.
Cook, Melissa. Anna & the Garden Fairy: Anna's Little Black Bear. 2009. (ENG., Illus.). 20p. (J). 14.95 *(978-1-57197-501-0(2)*, Ivy House Publishing Group) Pentland Pr., Inc.
Cooper, Helen S. Historias de Juguetes. (SPA., Illus.). 80p. (J). (gr. k-2). 23.95 *(978-84-261-3127-0(1)*, JV1108) Juventud, Editorial ESP. Dist: Lectorum Pubns., Inc.
—Tatty-Ratty. Cooper, Helen S., illus. 2004. (Illus.). 28p. (J). (gr. k-3). reprint ed. 19.00 *(978-0-7567-7214-7(1))* DIANE Publishing Co.
Corderoy, Tracey. It's Potty Time! Pedler, Caroline, illus. 2014. (ENG.). 22p. (J). (gr. -1-k). bds. 8.99 *(978-1-58925-574-6(7))* Tiger Tales.
Las Cosas Del Cuarto de Baño. (SPA.). 24p. 7.95 *(978-84-488-1110-5(0))* Beascoa, Ediciones S.A. ESP. Dist: Distribooks, Inc.
Cowell, Cressida. That Rabbit Belongs to Emily Brown. Layton, Neal, illus. 2007. (ENG.). 40p. (gr. -1-3). 16.99 *(978-1-4231-0645-6(8))* Hyperion Pr.
Cowley, Joy. Miss Doll & Friends: A Surprise for Miss Doll. Bordicchia, Gaia, illus. 2014. (ENG.). 8p. pap. *(978-0-927244-52-7(7)*, Joy Cowley Club) Flying Start Bks.
—Miss Doll & Friends: Old Jokes. Bordicchia, Gaia, illus. 2014. (ENG.). 8p. pap. *(978-0-927244-60-2(8)*, Joy Cowley Club) Flying Start Bks.
—Miss Doll & Friends: Red Lipstick. Bordicchia, Gaia, illus. 2014. (ENG.). 8p. pap. *(978-0-927244-78-7(0)*, Joy Cowley Club) Flying Start Bks.
—Miss Doll & Friends: Rocking Race. Bordicchia, Gaia, illus. 2014. (ENG.). 8p. pap. *(978-0-927244-64-0(0)*, Joy Cowley Club) Flying Start Bks.
—Miss Doll & Friends: The Rainbow Bird. Bordicchia, Gaia, illus. 2014. (ENG.). 8p. pap. *(978-0-927244-65-7(9)*, Joy Cowley Club) Flying Start Bks.
—Miss Doll & Friends: Tin Clown. Bordicchia, Gaia, illus. 2014. (ENG.). 8p. pap. *(978-0-927244-55-8(1)*, Joy Cowley Club) Flying Start Bks.
—Miss Doll & Friends: Tin Clown's Hat. Bordicchia, Gaia, illus. 2014. (ENG.). 8p. pap. *(978-0-927244-79-4(9)*, Joy Cowley Club) Flying Start Bks.
—Miss Doll & Friends: Toy Music. Bordicchia, Gaia, illus. 2014. (ENG.). 8p. pap. *(978-0-927244-59-6(4)*, Joy Cowley Club) Flying Start Bks.
—Miss Doll & Friends: Where Is Fire Engine? Bordicchia, Gaia, illus. 2014. (ENG.). 8p. pap. *(978-0-927244-57-2(8)*, Joy Cowley Club) Flying Start Bks.
—Miss Doll & Friends: Yellow Duck. Bordicchia, Gaia, illus. 2014. (ENG.). 8p. pap. *(978-0-927244-62-6(4)*, Joy Cowley Club) Flying Start Bks.
Cox, Katherine. The Missing Fox. Brantley Newton, Vanessa, illus. 2015. 32p. (J). *(978-1-4806-8800-1(2))* Scholastic, Inc.
Crimi, Carolyn. There Might Be Lobsters. Molk, Laurel, illus. 2017. (ENG.). 32p. (J). (gr. -1-2). 18.99 *(978-0-7636-7542-4(3))* Candlewick Pr.
Curious George Car Wash. 2013. (Curious George Ser.). (ENG., Illus.). 24p. (J). (gr. -1-3). pap. 5.99 *(978-0-547-94086-1(6)*, 1516996, Clarion Bks.) HarperCollins Pubs.
Curious George Saves His Pennies. 2014. (Curious George Ser.). (ENG., Illus.). 24p. (J). (gr. -1-3). pap. 5.99 *(978-0-547-81853-5(X)*, 1496643, Clarion Bks.) HarperCollins Pubs.
Curious George Takes a Trip (Reader Level 1) 2007. (Curious George TV Ser.). (ENG., Illus.). 24p. (J). (gr. -1-3). pap. 4.99 *(978-0-618-88403-2(3)*, 491698, Clarion Bks.) HarperCollins Pubs.
Curious George Tool Time (Cgtv Board Book) 2013. (Curious George Ser.). (ENG., Illus.). 12p. (J). (gr. -1 — 1). bds. 6.99 *(978-0-547-96818-6(3)*, 1521230, Clarion Bks.) HarperCollins Pubs.
Custer, Jason. Everyday Monsters. 2005. (J). lib. bdg. 19.95 *(978-0-9754728-3-5(6))* Big Ransom Studio.
Danowski, Sonja. Little Night Cat. Danowski, Sonja, illus. 2016. (ENG., Illus.). 48p. 19.95 *(978-0-7358-4266-3(3))* North-South Bks., Inc.
Davidson, Susanna. Nutcracker with Music. 2012. (Picture Books with Music Ser.). 24p. (J). bds. 18.99 *(978-0-7945-2646-7(2)*, Usborne) EDC Publishing.
Davies, Beth. Ninja in Action! 2018. (DK Readers Ser.). (ENG.). 23p. (J). (gr. -1-1). 13.89 *(978-1-64310-615-1(5))* Penworthy Co., LLC, The.
—Team Batman. 2017. (Illus.). 24p. (J). *(978-1-5182-3634-1(0))* Dorling Kindersley Publishing, Inc.
Davis, Jacky. Ladybug Girl & the Best Ever Playdate. Soman, David, illus. 2015. (Ladybug Girl Ser.). 40p. (J). (gr. -1-k). 17.99 *(978-0-8037-4030-3(1)*, Dial Bks) Penguin Young Readers Group.
Daywalt, Drew. The Epic Adventures of Huggie & Stick. Spencer, David, illus. 2018. 40p. (J). (gr. -1-3). 17.99 *(978-0-399-17276-2(9)*, Philomel Bks.) Penguin Young Readers Group.
de Sève, Randall & de Sève, Randall. Toy Boat. Long, Loren, illus. 2014. 32p. (J). (gr. -1 — 1). bds. 7.99 *(978-0-399-16797-3(8)*, Philomel Bks.) Penguin Young Readers Group.
—The Toy Boat. Long, Loren, illus. 2007. 40p. (J). (gr. -1-2). 18.99 *(978-0-399-24374-5(7)*, Philomel Bks.) Penguin Young Readers Group.
DeBord, Tina Ballon. Smell My Elephant. DeBord, Kim Jackson, illus. 2017. (ENG.). 32p. (J). (gr. k-3). 16.99 *(978-1-58536-992-8(6)*, 204235) Sleeping Bear Pr.
Deedman, Heidi. Too Many Toys! Deedman, Heidi, illus. 2015. (ENG., Illus.). 32p. (J). (gr. -1-1). 15.99 *(978-0-7636-7861-6(9))* Candlewick Pr.
deGroat, Diane. Happy Birthday to You, You Belong in a Zoo. deGroat, Diane, illus. 2007. (Gilbert & Friends Ser.). (Illus.). (gr. -1-3). 17.00 *(978-0-7569-8108-2(5))* Perfection Learning Corp.
Dempster, Al. Santa's Toy Shop (Disney) RH Disney, illus. 2015. (Little Golden Book Ser.). (ENG.). 24p. (J). (-k). 5.99 *(978-0-7364-3401-0(1)*, Golden/Disney) Random Hse. Children's Bks.
Depken, Kristen L. Merry Christmas, Woody. 2013. lib. bdg. 13.55 *(978-0-606-32213-3(2))* Turtleback.
—Merry Christmas, Woody (Disney/Pixar Toy Story) RH Disney, illus. 2013. (Pictureback(R) Ser.). (ENG.). 16p. (J). (gr. -1-2). 5.99 *(978-0-7364-3070-8(9)*, RH/Disney) Random Hse. Children's Bks.
—The Pet Problem (Disney/Pixar Toy Story) Egan, Caroline, illus. 2011. (Little Golden Book Ser.). (ENG.). 24p. (J). (gr. -1-2). 4.99 *(978-0-7364-2698-5(1)*, Golden/Disney) Random Hse. Children's Bks.
—A Roaring Adventure (Disney/Pixar Toy Story) Holtsclaw, Josh, illus. 2012. (Little Golden Book Ser.). (ENG.). 24p. (J). (gr. k-k). 5.99 *(978-0-7364-2907-8(7)*, Golden/Disney) Random Hse. Children's Bks.
—Scuffy the Tugboat. DiCicco, Sue, illus. 2017. (Step into Reading Ser.). 32p. (J). (gr. -1-1). 4.99 *(978-1-101-93929-1(X)*, Random Hse. Bks. for Young Readers) Random Hse. Children's Bks.
—Where's Woody? (Disney/Pixar Toy Story) RH Disney, illus. 2012. (Pictureback(R) Ser.). (ENG.). 16p. (J). (gr. -1-2). pap. 5.99 *(978-0-7364-2850-7(X)*, RH/Disney) Random Hse. Children's Bks.
Devargas, Casey Anthony. The Kindergarten Treasure. 2012. 44p. pap. 7.00 *(978-0-9859042-0-3(8))* CD Publishing.
deVet, L. J. Teddy's Christmas Wish. Zabarylo-Duma, Ewa, illus. 2013. 46p. (J). pap. *(978-0-9873686-5-2(6))* Print-Rite Publishers.
Dicamillo, Kate. The Miraculous Journey of Edward Tulane. 2012. 22.00 *(978-1-61383-813-6(1))* Perfection Learning Corp.
—The Miraculous Journey of Edward Tulane. 2015. lib. bdg. 17.20 *(978-0-606-37892-5(8))* Turtleback.
DiCamillo, Kate. The Miraculous Journey of Edward Tulane. Ibatoulline, Bagram, illus. (ENG.). (J). 2015. 240p. (gr. 2-5). pap. 8.99 *(978-0-7636-8090-9(7))* 2009. 228p. (gr. 2-5). pap. 14.99 *(978-0-7636-4783-4(7))* 2006. 228p. (gr. 1-4). 19.99 *(978-0-7636-2589-4(2))* Candlewick Pr.
Dicamillo, Kate. The Miraculous Journey of Edward Tulane. Ibatoulline, Bagram, illus. 2009. 198p. (gr. 8-12). 23.30 *(978-1-4178-0763-5(6))* Turtleback.
Dietrich, Christopher & Character Building Studio (Firm) Staff. Doc on Call. 2015. (Illus.). (J). *(978-1-4847-2292-3(2))* Disney Publishing Worldwide.
Disney Editors. Disney Zootopia Cinestory. 2016. (J). lib. bdg. 26.95 *(978-0-606-38728-6(5))* Turtleback.
Disney Press Editors. Dad's Favorite Toy. 2015. (Doc Mcstuffins 8X8 Ser.). (J). lib. bdg. 14.75 *(978-0-606-36898-8(1))* Turtleback.
—Training Army Al. 2014. (Doc Mcstuffins 8X8 Ser.). (J). lib. bdg. 13.55 *(978-0-606-35910-8(9))* Turtleback.
Disney/Pixar 6. 2010. bds. 12.99 *(978-1-4231-2789-5(7))* Disney Pr.
Dixon, Bob. Holiday Bunny. 2009. 28p. pap. 13.99 *(978-1-4490-0436-1(9))* AuthorHouse.
d'Lacey, Chris. Frankin's Bear. Taylor, Thomas, illus. 2005. (Red Go Bananas Ser.). (ENG.). 48p. (J). (gr. 2-3). *(978-0-7787-2696-8(7))* Crabtree Publishing Co.
Don, Freeman. Corduroy. 2014. (Corduroy Ser.). (ENG.). 32p. (J). (gr. k-12). 11.24 *(978-1-63245-291-7(X))* Lectorum Pubns., Inc.
Dorling Kindersley Publishing Staff. Attack of the Clones. 2013. (LEGO Star Wars DK Reader Ser.). lib. bdg. 13.55 *(978-0-606-32111-2(X))* Turtleback.
—Revenge of the Sith. 2013. (LEGO Star Wars DK Reader Ser.). lib. bdg. 13.55 *(978-0-606-32112-9(8))* Turtleback.
Drake, R. C. Let's Find a Toy for Moo Moo the Mutdog. 2011. 24p. pap. 24.95 *(978-1-4560-0881-9(1))* America Star Bks.
Drinnon, Sheila. Cuddles. 2008. 24p. pap. 24.95 *(978-1-60474-857-4(5))* America Star Bks.
Driscoll, Laura. A Mousy Mess. Melmon, Deborah, illus. 2014. (Mouse Math (r) Ser.). 32p. (J). (gr. -1-1). 22.60 *(978-1-57565-646-5(9))* Astra Publishing Hse.
—A Mousy Mess. 2018. (Mouse Math Ser.). (ENG.). 32p. (J). (gr. -1-1). lib. bdg. 34.28 *(978-1-4896-8295-6(3)*, AV2 by Weigl) Weigl Pubs., Inc.
—Real Heroes Don't Wear Capes. 2008. pap. 34.95 *(978-1-58013-764-5(4))* Astra Publishing Hse.
Dunrea, Olivier. Gideon & Otto Board Book. Dunrea, Olivier, illus. 2013. (Gossie & Friends Ser.). (ENG., Illus.). 32p. (J). (— 1). bds. 7.99 *(978-0-547-98398-1(0)*, 1524122, Clarion Bks.) HarperCollins Pubs.
Easton, Marilyn. New Girl in Town. 2013. (LEGO Friends Chapter Bks.: 1). lib. bdg. 14.75 *(978-0-606-31548-7(9))* Turtleback.
Elizabeth, Julie & Elizabeth, Annelise. Take Care of Our Friend, Baby Dog. 2012. 24p. pap. 13.95 *(978-1-61493-115-7(1))* Peppertree Pr., The.
Emma Treehouse Ltd. My Toys. Davis, Caroline, illus. 2007. (Easy Flaps Ser.). 10p. (J). (gr. -1). bds. 6.95 *(978-1-58925-825-9(8))* Tiger Tales.
Engler, Michael. Elephantastic! Tourlonias, Joëlle, illus. 2014. (ENG.). 32p. (J). 16.99 *(978-1-4413-0841-2(5)*, 9781441308412) Peter Pauper Pr. Inc.
Eshed, Tina. The Adventures of Bunzy: The Beginning. 2009. 60p. pap. 24.49 *(978-1-4389-2673-5(1))* AuthorHouse.
Everett, Clare. Henrietta - a Rabbit's Tale of Summer Time Fun. 2012. 116p. pap. *(978-1-84914-296-0(3))* CompletelyNovel.com.
Eyvindson, Peter. Chester Bear, Where Are You?, 1 vol. 2015. (ENG., Illus.). 32p. (J). (gr. -1-1). pap. 10.95 *(978-0-921827-08-5(3)*, f1112c31-5d85-49f9-9124-5c93634c7fb1) Pemmican Pubns., Inc. CAN. Dist: Firefly Bks., Ltd.
Fagan, Cary. Thing-Thing. Debon, Nicolas, illus. 2008. 32p. (J). (gr. -1-1). 18.95 *(978-0-88776-839-2(3)*, Tundra Bks.) Tundra Bks. CAN. Dist: Penguin Random Hse. LLC.
Falconer, Ian. Olivia ... & the Missing Toy. Falconer, Ian, illus. 2003. (ENG., Illus.). 42p. (J). (gr. -1-3). 19.99 *(978-0-689-85291-6(6)*, Atheneum Bks. for Young Readers) Simon & Schuster Children's Publishing.
—Olivia y el Juguete Desaparecido. Mlawer, Teresa, tr. from ENG. Falconer, Ian, illus. 2004. (Olivia Ser.).Tr. of Olivia & the Missing Toy. (SPA., Illus.). 30p. (J). 16.95 *(978-1-930332-71-3(8))* Lectorum Pubns., Inc.
Farshtey, Greg. The Doom Box. 2012. (LEGO Hero Factory Ser.: 1). lib. bdg. 16.00 *(978-0-606-26768-7(9))* Turtleback.
—Fire & Ice. 2014. (LEGO Legends of Chima Chapter Bks.: 6). lib. bdg. 14.75 *(978-0-606-36069-2(7))* Turtleback.
—Handbook: Updated Edition (LEGO DC Super Heroes) 2015. (LEGO DC Super Heroes Ser.). (ENG.). 144p. (J). (gr. -1-3). pap. 9.99 *(978-0-545-86800-6(9))* Scholastic, Inc.
—Lego DC Super Heroes. 2013. (LEGO DC Super Heroes Ser.). lib. bdg. 19.65 *(978-0-606-32019-1(9))* Turtleback.
—Mirror World, 5. 2013. (Lego Hero Factory: Secret Mission Ser.: 5). (ENG.). 144p. (J). (gr. 3-6). pap. 18.69 *(978-0-545-51271-8(9))* Scholastic, Inc.
—Mirror World. 2013. (LEGO Hero Factory Ser.: 5). lib. bdg. 16.00 *(978-0-606-32020-7(2))* Turtleback.
—Robot Rampage. 2013. (LEGO Hero Factory Ser.: 4). lib. bdg. 16.00 *(978-0-606-31542-5(X))* Turtleback.
Fellers, Tina. Toby & the Alien: In the Adventures of the Unusual Toys, 1 vol. Fellers, Cody, illus. 2009. 28p. pap. 24.95 *(978-1-60672-195-7(X))* America Star Bks.
Fentiman, David. The Lego Movie. 2013. (DK Reader Level 3 Ser.). lib. bdg. 13.55 *(978-0-606-35322-9(4))* Turtleback.
Fieber, Valerie. Three Caterpillars & a Lost Toy. 2012. (ENG.). 24p. pap. 14.93 *(978-1-4669-5573-8(2))* Trafford Publishing.
Field, Elaine. Toys (Cuddly Cuffs W/Hang Tag) Finn, Rebecca, illus. (Cuddly Cuffs Ser.). 12p. (J). tchr. ed. 5.95 *(978-1-58925-709-2(X))* Tiger Tales.
Filliozat, Isabelle. Jealousy: A Toy Story Tale. 2020. (J). *(978-1-5415-9859-1(8))* Lerner Publishing Group.
Fine, Anne. Jamie & Angus Together. Dale, Penny, illus. 2007. (Jamie & Angus Ser.). (ENG.). 112p. (J). (gr. -1-1). 15.99 *(978-0-7636-3374-5(7))* Candlewick Pr.
Finnegan, Evelyn M. My Little Friend Goes to a Baseball Game. Houghton, Diane R., illus. 2006. 32p. (J). (gr. -1-3). reprint ed. pap. 7.00 *(978-1-4223-5403-2(2))* DIANE Publishing Co.
Fitzgerald, Caroline. Animal Kingdom Goes to New York. 2011. 48p. pap. 18.46 *(978-1-4520-9966-8(9))* AuthorHouse.
Fleischman, Paul. Whirligig. 2010. (ENG.). 144p. (YA). (gr. 7-12). pap. 7.99 *(978-0-312-62911-3(7)*, 900066875) Square Fish.
Fontana, Shea & Nee, Chris. Smitten with a Kitten. 2016. (Doc Mcstuffins Ser.). (ENG., Illus.). 24p. (J). (gr. -1-1). 17.44 *(978-1-4844-8806-5(7))* Disney Pr.
Fontes, Justine. Toy Trouble. Hefferan, Rob, illus. 2003. 24p. (J). pap. *(978-1-59034-447-7(2))*; 14.95 *(978-1-59034-446-0(4))* Mondo Publishing.
Foreman, Michael. Scraps. (ENG., Illus.). 32p. (J). pap. 8.99 *(978-1-84270-003-7(0))* Andersen Pr. GBR. Dist: Trafalgar Square Publishing.
Fox, Mem. Tell Me about Your Day Today. Stringer, Lauren, illus. 2012. (ENG.). 40p. (J). (gr. -1-3). 17.99 *(978-1-4169-9006-2(2)*, Beach Lane Bks.) Beach Lane Bks.
Freedman, Claire. Night-Night, Emily! Massey, Jane, illus. 2005. 32p. (J). 6.95 *(978-1-58925-390-2(6))* Tiger Tales.
—Night-Night, Emily! Massey, Jane, tr. Massey, Jane, illus. 2003. 32p. (J). (gr. -1-1). tchr. ed. 15.95 *(978-1-58925-032-1(X))* Tiger Tales.

Freeman, Don. Corduroy: Giant Board Book. 2011. (Corduroy Ser.). 34p. (J). (gr. -1 — 1). bds. 11.99 *(978-0-670-01311-1(0),* Viking Books for Young Readers) Penguin Young Readers Group.
—Corduroy Book & Bear. 2008. (Corduroy Ser.). 32p. (J). (gr. -1-k). 22.99 *(978-0-670-06342-0(8),* Viking Books for Young Readers) Penguin Young Readers Group.
—A Pocket for Corduroy. 2015. (Corduroy Ser.). (Illus.). 34p. (J). (— 1). bds. 8.99 *(978-0-451-47113-0(X),* Viking Books for Young Readers) Penguin Young Readers Group.
Gaines, Isabel & Milne, Alan Alexander. Pooh's Halloween Parade. Wenzel, Paul & Enik, Ted, illus. 2012. (J). *(978-1-4351-4175-9(X))* Disney Publishing Worldwide.
Gail, Chris. The Littlest Train. (ENG., Illus.). (J). (gr. -1 — 1). 2018. 24p. bds. 8.99 *(978-0-316-44890-1(7))* 2017. 40p. 17.99 *(978-0-316-39286-0(3))* Little, Brown Bks. for Young Readers.
Garza, Xavier. The Great & Mighty Nikko! �el Gran y Poderoso Nikko!, 1 vol. Garza, Xavier, illus. 2015. (ENG., Illus.). 32p. (J). (gr. k-3). pap. 11.95 *(978-1-935955-83-2(7),* 23353382, Cinco Puntos Press) Lee & Low Bks., Inc.
Goss, Matt. Bear Crimbo. 2010. (ENG., Illus.). 72p. (J). 17.95 *(978-0-9815381-3-6(4))* Hilton Publishing Co.
Gould, Lorraine. Warren the Watchdog. 2010. 48p. pap. 19.49 *(978-1-4490-6845-5(6))* AuthorHouse.
Gracie's Lullaby Land. 2011. (ENG.). 24p. pap. 15.99 *(978-1-4568-9014-8(X))* Xlibris Corp.
Grange, Emma. The Empire Strikes Back. 2014. (LEGO Star Wars DK Reader Ser.). lib. bdg. 13.55 *(978-0-606-35734-0(3))* Turtleback.
—Lego Star Wars: The Return of the Jedi. 2014. (LEGO Star Wars DK Reader Ser.). lib. bdg. 13.55 *(978-0-606-35735-7(1))* Turtleback.
—A New Hope. 2014. (LEGO Star Wars DK Reader Ser.). lib. bdg. 13.55 *(978-0-606-35733-3(5))* Turtleback.
Gravett, Emily. Monkey & Me. Gravett, Emily, illus. 2008. (ENG., Illus.). 32p. (J). (gr. -1-3). 18.99 *(978-1-4169-5457-6(0),* Simon & Schuster Bks. For Young Readers) Simon & Schuster Bks. For Young Readers.
Greene, Stephanie. Princess Posey & the Tiny Treasure. Roth Sisson, Stephanie, illus. 2013. (Princess Posey, First Grader Ser.: 5). 96p. (J). (gr. k-3). pap. 5.99 *(978-0-14-242415-5(3),* Puffin Books) Penguin Young Readers Group.
Grey, Mini. Traction Man Is Here! 2012. (Traction Man Ser.). (ENG.). 32p. (J). (gr. -1-3). pap. 7.99 *(978-0-307-93111-5(0),* Dragonfly Bks.) Random Hse. Children's Bks.
Gurewitz, Samantha & Polay, Ellyn. Marvin Mcgunk & All of His Junk. 2012. (ENG.). 27p. (J). pap. 12.95 *(978-1-4327-9705-8(0))* Outskirts Pr., Inc.
H & T Imaginations Unlimited, Inc. Toy Trains with Professor Woodpecker. 2009. 12p. pap. 8.49 *(978-1-4389-5927-6(3))* AuthorHouse.
Hall, Tamony. Rick Brick & the Quest to Save Brickport: An Unofficial LEGO Novel. 2015. (ENG.). 112p. (J). (gr. 1-1). pap. 7.99 *(978-1-63450-149-1(7),* Sky Pony Pr.) Skyhorse Publishing Co., Inc.
Hancock, Chris. Starting Playschool- Mini-Pals Go, Too. 2013. 28p. pap. 16.09 *(978-1-4669-7906-2(2))* Trafford Publishing.
Hansen, Sue. Little Bitty Bella in a Big, Big World. 2012. 24p. pap. 10.99 *(978-1-4624-0272-4(0),* Inspiring Voices) Author Solutions, LLC.
Harper, Benjamin. Hot Wheels: To the Extreme. Wisinski, Ed & White, Dave, illus. 2007. (Scholastic Reader Ser.). 30p. (J). pap. *(978-0-545-02019-0(0))* Scholastic, Inc.
Hatton, Libby. Pete Puffin's Wild Ride Cruising Alaska's Currents. Hatton, Libby, illus. 2008. (Illus.). (J). pap. 16.95 *(978-0-930931-92-6(0))* Alaska Geographic Assn.
Havill, Juanita. Jamaica's Find Book & Cd. O'Brien, Anne Sibley, illus. 2009. (ENG.). 32p. (J). (gr. -1-3). audio compact disk 10.99 *(978-0-547-11961-8(5),* 1047233, Clarion Bks.) HarperCollins Pubs.
Hawksley, Gerald. Good Puppy. Stanley, Mandy, illus. 2005. (J). *(978-1-890647-14-8(4))* TOMY International, Inc.
Hazen, Barbara Shook. Babes in Toyland (Disney Classic) Walt Disney Studio & Marshall, Carol, illus. 2018. (Little Golden Book Ser.). (ENG.). 24p. (J). (-k). 4.99 *(978-0-7364-3879-7(3),* Golden/Disney) Random Hse. Children's Bks.
Henkes, Kevin. Waiting: A Caldecott Honor Award Winner. Henkes, Kevin, illus. 2015. (ENG., Illus.). 32p. (J). (gr. -1-3). 18.99 *(978-0-06-236843-0(5));* lib. bdg. 18.89 *(978-0-06-236844-7(3))* HarperCollins Pubs. (Greenwillow Bks.).
Hennessy, B. G. Claire & the Unicorn Happy Ever After. Mitchell, Susan, illus. 2006. (ENG.). 32p. (J). (gr. -1-3). 19.99 *(978-1-4169-0815-9(3),* Simon & Schuster Bks. For Young Readers) Simon & Schuster Bks. For Young Readers.
Hicer, Nancy. The Missing Block, 1 vol. 2015. (Rosen REAL Readers: STEM & STEAM Collection). (ENG.). 8p. (gr. k-1). pap. 5.46 *(978-1-4994-9554-6(4),* a52c05da-eb90-441b-84ef-3f72f15a74af, Rosen Classroom) Rosen Publishing Group, Inc., The.
Higgins, Jim. The Enchanted Nursery: Nessie's Friends. 2008. 24p. pap. 11.49 *(978-1-4343-8993-0(6))* AuthorHouse.
Higginson, Sheila Sweeny. Chilly Catches a Cold. 2013. (Doc Mcstuffins 8X8 Ser.). (J). lib. bdg. 13.55 *(978-0-606-35109-6(4))* Turtleback.
—A Very McStuffins Christmas. 2014. (Doc Mcstuffins 8X8 Ser.). (J). lib. bdg. 16.00 *(978-0-606-35908-5(7))* Turtleback.
Hill, Eric. Buenas Noches Spot. (SPA.). pap. 4.95 *(978-950-07-1964-3(9))* Editorial Sudamericana S.A. ARG. Dist: Distribooks, Inc.
—A Jugar Con Spot. (SPA.). pap. 4.95 *(978-950-07-1961-2(4))* Editorial Sudamericana S.A. ARG. Dist: Distribooks, Inc.
Hillert, Margaret. The Birthday Car. Girouard, Patrick, illus. 2016. (BeginningtoRead Ser.). (ENG.). 32p. (J). (gr. k-2). 22.60 *(978-1-59953-795-5(8))* Norwood Hse. Pr.
—The Purple Pussycat. Kate Cosgrove, illus. 2016. (Beginning-To-Read Ser.). (ENG.). 32p. (J). (gr. k-2). pap. 13.26 *(978-1-60357-944-5(3))* Norwood Hse. Pr.
—Purple Pussycat. 21st ed. 2016. (BeginningtoRead Ser.). (ENG., Illus.). 32p. (J). (gr. k-2). 22.60 *(978-1-59953-803-7(2))* Norwood Hse. Pr.
—Yellow Boat. 2016. (BeginningtoRead Ser.). (ENG., Illus.). 32p. (J). (gr. -1-2). 22.60 *(978-1-59953-811-2(3))* Norwood Hse. Pr.
Hinbest, Wendy. Frizzy Tizzy Cleans Up. 2011. (ENG.). 20p. 11.95 *(978-1-4583-5828-8(3))* Lulu Pr., Inc.
Holechek, Max. Edsel Mcfarlan's New Car. Toland, Darrell, illus. 2010. 52p. (J). *(978-1-935359-40-1(1))* Bk. Pubs. Network.
Holmes, Anna. Wyldstyle: The Search for the Special. 2014. lib. bdg. 13.55 *(978-0-606-36366-2(1))* Turtleback.
Holst, Jerome Alphonse. Gretchen & the Gremlins. Krajenbrink Hulin, Yvonne, illus. 2012. 48p. pap. 15.95 *(978-0-9794133-5-3(4))* Holst Bks.
Hood, Sue. Monkey Business. Chapman, Susan, illus. 2005. (J). bds. *(978-1-890647-17-9(9))* TOMY International, Inc.
Hope, Laura. The Story of a Plush Bear. 2005. pap. 9.95 *(978-1-55742-463-1(2))* Wildside Pr., LLC.
Hope, Laura Lee. The Story of a Nodding Donkey. rev. ed. 2006. 108p. 25.95 *(978-1-4218-1794-1(2));* pap. 10.95 *(978-1-4218-1894-8(9))* 1st World Publishing, Inc. (1st World Library - Literary Society).
Hopper, Bobby E. Bleep the Purple Bear. Hopper, Andy Lee, illus. 2009. 36p. pap. 18.99 *(978-1-4389-1908-9(5))* AuthorHouse.
Horse, Harry. Little Rabbit Goes to School, 1 vol. 2011. (Little Rabbit Ser.). (ENG., Illus.). 32p. (J). (gr. -1-k). pap. 7.95 *(978-1-56145-574-4(1))* Peachtree Publishing Co. Inc.
Howard, Kate. The LEGO Ninjago Movie: Junior Novel. 2017. (Illus.). 160p. (J). pap. *(978-1-4071-7752-6(4))* Scholastic, Inc.
—The Rescue Mission (LEGO Ninjago: Reader) 2015. (LEGO Ninjago Ser.: 11). (ENG., Illus.). 32p. (J). (gr. -1-3). pap. 3.99 *(978-0-545-74639-7(6))* Scholastic, Inc.
—Techno Strike! 2014. (Ninjago Readers Ser.: 9). lib. bdg. 13.55 *(978-0-606-35860-6(9))* Turtleback.
Howard, Kate, adapted by. Spy vs. Spy. 2015. (Illus.). 32p. (J). *(978-1-4806-9048-6(1))* Scholastic, Inc.
Howe, James. It Came from Beneath the Bed! 2004. (Tales from the House of Bunnicula Ser.). 112p. (J). (gr. 3-6). pap. 17.00 incl. audio *(978-1-4000-8632-0(9),* Listening Library) Random Hse. Audio Publishing Group.
Hughes, Shirley. Bobbo Goes to School. Hughes, Shirley, illus. 2013. (ENG., Illus.). 32p. (J). (gr. -1-2). 16.99 *(978-0-7636-6524-1(X))* Candlewick Pr.
—Jonadab & Rita. Hughes, Shirley, illus. 2010. (Alfie Ser.). (ENG., Illus.). 32p. (J). (gr. -1-k). pap. 11.99 *(978-1-86230-313-3(4),* Red Fox) Random House Children's Books GBR. Dist: Independent Pubs. Group.
Hunter, Sally. Humphrey's Playtime. 2013. (Illus.). (J). *(978-1-4351-4766-9(9))* Barnes & Noble, Inc.
Hunter, Todd H. Elf Night: A Christmas Story. Gavrilovskiy, Olga, illus. 2006. 52p. (J). (gr. -1-7). 16.95 *(978-0-9788085-0-1(9))* Tetoca Pr.
Huxman, K. D. Dragon Talk. 2007. (Illus.). 24p. (J). per. 11.99 *(978-0-9797574-9-5(5))* Dragonfly Publishing, Inc.
—Dragon Talk. Farrington, Teresa, illus. I.t. ed. 2006. 24p. (J). pap. 14.99 *(978-0-9765786-7-3(0))* Dragonfly Publishing, Inc.
Huxman, Karin (K. D.). Dragon Talk. 2006. (Illus.). 24p. (J). lib. bdg. 24.95 *(978-0-9778651-7-8(7))* Dragonfly Publishing, Inc.
I Can Say- Toys. 2005. (J). bds. *(978-1-4194-0033-9(9))* Paradise Pr., Inc.
Inches, Alison. Corduroy's Hike. 2019. (Penguin Young Readers Ser.). (ENG.). 31p. (J). (gr. 2-3). 14.89 *(978-0-87617-756-3(9))* Penworthy Co., LLC, The.
The Indian in the Cupboard. 2004. (J). *(978-1-59564-280-6(3))* Steps To Literacy, LLC.
Inkpen, Mick. Kipper's Toybox. (Illus.). 25p. (J). (CHI, ENG, URD, VIE & FRE.). *(978-1-85430-350-9(3),* 93452); (ENG, FRE, URD, VIE & CHI., *(978-1-85430-351-6(1),* 93453) Little Tiger Pr. Group.
Jeffers, Susan. The Nutcracker. Jeffers, Susan, illus. 2007. (Illus.). 40p. (J). (gr. -1-3). 17.89 *(978-0-06-074387-1(5))* HarperCollins Pubs.
—The Nutcracker. 2007. (ENG., Illus.). 40p. (J). (gr. -1-3). 18.99 *(978-0-06-074386-4(7),* HarperCollins) HarperCollins Pubs.
Jenkins, Emily. Toy Dance Party: Being the Further Adventures of a Bossyboots Stingray, a Courageous Buffalo, & a Hopeful Round Someone Called Plastic. Zelinsky, Paul O., illus. 2010. (Toys Go Out Ser.: 2). (ENG.). 176p. (J). (gr. 1-4). 6.99 *(978-0-375-85525-2(4),* Schwartz & Wade Bks.) Random Hse. Children's Bks.
—Toys Come Home: Being the Early Experiences of an Intelligent Stingray, a Brave Buffalo, & a Brand-New Someone Called Plastic. Zelinsky, Paul O., illus. 2011. (Toys Go Out Ser.: 3). 144p. (J). (gr. 1-4). 16.99 *(978-0-375-86200-7(5),* Schwartz & Wade Bks.) Random Hse. Children's Bks.
—Toys Go Out: Being the Adventures of a Knowledgeable Stingray, a Toughy Little Buffalo, & Someone Called Plastic. Zelinsky, Paul O., illus. 2008. (Toys Go Out Ser.: 1). (ENG.). 144p. (J). (gr. 1-4). 7.99 *(978-0-385-73661-9(4),* Yearling) Random Hse. Children's Bks.
—Toys Meet Snow: Being the Wintertime Adventures of a Curious Stuffed Buffalo, a Sensitive Plush Stingray, & a Book-Loving Rubber Ball. Zelinsky, Paul O., illus. 2015. 40p. (J). (gr. -1-2). 17.99 *(978-0-385-37330-2(9),* Schwartz & Wade Bks.) Random Hse. Children's Bks.
Jennings, Linda. Duna y Dan. Chapman, Jane, illus. (SPA.). 28p. (J). (gr. k-1). *(978-84-8418-027-2(1),* ZZ4481) Zendrera Zariquiey, Editorial ESP. Dist: Lectorum Pubns., Inc.
Jordan, Apple. The Bunny Surprise. 2012. (Step into Reading - Level 1 Ser.). lib. bdg. 13.55 *(978-0-606-23723-9(2))* Turtleback.
Joyce, Melanie. A New House, 1 vol. 2008. (Fred Bear & Friends Ser.). (ENG., Illus.). 24p. (gr. k-1). pap. 9.15 *(978-0-8368-8974-1(6),* 729ef204-73a0-4460-ae95-d8361712127e, Gareth Stevens Learning Library) Stevens, Gareth Publishing LLLP.
Joyce, William. Ollie's Odyssey. Joyce, William, illus. 2017. (ENG., Illus.). 304p. (J). (gr. 2-6). pap. 14.99 *(978-1-4424-7356-0(8))* Simon & Schuster, Inc.
Kamon. Playtoon & the Antpod. Krit, Joey, illus. 2012. 28p. pap. 24.95 *(978-1-4626-7346-9(5))* PublishAmerica, Inc.
Kao, Sleepless, illus. Monchan's Bag. 2010. (ENG.). 36p. (J). (gr. -1-3). 16.95 *(978-1-897476-32-1(9))* Simply Read Bks. CAN. Dist: Ingram Publisher Services.
Katschke, Judy. Hooray for Shoppywood! 2017. (Illus.). 62p. (J). *(978-1-5182-4211-3(1))* Scholastic, Inc.
Kehoe, Tim. Vincent Shadow: Toy Inventor. Wohnoutka, Mike & Francis, Guy, illus. 2011. (Vincent Shadow Ser.: 1). (ENG.). 224p. (J). (gr. 3-7). pap. 13.99 *(978-0-316-05666-3(9))* Little, Brown Bks. for Young Readers.
Kelly, Katherine, text. Albert Bear & the Big Celebration. 2005. (J). 12.95 *(978-0-9773481-0-7(5))* Kelly, Katherine.
Kelly, Mij. Lion's Lullaby. Clifton-Brown, Holly, illus. 2016. (ENG.). 32p. (J). (gr. -1 — 1). 16.99 *(978-1-4847-2526-9(3))* Disney Pr.
Kilgore, Mary & Kilgore, Mitchell. Where Is My Mommy? Coping When a Parent Leaves (and Doesn't Come Back) Pillo, Cary, illus. 2010. (ENG.). 32p. (J). (gr. -1-4). pap. 14.99 *(978-1-884734-46-5(4))* Parenting Pr., Inc.
Killen, Nicola. The Little Rabbit. Killen, Nicola, illus. 2019. (My Little Animal Friend Ser.). (ENG., Illus.). 32p. (J). (gr. -1-3). 17.99 *(978-1-5344-3828-6(9),* Simon & Schuster/Paula Wiseman Bks.) Simon & Schuster/Paula Wiseman Bks.
Kim, YeShil. We Are Proud of You. The Pope Twins, illus. rev. ed. 2014. (MySELF Bookshelf Ser.). (ENG.). 32p. (J). (gr. k-2). pap. 11.94 *(978-1-60357-651-2(7));* lib. bdg. 25.27 *(978-1-59953-642-2(0))* Norwood Hse. Pr.
King, Trey. Deep-Sea Treasure Dive. Wang, Sean & Hyland, Greg, illus. 2016. 24p. (J). *(978-1-5182-0031-1(1))* Scholastic, Inc.
—The Legend Begins. 2013. (LEGO Legends of Chima: Comic Reader Ser.: 1). lib. bdg. 13.55 *(978-0-606-32012-2(1))* Turtleback.
—Mystery on the LEGO Express. Wang, Sean, illus. 2014. 24p. (J). *(978-1-4242-6168-0(6))* Scholastic, Inc.
—Mystery on the Lego Express. 2014. (LEGO City 8X8 Ser.). (Illus.). 24p. (J). lib. bdg. 13.55 *(978-0-606-36068-5(9))* Turtleback.
—Sidekick Showdown! (LEGO DC Comics Super Heroes) Wang, Sean, illus. 2016. (LEGO DC Super Heroes Ser.). (ENG.). 24p. (J). (gr. -1-3). pap. 3.99 *(978-1-338-04742-4(6))* Scholastic, Inc.
King, Trey & Kiernan, Kenny. Cops, Crocs, & Crooks! 2015. (LEGO City 8X8 Ser.). lib. bdg. 13.55 *(978-0-606-36360-0(2))* Turtleback.
Kinra, Richa, illus. The Princess Panda Tea Party: A Cerebral Palsy Fairy Tale. 2014. 45p. (J). pap. 14.95 *(978-1-61599-219-5(7))* Loving Healing Pr., Inc.
Kirkland, Kim M. Car Cars Go Zoom Zoom Zoom. 2012. 24p. pap. 24.95 *(978-1-4626-6926-4(3))* America Star Bks.
Klein, Abby. Ready, Freddy #18: the Perfect Present. McKinley, John, illus. 2009. (Ready, Freddy! Ser.: 18). (ENG.). 96p. (J). (gr. -1-3). 5.99 *(978-0-545-13043-1(3),* Scholastic Paperbacks) Scholastic, Inc.
Korda, Lerryn. It's Vacation Time: Playtime with Little Nye. Korda, Lerryn, illus. 2010. (Playtime with Little Nye Ser.). (ENG., Illus.). 26p. (J). (— 1). 8.99 *(978-0-7636-4813-8(2))* Candlewick Pr.
Kreloff, Elliot, illus. Counting Duckies. 2010. 16p. (J). bds. *(978-1-60906-007-7(5))* Begin Smart LLC.
Kulick Triscila, Verne. Joel & the Magic Toy Tree. 2005. 36p. (J). 11.99 *(978-1-4116-6985-7(1))* Lulu Pr., Inc.
Lagonegro, Melissa & Redbank, Tennant. Five Toy Tales. 2012. (Step into Reading - Level 1 Ser.). lib. bdg. 18.40 *(978-0-606-23853-3(0))* Turtleback.
Landers, Ace. Arctic Blast. White, Dave, illus. 2012. 32p. (J). *(978-0-545-33455-6(1))* Scholastic, Inc.
—Empire Strikes Out. 2013. (LEGO Star Wars Chapter Bks.). lib. bdg. 14.75 *(978-0-606-31554-8(3))* Turtleback.
—The Lego Official Movie Handbook. 2013. lib. bdg. 16.00 *(978-0-606-35405-9(0))* Turtleback.
—Lego Star Wars: The Yoda Chronicles Trilogy. 2014. (LEGO Star Wars Chapter Bks.). lib. bdg. 18.40 *(978-0-606-35414-1(X))* Turtleback.
—The Padawan Menace. 2012. lib. bdg. 13.55 *(978-0-606-23975-2(8))* Turtleback.
—Revenge of the Sith. White, Dave, illus. 2015. (J). *(978-1-4806-9629-7(3))* Scholastic, Inc.
—Revenge of the Sith. 2015. (LEGO Star Wars 8X8 Ser.). lib. bdg. 13.55 *(978-0-606-37767-6(0))* Turtleback.
—Shark Attack. 2013. (Scholastic Reader Level 1 Ser.). (Illus.). 32p. (J). lib. bdg. 13.55 *(978-0-606-32391-8(0))* Turtleback.
—Start Your Engines. White, Dave, illus. 2007. (Scholastic Reader Ser.). (J). pap. *(978-0-545-02017-6(4))* Scholastic, Inc.
—Yoda's Secret Missions. 2014. (LEGO Star Wars Chapter Bks.: 1). (Illus.). 63p. (J). lib. bdg. 14.75 *(978-0-606-36070-8(0))* Turtleback.
Landers, Ace & White, Dave, illus. Drag Race! 2009. (Scholastic Reader Ser.). 32p. (J). *(978-0-545-11039-6(4))* Scholastic, Inc.
Lansley, Oliver. Holly & Ivan's Christmas Adventure. 2011. (Oberon Plays for Young People Ser.). (ENG., Illus.). 64p. (J). (gr. k-5). pap. *(978-1-84943-136-1(1),* 513368) Oberon Bks., Ltd.
LaReau, Kara. Rocko & Spanky Call It Quits. LaReau, Jenna, illus. 2008. (Rocko & Spanky Ser.). 40p. (J). 16.00 *(978-0-15-216611-3(4))* Harcourt Children's Bks.
Larson, Melissa J. It's Your Ball after All. Larson, Caleb A., illus. 2007. 20p. per. 24.95 *(978-1-4241-9046-1(0))* America Star Bks.
Last, Shari. Meet the Mixels. 2014. (DK Reader Level 1 Ser.). lib. bdg. 13.55 *(978-0-606-36276-4(2))* Turtleback.
Lee Green Pope. The Enchanted Toy Shop. 2009. 32p. pap. 16.49 *(978-1-4389-7320-3(9))* AuthorHouse.
Lee, Ingrid. George Most Wanted. Denis, Stephane, illus. 2005. 62p. (J). lib. bdg. 20.00 *(978-1-4242-1253-8(7))* Fitzgerald Bks.
—George, the Best of All!, 1 vol. Denis, Stephane, illus. 2006. (Orca Echoes Ser.). (ENG.). 64p. (J). (gr. 1-3). pap. 4.99 *(978-1-55143-623-4(X))* Orca Bk. Pubs. USA.
—The True Story of George. Denis, Stephane, illus. 2004. 62p. (J). lib. bdg. 20.00 *(978-1-4242-1262-0(6))* Fitzgerald Bks.
Lehman, Barbara. Trainstop. 2008. (ENG., Illus.). 32p. (J). (gr. -1-3). 17.99 *(978-0-618-75640-7(X),* 569198, Clarion Bks.) HarperCollins Pubs.
LeLeu, Lisa. Miss Moo-Moo the Cow: Puppet Show Play Set with 2 books & Crayons. 2004. (Lisa Leleu Puppet Show Books Ser.). 30p. 19.95 *(978-0-9710537-4-8(X))* LeLeu, Lisa Studios! Inc.
Leonard, Barry, ed. The Little Tin Soldier. 2003. (Illus.). 12p. (J). (gr. k-4). reprint ed. 17.00 *(978-0-7567-6867-6(5))* DIANE Publishing Co.
Let's Pretend: Individual Title Six-Packs. (gr. -1-2). 23.00 *(978-0-7635-9001-7(0))* Rigby Education.
Lewis, Kim. Hooray for Harry. 2006. (Illus.). (J). *(978-1-4156-7111-5(7))* Candlewick Pr.
Lewis, Michael. The Great Pirate Christmas Battle, 1 vol. Jaskiel, Stan, illus. 2014. (ENG.). 32p. (J). (gr. k-3). 16.99 *(978-1-4556-1934-4(5),* Pelican Publishing) Arcadia Publishing.
Linforth, Veda. More Toy Shop Tales. 2009. 124p. pap. 10.99 *(978-1-4389-0795-6(8))* AuthorHouse.
Liniers. Buenas Noches, Planeta: TOON Level 2. 2017. (SPA., Illus.). 36p. (J). (gr. k-1). 12.99 *(978-1-943145-21-8(0),* 9781943145218, TOON Books) Astra Publishing Hse.
—Buenas Noches, Planeta: TOON Level 2. 2017. (SPA., Illus.). 36p. (J). (gr. k-1). pap. 7.99 *(978-1-943145-19-5(9),* 9781943145195, Toon Books) Candlewick Pr.
—Good Night, Planet: TOON Level 2. 2017. (ENG., Illus.). 36p. (J). (gr. k-2). 12.99 *(978-1-943145-20-1(2),* 9781943145201, TOON Books) Astra Publishing Hse.
Lovell, Patty. Have Fun, Molly Lou Melon. Catrow, David, illus. 2012. (ENG.). 32p. (J). (gr. k-3). 18.99 *(978-0-399-25406-2(4),* G.P. Putnam's Sons Books for Young Readers) Penguin Young Readers Group.
Lucas, David. Christmas at the Toy Museum. Lucas, David, illus. 2012. (ENG., Illus.). 32p. (J). (gr. -1-2). 15.99 *(978-0-7636-5868-7(5))* Candlewick Pr.
—I Was Made for You. Lucas, David, illus. 2018. (ENG., Illus.). 32p. (J). (gr. -1-3). 17.99 *(978-1-5415-3559-6(6),* 61410c7f-c6e3-4f89-879f-d7fab81ce288) Lerner Publishing Group.
Luster, Bonnie. The Adventures of Mrs. Tibbles & Her Toys: Spots. 2012. 28p. pap. 16.95 *(978-1-4497-6929-1(2),* WestBow Pr.) Author Solutions, LLC.
Lynch, Brian. Ready for Action (Toy Academy #2) Taylor, Edwardian, illus. 2019. (ENG.). 192p. (J). (gr. 2-5). 14.99 *(978-1-338-14916-6(4),* Scholastic Pr.) Scholastic, Inc.
Lynn, Sarah. 1-2-3 Va-Va-Vroom! A Counting Book, 0 vols. Griffo, Daniel, illus. 2012. (ENG.). 32p. (J). (gr. -1-1). 16.99 *(978-0-7614-6162-3(0),* 9780761461623, Two Lions) Amazon Publishing.
Making Waves. 2004. (J). per. *(978-1-57657-460-7(1))* Paradise Pr., Inc.
Marcellino, Fred, illus. The Steadfast Tin Soldier. 2017.Tr. of Standhaftige Tinsoldat. (ENG.). 32p. (J). (gr. -1-3). 17.99 *(978-1-4814-7662-1(9),* Atheneum/Caitlyn Dlouhy Books) Simon & Schuster Children's Publishing.
March, Julia. Monster Battles. 2016. (Illus.). 63p. (J). *(978-1-5182-1852-1(0))* Dorling Kindersley Publishing, Inc.
—Power Up! 2015. (DK Reader Level 3 Ser.). lib. bdg. 13.55 *(978-0-606-36691-5(1))* Turtleback.
—Shark Attack! 2017. (Illus.). 24p. (J). *(978-1-5379-5701-2(5))* Dorling Kindersley Publishing, Inc.
Marsoli, Lisa Ann. Let's Go to the Zoo. Smitherton, Jeb, illus. 2005. (J). bds. 14.99 *(978-0-9767325-4-9(8))* Toy Quest.
Marzollo, Jean. I Spy Animals. 2012. (I Spy — Scholastic Ser.). lib. bdg. 13.55 *(978-0-606-23968-4(5))* Turtleback.
—I Spy Little Toys. Wick, Walter, photos by. 2011. (I Spy Ser.). (ENG., Illus.). 26p. (J). (gr. -1-k). bds. 7.99 *(978-0-545-22096-5(3),* Cartwheel Bks.) Scholastic, Inc.
Masterson, Josephine. Toy Box Trouble, 1 vol. 2015. (Rosen REAL Readers: STEM & STEAM Collection). (ENG.). 8p. (gr. k-1). pap. 5.46 *(978-1-4994-9599-7(4),* eb7f5698-5369-4122-8da7-19699494c18e, Rosen Classroom) Rosen Publishing Group, Inc., The.
Mayfield, Sue. The Four Franks. 2005. (Blue Go Bananas Ser.). (ENG., Illus.). 48p. (J). (gr. 1-2). lib. bdg. *(978-0-7787-2629-6(0))* Crabtree Publishing Co.
—The Four Franks. Parsons, Garry, illus. 2005. (Blue Go Bananas Ser.). (ENG.). 48p. (J). (gr. 1-2). *(978-0-7787-2651-7(7))* Crabtree Publishing Co.
McAllister, Angela. Brave Bitsy & the Bear. Beeke, Tiphanie, illus. 2006. (ENG.). 32p. (J). (gr. -1-3). 16.00 *(978-0-618-63994-6(2),* 100459, Clarion Bks.) HarperCollins Pubs.
Mccarthy, Rebecca L. Save This Christmas! 2012. (LEGO City 8X8 Ser.). lib. bdg. 13.55 *(978-0-606-26767-0(0))* Turtleback.
McClure, Brian D. The Bubble. 2006. (Illus.). 64p. (J). 14.95 *(978-1-933426-05-1(5))* Universal Flag Publishing.
McCue, Lisa, illus. Corduroy's Thanksgiving. 2006. (Corduroy Ser.). 16p. (J). (gr. -1 — 1). bds. 6.99 *(978-0-670-06108-2(5),* Viking Books for Young Readers) Penguin Young Readers Group.
McGougan, Kathy. Buddy's Toys. 2007. (J). pap. 5.00 *(978-0-9799980-2-7(6))* Buddy Bks. Publishing.
McNease, Mitzy. Chester's Presents. Cox, Kim, illus. 2006. 28p. (J). 10.95 *(978-0-9779488-0-2(3))* Blancmange Publishing LLC.
McPhail, David. Bella Loves Bunny. 2013. (ENG., Illus.). 22p. (J). (gr. -1 — 1). bds. 8.95 *(978-1-4197-0543-4(1),* 1037710, Abrams Appleseed) Abrams, Inc.
—Olivia Loves Owl. 2016. (ENG., Illus.). 20p. (J). (gr. -1 — 1). bds. 8.95 *(978-1-4197-2127-4(5),* 1128510, Abrams Appleseed) Abrams, Inc.
Meddaugh, Susan. Toy Trouble. 2010. (Martha Speaks Ser.). (ENG., Illus.). 24p. (J). (gr. -1-3). pap. 3.99 *(978-0-547-21078-0(7))* Houghton Mifflin Harcourt Publishing Co.
Meet the GiggleWings. 2005. (J). bds. 14.99 *(978-1-890647-13-1(6))* TOMY International, Inc.
Meyer, Susan. Matthew & Tall Rabbit Go Camping. Huntington, Amy, illus. 2008. (ENG.). 32p. (J). (gr. -1-3). 15.95 *(978-0-89272-769-8(1))* Down East Bks.
Michael, Melanie. Nerfnerd. Alderton, John, illus. 2011. (J). *(978-0-938467-07-6(7))* Headline Bks., Inc.
Michelini, Carlo A., ed. Blancanieves. (SPA., Illus.). 6p. pap. 5.95 *(978-84-414-0263-8(9))* Editorial Edaf, S.L. ESP. Dist: Spanish Pubs., LLC.
—Caperucita Roja. (SPA., Illus.). 6p. 5.95 *(978-84-414-0259-1(0))* Editorial Edaf, S.L. ESP. Dist: Spanish Pubs., LLC.

—La Cenicienta. (SPA., Illus.). 6p. 5.95 *(978-84-414-0261-4(2))* Editorial Edaf, S.L. ESP. Dist: Spanish Pubs., LLC.

Miller, Toby. The Magic Word. 2011. (Illus.). 24p. pap. 14.09 *(978-1-4567-7793-7(9))* AuthorHouse.

Milne, A. A. The House at Pooh Corner Deluxe Edition. Shepard, Ernest H., illus. deluxe ed. 2009. (Winnie-The-Pooh Ser.). (ENG.). 192p. (J). (gr. 3-7). 19.99 *(978-0-525-47856-0(6),* Dutton Books for Young Readers) Penguin Young Readers Group.

Milne, Alan Alexander. Tigger Tales. Shepard, Ernest H., illus. 2006. 36p. (J). (gr. k-4). reprint ed. 15.00 *(978-1-4223-5453-7(9))* DIANE Publishing Co.

—Winnie ille Pu. Lenardo, Alexandro, tr. from ENG. 2015.Tr. of Winnie-the-Pooh. (LAT., Illus.). 170p. (J). pap. 19.95 *(978-4-87187-394-9(3))* Ishi Pr. International.

Mitchell, Colleen. A Dinosaur under My Bed. Daly, Karen Anne, illus. 2013. 24p. (J). pap. 7.49 *(978-0-9853600-2-3(X))* Thistlewood Publishing.

Mitchell, Lee Ann. Milo the Mighty Protector. 2010. 32p. pap. 12.99 *(978-1-4490-5447-2(1))* AuthorHouse.

Miyares, Daniel. Float. Miyares, Daniel, illus. 2015. (ENG., Illus.). 48p. (J). (gr. -1-3). 18.99 *(978-1-4814-1524-8(7),* Simon & Schuster Bks. For Young Readers) Simon & Schuster Bks. For Young Readers.

Mlawer, Teresa, tr. Fix It!/¡a Reparar! Birkett, Georgie, illus. 2009. (Helping Hands English/Spanish Edition Ser.). (ENG.). 24p. (J). (gr. -1-k). pap. *(978-1-84643-571-3(4))* Child's Play International Ltd.

Morgan, Allen. Matthew & the Midnight Wrecker. 2004. (Illus.). (J). (gr. k-3). spiral bd. *(978-0-616-11123-9(1))* Canadian National Institute for the Blind/Institut National Canadien pour les Aveugles.

Morris, J. E. Flubby Will Not Play with That. Morris, J. E., illus. (Flubby Ser.). (Illus.). 32p. (J). 2020. (gr. k-2). 5.99 *(978-1-5247-9083-7(4))* 2019. (gr. -1-3). 9.99 *(978-1-5247-8778-3(7))* Penguin Young Readers Group. (Penguin Workshop).

Morrow, Ozzie. Bear Troubles. 2008. (ENG.). 92p. pap. 30.49 *(978-1-4343-4178-5(X))* AuthorHouse.

Mullican, Judy. My Toys. Bicking, Judith, illus. l.t. ed. 2005. (HRL Board Book Ser.). (J). (gr. -1-k). pap. 10.95 *(978-1-57332-307-9(1),* HighReach Learning, Incorporated) Carson-Dellosa Publishing, LLC.

Muñoz, Isabel. Now, What? / ¿Ahora, Qué? (Eric & Julieta) (Bilingual) (Bilingual Edition) Mazali, Gustavo, illus. 2006. (Eric & Julieta Ser.). (SPA & ENG.). 24p. (J). (gr. -1-3). pap. 3.99 *(978-0-439-78372-9(0))* Scholastic, Inc.

Murray, Helen. The Lego Movie. 2013. (DK Reader Level 2 Ser.). lib. bdg. 13.55 *(978-0-606-35321-2(6))* Turtleback.

—Stop the Stone Monsters! 2017. (Illus.). 24p. (J). *(978-1-5182-3635-8(9))* Dorling Kindersley Publishing, Inc.

My Yo-Yo. Date not set. pap. 3.95 *(978-0-89868-294-6(0))* ARO Publishing Co.

Nash, Sarah. Scaredy Bear. 1 vol. Everitt-Stewart, Andy, illus. 2009. (Stories to Grow With Ser.). (ENG.). 24p. (J). (gr. 1-2). 27.27 *(978-1-60754-472-2(5),* bf59d50c-0e89-4065-97dd-9028097bd68a, Windmill Bks.) Rosen Publishing Group, Inc., The.

Nash, Scott. Tuff Fluff: The Case of Duckie's Missing Brain. Nash, Scott, illus. 2004. (Illus.). (J). 101.94 *(978-0-7636-2503-0(5));* (ENG., 40p. (gr. 1-4). 17.99 *(978-0-7636-1882-7(9))* Candlewick Pr.

Nicholas, Christopher. Toy Story 2, Vol. 2. 2006. (Little Golden Book Ser.). (ENG., Illus.). 24p. (J). (gr. -1-2). 5.99 *(978-0-7364-2394-6(X),* Golden/Disney) Random Hse. Children's Bks.

Niddrie, June. Pom, the Pomegranate Pixie. 2010. 32p. pap. 16.10 *(978-0-557-31875-9(0))* Lulu Pr., Inc.

Nielsen-Fernlund, Susin. The Magic Beads. Côté, Geneviève, illus. 2007. (ENG.). 32p. (J). (gr. -1-3). 16.95 *(978-1-894965-47-7(7))* Simply Read Bks. CAN. Dist: Ingram Publisher Services.

Noisy Toys: Individual Title Six-Packs. (gr. -1-2). 23.00 *(978-0-7635-9002-4(9))* Rigby Education.

Noll, Amanda. Are You My Monster? McWilliam, Howard, illus. 2019. (I Need My Monster Ser.). 26p. (J). bds. 8.99 *(978-1-947277-32-8(4))* Flashlight Pr.

Novel Units. The Indian in the Cupboard Novel Units Student Packet. 2019. (Indian in the Cupboard Ser.: No. 1). (ENG.). (J). (gr. 4-7). pap. 13.99 *(978-1-56137-693-3(0),* NU6930SP, Novel Units, Inc.) Classroom Library Co.

—The Indian in the Cupboard Novel Units Teacher Guide. 2019. (Indian in the Cupboard Ser.: No. 1). (ENG.). (J). (gr. 4-7). pap. 12.99 *(978-1-56137-225-6(0),* Novel Units, Inc.) Classroom Library Co.

Odierno, Lisa. Bunny Hide-and-Seek. 2009. (Smithsonian Baby Animals Ser.). (ENG., Illus.). 16p. (J). (gr. -1-k). 6.95 *(978-1-60727-092-8(7))* Soundprints.

Odierno, Lisa & Soundprints Staff. Bunny Hide-and-Seek. 2009. (Smithsonian Baby Animals Ser.). (ENG., Illus.). 16p. (J). (gr. -1-k). 6.95 *(978-1-60727-105-5(2))* Soundprints.

Ogilvy, Ian. Measle & the Dragodon. 2006. 344p. (J). (gr. 3-8). per. 6.99 *(978-0-06-058690-4(7),* Harper Trophy) HarperCollins Pubs.

The Ooshes A Wish Comes True. 2005. (J). *(978-1-932233-05-6(9))* Aurora Libris Corp.

The Ooshes the Night Before Christmas. 2004. (J). mass mkt. *(978-1-932233-03-2(2))* Aurora Libris Corp.

Ottenbreit, Sharon. Only One Toy Allowed. 2010. 32p. pap. 15.99 *(978-0-557-36426-8(4))* Lulu Pr., Inc.

Panckridge, Michael & Daley, Laurie. Live Action. 2007. (ENG.). 224p. *(978-0-207-20053-3(X))* HarperCollins Pubs. Australia.

Paradine, Mike. King of Toys. 2006. 83p. pap. 19.95 *(978-1-4241-2694-1(0))* America Star Bks.

Parker, Danny. The Treasure Trove, Volume 3. Shield, Guy, illus. 2017. (Lola's Toy Box Ser.: 3). (ENG.). 96p. (J). (gr. k-2). pap. 6.99 *(978-1-76012-438-0(9))* Hardie Grant Children?s Publishing AUS. Dist: Independent Pubs. Group.

Parker, Danny & Shield, Guy. Plastic Palace, Volume 4. 2017. (Lola's Toy Box Ser.: 4). (ENG., Illus.). 96p. (J). (gr. k-2). pap. 6.99 *(978-1-76012-439-7(7))* Hardie Grant Children?s Publishing AUS. Dist: Independent Pubs. Group.

Parker, Theron J. June Bug & the Homemade Toys. 2013. 24p. 24.95 *(978-1-62709-397-2(4));* pap. 24.95 *(978-1-62709-158-9(0))* America Star Bks.

Parragon Staff. Celebrate the Year with Winnie the Pooh. 2010. (Disney Diecut Classics). (Illus.). 72p. (J). (gr. -1-1). *(978-1-4075-8902-2(4))* Parragon, Inc.

—Disney Toy Story 3: Toy Stars. 2010. (Disney Twinkly Lights Board Bks.). 6p. (J). (gr. -1-k). bds. *(978-1-4075-9341-8(2))* Parragon, Inc.

Paxton, Tom. The Marvelous Toy. Cox, Steve, illus. 2014. 22p. (J). (gr. -1-2). bds. 7.95 *(978-1-62354-043-2(7))* Charlesbridge Publishing, Inc.

Peacock, Lou. Oliver Elephant. Stephens, Helen, illus. 2018. (ENG.). 32p. (J). (-k). 16.99 *(978-1-5362-0266-3(5))* Candlewick Pr.

Pegg, Laura Wittman. The Patch Quilt Pony. 2006. 17.00 *(978-0-8059-7346-4(X))* Dorrance Publishing Co., Inc.

Pett, Mark. The Boy & the Airplane. Pett, Mark, illus. 2013. (ENG., Illus.). 40p. (J). (gr. -1). 18.99 *(978-1-4424-5123-0(8),* Simon & Schuster Bks. For Young Readers) Simon & Schuster Bks. For Young Readers.

PI Kids. Disney Pixar: Friends & Heroes First Look & Find. 2007. (ENG.). 16p. (J). bds. 12.99 *(978-1-4127-6848-1(9),* 4155, PIL Kids) Phoenix International Publications, Inc.

Pierce, Ricky. Bouncing Billy. 2008. 24p. per. 10.95 *(978-1-4327-1696-7(4))* Outskirts Pr., Inc.

Piggy Toes Press. Our Ballet Recital. Maddocks, Maria, illus. 2005. (ENG.). 12p. (J). (gr. -1-3). 12.95 *(978-1-58117-425-0(X),* Intervisual/Piggy Toes) Bendon, Inc.

Piggy Toes Press, creator. Toy Story 3. 2011. (Splish-Splash Stories Ser.). (ENG., Illus.). (gr. -1-k). 5.95 *(978-1-61524-419-5(0),* Intervisual/Piggy Toes) Bendon, Inc.

Pilutti, Deb. Ten Rules of Being a Superhero. Pilutti, Deb, illus. 2014. (ENG., Illus.). 32p. (J). (gr. -1-2). 19.99 *(978-0-8050-9759-7(7),* 900118487, Holt, Henry & Co. Bks. For Young Readers) Holt, Henry & Co.

Piper, Watty. The Little Engine That Could: Loren Long Edition. Long, Loren, illus. 2005. (Little Engine That Could Ser.). 48p. (J). (gr. -1-2). 18.99 *(978-0-399-24467-4(0),* Philomel Bks.) Penguin Young Readers Group.

Piper, Watty & Penguin / LeapFrog. The Little Engine That Could. Long, Loren, illus. 2008. (J). 13.99 *(978-1-59319-938-8(4))* LeapFrog Enterprises, Inc.

Posner-Sanchez, Andrea. As Big As a Whale (Disney Junior: Doc Mcstuffins) RH Disney, illus. 2014. (Little Golden Book Ser.). (ENG.). 24p. (J). (-k). 5.99 *(978-0-7364-3087-6(3),* Golden/Disney) Random Hse. Children's Bks.

—Bubble-Rific! (Disney Junior: Doc Mcstuffins) RH Disney, illus. 2014. (Little Golden Book Ser.). (ENG.). 24p. (J). (-k). 5.99 *(978-0-7364-3236-8(1),* Golden/Disney) Random Hse. Children's Bks.

—A Knight in Sticky Armor (Disney Junior: Doc Mcstuffins) RH Disney, illus. 2012. (Little Golden Book Ser.). (ENG.). 24p. (J). (-k). 5.99 *(978-0-7364-3030-2(X),* Golden/Disney) Random Hse. Children's Bks.

—Snowman Surprise (Disney Junior: Doc Mcstuffins) RH Disney, illus. 2013. (Little Golden Book Ser.). (ENG.). 24p. (J). (-k). 5.99 *(978-0-7364-3142-2(X),* Golden/Disney) Random Hse. Children's Bks.

Powers, Mark. Spy Toys: Out of Control! Wesson, Tim, illus. 2017. (Spy Toys Ser.). (ENG.). 208p. (J). pap. *(978-1-4088-7068-4(6),* 293748, Bloomsbury Children's Bks.) Bloomsbury Publishing Plc.

—Spy Toys: Out of Control. Wesson, Tim, illus. 2019. (Spy Toys Ser.). (ENG.). 208p. (J). 13.99 *(978-1-68119-960-3(2),* 900194411, Bloomsbury Children's Bks.) Bloomsbury Publishing USA.

Poyner, James R. Toy-Maker's Apprentice. 2006. 67p. per. 12.00 *(978-1-60002-282-1(0),* 4145) Mountain Valley Publishing, LLC.

Price, John. Quest. 2005. 37p. pap. 15.00 *(978-1-4116-5649-9(0))* Lulu Pr., Inc.

Price, Mathew. Tic, Tac Toc. (SPA.). pap. 3.95 *(978-950-07-2059-5(0))* Editorial Sudamericana S.A. ARG. Dist: Distribooks, Inc.

Publications International Ltd. Staff. Steering Wheel Sound Cars. 2007. 12p. (J). 17.98 *(978-1-4127-5884-0(X))* Phoenix International Publications, Inc.

Publications International Ltd. Staff, ed. Los Mejores Amigos. 2009.Tr. of Toy Story Best Friends. 12p. (J). bds. 10.98 *(978-1-4127-0269-0(0))* Phoenix International Publications, Inc.

—Sesame Street(r) Where Is Elmo's Friend? Play-A-Sound(r) Lift-a-Flap Sound Book. 2014. 10p. (J). bds. *(978-1-4508-8976-6(X),* 145088976X) Publications International, Ltd.

Pulford, Elizabeth. Finding Monkey Moon. Wilkinson, Kate, illus. 2015. (ENG.). 32p. (J). (gr. -1-2). 15.99 *(978-0-7636-6777-1(3))* Candlewick Pr.

R., Charlie. The Christmas Mama Santa Delivered the Toys. 2012. 36p. 19.95 *(978-1-4626-6824-3(0))* PublishAmerica, Inc.

Rack, Charlene. The Adventures of Delaware Bear & Young George Washington. 2011. 24p. (gr. 1-2). pap. 12.79 *(978-1-4567-5681-9(8))* AuthorHouse.

Rainey, L. E. Sad Sam, Glad Sam. 2006. (Illus.). 32p. (J). 16.95 *(978-0-9785521-0-7(5))* Shoetree Publishers, Inc.

Raitman, Ira. Amanda's Bunny. 2010. 16p. 8.99 *(978-1-4520-2021-1(3))* AuthorHouse.

Raley, Hugh W. Erin the Excellent Elf. 2013. 20p. pap. 12.95 *(978-1-4908-0533-7(8),* WestBow Pr.) Author Solutions, LLC.

Randall, Chuck. Curley's Wish Comes True. 2013. 28p. pap. 24.95 *(978-1-4626-9795-3(X))* America Star Bks.

Reasoner, Charles. Inside Santa's Toy Shop. Reasoner, Charles, illus. 2007. (Story Book Ser.). (Illus.). 12p. (J). (gr. k-3). bds. *(978-1-84666-151-8(X),* Tide Mill Pr.) Top That! Publishing PLC.

Rees, Susan A. P. The Pine Cone Wishing Tree. 2008. (Illus.). 20p. pap. 10.49 *(978-1-4343-7155-3(7))* AuthorHouse.

Rey, H. A. Curious Baby: My Favorite Things Padded Board Book. 2011. (Curious Baby Curious George Ser.). (ENG., Illus.). 14p. (J). (gr. -1 — 1). bds. 8.99 *(978-0-547-42893-2(6),* 1432083, Clarion Bks.) HarperCollins Pubs.

RH Disney. Toy Story (Disney/Pixar Toy Story) RH Disney, illus. 2009. (Little Golden Book Ser.). (ENG., Illus.). 24p. (J). (gr. -1-2). 5.99 *(978-0-7364-2596-4(9),* Golden/Disney) Random Hse. Children's Bks.

Rickards, Lynne. Jack's Bed. Beardshaw, Rosalind, illus. 2006. (Green Bananas Ser.). (ENG.). 48p. (J). (gr. -1-k). *(978-0-7787-1044-8(0))* Crabtree Publishing Co.

Rillo, Lori-Anne. Lorelei Finds a Home. 2010. 32p. pap. 13.49 *(978-1-4490-5890-6(6))* AuthorHouse.

Rinker, Gary W. The Very Best Toy. Rangel, Rawderson, illus. 2010. 28p. (J). (gr. -1). pap. 5.99 *(978-1-59188-881-9(6))* Maverick Bks., Inc.

Rippin, Sally. The Toy Sale. Spartels, Stephanie, illus. 2015. (Hey Jack! Ser.). (ENG.). 41p. (J). *(978-1-61067-454-6(5))* Kane Miller.

—The Toy Sale: Hey Jack! Spartels, Stephanie, illus. 2016. (ENG.). 48p. (J). pap. 4.99 *(978-1-61067-394-5(8))* Kane Miller.

Robinson, Marquita E. Teddy's Bear, 1 vol. Roscoe Robinson, illus. 2009. 15p. pap. 24.95 *(978-1-60749-249-8(0))* America Star Bks.

Rogers, Kenny & Junkerman, Kelly. Kenny Rogers Presents the Toy Shoppe. 2004. (Illus.). 30p. (J). (gr. 4-8). reprint ed. 16.00 *(978-0-7567-7758-6(5))* DIANE Publishing Co.

Rosen, Jonathan. Night of the Living Cuddle Bunnies: Devin Dexter #1. (Devin & Dexter Ser.: 1). (ENG.). (J). (gr. 2-7). 2018. 304p. pap. 9.99 *(978-1-5107-3487-6(2))* 2017. 256p. 15.99 *(978-1-5107-1523-3(1))* Skyhorse Publishing Co., Inc. (Sky Pony Pr.).

Rosenthal, Eileen. Bobo the Sailor Man! Rosenthal, Marc, illus. 2013. (ENG.). 40p. (J). (gr. -1-1). 15.99 *(978-1-4424-4443-0(6))* Simon & Schuster Children's Publishing.

—I Must Have Bobo! Rosenthal, Marc, illus. 2011. (ENG.). 40p. (J). (gr. -1-1). 14.99 *(978-1-4424-0377-2(2),* Atheneum Bks. for Young Readers) Simon & Schuster Children's Publishing.

Ross, Dev. We Both Read Bilingual Edition-Frank & the Tiger/Sapi y el Tigre. Canetti, Yanitzia, tr. from ENG. Reinhart, Larry, illus. 2014. (We Both Read - Level K-1 (Quality) Ser.). (ENG & SPA.). 44p. (J). (gr. k-1). pap. 5.99 *(978-1-60115-058-5(X))* Treasure Bay, Inc.

Roussey, Christine. My Funny Bunny. 2019. (ENG., Illus.). 32p. (J). (gr. -1-1). 16.99 *(978-1-4197-3618-6(3),* 1271001, Abrams Bks. for Young Readers) Abrams, Inc.

Rusu, Meredith. The New Ninja: (LEGO Ninjago: Chapter Book), Bk. 9. 2015. (LEGO Ninjago Ser.). (ENG., Illus.). 80p. (J). (gr. 2-5). pap. 4.99 *(978-0-545-90588-6(5))* Scholastic, Inc.

—Pythor's Revenge. 2018. (Lego Chapter Ser.). (ENG.). 78p. (J). (gr. 1-3). 15.96 *(978-1-64310-325-9(3))* Penworthy Co., LLC, The.

—Pythor's Revenge. 2017. 78p. (J). *(978-1-5182-3951-9(X))* Scholastic, Inc.

Ryherd, Tim. My Hurricane Book. 2006. (Illus.). (J). 12.95 *(978-0-9749974-1-4(2))* Ryherd, Tim Publishing.

Sakai, Komako, creator. The Velveteen Rabbit. 2012. (Illus.). 40p. (J). (gr. -1). 17.95 *(978-1-59270-128-5(0))* Enchanted Lion Bks., LLC.

Salane, Jeffrey. The Official Movie Handbook (the LEGO Movie) Kiernan, Kenny, illus. 2013. (LEGO Movie Ser.). (ENG.). 80p. (J). (gr. 2-5). pap. 5.99 *(978-0-545-62462-6(2))* Scholastic, Inc.

Salzmann, Mary Elizabeth. Here Are Toys! 2005. (First Words Ser.). (Illus.). 23p. (J). pap. 48.42 *(978-1-59679-375-0(9))* ABDO Publishing Co.

Samarrippas, Gloria. In Search for Lucky's Lost Toys. 2006. 17.00 *(978-0-8059-7329-7(X))* Dorrance Publishing Co., Inc.

San Souci, Robert D. Zigzag. Czernecki, Stefan, illus. 2005. (ENG.). 32p. (J). (gr. -1-2). 16.95 *(978-0-87483-764-3(2))* August Hse. Pubs., Inc.

Sanchez, Asa & Dumesnil, Phil. The Woollyhoodwinks: Vs. the Dark Patch. Root, Jeff, illus. 2008. (ENG.). 36p. (J). (gr. -1-3). 15.95 *(978-1-59702-012-1(5))* Immedium.

Sander, Sonia. Help Is on the Way! 2009. (LEGO City Adventures Scholastic Readers Level 1 Ser.: 2). lib. bdg. 13.55 *(978-0-606-07119-2(9))* Turtleback.

—LEGO City Reader Collection: LEGO City Emergency. 2012. (Illus.). 127p. (J). *(978-1-4351-3985-5(2))* Scholastic, Inc.

Sanschagrin, Joceline. El Osito de Peluche. 2004. (Caillou Ser.).Tr. of Where's Teddy? (SPA., Illus.). 24p. (J). (gr. -1-1). bds. 5.95 *(978-1-58728-404-5(9))* Cooper Square Publishing Llc.

Sansone, V. K. WANTED: Children for Toys. 2009. (ENG.). 32p. pap. 14.98 *(978-0-557-16717-3(5))* Lulu Pr., Inc.

Santillo, LuAnn. The Ball. Santillo, LuAnn, ed. 2003. (Half-Pint Kids Readers Ser.). (Illus.). 7p. (J). (gr. -1-1). pap. 1.00 *(978-1-59256-081-3(4))* Half-Pint Kids, Inc.

Santore, Charles. Velveteen Rabbit Board Book: The Classic Edition Board Book. 2014. (Classic Edition Ser.). (ENG., Illus.). 24p. (J). (gr. -1). bds. 8.95 *(978-1-60433-461-6(4),* Applesauce Pr.) Cider Mill Pr. Bk. Pubs., LLC.

—Velveteen Rabbit Hardcover: The Classic Edition. 2013. (Charles Santore Children's Classics Ser.). (ENG., Illus.). 48p. (J). (gr. -1). 19.95 *(978-1-60433-277-3(8),* Applesauce Pr.) Cider Mill Pr. Bk. Pubs., LLC.

Saunders, Catherine. Team Ninja. 2016. (DK Reader Level 4 Ser.). lib. bdg. 13.55 *(978-0-606-38712-5(9))* Turtleback.

Saunders, Kate. The Land of Neverendings. 2017. (ENG.). 336p. (J). 14.50 *(978-0-571-31084-5(2),* Faber & Faber Children's Bks.) Faber & Faber, Inc.

Schneider, Christine. I'm Bored! Pinel, Herve, illus. 2006. (ENG.). 40p. (J). (gr. -1-3). 15.00 *(978-0-618-65760-5(6),* 100467, Clarion Bks.) HarperCollins Pubs.

Scholastic. Space Justice! (LEGO DC Super Heroes) 2015. (LEGO DC Super Heroes Ser.). (ENG., Illus.). 80p. (J). (gr. -1-3). pap. 3.99 *(978-0-545-82556-6(3))* Scholastic, Inc.

Scholastic Editors, ed. Last Laugh! 2013. (LEGO DC Super Heroes Ser.). lib. bdg. 13.55 *(978-0-606-32018-4(0))* Turtleback.

Scholastic, Inc. Staff. Ready for Takeoff! 2010. (LEGO City Adventures Scholastic Readers Level 1 Ser.: 5). lib. bdg. 13.55 *(978-0-606-15057-6(9))* Turtleback.

Scholastic, Inc. Staff, ed. Save the Day. 2013. (LEGO DC Super Heroes Ser.). lib. bdg. 13.55 *(978-0-606-32017-7(2))* Turtleback.

Scholastic, Inc. Staff & Scholastic, Scholastic Scholastic. Adventures in LEGO City, Set. 2nd ed. 2015. (LEGO City Ser.). (ENG.). (J). (gr. -1-3). 24.99 *(978-0-545-80861-3(8))* Scholastic, Inc.

Schorr, Loretta Jean. Sash: The Life of a Little Toy Poodle. 2009. 32p. pap. 16.49 *(978-1-4490-0142-1(4))* AuthorHouse.

Schotter, Roni. Room for Rabbit. Moore, Cyd, illus. 2003. (ENG.). 32p. (J). (gr. k — 1). tchr. ed. 15.00 *(978-0-618-18183-4(0),* 111145, Clarion Bks.) HarperCollins Pubs.

Schwartz, Amy & Marcus, Leonard S. Oscar: The Big Adventure of a Little Sock Monkey. Schwartz, Amy, illus. 2006. (Illus.). 32p. (J). (gr. -1-2). 16.99 *(978-0-06-072622-5(9),* Tegen, Katherine Bks) HarperCollins Pubs.

Scraper, Katherine. Tag Sale Today. 2005. (J). pap. *(978-1-4108-4210-7(X))* Benchmark Education Co.

Seabrook, Heather. Lego Chima - Heroes' Quest. 2014. (DK Reader Level 3 Ser.). lib. bdg. 13.55 *(978-0-606-35732-6(7))* Turtleback.

Searl, Duncan. The Jamie & Angus Stories: A Study Guide. Friedland, Joyce & Kessler, Rikki, eds. 2008. (Novel-Ties Ser.). (Illus.). 23p. pap. 16.95 *(978-0-7675-1485-9(8))* Learning Links Inc.

The Secrets of Eastcliff-By-the-Sea: The Story of Annaliese Easterling & Throckmorton, Her Simply Remarkable Sock Monkey. 2014. (ENG., Illus.). 288p. (J). (gr. 3-7). 16.99 *(978-1-4424-9840-2(4),* Beach Lane Bks.) Beach Lane Bks.

Shannon, David. Too Many Toys. Shannon, David, illus. 2008. (ENG., Illus.). 32p. (J). (gr. -1-3). 18.99 *(978-0-439-49029-0(4),* Blue Sky Pr., The) Scholastic, Inc.

—Uh-Oh, David! A David Sticker Book. Shannon, David, illus. 2013. (ENG., Illus.). 16p. (J). (gr. -1-k). 6.99 *(978-0-545-43768-4(7),* Cartwheel Bks.) Scholastic, Inc.

Shay, Kenley. Marsha Mellow Goes Missing: An Unofficial Story for Shopkins Collectors. 2015. (Unofficial Shopkins Collectors Ser.). (ENG.). 112p. (J). (gr. 1-7). pap. 7.99 *(978-1-5107-0251-6(2),* Sky Pony Pr.) Skyhorse Publishing Co., Inc.

—Prommy Meets Her Match: An Unofficial Story for Shopkins Collectors. 2015. (Unofficial Shopkins Collectors Ser.). (ENG.). 112p. (J). (gr. 1-7). pap. 7.99 *(978-1-5107-0374-2(8),* Sky Pony Pr.) Skyhorse Publishing Co., Inc.

Sheninger, Rick. Buddy the Duck Gets Lost. 2012. 20p. pap. 15.99 *(978-1-4685-8371-7(9))* AuthorHouse.

Shepherd, Jodie. Merry Christmas, Rarity! Fletcher, Lyn, illus. 2006. (My Little Pony Ser.). 32p. (J). (gr. -1-1). pap., act. bk. ed. 3.99 *(978-0-06-079472-9(0),* HarperFestival) HarperCollins Pubs.

Shumate, Robert O. Snuffley. Sutherland, Nicholas, illus. 2008. 28p. pap. 24.95 *(978-1-60610-707-2(0))* America Star Bks.

Sills, Kathy & Sills, Karen. Feelings, Feelings, Feelings. 2012. 19p. 19.00 *(978-1-4349-8743-3(4),* RoseDog Bks.) Dorrance Publishing Co., Inc.

Silver Dolphin en Español Editors. Figuras Magicas: Disney Princesses Magical Magnets. 2005. (SPA., Illus.). 8p. (J). bds. *(978-970-718-241-7(5),* Silver Dolphin en Español) Advanced Marketing, S. de R. L. de C. V.

—Figuras Magicas: Disney Winnie the Pooh Magical Magnets. 2005. (SPA., Illus.). 8p. (J). bds. *(978-970-718-243-1(1),* Silver Dolphin en Español) Advanced Marketing, S. de R. L. de C. V.

Simonson, Audrey. Where Is Your Mousey? 2006. (ENG.). 40p. per. 22.65 *(978-1-4134-0270-4(4))* Xlibris Corp.

Simpson, Martha Seif. Esther's Gragger: A Toyshop Tale of Purim. 2019. (Illus.). 40p. (J). (gr. k-3). 16.95 *(978-1-937786-75-5(7),* Wisdom Tales) World Wisdom, Inc.

Slonim, David. Oh, Ducky! A Chocolate Calamity. Slonim, David, illus. 2006. (Illus.). 28p. (J). (gr. k-4). 16.00 *(978-1-4223-5259-5(5))* DIANE Publishing Co.

Smallman, Steve. Bumbletum. Warnes, Tim, illus. 2006. 24p. (J). (gr. -1-3). 15.95 *(978-1-58925-060-4(5))* Tiger Tales.

—A Very Special Hug. Warnes, Tim, illus. 2008. (ENG.). 32p. (gr. -1-1). 18.69 *(978-1-58925-410-7(4))* Tiger Tales.

Smith, Joel D. Santa's Secret Deal: Who Else Signed It, & Where You Can Find Proof of the Deal in Your Room Right Now. 2012. 30p. pap. 14.25 *(978-1-4575-1458-6(3))* Dog Ear Publishing, LLC.

Smith, John A. A Special Christmas for Oscar. 1 vol. 2010. 32p. 24.95 *(978-1-4512-0999-0(1))* PublishAmerica, Inc.

Smith, Maggie. My Blue Bunny, Bubbit. Smith, Maggie, illus. 2014. (ENG., Illus.). 40p. (J). (gr. -1-3). 16.99 *(978-0-547-55861-5(9),* 1453615, Clarion Bks.) HarperCollins Pubs.

Smith, Michael. My Ducky Buddy. Oliva, Octavio, illus. 2011. 23p. (J). *(978-0-9821675-4-0(7))* East West Discovery Pr.

—My Ducky Buddy. Oliva, Octavio, illus. 2015. (ARA & ENG.). 23p. (J). *(978-0-9913454-3-4(6))* East West Discovery Pr.

—My Ducky Buddy/Mi Amigo el Pato. Oliva, Octavio, illus. 2011. (ENG & SPA.). 24p. (J). (gr. -1-3). 12.95 *(978-0-9821675-5-7(5))* East West Discovery Pr.

Smith, Michael & Wang, Emily. My Ducky Buddy. Oliva, Octavio, illus. 2011. (CHI & ENG.). 23p. (J). *(978-0-9821675-7-1(1))* East West Discovery Pr.

Smith, Michael W. Nighty Night & Good Night. 1 vol. 2018. (Nurturing Steps Ser.). (ENG., Illus.). 22p. (J). bds. 9.99 *(978-0-310-76941-5(8))* Zonderkidz.

Smith, Michael W. & Nawrocki, Mike. Nighty Night & Good Night. 1 vol. 2018. (Nurturing Steps Ser.). (ENG., Illus.). 24p. (J). 12.99 *(978-0-310-76701-5(6))* Zonderkidz.

Snellenberger, Tracy. Tyler the Toddler Feeds the Cows. 2010. 28p. 13.99 *(978-1-4520-5169-7(0))* AuthorHouse.

Snider, Jesse Blaze. Return of Buzz Lightyear. 2. Watson, Nathan, illus. 2010. (Kaboom! Graphic Novels Ser.). (ENG.). 112p. (J). (gr. 4-7). 26.19 *(978-1-60886-557-4(6))* BOOM! Studios.

—Return of Buzz Lightyear Vol. 2. Watson, Nathan, illus. 2010. (Toy Story Ser.). (ENG.). 112p. (J). 24.99 *(978-1-60886-558-1(4))* BOOM! Studios.

—Toy Story: Some Assembly Required. Watson, Nathan, illus. 2010. (Toy Story Ser.). 112p. (J). pap. 9.99 *(978-1-60886-570-3(3))* BOOM! Studios.

—Toy Story: Toy Overboard. Watson, Nathan, illus. 2011. 128p. (J). pap. 9.99 *(978-1-60886-605-2(X))* BOOM! Studios.

Sowder, G. Wesley & Sowder, Joseph, told to. Hunter-Lee & the Toy Monster: Book One. 2008. 48p. pap. 16.95 *(978-1-60703-137-6(X))* America Star Bks.

T
U
V

Spiegelman, Art. Jack & the Box: Toon Books Level 1. 2008. (ENG., Illus.). 32p. (J). (gr. -1-3). 12.95 *(978-0-9799238-3-8(2)*, Toon Books) Astra Publishing Hse.

Spinelli, Eileen. Bath Time, 1 vol. Pedersen, Janet, illus. 2003. (ENG.). 32p. (J). 14.95 *(978-0-7614-5117-4(X))* Marshall Cavendish Corp.

Steele, Michael Anthony. Catch That Crook! Wang, Sean, illus. 2012. 23p. (J). *(978-1-4242-5333-3(0))* Scholastic, Inc.

—Catch That Crook! 2012. (LEGO City 8X8 Ser.). (Illus.). 23p. (J). lib. bdg. 13.55 *(978-0-606-23960-8(X))* Turtleback.

—Fix That Truck! 2012. (LEGO City 8X8 Ser.). lib. bdg. 13.55 *(978-0-606-26773-1(5))* Turtleback.

—LEGO City: Catch That Crook! 2012. (LEGO City Ser.). (ENG., Illus.). 24p. (J). (gr. -1-k). pap. 3.99 *(978-0-545-36991-6(6))* Scholastic, Inc.

Stein, Peter. Toys Galore. Staake, Bob, illus. 2013. (ENG.). 32p. (J). (gr. -1-3). 17.99 *(978-0-7636-6254-7(2))* Candlewick Pr.

Stevenson, James. Night after Christmas. 2003. (ENG.). 32p. (J). pap. 2.95 *(978-0-590-41600-9(6))* Scholastic, Inc.

Stierle, Cynthia. Together Forever. 2010. (Playbox Ser.). (ENG., Illus.). 32p. (J). bds. 19.99 *(978-0-7944-2026-0(5))* Reader's Digest Assn., Inc., The.

Stock, Lisa. Perfect Pets. 2014. (DK Reader Level 2 Ser.). lib. bdg. 13.55 *(978-0-606-35731-9(9))* Turtleback.

Stringer, Beverly. Joe the Dancing Spider. 2004. (ENG., Illus.). 26p. pap. 13.50 *(978-1-4120-2020-6(4))* Trafford Publishing.

Suen, Anastasia. Un Premio Adentro. Heck, Claudia M., tr. Laughead, Mike, illus. 2012. (Robot y Rico/Robot & Rico Ser.).Tr. of Prize Inside. (MUL.). 32p. (J). (gr. 1-2). lib. bdg. 22.65 *(978-1-4342-3780-4(X)*, 117077, Stone Arch Bks.) Capstone.

—A Prize Inside: A Robot & Rico Story, 1 vol. Laughead, Michael, illus. 2009. (Robot & Rico Ser.). (ENG.). 32p. (J). (gr. 1-2). 22.65 *(978-1-4342-1627-4(6)*, 95801, Stone Arch Bks.) Capstone.

—Test Drive: A Robot & Rico Story. Laughead, Michael, illus. 2010. (Robot & Rico Ser.). (ENG.). 32p. (J). (gr. 1-2). pap. 6.25 *(978-1-4342-2303-6(5)*, 103172, Stone Arch Bks.) Capstone.

Taylor, Sean. The World Champion of Staying Awake. Liao, Jimmy, illus. 2011. (ENG.). 32p. (J). (gr. -1-2). 15.99 *(978-0-7636-4957-9(0))* Candlewick Pr.

Terada, Junzo. A Good Home for Max. 2014. (ENG., Illus.). 40p. (J). (gr. -1-k). 16.99 *(978-1-4521-2702-6(6))* Chronicle Bks. LLC.

Tidhar, Lavie. Central Station, 1 vol. unabr. ed. 2017. (ENG.). 9.99 *(978-1-5436-2453-3(7)*, 9781543624533, Audible Studios on Brilliance Audio) Brilliance Publishing, Inc.

Tolley, Diane Stringam. Kris Kringle's Magic. 2012. 169p. (J). 14.99 *(978-1-4621-1105-3(X))* Cedar Fort, Inc./CFI Distribution.

Tootin' Around Town. (Magnets on the Move Ser.). 8p. (J). bds. *(978-2-7643-0101-2(4))* Phidal Publishing, Inc./Editions Phidal, Inc.

Tosten, S. Kennedy. Troy's Amazing Universe Bk. 2: T for Toy. 2004. (Illus.). 149p. (YA). (gr. 2-18). pap. 13.95 *(978-0-9743185-1-6(5))* Brite Pr.

Toy Box Innovations, creator. Disney/Pixar: Volume 2. abr. ed. 2006. (Disney's Read along Collection Ser.). (ENG.). 24p. (J). (gr. -1-3). pap. *(978-0-7634-2181-6(2))* Walt Disney Records.

Toy Town: Individual Title Six-Packs. (gr. -1-2). 23.00 *(978-0-7635-9003-1(7))* Rigby Education.

ToyBox Innovations, creator. Disney Pixar's Toy Story: Read-along. 2006. (Disney's Read Along Ser.). (ENG., Illus.). 24p. (J). (gr. -1-3). pap. *(978-0-7634-2179-3(0))* Walt Disney Records.

Trimmer, Christian. Teddy's Favorite Toy. Valentine, Madeline, illus. 2018. (ENG.). 40p. (J). (gr. -1-3). 17.99 *(978-1-4814-8079-6(0)*, Atheneum Bks. for Young Readers) Simon & Schuster Children's Publishing.

Tuma, Refe & Tuma, Susan. What the Dinosaurs Did Last Night: A Very Messy Adventure. 2015. (What the Dinosaurs Did Ser.: 1). (ENG., Illus.). 40p. (J). (gr. -1-1). 17.00 *(978-0-316-33562-1(2))* Little, Brown Bks. for Young Readers.

V, Vasanthi. The Toy-Gobbling Monster. Lee, Anais, illus. 2013. (ENG.). (J). 14.95 *(978-1-62086-330-5(8))* Amplify Publishing Group.

Vaitonis, Steven. Edison the Christmas Elf & the Imperfect Perfect Toy. Blue, Melissa, illus. 2014. 32p. (J). (gr. -1-1). pap. 12.95 *(978-1-939930-33-0(2)*, Belle Isle Bks.) Brandylane Pubs., Inc.

Valente, Shannon. Trucks, Trains & Worm Brains. 2009. 16p. pap. 10.79 *(978-1-4389-5411-0(5))* AuthorHouse.

Van Slyke, Rebecca. Monster's Trucks. Sutphin, Joe, illus. 2020. (ENG.). 40p. (J). 17.99 *(978-1-68119-301-4(9)*, 900165544, Bloomsbury Children's Bks.) Bloomsbury Publishing USA.

Varicak, Rebecca. The Journey of a Toys for Tots Toy! 2012. 24p. pap. 15.99 *(978-1-4772-8601-2(2))* AuthorHouse.

Vaughan, Richard & Crews, Marcia. Three Bears of the Pacific Northwest. Trammell, Jeremiah, illus. 2016. (Pacific Northwest Fairy Tales Ser.). 20p. (J). (—1). bds. 10.99 *(978-1-63217-076-7(0)*, Little Bigfoot) Sasquatch Bks.

Velasquez, Eric. Looking for Bongo. (ENG.). 32p. (J). (gr. -1-k). 2017. 7.99 *(978-0-8234-3767-2(1))* 2016. (Illus.). 17.99 *(978-0-8234-3565-4(2))* Holiday Hse., Inc.

Verrett, Michael. Cozmo the Elf. 2010. 86p. pap. 32.00 *(978-0-557-25717-1(4))* Lulu Pr., Inc.

Voigt, Cynthia. Teddy & Co. Zakimi, Paola, illus. 2018. (ENG.). 192p. (J). (gr. 2-5). 7.99 *(978-0-553-51163-5(7)*, Yearling) Random Hse. Children's Bks.

Voigtsberger, Sandra A. Jack's Pockets. 2008. 17p. pap. 24.95 *(978-1-60563-546-0(4))* America Star Bks.

Waldman, Debby & Feutl, Rita. Room Enough for Daisy, 1 vol. Revell, Cindy, illus. 2011. (ENG.). 32p. (J). (gr. -1-k). 19.95 *(978-1-55469-255-2(5))* Orca Bk. Pubs. USA.

Wallace, William H. Santa's Magic Key. 2010. 20p. (J). 10.49 *(978-1-4490-8924-5(0))* AuthorHouse.

Wang, Adria. My World: My Playtimes Toys. Nicholls, Paul, illus. 2005. 10p. (J). 4.95 *(978-1-58117-250-8(8)*, Intervisual/Piggy Toes) Bendon, Inc.

Ward, Helen. Twenty-five December Lane. Anderson, Wayne, illus. 2007. 17p. (J). *(978-1-74178-722-1(X))* Five Mile Australia.

Warnock, Chris. Toys Overboard!, 1 vol. 2009. (ENG.). 48p. 24.95 *(978-1-60672-197-1(6))* America Star Bks.

Watt, F. & Wells, R. That's Not My Dolly. 2004. (Illus.). 10p. (J). 7.95 *(978-0-7945-0635-3(6))* EDC Publishing.

Weinberger, David J. Answers to a Christmas Question. 2012. (ENG.). (J). pap. *(978-1-4675-2381-3(X))* Independent Pub.

—Answers to a Christmas Question Coloring Book. 2012. (ENG.). (J). pap. *(978-1-4675-2380-6(1))* Independent Pub.

Weisner, David. Mr. Wuffles! Weisner, David, illus. 2013. (Illus.). 14.99 *(978-0-9777098-8-5(4))*; 49.99 *(978-0-9777098-7-8(6))* Dreamscape Media, LLC.

Wells, Rosemary. Bunny Party. 2003. (Max & Ruby Ser.). (Illus.). 32p. (J). (gr. -1-k). pap. 7.99 *(978-0-14-250162-7(X)*, Puffin Books) Penguin Young Readers Group.

West, Tracey. The Golden Weapons. 2012. (Ninjago Readers Ser.: 3). lib. bdg. 13.55 *(978-0-606-26555-3(4))* Turtleback.

—The Green Ninja. 2013. (Ninjago Readers Ser.: 7). lib. bdg. 13.55 *(978-0-606-32027-6(X))* Turtleback.

—Masters of Spinjitzu. 2012. (Ninjago Readers Ser.: 2). lib. bdg. 13.55 *(978-0-606-23978-3(2))* Turtleback.

—A Ninja's Path (LEGO Ninjago: Reader) 2012. (LEGO Ninjago Ser.). (ENG.). 32p. (J). (gr. k-3). pap. 3.99 *(978-0-545-43593-2(5))* Scholastic, Inc.

—Pirates vs. Ninja. 2013. (Ninjago Readers Ser.: 6). lib. bdg. 13.55 *(978-0-606-32026-9(1))* Turtleback.

—Snake Attack!, Bk. 5. 2012. (LEGO Ninjago Ser.). (ENG.). 80p. (J). (gr. 2-5). pap. 4.99 *(978-0-545-46518-2(4))* Scholastic, Inc.

—A Team Divided. 2014. (LEGO Ninjago Chapter Bks.: 6). lib. bdg. 14.75 *(978-0-606-36367-9(X))* Turtleback.

West, Tracey & Howard, Kate. A Team Divided. 2015. 76p. (J). pap. *(978-0-545-79396-4(3))* Scholastic, Inc.

Weston Woods Staff, creator. Too Many Toys! 2011. 29.95 *(978-0-545-37421-7(9))* Weston Woods Studios, Inc.

Whybrow, Ian. Harry & the Bucketful of Dinosaurs. Reynolds, Adrian, illus. 2010. (Harry & the Dinosaurs Ser.). (ENG.). 32p. (J). (gr. -1-2). pap. 8.99 *(978-0-375-85119-3(4)*, Dragonfly Bks.) Random Hse. Children's Bks.

Wiesner, David. Mr. Wuffles! 2013. (CHI.). 40p. (J). *(978-986-189-418-8(7))* Grimm Cultural Ent., Co., Ltd.

—Mr. Wuffles! A Caldecott Honor Award Winner. Wiesner, David, illus. 2013. (ENG., Illus.). 32p. (J). (gr. -1-3). 19.99 *(978-0-618-75661-2(2)*, 100533, Clarion Bks.) HarperCollins Pubs.

Wilburn, Mary Lynne. Sam's Toy Museum. 2012. 24p. pap. 15.99 *(978-1-4653-4029-0(7))* Xlibris Corp.

Willems, Mo. A Cautionary Tale. Willems, Mo, illus. 2011. (Illus.). 40p. (J). (gr. -1-1). 19.99 *(978-1-4231-4449-6(X))* Hyperion Pr.

—El Conejito Knuffle: Un Cuento Aleccionador. rev. ed. 2007. (Knuffle Bunny Ser.). (SPA., Illus.). 40p. (J). (gr. -1-k). pap. 7.99 *(978-1-4231-0567-1(2)*, Hyperion Books for Children) Disney Publishing Worldwide.

—Hooray for Amanda & Her Alligator! Willems, Mo, illus. 2011. (ENG., Illus.). 72p. (J). (gr. -1-3). 19.99 *(978-0-06-200400-0(X)*, Balzer & Bray) HarperCollins Pubs.

—I Love My New Toy!-An Elephant & Piggie Book. 2008. (Elephant & Piggie Book Ser.). (ENG., Illus.). 64p. (J). (gr. -1-k). 9.99 *(978-1-4231-0961-7(9)*, Hyperion Books for Children) Disney Publishing Worldwide.

—Knuffle Bunny. 2014. 36p. pap. 8.00 *(978-1-61003-228-5(4))* Center for the Collaborative Classroom.

—Knuffle Bunny: A Cautionary Tale. Willems, Mo, illus. unabr. ed. 2006. (Illus.). (J). (gr. -1-1). 29.95 *(978-0-439-90583-1(4))* Weston Woods Studios, Inc.

—Knuffle Bunny Free: An Unexpected Diversion. Willems, Mo, illus. 2010. (ENG., Illus.). 52p. (J). (gr. -1-3). 19.99 *(978-0-06-192957-1(3)*, Balzer & Bray) HarperCollins Pubs.

—Knuffle Bunny Free: An Unexpected Diversion. 2012. *(978-0-545-44810-9(7))* Scholastic, Inc.

—Knuffle Bunny Free: Un Unexpected Diversion. Willems, Mo, illus. 2010. (ENG., Illus.). 52p. (J). (gr. -1-3). lib. bdg. 18.89 *(978-0-06-192958-8(1)*, Balzer & Bray) HarperCollins Pubs.

—Knuffle Bunny Too: A Case of Mistaken Identity. rev. ed. 2007. (Knuffle Bunny Ser.). (ENG., Illus.). 48p. (J). (gr. -1-k). 17.99 *(978-1-4231-0299-1(1)*, Hyperion Books for Children) Disney Publishing Worldwide.

Willems, Mo & Willems, Trixie, narrated by. Knuffle Bunny Too: A Case of Mistaken Identity. 2011. (J). (gr. -1-2). 29.95 *(978-0-545-13456-9(0))* Weston Woods Studios, Inc.

William H. Sadlier Staff. Tina's Toys: Big Book. 2005. (Emergent Library: Vol. 1). (gr. -1-1). 24.00 net. *(978-0-8215-8903-8(2))* Sadlier, William H. Inc.

Williams, Karen Lynn. Galimoto. Stock, Catherine, illus. 2015. 32p. pap. 7.00 *(978-1-61003-604-7(2))* Center for the Collaborative Classroom.

Williams, Margery. The Velveteen Rabbit. Felix, Monique, illus. 2005. 40p. pap. 8.95 *(978-0-89812-383-8(6))* Creative Co., The.

—The Velveteen Rabbit. Nicholson, William, illus. 2011. (Dover Children's Classics Ser.). (ENG.). 48p. (J). (gr. k-5). pap. 8.99 *(978-0-486-48606-2(0)*, 486060) Dover Pubns., Inc.

—The Velveteen Rabbit. 2003. (J). 9.99 *(978-0-9740847-3-2(5))* GiGi Bks.

—The Velveteen Rabbit. 2010. (CHI., Illus.). (J). *(978-957-762-476-5(6))* Hsin Yi Pubns.

—The Velveteen Rabbit. 2003. (ENG.). 16p. (C). pap. 10.00 *(978-0-582-77858-0(1))* Pearson Education.

—The Velveteen Rabbit. Nicholson, William, illus. 44p. (J). (gr. 2-3). pap. 3.50 *(978-0-8072-1346-9(2)*, Listening Library) Random Hse. Audio Publishing Group.

—The Velveteen Rabbit. Hague, Michael, illus. 2008. (ENG.). 48p. (J). (gr. -1-2). per. 7.99 *(978-0-312-37750-2(9)*, 900049139) Square Fish.

—The Velveteen Rabbit, 0 vols. Spirin, Gennady, illus. 2012. (ENG.). 48p. (J). (gr. 1-3). 17.99 *(978-0-7614-5848-7(4)*, 9780761458487, Two Lions) Amazon Publishing.

—The Velveteen Rabbit: The Classic Children's Book. Nicholson, William, illus. 2014. 48p. (J). (gr. -1-2). 19.99 *(978-0-385-37566-5(2)*, Doubleday Bks. for Young Readers) Random Hse. Children's Bks.

—The Velveteen Rabbit Board Book: An Easter & Springtime Book for Kids. Kliros, Thea, illus. 2004. (ENG.). 22p. (J). (gr. -1-1). bds. 7.99 *(978-0-06-052746-4(3)*, HarperFestival) HarperCollins Pubs.

Williams, Sam. Santa's Toys. Gill, Tim, illus. 2003. 14p. bds. *(978-1-85602-274-3(9)*, Pavilion Children's Books) Pavilion Bks.

Wilson, Karma. Princess Me. Unzner, Christa, illus. 2007. (ENG.). 32p. (J). (gr. -1-3). 19.99 *(978-1-4169-4098-2(7)*, McElderry, Margaret K. Bks.) McElderry, Margaret K. Bks.

Winnie the Pooh & a Day for Eeyore (Read-Along Ser.). (J). 7.99 incl. audio *(978-1-55723-176-5(1))* Walt Disney Records.

Wojtowycz, David, illus. Whatever the Weather, Clavde! 2004. 10p. (J). (gr. -1-2). reprint ed. 8.00 *(978-0-7567-8257-3(0))* DIANE Publishing Co.

Wolfe, Frances. The Little Toy Shop. Wolfe, Frances, illus. 2008. (Illus.). 32p. (J). (gr. -1-2). 19.95 *(978-0-88776-865-1(2)*, Tundra Bks.) Tundra Bks. CAN. Dist: Penguin Random Hse. LLC.

Wood, Courtney. Just the Way It Was. 2013. 28p. pap. 19.99 *(978-1-4817-0734-3(5))* AuthorHouse.

Woolf, Julia. Duck & Penguin Are NOT Friends, 1 vol. 2019. (ENG., Illus.). 32p. (J). (gr. -1-3). 16.95 *(978-1-68263-132-4(X))* Peachtree Publishing Co. Inc.

Wooten, Arthur. Wise Bear William: A New Beginning. Santora, Bud, illus. 2012. 44p. pap. 12.99 *(978-0-9850529-1-1(0))* Galaxias Productions.

Wrate, Richard. Din-o-mite in Aarons Closet. 2009. 28p. (J). 14.99 *(978-0-615-19210-9(6))* Show N' Tell Publishing.

Xiong, Kim, illus. The Clay General. 2008. (J). 18.95 *(978-1-60603-002-8(7))* Better Chinese LLC.

—Paper Horse. 2008. (ENG & CHI.). 37p. (J). 18.95 *(978-1-60603-003-5(5))* Better Chinese LLC.

Yaccarino, Dan. Journey to the Center of Town. 2017. (Class Pet Squad Ser.: 1). (J). lib. bdg. 17.20 *(978-0-606-39943-2(7))* Turtleback.

Yoon, Salina. Bear's Big Day. (ENG., Illus.). (J). 2017. 32p. bds. 7.99 *(978-1-68119-436-3(8)*, 900172658) 2016. 40p. 14.99 *(978-0-8027-3832-5(X)*, 900141994) Bloomsbury Publishing USA. (Bloomsbury USA Childrens).

—Found. 2014. (ENG., Illus.). 40p. (J). (gr. -1-1). 14.99 *(978-0-8027-3559-1(2)*, 900121351, Bloomsbury USA Childrens) Bloomsbury Publishing USA.

Yorinks, Arthur. Harry & Lulu. braille ed. 2004. (Illus.). (J). (gr. k-3). spiral bd. *(978-0-616-07249-3(X))*; spiral bd. *(978-0-616-07250-9(3))* Canadian National Institute for the Blind/Institut National Canadien pour les Aveugles.

Yuen, Dan. Charlie the Chopper & the Greatest Toymaker. Davis, Tim, illus. 2010. 26p. (J). *(978-0-88144-480-3(4))* Yorkshire Publishing Group.

Zagarenski, Pamela. Henry & Leo. 2016. (ENG., Illus.). 40p. (J). (gr. -1-3). 17.99 *(978-0-544-64811-1(0)*, 1621604, Clarion Bks.) HarperCollins Pubs.

Zak, Faith. Naptime Adventures: Train. 2012. 24p. 24.95 *(978-1-4626-5000-2(7))* America Star Bks.

Zolotow, Charlotte. Growing up Stories for 5-6 Year Olds. 114p. (J). (gr. -1-17). 19.99 *(978-0-7868-0519-8(6))* Disney Pr.

Zuber, Diane C. The Broken Doll. Firtl, Mary Meehan, illus. 2006. (ENG.). 32p. (J). (gr. -1-3). incl. audio compact disk *(978-0-9785551-1-5(2))* Zuber Publishing.

TOYS—POETRY

Bolocan, D. Stephie Learns about Animals: Funny Rhymes for Children about Toys & Animals. 2010. (Illus.). 56p. pap. 21.99 *(978-1-4490-9045-6(1))* AuthorHouse.

Evans, Olive. The Thrift Store Bears. Woolley, Patricia, illus. 2004. (ENG.). 41p. (J). 18.97 *(978-0-9748954-0-6(7))* Teddy Traveler Co.

Tanner, Suzy-Jane, illus. Nursery Rhymes. 2012. 24p. (J). 9.95 *(978-1-84135-743-0(X))* Award Pubns. Ltd. GBR. Dist: Parkwest Pubns., Inc.

TRACK AND FIELD

see also Walking

Amstutz, Lisa J. The Science Behind Track & Field. 2016. (Science of the Summer Olympics Ser.). (ENG., Illus.). 32p. (J). (gr. 3-9). lib. bdg. 28.65 *(978-1-4914-8158-5(7)*, 130637, Capstone Pr.) Capstone.

Belval, Brian. Olympic Track & Field. 2007. (Illus.). 52p. (gr. 3-7). pap. 26.50 *(978-1-4358-3779-9(7))* Rosen Publishing Group, Inc., The.

Bodden, Valerie. Running. 2009. (Active Sports Ser.). (ENG.). 24p. (J). (gr. 1-4). lib. bdg. 24.25 *(978-1-58341-700-3(1)*, 22078, Creative Education) Creative Co., The.

Chick, Chloe. Mighty Mira Based on the Story. 2016. (ENG., Illus.). 35p. (J). *(978-981-320-254-2(8))* World Scientific Publishing Co. Pte Ltd.

Clarke, Zoë. Collins Big Cat Phonics for Letters & Sounds - Big Mud Run: Band 02A/Red A, Bd. 2A. 2018. (Collins Big Cat Phonics Ser.). (ENG., Illus.). 16p. (J). (gr. -1-k). pap. 6.99 *(978-0-00-825144-4(4))* HarperCollins Pubs. Ltd. GBR. Dist: Independent Pubs. Group.

—The Modern Pentathlon: Band 04 Blue/Band 16 Sapphire (Collins Big Cat Progress) 2012. (Collins Big Cat Progress Ser.). (ENG., Illus.). 48p. (J). (gr. 4-5). pap. 6.99 *(978-0-00-742884-7(7))* HarperCollins Pubs. Ltd. GBR. Dist: Independent Pubs. Group.

Cohn, Jessica. Free Running, 1 vol. 2013. (Incredibly Insane Sports Ser.). (ENG., Illus.). 48p. (J). (gr. 4-5). 34.60 *(978-1-4339-8826-4(7)*, af0a6ac1-9927-4aba-8a59-99be4244f576); pap. 15.05 *(978-1-4339-8827-1(5)*, fd8e7044-c016-4e66-be1f-44cd2bd73ec3) Stevens, Gareth Publishing LLLP. (Gareth Stevens Learning Library).

Conklin, Wendy. No Way! Jolting Jumps. 2nd rev. ed. 2017. (TIME(r): Informational Text Ser.). (ENG., Illus.). 48p. (gr. 6-8). pap. 13.99 *(978-1-4938-3610-9(2))* Teacher Created Materials, Inc.

Crabtree Staff & Johnson, Robin. Take off Track & Field, 1 vol. 2012. (ENG., Illus.). 32p. (J). pap. *(978-0-7787-3181-8(2))* Crabtree Publishing Co.

Crossingham, John & Kalman, Bobbie. Track Events in Action. 2004. (Sports in Action Ser.). (ENG., Illus.). 32p. (J). pap. *(978-0-7787-0359-4(2))* Crabtree Publishing Co.

Doeden, Matt. Track & Field. 2015. (Summer Olympic Sports Ser.). (ENG., Illus.). 32p. (J). (gr. 2-4). 19.95 *(978-1-60753-810-3(5))* Amicus Learning.

Douglas, Peter. Track & Field: Conditioning for Greatness. 2017. (Preparing for Game Day Ser.: Vol. 10). (ENG., Illus.). 80p. (J). (gr. 7-12). 24.95 *(978-1-4222-3920-9(9))* Mason Crest.

Duling, Kaitlyn. Track & Field. 2017. (Illus.). 24p. (J). *(978-1-62031-824-9(5)*, Bullfrog Bks.) Jump! Inc.

Fleming, Sally. Rapid Runners. Underwood, Kay Povelite, illus. 2004. (It's Nature! Ser.). (ENG.). 32p. (J). (gr. 3-6). pap. 7.95 *(978-1-55971-789-2(0)*, NorthWord Bks. for Young Readers) T&N Children's Publishing.

Foster, John. Marathon: Band 06/Orange. 2006. (Collins Big Cat Ser.). (ENG., Illus.). 24p. (J). (gr. 2-2). pap. 8.99 *(978-0-00-718689-1(4))* HarperCollins Pubs. Ltd. GBR. Dist: Independent Pubs. Group.

Frederick, Shane. Track & Field. 2012. (Illus.). 48p. (J). 35.65 *(978-1-60818-212-1(6)*, Creative Education) Creative Co., The.

Gifford, Clive. Baseball, 1 vol. 2010. (Tell Me about Sports Ser.). (ENG.). 32p. (gr. 4-4). 31.21 *(978-0-7614-4453-4(X)*, b85b3e71-bfbc-48fa-bc6a-aba61b9ac99a) Cavendish Square Publishing LLC.

—The Inside Story of Track & Field, 1 vol. 2011. (Sports World Ser.). (ENG.). 48p. (YA). (gr. 5-5). lib. bdg. 34.47 *(978-1-4488-4846-1(6)*, 0e588318-fb27-4aee-9e68-73ff39a509c2) Rosen Publishing Group, Inc., The.

—Running, 1 vol. 2010. (Tell Me about Sports Ser.). (ENG.). 32p. (gr. 4-4). 31.21 *(978-0-7614-4459-6(9)*, b08933e2-6b99-4e1b-8466-19a6a2e8b2ea) Cavendish Square Publishing LLC.

—Track & Field. 2011. (Olympic Sports Ser.). (ENG.). 32p. (J). (gr. 4-8). lib. bdg. 28.50 *(978-1-60753-187-6(9)*, 17108) Amicus.

—Track & Field. 2011. (ENG., Illus.). 32p. (J). pap. 10.95 *(978-1-77092-040-8(4))* Saunders Bk. Co. CAN. Dist: RiverStream Publishing.

Glass, Maya. The Running Book / Correr. 2009. (Let's Get Moving / Diviértete en movimiento Ser.). (ENG & SPA.). 24p. (gr. k-1). 42.50 *(978-1-61514-236-1(3)*, Editorial Buenas Letras) Rosen Publishing Group, Inc., The.

Goodrow, Carol. Kids Running: Have Fun, Get Faster, & Go Farther. 2008. (ENG., Illus.). 88p. (J). (gr. 1-6). per. 10.95 *(978-1-891369-76-6(8))* Breakaway Bks.

Greek, Joe. Parkour, 1 vol. 2015. (Sports to the Extreme Ser.). (ENG., Illus.). 48p. (J). (gr. 5-6). 33.47 *(978-1-4994-3553-5(3)*, ffb961ac-6ea3-40e0-8a0a-621e589806d6, Rosen Central) Rosen Publishing Group, Inc., The.

—Zombie Runs, 1 vol., 1. 2015. (Role-Playing for Fun & Profit Ser.). (ENG.). 48p. (J). (gr. 5-5). pap. 12.75 *(978-1-4994-3736-2(6)*, 85954b2a-d109-459f-a72e-56134a1fbad6, Rosen Central) Rosen Publishing Group, Inc., The.

Griffis, Molly Levite. Great American Bunion Derby. 2003. (Illus.). viii, 87p. (J). 15.95 *(978-1-57168-801-9(3)*, Eakin Pr.) Eakin Pr.

Havelka, Jacqueline. STEM in Track & Field. 2019. (Connecting STEM & Sports Ser.). (Illus.). 80p. (J). (gr. 12). lib. bdg. 34.60 *(978-1-4222-4338-1(9))* Mason Crest.

Hayhurst, Chris. Ultra Marathon Running. 2009. (Ultra Sports Ser.). 64p. (gr. 5-8). 58.50 *(978-1-60854-609-1(8)*, Rosen Reference) Rosen Publishing Group, Inc., The.

Jackson, Demi. Parkour, 1 vol. 2015. (Daredevil Sports Ser.). (ENG., Illus.). 32p. (J). (gr. 1-1). pap. 11.50 *(978-1-4824-2993-0(4)*, 4f19ed8d-9985-41b7-9cfd-b85c30f10357) Stevens, Gareth Publishing LLLP.

Jankowski, Matt. The Greatest Track Stars of All Time, 1 vol. 2019. (Greatest of All Time: Sports Stars Ser.). (ENG.). 32p. (gr. 3-4). pap. 11.50 *(978-1-5382-4787-7(9)*, 952f41ce-5ad2-46b0-8037-bc093101b89a) Stevens, Gareth Publishing LLLP.

Johnson, Robin. Take off Track & Field. 2012. (ENG., Illus.). 32p. (J). lib. bdg. *(978-0-7787-3154-2(5))* Crabtree Publishing Co.

Kalman, Bobbie. Field Events in Action. 2004. (Sports in Action Ser.). (ENG., Illus.). 32p. (J). pap. *(978-0-7787-0360-0(6))* Crabtree Publishing Co.

—Field Events in Action. Crabtree, Marc & Rouse, Bonna, illus. Crabtree, Marc, photos by. 2004. (Sports in Action Ser.). (ENG.). 32p. (J). lib. bdg. *(978-0-7787-0340-2(1))* Crabtree Publishing Co.

Kortemeier, Todd. 12 Reasons to Love Track & Field. 2018. (Sports Report). (ENG.). 32p. (J). (gr. 3-6). 32.80 *(978-1-63235-431-0(4)*, 13794, 12-Story Library) Bookstaves, LLC.

—12 Reasons to Love Track & Field. 2018. (ENG.). 32p. (gr. 3-6). pap. 9.95 *(978-1-62143-552-5(0))* Pr. Room Editions LLC.

Lang, Heather. Fearless Flyer: Ruth Law & Her Flying Machine. ón, Raul, illus. 2016. (ENG.). 40p. (J). (gr. 2-5). 16.95 *(978-1-62091-650-6(9)*, Calkins Creek) Highlights Pr., c/o Highlights for Children, Inc.

Laughlin, Kara L. Parkour. 2018. (Neighborhood Sports Ser.). (ENG.). 24p. (J). (gr. k-3). lib. bdg. 32.79 *(978-1-5038-2371-6(7)*, 212214) Child's World, Inc, The.

Llanas, Sheila. Women in Track & Field. 2020. (She's Got Game Ser.). (ENG., Illus.). 32p. (J). (gr. 3-5). pap. 9.95 *(978-1-64493-144-8(3)*, 1644931443); lib. bdg. 31.35 *(978-1-64493-065-6(X)*, 164493065X) North Star Editions. (Focus Readers).

Loh-Hagan, Virginia. Extreme Ultra Running. 2016. (Nailed It! Ser.). (ENG., Illus.). 32p. (J). (gr. 4-8). 32.07 *(978-1-63470-484-7(3)*, 207667) Cherry Lake Publishing.

Luke, Andrew. Track & Field, Vol. 13. 2016. (Inside the World of Sports Ser.: Vol. 13). (ENG., Illus.). 80p. (J). (gr. 7-12). 24.95 *(978-1-4222-3467-9(3))* Mason Crest.

MacKay, Jennifer. Track & Field, 1 vol. 2012. (Science Behind Sports Ser.). (ENG., Illus.). 104p. (gr. 7-7). lib. bdg. 41.03 *(978-1-4205-0707-2(9)*, 00c78b03-6748-40f9-9073-73da01076cd9, Lucent Pr.) Greenhaven Publishing LLC.

Malaspina, Ann. Vivian & Victor Learn about Verbs. Prater, Linda, illus. 2014. (Language Builders Ser.). (ENG.). 32p. (J). (gr. 2-4). lib. bdg. 25.27 *(978-1-59953-667-5(6))* Norwood Hse. Pr.

Markovics, Pearl. Animals That Run. 2018. (Animals on the Move! Ser.). (ENG., Illus.). 16p. (J). (gr. -1-1). 6.99 *(978-1-64280-145-3(3))*; lib. bdg. 16.96 *(978-1-64280-006-7(6))* Bearport Publishing Co., Inc.

Marsico, Katie & Minden, Cecilia. Running. 2008. (21st Century Skills Library: Real World Math Ser.). (ENG., Illus.). 32p. (gr. 4-8). lib. bdg. 32.07 *(978-1-60279-249-4(6),* 200032) Cherry Lake Publishing.
Mason, Paul & Eason, Sarah. Free Running. 2011. (On the Radar: Sports Ser.). (ENG., Illus.). 32p. (gr. 4-8). lib. bdg. 26.60 *(978-0-7613-7759-7(X))* Lerner Publishing Group.
McDougall, Chros. Girls Play to Win Track & Field. 2011. (Girls Play to Win Ser.). 64p. (J). (gr. 3-6). lib. bdg. 27.93 *(978-1-59953-467-1(3))* Norwood Hse. Pr.
McGillivray, Dave & Feehrer, Nancy. Dream Big: A True Story of Courage & Determination. Himler, Ron, illus. 2018. (ENG.). 32p. (J). 16.95 *(978-1-61930-618-9(2),* d6b095db-9a57-41d0-968d-ef8d7bc7dbef) Nomad Pr.
Nitz, Kristin Wolden. Play-by-Play Field Events. King, Andy, illus. King, Andy, photos by. 2004. (Play-by-Play Ser.). 80p. (J). (gr. 4-8). lib. bdg. 23.93 *(978-0-8225-3933-9(0))* Lerner Publishing Group.
Osborne, M. K. El Atletismo. 2020. (Deportes Olímpicos de Verano Ser.). (SPA.). 32p. (J). (gr. 2-5). lib. bdg. *(978-1-68151-899-2(6),* 10703) Amicus.
—Track & Field. 2020. (Summer Olympic Sports Ser.). (ENG.). 32p. (J). (gr. 2-5). *(978-1-68151-825-1(2),* 10699) Amicus.
Payment, Simone. What Happens to Your Body When You Run, 1 vol. 2009. (How & Why of Exercise Ser.). (ENG., Illus.). 48p. (YA). (gr. 5-6). 34.47 *(978-1-4358-5306-5(7),* 213c9029-6f61-4a48-aaf4-30866cae4c4f) Rosen Publishing Group, Inc., The.
Poletti, Frances & Yee, Kristina. The Girl Who Ran: Bobbi Gibb, the First Woman to Run the Boston Marathon. Chapman, Susanna, illus. 2017. (J). *(978-1-943200-47-4(5))* Compendium, Inc., Publishing & Communications.
Richards-Ross, Sanya. Right on Track: Run, Race, Believe, 1 vol. 2018. (ENG.). 224p. (YA). 18.99 *(978-0-310-76090-0(9))* Zondervan.
A Robbie Reader-Extreme Sports, 4 vols., Set. Incl. Extreme Cycling with Dale Holmes. Hinman, Bonnie. lib. bdg. 25.70 *(978-1-58415-487-7(X));* Extreme Skateboarding with Paul Rodriquez JR. Kjelle, Marylou Morano. lib. bdg. 25.70 *(978-1-58415-489-1(6));* Ride the Giant Waves with Garrett Mcnamara. Smalley, Carol Parenzan. lib. bdg. 25.70 *(978-1-58415-486-0(1));* Ultra Running with Scott Jurek. Whiting, Jim. lib. bdg. 25.70 *(978-1-58415-484-6(5));* 32p. (J). (gr. 1-4). 2006. (Robbie Reader Ser.). (Illus.). 2006. lib. bdg. *(978-1-58415-485-3(3))* Mitchell Lane Pubs.
Royston, Angela. Why Do I Run? 2012. (My Body Ser.). (ENG., Illus.). 24p. (gr. k-4). pap. 7.95 *(978-1-77092-000-2(5))* Saunders Bk. Co. CAN. Dist: RiverStream Publishing.
Running, 6 vols. (Multicultural Programs Ser.). 16p. (gr. 1-3). 24.95 *(978-0-7802-9215-4(4))* Wright Group/McGraw-Hill.
Sisk, Siobhan. Would You Dare Run a Marathon?, 1 vol. 2016. (Would You Dare? Ser.). (ENG.). 32p. (J). (gr. 1-2). pap. 11.50 *(978-1-4824-5822-0(5),* 23efe255-d684-4ec1-b5be-1ec8096dd813) Stevens, Gareth Publishing LLLP.
Speno, Andrew. The Great American Foot Race: Ballyhoo for the Bunion Derby! 2017. (ENG., Illus.). 176p. (J). (gr. 5-12). 17.95 *(978-1-62979-602-4(6),* Calkins Creek) Highlights Pr., c/o Highlights for Children, Inc.
Teller, Jackson. Free Running. 2012. (Adrenaline Rush Ser.). (Illus.). 32p. (gr. 4-7). lib. bdg. 31.35 *(978-1-59920-682-0(X))* Black Rabbit Bks.
Thom, Kara Douglass. See Mom Run. Golden, Lilly, illus. 2003. (ENG.). 32p. (J). 15.00 *(978-1-891369-40-7(7))* Breakaway Bks.
Vanderhoof, Gabrielle. Track & Field. 2010. (Getting the Edge Ser.). 96p. (YA). lib. bdg. 24.95 *(978-1-4222-1740-5(X))* Mason Crest.
Wade, Alison. The Female Distance Runner's Training Log. 2003. 6.00 *(978-0-9701566-3-1(4))* Idea, Inc.
Way, Jennifer. The Running Book. (Let's Get Moving Ser.). 24p. (gr. k-k). 2009. 42.50 *(978-1-61514-230-9(4))* 2003. (ENG., Illus.). (J). lib. bdg. 26.27 *(978-1-4042-2512-1(9),* a9ba7c78-bd69-44ac-82fa-17ee7f13ff58) Rosen Publishing Group, Inc., The. (PowerKids Pr.).
—The Running Book: Correr, 1 vol. 2003. (Let's Get Moving / Diviértete en Movimiento Ser.). (ENG & SPA., Illus.). 24p. (J). (gr. k-1). lib. bdg. 26.27 *(978-1-4042-7512-6(6),* 5ac87a7c-aec7-42c8-a1bc-9b65d2f78a46) Rosen Publishing Group, Inc., The.

TRACK AND FIELD—FICTION

Almond, David. Harry Miller's Run. Rubbino, Salvatore, illus. 2017. (ENG.). 64p. (J). (gr. 2-4). 16.99 *(978-0-7636-8975-9(0))* Candlewick Pr.
Bari, Ellen. Jumping Jenny. García Maciá, Raquel, illus. 2011. (ENG.). 32p. (J). (gr. k-3). pap. 7.95 *(978-0-7613-5143-6(4),* f9babae4-19fc-4995-8a15-288015f0099f, Kar-Ben Publishing) Lerner Publishing Group.
—Jumping Jenny. Maciá, Raquel García, illus. 2011. (Kar-Ben Favorites Ser.). (ENG.). 32p. (J). (gr. k-3). lib. bdg. 17.95 *(978-0-7613-5141-2(8),* Kar-Ben Publishing) Lerner Publishing Group.
Cano, Fernando & Peters, Stephanie True. Track Team Titans, 1 vol. Aburto, Jesus & Esparza, Andres, illus. 2011. (Sports Illustrated Kids Graphic Novels Ser.). (ENG.). 56p. (J). (gr. 3-8). pap. 7.19 *(978-1-4342-3072-0(4),* 114688); lib. bdg. 26.65 *(978-1-4342-2224-4(1),* 103087) Capstone. (Stone Arch Bks.).
Cartier, Wesley. Marco's Run. Ruffins, Reynold, illus. 2003. (ENG.). 24p. (J). (gr. -1-3). pap. 4.99 *(978-0-15-204828-0(6),* 1194579, Clarion Bks.) HarperCollins Pubs.
Coniglio, Rebecca Perlman. Lily's Little Life Lessons: Lily's Laces. Mundy, Jen, illus. 2013. (ENG.). 24p. (J). (gr. -1-3). 14.95 *(978-1-62086-408-1(8))* Amplify Publishing Group.
Cotter, Steve. Cheesie Mack Is Running Like Crazy! Holgate, Douglas, illus. 2014. (Cheesie Mack Ser.: 3). 256p. (J). (gr. 3-7). pap. 7.99 *(978-0-307-97716-8(1),* Yearling) Random Hse. Children's Bks.
Covell, David. Run Wild. 2018. (Illus.). 40p. (J). (-k). 18.99 *(978-0-670-01411-8(7),* Viking Books for Young Readers) Penguin Young Readers Group.
Cross-country Race: Individual Title Six-Packs. (gr. 1-2). 22.00 *(978-0-7635-9169-4(6))* Rigby Education.
DelleCava, Karen. A Closer Look. 2011. 304p. (YA). (gr. 9-18). 16.95 *(978-1-934813-49-2(4))* Westside Bks.
Doyle, Bill. The Zombie at the Finish Line, 4. Lee, Jared, illus. 2013. (Scream Team Ser.). (ENG.). 96p. (J). (gr. 2-4). 17.44 *(978-0-545-47978-3(9))* Scholastic, Inc.
Driscoll, Laura. Slow down, Sara! O'Rourke, Page Eastburn, illus. 2003. (Science Solves It! Ser.). (ENG.). 32p. (J). (gr. 1-3). pap. 5.95 *(978-1-57565-125-5(4),* d9b4ea07-5fe7-46cf-84ca-95db3ae5272f, Kane Press) Astra Publishing Hse.
Fehlbaum, Beth. Hope in Patience. 2010. 312p. (YA). (gr. 8-18). 16.95 *(978-1-934813-41-6(9))* Westside Bks.
Fry, Erin. Losing It, 0 vols. 2013. (ENG.). 274p. (J). (gr. 4-6). pap. 9.99 *(978-1-4778-1668-4(2),* 9781477816684, Two Lions) Amazon Publishing.
Geary, Cailean McCarrick. Kelsey Shining Bright. 2012. 198p. pap. 12.95 *(978-1-934074-76-3(4))* Apprentice Hse.
Harkness, Karen. Coralee's Best Run Yet. 2007. (Illus.). 40p. (J). per. 7.99 net. *(978-0-9800934-0-7(6))* H&W Publishing Inc.
Hengel, Katherine. No Easy Race, 1 vol. unabr. ed. 2010. (District 13 Ser.). (ENG.). 47p. (YA). (gr. 9-12). 9.75 *(978-1-61651-277-4(6))* Saddleback Educational Publishing, Inc.
Jackson, Kyle. Back on Track. Rumble, Simon, illus. 2018. (Mac's Sports Report). (ENG.). 128p. (J). (gr. 3-4). pap. 7.99 *(978-1-63163-224-2(8),* 1631632248); lib. bdg. 27.13 *(978-1-63163-223-5(X),* 163163223X) North Star Editions. (Jolly Fish Pr.).
Kim, JiYu. Zippy the Runner. Seon, JeongHyeon, illus. rev. ed. 2014. (MySELF Bookshelf Ser.). (ENG.). 32p. (J). (gr. k-2). pap. 11.94 *(978-1-60357-656-7(8));* lib. bdg. 25.27 *(978-1-59953-647-7(1))* Norwood Hse. Pr.
Kuskowski, Alex. Line Up, 1 vol. unabr. ed. 2010. (District 13 Ser.). (ENG.). 48p. (YA). (gr. 9-12). pap. 9.75 *(978-1-61651-279-8(2))* Saddleback Educational Publishing, Inc.
M. Bergeron, Alain. Abby's Fabulous SeasonLa Fabuleuse Saison d'Abby Hoffman, 1 vol. 2014. Orig. Title: La Fabuleuse Saison d'Abby Hoffman. (ENG.). 312p. (J). (gr. 3-6). pap. 10.95 *(978-1-927583-47-0(0))* Second Story Pr. CAN. Dist: Orca Bk. Pubs. USA.
Maddox, Jake. Rookie Runner. 2018. (Jake Maddox JV Ser.). (ENG., Illus.). 96p. (J). (gr. 4-6). lib. bdg. 25.99 *(978-1-4965-6332-3(8),* 138063, Stone Arch Bks.) Capstone.
—Second Shot. Aburto, Jesus, illus. 2016. (Jake Maddox Sports Stories Ser.). (ENG.). 72p. (J). (gr. 3-6). lib. bdg. 25.99 *(978-1-4965-3052-3(7),* 131934, Stone Arch Bks.) Capstone.
Maddox, Jake & Maddox, Jake. Track & Field Takedown, 1 vol. Garcia, Eduardo, illus. 2012. (Jake Maddox Sports Stories Ser.). (ENG.). 72p. (J). (gr. 3-6). pap. 5.95 *(978-1-4342-3901-3(2),* 118086); lib. bdg. 25.99 *(978-1-4342-3287-8(5),* 116250) Capstone. (Stone Arch Bks.).
Malaspina, Ann. Touch the Sky: Alice Coachman, Olympic High Jumper. Velasquez, Eric, illus. 2012. (ENG.). 32p. (J). (gr. -1-3). 16.99 *(978-0-8075-8035-6(X),* 080758035X) Whitman, Albert & Co.
Molokie, Tom. Introducing Willy Mcspry. 2011. 36p. pap. 15.65 *(978-1-4634-3697-1(1))* AuthorHouse.
Montgomery, R. A. Track Star! Louie, Wes, illus. 2009. (ENG.). 144p. (J). (gr. 4-8). pap. 7.99 *(978-1-933390-31-4(X))* Chooseco LLC.
O'Connor, Jane. Fancy Nancy & the Mean Girl. Glasser, Robin Preiss, illus. 2011. (I Can Read Level 1 Ser.). (ENG.). 32p. (J). (gr. -1-3). 16.99 *(978-0-06-200178-8(7));* pap. 4.99 *(978-0-06-200177-1(9))* HarperCollins Pubs. (HarperCollins).
Reynolds, Jason. Ghost. 2018. (CHI.). (J). (gr. 5). pap. *(978-986-479-487-4(6))* Commonwealth Publishing Co., Ltd.
—Ghost, 1. 2018. (Penworthy Picks Middle School Ser.). (ENG.). 181p. (J). (gr. 5-7). 17.96 *(978-1-64310-441-6(1))* Penworthy Co., LLC, The.
—Ghost. (Track Ser.: 1). (ENG., Illus.). (J). (gr. 5). 2017. 208p. pap. 7.99 *(978-1-4814-5016-4(6))* 2016. 192p. 17.99 *(978-1-4814-5015-7(8),* Atheneum/Caitlyn Dlouhy Books) Simon & Schuster Children's Publishing.
—Ghost. l.t. ed. 2019. (ENG.). 196p. (J). (gr. 5). pap. 12.99 *(978-1-4328-6394-4(0),* Large Print Pr.) Thorndike Pr.
—Ghost. 2017. (Track Ser.: bk.1). (ENG.). (J). lib. bdg. 17.20 *(978-0-606-40160-9(1))* Turtleback.
—Lu. (Track Ser.: 4). (ENG.). (J). (gr. 5). 2019. 240p. pap. 7.99 *(978-1-4814-5025-6(5),* Atheneum Bks. for Young Readers) 2018. (Illus.). 224p. 16.99 *(978-1-4814-5024-9(7),* Atheneum/Caitlyn Dlouhy Books) Simon & Schuster Children's Publishing.
—Patina, 2. 2020. (Penworthy Picks YA Fiction Ser.). (ENG.). 235p. (J). (gr. 6-8). 18.49 *(978-1-64697-216-6(3))* Penworthy Co., LLC, The.
—Patina. (Track Ser.: 2). (ENG.). (J). (gr. 5). 2018. 256p. pap. 7.99 *(978-1-4814-5019-5(0))* 2017. (Illus.). 240p. 17.99 *(978-1-4814-5018-8(2),* Atheneum/Caitlyn Dlouhy Books) Simon & Schuster Children's Publishing.
—Patina. 2018. (Track Ser.: 2). lib. bdg. 18.40 *(978-0-606-41459-3(2))* Turtleback.
—Sunny. (Track Ser.: 3). (ENG., Illus.). (J). (gr. 5). 2019. 192p. pap. 7.99 *(978-1-4814-5022-5(0))* 2018. 176p. 16.99 *(978-1-4814-5021-8(2),* Atheneum/Caitlyn Dlouhy Books) Simon & Schuster Children's Publishing.
Richards, Katherine. My Favorite Run. Fieldhouse, Vicky, illus. 2013. (ENG.). 32p. (J). 16.99 *(978-0-9895095-2-7(4))* Fit Kids Publishing.
Robins, Eleanor. The Fastest Runner, 1 vol. unabr. ed. 2010. (Carter High Chronicles Ser.). (ENG.). 52p. (YA). (gr. 9-12). pap. 9.75 *(978-1-61651-308-5(X))* Saddleback Educational Publishing, Inc.
Schraff, Anne. A Boy Called Twister, 1 vol. unabr. ed. 2010. (Urban Underground Ser.). (ENG.). 180p. (YA). (gr. 9-12). pap. 11.95 *(978-1-61651-002-2(1))* Saddleback Educational Publishing, Inc.
—A Boy Called Twister. 2010. (Urban Underground — Harriet Tubman High School Ser.). (YA). lib. bdg. 20.80 *(978-0-606-14271-7(1))* Turtleback.
Scudamore, Beverly. Ready to Run, 1 vol. 2006. (Lorimer Sports Stories Ser.). (ENG.). 96p. (J). (gr. 4-8). 16.95 *(978-1-55028-915-2(2),* 915); 8.95 *(978-1-55028-914-5(4),* 914) James Lorimer & Co. Ltd., Pubs. CAN. Dist: Formac Lorimer Bks. Ltd.
Sommer, Carl. The Great Royal Race. 2003. (Another Sommer-Time Story Ser.). (Illus.). 48p. (J). (gr. k-4). lib. bdg. 23.95 incl. audio *(978-1-57537-758-2(6))* Advance Publishing, Inc.
—The Great Royal Race. Westbrook, Dick, illus. 2003. (Another Sommer-Time Story Ser.). 48p. (J). (gr. k-4). lib. bdg. 23.95 incl. audio compact disk *(978-1-57537-708-7(X))* Advance Publishing, Inc.
—The Great Royal Race. 2003. (Another Sommer-Time Story Ser.). (Illus.). 48p. (J). (gr. 1-4). 16.95 incl. audio *(978-1-57537-557-1(5))* Advance Publishing, Inc.
—The Great Royal Race. Westbrook, Dick, illus. 2003. (Another Sommer-Time Story Ser.). 48p. (J). (gr. 1-4). 16.95 incl. audio compact disk *(978-1-57537-508-3(7))* Advance Publishing, Inc.
—The Great Royal Race(La Gran Carrera Real) Westbrook, Dick, illus. 2009. (Another Sommer-Time Story Bilingual Ser.). (SPA & ENG.). 48p. (J). lib. bdg. 16.95 *(978-1-57537-152-8(9))* Advance Publishing, Inc.
Terrell, Brandon. Valor & Victory. Max, Iman, illus. 2016. (Time Machine Magazine Ser.). (ENG.). 128p. (J). (gr. 3-6). lib. bdg. 23.99 *(978-1-4965-2594-9(9),* 130723, Stone Arch Bks.) Capstone.
Voigt, Cynthia. The Runner. 2012. (Tillerman Cycle Ser.: 4). (ENG., Illus.). 240p. (YA). (gr. 7). pap. 7.99 *(978-1-4424-2881-2(3));*4. 18.99 *(978-1-4424-5066-0(5))* Simon & Schuster Children's Publishing. (Atheneum Bks. for Young Readers).
Wallace, Rich. Chasing the Baton, 1 vol. Heitz, Tim, illus. 2015. (Game Face Ser.). (ENG.). 112p. (J). (gr. 2-5). 38.50 *(978-1-62402-133-6(6),* 19194, Calico Chapter Bks.) ABDO Publishing Co.

TRACK AND FIELD ATHLETES

Baer, Peter. Wilma Rudolph: Gold-Medal Winner, 1 vol. 2013. (InfoMax Readers Ser.). (ENG.). 24p. (J). (gr. 2-2). pap. 8.25 *(978-1-4777-2381-4(1),* defcd7f1-a898-47df-9a31-df69535e32f8); pap. 49.50 *(978-1-4777-2383-8(8))* Rosen Publishing Group, Inc., The. (Rosen Classroom).
Baer, Peter & Castle, Grace. Olympic Champion: Wilma Rudolph, 1 vol. 2013. (Rosen Readers Ser.). (ENG.). 24p. (J). (gr. 2-2). pap. 8.25 *(978-1-4777-2385-2(4),* f1d8f54c-f98a-4788-9c86-4cf49f6347d3); pap. 49.50 *(978-1-4777-2386-9(2))* Rosen Publishing Group, Inc., The. (Rosen Classroom).
Benge, Janet & Benge, Geoff. Heroes of History - Louis Zamperini: Redemption. 2014. (ENG.). 218p. (J). pap. 11.99 *(978-1-62486-049-2(4))* Emerald Bks.
Buckley, James. Who Was Jesse Owens? Copeland, Gregory, illus. 2015. 106p. (J). *(978-1-4806-9215-2(8),* Grosset & Dunlap) Penguin Publishing Group.
—Who Was Jesse Owens? 2015. (Who Was...? Ser.). (Illus.). 106p. (J). lib. bdg. 16.00 *(978-0-606-36754-7(3))* Turtleback.
Burlingame, Jeff. Jesse Owens: I Always Loved Running, 1 vol. 2008. (African-American Biography Library). (ENG., Illus.). 128p. (gr. 6-7). lib. bdg. 35.93 *(978-0-7660-3497-6(6),* c6efb6b4-5e32-43da-8578-9363fa4e2314) Enslow Publishing, LLC.
Calkhoven, Laurie. Jesse Owens: Ready-To-Read Level 3. Vukovic, Elizabet, illus. 2017. (You Should Meet Ser.). (ENG.). 48p. (J). (gr. 1-3). pap. 4.99 *(978-1-4814-8095-6(2),* Simon Spotlight) Simon Spotlight.
Frederick, Shane. Track & Field. 2012. (Illus.). 48p. (J). 35.65 *(978-1-60818-212-1(6),* Creative Education) Creative Co., The.
Hoena, Blake. Jesse Owens: Athletes Who Made a Difference. Shephard, David, illus. 2020. (Athletes Who Made a Difference Ser.). (ENG.). 32p. (J). (gr. 3-6). 27.99 *(978-1-5415-7815-9(5),* 6f1177d5-000e-4572-8f43-0fa3db9ff35d); pap. 8.99 *(978-1-7284-0295-6(6),* 40623995-5723-437b-9ae3-f10d764102c0) Lerner Publishing Group. (Graphic Universe™).
Jankowski, Matt. The Greatest Track Stars of All Time, 1 vol. 2019. (Greatest of All Time: Sports Stars Ser.). (ENG.). 32p. (gr. 3-4). pap. 11.50 *(978-1-5382-4787-7(9),* 952f41ce-5ad2-46b0-8037-bc093101b89a) Stevens, Gareth Publishing LLLP.
Krull, Kathleen. Wilma Unlimited. Diaz, David, illus. 2015. 44p. pap. 7.00 *(978-1-61003-502-6(X))* Center for the Collaborative Classroom.
Lang, Heather. Queen of the Track: Alice Coachman, Olympic High-Jump Champion. Cooper, Floyd, illus. 2012. (ENG.). 40p. (J). (gr. k-4). 18.99 *(978-1-59078-850-9(8),* Astra Young Readers) Astra Publishing Hse.
Leed, Percy. Wilma Rudolph: Running for Gold. 2020. (Epic Sports Bios (Lerner (tm) Sports) Ser.). (ENG., Illus.). 32p. (J). (gr. 2-5). 30.65 *(978-1-5415-9744-0(3),* d02fb726-95e7-47ea-aa3b-c085bb381bd2, Lerner Pubns.) Lerner Publishing Group.
Mckissack, Patricia & Mckissack, Fredrick. Jesse Owens: Legendary Track Star, 1 vol. 2013. (Famous African Americans Ser.). (ENG.). 24p. (gr. 1-2). pap. 10.35 *(978-1-4644-0199-2(3),* 4261b8b0-7a97-4f86-92d0-a7b892e91f1e, Enslow Elementary); (Illus.). 25.27 *(978-0-7660-4104-2(2),* 99a92186-6ddf-45a7-a2b6-3866e32768d3) Enslow Publishing, LLC.
Mooney, Carla. Caitlyn Jenner, 1 vol. 2016. (Transgender Pioneers Ser.). (ENG., Illus.). 112p. (J). (gr. 7-7). 38.80 *(978-1-5081-7158-4(0),* 8c902777-750d-4810-bf21-b5d7db5b8ea7) Rosen Publishing Group, Inc., The.
Murray, John. Bolt - The Fastest Man on Earth. 2018. (Ultimate Sports Heroes Ser.). (ENG.). 176p. (J). (gr. 4-8). pap. 10.99 *(978-1-78606-467-7(7))* Blake, John Publishing, Ltd. GBR. Dist: Independent Pubs. Group.
Nardo, Don. The Science & Technology of Track & Field. 2019. (Science & Technology of Sports Ser.). (ENG.). 80p. (J). (gr. 6-12). 41.27 *(978-1-68282-657-7(0))* ReferencePoint Pr., Inc.
Offutt, Jason. Helen Stephens: The Fulton Flash. Hare, John, illus. 2014. (ENG.). 48p. (J). lib. bdg. 24.00 *(978-1-61248-114-2(0))* Truman State Univ. Pr.
Patrick, Jean L. S. Long-Armed Ludy & the First Women's Olympics. Gustavson, Adam, illus. 2017. 32p. (J). (gr. 1-4). lib. bdg. 16.99 *(978-1-58089-546-0(8))* Charlesbridge Publishing, Inc.
Pimentel, Annette Bay. Girl Running. Archer, Micha, illus. 2018. 32p. (J). (gr. k-3). 17.99 *(978-1-101-99668-3(4),* Nancy Paulsen Books) Penguin Young Readers Group.
Stanmyre, Jackie F. Jesse Owens: Facing down Hitler, 1 vol. 2015. (Game-Changing Athletes Ser.). (ENG., Illus.). 112p. (YA). (gr. 9-9). lib. bdg. 44.50 *(978-1-5026-1049-2(3),* a30ea382-851d-40c9-88f1-43a857e01970) Cavendish Square Publishing LLC.
Stone, Ken. Make Me the Best at Track & Field. 2016. (Make Me the Best Athlete Ser.). (ENG., Illus.). 48p. (J). (gr. 4-6). lib. bdg. 34.21 *(978-1-68078-485-5(4),* 23779, SportsZone) ABDO Publishing Co.
Williams, Heather. Jesse Owens. 2018. (21st Century Skills Library: Sports Unite Us Ser.). (ENG., Illus.). 32p. (J). (gr. 3-6). lib. bdg. 32.07 *(978-1-5341-2959-7(6),* 211880) Cherry Lake Publishing.

TRACK ATHLETICS

see Track and Field

TRACKING AND TRAILING

Graubart, Norman D. How to Track a Deer, 1 vol. 2014. (Scatalog: a Kid's Field Guide to Animal Poop Ser.). (ENG., Illus.). 24p. (J). (gr. 2-3). lib. bdg. 27.27 *(978-1-4777-5415-3(6),* 45f69167-28d8-44e3-b571-246f488c157d, Windmill Bks.) Rosen Publishing Group, Inc., The.
—How to Track a Rabbit, 1 vol. 2014. (Scatalog: a Kid's Field Guide to Animal Poop Ser.). (ENG., Illus.). 24p. (J). (gr. 2-3). lib. bdg. 27.27 *(978-1-4777-5434-4(2),* 1882a072-609e-4109-8356-dbbc29411ea0, Windmill Bks.) Rosen Publishing Group, Inc., The.
—How to Track a Turkey, 1 vol. 2014. (Scatalog: a Kid's Field Guide to Animal Poop Ser.). (ENG., Illus.). 24p. (J). (gr. 2-3). lib. bdg. 27.27 *(978-1-4777-5414-6(8),* 1a713d3c-c66a-44e8-9371-b1e14091374d, Windmill Bks.) Rosen Publishing Group, Inc., The.
Hall, Kirsten. True Tales: Tracking Animals. 2005. (True Tales Ser.). (ENG., Illus.). 48p. (J). (gr. 3-6). lib. bdg. 17.44 *(978-0-516-25186-8(4))* Scholastic Library Publishing.
Kavanagh, James & Waterford Press Staff. Australian Birds: An Introduction to Familiar Species. Leung, Raymond, illus. 2016. (Wildlife & Nature Identification Ser.). (ENG.). 12p. 7.95 *(978-1-58355-037-3(2))* Waterford Pr., Inc.
Kenney, Karen Latchana. Animal Tracks. 2011. (Amicus Readers. Our Animal World (Level 1) Ser.). (ENG.). 24p. (J). (gr. k-2). lib. bdg. 25.65 *(978-1-60753-142-5(9),* 17033) Amicus.
Mauro, Paul & Melton, H. Keith. Tracking & Surveillance. 2004. (Detective Academy Ser.). (Illus.). 48p. (J). *(978-0-439-57180-7(4))* Scholastic, Inc.
Maynard, Charles W. Going to the Great Smoky Mountains National Park. 2008. (Farcountry Explorer Bks.). (Illus.). 48p. (J). (gr. 3-7). per. 14.95 *(978-1-56037-477-0(2))* Farcountry Pr.
National Geographic Learning. Reading Expeditions (Science: on Assignment): Tracking Animal Migrators. 2007. (ENG., Illus.). 32p. (J). pap. 18.95 *(978-0-7922-8449-9(6))* CENGAGE Learning.
Oxlade, Chris. Be a Tracker. Sassin, Eva, illus. 2015. (Go Wild Ser.). (ENG.). 32p. (J). (gr. 3-6). pap. 7.99 *(978-1-4677-7650-9(5),* 24fb56df-735c-4ead-9afd-17731c178fd9, Hungry Tomato (r)) Lerner Publishing Group.
—Be an Explorer. Sassin, Eva, illus. 2015. (Go Wild Ser.). (ENG.). 32p. (J). (gr. 3-6). E-Book 42.65 *(978-1-4677-7223-5(2),* Hungry Tomato (r)) Lerner Publishing Group.
Patterson, Caroline. Who Pooped in the Zoo? Exploring the Weirdest, Wackiest, Grossest, & Most Surprising Facts about Zoo Poop. Rath, Robert, illus. 2011. 40p. (J). 14.95 *(978-1-56037-504-3(3))* Farcountry Pr.
Robson, Gary D. Who Pooped in the Northwoods? 2008. (Illus.). 48p. (J). pap. 11.95 *(978-1-56037-434-3(9))* Farcountry Pr.
—Who Pooped in the Park? Yellowstone. 2004. (Illus.). 48p. (J). pap. 11.95 *(978-1-56037-273-8(7))* Farcountry Pr.
—Who Pooped in the Park? Red Rock Canyon National Conservation Area: Scats & Tracks for Kids. Rath, Robert, illus. 2005. (Who Pooped in the Park? Ser.). 48p. (J). (gr. -1-3). pap. 9.95 *(978-1-56037-371-1(7))* Farcountry Pr.
—Who Pooped in the Park? Shenandoah National Park: Scats & Tracks for Kids. Rath, Robert, illus. 2006. (Who Pooped in the Park? Ser.). 48p. (J). (gr. -1-3). pap. *(978-1-56037-339-1(3))* Farcountry Pr.
—Who Pooped in the Sonoran Desert? Scats & Tracks for Kids. Rath, Robert, illus. 2006. (Who Pooped in the Park? Ser.). 48p. (J). (gr. -1-3). pap. 11.95 *(978-1-56037-349-0(0))* Farcountry Pr.
—Who Pooped on the Colorado Plateau? Scat & Tracks for Kids. Rath, Robert, illus. 2008. (Who Pooped in the Park? Ser.). 48p. (J). (gr. 1-7). pap. 11.95 *(978-1-56037-430-5(6))* Farcountry Pr.
Robson, Gary D. & Rath, Robert. Who Pooped in the Park? Olympic National Park. 2006. (Illus.). 48p. (J). pap. 11.95 *(978-1-56037-337-7(7))* Farcountry Pr.

TRACTION ENGINES

see Tractors

TRACTORS

Addison, D. R. Tractors at Work. 2009. (Big Trucks Ser.). 24p. (gr. 1-1). 42.50 *(978-1-61511-588-4(9),* PowerKids Pr.); (ENG., Illus.). (J). pap. 9.25 *(978-1-4358-3090-5(3),* 4679025f-e001-42a5-a242-c35d5621894f, PowerKids Pr.); (ENG., Illus.). (J). lib. bdg. 26.27 *(978-1-4358-2704-2(X),* 06bd021d-3e5b-4bc9-a1b4-18f984da70f1) Rosen Publishing Group, Inc., The.
Allan, John. Let's Look at Trucks & Tractors. 2019. (Mini Mechanics Ser.). (ENG., Illus.). 24p. (J). (gr. 1-3). 26.65 *(978-1-5415-5529-7(5),* 862c5358-e012-441a-a1c6-e67c9a1627bb, Hungry Tomato (r)) Lerner Publishing Group.
Alphabet Soup (Firm) Staff, contrib. by. Let's Look at Tractors. 2009. (Let's Go! Ser.). (Illus.). 18p. (J). (gr. -1-k). bds. 12.75 *(978-1-60754-418-0(0))* Windmill Bks.
Becker, Ann. Tractors, 1 vol. 2010. (Amazing Machines Ser.). (ENG.). 32p. (gr. 2-2). 31.21 *(978-0-7614-4406-0(8),* af23eb37-1db9-4f68-925d-ada36f86e673) Cavendish Square Publishing LLC.

T
U
V

Bell, Samantha. Four-Track Tractor. 2016. (21st Century Basic Skills Library: Welcome to the Farm Ser.). (ENG., Illus.). 24p. (J). (gr. k-3). 26.35 *(978-1-63471-033-6(9)*, 208212) Cherry Lake Publishing.
—Four-Wheel Drive Utility Tractor. 2016. (21st Century Basic Skills Library: Welcome to the Farm Ser.). (ENG., Illus.). 24p. (J). (gr. k-3). 26.35 *(978-1-63471-038-1(X)*, 208232) Cherry Lake Publishing.
Bender, Lionel. Diggers & Tractors. 2006. (J). *(978-1-59389-267-8(5))* Chrysalis Education.
Boothroyd, Jennifer. Tractors Go to Work. 2018. (Farm Machines at Work Ser.). (ENG., Illus.). 24p. (J). (gr. k-3). 26.65 *(978-1-5415-2601-3(5)*, 088324ed-a0ec-418c-9ce7-2e08c94c1d59, Lerner Pubns.) Lerner Publishing Group.
Bowman, Chris. Monster Tractors. 2014. (Monster Machines Ser.). (ENG., Illus.). 24p. (J). (gr. k-3). lib. bdg. 26.95 *(978-1-62617-055-1(X)*, Blastoff! Readers) Bellwether Media.
Brady, Peter. Tractors in Action. 2012. (Transportation Zone Ser.). (ENG.). 24p. (gr. 1-2). pap. 41.70 *(978-1-4296-8397-5(X))*; (Illus.). (J). lib. bdg. 25.99 *(978-1-4296-7693-9(0)*, 117290) Capstone. (Capstone Pr.).
Brooks, Felicity. Build a Picture Tractors Sticker Book. Lovell, Katie, illus. 2013. (Build a Picture Sticker Bks). 24p. (J). pap. 6.99 *(978-0-7945-3319-9(1)*, Usborne) EDC Publishing.
—Usborne Lift & Look Tractors. Van Wyk, Hanri, illus. 2007. (Lift & Look Board Bks.). 10p. (J). (gr. -1-k). bds. 9.99 *(978-0-7945-1597-3(5)*, Usborne) EDC Publishing.
Burch, Lynda S. Wicky Wacky Things that Go! Tractors. Burch, Lynda S., photos by. 2004. (Illus.). 28p. (J). E-Book 9.95 incl. cd-rom *(978-1-933090-09-2(X))* Guardian Angel Publishing, Inc.
Child's Play. Farm. Cocoretto, illus. 2017. (Wheels at Work (US Edition) Ser.: 4). (ENG.). 12p. (J). bds. *(978-1-78628-082-4(5))* Child's Play International Ltd.
Coming Soon. Tractors. 2018. (Eyediscover Ser.). (ENG., Illus.). 24p. (J). (gr. 3-7). 28.55 *(978-1-4896-8337-3(2)*, AV2 by Weigl) Weigl Pubs., Inc.
Dayton, Connor. Tractors. (Illus.). 24p. (J). 2012. 49.50 *(978-1-4488-5043-3(6)*, 1329062) 2011. (ENG., (gr. 1-1). pap. 9.25 *(978-1-4488-5042-6(8)*, f265e753-6972-4bd3-a1d0-5475e875fe3b) 2011. (ENG., (gr. 1-1). lib. bdg. 26.27 *(978-1-4488-4946-8(2)*, 807c483d-a6af-4e4b-ba98-3e105ab3ea3c) Rosen Publishing Group, Inc., The. (PowerKids Pr.).
Dieker, Wendy. Tractors. 2012. (ENG., Illus.). 24p. (J). lib. bdg. 25.65 *(978-1-62031-023-6(6))* Jump! Inc.
Disney, et al. The World of Cars: Tractor Tipping. 2008. (J). 13.99 *(978-1-59319-930-2(9))* LeapFrog Enterprises, Inc.
Dittmer, Lori. Tractors. 2018. (Seedlings Ser.). (ENG., Illus.). 24p. (J). (gr. -1-1). pap. 10.99 *(978-1-62832-528-7(3)*, 19659, Creative Paperbacks); *(978-1-60818-912-0(0)*, 19661, Creative Education) Creative Co., The.
DK. Baby Touch & Feel: Tractor. 2010. (Baby Touch & Feel Ser.). (ENG.). 14p. (J). (gr. -1 — 1). bds. 7.99 *(978-0-7566-7132-7(9)*, DK Children) Dorling Kindersley Publishing, Inc.
—Chug, Chug Tractor: Lots of Sounds & Loads of Flaps! 2013. (Super Noisy Bks.). (ENG.). 12p. (J). (gr. -1 — 1). bds. 14.99 *(978-1-4654-1426-7(6)*, DK Children) Dorling Kindersley Publishing, Inc.
—Farm Tractor. 2003. (Wheelie Bks.). (ENG., Illus.). 12p. (J). (gr. -1-k). bds. 8.99 *(978-0-7894-9713-0(1)*, DK Children) Dorling Kindersley Publishing, Inc.
—Touch & Feel: Tractor. 2011. (Touch & Feel Ser.). (ENG., Illus.). 12p. (J). (gr. -1-k). bds. 6.99 *(978-0-7566-9167-7(2)*, DK Children) Dorling Kindersley Publishing, Inc.
—Tractor. 2010. (ENG., Illus.). 10p. (J). (gr. -1-k). bds. 8.99 *(978-0-7566-6302-5(4)*, DK Children) Dorling Kindersley Publishing, Inc.
Dorling Kindersley Publishing Staff. See How They Go! Tractor. 2009. (See How They Go! Ser.). (ENG.). 20p. (J). (gr. -1-3). 16.19 *(978-0-7566-5540-2(4))* Dorling Kindersley Publishing, Inc.
Dufek, Holly. Big Tractors: With Casey & Friends. 2015. (Casey & Friends Ser.: 2). (ENG., Illus.). 32p. (J). (gr. k-3). 14.99 *(978-1-937747-53-4(0))* Octane Pr.
Ellis, Belinda. Tractor. 2007. (Pull-Alongs Ser.). (Illus.). 12p. (gr. -1). per. *(978-1-84610-443-5(2))* Make Believe Ideas.
Gifford, Clive. Tractors. 2013. (ENG.). 24p. (J). *(978-0-7787-1001-1(7))*; pap. *(978-0-7787-1005-9(X))* Crabtree Publishing Co.
Gilpin, Rebecca. Trucks & Tractors. 2005. (ENG.). 32p. (J). pap. 8.95 *(978-0-7945-1134-0(1)*, Usborne) EDC Publishing.
Glaser, Rebecca. Tractors Pull. 2016. (ENG., Illus.). 14p. (J). (gr. -1 — 1). bds. 7.99 *(978-1-68152-123-7(7)*, 15822) Amicus.
Glover, David & Glover, Penny. Tractors in Action, 1 vol. 2007. (On the Go Ser.). (ENG., Illus.). 24p. (J). (gr. 1-2). lib. bdg. 26.27 *(978-1-4042-4309-5(7)*, 589ef10d-6330-4e0b-be4e-aa220eb0878f, PowerKids Pr.) Rosen Publishing Group, Inc., The.
Gregory, Josh. What Does It Do? Tractor. 2011. (Community Connections: What Does It Do? Ser.). (ENG., Illus.). 24p. (gr. 2-5). lib. bdg. 29.21 *(978-1-60279-970-7(9)*, 200960) Cherry Lake Publishing.
Gunzi, Christiane. Big Noisy Tractors. 2015. (ENG., Illus.). 10p. (J). 9.99 *(978-1-904618-89-8(8))* Award Pubns. Ltd. GBR. Dist: Parkwest Pubns., Inc.
Hawes, Alison. The Tractor Pink a Band. Pérez-Cuadrado, Esther, illus. 2017. (Cambridge Reading Adventures Ser.). (ENG.). 16p. pap. 7.95 *(978-1-108-40069-5(8))* Cambridge Univ. Pr.
Hayes, Amy. Big Tractors, 1 vol. 2015. (Machines That Work Ser.). (ENG., Illus.). 24p. (gr. 1-1). 25.93 *(978-1-5026-0401-9(9)*, 30f506cb-814b-4879-8372-361e3f3b87de) Cavendish Square Publishing LLC.
Kawa, Katie. Tractors, 1 vol. 2011. (Big Machines Ser.). (Illus.). 24p. (gr. k-k). (ENG.). (J). 25.27 *(978-1-4339-5570-9(9)*, 6f34a979-f231-4ce7-a7c5-3980a2f238cd); (ENG., (J). pap. 9.15 *(978-1-4339-5572-3(5)*, 5d74906b-4c33-479a-bcc2-584afb717d10); 69.20 *(978-1-4339-6891-4(6))* Stevens, Gareth Publishing LLLP.
—Tractors / Tractores, 1 vol. 2011. (Big Machines / Grandes Máquinas Ser.). (SPA & ENG., Illus.). 24p. (J). (gr. k-k). 25.27 *(978-1-4339-5584-6(9)*, 8443c579-29d0-4b55-b265-9ced71f11f8d) Stevens, Gareth Publishing LLLP.
Lindeen, Mary. Tractors. 2007. (Mighty Machines Ser.). (ENG., Illus.). 24p. (J). (gr. k-3). lib. bdg. 26.95 *(978-1-60014-061-7(0))* Bellwether Media.
Litchfield, Jo & Brooks, F. Tractors. 2004. (ENG., Illus.). 10p. (J). bds. 4.95 *(978-0-7945-0588-2(0))* EDC Publishing.
Make Believe Ideas. Ultimate Sticker File Tractors & Trucks. Abbott, John A., illus. 2014. (ENG.). 56p. (J). pap. 6.99 *(978-1-78393-116-3(7))* Make Believe Ideas GBR. Dist: Scholastic, Inc.
Manolis, Kay. Big Rigs. 2008. (Mighty Machines Ser.). (ENG., Illus.). 24p. (J). (gr. k-3). lib. bdg. 26.95 *(978-1-60014-177-5(3))* Bellwether Media.
Mezzanotte, Jim. Giant Tractors, 1 vol. 2005. (Giant Vehicles Ser.). (ENG., Illus.). 24p. (gr. 2-4). pap. 9.15 *(978-0-8368-4922-6(1)*, e5822141-9b32-4984-a7d3-39cd7584f59f); lib. bdg. 25.67 *(978-0-8368-4915-8(9)*, 925d1060-c2a1-4954-a49d-95aba8f6060d) Stevens, Gareth Publishing LLLP. (Gareth Stevens Learning Library).
—Tractores (Giant Tractors), 1 vol. 2005. (Vehículos Gigantes (Giant Vehicles) Ser.). (SPA.). 24p. (gr. 2-4). lib. bdg. 25.67 *(978-0-8368-5986-7(3)*, c92091f3-c3f3-4d01-8248-3a655120dcf1, Gareth Stevens Learning Library) Stevens, Gareth Publishing LLLP.
Nelson, Kristin L. Farm Tractors on the Move. 2011. (Lightning Bolt Books Vroom-Vroom Ser.). 32p. pap. 45.32 *(978-0-7613-7617-0(8))* Lerner Publishing Group.
—Tractores Agrícolas. Translations.com Staff, tr. from ENG. 2006. (Libros para Avanzar-Potencia en Movimiento (Pull Ahead Books-Mighty Movers) Ser.). (SPA., Illus.). 32p. (gr. k-3). lib. bdg. 22.60 *(978-0-8225-6231-3(6)*, Ediciones Lerner) Lerner Publishing Group.
Nixon, James. Tractors. 2010. (Machines on the Move Ser.). (ENG.). 32p. (J). (gr. 1-3). lib. bdg. 28.50 *(978-1-60753-063-3(5)*, 17215) Amicus.
—Tractors. 2012. (ENG., Illus.). 32p. (gr. 1-3). pap. 8.95 *(978-1-926722-73-3(6))* Saunders Bk. Co. CAN. Dist: RiverStream Publishing.
Oachs, Emily Rose. Tractors. 2017. (Mighty Machines in Action Ser.). (ENG., Illus.). 24p. (J). (gr. k-3). lib. bdg. 26.95 *(978-1-62617-609-6(4)*, Blastoff! Readers) Bellwether Media.
Oxlade, Chris. This Is My Tractor. Lalla, Christine, photos by. 2008. (Mega Machine Drivers Ser.). (Illus.). 30p. (J). (gr. k). lib. bdg. 28.50 *(978-1-59771-106-7(3))* Sea-To-Sea Pubns.
Pearcey, Alice. Usborne Tractors & Trucks Stencil Book. Milbourne, Anna, ed. Tudor, Andy, illus. 2006. 10p. (J). bds. 12.99 *(978-0-7945-1139-5(2)*, Usborne) EDC Publishing.
Peppas, Lynn. Les Tracteurs. 2013. (FRE.). 32p. (J). pap. 9.95 *(978-2-89579-489-9(8))* Bayard Canada Livres CAN. Dist: Crabtree Publishing Co.
—Tractors at Work. 2010. (Vehicles on the Move Ser.). (ENG.). 32p. (J). (gr. k-3). pap. *(978-0-7787-3064-4(6))* Crabtree Publishing Co.
Reinke, Beth Bence. Tractors on the Go. 2018. (Bumba Books (r) — Machines That Go Ser.). (ENG., Illus.). 24p. (J). (gr. -1-1). 26.65 *(978-1-5124-8252-2(8)*, 4436ce8c-5127-4857-8177-55d65e3983f2, Lerner Pubns.); pap. 8.99 *(978-1-5415-1117-0(4)*, 0f2e4030-62b5-4588-b2f5-eee8203a9a39) Lerner Publishing Group.
Santos, Penelope. All about Tractors, 1 vol. 2015. (Rosen REAL Readers: STEM & STEAM Collection). (ENG.). 8p. (gr. k-1). pap. 5.46 *(978-1-4994-9690-1(7)*, 83f13ef8-81a8-4af7-a961-45f91e241770, Rosen Classroom) Rosen Publishing Group, Inc., The.
Schuh, Mari. La Course de Tracteur. 2016. (On Fait la Course? Ser.). (FRE., Illus.). 16p. (J). (gr. k-2). *(978-1-77092-345-4(4)*, 17640) Amicus.
—The Tractor Race. 2016. (Let's Race Ser.). (ENG., Illus.). 16p. (J). (gr. -1-1). lib. bdg. 17.95 *(978-1-60753-916-2(0)*, 15494) Amicus.
Small World Creations. Zippy Wheels: Tractors. 2016. (Zippy Wheels Ser.). (ENG., Illus.). 10p. (J). (gr. -1-k). bds. 8.99 *(978-0-7641-6828-4(2))* Sourcebooks, Inc.
Spaight, Anne J. Big Rigs on the Go. 2016. (Bumba Books (r) — Machines That Go Ser.). (ENG., Illus.). 24p. (J). (gr. -1-1). lib. bdg. 26.65 *(978-1-5124-1450-9(6)*, 2e20d3d1-2965-4983-903d-6bc54bb44bbf, Lerner Pubns.) Lerner Publishing Group.
Storey, Rita. Tractors & Trucks. 2013. (Have Fun with Arts & Crafts Ser.). (Illus.). 32p. (gr. 4-7). lib. bdg. 31.35 *(978-1-59920-901-2(2))* Black Rabbit Bks.
Tractor. 2010. (Illus.). (J). *(978-1-4654-5514-7(0))* Dorling Kindersley Publishing, Inc.
Tractors & Diggers. 2003. (Illus.). 32p. 12.98 *(978-1-4054-2005-1(7))* Parragon, Inc.
Watt, Fiona. Tractors. King, Sue, illus. 2009. (Luxury Touchy-Feely Board Bks). 10p. (J). bds. 15.99 *(978-0-7945-2432-6(X)*, Usborne) EDC Publishing.
Weingarten, E. T. Tractors, 1 vol. 2016. (Fantastic Farm Machines Ser.). (ENG.). 24p. (gr. 1-2). 24.27 *(978-1-4824-4586-2(7)*, bef5817d-08f2-4af8-b5d3-8a463eb2800d) Stevens, Gareth Publishing LLLP.
Williams, Michael. Power Tractors, 1 vol. 2006. (Cool Wheels Ser.). (ENG., Illus.). 32p. (gr. 3-5). lib. bdg. 28.67 *(978-0-8368-6828-9(5)*, e7b3e332-df52-4ea6-a895-949909d3d603, Gareth Stevens Learning Library) Stevens, Gareth Publishing LLLP.
Wiseman, Blaine. Tough Tractors. 2010. (World of Wonder Ser.). 24p. (J). (gr. 2-4). lib. bdg. 25.70 *(978-1-61690-148-6(9))* Weigl Pubs., Inc.
—Tractors: WOW: Big Machines. 2010. (J). pap. 9.95 *(978-1-61690-149-3(7))* Weigl Pubs., Inc.
Young, Caroline. Tractors. Lyon, Chris & Gower, Teri, illus. 2004. (Young MacHines Ser.). 32p. (J). (gr. k). lib. bdg. 14.95 *(978-1-58086-616-3(6)*, Usborne) EDC Publishing.
Young, Charles A. Tractors. rev. ed. 2004. (Young MacHines Ser.). (ENG., Illus.). 32p. (J). pap. 6.95 *(978-0-7945-0632-2(1))* EDC Publishing.

TRACTORS—FICTION

Amery, Heather. Red Tractor Board Book. Cartwright, Stephen, illus. 2004. (Young Farmyard Tales Board Books Ser.). 10p. (J). bds. 3.95 *(978-0-7945-0469-4(8)*, Usborne) EDC Publishing.
Amery, Heather & Doherty, Gillian. Wind-Up Tractor Book. 2007. (Wind-up Tractor Book Ser.). 14p. (J). bds. 25.99 *(978-0-7945-1861-5(3)*, Usborne) EDC Publishing.
Aumann, Jane & Ladage, Cindy. The Christmas Tractor. Freitag, Charles, illus. 2003. 30p. (J). (gr. k-4). pap. 8.95 *(978-0-9703319-2-2(4))* Roots & Wings.
Ayers, Sanda. Tommy Tractor Goes to the City, 1 vol. Young, Sue, illus. 2009. 29p. pap. 19.95 *(978-1-61582-054-2(X))* PublishAmerica, Inc.
Baggott, Stella, illus. Baby's Very First Tractor Book. 2018. (Baby's Very First Rolling Bks.). (ENG.). 8p. (J). 8.99 *(978-0-7945-4198-9(4)*, Usborne) EDC Publishing.
Baxter, Nicola. Stop That Tractor! Glover, Peter, illus. 2016. 24p. (J). (gr. -1-12). pap. 6.99 *(978-1-86147-758-3(9)*, Armadillo) Anness Publishing GBR. Dist: National Bk. Network.
Berrios, Frank. Tractor Trouble (Disney/Pixar Cars) RH Disney, illus. 2011. (Little Golden Book Ser.). (ENG.). 24p. (J). (gr. -1-2). 5.99 *(978-0-7364-2831-6(3)*, Golden/Disney) Random Hse. Children's Bks.
Brooks, Felicity. This Is My Tractor. Dimitri, Simona, illus. 2009. (Noisy Touchy-Feely Board Bks). 10p. (J). bds. 16.99 *(978-0-7945-2473-9(7)*, Usborne) EDC Publishing.
Bryant, Ann. Hurry Up! 2011. (Tadpoles Ser.). (ENG., Illus.). 24p. (J). (gr. k-2). *(978-0-7787-0580-2(3))*; pap. *(978-0-7787-0591-8(9))* Crabtree Publishing Co.
Burton, Virginia Lee. Katy & the Big Snow Board Book: A Winter & Holiday Book for Kids. 2010. (ENG., Illus.). 38p. (J). (gr. -1-k). bds. 7.99 *(978-0-547-37145-0(4)*, 1423786, Clarion Bks.) HarperCollins Pubs.
—Katy & the Big Snow Book & Cd: A Winter & Holiday Book for Kids, 1 vol. 2009. (ENG., Illus.). 40p. (J). (gr. -1-3). audio 10.99 *(978-0-547-25264-3(1)*, 1271216, Clarion Bks.) HarperCollins Pubs.
—Katy & the Big Snow Lap Board Book: A Christmas Holiday Book for Kids. 2014. (ENG., Illus.). 38p. (J). (— 1). bds. 11.99 *(978-0-544-31717-8(3)*, 1582016, Clarion Bks.) HarperCollins Pubs.
Clement, Nathan. Big Tractor. 2015. (ENG., Illus.). 32p. (J). (gr. k-3). 16.95 *(978-1-62091-790-9(4)*, Astra Young Readers) Astra Publishing Hse.
Cousins, Lucy. Maisy's Tractor. Cousins, Lucy, illus. 2015. (Maisy Ser.). (ENG., Illus.). 18p. (J). (— 1). bds. 7.99 *(978-0-7636-7305-5(6))* Candlewick Pr.
Crow, Melinda Melton. Brave Fire Truck, 1 vol. Thompson, Chad, illus. 2011. (Wonder Wheels Ser.). (ENG.). 32p. (J). (gr. -1-1). lib. bdg. 22.65 *(978-1-4342-3029-4(5)*, 114523, Stone Arch Bks.) Capstone.
—Busy, Busy Train, 1 vol. Thompson, Chad, illus. 2011. (Wonder Wheels Ser.). (ENG.). 32p. (J). (gr. -1-1). pap. 6.25 *(978-1-4342-3383-7(9)*, 116390); lib. bdg. 22.65 *(978-1-4342-3028-7(7)*, 114522) Capstone. (Stone Arch Bks.).
—Helpful Tractor, 1 vol. Thompson, Chad, illus. 2011. (Wonder Wheels Ser.). (ENG.). 32p. (J). (gr. -1-1). lib. bdg. 22.65 *(978-1-4342-3027-0(9)*, 114521, Stone Arch Bks.) Capstone.
Dobbins, Jan. Driving My Tractor. Sim, David, illus. 2009. 32p. (J). (gr. -1-3). 16.99 *(978-1-84686-358-5(9))* Barefoot Bks., Inc.
—Driving My Tractor Puzzle. Sim, David, illus. 2011. (J). (gr. -1-1). 14.99 *(978-1-84686-573-2(5))* Barefoot Bks., Inc.
Gabel, Stacey. The New Blue Tractor. Neuman, Richard, illus. 2007. 24p. per. 13.95 *(978-1-59858-424-0(3))* Dog Ear Publishing, LLC.
Garland, Michael. Grandpa's Tractor. 2011. (Life on the Farm Ser.). (ENG., Illus.). 32p. (J). (gr. -1-3). 17.99 *(978-1-59078-762-5(5)*, Astra Young Readers) Astra Publishing Hse.
Gould, Robert. Tractors. 2004. (Big Stuff Ser.). (ENG., Illus.). 16p. (J). bds. 7.95 *(978-1-929945-44-3(2))* Big Guy Bks., Inc.
Harris, Carrie. Sally Slick & the Steel Syndicate. Valentine, Amanda, ed. 2014. (Illus.). 200p. (YA). pap. 15.00 *(978-1-61317-063-2(7))* Evil Hat Productions LLC.
Hawksley, Gerald, illus. Patty Cow's Tractor: Press Out Parts Make a Tractor Carrying Patty Cow, 1 vol. 2009. (Toddler Make & Play Ser.). (ENG.). 10p. 6.95 *(978-1-59496-182-3(4))* Teora USA LLC.
Hillenbrand, Will. Down by the Barn, 0 vols. Hillenbrand, Will, illus. 2014. (ENG.). 32p. (J). (gr. -1-2). 16.99 *(978-1-4778-4731-2(6)*, 9781477847312, Two Lions) Amazon Publishing.
Ladage, Cindy & Aumann, Jane. My Name Is Huber. (Illus.). (J). 2013. (ENG.). 24p. pap. 10.00 *(978-1-61009-054-4(3))* 2012. *(978-1-61009-050-6(0))* Oak Tree Publishing. (Acorn).
Long, Loren. Otis. Long, Loren, illus. (Otis Ser.). (Illus.). (J). (gr. -1 — 1). 2011. 36p. bds. 9.99 *(978-0-399-25600-4(8))* 2009. 48p. 18.99 *(978-0-399-25248-8(7))* Penguin Young Readers Group. (Philomel Bks.).
—Otis & the Kittens. 2019. (Otis Ser.). (Illus.). 38p. (J). (-k). bds. 8.99 *(978-1-9848-3722-6(2)*, Philomel Bks.) Penguin Young Readers Group.
—Otis & the Kittens. Long, Loren, illus. 2016. (Otis Ser.). (Illus.). 40p. (J). (gr. -1-3). 18.99 *(978-0-399-16398-2(0)*, Philomel Bks.) Penguin Young Readers Group.
—Otis & the Puppy. Long, Loren, illus. 2013. (Otis Ser.: 3). (Illus.). 40p. (J). (gr. -1-2). 18.99 *(978-0-399-25469-7(2)*, Philomel Bks.) Penguin Young Readers Group.
—Otis & the Puppy: Board Book. Long, Loren, illus. 2014. (Otis Ser.: 3). (Illus.). 38p. (J). (gr. -1-k). bds. 8.99 *(978-0-399-17196-3(7)*, Philomel Bks.) Penguin Young Readers Group.
—Otis & the Scarecrow. Long, Loren, illus. 2014. (Otis Ser.). (ENG., Illus.). 40p. (J). (gr. -1-2). 19.99 *(978-0-399-16396-8(4)*, Philomel Bks.) Penguin Young Readers Group.
—Otis & the Tornado. Long, Loren, illus. 2011. (Otis Ser.: 2). (Illus.). 40p. (J). (gr. -1-2). 18.99 *(978-0-399-25477-2(3)*, Philomel Bks.) Penguin Young Readers Group.
—An Otis Christmas. Long, Loren, illus. 2016. (Otis Ser.). (Illus.). 36p. (J). (gr. -1-2). bds. 8.99 *(978-0-399-54811-6(4)*, Philomel Bks.) Penguin Young Readers Group.
—Otis (Spanish Edition) Long, Loren, illus. 2013. (Otis Ser.). (Illus.). 40p. (J). (gr. -1-k). 7.99 *(978-0-14-751124-9(0)*, Puffin Books) Penguin Young Readers Group.
Menges, Thais D. Granny & the Tractor. King, Joseph, illus. 2012. 36p. pap. 10.95 *(978-1-60920-047-3(0))* Ajoyin Publishing, Inc.
Mitton, Tony & Parker, Ant. Tremendous Tractors. 2005. (Amazing Machines Ser.). (ENG., Illus.). 24p. (J). (gr. -1-k). pap. 6.99 *(978-0-7534-5918-8(3)*, 900052727, Kingfisher) Roaring Brook Pr.
Oliver, Merlin. John Laughinghouse. 2007. 20.00 *(978-0-8059-7333-4(8))* Dorrance Publishing Co., Inc.
Pavon, Mar. A Very, Very Noisy Tractor. Brokenbrow, Jon, tr. Uya, Nivola, illus. 2013. (ENG.). 28p. (J). (gr. k-3). 15.95 *(978-84-15619-65-9(0))* Cuento de Luz SL ESP. Dist: Publishers Group West (PGW).
Publications International Ltd. Staff, ed. Tractor. 2010. 12p. (J). bds. 13.98 *(978-1-4508-0125-6(0))* Phoenix International Publications, Inc.
Rand, Johnathan. Freddie Fernortner #11: Tadpole Trouble. 2010. 95p. (J). pap. 4.99 *(978-1-893699-29-8(3))* AudioCraft Publishing, Inc.
Reader's Digest Staff. Tractor Trouble Drive Through Storybook. Pitt, Sarah, illus. 2011. (Drive-Through Storybooks Ser.). (ENG.). 10p. (J). (gr. -1-1). bds. 12.99 *(978-0-7944-2169-4(5))* Reader's Digest Assn., Inc., The.
Roberts, Margiad & Owen, Carys Eurwen. Tecwyn a Ffergi Lwyd. 2005. (WEL., Illus.). 35p. pap. *(978-0-86381-495-2(6))* Gwasg Carreg Gwalch.
—Tecwyn A'r Combein. 2005. (WEL., Illus.). 36p. pap. *(978-0-86381-368-9(2))* Gwasg Carreg Gwalch.
—Tecwyn A'r Moto-Beic. 2005. (WEL., Illus.). 36p. pap. *(978-0-86381-437-2(9))* Gwasg Carreg Gwalch.
—Tecwyn Yn Plannu Tatws. 2005. (WEL., Illus.). 36p. pap. *(978-0-86381-408-2(5))* Gwasg Carreg Gwalch.
—Tecwyn Yn Teilo. 2005. (WEL., Illus.). 36p. pap. *(978-0-86381-328-3(3))* Gwasg Carreg Gwalch.
Robinson, Michelle. Goodnight Tractor: The Perfect Bedtime Book! East, Nick, illus. 2015. (Goodnight Ser.). (ENG.). 32p. (J). (gr. -1 — 1). pap. 7.99 *(978-1-4380-0664-2(0))* Sourcebooks, Inc.
Rucker, Mike. Terry & the Beaver Dam Fiasco. 2003. (Terry the Tractor Ser.: Vol. 11). (Illus.). 63p. (J). (gr. -1-5). pap. 4.95 *(978-0-9711659-2-2(0))* Univ. Editions.
—Terry & the Earthquake. 2006. (Terry the Tractor Ser.: Vol. 14). 72p. (J). (gr. k-4). pap. 4.95 *(978-0-9711659-5-3(5))* Univ. Editions.
—Terry & the Elephant. pap. *(978-1-56002-746-1(0))* Univ. Editions.
—Terry & The South Pole Breakdown. pap. *(978-0-615-11379-1(6))* Univ. Editions.
—Terry & the Super Powerful Fuel. *(978-1-56002-673-0(1))* Univ. Editions.
Session, Garry. Odessa Bluegill - Out Shovels a Yellow Tractor. Warren, Pamela, ed. Redel, Nicole, illus. Gorman, Suzy, photos by. 2003. 42p. (J). pap. 9.95 *(978-0-9658006-2-4(8))* Session Family.
Shannon, David. Duck on a Tractor. 2017. 59.95 *(978-1-338-16188-5(1))* Scholastic, Inc.
—Duck on a Tractor. Shannon, David, illus. 2016. (ENG., Illus.). 40p. (J). (gr. -1-3). 18.99 *(978-0-545-61941-7(6)*, Blue Sky Pr., The) Scholastic, Inc.
—Un Pato en Tractor (Duck on a Tractor) 2016. (ENG & SPA.). 32p. (J). (gr. -1-3). 17.20 *(978-0-606-39157-3(6))* Turtleback.
Silcox, Beth Douglass. Little Rumely Man. Peters, Darcy, illus. 2012. 36p. pap. 12.99 *(978-0-9832514-2-2(8))* Courageous Heart Pr.
Spinelli, Jami. David's Tractor. Margolis, Lois, illus. l.t. ed. 2006. (J). 32p. 20.99 *(978-1-59879-242-3(3))*; 27p. (gr. -1-3). per. 11.99 *(978-1-59879-241-6(5))* Lifevest Publishing, Inc.
Steers, Billy. Farmers' Market. 2018. (Tractor Mac Ser.). (J). lib. bdg. 16.00 *(978-0-606-41117-2(8))* Turtleback.
—Tractor Mac: New Friend. 2019. (Tractor Mac Ser.). (J). lib. bdg. 16.00 *(978-0-606-41573-6(4))* Turtleback.
—Tractor Mac Arrives at the Farm. (Tractor Mac Ser.). (ENG., Illus.). (J). 2016. 24p. pap. 4.99 *(978-0-374-30536-9(6)*, 900163422) 2015. 32p. (gr. -1-k). 9.99 *(978-0-374-30102-6(6)*, 900138380) Farrar, Straus & Giroux. (Farrar, Straus & Giroux (BYR)).
—Tractor Mac: Autumn Is Here. Steers, Billy, illus. 2019. (Tractor Mac Ser.: 1). (ENG., Illus.). 40p. (J). 19.99 *(978-0-374-30920-6(5)*, 900189990, Farrar, Straus & Giroux (BYR)) Farrar, Straus & Giroux.
—Tractor Mac Builds a Barn. 2015. (Tractor Mac Ser.). (ENG., Illus.). 32p. (J). (gr. -1-2). 8.99 *(978-0-374-30105-7(0)*, 900138383, Farrar, Straus & Giroux (BYR)) Farrar, Straus & Giroux.
—Tractor Mac Colors on the Farm. Steers, Billy, illus. 2018. (Tractor Mac Ser.). (ENG., Illus.). 16p. (J). bds. 6.99 *(978-0-374-30633-5(8)*, 900175318, Farrar, Straus & Giroux (BYR)) Farrar, Straus & Giroux.
—Tractor Mac Family Reunion. 2015. (Tractor Mac Ser.). (ENG., Illus.). 32p. (J). (gr. -1-k). 8.99 *(978-0-374-30109-5(3)*, 900138387, Farrar, Straus & Giroux (BYR)) Farrar, Straus & Giroux.
—Tractor Mac Family Reunion. 2019. (Tractor Mac Ser.). (J). lib. bdg. 16.00 *(978-0-606-41574-3(2))* Turtleback.
—Tractor Mac Farm Days. 2016. (Tractor Mac Ser.). (ENG., Illus.). 16p. (J). bds. 7.99 *(978-0-374-30117-0(4)*, 900138398, Farrar, Straus & Giroux (BYR)) Farrar, Straus & Giroux.
—Tractor Mac Farmers' Market. 2015. (Tractor Mac Ser.). (ENG., Illus.). 32p. (J). (gr. -1-k). 9.99 *(978-0-374-30107-1(7)*, 900138385, Farrar, Straus & Giroux (BYR)) Farrar, Straus & Giroux.
—Tractor Mac Farmers Market: Farmer's Market: Steers, Billy, illus. 2009. (ENG., Illus.). (J). 7.95 *(978-0-9826870-1-7(X))* Tractor Mac Inc.
—Tractor Mac Harvest Time. (Tractor Mac Ser.). (ENG., Illus.). (J). 2017. 24p. pap. 5.99 *(978-0-374-30600-7(1)*, 900173474) 2015. 32p. (gr. -1-2). 8.99 *(978-0-374-30111-8(5)*, 900138389) Farrar, Straus & Giroux. (Farrar, Straus & Giroux (BYR)).
—Tractor Mac Learns to Fly. (Tractor Mac Ser.). (ENG., Illus.). (J). 2016. 24p. pap. 5.99 *(978-0-374-30537-6(4)*, 900163423) 2015. 32p. (gr. -1-2). 9.99 *(978-0-374-30103-3(4)*, 900138381) Farrar, Straus & Giroux. (Farrar, Straus & Giroux (BYR)).

—Tractor Mac Learns to Fly. 2016. (Tractor Mac Ser.). (J). lib. bdg. 14.75 *(978-0-606-39558-8(X))* Turtleback.
—Tractor Mac New Friend. 2015. (Tractor Mac Ser.). (ENG., Illus.). 32p. (J). (gr. -1-k). 9.99 *(978-0-374-30110-1(7),* 900138388, Farrar, Straus & Giroux (BYR)) Farrar, Straus & Giroux.
—Tractor Mac Parade's Best. 2015. (Tractor Mac Ser.). (ENG., Illus.). 32p. (J). (gr. -1-k). 9.99 *(978-0-374-30106-4(9),* 900138384, Farrar, Straus & Giroux (BYR)) Farrar, Straus & Giroux.
—Tractor Mac Saves Christmas. 24p. (J). 9.95 *(978-1-59445-461-5(2))* Dogs in Hats Children's Publishing Co.
—Tractor Mac Saves Christmas. 2015. (Tractor Mac Ser.). (ENG., Illus.). 32p. (J). (gr. -1-2). 9.99 *(978-0-374-30112-5(3),* 900138390, Farrar, Straus & Giroux (BYR)) Farrar, Straus & Giroux.
—Tractor Mac School Day. Steers, Billy, illus. 2018. (Tractor Mac Ser.). (ENG., Illus.). 40p. (J). 18.99 *(978-0-374-30635-9(4),* 900175320, Farrar, Straus & Giroux (BYR)) Farrar, Straus & Giroux.
—Tractor Mac Teamwork. 2016. (Tractor Mac Ser.). (ENG., Illus.). 32p. (J). 9.99 *(978-0-374-30113-2(1),* 900138395, Farrar, Straus & Giroux (BYR)) Farrar, Straus & Giroux.
—Tractor Mac Tune-Up. 2015. (Tractor Mac Ser.). (ENG., Illus.). 32p. (J). (gr. -1-2). 9.99 *(978-0-374-30108-8(5),* 900138386, Farrar, Straus & Giroux (BYR)) Farrar, Straus & Giroux.
—Tractor Mac Worth the Wait. 2017. (Tractor Mac Ser.). (ENG., Illus.). 32p. (J). 9.99 *(978-0-374-30115-6(8),* 900138396, Farrar, Straus & Giroux (BYR)) Farrar, Straus & Giroux.
—Tractor Mac You're a Winner. 2015. (Tractor Mac Ser.). (ENG., Illus.). 32p. (J). (gr. -1-k). 8.99 *(978-0-374-30104-0(2),* 900138382, Farrar, Straus & Giroux (BYR)) Farrar, Straus & Giroux.
—Tune-Up. 2018. (Tractor Mac Ser.). (J). lib. bdg. 16.00 *(978-0-606-41116-5(X))* Turtleback.
—You're a Winner. 2016. (Tractor Mac Ser.). (ENG.). 24p. (J). (gr. -1-k). 14.75 *(978-0-606-39283-9(1))* Turtleback.
Steers, Billy, illus. Tractor Mac Learns to Fly. 2007. (J). 7.95 *(978-0-9788496-2-7(0))* Tractor Mac Inc.
Stoddard, Jeffery. Skid & the Too Tiny Tunnel: A Story of Courage Based on Deuteronomy 31:6. Fogle, Robin & Rhodes, Karen, eds. Stoddard, Jeffery, illus. 2009. (ENG., Illus.). 32p. (J). (gr. -1-2). 12.99 *(978-1-59317-355-5(5))* Warner Pr., Inc.
Stone, Connie. A Tractor Green Day. Barnes, Garry, illus. 2008. 36p. pap. 24.95 *(978-1-60474-948-9(2))* PublishAmerica, Inc.
Sutton, Sally. Farmer John's Tractor. Belton, Robyn, illus. 2013. (ENG.). 32p. (J). (gr. -1-2). 15.99 *(978-0-7636-6430-5(8))* Candlewick Pr.
Terry & the Ecological Disaster. pap. *(978-1-56002-792-8(4))* Univ. Editions.
Watt, Fiona & Wells, Rachel. That's Not My Tractor. 2004. (Touchy-Feely Board Bks.). (SPA & ENG., Illus.). 1p. (J). bds. 7.99 *(978-0-7945-0011-5(0),* Usborne) EDC Publishing.

TRADE FAIRS
see Fairs

TRADE-MARKS
see Trademarks

TRADE ROUTES
Ceceri, Kathy. The Silk Road: Explore the World's Most Famous Trade Route with 20 Projects. Ceceri, Kathy, illus. 2011. (Build It Yourself Ser.). (Illus.). 128p. (J). (gr. 3-7). pap. 15.95 *(978-1-934670-62-0(6),* 73a69344-325b-4322-a632-9343fbcf8151) Nomad Pr.
Frankopan, Peter. The Silk Roads: The Extraordinary History That Created Your World - Illustrated Edition. Packer, Neil, illus. 2018. (ENG.). 128p. (J). 26.99 *(978-1-5476-0021-2(7),* 900195170, Bloomsbury Children's Bks.) Bloomsbury Publishing USA.
Heing, Bridey. Phoenician Trade Routes, 1 vol. 2017. (Routes of Cross-Cultural Exchange Ser.). (ENG., Illus.). 96p. (YA). (gr. 8-8). 44.50 *(978-1-5026-2861-9(9),* 264ba440-d2ad-455c-b0fe-046afd9c221f) Cavendish Square Publishing LLC.
—Trade Routes to India, 1 vol. 2017. (Routes of Cross-Cultural Exchange Ser.). (ENG.). 96p. (YA). (gr. 8-8). 44.50 *(978-1-5026-2694-3(2),* 637bfb2a-b1ae-45a7-b702-efc7f8987b26) Cavendish Square Publishing LLC.
Keranen, Rachel. The Northwest Passage, 1 vol. 2017. (Routes of Cross-Cultural Exchange Ser.). (ENG.). 96p. (YA). (gr. 8-8). 44.50 *(978-1-5026-2695-0(0),* af06c108-6b9b-46b8-a7b4-b40a85c938fd) Cavendish Square Publishing LLC.
Levy, Janey. The Silk Road: Using a Map Scale to Measure Distances, 1 vol. 2010. (Math for the REAL World Ser.). (ENG., Illus.). 32p. (gr. 5-6). pap. 10.00 *(978-1-4042-5140-3(5),* 799bfe4c-ef04-44b8-9d05-f9cd0955f09d) Rosen Publishing Group, Inc., The.
—The Silk Road: Using A Map Scale to Measure Distances, 1 vol. 2004. (PowerMath: Proficiency Plus Ser.). (ENG., Illus.). 32p. (J). (gr. 5-6). lib. bdg. 28.93 *(978-1-4042-2938-9(8),* ba7efad1-2e8e-4dc2-ae37-00966f217408, PowerKids Pr.) Rosen Publishing Group, Inc., The.

TRADE SCHOOLS
see Technical Education

TRADE UNIONS
see Labor Unions

TRADE-UNIONS
see Labor Unions

TRADE WASTE
see Waste Products

TRADEMARKS
Skinner, Tina. Trademarks of The 1950s, 1 vol. 2003. (ENG., Illus.). 160p. (gr. 10-13). pap. 29.95 *(978-0-7643-1828-3(4),* 2199) Schiffer Publishing, Ltd.

TRADITIONS
see Folklore; Legends; Superstition

TRAFFIC ACCIDENTS
Berry, Joy. Trauma. 2009. (ENG.). 52p. (J). (gr. k-7). pap. 7.95 *(978-1-60577-501-2(0))* Berry, Joy Enterprises.
Grosshandler, Janet. Drugs & Driving. 2009. (Drug Abuse Prevention Library). 64p. (gr. 5-5). 58.50 *(978-1-60853-429-6(4))* Rosen Publishing Group, Inc., The.
Mendralla, Valerie & Grosshandler, Janet. Drinking & Driving, Now What?, 1 vol. 2011. (Teen Life 411 Ser.). (ENG., Illus.). 112p. (YA). (gr. 7-7). lib. bdg. 39.80 *(978-1-4488-4654-2(4),* d3cc2489-4b9d-4361-9525-3b3d336f3e19) Rosen Publishing Group, Inc., The.
Walker, Niki. Transportation Disaster Alert! 2005. (Disaster Alert! Ser.). (ENG., Illus.). 32p. (J). (gr. 4-7). lib. bdg. *(978-0-7787-1584-9(1))* Crabtree Publishing Co.

TRAFFIC ACCIDENTS—FICTION
Applegate, Katherine & Grant, Michael. Eve & Adam. 2013. (ENG.). 304p. (YA). (gr. 8-12). pap. 15.99 *(978-1-250-03419-9(1),* 900120591) Square Fish.
Atwater-Rhodes, Amelia. Token of Darkness. 2011. (Den of Shadows Ser.: 6). (ENG.). 208p. (YA). (gr. 7). pap. 8.99 *(978-0-385-73751-7(3),* Ember) Random Hse. Children's Bks.
Barwin, Steven. Desert Slam, 1 vol. 2017. (Orca Soundings Ser.). (ENG.). 144p. (YA). (gr. 8-12). pap. 9.95 *(978-1-4598-1372-4(3))* Orca Bk. Pubs. USA.
Bruchac, Joseph. Whisper in the Dark. 2009. (ENG., Illus.). 192p. (J). (gr. 5). pap. 7.99 *(978-0-06-058089-6(5),* HarperCollins) HarperCollins Pubs.
Delacre, Lulu. Alicia Afterimage. 2008. (ENG.). 144p. (YA). (gr. 7-18). 19.95 *(978-1-60060-242-9(8))* Lee & Low Bks., Inc.
Easton, Kelly. Aftershock. 2007. (ENG.). 176p. (YA). (gr. 7-12). pap. 6.99 *(978-1-4169-0053-5(5),* McElderry, Margaret K. Bks.) McElderry, Margaret K. Bks.
Frank, E. R. Wrecked. (ENG., (YA). 2015. Illus.). 336p. (gr. 9). pap. 10.99 *(978-1-4814-5137-6(5))* 2007. 256p. (gr. 7-12). pap. 9.99 *(978-0-689-87384-3(0))* Simon & Schuster Children's Publishing. (Atheneum Bks. for Young Readers).
Glines, Abbi. As She Fades: A Novel. 2019. (ENG.). 272p. (YA). pap. 12.99 *(978-1-250-29467-8(3),* 900177590) Square Fish.
Grabenstein, Chris. The Crossroads. 2009. (Haunted Mystery Ser.: 1). (ENG.). 352p. (J). (gr. 3-7). 8.99 *(978-0-375-84698-4(0),* Yearling) Random Hse. Children's Bks.
Green, Tim. Lost Boy. 2015. (ENG.). 304p. (J). (gr. 3-7). 16.99 *(978-0-06-231708-7(3),* HarperCollins) HarperCollins Pubs.
Griffin, Adele. Loud Awake & Lost. 2015. (ENG.). 304p. (YA). (gr. 7). pap. 10.99 *(978-0-385-75275-6(X),* Ember) Random Hse. Children's Bks.
Grover, Lorie Ann. Hit, 1 vol. 2015. (ENG.). 224p. (YA). pap. 8.99 *(978-0-310-72938-9(6))* Blink.
Guest, Jacqueline. Racing Fear, 1 vol. 2004. (Lorimer SideStreets Ser.). (ENG.). 160p. (YA). (gr. 9-12). 16.95 *(978-1-55028-839-1(3),* 839) James Lorimer & Co. Ltd., Pubs. CAN. Dist: Formac Lorimer Bks. Ltd.
Jocelyn, Marthe. Would You. 2008. (ENG.). 176p. (J). (gr. 4-7). 19.99 *(978-0-88776-816-3(4),* Tundra Bks.) Tundra Bks. CAN. Dist: Penguin Random Hse. LLC.
Johnson, Terry Lynn. Falcon Wild. 2017. 176p. (J). (gr. 5). lib. bdg. 16.99 *(978-1-58089-788-4(6))* Charlesbridge Publishing, Inc.
Klein, Glasko. The Accident. 2019. (Do-Over Ser.). (ENG.). 96p. (YA). (gr. 6-12). 26.65 *(978-1-5415-4029-3(8),* 71255b39-86f8-44e8-b485-83b9e7d3b440, Darby Creek) Lerner Publishing Group.
Koertge, Ronald. Strays. 2007. (ENG.). 176p. (YA). (gr. 9-12). 16.99 *(978-0-7636-2705-8(4))* Candlewick Pr.
Lerangis, Peter. Wtf. (ENG., (YA). (gr. 9). 2013. Illus.). 288p. 17.99 *(978-1-4424-9369-8(0))* 2013. (Illus.). 288p. pap. 9.99 *(978-1-4424-9368-1(2))* 2009. 272p. pap. 8.99 *(978-1-4169-1360-3(2))* Simon Pulse. (Simon Pulse).
McGhee, Alison. All Rivers Flow to the Sea. 2005. (ENG.). 176p. (YA). (gr. 9-12). 15.99 *(978-0-7636-2591-7(4))* Candlewick Pr.
Messer, Celeste M. Three Miracles. 2004. (Adventures of Andi O'Malley Ser.). (Illus.). 82-92p. (J). (gr. 4-7). 4.95 *(978-0-9702171-4-1(5))* AshleyAlan Enterprises.
Meyers, Ann Marie. Up in the Air. 2013. 244p. (J). 22.99 *(978-1-939967-03-9(1),* Jolly Fish Pr.) North Star Editions.
Mitchard, Jacquelyn. All We Know of Heaven. 2008. (ENG.). 320p. (YA). (gr. 8-18). 16.99 *(978-0-06-134578-4(4),* HarperTeen) HarperCollins Pubs.
Phillips, Dee. Joyride, 1 vol. unabr. ed. 2010. (Right Now! Ser.). (ENG., Illus.). 45p. (YA). (gr. 9-12). pap. 10.75 *(978-1-61651-251-4(2))* Saddleback Educational Publishing, Inc.
Rice, Luanne. The Secret Language of Sisters. 2016. (ENG.). 352p. (YA). (gr. 7). 18.99 *(978-0-545-83955-6(6))* Scholastic, Inc.
Scieszka, Jon. Race from a to Z, No. 4. Shannon, David et al, illus. 2014. (Jon Scieszka's Trucktown Ser.). (ENG.). 48p. (J). (gr. -1-3). 19.99 *(978-1-4169-4136-1(3),* Simon & Schuster Bks. For Young Readers) Simon & Schuster Bks. For Young Readers.
—Uh-Oh, Max: Ready-To-Read Level 1. Shannon, David et al, illus. 2009. (Jon Scieszka's Trucktown Ser.). (ENG.). 24p. (J). (gr. -1-1). pap. 4.99 *(978-1-4169-4141-5(X),* Simon Spotlight) Simon Spotlight.
Scrimger, Richard. Me & Death: An Afterlife Adventure. 2010. (ENG.). 192p. (J). (gr. 5). pap. 12.95 *(978-0-88776-796-8(6),* Tundra Bks.) Tundra Bks. CAN. Dist: Penguin Random Hse. LLC.
Shelton, Donna. Lost in Time. 2018. (Monarch Jungle Ser.). lib. bdg. 19.60 *(978-0-606-41257-5(3))* Turtleback.
Sonneborn, Scott. Meet the South Police. Lozano, Omar, illus. 2015. (North Police Ser.). (ENG.). 32p. (J). (gr. k-2). lib. bdg. 21.32 *(978-1-4795-6486-6(9),* 128339, Picture Window Bks.) Capstone.
Stampler, Ann Redisch. Where It Began. 2013. (ENG.). 384p. (YA). (gr. 7-12). 26.19 *(978-1-4424-2321-3(8),* Simon Pulse) Simon Pulse.
Thompson, Michelle. Taming the Wind. 2010. 176p. pap. 12.99 *(978-1-59955-379-5(1))* Cedar Fort, Inc./CFI Distribution.
Walters, Eric. Overdrive. 2004. (Orca Soundings Ser.). 102p. (gr. 8-12). 19.95 *(978-0-7569-4320-2(5))* Perfection Learning Corp.
—A Toda Velocidad, 1 vol. 2008. (Spanish Soundings Ser.). (SPA.). 112p. (YA). (gr. 8-12). pap. 9.95 *(978-1-55469-055-8(2))* Orca Bk. Pubs. USA.

TRAFFIC REGULATIONS
see also Traffic Accidents
Beaver, Simon. Traffic Jams: the Road Ahead Beginning Book with Online Access, 1 vol. 2014. (ENG., Illus.). 24p. (J). pap., E-Book 9.50 *(978-1-107-67468-4(9))* Cambridge Univ. Pr.
Brezina, Corona. I've Gotten a DWI/DUI, Now What?, 1 vol. 2015. (Teen Life 411 Ser.). (ENG., Illus.). 112p. (J). (gr. 7-7). 38.80 *(978-1-4994-6146-6(1),* 06a623f9-3a52-4c8f-a3bc-3a76b05714fd, Rosen Young Adult) Rosen Publishing Group, Inc., The.
Crossing the Street: Individual Title Six-Packs. (gr. -1-2). 27.00 *(978-0-7635-9443-5(1))* Rigby Education.
Hemstock, Whitney M. The ABC's of Traffic Safety. 2010. 34p. pap. 16.95 *(978-0-557-28733-8(2))* Lulu Pr., Inc.
Jackson, Joann. Green Light, Red Light, Go! 2008. 20p. per. 24.95 *(978-1-60441-778-4(1))* America Star Bks.
McCaughtry, Keith. All about Street Signs & Laws. 2012. 16p. pap. 15.99 *(978-1-4772-5981-8(3))* AuthorHouse.
Moore, Elizabeth. Watch Out! 2011. (Wonder Readers Emergent Level Ser.). (ENG.). 8p. (gr. -1-1). pap. 35.94 *(978-1-4296-8237-4(X),* Capstone Pr.) Capstone.

TRAFFIC REGULATIONS—FICTION
Diggle, David Mark. Douglas: Pays the Price for Not Paying Attention. Preuss, Sarah Louise, illus. 2011. 24p. (J). pap. *(978-0-9871658-5-5(2))* Diggle de Doo Productions Pty, Ltd.
Harper, Charise Mericle. Go! Go! Go! Stop! 2014. (ENG.). 32p. (J). (-k). 18.99 *(978-0-375-86924-2(7),* Knopf Bks. for Young Readers) Random Hse. Children's Bks.
Judith Mader. I Went to Safety Town! 2009. 40p. pap. 16.99 *(978-1-4389-0129-9(1))* AuthorHouse.
McGovan, Michael. The Bobby Dazzlers. 2011. (Illus.). 28p. pap. 14.11 *(978-1-4567-8862-9(0))* AuthorHouse.
Molyneux, Caroline. Red for Stop. Green for Go. Yellow for Be Careful. 2010. 32p. 14.49 *(978-1-4490-5824-1(8))* AuthorHouse.
Sano, Gina. Traffic Lights. 2017. (ENG., Illus.). (J). pap. 24.14 *(978-1-5434-0348-0(4))* Xlibris Corp.
Scieszka, Jon. Pete's Party: Ready-To-Read Level 1. Gordon, David et al, illus. 2008. (Jon Scieszka's Trucktown Ser.). (ENG.). 24p. (J). (gr. -1-1). pap. 4.99 *(978-1-4169-4138-5(X),* Simon Spotlight) Simon Spotlight.
Taylor, Michael. Red Light, Green Light. Bassani, Srimalie, illus. 2017. (I Help My Friends Ser.). (ENG.). 24p. (gr. -1-2). pap. 9.95 *(978-1-68342-767-4(X),* 9781683427674) Rourke Educational Media.

TRAILERS
see Automobiles—Trailers

TRAILING
see Tracking and Trailing

TRAINING OF ANIMALS
see Animals—Training

TRAINING OF CHILDREN
see Child Rearing

TRAINING OF EMPLOYEES
see Employees—Training of

TRAINS, RAILROAD
see Railroads

TRAMPS—FICTION
Cory, Kim Delmar. Tending Ben's Garden. 2009. 121p. (J). pap. *(978-0-88092-778-9(X))* Royal Fireworks Publishing Co.
Guest, Jacqueline. Secret Signs, 1 vol. 2006. (Orca Young Readers Ser.). (ENG., Illus.). 144p. (J). (gr. 4-7). per. 8.95 *(978-1-55143-599-2(3))* Orca Bk. Pubs. USA.
Hoban, Russell. Charlie the Tramp. Hoban, Lillian, illus. 2016. (ENG.). 48p. 16.00 *(978-0-87486-780-0(0))* Plough Publishing Hse.
Mackall, Dandi Daley. Rudy Rides the Rails: A Depression Era Story. Ellison, Chris, illus. rev. ed. 2007. (Tales of Young Americans Ser.). (ENG.). 40p. (J). (gr. 1-4). 17.95 *(978-1-58536-286-8(7),* 202097) Sleeping Bear Pr.
Sweet, Melissa. Tupelo Rides the Rails. 2008. (ENG., Illus.). 40p. (J). (gr. 1-4). 17.00 *(978-0-618-71714-9(5),* 591982, Clarion Bks.) HarperCollins Pubs.
Waldman, Debby. Miriam's Secret, 1 vol. 2017. (ENG.). 208p. (J). (gr. 4-7). pap. 10.95 *(978-1-4598-1425-7(8))* Orca Bk. Pubs. USA.

TRANSATLANTIC FLIGHTS
see Aeronautics—Flights

TRANSCONTINENTAL JOURNEYS
see Overland Journeys to the Pacific

TRANSFORMERS (FICTITIOUS CHARACTERS)—FICTION
Ball, Georgia. Transformers Robots in Disguise Animated. 2016. lib. bdg. 26.95 *(978-0-606-38026-3(4))* Turtleback.
Burroughs, Caleb. Transformers. Mawhinney, Art, illus. 2007. (Look & Find (Publications International) Ser.). 16p. (J). (gr. -1-3). 7.98 *(978-1-4127-8673-7(8))* Publications International, Ltd.
Fox, Jennifer. Team of Heroes. 2014. (Transformers Passport to Reading Ser.). (J). lib. bdg. 13.55 *(978-0-606-35936-8(2))* Turtleback.
Foxe, Steve. Race to the Rescue. 2016. (Transformers 8x8 Ser.). (J). lib. bdg. 13.55 *(978-0-606-39192-4(4))* Turtleback.
Furman, Simon. Transformers: Spotlight - 6 Titles, 2 vols., Set. Musson, Robby, illus. Incl. Ultra Magnus. (ENG., Illus.). 24p. (gr. 2-7). 2008. 24.21 *(978-1-59961-479-3(0));* (Transformers: Spotlight Ser.: 6). (ENG.). Illus.). 24p. 2008. Set lib. bdg. 59.86 o.p. *(978-1-59961-473-1(1),* 14882, Graphic Novels) Spotlight.
Hasbro. Roll Out & Read Adventures. 2014. (Transformers Passport to Reading Ser.). (J). lib. bdg. 18.40 *(978-0-606-35294-9(5))* Turtleback.
Jakobs, D. Meet Blades the Copter-Bot. 2014. (Transformers Passport to Reading Ser.). (J). lib. bdg. 14.75 *(978-0-606-35295-6(3))* Turtleback.
Publications International Ltd. Staff. Interactive Sound Transformers. 2007. 24p. (J). 16.98 *(978-1-4127-6797-2(0),* PIL Kids) Publications International, Ltd.
—Look & Find Transformers. 2007. 24p. (J). 7.10 *(978-1-4127-6817-7(9),* PIL Kids) Publications International, Ltd.
Rau, Zachary. Autobots Versus Zombies. 2012. (Transformers 8x8 Ser.). (J). lib. bdg. 13.55 *(978-0-606-26687-1(9))* Turtleback.
Roe, David & Reader's Digest Editors. Mix & Match. Milne, Alex & Ruffolo, Rob, illus. 2007. (ENG.). 12p. (J). (gr. -1-1). bds. 14.99 *(978-0-7944-1286-9(6))* Reader's Digest Assn., Inc., The.
Sazaklis, John. The Ghosts of Griffin Rock. 2014. (Transformers 8x8 Ser.). (J). lib. bdg. 13.55 *(978-0-606-35935-1(4))* Turtleback.
—Optimus Prime Versus Predaking. 2013. (Transformers 8x8 Ser.). (J). lib. bdg. 13.55 *(978-0-606-32272-0(8))* Turtleback.
Snider, Brandon T., adapted by. Ghost in the Machine. 2017. (Illus.). (J). *(978-1-5379-5841-5(0))* Little, Brown Bks. for Young Readers.

TRANSISTORS
MacCarald, Clara. The Invention of the Transistor. 2017. (Engineering That Made America Ser.). (ENG.). 32p. (J). (gr. 3-6). lib. bdg. 35.64 *(978-1-5038-1638-1(9),* 211159) Child's World, Inc, The.
Roland, James. How Transistors Work. 2016. (Connect with Electricity Ser.). (ENG., Illus.). 40p. (J). (gr. 4-6). lib. bdg. 30.65 *(978-1-5124-0783-9(6),* 6346ba13-18e7-4c33-b79c-80349ee39cde); E-Book 46.65 *(978-1-5124-1011-2(X))* Lerner Publishing Group. (Lerner Pubns.).

TRANSMISSION OF POWER
see Electric Lines

TRANSPLANTATION OF ORGANS, TISSUES, ETC.
Abramovitz, Melissa. Organ Transplants, 1 vol. 2012. (Hot Topics Ser.). (ENG., Illus.). 128p. (gr. 7-7). lib. bdg. 41.03 *(978-1-4205-0816-1(4),* de58a3c6-ecd6-4d91-9d07-dc1373a0e0d2, Lucent Pr.) Greenhaven Publishing LLC.
Ballard, Carol. Organ Transplants, 1 vol. 2007. (Cutting Edge Medicine Ser.). (ENG., Illus.). 64p. (gr. 5-8). lib. bdg. 36.67 *(978-0-8368-7868-4(X),* 8c4418e8-5f53-40d2-b4ae-f85009d5edeb, Gareth Stevens Secondary Library) Stevens, Gareth Publishing LLLP.
Campbell, Andrew. Cosmetic Surgery. 2010. (J). 34.25 *(978-1-59920-322-5(7))* Black Rabbit Bks.
—Organ Transplants. 2010. (Illus.). 45p. (J). 34.25 *(978-1-59920-321-8(9))* Black Rabbit Bks.
Claybourne, Anna. What Are the Limits of Organ Transplants?, 1 vol. 2012. (Sci-Hi: Science Issues Ser.). (ENG., Illus.). 48p. (J). (gr. 6-10). lib. bdg. 35.99 *(978-1-4109-4466-5(2),* 117649, Raintree) Capstone.
Egendorf, Laura K., ed. Organ Donation, 1 vol. 2013. (Opposing Viewpoints Ser.). (ENG., Illus.). 184p. (gr. 10-12). lib. bdg. 50.43 *(978-0-7377-6332-4(9),* db925b84-cddb-4df0-9c03-c49ab326658f, Greenhaven Publishing) Greenhaven Publishing LLC.
Gray, Susan H. Transplants. 2008. (21st Century Skills Innovation Library: Innovation in Medicine Ser.). (ENG., Illus.). 32p. (gr. 4-8). lib. bdg. 32.07 *(978-1-60279-225-8(9),* 200156) Cherry Lake Publishing.
Kovacs, Vic. Organ Transplants, 1 vol. 2016. (Miracles of Medicine Ser.). (ENG.). 48p. (J). (gr. 6-6). pap. 15.05 *(978-1-4824-6100-8(5),* 7422eef8-9f24-43ca-b8b5-188dfac45657) Stevens, Gareth Publishing LLLP.
Small, Cathleen. Organ Transplants, 1 vol. 2018. (Great Discoveries in Science Ser.). (ENG.). 128p. (gr. 9-9). lib. bdg. 47.36 *(978-1-5026-4379-7(0),* 9c23f412-7a8c-4ed0-805e-8bf0eff85ede) Cavendish Square Publishing LLC.
Stearman, Kaye. The Debate about Cosmetic Surgery, 1 vol. 2010. (Ethical Debates Ser.). (ENG.). 48p. (YA). (gr. 6-6). lib. bdg. 34.47 *(978-1-4358-9650-5(5),* 8f609d1e-76aa-458b-960f-1a89fc900e8c, Rosen Reference) Rosen Publishing Group, Inc., The.
UNOS (Organization) Staff, contrib. by. Organ Transplants: What Every Kid Needs to Know. 2003. (Illus.). (J). *(978-1-886651-43-2(4))* United Network for Organ Sharing.
Wood, Ramona. Now Caitlin Can: A Donated Organ Helps a Child Get Well. 2004. (Illus.). 32p. (J). 16.00 *(978-0-9758622-0-9(0))* ABC Pr.
Wouk, Henry. Organ Transplants, 1 vol. 2013. (Advances in Medicine Ser.). (ENG.). 64p. (gr. 6-6). pap. 16.28 *(978-1-62712-010-4(6),* 59bec254-474c-44a8-9c90-187ec2c1e1da); (Illus.). 36.93 *(978-1-60870-467-5(X),* 34a568de-a134-4b1b-9d6f-a85196f8b8ee) Cavendish Square Publishing LLC.

TRANSPORTATION
see also Aeronautics, Commercial; Automobiles; Bridges; Buses; Canals; Commerce; Freight and Freightage; Harbors; Postal Service; Railroads; Roads; Steamboats; Streets; Subways; Trade Routes; Traffic Regulations; Trucks; Waterways
ABDO Publishing Company Staff & Murray, Julie. Transportation, 6 vols. 2014. (Transportation Ser.: 6). (ENG.). 24p. (J). (gr. -1-2). lib. bdg. 196.74 *(978-1-62970-077-9(0),* 1701, Abdo Kids) ABDO Publishing Co.
Aboff, Marcie. A Transportation Time Line from Feet to Cars & Beyond. 2016. (Spring Forward Ser.). (J). (gr. 1). *(978-1-4900-9407-6(5))* Benchmark Education Co.
Adams, Jennifer. Around the World in 80 Days: A BabyLit(TM) Transportation Primer, 1 vol. Oliver, Alison, illus. 2018. (BabyLit Ser.). 22p. (J). (— 1). bds. 9.99 *(978-1-4236-4746-1(7))* Gibbs Smith, Publisher.
Amstutz, L. J. How Can We Reduce Transportation Pollution? 2016. (Searchlight Books (tm) — What Can We Do about Pollution? Ser.). (ENG., Illus.). 40p. (J). (gr. 3-5). lib. bdg. 30.65 *(978-1-4677-9515-9(1),* a9e296ec-7845-4c32-9898-06a21242d0eb, Lerner Pubns.) Lerner Publishing Group.
Andrus, Aubre. National Geographic Readers: Let's Go! (Prereader) 2019. (Readers Ser.). (Illus.). 24p. (J). (gr. -1-k). pap. 4.99 *(978-1-4263-3335-4(8));* (ENG., lib. bdg. 14.90 *(978-1-4263-3336-1(6))* Disney Publishing Worldwide. (National Geographic Kids).

TUV

Animals at Work: Individual Title Six-Packs. (gr. k-1). 23.00 *(978-0-7635-9060-4(6))* Rigby Education.

Appleby, Alex. Dinosaurs on the Go, 1 vol. 2013. (Dinosaur School Ser.). 24p. (J). (gr. k-k). (ENG.). pap. 9.15 *(978-1-4339-9062-5(8),* ad5f4f50-705a-44c8-8b50-2b57f2abc8ad); pap. 48.90 *(978-1-4339-9063-2(6))*; (ENG., Illus.). lib. bdg. 25.27 *(978-1-4339-9061-8(X),* fa7ee29b-2ae5-4ecd-bb99-648c3c38e0bf) Stevens, Gareth Publishing LLLP.

Ard, Catherine. Origami on the Move, 1 vol. 2014. (Amazing Origami Ser.). (ENG., Illus.). 32p. (J). (gr. 2-3). 29.27 *(978-1-4824-2202-3(6),* 8f2d879d-bf21-4541-b109-25ea1972a95e) Stevens, Gareth Publishing LLLP.

Baer, Edith. This Is the Way We Go to School. 2014. 17.00 *(978-1-63419-734-2(8))* Perfection Learning Corp.

Ball, Jacqueline A. Traveling Green. (Going Green Ser.). 32p. 2016. (ENG.). (J). (gr. 2-7). pap. 7.99 *(978-1-944998-67-7(5))* 2009. (Illus.). (YA). (gr. 3-6). lib. bdg. 28.50 *(978-1-59716-964-6(1))* Bearport Publishing Co., Inc.

Barefoot Books. Fast & Slow. Teckentrup, Britta, illus. 2013. (ENG.). 16p. (J). (gr. -1-k). bds. 7.99 *(978-1-84686-952-5(8))* Barefoot Bks., Inc.

Barraclough, Sue. On the Move, 1 vol. 2009. (Me & My World Ser.). (ENG., Illus.). 24p. (J). (gr. -1-2). pap. 9.15 *(978-1-60754-064-9(9),* c576c3f3-4a86-4168-a56e-48aa81135323); lib. bdg. 27.27 *(978-1-60754-058-8(4),* faff1053-0eaa-401c-a610-e1e7b269ae5b) Rosen Publishing Group, Inc., The. (Windmill Bks.).

Barraclough, Sue, et al. Be an Eco Hero on the Move. 2013. (Be an Eco Hero Ser.). (ENG., Illus.). 24p. (J). (gr. 2-4). lib. bdg. 25.65 *(978-1-59771-380-1(5))* Sea-To-Sea Pubns.

Benchmark Education Company, LLC Staff, compiled by. Transportation. 2006. (J). 91.00 *(978-1-4108-7043-8(X))* Benchmark Education Co.

Bethea, Nikole Brooks. High-Tech Highways & Super Skyways: The Next 100 Years of Transportation. Pota, Giovanni et al, illus. 2016. (Our World: the Next 100 Years Ser.). (ENG.). 32p. (J). (gr. 3-9). lib. bdg. 31.32 *(978-1-4914-8266-7(4),* 130755, Capstone Pr.) Capstone.

Beylon, Cathy. Color Your Own Things That Go Stickers. 2006. (Dover Sticker Bks.). (ENG., Illus.). 2p. (J). (gr. 3-3). 2.95 *(978-0-486-44898-5(3))* Dover Pubns., Inc.

Bicknell, Joanna. Emergency. 2005. (Shimmer & Shine Bks.). 12p. (gr. -1-k). per., bds. *(978-1-905051-32-8(8))* Make Believe Ideas.

—My Digger Book. 2005. (Shimmer & Shine Books Ser.). 12p. (gr. -1-k). per., bds. *(978-1-905051-30-4(1))* Make Believe Ideas.

Biggs, Brian. Everything Goes: Blue Bus, Red Balloon: a Book of Colors. Biggs, Brian, illus. 2013. (ENG., Illus.). 24p. (J). (gr. -1 — 1). bds. 7.99 *(978-0-06-195814-4(X),* Balzer & Bray) HarperCollins Pubs.

Birch, Beverley. Transport. (ENG., Illus.). 128p. pap. 8.99 *(978-0-340-65698-3(0))* Hodder & Stoughton GBR. Dist: Trafalgar Square Publishing.

Bodden, Valerie. National Transportation Safety Board. 2016. (Agents of Government Ser.). (ENG.). 48p. (J). (gr. 4-7). pap. 12.00 *(978-1-62832-149-4(0),* 20847, Creative Paperbacks) Creative Co., The.

Boone, Mary. Transportation Inspired by Nature. 2019. (Inspired by Nature Ser.). (ENG., Illus.). 24p. (J). (gr. 1-3). pap. 7.95 *(978-1-9771-1009-1(6),* 140952); lib. bdg. 25.99 *(978-1-9771-0839-5(3),* 140459) Capstone. (Pebble).

Boothroyd, Jennifer. From the Model T to Hybrid Cars: How Transportation Has Changed. 2011. (Comparing Past & Present Ser.). pap. 45.32 *(978-0-7613-8392-5(1))*; pap. 7.95 *(978-0-7613-7837-2(5))* Lerner Publishing Group.

—Transportation. 2006. (First Step Nonfiction — We Are Alike & Different Ser.). (ENG., Illus.). 8p. (J). (gr. k-2). pap. 5.99 *(978-0-8225-5730-2(4),* b8ab8b3e-99ce-454a-9141-3b92d872c7d6) Lerner Publishing Group.

Brady, Peter. Transportation Zone. 2012. (Transportation Zone Ser.). (ENG.). 24p. (gr. 1-2). pap. 250.20 *(978-1-4296-8399-9(6),* Capstone Pr.) Capstone.

Broyles, Matthew. U. S. Air Marshals. (Extreme Careers Ser.). 64p. (gr. 5-5). 2009. 58.50 *(978-1-61512-416-9(0),* Rosen Reference) 2007. (ENG., Illus.). (J). lib. bdg. 37.13 *(978-1-4042-0942-8(5),* 8fa8bfbc-9017-41d4-90ce-81c18389abc5) Rosen Publishing Group, Inc., The.

Buckley, James. Things That Go! 2013. (Illus.). 32p. *(978-0-545-62399-5(5))* Scholastic, Inc.

Buckley Jr., James. Things That Go! (Scholastic Discover More Reader Level 1) 2013. (Scholastic Discover More Ser.). (ENG.). 32p. (J). (gr. -1-3). pap. 3.99 *(978-0-545-53376-8(7),* Scholastic Reference) Scholastic, Inc.

Bull, Peter, illus. Transport. (Music about Us Ser.). 64p. 9.95 *(978-1-85909-294-1(2),* Warner Bros. Pubns.) Alfred Publishing Co., Inc.

Burton, Margie, et al. Going Places. 2011. (Early Connections Ser.). (J). *(978-1-61672-490-0(0))* Benchmark Education Co.

Butterfield, Moira. Transportation Around the World, 1 vol. 2015. (Children Like Us Ser.). (ENG., Illus.). 32p. (gr. 3-3). pap. 11.58 *(978-1-5026-0854-3(5),* 73528b8b-ff84-477c-a660-e97d3b0573ea) Cavendish Square Publishing LLC.

Carle, Eric. My Very First Book of Motion. Carle, Eric, illus. 2007. (Illus.). 18p. (J). (gr. -1 — 1). bds. 6.99 *(978-0-399-24748-4(3))* Penguin Young Readers Group.

Catala, Ellen. How Do You Move? 2005. (Yellow Umbrella Fluent Level Ser.). (ENG., Illus.). 16p. (gr. k-1). pap. 35.70 *(978-0-7368-5295-1(6),* Capstone Pr.) Capstone.

Channing, Margot. On the Go. Claude, Jean, illus. 2017. (First Words & Pictures Ser.). (ENG.). 14p. (J). (gr. -1 — 1). bds. 9.99 *(978-1-68152-201-2(2),* 14731) Amicus.

Chappell, Jackie. When I Ride the Bus. 2006. (My Day at School (Rourke) Ser.). (Illus.). 8p. (J). (gr. 3-7). pap. 5.95 *(978-1-59515-939-7(8))* Rourke Educational Media.

Chmielewski, Gary. Let's Go in the Funny Zone: Jokes, Riddles, Tongue Twisters & Daffynitions. Caputo, Jim, illus. rev. ed. 2007. (Funny Zone Ser.). (ENG.). 24p. (J). (gr. 2-4). lib. bdg. 22.60 *(978-1-59953-182-3(8))* Norwood Hse. Pr.

Clark, Willow. Transportation Station, 12 vols., Set. Incl. Bikes on the Move. lib. bdg. 26.27 *(978-1-4358-9334-4(4),* 3b21c2d2-02c7-4131-8172-f36ca5f85cc0); Boats on the Move. lib. bdg. 26.27 *(978-1-4358-9336-8(0),* b51082dc-75da-4b6b-bbff-54e25d8c2041); Cars on the Move. lib. bdg. 26.27 *(978-1-4358-9333-7(6),* b0720a37-f204-4d59-bd1e-9e67aed69987); Motorcycles on the Move. lib. bdg. 26.27 *(978-1-4358-9335-1(2),* 0c0944d0-7e08-443e-bc21-89bb20db596a); Planes on the Move. lib. bdg. 26.27 *(978-1-4358-9332-0(8),* 93e936ae-bdb4-4dc5-a362-724485c63ae1); Trains on the Move. lib. bdg. 26.27 *(978-1-4358-9331-3(X),* 4012aa41-bf42-4f2e-9f66-255a4c910713); (J). (gr. 2-3). (Transportation Station Ser.). (ENG., Illus.). 24p. 2010. Set lib. bdg. 157.62 *(978-1-4358-9404-4(9),* 555b6a83-113e-458b-89d1-7b69f2f29467, PowerKids Pr.) Rosen Publishing Group, Inc., The.

Close, Edward. Wheels, Wings, & Motors, 1 vol., 1. 2014. (Discovery Education: How It Works). (ENG.). 32p. (gr. 4-5). 28.93 *(978-1-4777-6313-1(9),* 803af42f-58c3-43fd-81fa-5099de611187, PowerKids Pr.) Rosen Publishing Group, Inc., The.

Coleman, Miriam. Earth-Friendly Transportation, 1 vol. 2011. (How to Be Earth Friendly Ser.). (ENG., Illus.). 32p. (gr. 3-4). (J). pap. 11.00 *(978-1-4488-2769-5(8),* 73c73d5a-e605-4584-a7d4-20a4cfb42566, PowerKids Pr.); (YA). lib. bdg. 28.93 *(978-1-4488-2590-5(3),* 65b5a30c-3a70-4bfe-829a-25a6b2f95d03) Rosen Publishing Group, Inc., The.

de Seve, Karen. National Geographic Little Kids First Big Book of Things That Go. 2017. (National Geographic Little Kids First Big Bks.). (Illus.). 128p. (J). (gr. -1-k). 14.99 *(978-1-4263-2804-6(4))*; (ENG., lib. bdg. 24.90 *(978-1-4263-2805-3(2))* Disney Publishing Worldwide. (National Geographic Kids).

DeGezelle, Terri, et al. Mighty Machines: Construction (6 book Set) [NASCO]. 2012. (Mighty Machines Ser.). (ENG.). 24p. (gr. k-1). pap. 41.70 *(978-1-62065-474-3(1),* Capstone Pr.) Capstone.

Deibel, Zac. Racial Segregation: Plessy V. Ferguson, 1 vol. 2018. (Courting History Ser.). (ENG.). 64p. (gr. 6-6). pap. 16.87 *(978-1-5026-3591-4(7),* 4106d9cf-8657-4c82-98d3-f32be4fe6ad0) Cavendish Square Publishing LLC.

Depue, Anne. All Kinds of Transportation. Peattie, Cindy; Depue, ed. 2016. (Spring Forward Ser.). (ENG.). (J). (gr. 1). 6.84 net. *(978-1-4900-6022-4(7))* Benchmark Education Co.

DiSiena, Laura Lyn & Eliot, Hannah. Trains Can Float: And Other Fun Facts. Oswald, Pete & Spurgeon, Aaron, illus. 2014. (Did You Know? Ser.). (ENG.). 32p. (J). (gr. -1-3). 17.99 *(978-1-4814-0281-1(1),* Little Simon) Little Simon.

Dittmer, Lori. The Future of Transportation. 2012. (What's Next? Ser.). (Illus.). 48p. (J). (gr. 5-12). 23.95 *(978-1-60818-224-4(X),* Creative Education) Creative Co., The.

DK. Cars, Trains, Ships, & Planes: A Visual Encyclopedia of Every Vehicle. 2015. (DK Our World in Pictures Ser.). (ENG., Illus.). 256p. (J). (gr. 4-7). 24.99 *(978-1-4654-3805-8(X),* DK Children) Dorling Kindersley Publishing, Inc.

—Pop-Up Peekaboo! Things That Go: Pop-Up Surprise under Every Flap! 2012. (Pop-Up Peekaboo! Ser.). (ENG., Illus.). 12p. (J). (gr. -1 — 1). bds. 12.99 *(978-0-7566-9009-0(9),* DK Children) Dorling Kindersley Publishing, Inc.

Doman, Mary Kate. Big Military Machines, 1 vol. 2011. (All about Big Machines Ser.). (ENG., Illus.). 24p. (gr. -1-1). pap. 10.35 *(978-1-59845-243-3(6),* 13847093-d60d-4a47-bd72-f54ea6741012, Enslow Publishing) Enslow Publishing, LLC.

Dunn, Karen Lewit. Visiting Grandma. 2008. (Discovering & Exploring Science Ser.). (Illus.). 16p. (J). (gr. -1-3). lib. bdg. 12.95 *(978-0-7569-8434-2(3))* Perfection Learning Corp.

Eboch, M. M. The 12 Biggest Breakthroughs in Transportation Technology. 2014. (ENG.). 32p. (J). 32.80 *(978-1-63235-017-6(3),* 12-Story Library) Bookstaves, LLC.

Encyclopaedia Britannica, Inc. Staff, compiled by. Discover English with Ben & Bella: Series 2: Going Places. 2010. 180.00 *(978-1-61535-349-1(6))* Encyclopaedia Britannica, Inc.

Falk, Laine. This Is the Way We Go to School. 2009. (Scholastic News Nonfiction Readers: Kids Like Me Ser.). (ENG.). 24p. (J). (gr. k-3). lib. bdg. 21.19 *(978-0-531-21341-4(2),* Children's Pr.) Scholastic Library Publishing.

—This Is the Way We Go to School (Scholastic News Nonfiction Readers: Kids Like Me) 2009. (Scholastic News Nonfiction Readers Ser.). (ENG.). 24p. (J). (gr. 1-2). pap. 6.95 *(978-0-531-21440-4(0),* Children's Pr.) Scholastic Library Publishing.

Freedman, Jeri. Coding Careers in Transportation, 1 vol. 2019. (Coding Careers for Tomorrow Ser.). (ENG.). 80p. (gr. 8-8). pap. 18.64 *(978-1-5026-4590-6(4),* a020ef25-b153-4ddf-84f9-68f0bfc02825) Cavendish Square Publishing LLC.

Freudenthal. Ways to Go. 3rd ed. 2003. (Math in Context Ser.). (Illus.). 8.33 *(978-0-03-071614-0(4))* Holt McDougal.

Fridell, Ron. Seven Wonders of Transportation. 2010. (Seven Wonders Ser.). (Illus.). 80p. (J). (gr. 5-9). lib. bdg. 33.26 *(978-0-7613-4238-0(9))* Twenty First Century Bks.

Furgang, Kathy. On the Move: Green Transportation. 2009. (Your Carbon Footprint Ser.). 48p. (gr. 5-5). 53.00 *(978-1-60854-909-2(7),* Rosen Reference) Rosen Publishing Group, Inc., The.

Furgang, Kathy & Furgang, Adam. On the Move: Green Transportation, 1 vol. 2008. (Your Carbon Footprint Ser.). (ENG., Illus.). 48p. (YA). (gr. 5-5). lib. bdg. 34.47 *(978-1-4042-1773-7(8),* 4350af81-a9f6-4345-845b-09e5923144c1) Rosen Publishing Group, Inc., The.

Gaertner, Meg. Kim Takes a Trip: A Book about Transportation. 2018. (My Day Readers Ser.). (ENG.). 24p. (J). (gr. -1-2). lib. bdg. 32.79 *(978-1-5038-2750-9(X),* 212581) Child's World, Inc, The.

Gardner, Jane P. Travel Science, Vol. 11. Lewin, Russ, ed. 2015. (Science 24/7 Ser.). (Illus.). 48p. (J). (gr. 5). 20.95 *(978-1-4222-3415-0(0))* Mason Crest.

Gibbons, Gail. Transportation! How People Get Around. (Illus.). 32p. (J). (gr. -1-3). 2019. pap. 8.99 *(978-0-8234-4188-4(1))* 2017. (ENG., 18.99 *(978-0-8234-3425-1(7))* Holiday Hse., Inc.

Gillett, Jack & Gillett, Meg. Transportation-Network Maps, 1 vol. 2012. (Maps of the Environmental World Ser.). (ENG., Illus.). 32p. (J). (gr. 5-5). 30.27 *(978-1-4488-8613-5(9),* cc1156a7-01a5-45b0-8212-b55bc51e8426); pap. 11.60 *(978-1-4488-8619-7(8),* bf78b14a-bc85-43a2-93b0-77bbe55df12d) Rosen Publishing Group, Inc., The. (PowerKids Pr.).

Goldish, Meish & Parkhurst, Anthony. Horses, Donkeys, & Mules in the Marines. 2012. (America's Animal Soldiers Ser.). 24p. (J). (gr. 1-6). lib. bdg. 26.99 *(978-1-61772-453-4(X))* Bearport Publishing Co., Inc.

Goldsworthy, Steve. Travel Green. 2010. (Being Green Ser.). (Illus.). 32p. (YA). (gr. 3-6). lib. bdg. 27.13 *(978-1-61690-085-4(7))*; (J). (gr. 4-6). pap. 12.95 *(978-1-61690-086-1(5))* Weigl Pubs., Inc.

—Travelling Green. 2016. (Illus.). 32p. (J). *(978-1-5105-2223-7(9))* SmartBook Media, Inc.

Goodman, Polly. Transportation for the Future, 1 vol. 2011. (Earth Alert! Ser.). (ENG.). 32p. (YA). (gr. 3-4). lib. bdg. 29.27 *(978-1-4339-6011-6(7),* 6955fb73-f22a-48dd-b792-ae88cc3e61df) Stevens, Gareth Publishing LLLP.

Gordon, Bob. Touch & Sparkle Emergency. 2005. (Illus.). 12p. (gr. -1). bds. *(978-1-905051-58-8(1))* Make Believe Ideas.

Graham, Buck. My First Big Book of Questions & Answers: Things That Go. 2005. (Illus.). 10p. bds. 9.98 *(978-0-7853-7227-1(X),* 7171500) Publications International, Ltd.

Graham, Ian, et al. Firefly Encyclopedia of Transportation: A Comprehensive Look at the World of Transportation. Green, Oliver, ed. 2017. (ENG., Illus.). 160p. (J). (gr. 4-7). pap. 14.95 *(978-1-77085-931-9(4),* e40f5c35-f226-46e8-a492-1eb36dc12947) Firefly Bks., Ltd.

Greek, Joe. Solving Real World Problems with Transportation Engineering, 1 vol., 1. 2015. (Let's Find Out! Engineering Ser.). (ENG., Illus.). 32p. (J). (gr. 2-3). pap. 13.90 *(978-1-5081-0071-3(3),* d99676dd-f164-47f4-a80c-cea39e6ce4e8, Britannica Educational Publishing) Rosen Publishing Group, Inc., The.

Gregory, Helen. Getting There, 1 vol. 2011. (Wonder Readers Early Level Ser.). (ENG.). 16p. (gr. -1-1). (J). pap. 6.25 *(978-1-4296-7805-6(4),* 117977); pap. 35.94 *(978-1-4296-8091-2(1),* Capstone Pr.) Capstone.

Grossbard, H. A. Driving in Florida: The Politically Incorrect Guide to Surviving the Roadways of the Sunshine State. 2011. 40p. (gr. -1). pap. 16.99 *(978-1-4520-9741-1(0))* AuthorHouse.

Guin, Valerie. On the Move. 2005. (One World (Smart Apple Media) Ser.). (Illus.). 30p. (J). (gr. 3-6). lib. bdg. 27.10 *(978-1-58340-699-1(9))* Black Rabbit Bks.

Harrier Jump Jet. 2004. (Press-Out & Build Ser.). (Illus.). 24p. (J). per. *(978-1-84229-725-4(2))* Top That! Publishing PLC.

Harrison, Paul. On the Move. 2011. (Window on the World Ser.). (Illus.). 32p. *(978-1-84089-660-2(4))* Zero to Ten, Ltd.

—Speed Machines. (Up Close Ser.). 24p. (gr. 3-3). 2009. 47.90 *(978-1-60854-705-0(1))* 2007. (ENG., Illus.). (J). lib. bdg. 28.93 *(978-1-4042-4222-7(8),* 0cc7297d-c4a0-451f-b09e-2535c2a0696c) Rosen Publishing Group, Inc., The. (PowerKids Pr.).

Hergé. Tintín: Descubro Los Transportes. 2004. (SPA., Illus.). 24p. 19.95 *(978-1-59497-064-1(5))* Public Square Bks.

Hewitt, Sally. Transportation. 2010. (Starting Geography Ser.). 32p. (J). (gr. 2-5). 28.50 *(978-1-60753-129-6(1))* Amicus Learning.

—Transportation. 2012. (Map Smart Ser.). 32p. (gr. 2-6). lib. bdg. 27.10 *(978-1-59920-415-4(0))* Black Rabbit Bks.

Hinkler Books, creator. 101 First Words: Things That Go. 2011. (101 First Words Ser.). (Illus.). 16p. (J). (gr. -1). bds. 7.99 *(978-1-74184-818-2(0))* Hinkler Bks. Pty, Ltd. AUS. Dist: Ideals Pubns.

Hinote Lanier, Wendy. Transportation Technology Inspired by Nature. 2018. (Technology Inspired by Nature Ser.). (ENG., Illus.). 32p. (J). (gr. 3-5). pap. 9.95 *(978-1-64185-046-9(9),* 1641850469); lib. bdg. 31.35 *(978-1-63517-944-6(0),* 1635179440) North Star Editions. (Focus Readers).

HOP, LLC. Hooked on Trains, Planes, & Cars Super Activity Kit. 2006. (J). (gr. -1). 9.99 *(978-1-933863-21-4(8))* HOP, LLC.

—Super Activity 3-pack - Hooked on Things That Go. 2006. (J). (gr. -1). 24.99 *(978-1-933863-96-2(X))* HOP, LLC.

Hudak, Heather C. Pathways Through Africa. 2019. (Human Path Across the Continents Ser.). (ENG.). 32p. (J). (gr. 5-5). pap. *(978-0-7787-6644-5(6),* fd934af9-9fec-4617-81ed-d62e1d13d015) Crabtree Publishing Co.

Ieda, Hitoshi, ed. Sustainable Urban Transport in an Asian Context, 1 vol. 2010. (CSUR-UT Series: Library for Sustainable Urban Regeneration Ser.: 9). (ENG., Illus.). xviii, 422p. 169.99 *(978-4-431-93953-5(9),* 978-4-431-93953-5, Springer) Springer Japan JPN. Dist: Springer.

Imperato, Teresa. On the Go! A Transportation Book. Rayner, Olivia, illus. 2005. 10p. (J). 7.95 *(978-1-58117-271-3(0),* Intervisual/Piggy Toes) Bendon, Inc.

—Speed Machines: A Pop-up Book with Moving Gears. Robinson, Keith, illus. 2005. 8p. (J). 14.95 *(978-1-58117-323-9(7),* Intervisual/Piggy Toes) Bendon, Inc.

Iyer, Rani. Green Transport: Exploring Eco-Friendly Travel for a Better Tomorrow. 2016. (ENG.). 120p. (gr. 8-12). *(978-81-7993-444-9(6))* Energy and Resources Institute, The IND. Dist: Motilal (UK) Bks. of India.

Kalman, Bobbie. Animals Move Like This. 2011. (ENG.). 24p. (J). *(978-0-7787-9564-3(0))*; pap. *(978-0-7787-9589-6(6))* Crabtree Publishing Co.

—Getting from Place to Place in My Community. 2017. (My World Ser.). (Illus.). 24p. (J). (gr. 1-1). *(978-0-7787-9596-4(9))*; pap. *(978-0-7787-9604-6(3))* Crabtree Publishing Co.

—I Like Riding. 2011. (ENG.). 16p. (J). *(978-0-7787-9550-6(0))*; (My World Ser.: No. 52). pap. *(978-0-7787-9575-9(6))* Crabtree Publishing Co.

—Travel Then & Now. 2013. (ENG., Illus.). 24p. (J). *(978-0-7787-0129-3(8))*; pap. *(978-0-7787-0211-5(1))* Crabtree Publishing Co.

Kawa, Katie. My First Trip on an Airplane, 1 vol. 2012. (My First Adventures Ser.). (ENG., Illus.). 24p. (J). (gr. k-k). pap. 9.15 *(978-1-4339-7297-3(2),* 0d6b57c0-466a-42b7-a998-b211a6af6485); lib. bdg. 25.27 *(978-1-4339-7296-6(4),* 20a971c6-2c7f-413f-8afe-5f8b5242fc2e) Stevens, Gareth Publishing LLLP.

Kemp, Kristin. Amazing Americans: Rosa Parks, 1 vol. rev. ed. 2014. (Social Studies: Informational Text Ser.). (ENG., Illus.). 32p. (gr. 3-4). pap. 11.99 *(978-1-4333-7375-6(0))* Teacher Created Materials, Inc.

Kent, Lorna, illus. On the Move. 2004. 8p. (J). pap. 3.99 *(978-1-85854-089-4(5))* Brimax Books Ltd. GBR. Dist: Byeway Bks.

Kopp, Megan. Top Secret Science in Transportation. 2019. (Top Secret Science Ser.). (Illus.). 48p. (J). (gr. 5-5). *(978-0-7787-5997-3(0))*; pap. *(978-0-7787-6035-1(9))* Crabtree Publishing Co.

Lake, Joss. The Evolution of Transportation Technology, 1 vol. 2018. (Evolving Technology Ser.). (ENG.). 64p. (gr. 6-7). lib. bdg. 34.29 *(978-1-5383-0287-3(X),* fe1e2690-75e4-45e2-8e0c-c82ce7519171, Britannica Educational Publishing) Rosen Publishing Group, Inc., The.

Lanier, Wendy Hinote. Transportation Technology: Designed by Nature. 2018. (Illus.). 32p. (J). *(978-1-4896-9733-2(0),* AV2 by Weigl) Weigl Pubs., Inc.

Leitten, Amanda. Transportation Then & Now, 1 vol. 2008. (Real Life Readers Ser.). (ENG.). 12p. (gr. 1-2). pap. 5.90 *(978-1-4042-7903-2(2),* 71e7d69c-dd11-49c0-9dbe-b1a7882bfcb2, Rosen Classroom) Rosen Publishing Group, Inc., The.

Lerner Publishing Group Staff. Lightning Bolt Books: Vroom-Vroom, 6 vols., Set. 2011. (J). (gr. k-2). lib. bdg. 151.56 *(978-0-7613-7481-7(7))* Lerner Publishing Group.

Let's Find Out! Transportation, 16 vols. 2016. (Let's Find Out! Transportation Ser.). 32p. (ENG.). (gr. 2-3). 208.48 *(978-1-5081-0217-5(1),* 7a620a9f-d25e-4a9a-8a13-7d919ab4e1aa); (gr. 3-2). pap. 103.20 *(978-1-68048-598-1(9))* Rosen Publishing Group, Inc., The. (Britannica Educational Publishing).

Light, Kate. Weird Transportation Inventions, 1 vol. 2018. (Wild & Wacky Inventions Ser.). (ENG.). 32p. (gr. 4-5). 28.27 *(978-1-5382-2087-0(3),* 5821d0b5-a76a-465f-83f4-b42f5f2f5e67) Stevens, Gareth Publishing LLLP.

Light, Steve. Trucks Go: (Board Books about Trucks, Go Trucks Books for Kids) 2008. (Vehicles Go! Ser.). (ENG., Illus.). 16p. (J). (gr. -1 — 1). bds. 9.99 *(978-0-8118-6542-5(8))* Chronicle Bks. LLC.

Lomberg, Michelle. Avoiding Gridlock. Schwartzenberger, Tina, ed. 2004. (Understanding Global Issues). (Illus.). 56p. (J). (gr. 10-12). lib. bdg. 28.50 *(978-1-58340-357-0(4))* Weigl Pubs., Inc.

Lyons, Shelly. Transportation in My Neighborhood. 2013. (My Neighborhood Ser.). (ENG.). 24p. (J). (gr. k-1). pap. 43.74 *(978-1-62065-892-5(5),* 19445); (Illus.). (gr. -1-2). pap. 7.29 *(978-1-62065-891-8(7),* 121805); (Illus.). (gr. -1-2). lib. bdg. 27.32 *(978-1-62065-101-8(7),* 120798) Capstone. (Capstone Pr.).

Manolis, Kay. Big Rigs. 2008. (Mighty Machines Ser.). (ENG., Illus.). 24p. (J). (gr. k-3). lib. bdg. 26.95 *(978-1-60014-177-5(3))* Bellwether Media.

Marks, Aaron. Transportation: Then & Now. 2008. (Discovering & Exploring Science Ser.). (Illus.). 16p. (J). (gr. -1-3). lib. bdg. 12.95 *(978-0-7569-8420-5(3))* Perfection Learning Corp.

Mason, Paul. How Big Is Your Travel Footprint?, 1 vol. 2010. (Environmental Footprints Ser.). (ENG., Illus.). 32p. (gr. 4-4). 31.21 *(978-0-7614-4415-2(7),* 27c4c20d-a497-492c-b038-7a9ae9e4b132) Cavendish Square Publishing LLC.

Mattern, Joanne. Staying Safe in the Car, 1 vol. 2007. (Safety First Ser.). (ENG., Illus.). 24p. (gr. k-2). pap. 9.15 *(978-0-8368-7800-4(0),* 4ff21788-c148-46db-b290-5273f980bfa1); lib. bdg. 24.67 *(978-0-8368-7793-9(4),* 9b042e38-44fd-4479-9be2-5ab8d55cccc6) Stevens, Gareth Publishing LLLP. (Weekly Reader Leveled Readers).

—Staying Safe in the Car / la Seguridad en el Auto, 1 vol. 2007. (Safety First / la Seguridad Es lo Primero Ser.). (ENG & SPA.). 24p. (gr. k-2). pap. 9.15 *(978-0-8368-8065-6(X),* 2e9877ca-d766-4a98-814a-27c1650015d8); (Illus.). lib. bdg. 24.67 *(978-0-8368-8058-8(7),* fe3ec959-a3e3-445d-ac8d-30d68071c0d5) Stevens, Gareth Publishing LLLP. (Weekly Reader Leveled Readers).

Maynard, Chris. I Wonder Why Planes Have Wings: And Other Questions about Transportation. 2012. (I Wonder Why Ser.). (ENG., Illus.). 32p. (J). (gr. k-3). pap. 6.99 *(978-0-7534-6703-9(8),* 900076420, Kingfisher) Roaring Brook Pr.

McGill, Jordan. Medios de Transporte. 2012. (SPA.). (J). *(978-1-61913-213-9(3))* Weigl Pubs., Inc.

—Transportation. 2011. (J). *(978-1-61690-598-9(0))*; lib. bdg. 27.13 *(978-1-61690-952-9(8))* Weigl Pubs., Inc.

McIntosh, Kenneth. Buggies, Bicycles & Iron Horses: Transportation in the 1800s. 2009. (Daily Life in America in the 1800s Ser.). 64p. (YA). (gr. 7-18). pap. 9.95 *(978-1-4222-1849-5(X))*; lib. bdg. 22.95 *(978-1-4222-1776-4(0))* Mason Crest.

Meachen Rau, Dana. Bookworms We Go!, 6 vols., Set. Incl. Boats. 25.50 *(978-0-7614-4076-5(3),* ef184f46-2770-4614-b016-6537d3791756); Buses. 25.50 *(978-0-7614-4077-2(1),* eea2f55d-024c-43d2-9d2a-acea585e8529); Cars. 25.50 *(978-0-7614-4078-9(X),* 02ef01ab-3617-449d-91f8-83f01663c5fc); Planes. 25.50 *(978-0-7614-4080-2(1),* b2729cc4-016f-47db-9632-fb08630242cf); Trains. 25.50 *(978-0-7614-4081-9(X),* 78dda8aa-fca5-4aaa-994a-50ffb6c1398f); Trucks. 25.50 *(978-0-7614-4083-3(6),* e39860e8-c66f-4bd7-9353-028bb5c0dd04); 24p. (gr. 3-3). 2010. (Bookworms: We Go! Ser.). 2009. Set lib. bdg. 95.70 o.p. *(978-0-7614-4075-8(5),* Cavendish Square) Cavendish Square Publishing LLC.

—Safety on the Go, 1 vol. 2010. (Safe Kids Ser.). (ENG.). 32p. (gr. k-1). 25.50 *(978-0-7614-4085-7(2),* b72f31f1-6813-4147-9dda-93aaf7c04e6a) Cavendish Square Publishing LLC.

—Seguridad en el Viaje / Safety on the Go, 1 vol. 2010. (Niños Seguros / Safe Kids Ser.). (ENG & SPA.). 32p. (gr. k-2). lib. bdg. 25.50 *(978-0-7614-4776-4(8),* 815d4494-f4d6-42a8-9a10-ccf4d57c672f) Cavendish Square Publishing LLC.
—Travel in American History, 1 vol. 2006. (How People Lived in America Ser.). (ENG., Illus.). 24p. (gr. 2-4). lib. bdg. 24.67 *(978-0-8368-7210-1(X),* 5b46d85b-a64e-428a-a9df-918d06762c48, Weekly Reader Leveled Readers) Stevens, Gareth Publishing LLLP.
Mitten, Ellen. Moving People, Moving Stuff. 2011. (Little World Social Studies). (ENG., Illus.). 24p. (gr. k-2). pap. 9.95 *(978-1-61741-994-2(X),* 9781617419942) Rourke Educational Media.
Mitton, Tony & Parker, Ant. Cool Cars. (Amazing Machines Ser.). (ENG.). (J). 2018. 20p. bds. 6.99 *(978-0-7534-7395-5(X),* 900183777) 2014. (Illus.). 24p. (gr. -1-k). 6.99 *(978-0-7534-7207-1(4),* 900143118) Roaring Brook Pr. (Kingfisher).
—Cool Cars. 2014. (Amazing Machines Ser.). (J). lib. bdg. 14.75 *(978-0-606-36132-3(4))* Turtleback.
Moore, Andrew. Traveling in New York City, 1 vol. 2011. (My Community Ser.). (ENG., Illus.). 12p. (gr. 2-2). pap. 6.95 *(978-1-4488-5719-7(8),* 981569f2-163d-44c2-8621-fa202567b4a1, Rosen Classroom) Rosen Publishing Group, Inc., The.
Morris, Ann. On the Go. Heyman, Ken, photos by. 2015. (Illus.). 32p. pap. 7.00 *(978-1-61003-611-5(5))* Center for the Collaborative Classroom.
Morrison, Heather S. Inventors of Transportation Technology, 1 vol. 2015. (Designing Engineering Solutions Ser.). (ENG.). 144p. (YA). (gr. 8-8). lib. bdg. 44.50 *(978-1-5026-0662-4(3),* 21e62a19-f136-4428-aabb-dfeebecd5a30) Cavendish Square Publishing LLC.
Nardo, Don. Roman Roads & Aqueducts. 2014. (History's Great Structures). (ENG., Illus.). 80p. (J). lib. bdg. *(978-1-60152-634-2(2))* ReferencePoint Pr., Inc.
National Geographic. National Geographic Readers: Things That Go Collection. 2015. (Readers Ser.). 120p. (J). (gr. 1-3). pap. 7.99 *(978-1-4263-1972-3(X));* (ENG., Illus.). lib. bdg. 16.90 *(978-1-4263-1973-0(8))* Disney Publishing Worldwide. (National Geographic Kids).
Noll, Elizabeth. Coding in Transportation. 2018. (Coding Is Everywhere Ser.). (ENG., Illus.). 24p. (J). (gr. k-3). lib. bdg. 26.95 *(978-1-62617-835-9(6),* Blastoff! Readers) Bellwether Media.
Nunn, Daniel. True or False? Transportation. 2013. (True or False? Ser.). (ENG.). 24p. (J). (gr. -1-1). pap. 6.29 *(978-1-4109-5075-8(1),* 121304, Raintree) Capstone.
O'Brien, Cynthia. Dream Jobs in Transportation, Distribution & Logistics. 2018. (Cutting-Edge Careers in Technical Education Ser.). (ENG., Illus.). 32p. (J). (gr. 5-5). *(978-0-7787-4447-4(7));* pap. *(978-0-7787-4458-0(2))* Crabtree Publishing Co.
O'Connell, Eleanor. Transportation Around the World, 1 vol. 2016. (Adventures in Culture Ser.). (ENG.). 24p. (J). (gr. 1-2). pap. 9.15 *(978-1-4824-5593-9(5),* 7398e61b-9ff5-4853-8479-b6b2b4683eca) Stevens, Gareth Publishing LLLP.
Orr, Tamra B. The Department of Transportation, 1 vol. 2005. (This Is Your Government Ser.). (ENG., Illus.). 64p. (J). (gr. 4-6). lib. bdg. 37.13 *(978-1-4042-0211-5(0),* 6d7167b8-0f5b-43bc-af08-8e793ba5c503) Rosen Publishing Group, Inc., The.
Owens, Tom. Traveling on the Freedom Machines of the Transportation Age. 2003. (Reading Essentials in Social Studies). (Illus.). 40p. pap. 8.00 *(978-0-7891-5873-4(6))* Perfection Learning Corp.
Oxlade, Chris. Hands-on Science Projects: Transport. 2008. (ENG., Illus.). 64p. (J). (gr. 4-7). pap. 7.99 *(978-1-84476-533-1(4))* Anness Publishing GBR. Dist: National Bk. Network.
—Transportation Around the World: How Do We Get Where We're Going?, 8 bks. (Illus.). (gr. k-2). Set lib. bdg. 170.88 *(978-1-57572-310-5(7))*Set 1. (J). lib. bdg. 85.44 *(978-1-57572-304-4(2))*Set 2. lib. bdg. 85.44 *(978-1-57572-309-9(3))* Heinemann-Raintree.
Page, Robin. Move! Jenkins, Steve, illus. 2018. (ENG.). 32p. (J). (gr. -1-3). pap. 8.99 *(978-1-328-89573-8(4),* 1699519, Clarion Bks.) HarperCollins Pubs.
Pebble Books: Transportation: Who, Where, & What. 2005. (YA). (gr. k-3). 475.20 *(978-0-7368-4216-7(0),* Pebble) Capstone.
Perritano, John. Revolution in Transportation, 1 vol. 2010. (It Works! Ser.). (ENG.). 32p. (gr. 3-3). 31.21 *(978-0-7614-4379-7(7),* 5b6d16ae-f4d8-43c3-9810-47996785a375) Cavendish Square Publishing LLC.
—Stem in Current Events: Transportation, Vol. 10. 2016. (Stem in Current Events Ser.: Vol. 10). (ENG., Illus.). 64p. (J). (gr. 7-12). 23.95 *(978-1-4222-3596-6(3))* Mason Crest.
Peters, Elisa. Let's Ride the City Bus!, 1 vol. 2014. (Public Transportation Ser.). (ENG.). 24p. (J). (gr. 1-2). 25.27 *(978-1-4777-6482-4(8),* 79ef7210-e3fa-4d5d-9f1b-46aa9c46d69e, PowerKids Pr.) Rosen Publishing Group, Inc., The.
—Let's Ride the Streetcar! 2014. (Public Transportation Ser.). 24p. (J). (gr. k-2). pap. 49.50 *(978-1-4777-6513-5(1),* PowerKids Pr.) Rosen Publishing Group, Inc., The.
—Let's Take the Train! 2014. (Public Transportation Ser.). (Illus.). 24p. (J). (gr. k-2). pap. 49.50 *(978-1-4777-6514-2(X),* PowerKids Pr.) Rosen Publishing Group, Inc., The.
—¡Vamos a Tomar el Autobús! / Let's Ride the City Bus!, 1 vol. de la Vega, Eida, ed. 2014. (Transporte Público / Public Transportation Ser.). (SPA & ENG.). 24p. (J). (gr. 1-2). 25.27 *(978-1-4777-6777-1(0),* 5d39f642-7088-4721-b358-453a2a1d9cc5, PowerKids Pr.) Rosen Publishing Group, Inc., The.
—¡Vamos a Tomar el Tranvía! / Let's Ride the Streetcar!, 1 vol. de la Vega, Eida, ed. 2014. (Transporte Público / Public Transportation Ser.). (SPA & ENG.). 24p. (J). (gr. 1-2). 25.27 *(978-1-4777-6779-5(7),* 830ed458-f9ed-413d-9aff-34c977d56703, PowerKids Pr.) Rosen Publishing Group, Inc., The.
—¡Vamos a Tomar el Tren! / Let's Take the Train!, 1 vol. de la Vega, Eida, ed. 2014. (Transporte Público / Public Transportation Ser.). (SPA & ENG.). 24p. (J). (gr. 1-2). 25.27 *(978-1-4777-6781-8(9),* 3e6a6f3a-d9b9-438b-9687-58e1d9b15ea4, PowerKids Pr.) Rosen Publishing Group, Inc., The.
Peters, Jennifer. Inside the Department of Transportation, 1 vol. 2018. (Understanding the Executive Branch Ser.). (ENG.). 48p. (gr. 5-5). 29.60 *(978-0-7660-9899-2(0),* be00994c-fc8a-4528-8617-2537323b01ee) Enslow Publishing, LLC.
Phillips, Jessica, illus. Zoom Along. 2018. (Zoom Along Ser.). (ENG.). 16p. (J). (gr. -1 — 1). bds. 15.99 *(978-1-77138-797-2(1))* Kids Can Pr., Ltd. CAN. Dist: Hachette Bk. Group.
Picthall, Chez. My Top 100 on the Move. 2015. (ENG., Illus.). 16p. (J). pap. 7.99 *(978-1-907604-81-2(2))* Award Pubns. Ltd. GBR. Dist: Parkwest Pubns., Inc.
Priddy, Roger. Lift-The-Flap Tab: on the Go. 2014. (Lift-The-Flap Tab Bks.). (ENG., Illus.). 16p. (J). (gr. -1 — 1). bds. 8.99 *(978-0-312-51731-1(9),* 900132617) St. Martin's Pr.
Public Transportation. 2014. (Public Transportation Ser.). 24p. (J). (gr. k-2). pap. 49.50 *(978-1-4777-7238-6(3));* (ENG.). (gr. 1-2). 151.62 *(978-1-4777-6478-7(X),* 50d412f4-0dc5-4c6b-99a9-bec2f79ac988) Rosen Publishing Group, Inc., The. (PowerKids Pr.).
Rauf, Don & Fireside, Harvey. Separate but Equal: Plessy V. Ferguson, 1 vol. 2016. (U. S. Supreme Court Landmark Cases Ser.). (ENG., Illus.). 128p. (gr. 7-7). 38.93 *(978-0-7660-8434-6(5),* f5084a60-474b-4f82-85ef-b3531537a699) Enslow Publishing, LLC.
Raum, Elizabeth. The Scoop on Clothes, Homes, & Daily Life in Colonial America. rev. ed. 2017. (Life in the American Colonies Ser.). (ENG.). 32p. (J). (gr. 3-6). pap. 8.10 *(978-1-5157-9746-3(5),* 136863) Capstone.
Reich, Kass. Hamsters on the Go, 1 vol. 2016. (ENG., Illus.). 24p. (J). (gr. -1 — 1). bds. 9.95 *(978-1-4598-1016-7(3))* Orca Bk. Pubs. USA.
Reis, Ronald A. The New York City Subway System. 2009. (ENG., Illus.). 144p. (gr. 5-8). 35.00 *(978-1-60413-046-1(6),* P162091, Facts On File) Infobase Holdings, Inc.
Richard, John. Big Book of Transport. Leeks, David, illus. 2004. 48p. (J). 7.99 *(978-1-85854-550-9(1))* Brimax Books Ltd. GBR. Dist: Byeway Bks.
Richards, Jon. Transportation. 2005. (How Things Have Changed Ser.). (Illus.). 32p. (J). (gr. 3-7). lib. bdg. 27.10 *(978-1-59389-196-1(2))* Chrysalis Education.
RIGBY. Transportation: Then & Now: Third Grade Big Books. 2003. (Rigby on Our Way to English Ser.). (ENG.). 24p. (gr. 3-3). pap. 50.70 *(978-0-7578-4209-2(7))* Rigby Education.
Ripley Entertainment. Life in the Fast Lane. 2010. (Ripley's Believe It or Not Ser.). 36p. (YA). (gr. 3-18). lib. bdg. 19.95 *(978-1-4222-1538-8(5))* Mason Crest.
Roberts, Sheena. We All Go Traveling By. Bell, Siobhan, illus. 2003. (ENG.). 24p. (J). 17.99 *(978-1-84148-168-5(8))* Barefoot Bks., Inc.
Roza, Greg. Gross Things on Buses, Trains, & Planes, 1 vol. 2012. (That's Gross! Ser.). (ENG., Illus.). 24p. (J). (gr. 2-3). 25.27 *(978-1-4339-7127-3(5),* 9bd53492-e49c-4e66-987e-d67b72620c7c); pap. 9.15 *(978-1-4339-7128-0(3),* 5f2d2c0c-e794-4a37-a1b3-36280b294bac) Stevens, Gareth Publishing LLLP. (Gareth Stevens Learning Library).
Rozines Roy, Jennifer & Roy, Gregory. Shapes in Transportation, 1 vol. (Math All Around Ser.). (ENG., Illus.). 32p. (gr. 2-2). 2008. pap. 9.23 *(978-0-7614-3387-3(2),* 6f295ceb-6ea9-4f86-ac9a-86411c9ee12d) 2007. lib. bdg. 32.64 *(978-0-7614-2265-5(X),* 3ce6ec45-cd78-4dc2-bf97-36b786ae4847) Cavendish Square Publishing LLC.
Rustad, Martha E. H. Across the Country 18, 19, 20: A Transportation Counting Book. 2016. (1, 2, 3 Count with Me Ser.). (ENG., Illus.). 24p. (J). (gr. k-2). pap. 8.99 *(978-1-68152-110-7(5),* 15521); lib. bdg. 20.95 *(978-1-60753-919-3(5),* 15515) Amicus.
—Je Compte 20 Moyens de Transport. 2016. (1, 2, 3 Compte Avec Moi Ser.). (FRE., Illus.). 24p. (J). (gr. k-2). *(978-1-77092-348-5(9),* 17623) Amicus.
—Transportation in Many Cultures. rev. ed. 2016. (Life Around the World Ser.). (ENG.). 24p. (J). (gr. -1-2). pap. 7.29 *(978-1-5157-4241-8(5),* 133999, Capstone Pr.) Capstone.
Salazar, Julia. Spanish Words on the Road, 1 vol., Vol. 1. 2013. (Learn My Language! Spanish Ser.). (ENG., Illus.). 24p. (J). (gr. 1-2). 25.27 *(978-1-4824-0365-7(X),* 19b4adc3-af80-4fc0-bd13-e7f4a671247f) Stevens, Gareth Publishing LLLP.
Scholastic. First 100 Things That Go: Scholastic Early Learners (Touch & Lift) 2016. (Scholastic Early Learners Ser.). (ENG.). 12p. (J). (gr. -1 — 1). bds. 6.99 *(978-0-545-90343-1(2))* Scholastic, Inc.
Sebastiani, Laura, creator. Penny & Drew's Penciltips: Transportation. 2006. 80p. (J). 4.95 *(978-0-9766793-3-2(7))* ThoughtRockets, Inc.
Shackleton, Caroline. Down to Earth Intermediate Book with Online Access, 1 vol. 2014. (ENG., Illus.). 28p. pap., E-Book, E-Book 9.50 *(978-1-107-66117-2(X))* Cambridge Univ. Pr.
Sheen, Barbara. Cutting Edge Transportation Technology. 2016. (ENG.). 80p. (J). (gr. 5-12). lib. bdg. *(978-1-68282-046-9(7))* ReferencePoint Pr., Inc.
Smith, Alastair, ed. Travel & Transport Then & Now. 2004. (Then & Now Flip Flaps Ser.). (ENG., Illus.). 1p. (J). (gr. 2-18). pap. 7.95 *(978-0-7460-3102-5(5))* EDC Publishing.
Smith, Paula. Transportation in Different Places. 2015. (Learning about Our Global Community Ser.). (ENG., Illus.). 24p. (J). (gr. 2-2). *(978-0-7787-2014-0(4))* Crabtree Publishing Co.
Smith, Robin Wayne. If You Got It, a Truck Brought It. Smith, Robin Wayne, illus. 2012. (Illus.). 20p. pap. 6.00 *(978-0-615-63721-1(3))* Bright Tyke Creations LLC.
Star Bright Books. Carry Me, 1 vol. 2009. (Babies Everywhere Ser.). (ENG.). 32p. (J). (gr. -1). bds. 6.95 *(978-1-59572-180-8(0))* Star Bright Bks., Inc.
Starke, John. Speed Machines: Mission Xtreme 3D. 2004. (Mission Xtreme 3D Ser.). (Illus.). 18p. (J). pap. 5.95 *(978-1-902626-50-5(8))* Red Bird Publishing GBR. Dist: Weatherhill, Inc.
Sterling Publishing Co., Inc. Things That Go/Cosas Que Se Mueven. 2013. (Say & Play Ser.). (ENG & SPA., Illus.). 28p. (J). (— 1). bds. 6.95 *(978-1-4549-1042-8(9))* Sterling Publishing Co., Inc.
Summers, Alex. Taxi Cab. 2017. (Transportation & Me! Ser.). (ENG.). 24p. (gr. -1-1). pap. 9.95 *(978-1-68342-203-7(1),* 9781683422037) Rourke Educational Media.
Sundance/Newbridge LLC Staff. On the Move! 2004. (Reading PowerWorks Ser.). (gr. 1-3). 37.50 *(978-0-7608-8928-2(7));* pap. 6.10 *(978-0-7608-8929-9(5))* Sundance/Newbridge Educational Publishing.
Szymanski, Jennifer. National Geographic Readers: Here to There (L1/Coreader) 2019. (Readers Ser.). (Illus.). 48p. (J). (gr. -1-k). pap. 4.99 *(978-1-4263-3495-5(8));* (ENG., lib. bdg. 14.90 *(978-1-4263-3496-2(6))* Disney Publishing Worldwide. (National Geographic Kids).
Teckentrup, Britta, illus. Fast & Slow Spanish. 2013. 14p. (J). (gr. -1-k). bds. 6.99 *(978-1-78285-035-9(X))* Barefoot Bks., Inc.
Ticktock Media, Ltd. Staff. Guess What? Things That Go. 2008. (Mini Flap Ser.). (ENG.). 10p. (J). (gr. k — 1). bds. 5.95 *(978-1-84696-819-8(4),* TickTock Books) Octopus Publishing Group GBR. Dist: Independent Pubs. Group.
Top That! Kids, creator. Things That Go. 2008. (Magnetic Play & Learn Ser.). (ENG., Illus.). 12p. (J). (gr. -1-k). *(978-1-84510-726-0(8))* Top That! Publishing PLC.
Transportation. 2010. (Mighty Machines Ser.). 24p. 191.92 *(978-1-4296-5197-4(0),* Capstone Pr.) Capstone.
Transportation. (Butterfly Bks.). (Illus.). 15p. (J). 11.95 *(978-0-86685-613-3(7))* International Bk. Ctr., Inc.
Transportation & Communication. (J). (gr. k-1). *(978-84-342-2418-6(6),* PR30572) Parramon Ediciones S.A. ESP. Dist: Lectorum Pubns., Inc.
Transportation Technology Systems. 2nd rev. ed. 2004. 55p. pap. *(978-0-86657-514-0(6))* Lab-Volt Systems, Inc.
Varonka, Steve. Hard Coal Times Vol. 3: Early Coal Transportation. 2004. (Illus.). 24p. (YA). 4.72 *(978-0-9709630-5-5(X))* Coal Hole Productions.
Vehiculos de Alta Tecnologia Series, 12 vols., Set. 2003. (Vehiculos de Alta Tecnologia (High-Tech Vehicles) Ser.). (SPA., Illus.). (J). (gr. 2-2). lib. bdg. 157.62 *(978-0-8239-6919-7(3),* a517a17f-324d-46e8-83e3-748892fe7524, Editorial Buenas Letras) Rosen Publishing Group, Inc., The.
Verstraete, Larry. Innovations in Transportation. 2016. (Problem Solved! Your Turn to Think Big Ser.). (ENG., Illus.). 32p. (J). (gr. 3-6). *(978-0-7787-2680-7(0))* Crabtree Publishing Co.
Vous, Nous. Show + Tell Transport Activities: With 3 Posters, 40 Stickers & Colouring + Activity Book. 2017. (ENG., Illus.). 10p. (J). pap. 9.99 *(978-1-84780-731-1(3),* Wide Eyed Editions) Quarto Publishing Group UK GBR. Dist: Littlehampton Bk Services, Ltd.
Wainewright, Max. Scratch Code Transportation. 2019. (Scratch Code Challenge Ser.). (ENG.). 32p. (J). (gr. 5-5). pap. *(978-0-7787-6570-7(9),* 9a5cc93c-4ebc-414b-b50d-ba9b4abf6a3a); lib. bdg. *(978-0-7787-6542-4(3),* 0e770f69-7e5b-4d5f-84fe-13470b580bb2) Crabtree Publishing Co.
Walker, Niki. Transportation Disaster Alert! 2005. (Disaster Alert! Ser.). (ENG., Illus.). 32p. (J). (gr. 4-7). lib. bdg. *(978-0-7787-1584-9(1))* Crabtree Publishing Co.
Walker, Robert. Transportation Inventions, 1 vol. 2013. (ENG., Illus.). 48p. (J). pap. *(978-0-7787-0240-5(5))* Crabtree Publishing Co.
—Transportation Inventions: Moving Our World Forward. 2013. (ENG., Illus.). 48p. (J). *(978-0-7787-0223-8(5))* Crabtree Publishing Co.
Waxman, Laura Hamilton. Ambulances. 2004. (Pull Ahead Bks.). (Illus.). 32p. (J). (gr. k-2). lib. bdg. 22.60 *(978-0-8225-0769-7(2))* Lerner Publishing Group.
Waxman, Laura Hamilton & Levine, Michelle. Ambulances. 2004. (Pull Ahead Bks.). (Illus.). 32p. (J). (gr. k-2). pap. 6.95 *(978-0-8225-9923-4(6))* Lerner Publishing Group.
Way, Steve & Bailey, Gerry. Land Transportation, 1 vol. 2008. (Simply Science Ser.). (ENG., Illus.). 32p. (YA). (gr. 3-5). lib. bdg. 28.67 *(978-0-8368-9228-4(3),* b49a5b54-7230-4d20-9dfd-ba36cf8eabb9) Stevens, Gareth Publishing LLLP.
Weakland, Mark. On My Way to School. Zhai, Rea, illus. 2019. (School Rules Ser.). (ENG.). 24p. (J). (gr. k-2). pap. 8.95 *(978-1-5158-4063-3(8),* 140057, Picture Window Bks.) Capstone.
Welvaert, Scott R. Follow That Crop: From the Farmer's Field to Our Grocery Store. 2003. (From Here to There Ser.). (J). *(978-1-58417-194-2(4));* pap. *(978-1-58417-195-9(2))* Lake Street Pubs.
Wheels & Rockets. (J). (gr. 4). 42.95 *(978-0-673-72657-5(6),* Scott Foresman) Addison Wesley Schl.
Will, Sandra. Transportation Inventions: From Subways to Submarines. 2006. (Which Came First? Ser.). (Illus.). 32p. (YA). (gr. 3-6). lib. bdg. 28.50 *(978-1-59716-133-6(0))* Bearport Publishing Co., Inc.
Wood, John. Travel Technology: Maglev Trains, Hovercrafts, & More, 1 vol. 2018. (STEM in Our World Ser.). (ENG.). 32p. (gr. 4-5). lib. bdg. 28.27 *(978-1-5382-2654-4(5),* 78bfafe4-2978-4d79-a5d5-cf163481174b) Stevens, Gareth Publishing LLLP.
World Book, Inc. Staff, contrib. by. Flying Cars & Other Transportation Tech. 2019. (Illus.). 48p. (J). *(978-0-7166-2430-1(3))* World Bk., Inc.
—On the Move. 2007. *(978-0-7166-7728-4(8))* World Bk., Inc.
A World of Wheels, 8 vols., Set. (Illus.). 104,132p. (gr. 7-18). lib. bdg. *(978-1-59084-483-0(1))* Mason Crest.
Yaun, Katherine. Getting a Job in the Transportation Industry, 1 vol. 2016. (Job Basics: Getting the Job You Need Ser.). (ENG.). 80p. (J). (gr. 8-8). 38.41 *(978-1-4777-8568-3(X),* a2927edc-a51c-421a-a0bd-5e76a1b4c3a5) Rosen Publishing Group, Inc., The.
Yomtov, Nel. Troop Transport. 2016. (Military Missions Ser.). (ENG., Illus.). 24p. (J). (gr. 3-7). 26.95 *(978-1-62617-440-5(7),* Epic Bks.) Bellwether Media.
Yoyo Books, creator. Vroom. 2011. (Baby's First Library). (ENG., Illus.). 38p. (gr. -1-k). bds. 6.99 *(978-90-8622-910-9(7))* YoYo Bks.
Zobel, Derek. Blastoff! Readers - Mighty Machines, 4 vols., Set. Incl. Bucket Trucks. 20.00 *(978-0-531-21707-8(8));* Diggers. 20.00 *(978-0-531-21708-5(6));* Pickup Trucks. 20.00 *(978-0-531-21709-2(4));* Wheel Loaders. 20.00 *(978-0-531-21710-8(8));* (Illus.). 24p. (J). (gr. k-3). 2009. 2009. Set lib. bdg. 80.00 *(978-0-531-26127-9(1),* Children's Pr.) Scholastic Library Publishing.

TRANSPORTATION, AUTOMOTIVE

see also Automobiles; Buses; Trucks

Bozzo, Linda. Getting Around in the Past, Present, & Future, 1 vol. 2010. (Imagining the Future Ser.). (ENG., Illus.). 24p. (gr. k-2). lib. bdg. 25.27 *(978-0-7660-3437-2(2),* 02ebbfba-dcd2-4a1d-8eb4-0be67092261a, Enslow Elementary) Enslow Publishing, LLC.
Brown Bear Books. Land & Water Transportation. 2012. (Invention & Technology Ser.). (ENG.). 64p. (J). (gr. 8-11). lib. bdg. 39.95 *(978-1-936333-42-4(2),* 16522) Brown Bear Bks.
Doeden, Matt. Lowriders. 2009. pap. 8.95 *(978-0-8225-6664-9(8))* Lerner Publishing Group.
Edwards, Pamela Duncan. The Bus Ride That Changed History. Shanahan, Danny, illus. 2009. (ENG.). 32p. (J). (gr. -1-3). pap. 7.99 *(978-0-547-07674-4(6),* 1042031, Clarion Bks.) HarperCollins Pubs.
Flounders, Anne. Cars. 2013. (Machines in Motion Ser.). 48p. (J). (gr. 3-5). pap. 84.30 *(978-1-4339-9598-9(0));* (ENG., Illus.). lib. bdg. 34.61 *(978-1-4339-9596-5(4),* 02034d19-781a-4161-b168-2312776d351a) Stevens, Gareth Publishing LLLP.
Gilpin, Daniel. Record Breakers, 1 vol. Pang, Alex, illus. 2011. (Machines Close-Up Ser.). (ENG.). 32p. (gr. 4-4). 31.21 *(978-1-60870-113-1(1),* 4582474e-2edb-4155-a62a-6f9144194f4c) Cavendish Square Publishing LLC.
—Rescue Vehicles, 1 vol. Pang, Alex, illus. 2011. (Machines Close-Up Ser.). (ENG.). 32p. (gr. 4-4). 31.21 *(978-1-60870-111-7(5),* 2b5c3164-2cb9-466b-80f6-484ba3f35644) Cavendish Square Publishing LLC.
Gustaitis, Joseph Alan. Arctic Trucker, 1 vol. 2011. (Dirty & Dangerous Jobs Ser.). (ENG., Illus.). 32p. (gr. 3-3). 31.21 *(978-1-60870-169-8(7),* 7ef75d26-21d1-484b-a635-d1be48f1168c) Cavendish Square Publishing LLC.
Hemstock, Whitney M. The ABC's of Traffic Safety. 2010. 34p. pap. 16.95 *(978-0-557-28733-8(2))* Lulu Pr., Inc.
Idzikowski, Lisa & Schauer, Pete, compiled by. Self-Driving Cars, 1 vol. 2018. (Introducing Issues with Opposing Viewpoints Ser.). (ENG.). 120p. (J). (gr. 7-10). 43.63 *(978-1-5345-0363-2(3),* 7fb6863d-2f06-402e-ac8b-d9103836bd24) Greenhaven Publishing LLC.
Kelly, Tracey. Space Exploration: From Rockets to Space Stations. 2019. (History of Inventions Ser.). (ENG.). 24p. (J). (gr. 2-4). lib. bdg. *(978-1-78121-453-4(0),* 16732) Brown Bear Bks.
Mean Machines Series, 4 bks., Set 2. 2004. (Illus.). (J). pap. 32.20 *(978-1-4109-1200-8(0))* Harcourt Schl. Pubs.
Moore, Elizabeth. Watch Out!, 1 vol. 2011. (Wonder Readers Emergent Level Ser.). (ENG.). 8p. (J). (gr. -1-1). pap. 6.25 *(978-1-4296-7852-0(6),* 118165, Capstone Pr.) Capstone.
National Geographic Learning. Windows on Literacy Step up (Social Studies: Out & about): Where Is It Going. 2007. (ENG., Illus.). 12p. (J). pap. 11.95 *(978-0-7922-8476-5(3))* National Geographic School Publishing, Inc.
Oachs, Emily Rose. The Automobile. 2019. (Inventions That Changed the World Ser.). (ENG., Illus.). 32p. (J). (gr. 3-8). pap. 8.99 *(978-1-61891-509-2(6),* 12159, Blastoff! Discovery) Bellwether Media.
Rosa-Mendoza, Gladys. Cars, Trucks, & Planes, 1 vol. Tugeau, Jeremy, illus. 2010. (My World Ser.). (ENG.). 24p. (J). (gr. k-1). lib. bdg. 27.27 *(978-1-60754-949-9(2),* f1d5f54f-3fad-4227-8b51-2df409f392e9, Windmill Bks.) Rosen Publishing Group, Inc., The.
Schuh, Mari. Bus Drivers. 2018. (Community Helpers Ser.). (ENG., Illus.). 24p. (J). (gr. k-3). lib. bdg. 26.95 *(978-1-62617-742-0(2),* Blastoff! Readers) Bellwether Media.
Stephens, Ronald, ed. Road Safety. 2014. (Safety First Ser.: 11). 48p. (J). (gr. 5-18). 20.95 *(978-1-4222-3052-7(X))* Mason Crest.
Winget, Mary. Taxis. 2007. (Pull Ahead Books-Mighty Movers Ser.). (ENG., Illus.). 32p. (gr. k-3). lib. bdg. 22.60 *(978-0-8225-6419-5(X),* Lerner Pubns.) Lerner Publishing Group.
Woods, Bob. Wild Racers, 1 vol. 2010. (Racing Mania Ser.). (ENG.). 48p. (gr. 4-4). lib. bdg. 34.07 *(978-0-7614-4389-6(4),* 84e59eb8-835a-4c9c-b9c8-4a92797537e2) Cavendish Square Publishing LLC.

TRANSPORTATION, AUTOMOTIVE—FICTION

Alexander, Jenny. The Rugged Off-Roader. 2010. (ENG., Illus.). 64p. (J). *(978-0-340-98150-4(4),* Hodder Children's Books) Hachette Children's Group GBR. Dist: Hachette Bk. Group.
Gutman, Dan. The Genius Files #2: Never Say Genius. 2012. (Genius Files Ser.: 2). (ENG., Illus.). 288p. (J). (gr. 3-7). 16.99 *(978-0-06-182767-9(3),* HarperCollins) HarperCollins Pubs.
—The Genius Files: Mission Unstoppable. 2011. (Genius Files Ser.: 1). (ENG.). 304p. (J). (gr. 3-7). pap. 7.99 *(978-0-06-182766-2(5));* (Illus.). 16.99 *(978-0-06-182764-8(9))* HarperCollins Pubs. (HarperCollins).
—Mission Unstoppable. 2011. (Genius Files Ser.: 1). (J). lib. bdg. 17.20 *(978-0-606-23559-4(0))* Turtleback.
Horacek, Petr. Beep Beep. Horacek, Petr, illus. 2008. (ENG., Illus.). 16p. (J). (gr. k-k). bds. 6.99 *(978-0-7636-3482-7(4))* Candlewick Pr.

TRANSPORTATION—FICTION

Angleberger, Tom. McToad Mows Tiny Island. Hendrix, John, illus. 2015. (ENG.). 40p. (J). (gr. -1-3). 16.95 *(978-1-4197-1650-8(6),* 1088401, Abrams Bks. for Young Readers) Abrams, Inc.
Arnold, Tedd. Ride, Fly Guy, Ride! 2012. (Fly Guy Ser.: 11). lib. bdg. 17.20 *(978-0-606-23904-2(9))* Turtleback.
—Ride, Fly Guy, Ride! (Fly Guy #11) Arnold, Tedd, illus. 2012. (Fly Guy Ser.: 11). (ENG., Illus.). 32p. (J). (gr. -1-3). 6.99 *(978-0-545-22276-1(1),* Cartwheel Bks.) Scholastic, Inc.
Awdry, W. Blue Mountain Mystery (Thomas & Friends) Golden Books, illus. 2012. (Little Golden Book Ser.). (ENG.). 24p. (J). (gr. k-k). 5.99 *(978-0-307-97590-4(8),* Golden Bks.) Random Hse. Children's Bks.

TUV

AZ Books Staff. Fast Vehicles Moving & Talking. Harko, Lubov, ed. 2012. (Funny Trails Ser.). (ENG.). 10p. (J). (gr. -1-k). bds. 9.95 *(978-1-61889-177-8(4))* AZ Bks. LLC.

Barton, Byron. My Bus Board Book. Barton, Byron, illus. 2015. (ENG., Illus.). 38p. (J). (gr. -1 — 1). bds. 8.99 *(978-0-06-228738-0(9),* Greenwillow Bks.) HarperCollins Pubs.

Bianchini, Bob. Charlie Rides: Planes, Trains, Bikes, & More! 2017. (ENG., Illus.). 20p. (J). (gr. -1-k). bds. 8.95 *(978-1-4197-2292-9(1),* 1156010, Abrams Appleseed) Abrams, Inc.

Biggs, Brian. Everything Goes: 123 Beep Beep Beep!: a Counting Book. Biggs, Brian, illus. 2012. (ENG., Illus.). 24p. (J). (gr. -1 — 1). bds. 8.99 *(978-0-06-195812-0(3),* Balzer & Bray) HarperCollins Pubs.

—Everything Goes: in the Air. Biggs, Brian, illus. 2012. (ENG., Illus.). 56p. (J). (gr. -1-3). 16.99 *(978-0-06-195810-6(7),* Balzer & Bray) HarperCollins Pubs.

—Everything Goes: on Land. Biggs, Brian, illus. 2011. (ENG., Illus.). 56p. (J). (gr. -1-3). 14.99 *(978-0-06-195809-0(3),* Balzer & Bray) HarperCollins Pubs.

—Everything Goes: Stop! Go!: a Book of Opposites. Biggs, Brian, illus. 2012. (ENG., Illus.). 24p. (J). (gr. -1 — 1). bds. 7.99 *(978-0-06-195813-7(1),* Balzer & Bray) HarperCollins Pubs.

Blackstone, Stella. Bear on a Bike / Oso en Bicicleta. Harter, Debbie, illus. 2014. (Bear Ser.). (ENG.). 32p. (J). (gr. -1-1). pap. 8.99 *(978-1-78285-079-3(1))* Barefoot Bks., Inc.

Book Company Staff. Beep Beep. 2003. (Novelty Bks.). (Illus.). (J). 15.95 *(978-1-74047-232-6(2))* Book Co. Publishing Pty, Ltd., The AUS. Dist: Penton Overseas, Inc.

Boyd, Bentley. Moving & Grooving. 2009. (Chester Comix Ser.). (Illus.). 24p. pap. 6.95 *(978-1-933122-36-6(6))* Chester Comix, LLC.

Brooks, Susie. Choose Your Own Journey. Cottingham, Tracy, illus. 2017. (J). 11.99 *(978-1-61067-537-6(1))* Kane Miller.

Burleigh, Robert. Zoom! Zoom! Sounds of Things That Go in the City. Carpenter, Tad, illus. 2014. (ENG.). 32p. (J). (gr. -1-3). 18.99 *(978-1-4424-8315-6(6),* Simon & Schuster Bks. For Young Readers) Simon & Schuster Bks. For Young Readers.

Calmenson, Stephanie. Late for School! 2008. (ENG., Illus.). 32p. (J). (gr. -1-2). lib. bdg. 16.95 *(978-1-57505-935-8(5))* Lerner Publishing Group.

Chapman, Allen. Bart Stirling's Road to Success; or, the Young Express Agent. 2007. 112p. per. *(978-1-4068-4512-9(4))* Echo Library.

Collicutt, Paul. Murder on the Robot City Express. Collicutt, Paul, illus. 2010. (Robot City Ser.: 4). (ENG., Illus.). 48p. (J). (gr. 3-7). pap. 8.99 *(978-0-7636-5015-5(3),* Templar) Candlewick Pr.

Cordsen, Carol Foskett. The Milkman. Jones, Douglas B., illus. 2007. (gr. -1-3). 17.00 *(978-0-7569-8148-8(4))* Perfection Learning Corp.

Crampton, Gertrude. Tootle: Classic Edition. Gergely, Tibor, illus. Date not set. 21p. (J). (gr. -1-1). *(978-1-929566-53-2(0))* Cronies.

Crisp, Dan. Trabajo/ Work. 2007. 14p. 10.95 *(978-84-263-6452-4(7))* Vives, Luis Editorial (Edelvives) ESP. Dist: Baker & Taylor Bks.

Dale, Jay. I Go up & Down. Dybing, Michelle, illus. 2012. (Wonder Words Ser.). (ENG.). 16p. (J). (gr. k-2). pap. 36.94 *(978-1-4296-8895-6(5),* 18343, Capstone Pr.) Capstone.

Dale, Jay & Scott, Kay. I Go up & Down. Dybing, Michelle, illus. 2012. (Wonder Words Ser.). (ENG.). 16p. (J). (gr. k-2). pap. 6.99 *(978-1-4296-8894-9(7),* 119950, Capstone Pr.) Capstone.

Davies, Benji, illus. Bizzy Bear: off We Go! 2012. (Bizzy Bear Ser.). (ENG.). 8p. (J). (gr. k — 1). bds. 7.99 *(978-0-7636-5900-4(2))* Candlewick Pr.

DeLand, M. Maitland. Baby Santa's Worldwide Christmas Adventure. Wilson, Phil, illus. 2010. 32p. (J). 14.95 *(978-1-60832-062-2(6))* Greenleaf Book Group.

Derubertis, Barbara. Walter Warthog's Wonderful Wagon. Alley, R. W., illus. 2011. (Animal Antics A to Z Set III Ser.). pap. 45.32 *(978-0-7613-8432-8(4))* Astra Publishing Hse.

Dopirak, Kate. Twinkle, Twinkle, Little Car. Peterson, Mary, illus. 2018. (ENG.). 40p. (J). (gr. -1-3). 18.99 *(978-1-4814-8803-7(1),* Beach Lane Bks.) Beach Lane Bks.

Durango, Julia. Go-Go Gorillas. Taylor, Eleanor, illus. 2010. (ENG.). 32p. (J). (gr. -1-3). 19.99 *(978-1-4169-3779-1(X),* Simon & Schuster Bks. For Young Readers) Simon & Schuster Bks. For Young Readers.

Eastman, P. D. Ve, Perro. Ve! (Go, Dog. Go! Spanish Edition) Perdomo, Adolfo Perez, tr. from ENG. 2003. (Bright & Early Board Books(TM) Ser.).Tr. of Go, Dog. Go! (SPA., Illus.). 24p. (J). (— 1). bds. 4.99 *(978-0-375-82361-9(1),* Random House Para Ninos) Random Hse. Children's Bks.

Franco, Betsy. Going to Grandma's Farm. 2004. (Rookie Reader Español Ser.). (ENG., Illus.). 24p. (J). (gr. k-2). pap. 4.95 *(978-0-516-27787-5(1),* Children's Pr.) Scholastic Library Publishing.

Friday, Stormy. Signal's Airport Adventure. Saroff, Phyllis, illus. 2006. (J). 14.95 *(978-0-9717047-5-6(9))* Bay Media, Inc.

Gergely, Tibor, illus. Tootle. Golden Books Staff, photos by. deluxe ed. Date not set. (J). (gr. -1-2). reprint ed. *(978-1-929566-58-7(1))* Cronies.

Hajdusiewicz, Babs Bell. The Bridge Is Up! Hefferan, Rob, illus. 2006. (J). pap. 7.99 *(978-0-15-365089-5(3))* Houghton Mifflin Harcourt School Pubs.

Harper, Benjamin. All Around Trucktown. Shannon, David et al, illus. 2008. (Jon Scieszka's Trucktown Ser.). (ENG.). 32p. (J). (gr. -1-1). 3.99 *(978-1-4169-4194-1(0),* Simon Scribbles) Simon Scribbles.

Holden, Pam. See Me Ride, 1 vol. East, Jacqueline, illus. 2009. (Red Rocket Readers Ser.). (ENG.). 16p. (J). (gr. -1-1). pap. *(978-1-877363-30-6(8),* Red Rocket Readers) Flying Start Bks.

Hopgood, Sally. A Trip to Busy Town: A Pull-The-Tab Book. Hinton, Stephanie, illus. 2014. (J). *(978-1-4351-5690-6(0))* Barnes & Noble, Inc.

Lamb, Jenny. A Long Car Ride. Piwowarski, Marcin, illus. 2017. (Family Time Ser.). (ENG.). 24p. (gr. -1-2). pap. 9.95 *(978-1-68342-780-3(7),* 9781683427803) Rourke Educational Media.

Let's Go Downtown: Individual Title Six-Packs. (gr. -1-2). 27.00 *(978-0-7635-9458-9(X))* Rigby Education.

Liwska, Renata. Red Wagon. Liwska, Renata, illus. 2013. (Illus.). 34p. (J). (gr. -1 — 1). bds. 8.99 *(978-0-399-16239-8(9),* Philomel Bks.) Penguin Young Readers Group.

Lord, Janet. Here Comes Grandma! Paschkis, Julie, illus. rev. ed. 2005. (ENG.). 32p. (J). (gr. -1-k). 18.99 *(978-0-8050-7666-0(2),* 900030219, Holt, Henry & Co. Bks. For Young Readers) Holt, Henry & Co.

Maccarone, Grace. Bunny Race! Long, Ethan, illus. 2009. (J). *(978-0-545-11290-1(7))* Scholastic, Inc.

McOmber, Rachel B., ed. McOmber Phonics Storybooks: The Tan Cab. rev. ed. (Illus.). (J). *(978-0-944991-04-6(1))* Swift Learning Resources.

Meachen Rau, Dana. Riding, 1 vol. 2007. (On the Move Ser.). (ENG., Illus.). 24p. (gr. k-1). lib. bdg. 25.50 *(978-0-7614-2317-1(6),* fe9446d0-0ac9-46da-8382-235cc6d7db07) Cavendish Square Publishing LLC.

Meshon, Aaron. Delivery. Meshon, Aaron, illus. 2017. (ENG., Illus.). 48p. (J). (gr. -1-3). 17.99 *(978-1-4814-4175-9(2))* Simon & Schuster Children's Publishing.

Mok, Carmen. Ride the Big Machines Across Canada. 2015. (My Big Machines Ser.). (ENG.). 14p. (J). bds. 10.50 *(978-1-4434-3810-0(3),* HarperCollins) HarperCollins Pubs.

My Big Book of Beginner Books about Me. 2011. (Beginner Books(R) Ser.). (ENG., Illus.). 208p. (J). (gr. -1-2). 16.99 *(978-0-307-93183-2(8),* Random Hse. Bks. for Young Readers) Random Hse. Children's Bks.

Pallotta, Jerry. How Will I Get to School This Year? Biedrzycki, David, illus. 2011. (J). *(978-0-545-26659-8(9))* Scholastic, Inc.

Parker, Emma. How Shall I Get to School Today? 2010. (Illus.). pap. *(978-1-877547-84-3(0))* First Edition Ltd.

PAW Patrol on the Roll! 2016. (Illus.). (J). *(978-1-5182-2638-0(8))* Random House Children's Books.

Perlman, Rhea. Water Balloon Doom. Santat, Dan, illus. 2006. (Otto Undercover Ser.: No. 3). 124p. (J). (gr. 2-6). 14.99 *(978-0-06-075500-3(8),* Tegen, Katherine Bks) HarperCollins Pubs.

Reynolds, Aaron. Back of the Bus. Cooper, Floyd, illus. 2010. 32p. (J). (gr. 1-3). 16.99 *(978-0-399-25091-0(3),* Philomel Bks.) Penguin Young Readers Group.

Rosa-Mendoza, Gladys. Cars, Trucks & Planes/Carros, Camiones y Aviones. Tugeau, Jeremy, illus. 2004. (English-Spanish Foundations Ser.). (SPA & ENG.). 20p. (J). (gr. -1). bds. 6.95 *(978-1-931398-14-5(3))* Me+Mi Publishing.

Santoro, Christopher. Open the Garage Door. 2018. (Lift-The-Flap Ser.). (Illus.). 22p. (J). (— 1). bds. 6.99 *(978-1-5247-6778-5(6),* Random Hse. Bks. for Young Readers) Random Hse. Children's Bks.

Scarry, Richard. Cosas Que Se Mueven.Tr. of Things That Move. (SPA., Illus.). (J). pap. 6.95 *(978-950-04-1042-7(7))* Emecé Editores S.A. ARG. Dist: Planeta Publishing Corp.

—Cosas Que Se Mueven. 2003. (Richard Scarry Ser.).Tr. of Things That Move. (SPA.). (J). pap. *(978-970-690-847-6(1))* Planeta Mexicana Editorial S. A. de C. V.

Schertle, Alice. Little Blue Truck Leads the Way. McElmurry, Jill, illus. 2009. (ENG.). 40p. (J). (gr. -1-3). 18.99 *(978-0-15-206389-4(7),* 1199129, Clarion Bks.) HarperCollins Pubs.

Sharpe, Jeannie w. Once There Was an Orange Truck. 2005. 37p. (J). 15.95 *(978-0-9763117-0-6(4))* Sharpe, Jeannie W.

Tibo, Gilles & Vaillancourt, Francois. El Senor Patapum. (Barril Sin Fondo Ser.). (SPA.). (J). (gr. 3-5). pap. *(978-968-6465-58-7(8))* Casa de Estudios de Literatura y Talleres Artisticos Amaquemecan A.C. MEX. Dist: Lectorum Pubns., Inc.

Ticktock Media, Ltd. Staff. Under the Ocean with the Little Yellow Submarine. 2009. (Touch & Feel Fun Ser.). (ENG.). 10p. (J). (gr. k — 1). bds. 5.95 *(978-1-84696-811-2(9),* TickTock Books) Octopus Publishing Group GBR. Dist: Independent Pubs. Group.

Transportation Board Books 800618, 4. 2005. (J). bds. *(978-1-59794-035-1(6))* Environments, Inc.

Upton, Elizabeth. Maxi the Little Taxi. Cole, Henry, illus. 2016. (ENG.). 32p. (J). (gr. -1-k). 17.99 *(978-0-545-79860-0(4),* Scholastic Pr.) Scholastic, Inc.

Yang, James, illus. Bus! Stop! 2018. (ENG.). 32p. (J). (-k). 17.99 *(978-0-425-28877-1(3),* Viking Books for Young Readers) Penguin Young Readers Group.

TRANSPORTATION, HIGHWAY

see Transportation, Automotive

TRANSPORTATION—HISTORY

Brown Bear Books. Land & Water Transportation. 2012. (Invention & Technology Ser.). (ENG.). 64p. (J). (gr. 8-11). lib. bdg. 39.95 *(978-1-936333-42-4(2),* 16522) Brown Bear Bks.

Edison, Erin. Rosa Parks, 1 vol. 2013. (Great Women in History Ser.). (ENG.). 24p. (J). (gr. -1-2). pap. 6.29 *(978-1-62065-863-5(1),* 121794); (gr. k-1). pap. 38.74 *(978-1-62065-864-2(X),* 19429) Capstone. (Pebble).

El transporte ayer y hoy/ Transportation Through the Ages, 12 vols., Set. 2003. (Transporte Ayer y Hoy (Transportation Through the Ages) Ser.). (SPA., Illus.). (J). (gr. 1-2). lib. bdg. 157.62 *(978-0-8239-6916-6(9),* 8db7160d-468d-4a6a-8f16-1da60a70e75e, Editorial Buenas Letras) Rosen Publishing Group, Inc., The.

From There to Here: a Transportation Time Line: Individual Title Six-Packs. (Discovery World Ser.). 24p. (gr. 1-2). 33.00 *(978-0-7635-8484-9(3))* Rigby Education.

Harris, Joseph. Transportation: The Impact of Science & Technology, 1 vol. 2009. (Pros & Cons Ser.). (ENG.). 64p. (YA). (gr. 5-8). lib. bdg. 37.67 *(978-1-4339-1990-9(7),* 0da50825-d40e-4526-a54d-f1b73cd44e16) Stevens, Gareth Publishing LLLP.

Harris, Tim. Transportation Technology, 1 vol. 2015. (Science Q & A Ser.). (ENG., Illus.). 32p. (gr. 3-3). pap. 11.58 *(978-1-5026-0627-3(5),* 41d070c5-418a-494f-8764-16e8f71447d7) Cavendish Square Publishing LLC.

Isaacs, Sally Senzell. Stagecoaches & Railroads. 2012. (All about America Ser.). (ENG., Illus.). 32p. (J). (gr. 4-7). 26.19 *(978-0-7534-6696-4(1),* 9780753466964) Kingfisher Publications, plc GBR. Dist: Children's Plus, Inc.

Jackson, Tom. Machines in Motion: The Amazing History of Transportation. Mould, Chris, illus. 2020. 64p. (J). *(978-1-5476-0338-1(0))* Bloomsbury Pr.

—Machines in Motion: The Amazing History of Transportation. 2020. (ENG., Illus.). 64p. (J). 19.99 *(978-1-5476-0337-4(2),* 900211327, Bloomsbury Children's Bks.) Bloomsbury Publishing USA.

Kelly, Tracey. Air Transportation: From Balloons to Superjets. 2019. (History of Inventions Ser.). (ENG.). 24p. (J). (gr. 2-4). lib. bdg. *(978-1-78121-452-7(2),* 16728) Brown Bear Bks.

—Space Exploration: From Rockets to Space Stations. 2019. (History of Inventions Ser.). (ENG.). 24p. (J). (gr. 2-4). lib. bdg. *(978-1-78121-453-4(0),* 16732) Brown Bear Bks.

Meachen Rau, Dana. Los Viajes en la Historia de América (Travel in American History), 1 vol. 2006. (Cómo Era la Vida en América (How People Lived in America) Ser.). (SPA., Illus.). 24p. (gr. 2-4). pap. 9.15 *(978-0-8368-7441-9(2),* 3bfd5f74-eb8b-4d2b-933d-68201d92822d); lib. bdg. 24.67 *(978-0-8368-7434-1(X),* aed14468-7e70-470f-9f29-a37b12449b48) Stevens, Gareth Publishing LLLP. (Weekly Reader Leveled Readers).

—Travel in American History, 1 vol. 2006. (How People Lived in America Ser.). (ENG., Illus.). 24p. (gr. 2-4). pap. 9.15 *(978-0-8368-7217-0(7),* d105dd4f-b179-4164-8e04-27a969131b5e, Weekly Reader Leveled Readers) Stevens, Gareth Publishing LLLP.

Murdico, Suzanne J. Railroads & Steamships: Important Developments in American Transportation. (America's Industrial Society in the 19th Century Ser.). 32p. (gr. 4-4). 2009. 47.90 *(978-1-61511-340-8(1))* 2003. (ENG., Illus.). (J). pap. 10.00 *(978-0-8239-4278-7(3),* 44a84b6b-b256-4ad5-a2e0-5367fe9c4a95) 2003. (ENG., Illus.). (J). lib. bdg. 29.13 *(978-0-8239-4024-0(1),* 9c5f4762-c197-4003-b7e8-465e5458522a, Rosen Reference) Rosen Publishing Group, Inc., The.

Orme, David. Speed. 2009. (Fact to Fiction Grafx Ser.). (Illus.). 36p. (J). pap. 6.95 *(978-0-7891-7906-7(7))* Perfection Learning Corp.

Orr, Tamra. The Department of Transportation. 2009. (This Is Your Government Ser.). 64p. (gr. 5-6). 58.50 *(978-1-60854-377-9(3),* Rosen Reference) Rosen Publishing Group, Inc., The.

Orr, Tamra B. The Department of Transportation, 1 vol. 2005. (This Is Your Government Ser.). (ENG., Illus.). 64p. (gr. 4-6). per. 12.95 *(978-1-4042-0664-9(7),* a8f81d80-a822-47eb-90dd-5ae99b5dd93b) Rosen Publishing Group, Inc., The.

Oxlade, Chris. The History of Transportation. 2017. (History of Technology Ser.). (ENG., Illus.). 32p. (J). (gr. 2-5). lib. bdg. 29.99 *(978-1-4846-4038-8(1),* 135139, Heinemann) Capstone.

Petersen, Christine. The Wheelwright, 1 vol. 2013. (Colonial People Ser.). (ENG.). 48p. (gr. 4-4). pap. 13.93 *(978-1-62712-049-4(1),* bdf2b57d-e06b-4052-a881-9886cdfa4cde) Cavendish Square Publishing LLC.

Raum, Elizabeth. The Scoop on Clothes, Homes, & Daily Life in Colonial America. 2011. (Life in the American Colonies Ser.). (ENG.). 32p. (gr. 3-4). pap. 47.70 *(978-1-4296-7214-6(5),* Capstone Pr.) Capstone.

Ray, Kurt. New Roads, Canals, & Railroads in Early 19th-Century America: The Transportation Revolution. (Life in the New American Nation Ser.). 32p. (gr. 4-4). 2009. 47.90 *(978-1-61514-281-1(9))* 2003. (ENG., Illus.). pap. 10.00 *(978-0-8239-4254-1(6),* a1f0d882-6e43-4123-ac36-7015b8fc06c8) 2003. (ENG., Illus.). lib. bdg. 29.13 *(978-0-8239-4036-3(5),* a4ee531f-1616-45f0-bb56-6f4a8a9fad93, Rosen Reference) Rosen Publishing Group, Inc., The.

Ruiz, Rachel. When Rosa Parks Went Fishing. Fedele, Chiara, illus. 2017. (Leaders Doing Headstands Ser.). (ENG.). 32p. (J). (gr. 1-4). lib. bdg. 28.65 *(978-1-5158-1574-7(9),* 136244, Picture Window Bks.) Capstone.

Spengler, Kremena T. An Illustrated Timeline of Transportation, 1 vol. Doty, Eldon, illus. 2011. (Visual Timelines in History Ser.). (ENG.). 32p. (J). (gr. 2-4). pap. 7.49 *(978-1-4048-7019-2(9),* 116799, Picture Window Bks.) Capstone.

Stott, Colin. Victorian Transport. (ENG., Illus.). 32p. pap. *(978-0-7502-3752-9(X),* Wayland) Hachette Children's Group.

Suen, Anastasia. Finding a Way: Six Historic U.S. Routes. 2004. (ENG., Illus.). 32p. (J). (gr. 5-5). pap. 13.00 net. *(978-0-7652-5239-5(2))* Celebration Pr.

Tracy, Kathleen. The Life & Times of Rosa Parks. 2008. (Illus.). 48p. (J). (gr. 4-8). lib. bdg. 29.95 *(978-1-58415-666-6(X))* Mitchell Lane Pubs.

Wirkner, Linda. Learning about America's Industrial Growth with Graphic Organizers, 1 vol. 2004. (Graphic Organizers in Social Studies). (ENG., Illus.). 24p. (J). (gr. 4-5). lib. bdg. 26.27 *(978-1-4042-2812-2(8),* 4cef37cd-1393-49ee-a5b5-bbf019d5342e, PowerKids Pr.) Rosen Publishing Group, Inc., The.

Woods, Michael & Woods, Mary B. Ancient Transportation: From Camels to Canals. 2005. (Ancient Technology Ser.). (Illus.). 96p. (gr. 6-12). 25.26 *(978-0-8225-2993-4(9))* Lerner Publishing Group.

World Book, Inc. Staff, contrib. by. Transportation. 2009. (J). *(978-0-7166-0381-8(0))* World Bk., Inc.

TRANSPORTATION—POETRY

Scieszka, Jon. Truckery Rhymes. 2009. (ENG., Illus.). 24p. (J). (gr. k-k). pap. 6.25 *(978-0-328-50050-5(X),* Scott Foresman) Savvas Learning Co.

—Truckery Rhymes. Shannon, David et al, illus. 2009. (Jon Scieszka's Trucktown Ser.). (ENG.). 64p. (J). (gr. -1-3). 19.99 *(978-1-4169-4135-4(5),* Simon & Schuster Bks. For Young Readers) Simon & Schuster Bks. For Young Readers.

TRANSPORTATION—VOCATIONAL GUIDANCE

Dakers, Diane. Green Ways of Getting Around: Careers in Transportation. 2011. (ENG., Illus.). 64p. (J). pap. *(978-0-7787-4867-0(7),* 1331598); (gr. 5-9). *(978-0-7787-4856-4(1),* 1331598) Crabtree Publishing Co.

Greek, Joe. A Career in Transportation & Warehousing, 1 vol. 2018. (Jobs for Rebuilding America Ser.). (ENG., Illus.). 80p. (J). (gr. 6-6). 38.80 *(978-1-5081-8005-0(9),* bd33d587-7269-4bd3-9734-2695cd4362d3) Rosen Publishing Group, Inc., The.

Kamberg, Mary-Lane. Working in Public Transportation in Your Community, 1 vol. 2018. (Careers in Your Community Ser.). (ENG.). 80p. (gr. 7-7). 37.47 *(978-1-4994-6732-1(X),* 82958b15-133d-4f21-87cb-30bc45763d8c) Rosen Publishing Group, Inc., The.

Lewis, Daniel. Transportation & Manufacturing, Vol. 10. 2018. (Careers in Demand for High School Graduates Ser.). 112p. (J). (gr. 7). 34.60 *(978-1-4222-4139-4(4))* Mason Crest.

Miller, Malinda. Tomorrow's Transportation: Green Solutions for Air, Land & Sea. 2010. (New Careers for the 21st Century Ser.). 64p. (YA). (gr. 7-18). lib. bdg. 22.95 *(978-1-4222-1824-2(4))* Mason Crest.

—Tomorrow's Transportation: Green Solutions for Air, Land, & Sea. 2010. (New Careers for the 21st Century Ser.). 64p. (YA). (gr. 7-18). pap. 9.95 *(978-1-4222-2045-0(1))* Mason Crest.

Reeves, Diane Lindsey. Transportation. 2017. (Bright Futures Press: World of Work Ser.). (ENG., Illus.). 32p. (J). (gr. 4-7). lib. bdg. 32.07 *(978-1-63472-629-0(4),* 209550) Cherry Lake Publishing.

Yomtov, Nel. Transportation Planner. 2013. (21st Century Skills Library: Cool STEM Careers Ser.). (ENG., Illus.). 32p. (J). (gr. 4-8). 32.07 *(978-1-62431-008-9(7),* 202483); pap. 14.21 *(978-1-62431-032-4(X),* 202485) Cherry Lake Publishing.

TRAPP FAMILY SINGERS

Anderson, William. V Is for Von Trapp: A Musical Family Alphabet. Graves, Linda, illus. 2010. (ENG.). 32p. (J). (gr. 1-4). 18.99 *(978-1-58536-531-9(9),* 202214) Sleeping Bear Pr.

Ransom, Candice. Maria von Trapp: Beyond the Sound of Music. 2005. (Trailblazers Biographies Ser.). (Illus.). 112p. (J). (gr. 5-9). lib. bdg. 27.93 *(978-1-57505-444-5(2))* Lerner Publishing Group.

TRAPPING

see also Fur Trade; Game and Game Birds; Hunting

Gilsvik, Bob. The Complete Book of Trapping. Gilsvik, David, illus. 172p. (J). (gr. 7). reprint ed. 14.95 *(978-0-936622-29-3(6))* A.R. Harding Publishing Co.

TRAPPING—FICTION

Anderson, Laurie Halse. Trapped. 2009. (Vet Volunteers Ser.: 8). (ENG.). 144p. (J). (gr. 3-7). 7.99 *(978-0-14-241223-7(6),* Puffin Books) Penguin Young Readers Group.

Dalton, Matthew. The Next Steve Erwin, 1 vol. Cavanaugh, Stacy, illus. 2009. 16p. pap. 24.95 *(978-1-60836-635-4(9))* America Star Bks.

Kehret, Peg & the Cat, Pete. Trapped! 2008. (Pete the Cat Ser.: 3). (ENG.). 192p. (J). (gr. 3-7). 7.99 *(978-0-14-241189-6(2),* Puffin Books) Penguin Young Readers Group.

Lindsey, Stephanie. Crabs in a Bucket. 2013. 28p. pap. 24.95 *(978-1-63000-538-2(X))* America Star Bks.

Smelcer, John. The Trap. 2007. (ENG.). 176p. (YA). (gr. 7-9). per. 10.99 *(978-0-312-37755-7(X),* 900049151) Square Fish.

TRAVEL

see also Automobile Travel; Games for Travelers; Tourism; Voyages and Travels; Voyages around the World

also names of countries, states, etc. with the subdivision Description and Travel, e.g. United States—Description and travel

Aguilera, Rich. Passport to Adventure: Daily Devotions for Juniors. 2016. 369p. (J). pap. *(978-0-8163-6189-2(4))* Pacific Pr. Publishing Assn.

Andrus, Aubre. A Smart Girl's Guide: Travel: Everything You Need to Know about Adventuring near & Far. Lewis, Stevie, illus. 2019. (American Girl(r) Wellbeing Ser.). (ENG.). 96p. (J). pap. 12.99 *(978-1-68337-123-6(2))* American Girl Publishing, Inc.

Awal, Pia. Travel Math, 1 vol. 2009. (Math Alive! Ser.). (ENG., Illus.). 32p. (J). (gr. 4-4). lib. bdg. 31.21 *(978-0-7614-3217-3(5),* d4112795-25d1-4f4b-819b-d56afdd269e8) Cavendish Square Publishing LLC.

Ball, Jacqueline A. Traveling Green. (Going Green Ser.). 32p. 2016. (ENG.). (J). (gr. 2-7). pap. 7.99 *(978-1-944998-67-7(5))* 2009. (Illus.). (YA). (gr. 3-6). lib. bdg. 28.50 *(978-1-59716-964-6(1))* Bearport Publishing Co., Inc.

Barbas, Keri, des. Travel Scratch & Sketch. 2005. (Activity Journal Ser.). (J). 12.99 *(978-0-88088-486-0(X))* Peter Pauper Pr. Inc.

Bardswich, Elizabeth & Bardswich, Miriam. Out There - Travel. 2007. (Steck-Vaughn BOLDPRINT Anthologies Ser.). (ENG., Illus.). 48p. (gr. 8-10). pap. 16.90 *(978-1-4190-4030-6(8))* Houghton Mifflin Harcourt Publishing Co.

Barnham, Kay. Journeys. 2004. (Starters Ser.). (Illus.). 24p. (J). lib. bdg. 22.80 *(978-1-58340-566-6(6))* Black Rabbit Bks.

Baxter, Nicola. Lonely Planet Kids My Travel Journal 1. Mansfield, Andy, illus. 2016. (Lonely Planet Kids Ser.). (ENG.). 72p. (J). (gr. 1-3). 12.99 *(978-1-76034-100-8(2),* 5184) Lonely Planet Global Ltd. IRL. Dist: Hachette Bk. Group.

Bernardo, Kat. Stem: The Science of Travel: Multiplication (Grade 3) 2017. (Mathematics in the Real World Ser.). (ENG., Illus.). 32p. (J). (gr. 3-4). pap. 11.99 *(978-1-4807-5797-4(7))* Teacher Created Materials, Inc.

Calfee, Susan. St. Augustine a to Z: A Young Reader's Guide to America's Oldest City. Senn, Oscar, illus. 2016. (ENG.). (J). pap. 12.95 *(978-0-9895487-1-7(6))* Wordwhittler Bks.

Cargile, Phillip & Miss Cheryl. The Wagon Man: The Untold Story of the Go-Burn Kids. 2009. 54p. pap. 16.95 *(978-1-60703-939-6(7))* America Star Bks.

Cascone, Gina & Sheppard, Bryony Williams. Around the World Right Now. Beckman, Olivia, illus. 2017. (ENG.). 32p. (J). (gr. k-3). 16.99 *(978-1-58536-976-8(4),* 204230) Sleeping Bear Pr.

Daniels, Jimmy. The Dusty Road. 2008. (ENG.). 26p. pap. 11.00 *(978-1-4196-2664-7(7))* CreateSpace Independent Publishing Platform.

Doering Tourville, Amanda. Manners on the School Bus. Lensch, Chris, illus. 2009. (Way to Be!: Manners Ser.). 24p. (gr. -1-2). pap. 2.76 *(978-1-4048-6052-0(5),* Picture Window Bks.) Capstone.

Downing, Sue. Lost in the City: Daytime. 2020. (Lost in the City Ser.). (ENG.). 12p. (J). (— 1). bds. 15.99 *(978-1-76040-935-7(9))* Little Hare Bks. AUS. Dist: Independent Pubs. Group.

—Lost in the City: Night Time. 2020. (Lost in the City Ser.). (ENG.). 12p. (J). (— 1). bds. 15.99 *(978-1-76040-936-4(7))* Little Hare Bks. AUS. Dist: Independent Pubs. Group.
Dyan, Penelope. I Remember Still, a Kid's Guide to Seville, Spain. Weigand, John D., photos by. 2012. (Illus.). 34p. pap. 11.95 *(978-1-61477-034-3(4))* Bellissima Publishing, LLC.
—Turkish Delight — A Kid's Guide to Istanbul, Turkey. Weigand, John D., photos by. 2011. (Illus.). 44p. pap. 12.95 *(978-1-935630-54-8(7))* Bellissima Publishing, LLC.
Enchantment of the World, Second Series (Fall 2014 Set Of 6) 2014. (Enchantment of the World, Second Ser.). (J). lib. bdg. 240.00 *(978-0-531-24351-0(6))* Scholastic Library Publishing.
Givens, David, ed. For the Kids! A Family-Friendly Guide to Outings & Activities. 2003. (ENG., Illus.). 220p. pap. 24.95 *(978-1-904148-27-2(1))* Liffey Pr., The IRL. Dist: Dufour Editions, Inc.
Glencoe Staff. Off We Go '83, Level 3. (J). *(978-0-02-131640-3(6))* Macmillan Publishing Co., Inc.
—Opening Doors '83: Level 7-8. (J). *(978-0-02-131700-4(3))* Macmillan Publishing Co., Inc.
Going Out: KinderWords Individual Title Six-Packs. (Kinderstarters Ser.). 8p. (gr. -1-1). 21.00 *(978-0-7635-8696-6(X))* Rigby Education.
Goldsworthy, Steve. Travelling Green. 2016. (Illus.). 32p. (J). *(978-1-5105-2223-7(9))* SmartBook Media, Inc.
Hamilton, Robert M. On a Bus, 1 vol. 2012. (Going Places (New Edition) Ser.). (ENG.). 24p. (J). (gr. k-k). pap. 9.15 *(978-1-4339-6275-2(6),* f7ea49bb-f4e4-4eae-9e82-f2d8a84f11ce); lib. bdg. 25.27 *(978-1-4339-6273-8(X),* b0e4b1d8-2298-41d4-8618-bed062c1c234) Stevens, Gareth Publishing LLLP.
—On a Plane, 1 vol. 2012. (Going Places (New Edition) Ser.). (ENG.). 24p. (J). (gr. k-k). pap. 9.15 *(978-1-4339-6279-0(9),* 66c9822f-604f-4159-ad55-67c5ac8c265a); lib. bdg. 25.27 *(978-1-4339-6277-6(2),* 03e48fbf-ed0c-42a9-9a64-5ecbdb1e516b) Stevens, Gareth Publishing LLLP.
—On a Train, 1 vol. 2012. (Going Places (New Edition) Ser.). (ENG.). 24p. (J). (gr. k-k). pap. 9.15 *(978-1-4339-6283-7(7),* 71a425e6-b89b-4369-8a84-d3e96f0049c9); lib. bdg. 25.27 *(978-1-4339-6281-3(0),* 0e950fe3-4e8e-40e5-9e50-87be54942ce3) Stevens, Gareth Publishing LLLP.
Hammond World Atlas Corporation Staff, ed. World Passport Atlas & Travelmate. 2nd rev. ed. 2008. 128p. 6.95 *(978-0-8437-1350-3(X))* Hammond World Atlas Corp.
Hawkins, Emily. Atlas of Miniature Adventures: A Pocket-Sized Collection of Small-scale Wonders - Because Bigger Isn't Always Better. Letherland, Lucy, illus. 2016. (Atlas Of Ser.). (ENG.). 64p. (J). 9.99 *(978-1-84780-909-4(X),* Wide Eyed Editions) Quarto Publishing Group UK GBR. Dist: Littlehampton Bk Services, Ltd.
Heuer, Steve. Spectacular Experiments & Mad Science Kids Love: Science That Dazzles @ Home, School or on the Go! 2010. 204p. pap. 19.99 *(978-1-4490-7041-0(8))* AuthorHouse.
Hewitt, Sally. Transportation. 2010. (Starting Geography Ser.). 32p. (J). (gr. 2-5). 28.50 *(978-1-60753-129-6(1))* Amicus Learning.
—Transportation. 2012. (Map Smart Ser.). 32p. (gr. 2-6). lib. bdg. 27.10 *(978-1-59920-415-4(0))* Black Rabbit Bks.
Higgins, Melissa. A Traveler's Guide to a Smooth Roadtrip. 2017. (Go-To Guides). (ENG., Illus.). 32p. (J). (gr. 3-9). lib. bdg. 28.65 *(978-1-5157-3661-5(X),* 133646, Capstone Pr.) Capstone.
Hood, Karen Jean Matsko. Adventure Travel: A Daily Journal, Vol. 1. Whispering Pine Press International, Inc. Staff, ed. Artistic Design Services Staff, illus. 2014. (Hood Journal Ser.). (ENG.). 130p. (J). 19.95 *(978-1-59210-428-4(2));* per. 13.95 *(978-1-59210-134-4(8),* 1-59210-134-8) Whispering Pine Pr. International, Inc.
—Adventure Travel Activity & Coloring Book. Whispering Pine Press International, ed. Hatakeyama, Hiroshi, tr. Hatakeyama, Hiroshi, illus. 2014. (Hood Activity & Coloring Book Ser.). (ENG & JPN.). 160p. (J). spiral bd. 19.95 *(978-1-59649-334-6(8));* per. 19.95 *(978-1-59210-590-8(4))* Whispering Pine Pr. International, Inc.
—Adventure Travel Activity & Coloring Book: Activity & Coloring Book Series. 2006. (Educational Activity & Coloring Book Ser.). (Illus.). (J). 17.95 *(978-1-930948-58-7(1))* Whispering Pine Pr. International, Inc.
James, Trisha. I Know Things That Go, 1 vol. 2017. (What I Know Ser.). (ENG.). 24p. (J). (gr. k-k). pap. 9.15 *(978-1-4824-6309-5(1),* c2580a63-e184-4ac8-b41b-65f77a4ae94c) Stevens, Gareth Publishing LLLP.
Jocelyn, Marthe. Which Way? Slaughter, Tom, illus. 2010. 24p. (J). (gr. k-k). 15.95 *(978-0-88776-970-2(5),* Tundra Bks.) Tundra Bks. CAN. Dist: Penguin Random Hse. LLC.
Johnson, Allen L. Kayaking Around Iceland: Adventures with Grandchildren. 2003. (Illus.). 196p. 15.00 *(978-1-880675-07-6(2))* Creative Enterprises.
Ko, Hannah. Where Do You Want to Travel? Piwowarski, Marcin, illus. 2017. (Field Trip Fun Ser.). (ENG.). 24p. (gr. -1-2). pap. 9.95 *(978-1-68342-794-0(7),* 9781683427940) Rourke Educational Media.
Krebs, Laurie. Off We Go to Mexico. Corr, Christopher, illus. 2008. (ENG.). 32p. (J). (gr. k-5). pap. 9.99 *(978-1-84686-159-8(4))* Barefoot Bks., Inc.
Ledieux, Jack. The Worst Trip EVER! 2017. (Text Connections Guided Close Reading Ser.). (J). (gr. 2). *(978-1-4900-1853-9(0))* Benchmark Education Co.
Macdonald, Fiona. Travel & Trade in the Middle Ages, 1 vol. 2005. (World Almanac(r) Library of the Middle Ages Ser.). (ENG., Illus.). 48p. (gr. 5-8). pap. 15.05 *(978-0-8368-5908-9(1),* f8b81ad4-1e2f-4855-ab46-eb8791a8108a); lib. bdg. 33.67 *(978-0-8368-5899-0(9),* 26f8e42e-103d-4545-85e0-d9f049292d64) Stevens, Gareth Publishing LLLP. (Gareth Stevens Secondary Library).
MacLaine, James. The Usborne Little Children's Travel Activity Book. Watt, Fiona, ed. Harrison, Erica et al, illus. 2013. (Activity Books for Little Children Ser.). (ENG.). 63p. (J). pap. 9.99 *(978-0-7945-3127-0(X),* Usborne) EDC Publishing.
Maloney, Brenna. This Is Mouse - An Adventure in Sewing: Make Mouse & Friends * Travel with Them from Africa to Outer Space. 2015. (ENG., Illus.). 112p. (J). (gr. -1-12). pap. 16.95 *(978-1-60705-977-6(0),* FunStitch Studio) C & T Publishing.
Mason, Paul. How Big Is Your Travel Footprint?, 1 vol. 2010. (Environmental Footprints Ser.). (ENG., Illus.). 32p. (gr. 4-4). 31.21 *(978-0-7614-4415-2(7),* 27c4c20d-a497-492c-b038-7a9ae9e4b132) Cavendish Square Publishing LLC.
Mattern, Joanne. I Use Math on a Trip, 1 vol. 2005. (I Use Math Ser.). (ENG., Illus.). 24p. (J). (gr. k-2). pap. 9.15 *(978-0-8368-4866-3(7),* 895d92ef-3d72-4133-85ab-993d72f5273d); lib. bdg. 24.67 *(978-0-8368-4859-5(4),* 6d2dcd22-2c4d-45f0-8797-d0010a4e526d) Stevens, Gareth Publishing LLLP. (Weekly Reader Leveled Readers).
Mayo Clinic Staff, contrib. by. Healthy Traveler: Answers on Staying Well While Away from Home. 2004. (Mayo Clinic on Health Ser.). (Illus.). 36.52p. (YA). (gr. 8-18). lib. bdg. 15.95 *(978-1-59084-253-9(7))* Mason Crest.
Meachen Rau, Dana. Los Viajes en la Historia de América (Travel in American History), 1 vol. 2006. (Cómo Era la Vida en América (How People Lived in America) Ser.). (SPA., Illus.). 24p. (gr. 2-4). pap. 9.15 *(978-0-8368-7441-9(2),* 3bfd5f74-eb8b-4d2b-933d-68201d92822d); lib. bdg. 24.67 *(978-0-8368-7434-1(X),* aed14468-7e70-470f-9f29-a37b12449b48) Stevens, Gareth Publishing LLLP. (Weekly Reader Leveled Readers).
—Travel in American History, 1 vol. 2006. (How People Lived in America Ser.). (ENG., Illus.). 24p. (gr. 2-4). lib. bdg. 24.67 *(978-0-8368-7210-1(X),* 5b46d85b-a64e-428a-a9df-918d06762c48, Weekly Reader Leveled Readers) Stevens, Gareth Publishing LLLP.
Michel, June, illus. Going Places: True Tales from Young Travelers. 2003. 160p. (J). (gr. 4-12). pap. *(978-1-58270-070-0(2))* Beyond Words Publishing, Inc.
Newman-D'Amico, Fran. Travel Fun. 2004. (Dover Little Activity Bks.). (ENG., Illus.). 64p. (J). (gr. k-3). pap., act. bk. ed. 2.50 *(978-0-486-43532-9(6),* 435326) Dover Pubns., Inc.
Ortiz, Rafael. Road Trip Across America. 2017. (Text Connections Guided Close Reading Ser.). (J). (gr. 2). *(978-1-4900-1841-6(7))* Benchmark Education Co.
Otowa, Rebecca. My Awesome Japan Adventure: A Diary about the Best 4 Months Ever! 2013. (Illus.). 48p. (J). (gr. 2-6). 14.95 *(978-4-8053-1216-2(5))* Tuttle Publishing.
Peters, Scott. How I Go. 2011. (Early Connections Ser.). (J). *(978-1-61672-322-4(X))* Benchmark Education Co.
Quan, Elizabeth. Once upon a Full Moon. 2007. (Illus.). 48p. (J). (gr. 1-4). 19.95 *(978-0-88776-813-2(X),* Tundra Bks.) Tundra Bks. CAN. Dist: Penguin Random Hse. LLC.
Rice, Dona Herweck. Places to Go, 1 vol. 2nd rev. ed. (TIME for KIDS(r): Informational Text Ser.). (ENG.). 12p. (gr. k-1). 2013. Illus.). (J). lib. bdg. 15.96 *(978-1-4807-1012-2(1))* 2011. 7.99 *(978-1-4333-3573-0(5))* Teacher Created Materials, Inc.
Rissman, Rebecca. Taking a Trip: Comparing Past & Present, 1 vol. 2014. (Comparing Past & Present Ser.). (ENG.). 24p. (J). (gr. -1-1). lib. bdg. 25.32 *(978-1-4329-8994-1(4),* 124791, Heinemann) Capstone.
Road Trip: Famous Routes, 12 vols. 2016. (Road Trip: Famous Routes Ser.). 24p. (ENG.). (gr. 2-3). lib. bdg. 151.62 *(978-1-4824-4603-6(0),* 8efb1200-0b21-429a-bf5a-ab9eed8506c6); (gr. 3-2). pap. 48.90 *(978-1-4824-5300-3(2))* Stevens, Gareth Publishing LLLP.
Sánchez, Gervasio. Cinco Anos Despues: Vidas Minadas. 2004. (SPA., Illus.). 80p. pap. 24.95 *(978-84-95939-33-3(9))* Blume ESP. Dist: Independent Pubs. Group.
Sasek, Miroslav. This Is the World: A Global Treasury. 2014. (This Is ... Ser.). (ENG., Illus.). 234p. (J). (gr. 5). 37.50 *(978-0-8478-4396-1(3))* Universe Publishing.
Scillian, Devin. P Is for Passport: A World Alphabet. Rose, Melanie & Guy, Susan, illus. 2003. (Discover the World Ser.). (ENG.). 48p. (J). (gr. 1-3). 19.95 *(978-1-58536-157-1(7),* 202017) Sleeping Bear Pr.
Smith, Aimee & Johnston, Deon. My Hometown Is the Best Place to Visit. 2017. (Text Connections Guided Close Reading Ser.). (J). (gr. 1). *(978-1-4900-1824-9(7))* Benchmark Education Co.
Smith, Sarah. Traveling Abroad, Vol. 7. 2018. (Etiquette for Success Ser.). 64p. (J). (gr. 7). 31.93 *(978-1-4222-3975-9(6))* Mason Crest.
Spenser & Mom. Spenser Goes to Portland. Jacobsen, Amie, illus. 2008. (ENG.). 32p. (J). 14.95 *(978-0-9817598-0-7(7),* cf47a802-b05d-4aa8-9dd0-abec385a8af9) Simple Fish Bk. Co., LLC.
Suen, Anastasia. Finding a Way: Six Historic U.S. Routes. 2004. (ENG., Illus.). 32p. (J). (gr. 5-5). pap. 13.00 net. *(978-0-7652-5239-5(2))* Celebration Pr.
Thomson, Ruth. Countries, 8 vols., Set. Incl. France. lib. bdg. 26.27 *(978-1-4488-3275-0(6),* eeed21c9-04b5-4d97-a14d-81867f8164f0); India. lib. bdg. 26.27 *(978-1-4488-3276-7(4),* caa0ed04-d37e-4776-887d-fa9d0f0ac027); Poland. lib. bdg. 26.27 *(978-1-4488-3277-4(2),* 9c9e6b45-8545-4c19-bc0d-488f655b0a25); Spain. lib. bdg. 26.27 *(978-1-4488-3278-1(0),* a4af7158-1d17-452e-ade1-e84c95f00e39); (J). (gr. 2-2). (Countries Ser.). (ENG., Illus.). 24p. 2011. Set lib. bdg. 105.08 *(978-1-4488-3304-7(3),* 425c85d5-99bd-47b7-a720-11f5c45fe719, PowerKids Pr.) Rosen Publishing Group, Inc., The.
Timmerman, Charles. The Everything Large-Print Travel Word Search Book: Find Your Way Through 150 Easy-To-read Puzzles. l.t. ed. 2011. (Everything(r) Ser.). (ENG.). 352p. pap. 15.95 *(978-1-4405-2736-4(9))* Adams Media Corp.
Tweh, Steven R. Traveling Abroad: How to Proceed & Succeed. 2011. 132p. (gr. -1). pap. 10.99 *(978-1-4343-3933-1(5))* AuthorHouse.
Watson, Hannah. First Sticker Book Travel. 2018. (First Sticker Bks.). (ENG.). 16p. (J). pap. 6.99 *(978-0-7945-4123-1(2),* Usborne) EDC Publishing.
Williams, John Matthew. Planes Go!, 1 vol. 2017. (Ways to Go Ser.). (ENG.). 24p. (J). (gr. k-k). pap. 9.15 *(978-1-5382-1020-8(7),* e7632cf6-6da0-40ac-bdba-776df62f0088) Stevens, Gareth Publishing LLLP.
Wood, Anita. Travel Doodles for Kids, 1 vol. Sabatino, Chris, illus. 2012. (ENG.). 272p. (J). pap. 9.99 *(978-1-4236-2454-7(8))* Gibbs Smith, Publisher.
Woods, Michael & Woods, Mary B. Ancient Transportation Technology: From Oars to Elephants. 2011. (Technology in Ancient Cultures Ser.). (ENG., Illus.). 96p. (J). (gr. 6-12). lib. bdg. 31.93 *(978-0-7613-6524-2(9))* Lerner Publishing Group.
Zannos, Susan. The Life & Times of Marco Polo. 2004. (Biography from Ancient Civilizations Ser.). (Illus.). 48p. (J). (gr. 4-8). lib. bdg. 29.95 *(978-1-58415-264-4(8))* Mitchell Lane Pubs.

TRAVEL—FICTION

Abbott, Jacob. Aunt Margaret; or, How John True Kept His Resolutions. 2013. 160p. pap. 19.95 *(978-1-4455-2937-0(8))* Research Pr.
—Rollo in Holland. 2008. 108p. 23.95 *(978-1-60664-820-9(9));* pap. 9.95 *(978-1-60664-065-4(8))* Aegypan.
—Rollo in London. 2008. 124p. 23.95 *(978-1-60664-942-8(6));* pap. 10.95 *(978-1-60312-492-8(6))* Aegypan.
—Rollo in Naples. 2008. 108p. 23.95 *(978-1-60664-821-6(7));* pap. 9.95 *(978-1-60664-066-1(6))* Aegypan.
—Rollo in Paris. 2008. 116p. 22.95 *(978-1-60664-943-5(4));* pap. 9.95 *(978-1-60312-493-5(4))* Aegypan.
Abraham, Arnetta. Miss Robbie's House. 2009. 64p. pap. 23.49 *(978-1-4490-4571-5(5))* AuthorHouse.
Abshier, Stan. Teddy's Journal: Cruise to Japan, China, & Singapore. 2012. 96p. pap. 31.99 *(978-1-4685-2319-5(8))* AuthorHouse.
Ahern, Carolyn L. Tino Turtle Travels to Beijing, China. Burt-Sullivan, Neallia, illus. 2011. (ENG.). 56p. (J). (gr. -1-4). 19.95 incl. audio compact disk *(978-0-9793158-4-8(0))* Tino Turtle Travels, LLC.
—Tino Turtle Travels to Kenya - the Great Safari. Burt Sullivan, Neallia, illus. 2009. (ENG & SWA.). 32p. (J). (gr. -1-4). 19.95 incl. audio compact disk *(978-0-9793158-3-1(2))* Tino Turtle Travels, LLC.
—Tino Turtle Travels to London, England. Burt Sullivan, Neallia, illus. (J). 2007. 36p. 17.95 incl. audio compact disk *(978-0-9793158-0-0(8))* 2008. (ENG.). 32p. 19.95 incl. audio compact disk *(978-0-9816297-0-4(9))* Tino Turtle Travels, LLC.
—Tino Turtle Travels to Mexico City, Mexico. Burt Sullivan, Neallia, illus. 2008. (ENG & SPA.). 32p. (J). (gr. -1-4). 19.95 incl. audio compact disk *(978-0-9793158-2-4(4))* Tino Turtle Travels, LLC.
—Tino Turtle Travels to Paris, France. Burt Sullivan, Neallia, illus. 2007. 36p. (J). (gr. -1-4). 17.95 incl. audio compact disk *(978-0-9793158-1-7(6))* Tino Turtle Travels, LLC.
Alonso Gómez, Manuel Luis. Rumbo Sur. 2005. (SPA.). *(978-84-263-5948-3(5))* Vives, Luis Editorial (Edelvives).
Alter, Anna. Sprout Street Neighbors: Bon Voyage. 2017. (Sprout Street Neighbors Ser.: 3). (ENG., Illus.). 96p. (J). (gr. 1-4). pap. 6.99 *(978-1-5247-0053-9(3),* Yearling) Random Hse. Children's Bks.
Anderson, Nancy. Jeff's Trip to Holland, 1 vol. 2016. (Rosen REAL Readers: STEM & STEAM Collection). (ENG.). 12p. (gr. 1-2). pap. 6.33 *(978-1-5081-2679-9(8),* a15ab0b7-d567-4e08-b4cc-2c81570e431a, Rosen Classroom) Rosen Publishing Group, Inc., The.
Asher, Penny & Booker, Ricki. Mommy & Daddy Are Going on a Trip. Kassab, Selena, illus. 2006. 32p. (J). 12.95 *(978-0-9755902-1-8(9))* Change Is Strange, Inc.
Auerbach, Annie. My Race into Space! A Water Wonder Book. Garofoli, Viviana, illus. 2005. 18p. (J). 9.95 *(978-1-58117-351-2(2),* Intervisual/Piggy Toes) Bendon, Inc.
AZ Books, creator. Tyler Turtle Travels to Australia. 2013. (Pop-Up: Play & Listen Ser.). (ENG., Illus.). 10p. (J). (gr. -1-k). bds. 16.95 *(978-1-61889-036-8(0))* AZ Bks. LLC.
Barchers, Suzanne I. Pack a Bag!, 1 vol. rev. ed. 2011. (Phonics Ser.). (ENG.). 16p. (gr. k-1). 6.99 *(978-1-4333-2409-3(1))* Teacher Created Materials, Inc.
Barton, Bob. Trouble on the Voyage. 2010. (ENG., Illus.). 240p. (J). (gr. 4-7). pap. 10.95 *(978-1-926607-10-8(4),* Napoleon & Co.) Dundurn Pr. CAN. Dist: Publishers Group West (PGW).
Benchimol, Brigitte. Jadyn & the Magic Bubble: I Met Gandhi. Adams, Mark Wayne, illus. 2008. (J). 24.95 *(978-0-9799339-7-4(8))* East West Discovery Pr.
Benchmark Education Co., LLC. A Trip to Washington, D. C. A Capital Idea Teacher's Guide. 2013. (Reader's Theater Word Plays Ser.). *(978-1-4509-9037-0(1))* Benchmark Education Co.
Berenstain, Mike. The Berenstain Bears Around the World. 2016. (Illus.). 27p. (J). *(978-1-5182-1952-8(7))* Harper & Row Ltd.
Bidzilya, Kristin. Two Girls Dreams Come True. 2007. 64p. per. 9.95 *(978-1-934246-87-0(5))* Peppertree Pr., The.
Bilbrey, Heather. The Cookie Man. Green, Megan, illus. 2008. 20p. pap. 24.95 *(978-1-60703-328-8(3))* America Star Bks.
Bilik-Franklin, MidiAna & Griffith, Indigo, photos by. The Carseat Tourist. 2006. (Illus.). (J). bds. 7.95 *(978-0-9772825-0-0(3))* Critter Camp Inc.
Blabey, Aaron. Pig the Tourist. Blabey, Aaron, illus. 2020. (Pig the Pug Ser.). (ENG., Illus.). 32p. (J). (gr. -1-k). 14.99 *(978-1-338-59339-6(0),* Scholastic Pr.) Scholastic, Inc.
Blake, Christine & Lopez, Jill. Signs, Signs, Everywhere Signs. 2008. 32p. pap. 15.95 *(978-1-4327-2523-5(8))* Outskirts Pr., Inc.
Bond, Michael. Love from Paddington. Fortnum, Peggy & Alley, R. W., illus. 2016. (Paddington Ser.). (ENG.). 144p. (J). (gr. 3-7). pap. 5.99 *(978-0-06-242526-3(9),* HarperCollins) HarperCollins Pubs.
Bowater, Alan. A Pig Called Pete, 1 vol. Pascoe, Pete, illus. 2009. (Pig Called Pete Ser.). (ENG.). 32p. (J). (gr. 1-2). 27.27 *(978-1-60754-558-3(6),* 666020cf-7837-4b2a-b12e-20b4a79ed0be); pap. 11.55 *(978-1-60754-559-0(4),* cb0d11a6-5d4a-4d60-b1ce-61000758511e) Rosen Publishing Group, Inc., The. (Windmill Bks.).
Bradbury, Jennifer. Shift. (ENG., Illus.). (YA). (gr. 7). 2012. 272p. pap. 12.99 *(978-1-4424-0852-4(9))* 2008. 256p. 17.99 *(978-1-4169-4732-5(9))* Simon & Schuster Children's Publishing. (Atheneum Bks. for Young Readers).
Bridwell, Norman. Clifford Takes a Trip (Classic Storybook) Bridwell, Norman, illus. 2011. (ENG., Illus.). 32p. (J). (gr. -1-k). pap. 4.99 *(978-0-545-21591-6(9),* Cartwheel Bks.) Scholastic, Inc.
Brooks, Walter R. Freddy Goes to Florida. Wiese, Kurt, illus. 2012. (ENG.). 224p. (YA). (gr. 4-13). 11.99 *(978-1-59020-741-3(6),* 1452703, Amulet Bks.) Abrams, Inc.
Brown, Amanda C. Flying Courage. Archeval, Jose, illus. 2012. (ENG.). 26p. (J). pap. 9.99 *(978-1-62006-121-3(X))* Sunbury Press, Inc.
Brown, Rosie L. Zach & Rob's Journey: The Lost Eggs. 2007. 24p. per. 24.95 *(978-1-4241-8401-9(0))* America Star Bks.
Bunting, Eve. The Man with the Red Bag. 2007. 230p. (J). (gr. 5-9). 15.99 *(978-0-06-081828-9(X),* Cotler, Joanna Books) HarperCollins Pubs.
Burleigh, Robert. Hit the Road, Jack. MacDonald, Ross, illus. 2012. (ENG.). 48p. (J). (gr. -1-3). 17.95 *(978-1-4197-0399-7(4),* 689701, Abrams Bks. for Young Readers) Abrams, Inc.
Burt, Marissa. The 12 Dares of Christa. 2017. (ENG.). 304p. (J). (gr. 3-7). 16.99 *(978-0-06-241618-6(9),* Tegen, Katherine Bks) HarperCollins Pubs.
Butler, Ethel And Steven, creator. Callie the Kangie Traveling America. 2012. 32p. pap. 15.99 *(978-1-4685-6197-5(9))* AuthorHouse.
Cameron, Thomas "Tom". Freddy's Adventure on the Safari River. 2012. 36p. pap. 24.95 *(978-1-4626-7436-7(4))* America Star Bks.
Campbell, Aileen. The Wee Scot Travels. 2003. 32p. pap. 7.95 *(978-1-56554-873-2(6),* Pelican Publishing) Arcadia Publishing.
Carbonell Penichet, Paula. BUTTERFLY TRIP. 2007. (ENG., Illus.). 48p. (J). 18.95 *(978-84-96788-85-5(7))* OQO, Editora ESP. Dist: Baker & Taylor Bks.
Carlon, Mick. Riding on Duke's Train. 2011. (LeapKids Ser.). (ENG.). 160p. (J). (gr. k-7). pap. 9.95 *(978-1-935248-06-4(5))* Leapfrog Pr.
Chalifoux, Lisa M. Spotty & Eddie Visit Percé. 2010. 24p. pap. 14.95 *(978-1-4269-2660-0(X))* Trafford Publishing.
Chapman, Nancy Kapp & Chapman, Nancy. Tripper's Travels: An International Scrapbook, 1 vol. Chapman, Lee, illus. 2005. (ENG.). 32p. (J). (gr. 1-5). 16.95 *(978-0-7614-5240-9(0))* Marshall Cavendish Corp.
Chesne, Sabrina. Lillie's Treasures/Los tesoros de Lili. Capasso, Diana, tr. Patagonia School, illus. 2004. (ENG & SPA.). 32p. per. 15.00 *(978-0-9630310-9-9(0))* Will Hall Bks.
Church, Anna. Hug-A-Bug Travels to Peru. Church, Anna & Taylor, Nicole, illus. 2013. 44p. pap. 12.00 *(978-0-9831449-4-6(X))* Mighty Lion Ventures.
Clark, Ruth E. Airport Mouse Becomes a VIP/VIM World Traveler. Jones, Phil, illus. 2009. 32p. (J). 15.95 *(978-0-9792963-5-2(8))* Hibiscus Publishing.
Cohen, Deborah Bodin. Engineer Ari & the Rosh Hashanah Ride. Kober, Shahar, illus. 2008. (ENG.). 32p. (J). (gr. k-3). pap. 7.95 *(978-0-8225-8650-0(9),* 37414485-35cb-4009-8244-ca373dec1e78, Kar-Ben Publishing) Lerner Publishing Group.
Colato Laínez, René & Vanden Broeck, Fabricio. My Shoes & I / Mis Zapatos y Yo: Crossing Three Borders / Cruzando Tres Fronteras. Vanden Broeck, Fabricio, illus. 2019. (ENG & SPA., Illus.). 32p. (J). (gr. 1-3). 17.95 *(978-1-55885-884-8(9),* Piñata Books) Arte Publico Pr.
Cole, Dina. Are There Alligators at the Equator? An Eddie the Equator Adventure. 2012. 40p. pap. 20.99 *(978-1-4772-6819-3(7))* AuthorHouse.
Conklin, Wendy. Dos Amigos Planos Viajan por el Mundo. rev. ed. 2007. (Reader's Theater Ser.).Tr. of Two Flat Friends Travel the World. (SPA.). 24p. (gr. 3-4). pap. 8.99 *(978-1-4333-0022-6(2))* Teacher Created Materials, Inc.
Cowan, Sarah & Kitchen. A Trip to the Beach. 2009. 60p. pap. *(978-1-84923-198-5(2))* YouWriteOn.
Crawford, Quinton. Moochie the Soochie - Visits the Peace People. 2009. 42p. pap. 17.98 *(978-0-557-07714-4(1))* Lulu Pr., Inc.
Creek, Silent. All the Ice of Afric. 2009. 160p. 22.95 *(978-1-4401-2118-0(4))* iUniverse, Inc.
Cunningham, Mary. The Missing Locket. 2005. (Cynthia's Attic Ser.). 152p. (J). (gr. 5). per. 9.99 *(978-1-59080-441-4(4))* Echelon Press Publishing.
Czerw, Nancy Carpenter. Itty & Bitty - On the Road. Berlin, Rose Mary, illus. 2008. (Itty & Bitty Ser.: 3). (ENG.). 32p. (J). (gr. -1-3). 16.95 *(978-0-9755618-4-3(7))* McWitty Pr., Inc.
Darrington, Rebecca. Doodletoot- a Happy Little Basset Hound Dog. 2012. 24p. pap. 17.99 *(978-1-61996-337-5(X))* Salem Author Services.
Davies, Lewis. Tai, Troll & the Black & White Cow. 2009. (ENG., Illus.). 30p. (J). pap. 7.95 *(978-1-905762-64-4(X))* Parthian Bks. GBR. Dist: Independent Pubs. Group.
Davis, Pat. Estelle & the Escape from Mars: A Children's Novel By. 2009. 136p. pap. 10.99 *(978-1-4389-5432-5(8))* AuthorHouse.
Day, Nick. Vegas. 2017. (Summer Road Trip Ser.). (ENG.). 184p. (YA). (gr. 5-12). 31.42 *(978-1-68076-727-8(5),* 27442, Epic Escape) EPIC Pr.
De Haven, Amanda. Queen Elizabeth's Travel. 2012. 24p. pap. 15.99 *(978-1-4691-6388-8(8))* Xlibris Corp.
DeLand, M. Maitland. Baby Santa's Worldwide Christmas Adventure. Wilson, Phil, illus. 2010. 32p. (J). 14.95 *(978-1-60832-062-2(6))* Greenleaf Book Group.
DeMico, Judy. The Bus Trip, 1 vol. Johnson, Catherine LeAnn, illus. 2010. 26p. pap. 24.95 *(978-1-4489-2767-8(6))* PublishAmerica, Inc.
Denofsky, Howard. Sillyishis, Beanie & the Hobblebobs. 2012. 32p. 24.95 *(978-1-4626-6211-1(0))* America Star Bks.
DeNucci, Sharon. Ava Goes to Africa. DeNucci, Corinne, illus. 2010. (ENG.). 30p. pap. 16.99 *(978-1-4520-4091-2(5))* AuthorHouse.
Diesen, Deborah. The Pout-Pout Fish, Far, Far from Home. Hanna, Dan, illus. (Pout-Pout Fish Adventure Ser.). (ENG.). 32p. (J). 2019. bds. 8.99 *(978-0-374-31078-3(5),* 900194752) 2017. 16.99 *(978-0-374-30194-1(8),* 900141733) Farrar, Straus & Giroux. (Farrar, Straus & Giroux (BYR)).
Diller, Janelle. Mystery at the Christmas Market. Travis, Lisa, ed. Turner, Adam, illus. 2014. 110p. (J). (gr. 1-4). pap. 5.99 *(978-1-936376-18-6(0))* WorldTrek Publishing.
Dodson, Shon. All I Need. 2010. (ENG.). 36p. pap. 16.99 *(978-1-4520-1053-3(6))* AuthorHouse.

T U V

Dotlich, Rebecca Kai. The Knowing Book. Cordell, Matthew, illus. 2016. (ENG.). 32p. (J). (gr. 2). 16.99 *(978-1-59078-926-1(1),* Astra Young Readers) Astra Publishing Hse.

Downey, Tika. Tracks in the Snow, 1 vol. 2006. (Neighborhood Readers Ser.). (ENG.). 16p. (gr. 1-2). pap. 6.50 *(978-1-4042-7180-7(5),* 510446d8-1f90-41d2-ac8b-45d75e748255, Rosen Classroom) Rosen Publishing Group, Inc., The.

Dream Catchers - Evaluation Guide: Evaluation Guide. 2006. (J). *(978-1-55942-403-5(6))* Witcher Productions.

du Bois, William Pène. Twenty-One Balloons. du Bois, William Pène, illus. 2005. (Illus.). 180p. (J). lib. bdg. 15.00 *(978-1-4242-2270-4(2))* Fitzgerald Bks.

Dubyn, Bj. The Thrilling & Dynamic Adventures of Barbara Ann, Her Kid Brother, Billy, Jr, & Manfred the Magnificent, Their Parrot. 2008. 104p. pap. 15.99 *(978-1-4363-2652-0(4))* Xlibris Corp.

DuPrau, Jeanne. Car Trouble. 2005. 288p. (J). 15.99 *(978-0-06-073672-9(0));* lib. bdg. 16.89 *(978-0-06-073674-3(7))* HarperCollins Pubs.

Duthaluru, Vidhya. Michael's Field Trip. 2007. (Illus.). 18p. (J). 3.99 *(978-0-9797657-0-4(6))* Duthaluru, Vidhya.

Earp-Bridgmon, Krista D. The Adventures of Jim-Bob: A Bearography. 2013. 24p. pap. 10.99 *(978-1-4582-1005-0(7),* Abbott Pr.) Author Solutions, LLC.

Eastman, P. D. Ve, Perro, Ve! (Go, Dog, Go! Spanish Edition) Perdomo, Adolfo Perez, tr. from ENG. 2003. (Bright & Early Board Books(TM) Ser.) Tr. of Go, Dog, Go! (SPA., Illus.). 24p. (J). (— 1). bds. 4.99 *(978-0-375-82361-9(1),* Random House Para Ninos) Random Hse. Children's Bks.

Edman Lamote, Lisa. A Day Out for Opus. Wilson, Alisha, illus. 2006. (Bookmann Family Presents Ser.). 32p. (J). (gr. k-3). 15.99 *(978-1-933673-03-5(6),* BookMann Pr.) Mann Publishing Group.

Eller, Sylvia Klope. The Squirrel Who Hitchhiked to Atlanta. 2007. (Illus.). 32p. (J). pap. 8.00 *(978-0-8059-7596-3(9))* Dorrance Publishing Co., Inc.

Errico, Jessica / C. Grandpa's Magical Accordion. Star, Brenda, illus. 2007. 28p. (J). pap. 17.95 incl. cd-rom *(978-0-9800577-0-6(1))* Three Part Harmony LLC.

Fath, Teresa. The Train Track Trolley & the Bell Dogs. 2009. 32p. pap. 21.99 *(978-1-4415-4350-9(3))* Xlibris Corp.

Fenn, George. Yussuf the Guide or the Mountain Bandits: Being the Strange Story of the Travels in Asia Minor of Burne the Lawyer, Preston the Professor, & Lawren. Schönberg, John, illus. 2007. 424p. 26.95 *(978-0-9776786-6-2(0))* Salem Ridge Press LLC.

Figorito, Marcus. Tara Takes the Train, 1 vol. 2006. (Neighborhood Readers Ser.). (ENG.). 16p. (gr. 1-2). pap. 6.50 *(978-1-4042-7208-8(9),* 6defb4c6-988b-44df-bcfb-a804e6b6e432, Rosen Classroom) Rosen Publishing Group, Inc., The.

Finley, Martha. Elsie's Winter Trip, Vol. 26. 320p. (gr. 4-7). pap. 5.95 *(978-1-58182-181-9(6),* Cumberland Hse.) Sourcebooks, Inc.

Flack, Annie. Mysteries of the Lake. 2009. 92p. pap. 10.49 *(978-1-4389-6264-1(9))* AuthorHouse.

Florence, Leigh Anne. Mr. Dogwood Goes to Washington. Asher, James, illus. 2008. (Woody the Kentucky Wiener Ser.). 56p. (J). (gr. 2-8). pap. 12.95 *(978-0-9741417-5-6(5))* HotDiggetyDog Pr.

Floyd, Belinda D. Going to America. 2005. 28p. per. 25.49 *(978-1-4208-8693-1(2))* AuthorHouse.

Foster, Tim & Foster, Tina. Abap the Ambulance in Happy to Help! 2008. 28p. 18.95 *(978-0-9556910-0-3(1))* Eclipse Solutions (UK) Ltd. GBR. Dist: Lulu Pr., Inc.

Francia, Giada. In the Wild West on MacKenzie's Trail. McCloskey, Erin, ed. Howard, Catherine, tr. 2007. (Alex & Penny Ser.). (ENG., Illus.). 80p. (gr. 2-5). pap. 14.95 *(978-88-544-0245-4(1))* White Star Publishers ITA. Dist: Random Hse., Inc.

Franco, Betsy. Going to Grandma's Farm. 2004. (Rookie Reader Español Ser.). (ENG., Illus.). 24p. (J). (gr. k-2). pap. 4.95 *(978-0-516-27787-5(1),* Children's Pr.) Scholastic Library Publishing.

George, Audra. Vagabonding. George, Audra, illus. 2006. (Illus.). 32p. (J). (gr. -1-3). 17.95 *(978-1-60108-010-3(7))* Red Cygnet Pr.

George, Sandy. Anika's Travel Diaries: The Lava Island Trip. 2012. 28p. pap. 17.99 *(978-1-4772-9297-6(7))* AuthorHouse.

Gershator, Phillis. Time for a Trip. Walker, David, illus. 2018. (Snuggle Time Stories Ser.: 10). 22p. (J). (— 1). bds. 7.99 *(978-1-4549-3016-7(0))* Sterling Publishing Co., Inc.

Gill, Heidi. Egypt. Carter, Kris, illus. 2012. (2 Kurious Kids Ser.: Vol. 5). (ENG.). 24p. (J). (gr. -1-5). 14.95 *(978-1-936319-93-0(4))* Amplify Publishing Group.

—2 Kurious Kids: France. Carter, Kris, illus. 2012. 38p. (J). 14.95 *(978-1-936319-90-9(X))* Amplify Publishing Group.

—2 Kurious Kids: India. Carter, Kris, illus. 2012. 38p. (J). 14.95 *(978-1-936319-92-3(6))* Amplify Publishing Group.

Gill, Heidi & Carter, Kris. 2 Kurious Kids: Mexico. 2012. (Illus.). 38p. (J). 14.95 *(978-1-936319-91-6(8))* Amplify Publishing Group.

Ginn, Jennifer. My Father Flies, 1 vol. 2013. (ENG., Illus.). 32p. (J). (gr. -1-3). 16.99 *(978-0-7643-4385-8(8),* 4799) Schiffer Publishing, Ltd.

Gramberg, J. E. Pakrat Bill. 2006. (ENG.). 36p. per. 21.32 *(978-1-4257-3117-5(1))* Xlibris Corp.

Grant, Natalie. Light up New York, 1 vol. 2017. (Faithgirlz / Glimmer Girls Ser.: 4). (ENG., Illus.). 208p. (J). pap. 8.99 *(978-0-310-75274-5(4))* Zonderkidz.

Greene, Reggie. The Adventures of Swami Somewhere- the Supermarket. Graham, Michael, illus. 2011. 32p. (J). 14.95 *(978-1-60131-095-8(1))* Big Tent Bks.

Gregerson, Lajuan. A Child's Tour of the Holy Land. 2008. 73p. pap. 19.95 *(978-1-60610-367-8(9))* America Star Bks.

Haddix, Margaret Peterson. Takeoffs & Landings. 2004. 201p. (gr. 5-9). 17.00 *(978-0-7569-4255-7(1))* Perfection Learning Corp.

Haidar, Hanna. Earl's Big Adventure in Costa Rica. Hutcheson, Meredith, ed. Newton, Kimberly, illus. 2007. 22p. (J). per. 7.99 *(978-0-9800975-0-4(9))* Old Silver Pr.

Harley, Bill. The Amazing Flight of Darius Frobisher, 1 vol. 2009. 160p. (J). (gr. 3-7). pap. 7.95 *(978-1-56145-494-5(X))* Peachtree Publishing Co. Inc.

Harrington, Jane. Four Things My Geeky-Jock-of-a-Best-Friend Must Do in Europe. 2006. (ENG.). 160p. (J). (gr. 6-9). 15.95 *(978-1-58196-041-9(7),* Darby Creek) Lerner Publishing Group.

Harrison, Troon. Poetry & Potatoes. Heliard, Susan, illus. 2003. 32p. (YA). *(978-1-84365-020-1(7),* Pavilion Children's Books) Pavilion Bks.

Harvey, Jacqueline & Yi Anne, Anne. Alice-Miranda in Hollywood. 2018. (Alice-Miranda Ser.: 16). (ENG.). 362p. (J). (gr. 3-7). 10.99 *(978-0-14-378061-8(1))* Random Hse. Australia AUS. Dist: Independent Pubs. Group.

Hathorn, Sarah Alexandra. Teenagents: World Challenge. 2012. 240p. pap. 12.99 *(978-2-9700738-2-6(X))* Simon & Schuster, Inc.

Henisz, Jerzy E. SOPHIE in PARIS & other Stories. 2009. (ENG.). 99p. pap. 9.46 *(978-0-557-09520-9(4))* Lulu Pr., Inc.

Henisz, Jerzy E. & Henisz, Sophie, illustrator. TEDDY BEAR who went on a Trip around the World & other Stories. 2006. (ENG.). 88p. (J). pap. *(978-0-615-13851-0(9))* Henisz, Jerzy E.

Hensley, Tana. Ellie's Trip to Ellis Island: Collecting Data, 1 vol. 2017. (Computer Kids: Powered by Computational Thinking Ser.). (ENG.). 24p. (J). (gr. 3-4). 25.27 *(978-1-5383-2392-2(3),* 0daffc28-8127-435d-94b6-20e545e0c9e4, PowerKids Pr.); pap. *(978-1-5081-3778-8(1),* fba8d102-3686-4098-9cf1-5347d3ca654d, Rosen Classroom) Rosen Publishing Group, Inc., The.

Hersh, Kristin. Toby Snax. 2016. (ENG., Illus.). 40p. (J). (gr. 1-5). 14.95 *(978-1-4773-1127-1(0))* Univ. of Texas Pr.

Hill, Eveline. Hugo & Oscar Go Travelling: Continuing the Adventures of Hugo & Oscar. 2012. (Illus.). 52p. pap. 27.45 *(978-1-4772-2733-6(4))* AuthorHouse.

Hirota, Denise. Little Zippy Duffelbag Goes to France. 2012. 24p. pap. 12.45 *(978-1-4624-0443-8(X),* Inspiring Voices) Author Solutions, LLC.

Hobbie, Holly. Toot & Puddle. (Toot & Puddle Ser.: 1). (ENG., Illus.). 32p. (J). (gr. -1-3). 2010. 8.99 *(978-0-316-08080-4(2))* 2007. 18.99 *(978-0-316-16702-4(9))* Little, Brown Bks. for Young Readers.

Hobbs, Leigh. Mr Chicken Arriva a Roma. 2017. (Mr Chicken Ser.). (ENG., Illus.). 32p. (J). (gr. -1-3). 18.99 *(978-1-925266-77-1(X))* Allen & Unwin AUS. Dist: Independent Pubs. Group.

Hobbs, Will. Changes in Latitudes. 2004. (ENG.). 176p. (YA). (gr. 7). pap. 9.95 *(978-0-689-87069-9(8),* Simon Pulse) Simon Pulse.

Hoffman, Amalia. Klezmer Bunch. 2009. (ENG.). 36p. 15.95 *(978-965-229-447-0(0))* Gefen Publishing Hse., Ltd ISR. Dist: Strauss Consultants.

Hoffman, Mary Ann. Elbert Takes a Trip, 1 vol. 2006. (Neighborhood Readers Ser.). (ENG., Illus.). 12p. (gr. 1-2). pap. 5.90 *(978-1-4042-6847-0(2),* 63f8bd14-9afd-4550-accd-46efdd3dcaee, Rosen Classroom) Rosen Publishing Group, Inc., The.

Hofmeister, Alan, et al. A Trip. (Reading for All Learners Ser.). (Illus.). (J). pap. *(978-1-56861-130-3(7))* Swift Learning Resources.

Hooray for Boys & Girls! 2006. (J). 15.95 *(978-0-9776837-0-3(2))* West Woods Pr.

Hubbard, Kirsten. Wanderlove. 2013. (ENG.). 352p. (YA). (gr. 9). pap. 9.99 *(978-0-385-73938-2(9),* Ember) Random Hse. Children's Bks.

Hudson, Cheryl Willis. Sights I Love to See. 2009. 24p. 3.99 *(978-1-60349-009-2(4),* Marimba Bks.) Just Us Bks., Inc.

Hunter, K. N. Hollow: N2 the Hollow World. 2008. 62p. pap. 16.95 *(978-1-4241-0220-4(0))* PublishAmerica, Inc.

I Am A Dog. 2008. (Illus.). 26p. 24.95 *(978-0-9801054-0-7(4))* Teahouse of Danger.

Inzer, Christine Mari. Diary of a Tokyo Teen: A Japanese-American Girl Travels to the Land of Trendy Fashion, High-Tech Toilets & Maid Cafes. 2016. (Illus.). 128p. (gr. 6-12). pap. 14.99 *(978-4-8053-1396-1(X))* Tuttle Publishing.

Islam, M. N. Hamza's Journey of a Lifetime. 2012. 124p. pap. *(978-1-909395-70-1(6))* Legend Pr.

Jackson, Ciandress. Chloe the Jumbo Jet: A Problem of Olympic Proportions. 2012. 26p. (-18). pap. 8.99 *(978-1-61286-131-9(8))* Avid Readers Publishing Group.

Jacquemain, Patti. Journey of the Great Bear: Through California's Golden Past. Jacquemain, Patti, illus. 2006. (Illus.). (J). *(978-0-929702-10-0(7))* Mission Creek Studios.

Jebiwool Art Museum Staff. Destination Blackbeard: Destinations in Time, Book 2, 1 vol. 2009. 101p. pap. 19.95 *(978-1-60749-626-7(7))* America Star Bks.

Jofre, Paola. Lilliput Blasts Off! 2010. 36p. 17.50 *(978-1-4490-7450-0(2))* AuthorHouse.

Johnson, Mary Victoria. Golden. 2017. (Summer Road Trip Ser.). (ENG.). 184p. (YA). (gr. 5-12). 31.42 *(978-1-68076-722-3(4),* 27437, Epic Escape) EPIC Pr.

Johnston-Thomas, Lee Ann. The Hidden Treasure of the Forgotten Pharaoh. 2008. 136p. 21.95 *(978-0-595-71157-4(X));* pap. 11.95 *(978-0-595-47552-0(3))* iUniverse, Inc.

Jones, V. C. Anna Banana Goes to Louisiana. 2010. 16p. 8.49 *(978-1-4490-8390-8(0))* AuthorHouse.

Joy, Brenda. Kaweah's Journey to New Mexico. 2005. 57p. pap. 16.95 *(978-1-4137-9549-3(8))* America Star Bks.

Jules. Bubble's World: Book Four Enchanted England. 2010. 40p. 16.99 *(978-1-4520-5407-0(X))* AuthorHouse.

Kent, Elizabeth. The Enchanted Adventures of the Caroline Kemps. 2007. 148p. pap. 24.95 *(978-1-4241-9915-0(8))* America Star Bks.

Kincaid, Tracy. The Adventures of Casey the Lost Suitcase. 2007. (Illus.). 32p. (J). (gr. -1-3). 16.95 *(978-0-929915-67-8(4))* Headline Bks., Inc.

King, Philip. Bluey, the Little Drip. King, Janet, illus. 2011. 40p. pap. 14.95 *(978-1-60976-661-0(X),* Eloquent Bks.) Strategic Book Publishing & Rights Agency (SBPRA).

Knight, Grover. Ahzar's Travels & Life Lessons - Meet Ahzar: Book One. 2003. (Illus.). 40p. (J). 16.95 *(978-0-9746130-0-0(2))* Ahzar's Bk. Co. Publishing.

Kostecki-Shaw, Jenny Sue. Papa Brings Me the World. Kostecki-Shaw, Jenny Sue, illus. 2020. (ENG., Illus.). 40p. (J). 18.99 *(978-1-250-15925-0(3),* 900185620, Holt, Henry & Co. Bks. For Young Readers) Holt, Henry & Co.

Kovacs, Deborah. Catie Copley's Great Escape. Williams, Jared T., illus. 2009. (ENG.). 32p. (J). (gr. -1-3). 17.95 *(978-1-56792-379-7(8))* Godine, David R. Pub.

Kurchinski, Alessandra. Disney Story. 2010. 36p. pap. 17.30 *(978-0-557-25447-7(7))* Lulu Pr., Inc.

Laberje, Reji. Max Explores Chicago. Fenech, Liza, illus. 2014. (Max Explores Ser.). (ENG.). 20p. (J). (— 1). bds. 9.95 *(978-1-62937-003-3(7))* Triumph Bks.

—Max Explores New York. Fenech, Liza, illus. 2014. (Max Explores Ser.). (ENG.). 20p. (J). (— 1). bds. 9.95 *(978-1-62937-004-0(5))* Triumph Bks.

—Max Explores San Francisco. Fenech, Liza, illus. 2014. (Max Explores Ser.). (ENG.). 20p. (J). (— 1). bds. 9.95 *(978-1-62937-005-7(3))* Triumph Bks.

Langen, Annette. Felix Explores Planet Earth. Droop, Constanza, illus. 2004. (Perfect for Earth Day Promotions! Ser.). 47p. (J). 14.99 *(978-1-59384-030-3(6))* Parklane Publishing.

Lay, Kathryn. The Curse of Time. Bardin, Dave, illus. 2016. (Time Twisters Ser.). (ENG.). 112p. (J). (gr. 2-5). lib. bdg. 38.50 *(978-1-62402-179-4(4),* 24537, Calico Chapter Bks.) ABDO Publishing Co.

—Haunted Time. Bardin, Dave, illus. 2016. (Time Twisters Ser.). (ENG.). 112p. (J). (gr. 2-5). lib. bdg. 38.50 *(978-1-62402-178-7(6),* 24535, Calico Chapter Bks.) ABDO Publishing Co.

—Time & Space. Bardin, Dave, illus. 2016. (Time Twisters Ser.). (ENG.). 112p. (J). (gr. 2-5). lib. bdg. 38.50 *(978-1-62402-177-0(8),* 24533, Calico Chapter Bks.) ABDO Publishing Co.

Le Guin, Ursula K. Tom Mouse. 2004. (Illus.). (J). (gr. k-3). spiral bd. *(978-0-616-14584-5(5))* Canadian National Institute for the Blind/Institut National Canadien pour les Aveugles.

Learning Company Books Staff, ed. Westward Bound! 2004. (Oregon Trail Adventures Ser.). (Illus.). 96p. (J). pap. *(978-0-7630-7724-2(0))* Magma.

Leckey, Carl. Pop up & Go. 2012. (Illus.). 176p. (gr. -1). 30.51 *(978-1-4685-7851-5(0));* pap. 18.24 *(978-1-4685-7852-2(9))* AuthorHouse.

Lewis, J. Patrick & Zappitello, Beth. First Dog. Bowers, Tim, illus. 2009. (ENG.). 32p. (J). (gr. 1-4). 15.95 *(978-1-58536-467-1(3),* 202187) Sleeping Bear Pr.

Lewis, K. s. & Lewis, K. S. Happiness: A Charlie Travel Adventure Story. 2009. (ENG.). 24p. 21.20 *(978-0-557-12094-9(2))* Lulu Pr., Inc.

Loesch, Joe. The Tuskegee Airmen: Raiders of the Skies with Buffalo Biff & Farley's Raiders. Hutchinson, Cheryl, ed. 2004. (Backyard Adventure Ser.). (Illus.). 56p. (J). bds. 16.95 incl. audio compact disk *(978-1-932332-27-8(8))* Toy Box Productions.

London, Olivia. Welcome to Equestria! 2013. (My Little Pony 8X8 Picture Bks.). (J). lib. bdg. 13.55 *(978-0-606-31731-3(7))* Turtleback.

Lopez, Sixto. Snarloff Duwaki's Adventures. 2011. 24p. pap. 24.95 *(978-1-4626-2557-4(6))* America Star Bks.

Lorraine. The Adventures of Ruthy: Ruthy Gets Lost. 2012. 32p. pap. 19.99 *(978-1-4772-6000-5(5))* AuthorHouse.

Lowery, Mark. Charlie & Me: 421 Miles from Home. 2018. (ENG.). 320p. (J). (gr. 4-9). 16.99 *(978-1-4998-0756-1(2),* Yellow Jacket) Bonnier Publishing USA.

Luedtke, Courtney. Baby Boo: The Happy Beginning. 2009. (Illus.). 72p. pap. 27.49 *(978-1-4389-2696-4(0))* AuthorHouse.

Lund, Celia. Square Sails & Dragons. 2006. 284p. per. 19.95 *(978-1-4120-5758-5(2))* Trafford Publishing.

Lund, Deb. All Aboard the Dinotrain. Fine, Howard, illus. 2009. (ENG.). 40p. (J). (gr. -1-3). pap. 9.99 *(978-0-547-24825-7(3),* 1100733, Clarion Bks.) HarperCollins Pubs.

—All Aboard the Dinotrain Board Book. Fine, Howard, illus. 2011. (ENG.). 30p. (J). (gr. -1 — 1). bds. 7.99 *(978-0-547-55415-0(X),* 1452006, Clarion Bks.) HarperCollins Pubs.

Maldonado, Cristina Falcon. 1, 2, 3 Suddenly in Brazil: The Ribbons of Bonfim. Fabrega, Marta, illus. 2011. (1, 2, 3 Suddenly In... Ser.). (ENG.). 35p. (J). (gr. 1-3). 22.44 *(978-0-7641-4582-7(7),* B.E.S. Publishing) Peterson's.

Malone, Jen. Wanderlost. 2016. (ENG.). 352p. (YA). (gr. 9). pap. 10.99 *(978-0-06-238015-9(X),* HarperTeen) HarperCollins Pubs.

Mancuso, Jackie Clark. Hudson in Provence. l.t. ed. 2015. (Paris-Chien Adventure Ser.: 2). (ENG., Illus.). 32p. (J). (gr. k-2). 17.95 *(978-0-9886058-4-8(8))* La Librairie Parisienne.

—Paris-Chien: Adventures of an Expat Dog. 2013. (Paris-Chien Adventure Ser.: 1). (ENG., Illus.). 32p. (J). (gr. k-2). 17.95 *(978-0-615-54542-4(4))* La Librairie Parisienne.

Manzano, Sonia. No Dogs Allowed! Muth, Jon J., illus. 2004. (ENG.). 32p. (J). (gr. -1-2). 19.99 *(978-0-689-83088-4(2),* Atheneum Bks. for Young Readers) Simon & Schuster Children's Publishing.

Marsh, Carole. The Curse of the Ancient Acropolis: Athens, Greece. 2008. (Carole Marsh Mysteries Ser.). 133p. (J). (gr. 3-5). per. 7.99 *(978-0-635-06470-7(7),* Marsh, Carole Bks.) Gallopade International.

—The Rip-Roaring Mystery on the African Safari, 13. 2009. (Carole Marsh Mysteries: Around the World in 80 Mysteries Ser.). (ENG., Illus.). 123p. (J). (gr. 4-6). 22.44 *(978-0-635-06829-3(X))* Gallopade International.

—The Wild Water Mystery of Niagra Falls, 25. 2009. (Carole Marsh Mysteries: Real Kids, Real Places Ser.). (ENG., Illus.). 146p. (J). (gr. 4-6). 18.69 *(978-0-635-06825-5(7))* Gallopade International.

Martin, Lance. The Little Hermit. 2008. 56p. pap. 14.95 *(978-0-9815573-1-1(7))* Highland Pr.

Mayer, Mercer & Mayer, Gina. On the Go. 2013. (Big Little Critter Ser.: 4). (ENG., Illus.). 96p. (J). 12.95 *(978-1-60746-983-4(9),* Premiere) FastPencil, Inc.

McGovern, DeeDee Jean. The Heartland of Home: Tight Quarters in the City. 2008. 58p. pap. 16.95 *(978-1-60610-058-5(0))* America Star Bks.

McKennon, Tony. You're Moving Where?! 2008. 40p. pap. 18.55 *(978-1-4389-1397-1(4))* AuthorHouse.

Mcleod-Stecy, Tracey. The Stone Guardian. 2011. 144p. (gr. 4-6). pap. 11.95 *(978-1-4620-3954-8(5))* iUniverse, Inc.

McMiller, Theresa R. Bessie Goes All over the World. 2012. 28p. pap. 24.95 *(978-1-4626-9464-8(0))* America Star Bks.

McPherson, Missie & O'Neill, Elizabeth. Alfred Visits Washington, D. C. 2005. (ENG., Illus.). 24p. (J). (gr. -1-3). pap. 12.00 *(978-0-9771836-1-6(0))* Funny Bone Bks.

Medina, Sylvia M. & Ballock-Dixon, Saige J. Jade Elephant. Eagle, Joy, illus. 2012. 36p. pap. 11.49 *(978-0-9836602-4-8(7))* Green Kids Club, Inc.

Mims-Word, Marsha. The Great Vacation. 2011. 36p. pap. 21.99 *(978-1-4568-9675-1(X))* Xlibris Corp.

Miner, Deb. I get Around. Miner, Deb, illus. 2007. (ENG., Illus.). 32p. (J). bds. 11.00 *(978-0-9794262-0-9(0))* do be you.

Mitchell, Jack. The Ancient Ocean Blues. 2008. 200p. (J). (gr. 5-8). pap. 9.95 *(978-0-88776-832-3(6),* Tundra Bks.) Tundra Bks. CAN. Dist: Penguin Random Hse. LLC.

Mitchell, Julie & Rinkel, Ken. Slow down, Mrs. Brown! 2008. (Rigby Focus Forward: Level F Ser.). (Illus.). 24p. (J). (gr. 4-7). pap. *(978-1-4190-3700-9(5),* Rigby) Pearson Education Australia.

Mitchell, Trish. Noah Pals: Journey to the Apple Tree. 2011. 32p. pap. 16.99 *(978-1-4567-9939-7(8))* AuthorHouse.

Miyakoshi, Akiko. I Dream of a Journey. Miyakoshi, Akiko, illus. 2020. (ENG., Illus.). 32p. (J). (gr. -1-3). 16.99 *(978-1-5253-0478-1(X))* Kids Can Pr., Ltd. CAN. Dist: Hachette Bk. Group.

Montague, Chester. Timmy's Vacation. 2008. 40p. pap. 24.95 *(978-1-60441-225-3(9))* America Star Bks.

Montes, Marisa. Get Ready for Gabi No. 5: All in the Familia. Cepeda, Joe, illus. 2004. (ENG.). 112p. (J). (gr. 2-5). pap. *(978-0-439-66156-0(0),* Scholastic Paperbacks) Scholastic, Inc.

Morrill, Lauren. Meant to Be. 2014. (ENG.). 304p. (YA). (gr. 7). pap. 9.99 *(978-0-385-74178-1(2),* Ember) Random Hse. Children's Bks.

Mullican, Judy. Let's Take a Ride. Gillen, Lisa P., illus. l.t. ed. 2004. (HRL Little Book Ser.). (J). (gr. -1-k). pap. 10.95 *(978-1-57332-319-2(5));* pap. 10.95 *(978-1-57332-318-5(7))* Carson-Dellosa Publishing, LLC. (HighReach Learning, Incorporated).

Murray, Scott. Granny's Christmas Blunder. 2012. 28p. pap. 18.00 *(978-1-4772-0990-5(5))* AuthorHouse.

Newcomb, Kristene. Molly Q's Trash Travels Through the Water Cycle. Paschall, Patricia, ed. Newcomb, Kristene, illus. 2007. (Illus.). 32p. (J). per. 8.00 *(978-0-9760790-9-5(7))* Folsom Fallies Pr.

North, Merry. My Vacation: Picture, Play, & Tote. 2003. (Picture, Play & Tote-Book Ser.). (Illus.). 10p. (J). (gr. -1-18). bds. 5.99 *(978-1-57151-720-3(0))* Playhouse Publishing.

O'Connor, Jane & Glasser, Robin Preiss. Fancy Nancy: Girl on the Go: a Doodle & Draw Book. 2012. (Fancy Nancy Ser.). (ENG., Illus.). 64p. (J). (gr. -1-3). pap. 6.99 *(978-0-06-188282-1(8),* HarperFestival) HarperCollins Pubs.

O'Dell, Kathryn L. From Wagon to Train. Chalk, Chris, illus. 2017. (Text Connections Guided Close Reading Ser.). (J). (gr. 2). *(978-1-4900-1854-6(9))* Benchmark Education Co.

O'Neill, Elizabeth. Alfred Visits Georgia. 2007. (Illus.). 24p. (gr. -1-3). pap. 12.00 *(978-0-9799121-0-8(5))* Funny Bone Bks.

—Alfred Visits Hawaii. 2009. 24p. (J). pap. 12.00 *(978-0-9822288-5-2(6))* Funny Bone Bks.

—Alfred Visits Maine. 2008. (Illus.). 24p. (J). pap. 12.00 *(978-0-9799121-3-9(X))* Funny Bone Bks.

—Alfred Visits Minnesota. 2007. (Illus.). 24p. (J). pap. 12.00 *(978-0-9799121-2-2(1))* Funny Bone Bks.

—Alfred Visits Missouri. 2008. 24p. (J). pap. 12.00 *(978-0-9799121-4-6(8))* Funny Bone Bks.

—Alfred Visits Montana. 2009. 24p. pap. 12.00 *(978-0-9822288-6-9(4))* Funny Bone Bks.

—Alfred Visits Nevada. 2007. (ENG., Illus.). 24p. (J). pap. 12.00 *(978-0-9799121-1-5(3))* Funny Bone Bks.

—Alfred Visits New Jersey. 2007. 24p. (J). pap. 12.00 *(978-0-9790240-7-8(2))* Funny Bone Bks.

—Alfred Visits Rhode Island. 2007. (Illus.). 24p. (J). pap. 12.00 *(978-0-9790240-6-1(4))* Funny Bone Bks.

—Alfred Visits Texas. 2007. 24p. (J). pap. 12.00 *(978-0-9790240-9-2(9))* Funny Bone Bks.

—Alfred Visits Utah. 2009. 24p. (J). pap. 12.00 *(978-0-9822288-3-8(X))* Funny Bone Bks.

—Alfred Visits Washington State. 2009. 24p. (J). pap. 12.00 *(978-0-9822288-4-5(8))* Funny Bone Bks.

Oneill, Elizabeth. Alfred Visits West Virginia. 2009. 24p. (J). pap. 12.00 *(978-0-9822288-2-1(1))* Funny Bone Bks.

—Alfred Visits Wyoming. 2008. 24p. (J). pap. 12.00 *(978-0-9822288-1-4(3))* Funny Bone Bks.

O'Reilly, Basha. Count Pompeii - Stallion of the Steppes. 2005. (Illus.). pap. 9.99 *(978-1-59048-007-6(4))* Long Riders' Guild Pr., The.

Otis, James. Ruth of Boston: A story of the Massachusetts Bay Colony. 2007. 140p. per. 9.95 *(978-0-9790876-3-9(5))* Living Bks. Pr.

Owens, L. L. The Longest Car Ride Ever. Tolson, Scott, illus. 2004. 28p. *(978-1-57021-032-7(2))* Comprehensive Health Education Foundation.

Page, Cecelia Frances. Phenomenal Experiences. 2007. 144p. per. 11.95 *(978-0-595-46360-2(6))* iUniverse, Inc.

Parker, Sandy. What Month Is It? Hofner, Cathy, illus. l.t. ed. 2004. 32p. (J). 15.95 *(978-0-9643462-5-3(7),* Just Think Bks.) Canary Connect Pubns.

Pati, Geeta. Finny's Voyage Through the Universe: The. 2005. (ENG.). 64p. per. 10.95 *(978-1-59526-019-2(6))* Aeon Publishing Inc.

Pattison, Darcy. The Journey of Oliver K. Woodman. Cepeda, Joe, illus. 2009. (ENG.). 52p. (J). (gr. -1-3). pap. 8.99 *(978-0-15-206118-0(5),* 1099013, Clarion Bks.) HarperCollins Pubs.

Paulsen, Gary. The Car. 2006. (ENG., Illus.). 192p. (YA). (gr. 7-12). pap. 9.99 *(978-0-15-205827-2(3),* 253004, Clarion Bks.) HarperCollins Pubs.

—The Car. 2006. 182p. (gr. 7-12). 17.00 *(978-0-7569-6685-0(X))* Perfection Learning Corp.

Payne, Rachel. Summer of Circles & Sapphires: Iggy Colvin Adventure Series. 2003. 194p. 23.95 *(978-0-595-74705-4(1));* pap. 13.95 *(978-0-595-27915-9(5))* iUniverse, Inc.

Penn, Linda M. Is Kentucky in the Sky? 2012. 36p. pap. 9.95 *(978-0-9852488-0-2(7))* Linda M. Penn Author.

Perry, Shelly. Duckling's First Adventure. Loebel, Bonnie, illus. 2006. (ENG.). 56p. (J). per. 9.95 *(978-0-9787740-3-5(5))* Peppertree Pr., The.

Pla, Sally J. The Someday Birds. McLaughlin, Julie, illus. 2018. (ENG.). 352p. (J). (gr. 3-7). pap. 6.99 *(978-0-06-244577-3(4),* HarperCollins) HarperCollins Pubs.
—The Someday Birds. 2017. (ENG., Illus.). 336p. (J). (gr. 3-7). 16.99 *(978-0-06-244576-6(6),* HarperCollins) HarperCollins Pubs.
Player, Micah. Lately Lily ABC Travel Flash Cards. 2014. (Lately Lily Ser.). (ENG., Illus.). 26p. (J). (gr. -1-17). 14.99 *(978-1-4521-1524-5(9))* Chronicle Bks. LLC.
Ponnay, Brenda & Ponnay, Brenda. Secret Agent Josephine in Paris. 2013. 32p. pap. 9.99 *(978-1-62395-552-6(1))* Xist Publishing.
Potter, Ellen. Piper Green & the Fairy Tree: Going Places. Leng, Qin, illus. 2017. (Piper Green & the Fairy Tree Ser.). (ENG.). (J). (gr. 2-4). 20.95 *(978-1-4301-2680-5(9))* Live Oak Media.
—Piper Green & the Fairy Tree: Going Places. Leng, Qin, illus. 2017. (Piper Green & the Fairy Tree Ser.: 4). (ENG.). 128p. (J). (gr. 2-4). lib. bdg. 17.99 *(978-1-101-93962-8(1),* Knopf Bks. for Young Readers) Random Hse. Children's Bks.
Powell, Gail. The Adventures of Harold J. Kat. 2008. 40p. pap. 16.99 *(978-1-4259-6334-7(X))* AuthorHouse.
Priceman, Marjorie. How to Make a Cherry Pie & See the U. S. A. Priceman, Marjorie, illus. 2013. (Illus.). 40p. (J). (gr. k-3). 8.99 *(978-0-385-75293-0(8),* Dragonfly Bks.) Random Hse. Children's Bks.
Rangel, Graciela. Anthony's Christmas Journey. 2006. (ENG.). 80p. pap. 9.95 *(978-1-59526-650-7(X),* Llumina Christian Bks.) Aeon Publishing Inc.
Raphael, Akili & Lewis, Harriet. Malik & the Malaria-Carrying Mosquito. 2012. 32p. pap. 19.99 *(978-1-4772-8813-9(9))* AuthorHouse.
—Malik Says, Turn off the Water! 2012. 36p. pap. 20.99 *(978-1-4772-9541-0(0))* AuthorHouse.
Rapoport, Cindy. The Adventures of Poca & Flea Bert. 2008. 64p. pap. 19.95 *(978-1-60672-901-4(2))* America Star Bks.
Reece, Eva. The Boinking Bubble MacHine. Davis, Shelley L. A., illus. 2013. 24p. pap. 12.99 *(978-0-9886360-2-6(6))* Kids At Heart Publishing, LLC.
Rey, H. A. Curious George Travel Activity Kit. 2010. (Curious George Ser.). (ENG., Illus.). 64p. (J). (gr. -1-3). pap. 12.99 *(978-0-547-25875-1(5),* 1402329, Clarion Bks.) HarperCollins Pubs.
Rigby Education Staff. The Island of Wingo. (Sails Literacy Ser.). (Illus.). 16p. (gr. 2-3). 27.00 *(978-0-7635-9946-1(8),* 699468C99) Rigby Education.
Riordan, Betty J. The Imaginary Journeys of Bj & Dobbin. 2008. 108p. pap. 11.99 *(978-1-60647-432-7(4))* Salem Author Services.
Ripley's Believe It Or Not! Ripley's Bureau of Investigation 7: Shock Horror, 7. 2010. (Rbi Ser.: 7). (ENG.). 128p. (J). (gr. 2-5). pap. 4.99 *(978-1-893951-58-7(8))* Ripley Entertainment, Inc.
Roberts, Sheena. We All Go Traveling By. Bell, Siobhan, illus. 2004. (ENG.). 24p. (J). pap. 9.99 *(978-1-84148-410-5(5))* Barefoot Bks., Inc.
Roberts, Willo Davis. What Could Go Wrong? 2012. (ENG., Illus.). 176p. (J). (gr. 3-7). reprint ed. pap. 9.99 *(978-0-689-71690-4(7),* Simon & Schuster/Paula Wiseman Bks.) Simon & Schuster/Paula Wiseman Bks.
Rogers, Carol J. The Adventures of Buttonbals' Trails. 2012. 28p. pap. 19.99 *(978-1-4772-4481-4(6))* AuthorHouse.
Ruellan, Susan. The Lost Treasure of Finistere. 2008. (ENG & FRE., Illus.). 83p. (J). (gr. 4-7). pap. 9.95 *(978-1-933916-24-8(9))* Nelson Publishing & Marketing.
Runholt, Susan. The Mystery of the Third Lucretia. 2009. (Kari & Lucas Mystery Ser.: 1). (ENG.). 304p. (J). (gr. 5-18). pap. 6.99 *(978-0-14-241338-8(0),* Puffin Books) Penguin Young Readers Group.
Saha, Tulika. 'Kosho & Sid on the Rainbow' 2014. 22p. pap. 13.99 *(978-1-4828-1762-1(4))* Partridge Pub.
Samoun, Abigail. How Hippo Says Hello! Watts, Sarah, illus. 2014. (Little Traveler Ser.). 22p. (J). (gr. -1-k). bds. 6.95 *(978-1-4549-0820-3(3))* Sterling Publishing Co., Inc.
Santillo, LuAnn. The Trip. Santillo, LuAnn, ed. 2003. (Half-Pint Kids Readers Ser.). (Illus.). 7p. (J). (gr. -1-1). pap. 1.00 *(978-1-59256-057-8(1))* Half-Pint Kids, Inc.
Sayle, Stephen. Cam & Zara the Travel Bugs. 2011. (ENG.). 20p. 11.70 *(978-1-105-42214-0(3))* Lulu Pr., Inc.
—Cam & Zara the Travel Bugs: Egypt. 2011. 36p. pap. 15.25 *(978-1-4567-6978-9(2))* AuthorHouse.
Scala, Vincent. Beep Beep Goes the Bus Driver, 1 vol. 2013. (ENG., Illus.). 32p. (J). (gr. -1-3). 16.99 *(978-0-7643-4493-0(5),* 4934) Schiffer Publishing, Ltd.
Scherer, Catherine W. Simon & Barklee in China, Book 2 - the Mountains. 2008. (Another Country Calling Ser.). (J). per. 15.00 *(978-0-9714502-7-1(7),* Explorer Media) Simon & Barklee, Inc./ExplorerMedia.
—Simon & Barklee in China, Book 3 - the North. 2008. (Another Country Calling Ser.). (J). per. 15.00 *(978-0-9714502-8-8(5),* Explorer Media) Simon & Barklee, Inc./ExplorerMedia.
Schomer-Wendel, Gretchen & Schomer, Adam Anthony. Becka Goes to the North Pole, 1 vol. Renthrope, Damon, illus. 2009. (Becka & the Big Bubble Ser.). (ENG.). 32p. (J). (gr. 1-2). pap. 11.55 *(978-1-60754-117-2(3),* c00b48e1-07cf-4ffd-b439-e3a8068d929d, Windmill Bks.) Rosen Publishing Group, Inc., The.
Scott, Shirley A. The Adventures of Jack & Dobbie: Traveling Buddies. 2012. 30p. pap. 18.99 *(978-1-4772-7851-2(6))* AuthorHouse.
Sedgwick, Chantele. Interlude. 2018. (Love, Lucas Novel Ser.: 3). (ENG.). 284p. (YA). (gr. 7-13). 16.99 *(978-1-5107-1515-8(0),* Sky Pony Pr.) Skyhorse Publishing Co., Inc.
Seerattan, Tanya. Uncle Noel's Journey to Americ. 2011. 28p. pap. 15.99 *(978-1-4568-3065-6(1))* Xlibris Corp.
Sempe, Goscinny. Las Vacaciones del Pequeno Nicolas. 2003. (SPA., Illus.). 150p. (J). (gr. 5-8). pap. 9.95 *(978-84-204-4813-8(3))* Santillana USA Publishing Co., Inc.
Shea, Therese. A Trip to the White House, 1 vol. 2006. (Neighborhood Readers Ser.). (ENG.). 16p. (gr. 1-2). pap. 6.50 *(978-1-4042-7204-0(6),* e45cdfbc-8f15-4bce-b753-7d66fa6cae83, Rosen Classroom) Rosen Publishing Group, Inc., The.
Shin, Ami & Harris, Jamie. Mice in the City: Around the World. 2018. (Mice in the City Ser.: 0). (Illus.). 40p. (J). (gr. k-3). 19.95 *(978-0-500-65152-0(3),* 565152) Thames & Hudson.
Shirley Russak Wachtel. Howie Rocket — World Traveler-Detective: The Search for the Lovely Precious. 2010. 100p. pap. 9.95 *(978-1-4401-9993-6(0))* iUniverse, Inc.
Shreeve, Elizabeth. Hector Finds a Fortune. Levy, Pamela R., illus. 2004. 68p. (J). lib. bdg. 15.00 *(978-1-4242-0903-3(X))* Fitzgerald Bks.
—Hector Finds a Fortune. Levy, Pamela R., illus. 2004. (Adventures of Hector Fuller Ser.). 68p. (J). (gr. 1-4). 11.65 *(978-0-7569-5527-4(0))* Perfection Learning Corp.
Shrum, Brianna R. How to Make Out. (ENG.). (gr. 6-12). 2018. 296p. (YA). pap. 9.99 *(978-1-5107-3204-9(7))* 2016. 284p. (J). 16.99 *(978-1-5107-0167-0(2))* Skyhorse Publishing Co., Inc. (Sky Pony Pr.).
Simpson, Wanda. Sammy, the Earth Traveling Turtle, 1 vol. 2010. 16p. pap. 24.95 *(978-1-4489-9844-9(1))* PublishAmerica, Inc.
Smith, Jeff & Robertson, Barry. Pirates of the 'I Don't Care'-Ibbean: A Kids' Musical about Storing up Treasures in Heaven. 2007. (ENG.). 104p. pap. 7.99 *(978-0-8341-7595-2(9),* 0834175959) Lillenas Publishing Co.
Smith, Jennifer E. Field Notes on Love. 2020. (ENG.). 288p. (YA). (gr. 7). pap. 10.99 *(978-0-399-55944-0(2),* Ember) Random Hse. Children's Bks.
Smith, Vicki. Jamaican Adventure with Tori & Paul. 2012. (ENG., Illus.). 24p. (J). pap. 13.95 *(978-1-4327-8578-9(8))* Outskirts Pr., Inc.
Southall, Donna. The Bubble Trailer. 2004. (J). 15.00 *(978-0-8059-6585-8(8))* Dorrance Publishing Co., Inc.
Stanek, Robert, pseud. Journey Beyond the Beyond. 2007. (ENG., Illus.). 156p. (J). 18.95 *(978-1-57545-133-6(6))* RP Media.
Stewart, Dianne C. Longitude - Zero Degrees. 2009. (ENG.). 200p. pap. 8.95 *(978-0-9667359-4-9(3),* BeanPole Bks.) OH Industries.
Still, Cynthia W. Gypsy Travels the World. 2012. 48p. pap. 21.99 *(978-1-4685-5839-5(0))* AuthorHouse.
Stilton, Gerónimo. The Race Across America. 2009. (Geronimo Stilton Ser.: 37). lib. bdg. 18.40 *(978-0-606-00228-8(6))* Turtleback.
Stilton, Thea. Thea Stilton & the Frozen Fiasco (Thea Stilton #25) A Geronimo Stilton Adventure. (Thea Stilton Ser.: 25). (ENG., 176p. (J). (gr. 2-5). 2017. Illus.). pap. 8.99 *(978-1-338-08786-4(X))* 2016. E-Book 5.99 *(978-1-338-08787-1(8))* Scholastic, Inc. (Scholastic Paperbacks).
—Thea Stilton & the Ghost of the Shipwreck (Thea Stilton #3) A Geronimo Stilton Adventure. 2010. (Thea Stilton Ser.: 3). Orig. Title: Il Vascello Fantasma. (ENG., Illus.). 176p. (J). (gr. 2-5). pap. 8.99 *(978-0-545-15059-0(0),* Scholastic Paperbacks) Scholastic, Inc.
Stockdale, Stephanie. Sidney Visits Australi. 2009. 44p. pap. 18.99 *(978-1-4389-8698-2(X))* AuthorHouse.
Sundstrom, Dainel H. The Return of Oz. 2007. pap. 10.00 *(978-0-8059-8944-1(7))* Dorrance Publishing Co., Inc.
Szymanski, Lois K. The True Story of Sea Feather, 1 vol. 2010. (ENG., Illus.). 48p. (gr. 3-6). pap. 14.99 *(978-0-7643-3609-6(6),* 4019) Schiffer Publishing, Ltd.
Takara, Kathryn Waddell. Timmy Turtle Teaches. Driver, Audrey, illus. 2012. 54p. pap. 29.95 *(978-0-9840204-3-0(8))* Pacific Raven Pr.
Taylor, Pearl Fleming. Snowbird Weenie, 1 vol. 2009. 59p. pap. 16.95 *(978-1-60836-745-0(2))* America Star Bks.
Tillis, Doris. Rudy the Rabbit. Tillis, Carrie, illus. 2005. 32p. per. 17.95 *(978-1-58961-410-9(0))* PageFree Publishing, Inc.
Time, Nicholas O. Stay a Spell. 2016. (In Due Time Ser.: 2). lib. bdg. 17.20 *(978-0-606-38986-0(5))* Turtleback.
Tolan, Stephanie S. & Tolan, R. J. Applewhites Coast to Coast. 2017. (ENG.). 320p. (J). (gr. 3-7). 16.99 *(978-0-06-213320-5(9),* HarperCollins) HarperCollins Pubs.
Travis, Lisa. Mystery of the Troubled Toucan. Diller, Janelle, ed. Turner, Adam, illus. 2015. (Pack-N-Go Girls Adventures - Brazil 1 Ser.). (ENG.). 128p. (J). (gr. 1-3). pap. 5.99 *(978-1-936376-24-7(5))* WorldTrek Publishing.
Turnage, Cyndy. A Trip to Washington, D. C. A Capital Idea. Fagan, Martin, illus. 2013. (Reader's Theater Word Plays Ser.). (J). (gr. 1-2). *(978-1-4509-8941-1(1))* Benchmark Education Co.
Uncle Markie. Pigletté & Bobo in Berkeley. 2003. (YA). ring bd. 9.95 *(978-1-933129-07-5(7))* Studio 403.
—Pigletté & Bobo in Kansas City. 2003. (YA). ring bd. 9.95 *(978-1-933129-08-2(5))* Studio 403.
—Pigletté & Bobo in Sud Africa. 2003. (YA). ring bd. 9.95 *(978-1-933129-15-0(8))* Studio 403.
—Pigletté & Bobo Join the Manscouts. 2003. (YA). ring bd. 9.95 *(978-1-933129-05-1(0))* Studio 403.
—Pigletté & Bobo on Safari. 2003. (YA). ring bd. 9.95 *(978-1-933129-16-7(6))* Studio 403.
—Pigletté & Bobo Winter in Zagreb. 2003. (YA). ring bd. 9.95 *(978-1-933129-11-2(5))* Studio 403.
—Pigletté & BoBoTrash Orange County. 2003. (YA). ring bd. 9.95 *(978-1-933129-09-9(3))* Studio 403.
Van Straaten, Harmen. TIM & the FLYING MACHINE. 2008. (ENG.). 28p. (J). (gr. 1-7). 12.95 *(978-1-60136-003-8(7))* Audio Holdings, LLC.
Vancil, Marybelle. Adventures with Macy & the Sneezy, Sneezy Dog: First Adventure: We Visit Indians. 2010. (Illus.). 43p. (J). pap. 23.95 *(978-1-4327-5038-1(0))* Outskirts Pr., Inc.
Vasquez, Elisa Irene. My Little Piggy: A Bilingual English-Spanish Children's Book. 2010. 28p. 14.95 *(978-1-4490-8716-6(7))* AuthorHouse.
Verdick, Elizabeth. On-The-Go Time. Heinlen, Marieka, illus. 2011. (Toddler Tools(r) Ser.). (ENG.). 26p. (J). (— 1). bds. 9.99 *(978-1-57542-379-1(0),* 23791) Free Spirit Publishing Inc.
Vern, Jules. The Adventures of a Special Correspondent. 2009. 180p. pap. 13.95 *(978-1-60664-377-8(0))* Rodgers, Alan Bks.
Vern, Jules, ed. Cinco Semanas en Globo.Tr. of Around the World in Eighty Days. (SPA., Illus.). 142p. (YA). 14.95 *(978-84-7281-102-7(6),* AF1102) Auriga, Ediciones S.A. ESP. Dist: Continental Bk. Co., Inc.
—Cinco Semanas en Globo. 2003. (Advanced Reading Ser.).Tr. of Around the World in Eighty Days. (SPA., Illus.). 240p. (J). 11.95 *(978-84-239-5898-6(1))* Espasa Calpe, S.A. ESP. Dist: Planeta Publishing Corp.
Waldron, Douglas E. Cody Sackett of Montana: Tales of Adventure. 2008. 188p. per. 24.95 *(978-1-4241-9781-1(3))* America Star Bks.
Watt, Fiona. Complete Book of First Experiences. rev. ed. 2011. (First Experiences Ser.). 144p. (J). ring bd. 19.99 *(978-0-7945-2948-2(8),* Usborne) EDC Publishing.
Watts, Tammy E. From Libya to Namibi. 2012. 24p. 24.95 *(978-1-4626-5928-9(4))* America Star Bks.
Wendel, Gretchen Schomer & Schomer, Adam Anthony. Becka & the Big Bubble: Becka Goes to San Diego. Renthrope, Damon, illus. 2008. 32p. (J). (gr. -1-3). 11.99 *(978-1-933754-51-2(6))* Waterside Pr.
Wendel, Gretchen Schomer & Schomer, Adam Anthony. Becka Goes to Chicago. Renthrope, Damon, illus. 2008. (ENG.). 36p. (J). (gr. -1-3). 11.99 *(978-1-933754-52-9(4))* Waterside Publishing.
Weston Woods Staff, creator. Henry Hikes to Fitchburg. 2011. 18.95 *(978-0-439-90696-8(2));* 38.75 *(978-0-439-90698-2(9))* Weston Woods Studios, Inc.
Wheelie, P. Tommy's Triumph: The tales of Tommy the tortoise & Friends. 2009. (Illus.). 28p. pap. 12.49 *(978-1-4389-2718-3(5))* AuthorHouse.
Whint, Ana Lee. Espalemit. 2003. (ENG.). 112p. pap. 9.95 *(978-0-595-26259-5(7),* Writers Club Pr.) iUniverse, Inc.
White-Adams, Beverly. The Adventures of Rusty: Rusty Goes to Maine Vol. 3. 2012. 40p. pap. 19.57 *(978-1-4669-5442-7(6))* Trafford Publishing.
Wightman, Jillian C. The Adventures of Erin Mctavitt. 2008. 68p. pap. 19.95 *(978-1-4327-3164-9(5))* Outskirts Pr., Inc.
Wilhelm, Kj. Grandma Coocoonutts Goes to Boston. 2009. 28p. pap. 15.99 *(978-1-4363-9933-3(5))* Xlibris Corp.
Williams, M. J. Alora & the Howling Guff. 2010. 132p. pap. 10.68 *(978-1-4520-3207-8(6))* AuthorHouse.
Williams, Rozanne Lanczak. Captain Jack's Journal. Grayson, Rick, illus. 2006. (Learn to Write Ser.). 16p. (J). (gr. k-2). pap. 2.99 *(978-1-59198-303-3(7),* 6197) Creative Teaching Pr., Inc.
—Captain Jack's Journal. Maio, Barbara, ed. Grayson, Rick, illus. 2006. (J). per. 8.99 *(978-1-59198-361-3(4))* Creative Teaching Pr., Inc.
—Postcards from Barney Bear. Maio, Barbara & Faulkner, Stacey, eds. Thelen, Mary, illus. 2006. (Learn to Write Ser.). 8p. (J). pap. 3.49 *(978-1-59198-287-6(1),* 6181) Creative Teaching Pr., Inc.
Williams, Will. Dog Called Doogo & His Friends. 2006. (ENG.). 48p. (J). pap. 15.96 *(978-1-84753-901-4(7))* Lulu Pr., Inc.
Wolff, Tracy. Book 1: Crisis. Kinsella, Pat, illus. 2016. (Mars Bound Ser.). (ENG.). 48p. (J). (gr. 3-7). lib. bdg. 34.21 *(978-1-62402-197-8(2),* 24573, Spellbound) Magic Wagon.
Worcester, Daryl D. The Story of the Famous Traves Travlslot. 2006. 48p. pap. 16.95 *(978-1-4241-2417-6(4))* America Star Bks.
Yansky, Brian. My Road Trip to the Pretty Girl Capital of the World. 2003. (ENG.). 160p. (J). 16.95 *(978-0-8126-2691-9(5))* Cricket Bks.
Zachary, Ken. Missions of Big Zach. Waytula, Brian, illus. 2005. 36p. (J). (gr. -1-3). per. 9.95 *(978-1-59879-061-0(7))* Lifevest Publishing, Inc.
Zschock, Martha. Hello, San Francisco! 2012. (Hello Ser.). (ENG., Illus.). 16p. (J). (gr. -1-k). bds. 9.99 *(978-1-933212-65-4(9),* Commonwealth Editions) Applewood Bks.

TRAVEL GAMES

see Games for Travelers

TRAVELERS

see also Explorers

A Yusuf, Ali. Three Travellers to India. 2006. 108p. per. *(978-1-4067-3192-7(7),* Hesperides Pr.) Read Bks.
Albert, Edoardo. Ibn Battuta: The Journey of a Medieval Muslim. 2019. (Concise Life Ser.). (ENG., Illus.). 80p. (J). pap. 9.95 *(978-1-84774-047-2(2))* Kube Publishing Ltd. GBR. Dist: Consortium Bk. Sales & Distribution.
Comerciantes Y Viajeros, 6 vols., Vol. 2. (Explorers. Exploradores Nonfiction Sets Ser.). (SPA.). 32p. (gr. 3-6). 44.95 *(978-0-7699-0647-8(8))* Shortland Pubns. (U. S. A.) Inc.
Cooke, Tim. Explore with Gertrude Bell. 2017. (Travel with the Great Explorers Ser.). (Illus.). 32p. (J). (gr. 4-5). *(978-0-7787-3910-4(4));* pap. *(978-0-7787-3925-8(2))* Crabtree Publishing Co.
Harmon, Daniel E. Ibn Battuta: The Medieval World's Greatest Traveler Throughout Africa, Asia, the Middle East, & Europe, 1 vol. 2016. (Silk Road's Greatest Travelers Ser.). (ENG., Illus.). 112p. (J). (gr. 6-6). lib. bdg. 38.80 *(978-1-5081-7150-8(5),* 237a9da8-4384-49c2-b4d3-ab788ab5893a) Rosen Publishing Group, Inc., The.
McLean, Jacqueline. Women of Adventure. 2003. (Profiles Ser.). (Illus.). 160p. (gr. 5-18). lib. bdg. 19.95 *(978-1-881508-73-1(0))* Oliver Pr., Inc.
Mortensen, Lori. Away with Words: The Daring Story of Isabella Bird. Caldwell, Kristy, illus. 2019. 36p. (J). (gr. 1-4). 17.95 *(978-1-68263-005-1(6))* Peachtree Publishing Co. Inc.
Porterfield, Jason. Marco Polo, 1 vol. 2016. (Silk Road's Greatest Travelers Ser.). (ENG.). 112p. (gr. 6-6). 38.80 *(978-1-5081-7152-2(1),* a388d701-fba5-41e0-bcba-5a0e27a2b525) Rosen Publishing Group, Inc., The.
Stuckey, Rachel. Explore with Ibn Battuta. 2017. (Travel with the Great Explorers Ser.). (Illus.). 32p. (J). (gr. 4-5). *(978-0-7787-3908-1(2));* pap. *(978-0-7787-3924-1(4))* Crabtree Publishing Co.
Toth, Henrietta. Ibn Battuta: The Greatest Traveler of the Muslim World, 1 vol. 2017. (Spotlight on Explorers & Colonization Ser.). (ENG.). 48p. (gr. 6-6). pap. 12.75 *(978-1-5081-7499-8(7),* 7a8e7250-4c64-409b-9ec6-54a1b7b69426, Rosen Young Adult) Rosen Publishing Group, Inc., The.

TRAVELERS—FICTION

Aesop, Aesop. Two Travelers & a Bear. 2012. (J). *(978-1-61913-102-6(1))* Weigl Pubs., Inc.
Fenn, George Manville. Yussuf the Guide or the Mountain Bandits: Being the Strange Story of the Travels in Asia Minor of Burne the Lawyer, Preston the Professor, & Lawrenc. Schönberg, John, illus. 2008. 432p. pap. 16.95 *(978-1-934671-20-7(7))* Salem Ridge Press LLC.
Friedman, J. S. Casablanca. Beatrice, Chris, illus. 2013. (Maurice's Valises Ser.: Vol. 3). (ENG.). 53p. (J). (gr. k-4). 16.95 *(978-94-91613-09-8(X))* Mouse Prints Pr. NLD. Dist: Ingram Publisher Services.
Garis, Howard Roger. Uncle Wiggily's Travels. Date not set. 192p. (J). 20.95 *(978-0-8488-2278-1(1))* Amereon Ltd.
Gentile, Joe. Mysterious Traveler. 2003. (ENG., Illus.). 48p. (gr. 12-18). pap. 5.50 *(978-0-9721668-5-0(8),* 69962463-033c-4c38-aadd-6cd41685080a) Moonstone.
Hunsaker, Joan. A Dagger in Time - the Web of Spies. 2010. 200p. 25.99 *(978-1-58930-247-1(8));* pap. 15.99 *(978-1-58930-248-8(6))* Selah Publishing Group, LLC.
Hunt, Wayne. Zack & the Validators: Good As Gold. 2011. 138p. pap. 19.99 *(978-1-4653-5816-5(1))* Xlibris Corp.
Jackson, Lyn D. The Perilous Journey Home. 2009. 200p. pap. 14.49 *(978-1-4389-4651-1(1))* AuthorHouse.
Joan, Marler. Secrets of the Wind. 2006. pap. *(978-1-888251-37-1(9))* Voice & Vision Pubns.
Lang, Andrew, ed. & compiled by. The Orange Fairy Book. Lang, Andrew, compiled by. 2011. 234p. 27.95 *(978-1-4638-9520-4(8))* Rodgers, Alan Bks.
Mahy, Margaret. Maddigan's Fantasia. 2005. 320p. *(978-1-86950-561-5(1))* HarperCollins Pubs. Australia.
Stokes, Katherine. Motor Maids in Fair Japan. 2006. pap. *(978-1-4068-3090-3(9))* Echo Library.
Webster, Jean. Jerry. 2008. 108p. 22.95 *(978-1-60664-939-8(6))* Aegypan.
Wiggin, Kate Douglas. Penelope Travels Abroad. 2008. 460p. 34.95 *(978-1-60664-818-6(7))* Aegypan.

TRAVELERS—POETRY

Capildeo, Vahni. No Traveller Returns. 2004. (Salt Modern Poets). (ENG.). 184p. pap. *(978-1-876857-88-2(9))* Salt Publishing.

TRAVELS

see Overland Journeys to the Pacific; Scientific Expeditions; Voyages and Travels; Voyages around the World

TRAVESTIES

see Parodies

TRAY GARDENS

see Gardens, Miniature

TREASURE ISLAND (IMAGINARY PLACE)—FICTION

Cole, Bob. Power Reading: Classics/Treasure Island. Lee, Joe, illus. 2004. 94p. (J). (gr. 5-6). vinyl bd. 39.95 *(978-1-883186-59-3(5),* PPCL3) National Reading Styles Institute, Inc.
Dennis, Peter & Rawson, Christopher. Treasure Island. 2004. (Young Reading Ser.). (Illus.). 64p. (J). (gr. 2-18). pap. 5.95 *(978-0-7945-0411-3(6),* Usborne) EDC Publishing.
Francis, Pauline, retold by. Treasure Island. 2010. (Essential Classics - Adventure Ser.). (Illus.). 48p. pap. *(978-0-237-54085-2(1))* Evans Brothers, Ltd.
Fuerst, Jeffrey B. & Benchmark Education Co., LLC. Robert Louis Stevenson's Treasure Island: My Sea Adventure Israel Hands. Hondru, Ovi, illus. 2014. (Text Connections Ser.). (J). (gr. 3). *(978-1-4509-9652-5(3))* Benchmark Education Co.
Publications International Ltd. Staff, ed. Treasure Hunt. 2010. 12p. (J). bds. 9.98 *(978-1-4127-9885-3(X))* Phoenix International Publications, Inc.
Stevenson, Robert Louis. Treasure Island. 2003. (More for Teens Ser.). 64p. (Orig.). (YA). (gr. 6-12). pap. 6.00 *(978-0-88734-412-1(7))* Players Pr., Inc.
—Treasure Island, 1 vol. 2009. (Foundation Classics Ser.). (ENG., Illus.). 56p. (J). (gr. 5-5). lib. bdg. 32.60 *(978-1-60754-543-9(8),* 6b653e76-88e4-4e0d-8b9e-9c203184819d, Windmill Bks.) Rosen Publishing Group, Inc., The.
—Treasure Island. Blum, Alex A., illus. 2015. (Classics Illustrated Ser.: 21). 48p. pap. 9.95 *(978-1-906814-47-2(3))* Classic Comic Store, Ltd. GBR. Dist: Casemate Pubs. & Bk. Distributors, LLC.
—Treasure Island. (Young Collector's Illustrated Classics Ser.). (Illus.). 192p. (J). (gr. 3-7). 9.95 *(978-1-56156-456-9(7))* Kidsbooks, LLC.
—Treasure Island. Todd, Justin, illus. unabr. ed. 2003. (Chrysalis Childrens Classics Ser.). (ENG.). 208p. (YA). pap. *(978-1-84365-037-9(1),* Pavilion Children's Books) Pavilion Bks.
—Treasure Island. Wyeth, N. C., illus. abr. ed. 2003. (Scribner Storybook Classics Ser.). (ENG.). 64p. (J). (gr. 3-7). 21.99 *(978-0-689-85468-2(4),* Atheneum Bks. for Young Readers) Simon & Schuster Children's Publishing.
—Treasure Island: A Classic Story about Responsibility. 2003. (Illus.). 32p. per. 3.95 *(978-0-9747133-4-2(1),* Values to Live By Classic Stories) Thomas, Frederic Inc.
—Treasure Island: With Story of the Treasure of Normon Island. Date not set. (J). (gr. 5-6). reprint ed. lib. bdg. 22.95 *(978-0-89190-236-2(8),* American Reprint Co.) Amereon Ltd.
Stilton, Gerónimo. El Misterio Del Ojo Esmeralda. (SPA., Illus.). 128p. (J). (gr. 3-5). pap. 7.95 *(978-1-59437-453-1(8))* Santillana USA Publishing Co., Inc.
Stratemeyer, Edward. The Rover Boys on Treasure Isle. 2007. 268p. 27.95 *(978-1-4218-4148-9(7));* per. 12.95 *(978-1-4218-4246-2(7))* 1st World Publishing, Inc. (1st World Library - Literary Society).

TREASURE TROVES

see Buried Treasure

TREE HOUSES—FICTION

Adams, Jennifer. Edgar & the Tree House of Usher: Inspired by Edgar Allan Poe's the Fall of the House of Usher, 1 vol. Stucki, Ron, illus. (Edgar the Raven Ser.). (J). 2016. 22p. (— 1). bds. 9.99 *(978-1-4236-4493-4(X))* 2015. (ENG.). 32p. (gr. -1-k). 16.99 *(978-1-4236-4043-1(8))* Gibbs Smith, Publisher.
Apted, Violet. Tommy & Jacqui: Laughing with Kookaburras. 2011. 32p. pap. 13.00 *(978-1-61204-118-6(3),* Eloquent Bks.) Strategic Book Publishing & Rights Agency (SBPRA).
Arena, Felice & Kettle, Phil. The Tree House. Vane, Mitch, illus. 2004. (J). pap. *(978-1-59336-357-4(5))* Mondo Publishing.
Atwood, Margaret. Up in the Tree, 1 vol. 2010. (ENG., Illus.). 32p. (J). (gr. k-k). 19.95 *(978-1-55498-080-2(1))*

T U V

Groundwood Bks. CAN. Dist: Publishers Group West (PGW).
Banning, Gail. Out on a Limb. 2008. (ENG.). 256p. (YA). (gr. 6-9). *(978-1-55470-012-7(4))* Me to We.
Bauer, Carole. The Tree House Kids. 2013. 40p. pap. 15.95 *(978-1-4624-0849-8(4)*, Inspiring Voices) Author Solutions, LLC.
Bishop, Clive. Trophy Trouble. 2009. 74p. pap. 9.99 *(978-1-60860-547-7(7)*, Strategic Bk. Publishing) Strategic Book Publishing & Rights Agency (SBPRA).
Blyton, Enid. Hollow Tree House. 160p. (J). (gr. k-6). pap. 5.95 *(978-0-09-947220-9(1))* Penguin Random Hse. GBR. Dist: Trafalgar Square Publishing.
Bowlin, Serina. Wandering Sam. Thrasher, Brian, illus. 2011. 20p. pap. 9.97 *(978-1-61204-280-0(5)*, Eloquent Bks.) Strategic Book Publishing & Rights Agency (SBPRA).
Brown, Marc. Arthur's Tree House. 2007. (ENG., Illus.). 24p. (J). (gr. -1-1). pap. 3.99 *(978-0-316-05776-9(2))* Little, Brown Bks. for Young Readers.
Burk, Rachelle. Tree House in a Storm. Schneider, Rex, illus. 2009. (ENG.). 42p. (J). (gr. k-4). 16.95 *(978-0-916144-23-4(2))* Stemmer Hse. Pubs.
Dahlstrom, Halene. Raven Cove Mystery: A Rennie of Alaska Mystery. 2003. (YA). pap. 12.95 *(978-1-59433-001-8(8))* Publication Consultants.
Dean, James & Dean, Kimberly. Pete the Cat & the Tip-Top Tree House. Dean, James, illus. 2017. (My First I Can Read Ser.). (ENG., Illus.). 32p. (J). (gr. -1-3). pap. 4.99 *(978-0-06-240431-2(8)*, HarperCollins) HarperCollins Pubs.
Dixon, Joyce Ann. Katie's Tree House. 2009. 48p. pap. 16.95 *(978-1-60836-626-2(X))* America Star Bks.
Durbin, Amanda. Tree Houses & Treasures. 2013. 24p. pap. 24.95 *(978-1-63004-353-7(2))* America Star Bks.
Edwards, Jean E. Adventure Tales: For Kids Who Want to Become Better Readers. 2012. 102p. 24.99 *(978-1-4771-4118-2(9))* Xlibris Corp.
Edwards, Pamela Duncan. Jack & Jill's Treehouse. Cole, Henry & Bond, Felicia, illus. 2008. 24p. (J). (gr. -1-2). lib. bdg. 17.89 *(978-0-06-009078-4(2)*, Tegen, Katherine Bks) HarperCollins Pubs.
Eliot, Ethel Cook. The House above the Trees. 2003. (Illus.). 140p. (J). 20.00 *(978-0-9615961-7-0(1))*; 2nd ed. pap. 12.00 *(978-0-9615961-6-3(3))* Raven Rocks Pr.
Esenwine, Matt Forrest. Flashlight Night. Koehler, Fred, illus. 2017. (ENG.). 32p. (J). (gr. -1-3). 16.95 *(978-1-62979-493-8(7)*, Astra Young Readers) Astra Publishing Hse.
Foster, Marilyn. Moon Tricks. Vega, Alison, illus. 2012. 48p. pap. *(978-1-77097-960-4(3))* FriesenPress.
Garant, Andre J. Jake's Tree House. 2010. 128p. pap. 10.99 *(978-1-4490-8369-4(2))* AuthorHouse.
Graff, Lisa. The Great Treehouse War. 2018. (ENG.). 304p. (J). (gr. 3-7). 8.99 *(978-0-14-751671-8(4)*, Puffin Books) Penguin Young Readers Group.
—The Great Treehouse War. 2018. lib. bdg. 19.65 *(978-0-606-41308-4(1))* Turtleback.
Griffiths, Andy. The 13-Story Treehouse: Monkey Mayhem! Denton, Terry, illus. 2015. (Treehouse Bks.: 1). (ENG.). 272p. (J). (gr. 1-5). pap. 8.99 *(978-1-250-07065-4(1)*, 900148615) Square Fish.
—The 26-Story Treehouse: Pirate Problems! Denton, Terry, illus. 2014. (Treehouse Bks.: 2). (ENG.). 352p. (J). (gr. 1-5). 14.99 *(978-1-250-02691-0(1)*, 900098156) Feiwel & Friends.
—The 39-Story Treehouse: Mean Machines & Mad Professors! Denton, Terry, illus. 2015. (Treehouse Bks.: 3). (ENG.). 352p. (J). (gr. 1-5). 15.99 *(978-1-250-02692-7(X)*, 900098157) Feiwel & Friends.
—The 39-Story Treehouse: Mean Machines & Mad Professors! Denton, Terry, illus. 2016. (Treehouse Bks.: 3). (ENG.). 368p. (J). pap. 8.99 *(978-1-250-07511-6(4)*, 900151529) Square Fish.
—The 52-Story Treehouse. 2017. (Treehouse Adventures Ser.: 4). (J). lib. bdg. 17.20 *(978-0-606-40350-4(7))* Turtleback.
—The 52-Story Treehouse: Vegetable Villains! Denton, Terry, illus. 2016. (Treehouse Bks.: 4). (ENG.). 336p. (J). (gr. 2-5). 17.99 *(978-1-250-02693-4(8)*, 900098158) Feiwel & Friends.
—The 52-Story Treehouse: Vegetable Villains! Denton, Terry, illus. 2017. (Treehouse Bks.: 4). (ENG.). 352p. (J). pap. 8.99 *(978-1-250-10379-6(7)*, 900163638) Square Fish.
—The 65-Story Treehouse: Time Travel Trouble! Denton, Terry, illus. 2018. (Treehouse Bks.: 5). (ENG.). 400p. (J). pap. 8.99 *(978-1-250-10247-8(2)*, 900163128) Square Fish.
—The 78-Story Treehouse: Moo-Vie Madness! Denton, Terry, illus. 2018. (Treehouse Bks.: 6). (ENG.). 384p. (J). 13.99 *(978-1-250-10485-4(8)*, 900164004) Feiwel & Friends.
—The 91-Story Treehouse: Babysitting Blunders! Denton, Terry, illus. 2018. (Treehouse Bks.: 7). (ENG.). 384p. (J). 15.99 *(978-1-250-10488-5(2)*, 900164007) Feiwel & Friends.
—The 91-Story Treehouse: Babysitting Blunders! Denton, Terry, illus. 2022. (Treehouse Bks.: 7). (ENG.). 384p. (J). pap. 8.99 *(978-1-250-10486-1(6)*, 900164008) Square Fish.
—The 104-Story Treehouse: Dental Dramas & Jokes Galore! Denton, Terry, illus. 2019. (Treehouse Bks.: 8). (ENG.). 368p. (J). 14.99 *(978-1-250-30149-9(1)*, 900196710) Feiwel & Friends.
—The 117-Story Treehouse: Dots, Plots & Daring Escapes! Denton, Terry, illus. 2019. (Treehouse Bks.: 9). (ENG.). 384p. (J). 14.99 *(978-1-250-31720-9(7)*, 900199916) Feiwel & Friends.
Guest, Elissa Haden. Iris & Walter. Davenier, Christine, illus. alt. ed. 2012. (Iris & Walter Ser.). (ENG.). 44p. (J). (gr. 1-4). pap. 4.99 *(978-0-547-74555-8(9)*, 1486268, Clarion Bks.) HarperCollins Pubs.
Hibbeler, Stephen Paul. A Wonderful, Magical World. 2006. 48p. pap. 16.95 *(978-1-4241-2631-6(2))* PublishAmerica, Inc.
Higgins, Carter. Everything You Need for a Treehouse: (Children?s Treehouse Book, Story Book for Kids, Nature Book for Kids) Hughes, Emily, illus. 2018. (ENG.). 40p. (J). (gr. -1-k). 17.99 *(978-1-4521-4255-5(6))* Chronicle Bks. LLC.
Hoenecke, Karen. Tree House. Graves, Dennis, illus. 2005. (ENG.). 12p. (gr. k-1). pap. 7.95 *(978-1-57874-090-1(8)*, Kaeden Bks.) Kaeden Corp.
Hughes, Jenny. Audrey's Tree House. Bentley, Jonathan, illus. 2015. (J). pap. *(978-0-545-81405-8(7)*, Scholastic Pr.) Scholastic, Inc.
Kerrin, Jessica Scott. The Better Tree Fort. Leng, Qin, illus. 2018. (ENG.). 32p. E-Book *(978-1-55498-864-8(0))* Groundwood Bks.
Kreidler, Shannon. The Adventures of Sally the Squirrel: Interactive... Educational & Earn Gold Stars. 2013. 28p. pap. 15.99 *(978-1-4797-7674-0(2))* Xlibris Corp.
Lee, Shell. Teenie's Treehouse Adventures: The Magic Begins. 2004. 37p. pap. 24.95 *(978-1-4137-2879-8(0))* PublishAmerica, Inc.
Leyh, Kat. Lumberjanes 9. 2018. (Lumberjanes (Graphic Novels) Ser.: 9). lib. bdg. 26.95 *(978-0-606-41295-7(6))* Turtleback.
London, Jonathan. Froggy Builds a Tree House. 2013. (Froggy Ser.). 32p. (J). (-k). pap. 7.99 *(978-0-14-242533-6(8)*, Puffin Books) Penguin Young Readers Group.
—Froggy Builds a Tree House. 2013. (Froggy Ser.). lib. bdg. 17.20 *(978-0-606-30518-1(1))* Turtleback.
Mercer, M. J. O'No It's Henry. 2010. 24p. 12.99 *(978-1-4520-2125-6(2))* AuthorHouse.
Miyares, Daniel. That Neighbor Kid. Miyares, Daniel, illus. 2017. (ENG., Illus.). 32p. (J). (gr. -1-3). 19.99 *(978-1-4814-4979-3(6)*, Simon & Schuster Bks. For Young Readers) Simon & Schuster Bks. For Young Readers.
Moore, Natascha. Lost Verloren. 2013. 28p. pap. 19.99 *(978-1-4817-0664-3(0))* AuthorHouse.
Munoz, Norma. Los Cuentos de la Casa del Arbol. Olson, John & Olson, Johan, illus. rev. ed. 2005. (Castillo de la Lectura Blanca Ser.). (SPA & ENG.). 72p. (J). (gr. -1-3). pap. 6.95 *(978-970-20-0124-9(2))* Castillo, Ediciones, S. A. de C. V. MEX. Dist: Macmillan.
O'Hagan, William. Anything Else but Me. 2008. 36p. pap. 24.95 *(978-1-60563-701-3(7))* America Star Bks.
Osborne, Mary Pope. Balto of the Blue Dawn. Murdocca, Sal, illus. (Magic Tree House (R) Merlin Mission Ser.: 26). 128p. (J). (gr. 2-5). 2017. 6.99 *(978-0-553-51088-1(6))* 2016. 13.99 *(978-0-553-51085-0(1))* Random Hse. Children's Bks. (Random Hse. Bks. for Young Readers).
—Barcos Vikingos Al Amanecer. Brovelli, Marcela, tr. from ENG. Murdocca, Sal, illus. 2007. (Casa del Arbol Ser.: 15). (SPA.). 73p. (J). per. 6.99 *(978-1-933032-21-4(9))* Lectorum Pubns., Inc.
—A Big Day for Baseball. Ford, A. G., illus. 2017. (Magic Tree House (R) Ser.: 29). (J). (gr. 1-4). 80p. 13.99 *(978-1-5247-1308-9(2))*; (ENG.). 96p. lib. bdg. 16.99 *(978-1-5247-1309-6(0))* Random Hse. Children's Bks. (Random Hse. Bks. for Young Readers).
—Blizzard of the Blue Moon. Murdocca, Sal, illus. 2007. (Magic Tree House (R) Merlin Mission Ser.: 8). 144p. (J). (gr. 2-5). 5.99 *(978-0-375-83038-9(3)*, Random Hse. Bks. for Young Readers) Random Hse. Children's Bks.
—Buffalo Before Breakfast. 2004. (Magic Tree House Ser.: No. 18). 72p. (J). (gr. k-3). pap. 17.00 incl. audio *(978-0-8072-0927-1(9)*, Listening Library) Random Hse. Audio Publishing Group.
—El Caballero Del Alba. 2004. (Casa del Arbol Ser.: 2). (SPA.). (J). pap. 6.99 *(978-1-930332-50-8(5))* Lectorum Pubns., Inc.
—Carnival at Candlelight, Vol. 5. Murdocca, Sal, illus. 2006. (Magic Tree House (R) Merlin Mission Ser.: 5). 144p. (J). (gr. 2-5). 6.99 *(978-0-375-83034-1(0)*, Random Hse. Bks. for Young Readers) Random Hse. Children's Bks.
—Un Castillo Embrujado en la Noche de Halloween. 2015. (Casa De árbol Ser.: 30). (SPA., Illus.). 144p. (J). (gr. 2-4). pap. 6.99 *(978-1-63245-533-8(1))* Lectorum Pubns., Inc.
—Christmas in Camelot. Murdocca, Sal, illus. 2009. (Magic Tree House (R) Merlin Mission Ser.: 1). 144p. (J). (gr. 2-5). 6.99 *(978-0-375-85812-3(1)*, Random Hse. Bks. for Young Readers) Random Hse. Children's Bks.
—Christmas in Camelot. 2009. (Magic Tree House Merlin Missions Ser.: 1). lib. bdg. 16.00 *(978-0-606-06386-9(2))* Turtleback.
—Civil War on Sunday. unabr. ed. 2004. (Magic Tree House Ser.: No. 21). 76p. (J). (gr. k-3). pap. 17.00 incl. audio *(978-0-8072-0930-1(9)*, S FTR 253 SP, Listening Library) Random Hse. Audio Publishing Group.
—A Crazy Day with Cobras. Murdocca, Sal, illus. 2012. (Magic Tree House (R) Merlin Mission Ser.: 17). 144p. (J). (gr. 2-5). 5.99 *(978-0-375-86795-8(3)*, Random Hse. Bks. for Young Readers) Random Hse. Children's Bks.
—A Crazy Day with Cobras. 2012. (Magic Tree House Merlin Missions Ser.: 17). lib. bdg. 16.00 *(978-0-606-26997-1(5))* Turtleback.
—Dark Day in the Deep Sea. Murdocca, Sal, illus. 2009. (Magic Tree House (R) Merlin Mission Ser.: 11). 144p. (J). (gr. 2-5). 6.99 *(978-0-375-83732-6(9)*, Random Hse. Bks. for Young Readers) Random Hse. Children's Bks.
—Dark Day in the Deep Sea. 2009. (Magic Tree House Merlin Missions Ser.: 11). lib. bdg. 16.00 *(978-0-606-01778-7(X))* Turtleback.
—Das magische Baumhaus 09. Der Ruf der Delfine. 18.95 *(978-3-7855-4185-2(6))* Loewe Verlag GmbH DEU. Dist: Distribooks, Inc.
—Day of the Dragon King. unabr. ed. 2004. (Magic Tree House Ser.: No. 14). 68p. (J). (gr. k-3). pap. 17.00 incl. audio *(978-0-8072-0783-3(7)*, S FTR 242 SP, Listening Library) Random Hse. Audio Publishing Group.
—Dinosaurs Before Dark. unabr. ed. 2004. (Magic Tree House Ser.: No. 1). 68p. (J). (gr. k-5). pap. 17.00 incl. audio *(978-0-8072-0330-9(0)*, FTR208SP, Listening Library) Random Hse. Audio Publishing Group.
—Earthquake in the Early Morning. unabr. ed. 2004. (Magic Tree House Ser.: No. 24). 71p. (J). (gr. k-3). pap. 17.00 incl. audio *(978-0-8072-0933-2(3)*, S FTR 256 SP, Listening Library) Random Hse. Audio Publishing Group.
—Eve of the Emperor Penguin. Murdocca, Sal, illus. 2009. (Magic Tree House (R) Merlin Mission Ser.: 12). (ENG.). 144p. (J). (gr. 2-5). 6.99 *(978-0-375-83734-0(5)*, Random Hse. Bks. for Young Readers) Random Hse. Children's Bks.
—Ghost Town at Sundown. unabr. ed. 2004. (Magic Tree House Ser.: No. 10). 73p. (J). (gr. k-3). pap. 17.00 incl. audio *(978-0-8072-0535-8(4)*, Listening Library) Random Hse. Audio Publishing Group.
—Haunted Castle on Hallows Eve. Murdocca, Sal, illus. 2010. (Magic Tree House (R) Merlin Mission Ser.: 2). 144p. (J). (gr. 2-5). pap. 5.99 *(978-0-375-86090-4(8)*, Random Hse. Bks. for Young Readers) Random Hse. Children's Bks.
—Haunted Castle on Hallows Eve. 2010. (Magic Tree House Merlin Missions Ser.: 2). lib. bdg. 16.00 *(978-0-606-13992-2(3))* Turtleback.
—High Tide in Hawaii. Murdocca, Sal, illus. 2003. (Magic Tree House (R) Ser.: 28). 96p. (J). (gr. 1-4). pap. 6.99 *(978-0-375-80616-2(4)*, Random Hse. Bks. for Young Readers) Random Hse. Children's Bks.
—High Tide in Hawaii. 2003. (Magic Tree House Ser.: 28). (gr. k-3). lib. bdg. 16.00 *(978-0-613-62386-5(X))* Turtleback.
—High Time for Heroes. Murdocca, Sal, illus. 2016. (Magic Tree House (R) Merlin Mission Ser.: 23). 144p. (J). (gr. 2-5). 6.99 *(978-0-307-98052-6(9)*, Random Hse. Bks. for Young Readers) Random Hse. Children's Bks.
—La Hora de Los Juegos Olimpicos. Brovelli, Marcela, tr. Murdocca, Sal, illus. 2007. (Casa del Arbol Ser.: 16).Tr. of Hour of the Olympics Games. (ENG & SPA.). 68p. (J). per. 6.99 *(978-1-933032-22-1(7))* Lectorum Pubns., Inc.
—Hour of the Olympics. unabr. ed. 2004. (Magic Tree House Ser.: No. 16). 70p. (J). (gr. k-3). pap. 17.00 incl. audio *(978-0-8072-0785-7(3)*, LFTR 244 SP, Listening Library) Random Hse. Audio Publishing Group.
—Hurricane Heroes in Texas. Ford, A. G., illus. 2018. (Magic Tree House (R) Ser.: 30). 112p. (J). (gr. 1-4). 13.99 *(978-1-5247-1312-6(0)*, Random Hse. Bks. for Young Readers) Random Hse. Children's Bks.
—Hurry up, Houdini! Murdocca, Sal, illus. 2015. (Magic Tree House (R) Merlin Mission Ser.: 22). 144p. (J). (gr. 2-5). 6.99 *(978-0-307-98048-9(0)*, Random Hse. Bks. for Young Readers) Random Hse. Children's Bks.
—The Knight at Dawn. unabr. ed. 2004. (Magic Tree House Ser.: No. 2). 66p. (J). (gr. k-3). pap. 17.00 incl. audio *(978-0-8072-0331-6(9)*, Listening Library) Random Hse. Audio Publishing Group.
—Leprechaun in Late Winter. Murdocca, Sal, illus. 2012. (Magic Tree House (R) Merlin Mission Ser.: 15). 144p. (J). (gr. 2-5). 6.99 *(978-0-375-85651-8(X)*, Random Hse. Bks. for Young Readers) Random Hse. Children's Bks.
—Leprechaun in Late Winter. 2012. (Magic Tree House Merlin Missions Ser.: 15). lib. bdg. 16.00 *(978-0-606-23860-1(3))* Turtleback.
—Una Momia Al Amanecer. 2004. (Casa del Arbol Ser.: 3). (SPA.). (J). pap. 6.99 *(978-1-930332-51-5(3))* Lectorum Pubns., Inc.
—Una Momia en la Manana. 2003. (Magic Tree House Ser.: 3). (SPA.). (gr. 3-6). lib. bdg. 16.00 *(978-0-613-64609-3(6))* Turtleback.
—Navidad en Camelot. 2015. (Casa De árbol Ser.: 29). (SPA., Illus.). 144p. (J). (gr. 2-4). pap. 6.99 *(978-1-63245-532-1(3))* Lectorum Pubns., Inc.
—Night of the Ninth Dragon. Murdocca, Sal, illus. (Magic Tree House (R) Merlin Mission Ser.: 27). 144p. (J). (gr. 2-5). 2018. 6.99 *(978-0-553-51092-8(4))* 2016. 13.99 *(978-0-553-51089-8(4))* Random Hse. Children's Bks. (Random Hse. Bks. for Young Readers).
—Osos Polares Despues de la Medianoche. 2005. (Casa del Arbol Ser.: 12).Tr. of Polar Bears Past Bedtime. (SPA., Illus.). 71p. (J). pap. 6.99 *(978-1-930332-99-7(8))* Lectorum Pubns., Inc.
—Piratas Despues Del Mediodia. 2004. (Casa del Arbol Ser.: 4). (SPA.). (J). pap. 6.99 *(978-1-930332-52-2(1))* Lectorum Pubns., Inc.
—Revolutionary War on Wednesday. unabr. ed. 2004. (Magic Tree House Ser.: No. 22). 69p. (J). (gr. k-3). pap. 17.00 incl. audio *(978-0-8072-0931-8(7)*, S FTR 254 SP, Listening Library) Random Hse. Audio Publishing Group.
—Summer of the Sea Serpent, Bk. 3. Murdocca, Sal, illus. 2011. (Magic Tree House (R) Merlin Mission Ser.: 3). 144p. (J). (gr. 2-5). 6.99 *(978-0-375-86491-9(1)*, Random Hse. Bks. for Young Readers) Random Hse. Children's Bks.
—Twister on Tuesday. 2004. (Magic Tree House Ser.: No. 23). 70p. (J). (gr. k-3). pap. 17.00 incl. audio *(978-0-8072-9932-6(4)*, Listening Library) Random Hse. Audio Publishing Group.
—Vacaciones Al Pie de un Volcan. Brovelli, Marcela, tr. from ENG. Murdocca, Sal, illus. 2007. (Casa del Arbol Ser.: 13).Tr. of Vacation under the Colcano. (SPA.). 74p. (J). per. 6.99 *(978-1-933032-19-1(7))* Lectorum Pubns., Inc.
—Vacation under the Volcano. unabr. ed. 2004. (Magic Tree House Ser.: No. 13). 74p. (J). (gr. k-3). pap. 17.00 incl. audio *(978-0-8072-0782-6(9)*, LFTR 241 SP, Listening Library) Random Hse. Audio Publishing Group.
—Viking Ships at Sunrise. unabr. ed. 2004. (Magic Tree House Ser.: No. 15). 71p. (J). (gr. k-3). pap. 17.00 incl. audio *(978-0-8072-0784-0(5)*, LFTR 243 SP, Listening Library) Random Hse. Audio Publishing Group.
—Winter of the Ice Wizard. Murdocca, Sal, illus. 2011. (Magic Tree House (R) Merlin Mission Ser.: 4). 144p. (J). (gr. 2-5). 6.99 *(978-0-375-87395-9(3)*, Random Hse. Bks. for Young Readers) Random Hse. Children's Bks.
Osborne, Mary Pope & PLC Editors Staff. Carnival at Candlelight. Murdocca, Sal, illus. 2006. (Magic Tree House Merlin Missions Ser.: No. 5). 105p. (gr. 2-6). 15.00 *(978-0-7569-6690-4(6))* Perfection Learning Corp.
Osborne, Mary Pope, et al. Buenos Días, Gorilas. Murdocca, Sal, illus. 2014. (SPA.). 88p. (J). (gr. 2-4). pap. 6.99 *(978-1-933032-93-1(6))* Lectorum Pubns., Inc.
—Búfalos Antes Del Desayuno. Murdocca, Sal, illus. 2008. (Casa del Arbol Ser.: 18).Tr. of Buffalo Before Breakfast. (SPA.). (J). (gr. 2-4). pap. 6.99 *(978-1-933032-48-1(0))* Lectorum Pubns., Inc.
—Carnaval a Media Luz. Murdocca, Sal, illus. 2016. (SPA.). 113p. (J). (gr. 2-4). pap. 6.99 *(978-1-63245-643-4(5))* Lectorum Pubns., Inc.
—Día Negro en el Fondo Del Mar. Murdocca, Sal, illus. 2018. (SPA.). 118p. (J). (gr. 2-4). pap. 6.99 *(978-1-63245-682-3(6))* Lectorum Pubns., Inc.
—El Dragon Del Amanecer Rojo. Murdocca, Sal, illus. 2018. (SPA.). 132p. (J). (gr. 2-4). pap. 6.99 *(978-1-63245-680-9(X))* Lectorum Pubns., Inc.
—The Fun Starts Here! Four Favorite Chapter Books in One: Junie B. Jones, Magic Tree House, Purrmaids, & a to Z Mysteries. Murdocca, Sal, illus. 2018. (ENG.). 336p. (J). (gr. 1-4). 9.99 *(978-1-9848-3059-3(7)*, Random Hse. Bks. for Young Readers) Random Hse. Children's Bks.
—Maremoto en Hawái. Murdocca, Sal, illus. 2014. (SPA.). 88p. (J). (gr. 2-4). pap. 6.99 *(978-1-933032-95-5(2))* Lectorum Pubns., Inc.
—Miedo Escénico en una Noche de Verano. Murdocca, Sal, illus. 2014. (SPA.). 86p. (J). (gr. 2-4). pap. 6.99 *(978-1-933032-92-4(8))* Lectorum Pubns., Inc.
—El Regalo Del Pingüino Emperador. Murdocca, Sal, illus. 2018. (SPA.). 118p. (J). (gr. 2-4). pap. 6.99 *(978-1-63245-683-0(4))* Lectorum Pubns., Inc.
—Tigres Al Anochecer. Murdocca, Sal, illus. 2008. (Casa del Arbol Ser.: 19).Tr. of Tigers at Twilight. (SPA.). (J). (gr. 2-4). pap. 8.99 *(978-1-933032-49-8(9))* Lectorum Pubns., Inc.
—Tormenta de Nieve en Luna Azul. Murdocca, Sal, illus. 2016. (SPA.). (J). (gr. 2-4). pap. 6.99 *(978-1-63245-646-5(X))* Lectorum Pubns., Inc.
Parish, Herman. Amelia Bedelia Chapter Book #6: Amelia Bedelia Cleans Up. Avril, Lynne, illus. 2015. (Amelia Bedelia Ser.). (ENG.). 160p. (J). (gr. 1-5). pap. 6.99 *(978-0-06-233400-8(X)*, Greenwillow Bks.) HarperCollins Pubs.
—Amelia Bedelia Chapter Book #6: Amelia Bedelia Cleans Up (POB) Avril, Lynne, illus. 2015. (Amelia Bedelia Ser.). (ENG.). 160p. (J). (gr. 1-5). 9.99 *(978-0-06-233403-9(4)*, Greenwillow Bks.) HarperCollins Pubs.
Pittar, Gill. Milly, Molly & the Tree Hut (book W/dolls) 2006. 28p. pap. *(978-1-86972-096-4(2))* Milly Molly Bks.
Plume, Ken, et al. There's a Zombie in My Treehouse! 2010. 52p. pap. 10.00 *(978-0-557-28932-5(7))* Lulu Pr., Inc.
Rey, H. A. Curious George Builds Tree House/Jorge el Curioso Construye una Casa en Un árbol: Bilingual English-Spanish. 2017. (Curious George TV Ser.). (ENG., Illus.). 24p. (J). (gr. -1-3). 12.99 *(978-0-544-97461-6(1)*, 1663440, Clarion Bks.) HarperCollins Pubs.
Rouillard, Wendy W. Barnaby's Tree House. 2005. (Illus.). 30p. (J). *(978-0-9651070-4-4(3))* Barnaby & Co.
Rylant, Cynthia. Henry & Mudge & the Tall Tree House. 2003. (Henry & Mudge Ready-To-Read Ser.: 21). (gr. k-3). lib. bdg. 13.55 *(978-0-613-90605-0(5))* Turtleback.
—Henry & Mudge & the Tall Tree House: Ready-To-Read Level 2. Bracken, Carolyn, illus. 2003. (Henry & Mudge Ser.). (ENG.). 40p. (J). (gr. k-2). pap. 4.99 *(978-0-689-83445-5(4)*, Simon Spotlight) Simon Spotlight.
Shoesmith-Bateman, Amanda. The Magic Tree House, 1 vol. Beitz-Grant, Heather, illus. 2010. 22p. 24.95 *(978-1-4489-3866-7(X))* PublishAmerica, Inc.
Simon, Nadine. Flickers of True Destiny. 2010. 58p. pap. 11.95 *(978-1-60860-948-2(0)*, Eloquent Bks.) Strategic Book Publishing & Rights Agency (SBPRA).
The Tree House Lab. 2003. (J). per. *(978-1-57657-826-1(7))* Paradise Pr., Inc.
The Treehouse Club: Individual Title Six-Packs. (gr. -1-2). 23.00 *(978-0-7635-8821-2(0))* Rigby Education.
Verburg, Bonnie. The Tree House That Jack Built. Teague, Mark, illus. 2014. (ENG.). 40p. (J). (gr. -1-k). 17.99 *(978-0-439-85338-5(9)*, Orchard Bks.) Scholastic, Inc.
Volker, Kerstin. Henry Builds a Tree House. 2003. (Funny Friends Lift-and-Learn Bks.). (Illus.). 14p. (J). 5.99 *(978-1-59384-023-5(3))* Parklane Publishing.
Weakland, Mark. The West End Treehouse Mystery, 1 vol. 2018. (ENG., Illus.). 160p. (J). (gr. 3-7). pap. 9.95 *(978-1-4556-2384-6(9)*, Pelican Publishing) Arcadia Publishing.
Weitzman, Jacqueline Preiss. Superhero Joe & the Creature Next Door. Barrett, Ron, illus. 2013. (ENG.). 32p. (J). (gr. -1-3). 16.99 *(978-1-4424-1268-2(2)*, Simon & Schuster Bks. For Young Readers) Simon & Schuster Bks. For Young Readers.
Wolfe, Bradley W. Upside Downside Up. 2009. (ENG.). 144p. 27.99 *(978-0-557-11670-6(8))* Lulu Pr., Inc.

TREE PLANTING

see also Trees

Cullerton Johnson, Jen. Seeds of Change: Wangari's Gift to the World, 1 vol. Sadler, Sonia Lynn, illus. 2013. (ENG.). 32p. (J). (gr. 1-6). 19.95 *(978-1-60060-367-9(X)*, leelowbooks) Lee & Low Bks., Inc.
Stamper, Judith Bauer. Growing Trees. Lowe, Wesley, illus. 2010. (J). *(978-1-60617-127-1(5))* Teaching Strategies, LLC.
Swanson, Jennifer. Environmental Activist Wangari Maathai. 2018. (STEM Trailblazer Bios Ser.). (ENG., Illus.). 32p. (J). (gr. 2-5). pap. 8.99 *(978-1-5415-1215-3(4)*, f4632edc-ce4f-4012-b76a-c2d9b6afb0fd); lib. bdg. 26.65 *(978-1-5124-9982-7(X)*, c99e835f-9a46-418c-9012-40ad8b652ff3, Lerner Pubns.) Lerner Publishing Group.

TREES

see also Forests and Forestry; Fruit Culture; Landscape Gardening; Leaves; Lumber and Lumbering; Nuts; Shrubs; Tree Planting; Wood

Aldrich, William & Williamson, Don. Tree & Shrub Gardening for Illinois, 1 vol., Vol. 1. rev. ed. 2004. (ENG., Illus.). 352p. (gr. 4). pap. 18.95 *(978-1-55105-404-9(3)*, 78116449-5f28-42de-b982-e75dedb9047c) Lone Pine Publishing USA.
Andrews, Alexa. In the Forest. Keimig, Candice, illus. 2013. (Penguin Young Readers, Level 1 Ser.). 32p. (J). (gr. k-1). pap. 4.99 *(978-0-448-46719-1(4)*, Penguin Young Readers) Penguin Young Readers Group.
Ashley, Michele. When Do Trees Look Different? 2012. (Level D Ser.). (ENG., Illus.). 16p. (J). (gr. k-2). pap. 7.95 *(978-1-927136-38-6(5)*, 19433) RiverStream Publishing.
Bachmann, Elaine Rice. While a Tree Grew, the Story of Maryland's Wye Oak, 1 vol. 2009. (ENG., Illus.). 30p. (gr. -1-3). 10.00 *(978-0-87033-577-8(4)*, 7335, Cornell Maritime Pr./Tidewater Pubs.) Schiffer Publishing, Ltd.
Baumbusch, Brigitte. Trees in Art, 1 vol. 2004. (What Makes a Masterpiece? Ser.). (ENG., Illus.). 32p. (gr. 2-4). lib. bdg. 25.67 *(978-0-8368-4449-8(1)*, b39cd59b-4ec2-482b-bcf4-e2a92c3713d0, Gareth Stevens Learning Library) Stevens, Gareth Publishing LLLP.
Bernhard, Durga Yael. Just Like Me, Climbing a Tree: Exploring Trees Around the World. 2015. (Illus.). 32p. (J). (gr. k-2). 16.95 *(978-1-937786-34-2(X)*, Wisdom Tales) World Wisdom, Inc.
Boothroyd, Jennifer. In a Tree. 2006. (First Step Nonfiction — Animal Homes Ser.). (ENG., Illus.). 8p. (J). (gr. k-2). pap. 5.99 *(978-0-8225-5663-3(4)*, f9f1ef0e-4d88-4bfc-8ad5-63eb062406f8) Lerner Publishing Group.
Bowman, Debbie. The Happy Tree. 2013. 20p. pap. 8.99 *(978-1-62509-760-6(3))* Salem Author Services.

Bredeson, Carmen & Cousins, Lindsey. Can You Find These Trees?, 1 vol. 2012. (All about Nature Ser.). (ENG.). 24p. (gr. -1-1). 25.27 *(978-0-7660-3981-0(1),* 3c202212-df4e-47d3-b2e1-54e0d179776a); (Illus.). pap. 10.35 *(978-1-4644-0070-4(9),* 5959afcd-c18a-43d6-b809-35a09c0e0593) Enslow Publishing, LLC. (Enslow Publishing).

Broutin, Christian. Trees. Broutin, Christian, illus. 2012. (ENG., Illus.). 36p. (J). (gr. -1-k). spiral bd. 19.99 *(978-1-85103-401-7(3))* Moonlight Publishing, Ltd. GBR. Dist: Independent Pubs. Group.

Broutin, Christian & de Bourgoing, Pascale. El Arbol. (Coleccion Mundo Maravilloso). (SPA., Illus.). 40p. (J). (gr. 2-4). *(978-84-348-4056-0(1),* AR9290) SM Ediciones.

Brown, Carron. Secrets of the Apple Tree. 2014. (ENG., Illus.). 36p. (J). 12.99 *(978-1-61067-243-6(7))* Kane Miller.

Buckley, Arabella B. Trees & Shrubs. 2008. (Illus.). 88p. pap. 11.95 *(978-1-59915-275-2(4))* Yesterday's Classics.

Burnie, David. Eyewitness Tree: Discover the Fascinating World of Trees — From Tiny Seeds to Mighty Forest Giants. 2015. (DK Eyewitness Ser.). (ENG., Illus.). 72p. (J). (gr. 3-7). pap. 9.99 *(978-1-4654-3847-8(5),* DK Children) Dorling Kindersley Publishing, Inc.

Butterworth, Chris & Voake, Charlotte. The Things That I LOVE about TREES. 2018. (Illus.). 32p. (J). *(978-1-4063-4940-5(2))* Candlewick Pr.

Cain, Marie Mowery. Tremendous Trees. 2013. (Big Books, Red Ser.). (ENG & SPA., Illus.). 16p. pap. 33.00 *(978-1-59246-219-3(7))* Big Books, by George!

Cardenas, Ernesto A. Wood or Paper? 2009. 23.95 *(978-1-60698-059-0(9))*; pap. 4.95 *(978-1-60698-057-6(2))* Milo Educational Bks. & Resources.

Carlson-Berne, Emma. From Cone to Pine Tree. 2017. (Start to Finish, Second Ser.). (ENG., Illus.). 24p. (J). (gr. k-3). 23.99 *(978-1-5124-3444-6(2),* 194690a3-7c6e-487a-9341-7c25f8e0f17a, Lerner Pubns.); pap. 7.99 *(978-1-5124-5622-6(5),* 28637ad3-bba3-46ca-ace4-1632df312229) Lerner Publishing Group.

Chapman. Seasons & Woodman. 2010. (ENG., Illus.). 88p. pap. 32.99 *(978-0-521-14142-0(7))* Cambridge Univ. Pr.

Churnin, Nancy. The Queen & the First Christmas Tree: Queen Charlotte's Gift to England. Uribe, Luisa, illus. 2018. (ENG.). 32p. (J). (gr. -1-3). 16.99 *(978-0-8075-6636-7(5),* 807566365) Whitman, Albert & Co.

Colby, Jennifer. Trees. 2014. (21st Century Junior Library: Plants Ser.). (ENG., Illus.). 24p. (J). (gr. 2-5). 29.21 *(978-1-63188-041-4(1),* 205571) Cherry Lake Publishing.

Conroy, Jim & Alexander, Basia. Messages from Trees Set 1: A Coloring Book for the Young & Young-At-Heart. 2013. (ENG., Illus.). 32p. (J). pap. 8.00 *(978-0-9834114-5-1(X))* Plant Kingdom Communications.

Cornell, Kari. Big Trees. 2016. (Illus.). 24p. (J). *(978-0-87659-702-6(9))* Gryphon Hse., Inc.

Daniels, Patricia. Trees. 2017. (Illus.). 160p. (J). (gr. 3-7). pap. 12.99 *(978-1-4263-2891-6(5),* National Geographic Kids) Disney Publishing Worldwide.

—Ultimate Explorer Field Guide: Trees. 2017. (ENG., Illus.). 160p. (J). (gr. 3-7). 22.90 *(978-1-4263-2892-3(3),* National Geographic Kids) Disney Publishing Worldwide.

Dawson, Emily C. Birds & Trees. 2010. (Amicus Readers. Our Animal World (Level 1) Ser.). (ENG.). 24p. (J). (gr. k-2). lib. bdg. 25.65 *(978-1-60753-010-7(4),* 17165) Amicus.

De la Bédoyère, Camilla & Gallagher, Belinda. British Wildflowers & Trees Handbook: Identify & Record 100 Species. Kelly, Richard, ed. 2017. (ENG., Illus.). 224p. (J). pap. 14.99 *(978-1-78209-129-5(7))* Miles Kelly Publishing, Ltd. GBR. Dist: Parkwest Pubns., Inc.

Delano, Marfe Ferguson. Explore My World a Tree Grows Up. 2016. (Explore My World Ser.). (Illus.). 32p. (J). (gr. -1-k). pap. 4.99 *(978-1-4263-2429-1(4),* National Geographic Kids) Disney Publishing Worldwide.

DePalma, Mary Newell. A Grand Old Tree. DePalma, Mary Newell, illus. 2005. (ENG., Illus.). 32p. (J). (gr. -1-3). 18.99 *(978-0-439-62334-6(0),* Levine, Arthur A. Bks.) Scholastic, Inc.

Dorion, Christiane. How Plants & Trees Work: A Hands-On Guide to the Natural World. Young, Beverley, illus. 2017. (Explore the Earth Ser.). (ENG.). 18p. (J). (gr. 2-5). 19.99 *(978-0-7636-9298-8(0),* Templar) Candlewick Pr.

Dreyer, Ellen. Grow, Tree, Grow! Swanson, Maggie, tr. Swanson, Maggie, illus. 2003. (Hello Reader! Ser.). (J). *(978-0-439-43964-0(7))* Scholastic, Inc.

Edwards, Nicola. Trees, 1 vol. 2007. (See How Plants Grow Ser.). (ENG., Illus.). 24p. (J). (gr. 2-2). lib. bdg. 26.27 *(978-1-4042-3571-7(X),* f12c5a9d-9599-4a78-b730-c514a84f5aae) Rosen Publishing Group, Inc., The.

Filippucci, Laura. The Universe Is a Tree. 2018. (ENG.). 32p. (J). (gr. 4-7). 18.99 *(978-1-56846-304-9(9),* 19709, Creative Editions) Creative Co., The.

Fletcher, Patricia. Bristlecone Pines Are Ancient!, 1 vol. 2016. (World's Weirdest Plants Ser.). (ENG., Illus.). 24p. (J). (gr. 2-3). pap. 9.15 *(978-1-4824-5599-1(4),* 84369da1-015c-41c1-b6d0-90e8a2fbe3d1) Stevens, Gareth Publishing LLLP.

Fredericks, Anthony D. Around One Log: Chipmunks, Spiders, & Creepy Insiders, 1 vol. DiRubbio, Jennifer, illus. 2011. (ENG.). 32p. (J). (gr. -1-5). 16.95 *(978-1-58469-137-2(9))* Take Heart Pubns.

Fretland VanVoorst, Jenny. Los árboles en la Primavera. 2015.Tr. of Trees in Spring. (SPA., Illus.). 24p. (J). lib. bdg. *(978-1-62031-251-3(4),* Bullfrog Bks.) Jump! Inc.

—Trees in Spring. 2015. (Illus.). 24p. (J). lib. bdg. *(978-1-62031-237-7(9),* Bullfrog Bks.) Jump! Inc.

Gardner, Robert. Temperate Forest Experiments: 8 Science Experiments in One Hour or Less, 1 vol. 2014. (Last Minute Science Projects with Biomes Ser.). (ENG.). 48p. (gr. 5-6). 26.93 *(978-0-7660-5922-1(7),* f6dd3daf-1662-4970-9e07-34fd8e1e6c9d); (Illus.). pap. 11.53 *(978-0-7660-5923-8(5),* fddb4e6b-2498-48d6-8d42-b5cd0a0f260b, Enslow Elementary) Enslow Publishing, LLC.

Gerber, Carole. Leaf Jumpers. Evans, Leslie, illus. (J). 2017. 28p. (— 1). bds. 7.99 *(978-1-58089-782-2(7))* 2006. (ENG.). 32p. (gr. -1-2). per. 7.95 *(978-1-57091-498-0(2))* Charlesbridge Publishing, Inc.

Gillespie, Lisa. Trees. 2009. (Beginners Nature Ser.). 32p. (J). (gr. 1). 4.99 *(978-0-7945-2156-1(8),* Usborne) EDC Publishing.

Gould, Margee. Giant Plants, 1 vol. 2011. (Strangest Plants on Earth Ser.). (ENG., Illus.). 24p. (J). (gr. 2-3). lib. bdg. 26.27 *(978-1-4488-4990-1(X),* 28910091-cf77-4979-bb47-8b5871fbdd8c) Rosen Publishing Group, Inc., The.

Green, Jen. The Magic & Mystery of Trees. McElfatrick, Claire, illus. 2019. (Magic & Mystery of Nature Ser.). (ENG.). 80p. (J). (gr. 2-4). 16.99 *(978-1-4654-7936-5(8),* DK Children) Dorling Kindersley Publishing, Inc.

Gregoire, Maryellen. Trees, 1 vol. 2011. (Wonder Readers Early Level Ser.). (ENG.). 16p. (gr. -1-1). (J). pap. 6.25 *(978-1-4296-7830-8(5),* 118117); pap. 35.94 *(978-1-4296-8196-4(9))* Capstone. (Capstone Pr.).

Gregory, Cam. Where Do Tall Trees Grow? 2012. (Level C Ser.). (ENG., Illus.). 16p. (J). (gr. k-2). pap. 7.95 *(978-1-927136-28-7(8),* 19445) RiverStream Publishing.

Gregson, Margaret M. The Story of Our Trees: In Twenty-Four Lessons. 2013. (ENG., Illus.). 174p. pap. 41.99 *(978-1-107-66278-0(8))* Cambridge Univ. Pr.

Hall, Katharine. Trees: a Compare & Contrast Book, 1 vol. 2015.Tr. of Trees: a Compare & Contrast Book. (SPA., Illus.). 32p. (J). (gr. 2-3). pap. 11.95 *(978-1-62855-469-4(X),* 62c348ab-6a1b-4b16-9313-6395be0cb12c) Arbordale Publishing.

Halter, Loretta. A Voice for the Redwoods. Bartczak, Peter, illus. 2010. (ENG.). 64p. (J). 18.95 *(978-0-9822942-0-8(4))* Nature's Hopes & Heroes.

Hawk, Fran. Count down to Fall, 1 vol. Neidigh, Sherry, illus. 2009. (ENG.). 32p. (J). (gr. -1-3). 16.95 *(978-1-934359-94-5(7))* Arbordale Publishing.

Henderson, Dave, illus. A Story of Three Trees: And the miracle of Prayer. 2005. (ENG.). 12p. (J). bds. 5.99 *(978-1-4037-1197-7(6),* Spirit Pr.) Bendon, Inc.

Heos, Bridget. So You Want to Grow a Pie? Fabbri, Daniele, illus. 2015. (Grow Your Food Ser.). (ENG.). 24p. (J). (gr. 1-4). lib. bdg. 19.95 *(978-1-60753-739-7(7),* 15269) Amicus.

Hibbert, Clare. Trees, 1 vol., 1. 2015. (Adventures in Nature Ser.). (ENG.). 32p. (J). (gr. 3-4). pap. 11.00 *(978-1-5081-4591-2(1),* b3ad0bd4-30f0-4e4c-8304-859a117d3003, PowerKids Pr.) Rosen Publishing Group, Inc., The.

Hickman, Pamela. Nature All Around: Trees. Gavin, Carolyn, illus. 2019. (ENG.). 32p. (J). (gr. 2-5). 18.99 *(978-1-77138-804-7(8))* Kids Can Pr., Ltd. CAN. Dist: Hachette Bk. Group.

Hipp, Andrew. El Árbol del Olivo: Por Dentro y Por fuera, 1 vol. 2003. (Explora la Naturaleza (Getting into Nature) Ser.). (SPA., Illus.). 32p. (gr. 3-4). lib. bdg. 28.93 *(978-1-4042-2865-8(9),* e467edee-4ace-44a0-970b-5934cc25693f) Rosen Publishing Group, Inc., The.

—Oak, 1 vol. 2004. (Getting into Nature Ser.). (ENG., Illus.). 32p. (J). (gr. 3-4). lib. bdg. 28.93 *(978-0-8239-4206-0(6),* ce5f4eec-5093-43f9-9f90-94d8b1908bf1) Rosen Publishing Group, Inc., The.

—Olive Tree, 1 vol. 2004. (Getting into Nature Ser.). (ENG., Illus.). 32p. (J). (gr. 3-4). lib. bdg. 28.93 *(978-0-8239-4207-7(4),* 7cd53f31-eeb8-438a-8a8d-915f5f17d6a7) Rosen Publishing Group, Inc., The.

—Olive Trees: Inside & Out. 2009. (Getting into Nature Ser.). 32p. (gr. 3-4). 47.90 *(978-1-61512-723-8(2),* PowerKids Pr.) Rosen Publishing Group, Inc., The.

Hirsch, Andy. Science Comics: Trees: Kings of the Forest. Hirsch, Andy, illus. 2018. (Science Comics Ser.). (ENG., Illus.). 128p. (J). 19.99 *(978-1-250-14311-2(X),* 900180428); pap. 12.99 *(978-1-250-14310-5(1),* 900180429) Roaring Brook Pr. (First Second Bks.).

Holden, Pam. Good Things from Trees, 1 vol. 2015. (ENG., Illus.). 16p. (-1). pap. *(978-1-77654-079-2(4),* Red Rocket Readers) Flying Start Bks.

Holland, Trish. Trees: Count. 2010. (J). *(978-1-60617-128-8(3))* Teaching Strategies, LLC.

Howse, Jennifer. Trees. 2010. pap. 9.95 *(978-1-60596-917-6(6))*; 24p. (J). (gr. 2-4). lib. bdg. 25.70 *(978-1-60596-916-9(8))* Weigl Pubs., Inc.

Hubbell, Patricia. Every Orchard Tree. Broxon, Janet, illus. 2008. (J). *(978-1-55971-986-5(9),* NorthWord Bks. for Young Readers) T&N Children's Publishing.

Hudd, Emily. How Long Does a Redwood Tree Live? 2019. (How Long Does It Take? Ser.). (ENG., Illus.). 32p. (J). (gr. 3-6). pap. 7.95 *(978-1-5435-7540-8(4),* 141072); lib. bdg. 27.99 *(978-1-5435-7295-7(2),* 140612) Capstone.

Hughes, Meredith Sayles. Hard to Crack: Nut Trees. 2005. (Plants We Eat Ser.). (Illus.). 104p. (gr. 6-9). 26.60 *(978-0-8225-2838-8(X))* Lerner Publishing Group.

—Tall & Tasty: Fruit Trees. 2005. (Plants We Eat Ser.). (Illus.). 104p. (gr. 6-9). 26.60 *(978-0-8225-2837-1(1))* Lerner Publishing Group.

Ingoglia, Gina. The Tree Book for Kids & Their Grown-Ups. 2013. (ENG., Illus.). 96p. (J). 15.95 *(978-1-889538-86-0(8))* Brooklyn Botanic Garden.

Julivert, Maria Angeles. Trees, 1 vol. 2006. (Field Guides). (ENG., Illus.). 64p. (J). (gr. 3-3). 26.93 *(978-1-59270-065-3(9),* 1ba34602-58fd-4e97-b7cb-d191181e7d8c, Cavendish Square) Cavendish Square Publishing LLC.

Kalman, Bobbie. El Ciclo de Vida del Árbol. 2005. (Serie Ciclos de Vida Ser.). (SPA., Illus.). 32p. (J). lib. bdg. *(978-0-7787-8665-8(X))* Crabtree Publishing Co.

Kalman, Bobbie, et al. Les Arbres. 2005. (Petit Monde Vivant Ser.). (FRE., Illus.). 32p. (J). pap. 9.95 *(978-2-89579-052-5(3))* Bayard Canada Livres CAN. Dist: Crabtree Publishing Co.

Kavanagh, James & Waterford Press Staff. Hawaii Trees & Wildflowers: A Folding Pocket Guide to Familiar Species. Leung, Raymond, illus. 2017. (Wildlife & Nature Identification Ser.). (ENG.). 12p. 7.95 *(978-1-58355-509-5(9))* Waterford Pr., Inc.

Kelley, K. C. Trees. 2018. (Spot Awesome Nature Ser.). (ENG.). 16p. (J). (gr. -1-2). pap. 7.99 *(978-1-68152-246-3(2),* 14826) Amicus.

Kim, Tae-yeon. Mango Trees: Philippines. Cowley, Joy, ed. Muhn, Gu-seon, illus. 2015. (Global Kids Storybooks Ser.). (ENG.). 32p. (gr. 1-4). 26.65 *(978-1-925246-33-9(7))*; 26.65 *(978-1-925246-07-0(8))*; 7.99 *(978-1-925246-59-9(0))* ChoiceMaker Pty. Ltd., The AUS. (Big and SMALL). Dist: Lerner Publishing Group.

—Mango Trees: Philippines. Muhn, Gu-seon, illus. 2015. (Global Kids Storybooks Ser.). (ENG.). 32p. (J). (gr. 1-4). pap. 8.99 *(978-1-925233-46-9(4),* 8bd14744-4a86-4723-b7e3-b672d8026c10, Big and SMALL) ChoiceMaker Pty. Ltd., The AUS. Dist: Lerner Publishing Group.

Klepeis, Alicia Z. Deciduous Trees & Coniferous Trees Explained, 1 vol. 2016. (Distinctions in Nature Ser.). (ENG., Illus.). 32p. (gr. 3-3). 30.21 *(978-1-5026-1743-9(9),* 37084d28-5c02-4e44-b87e-eadc430d495b) Cavendish Square Publishing LLC.

Knowles, Laura. It Starts with a Seed. Webber, Jennie, illus. 2017. (It Starts with A Ser.). (ENG.). 32p. (J). (gr. 1-4). 22.99 *(978-1-910277-26-3(6),* Words & Pictures) Quarto Publishing Group UK GBR. Dist: Hachette Bk. Group.

Lawley, Lacy. The Life Cycle of a Tree, 1 vol. 2013. (Rosen Readers Ser.). (ENG.). 24p. (J). (gr. 3-3). pap. 8.25 *(978-1-4777-2565-8(2),* a48e9b85-575d-43d1-bb95-1206a451c70c); pap. 49.50 *(978-1-4777-2566-5(0))* Rosen Publishing Group, Inc., The. (Rosen Classroom).

Lawrence, Ellen. Extreme Trees. 2015. (Illus.). 24p. (J). lib. bdg. 26.99 *(978-1-62724-306-3(2))* Bearport Publishing Co., Inc.

Lemniscates, Carme. Trees. Lemniscates, Carme, illus. 2017. (ENG., Illus.). 40p. (J). (-k). 15.99 *(978-0-7636-9001-4(5))* Candlewick Pr.

Levy, Janey. Banyan Trees Strangle Their Host!, 1 vol. 2019. (World's Weirdest Plants Ser.). (ENG.). 24p. (gr. 2-3). pap. 9.15 *(978-1-5382-4630-6(9),* 14bc1603-7743-4e47-9ba3-e2a7fac629f8) Stevens, Gareth Publishing LLLP.

Lowery, Lawrence F. The Tree by Diane's House. 2015. (I Wonder Why Ser.). (ENG., Illus.). 36p. (J). (gr. k-3). pap. 11.95 *(978-1-941316-25-2(5))* National Science Teachers Assn.

MacDonald, Margaret. Deciduous & Evergreen Trees. 2011. (Learn-Abouts: Level 10 Ser.). (Illus.). 16p. (J). pap. 7.95 *(978-1-59920-603-5(X))* Black Rabbit Bks.

—When Does This Tree Grow Best? 2012. (Level A Ser.). (ENG., Illus.). 16p. (J). (gr. k-2). pap. 7.95 *(978-1-927136-04-1(0),* 19435) RiverStream Publishing.

Marsico, Katie. A True Book Extreme Places: the Oldest & the Newest. 2015. (True Book — Extreme Places Ser.). (ENG., Illus.). 48p. (J). pap. 6.95 *(978-0-531-21785-6(X),* Children's Pr.) Scholastic Library Publishing.

Matinkhah, Sue Ann. Plant a Tree & Watch It Grow. 2013. 28p. pap. 16.95 *(978-1-4624-0676-0(9),* Inspiring Voices) Author Solutions, LLC.

Mattern, Joanne. How Pine Trees Grow, 1 vol. 2005. (How Plants Grow Ser.). (ENG., Illus.). 24p. (gr. k-k). pap. 9.15 *(978-0-8368-6340-6(2),* 583b6cb1-38b2-41e6-bc40-0231d74de987); lib. bdg. 24.67 *(978-0-8368-6333-8(X),* 88909f88-523c-4145-9bca-ae8fe2312ee7) Stevens, Gareth Publishing LLLP. (Weekly Reader Leveled Readers).

—How Pine Trees Grow / Cómo Crecen Los Pinos, 1 vol. 2005. (How Plants Grow / Cómo Crecen Las Plantas Ser.). (ENG & SPA., Illus.). 24p. (gr. k-2). pap. 9.15 *(978-0-8368-6471-7(9),* 21805ac3-50bc-49fe-af51-2598497fff4b, Weekly Reader Leveled Readers) Stevens, Gareth Publishing LLLP.

McGinlay, Richard. My First Encyclopedia of Trees: A Great Big Book of Amazing Plants to Discover. 2017. (Illus.). 24p. (J). (gr. -1-12). pap. 7.99 *(978-1-86147-825-2(9),* Armadillo) Anness Publishing GBR. Dist: National Bk. Network.

Meierhenry, Mark, et al. The Mystery of the Tree Rings. 2008. (Mystery Ser.). (ENG., Illus.). 44p. 13.95 *(978-0-9798940-0-8(X),* P240883, South Dakota State Historical Society Pr.) South Dakota Historical Society Pr.

Mellet, Peter. Find Out about Trees: With 18 Projects & More Than 250 Pictures. 2013. (ENG., Illus.). 64p. (J). (gr. 3-7). 9.99 *(978-1-84322-897-4(1))* Anness Publishing GBR. Dist: National Bk. Network.

Miller, Debbie S. Are Trees Alive? Schuett, Stacey, illus. 2003. (ENG.). 32p. (J). (gr. -1-3). 17.99 *(978-0-8027-8801-6(7),* 900034837, Bloomsbury USA Childrens) Bloomsbury Publishing USA.

Mitchell, Melanie S. Oak Trees. (First Step Nonfiction Ser.). (Illus.). (gr. k-2). 2005. 24p. lib. bdg. 17.27 *(978-0-8225-4610-8(8))* 2003. 23p. (J). pap. 5.95 *(978-0-8225-4611-5(6),* Lerner Pubns.) Lerner Publishing Group.

Moore, David. National Geographic Science 1-2 (Life Science: Plants & Animals): Explore on Your Own: Trees, Seeds, & Leaves. 2009. (C). pap. 8.95 *(978-0-7362-5563-9(X))* National Geographic School Publishing, Inc.

Munson, Victoria. Nature Detective: British Trees. 2016. (Nature Detective Ser.). (ENG., Illus.). 64p. (J). (gr. 2-4). pap. 9.99 *(978-0-7502-9325-9(X),* Wayland) Hachette Children's Group GBR. Dist: Hachette Bk. Group.

National Geographic Learning. Windows on Literacy Step up (Science: Plants Around Us): in the Tree. 2007. (ENG., Illus.). 12p. (J). pap. 11.95 *(978-0-7922-8461-1(5))* CENGAGE Learning.

—World Windows 1 (Science): Parts of a Tree: Content Literacy, Nonfiction Reading, Language & Literacy. 2011. (World Windows Ser.). (ENG., Illus.). 16p. (J). pap., stu. ed. 10.95 *(978-1-133-31082-2(6))* Cengage Heinle.

Owen, Ruth. Science & Craft Projects with Trees & Leaves, 1 vol. 2013. (Get Crafty Outdoors Ser.). (ENG., Illus.). 32p. (J). (gr. 2-3). 30.27 *(978-1-4777-0248-2(2),* 4ec901d9-4d27-4a64-8507-e1ed446eed8f); pap. 12.75 *(978-1-4777-0259-8(8),* be0f4e5a-740f-4a00-8387-bffd8afc2443) Rosen Publishing Group, Inc., The. (PowerKids Pr.).

Pallotta, Jerry. Who Will Plant a Tree? Leonard, Tom, illus. 2010. (ENG.). 32p. (J). (gr. 1-4). 16.99 *(978-1-58536-502-9(5),* 202196) Sleeping Bear Pr.

Payne, Kimberley J. Trees of the Book: Learning from God's Creation. 2013. 28p. pap. *(978-1-896213-73-6(1))* Praise Publishing.

Peanuckle. Mrs. Peanuckle's Tree Alphabet. Ford, Jessie, illus. 2018. (Mrs. Peanuckle's Alphabet Ser.: 6). 28p. (J). (— 1). 7.99 *(978-1-62336-943-9(6),* 9781623369439, Rodale Kids) Random Hse. Children's Bks.

Pearson Learning Staff, creator. Trees & Leaves. 2004. (ENG.). (J). (gr. k-k). pap. 7.56 *(978-0-7652-5136-7(1),* Celebration Pr.) Savvas Learning Co.

Petersen, Christine. Trees. 2008. (21st Century Junior Library: Plants Ser.). (ENG., Illus.). 24p. (gr. 2-5). lib. bdg. 29.21 *(978-1-60279-274-6(7),* 200179) Cherry Lake Publishing.

Pipe, Jim. You Wouldn't Want to Live Without Trees! 2016. (You Wouldn't Want to Live Without Ser.). lib. bdg. 20.80 *(978-0-606-38720-0(X))* Turtleback.

Pourquie, Bernadette & Gambini, Cécile. Strange Trees: And the Stories Behind Them. Broad, Yolanda Stern, tr. 2016. (ENG., Illus.). 40p. (J). (gr. k-3). 17.95 *(978-1-61689-459-7(8))* Princeton Architectural Pr.

Pugliano-Martin, Carol. Discover the Life Cycle of Pine Trees. 2006. (English Explorers Ser.). (J). pap. *(978-1-4108-6473-4(1))* Benchmark Education Co.

—The Life Cycle of Pine Trees. 2006. (English Explorers Ser.). (J). pap. *(978-1-4108-6470-3(7))* Benchmark Education Co.

Rechenbaeume-Terme-Texte. (Duden-Schuelerhilfen Ser.). (GER.). 96p. (J). (gr. 5-6). *(978-3-411-02621-0(9))* Bibliographisches Institut & F. A. Brockhaus AG DEU. Dist: International Bk. Import Service, Inc.

Rushworth, Gary. The Life Cycle of Trees: Set Of 6. 2011. (Navigators Ser.). (J). pap. 44.00 net. *(978-1-4108-6223-5(2))* Benchmark Education Co.

—The Life Cycle of Trees: Text Pairs. 2008. (Bridges/Navigators Ser.). (J). (gr. 3). 94.00 *(978-1-4108-8364-3(7))* Benchmark Education Co.

Russo, Monica. Treecology: 30 Activities & Observations for Exploring the World of Trees & Forests. 2016. (Young Naturalists Ser.: 4). (ENG., Illus.). 144p. (J). (gr. 2). pap. 17.99 *(978-1-61373-396-7(8))* Chicago Review Pr., Inc.

Saunders, Gary L. My Life with Trees: A Sylvan Journey. 2015. (ENG.). 256p. pap. *(978-1-55447-151-5(6))* Gaspereau Pr.

Schuh, Mari. Apples Grow on a Tree. 2010. (How Fruits & Vegetables Grow Ser.). (ENG.). 24p. (J). (gr. k-1). pap. 37.74 *(978-1-4296-6182-9(8),* 16059, Pebble) Capstone.

Shapiro, Sara. What Do You See? A Book about the Seasons. 2009. (Illus.). 16p. (J). pap. *(978-0-545-16154-1(1))* Scholastic, Inc.

Shea, Therese M. Watch Pine Trees Grow, 1 vol. 2011. (Watch Plants Grow! Ser.). (ENG., Illus.). 24p. (J). (gr. k-k). pap. 9.15 *(978-1-4339-4840-4(0),* 835cb28d-5c96-457e-a7b2-1ec87bd960fc); lib. bdg. 25.27 *(978-1-4339-4839-8(7),* edeb0a01-157d-461d-a791-b07908609cdb) Stevens, Gareth Publishing LLLP.

Singley, Judith M. A B C Trees. 2012. 32p. pap. 17.25 *(978-1-4669-4640-8(7))* Trafford Publishing.

Snow, Wesley. A Tree's Life. 2013. (InfoMax Readers Ser.). (ENG.). 24p. (J). (gr. 3-4). pap. 49.50 *(978-1-4777-2629-7(2),* Rosen Classroom) Rosen Publishing Group, Inc., The.

Socha, Piotr & Grajkowski, Wojciech. Trees: A Rooted History. 2019. (ENG., Illus.). 80p. (J). 25.99 *(978-1-4197-3723-7(6),* 1277301) Abrams, Inc.

Sohn, Emily. Trees. 2019. (IScience Ser.). (ENG., Illus.). 24p. (J). (gr. k-2). pap. 13.26 *(978-1-68404-365-1(4))* Norwood Hse. Pr.

Stamper, Judith Bauer. Growing Trees. Lowe, Wesley, illus. 2010. (J). *(978-1-60617-127-1(5))* Teaching Strategies, LLC.

—A Tree Is For- 2010. (J). *(978-1-60617-126-4(7))* Teaching Strategies, LLC.

Stockland, Patricia M. Look at a Palm Tree. 2012. (First Step Nonfiction — Look at Trees Ser.). (ENG., Illus.). 8p. (J). (gr. k-2). pap. 4.99 *(978-1-4677-0523-3(3))* Lerner Publishing Group.

Stone, Tiffany. Tree Song. Hatam, Holly, illus. 2018. (ENG.). 32p. (J). (gr. k-2). 18.95 *(978-1-77321-001-8(7))* Annick Pr., Ltd. CAN. Dist: Publishers Group West (PGW).

Sundance/Newbridge LLC Staff. Life in a Tree. 2007. (Early Science Ser.). (gr. k-3). 18.95 *(978-1-4007-6459-4(9))*; pap. 6.10 *(978-1-4007-6455-6(6))* Sundance/Newbridge Educational Publishing.

Tanem, Bob & Williamson, Don. Tree & Shrub Gardening for Northern California, 1 vol. rev. ed. 2003. (ENG., Illus.). 360p. (gr. 4). pap. 18.95 *(978-1-55105-275-5(X),* c3c657e4-5407-4355-b04b-f7bf0ec93f92) Lone Pine Publishing USA.

Tate, Nikki. Deep Roots: How Trees Sustain Our Planet, 1 vol. 2016. (Orca Footprints Ser.: 8). (ENG., Illus.). 48p. (J). (gr. 4-7). 19.95 *(978-1-4598-0582-8(8))* Orca Bk. Pubs. USA.

Tree. 2005. (J). *(978-0-9767139-0-6(X))* Britt Allcroft Productions.

Trees, Please! Level M, 6 vols. 128p. (gr. 2-3). 40.50 *(978-0-7699-1034-5(3))* Shortland Pubns. (U. S. A.) Inc.

Udry, Janice May. Un Arbol Es Hermoso: A Caldecott Award Winner. Simont, Marc, illus. 2006.Tr. of Tree Is Nice. (SPA.). 32p. (J). (gr. -1-3). pap. 7.99 *(978-0-06-088708-7(7))* HarperCollins Español.

Veitch, Catherine. Learning about Trees, 1 vol. 2013. (Natural World Ser.). (ENG., Illus.). 24p. (J). (gr. -1-1). pap. 6.95 *(978-1-4109-5407-7(2),* 123358, Raintree) Capstone.

Voake, Charlotte, et al. A Little Guide to Trees. 2011. (ENG., Illus.). 80p. (J). (gr. -1-2). pap. 19.95 *(978-1-903919-82-8(7))* Transworld Publishers Ltd. GBR. Dist: Independent Pubs. Group.

Volant, Iris. Under the Canopy: Trees Around the World. Alonso, Cynthia, illus. 2018. (ENG.). 56p. (J). (gr. 2). 19.95 *(978-1-911171-42-3(9))* Flying Eye Bks. GBR. Dist: Penguin Random Hse. LLC.

Webb, Barbara & Webb, Barbara L. Trees: Earth's Lungs. 2010. (Green Earth Science Discovery Library). (ENG., Illus.). 24p. (gr. k-2). pap. 9.95 *(978-1-61590-543-0(X),* 9781615905430) Rourke Educational Media.

Weil, Susan. Trees, 1 vol. 2018. (My First Book of Nature Ser.). (ENG.). 24p. (gr. 2-2). 26.27 *(978-1-5081-9623-5(0),* 77cb198c-d382-41ba-95bc-11231d22098b, Windmill Bks.) Rosen Publishing Group, Inc., The.

Weiss, Ellen. From Pinecone to Pine Tree. 2007. (Scholastic News Nonfiction Readers Ser.). (ENG., Illus.). 24p. (J). (gr. 1-2). 22.00 *(978-0-531-18537-7(0))* Scholastic Library Publishing.

—From Pit to Peach Tree. 2007. (Scholastic News Nonfiction Readers Ser.). (ENG., Illus.). 24p. (J). (gr. 1-2). pap. 6.95 *(978-0-531-18791-3(8))* Scholastic Library Publishing.
Whelan, Piper. Trees. (Illus.). 24p. (J). 2017. *(978-1-5105-1408-9(2))* 2016. *(978-1-5105-1411-9(2))* SmartBook Media, Inc.
Williams, Nancy Noel. Don't Lose It, Reuse It. 2010. *(978-1-60617-130-1(5))* Teaching Strategies, LLC.
Williams, Rachel. Little Pear Tree. Bowers, Jenny, illus. 2014. (ENG.). 12p. (J). (-k). bds. 14.99 *(978-0-7636-7126-6(6)*, Big Picture Press) Candlewick Pr.
Wood, Tim & Beck, Alison. Tree & Shrub Gardening for Michigan, 1 vol. rev. ed. 2003. (ENG., Illus.). 352p. (gr. 4). pap. 18.95 *(978-1-55105-347-9(0)*, 9d32c73f-cb05-4a97-b30a-b85221c344d0) Lone Pine Publishing USA.
World Book, Inc. Staff, contrib. by. Terrific Trees. 2017. *(978-0-7166-7953-0(1))* World Bk., Inc.
—Trees of the United States & Canada. 2004. (World Book's Science & Nature Guides Ser.). (Illus.). 80p. (J). *(978-0-7166-4219-0(0))* World Bk., Inc.
Worth, Bonnie. I Can Name 50 Trees Today! All about Trees. Ruiz, Aristides & Mathieu, Joe, illus. 2006. (Cat in the Hat's Learning Library). (ENG.). 48p. (J). (gr. -1-3). 9.99 *(978-0-375-82277-3(1)*, Random Hse. Bks. for Young Readers) Random Hse. Children's Bks.

TREES—FICTION

Abel, Melanie. Kitten up a Tree. Lederhos, Anne, illus. 2008. 24p. (J). pap. 15.95 *(978-0-9791606-4-6(2))* E & E Publishing.
Adams, Lacole Sessions. Maggie & Her Tree. 2011. 28p. (gr. -1). pap. 15.29 *(978-1-4567-2416-0(9))* AuthorHouse.
Aguirre, Jorge. Trees for the Okapis: Little Green Nickelodeon. Mawhinney, Art, illus. 2010. (Go Diego Go! Ser.). (ENG.). 24p. (J). (gr. -1-1). 17.44 *(978-1-4169-9090-1(9))* Simon & Schuster, Inc.
Alexander, Carol. The Bean Trees. Friedland, Joyce & Kessler, Rikki, eds. 2007. (Novel-Ties Ser.). (Illus.). 35p. pap. 16.95 *(978-0-7675-3554-0(5))* Learning Links Inc.
Allamand, Maite. Alamito el Largo. (SPA.). (J). (gr. 2-3). pap. *(978-956-13-1428-3(2)*, AB3840) Bello, Andres CHL. Dist: Lectorum Pubns., Inc.
Alonso, Fernando. El Arbol de los Suenos. Urberuaga, Emilio, illus. 2005. (Alfaguara Juvenil Ser.).Tr. of Dream Trees. (SPA.). 124p. (J). (gr. 5-8). pap. 10.95 *(978-968-19-0978-9(X))* Santillana USA Publishing Co., Inc.
—El Arbol Que No Tenia Hojas (The Tree Without Leaves) (Superbks./Superlibros). (J). (gr. k-1). (SPA.). pap. 6.95 *(978-0-88272-469-0(X))*;Big Book. (SPA.). 21.95 *(978-0-88272-459-1(2))*;Big Book. 21.95 *(978-0-88272-460-7(6))* Santillana USA Publishing Co., Inc.
—The Tree Without Leaves. (Superbks./Superlibros). (Illus.). 16p. (J). (gr. k-3). pap. 6.95 *(978-0-88272-470-6(3))* Santillana USA Publishing Co., Inc.
Amo, Montserrat del. Montes, Pájaros y Amigos. 2007. (SPA.). 104p. (gr. 5-8). pap. 13.99 *(978-84-207-2788-2(1)*, GS6293) Grupo Anaya, S.A. ESP. Dist: Lectorum Pubns., Inc.
Ann. My Name Is Oak... Daytona Oak. 2013. 28p. pap. 24.95 *(978-1-63004-172-4(6))* America Star Bks.
Anna. The Magic Money Tree. 2009. (Illus.). 20p. pap. 15.49 *(978-1-4389-0472-6(X))* AuthorHouse.
Anna's Tree: Individual Title Six-Packs. (gr. 1-2). 25.00 *(978-0-7635-9134-2(3))* Rigby Education.
Applegate, Katherine. Wishtree. Lt. ed. 2018. (ENG.). 226p. 22.99 *(978-1-4328-4821-7(6))* Cengage Gale.
—Wishtree. (ENG., Illus.). 224p. 2019. pap. 15.99 *(978-1-250-30686-9(8)*, 900197882) 2017. (J). 16.99 *(978-1-250-04322-1(0)*, 900127764) Feiwel & Friends.
—Wishtree. 2023. (ENG.). 240p. (gr. 3-6). 24.94 ***(978-1-5364-7846-4(6))*** Square Fish.
Araque, Ana. My little Seed. 2009. 36p. pap. 21.99 *(978-1-4415-8537-0(0))* Xlibris Corp.
Arnold, Tedd. Dirty Gert. 2014. (ENG., Illus.). 32p. (J). (gr. -1-3). 7.99 *(978-0-8234-3054-3(5))* Holiday Hse., Inc.
Arrington, Linda. Ugly Trees. Arrington, Linda, photos by. 2012. (Illus.). 24p. pap. 24.95 *(978-1-4626-8925-5(6))* America Star Bks.
Atwood, Margaret. Up in the Tree, 1 vol. (ENG., Illus.). 32p. (J). 2010. (gr. k-k). 19.95 *(978-1-55498-080-2(1))* 2006. (gr. -1-1). 16.95 *(978-0-88899-729-6(9))* Groundwood Bks. CAN. Dist: Publishers Group West (PGW).
Babel, Ann. Little Tree. 2011. 32p. pap. 12.99 *(978-1-4520-8781-8(4))* AuthorHouse.
Babin, Claire. Gus Is a Tree. Tallec, Olivier, illus. 2009. (ENG.). 32p. (J). (gr. -1-2). 14.95 *(978-1-59270-078-3(0))* Enchanted Lion Bks., LLC.
Bailey, David J. The Storm. 2016. (ENG.). 190p. (J). pap. 11.95 *(978-1-78554-826-0(3)*, 117c8019-8df2-4fc5-9774-fbb9e767038b) Austin Macauley Pubs. Ltd. GBR. Dist: Baker & Taylor Publisher Services (BTPS).
Bailey, Dawn Wentz. Joey & the Mighty Oak. 2008. 20p. pap. 24.95 *(978-1-60813-377-2(X))* PublishAmerica, Inc.
Bang, Molly. When Sophie's Feelings Are Really, Really Hurt. Bang, Molly, illus. 2015. (ENG., Illus.). 40p. (J). (gr. -1-3). 18.99 *(978-0-545-78831-1(5)*, Blue Sky Pr., The) Scholastic, Inc.
Barganier, Jeff S. The Crooked Tree. 2010. (ENG.). 24p. pap. 15.99 *(978-1-4500-4396-0(8))* Xlibris Corp.
Barr, Carolyn Mims. The Waiting Tree. 2012. 20p. pap. 13.77 *(978-1-4669-5538-7(4))* Trafford Publishing.
Barron, T. A. Tree Girl. 2013. (ENG.). 144p. (J). (gr. 3-7). pap. 7.99 *(978-0-14-242708-8(X)*, Puffin Books) Penguin Young Readers Group.
Barroux. How Many Trees? 2018. (ENG., Illus.). 32p. (J). (gr. -1-k). pap. 7.99 *(978-1-4052-8055-6(7))* Farshore GBR. Dist: HarperCollins Pubs.
Beamish, Diane. The Treefellows. 2006. 35p. (J). pap. 14.28 *(978-1-4116-5967-4(8))* Lulu Pr., Inc.
Beard, Darleen Bailey & Malone, Heather. Annie Glover Is NOT a Tree Lover. 2009. (ENG., Illus.). 128p. (J). (gr. 2-5). 18.99 *(978-0-374-30351-8(7)*, 900049730, Farrar, Straus & Giroux (BYR)) Farrar, Straus & Giroux.
Beedie, Duncan. The Lumberjack's Beard. Beedie, Duncan, illus. 2017. (ENG., Illus.). 40p. (J). (gr. k-3). 16.99 *(978-0-7636-9649-8(8)*, Templar) Candlewick Pr.
Below, Halina. Chestnut Dreams, 1 vol. 2003. (ENG., Illus.). 40p. (J). (gr. -1-2). pap. 5.95 *(978-1-55041-690-9(1)*, 4cc85dad-60ec-42a1-8cce-6eb02c85b388) Clockwise Pr. CAN. Dist: Firefly Bks., Ltd.
Bennett, Earl. The Legend of Bucky the Beaver. 2009. 44p. pap. 12.95 *(978-1-4269-1669-4(8))* Trafford Publishing.
Bennett-Minnerly, Denise. The Color Tree. Bennett-Minnerly, Denise, illus. 2005. (Illus.). (J). 14.95 *(978-1-56290-328-2(4))* Crystal Productions.
Berger, Carin. The Little Yellow Leaf. Berger, Carin, illus. 2008. (ENG., Illus.). 40p. (J). (gr. -1-3). 18.99 *(978-0-06-145223-9(8)*, Greenwillow Bks.) HarperCollins Pubs.
Berkes, Marianne. The Tree That Bear Climbed, 1 vol. Rietz, Kathleen, illus. 2012. 32p. (J). (gr. -1-3). (ENG.). 17.95 *(978-1-60718-528-4(8))*; (SPA.). pap. 11.95 *(978-1-62855-426-7(6)*, 9f77be8a-74b8-4060-9de5-9f55de276c05); (ENG.). pap. 9.95 *(978-1-60718-537-6(7))* Arbordale Publishing.
Bishop, Helena Edwards. Simon & the Money Tree. 2012. (ENG., Illus.). 40p. 18.95 *(978-1-4709-9783-0(5))* Lulu Pr., Inc.
Blackdog, J. M. Loni Talltree: The world's greatest tree Climber. 2012. 24p. pap. 14.99 *(978-1-4685-5319-2(4))* AuthorHouse.
Blyton, Enid. Up the Faraway Tree. (Illus.). 96p. (J). pap. 5.95 *(978-0-09-942720-9(6))* Penguin Random Hse. GBR. Dist: Trafalgar Square Publishing.
Boger-Bass, Vallerie. The Mustard Seed: A Christian Promise. Boger-Bass, Vallerie, illus. 2003. (Illus.). 40p. pap. 10.00 *(978-0-8059-5640-5(9))* Dorrance Publishing Co., Inc.
Boss, S. Up in the Leaves. 2018. (ENG., Illus.). 40p. (J). (gr. k-3). 18.99 *(978-1-4549-2071-7(8))* Sterling Publishing Co., Inc.
Braillier, Jess M. Tess's Tree. Reynolds, Peter H., illus. 2010. (JPN.). 28p. (J). *(978-4-07-269392-6(8))* Shufunotomo Company, Limited.
Brodsky, Kathy. My Bent Tree. Bennett, Cameron, illus. 2008. (ENG.). 44p. (J). 19.95 *(978-0-615-16066-5(2))* Helpingwords.
Brooke, Samantha. Apple-Picking Day! Durk, Jim, illus. 2007. (Clifford's Puppy Days Ser.). (J). *(978-0-545-02841-7(8))* Scholastic, Inc.
Brown, Margaret Wise. The Little Fir Tree. LaMarche, Jim, illus. 2005. 32p. (J). (gr. -1-1). lib. bdg. 16.89 *(978-0-06-028190-8(1))* HarperCollins Pubs.
—The Little Fir Tree: A Christmas Holiday Book for Kids. LaMarche, Jim, illus. (ENG.). 32p. (J). (gr. -1-1). 2009. pap. 9.99 *(978-0-06-443529-1(6))* 2005. 15.99 *(978-0-06-028189-2(8))* HarperCollins Pubs. (HarperCollins).
Brown, Palmer. The Silver Nutmeg: The Story of Anna Lavinia & Toby. 2012. (Anna Lavinia Ser.). (ENG., Illus.). 152p. (J). (gr. k-4). 15.95 *(978-1-59017-500-2(X)*, NYR Children's Collection) New York Review of Bks., Inc., The.
Bryant, Clorinda. Imaginary World: The Stone of Amajara. 2011. (ENG.). 252p. 30.50 *(978-0-557-54922-1(1))* Lulu Pr., Inc.
Burgess, Thornton W. Blacky the Crow. 2011. 132p. 25.95 *(978-1-4638-9575-4(5))* Rodgers, Alan Bks.
—Happy Jack. 2011. 140p. 25.95 *(978-1-4638-9558-7(5))* Rodgers, Alan Bks.
Busheri, Devora. The Abba Tree. Shkedi, Gal, illus. 2020. (ENG.). 24p. (J). (gr. -1-3). 17.99 *(978-1-5415-3466-7(2)*, 16b82cf6-5bb3-486a-b02b-85d4be5457a6, Kar-Ben Publishing) Lerner Publishing Group.
Bushweller, Ellie. The Tree with A Hundred Hands. 2008. 40p. 18.50 *(978-0-615-24478-5(5))* Bushweller, Ellie.
Butterworth, Chris. The Things That I Love about Trees. Voake, Charlotte, illus. 2018. (ENG.). 32p. (J). (gr. k-3). 15.99 *(978-0-7636-9569-9(6))* Candlewick Pr.
Cabral, Jeane. Tree Hugs. 2009. (Jeane Cabral Bks.). (Illus.). (J). bds. 12.99 *(978-1-934650-08-0(0))* Just For Kids Pr., LLC.
Candy, Wolf. The Tree, the House & the Hurricane. Lt. ed. 2005. (Illus.). 24p. (J). 7.00 *(978-0-9762292-3-0(4))* New Global Publishing.
Cannon, K. L. Mr. Mortimer: The Grapevine That Wouldn't Die. 2005. (J). 4.95 *(978-0-9675594-2-1(1))* Cannon, K. L.
Cano, Carles & Cano Peiró, Carles. El Arbol de las Hojas Din A-4. (SPA., Illus.). 28p. (J). (gr. k-2). *(978-84-8464-027-1(2)*, KA30310) Kalandraka Editora, S.L. ESP. Dist: Lectorum Pubns., Inc.
Caprara, Rebecca. The Magic of Melwick Orchard. 2018. (ENG.). 376p. (J). (gr. 4-8). 17.99 *(978-1-5124-6687-4(5)*, cbdf4843-d3d6-457a-9fa0-9e41212c3008, Carolrhoda Bks.) Lerner Publishing Group.
Cardin, Beth W. Little Red Leaf. 2010. (ENG.). 24p. pap. 12.99 *(978-1-4520-7414-6(3))* AuthorHouse.
Caron, Susie. Twee' Eckstein, Joe, illus. 2013. 24p. (J). pap. 12.99 *(978-0-9889113-0-7(2))* Coda Grove Publishing.
Carr, Lawrence. Under the Peach Tree. 2006. pap. 8.00 *(978-0-8059-7019-7(3))* Dorrance Publishing Co., Inc.
Carrasco, José Manuel, illus. El viaje de las semillas. 2008. 48p. *(978-84-95225-83-2(2))* Saure, Jean-Francois Editor.
Carver, David. Leafy Leafs Where Is Lester?, 1 vol. Carver, Erin, illus. 2009. 34p. pap. 19.95 *(978-1-4489-2203-1(8))* PublishAmerica, Inc.
—Lester Returns Home with His New Friend La'doo, 1 vol. Carver, Erin, illus. 2010. 28p. 24.95 *(978-1-4489-6340-9(0))* PublishAmerica, Inc.
Cerimele, Ron. Winup. 2012. 28p. pap. 21.99 *(978-1-4771-1144-4(1))* Xlibris Corp.
Charley, Grace. The Trouble with Benny Bubble. 2007. (Illus.). 72p. per. 9.76 *(978-1-4251-0147-3(X))* Trafford Publishing.
Chase, et al. Angel in a Gum Tree. (Illus.). 32p. pap. 13.95 *(978-1-86368-222-0(8))* Fremantle Pr. AUS. Dist: Independent Pubs. Group.
Chering, Don. The Acorn That Doubted. 2008. 32p. pap. 14.49 *(978-1-4389-0493-1(2))* AuthorHouse.
Christmas Book - Christmas Tree. 2005. (J). bds. *(978-1-4194-0073-5(8))* Paradise Pr., Inc.
Church, Bryan. The Dreamcatcher Bowl. 2009. (ENG.). 54p. pap. 9.99 *(978-0-557-07517-1(3))* Lulu Pr., Inc.
Clauson, Marilyn & Drake, Lana. Woody Acorn. Drake, Lana, illus. 2012. (Illus.). 48p. 24.95 *(978-1-4626-9647-5(3))* America Star Bks.
Coffey, Joe. Lynnie Leonardson & the Weeping Willow. Selby, Shannon, illus. 2011. 44p. pap. 24.95 *(978-1-4560-6487-7(8))* America Star Bks.
Cole, Henry. The Littlest Evergreen. 2010. (J). lib. bdg. 18.89 *(978-0-06-114620-6(X))* HarperCollins Pubs.
—The Littlest Evergreen: A Christmas Holiday Book for Kids. Cole, Henry, illus. 2011. (ENG., Illus.). 32p. (J). (gr. -1-2). 16.99 *(978-0-06-114619-0(6)*, Tegen, Katherine Bks) HarperCollins Pubs.
Colfer, Chris. The Curvy Tree: A Tale from the Land of Stories. Dorman, Brandon, illus. 2015. (Land of Stories Ser.). (ENG.). 32p. (J). (gr. -1-3). 18.99 *(978-0-316-40685-7(6))* Little, Brown Bks. for Young Readers.
Coll-Seck, Jayden. A Tree's Tale, 1 vol., 1. 2015. (Rosen REAL Readers: STEM & STEAM Collection). (ENG.). 8p. (J). (gr. k-1). pap. 5.46 *(978-1-5081-1397-3(1)*, df168516-ce9e-4285-9bc1-c690d6136d51, Rosen Classroom) Rosen Publishing Group, Inc., The.
Corley, Sandra J. The Scrawny Little Tree. 2011. 28p. pap. 16.95 *(978-1-4497-1274-7(6)*, WestBow Pr.) Author Solutions, LLC.
Coulton, Mia. Danny's Special Tree. Coulton, Mia, photos by. 2008. (ENG., Illus.). pap. 6.95 *(978-1-933624-25-9(6))* Maryruth Bks., Inc.
Coutin, Gustavo. When I climb a Tree. 2011. 20p. 12.00 *(978-1-4567-4303-1(1))* AuthorHouse.
Cruikshank, Fran. The Tale of the Not-So-Perfect Christmas Tree. Olson, Tom, illus. 2005. 17p. (J). 9.95 *(978-1-59971-055-6(2))* Aardvark Global Publishing.
Cuccia, Louis J. The Bottle Tree. 2003. (Illus.). 106p. (J). per. *(978-0-9727415-1-4(8))* Cuccia, Louis.
Cunliffe, April. Willy the Weeping Willow. 2008. 36p. pap. 24.95 *(978-1-60441-613-8(0))* America Star Bks.
Curious George at the Park Touch-And-Feel (Cgtv Board Book) 2010. (Curious George Ser.). (ENG., Illus.). 10p. (J). (gr. -1 — 1). bds. 6.99 *(978-0-547-24300-9(6)*, 1099424, Clarion Bks.) HarperCollins Pubs.
Curious George Plants a Tree. 2010. (Curious George Ser.). (ENG., Illus.). 24p. (J). (gr. -1-3). pap. 5.99 *(978-0-547-29776-7(9)*, 1413169, Clarion Bks.) HarperCollins Pubs.
Curry, Kenneth. The Legend of the Dancing Trees: An African American Folk Tale. 2007. 111p. (J). per. 14.95 *(978-0-9798364-0-4(9))* Curry Brothers Publishing Group.
Curry, Kenneth, et al. The Legend of the Dancing Tees Teachers Resource: The Legend of the Dancing Trees. 2007.Tr. of Teachers Resource. per. 19.95 *(978-0-9798364-1-1(7))* Curry Brothers Publishing Group.
Curto Family, The & Fischer, Rusty. One Little Christmas Tree. 2012. 26p. pap. 9.99 *(978-0-9840338-1-2(5))* Good Times at Home LLC.
Cyr, Joe. Magical Trees & Crayons: Great Stories. 2006. (Illus.). pap. 9.95 *(978-0-9778525-6-7(3))* Peppertree Pr., The.
Dale, Jay. Up Here. Hancock, Anna, illus. 2012. (Engage Literacy Magenta Ser.). (ENG.). 16p. (J). (gr. k-2). pap. 36.94 *(978-1-4296-8863-5(7)*, 18327, Capstone Pr.) Capstone.
Darling, Pollyanna. Heartwood. Chalmers, Kirsty, illus. 2013. 66p. (J). pap. *(978-0-9871164-4-4(4))* Imaginaria.
Daugherty, Doug. Boxy: A Tree of the Prairie. Gasal, Ben, illus. 2008. 24p. pap. 24.95 *(978-1-60610-808-6(5))* PublishAmerica, Inc.
Davenport, Kelly. Do Hotdogs Grow on Trees? 2010. 32p. pap. 17.99 *(978-1-4520-6636-3(1))* AuthorHouse.
Davis, Lynda S. & Weisel, Kaitlyn E. Christopher James Mcabee & the Wonderful Tree. Trone, Melody Kams, illus. 2013. 54p. pap. 6.99 *(978-0-9889907-0-8(3))* Sruvis Publishing.
Davis, Rachayl Eckstein & Schram, Peninnah. The Apple Tree's Discovery. Lee, Wendy W., illus. 2012. (ENG.). 24p. (J). (gr. -1-2). pap. 7.99 *(978-0-7613-5132-0(9)*, 6adca0a0-d419-4ca4-82b0-6ee930438a2e, Kar-Ben Publishing) Lerner Publishing Group.
Dawson, Jennifer. Silly Sally Sue. 2013. 24p. pap. 24.95 *(978-1-62709-938-7(7))* America Star Bks.
De Lint, Charles. The Cats of Tanglewood Forest. 2014. (J). lib. bdg. 22.10 *(978-0-606-36532-1(X))* Turtleback.
Decola, Diane. Butterfly. 2008. 180p. pap. 15.99 *(978-1-4389-0715-4(X))* AuthorHouse.
Dee, Carolyn. The Tree Who Couldn't Choose. 2008. 36p. pap. 15.49 *(978-1-4389-2950-7(1))* AuthorHouse.
Deluna, Alicia C. Tippy Gets a Friend. 2012. 20p. pap. 17.99 *(978-1-4685-5513-4(8))* AuthorHouse.
Derrick, Patricia. Farley the Ferret of Farkleberry Farm. Martinez, J-P Loppo, illus. 2007. 32p. (J). (gr. -1-3). 18.95 incl. audio compact disk *(978-1-933818-12-2(3))* Animalations.
Desrochers, Diane O. The Little Tree That Would Be Great. Boucher, Julie, illus. 2009. 36p. pap. 14.95 *(978-0-9819727-7-0(2))* Fiction Publishing, Inc.
Dixon, Bob. Rooty the Tree Troll. 2009. 28p. pap. 13.99 *(978-1-4389-0129-0(0))* AuthorHouse.
Doman, Dave. Tree Talkers: A Christmas Story, 1 vol. Swope, Brenda, illus. 2009. 32p. pap. 24.95 *(978-1-61546-180-6(9))* America Star Bks.
Drane, John Wanzer. Sassafras & Chicory. 2012. 32p. pap. 13.00 *(978-0-578-10633-5(7))* Drane, John Wanzer.
Duvall, John. The Great Spruce. Gibbon, Rebecca, illus. 2016. 40p. (J). (gr. k-3). 18.99 *(978-0-399-16084-4(1)*, G.P. Putnam's Sons Books for Young Readers) Penguin Young Readers Group.
Edgren, Elizabeth. Little Tree's Mightiest Deed. Penk, Kathryn, illus. 2009. 36p. pap. 12.95 *(978-1-59858-825-5(7))* Dog Ear Publishing, LLC.
Ehlert, Lois. Pie in the Sky. Ehlert, Lois, illus. 2004. (ENG., Illus.). 40p. (J). (gr. -1-3). 17.99 *(978-0-15-216584-0(3)*, 1201415, Clarion Bks.) HarperCollins Pubs.
Ellen, Connie. Marvel Mansion Gang. 2012. 114p. 22.19 *(978-1-4269-6666-8(0))* Trafford Publishing.
Ellis, Leanne Statland. Tree Huggers. 2010. (J). pap. *(978-0-88092-521-1(3))* Royal Fireworks Publishing Co.
Emma's Problem, 6 Pack. (Literatura 2000 Ser.). (gr. 1-2). 28.00 *(978-0-7635-0131-0(X))* Rigby Education.
Erickson, Patricia. The Little Christmas Tree. 2012. 24p. (-18). pap. 17.99 *(978-1-4772-8610-4(1))* AuthorHouse.
Evert, Jeffrey. The Tree That Didn't Want to Be. 2004. pap. 9.00 *(978-0-8059-6189-8(5))* Dorrance Publishing Co., Inc.
Evyindson, Peter. Jen & the Great One, 1 vol. Brynjolson, Rhian, illus. 2015. (ENG.). 32p. (J). (gr. k-4). mass mkt. 10.95 *(978-1-921827-19-1(9)*, 51e37bea-0bcb-45c0-b2b8-9f0475be003) Pemmican Pubns., Inc. CAN. Dist: Firefly Bks., Ltd.
Fields, Trisha A. Eggbert, the Hero. 2012. 44p. pap. 21.99 *(978-1-4771-3548-8(0))* Xlibris Corp.
Fischer, Lavanya Regunathan. One Tree, One King & the Open Road. 2015. 212p. 14.99 *(978-93-5177-028-2(1)*, HarperCollins) HarperCollins Pubs.
Fitzgerald, J. Rupert, the Sturdy Oak Tree: Who thought he was a little better than the other Trees. 2010. 16p. (J). pap. 14.95 *(978-1-4327-5734-2(2))* Outskirts Pr., Inc.
Fitzmartin, Elisa D. God's Silent Soldier. 2012. 32p. pap. 13.99 *(978-1-4497-3913-3(X)*, WestBow Pr.) Author Solutions, LLC.
Fleischman, Paul. The Birthday Tree. Root, Barry, illus. 2008. (ENG.). 40p. (J). (gr. -1-3). 16.99 *(978-0-7636-2604-4(X))* Candlewick Pr.
Fleming, Chula. Spooky Old Tree, 1 vol. 2010. 26p. pap. 24.95 *(978-1-4489-9166-2(8))* PublishAmerica, Inc.
Forbes, Chris. El Tronco de Arbol, Level 1. Flor Ada, Alma, tr. Sullivan, Don, illus. 2003. (Dejame Leer Ser.). (SPA.). 8p. (J). (gr. -1-k). 6.50 *(978-0-673-36300-8(7)*, Good Year Bks.) Celebration Pr.
Ford, RoShawn T. Marty & the Magical Christmas Tree. 2012. 24p. pap. 17.99 *(978-1-4772-3719-9(4))* AuthorHouse.
Formento, Alison. This Tree Counts! Snow, Sarah, illus. 2013. (AV2 Fiction Readalong Ser.: Vol. 72). (ENG.). (J). (gr. k-3). 34.28 *(978-1-62127-902-0(2)*, AV2 by Weigl) Weigl Pubs., Inc.
—This Tree Counts! Snow, Sarah, illus. 2019. (These Things Count! Ser.). (ENG.). 32p. (J). (gr. -1-3). pap. 7.99 *(978-0-8075-7897-1(5)*, 807578975) Whitman, Albert & Co.
Fortuna, Loma. When God Spoke to Trees. 2006. 17.00 *(978-0-8059-9884-9(5))* Dorrance Publishing Co., Inc.
Fowler, Greg. T Is for Tree. 2017. (ENG.). 388p. (YA). (gr. 7). pap. 12.95 *(978-1-78530-126-1(8))* Black and White Publishing Ltd. GBR. Dist: Independent Pubs. Group.
Freedman, Georgene. The Olive Tree. 2nd num. ed. 2006. (J). per. 12.95 *(978-0-9771322-1-8(8))* Simpatico Bks.
French, Joyce. The Popcorn Tree. Hansen, Paisley, illus. 2012. 22p. 15.95 *(978-1-60414-639-4(7))* Fideli Publishing, Inc.
French, S. Terrell. Operation Redwood. 2011. (ENG.). 368p. (J). (gr. 3-7). pap. 9.95 *(978-0-8109-9720-2(7)*, 634703) Abrams, Inc.
French, Vivian. Morris in the Apple Tree. Villet, Olivia, illus. 2011. (ENG.). 64p. pap. 5.99 *(978-0-00-718027-1(6)*, HarperCollins Children's Bks.) HarperCollins Pubs. Ltd. GBR. Dist: HarperCollins Pubs.
Frisch, Aaron. The Lonely Pine. Delessert, Etienne, illus. 2011. (ENG.). 32p. (J). (gr. 1-3). 17.99 *(978-1-56846-214-1(X)*, 22066, Creative Editions) Creative Co., The.
Fuggle, Debbie. The Two Little Fir Trees. 2012. 28p. pap. 32.70 *(978-1-4691-3253-2(2))* Xlibris Corp.
Galbraith, Kathryn O. Arbor Day Square, 1 vol. Moore, Cyd, illus. 2016. 32p. (J). (gr. -1-3). pap. 7.99 *(978-1-56145-922-3(4))* Peachtree Publishing Co. Inc.
Galjanic, Lisa. When Leaves Die. Hope, Michelle, illus. 2007. (J). 9.95 *(978-1-933532-00-4(9))* LSG Pubns.
Gardner, Yvonne. Scrawny the Tree. 2005. 12p. 11.33 *(978-1-4116-6413-5(2))* Lulu Pr., Inc.
Gates, Pat. The Apple Tree's Secret, 1 vol. Hosselkus, Devin, illus. 2009. 47p. pap. 24.95 *(978-1-60836-637-8(5))* America Star Bks.
Gault, Linda Fulford. The Chosen Tree. 2011. 28p. pap. 12.95 *(978-1-4567-1561-8(5))* AuthorHouse.
Gentner, Norma L. & Young, Steve. Save a Tree for Me. (Song Box Ser.). (Illus.). 16p. (gr. 1-2). 31.50 *(978-0-7802-2264-9(4))* Wright Group/McGraw-Hill.
George, Lynn. The Leaf Pile, 1 vol. 2006. (Neighborhood Readers Ser.). (ENG.). 16p. (gr. 1-2). pap. 6.50 *(978-1-4042-7120-3(1)*, eb28fcd8-46b5-4310-bbff-9d8e2396137c, Rosen Classroom) Rosen Publishing Group, Inc., The.
George, Olivia. The Weather. Fletcher, Rusty, illus. 2005. (My First Reader Ser.). (ENG.). 32p. (J). (gr. k-1). lib. bdg. 18.50 *(978-0-516-24880-6(4)*, Children's Pr.) Scholastic Library Publishing.
Gettman, Cheryl. Molly Magee & the Jelly Bean Tree. 2011. 24p. pap. 12.99 *(978-1-4634-3770-1(6))* AuthorHouse.
Gibbs, D. Renee. The Special Little Christmas Tree. 2003. (Illus.). (J). bds. 14.95 *(978-0-9741406-0-5(0))* Cranberry Quill Publishing Co.
Gile, John. El Primer Bosque. Kohen-Klieman, Clarita, tr. 2006.Tr. of First Forest. (SPA., Illus.). 40p. per. 9.95 *(978-0-910941-15-0(7))* JGC/United Publishing Corps.
Gillen, Lisa P. Spring Time. Gillen, Lisa P., illus. Lt. ed. 2006. (Illus.). 12p. (J). (gr. -1-k). pap. 10.95 *(978-1-57332-351-2(9)*, HighReach Learning, Incorporated) Carson-Dellosa Publishing, LLC.
Gilman, Phoebe. The Balloon Tree. 2011. (ENG., Illus.). 32p. (J). (gr. -1-k). 16.95 *(978-1-61608-454-7(5)*, 608454, Sky Pony Pr.) Skyhorse Publishing Co., Inc.
Givens, Ed. Molly Maple: The Wishing Star. 2004. (Illus.). 32p. (J). bds. 14.95 *(978-1-59094-053-2(9)*, Jawbreakers for Kids) Jawbone Publishing Corp.
Goebel, Kelly. Adventures in the Weeping Willow Tree. Murfield, Anna, illus. 2013. 26p. pap. 9.99 *(978-1-937165-49-9(3))* Orange Hat Publishing.
Goertzen, Angelina. Tinsel the Christmas Tree. 2009. 32p. pap. 12.49 *(978-1-4389-8569-5(X))* AuthorHouse.
Goldstyn, Jacques. Bertolt. Bedrick, Claudia Zoe, tr. 2017. (Illus.). 80p. (J). (gr. -1-4). 15.95 *(978-1-59270-229-9(5))* Enchanted Lion Bks., LLC.
Grandfather Pine & His Special Place: Book One - Spring. 2013. 48p. *(978-1-4602-2520-2(1))* FriesenPress.
Grant, Carolyn E. Christmas in Maggie's Neighborhood. 2009. 24p. pap. 12.99 *(978-1-4490-0633-4(7))* AuthorHouse.
Greathouse, Lisa. Johnny Appleseed, 1 vol. rev. ed. 2009. (Reader's Theater Ser.). (ENG.). 24p. (gr. 2-4). pap. 8.99 *(978-1-4333-0990-8(4))* Teacher Created Materials, Inc.
Green, M. L. Underneath My Favorite Tree. 2008. 20p. pap. 24.95 *(978-1-60474-858-1(3))* America Star Bks.
Greenwood, Chris. Tanya Talia Plants A Tree. 2007. (Illus.). 32p. (J). 12.95 *(978-0-9799540-1-6(0))* E Innovative Ideas.

—Tanya Talia Plats a Tree. 2007. (Illus.). 32p. (J). pap. 10.95 *(978-0-9799540-0-9(2))* E Innovative Ideas.
Griffin, Saundra J. Which Should I Be? 2004. 21p. pap. 24.95 *(978-1-4137-3167-5(8))* PublishAmerica, Inc.
Grime, L. L. Little Tree. 2007. 48p. pap. 22.95 *(978-1-4357-0092-5(9))* Lulu Pr., Inc.
Guarneri, Cristina. The Magic Tree. 2005. 50p. pap. 10.95 *(978-0-7414-2336-8(7))* Infinity Publishing.
Gurney, Stella. Not so Silly Sausage. Million, Liz, illus. 2011. 32p. pap. *(978-1-84089-707-4(4))* Zero to Ten, Ltd.
Haen, Teri R. Treasure to Love. 2012. 74p. pap. 27.95 *(978-1-4497-4207-2(6),* WestBow Pr.) Author Solutions, LLC.
Hahn, Molly. Under the Sneep Tree: The Wamboozling of a Village. 2009. pap. *(978-1-61623-907-7(7))* Independent Pub.
Hale, Shannon. Forest Born. 2017. (Books of Bayern Ser.). (ENG.). 400p. (YA). pap. 10.99 *(978-1-68119-319-9(1),* 900165750, Bloomsbury USA Childrens) Bloomsbury Publishing USA.
Hall, Michael. Wonderfall. 2016. (ENG., Illus.). 40p. (J). (gr. -1-3). 17.99 *(978-0-06-238298-6(5),* Greenwillow Bks.) HarperCollins Pubs.
Hannah, Helen Elizabeth. Let's Help Little Polka Dot Find His Way Home. 2011. 32p. pap. 21.99 *(978-1-4568-5194-1(2))* Xlibris Corp.
Harman, Ian. The Adventures of Terry Tool Bench: Book 1 Terry Is Born. 2009. 36p. pap. 16.99 *(978-1-4490-0048-6(7))* AuthorHouse.
Harman, Michael. The Parrot & the Fig Tree: A Story about Friendship & Respect for Nature. 2nd ed. 2009. (Jataka Tales Ser.). (Illus.). 32p. (J). (gr. -1-5). pap. 8.95 *(978-0-89800-430-4(6))* Dharma Publishing.
Harris, Odis Clinton. Wee Willie & the Lonely Pine. 2008. 23p. pap. 24.95 *(978-1-60563-741-9(6))* America Star Bks.
Harrison, Francesca. Obus the Eucalyptus Tree Fairy. 2012. 26p. pap. *(978-1-909381-03-2(9))* Foote, Douglas.
Hartwell, Dana S. The Angry Tree. 2011. 24p. pap. 24.95 *(978-1-4626-3671-6(3))* America Star Bks.
Haxhia, Miranda. Andy's Cherry Tree. Deisadze, Zaur, illus. 2007. (POL & ENG.). 32p. (J). pap. 12.95 *(978-1-60195-094-9(2))* International Step by Step Assn.
Haynes, Anne S. Little Tree Makes a New Year's Resolution. 2013. 28p. pap. 24.95 *(978-1-4241-0479-6(3))* America Star Bks.
Henderson, Brandon. The Legend of the Kukui Nut. 2008. 32p. (J). 15.99 *(978-1-59955-119-7(5))* Cedar Fort, Inc./CFI Distribution.
Higgs, Liz Curtis. The Pine Tree Parable. 2005. (Parable Ser.). 32p. (J). pap. 3.99 *(978-1-4003-0685-5(X))* Nelson, Thomas Inc.
Hoedl, Lee. Jesse the Wait of the Wood. Hoedl, Lee, photos by. 2006. (Illus.). 30p. (J). per. 12.95 *(978-1-59879-139-6(7))* Lifevest Publishing, Inc.
Hoffman, Mary Ann. The Maple Tree Mystery. (Neighborhood Readers Ser.). (ENG.). 16p. 2007. 37.95 *(978-1-4042-7342-9(5))* 2006. (gr. 1-2). pap. 6.50 *(978-1-4042-7220-0(8),* d2f27e77-c054-4adc-ba36-4f0206c429a1) Rosen Publishing Group, Inc., The. (Rosen Classroom).
—El misterio en el árbol (the Maple Tree Mystery) 2007. (Lecturas del barrio (Neighborhood Readers) Ser.). (SPA.). 16p. 37.95 *(978-1-4042-7343-6(3),* Rosen Classroom) Rosen Publishing Group, Inc., The.
Hofmeister, Alan, et al. Bud & the Tree. (Reading for All Learners Ser.). (Illus.). (J). pap. *(978-1-56861-135-8(8))* Swift Learning Resources.
Holm, M. S. The Arborist. Sayles, Susana, illus. 2007. (ENG.). 104p. (J). 16.95 *(978-0-9796199-1-5(2));* pap. 11.95 *(978-0-9796199-3-9(9))* Great West Publishing. (Sentry Bks.).
Holston-Holloway, Angela M. The Apple Pie Kids. 2006. (J). pap. 8.00 *(978-0-8059-6899-6(7))* Dorrance Publishing Co., Inc.
Hopkins, Leslie. A World Apart. 2012. 20p. pap. 17.99 *(978-1-4772-6783-7(2))* AuthorHouse.
Hopkinson, Deborah. Apples to Oregon. 2014. 17.00 *(978-1-63419-642-0(2))* Perfection Learning Corp.
—Apples to Oregon: Being the (Slightly) True Narrative of How a Brave Pioneer Father Brought Apples, Peaches, Pears, Plums, Grapes, & Cherries (and Children) Across the Plains. Carpenter, Nancy, illus. 2008. (ENG.). 40p. (J). (gr. -1-3). 8.99 *(978-1-4169-6746-0(X),* Aladdin) Simon & Schuster Children's Publishing.
—Apples to Oregon: Being the (Slightly) True Narrative of How a Brave Pioneer Father Brought Apples, Peaches, Pears, Plums, Grapes, & Cherries (and Children) Across the Plains. Carpenter, Nancy, illus. 2004. (ENG.). 40p. (J). (gr. -1-3). 19.99 *(978-0-689-84769-1(6))* Simon & Schuster, Inc.
Horman, Mamie. Carrie's Silver Christmas Tree. 2007. 32p. per. 12.95 *(978-1-4327-1615-8(8))* Outskirts Pr., Inc.
Houts, Michelle. Nuts about Science: Lucy's Lab #1. Zechel, Elizabeth, illus. 2017. (Lucy's Lab Ser.: 1). (ENG.). 112p. (J). (gr. 1-4). 13.99 *(978-1-5107-1064-1(7),* Sky Pony Pr.) Skyhorse Publishing Co., Inc.
Howell, Julie Ann. The Pepper Tree, How the Seeds Were Planted! LaGrange, Tiffany, illus. 2008. 28p. pap. 12.95 *(978-0-9820479-0-3(8))* Peppertree Pr., The.
—The Pepper Tree, How the Seeds Were Planted. LaGrange, Tiffany, illus. 2012. 28p. pap. 24.95 *(978-1-61493-059-4(7))* Peppertree Pr., The.
Hughes, David Pierce & Perot, Richard. The One Tree. 2006. (Illus.). 48p. (J). pap. 7.99 *(978-1-905470-18-1(5))* SeaSquirt Pubns. GBR. Dist: Basic Distribution, Inc.
Hunt, Zoe. Azarels Christmas Wish. 2007. (J). per. 10.95 *(978-1-934345-20-7(2))* GoodLife Publishing.
Hunt, Zoe Paton. Azrael's Magical Moment. 2008. 24p. pap. 18.95 *(978-1-60693-070-0(2),* Strategic Bk. Publishing) Strategic Book Publishing & Rights Agency (SBPRA).
I Am Twee' 2013. (Illus.). 24p. (J). pap. 12.99 *(978-0-9889113-2-1(9))* Coda Grove Publishing.
Ikeda, Daisaku. The Cherry Tree. McCaughrean, Geraldine, tr. from JPN. Wildsmith, Brian, illus. 2013. 6.95 *(978-1-935523-57-4(0))* World Tribune Pr.
Irene's Wish. 2014. (ENG., Illus.). 32p. (J). (gr. k-4). 18.99 *(978-0-689-86300-4(4),* Simon & Schuster/Paula Wiseman Bks.) Simon & Schuster/Paula Wiseman Bks.
Irish, Terry. Tree Secrets. 2012. (ENG.). (J). pap. *(978-1-4675-4341-5(1))* Independent Pub.
Iverson, Diane. My Favorite Tree: Terrific Trees of North America. 2004. (Sharing Nature with Children Book Ser.). (Illus.). 64p. (YA). (gr. -1-3). pap. 9.95 *(978-1-883220-93-8(9))* Take Heart Pubns.
Ives, Suzanne Lintz. Bob, the Tree who Became a Star. 2010. 16p. (J). pap. 14.95 *(978-1-4327-2748-2(6))* Outskirts Pr., Inc.
Jackson, Tyrone. Save Our Home. 2006. (ENG.). 88p. per. 16.95 *(978-1-4241-0875-6(6))* PublishAmerica, Inc.
Jacobs, Jaco. A Good Day for Climbing Trees. Geldenhuys, Kobus, tr. 2018. (ENG., Illus.). 160p. (J). pap. 11.99 *(978-1-78607-317-4(X),* 178607317X, Rock the Boat) Oneworld Pubns. GBR. Dist: Grantham Bk. Services.
Jamieson, Mark. Ico Island. 2007. (J). pap. 11.95 *(978-0-9792518-0-1(X))* Gequalsa.
Jeanfield. Twinkle, a Christmas Story. 2009. 36p. pap. 13.95 *(978-1-60693-745-7(6),* Eloquent Bks.) Strategic Book Publishing & Rights Agency (SBPRA).
Jeffers, Oliver. The Great Paper Caper. Jeffers, Oliver, illus. 2009. (ENG., Illus.). 40p. (J). (gr. -1-k). 19.99 *(978-0-399-25097-2(2),* Philomel Bks.) Penguin Young Readers Group.
Jo-Marie. Adi's World. 2013. 198p. 33.99 *(978-1-4497-9417-0(3));* pap. 17.99 *(978-1-4497-9416-3(5))* Author Solutions, LLC. (WestBow Pr.).
Johns, Eric. The Giraffe Tree & Other Tall Stories. 2012. (ENG.). 179p. (-18). pap. 12.95 *(978-1-291-03279-6(7))* Lulu Pr., Inc.
Johnson-Carrigan, Ettarose. Old Rugged: How the Tree Became the Cross. 2008. 24p. pap. 11.99 *(978-1-4389-2781-7(9))* AuthorHouse.
Johnson, Dennis. The Tree That Went Sailing. 2009. (J). pap. *(978-1-61623-539-0(X))* Independent Pub.
—The Tree That Went Sailing: (Based on a true story - Palm Beach, Florida) 2009. (ENG.). 40p. pap. 21.99 *(978-1-4415-0181-3(9))* Xlibris Corp.
Johnson, Donna. The Story of the Little Red Leaf. Johnson, Emily, illus. l.t. ed. 2006. (ENG.). 22p. (J). 25.00 *(978-0-9778774-0-9(X))* Choice Point Editions.
Johnson, Grant. Big Tree Bob. 2012. 20p. pap. 12.50 *(978-1-61897-208-8(1),* Strategic Bk. Publishing) Strategic Book Publishing & Rights Agency (SBPRA).
Johnson, Lafayette, Jr. & Liberty, Dendron. Tyler's Wise Old Tree. 2012. (Illus.). 65p. (J). pap. 12.99 *(978-0-9817448-1-0(8))* MaMbabooks.com.
Johnson, Penny, illus. Here Comes Santa! 2016. (J). *(978-1-4351-6387-4(7))* Barnes & Noble, Inc.
Johnson, William C. Little Tree. 2007. pap. 9.00 *(978-0-8059-8486-6(0))* Dorrance Publishing Co., Inc.
Johnston, Tony. Isabel's House of Butterflies. Guevara, Susan, illus. 2005. 32p. pap. 6.95 *(978-1-58685-844-5(0))* Gibbs Smith, Publisher.
Karas, G. Brian. As an Oak Tree Grows. Karas, G. Brian, illus. 2014. (Illus.). 32p. (J). (gr. k-3). 19.99 *(978-0-399-25233-4(9),* Nancy Paulsen Books) Penguin Young Readers Group.
Kaufile, Christa. The Little Acorn. Natural Resources Conservation Service (U.S.), ed. Tannehill, Mary Jo, illus. 2008. (ENG.). 24p. (gr. -1-4). pap. 5.00 *(978-0-16-081701-4(3),* Forest Service) United States Government Printing Office.
Kayler, Ralph. The Tea Party in the Tree Tops. 2009. 48p. pap. 19.49 *(978-1-4389-8000-3(0))* AuthorHouse.
Kelley, Alden. A Tree Is a Home. 2017. (Learn-To-Read Ser.). (ENG., Illus.). (J). pap. 3.49 *(978-1-68310-302-8(5))* Pacific Learning, Inc.
Kellis, Michael. The Grubkins. 2008. 36p. pap. 17.49 *(978-1-4343-8708-0(9))* AuthorHouse.
Kelly, Erin Entrada. Maybe Maybe Marisol Rainey. Kelly, Erin Entrada, illus. 2021. (Maybe Marisol Ser.: 1). (ENG., Illus.). 160p. (J). (gr. 3-7). 18.99 *(978-0-06-297042-8(9),* Greenwillow Bks.) HarperCollins Pubs.
Kelly, Karen. Angel Tree. 2012. (Illus.). 24p. pap. 19.82 *(978-1-4678-9637-5(3))* AuthorHouse.
Kelso, Mary Jean. One Family's Christmas. Snider, K. C., illus. 2012. 24p. 19.95 *(978-1-61633-308-9(1))* Guardian Angel Publishing, Inc.
Kendall, Jack. The Magic Apple Tree. Bostrom, Sally, illus. l.t. ed. 2006. (ENG.). 48p. (J). per. 9.95 *(978-0-9787740-4-2(3))* Peppertree Pr., The.
King, Jo. A Flight of Fancy. 2011. 58p. 24.99 *(978-1-4691-3665-3(1));* pap. 15.99 *(978-1-4653-9298-5(X))* Xlibris Corp.
Kirk, Janice. The Christmas Redwood. Kirk, Janice, illus. 2007. (Illus.). 56p. per. 18.95 *(978-1-60290-147-6(3))* Nassau-Street.com.
Kisson, Nisha. Leah - the Fairy of the Lime Tree. KecskTs, Anna, illus. 2008. 36p. pap. *(978-1-904312-39-0(X))* MX Publishing, Ltd.
Klise, Kate & Klise, M. Sarah. Regarding the Trees: A Splintered Saga Rooted in Secrets. Klise, Kate & Klise, M. Sarah, illus. 2007. (Regarding The ... Ser.: Bk. 3). (ENG., Illus.). 160p. (J). (gr. 3-7). pap. 7.99 *(978-0-15-206090-9(1),* 1198293, Clarion Bks.) HarperCollins Pubs.
Knights, David. Stumpy the Tree. 2013. 28p. pap. 24.95 *(978-1-62709-375-0(3))* America Star Bks.
Korten, Gerri. The Parakeets & the Ginkgo Tree at Hide Park. l.t. ed. 2006. (Illus.). 36p. (J). 18.85 *(978-0-9785609-7-3(3))* New Global Publishing.
Koumjian, Gay Melanie. Mojo's Mojo. 2013. (ENG.). 23p. (J). pap. 12.95 *(978-1-4787-1623-5(1))* Outskirts Pr., Inc.
Krensky, Stephen. My Pet Tree. Albert, Hobai, Ioana, illus. 2016. (J). *(978-0-7680-8372-9(9))* SAE Intl.
—Once upon a Time in the Woods. Shortley, Michele, illus. 2011. (J). pap. *(978-0-7680-3488-2(4))* SAE Intl.
Krishnaswami, Uma. Out of the Way! Out of the Way!, 1 vol. Krishnaswamy, Uma, illus. 2012. (ENG.). 28p. (J). (gr. -1-2). 17.95 *(978-1-55498-130-4(1))* Groundwood Bks. CAN. Dist: Publishers Group West (PGW).
—Out of the Way! Out of the Way!, 1 vol. Uma Krishnaswamy, illus. 2022. (ENG.). 24p. (J). (gr. k-2). pap. 11.99 ***(978-81-8146-792-8(2))*** Tulika Pubs. IND. Dist: Independent Pubs. Group.
Kruusval, Catarina. Ellen's Apple Tree. Sandin, Joan, tr. from SWE. 2008. (Illus.). 32p. (J). (gr. -1-3). 16.00 *(978-91-29-66905-3(7))* R & S Bks. SWE. Dist: Macmillan.
L. Ray. Lady Bugs 3. 2005. (ENG.). 24p. per. 12.99 *(978-1-4134-8583-7(9))* Xlibris Corp.
Laing, Amy Wilson. Ginger Helps Spikey. 2011. (Illus.). 28p. pap. 15.99 *(978-1-4568-5912-1(9))* Xlibris Corp.
Langton, Jane. The Dragon Tree. 2008. (Hall Family Chronicles). 176p. (J). (gr. 3-7). lib. bdg. 16.89 *(978-0-06-082342-9(9))* HarperCollins Pubs.
Lanqcaon, Jeff. Grandpa's Magic Banyan Tree. 2005. 32p. (J). 12.95 *(978-1-56647-740-6(9))* Mutual Publishing LLC.
Lasky, Kathryn. The Golden Tree. 2007. (Guardians of Ga'Hoole Ser.: 12). (Illus.). 192p. lib. bdg. 17.20 *(978-1-4177-8260-4(9))* Turtleback.
Lawless, Mary Ann. The Proud Christmas Tree. McCool, Arlene, illus. 2006. (J). 12.95 *(978-0-9772795-0-0(2))* Tuesday's Child.
Lawlor, Laurie. Big Tree Down! Gordon, David, illus. 2018. (ENG.). 32p. (J). (gr. -1-3). 17.95 *(978-0-8234-3661-3(6))* Holiday Hse., Inc.
Layton, Neal. The Tree: An Environmental Fable. Layton, Neal, illus. 2017. (ENG., Illus.). 40p. (J). (-k). 17.99 *(978-0-7636-8952-0(1))* Candlewick Pr.
Leavey, Peggy Dymond. The Path Through the Trees. 2005. (ENG., Illus.). 136p. (J). pap. 8.95 *(978-1-894917-21-6(9),* Napoleon & Co.) Dundurn Pr. CAN. Dist: Publishers Group West (PGW).
Lee, Glenda. Alexander's Tree. 2012. 28p. pap. 24.95 *(978-1-4626-9734-2(8))* America Star Bks.
Leigh, Autumn. The Apple Tree. (Neighborhood Readers Ser.). (ENG.). 16p. 2007. 33.50 *(978-1-4042-7328-3(X))* 2006. (gr. 1-2). pap. 6.50 *(978-1-4042-7128-9(7),* e3b3cedf-a072-4b5b-89a1-89173083a724) Rosen Publishing Group, Inc., The. (Rosen Classroom).
—El manzano (the Apple Tree) 2007. (Lecturas del barrio (Neighborhood Readers) Ser.). (SPA.). 16p. 33.50 *(978-1-4042-7329-0(8),* Rosen Classroom) Rosen Publishing Group, Inc., The.
Leon, Georgina Lazaro & León, Georgina Lázaro. El Flamboyan Amarillo. Delacre, Lulu, illus. 2nd ed. 2016.Tr. of Yellow Flame Tree. (SPA.). 32p. (J). 14.99 *(978-1-930332-55-3(6))* Lectorum Pubns., Inc.
Lester, Julius. The Girl Who Saved Yesterday. Angel, Carl, illus. 2016. (ENG.). 32p. (J). (gr. 2-5). 16.99 *(978-1-939547-24-8(5),* 13dc2969-1695-493e-a2a3-10c58eaf602d) Creston Bks.
Lindquist, Jennie D. The Crystal Tree. Chalmers, Mary, illus. 2008. (J). (gr. 2-6). 25.00 *(978-0-8446-6287-9(9))* Smith, Peter Pub., Inc.
Linsley, Sonja Paschal. The Conifer Court Competition. Linsley, Paul, illus. 2006. 26p. (J). 18.95 *(978-0-9766062-1-5(6),* HGP 2005-2) Higher Ground Pr.
Little Tree. Date not set. *(978-0-517-80134-5(5))* Random Hse. Value Publishing.
The Littlest Christmas Tree. 2005. 45.00 *(978-0-916773-85-4(X))* Book Peddlers.
Long, Loren. Little Tree. Long, Loren, illus. 2015. (Illus.). 40p. (J). (gr. k-3). 18.99 *(978-0-399-16397-5(2),* Philomel Bks.) Penguin Young Readers Group.
Lucado, Max. Best of All. Martinez, Sergio, illus. 2003. (Max Lucado's Wemmicks Ser.: 4). (ENG.). 32p. (J). 16.99 *(978-1-58134-501-8(1))* Crossway.
Lucken, Eve M. The Tree, the Crazy Leaf, & Me. 2012. 64p. pap. 20.99 *(978-1-4525-5016-9(6))* Balboa Pr.
Luyken, Corinna. The Tree in Me. 2021. (Illus.). 56p. (J). (gr. -1-3). 18.99 *(978-0-593-11259-5(8),* Dial Bks) Penguin Young Readers Group.
Lynn, Michelle. Fall Leaves. 2008. 17p. pap. 24.95 *(978-1-60672-027-1(9))* America Star Bks.
MacKay, Elly, illus. If You Hold a Seed. 2013. (ENG.). 32p. (J). (gr. -1-1). 17.99 *(978-0-7624-4721-3(4),* Running Pr. Kids) Running Pr.
Macor, Jim. Frazier Fir, A Christmas Fable. Macor, Jim, illus. 2007. (Illus.). 32p. (J). 17.95 *(978-0-9785551-3-9(9))* Zuber Publishing.
Maddock-Cowart, Donna. The Anhinga Tree. Mann, William A., illus. 2012. 74p. pap. 9.95 *(978-0-9836484-3-7(3))* Miglior Pr.
Madhu, Kailash. The Wise Tree & Meu: Mind & Spirit. 2012. 108p. pap. 40.81 *(978-1-4669-2744-5(5))* Trafford Publishing.
Mahon, Matthew. The Defenders of All Thats Fall. 2008. 56p. pap. 24.95 *(978-1-4327-3169-4(6))* Outskirts Pr., Inc.
Markarian, Marianne. The Pesky Bird Wasielewski, Margaret M., illus. l.t. ed. 2005. 32p. (J). 16.00 *(978-0-9767377-0-4(1))* Pomegranate Publishing.
Marshall, Jane Garrett. The Christmas Tree That Cried. Tomasek, Dean, illus. 2013. 106p. pap. 24.99 *(978-0-9896247-0-1(6))* WRB Pub.
Marston, Elsa. The Olive Tree. Ewart, Claire, illus. 2014. 32p. (J). (gr. -1-2). 16.95 *(978-1-937786-29-8(3),* Wisdom Tales) World Wisdom, Inc.
Martin, Bill, Jr. & Archambault, John. Chicka Chicka ABC: Lap Edition. Ehlert, Lois, illus. 2009. (Chicka Chicka Book Ser.). (ENG.). 16p. (J). (gr. -1-1). bds. 11.99 *(978-1-4169-8447-4(X),* Little Simon) Little Simon.
—Chicka Chicka Boom Boom: Book & CD. Ehlert, Lois, illus. 2006. (Chicka Chicka Book Ser.). (ENG.). 40p. (J). (gr. -1-3). 10.99 *(978-1-4169-2718-1(2),* Little Simon) Little Simon.
Martin, David. Christmas Tree. Sweet, Melissa, illus. 2009. (ENG.). 26p. (J). (— 1). bds. 5.99 *(978-0-7636-3030-0(6))* Candlewick Pr.
Martin, Jayme. Skinny Little Tree. 2013. (ENG.). 28p. (J). 18.95 *(978-1-4787-0813-1(1));* pap. 13.95 *(978-1-4787-0870-4(0))* Outskirts Pr., Inc.
Martin, T. J. Why Do the Leaves Fall? 2008. (ENG.). 20p. 12.49 *(978-1-4389-4329-9(6))* AuthorHouse.
Marvelous Marty. 2008. (J). *(978-0-9778113-4-2(4));* pap. *(978-0-9778113-5-9(2))* HeartFelt Stories LLC.
Mason, Charlene. Mr Wilson's Tree. 2012. 28p. pap. 24.95 *(978-1-4626-7975-1(7))* America Star Bks.
Matheson, Christie. Tap the Magic Tree. Matheson, Christie, illus. 2013. (ENG., Illus.). 40p. (J). (gr. -1-3). 18.99 *(978-0-06-227445-8(7),* Greenwillow Bks.) HarperCollins Pubs.
Matsuura, Richard & Matsuura, Ruth. Fruit, the Tree & the Flower. (J). 8.95 *(978-1-887916-02-8(4))* Orchid Isle Publishing Co.
Maylin, Grace B. There Will Come Another: A Lesson from the Trees. Maylin, Grace B., photos by. 2007. (Illus.). per. *(978-0-9792384-0-6(4))* Maylin, Grace.
Mazzola, Lori. Tales of the Tree People to Tree... or. 2006. 48p. pap. 16.95 *(978-1-4241-5065-6(5))* PublishAmerica, Inc.
McAllister, Ava. The Honor Tree. 2011. 24p. 15.00 *(978-1-4567-3524-1(1))* AuthorHouse.
McEvoy, Grace. The Tiniest Tepee. 2005. 9.00 *(978-0-8059-8040-0(7))* Dorrance Publishing Co., Inc.
McLeod, Rona. Big Daddy Chinaberry: Love Given - Love Returned. McLeod, Herbert, illus. 2012. 24p. pap. 24.95 *(978-1-4626-7700-9(2))* America Star Bks.
McPhail, David. The Searcher & Old Tree. McPhail, David, illus. 2011. (ENG., Illus.). 32p. (J). (gr. -1-2). pap. 7.95 *(978-1-58089-224-7(8))* Charlesbridge Publishing, Inc.
McVay, Elizabeth. Baby Bun & the Littlest Tree. 2004. (Illus.). 31p. (J). pap. 9.95 *(978-0-9759621-0-7(8))* Koenisha Pubns.
Meister, Cari. I Love Trees. Sirrell, Terry, illus. 2011. (Rookie Ready to Learn Ser.). 40p. (J). pap. 5.95 *(978-0-531-26733-2(4),* Children's Pr.) Scholastic Library Publishing.
—Rookie Ready to Learn en Español: Me Fascinan Los árboles. Sirrell, Terry, illus. 2011. (Rookie Ready to Learn Español Ser.). Orig. Title: Rookie Ready to Learn: I Love Trees. (SPA.). 40p. (J). pap. 5.95 *(978-0-531-26786-8(5),* Children's Pr.) Scholastic Library Publishing.
Meister, Cari & Sirrell, Terry. Me Fascinan Los Arboles. Sirrell, Terry, illus. 2005. (Rookie Reader Español Ser.). (ENG & SPA., Illus.). 32p. (J). (gr. k-2). 19.50 *(978-0-516-25253-7(4),* Children's Pr.) Scholastic Library Publishing.
Mellon, Nancy. The Knottles, 1 vol. Lieberherr, Ruth, illus. 2012. 32p. (J). pap. 11.95 *(978-1-62148-003-7(8))* SteinerBooks, Inc.
Mercer, Steven A. Florence the Fir Tree: (and the Angels of the Forest) 2012. 36p. 24.95 *(978-1-4560-6659-8(5))* America Star Bks.
Meron, Renato Mas. Why Mangrove Roots Float. 2013. 20p. pap. 24.95 *(978-1-63000-427-9(8))* America Star Bks.
Mesibere, Ellen. The Curse of the Laulau Tree. Manasau, Amos, illus. 2012. 34p. pap. *(978-9980-945-67-9(2))* Univ. of Papua New Guinea Pr.
Messier, Mireille. The Branch. Pratt, Pierre, illus. 2016. (ENG.). 32p. (J). (gr. -1-2). 16.95 *(978-1-77138-564-0(2))* Kids Can Pr., Ltd. CAN. Dist: Hachette Bk. Group.
Messner, Kate. The Brilliant Fall of Gianna Z. 2017. (ENG.). 224p. (J). pap. 8.99 *(978-1-68119-547-6(X),* 900177249, Bloomsbury USA Childrens) Bloomsbury Publishing USA.
—The Brilliant Fall of Gianna Z. 2017. (J). lib. bdg. 19.65 *(978-0-606-40595-9(X))* Turtleback.
—The Brilliant Fall of Gianna Z. 2010. (ENG.). 208p. (YA). (gr. 4-6). 24.94 *(978-0-8027-9842-8(X),* 9780802798428) Walker & Co.
Metzger, Steve. Under the Apple Tree. Girasole, Alessia, illus. 2009. (J). *(978-0-545-14200-7(8))* Scholastic, Inc.
Micklos, John, Jr. & Micklos, John. One Leaf, Two Leaves, Count with Me! McFarland, Clive, illus. 2017. 32p. (J). (— 1). 16.99 *(978-0-399-54471-2(2),* Nancy Paulsen Books) Penguin Young Readers Group.
Migliore, R. Elizabeth. Stanley, 1 vol. 2009. 13p. pap. 24.95 *(978-1-61546-829-4(3))* America Star Bks.
Mill, Lynda. Let's Climb the Apple Tree. 2012. 44p. pap. 17.45 *(978-1-4669-6871-4(0))* Trafford Publishing.
Mills, Joyce C. Gentle Willow: A Story for Children about Dying. Pillo, Cary, illus. 2nd ed. 2003. 32p. (J). pap. 9.95 *(978-1-59147-072-4(2));* 14.95 *(978-1-59147-071-7(4))* American Psychological Assn. (Magination Pr.).
—Little Tree: A Story for Children with Serious Medical Illness. Sebern, Brian, illus. 2nd ed. 2003. 32p. (J). pap. 9.95 *(978-1-59147-042-7(0));* 14.95 *(978-1-59147-041-0(2))* American Psychological Assn. (Magination Pr.).
Mills, Patricia Anne. Stevie's First Christmas. 2009. 28p. pap. 12.49 *(978-1-4490-3452-8(7))* AuthorHouse.
Milson, Matthew R. Young Arcan & the Garden of Loc. 2007. (Tales from Emberthel Ser.). 221p. (J). (gr. 3-7). per. 14.95 *(978-1-933770-03-1(1))* Avari Pr.
Miranda, Patricia J. Leaf Man. O'Leary, Chris, illus. 2019. (ENG.). 32p. (J). (gr. -1-3). 16.99 *(978-0-8075-4416-7(7),* 807544167) Whitman, Albert & Co.
Mitchell, Trish. Noah Pals: Journey to the Apple Tree. 2011. 32p. pap. 16.99 *(978-1-4567-9939-7(8))* AuthorHouse.
Mohler, Marie. Hearts of Trees. 2008. 32p. pap. 18.95 *(978-1-4357-4614-5(7))* Lulu Pr., Inc.
Mollis Lindquist, Melody Rose. Oak Tree. 2009. 16p. pap. 10.99 *(978-1-4490-0859-8(3))* AuthorHouse.
Monaghan, Joseph. The Boy Who Loved Trees. 2013. (Illus.). 24p. pap. 19.82 *(978-1-4817-8225-8(8))* AuthorHouse.
Moore, Sandra. The Peace Tree from Hiroshima: The Little Bonsai with a Big Story. Wilds, Kazumi, illus. 2015. 32p. (J). (gr. 2-6). 14.95 *(978-4-8053-1347-3(1))* Tuttle Publishing.
Moran, Kelly. The Tiny Caterpillar & the Great Big Tree. 2009. 50p. pap. 19.50 *(978-0-557-09498-1(4))* Lulu Pr., Inc.
Morgan, Melissa. The Tip Trip. 2008. 36p. pap. 24.95 *(978-1-4241-9226-7(9))* America Star Bks.
Morse, Rose. The Everlasting Evergreen. 2009. (ENG.). 32p. pap. 18.01 *(978-0-557-21209-5(X))* Lulu Pr., Inc.
Moulton, Mark Kimball. Miss Sadie Mcgee Who Lived in a Tree. Good, Karen H., illus. 2008. (ENG.). 32p. (J). (gr. k-3). 16.95 *(978-0-8249-5152-8(2),* Ideals Pubns.) Worthy Publishing.
Munoz, R. C. In Honor of the Oak Tree. 2012. 20p. pap. 24.95 *(978-1-4626-6454-2(7))* America Star Bks.
Munsch, Robert. Up, up, Down. 2004. (Illus.). (J). (gr. k-3). spiral bd. *(978-0-616-11127-7(4));* spiral bd. *(978-0-616-11126-0(6))* Canadian National Institute for the Blind/Institut National Canadien pour les Aveugles.
—Up, up, Down. Martchenko, Michael, illus. 2023. (ENG.). 32p. (J). (gr. -1-3). pap. 8.99 *(978-0-439-98815-5(2))* Scholastic Canada, Ltd. CAN. Dist: Publishers Group West (PGW).
Murphy, Susan White. D. J. 's Special Tree. 2012. 50p. (-18). pap. 8.95 *(978-1-4759-5983-3(4))* iUniverse, Inc.
Musariri, Blessing. Going Home: A Tree's Story. 2005. (Illus.). 29p. pap. *(978-1-77922-042-4(1))* Weaver Pr. ZWE. Dist: Michigan State Univ. Pr.

My Apple Tree. 2003. (J). per. (978-1-57657-899-5(2)) Paradise Pr., Inc.

Nan, Carol. Nana the Baby Pine Tree. 2012. 24p. pap. 24.95 (978-1-4626-8944-6(2)) America Star Bks.

Navarro, Cece P. My Cherry Tree House. 2008. 16p. pap. 24.95 (978-1-60474-415-6(4)) America Star Bks.

Neff, Fred. The Memory Tree. Montmeat, Jack, illus. 2008. 36p. pap. 14.99 (978-1-59858-854-5(0)) Dog Ear Publishing, LLC.

Neimark, Jill. The Hugging Tree: A Story about Resilience. Wong, Nicole, illus. 2015. 32p. (J). (978-1-4338-1907-0(4), Magination Pr.) American Psychological Assn.

Nelson, Holly. Ig's Apples. I.t. ed. 2003. (Illus.). (J). 28p. lib. bdg. 14.95 (978-1-932338-32-4(2)); 15p. per. 9.99 (978-1-932338-17-1(9)) Lifevest Publishing, Inc.

The Nevergreen. 2003. (J). 15.99 (978-0-9744565-9-1(4)) Heart-to-Heart Pubns.

Newman, C. Edward. The Enchanted Bat. 2007. pap. 0.01 net. (978-1-60402-471-5(2)) Independent Pub.

Nichols, Lori. Maple. Nichols, Lori, illus. (Illus.). 32p. (J). 2019. (— 1). bds. 8.99 (978-1-9848-1298-8(X)) 2014. (gr. -1-k). 17.99 (978-0-399-16085-1(X)) Penguin Young Readers Group. (Nancy Paulsen Books).

Niddrie, June. Pom, the Pomegranate Pixie. 2010. 32p. pap. 16.10 (978-0-557-31875-9(0)) Lulu Pr., Inc.

Noble, Trinka Hakes. Apple Tree Christmas. Noble, Trinka Hakes, illus. 2005. (Holiday Ser.). (ENG., Illus.). 32p. (J). (gr. 1-4). 16.95 (978-1-58536-270-7(0), 202083) Sleeping Bear Pr.

Nolan, Allia Zobel. God's Oak Tree. Chung, Chi, illus. 2007. 16p. (J). (gr. -1). 12.99 (978-0-8254-5536-0(7)) Kregel Pubns.

Nunnery, Donna. The Leaf That Was Afraid to Fall, 1 vol. Scardina, Tom, illus. 2010. 26p. 24.95 (978-1-4489-5927-3(6)) PublishAmerica, Inc.

Nye, Donna Kight. Sammi & the Tree. 2011. 12p. pap. 8.32 (978-1-4634-4659-8(4)) AuthorHouse.

O'Connor, Jane. Fancy Nancy: Poison Ivy Expert. Glasser, Robin Preiss, illus. 2008. (I Can Read Level 1 Ser.). (ENG.). 32p. (J). (gr. -1-3). 16.99 (978-0-06-123614-3(4)); pap. 4.99 (978-0-06-123613-6(6)) HarperCollins Pubs. (HarperCollins).

Oram, Hiawyn. Snowboy & the Last Tree Standing. Sif, Birgitta, illus. 2018. (ENG.). 32p. (J). (gr. -1-2). 16.99 (978-0-7636-9572-9(6)) Candlewick Pr.

Ortiac, Catherine. Te Tumu o Rapa Nui: El Arbolito de Rapa Nui. the Little Tree of Rapa Nui. le Petit Arbre de Rapa Nui. Haoa Cardinali, Viki et al, trs. Willemin, Veronique, illus. 2005. (FRE, SPA & ENG.). 40p. (J). spiral bd. 12.00 (978-1-880636-02-2(6)) Easter Island Foundation.

Ornelas, Martin. Little Needles the Christmas Tree. 2007. (ENG.). 24p. per. 10.49 (978-1-4343-4122-8(4)) AuthorHouse.

Osborne, Mary Pope. To the Future, Ben Franklin! Ford, A. G., illus. 2019. (Magic Tree House (R) Ser.: 32). (J). (gr. 1-4). 96p. 13.99 (978-0-525-64832-1(1)); (ENG.). 112p. lib. bdg. 16.99 (978-0-525-64833-8(X)) Random Hse. Children's Bks. (Random Hse. Bks. for Young Readers).

Our Shinning Christmas Tree. 2003. (J). per. (978-1-57657-911-4(5)) Paradise Pr., Inc.

Ozment, Jones. The Tree. 2012. (ENG.). pap. (978-1-4675-2966-2(4)) Independent Pub.

Page, Lawana. The Weeping Willow Tree. Amaya, Laura, tr. Heaton, Layce, illus. 2006. (SPA.). 32p. 10.95 (978-0-9761128-2-2(5)) KB Bks. & More.

Pappas, Charles. The Tree That Loved the Eagle. Schlueter, Rachel, illus. 2013. 56p. (J). 19.95 (978-1-58790-175-1(7)) Regent Pr.

Parent, Nancy. A Tree for Me. 15 vols. Harchy, Atelier Philippe, illus. 2003. (It's Fun to Learn Ser.). 32p. (J). (gr. -1-3). 3.99 (978-1-57973-138-0(4)) Advance Pubs. LLC.

Parish, Alex. Peter & the Flying Sergeant. 2009. 30p. 21.50 (978-0-9561613-0-7(8)) Parish, Alex GBR. Dist: Lulu Pr., Inc.

Park, Barbara & Wotherspoon, John. The Adventures of Lily Leaf. 2011. (Illus.). 28p. pap. 11.36 (978-1-4567-8648-9(2)) AuthorHouse.

Parker, Emma. The Spaghetti Tree. 2010. (Illus.). pap. (978-1-877561-02-3(9)) First Edition Ltd.

Patterson, Jim. Lisa B's Cookie Tree. 2011. 36p. pap. 24.95 (978-1-4560-3599-0(1)) America Star Bks.

peddi, radhika. Kichkide. 2010. 44p. pap. 19.70 (978-0-557-16435-6(4)) Lulu Pr., Inc.

Percival, Tom. The Story Tree. 2018. (Little Legends Ser.: 6). (ENG., Illus.). 192p. (J). (gr. 2-5). pap. 8.99 (978-1-4926-6573-1(8), Sourcebooks Jabberwocky) Sourcebooks, Inc.

Pfitsch, Patricia Curtis. Riding the Flume. 2004. (Aladdin Historical Fiction Ser.). 232p. (gr. 5-9). 15.00 (978-0-7569-2938-1(5)) Perfection Learning Corp.

Phillips, Dixie & Phillips, Sharon. Once upon an Empty Tomb. 2013. 24p. pap. 7.95 (978-1-61633-380-5(4)) Guardian Angel Publishing, Inc.

Pitt, Tamina & Terri, Janke. What Makes a Tree Smile? Francine Ngardab, Riches, illus. 2003. (Uupababa Ser.). 24p. (J). pap. (978-1-875641-80-2(7)) Magabala Bks.

Poehler, S. Applecheeks & the Pop E. Tree. 2012. 12p. pap. 15.99 (978-1-4772-8180-2(0)) AuthorHouse.

Polwart, Karine. A Wee Bird Was Watching. Leiper, Kate, illus. 2018. (ENG.). 32p. pap. 10.95 (978-1-78027-532-1(3), BC Bks.) Birlinn, Ltd. GBR. Dist: Casemate Pubs. & Bk. Distributors, LLC.

Postma, Carryl. The Tree That Could Be Green. 2009. 20p. pap. 14.99 (978-1-4389-5842-2(0)) AuthorHouse.

Potter, Dawn. Isobel's Tree. 2010. 16p. pap. 9.99 (978-1-60860-966-6(9), Eloquent Bks.) Strategic Book Publishing & Rights Agency (SBPRA).

Power, Eloise. The Apple Tree Inside of Me. 2012. 36p. pap. 16.95 (978-1-4525-5522-5(2)) Balboa Pr.

Price, Cheryl. The Golden Aspen. 2009. 36p. pap. 15.95 (978-1-4490-2855-8(1)) AuthorHouse.

Pugliano-Martin, Carol. Ready for Fall! 2006. (Early Explorers Ser.). (J). pap. (978-1-4108-6103-0(1)) Benchmark Education Co.

Rabe, Tish. The Tree Doctor. 2013. (Step into Reading Level 2 Ser.). lib. bdg. 13.55 (978-0-606-26965-0(7)) Turtleback.

Ramsey, Byra L. Little Stick. 2009. 28p. pap. 13.99 (978-1-4490-3371-2(7)) AuthorHouse.

Randolph, Joanne. Greenley: a Tree's Story, 1 vol. 2009. (Nature Stories Ser.). (ENG., Illus.). 24p. (J). (gr. 1-2). pap. 9.15 (978-1-60754-090-8(8), 60456d2c-8439-41f0-a842-df31f29b5f2e); lib. bdg. 27.27 (978-1-60754-089-2(4), f8e3b980-7b75-4d78-a8fc-c9fefa8a02b2) Rosen Publishing Group, Inc., The. (Windmill Bks.).

Random House. Nickelodeon 5-Minute Christmas Stories (Nickelodeon) Random House, illus. 2017. (ENG., Illus.). 160p. (J). (gr. -1-2). 12.99 (978-1-5247-6398-5(5), Random Hse. Bks. for Young Readers) Random Hse. Children's Bks.

Ranganathan, Babu G. The Selfish Apple Tree. 2010. 12p. 7.95 (978-1-4497-0312-7(7), WestBow Pr.) Author Solutions, LLC.

Ransburg, Ashley B. Evie Finds Her Family Tree. 2006. (Illus.). 34p. (J). (gr. -1-3). 14.95 (978-0-87195-187-8(8)) Indiana Historical Society.

Rawlinson, Julia. Fletcher & the Falling Leaves. Beeke, Tiphanie, illus. 2006. (ENG.). 32p. (J). (gr. -1-2). 19.99 (978-0-06-113401-2(5), Greenwillow Bks.) HarperCollins Pubs.

—Fletcher & the Falling Leaves. 2011. (J). (gr. -1-2). 18.95 (978-0-545-19705-2(8)); 29.95 (978-0-545-19699-4(X)) Weston Woods Studios, Inc.

—Fletcher & the Falling Leaves: A Fall Book for Kids. Beeke, Tiphanie, illus. 2008. (ENG.). 32p. (J). (gr. -1-2). pap. 9.99 (978-0-06-157397-2(3), Greenwillow Bks.) HarperCollins Pubs.

Ray, Mary Lyn. Christmas Farm: A Christmas Holiday Book for Kids. Root, Barry, illus. alt. ed. 2013. (ENG.). 40p. (J). (gr. -1-3). 7.99 (978-0-544-10509-6(5), 1540809, Clarion Bks.) HarperCollins Pubs.

Razilov, Evelyn. The Little Ant & the Apple Tree. 2013. 24p. pap. 12.56 (978-1-4669-7729-7(9)) Trafford Publishing.

Reardon, John. The South Overlook Oaks. Youngbluth, Chris, illus. 2006. 119p. (J). (gr. 4-7). 16.95 (978-1-931643-91-7(1)) Seven Locks Pr.

Redwine, Connie. A Story from Graandfather Tree. Keithline, Brian, illus. 2005. 25p. (J). (gr. k-2). pap. 7.95 (978-0-88100-135-8(X)) National Writers Pr., The.

Reed, Jennifer. The Falling Flowers. Cole, Dick, illus. 2005. (Falling Flowers Ser.). 32p. (J). (gr. -1-3). 16.95 (978-1-885008-28-2(7), Shen's Bks.) Lee & Low Bks., Inc.

Reid, Barbara. Picture a Tree. Reid, Barbara, illus. 2013. (ENG., Illus.). 32p. (J). (gr. -1-3). 16.99 (978-0-8075-6526-1(1), 807565261) Whitman, Albert & Co.

Reilly, Carmel & Wallace-Mitchell, Jane. Mercury & the Woodcutter. 2008. (Rigby Focus Forward: Level J Ser.). (Illus.). 24p. (J). (gr. 4-7). pap. (978-1-4190-3765-8(X), Rigby) Pearson Education Australia.

Reinertson, Bob. The Mysterious Visitor. 2012. 28p. pap. 21.99 (978-1-4771-0006-6(7)) Xlibris Corp.

Rey, H. A. Curious George Plants a Tree. 2009. (Curious George Ser.). (ENG., Illus.). 32p. (J). (gr. -1-3). 14.99 (978-0-547-15087-1(3), 1051758, Clarion Bks.) HarperCollins Pubs.

Rhiger, Tenna. The Story about How the Spotted Wobblepig Got Its Spots. 2012. 40p. pap. (978-1-84903-152-3(5)) Schiel & Denver Publishing Ltd.

Rhode, Paul. Presents for Phoebe: Growing Independent. Margolis, Al, illus. 2011. 24p. (YA). pap. 9.95 (978-1-935706-05-2(5)) Wiggles Pr.

Rice, June K. The Little Blue Tree. 2009. 20p. pap. 10.99 (978-1-4389-4806-5(9)) AuthorHouse.

Rie, Jannie. The Community Food Tree. 2012. (ENG.). (J). pap. (978-1-4675-5240-0(2)) Independent Pub.

Ringgold, Robyn. My Mom Hugs Trees. Vasudevan, Vidya, illus. 2006. 24p. (J). per. 15.95 (978-0-9785326-1-1(9)) Solar Publishing LLC.

Ripton, Kyle. The Mourning Tree. 2012. 74p. pap. 9.97 (978-1-300-31829-3(5)) Lulu Pr., Inc.

Rocklin, Joanne. One Day & One Amazing Morning on Orange Street. 2012. (ENG., Illus.). 224p. (J). (gr. 3-7). pap. 8.95 (978-1-4197-0181-8(9), 690103, Amulet Bks.) Abrams, Inc.

Rodhe, Paul & Wallas Reidy, Sarah. The Little Plum Tree. Margolis, Al & Young, Bill, illus. 2010. 24p. (J). pap. 9.95 (978-1-935706-06-9(3)) Wiggles Pr.

Rodman, Mary Ann. A Tree for Emmy. Mai-Wyss, Tatjana, illus. 32p. (J). (gr. -1-3). 2018. (ENG.). pap. 7.99 (978-1-68263-037-2(4)) 2009. 16.99 (978-1-56145-475-4(3)) Peachtree Publishing Co. Inc.

Roman, Celso. El Arbol de los Tucanes. 2012. 44p. (J). (gr. 2-4). pap. 12.99 (978-958-30-3662-0(5)) Panamericana Editorial COL. Dist: Lectorum Pubns., Inc.

Rothman, Lorne. Southcrop Forest. 2008. 184p. pap. 13.95 (978-0-595-49588-7(5)) iUniverse, Inc.

Rouss, Sylvia. The Littlest Tree. Binus, Ari, illus. 2005. 32p. (J). 16.95 (978-1-932687-25-5(4), Devora Publishing) Simcha Media Group.

Ruben, Pamela. Lessons from the Bubbe & Zayde Tree. 2004. (Illus.). 33p. (J). 12.95 (978-0-9764813-2-4(4)) Peppery Pr.

—Lessons from the Grandma & Grandpa Tree. 2004. (J). 12.95 (978-0-9764813-3-1(2)) Peppery Pr.

Rucker, David. The Valley of the Christmas Trees: A Legend. Laster, Brenda, illus. 2007. 41p. (J). (gr. -1-3). 14.95 (978-1-931643-94-8(6)) Seven Locks Pr.

Ruiz-Flores, Lupe. The Woodcutter's Gift/el Regalo del Lenador. Ventura, Gabriela Baeza, tr. from ENG. Jerome, Elaine, illus. 2007. (SPA & ENG.). 32p. (J). (gr. -1-2). 16.95 (978-1-55885-489-5(4), Piñata Books) Arte Publico Pr.

Ryan, Mary C., illus. & text. Twitcher Mcgee & the Wonderful Tree. Ryan, Mary C., text. 2008. 12p. (J). 4.95 (978-0-9678115-3-6(8)) Dragonseed Pr.

Saito, Ryusuke & Takidaira, Jiro. The Tree of Courage. Laughlin, Sako, tr. 2008. (Illus.). 32p. (J). 14.95 incl. audio compact disk (978-4-74126-442-5(1)) R.I.C. Pubns. AUS. Dist: SCB Distributors.

Salib Salibi, Nuha. The Palm Tree & the Fir. 2009. 24p. pap. 11.49 (978-1-4389-9419-2(2)) AuthorHouse.

San Giacomo, Renee. Herbie's Star. 2012. 24p. pap. 24.95 (978-1-4626-7596-8(4)) America Star Bks.

Sanders, Nancy I. The Very Oldest Pear Tree. Imamura, Yas, illus. 2020. (ENG.). 32p. (J). (gr. -1-3). 16.99 (978-0-8075-6681-7(0), 807566810) Whitman, Albert & Co.

Schexnayder, Paul, illus. In the Time of Joy & Wonder. 2017. (J). (978-1-946160-08-9(3)) Univ. of Louisiana at Lafayette Pr.

Schneider, Richard H. Why Christmas Trees Aren't Perfect. 2016. (ENG.). 32p. 14.99 (978-1-5018-2583-5(6), 15307) Abingdon Pr.

Schorr, Titus. Tony's Tree, 1 vol., 1. 2015. (Rosen REAL Readers: Social Studies Nonfiction / Fiction: Myself, My Community, My World Ser.). (ENG.). 12p. (J). (gr. k-1). pap. 6.33 (978-1-5081-2000-1(5), ac0abb90-d1f7-4d10-9929-8dafc65ea508, Rosen Classroom) Rosen Publishing Group, Inc., The.

Schouest, Stacey. The Very 1st Christmas Tree. 2011. 44p. pap. 16.95 (978-1-4497-2528-0(7), WestBow Pr.) Author Solutions, LLC.

Schram, Peninnah & Davis, Rachayl Eckstein. The Apple Tree's Discovery. Lee, Wendy W., illus. 2012. (Kar-Ben Favorites Ser.). (ENG.). 24p. (J). (gr. -1-2). lib. bdg. 16.95 (978-0-7613-5130-6(2), Kar-Ben Publishing) Lerner Publishing Group.

Schultz, Agnes Szenozicska. The Little Tree. 2007. 32p. (J). 14.00 (978-0-8059-7211-5(0)) Dorrance Publishing Co., Inc.

Schwartz, Suzanne & Schwartz, Robert. The Christmas Palm Tree: A Storybook to Color. Schwartz, Suzanne & Schwartz, Robert, illus. I.t. ed. 2005. (Illus.). 22p. (J). spiral bd. 3.99 (978-0-9764152-3-7(2)) Seascay Productions.

Scott-Branagan, Brownen. The Pandanuspeople. 2009. 32p. pap. 13.75 (978-1-60860-006-9(8), Strategic Bk. Publishing) Strategic Book Publishing & Rights Agency (SBPRA).

Scott, Earnestine E. Little Mike's Family: A Novel for Second & Third Graders. 2012. 30p. 24.95 (978-1-4626-6018-6(5)) America Star Bks.

Scott, Leah. Tincup & the Tornado. 2012. (ENG.). 34p. (J). pap. 12.95 (978-1-4327-8695-3(4)); pap. 18.95 (978-1-4327-8826-1(4)) Outskirts Pr., Inc.

Selznick, Brian. Big Tree. Selznick, Brian, illus. 2023. (ENG., Illus.). 528p. (J). (gr. 2). 32.99 (978-1-338-18063-3(0), Scholastic Pr.) Scholastic, Inc.

Sera, Lucia. Another Tree in the Yard. Lonergan Iorio, John, illus. 2004. 32p. (J). per. 16.95 (978-1-932653-36-6(8)) Vocalis, Ltd.

Seredy, Kate. A Tree for Peter. Seredy, Kate, illus. 2004. (Illus.). 112p. (J). reprint ed. 19.95 (978-1-930900-26-4(0)) Purple Hse. Pr.

Sevonna, Simon. the Christmas Tree Fle. 2012. 32p. pap. 21.99 (978-1-4771-3105-3(1)) Xlibris Corp.

Shankman, Ed. Champ & Me by the Maple Tree: A Vermont Tale. O'Neill, Dave, illus. 2010. (Shankman & O'Neill Ser.). (ENG.). 32p. (J). (gr. -1-3). 14.95 (978-0-9819430-5-3(5), Commonwealth Editions) Applewood Bks.

Shannon, Terry Miller. George & the Cherry Tree. 2016. (Spring Forward Ser.). (J). (gr. 1). (978-1-4900-9408-3(3)) Benchmark Education Co.

Shapiro, Lindy. Moon Mangoes. Peterson, Kathleen, illus. 2011. (ENG.). 36p. (J). (gr. -1-2). 14.95 (978-1-933067-42-1(X)) Beachhouse Publishing, LLC.

Sharp, Euan. Diggedy Dozer in Treetop Troubles. 2008. 34p. 15.95 (978-1-4357-0982-9(9)) Lulu Pr., Inc.

Shelby, Anne. The Man Who Lived in a Hollow Tree. Hazelaar, Cor, illus. 2009. (ENG.). 40p. (J). (gr. -1-2). 19.99 (978-0-689-86169-7(9), Atheneum/Richard Jackson Bks.) Simon & Schuster Children's Publishing.

Shoen, Melinda. Invisible Me: A Walking Stick's Wish. 2009. 24p. pap. 11.79 (978-1-4389-4851-5(4)) AuthorHouse.

Shuff, Chrissi. The Dancing Tree & other Stories. 2010. (Illus.). 80p. pap. 28.99 (978-1-4520-0054-1(9)) AuthorHouse.

Silverstein, Shel. The Giving Tree. (Illus.). 95.94 (978-0-06-056897-9(6)) HarperCollins Pubs.

—The Giving Tree. Silverstein, Shel, illus. (Illus.). 64p. 2003. (ENG.). (J). (gr. -1-3). lib. bdg. 18.89 (978-0-06-025666-1(4), HarperCollins) gif. ed. 2007. 16.99 (978-0-06-124001-0(X)) 50th anniv. ed. 2014. (ENG.). (J). (gr. -1-3). 19.99 (978-0-06-025665-4(6), HC5567, HarperCollins) HarperCollins Pubs.

—The Giving Tree with CD. Silverstein, Shel, illus. anniv. ed. 2014. (ENG., Illus.). 64p. (J). (gr. -1-3). 19.99 (978-0-06-058675-1(3), HarperCollins) HarperCollins Pubs.

Simmons, Mary Louise. The Little Fir Tree Who Wanted a Friend. 2008. 28p. per. 24.95 (978-1-60441-391-5(3)) America Star Bks.

Smith, Jodene Lynn & Rice, Dona Herweck. If I Were a Tree. 2010. (Early Literacy Ser.). (ENG., Illus.). 16p. (gr. k-1). 19.99 (978-1-4333-1488-9(6)); 6.99 (978-1-4333-1487-2(8)) Teacher Created Materials, Inc.

Smith, Linda. The Inside Tree. Brown, Kathryn, illus. Date not set. 32p. (J). (gr. -1-3). 5.99 (978-0-06-443542-0(3)) HarperCollins Pubs.

Smith, Roy. Louphole Forest Tells Its Tale of Enchantment. Magpie, ed. Burnell Walsh, Avenda, illus. 2012. 38p. (978-1-908000-18-7(X)) Pyjama Pr.

Speed, Bryan W. Little Bent Cedar. Todd, Sheri, illus. 2007. (ENG.). 24p. (J). (gr. 2-4). per. (978-1-933255-38-5(2)) DNA Pr.

Stack, Kevin W. The Great Oak Tree. 2008. (Illus.). 32p. pap. 12.99 (978-1-4389-1856-3(9)) AuthorHouse.

Standiford, Natalie. The Secret Tree. (J). 2014. (ENG.). 256p. (gr. 3-7). pap. 7.99 (978-0-545-33480-8(2), Scholastic Paperbacks) 2012. 245p. pap. (978-0-545-48976-8(8), Scholastic Pr.) Scholastic, Inc.

Starks-Johnson, Annie. Dottie Meets Gilda the Old Oak Tree. 2009. 28p. pap. 12.49 (978-1-4389-5361-8(5)) AuthorHouse.

Strange, J. R. The Tree & the Light. Massivebrain.com, illus. 2013. 48p. pap. 11.99 (978-0-9887214-0-1(6)) Firesidenook.

Strathie, Chae. The Tickle Tree. Bernatene, Poly, illus. 2008. 24p. (J). (gr. -1-1). (978-1-84539-344-1(9)); (978-1-84539-345-8(7)) Meadowside Children's Bks.

Stuart & McArthur, Amanda. Humphry & the Tree. 2012. 24p. pap. 15.99 (978-1-4691-5082-6(4)) Xlibris Corp.

Suchy, Julianne. Leaf Me Alone. 2009. 36p. pap. 13.95 (978-1-60693-300-8(0), Eloquent Bks.) Strategic Book Publishing & Rights Agency (SBPRA).

Sullivan, Kathryn. Talking to Trees. 2017. (J). pap. (978-1-61271-356-4(4)) Zumaya Pubns. LLC.

Surratt, Tereasa & Charlton-Perrin, Donna. The Forever Tree. Roode, Daniel, illus. 2018. (J). pap. (978-0-553-52395-9(3)) Bantam Doubleday Dell Large Print Group, Inc.

Surratt, Tereasa & Lukas, Donna. The Forever Tree. Slater, Nicola, illus. 2018. 40p. (J). (gr. -1-2). 18.99 (978-0-553-52392-8(9), Crown Books For Young Readers) Random Hse. Children's Bks.

The Talking Christmas Tree. 2003. (J). per. (978-1-57657-925-1(5)) Paradise Pr., Inc.

Tatsuyama, Sayuri. Happy Happy Clover, Vol. 4. Tatsuyama, Sayuri, illus. 2010. (Happy Happy Clover Ser.: 4). (ENG., Illus.). 192p. (J). pap. 7.99 (978-1-4215-2735-2(9)) Viz Media.

Taylor, Mildred D. Song of the Trees. 2003. (ENG., Illus.). 80p. (J). (gr. 5-7). 7.99 (978-0-14-250075-0(5), Puffin Books) Penguin Young Readers Group.

Teckentrup, Britta. Tree: a Peek-Through Picture Book. 2016. (ENG.). 32p. (J). (gr. -1-2). 16.99 (978-1-101-93242-1(2), Doubleday Bks. for Young Readers) Random Hse. Children's Bks.

The Library Fairy. The Magical Tree & Musical Wind. Faust, Laurie A., illus. 2008. 32p. pap. 16.95 (978-1-59858-604-6(1)) Dog Ear Publishing, LLC.

Thomas, John & Rowe, Susan. Mynydd y Brain. 2005. (WEL., Illus.). 32p. pap. (978-1-85596-221-7(7)) Dref Wen.

Thompson, Lauren. The Apple Pie That Papa Baked. Bean, Jonathan, illus. 2007. (ENG.). 32p. (J). (gr. k-3). 19.99 (978-1-4169-1240-8(1), Simon & Schuster Bks. For Young Readers) Simon & Schuster Bks. For Young Readers.

Tim Todd. The Town of Ill. 2009. 36p. pap. 18.99 (978-1-4389-2778-7(9)) AuthorHouse.

Toombs, Tom. The Mysterious Money Tree: Little Tommy Learns a Lesson in Giving. Smith, Abby, illus. 2012. 28p. (J). pap. 12.95 (978-1-61314-033-8(9), Innovo Pr.) Innovo Publishing, LLC.

Torrance-Matthews, Armer, et al. Miss Bertha, the Talking Tree: A Delightful Story of a Talking Tree. 2010. 36p. pap. 18.95 (978-1-4269-2051-6(2)) Trafford Publishing.

Trembley, Skip & Ochs, Susan A. You'll See, Little Tree. Hollis, Michael, illus. 2003. (J). pap. 7.95 (978-0-9643452-2-5(6)) Graphics North.

Trinco, Trish. The Leaf That Wouldn't Leave. Langdo, Bryan, illus. 2008. (ENG.). 32p. (J). 16.95 (978-0-931674-90-7(5), Waldman House Pr.) TRISTAN Publishing, Inc.

Trites, Judy. Charlie's Challenge. 2011. 24p. pap. 15.99 (978-1-4628-4568-2(1)) Xlibris Corp.

Tu, Tzu Hui. Traveling Tree. 2012. 36p. pap. 20.99 (978-1-4685-9594-9(6)) AuthorHouse.

Tukel, Onur. Little Friends, 0 vols. Tukel, Onur, illus. 2012. (ENG.). 64p. (J). (gr. 1-4). 14.99 (978-0-7614-6260-6(0), 9780761462606, Two Lions) Amazon Publishing.

Tunbridge, J. L. The Jellybean Tree. 2012. 40p. pap. 15.95 (978-1-4525-0813-9(5)) Balboa Pr.

Uncle Chuck. The Monkey Puzzle Tree. 2011. 32p. pap. 24.95 (978-1-4560-6992-6(6)) America Star Bks.

Van, Muon. The Little Tree. Adinolfi, JoAnn, illus. 2015. (ENG.). 32p. (J). (gr. k-3). 16.95 (978-1-939547-19-4(9), 1405f785-4f8e-4f2f-adbe-93dcf2ee9cb1) Creston Bks.

Vance, L. K. Jennadi. 2006. 73p. pap. 16.95 (978-1-4241-1574-7(4)) PublishAmerica, Inc.

VanDerlinden, Jean A. The Family Tree: The Secret Door. 2013. 64p. pap. 24.99 (978-1-4772-7941-0(5)) AuthorHouse.

Verrett, Michael. Galid's Christmas Wish. 2010. 44p. pap. 22.90 (978-0-557-29109-0(7)) Lulu Pr., Inc.

Violet Mackerel's Pocket Protest. 2014. (Violet Mackerel Ser.). (ENG., Illus.). 128p. (J). (gr. 1-5). 17.99 (978-1-4424-9458-9(1), Atheneum Bks. for Young Readers) Simon & Schuster Children's Publishing.

Vos, Sharon. Neddy the Nutty Acorn. Rosenfelder, Cheryl, illus. 2008. 40p. per. 24.95 (978-1-60441-232-1(1)) America Star Bks.

Wahl, Charis. Rosario's Fig Tree, 1 vol. Melanson, Luc, illus. 2015. (ENG.). 32p. (J). (gr. -1-2). 18.95 (978-1-55498-341-4(X)) Groundwood Bks. CAN. Dist: Publishers Group West (PGW).

Wales, Amy S. Fiona & the Fiddle Tree. 2012. 32p. pap. 21.99 (978-1-4691-5485-5(4)) Xlibris Corp.

Walker, Crystal. Maceys Magic Tree. 2009. 28p. pap. 12.49 (978-1-4490-4916-4(8)) AuthorHouse.

Walker, Mary. The Flower Tree. 2010. (Illus.). 50p. pap. 12.95 (978-1-4327-3588-3(8)) Outskirts Pr., Inc.

Ward, Jennifer. The Busy Tree, 0 vols. Falkenstern, Lisa, illus. 2012. (ENG.). 32p. (J). (gr. -1-2). 17.99 (978-0-7614-5550-9(7), 9780761455509, Two Lions) Amazon Publishing.

Waszak, Madonna. Mason's Mashed Potato Tree. Johnston, Lisa Harp, illus. 2011. 34p. pap. 14.95 (978-1-4575-0159-3(7)) Dog Ear Publishing, LLC.

Watkins, Albert. The Brothers Three. I.t. ed. 2004. (Illus.). 48p. (J). pap. 22.95 (978-0-9629124-4-3(1)) Floppinfish Publishing Co., Ltd.

Watkins, Samuel R. Precious Palm Tree. 2011. 32p. (gr. -1). pap. 17.25 (978-1-4269-5267-8(8)) Trafford Publishing.

Weber, Rivka Doba. Dear Tree. Rosenfeld, D. L., ed. Saroff, Phyllis, illus. 2010. (ENG.). 24p. (YA). 11.99 (978-1-929628-48-3(X)) Hachai Publishing.

Weinberger, David J. Answers to a Christmas Question. 2012. (ENG.). (J). pap. (978-1-4675-2381-3(X)) Independent Pub.

—Answers to a Christmas Question Coloring Book. 2012. (ENG.). (J). pap. (978-1-4675-2380-6(1)) Independent Pub.

Wells, Rita. Janie Plants a Tree. 2013. 26p. pap. 16.95 (978-1-4497-8903-9(X), WestBow Pr.) Author Solutions, LLC.

Welsh, Kenneth Wilbur. The Oak Brothers. 2011. 16p. 12.00 (978-1-4520-6079-8(7)) AuthorHouse.

Wentz, Andrea, illus. Nora & the Growing Tree: An Owlegories Tale. 2018. (Owlegories Ser.). 32p. (J). (gr. -1-3). 12.99 (978-1-5064-3309-7(X), Sparkhouse Family) 1517 Media.

Weston Woods Staff, creator. Fletcher & the Falling Leaves. 2011. 38.75 (978-0-545-19710-6(4)) Weston Woods Studios, Inc.

The Whispering Sycamore. 2012. (Illus.). 24p. pap. 8.99 (978-1-938768-02-6(7)) Gypsy Pubns.

Williams, Karen Lynn. Circles of Hope. 2005. (ENG., Illus.). 32p. (J). 16.00 (978-0-8028-5276-2(9)) Eerdmans, William B. Publishing Co.

Williams, Mercedes. The Little Tree. 2011. (ENG.). 14p. 18.95 (978-0-557-84137-0(2)) Lulu Pr., Inc.

Wilson, Melissa Anne. Nalyn & the Indigo Pearl. 2008. (Illus.). 24p. (J). pap. 8.00 *(978-0-8059-7409-6(1))* Dorrance Publishing Co., Inc.
Wilson, N. D. The Door Before (100 Cupboards Prequel) 2018. (100 Cupboards Ser.). 256p. (J). (gr. 3-7). 8.99 *(978-0-449-81680-6(X),* Yearling) Random Hse. Children's Bks.
Wilson, Wendy. The First Book of Red. 2005. 99p. pap. 19.95 *(978-1-4137-5570-1(4))* America Star Bks.
Witek, Jo. My Tree & Me: A Book of Seasons. 2019. (Growing Hearts Ser.). (ENG., Illus.). 32p. (J). (gr. -1 — 1). 16.99 *(978-1-4197-3503-5(9),* 1268201) Abrams, Inc.
Woebkenberg, Valerie. The Story the Little Christmas Tree Told. 2013. 26.95 *(978-0-7414-8367-6(X))* Infinity Publishing.
Woebkenberg, Valerie & Ingels, Diane. The Story the Little Christmas Tree Told. 2012. pap. 11.95 *(978-0-7414-8095-8(6))* Infinity Publishing.
Youngs, Puma Wun. Dreamtime. 2010. 28p. pap. 13.99 *(978-1-4490-8378-6(1))* AuthorHouse.
Zhou, Carmen. A Tree's Dream. 2012. 24p. pap. 15.99 *(978-1-4691-8958-1(5))* Xlibris Corp.
Ziskind, Hélio & Duchesne, Christiane. Le Géant de la Forêt: Un Voyage Musical. Pratt, Pierre, illus. 2014. (ENG.). 48p. (J). (gr. k-2). 16.95 *(978-2-923163-36-9(2))* La Montagne Secrete CAN. Dist: Independent Pubs. Group.
Zito, Ann R. Rock, Stream, Tree. Matheny, Melody, illus. 2010. 52p. pap. 11.00 *(978-1-4520-7822-9(X))* AuthorHouse.
Zommer, Yuval. The Tree That's Meant to Be. 2019. (ENG., Illus.). 32p. (J). (gr. -1-2). 17.99 *(978-0-593-11967-9(3),* Doubleday Bks. for Young Readers) Random Hse. Children's Bks.
Zweibel, Alan. Our Tree Named Steve. Catrow, David, illus. 2007. 32p. (J). (gr. -1-k). pap. 8.99 *(978-0-14-240743-1(7),* Puffin Books) Penguin Young Readers Group.
—Our Tree Named Steve. 2007. 16.00 *(978-1-4177-6974-2(2))* Turtleback.

TREES—POETRY

Florian, Douglas. Poetrees. Florian, Douglas, illus. 2010. (ENG., Illus.). 48p. (J). (gr. 1-5). 18.99 *(978-1-4169-8672-0(3),* Beach Lane Bks.) Beach Lane Bks.
George, Kristine O'Connell. Old Elm Speaks: Tree Poems. Kiesler, Kate, illus. 2007. (ENG.). 48p. (J). (gr. -1-3). 7.99 *(978-0-618-75242-3(0),* 100524, Clarion Bks.) HarperCollins Pubs.
Hutchens, Verlie. Trees. Tsong, Jing Jing, illus. 2019. (ENG.). 40p. (J). (gr. -1-3). 17.99 *(978-1-4814-4707-2(6),* Beach Lane Bks.) Beach Lane Bks.
Mervyn, Catherine Antolino. A Lesson from a Tree. Carr, Tabatha, illus. 2008. 32p. pap. 12.95 *(978-0-9821153-2-9(6))* Living Waters Publishing Co.
Singh, Rina. A Forest of Stories: Magical Tree Tales from Around the World. Cann, Helen, illus. 2003. (ENG.). 64p. (J). 19.99 *(978-1-84148-963-6(8))* Barefoot Bks., Inc.

TRIAL BY JURY

see Jury

TRIALS

Alphin, Elaine Marie. An Unspeakable Crime: The Prosecution & Persecution of Leo Frank. 2009. 152p. (YA). (gr. 9-12). lib. bdg. 22.95 *(978-0-8225-8944-0(3))* Lerner Publishing Group.
Bailey, Budd. School Desegregation: Brown V. Board of Education of Topeka, 1 vol. 2018. (Courting History Ser.). (ENG.). 64p. (J). (gr. 6-6). pap. 16.87 *(978-1-5026-3952-3(1),* 8019b94c-0e9d-4c56-8df5-3bff1cbd30c8) Cavendish Square Publishing LLC.
Blohm, Craig E. The O. J. Simpson Murder Trial, 1 vol. 2008. (Crime Scene Investigations Ser.). (ENG., Illus.). 104p. (gr. 7-7). lib. bdg. 42.03 *(978-1-4205-0038-7(4),* 73fed46b-f168-4dd6-adfa-8cf3fa02c260, Lucent Pr.) Greenhaven Publishing LLC.
Blumenthal, Karen. Jane Against the World: Roe V. Wade & the Fight for Reproductive Rights. 2020. (ENG., Illus.). 384p. (YA). 19.99 *(978-1-62672-165-4(3),* 900141057) Roaring Brook Pr.
Brimner, Larry Dane. Accused! The Trials of the Scottsboro Boys: Lies, Prejudice, & the Fourteenth Amendment. 2019. (Illus.). 192p. (YA). (gr. 8-12). 18.99 *(978-1-62979-775-5(8),* Calkins Creek) Highlights Pr., c/o Highlights for Children, Inc.
Coleman, Wim & Perrin, Pat. Racism on Trial: From the Medgar Evers Murder Case to Ghosts of Mississippi, 1 vol. 2009. (Famous Court Cases That Became Movies Ser.). (ENG., Illus.). 112p. (gr. 6-7). lib. bdg. 35.93 *(978-0-7660-3059-6(8),* fdc7ea56-35b4-4971-bb05-2efa75ae67aa) Enslow Publishing, LLC.
Crewe, Sabrina & Uschan, Michael V. The Scottsboro Case, 1 vol. 2004. (Events That Shaped America Ser.). (ENG., Illus.). 32p. (gr. 3-5). lib. bdg. 28.67 *(978-0-8368-3407-9(0),* abf6512b-1918-46fb-9619-7a4ac644103a, Gareth Stevens Learning Library) Stevens, Gareth Publishing LLLP.
Currie, Stephen. The Struggle for Equality: Landmark Court Cases, 1 vol. 2009. (Lucent Library of Black History Ser.). (ENG., Illus.). 104p. (J). (gr. 7-7). 41.03 *(978-1-4205-0122-3(4),* 25ad6ee3-f4e5-43a8-847b-53269fef3353, Lucent Pr.) Greenhaven Publishing LLC.
D'Costa, Jasmine. Real Justice: Branded a Baby Killer: The Story of Tammy Marquardt. 2015. (Lorimer Real Justice Ser.). (ENG., Illus.). 120p. (YA). (gr. 9-12). pap. 12.95 *(978-1-4594-0993-4(0))* James Lorimer & Co. Ltd., Pubs. CAN. Dist: Casemate Pubs. & Bk. Distributors, LLC.
Doeden, Matt. The Salem Witch Trials: An Interactive History Adventure. 2010. (You Choose: History Ser.). (ENG.). 112p. (J). (gr. 3-4). pap. 41.70 *(978-1-4296-6440-0(1),* 16180); (Illus.). 32.65 *(978-1-4296-5478-4(3),* 113878) Capstone. (Capstone Pr.).
Don Nardo. The Trial of Galileo. 2003. (Famous Trials Ser.). (ENG., Illus.). 112p. (J). 29.95 *(978-1-59018-423-3(8))* Cengage Gale.
Donnelly, Karen J. Cruzan v. Missouri: The Right to Die, 1 vol. 2003. (Supreme Court Cases Through Primary Sources Ser.). (ENG., Illus.). 64p. (YA). (gr. 5-8). lib. bdg. 37.13 *(978-0-8239-4014-1(4),* 440627a3-2822-4bcd-9cd8-62f407eac8ae) Rosen Publishing Group, Inc., The.
Dudley Gold, Susan. Clear & Present Danger: Schenck V. United States, 1 vol. 2014. (First Amendment Cases Ser.). (ENG., Illus.). 144p. (J). (gr. 9-9). lib. bdg. 45.50 *(978-1-62712-387-5(3),* f343c335-f811-4ea5-b1e7-80f9199de87f) Cavendish Square Publishing LLC.
Ferguson, Amanda. The Attack Against the U. S. Embassies in Kenya & Tanzania. 2009. (Terrorist Attacks Ser.). 64p. (gr. 5-5). 58.50 *(978-1-60853-309-1(3))* Rosen Publishing Group, Inc., The.
Ford, Jeanne Marie. Freedom of the Press: Crown V. John Peter Zenger, 1 vol. 2018. (Courting History Ser.). (ENG.). 64p. (gr. 6-6). lib. bdg. 37.36 *(978-1-5026-3583-9(6),* f0d93165-5787-4171-9a1e-851a4a4bef81) Cavendish Square Publishing LLC.
Graves, Renee. Cornerstones of Freedom: the Scopes Trial. 2003. (Cornerstones of Freedom Ser.). (ENG., Illus.). 48p. (YA). (gr. 4-7). 26.00 *(978-0-516-24221-7(0))* Scholastic Library Publishing.
Heing, Bridey. What Does a Juror Do?, 1 vol. 2018. (What Does a Citizen Do? Ser.). (ENG.). 48p. (gr. 5-5). 30.93 *(978-0-7660-9863-3(X),* a29916be-0415-41ff-81b1-b4c674cdf298) Enslow Publishing, LLC.
Herda, D. J. Fighting Censorship: New York Times V. United States, 1 vol. 2016. (U. S. Supreme Court Landmark Cases Ser.). (ENG., Illus.). 128p. (gr. 7-7). 38.93 *(978-0-7660-8432-2(9),* 8318c2c7-9ecd-4156-8dad-11bfd88263ae) Enslow Publishing, LLC.
—A Woman's Right to an Abortion: Roe V. Wade, 1 vol. 2016. (U. S. Supreme Court Landmark Cases Ser.). (ENG., Illus.). 128p. (gr. 7-7). 38.93 *(978-0-7660-8424-7(8),* 887bcdd0-580f-4598-bc48-bd01e3adec12) Enslow Publishing, LLC.
Hinton, Kerry. The Trial of Sacco & Vanzetti: A Primary Source Account. (Great Trials of the Twentieth Century Ser.). 64p. (gr. 5-8). 2009. 58.50 *(978-1-61513-220-1(1))* 2003. (ENG., Illus.). lib. bdg. 37.13 *(978-0-8239-3973-2(1),* 859f69c0-9e85-472e-9cac-f71d4dec37f0, Rosen Reference) Rosen Publishing Group, Inc., The.
Hitchcock, Susan Tyler. Roe V. Wade. McNeese, Tim, ed. 2006. (ENG., Illus.). 128p. (gr. 5-9). lib. bdg. 32.95 *(978-0-7910-9239-2(9),* P114573, Facts On File) Infobase Holdings, Inc.
Landau, Elaine. Sacco & Vanzetti. 2004. (Cornerstones of Freedom Ser.). (ENG., Illus.). 48p. (YA). (gr. 4-7). 26.00 *(978-0-516-24237-8(7))* Scholastic Library Publishing.
Light, Kate. Questions & Answers about the Salem Witch Trials, 1 vol. 2018. (Eye on Historical Sources Ser.). (ENG.). 32p. (gr. 4-4). 27.93 *(978-1-5383-4123-0(9),* 3f08d66a-28ec-44e9-a1b1-a3a68d59a8c8, PowerKids Pr.) Rosen Publishing Group, Inc., The.
Lock, Joan. Famous Trials. 2004. (Crime & Detection Ser.). (Illus.). 96p. (YA). (gr. 7-18). lib. bdg. 22.95 *(978-1-59084-381-9(9))* Mason Crest.
Lowery, Zoe & MacBain, Jenny. A Primary Source Investigation of the Salem Witch Trials, 1 vol. 2015. (Uncovering American History Ser.). (ENG., Illus.). 64p. (J). (gr. 5-6). 36.13 *(978-1-4994-3513-9(4),* b252eb53-85d0-40f3-ba81-a4f644734d72, Rosen Central) Rosen Publishing Group, Inc., The.
Malaspina, Ann. Heart on Fire: Susan B. Anthony Votes for President. James, Steve, illus. 2012. (ENG.). 32p. (J). (gr. 1-3). 17.99 *(978-0-8075-3188-4(X),* 080753188X) Whitman, Albert & Co.
Meter, Larry A. Van. Miranda V. Arizona. McNeese, Tim, ed. 2006. (ENG., Illus.). 112p. (gr. 5-9). 32.95 *(978-0-7910-9259-0(3),* P114592, Facts On File) Infobase Holdings, Inc.
Midland, C. J. Found Guilty. 2011. (J). pap. *(978-0-531-22555-4(0))* Scholastic, Inc.
Miller, Sarah. The Borden Murders: Lizzie Borden & the Trial of the Century. 2019. 336p. (J). (gr. 5). pap. 9.99 *(978-1-9848-9244-7(4),* Schwartz & Wade Bks.) Random Hse. Children's Bks.
Morrison, Toni. Remember: the Journey to School Integration. 2004. (ENG., Illus.). 80p. (J). (gr. -1-3). tchr. ed. 19.99 *(978-0-618-39740-2(X),* 591875, Clarion Bks.) HarperCollins Pubs.
Payment, Simone. Roe V. Wade: The Right to Choose, 1 vol. 2003. (Supreme Court Cases Through Primary Sources Ser.). (ENG., Illus.). 64p. (J). (gr. 5-8). lib. bdg. 36.13 *(978-0-8239-4012-7(8),* 4fb18163-d562-40a8-8de5-52d12b91fe6f, Rosen Reference) Rosen Publishing Group, Inc., The.
Perl, Lila. Cruzan V. Missouri: The Right to Die, 1 vol. 2008. (Supreme Court Milestones Ser.). (ENG., Illus.). 128p. (YA). (gr. 8-8). lib. bdg. 45.50 *(978-0-7614-2581-6(0),* a2b22d8e-f4bb-4621-87a0-23552342b64f) Cavendish Square Publishing LLC.
Randolph, Ryan P. Marbury V. Madison: The New Supreme Court Gets More Power, 1 vol. 2003. (Primary Sources of Life in the New American Nation Ser.). (ENG., Illus.). 32p. (gr. 4-5). pap. 10.00 *(978-0-8239-4252-7(X),* abe9cb63-e713-415d-8c3c-f5dc7ba5b5ea); (J). lib. bdg. 29.13 *(978-0-8239-4034-9(9),* ff5a4f36-2411-457d-8ff2-6a604f6e110b, Rosen Reference) Rosen Publishing Group, Inc., The.
Roensch, Greg. The Lindbergh Baby Kidnapping Trial: A Primary Source Account, 1 vol. 2003. (Great Trials of the Twentieth Century Ser.). (ENG., Illus.). 64p. (gr. 5-8). lib. bdg. 37.13 *(978-0-8239-3971-8(5),* 16c459b2-818a-403a-8400-724858aeafa6, Rosen Reference) Rosen Publishing Group, Inc., The.
Smith, Andrea P. The Salem Witch Trials. (Illus.). 24p. 2012. 63.60 *(978-1-4488-5215-4(3))* 2011. (ENG., (gr. 2-3). pap. 11.60 *(978-1-4488-5214-7(5)),* 361277c1-75d9-4d13-aef9-4cbffbd3e9c5) 2011. (ENG., (gr. 2-3). lib. bdg. 28.93 *(978-1-4488-5188-1(2),* f2f49013-fd8c-4d4a-b602-c5f1b365aff3) Rosen Publishing Group, Inc., The. (PowerKids Pr.).
Toth, Henrietta. The Murder of Emmett Till, 1 vol. 2017. (Spotlight on the Civil Rights Movement Ser.). (ENG., Illus.). 48p. (J). (gr. 6-6). pap. 12.75 *(978-1-5383-8054-3(4),* 3b16bc12-3c08-48ab-bbe3-b39c57cdc263) Rosen Publishing Group, Inc., The.
Uschan, Michael V. The Salem Witch Trials, 1 vol. 2004. (Landmark Events in American History Ser.). (ENG., Illus.). 48p. (gr. 5-8). pap. 15.05 *(978-0-8368-5415-2(2),* c80ebd89-e501-4720-8818-457470b372e2); lib. bdg. 33.67 *(978-0-8368-5387-2(3),* ec56240d-e910-4b70-991f-b0a25161bb6b) Stevens, Gareth Publishing LLLP. (Gareth Stevens Secondary Library).
—The Scottsboro Case, 1 vol. 2004. (Landmark Events in American History Ser.). (ENG., Illus.). 48p. (gr. 5-8). lib. bdg. 33.67 *(978-0-8368-5388-9(1),* 3e142ddb-25bb-4aad-a1f6-2ab370d96d45, Gareth Stevens Secondary Library) Stevens, Gareth Publishing LLLP.
von Zumbusch, Amelie. The True Story of the Salem Witch Hunts. 2009. (What Really Happened? Ser.). 24p. (gr. 2-3). 42.50 *(978-1-60854-770-8(1),* PowerKids Pr.) Rosen Publishing Group, Inc., The.

TRIALS—FICTION

Basye, Dale E. Snivel. 5. Dob, Bob, illus. 2013. (Heck Ser.). (ENG.). 448p. (J). (gr. 6-8). lib. bdg. 22.44 *(978-0-375-96834-1(2))* Random Hse. Bks. for Young Readers.
—Snivel: the Fifth Circle of Heck. Dob, Bob, illus. 2013. (Heck Ser.: 5). 448p. (J). (gr. 4-7). 8.99 *(978-0-375-86806-1(2),* Yearling) Random Hse. Children's Bks.
Bond, Douglas. Hand of Vengeance. 2012. (J). pap. *(978-1-59638-215-2(5))* P & R Publishing.
Bryant, Jen. The Trial. 2005. (Illus.). 176p. (J). (gr. 3-7). 7.99 *(978-0-440-41986-0(7),* Yearling) Random Hse. Children's Bks.
Davies, Jacqueline. The Lemonade Crime. 2011. (Lemonade War Ser.: 2). (ENG., Illus.). 160p. (J). (gr. 3-7). 16.99 *(978-0-547-27967-1(1),* 1411007, Clarion Bks.) HarperCollins Pubs.
—The Lemonade Crime. 2012. (Lemonade War Ser.: 2). lib. bdg. 18.40 *(978-0-606-24518-0(9))* Turtleback.
Grisham, John. The Accused. 2013. (Theodore Boone Ser.: 3). lib. bdg. 18.40 *(978-0-606-31696-5(5))* Turtleback.
—Kid Lawyer. l.t. ed. 2010. (Theodore Boone Ser.: Bk. 1). (ENG.). 278p. (J). 24.99 *(978-1-4104-3050-2(2))* Thorndike Pr.
—Kid Lawyer. 2011. (Theodore Boone Ser.: 1). lib. bdg. 19.65 *(978-0-606-23071-1(8))* Turtleback.
—Theodore Boone: Kid Lawyer. 2014. lthr. 79.00 *(978-1-62715-259-4(8))* Leatherbound Bestsellers.
—Theodore Boone: Kid Lawyer. 2011. 18.00 *(978-1-60686-999-4(X))* Perfection Learning Corp.
—Theodore Boone: Kid Lawyer. 2011. (Theodore Boone Ser.: 1). (ENG.). 288p. (J). (gr. 3-7). 8.99 *(978-0-14-241722-5(X),* Puffin Books) Penguin Young Readers Group.
—Theodore Boone: the Accused. 2013. (Theodore Boone Ser.: 3). (ENG.). 304p. (J). (gr. 3-7). pap. 8.99 *(978-0-14-242613-5(X),* Puffin Books) Penguin Young Readers Group.
Lee, J. A. The Trials of Edward Finlay. 2010. 223p. pap. 15.99 *(978-0-557-36757-3(3))* Lulu Pr., Inc.
Lehr, Dick. Trell. 2017. (ENG.). 320p. (YA). (gr. 7). 17.99 *(978-0-7636-9275-9(1))* Candlewick Pr.
—Trell: Nothing but the Truth. 2019. (ENG.). 320p. (J). (gr. 7). pap. 8.99 *(978-1-5362-0490-2(0))* Candlewick Pr.
Miller, Marvin. You Be the Jury: Courtroom Collection. Roper, Bob, illus. 2005. 361p. pap. *(978-0-439-77480-2(2))* Scholastic, Inc.
Montgomery, Lewis B. The Case of the Locked Box. Wummer, Amy, illus. 2013. (Milo & Jazz Mysteries Ser.: Vol. 11). (ENG.). 106p. (J). (gr. 2-4). lib. bdg. 22.60 *(978-1-57565-625-0(6))* Astra Publishing Hse.
—The Case of the Locked Box (Book 11), No. 11. Wummer, Amy, illus. 2013. (Milo & Jazz Mysteries Ser.: 11). 112p. (J). (gr. 2-6). pap. 6.99 *(978-1-57565-626-7(4),* 4eb267cb-73d0-4237-8cdc-45a0c519fde1, Kane Press) Astra Publishing Hse.
Myers, Walter Dean. Monster. 2019. (ENG., Illus.). 336p. (YA). (gr. 8). reprint ed. pap. 12.99 *(978-0-06-440731-1(4),* Amistad) HarperCollins Pubs.
Neri, G. Tru & Nelle: a Christmas Tale: A Christmas Holiday Book for Kids. 2017. (ENG.). 304p. (J). (gr. 5-7). 16.99 *(978-1-328-68598-8(5),* 1670543, Clarion Bks.) HarperCollins Pubs.
Pearsall, Shelley. Crooked River. 2007. (ENG.). 272p. (J). (gr. 3-7). 8.99 *(978-0-440-42101-6(2),* Yearling) Random Hse. Children's Bks.
Rothenberg, Jess. The Kingdom. 2019. (Illus.). 340p. (YA). *(978-1-250-25935-6(5))* Holt, Henry & Co.
Smith-Ready, Jeri. Shade. (ENG.). (YA). (gr. 9). 2011. 336p. pap. 9.99 *(978-1-4169-9407-7(6))* 2010. 320p. 17.99 *(978-1-4169-9406-0(8))* Simon Pulse. (Simon Pulse).
Thompson, Paul B. The Devil's Door: A Salem Witchcraft Story, 1 vol. 2011. (Historical Fiction Adventures Ser.). (ENG., Illus.). 160p. (J). (gr. 3-5). 31.93 *(978-0-7660-3387-0(2),* b032300a-5660-4f10-8e33-a57d5745824e) Enslow Publishing, LLC.

TRIBES

Gachot, Lynn. June-Ah-Vee's Blessing. 2010. 24p. 14.50 *(978-1-4520-7747-5(9))* AuthorHouse.

TRIBES AND TRIBAL SYSTEM

see Tribes

TRICKS

see also Card Tricks; Magic

Amazing Tricks: Level L, 6 vols. 128p. (gr. 2-3). 40.50 *(978-0-7699-0996-7(5))* Shortland Pubns. (U. S. A.) Inc.
Barnhart, Norm. Fantastically Funny Tricks, 1 vol. 2013. (Magic Manuals Ser.). (ENG.). 32p. (J). (gr. 3-9). 28.65 *(978-1-4765-0136-9(X),* 122213, Capstone Pr.) Capstone.
—Marvelous Money Tricks, 1 vol. 2013. (Magic Manuals Ser.). (ENG.). 32p. (J). (gr. 3-9). 28.65 *(978-1-4765-0134-5(3),* 122211, Capstone Pr.) Capstone.
—Stunning Stage Tricks, 1 vol. 2013. (Magic Manuals Ser.). (ENG.). 32p. (J). (gr. 3-9). 28.65 *(978-1-4765-0135-2(1),* 122212, Capstone Pr.) Capstone.
Charney, Steve. Awesome Coin Tricks, 1 vol. 2010. (Easy Magic Tricks Ser.). (ENG.). 24p. (J). (gr. 1-3). lib. bdg. 25.99 *(978-1-4296-4514-0(8),* 103007, Capstone Pr.) Capstone.
Cooke, Tim. Magic & Illusions. 2015. (Mystery Files Ser.). (ENG., Illus.). 32p. (J). (gr. 4-4). *(978-0-7787-8072-4(4))* Crabtree Publishing Co.
Crompton, Richmal. Just William's Tricks. 2003. (ENG., Illus.). 64p. (J). pap. 2.95 *(978-0-333-62679-5(6))* Macmillan Pubs., Ltd. GBR. Dist: Trafalgar Square Publishing.
Hamilton, S. L. Daredevil. 2015. (Xtreme Jobs Ser.). (ENG., Illus.). 32p. (J). (gr. 3-9). 32.79 *(978-1-62403-757-3(7),* 17748, Abdo & Daughters) ABDO Publishing Co.
Leet, Karen M. Gross Pranks, 1 vol. 2013. (Gross Guides). (ENG., Illus.). 32p. (J). (gr. 3-9). 28.65 *(978-1-4296-9922-8(1),* 120633, Capstone Pr.) Capstone.
Mason, Tom, et al. Funny Magic: How to Do Tricks That Make People Laugh! 2007. (Illus.). 48p. (J). pap. *(978-0-439-90714-9(4))* Scholastic, Inc.
Moore, Gareth. Not So Ordinary. 2015. (Brain Benders Ser.). (ENG., Illus.). 32p. (J). (gr. 3-6). pap. 7.99 *(978-1-4677-7199-3(6),* 367402b5-bdbd-4551-8540-53abcb818914, Hungry Tomato (r)) Lerner Publishing Group.
Owen, Ruth. Pranks, Tricks, & Practical Jokes, 1 vol., 1. 2014. (DIY for Boys Ser.). (ENG.). 32p. (J). (gr. 4-4). 30.17 *(978-1-4777-6294-3(9),* dbe28306-b0a8-435b-b4f8-b280e4a43830, PowerKids Pr.) Rosen Publishing Group, Inc., The.
Ransford, Sandy. Jokes & Pranks, 3 vols. 2003. (Wicked Wallets Ser.). (ENG., Illus.). 24p. (YA). *(978-1-84347-040-3(3),* Pavilion Children's Books) Pavilion Bks.
Roff, Don. Holiday Magic. 2012. (Illus.). 32p. (J). *(978-0-545-52106-2(8))* Scholastic, Inc.
Stephens, Sarah Hines & Mann, Bethany. Do It Now! Tricks: Rad Stunts & Sneaky Pranks. 2012. (ENG.). 80p. (J). pap. 6.99 *(978-1-61628-391-9(2))* Weldon Owen, Inc.
Turnbull, Stephanie. Easy Coin Tricks. 2014. (Beginner Magic Ser.). (ENG., Illus.). 24p. (J). (gr. 2-5). 28.50 *(978-1-62588-007-9(3),* 17260) Black Rabbit Bks.
—Easy Scarf & Rope Tricks. 2014. (Beginner Magic Ser.). (ENG.). 24p. (J). (gr. 2-5). 28.50 *(978-1-62588-008-6(1),* 17263) Black Rabbit Bks.
Zenon, Paul. Gimmicks & Card Tricks: Illusions for the Intermediate Magician, 1 vol. 2007. (Amazing Magic Ser.). (ENG., Illus.). 64p. (gr. 6-6). pap. 15.05 *(978-1-4042-1758-4(4),* ff0d689b-0939-4cf5-a660-2cc6678173f7, Rosen Reference) Rosen Publishing Group, Inc., The.

TRICYCLES

see Bicycles and Bicycling

TRIGONOMETRY

Accelerated Math West Virginia State Tagged Pre-Calculus Library. 2004. cd-rom 1199.00 *(978-1-59455-116-1(2))* Renaissance Learning, Inc.
Algebra & Trigonometry: Complete Solutions Guide. 6th ed. 2004. (gr. 11-12). *(978-0-618-31785-1(6),* 3-32723) CENGAGE Learning.
Algebra & Trigonometry: Learning Tools. 6th ed. 2004. (gr. 11-12). stu. ed. incl. cd-rom *(978-0-618-31794-3(5),* 3-32732) CENGAGE Learning.
Algebra & Trigonometry: Test Item File. 6th ed. 2004. (gr. 11-12). *(978-0-618-31786-8(4),* 3-32724) CENGAGE Learning.
Andreescu, Titu & Tetiva, Marian. Sums & Products. 2018. (ENG.). 340p. 54.95 *(978-0-9993428-1-7(9),* P586376) XYZ Pr.
Faulkner, Nicholas & Hosch, William L., eds. Algebra & Trigonometry, 1 vol. 2017. (Foundations of Math Ser.). (ENG., Illus.). 312p. (J). (gr. 10-10). lib. bdg. 55.59 *(978-1-68048-774-9(4),* 2cdca200-24cf-448b-8a3d-0b0ffe8f85a3) Rosen Publishing Group, Inc., The.
Holt, Rinehart and Winston Staff. Precalculus: A Graphing Approach. 4th ed. 2004. (Holt Precalculus: a Graphing Approach Ser.). (ENG.). 1184p. (gr. 9-12). 133.65 *(978-0-03-069608-4(9))* Houghton Mifflin Harcourt Publishing Co.
Hostetler, Robert P. & Larson, Ron. Trigonometry. 6th ed. 2003. (ENG.). (C). 156.95 *(978-0-618-37393-2(4),* 332774) Brooks/Cole.
Hungerford, Thomas W. Contemporary College Algebra & Trigonometry: A Graphing Approach. 2nd ed. 2004. (ENG.). 496p. (C). pap. 111.95 *(978-0-534-46792-0(X))* Brooks/Cole.
Larson, Ron. Study & Solutions Guide: Used with ... Larson-Precalculus. 6th ed. 2003. (YA). (gr. 11-12). stu. ed. 54.36 *(978-0-618-31437-9(7),* 332743) CENGAGE Learning.
—Trigonometry AP Version 6ed. 6th ed. 2003. (ENG.). 640p. (YA). (gr. 11-12). 137.96 *(978-0-618-31797-4(X),* 332762) CENGAGE Learning.
—Trigonometry Computer Solutions. (J). 7.00 *(978-0-669-12001-1(4))* Houghton Mifflin Harcourt School Pubs.
—Trigonometry IG. (J). 2.00 *(978-0-669-08612-6(6))* Houghton Mifflin Harcourt School Pubs.
Larson, Ron, et al. Precalculus with Limits: A Graphing Approach. 4th rev. ed. 2004. (ENG.). 1104p. (C). 199.95 *(978-0-618-39478-4(8),* 333050) CENGAGE Learning.
Precalculus: Complete Solutions Guide. 6th ed. 2004. (gr. 11-12). *(978-0-618-31438-6(5),* 3-32744) CENGAGE Learning.
Precalculus: HM MathSpace Technology Package. 3rd ed. 2004. (gr. 6-12). tchr. ed. *(978-0-618-35699-7(1),* 3-02981) Holt McDougal.
Precalculus with Limits: a Graphing Approach: Learning Tools. 6th ed. 2004. (gr. 11-12). stu. ed. incl. cd-rom *(978-0-618-31447-8(4),* 3-32754) CENGAGE Learning.
Reeves, Brian & Robinson, Craig. Pre-Calculus Student Activity Book. Matthews, Douglas L., ed. 2003. (Illus.). stu. ed., per., wbk. ed. *(978-1-931680-24-0(8),* Expert Systems for Teachers) Teaching Point, Inc.
Ssm Precalc: Func/Graphs. 10th ed. 2005. (C). pap. 37.95 *(978-0-534-99995-7(6))* Brooks/Cole.
Trigonometrie. 2nd ed. (Duden-Schuelerhilfen Ser.). (GER.). 112p. (YA). (gr. 10). *(978-3-411-70892-5(1))* Bibliographisches Institut & F. A. Brockhaus AG DEU. Dist: International Bk. Import Service, Inc.

TRINIDAD AND TOBAGO

Greenwood, Mark. Drummer Boy of John John. Lessac, Frané, illus. 2006. (ENG.). 40p. (J). 18.95 *(978-1-60060-652-6(0))* Lee & Low Bks., Inc.

TUV

Hernandez, Romel. Trinidad & Tobago. 2010. (Caribbean Today Ser.). (Illus.). 64p. (YA). (gr. 9-12). 21.95 *(978-1-4222-0629-4(7))* Mason Crest.
—Trinidad & Tobago, Vol. 11. Henderson, James D., ed. 2015. (Discovering the Caribbean: History, Politics, & Culture Ser.). (Illus.). 64p. (J). (gr. 7). lib. bdg. 22.95 *(978-1-4222-3317-7(0))* Mason Crest.
Sheehan, Sean & Lin, Yong Jui. Trinidad & Tobago, 1 vol. 2nd rev. ed. 2011. (Cultures of the World (Second Edition)(r) Ser.). (ENG.). 144p. (gr. 5-5). 49.79 *(978-1-60870-456-9(4)*, aef4a4a6-a9bb-4bf3-9dd6-cc135c313e9a) Cavendish Square Publishing LLC.
Williams, Heather DiLorenzo. Trinidad & Tobago. 2019. (Countries We Come From Ser.). (ENG., Illus.). 32p. (J). (gr. k-3). 19.95 *(978-1-64280-193-4(3))* Bearport Publishing Co., Inc.

TRINIDAD AND TOBAGO—FICTION

Baptiste, Tracey. Angel's Grace. 2009. (ENG.). 176p. (YA). (gr. 7). pap. 9.99 *(978-1-4169-9537-1(4)*, Simon & Schuster/Paula Wiseman Bks.) Simon & Schuster/Paula Wiseman Bks.
Benjamin, Floella. My Two Grannies. Chamberlain, Margaret, illus. 2009. (ENG.). 32p. (J). (gr. k-3). pap. 9.99 *(978-1-84780-034-3(3)*, Frances Lincoln Children's Bks.) Quarto Publishing Group UK GBR. Dist: Hachette Bk. Group.
Platt, Christine. Dancing at Carnival. Sordo, Sharon, illus. 2018. (Ana & Andrew Ser.). (ENG.). 32p. (J). (gr. -1-3). lib. bdg. 32.79 *(978-1-5321-3351-0(0)*, 31125, Calico Chapter Bks) Magic Wagon.

TRIPLETS—FICTION

Bennett, Paul. Freddie, Bill & Irving. Shannon, Kate, illus. 2009. 112p. (gr. 2-2). pap. 25.16 *(978-1-4251-7692-1(5))* Trafford Publishing.
Blake, Kendare. One Dark Throne. (YA). 2019. (Three Dark Crowns Ser.: 2). (ENG.). 480p. (gr. 9). pap. 12.99 *(978-0-06-238547-5(X)*, Quill Tree Bks.) 2017. (Three Dark Crowns Ser.: 2). (ENG., Illus.). 464p. (gr. 9). 18.99 *(978-0-06-238546-8(1)*, Quill Tree Bks.) 2017. (Illus.). 448p. *(978-0-06-279729-2(8)*, HarperTeen) 2017. (Illus.). 448p. *(978-0-06-274764-8(9)*, HarperTeen) 2017. (Illus.). 448p. *(978-0-06-269935-0(0)*, HarperTeen) 2017. (Illus.). 448p. *(978-0-06-269045-6(0)*, HarperTeen) 2017. (Illus.). 448p. *(978-0-06-269730-1(7)*, HarperTeen) HarperCollins Pubs.
—Three Dark Crowns. (Three Dark Crowns Ser.: 1). (ENG.). (YA). (gr. 9). 2018. 432p. pap. 15.99 *(978-0-06-238544-4(5))* 2016. (Illus.). 416p. 17.99 *(978-0-06-238543-7(7))* HarperCollins Pubs. (Quill Tree Bks.).
—Three Dark Crowns. 2018. (YA). lib. bdg. 22.10 *(978-0-606-40404-4(X))* Turtleback.
—Two Dark Reigns. 2018. (Three Dark Crowns Ser.: 3). (ENG., Illus.). 464p. (YA). (gr. 9). 18.99 *(978-0-06-268614-5(3)*, Quill Tree Bks.) HarperCollins Pubs.
—Two Dark Reigns: Three Dark Crowns Book 3. 2018. (ENG., Illus.). 432p. (J). *(978-1-5098-7649-5(9)*, HarperTeen) HarperCollins Pubs.
Carpenter, Donna. A Triple Treat. 2007. (Illus.). 20p. (J). 14.95 *(978-0-9793987-0-4(3))* DFC Pubs.
Childs, Tera Lynn. Sweet Legacy. 2013. (Sweet Venom Ser.: 3). (ENG.). 384p. (YA). (gr. 8). 17.99 *(978-0-06-200185-6(X)*, Tegen, Katherine Bks) HarperCollins Pubs.
—Sweet Shadows. (Sweet Venom Ser.: 2). (ENG.). (YA). (gr. 8). 2013. 352p. pap. 9.99 *(978-0-06-200184-9(1))* 2012. 336p. 17.99 *(978-0-06-200183-2(3))* HarperCollins Pubs. (Tegen, Katherine Bks).
Cooney, Caroline B. Three Black Swans. 2012. (ENG.). 288p. (YA). (gr. 7). pap. 9.99 *(978-0-385-73868-2(4)*, Ember) Random Hse. Children's Bks.
DeVillers, Julia & Roy, Jennifer. Triple Trouble. 2014. (Mix Ser.). (ENG., Illus.). 240p. (J). (gr. 4-8). pap. 7.99 *(978-1-4424-3406-6(6)*, Aladdin) Simon & Schuster Children's Publishing.
Fishbone, Greg. The Penguins of Doom. 2007. (From the Desk of Septina Nash Ser.). (ENG., Illus.). 182p. (J). (gr. 2-7). 13.95 *(978-1-933831-03-9(0))* Blooming Tree Pr.
Goulbourne, Nathaniel. The Aliens Zoo. 2013. (Illus.). 28p. pap. 21.35 *(978-1-4817-8198-5(7))* AuthorHouse.
Horse, Harry. Little Rabbit's New Baby, 1 vol. 2016. (Little Rabbit Ser.). (ENG., Illus.). 32p. (J). (gr. -1-k). pap. 7.95 *(978-1-56145-915-5(1))* Peachtree Publishing Co. Inc.
—Little Rabbit's New Baby / Book & Doll Package. 2008. (Illus.). 32p. (J). (gr. k-1). pap. 22.90 *(978-1-56145-453-2(2))* Peachtree Publishing Co. Inc.
Huelin, Jodi. Alvin's Easter Break. 2014. (ENG., Illus.). 24p. (J). (gr. -1-3). pap. 3.99 *(978-0-06-225222-7(4)*, HarperFestival) HarperCollins Pubs.
Landis, Mary M. Winter Days with the Treelo Triplets. 2012. (Illus.). 218p. (J). *(978-0-7399-2447-1(8))* Rod & Staff Pubs., Inc.
Lindman. Flicka, Ricka, Dicka & the Little Dog. Lindman, illus. 2013. (Flicka, Ricka, Dicka Ser.). (ENG., Illus.). 32p. (J). (gr. -1-3). 9.99 *(978-0-8075-2509-8(X)*, 080752509X) Whitman, Albert & Co.
—Flicka, Ricka, Dicka & the New Dotted Dresses. Lindman, illus. 2012. (Flicka, Ricka, Dicka Ser.). (ENG., Illus.). 32p. (J). (gr. -1-3). 9.99 *(978-0-8075-2484-8(0)*, 807524840) Whitman, Albert & Co.
—Flicka, Ricka, Dicka & the Strawberries. Lindman, illus. 2013. (Flicka, Ricka, Dicka Ser.). (ENG., Illus.). 32p. (J). (gr. -1-3). 9.99 *(978-0-8075-2512-8(X)*, 080752512X) Whitman, Albert & Co.
—Flicka, Ricka, Dicka & the Three Kittens. Lindman, illus. 2013. (Flicka, Ricka, Dicka Ser.). (ENG., Illus.). 32p. (J). (gr. -1-3). 9.99 *(978-0-8075-2515-9(4)*, 807525154) Whitman, Albert & Co.
—Flicka, Ricka, Dicka & Their New Skates. Lindman, illus. 2011. (Flicka, Ricka, Dicka Ser.). (ENG., Illus.). 32p. (J). (gr. -1-3). 9.99 *(978-0-8075-2491-6(3)*, 807524913) Whitman, Albert & Co.
—Flicka, Ricka, Dicka Bake a Cake. Lindman, illus. 2013. (Flicka, Ricka, Dicka Ser.). (ENG., Illus.). 32p. (J). (gr. -1-3). 9.99 *(978-0-8075-2506-7(5)*, 807525065) Whitman, Albert & Co.
—Flicka, Ricka, Dicka Go to Market. Lindman, illus. 2012. (Flicka, Ricka, Dicka Ser.). (ENG., Illus.). 32p. (J). (gr. -1-3). 9.99 *(978-0-8075-2478-7(6)*, 807524786) Whitman, Albert & Co.
Lindman, Maj. Flicka, Ricka, Dicka & the New Dotted Dresses. 2012. (J). *(978-0-8075-2495-4(6))* Whitman, Albert & Co.
May, Maggie. Times Three. L, Joe, illus. 2011. 36p. pap. 24.95 *(978-1-4626-2504-8(5))* America Star Bks.
Novak, Ali. The Heartbreakers. 2015. (Heartbreak Chronicles Ser.: 1). 336p. (YA). (gr. 6-12). pap. 12.99 *(978-1-4926-1256-8(1)*, 9781492612568) Sourcebooks, Inc.
Pearce, Jackson. Fathomless. 2013. (Fairy Tale Retelling Ser.). (ENG.). 320p. (YA). (gr. 10-17). pap. 8.99 *(978-0-316-20777-5(2))* Little, Brown Bks. for Young Readers.
Rhoton, Lesa. Angus & the Triplets. Switzer, Bobby, illus. 2006. 28p. (J). (gr. -1-3). per. 13.95 *(978-1-58939-852-8(1))* Virtualbookworm.com Publishing, Inc.
Rinehart, J. D. Crown of Three. (Crown of Three Ser.: 1). (ENG., (J). (gr. 4-8). 2016. Illus.). 432p. pap. 8.99 *(978-1-4814-2444-8(0))* 2015. 416p. 17.99 *(978-1-4814-2443-1(2))* Simon & Schuster Children's Publishing. (Aladdin).
—The Lost Realm. 2016. (Crown of Three Ser.: 2). (ENG., Illus.). 496p. (J). (gr. 4-8). 17.99 *(978-1-4814-2446-2(7)*, Aladdin) Simon & Schuster Children's Publishing.
The T-Shirt Triplets: Individual Title Six-Packs. (Literatura 2000 Ser.). (gr. 2-3). 33.00 *(978-0-7635-0187-7(5))* Rigby Education.
Ziegler, Jennifer. Revenge of the Angels: a Wish Novel (the Brewster Triplets) 2017. (Brewster Triplets Ser.). (ENG.). 256p. (J). (gr. 3-7). pap. 6.99 *(978-0-545-83902-0(5)*, Scholastic Pr.) Scholastic, Inc.
—Revenge of the Teacher's Pets. 2018. (ENG.). 256p. (J). (gr. 3-7). 16.99 *(978-1-338-09123-6(9)*, Scholastic Pr.) Scholastic, Inc.
Zirkind, Chaya Sara. Bas Mitzvah X 3. 2008. 156p. (J). *(978-1-56871-448-6(3))* Targum Pr., Inc.

TROJAN WAR

Black Ships Before Troy. 2011. 8.80 *(978-0-7848-3649-1(3)*, Everbind) Marco Bk. Co.
Bornemann Spies, Karen. Mythology of the Iliad & the Odyssey, 1 vol. 2014. (Mythology, Myths, & Legends Ser.). (ENG.). 96p. (gr. 6-7). 31.61 *(978-0-7660-6172-9(8)*, d2f57f38-2bed-4654-ba55-2672efdd2dc9) Enslow Publishing, LLC.
Bowman, Patrick. Torn from Troy. 2011. (ENG., Illus.). 200p. (YA). (gr. 5-18). pap. 11.95 *(978-1-55380-110-8(5))* Ronsdale Pr. CAN. Dist: SPD-Small Pr. Distribution.
Capaldi, Mario, illus. Odysseus & the Wooden Horse: A Greek Legend. 2003. (Dominie Collection of Myths & Legends). (SPA.). 20p. (J). lib. bdg. *(978-0-7685-2425-3(3))* Dominie Pr., Inc.
—Odysseus & the Wooden Horse: A Greek Legend. 2004. (ENG.). 20p. (J). (gr. 3-3). pap. 6.47 net. *(978-0-7685-2128-3(9)*, Dominie Elementary) Savvas Learning Co.
Church, Alfred John. The Story of the Iliad. 2005. reprint ed. pap. 31.95 *(978-1-4191-5466-9(4))* Kessinger Publishing, LLC.
Clarke, M. The Story of Troy. 2007. (Illus.). 184p. per. *(978-1-4065-1381-3(4))* Dodo Pr.
Clarke, Michael. The Story of Troy. 2007. 192p. 25.95 *(978-1-4218-4207-3(6))*; per. 10.95 *(978-1-4218-4305-6(6))* 1st World Publishing, Inc. (1st World Library - Literary Society).
—The Story of Troy. 2017. (ENG., Illus.). (J). 23.95 *(978-1-374-81990-0(5))*; pap. 13.95 *(978-1-374-81989-4(1))* Capital Communications, Inc.
Claybourne, A. & Khanduri, K. Greek Myths: Ulysses & the Trojan War: Mini-Edition. 2004. (Spotter's Guides). 160p. (J). 8.95 *(978-0-7945-0535-6(X))* EDC Publishing.
Colum, Padraic. The Adventures of Odysseus & the Tale of Troy. Pogány, Willy, illus. 2008. 164p. pap. *(978-1-4068-2730-9(4))* Echo Library.
—The Adventures of Odysseus & the Tales of Troy. l.t. ed. 2007. (ENG.). 220p. pap. 22.99 *(978-1-4346-0648-8(1))* Creative Media Partners, LLC.
—The Children's Homer: The Adventures of Odysseus & the Tale of Troy. Pogany, Willy, illus. 2004. (ENG.). 256p. (J). (gr. 5-9). pap. 10.99 *(978-0-689-86883-2(9)*, Aladdin) Simon & Schuster Children's Publishing.
—The Children's Homer: The Adventures of Odysseus & the Tale of Troy. 2015. (ENG., Illus.). (J). 25.95 *(978-1-298-49026-1(X))* Creative Media Partners, LLC.
—The Children's Homer: The Adventures of Odysseus & the Tale of Troy. 2018. (ENG., Illus.). 176p. (J). 24.68 *(978-1-7317-0502-0(6))* 2018. (ENG., Illus.). 176p. (J). pap. 12.62 *(978-1-7317-0503-7(4))* 2018. (ENG., Illus.). 176p. (J). 12.64 *(978-1-7317-0085-6(7))* 2018. (ENG., Illus.). 176p. (J). pap. 5.85 *(978-1-7317-0086-5(5))* 2012. (ENG., Illus.). 176p. (J). pap. 8.50 *(978-1-61382-346-0(0))* 2011. 144p. pap. 7.95 *(978-1-61382-004-9(6))* Simon & Brown.
—The Children's Homer: The Adventures of Odysseus & the Tale of Troy. Pogany, Willy. illus. 2019. (ENG.). 256p. (J). (gr. 5-9). 18.99 *(978-1-5344-5037-0(8)*, Aladdin) Simon & Schuster Children's Publishing.
Ferrell, David L. Achilles & the Trojan War, 1 vol., 1. 2013. (Jr. Graphic Myths: Greek Heroes Ser.). (ENG.). 24p. (J). (gr. 2-3). 28.93 *(978-1-4777-6240-0(X)*, 2ddcda8f-429b-4dfd-b3cd-522268eb6239, PowerKids Pr.) Rosen Publishing Group, Inc., The.
Hoena, Blake. The Trojan War: An Interactive Mythological Adventure. Takvorian, Nadine, illus. 2017. (You Choose: Ancient Greek Myths Ser.). (ENG.). 112p. (J). (gr. 3-7). lib. bdg. 32.65 *(978-1-5157-4822-9(7)*, 134438, Capstone Pr.) Capstone.
Holub, Joan. Surprise, Trojans! The Story of the Trojan Horse (Ready-To-Read Level 2) Jones, Dani, illus. 2014. (Ready-To-Read Ser.). (ENG.). 32p. (J). (gr. k-2). 16.99 *(978-1-4814-2087-7(9))*; pap. 4.99 *(978-1-4814-2086-0(0))* Simon Spotlight. (Simon Spotlight).
Jeffrey, Gary. Achilles & the Trojan War, 1 vol. Spender, Nick, illus. 2012. (Graphic Mythical Heroes Ser.). (ENG.). 24p. (J). (gr. 3-3). pap. 9.15 *(978-1-4339-7508-0(4)*, 1e5a4b63-0298-444c-9d2a-0e2f5c08d65a); lib. bdg. 26.60 *(978-1-4339-7507-3(6)*, c2476a4c-35f1-48e1-8f09-42ee80f389e2) Stevens, Gareth Publishing LLLP.
Lang, Andrew. Tales of Troy: Ulysses the Sacker of Cities. 2004. reprint ed. pap. 1.99 *(978-1-4192-5072-9(6))* Kessinger Publishing, LLC.
—Tales of Troy & Greece. Ford, H. J., illus. 2006. (Dover Children's Classics Ser.). (ENG.). 336p. (gr. 9-12). per. 9.95 *(978-0-486-44917-3(3))* Dover Pubns., Inc.
McCarty, Nick. Troy: The Myth & Reality Behind the Epic Legend, 1 vol. 2008. (Prime Time History Ser.). (ENG., Illus.). 128p. (YA). (gr. 10-10). lib. bdg. 47.80 *(978-1-4042-1365-4(1)*, 32d3a0e1-a289-4c81-b3fa-931fedea771a) Rosen Publishing Group, Inc., The.
O'Connor, George. Ares: Bringer of War. 2015. (Olympians Ser.: 7). (ENG., Illus.). 80p. (J). (gr. 4-9). pap. 12.99 *(978-1-62672-013-8(4)*, 900131512, First Second Bks.) Roaring Brook Pr.
Rosemary, Sutcliff. Black Ships Before Troy: The Story of the Iliad. 2014. (ENG.). 160p. (YA). 11.24 *(978-1-63245-187-3(5))* Lectorum Pubns., Inc.
Sheppard, Si. Heroes of the Trojan War, 1 vol. 2015. (Heroes & Legends Ser.). (ENG., Illus.). 88p. (J). (gr. 8-8). 38.80 *(978-1-4994-6172-5(0)*, 5add6ebf-2b69-4f6f-a2a3-82ddb2bb0bfe, Rosen Young Adult) Rosen Publishing Group, Inc., The.
Sutcliff, Rosemary. Black Ships Before Troy: The Story of the Iliad. 2005. (ENG.). 176p. (YA). (gr. 7). mass mkt. 8.99 *(978-0-553-49483-9(X)*, Laurel Leaf) Random Hse. Children's Bks.
Tracy, Kathleen. The Life & Times of Homer. 2004. (Biography from Ancient Civilizations Ser.). (Illus.). 48p. (J). (gr. 4-8). lib. bdg. 29.95 *(978-1-58415-260-6(5))* Mitchell Lane Pubs.
—Odysseus. 2008. (Profiles in Greek & Roman Mythology Ser.). (Illus.). 48p. (J). (gr. 4-7). lib. bdg. 29.95 *(978-1-58415-705-2(4))* Mitchell Lane Pubs.
World Book, Inc. Staff, contrib. by. The Mysteries of the Trojan War. 2014. (J). *(978-0-7166-2668-8(3))* World Bk., Inc.

TROLLS

see Fairies

TROPICAL FISH

Hawes, Alison. Collins Big Cat Phonics for Letters & Sounds - in the Fish Tank: Band 02A/Red A, Bd. 2A. John and Gus art, illus. 2018. (Collins Big Cat Phonics Ser.). (ENG.). 16p. (J). (gr. -1-k). pap. 6.99 *(978-0-00-825142-0(8))* HarperCollins Pubs. Ltd. GBR. Dist: Independent Pubs. Group.
Tropical Fish. 2017. (J). *(978-0-7166-7954-7(X))* World Bk., Inc.

TROPICAL RAIN FOREST ECOLOGY

see Rain Forest Ecology

TROPICAL RAIN FORESTS

see Rain Forests

TROPICS

Baker, Stuart. In the Tropics, 1 vol. 2010. (Climate Change Ser.). (ENG.). 32p. (gr. 4-4). 31.21 *(978-0-7614-4440-4(8)*, 792688c1-3703-4111-9169-a217a588ee43) Cavendish Square Publishing LLC.
Benduhn, Tea. Living in Tropical Rain Forests, 1 vol. 2007. (Life on the Edge Ser.). (ENG., Illus.). 24p. (gr. 2-4). pap. 9.15 *(978-0-8368-8349-7(7)*, 255750a9-1115-4bd4-8574-b4a045c6c3ec); lib. bdg. 24.67 *(978-0-8368-8344-2(6)*, 3f407531-1650-49a6-adef-8e3f8c2ce084) Stevens, Gareth Publishing LLLP. (Weekly Reader Leveled Readers).
Bradley, Timothy J. Terror in the Tropics, 1 vol. 2nd rev. ed. 2013. (TIME for KIDS(r): Informational Text Ser.). (ENG., Illus.). 64p. (J). (gr. 4-8). pap. 14.99 *(978-1-4333-4898-3(5))* Teacher Created Materials, Inc.
Dawson, Emily C. Wet & Dry Places. 2011. (Amicus Readers. Let's Compare (Level A) Ser.). (ENG.). 24p. (J). (gr. -1-2). lib. bdg. 25.65 *(978-1-60753-004-6(X)*, 17025) Amicus.
First Discovery Staff & Mettler, René. Jungle. Mettler, René, illus. 2006. (ENG., Illus.). 36p. (J). (gr. k-3). spiral bd. 11.99 *(978-1-85103-183-2(9))* Moonlight Publishing, Ltd. GBR. Dist: Independent Pubs. Group.
Gifford, Clive. In Focus: Tropical Lands. 2017. (In Focus Ser.). (ENG.). 64p. (J). 17.99 *(978-0-7534-7366-5(6)*, 9780753473665, Kingfisher) Roaring Brook Pr.
Lazor, Stephanie. Life on the Equator, 1 vol. 2003. (Life in Extreme Environments Ser.). (ENG., Illus.). 64p. (gr. 5-8). lib. bdg. 37.13 *(978-0-8239-3986-2(3)*, fe1cd37d-a67a-472c-b5b1-0e0cda3e8d96, Rosen Reference) Rosen Publishing Group, Inc., The.
Rustad, Martha E. H. The Wettest Places on Earth, 1 vol. 2010. (Extreme Planet Ser.). (ENG.). 24p. (J). (gr. 1-3). lib. bdg. 25.99 *(978-1-4296-3966-8(0)*, 102576, Capstone Pr.) Capstone.
Senker, Cath. Tropical Climates. 2017. (Focus on Climate Zones Ser.). (ENG., Illus.). 48p. (J). (gr. 4-6). lib. bdg. 35.99 *(978-1-4846-3783-8(6)*, 134493, Heinemann) Capstone.
Soll, Karen. Hottest Places on the Planet. 2016. (Extreme Earth Ser.). (ENG., Illus.). 24p. (J). (gr. -1-2). lib. bdg. 27.32 *(978-1-4914-8341-1(5)*, 130811, Capstone Pr.) Capstone.

TROPICS—FICTION

Billups, Ruth A. No Place for a Horse. 2008. 48p. pap. 16.95 *(978-1-60703-118-5(3))* America Star Bks.
Collins, Pat Lowery. The Fattening Hut. 2005. (ENG.). 192p. (YA). (gr. 7). pap. 12.95 *(978-0-618-55209-2(X)*, 491911, Clarion Bks.) HarperCollins Pubs.

TROUT

Statts, Leo. Trout. 2018. (Freshwater Fish Ser.). (ENG., Illus.). 24p. (J). (gr. -1-2). lib. bdg. 31.36 *(978-1-5321-2292-7(6)*, 28351, Abdo Zoom-Launch) ABDO Publishing Co.

TROY (EXTINCT CITY)

Capaldi, Mario, illus. Odysseus & the Wooden Horse: A Greek Legend. 2003. (Dominie Collection of Myths & Legends). (SPA.). 20p. (J). lib. bdg. *(978-0-7685-2425-3(3))* Dominie Pr., Inc.
—Odysseus & the Wooden Horse: A Greek Legend. 2004. (ENG.). 20p. (J). (gr. 3-3). pap. 6.47 net. *(978-0-7685-2128-3(9)*, Dominie Elementary) Savvas Learning Co.
Clarke, Michael. The Story of Troy. 2007. 192p. 25.95 *(978-1-4218-4207-3(6))*; per. 10.95 *(978-1-4218-4305-6(6))* 1st World Publishing, Inc. (1st World Library - Literary Society).
Crompton. Troy (Lost Worlds & Mysterious Civilizations) 2012. (ENG., Illus.). 104p. (gr. 6-12). 35.00 *(978-1-60413-974-7(9)*, P200201, Facts On File) Infobase Holdings, Inc.
Kerns, Ann. Troy. 2008. (Unearthing Ancient Worlds Ser.). (ENG.). 80p. (gr. 5-8). lib. bdg. 30.60 *(978-0-8225-7582-5(5))* Lerner Publishing Group.
McCarty, Nick. Troy: The Myth & Reality Behind the Epic Legend, 1 vol. 2008. (Prime Time History Ser.). (ENG., Illus.). 128p. (YA). (gr. 10-10). lib. bdg. 47.80 *(978-1-4042-1365-4(1)*, 32d3a0e1-a289-4c81-b3fa-931fedea771a) Rosen Publishing Group, Inc., The.
Schlitz, Laura Amy. The Hero Schliemann: The Dreamer Who Dug for Troy. Byrd, Robert, illus. 2013. (ENG.). 80p. (J). (gr. 4-7). pap. 8.99 *(978-0-7636-6504-3(5))* Candlewick Pr.

TROY (EXTINCT CITY)—FICTION

Alexander, Lloyd. The Xanadu Adventure. 2007. (Vesper Holly Ser.). (ENG.). 160p. (J). (gr. 5-18). 5.99 *(978-0-14-240786-8(0)*, Puffin Books) Penguin Young Readers Group.
Bowler, Bill. Troy. 2nd ed. 2013. (ENG., Illus.). 40p. pap. 11.00 *(978-0-19-424970-6(0))* Oxford Univ. Pr., Inc.
Gabrielson, Ernest & Gabrielson, Brian. Home in Ithaca: A novel of Ancient Greece & Troy. 2004. 120p. (YA). pap. 10.95 *(978-0-595-30889-7(9))* iUniverse, Inc.
Geras, Adèle. Troy. 2004. 368p. (J). (gr. 8-18). pap. 48.00 incl. audio *(978-0-8072-2288-1(7)*, Listening Library) Random Hse. Audio Publishing Group.
Geras, Adèle & Geras, Adèle. Troy. 2017. (ENG., Illus.). 368p. (YA). (gr. 9). pap. 11.99 *(978-0-544-92546-5(7)*, 1656861, Clarion Bks.) HarperCollins Pubs.
McLaren, Clemence. Inside the Walls of Troy: A Novel of the Women Who Lived the Trojan War. 2004. (ENG., Illus.). 208p. (YA). (gr. 7-12). mass mkt. 8.99 *(978-0-689-87397-3(2)*, Simon Pulse) Simon Pulse.
Peacock, L. A. Terror at Troy. Hale, Nathan, illus. 2012. 90p. (J). *(978-0-545-34063-2(2))* Scholastic, Inc.

TRUANCY (SCHOOLS)

see School Attendance

TRUCK DRIVERS

Barrington, Richard. Careers in Trucking, 1 vol. 2013. (Essential Careers Ser.). (ENG., Illus.). 80p. (YA). (gr. 6-6). lib. bdg. 37.47 *(978-1-4488-9473-4(5)*, 2ea4fb75-5c2b-4f23-b0df-5623d41a0aff, Rosen Classroom) Rosen Publishing Group, Inc., The.
Gordon, Nick. Ice Road Trucker. 2013. (Dangerous Jobs Ser.). (ENG., Illus.). 24p. (J). (gr. 3-7). lib. bdg. 26.95 *(978-1-60014-895-8(6)*, Torque Bks.) Bellwether Media.
Gustaitis, Joseph Alan. Arctic Trucker, 1 vol. 2011. (Dirty & Dangerous Jobs Ser.). (ENG., Illus.). 32p. (gr. 3-3). 31.21 *(978-1-60870-169-8(7)*, 7ef75d26-21d1-484b-a635-d1be48f1168c) Cavendish Square Publishing LLC.
Honders, Christine. Truck Drivers, 1 vol. 2019. (Helpers in Our Community Ser.). (ENG.). 24p. (gr. 1-2). pap. 9.25 *(978-1-7253-0830-5(4)*, 53d3216e-53a0-4377-bc6f-d63b27f4c2d9, PowerKids Pr.) Rosen Publishing Group, Inc., The.
Liebman, Dan & Liebman, Dan. I Want to Be a Truck Driver. 2nd rev. ed. 2018. (I Want to Be Ser.). (ENG., Illus.). 24p. (J). (gr. -1-2). pap. 3.99 *(978-0-2281-0103-1(4)*, 00cb6b7b-59dc-42d5-a722-63c10c427b93) Firefly Bks., Ltd.
Mara, Wil. Motor Transport Operator. 2012. (21st Century Skills Library: Cool Military Careers Ser.). (ENG.). 32p. (gr. 4-8). pap. 14.21 *(978-1-61080-624-4(7)*, 202234); (Illus.). 32.07 *(978-1-61080-450-9(3)*, 202060) Cherry Lake Publishing.
Rathburn, Betsy. Truck Drivers. 2020. (Community Helpers Ser.). (ENG., Illus.). 24p. (J). (gr. k-3). pap. 7.99 *(978-1-61891-789-8(7)*, 12574, Blastoff! Readers) Bellwether Media.
Syrewicz, Connor. Truck Driver. 2013. (Earning $50,000 - $100,000 with a High School Diploma or Less Ser.: 14). 64p. (J). (gr. 7-18). 22.95 *(978-1-4222-2900-2(9))* Mason Crest.
Thomas, William David. Truck Driver, 1 vol. 2009. (Cool Careers: on the Go Ser.). (ENG.). 32p. (gr. 3-3). pap. 11.50 *(978-1-4339-0169-0(2)*, eb40b724-844e-46e6-97a3-7ea175c0b0f5); (YA). lib. bdg. 28.67 *(978-1-4339-0005-1(X)*, 434a477c-42f6-4db9-ab65-a1739d0970c4) Stevens, Gareth Publishing LLLP.

TRUCK DRIVERS—FICTION

Iverson, Gregory. Tyler's Big Blue Truck. Fritz, Siegfried, illus. 2006. 40p. (J). *(978-0-9755184-0-3(2))* Sandbox Bks.
Jones, Kristy. The Adventures of Ziggy the Trucker Dog. 2010. (ENG.). 24p. pap. 15.99 *(978-1-4500-8751-3(5))* Xlibris Corp.
London, Jonathan. My Big Rig, 0 vols. Garofoli, Viviana, illus. 2013. (ENG.). 32p. (J). (gr. -1-1). pap. 9.99 *(978-1-4778-1673-8(9)*, 9781477816738, Two Lions) Amazon Publishing.
Royston, Angela. Truck Trouble. 2013. (DK Readers Level 1 Ser.). (ENG.). 32p. (J). (gr. k-2). 16.19 *(978-1-4654-0244-8(6))* Dorling Kindersley Publishing, Inc.
Venning, Edward W. The Truck & a Boy: The Truck with a big Heart. 2007. 48p. (YA). per. 15.95 *(978-1-4327-0738-5(8))* Outskirts Pr., Inc.

TRUCK FARMING

see Vegetable Gardening

TRUCKS

Abbot, Henry. I Want to Drive a Snowplow, 1 vol. 2016. (At the Wheel Ser.). (ENG.). 24p. (J). (gr. 1-1). pap. 9.25 *(978-1-4994-2666-3(6)*, 45e1bd80-406e-4a44-beb3-874fc2328a59, PowerKids Pr.) Rosen Publishing Group, Inc., The.
Abdo, Kenny. Monster Truck Rallies. 2018. (Arena Events Ser.). (ENG., Illus.). 24p. (J). (gr. 2-8). lib. bdg. 31.36 *(978-1-5321-2535-5(6)*, 30079, Abdo Zoom-Fly) ABDO Publishing Co.
ABDO Publishing Company Staff. Mighty Movers. 2005. (Mighty Movers Ser.). (gr. k-4). 153.90 *(978-1-59197-824-4(6)*, Buddy Bks.) ABDO Publishing Co.
Abramovitz, Melissa. Military Trucks, 1 vol. 2012. (Military Machines Ser.). (ENG.). 24p. (J). (gr. -1-2). lib. bdg. 27.32 *(978-1-4296-7570-3(5)*, 117167); (gr. k-1). pap. 41.70 *(978-1-4296-8317-3(1))* Capstone. (Capstone Pr.).

Addison, D. R. Garbage Trucks at Work, 1 vol. 2009. (Big Trucks Ser.). (ENG., Illus.). 24p. (J). (gr. 1-1). pap. 9.25 (978-1-4358-3085-1(7), d1ce0bbc-57ef-4a37-a3c0-a07da30b143f, PowerKids Pr.) Rosen Publishing Group, Inc., The.

Allan, John. Let's Look at Diggers & Dumpers. 2019. (Mini Mechanics Ser.). (ENG., Illus.). 24p. (J). (gr. 1-3). 26.65 (978-1-5415-5533-4(3), 3f9f0141-dc97-4206-a7cf-c476072f5dc7, Hungry Tomato (r)) Lerner Publishing Group.

—Let's Look at Trucks & Tractors. 2019. (Mini Mechanics Ser.). (ENG., Illus.). 24p. (J). (gr. 1-3). 26.65 (978-1-5415-5529-7(5), 862c5358-e012-441a-a1c6-e67c9a1627bb, Hungry Tomato (r)) Lerner Publishing Group.

Aloian, Molly. Fire Trucks: Racing to the Scene. 2010. (Vehicles on the Move Ser.). (ENG.). 32p. (J). (gr. k-3). pap. (978-0-7787-3060-6(3)) Crabtree Publishing Co.

Anderson, Jill, ed. Let's Get to Work! Vamos a Trabajar! Evrard, Gaetan, illus. 2005. (Word Play/Juegos con Pala Ser.). (ENG.). 20p. (J). (gr. -1-17). bds. 6.95 (978-1-58728-512-7(6)) Cooper Square Publishing Llc.

Ardagh, Philip. All at Sea. (Mighty Machines Ser.). (Illus.). 32p. (J). lib. bdg. 24.25 (978-1-931983-04-4(6)) Chrysalis Education.

—On the Farm. (Mighty Machines Ser.). (Illus.). 32p. lib. bdg. 24.25 (978-1-931983-05-1(4)) Chrysalis Education.

Arnold, Quinn M. Big Rigs. 2017. (Seedlings Ser.). (ENG., Illus.). 24p. (J). (gr. -1-k). (978-1-60818-789-8(6), 20107, Creative Education) Creative Co., The.

—Dump Trucks. 2018. (Amazing Machines Ser.). (ENG., Illus.). 24p. (J). (gr. 1-4). (978-1-60818-890-1(6), 19540, Creative Education); pap. 8.99 (978-1-62832-506-5(2), 19538, Creative Paperbacks) Creative Co., The.

—Garbage Trucks. 2017. (Seedlings Ser.). (ENG., Illus.). 24p. (J). (gr. -1-k). (978-1-60818-790-4(X), 20110, Creative Education) Creative Co., The.

—Monster Trucks. 2017. (Seedlings Ser.). (ENG., Illus.). 24p. (J). (gr. -1-k). (978-1-60818-791-1(8), 20113, Creative Education) Creative Co., The.

—Seedlings: Big Rigs. 2017. (Seedlings Ser.). (ENG., Illus.). 24p. (J). (gr. -1-1). pap. 10.99 (978-1-62832-385-6(X), 20105, Creative Paperbacks) Creative Co., The.

—Seedlings: Garbage Trucks. 2017. (Seedlings Ser.). (ENG., Illus.). 24p. (J). (gr. -1-1). pap. 10.99 (978-1-62832-386-3(8), 20108, Creative Paperbacks) Creative Co., The.

—Seedlings: Monster Trucks. 2017. (Seedlings Ser.). (ENG., Illus.). 24p. (J). (gr. -1-1). pap. 10.99 (978-1-62832-387-0(6), 20111, Creative Paperbacks) Creative Co., The.

Award, Anna. Working Trucks. 2012. (ENG., Illus.). 16p. (J). pap. 3.95 (978-0-86163-969-4(3)) Award Pubns. Ltd. GBR. Dist: Parkwest Pubns., Inc.

Bach, Rachel. La Course de Camion Monstre. 2016. (On Fait la Course? Ser.). (FRE., Illus.). 16p. (J). (gr. k-2). (978-1-77092-346-1(2), 17641) Amicus.

—The Monster Truck Race. 2016. (Let's Race Ser.). (ENG.). 16p. (J). (gr. -1-1). pap. 7.99 (978-1-68152-134-3(2), 15500) Amicus.

—The Monster Truck Race. 2016. (Let's Race Ser.). (ENG.). 16p. (J). (gr. k-3). 17.95 (978-1-60753-917-9(9)) Amicus Learning.

Becker, Ann. Monster Trucks. 2009. (Illus.). 24p. (J). pap. 7.95 (978-1-60694-838-5(5)) Rourke Educational Media.

Bell, Samantha. Dump Truck. 2018. (21st Century Basic Skills Library: Level 1: Welcome to the Construction Site Ser.). (ENG., Illus.). 24p. (J). (gr. k-3). lib. bdg. 30.64 (978-1-5341-2918-4(9), 211716) Cherry Lake Publishing.

Benchmark Education Co., LLC. Big Trucks Big Book. 2014. (Shared Reading Foundations Ser.). (J). (gr. -1). (978-1-4509-9445-3(8)) Benchmark Education Co.

Bender, Lionel. Trucks & Trailers. 2006. (J). (978-1-59389-270-8(5)) Chrysalis Education.

Bingham, Caroline. Truck-Mania!, 1 vol. 2003. (Vehicle-Mania! Ser.). (ENG., Illus.). 32p. (gr. 2-4). lib. bdg. 26.67 (978-0-8368-3785-8(1), 22869ec1-8310-478f-8745-736746c563fc, Gareth Stevens Learning Library) Stevens, Gareth Publishing LLLP.

Bowman, Chris. Monster Bulldozers. 2014. (Monster Machines Ser.). (ENG., Illus.). 24p. (J). (gr. k-3). lib. bdg. 26.95 (978-1-62617-053-7(3), Blastoff! Readers) Bellwether Media.

—Monster Tractors. 2014. (Monster Machines Ser.). (ENG., Illus.). 24p. (J). (gr. k-3). lib. bdg. 26.95 (978-1-62617-055-1(X), Blastoff! Readers) Bellwether Media.

—Monster Trucks. 2017. (Mighty Machines in Action Ser.). (ENG., Illus.). 24p. (J). (gr. k-3). lib. bdg. 26.95 (978-1-62617-606-5(X), Blastoff! Readers) Bellwether Media.

—Pickup Trucks. 2018. (Mighty Machines in Action Ser.). (ENG., Illus.). 24p. (J). (gr. k-3). lib. bdg. 26.95 (978-1-62617-757-4(0), Blastoff! Readers) Bellwether Media.

Brack, Amanda. Big Book of Brick Trucks. 2015. (ENG., Illus.). 32p. (J). (-k). 14.99 (978-1-63220-598-8(X), Sky Pony Pr.) Skyhorse Publishing Co., Inc.

Bradley, Michael. Escalade. 2009. (Cars 2 Ser.). 32p. (gr. 3). 28.50 (978-0-7614-4101-4(8)) Marshall Cavendish GBR. Dist: Marshall Cavendish Corp.

—The Hummer. 2008. (Cars Ser.). (Illus.). 32p. (J). (gr. 3-18). lib. bdg. 28.50 (978-0-7614-2981-4(6)) Marshall Cavendish Corp.

Brill, Marlene Targ. Garbage Trucks. 2004. (Pull Ahead Books — Mighty Movers Ser.). (ENG., Illus.). 32p. (gr. k-3). (J). pap. 7.99 (978-0-8225-2381-9(7), c7272054-390b-49b0-a4ac-3fb2fa8f9e37, First Avenue Editions); lib. bdg. 22.60 (978-0-8225-1539-5(3)) Lerner Publishing Group.

Brooks, Felicity, des. Build a Picture Trucks Sticker Book. 2012. (Build a Picture Sticker Bks). 24p. (J). pap. 6.99 (978-0-7945-3248-2(9), Usborne) EDC Publishing.

Brooks, Felicity & Durber, Matt. Trucks & Diggers. Mazali, Gustavo, illus. 2008. (Magnet Bks.). 10p. (J). (gr. -1-3). bds. 19.99 (978-0-7945-1907-0(5), Usborne) EDC Publishing.

Burch, Lynda S. Wicky Wacky Things That Go! Trucks. Burch, Lynda S., photos by. 2004. (Illus.). 28p. (J). E-Book 9.95 incl. cd-rom (978-1-933090-11-5(1)) Guardian Angel Publishing, Inc.

Buzzeo, Toni. Whose Truck? (a Guess-The-Job Book) Datz, Jim, illus. 2015. (Guess-The-Job Book Ser.). (ENG.). 16p. (J). (gr. -1 — 1). bds. 10.99 (978-1-4197-1612-6(3), 1098610) Abrams, Inc.

Byerly, Robbie. Trucks in the City. 2015. (1-3Y Getting Around Ser.). (ENG., Illus.). 16p. (J). pap. 8.00 (978-1-63437-719-5(2)) American Reading Co.

Camionetas Gigantes (Monster Trucks) 2006. (J). pap. 6.95 (978-0-8225-6646-5(X), Ediciones Lerner) Lerner Publishing Group.

Carr, Aaron. Semi Trucks. 2014. (Illus.). 24p. (J). (978-1-4896-3232-6(8)) Weigl Pubs., Inc.

Carrière, Nicholle. Big Trucks, 1 vol. 2016. (Mega Machines Ser.). (ENG., Illus.). 64p. (J). pap. 6.99 (978-1-926700-64-9(3), c03b1e22-441f-41bc-9899-2a56ace803f4) Blue Bike Bks. CAN. Dist: Lone Pine Publishing USA.

Cars & Trucks. Date not set. (Illus.). (J). bds. 9.98 (978-0-7525-9892-5(9)) Parragon, Inc.

Castor, Harriet. Trucks. Lyon, Chris, illus. 2006. (Big MacHines Ser.). 32p. (J). (gr. k). lib. bdg. 14.95 (978-1-58086-847-1(9)) EDC Publishing.

—Trucks. Lyon, Chris et al, illus. rev. ed. 2004. (Usborne Big Machines Ser.). 31p. (J). (gr. -1). per. 6.95 (978-0-7945-0839-5(1), Usborne) EDC Publishing.

Clay, Kathryn. Dump Trucks. 2016. (Construction Vehicles at Work Ser.). (ENG., Illus.). 24p. (J). (gr. -1-2). lib. bdg. 22.65 (978-1-5157-2526-8(X), 132897, Pebble) Capstone.

Cohn, Jessica. Trucks, 1 vol. 2013. (Machines in Motion Ser.). 48p. (J). (gr. 3-3). (ENG.). 34.61 (978-1-4339-9616-0(2), 5cf25482-7ce4-4eb8-8391-56c19f76229a); (ENG.). pap. 15.05 (978-1-4339-9617-7(0), a971b614-8616-4bad-912e-3c9ad4c6a93b); pap. 84.30 (978-1-4339-9618-4(9)) Stevens, Gareth Publishing LLLP.

Colson, Rob Scott. Trucks, 1 vol. 2013. (Ultimate Machines Ser.). (ENG., Illus.). 24p. (J). (gr. 5-5). pap. 9.25 (978-1-4777-0121-8(4), 0a241421-5dd4-4a80-8c3a-36d73d70be9a); lib. bdg. 26.27 (978-1-4777-0068-6(4), 5bf1964b-4ebc-417a-ac90-5420cc46a27c) Rosen Publishing Group, Inc., The. (PowerKids Pr.).

Coming Soon. Monster Trucks. 2018. (Eyediscover Ser.). (ENG., Illus.). 24p. (J). (gr. 1-2). 28.55 (978-1-4896-8005-1(5), AV2 by Weigl) Weigl Pubs., Inc.

Construction Trucks. 2004. (Mega MacHines Ser.). (Illus.). 16p. (J). (978-2-7643-0198-2(7)) Phidal Publishing, Inc./Editions Phidal, Inc.

Coppendale, Jean. Trucks. 2010. (Mighty Machines Ser.). (ENG., Illus.). 24p. (J). (gr. -1-2). pap. 5.95 (978-1-55407-619-2(6), c0934390-d777-4e1c-96e2-240c0bdd3eca) Firefly Bks., Ltd.

Dalmatian Press Staff. Pop & Shine Trucks. 2008. (ENG.). 12p. (J). 10.95 (978-1-58117-672-8(4), Intervisual/Piggy Toes) Bendon, Inc.

David, Jack. Humvees. 2009. (Military Machines Ser.). (ENG., Illus.). 24p. (J). (gr. 3-7). lib. bdg. 26.95 (978-1-60014-260-4(5), 10283, Torque Bks.) Bellwether Media.

—Torque: Humvees. 2009. (Torque Ser.). 24p. (J). (gr. 3-7). 20.00 (978-0-531-21734-4(5), Children's Pr.) Scholastic Library Publishing.

Daynes, Katie. Trucks. 2004. (Beginners Ser.). 32p. (J). (gr. 1-18). (ENG.). pap. 4.95 (978-0-7945-0365-9(9)); lib. bdg. 12.95 (978-1-58086-511-1(9)) EDC Publishing.

Devera, Czeena. Go Truck! 2019. (Watch It Go Ser.). (ENG.). 16p. (J). (gr. -1-2). pap. 11.36 (978-1-5341-3918-3(4), 212504, Cherry Blossom Press) Cherry Lake Publishing.

Dickason, Chris. The Diggers & Trucks Colouring Book. Dickason, Chris, illus. 2017. (ENG., Illus.). 64p. (J). (gr. k-2). pap. 10.99 (978-1-78055-250-7(5)) O'Mara, Michael Bks., Ltd. GBR. Dist: Independent Pubs. Group.

Dieker, Wendy Strobel. Big Rigs. 2018. (Spot Mighty Machines Ser.). (ENG.). 16p. (J). (gr. -1-2). lib. bdg. (978-1-68151-372-0(2), 14976) Amicus.

—Garbage Trucks. 2018. (Spot Mighty Machines Ser.). (ENG.). 16p. (J). (gr. -1-2). lib. bdg. (978-1-68151-374-4(9), 14978) Amicus.

—Las Camionetas. 2018. (Máquinas Poderosas Ser.). (SPA.). 16p. (J). (gr. -1-2). lib. bdg. (978-1-68151-607-3(1), 15215) Amicus.

—Los Camiones Cisterna. 2018. (Máquinas Poderosas Ser.). (SPA.). 16p. (J). (gr. -1-2). (978-1-68151-608-0(X), 15216) Amicus.

—Los Camiones Grandes. 2018. (Máquinas Poderosas Ser.). (SPA.). 16p. (J). (gr. -1-2). lib. bdg. (978-1-68151-604-2(7), 15212) Amicus.

—Pickup Trucks. 2018. (Spot Mighty Machines Ser.). (ENG.). 16p. (J). (gr. -1-2). pap. 7.99 (978-1-68152-295-1(0), 14985); lib. bdg. (978-1-68151-375-1(7), 14979) Amicus.

—Tanker Trucks. 2018. (Spot Mighty Machines Ser.). 16p. (J). (gr. -1-2). pap. 7.99 (978-1-68152-296-8(9), 14986); (ENG.). lib. bdg. (978-1-68151-376-8(5), 14980) Amicus.

Dinmont, Kerry. Monster Trucks on the Go. 2016. (Bumba Books (r) — Machines That Go Ser.). (ENG., Illus.). 24p. (J). (gr. -1-1). lib. bdg. 26.65 (978-1-5124-1445-5(X), c9481e44-147d-421e-8b14-24c2d5623829, Lerner Pubns.) Lerner Publishing Group.

DK. Baby Touch & Feel: Tractor. 2010. (Baby Touch & Feel Ser.). (ENG.). 14p. (J). (gr. -1 — 1). bds. 7.99 (978-0-7566-7132-7(9), DK Children) Dorling Kindersley Publishing, Inc.

—Baby Touch & Feel: Trucks. 2008. (Baby Touch & Feel Ser.). (ENG., Illus.). 14p. (J). (gr. -1 — 1). bds. 7.99 (978-0-7566-3465-0(2), DK Children) Dorling Kindersley Publishing, Inc.

—Big Dump Truck. 2003. (Wheelie Bks.). (ENG., Illus.). 12p. (J). (gr. -1-k). bds. 8.99 (978-0-7894-9714-7(X), DK Children) Dorling Kindersley Publishing, Inc.

—Follow the Trail: Trucks. 2016. (Follow the Trail Ser.). (ENG., Illus.). 14p. (J). (-k). bds. 9.99 (978-1-4654-5126-2(9), DK Children) Dorling Kindersley Publishing, Inc.

—My First Trucks. 2015. (My First Board Bks.). (ENG.). 36p. (J). (gr. -1 — 1). bds. 5.99 (978-1-4654-2904-9(2), DK Children) Dorling Kindersley Publishing, Inc.

—Really Feely Trucks. 2017. (Really Feely Board Bks.). (ENG., Illus.). 12p. (J). (— 1). bds. 7.99 (978-1-4654-6204-6(X), DK Children) Dorling Kindersley Publishing, Inc.

—Tabbed Board Books: My First Trucks & Diggers: Let's Get Driving! 2013. (My First Tabbed Board Book Ser.). (ENG.). 28p. (J). (gr. -1 — 1). bds. 12.99 (978-1-4654-1673-5(0), DK Children) Dorling Kindersley Publishing, Inc.

—Ultimate Sticker Book: Truck: Over 60 Reusable Full-Color Stickers. 2004. (Ultimate Sticker Book Ser.). (ENG.). 16p. (J). (gr. k-3). pap. 6.99 (978-0-7566-0239-0(4), DK Children) Dorling Kindersley Publishing, Inc.

Doeden, Matt. Monster Trucks. 2007. (J). lib. bdg. 26.60 (978-0-8225-6567-3(6), Lerner Pubns.) Lerner Publishing Group.

Doman, Mary Kate. Big Trucks, 1 vol. 2011. (All about Big Machines Ser.). (ENG., Illus.). 24p. (gr. -1-1). pap. 10.35 (978-1-59845-241-9(X), 4c2d11a5-249b-4452-b1bb-eecd74161ff3); lib. bdg. 25.27 (978-0-7660-3929-2(3), 9e5ae066-bbcf-44a7-a433-b57626fa9651) Enslow Publishing, LLC. (Enslow Publishing).

Dos Santos, Julie. Trucks, 1 vol. 2010. (Amazing Machines Ser.). (ENG.). 32p. (gr. 2-2). 31.21 (978-0-7614-4407-7(6), d35ace72-840f-4b24-83a5-195d173fca84) Cavendish Square Publishing LLC.

Ellis, Catherine. Cars & Trucks. 2009. (Mega Military Machines Ser.). 24p. (gr. 1-1). 42.50 (978-1-61514-634-5(2), PowerKids Pr.) Rosen Publishing Group, Inc., The.

—Cars & Trucks/Autos y Camiones. 2009. (Mega Military Machines/Megamaquinas militares Ser.). (ENG & SPA.). 24p. (gr. 1-1). 42.50 (978-1-61514-639-0(3), Editorial Buenas Letras) Rosen Publishing Group, Inc., The.

Emberley, Ed. Ed Emberley's Drawing Book of Trucks & Trains. Emberley, Ed, illus. 2005. (ENG., Illus.). 32p. (J). (gr. 2-17). pap. 8.99 (978-0-316-78967-7(4)) Little, Brown Bks. for Young Readers.

Falligant, Erin. Dump Trucks / Camiones de Volteo. Sánchez, Sr., illus. 2019. (Machines! / ¡Las Máquinas! Ser.). (MUL.). 24p. (J). (gr. -1-2). lib. bdg. 33.99 (978-1-68410-338-6(X), 140258) Cantata Learning.

Farndon, John. Megafast Trucks. Edwards, Mat & Pyke, Jeremy, illus. 2016. (Megafast Ser.). (ENG.). 32p. (J). (gr. 3-6). lib. bdg. 27.99 (978-1-4677-9366-7(3), 6446f51e-b64b-4605-b835-179a9d071911, Hungry Tomato (r)) Lerner Publishing Group.

Finn, Denny Von. Humvees. 2013. (Military Vehicles Ser.). (ENG., Illus.). 24p. (J). (gr. 3-7). lib. bdg. 26.95 (978-1-60014-886-6(7), Epic Bks.) Bellwether Media.

—4x4 Trucks. 2009. (Cool Rides Ser.). (ENG., Illus.). 24p. (J). (gr. 3-7). lib. bdg. 26.95 (978-1-60014-254-3(0)) Bellwether Media.

Fishman, Jon M. Cool Pickup Trucks. 2018. (Lightning Bolt Books (r) — Awesome Rides Ser.). (ENG., Illus.). 24p. (J). (gr. 1-3). lib. bdg. 29.32 (978-1-5415-1995-4(7), e99c3422-3714-4f56-a361-4410153542fc, Lerner Pubns.) Lerner Publishing Group.

Frisch, Aaron. Dump Trucks. 2013. 24p. 20.57 (978-1-60818-341-8(6)) Creative Co., The.

—Seedlings: Dump Trucks. 2014. (Seedlings Ser.). (ENG.). 24p. (J). (gr. -1-k). pap. 9.99 (978-0-89812-886-4(2), 21675, Creative Paperbacks) Creative Co., The.

Galvin, Laura Gates. First Look at Trucks. Eaddy, Susan, illus. 2008. (ENG.). 16p. (J). (gr. -1-k). 6.95 (978-1-59249-861-1(2)) Soundprints.

Geddis, Norm. Concept Cars: Past & Future. 2018. (J). (978-1-4222-4086-1(X)) Mason Crest.

—Toughest Trucks from the Streets to Showtime, Vol. 5. 2018. (World of Automobiles Ser.). (Illus.). 80p. (J). (gr. 7). lib. bdg. 33.27 (978-1-4222-4091-5(6)) Mason Crest.

Giants on the Road, 12 vols. 2014. (Giants on the Road Ser.). (ENG.). 24p. (J). (gr. 1-2). lib. bdg. 151.62 (978-1-4777-5744-4(9), a2d24ebe-38d7-4a26-9181-cde89ff83c96, PowerKids Pr.) Rosen Publishing Group, Inc., The.

Gibbons, Gail. Trucks. 2019. (Illus.). 24p. (J). (— 1). bds. 7.99 (978-0-8234-4149-5(0)) Holiday Hse., Inc.

Gibbs, Lynne. Mega Book of Trucks: Discover the Most Amazing Trucks on Earth! 2003. (Illus.). 32p. (YA). pap. (978-1-904516-21-7(1), Pavilion Children's Books) Pavilion Bks.

Gifford, Clive. Monster Trucks. 2nd rev. ed. 2019. (Mighty Machines Ser.). (ENG., Illus.). 32p. (J). (gr. 2-5). pap. 6.95 (978-0-2281-0221-2(9), 2eef9599-0154-43d4-867b-bdd7db77dbf4) Firefly Bks., Ltd.

—Trucks. 2012. (ENG.). 24p. (J). lib. bdg. (978-0-7787-7477-8(5)); (Illus.). pap. (978-0-7787-7482-2(1)) Crabtree Publishing Co.

Gigliotti, Jim. Monster Trucks, 1 vol. 2010. (Racing Mania Ser.). (ENG.). 48p. (gr. 4-4). lib. bdg. 34.07 (978-0-7614-4385-8(1), 244487bb-37c3-44ff-a4ea-3964dfbce05c) Cavendish Square Publishing LLC.

Gilpin, Rebecca. Trucks & Tractors. 2005. (ENG.). 32p. (J). pap. 8.95 (978-0-7945-1134-0(1), Usborne) EDC Publishing.

Glaser, Rebecca. Dump Truck. 2012. (ENG., Illus.). 24p. (J). lib. bdg. 25.65 (978-1-62031-019-9(8)) Jump! Inc.

—Trucks Haul. 2016. (ENG., Illus.). 14p. (J). (gr. -1 — 1). bds. 7.99 (978-1-68152-124-4(5), 15823) Amicus.

Glover, David & Glover, Penny. Trucks in Action, 1 vol. 2007. (On the Go Ser.). (ENG., Illus.). 24p. (J). (gr. 1-2). lib. bdg. 26.27 (978-1-4042-4310-1(0), a506bd8b-8f7d-4ec9-9db9-b219181505e0, PowerKids Pr.) Rosen Publishing Group, Inc., The.

Goldish, Meish. Titanic Trucks. 2009. (World's Biggest Ser.). (Illus.). 24p. (J). (gr. 1-6). lib. bdg. 26.99 (978-1-59716-957-8(9)) Bearport Publishing Co., Inc.

Goodman, Susan E. Monster Trucks! Doolittle, Michael J., illus. 2010. (Step into Reading Ser.). (ENG.). 48p. (J). (gr. k-3). pap. 5.99 (978-0-375-86208-3(0), Random Hse. Bks. for Young Readers) Random Hse. Children's Bks.

Gordon, Nick. Monster Dump Trucks. 2013. (Monster Machines Ser.). (ENG., Illus.). 24p. (J). (gr. k-3). lib. bdg. 26.95 (978-1-60014-938-2(3), Blastoff! Readers) Bellwether Media.

—Monster Trucks. 2013. (Monster Machines Ser.). (ENG., Illus.). 24p. (J). (gr. k-3). lib. bdg. 26.95 (978-1-60014-940-5(5), Blastoff! Readers) Bellwether Media.

Graham, Ian. Super Trucks. Bergin, Mark & Hewetson, N. J., illus. 2014. (Time Shift Speed Ser.). 32p. (gr. 3-6). 31.35 (978-1-908973-97-9(8)) Book Hse. GBR. Dist: Black Rabbit Bks.

—Trucks. 2007. (Extreme Machines/Watts Ser.). (Illus.). 32p. (YA). (gr. 4-7). lib. bdg. 28.50 (978-1-59920-043-9(0)) Black Rabbit Bks.

Graubart, Norman D. Tractor-Trailers, 1 vol. 2014. (Giants on the Road Ser.). (ENG.). 24p. (J). (gr. 1-2). lib. bdg. 25.27 (978-1-4994-0219-3(8), 72e7e8c7-1cae-4c22-96f3-b5ba7e97cd3e, PowerKids Pr.) Rosen Publishing Group, Inc., The.

Greve, Meg & Robertson, J. Jean. Camiones: Trucks. 2008. (Mis Primeros Descubrimientos = My First Discovery Ser.). (ENG & SPA., Illus.). 24p. (J). (gr. k-2). 19.44 (978-1-60472-504-9(4)) Rourke Educational Media.

—Trucks. 2008. (My First Discovery Library). (ENG., Illus.). 24p. (gr. k-1). bds. 5.99 (978-1-60472-433-2(1), 9781604724332) Rourke Educational Media.

Gunzi, Christiane. Big Noisy Trucks. 2015. (ENG., Illus.). 10p. (J). 9.99 (978-1-904618-88-1(X)) Award Pubns. Ltd. GBR. Dist: Parkwest Pubns., Inc.

Hankin, Rosie. Cut & Paste Trucks, Trains, & Big Machines, 1 vol. 2007. (Cut, Paste, & Create Ser.). (ENG., Illus.). 32p. (gr. 1-3). lib. bdg. 28.67 (978-0-8368-7721-2(7), 36f28e3c-f97d-453a-af3c-291be27279ba, Gareth Stevens Learning Library) Stevens, Gareth Publishing LLLP.

Harrison, Paul. Monster Trucks. (Up Close Ser.). 24p. (gr. 3-3). 2009. 47.90 (978-1-60854-697-8(7)) 2007. (ENG., Illus.). (J). lib. bdg. 28.93 (978-1-4042-4223-4(6), a3757533-c760-4f3d-9d7c-0367514cbac1) Rosen Publishing Group, Inc., The. (PowerKids Pr.).

—Supertrucks. 2013. (Illus.). 32p. (J). (978-1-84858-566-9(7)) Arcturus Pubs., Inc.

Hayes, Amy. Big Dump Trucks, 1 vol. 2015. (Machines That Work Ser.). (ENG., Illus.). 24p. (gr. 1-1). pap. 9.23 (978-1-5026-0394-4(2), 7f889a43-9425-4477-a328-202e5677c255) Cavendish Square Publishing LLC.

Helbrough, Emma & Brooks, Felicity. First Picture Trucks. Van Wyk, Hanri & Newell, Keith, illus. MMStudios, photos by. 2007. (First Picture Board Bks.). 16p. (J). (gr. -1-k). bds. 11.99 (978-0-7945-1454-9(5), Usborne) EDC Publishing.

Heller, Daryl. Let's Make a Dump Truck with Everyday Materials, 1 vol. 2005. (Let's Do Arts & Crafts Ser.). (ENG., Illus.). 24p. (J). (gr. 2-2). lib. bdg. 26.27 (978-1-4042-3059-0(9), fa9d4e85-fa73-4ffd-a570-35f0f2f4e475) Rosen Publishing Group, Inc., The.

Higgins, Nadia. Garbage Trucks / Camiones de Basura. Sánchez, Sr., illus. 2019. (Machines! / ¡Las Máquinas! Ser.). (MUL.). 24p. (J). (gr. -1-2). lib. bdg. 33.99 (978-1-68410-340-9(1), 140260) Cantata Learning.

HOP, LLC. Hooked on Trucks Super Activity Kit. 2006. (J). (gr. -1). 9.99 (978-1-933863-18-4(8)) HOP, LLC.

Hudson, Amanda. This Is My Truck, 1 vol. 2008. (Our Toys Ser.). (ENG., Illus.). 16p. (gr. k-1). (J). lib. bdg. 21.67 (978-0-8368-9255-0(0), 9a459ed5-b893-4005-941d-f51b843fa30d); pap. 6.30 (978-0-8368-9354-0(9), 8bc04754-a818-4aa3-93e1-1d0a2d98565a) Stevens, Gareth Publishing LLLP. (Weekly Reader Leveled Readers).

—This Is My Truck / Éste Es Mi Camión, 1 vol. 2008. (Our Toys / Nuestros Juguetes Ser.). 16p. (gr. k-k). (SPA & ENG.). pap. 6.30 (978-0-8368-9358-8(1), b2327768-06b6-4484-be62-c9e780c2413c); (ENG & SPA., Illus.). (J). lib. bdg. 21.67 (978-0-8368-9259-8(3), 14899ea7-40e8-49a1-a34b-ab1675379817) Stevens, Gareth Publishing LLLP. (Weekly Reader Leveled Readers).

Ikids Staff. Soft Shapes: Trucks (Baby's First Book + Puzzle) Ski, Jenn, illus. 2010. (ENG.). 8p. (J). (gr. -1 — 1). 10.99 (978-1-60169-044-9(4)) Innovative Kids.

—Trucks. Larranaga, Ana Martin, illus. 2009. (ENG.). 12p. (J). (gr. -1 — 1). bds. 5.99 (978-1-58476-936-1(X)) Innovative Kids.

Jango-Cohen, Judith. Fire Trucks on the Move. 2010. (Lightning Bolt Books (r) — Vroom-Vroom Ser.). (ENG., Illus.). 32p. (J). (gr. 1-3). pap. 9.99 (978-0-7613-6119-0(7), 74c0b7b4-6df2-463f-9070-c2af13a16e3c) Lerner Publishing Group.

—Volquetes. Translations.com Staff, tr. from ENG. 2006. (Libros para Avanzar-Potencia en Movimiento (Pull Ahead Books-Mighty Movers) Ser.). (SPA., Illus.). 32p. (gr. k-3). lib. bdg. 22.60 (978-0-8225-6228-3(6), Ediciones Lerner) Lerner Publishing Group.

Jennings, Terry. Trucks. 2009. (J). 28.50 (978-1-59920-291-4(3)) Black Rabbit Bks.

—Trucks. 2009. (How Machines Work Ser.). (ENG., Illus.). 32p. (J). (gr. 3-7). pap. (978-1-897563-45-8(0)) Saunders Bk. Co.

Johansen, Heidi Leigh. My Book of Trucks. 2005. (Early Learning Collections Ser.). (Illus.). (J). 8.95 (978-1-4042-2800-9(4), PowerKids Pr.) Rosen Publishing Group, Inc., The.

Johnson, Earl L. & Hawkins, Grace. The World's Greatest Working Trucks Vol. 5: The Best of the Northeast. 2003. 100p. (Orig.). (YA). (gr. 8-12). pap. 19.95 (978-0-9649645-1-8(1)) Johnson, Earl Photography.

Johnstone, Michael. Monster Trucks. 2005. (Need for Speed Ser.). (Illus.). 32p. (gr. 3-5). lib. bdg. 23.93 (978-0-8225-0388-0(3)) Lerner Publishing Group.

Kalman, Bobbie. Camiones Robustos. 2007. (Vehículos en Acción Ser.). (SPA & ENG., Illus.). 32p. (J). (gr. 4-7). pap. (978-0-7787-8316-9(2)); lib. bdg. (978-0-7787-8306-0(5)) Crabtree Publishing Co.

—Tough Trucks. 2007. (Vehicles on the Move Ser.). (ENG., Illus.). 32p. (J). (gr. 3-7). lib. bdg. (978-0-7787-3044-6(1)); (gr. 1-5). pap. (978-0-7787-3058-3(1)) Crabtree Publishing Co.

Kawa, Katie. Dump Trucks, 1 vol. 2011. (Big Machines Ser.). (Illus.). 24p. (ENG.). (J). pap. 9.15 (978-1-4339-5564-8(4), 4653d2dd-d391-444b-ac5d-49a122868d8e); (ENG., (J). lib. bdg. 25.27 (978-1-4339-5562-4(8), 00fab2c3-f54f-4d56-832d-48272246404c); 69.20 (978-1-4339-6889-1(4)) Stevens, Gareth Publishing LLLP.

—Dump Trucks / Camiones de Volteo, 1 vol. 2011. (Big Machines / Grandes Máquinas Ser.). (SPA & ENG., Illus.). 24p. (J). (gr. k-k). lib. bdg. 25.27 (978-1-4339-5580-8(6),

TUV

b0c3f82c-9c6c-4e63-9fff-0f1cc2419321) Stevens, Gareth Publishing LLLP.

Kilby, Don. On the Road. 2003. (Wheels at Work Ser.). (Illus.). 24p. (J). (gr. -1-k). *(978-1-55337-043-7(0))* Kids Can Pr., Ltd.

—On the Road. Kilby, Don, illus. 2006. (Wheels at Work Ser.). (Illus.). 24p. (J). (gr. -1-2). 5.95 *(978-1-55337-986-7(1))* Kids Can Pr., Ltd. CAN. Dist: Hachette Bk. Group.

LaFontaine, Bruce. History of Trucks. 2013. (Dover Planes Trains Automobiles Coloring Ser.). (ENG., Illus.). 48p. (J). (gr. 3-12). pap. 4.99 *(978-0-486-29278-6(9)*, 292789) Dover Pubns., Inc.

Landers, Ace. I Am a Garbage Truck. Migliari, Paola, illus. 2008. (ENG.). 8p. (J). (gr. -1 — 1). bds. 4.99 *(978-0-545-07963-1(2)*, Cartwheel Bks.) Scholastic, Inc.

Latham, Donna. Superfast Trucks. 2006. (Ultimate Speed Ser.). (Illus.). 32p. (J). (gr. 3-6). lib. bdg. 28.50 *(978-1-59716-253-1(1))* Bearport Publishing Co., Inc.

Leonard, Barry, ed. Drawing Trucks & Diggers: A Book of 10 Stencils. 2004. (Illus.). 34p. (J). (gr. k-4). reprint ed. ring bd. 10.00 *(978-0-7567-8505-5(7))* DIANE Publishing Co.

Levete. Monster Trucks 6-Pack. 2004. (Mean Machines Ser.). (Illus.). (J). pap. 48.30 *(978-1-4109-1202-2(7))* Harcourt Schl. Pubs.

Light, Steve. Trucks Go: (Board Books about Trucks, Go Trucks Books for Kids) 2008. (Vehicles Go! Ser.). (ENG., Illus.). 16p. (J). (gr. -1 — 1). bds. 9.99 *(978-0-8118-6542-5(8))* Chronicle Bks. LLC.

Lindeen, Mary. Garbage Trucks. 2007. (Mighty Machines Ser.). (ENG., Illus.). 24p. (J). (gr. k-3). lib. bdg. 26.95 *(978-1-60014-117-1(X))* Bellwether Media.

—Trucks. 2007. (Mighty Machines Ser.). (ENG., Illus.). 24p. (J). (gr. k-3). lib. bdg. 26.95 *(978-1-60014-063-1(7))* Bellwether Media.

Litchfield, Jo & Brooks, F. Trucks. 2004. (Chunky Board Bks.). (ENG., Illus.). 6p. (J). bds. 4.95 *(978-0-7945-0349-9(7)*, Usborne) EDC Publishing.

Llewellyn, Claire. Trucks. 2015. (Wonderwise Ser.). (Illus.). 32p. (gr. 2-6). 31.35 *(978-1-62588-363-6(3))* Black Rabbit Bks.

Lock, Deborah. Big Trucks. 2013. (DK Reader Pre Level Ser.). lib. bdg. 13.55 *(978-0-606-32459-5(3))* Turtleback.

Lynch, Seth. Chevrolet Trucks, 1 vol. 2018. (Tough Trucks Ser.). (ENG.). 32p. (gr. 1-2). 28.27 *(978-1-5382-3035-0(6)*, 874ff60c-28bf-41c0-b3fd-ab18a9dcbd44) Stevens, Gareth Publishing LLLP.

—GMC Trucks, 1 vol. 2018. (Tough Trucks Ser.). (ENG.). 32p. (gr. 1-2). 28.27 *(978-1-5382-3033-6(X)*, a3bb6105-f0e0-4ddc-b58d-bff5fbb49cef) Stevens, Gareth Publishing LLLP.

—Honda Trucks, 1 vol. 2018. (Tough Trucks Ser.). (ENG.). 32p. (gr. 1-2). 28.27 *(978-1-5382-3037-4(2)*, 151911f7-f143-484d-a184-55fe19dd5b50) Stevens, Gareth Publishing LLLP.

—Ram Trucks, 1 vol. 2018. (Tough Trucks Ser.). (ENG.). 32p. (gr. 1-2). 28.27 *(978-1-5382-3036-7(4)*, b834c24d-ead6-4db6-8586-0069de71c95a) Stevens, Gareth Publishing LLLP.

—Toyota Trucks, 1 vol. 2018. (Tough Trucks Ser.). (ENG.). 32p. (gr. 1-2). 28.27 *(978-1-5382-3032-9(1)*, d821e6f1-25aa-4aa3-88fe-ae88744014a0) Stevens, Gareth Publishing LLLP.

MacDumont, Sean. Trucks Go! 2017. (Ways to Go Ser.). 24p. (J). (gr. k-k). 48.90 *(978-1-5382-0847-2(4))* Stevens, Gareth Publishing LLLP.

Mack, Larry. Chevrolet Silverado. 2018. (Tough Trucks Ser.). (ENG., Illus.). 24p. (J). (gr. 3-7). lib. bdg. 26.95 *(978-1-62617-891-5(7)*, Torque Bks.) Bellwether Media.

—Ford F-150. 2018. (Tough Trucks Ser.). (ENG., Illus.). 24p. (J). (gr. 3-7). lib. bdg. 26.95 *(978-1-62617-892-2(5)*, Torque Bks.) Bellwether Media.

—Honda Ridgeline. 2018. (Tough Trucks Ser.). (ENG., Illus.). 24p. (J). (gr. 3-7). lib. bdg. 26.95 *(978-1-62617-893-9(3)*, Torque Bks.) Bellwether Media.

—Nissan Frontier. 2018. (Tough Trucks Ser.). (ENG., Illus.). 24p. (J). (gr. 3-7). lib. bdg. 26.95 *(978-1-62617-894-6(1)*, Torque Bks.) Bellwether Media.

—Ram 1500. 2018. (Tough Trucks Ser.). (ENG., Illus.). 24p. (J). (gr. 3-7). lib. bdg. 26.95 *(978-1-62617-895-3(X)*, Torque Bks.) Bellwether Media.

Manolis, Kay. Big Rigs. 2008. (Mighty Machines Ser.). (ENG., Illus.). 24p. (J). (gr. k-3). lib. bdg. 26.95 *(978-1-60014-177-5(3))* Bellwether Media.

—Tow Trucks. 2008. (Mighty Machines Ser.). (ENG., Illus.). 24p. (J). (gr. k-3). lib. bdg. 26.95 *(978-1-60014-182-9(X))* Bellwether Media.

Mara, Wil. National Geographic Readers: Trucks. 2009. (Readers Ser.). (Illus.). 32p. (J). (gr. -1-k). (ENG.). 13.90 *(978-1-4263-0527-6(3))*; pap. 4.99 *(978-1-4263-0526-9(5))* Disney Publishing Worldwide. (National Geographic Kids).

Marshall, Jane. Trucks & Diggers. 2013. (Wild Rides Ser.). 32p. (J). (gr. k-2). *(978-1-84898-623-7(8)*, TickTock Books) Octopus Publishing Group.

Mason, Paul. Monster Trucks. 2010. (Motorsports Ser.). 32p. (J). (gr. 3-6). 28.50 *(978-1-60753-120-3(8))* Amicus Learning.

Masters, Neil. Trucks Coloring Book. 2013. (ENG.). 32p. 12.48 *(978-1-62884-654-6(2)*, Baby Professor (Education Kids)) Speedy Publishing LLC.

Matthies, Janna. Monster Trucks. Barretta, Gene, illus. 2009. (ENG.). 14p. (J). (gr. -1-k). 9.95 *(978-1-58117-853-1(0)*, Intervisual/Piggy Toes) Bendon, Inc.

Maurer, Tracy Nelson. Land Rover. 2006. (Full Throttle Ser.). (Illus.). 32p. (J). (gr. -1-3). lib. bdg. 28.50 *(978-1-60044-225-4(0))* Rourke Educational Media.

McClellan, Ray. Dump Trucks. 2006. (Mighty Machines Ser.). (ENG., Illus.). 24p. (J). (gr. k-3). lib. bdg. 26.95 *(978-1-60014-046-4(7))* Bellwether Media.

Meachen Rau, Dana. En Camiones / Trucks, 1 vol. 2010. (¡Viajamos! / We Go! Ser.). (ENG & SPA.). 24p. (gr. k-1). lib. bdg. 25.50 *(978-0-7614-4774-0(1)*, 0ff96e09-e7f0-4ac2-a270-edf5b05e2b4f) Cavendish Square Publishing LLC.

—Trucks, 1 vol. 2010. (We Go! Ser.). (ENG.). 24p. (gr. 3-3). 25.50 *(978-0-7614-4083-3(6)*, e39860e8-c66f-4bd7-9353-028bb5c0dd04) Cavendish Square Publishing LLC.

Meister, Cari. Trucks. 2019. (Transportation in My Community Ser.). (ENG., Illus.). 32p. (J). (gr. -1-2). lib. bdg. 27.99 *(978-1-9771-0247-8(6)*, 139253, Pebble) Capstone.

Mezzanotte, Jim. Camiones Basculantes (Giant Dump Trucks), 1 vol. 2005. (Vehículos Gigantes (Giant Vehicles) Ser.). (SPA.). 24p. (gr. 2-4). lib. bdg. 25.67 *(978-0-8368-5985-0(5)*, fd75d804-d2fb-4ba7-b79b-1c241dbc39e3, Gareth Stevens Learning Library) Stevens, Gareth Publishing LLLP.

—Giant Dump Trucks, 1 vol. 2005. (Giant Vehicles Ser.). (ENG., Illus.). 24p. (gr. 2-4). pap. 9.15 *(978-0-8368-4919-6(1)*, 573b6c2b-a7c7-46f4-aea5-43aafb62eac2); lib. bdg. 25.67 *(978-0-8368-4912-7(4)*, c4fe8f93-4b4e-424c-98dc-42f6dce786ed) Stevens, Gareth Publishing LLLP. (Gareth Stevens Learning Library).

Mikoley, Kate. Monster Trucks, 1 vol. 2019. (Motorsports Maniacs Ser.). (ENG.). 32p. (gr. 1-2). pap. 11.50 *(978-1-5382-4090-8(4)*, 65122718-d6db-4ba1-b7c8-957f447f3c60) Stevens, Gareth Publishing LLLP.

Miller, Connie Colwell. I'll Be a Truck Driver. Baroncelli, Silvia, illus. 2018. (When I Grow Up Ser.). (ENG.). 24p. (J). (gr. 1-4). pap. 8.99 *(978-1-68152-320-0(5)*, 15061); lib. bdg. *(978-1-68151-400-0(1)*, 15055) Amicus.

Morganelli, Adrianna. Trucks: Pickups to Big Rigs. 2007. (Automania! Ser.). (ENG., Illus.). 32p. (J). (gr. 3-7). lib. bdg. *(978-0-7787-3015-6(8))*; (gr. 2-9). pap. *(978-0-7787-3037-8(9))* Crabtree Publishing Co.

Morrison, Marie. Dump Trucks, 1 vol. 2019. (XL Machines! Ser.). (ENG.). 24p. (gr. 1-2). pap. 9.25 *(978-1-7253-1146-6(1)*, 2bbb0af1-665e-4cd1-ae24-ac2a34c60e1e, PowerKids Pr.) Rosen Publishing Group, Inc., The.

—Garbage Trucks, 1 vol. 2019. (XL Machines! Ser.). (ENG.). 24p. (gr. 1-2). pap. 9.25 *(978-1-7253-1154-1(2)*, 042e1794-2cdc-4565-bb2b-e7c60b771148, PowerKids Pr.) Rosen Publishing Group, Inc., The.

Mullins, Matt. Trucks. 2008. (21st Century Skills Innovation Library: Innovation in Transportation Ser.). (ENG., Illus.). 32p. (gr. 4-8). lib. bdg. 32.07 *(978-1-60279-237-1(2)*, 200167) Cherry Lake Publishing.

Murray, Julie. Dump Trucks. 2018. (Construction Machines (Dash!) Ser.). (ENG., Illus.). 24p. (J). (gr. k-4). lib. bdg. 31.36 *(978-1-5321-2516-4(X)*, 30041, Abdo Zoom-Dash) ABDO Publishing Co.

—Trucks, 1 vol. 2014. (Transportation Ser.). (ENG.). 24p. (J). (gr. -1-2). lib. bdg. 32.79 *(978-1-62970-083-0(5)*, 1707, Abdo Kids) ABDO Publishing Co.

My First Book of Trucks. 2004. (Illus.). 18p. (J). bds. 5.99 *(978-1-85854-431-1(9))* Brimax Books Ltd. GBR. Dist: Byeway Bks.

National Geographic. National Geographic Readers: Things That Go Collection. 2015. (Readers Ser.). (ENG., Illus.). 120p. (J). (gr. 1-3). lib. bdg. 16.90 *(978-1-4263-1973-0(8)*, National Geographic Kids) Disney Publishing Worldwide.

Nelson, Kristin L. Camionetas Gigantes. Translations.com Staff, tr. from ENG. 2006. (Libros para Avanzar-Potencia en Movimiento (Pull Ahead Books-Mighty Movers) Ser.). (SPA., Illus.). 32p. (gr. k-3). lib. bdg. 22.60 *(978-0-8225-6227-6(8)*, Ediciones Lerner) Lerner Publishing Group.

—Monster Trucks on the Move. 2010. (Lightning Bolt Books (r) — Vroom-Vroom Ser.). (ENG., Illus.). 32p. (J). (gr. 1-3). pap. 9.99 *(978-0-7613-6120-6(0)*, 388948ac-9c9d-4149-9d7d-97a990b33dfe); pap. 45.32 *(978-0-7613-6939-4(2))* Lerner Publishing Group.

Nixon, James. Trucks. 2010. (Machines on the Move Ser.). (ENG.). 32p. (J). (gr. 1-3). lib. bdg. 28.50 *(978-1-60753-064-0(3)*, 17216) Amicus.

—Trucks. 2012. (ENG., Illus.). 32p. (gr. 1-3). pap. 8.95 *(978-1-926722-74-0(4))* Saunders Bk. Co. CAN. Dist: RiverStream Publishing.

Oachs, Emily Rose. Dump Trucks. 2017. (Mighty Machines in Action Ser.). (ENG., Illus.). 24p. (J). (gr. k-3). lib. bdg. 26.95 *(978-1-62617-603-4(5)*, Blastoff! Readers) Bellwether Media.

Osier, Dan. Dump Trucks, 1 vol., 1. 2014. (Construction Site Ser.). (ENG.). 24p. (J). (gr. 1-2). 26.27 *(978-1-4777-2862-8(7)*, 87bfb648-8e1e-45f5-b21c-a3ebf0f275cf, PowerKids Pr.) Rosen Publishing Group, Inc., The.

—Forklifts, 1 vol., 1. 2014. (Construction Site Ser.). (ENG.). 24p. (J). (gr. 1-2). pap. 9.25 *(978-1-4777-2956-4(9)*, 016515c6-9d36-4446-9193-50e0f603230e, PowerKids Pr.) Rosen Publishing Group, Inc., The.

Oxlade, Chris. This Is My Dump Truck. Crawford, Andy, photos by. 2008. (Mega Machine Drivers Ser.). (Illus.). 30p. (J). (gr. k). lib. bdg. 28.50 *(978-1-59771-105-0(5))* Sea-To-Sea Pubns.

—Trucks. 2009. (Mighty Machines Ser.). (Illus.). 31p. (J). (gr. 4-7). pap. 7.95 *(978-1-59920-256-3(5))* Black Rabbit Bks.

—Trucks Inside & Out, 1 vol. 2009. (Machines Inside Out Ser.). (ENG.). 32p. (J). (gr. 4-4). pap. 11.00 *(978-1-4358-2940-4(9)*, b5e5daa8-c961-4f74-883c-bb7a155e5473, PowerKids Pr.) Rosen Publishing Group, Inc., The.

Page, Josephine. I Am a Dump Truck. Migliari, Paola, illus. 2007. (ENG.). 10p. (J). (gr. -1 — 1). bds. 4.99 *(978-0-439-91617-2(8)*, Cartwheel Bks.) Scholastic, Inc.

Parker, Steve. Cars Trucks & Bikes. 2010. (How It Works Ser.). (Illus.). 40p. (J). (gr. 3-18). lib. bdg. 19.95 *(978-1-4222-1792-4(2)*, 1317905) Mason Crest.

—Giant Machines. 2010. (How It Works Ser.). 40p. (J). (gr. 3-18). lib. bdg. 19.95 *(978-1-4222-1796-2(5))* Mason Crest.

Pearcey, Alice. Usborne Tractors & Trucks Stencil Book. Milbourne, Anna, ed. Tudor, Andy, illus. 2006. 10p. (J). bds. 12.99 *(978-0-7945-1139-5(2)*, Usborne) EDC Publishing.

Peppas, Lynn. Monster Trucks. 2012. (ENG., Illus.). 32p. (J). *(978-0-7787-3019-4(0))*; pap. *(978-0-7787-3024-8(7))* Crabtree Publishing Co.

Perez, Jessica. Under Construction: A Moving Track Book. Schneider, Christine, illus. 2005. (ENG.). 12p. (J). 12.95 *(978-1-58117-272-0(9)*, Intervisual/Piggy Toes) Bendon, Inc.

Petruccio, Steven James. BOOST Trucks Coloring Book. 2013. (Dover Planes Trains Automobiles Coloring Ser.). (ENG.). 32p. (J). (gr. 1-2). pap. 4.99 *(978-0-486-49411-1(X)*, 49411X) Dover Pubns., Inc.

—Create Your Own Construction Truck Sticker Activity Book. 2011. (Dover Little Activity Books Stickers Ser.). (ENG., Illus.). 4p. (J). (gr. k-3). 1.99 *(978-0-486-47232-4(9)*, 472329) Dover Pubns., Inc.

—Create Your Own Fire Truck. 2010. (Dover Little Activity Books Stickers Ser.). (ENG., Illus.). 4p. (J). (gr. 1-4). 2.50 *(978-0-486-47548-6(4)*, 475484) Dover Pubns., Inc.

Pettiford, Rebecca. Big Rigs. 2017. (Mighty Machines in Action Ser.). (ENG., Illus.). 24p. (J). (gr. k-3). lib. bdg. 26.95 *(978-1-62617-629-4(9)*, Blastoff! Readers) Bellwether Media.

Picthall, Chez. My Favourite Trucks Sticker Book. Rayner, Katy, ed. 2015. (Illus.). 20p. (J). pap. 7.99 *(978-1-906572-83-9(6))* Award Pubns. Ltd. GBR. Dist: Parkwest Pubns., Inc.

Poolos, J. Monster Trucks/Camionetas Gigantes, 1 vol. Alaman, Eduardo, tr. 2007. (Wild Rides / Autos de Locura Ser.). (SPA & ENG., Illus.). 24p. (YA). (gr. 2-3). lib. bdg. 26.27 *(978-1-4042-7640-6(8)*, 92cb1c5e-6bbc-4ba7-8432-f89798251e17) Rosen Publishing Group, Inc., The.

—Wild about Monster Trucks. 2009. (Wild Rides Ser.). 24p. (gr. 2-3). 42.50 *(978-1-60854-801-9(5)*, PowerKids Pr.) Rosen Publishing Group, Inc., The.

—Wild about Monster Trucks/Camionetas Gigantes. 2009. (Wild Rides/Autos de locura Ser.). 24p. (gr. 2-3). 42.50 *(978-1-60854-808-8(2)*, Editorial Buenas Letras) Rosen Publishing Group, Inc., The.

Powell, Patricia Hruby. Struttin' with Some Barbecue: Lil Hardin Armstrong Becomes the First Lady of Jazz. Himes, Rachel, illus. 2018. (ENG.). 96p. (J). (gr. 4-7). 18.99 *(978-1-58089-740-2(1))* Charlesbridge Publishing, Inc.

Priddy, Roger. Bilingual Bright Baby Trucks / Camiones: English-Spanish Bilingual. 2007. (Bright Baby Ser.). (SPA., Illus.). 26p. (J). (gr. -1 — 1). bds. 6.99 *(978-0-312-50299-7(0)*, 900051445) St. Martin's Pr.

—Bright Baby Trucks. rev. ed. 2004. (Bright Baby Ser.). (ENG., Illus.). 26p. (J). (gr. -1 — 1). bds. 5.99 *(978-0-312-49389-9(4)*, 900028209) St. Martin's Pr.

—First 100 Stickers: Trucks & Things That Go: Sticker Book, with over 500 Stickers. 2016. (First 100 Ser.). (ENG.). 80p. (J). pap. 9.99 *(978-0-312-52145-5(6)*, 900165282) St. Martin's Pr.

—First 100 Trucks: And Things That Go. 2011. (First 100 Ser.). (ENG., Illus.). 24p. (J). (gr. -1 — 1). bds. 5.99 *(978-0-312-51080-0(2)*, 900075563) St. Martin's Pr.

—First 100 Trucks & Things That Go Lift-The-Flap: Over 50 Fun Flaps to Lift & Learn. 2015. (First 100 Ser.). (ENG., Illus.). 14p. (J). (gr. -1 — 1). bds. 9.99 *(978-0-312-51782-3(3)*, 900141264) St. Martin's Pr.

—Lift-The-Flap Tab: Trucks. 2013. (Lift-The-Flap Tab Bks.). (ENG., Illus.). 16p. (J). (gr. -1 — 1). bds. 8.99 *(978-0-312-51582-9(0)*, 900118542) St. Martin's Pr.

—My Big Truck Book. 2011. (My Big Board Bks.). (ENG., Illus.). 10p. (J). (gr. -1 — 1). bds. 8.99 *(978-0-312-51106-7(X)*, 900075566) St. Martin's Pr.

—Slide & Find - Trucks. 2007. (Slide & Find Ser.). (ENG., Illus.). 8p. (J). (gr. -1 — 1). bds. 8.99 *(978-0-312-49909-9(4)*, 900044117) St. Martin's Pr.

QEB Publishing Staff, contrib. by. My Little Book of Dump Trucks & Diggers. 2016. (Illus.). 64p. (J). *(978-1-4351-6348-5(6))* Barnes & Noble, Inc.

Racing Mania, 12 vols., Set. Incl. Drag Racing. Kelley, K. C. lib. bdg. 34.07 *(978-0-7614-4384-1(3)*, ab59e927-96fd-40a0-ba3f-ecccf8ef3d9a); Monster Trucks. Gigliotti, Jim. lib. bdg. 34.07 *(978-0-7614-4385-8(1)*, 244487bb-37c3-44ff-a4ea-3964dfbce05c); Motorcross. Stealey, Bryan. lib. bdg. 34.07 *(978-0-7614-4386-5(X)*, 6f7b6a63-c7b6-400a-8871-54c4840a402d); Nascar. Kelley, K. C. lib. bdg. 34.07 *(978-0-7614-4387-2(8)*, c342161d-5b34-4ce1-bd61-2bb0f1f76084); Off-Road Racing. Gigliotti, Jim. lib. bdg. 34.07 *(978-0-7614-4388-9(6)*, 8c81bd3a-67ee-41ad-93af-45e3968cbe25); Wild Racers. Woods, Bob. lib. bdg. 34.07 *(978-0-7614-4389-6(4)*, 84e59eb8-835a-4c9c-b9c8-4a92797537e2); 48p. (gr. 4-4). (Racing Mania Ser.). (ENG.). 2010. Set lib. bdg. 204.42 *(978-0-7614-4380-3(0)*, 375b0446-28f0-494a-9619-018be333f5f8, Cavendish Square) Cavendish Square Publishing LLC.

Randolph, Joanne. Concrete Mixers. 2009. (Road Machines Ser.). 24p. (gr. k-1). 37.50 *(978-1-60852-461-7(2)*, PowerKids Pr.) Rosen Publishing Group, Inc., The.

—Tow Trucks. 2009. (To the Rescue! Ser.). 24p. (gr. 1-1). 42.50 *(978-1-60854-399-1(4)*, PowerKids Pr.) Rosen Publishing Group, Inc., The.

—Tow Trucks/Gruas. 2009. (To the Rescue! / ¡Al rescate! Ser.). (ENG & SPA.). 24p. (gr. 1-1). 42.50 *(978-1-60854-405-9(2)*, Editorial Buenas Letras) Rosen Publishing Group, Inc., The.

Ransom, Candice. Big Rigs on the Move. 2010. pap. 45.32 *(978-0-7613-6937-0(6))* Lerner Publishing Group.

—Monster Trucks. 2017. (Let's Roll Ser.). (ENG., Illus.). 32p. (J). (gr. 2-3). pap. 9.95 *(978-1-63517-103-7(2)*, 1635171032); lib. bdg. 31.35 *(978-1-63517-047-4(8)*, 1635170478) North Star Editions. (Focus Readers).

Rayner, Katy. Trucks. 2014. (ENG., Illus.). 22p. 8.95 *(978-1-906572-11-2(9))* Award Pubns. Ltd. GBR. Dist: Parkwest Pubns., Inc.

Richards, M. & Creese, S. Carry Me Rough N Tough - Trucks. 2009. 12p. pap. *(978-1-84610-871-6(3))* Make Believe Ideas.

Riggs, Kate. Seedlings: Pickup Trucks. 2017. (Seedlings Ser.). (ENG., Illus.). 24p. (J). (gr. -1-1). pap. 7.99 *(978-1-62832-388-7(4)*, 20114, Creative Paperbacks) Creative Co., The.

—Seedlings: Tanker Trucks. 2017. (Seedlings Ser.). (ENG., Illus.). 24p. (J). (gr. -1-1). pap. 7.99 *(978-1-62832-389-4(2)*, 20117, Creative Paperbacks) Creative Co., The.

—Seedlings: Tow Trucks. 2017. (Seedlings Ser.). (ENG., Illus.). 24p. (J). (gr. -1-1). pap. 7.99 *(978-1-62832-390-0(6)*, 20120, Creative Paperbacks) Creative Co., The.

—Tanker Trucks. 2017. (Seedlings Ser.). (ENG., Illus.). 24p. (J). (gr. -1-k). *(978-1-60818-793-5(4)*, 20119, Creative Education) Creative Co., The.

—Tow Trucks. 2017. (Seedlings Ser.). (ENG., Illus.). 24p. (J). (gr. -1-k). *(978-1-60818-794-2(2)*, 20122, Creative Education) Creative Co., The.

Ruck, Colleen. Trucks. 2011. (My Favorite Machines Ser.). 24p. (gr. 2-5). 28.50 *(978-1-59920-680-6(3))* Black Rabbit Bks.

Sautter, Aaron. How to Draw Monster Trucks, 1 vol. 2007. (Drawing Cool Stuff Ser.). (ENG., Illus.). 32p. (J). (gr. 3-9). 28.65 *(978-1-4296-0079-8(9)*, 94094, Capstone Pr.) Capstone.

Savage, Jeff. Monster Trucks, 1 vol. 2010. (Full Throttle Ser.). (ENG.). 32p. (J). (gr. 3-9). lib. bdg. 28.65 *(978-1-4296-3943-9(1)*, 102553, Capstone Pr.) Capstone.

Schaefer, Lola M. Semitrucks in Action, 1 vol. 2011. (Transportation Zone Ser.). (ENG.). 24p. (J). (gr. 1-3). lib. bdg. 25.99 *(978-1-4296-6826-2(1)*, 116356, Capstone Pr.) Capstone.

Scheff, Matt. Humvees: A 4D Book. 2018. (Mighty Military Machines Ser.). (ENG., Illus.). 24p. (J). (gr. -1-2). lib. bdg. 24.65 *(978-1-9771-0109-9(7)*, 138300, Pebble) Capstone.

Scholastic Early Learners Staff. Noisy Touch & Lift Truck. 2018. (Scholastic Early Learners Ser.). (ENG.). 14p. (J). (gr. -1-k). 12.99 *(978-1-338-28398-3(7)*, Cartwheel Bks.) Scholastic, Inc.

Schuh, Mari. Dump Trucks. (Spot Ser.). (ENG.). 16p. (J). (gr. -1-1). 2018. pap. 7.99 *(978-1-68152-213-5(6)*, 14744) 2017. 17.95 *(978-1-68151-102-3(9)*, 14625) Amicus.

—Los Camiones Volquetes (Dump Trucks) 2017. (Spot Mighty Machines Ser.). (ENG & SPA., Illus.). 16p. (J). (gr. k-3). 17.95 *(978-1-68151-268-6(8)*, Amicus Readers) Amicus Learning.

—Trucks. 2017. (Transportation Ser.). (ENG., Illus.). 24p. (J). (gr. -1-2). lib. bdg. 22.65 *(978-1-5157-7300-9(0)*, 135644, Pebble) Capstone.

Shaffer, Lindsay. 4x4 Trucks. 2018. (Full Throttle Ser.). (ENG., Illus.). 24p. (J). (gr. 3-7). lib. bdg. 26.95 *(978-1-62617-869-4(0)*, Epic Bks.) Bellwether Media.

Shealy, Dennis R. I'm a Truck. Staake, Bob, illus. 2006. (Little Golden Book Ser.). 32p. (J). (gr. -1-2). 5.99 *(978-0-375-83263-5(7)*, Golden Bks.) Random Hse. Children's Bks.

Silverman, Buffy. How Do Monster Trucks Work? 2016. (Lightning Bolt Books (r) — How Vehicles Work Ser.). (ENG., Illus.). 32p. (J). (gr. 1-3). lib. bdg. 29.32 *(978-1-4677-9499-2(6)*, 9c2690b4-39c6-452c-9568-0c46d17338c7, Lerner Pubns.) Lerner Publishing Group.

Small World Creations. Zippy Wheels: Diggers. 2016. (Zippy Wheels Ser.). (ENG., Illus.). 10p. (J). (gr. -1-k). bds. 8.99 *(978-0-7641-6825-3(8))* Sourcebooks, Inc.

Storey, Rita. Tractors & Trucks. 2013. (Have Fun with Arts & Crafts Ser.). (Illus.). 32p. (gr. 4-7). lib. bdg. 31.35 *(978-1-59920-901-2(2))* Black Rabbit Bks.

Sturges, Philemon. I Love Trucks! Board Book. Halpern, Shari, illus. 2003. (ENG.). 26p. (J). (gr. -1-3). bds. 7.99 *(978-0-06-052666-5(1)*, HarperFestival) HarperCollins Pubs.

Sutton, Sally. Roadwork. Lovelock, Brian, illus. 2011. (Construction Crew Ser.). (ENG.). 28p. (J). (gr. k-k). bds. 8.99 *(978-0-7636-4653-0(9))* Candlewick Pr.

Tatge, Cathy. Trucks. 2007. (My First Look at: Vehicles Ser.). (Illus.). 24p. (J). (gr. -1-3). lib. bdg. 24.25 *(978-1-58341-530-6(0)*, Creative Education) Creative Co., The.

Taylor, Trace. The Tree Truck. Taylor, Trace, illus. 2015. (1-3Y Jobs & Careers Ser.). (ENG., Illus.). 24p. (J). (gr. k-2). pap. 8.00 *(978-1-59301-463-6(5))* American Reading Co.

Teitelbaum, Michael & Kiland, Taylor Baldwin. Military Humvees: Armored Mobility, 1 vol. 2015. (Military Engineering in Action Ser.). (ENG., Illus.). 48p. (gr. 6-6). 29.60 *(978-0-7660-6914-5(1)*, c901ab4e-c940-4495-b0ed-72bf3fa7976b) Enslow Publishing, LLC.

Tiner, John Hudson. Trucks. (Illus.). 32p. 2004. pap. 8.95 *(978-0-89812-392-0(5)*, Creative Paperbacks) 2003. (J). lib. bdg. 18.95 *(978-1-58341-259-6(X)*, Creative Education) Creative Co., The.

Trucks & Cars. 2003. 32p. 12.98 *(978-1-4054-2006-8(5))* Parragon, Inc.

Tudhope, Simon. Build Your Own Monster Trucks. 2018. (Build Your Own Sticker Bks.). (ENG.). 24p. pap. 8.99 *(978-0-7945-4213-9(1)*, Usborne) EDC Publishing.

Tuxworth, Nicola. Diggers & Dumpers. 2015. (Illus.). 20p. (J). (gr. -1 — 1). bds. 6.99 *(978-1-86147-383-7(4)*, Armadillo) Anness Publishing GBR. Dist: National Bk. Network.

Von Finn, Denny. Torque: 4X4 Trucks. 2009. (Torque Ser.). (ENG.). 24p. (J). (gr. 3-7). 20.00 *(978-0-531-21741-2(8)*, Children's Pr.) Scholastic Library Publishing.

Watt, Fiona. That's Not My Truck. 2009. (Touchy-Feely Board Bks). 10p. (J). bds. 8.99 *(978-0-7945-2188-2(6)*, Usborne) EDC Publishing.

Watt, Fiona & Wells, Rachel. Trucks. 2004. (Ultimate Touchy-Feely Ser.). (ENG., Illus.). 12p. (J). bds. 15.95 *(978-0-7945-0228-7(8)*, Usborne) EDC Publishing.

Weldon Owen Inc Staff, contrib. by. The Mighty World of Trucks. 2016. (Illus.). 46p. (J). *(978-1-68188-097-6(0))* Fog City Pr.

West, David. Trucks. 2014. (Mechanic Mike's Machines Ser.). 24p. (gr. k-3). 28.50 *(978-1-62588-061-1(8))* Black Rabbit Bks.

Wilson, CeCe. My Dad's Truck, 1 vol. 2015. (Rosen REAL Readers: STEM & STEAM Collection). (ENG.). 8p. (gr. k-1). pap. 5.46 *(978-1-4994-9672-7(9)*, 1e1ed4a7-f900-4bf1-b24b-bfcf0affd9b9, Rosen Classroom) Rosen Publishing Group, Inc., The.

Wiseman, Blaine. Dump Trucks. 2010. (World of Wonder Ser.). (Illus.). 24p. (J). (gr. 2-4). lib. bdg. 25.70 *(978-1-61690-145-5(4)*, 1315074) Weigl Pubs., Inc.

—Dump Trucks: WOW: Big Machines. 2010. (Illus.). 24p. (J). pap. 9.95 *(978-1-61690-146-2(2)*, 1315074) Weigl Pubs., Inc.

—Monster Trucks. 2010. (World of Wonder Ser.). 24p. (J). (gr. 2-4). lib. bdg. 25.70 *(978-1-61690-139-4(X))* Weigl Pubs., Inc.

—Monster Trucks: WOW: Big Machines. 2010. (J). pap. 9.95 *(978-1-61690-140-0(3))* Weigl Pubs., Inc.

World Book, Inc. Staff, contrib. by. Tough Trucks. 2007. (J). *(978-0-7166-7730-7(X))* World Bk., Inc.

Worms, Penny. Trucks. 2016. (Motormania Ser.). 32p. (gr. 2-7). 31.35 *(978-1-59920-997-5(7)*, Smart Apple Media) Black Rabbit Bks.

Young, Jeff C. Trucks: The Ins & Outs of Monster Trucks, Semis, Pickups, & Other Trucks. 2010. (Rpm Ser.). (ENG.). 48p. (gr. 3-4). pap. 59.70 *(978-1-4296-5129-5(6))* Capstone.

Yoyo Books, creator. Vroom. 2011. (Baby's First Library). (ENG., Illus.). 38p. (gr. -1-k). bds. *(978-90-8622-910-9(7))* YoYo Bks.

Zeiger, Jennifer. What Does It Do? Dump Truck. 2011. (Community Connections: What Does It Do? Ser.). (ENG., Illus.). 24p. (gr. 2-5). lib. bdg. 29.21 *(978-1-60279-974-5(1),* 200962) Cherry Lake Publishing.

Zobel, Derek. Bucket Trucks. 2009. (Mighty Machines Ser.). (ENG., Illus.). 24p. (J). (gr. k-3). lib. bdg. 26.95 *(978-1-60014-234-5(6))* Bellwether Media.

—Bucket Trucks. 2009. (Blastoff! Readers Ser.). (ENG., Illus.). 24p. (J). (gr. k-3). 20.00 *(978-0-531-21707-8(8),* Children's Pr.) Scholastic Library Publishing.

—Diggers. 2009. (Mighty Machines Ser.). (ENG., Illus.). 24p. (J). (gr. k-3). lib. bdg. 26.95 *(978-1-60014-235-2(4))* Bellwether Media.

—Monster Vehicles. 2008. (Cool Rides Ser.). (ENG., Illus.). 24p. (J). (gr. 3-7). lib. bdg. 26.95 *(978-1-60014-151-5(X))* Bellwether Media.

—Pickup Trucks. 2009. (Mighty Machines Ser.). (ENG., Illus.). 24p. (J). (gr. k-3). lib. bdg. 26.95 *(978-1-60014-236-9(2))* Bellwether Media.

—Pickup Trucks. 2009. (Blastoff! Readers Ser.). (ENG., Illus.). 24p. (J). (gr. k-3). 20.00 *(978-0-531-21709-2(4),* Children's Pr.) Scholastic Library Publishing.

—Wheel Loaders. 2009. (Mighty Machines Ser.). (ENG., Illus.). 24p. (J). (gr. k-3). lib. bdg. 26.95 *(978-1-60014-237-6(0))* Bellwether Media.

Zuehlke, Jeffrey. Camionetas. Translations.com Staff, tr. from ENG. 2006. (Libros para Avanzar-Potencia en Movimiento (Pull Ahead Books-Mighty Movers) Ser.). (ENG & SPA., Illus.). 32p. (gr. k-3). lib. bdg. 22.60 *(978-0-8225-6499-7(8),* Ediciones Lerner) Lerner Publishing Group.

—Forklifts. 2006. (Pull Ahead Bks.). (Illus.). 32p. (J). (gr. 3-7). lib. bdg. 22.60 *(978-0-8225-6008-1(9),* Lerner Pubns.) Lerner Publishing Group.

—Pickup Trucks. Mueller, Mike, photos by. 2007. (Motor Mania Ser.). (ENG., Illus.). 48p. (J). (gr. 4-7). lib. bdg. 26.60 *(978-0-8225-6564-2(1))* Lerner Publishing Group.

—Pickup Trucks. 2004. (Pull Ahead Books-Mighty Movers Ser.). (ENG., Illus.). 32p. (gr. k-3). lib. bdg. 22.60 *(978-0-8225-1542-5(3))* Lerner Publishing Group.

—Pickup Trucks on the Move. 2010. pap. 45.32 *(978-0-7613-6941-7(4))* Lerner Publishing Group.

TRUCKS—FICTION

Accord Publishing, Accord. Trucks: A Mini Animotion Book. 2010. (ENG., Illus.). 12p. (J). (gr. -1). 9.99 *(978-0-7407-9200-7(8))* Andrews McMeel Publishing.

Accord Publishing Staff. Trucks: A Mini Animotion Book. 2013. (ENG.). 12p. (J). bds. 5.99 *(978-1-4494-3558-5(0))* Andrews McMeel Publishing.

Allen, Francesca & Brooks, Felicity. Busy Truck. Crisp, Dan, illus. 2007. (Usborne Play Bks.). 10p. (J). (gr. -1-k). bds. 10.99 *(978-0-7945-1453-2(7),* Usborne) EDC Publishing.

Andrews, Julie. Dumpy's Apple Shop. Walton, Tony, illus. 2004. (My First I Can Read Bks.). 32p. (J). (gr. -1-18). lib. bdg. 15.89 *(978-0-06-052693-1(9))* HarperCollins Pubs.

—Dumpy's Happy Holiday. Walton, Tony, illus. 2005. (Julie Andrews Collection). 32p. (J). lib. bdg. 16.89 *(978-0-06-052685-6(8),* Julie Andrews Collection) HarperCollins Pubs.

Andrews, Julie & Hamilton, Emma Walton. Dumpy & the Firefighters. Walton, Tony, illus. 2003. (Julie Andrews Collection). (ENG.). 32p. (J). (gr. -1-2). 15.99 *(978-0-06-052681-8(5),* Julie Andrews Collection) HarperCollins Pubs.

—Dumpy to the Rescue! Walton, Tony, illus. 2004. 24p. (J). lib. bdg. 13.85 *(978-1-4242-0707-7(X))* Fitzgerald Bks.

Arnold, Janet. The Special Number. 2011. 28p. pap. 15.99 *(978-1-4568-8982-1(6))* Xlibris Corp.

Back-Canevaro, Vanessa. The Other Side of Yesterday. 2006. 20p. per. 12.00 *(978-0-9769132-8-3(3))* Capri Publishing.

Barton, Chris. Mighty Truck. Cummings, Troy, illus. 2016. (ENG.). 32p. (J). (gr. -1-3). 17.99 *(978-0-06-234478-6(1),* HarperCollins) HarperCollins Pubs.

—Mighty Truck: Muddymania! Cummings, Troy, illus. 2017. (ENG.). 32p. (J). (gr. -1-3). 17.99 *(978-0-06-234479-3(X),* HarperCollins) HarperCollins Pubs.

—Mighty Truck: The Traffic Tie-Up. Cummings, Troy, illus. 2018. (I Can Read Level 1 Ser.). (ENG.). 32p. (J). (gr. -1-3). 16.99 *(978-0-06-234470-0(6),* HarperCollins) HarperCollins Pubs.

—Mighty Truck on the Farm. Cummings, Troy, illus. 2018. (I Can Read Level 1 Ser.). (ENG.). 32p. (J). (gr. -1-3). 16.99 *(978-0-06-234467-0(6));* pap. 4.99 *(978-0-06-234466-3(8))* HarperCollins Pubs. (HarperCollins).

—Mighty Truck on the Farm. 2019. (I Can Read 88 Ser.). (ENG.). 32p. (J). (gr. k-1). 14.96 *(978-1-64310-977-0(4))* Penworthy Co., LLC, The.

—Mighty Truck: the Traffic Tie-Up. Cummings, Troy, illus. 2018. (I Can Read Level 1 Ser.). (ENG.). 32p. (J). (gr. -1-3). pap. 5.99 *(978-0-06-234469-4(2),* HarperCollins) HarperCollins Pubs.

Baxter, Nicola. The Trouble with Trucks. Ball, Geoff, illus. 2012. (ENG.). 24p. (J). (gr. -1-k). pap. 6.99 *(978-1-84322-786-1(X),* Armadillo) Anness Publishing GBR. Dist: National Bk. Network.

Bedford, David. Tipper, Tipper! Watson, Judy, illus. 2008. 9p. bds. *(978-1-921272-26-4(0))* Little Hare Bks. AUS. Dist: HarperCollins Pubs. Australia.

Beil, Karen Magnuson. Jack's House. Wohnoutka, Mike, illus. 2009. (ENG.). 32p. (J). (gr. -1-3). pap. 8.99 *(978-0-8234-2242-5(9))* Holiday Hse., Inc.

Beinstein, Phoebe. Dora & the Stuck Truck. Roper, Robert, illus. 2008. (Dora the Explorer Ser.: 25). (ENG & SPA.). 24p. (J). (gr. -1-2). pap. 3.99 *(978-1-4169-4799-8(X),* Simon Spotlight/Nickelodeon) Simon Spotlight/Nickelodeon.

Berenstain, Jan & Berenstain, Mike. The Berenstain Bears: We Love Trucks! Berenstain, Jan & Berenstain, Mike, illus. 2013. (I Can Read Level 1 Ser.). (ENG., Illus.). 32p. (J). (gr. -1-3). 16.99 *(978-0-06-207536-9(5));* pap. 4.99 *(978-0-06-207535-2(7))* HarperCollins Pubs. (HarperCollins).

—We Love Trucks! 2013. (Berenstain Bears — I Can Read Ser.). (J). lib. bdg. 13.55 *(978-0-606-27159-2(7))* Turtleback.

Bergen, Lara. Let's Dig It! Shannon, David et al, illus. 2010. (Jon Scieszka's Trucktown Ser.). (ENG.). 12p. (J). (gr. -1-k). bds. 5.99 *(978-1-4169-4190-3(8),* Little Simon) Little Simon.

Berneger, Marcia. Buster the Little Garbage Truck. Zimmer, Kevin, illus. 2015. (ENG.). 32p. (J). (gr. -1-1). 14.99 *(978-1-58536-894-5(6),* 203814) Sleeping Bear Pr.

Berrios, Frank. The Easter Buggy. 2014. lib. bdg. 14.75 *(978-0-606-35543-8(X))* Turtleback.

Biggs, Brian. Everything Goes: Good Night, Trucks: a Bedtime Book. Biggs, Brian, illus. 2013. (ENG., Illus.). 24p. (J). (gr. -1 — 1). bds. 7.99 *(978-0-06-195815-1(8),* Balzer & Bray) HarperCollins Pubs.

Bob Goldstein. Josh the Firetruck. 2006. (ENG.). 38p. per. 15.99 *(978-1-4257-1684-4(9))* Xlibris Corp.

Bourgeois, Paulette. Police Workers. LaFave, Kim, illus. 2004. 32p. (J). lib. bdg. 15.38 *(978-1-4242-1191-3(3))* Fitzgerald Bks.

Bowser, Ken. Bobbi's Big Brake: Self-Confidence. Bowser, Ken, illus. 2016. (Funny Bone Readers (tm) — Truck Pals on the Job Ser.). (ENG., Illus.). 24p. (J). (gr. k-2). E-Book 30.65 *(978-1-63440-064-0(X))* Red Chair Pr.

—Hal & Al: Self-Esteem. Bowser, Ken, illus. 2016. (Funny Bone Readers (tm) — Truck Pals on the Job Ser.). (ENG., Illus.). 24p. (J). (gr. k-2). E-Book 30.65 *(978-1-63440-070-1(4))* Red Chair Pr.

—Hitch Takes Off: Perseverance. Bowser, Ken, illus. 2016. (Funny Bone Readers (tm) — Truck Pals on the Job Ser.). (ENG., Illus.). 24p. (J). (gr. k-2). E-Book 30.65 *(978-1-63440-073-2(9))* Red Chair Pr.

—Lawni Takes the Field: Teamwork. Bowser, Ken, illus. 2016. (Funny Bone Readers (tm) — Truck Pals on the Job Ser.). (ENG., Illus.). 24p. (J). (gr. k-2). E-Book 30.65 *(978-1-63440-076-3(3))* Red Chair Pr.

—One Wrong Turn: Helping Those in Need. Bowser, Ken, illus. 2016. (Funny Bone Readers (tm) — Truck Pals on the Job Ser.). (ENG., Illus.). 24p. (J). (gr. k-2). E-Book 30.65 *(978-1-63440-079-4(8))* Red Chair Pr.

Brown, Renee. The Big Rig Kids. Taylor, JaRabia, illus. 2016. 119p. (J). *(978-0-692-79625-2(8))* Big Rig LLC.

Bryant, Megan E. Dump Truck Duck. de Ruiter, Jo, illus. 2016. (ENG.). 32p. (J). (gr. -1-3). 16.99 *(978-0-8075-1736-9(4),* 807517364) Whitman, Albert & Co.

Bunting, Eve. Little Yellow Truck. Zimmer, Kevin, illus. 2019. (ENG.). 32p. (J). (gr. k-3). 16.99 *(978-1-58536-407-7(X),* 204649) Sleeping Bear Pr.

Burton, Jeffrey. Delivery Trucks! Cooper, Jay, illus. 2017. (ENG.). 12p. (J). (gr. -1). bds. 7.99 *(978-1-4814-9219-5(5),* Little Simon) Little Simon.

—Food Trucks! A Lift-The-Flap Meal on Wheels! Cooper, Jay, illus. 2016. (ENG.). 12p. (J). (gr. -1). bds. 8.99 *(978-1-4814-6521-2(X),* Little Simon) Little Simon.

Cammy Fox Riley. Truckee's Adventures: Book One. 2009. 24p. pap. 11.49 *(978-1-4389-4023-6(8))* AuthorHouse.

Cassidy, Colette. DIVCO, the Little Milk Truck. 2007. (Illus.). 28p. (J). pap. 7.99 *(978-0-615-17346-7(2))* Redcay Publishing.

Cena, John. Elbow Grease. McWilliam, Howard, illus. (Elbow Grease Ser.). (ENG.). (J). 2019. 34p. (— 1). bds. 8.99 *(978-1-5247-7356-4(5))* 2018. 40p. (gr. -1-2). 17.99 *(978-1-5247-7350-2(6))* 2018. 40p. (gr. -1-2). lib. bdg. 20.99 *(978-1-5247-7351-9(4))* Random Hse. Children's Bks. (Random Hse. Bks. for Young Readers).

Clement, Nathan. Drive. (ENG., Illus.). 32p. (J). (— 1). 2016. bds. 7.99 *(978-1-62979-692-5(1))* 2013. pap. 6.99 *(978-1-62091-030-6(6))* 2008. 16.95 *(978-1-59078-517-1(7))* Astra Publishing Hse. (Astra Young Readers).

Cochran, Jean M. Farmer Brown & His Little Red Truck. Enos, Daryl, illus. 2009. (ENG.). 32p. (J). (gr. -1-k). 16.95 *(978-0-9792035-0-3(3))* Pleasant St. Pr.

Crisp, Dan. Trabajo/ Work. 2007. 14p. 10.95 *(978-84-263-6452-4(7))* Vives, Luis Editorial (Edelvives) ESP. Dist: Baker & Taylor Bks.

Crooks, Andrea Syvrud. Little Truck Without a Load. 2013. 40p. pap. 16.95 *(978-1-4497-9737-9(7),* WestBow Pr.) Author Solutions, LLC.

Crow, Melinda Melton. Drive Along, 1 vol. Girouard, Patrick & Girouard, Patrick, illus. 2010. (Truck Buddies Ser.). (ENG.). 32p. (J). (gr. -1-1). pap. 6.25 *(978-1-4342-2296-1(9),* 103165, Stone Arch Bks.) Capstone.

—Líos en el Lodo/Mud Mess. Heck, Claudia, tr. Rooney, Veronica, illus. 2012. (Camiones Amigos/Truck Buddies Ser.). (MUL.). 32p. (J). (gr. -1-1). pap. 5.05 *(978-1-4342-3916-7(0),* 118103, Stone Arch Bks.) Capstone.

—Líos en la Nieve. Heck, Claudia M., tr. Rooney, Ronnie, illus. 2012. (Camiones Amigos/Truck Buddies Ser.).Tr. of Snow Trouble. (MUL.). 32p. (J). (gr. -1-1). pap. 5.05 *(978-1-4342-3914-3(4),* 118101, Stone Arch Bks.) Capstone.

—Little Wheels, 1 vol. Girouard, Patrick & Girouard, Patrick, illus. 2010. (Truck Buddies Ser.). (ENG.). 32p. (J). (gr. -1-1). pap. 6.25 *(978-1-4342-2297-8(7),* 103166, Stone Arch Bks.) Capstone.

—Mud Mess, 1 vol. Rooney, Veronica, illus. 2009. (Truck Buddies Ser.). (ENG.). 32p. (J). (gr. -1-1). pap. 6.25 *(978-1-4342-1753-0(1),* 102225, Stone Arch Bks.) Capstone.

—Ride & Seek, 1 vol. Girouard, Patrick, illus. 2010. (Truck Buddies Ser.). (ENG.). 32p. (J). (gr. -1-1). pap. 6.25 *(978-1-4342-2298-5(5),* 103168, Stone Arch Bks.) Capstone.

—Road Race, 1 vol. Rooney, Veronica, illus. 2009. (Truck Buddies Ser.). (ENG.). 32p. (J). (gr. -1-1). 22.65 *(978-1-4342-1623-6(3),* 95797); pap. 6.25 *(978-1-4342-1754-7(X),* 102226) Capstone. (Stone Arch Bks.).

—Snow Trouble, 1 vol. Rooney, Veronica, illus. 2009. (Truck Buddies Ser.). (ENG.). 32p. (J). (gr. -1-1). pap. 6.25 *(978-1-4342-1755-4(8),* 102227, Stone Arch Bks.) Capstone.

—Tired Trucks, 1 vol. Girouard, Patrick & Girouard, Patrick, illus. 2010. (Truck Buddies Ser.). (ENG.). 32p. (J). (gr. -1-1). pap. 6.25 *(978-1-4342-2299-2(3),* 103167); lib. bdg. 22.65 *(978-1-4342-1864-3(3),* 102313) Capstone. (Stone Arch Bks.).

—Truck Buddies, 1 vol. Rooney, Veronica, illus. 2009. (Truck Buddies Ser.). (ENG.). 32p. (J). (gr. -1-1). 22.65 *(978-1-4342-1625-0(X),* 95799); pap. 6.25 *(978-1-4342-1756-1(6),* 102228) Capstone. (Stone Arch Bks.).

—Truck Parade, 1 vol. Thompson, Chad, illus. 2012. (Wonder Wheels Ser.). (ENG.). 32p. (J). (gr. -1-1). pap. 6.25 *(978-1-4342-4240-2(4),* 120298); lib. bdg. 22.65 *(978-1-4342-4017-0(7),* 118398) Capstone. (Stone Arch Bks.).

Cuyler, Margery. The Little Dump Truck. Kolar, Bob, illus. 2014. (Little Vehicles Ser.: 1). (ENG.). 24p. (J). (gr. -1-1). bds. 8.99 *(978-0-8050-9990-4(5),* 900129326, Holt, Henry & Co. Bks. For Young Readers) Holt, Henry & Co.

—The Little Fire Truck. Kolar, Bob, illus. 2017. (Little Vehicles Ser.: 3). (ENG.). 32p. (J). 14.99 *(978-1-62779-805-1(6),* 900160047, Holt, Henry & Co. Bks. For Young Readers) Holt, Henry & Co.

—The Little Ice Cream Truck. Kolar, Bob, illus. 2018. (Little Vehicles Ser.: 4). (ENG.). 32p. (J). 17.99 *(978-1-62779-806-8(4),* 900160050, Holt, Henry & Co. Bks. For Young Readers) Holt, Henry & Co.

Delco, Bobby. Lil Mack Jr. 2009. 108p. pap. 11.99 *(978-1-4389-0473-3(8))* AuthorHouse.

Denise, Anika. Monster Trucks Board Book. Wragg, Nate, illus. 2018. (ENG.). 32p. (J). (gr. -1 — 1). bds. 7.99 *(978-0-06-274162-2(4),* HarperFestival) HarperCollins Pubs.

Diaz, T. Richard. Little Growler, Big Heart. l.t. ed. 2003. (Illus.). 12p. (J). lib. bdg. 11.95 *(978-1-932338-21-8(7));* per. 8.95 *(978-1-932338-15-7(2))* Lifevest Publishing, Inc.

Doeden, Matt. Monster Trucks. 2018. (Horsepower Ser.). (ENG., Illus.). 32p. (J). (gr. 3-9). lib. bdg. 27.32 *(978-1-5435-2456-7(7),* 137959, Capstone Pr.) Capstone.

Dronsfield, Paul, illus. The Bulldozer. 2009. (My Shiny Little Truck Bks.). (ENG.). 10p. (J). bds. 3.95 *(978-1-58117-858-6(1),* Intervisual/Piggy Toes) Bendon, Inc.

—The Concrete Mixer. 2009. (My Shiny Little Truck Bks.). (ENG.). 10p. (J). bds. 3.95 *(978-1-58117-859-3(X),* Intervisual/Piggy Toes) Bendon, Inc.

—The Digger. 2009. (My Shiny Little Truck Bks.). (ENG.). 10p. (J). bds. 3.95 *(978-1-58117-860-9(3),* Intervisual/Piggy Toes) Bendon, Inc.

—The Dump Truck. 2009. (My Shiny Little Truck Bks.). (ENG.). 10p. (J). bds. 3.95 *(978-1-58117-861-6(1),* Intervisual/Piggy Toes) Bendon, Inc.

Fliess, Sue. Tons of Trucks. Snyder, Betsy, illus. 2012. (ENG.). 18p. (J). (gr. k — 1). bds. 13.99 *(978-0-547-44927-2(5),* 1435126, Clarion Bks.) HarperCollins Pubs.

Floca, Brian. Five Trucks. Floca, Brian, illus. 2014. (ENG., Illus.). 32p. (J). (gr. -1-3). 17.99 *(978-1-4814-0593-5(4),* Atheneum Bks. for Young Readers) Simon & Schuster Children's Publishing.

Frost, Maddie. Animobiles: Animals on the Mooove. 2018. (ENG., Illus.). 40p. (J). (gr. -1-3). 17.99 *(978-1-4926-5671-5(2),* Sourcebooks Jabberwocky) Sourcebooks, Inc.

Gall, Chris. Dinotrux. 2009. (Dinotrux Ser.: 1). (ENG., Illus.). 32p. (J). (gr. -1-3). 18.99 *(978-0-316-02777-9(4))* Little, Brown Bks. for Young Readers.

—Dinotrux. 2012. (J). lib. bdg. 17.20 *(978-0-606-26144-9(3))* Turtleback.

—Dinotrux Go to School. 2014. (Passport to Reading Level 1 Ser.). (ENG., Illus.). 32p. (J). (gr. -1-3). 4.99 *(978-0-316-40061-9(0))* Little, Brown Bks. for Young Readers.

Gamble, Adam & Jasper, Mark. Good Night Dump Truck. Stevenson, Harvey, illus. 2014. (Good Night Our World Ser.). (ENG.). 26p. (J). (— 1). bds. 9.95 *(978-1-60219-189-1(1))* Good Night Bks.

Goetz, Steve. Old MacDonald Had a Truck. Kaban, Eda, illus. 2019. (ENG.). 30p. (J). (gr. -1-k). bds. 8.99 *(978-1-4521-8176-9(4))* Chronicle Bks. LLC.

—Old MacDonald Had a Truck: (Preschool Read Aloud Books, Books for Kids, Kids Construction Books) Kaban, Eda, illus. 2016. (ENG.). 40p. (J). (gr. -1-k). 16.99 *(978-1-4521-3260-0(7))* Chronicle Bks. LLC.

Golden Books. Mighty Monster Machines (Blaze & the Monster Machines) Lambe, Steve, illus. 2015. (Little Golden Book Ser.). (ENG.). 24p. (J). (-k). 5.99 *(978-0-553-52456-7(9),* Golden Bks.) Random Hse. Children's Bks.

—Wind Power! (Blaze & the Monster Machines) Burch, Benjamin, illus. 2016. (Little Golden Book Ser.). (ENG.). 24p. (J). (-k). 5.99 *(978-1-101-93682-5(7),* Golden Bks.) Random Hse. Children's Bks.

Golden Books, illus. Blaze & the Monster Machines Little Golden Book Library (Blaze & the Monster Machines) Five of Nickeoldeon's Blaze & the Monster Machines Little Golden Books, 5 vols. 2017. (Little Golden Book Ser.). (ENG.). 120p. (J). (-k). 29.95 *(978-1-5247-6410-4(8),* Golden Bks.) Random Hse. Children's Bks.

Gomi, Taro. Little Truck: (Transportation Books for Toddlers, Board Book for Toddlers) 2018. (Taro Gomi by Chronicle Bks.). (ENG., Illus.). 22p. (J). (gr. -1 — 1). bds. 6.99 *(978-1-4521-6300-0(6))* Chronicle Bks. LLC.

Gordon, David. Three Little Rigs. 2005. (ENG., Illus.). 32p. (J). (gr. -1-3). 17.99 *(978-0-06-058118-3(2),* HarperCollins) HarperCollins Pubs.

—The Ugly Truckling. Gordon, David, illus. 2004. (Illus.). 32p. (J). (gr. -1-2). lib. bdg. 16.89 *(978-0-06-054601-4(8),* Geringer, Laura Book) HarperCollins Pubs.

Gould, Robert. Monster Trucks. 2004. (Big Stuff Ser.). (ENG., Illus.). 16p. (J). bds. 7.95 *(978-1-929945-43-6(4))* Big Guy Bks., Inc.

Greene, Rhonda Gowler. Push! Dig! Scoop! A Construction Counting Rhyme. Kirk, Daniel, illus. 2017. (ENG.). 26p. (J). bds. 7.99 *(978-1-68119-085-3(0),* 900158430, Bloomsbury USA Childrens) Bloomsbury Publishing USA.

H & T Imaginations Unlimited, Inc. Kid's Sand Box Fun with Professor Woodpecker: Good Old Fashion Wholesome Fun Children's Story. 2008. 12p. pap. 8.49 *(978-1-4389-1116-8(5))* AuthorHouse.

Hamilton, Kersten. Red Truck. Petrone, Valeria, illus. 2012. (Red Truck & Friends Ser.). 26p. (J). (gr. -1 — 1). bds. 8.99 *(978-0-670-01467-5(2),* Viking Books for Young Readers) Penguin Young Readers Group.

Hardyment, Christina. Arthur Ransome & Captain Flint's Trunk. (Illus.). 224p. (J). *(978-0-224-02989-6(4))* Penguin Random Hse.

Harper, Benjamin. All Around Trucktown. Shannon, David et al, illus. 2008. (Jon Scieszka's Trucktown Ser.). (ENG.). 32p. (J). (gr. -1-1). 3.99 *(978-1-4169-4194-1(0),* Simon Scribbles) Simon Scribbles.

Hoena, Blake. Colossal Course! A Monster Truck Myth. Cano, Fern, illus. 2018. (ThunderTrucks! Ser.). (ENG.). 56p. (J). (gr. k-2). lib. bdg. 21.99 *(978-1-4965-5735-3(2),* 136725, Stone Arch Bks.) Capstone.

—Freestyle Fun. 2018. (ThunderTrucks! Ser.). (ENG., Illus.). 56p. (J). (gr. k-2). lib. bdg. 21.99 *(978-1-4965-6493-1(6),* 138394, Stone Arch Bks.) Capstone.

—Gas Guzzler! A Monster Truck Myth. Cano, Fern, illus. 2018. (ThunderTrucks! Ser.). (ENG.). 56p. (J). (gr. k-2). lib. bdg. 21.99 *(978-1-4965-5737-7(9),* 136727, Stone Arch Bks.) Capstone.

—Maximum Horsepower! A Monster Truck Myth. Cano, Fern, illus. 2018. (ThunderTrucks! Ser.). (ENG.). 56p. (J). (gr. k-2). lib. bdg. 21.99 *(978-1-4965-5738-4(7),* 136728, Stone Arch Bks.) Capstone.

—Monster Maze! A Monster Truck Myth. Cano, Fern, illus. 2018. (ThunderTrucks! Ser.). (ENG.). 56p. (J). (gr. k-2). lib. bdg. 21.99 *(978-1-4965-5736-0(0),* 136726, Stone Arch Bks.) Capstone.

—Speed Dash. 2018. (ThunderTrucks! Ser.). (ENG., Illus.). 56p. (J). (gr. k-2). lib. bdg. 21.99 *(978-1-4965-6492-4(8),* 138393, Stone Arch Bks.) Capstone.

—ThunderTrucks! Monster Truck Myths. Cano, Fernando, illus. 2018. (ThunderTrucks! Ser.). (ENG.). (J). (gr. k-2). 56p. 186.56 *(978-1-4965-6498-6(7),* 28379); 144p. pap., pap., pap. 7.95 *(978-1-68436-000-0(5),* 136729) Capstone. (Stone Arch Bks.).

—Trojan Horse Power. 2018. (ThunderTrucks! Ser.). (ENG., Illus.). 56p. (J). (gr. k-2). lib. bdg. 21.99 *(978-1-4965-6490-0(1),* 138391, Stone Arch Bks.) Capstone.

—Underworld Clash. 2018. (ThunderTrucks! Ser.). (ENG., Illus.). 56p. (J). (gr. k-2). lib. bdg. 21.99 *(978-1-4965-6491-7(X),* 138392, Stone Arch Bks.) Capstone.

Holmes, Andy. Tipper Tells a Lie, 1 vol. de Giorgi, Sergio, illus. 2014. (ENG.). 22p. (J). bds. 9.99 *(978-0-529-11213-2(2),* Tommy Nelson) Nelson, Thomas Inc.

Houghton Mifflin Company Staff. Fire Truck Fun with Curious George. 2005. (J). (gr. -1-k). pap. *(978-0-618-70499-6(X))* Houghton Mifflin Harcourt Trade & Reference Pubs.

Hubbell, Patricia. Trucks: Whizz! Zoom! Rumble!, 0 vols. Halsey, Megan, illus. 2012. (ENG.). 32p. (J). (gr. -1-1). per. 9.99 *(978-0-7614-5328-4(8),* 9780761453284, Two Lions) Amazon Publishing.

Hundal, Nancy. Number 21, 1 vol. Denes, Brian, illus. 2004. (ENG.). 32p. (J). (gr. -1-k). pap. 9.95 *(978-1-55041-905-4(6),* ee2e48d4-a9bc-4384-8ca6-6e5o44ced503) Trifolium Bks., Inc. CAN. Dist: Firefly Bks., Ltd.

Hurt, Laurie. Jay & the Old Big Blue Truck. Parker, Natasha, illus. 2008. (ENG.). 44p. pap. 21.99 *(978-1-4363-5487-5(0))* Xlibris Corp.

The Ice cream Truck. 2004. (J). per. 15.95 *(978-0-9778937-4-4(X))* Priceless Ink Publishing Co., Inc.

Iverson, Gregory. Tyler's Big Blue Truck. Fritz, Siegfried, illus. 2006. 40p. (J). *(978-0-9755184-0-3(2))* Sandbox Bks.

James, Martin. William Is Going Green. 2008. 38p. 14.95 *(978-0-9799465-1-6(4))* Martin, James Jr.

Katz, Karen. Vroom, Vroom, Trucks! Katz, Karen, illus. 2016. (ENG., Illus.). 14p. (J). (gr. -1 — 1). bds. 6.99 *(978-1-4814-4209-1(0),* Little Simon) Little Simon.

Keeler, Patricia. Scoop the Ice Cream Truck. 2018. (ENG., Illus.). 32p. (J). (gr. -1-k). 16.99 *(978-1-5107-0631-6(3),* Sky Pony Pr.) Skyhorse Publishing Co., Inc.

Krensky, Stephen. Trucks: Ready-To-Read Level 1. Ivanke & Lola, Ivanke &, illus. 2009. (Ready-To-Read Ser.). (ENG.). 32p. (J). (gr. -1-1). pap. 4.99 *(978-1-4169-0236-2(8),* Simon Spotlight) Simon Spotlight.

Lagonegro, Melissa. Mater's Birthday Surprise. 2012. (Cars Step into Reading Ser.). lib. bdg. 13.55 *(978-0-606-23724-6(0))* Turtleback.

—Mater's Birthday Surprise (Disney/Pixar Cars) RH Disney, illus. 2012. (Step into Reading Ser.). (ENG.). 32p. (J). (gr. -1-1). pap. 5.99 *(978-0-7364-2858-3(5),* RH/Disney) Random Hse. Children's Bks.

Lee, Mark. Twenty Big Trucks in the Middle of the Street. Cyrus, Kurt, illus. 2015. (ENG.). 30p. (J). (-k). bds. 8.99 *(978-0-7636-7650-6(0))* Candlewick Pr.

Lewis, Kevin. My Truck Is Stuck! Kirk, Daniel, illus. 2006. (ENG.). 30p. (J). (gr. -1-k). bds. 7.99 *(978-0-7868-3739-7(X))* Little, Brown Bks. for Young Readers.

Liberts, Jennifer. Go, Go, Trucks! Yamada, Mike, illus. 2017. (Step into Reading Ser.). 32p. (J). (gr. -1-1). 5.99 *(978-0-399-54951-9(X),* Random Hse. Bks. for Young Readers) Random Hse. Children's Bks.

London, Jonathan. I'm a Truck Driver. Parkins, David, illus. 2018. (ENG.). 24p. (J). bds. 7.99 *(978-1-250-17506-9(2),* 900189297, Holt, Henry & Co. Bks. For Young Readers) Holt, Henry & Co.

Lyon, George Ella. Trucks Roll! Frazier, Craig, illus. 2007. (ENG.). 40p. (J). (gr. -1-2). 19.99 *(978-1-4169-2435-7(3),* Atheneum/Richard Jackson Bks.) Simon & Schuster Children's Publishing.

Maddox, Jake. Striker Assist, 1 vol. Tiffany, Sean, illus. 2012. (Jake Maddox Sports Stories Ser.). (ENG.). 72p. (J). (gr. 3-6). pap. 5.95 *(978-1-4342-4208-2(0),* 120267, Stone Arch Bks.) Capstone.

Manushkin, Fran. Pedro's Monster. Lyon, Tammie, illus. 2018. (Pedro Ser.). (ENG.). 32p. (J). (gr. k-2). lib. bdg. 21.32 *(978-1-5158-2821-1(2),* 137986, Picture Window Bks.) Capstone.

Marshall, Amelia. Big Truck's Road Adventure, 1 vol. 2016. (Big Machines Ser.). (ENG.). 32p. (gr. 1-2). pap. 11.00 *(978-1-4994-8099-3(7),* c257934b-f174-4b4c-b032-fd3fafdb162d, Windmill Bks.) Rosen Publishing Group, Inc., The.

Martinez, Heather, illus. Ready, Set, Tow! 2018. (J). *(978-1-5444-0206-2(6),* Golden Bks.) Random Hse. Children's Bks.

Mason, Tom & Danko, Dan. A Christmas Surprise: A Lift-The-Flap Adventure. Shannon, David et al, illus. 2011. (Jon Scieszka's Trucktown Ser.). (ENG.). 12p. (J). (gr. -1-k). 8.99 *(978-1-4169-4193-4(2),* Simon & Schuster Bks. For Young Readers) Simon & Schuster Bks. For Young Readers.

Mason, Tom, et al. Who's That Truck? Shannon, David et al, illus. 2008. (Jon Scieszka's Trucktown Ser.). (ENG.). 14p. (J).

(gr. -1-1). bds. 7.99 *(978-1-4169-4175-0(4)*, Little Simon) Little Simon.

Masterson, Josephine. Toy Box Trouble, 1 vol. 2015. (Rosen REAL Readers: STEM & STEAM Collection). (ENG.). 8p. (gr. k-1). pap. 5.46 *(978-1-4994-9599-7(4)*, eb7f5698-5369-4122-8da7-19699494c18e, Rosen Classroom) Rosen Publishing Group, Inc., The.

McEwen, James. Westley, the Big Truck. 2006. (ENG., Illus.). 52p. (J). (gr. -1). 12.99 *(978-0-89051-410-8(0)*, Master Books) New Leaf Publishing Group.

McKown, Hunter. Sand Castle Bash: Counting from 1 To 10. Shannon, David et al, illus. 2009. (Jon Scieszka's Trucktown Ser.). (ENG.). 26p. (J). (gr. -1-k). bds. 5.99 *(978-1-4169-4179-8(7)*, Little Simon) Little Simon.

McMullan, Kate. I'm Brave! McMullan, Jim, illus. 2014. (ENG.). 40p. (J). (gr. -1-3). 18.99 *(978-0-06-220318-2(5)*, Balzer & Bray) HarperCollins Pubs.

—I'm Dirty! 2015. (J). lib. bdg. 17.20 *(978-0-606-36466-9(8))* Turtleback.

Meister, Cari. Dump Truck Day, 1 vol. Emmerson, Michael, illus. 2010. (My First Graphic Novel Ser.). (ENG.). 32p. (J). (gr. k-2). pap. 6.25 *(978-1-4342-2288-6(8)*, 103157, Stone Arch Bks.) Capstone.

Melendez, Renee. The Great Ice Race. Aikins, Dave, illus. 2017. 24p. (J). *(978-1-5182-5217-4(6))* Random Hse., Inc.

—The Great Ice Race (Blaze & the Monster Machines) Aikins, Dave, illus. 2017. (Step into Reading Ser.). (ENG.). 24p. (J). (gr. -1-1). pap. 5.99 *(978-1-5247-6384-8(5)*, Random Hse. Bks. for Young Readers) Random Hse. Children's Bks.

Mellor, Colleen Kelly. Grandpa & the Truck Book 2. Irwin, Dana M., illus. 2012. 34p. pap. 9.99 *(978-0-9856770-2-2(3))* truckerkidzPr.

—Grandpa & the Truck Book One. Irwin, Dana, illus. 2012. 34p. pap. 9.99 *(978-0-9856770-0-8(7))* truckerkidzPr.

Merrill, Jean. The Pushcart War. 2006. (J). 1.25 *(978-1-4193-8348-9(5))* Recorded Bks., Inc.

Miller, Cindy M. The Little Green Truck: The Adventures of a 1998 Ford Ranger & Its Owner. 2012. 20p. pap. 15.00 *(978-1-4772-0319-4(2))* AuthorHouse.

Milton, Elizabeth. Rolling with the Rollodons! 2017. (Dinotrux 8X8 Ser.). (J). lib. bdg. 14.75 *(978-0-606-39909-8(7))* Turtleback.

Mitton, Tony & Parker, Ant. Tough Trucks. 2005. (Amazing Machines Ser.). (ENG., Illus.). 24p. (J). (gr. -1-k). 6.99 *(978-0-7534-5917-1(5)*, 900052726, Kingfisher) Roaring Brook Pr.

Mok, Carmen. Ride the Big Machines Across Canada. 2015. (My Big Machines Ser.). (ENG.). 14p. (J). bds. 10.50 *(978-1-4434-3810-0(3)*, HarperCollins) HarperCollins Pubs.

Mr. Cheesehead Goes for a Ride... 2nd rev. ed. 2005. (Illus.). 32p. (J). 12.99 *(978-0-9764463-1-6(6))* Vertigo Publishing.

Nelson, Suzanne. You're Bacon Me Crazy. 2014. 248p. (J). pap. *(978-0-545-65268-1(5))* Scholastic, Inc.

Nelson, Thomas. Big Trucks: A Touch-And-Feel Book, 1 vol. 2018. (ENG., Illus.). 12p. (J). bds. 9.99 *(978-1-4003-1058-6(X)*, Tommy Nelson) Nelson, Thomas Inc.

Novesky, Amy. Love Is a Truck. Gillingham, Sara, illus. 2016. (ENG.). 24p. (J). (gr. -1-1). bds. 13.99 *(978-1-937359-86-7(7)*, 1330001) Abrams, Inc.

Ode, Eric. Busy Trucks on the Go. 2014. (ENG., 32p. (J). Illus.). pap. 6.99 *(978-1-61067-287-0(9))*; 11.99 *(978-1-61067-313-6(1))* Kane Miller.

Parr, todd. The Cars & Trucks Book. 2018. (ENG., Illus.). 32p. (J). (gr. -1-1). 18.99 *(978-0-316-50662-5(1))* Little, Brown Bks. for Young Readers.

Pearson, Peter. How to Walk a Dump Truck. Catusanu, Mircea, illus. 2019. (ENG.). 40p. (J). (gr. -1-3). 17.99 *(978-0-06-232063-6(7)*, HarperCollins) HarperCollins Pubs.

Petrie, Catherine. Joshua James Likes Trucks. Snyder, Joel, illus. 2011. (Rookie Ready to Learn: Out & about in My Community Ser.). (ENG.). 32p. (J). (gr. -1-k). lib. bdg. 18.69 *(978-0-531-27177-3(3))*; pap. 5.95 *(978-0-531-26827-8(6))* Scholastic Library Publishing. (Children's Pr.).

Pinkney, Brian. Puppy Truck. Pinkney, Brian, illus. 2019. (ENG., Illus.). 40p. (J). (gr. k-3). 17.99 *(978-1-5344-2687-0(6))* Simon & Schuster Children's Publishing.

Priddy, Roger. What's in My Truck? A Slide & Find Book. 2018. (What's in My? Ser.). (ENG., Illus.). 10p. (J). bds. 12.99 *(978-0-312-52556-9(7)*, 900180420) St. Martin's Pr.

Pumphrey, Jarrett & Pumphrey, Jerome. The Old Truck. 2020. (ENG., Illus.). 48p. (J). (gr. -1-3). 17.95 *(978-1-324-00519-3(X)*, 340519, Norton Young Readers) Norton, W. W. & Co., Inc.

Random House. Nickelodeon 5-Minute Christmas Stories (Nickelodeon) Random House, illus. 2017. (ENG., Illus.). 160p. (J). (gr. -1-2). 12.99 *(978-1-5247-6398-5(5)*, Random Hse. Bks. for Young Readers) Random Hse. Children's Bks.

—Pop the Hood! (Blaze & the Monster Machines) Hechtenkopf, Omar, illus. 2016. (Lift-The-Flap Ser.). (ENG.). 12p. (J). (gr. -1 — 1). bds. 6.99 *(978-0-553-53893-9(4)*, Random Hse. Bks. for Young Readers) Random Hse. Children's Bks.

—Ready to Race! (Blaze & the Monster Machines) Kobasic, Kevin, illus. 2015. (Step into Reading Ser.). (ENG.). 24p. (J). (gr. -1-1). 5.99 *(978-0-553-52460-4(7)*, Random Hse. Bks. for Young Readers) Random Hse. Children's Bks.

Random House Staff & Disney Editors. Five Tales from the Road. 2013. (Cars Step into Reading Ser.). lib. bdg. 18.40 *(978-0-606-32198-3(5))* Turtleback.

Rao, Lisa. Playtime in Trucktown. Shannon, David et al, illus. 2008. (Jon Scieszka's Trucktown Ser.). (ENG.). 24p. (J). (gr. -1-1). 5.99 *(978-1-4169-4197-2(5)*, Simon Scribbles) Simon Scribbles.

Rey and others, Rey and. Start Your Engines 5-Minute Stories. 2014. (5-Minute Stories Ser.). (ENG., Illus.). 224p. (J). (gr. -1-3). 12.99 *(978-0-544-15881-8(4)*, 1550258, Clarion Bks.) HarperCollins Pubs.

Riley, J. D. Axel the Truck: Beach Race. 2013. (My First I Can Read Ser.). (ENG., Illus.). 32p. (J). (gr. -1-3). 16.99 *(978-0-06-222230-5(9)*, Greenwillow Bks.) HarperCollins Pubs.

—Axel the Truck: Rocky Road. 2013. (My First I Can Read Ser.). (J). lib. bdg. 13.55 *(978-0-606-32163-1(2))* Turtleback.

—Axel the Truck: Beach Race. Dorman, Brandon, illus. 2013. (My First I Can Read Ser.). (ENG.). 32p. (J). (gr. -1-3). pap. 4.99 *(978-0-06-222229-9(5)*, Greenwillow Bks.) HarperCollins Pubs.

—Axel the Truck: Field Trip. Dorman, Brandon, illus. 2019. (My First I Can Read Ser.). (ENG.). 24p. (J). (gr. -1-3). 16.99 *(978-0-06-269281-8(X))*; pap. 5.99 *(978-0-06-269280-1(1))* HarperCollins Pubs. (Greenwillow Bks.).

—Axel the Truck: Rocky Road. Dorman, Brandon, illus. 2013. (My First I Can Read Ser.). (ENG.). 32p. (J). (gr. -1-3). 16.99 *(978-0-06-222232-9(5))*; pap. 5.99 *(978-0-06-222231-2(7))* HarperCollins Pubs. (Greenwillow Bks.).

Rinker, Sherri Duskey. Buenas Noches, ConstruccióN. Buenas Noches, DiversióN. (Goodnight, Goodnight, Construction Site Spanish Language Edition) (Bilingual Children's Book, Spanish Books for Kids) Lazaro, Georgina, tr. Lichtenheld, Tom, illus. 2019. (Goodnight, Goodnight Construction Site Ser.). (SPA.). 32p. (J). (gr. -1 — 1). 16.99 *(978-1-4521-7037-4(1))* Chronicle Bks. LLC.

—Construction Site: Farming Strong, All Year Long. Ford, A. G., illus. 2022. (Goodnight, Goodnight, Construc Ser.). (ENG.). 40p. (J). (gr. -1 — 1). 17.99 *(978-1-7972-1387-3(3))* Chronicle Bks. LLC.

—Goodnight, Goodnight, Construction Site. Lichtenheld, Tom, illus. 2024. (J). **(978-1-64549-816-2(6))** Amicus Learning.

—Goodnight, Goodnight, Construction Site. Lichtenheld, Tom, illus. 2017. (Goodnight, Goodnight, Construc Ser.). (ENG.). 30p. (J). (gr. -1 — 1). bds. 7.99 *(978-1-4521-1173-5(1))* Chronicle Bks. LLC.

—Goodnight, Goodnight, Construction Site. 2011. (Goodnight, Goodnight, Construc Ser.). (ENG., Illus.). 32p. (J). (gr. -1 — 1). 16.99 *(978-0-8118-7782-4(5))* Chronicle Bks. LLC.

—Goodnight, Goodnight, Construction Site & Steam Train, Dream Train Board Books Boxed Set, 1 vol. Lichtenheld, Tom, illus. 2015. (Goodnight, Goodnight, Construc Ser.). (ENG.). 66p. (J). (gr. -1 — 1). bds. 15.99 *(978-1-4521-4698-0(5))* Chronicle Bks. LLC.

—Goodnight, Goodnight, Construction Site Glow in the Dark Growth Chart. Lichtenheld, Tom, illus. 2016. (Goodnight, Goodnight Construction Site Ser.). (ENG.). 20p. (J). (gr. -1-7). 12.99 *(978-1-4521-5463-3(5))* Chronicle Bks. LLC.

—Goodnight Goodnight Construction Site Sound Book: (Construction Books for Kids, Books with Sound for Toddlers, Children's Truck Books, Read Aloud Books) Lichtenheld, Tom, illus. 2014. (Goodnight, Goodnight Construction Site Ser.). (ENG.). 12p. (J). (gr. -1 — 1). 12.99 *(978-1-4521-2824-5(3))* Chronicle Bks. LLC.

—Mighty, Mighty Construction Site. Lichtenheld, Tom, illus. 2024. (J). **(978-1-64549-817-9(4))** Amicus Learning.

—Mighty, Mighty Construction Site. Lichtenheld, Tom, illus. 2017. (Goodnight, Goodnight, Construc Ser.). (ENG.). 40p. (J). (gr. -1 — 1). 16.99 *(978-1-4521-5216-5(0))* Chronicle Bks. LLC.

—Mighty, Mighty Construction Site. 2019. (CHI.). (gr. -1). *(978-986-479-602-1(X))* Commonwealth Publishing Co., Ltd.

—Three Cheers for Kid Mcgear! (Family Read Aloud Books, Construction Books for Kids, Children's New Experiences Books, Stories in Verse) Ford, A. G., illus. 2019. (Goodnight, Goodnight, Construc Ser.). (ENG.). 40p. (J). (gr. -1 — 1). 17.99 *(978-1-4521-5582-1(8))* Chronicle Bks. LLC.

Rinker, Sherri Duskey & Lichtenheld, Tom. Goodnight, Goodnight, Construction Site. 2012. 12.95 *(978-0-545-50222-1(5))* Scholastic, Inc.

Rips, Nancy. Noah & the Eight Trucks of Hanukkah, 1 vol. Kerr, Thomas & Hierstein, Judith, illus. 2019. (ENG.). 32p. (J). 16.99 *(978-1-4556-2203-0(6)*, Pelican Publishing) Arcadia Publishing.

Robertson, Ruth. The Truck That Wouldn't! 2004. pap. 9.00 *(978-0-8059-6316-8(2))* Dorrance Publishing Co., Inc.

Royston, Angela. Truck Trouble. 2013. (DK Readers Level 1 Ser.). (ENG.). 32p. (J). (gr. k-2). 16.19 *(978-1-4654-0244-8(6))* Dorling Kindersley Publishing, Inc.

Salzano, Tammi. Truck Party. Wood, Hannah, illus. 2011. (ENG.). 20p. (J). bds. 7.95 *(978-1-58925-865-5(7))* Tiger Tales.

Sander, Sonia. Smash That Trash! Shannon, David et al, illus. 2009. (Jon Scieszka's Trucktown Ser.). (ENG.). 14p. (J). (gr. -1-k). 7.99 *(978-1-4169-4180-4(0)*, Little Simon) Little Simon.

Sauer, Tammi. Truck, Truck, Goose! Waring, Zoe, illus. 2017. (ENG.). 40p. (J). (gr. -1 — 1). 14.99 *(978-0-06-242153-1(0)*, HarperCollins) HarperCollins Pubs.

—Truck, Truck, Goose! Board Book. Waring, Zoe, illus. 2018. (ENG.). 40p. (J). (gr. -1 — 1). bds. 7.99 *(978-0-06-242154-8(9)*, HarperFestival) HarperCollins Pubs.

Savage, Stephen. The Mixed-Up Truck. 2016. (ENG., Illus.). 32p. (J). 19.99 *(978-1-62672-153-1(X)*, 900140585) Roaring Brook Pr.

—Supertruck. Savage, Stephen, illus. (ENG., Illus.). (J). 2018. 34p. bds. 7.99 *(978-1-250-14154-5(0)*, 900179942) 2015. 32p. (gr. -1-1). 15.99 *(978-1-59643-821-7(5)*, 900087176) Roaring Brook Pr.

Sayres, Brianna Caplan. Where Do Diggers Sleep at Night? Slade, Christian, illus. (Where Do... Ser.). (J). (— 1). 2014. 26p. bds. 8.99 *(978-0-385-37415-6(1))* 2012. 32p. 18.99 *(978-0-375-86848-1(8))* Random Hse. Children's Bks. (Random Hse. Bks. for Young Readers).

Scarry, Richard. Richard Scarry's Trucks. 2015. (Illus.). 24p. (J). (— 1). bds. 4.99 *(978-0-385-38925-9(6)*, Golden Bks.) Random Hse. Children's Bks.

Schertle, Alice. El Camioncito Azul: Little Blue Truck (Spanish Edition) McElmurry, Jill, illus. 2013.Tr. of Little Blue Truck. (SPA.). 30p. (J). (gr. -1 — 1). bds. 9.99 *(978-0-547-98397-4(2)*, 1524121, Clarion Bks.) HarperCollins Pubs.

—Good Night, Little Blue Truck. McElmurry, Jill, illus. 2019. (ENG.). 32p. (J). (gr. -1-3). 17.99 *(978-1-328-85213-7(X)*, 1711385, Clarion Bks.) HarperCollins Pubs.

—Little Blue Truck. McElmurry, Jill, illus. 2008. (ENG.). 32p. (J). (gr. -1-3). 18.99 *(978-0-15-205661-2(0)*, 1197021, Clarion Bks.) HarperCollins Pubs.

—Little Blue Truck. (J). 194.75 *(978-1-4703-3555-7(7))*; 37.75 *(978-1-4703-3557-1(3))*; 2012. 37.75 *(978-1-4703-3558-8(1))*; 2012. 39.75 *(978-1-4703-3013-2(X))* Recorded Bks., Inc.

—Little Blue Truck Big Book. McElmurry, Jill, illus. 2010. (ENG.). 32p. (J). (gr. -1-3). pap. 26.99 *(978-0-547-48248-4(5)*, 1439681, Clarion Bks.) HarperCollins Pubs.

—Little Blue Truck Lap Board Book. McElmurry, Jill, illus. 2015. (ENG.). 30p. (J). (— 1). bds. 12.99 *(978-0-544-05685-5(X)*, 1533603, Clarion Bks.) HarperCollins Pubs.

—Little Blue Truck Leads the Way. McElmurry, Jill, illus. 2009. (ENG.). 40p. (J). (gr. -1-3). 18.99 *(978-0-15-206389-4(7)*, 1199129, Clarion Bks.) HarperCollins Pubs.

—Little Blue Truck Leads the Way Big Book. McElmurry, Jill, illus. 2012. (ENG.). 40p. (J). (gr. -1-3). pap. 26.99 *(978-0-547-85060-3(3)*, 1501044, Clarion Bks.) HarperCollins Pubs.

—Little Blue Truck Leads the Way Board Book. McElmurry, Jill, illus. 2015. (ENG.). 38p. (J). (— 1). bds. 8.99 *(978-0-544-56805-1(2)*, 1611971, Clarion Bks.) HarperCollins Pubs.

—Little Blue Truck Leads the Way Lap Board Book. McElmurry, Jill, illus. 2016. (ENG.). 38p. (J). (— 1). bds. 12.99 *(978-0-544-70899-0(7)*, 1628910, Clarion Bks.) HarperCollins Pubs.

—Little Blue Truck Makes a Friend: A Friendship Book for Kids. McElmurry, Jill, illus. 2022. (Little Blue Truck Ser.). (ENG.). 40p. (J). (gr. -1-3). 18.99 *(978-0-358-72282-3(9)*, Clarion Bks.) HarperCollins Pubs.

—Little Blue Truck's Beep-Along Book. McElmurry, Jill, illus. 2015. (ENG.). 8p. (J). (— 1). bds. 14.99 *(978-0-544-56812-9(5)*, 1611972, Clarion Bks.) HarperCollins Pubs.

—Little Blue Truck's Christmas: A Christmas Holiday Book for Kids. McElmurry, Jill, illus. 2014. (ENG.). 24p. (J). (— 1). 18.99 *(978-0-544-32041-3(7)*, 1582526, Clarion Bks.) HarperCollins Pubs.

—Little Blue Truck's Halloween: A Halloween Book for Kids. McElmurry, Jill, illus. 2016. (Little Blue Truck Ser.). (ENG.). 16p. (J). (— 1). bds. 13.99 *(978-0-544-77253-3(9)*, 1636990, Clarion Bks.) HarperCollins Pubs.

—Little Blue Truck's Springtime: An Easter & Springtime Book for Kids. McElmurry, Jill, illus. 2018. (ENG.). 16p. (J). (gr. -1 — 1). bds. 13.99 *(978-0-544-93809-0(7)*, 1658575, Clarion Bks.) HarperCollins Pubs.

—Little Blue Truck's Valentine. McElmurry, Jill, illus. 2020. (ENG.). 20p. (J). (gr. -1). 13.99 *(978-0-358-27244-1(0)*, 1771924, Clarion Bks.) HarperCollins Pubs.

—Time for School, Little Blue Truck: A Back to School Book for Kids. McElmurry, Jill, illus. 2021. (Little Blue Truck Ser.). (ENG.). 32p. (J). (gr. -1-3). 18.99 *(978-0-358-41224-3(2)*, 1790429, Clarion Bks.) HarperCollins Pubs.

—Time for School, Little Blue Truck Big Book. McElmurry, Jill, illus. 2022. (ENG.). 32p. (J). (gr. -1-3). pap. 26.99 *(978-0-358-66599-1(X)*, 1822616, Clarion Bks.) HarperCollins Pubs.

Scholastic. Build This City! (LEGO City) 2010. (LEGO City Ser.). (ENG.). 24p. (J). (gr. -1-3). pap. 3.99 *(978-0-545-17765-8(0))* Scholastic, Inc.

—Let's Go, Rescue Trucks! 2018. (Spin Me! Ser.). (ENG.). 12p. (J). (gr. -1 — 1). bds. 7.99 *(978-1-338-25680-2(7)*, Cartwheel Bks.) Scholastic, Inc.

Schorr, Titus. The Truck Parade, 1 vol., 1. 2015. (Rosen REAL Readers: STEM & STEAM Collection). (ENG.). 8p. (J). (gr. k-1). pap. 5.46 *(978-1-5081-1401-7(3)*, 45fd0d7c-9e4f-41d2-874d-8b4333bd0283, Rosen Classroom) Rosen Publishing Group, Inc., The.

Schwartz, Corey Rosen & Gomez, Rebecca J. Two Tough Trucks. Leung, Hilary, illus. 2019. (ENG.). 40p. (J). (gr. -1-k). 17.99 *(978-1-338-23654-5(7)*, Orchard Bks.) Scholastic, Inc.

Scieszka, Jon. Dizzy Izzy: Ready-To-Read Level 1. Shannon, David et al, illus. (Jon Scieszka's Trucktown Ser.). (ENG.). 24p. (J). (gr. -1-1). 2014. 17.99 *(978-1-4814-1460-9(7))* 2010. pap. 4.99 *(978-1-4169-4145-3(2))* Simon Spotlight. (Simon Spotlight).

—The Great Truck Rescue. Shannon, David et al, illus. 2010. (Jon Scieszka's Trucktown Ser.). (ENG.). 40p. (J). (gr. -1-3). pap. 4.99 *(978-1-4424-0932-3(0)*, Simon & Schuster Bks. For Young Readers) Simon & Schuster Bks. For Young Readers.

—Kat's Maps: Ready-To-Read Level 1. Shannon, David et al, illus. 2011. (Jon Scieszka's Trucktown Ser.). (ENG.). 24p. (J). (gr. -1-1). pap. 4.99 *(978-1-4169-4148-4(7)*, Simon Spotlight) Simon Spotlight.

—Kat's Mystery Gift: Ready-To-Read Level 1. Shannon, David et al, illus. 2009. (Jon Scieszka's Trucktown Ser.). (ENG.). 24p. (J). (gr. -1-1). pap. 4.99 *(978-1-4169-4143-9(6)*, Simon Spotlight) Simon Spotlight.

—Melvin Might? Shannon, David et al, illus. 2008. (Jon Scieszka's Trucktown Ser.). (ENG.). 44p. (J). (gr. -1-3). 19.99 *(978-1-4169-4134-7(7)*, Simon & Schuster Bks. For Young Readers) Simon & Schuster Bks. For Young Readers.

—Melvin's Valentine: Ready-To-Read Level 1. Shannon, David et al, illus. (Jon Scieszka's Trucktown Ser.). (ENG.). 24p. (J). (gr. -1-1). 2014. 17.99 *(978-1-4814-1458-6(5))* 2009. pap. 4.99 *(978-1-4169-4144-6(4))* Simon Spotlight. (Simon Spotlight).

—Pete's Party: Ready-To-Read Level 1. Gordon, David et al, illus. 2008. (Jon Scieszka's Trucktown Ser.). (ENG.). 24p. (J). (gr. -1-1). pap. 4.99 *(978-1-4169-4138-5(X)*, Simon Spotlight) Simon Spotlight.

—Race from a to Z, No. 4. Shannon, David et al, illus. 2014. (Jon Scieszka's Trucktown Ser.). (ENG.). 48p. (J). (gr. -1-3). 19.99 *(978-1-4169-4136-1(3)*, Simon & Schuster Bks. For Young Readers) Simon & Schuster Bks. For Young Readers.

—Smash!Crash! Shannon, David et al, illus. 2008. (Jon Scieszka's Trucktown Ser.). (ENG.). 42p. (J). (gr. -1-3). 19.99 *(978-1-4169-4133-0(9)*, Simon & Schuster Bks. For Young Readers) Simon & Schuster Bks. For Young Readers.

—Snow Trucking! Ready-To-Read Level 1. Gordon, David et al, illus. 2008. (Jon Scieszka's Trucktown Ser.). (ENG.). 24p. (J). (gr. -1-1). pap. 4.99 *(978-1-4169-4140-8(1)*, Simon Spotlight) Simon Spotlight.

—The Spooky Tire: Ready-To-Read Level 1. Shannon, David et al, illus. 2009. (Jon Scieszka's Trucktown Ser.). (ENG.). 24p. (J). (gr. -1-k). lib. bdg. 17.99 *(978-1-4169-4153-8(3))*; pap. 4.99 *(978-1-4169-4142-2(8))* Simon Spotlight. (Simon Spotlight).

—Trucks Line Up: Ready-To-Read Level 1. Shannon, David et al, illus. 2011. (Jon Scieszka's Trucktown Ser.). (ENG.). 24p. (J). (gr. -1-1). 17.99 *(978-1-4169-4158-3(4))*; pap. 4.99 *(978-1-4169-4147-7(9))* Simon Spotlight. (Simon Spotlight).

—Trucksgiving: Ready-To-Read Level 1. Shannon, David et al, illus. 2010. (Jon Scieszka's Trucktown Ser.). (ENG.). 24p. (J). (gr. -1-1). 16.99 *(978-1-4169-4157-6(6))*; pap. 4.99 *(978-1-4169-4146-0(0))* Simon Spotlight. (Simon Spotlight).

—Uh-Oh, Max: Ready-To-Read Level 1. Shannon, David et al, illus. (Jon Scieszka's Trucktown Ser.). (ENG.). 24p. (J). (gr. -1-1). 2014. 17.99 *(978-1-4814-1461-6(5))* 2009. pap. 4.99 *(978-1-4169-4141-5(X))* Simon Spotlight. (Simon Spotlight).

—Welcome to Trucktown! Shannon, David et al, illus. 2010. (Jon Scieszka's Trucktown Ser.). (ENG.). 40p. (J). (gr. -1-3). pap. 4.99 *(978-1-4424-1271-2(2)*, Simon & Schuster Bks. For Young Readers) Simon & Schuster Bks. For Young Readers.

—Zoom! Boom! Bully: Ready-To-Read Level 1. Shannon, David et al, illus. 2008. (Jon Scieszka's Trucktown Ser.). (ENG.). 24p. (J). (gr. -1-1). pap. 4.99 *(978-1-4169-4139-2(8)*, Simon Spotlight) Simon Spotlight.

Shea, Christine. Las Aventuras de Max, el Camión Volteador: El Mejor Día de Nieve! = the Adventures of Max the Dump Truck: The Greatest Snow Day Ever! Chase, Michelle B. & Chase, Tanor R., illus. 2007. (ENG & SPA.). (J). *(978-1-933002-01-9(8))* PublishingWorks.

Shealy, Dennis R. I'm a Monster Truck. Staake, Bob, illus. 2011. (Little Golden Book Ser.). 24p. (J). (gr. -1-2). 5.99 *(978-0-375-86132-1(7)*, Golden Bks.) Random Hse. Children's Bks.

Silver Dolphin en Español Editors. Tonka Vehiculos Robustos y Sensacionales. 2006. (Tonka Board Bks.). (Illus.). 22p. (J). (gr. -1). bds. *(978-970-718-362-9(4)*, Silver Dolphin en Español) Advanced Marketing, S. de R. L. de C. V.

Silver Dolphin en Español Editors, creator. Camiones a la Obra! 2006. (Tonka Figuras Magicas Ser.). (Illus.). 8p. (J). (gr. -1). *(978-970-718-360-5(8)*, Silver Dolphin en Español) Advanced Marketing, S. de R. L. de C. V.

Sís, Peter. Trucks Trucks Trucks Board Book. Sís, Peter, illus. 2004. (ENG., Illus.). 28p. (J). (gr. -1-1). bds. 8.99 *(978-0-06-056258-8(7)*, Greenwillow Bks.) HarperCollins Pubs.

Sisler, Celeste. Robot Power! (Blaze & the Monster Machines) Aikins, Dave, illus. 2018. (Step into Reading Ser.). (ENG.). 24p. (J). (gr. -1-1). pap. 5.99 *(978-0-525-57820-8(X)*, Random Hse. Bks. for Young Readers) Random Hse. Children's Bks.

Sollinger, Emily. Dare to Repair! 2016. (Dinotrux 8X8 Ser.). (Illus.). (J). lib. bdg. 13.55 *(978-0-606-38318-9(2))* Turtleback.

—Dinotrux to the Rescue! 2016. (Dinotrux Passport Reading Level 1 Ser.). (J). lib. bdg. 13.55 *(978-0-606-38320-2(4))* Turtleback.

Spelvin, Justin. Honk That Horn! Shannon, David et al, illus. 2011. (Jon Scieszka's Trucktown Ser.). (ENG.). 24p. (J). (gr. -1-k). pap. 4.99 *(978-1-4169-4184-2(3)*, Simon & Schuster Bks. For Young Readers) Simon & Schuster Bks. For Young Readers.

—Take a Trip with Trucktown! Shannon, David et al, illus. 2011. (Jon Scieszka's Trucktown Ser.). (ENG.). 24p. (J). (gr. -1-3). pap. 4.99 *(978-1-4169-4181-1(9)*, Simon & Schuster Bks. For Young Readers) Simon & Schuster Bks. For Young Readers.

Stark, Hannah. Trucker & Train. Kolar, Bob, illus. 2019. (ENG.). 40p. (J). (gr. -1-3). 17.99 *(978-0-544-80181-3(4)*, 1640534, Clarion Bks.) HarperCollins Pubs.

Staunton, Ted. Morgan on Ice, 1 vol. Slavin, Bill, illus. 2013. (Formac First Novels Ser.). (ENG.). 56p. (J). (gr. 2-3). 14.95 *(978-1-4595-0289-5(2)*, 0289) Formac Publishing Co., Ltd. CAN. Dist: Formac Lorimer Bks. Ltd.

Steele, Michael Anthony. Fix That Truck! 2012. (LEGO City 8X8 Ser.). lib. bdg. 13.55 *(978-0-606-26773-1(5))* Turtleback.

Stein, Peter. Trucks Galore. Staake, Bob, illus. 2017. (ENG.). 32p. (J). (gr. -1-3). 17.99 *(978-0-7636-8978-0(5))* Candlewick Pr.

Stoddard, Jeffery. Pete & Pillar: A Story of Friendship Based on John 15:13: the Big Rain. Stoddard, Jeffery, illus. 2007. (Pete & Pillar Ser.). (ENG., Illus.). 32p. (J). (gr. -1-2). 12.99 *(978-1-59317-203-9(6))* Warner Pr., Inc.

Stott, Ann. Want to Play Trucks? Graham, Bob, illus. 2018. (ENG.). 32p. (J). (gr. -1-2). 17.99 *(978-0-7636-8173-9(3))* Candlewick Pr.

Sutton, Sally. Roadwork. Lovelock, Brian, illus. 2017. (Construction Crew Ser.). (ENG.). 32p. (J). (-k). 7.99 *(978-0-7636-9870-6(9))* Candlewick Pr.

Sweeney, Kathleen. Matty Monster Truck. 2008. 14p. pap. 24.95 *(978-1-60672-865-9(2))* America Star Bks.

Swenson, Jamie A. Big Rig. Young, Ned, illus. 2014. (ENG.). 32p. (J). (gr. -1-k). 16.99 *(978-1-4231-6330-5(3))* Hyperion Bks. for Children.

Teitelbaum, Michael. On the Move! Shannon, David et al, illus. 2009. (Jon Scieszka's Trucktown Ser.). (ENG.). 10p. (J). (gr. -1-k). bds. 6.99 *(978-1-4169-4178-1(9)*, Little Simon) Little Simon.

—Steer the Wheel! Shannon, David et al, illus. 2011. (Jon Scieszka's Trucktown Ser.). (ENG.). 12p. (J). (gr. -1-1). bds. 7.99 *(978-1-4169-4185-9(1)*, Simon & Schuster Bks. For Young Readers) Simon & Schuster Bks. For Young Readers.

Tillworth, Mary. Bouncy Tires! (Blaze & the Monster Machines) Burch, Benjamin, illus. 2016. (Little Golden Book Ser.). (ENG.). 24p. (J). (gr. -1-k). 5.99 *(978-0-553-53891-5(8)*, Golden Bks.) Random Hse. Children's Bks.

—Zeg & the Egg. Foley, Niki, illus. 2016. 18p. (J). *(978-1-4806-9878-9(4))* Random Hse., Inc.

Todd, Mark. Food Trucks! 2014. (ENG., Illus.). 32p. (J). (gr. -1-3). 17.99 *(978-0-544-15784-2(2)*, 1550624, Clarion Bks.) HarperCollins Pubs.

Torres, Jennifer. Stef Soto, Taco Queen. 2018. (ENG.). 192p. (J). (gr. 3-7). pap. 7.99 *(978-0-316-30684-3(3))* Little, Brown Bks. for Young Readers.

Valentine, Tanya. Little Taco Truck. Martin, Jorge, illus. 2019. 40p. (J). (gr. -1-2). 18.99 *(978-1-5247-6585-9(6))* Random Hse. Children's Bks.

Van Slyke, Rebecca. Monster's Trucks. Sutphin, Joe, illus. 2020. (ENG.). 40p. (J). 17.99 *(978-1-68119-301-4(9)*, 900165544, Bloomsbury Children's Bks.) Bloomsbury Publishing USA.

Venning, Edward W. The Story of Pete & Ralph. 2008. 56p. pap. 16.95 *(978-1-4327-2237-1(9))* Outskirts Pr., Inc.

Verdick, Elizabeth. Small Walt. Rosenthal, Marc, illus. 2017. (ENG.). 40p. (J). (gr. -1-3). 17.99 *(978-1-4814-4845-1(5)*, Simon & Schuster Bks. For Young Readers) Simon & Schuster Bks. For Young Readers.

—Small Walt & Mo the Tow. Rosenthal, Marc, illus. 2018. (ENG.). 40p. (J). (gr. -1-3). 17.99 *(978-1-4814-6660-8(7)*, Simon & Schuster/Paula Wiseman Bks.) Simon & Schuster/Paula Wiseman Bks.

Weldon, Stayton. Whitey on the Ranch. Anderson-Shorter, Susan, illus. 2010. 52p. pap. 12.95 *(978-1-4490-5474-8(9))* AuthorHouse.

Wheeler, Lisa. Farmer Dale's Red Pickup Truck Board Book. Bates, Ivan, illus. 2014. (ENG.). 32p. (J). (— 1). bds. 7.99 *(978-0-544-24765-9(5)*, 1566128, Clarion Bks.) HarperCollins Pubs.

Whybrow, Ian. The Flying Diggers. Melling, David, illus. 2009. (J). *(978-1-4351-6500-7(4))* Barnes & Noble, Inc.

Wildman, Dale. Big Rig Daddy: A Ride in the Truck of All Trucks. Dickson, Bill, illus. 2006. 24p. (J). per. 2.99 *(978-1-59958-007-4(1))* Journey Stone Creations, LLC.

Williamson, Jennifer. Timmy the Tow Truck, 6 vols. Williamson, Alan, 8th, illus. 2005. 28p. (J). pap. *(978-0-9771678-1-4(X))* Theee Hole Punch Publishing.

Wolf, Sallie. Peter's Trucks. 2013. 26p. 26.95 *(978-1-62352-033-5(9))* IntoPrint Publishing LLC.

—Truck Stuck. Davies, Andy Robert, illus. (J). (— 1). 2017. 28p. bds. 7.99 *(978-1-58089-781-5(9))* 2009. 32p. pap. 7.95 *(978-1-58089-257-5(4))* Charlesbridge Publishing, Inc.

Wyre, Yvonne. The Adventures of Cuthbert the Coal Lorry. 2005. 160p. pap. *(978-1-84401-500-9(9))* Athena Pr.

Zandman, Herm. It's Not a Truck! It's a B-Double! 2012. 40p. pap. 32.70 *(978-1-4797-0543-6(8))* Xlibris Corp.

TRUMAN, HARRY S., 1884-1972

Blake, Kevin. Harry S. Truman: The 33rd President. 2016. (First Look at America's Presidents Ser.). (ENG., Illus.). 24p. (J). (gr. -1-3). 26.99 *(978-1-943553-29-7(7))* Bearport Publishing Co., Inc.

Elston, Heidi. Harry S. Truman, 1 vol. 2016. (United States Presidents *2017 Ser.). (ENG., Illus.). 40p. (J). (gr. 2-5). 35.64 *(978-1-68078-119-9(7)*, 21855, Big Buddy Bks.) ABDO Publishing Co.

Etingoff, Kim. Harry Truman: From Farmer to President. 2012. (J). pap. *(978-1-4222-2485-4(6))*; lib. bdg. 64p. (gr. 7-8). 22.95 *(978-1-4222-2482-3(1))* Mason Crest.

Geller, Kevin. Harry S. Truman, 1 vol. 2017. (Pivotal Presidents: Profiles in Leadership Ser.). (ENG., Illus.). 80p. (J). (gr. 8-8). lib. bdg. 36.47 *(978-1-68048-633-9(0)*, 6fbd2e3d-226b-4f14-9f06-044fc28f431d, Britannica Educational Publishing) Rosen Publishing Group, Inc., The.

Lazo, Caroline Evensen. Harry S. Truman. 2003. (Presidential Biography Ser.). (Illus.). 112p. (J). (gr. 6-12). lib. bdg. 29.27 *(978-0-8225-0096-4(5))* Lerner Publishing Group.

Mara, Wil. Harry Truman, 1 vol. 2012. (Presidents & Their Times Ser.). (ENG., Illus.). 96p. (gr. 6-6). 36.93 *(978-1-60870-185-8(9)*, 1e388eab-e112-43b3-81e4-33d929da8328) Cavendish Square Publishing LLC.

Parker, Lewis. How to Draw the Life & Times of Harry S. Truman. 2009. (Kid's Guide to Drawing the Presidents of the United States of America Ser.). 32p. (gr. 4-4). 50.50 *(978-1-61511-143-5(3)*, PowerKids Pr.) Rosen Publishing Group, Inc., The.

Parker, Lewis K. How to Draw the Life & Times of Harry S. Truman, 1 vol. 2005. (Kid's Guide to Drawing the Presidents of the United States of America Ser.). (ENG., Illus.). 32p. (YA). (gr. 4-4). lib. bdg. 30.27 *(978-1-4042-3009-5(2)*, 5bcc9da0-a969-4832-8968-c374049d2fcc) Rosen Publishing Group, Inc., The.

Saffer, Barbara. Harry S. Truman. 2004. (Childhoods of the Presidents Ser.). (Illus.). 48p. (J). (gr. 4-18). lib. bdg. 17.95 *(978-1-59084-282-9(0))* Mason Crest.

Stanley, George E. Harry S. Truman: Thirty-Third President of the United States. Henderson, Meryl, illus. 2004. (Childhood of Famous Americans Ser.). (ENG.). 256p. (J). (gr. 3-7). pap. 7.99 *(978-0-689-86247-2(4)*, Aladdin) Simon & Schuster Children's Publishing.

Venezia, Mike. Harry S. Truman: Thirty-Third President. Venezia, Mike, illus. 2007. (Getting to Know the U. S. Presidents Ser.). (Illus.). 32p. (J). (gr. 3-4). 28.00 *(978-0-516-22637-8(1)*, Children's Pr.) Scholastic Library Publishing.

TRUMBULL, JOHN, 1756-1843

Murray, Stuart A. P. John Trumbull: Painter of the Revolutionary War: Painter of the Revolutionary War. 2008. (ENG., Illus.). 83p. (C). (gr. 6-18). lib. bdg. 180.00 *(978-0-7656-8150-8(1)*, Y182501) Routledge.

TRUMP, DONALD, 1946-

Allen, John. The Trump Presidency. 2020. (ENG.). 80p. (J). (gr. 6-12). 41.27 *(978-1-68282-759-8(3))* ReferencePoint Pr., Inc.

Carser, A. R. Donald Trump: 45th US President. 2016. (Essential Lives Set 10 Ser.). (ENG., Illus.). 112p. (J). (gr. 6-12). lib. bdg. 41.36 *(978-1-68078-366-7(1)*, 23222, Essential Library) ABDO Publishing Co.

Hinman, Bonnie. Donald Trump: 45th President of the United States. 2017. (Newsmakers Set 2 Ser.). (ENG., Illus.). 48p. (J). (gr. 4-8). lib. bdg. 35.64 *(978-1-5321-1185-3(1)*, 25946) ABDO Publishing Co.

—Donald Trump: 45th President of the United States. 2017. (Newsmakers Set 2 Ser.). (ENG., Illus.). 48p. (J). (gr. 4-8). 55.65 *(978-1-68078-970-6(8)*, 26371) ABDO Publishing Co.

Lee, Jake. Donald Trump: Tbd. 2016. (United States Presidents *2017 Ser.). (ENG., Illus.). 40p. (J). (gr. 2-5). lib. bdg. 31.35 *(978-1-68078-362-9(9)*, 21865, Big Buddy Bks.) ABDO Publishing Co.

Marsh, Carole. Donald Trump: Presidential Coloring & Activity Book. 2017. (Here & Now Ser.). (ENG., Illus.). (J). (gr. 3-7). 5.99 *(978-0-635-12561-3(7))* Gallopade International.

—I'm Reading about Donald Trump: America's 45th President. 2017. (I'm Reading About Ser.). (ENG., Illus.). (J). pap. 7.99 *(978-0-635-12564-4(1))*; lib. bdg. 24.99 *(978-0-635-12565-1(X))* Gallopade International.

Mattern, Joanne. President Donald Trump. 2017. (Rookie Biographies(tm) Ser.). (ENG., Illus.). 32p. (J). lib. bdg. 25.00 *(978-0-531-23226-2(3)*, Children's Pr.) Scholastic Library Publishing.

—Rookie Biographies: President Donald Trump. 2017. (Rookie Biographies Ser.). (ENG., Illus.). 32p. (J). pap. 5.95 *(978-0-531-23860-8(1)*, Children's Pr.) Scholastic Library Publishing.

—A True Book: President Donald Trump. 2017. (True Book(tm), A — Biographies Ser.). (ENG., Illus.). 48p. (J). 31.00 *(978-0-531-22718-3(9))*; pap. 7.95 *(978-0-531-23014-5(7))* Scholastic Library Publishing. (Children's Pr.).

Mcintosh Wooten, Sara. Donald Trump: Real Estate Mogul & President, 1 vol. 2017. (Influential Lives Ser.). (ENG., Illus.). 128p. (gr. 7-7). lib. bdg. 40.27 *(978-0-7660-8499-5(X)*, 9a36aa24-fde2-41d1-abe9-f162ce87fbcc) Enslow Publishing, LLC.

Nagelhout, Ryan. Before Donald Trump Was President, 1 vol. 2017. (Before They Were President Ser.). (ENG.). 24p. (J). (gr. 2-3). pap. 9.15 *(978-1-5382-1064-2(9)*, 3e0a1dcc-caeb-4c75-a338-e2a712d99cd5); lib. bdg. 24.27 *(978-1-5382-1066-6(5)*, 7d4d45f5-1c41-432c-a773-1fda7f91527c) Stevens, Gareth Publishing LLLP.

Robison, Nick. President Donald Trump. 2017. (Pebble Plus Ser.). (ENG., Illus.). 32p. (J). (gr. -1-2). lib. bdg. 27.32 *(978-1-5157-7895-0(9)*, 136018, Capstone Pr.) Capstone.

Santos, Rita. Donald Trump: Businessman & President, 1 vol. 2017. (Junior Biographies Ser.). (ENG.). 24p. (gr. 3-4). lib. bdg. 24.27 *(978-0-7660-8666-1(6)*, 7385afec-7721-4292-9a52-5bf2e66ecba6) Enslow Publishing, LLC.

TRUMPET—FICTION

Acampora, Paul. Rachel Spinelli Punched Me in the Face. 2013. (ENG.). 192p. (J). (gr. 8-12). pap. 14.99 *(978-1-250-01669-0(X)*, 900087083) Square Fish.

Dorie & Me. 2003. (YA). per. *(978-1-59431-071-3(8)*, Ebks. On The Net) Write Words, Inc.

Lipsyte, Robert. Yellow Flag. 2009. (ENG.). 256p. (YA). (gr. 8). pap. 10.99 *(978-0-06-055709-6(5)*, HarperCollins) HarperCollins Pubs.

Polizzotto, Carolyn & Spinks, Sarah. Trumpet's Kittens. Duke, Marion, illus. 2003. 32p. (YA). 22.50 *(978-1-86368-331-9(3))* Fremantle Pr. AUS. Dist: Independent Pubs. Group.

Ritter, John H. Under the Baseball Moon. 2008. (Illus.). 283p. (gr. 8-12). 17.00 *(978-0-7569-8934-7(5))* Perfection Learning Corp.

Torres, Jos A. & Torres, Jose A. Joey Kanga Roo: Plays the Trumpet. 2009. 36p. pap. 15.99 *(978-1-4389-7434-7(5))* AuthorHouse.

Townsend, Daniel. Trumpet. 2008. 24p. pap. 24.95 *(978-1-4241-9387-5(7))* America Star Bks.

Willems, Mo. Listen to My Trumpet!-An Elephant & Piggie Book. 2012. (Elephant & Piggie Book Ser.: 17). (ENG., Illus.). 64p. (J). (gr. -1-k). 9.99 *(978-1-4231-5404-4(5)*, Hyperion Books for Children) Disney Publishing Worldwide.

TRUST IN GOD

see Faith

TRUTH, SOJOURNER, 1799-1883

Butler, Mary. Sojourner Truth: From Slave to Activist for Freedom. 2009. (Library of American Lives & Times Ser.). 112p. (gr. 5-5). 69.20 *(978-1-60853-505-7(3))* Rosen Publishing Group, Inc., The.

Clinton, Catherine. When Harriet Met Sojourner. Evans, Shane W., illus. 2007. (ENG.). 32p. (J). (gr. k-3). 16.99 *(978-0-06-050425-0(0)*, Tegen, Katherine Bks) HarperCollins Pubs.

Collins, Kathleen. Sojourner Truth: Defensora de los derechos Civiles, 1 vol. 2003. (Grandes Personajes en la Historia de Los Estados Unidos (Famous People in American History) Ser.). (SPA.). 32p. (gr. 3-4). pap. 10.00 *(978-0-8239-4239-8(2)*, 6f31c133-2276-4b5a-816a-e9203a1295c1, Rosen Classroom) Rosen Publishing Group, Inc., The.

—Sojourner Truth: Defensora de los derechos civiles (Sojourner Truth: Equal Rights Advocate) 2009. (Grandes personajes en la historia de los Estados Unidos (Famous People in American History) Ser.). (SPA.). 32p. (gr. 2-3). 47.90 *(978-1-61512-808-2(5)*, Editorial Buenas Letras) Rosen Publishing Group, Inc., The.

—Sojourner Truth: Equal Rights Advocate. (Primary Sources of Famous People in American History Ser.). 32p. 2009. (gr. 2-3). 47.90 *(978-1-60851-727-5(6))* 2003. (ENG., Illus.). (gr. 3-4). pap. 10.00 *(978-0-8239-4193-3(0)*, a3e0d003-2b16-455d-a83a-e5c1a3908d7c) Rosen Publishing Group, Inc., The.

—Sojourner Truth: Equal Rights Advocate / Defensora de los derechos Civiles. 2009. (Famous People in American History/Grandes personajes en la historia de los Estados Unidos Ser.). (ENG & SPA.). 32p. (gr. 2-3). 47.90 *(978-1-61512-556-2(6)*, Editorial Buenas Letras) Rosen Publishing Group, Inc., The.

Krass, Peter. Sojourner Truth: Antislavery Activist. 2004. (Black Americans of Achievement Legacy Edition Ser.). (ENG., Illus.). 112p. (gr. 6-12). 35.00 *(978-0-7910-8165-5(6)*, P114169, Facts On File) Infobase Holdings, Inc.

Kudlinski, Kathleen. Sojourner Truth. Wooden, Lenny, illus. 2003. (Childhood of Famous Americans Ser.). (ENG.). 160p. (J). (gr. 3-7). mass mkt. 7.99 *(978-0-689-85274-9(6)*, Simon & Schuster/Paula Wiseman Bks.) Simon & Schuster/Paula Wiseman Bks.

Lantier, Patricia & Michael Hom, Geoffrey. Sojourner Truth: Speaking up for Freedom. 2009. (Voices for Freedom Ser.). (ENG.). 64p. (J). (gr. 5-8). pap. *(978-0-7787-4840-3(5))*; lib. bdg. *(978-0-7787-4824-3(3))* Crabtree Publishing Co.

Marsh, Carole. Sojourner Truth. 2003. 12p. (gr. k-4). 2.95 *(978-0-635-02355-1(5))* Gallopade International.

Mattern, Joanne. Sojourner Truth: Early Abolitionist. 2009. (Women Who Shaped History Ser.). 24p. (gr. 2-3). 42.50 *(978-1-60854-821-7(X)*, PowerKids Pr.) Rosen Publishing Group, Inc., The.

Mcdonough, Yona Zeldis. Who Was Sojourner Truth? 2015. (Who Was... ? Ser.). lib. bdg. 16.00 *(978-0-606-37560-3(0))* Turtleback.

McDonough, Yona Zeldis & Who HQ. Who Was Sojourner Truth? Eldridge, Jim, illus. 2015. (Who Was? Ser.). 112p. (J). (gr. 3-7). 5.99 *(978-0-448-48678-9(4)*, Penguin Workshop) Penguin Young Readers Group.

McKissack, Patricia C. & McKissack, Fredrick, Jr. Sojourner Truth: Ain't I a Woman? 2003. (Illus.). 186p. (gr. 4-7). 17.20 *(978-0-7857-2515-2(6))* Turtleback.

Moore, Barbara R. Sojourner Truth. 2005. (Illus.). 16p. (J). *(978-0-618-56039-4(4))* Houghton Mifflin Harcourt Publishing Co.

Ruffin, Frances E. Her Story, Her Words: The Narrative of Sojourner Truth. (Great Moments in American History Ser.). 32p. (gr. 3-3). 2009. 47.90 *(978-1-61513-144-0(2))* 2003. (ENG., Illus.). lib. bdg. 29.13 *(978-0-8239-4387-6(9)*, b981b6e9-653c-4bc0-b07c-deb6aeab09a2, Rosen Reference) Rosen Publishing Group, Inc., The.

—Sojourner Truth: Early Abolitionist. 2009. (American Legends Ser.). 24p. (gr. 3-3). 42.50 *(978-1-61511-387-3(8)*, PowerKids Pr.) Rosen Publishing Group, Inc., The.

Schmidt, Gary D. So Tall Within: Sojourner Truth's Long Walk Toward Freedom. Minter, Daniel, illus. 2018. (ENG.). 48p. (J). 18.99 *(978-1-62672-872-1(0)*, 900176273) Roaring Brook Pr.

Swain, Gwenyth. Sojourner Truth. Archambault, Matthew, illus. 2005. (On My Own Biography Ser.). 48p. (J). (gr. 1-3). pap. 6.95 *(978-1-57505-827-6(8))* Lerner Publishing Group.

—Sojourner Truth. 2005. (On My Own Biography Ser.). (Illus.). 48p. (J). 25.26 *(978-1-57505-651-7(8)*, Carolrhoda Bks.) Lerner Publishing Group.

Taylor, Charlotte. Sojourner Truth: Abolitionist & Activist, 1 vol. 2015. (Exceptional African Americans Ser.). (ENG.). 24p. (gr. 3-3). pap. 10.35 *(978-0-7660-7370-8(X)*, 74c8a009-54b8-46a8-9618-17684d1cbaff); (Illus.). (J). 24.27 *(978-0-7660-7372-2(6)*, 0875ecb8-6d51-4bdc-b90d-0fb514a78530) Enslow Publishing, LLC.

Waxman, Laura Hamilton. Sojourner Truth. 2008. pap. 52.95 *(978-0-8225-9396-6(3))*; (ENG., Illus.). 48p. (gr. 3-6). lib. bdg. 27.93 *(978-0-8225-7172-8(2)*, Lerner Pubns.) Lerner Publishing Group.

TRUTHFULNESS AND FALSEHOOD

see also Honesty

Amos, Janine & Spenceley, Annabel. Let's Own Up, 1 vol. 2009. (Best Behavior Ser.). (ENG., Illus.). 32p. (J). (gr. -1-2). 27.27 *(978-1-60754-503-3(9)*, b379773b-ff8b-4943-a198-52afff231c36); pap. 11.55 *(978-1-60754-505-7(5)*, b3a94595-c243-4053-b9e9-8c11f7c2ea20) Rosen Publishing Group, Inc., The. (Windmill Bks.).

Beeson, Sam. White Lies. 2009. 9.99 *(978-1-59955-343-6(0))* Cedar Fort, Inc./CFI Distribution.

Berry, Joy. Help Me Be Good about Lying. 2009. (Help Me Be Good Ser.). 32p. pap. 7.95 *(978-1-60577-113-7(9))* Berry, Joy Enterprises.

Berry, Joy Wilt. A Book about Cheating. 2005. (Illus.). (J). *(978-0-7172-8583-9(9))* Scholastic, Inc.

—A Book about Lying. 2005. (Illus.). (J). *(978-0-7172-8576-1(6))* Scholastic, Inc.

Gerber, Larry. The Distortion of Facts in the Digital Age, 1 vol. 2012. (Digital & Information Literacy Ser.). (ENG., Illus.). 48p. (YA). (gr. 6-6). 33.47 *(978-1-4488-8357-8(1)*, 277f2634-5014-4225-9fe2-01ead6459e2a); pap. 12.75 *(978-1-4488-8368-4(7)*, e5d5507e-d10b-42a8-9453-32c99c56992a) Rosen Publishing Group, Inc., The. (Rosen Reference).

Graves, Sue. I Didn't Do It! A Book about Telling the Truth. Guicciardini, Desideria, illus. 2013. (Our Emotions & Behavior Ser.). (ENG.). 28p. (J). (gr. -1-3). 15.99 *(978-1-57542-445-3(2))* Free Spirit Publishing Inc.

Gresh, Dannah K. Lies Girls Believe: And the Truth That Sets Them Free. 2019. (ENG., Illus.). 176p. (J). pap. 14.99 *(978-0-8024-1447-2(8))* Moody Pubs.

Kiesbye, Stefan, ed. Cheating, 1 vol. 2010. (Social Issues Firsthand Ser.). (ENG.). 112p. (gr. 10-12). 39.93 *(978-0-7377-5009-6(X)*, 54f73f30-a58a-4da3-8bb8-138e64c1f6fa, Greenhaven Publishing) Greenhaven Publishing LLC.

Larsen, Carolyn. Telling the Truth: A Book about Lying. O'Connor, Tim, illus. 2016. (Growing God's Kids Ser.). (ENG.). 32p. (J). pap. 5.99 *(978-0-8010-0926-6(X))* Baker Bks.

Lynette, Rachel. How to Deal with Lying. (Let's Work It Out Ser.). 24p. (gr. 2-3). 2009. 42.50 *(978-1-61514-265-1(7)*, PowerKids Pr.) 2008. (ENG., Illus.). (J). lib. bdg. 26.27 *(978-1-4042-4517-4(0)*, 328ab07f-49c9-4b2d-a54e-18f1727749b6) Rosen Publishing Group, Inc., The.

Miller, Connie Colwell. You're in Trouble: Fib or Truth? Assanelli, Victoria, illus. 2017. (Making Good Choices Ser.). (ENG.). 24p. (J). (gr. 1-4). lib. bdg. 20.95 *(978-1-68151-163-4(0)*, 14660) Amicus.

—You're in Trouble: Fib or Truth? 2018. (Making Good Choices Ser.). (ENG., Illus.). 24p. (J). (gr. k-3). pap. 10.99 *(978-1-68152-232-6(2)*, 14779) Amicus.

Naish, Sarah & Jefferies, Rosie. Charley Chatty & the Disappearing Pennies: A Story about Lying & Stealing. Evans, Megan, illus. 2017. (Therapeutic Parenting Bks.). (ENG.). 32p. (C). pap. 17.95 *(978-1-78592-303-6(X)*, 696533) Kingsley, Jessica Pubs. GBR. Dist: Hachette UK Distribution.

Perl, Erica S. Truth or Lie: Presidents! Slack, Michael, illus. 2019. (Step into Reading Ser.). (ENG.). 48p. (J). (gr. k-3). pap. 4.99 *(978-1-9848-9391-8(2)*, Random Hse. Bks. for Young Readers) Random Hse. Children's Bks.

Prather, Michelle Reneé. Deception: Why Do People Lie? 2018. (TIME(r): Informational Text Ser.). (ENG., Illus.). 48p. (J). (gr. 7-8). pap. 13.99 *(978-1-4258-5010-4(3))* Teacher Created Materials, Inc.

Rondina, Catherine. Lying: Deal with It Straight Up, 1 vol. Workman, Dan, illus. 2006. (Lorimer Deal with It Ser.). (ENG.). 32p. (J). (gr. 4-9). pap. 12.95 *(978-1-55028-906-0(3)*, a38dacf7-2e21-4b79-9de7-2e1eff41a717) James Lorimer & Co. Ltd., Pubs. CAN. Dist: Lerner Publishing Group.

Rothschild, Jennifer. Me, Myself, & Lies for Young Women: What to Say When You Talk to Yourself. 2017. (ENG.). 192p. (YA). (gr. 7-13). pap. 13.99 *(978-0-7369-6421-0(5)*, 6964210) Harvest Hse. Pubs.

Vermond, Kira & Hanmer, Clayton. Half-Truths & Brazen Lies: An Honest Look at Lying. 2016. (ENG., Illus.). 48p. (J). (gr. 3-7). 16.95 *(978-1-77147-146-6(8)*, Owlkids) Owlkids Bks. Inc. CAN. Dist: Publishers Group West (PGW).

Vranich, Belisa & Eagleson, Holly. Boys Lie: How Not to Get Played. 2010. (ENG.). 264p. (YA). (gr. 13-18). pap. 12.95 *(978-0-7573-1364-6(7)*, HCI Teens) Health Communications, Inc.

TRUTHFULNESS AND FALSEHOOD—FICTION

Alexan, Julie. Nolia Fasolia: Read-Along Book: Arabic & English. El-Ahraf, Amer, ed. Ceasar, Fady, illus. 2011. (ARA & ENG.). 48p. pap. 5.99 *(978-0-9844310-1-4(2))* BigKids Bilingual Bks.

Atwood, Megan. Olive Spins a Tale (and It's a Doozy!) Fleming, Lucy, illus. 2016. (Dear Molly, Dear Olive Ser.). (ENG.). 96p. (J). (gr. 1-3). lib. bdg. 21.99 *(978-1-4795-8695-0(1)*, 130931, Picture Window Bks.) Capstone.

Banning, Gail. Out on a Limb. 2008. (ENG.). 256p. (YA). (gr. 6-9). *(978-1-55470-012-7(4))* Me to We.

Beifus, Ruth. Shlavim Classics 2-in-1 Vol. 1: The Best Reward & the Taste of Truth. 2009. 32p. 14.99 *(978-1-59826-329-9(3))* Feldheim Pubs.

Blabey, Aaron. Pig the Fibber. 2018. (Pig the Pug Ser.). (ENG.). 32p. (J). (gr. -1-k). 14.99 *(978-1-338-29176-6(9)*, Scholastic Pr.) Scholastic, Inc.

Bodeen, S. A. The Compound. 2009. (Compound Ser.: 1). (ENG.). 272p. (YA). (gr. 7-12). pap. 10.99 *(978-0-312-57860-2(1)*, 900061807) Square Fish.

Bogart, Jo Ellen. The White Cat & the Monk: A Retelling of the Poem Pangur Bán, 1 vol. Smith, Sydney, illus. 2016. (ENG.). 36p. (J). (gr. -1-3). 18.95 *(978-1-55498-780-1(6))* Groundwood Bks. CAN. Dist: Publishers Group West (PGW).

Bourgeois, Paulette. Franklin Fibs. Clark, Brenda, illus. 2nd ed. 2011. (Franklin Ser.). (ENG.). 32p. (J). (gr. -1-3). pap. 6.99 *(978-1-55453-774-7(6))* Kids Can Pr., Ltd. CAN. Dist: Hachette Bk. Group.

Braxton-Smith, Ananda. Merrow. 2016. (ENG.). 240p. (YA). (gr. 9). 16.99 *(978-0-7636-7924-8(0))* Candlewick Pr.

Bright, J. E. The Brave Little Tailor: A Grimm & Gross Retelling. Banks, Timothy, illus. 2018. (Michael Dahl Presents: Grimm & Gross Ser.). (ENG.). 64p. (J). (gr. 3-5). lib. bdg. 21.99 *(978-1-4965-7315-5(3)*, 138919, Stone Arch Bks.) Capstone.

Carlson, Melody. Grover Tells a Whopper: A Scoozie Tale about Honesty. Fincher, Kathryn Andrews, illus. Date not set. 32p. (J). 9.99 *(978-0-7369-0733-0(5))* Harvest Hse. Pubs.

Cook, Julia. Well, I Can Top That!, Volume 1. DuFalla, Anita, illus. 2014. (Communicate with Confidence Ser.). (ENG.). 31p. (J). (gr. k-6). pap. 11.95 *(978-1-934490-57-0(1))* Boys Town Pr.

Curry, Kenneth. Chuka & the Drum. 2007. (Illus.). 22p. (J). 10.95 *(978-0-9798364-4-2(1))* Curry Brothers Publishing Group.

Dimplechin, Lord Reginald. McKenzie Was Here. 2012. 24p. pap. 24.95 *(978-1-4626-8674-2(5))* America Star Bks.

Dyan, Penelope. I Did It, & I Hid It! a Book about Taking Responsibility. Dyan, Penelope, illus. 2009. (Illus.). 44p. pap. 11.95 *(978-1-935118-68-8(4))* Bellissima Publishing, LLC.

Eason, Sarah. Come Clean, Carlos, 1 vol. 2013. (You Choose Ser.). (ENG.). 32p. (gr. 2-2). pap. 11.52 *(978-1-4644-0557-0(3)*, 1cb8a488-72d0-4cb3-8b02-ead9cb9a7320, Enslow Elementary) Enslow Publishing, LLC.

Garrelts, Christopher. Squarey Head Tells a Lie. Mayabb, Darrell, ed. 2003. (Adventures of Squarey Head Ser.: Bk. 1). (Illus.). 30p. (J). (gr. k-6). 4.95 *(978-0-9742003-0-9(1))* Squarey Head, Inc.

Gewirtz, Adina Rishe. Zebra Forest. 208p. (J). (gr. 4-7). 2014. (Illus.). pap. 8.99 *(978-0-7636-7166-2(5))* 2013. (ENG.). 15.99 *(978-0-7636-6041-3(8))* Candlewick Pr.

Hall, Kirsten. Little Lies: All about Math. Luedecke, Bev, illus. 2004. (Beastieville Ser.). (ENG.). 32p. (J). (gr. k-1). pap. 3.95 *(978-0-516-24656-7(9)*, Children's Pr.) Scholastic Library Publishing.

Hamilton, Martha & Weiss, Mitch. The Well of Truth: A Folktale from Egypt. Wrenn, Tom, illus. 2008. (Story Cove Ser.). (ENG.). 32p. (J). (gr. -1-3). pap. 4.95 *(978-0-87483-880-0(0))* August Hse. Pubs., Inc.

Hennessy, B. G. The Boy Who Cried Wolf. Kulikov, Boris, illus. 2006. (ENG.). 40p. (J). (gr. -1-3). 19.99 *(978-0-689-87433-8(2)*, Simon & Schuster Bks. For Young Readers) Simon & Schuster Bks. For Young Readers.

—The Boy Who Cried Wolf. Kulikov, Boris, illus. 2011. (J). (gr. -1-2). 29.95 *(978-0-545-09452-8(6))* Weston Woods Studios, Inc.

Hopkins, Cathy. The Princess of Pop. 2012. (Truth or Dare Ser.). (ENG.). 224p. (YA). (gr. 7). pap. 10.99 *(978-1-4424-6057-7(1)*, Simon Pulse) Simon Pulse.

House, E. A. The Truth #5. 2017. (Treasure Hunters Ser.). (ENG.). 184p. (YA). (gr. 5-12). 32.84 *(978-1-68076-880-0(8)*, 27448, Epic Escape) EPIC Pr.

Hughes, Huw John, tr. Cadi Deud Celwydd. 2005. (Storiau Crefyddol Religious Stories Ser.). (WEL., Illus.). 24p. pap. *(978-1-85994-517-9(1))* Cyhoeddiadau'r Gair.

Ivey, Lisa. The Christmas Tree That Didn't Get Picked. 2007. 64p. per. 19.95 *(978-1-4241-8276-3(X))* America Star Bks.

Keplinger, Kody. That's Not What Happened, 1 vol. (ENG.). 336p. (YA). (gr. 7). 2020. pap. 10.99 *(978-1-338-18653-6(1))* 2018. 18.99 *(978-1-338-18652-9(3)*, Scholastic Pr.) Scholastic, Inc.

Kropp, Paul. Winner! *(978-1-897039-31-1(X))* High Interest Publishing (HIP).

Kulick Triscila, Verne. Joel & the Magic Toy Tree. 2005. 36p. (J). 11.99 *(978-1-4116-6985-7(1))* Lulu Pr., Inc.

Kyi, Tanya Lloyd. Truth. 2004. (Orca Soundings Ser.). 108p. 19.95 *(978-0-7569-4346-2(9))* Perfection Learning Corp.

Lamb, Lenny. The Truth about Lying: Greener Grass Volume 3. 2012. 48p. 24.95 *(978-1-4626-5046-0(5))* America Star Bks.

Loewen, Nancy. The Boy Who Cried Wolf, Narrated by the Sheepish but Truthful Wolf. Moreno, Juan M., illus. 2018. (Other Side of the Fable Ser.). (ENG.). 24p. (J). (gr. -1-3). lib. bdg. 27.99 *(978-1-5158-2869-3(7)*, 138407, Picture Window Bks.) Capstone.

Mackinnon, Mairi. The Boy Who Cried Wolf. 2009. (First Reading Level 3 Ser.). 48p. (J). 6.99 *(978-0-7945-2472-2(9)*, Usborne) EDC Publishing.

T
U
V

McClintock, Norah. Tell. 2007. (Orca Soundings Ser.). 100p. (gr. 4-7). 19.95 *(978-0-7569-8069-6(0))* Perfection Learning Corp.

McConnaughhay, JoDee H. Tell the Truth, Tyler. Urbanovic, Jackie, illus. 2014. (Happy Day Ser.). (ENG.). 16p. (J). pap. 2.49 *(978-1-4143-9468-8(3)*, 4608458, Happy Day) Tyndale Hse. Pubs.

Moranville, Sharelle Byars. 27 Magic Words. (ENG.). 208p. (J). (gr. 3-7). 2018. pap. 7.99 *(978-0-8234-4034-4(6))* 2016. 16.95 *(978-0-8234-3657-6(8))* Holiday Hse., Inc.

O'Dell, Patrick Timothy Wayne. Elvin. 2009. 58p. pap. 16.95 *(978-1-61546-576-7(6))* America Star Bks.

Penn, Tony. The Misadventures of Michael McMichaels: The Creepy Campers, Vol. 3. Martin, Brian, illus. 2017. (Misadventures of Michael Mcmichaels Ser.: 3). (ENG.). 83p. (J). (gr. 1-6). pap. 7.95 *(978-1-944882-10-5(3))* Boys Town Pr.

Petrucci, Lou. Heart of the Hide. 2008. 320p. 22.95 *(978-1-4401-0102-1(7)*, iUniverse Star) iUniverse, Inc.

Picou, Lin. Who's Right. DuFalla, Anita, illus. 2012. (Little Birdie Bks.). (ENG.). 24p. (gr. 2-3). pap. 9.95 *(978-1-61810-323-9(7)*, 9781618103239) Rourke Educational Media.

Pincus, Greg. The 14 Fibs of Gregory K. 2013. (ENG.). 240p. (J). (gr. 3-7). 17.99 *(978-0-439-91299-0(7)*, Levine, Arthur A. Bks.) Scholastic, Inc.

Pincus, Gregory K. The 14 Fibs of Gregory K. 2013. 226p. (J). pap. *(978-0-439-91300-3(4)*, Levine, Arthur A. Bks.) Scholastic, Inc.

Rayner, Robert. Suspended, 1 vol. 2004. (Lorimer Sports Stories Ser.). (ENG.). 112p. (J). (gr. 4-8). 16.95 *(978-1-55028-861-2(X)*, 861) James Lorimer & Co. Ltd., Pubs. CAN. Dist: Formac Lorimer Bks. Ltd.

Reynolds, Betty. Little Lies. 2012. 102p. pap. 7.99 *(978-0-9856724-0-9(4))* Personal.

Rippin, Sally. The Little Lie. Fukuoka, Aki, illus. 2014. (Billie B. Brown Ser.). (ENG.). 43p. (J). *(978-1-61067-291-7(7))* Kane Miller.

Robins, Eleanor. No Limits, 1 vol. unabr. ed. 2011. (Choices Ser.). (ENG.). 52p. (YA). (gr. 5-12). 9.75 *(978-1-61651-598-0(8))* Saddleback Educational Publishing, Inc.

Ross, Jill. What's the Matter, Mr. Ticklebritches? Pruitt, Gwendolyn, illus. 2010. (ENG.). 70p. (J). (gr. 3-7). pap. 9.95 *(978-1-59825-948-3(2))* Shenanigans Series.

Sargeant, Glen. Finders Keepers, 1 vol. 2009. 142p. pap. 24.95 *(978-1-61582-202-7(X))* America Star Bks.

Seal, Vickie Di-Ann. Edgar Tells the Truth. 2012. 26p. 24.95 *(978-1-4626-0976-5(7))* America Star Bks.

Self, Jeffery. A Very, Very Bad Thing. 2017. (ENG.). 240p. (YA). (gr. 9). 17.99 *(978-1-338-11840-7(4)*, PUSH) Scholastic, Inc.

Shepard, Sara. Ali's Pretty Little Lies. 2013. (Pretty Little Liars Ser.). (YA). lib. bdg. 20.85 *(978-0-606-35048-8(9))* Turtleback.

—Pretty Little Liars: Ali's Pretty Little Lies. 2013. (Pretty Little Liars Companion Novel Ser.). (ENG.). (YA). (gr. 9). 320p. pap. 10.99 *(978-0-06-223337-0(8))*; 304p. 17.99 *(978-0-06-223336-3(X))* HarperCollins Pubs. (HarperTeen).

Simon, Mary Manz. Piglet Tells the Truth. Stott, Dorothy, illus. 2006. (First Virtues for Toddlers Ser.). 20p. (J). 5.99 *(978-0-7847-1407-2(X)*, 04035) Standard Publishing.

Sommer, Carl. No One Will Ever Know. Westbrook, Dick, illus. 2003. (Another Sommer-Time Story Ser.). (ENG.). 48p. (J). (gr. 1-4). 16.95 incl. audio compact disk *(978-1-57537-506-9(0))* Advance Publishing, Inc.

—Tied up in Knots. Budwine, Greg, illus. 2003. (Another Sommer-Time Story Ser.). (ENG.). 48p. (J). 16.95 incl. audio compact disk *(978-1-57537-503-8(6))* Advance Publishing, Inc.

—Tied up in Knots. 2003. (Another Sommer-Time Story Ser.). (Illus.). 48p. (J). (gr. 1-4). 16.95 incl. audio *(978-1-57537-552-6(4))* Advance Publishing, Inc.

Staunton, Ted. Morgan & the Money. Slavin, Bill, illus. 2008. (First Novel Ser.). (ENG.). 64p. (J). (gr. 1-5). *(978-0-88780-776-3(3))* Formac Publishing Co., Ltd.

—Morgan & the Money, 1 vol. 2008. (Formac First Novels Ser.). (ENG., Illus.). 64p. (gr. 1-5). 4.95 *(978-0-88780-774-9(7)*, 774) Formac Publishing Co., Ltd. CAN. Dist: Formac Lorimer Bks. Ltd.

Undercuffler, Gary, illus. The Boy Who Cried Wolf: A Tale about Telling the Truth. 2006. (Famous Fables Ser.). (J). 6.99 *(978-1-59939-026-0(4))* Cornerstone Pr.

Weigl Publishers, creator. The Shoemaker & His Medicine: Why Should You Tell the Truth? 2013. (AV2 Animated Storytime Ser.: Vol. 18). (ENG., Illus.). 32p. (J). (gr. -1-3). lib. bdg. 29.99 *(978-1-62127-922-8(7)*, AV2 by Weigl) Weigl Pubs., Inc.

Winter, Jonah. The Sad Little Fact. Oswald, Pete, illus. 2019. 40p. (J). (gr. -1-2). 17.99 *(978-0-525-58179-6(0)*, Schwartz & Wade Bks.) Random Hse. Children's Bks.

TUAREGS

Reynolds, Jan. Sahara, 1 vol. 2007. (Vanishing Cultures Ser.). (ENG., Illus.). 32p. *(978-1-60060-146-0(4))*; (J). 11.95 *(978-1-60060-131-6(6)*, leelowbooks) Lee & Low Bks., Inc.

TUBA—FICTION

Bartlett, T. C. Tuba Lessons. Felix, Monique, illus. 2010. (ENG.). 32p. (J). (gr. k-3). 17.95 *(978-1-56846-209-7(3)*, 22071, Creative Editions) Creative Co., The.

Tripp, Paul. Tubby the Tuba. Cole, Henry, illus. 2006. 32p. (J). (gr. -1-3). 17.99 *(978-0-525-47717-4(9)*, Dutton Books for Young Readers) Penguin Young Readers Group.

Wilbur, Helen L. A Tuba Christmas. Uhles, Mary Reaves, illus. 2018. (ENG.). 32p. (J). (gr. k-2). 16.99 *(978-1-58536-384-1(7)*, 204580) Sleeping Bear Pr.

Zeppa, Talaylin. Teddy the Tub. 2011. 32p. pap. 32.70 *(978-1-4568-6908-3(6))* Xlibris Corp.

TUBMAN, HARRIET, 1822-1913

Abnett, Dan. Harriet Tubman & the Underground Railroad. (Jr. Graphic Biographies Ser.). (ENG.). 24p. (J). (gr. 2-3). 2009. 47.90 *(978-1-61513-816-6(1)*, PowerKids Pr.) 2006. (Illus.). pap. 10.60 *(978-1-4042-2146-8(8)*, 1e1e4fac-305d-4a55-a5ea-272406655f1b, PowerKids Pr.) 2006. (Illus.). lib. bdg. 28.93 *(978-1-4042-3393-5(8)*, faf3f8b3-291f-45bf-a467-b7772adb82ea) Rosen Publishing Group, Inc., The.

—Harriet Tubman y el Ferrocarril Clandestino, 1 vol. 2009. (Historietas Juveniles: Biografías (Jr. Graphic Biographies) Ser.). (SPA., Illus.). 24p. (J). (gr. 2-3). 28.93 *(978-1-4358-8563-9(5)*, 23c71f0e-1635-4a3c-be85-311206bd48c0); pap. 10.60 *(978-1-4358-3320-3(1)*, c5f7e9e3-e763-46ae-87d5-410dd4478a6b) Rosen Publishing Group, Inc., The.

Adler, David A. A Picture Book of Harriet Tubman. Byrd, Samuel, illus. unabr. ed. 2005. (Picture Book Readalong Ser.). (J). (gr. k-4). 25.95 incl. audio *(978-1-59519-381-0(2))*; 28.95 incl. audio compact disk *(978-1-59519-385-8(5))*;Set. pap. 37.95 incl. audio *(978-1-59519-382-7(0))*;Set. pap. 39.95 incl. audio compact disk *(978-1-59519-386-5(3))* Live Oak Media.

Agard, Sandra A. Trailblazers: Harriet Tubman: A Journey to Freedom. 2019. (Trailblazers Ser.). (ENG., Illus.). 192p. (J). (gr. 3-7). 7.99 *(978-0-593-12407-9(3))*; lib. bdg. 12.99 *(978-0-593-12408-6(1))* Random Hse. Children's Bks. (Random Hse. Bks. for Young Readers).

Allen, Thomas B. Harriet Tubman, Secret Agent: How Daring Slaves & Free Blacks Spied for the Union During the Civil War. 2008. (Illus.). 192p. (J). (gr. 5-9). 5.95 *(978-1-4263-0401-9(3)*, National Geographic Kids) Disney Publishing Worldwide.

Allen, Thomas B. & Allen, Thomas. Harriet Tubman, Secret Agent (Direct Mail Edition) How Daring Slaves & Free Blacks Spied for the Union During the Civil War. 2006. (ENG., Illus.). 192p. (J). (gr. 5-9). 16.95 *(978-0-7922-7889-4(5))* National Geographic Society.

Anderson, Jane. Harriet Tubman & the Underground Railroad. 2005. (J). pap. *(978-1-4108-4202-2(9))* Benchmark Education Co.

Auch, Allison. Women Who Dared & Mujeres que se Atrevieron: 6 English, 6 Spanish Adaptations. 2011. (ENG & SPA.). (J). 97.00 net. *(978-1-4108-5692-0(5))* Benchmark Education Co.

Bauer, Marion Dane. Harriet Tubman. Lyon, Tammie, illus. 2010. (My First Biography Ser.). (ENG.). 32p. (J). (gr. -1-3). 16.19 *(978-0-545-23257-9(0))* Scholastic, Inc.

Baumann, Susan K. Harriet Tubman, 1 vol. 2013. (Jr. Graphic African American History Ser.). (ENG., Illus.). 24p. (J). (gr. 2-3). 28.93 *(978-1-4777-1312-9(3)*, 5857a12b-5a9e-48cd-8def-0baf9168c30b); pap. 11.60 *(978-1-4777-1449-2(9)*, 6d3e3e76-88e9-4073-a428-cdc6f9f55c07) Rosen Publishing Group, Inc., The. (PowerKids Pr.).

—Harriet Tubman: Conductor of the Underground Railroad. 2013. (Jr. Graphic African American History Ser.). (Illus.). 24p. (J). (gr. 3-6). pap. 63.60 *(978-1-4777-1450-8(2)*, PowerKids Pr.) Rosen Publishing Group, Inc., The.

Bennett, Doraine. Harriet Tubman. 2012. (Illus.). 24p. (J). *(978-1-935884-44-6(1))* State Standards Publishing, LLC.

Blue, Rose, et al. Harriet Tubman: Riding the Freedom Train. 2003. (Gateway Biographies Ser.: 4). (ENG., Illus.). 48p. (J). (gr. 4-8). lib. bdg. 26.60 *(978-0-7613-2571-0(9)*, Millbrook Pr.) Lerner Publishing Group.

Chipley Slavicek, Louise. Harriet Tubman & the Underground Railroad, 1 vol. 2006. (Lucent Library of Black History Ser.). (ENG., Illus.). 104p. (gr. 7-7). lib. bdg. 36.43 *(978-1-59018-927-6(2)*, 57368502-a57f-4f41-a791-2010e42c49f1, Lucent Pr.) Greenhaven Publishing LLC.

Cipriano, Jeri. Harriet Tubman: Union Spy. Brooks, Scott R., illus. 2018. (Hidden History — Spies Ser.). (ENG.). 32p. (J). (gr. 2-5). pap. 8.99 *(978-1-63440-297-2(9)*, 5e2c1d5c-d773-44e5-88c4-8055f5dbaba1); lib. bdg. 26.65 *(978-1-63440-284-2(7)*, 4952045c-b015-4ac4-8fd8-61bdf73e9075) Red Chair Pr.

Cline-Ransome, Lesa. Before She Was Harriet. Ransome, James E., illus. (ENG.). 32p. (J). (gr. -1-3). 2019. pap. 8.99 *(978-0-8234-4429-8(5))* 2017. 18.99 *(978-0-8234-2047-6(7))* Holiday Hse., Inc.

Clinton, Catherine. When Harriet Met Sojourner. Evans, Shane W., illus. 2007. (ENG.). 32p. (J). (gr. k-3). 16.99 *(978-0-06-050425-0(0)*, Tegen, Katherine Bks) HarperCollins Pubs.

Connors, Kathleen. The Life of Harriet Tubman, 1 vol., Vol. 1. 2013. (Famous Lives Ser.). (ENG., Illus.). 24p. (J). (gr. 1-2). 25.27 *(978-1-4824-0412-8(5)*, fec7aad9-ab27-4cc4-9ace-7cd2daa329e2) Stevens, Gareth Publishing LLLP.

Cosson, M. J. Harriet Tubman, 1 vol. 2007. (Essential Lives Set 1 Ser.). (ENG., Illus.). 112p. (YA). (gr. 6-12). lib. bdg. 41.36 *(978-1-59928-842-0(7)*, 6637, Essential Library) ABDO Publishing Co.

DeFord, Diane. Harriet Tubman. 2009. pap. 13.25 *(978-1-60559-061-5(4))* Hameray Publishing Group, Inc.

Devera, Czeena. Harriet Tubman SP. Bane, Jeff, illus. 2018. (My Early Library: Mi Mini Biografía (My Itty-Bitty Bio) Ser.). (SPA.). 24p. (J). (gr. k-1). lib. bdg. 30.64 *(978-1-5341-2997-9(9)*, 212036) Cherry Lake Publishing.

Dudley Gold, Susan. Harriet Tubman & the Underground Railroad, 1 vol. 2015. (Primary Sources of the Abolitionist Movement Ser.). (ENG., Illus.). 64p. (J). (gr. 6-6). 35.93 *(978-1-5026-0522-1(8)*, b2a4f659-f06c-40f8-acad-53f206119593) Cavendish Square Publishing LLC.

Edison, Erin. Harriet Tubman, 1 vol. 2013. (Great Women in History Ser.). (ENG.). 24p. (J). (gr. -1-2). pap. 6.29 *(978-1-62065-859-8(3)*, 121792); (gr. k-1). pap. 37.74 *(978-1-62065-860-4(7)*, 19427, Pebble) Capstone.

Feinstein, Stephen & Taylor, Charlotte. Harriet Tubman: Hero of the Underground Railroad, 1 vol. 2015. (Exceptional African Americans Ser.). (ENG.). 24p. (gr. 3-4). pap. 10.35 *(978-0-7660-7126-1(X)*, a9f5fbde-29ae-491f-83d3-78968c658080) Enslow Publishing, LLC.

Ganeri, Anita. Harriet Tubman: The Life of an African-American Abolitionist, 1 vol. Shone, Rob, illus. 2004. (Graphic Nonfiction Biographies Ser.). (ENG.). 48p. (gr. 4-6). pap. 14.05 *(978-1-4042-5172-4(3)*, c18f7686-5d5e-4423-a6ef-da0119694c22) Rosen Publishing Group, Inc., The.

Gateway Christian Academy (Fort Lauderdale, Fla.) Staff & Juvenile Collection Staff, contrib. by. Letters from Minty: An Imaginative Look into the Life & Thoughts of a Young Harriet Tubman. 2016. (Illus.). 31p. (J). *(978-1-338-13424-7(8))* Scholastic, Inc.

Gayle, Sharon. Harriet Tubman & the Freedom Train. Marshall, Felicia, illus. 2005. (Ready-to-Read Ser.). 32p. (J). lib. bdg. 15.00 *(978-1-59054-960-5(0))* Fitzgerald Bks.

—Harriet Tubman & the Freedom Train: Ready-To-Read Level 3. Marshall, Felicia, illus. 2003. (Ready-To-Read Stories of Famous Americans Ser.). (ENG.). 32p. (J). (gr. 1-3). pap. 4.99 *(978-0-689-85480-4(3)*, Simon Spotlight) Simon Spotlight.

Gosman, Gillian. Harriet Tubman, 1 vol. 2011. (Life Stories Ser.). (ENG., Illus.). 24p. (J). (gr. 3-3). pap. 9.25 *(978-1-4488-2761-9(2)*, 81b82e2d-02e3-45ed-bd92-6f617d19e0c0, PowerKids Pr.); lib. bdg. 26.27 *(978-1-4488-2586-8(5)*, 2b2679ea-cfb1-4eca-836c-8a5dfb5868f9, PowerKids Pr.); lib. bdg. 26.27 *(978-1-4488-3220-0(9)*, 97d663d2-94f7-478c-b5fa-c7679ce2a0f5) Rosen Publishing Group, Inc., The.

Hale, Nathan. The Underground Abductor. 2017. (Nathan Hale's Hazardous Tales Ser.). (J). lib. bdg. 24.45 *(978-0-606-40708-3(1))* Turtleback.

—The Underground Abductor (Nathan Hale's Hazardous Tales #5) An Abolitionist Tale about Harriet Tubman. 2015. (Nathan Hale's Hazardous Tales Ser.). (ENG., Illus.). 128p. (J). (gr. 3-9). 14.99 *(978-1-4197-1536-5(4)*, 1103801) Abrams, Inc.

Hohn, Nadia L. Harriet Tubman: Freedom Fighter. Mazali, Gustavo, illus. 2018. (I Can Read Level 2 Ser.). (ENG.). 32p. (J). (gr. -1-3). 16.99 *(978-0-06-243285-8(0))*; pap. 4.99 *(978-0-06-243284-1(2))* HarperCollins Pubs. (HarperCollins).

Kernan, Elizabeth. Harriet Tubman: A Lesson in Bravery. 2009. (Reading Room Collection 2 Ser.). 24p. (gr. 3-4). 42.50 *(978-1-60851-966-8(X)*, PowerKids Pr.) Rosen Publishing Group, Inc., The.

Kramer, Barbara. National Geographic Readers: Harriet Tubman (L2) 2019. (Readers Ser.). (Illus.). 32p. (J). (gr. 1-3). pap. 4.99 *(978-1-4263-3721-5(3)*, National Geographic Kids) Disney Publishing Worldwide.

Lantier, Patricia. Harriet Tubman: Conductor on the Underground Railroad, 1 vol. 2009. (Voices for Freedom Ser.). (ENG., Illus.). 64p. (J). (gr. 5-8). pap. *(978-0-7787-4838-0(3))*; lib. bdg. *(978-0-7787-4822-9(7))* Crabtree Publishing Co.

Leavitt, Amie Jane. Harriet Tubman. 2007. (What's So Great About... ? Ser.). (Illus.). 32p. (J). (gr. 2-4). lib. bdg. 25.70 *(978-1-58415-577-5(9))* Mitchell Lane Pubs.

Levy, Janey. Harriet Tubman, 1 vol. 2020. (Heroes of Black History Ser.). (ENG.). 32p. (J). (gr. 3-4). pap. 11.50 *(978-1-5382-5814-9(5)*, 20d86b14-ede0-4eff-8674-8fe38633554b) Stevens, Gareth Publishing LLLP.

Maloof, Torrey. Harriet Tubman: Leading Others to Liberty. rev. ed. 2017. (Social Studies: Informational Text Ser.). (ENG., Illus.). 32p. (J). (gr. 4-8). pap. 11.99 *(978-1-4938-3802-8(4))* Teacher Created Materials, Inc.

Mara, Wil. Rookie Biographies: Harriet Tubman. 2013. (Rookie Biographies(r) Ser.). (ENG., Illus.). 32p. (J). lib. bdg. 23.00 *(978-0-531-24737-2(6))* Scholastic Library Publishing.

Martin, Michael J. Harriet Tubman & the Underground Railroad, 1 vol. Hoover, Dave & Anderson, Bill, illus. 2005. (Graphic History Ser.). (ENG.). 32p. (J). (gr. 3-9). per. 8.10 *(978-0-7368-5245-6(X)*, 86991, Capstone Pr.) Capstone.

McDonnell, Julia. Harriet Tubman in Her Own Words, 1 vol. 2015. (Eyewitness to History Ser.). (ENG., Illus.). 32p. (J). (gr. 4-5). pap. 11.50 *(978-1-4824-4066-9(0)*, ab6258de-79e3-425e-b245-fc71bfbeadb3) Stevens, Gareth Publishing LLLP.

McDonough, Yona Zeldis. Who Was Harriet Tubman? 2004. (ENG., Illus.). 106p. (J). lib. bdg. 13.00 *(978-1-4242-2135-6(8))* Dingles & Co.

—Who Was Harriet Tubman? Harrison, Nancy, illus. 2003. (Who Was... ? Ser.). 106p. (gr. 4-7). 15.00 *(978-0-7569-1590-2(2))* Perfection Learning Corp.

McDonough, Yona Zeldis & Who HQ. Who Was Harriet Tubman? Harrison, Nancy, illus. 2019. (Who Was? Ser.). 112p. (J). (gr. 3-7). 5.99 *(978-0-593-09722-9(X))*; 15.99 *(978-0-593-09723-6(8))* Penguin Young Readers Group. (Penguin Workshop).

Meltzer, Brad. I Am Harriet Tubman. Eliopoulos, Christopher, illus. 2018. (Ordinary People Change the World Ser.). 40p. (J). (gr. k-4). 16.99 *(978-0-7352-2871-9(X)*, Dial Bks) Penguin Young Readers Group.

Norwich, Grace. I Am Harriet Tubman. Simon, Ute, illus. 2013. 127p. (J). *(978-0-545-61344-6(2))* Scholastic, Inc.

—I Am Harriet Tubman (I Am #6) Simon, Ute, illus. 2013. (I Am Ser.: 6). (ENG.). 128p. (J). (gr. 3-5). pap. 5.99 *(978-0-545-48436-7(7)*, Scholastic Paperbacks) Scholastic, Inc.

Pace, Lorenzo. Harriet Tubman & My Grandmother's Quilts, 1 vol. 2015. (African American Quartet Ser.). (ENG., Illus.). 48p. (J). (gr. 2-3). 32.93 *(978-1-4777-9289-6(9)*, 809f909e-11f1-4769-91da-ad44e05b152a, Windmill Bks.) Rosen Publishing Group, Inc., The.

Patterson, Marie. Harriet Tubman, 1 vol. rev. ed. 2005. (Social Studies: Informational Text Ser.). (ENG.). 24p. (gr. 4-8). pap. 10.99 *(978-0-7439-8912-1(0))* Teacher Created Materials, Inc.

Petry, Ann. Harriet Tubman: Conductor on the Underground Railroad. 2018. (ENG.). 272p. (J). (gr. 3-7). 16.99 *(978-0-06-269130-9(9))*; pap. 9.99 *(978-0-06-266826-4(9))* HarperCollins Pubs. (Amistad).

Petry, Ann & Reynolds, Jason. Harriet Tubman: Conductor on the Underground Railroad. 2007. (ENG.). 256p. (J). (gr. 3-7). pap. 7.99 *(978-0-06-446181-8(5)*, Amistad) HarperCollins Pubs.

Raum, Elizabeth. The Life of Harriet Tubman. 2019. (Sequence Change Maker Biographies Ser.). (ENG.). 32p. (J). (gr. 2-5). lib. bdg. *(978-1-68151-676-9(4)*, 10808) Amicus.

Rausch, Monica. Harriet Tubman, 1 vol. 2007. (Great Americans Ser.). 24p. (J). (gr. 2-4). (ENG.). pap. 9.15 *(978-0-8368-7693-2(8)*, 4353d179-8f76-4e6a-a060-e37e98de4633, Weekly Reader Leveled Readers); (SPA & ENG., Illus.). lib. bdg. 24.67 *(978-0-8368-7985-8(6)*, 37c3334d-c56d-49f8-a22f-710f4fba4f8b); (ENG., Illus.). lib. bdg. 24.67 *(978-0-8368-7686-4(5)*, 71172d49-c35b-42d9-9142-6c544f8c12fc, Weekly Reader Leveled Readers) Stevens, Gareth Publishing LLLP.

Sawyer, Kem Knapp. Harriet Tubman. 2010. (DK Biography Ser.). (ENG., Illus.). 128p. (J). (gr. 5-8). 18.69 *(978-0-7566-5807-6(1))* Dorling Kindersley Publishing, Inc.

Schraff, Anne. The Life of Harriet Tubman: Moses of the Underground Railroad, 1 vol. 2014. (Legendary African Americans Ser.). (ENG., Illus.). 96p. (J). (gr. 6-7). 31.61 *(978-0-7660-6137-8(X)*, 5842c0c2-69d9-4654-adef-59a5d8989371) Enslow Publishing, LLC.

Shone, Rob. Harriet Tubman: The Life of an African-American Abolitionist. 2009. (Graphic Nonfiction Biographies Ser.). (ENG.). 48p. (YA). (gr. 4-5). 58.50 *(978-1-61513-018-4(7)*, Rosen Reference) Rosen Publishing Group, Inc., The.

Shone, Rob & Ganeri, Anita. Harriet Tubman: The Life of an African-American Abolitionist, 1 vol. 2004. (Graphic Nonfiction Biographies Ser.). (ENG., Illus.). 48p. (J). (gr. 4-6). lib. bdg. 37.13 *(978-1-4042-0245-0(5)*, ba8a5d50-aee5-4c2c-802b-2ead9f0d0c2a) Rosen Publishing Group, Inc., The.

Skelton, Renee. Harriet Tubman A Woman of Courage. 2005. 2005p. (J). lib. bdg. 15.00 *(978-1-4242-0849-4(1))* Fitzgerald Bks.

—A Woman of Courage. 2005. (Time for Kids Ser.). (ENG., Illus.). 48p. (J). (gr. 2-4). pap. 3.99 *(978-0-06-057607-3(3))* HarperCollins Pubs.

Skelton, Renee & Time for Kids Editors. Time for Kids: A Woman of Courage. 2005. (Time for Kids Ser.). (ENG., Illus.). 48p. (J). 16.99 *(978-0-06-057608-0(1))* HarperCollins Pubs.

Stearns, Dan. Harriet Tubman & the Underground Railroad, 1 vol. 2005. (In the Footsteps of American Heroes Ser.). (ENG., Illus.). 64p. (J). (gr. 5-8). lib. bdg. 36.67 *(978-0-8368-6428-1(X)*, 0c93b9fc-79bf-476e-a6cc-85a9c820bfac, Gareth Stevens Secondary Library) Stevens, Gareth Publishing LLLP.

Stein, R. Conrad. Harriet Tubman: On My Underground Railroad I Never Ran My Train off the Track, 1 vol. 2008. (Americans: the Spirit of a Nation Ser.). (ENG., Illus.). 128p. (J). (gr. 5-6). lib. bdg. 35.93 *(978-0-7660-3481-5(X)*, f1675bad-1c07-4b76-adc6-eb89aa02c903) Enslow Publishing, LLC.

Stoltman, Joan. Harriet Tubman, 1 vol. 2017. (Little Biographies of Big People Ser.). (ENG.). 24p. (J). (gr. 1-2). pap. 9.15 *(978-1-5382-0923-3(3)*, 019cd048-f5b7-4135-9d4e-0594639408d7) Stevens, Gareth Publishing LLLP.

—Harriet Tubman, 1 vol. Garcia, Ana Maria, tr. 2017. (Pequeñas Biografías de Grandes Personajes (Little Biographies of Big People) Ser.). (SPA.). 24p. (J). (gr. 1-2). pap. 9.15 *(978-1-5382-1559-3(4)*, 885f27e3-a953-4d2e-9705-f3a7f168bf4c); lib. bdg. 24.27 *(978-1-5382-1532-6(2)*, 2e5b2b7a-3997-4773-aecd-9f20f001c9fc) Stevens, Gareth Publishing LLLP.

Susienka, Kristen. Harriet Tubman, 1 vol. 2019. (African American Leaders of Courage Ser.). (ENG.). 24p. (J). (gr. 1-2). pap. 9.25 *(978-1-7253-0838-1(X)*, bd382e70-5850-4e81-a8f1-6f6b909b71f2, PowerKids Pr.) Rosen Publishing Group, Inc., The.

Taylor, Marion. Harriet Tubman. 2004. (Black Americans of Achievement Legacy Edition Ser.). (ENG., Illus.). 112p. (J). (gr. 6-12). 35.00 *(978-0-7910-8166-2(4)*, P114170, Facts On File) Infobase Holdings, Inc.

Turner, Glennette Tilley. An Apple for Harriet Tubman. Keeter, Susan, illus. 2016. (ENG.). 24p. (J). (gr. -1-3). pap. 7.99 *(978-0-8075-0396-6(7)*, 807503967) Whitman, Albert & Co.

Waxman, Laura Hamilton. How Did Slaves Find a Route to Freedom? And Other Questions about the Underground Railroad. 2011. (Six Questions of American History Ser.). (ENG.). 48p. (gr. 4-6). pap. 56.72 *(978-0-7613-7641-5(0))*; (Illus.). (J). lib. bdg. 30.65 *(978-0-7613-5229-7(5)*, c97e1afb-3b6e-49d9-bb44-63d8c24cf045, Lerner Pubns.) Lerner Publishing Group.

Weatherford, Carole Boston. Moses: When Harriet Tubman Led Her People to Freedom (Caldecott Honor Book) Nelson, Kadir, illus. 2006. (ENG.). 48p. (J). (gr. -1-3). 18.99 *(978-0-7868-5175-1(9)*, Jump at the Sun) Hyperion Bks. for Children.

Weidt, Maryann N. Harriet Tubman. 2003. (History Maker Bios Ser.). (Illus.). 47p. (J). 26.60 *(978-0-8225-4676-4(0)*, Lerner Pubns.) Lerner Publishing Group.

Wheeler, Jill C. Harriet Tubman. 2003. (Breaking Barriers Ser.). (Illus.). 64p. (J). (gr. 3-8). 27.07 *(978-1-57765-908-2(2)*, Abdo & Daughters) ABDO Publishing Co.

TUBMAN, HARRIET, 1822-1913—FICTION

Grimes, Nikki. Chasing Freedom: the Life Journeys of Harriet Tubman & Susan B. Anthony, Inspired by Historical Facts. Wood, Michele, illus. 2015. (ENG.). 56p. (J). (gr. 1-5). 21.99 *(978-0-439-79338-4(6)*, Orchard Bks.) Scholastic, Inc.

Hedstrom-Page, Deborah. From Slavery to Freedom with Harriet Tubman. Martinez, Sergio, illus. 2007. (My American Journey Ser.). 84p. (J). (gr. 3-9). 9.99 *(978-0-8054-3268-8(X))* B&H Publishing Group.

TUGBOATS

Garland, Michael. Tugboat. (I Like to Read Ser.). (ENG.). 32p. (J). (gr. -1-3). 2018. 7.99 *(978-0-8234-3981-2(X))* 2014. (Illus.). 16.95 *(978-0-8234-2866-3(4))* Holiday Hse., Inc.

TUGBOATS—FICTION

Braun, Sebastien. Toot & Pop! Braun, Sebastien, illus. 2012. (ENG., Illus.). 32p. (J). (gr. -1-2). 12.99 *(978-0-06-207750-9(3)*, HarperCollins) HarperCollins Pubs.

Capucilli, Alyssa Satin. Mighty Tug. Mottram, David, illus. 2018. (ENG.). 40p. (J). (gr. -1-3). 17.99 *(978-1-4814-7681-2(5)*, Simon & Schuster/Paula Wiseman Bks.) Simon & Schuster/Paula Wiseman Bks.

Depken, Kristen L. Scuffy the Tugboat. DiCicco, Sue, illus. 2017. (Step into Reading Ser.). 32p. (J). (gr. -1-1). 4.99 *(978-1-101-93929-1(X)*, Random Hse. Bks. for Young Readers) Random Hse. Children's Bks.

Donaldson, Leo. Toby's Big Surprise. 2009. (Illus.). 52p. pap. 20.49 *(978-1-4389-4739-6(9))* AuthorHouse.

Edgar, Robert. Tom Tuff to the Rescue. Sharp, Todd, illus. 2013. 26p. pap. *(978-0-9874832-0-1(X))* MoshPit Publishing.

Gramatky, Hardie. Little Toot. Gramatky, Hardie, illus. 2007. (Little Toot Ser.). (Illus.). 104p. (J). (gr. -1-2). 17.99 *(978-0-399-24713-2(0),* G.P. Putnam's Sons Books for Young Readers) Penguin Young Readers Group.

Harris-Davies, Dafydd, et al. Caleb a Tyg. 2005. (WEL., Illus.). 24p. pap. *(978-0-86381-854-7(4))* Gwasg Carreg Gwalch.

McMullan, Kate. I'm Mighty! McMullan, Jim, illus. 2003. (ENG.). 40p. (J). (gr. -1-3). 17.99 *(978-0-06-009290-0(4),* HarperCollins) HarperCollins Pubs.

Watts, Kevin Bradley. Ben & the Mysterious Sound: Series: the Adventures of Tug Boat Ben. 2007. (Illus.). 32p. (J). *(978-0-9782625-2-5(2));* pap. *(978-0-9782625-1-8(4))* Alderney Publishing, Inc.

TUMBLING

Mullarkey, Lisa. Cheerleading Stunts & Tumbling, 1 vol. 2010. (Ready, Set, Cheer! Ser.). (ENG., Illus.). 48p. (gr. 5-7). pap. 11.53 *(978-1-59845-200-6(2),* 34319198-6eb3-4876-bc55-e5d4252f4d04); lib. bdg. 27.93 *(978-0-7660-3537-9(9),* aa963598-ceb8-4c48-969a-17826886ac45) Enslow Publishing, LLC.

TUNISIA

Carew-Miller, Anna. Tunisia. 2010. (Major Muslim Nations Ser.). 120p. (YA). (gr. 5-18). lib. bdg. 25.95 *(978-1-4222-1393-3(5))* Mason Crest.

Grolier Educational Staff, contrib. by. Argentina. 2003. (Illus.). 32p. (J). 309.00 *(978-0-7172-5788-1(6),* Grolier) Scholastic Library Publishing.

Newsome, Joel. Hannibal, 1 vol. 2017. (Great Military Leaders Ser.). (ENG.). 128p. (YA). (gr. 9-9). 47.36 *(978-1-5026-2869-5(4),* 5a9f24ae-5483-45ea-b2fb-6d1680e49a8f) Cavendish Square Publishing LLC.

Varghese Brown, Roslind & Spilling, Michael. Tunisia, 1 vol. 2nd rev. ed. 2009. (Cultures of the World (Second Edition)(r) Ser.). (ENG., Illus.). 144p. (gr. 5-5). lib. bdg. 49.79 *(978-0-7614-3037-7(7),* 3fe5e37b-ba2f-4eef-ab93-b6e9168addff) Cavendish Square Publishing LLC.

Varghese Brown, Roslind, et al. Tunisia, 1 vol. 2017. (Cultures of the World (Third Edition)(r) Ser.). (ENG.). 144p. (gr. 5-5). lib. bdg. 48.79 *(978-1-5026-3235-7(7),* e5f1c97a-d6b8-4b65-8593-1ff15156c53a) Cavendish Square Publishing LLC.

TUNISIA—FICTION

Colfer, Eoin. Benny & Omar. 2003. (ENG.). 240p. (YA). (gr. 5-18). pap. 7.95 *(978-0-86278-567-3(7))* O'Brien Pr., Ltd., The IRL. Dist: Independent Pubs. Group.

TUNNELS

see also Excavation; Subways

Bernhardt, Carolyn. Engineer It! Tunnel Projects. 2017. (Super Simple Engineering Projects Ser.). (ENG., Illus.). 32p. (J). (gr. k-4). lib. bdg. 34.21 *(978-1-5321-1127-3(4),* 25830, Super SandCastle) ABDO Publishing Co.

Blankenship, LeeAnn. 21st-Century Tunnels, 1 vol. 2018. (Feats of 21st-Century Engineering Ser.). (ENG.). 48p. (gr. 4-4). 29.60 *(978-0-7660-9712-4(9),* 359803a9-6c17-4cca-ae86-bf93e14000cf) Enslow Publishing, LLC.

Borchelt, Kelly L. The Longest Tunnel. 2004. (Extreme Places Ser.). (ENG., Illus.). 48p. (J). 27.50 *(978-0-7377-1882-9(X),* Greenhaven Pr., Inc.) Cengage Gale.

Crowther, Robert. Deep down under Ground: A Pop-up Book of Amazing Facts & Feats. Crowther, Robert, illus. 2004. (Illus.). 18p. (J). (gr. 3-8). reprint ed. pap. 22.00 *(978-0-7567-7179-9(X))* DIANE Publishing Co.

Donovan, Sandy. The Channel Tunnel. 2003. (Great Building Feats Ser.). (Illus.). 96p. (J). (gr. 5-9). 27.93 *(978-0-8225-4692-4(2))* Lerner Publishing Group.

Fine, Jil. The Chunnel: The Building of a 200-Year-Old Dream. 2004. (High Interest Bks.). (ENG.). 48p. (J). (gr. 7-12). pap. 6.95 *(978-0-516-25906-2(7),* Children's Pr.) Scholastic Library Publishing.

Franchino, Vicky. How Did They Build That? Tunnel. 2009. (Community Connections: How Did They Build That? Ser.). (ENG.). 24p. (gr. 2-5). lib. bdg. 29.21 *(978-1-60279-484-9(7),* 200260) Cherry Lake Publishing.

Graham, Ian. The Science of Bridges & Tunnels: the Art of Engineering (the Science of Engineering) (Library Edition) Vaisberg, Diego & Beach, Bryan, illus. 2019. (Science Of... Ser.). (ENG.). 32p. (J). (gr. 3-3). lib. bdg. 29.00 *(978-0-531-13199-2(8),* Watts, Franklin) Scholastic Library Publishing.

—Tremendous Tunnels. 2010. (Superstructures Ser.). 32p. (YA). (gr. 4-7). 28.50 *(978-1-60753-134-0(8))* Amicus Learning.

—Tremendous Tunnels. 2012. (What's in My Food Ser.). 32p. (gr. 1-4). lib. bdg. 27.10 *(978-1-59920-420-8(7))* Black Rabbit Bks.

Hardyman, Robyn. Tunnels, 1 vol. 2016. (Engineering Eurekas Ser.). (ENG.). 32p. (J). (gr. 3-4). pap. 11.00 *(978-1-4994-3109-4(0),* 268c28d5-0400-430a-91eb-9b7e2aee5436, PowerKids Pr.) Rosen Publishing Group, Inc., The.

Kenney, Karen Latchana. Building a Highway. 2020. (Sequence Amazing Structures Ser.). (ENG.). 32p. (J). (gr. 2-5). pap. 12.00 *(978-1-68152-560-0(7),* 10761) Amicus.

—Building a Tunnel. 2018. (Sequence Amazing Structures Ser.). (ENG.). 32p. (J). (gr. 2-5). pap. 9.99 *(978-1-68152-353-8(1),* 15168); lib. bdg. *(978-1-68151-433-8(8),* 15162) Amicus.

Loh-Hagan, Virginia. Tunnels. 2017. (21st Century Junior Library: Extraordinary Engineering Ser.). (ENG., Illus.). 24p. (J). (gr. 2-5). lib. bdg. 29.21 *(978-1-63472-167-7(5),* 209240) Cherry Lake Publishing.

Lusted, Marcia Amidon. Infrastructure of America's Tunnels. 2018. lib. bdg. 29.95 *(978-1-68020-150-5(6))* Mitchell Lane Pubs.

MacLeod, Elizabeth. Secrets Underground: North America's Buried Past. 2014. (ENG., Illus.). 96p. (YA). (gr. 5-12). pap. 14.95 *(978-1-55451-630-8(7),* 9781554516308) Annick Pr., Ltd. CAN. Dist: Publishers Group West (PGW).

—Secrets Underground: North America's Buried Past. Martchenko, Michael, illus. 2014. (ENG.). 96p. (YA). (gr. 5-12). 24.95 *(978-1-55451-631-5(5),* 9781554516315) Annick Pr., Ltd. CAN. Dist: Publishers Group West (PGW).

Mattern, Joanne. Tunnels. 2015. (Engineering Wonders Ser.). (ENG.). 48p. (gr. 3-6). 35.64 *(978-1-63430-420-7(9),* 9781634304207) Rourke Educational Media.

Mitchell, Susan. The Longest Tunnels, 1 vol. 2007. (Megastructures Ser.). (ENG., Illus.). 32p. (gr. 3-3). lib. bdg. 28.67 *(978-0-8368-8365-7(9),* e7ec3b9c-b9ea-4c96-9180-24682491f5a4) Stevens, Gareth Publishing LLLP.

Moore, Jeanette. Explore Tunnels! With 25 Great Projects. Crosier, Mike, illus. 2018. (Explore Your World Ser.). (ENG.). 96p. (J). (gr. 3-5). 19.95 *(978-1-61930-648-6(4),* caa42fb5-82d0-4a7f-a0bb-91bf3105286f) Nomad Pr.

Pettiford, Rebecca. Tunnels. 2015. (Illus.). 24p. (J). lib. bdg. *(978-1-62031-212-4(3))* Jump! Inc.

Polinsky, Paige V. Tunnels. 2017. (Engineering Super Structures Ser.). (ENG., Illus.). 24p. (J). (gr. -1-3). lib. bdg. 29.93 *(978-1-5321-1106-8(1),* 25788, SandCastle) ABDO Publishing Co.

Reilly, Kevin. Tunnels, 1 vol. 2019. (Exploring Infrastructure Ser.). (ENG.). 48p. (gr. 3-4). 29.60 *(978-1-9785-0338-0(5),* ed25b967-c665-4a07-880e-63232cc112c5) Enslow Publishing, LLC.

—Zoom in on Tunnels, 1 vol. 2017. (Zoom in on Engineering Ser.). (ENG.). 24p. (gr. 2-2). lib. bdg. 25.60 *(978-0-7660-8712-5(3),* f1c265c5-f6bb-4c8d-ac52-b73a702ad39a) Enslow Publishing, LLC.

Rose, Simon. Underground Transportation Systems. 2018. (Underground Worlds Ser.). (Illus.). 32p. (J). (gr. 4-4). *(978-0-7787-6127-3(4))* Crabtree Publishing Co.

Sikkens, Crystal. A Tunnel Runs Through. 2017. (Be an Engineer! Designing to Solve Problems Ser.). 24p. (J). (gr. 2-2). *(978-0-7787-2903-7(6))* Crabtree Publishing Co.

Spray, Sally. Awesome Engineering Tunnels. 2018. (Awesome Engineering Ser.). (ENG., Illus.). 32p. (J). (gr. 3-6). lib. bdg. 27.99 *(978-1-5435-1338-7(7),* 137769, Capstone Pr.) Capstone.

Stefoff, Rebecca. Building Tunnels, 1 vol. 2015. (Great Engineering Ser.). (ENG.). 32p. (gr. 3-3). pap. 11.58 *(978-1-5026-0600-6(3),* 4ec93daa-24c4-4857-902d-0df335e042d2) Cavendish Square Publishing LLC.

Tan, Richard. The Bridges & Tunnels of New York City, 1 vol. 2011. (My Community Ser.). (ENG., Illus.). 12p. (gr. 2-2). pap. 6.95 *(978-1-4488-5717-3(1),* eadfb852-7d71-42eb-8d5d-e46d36f2c213, Rosen Classroom) Rosen Publishing Group, Inc., The.

Thomas, Mark. The Seikan Railroad Tunnel: World's Longest Tunnel. 2009. (Record-Breaking Structures Ser.). 24p. (gr. 1-2). 42.50 *(978-1-60852-458-7(2),* PowerKids Pr.) Rosen Publishing Group, Inc., The.

—El Tunel Ferroviario Seikan: El Tunel Mas Largo Del Mundo, 1 vol. 2003. (Estructuras Extraordinarias (Record-Breaking Structures) Ser.). (SPA., Illus.). 24p. (J). (gr. 2-2). lib. bdg. 26.27 *(978-0-8239-6867-1(7),* 03dd83b8-80c6-4ca1-b28d-08b3cf62f7fe, Editorial Buenas Letras) Rosen Publishing Group, Inc., The.

—El túnel ferroviario Seikan: El túnel más largo del mundo (the Seikan Railroad Tunnel: World's Longest Tunnel) 2009. (Estructuras extraordinarias (Record-Breaking Structures) Ser.). (SPA.). 24p. (gr. 1-2). 42.50 *(978-1-61512-312-4(1),* Editorial Buenas Letras) Rosen Publishing Group, Inc., The.

Tunnels: Early Level Satellite Individual Title Six-Packs. (Sails Literacy Ser.). 16p. (gr. 1-2). 27.00 *(978-0-7578-2942-0(2))* Rigby Education.

Wolny, Philip. High Risk Construction Work: Life Building Skyscrapers, Bridges, & Tunnels, 1 vol. 2008. (Extreme Careers Ser.). (ENG., Illus.). 64p. (YA). (gr. 5-5). lib. bdg. 37.13 *(978-1-4042-1789-8(4),* 0960af74-fa6b-4f71-aea5-51c5e2f3c888) Rosen Publishing Group, Inc., The.

—High-Risk Construction Work: Life Building Skyscrapers, Bridges, & Tunnels. 2009. (Extreme Careers Ser.). 64p. (gr. 5-5). 58.50 *(978-1-61512-397-1(0),* Rosen Reference) Rosen Publishing Group, Inc., The.

TURKEY

Blomquist, Christopher. A Primary Source Guide to Turkey. (Countries of the World). 24p. (gr. 2-3). 2009. 42.50 *(978-1-61512-048-2(3))* 2004. (ENG., Illus.). (J). lib. bdg. 26.27 *(978-1-4042-2759-0(8),* 434cbb72-b538-41bb-b53d-f17749caf2d6) Rosen Publishing Group, Inc., The. (PowerKids Pr.).

Canino, Kate. Turkey Hunting, 1 vol. 2011. (Hunting: Pursuing Wild Game! Ser.). (ENG.). 64p. (YA). (gr. 5-5). pap. 13.95 *(978-1-4488-2274-4(2),* 56288cea-6e87-4b86-af69-debf55cc981b, Rosen Reference); (Illus.). lib. bdg. 37.13 *(978-1-4488-1244-8(5),* 8048d783-6bce-4538-bb03-ec2ab2c91b84) Rosen Publishing Group, Inc., The.

Cornell, Kari & Turkoglu, Nurcay. Cooking the Turkish Way. 2nd rev. ed. 2004. (Easy Menu Ethnic Cookbooks 2nd Edition Ser.). (ENG., Illus.). 72p. (gr. 5-12). 25.26 *(978-0-8225-4123-3(8),* Carolrhoda Bks.) Lerner Publishing Group.

Donaldson, Madeline. Turkey. 2011. (Country Explorers Ser.). 48p. pap. 51.02 *(978-0-7613-7628-6(3));* (ENG.). (gr. 2-4). 29.27 *(978-0-7613-6409-2(9))* Lerner Publishing Group.

Dyan, Penelope. A Step in Time — A Kid's Guide to Ephesus, Turkey. Weigand, John D., photos by. 2011. (Illus.). 40p. pap. 12.95 *(978-1-935630-57-9(1))* Bellissima Publishing, LLC.

—Turkish Delight — A Kid's Guide to Istanbul, Turkey. Weigand, John D., photos by. 2011. (Illus.). 44p. pap. 12.95 *(978-1-935630-54-8(7))* Bellissima Publishing, LLC.

Franchino, Vicky. It's Cool to Learn about Countries: Turkey. 2012. (Explorer Library: Social Studies Explorer Ser.). (ENG.). 48p. (gr. 4-8). pap. 15.64 *(978-1-61080-616-9(6),* 202226) Cherry Lake Publishing.

—It's Cool to Learn about Countries: Turkey. 2012. (Explorer Library: Social Studies Explorer Ser.). (ENG., Illus.). 48p. (gr. 4-8). 34.93 *(978-1-61080-442-4(2),* 202052) Cherry Lake Publishing.

Ganeri, Anita. Focus on Turkey, 1 vol. 2007. (World in Focus Ser.). (ENG.). 64p. (gr. 5-8). pap. 15.05 *(978-0-8368-6760-2(2),* 72804b90-b3b3-4422-aefc-b6b63b3a2ad9); (Illus.). lib. bdg. 36.67 *(978-0-8368-6753-4(X),* c58fac85-b228-47c6-a25c-d1702999deb1) Stevens, Gareth Publishing LLLP. (Gareth Stevens Secondary Library).

Harmon, Daniel E. Turkey. rev. ed. 2010. (Major Muslim Nations Ser.). (Illus.). 119p. (J). (gr. 4-8). 25.95 *(978-1-4222-1399-5(4))* Mason Crest.

Jackson, Elaine. Discover Turkey, 1 vol. 2011. (Discover Countries Ser.). (ENG., Illus.). 32p. (YA). (gr. 4-4). lib. bdg. 30.27 *(978-1-4488-5272-7(2),* 9cd5e0db-9f3d-4cbd-b78c-45cbdacf262e) Rosen Publishing Group, Inc., The.

Klepeis, Alicia. Understanding Turkey Today. 2014. (Illus.). 63p. (J). (gr. 3-6). 33.95 *(978-1-61228-649-5(6))* Mitchell Lane Pubs.

Kneib, Martha. Turkey: A Primary Source Cultural Guide, 1 vol. 2003. (Primary Sources of World Cultures Ser.). (ENG., Illus.). 128p. (J). (gr. 4-5). lib. bdg. 43.60 *(978-0-8239-3842-1(5),* cdb5ca12-84bc-4dd4-a712-81d74f7cbb84) Rosen Publishing Group, Inc., The.

Mattern, Joanne. Turkey, 1 vol. 2018. (Exploring World Cultures (First Edition) Ser.). (ENG.). 32p. (gr. 3-3). 31.64 *(978-1-5026-3818-2(5),* 45f1f854-73be-4121-9c2a-0ead5ead2870) Cavendish Square Publishing LLC.

McNeil, Niki, et al. HOCPP 1117 Turkey Time. 2006. spiral bd. 14.00 *(978-1-60308-117-7(8))* In the Hands of a Child.

Pavlovic, Zoran. Turkey. 2004. (Modern World Nations Ser.). (ENG., Illus.). 120p. (gr. 6-12). 35.00 *(978-0-7910-7916-4(3),* P114070, Facts On File) Infobase Holdings, Inc.

Roome, Hugh. Turkey. 2018. (Follow Me Around Ser.). (J). pap. 7.95 *(978-0-531-13861-8(5));* lib. bdg. 27.00 *(978-0-531-12919-7(5))* Scholastic Library Publishing. (Children's Pr.).

Schlitz, Laura Amy. The Hero Schliemann: The Dreamer Who Dug for Troy. Byrd, Robert, illus. 2013. (ENG.). 80p. (J). (gr. 4-7). pap. 8.99 *(978-0-7636-6504-3(5))* Candlewick Pr.

Sheehan, Sean. Turkey, 1 vol. 2nd rev. ed. 2004. (Cultures of the World (Second Edition)(r) Ser.). (ENG., Illus.). 144p. (gr. 5-5). lib. bdg. 49.79 *(978-0-7614-1705-7(2),* b0060e39-5440-49e0-85ce-3c080da5cd99) Cavendish Square Publishing LLC.

Stefoff, Rebecca. The Asian Empires, 1 vol. 2006. (World Historical Atlases Ser.). (ENG., Illus.). 48p. (gr. 5-5). 34.07 *(978-0-7614-1643-2(9),* a52d1b3a-98dc-4b83-b800-ac857b13767a) Cavendish Square Publishing LLC.

Zocchi, Judy. In Turkey. Brodie, Neale, illus. 2005. (Global Adventures II Ser.). 32p. (J). per. 10.95 *(978-1-59646-153-6(5))* Dingles & Co.

—In Turkey/en Turquía. Brodie, Neale, illus. 2005. (Global Adventures II Ser.).Tr. of En Turquía. (ENG & SPA.). 32p. (J). per. 10.95 *(978-1-59646-155-0(1))* Dingles & Co.

TURKEY—BIOGRAPHY

Kazerooni, Abbas. On Two Feet & Wings, 0 vols. 2014. (ENG.). 256p. (YA). (gr. 7-12). pap. 9.99 *(978-1-4778-2037-7(X),* 9781477820377, Skyscape) Amazon Publishing.

Samanci, Ozge. Dare to Disappoint: Growing up in Turkey. 2015. (ENG., Illus.). 200p. (YA). (gr. 9). pap. 21.99 *(978-0-374-31698-3(8),* 900078947, Farrar, Straus & Giroux (BYR)) Farrar, Straus & Giroux.

Schlesinger, Arthur M., ed. Recep Tayyip Erdogan. 2005. (Major World Leaders Ser.). (ENG., Illus.). 144p. (gr. 6-12). 30.00 *(978-0-7910-8263-8(6),* P114247, Facts On File) Infobase Holdings, Inc.

Stefoff, Rebecca. Redbeard. 2015. (J). lib. bdg. *(978-1-62713-533-7(2))* 2014. (ENG.). 48p. (gr. 4-4). 33.07 *(978-1-5026-0199-5(0),* e4b135dd-9834-4a92-bf28-59f105628332) Cavendish Square Publishing LLC.

Weintraub, Aileen. The Barbarossa Brothers: 16th-Century Pirates of the Barbary Coast. 2009. (Library of Pirates Ser.). 24p. (gr. 3-3). 42.50 *(978-1-60853-814-0(1),* PowerKids Pr.) Rosen Publishing Group, Inc., The.

TURKEY—FICTION

Alexander, Lloyd. The Xanadu Adventure. 2007. (Vesper Holly Ser.). (ENG.). 160p. (J). (gr. 5-18). 5.99 *(978-0-14-240786-8(0),* Puffin Books) Penguin Young Readers Group.

Amosky, Jim. I'm a Turkey! 2009. (Illus.). (J). *(978-0-545-22631-8(7),* Scholastic Pr.) Scholastic, Inc.

Cameron, Kristy. The Adventures of Herb the Wild Turkey - Herb Goes Camping. Shickle, Ian, illus. 2012. 38p. pap. *(978-0-9859790-0-3(3))* LP Publishing.

Duder, Tessa. Carpet of Dreams. Wilson, Mark, illus. 2008. 32p. pap. *(978-0-207-19991-2(4))* HarperCollins Pubs. Australia.

Durmush, F. Ayshe, an Anatolian Tale. 2007. (ENG.). 84p. per. *(978-1-84747-171-0(4))* Chipmunkapublishing.

Durston, George. Boy Scouts' Victory. 2005. pap. 26.95 *(978-1-885529-58-9(9))* Stevens Publishing.

Fenn, George. Yussuf the Guide or the Mountain Bandits: Being the Strange Story of the Travels in Asia Minor of Burne the Lawyer, Preston the Professor, & Lawrenn. Schönberg, John, illus. 2007. 424p. 26.95 *(978-0-9776786-6-2(0))* Salem Ridge Press LLC.

Fenn, George Manville. Yussuf the Guide or the Mountain Bandits: Being the Strange Story of the Travels in Asia Minor of Burne the Lawyer, Preston the Professor, & Lawrenc. Schönberg, John, illus. 2008. 432p. pap. 16.95 *(978-1-934671-20-7(7))* Salem Ridge Press LLC.

Katz, Karen. Where Is Baby's Turkey? A Karen Katz Lift-The-Flap Book. Katz, Karen, illus. 2017. (ENG., Illus.). 14p. (J). (gr. -1 — 1). bds. 7.99 *(978-1-5344-0089-4(3),* Little Simon) Little Simon.

Mandel, Muriel. A Donkey Reads, 1 vol. Letria, Andre, illus. 2011. (ENG.). 32p. (J). (gr. k-3). 16.95 *(978-1-59572-255-3(6));* pap. 6.95 *(978-1-59572-256-0(4))* Star Bright Bks., Inc.

Mein eigenes Auto. 2005. (GER.). 4.95 net. *(978-0-929724-89-8(5))* Command Performance Language Institute.

Mitchell, Jane. Without Refuge. 2018. (ENG.). 288p. (J). (gr. 4-7). 16.99 *(978-1-5415-0050-1(4),* bbf255d3-caab-431e-aef2-238a34400f75, Carolrhoda Bks.) Lerner Publishing Group.

Rains, Deborah Jane. Cuddles & Snuggles. 2011. 24p. pap. 24.95 *(978-1-4489-3917-6(8))* America Star Bks.

Sargent, Dave & Sargent, David, Jr. Tom Turkey: Don't Bully, 19, 20. Lenoir, Jane, illus. 2003. (Feather Tales Ser.: 20). 42p. (J). pap. 6.95 *(978-1-56763-758-8(2))* Ozark Publishing.

Skrypuch, Marsha Forchuk. Call Me Aram, 1 vol. Wood, Muriel, illus. 2008. (New Beginnings Ser.). (ENG.). 86p. (J). (gr. 4-6). 16.95 *(978-1-55455-000-5(9),* 7c62f834-f311-47df-9b12-d300eb5d35c9) Fitzhenry & Whiteside, Ltd. CAN. Dist: Firefly Bks., Ltd.

—Call Me Aram, 1 vol. Wood, Muriel, illus. 2008. (New Begininngs Ser.). (ENG.). 86p. (J). (gr. 4-6). pap. 9.95 *(978-1-55455-001-2(7),* db65e2ae-6abd-4783-9938-9a307fa1f9e3) Trifolium Bks., Inc. CAN. Dist: Firefly Bks., Ltd.

Thompson, Emma. The Christmas Tale of Peter Rabbit. Taylor, Eleanor, illus. 2013. (Peter Rabbit Ser.). (ENG.). 72p. (J). (gr. -1-2). 20.00 *(978-0-7232-7694-4(3),* Warne) Penguin Young Readers Group.

Whelan, Gloria. Parade of Shadows. 2007. 304p. (J). (gr. 5-18). lib. bdg. 16.89 *(978-0-06-089029-2(0))* HarperCollins Pubs.

White, Kiersten. Bright We Burn. 2019. (And I Darken Ser.: 3). (ENG., Illus.). 432p. (YA). (gr. 7). pap. 10.99 *(978-0-553-52242-6(6),* Ember) Random Hse. Children's Bks.

Winter, Barbara. Trapped in Gallipoli. 2007. (Illus.). 48p. (YA). lib. bdg. 15.00 *(978-1-4242-1643-7(5))* Dingles & Co.

TURKEY—HISTORY

Cline, Bev. Turkey. 2018. (J). *(978-1-5105-3570-1(5))* SmartBook Media, Inc.

—Turkey. 2014. (J). *(978-1-4896-3070-4(8))* Weigl Pubs., Inc.

Freedman, Jeri. The Armenian Genocide. 2009. (Genocide in Modern Times Ser.). 64p. (gr. 6-6). 58.50 *(978-1-61512-676-7(7))* Rosen Publishing Group, Inc., The.

Galat, Joan Marie. Cultural Traditions in Turkey. 2017. (Cultural Traditions in My World Ser.). (Illus.). 32p. (J). (gr. 2-3). *(978-0-7787-8100-4(3))* Crabtree Publishing Co.

Greenblatt, Miriam. Süleyman the Magnificent & the Ottoman Empire, 1 vol. 2003. (Rulers & Their Times Ser.). (ENG., Illus.). 80p. (gr. 6-6). 36.93 *(978-0-7614-1489-6(4),* 48cdd3b8-efa7-4e6c-9607-c7284779278c) Cavendish Square Publishing LLC.

Greenwood, Mark. The Donkey of Gallipoli: A True Story of Courage in World War I. Lessac, Frane, illus. 2008. (ENG.). 32p. (J). (gr. 1-4). 17.99 *(978-0-7636-3913-6(3))* Candlewick Pr.

Harmon, Daniel E. Turkey, Vol. 13. 2015. (Major Nations of the Modern Middle East Ser.). (Illus.). 120p. (J). (gr. 7). lib. bdg. 25.95 *(978-1-4222-3452-5(5))* Mason Crest.

Hawker, Frances & Alicavusoglu, Leyla. Islam in Turkey. Campbell, Bruce, photos by. 2009. (ENG., Illus.). 32p. (J). (gr. 3-6). *(978-0-7787-5009-3(4))* Crabtree Publishing Co.

Jeffrey, Gary. Gallipoli & the Southern Theaters, 1 vol. 2013. (ENG., Illus.). 48p. (J). pap. *(978-0-7787-0917-6(5))* Crabtree Publishing Co.

Kalman, Bobbie & Jeffrey, Gary. Gallipoli & the Southern Theaters. 2013. (ENG.). 48p. (J). *(978-0-7787-0911-4(6))* Crabtree Publishing Co.

Kneib, Martha. Turkey: A Primary Source Cultural Guide. 2009. (Primary Sources of World Cultures Ser.). 128p. (gr. 4-5). 79.90 *(978-1-60851-931-6(7))* Rosen Publishing Group, Inc., The.

LaRoche, Amelia. We Visit Turkey. 2011. (Your Land & My Land Ser.). (Illus.). 64p. (J). (gr. 4-7). lib. bdg. 33.95 *(978-1-58415-956-8(1))* Mitchell Lane Pubs.

Marsico, Katie. Farm Animals: Turkey. 2011. (21st Century Junior Library: Farm Animals Ser.). (ENG., Illus.). 24p. (gr. 2-4). lib. bdg. 29.21 *(978-1-60279-976-9(8),* 200942) Cherry Lake Publishing.

Murray, Julie. Turkey, 1 vol. 2014. (Explore the Countries Ser.). (ENG.). 40p. (J). (gr. 2-5). lib. bdg. 35.64 *(978-1-62403-348-3(2),* 1372, Big Buddy Bks.) ABDO Publishing Co.

Owings, Lisa. Turkey. 2011. (Exploring Countries Ser.). (ENG., Illus.). 32p. (J). (gr. 3-7). lib. bdg. 27.95 *(978-1-60014-625-1(2),* Blastoff! Readers) Bellwether Media.

Robbins, Gerald. The Ottoman & Qajar Empires in the Age of Reform. 2009. (Making of the Middle East Ser.). (Illus.). 80p. (YA). (gr. 7-18). lib. bdg. 22.95 *(978-1-4222-0167-1(8))* Mason Crest.

Steele, Philip. Turkey. 2015. (Emerging Nations Ser.). (ENG., Illus.). 48p. (J). (gr. 4-9). 37.10 *(978-1-59920-991-3(8))* Black Rabbit Bks.

Van Cleaf, Kristin. Turkey. 2008. (Countries Set 6 Ser.). 40p. (gr. k-6). 27.07 *(978-1-59928-787-4(0),* Checkerboard Library) ABDO Publishing Co.

World Book, Inc. Staff, contrib. by. Carved by Time. 2017. (Illus.). 40p. (J). *(978-0-7166-3365-5(5))* World Bk.-Childcraft International.

—The Mysteries of the Trojan War. 2014. (J). *(978-0-7166-2668-8(3))* World Bk., Inc.

Zocchi, Judy. In Turkey. Brodie, Neale, illus. 2005. (Global Adventures I Ser.). 32p. (J). pap. 10.95 *(978-1-59646-152-9(7));* lib. bdg. 21.65 *(978-1-59646-031-7(8))* Dingles & Co.

—In Turkey/en Turquía. Brodie, Neale, illus. 2005. (Global Adventures I Ser.).Tr. of En Turquía. (ENG & SPA.). 32p. (J). pap. 10.95 *(978-1-59646-154-3(3));* lib. bdg. 21.65 *(978-1-59646-032-4(6))* Dingles & Co.

TURKEYS

Carr, Aaron. Turkey. 2014. (Illus.). 24p. (J). *(978-1-62127-233-5(8))* Weigl Pubs., Inc.

Carter, Denzel T. All about Turkeys, 1 vol. 2015. (Rosen REAL Readers: STEM & STEAM Collection). (ENG.). 8p. (gr. k-1). pap. 5.46 *(978-1-4994-9692-5(3),* f87fa781-ce68-4970-b49b-294513f1c918, Rosen Classroom) Rosen Publishing Group, Inc., The.

Coffelt, Soraya Diase. It's Not about You, Mrs. Turkey: A Love Letter about the True Meaning of Thanksgiving. 2015. (Love Letters Book Ser.). (ENG., Illus.). 32p. (J). pap. 8.99 *(978-1-63047-636-6(6))* Morgan James Publishing.

Dicker, Katie. Turkeys. 2014. (Farm Animals Ser.). (Illus.). 24p. (gr. 2-5). 28.50 *(978-1-62588-025-3(1))* Black Rabbit Bks.

Dieker, Wendy. Turkeys. 2012. (Illus.). 24p. (J). lib. bdg. 25.65 *(978-1-62031-007-6(4))* Jump! Inc.

Endres, Hollie. Turkeys. 2007. (Farm Animals Ser.). (ENG., Illus.). 24p. (J). (gr. k-3). lib. bdg. 26.95 *(978-1-60014-086-0(6))* Bellwether Media.

Graubart, Norman D. How to Track a Turkey, 1 vol. 2014. (Scatalog: a Kid's Field Guide to Animal Poop Ser.). (ENG., Illus.). 24p. (J). (gr. 2-3). lib. bdg. 27.27 *(978-1-4777-5414-6(8),* 1a713d3c-c66a-44e8-9371-b1e14091374d, Windmill Bks.) Rosen Publishing Group, Inc., The.

Magby, Meryl. Wild Turkeys. 2013. (American Animals Ser.). 24p. (J). (gr. k-5). pap. 49.50 *(978-1-4777-0947-4(9));* (ENG.). (gr. 2-3). 26.27 *(978-1-4777-0787-6(5),* 3c743be6-1380-44a0-96db-428b0fa919b3); (ENG.). (gr. 2-3). pap. 9.25 *(978-1-4777-0946-7(0),* 170f93d2-050b-412c-bace-86c565668a9d) Rosen Publishing Group, Inc., The. (PowerKids Pr.).

Murray, Julie. Turkeys. 2019. (Animal Kingdom Ser.). (ENG.). 32p. (J). (gr. 2-5). lib. bdg. 34.21 *(978-1-5321-1656-8(X),* 32423, Big Buddy Bks.) ABDO Publishing Co.

Sabelko, Rebecca. Wild Turkeys. 2019. (North American Animals Ser.). (ENG., Illus.). 24p. (J). (gr. k-3). lib. bdg. 26.95 *(978-1-62617-914-1(X),* Blastoff! Readers) Bellwether Media.

Schuetz, Kari. Turkeys. 2018. (Animals on the Farm Ser.). (ENG., Illus.). 24p. (J). (gr. k-3). lib. bdg. 26.95 *(978-1-62617-727-7(9),* Blastoff! Readers) Bellwether Media.

Schuetz, Kristin. Wild Turkeys. 2014. (Backyard Wildlife Ser.). (ENG.). 24p. (J). (gr. k-3). lib. bdg. 26.95 *(978-1-60014-972-6(3),* Blastoff! Readers) Bellwether Media.

Siemens, Jared. Turkeys. 2017. (Illus.). 24p. (J). *(978-1-5105-0626-8(8))* SmartBook Media, Inc.

Statts, Leo. Turkeys. 2016. (Farm Animals Ser.). (ENG., Illus.). 24p. (J). (gr. -1-2). lib. bdg. 31.36 *(978-1-68079-908-8(8),* 24120, Abdo Zoom-Launch) ABDO Publishing Co.

Stiefel, Chana. Turkeys on the Family Farm, 1 vol. 2013. (Animals on the Family Farm Ser.). (ENG.). 24p. (gr. k-2). pap. 10.35 *(978-1-4644-0357-6(0),* ef852893-7f23-42f4-8e88-088d6b77ff87, Enslow Elementary); lib. bdg. 25.27 *(978-0-7660-4207-0(3),* 643a090c-aa9c-4318-8d4f-a3ada223fce2) Enslow Publishing, LLC.

Woodland, Faith. Turkeys. 2019. (J). *(978-1-7911-1644-6(2),* AV2 by Weigl) Weigl Pubs., Inc.

TURKEYS—FICTION

Allen, Christina. A Micro-Chip on my Shoulder: A True Story of a Little Poult. 2010. 28p. pap. 13.99 *(978-1-4490-6681-9(X))* AuthorHouse.

Balian, Lorna. Sometimes It's Turkey, Sometimes It's Feathers, 1 vol. Balian, Lecia, illus. 2003. (ENG.). 32p. (J). 14.95 *(978-1-932065-33-6(4));* pap. 5.95 *(978-1-932065-41-1(5))* Star Bright Bks., Inc.

Balsley, Tilda. Ten Hungry Turkeys, 1 vol. Stott, Dorothy & Richard, Ilene, illus. 2018. (ENG.). 32p. (J). (gr. -1-3). 16.99 *(978-1-4556-2235-1(4),* Pelican Publishing) Arcadia Publishing.

Bateman, Teresa. A Plump & Perky Turkey, 0 vols. Shelly, Jeff, illus. 2013. (ENG.). 32p. (J). (gr. -1-3). pap. 9.99 *(978-0-7614-5188-4(9),* 9780761451884, Two Lions) Amazon Publishing.

Berenstain, Mike, et al. The Berenstain Bears Give Thanks, 1 vol. Berenstain, Stan, illus. 2009. (Berenstain Bears/Living Lights: a Faith Story Ser.). (ENG.). 32p. (J). (gr. -1-2). pap. 4.99 *(978-0-310-71251-0(3))* Zonderkidz.

Bishop, Kimberly & Gray, Joyce. Sam, the Lollipop Turkey. 2018. (ENG., Illus.). 26p. (J). pap. 9.95 *(978-1-949231-58-8(5))* Yorkshire Publishing Group.

Bishop, Rhonda. Felix's Fabulous Feathers, 1 vol. Roberts, Gaylia, illus. 2009. 23p. pap. 24.95 *(978-1-60836-890-7(4))* America Star Bks.

Cazet, Denys. Bob & Tom. Cazet, Denys, illus. 2017. (ENG., Illus.). 40p. (J). (gr. -1-3). 17.99 *(978-1-4814-6140-5(0),* Atheneum/Richard Jackson Bks.) Simon & Schuster Children's Publishing.

Colandro, Lucille. There Was an Old Lady Who Swallowed a Turkey! Lee, Jared, illus. 2016. (ENG.). 32p. (J). (gr. -1-1). 6.99 *(978-0-545-93190-8(8),* Cartwheel Bks.) Scholastic, Inc.

Crissey, Brian L. The Loneliest Christmas Tree. Crissey, Noah, illus. 2004. (J). *(978-1-930724-12-9(8));* *(978-1-930724-13-6(6))* Granite Publishing, LLC.

Cumming, Wendy. How to Soar Like an Eagle When You Are Standing with the Turkeys. 2012. 32p. pap. 21.99 *(978-1-4797-2934-0(5))* Xlibris Corp.

Fronis, Aly. This Little Turkey. Blanco, Migy, illus. 2016. (ENG.). 16p. (J). (gr. -1-k). bds. 5.99 *(978-1-4998-0302-0(8))* Little Bee Books Inc.

Goodspeed, Jjdy. Perky Turkey's 4th of July Adventure. 2008. (Illus.). 24p. (J). per. *(978-0-9801376-1-3(6))* Dragonfly Publishing, Inc.

Goodspeed, Judy. Perky Turkey Finds a Friend. (Illus.). 24p. (J). 2007. per. 11.99 *(978-0-9797574-2-6(8))* 2006. lib. bdg. 24.95 *(978-0-9778651-2-3(6))* Dragonfly Publishing, Inc.

—Perky Turkey's 4th of July Adventure. 2008. (Illus.). 24p. (J). lib. bdg. *(978-0-9801376-0-6(8))* Dragonfly Publishing, Inc.

—Perky Turkey's Perfect Plan. (Illus.). 22p. (J). 2007. per. 11.99 *(978-0-9797574-3-3(6))* 2006. lib. bdg. 24.95 *(978-0-9778651-1-6(8))* Dragonfly Publishing, Inc.

—Perky Turkey's Perfect Plan. Taylor, Chet, illus. 2005. 22p. (J). 18.99 *(978-0-9765786-0-4(3))* Dragonfly Publishing, Inc.

Griechen, Jane M. Theodore B a Turkey. 2008. 68p. pap. 41.99 *(978-1-4363-2703-9(2))* Xlibris Corp.

Halverson, Barbara. Farm Friends Forever: Everyone Needs Friends. 2013. (ENG.). 27p. (J). pap. 13.95 *(978-1-4787-1380-7(1))* Outskirts Pr., Inc.

Harris, Nikki. Adventures in Friendship for Benji Butterfly & Tom Turkey. 2013. 24p. pap. 24.95 *(978-1-63004-741-2(4))* America Star Bks.

Honeycutt, Scarlet. Turkeys in Disguise. Aarvig, Cindy, illus. 2007. 48p. per. 24.95 *(978-1-4137-4035-6(9))* America Star Bks.

Hooper, Carrie Lynn. Andrew & the Wild Turkey. 2018. (ENG., Illus.). 24p. (J). 12.99 *(978-1-948653-45-9(1));* pap. 6.99 *(978-1-948653-44-2(3))* Authors Pr.

Hubble, Miles & Bryant, Justin. Bob & the Fowl War: Book One in the Poultry Series. 2008. 140p. pap. 11.95 *(978-1-4401-0857-0(9))* iUniverse, Inc.

Isbell, Tessa J. Animal Adventures: Goosey & Beauty Take a Mystery Magic Carpet Ride to Jamaica. 2013. 48p. pap. 21.99 *(978-1-4669-7217-9(3))* Trafford Publishing.

Johnston, Tony. 10 Fat Turkeys. Deas, Rich, illus. (ENG.). (J). (gr. -1-k). 2009. 28p. bds. 6.99 *(978-0-545-16469-6(9))* 2004. 32p. pap. 3.99 *(978-0-439-45948-8(6))* Scholastic, Inc. (Cartwheel Bks.).

Kane, Bob. Sandwich Day & Our Family Album. Nguyen, Dustin, illus. 2015. (Batman: Li'l Gotham Ser.). (ENG.). 32p. (J). (gr. 1-5). lib. bdg. 22.60 *(978-1-4342-9737-2(3),* 127069, Stone Arch Bks.) Capstone.

Karr, Kathleen. The Great Turkey Walk. 2004. 199p. (gr. 4-7). 18.00 *(978-0-7569-4124-6(5))* Perfection Learning Corp.

Kenah, Katharine. The Very Stuffed Turkey. Talib, Binny, illus. 2015. (ENG.). 32p. (J). (gr. -1-k). pap. 6.99 *(978-0-545-76109-3(3),* Cartwheel Bks.) Scholastic, Inc.

King, Lisa. Lurkey the Proud Turkey. 2013. 24p. pap. 24.95 *(978-1-63004-113-7(0))* America Star Bks.

Langlois, Annie. L' Evasion d'Alfred le Dindon. Beaulieu, Jimmÿ, illus. 2004. (Roman Jeunesse Ser.). (FRE.). 96p. (J). (gr. 4-7). pap. *(978-2-89021-687-7(X))* Diffusion du livre Mirabel (DLM).

Langlois, Suzanne. Mia, Matt & the Turkey Chase, 1 vol. Cummins, Sarah, tr. Beaulieu, Jimmy, illus. 2008. (Formac First Novels Ser.). (ENG.). 64p. (J). (gr. 2-5). 5.95 *(978-0-88780-763-3(1),* 763); 14.95 *(978-0-88780-765-7(8),* 765) Formac Publishing Co., Ltd. CAN. Dist: Formac Lorimer Bks. Ltd.

Lonsdale, Cathy. Bill the Brush Turkey. 2008. (ENG.). 24p. 13.95 *(978-1-4092-0414-5(6))* Lulu Pr., Inc.

Mayr, Diane. Run, Turkey, Run! Rader, Laura, illus. 2009. (ENG.). 32p. (J). (gr. -1-2). pap. 7.99 *(978-0-8027-8481-0(X),* 900062746, Bloomsbury USA Childrens) Bloomsbury Publishing USA.

Metzger, Steve. The Great Turkey Race. Paillot, Jim, illus. 2006. (J). *(978-0-439-85930-1(1))* Scholastic, Inc.

—The Turkey Train. Paillot, Jim, illus. 2013. (ENG.). 32p. (J). (gr. -1-k). 6.99 *(978-0-545-49229-4(7),* Cartwheel Bks.) Scholastic, Inc.

Neimark, Jill & Weiner, Marcella Bakur. Toodles & Teeny: A Story about Friendship. Adinolfi, JoAnn, illus. 2012. 32p. (J). 14.95 *(978-1-4338-1198-2(7));* pap. 9.95 *(978-1-4338-1199-9(5))* American Psychological Assn. (Magination Pr.).

Nielsen, Gwyn English. Torey the Turkey Goes Skiing. 2003. (Illus.). 24p. (Orig.). (gr. -1-4). pap. 5.99 *(978-0-9660726-0-0(X))* C.G.S. Pr.

Park, Barbara. Junie B. Jones #28: Turkeys We Have Loved & Eaten (and Other Thankful Stuff) Brunkus, Denise, illus. 2014. (Junie B. Jones Ser.: 28). (ENG.). 144p. (J). (gr. 1-4). 5.99 *(978-0-375-87115-3(2),* Random Hse. Bks. for Young Readers) Random Hse. Children's Bks.

Parnell, Declan. Tina & the Turkeys, 1 vol., 1. 2015. (Rosen REAL Readers: STEM & STEAM Collection). (ENG.). 8p. (J). (gr. k-1). pap. 5.46 *(978-1-5081-1458-1(7),* d4bbe2aa-48b9-4c40-a622-a33ef50a4b37, Rosen Classroom) Rosen Publishing Group, Inc., The.

Phillips, Tikera M. Thanksgiving Turkey. 2012. 16p. pap. 12.70 *(978-1-4669-4053-6(0))* Trafford Publishing.

Priddy, Roger. Shiny Shapes: Hooray for Thanksgiving! 2018. (Shiny Shapes Ser.). (ENG., Illus.). 10p. (J). bds. 7.99 *(978-0-312-52724-2(1),* 900189781) St. Martin's Pr.

Reynolds Naylor, Phyllis. Zack & the Turkey Attack! To, Vivienne, illus. (ENG.). (J). (gr. 2-6). 2018. 192p. pap. 7.99 *(978-1-4814-3780-6(1))* 2017. 176p. 16.99 *(978-1-4814-3779-0(8),* Atheneum/Caitlyn Dlouhy Books) Simon & Schuster Children's Publishing.

—Zack & the Turkey Attack. 2018. lib. bdg. 18.40 *(978-0-606-41461-6(4))* Turtleback.

Roesser, Griffin. Who Ate the Turkey?, 1 vol. 2006. (Neighborhood Readers Ser.). (ENG.). 12p. (gr. k-1). pap. 5.90 *(978-1-4042-6457-1(4),* afed3ba8-a504-4cf7-a0e6-42a7b323526e, Rosen Classroom) Rosen Publishing Group, Inc., The.

Ross, Patrick. Runt River Rat's Wild Ride, 1 vol. Burcham, David, illus. 2010. 24p. 24.95 *(978-1-4512-0067-6(6))* PublishAmerica, Inc.

Roy, Ron. Capital Mysteries #14: Turkey Trouble on the National Mall. Bush, Timothy, illus. 2012. (Capital Mysteries Ser.: 14). 96p. (J). (gr. 1-4). 6.99 *(978-0-307-93220-4(6),* Random Hse. Bks. for Young Readers) Random Hse. Children's Bks.

Roy, Ronald. Capital Mysteries #14: Turkey Trouble on the National Mall, 14. Bush, Timothy, illus. 2012. (Capital Mysteries Ser.). (ENG.). 96p. (J). (gr. 1-4). lib. bdg. 17.44 *(978-0-375-87004-0(0))* Random House Publishing Group.

—Turkey Trouble on the National Mall. 2012. (Capital Mysteries Ser.: 14). lib. bdg. 14.75 *(978-0-606-26809-7(X))* Turtleback.

Shannon, George. Turkey Tot. Mann, Jennifer K., illus. 2014. (ENG.). 32p. (J). (gr. -1-k). 6.99 *(978-0-8234-3175-5(4))* Holiday Hse., Inc.

Sharmat, Marjorie Weinman & Sharmat, Mitchell. Nate the Great Talks Turkey. Wheeler, Jody, illus. 2007. (Nate the Great Ser.: No. 25). 96p. (J). (gr. 1-4). per. 5.99 *(978-0-440-42126-9(8),* Yearling) Random Hse. Children's Bks.

—Nate the Great Talks Turkey: With Help from Olivia Sharp. Wheeler, Jody, illus. 2007. (Nate the Great Ser.: Bk. 25). (gr. -1-3). lib. bdg. 16.00 *(978-1-4177-9248-1(5))* Turtleback.

Silvano, Wendi. Turkey Claus, 0 vols. Harper, Lee, illus. 2012. (Turkey Trouble Ser.: 2). (ENG.). 40p. (J). (gr. -1-2). 16.99 *(978-0-7614-6239-2(2),* 9780761462392, Two Lions) Amazon Publishing.

—Turkey Trouble, 0 vols. Harper, Lee, illus. 2012. (Turkey Trouble Ser.: 1). (ENG.). 40p. (J). (gr. -1-2). 15.99 *(978-0-7614-5529-5(9),* 9780761455295, Two Lions) Amazon Publishing.

Sommerset, Mark. Baa Baa Smart Sheep. Sommerset, Rowan, illus. 2016. (ENG.). 32p. (J). (gr. k-3). 14.00 *(978-0-7636-8066-4(4))* Candlewick Pr.

—I Love Lemonade. Sommerset, Rowan, illus. 2016. (ENG.). 32p. (J). (gr. k-3). 14.00 *(978-0-7636-8067-1(2))* Candlewick Pr.

Steinberg, Jessica. Not This Turkey! 2018. (2019 Av2 Fiction Ser.). (ENG.). 32p. (J). (gr. k-3). lib. bdg. 34.28 *(978-1-4896-8273-4(2),* AV2 by Weigl) Weigl Pubs., Inc.

—Not This Turkey! Pike, Amanda, illus. 2016. (ENG.). 32p. (J). (gr. -1-3). 16.99 *(978-0-8075-7908-4(4),* 807579084) Whitman, Albert & Co.

Suhay, Lisa. Pardon Me, It's Ham, Not Turkey. Barcita, Pamela, illus. 2007. (J). (gr. -1-3). 17.95 *(978-1-933982-01-4(2))* Bumble Bee Publishing.

Turkey in the Straw. (J). (gr. -1-1). pap. 7.50 *(978-0-932970-93-0(1))* Prinit Pr.

Weiner, Marcella Bakur & Neimark, Jill. I Want Your Moo: A Story for Children about Self-Esteem. Adinolfi, JoAnn, illus. 2nd ed. 2009. 32p. (J). (gr. -1-3). 14.95 *(978-1-4338-0542-4(1));* pap. 9.95 *(978-1-4338-0552-3(9))* American Psychological Assn. (Magination Pr.).

Wheeler, Lisa. Turk & Runt: A Thanksgiving Comedy. Ansley, Frank, illus. 2005. (ENG.). 32p. (J). (gr. -1-2). 7.99 *(978-1-4169-0714-5(9),* Atheneum Bks. for Young Readers) Simon & Schuster Children's Publishing.

Wigden, Susan. I Want to Learn to Dance. Franzese, Nora Tapp, illus. 2012. 36p. pap. 11.99 *(978-1-60820-725-1(0))* MLR Pr., LLC.

Yoon, Salina. Five Silly Turkeys. Yoon, Salina, illus. 2005. (Illus.). 12p. (J). (gr. -1-k). bds. 7.99 *(978-0-8431-1416-4(9),* Price Stern Sloan) Penguin Young Readers Group.

TURNER, J. M. W. (JOSEPH MALLORD WILLIAM), 1775-1851

Stewart, Lizzy. Meet the Artist: JMW Turner. 2018. (Tate Meet the Artist Ser.). (ENG., Illus.). 32p. (J). (gr. k-17). 12.95 *(978-1-84976-518-3(9),* 1325003) Tate Publishing, Ltd. GBR. Dist: Abrams, Inc.

TURNER, NAT, 1800?-1831

Roxburgh, Ellis. Nat Turner's Slave Rebellion. 2017. (Rebellions, Revolts, & Uprisings Ser.). 48p. (gr. 5-5). pap. 84.30 *(978-1-5382-0753-6(2))* Stevens, Gareth Publishing LLLP.

Schmid, Katie Kelley. Nat Turner & Slave Life on a Southern Plantation, 1 vol. 2013. (Jr. Graphic African American History Ser.). (Illus.). 24p. (J). (ENG.). (gr. 2-3). pap. 11.60 *(978-1-4777-1453-9(7),* 8bc536b5-87fd-4812-ba81-35b2ae4fa79e); (ENG.). (gr. 2-3). lib. bdg. 28.93 *(978-1-4777-1314-3(X),* 92a828d3-4636-48db-8581-fb3bf864f169); (gr. 3-6). pap. 63.60 *(978-1-4777-1454-6(5))* Rosen Publishing Group, Inc., The. (PowerKids Pr.).

TURTLES

Albertson, Al. Common Box Turtles. 2019. (North American Animals Ser.). (ENG., Illus.). 24p. (J). (gr. k-3). lib. bdg. 26.95 *(978-1-62617-982-0(4),* Blastoff! Readers) Bellwether Media.

Arnold, Quinn M. Sea Turtles. 2017. (Seedlings Ser.). (ENG., Illus.). 24p. (J). (gr. -1-k). pap. 8.99 *(978-1-62832-400-6(7),* 20150, Creative Paperbacks); *(978-1-60818-780-5(2),* 20152, Creative Education) Creative Co., The.

Arnosky, Jim. All about Turtles. Arnosky, Jim, illus. 2008. (ENG., Illus.). 32p. (J). (gr. -1-3). pap. 6.99 *(978-0-590-69781-1(1))* Scholastic, Inc.

Ashton, Ray E., Jr. The Gopher Tortoise: A Life History. 2004. (Life History Ser.). (ENG., Illus.). 67p. (J). (gr. -1-12). 19.95 *(978-1-56164-303-5(3))* Pineapple Pr., Inc.

Ashton, Ray E., Jr. & Ashton, Ray E. The Gopher Tortoise: A Life Story. 2004. (Life History Ser.). (ENG., Illus.). 74p. (J). (gr. -1-12). pap. 14.95 *(978-1-56164-301-1(7))* Pineapple Pr., Inc.

Barrett, Tracy. Turtles & Tortoises, 1 vol. 2007. (Animals, Animals Ser.). (ENG., Illus.). 48p. (gr. 5-5). lib. bdg. 32.64 *(978-0-7614-2239-6(0),* 360df613-b3a6-4733-937a-ab5dc8b8eb03) Cavendish Square Publishing LLC.

Baxter, Bethany. Snapping Turtles. 2013. (Awesome Armored Animals Ser.). 24p. (J). (gr. k-5). pap. 49.50 *(978-1-4777-0963-4(0));* (ENG.). (gr. 2-3). pap. 9.25 *(978-1-4777-0962-7(2),* 001e5490-8c63-4d39-8d20-a937039bbd70); (ENG.). (gr. 2-3). lib. bdg. 26.27 *(978-1-4777-0795-1(6),* 85dc72fb-0f19-45e7-b636-a8040dfc2430) Rosen Publishing Group, Inc., The. (PowerKids Pr.).

Becker, John E. Green Sea Turtles. 2003. (Returning Wildlife Ser.). (Illus.). 48p. (J). 26.20 *(978-0-7377-1831-7(5),* Greenhaven Pr., Inc.) Cengage Gale.

Bell, Samantha. Sea Turtles. 2014. (21st Century Skills Library: Exploring Our Oceans Ser.). (ENG., Illus.). 32p. (J). (gr. 3-6). 32.07 *(978-1-62431-602-9(6),* 203192) Cherry Lake Publishing.

Benrali. The turtle's dream & Keys. 2009. (Illus.). 32p. (YA). 19.99 net. *(978-0-9763354-2-9(5))* ONLY1EARTH, LLC.

Best, B. J. Sea Turtles, 1 vol. 2016. (Migrating Animals Ser.). (ENG.). 24p. (gr. 1-1). pap. 9.81 *(978-1-5026-2094-1(4),* cba47255-7249-487c-ab11-0eb5d803d5af) Cavendish Square Publishing LLC.

Biel, Timothy Levi. Turtles. rev. ed. 2003. (Illus.). 24p. (J). (gr. 1-7). 10.95 *(978-1-888153-99-6(7),* Zoo Bks.) National Wildlife Federation.

Blomquist, Christopher. Box Turtles, 1 vol. 2003. (Library of Turtles & Tortoises Ser.). (ENG., Illus.). 24p. (J). (gr. 3-3). lib. bdg. 26.27 *(978-0-8239-6735-3(2),* d2cbdc49-b8d3-4479-9309-321a940fde30, PowerKids Pr.) Rosen Publishing Group, Inc., The.

—Desert Tortoises. (Library of Turtles & Tortoises Ser.). 24p. (gr. 3-3). 2009. 42.50 *(978-1-60853-946-8(6),* PowerKids Pr.) 2003. (ENG., Illus.). (J). lib. bdg. 26.27 *(978-0-8239-6739-1(5),* dfbb65c1-4c40-47cd-b7c0-53fdfc8747a2) Rosen Publishing Group, Inc., The.

—Gopher Tortoises, 1 vol. 2003. (Library of Turtles & Tortoises Ser.). (ENG., Illus.). 24p. (J). (gr. 3-3). lib. bdg. 26.27 *(978-0-8239-6740-7(9),* d7f492f5-c965-46d5-98ae-e95fbeea6726, PowerKids Pr.) Rosen Publishing Group, Inc., The.

—Snapping Turtles. 2009. (Library of Turtles & Tortoises Ser.). 24p. (gr. 3-3). 42.50 *(978-1-60853-948-2(2),* PowerKids Pr.) Rosen Publishing Group, Inc., The.

—Spiny Soft Shell Turtles, 1 vol. 2003. (Library of Turtles & Tortoises Ser.). (ENG.). 24p. (J). (gr. 3-3). lib. bdg. 26.27 *(978-0-8239-6737-7(9),* 91b86db9-59d3-47af-aee3-a97b9a9be968, PowerKids Pr.) Rosen Publishing Group, Inc., The.

—Spiny Softshell Turtles. 2009. (Library of Turtles & Tortoises Ser.). 24p. (gr. 3-3). 42.50 *(978-1-60853-949-9(0),* PowerKids Pr.) Rosen Publishing Group, Inc., The.

Boothroyd, Jennifer. Shells. 2011. (First Step Nonfiction — Body Coverings Ser.). (gr. k-2). (ENG., Illus.). 24p. (J). pap. 6.99 *(978-0-7613-7830-3(8),* cd062e6f-906d-457c-8a42-d66b6571ce41); pap. 33.92 *(978-0-7613-8610-0(6));* (ENG., Illus.). 24p. lib. bdg. 23.93 *(978-0-7613-5788-9(2))* Lerner Publishing Group.

Borgert-Spaniol, Megan. Baby Turtles. 2016. (Super Cute! Ser.). (ENG., Illus.). 24p. (J). (gr. k-3). 26.95 *(978-1-62617-390-3(7),* Blastoff! Readers) Bellwether Media.

Box Turtle, Earth & Time. 2007. 34p. (YA). *(978-0-9763354-3-6(3))* ONLY1EARTH, LLC.

Bozzo, Linda. How Turtles Grow Up, 1 vol. 2019. (Animals Growing Up Ser.). (ENG.). 24p. (gr. 1-2). 24.27 *(978-1-9785-0723-4(2),* 8d1eda05-efeb-47d8-84f8-b59733f7efc8) Enslow Publishing, LLC.

Brannon, Cecelia H. Baby Turtles at the Zoo, 1 vol. 2015. (All about Baby Zoo Animals Ser.). (ENG.). 24p. (gr. k-1). pap. 10.35 *(978-0-7660-7158-2(8),* 4ed21be0-12c3-4927-b0a5-0e5de4d3d259); (Illus.). lib. bdg. 24.27 *(978-0-7660-7160-5(X),* 9e85e27e-7cbb-4acb-9d32-a2521d1441bb) Enslow Publishing, LLC.

Braun, Eric. Cheetah vs. Tortoise. 2018. (Versus! Ser.). (ENG.). 24p. (gr. 4-6). pap. 9.99 *(978-1-64466-329-5(5),* 12151); (Illus.). lib. bdg. *(978-1-68072-346-5(4),* 12150) Black Rabbit Bks. (Hi Jinx).

Bronson, Wilfrid S., illus. Turtles. 2008. 68p. (J). pap. 18.95 *(978-0-86534-651-2(8))* Sunstone Pr.

Carr, Aaron. Sea Turtles. 2014. (Illus.). 24p. (J). *(978-1-4896-3212-8(3))* Weigl Pubs., Inc.

Carraway, Rose. Terrific Turtles, 1 vol. 2012. (Pet Corner Ser.). (ENG., Illus.). 24p. (J). (gr. k-k). pap. 9.15 *(978-1-4339-6311-7(6),* fb854867-ac66-4842-a000-00341ea1021e); lib. bdg. 25.27 *(978-1-4339-6309-4(4),* 38801156-4bf0-47e7-b864-818ae0c37555) Stevens, Gareth Publishing LLLP.

—Terrific Turtles / Tortugas Asombrosas, 1 vol. 2012. (Pet Corner / Rincón de Las Mascotas Ser.). (SPA & ENG.). 24p. (J). (gr. k-k). lib. bdg. 25.27 *(978-1-4339-6647-7(6),* 43d01710-5eaa-45b9-a6fb-88b8d9c8f7be) Stevens, Gareth Publishing LLLP.

Carroll, D. Year of the Turtle. (Illus.). 160p. (J). 21.95 *(978-0-8048-7036-8(5))* Tuttle Publishing.

Carstairs, Sue. Saving Turtles: A Kids' Guide to Helping Endangered Creatures. 2014. (ENG., Illus.). 64p. (J). (gr. 4-7). pap. 9.95 *(978-1-77085-290-7(5),* b96cddfb-0fd1-45ee-93c9-da39db98af47) Firefly Bks., Ltd.

Chang, Kirsten. Turtle or Tortoise? 2019. (Spotting Differences Ser.). (ENG., Illus.). 24p. (J). (gr. k-3). lib. bdg. 26.95 *(978-1-64487-036-5(3),* Blastoff! Readers) Bellwether Media.

Cohen Christopherson, Sara. Top 50 Reasons to Care about Marine Turtles: Animals in Peril, 1 vol. 2010. (Top 50 Reasons to Care about Endangered Animals Ser.). (ENG., Illus.). 104p. (gr. 5-6). 35.93 *(978-0-7660-3455-6(0),* fb152d80-f230-49d4-861d-8fc06c518543) Enslow Publishing, LLC.

Coleman, Miriam. Swimming with Sea Turtles, 1 vol. 2009. (Flippers & Fins Ser.). (ENG., Illus.). 24p. (J). (gr. 2-3). pap. 9.25 *(978-1-4358-3243-5(4),* 46299728-79b4-47d2-be91-ef5c4fc820cb, PowerKids Pr.); lib. bdg. 26.27 *(978-1-4042-8093-9(6),* 1ecbbce4-a525-44b1-a972-2c7f008f3dd3) Rosen Publishing Group, Inc., The.

Connors, Kathleen. Snapping Turtles, 1 vol. 2013. (Really Wild Reptiles Ser.). (ENG., Illus.). 24p. (gr. 2-3). 25.27 *(978-1-4339-8384-9(2),* c8e0ddff-9bbd-4fe6-9735-b9e072d18f8d); pap. 9.15 *(978-1-4339-8385-6(0),* 2171cac7-ff32-4ce4-93b2-491db7178690) Stevens, Gareth Publishing LLLP. (Gareth Stevens Learning Library).

Cousteau, Philippe & Hopkinson, Deborah. Follow the Moon Home: A Tale of One Idea, Twenty Kids, & a Hundred Sea Turtles (Children's Story Books, Sea Turtle Gifts, Moon Books for Kids, Children's Environment Books, Kid's Turtle Books) So, Meilo, illus. 2016. (ENG.). 48p. (J). (gr. k-3). 16.99 *(978-1-4521-1241-1(X))* Chronicle Bks. LLC.

Cunningham, Kevin. Sea Turtles & Yellow Tang Fish. 2016. (21st Century Junior Library: Better Together Ser.). (ENG., Illus.). 24p. (J). (gr. 2-5). 29.21 *(978-1-63471-088-6(6),* 208431) Cherry Lake Publishing.

Cussen, Sarah. Those Terrific Turtles. Weaver, Steve, illus. 2006. (Those Amazing Animals Ser.). (ENG.). 58p. (J). (gr. -1-12). per. 11.95 *(978-1-56164-364-6(5))* Pineapple Pr., Inc.

Dahlen, Kirsten. Wrong Way Peach Fuzz: A Turtle Tale. 2008. 108p. pap. 9.95 *(978-1-4357-1273-7(0))* Lulu Pr., Inc.

Davies, Nicola. One Tiny Turtle: Read & Wonder. Chapman, Jane, illus. 2005. (Read & Wonder Ser.). (ENG.). 32p. (J). (gr. -1-3). reprint ed. pap. 8.99 *(978-0-7636-2311-1(3))* Candlewick Pr.

Davis, Patricia. Turtles. 2008. (Nature's Children Ser.). (Illus.). 52p. (J). *(978-0-7172-6288-5(X))* Grolier, Ltd.

Dennard, Deborah. Turtles. Dewey, Jennifer Owings, illus. 2003. (Our Wild World Ser.). (ENG.). 48p. (J). (gr. 2-5). pap. 7.95 *(978-1-55971-861-5(7))* Cooper Square Publishing Llc.

Devers, Marie. Turtles. 2009. (Illus.). 112p. (J). 14.95 *(978-1-932904-42-0(5))* Eldorado Ink.

Duhaime, Darla. Turtles. 2017. (Reptiles! Ser.). (ENG.). 24p. (gr. -1-1). 28.50 *(978-1-68342-157-3(4),* 9781683421573); pap. 9.95 *(978-1-68342-199-3(X),* 9781683421993) Rourke Educational Media.

Dunn, Mary R. A Turtle's Life Cycle. 2017. (Explore Life Cycles Ser.). (ENG., Illus.). 24p. (J). (gr. -1-2). pap. 6.95 *(978-1-5157-7060-2(5),* 135490); lib. bdg. 27.32 *(978-1-5157-7054-1(0),* 135484) Capstone. (Capstone Pr.).

Dunphy, Madeleine. At Home with the Gopher Tortoise: The Story of a Keystone Species. Rothman, Michael, illus. 2010. (Story of a Keystone Species Ser.: 1). (ENG.). 32p. (J). (gr. k-4). pap. 11.95 *(978-0-9777539-5-6(6))* Web of Life Children's Bks.

Edwards, Roberta. Best Friends: The True Story of Owen & Mzee. Schwartz, Carol, illus. 2007. (Penguin Young Readers, Level 2 Ser.). 32p. (J). (gr. 1-2). mass mkt. 5.99

(978-0-448-44567-0(0), Penguin Young Readers) Penguin Young Readers Group.

—Best Friends: The True Story of Owen & Mzee. Schwartz, Carol, illus. 2007. (All Aboard Science Reader Ser.). 32p. (gr. -1-3). 14.00 *(978-0-7569-8167-9(0))* Perfection Learning Corp.

Evans, Topper. 100-Year-Old Tortoises, 1 vol. 2016. (World's Longest-Living Animals Ser.). (ENG., Illus.). 24p. (J). (gr. 1-2). pap. 9.15 *(978-1-4824-5620-2(6)*, 6447536b-c57c-4b0f-8461-c1ec71a0a2a6) Stevens, Gareth Publishing LLLP.

Findley, Violet. Sea Turtles. 2011. (Illus.). 16p. (J). pap. *(978-0-545-24791-7(8))* Scholastic, Inc.

Franchino, Vicky. Sea Turtles. 2013. (Nature's Children Ser.). (ENG.). 48p. (J). 28.00 *(978-0-531-20981-3(4))*; pap. 6.95 *(978-0-531-24307-7(9))* Scholastic Library Publishing. (Children's Pr.).

Franks, Katie. Turtles up Close. (Nature up Close Ser.). 24p. 2009. (gr. k-1). 42.50 *(978-1-61514-830-1(2))* 2007. (ENG., Illus.). (J). (gr. 1-1). lib. bdg. 26.27 *(978-1-4042-4139-8(6)*, 43e0dfd9-c3f0-479e-b015-403bd3b79412) Rosen Publishing Group, Inc., The. (PowerKids Pr.).

—Turtles up Close / Las Tortugas. 2009. (Nature up Close / la naturaleza de cerca Ser.). (ENG & SPA.). 24p. (gr. k-1). 42.50 *(978-1-61514-836-3(1)*, Editorial Buenas Letras) Rosen Publishing Group, Inc., The.

—Turtles up Close/Las Tortugas, 1 vol. Sanz, Pilar, tr. 2007. (Nature up Close / la Naturaleza de Cerca Ser.). (ENG & SPA., Illus.). 24p. (J). (gr. 1-1). lib. bdg. 26.27 *(978-1-4042-7681-9(5)*, 09cd1445-12c7-49e4-9250-6f8c9febdc97, Editorial Buenas Letras) Rosen Publishing Group, Inc., The.

Freeman, Debby. Turtle. 2016. (See Them Grow Ser.). (ENG., Illus.). 24p. (J). (gr. -1-3). 26.99 *(978-1-68402-041-6(7))* Bearport Publishing Co., Inc.

Furstinger, Nancy. Sea Turtles, 1 vol. 2014. (Amazing Reptiles Ser.). (ENG.). 48p. (J). (gr. 4-8). lib. bdg. 35.64 *(978-1-62403-375-9(X)*, 1195) ABDO Publishing Co.

Gaertner, Meg. Turtles. 2019. (Pond Animals Ser.). (ENG., Illus.). 24p. (J). (gr. 1-1). pap. 8.95 *(978-1-64185-582-2(7)*, 1641855827) North Star Editions.

—Turtles. 2018. (Pond Animals Ser.). (ENG., Illus.). 24p. (J). (gr. k-3). lib. bdg. 31.36 *(978-1-5321-6211-4(1)*, 30205, Pop! Cody Koala) Pop!

Gagne, Tammy. Giant Galápagos Tortoise. 2016. (Back from near Extinction Ser.). (ENG., Illus.). 48p. (J). (gr. 4-8). lib. bdg. 35.64 *(978-1-68078-466-4(8)*, 23869) ABDO Publishing Co.

George, Jean Craighead. Galapagos George. Minor, Wendell, illus. 2014. (ENG.). 40p. (J). (gr. k-3). 16.99 *(978-0-06-028793-1(4)*, HarperCollins) HarperCollins Pubs.

—Galapagos Picture Book. Minor, Wendell, illus. Date not set. 32p. (J). (gr. k-3). 5.99 *(978-0-06-443648-9(9))* HarperCollins Pubs.

Gibson. Sail Yel Nf Out of the Egg. 2003. (Rigby Sails Early Ser.). (ENG.). 16p. (gr. 1-2). pap. 6.95 *(978-0-7578-8892-2(5))* Rigby Education.

Gilkerson, Patricia. My Adventure with Sea Turtles. 2009. (ENG.). 44p. (J). 8.99 *(978-1-59092-466-2(5))* Blue Forge Pr.

Gish, Ashley. Sea Turtles. 2019. (X-Books: Reptiles Ser.). (ENG.). 32p. (J). (gr. 3-5). pap. 9.99 *(978-1-62832-672-7(7)*, 18888, Creative Paperbacks); *(978-1-64026-084-9(6)*, 18887) Creative Co., The.

Gish, Melissa. Sea Turtle. 2019. (Spotlight on Nature Ser.). (ENG.). 32p. (J). (gr. 4-7). pap. 9.99 *(978-1-62832-748-9(0)*, 19193, Creative Paperbacks) Creative Co., The.

—Sea Turtles. 2014. (Living Wild Ser.). (ENG.). 48p. (J). (gr. 4-7). *(978-1-60818-419-4(6)*, 21382, Creative Education) Creative Co., The.

—Tortoises. 2012. (Living Wild Ser.). (ENG.). 48p. (J). (gr. 4-7). 23.95 *(978-1-60818-170-4(7)*, 21896, Creative Education) Creative Co., The.

Gladstone, James. Turtle Pond, 1 vol. Reczuch, Karen, illus. 2018. (ENG.). 32p. (J). (gr. k-3). 18.95 *(978-1-55498-910-2(8))* Groundwood Bks. CAN. Dist: Publishers Group West (PGW).

—Turtle Pond. Reczuch, Karen, illus. 2018. (ENG.). 32p. E-Book *(978-1-55498-911-9(6))* Groundwood Bks.

Gordon, Sharon. Guess Who Hides, 1 vol. 2005. (Guess Who? Ser.). (ENG., Illus.). 32p. (gr. k-1). lib. bdg. 25.50 *(978-0-7614-1555-8(6)*, 2a372b1f-a8f8-4a3f-b936-bbbe2f1455b2) Cavendish Square Publishing LLC.

Graubart, Norman D. Mi Tortuga / My Turtle, 1 vol., 1. Green, Christina, ed. 2013. (¡Las Mascotas Son Geniales! / Pets Are Awesome! Ser.). (SPA & ENG.). 24p. (J). (gr. 1-2). 26.27 *(978-1-4777-3316-5(7)*, d6e9d08e-9e3f-42c2-a1e2-88811687d4c1, PowerKids Pr.) Rosen Publishing Group, Inc., The.

—My Turtle, 1 vol., 1. 2013. (Pets Are Awesome! Ser.). (ENG.). 24p. (J). (gr. 1-2). 26.27 *(978-1-4777-2869-7(4)*, 7b4bf9fc-f983-47e3-a8c3-3e755f4e187c, PowerKids Pr.) Rosen Publishing Group, Inc., The.

Green, Emily. Turtles. 2010. (Backyard Wildlife Ser.). (ENG., Illus.). 24p. (J). (gr. k-3). lib. bdg. 26.95 *(978-1-60014-448-6(9)*, Blastoff! Readers) Bellwether Media.

Group/McGraw-Hill, Wright. The Turtle: Collection 2. (Storyteller Interactive Writing Cards Ser.). (gr. k-3). *(978-0-322-09340-9(6))* Wright Group/McGraw-Hill.

—Turtles, Tortoises & Terrapins: Level M, 6 vols. (Summer Skies Ser.). 128p. (gr. 3-6). 36.95 *(978-0-322-06723-3(5))* Wright Group/McGraw-Hill.

Grunbaum, Mara. Sea Turtles (Nature's Children) (Library Edition) 2018. (Nature's Children, Fourth Ser.). (ENG., Illus.). 48p. (J). (gr. 3-5). lib. bdg. 30.00 *(978-0-531-23480-8(0)*, Children's Pr.) Scholastic Library Publishing.

Guiberson, Brenda Z. Into the Sea. Berenzy, Alix, illus. 2014. 32p. pap. 9.00 *(978-1-61003-227-8(6))* Center for the Collaborative Classroom.

Hall, Kirsten. Leatherback Turtle: The World's Heaviest Reptile. 2007. (SuperSized! Ser.). (Illus.). 24p. (J). (gr. k-3). lib. bdg. 26.99 *(978-1-59716-393-4(7)*, 1265938) Bearport Publishing Co., Inc.

Hamilton, Lynn. Caring for Your Turtle. 2004. (Caring for Your Pet Ser.). (Illus.). 32p. (J). per. 9.95 *(978-1-59036-153-5(9))* Weigl Pubs., Inc.

—Turtle. 2009. (My Pet Ser.). (Illus.). 32p. (J). (gr. 3-5). lib. bdg. 26.00 *(978-1-60596-088-3(8))* Weigl Pubs., Inc.

—Turtle: My Pet. 2009. (Illus.). 32p. (J). pap. 9.95 *(978-1-60596-089-0(6))* Weigl Pubs., Inc.

Hamilton, Lynn & Gillespie, Katie. Turtle. (J). 2019. *(978-1-7911-1928-7(X)*, AV2 by Weigl) 2015. *(978-1-4896-2974-6(2))* Weigl Pubs., Inc.

Hamilton, Lynn A. Caring for Your Turtle. 2005. (Caring for Your Pet Ser.). (Illus.). 32p. (J). (gr. -1-3). lib. bdg. 26.00 *(978-1-59036-118-4(0))* Weigl Pubs., Inc.

Haney, Johannah. Turtles, 1 vol. 2008. (Great Pets Ser.). (ENG., Illus.). 48p. (gr. 3-3). lib. bdg. 32.64 *(978-0-7614-2709-4(0)*, f4cc7c40-3b15-4dbe-a645-f7deae1ba302) Cavendish Square Publishing LLC.

Hansen, Grace. Leatherback Turtle Migration. 2017. (Animal Migration Ser.). (ENG., Illus.). 24p. (J). (gr. -1-2). lib. bdg. 32.79 *(978-1-5321-0029-1(9)*, 25138, Abdo Kids) ABDO Publishing Co.

—Turtles, 1 vol. 2014. (Reptiles (Abdo Kids) Ser.). (ENG.). 24p. (J). (gr. -1-2). lib. bdg. 32.79 *(978-1-62970-062-5(2)*, 1615, Abdo Kids) ABDO Publishing Co.

Harris, Terrell. Turtles, 1 vol. 2010. (Slimy, Scaly, Deadly Reptiles & Amphibians Ser.). (ENG., Illus.). 32p. (J). (gr. 3-4). pap. 11.50 *(978-1-4339-3439-1(6)*, 440e6041-b61d-498e-8f5b-e99705b6443e); lib. bdg. 28.67 *(978-1-4339-3438-4(8)*, 86b29150-444c-41c0-a127-30bd61400abb) Stevens, Gareth Publishing LLLP. (Gareth Stevens Learning Library).

Hatkoff, Isabella, et al. Owen & Mzee: the True Story of a Remarkable Friendship. Greste, Peter, photos by. 2006. (ENG., Illus.). 40p. (J). (gr. -1-3). 18.99 *(978-0-439-82973-1(9)*, Scholastic Pr.) Scholastic, Inc.

Heller, Ruth. Galapagos Means Tortoises. Heller, Ruth, illus. 2003. (ENG., Illus.). 48p. (J). (gr. k-4). reprint ed. pap. 7.95 *(978-1-57805-101-4(0))* Gibbs Smith, Publisher.

Heos, Bridget. Do You Really Want a Turtle? Longhi, Katya, illus. 2015. (Do You Really Want a Pet? Ser.). (ENG.). 24p. (J). (gr. 1-3). 19.95 *(978-1-60753-752-6(4))* Amicus Learning.

Herriges, Ann. Sea Turtles. 2006. (Oceans Alive Ser.). (ENG., Illus.). 24p. (J). (gr. k-3). lib. bdg. 26.95 *(978-1-60014-022-8(X))* Bellwether Media.

Hicer, Nancy. My Sister's Turtle, 1 vol. 2015. (Rosen REAL Readers: STEM & STEAM Collection). (ENG.). 8p. (gr. k-1). pap. 5.46 *(978-1-4994-9675-8(3)*, a2d8c309-eea6-48a3-af9c-06ba27103092, Rosen Classroom) Rosen Publishing Group, Inc., The.

Hickman, Pamela. Turtle Rescue: Changing the Future for Endangered Wildlife. 2005. (Firefly Animal Rescue Ser.). (ENG., Illus.). 64p. (J). (gr. 5-12). 19.95 *(978-1-55297-916-7(4)*, 93280d78-a9bb-4d4f-9282-4068af36a3ca); pap. 9.95 *(978-1-55297-915-0(6)*, 12e125df-95a3-401a-abb4-007397ec8220) Firefly Bks., Ltd.

Hinman, Bonnie. Threat to the Leatherback Turtle. 2008. (On the Verge of Extinction Ser.). (Illus.). 32p. (YA). (gr. 2-5). lib. bdg. 25.70 *(978-1-58415-690-1(2))* Mitchell Lane Pubs.

Hipp, Andrew. The Life Cycle of a Painted Turtle. 2009. (Life Cycles Library). 24p. (gr. 3-4). 42.50 *(978-1-60853-996-3(2)*, PowerKids Pr.) Rosen Publishing Group, Inc., The.

Hirsch, Rebecca E. Galápagos Tortoises: Long-Lived Giant Reptiles. 2015. (Comparing Animal Traits Ser.). (ENG., Illus.). 32p. (J). (gr. 2-4). 26.65 *(978-1-4677-7982-1(2)*, 6a0cc49b-ddad-4d02-902d-eb6165c34bff, Lerner Pubns.) Lerner Publishing Group.

Hirschmann, Kris. Sea Turtles. 2005. (Creatures of the Sea Ser.). (ENG., Illus.). 48p. (J). (gr. 4-8). 29.15 *(978-0-7377-3011-1(0)*, Greenhaven Pr., Inc.) Cengage Gale.

Houghton, Gillian. Tortugas: Por Dentro y Por Fuera, 1 vol. Gonzalez, Tomas, tr. Studio Stalio, illus. 2003. (Explora la Naturaleza (Getting into Nature) Ser.). (SPA.). 32p. (J). (gr. 3-4). lib. bdg. 28.93 *(978-1-4042-2869-6(1)*, 4ef3de6b-f7ef-4736-967f-f65757634c04) Rosen Publishing Group, Inc., The.

—Tortugas: Por dentro y por fuera (Turtles: Inside & Out) 2009. (Explora la Naturaleza (Getting into Nature) Ser.). (SPA.). 32p. (gr. 3-4). 47.90 *(978-1-61512-339-1(3)*, Editorial Buenas Letras) Rosen Publishing Group, Inc., The.

—Turtle, 1 vol. 2004. (Getting into Nature Ser.). (ENG., Illus.). 32p. (J). (gr. 3-4). lib. bdg. 28.93 *(978-0-8239-4211-4(2)*, c7fcf848-312b-479c-94d9-ad345bff0c6a) Rosen Publishing Group, Inc., The.

—Turtles: Inside & Out. 2009. (Getting into Nature Ser.). 32p. (gr. 3-4). 47.90 *(978-1-61512-727-6(5)*, PowerKids Pr.) Rosen Publishing Group, Inc., The.

Huelin, Jodi. Turtles. Gonzalez, Pedro Julio, illus. 2003. (Penguin Young Readers, Level 2 Ser.). (ENG.). 32p. (J). (gr. 1-2). 4.99 *(978-0-448-43117-8(3)*, Penguin Young Readers) Penguin Young Readers Group.

Jacobs, Lee. Turtle. 2003. (Wild America Ser.). (Illus.). 24p. (J). 24.94 *(978-1-56711-571-0(3)*, Blackbirch Pr., Inc.) Cengage Gale.

Johnson, Gee, et al. Sea Turtles. Dibble, Traci, illus. 2010. (2G Marine Life Ser.). (ENG.). 32p. (J). (gr. k-2). pap. 9.60 *(978-1-61541-399-7(5))* American Reading Co.

Johnson, Nancy Carole. Pierre, the Turtle Who Went to College. 2008. 24p. pap. 10.95 *(978-1-4327-2614-0(5))* Outskirts Pr., Inc.

Jopp, Kelsey. Leatherback Sea Turtle Migration. 2018. (Natural Phenomena Ser.). (ENG., Illus.). 32p. (J). (gr. 3-5). pap. 9.95 *(978-1-64185-011-7(6)*, 1641850116); lib. bdg. 31.35 *(978-1-63517-909-5(2)*, 1635179092) North Star Editions. (Focus Readers).

Kalman, Bobbie. Endangered Sea Turtles. 2004. (Earth's Endangered Animals Ser.). (ENG., Illus.). 32p. (J). pap. *(978-0-7787-1899-4(9))* Crabtree Publishing Co.

—Les Tortues de Mer. Briere, Marie-Josee, tr. from ENG. 2007. (Petit Monde Vivant Ser.). (FRE., Illus.). 32p. (J). (gr. -1-3). pap. 9.95 *(978-2-89579-164-5(3))* Bayard Canada Livres CAN. Dist: Crabtree Publishing Co.

Kingston, Anna. The Life Cycle of a Sea Turtle, 1 vol. 2011. (Nature's Life Cycles Ser.). (ENG., Illus.). 24p. (J). (gr. 2-3). pap. 9.15 *(978-1-4339-4688-2(2)*, 6c7c61e5-fc0d-49c0-9857-869f32c51486); lib. bdg. 25.27 *(978-1-4339-4687-5(4)*, 7ef93d2c-41a0-4898-9259-6b84f38a9caf) Stevens, Gareth Publishing LLLP. (Gareth Stevens Learning Library).

Kishel, Ann-Marie. Turtles & Hatchlings. 2006. (First Step Nonfiction — Animal Families Ser.). (ENG., Illus.). 8p. (J). (gr. k-2). pap. 5.99 *(978-0-8225-5647-3(2)*, 8a106d42-869c-4082-bf5e-78c0b1436b5a) Lerner Publishing Group.

Klukow, Mary Ellen. A Turtle's Dangerous Journey. Pinilla, Albert, illus. 2019. (Animal Habitats at Risk Ser.). (ENG.). 24p. (J). (gr. 1-3). pap. 9.99 *(978-1-68152-491-7(0)*, 11077) Amicus.

Korman, Susan. Box Turtle at Silver Pond Lane. Marchesi, Stephen, illus. 2005. (Smithsonian's Backyard Ser.). (ENG.). 32p. (J). (gr. -1-2). 15.95 *(978-1-56899-860-2(0)*, B5020) Soundprints.

Kosara, Victoria & Kosara, Tori. Lonesome George Finds His Friends. 2011. (Scholastic Reader: Level 3 Ser.). (ENG., Illus.). 32p. (J). (gr. 1-3). 16.19 *(978-0-545-26129-6(5))* Scholastic, Inc.

Kuzio, Daisy Williams. All about Annie: (A True Story) 2006. 9.00 *(978-0-8059-9118-5(2))* Dorrance Publishing Co., Inc.

Lang, Aubrey. Baby Sea Turtle, 1 vol. Lynch, Wayne, illus. 2007. (Nature Babies Ser.). (ENG.). 32p. (J). (gr. k-3). pap. 7.95 *(978-1-55041-746-3(0)*, d6d13ec6-8851-43bb-ac7d-dd32d12d7cae) Trifolium Bks., Inc. CAN. Dist: Firefly Bks., Ltd.

Lasky, Kathryn. Interrupted Journey: Saving Endangered Sea Turtles. Knight, Christopher G., photos by. 2006. (ENG., Illus.). 48p. (J). (gr. 1-4). 7.99 *(978-0-7636-2883-3(2))* Candlewick Pr.

Laughlin, Kara L. Sea Turtles. 2017. (In the Deep Blue Sea Ser.). (ENG.). 24p. (J). (gr. k-3). lib. bdg. 32.79 *(978-1-5038-1690-9(7)*, 211523) Child's World, Inc, The.

Lawrence, Ellen. A Sea Turtle's Life. 2016. (Animal Diaries: Life Cycles Ser.). (ENG., Illus.). 24p. (J). (gr. -1-3). 26.99 *(978-1-944102-48-7(5))* Bearport Publishing Co., Inc.

Lindeen, Carol K. & Lugtu, Carol J. Sea Turtles [Scholastic]. 2010. (Under the Sea Ser.). 24p. pap. 0.50 *(978-1-4296-5067-0(2)*, Capstone Pr.) Capstone.

Loh-Hagan, Virginia. Discover Sea Turtles. 2015. (21st Century Basic Skills Library: Splash! Ser.). (ENG., Illus.). 24p. (J). (gr. 2-4). 26.35 *(978-1-63362-607-2(5)*, 206612) Cherry Lake Publishing.

Machajewski, Sarah. Saving the Endangered Green Sea Turtle, 1 vol., 1. 2015. (Conservation of Endangered Species Ser.). (ENG., Illus.). 32p. (J). (gr. 2-3). pap. 13.90 *(978-1-5081-0056-0(X)*, 9be020f9-9ad6-4cc2-b9c4-67df338ca333, Britannica Educational Publishing) Rosen Publishing Group, Inc., The.

Macheske, Felicia. Flying Flippers: Sea Turtle. 2016. (Guess What Ser.). (ENG., Illus.). 24p. (J). (gr. k-2). 30.64 *(978-1-63470-716-9(8)*, 207575) Cherry Lake Publishing.

Marsh, Laura. National Geographic Readers: Sea Turtles. 2011. (Readers Ser.). (Illus.). 32p. (J). (gr. 1-3). pap. 5.99 *(978-1-4263-0853-6(1))*; (ENG., lib. bdg. 14.90 *(978-1-4263-0854-3(X))* Disney Publishing Worldwide. (National Geographic Kids).

—National Geographic Readers: Turtles. 2016. (Readers Ser.). (Illus.). 32p. (J). (gr. -1-k). pap. 4.99 *(978-1-4263-2293-8(3)*, National Geographic Kids) Disney Publishing Worldwide.

Marsico, Katie. How Do We Live Together? Turtles. 2010. (Community Connections: How Do We Live Together? Ser.). (ENG., Illus.). 24p. (gr. 2-5). lib. bdg. 29.21 *(978-1-60279-623-2(8)*, 200332) Cherry Lake Publishing.

McDonnell, Mary Rose. Tell Time with Turtles, 1 vol. 2011. (Animal Math Ser.). (ENG., Illus.). 24p. (J). (gr. 1-2). 25.27 *(978-1-4339-5674-4(8)*, aec48123-cf47-4a39-b130-e29aa69b5355); pap. 9.15 *(978-1-4339-5676-8(4)*, b23017fd-e95d-42af-9379-bfce2d66919e) Stevens, Gareth Publishing LLLP.

Meister, Cari. Sea Turtles. 2013. (ENG.). 24p. (J). lib. bdg. 25.65 *(978-1-62031-034-2(1))* Jump! Inc.

—Snapping Turtles. 2015. (Illus.). 24p. (J). lib. bdg. *(978-1-62031-199-8(2)*, Bullfrog Bks.) Jump! Inc.

—Turtles. 2014. (Illus.). 24p. (J). lib. bdg. 25.65 *(978-1-62031-126-4(7)*, Bullfrog Bks.) Jump! Inc.

Merwin, E. Matamata. 2018. (Even Weirder & Cuter Ser.). (ENG.). 24p. (J). (gr. -1-3). 17.95 *(978-1-68402-464-3(1))* Bearport Publishing Co., Inc.

Miller, Mirella S. Sea Turtles Are Awesome. 2018. (Animals Are Awesome Ser.). (ENG., Illus.). 32p. (J). (gr. 3-6). 32.80 *(978-1-63235-437-2(3)*, 13815, 12-Story Library) Bookstaves, LLC.

Monroe, Mary Alice. Turtle Summer: a Journal for My Daughter, 1 vol. Bergwerf, Barbara J., illus. 2007. (ENG.). 32p. (J). (gr. k-4). 16.95 *(978-0-9777423-5-6(0))* Arbordale Publishing.

Morgan, Sally. Turtles. 2006. (Animal Lives (QEB Publishing) Ser.). (Illus.). 32p. (J). (gr. 4-7). lib. bdg. 18.95 *(978-1-59566-206-4(5))* QEB Publishing Inc.

Morgan, Sally & Teacher Created Resources Staff. Tortoises & Turtles. 2007. (Animal Lives (QEB Publishing) Ser.). (ENG., Illus.). 32p. (gr. 2-9). pap. 7.99 *(978-1-4206-8110-9(9))* Teacher Created Resources, Inc.

Murray, Julie. Turtles. 2019. (Animal Kingdom Ser.). (ENG.). 32p. (J). (gr. 2-5). lib. bdg. 34.21 *(978-1-5321-1657-5(8)*, 32425, Big Buddy Bks.) ABDO Publishing Co.

Nagelhout, Ryan. Turtles, 1 vol. 2013. (Underwater World Ser.). (ENG., Illus.). 24p. (J). (gr. k-k). pap. 9.15 *(978-1-4339-8579-9(9)*, 264519b3-382c-4b78-b12d-d82ef74cc17f); lib. bdg. 25.27 *(978-1-4339-8578-2(0)*, 7d897272-5b79-4d4c-8b99-146bea4dab2e) Stevens, Gareth Publishing LLLP.

—Turtles / Tortugas, 1 vol. 2013. (Underwater World / el Mundo Submarino Ser.). (SPA & ENG., Illus.). 24p. (J). (gr. k-k). lib. bdg. 25.27 *(978-1-4339-8786-1(4)*, cc345107-eeec-4011-93b6-1b856779f06d) Stevens, Gareth Publishing LLLP.

Northeast Editing, Inc Staff, contrib. by. Turtles. 2008. (J). *(978-1-932904-34-5(4))* Eldorado Ink.

Oczkus, Lori. Close Reading with Paired Texts Level 1: Engaging Lessons to Improve Comprehension. rev. ed. 2015. (Close Reading with Paired Texts). (ENG., Illus.). 128p. (gr. 1-1). pap. 19.99 *(978-1-4258-1357-4(7))* Shell Educational Publishing.

Owen, Ruth. Sea Turtle Hatchlings. 2012. (Water Babies Ser.). 24p. (J). (gr. -1-3). lib. bdg. 25.65 *(978-1-61772-603-3(6))* Bearport Publishing Co., Inc.

Owings, Lisa. From Egg to Sea Turtle. 2016. (Start to Finish, Second Ser.). (ENG., Illus.). 24p. (J). (gr. k-3). 23.99 *(978-1-5124-1827-9(7)*, 385fcb44-1ae0-4830-b871-351293a990ba, Lerner Pubns.) Lerner Publishing Group.

Phillips, Dee. Desert Tortoise's Burrow. 2015. (Illus.). 24p. (J). lib. bdg. 26.99 *(978-1-62724-308-7(9))* Bearport Publishing Co., Inc.

Picayo, Mario. Sea Turtles of the Virgin Islands. 2017. (J). pap. *(978-1-934370-66-7(5))* Editorial Campana.

Pohl, Kathleen. Sea Turtles, 1 vol. 2007. (Let's Read about Animals Ser.). (ENG., Illus.). 24p. (gr. k-2). pap. 9.15 *(978-0-8368-7827-1(2)*, a9acc54b-16b2-4267-b418-0010007d17c3); lib. bdg. 24.67 *(978-0-8368-7820-2(5)*, 60f3e003-0d8f-4cce-8fad-48c0c5c7b928) Stevens, Gareth Publishing LLLP. (Weekly Reader Leveled Readers).

—Sea Turtles / Tortugas Marinas, 1 vol. 2007. (Let's Read about Animals / Conozcamos a Los Animales Ser.). (SPA & ENG., Illus.). 24p. (gr. k-2). pap. 9.15 *(978-0-8368-8016-8(1)*, a324b9a3-3cb3-46e2-a9e8-98c3d96927f3); lib. bdg. 24.67 *(978-0-8368-8009-0(9)*, dffbbdd8-bce0-4776-bfbe-9f1a48e5a8a4) Stevens, Gareth Publishing LLLP. (Weekly Reader Leveled Readers).

Portman, Michael. Sea Turtles in Danger, 1 vol. 2011. (Animals at Risk Ser.). (ENG., Illus.). 24p. (J). (gr. 2-3). 25.27 *(978-1-4339-5802-1(3)*, 41685d56-5316-4dbb-9884-30984db0f983); pap. 9.15 *(978-1-4339-5804-5(X)*, c55aa3ab-7a2f-4619-9bbc-3e4ee598d4e3) Stevens, Gareth Publishing LLLP. (Gareth Stevens Learning Library).

Randolph, Joanne. My Friend the Box Turtle, 1 vol. 2010. (Curious Pet Pals Ser.). (ENG.). 24p. (J). (gr. 2-3). lib. bdg. 27.27 *(978-1-60754-979-6(4)*, 89c1a1bc-0e5e-44fc-8d47-63f77c9e7c6e); (Illus.). pap. 9.15 *(978-1-60754-989-5(1)*, 28a52e21-d7ae-4966-bf17-b2b2d55980b5) Rosen Publishing Group, Inc., The. (Windmill Bks.).

—Turtles. (Classroom Pets Ser.). 24p. (gr. 2-3). 2009. 42.50 *(978-1-61511-863-2(2))* 2006. (ENG., Illus.). (J). lib. bdg. 26.27 *(978-1-4042-3677-6(5)*, 08610ce0-8943-482b-bc7f-aa563c1e7c3b) Rosen Publishing Group, Inc., The. (PowerKids Pr.).

Rathmell, Donna. Carolina's Story: Sea Turtles Get Sick Too!, 1 vol. Bergwerf, Barbara J., illus. 2005. (ENG.). 32p. (J). (gr. -1-3). 15.95 *(978-0-9764943-0-0(2))*; pap. 8.95 *(978-1-934359-00-6(9))* Arbordale Publishing.

Reid, Siuna A. Reptiles Are Cool- Understanding My Tortoise. Lodge, Vivienne E., ed. 2013. (Illus.). 76p. pap. *(978-0-9576568-2-6(3))* Siuna A Reid.

Ricciuti, Edward R. Adivina Quién Se Esconde / Guess Who Hides, 1 vol. 2008. (Adivina Quién / Guess Who? Ser.). (ENG & SPA., Illus.). 32p. (gr. k-2). lib. bdg. 25.50 *(978-0-7614-2465-9(2)*, dea09a7a-025d-48a7-b1a4-7dcce4919bcf) Cavendish Square Publishing LLC.

—Adivina Quién Se Esconde (Guess Who Hides), 1 vol. 2008. (Adivina Quién (Guess Who?) Ser.). (SPA., Illus.). 32p. (gr. k-2). lib. bdg. 25.50 *(978-0-7614-2385-0(0)*, 2ed3baec-9e12-4aac-ba75-10f2697eeeab) Cavendish Square Publishing LLC.

—Guess Who Hides, 1 vol. 2008. (Guess Who? Ser.). (ENG.). 32p. (gr. k-1). pap. 9.23 *(978-0-7614-3321-7(X)*, f24f8eb0-d738-4a41-baff-5392de24b47d) Cavendish Square Publishing LLC.

Riggs, Kate. Amazing Animals: Tortoises. 2014. (Amazing Animals Ser.). (ENG.). 24p. (J). (gr. 1-3). pap. 9.99 *(978-0-89812-929-8(X)*, 21479, Creative Paperbacks) Creative Co., The.

—Sea Turtles. 2015. (J). *(978-1-60818-491-0(9)*, Creative Education) Creative Co., The.

—Tortoises. (Seedlings Ser.). (ENG., 24p. (J). 2017. Illus.). (gr. k-2). pap. 9.99 *(978-1-62832-336-8(1)*, 20748, Creative Paperbacks) 2016. (Illus.). (gr. -1-k). *(978-1-60818-740-9(3)*, 20750, Creative Education) 2014. (gr. 1-4). 25.65 *(978-1-60818-350-0(5)*, 21478, Creative Education) Creative Co., The.

Rudenko, Dennis. Sea Turtles, 1 vol., 1. 2015. (Ocean Friends Ser.). (ENG., Illus.). 24p. (J). (gr. 1-1). pap. 9.25 *(978-1-5081-4185-3(1)*, 0426c705-89f6-43da-be3b-9ce44a27cc88, PowerKids Pr.) Rosen Publishing Group, Inc., The.

Rustad, Martha E. Sea Turtles [Scholastic]. 2009. (Ocean Life Ser.). 24p. (gr. k-1). pap. 2.99 *(978-1-4296-3676-6(9)*, Pebble) Capstone.

Ryndak, Rob. Turtle or Tortoise?, 1 vol. 2015. (Animal Look-Alikes Ser.). (ENG., Illus.). 24p. (J). (gr. 1-2). pap. 9.15 *(978-1-4824-2728-8(1)*, eec3c11b-bb3d-4feb-a5d9-b9e88059d498) Stevens, Gareth Publishing LLLP.

Sabelko, Rebecca. Common Snapping Turtles. 2019. (North American Animals Ser.). (ENG., Illus.). 24p. (J). (gr. k-3). lib. bdg. 26.95 *(978-1-62617-911-0(5)*, Blastoff! Readers) Bellwether Media.

Schreyer, Karmel. Turtles: Ancient Symbol/Modern Survivor Upper Intermediate Book with Online Access, 1 vol. 2014. (ENG., Illus.). 28p. (J). pap., E-Book, E-Book 9.50 *(978-1-107-66057-1(2))* Cambridge Univ. Pr.

Schuetz, Kari. Leatherback Sea Turtle Migration. 2018. (Animals on the Move Ser.). (ENG., Illus.). 24p. (J). (gr. k-3). lib. bdg. 26.95 *(978-1-62617-817-5(8)*, Blastoff! Readers) Bellwether Media.

—Sea Turtles. 2016. (Ocean Life up Close Ser.). (ENG., Illus.). 24p. (J). (gr. k-3). 26.95 *(978-1-62617-422-1(9)*, Blastoff! Readers) Bellwether Media.

Schuh, Mari. Sea Turtles. 2018. (Spot Ocean Animals Ser.). (ENG.). 16p. (J). (gr. -1-2). pap. 7.99 *(978-1-68152-302-6(7)*, 15004); lib. bdg. *(978-1-68151-382-9(X)*, 14998) Amicus.

—Turtles. 2018. (Spot Pets Ser.). (ENG.). 16p. (J). (gr. -1-2). *(978-1-68151-371-3(4)*, 14951); pap. 7.99 *(978-1-68152-291-3(8)*, 14959) Amicus.

Sexton, Colleen. Caring for Your Turtle. 2010. (Pet Care Library). (ENG., Illus.). 24p. (J). (gr. 2-5). lib. bdg. 26.95 *(978-1-60014-472-1(1),* Blastoff! Readers) Bellwether Media.
—The Life Cycle of a Turtle. 2010. (Life Cycles Ser.). (ENG., Illus.). 24p. (J). (gr. k-3). lib. bdg. 26.95 *(978-1-60014-452-3(7),* Blastoff! Readers) Bellwether Media.
Shea, Therese M. Is a Turtle a Good Pet for Me? 2019. (Best Pet for Me Ser.). (ENG.). 24p. (gr. 3-3). 49.50 *(978-1-7253-0121-4(0),* PowerKids Pr.) Rosen Publishing Group, Inc., The.
Speed Shaskan, Trisha. What's the Difference Between a Turtle & a Tortoise?, 1 vol. Bandelin Dacey Studios, Bandelin Dacey, illus. 2010. (What's the Difference? Ser.). (ENG.). 24p. (J). (gr. k-3). lib. bdg. 27.32 *(978-1-4048-5546-5(7),* 96038, Picture Window Bks.) Capstone.
Staff, Gareth Editorial Staff. Turtles, 1 vol. 2004. (All about Wild Animals Ser.). (ENG., Illus.). 32p. (gr. 2-4). lib. bdg. 28.67 *(978-0-8368-4123-7(9),* 0023390b-bc18-4e11-8df0-8d5daa50df04, Gareth Stevens Learning Library) Stevens, Gareth Publishing LLLP.
Stefoff, Rebecca. Turtles, 1 vol. 2009. (Animal Ways Ser.). (ENG., Illus.). 112p. (gr. 6-6). lib. bdg. 38.36 *(978-0-7614-2539-7(X),* 9788a317-b99e-442e-ab0c-cef1041ce0f5) Cavendish Square Publishing LLC.
Stewart, Melissa. A Place for Turtles. Bond, Higgins, illus. rev. ed. 2019. (Place For... Ser.: 6). 32p. (J). (gr. 2-6). 16.95 *(978-1-68263-096-9(X));* pap. 7.99 *(978-1-68263-097-6(8))* Peachtree Publishing Co. Inc.
Stone, Lynn M. Box Turtles. Stone, Lynn M., photos by. 2007. (Nature Watch Ser.). (ENG., Illus.). 48p. (gr. 4-8). lib. bdg. 27.93 *(978-1-57505-869-6(3),* Lerner Pubns.) Lerner Publishing Group.
Storad, Conrad J. Galápagos Tortoises. 2009. (Early Bird Nature Bks.). (ENG., Illus.). 48p. (J). (gr. 2-5). 26.60 *(978-0-8225-9431-4(5),* Lerner Pubns.) Lerner Publishing Group.
Swinburne, Stephen R. Sea Turtle Scientist. (Scientists in the Field Ser.). (ENG., Illus.). 80p. (J). (gr. 5-7). 2015. pap. 10.99 *(978-0-544-58240-8(3),* 1613826) 2014. 18.99 *(978-0-547-36755-2(4),* 1422686) HarperCollins Pubs. (Clarion Bks.).
Taylor, Barbara. Turtles & Tortoises: An In-Depth Look at Chelonians, the Shelled Reptiles That Have Existed since the Time of the Dinosaurs. 2016. (Illus.). 64p. (J). (gr. -1-12). 12.99 *(978-1-86147-643-2(4),* Armadillo) Anness Publishing GBR. Dist: National Bk. Network.
Taylor, Trace. Sea Turtles. Taylor, Trace, illus. 2010. (1-3Y Marine Life Ser.). (ENG., Illus.). 16p. (J). pap. 8.00 *(978-1-61541-483-3(5))* American Reading Co.
Terp, Gail. Is It a Turtle or a Tortoise? 2019. (Can You Tell the Difference? Ser.). (ENG., Illus.). 24p. (J). (gr. 4-6). lib. bdg. *(978-1-68072-901-6(2),* 12920, Hi Jinx) Black Rabbit Bks.
—Sea Turtles. 2017. (Wild Animal Kingdom Ser.). (ENG.). (J). (gr. 4-7). pap. 9.95 *(978-1-68072-489-9(4));* 32p. pap. 9.99 *(978-1-64466-226-7(4),* 11505); (Illus.). 32p. lib. bdg. *(978-1-68072-192-8(5),* 10567) Black Rabbit Bks. (Bolt).
Thivierge, Claude. The World of Turtles. 2009. (Dover Animal Coloring Bks.). (ENG., Illus.). 32p. (J). (gr. 1-5). pap. 3.99 *(978-0-486-46854-9(2),* 468542) Dover Pubns., Inc.
Tobler, Elise. Snapping Turtles Eat Anything!, 1 vol. 2020. (Reptiles Rock! Ser.). (ENG.). 32p. (gr. 2-3). pap. 11.53 *(978-1-9785-1832-2(3),* 2c64a105-7677-4b50-b7a0-1366cdb1adfa) Enslow Publishing, LLC.
Trifer, Jen. Turtles from Head to Tail, 1 vol. 2016. (Animals from Head to Tail Ser.). (ENG.). 24p. (J). (gr. k-2). lib. bdg. 24.27 *(978-1-4824-4540-4(9),* 1736eca0-eeec-4163-acb3-9eba597e887b) Stevens, Gareth Publishing LLLP.
Wang, Margaret. Turtles Take Their Time. 2007. 6p. 14.95 *(978-1-58117-601-8(5),* Intervisual/Piggy Toes) Bendon, Inc.
Watt, E. Melanie. Leatherback Turtles, with Code. 2012. (Animals on the Brink Ser.). (ENG., Illus.). 48p. (J). (gr. 3-7). pap. 14.95 *(978-1-61913-428-7(4),* AV2 by Weigl) Weigl Pubs., Inc.
Watt, Mélanie. Leatherback Turtles. 2013. (Illus.). 48p. *(978-1-61913-427-0(6))* Weigl Pubs., Inc.
Wearing, Judy. Sea Turtle: World of Wonder: Underwater Life. 2009. (Illus.). 24p. (J). pap. 8.95 *(978-1-60596-107-1(8))* Weigl Pubs., Inc.
—Sea Turtles. 2009. (World of Wonder Ser.). (Illus.). 24p. (J). (gr. 2-4). lib. bdg. 24.45 *(978-1-60596-106-4(X))* Weigl Pubs., Inc.
Weber, Valerie J. Sea Turtles, 1 vol. 2008. (Animals That Live in the Ocean Ser.). (ENG., Illus.). 24p. (J). (gr. 1-1). pap. 9.15 *(978-0-8368-9343-4(3),* 45ac725e-e304-4e76-a3b6-9ff415d0ed9c, Weekly Reader Leveled Readers) Stevens, Gareth Publishing LLLP.
—Sea Turtles, 1 vol. 2008. (Animals That Live in the Ocean Ser.). (ENG., Illus.). 24p. (J). (gr. 1-1). lib. bdg. 25.27 *(978-0-8368-9244-4(5),* ae2dd165-8622-4bff-8450-bb29abd5b218, Weekly Reader Leveled Readers) Stevens, Gareth Publishing LLLP.
—Sea Turtles / Tortugas Marinas, 1 vol. 2008. (Animals That Live in the Ocean / Animales Que Viven en el Océano Ser.). (SPA & ENG.). 24p. (gr. 1-1). (J). lib. bdg. 25.27 *(978-0-8368-9250-5(X),* d833269d-dc68-452e-b9eb-7011da8449ec); pap. 9.15 *(978-0-8368-9349-6(2),* d4eeedee-5c3a-4092-806d-0ec3df50ee91) Stevens, Gareth Publishing LLLP. (Weekly Reader Leveled Readers).
Webster, Christine. Who on Earth Is Archie Carr? Protector of Sea Turtles, 1 vol. 2009. (Scientists Saving the Earth Ser.). (ENG., Illus.). 112p. (J). (gr. 5-6). lib. bdg. 35.93 *(978-1-59845-120-7(0),* c0c9a912-9d14-44cd-895e-e4892875f9a3) Enslow Publishing, LLC.
Whitt, Stephen. The Turtle & the Universe. Hernandez, Stephanie, illus. 2008. 86p. (J). (gr. 3-7). pap. 14.99 *(978-1-59102-626-6(1))* Prometheus Bks., Pubs.
Wildlife Education, compiled by. Turtles. 2007. (Illus.). 12p. (J). 5.99 *(978-1-932396-40-9(3),* Critters Up Close) National Wildlife Federation.
Wilsdon, Christina. Turtles, 1 vol. 2009. (Amazing Animals Ser.). (ENG.). 48p. (gr. 3-5). (J). pap. 11.50 *(978-1-4339-2127-8(8),* d7e9f38c-4409-42f0-883d-3ba785df6096, Gareth Stevens Learning Library); (YA). lib. bdg. 30.67 *(978-0-8368-9123-2(6),* 06c39532-b416-4b01-a1ad-cc56bcefee31) Stevens, Gareth Publishing LLLP.
—Turtles. 2007. (J). *(978-1-59939-112-0(0),* Reader's Digest Young Families, Inc.) Studio Fun International.
World Book, Inc. Staff. Box Turtles & Other Pond & Marsh Turtles. 2007. (World Book's Animals of the World Ser.). (Illus.). 64p. (J). *(978-0-7166-1326-8(3))* World Bk., Inc.
Young, Karen Romano. National Geographic Kids Mission: Sea Turtle Rescue: All about Sea Turtles & How to Save Them. 2015. (NG Kids Mission: Animal Rescue Ser.). (ENG., Illus.). 112p. (J). (gr. 5-9). lib. bdg. 21.90 *(978-1-4263-1894-8(4),* National Geographic Kids) Disney Publishing Worldwide.

TURTLES—FICTION

Abbott, Monica. L T Makes New Friends. 2010. 24p. pap. 13.50 *(978-1-4520-6128-3(9))* AuthorHouse.
Abrahams, Marlon. Thomas Goes to the Se. 2009. 24p. pap. 14.50 *(978-1-60693-831-7(2),* Eloquent Bks.) Strategic Book Publishing & Rights Agency (SBPRA).
Achrafi, Sherihan. Turtles' Day Out. 2017. (ENG., Illus.). 28p. pap. 28.22 *(978-1-5245-6081-2(2))* AuthorHouse.
Adams, Alison. How the Turtle Cracked Its Shell: Classic Tales Edition. Greenhead, Bill, illus. 2011. (Classic Tales Ser.). (J). *(978-1-936258-58-1(7))* Benchmark Education Co.
Ahern, Carolyn L. Tino Turtle Travels to Beijing, China. Burt-Sullivan, Neallia, illus. 2011. (ENG.). 56p. (J). (gr. -1-4). 19.95 incl. audio compact disk *(978-0-9793158-4-8(0))* Tino Turtle Travels, LLC.
—Tino Turtle Travels to Kenya - the Great Safari. Burt Sullivan, Neallia, illus. 2009. (ENG & SWA.). 32p. (J). (gr. -1-4). 19.95 incl. audio compact disk *(978-0-9793158-3-1(2))* Tino Turtle Travels, LLC.
—Tino Turtle Travels to London, England. Burt Sullivan, Neallia, illus. (J). 2007. 36p. 17.95 incl. audio compact disk *(978-0-9793158-0-0(8))* 2008. (ENG.). 32p. 19.95 incl. audio compact disk *(978-0-9816297-0-4(9))* Tino Turtle Travels, LLC.
—Tino Turtle Travels to Mexico City, Mexico. Burt Sullivan, Neallia, illus. 2008. (ENG & SPA.). 32p. (J). (gr. -1-4). 19.95 incl. audio compact disk *(978-0-9793158-2-4(4))* Tino Turtle Travels, LLC.
—Tino Turtle Travels to Paris, France. Burt Sullivan, Neallia, illus. 2007. 36p. (J). (gr. -1-4). 17.95 incl. audio compact disk *(978-0-9793158-1-7(6))* Tino Turtle Travels, LLC.
Aina, Olaiya E. Ijapa, the Lion, & the Boar. 2010. 20p. 13.80 *(978-1-4269-3183-3(2))* Trafford Publishing.
Ajdari, Fereshteh. The turtle & the Rabbit: A Story for children, parents & grand Parents. 2009. (ENG.). 26p. pap. 15.99 *(978-1-4415-6424-5(1))* Xlibris Corp.
Allen, Jean M. A Tangled Web. 2012. 26p. 24.95 *(978-1-4512-9475-0(1))* America Star Bks.
Amar, Cindy. Tommy's Discovery. 2012. 28p. pap. 16.99 *(978-1-4525-5399-3(8))* Balboa Pr.
Ananthanarayanan, Ashraya. Ring of Hope. 2011. pap. 10.95 *(978-0-7414-6492-7(6))* Infinity Publishing.
Anastasio, Dina. The Magic Turtle: Set Of 6. 2011. (Early Connections Ser.). (J). pap. 37.00 net. *(978-1-4108-1366-4(5))* Benchmark Education Co.
—The Magic Turtle & la tortuga Mágica: 6 English, 6 Spanish Adaptations. 2011. (ENG & SPA.). (J). 75.00 net. *(978-1-4108-5650-0(X))* Benchmark Education Co.
Arai, Shizuko. The Turtle & the Warrior. Maeda, Matsuo, illus. 2014. (J). 8.95 *(978-1-935523-69-7(4))* World Tribune Pr.
Armitage, Kimo. Limu: The Blue Turtle & His Hawaiian Garden. Kaneshiro, Scott, illus. 2004. 28p. (J). 11.95 *(978-0-931548-64-2(0))* Island Heritage Publishing.
Atkins, Jill. Tortoise Races Home. Blake, Beccy, illus. 2009. (Tadpoles Ser.). (ENG.). 24p. (J). (gr. -1-2). pap. *(978-0-7787-3902-9(3))* Crabtree Publishing Co.
Austin, K. B. Old Mother Turtle & the Three Frogs. 2005. (J). lib. bdg. *(978-0-9772027-0-6(4))* Dream Star Productions.
Award, Anna & Biro, Val. The Bear & the Travellers & the Ducks & the Tortoise. 2014. (ENG.). 24p. (J). pap. 6.95 *(978-1-84135-959-5(9))* Award Pubns. Ltd. GBR. Dist: Parkwest Pubns., Inc.
Award, Anna, et al. The Hare & the Tortoise & The Sick Lion. 2014. (ENG.). (J). pap. 6.95 *(978-1-84135-954-0(8))* Award Pubns. Ltd. GBR. Dist: Parkwest Pubns., Inc.
AZ Books, creator. Tyler Turtle Travels to Australia. 2013. (Pop-Up: Play & Listen Ser.). (ENG., Illus.). 10p. (J). (gr. -1-k). bds. 16.95 *(978-1-61889-036-8(0))* AZ Bks. LLC.
Barker, Leslie. Bailey's Turtle. 2011. 20p. 12.49 *(978-1-4520-8762-7(8))* AuthorHouse.
Barnhouse Ms Ncc, Natalie. Shimmy Saves the Day: A Tale about Embracing Your Differences. 2012. 28p. pap. 19.99 *(978-1-4772-9933-3(5))* AuthorHouse.
Barr, Carolyn Mims. Blue Turtle. 2013. 24p. pap. 14.93 *(978-1-4669-8231-4(4))* Trafford Publishing.
Barsy, Kalman. Los Tres Naufragos. Perez-Moliere, Mamie, illus. 2004. (Orange Ser.). (SPA.). 40p. (J). (gr. 3-5). pap. 5.95 *(978-1-57581-469-8(2))* Santillana USA Publishing Co., Inc.
Bauer, Marion Dane. Mama for Owen. Butler, John, illus. 2007. (ENG.). 32p. (J). (gr. -1-3). 19.99 *(978-0-689-85787-4(X),* Simon & Schuster Bks. For Young Readers) Simon & Schuster Bks. For Young Readers.
Bennett, Katrina. Pandora the Sea Turtle. 2012. 28p. pap. 21.99 *(978-1-4797-0537-5(3))* Xlibris Corp.
Benson, Donald. Tommy Turtle Turns Blue. 2007. 28p. (J). pap. 12.78 *(978-1-4251-2087-0(3))* Trafford Publishing.
Berkes, Marianne. The Tortoise & Hare's Amazing Race, 1 vol. Morrison, Cathy, illus. 2015. (ENG & SPA.). 32p. (J). (gr. k-3). 17.95 *(978-1-62855-635-3(8))* Arbordale Publishing.
Bernstein, Owen. My Turtle & Me. Thompson, Carol, illus. 2012. (ENG.). 10p. (J). (— 1). bds. 9.99 *(978-0-545-43387-7(8))* Scholastic, Inc.
Biachi, Kelvin K. Tortoise the King. 2010. 74p. pap. 21.50 *(978-1-60911-875-4(8),* Eloquent Bks.) Strategic Book Publishing & Rights Agency (SBPRA).
Bieber Domm, Kristin. Hatchling's Journey, 1 vol. Domm, Jeffrey, illus. 2003. (ENG.). 40p. (J). (gr. -1-3). pap. 10.95 *(978-1-55109-438-0(X),* f57d42de-ae15-4d0b-b10c-3384cc83a12d) Nimbus Publishing, Ltd. CAN. Dist: Baker & Taylor Publisher Services (BTPS).
Biehn, Lesley. Humphrey & His Not So Lonely Shell. 2012. 20p. (-18). pap. 17.99 *(978-1-4772-8334-9(X))* AuthorHouse.
Birt, Michael. Kody the Conservation Pup: Helps Tori Cross the Road. Trammell, Brandon, illus. 2012. 58p. 27.95 *(978-0-578-11315-9(5));* pap. 19.95 *(978-0-578-11306-7(6))* Birt Hse. Publishing.
Blotnick, Elihu. Blue Turtle Moon Queen: The September Book. Robinson, Barbara J., illus. 2009. (ENG.). 114p. (J). (gr. 6-12). pap. 7.25 *(978-0-915090-20-4(1),* California Street) Firefall Editions.
Bodenstein, Dan. The Tale of Eartha the Sea Turtle. 2009. (Illus.). 36p. (J). pap. 12.99 *(978-0-9843228-0-0(9))* Totem Tales Publishing.
—The Tale of Eartha the Sea Turtle - Special Edition. 2011. (Illus.). 36p. (YA). pap. 12.99 *(978-0-9843228-1-7(7))* Totem Tales Publishing.
Bourgeois, Paulette. Benjamin et Sa Petite Soeur. 2004.Tr. of Franklin's Baby Sister. (FRE., Illus.). (J). (gr. k-3). spiral bd. *(978-0-616-14597-5(7))* Canadian National Institute for the Blind/Institut National Canadien pour les Aveugles.
—Franklin & the Computer. Clark, Brenda, illus. 2003. (Franklin Ser.: Bk. 16). 32p. (J). pap. 4.50 *(978-0-439-43121-7(2))* Scholastic, Inc.
—Franklin Es un Mandon. Varela, Alejandra López, tr. Clark, Brenda, illus.Tr. of Franklin Is Bossy. (SPA.). 10.95 *(978-1-930332-16-4(5),* LC6564) Lectorum Pubns., Inc.
—Franklin Fibs. Clark, Brenda, illus. 2nd ed. 2011. (Franklin Ser.). (ENG.). 32p. (J). (gr. -1-3). pap. 6.99 *(978-1-55453-774-7(6))* Kids Can Pr., Ltd. CAN. Dist: Hachette Bk. Group.
—Franklin in the Dark. 2004. (Illus.). (J). (gr. -1-2). spiral bd. *(978-0-616-01575-9(5));* spiral bd. *(978-0-616-01574-2(7))* Canadian National Institute for the Blind/Institut National Canadien pour les Aveugles.
—Franklin Says I Love You. 2004. (Illus.). (J). (gr. k-3). spiral bd. *(978-0-616-14562-3(4));* spiral bd. *(978-0-616-14561-6(6))* Canadian National Institute for the Blind/Institut National Canadien pour les Aveugles.
—Franklin Wants a Pet. Clark, Brenda, illus. 2013. (Franklin Ser.). (ENG.). 32p. (J). (gr. -1-3). pap. 6.99 *(978-1-77138-004-1(7))* Kids Can Pr., Ltd. CAN. Dist: Hachette Bk. Group.
—Franklin's Baby Sister. Clark, Brenda, illus. (Franklin Ser.). (ENG.). 32p. (J). (gr. -1-3). *(978-1-55074-858-1(0))* Kids Can Pr., Ltd.
—Franklin's Family Treasury. Clark, Brenda, illus. 2003. (Franklin Ser.). (ENG.). 128p. (J). (gr. -1-3). 15.95 *(978-1-55337-479-4(7))* Kids Can Pr., Ltd. CAN. Dist: Hachette Bk. Group.
—Franklin's New Friend. Clark, Brenda, illus. (Franklin Ser.). (ENG.). 32p. (J). (gr. -1-3). *(978-1-55074-363-0(5))* Kids Can Pr., Ltd.
—Franklin's New Friend. 2004. (Illus.). (J). (gr. k-3). spiral bd. *(978-0-616-01591-9(7));* spiral bd. *(978-0-616-01590-2(9))* Canadian National Institute for the Blind/Institut National Canadien pour les Aveugles.
—Fun with Franklin: A Learning to Read Book. Clark, Brenda, illus. (Franklin Ser.). (J). (gr. -1-3). pap. *(978-1-55074-646-4(4))* Kids Can Pr., Ltd.
—Neighborhood. 2004. (Illus.). (J). (gr. k-3). spiral bd. *(978-0-616-01589-6(5));* spiral bd. *(978-0-616-01588-9(7))* Canadian National Institute for the Blind/Institut National Canadien pour les Aveugles.
—Un Nouvel Ami pour Benjamin. 2004.Tr. of Franklin's New Friend. (FRE., Illus.). (J). (gr. -1-2). spiral bd. *(978-0-616-01828-6(2))* Canadian National Institute for the Blind/Institut National Canadien pour les Aveugles.
Brett, Jan. Mossy. Brett, Jan, illus. 2012. (Illus.). 32p. (J). (gr. -1-k). 19.99 *(978-0-399-25782-7(9),* G.P. Putnam's Sons Books for Young Readers) Penguin Young Readers Group.
Briceno, Carole. Turtle's Journey, 1 vol. White, Tina Jorgenson, illus. 2009. 28p. pap. 24.95 *(978-1-60813-934-7(4))* America Star Bks.
Brightwood, Laura, illus. Anansi & the Turtle. Brightwood, Laura, . 2006. (J). *(978-0-9779290-0-9(0))* 3-C Institute for Social Development.
Brown, Dolores. A Wave of Stars. Wimmer, Sonja, illus. 2020. 44p. (J). 16.95 *(978-84-17673-41-3(5))* NubeOcho Ediciones ESP. Dist: Consortium Bk. Sales & Distribution.
Browning, Barbara T. Taru's Exciting Journey. 2009. (ENG.). 30p. pap. 21.99 *(978-1-4415-3428-6(8))* Xlibris Corp.
Bruchac, Joseph. Turtle's Race with Beaver. Dewey, Ariane & Aruego, Jose, illus. 2005. (ENG.). 32p. (J). (gr. k-3). pap. 7.99 *(978-0-14-240466-9(7),* Puffin Books) Penguin Young Readers Group.
Buckley, Richard. The Foolish Tortoise. Carle, Eric, illus. 2009. (World of Eric Carle Ser.). (ENG.). 24p. (J). (gr. -1-k). bds. 8.99 *(978-1-4169-7916-6(6),* Little Simon) Little Simon.
—The Foolish Tortoise: Book & CD. Carle, Eric, illus. 2013. (World of Eric Carle Ser.). (ENG.). 24p. (J). (gr. -1-3). pap. 10.99 *(978-1-4424-6638-8(3),* Little Simon) Little Simon.
—The Foolish Tortoise: Lap Edition. Carle, Eric, illus. 2013. (World of Eric Carle Ser.). (ENG.). 24p. (J). (gr. -1-k). bds. 12.99 *(978-1-4424-8990-5(1),* Little Simon) Little Simon.
—The Foolish Tortoise/Ready-To-Read Level 2, 1 vol. Carle, Eric, illus. 2015. (World of Eric Carle Ser.). (ENG.). 24p. (J). (gr. k-2). pap. 4.99 *(978-1-4814-3577-2(9),* 7a3ea40d-9930-41c6-98ec-71785d7c50af, Simon Spotlight) Simon Spotlight.
Bullock, Miranda. Mama Where Are You? 2008. 36p. pap. 16.99 *(978-1-4389-2962-0(5))* AuthorHouse.
Bumpsie the Red-Footed Tortoise. 2005. (J). bds. 5.99 *(978-0-9770957-0-4(3))* Turtle Time Bks.
Bumpsie's Neighborhood. 2006. (J). bds. 6.99 *(978-0-9770957-2-8(X))* Turtle Time Bks.
Bunting, Eve. Emma's Turtle. Winborn, Marsha, illus. 2014. (ENG.). 32p. (J). (gr. -1-3). pap. 6.99 *(978-1-62091-735-0(1),* Astra Young Readers) Astra Publishing Hse.
—I Love You, Too! Sweet, Melissa, illus. 2015. (ENG.). 24p. (J). (— 1). bds. 7.99 *(978-0-545-81390-7(5),* Cartwheel Bks.) Scholastic, Inc.
Burgess, Thornton W. The Adventures of Jerry Muskrat. 2004. reprint ed. pap. 1.99 *(978-1-4192-5151-1(1));* pap. 15.95 *(978-1-4191-5151-4(7))* Kessinger Publishing, LLC.
Butler, Dori. The Tortoise & the Hare: An Aesop's Fable. 2006. (J). pap. *(978-1-4108-6167-2(8))* Benchmark Education Co.
Cain, Sheridan. La Pequena Tortuga y la Cancion del Mar. Burgin, Norma, illus. 2003. (SPA.). 24p. (J). (gr. k-2). *(978-84-8418-037-1(9),* ZZ30445) Zendrera Zariquiey, Editorial ESP. Dist: Lectorum Pubns., Inc.
Canby, Kelly. Rodney. 2019. (Illus.). 32p. (J). (gr. -1-k). 17.95 *(978-1-925815-32-0(3))* Fremantle Pr. AUS. Dist: Independent Pubs. Group.
Caplin, Daniel. Grandfather Turtle. 2003. pap. 14.95 *(978-0-9726781-0-0(7))* Evening Sun Pr.
Carle, Eric. Rooster Is off to See the World. 2013. (Eric Carle Ready-To-Read Ser.). lib. bdg. 13.55 *(978-0-606-32063-4(6))* Turtleback.
Chaconas, Dori. Best Friends No. 1. McCue, Lisa, illus. 2010. (Cork & Fuzz Ser.: 1). 32p. (J). (gr. 1-3). mass mkt. 4.99 *(978-0-14-241593-1(6),* Penguin Young Readers) Penguin Young Readers Group.
Chalifoux, Lisa M. Spotty & Eddie Visit Percé. 2010. 24p. pap. 14.95 *(978-1-4269-2660-0(X))* Trafford Publishing.
Chanda, J-P. Turtle Rescue! Redondo, Jesus, illus. 2004. (Teenage Mutant Ninja Turtles Ser.). 32p. (J). (gr. 4-7). 11.65 *(978-0-7569-5371-3(5))* Perfection Learning Corp.
Cheek, Stephen. Catfish Cowboy & Mr. Turtle. 2008. 35p. pap. 21.80 *(978-0-557-02684-5(9))* Lulu Pr., Inc.
Chidebelu-Eze/Dove Publishing, Chibueze / Obi. The Tales of Tortoise: Inspirational Stories of Wisdom. Newborne, David / F., illus. 2005. (ENG.). 76p. (J). 16.00 *(978-0-9766578-0-4(5))* Dove Publishing, Inc.
Chronicle Books & ImageBooks. Little Sea Turtle: Finger Puppet Book: (Finger Puppet Book for Toddlers & Babies, Baby Books for First Year, Animal Finger Puppets) 2014. (Little Finger Puppet Board Bks.). (ENG., Illus.). 12p. (J). (gr. -1 — 1). 7.99 *(978-1-4521-2913-6(4))* Chronicle Bks. LLC.
Cockburn, Gerrie L. Why Turtles Have Shells. Cockburn, Ian, ed. Cockburn, Gerrie L., illus. (Friendship Ser.). (Illus.). 31p. (Orig.). (J). (gr. k-4). pap. 5.95 *(978-1-887461-00-9(0))* GoFindHome.
Coll-Seck, Jayden. A Turtle for Malia, 1 vol., 1. 2015. (Rosen REAL Readers: STEM & STEAM Collection). (ENG.). 8p. (J). (gr. k-1). pap. 5.46 *(978-1-5081-1441-3(2),* 36290bef-ecf4-4436-a43a-5512c10a7319, Rosen Classroom) Rosen Publishing Group, Inc., The.
Collier, Kevin Scott. Esther's Channel. 2005. (Illus.). 160p. pap. 10.95 *(978-0-9752880-6-1(7))* Baker Trittin Pr.
Collier, Talina L. Jacob & the Turtle Race. 2012. 28p. pap. 24.95 *(978-1-4626-8045-0(3))* America Star Bks.
Conlin, Laura E. Winston's Wild Journeys: Live Outside Your Shell. 2011. 43p. (J). 18.95 *(978-1-4327-6885-0(9))* Outskirts Pr., Inc.
Conway, Aaron, illus. Alex the Sea Turtle. 2007. 26p. (J). *(978-0-9777923-0-6(7))* Shiloh Children's Bks.
Cook, Sherry & Johnson, Terri. Timothy Tornado, 26. Kuhn, Jesse, illus. I.t. ed. 2006. (Quirkles — Exploring Phonics through Science Ser.: 20). 32p. 7.99 *(978-1-933815-19-0(1),* Quirkles, The) Creative 3, LLC.
Corwin, Katherine A. R. Greg the Bearded Dragon & Thomas the Sea Turtle: A Tale of Adventure, Discovery, & Friendship. 2012. 28p. pap. 19.99 *(978-1-4685-7958-1(4))* AuthorHouse.
Costello, Judi. Gertrude & the Creature. Bouthyette, Valerie, illus. 2008. 28p. pap. 24.95 *(978-1-60672-737-9(0))* America Star Bks.
Councilman, Janet H. Rocky & His Responsible Band of Cowboys, 1 vol. 2009. pap. 24.95 *(978-1-60749-384-6(5))* America Star Bks.
Courter, John. The Cheetah & the Turtle. 2011. 28p. pap. 15.99 *(978-1-4628-2952-1(X))* Xlibris Corp.
Courtney, Suzanne Gene. Ride to the Stars, a Story for Children about Life, Loss, & Love. 2009. 32p. pap. 16.50 *(978-1-60860-164-6(1),* Eloquent Bks.) Strategic Book Publishing & Rights Agency (SBPRA).
Cox, Janis. Tadeo Turtle. 2012. *(978-1-77069-695-2(4))* Word Alive Pr.
Crawford, Deborah. Tyler the Turtle Is Afraid of the Dark. Balzer, Jeremy, illus. 2006. 32p. (J). 14.95 *(978-0-9770516-1-8(7))* Laffin Minor Pr.
Crawford, Deborah & Crawford, Ryan. Pity's Porch. Ballard, Merry, illus. 2012. 24p. pap. 11.50 *(978-1-60976-796-9(9),* Strategic Bk. Publishing) Strategic Book Publishing & Rights Agency (SBPRA).
Crays, Lettie L. Timmy the Turtle Learns to Swim. Rollins, Joe, illus. 2011. 44p. (J). pap. 11.95 *(978-1-937089-06-1(1))* Truth Bk. Pubs.
Crowe, Ellie. Go to Sleep, Hide & Seek. Wu, Julie, illus. 2009. 10p. (J). bds. 11.95 *(978-1-59700-759-7(5))* Island Heritage Publishing.
Cuevas, Michelle. The Town of Turtle. Chien, Cátia, illus. 2018. (ENG.). 40p. (J). (gr. -1-3). 17.99 *(978-0-544-74982-5(0),* 1633373, Clarion Bks.) HarperCollins Pubs.
Curriculum Corporation. Tai Hao Le! 2005. pap. 79.95 incl. audio compact disk *(978-1-86366-402-8(5))* Education Services Australia Ltd. AUS. Dist: Cheng & Tsui Co.
Dadey, Debbie. Dream of the Blue Turtle. Avakyan, Tatevik, illus. 2014. (Mermaid Tales Ser.: 7). (ENG.). 128p. (J). (gr. 1-4). 17.99 *(978-1-4424-8264-7(8),* Aladdin) Simon & Schuster Children's Publishing.
Dahl, Roald. Esio Trot. 2009. 8.32 *(978-0-7848-2293-7(X),* Everbind) Marco Bk. Co.
—Esio Trot. Blake, Quentin, illus. 2009. (ENG.). 96p. (J). (gr. 3-7). 7.99 *(978-0-14-241382-1(8),* Puffin Books) Penguin Young Readers Group.
—Esio Trot. 2004. (CHI.). (J). pap. 11.70 *(978-957-574-477-9(2))* Youth Cultural Publishing Co. CHN. Dist: Chinasprout, Inc.
Davis, Laura. No! No! I Won't Be Slow! 2012. 24p. pap. 17.99 *(978-1-4772-5491-2(9))* AuthorHouse.
DeDonato, Rick. Pipsie, Nature Detective: the Lunchnapper, 0 vols. Bishop, Tracy, illus. 2016. (Pipsie, Nature Detective Ser.). (ENG.). 40p. (J). (gr. -1-2). 17.99 *(978-1-5039-5061-0(1),* 9781503950610, Two Lions) Amazon Publishing.
Demas, Corinne. Returning to Shore. 2014. (ENG.). 208p. (YA). (gr. 6-12). 17.95 *(978-1-4677-1328-3(7),* f1305577-556b-4ab1-bbd3-6087cb98b8e1, Carolrhoda Lab™) Lerner Publishing Group.

Dembicki, Carol & Dembicki, Matt. Mr. Big: A Tale of Pond Life. 2012. (ENG., Illus.). 160p. (J). (gr. 1-7). pap. 12.95 (978-1-61608-967-2(9), 608967, Sky Pony Pr.) Skyhorse Publishing Co., Inc.
Dillon-Butler, Marybeth. Myrtle the Hurdler: And Her Pink & Purple Polka-Dotted Girdle. Messing, David, illus. 2005. (ENG.). 32p. (J). (gr. -1-2). pap. 11.95 (978-0-9785075-9-6(2), Ferne Pr.) Nelson Publishing & Marketing.
Dixon, Kirstie. Pickles Helps a Friend. 2012. 16p. pap. 15.99 (978-1-4772-6445-4(0)) AuthorHouse.
Doder, Joshua. Grk: Operation Tortoise. 2009. 219p. (J). pap. (978-0-440-42152-8(7), Delacorte Pr) Random House Publishing Group.
Doerr, Bonnie J. Stakeout. Edwards, Laurie J. & Britt, Joanna, illus. 2011. 310p. pap. 12.99 (978-1-61603-007-0(0)) Leap Bks.
Dub-u-el. Zoom-Zoom & Slo-Poke. 2005. (J). pap. 15.00 (978-0-8059-6808-8(3)) Dorrance Publishing Co., Inc.
Duncan, Tisha Admire. Myrtle the Blue Eyed Turtle: A My Dirty Cat Mutt Adventure. 2012. 28p. pap. 14.95 (978-1-4497-5727-4(8), WestBow Pr.) Author Solutions, LLC.
Dunkwu, Jude. The Tortoise Tales Niki the Tortoise & the Birds: Why the Tortoise's Shell Is Cracked. 2013. (Illus.). 54p. pap. (978-0-9573727-2-6(8)) Sahara Media, Ltd.
Dunrea, Olivier. Gus Board Book. Dunrea, Olivier, illus. 2016. (Gossie & Friends Ser.). (ENG., Illus.). 32p. (J). (— 1). bds. 7.99 (978-0-544-64102-0(7), 1620822, Clarion Bks.) HarperCollins Pubs.
Duracell and the National Center for Missing & Exploited Children (NCMEC), creator. The Great Tomato Adventure: A Story about Smart Safety Choices. 2007. 0.00 (978-0-9795307-0-8(9)) Duracell & the National Ctr. for Missing & Exploited Children (NCMEC).
Durrell, Gerald. Toby the Tortoise. (Illus.). 32p. (J). 15.95 (978-1-85479-032-3(3)) O'Mara, Michael Bks., Ltd. GBR. Dist: Trans-Atlantic Pubns., Inc.
Dutton, Maude Barrows. The Tortoise & the Geese & Other Fables of Bidpai. Smith, E. Boyd, illus. 2008. 104p. pap. 7.95 (978-1-59915-249-3(5)) Yesterday's Classics.
Eggleton, Jill. Turtle's Trouble. Cammell, Sandra, illus. 2003. (Rigby Sails Early Ser.). (ENG.). 16p. (gr. 1-2). pap. 6.95 (978-0-7578-8672-0(8)) Houghton Mifflin Harcourt Publishing Co.
Eke, Vincent. The Turtle's Shell. 2013. (Illus.). 46p. pap. (978-1-909688-00-1(2)) Lionpen Publishing.
Elk, Ronit. A Surprise at Dancing Fields. 2009. 76p. pap. 10.49 (978-1-4490-2064-4(X)) AuthorHouse.
Ende, Michael. Tranquila Tragaleguas: La Tortuga Cabezota. Asensio, Agusti, illus. 2003.Tr. of Tranquila Trampeltreu. (SPA.). 42p. (J). (gr. k-3). pap. 8.95 (978-84-204-3709-5(3)) Santillana USA Publishing Co., Inc.
Fable, Aesop. The Tortoise & the Hare. 2012. (J). 29.99 (978-1-61913-103-3(X)) Weigl Pubs., Inc.
Falwell, Cathryn. Turtle Splash! Countdown at the Pond. Falwell, Cathryn, illus. 2008. (ENG., Illus.). 32p. (J). (gr. -1-3). pap. 7.99 (978-0-06-142927-9(9), Greenwillow Bks.) HarperCollins Pubs.
Finally, Lil Rose. Slowpoke the Turtle & Company. Drape, Kaitlin, illus. 2005. (J). pap. 8.00 (978-0-8059-6778-4(8)) Dorrance Publishing Co., Inc.
Finn, Ann-Marie. Captain Kieron. Finn, Ann-Marie, illus. 2013. (Illus.). 32p. pap. (978-0-9874160-3-2(0)) Wybble Publishing.
Floyd, Lucy. Rabbit & Turtle Go to School/Conejo y Tortuga Van a la Escuela: Bilingual English-Spanish. Ada, Alma Flor & Campoy, F. Isabel, trs. Denise, Christopher, illus. 2010. (Green Light Readers Level 1 Ser.).Tr. of Rabbit & Turtle Go to School. (ENG.). 28p. (J). (gr. -1-3). pap. 5.99 (978-0-547-33898-9(8), 1418429, Clarion Bks.) HarperCollins Pubs.
For the Love of Turtles: Six-Pack. (Greetings Ser.: Vol. 1). 24p. (gr. 2-3). 31.00 (978-0-7635-9423-7(7)) Rigby Education.
Ford, Carole S. Timothy Turtle & Sammy Scallop. Edwin, Kimberly, illus. 30p. (J). (gr. -1-k). pap. 4.95 (978-1-891533-02-0(9)) Calvin Partnership, LLC.
Frances Holloway. The Turtle That Lived in the Sand. 2010. 28p. pap. 21.99 (978-1-4535-4845-5(9)) Xlibris Corp.
Fusek Peters, Andrew. Bear & Turtle & the Great Lake Race. Edgson, Alison, illus. 2005. (Traditional Tales with a Twist Ser.). 32p. (J). (gr. 2-2). per. (978-1-904550-91-4(6)) Child's Play International Ltd.
—The Talkative Tortoise. 2011. (Traditional Tales with a Twist Ser.). (Illus.). 32p. (J). (978-1-84643-418-1(1)) Child's Play International Ltd.
Fuson, Robin Densmore. Rosita Valdez: And the Giant Sea Turtle. 2012. 108p. 28.99 (978-1-4497-6487-6(8)); pap. 11.99 (978-1-4497-6486-9(X)) Author Solutions, LLC. (WestBow Pr.).
Galera Staff. La Liebre y la Tortuga. (SPA.). 24p. (J). 9.95 (978-84-246-1555-0(7), GL3096) La Galera, S.A. Editorial ESP. Dist: AIMS International Bks., Inc.
Gamlin, Jim. Lucky Nickel: The Story of Nickel the Sea Turtle. 2012. 44p. pap. 21.99 (978-1-4691-9662-6(X)) Xlibris Corp.
Gaona, Gloria. Dominic & His Turtle Michael Angelo. 2003. 32p. (J). pap. 9.00 (978-0-8059-5764-8(2)) Dorrance Publishing Co., Inc.
Garcia, R. M. The Steamer Trunk Adventures #1: The Trunk & the Tortoise. 2006. 76p. pap. 16.95 (978-1-4241-0614-1(1)) PublishAmerica, Inc.
Gates, Margo. Turtles in the Sun. Hartley, Brian, illus. 2019. (Let's Look at Weather (Pull Ahead Readers — Fiction) Ser.). (ENG.). 16p. (J). (gr. -1-1). 27.99 (978-1-5415-5842-7(1), 42323cb5-f653-4387-aa19-f6d8c3f03a94, Lerner Pubns.) Lerner Publishing Group.
Gehl, Laura. Hare & Tortoise Race Across Israel. Goodreau, Sarah, illus. 2015. (ENG.). 32p. (J). (gr. -1-1). E-Book 23.99 (978-1-4677-6202-1(4), Kar-Ben Publishing) Lerner Publishing Group.
Gerver, Jane E. The Santa Snatcher. Spaziante, Patrick, illus. 2004. 32p. (J). lib. bdg. 15.00 (978-1-4242-0959-0(5)) Fitzgerald Bks.
Gewirtz, Allen. The Magic Turtle. 2008. (ENG.). 42p. per. 16.99 (978-1-4257-9134-6(4)) Xlibris Corp.
Geyer, Clyde. The Awesome Adventures of Chuckie Chopper & Friends. 2012. 52p. pap. 15.95 (978-1-4575-0741-0(2)) Dog Ear Publishing, LLC.
Gilland, Gary P. The Turtle Train Troop. 2011. 24p. pap. 24.95 (978-1-4626-3210-7(6)) America Star Bks.
Gipson, Crash. Sheldon's Favorite Game. 2011. 36p. pap. 24.95 (978-1-4626-4578-7(X)) America Star Bks.
Glick, Susan. Jemma's Got the Travel Bug, 1 vol. 2010. (ENG., Illus.). 32p. (J). (gr. -1-3). 14.99 (978-0-7643-3632-4(0), 3968) Schiffer Publishing, Ltd.
Golden Books. Follow the Ninja! (Teenage Mutant Ninja Turtles) Lambe, Steve, illus. 2015. (Little Golden Book Ser.). (ENG.). 24p. (J). (-k). 5.99 (978-0-553-51204-5(8), Golden Bks.) Random Hse. Children's Bks.
Gorbachev, Valeri. Ms. Turtle the Babysitter. Gorbachev, Valeri, illus. 2005. (I Can Read Bks.). (Illus.). 64p. (J). (gr. k-3). (ENG.). 15.99 (978-0-06-058073-5(9)); lib. bdg. 16.89 (978-0-06-058074-2(7)) HarperCollins Pubs.
—Whose Hat Is It? 2004. 30p. (J). lib. bdg. 13.85 (978-1-4242-0713-8(4)) Fitzgerald Bks.
—Whose Hat Is It? Gorbachev, Valeri, illus. (My First I Can Read Ser.). (Illus.). 32p. (J). (gr. -1 — 1). 2005. (ENG.). pap. 4.99 (978-0-06-053436-3(2), HarperCollins) 2004. (ENG., 14.99 (978-0-06-053434-9(6)) 2004. lib. bdg. 15.89 (978-0-06-053435-6(4)) HarperCollins Pubs.
Greenberg, Penny. The Adventures of Toby the Turtle & Mighty Magoo. 2008. 16p. pap. 8.49 (978-1-4389-1014-7(2)) AuthorHouse.
Grubnedor Press. Tuppy the Turtle Puppy. 2007. (Illus.). 32p. (J). 10.95 (978-0-9795407-0-7(4)) Grubnedor Pr.
Gumbs, Al-Tariq. The Turtle Who Bullied. 2012. (ENG.). pap. 10.00 (978-1-4675-1785-0(2)) Independent Pub.
Haltigan, Susanne. Seymour the Sea Turtle Saves His Sea Friends. 2011. 28p. pap. 11.95 (978-1-4567-6549-1(3)) AuthorHouse.
Hamilton, Linda. The Wise Old Turtle. 2005. (J). (978-1-933248-06-6(8)) World Quest Learning.
Harder, Christopher. It's Tough to Nap on a Turtle. Harder, Rolf, illus. 2008. (ENG.). 11p. (J). (gr. -1). bds. 5.95 (978-0-9726614-9-2(2)) Shenanigan Bks.
harkins, charles. Naptime Adventures of Luksi the Turtle. 2010. (ENG.). 174p. pap. 20.96 (978-0-557-28695-9(6)) Lulu Pr., Inc.
Hausman, Gerald. Timeswimmer. 2009. (Island Fiction Ser.). 187p. (J). (gr. 5-16). pap. (978-1-4050-9898-4(8)) Macmillan Caribbean.
Heckt, Jackie. Tilly the Turtle, 1 vol. 2017. (Pet Tales! Ser.). (ENG.). 24p. (J). (gr. 1-1). pap. 9.25 (978-1-5081-5676-5(X), dae0fb68-6940-4774-9d3d-bbceb149e20a, PowerKids Pr.) Rosen Publishing Group, Inc., The.
Heder, Thyra. Alfie: (the Turtle That Disappeared) 2017. (ENG., Illus.). 48p. (J). (gr. -1-3). 18.99 (978-1-4197-2529-6(7), 1165701, Abrams Bks. for Young Readers) Abrams, Inc.
Helean, April K. Love Can Build a Bridge. 2012. 24p. pap. 15.99 (978-1-4691-5621-7(0)) Xlibris Corp.
Henry, Kristina. The Turtle Tank, 1 vol. 2011. (ENG., Illus.). 32p. (J). (gr. -1-3). 16.99 (978-0-7643-3843-4(9), 4272, Schiffer Publishing Ltd) Schiffer Publishing, Ltd.
Hensley, Terri Anne. Tobias Andrew Bartholomew. Hall, Norris, illus. 2007. 32p. per. 8.99 (978-0-9789057-6-7(8)) Huntington Ludlow Media Group.
Hicks, Robert Z. Tommie Turtle's Secret. Rolseth, Ruthie, illus. 2007. (ENG.). 40p. (J). 16.95 (978-0-9792031-0-7(4)) R.Z. Enterprises of Florida.
Himes, John. Everyone Is Special. 2012. 24p. pap. 24.95 (978-1-4626-7462-6(3)) America Star Bks.
Himmelman, John. Box Turtle. 2018. (Illus.). 32p. (J). (gr. -1-12). 15.95 (978-1-63076-331-2(4)) Taylor Trade Publishing.
—Tudley Didn't Know, 1 vol. Himmelman, John, illus. 2006. (ENG., Illus.). 32p. (J). (gr. -1-3). 15.95 (978-0-9764943-6-2(1)); pap. 8.95 (978-1-934359-04-4(1)) Arbordale Publishing.
Hixon, Mara Uman. Turtle's Way: Loggy, Greeny & Leather. Harris, Steve J., illus. 2004. 25p. (J). (gr. -1-3). 16.00 (978-1-887774-20-8(3), Wynden) Canmore Pr.
Holden, Pam. Turtle Is Lost, 1 vol. 2015. (ENG., Illus.). 16p. (-1). pap. (978-1-77654-074-7(3), Red Rocket Readers) Flying Start Bks.
Holyoak, Kathleen & Summers, Sherry. Flowers in Heaven. 2009. 32p. pap. 14.49 (978-1-4389-4607-8(4)) AuthorHouse.
Hong, Catherine Thao. The Adventures of Miss Turtle. Pipe, Jasper, illus. 2012. 24p. (J). pap. (978-0-9873790-0-9(3)) Icky Grass Books.
Hoobler, David. Zonk & the Secret Lagoon: The Further Adventures of Zonk the Dreaming Tortoise. Hoobler, David, illus. l.t. ed. 2005. (Illus.). 32p. (J). lib. bdg. 18.95 (978-0-9706537-1-0(9)) Zonk Galleries and Pubns.
Hooray for Boys & Girls! 2006. (J). 15.95 (978-0-9776837-0-3(2)) West Woods Pr.
Horn, Peter. When I Grow Up... Kadmon, Cristina, illus. 2014. 32p. pap. 8.00 (978-1-61003-370-1(1)) Center for the Collaborative Classroom.
Howell, Gill. Tortoise & the Baboon. Woody, illus. 2004. (ENG.). 16p. (J). lib. bdg. 23.65 (978-1-59646-686-9(3)) Dingles & Co.
Hsia, Pei Chen. The Little Dumpling. 2012. 82p. pap. 19.95 (978-1-4626-8041-2(0)) America Star Bks.
Hughes, John P. A Wish for Little Tommy Turtle. White, Tara B., illus. 2011. 48p. pap. 24.95 (978-1-4626-0011-3(5)) America Star Bks.
I Am A Dog. 2008. (Illus.). 26p. 24.95 (978-0-9801054-0-7(4)) Teahouse of Danger.
Ikids Staff. Little Turtles. Larranaga, Ana, illus. 2008. (iBaby Float-Alongs Ser.). (ENG.). 6p. (J). (gr. -1). 12.99 (978-1-58476-808-1(8)) Innovative Kids.
Ikpe, Ernest & Madge. African Stories about the Tortoise. 2011. 32p. pap. 17.00 (978-1-4634-2726-9(3)) AuthorHouse.
Ingram, Jacquelyn. Dakota's Doggie Tale. 2009. 32p. pap. 14.99 (978-1-4490-1327-1(9)) AuthorHouse.
Irvin-Marston, Hope. My Little Book of Painted Turtles. Magdalena-Brown, Maria, illus. 2nd ed. 2004. (ENG.). 32p. (J). pap. 7.95 (978-0-89317-055-4(0), WW-0550, Windward Publishing) Finney Co., Inc.
Irwin, Bindi & Black, Jess. Surfing with Turtles: Bindi Wildlife Adventures, 8. 2013. (Bindi's Wildlife Adventures Ser.: 8). (ENG.). 112p. (J). (gr. 3-6). pap. 8.99 (978-1-4022-8094-8(7), Sourcebooks Jabberwocky) Sourcebooks, Inc.
Itoh, Shimpei. Hyper Dolls, Vol. 5. 2003. (Illus.). 208p. pap. 15.95 (978-1-929090-67-9(6)) International Comics & Entertainment L.L.C.
James, Hollis. Mikey's Monster (Teenage Mutant Ninja Turtles) Spaziante, Patrick, illus. 2013. (Step into Reading Ser.). (ENG.). 48p. (J). (gr. k-3). 5.99 (978-0-449-81826-8(8), Random Hse. Bks. for Young Readers) Random Hse. Children's Bks.
Javernick, Ellen. The Birthday Pet, 0 vols. O'Malley, Kevin, illus. 2012. (ENG.). 34p. (J). (gr. -1-2). pap. 9.99 (978-0-7614-6238-5(4), 9780761462385, Two Lions) Amazon Publishing.
Jay, Lorraine A. Sea Turtle Journey: The Story of a Loggerhead Turtle. Lee, Katie, illus. 2011. (Smithsonian Oceanic Collection Ser.). (ENG.). 32p. (J). (gr. -1-3). 19.95 (978-1-60727-660-9(7)) Soundprints.
Jeffords, Stephanie & Branum, Anita. Jumpy the Turtle. May, Ashley, illus. 2012. 92p. pap. 20.00 (978-1-936750-80-1(5)) Yorkshire Publishing Group.
Jenkins, Amanda. How the Turtle Cracked its Shell: A Tale from Guatemala. 2006. (J). pap. (978-1-4108-6171-9(6)) Benchmark Education Co.
Jennings, Sharon. Franklin Stays Up. Jeffrey, Sean et al, illus. 2003. 32p. (J). pap. (978-0-439-41815-7(1)) Scholastic, Inc.
Jennings, Sharon, et al, adapted by. Franklin & the Bubble Gum. 2006. (Kids Can Read Ser.). (ENG., Illus.). 32p. (J). (gr. 1-2). 3.95 (978-1-55337-817-4(2)); 14.95 (978-1-55337-816-7(4)) Kids Can Pr., Ltd. CAN. Dist: Hachette Bk. Group.
—Franklin & the Computer. 2003. (Franklin TV Storybook Ser.). (ENG., Illus.). 32p. (J). (gr. -1-3). 4.95 (978-1-55337-363-6(4)); 10.95 (978-1-55337-362-9(6)) Kids Can Pr., Ltd. CAN. Dist: Hachette Bk. Group.
—Franklin & the Cookies. 2005. (Kids Can Read Ser.). (ENG., Illus.). 32p. (J). (gr. 1-2). 3.95 (978-1-55337-717-7(6)); 14.95 (978-1-55337-716-0(8)) Kids Can Pr., Ltd. CAN. Dist: Hachette Bk. Group.
—Franklin & the Tin Flute. 2005. (Kids Can Read Ser.). (ENG., Illus.). 32p. (J). (gr. 1-2). 3.95 (978-1-55337-801-3(6)); 14.95 (978-1-55337-800-6(8)) Kids Can Pr., Ltd. CAN. Dist: Hachette Bk. Group.
—Franklin Celebrates. 2005. (Franklin TV Storybook Ser.). (ENG., Illus.). 32p. (J). (gr. -1-3). 4.95 (978-1-55337-502-9(5)) Kids Can Pr., Ltd. CAN. Dist: Hachette Bk. Group.
—Franklin Stays Up. 2003. (Kids Can Read Ser.). (ENG., Illus.). 32p. (J). (gr. 1-2). 3.95 (978-1-55337-372-8(3)); 14.95 (978-1-55337-371-1(5)) Kids Can Pr., Ltd. CAN. Dist: Hachette Bk. Group.
—Franklin Wants a Badge. 2003. (Franklin TV Storybook Ser.). (ENG., Illus.). 32p. (J). (gr. -1-3). 4.95 (978-1-55337-468-8(1)); 10.95 (978-1-55337-467-1(3)) Kids Can Pr., Ltd. CAN. Dist: Hachette Bk. Group.
—Franklin's Picnic. 2006. (Kids Can Read Ser.). (ENG., Illus.). 32p. (J). (gr. 1-2). 3.95 (978-1-55337-715-3(X)) Kids Can Pr., Ltd. CAN. Dist: Hachette Bk. Group.
—Franklin's Pond Phantom. 2005. (Kids Can Read Ser.). (ENG., Illus.). 32p. (J). (gr. 1-2). 3.95 (978-1-55337-719-1(2)); 14.95 (978-1-55337-718-4(4)) Kids Can Pr., Ltd. CAN. Dist: Hachette Bk. Group.
—Franklin's Soapbox Derby. 2006. (Kids Can Read Ser.). (ENG., Illus.). 32p. (J). (gr. 1-2). 3.95 (978-1-55337-819-8(9)); 14.95 (978-1-55337-818-1(0)) Kids Can Pr., Ltd. CAN. Dist: Hachette Bk. Group.
—Franklin's Surprise. 2003. (Kids Can Read Ser.). (ENG., Illus.). 32p. (J). (gr. 1-2). 3.95 (978-1-55337-466-4(5)) Kids Can Pr., Ltd. CAN. Dist: Hachette Bk. Group.
Jepson, Jeanette. The Adventures of Theodore Tortoise - Claude's Big Adventure: Claude's Big Adventure. 2011. 24p. pap. 15.99 (978-1-4628-8646-3(9)) Xlibris Corp.
Johanson, Rhonda. The Great Tempo Race. 2011. 32p. pap. 21.99 (978-1-4568-5363-1(5)) Xlibris Corp.
John, Jory. Giraffe Problems. Smith, Lane, illus. 2018. (Animal Problems Ser.). (ENG.). 42p. (J). (gr. -1-2). 17.99 (978-1-5247-7203-1(8), Random Hse. Bks. for Young Readers) Random Hse. Children's Bks.
Johnson, Rebecca. Grace the Green Sea Turtle, 1 vol. 2017. (Reptile Adventures Ser.). (ENG.). 24p. (J). (gr. 1-2). 26.27 (978-1-5081-9358-6(4), 99c0b084-6b9a-4fb1-b488-64b9960476e9); pap. 9.25 (978-1-5081-9362-3(2), cd849d35-a777-4c3f-a929-dc68003c518f) Rosen Publishing Group, Inc., The. (Windmill Bks.).
—Sea Turtle's Clever Plan, 1 vol. 2005. (Animal Storybooks Ser.). (ENG., Illus.). 24p. (gr. k-2). lib. bdg. 24.67 (978-0-8368-5975-1(8), 85df11cc-cd7f-448c-b0b2-d5dab7c71562, Gareth Stevens Learning Library) Stevens, Gareth Publishing LLLP.
Jonas, Debbie Sue. The Key Lime Candies Clubt in Two Turtles' Tales. 2012. 44p. pap. 17.49 (978-1-4691-5283-7(5)) Xlibris Corp.
Jones, Shelley V. & Sprick, Marilyn. Turtle in the Tuba: Read Well Level K Unit 8 Storybook. McDonnell, Kevin, illus. 2004. (Read Well Level K Ser.). 20p. (978-1-57035-672-8(6)) Cambium Education, Inc.
Keane, Sarah. The Hare & the Tortoise: An Aesop's Fable Retold by Sarah Keane, 1 vol. rev. ed. 2013. (Literary Text Ser.). (ENG., Illus.). 28p. (J). (gr. 2-3). pap. 9.99 (978-1-4333-5572-1(8)) Teacher Created Materials, Inc.
Keats Curtis, Jennifer. Turtles in My Sandbox, 1 vol. Schongut, Emanuel, illus. 2006. (ENG.). 32p. (J). (gr. 1-5). 16.95 (978-0-9768823-7-4(X)) Arbordale Publishing.
Keene, Carolyn. The Tortoise & the Scare. Francis, Peter, illus. 2019. (Nancy Drew Clue Book Ser.: 11). (ENG.). 96p. (J). (gr. 1-4). 16.99 (978-1-5344-1483-9(5)); pap. 5.99 (978-1-5344-1482-2(7)) Simon & Schuster Children's Publishing. (Aladdin).
Keith, Brooke. Chrissie's Shell. Bausman, Mary, illus. 2010. 32p. (J). 14.99 (978-1-59317-398-2(9)) Warner Pr., Inc.
Kennedy, Geno. Tiny Takes a Trip. Engler, Lori, illus. 2011. 24p. pap. 24.95 (978-1-4560-8523-0(9)) America Star Bks.
Kessler, Liz. Poppy the Pirate Dog & the Missing Treasure. Phillips, Mike, illus. (Candlewick Sparks Ser.). (ENG.). 64p. (J). (gr. k-4). 2016. pap. 5.99 (978-0-7636-8772-4(3)) 2015. 14.99 (978-0-7636-7497-7(4)) Candlewick Pr.
Kim, Melissa. A Blanding's Turtle Story, 1 vol. Fitch, Jada, illus. 2016. (Wildlife on the Move Ser.). (ENG.). 24p. (J). bds. 10.95 (978-1-939017-92-5(0), 01b48992-e322-45a8-bf26-dbad0b60965e) Islandport Pr., Inc.
Kim, YeShil. Tortoise & Hare. Kheiriyeh, Rashin, illus. 2014. (MySELF Bookshelf Ser.). (ENG.). 32p. (J). (gr. k-2). pap. 11.94 (978-1-60357-700-7(9)); lib. bdg. 25.27 (978-1-59953-665-1(X)) Norwood Hse. Pr.
Kimmel, Eric A. The Fisherman & the Turtle, 0 vols. Aviles, Martha, illus. 2013. (ENG.). 32p. (J). (gr. k-3). pap. 9.99 (978-1-4778-1672-1(0), 9781477816721, Two Lions) Amazon Publishing.
King, Jerry. Tommy the Turtle. 2009. 16p. pap. 9.95 (978-1-4389-7551-1(1)) AuthorHouse.
Klassen, Jon. We Found a Hat. Klassen, Jon, illus. 2016. (Hat Trilogy Ser.). (ENG., Illus.). 56p. (J). (gr. -1-3). 18.99 (978-0-7636-5600-3(3)) Candlewick Pr.
Kleemann, Linda. Larry the Turtle When Everyone Helps, Everyone Wins! Malkowski, Melissa, illus. 2005. (J). pap. 7.95 (978-0-9776487-0-2(2)) Fencepost Communications Inc.
Klise, Kate. The Loch Ness Punster. Klise, M. Sarah, illus. 2016. (43 Old Cemetery Road Ser.: 7). (ENG.). 144p. (J). (gr. 3-7). pap. 7.99 (978-0-544-81085-3(6), 1641667, Clarion Bks.) HarperCollins Pubs.
Korman, Susan. Box Turtle at Silver Pond Lane: Smithsonians Backyard. Marchesi, Stephen, illus. 2005. (Smithsonian's Backyard Ser.). (ENG.). 32p. (J). (gr. -1-2). pap. 6.95 (978-1-56899-935-7(6), S5020) Soundprints.
Kreitz, Tina. Rocky the Sea Turtle. Triplett, Chris Harper, illus. 2013. (ENG.). (J). 14.95 (978-1-62086-132-5(1)) Amplify Publishing Group.
Kruse, Robyn A. Sammy the Sea Turtle, 1 vol. Litteral, Christopher, illus. 2010. 18p. 24.95 (978-1-4489-4020-2(6)) PublishAmerica, Inc.
Kuperman, Marina. Turtle Feet, Surfer's Beat. 2007. 164p. (J). pap. 9.99 (978-0-9801109-0-6(4)) Kuperman, Marina.
Labadie, Sally. Tanner's Turtle. Jeremiah, illus. 2012. 32p. pap. 12.95 (978-1-61244-085-9(1)) Halo Publishing International.
Lampley, David Gerald. Shorty's Dilemm. 2011. 74p. pap. 19.95 (978-1-4560-4189-2(4)) America Star Bks.
Larsen, Alison. My Turtle. Larsen, Alison, illus. 2006. (Illus.). 24p. (J). (gr. -1-3). per. 11.95 (978-1-60002-095-7(X), 3963) Mountain Valley Publishing, LLC.
—Thomas the Turtle. 2006. (Illus.). 21p. (J). per. 14.95 (978-1-60002-097-1(6), 3961) Mountain Valley Publishing, LLC.
—Thomas the Turtle's Adventures. 2006. (Illus.). 23p. (J). per. 14.95 (978-1-60002-096-4(8), 3962) Mountain Valley Publishing, LLC.
LeapFrog Staff. Pirates: The Treasure of Turtle Island. 2008. (J). 13.99 (978-1-59319-927-2(9)) LeapFrog Enterprises, Inc.
Lee, Ginger. Tessa T's Treasures, 1 vol. 2010. 22p. 29.95 (978-1-4489-4526-9(7)) America Star Bks.
Lee, Taekwon & Nodelman, Jeffrey. Baeoh & the Bully. Beavers, Ethen, illus. 2018. (Team Taekwondo Ser.: 2). 96p. (J). (gr. 1-4). pap. 9.99 (978-1-62336-945-3(2), 9781623369453, Rodale Kids) Random Hse. Children's Bks.
León, Georgina Lázaro. ¡Viva la Tortuga! Torres, Walter, illus. (SPA.). 30p. (J). (gr. 3-5). 12.95 (978-1-57581-605-0(9)) Santillana USA Publishing Co., Inc.
Libby, Lori Ann. The Adventures of Henry Hamper & the Flying Fish. Lee, Tricia Ting, illus. 2010. 34p. pap. 13.95 (978-1-60911-493-0(0), Eloquent Bks.) Strategic Book Publishing & Rights Agency (SBPRA).
Lievre et la Tortue. pap. 5.95 (978-88-8148-779-0(9)) EMC/Paradigm Publishing.
Limu the Blue Turtle. 2003. (J). 15.95 (978-0-89610-549-2(0)) Island Heritage Publishing.
Lin, Joyce, tr. The frog in the Well. Caprio, Pattie, illus. 2008. (ENG & CHI.). 36p. (J). 14.95 (978-0-9801305-1-5(4)) CE Bilingual Bks. LLC.
Lloyd, Sylvia. A Little Turtle's Tale. 2005. pap. (978-1-932077-96-4(0)) Athena Pr.
Lockaby, Angie. Tad the Turtle It's Okay to Be Different. 2012. 28p. pap. 19.99 (978-1-4772-7295-4(X)) AuthorHouse.
Lockard, Donna Lee. Sasha the Tortoise's Summer Vacation. 2013. (ENG.). 36p. (J). pap. 19.95 (978-1-4787-0938-1(3)) Outskirts Pr., Inc.
Loewen, Nancy. The Tortoise & the Hare, Narrated by the Silly but Truthful Tortoise. Cox, Russ & Cox, Thomas, illus. 2018. (Other Side of the Fable Ser.). (ENG.). 24p. (J). (gr. -1-3). lib. bdg. 27.99 (978-1-5158-2867-9(0), 138405, Picture Window Bks.) Capstone.
The Long Legged Turtle. 2013. 44p. pap. 16.99 (978-1-4808-0460-9(6)) Archway Publishing.
Lordon, Claire. Lorenzo, the Pizza-Loving Lobster. 2016. (ENG., Illus.). 32p. (J). (gr. -1-3). 16.99 (978-1-4998-0228-3(5)) Little Bee Books Inc.
Lowe, Lana. The Three Little Girls & the Giant Sea Turtle. Beaumont, Peter, illus. 2006. (J). (978-0-9777274-0-7(8)) Lone Star Publishing Co.
Lowell, Susan. The Tortoise & the Jackrabbit: La Tortuga y la Liebre. Harris, Jim, illus. 2004. (New Bilingual Picture Book Ser.). (ENG.). 32p. (J). (gr. -1-3). pap. 7.95 (978-0-87358-869-0(X)) Cooper Square Publishing Llc.
Lowery, Paul. Do You Know Where Sea Turtles Go? 2007. (J). 15.99 (978-0-9792379-0-4(4)) PBL Stories LLC.
—Do You Know Where Sea Turtles Go? Thomas, Tim, illus. 2005. (J). lib. bdg. 15.99 (978-0-9771059-9-1(7)) Thomas Expressions, LLC.
Lueders, Tamara Devitre. Hoagie, the Hockey Turtle. 2005. (ENG., Illus.). 34p. per. 15.99 (978-1-4257-0169-7(8)) Xlibris Corp.
Lynch, Stephen D. The Travels of Kui, the African Spurred Tortoise. Richard, Keisha Luana, illus. 2007. 36p. per. 24.95 (978-1-4137-1802-7(7)) America Star Bks.
MacGregor, Doug. Turtellini the Turbo-Charged Turtle. 2011. (ENG., Illus.). 52p. (J). lib. bdg. 14.95 (978-0-9654843-8-1(6)) MacGregor, Doug.
MacKinnon, Mairi, ed. The Hare & the Tortoise. Howarth, Daniel, illus. 2007. (First Reading Level 4 Ser.). 48p. (J). (gr.

-1-3). 8.99 *(978-0-7945-1612-3(2)*, Usborne) EDC Publishing.

Mainor, Carol L. On Kiki's Reef, 1 vol. Hunner, Trina L., illus. 2014. (ENG.). 32p. (J). (gr. k-4). 16.95 *(978-1-58469-476-2(9)*, Dawn Pubns.) Sourcebooks, Inc.

Mangual, C. Ines. Bug Battle! Spaziante, Patrick, illus. 2017. 20p. (J). *(978-1-5182-2750-9(3))* Random Hse., Inc.

Mangual, Cynthia Ines. Bug Battle! 2017. (Step into Reading Level 2 Ser.). lib. bdg. 14.75 *(978-0-606-39863-3(5))* Turtleback.

March, Julia. Lego Ninjago - Ninja, Go! 2015. (DK Reader Level 2 Ser.). lib. bdg. 13.55 *(978-0-606-36924-4(4))* Turtleback.

Martin, Candice J. Theo's Special Gift. Bonavita, Madison M., illus. l.t. ed. 2006. 12p. (J). per. 12.99 *(978-1-59879-190-7(7))* Lifevest Publishing, Inc.

Mason, Craig. Turtle Games. Mason, Bergetta, illus. 2003. 32p. (J). 4.99 *(978-0-9729153-0-4(3))* 1 Sleeve Publishing.

Matsumoto, Lisa. The Adventures of Gary & Harry: A Tale of Two Turtles. Furuya, Michael, illus. 2006. (J). 16.95 *(978-0-9647491-4-6(9))* Lehua, Inc.

Matter, Sandy. The Great Sea Chase. 2011. 20p. pap. 24.95 *(978-1-4626-2488-1(X))* America Star Bks.

Mau, Connie. Catch me if you Can. Lemus, Kristina, illus. l.t. ed. 2006. 28p. (J). 14.95 *(978-0-9778843-0-8(9))* Mau, C. Publishing Co.

May, Karen. Thelma the Tiny Sea Turtle. 2011. 26p. pap. *(978-1-908481-78-8(1))* YouWriteOn.

Mbe na Nkita: The Tortoise & the Dog. 2008. (YOR & ENG., Illus.). 36p. 16.00 *(978-0-9801243-1-6(X))* Blazing Ideas Ltd.

McCall, Val. Twelve Rabbits & a Turtle: Bilingual English French. 2012. 46p. pap. 9.95 *(978-1-938367-00-7(6))* Destinee Media.

McCune, Susan. Rabbit & Turtle, 1 vol., 1. 2015. (Rosen REAL Readers: STEM & STEAM Collection). (ENG.). 8p. (J). (gr. k-1). pap. 5.46 *(978-1-5081-1409-3(9)*, aaa38a43-2ffa-49d7-8ad0-a88ba4792a86, Rosen Classroom) Rosen Publishing Group, Inc., The.

McDermott, Gerald. Jabutí the Tortoise: A Trickster Tale from the Amazon. McDermott, Gerald, illus. 2005. (ENG., Illus.). 32p. (J). (gr. -1-3). pap. 8.99 *(978-0-15-205374-1(3)*, 1196181, Clarion Bks.) HarperCollins Pubs.

McGovern, Suzanne. Gator & Pete - More Alike Than It Seems. Bizjak, Donna, illus. 2007. (J). 13.99 *(978-0-9792558-0-9(5))* Hatch Ideas, Inc.

McKelvie, Melissa, told to. Serena & the Turtle Eggs. 2007. (ENG.). 28p. pap. 15.99 *(978-1-4196-7780-9(2))* CreateSpace Independent Publishing Platform.

McLellan, Joseph. How the Turtle Got Its Shell: A Nanabosho Legend. Brynjolson, Rhian, illus. 2015. (ENG.). 32p. (J). mass mkt. 10.95 *(978-0-921827-40-5(7)*, ae600540-de47-46be-be3d-c8478474bf69) Pemmican Pubns., Inc. CAN. Dist: Firefly Bks., Ltd.

McMurtrie, Kevin. The Very Thoughtful Turtle. 2013. (ENG.). 24p. (YA). pap. 13.77 *(978-1-4907-0940-6(1))* Trafford Publishing.

McVicar, William E. Turtle Tries. 2008. 16p. pap. 24.95 *(978-1-60563-180-6(9))* America Star Bks.

Meadows, Daisy. Tess the Sea Turtle Fairy. 2011. (Illus.). 65p. (J). *(978-0-545-28874-3(6))* Scholastic, Inc.

Melancon, Lenell Levy. Tooties the Turtle Tells the Truth: An Interactive Tale about Secrets. 2013. 40p. pap. 15.99 *(978-1-4525-7900-9(8)*, Balboa Pr.) Author Solutions, LLC.

Meng, Cece. Always Remember. Jago, illus. 2016. 32p. (J). (gr. -1-2). 17.99 *(978-0-399-16809-3(5)*, Philomel Bks.) Penguin Young Readers Group.

Meredith, Amberley. Bessie Bump Gets a New Family. Lee, Nikita, illus. 2010. 26p. pap. 13.95 *(978-1-60911-901-0(0)*, Eloquent Bks.) Strategic Book Publishing & Rights Agency (SBPRA).

Michalak, Jamie. Joe & Sparky Get New Wheels: Candlewick Sparks. Remkiewicz, Frank, illus. 2013. (Candlewick Sparks Ser.). (ENG.). 48p. (J). (gr. k-4). pap. 5.99 *(978-0-7636-6641-5(6))* Candlewick Pr.

—Joe & Sparky Go to School. Remkiewicz, Frank, illus. 2014. (Candlewick Sparks Ser.). (ENG.). 48p. (J). (gr. k-4). pap. 5.99 *(978-0-7636-7181-5(9))* Candlewick Pr.

—Joe & Sparky, Superstars! Candlewick Sparks. Remkiewicz, Frank, illus. 2013. (Candlewick Sparks Ser.). (ENG.). 48p. (J). (gr. k-4). pap. 5.99 *(978-0-7636-6642-2(4))* Candlewick Pr.

Monroe, Mary Alice. The Islanders. (Islanders Ser.: 1). (ENG.). (J). (gr. 3-7). 2022. 320p. pap. 8.99 *(978-1-5344-2728-0(7))* 2021. (Illus.). 304p. 17.99 *(978-1-5344-2727-3(9))* Simon & Schuster Children's Publishing. (Aladdin).

Moore, Ginny. Fast. 2011. 28p. pap. 24.95 *(978-1-4626-2254-2(2))* America Star Bks.

Moran, Martin, V, ed. The Town Turtles of Sandy Springs: The Stories Behind the Turtles by the Children Who Saw Them. 2006. (Illus.). 64p. (J). 24.00 *(978-0-9742704-1-8(5))* Hardin Publishing, LLC.

Moriarty, Ros. Who Saw Turtle? 2019. (ENG., Illus.). 24p. (J). (gr. -1-k). pap. 9.99 *(978-1-76029-780-0(1))* Allen & Unwin AUS. Dist: Independent Pubs. Group.

Morrison, Toni & Morrison, Slade. The Tortoise or the Hare. Cepeda, Joe, illus. (ENG.). 32p. (J). (gr. -1-3). 2014. 8.99 *(978-1-4169-8335-4(X))* 2010. 19.99 *(978-1-4169-8334-7(1))* Simon & Schuster/Paula Wiseman Bks. (Simon & Schuster/Paula Wiseman Bks.).

Moses, Albert. The Hawk & the Turtles. Roberts, Pam, illus. 2011. 16p. pap. 24.95 *(978-1-4626-4261-8(6))* America Star Bks.

Moss, Deborah. Shelley, the Hyperactive Turtle. Schwartz, Carol, illus. 2nd ed. 2006. (ENG.). 20p. (J). (gr. -1-2). *(978-1-890627-75-1(5))* Woodbine Hse.

Müller, Isabel & Müller, Isabel. The Green Sea Turtle. 2014. (ENG., Illus.). 40p. (J). (gr. k-2). 18.95 *(978-0-7358-4189-5(6))* North-South Bks., Inc.

Murcray, Rod. Tuttle Stories. McDaniel, Rick, illus. 2012. 40p. pap. 14.95 *(978-1-61897-654-3(0)*, Strategic Bk. Publishing) Strategic Book Publishing & Rights Agency (SBPRA).

Murphy, Bobby. Ted the Turtle's Trip to the Moon. 2013. 24p. pap. 11.50 *(978-1-62212-431-2(6)*, Strategic Bk. Publishing) Strategic Book Publishing & Rights Agency (SBPRA).

Murphy, Steve & Murphy, Sonia. The Secret. Ostrom, Bob, illus. 2004. (Teenage Mutant Ninja Turtles Ser.). 32p. (J). (gr. k-2). 11.65 *(978-0-7569-5401-7(0))* Perfection Learning Corp.

Murray, Alison. Hare & Tortoise. Murray, Alison, illus. 2016. (ENG., Illus.). 32p. (J). (-k). 18.99 *(978-0-7636-8721-2(9))* Candlewick Pr.

Myracle, Lauren. Thirteen Plus One. 2011. (Winnie Years Ser.: 5). (ENG.). 304p. (J). (gr. 5-18). 8.99 *(978-0-14-241901-4(X)*, Puffin Books) Penguin Young Readers Group.

Nelson, Sean. Bungles Loses His Marbles. 2008. 36p. pap. 16.95 *(978-1-59858-605-3(X))* Dog Ear Publishing, LLC.

Nieting, Sherry. Adventures in Hope Forest: Isabelle's Search for God. 2011. (Illus.). 24p. (J). pap. 10.95 *(978-1-4497-2518-1(X)*, WestBow Pr.) Author Solutions, LLC.

Norfolk, Bobby & Norfolk, Sherry. Anansi & Turtle Go to Dinner. Hoffmire, Baird, illus. 2007. (Story Cove Ser.). (ENG.). 32p. (J). (gr. -1-3). pap. 4.95 *(978-0-87483-856-5(8))* August Hse. Pubs., Inc.

Nye, Naomi Shihab. The Turtle of Oman: A Novel. 2014. (ENG.). 304p. (J). (gr. 3-7). 16.99 *(978-0-06-201972-1(4)*, Greenwillow Bks.) HarperCollins Pubs.

Nyirenda, Vukani G. The Wise Old Tortoise & the Monkey. 2011. 24p. pap. 15.99 *(978-1-4568-9133-6(2))* Xlibris Corp.

O Flatharta, Antoine. Hurry & the Monarch. So, Meilo, illus. 2009. (ENG.). 40p. (J). (gr. k-3). pap. 8.99 *(978-0-385-73719-7(X)*, Dragonfly Bks.) Random Hse. Children's Bks.

Oduwole, Ben. The Flying Tortoise. 2009. 182p. pap. 43.50 *(978-1-60693-611-5(5)*, Eloquent Bks.) Strategic Book Publishing & Rights Agency (SBPRA).

Oliver, Sheila. Tinky Turtle Finds the Word. McQuitty, LaVonia Corbin, illus. 2011. (ENG.). 16p. (J). 6.00 *(978-0-9801269-4-5(0))* Scribe's Closet Pubns., The.

Orr, Wendy. Nim's Island. Millard, Kerry, illus. 2008. (Nim Ser.). (ENG.). 128p. (J). (gr. 3-7). 7.99 *(978-0-385-73606-0(1)*, Yearling) Random Hse. Children's Bks.

Ostrom, Bob, illus. Friends till the End! 2005. (Teenage Mutant Ninja Turtles Ser.: No. 3). 24p. (J). lib. bdg. 15.00 *(978-1-59054-833-2(7))* Fitzgerald Bks.

Otitoloju/Blazing Ideas Ltd, Ololade/Adewunmi, retold by. Kunkuru Da Kare: The Tortoise & the Dog. 2008. (YOR & ENG., Illus.). 36p. 16.00 *(978-0-9801243-6-1(0))* Blazing Ideas Ltd.

Otitoloju/Blazing Ideas ltd, Ololade/Adewunmi, retold by. Kunkuru, Jaba Da Kurege: The Tortoise, the Rat & the Squirrel. 2008. (YOR & ENG., Illus.). 36p. 16.00 *(978-0-9801243-7-8(9))* Blazing Ideas Ltd.

—Mbe, Nkapi na Osa. 2008. (YOR & ENG., Illus.). 36p. 16.00 *(978-0-9801243-3-0(6))* Blazing Ideas Ltd.

Paige, Nancy. Myrtle the Turtle, 1 vol. Green, Megan, illus. 2009. 19p. pap. 24.95 *(978-1-60836-085-7(7))* America Star Bks.

Parker, Beth. The Tale of Tom Turtle, 1 vol. 2009. 24p. pap. 24.95 *(978-1-61546-887-4(0))* America Star Bks.

—Tom Turtle Visits Grandma's Farm. 2011. 28p. pap. 24.95 *(978-1-4560-1000-3(X))* America Star Bks.

Pashilk, Meri. Pearl the Turtle. 2013. 32p. pap. 13.99 *(978-1-4525-6658-0(5))* Balboa Pr.

A Path of Clouds: The Book off Rhymes. 2013. 50p. pap. *(978-965-550-241-1(4))* Contento De Semrik.

Pellant, Terry. The Real Valentine's Story. 2004. 27p. (J). pap. 24.95 *(978-1-4137-2146-1(X))* PublishAmerica, Inc.

Pelton, Deena. My Turtle. 2012. 20p. pap. 24.95 *(978-1-4626-8210-2(3))* America Star Bks.

Peters, Lou. The Owl & the Turtle. 2010. 32p. pap. 15.95 *(978-0-557-51727-5(3))* Lulu Pr., Inc.

Peters, Stephanie True. The Robo-Battle of Mega Tortoise vs. Hazard Hare: A Graphic Novel. Cano, Fernando, illus. 2017. (Far Out Fables Ser.). (ENG.). 40p. (J). (gr. 3-6). pap. 4.95 *(978-1-4965-5424-6(8)*, 136357); lib. bdg. 25.32 *(978-1-4965-5420-8(5)*, 136353) Capstone. (Stone Arch Bks.).

Petersen, Pat. The Turtle Who Couldn't Swim. Pham, Xuan, illus. 2012. 28p. 24.95 *(978-1-4626-8615-5(X))*; pap. 24.95 *(978-1-4626-4847-4(9))* America Star Bks.

Peterson, Kay. Tillie the Turtle. 2012. 24p. pap. 15.99 *(978-1-4691-8414-2(1))* Xlibris Corp.

Peterson, Kevan. Turtle Takes the Bus. 2005. (Illus.). 32p. (J). 12.99 *(978-0-9767661-0-0(8))* Red Giant Publishing.

Peterson, Scott. Blackout! Spaziante, Patrick, illus. 2005. (Teenage Mutant Ninja Turtles Ser.: Garden & No. 6). 24p. (J). lib. bdg. 15.00 *(978-1-59054-831-8(0))* Fitzgerald Bks.

Piggy Toes Press Staff, creator. Little Feet Like: A Tiny Tootsie Touch & Feel Book. 2008. (ENG., Illus.). 12p. (gr. -1-k). 9.95 *(978-1-58117-692-6(9)*, Intervisual/Piggy Toes) Bendon, Inc.

Pinkney, Jerry. The Tortoise & the Hare. 2013. (ENG., Illus.). 40p. (J). (gr. -1-3). 18.99 *(978-0-316-18356-7(3))* Little, Brown Bks. for Young Readers.

Pinkwater, Daniel M. The Neddiad: How Neddie Took the Train, Went to Hollywood, & SavedCivilization. 2009. (ENG., Illus.). 320p. (J). (gr. 5-7). pap. 8.99 *(978-0-547-13367-6(7)*, 1048766, Clarion Bks.) HarperCollins Pubs.

Police, Gerard. Herbert the Frog Goes to the Store. 2008. 20p. pap. 13.50 *(978-1-60693-066-3(4)*, Eloquent Bks.) Strategic Book Publishing & Rights Agency (SBPRA).

Poling Kilough, Melissa. Titus the Turtle & the Hard Shell Story. 2009. 28p. pap. 13.99 *(978-1-4490-0962-5(X))* AuthorHouse.

Powell, Pamela. La Patrulla de las Tortugas. 2003. (SPA., Illus.). 190p. (YA). (gr. 5-8). *(978-84-236-3791-1(3)*, ED1183) Edebé ESP. Dist: Lectorum Pubns., Inc.

Pritchard, Gabby. Turtle Is a Hero Green Band. Di Baldo, Fabrizio, illus. 2016. (Cambridge Reading Adventures Ser.). (ENG.). 16p. pap. 7.95 *(978-1-107-55046-9(7))* Cambridge Univ. Pr.

Pugliano-Martin, Carol. The Earth on Turtles Back. 2011. (Early Connections Ser.). (J). *(978-1-61672-674-4(1))* Benchmark Education Co.

Puglisi, Salvatore. It's best to be Me. 2008. (ENG.). 36p. pap. 14.99 *(978-1-4196-8330-5(6))* CreateSpace Independent Publishing Platform.

Quail, Annette. Lucy & Coco. 2008. 44p. pap. 24.95 *(978-1-60441-854-5(0))* America Star Bks.

Random House. Pizza Party! (Teenage Mutant Ninja Turtles) Random House, illus. 2017. (Step into Reading Ser.). (ENG., Illus.). 24p. (J). (gr. -1-1). pap. 5.99 *(978-1-5247-6982-6(7)*, Random Hse. Bks. for Young Readers) Random Hse. Children's Bks.

Random House Staff. Saved by the Shell! 2012. lib. bdg. 13.55 *(978-0-606-26800-4(6))* Turtleback.

Rao, Lisa. Diego & the Baby Sea Turtles. McGee, Warner, illus. 2008. (Go, Diego, Go! Ser.: 8). (ENG.). 24p. (J). pap. 3.99 *(978-1-4169-5450-7(3)*, Simon Spotlight/Nickelodeon) Simon Spotlight/Nickelodeon.

Raun, Robert L. Tales of the Clam Club: Turtle Soup. 2012. (ENG.). pap. *(978-1-4675-1923-6(5))* Independent Pub.

Reason, Diane. Travis the Traveling Turtle & the Beautiful Butterfly. 2011. 32p. pap. 14.98 *(978-1-4634-0206-8(6))* AuthorHouse.

Rebecca, Rebecca. The Turtle Who Did His Best. 2016. (ENG., Illus.). 26p. pap. 5.99 *(978-1-61984-471-1(0)*, Gatekeeper Pr.) Gatekeeper Pr.

Reidy, Jean. Truman. Cummins, Lucy Ruth, illus. 2019. (ENG.). 48p. (J). (gr. -1-3). 17.99 *(978-1-5344-1664-2(1))* Simon & Schuster Children's Publishing.

Reis, Jason & Hurley, Meagan. The Adventures of Burt: Burt & the Big Race. 2012. 28p. pap. 19.99 *(978-1-4634-4126-5(6))* AuthorHouse.

Reiss, Mike. Turtle & Tortoise Are Not Friends. Spires, Ashley, illus. 2019. (ENG.). 32p. (J). (gr. -1-3). 17.99 *(978-0-06-074031-3(0)*, HarperCollins) HarperCollins Pubs.

Ricci, Christine. Diego's Sea Turtle Adventure. Maher, Alex, illus. 2006. 26p. (J). *(978-0-7172-9870-9(1))* Scholastic, Inc.

Rice, Dona Herwick. The Tortoise & the Hare, 1 vol. rev. ed. 2008. (Reader's Theater Ser.). (ENG.). 24p. (gr. 1-3). pap. 8.99 *(978-1-4333-0290-9(X))* Teacher Created Materials, Inc.

Richard Scott Morris. Irving the Duck in the Tortoise Shell Suit. 2009. 36p. pap. 20.00 *(978-1-4389-5356-4(9))* AuthorHouse.

Rider, Cynthia. Chatterbox Turtle. Petrlik, Andrea, illus. 2004. (ENG.). 24p. (J). lib. bdg. 23.65 *(978-1-59646-696-8(0))* Dingles & Co.

Ridgell, Regina. Baby Loggerhead's Long Journey. 2008. 28p. pap. 15.99 *(978-1-4363-2087-0(9))* Xlibris Corp.

Ritchie, Alison. The Tortoise & the Hare. Noj, Nahta, illus. 2015. (ENG.). 32p. (J). (-k). 15.99 *(978-0-7636-7601-8(2)*, Templar) Candlewick Pr.

Robert, Quackenbush & Robert Quackenbush. Calling Doctor Quack. 2010. 68p. (J). (gr. k-4). pap. 8.95 *(978-1-4502-1379-0(0))* iUniverse, Inc.

Robertson, Allen. Timothy Tuttles Story Book. 2005. 27p. 11.58 *(978-1-4116-6352-7(7))* Lulu Pr., Inc.

—Timothy Tuttles Story Book 11. 2005. 32p. 13.83 *(978-1-4116-8045-6(6))* Lulu Pr., Inc.

Rogers, Alan. En Forme de Bateau. 2003. (Little Giants Ser.). (FRE., Illus.). 16p. (J). (gr. -1-k). 5.95 *(978-1-58728-177-8(5)*, Two-Can Publishing) T&N Children's Publishing.

Roh, Grace S. Booyoung & Sea Turtle's Adventure: God's Creatures' Adventures Series 1. Park, Mi-Ok, illus. 2013. 52p. pap. 17.50 *(978-1-62212-718-4(8)*, Strategic Bk. Publishing) Strategic Book Publishing & Rights Agency (SBPRA).

Ron Chemey With Angel Logan. Coming Out of Her Shell. 2011. 72p. pap. 33.32 *(978-1-4568-7141-3(2))* Xlibris Corp.

Ross, Andrea. Turtles Go Slow. Ross, Andrea, illus. 2003. (Illus.). 25p. (J). (gr. 1-3). pap. 7.95 *(978-1-887683-45-6(3))* Storybook Pr. & Productions.

Russell, Bill. Bruno the Red Ear Slider. 2013. 24p. pap. 24.95 *(978-1-62709-547-1(0))* America Star Bks.

Rutt, Preston. Tortoise vs. Hare: The Rematch. Redlich, Ben, illus. 2015. (ENG.). 24p. (J). (gr. -1-3). 7.99 *(978-1-85733-722-8(0))* Lerner Publishing Group.

Rylant, Cynthia. The Turtle. McDaniels, Preston, illus. 2006. (Lighthouse Family Ser.). 47p. (J). (gr. -1-3). 11.65 *(978-0-7569-6611-9(6))* Perfection Learning Corp.

—The Turtle. McDaniels, Preston, illus. (Lighthouse Family Ser.: 4). (ENG.). 48p. (J). (gr. 1-5). 2006. pap. 5.99 *(978-0-689-86312-7(8))* 2005. 17.99 *(978-0-689-86244-1(X))* Simon & Schuster Bks. For Young Readers. (Simon & Schuster Bks. For Young Readers).

Salzmann, Mary Elizabeth. Turtle Shells. Nobens, C. A., illus. 2006. (Fact & Fiction Ser.). 24p. (J). pap. 48.42 *(978-1-59679-970-7(6))* ABDO Publishing Co.

Sampson, Brent. One Wacky Wasp: The Perfect Children's Book for Kids Ages 3-6 Who Are Learning to Read. 2010. 24p. (J). 14.95 *(978-1-4327-6217-9(6))*; pap. 9.95 *(978-1-4327-0465-0(6))* Outskirts Pr., Inc.

Samuel, Josiah C. Mr. Tortoise Funny Life, Bk. 1. 2013. 132p. pap. 45.07 *(978-1-4669-9904-6(7))* Trafford Publishing.

Sapre, Reshme. The Unfortunate Tale of Kachuva the Tortoise: As Told by Chukwa Sulcata. Robinson, Jayme, illus. 2012. (ENG.). 40p. 16.95 *(978-0-9829362-0-7(6))* Hathi Chiti Bks. for Kids.

Sargent, Dave & Sargent, Pat. Tunnel King: I Work Hard, 15 vols., Vol. 11. Huff, Jeane, illus. 2nd rev. ed. 2003. (Animal Pride Ser.: No. 11). 42p. (J). pap. 10.95 *(978-1-56763-780-9(9))*; lib. bdg. 20.95 *(978-1-56763-779-3(5))* Ozark Publishing.

Sayre, April Pulley. Turtle, Turtle, Watch Out! Patterson, Annie, illus. 2010. (ENG.). 32p. (J). (gr. k-3). pap. 8.99 *(978-1-58089-149-3(7))* Charlesbridge Publishing, Inc.

Sazaklis, John. Salamander Smackdown! Baltazar, Art, illus. 2011. (DC Super-Pets Ser.). (ENG.). 56p. (J). (gr. 1-3). pap. 4.95 *(978-1-4048-6844-1(5)*, 116401); lib. bdg. 25.32 *(978-1-4048-6478-8(4)*, 114159) Capstone. (Stone Arch Bks.).

Schacht, Carol. Timmy Turtle's Journey to the Light. 2009. 20p. pap. 11.75 *(978-1-4490-0503-0(9))* AuthorHouse.

Scholastic. Animal Antics e-J First Grade Reader Box Set: Scholastic Early Learners (Guided Reader), 1 vol. 2019. (Scholastic Early Learners Ser.).Tr. of Guided Reader. (ENG.). 256p. (J). (gr. -1-1). 16.99 *(978-1-338-36086-8(8)*, Cartwheel Bks.) Scholastic, Inc.

Scholastic Editors. The Rescue Mission. 2015. (Ninjago Readers Ser.: 11). lib. bdg. 13.55 *(978-0-606-36373-0(4))* Turtleback.

Scholastic, Inc. Staff. Spy vs. Spy. 2015. (Ninjago Readers Ser.: 13). lib. bdg. 13.55 *(978-0-606-37080-6(3))* Turtleback.

Seigel, Jonathan & Rother, Beverly S. Myrtle the Turtle & Popeye the Mouse: Learning about Our Solar System. 2012. 40p. pap. 24.95 *(978-1-4626-6587-7(X))* America Star Bks.

Senkungu, Dinah. How the Tortoise Got His Scars. 2011. 40p. pap. 18.66 *(978-1-4567-1811-4(8))* AuthorHouse.

Sheffer, Donnel Gloster. Seacil the Sea Turtle. 2003. (J). pap. 8.00 *(978-0-8059-5288-9(8))* Dorrance Publishing Co., Inc.

Silvernetz, Marcia A. Gertrude the Albino Frog & Her Friend Rupert the Turtle. Doyel, Ginger, illus. 2003. 48p. (J). (gr. 2-3). 19.95 *(978-0-9718724-0-0(6))* Hiccup Cottage Pubns.

Simpson, Wanda. Sammy, the Earth Traveling Turtle, 1 vol. 2010. 16p. pap. 24.95 *(978-1-4489-9844-9(1))* PublishAmerica, Inc.

Smiley, Jeremy. Chester: Little Turtle, Big Adventure, 1 vol. 2009. 36p. pap. 24.95 *(978-1-60703-489-6(1))* America Star Bks.

Smith, Carrie. Tortoise & Hare Run a Race: Lap Book Edition. Berchtold, Lauren, illus. 2016. (My First Reader's Theater Tales Ser.). (J). (gr. k). *(978-1-5021-5509-2(5))* Benchmark Education Co.

—Tortoise & Hare Run a Race: Small Book Edition. Berchtold, Lauren, illus. 2016. (My First Reader's Theater Tales Ser.). (J). (gr. k). *(978-1-5021-5514-6(1))* Benchmark Education Co.

Smith, James J. Mikey's Monster. 2013. (Step into Reading Level 4 Ser.). lib. bdg. 13.55 *(978-0-606-32223-2(X))* Turtleback.

The Snappy Turtle. 2003. (J). per. *(978-1-57657-938-1(7))* Paradise Pr., Inc.

Soisson, Chelsea. Tate's Wayward Voyage. 2012. (ENG.). (J). pap. 17.99 *(978-1-4675-2650-0(9))*; pap. 17.99 *(978-1-4675-2651-7(7))* Independent Pub.

Solis, Javier Rene. The Adventures of Tony the Turtle: La Familia the Family. 2008. 24p. pap. 14.99 *(978-1-4389-1421-3(0))* AuthorHouse.

Southern, Shelley, et al, adapted by. Franklin & the New Teacher. 2004. (Franklin TV Storybook Ser.). (ENG., Illus.). 32p. (J). (gr. -1-3). 4.95 *(978-1-55337-500-5(9))* Kids Can Pr., Ltd. CAN. Dist: Hachette Bk. Group.

Spaziante, Patrick. Too Much Ooze! 2015. (Step into Reading Level 2 Ser.). lib. bdg. 14.75 *(978-0-606-36399-0(8))* Turtleback.

Spero, Mitch & Spero, Maria. Florida the Turtle: Who Thinks He's a Dog Finds His Feelings. 2012. 28p. pap. 21.99 *(978-1-4771-0184-1(5))* Xlibris Corp.

Spin & Match - Kings, Cookies, & Quakers: The Cookie Man, New Clothes for the King, the Ugly Baby Duck. 2006. (ENG.). 66p. (J). 9.99 *(978-1-59204-203-6(1))* Learning Wrap-Ups, Inc.

Spohn, Kate. Turtle & Snake's Day at the Beach. Spohn, Kate, illus. 2004. (Penguin Young Readers, Level 2 Ser.). (Illus.). 32p. (J). (gr. 1-2). mass mkt. 4.99 *(978-0-14-240157-6(9)*, Penguin Young Readers) Penguin Young Readers Group.

—Turtle & Snake's Day at the Beach. Spohn, Kate, illus. 2004. (Puffin Easy-to-Read Ser.). (Illus.). 32p. (gr. k-3). 14.00 *(978-0-7569-2826-1(5))* Perfection Learning Corp.

—Turtle & Snake's Spooky Halloween. Spohn, Kate, illus. 2003. (Easy-to-Read Ser.). (Illus.). 32p. (J). (gr. -1-3). 11.65 *(978-0-7569-1949-8(5))* Perfection Learning Corp.

Sprick, Marilyn & Lemieux, Aurora, adapted by. The Race: Read Well Level K Unit 13 Storybook. 2003. (Read Well Level K Ser.). (Illus.). 20p. (J). *(978-1-57035-684-1(X)*, 55538) Cambium Education, Inc.

Stark, Barbara. Blue Dinosaur's Friends. l.t. ed. 2006. (Illus.). 24p. (J). E-Book 9.95 incl. cd-rom *(978-1-933090-20-7(0))* Guardian Angel Publishing, Inc.

Stewart, Chantal, illus. Tortoise Soup! 2009. 24p. pap. 10.67 *(978-1-4190-5523-2(2))* Rigby Education.

Stickler, John C. & Han, Soma. Maya & the Turtle: A Korean Fairy Tale. Han, Soma, illus. 2012. (ENG., Illus.). 32p. (J). (gr. -1-3). 14.95 *(978-0-8048-4277-8(9))* Tuttle Publishing.

Stone, Laura. Tulia Turtle Finds Her Talents. 2010. 33p. pap. 16.95 *(978-0-557-33227-4(3))* Lulu Pr., Inc.

Stone, Pam. Oscar's Adventures in the Woods: True story about a turtle that comes back every year to find his Friend. 2011. 15p. (J). pap. 14.95 *(978-1-4327-6382-4(2))* Outskirts Pr., Inc.

Stuart, Janet. Something New in Cloverville? 2010. 20p. 12.49 *(978-1-4520-7701-7(0))* AuthorHouse.

Syrstad, Suzi. Timmy the Tiny Troubled Turtle, 1 vol. Maki, Tab, illus. 2009. 13p. pap. 24.95 *(978-1-61546-455-5(7))* PublishAmerica, Inc.

Tagliere, Georgina. Turtle Tales - Book One: The Baby Turtle who Wanted to Fly. 2009. (Illus.). 60p. pap. *(978-1-84748-406-2(9))* Athena Pr.

Takara, Kathryn Waddell. Timmy Turtle Teaches. Driver, Audrey, illus. 2012. 54p. pap. 29.95 *(978-0-9840204-3-0(8))* Pacific Raven Pr.

Talbot, Amy. Deer & His Dear Friends: A Tale from India. 2006. (J). pap. *(978-1-4108-6173-3(2))* Benchmark Education Co.

Tate, Suzanne. Tammy Turtle: A Tale of Saving Sea Turtles. Melvin, James, illus. 2004. (Suzanne Tate's Nature Ser.: No. 11). 32p. (J). per. 10.95 *(978-1-878405-45-6(4))* Nags Head Art, Inc.

Tatro, MaryAnn. Milton the Square Shell Turtle. Lucas, Diane, illus. 2013. 24p. pap. 11.95 *(978-1-61244-106-1(8))* Halo Publishing International.

Taylor, Emma. Adventures of Bunting, the Turtle. 2011. 24p. pap. 15.99 *(978-1-4568-5911-4(0))* Xlibris Corp.

Teitelbaum, Michael. Teenage Mutant Ninja Turtles Wheel Power Book & Skateboard. 2013. (ENG.). 48p. (J). 12.99 *(978-0-7944-2796-2(0))* Reader's Digest Assn., Inc., The.

Tewkesbury, Alexa. The Perfect Christmas Present. 2008. (ENG.). 32p. (J). *(978-1-85345-476-9(1))* Crusade for World Revival.

Tharp, Barbara, et al. Tillena Lou's Day in the Sun. Denk, James, ed. Lewis, T., illus. 2nd ed. 2013. (My World & Me Ser.). (ENG.). 32p. (J). (gr. k-2). pap. *(978-1-888997-44-6(3)*, BioEd) Baylor College of Medicine.

Theval, Lio. Angela's Lost Turtle. 2007. 20p. 23.70 *(978-1-4357-0020-8(1))* Lulu Pr., Inc.

The Thirsty Turtle. 2003. 32p. (J). per. 14.95 *(978-1-59094-049-5(0))* Jawbone Publishing Corp.

Thomas, Jim. Comic Book Heroes. Ruiz, Aristides & Giles, Mike, illus. 2005. 32p. (J). lib. bdg. 15.00 *(978-1-59054-990-2(2))* Fitzgerald Bks.

Thompson, Kay. Eloise & Friends. Knight, Hilary, illus. 2015. (Eloise Ser.). (ENG.). 26p. (J). (gr. -1-2). bds. 8.99 *(978-1-4814-5158-1(8)*, Little Simon) Little Simon.

Thwin, Soe Soe. The Story of Inle in the Galapagos. 2009. 44p. pap. 15.95 *(978-1-60860-361-9(X)*, Strategic Bk. Publishing) Strategic Book Publishing & Rights Agency (SBPRA).

Tikki Turtle's Quest. (J). 8.95 *(978-0-9701528-0-0(9))* Ruwanga Trading.

Towle, Barbara E. How Timbo & Trevor Got Together. Spellman, Susan, illus. 2007. (ENG.). 38p. (J). (gr. -1-3). 19.95 *(978-1-933002-21-7(2))* PublishingWorks.

Tracy, Kathleen. The Turtle in Our Class. 2011. (Randy's Corner Ser.). (Illus.). 32p. (J). (gr. -1-2). lib. bdg. 25.70 *(978-1-58415-979-7(0))* Mitchell Lane Pubs.

Tucker, Sally A. Leo & Apollo: The Forbidden Land. 2012. (ENG.). 25p. 15.00 *(978-1-105-60121-7(8))* Lulu Pr., Inc.

Turín, Adela. Arturo y Clementina. Bosnia, Nella, illus. (SPA.). 40p. (J). (gr. 3-5). *(978-84-264-3801-0(6))* Editorial Lumen ESP. Dist: Lectorum Pubns., Inc.

The Turtle Race. 2003. (J). per. *(978-1-57657-891-9(7))* Paradise Pr., Inc.

Twohy, Mike. Poindexter Makes a Friend. Twohy, Mike, illus. 2011. (ENG., Illus.). 32p. (J). (gr. -1-3). 15.99 *(978-1-4424-0965-1(7)*, Simon & Schuster/Paula Wiseman Bks.) Simon & Schuster/Paula Wiseman Bks.

Van Wemmer, Deby. Wishes & Walnuts. 2009. 28p. pap. 14.50 *(978-1-60860-723-5(2)*, Eloquent Bks.) Strategic Book Publishing & Rights Agency (SBPRA).

Verrett, Michael. The White Alligator Crown Quatro. 2010. 147p. pap. 13.95 *(978-0-557-58121-4(4))* Lulu Pr., Inc.

—The White Alligator (paper Back) 2010. 116p. pap. 17.30 *(978-0-557-28042-1(7))* Lulu Pr., Inc.

—The White Alligator (paperback full Color) 2010. 116p. pap. 42.00 *(978-0-557-36924-9(X))* Lulu Pr., Inc.

Wacker, Eileen. Black Tortoise & the Dynasty Dragon. Low, Alan M., illus. 2012. (ENG.). 40p. (J). (gr. -1-3). 10.99 *(978-1-4675-1741-6(0)*, 232e8e58-28e5-4b56-9270-e7e7a6090f86) Oncekids.

Wagenbach, Debbie. Big Brave Bold Sergio. Tablason, Jamie, illus. 2018. 32p. (J). *(978-1-4338-2794-5(8))* American Psychological Assn.

Ward, Helen. Hare & Tortoise. 2005. (Illus.). 32p. (J). (ARA, ENG & MUL.). pap. *(978-1-84444-780-0(4))*; (ALB & ENG., pap. *(978-1-84444-779-4(0))*; (POL & ENG., pap. *(978-1-84444-794-7(4))*; (ENG., pap. *(978-1-84444-801-2(0))*; (POR., pap. *(978-1-84444-795-4(2))*; (ENG & RUM., pap. *(978-1-84444-796-1(0))*; (VIE, ENG & MUL., pap. *(978-1-84444-806-7(1))*; (URD, ENG & MUL., pap. *(978-1-84444-805-0(3))*; (TUR & ENG., pap. *(978-1-84444-803-6(7))*; (BEN, ENG & MUL., pap. *(978-1-84444-781-7(2))*; (CHI, ENG & MUL., pap. *(978-1-84444-783-1(9))*; (PER, ENG & MUL., pap. *(978-1-84444-786-2(3))*; (FRE & ENG., pap. *(978-1-84444-787-9(1))*; (GUJ, ENG & MUL., pap. *(978-1-84444-789-3(8))*; (HIN, ENG & MUL., pap. *(978-1-84444-790-9(1))*; (SOM & ENG., pap. *(978-1-84444-799-2(5))*; (SPA & ENG., pap. *(978-1-84444-800-5(2))*; (PAN, ENG & MUL., pap. *(978-1-84444-793-0(6))*; (RUS & ENG., pap. *(978-1-84444-797-8(9))* Mantra Lingua.

Ward, Helen & Aesop, Aesop. Hare & Tortoise. 2005. (Illus.). 32p. (J). (GRE, ENG & MUL.). pap. *(978-1-84444-788-6(X))*; (CHI, ENG & MUL., pap. *(978-1-84444-784-8(7))*; (JPN & ENG., pap. *(978-1-84444-791-6(X))* Mantra Lingua.

Ward, Jean Elizabeth. A Barbara Anne Bushy Tale: Book #2 in a Series. 2007. 188p. per. 16.95 *(978-0-595-45726-7(6))* iUniverse, Inc.

Washer, Mark Gregory. Blue Bonnie Butterfly: Tale of Two Tails. 2013. 36p. pap. 18.41 *(978-1-4669-8434-9(1))* Trafford Publishing.

Watson, J. A. Hatchling Hero: A Sea Turtle Defender's Journal. Olbey, Arpad, illus. 2018. (Science Squad Ser.). (ENG.). 192p. (J). (gr. 3-4). 28.50 *(978-1-63163-160-3(8)*, 1631631608); pap. 9.99 *(978-1-63163-161-0(6)*, 1631631616) North Star Editions. (Jolly Fish Pr.).

Wax, Wendy. Meet Leatherhead. Spaziante, Patrick, illus. 2005. 22p. (J). lib. bdg. 15.00 *(978-1-4242-0972-9(2))* Fitzgerald Bks.

Webster, Christy. Double-Team! (Teenage Mutant Ninja Turtles) Spaziante, Patrick, illus. 2014. (Step into Reading Ser.). (ENG.). 48p. (J). (gr. 2-4). 5.99 *(978-0-385-37434-7(8)*, Random Hse. Bks. for Young Readers) Random Hse. Children's Bks.

—Green Team! 2012. (Step into Reading Level 4 Ser.). lib. bdg. 13.55 *(978-0-606-26801-1(4))* Turtleback.

—Robot Rampage! 2013. (Step into Reading Level 4 Ser.). lib. bdg. 13.55 *(978-0-606-26985-8(1))* Turtleback.

—Robot Rampage! (Teenage Mutant Ninja Turtles) Spaziante, Patrick, illus. 2013. (Step into Reading Ser.). (ENG.). 48p. (J). (gr. k-3). pap. 5.99 *(978-0-307-98212-4(2)*, Random Hse. Bks. for Young Readers) Random Hse. Children's Bks.

Weeks, Sarah. Follow the Moon Book & CD. Duranceau, Suzanne, illus. 2003. (ENG.). 32p. (J). (gr. -1-3). audio compact disk 17.99 *(978-0-06-055744-7(3)*, HarperCollins) HarperCollins Pubs.

Weiss, Flo. Little Bit Is Big Enough. 2012. 28p. pap. 16.09 *(978-1-4669-4074-1(3))* Trafford Publishing.

Weller, Sadie Bedoka. Tsa Ch'ayah How the Turtle Got Its Squares: A Traditional Caddo Indian Children's Story. Chafe, Wallace, tr. Montoya, Robin Michelle, illus. 2005. (ENG.). 42p. (gr. 3-7). per. 16.99 *(978-1-4134-8836-4(6))* Xlibris Corp.

West, Tracey. Lego Ninjago: Breakout. 2015. (LEGO Ninjago Chapter Bks.: 8). lib. bdg. 14.75 *(978-0-606-37078-3(1))* Turtleback.

—Lego Ninjago: Chronicles of Ninjago: an Official Handbook. 2014. lib. bdg. 16.00 *(978-0-606-36371-6(8))* Turtleback.

—Titanium Ninja. 2014. (Ninjago Readers Ser.: 10). lib. bdg. 13.55 *(978-0-606-36372-3(6))* Turtleback.

Westheimer, Ruth K. Leopold. (ENG., Illus.). 2017. 36p. pap. 11.99 *(978-1-68336-709-3(X))* 2015. 34p. (J). 24.95 *(978-1-63026-918-0(2))* Turner Publishing Co.

Wheelie, P. Tommy's Triumph: The tales of Tommy the tortoise & Friends. 2009. (Illus.). 28p. pap. 12.49 *(978-1-4389-2718-3(5))* AuthorHouse.

Whitfield, Peter. Zen Tails up & Down. Bevington, Nancy, illus. 2005. (ENG.). 28p. (J). (gr. -1-3). 15.95 *(978-1-894965-22-4(1))* Simply Read Bks. CAN. Dist: Ingram Publisher Services.

Williams, Barbara A. Tilli's Tale. Lewis, Rebecca, illus. 2004. 48p. (J). per. *(978-1-932077-52-0(9))* Athena Pr.

Wilson, Angela. Tara the Terrified Turtle. Basta, Stormie, illus. 2012. 28p. pap. 24.95 *(978-1-4626-7454-1(2))* America Star Bks.

Winderman, Jay B. Thunder on the Desert. Becker, LuAnne E. & Becker, Lisa E., illus. 2005. 152p. (J). (gr. 3-7). per. 13.95 *(978-0-9761623-1-5(8))* Pill Bug Pr.

—Thunder on the Reservation. Becker, LuAnne E., illus. 2007. 147p. (J). (gr. 3-7). per. 13.95 *(978-0-9761623-2-2(6))* Pill Bug Pr.

Winn, Don M. The Tortoise & the Hairpiece. Hefflin, Toby, illus. 2009. 20p. pap. 7.99 *(978-0-88144-452-0(9))* Yorkshire Publishing Group.

Winningham, Barbara. The Turtle Pit. 2013. 36p. 24.95 *(978-1-62709-875-5(5))*; pap. 24.95 *(978-1-62709-493-1(8))* America Star Bks.

Winship, Daniel, illus. The Tortoise & the Hare: The Tortoise & the Hare. 2012. (SGN, ARA, BOS, CHI & FRE.). 32p. (J). pap. 19.95 incl. DVD *(978-0-9818139-2-9(5))* ASL Tales.

Wise, Alicia. Myrtle's True Friend. Wise, Jesse D., illus. 2008. 15p. pap. 24.95 *(978-1-60610-626-6(0))* America Star Bks.

Wohnoutka, Mike. Croc & Turtle. 2019. (ENG., Illus.). 40p. (J). 17.99 *(978-1-68119-634-3(4)*, 900179787, Bloomsbury Children's Bks.) Bloomsbury Publishing USA.

—Croc & Turtle! 2020. (ENG., Illus.). 32p. (J). bds. 7.99 *(978-1-5476-0312-1(7)*, 900221450, Bloomsbury Children's Bks.) Bloomsbury Publishing USA.

Wood, Douglas. Old Turtle: Questions of the Heart: From the Lessons of Old Turtle #2. Ruth, Greg, illus. 2017. (ENG.). 56p. (J). (gr. -1-3). 19.99 *(978-0-439-32111-2(5)*, Scholastic Pr.) Scholastic, Inc.

Wright-McAdoo, Joyce & Wright-Mcadoo, Joyce. Zimb: Believe. 2009. (Illus.). 28p. pap. 15.99 *(978-1-4415-8051-1(4))* Xlibris Corp.

Wyllie, Ruth G. The Adventures of George the Turtle. 2012. 16p. pap. 15.99 *(978-1-4772-5284-0(3))* AuthorHouse.

Yerger, Susan M. Mighty Little Samuel Seagull. 2013. 20p. pap. 24.95 *(978-1-4626-9941-4(3))* America Star Bks.

Young, Steve. Winchell Mink: The Misadventure Begins. 2004. 144p. (J). 16.89 *(978-0-06-053500-1(8))* HarperCollins Pubs.

Zagorski, Steve. The River of Wisdom. 2010. pap. 17.95 *(978-0-578-05364-6(0))* Zagorski, Steve.

Zambak Çucok Publishing Staff, ed. The Onion: Niloya 2. 2016. (J). pap. 4.99 *(978-1-4621-1863-2(1)*, Horizon Pubs.) Cedar Fort, Inc./CFI Distribution.

—The Rainbow: Niloya 1. 2016. (J). pap. 4.99 *(978-1-4621-1862-5(3)*, Horizon Pubs.) Cedar Fort, Inc./CFI Distribution.

TUSKEGEE INSTITUTE

Hurt, Avery Elizabeth. Booker T. Washington: Civil Rights Leader & Education Advocate, 1 vol. 2019. (African American Trailblazers Ser.). (ENG.). 128p. (gr. 9-9). pap. 22.16 *(978-1-5026-4557-9(2)*, 40dea83a-65cc-4a3c-87e7-9270ea1546b1) Cavendish Square Publishing LLC.

Thomas, Peggy. George Washington Carver for Kids: His Life & Discoveries, with 21 Activities. 2019. (For Kids Ser.: 73). (ENG., Illus.). 144p. (J). (gr. 4). pap. 18.99 *(978-0-915864-00-3(2))* Chicago Review Pr., Inc.

TUTANKHAMEN, KING OF EGYPT

Burgan, Michael. The Curse of King Tut's Tomb, 1 vol. Schulz, Barbara, illus. 2005. (Graphic History Ser.). (ENG.). 32p. (J). (gr. 3-9). per. 8.10 *(978-0-7368-5244-9(1)*, 86990, Capstone Pr.) Capstone.

Conkin, Wendy. You Are There! Ancient Egypt 1535 BC. 2nd rev. ed. 2016. (TIME(r): Informational Text Ser.). (ENG., Illus.). 32p. (gr. 5-8). pap. 13.99 *(978-1-4938-3602-4(1))* Teacher Created Materials, Inc.

Cottrell, Leonard. Land of the Pharaohs. Powers, Richard M., illus. 2012. 130p. 40.95 *(978-1-258-23853-7(5))*; pap. 25.95 *(978-1-258-24652-5(X))* Literary Licensing, LLC.

Demi. Tutankhamun. 0 vols. Demi, illus. 2012. (ENG., Illus.). 64p. (J). (gr. 3-6). 19.99 *(978-0-7614-5558-5(2)*, 9780761455585, Two Lions) Amazon Publishing.

Harkins, Susan Sales & Harkins, William H. King Tut. 2008. (What's So Great About... ? Ser.). (Illus.). 32p. (YA). (gr. 2-4). lib. bdg. 25.70 *(978-1-58415-681-9(3))* Mitchell Lane Pubs.

Harvey, Gill. Tutankhamun. McNee, Ian, illus. 2006. (Usborne Young Reading Ser.). 64p. (J). (gr. 3-7). 8.99 *(978-0-7945-1271-2(2)*, Usborne) EDC Publishing.

Hirschmann, Kris. The Curse of King Tut. 2019. (Historic Disasters & Mysteries Ser.). (ENG.). 64p. (J). (gr. 6-12). 41.27 *(978-1-68282-631-7(7))* ReferencePoint Pr., Inc.

Hyde, Natalie. King Tut. 2013. (ENG., Illus.). 48p. (J). *(978-0-7787-1172-8(2))*; pap. *(978-0-7787-1181-0(1))* Crabtree Publishing Co.

Lace, William W. The Curse of King Tut. 2007. (Mysterious & Unknown Ser.). (Illus.). 104p. (YA). (gr. 7-12). lib. bdg. 41.27 *(978-1-60152-024-1(7))* ReferencePoint Pr., Inc.

Loh-Hagan, Virginia. The Real King Tut. 2018. (History Uncut Ser.). (ENG., Illus.). 32p. (J). (gr. 4-8). lib. bdg. 32.07 *(978-1-5341-2954-2(5)*, 211860, 45th Parallel Press) Cherry Lake Publishing.

Lunis, Natalie. Tut's Deadly Tomb. 2010. (HorrorScapes Ser.). 32p. (YA). (gr. 4-7). lib. bdg. 28.50 *(978-1-936087-98-3(7))* Bearport Publishing Co., Inc.

Málek, Jaromír. Tutankhamun: The Story of Egyptology's Greatest Discovery. 2013. (Illus.). 63p. (J). *(978-1-4351-4689-1(1))* Metro Bks.

Morley, Jacqueline. Inside the Tomb of Tutankhamun. James, John, illus. 2005. (ENG.). 48p. (J). (gr. 3-7). 19.95 *(978-1-59270-042-4(X))* Enchanted Lion Bks., LLC.

—You Wouldn't Want to Be Cursed by King Tut! Antram, David, illus. 2012. (You Wouldn't Want to... Ser.). (ENG.). 32p. (J). pap. 9.95 *(978-0-531-20949-3(0)*, Watts, Franklin) Scholastic Library Publishing.

—You Wouldn't Want to Be Cursed by King Tut! A Mysterious Death You'd Rather Avoid. Antram, David, illus. 2012. (ENG.). 32p. (J). (gr. 3-12). lib. bdg. 29.00 *(978-0-531-20874-8(5))* Scholastic Library Publishing.

Oachs, Emily Rose. King Tut's Tomb. 2019. (Digging up the Past Ser.). (ENG., Illus.). 24p. (J). (gr. 3-7). lib. bdg. 26.95 *(978-1-64487-067-9(3)*, Torque Bks.) Bellwether Media.

Peterson, Megan Cooley. King Tut: Is His Tomb Really Cursed? 2018. (History's Mysteries Ser.). (ENG.). 32p. (J). (gr. 4-6). pap. 9.99 *(978-1-64466-258-8(2)*, 12285); (Illus.). lib. bdg. *(978-1-68072-411-0(8)*, 12284) Black Rabbit Bks. (Bolt).

Stewart, David. Tutankhamen! A Mummy Who Really Got Meddled With. Antram, David, illus. 2007. (You Wouldn't Want to... Ser.). (ENG.). 32p. (J). (gr. 2-5). 29.00 *(978-0-531-18725-8(X))* Scholastic Library Publishing.

The Treasures of Tutankhamun. (Butterfly Bks.). (ARA.). 48p. (YA). (gr. 5-8). 9.95 *(978-0-86685-485-6(1))* International Bk. Ctr., Inc.

Westphal, Jeremy. The Mummy's Curse. 2011. (Unexplained Ser.). (ENG., Illus.). 24p. (J). (gr. 3-7). lib. bdg. 26.95 *(978-1-60014-643-5(0)*, Torque Bks.) Bellwether Media.

Woods, Michael & Woods, Mary B. The Tomb of King Tutankhamen. 2008. (Unearthing Ancient Worlds Ser.). (ENG., Illus.). 80p. (gr. 5-8). lib. bdg. 30.60 *(978-0-8225-7506-1(X))* Lerner Publishing Group.

World Book, Inc. Staff, contrib. by. The Mystery of Tutankhamun. 2015. (Illus.). 48p. (J). *(978-0-7166-2678-7(0))* World Bk., Inc.

Wynne, Patricia J. King Tut Coloring Book. 2005. (Dover Ancient History Coloring Bks.). (ENG., Illus.). 32p. (J). (gr. 3-5). 4.99 *(978-0-486-44444-4(9)*, 444449) Dover Pubns., Inc.

Zoehfeld, Kathleen Weidner. The Curse of King Tut's Mummy (Totally True Adventures) How a Lost Tomb Was Found. Nelson, Jim, illus. 2007. (Totally True Adventures Ser.). 112p. (J). (gr. 2-5). per. 5.99 *(978-0-375-83862-0(7)*, Random Hse. Bks. for Young Readers) Random Hse. Children's Bks.

TV

see Television

TWAIN, MARK, 1835-1910

Aller, Susan Bivin. Mark Twain. (Just the Facts Biographies Ser.). (Illus.). 112p. (J). 2006. 27.93 *(978-0-8225-3425-9(8)*, Lerner Pubns.) 2006. (gr. 3-7). pap. 9.95 *(978-0-8225-5998-6(6)*, Lerner Pubns.) 2003. (gr. 6-18). pap. 7.95 *(978-0-8225-9696-7(2))* Lerner Publishing Group.

Armentrout, David & Armentrout, Patricia. Mark Twain. 2003. (Discover the Life of an American Legend Ser.). (Illus.). 24p. (gr. 2-5). lib. bdg. *(978-1-58952-660-0(0))* Rourke Educational Media.

Ashmore, Wayne & Nault, Jennifer. The Adventurous World of Mark Twain. 2016. (J). *(978-1-5105-1955-8(6))* SmartBook Media, Inc.

—Mark Twain. 2008. (My Favorite Writer Ser.). (Illus.). 32p. (YA). (gr. 5-18). pap. 9.95 *(978-1-59036-931-9(9))*; lib. bdg. 26.00 *(978-1-59036-930-2(0))* Weigl Pubs., Inc.

Bloom, Harold, ed. Mark Twain. 2nd rev. ed. 2006. (Modern Critical Views Ser.). (ENG.). 300p. (gr. 9). 45.00 *(978-0-7910-8569-1(4)*, P114302, Facts On File) Infobase Holdings, Inc.

—Mark Twain's the Adventures of Huckleberry Finn. 2nd rev. ed. 2007. (Bloom's Modern Critical Interpretations Ser.). (ENG.). 248p. (gr. 9-18). lib. bdg. 45.00 *(978-0-7910-9426-6(X)*, P125509, Facts On File) Infobase Holdings, Inc.

Burleigh, Robert. The Adventures of Mark Twain by Huckleberry Finn. Blitt, Barry, illus. 2011. (ENG.). 48p. (J). (gr. 2-5). 19.99 *(978-0-689-83041-9(6)*, Atheneum Bks. for Young Readers) Simon & Schuster Children's Publishing.

Caravantes, Peggy. A Great & Sublime Fool: The Story of Mark Twain. 2010. (World Writers Ser.). (Illus.). 176p. (YA). (gr. 8-18). lib. bdg. 28.95 *(978-1-59935-088-2(2))* Reynolds, Morgan Inc.

Carew-Miller, Anna. Mark Twain. Di Gennaro, Andrea, illus. 2003. (Great Names Ser.). (J). 19.95 *(978-957-745-414-0(3))* Mason Crest.

—Mark Twain: Great American Fiction Writer. 2004. (Great Names Ser.). (Illus.). 32p. (J). (gr. 3-18). lib. bdg. 19.95 *(978-1-59084-158-7(1))* Mason Crest.

Diorio, Mary Ann L. A Student's Guide to Mark Twain, 1 vol. 2008. (Understanding Literature Ser.). (ENG., Illus.). 160p. (gr. 9-10). lib. bdg. 31.93 *(978-0-7660-2438-0(5)*, 6e218b03-de6a-42a3-b29f-35fe938b14c5) Enslow Publishing, LLC.

Fleischman, Sid. The Trouble Begins At 8: A Life of Mark Twain in the Wild, Wild West. 2008. (ENG., Illus.). 224p. (J). (gr. 4-7). 18.99 *(978-0-06-134431-2(1)*, Greenwillow Bks.) HarperCollins Pubs.

Goldsmith, Howard. Mark Twain at Work! Habbas, Frank, illus. 2005. 32p. (J). lib. bdg. 15.00 *(978-1-59054-951-3(1))* Fitzgerald Bks.

—Mark Twain at Work! Ready-To-Read Level 2. Habbas, Frank, illus. 2003. (Ready-To-Read Childhood of Famous Americans Ser.). (ENG.). 32p. (J). (gr. k-2). pap. 4.99 *(978-0-689-85399-9(8)*, Simon Spotlight) Simon Spotlight.

Helms, Neil. Reading the Adventures of Tom Sawyer. 2005. (Engaged Reader Ser.). (ENG., Illus.). 96p. (gr. 5-8). lib. bdg. 25.00 *(978-0-7910-8828-9(6)*, P114440, Facts On File) Infobase Holdings, Inc.

Hermann, Spring. Reading & Interpreting the Works of Mark Twain, 1 vol. 2017. (Lit Crit Guides). (ENG.). 160p. (gr. 8-8). lib. bdg. 41.60 *(978-0-7660-8493-3(0)*, 8ebb5855-0a1f-48bd-8728-9675743e99be) Enslow Publishing, LLC.

Houle, Michelle M. Mark Twain: Banned, Challenged, & Censored, 1 vol. 2008. (Authors of Banned Bks.). (ENG., Illus.). 160p. (gr. 9-10). lib. bdg. 38.60 *(978-0-7660-2689-6(2)*, 35638c06-5cb3-440c-abe0-b9ce1f662f61) Enslow Publishing, LLC.

Lázaro León, Georgina. Mark Twain. Lindmark, Margaret, illus. 2019. (SPA.). 32p. (J). (gr. 4-6). 14.99 *(978-1-63245-762-2(8))* Lectorum Pubns., Inc.

MacLeod, Elizabeth. Mark Twain: An American Star. 2008. (Snapshots: Images of People & Places in History Ser.). (Illus.). 32p. (J). (gr. 3-6). 21.19 *(978-1-55337-908-9(X))* Kids Can Pr., Ltd. CAN. Dist: Children's Plus, Inc.

Maloof, Torrey. Stepping into Mark Twain's World. 2nd rev. ed. 2017. (TIME(r): Informational Text Ser.). (ENG., Illus.). 48p. (J). (gr. 6-8). pap. 13.99 *(978-1-4938-3620-8(X))* Teacher Created Materials, Inc.

—Stepping into Mark Twain's World. 2017. (Time for Kids Nonfiction Readers Ser.). lib. bdg. 20.85 *(978-0-606-40285-9(3))* Turtleback.

Mark Twain. 2010. (ENG., Illus.). 128p. (gr. 6-12). 35.00 *(978-1-60413-728-6(2)*, P179353, Facts On File) Infobase Holdings, Inc.

North, Sterling. Mark Twain & the River. 2009. 192p. (J). (gr. 3-7). 6.99 *(978-0-14-241235-0(X)*, Puffin) Penguin Young Readers Group.

Prince, April Jones. Who Was Mark Twain? O'brien, John, illus. 2004. (Who Was... ? Ser.). 105p. (gr. 3-7). 16.00 *(978-0-7569-4590-9(9))* Perfection Learning Corp.

Prince, April Jones & Who HQ. Who Was Mark Twain? O'Brien, John, illus. 2004. (Who Was? Ser.). 112p. (J). (gr. 3-7). pap. 5.99 *(978-0-448-43319-6(2)*, Penguin Workshop) Penguin Young Readers Group.

Rasmussen, R. Kent. Mark Twain for Kids: His Life & Times, 21 Activities. 2004. (For Kids Ser.: 7). (ENG., Illus.). 160p. (J). (gr. 4). pap. 14.95 *(978-1-55652-527-8(3))* Chicago Review Pr., Inc.

Sherman, Josepha. Mark Twain. 2005. (Classic Storytellers Ser.). (Illus.). 48p. (J). (gr. 4-8). lib. bdg. 29.95 *(978-1-58415-374-0(1))* Mitchell Lane Pubs.

Wallace, Elise. The Prehistoric Masters of Literature Volume 1: Discover Literary History with a Prehistoric Twist! Isik, Semur, illus. 2018. (Jurassic Classics Ser.). (ENG.). 32p. (J). (gr. 4-7). lib. bdg. 26.65 *(978-1-942875-55-0(X)*, 5dd27ad0-30fb-4ce7-a68e-d1ced05396be, Walter Foster Jr) Quarto Publishing Group USA.

—The Prehistoric Masters of Literature Volume 2: Discover Literary History with a Prehistoric Twist! Isik, Semur, illus. 2018. (Jurassic Classics Ser.). (ENG.). 32p. (J). (gr. 4-7). lib. bdg. 26.65 *(978-1-942875-56-7(8)*, 83333adc-1433-4bd6-b1f8-7de331dd16e6, Walter Foster Jr) Quarto Publishing Group USA.

Wilson, Douglas. Adventures of Huckleberry Finn. 2016. (J). pap. *(978-1-944503-41-3(2))* Canon Pr.

Youngblood, Wayne. Mark Twain along the Mississippi, 1 vol. 2005. (In the Footsteps of American Heroes Ser.). (ENG., Illus.). 64p. (gr. 5-8). pap. 15.05 *(978-0-8368-6435-9(2)*, fc650921-fafb-4dde-ae34-50f8069dd1ae); lib. bdg. 36.67 *(978-0-8368-6430-4(1)*, 075f253e-b58f-4ce9-9e41-a0fcee83e823) Stevens, Gareth Publishing LLLP. (Gareth Stevens Secondary Library).

TWAIN, MARK, 1835-1910—FICTION

Howard, Joan. The Story of Mark Twain. Meadowcroft, Enid Lamonte, ed. McKay, Donald, illus. 2011. 186p. 42.95 *(978-1-258-05565-3(1))* Literary Licensing, LLC.

Kerley, Barbara. The Extraordinary Mark Twain (According to Susy) Fotheringham, Edwin, illus. 2010. (ENG.). 48p. (J). (gr. 2-6). 21.99 *(978-0-545-12508-6(1)*, Scholastic Pr.) Scholastic, Inc.

—The "Extrodinary" Mark Twain (According to Susy) Fotheringham, Edwin, illus. 2010. (J). *(978-0-545-12509-3(X)*, Scholastic Pr.) Scholastic, Inc.

TWENTIETH CENTURY

Hunter, Rebecca & Walker, Kathryn. Growing up in the Forties. 2003. (ENG., Illus.). 32p. pap. *(978-0-7502-3434-4(2)*, Wayland) Hachette Children's Group.

—Growing up in the Thirties. 2003. (ENG., Illus.). 32p. pap. *(978-0-7502-3433-7(4)*, Wayland) Hachette Children's Group.

National Geographic Learning. Reading Expeditions (Social Studies: Voices from America's Past): the Roaring 20s. 2007. (ENG., Illus.). 40p. (J). pap. 21.95 *(978-0-7922-4551-3(2))* National Geographic School Publishing, Inc.

Parker, Janice. 1980: Canadian Decades. 2011. 48p. (C). (gr. 4-6). pap. *(978-1-77071-729-9(3))* Weigl Educational Pubs. Ltd.

Ryan, James Gilbert & Schlup, Leonard C. Historical Dictionary of The 1940s. 2006. (ENG., Illus.). 648p. (C). 180.00 *(978-0-7656-0440-8(X)*, Y182788) Routledge.

Sandler, Martin W. 1919 the Year That Changed America. 2019. (ENG., Illus.). 192p. (J). 24.99 *(978-1-68119-801-9(0)*, 900187333, Bloomsbury Children's Bks.) Bloomsbury Publishing USA.

Sharman, Margaret. 1950s. (Illus.). 47p. (J). pap. *(978-0-237-51664-2(0))* Evans Brothers, Ltd.

1900s: Decades of the 20th Century, 10 vols. 2005. (Illus.). 64p. (YA). 29.95 *(978-1-932904-00-0(X))* Eldorado Ink.

1910s: Decades of the 20th Century, 10 vols. 2005. (Illus.). 64p. (YA). 29.95 *(978-1-932904-01-7(8))* Eldorado Ink.

1920s: Decades of the 20th Century, 10 vols. 2005. (Illus.). 64p. (YA). 29.95 *(978-1-932904-02-4(6))* Eldorado Ink.

1930s: Decades of the 20th Century, 10 vols. 2005. (Illus.). 64p. (YA). 29.95 *(978-1-932904-03-1(4))* Eldorado Ink.

1940s: Decades of the 20th Century, 10 vols. 2005. (Illus.). 64p. (YA). 29.95 *(978-1-932904-04-8(2))* Eldorado Ink.

1950s: Decades of the 20th Century, 10 vols. 2005. (Illus.). 64p. (YA). 29.95 *(978-1-932904-05-5(0))* Eldorado Ink.

1960s: Decades of the 20th Century, 10 vols. 2005. (Illus.). 64p. (YA). 29.95 *(978-1-932904-06-2(9))* Eldorado Ink.

1970s: Decades of the 20th Century, 10 vols. 2005. (Illus.). 64p. (YA). 29.95 *(978-1-932904-07-9(7))* Eldorado Ink.

1980s: Decades of the 20th Century, 10 vols. 2005. (Illus.). 64p. (YA). 29.95 *(978-1-932904-08-6(5))* Eldorado Ink.

1990s: Decades of the 20th Century, 10 vols. 2005. (Illus.). 64p. (YA). 29.95 *(978-1-932904-09-3(3))* Eldorado Ink.

TWINS

Kongyin. Sungrass. 2011. 344p. pap. *(978-0-9869858-5-0(6))* Kima Global Pubs.

Kor, Eva Mozes & Buccieri, Lisa Rojany. Surviving the Angel of Death: The True Story of a Mengele Twin in Auschwitz. 2012. lib. bdg. 19.60 *(978-0-606-23838-0(7))* Turtleback.

Look A-Likes Don't Act A-Like. 2007. (Illus.). 40p. (J). 12.95 *(978-0-9776711-4-4(3)*, Blue Marble Bks.) Sphinx Publishing.

Markham, Lauren. The Far Away Brothers (Adapted for Young Adults) Two Teenage Immigrants Making a Life in America. 2019. (ENG.). 288p. (YA). (gr. 7). 17.99 *(978-1-9848-2977-1(7)*, Delacorte Pr.) Random Hse. Children's Bks.

Miller, Kerri. My Twin & Me - Fun with Twin Brothers & Sisters. 2013. (Illus.). 20p. pap. *(978-0-9576753-0-8(5))* Hot Tub Publishing, Ltd.

Olsen, Mary-Kate & Olsen, Ashley. The Ultimate Guide to Mary-Kate & Ashley. 2004. (Illus.). 93p. *(978-0-00-718136-0(1))* HarperCollins Pubs. Australia.

TWINS—FICTION

Abbott, Tony. Denis Ever After. 2018. (ENG.). 320p. (J). (gr. 5-7). 16.99 *(978-0-06-249122-0(9)*, Tegen, Katherine Bks) HarperCollins Pubs.

Abel, Cheyanne. It's Better by Far, When You Are Who You Are. 2012. 24p. pap. 17.99 *(978-1-4685-7492-0(2))* AuthorHouse.

Adventures with Kat & Dex: The search for the key to Golden Gate Park. Lt. ed. 2004. (Illus.). 32p. (J). lib. bdg. 22.95 *(978-0-9754853-0-9(X))* DeAngelis, Anthony.

Aldridge, Ethan M. Estranged. Aldridge, Ethan M., illus. 2018. (ENG., Illus.). 224p. (J). (gr. 3-7). 21.99 *(978-0-06-265387-1(3))*; pap. 13.99 *(978-0-06-265386-4(5))* HarperCollins Pubs. (Quill Tree Bks.).

Alexander, Kwame. The Crossover. 2020. (ENG., Illus.). 218p. (J). (gr. 4-5). 24.19 *(978-1-64697-344-6(5))* Penworthy Co., LLC, The.

—The Crossover. 2014. lib. bdg. 29.40 *(978-0-606-37975-5(4))* Turtleback.

—The Crossover: A Newbery Award Winner. Anyabwile, Dawud, illus. (Crossover Ser.). (ENG.). (J). (gr. 3-7). 2019. 256p. pap. 10.99 *(978-0-544-93520-4(9)*, 1658124) 2014. 240p. 17.99 *(978-0-544-10771-7(3)*, 1540363) HarperCollins Pubs. (Clarion Bks.).

—El Crossover: Crossover (Spanish Edition), a Newbery Award Winner. Herrera, Juan Felipe, tr. Anyabwile, Dawud, illus. 2019. (Crossover Ser.). (SPA.). 256p. (J). (gr. 5-7). pap. 9.99 *(978-0-358-06473-2(2)*, 1743975, Clarion Bks.) HarperCollins Pubs.

Amato, Carol J. The Lost Treasure of the Golden Sun. 2005. 172p. (J). *(978-0-9713756-3-5(1))* Stargazer Publishing Co.

—The Secret of Blackhurst Manor. 2017. (ENG.). 232p. (J). pap. 9.95 *(978-1-933277-02-8(5))* Stargazer Publishing Co.

Amirkhan, Michele. Princess Elian's Quest. 2008. 112p. 20.95 *(978-0-595-50870-9(7))*; pap. 10.95 *(978-0-595-51400-7(6))* iUniverse, Inc.

Anderson, Laurie Halse. New Beginnings, 13 vols., 13. 2012. (Vet Volunteers Ser.: 13). (ENG.). 192p. (J). (gr. 3-7). 7.99 *(978-0-14-241675-4(4)*, Puffin) Penguin Young Readers Group.

Anderson, Patricia. It's Time for Kindergarten PJ & Parker. 2012. (Illus.). 26p. (J). 19.95 *(978-1-61863-379-8(1))* Bookstand Publishing.

Apte, Sunita. Ride the Whale: A Surfer Tall Tale. Reed, Kyle, illus. 2006. 16p. (J). pap. *(978-0-439-74638-0(8))* Scholastic, Inc.

Arcos, Carrie. There Will Come a Time. 2014. (ENG., Illus.). 320p. (YA). (gr. 9). 17.99 *(978-1-4424-9585-2(5)*, Simon Pulse) Simon Pulse.

Armstrong, Kelley. Sea of Shadows. (Age of Legends Trilogy Ser.: 1). (ENG.). (YA). (gr. 8). 2015. 432p. pap. 9.99 *(978-0-06-207125-5(4))* 2014. 416p. 17.99 *(978-0-06-207124-8(6))* HarperCollins Pubs. (HarperCollins).

—Sea of Shadows. 2015. (Age of Legends Ser.: 1). (YA). lib. bdg. 20.85 *(978-0-606-36511-6(7))* Turtleback.

Arnold, David. The Strange Fascinations of Noah Hypnotik. 2019. 448p. (YA). (gr. 9). pap. 10.99 *(978-0-425-28887-0(0)*, Penguin Books) Penguin Young Readers Group.

Ashburn, Boni. A Twin Is to Hug. 2019. (ENG., Illus.). 32p. (J). (gr. -1-1). 14.99 *(978-1-4197-3158-7(0)*, 1195301, Abrams Bks. for Young Readers) Abrams, Inc.

Astrotwins — Project Blastoff. 2015. (Astrotwins Ser.). (ENG., Illus.). 224p. (J). (gr. 3-7). 18.99 *(978-1-4814-1545-3(X)*, Simon & Schuster/Paula Wiseman Bks.) Simon & Schuster/Paula Wiseman Bks.

Atwood, Megan. Once upon a Winter. Andrewson, Natalie, illus. 2017. (Orchard Novel Ser.: 2). (ENG.). 240p. (J). (gr. 2-6). 12.99 *(978-1-4814-9049-8(4)*, Aladdin) Simon & Schuster Children's Publishing.

Auerbach, Annie. The Grosse Adventures: The Good, the Bad, & the Gassy, Vol. 1. Norton, Mike, illus. 2006. (Grosse Adventures Manga Ser.: 1). (ENG.). 96p. (J). (gr. 4-1). pap. 9.99 *(978-1-59816-049-9(4))* TOKYOPOP, Inc.

—The Grosse Adventures Vol. 3: Trouble at Twilight Cave, 1 vol. Nicholas, Jamar, illus. 2008. (Tokyopop Ser.). (ENG.). 96p. (J). (gr. 2-6). 32.79 *(978-1-59961-562-2(2)*, 14806, Graphic Novels) Spotlight.

Avery, Lara. A Million Miles Away. 2016. (ENG.). 336p. (YA). (gr. 10-17). pap. 17.99 *(978-0-316-28372-4(X)*, Poppy) Little, Brown Bks. for Young Readers.

Avi & Vail, Rachel. Never Mind! 2005. (Twin Novels Ser.). 200p. (gr. 5-9). 16.00 *(978-0-7569-5667-7(6))* Perfection Learning Corp.

—Never Mind! A Twin Novel. 2005. (ENG.). 208p. (J). (gr. 5-18). reprint ed. pap. 6.99 *(978-0-06-054316-7(7)*, HarperCollins) HarperCollins Pubs.

Azmitia, M. The Same Blood, 1 vol. 2018. (YA Verse Ser.). (ENG.). 200p. (YA). (gr. 3-4). 25.80 *(978-1-5383-8252-3(0)*, 873f0b82-85b1-4d42-8166-a153a96bd440); pap. 16.35 *(978-1-5383-8251-6(2)*, 3f5a2881-e090-4972-b7b7-1e5e74b46e79) Enslow Publishing, LLC.

Baggott, Julianna. The Ever Breath. 2011. (ENG.). 240p. (J). (gr. 4-6). lib. bdg. 21.19 *(978-0-385-90676-0(5)*, Delacorte Pr.) Random Hse. Children's Bks.

Baier, Jeanne M. The Twins Jeffrey & Jeanne. 2012. 28p. pap. 16.00 *(978-1-4669-5194-5(X))* Trafford Publishing.

Bailey, Ethel M. T. Lily Pond Village, 1 vol. 2009. 57p. pap. 16.95 *(978-1-60703-379-0(8))* America Star Bks.

Bair, Sheila. Rock, Brock, & the Savings Shock. Gott, Barry, illus. 2017. (Money Tales Ser.). (ENG.). 32p. (J). (gr. -1-3). pap. 8.99 *(978-0-8075-7095-1(8)*, 807570958) Whitman, Albert & Co.

Balasubramanian, Lalitha. The Twins at the Ancient Villa, 1 vol. 2009. 48p. pap. 16.95 *(978-1-61582-601-8(7))* America Star Bks.

Banks, Jacqueline Turner. Egg-Drop Blues. 2003. (ENG.). 128p. (J). (gr. 5-7). pap. 10.95 *(978-0-618-25080-6(8)*, 481193, Clarion Bks.) HarperCollins Pubs.

Banks, Lynne Reid. Angela & Diabola. 163p. (J). (gr. 4-6). pap. 4.50 *(978-0-8072-1515-9(5)*, Listening Library) Random Hse. Audio Publishing Group.

Barber, Ronde & Barber, Tiki. Go Long! 2011. (Barber Game Time Bks.). (ENG.). 160p. (J). (gr. 3-7). pap. 7.99 *(978-1-4169-8573-0(5)*, Simon & Schuster/Paula Wiseman Bks.) Simon & Schuster/Paula Wiseman Bks.

Barber, Tiki & Barber, Ronde. End Zone. (Barber Game Time Bks.). (ENG., Illus.). (J). (gr. 3-7). 2014. 192p. pap. 7.99 *(978-1-4169-9098-7(4))* 2012. 176p. 15.99 *(978-1-4169-9097-0(6))* Simon & Schuster/Paula Wiseman Bks. (Simon & Schuster/Paula Wiseman Bks.).

—Extra Innings. 2014. (Barber Game Time Bks.). (ENG., Illus.). 160p. (J). (gr. 3-7). 16.99 *(978-1-4424-5726-3(0)*, Simon & Schuster/Paula Wiseman Bks.) Simon & Schuster/Paula Wiseman Bks.

—Goal Line. (Barber Game Time Bks.). (ENG., Illus.). 176p. (J). (gr. 3-7). 2013. pap. 7.99 *(978-1-4169-9096-3(8))* 2011. 15.99 *(978-1-4169-9095-6(X))* Simon & Schuster/Paula Wiseman Bks. (Simon & Schuster/Paula Wiseman Bks.).

—Jump Shot. 2013. (Barber Game Time Bks.). (ENG., Illus.). 160p. (J). (gr. 3-7). 16.99 *(978-1-4424-5729-4(5)*, Simon & Schuster/Paula Wiseman Bks.) Simon & Schuster/Paula Wiseman Bks.

—Red Zone. (Barber Game Time Bks.). (ENG., 176p. (J). (gr. 3-7). 2013. Illus.). pap. 7.99 *(978-1-4169-6861-0(X))* 2010. 15.99 *(978-1-4169-6860-3(1))* Simon & Schuster/Paula Wiseman Bks. (Simon & Schuster/Paula Wiseman Bks.).

—Wild Card. (Barber Game Time Bks.). (ENG.). 160p. (J). (gr. 3-7). 2012. pap. 7.99 *(978-1-4169-6859-7(8))* 2009. 15.99 *(978-1-4169-6858-0(X))* Simon & Schuster/Paula Wiseman Bks. (Simon & Schuster/Paula Wiseman Bks.).

Barnhill, Kelly. The Witch's Boy. 2014. (ENG.). 400p. (J). (gr. 4-7). 37.99 *(978-1-61620-351-1(X)*, 73351) Algonquin Young Readers.

Barrett, Tracy. Marabel & the Book of Fate. 2018. (Marabel Novel Ser.). (ENG.). 304p. (J). (gr. 3-7). 16.99 *(978-0-316-43399-0(3))* Little, Brown Bks. for Young Readers.

Barrowman, John & Barrowman, Carole. Conjuror. 2016. (Orion Chronicles Ser.). (ENG.). 320p. (YA). (gr. 7). 16.99 *(978-1-78185-637-6(0))* Head of Zeus GBR. Dist: Independent Pubs. Group.

—Inquisitor. 2018. (Orion Chronicles Ser.: 3). (ENG.). 320p. (YA). (gr. 7). 19.99 *(978-1-78185-645-1(1))* Head of Zeus GBR. Dist: Independent Pubs. Group.

Barrowman, John & Barrowman, Carole E. Bone Quill. 2014. (Hollow Earth Ser.). (ENG., Illus.). 304p. (J). (gr. 3-7). pap. 8.99 *(978-1-4424-8929-5(4)*, Aladdin) Simon & Schuster Children's Publishing.

—Hollow Earth. (Hollow Earth Ser.). (ENG., (J). (gr. 3-7). 2013. Illus.). 416p. pap. 8.99 *(978-1-4424-5853-6(4))* 2012. 400p. 16.99 *(978-1-4424-5852-9(6))* Simon & Schuster Children's Publishing. (Aladdin).

Barrows, Annie. Magic in the Mix. 2015. (ENG.). 288p. (YA). (gr. 3-6). pap. 8.99 *(978-1-61963-798-6(7)*, 900148899, Bloomsbury USA Childrens) Bloomsbury Publishing USA.

Bateman, Anya. The Makeover of James Orville Wickenbee. 2007. 262p. (J). pap. *(978-1-59038-707-8(4))* Deseret Bk. Co.

Bath, K. P. Flip Side. 2009. (YA). 16.99 *(978-0-316-03836-2(9))* Little Brown & Co.

Bauer, Deidre. Silver Mountain. 2008. 38p. pap. 8.00 *(978-0-8059-7672-4(8))* Dorrance Publishing Co., Inc.

Baxter, David. The Tournesol Twins. 2006. 68p. pap. *(978-1-84401-901-4(2))* Athena Pr.

Beaty, Andrea. Attack of the Fluffy Bunnies. 2012. (Fluffy Bunnies Ser.). (ENG.). 192p. (YA). (gr. 2-8). pap. 7.95 *(978-1-4197-0519-9(9)*, 670903, Amulet Bks.) Abrams, Inc.

—Fluffy Bunnies 2: The Schnoz of Doom. 2016. (ENG., Illus.). 208p. (J). (gr. 3-7). pap. 7.95 *(978-1-4197-1942-4(4)*, 1068603, Amulet Bks.) Abrams, Inc.

—Fluffy Bunnies 2: The Schnoz of Doom. Santat, Dan, illus. 2015. (Fluffy Bunnies Ser.). (ENG.). 192p. (J). (gr. 3-7). 12.95 *(978-1-4197-1051-3(6)*, 1068601, Amulet Bks.) Abrams, Inc.

BEEBE, Diane. School's Out. 2006. (J). *(978-1-4276-0238-1(7))* Aardvark Global Publishing.

Bell, Michele Ashman. Dragon's Jaw: A Heart-Pounding Adventure. 2005. 241p. (J). *(978-1-59156-880-3(3))* Covenant Communications.

—Spyhunt: A Heart-Pounding Adventure: A Novel. 2004. 187p. (J). *(978-1-59156-457-7(3))* Covenant Communications.

Bellino, Sarah. The Little Miss Detectives: Case Number 1. 2012. 32p. pap. 14.51 *(978-1-4669-6867-7(2))* Trafford Publishing.

Bellisario, Gina. Camp Hero Double Trouble. von Innerebner, Jessika, illus. 2018. (Ellie Ultra Ser.). (ENG.). 128p. (J). (gr. 1-3). pap. 6.95 *(978-1-4965-6517-4(7)*, 138521); lib. bdg. 25.99 *(978-1-4965-6513-6(4)*, 138519) Capstone. (Stone Arch Bks.).

Bergen, Lara. Tutu Twins. Pastel, Elyse & Pastel, Elyse, illus. 2008. (ENG.). 24p. (J). (gr. k-17). per. 3.99 *(978-1-58476-615-5(8))* Innovative Kids.

Betancourt, Jeanne. Pony Mysteries #1: Penny & Pepper (Scholastic Reader, Level 3) Riley, Kellee, illus. 2011. (Scholastic Reader, Level 3 Ser.). (ENG.). 48p. (J). (gr. 1-3). pap. 3.99 *(978-0-545-11508-7(6)*, Cartwheel Bks.) Scholastic, Inc.

Billingsley, Franny. Chime. 2011. (Playaway Young Adult Ser.). (YA). 59.99 *(978-1-61707-143-0(9))* Findaway World, LLC.

—Chime. 2012. (ENG.). 320p. (YA). (gr. 7-12). 26.19 *(978-0-8037-3552-1(9)*, Dial) Penguin Publishing Group.

—Chime. 2012. (ENG.). 384p. (YA). (gr. 7-18). 8.99 *(978-0-14-242092-8(1)*, Speak) Penguin Young Readers Group.

Bingham, Laura. Alvor. 2009. 277p. (J). pap. 17.99 *(978-1-59955-272-9(8))* Cedar Fort, Inc./CFI Distribution.

—Wings of Light. 2011. 240p. (J). pap. 15.99 *(978-1-59955-492-1(5)*, Sweetwater Bks.) Cedar Fort, Inc./CFI Distribution.

Bitterman, Kevin. BD's Big Hit, 1 vol. 2009. (ENG.). 63p. pap. 19.95 *(978-1-60836-366-7(X))* America Star Bks.

Bjork, Linda. Salmon Cavern. 2006. 92p. pap. 10.95 *(978-1-59800-546-2(4))* Outskirts Pr., Inc.

Black, Holly. The Queen of Nothing. (Folk of the Air Ser.: 3). (ENG., Illus.). (YA). (gr. 9-17). 2020. 336p. pap. 12.99 *(978-0-316-31037-6(9))* 2019. 320p. 19.99 *(978-0-316-31042-0(5))* Little, Brown Bks. for Young Readers.

Blake, Ashley Herring. Girl Made of Stars. (ENG.). 304p. (YA). (gr. 9). 2019. pap. 9.99 *(978-0-358-10822-1(5)*, 1748885) 2018. 17.99 *(978-1-328-77823-9(1)*, 1681853) HarperCollins Pubs. (Clarion Bks.).

Blake-Garrett, Andrea. The Adventures of Izzy & Juju: Twin Detective Investigators (T. D. I.) 2012. 28p. pap. 19.99 *(978-1-4685-0683-9(8))* AuthorHouse.

—Las Aventuras de Izzy y Juju: Gemelos Detectives Investigadores (G. D. I.) 2012. 28p. pap. 19.99 *(978-1-4772-2523-3(4))* AuthorHouse.

Bliss, Bryan. No Parking at the End Times. 2015. (ENG.). 272p. (YA). (gr. 9). 17.99 *(978-0-06-227541-7(0)*, Greenwillow Bks.) HarperCollins Pubs.

Bloumis, Joy. An Adventure in Fairyland. 2013. 84p. pap. 10.50 *(978-1-62212-835-8(4)*, Strategic Bk. Publishing) Strategic Book Publishing & Rights Agency (SBPRA).

Blyton, Enid. House at the Corner: Family Adventure. 2013. 271p. (J). pap. 9.99 *(978-1-84135-647-1(6))* Award Pubns. Ltd. GBR. Dist: Parkwest Pubns., Inc.

Bo, Ben. Skullcrack. 2003. (ENG.). 168p. (YA). (gr. 5-12). pap. 6.95 *(978-0-8225-3311-5(1))* Lerner Publishing Group.

Bodeen, S. A. The Compound. 2011. 9.46 *(978-0-7848-3490-9(3)*, Everbind) Marco Bk. Co.

—The Compound. 2009. (Compound Ser.: 1). (ENG.). 272p. (YA). (gr. 7-12). pap. 10.99 *(978-0-312-57860-2(1)*, 900061807) Square Fish.

Boeve, Eunice. Echoes of Kansas Past. Peterson-Shea, Julie, illus. 2012. 176p. pap. 10.99 *(978-0-9851196-9-0(1))* Rowe Publishing.

Bogart, Mike. The Henderson Twins in Muckleball! 2006. 107p. pap. 16.95 *(978-1-4241-3050-4(6))* PublishAmerica, Inc.

—Ice Warriors, 1 vol. 2010. 72p. pap. 19.95 *(978-1-4489-3885-8(6))* America Star Bks.

Boling, Katharine. January 1905: a Novel. 2006. (ENG., Illus.). 192p. (J). (gr. 5-7). pap. 11.99 *(978-0-15-205121-1(X)*, 1195464, Clarion Bks.) HarperCollins Pubs.

Bollback, Anthony G. Capture of the Twin Dragon. 2012. 152p. pap. 8.99 *(978-0-9849359-1-8(6))* Finding the Cause, LLC.

—Hijacked. 2012. 176p. pap. 8.99 *(978-0-9849359-5-6(9))* Finding the Cause, LLC.

—Mystery of the Counterfeit Money. 2012. 170p. (gr. 4-7). pap. 8.99 *(978-0-9849359-2-5(4))* Finding the Cause, LLC.

—Rescue at Cripple Creek. 2012. 178p. pap. 8.99 *(978-0-9849359-3-2(2))* Finding the Cause, LLC.

—Smugglers in Hong Kong. 2012. 156p. pap. 8.99 *(978-0-9849359-0-1(8))* Finding the Cause, LLC.

—The Tiger Shark Strikes Again. 2012. 172p. pap. 8.99 *(978-0-9849359-4-9(0))* Finding the Cause, LLC.

Bosworth, Jennifer. The Killing Jar. 2016. (ENG.). 352p. (YA). 34.99 *(978-0-374-34137-4(0)*, 900126267, Farrar, Straus & Giroux (BYR)) Farrar, Straus & Giroux.

Boykin, Antonee. Alex & Tony Learn to Be Gentlemen. 2011. 31p. (J). pap. 13.95 *(978-1-4327-5255-2(3))* Outskirts Pr., Inc.

Bradford, Chris. Bodyguard: Hostage (Book 2), Bk. 2. 2017. (Bodyguard Ser.: 2). (ENG.). 224p. (J). (gr. 5). pap. 8.99 *(978-1-5247-3699-6(6)*, Philomel Bks.) Penguin Young Readers Group.

—Bodyguard: Ransom (Book 4), Bk. 4. 2017. (Bodyguard Ser.: 4). (ENG.). 224p. (J). (gr. 5). pap. 9.99 *(978-1-5247-3703-0(8)*, Philomel Bks.) Penguin Young Readers Group.

Brehm, David L. Willy Nilly Volume 1. Claerhout, Paul, illus. 2013. 94p. (J). pap. 19.95 *(978-0-9860669-0-0(7))* Blue Logic Publishing.

Brewer, Heather. The Cemetery Boys. 2016. (YA). lib. bdg. 20.85 *(978-0-606-38741-5(2))* Turtleback.

Bronte, Jules & Oapos, Jem, illus. The Castle Adventure. 2013. 171p. pap. *(978-1-908804-08-2(4))* Bingham Mayne & Smith, Ltd.

Brooks, Grace. The Asquinn Twins & Grant. 2010. 111p. pap. 9.94 *(978-0-557-26972-3(5))* Lulu Pr., Inc.

Brooks, Linda Grace. The Asquinn Twins & Where the Trail Forks. 2005. 119p. pap. 16.95 *(978-0-7414-2445-7(2))* Infinity Publishing.

Brown, Jim. The Foster Twins in the Mystery at Moore's Lake. 2005. 164p. 22.95 *(978-0-595-67087-1(3))* iUniverse, Inc.

Brown, Jim D. The Foster Twins in the Mystery of the House on Joiner Lane. 2003. 160p. pap. 11.95 *(978-0-595-26504-6(9)*, Writers Club Pr.) iUniverse, Inc.

Brown, Jim D. & Brown, Ina M. The Foster Twins in the Mystery of the House on Joiner Lane. 2003. (ENG.). 164p. 21.95 *(978-0-595-74653-8(5)*, Writers Club Pr.) iUniverse, Inc.

Brunstetter, Wanda E. Humble Pie. Madden, Colleen M., illus. 2014. 158p. (J). *(978-1-63058-967-7(5))* Barbour Publishing, Inc.

Bruzon, Louise A. The Grimstone Galleries. 2010. 192p. pap. *(978-1-907652-17-2(5))* Grosvenor Hse. Publishing Ltd.

Bush, Rosetta Bowman. The Coal Dust Twins. 2013. 36p. pap. 24.95 *(978-1-62709-920-2(4))* America Star Bks.

But... Why? 2006. (Illus.). 32p. (J). 14.95 *(978-0-9773651-0-4(7))* Coleman, CJ.

Butcher, Kristin. Zach & Zoe & the Bank Robber, 1 vol. 2008. (Lorimer Streetlights Ser.). (ENG.). 112p. (J). (gr. 2-4). 8.95 *(978-1-55277-015-3(X)*, 015) James Lorimer & Co. Ltd., Pubs. CAN. Dist: Formac Lorimer Bks. Ltd.

Butcher, Nancy, et al. It's Snow Problem, 3 vols. 2003. (ENG., Illus.). 112p. *(978-0-00-714466-2(0)*, HarperCollins Children's Bks.) HarperCollins Pubs. Ltd.

—Two for the Road. 2003. (ENG., Illus.). 112p. *(978-0-00-714463-1(6)*, HarperCollins Children's Bks.) HarperCollins Pubs. Ltd.

Butler, Dori Hillestad. Yes, I Know the Monkey Man, 1 vol. 2018. 224p. (J). (gr. 5-9). pap. 7.95 *(978-1-68263-060-0(9))* Peachtree Publishing Co. Inc.

Bybee, Linda & Lawless, Laura. Untwin. 2011. 32p. pap. 14.99 *(978-1-4567-5365-8(7))* AuthorHouse.

Byng, Georgia. Molly Moon, Micky Minus, & the Mind Machine. (Molly Moon Ser.). (ENG.). (J). (gr. 3-7). 2007. 384p. 16.99 *(978-0-06-075036-7(7))*; 2008. 416p. pap. 7.99 *(978-0-06-075038-1(3)*, HarperCollins) HarperCollins Pubs.

Calonita, Jen. Summer State of Mind. 2014. (ENG.). 256p. (YA). (gr. 7-17). pap. 10.00 *(978-0-316-09115-2(4)*, Poppy) Little, Brown Bks. for Young Readers.

Cannon, Sarah. Oddity. 2019. (ENG.). 320p. (J). pap. 7.99 *(978-1-250-17906-7(8)*, 900174055) Square Fish.

Caring, Angela. Becoming Bryn. 2013. (ENG.). 297p. (YA). (gr. 7). pap. 11.95 *(978-1-935089-66-7(8))* Acacia Publishing, Inc.

Carkhuff, Denise. Mama's Heart Fits Two. 2015. (ENG., Illus.). 32p. (J). (gr. -1-2). 16.95 *(978-1-62634-222-4(9))* Greenleaf Book Group.

Carmichael, Clay. Brother, Brother. 2013. (ENG.). 320p. (YA). (gr. 7). 22.99 *(978-1-59643-743-2(X)*, 900077700) Roaring Brook Pr.

Casella, Jody. Thin Space. 2013. (ENG.). 256p. (YA). (gr. 7). 16.99 *(978-1-58270-435-7(X))*; pap. 10.99 *(978-1-58270-392-3(2))* Simon Pulse. (Simon Pulse).

Casey, Carin Jayne. Granny Babysits: The Mischievous Five. 2012. 62p. 31.95 *(978-1-4582-0474-5(X)*, Abbott Pr.) Author Solutions, LLC.

Cassidy, Anne & Durant, Alan. Doing the Double. 2007. (Sharp Shades Ser.). (ENG., Illus.). 64p. (J). (gr. 6-8). pap. 8.99 *(978-0-237-53447-9(9))* Evans Brothers, Ltd. GBR. Dist: Independent Pubs. Group.

Catanese, P. W. The Mirror's Tale. 2017. (ENG., Illus.). 304p. (J). (gr. 4-8). 17.99 *(978-1-4814-7636-2(X))*; pap. 8.99 *(978-1-4814-7635-5(1))* Simon & Schuster/Paula Wiseman Bks. (Simon & Schuster/Paula Wiseman Bks.).

Cento, Nucci. Maverick & Miss Murphy at Rascal's Rescue Ranch. 2009. 48p. pap. 12.50 *(978-1-60860-388-6(1)*, Eloquent Bks.) Strategic Book Publishing & Rights Agency (SBPRA).

Chadwick, Jennie. The Peach Tree Kids: Circus Fleas. 2012. 96p. pap. 9.99 *(978-1-61897-455-6(6)*, Strategic Bk. Publishing) Strategic Book Publishing & Rights Agency (SBPRA).

Chan, Queenie. The Dreaming Collection. 2010. (ENG., Illus.). 576p. pap. 19.99 *(978-1-4278-1871-3(1))* TOKYOPOP, Inc.

Chankhamma, Shari. The Sisters' Luck. 2010. (ENG., Illus.). 144p. (YA). pap. 12.95 *(978-1-59362-190-2(6)*, 7ad4c114-07c1-44ee-a74e-6f5f42969ae6) Slave Labor Bks.

Chapman, Allan W. Mr Wugidgem & the Dark Journey. 2012. 40p. pap. 7.99 *(978-0-9796780-3-5(X))* AC Writings.

—Mr. Wugidgem & the Phoenix Journey. 2012. 74p. pap. 7.99 *(978-0-9796780-4-2(8))* AC Writings.

Chapman, Elsie. Divided (Dualed Sequel) 2015. (Dualed Ser.: 2). (ENG.). 336p. (YA). (gr. 7). pap. 9.99 *(978-0-449-81298-3(7)*, Ember) Random Hse. Children's Bks.

Charbonneau, Joelle. Dividing Eden. (YA). 2018. (ENG.). 432p. (gr. 8). pap. 9.99 *(978-0-06-245385-3(8))* 2017. 318p. *(978-0-06-274088-5(1))* HarperCollins Pubs. (HarperTeen).

Choo, Choo, Choo, Me & You & You! 2005. (J). bds. *(978-0-9769910-5-2(5))* Terrific Twins LLC.

Christopher, Matt. The Great Quarterback Switch. 2008. (New Matt Christopher Sports Library). 144p. (J). (gr. 4-6). lib. bdg. 26.60 *(978-1-59953-216-5(6))* Norwood Hse. Pr.

Ciencin, Scott. Point-Blank Paintball, 1 vol. Aburtov, illus. 2010. (Sports Illustrated Kids Graphic Novels Ser.). (ENG.). 32p. pap. 1.00 *(978-1-4342-2137-7(7)*, Stone Arch Bks.) Capstone.

Ciencin, Scott, et al. Point-Blank Paintball, 1 vol. Aburto, Jesus, illus. 2010. (Sports Illustrated Kids Graphic Novels Ser.). (ENG.). 56p. (J). (gr. 3-8). 26.65 *(978-1-4342-1914-5(3)*, 102373); pap. 7.19 *(978-1-4342-2293-0(4)*, 103162) Capstone. (Stone Arch Bks.).

Clairmont, Patsy. 5 Cheesy Stories: About Friendship, Bravery, Bullying, & More, 1 vol. Oeltjenbruns, Joni, illus. 2007. (Tails from the Pantry Ser.). (ENG.). 144p. (J). (gr. -1-2). 15.99 *(978-1-4003-1042-5(3)*, Tommy Nelson) Nelson, Thomas Inc.

Clare, Mimi St. The Fairbluffs of Pennington Island. 2013. 36p. pap. 12.99 *(978-1-935986-49-2(X))* Liberty University Press.

Clark-Elliott, Mary. The Day Ms. Qualbaum Came to Visit. 2013. 44p. pap. 20.72 *(978-1-4907-0921-5(5))* Trafford Publishing.

Clayton, Emma. The Whisper. 2012. 309p. *(978-0-545-43365-5(7)*, Chicken Hse., The) Scholastic, Inc.

Cleary, Beverly. Two Times the Fun. 2005. (ENG., Illus.). 96p. (J). (gr. -1-2). 16.99 *(978-0-06-057921-0(8)*, HarperCollins) HarperCollins Pubs.

Clements, Andrew. Lost & Found. Elliott, Mark, illus. (ENG.). (J). (gr. 3-7). 2010. 192p. pap. 7.99 *(978-1-4169-0986-6(9))* 2008. 176p. 18.99 *(978-1-4169-0985-9(0))* Simon & Schuster Children's Publishing. (Atheneum Bks. for Young Readers).

Cleverly, Sophie. The Curse in the Candlelight: a Scarlet & Ivy Mystery. 2019. (ENG.). 384p. (J). 7.99 *(978-0-00-830822-3(5)*, HarperCollins Children's Bks.) HarperCollins Pubs. Ltd. GBR. Dist: HarperCollins Pubs.

—The Dance in the Dark. 2018. (Scarlet & Ivy Ser.: 3). (ENG.). 320p. (J). (gr. 5-8). pap. 7.99 *(978-1-4926-3409-6(3))* Sourcebooks, Inc.

—The Last Secret: a Scarlet & Ivy Mystery. 2019. (ENG.). 320p. (J). 7.99 *(978-0-00-830823-0(3)*, HarperCollins Children's Bks.) HarperCollins Pubs. Ltd. GBR. Dist: HarperCollins Pubs.

—The Lights under the Lake: a Scarlet & Ivy Mystery. 2018. (ENG.). 304p. (J). 7.99 *(978-0-00-830821-6(7)*, HarperCollins Children's Bks.) HarperCollins Pubs. Ltd. GBR. Dist: HarperCollins Pubs.

—The Lost Twin. 2017. (Scarlet & Ivy Ser.: 1). (ENG.). 320p. (J). (gr. 5-8). 7.99 *(978-1-4926-4792-8(6)*, 9781492647928) Sourcebooks, Inc.

—The Whispers in the Walls. 2017. (Scarlet & Ivy Ser.: 2). (ENG.). 288p. (J). (gr. 5-8). pap. 12.99 *(978-1-4926-3406-5(9)*, 9781492634065) Sourcebooks, Inc.

Cohn, Rachel & Levithan, David. Sam & Ilsa's Last Hurrah. 2018. (ENG.). 224p. (YA). (gr. 7). 17.99 *(978-0-399-55384-4(3)*, Knopf Bks. for Young Readers) Random Hse. Children's Bks.

Coleman, K. R. Off Course. 2020. (Road Trip Ser.). (ENG.). 112p. (YA). (gr. 6-12). 26.65 *(978-1-5415-5688-1(7)*, 9357fa30-bd0d-473d-a077-2f69a92d5727, Darby Creek) Lerner Publishing Group.

Colfer, Chris. An Author's Odyssey. 2016. (Land of Stories Ser.: 5). (ENG.). 496p. (J). (gr. 3-7). pap. 11.99 *(978-0-316-27214-8(0))* Little, Brown Bks. for Young Readers.

—The Curvy Tree: A Tale from the Land of Stories. Dorman, Brandon, illus. 2015. (Land of Stories Ser.). (ENG.). 32p. (J). (gr. -1-3). 18.99 *(978-0-316-40685-7(6))* Little, Brown Bks. for Young Readers.

—The Enchantress Returns. 2014. (Land of Stories Ser.: 2). (J). lib. bdg. 20.85 *(978-0-606-37229-9(6))* Turtleback.

—A Grimm Warning. 2015. (Land of Stories Ser.: 3). (J). lib. bdg. 20.85 *(978-0-606-37230-5(X))* Turtleback.
—The Land of Stories: a Grimm Warning. (Land of Stories Ser.: 3). (ENG.). (J). (gr. 3-7). 2015. 496p. pap. 9.99 *(978-0-316-40682-6(1))* 2014. 480p. 19.99 *(978-0-316-40681-9(3))* 2014. 768p. 50.99 *(978-0-316-40964-3(2))* Little, Brown Bks. for Young Readers.
—The Land of Stories: an Author's Odyssey. (Land of Stories Ser.: 5). (ENG., Illus.). 464p. (J). (gr. 3-7). 2017. pap. 9.99 *(978-0-316-38321-9(X))* 2016. 19.99 *(978-0-316-38329-5(5))* Little, Brown Bks. for Young Readers.
—The Land of Stories: Beyond the Kingdoms. 2015. (Land of Stories Ser.: 4). (ENG., Illus.). 432p. (J). (gr. 3-7). 19.99 *(978-0-316-40689-5(9))* Little, Brown Bks. for Young Readers.
—The Land of Stories: the Enchantress Returns. (Land of Stories Ser.: 2). (ENG.). (J). (gr. 3-7). 2014. 544p. pap. 9.99 *(978-0-316-20155-1(3))* 2013. (Illus.). 528p. 19.99 *(978-0-316-20154-4(5))* 2013. 832p. 52.99 *(978-0-316-24235-6(7))* Little, Brown Bks. for Young Readers.
—The Land of Stories: the Wishing Spell. (Land of Stories Ser.: 1). (ENG., Illus.). (J). (gr. 3-7). 2013. 464p. pap. 9.99 *(978-0-316-20156-8(1))* 2012. 448p. 19.99 *(978-0-316-20157-5(X))* 2013. 672p. pap. 28.99 *(978-0-316-24236-3(5))* Little, Brown Bks. for Young Readers.
—The Land of Stories: Worlds Collide. 2018. (Land of Stories Ser.: 6). (ENG.). 464p. (J). (gr. 3-7). pap. 9.99 *(978-0-316-35588-9(7))* Little, Brown Bks. for Young Readers.
—The Wishing Spell. Dorman, Brandon, illus. 2012. 438p. (J). pap. *(978-0-316-45393-6(5))* Little Brown & Co.
—The Wishing Spell. 2013. (Land of Stories Ser.: 1). (J). lib. bdg. 20.85 *(978-0-606-31746-7(5))* Turtleback.
—Worlds Collide. Dorman, Brandon, illus. 2017. 434p. (J). *(978-0-316-43920-6(7))* Little Brown & Co.
Colfer, Chris & Dorman, Brandon. The Land of Stories the Wishing Spell. 2013. pap. *(978-0-545-64793-9(2))* Scholastic, Inc.
Colfer, Eoin. Fowl Twins, the-A Fowl Twins Novel, Book 1. 2019. (Artemis Fowl Ser.). (ENG.). 368p. (J). (gr. 5-9). 18.99 *(978-1-368-04375-5(5)*, Disney-Hyperion) Disney Publishing Worldwide.
Collins, Wendy Jane. The Adventure Door: Book 1 'How it all began' & Book 2 'Return to Courtney Bay' 2010. 112p. pap. 10.99 *(978-1-4520-4228-2(4))* AuthorHouse.
Common, Gabriel. The Demon of Basile High: The Return of Cassius. 2007. 132p. per. 11.95 *(978-1-4327-0664-7(0))* Outskirts Pr., Inc.
Condie, Ally. Atlantia. 2015. (ENG.). 320p. (YA). (gr. 7). pap. 10.99 *(978-0-14-751065-5(1)*, Speak) Penguin Young Readers Group.
—Atlantia. 2015. lib. bdg. 22.10 *(978-0-606-37576-4(7))* Turtleback.
Cotter, Charis. The Ghost Road. 368p. (J). (gr. 4-7). 2019. (ENG.). pap. 9.99 *(978-0-7352-6325-3(6))* 2018. (Illus.). 16.99 *(978-1-101-91889-0(6))* Tundra Bks. CAN. (Tundra Bks.). Dist: Penguin Random Hse. LLC.
Covey, Sean. Sammy & the Pecan Pie: Habit 4. Curtis, Stacy, illus. (7 Habits of Happy Kids Ser.: 4). (ENG.). 32p. (J). (gr. -1-1). 2018. 6.99 *(978-1-5344-1581-2(5))* 2013. 7.99 *(978-1-4424-7647-9(8))* Simon & Schuster Bks. For Young Readers. (Simon & Schuster Bks. For Young Readers).
—Sammy & the Pecan Pie: Habit 4 (Ready-To-Read Level 2) Curtis, Stacy, illus. 2019. (7 Habits of Happy Kids Ser.: 4). (ENG.). 32p. (J). (gr. k-2). 17.99 *(978-1-5344-4454-6(8))*; pap. 4.99 *(978-1-5344-4453-9(X))* Simon Spotlight. (Simon Spotlight).
Creech, Sharon. Ruby Holler. 2012. (ENG.). 288p. (J). (gr. 3-7). pap. 7.99 *(978-0-06-056015-7(0)*, HarperCollins) HarperCollins Pubs.
—Ruby Holler. 2004. (Joanna Cotler Bks.). 310p. (gr. 3-7). 17.00 *(978-0-7569-1940-5(1))* Perfection Learning Corp.
—Ruby Holler. 2012. (J). (gr. 3-6). 17.20 *(978-0-613-86272-1(4))* Turtleback.
Cross, Kady. Sisters of Salt & Iron. 2016. (Sisters of Blood & Spirit Ser.: 2). (ENG.). 352p. (YA). 18.99 *(978-0-373-21176-0(7)*, Harlequin Teen) Harlequin Enterprises ULC CAN. Dist: HarperCollins Pubs.
Crossan, Sarah. One. 2015. (ENG.). 400p. (YA). (gr. 8). 17.99 *(978-0-06-211875-2(7)*, Greenwillow Bks.) HarperCollins Pubs.
Crowley, James. The Magic Hour. 2003. (Illus.). 280p. (J). pap. 17.95 *(978-1-55517-713-3(1)*, 77131) Cedar Fort, Inc./CFI Distribution.
Cry of the Falcon. 2006. 208p. (J). pap. 9.95 *(978-0-9788541-0-2(1))* m.d. hughes.
Cusack, Dale. Gwen & the Dragon. 2007. (Illus.). 114p. pap. 9.95 *(978-1-4303-1080-8(4))* Lulu Pr., Inc.
Cussler, Clive. The Adventures of Hotsy Totsy. 2011. (ENG., Illus.). 166p. (J). (gr. 3-7). 7.99 *(978-0-14-241873-4(0)*, Puffin Books) Penguin Young Readers Group.
Cuyler, Margery. Tick Tock Clock. Neubecker, Robert, illus. 2012. (My First I Can Read Ser.). (ENG.). 32p. (J). (gr. -1 — 1). pap. 4.99 *(978-0-06-136311-5(1)*, HarperCollins) HarperCollins Pubs.
Cuyler, Margery & Neubecker, Robert. Tick Tock Clock. 2012. (My First I Can Read Ser.). (ENG., Illus.). 32p. (J). (gr. -1 — 1). 16.99 *(978-0-06-136309-2(X)*, HarperCollins) HarperCollins Pubs.
Daddy! 2005. (J). bds. *(978-0-9769910-6-9(3))* Terrific Twins LLC.
Daily, Lorrie Ann. The Castlewood Twins, the Magic Begins. 2008. 196p. pap. 12.95 *(978-0-9820479-8-9(3))* Peppertree Pr., The.
Daly, Catherine. Double or Nothing: A Makers Story about 3D Printing. Lyon, Tammie, illus. 2018. (Makers Make It Work Ser.). 32p. (J). (gr. k-3). pap. 6.99 *(978-1-57565-989-3(1)*, 1b82b37e-f971-49a5-bd2a-c3b5e07aa673, Kane Press) Astra Publishing Hse.
Danna, Natasha. Any Two Can Be Twindollicious. Dye, Jerel, illus. 2013. 32p. (J). 17.95 *(978-1-60131-154-2(0)*, Castlebridge Bks.) Big Tent Bks.
Danticat, Edwidge. Untwine. 2017. (ENG.). 320p. (J). (gr. 7). pap. 11.99 *(978-0-545-42304-5(X))* Scholastic, Inc.
Darke, J. A. The Grin in the Dark. Evergreen, Nelson, illus. 2015. (Spine Shivers Ser.). (ENG.). 128p. (J). (gr. 4-6). lib. bdg. 27.32 *(978-1-4965-0217-9(5)*, 128031, Stone Arch Bks.) Capstone.
Darlison, Aleesah. Quinn's Riddles. Brailsford, Jill, illus. 2017. (Unicorn Riders Ser.). (ENG.). 112p. (J). (gr. 3-5). pap. 5.95 *(978-1-4795-6552-8(0)*, 128542, Picture Window Bks.) Capstone.
—Quinn's Truth. Brailsford, Jill, illus. 2017. (Unicorn Riders Ser.). (ENG.). 112p. (J). (gr. 3-5). pap. 5.95 *(978-1-4795-6556-6(3)*, 128546, Picture Window Bks.) Capstone.
Dasilva, D. Mom Has Left & Gone to Vegas. Craig, Dan, illus. 2008. 32p. pap. 19.95 *(978-1-59858-603-9(3))* Dog Ear Publishing, LLC.
David, Jamie. Johann Sebastian Humpbach. David, Jamie, illus. 2009. (Illus.). 167p. pap. 14.95 *(978-0-615-31840-0(1))* Chai Yo Maui Pr.
Davis, Tanita S. Happy Families. 2013. (ENG.). 240p. (YA). (gr. 7). pap. 9.99 *(978-0-375-87170-2(5)*, Ember) Random Hse. Children's Bks.
Dearle, Anne Crofton. Ginger Cat. 2011. (Illus.). 92p. pap. 12.10 *(978-1-4567-7484-4(0))* AuthorHouse.
Deen, Natasha. Lark & the Diamond Caper, 1 vol. Cutler, Marcus, illus. 2017. (Orca Echoes Ser.: 2). (ENG.). 96p. (J). (gr. 1-3). pap. 7.95 *(978-1-4598-1400-4(2))* Orca Bk. Pubs. USA.
—Lark Takes a Bow, 1 vol. Cutler, Marcus, illus. 2018. (Orca Echoes Ser.: 3). (ENG.). 96p. (J). (gr. 1-3). pap. 7.95 *(978-1-4598-1715-9(X))* Orca Bk. Pubs. USA.
Deering, Leta. Patriotic Samáand the Mendez Twins at the Alamo. 2008. 112p. pap. 19.95 *(978-1-60610-689-1(9))* America Star Bks.
dePaola, Tomie. Meet the Barkers. dePaola, Tomie, illus. 2003. (Barker Twins Ser.). (Illus.). 32p. (J). (gr. -1-3). 7.99 *(978-0-14-250083-5(6)*, Puffin Books) Penguin Young Readers Group.
—Meet the Barkers: Morgan & Moffat Go to School. 2005. (J). (gr. k-3). pap. 17.95 incl. audio *(978-0-8045-6934-7(7)*, SAC6934) Spoken Arts, Inc.
—Strega Nona & the Twins. 2017. (Simon & Schuster Ready-To-Read Level 1 Ser.). lib. bdg. 13.55 *(978-0-606-40215-6(2))* Turtleback.
—Strega Nona & the Twins: Ready-To-Read Level 1. dePaola, Tomie, illus. 2017. (Strega Nona Book Ser.). (ENG., Illus.). 32p. (J). (gr. -1-1). pap. 4.99 *(978-1-4814-8137-3(1)*, Simon Spotlight) Simon Spotlight.
dePaola, Tomie, illus. Strega Nona & the Twins. 2017. (J). *(978-1-5379-5057-0(6)*, Simon Spotlight) Simon Spotlight.
dePaola, Tomie, et al. Triple Checkup. 2004. (Barker Twins Ser.). (ENG., Illus.). 32p. (J). (gr. k-3). 16.19 *(978-0-448-43484-1(9))* Penguin Young Readers Group.
Depken, Kristen L. Happy Birthday to You! (Shimmer & Shine) Aikins, Dave, illus. 2018. (Step into Reading Ser.). (ENG.). 24p. (J). (gr. -1-1). pap. 5.99 *(978-1-5247-6799-0(9)*, Random Hse. Bks. for Young Readers) Random Hse. Children's Bks.
—Winter Wishes! Aikins, Dave, illus. 2017. 23p. (J). *(978-1-5182-5212-9(5))* Random Hse., Inc.
DeVillers, Julia & Roy, Jennifer. Double Feature. 2012. (Mix Ser.). (ENG.). (J). (gr. 4-8). 288p. pap. 7.99 *(978-1-4424-3403-5(1))*; 272p. 16.99 *(978-1-4424-3402-8(3))* Simon & Schuster Children's Publishing. (Aladdin).
—Take Two. 2010. (Mix Ser.). (ENG.). 304p. (J). (gr. 4-8). pap. 8.99 *(978-1-4169-6731-6(1)*, Aladdin) Simon & Schuster Children's Publishing.
—Times Squared. 2011. (Mix Ser.). (ENG.). (J). (gr. 4-8). 272p. pap. 8.99 *(978-1-4169-6732-3(X))*; 240p. 16.99 *(978-1-4169-7532-8(2))* Simon & Schuster Children's Publishing. (Aladdin).
—Trading Faces. 2008. (Mix Ser.). (ENG.). 304p. (J). (gr. 4-8). 16.99 *(978-1-4169-7531-1(4)*, Simon & Schuster/Paula Wiseman Bks.) Simon & Schuster/Paula Wiseman Bks.
—Triple Trouble. 2014. (Mix Ser.). (ENG., Illus.). 240p. (J). (gr. 4-8). pap. 7.99 *(978-1-4424-3406-6(6)*, Aladdin) Simon & Schuster Children's Publishing.
Diane, Rachel And Rebecca Sall. Mother Earth's Message. 2009. 28p. pap. 15.99 *(978-1-4363-8613-5(6))* Xlibris Corp.
Dinardo, Jeff. Field Trip to Mars (Book 1) Clegg, Dave, illus. 2018. (Funny Bone Books (tm) First Chapters — the Jupiter Twins Ser.). (ENG.). 32p. (J). (gr. k-2). pap. 4.99 *(978-1-63440-253-8(7)*, a36c3066-7240-49c6-8199-6603c4e655a8); lib. bdg. 19.99 *(978-1-63440-249-1(9)*, 6e39dd05-728c-4f2b-a77c-a147a05d70b4) Red Chair Pr.
—Lost on Earth (Book 2) Clegg, Dave, illus. 2018. (Funny Bone Books (tm) First Chapters — the Jupiter Twins Ser.: Vol. 2). (ENG.). 32p. (J). (gr. k-2). lib. bdg. 19.99 *(978-1-63440-250-7(2)*, 2095c0c4-de74-4dce-8ea1-005fdbc5304d) Red Chair Pr.
—Party on Pluto (Book 4) Clegg, Dave, illus. 2018. (Funny Bone Books (tm) First Chapters — the Jupiter Twins Ser.). (ENG.). 32p. (J). (gr. k-2). pap. 4.99 *(978-1-63440-256-9(1)*, 87d1a80e-6152-46fc-9771-54bebed1096c); lib. bdg. 19.99 *(978-1-63440-252-1(9)*, 089f8f27-9295-4aac-8f56-a859d89d15a0) Red Chair Pr.
—Scout Trip to Saturn (Book 3) Clegg, Dave, illus. 2018. (Funny Bone Books (tm) First Chapters — the Jupiter Twins Ser.). (ENG.). 32p. (J). (gr. k-2). pap. 4.99 *(978-1-63440-255-2(3)*, bac7dde8-6758-450f-824b-41607ade5c01); lib. bdg. 19.99 *(978-1-63440-251-4(0)*, 2209adee-6f57-4c9f-9075-4e7d59fa6385) Red Chair Pr.
DiTerlizzi, Tony & Black, Holly. The Ironwood Tree. l.t. ed. 2006. (Spiderwick Chronicles: Bk. 4). 90p. (YA). (gr. 2-18). 23.95 *(978-0-7862-8583-9(4))* Thorndike Pr.
Dixon, Franklin W. Double Deception: Book Three in the Double Danger Trilogy, 27. 2009. (Hardy Boys (All New) Undercover Brothers Ser.: 27). (ENG.). 176p. (J). (gr. 3-7). pap. 6.99 *(978-1-4169-6766-8(4))* Simon & Schuster, Inc.
—Double Down: Book Two in the Double Danger Trilogy, 26. 26th ed. 2008. (Hardy Boys (All New) Undercover Brothers Ser.: 26). (ENG.). 172p. (J). (gr. 3-7). pap. 7.99 *(978-1-4169-7446-8(6))* Simon & Schuster, Inc.
Dokey, Cameron. The World Above. 2010. (Once upon a Time Ser.). (ENG.). 208p. (YA). (gr. 7-18). pap. 6.99 *(978-1-4424-0337-6(3)*, Simon Pulse) Simon Pulse.
Doktorski, Jennifer. The Summer after You & Me. 2015. 304p. (YA). (gr. 8-12). pap. 12.99 *(978-1-4926-1903-1(5))* Sourcebooks, Inc.
Double or Nothing. 2014. (It Takes Two Ser.: 3). (ENG., Illus.). 160p. (J). (gr. 3-7). pap. 6.99 *(978-1-4814-1652-8(9)*, Simon Spotlight) Simon Spotlight.
Doyle, Marissa. Bewitching Season. 2009. (ENG.). 368p. (YA). (gr. 9-12). 24.94 *(978-0-312-59695-8(2)*, 9780312596958) Square Fish.
Driscoll, Laura. We Are Twins. Campion, Pascal, illus. 2012. (Penguin Young Readers, Level 1 Ser.). 32p. (J). (gr. k-1). mass mkt. 4.99 *(978-0-448-46157-1(9)*, Penguin Young Readers) Penguin Young Readers Group.
—We Are Twins. 2012. (Penguin Young Readers: Level 1 Ser.). lib. bdg. 13.55 *(978-0-606-26641-3(0))* Turtleback.
Duncan, Lois. Stranger with My Face. 2011. (ENG.). 320p. (YA). (gr. 7-17). pap., pap. 17.99 *(978-0-316-09904-2(X))* Little, Brown Bks. for Young Readers.
Durant, Alan. Doing the Double. 2004. (Shades Ser.). (ENG.). 64p. (J). pap. *(978-0-237-52846-1(0))* Evans Brothers, Ltd.
Durrant, Geraldine. Twinbane: an Appalling True History. 2010. 142p. pap. 16.95 *(978-1-4457-7998-0(6))* Lulu Pr., Inc.
Durst, Sarah Beth. Journey Across the Hidden Islands. 2017. (ENG., Illus.). 352p. (J). (gr. 5-7). 16.99 *(978-0-544-70679-8(X)*, 1628641, Clarion Bks.) HarperCollins Pubs.
Dyan, Penelope. Mikey & Me & the Se. 2011. 36p. pap. 11.95 *(978-1-935630-63-0(6))* Bellissima Publishing, LLC.
Dyer, Heather. The Girl with the Broken Wing. Bailey, Peter, illus. 2005. 147p. (J). *(978-1-4156-3468-4(8))* Scholastic, Inc.
Eaddy, Susan. Poppy's Best Babies. Bonnet, Rosalinde, illus. 2018. 40p. (J). (gr. k-3). 15.99 *(978-1-58089-770-9(3))* Charlesbridge Publishing, Inc.
Easley, Sean. The Hotel Between. 2018. (ENG., Illus.). 352p. (J). (gr. 4-7). 19.99 *(978-1-5344-1697-0(8)*, Simon & Schuster Bks. For Young Readers) Simon & Schuster Bks. For Young Readers.
—The Key of Lost Things. 2020. (ENG.). 400p. (J). (gr. 4-7). pap. 8.99 *(978-1-5344-3788-3(6)*, Simon & Schuster Bks. For Young Readers) Simon & Schuster Bks. For Young Readers.
Eaton, Jason Carter. The Facttracker. Constantin, Pascale, illus. 2008. 272p. (J). (gr. 3-7). 16.99 *(978-0-06-056434-6(2))* HarperCollins Pubs.
Echols, Jennifer. Such a Rush. 2012. (ENG.). 336p. (YA). (gr. 7). pap. 20.99 *(978-1-4516-5802-6(8)*, Gallery Bks.) Gallery Bks.
Eddy, Catherine J. Sandbox Sandshoes. Krupnek, Joann J., illus. 2009. 38p. pap. 10.95 *(978-0-9818488-5-3(0))* Ajoyin Publishing, Inc.
Edwards, Christine. The Charmed Enchanted Book. 2010. 24p. pap. 16.49 *(978-1-4490-7091-5(4))* AuthorHouse.
Ehrlich, Nikki. Twindergarten. Wagner, Zoey Abbott, illus. 2017. (ENG.). 32p. (J). (gr. -1-3). 16.99 *(978-0-06-256423-8(4)*, HarperCollins) HarperCollins Pubs.
Elizabeth's Story 1848. 2014. (Secrets of the Manor Ser.: 3). (ENG., Illus.). 160p. (J). (gr. 3-7). pap. 7.99 *(978-1-4814-1840-9(8)*, Simon Spotlight) Simon Spotlight.
Emerson, Alice B. Ruth Fielding at Snow Camp or Lost in the Backwoods. 2005. reprint ed. pap. 24.95 *(978-1-4179-3132-3(9))* Kessinger Publishing, LLC.
Erickson, Mary Ellen. Who Jinxed the CG Ranch? 2009. 196p. 24.95 *(978-1-4401-4218-5(1))*; pap. 14.95 *(978-1-4401-4216-1(5))* iUniverse, Inc.
Farnsworth, Frances Joyce. Tike & Tiny in the Tetons. 2007. (Illus.). 172p. (J). pap. 14.95 *(978-0-943972-79-4(5))* Homestead Publishing.
Faust, Jon. Helicopter Harry & the Copter Kids. 2016. (ENG., Illus.). (J). pap. 9.95 *(978-0-692-78184-5(6))* Mother Lode Pr. LLC.
Finch, Kate. Calling All Pets! 2013. (Pet Hotel Ser.: 1). lib. bdg. 14.75 *(978-0-606-31984-3(0))* Turtleback.
Finkelstein, Ruth. The Thankyou Twins. Rubenstein, Reva, illus. 2006. 24p. (J). *(978-0-9628157-5-1(6))* Finkelstein, Ruth.
Finnegan, Marco. Lizard in a Zoot Suit. Finnegan, Marco, illus. 2020. (ENG., Illus.). 144p. (YA). (gr. 7-12). 31.99 *(978-1-5415-2365-4(2)*, a6f85d3f-7999-47b7-b6d3-96fccb4d533f, Graphic Universe™) Lerner Publishing Group.
Fischel, Ana. The Twelve Quests - Book 2, a Dragon's Tooth. 2009. 158p. pap. *(978-1-84923-874-8(X))* YouWriteOn.
—The Twelve Quests - Book 3, the Pied Piper's Flute. 2009. 158p. pap. *(978-1-84923-875-5(8))* YouWriteOn.
—The Twelve Quests - Book 4, Rapunzel's Hair. 2009. 158p. pap. *(978-1-84923-876-2(6))* YouWriteOn.
—The Twelve Quests - Book 5, a Firebird's Feather. 2009. 158p. pap. *(978-1-84923-877-9(4))* YouWriteOn.
—The Twelve Quests - Book 6, the Enchanted Harp. 2009. 158p. pap. *(978-1-84923-878-6(2))* YouWriteOn.
Fontenot, Mary Alice & Fontenot Landry, Julie. Clovis Crawfish & the Twin Sister, 1 vol. Butler, Julie Dupre & Buckner, Julie Dupre, illus. 2007. (Clovis Crawfish Ser.). (ENG.). 32p. (J). (gr. k-3). 16.99 *(978-1-58980-467-8(8)*, Pelican Publishing) Arcadia Publishing.
Foresman, Timothy. The Last Little Polar Bear: A Global Change Adventure Story. Laura Lee, Cundiff, illus. 2007. 60p. (J). per. 19.95 *(978-0-9776906-2-6(8))* Blueline Publishing.
Foster, Kia. Tom & Rondy. 2012. 24p. pap. 17.99 *(978-1-4772-0134-3(3))* AuthorHouse.
Francia, Giada. Alex & Penny in China Jigsaw Book. 2011. (ENG., Illus.). 14p. 14.95 *(978-88-544-0310-9(5))* White Star Publishers ITA. Dist: Random Hse., Inc.
—Alex & Penny in Egypt Jigsaw Book. 2011. (ENG., Illus.). 14p. 14.95 *(978-88-544-0240-9(0))* White Star Publishers ITA. Dist: Random Hse., Inc.
—In the Wild West on MacKenzie's Trail. McCloskey, Erin, ed. Howard, Catherine, tr. 2007. (Alex & Penny Ser.). (ENG., Illus.). 80p. (gr. 2-5). pap. 14.95 *(978-88-544-0245-4(1))* White Star Publishers ITA. Dist: Random Hse., Inc.
Francois, Rose Darlie. Little Miss Daring Evelynne. 2009. (ENG.). 47p. pap. 19.10 *(978-0-557-07136-4(4))* Lulu Pr., Inc.
Franklin, Shirley A. Emma's Fantastique Word Play. 2009. 80p. pap. 8.95 *(978-1-4401-3824-9(9))* iUniverse, Inc.
Frazier, Sundee T. The Other Half of My Heart. 2011. 304p. (J). (gr. 3-7). 8.99 *(978-0-440-24006-8(9)*, Yearling) Random Hse. Children's Bks.
Frazier, Sundee Tucker. The Other Half of My Heart. 2011. (ENG.). 304p. (J). (gr. 4-6). lib. bdg. 21.19 *(978-0-385-90446-9(0)*, Delacorte Pr.) Random Hse. Children's Bks.
Friday, Anita. Twins. Branman, Liz, illus. 2013. 34p. pap. 11.99 *(978-0-9899544-0-2(4))* Two Chicks.
Fukui, Isamu. Truancy Origins: A Novel. 2011. (Truancy Ser.: 2). (ENG.). 384p. (YA). (gr. 8-12). pap. 19.99 *(978-0-7653-2264-7(1)*, 900055685, Tor Teen) Doherty, Tom Assocs., LLC.
Fuss, Kevin. The Brothers Geek. 2010. 180p. 24.99 *(978-1-4490-7366-4(2))*; pap. 14.49 *(978-1-4490-7365-7(4))* AuthorHouse.
Gaffney, Linda. My Daddy Does GOOD Things, Too! Dabney, Undra & Goettling, Nickalas, illus. 2006. 55p. per. 10.99 *(978-0-9787501-0-7(1))* Gaffney, Linda.
Gallagher, Mary. Mulhern Twins. 2007. (ENG., Illus.). 126p. (J). pap. 11.95 *(978-1-905172-17-7(6)*, Collins Pr., The) M.H. Gill & Co. U. C. IRL. Dist: Dufour Editions, Inc.
Gantos, Jack. The Love Curse of the Rumbaughs. 2008. (ENG.). 192p. (YA). (gr. 9-12). pap. 15.99 *(978-0-312-38052-6(6)*, 900050683) Square Fish.
Garcia, Maria. Las Aventuras de Connie y Diego. 2004. (ENG & SPA., Illus.). (J). (gr. k-3). spiral bd. *(978-0-616-14605-7(1))* Canadian National Institute for the Blind/Institut National Canadien pour les Aveugles.
Gauthier, Bertrand. Abracadabra, les Jumeaux Sont La! 2003. (Premier Roman Ser.). (FRE.). 64p. (J). (gr. 2-5). pap. *(978-2-89021-144-5(4))* Diffusion du livre Mirabel (DLM).
Gifford, Peggy. Moxy Maxwell Does Not Love Stuart Little. Fisher, Valorie, photos by. 2008. (Moxy Maxwell Ser.: 1). (ENG., Illus.). 112p. (J). (gr. 2-5). 6.99 *(978-0-440-42230-3(2)*, Yearling) Random Hse. Children's Bks.
—Moxy Maxwell Does Not Love Writing Thank-You Notes. Fisher, Valorie, illus. 2009. (Moxy Maxwell Ser.: 2). (ENG.). 192p. (J). (gr. 2-5). 6.99 *(978-0-375-84343-3(4)*, Yearling) Random Hse. Children's Bks.
Gifford, Peggy Elizabeth. Moxy Maxwell Does Not Love Practicing the Piano: (But She Does Love Being in Recitals) Fisher, Valorie, illus. Fisher, Valorie, photos by. 2009. (Moxy Maxwell Ser.). (ENG.). 192p. (J). (gr. 4-6). lib. bdg. 21.19 *(978-0-375-96688-0(9)*, Yearling) Random Hse. Children's Bks.
—Moxy Maxwell Does Not Love Writing Thank-You Notes. Fisher, Valorie, illus. Fisher, Valorie, photos by. 2008. (Moxy Maxwell Ser.). (ENG.). 176p. (J). (gr. 4-6). lib. bdg. 18.69 *(978-0-375-94552-6(0)*, Yearling) Random Hse. Children's Bks.
Gilbert, Wendy June. Our Beds Are Cars. 2008. 44p. per. 24.95 *(978-1-60441-749-4(8))* America Star Bks.
Gill, Timothy. Flip & Fin: Super Sharks to the Rescue! 2016. (ENG., Illus.). 32p. (J). (gr. -1-3). 15.99 *(978-0-06-224301-0(2)*, Greenwillow Bks.) HarperCollins Pubs.
—Flip & Fin: We Rule the School! 2014. (ENG., Illus.). 32p. (J). (gr. -1-3). 14.99 *(978-0-06-224300-3(4)*, Greenwillow Bks.) HarperCollins Pubs.
Gleitzman, Morris;Gleitzman. Grace. 2018. 192p. (J). (gr. 3-7). 15.99 *(978-0-14-378818-8(3))* Random Hse. Australia AUS. Dist: Independent Pubs. Group.
Go! Fight! Twin! 2014. (It Takes Two Ser.: 4). (ENG., Illus.). 160p. (J). (gr. 3-7). 17.99 *(978-1-4814-1656-6(1))*; pap. 6.99 *(978-1-4814-1655-9(3))* Simon Spotlight. (Simon Spotlight).
Godby, Ron. The King of Imperial Hill. 2006. 76p. pap. 16.95 *(978-1-4241-1061-2(0))* PublishAmerica, Inc.
Golden Books. Shimmer & Shine Little Golden Book Favorites (Shimmer & Shine) Golden Books, illus. 2017. (ENG., Illus.). 80p. (J). (gr. -1-2). 7.99 *(978-1-5247-1720-9(7)*, Random Hse. Bks. for Young Readers) Random Hse. Children's Bks.
Gordon, Pauline C. The Adventures of the Droplet Twins. 2013. 136p. *(978-1-4602-1343-8(2))*; pap. *(978-1-4602-1344-5(0))* FriesenPress.
Gormally, Eleanor. The Little Flower Bulb: Helping Children Bereaved by Suicide. Loki, #VALUE! & Splink, illus. 2011. (ENG.). 32p. (J). (gr. -1-3). pap. 21.95 *(978-1-84730-260-1(2))* Veritas Pubns. IRL. Dist: Casemate Pubs. & Bk. Distributors, LLC.
Gosling, Sharon. The Sapphire Cutlass. 2016. (Diamond Thief Ser.). (ENG.). 336p. (J). (gr. 9-12). 16.95 *(978-1-63079-041-7(9)*, 131432, Switch Pr.) Capstone.
Grace, Amanda. No One Needs to Know. 2014. (ENG.). 240p. (YA). (gr. 9-12). pap. 9.99 *(978-0-7387-3625-9(2)*, 0738736252, Flux) North Star Editions.
Graff, Keir. The Phantom Tower. 2021. 288p. (J). (gr. 3-7). 8.99 *(978-1-5247-3954-6(5)*, Puffin Books) Penguin Young Readers Group.
Grant, Michael. Bzrk. (Bzrk Ser.). (ENG.). 400p. (YA). (gr. 9-12). 2013. pap. 9.99 *(978-1-60684-418-2(0)*, be48eae0-186e-42f3-9a8f-7a9a80661ce8) 2012. 17.99 *(978-1-60684-312-3(5)*, ba9d46d5-5aa2-4bc4-bb35-da33ac28de6c) Lerner Publishing Group. (Carolrhoda Lab™).
—BZRK Reloaded. 2013. (Bzrk Ser.). (ENG.). 432p. (YA). (gr. 9-12). 18.99 *(978-1-60684-394-9(X)*, 20fe8bbb-63fa-40af-8c0e-54890e077fe3, Carolrhoda Lab™) Lerner Publishing Group.
Grant, Natalie. Light up New York, 1 vol. 2017. (Faithgirlz / Glimmer Girls Ser.: 4). (ENG., Illus.). 208p. (J). pap. 8.99 *(978-0-310-75274-5(4))* Zonderkidz.
—Miracle in Music City, 1 vol. 2016. (Faithgirlz / Glimmer Girls Ser.: 3). (ENG.). 208p. (J). pap. 8.99 *(978-0-310-75250-9(7))* Zonderkidz.
Green, Paige. Family over Everything: A Novel. 2013. (ENG., Illus.). 216p. pap. 15.99 *(978-1-59309-501-7(5)*, Strebor Bks.) Strebor Bks.
Green, Tim. Pinch Hit. (ENG.). (J). (gr. 3-7). 2013. 336p. pap. 9.99 *(978-0-06-201247-0(9))* 2012. 320p. 16.99 *(978-0-06-201246-3(0))* HarperCollins Pubs. (HarperCollins).
Greenburg, Dan. Secrets of Dripping Fang, Book Eight: When Bad Snakes Attack Good Children. Fischer, Scott M., illus. 2007. (Secrets of Dripping Fang Ser.: Bk. 8). (ENG.). 144p.

TUV

(J). (gr. 3-7). 11.99 *(978-0-15-206056-5(1)*, 1198190, Clarion Bks.) HarperCollins Pubs.
—Secrets of Dripping Fang, Book Six: Attack of the Giant Octopus. Fischer, Scott M., illus. 2007. (Secrets of Dripping Fang Ser.: Bk. 6). (ENG.). 160p. (J). (gr. 3-7). 12.99 *(978-0-15-206041-1(3)*, 1198144, Clarion Bks.) HarperCollins Pubs.
—Secrets of Dripping Fang, Book Three: The Vampire's Curse, Bk. 3. Fischer, Scott M., illus. 2006. (Secrets of Dripping Fang Ser.: Bk. 3). (ENG.). 144p. (J). (gr. 3-7). 12.99 *(978-0-15-205469-4(3)*, 1196455, Clarion Bks.) HarperCollins Pubs.
—Secrets of Dripping Fang, Book Two: Treachery & Betrayal at Jolly Days. Fischer, Scott M., illus. 2006. (Secrets of Dripping Fang Ser.: Bk. 2). (ENG.). 144p. (J). (gr. 3-7). 12.99 *(978-0-15-205463-2(4)*, 1196437, Clarion Bks.) HarperCollins Pubs.
Greer, Hannah. The Lighthouse Summer Greer, Tica, illus. 2009. 156p. pap. 24.95 *(978-1-60813-493-9(8))* America Star Bks.
—The Velvet Bag Memoirs, Bk. 1. 2008. 132p. pap. 24.95 *(978-1-60672-190-2(9))* America Star Bks.
Griffin, Sarah Maria. Other Words for Smoke. 2019. (ENG.). 352p. (YA). (gr. 9). 17.99 *(978-0-06-240891-4(7)*, Greenwillow Bks.) HarperCollins Pubs.
Grill-Merrill, Karen. The Muk & Tuk Tales. 2006. 65p. 20.00 *(978-1-4257-0795-8(5))*; pap. 10.00 *(978-1-4257-0794-1(7))* Xlibris Corp.
Griner, Sophia Maria. Hooray for Saturday! 2013. 24p. pap. *(978-1-4602-1806-8(X))* FriesenPress.
Groth, Darren. Are You Seeing Me?, 1 vol. 2015. (ENG., Illus.). 288p. (YA). (gr. 8-12). 19.95 *(978-1-4598-1079-2(1))* Orca Bk. Pubs. USA.
Guillory, Sarah. Reclaimed. 2013. (ENG.). 306p. (YA). (gr. 7-9). pap. 9.95 *(978-1-937053-88-8(1)*, Spencer Hill Contemporary) Spencer Hill Pr.
Gutman, Dan. From Texas with Love. 2014. (Genius Files Ser.: 4). (J). lib. bdg. 17.20 *(978-0-606-36462-1(5))* Turtleback.
—The Genius Files #2: Never Say Genius. 2012. (Genius Files Ser.: 2). (ENG.). (J). (gr. 3-7). 304p. pap. 6.99 *(978-0-06-182769-3(X))*; (Illus.). 288p. 16.99 *(978-0-06-182767-9(3))* HarperCollins Pubs. (HarperCollins).
—The Genius Files #3: You Only Die Twice. 2013. (Genius Files Ser.: 3). (ENG.). (J). (gr. 3-7). 320p. pap. 7.99 *(978-0-06-182772-3(X))*; (Illus.). 304p. 16.99 *(978-0-06-182770-9(3))* HarperCollins Pubs. (HarperCollins).
—The Genius Files #4: from Texas with Love. 2014. (Genius Files Ser.: 4). (ENG.). (J). (gr. 3-7). 304p. pap. 9.99 *(978-0-06-182775-4(4))*; (Illus.). 288p. 16.99 *(978-0-06-182773-0(8))* HarperCollins Pubs. (HarperCollins).
—The Genius Files: Mission Unstoppable. 2011. (Genius Files Ser.: 1). (ENG.). 304p. (J). (gr. 3-7). pap. 7.99 *(978-0-06-182766-2(5))*; (Illus.). 16.99 *(978-0-06-182764-8(9))* HarperCollins Pubs. (HarperCollins).
—Mission Unstoppable. 2011. (Genius Files Ser.: 1). (J). lib. bdg. 17.20 *(978-0-606-23559-4(0))* Turtleback.
—Never Say Genius. 2012. (Genius Files Ser.: 2). (J). lib. bdg. 17.20 *(978-0-606-27128-8(7))* Turtleback.
—You Only Die Twice. 2013. (Genius Files Ser.: 3). (J). lib. bdg. 17.20 *(978-0-606-35043-3(8))* Turtleback.
Haddix, Margaret Peterson. In over Their Heads. 2017. (Under Their Skin Ser.: 2). (ENG., Illus.). 320p. (J). (gr. 3-7). 18.99 *(978-1-4814-1761-7(4)*, Simon & Schuster Bks. For Young Readers) Simon & Schuster Bks. For Young Readers.
—Redeemed. 2015. (Missing Ser.: 8). (ENG.). 416p. (J). (gr. 3-7). 19.99 *(978-1-4424-9756-6(4)*, Simon & Schuster Bks. For Young Readers) Simon & Schuster Bks. For Young Readers.
—Redeemed. 2016. (Missing Ser.: 8). lib. bdg. 18.40 *(978-0-606-39234-1(3))* Turtleback.
—Under Their Skin. 2016. (Under Their Skin Ser.: 1). (ENG., Illus.). 320p. (J). (gr. 3-7). 18.99 *(978-1-4814-1758-7(4)*, Simon & Schuster Bks. For Young Readers) Simon & Schuster Bks. For Young Readers.
Hale, Bruce. Pirates of Underwhere. Hillman, Shane, illus. 2008. (Underwhere Ser.). 164p. (J). (gr. 3-7). lib. bdg. 16.89 *(978-0-06-085128-6(7))* HarperCollins Pubs.
—Prince of Underwhere. Hillman, Shane, illus. 2009. (Underwhere Ser.: 1). (ENG.). 176p. (J). (gr. 3-7). pap. 5.99 *(978-0-06-085126-2(0)*, HarperCollins) HarperCollins Pubs.
Hale, Nathan. Apocalypse Taco. 2019. (ENG., Illus.). 128p. (YA). (gr. 3-7). 14.99 *(978-1-4197-3373-4(7)*, 1256501, Amulet Bks.) Abrams, Inc.
Hall, Angela Marie. Priscilla Pennybrook: Hello World, I Have Arrived!, 1 vol. 2009. 55p. pap. 16.95 *(978-1-61582-899-9(0))* America Star Bks.
Hamilton, Elizabeth L. Lost on Superstition Mountain. 2004. (Character Mystery Ser.: No. 3). (Illus.). 144p. (J). per. 9.95 *(978-0-9754629-5-9(4)*, Character-in-Action) Quiet Impact, Inc.
—Mystery at Lake Cachuma. 2003. (Character Mystery Ser.: No. 1). (Illus.). 114p. (J). (gr. 3-6). per. 9.95 *(978-0-9713749-4-2(5)*, Character-in-Action) Quiet Impact, Inc.
—Surprise at Pearl Harbor. 2004. (Character Mystery Ser.: No. 2). (Illus.). 144p. (J). per. 9.95 *(978-0-9754629-2-8(X)*, Character-in-Action) Quiet Impact, Inc.
Hassler, Kurt. Diva V Poe. 2006. (Illus.). 32p. (J). 16.95 *(978-1-933164-29-8(8))* Seven Seas Entertainment, LLC.
Haydu, Corey Ann. Eventown. 2019. (ENG.). 336p. (J). (gr. 3-7). 16.99 *(978-0-06-268980-1(0)*, Tegen, Katherine Bks) HarperCollins Pubs.
Hayes, Sadie. The Social Code: A Novel. 2013. (Start-Up Ser.: 1). (ENG., Illus.). 320p. (YA). (gr. 7-12). pap. 22.99 *(978-1-250-03565-3(1)*, 900121146, St. Martin's Griffin) St. Martin's Pr.
Hays, Sharon. The Tumbleweed Family. 2011. 28p. pap. 15.99 *(978-1-4568-6825-3(X))* Xlibris Corp.
Hayton, Althea. Two Little Birds. Schlitt, RaRa, illus. 2012. 38p. pap. *(978-0-9557808-1-3(0))* Wren Pubns.
Heller, Andrew. A Fine Mess. 2003. (J). 7.99 *(978-0-9722038-6-9(9))* Mr Do It All, Inc.
Heuiser Hill, Melanie. Giant Pumpkin Suite. 2017. (ENG.). 448p. (J). (gr. 4-7). 18.99 *(978-0-7636-9155-4(0))* Candlewick Pr.
Higgins, B. T. The Master of Disaster. 2005. 103p. pap. 10.00 *(978-1-4116-3121-2(8))* Lulu Pr., Inc.
Higgins, Jack. Sure Fire. 2007. (ENG.). 304p. (YA). ***(978-0-00-724409-6(6))*** Penguin Publishing Group.
Higgins, Jack & Richards, Justin. Death Run. 2009. (ENG.). 288p. (YA). (gr. 7-18). 8.99 *(978-0-14-241475-0(1)*, Speak) Penguin Young Readers Group.
—First Strike. 2011. (Chance Twins Ser.: Bk. 4). (ENG.). 240p. (YA). (gr. 7-12). 24.94 *(978-0-399-25240-2(1))* Penguin Young Readers Group.
—Sharp Shot. 2010. (ENG.). 240p. (YA). (gr. 7-18). 8.99 *(978-0-14-241730-0(0)*, Speak) Penguin Young Readers Group.
—Sure Fire. 2008. (ENG.). 272p. (YA). (gr. 7-18). 8.99 *(978-0-14-241213-8(9)*, Speak) Penguin Young Readers Group.
Higgins, Lawrence. Demons & Dragons: Time, Space & Magic. 2010. (ENG., Illus.). 93p. pap. 20.99 *(978-1-906791-68-1(6))* Arena Bks. GBR. Dist: Lightning Source UK, Ltd.
Hill, C. J. Echo in Time. 2014. 387p. (YA). *(978-0-06-212395-4(5))* HarperCollins Pubs.
Hill, Janet Muirhead. Kendall & Kyleah. Leonhard, Herb, illus. 2012. (J). pap. 14.00 *(978-1-937849-05-4(8))* Raven Publishing Inc. of Montana.
Hirsch, Alex. Gravity Falls: Journal 3. 2016. (ENG., Illus.). 288p. (J). (gr. 3-7). 19.99 *(978-1-4847-4669-1(4)*, Disney Press Books) Disney Publishing Worldwide.
—Gravity Falls:: Lost Legends: 4 All-New Adventures! 2018. (ENG., Illus.). 144p. (J). (gr. 3-7). 19.99 *(978-1-368-02142-5(5)*, Disney Press Books) Disney Publishing Worldwide.
Hodgson, Mona. The Princess Twins & the Birthday Party, 1 vol. Olson, Julie, illus. 2016. (I Can Read! / Princess Twins Ser.). (ENG.). 32p. (J). pap. 4.99 *(978-0-310-75067-3(9))* Zonderkidz.
—The Princess Twins Collection, 1 vol. Olson, Julie, illus. 2017. (I Can Read! / Princess Twins Ser.). (ENG.). 128p. (J). 12.99 *(978-0-310-75319-3(8))* Zonderkidz.
Hole, Stian. Garmann's Secret. 2011. (ENG., Illus.). 56p. (J). 17.00 *(978-0-8028-5400-1(1)*, Eerdmans Bks For Young Readers) Eerdmans, William B. Publishing Co.
Holm, H. R. Forever Santa. 2009. 14p. (J). pap. 2.99 *(978-1-59955-345-0(7))* Cedar Fort, Inc./CFI Distribution.
Hood, Ann. Crazy Horse: Brave Warrior, 5. Altmann, Scott, illus. 2013. (Treasure Chest: the Time-Traveling Adventures of the Robbins Twins Ser.: 5). (ENG.). 192p. (J). (gr. 4-6). 18.69 *(978-0-448-45738-3(5))* Penguin Young Readers Group.
—Prince of Air, 4. Altmann, Scott & Zilber, Denis, illus. 2012. (Treasure Chest: the Time-Traveling Adventures of the Robbins Twins Ser.: 4). 208p. (J). (gr. 4-6). 21.19 *(978-0-448-45474-0(2))* Penguin Young Readers Group.
Hope, Laura. The Bobbsey Twins on Blueberry Island. 2007. 112p. (gr. 3-9). per. 11.95 *(978-1-4344-0033-8(6))* Wildside Pr., LLC.
Hope, Laura Lee. Bobbsey Twins. 2006. 25.95 *(978-1-4218-2978-4(9))*; pap. 10.95 *(978-1-4218-3078-0(7))* 1st World Publishing, Inc.
—The Bobbsey Twins: The First Fifteen Stories, Including Merry Days Indoors & Out, in the Country, at the Seashore, at School, at Snow Lodge, on A. 2013. 1080p. *(978-1-78139-372-7(9))* Benediction Classics.
—The Bobbsey Twins at Home. 2007. (ENG.). 134p. pap. 18.99 *(978-1-4264-5199-7(7))* Creative Media Partners, LLC.
—The Bobbsey Twins at Meadow Brook. 2005. 200p. 27.95 *(978-1-4218-0653-2(3)*, 1st World Library - Literary Society) 1st World Publishing, Inc.
—The Bobbsey Twins at Snow Lodge. 2005. 26.95 *(978-1-4218-0973-1(7)*, 1st World Library - Literary Society) 1st World Publishing, Inc.
—The Bobbsey Twins at the Seashore. 2005. 26.95 *(978-1-4218-1070-6(0))*; 176p. pap. 11.95 *(978-1-4218-1170-3(7))* 1st World Publishing, Inc. (1st World Library - Literary Society).
—The Bobbsey Twins in a Great City. 2005. 27.95 *(978-1-4218-1482-7(X))*; 204p. pap. 12.95 *(978-1-4218-1582-4(6))* 1st World Publishing, Inc. (1st World Library - Literary Society).
—The Bobbsey Twins in the Country. 2005. 208p. 27.95 *(978-1-4218-0655-6(X)*, 1st World Library - Literary Society) 1st World Publishing, Inc.
—The Bobbsey Twins in the Great West. 2005. 27.95 *(978-1-4218-0365-4(8)*, 1st World Library - Literary Society) 1st World Publishing, Inc.
—The Bobbsey Twins in Volcano Land. 2011. 190p. 42.95 *(978-1-258-04953-9(8))* Literary Licensing, LLC.
—The Bobbsey Twins in Washington. 2005. 27.95 *(978-1-4218-0974-8(5)*, 1st World Library - Literary Society) 1st World Publishing, Inc.
—The Bobbsey Twins in Washington. 2007. 256p. 29.95 *(978-1-4344-8591-5(9))*; per. 17.95 *(978-1-4344-8590-8(0))* Wildside Pr., LLC.
—The Bobbsey Twins on a House Boat. 2005. 204p. pap. 12.95 *(978-1-4218-1167-3(7)*, 1st World Library - Literary Society) 1st World Publishing, Inc.
—The Bobbsey Twins on A House Boat. 2005. 27.95 *(978-1-4218-1067-6(0)*, 1st World Library - Literary Society) 1st World Publishing, Inc.
—Freddie & Flossie. Pyle, Chuck, illus. 2005. (Bobbsey Twins Ser.). (ENG.). 32p. (J). (gr. -1-k). pap. 3.99 *(978-1-4169-0270-6(8)*, Simon Spotlight) Simon Spotlight.
—Freddie & Flossie. Pyle, Chuck, illus. 2006. (Bobbsey Twins Ser.). 32p. (J). (gr. -1-2). 22.78 *(978-1-59961-095-5(7))* Spotlight.
—Freddie & Flossie & Snap: Ready-To-Read Pre-Level 1. Pyle, Chuck, illus. 2005. (Bobbsey Twins Ser.). (ENG.). 32p. (J). (gr. -1-k). pap. 13.99 *(978-1-4169-0267-6(8)*, Simon Spotlight) Simon Spotlight.
—Freddie & Flossie & the Easter Egg Hunt. Downer, Maggie, illus. 2006. (Ready-To-Read Pre-Level 1 Ser.). (ENG.). 32p. (J). (gr. -1-1). 16.19 *(978-1-4169-1029-9(8))* Simon & Schuster, Inc.
—Freddie & Flossie & the Train Ride: Ready-To-Read Pre-Level 1. Pyle, Chuck, illus. 2005. (Bobbsey Twins Ser.). (ENG.). 32p. (J). (gr. -1-k). pap. 13.99 *(978-1-4169-0269-0(4)*, Simon Spotlight) Simon Spotlight.
—Freddie & Flossie at the Beach: Ready-To-Read Pre-Level 1. Pyle, Chuck, illus. 2005. (Bobbsey Twins Ser.). (ENG.). 32p. (J). (gr. -1-k). pap. 13.99 *(978-1-4169-0268-3(6)*, Simon Spotlight) Simon Spotlight.
Hopkins, Ellen. Identical. (ENG.). (YA). (gr. 9-18). 2010. 592p. pap. 14.99 *(978-1-4169-5006-6(0))* 2008. 576p. 24.99 *(978-1-4169-5005-9(2))* McElderry, Margaret K. Bks. (McElderry, Margaret K. Bks.).
Hosie, Donna. The 48. 2018. 360p. (YA). (gr. 9). 17.99 *(978-0-8234-3856-3(2))* Holiday Hse., Inc.
Hostetter, Joyce Moyer. Drive. 2018. (Bakers Mountain Stories Ser.). (Illus.). 352p. (J). (gr. 5-9). 18.95 *(978-1-62979-865-3(7)*, Calkins Creek) Highlights Pr., c/o Highlights for Children, Inc.
Howson, Imogen. Linked. 2014. (ENG., Illus.). 384p. (YA). (gr. 7). pap. 9.99 *(978-1-4424-4660-1(9)*, Simon & Schuster Bks. For Young Readers) Simon & Schuster Bks. For Young Readers.
—Unravel. 2014. (ENG., Illus.). 480p. (YA). (gr. 7). 17.99 *(978-1-4424-4658-8(7)*, Simon & Schuster Bks. For Young Readers) Simon & Schuster Bks. For Young Readers.
Hulme-Cross, Benjamin. Grayfields. 2018. (Mission Alert Ser.). (ENG., Illus.). 72p. (J). (gr. 5-8). pap. 7.99 *(978-1-5415-2632-7(5)*, a52730cf-d72c-4750-9477-584023c33d5b, Darby Creek) Lerner Publishing Group.
—Island X. 2018. (Mission Alert Ser.). (ENG., Illus.). 72p. (J). (gr. 5-8). pap. 7.99 *(978-1-5415-2633-4(3)*, ac1afa40-f139-4730-918c-fb6bac75511b, Darby Creek) Lerner Publishing Group.
—Lab 101. 2018. (Mission Alert Ser.). (ENG., Illus.). 72p. (J). (gr. 5-8). pap. 7.99 *(978-1-5415-2634-1(1)*, e0aa8cce-4b5c-4c27-ab6d-9182c2e44a05); lib. bdg. 26.65 *(978-1-5415-2581-8(7)*, 8b70c8b2-a5c4-4888-8800-441922b9cd6b) Lerner Publishing Group. (Darby Creek).
—Viper Attack. 2018. (Mission Alert Ser.). (ENG., Illus.). 72p. (J). (gr. 5-8). pap. 7.99 *(978-1-5415-2635-8(X)*, 37ed1a29-87bb-4c86-8008-c787d7fb4c3f); lib. bdg. 26.65 *(978-1-5415-2582-5(5)*, 20dc948f-9702-402f-9a96-e489206343b6) Lerner Publishing Group. (Darby Creek).
Hunt, Bonnie. Danger! Keep Out! The Grayson Twins Adventures. 2008. 96p. pap. 19.95 *(978-1-60563-202-5(3))* America Star Bks.
—The Missing Chimp: A Grayson Twins Adventures, 1 vol. 2009. 100p. pap. 19.95 *(978-1-60813-481-6(4))* America Star Bks.
Hurwitz, Johanna. Double or Nothing with the Two & Only Kelly Twins. Mourning, Tuesday, illus. (ENG.). 80p. (J). (gr. 1-4). 2019. pap. 4.99 *(978-1-5362-0372-1(6))* 2017. 14.99 *(978-0-7636-8808-0(8))* Candlewick Pr.
—The Two & Only Kelly Twins. Mourning, Tuesday, illus. (ENG.). 96p. (J). (gr. 1-4). 2018. pap. 4.99 *(978-1-5362-0050-8(6))* 2013. 14.99 *(978-0-7636-5602-7(X))* Candlewick Pr.
—The Two & Only Kelly Twins. 2018. lib. bdg. 14.75 *(978-0-606-40911-7(4))* Turtleback.
Hutton, Clare. Emma Moves In, 1. 2018. (American Girl Contemporary Ser.). (ENG.). 188p. (J). (gr. 4-5). 16.96 *(978-1-64310-229-0(X))* Penworthy Co., LLC, The.
I'm Not a Rerun! 2005. (J). bds. *(978-0-9769910-4-5(7))* Terrific Twins LLC.
Imfeld, Robert. Baylor's Guide to Dreadful Dreams. (ENG., Illus.). 320p. (J). (gr. 5-9). 2018. pap. 7.99 *(978-1-4814-6640-0(2))* 2017. 16.99 *(978-1-4814-6639-4(9))* Simon & Schuster Children's Publishing. (Aladdin).
—A Guide to the Other Side. 2016. (Beyond Baylor Ser.: 1). (ENG., Illus.). 320p. (J). (gr. 5-9). 17.99 *(978-1-4814-6636-3(4)*, Aladdin) Simon & Schuster Children's Publishing.
Irvin, William. The Adventures of Winston & Hazel: Episode 1: the Silver Medallion. 2006. 11.00 *(978-0-8059-8220-6(5))* Dorrance Publishing Co., Inc.
Isbell, Tom. The Capture. 2016. (Prey Trilogy Ser.: 2). (ENG.). 448p. (YA). (gr. 8). 17.99 *(978-0-06-221605-2(8)*, HarperTeen) HarperCollins Pubs.
—The Prey. 2015. (Prey Trilogy Ser.: 1). (ENG.). 416p. (YA). (gr. 8). 17.99 *(978-0-06-221601-4(5)*, HarperTeen) HarperCollins Pubs.
Island of Legends. 2014. (Unwanteds Ser.: 4). (ENG., Illus.). 496p. (J). (gr. 3-7). 19.99 *(978-1-4424-9328-5(3)*, Aladdin) Simon & Schuster Children's Publishing.
It's Dark! 2005. (J). bds. *(978-0-9769910-1-4(2))* Terrific Twins LLC.
Jesus, Opal De. The Golden Apple Kingdom, 1 vol. 2009. 48p. pap. 16.95 *(978-1-60749-414-0(0))* America Star Bks.
Johnson, Allen, Jr. The Dead House. McMorris, Kelley, illus. 2014. (Blackwater Novels Ser.: Vol. 2). (ENG.). 212p. (J). (gr. 4-7). 14.99 *(978-1-933725-34-5(6))* Premium Pr. America.
—My Brother's Story. McMorris, Kelley, illus. 2014. (Blackwater Novels Ser.: Vol. 1). (ENG.). 191p. (J). (gr. 4-7). 14.99 *(978-1-933725-37-6(0))* Premium Pr. America.
Johnson, C. Homecoming. 2007. (Illus.). 64p. per. 10.00 *(978-1-4251-1358-2(3))* Trafford Publishing.
Johnson, Terry Lynn. Avalanche! Orban, Jani, illus. 2018. (Survivor Diaries). (ENG.). 112p. (J). (gr. 1-5). pap. 6.99 *(978-1-328-51906-1(6)*, 1720632); 9.99 *(978-0-544-97039-7(X)*, 1662544) HarperCollins Pubs. (Clarion Bks.).
Jolley, Dan. The Hero Twins: Against the Lords of Death [a Mayan Myth]. Witt, David, illus. 2009. (Graphic Myths & Legends Ser.). (ENG.). 48p. (J). (gr. 4-8). pap. 9.99 *(978-1-58013-892-5(6)*, 6f846b77-3d0c-4698-8bb2-7500d90f8f23, Graphic Universe™) Lerner Publishing Group.
Jones, Jen. Maren's New Family. Franco, Paula, illus. 2015. (Sleepover Girls Ser.). (ENG.). 128p. (J). (gr. 3-5). lib. bdg. 22.65 *(978-1-4965-0540-8(9)*, 128612, Stone Arch Bks.) Capstone.
—Willow's Boy-Crazy Birthday. Franco, Paula, illus. 2014. (Sleepover Girls Ser.). (ENG.). 128p. (J). (gr. 3-5). lib. bdg. 22.65 *(978-1-4342-9757-0(8)*, 127105, Stone Arch Bks.) Capstone.
Jones, Sandra O. A Voice on the Wind: I Know about the Apple... do You? 2012. 24p. pap. 17.99 *(978-1-4567-3553-1(5))* AuthorHouse.
Jump Shot. 2014. (Barber Game Time Bks.). (ENG., Illus.). 160p. (J). (gr. 3-7). pap. 7.99 *(978-1-4424-5730-0(9)*, Simon & Schuster/Paula Wiseman Bks.) Simon & Schuster/Paula Wiseman Bks.
Kade, Stacey. For This Life Only. 2016. (ENG., Illus.). 320p. (YA). (gr. 9). 17.99 *(978-1-4814-3248-1(6)*, Simon & Schuster Bks. For Young Readers) Simon & Schuster Bks. For Young Readers.
Kassel, Roger de. Mr P & the Bully Birds. 2013. (ENG., Illus.). 12p. pap. 8.75 *(978-1-78035-677-8(3)*, Fastprint Publishing) Upfront Publishing Ltd. GBR. Dist: Printondemand-worldwide.com.
Kastner, Erich. Lisa & Lottie. 2015. (ENG.). 168p. (gr. 3). pap. 12.95 *(978-1-939601-33-9(9))* Ig Publishing, Inc.
Katherine's Story 1848. 2014. (Secrets of the Manor Ser.: 4). (ENG., Illus.). 160p. (J). (gr. 3-7). pap. 6.99 *(978-1-4814-1843-0(2)*, Simon Spotlight) Simon Spotlight.
Katschke, Judy. The Facts about Flirting. 2003. (Two of a Kind Ser.: Vol. 27). (Illus.). 112p. mass mkt. 4.99 *(978-0-06-009323-5(4)*, Harper Entertainment) HarperCollins Pubs.
Katschke, Judy, et al. Bye-Bye Boyfriend, 3 vols. 2003. (ENG., Illus.). 112p. *(978-0-00-714467-9(9)*, HarperCollins Children's Bks.) HarperCollins Pubs. Ltd.
Kaufman, Amie. Elementals: Scorch Dragons. (Elementals Ser.: 2). (ENG.). (J). (gr. 3-7). 2020. 384p. pap. 9.99 *(978-0-06-245802-5(7))* 2019. (Illus.). 368p. 16.99 *(978-0-06-245801-8(9))* HarperCollins Pubs. (HarperCollins).
Keating, Jess. How to Outrun a Crocodile When Your Shoes Are Untied. 2014. (My Life Is a Zoo Ser.: 1). 288p. (J). (gr. 4-7). pap. 11.99 *(978-1-4022-9755-7(6)*, 9781402297557) Sourcebooks, Inc.
—How to Outswim a Shark Without a Snorkel. 2015. (My Life Is a Zoo Ser.: 2). 304p. (J). (gr. 4-7). pap. 11.99 *(978-1-4022-9758-8(0)*, 9781402297588) Sourcebooks, Inc.
Kehret, Peg. Runaway Twin. 2011. (ENG.). 208p. (J). (gr. 5-18). 8.99 *(978-0-14-241849-9(8)*, Puffin Books) Penguin Young Readers Group.
Kelley, Jane. The Girl Behind the Glass. 2012. (ENG.). 192p. (J). (gr. 4-7). pap. 6.99 *(978-0-375-86219-9(6)*, Yearling) Random Hse. Children's Bks.
Kelly, Erin Entrada. We Dream of Space: A Newbery Honor Award Winner. 2020. (ENG., Illus.). 400p. (J). (gr. 3-7). 16.99 *(978-0-06-274730-3(4)*, Greenwillow Bks.) HarperCollins Pubs.
Kelly, J. M. Speed of Life. 2016. (ENG.). 352p. (YA). (gr. 9). 17.99 *(978-0-544-74782-1(8)*, 1633256, Clarion Bks.) HarperCollins Pubs.
Kelly, Mark. Astrotwins — Project Rescue. 2016. (Astrotwins Ser.). (ENG., Illus.). 256p. (J). (gr. 3-7). 16.99 *(978-1-4814-2458-5(0)*, Simon & Schuster/Paula Wiseman Bks.) Simon & Schuster/Paula Wiseman Bks.
Kemnitz, Dianna. Meet Jack & His New Friend. 2011. 36p. pap. 24.95 *(978-1-4560-8776-0(2))* America Star Bks.
Kent, Jaden. Ella & Owen 1: the Cave of Aaaaah! Doom! Bodnaruk, Iryna, illus. 2017. (Ella & Owen Ser.: 1). (ENG.). 112p. (J). (gr. k-3). pap. 5.99 *(978-1-4998-0368-6(0))* Little Bee Books Inc.
—Ella & Owen 10: the Dragon Games! Bodnaruk, Iryna, illus. 2018. (Ella & Owen Ser.: 10). (ENG.). 112p. (J). (gr. k-3). 16.99 *(978-1-4998-0617-5(5))*; pap. 5.99 *(978-1-4998-0616-8(7))* Little Bee Books Inc.
—Ella & Owen 2: Attack of the Stinky Fish Monster! Bodnaruk, Iryna, illus. 2017. (Ella & Owen Ser.: 2). (ENG.). 112p. (J). (gr. k-3). pap. 5.99 *(978-1-4998-0369-3(9))* Little Bee Books Inc.
—Ella & Owen 5: the Great Troll Quest. Bodnaruk, Iryna, illus. 2017. (Ella & Owen Ser.: 5). (ENG.). 112p. (J). (gr. k-3). 16.99 *(978-1-4998-0474-4(1))*; pap. 5.99 *(978-1-4998-0473-7(3))* Little Bee Books Inc.
—Ella & Owen 6: Dragon Spies! Bodnaruk, Iryna, illus. 2017. (Ella & Owen Ser.: 6). (ENG.). 112p. (J). (gr. k-3). 16.99 *(978-1-4998-0476-8(8))*; pap. 5.99 *(978-1-4998-0475-1(X))* Little Bee Books Inc.
—Ella & Owen 7: Twin Trouble. Bodnaruk, Iryna, illus. 2018. (Ella & Owen Ser.: 7). (ENG.). 112p. (J). (gr. k-3). 16.99 *(978-1-4998-0611-3(6))*; pap. 5.99 *(978-1-4998-0610-6(8))* Little Bee Books Inc.
—Ella & Owen 8: the Worst Pet. Bodnaruk, Iryna, illus. 2018. (Ella & Owen Ser.: 8). (ENG.). 112p. (J). (gr. k-3). 16.99 *(978-1-4998-0613-7(2))*; pap. 5.99 *(978-1-4998-0612-0(4))* Little Bee Books Inc.
—Ella & Owen 9: Grumpy Goblins. Bodnaruk, Iryna, illus. 2018. (Ella & Owen Ser.: 9). (ENG.). 112p. (J). (gr. k-3). 16.99 *(978-1-4998-0615-1(9))*; pap. 5.99 *(978-1-4998-0614-4(0))* Little Bee Books Inc.
Kiernan, Celine. Into the Grey. 2014. (ENG.). 304p. (YA). (gr. 7). 16.99 *(978-0-7636-7061-0(8))* Candlewick Pr.
Kimmel, Eric A. Escape from Egypt. Stevanovic, Ivica, illus. 2015. (Scarlett & Sam Ser.). (ENG.). 168p. (J). (gr. 1-3). E-Book 23.99 *(978-1-4677-6207-6(5)*, Kar-Ben Publishing) Lerner Publishing Group.
—Search for the Shamir. Stevanovic, Ivica, illus. 2018. (Scarlett & Sam Ser.). (ENG.). 152p. (J). (gr. 1-3). pap. 6.99 *(978-1-5124-2938-1(4)*, fa05c70d-97fc-4c41-af59-93be9cd9769f, Kar-Ben Publishing) Lerner Publishing Group.
Kleiman, Deanna M. My Twin Brother. Greenes, Shimra, illus. 2012. 24p. pap. 9.13 *(978-0-615-35370-8(3))* TwinsBooks.
Knutsson, Catherine. Shadows Cast by Stars. 2013. (ENG., Illus.). 464p. (YA). (gr. 7). pap. 13.99 *(978-1-4424-0192-1(3)*, Atheneum Bks. for Young Readers) Simon & Schuster Children's Publishing.
Kogler, Jennifer. The Otherworldlies. 2008. 400p. (J). lib. bdg. 17.89 *(978-0-06-073960-7(6))*; (ENG.). (gr. 5-18). 16.99 *(978-0-06-073959-1(2))* HarperCollins Pubs. (Eos).
Kraft, Erik P. Lenny & Mel. Kraft, Erik P., illus. 2012. (Ready-For-Chapters Ser.). (ENG., Illus.). 64p. (J). (gr. 2-5). pap. 6.99 *(978-0-689-85891-8(4)*, Aladdin) Simon & Schuster Children's Publishing.
—Lenny & Mel after-School Confidential. Kraft, Erik P., illus. 2012. (Lenny & Mel Ser.). (ENG., Illus.). 64p. (J). (gr. 2-5). pap. 6.99 *(978-1-4424-6314-1(7)*, Simon & Schuster/Paula Wiseman Bks.) Simon & Schuster/Paula Wiseman Bks.
—Lenny & Mel's Summer Vacation. Kraft, Erik P., illus. 2012. (Ready-For-Chapters Ser.). (ENG., Illus.). 64p. (J). (gr. 2-5).

pap. 6.99 *(978-0-689-86874-0(X)*, Simon & Schuster/Paula Wiseman Bks.) Simon & Schuster/Paula Wiseman Bks.

Kuhlman, Evan. Great Ball of Light. Holmes, Jeremy, illus. 2015. (ENG.). 304p. (J). (gr. 5-9). 16.99 *(978-1-4169-6461-2(4))* Simon & Schuster Children's Publishing.

Lamb, Charles, et al. Tales from Shakespeare: "Twelfth Night" Strang, Kay, ed. rev. ed. 2005. (Illus.). 40p. pap. 4.95 *(978-0-9542905-7-3(7))* Capercaillie Bks., Ltd GBR. Dist: Gatewood Pr.

Lambert, Clercina. The Indifferent Twin: Outside Beauty Will Fade Away but Inside Beauty Will Last for a Lifetime. 2012. 28p. (-18). pap. 15.99 *(978-1-4771-1647-0(8))* Xlibris Corp.

Lampman, Evelyn Sibley. The Shy Stegosaurus of Cricket Creek. Buel, Hubert, illus. 2007. 218p. (J). (gr. 4-7). per. 12.00 *(978-1-930900-37-0(6))* Purple Hse. Pr.

Langdale, Mark Roland. Professor Doppelganger & the Fantastical Cloud Factory. 2012. 106p. pap. *(978-1-78003-267-2(6))* Pen Pr. Pubs., Ltd.

Langlois, Suzanne. Mia, Matt & the Turkey Chase, 1 vol. Cummins, Sarah, tr. Beaulieu, Jimmy, illus. 2008. (Formac First Novels Ser.). (ENG.). 64p. (J). (gr. 2-5). 5.95 *(978-0-88780-763-3(1)*, 763); 14.95 *(978-0-88780-765-7(8)*, 765) Formac Publishing Co., Ltd. CAN. Dist: Formac Lorimer Bks. Ltd.

Langrish, Katherine. Troll Fell. 2004. (Illus.). 272p. (J). (gr. 5-18). (ENG.). 16.99 *(978-0-06-058304-0(5))*; lib. bdg. 16.89 *(978-0-06-058305-7(3))* HarperCollins Pubs.

Larson, Hope. Compass South. 2017. (Four Points Ser.: 1). (J). lib. bdg. 24.50 *(978-0-606-39953-1(4))* Turtleback.

Lasky, Kathryn. Double Trouble Squared: A Starbuck Twins Mystery, Book One. 2008. (ENG., Illus.). 240p. (J). (gr. 3-7). pap. 14.99 *(978-0-15-205878-4(8)*, 1197650, Clarion Bks.) HarperCollins Pubs.

—Shadows in the Water: A Starbuck Twins Mystery, Book Two. 2008. (ENG., Illus.). 224p. (J). (gr. 3-7). pap. 14.95 *(978-0-15-205874-6(5)*, 1197638, Clarion Bks.) HarperCollins Pubs.

—A Voice in the Wind: A Starbuck Twins Mystery, Book Three. 2008. (ENG., Illus.). 272p. (J). (gr. 3-7). pap. 15.95 *(978-0-15-205875-3(3)*, 1197642, Clarion Bks.) HarperCollins Pubs.

Lathan, Betty Jean. Sierra, the Unwanted Cat. 2011. 28p. pap. 13.59 *(978-1-4567-3297-4(8))* AuthorHouse.

Lawson, Jessica. Nooks & Crannies. Andrewson, Natalie, illus. 2015. (ENG.). 336p. (J). (gr. 3-7). 19.99 *(978-1-4814-1921-5(8)*, Simon & Schuster Bks. For Young Readers) Simon & Schuster Bks. For Young Readers.

Lay, Kathryn. The Substitutes: An Up2U Action Adventure, 1 vol. Calo, Marcos, illus. 2015. (Up2U Adventures Ser.). (ENG.). 80p. (J). (gr. 2-5). 35.64 *(978-1-62402-095-7(X)*, 17359, Calico Chapter Bks.) ABDO Publishing Co.

Leder, Meg. Letting Go of Gravity. (ENG.). (YA). (gr. 7). 2019. 448p. pap. 12.99 *(978-1-5344-0317-8(5))* 2018. (Illus.). 432p. 19.99 *(978-1-5344-0316-1(7))* Simon Pulse. (Simon Pulse).

Ledger, Kate. Twin Magic: School Bully, Beware! 2013. (Scholastic Reader Level 2 Ser.). (Illus.). 32p. (J). lib. bdg. 13.55 *(978-0-606-31972-0(7))* Turtleback.

Lee Hope, Laura. The Bobbsey Twins in the Great West. 2005. 200p. pap. 12.95 *(978-1-4218-0465-1(4)*, 1st World Library - Literary Society) 1st World Publishing, Inc.

—The Bobbsey Twins in the Great West. 2004. reprint ed. pap. 1.99 *(978-1-4192-5444-4(8))*; pap. 20.95 *(978-1-4191-5444-7(3))* Kessinger Publishing, LLC.

Lee, J. M. Shadows of the Dark Crystal #1. Froud, Brian, illus. 2016. (Jim Henson's the Dark Crystal Ser.: 1). 272p. (YA). (gr. 7). 17.99 *(978-0-448-48289-7(4)*, Grosset & Dunlap) Penguin Young Readers Group.

Lee, Shari. Mandie's & Mindie's Adventure under the Sea, 1 vol. 2009. 63p. pap. 19.95 *(978-1-4489-9977-4(4))* America Star Bks.

Lee, Wan, et al. A Fish Wish - Lunch for Patch - Squid Twins: BuildUp Unit 4 Lap Book. Moor, Beka et al, illus. 2015. (Build up Core Phonics Ser.). (J). (gr. 1). *(978-1-4900-2603-9(7))* Benchmark Education Co.

Leigh, Savanah-Rose. Trunks & Amelia. 2012. 48p. pap. 9.89 *(978-1-4669-3803-8(X))* Trafford Publishing.

Leitich Smith, Greg. Chronal Engine. Henry, Blake, illus. 2013. (ENG.). 192p. (J). (gr. 5-7). pap. 6.99 *(978-0-544-02277-5(7)*, 1528498, Clarion Bks.) HarperCollins Pubs.

L'Engle, Madeleine. Many Waters. 2007. (Wrinkle in Time Quintet Ser.: 3). (ENG.). 368p. (J). (gr. 5-9). per. 7.99 *(978-0-312-36857-9(7)*, 900042674) Square Fish.

Leonard, Marcia. Trae la Pelota, Tito. Handelman, Dorothy, photos by. 2005.Tr. of Get the Ball, Slim. (Illus.). 32p. (J). (ENG & SPA.). (gr. -1-1). pap. 4.99 *(978-0-8225-3293-4(X))*; (SPA., (gr. 1-1). per. 5.95 *(978-0-8225-3292-7(1)*, Ediciones Lerner) Lerner Publishing Group.

Leprechaun, Seamus T. The o'Shea Chronicles. 2013. 312p. pap. *(978-1-78407-190-5(0))* FeedARead.com.

Lerangis, Peter. The Code. 2004. (Spy X Ser.: No. 1). 139p. (Orig.). (J). *(978-0-439-70242-3(9))* Scholastic, Inc.

Let's Celebrate!, 10 bks. 2005. (Illus.). (J). bds. *(978-0-9769910-9-0(8))* Terrific Twins LLC.

Lewis. Want to Trade Two Brothers for a Cat? 2008. (ENG.). 112p. (YA). (gr. 7). pap. 7.95 *(978-1-4169-7538-0(1)*, Simon Pulse) Simon Pulse.

Lewison, Wendy Cheyette. Two Is for Twins. Nakata, Hiroe, illus. 2011. 28p. (J). (gr. -1 — 1). bds. 8.99 *(978-0-670-01310-4(2)*, Viking Books for Young Readers) Penguin Young Readers Group.

Lin, Grace. Ling & Ting: Not Exactly the Same! 2011. (Passport to Reading Level 3 Ser.). (ENG.). 48p. (J). (gr. 1-4). pap. 4.99 *(978-0-316-02453-2(8))* Little, Brown Bks. for Young Readers.

—Ling & Ting: Together in All Weather. 2016. (Passport to Reading Level 3 Ser.). (J). lib. bdg. 14.75 *(978-0-606-39187-0(8))* Turtleback.

—Ling & Ting Share a Birthday. 2014. (ENG.). 48p. (J). (gr. 1-4). pap. 4.99 *(978-0-316-18404-5(7))* Little, Brown Bks. for Young Readers.

—Ling & Ting Share a Birthday. 2014. (Passport to Reading Level 3 Ser.). (J). lib. bdg. 14.75 *(978-0-606-35932-0(X))* Turtleback.

—Ling & Ting: Together in All Weather. 2016. (ENG.). 48p. (J). (gr. 1-4). pap. 4.99 *(978-0-316-33548-5(7))* Little, Brown Bks. for Young Readers.

—Twice as Silly. 2015. (Passport to Reading Level 3 Ser.). (J). lib. bdg. 14.75 *(978-0-606-37464-4(7))* Turtleback.

Linko, Gina. Flower Moon. 2018. (ENG.). 256p. (J). (gr. 4-8). 15.99 *(978-1-5107-2274-3(2)*, Sky Pony Pr.) Skyhorse Publishing Co., Inc.

Lipsyte, Robert. The Twinning Project. 2014. (ENG.). 288p. (J). (gr. 5-7). pap. 16.99 *(978-0-544-22522-0(8)*, 1563389, Clarion Bks.) HarperCollins Pubs.

Locke, Thomas, pseud. Renegades. 2017. (Recruits Ser.). (ENG.). 288p. pap. 16.00 *(978-0-8007-2790-1(8))* Revell.

Loewen, Nancy. The Lion & the Mouse, Narrated by the Timid but Truthful Mouse. Bernardini, Cristian, illus. 2018. (Other Side of the Fable Ser.). (ENG.). 24p. (J). (gr. -1-3). lib. bdg. 27.99 *(978-1-5158-2866-2(2)*, 138404, Picture Window Bks.) Capstone.

London, Alex. Black Wings Beating. 2019. (Skybound Saga Ser.: 1). (ENG., Illus.). 448p. (YA). pap. 17.99 *(978-1-250-21148-4(4)*, 900177982) Square Fish.

London, C. Alexander. We Are Not Eaten by Yaks. 2013. (Accidental Adventure Ser.: 1). 384p. (J). (gr. 3-7). pap. 8.99 *(978-0-14-242056-0(5)*, Puffin Books) Penguin Young Readers Group.

—We Dine with Cannibals. 2013. (Accidental Adventure Ser.: 2). 384p. (J). (gr. 3-7). pap. 7.99 *(978-0-14-242474-2(9)*, Puffin Books) Penguin Young Readers Group.

—We Give a Squid a Wedgie. 3. Duddle, Jonny, illus. 2013. (Accidental Adventure Ser.: 3). 400p. (J). (gr. 3-7). 7.99 *(978-0-14-242475-9(7)*, Puffin) Penguin Young Readers Group.

Lord, Gabrielle. Black Ops Hunted: Conspiracy 365. 2014. 192p. (J). 10.99 *(978-1-61067-171-2(6))* Kane Miller.

Love, D. Anne. The Secret Prince. 2012. (ENG.). 240p. (J). (gr. 3-7). pap. 11.99 *(978-1-4424-5931-1(X)*, McElderry, Margaret K. Bks.) McElderry, Margaret K. Bks.

Lowell, Susan. The Great Grand Canyon Time Train. Shroades, John / W., illus. 2011. 32p. (J). 15.95 *(978-1-933855-63-9(0))* Rio Nuevo Pubs.

Luces-Tucker, Max. Bobby & Chrissy: One Gift. 2008. (ENG.). 36p. pap. 17.99 *(978-1-4343-8199-6(4))* AuthorHouse.

Lucy Fitch Perkins. The Dutch Twins. 2005. pap. *(978-1-905432-05-9(4))* Dodo Pr.

Lundquist, Jenny. The Opal Crown. 2014. (ENG., Illus.). 368p. (J). (gr. 7-17). pap. 9.95 *(978-0-7624-5422-8(9)*, Running Pr. Kids) Running Pr.

Lupica, Mike. The Football Fiasco. 2018. (Zach & Zoe Mysteries Ser.: 3). (ENG., Illus.). 80p. (J). (gr. 1-4). 6.99 *(978-0-425-28943-3(5)*, Puffin Books); 14.99 *(978-0-425-28942-6(7)*, Philomel Bks.) Penguin Young Readers Group.

—The Half-Court Hero. 2018. (Zach & Zoe Mysteries Ser.: 2). (ENG., Illus.). 96p. (J). (gr. 1-4). 6.99 *(978-0-425-28940-2(0)*, Puffin Books) Penguin Young Readers Group.

—The Hockey Rink Hunt. 2019. (Zach & Zoe Mysteries Ser.: 5). (ENG., Illus.). 80p. (J). (gr. 1-4). 14.99 *(978-0-425-28948-8(6)*, Philomel Bks.) Penguin Young Readers Group.

—The Missing Baseball. 2018. (Zach & Zoe Mysteries Ser.: 1). (ENG., Illus.). 80p. (J). (gr. 1-4). 6.99 *(978-0-425-28937-2(0)*, Puffin Books) Penguin Young Readers Group.

Lyga, Barry. The Flash: the Tornado Twins (the Flash Book 3) 2018. (ENG.). 272p. (J). (gr. 5-9). 13.99 *(978-1-4197-3124-2(6)*, 1202401, Amulet Bks.) Abrams, Inc.

Lynch, Jay. Mo & Jo Fighting Together Forever: Toon Books Level 3. Haspiel, Dean, illus. (Toon Ser.). (ENG.). 40p. (J). (gr. -1-3). 2013. pap. 4.99 *(978-1-935179-37-5(3)*, Toon Books) 2008. 12.95 *(978-0-9799238-5-2(9)*, TOON Books) Astra Publishing Hse.

Lynch, Jay & Haspiel, Dean. Mo & Jo: Fighting Together Forever, 1 vol. Lynch, Jay, illus. 2013. (Toon Bks.). (ENG., Illus.). 40p. (J). (gr. 2-3). lib. bdg. 32.79 *(978-1-61479-152-2(X)*, 14844) Spotlight.

MacAndrew, Richard & Morgan, Richard. A Little Trouble in California. 2012. (Cambridge Experience Readers Ser.). (ENG., Illus.). 48p. pap. 14.75 *(978-1-107-68322-8(X))* Cambridge Univ. Pr.

MacAndrewRichard. A Little Trouble in California Level Starter/Beginner, 1 vol. 2011. (Cambridge Experience Readers Ser.). (ENG., Illus.). 48p. pap. 14.75 *(978-84-8323-982-7(5))* Cambridge Univ. Pr.

—A Little Trouble in the Yorkshire Dales Level 3 Lower Intermediate. 2009. (Cambridge Experience Readers Ser.). (ENG.). 80p. pap. 14.75 *(978-84-8323-584-3(6))* Cambridge Univ. Pr.

Mack, W. C. Athlete vs. Mathlete. 2013. (ENG., 208p. (YA). Illus.). (gr. 3-6). pap. 8.99 *(978-1-59990-858-8(1)*, 900081981); 1. (gr. 4-6). 16.99 *(978-1-59990-915-8(4)*, 900084829) Bloomsbury Publishing USA. (Bloomsbury USA Childrens).

Maddox, Jake. Gear Hero. Garcia, Eduardo, illus. 2018. (Jake Maddox Graphic Novels Ser.). (ENG.). 72p. (J). (gr. 3-8). pap. 6.95 *(978-1-4965-6049-0(3)*, 137430); lib. bdg. 26.65 *(978-1-4965-6045-2(0)*, 137426) Capstone. (Stone Arch Bks.).

—Rebound Time, 1 vol. Wood, Katie, illus. 2013. (Jake Maddox Girl Sports Stories Ser.). (ENG.). 72p. (J). (gr. 3-6). pap. 5.95 *(978-1-4342-4202-0(1)*, 120260); lib. bdg. 25.32 *(978-1-4342-4013-2(4)*, 118394) Capstone. (Stone Arch Bks.).

—Rookie Runner. 2018. (Jake Maddox JV Ser.). (ENG., Illus.). 96p. (J). (gr. 4-6). pap. 5.95 *(978-1-4965-6334-7(4)*, 138064); lib. bdg. 25.99 *(978-1-4965-6332-3(8)*, 138063) Capstone. (Stone Arch Bks.).

—Speedway Switch. Tiffany, Sean, illus. 2007. (Jake Maddox Sports Stories Ser.). (ENG.). 72p. (J). (gr. 3-6). pap. 5.95 *(978-1-59889-416-5(1)*, 93563); lib. bdg. 25.99 *(978-1-59889-321-2(1)*, 93517) Capstone. (Stone Arch Bks.).

—Spinning Away. 2017. (Jake Maddox JV Girls Ser.). (ENG., Illus.). 96p. (J). (gr. 4-8). lib. bdg. 26.65 *(978-1-4965-4927-3(9)*, 135824, Stone Arch Bks.) Capstone.

Maguire, Gregory. Missing Sisters. 2009. 192p. (J). 16.99 *(978-0-06-123204-6(1))*; (ENG.). (gr. 3-7). pap. 6.99 *(978-0-06-123203-9(3)*, HarperCollins) HarperCollins Pubs.

Mahoney, Tammy. Eddie the Eagle Learns to Fly. 2012. 24p. pap. 19.99 *(978-1-4772-1747-4(9))* AuthorHouse.

Mak, D P. Invisible Pill. 2005. 44p. pap. *(978-1-84401-210-7(7))* Athena Pr.

Manley, Francis G. Tellin Twins: The Great Art Scam. 2004. (Illus.). 132p. pap. *(978-1-84401-292-3(1))* Athena Pr.

Manson, Sheri. Bumpy & Boo Visits the Eye Doctor: Guess Who Needs Glasses? Cabrera, Marcela, illus. 2006. 32p. (J). 15.95 *(978-0-9744307-3-7(0))* Merry Lane Pr.

Margallo, Ramon. The MANGER, the CROSS, & the EMPTY TOMB Christian Apologetics for Young Readers: A Short Story. 2006. 108p. pap. 9.99 *(978-1-4116-5751-9(9))* Lulu Pr., Inc.

Margolis, Leslie. Girl's Best Friend. 2011. (Maggie Brooklyn Mystery Ser.). (ENG.). 288p. (J). (gr. 3-12). pap. 7.99 *(978-1-59990-690-4(2)*, 900076050, Bloomsbury USA Childrens) Bloomsbury Publishing USA.

—Secrets at the Chocolate Mansion. 2014. (Maggie Brooklyn Mystery Ser.). (ENG.). 272p. (J). (gr. 3-6). pap. 7.99 *(978-1-61963-493-0(7)*, 900138595, Bloomsbury USA Childrens) Bloomsbury Publishing USA.

—Vanishing Acts. 2013. (Maggie Brooklyn Mystery Ser.). (ENG.). 256p. (J). (gr. 3-6). pap. 7.99 *(978-1-59990-981-3(2)*, 900096404, Bloomsbury USA Childrens) Bloomsbury Publishing USA.

Martinez Jover, Carmen. The Twin Kangaroo Treasure Hunt, a Gay Parenting Story. Martinez, Rosemary, illus. 2013. 32p. pap. *(978-607-00-6545-3(X))* Martinez Jover, María del Carmen Dorotea.

Massie, Elizabeth. Ameri-Scares: New York. 2013. 148p. pap. 12.99 *(978-1-937530-55-6(8))* Crossroad Pr.

Matthews, L. S. Lexi. 2008. 200p. (J). pap. *(978-0-385-73575-9(8)*, Delacorte Pr) Random House Publishing Group.

Mawter, J. A. Launched! 2007. (ENG.). 258p. *(978-0-207-20073-1(4))* HarperCollins Pubs. Australia.

McAlpine, Gordon. The Tell-Tale Start. Zuppardi, Sam, illus. 2013. (Misadventures of Edgar & Allan Poe Ser.: 1). 208p. (J). (gr. 3-7). pap. 7.99 *(978-0-14-242346-2(7)*, Puffin Books) Penguin Young Readers Group.

McCafferty, Megan. Bumped. 2012. (Bumped Ser.: 1). (ENG.). 352p. (YA). (gr. 9). pap. 9.99 *(978-0-06-196275-2(9)*, Balzer & Bray) HarperCollins Pubs.

—Thumped. 2013. (Bumped Ser.: 2). (ENG.). 304p. (YA). (gr. 8). pap. 8.99 *(978-0-06-196277-6(5)*, Balzer & Bray) HarperCollins Pubs.

McCall Smith, Alexander. School Ship Tobermory. 2016. (School Ship Tobermory Ser.: 1). (ENG., Illus.). 224p. (J). (gr. 3-7). 15.99 *(978-0-399-55261-8(8)*, Delacorte Bks. for Young Readers) Random Hse. Children's Bks.

McClymer, Kelly. Must Love Black. 2008. (ENG.). 192p. (YA). (gr. 7-18). pap. 8.99 *(978-1-4169-4903-9(8)*, Simon Pulse) Simon Pulse.

McDonald, Kirsten. The Big Rain, 1 vol. Meza, Erika, illus. 2015. (Carlos & Carmen Ser.). (ENG.). 32p. (J). (gr. k-3). 32.79 *(978-1-62402-137-4(9)*, 19071, Calico Chapter Bks) Magic Wagon.

—Carlos & Carmen Set 2, 4 vols. Meza, Erika, illus. 2016. (Carlos & Carmen Ser.). (ENG.). 32p. (J). (gr. -1-3). 131.16 *(978-1-62402-141-1(7)*, 21549, Calico Chapter Bks) Magic Wagon.

—The Costume Contest. Meza, Erika, illus. 2016. (Carlos & Carmen Ser.). (ENG.). 32p. (J). (gr. -1-3). lib. bdg. 32.79 *(978-1-62402-182-4(4)*, 24543, Calico Chapter Bks) Magic Wagon.

—El Error Rico (the Yummy Mistake) Meza, Erika, illus. 2018. (Carlos & Carmen (Spanish Version) (Calico Kid) Ser.). (SPA.). 32p. (J). (gr. -1-3). lib. bdg. 32.79 *(978-1-5321-3324-4(3)*, 28511, Calico Chapter Bks) Magic Wagon.

—El Fin de Semana Arenoso (the Sandy Weekend) Meza, Erika, illus. 2018. (Carlos & Carmen (Spanish Version) (Calico Kid) Ser.). (SPA.). 32p. (J). (gr. -1-3). lib. bdg. 32.79 *(978-1-5321-3321-3(9)*, 28505, Calico Chapter Bks) Magic Wagon.

—The Fun Fort. Anaya, Fátima, illus. 2017. (Carlos & Carmen Ser.). (ENG.). 32p. (J). (gr. -1-3). lib. bdg. 32.79 *(978-1-5321-3033-5(3)*, 27035, Calico Chapter Bks) Magic Wagon.

—The Green Surprise, 1 vol. Meza, Erika, illus. 2015. (Carlos & Carmen Ser.). (ENG.). 32p. (J). (gr. k-3). 32.79 *(978-1-62402-138-1(7)*, 19073, Calico Chapter Bks) Magic Wagon.

—Las Ruedas Tambaleantes (the Wobbly Wheels) Meza, Erika, illus. 2018. (Carlos & Carmen (Spanish Version) (Calico Kid) Ser.). (SPA.). 32p. (J). (gr. -1-3). lib. bdg. 32.79 *(978-1-5321-3323-7(5)*, 28509, Calico Chapter Bks) Magic Wagon.

—The Nighttime Noise, 1 vol. Meza, Erika, illus. 2015. (Carlos & Carmen Ser.). (ENG.). 32p. (J). (gr. k-3). 32.79 *(978-1-62402-139-8(5)*, 19075, Calico Chapter Bks) Magic Wagon.

—The One-Tire House, 1 vol. Meza, Erika, illus. 2015. (Carlos & Carmen Ser.). (ENG.). 32p. (J). (gr. k-3). 32.79 *(978-1-62402-140-4(9)*, 19077, Calico Chapter Bks) Magic Wagon.

—The Perfect Piñatas. Meza, Erika, illus. 2016. (Carlos & Carmen Ser.). (ENG.). 32p. (J). (gr. -1-3). lib. bdg. 32.79 *(978-1-62402-183-1(2)*, 24545, Calico Chapter Bks) Magic Wagon.

—The Pet Show Problem. Meza, Erika, illus. 2016. (Carlos & Carmen Ser.). (ENG.). 32p. (J). (gr. -1-3). lib. bdg. 32.79 *(978-1-62402-184-8(0)*, 24547, Calico Chapter Bks) Magic Wagon.

—The Sandy Weekend, 1 vol. Meza, Erika, illus. 2016. (Carlos & Carmen Ser.). (ENG.). 32p. (J). (gr. -1-3). 32.79 *(978-1-62402-142-8(5)*, 21551, Calico Chapter Bks) Magic Wagon.

—The Sparkly Night. Meza, Erika, illus. 2016. (Carlos & Carmen Ser.). (ENG.). 32p. (J). (gr. -1-3). lib. bdg. 32.79 *(978-1-62402-185-5(9)*, 24549, Calico Chapter Bks) Magic Wagon.

—Tío Time, 1 vol. Meza, Erika, illus. 2016. (Carlos & Carmen Ser.). (ENG.). 32p. (J). (gr. -1-3). 32.79 *(978-1-62402-143-5(3)*, 21553, Calico Chapter Bks) Magic Wagon.

—Too Many Valentines. Anaya, Fátima, illus. 2017. (Carlos & Carmen Ser.). (ENG.). 32p. (J). (gr. -1-3). lib. bdg. 32.79 *(978-1-5321-3035-9(X)*, 27037, Calico Chapter Bks) Magic Wagon.

—The Wobbly Wheels, 1 vol. Meza, Erika, illus. 2016. (Carlos & Carmen Ser.). (ENG.). 32p. (J). (gr. -1-3). 32.79 *(978-1-62402-144-2(1)*, 21555, Calico Chapter Bks) Magic Wagon.

—The Yummy Mistake. Meza, Erika, illus. 2016. (Carlos & Carmen Ser.). (ENG.). 32p. (J). (gr. -1-3). 32.79 *(978-1-62402-145-9(X)*, 21557, Calico Chapter Bks) Magic Wagon.

McIntosh, Will. Watchdog. 2019. (ENG.). 192p. (J). (gr. 5). 8.99 *(978-1-5247-1387-4(2)*, Yearling) Random Hse. Children's Bks.

McKenzie, Precious. A Vacation in Ruins. 2015. (Rourke's World Adventure Chapter Bks.). (ENG.). 96p. (gr. 3-5). 29.93 *(978-1-63430-393-4(8)*, 9781634303934) Rourke Educational Media.

McMann, Lisa. Dragon Bones. (Unwanteds Quests Ser.: 2). (ENG., Illus.). (J). (gr. 3-7). 2019. 432p. pap. 9.99 *(978-1-4814-5685-2(7))* 2018. 416p. 19.99 *(978-1-4814-5684-5(9))* Simon & Schuster Children's Publishing. (Aladdin).

—Dragon Captives. 2017. (Unwanteds Quests Ser.: 1). (ENG., Illus.). 432p. (J). (gr. 3-7). 19.99 *(978-1-4814-5681-4(4)*, Simon & Schuster/Paula Wiseman Bks.) Simon & Schuster/Paula Wiseman Bks.

—Dragon Captives. 2018. (Unwanteds Quests Ser.: 1). lib. bdg. 18.40 *(978-0-606-40846-2(0))* Turtleback.

—Dragon Curse. 2019. (Unwanteds Quests Ser.: 4). (ENG., Illus.). 432p. (J). (gr. 3-7). 18.99 *(978-1-5344-1601-7(3)*, Simon & Schuster/Paula Wiseman Bks.) Simon & Schuster/Paula Wiseman Bks.

—Dragon Ghosts. 2019. (Unwanteds Quests Ser.: 3). (ENG., Illus.). 528p. (J). (gr. 3-7). 19.99 *(978-1-5344-1598-0(X)*, Aladdin) Simon & Schuster Children's Publishing.

—Island of Dragons. (Unwanteds Ser.: 7). (ENG., Illus.). 544p. (J). (gr. 3-7). 2017. pap. 9.99 *(978-1-4424-9338-4(0))* 2016. 19.99 *(978-1-4424-9337-7(2))* Simon & Schuster Children's Publishing. (Aladdin).

—Island of Fire. (Unwanteds Ser.: 3). (ENG., Illus.). (J). (gr. 3-7). 2014. 480p. pap. 9.99 *(978-1-4424-5846-8(1))* 2013. 464p. 19.99 *(978-1-4424-5845-1(3))* Simon & Schuster Children's Publishing. (Aladdin).

—Island of Fire. 2014. (Unwanteds Ser.: 3). lib. bdg. 19.65 *(978-0-606-35796-8(3))* Turtleback.

—Island of Graves. (Unwanteds Ser.: 6). (ENG., Illus.). (J). (gr. 3-7). 2016. 560p. pap. 9.99 *(978-1-4424-9335-3(6))* 2015. 528p. 21.99 *(978-1-4424-9334-6(8))* Simon & Schuster Children's Publishing. (Aladdin).

—Island of Graves. 2016. (Unwanteds Ser.: 6). lib. bdg. 19.65 *(978-0-606-38497-1(9))* Turtleback.

—Island of Shipwrecks. 2015. (Unwanteds Ser.: 5). (ENG., Illus.). 480p. (J). (gr. 3-7). pap. 9.99 *(978-1-4424-9332-2(1)*, Aladdin) Simon & Schuster Children's Publishing.

—Island of Silence. (Unwanteds Ser.: 2). (ENG., (J). (gr. 3-7). 2013. Illus.). 432p. pap. 8.99 *(978-1-4424-0772-5(7))* 2012. 416p. 19.99 *(978-1-4424-0771-8(9))* Simon & Schuster Children's Publishing. (Aladdin).

—Island of Silence. 2013. (Unwanteds Ser.: 2). lib. bdg. 18.40 *(978-0-606-32044-3(X))* Turtleback.

—The Unwanteds. 2011. (Unwanteds Ser.: Bk. 1). (J). 1.25 *(978-1-4640-2489-4(8))* Recorded Bks., Inc.

—The Unwanteds. (Unwanteds Ser.: 1). (ENG., Illus.). (J). (gr. 3-7). 2012. 416p. pap. 8.99 *(978-1-4424-0769-5(7))* 2011. 400p. 19.99 *(978-1-4424-0768-8(9))* Simon & Schuster Children's Publishing. (Aladdin).

—The Unwanteds. 2012. (Unwanteds Ser.: 1). lib. bdg. 18.40 *(978-0-606-26953-7(3))* Turtleback.

McManus, Karen M. Two Can Keep a Secret. 2019. (ENG.). 352p. lib. bdg. 21.80 *(978-1-6636-2970-8(6))* Perfection Learning Corp.

—Two Can Keep a Secret. (ENG.). 352p. (YA). (gr. 9). 2021. pap. 12.99 *(978-1-5247-1471-0(2)*, Ember) 2019. 19.99 *(978-1-5247-1472-7(0)*, Delacorte Pr.) Random Hse. Children's Bks.

McNicoll, Sylvia. Dying to Go Viral, 1 vol. 2013. (ENG.). 255p. (YA). (gr. 6-10). pap. 12.95 *(978-1-55455-271-9(0)*, 9d8b3716-4fd7-4704-8b1d-7989b70be74b) Trifolium Bks., Inc. CAN. Dist: Firefly Bks., Ltd.

Meadows, Daisy. Lila & Myla, the Twins Fairies. 2015. (Rainbow Magic — Special Edition Ser.). lib. bdg. 17.20 *(978-0-606-36341-9(6))* Turtleback.

—Violet the Painting Fairy. 2015. (Illus.). 65p. (J). *(978-0-545-72413-5(9))* Scholastic, Inc.

Meehl, Brian. Blowback '07: When the Only Way Forward Is Back. 2016. (Illus.). 346p. (J). pap. 12.95 *(978-1-63505-185-8(1))* Salem Author Services.

Mellon, David. Silent. 2017. (ENG.). 320p. (YA). (gr. 9-12). 17.99 *(978-1-5072-0168-8(0)*, Simon Pulse) Simon Pulse.

Menon, Sandhya. From Twinkle, with Love. 2018. (ENG., Illus.). 336p. (YA). (gr. 7). 18.99 *(978-1-4814-9540-0(2)*, Simon Pulse) Simon Pulse.

Mercer, Sienna. My Sister the Vampire #2: Fangtastic! 2007. (My Sister the Vampire Ser.: 2). (ENG.). 208p. (J). (gr. 3-7). per. 6.99 *(978-0-06-087115-4(6)*, HarperCollins) HarperCollins Pubs.

Messer, Celeste M. The Ghost of Piper's Landing. Hoeffner, Deb, illus. 2004. 82-92p. 4.95 *(978-0-9702171-7-2(X))* AshleyAlan Enterprises.

Meyer, C. The Very First Unicorn. 2013. 24p. pap. 24.95 *(978-1-63004-317-9(6))* America Star Bks.

Michaels, Rune. Fix Me. 2011. (ENG., Illus.). 160p. (YA). (gr. 9). 16.99 *(978-1-4169-5772-0(3)*, Atheneum Bks. for Young Readers) Simon & Schuster Children's Publishing.

Miller, Gary & Miller, Lynda. The Adventures of Bob & Betty. 2006. (J). spiral bd. *(978-1-933594-92-7(6))* FBC Pubns. & Printing.

Miller, Stefne & Madison, Bailee. Losing Brave, 1 vol. 2018. (ENG.). 352p. (YA). 17.99 *(978-0-310-76054-2(2))* Blink.

Millner, Denene & Miller, Mitzi. If Only You Knew, Bk. 2. 2008. (Hotlanta Ser.: 2). (ENG.). 254p. (J). (gr. 7-18). 24.94 *(978-0-545-00309-4(1))* Scholastic, Inc.

Mishica, C. Twins. 2007. (gr. k-3). pap. 5.50 *(978-0-8454-1692-1(8)*, Seedling Pubns.) Continental Pr., Inc.

T U V

Monson, Marianne. The Enchanted Tunnel Vol. 3: Journey to Jerusalem. Burr, Dan, illus. 2011. 85p. (YA). (gr. 3-6). pap. 7.99 *(978-1-60908-068-6(8))* Deseret Bk. Co.
—The Enchanted Tunnel Vol. 4: Wandering in the Wilderness. Burr, Dan, illus. 2011. 85p. (YA). (gr. 3-6). pap. 7.99 *(978-1-60908-069-3(6))* Deseret Bk. Co.
—Pioneer Puzzle. 2010. (Illus.). 84p. (J). *(978-1-60641-669-3(3))* Deseret Bk. Co.
Moore, Mykela. Meet the Super Sisters. Garrett, Myers, illus. 2013. (J). 9.99 *(978-0-9852746-9-6(7))* Hope of Vision Publishing.
Moore, Tessa. Dad & the Mad Cow Roundabout. 2007. (ENG.). 64p. (J). pap. *(978-1-901737-54-7(3),* Anvil Bks.) Mercier Pr., Ltd., The.
Morah, Chizoba. The Anderson Twins. 2007. 76p. per. 19.95 *(978-1-60441-015-0(9))* America Star Bks.
Morgan, C. M. Silver Doorway #1: A Gnome Away from Home. 2003. 104p. (J). pap. 6.99 *(978-0-9702189-2-6(3))* Sabledrake Enterprises.
—Silver Doorway #6: The Alchemist's Girl. 2008. 108p. pap. 6.99 *(978-0-9771005-2-1(9))* Sabledrake Enterprises.
Morgan, Melissa J. A Fair to Remember #13. 2007. (Camp Confidential Ser.: 13). 160p. (J). (gr. 3-7). pap. 4.99 *(978-0-448-44451-2(8),* Grosset & Dunlap) Penguin Young Readers Group.
Morris, Chad. Cragbridge Hall, Book 2: The Avatar Battle. 2014. (Cragbridge Hall Ser.: 2). (ENG., Illus.). 360p. (J). (gr. 3-9). 17.99 *(978-1-60907-809-6(8),* Shadow Mountain) Shadow Mountain Publishing.
—Cragbridge Hall, Book 3: The Impossible Race. 2015. (Cragbridge Hall Ser.: 3). (ENG., Illus.). 432p. (J). (gr. 3-9). 18.99 *(978-1-60907-979-6(5),* 5127575, Shadow Mountain) Shadow Mountain Publishing.
Morris, David. My Twins First Christmas. 2008. (Illus.). 24p. (J). pap. 14.95 *(978-0-9799885-0-9(0))* New Year Publishing.
Morris, Paris. My Twins First Halloween. 2008. (J). pap. 12.95 *(978-0-9760095-9-7(5))* New Year Publishing.
Morris, Paris & Florzak, Douglas. My Twins Are Coming Home. 2010. (ENG., Illus.). 24p. (J). pap. 12.95 *(978-0-9760095-5-9(2))* New Year Publishing.
—My Twins First Birthday. 2010. (ENG., Illus.). 24p. (J). pap. 12.95 *(978-0-9760095-8-0(7))* New Year Publishing.
Morris, Paris & Singer, Thom. I'm Having Twins, 1 vol. 2010. (ENG., Illus.). 24p. (J). pap. 12.95 *(978-0-9760095-4-2(4))* New Year Publishing.
Moses, Shelia P. The Baptism. 2008. (ENG., Illus.). 144p. (J). (gr. 5-9). pap. 7.99 *(978-1-4169-5833-8(9),* McElderry, Margaret K. Bks.) McElderry, Margaret K. Bks.
Moss, Christopher Hawthorne. Beloved Pilgrim. 2nd ed. (ENG., 2016. Illus.). (J). 29.99 *(978-1-63477-939-5(8))* 2014. 304p. (YA). pap. 17.99 *(978-1-62798-538-3(7))* Dreamspinner Pr. (Harmony Ink Pr.).
Mowry, Tia & Mowry, Tamera. Twintuition: Double Cross. 2018. (Twintuition Ser.: 4). (ENG.). 208p. (J). (gr. 3-7). 16.99 *(978-0-06-237295-6(5),* HarperCollins) HarperCollins Pubs.
—Twintuition: Double Dare. (Twintuition Ser.: 3). (ENG.). (J). (gr. 3-7). 2018. 224p. pap. 6.99 *(978-0-06-237293-2(9))* 2017. 208p. 16.99 *(978-0-06-237292-5(0))* HarperCollins Pubs. (HarperCollins).
—Twintuition: Double Vision. 2015. (Twintuition Ser.: 1). (ENG.). 208p. (J). (gr. 3-7). 16.99 *(978-0-06-237286-4(6),* HarperCollins) HarperCollins Pubs.
Mudrovich, Jane. Exorcising the Google. 2012. 154p. pap. 14.97 *(978-1-61897-939-1(6),* Strategic Bk. Publishing) Strategic Book Publishing & Rights Agency (SBPRA).
Muir, Suzanne. The Magic Tile. 2007. (Illus.). 48p. (J). lib. bdg. 15.00 *(978-1-4242-1619-2(2))* Dingles & Co.
Murray, Tamsyn. Instructions for a Secondhand Heart. 2017. (ENG.). 320p. (YA). (gr. 9-17). 17.99 *(978-0-316-47178-7(X),* Poppy) Little, Brown Bks. for Young Readers.
My Day! 2005. (J). bds. *(978-0-9769910-0-7(4))* Terrific Twins LLC.
The Mystery of the Lion's Tail. 2014. (Greetings from Somewhere Ser.: 5). (ENG., Illus.). 128p. (J). (gr. -1-4). pap. 6.99 *(978-1-4814-1464-7(X),* Little Simon) Little Simon.
National Children's Book and Literacy Alliance Staff, contrib. by. The Exquisite Corpse Adventure. 2011. (ENG., Illus.). 288p. (J). (gr. 4-6). 22.44 *(978-0-7636-5149-7(4))* Candlewick Pr.
Natl Children's Book & Literacy Alliance. The Exquisite Corpse Adventure. 2011. (ENG., Illus.). 288p. (J). (gr. 4-7). pap. 9.99 *(978-0-7636-5773-4(5))* Candlewick Pr.
Neasi, Barbara J. Just Like Me. Hantel, Johanna, illus. 2011. (Rookie Ready to Learn — All about Me! Ser.). 40p. (J). (gr. -1-k). lib. bdg. 25.00 *(978-0-531-26371-6(1),* Children's Pr.) Scholastic Library Publishing.
—Just Like Me (Rookie Ready to Learn - All about Me!) Hantel, Johanna, illus. 2011. (Rookie Ready to Learn Ser.). (ENG.). 40p. (J). (gr. -1-k). pap. 5.95 *(978-0-531-26676-2(1),* Children's Pr.) Scholastic Library Publishing.
Nelson, Jandy. I'll Give You the Sun. 2015. (CHI.). 384p. (YA). (gr. 9). pap. *(978-986-359-180-1(7))* Ecus Publishing Hse.
—I'll Give You the Sun. (ENG.). (YA). (gr. 9-12). 2015. 400p. pap. 11.99 *(978-0-14-242576-3(1),* Speak) 2014. 384p. 18.99 *(978-0-8037-3496-8(4),* Dial Bks) Penguin Young Readers Group.
—I'll Give You the Sun. 2015. (ENG.). 400p. (YA). (gr. 9). 21.30 *(978-1-68065-512-4(4))* Perfection Learning Corp.
—I'll Give You the Sun. 2015. lib. bdg. 22.10 *(978-0-606-37572-6(4))* Turtleback.
Night, P. J. Together Forever. 2012. (You're Invited to a Creepover Ser.: 8). (ENG.). 160p. (J). (gr. 3-7). pap. 6.99 *(978-1-4424-5159-9(9),* Simon Spotlight) Simon Spotlight.
—Together Forever. 2012. (Creepover Ser.: 8). lib. bdg. 16.00 *(978-0-606-26339-9(X))* Turtleback.
Nolen, Jerdine. Block Party Surprise. Henninger, Michelle, illus. 2015. 41p. (J). *(978-1-4806-8574-1(7))* Harcourt.
—Bradford Street Buddies: Block Party Surprise. Henninger, Michelle, illus. 2015. (ENG.). 48p. (J). (gr. 1-4). pap. 4.99 *(978-0-544-35863-8(5),* 1587297, Clarion Bks.) HarperCollins Pubs.
Noonan, Rosalind, et al. The Love Factor. 2003. (ENG., Illus.). 128p. *(978-0-00-714454-9(7),* HarperCollins Children's Bks.) HarperCollins Pubs. Ltd.
Noyes, Deborah. Plague in the Mirror. 2013. (ENG.). 272p. (YA). (gr. 9). 16.99 *(978-0-7636-5980-6(0))* Candlewick Pr.
Nuri, Alya & Nuri, Alya. Amr's Adventure in Europe. 2013. 68p. pap. *(978-1-935948-29-2(6))* Roxby Media Ltd.
Odentz, Howard. Dead. 2013. 272p. pap. 14.95 *(978-1-61194-299-6(3),* Bell Bridge Bks.) BelleBks., Inc.
—Wicked Dead. 2016. (ENG., Illus.). (YA). pap. 15.95 *(978-1-61194-712-0(X))* BelleBks., Inc.
Ogden, Charles. Frost Bites. Carton, Rick, illus. 2008. (Edgar & Ellen Nodyssey Ser.: 2). (ENG.). 192p. (J). (gr. 3-7). 23.99 *(978-1-4169-5464-4(3),* Simon & Schuster/Paula Wiseman Bks.) Simon & Schuster/Paula Wiseman Bks.
—High Wire. Carton, Rick, illus. 2006. (Edgar & Ellen Ser.: 5). (ENG.). 208p. (J). (gr. 3-7). 24.99 *(978-1-4169-1500-3(1),* Simon & Schuster/Paula Wiseman Bks.) Simon & Schuster/Paula Wiseman Bks.
—Hot Air. Carton, Rick, illus. 2008. (Edgar & Ellen Nodyssey Ser.: 1). (ENG.). 192p. (J). (gr. 3-7). 9.99 *(978-1-4169-5465-1(1),* Aladdin) Simon & Schuster Children's Publishing.
—Nod's Limbs. Carton, Rick, illus. 2007. (Edgar & Ellen Ser.: 6). (ENG.). 224p. (J). (gr. 3-7). 24.99 *(978-1-4169-1501-0(X),* Simon & Schuster/Paula Wiseman Bks.) Simon & Schuster/Paula Wiseman Bks.
—Pet's Revenge. Carton, Rick, illus. 2006. (Edgar & Ellen Ser.: 4). (ENG.). 192p. (J). (gr. 3-7). 23.99 *(978-1-4169-1408-2(0),* Simon & Schuster/Paula Wiseman Bks.) Simon & Schuster/Paula Wiseman Bks.
O'Hair, Margaret. Twin to Twin. Courtin, Thierry, illus. 2003. (ENG.). 32p. (J). (gr. -1-3). 17.99 *(978-0-689-84494-2(8),* McElderry, Margaret K. Bks.) McElderry, Margaret K. Bks.
Oldfield, Jenny. Skye - The Champion, Bk. 13. (ENG., Illus.). 122p. (J). pap. 7.99 *(978-0-340-69985-0(X))* Hodder & Stoughton GBR. Dist: Trafalgar Square Publishing.
—Sorrel the Substitute, Bk. 12. (ENG., Illus.). 120p. (J). pap. 7.99 *(978-0-340-69984-3(1))* Hodder & Stoughton GBR. Dist: Trafalgar Square Publishing.
—Stanley the Troublemaker. (ENG., Illus.). 120p. (J). pap. 8.99 *(978-0-340-72675-4(X))* Hodder & Stoughton GBR. Dist: Trafalgar Square Publishing.
—Stevie the Rebel. (Home Farm Twins Ser.: Vol. 9). (ENG., Illus.). 128p. (J). pap. 7.99 *(978-0-340-68992-9(7))* Hodder & Stoughton GBR. Dist: Trafalgar Square Publishing.
—Sultan the Patient, Vol. 2. (ENG., Illus.). 119p. (J). pap. 7.99 *(978-0-340-69983-6(3))* Hodder & Stoughton GBR. Dist: Trafalgar Square Publishing.
—Sunny the Hero. (Home Farm Twins Ser.: No. 7). (ENG., Illus.). 120p. (J). pap. 7.99 *(978-0-340-68990-5(0))* Hodder & Stoughton GBR. Dist: Trafalgar Square Publishing.
Oliver, Lin. Attack of the Growling Eyeballs. Gilpin, Stephen, illus. 2009. (Who Shrunk Daniel Funk? Ser.: 1). (ENG.). 160p. (J). (gr. 3-7). pap. 7.99 *(978-1-4169-0958-3(3),* Simon & Schuster Bks. For Young Readers) Simon & Schuster Bks. For Young Readers.
—Double-Crossed #3. 2013. (Almost Identical Ser.: 3). 224p. (J). (gr. 3-7). pap. 7.99 *(978-0-448-45193-0(X),* Grosset & Dunlap) Penguin Young Readers Group.
—Double-Crossed #3 (HC), 3. 2013. (Almost Identical Ser.). (ENG.). 224p. (J). (gr. 4-6). 22.44 *(978-0-448-46161-8(7))* Penguin Young Readers Group.
—Escape of the Mini-Mummy. Gilpin, Stephen, illus. 2009. (Who Shrunk Daniel Funk? Ser.: 2). (ENG.). 160p. (J). (gr. 3-7). pap. 8.99 *(978-1-4169-0960-6(5),* Simon & Schuster Bks. For Young Readers) Simon & Schuster Bks. For Young Readers.
—Revenge of the Itty-Bitty Brothers. Gilpin, Stephen, illus. 2010. (Who Shrunk Daniel Funk? Ser.: 3). (ENG.). 176p. (J). (gr. 3-7). pap. 6.99 *(978-1-4169-0962-0(1),* Simon & Schuster Bks. For Young Readers) Simon & Schuster Bks. For Young Readers.
—Revenge of the Itty-Bitty Brothers, 3. Gilpin, Stephen, illus. 2009. (Who Shrunk Daniel Funk? Ser.: 3). (ENG.). 112p. (J). (gr. 2-4). 21.19 *(978-1-4169-0961-3(3))* Simon & Schuster, Inc.
—Secret of the Super-Small Superstar. Gilpin, Stephen, illus. 2010. (Who Shrunk Daniel Funk? Ser.: 4). (ENG.). 160p. (J). (gr. 3-7). 14.99 *(978-1-4169-0963-7(X),* Simon & Schuster Bks. For Young Readers) Simon & Schuster Bks. For Young Readers.
Olsen, Mary-Kate & Olsen, Ashley. Beach Collection, 3 vols. 2004. (ENG., Illus.). 320p. pap., pap., pap. *(978-0-00-718443-9(3))* HarperCollins Pubs. Australia.
—The Cool Club. 2003. (ENG., Illus.). 112p. *(978-0-00-714469-3(5),* HarperCollins Children's Bks.) HarperCollins Pubs. Ltd.
—Dare to Scare. 2005. (ENG., Illus.). 112p. *(978-0-00-715887-4(4))* HarperCollins Pubs. Australia.
—Dating Game, 2 vols. 2003. (ENG., Illus.). 128p. *(978-0-00-714447-1(4),* HarperCollins Children's Bks.) HarperCollins Pubs. Ltd.
—The Facts about Flirting. 2005. (ENG., Illus.). 112p. *(978-0-00-715883-6(1),* HarperCollins Children's Bks.) HarperCollins Pubs. Ltd.
—A Girl's Guide to Guys. 2003. (ENG., Illus.). 128p. *(978-0-00-714455-6(5),* HarperCollins Children's Bks.) HarperCollins Pubs. Ltd.
—Let's Party, 3 vols. 2003. (ENG., Illus.). 112p. *(978-0-00-714473-0(3))* HarperCollins Pubs. Australia.
—Love-Set-Match. 2005. (ENG., Illus.). 112p. *(978-0-00-715885-0(8))* HarperCollins Pubs. Australia.
—P. S Wish You Were Here. 2003. (ENG., Illus.). 112p. *(978-0-00-714470-9(9),* HarperCollins Children's Bks.) HarperCollins Pubs. Ltd.
—Santa Girls, 3 vols. 2005. (ENG., Illus.). 112p. *(978-0-00-715888-1(2))* HarperCollins Pubs. Australia.
—Surf, Sand & Secrets. 2004. (ENG., Illus.). 112p. *(978-0-00-714459-4(8),* HarperCollins Children's Bks.) HarperCollins Pubs. Ltd.
—Tell Me about It. 2003. (ENG., Illus.). 128p. *(978-0-00-714451-8(2),* HarperCollins Children's Bks.) HarperCollins Pubs. Ltd.
—Winner Take All. 2003. (ENG., Illus.). 112p. *(978-0-00-714471-6(7),* HarperCollins Children's Bks.) HarperCollins Pubs. Ltd.
Oppel, Kenneth. Such Wicked Intent: The Apprenticeship of Victor Frankenstein, Book Two. (ENG., 320p. (YA). (gr. 7). 2012. Illus.). 16.99 *(978-1-4424-0318-5(7))*Bk. 2. 2013. pap. 12.99 *(978-1-4424-0319-2(5))* Simon & Schuster Bks. For Young Readers. (Simon & Schuster Bks. For Young Readers).
—This Dark Endeavor: The Apprenticeship of Victor Frankenstein. 2011. (Apprenticeship of Victor Frankenstein Ser.: Bk. 1). (ENG.). (YA). (gr. 7-12). 64.99 *(978-1-4558-2316-1(3))* Findaway World, LLC.
—This Dark Endeavor: The Apprenticeship of Victor Frankenstein. (ENG., (YA). (gr. 7). 2012. Illus.). 320p. pap. 12.99 *(978-1-4424-0316-1(0))* 2011. 304p. lib. bdg. 17.99 *(978-1-4424-0315-4(2))* Simon & Schuster Bks. For Young Readers. (Simon & Schuster Bks. For Young Readers).
Ormsbee, K. E. The House in Poplar Wood: (Fantasy Middle Grade Novel, Mystery Book for Middle School Kids) 2018. (ENG., Illus.). 344p. (J). (gr. 3-7). 16.99 *(978-1-4521-4986-8(0))* Chronicle Bks. LLC.
O'Ryan, Ray. Operation Twin Trouble. Kraft, Jason, illus. 2015. (Galaxy Zack Ser.: 12). (ENG.). 128p. (J). (gr. k-4). pap. 5.99 *(978-1-4814-4399-9(2),* Little Simon) Little Simon.
Owens, Bettina. Athena, Never A Bite. 2010. 32p. 18.99 *(978-1-4520-6381-2(8))* AuthorHouse.
Page, Nathan. The Montague Twins: the Witch's Hand: (a Graphic Novel) Shannon, Drew, illus. 2020. (Montague Twins Ser.: 1). 352p. (YA). (gr. 7). pap. 17.99 *(978-0-525-64677-8(9),* Knopf Bks. for Young Readers) Random Hse. Children's Bks.
Pandanas, Ms L. A. The Slinky Luminescence: Two Plus Who? 2013. 84p. pap. *(978-0-9870702-9-6(0))* Reed, Laura.
Papa's Gold. 2013. 196p. pap. 11.97 *(978-0-9851274-4-2(9))* Pen-L Publishing.
Paris, Harper. The Mystery Across the Secret Bridge. Calo, Marcos, Illus. 2015. (Greetings from Somewhere Ser.: 7). (ENG.). 128p. (J). (gr. k-4). pap. 6.99 *(978-1-4814-2367-0(3),* Little Simon) Little Simon.
—The Mystery at the Coral Reef. Calo, Marcos, illus. 2015. (Greetings from Somewhere Ser.: 8). (ENG.). 128p. (J). (gr. k-4). pap. 6.99 *(978-1-4814-2370-0(3),* Little Simon) Little Simon.
—The Mystery in the Forbidden City. Calo, Marcos, illus. 2014. (Greetings from Somewhere Ser.: 4). (ENG.). 128p. (J). (gr. k-4). pap. 6.99 *(978-1-4814-0299-6(4),* Little Simon) Little Simon.
—The Mystery of the Gold Coin. Calo, Marcos, illus. 2014. (Greetings from Somewhere Ser.: 1). (ENG.). 128p. (J). (gr. k-4). pap. 5.99 *(978-1-4424-9718-4(1),* Little Simon) Little Simon.
—The Mystery of the Icy Paw Prints. Calo, Marcos, illus. 2015. (Greetings from Somewhere Ser.: 9). (ENG.). 128p. (J). (gr. k-4). pap. 5.99 *(978-1-4814-2373-1(8),* Little Simon) Little Simon.
—The Mystery of the Mosaic. Calo, Marcos, illus. 2014. (Greetings from Somewhere Ser.: 2). (ENG.). 128p. (J). (gr. k-2). pap. 6.99 *(978-1-4424-9721-4(1),* Little Simon) Little Simon.
—The Mystery of the Mosaic. Calo, Marcos, illus. 2014. (Greetings from Somewhere Ser.: Vol. 2). (ENG.). 115p. (J). (gr. k-2). lib. bdg. 16.80 *(978-1-62765-837-9(8))* Perfection Learning Corp.
—The Mystery of the Secret Society. Calo, Marcos, illus. 2016. (Greetings from Somewhere Ser.: 10). (ENG.). 128p. (J). (gr. k-4). pap. 5.99 *(978-1-4814-5171-0(5),* Little Simon) Little Simon.
—The Mystery of the Stolen Painting. Calo, Marcos, illus. 2014. (Greetings from Somewhere Ser.: 3). (ENG.). 128p. (J). (gr. k-4). pap. 6.99 *(978-1-4814-0296-5(X),* Little Simon) Little Simon.
—The Mystery of the Suspicious Spices. Calo, Marcos, illus. 2014. (Greetings from Somewhere Ser.: 6). (ENG.). 128p. (J). (gr. k-4). pap. 6.99 *(978-1-4814-1467-8(4),* Little Simon) Little Simon.
Pascal, Francine. Amigacho de Pluma del Amy. Orig. Title: Amy's Pen Pal. (SPA.). 144p. (YA). 6.95 *(978-84-272-3596-0(8))* Molino, Editorial ESP. Dist: AIMS International Bks., Inc.
—Centro de Atencion. (Gemelas de Sweet Valley Ser.: No. 18).Tr. of Center of Attention. (SPA.). (J). (gr. 3-7). 6.95 *(978-84-272-3788-9(X))* Molino, Editorial ESP. Dist: AIMS International Bks., Inc.
—Demasiado Perfecta.Tr. of Too Good to be True. (SPA.). 160p. (J). 7.95 *(978-84-272-3881-7(9))* Molino, Editorial ESP. Dist: AIMS International Bks., Inc.
—Esa Clase de Chica.Tr. of Wrong Kind of Girl. (SPA.). 168p. (J). 7.95 *(978-84-272-3880-0(0))* Molino, Editorial ESP. Dist: AIMS International Bks., Inc.
—Estrella del Rock. Orig. Title: Jessica the Rock Star. (SPA.). (J). 6.95 *(978-84-272-3595-3(X))* Molino, Editorial ESP. Dist: AIMS International Bks., Inc.
—Los Gemelos Consiguen Cogidos. Orig. Title: The Twins Get Caught. (SPA.). 136p. (J). 6.95 *(978-84-272-4641-6(2))* Molino, Editorial ESP. Dist: AIMS International Bks., Inc.
—Una Gran Luchadora. (Gemelas de Sweet Valley Ser.: No. 10).Tr. of One of the Gang. (SPA.). 128p. (J). (gr. 3-7). 6.95 *(978-84-272-3780-3(4))* Molino, Editorial ESP. Dist: AIMS International Bks., Inc.
—Una Larga Noche.Tr. of All Night Long. (SPA.). 128p. (J). 7.95 *(978-84-272-3875-6(4))* Molino, Editorial ESP. Dist: AIMS International Bks., Inc.
—Lo Que los Padres Ignoran.Tr. of What Your Parents Don't Know.... (SPA.). 224p. (J). 10.50 *(978-84-272-3163-4(6))* Molino, Editorial ESP. Dist: AIMS International Bks., Inc.
—Mala Idea de Jessica.Tr. of Jessica's Bad Idea. (SPA.). 112p. (J). 6.95 *(978-84-272-3593-9(3))* Molino, Editorial ESP. Dist: AIMS International Bks., Inc.
—Maria Falta. Orig. Title: Mary Is Missing. (SPA.). 128p. (YA). 6.95 *(978-84-272-3597-7(6))* Molino, Editorial ESP. Dist: AIMS International Bks., Inc.
—Peligrosa Tentacion.Tr. of Dangerous Love. (SPA., Illus.). 136p. (J). 7.95 *(978-84-272-3876-3(2))* Molino, Editorial ESP. Dist: AIMS International Bks., Inc.
—Querida Hermana.Tr. of Dear Sister. (SPA., Illus.). 168p. (J). 7.95 *(978-84-272-3877-0(0))* Molino, Editorial ESP. Dist: AIMS International Bks., Inc.
—Trabajo del Equipo. Orig. Title: Team Work. (SPA.). 120p. (J). 6.95 *(978-84-272-3797-1(9))* Molino, Editorial ESP. Dist: AIMS International Bks., Inc.
Pascal, Francine & Suzanne, Jamie. Señorita Jessica. (Sweet Valley Twins Ser.: No. 46). Orig. Title: Mademoiselle Jessica. (SPA.). 160p. (J). (gr. 3-7). 6.95 *(978-84-272-4646-1(3))* Molino, Editorial ESP. Dist: AIMS International Bks., Inc.
Paterson, Katherine. Jacob Have I Loved: A Newbery Award Winner. 2020. (ENG.). 272p. (YA). (gr. 8-8). pap. 7.99 *(978-0-06-440368-9(8),* HarperCollins) HarperCollins Pubs.
Patterson, James. Crazy House. 2019. (Crazy House Ser.: 1). (ENG.). 352p. mass mkt. 8.99 *(978-1-5387-1406-5(X))* Grand Central Publishing.
—Crazy House. 2018. (Crazy House Ser.: 1). (ENG.). 384p. (YA). (gr. 9-17). pap. 9.99 *(978-0-316-51499-6(3),* Jimmy Patterson) Little Brown & Co.
—Treasure Hunters: Quest for the City of Gold. Neufeld, Juliana, illus. 2018. (Treasure Hunters Ser.: 5). (ENG.). 384p. (J). (gr. 3-7). 14.99 *(978-0-316-34955-0(0),* Jimmy Patterson) Little Brown & Co.
Patterson, James & Grabenstein, Chris. Katt vs. Dogg. López, Anuki, illus. (ENG.). (J). (gr. 3-7). 2021. (Katt vs. Dogg Ser.: 1). 336p. pap. 8.99 *(978-0-316-39712-4(1))* 2019. 320p. 13.99 *(978-0-316-41156-1(6))* Little Brown & Co. (Jimmy Patterson).
—Treasure Hunters. Neufeld, Juliana, illus. (Treasure Hunters Ser.: 1). (ENG.). 480p. (J). (gr. 3-7). 2015. pap. 9.99 *(978-0-316-20757-7(8))* 2013. 14.99 *(978-0-316-20756-0(X))* Little Brown & Co. (Jimmy Patterson).
—Treasure Hunters. 2015. (Treasure Hunters Ser.: 1). (J). lib. bdg. 18.45 *(978-0-606-37305-0(5))* Turtleback.
—Treasure Hunters: Danger down the Nile. Neufeld, Juliana, illus. (Treasure Hunters Ser.: 2). (ENG.). 480p. (J). (gr. 3-7). 2018. pap. 8.99 *(978-0-316-51510-8(8))* 2014. 14.99 *(978-0-316-37086-8(X))* Little Brown & Co. (Jimmy Patterson).
—Treasure Hunters: Peril at the Top of the World. Neufeld, Juliana, illus. 2016. (Treasure Hunters Ser.: 4). (ENG.). 384p. (J). (gr. 3-7). 14.99 *(978-0-316-34693-1(4),* Jimmy Patterson) Little Brown & Co.
—Treasure Hunters: Secret of the Forbidden City. Neufeld, Juliana, illus. 2015. (Treasure Hunters Ser.: 3). (ENG.). 448p. (J). (gr. 3-7). 14.99 *(978-0-316-28480-6(7),* Jimmy Patterson) Little Brown & Co.
Patterson, James & Paetro, Maxine. Confessions of a Murder Suspect. (YA). 2013. (Confessions Ser.: 1). (ENG.). 400p. (gr. 7-17). pap. 10.99 *(978-0-316-20700-3(4),* Jimmy Patterson) 2012. (Confessions Ser.: 1). (ENG.). 384p. (gr. 7-17). 19.99 *(978-0-316-20698-3(9),* Jimmy Patterson) 2012. 372p. 11.99 *(978-0-316-22641-7(6))* 2012. (Confessions Ser.: 1). (ENG.). 400p. (gr. 7-17). 36.99 *(978-0-316-22418-5(9),* Jimmy Patterson) Little Brown & Co.
—Confessions of a Murder Suspect. 2013. (Confessions Ser.: 1). lib. bdg. 20.85 *(978-0-606-32278-2(7))* Turtleback.
—Confessions: the Paris Mysteries. 2014. (Confessions Ser.: 3). (ENG.). (YA). (gr. 7-17). 320p. 33.99 *(978-0-316-37084-4(3));* 352p. 35.99 *(978-0-316-40963-6(4))* Little Brown & Co. (Jimmy Patterson).
—The Paris Mysteries. 2015. (Confessions Ser.: 3). (YA). lib. bdg. 20.85 *(978-0-606-37526-9(0))* Turtleback.
Patterson, James, et al. Treasure Hunters. Neufeld, Juliana, illus. 2013. 451p. (J). *(978-0-316-24262-2(4))* Little Brown & Co.
Paull, John W. The Great Stampede: A Jimmy James Story. 2010. 28p. 16.09 *(978-1-4269-4698-1(8))* Trafford Publishing.
Paulson, Ingrid. Why I Loathe Sterling Lane. 2017. (ENG.). 150p. (YA). pap. 9.99 *(978-1-63375-700-4(5),* 9781633757004) Entangled Publishing, LLC.
Payton, Belle. Are You Thinking What I'm Thinking? 2015. (It Takes Two Ser.: 8). (ENG., Illus.). 160p. (J). (gr. 3-7). pap. 6.99 *(978-1-4814-3137-8(4),* Simon Spotlight) Simon Spotlight.
—Even the Score. 2015. (It Takes Two Ser.: 5). (ENG., Illus.). 160p. (J). (gr. 3-7). pap. 6.99 *(978-1-4814-1951-2(X),* Simon Spotlight) Simon Spotlight.
—May the Best Twin Win. 2015. (It Takes Two Ser.: 7). (ENG., Illus.). 160p. (J). (gr. 3-7). pap. 6.99 *(978-1-4814-3134-7(X),* Simon Spotlight) Simon Spotlight.
—'Tis the Off-Season. 2015. (It Takes Two Ser.: 10). (ENG., Illus.). 160p. (J). (gr. 3-7). pap. 6.99 *(978-1-4814-4205-3(8),* Simon Spotlight) Simon Spotlight.
—Two Cool for School. 2014. (It Takes Two Ser.: 2). (ENG., Illus.). 160p. (J). (gr. 3-7). 16.99 *(978-1-4814-0645-1(0),* Simon Spotlight) Simon Spotlight.
—Two Steps Back. 2015. (It Takes Two Ser.: 6). (ENG., Illus.). 160p. (J). (gr. 3-7). 17.99 *(978-1-4814-2519-3(6),* Simon Spotlight) Simon Spotlight.
—A Whole New Ball Game. 2014. (It Takes Two Ser.: 1). (ENG., Illus.). 160p. (J). (gr. 3-7). 16.99 *(978-1-4814-0642-0(6));* pap. 7.99 *(978-1-4814-0641-3(8))* Simon Spotlight. (Simon Spotlight).
Peacock, L. A. Panic in Pompeii. Hale, Nathan, illus. 2011. 92p. (J). pap. *(978-0-545-34062-5(4))* Scholastic, Inc.
—Terror at Troy. Hale, Nathan, illus. 2012. 90p. (J). *(978-0-545-34063-2(2))* Scholastic, Inc.
Pederson, Katie. The Point of No Return. 2006. 304p. pap. 29.95 *(978-1-4137-9945-3(0))* PublishAmerica, Inc.
Peete, Holly Robinson & Peete, Ryan Elizabeth. My Brother Charlie. Evans, Shane, illus. 2010. (ENG.). 40p. (J). (gr. 1-5). 18.99 *(978-0-545-09466-5(6),* Scholastic Pr.) Scholastic, Inc.
Percival, Tom. The Magic Looking Glass. 2017. (Little Legends Ser.: 4). (ENG.). 192p. (J). (gr. 2-5). pap. 8.99 *(978-1-4926-4259-6(2),* Sourcebooks Jabberwocky) Sourcebooks, Inc.
Perkins, Lucy Fitch. The Belgian Twins. 2004. reprint ed. pap. 15.95 *(978-1-4191-5388-4(9));* pap. 1.99 *(978-1-4192-5388-1(3))* Kessinger Publishing, LLC.
—The Dutch Twins. 2004. reprint ed. pap. 1.99 *(978-1-4192-6040-7(5))* Kessinger Publishing, LLC.
—The Eskimo Twins. 2004. reprint ed. pap. 1.99 *(978-1-4192-6126-8(6));* pap. 15.95 *(978-1-4191-6126-1(1))* Kessinger Publishing, LLC.
—The Eskimo Twins (Yesterday's Classics) 2006. (J). per. 9.95 *(978-1-59915-059-8(X))* Yesterday's Classics.
—The Japanese Twins. 2005. 26.95 *(978-1-4218-0369-2(0),* 1st World Library - Literary Society) 1st World Publishing, Inc.
—The Japanese Twins. 2004. reprint ed. pap. 1.99 *(978-1-4192-6781-9(7));* pap. 15.95 *(978-1-4191-6781-2(2))* Kessinger Publishing, LLC.

—The Japanese Twins (Yesterday's Classics) 2006. (J). per. 9.95 *(978-1-59915-058-1(1))* Yesterday's Classics.
—Rhe Japanese Twins. 2005. 96p. pap. 10.95 *(978-1-4218-0469-9(7)*, 1st World Library - Literary Society) 1st World Publishing, Inc.
—The Scotch Twins. 2004. reprint ed. pap. 15.95 *(978-1-4191-8160-3(2))*; pap. 1.99 *(978-1-4192-8160-0(7))* Kessinger Publishing, LLC.
—The Swiss Twins. 2004. reprint ed. pap. 1.99 *(978-1-4192-8467-0(3))*; pap. 15.95 *(978-1-4191-8467-3(9))* Kessinger Publishing, LLC.
Peterson, Will. Triskellion 2: the Burning. 2009. (Triskellion Ser.: 2). (ENG., Illus.). 480p. (J). (gr. 9-8). 16.99 *(978-0-7636-4223-5(1))* Candlewick Pr.
—Triskellion 3: the Gathering. 2010. (Triskellion Ser.: 3). (ENG., Illus.). 384p. (J). (gr. 9-18). 16.99 *(978-0-7636-4847-3(7))* Candlewick Pr.
Petreman, Gwen. Who Laid Those Eggs? 2013. 20p. pap. 11.59 *(978-1-4669-7633-7(0))* Trafford Publishing.
Phillips, Leigh Hope. Birthday Wishes. Fountain, John, illus. 2005. (J). pap. *(978-1-933156-10-1(4))*; per. *(978-1-933156-03-3(1))* GSVQ Publishing. (VisionQuest Kids).
Pollak, Dale. Velocity: From the Front Line to the Bottom Line. 2010. (ENG.). 144p. 29.95 *(978-0-9760095-7-3(9))* New Year Publishing.
Pollock, Tom. This Story Is a Lie. 2019. (ENG.). 336p. (YA). (gr. 9). pap. 10.99 *(978-1-64129-032-6(3)*, Soho Teen) Soho Pr., Inc.
Pont, Beattie. Grandma, Tell Me More: Fishing with Grandpa. 2013. 80p. (gr. 2-4). pap. 19.95 *(978-1-4817-2073-1(2))* AuthorHouse.
Popovic, Lana. Wicked Like a Wildfire. (ENG.). (YA). (gr. 9). 2018. 432p. 10.99 *(978-0-06-243684-9(8))* 2017. 416p. 17.99 *(978-0-06-243683-2(X))* HarperCollins Pubs. (Tegen, Katherine Bks).
Prime, Derek. Sarah & Paul Go Back to School Bk. 1. 2006. (Sarah & Paul Ser.). (ENG., Illus.). 128p. (J). (gr. 2-5). per. 6.99 *(978-1-84550-157-0(8)*, 607ff22b-e8f5-4688-a389-9c7f700cd974) Christian Focus Pubns. GBR. Dist: Baker & Taylor Publisher Services (BTPS).
—Sarah & Paul Go on Holiday Again. 2006. (Sarah & Paul Ser.). (ENG., Illus.). 128p. (J). per. 6.99 *(978-1-84550-162-4(4)*, 95f5f241-ee1b-4c61-ac27-024da165813d) Christian Focus Pubns. GBR. Dist: Baker & Taylor Publisher Services (BTPS).
—Sarah & Paul Go to the Museum. 2006. (Sarah & Paul Ser.). (ENG., Illus.). 128p. (J). (gr. 2-5). per. 6.99 *(978-1-84550-161-7(6)*, 2998b457-4155-49a3-83f2-dd09f61c5ae7) Christian Focus Pubns. GBR. Dist: Baker & Taylor Publisher Services (BTPS).
—Sarah & Paul Go to the Seaside. 2006. (Sarah & Paul Ser.). (ENG., Illus.). 128p. (J). (gr. 2-5). per. 6.99 *(978-1-84550-159-4(4)*, a2b05462-add2-45ac-a5a9-d8af42a15091) Christian Focus Pubns. GBR. Dist: Baker & Taylor Publisher Services (BTPS).
—Sarah & Paul Have a Visitor. 2006. (Sarah & Paul Ser.). (ENG., Illus.). 128p. (J). (gr. 2-5). per. 6.99 *(978-1-84550-158-7(6)*, 1ad56387-6385-442a-b604-98ae55b8f5f4) Christian Focus Pubns. GBR. Dist: Baker & Taylor Publisher Services (BTPS).
—Sarah & Paul Make a Scrapbook. 2006. (Sarah & Paul Ser.). (ENG., Illus.). 128p. (J). (gr. 2-5). per. 6.99 *(978-1-84550-160-0(8)*, 0bc9cf8e-fad2-467a-ae59-256edcd69a52) Christian Focus Pubns. GBR. Dist: Baker & Taylor Publisher Services (BTPS).
Promise 2012. 218p. pap. *(978-1-78176-337-7(2))* FeedARead.com.
Pyles, Mary Kay. Rise & Shine Rosie. 2013. 134p. pap. 11.95 *(978-0-9887836-9-0(X))* Taylor and Seale Publishing.
Pyros, Andrea. Pink Hair & Other Terrible Ideas. 2019. (ENG.). 256p. (J). (gr. 4-7). lib. bdg. 15.95 *(978-1-68446-028-1(X)*, 139700, Capstone Editions) Capstone.
Radford, Heather. The Asquinn Twins: Frontier Life. Oakley, Darlene, ed. 2012. 104p. *(978-1-77097-693-1(0))*; pap. *(978-1-77097-694-8(9))* FriesenPress.
Raines, Jennifer. Alex & Andrew Swap Places. 2008. 32p. per. 24.95 *(978-1-4241-8938-0(1))* America Star Bks.
Ramos, Ramona J. A Summer with Kaitlyn & Lexi. 2011. 48p. pap. 16.95 *(978-1-4626-1890-3(1))* America Star Bks.
Random House. Meet Shimmer & Shine! (Shimmer & Shine) Cardona, Jose Maria, illus. 2016. (Step into Reading Ser.). (ENG.). 24p. (J). (gr. -1-1). 4.99 *(978-0-553-52203-7(5)*, Random Hse. Bks. for Young Readers) Random Hse. Children's Bks.
Rex, Adam. Cold Cereal, 1. 2013. (Cold Cereal Saga Ser.: 1). (ENG.). 448p. (J). (gr. 3-7). pap. 7.99 *(978-0-06-206003-7(1)*, Balzer & Bray) HarperCollins Pubs.
Reynolds, Paul A. Sydney & Simon: Full Steam Ahead! Reynolds, Peter H., illus. 2014. (Sydney & Simon Ser.: 1). (ENG.). 48p. (J). (gr. 1-4). 12.95 *(978-1-58089-675-7(8))* Charlesbridge Publishing, Inc.
—Sydney & Simon: Go Green! Reynolds, Peter H., illus. 2015. (Sydney & Simon Ser.: 2). 48p. (J). (gr. 1-4). lib. bdg. 12.95 *(978-1-58089-677-1(4))* Charlesbridge Publishing, Inc.
—Sydney & Simon: to the Moon! Reynolds, Peter H., illus. 2017. (Sydney & Simon Ser.: 3). 48p. (J). (gr. 1-4). lib. bdg. 12.99 *(978-1-58089-679-5(0))* Charlesbridge Publishing, Inc.
Richards, Stephen J. The Twins First Snow. 2010. 28p. pap. 13.99 *(978-1-4490-8853-8(8))* AuthorHouse.
Rivers, Karen. Finding Ruby Starling. 2014. (ENG.). 304p. (J). (gr. 5-9). 17.99 *(978-0-545-53479-6(8)*, Levine, Arthur A. Bks.) Scholastic, Inc.
Roberts, Stacey. Reggie He Came from Zarzieville. 2006. (ENG.). 74p. pap. 25.99 *(978-1-4257-1120-7(0))* Xlibris Corp.
Roberts, Willo Davis. The One Left Behind. 2007. (ENG., Illus.). 144p. (J). (gr. 3-7). pap. 8.99 *(978-0-689-85083-7(2)*, Aladdin) Simon & Schuster Children's Publishing.
Robinson, Keith. Valley of Monsters. 2013. 212p. pap. *(978-0-9843906-6-3(9))* Roxby Media Ltd.
Rodkey, Geoff. The Tapper Twins Go to War (with Each Other) 2016. (Tapper Twins Ser.: 1). (ENG., Illus.). 240p. (J). (gr. 3-7). pap. 7.99 *(978-0-316-31597-5(4))* Little, Brown Bks. for Young Readers.
—The Tapper Twins Go Viral. (Tapper Twins Ser.: 4). (ENG., Illus.). 256p. (J). (gr. 3-7). 2018. pap. 7.99 *(978-0-316-47893-9(8))* 2017. 13.99 *(978-0-316-29784-4(4))* Little, Brown Bks. for Young Readers.
—The Tapper Twins Go Viral. 2018. (Tapper Twins Ser.: 4). (J). lib. bdg. 17.20 *(978-0-606-40992-6(0))* Turtleback.
—The Tapper Twins Run for President. 2016. (Tapper Twins Ser.: 3). (ENG., Illus.). 304p. (J). (gr. 3-7). 13.99 *(978-0-316-29785-1(2))* Little, Brown Bks. for Young Readers.
—The Tapper Twins Tear up New York. 2016. (Tapper Twins Ser.: 2). (ENG., Illus.). 288p. (J). (gr. 3-7). pap. 8.99 *(978-0-316-31601-9(6))* Little, Brown Bks. for Young Readers.
Rogers, Blessing. Gabby & Ralph Meet Their New Teacher. 2010. 24p. 11.49 *(978-1-4520-5447-6(9))* AuthorHouse.
Roland, Timothy. Monkey Me & the New Neighbor. 2014. (Monkey Me Ser.: 3). lib. bdg. 14.75 *(978-0-606-35360-1(7))* Turtleback.
—Monkey Me & the New Neighbor: a Branches Book (Monkey Me #3) Roland, Timothy, illus. 2014. (Monkey Me Ser.: 3). (ENG., Illus.). 96p. (J). (gr. 1-3). pap. 4.99 *(978-0-545-55984-3(7))* Scholastic, Inc.
—Monkey Me & the Pet Show. 2014. (Monkey Me Ser.: 2). lib. bdg. 14.75 *(978-0-606-35359-5(3))* Turtleback.
—Monkey Me & the Pet Show: a Branches Book (Monkey Me #2) Roland, Timothy, illus. 2014. (Monkey Me Ser.: 2). (ENG., Illus.). 96p. (J). (gr. 1-3). pap. 4.99 *(978-0-545-55980-5(4))* Scholastic, Inc.
—Monkey Me & the School Ghost. Roland, Timothy, illus. 2014. (Monkey Me Ser.: 4). (ENG., Illus.). 96p. (J). (gr. 1-3). pap. 4.99 *(978-0-545-55989-8(8))* Scholastic, Inc.
—Monkey Me & the School Ghost. 2014. (Monkey Me Ser.: 4). lib. bdg. 14.75 *(978-0-606-36053-1(0))* Turtleback.
Rose, Valerie. The Family Reunion Is Not A Real Vacation. 2003. 28p. (J). 9.95 *(978-0-9703489-2-0(4)*, Little Petals) Roses Are READ Productions.
Rosenberg, Michael. The Little Lost Tune: More Adventures from Bendalot. 2010. 30p. pap. 13.00 *(978-1-60911-881-5(2)*, Eloquent Bks.) Strategic Book Publishing & Rights Agency (SBPRA).
—The Story of Bendalot Part: The Return Home. 2009. (Illus.). 36p. pap. 15.49 *(978-1-4389-8294-6(1))* AuthorHouse.
Rowe, Jeffrey. Gravity Falls: Dipper & Mabel & the Curse of the Time Pirates' Treasure! A Select Your Own Choose-Venture! 2016. (ENG., Illus.). 288p. (J). (gr. 3-7). 12.99 *(978-1-4847-4668-4(6)*, Disney Press Books) Disney Publishing Worldwide.
Roy, Arundhati. Le Dieu des Petits Riens. pap. 19.95 *(978-2-07-041172-6(9))* Gallimard, Editions FRA. Dist: Distribooks, Inc.
Roy, Ron. April Adventure. 2010. (Calendar Mysteries Ser.: 4). lib. bdg. 14.75 *(978-0-606-12465-2(9))* Turtleback.
—August Acrobat. 2012. (Calendar Mysteries Ser.: 8). lib. bdg. 14.75 *(978-0-606-26403-7(5))* Turtleback.
—Calendar Mysteries #1: January Joker. Gurney, John Steven, illus. 2009. (Calendar Mysteries Ser.: 1). 96p. (J). (gr. 1-4). 6.99 *(978-0-375-85661-7(7)*, Random Hse. Bks. for Young Readers) Random Hse. Children's Bks.
—Calendar Mysteries #10: October Ogre. Gurney, John Steven, illus. 2013. (Calendar Mysteries Ser.: 10). 80p. (J). (gr. 1-4). 7.99 *(978-0-375-86888-7(7)*, Random Hse. Bks. for Young Readers) Random Hse. Children's Bks.
—Calendar Mysteries #11: November Night. Gurney, John Steven, illus. 2014. (Calendar Mysteries Ser.: 11). 80p. (J). (gr. 1-4). 7.99 *(978-0-385-37165-0(9)*, Random Hse. Bks. for Young Readers) Random Hse. Children's Bks.
—Calendar Mysteries #2: February Friend. Gurney, John Steven, illus. 2009. (Calendar Mysteries Ser.: 2). 80p. (J). (gr. 1-4). 6.99 *(978-0-375-85662-4(5)*, Random Hse. Bks. for Young Readers) Random Hse. Children's Bks.
—Calendar Mysteries #3: March Mischief. Gurney, John Steven, illus. 2010. (Calendar Mysteries Ser.: 3). 80p. (J). (gr. 1-4). 6.99 *(978-0-375-85663-1(3)*, Random Hse. Bks. for Young Readers) Random Hse. Children's Bks.
—Calendar Mysteries #4: April Adventure. Gurney, John Steven, illus. 2010. (Calendar Mysteries Ser.: 4). 80p. (J). (gr. 1-4). 6.99 *(978-0-375-86116-1(5)*, Random Hse. Bks. for Young Readers) Random Hse. Children's Bks.
—Calendar Mysteries #5: May Magic. Gurney, John Steven, illus. 2011. (Calendar Mysteries Ser.: 5). 80p. (J). (gr. 1-4). 6.99 *(978-0-375-86111-6(4)*, Random Hse. Bks. for Young Readers) Random Hse. Children's Bks.
—Calendar Mysteries #6: June Jam. Gurney, John Steven, illus. 2011. (Calendar Mysteries Ser.: 6). 80p. (J). (gr. 1-4). 6.99 *(978-0-375-86112-3(2)*, Random Hse. Bks. for Young Readers) Random Hse. Children's Bks.
—Calendar Mysteries #7: July Jitters. Gurney, John Steven, illus. 2012. (Calendar Mysteries Ser.: 7). 80p. (J). (gr. 1-4). 7.99 *(978-0-375-86882-5(8)*, Random Hse. Bks. for Young Readers) Random Hse. Children's Bks.
—Calendar Mysteries #8: August Acrobat. Gurney, John Steven, illus. 2012. (Calendar Mysteries Ser.: 8). 80p. (J). (gr. 1-4). 6.99 *(978-0-375-86886-3(0)*, Random Hse. Bks. for Young Readers) Random Hse. Children's Bks.
—Calendar Mysteries #9: September Sneakers. Gurney, John Steven, illus. 2013. (Calendar Mysteries Ser.: 9). (ENG.). 80p. (J). (gr. 1-4). 7.99 *(978-0-375-86887-0(9)*, Random Hse. Bks. for Young Readers) Random Hse. Children's Bks.
—July Jitters. 2012. (Calendar Mysteries Ser.: 7). lib. bdg. 14.75 *(978-0-606-26402-0(7))* Turtleback.
—June Jam, 6. Gurney, John, illus. 2011. (Calendar Mysteries Ser.). (ENG.). 80p. (J). (gr. 1-4). lib. bdg. 18.69 *(978-0-375-96112-0(7))* Random House Publishing Group.
—June Jam. 2011. (Calendar Mysteries Ser.: 6). lib. bdg. 14.75 *(978-0-606-16114-5(7))* Turtleback.
—March Mischief. 2010. (Calendar Mysteries Ser.: 3). lib. bdg. 14.75 *(978-0-606-12460-7(8))* Turtleback.
—October Ogre. 2013. (Calendar Mysteries Ser.: 10). lib. bdg. 14.75 *(978-0-606-32232-4(9))* Turtleback.
—September Sneakers. 2013. (Calendar Mysteries Ser.: 9). lib. bdg. 14.75 *(978-0-606-32231-7(0))* Turtleback.
Royal, Stephen. The Journey Inside the Womb. 2012. (Illus.). 16p. pap. 18.30 *(978-1-4772-2604-9(4))* AuthorHouse.
Ruby, Laura. York: The Clockwork Ghost. 2019. (Illus.). 464p. (YA). *(978-0-06-293755-1(3)*, Waldon Pond Pr.) HarperCollins Pubs.
—York: the Clockwork Ghost. 2019. (York Ser.: 2). (ENG., Illus.). 464p. (J). (gr. 3-7). 17.99 *(978-0-06-230696-8(0)*, Waldon Pond Pr.) HarperCollins Pubs.
Ryder, Michael Todd, illus. Twins. 2012. 32p. (J). pap. 12.00 *(978-0-9847836-0-1(1))* Celtic Cat Publishing.
S., Lisa Hamilton Ed. The Tale of the Talking Trees: The Tale of the Talking Trees a Story of Suspense & Surprise. 2012. 32p. pap. 21.99 *(978-1-4691-7846-2(X))* Xlibris Corp.
Saddlewick, A. B. Monstrous Maud: Big Fright. 2017. (ENG., Illus.). 128p. (J). (gr. 1-5). pap. 7.99 *(978-1-5107-1698-8(X)*, Sky Pony Pr.) Skyhorse Publishing Co., Inc.
Salom, Susie. Kyle Finds Her Way. 2016. (ENG.). 256p. (J). (gr. 5-9). 16.99 *(978-0-545-85266-1(8)*, Levine, Arthur A. Bks.) Scholastic, Inc.
Same Day, Different Way! 2005. (J). pap. *(978-0-9769910-3-8(9))* Terrific Twins LLC.
Sansone, V. K. A Daunting Quest for Quincy & Quigley. 2008. (ENG.). 32p. pap. 8.98 *(978-0-557-03594-6(5))* Lulu Pr., Inc.
Sargeant, Theresa. The Drainpipe Gang - the Adventures of Chris & Andy Smy. 2011. 112p. pap. *(978-1-907256-80-6(6))* Abela Publishing.
Sateren, Shelley Swanson. Fearless Freddie. Melmon, Deborah, illus. 2015. (Adventures at Hound Hotel Ser.). (ENG.). 72p. (J). (gr. 1-3). lib. bdg. 25.32 *(978-1-4795-5898-8(2)*, 127044, Picture Window Bks.) Capstone.
—Growling Gracie. Melmon, Deborah, illus. 2015. (Adventures at Hound Hotel Ser.). (ENG.). 72p. (J). (gr. 1-3). lib. bdg. 25.32 *(978-1-4795-5899-5(0)*, 127045, Picture Window Bks.) Capstone.
—Homesick Herbie. Melmon, Deborah, illus. 2015. (Adventures at Hound Hotel Ser.). (ENG.). 72p. (J). (gr. 1-3). lib. bdg. 25.32 *(978-1-4795-5897-1(4)*, 127043, Picture Window Bks.) Capstone.
—Mudball Molly. Melmon, Deborah, illus. 2015. (Adventures at Hound Hotel Ser.). (ENG.). 72p. (J). (gr. 1-3). lib. bdg. 25.32 *(978-1-4795-5900-8(8)*, 127046, Picture Window Bks.) Capstone.
Saunders, Kate. The Whizz Pop Chocolate Shop. 2014. (ENG.). 304p. (J). (gr. 5). 7.99 *(978-0-385-74302-0(5)*, Yearling) Random Hse. Children's Bks.
Schuster, Judith A. No Place to Call Home: Book Two-the Eddie Brewster Adventures. 2008. 196p. pap. 24.95 *(978-1-60563-559-0(6))* PublishAmerica, Inc.
Schwartz, Corey Rosen. Twinderella, a Fractioned Fairy Tale. Marcero, Deborah, illus. 2017. 32p. (J). (gr. -1-3). 17.99 *(978-0-399-17633-3(0)*, G.P. Putnam's Sons Books for Young Readers) Penguin Young Readers Group.
Schwarzkopf, Tom. Trouble Twins Save Christmas, 1 vol. 2007. (ENG.). 96p. (J). (gr. 4-7). pap. 10.95 *(978-1-55109-619-3(6))* Nimbus Publishing, Ltd. CAN. Dist: Orca Bk. Pubs. USA.
Sclafani, Terry. The Thompson Twins Cruise Adventure. 2007. 84p. per. 10.95 *(978-1-4327-1542-7(9))* Outskirts Pr., Inc.
—The Thompson Twins Western Adventure. 2009. 114p. pap. 11.95 *(978-1-4327-3783-2(X))* Outskirts Pr., Inc.
Scollon, Bill. Minnie: Case of the Missing Sparkle-Izer. Loter Inc. Staff, illus. 2014. (World of Reading Level Pre-1 (Leveled Readers) Ser.). (ENG.). 32p. (J). (gr. -1-2). lib. bdg. 31.36 *(978-1-61479-248-2(8)*, 1762) Spotlight.
Scollon, William. The Case of the Missing Sparkle-Izer. 2013. (Mickey & Friends World of Reading Ser.). (J). lib. bdg. 13.55 *(978-0-606-32292-8(2))* Turtleback.
Scott, Michael. The Alchemyst. 2009. (ENG., Illus.). 375p. (gr. 6-10). 19.00 *(978-1-60686-514-9(5))* Perfection Learning Corp.
—The Alchemyst. (Secrets of the Immortal Nicholas Flamel Ser.: 1). (ENG.). 400p. (YA). (gr. 7). 2008. pap. 11.99 *(978-0-385-73600-8(2)*, Ember) 2007. (Illus.). 18.99 *(978-0-385-73357-1(7)*, Delacorte Bks. for Young Readers) Random Hse. Children's Bks.
—The Enchantress. 2013. (Secrets of the Immortal Nicholas Flamel Ser.: 6). (ENG.). 528p. (YA). (gr. 7). pap. 10.99 *(978-0-385-73536-0(7)*, Ember) Random Hse. Children's Bks.
—The Enchantress. 2013. (Secrets of the Immortal Nicholas Flamel Ser.: 6). lib. bdg. 22.10 *(978-0-606-31947-8(6))* Turtleback.
—The Magician. 2009. (Secrets of the Immortal Nicholas Flamel Ser.: 2). (ENG.). 496p. (YA). (gr. 7). pap. 11.99 *(978-0-385-73728-9(9)*, Ember) Random Hse. Children's Bks.
—The Necromancer. 2011. (Secrets of the Immortal Nicholas Flamel Ser.: 4). (ENG.). 416p. (YA). (gr. 7). pap. 11.99 *(978-0-385-73532-2(4)*, Ember) Random Hse. Children's Bks.
—The Necromancer. l.t. ed. 2010. (Secrets of the Immortal Nicholas Flamel Ser.). (ENG.). 690p. pap. 23.99 *(978-1-4104-2851-6(6))* Thorndike Pr.
—The Sorceress. 2010. (Secrets of the Immortal Nicholas Flamel Ser.: 3). (ENG.). 512p. (YA). (gr. 7-18). pap. 11.99 *(978-0-385-73530-8(8)*, Ember) Random Hse. Children's Bks.
—The Sorceress. 2010. (Secrets of the Immortal Nicholas Flamel Ser.: 3). lib. bdg. 22.10 *(978-0-606-14133-8(2))* Turtleback.
—The Sorceress the Secrets of the Immortal Nicholas Flamel. l.t. ed. 2009. (Secrets of the Immortal Nicholas Flamel Ser.). (ENG.). 614p. (YA). 23.95 *(978-1-4104-2092-3(2))* Thorndike Pr.
—The Warlock. 2012. (Secrets of the Immortal Nicholas Flamel Ser.: 5). (ENG.). 400p. (YA). (gr. 7). pap. 11.99 *(978-0-385-73534-6(0)*, Ember) Random Hse. Children's Bks.
—The Warlock. l.t. ed. 2011. (Secrets of the Immortal Nicholas Flamel Ser.). (ENG.). 545p. 23.99 *(978-1-4104-4157-7(1))* Thorndike Pr.
—The Warlock. 2012. (Secrets of the Immortal Nicholas Flamel Ser.: 5). lib. bdg. 22.10 *(978-0-606-26411-2(6))* Turtleback.
Seeger, K R. Asa-Birdie Corn. 2007. 244p. 26.95 *(978-0-595-69522-5(1))*; per. 16.95 *(978-0-595-45553-9(0))* iUniverse, Inc.
Segal, Andrew. Clarissa the Clown. Scott, Peter & JessT, Grant, illus. 2007. 32p. per. *(978-1-905823-20-8(7))* Panoma Pr. Ltd.
Self, Adam, creator. Tacos, Beans & Rice... the Episodes: From the Beginning. l.t. ed. 2006. (Illus.). 32p. (J). *(978-0-9719518-0-8(2))* Doodle Publishing.
Senior, Patricia. Mischief on Mumpit Mountain. 2009. 36p. pap. 14.75 *(978-1-60693-661-0(1)*, Eloquent Bks.) Strategic Book Publishing & Rights Agency (SBPRA).
Sgarlato, Dawn. Big Sister. 2012. 24p. pap. 17.99 *(978-1-4685-9426-3(5))* AuthorHouse.
Shaw, LaVerne. Mesa Magic. 2006. 184p. per. 19.95 *(978-1-59879-238-6(5))* Lifevest Publishing, Inc.
Shearer, Alex. Sea Legs. 2006. (ENG.). 320p. (J). (gr. 5-9). per. 17.99 *(978-0-689-87144-3(9)*, Simon & Schuster/Paula Wiseman Bks.) Simon & Schuster/Paula Wiseman Bks.
Sheinmel, Courtney. Twinsanity. Bell, Jennifer A., illus. 2017. (Zacktastic Ser.). (ENG.). 272p. (J). (gr. 2-4). 11.99 *(978-1-58536-936-2(5)*, 204319); pap. 6.99 *(978-1-58536-937-9(3)*, 204333) Sleeping Bear Pr.
—Zacktastic. 2015. (Zacktastic Ser.). (ENG.). 272p. (J). (gr. 2-5). 11.99 *(978-1-58536-934-8(9)*, 203947) Sleeping Bear Pr.
Sheinmel, Courtney & Turetsky, Bianca. Magic on the Map #1: Let's Mooove! Lewis, Stevie, illus. 2019. (Magic on the Map Ser.: 1). 128p. (J). (gr. 2-5). 6.99 *(978-1-63565-166-9(2)*, Random Hse. Bks. for Young Readers) Random Hse. Children's Bks.
—Magic on the Map #2: the Show Must Go On. Lewis, Stevie, illus. 2019. (Magic on the Map Ser.: 2). 128p. (J). (gr. 2-5). 5.99 *(978-1-63565-169-0(7)*, Random Hse. Bks. for Young Readers) Random Hse. Children's Bks.
—Magic on the Map #3: Texas Treasure, 3. Lewis, Stevie, illus. 2020. (Magic on the Map Ser.: 3). 128p. (J). (gr. 2-5). 5.99 *(978-1-9848-9569-1(9)*, Random Hse. Bks. for Young Readers) Random Hse. Children's Bks.
Shepard, Sara. Hide & Seek. 2012. (Lying Game Ser.: Bk. 4). 289p. (YA). 9.99 *(978-0-06-219369-8(4)*, HarperTeen) HarperCollins Pubs.
—The Lying Game. (Lying Game Ser.: 1). (ENG.). (YA). (gr. 9-18). 2010. 320p. 17.99 *(978-0-06-186970-9(8))*1. 2011. 336p. pap. 11.99 *(978-0-06-186971-6(6))* HarperCollins Pubs. (HarperTeen).
—The Lying Game. 2011. (Lying Game (Quality) Ser.: Vol. 1). (ENG.). (YA). (gr. 9). lib. bdg. 20.60 *(978-1-61383-667-5(8))* Perfection Learning Corp.
—The Lying Game #2: Never Have I Ever. (Lying Game Ser.: 2). (ENG.). (YA). (gr. 9). 2012. 336p. pap. 10.99 *(978-0-06-186973-0(2))* 2011. 320p. 16.99 *(978-0-06-186972-3(4))* HarperCollins Pubs. (HarperTeen).
—The Lying Game #3: Two Truths & a Lie. (Lying Game Ser.: 3). (ENG.). (YA). (gr. 9). 2013. 320p. pap. 10.99 *(978-0-06-186975-4(9))* 2012. 304p. 17.99 *(978-0-06-186974-7(0))* HarperCollins Pubs. (HarperTeen).
—The Lying Game #4: Hide & Seek. 2013. (Lying Game Ser.: 4). (ENG.). 320p. (YA). (gr. 9). pap. 10.99 *(978-0-06-186977-8(5)*, HarperTeen) HarperCollins Pubs.
—The Lying Game #6: Seven Minutes in Heaven. 2014. (Lying Game Ser.: 6). (ENG.). 400p. (YA). (gr. 9). pap. 11.99 *(978-0-06-212823-2(X)*, HarperTeen) HarperCollins Pubs.
Shepherd, Kat. The Gemini Mysteries: the Cat's Paw (the Gemini Mysteries Book 2) 2021. (Gemini Mysteries Ser.: 2). (ENG., Illus.). 304p. (J). (gr. 3-7). 16.99 *(978-1-4998-0810-0(0)*, Yellow Jacket) Bonnier Publishing USA.
Shickman, Allan Richard. Dael & the Painted People. 2011. (Zan-Gah Ser.). 155p. (YA). pap. 9.95 *(978-0-9790357-6-0(7))* Earthshaker Bks.
—Zan-Gah & the Beautiful Country. 2009. 151p. pap. 9.95 *(978-0-9790357-1-5(6))* Earthshaker Bks.
Shimokawa, Melanie. A Family for Madison. 2008. 53p. pap. 16.95 *(978-1-60672-701-0(X))* America Star Bks.
Shusterman, Neal. Bruiser. 2010. (ENG.). 336p. (YA). (gr. 9-18). 17.99 *(978-0-06-113408-1(2)*, Quill Tree Bks.) HarperCollins Pubs.
Siamon, Sharon. Heartbreak Hills, 1 vol. 2011. (Wild Horse Creek Ser.: 0). (ENG., Illus.). 144p. (J). (gr. 2-7). pap. 6.95 *(978-1-55285-998-8(3)*, f09adab9-19c4-44bb-aa66-3294791dc574) Whitecap Bks., Ltd. CAN. Dist: Firefly Bks., Ltd.
Silvey, Diane. Spirit Quest. 2009. (ENG., Illus.). 64p. (J). (gr. 6). pap. 11.99 *(978-1-55002-831-7(6))* Dundurn Pr. CAN. Dist: Publishers Group West (PGW).
—Time of the Thunderbird. Mantha, John, illus. 2008. (ENG.). 88p. (J). (gr. 6-5). pap. 11.99 *(978-1-55002-792-1(1))* Dundurn Pr. CAN. Dist: Publishers Group West (PGW).
Simon, Francesca. Hack & Whack. Cotterill, Charlotte, illus. 2017. (ENG.). 32p. (gr. -1-k). 16.95 *(978-0-571-32871-0(7)*, Faber & Faber Children's Bks.) Faber & Faber, Inc.
Skead, Robert A. Patriots Redcoats & Spies, 1 vol. 2015. (American Revolutionary War Adventures Ser.). (ENG.). 192p. (J). 14.99 *(978-0-310-74841-0(0))* Zonderkidz.
Skelton, Vonda Skinner. Bitsy & the Mystery at Amelia Island. 2005. (Bitsy Burroughs Mysteries Ser.). 183p. (J). (gr. 3-7). per. 8.95 *(978-1-57072-307-0(9)*, Silver Dagger Mysteries) Overmountain Pr.
Skurzynski, Gloria. Afterwar. 2011. (ENG., Illus.). 528p. (YA). (gr. 7). pap. 9.99 *(978-1-4424-1681-9(5)*, Atheneum Bks. for Young Readers) Simon & Schuster Children's Publishing.
Smith, Jennifer E. The Storm Makers. Helquist, Brett, illus. 2013. (ENG.). 384p. (J). (gr. 3-7). pap. 19.99 *(978-0-316-17959-1(0))* Little, Brown Bks. for Young Readers.
Smith, Roland. Cryptid Hunters. 2006. (ENG.). 352p. (J). (gr. 5-9). pap. 7.99 *(978-0-7868-5162-1(7))* Little, Brown Bks. for Young Readers.
Soderberg, Erin. The Quirks & the Quirkalicious Birthday. 2015. (Quirks Ser.). (ENG., Illus.). 208p. (J). (gr. 3-6). 13.99 *(978-1-61963-370-4(1)*, 9781619633704, Bloomsbury USA Childrens) Bloomsbury Publishing USA.
Solomon, Rachel Lynn. You'll Miss Me When I'm Gone. 2018. (ENG., Illus.). 384p. (YA). (gr. 9). 19.99 *(978-1-4814-9773-2(1)*, Simon Pulse) Simon Pulse.

T
U
V

Sommers, Jackie Lea. Truest. 2015. (ENG.). 384p. (YA). (gr. 8). 17.99 *(978-0-06-234825-8(6),* HarperCollins) HarperCollins Pubs.
Somper, Justin. Demons of the Ocean. 2006. 1.00 *(978-1-4294-1974-1(1))* Recorded Bks., Inc.
—Demons of the Ocean. 2007. (Vampirates Ser.: 1). (Illus.). 330p. (J). 19.65 *(978-1-4177-8287-1(0))* Turtleback.
—Immortal War. 2013. (Vampirates Ser.: 6). (J). lib. bdg. 22.10 *(978-0-606-26696-3(8))* Turtleback.
—Vampirates: Demons of the Ocean. 2007. (Vampirates Ser.: 1). (ENG.). 352p. (J). (gr. 3-7). per. 18.99 *(978-0-316-01444-1(3))* Little, Brown Bks. for Young Readers.
—Vampirates: Black Heart. 2010. (Vampirates Ser.: 4). (ENG.). 512p. (J). (gr. 3-7). pap. 22.99 *(978-0-316-02088-6(5))* Little, Brown Bks. for Young Readers.
—Vampirates: Blood Captain. 2009. (Vampirates Ser.: 3). (ENG.). 592p. (J). (gr. 3-7). pap. 26.99 *(978-0-316-02086-2(9))* Little, Brown Bks. for Young Readers.
—Vampirates: Empire of Night. 2011. (Vampirates Ser.: 5). (ENG.). 512p. (J). (gr. 3-7). pap. 22.99 *(978-0-316-03323-7(5))* Little, Brown Bks. for Young Readers.
—Vampirates: Immortal War. 2013. (Vampirates Ser.: 6). (ENG.). 512p. (J). (gr. 3-7). pap. 23.99 *(978-0-316-03325-1(1))* Little, Brown Bks. for Young Readers.
—Vampirates: Tide of Terror. 2008. (Vampirates Ser.: 2). (ENG.). 480p. (J). (gr. 3-7). pap. 21.99 *(978-0-316-01445-8(1))* Little, Brown Bks. for Young Readers.
Sparkes, Ali. Alligator Action, No. 14. Collins, Ross, illus. 2014. (S. W. I. T. C. H. Ser.: 14). (ENG.). 112p. (J). (gr. 2-5). lib. bdg. 27.99 *(978-1-4677-2117-2(4),* a29ee350-23b8-409b-9c6f-f08687ada878, Darby Creek) Lerner Publishing Group.
—Gecko Gladiator, No. 12. Collins, Ross, illus. 2014. (S. W. I. T. C. H. Ser.: 12). (ENG.). 104p. (J). (gr. 2-5). lib. bdg. 27.99 *(978-1-4677-2115-8(8),* cc532572-06e9-4568-a918-8e1b276481a3, Darby Creek) Lerner Publishing Group.
—Lizard Loopy, Bk. 9. Collins, Ross, illus. 2014. (S. W. I. T. C. H. Ser.: 9). (ENG.). 104p. (J). (gr. 2-5). lib. bdg. 27.99 *(978-1-4677-2112-7(3),* b130a932-7a79-4525-84ae-ef15db1971ce, Darby Creek) Lerner Publishing Group.
—Newt Nemesis, No. 8. Collins, Ross, illus. 2014. (S. W. I. T. C. H. Ser.: 8). (ENG.). 88p. (J). (gr. 2-5). lib. bdg. 27.99 *(978-1-4677-3233-8(8),* 929674af-dfcb-4fe0-abb2-b77ab1d219ad, Darby Creek) Lerner Publishing Group.
Spinelli, Jerry. Jake & Lily. 2012. (ENG.). 352p. (J). (gr. 3-7). 16.99 *(978-0-06-028135-9(9),* Balzer & Bray) HarperCollins Pubs.
Stadelmann, Amy Marie. Olive & Beatrix: The Super-Smelly Moldy Blob, Vol. 2. Stadelmann, Amy Marie, illus. 2016. (Olive & Beatrix Ser.: 2). (ENG., Illus.). 80p. (J). (gr. k-2). 15.99 *(978-0-545-81485-0(5))* Scholastic, Inc.
Stamper, Judith Bauer. Breakfast at Danny's Diner: A Book about Multiplication. Demarest, Chris, illus. 2003. (All Aboard Math Reader Ser.). 48p. (J). (gr. 2-4). 11.65 *(978-0-7569-1695-4(X))* Perfection Learning Corp.
Standish, Joyce, ed. The Adventures of Ryan Lincoln. Cooper, Nicole, illus. 2012. 46p. (J). pap. 10.00 *(978-0-9716244-5-0(3))* TLS Publishing.
Starrenburg, Hasko. The Queen's Orb. 2012. (Illus.). 144p. pap. 8.00 *(978-1-4349-8782-2(5),* RoseDog Bks.) Dorrance Publishing Co., Inc.
Stein, A. K. EZEKIEL MAYHILL & the Crystal of God. 2007. 196p. pap. 16.96 *(978-1-4303-2540-6(2))* Lulu Pr., Inc.
Sterling, L. E. True North. 2018. (True Born Ser.: 2). (ENG.). 304p. (YA). pap. 9.99 *(978-1-63375-915-2(6),* 900185555) Entangled Publishing, LLC.
Sternick, Michele J. The Charged up Twins. 2005. 29p. 9.98 *(978-1-4116-3475-6(6))* Lulu Pr., Inc.
Stine, Megan, et al. Sealed with a Kiss. 2003. (ENG., Illus.). 112p. *(978-0-00-714461-7(X),* HarperCollins Children's Bks.) HarperCollins Pubs. Ltd.
—Surprise, Surprise! 2003. (ENG., Illus.). 112p. *(978-0-00-714462-4(8),* HarperCollins Children's Bks.) HarperCollins Pubs. Ltd.
—War of the Wardrobes. 2003. (ENG., Illus.). 112p. *(978-0-00-714468-6(7),* HarperCollins Children's Bks.) HarperCollins Pubs. Ltd.
Stine, R. L. Dangerous Girls. 2003. 256p. (J). 111.92 *(978-0-06-056909-9(3));* 111.92 *(978-0-06-056910-5(7));* (ENG., Illus.). (gr. 7-18). 13.99 *(978-0-06-053080-8(4))* HarperCollins Pubs.
—Escape from Shudder Mansion (Goosebumps SlappyWorld #5) 2018. (Goosebumps SlappyWorld Ser.: 5). (ENG.). 160p. (J). (gr. 3-7). pap. 6.99 *(978-1-338-22299-9(6),* Scholastic Paperbacks) Scholastic, Inc.
—First Evil. 2011. (Fear Street Cheerleaders Ser.: 1). (ENG.). 176p. (YA). (gr. 9). pap. 9.99 *(978-1-4424-3086-0(9),* Simon Pulse) Simon Pulse.
—Help! We Have Strange Powers! 2009. (Goosebumps HorrorLand Ser.: 10). lib. bdg. 17.20 *(978-0-606-05347-1(6))* Turtleback.
—Night of the Living Dummy (Classic Goosebumps #1) 2008. (Classic Goosebumps Ser.: 1). (ENG.). 160p. (J). (gr. 3-7). 7.99 *(978-0-545-03517-0(1),* Scholastic Paperbacks) Scholastic, Inc.
—Night of the Puppet People. 2015. 136p. (J). *(978-1-4806-9296-1(4))* Scholastic, Inc.
—Weirdo Halloween. 2010. (Goosebumps HorrorLand Ser.: No. 16). 240p. (J). pap. *(978-1-4071-1637-2(1))* Scholastic, Inc.
—Weirdo Halloween (Goosebumps HorrorLand #16) Special Edition. 2010. (Goosebumps Horrorland Ser.: 16). (ENG.). 240p. (J). (gr. 3-7). 8.99 *(978-0-545-16197-8(5),* Scholastic Paperbacks) Scholastic, Inc.
Stirnkorb, Patricia. All about Me! Inspirational Version, 1. 2005. (Illus.). 12p. (J). bds. 12.99 *(978-0-9758709-7-6(1),* A.W.A. Gang) Journey Stone Creations, LLC.
Stohl, Margaret & Peterson, Lewis. Cats vs. Robots #1: This Is War. Peterson, Kay, illus. (ENG.). (J). (gr. 3-7). 2019. 336p. pap. 6.99 *(978-0-06-266571-3(5))* 2018. 320p. 16.99 *(978-0-06-266570-6(7))* HarperCollins Pubs. (Tegen, Katherine Bks).
The Strange & Beautiful Sorrows of Ava Lavender. 2014. (ENG.). 320p. (YA). (gr. 9). E-Book 12.99 *(978-0-7636-7034-4(0),* 28917) Candlewick Pr.
Strasnick, Lauren. Her & Me & You. (ENG.). 208p. (YA). (gr. 9). 2011. pap. 9.99 *(978-1-4169-9267-8(1))* 2010. 16.99 *(978-1-4169-8266-1(3))* Simon Pulse. (Simon Pulse).
Streib, Sally. Octopus Encounter. 2007. (Illus.). 126p. (J). 6.97 *(978-0-8163-2210-7(4))* Pacific Pr. Publishing Assn.
Sullivan, Kathryn. Talking to Trees. 2017. (J). pap. *(978-1-61271-356-4(4))* Zumaya Pubns. LLC.
Surget, Alain. Escape from Veracruz. 2015. (Jolly Roger Ser.). (Illus.). 96p. (gr. 3-6). 28.50 *(978-1-909645-44-8(3))* Book Hse. GBR. Dist: Black Rabbit Bks.
—The Plumed Serpent's Gold. 2015. (Jolly Roger Ser.). (Illus.). 96p. (gr. 3-6). 28.50 *(978-1-909645-43-1(5))* Book Hse. GBR. Dist: Black Rabbit Bks.
—Shark Island. 2015. (Jolly Roger Ser.). (Illus.). 96p. (gr. 3-6). 28.50 *(978-1-909645-42-4(7))* Book Hse. GBR. Dist: Black Rabbit Bks.
Swanson, Matthew. The Real Mccoys: Wonder Undercover. Behr, Robbi, illus. 2019. (Real Mccoys Ser.: 3). (ENG.). 352p. (J). 16.99 *(978-1-250-30782-8(1),* 900198140) Imprint IND. Dist: Macmillan.
Swanson Sateren, Shelley. Cool Crosby. Melmon, Deborah, illus. 2016. (Adventures at Hound Hotel Ser.). (ENG.). 72p. (J). (gr. 1-3). lib. bdg. 25.32 *(978-1-5158-0066-8(0),* 131911, Picture Window Bks.) Capstone.
—Mighty Murphy. Melmon, Deborah, illus. 2016. (Adventures at Hound Hotel Ser.). (ENG.). 72p. (J). (gr. 1-3). lib. bdg. 25.32 *(978-1-5158-0067-5(5),* 131916, Picture Window Bks.) Capstone.
—Stinky Stanley. Melmon, Deborah, illus. 2016. (Adventures at Hound Hotel Ser.). (ENG.). 72p. (J). (gr. 1-3). lib. bdg. 25.32 *(978-1-5158-0221-1(3),* 132456, Picture Window Bks.) Capstone.
Taddonio, Lea. The Curse of Deadwood Hill: Book 2. Trunfio, Alessia, illus. 2017. (Lucky 8 Ser.). (ENG.). 48p. (J). (gr. 3-7). lib. bdg. 34.21 *(978-1-5321-3054-0(6),* 27061, Spellbound) Magic Wagon.
—Deadwood Hill Strikes Back: Book 3. Trunfio, Alessia, illus. 2017. (Lucky 8 Ser.). (ENG.). 48p. (J). (gr. 3-7). lib. bdg. 34.21 *(978-1-5321-3055-7(4),* 27062, Spellbound) Magic Wagon.
—The Deadwood Hill Trap: Book 4. Trunfio, Alessia, illus. 2017. (Lucky 8 Ser.). (ENG.). 48p. (J). (gr. 3-7). lib. bdg. 34.21 *(978-1-5321-3056-4(2),* 27063, Spellbound) Magic Wagon.
Tagert-Paul, Kimberley. God's Ten Promises: Helping Children Understand the Ten Commandments. 2010. (J). 12.99 *(978-0-8163-2379-1(8))* Pacific Pr. Publishing Assn.
Tapia, Jeff. Hippomobile! 2013. (ENG., Illus.). 240p. (J). (gr. 5-7). 16.99 *(978-0-547-99548-9(2),* 1525383, Clarion Bks.) HarperCollins Pubs.
Taylor, G. P. The Tizzle Sisters & Erik. 2007. 188p. *(978-1-905692-22-4(6))* Markosia Enterprises, Ltd.
Terrell, Brandon. The Cursed Stage. Epelbaum, Mariano, illus. 2017. (Snoops, Inc Ser.). (ENG.). 112p. (J). (gr. 4-8). lib. bdg. 27.32 *(978-1-4965-4346-2(7),* 134263, Stone Arch Bks.) Capstone.
—Phantom of the Library. Epelbaum, Mariano, illus. 2017. (Snoops, Inc Ser.). (ENG.). 112p. (J). (gr. 4-8). lib. bdg. 27.32 *(978-1-4965-5060-6(9),* 135986, Stone Arch Bks.) Capstone.
—Science Fair Sabotage. Epelbaum, Mariano, illus. 2017. (Snoops, Inc Ser.). (ENG.). 112p. (J). (gr. 4-8). lib. bdg. 27.32 *(978-1-4965-4347-9(5),* 134264, Stone Arch Bks.) Capstone.
—Tracking Champ. Epelbaum, Mariano, illus. 2017. (Snoops, Inc Ser.). (ENG.). 112p. (J). (gr. 4-8). lib. bdg. 27.32 *(978-1-4965-4348-6(3),* 134265, Stone Arch Bks.) Capstone.
—The Vanishing Treasure. Epelbaum, Mariano, illus. 2017. (Snoops, Inc Ser.). (ENG.). 112p. (J). (gr. 4-8). lib. bdg. 27.32 *(978-1-4965-4345-5(9),* 134262, Stone Arch Bks.) Capstone.
Terry, Gail Contreina. Twins. 2005. pap. 8.00 *(978-0-8059-6818-7(0))* Dorrance Publishing Co., Inc.
Terry, Teri. The Book of Lies. 2017. (ENG.). 384p. (YA). (gr. 7). 17.99 *(978-0-544-90048-6(0),* 1654927, Clarion Bks.) HarperCollins Pubs.
Thomas, Dee. Silly, Silly, Eggleton Egg: Meet the Egg's of Eggville. 2012. 28p. pap. 21.99 *(978-1-4771-5325-3(X))* Xlibris Corp.
Thompson, Colleen. Claudine & Claudette: A Bug Story. 2010. 12p. 8.49 *(978-1-4520-7902-8(1))* AuthorHouse.
—Claudine & Claudette a Bug Story. 2011. 12p. pap. 8.32 *(978-1-4634-2286-8(5))* AuthorHouse.
Tillworth, Mary. Leah's Dream Dollhouse (Shimmer & Shine) Yum, Heekyoung & Aikins, Dave, illus. 2016. (Pictureback(R) Ser.). (ENG.). 16p. (J). (gr. -1-2). 4.99 *(978-1-101-93249-0(X),* Random Hse. Bks. for Young Readers) Random Hse. Children's Bks.
Tossell, David H. Charlie & Chippo Meet a Ghost. Pritchard, Louise, illus. 2012. 24p. pap. *(978-1-908773-25-8(1))* Iponymous Publishing, Ltd.
Trees, Annie Mae. The Old Apartment Building: A Tale from the Trees. 2012. 24p. 24.95 *(978-1-4626-6093-3(2))* America Star Bks.
Tremblay, Amanda. The Tornado Trial. 2010. 65p. pap. 12.00 *(978-0-557-14051-0(X))* Lulu Pr., Inc.
Trevia, Rick & Benchmark Education Co., LLC Staff. Squid Twins. 2015. (BuildUp Ser.). (J). (gr. 1). *(978-1-4900-0724-3(5))* Benchmark Education Co.
Troulis, Jennifer. Penelope & Priscilla: And the Enchanted House of Whispers. 2nd ed. 2004. (Illus.). 229p. per. 13.95 *(978-0-9768602-0-4(1))* Twin Monkeys Pr.
—Penelope & Priscilla & the City of the Banished. 2007. (J). per. 14.95 *(978-0-9768602-1-1(X))* Twin Monkeys Pr.
Troupe, Thomas Kingsley. Darling Doll. Faber, Rudy, illus. 2016. (Hauntiques Ser.). (ENG.). 128p. (J). (gr. 4-6). lib. bdg. 25.32 *(978-1-4965-3548-1(0),* 132657, Stone Arch Bks.) Capstone.
—Ghostly Goalie. Faber, Rudy, illus. 2016. (Hauntiques Ser.). (ENG.). 128p. (J). (gr. 4-6). lib. bdg. 25.32 *(978-1-4965-3544-3(8),* 132654, Stone Arch Bks.) Capstone.
—Phantom's Favorite. Faber, Rudy, illus. 2016. (Hauntiques Ser.). (ENG.). 128p. (J). (gr. 4-6). lib. bdg. 25.32 *(978-1-4965-3546-7(4),* 132655, Stone Arch Bks.) Capstone.
—Wandering Wagon. Faber, Rudy, illus. 2016. (Hauntiques Ser.). (ENG.). 128p. (J). (gr. 4-6). lib. bdg. 25.32 *(978-1-4965-3547-4(2),* 132656, Stone Arch Bks.) Capstone.
Trueit, Trudi. Mom, There's a Dinosaur in Beeson's Lake. Paillot, Jim, illus. 2011. (Secrets of a Lab Rat Ser.). (ENG.). 160p. (J). (gr. 3-7). pap. 6.99 *(978-1-4169-6112-3(7),* Aladdin) Simon & Schuster Children's Publishing.
—Mom, There's a Dinosaur in Beeson's Lake, 2. Paillot, Jim, illus. 2010. (Secrets of a Lab Rat Ser.). (ENG.). 160p. (J). (gr. 3-7). 14.99 *(978-1-4169-7593-9(4))* Simon & Schuster, Inc.
—My Top Secret Dares & Don'ts. 2017. (Mix Ser.). (ENG., Illus.). 272p. (J). (gr. 4-8). 17.99 *(978-1-4814-6905-0(3));* pap. 7.99 *(978-1-4814-6904-3(5))* Simon & Schuster/Paula Wiseman Bks. (Simon & Schuster/Paula Wiseman Bks.).
—No Girls Allowed (Dogs Okay) Paillot, Jim, illus. 2010. (Secrets of a Lab Rat Ser.). (ENG.). 144p. (J). (gr. 3-7). pap. 5.99 *(978-1-4169-6111-6(9),* Aladdin) Simon & Schuster Children's Publishing.
—No Girls Allowed (Dogs Okay) Paillot, Jim, illus. 2009. (Secrets of a Lab Rat Ser.). (ENG.). 128p. (J). (gr. 3-7). 14.99 *(978-1-4169-7592-2(6),* Simon & Schuster/Paula Wiseman Bks.) Simon & Schuster/Paula Wiseman Bks.
Trussell-Cullen, Alan. The Twin Competition. Hurst, Elise, illus. 2009. (Rigby PM Stars Bridge Bks.). (ENG.). 16p. (gr. 2-3). pap. 8.25 *(978-1-4190-5510-2(0))* Rigby Education.
Tuck, Justin. Home-Field Advantage. Rodriguez, Leonardo, illus. 2011. (ENG.). 40p. (J). (gr. -1-3). 16.99 *(978-1-4424-0369-7(1),* Simon & Schuster Bks. For Young Readers) Simon & Schuster Bks. For Young Readers.
Tym, Kate. Time to Share. 2008. (Manners Ser.). (Illus.). 24p. (J). (gr. -1-1). lib. bdg. 16.95 *(978-1-59566-591-1(9))* QEB Publishing Inc.
Ure, Jean. Shrinking Violet. 2011. (ENG., Illus.). 176p. (gr. 4-7). pap. 7.99 *(978-0-00-714390-0(7),* HarperCollins Children's Bks.) HarperCollins Pubs. Ltd. GBR. Dist: HarperCollins Pubs.
Ursu, Anne. The Lost Girl. 2019. (ENG., Illus.). 368p. (J). (gr. 3-7). 16.99 *(978-0-06-227509-7(7),* Walden Pond Pr.) HarperCollins Pubs.
Van Stockum, Hilda. A Day on Skates: The Story of a Dutch Picnic. Van Stockum, Hilda, illus. 2007. (Illus.). 40p. (J). (gr. 1). 19.95 *(978-1-932350-18-0(7))* Bethlehem Bks.
Van Wyk, Tasja. Twins: Meet the Doctor. 2011. (Illus.). 28p. pap. 13.78 *(978-1-4567-7813-2(7))* AuthorHouse.
Venable, Alan. The Man in the Iron Mask. 2007. (Classic Adventures Ser.). pap. 9.95 *(978-1-4105-0860-7(9))* Building Wings LLC.
Vick, Mamie Farrar. Someone's Near. 2012. 24p. pap. 17.99 *(978-1-4670-4124-9(6))* AuthorHouse.
Vogiel, Eva. Facing the Music. 2003. 284p. 19.95 *(978-1-880582-94-7(5))* Judaica Pr., Inc., The.
Walker, Lane. The Hunt for Scarface. 2014. (ENG.). 161p. (YA). (gr. 7-13). pap. 9.99 *(978-1-58169-518-2(7),* Evergreen Pr.) Genesis Communications, Inc.
Walters, Eric. Visions. 2011. (ENG.). 208p. (J). pap. *(978-1-55455-122-4(6))* Fitzhenry & Whiteside, Ltd.
Walton, Leslye. The Strange & Beautiful Sorrows of Ava Lavender. (ENG.). 320p. (YA). (gr. 9). 2015. pap. 12.99 *(978-0-7636-8027-5(3))* 2014. 17.99 *(978-0-7636-6566-1(5))* Candlewick Pr.
—The Strange & Beautiful Sorrows of Ava Lavender. 2015. lib. bdg. 19.65 *(978-0-606-36879-7(5))* Turtleback.
Watson, Jude. Loot. 2015. (ENG.). 272p. (J). (gr. 3-7). pap. 8.99 *(978-0-545-46803-9(5),* Scholastic Paperbacks) Scholastic, Inc.
Watson, Renee. This Side of Home. 2015. (ENG.). 336p. (YA). (gr. 7). 18.99 *(978-1-59990-668-3(6),* 900074806, Bloomsbury USA Childrens) Bloomsbury Publishing USA.
Watts, Robin Queen. The Adventures of Beauty & Sam. 2009. 20p. pap. 10.50 *(978-1-4269-1286-3(2))* Trafford Publishing.
Webb, Holly. The Rescued Puppy. Williams, Sophy, illus. 2017. 124p. (J). *(978-1-5182-4904-4(3))* Tiger Tales.
Weiner, Ellis. The Templeton Twins Have an Idea: Book 1. Holmes, Jeremy, illus. 2013. (Templeton Twins Ser.). (ENG.). 240p. (J). (gr. 3-7). pap. 7.99 *(978-1-4521-2704-0(2))* Chronicle Bks. LLC.
Weiss, Ellen. Bathtime for Twins. Williams, Sam, illus. 2012. (ENG.). 30p. (J). (gr. -1 — 1). bds. 7.99 *(978-1-4424-3026-6(5),* Little Simon) Little Simon.
—Playtime for Twins. Williams, Sam, illus. 2012. (ENG.). 30p. (J). (gr. -1 — 1). bds. 7.99 *(978-1-4424-3027-3(3),* Little Simon) Little Simon.
—Twins in the Park: Ready-To-Read Pre-Level 1. Williams, Sam, illus. 2003. (Ready-To-Read Ser.). (ENG.). 24p. (J). (gr. -1-k). pap. 4.99 *(978-0-689-85742-3(X),* Simon Spotlight) Simon Spotlight.
Wells, Rosemary. Max & Ruby & Twin Trouble. Wells, Rosemary, illus. 2019. (Max & Ruby Adventure Ser.). (ENG., Illus.). 32p. (J). (gr. -1-3). 17.99 *(978-1-5344-4365-5(7),* Simon & Schuster Bks. For Young Readers) Simon & Schuster Bks. For Young Readers.
We're a Team! 2005. (J). bds. *(978-0-9769910-7-6(1))* Terrific Twins LLC.
Wescott, Derek. Terry & Thomas the Tandem Twins. 2007. 160p. pap. *(978-1-84401-875-8(X))* Athena Pr.
Westerfeld, Scott. Impostors, 1 vol. (Impostors Ser.). (ENG.). 416p. (YA). (gr. 7-7). 2021. 12.99 *(978-1-338-75790-3(3))* 2018. 18.99 *(978-1-338-15151-0(7),* Scholastic Pr.) Scholastic, Inc.
—Shatter City (Impostors, Book 2) 2019. (Impostors Ser.: 2). (ENG.). 416p. (YA). (gr. 7-7). 18.99 *(978-1-338-15041-4(3),* Scholastic Pr.) Scholastic, Inc.
Weston, Paula. Shadows. 2013. (Rephaim Ser.: 1). (ENG.). 400p. (YA). (gr. 9). 17.99 *(978-1-77049-547-0(9),* Tundra Bks.) Tundra Bks. CAN. Dist: Penguin Random Hse. LLC.
Wiggin, Kate Douglas. Marm Lisa. 2004. reprint ed. pap. 1.99 *(978-1-4192-3278-7(9));* pap. 15.95 *(978-1-4191-3278-0(4))* Kessinger Publishing, LLC.
Wiggins, Bethany. Cured: A Stung Novel. 2015. (ENG.). 320p. (YA). (gr. 7). pap. 10.99 *(978-0-8027-3787-8(0),* 900139083, Bloomsbury USA Childrens) Bloomsbury Publishing USA.
Wilce, Colin. The Valley & Daffodils (Rabbit Brook T. 2007. 80p. pap. 11.34 *(978-1-4116-8792-9(2))* Lulu Pr., Inc.
Wild, Ailsa. Squishy Taylor & the Vase That Wasn't. 2018. (Squishy Taylor Ser.). (ENG., Illus.). 128p. (J). (gr. 2-4). pap. 6.95 *(978-1-5158-1974-5(4),* 136644, Picture Window Bks.) Capstone.
—Squishy Taylor in Zero Gravity. 2018. (Squishy Taylor Ser.). (ENG., Illus.). 128p. (J). (gr. 2-4). lib. bdg. 25.32 *(978-1-5158-1980-6(9),* 136647, Picture Window Bks.) Capstone.
Wild, Alisa. Squishy Taylor & the Vase That Wasn't. Wood, Ben, illus. 2017. (Squishy Taylor Ser.). (ENG.). 128p. (J). (gr. 2-4). lib. bdg. 25.32 *(978-1-5158-1958-5(2),* 136641, Picture Window Bks.) Capstone.
Wildavsky, Rachel. The Secret of Rover. Caparo, Antonio, illus. 2015. (ENG.). 360p. (J). (gr. 4-8). pap. 7.95 *(978-1-4197-1968-4(8),* 681103, Amulet Bks.) Abrams, Inc.
Willard, Eliza, et al. Love Is in the Air. 2004. (ENG.). 128p. *(978-0-00-718094-3(2))* HarperCollins Pubs. Australia.
Williams, Geoffrey T. The Great White Red Alert. Artful Doodlers, illus. Campbell, Tom, photos by. 2008. (Save Our Seas Adventure Bks.). (ENG.). 64p. (J). (gr. 4-7). 8.95 *(978-0-9800444-0-9(5))* Save Our Seas, Ltd.
—The Hammerheads of Treasure Island. 2010. (ENG., Illus.). 64p. (J). (gr. 3-7). 8.95 *(978-0-9800444-2-3(1))* Save Our Seas, Ltd.
Williamson, Linda. Groundhog Breakfast, Soft Petals, & a Roof That Don't Leak Too Much, 1 vol. Mollett, Irene, illus. 2009. 23p. pap. 24.95 *(978-1-60749-618-2(6))* America Star Bks.
Wilson, Tony, et al. Battle Royale (the Selwood Boys, #1) 2018. (Selwood Boys Ser.: 01). 160p. 5.99 *(978-0-7333-3545-7(4))* ABC Bks. AUS. Dist: HarperCollins Pubs.
—Hit the Road (the Selwood Boys, #3) 2018. (Selwood Boys Ser.: 03). 162p. 5.99 *(978-0-7333-3547-1(0))* ABC Bks. AUS. Dist: HarperCollins Pubs.
—The Miracle Goal (the Selwood Boys, #2) 2018. (Selwood Boys Ser.: 02). 160p. 5.99 *(978-0-7333-3546-4(2))* ABC Bks. AUS. Dist: HarperCollins Pubs.
Wilson, Troy. Liam Takes a Stand. Holinaty, Josh, illus. 2017. (ENG.). 32p. (J). (gr. k-4). 16.95 *(978-1-77147-161-9(1))* Owlkids Bks. Inc. CAN. Dist: Publishers Group West (PGW).
Winter, Ariel S. One of a Kind. Hitch, David, illus. 2012. (ENG.). 32p. (J). (gr. -1-2). 15.99 *(978-1-4424-2016-8(2),* Aladdin) Simon & Schuster Children's Publishing.
Wood, Brian. The Cramp Twins: Lucien's Little. 2005. (Illus.). 112p. 13.95 *(978-1-904674-01-6(1))* Reynolds & Hearn GBR. Dist: Trafalgar Square Publishing.
Wylie, Sarah. All These Lives, 1 vol. 2012. (ENG.). 256p. (YA). (gr. 7-12). 24.99 *(978-0-374-30208-5(1),* 900072205, Farrar, Straus & Giroux (BYR)) Farrar, Straus & Giroux.
Yang, Belle. Always Come Home to Me. Yang, Belle, illus. 2007. (ENG., Illus.). 32p. (J). (gr. -1-3). 16.99 *(978-0-7636-2899-4(9))* Candlewick Pr.
Yang, Belle & Williams, Marcia. Archie's War: My Scrapbook of the First World War. Williams, Marcia, illus. 2007. (ENG., Illus.). 48p. (J). (gr. 3-7). 18.99 *(978-0-7636-3532-9(4))* Candlewick Pr.
Young, Moira. Blood Red Road. (Dust Lands Ser.: 1). (ENG.). (YA). (gr. 9). 2012. 480p. pap. 12.99 *(978-1-4424-2999-4(2))* 2011. (Illus.). 464p. 17.99 *(978-1-4424-2998-7(4))* McElderry, Margaret K. Bks. (McElderry, Margaret K. Bks.).
—Blood Red Road, 9 vols. 2011. (YA). 122.75 *(978-1-4618-0629-5(1));* 1.25 *(978-1-4640-2632-4(7));* 120.75 *(978-1-4618-0633-2(X));* 120.75 *(978-1-4618-0630-1(5));* 286.75 *(978-1-4618-0634-9(8))* Recorded Bks., Inc.
—Raging Star. (Dust Lands Ser.: 3). (ENG., Illus.). 448p. (YA). (gr. 9). 2015. pap. 13.99 *(978-1-4424-3003-7(6))* 2014. 17.99 *(978-1-4424-3002-0(8))* McElderry, Margaret K. Bks. (McElderry, Margaret K. Bks.).
—Rebel Heart. 2013. (Dust Lands Ser.: 2). (ENG., Illus.). 448p. (YA). (gr. 9). pap. 13.99 *(978-1-4424-3001-3(X),* McElderry, Margaret K. Bks.) McElderry, Margaret K. Bks.
Yum, Hyewon. The Twins' Blanket. Yum, Hyewon, illus. 2011. (ENG., Illus.). 40p. (J). (gr. -1-1). 19.99 *(978-0-374-37972-8(6),* 900068267, Farrar, Straus & Giroux (BYR)) Farrar, Straus & Giroux.
Zafon, Carlos Ruiz. The Midnight Palace. 2012. (ENG.). 320p. (YA). (gr. 7-17). pap. 17.99 *(978-0-316-04474-5(1))* Little, Brown Bks. for Young Readers.
Zaugg, Sandra L. Hidden Notes & High Seas. 2005. (Illus.). 95p. (J). *(978-0-8163-2052-3(7))* Pacific Pr. Pubns.
—Secret of the Desert Lights: A Story about Following God's Laws. 2009. (J). pap. 9.99 *(978-0-8163-2294-7(5))* Pacific Pr. Publishing Assn.
Zimmer, Tracie Vaughn. Sketches from a Spy Tree. Glass, Andrew, illus. 2005. (ENG.). 64p. (J). (gr. 5-7). 16.00 *(978-0-618-23479-0(9),* 111177, Clarion Bks.) HarperCollins Pubs.
Zink, Michelle. Circle of Fire. 2012. (Prophecy of the Sisters Ser.: 3). (ENG.). 368p. (YA). (gr. 7-17). pap. 19.99 *(978-0-316-03446-3(0))* Little, Brown Bks. for Young Readers.
—Guardian of the Gate. 2011. (Prophecy of the Sisters Ser.: 2). (ENG.). 368p. (YA). (gr. 7-17). pap. 18.99 *(978-0-316-02740-3(5))* Little, Brown Bks. for Young Readers.
—Prophecy of the Sisters. 2010. (Prophecy of the Sisters Ser.: 1). (ENG.). 368p. (YA). (gr. 7-17). pap. 18.99 *(978-0-316-02741-0(3))* Little, Brown Bks. for Young Readers.
1, 2, 3 Happy Family. 2005. (J). bds. *(978-0-9769910-2-1(0))* Terrific Twins LLC.

TWINS—POETRY

Lewis, J. Patrick & Yolen, Jane. Take Two! A Celebration of Twins. Blackall, Sophie, illus. 2012. (ENG.). 72p. (J). (gr. -1-3). 18.99 *(978-0-7636-3702-6(5))* Candlewick Pr.

TYLER, JOHN, 1790-1862

Gunderson, Megan M. John Tyler, 1 vol. 2016. (United States Presidents *2017 Ser.). (ENG., Illus.). 40p. (J). (gr. 2-5). lib. bdg. 35.64 *(978-1-68078-120-5(0),* 21857, Big Buddy Bks.) ABDO Publishing Co.

Havelin, Kate. John Tyler. 2005. (Presidential Leaders Ser.). (Illus.). 112p. (J). (gr. 3-7). lib. bdg. 29.27 *(978-0-8225-1395-7(1))* Lerner Publishing Group.

Venezia, Mike. Getting to Know the U. S. Presidents: John Tyler. Venezia, Mike, illus. 2005. (Getting to Know the U. S. Presidents Ser.). (ENG., Illus.). 32p. (J). (gr. 3-4). per. 7.95 *(978-0-516-27484-3(8),* Children's Pr.) Scholastic Library Publishing.

—John Tyler: Tenth President, 1841-1845. Venezia, Mike, illus. 2005. (Getting to Know the U. S. Presidents Ser.). (ENG., Illus.). 32p. (J). (gr. 3-4). 28.00 *(978-0-516-22615-6(0),* Children's Pr.) Scholastic Library Publishing.

Zamora, Dulce. How to Draw the Life & Times of John Tyler. 2009. (Kid's Guide to Drawing the Presidents of the United States of America Ser.). 32p. (gr. 4-4). 50.50 *(978-1-61511-153-4(0),* PowerKids Pr.) Rosen Publishing Group, Inc., The.

TYPEWRITERS—FICTION

Ackerman, Peter. The Lonely Typewriter. Dalton, Max, illus. 2014. (ENG.). 32p. (J). 16.95 *(978-1-56792-518-0(9))* Godine, David R. Pub.

Cronin, Doreen. Click, Clack, Moo: Cows That Type. Lewin, Betsy, illus. 2010. (Click Clack Book Ser.). (ENG.). 34p. (J). (gr. -1-k). bds. 8.99 *(978-1-4424-0889-0(8),* Little Simon) Little Simon.

—Click, Clack, Moo: Cows That Type. Lewin, Betsy, illus. 2016. (J). *(978-0-605-96664-2(8),* Simon Spotlight) Simon Spotlight.

—Click, Clack, Moo: Cows That Type. 2004. 29.95 *(978-1-55592-104-0(3))* Weston Woods Studios, Inc.

—Click, Clack, Moo: Cows That Type/ Book & CD. Lewin, Betsy, illus. 2011. (Click Clack Book Ser.). (ENG.). 32p. (J). (gr. -1-3). pap. 10.99 *(978-1-4424-3370-0(1),* Little Simon) Little Simon.

Cronin, Doreen & Lewin, Betsy. Click, Clack, Moo: Cows That Type. 2014. 32p. pap. 8.00 *(978-1-61003-342-8(6))* Center for the Collaborative Classroom.

Cronin, Doreen & Simon and Schuster/LeapFrog Staff. Click, Clack, Moo: Cows That Type. Lewin, Betsy, illus. 2008. (J). 13.99 *(978-1-59319-936-4(8))* LeapFrog Enterprises, Inc.

Dorie & Me. 2003. (YA). per. *(978-1-59431-071-3(8),* Ebks. On The Net) Write Words, Inc.

TYPEWRITING

Scholastic, Inc. Staff. Brain Play 1st-3rd. 2008. (J). 29.99 *(978-0-545-05207-8(6))* Scholastic, Inc.

—Brain Play Preschool-1st. 2008. (J). 29.99 *(978-0-439-81350-1(6))* Scholastic, Inc.

TYPOGRAPHY

see Printing

TYROL (AUSTRIA)—FICTION

de la Ramée, Louise & Ouida. Bimbi. 2007. 152p. per. 13.95 *(978-1-60312-344-0(X));* 24.95 *(978-1-60312-682-3(1))* Aegypan.

U

U BOATS

see Submarines (Ships)

UFOS

see Unidentified Flying Objects

U. N.

see United Nations

UGANDA

Barlas, Robert & Lin, Yong Jui. Uganda, 1 vol. 2nd rev. ed. 2010. (Cultures of the World (Second Edition)(r) Ser.). (ENG.). 144p. (gr. 5-5). 49.79 *(978-0-7614-4859-4(4),* d118f41f-c688-44c0-b6cb-9d23e3c39a1d) Cavendish Square Publishing LLC.

Barter, James. Idi Amin. 2004. (Heroes & Villains Ser.). (ENG., Illus.). 112p. (J). (gr. 7-10). 32.10 *(978-1-59018-553-7(6),* Lucent Bks.) Cengage Gale.

Blauer, Ettagale & Lauré, Jason. Uganda. 2nd rev. ed. 2009. (Enchantment of the World Ser.). (ENG.). 144p. (J). (gr. 5-9). 40.00 *(978-0-531-20655-3(6))* Scholastic Library Publishing.

Braun, Eric. Uganda in Pictures. 2nd ed. 2005. (Visual Geography Series, Second Ser.). (ENG., Illus.). 80p. (gr. 5-12). lib. bdg. 31.93 *(978-0-8225-2397-0(3))* Lerner Publishing Group.

Dougherty, Steve. Idi Amin. 2010. (Wicked History Ser.). 128p. (J). (gr. 6-12). pap. 5.95 *(978-0-531-22354-3(X));* (ENG., Illus.). (gr. 7-12). 18.69 *(978-0-531-20754-3(4))* Scholastic Library Publishing. (Watts, Franklin).

Griffin, Brett, et al. Uganda, 1 vol. 2019. (Cultures of the World (Third Edition)(r) Ser.). (ENG.). 144p. (gr. 5-5). lib. bdg. 48.79 *(978-1-5026-4740-5(0),* 4ea162df-7eb6-4d8f-b6a5-d5d42910c3e8) Cavendish Square Publishing LLC.

Immell, Myra, ed. Uganda, 1 vol. 2012. (Genocide & Persecution Ser.). (ENG., Illus.). 248p. (gr. 10-12). lib. bdg. 43.63 *(978-0-7377-6258-7(6),* 17a6f05b-1ceb-4980-9b60-09b487ae5b95, Greenhaven Publishing) Greenhaven Publishing LLC.

Kubuitsile, Lauri. Uganda. Rotberg, Robert I., ed. 2012. (Evolution of Africa's Major Nations Ser.). (Illus.). 80p. (J). (gr. 7). 22.95 *(978-1-4222-2187-7(3))* Mason Crest.

—Uganda. 2011. (J). pap. *(978-1-4222-2215-7(2))* 2006. (Illus.). 79p. (YA). lib. bdg. 21.95 *(978-1-59084-816-6(0))* Mason Crest.

Lewin, Ted & Lewin, Betsy. Gorilla Walk, 1 vol. 2014. (Adventures Around the World Ser.). (ENG., Illus.). 48p. (J). (gr. 1-6). pap. 12.95 *(978-1-62014-182-3(5),* leelowbooks) Lee & Low Bks., Inc.

McCollum, Sean. Deadly Despot: Idi Amin Rains Terror on Uganda. 2011. (J). pap. *(978-0-545-32936-1(1))* Scholastic, Inc.

Oghojafor, Kingsley. Uganda, 1 vol. 2004. (Countries of the World Ser.). (ENG., Illus.). 96p. (gr. 6-8). lib. bdg. 33.67 *(978-0-8368-3112-2(8),* 5c40505d-6bbe-4860-a478-b006b5f13303) Stevens, Gareth Publishing LLLP.

Sawyer, Kem Knapp. Grace Akallo & the Pursuit of Justice for Child Soldiers. 2015. (J). *(978-1-59935-456-9(X))* Reynolds, Morgan Inc.

Sobol, Richard. Breakfast in the Rainforest: A Visit with Mountain Gorillas. Sobol, Richard, photos by. 2010. (Traveling Photographer Ser.). (ENG., Illus.). 48p. (J). (gr. 1-4). pap. 7.99 *(978-0-7636-5134-3(6))* Candlewick Pr.

—Growing Peace, 1 vol. 2016. (ENG., Illus.). 40p. (J). (gr. 2-7). 20.95 *(978-1-60060-450-8(1),* leelowbooks) Lee & Low Bks., Inc.

UKRAINE

Abrams, Dennis. Viktor Yushchenko. 2007. (Modern World Leaders Ser.). (ENG., Illus.). 120p. (gr. 7-12). lib. bdg. 30.00 *(978-0-7910-9266-8(6),* P114597, Facts On File) Infobase Holdings, Inc.

Bassis, Volodymyr. Ukraine, 1 vol. 2017. (Cultures of the World (Third Edition)(r) Ser.). (ENG.). 144p. (gr. 5-5). lib. bdg. 48.79 *(978-1-5026-2744-5(2),* 156b93f3-8ce4-40e1-a8bb-c11ea95bb6aa) Cavendish Square Publishing LLC.

Bassis, Volodymyr & Dhilawala, Sakina. Ukraine, 1 vol. 2nd rev. ed. 2008. (Cultures of the World (Second Edition)(r) Ser.). (ENG.). 144p. (gr. 5-5). lib. bdg. 49.79 *(978-0-7614-2090-3(8),* 9ecdef87-d7cd-41eb-89de-9a9a91e9b69a) Cavendish Square Publishing LLC.

Cooper, Catherine W. & Pavlovic, Zoran. Ukraine. Gritzner, Charles F., ed. 2nd rev. ed. 2006. (ENG., Illus.). 120p. (gr. 7-12). lib. bdg. 35.00 *(978-0-7910-9207-1(0),* P114543, Facts On File) Infobase Holdings, Inc.

Cruise, Robin. The Nuclear Disaster at Chernobyl. Taylor, Marjorie, illus. rev. ed. 2003. (Take Ten Ser.). 46p. (J). (gr. 4-18). pap. 4.95 *(978-1-58659-022-2(7))* Artesian Pr.

Grimberg, Tina. Out of Line: Growing up Soviet. 2007. (Illus.). 128p. (J). (gr. 5-18). 22.95 *(978-0-88776-803-3(2),* Tundra Bks.) Tundra Bks. CAN. Dist: Penguin Random Hse. LLC.

Johnson, Rebecca L. Chernobyl's Wild Kingdom: Life in the Dead Zone. 2014. (ENG., Illus.). 64p. (YA). (gr. 6-12). lib. bdg. 34.65 *(978-1-4677-1154-8(3),* 562951a0-3ba4-42c1-bd72-e01d771e818e, Twenty-First Century Bks.) Lerner Publishing Group.

Kent, Deborah. Ukraine. 2015. (ENG., Illus.). 144p. (J). lib. bdg. 40.00 *(978-0-531-21251-6(3),* Orchard Bks.) Scholastic Library Publishing.

Murray, Julie. Ukraine. 2017. (Explore the Countries Set 4 Ser.). (ENG., Illus.). 40p. (J). (gr. 2-5). lib. bdg. 35.64 *(978-1-5321-1053-5(7),* 25682, Big Buddy Bks.) ABDO Publishing Co.

Nicola, Christos & Taylor, Peter Lane. The Secret of Priest's Grotto: A Holocaust Survival Story. Nicola, Christos & Taylor, Peter Lane, photos by. 2007. (ENG., Illus.). 64p. (YA). (gr. 5-12). per. 8.95 *(978-1-58013-261-9(8),* 7cacf770-a778-4fb5-b90e-a2031c561994, Kar-Ben Publishing) Lerner Publishing Group.

Owings, Lisa. Pripyat: The Chernobyl Ghost Town. 2017. (Abandoned Places Ser.). (ENG., Illus.). 24p. (J). (gr. 3-7). lib. bdg. 26.95 *(978-1-62617-697-3(3),* Torque Bks.) Bellwether Media.

Owings, Lisa & Borgert-Spaniol, Megan. Ukraine. 2014. (Exploring Countries Ser.). (ENG., Illus.). 32p. (J). (gr. 3-7). lib. bdg. 27.95 *(978-1-62617-071-1(1),* Blastoff! Readers) Bellwether Media.

Rissman, Rebecca. Chernobyl Disaster, 1 vol. 2013. (History's Greatest Disasters Ser.). (ENG.). 48p. (J). (gr. 4-8). lib. bdg. 35.64 *(978-1-61783-955-9(8),* 9481) ABDO Publishing Co.

—Chernobyl Disaster Paperback. 2013. (History's Greatest Disasters Ser.). (ENG.). (J). (gr. 4-8). pap. 18.50 *(978-1-62403-020-8(3),* 10769) ABDO Publishing Co.

Rodger, Ellen. A Refugee's Journey from Ukraine. 2018. (Leaving My Homeland Ser.). (Illus.). 32p. (J). (gr. 4-4). *(978-0-7787-4689-8(5))* Crabtree Publishing Co.

Savery, Annabel. Ukraine. 2014. (My Country Ser.). 24p. (gr. k-3). lib. bdg. 28.50 *(978-1-59920-908-1(X))* Black Rabbit Bks.

Stewart, Gail B. Ukraine: Then & Now. 2014. (The Former Soviet Union: Then & Now). (ENG., Illus.). 80p. (J). lib. bdg. *(978-1-60152-708-0(X))* ReferencePoint Pr., Inc.

Taylor, Peter Lane. The Secret of Priest's Grotto: A Holocaust Survival Story. 2007. (Holocaust Ser.). (Illus.). 64p. (J). (gr. 3-7). lib. bdg. 18.95 *(978-1-58013-260-2(X),* Kar-Ben Publishing) Lerner Publishing Group.

Toll, Nelly S. Behind the Secret Window. 2003. 176p. (J). (gr. 3-7). 5.99 *(978-0-14-230241-5(4),* Puffin Books) Penguin Young Readers Group.

Van Cleaf, Kristin. Ukraine. 2008. (Countries Set 6 Ser.). 40p. (gr. k-6). 27.07 *(978-1-59928-788-1(9),* Checkerboard Library) ABDO Publishing Co.

Vasilyeva, Anastasiya. Ukraine. 2016. (Countries We Come From Ser.). (ENG., Illus.). 32p. (J). (gr. -1-3). 28.50 *(978-1-68402-059-1(X))* Bearport Publishing Co., Inc.

Weber, Valerie J. I Come from Ukraine, 1 vol. 2006. (This Is My Story Ser.). (ENG., Illus.). 24p. (gr. 2-4). pap. 9.15 *(978-0-8368-7245-3(2),* e99cfde8-c255-43ce-8568-f40c710999ce, Weekly Reader Leveled Readers) Stevens, Gareth Publishing LLLP.

—I Come from Ukraine, 1 vol. 2006. (This Is My Story Ser.). (ENG., Illus.). 24p. (gr. 2-4). lib. bdg. 24.67 *(978-0-8368-7238-5(X),* 645c9201-c314-4ca6-bb39-fa7a1c408d74, Weekly Reader Leveled Readers) Stevens, Gareth Publishing LLLP.

Wolny, Philip. Holodomor: The Ukrainian Famine-Genocide, 1 vol. 2017. (Bearing Witness: Genocide & Ethnic Cleansing Ser.). (ENG.). 64p. (J). (gr. 6-6). 36.13 *(978-1-5081-7732-6(5),* 65a42909-1453-465e-8d51-639d86346ffe, Rosen Young Adult) Rosen Publishing Group, Inc., The.

UKRAINE—FICTION

Hyde, Lily. Dream Land. 2008. (Illus.). 277p. pap. *(978-1-4063-0765-8(3))* Walker Bks., Ltd.

Landau, Natasha, illus. Misha Loves to Sing. 2004. (J). *(978-0-615-12595-4(6))* Tikva Corp.

Masih, Tara Lynn. My Real Name Is Hanna. 3rd ed. 2018. 224p. (YA). (gr. 6-16). pap. 16.95 *(978-1-942134-51-0(7))* Mandel Vilar Pr.

Parker, Derek. Children of Zone. 2015. (ENG., Illus.). 142p. pap. *(978-1-925138-91-7(7))* Connor Court Publishing Pty Ltd.

Skrypuch, Marsha Forchuk. The War Below. 2018. (ENG.). 256p. (J). (gr. 3-7). 17.99 *(978-1-338-23302-5(5),* Scholastic Pr.) Scholastic, Inc.

The Trail of the Wooden Horse. 2007. 32p. pap. 4.50 *(978-0-8341-2284-0(7),* 083-412-2847) Beacon Hill Pr. of Kansas City.

Watts, Irene N. Touched by Fire. 2013. (Illus.). 208p. (J). (gr. 5-9). 17.95 *(978-1-77049-524-1(X),* Tundra Bks.) Tundra Bks. CAN. Dist: Penguin Random Hse. LLC.

White, Andrea. Radiant Girl. 2008. (J). *(978-1-933979-35-9(6))* Night Heron Media.

Zemko Tetro, Maria, tr. from UKR. How the Animals Built their House & Other Stories. 2008. (Illus.). 40p. (J). 14.95 *(978-0-9797372-5-1(7))* Winter Light Bks., Inc.

ULTRASONIC WAVES

Jennings, Terry J. Sound. 2009. (J). 28.50 *(978-1-59920-275-4(1))* Black Rabbit Bks.

ULYSSES (GREEK MYTHOLOGY)

see Odysseus (Greek Mythology)

UMBRELLAS AND PARASOLS—FICTION

Bates, Amy June & Bates, Juniper. The Big Umbrella. Bates, Amy June, illus. 2018. (ENG., Illus.). 40p. (J). (gr. -1-3). 18.99 *(978-1-5344-0658-2(1),* Simon & Schuster/Paula Wiseman Bks.) Simon & Schuster/Paula Wiseman Bks.

Baum, L. Frank. Sky Island. 2007. 144p. (gr. 4-7). per. 11.95 *(978-1-60312-253-5(2))* Aegypan.

Bennett, Marcia Allen. Umbrella Town. 2012. (ENG.). 33p. (J). pap. 15.95 *(978-1-4327-8439-3(0))* Outskirts Pr., Inc.

Blyton, Enid. The Strange Umbrella: And Other Stories. Gregory, Sally, illus. 2013. 192p. (J). 9.95 *(978-1-84135-461-3(9))* Award Pubns. Ltd. GBR. Dist: Parkwest Pubns., Inc.

Brett, Jan. The Umbrella. Brett, Jan, illus. 2004. (Illus.). 32p. (J). (gr. -1-3). 18.99 *(978-0-399-24215-1(5),* G.P. Putnam's Sons Books for Young Readers) Penguin Young Readers Group.

—The Umbrella. 2005. (Illus.). (J). (gr. k-3). 27.95 incl. audio *(978-0-8045-6931-6(2),* SAC6931) Spoken Arts, Inc.

Bridges, Shirin Yim. The Umbrella Queen. 2008. (ENG., Illus.). 40p. (J). (gr. k-3). 17.99 *(978-0-06-075040-4(5),* Greenwillow Bks.) HarperCollins Pubs.

Burnell, Cerrie. Harper & the Scarlet Umbrella. Anderson, Laura Ellen, illus. 2017. (ENG.). 128p. (J). (gr. 1-4). 14.99 *(978-1-5107-1566-0(5),* Sky Pony Pr.) Skyhorse Publishing Co., Inc.

Carlton, Glenis. Four Snails & an Umbrella. 2016. (ENG., Illus.). 22p. (J). 23.95 *(978-1-78612-332-9(0),* 6c37e2f4-5144-43d4-8c65-5bd5a8655cd9) Austin Macauley Pubs. Ltd. GBR. Dist: Baker & Taylor Publisher Services (BTPS).

Dahl, Michael. The Penguin's Power Parasol. Vecchio, Luciano, illus. 2016. (Batman Tales of the Batcave Ser.). (ENG.). 40p. (J). (gr. 4-8). lib. bdg. 24.65 *(978-1-4965-4012-6(3),* 133211, Stone Arch Bks.) Capstone.

Delcoglin, Gwen. Bella's Umbrella. Delcoglin, Nathan, illus. 2007. 28p. (J). (gr. -1-3). per. 10.99 *(978-1-59879-315-4(2))* Lifevest Publishing, Inc.

Derubertis, Barbara. Umma Ungka's Unusual Umbrella. Alley, R. W., illus. 2011. (Animal Antics A to Z Set III Ser.). pap. 45.32 *(978-0-7613-8430-4(8))* Astra Publishing Hse.

deRubertis, Barbara & DeRubertis, Barbara. Umma Ungka's Unusual Umbrella. Alley, R. W., illus. 2012. (Animal Antics A to Z Ser.). 32p. (J). (gr. 2 — 1). cd-rom 7.95 *(978-1-57565-414-0(8))* Astra Publishing Hse.

Grace, Elora. Umbrellas Everywhere!, 1 vol. 2006. (Neighborhood Readers Ser.). (ENG.). 8p. (gr. 1-2). pap. 5.15 *(978-1-4042-6791-6(3),* 6617174c-4804-4004-934c-cad40c81ac46, Rosen Classroom) Rosen Publishing Group, Inc., The.

Holden, Pam. Umbrellas Go Up, 1 vol. 2015. (ENG., Illus.). 16p. (-1). pap. *(978-1-77654-073-0(5),* Red Rocket Readers) Flying Start Bks.

Kahanek, Kristine Elizabeth. Katie & the Magic Umbrella: A Stormy Adventure. 2008. (Katie & the Magic Umbrella Ser.). (Illus.). 44p. (J). (gr. -1-4). 14.95 *(978-0-9801423-0-3(X))* K.Co.Kids, LLC.

Levine, Rhoda. Harrison Loved His Umbrella. Kuskin, Karla, illus. 2016. 56p. (J). (-k). 14.95 *(978-1-59017-991-8(9),* NYR Children's Collection) New York Review of Bks., Inc., The.

Lloyd, Jennifer. Ella's Umbrellas. Spires, Ashley, illus. 2010. (ENG.). 32p. (J). (gr. -1-3). 16.95 *(978-1-897476-23-9(X))* Simply Read Bks. CAN. Dist: Ingram Publisher Services.

Robertson, Charmaine. Nancy's Beach Umbrella, 1 vol. 2016. (Rosen REAL Readers: STEM & STEAM Collection). (ENG.). 12p. (gr. 1-2). pap. 6.33 *(978-1-5081-2658-4(5),* f251fd2f-0a5c-4c6d-80e1-223d3e10814c, Rosen Classroom) Rosen Publishing Group, Inc., The.

Robertson, Chris. My Yellow Umbrella. Robertson, Chris, illus. 2013. (ENG., Illus.). 36p. (J). (gr. -1-2). pap. 9.99 *(978-1-62395-543-4(2))* Xist Publishing.

Stevens, Terry. Tommy, the Wizard & the Magic Umbrella. 2006. (Illus.). 60p. pap. *(978-1-84401-752-2(4))* Athena Pr.

Thomas, Gerry. The Umbrella Race. 2010. 25p. (J). pap. 25.95 *(978-1-4327-6006-9(8))* Outskirts Pr., Inc.

Tremblay, Carole. Floop's New Umbrella, 1 vol. Beshwaty, Steve, illus. 2009. (Floop Ser.). (ENG.). 24p. (J). (gr. -1-k). 27.27 *(978-1-60754-347-3(8),* 506866a0-14a4-4c13-9e62-69e155ee53fc); pap. 9.15 *(978-1-60754-348-0(6),* 1851b8a0-f2cc-431b-bb8e-81d6fdf06de1) Rosen Publishing Group, Inc., The. (Windmill Bks.).

Under the Big Green Umbrella. 2008. (J). spiral bd. *(978-0-9793930-4-4(3))* Dandelion Publishing.

Weeks, Sarah. Ella, of Course! Cushman, Doug, illus. 2007. (ENG.). 32p. (J). (gr. -1-3). 16.00 *(978-0-15-204943-0(6),* 1194927, Clarion Bks.) HarperCollins Pubs.

Wilder, Vickie. The Umbrella. 2013. 24p. pap. 11.97 *(978-1-62212-534-0(7),* Strategic Bk. Publishing) Strategic Book Publishing & Rights Agency (SBPRA).

UNDERGROUND, ANTI-COMMUNIST

see Anti-Communist Movements

UNDERGROUND MOVEMENTS (WORLD WAR, 1939-1945)

see World War, 1939-1945—Underground Movements

UNDERGROUND RAILROAD

see also Slavery—United States

Abnett, Dan. Harriet Tubman & the Underground Railroad. (Jr. Graphic Biographies Ser.). (ENG.). 24p. (J). (gr. 2-3). 2009. 47.90 *(978-1-61513-816-6(1),* PowerKids Pr.) 2006. (Illus.). pap. 10.60 *(978-1-4042-2146-8(8),* 1e1e4fac-305d-4a55-a5ea-272406655f1b, PowerKids Pr.) 2006. (Illus.). lib. bdg. 28.93 *(978-1-4042-3393-5(8),* faf3f8b3-291f-45bf-a467-b7772adb82ea) Rosen Publishing Group, Inc., The.

—Harriet Tubman y el Ferrocarril Clandestino, 1 vol. 2009. (Historietas Juveniles: Biografías (Jr. Graphic Biographies) Ser.). (SPA., Illus.). 24p. (J). (gr. 2-3). 28.93 *(978-1-4358-8563-9(5),* 23c71f0e-1635-4a3c-be85-311206bd48c0); pap. 10.60 *(978-1-4358-3320-3(1),* c5f7e9e3-e763-46ae-87d5-410dd4478a6b) Rosen Publishing Group, Inc., The.

Agard, Sandra A. Trailblazers: Harriet Tubman: A Journey to Freedom. 2019. (Trailblazers Ser.). (ENG., Illus.). 192p. (J). (gr. 3-7). 7.99 *(978-0-593-12407-9(3));* lib. bdg. 12.99 *(978-0-593-12408-6(1))* Random Hse. Children's Bks. (Random Hse. Bks. for Young Readers).

Allen, Thomas B. Harriet Tubman, Secret Agent: How Daring Slaves & Free Blacks Spied for the Union During the Civil War. 2008. (Illus.). 192p. (J). (gr. 5-9). 5.95 *(978-1-4263-0401-9(3),* National Geographic Kids) Disney Publishing Worldwide.

Anderson, Jane. Harriet Tubman & the Underground Railroad. 2005. (J). pap. *(978-1-4108-4202-2(9))* Benchmark Education Co.

Améz, Lynda. My Journey on the Underground Railroad, 1 vol. 2015. (My Place in History Ser.). (ENG., Illus.). 24p. (J). (gr. 2-3). 24.27 *(978-1-4824-3997-7(2),* 0db0d968-c6f2-4dac-bd95-9eb248fbb175); pap. 9.15 *(978-1-4824-4010-2(5),* 8a49b461-5176-463b-bfa9-0d362da284d1) Stevens, Gareth Publishing LLLP.

Ashby, Ruth. The Underground Railroad. 2016. (Civil War Chronicles Ser.: Vol. 1). (ENG., Illus.). 48p. (J). (gr. 4-6). pap. 23.95 *(978-1-59687-515-9(1),* ipicturebooks) ibooks, Inc.

Bauer, Marion Dane. Harriet Tubman. Lyon, Tammie, illus. 2010. (My First Biography Ser.). (ENG.). 32p. (J). (gr. -1-3). 16.19 *(978-0-545-23257-9(0))* Scholastic, Inc.

Baumann, Susan K. Harriet Tubman, 1 vol. 2013. (Jr. Graphic African American History Ser.). (ENG., Illus.). 24p. (J). (gr. 2-3). 28.93 *(978-1-4777-1312-9(3),* 5857a12b-5a9e-48cd-8def-0baf9168c30b); pap. 11.60 *(978-1-4777-1449-2(9),* 6d3e3e76-88e9-4073-a428-cdc6f9f55c07) Rosen Publishing Group, Inc., The. (PowerKids Pr.).

—Harriet Tubman: Conductor of the Underground Railroad. 2013. (Jr. Graphic African American History Ser.). (Illus.). 24p. (J). (gr. 3-6). pap. 63.60 *(978-1-4777-1450-8(2),* PowerKids Pr.) Rosen Publishing Group, Inc., The.

Bennett, Doraine. Harriet Tubman. 2012. (Illus.). 24p. (J). *(978-1-935884-44-6(1))* State Standards Publishing, LLC.

Blue, Rose, et al. Harriet Tubman: Riding the Freedom Train. 2003. (Gateway Biographies Ser.: 4). (ENG., Illus.). 48p. (J). (gr. 4-8). lib. bdg. 26.60 *(978-0-7613-2571-0(9),* Millbrook Pr.) Lerner Publishing Group.

Bolte, Mari. Flight to Freedom! Nickolas Flux & the Underground Railroad, 1 vol. Simmons, Mark, illus. 2014. (Nickolas Flux History Chronicles Ser.). (ENG.). 32p. (J). (gr. 3-9). lib. bdg. 31.32 *(978-1-4914-0254-2(7),* 125809) Capstone.

Brill, Marlene Targ. Allen Jay Y el Ferrocarril Subterraneo; Allen Jay & the Underground Railroad. 2008. pap. 40.95 *(978-0-8225-9679-0(2))* Lerner Publishing Group.

Brindell Fradin, Dennis. The Underground Railroad, 1 vol. (Great Escapes Ser.). (ENG.). 2012. 80p. (gr. 6-6). 36.93 *(978-1-60870-476-7(9),* 6bfe942d-9f47-4295-a9b2-e50357064da3) 2009. 48p. (gr. 4-4). lib. bdg. 34.07 *(978-0-7614-3014-8(8),* 9dc92785-4a3d-4835-bf07-5679dd35196f) Cavendish Square Publishing LLC.

Brooks-Simon, Barbara. Escape to Freedom: The Underground Railroad Adventures of Callie & William. 2004. (I Am American Ser.). (Illus.). 40p. (J). (gr. 3-7). pap. 6.99 *(978-0-7922-6551-1(3),* National Geographic Kids) Disney Publishing Worldwide.

Carson, Mary Kay. The Underground Railroad for Kids: From Slavery to Freedom with 21 Activities. 2005. (For Kids Ser.: 3). (ENG., Illus.). 176p. (J). (gr. 4). pap. 19.99 *(978-1-55652-554-4(0))* Chicago Review Pr., Inc.

Cary, Lorene. Free! Great Escapes from Slavery on the Underground Railroad. 2011. (J). pap. 15.00 *(978-0-9819560-3-9(3))* New City Community Pr.

Chipley Slavicek, Louise. Harriet Tubman & the Underground Railroad, 1 vol. 2006. (Lucent Library of Black History Ser.). (ENG., Illus.). 104p. (gr. 7-7). lib. bdg. 36.43 *(978-1-59018-927-6(2),* 57368502-a57f-4f41-a791-2010e42c49f1, Lucent Pr.) Greenhaven Publishing LLC.

Cline-Ransome, Lesa. Before She Was Harriet. Ransome, James E., illus. (ENG.). 32p. (J). (gr. -1-3). 2019. pap. 8.99 *(978-0-8234-4429-8(5))* 2017. 18.99 *(978-0-8234-2047-6(7))* Holiday Hse., Inc.

Conkling, Winifred. Passenger on the Pearl: The True Story of Emily Edmonson's Flight from Slavery. 2016. (ENG., Illus.). 176p. (YA). (gr. 7-10). pap. 10.95 *(978-1-61620-550-8(4),* 73550) Algonquin Young Readers.

Conley, Kate. Engineering the London Underground. 2017. (Building by Design Set 2 Ser.). (ENG., Illus.). 48p. (J). (gr. 4-8). lib. bdg. 35.64 *(978-1-5321-1374-1(9),* 27672) ABDO Publishing Co.

Connors, Kathleen. The Life of Harriet Tubman, 1 vol., Vol. 1. 2013. (Famous Lives Ser.). (ENG., Illus.). 24p. (J). (gr. 1-2). 25.27 *(978-1-4824-0412-8(5),* fec7aad9-ab27-4cc4-9ace-7cd2daa329e2) Stevens, Gareth Publishing LLLP.

Cosson, M. J. Harriet Tubman, 1 vol. 2007. (Essential Lives Set 1 Ser.). (ENG., Illus.). 112p. (YA). (gr. 6-12). lib. bdg. 41.36 *(978-1-59928-842-0(7),* 6637, Essential Library) ABDO Publishing Co.

DeFord, Diane. Harriet Tubman. 2009. pap. 13.25 *(978-1-60559-061-5(4))* Hameray Publishing Group, Inc.

TUV

Dendy, Christina. Underground Railroad: Defining Moments in Canadian History. 2011. (Illus.). 32p. (gr. 5-8). (978-1-77071-691-9(2)) Weigl Educational Pubs. Ltd.

Devera, Czeena. Harriet Tubman SP. Bane, Jeff, illus. 2018. (My Early Library: Mi Mini Biografía (My Itty-Bitty Bio) Ser.). (SPA.). 24p. (J). (gr. k-1). lib. bdg. 30.64 (978-1-5341-2997-9(9), 212036) Cherry Lake Publishing.

Dodge Cummings, Judy. The Underground Railroad: Navigate the Journey from Slavery to Freedom. Casteel, Tom, illus. 2017. (Build It Yourself Ser.). (ENG.). 128p. (J). (gr. 4-7). 22.95 (978-1-61930-486-4(4), e3d6f9a9-2860-4192-b376-74bb2cb1fe44); pap. 17.95 (978-1-61930-490-1(2), d95113fe-daff-4a4f-b949-a7dd29f0b56c) Nomad Pr.

Dudley Gold, Susan. Harriet Tubman & the Underground Railroad, 1 vol. 2015. (Primary Sources of the Abolitionist Movement Ser.). (ENG., Illus.). 64p. (J). (gr. 6-6). 35.93 (978-1-5026-0522-1(8), b2a4f659-f06c-40f8-acad-53f206119593) Cavendish Square Publishing LLC.

Dunn, Joe. The Underground Railroad. 1 vol. 2007. (Graphic History Ser.). (ENG., Illus.). 32p. (J). (gr. 3-8). 32.79 (978-1-60270-080-2(X), 9046, Graphic Planet - Fiction) Magic Wagon.

Edison, Erin. Harriet Tubman, 1 vol. 2013. (Great Women in History Ser.). (ENG.). 24p. (J). (gr. -1-2). pap. 6.29 (978-1-62065-859-8(3), 121792); (gr. k-1). pap. 37.74 (978-1-62065-860-4(7), 19427, Pebble) Capstone.

Feinstein, Stephen & Taylor, Charlotte. Harriet Tubman: Hero of the Underground Railroad, 1 vol. 2015. (Exceptional African Americans Ser.). (ENG.). 24p. (gr. 3-4). pap. 10.35 (978-0-7660-7126-1(X), a9f5fbde-29ae-491f-83d3-78968c658080); (Illus.). (J). 24.27 (978-0-7660-7128-5(6), cf2c9f02-bc5b-4c9a-8a5b-0b63839c3f25) Enslow Publishing, LLC.

Flatt, Lizann. The Underground Railroad. 2015. (Uncovering the Past: Analyzing Primary Sources Ser.). (ENG., Illus.). 48p. (J). (gr. 5-6). (978-0-7787-1551-1(5)) Crabtree Publishing Co.

Ford, Carin T. The Underground Railroad & Slavery Through Primary Sources, 1 vol. 2013. (Civil War Through Primary Sources Ser.). (ENG.). 48p. (gr. 4-6). pap. 11.53 (978-1-4644-0185-5(3), cf8e5917-daa9-4221-aab6-93e96218af39); lib. bdg. 27.93 (978-0-7660-4127-1(1), a9f3a436-595a-4fd6-aa17-0fcf3ef94920) Enslow Publishing, LLC.

Ganeri, Anita. Harriet Tubman: The Life of an African-American Abolitionist, 1 vol. Shone, Rob, illus. 2004. (Graphic Nonfiction Biographies Ser.). (ENG.). 48p. (gr. 4-6). pap. 14.05 (978-1-4042-5172-4(3), c18f7686-5d5e-4423-a6ef-da0119694c22) Rosen Publishing Group, Inc., The.

Gateway Christian Academy (Fort Lauderdale, Fla.) Staff & Juvenile Collection Staff, contrib. by. Letters from Minty: An Imaginative Look into the Life & Thoughts of a Young Harriet Tubman. 2016. (Illus.). 31p. (J). (978-1-338-13424-7(8)) Scholastic, Inc.

Gayle, Sharon. Harriet Tubman & the Freedom Train: Ready-To-Read Level 3. Marshall, Felicia, illus. 2003. (Ready-To-Read Stories of Famous Americans Ser.). (ENG.). 32p. (J). (gr. 1-3). pap. 4.99 (978-0-689-85480-4(3), Simon Spotlight) Simon Spotlight.

Glatzer, Jenna. Beacon to Freedom: The Story of a Conductor on the Underground Railroad. Glenn, Ebony, illus. 2017. (Encounter: Narrative Nonfiction Picture Bks.). (ENG.). 40p. (J). (gr. 1-5). lib. bdg. 29.32 (978-1-5157-3496-3(X), 133465, Capstone Pr.) Capstone.

Gorrell, Gena. North Star to Freedom: The Story of the Underground Railroad, 1 vol. 2004. (ENG., Illus.). 184p. (J). (gr. 4-7). pap. 14.95 (978-1-55005-068-4(0), 92678a78-63f9-4b88-8ce6-a684ef8d1f15) éditeur, Annika Parance CAN. Dist: Firefly Bks., Ltd.

Hansen, Joyce & McGowan, Gary. Freedom Roads: Searching for the Underground Railroad. Ransome, James, illus. 2003. (ENG.). 166p. (J). (gr. 5-9). 18.95 (978-0-8126-2673-5(7)) Cricket Bks.

Hohn, Nadia L. Harriet Tubman: Freedom Fighter. Mazali, Gustavo, illus. 2018. (I Can Read Level 2 Ser.). (ENG.). 32p. (J). (gr. -1-3). 16.99 (978-0-06-243285-8(0)); pap. 4.99 (978-0-06-243284-1(2)) HarperCollins Pubs. (HarperCollins).

Hudson, Wade. The Underground Railroad. 2005. (Cornerstones of Freedom Ser.). (ENG., Illus.). 48p. (J). (gr. 4-6). 26.00 (978-0-516-23630-8(X), Children's Pr.) Scholastic Library Publishing.

Hyde, Natalie. The Underground Railroad. 2015. (Uncovering the Past: Analyzing Primary Sources Ser.). (ENG.). 48p. (J). (gr. 6-9). 21.75 (978-1-5311-8692-0(0)) Perfection Learning Corp.

Jones, Viola & Wolny, Philip. A Primary Source Investigation of the Underground Railroad, 1 vol. 2015. (Uncovering American History Ser.). (ENG.). 64p. (J). (gr. 5-6). 36.13 (978-1-4994-3517-7(7), 2b24fc5b-21a8-43f0-a494-b1a33286099c, Rosen Central) Rosen Publishing Group, Inc., The.

Kennon, Caroline. Depots of the Underground Railroad, 1 vol. 2016. (Hidden History Ser.). (ENG.). 32p. (J). (gr. 4-5). pap. 11.50 (978-1-4824-5794-0(6), 76949546-b4df-4a3d-9e0e-71323d1b42c0) Stevens, Gareth Publishing LLLP.

Kernan, Elizabeth. Harriet Tubman: A Lesson in Bravery. 2009. (Reading Room Collection 2 Ser.). 24p. (gr. 3-4). 42.50 (978-1-60851-966-8(X), PowerKids Pr.) Rosen Publishing Group, Inc., The.

Knapp Sawyer, Kem. The Amazing Underground Railroad, 1 vol. 2012. (Stories in American History Ser.). (ENG., Illus.). 128p. (gr. 5-6). E-Book 35.93 (978-1-4645-0470-9(9), d90c9d9b-691e-4bc5-b144-d8a8730b24de); E-Book 35.93 (978-1-4646-0470-6(3), d34e13c2-99b4-4f78-9972-08a5b2523880) Enslow Publishing, LLC.

—The Amazing Underground Railroad: Stories in American History, 1 vol. 2012. (Stories in American History Ser.). (ENG., Illus.). 128p. (gr. 5-6). 35.93 (978-0-7660-3951-3(X), fdaea571-02ee-49a7-96ae-9cff1ff26e2a); pap. 13.88 (978-1-4644-0021-6(0), a08e7a9b-deda-4afa-9622-2d1b019f26b7) Enslow Publishing, LLC.

Kramer, Barbara. National Geographic Readers: Harriet Tubman (L2) 2019. (Readers Ser.). (Illus.). 32p. (J). (gr. 1-3). pap. 4.99 (978-1-4263-3721-5(3), National Geographic Kids) Disney Publishing Worldwide.

Krasner, Barbara. Harriet Tubman: Abolitionist & Conductor of the Underground Railroad, 1 vol. 2017. (Women Who Changed History Ser.). (ENG., Illus.). 48p. (J). (gr. 6-7). lib. bdg. 28.41 (978-1-68048-659-9(4), 611d4e7b-3922-4555-9e42-c5a184b72b18, Britannica Educational Publishing) Rosen Publishing Group, Inc., The.

Landau, Elaine. Fleeing to Freedom on the Underground Railroad: The Courageous Slaves, Agents, & Conductors. 2006. (People's History Ser.). (ENG., Illus.). 88p. (gr. 5-12). lib. bdg. 33.26 (978-0-8225-3490-7(8)) Lerner Publishing Group.

—The Underground Railroad: Would You Help Them Escape?, 1 vol. 2014. (What Would You Do? Ser.). (ENG., Illus.). 48p. (gr. 3-3). 27.93 (978-0-7660-4225-4(1), 5f3aaa1d-72e8-444b-833a-bd13daeb04dc) Enslow Publishing, LLC.

Lantier, Patricia. Harriet Tubman: Conductor on the Underground Railroad, 1 vol. 2009. (Voices for Freedom Ser.). (ENG., Illus.). 64p. (J). (gr. 5-8). pap. (978-0-7787-4838-0(3)); lib. bdg. (978-0-7787-4822-9(7)) Crabtree Publishing Co.

Leavitt, Amie Jane. Harriet Tubman. 2007. (What's So Great About... ? Ser.). (Illus.). 32p. (J). (gr. 2-4). lib. bdg. 25.70 (978-1-58415-577-5(9)) Mitchell Lane Pubs.

Levy, Janey. Harriet Tubman, 1 vol. 2020. (Heroes of Black History Ser.). (ENG.). 32p. (J). (gr. 3-4). pap. 11.50 (978-1-5382-5814-9(5), 20d86b14-ede0-4eff-8674-8fe38633554b) Stevens, Gareth Publishing LLLP.

Llanas, Sheila Griffin. The Underground Railroad: A History Perspectives Book. 2013. (Perspectives Library). (ENG., Illus.). 32p. (J). (gr. 4-8). 32.07 (978-1-62431-423-0(6), 202812); pap. 14.21 (978-1-62431-499-5(6), 202814) Cherry Lake Publishing.

Loh-Hagan, Virginia. Escape North: Underground Railroad. 2019. (Behind the Curtain Ser.). (ENG.). 32p. (J). (gr. 4-8). pap. 14.21 (978-1-5341-3997-8(4), 212817); (Illus.). lib. bdg. 32.07 (978-1-5341-4341-8(6), 212816) Cherry Lake Publishing. (45th Parallel Press).

Maloof, Torrey. Harriet Tubman: Leading Others to Liberty. rev. ed. 2017. (Social Studies: Informational Text Ser.). (ENG., Illus.). 32p. (J). (gr. 4-8). pap. 11.99 (978-1-4938-3802-8(4)) Teacher Created Materials, Inc.

Mara, Wil. Rookie Biographies: Harriet Tubman. 2013. (Rookie Biographies(r) Ser.). (ENG., Illus.). 32p. (J). lib. bdg. 23.00 (978-0-531-24737-2(6)) Scholastic Library Publishing.

Marsh, Carole. Underground Railroad: Path to Freedom. 2006. 28p. pap. 5.95 (978-0-635-06359-5(X)) Gallopade International.

McConaghy, Lorraine & Bentley, Judy. Free Boy: A True Story of Slave & Master. 2013. (V Ethel Willis White Bks.). (ENG., Illus.). 112p. (J). pap. 18.95 (978-0-295-99271-6(9)) Univ. of Washington Pr.

McDonnell, Julia. Harriet Tubman in Her Own Words, 1 vol. 2015. (Eyewitness to History Ser.). (ENG., Illus.). 32p. (J). (gr. 4-5). pap. 11.50 (978-1-4824-4066-9(0), ab6258de-79e3-425e-b245-fc71bfbeadb3) Stevens, Gareth Publishing LLLP.

McDonough, Yona Zeldis. What Was the Underground Railroad? 2013. (What Was... Ser.). lib. bdg. 16.00 (978-0-606-32130-3(6)) Turtleback.

—Who Was Harriet Tubman? 2004. (ENG., Illus.). 106p. (J). lib. bdg. 13.00 (978-1-4242-2135-6(8)) Dingles & Co.

—Who Was Harriet Tubman? Harrison, Nancy, illus. 2003. (Who Was... ? Ser.). 106p. (gr. 4-7). 15.00 (978-0-7569-1590-2(2)) Perfection Learning Corp.

McDonough, Yona Zeldis & Who HQ. What Was the Underground Railroad? Mortimer, Lauren, illus. 2013. (What Was? Ser.). 112p. (J). (gr. 3-7). 5.99 (978-0-448-46712-2(7), Penguin Workshop) Penguin Young Readers Group.

—Who Was Harriet Tubman? Harrison, Nancy, illus. 2019. (Who Was? Ser.). 112p. (J). (gr. 3-7). 5.99 (978-0-593-09722-9(X)); 15.99 (978-0-593-09723-6(8)) Penguin Young Readers Group. (Penguin Workshop).

McGraw Hill. American History Ink the Underground Railroad Bk. 4. 2007. (Jt Am Hist Graph Novel Ser.). (ENG.). 24p. (gr. 6-12). spiral bd. 15.08 (978-0-07-878026-4(8), 0078780268) McGraw-Hill Education.

McKinney, Louise Chessi. The Journey to Freedom on the Underground Railroad. 2006. (ENG.). 32p. pap. 14.99 (978-1-4257-2304-0(7)) Xlibris Corp.

McNamara, Margaret. Discover the Underground Railroad. 2006. (J). pap. (978-1-4108-6449-9(9)) Benchmark Education Co.

—The Underground Railroad. 2006. (J). pap. (978-1-4108-6446-8(4)) Benchmark Education Co.

Meltzer, Brad. I Am Harriet Tubman. Eliopoulos, Christopher, illus. 2018. (Ordinary People Change the World Ser.). 40p. (J). (gr. k-4). 16.99 (978-0-7352-2871-9(X), Dial Bks) Penguin Young Readers Group.

Miner Huey, Lois. American Archaeology Uncovers the Underground Railroad, 1 vol. 2010. (American Archaeology Ser.). (ENG.). 64p. (gr. 5-5). 34.07 (978-0-7614-4267-7(7), b8da61e8-ecb8-414b-8eab-1704282f1b52) Cavendish Square Publishing LLC.

Moore Niver, Heather. Questions & Answers about the Underground Railroad, 1 vol. 2018. (Eye on Historical Sources Ser.). (ENG.). 32p. (gr. 4-4). 27.93 (978-1-5383-4131-5(X), 16bb0644-dc74-4efa-9ce8-17f9e5dcfc42, PowerKids Pr.) Rosen Publishing Group, Inc., The.

National Geographic Learning. Reading Expeditions (Social Studies: Voices from America's Past): the Underground Railroad. 2007. (Nonfiction Reading & Writing Workshops Ser.). (ENG., Illus.). 40p. (J). pap. 21.95 (978-0-7922-4549-0(0)) National Geographic School Publishing, Inc.

Norwich, Grace. I Am Harriet Tubman. Simon, Ute, illus. 2013. 127p. (J). (978-0-545-61344-6(2)) Scholastic, Inc.

—I Am Harriet Tubman (I Am #6) Simon, Ute, illus. 2013. (I Am Ser.: 6). (ENG.). 128p. (J). (gr. 3-5). pap. 5.99 (978-0-545-48436-7(7), Scholastic Paperbacks) Scholastic, Inc.

Otfinoski, Steven. From Fugitive to Freedom: The Story of the Underground Railroad. 2017. (Tangled History Ser.). (ENG., Illus.). 112p. (J). (gr. 3-9). lib. bdg. 32.65 (978-1-5157-3604-2(0), 133594, Capstone Pr.) Capstone.

Pace, Lorenzo. Harriet Tubman & My Grandmother's Quilts, 1 vol. 2015. (African American Quartet Ser.). (ENG., Illus.). 48p. (J). (gr. 2-3). 32.93 (978-1-4777-9289-6(9), 809f909e-11f1-4769-91da-ad44e05b152a, Windmill Bks.) Rosen Publishing Group, Inc., The.

Perrin, Pat & Coleman, Wim. The Mystery of the Vanishing Slaves. 2004. (Cover-To-Cover Books). (Illus.). 64p. pap. 9.00 (978-0-7891-5874-1(4)); (J). (gr. 4-7). lib. bdg. 17.95 (978-0-7569-1041-9(2)) Perfection Learning Corp.

Petry, Ann. Harriet Tubman: Conductor on the Underground Railroad. 2018. (ENG.). 272p. (J). (gr. 3-7). 16.99 (978-0-06-269130-9(9)); pap. 9.99 (978-0-06-266826-4(9)) HarperCollins Pubs. (Amistad).

Petry, Ann & Reynolds, Jason. Harriet Tubman: Conductor on the Underground Railroad. 2007. (ENG.). 256p. (J). (gr. 3-7). pap. 7.99 (978-0-06-446181-8(5), Amistad) HarperCollins Pubs.

Pferdehirt, Julia. Caroline Quarlls & the Underground Railroad. 2008. (Badger Biographies Ser.). (ENG., Illus.). 120p. (J). (gr. 3-7). per. 12.95 (978-0-87020-388-6(6)) Wisconsin Historical Society.

—Freedom Train North: Stories of the Underground Railroad in Wisconsin. Butler, Jerry, illus. Date not set. (J). (gr. 3-8). pap. 10.00 (978-0-9664925-0-7(1)) Living History Pr.

Prince, Bryan. I Came As a Stranger: The Underground Railroad. 2004. (Illus.). 168p. (J). (gr. 5). pap. 15.95 (978-0-88776-667-1(6), Tundra Bks.) Tundra Bks. CAN. Dist: Penguin Random Hse. LLC.

Raatma, Lucia. The Underground Railroad. 2011. (Cornerstones of Freedom, Third Ser.). (Illus.). 64p. (J). lib. bdg. 30.00 (978-0-531-25043-3(1), Children's Pr.) Scholastic Library Publishing.

Rajczak, Michael. The Underground Railroad, 1 vol., Vol. 1. 2013. (What You Didn't Know about History Ser.). (ENG.). 24p. (J). (gr. 2-3). 25.27 (978-1-4824-0601-6(2), 1f0c597d-26a2-49b3-9bd4-248456af2510) Stevens, Gareth Publishing LLLP.

Rausch, Monica. Harriet Tubman, 1 vol. 2007. (Great Americans Ser.). 24p. (J). (gr. 2-4). (ENG.). pap. 9.15 (978-0-8368-7693-2(8), 4353d179-8f76-4e6a-a060-e37e98de4633, Weekly Reader Leveled Readers); (SPA & ENG., Illus.). lib. bdg. 24.67 (978-0-8368-7985-8(6), 37c3334d-c56d-49f8-a22f-710f4fba4f8b); (ENG., Illus.). lib. bdg. 24.67 (978-0-8368-7686-4(5), 71172d49-c35b-42d9-9142-6c544f8c12fc, Weekly Reader Leveled Readers) Stevens, Gareth Publishing LLLP.

Roop, Peter & Roop, Connie. Who Conducted the Underground Railroad? And Other Questions about the Path to Freedom. 2008. (Illus.). 44p. (J). pap. (978-0-439-02524-9(9)) Scholastic, Inc.

Russo, Kristin J. Viewpoints on the Underground Railroad. 2018. (Perspectives Library: Viewpoints & Perspectives Ser.). (ENG., Illus.). 48p. (J). (gr. 5-8). lib. bdg. 39.21 (978-1-5341-2969-6(3), 211920) Cherry Lake Publishing.

Sawyer, Kem Knapp. Harriet Tubman. 2010. (DK Biography Ser.). (ENG., Illus.). 128p. (J). (gr. 5-8). 18.69 (978-0-7566-5807-6(1)) Dorling Kindersley Publishing, Inc.

Schraff, Anne. The Life of Harriet Tubman: Moses of the Underground Railroad, 1 vol. 2014. (Legendary African Americans Ser.). (ENG., Illus.). 96p. (J). (gr. 6-7). 31.61 (978-0-7660-6137-8(X), 5842c0c2-69d9-4654-adef-59a5d8989371) Enslow Publishing, LLC.

Shone, Rob. Harriet Tubman: The Life of an African-American Abolitionist. 2009. (Graphic Nonfiction Biographies Ser.). (ENG.). 48p. (YA). (gr. 4-5). 58.50 (978-1-61513-018-4(7), Rosen Reference) Rosen Publishing Group, Inc., The.

Shone, Rob & Ganeri, Anita. Harriet Tubman: The Life of an African-American Abolitionist, 1 vol. 2004. (Graphic Nonfiction Biographies Ser.). (ENG., Illus.). 48p. (J). (gr. 4-6). lib. bdg. 37.13 (978-1-4042-0245-0(5), ba8a5d50-aee5-4c2c-802b-2ead9f0d0c2a) Rosen Publishing Group, Inc., The.

Simons, Barbara Brooks. Escape to Freedom the Underground Railroad: Set Of 6. 2011. (Navigators Ser.). (J). pap. 48.00 net. (978-1-4108-6261-7(5)) Benchmark Education Co.

—Escape to Freedom: the Underground Railroad: Text Pairs. 2008. (Bridges/Navigators Ser.). (J). (gr. 5). 81.00 (978-1-4108-8415-2(5)) Benchmark Education Co.

Skelton, Renee. Harriet Tubman A Woman of Courage. 2005. 2005p. (J). lib. bdg. 15.00 (978-1-4242-0849-4(1)) Fitzgerald Bks.

—A Woman of Courage. 2005. (Time for Kids Ser.). (ENG., Illus.). 48p. (J). (gr. 2-4). pap. 3.99 (978-0-06-057607-3(3)) HarperCollins Pubs.

Skelton, Renee & Time for Kids Editors. Time for Kids: A Woman of Courage. 2005. (Time for Kids Ser.). (ENG., Illus.). 48p. (J). 16.99 (978-0-06-057608-0(1)) HarperCollins Pubs.

Stearns, Dan. Harriet Tubman & the Underground Railroad, 1 vol. 2005. (In the Footsteps of American Heroes Ser.). (ENG., Illus.). 64p. (J). (gr. 5-8). lib. bdg. 36.67 (978-0-8368-6428-1(X), 0c93b9fc-79bf-476e-a6cc-85a9c820bfac, Gareth Stevens Secondary Library) Stevens, Gareth Publishing LLLP.

Stein, R. Conrad. Escaping Slavery on the Underground Railroad, 1 vol. 2008. (From Many Cultures, One History Ser.). (ENG., Illus.). 128p. (gr. 5-6). lib. bdg. 35.93 (978-0-7660-2799-2(6), 6824421d-86d0-4c2b-880d-c9848439e5d1) Enslow Publishing, LLC.

—Harriet Tubman: On My Underground Railroad I Never Ran My Train off the Track, 1 vol. 2008. (Americans: the Spirit of a Nation Ser.). (ENG., Illus.). 128p. (J). (gr. 5-6). lib. bdg. 35.93 (978-0-7660-3481-5(X), f1675bad-1c07-4b76-adc6-eb89aa02c903) Enslow Publishing, LLC.

Stein, R. Conrad & Taylor, Charlotte. The Underground Railroad, 1 vol. 2015. (Our Shared History Ser.). (ENG., Illus.). 128p. (gr. 7-7). lib. bdg. 38.93 (978-0-7660-7014-1(X), d87cd6fa-e11a-4f30-bf07-1a26491132a5) Enslow Publishing, LLC.

Stoltman, Joan. Harriet Tubman, 1 vol. 2017. (Little Biographies of Big People Ser.). (ENG.). 24p. (J). (gr. 1-2). pap. 9.15 (978-1-5382-0923-3(3), 019cd048-f5b7-4135-9d4e-0594639408d7) Stevens, Gareth Publishing LLLP.

—Harriet Tubman, 1 vol. Garcia, Ana Maria, tr. 2017. (Pequeñas Biografías de Grandes Personajes (Little Biographies of Big People) Ser.). (SPA.). 24p. (J). (gr. 1-2). pap. 9.15 (978-1-5382-1559-3(4), 885f27e3-a953-4d2e-9705-f3a7f168bf4c); lib. bdg. 24.27 (978-1-5382-1532-6(2), 2e5b2b7a-3997-4773-aecd-9f20f001c9fc) Stevens, Gareth Publishing LLLP.

Susienka, Kristen. Harriet Tubman, 1 vol. 2019. (African American Leaders of Courage Ser.). (ENG.). 24p. (J). (gr. 1-2). pap. 9.25 (978-1-7253-0838-1(X), bd382e70-5850-4e81-a8f1-6f6b909b71f2, PowerKids Pr.) Rosen Publishing Group, Inc., The.

Tate, Don. William Still & His Freedom Stories: The Father of the Underground Railroad. 2020. (Illus.). 40p. (J). (gr. 1-4). 18.99 (978-1-56145-935-3(6)) Peachtree Publishing Co. Inc.

Taylor, Marion. Harriet Tubman. 2004. (Black Americans of Achievement Legacy Edition Ser.). (ENG., Illus.). 112p. (J). (gr. 6-12). 35.00 (978-0-7910-8166-2(4), P114170, Facts On File) Infobase Holdings, Inc.

Troupe, Thomas Kingsley. Harriet Tubman's Escape: a Fly on the Wall History. Tejido, Jomike, illus. 2017. (Fly on the Wall History Ser.). (ENG.). 32p. (J). (gr. 1-3). lib. bdg. 27.99 (978-1-4795-9788-8(0), 133417, Picture Window Bks.) Capstone.

Waxman, Laura Hamilton. How Did Slaves Find a Route to Freedom? And Other Questions about the Underground Railroad. 2011. (Six Questions of American History Ser.). (ENG.). 48p. (gr. 4-6). pap. 56.72 (978-0-7613-7641-5(0)); (Illus.). (J). lib. bdg. 30.65 (978-0-7613-5229-7(5), c97e1afb-3b6e-49d9-bb44-63d8c24cf045, Lerner Pubns.) Lerner Publishing Group.

Weidt, Maryann N. Harriet Tubman. 2003. (History Maker Bios Ser.). (Illus.). 47p. (J). 26.60 (978-0-8225-4676-4(0), Lerner Pubns.) Lerner Publishing Group.

Weymouth Seguin, Marilyn. The Freedom Stairs: The Story of Adam Lowry Rankin, Underground Railroad Conductor. 2004. (ENG., Illus.). 93p. (J). (gr. 3-7). per. 12.95 net. (978-0-8283-2084-9(5)) Branden Bks.

Wheeler, Jill C. Harriet Tubman. 2003. (Breaking Barriers Ser.). (Illus.). 64p. (J). (gr. 3-8). 27.07 (978-1-57765-908-2(2), Abdo & Daughters) ABDO Publishing Co.

Winters, Kay. Voices from the Underground Railroad. Day, Larry, illus. 2018. 48p. (J). (gr. 2-4). 18.99 (978-0-8037-4092-1(1), Dial Bks) Penguin Young Readers Group.

Wolny, Philip. The Underground Railroad: A Primary Source History of the Journey to Freedom. (Primary Sources in American History Ser.). 64p. (gr. 5-8). 2009. 58.50 (978-1-60851-505-9(2)) 2004. (ENG., Illus.). (J). lib. bdg. 37.13 (978-0-8239-4008-0(X), 9edec6a4-1163-41a6-b9ed-75ecfb826a0e, Rosen Reference) Rosen Publishing Group, Inc., The.

UNDERGROUND RAILROAD—FICTION

Alonso, Harriet Hyman. Martha & the Slave Catchers. Zunon, Elizabeth, illus. 2017. 256p. (J). (gr. 3-7). 17.95 (978-1-60980-800-6(2), Triangle Square) Seven Stories Pr.

Bradbury, Jennifer. River Runs Deep. 2015. (ENG., Illus.). 336p. (J). (gr. 4-8). 17.99 (978-1-4424-6824-5(6), Atheneum Bks. for Young Readers) Simon & Schuster Children's Publishing.

Brill, Marlene Targ. Allen Jay & the Undergound Railroad, 4 bks., Set. Porter, Janice Lee, illus. 2007. (Readalongs for Beginning Readers Ser.). (J). (gr. 1-3). pap. 37.95 incl. audio (978-1-59519-947-8(0)) Live Oak Media.

—Allen Jay y el Ferrocarril Subterraneo. Porter, Janice Lee, illus. 2007. (Yo Solo - Historia (on My Own - History) Ser.). 48p. (J). (gr. 4-7). per. 6.95 (978-0-8225-7787-4(9)) Lerner Publishing Group.

—The Underground Railroad Adventure of Allen Jay, Antislavery Activist. Hammond, Ted & Carbajal, Richard Pimentel, illus. 2011. (History's Kid Heroes Set III Ser.). pap. 51.02 (978-0-7613-8622-3(X), Graphic Universe™) Lerner Publishing Group.

Carbone, Elisa. Stealing Freedom. 2003. (EMC Masterpiece Series Access Editions). (Illus.). xix, 284p. (J). 12.99 (978-0-8219-2507-2(5)) EMC/Paradigm Publishing.

Cole, Henry. Unspoken: a Story from the Underground Railroad. Cole, Henry, illus. 2012. (ENG., Illus.). 40p. (J). (gr. k-2). 19.99 (978-0-545-39997-5(1), Scholastic Pr.) Scholastic, Inc.

Dowell, Frances O'Roark. Trouble the Water. (ENG., Illus.). (J). (gr. 4-8). 2017. 304p. pap. 8.99 (978-1-4814-2464-6(5)) 2016. 288p. 16.99 (978-1-4814-2463-9(7)) Simon & Schuster Children's Publishing.

Draper, Sharon M. Lost in the Tunnel of Time. Watson, Jesse Joshua, illus. 2011. (Clubhouse Mysteries Ser.: 2). (ENG.). 112p. (J). (gr. 3-7). pap. 6.99 (978-1-4424-2704-4(3), Aladdin) Simon & Schuster Children's Publishing.

—Lost in the Tunnel of Time. Watson, Jesse Joshua, illus. 2011. (Clubhouse Mysteries Ser.: 2). (ENG.). 112p. (J). (gr. 3-7). lib. bdg. 16.99 (978-1-4424-2703-7(5), Simon & Schuster/Paula Wiseman Bks.) Simon & Schuster/Paula Wiseman Bks.

Evatt, Harriet. The Secret of the Old Coach Inn. Stone, David, illus. 2011. 190p. 42.95 (978-1-258-08239-0(X)) Literary Licensing, LLC.

Falk, Elizabeth Sullivan. Lettie's North Star. Wolf, Elizabeth, illus. 2006. (J). (978-1-59336-694-0(9)) Mondo Publishing.

Frazier, Jan. Prairie Points:: a Civil War Sanctuary. 2017. (ENG., Illus.). (J). pap. 12.95 (978-1-55571-864-0(7), Hellgate Pr.) L & R Publishing, LLC.

Gayle, Sharon Shavers. Emma's Escape: A Story of America's Underground Railroad. Velasquez, Eric, illus. 3rd ed. 2003. (Soundprints' Read-and-Discover Ser.). (ENG.). 48p. (J). (gr. -1-3). pap. 3.95 (978-1-59249-021-9(2), S2009) Soundprints.

Gilfert, Shirley Tankersley. The Other Side of Jordan: A Story of the Underground Railroad. 2007. 140p. 21.95

(978-0-595-70289-3(9)); per. 11.95 (978-0-595-46274-2(X)) iUniverse, Inc.

Griffiths, Robert. Adventures of Clive. 2005. 89p. pap. 8.81 (978-1-4116-5191-3(X)) Lulu Pr., Inc.

Grimes, Nikki. Chasing Freedom: the Life Journeys of Harriet Tubman & Susan B. Anthony, Inspired by Historical Facts. Wood, Michele, illus. 2015. (ENG.). 56p. (J). (gr. 1-5). 21.99 (978-0-439-79338-4(6), Orchard Bks.) Scholastic, Inc.

Hamilton, Virginia. The House of Dies Drear. 8.97 (978-0-13-437491-8(6)) Prentice Hall PTR.

—The House of Dies Drear. 2006. (ENG., Illus.). 256p. (J). (gr. 6-9). pap. 8.99 (978-1-4169-1405-1(6), Aladdin) Simon & Schuster Children's Publishing.

Hedstrom-Page, Deborah. From Slavery to Freedom with Harriet Tubman. Martinez, Sergio, illus. 2007. (My American Journey Ser.). 84p. (J). (gr. 3-9). 9.99 (978-0-8054-3268-8(X)) B&H Publishing Group.

Hopkinson, Deborah. Under the Quilt of Night. Ransome, James E., illus. 2005. (gr. k-5). 18.00 (978-0-7569-5077-4(5)) Perfection Learning Corp.

—Under the Quilt of Night. Ransome, James E., illus. 2005. (ENG.). 40p. (J). (gr. k-5). reprint ed. 7.99 (978-0-689-87700-1(5), Aladdin) Simon & Schuster Children's Publishing.

Hulme, Lucy V. Passages, 1 bk. Redpath, Dale, illus. 2005. 40p. (J). 7.95 (978-0-9769854-0-2(3), 001) Combs-Hulme Publishing.

Landau, Elaine. The Underground Railroad: Would You Help Them Escape?, 1 vol. 2014. (What Would You Do? Ser.). (ENG., Illus.). 48p. (gr. 3-3). pap. 11.53 (978-1-4644-0393-4(7), 29c78e8a-1c2f-4772-b420-98ae07f9cadc, Enslow Elementary) Enslow Publishing, LLC.

LeSourd, Nancy. Escape on the Underground Railroad, 1 vol. 2008. (Liberty Letters Ser.). (ENG.). 224p. (J). pap. 7.99 (978-0-310-71391-3(9)) Zonderkidz.

—Secrets of Civil War Spies, 1 vol. 2008. (Liberty Letters Ser.). (ENG.). 224p. (J). pap. 7.99 (978-0-310-71390-6(0)) Zonderkidz.

Levine, Ellen. Henry's Freedom Box, 1 vol. Nelson, Kadir, illus. 2007. (ENG.). 40p. (J). (gr. -1-3). 18.99 (978-0-439-77733-9(X), Scholastic Pr.) Scholastic, Inc.

MacColl, Michaela. The Revelation of Louisa May: A Novel of Intrigue & Romance. 2015. (ENG.). 272p. (J). (gr. 7-12). 16.99 (978-1-4521-3357-7(3)) Chronicle Bks. LLC.

Marsh, Carole. The Mystery on the Underground Railroad. 2009. (Real Kids, Real Places Ser.). (Illus.). 146p. (J). lib. bdg. 18.99 (978-0-635-06991-7(1), Marsh, Carole Mysteries) Gallopade International.

—The Mystery on the Underground Railroad (Hardcover) 2003. 160p. (gr. 2-8). 14.95 (978-0-635-02110-6(2)) Gallopade International.

McKissack, Patricia C. A Picture of Freedom (Dear America) 2011. (Dear America Ser.). (ENG.). 240p. (J). (gr. 3-9). 14.99 (978-0-545-24253-0(3), Scholastic Pr.) Scholastic, Inc.

McMann, Lisa. The Trap Door. 2015. (Infinity Ring Ser.: 3). lib. bdg. 17.20 (978-0-606-37788-1(3)) Turtleback.

Meltzer, Milton. Underground Man. 2006. (ENG.). 288p. (J). (gr. 5-7). pap. 15.99 (978-0-15-205524-0(X), 1196611, Clarion Bks.) HarperCollins Pubs.

Messner, Kate. Long Road to Freedom (Ranger in Time #3) McMorris, Kelley, illus. 2015. (Ranger in Time Ser.: 3). (ENG.). 160p. (J). (gr. 2-5). pap. 5.99 (978-0-545-63920-0(4), Scholastic Pr.) Scholastic, Inc.

Nelson, Vaunda Micheaux. Almost to Freedom. Bootman, Colin, illus. 2003. (ENG.). 40p. (J). (gr. k-3). 19.99 (978-1-57505-342-4(X), be180074-5c10-415a-9c04-ab11908ca27f, Carolrhoda Bks.) Lerner Publishing Group.

Novel Units. The House of Dies Drear Novel Units Teacher Guide. 2019. (ENG.). (J). pap. 12.99 (978-1-56137-516-5(0), NU5168, Novel Units, Inc.) Classroom Library Co.

Orzechowski, Shawneen. Midnight Journey: Running for Freedom on the Underground Railroad. 2006. 112p. (J). (gr. 3-7). per. 8.95 (978-1-57249-379-7(8), White Mane Kids) White Mane Publishing Co., Inc.

Pearsall, Shelley. Trouble Don't Last. 2003. (ENG.). 256p. (J). (gr. 3-7). reprint ed. 7.99 (978-0-440-41811-5(9), Yearling) Random Hse. Children's Bks.

Phillips, Dee. Runaway. 2014. (Yesterday's Voices Ser.). (YA). lib. bdg. 19.60 (978-0-606-35584-1(7)) Turtleback.

Pignat, Caroline. The Gospel Truth, 1 vol. 2014. (ENG.). 328p. (YA). (gr. 9-12). pap. 12.95 (978-0-88995-493-9(3), 6f9201cc-ee51-4595-847d-0fb9335d7ae7) Trifolium Bks., Inc. CAN. Dist: Firefly Bks., Ltd.

Plaxton, Judith. Morning Star, 1 vol. 2011. (ENG.). 278p. (J). (gr. 5-8). pap. 10.95 (978-1-897187-97-5(1)) Second Story Pr. CAN. Dist: Orca Bk. Pubs. USA.

Polacco, Patricia. January's Sparrow. Polacco, Patricia, illus. 2009. (Illus.). 96p. (J). (gr. 3-7). 23.99 (978-0-399-25077-4(8), Philomel Bks.) Penguin Young Readers Group.

Porter, Janice Lee, illus. Allen Jay & the Underground Railroad, 4 bks., Set. 2006. (Readalongs for Beginning Readers Ser.). (J). (gr. 2-5). pap. 39.95 incl. audio compact disk (978-1-59519-951-5(9)) Live Oak Media.

Raven, Margot Theis. Night Boat to Freedom. Lewis, E. B., illus. 2008. (ENG.). 40p. (J). (gr. 1-4). pap. 10.99 (978-0-312-55018-9(9), 900055951) Square Fish.

Reed, Stephanie. The Light Across the River, 1 vol. 2008. (Illus.). 216p. (J). (gr. 4-7). pap. 10.99 (978-0-8254-3574-4(9)) Kregel Pubns.

Reese Martin, Faith. Ghost Train to Freedom: An Adventure on the Underground Railroad. Sachs, Barry, illus. 2012. (JMP Mystery Ser.: Bk. 3). (ENG.). 416p. (YA). pap. 14.99 (978-1-60800-014-2(1), American Literary Publishing) LifeReloaded Specialty Publishing LLC.

Roop, Peter. Lead Us to Freedom, Harriet Tubman! 2006. (Illus.). 58p. (J). pap. (978-0-439-79255-4(X)) Scholastic, Inc.

Rubenstein, Dan. Railroad of Courage. 2017. (ENG.). 162p. pap. 11.95 (978-1-55380-514-4(3)) Ronsdale Pr. CAN. Dist: SPD-Small Pr. Distribution.

Sargent, Dave & Sargent, Pat. Nubbin: (Linebacked Apricot Dun) Freedom, 30 vols., Vol. 43. Lenoir, Jane, illus. 2003. (Saddle up Ser.: Vol. 43). 42p. (J). pap. 10.95 (978-1-56763-704-5(3)); lib. bdg. 23.60 (978-1-56763-703-8(5)) Ozark Publishing.

Smith, Nikki Shannon. Ann Fights for Freedom: An Underground Railroad Survival Story. Trunfio, Alessia, illus. 2019. (Girls Survive Ser.). (ENG.). 112p. (J). (gr. 3-7). lib. bdg. 25.99 (978-1-4965-7853-2(8), 139371, Stone Arch Bks.) Capstone.

Squier, Robert, illus. Follow the Drinking Gourd: An Underground Railroad Story, 1 vol. 2012. (Night Sky Stories Ser.). (ENG.). 24p. (J). (gr. 2-4). pap. 8.95 (978-1-4048-7714-6(2), 120446, Picture Window Bks.) Capstone.

Swain, Gwenyth & Whelan, Gloria. Voices for Freedom. Geister, David et al, illus. 2013. (American Adventures Ser.). (ENG.). 72p. (J). (gr. 3-6). 6.99 (978-1-58536-886-0(5), 202900) Sleeping Bear Pr.

Vande Velde, Vivian. There's a Dead Person Following My Sister Around. 2008. (ENG., Illus.). 160p. (J). (gr. 5-7). pap. 11.95 (978-0-15-206467-9(2), 1199316, Clarion Bks.) HarperCollins Pubs.

Walker, Sally M. Freedom Song: The Story of Henry Box Brown. Qualls, Sean, illus. 2012. (ENG.). 40p. (J). (gr. -1-3). 18.99 (978-0-06-058310-1(X), HarperCollins) HarperCollins Pubs.

Warburton, Carol. Edge of Night: A Novel. 2004. (Illus.). 278p. pap. 14.95 (978-1-59156-013-5(6)) Covenant Communications, Inc.

Weston Woods Staff, creator. Henry's Freedom Box. 2011. 38.75 (978-0-545-31403-9(8)); 18.95 (978-0-545-31402-2(X)) Weston Woods Studios, Inc.

Wisehart, Randall. Luke's Summer Secret. 2017. 135p. (YA). pap. 12.00 (978-0-913408-45-2(X)) Friends United Pr.

Wyeth, Sharon Dennis. Message in the Sky Bk. 3: Corey's Underground Railroad Diary. 2003. (My America Ser.). (ENG.). 112p. (J). 10.95 (978-0-439-37057-8(4), Scholastic Pr.) Scholastic, Inc.

UNDERGROUND RAILROADS

see Subways

UNDERSEA EXPLORATION

see Underwater Exploration

UNDERSEA TECHNOLOGY

see Oceanography

UNDERSTANDING

see Intellect; Knowledge, Theory of

UNDERWATER EXPLORATION

see also Marine Biology; Skin Diving

Bodden, Valerie. To the Ocean Deep. 2011. (Great Expeditions Ser.). (ENG., Illus.). 48p. (J). (gr. 5-8). 35.65 (978-1-60818-067-7(0), 22154, Creative Education); pap. 12.00 (978-0-89812-665-5(7), 22160, Creative Paperbacks) Creative Co., The.

Chapman, Simon. Under the Sea. Chapman, Simon, illus. 2005. (Illus.). 112p. (J). lib. bdg. 20.00 (978-1-4242-0631-5(6)) Fitzgerald Bks.

Collins, Luke. Underwater Robots. 2020. (World of Robots Ser.). (ENG.). 24p. (J). (gr. k-3). lib. bdg. (978-1-62310-167-1(0), 14438, Bolt Jr.) Black Rabbit Bks.

Cusolito, Michelle. Flying Deep: Climb Inside Deep-Sea Submersible Alvin. Wong, Nicole, illus. 2018. 32p. (J). (gr. k-4). 17.99 (978-1-58089-811-9(4)); pap. 7.99 (978-1-58089-841-6(6)) Charlesbridge Publishing, Inc.

Fertig, Dennis. Sylvia Earle: Ocean Explorer, 1 vol. 2014. (Women in Conservation Ser.). (ENG., Illus.). 48p. (J). (gr. 3-6). 35.99 (978-1-4846-0470-0(9), 126602); pap. 8.99 (978-1-4846-0475-5(X), 126606) Capstone. (Heinemann).

Gibbons, Gail. Exploring the Deep, Dark Sea. (Illus.). 32p. (J). (gr. -1-3). 2020. pap. 8.99 (978-0-8234-4602-5(6)) 2019. 18.99 (978-0-8234-4152-5(0)) Holiday Hse., Inc.

Graham, Ian. Be in the First Submarine! An Undersea Expedition You'D Rather Avoid. Antram, David, illus. 2008. (You Wouldn't Want to...: American History Ser.). (ENG.). 32p. (J). 29.00 (978-0-531-20702-4(1), Watts, Franklin) Scholastic Library Publishing.

—You Wouldn't Want to Be in the First Submarine! An Undersea Expedition You'd Rather Avoid. Antram, David, illus. 2008. (You Wouldn't Want to...: American History Ser.). (ENG.). 32p. (J). (gr. 3-18). pap. 9.95 (978-0-531-21912-6(7), Watts, Franklin) Scholastic Library Publishing.

Hall, Kirsten. Deep Sea Adventures: A Chapter Book. 2003. (True Tales Ser.). (ENG., Illus.). 48p. (J). 22.50 (978-0-516-22917-1(6), Children's Pr.) Scholastic Library Publishing.

Labrecque, Ellen. Sarah Mather & Underwater Telescopes. 2017. (21st Century Junior Library: Women Innovators Ser.). (ENG., Illus.). 24p. (J). (gr. 2-5). lib. bdg. 29.21 (978-1-63472-181-3(0), 209296) Cherry Lake Publishing.

MacCarald, Clara. Exploring Ocean Depths. 2019. (Science for the Future Ser.). (ENG., Illus.). 48p. (J). (gr. 5-6). pap. 11.95 (978-1-64185-848-9(6), 1641858486); lib. bdg. 34.21 (978-1-64185-779-6(X), 164185779X) North Star Editions. (Focus Readers).

Mara, Wil. Deep-Sea Exploration: Science, Technology, Engineering (Calling All Innovators: a Career for You) 2015. (Calling All Innovators: a Career for You Ser.). (ENG., Illus.). 64p. (J). (gr. 5-8). pap. 8.95 (978-0-531-21173-1(8), Children's Pr.) Scholastic Library Publishing.

Marx, Christy. Life in the Ocean Depths. (Life in Extreme Environments Ser.). 64p. (gr. 5-8). 2009. 53.00 (978-1-61514-272-9(X)) 2003. (ENG.). (YA). pap. 13.95 (978-1-4358-3265-7(5), cf7d2f7a-5334-4406-9410-309b306f5853) Rosen Publishing Group, Inc., The. (Rosen Reference).

Mizielinska, Aleksandra & Mizielinski, Daniel. Under Water, under Earth. 2016. (ENG., Illus.). 112p. (J). (gr. 2-4). 37.99 (978-0-7636-8922-3(X), Big Picture Press) Candlewick Pr.

National Geographic Learning. Reading Expeditions (Science: Scientists in the Field): Robert Ballard: Discovering Underwater Treasures. 2007. (Rise & Shine Ser.). (ENG., Illus.). 32p. (J). pap. 18.95 (978-0-7922-8881-7(5)) CENGAGE Learning.

Peterson, Christy. Into the Deep: Science, Technology, & the Quest to Protect the Ocean. 2020. (ENG., Illus.). 152p. (YA). (gr. 6-12). lib. bdg. 39.99 (978-1-5415-5555-6(4), 146760ff-0ad5-44c7-8434-6d8a84d3d8ab, Twenty-First Century Bks.) Lerner Publishing Group.

Prather, Michelle. On the Job: Underwater Investigators: Plotting Rational Numbers (Grade 6) 2019. (Mathematics in the Real World Ser.). (ENG., Illus.). 32p. (gr. 5-8). pap. 11.99 (978-1-4258-5884-1(8)) Teacher Created Materials, Inc.

Reichard, Susan E. Who on Earth Is Sylvia Earle? Undersea Explorer of the Ocean, 1 vol. 2009. (Scientists Saving the Earth Ser.). (ENG., Illus.). 112p. (J). (gr. 5-6). lib. bdg. 35.93 (978-1-59845-118-4(9), dae42add-b697-4162-b665-6aa14bed4142) Enslow Publishing, LLC.

Rhodes, Mary Jo & Hall, David. Undersea Encounters, 5 bks., Set. Hall, David, photos by. Incl. Seahorses & Sea Dragons. (Illus.). 48p. (J). (gr. 3-7). 2005. lib. bdg. 27.00 (978-0-516-24393-1(4), Children's Pr.); (Illus.). 2005. 125.00 o.p. (978-0-516-24439-6(6), Children's Pr.) Scholastic Library Publishing.

Rice, Racheal & Benchmark Education Co., LLC. Robert Ballard: Deepwater Explorer. 2014. (Text Connections Ser.). (J). (gr. 3). (978-1-4509-9650-1(7)) Benchmark Education Co.

Rosenstock, Barb. Otis & Will Discover the Deep: The Record-Setting Dive of the Bathysphere. Roy, Katherine, illus. 2018. (ENG.). 48p. (J). (gr. -1-3). 18.99 (978-0-316-39382-9(7)) Little, Brown Bks. for Young Readers.

Sheehan, Robert. The Undersea Lab: Exploring the Oceans, 1 vol., 1. 2014. (Discovery Education: Earth & Space Science Ser.). (ENG.). 32p. (gr. 4-5). 28.93 (978-1-4777-6166-3(7), 6a769a12-03d4-48cc-a641-d87d763751bd, PowerKids Pr.) Rosen Publishing Group, Inc., The.

Spilsbury, Richard. Deep Sea Exploration. 2010. (ENG.). 32p. (J). (978-0-7787-9893-4(3)); (gr. 3-6). pap. (978-0-7787-9914-6(X)) Crabtree Publishing Co.

Swanson, Jennifer. Astronaut-Aquanaut: How Space Science & Sea Science Interact. 2018. (Illus.). 96p. (J). (gr. 3-7). 18.99 (978-1-4263-2867-1(2), National Geographic Kids) Disney Publishing Worldwide.

Tief im Meer. (GER.). 19.95 (978-3-411-09271-0(8)) Bibliographisches Institut & F. A. Brockhaus AG DEU. Dist: Distribooks, Inc.

Troupe, Thomas Kingsley. Underwater Robots. 2017. (Mighty Bots Ser.). (ENG.). 32p. (J). (gr. 4-6). pap. 9.99 (978-1-64466-201-4(9), 11450); (Illus.). lib. bdg. (978-1-68072-161-4(5), 10506) Black Rabbit Bks. (Bolt).

Vogel, Carole Garbuny. Underwater Exploration. 2003. (Restless Sea Ser.). (ENG., Illus.). 80p. (J). 30.50 (978-0-531-12327-0(8), Watts, Franklin) Scholastic Library Publishing.

Westerskov, Kim, photos by. Diving in Antarctica. 2004. (Illus.). 32p. (J). (978-0-7685-2384-3(2)) Dominie Pr., Inc.

White, Katherine. Sylvia Earle: Deep Sea Explorer & Ocean Activist. (Women Hall of Famers in Mathematics & Science Ser.). 112p. (gr. 5-8). 2009. 63.90 (978-1-60854-814-9(7)) 2003. (ENG., Illus.). lib. bdg. 39.80 (978-0-8239-3879-7(4), 605a1e36-bafd-4ce1-86f8-a6c460e534d4) Rosen Publishing Group, Inc., The. (Rosen Reference).

UNDERWATER EXPLORATION—FICTION

Bardhan-Quallen, Sudipta. Purrmaids #1: the Scaredy Cat. Wu, Vivien, illus. 2017. (Purrmaids Ser.: 1). (ENG.). 96p. (J). (gr. 1-4). 6.99 (978-1-5247-0161-1(0), Random Hse. Bks. for Young Readers) Random Hse. Children's Bks.

Belcher, Angie & Belcher, Andy. Swimming with Dolphins. 2005. (Big Cat Ser.). pap. 6.50 (978-1-60457-102-8(0)) Pacific Learning, Inc.

Berardy, Lloyd, 1st. A Tropical Bear in Hawaii Goes Underwater. 2006. (J). 12.95 (978-1-4276-0212-1(3)) Aardvark Global Publishing.

Bonnell, Kris. Down in the Sea. 2006. (J). pap. 5.95 (978-1-933727-38-7(1)) Reading Reading Bks., LLC.

Chiarello, Robin Taylor. The Clam Diggers Ball. Bohart, Lisa, illus. 2011. 40p. pap. 15.95 (978-1-61493-013-6(9)) Peppertree Pr., The.

Cookson, Jan. Ant on the Run. 2003. 84p. pap. 8.95 (978-0-595-29440-4(5)) iUniverse, Inc.

Davies, Benji, illus. Bizzy Bear: Deep-Sea Diver. 2016. (Bizzy Bear Ser.). (ENG.). 8p. (J). (— 1). bds. 7.99 (978-0-7636-8647-5(6)) Candlewick Pr.

de Lesseps, Ferdinand Zoticus. Oceanology: The True Account of the Voyage of the Nautilus. Hawkins, Emily, ed. 2009. (Ologies Ser.: 8). (ENG., Illus.). 32p. (J). (gr. 3-7). 29.99 (978-0-7636-4290-7(8)) Candlewick Pr.

Fraioli, James O. Polar Ice Expedition: With Jean-Michel Cousteau. 2009. (J). (gr. 4-7). (978-1-4236-0550-8(0)) Gibbs Smith, Publisher.

Greenburg, J. C. Andrew Lost #5: under Water. Reed, Mike, illus. 2003. (Andrew Lost Ser.: 5). (ENG.). 96p. (J). (gr. 1-4). mass mkt. 4.99 (978-0-375-82523-1(1), Random Hse. Bks. for Young Readers) Random Hse. Children's Bks.

King, Trey. Deep-Sea Treasure Dive. Wang, Sean & Hyland, Greg, illus. 2016. 24p. (J). (978-1-5182-0031-1(1)) Scholastic, Inc.

Meomi. The Octonauts: Underwater Adventures Box Set. 2017. (Octonauts Ser.). (Illus.). 160p. (J). (gr. -1-3). 59.95 (978-1-59702-135-7(0)) Immedium.

—The Octonauts & the Frown Fish. 2008. (Octonauts Ser.). (Illus.). 36p. (J). (gr. -1-3). 15.95 (978-1-59702-014-5(1)) Immedium.

—The Octonauts & the Great Ghost Reef. 2009. (Octonauts Ser.). (Illus.). 36p. (J). (gr. -1-3). 15.95 (978-1-59702-019-0(2)) Immedium.

—The Octonauts & the Only Lonely Monster. 2006. (Octonauts Ser.). (ENG., Illus.). 36p. (J). (gr. -1-3). 15.95 (978-1-59702-005-3(2)) Immedium.

—The Octonauts & the Sea of Shade. 2007. (Octonauts Ser.). (Illus.). 36p. (J). (gr. k-2). 15.95 (978-1-59702-010-7(9)) Immedium.

Montgomery, R. A. Journey under the Sea. Sundaravej, Sittisan, illus. 2006. (ENG.). 144p. (J). (gr. 4-8). per. 7.99 (978-1-933390-02-4(6), CHCL02) Chooseco LLC.

—Journey under the Sea. 2006. (Choose Your Own Adventure Ser.: 2). 17.20 (978-1-4177-6410-5(4)) Turtleback.

—Return to Atlantis. 2005. (Choose Your Own Adventure Ser.). (Illus.). 119p. (gr. 4-8). pap. 5.50 (978-0-7608-9706-5(9)) Sundance/Newbridge Educational Publishing.

—Return to Atlantis. Sundaravej, Sittisan & Thongmoon, Kriangsak, illus. 2006. (ENG.). 144p. (J). (gr. 4-8). per. 7.99 (978-1-933390-18-5(2), CHCL18) Chooseco LLC.

Riordan, Rick. Daughter of the Deep. Naidu, Lavanya, illus. 2021. xii, 336p. (J). (978-1-368-08084-2(7)) Disney Pr.

—Daughter of the Deep. (ENG.). 2023. 368p. (J). (gr. 5-9). pap. 9.99 (978-1-368-07793-4(5), Disney-Hyperion) 2023. 368p. (gr. 6-8). 26.19 (978-1-5364-7874-7(1)) 2021. (Illus.). 352p. (J). (gr. 5-9). 19.99 (978-1-368-07792-7(7), Disney-Hyperion) Disney Publishing Worldwide.

Scott, Jeff. The Discovery of Monkey Island. 2008. 64p. pap. 19.95 (978-1-60610-921-2(9)) America Star Bks.

Sesso, Karen A. Off They Swam, 1 vol. 2009. 37p. pap. 19.95 (978-1-61546-453-1(0)) PublishAmerica, Inc.

Treasures of the Barrier Reef. 2005. (J). audio, cd-rom 24.95 (978-0-9771381-7-3(8)) Williams, Geoffrey T.

Vern, Jules. Twenty Thousand Leagues under the Sea. abr. ed. 2019. (ENG.). (J). 232p. 19.95 (978-1-61895-531-9(4)); 230p. pap. 12.95 (978-1-61895-530-2(6)) Bibliotech Pr.

—Twenty Thousand Leagues under the Sea. 2018. (ENG., Illus.). 170p. (J). (gr. 5). pap. 7.99 (978-1-9779-9837-8(2)) CreateSpace Independent Publishing Platform.

—Twenty Thousand Leagues under the Sea. (ENG., Illus.). (J). 2017. (gr. 5). pap. 17.95 (978-1-376-13408-7(X)) 2015. (gr. 3-7). 27.95 (978-1-296-82308-5(3)) Creative Media Partners, LLC.

—Twenty Thousand Leagues under the Sea. 2019. (ENG.). 238p. (J). (gr. 5). pap. (978-1-989201-88-6(1)) East India Publishing Co.

—Twenty Thousand Leagues under the Sea. l.t. ed. 2006. 592p. pap. (978-1-84702-222-6(7)) Echo Library.

—Twenty Thousand Leagues under the Sea. 2019. (ENG.). 662p. (J). (gr. 3-7). pap. 25.99 (978-1-7033-4221-5(6)) Independently Published.

—Twenty Thousand Leagues under the Sea. 2020. (ENG.). 230p. (J). (gr. 3-7). 19.95 (978-1-64439-407-6(3)) IndoEuropeanPublishing.com.

—Twenty Thousand Leagues under the Sea. 2018. (ENG., Illus.). 254p. (J). (gr. 5). (978-3-7326-2412-6(9)) Klassik Literatur. ein Imprint der Salzwasser Verlag GmbH.

—Twenty Thousand Leagues under the Sea. 2018. (ENG., Illus.). 388p. (J). (gr. 5). pap. 16.95 (978-0-940075-35-1(0)) Quillquest Books.

—Twenty Thousand Leagues under the Sea. 2016. (ENG.). 376p. (J). (gr. 3-7). pap. (978-93-5304-941-6(5)) Rupa & Co.

—20,000 Leagues under the Sea. 2004. (Fast Track Classics Ser.). (Illus.). 48p. (J). pap. (978-0-237-52688-7(3)) Evans Brothers, Ltd.

Verne, Julio & Vern, Jules. Veinte Mil Leguas de Viaje Submarino. 2019. (Brújula y la Veleta Ser.).Tr. of Twenty Thousand Leagues under the Sea. (SPA.). 64p. (J). (gr. 2-4). pap. 9.95 (978-987-718-566-9(0)) Ediciones Lea S.A. ARG. Dist: Independent Pubs. Group.

Wang, M. S. Rosie. Seeing the Underwater World with Abby & Josh. Grijalva, M. S. Laurah, illus. 2018. (ENG.). 28p. pap. (978-0-646-97449-1(1)) arima publishing.

Wang, Rosie C. Seeing the Underwater World with Abby & Josh. 2018. (Sight Test Book Ser.: Vol. 1). (ENG., Illus.). 28p. (J). (gr. 1-4). (978-0-646-98372-1(5)) Wang, Rosie.

Zindel, Paul. Loch. 2005. 209p. (YA). (gr. 7-12). 13.65 (978-0-7569-6001-8(0)) Perfection Learning Corp.

UNDERWATER GEOLOGY

see Submarine Geology

UNDERWATER SWIMMING

see Skin Diving

UNDERWRITING

see Insurance

UNICEF

Connolly, Sean. UNICEF. 2009. 32.80 (978-1-59920-303-4(0)) Black Rabbit Bks.

—Unicef. 2009. (Global Organizations Ser.). (ENG., Illus.). 48p. (J). (gr. 4-7). pap. (978-1-897563-37-3(X)) Saunders Bk. Co.

Marsico, Katie. Unicef. 2014. (Community Connections: How Do They Help? Ser.). (ENG., Illus.). 24p. (J). (gr. 2-5). 29.21 (978-1-63188-031-5(4), 205531) Cherry Lake Publishing.

Suen, Anastasia. UNICEF, 1 vol. 2003. (Organizaciones de Ayuda (Helping Organizations) Ser.). (SPA., Illus.). 24p. (J). (gr. 2-2). lib. bdg. 26.27 (978-0-8239-6858-9(8), 115b197a-299a-4ed8-afbb-debaa8f1900a) Rosen Publishing Group, Inc., The.

—Unicef. 2009. (Helping Organizations Ser.). 24p. (gr. 2-2). 42.50 (978-1-61513-263-8(5), PowerKids Pr.) Rosen Publishing Group, Inc., The.

—Unicef (unicef) 2009. (Organizaciones de ayuda (Helping Organizations) Ser.). (SPA.). 24p. (gr. 2-2). 42.50 (978-1-60851-148-8(0), Editorial Buenas Letras) Rosen Publishing Group, Inc., The.

Verloren, Ada. The United Nations Children's Fund (UNICEF) 2009. (Global Organizations Ser.). (ENG., Illus.). 128p. (gr. 7-12). 35.00 (978-0-7910-9566-9(5), P165049, Facts On File) Infobase Holdings, Inc.

UNICORNS

Accord Publishing, Accord. Go Fun! Unicorns. 2014. (ENG.). 72p. (J). pap. 9.99 (978-1-4494-3176-1(3)) Andrews McMeel Publishing.

Alberti, Theresa Jarosz. Unicorns. 2019. (Illus.). 32p. (978-1-64185-107-7(4), Focus Readers) North Star Editions.

Carlson-Berne, Emma. A First Look at Unicorns. 2020. (Bumba Books (r) — Fantastic Creatures Ser.). (ENG., Illus.). 24p. (J). (gr. -1-1). 26.65 (978-1-5415-9681-8(1), 90ac2777-0aed-45e4-a236-810c5d03be41, Lerner Pubns.) Lerner Publishing Group.

Dudley, William. Unicorns. 2008. (Mysterious & Unknown Ser.). (Illus.). 104p. (YA). (gr. 3-7). lib. bdg. 43.93 (978-1-60152-028-9(X)) ReferencePoint Pr., Inc.

Farshore. The Ultimate Unicorn Joke Book. 2018. (ENG., Illus.). 96p. (J). (gr. k-2). pap. 7.99 (978-1-4052-9433-1(7), Red Shed) Farshore GBR. Dist: HarperCollins Pubs.

Gish, Ashley. Unicorns. 2019. (X-Books: Mythical Creatures Ser.). (ENG.). 32p. (J). (gr. 3-5). pap. 9.99 (978-1-62832-761-8(8), 19245, Creative Paperbacks) Creative Co., The.

Hinds, Kathryn. Unicorns, 1 vol. 2013. (Creatures of Fantasy Ser.). (ENG.). 64p. (gr. 6-6). pap. 16.28 (978-1-62712-055-5(6), 2b76cc8a-0d17-4b9d-ad64-31cba9d9a0b6); (Illus.). 36.93 (978-0-7614-4928-7(0), aab58bb9-ac97-4884-bfca-f3db07291026) Cavendish Square Publishing LLC.

Jarosz Alberti, Theresa. Unicorns. 2018. (Mythical Creatures Ser.). (ENG., Illus.). 32p. (J). (gr. 2-3). pap. 9.95 (978-1-64185-006-3(X), 164185006X); lib. bdg. 31.35 (978-1-63517-904-0(1), 1635179041) North Star Editions. (Focus Readers).

Jeffrey, Gary. Unicorns, 1 vol. Verma, Dheeraj, illus. 2012. (Graphic Mythical Creatures Ser.). (ENG.). 24p. (J). (gr. 3-3). pap. 9.15 (978-1-4339-6769-6(3), 4069baef-3409-47ee-be5f-d24f6130ebb2); lib. bdg. 26.60 (978-1-4339-6767-2(7), 044a2e8f-460f-4636-b8e6-7abcbbe50764) Stevens, Gareth Publishing LLLP. (Gareth Stevens Learning Library).

Loh-Hagan, Virginia. Unicorns. 2016. (Magic, Myth, & Mystery Ser.). (ENG., Illus.). 32p. (J). (gr. 4-8). 32.07 (978-1-63471-115-9(7), 208571, 45th Parallel Press) Cherry Lake Publishing.

Mahoney, Emily. Learn Compound Sentences with Unicorns, 1 vol. 2020. (Grammar Magic! Ser.). (ENG.). 24p. (J). (gr. 2-3). pap. 9.15 (978-1-5382-4739-6(9), 5343a356-8c2d-49c8-8a0e-d85ad57445d7) Stevens, Gareth Publishing LLLP.

Meachen Rau, Dana. Unicorns, 1 vol. 2011. (For Real? Ser.). (ENG.). 24p. (gr. 3-3). 25.50 (978-0-7614-4864-8(0), f76c18c9-cc5a-45fd-9656-0716b838952b) Cavendish Square Publishing LLC.

Meister, Cari. Unicorns. Whisker, Dan A., illus. 2019. (Mythical Creatures Ser.). (ENG.). 32p. (J). (gr. k-2). lib. bdg. 29.99 (978-1-5158-4441-9(2), 140561, Picture Window Bks.) Capstone.

More Unicorns. 2007. (Illus.). 20p. (J). 10.00 (978-0-9795206-6-2(5)) Unseen Gallery.

Potter, Joe. My First Unicorn Dot-To-Dot: Over 50 Fantastic Puzzles. Buckingham, Faye, illus. 2019. (My First Activity Bks.). (ENG.). 64p. (J). (gr. -1-2). pap. 8.99 (978-1-4380-1272-8(1)) Sourcebooks, Inc.

Renison, Jessica. The Secret History of Unicorns. 2008. (Illus.). 96p. (978-1-904756-97-2(2)) Kandour Ltd.

Seraphini, Temisa. The Secret Lives of Unicorns. Robin, Sophie, illus. 2019. (Secret Lives Ser.: 1). (ENG.). 64p. (J). (gr. 2-4). 18.95 (978-1-911171-95-9(X)) Flying Eye Bks. GBR. Dist: Penguin Random Hse. LLC.

Shaffer, Christy. Glitter Unicorns Stickers. 2004. (Dover Little Activity Books Stickers Ser.). (ENG., Illus.). 2p. (J). (gr. 1-4). pap. 2.99 (978-0-486-43538-1(5), 435385) Dover Pubns., Inc.

Summers, Portia & Meachen Rau, Dana. Are Unicorns Real?, 1 vol. 2016. (I Want to Know Ser.). (ENG., Illus.). 32p. (gr. 3-3). pap. 11.52 (978-0-7660-8248-9(2), a91c2f9e-44cf-49af-b51c-60bd984ace68) Enslow Publishing, LLC.

Watt, Fiona. Unicorns Sticker Book. 2018. (Unicorns Sticker Book Ser.). (ENG.). 24p. (J). pap. 9.99 (978-0-7945-4208-5(5), Usborne) EDC Publishing.

Wonderland Unicorns: Coloring book by Darla Hallmark. 2007. (Illus.). 20p. (YA). 10.00 (978-0-9795206-1-7(4)) Unseen Gallery.

UNICORNS—FICTION

Arrhenius, Ingela P., illus. Where's the Unicorn? 2018. (Where's The Ser.). (ENG.). 10p. (J). (— 1). bds. 9.99 (978-1-5362-0696-8(2)) Candlewick Pr.

Atkinson, Cale. Unicorns 101. 2019. (Illus.). 32p. (J). (gr. -1-2). 17.99 (978-1-9848-3036-4(8), Doubleday Bks. for Young Readers) Random Hse. Children's Bks.

Augenstein, Marianne R. The Quest for Kair, 1 vol. 2009. 152p. pap. 24.95 (978-1-60813-899-9(2)) America Star Bks.

Bardhan-Quallen, Sudipta. Purrmaids #4: Search for the Mermicorn. Wu, Vivien, illus. 2018. (Purrmaids Ser.: 4). (ENG.). 96p. (J). (gr. 1-4). pap. 5.99 (978-1-5247-0170-3(X), Random Hse. Bks. for Young Readers) Random Hse. Children's Bks.

Bell, Hilari. The Prophecy. 2006. (ENG., Illus.). 208p. (J). (gr. 5-9). 15.99 (978-0-06-059943-0(X)) HarperCollins Pubs.

Benko, Kamilla. Fire in the Star. 2020. (Unicorn Quest Ser.). (ENG., Illus.). 384p. (J). 16.99 (978-1-68119-249-9(7), 900164375, Bloomsbury Children's Bks.) Bloomsbury Publishing USA.

—Secret in the Stone. (Unicorn Quest Ser.). (ENG.). (J). 2020. 352p. pap. 8.99 (978-1-5476-0310-7(0), 900211266) 2019. (Illus.). 336p. 16.99 (978-1-68119-247-5(0), 900164378) Bloomsbury Publishing USA. (Bloomsbury Children's Bks.).

—The Unicorn Quest. (Unicorn Quest Ser.). (ENG.). 336p. (J). 2019. pap. 8.99 (978-1-68119-983-2(1), 900194729, Bloomsbury Children's Bks.) 2018. 16.99 (978-1-68119-245-1(4), 900164376, Bloomsbury USA Childrens) Bloomsbury Publishing USA.

Bharadwaj, Meenakshi. Lonely Unicorn. 2004. (Illus.). 20p. (J). pap. (978-81-87649-89-2(5)) Katha.

Blabey, Aaron. The Return of Thelma the Unicorn. Blabey, Aaron, illus. 2019. (ENG., Illus.). 36p. (J). (gr. -1-k). 14.99 (978-1-338-60889-2(4), Scholastic Pr.) Scholastic, Inc.

—Thelma the Unicorn. 2017. (ENG., Illus.). 28p. (J). (gr. -1-k). 14.99 (978-1-338-15842-7(2), Scholastic Pr.) Scholastic, Inc.

Black, Holly. Zombies vs. Unicorns. 2012. lib. bdg. 22.10 (978-0-606-23686-7(4)) Turtleback.

Black, Holly & Larbalestier, Justine, eds. Zombies vs. Unicorns. 2012. (ENG.). 432p. (YA). (gr. 9). pap. 12.99 (978-1-4169-8954-7(4), McElderry, Margaret K. Bks.) McElderry, Margaret K. Bks.

Bliss, Emily. Unicorn Princesses 2: Flash's Dash. Hanson, Sydney, illus. 2017. (Unicorn Princesses Ser.: 2). (ENG.). 128p. (J). 15.99 (978-1-68119-329-8(9), 900170030, Bloomsbury USA Childrens) Bloomsbury Publishing USA.

—Unicorn Princesses 3: Bloom's Ball. Hanson, Sydney, illus. 2017. (Unicorn Princesses Ser.: 3). (ENG.). 128p. (J). pap. 5.99 (978-1-68119-334-2(5), 900170042, Bloomsbury USA Childrens) Bloomsbury Publishing USA.

—Unicorn Princesses 4: Prism's Paint. Hanson, Sydney, illus. 2017. (Unicorn Princesses Ser.: 4). (ENG.). 128p. (J). pap. 5.99 (978-1-68119-338-0(8), 900170045, Bloomsbury USA Childrens) Bloomsbury Publishing USA.

—Unicorn Princesses 5: Breeze's Blast. Hanson, Sydney, illus. 2018. (Unicorn Princesses Ser.: 5). (ENG.). 128p. (J). 16.99 (978-1-68119-650-3(6), 900179833); pap. 5.99 (978-1-68119-649-7(2), 900179849) Bloomsbury Publishing USA. (Bloomsbury USA Childrens).

—Unicorn Princesses 6: Moon's Dance. Hanson, Sydney, illus. 2018. (Unicorn Princesses Ser.: 6). (ENG.). 128p. (J). pap. 6.99 (978-1-68119-652-7(2), 900179844, Bloomsbury USA Childrens) Bloomsbury Publishing USA.

—Unicorn Princesses 7: Firefly's Glow. Hanson, Sydney, illus. 2018. (Unicorn Princesses Ser.: 7). (ENG.). 128p. (J). 16.99 (978-1-68119-927-6(0), 900192376); pap. 5.99 (978-1-68119-926-9(2), 900192401) Bloomsbury Publishing USA. (Bloomsbury Children's Bks.).

—Unicorn Princesses 8: Feather's Flight. Hanson, Sydney, illus. 2018. (Unicorn Princesses Ser.: 8). (ENG.). 128p. (J). 16.99 (978-1-68119-930-6(0), 900192387); pap. 5.99 (978-1-68119-929-0(7), 900192375) Bloomsbury Publishing USA. (Bloomsbury Children's Bks.).

Bohn, Kendall. Fantasy Adventure. 2008. (Kaleidoscopia Coloring Book Ser.). (Illus.). 56p. (J). (gr. -1-7). 8.95 (978-0-929636-83-2(X)) Syren Bk. Co.

Braun, Eric. Taking Care of Your Unicorn. 2019. (Caring for Your Magical Pets Ser.). (ENG., Illus.). 24p. (J). (gr. 2-4). pap. 8.99 (978-1-64466-092-8(X), 12941); (gr. 4-6). lib. bdg. (978-1-68072-913-9(6), 12940) Black Rabbit Bks. (Hi Jinx).

Burkhart, Jessica. Bella's Birthday Unicorn. Ying, Victoria, illus. 2014. (Unicorn Magic Ser.: 1). (ENG.). 144p. (J). (gr. 1-4). pap. 6.99 (978-1-4424-9822-8(6), Aladdin) Simon & Schuster Children's Publishing.

—The Hidden Treasure. Ying, Victoria, illus. 2015. (Unicorn Magic Ser.: 4). (ENG.). 112p. (J). (gr. 1-4). pap. 6.99 (978-1-4424-9829-7(3), Aladdin) Simon & Schuster Children's Publishing.

—Unicorn Magic 3-Books-In-1!: Bella's Birthday Unicorn; Where's Glimmer?; Green with Envy, 3 Bks. in 1. Ying, Victoria, illus. 2018. (Unicorn Magic Ser.). (ENG.). 384p. (J). (gr. 1-4). pap. 8.99 (978-1-5344-0998-9(X), Aladdin) Simon & Schuster Children's Publishing.

—Where's Glimmer? Ying, Victoria, illus. 2014. (Unicorn Magic Ser.: 2). (ENG.). 144p. (J). (gr. 1-4). pap. 6.99 (978-1-4424-9824-2(2), Aladdin) Simon & Schuster Children's Publishing.

Burnell, Heather Ayris. Friends Rock: an Acorn Book (Unicorn & Yeti #3) Quintanilla, Hazel. illus. 2019. (Unicorn & Yeti Ser.: 3). (ENG.). 64p. (J). (gr. k-2). pap., act. bk. ed. 4.99 (978-1-338-32907-0(3)) Scholastic, Inc.

—Friends Rock: an Acorn Book (Unicorn & Yeti #3) (Library Edition) Quintanilla, Hazel, illus. 2019. (Unicorn & Yeti Ser.: 3). (ENG.). 64p. (J). (gr. k-2). 23.99 (978-1-338-32908-7(1)) Scholastic, Inc.

—A Good Team: an Acorn Book (Unicorn & Yeti #2) Quintanilla, Hazel, illus. 2019. (Unicorn & Yeti Ser.: 2). (ENG.). 64p. (J). (gr. k-2). pap. 4.99 (978-1-338-32904-9(9)) Scholastic, Inc.

—Sparkly New Friends: an Acorn Book (Unicorn & Yeti #1) Quintanilla, Hazel, illus. 2019. (Unicorn & Yeti Ser.: 1). (ENG.). 64p. (J). (gr. k-2). pap. 4.99 (978-1-338-32901-8(4)) Scholastic, Inc.

Carter, Lou. Oscar the Hungry Unicorn. Dyson, Nikki, illus. 2020. (Oscar the Hungry Unicorn Ser.). (ENG.). 32p. (J). (gr. -1-k). pap. 10.99 (978-1-4083-5575-6(2), Orchard Bks.) Hachette Children's Group GBR. Dist: Hachette Bk. Group.

Chapman, Linda. Flying High. Hull, Biz & Farley, Andrew, illus. 2004. (My Secret Unicorn Ser.). 118p. (J). (978-0-439-65273-5(1)) Scholastic, Inc.

—Starlight Surprise, Vol. 4. 4th ed. 2003. (ENG., Illus.). 144p. pap. (978-0-14-131344-3(7), Puffin) Penguin Bks., Ltd.

—Starlight Surprise. Hull, Biz. illus. 2003. (My Secret Unicorn Ser.). 130p. (J). (978-0-439-65275-9(8)) Scholastic, Inc.

—Twilight Magic. Kronheimer, Ann, illus. 2008. 149p. (J). pap. (978-0-545-03160-8(5)) Scholastic, Inc.

Chien Chow Chine, Aurélie. Little Unicorn Is Angry. 2019. (Little Unicorn Ser.: 1). (ENG., Illus.). 32p. (J). (gr. -1-3). 12.99 (978-0-316-53178-8(2)) Little, Brown Bks. for Young Readers.

—Little Unicorn Is Sad. 2020. (Little Unicorn Ser.: 3). (ENG., Illus.). 32p. (J). (gr. -1-3). 12.99 (978-0-316-53190-0(1)) Little, Brown Bks. for Young Readers.

—Little Unicorn Is Scared. 2019. (Little Unicorn Ser.: 2). (ENG., Illus.). 32p. (J). (gr. -1-3). 12.99 (978-0-316-53185-6(5)) Little, Brown Bks. for Young Readers.

—Little Unicorn Is Shy. 2020. (Little Unicorn Ser.: 4). (ENG., Illus.). 32p. (J). (gr. -1-3). 12.99 (978-0-316-53210-5(X)) Little, Brown Bks. for Young Readers.

Chronicle Books. Baby Unicorn: Finger Puppet Book: (Unicorn Puppet Book, Unicorn Book for Babies, Tiny Finger Puppet Books) Ying, Victoria, illus. 2018. (Baby Animal Finger Puppets Ser.: 13). (ENG.). 12p. (J). (gr. -1 — 1). 7.99 (978-1-4521-7076-3(2)) Chronicle Bks. LLC.

Citro, Asia. Unicorn & Germs: Zoey & Sassafras #6. Lindsay, Marion, illus. 2018. (Zoey & Sassafras Ser.: 6). 96p. (J). (gr. 1-5). pap. 5.99 (978-1-943147-47-2(7), 28266b15-d47f-4eb9-a5f7-47058f41d3fc) Innovation Pr., The.

Clark, Isabelle. The Enchanted Forest of Hope. 2009. 44p. pap. 18.50 (978-1-4389-7781-2(6)) AuthorHouse.

Clark, Platte F. Bad Unicorn. 2013. (Bad Unicorn Trilogy Ser.: 1). (ENG., Illus.). 432p. (J). (gr. 3-7). 18.99 (978-1-4424-5012-7(6), Aladdin) Simon & Schuster Children's Publishing.

—Good Ogre. 2015. (Bad Unicorn Trilogy Ser.: 3). (ENG., Illus.). 384p. (J). (gr. 3-7). 17.99 (978-1-4424-5018-9(5), Aladdin) Simon & Schuster Children's Publishing.

Clarke, Phillip. Unicorns. Scott, Peter, illus. 2006. (Luxury Lift-the-Flap Learners Ser.). 16p. (J). (gr. -1-3). 11.99 (978-0-7945-1280-4(1), Usborne) EDC Publishing.

Coats, Lucy. The Unicorn Emergency #8. Bean, Brett, illus. 2018. (Beasts of Olympus Ser.: 8). (ENG.). 144p. (J). (gr. 2-4). 6.99 (978-0-515-15952-3(2), Penguin Workshop) Penguin Young Readers Group.

Cole, Dina. Maggie's Magic Unicorn. 2012. 28p. pap. 19.99 (978-1-4685-7734-1(4)) AuthorHouse.

Coville, Bruce. Into the Land of the Unicorns. 2008. (Unicorn Chronicles Ser.). (Illus.). 159p. (J). (gr. 4-7). 14.65 (978-0-7569-9061-9(0)) Perfection Learning Corp.

—Song of the Wanderer, 2. 2008. (Unicorn Chronicles Ser.: 2). 352p. (J). (gr. 4-6). 21.19 (978-0-545-06825-3(8)) Scholastic, Inc.

—The Unicorn Treasury: Stories, Poems, & Unicorn Lore. 2004. (ENG., Illus.). 224p. (J). (gr. 3-7). pap. 7.99 (978-0-15-205216-4(X), 1195730, Clarion Bks.) HarperCollins Pubs.

Coxe, Molly. Blues for Unicorn. 2019. (Bright Owl Bks.). (Illus.). 40p. (J). (gr. -1-2). 17.99 (978-1-63592-109-0(0), 4d7b72dd-81cd-4c1e-814c-6500c4591452); pap. 6.99 (978-1-63592-110-6(4), 52e6d08c-51b4-4aad-91f4-67b0c8896404) Astra Publishing Hse. (Kane Press).

Cross, Frances. Butternut Blobber & the Blue Jade. 2007. (Blobber Ser.). (ENG.). 84p. pap. (978-1-84167-561-9(X)) Ransom Publishing Ltd.

Currey, Anna. The Christmas Unicorn. 2013. (Illus.). (J). (978-1-4351-5017-1(1)) Barnes & Noble, Inc.

Darlison, Aleesah. Ellabeth's Light. Brailsford, Jill, illus. 2017. (Unicorn Riders Ser.). (ENG.). 112p. (J). (gr. 3-5). pap. 5.95 (978-1-4795-6559-7(8), 128549, Picture Window Bks.) Capstone.

—Ellabeth's Test. Brailsford, Jill, illus. 2017. (Unicorn Riders Ser.). (ENG.). 112p. (J). (gr. 3-5). pap. 5.95 (978-1-4795-6555-9(5), 128545, Picture Window Bks.) Capstone.

—Krystal's Charge. Brailsford, Jill, illus. 2017. (Unicorn Riders Ser.). (ENG.). 112p. (J). (gr. 3-5). pap. 5.95 (978-1-4795-6558-0(X), 128548, Picture Window Bks.) Capstone.

—Krystal's Choice. Brailsford, Jill, illus. 2017. (Unicorn Riders Ser.). (ENG.). 112p. (J). (gr. 3-5). pap. 5.95 (978-1-4795-6554-2(7), 128544, Picture Window Bks.) Capstone.

—Quinn's Riddles. Brailsford, Jill, illus. 2017. (Unicorn Riders Ser.). (ENG.). 112p. (J). (gr. 3-5). pap. 5.95 (978-1-4795-6552-8(0), 128542, Picture Window Bks.) Capstone.

—Quinn's Truth. Brailsford, Jill, illus. 2017. (Unicorn Riders Ser.). (ENG.). 112p. (J). (gr. 3-5). pap. 5.95 (978-1-4795-6556-6(3), 128546, Picture Window Bks.) Capstone.

—Willow's Challenge. Brailsford, Jill, illus. 2017. (Unicorn Riders Ser.). (ENG.). 112p. (J). (gr. 3-5). pap. 5.95 (978-1-4795-6553-5(9), 128543, Picture Window Bks.) Capstone.

—Willow's Victory. Brailsford, Jill, illus. 2017. (Unicorn Riders Ser.). (ENG.). 112p. (J). (gr. 3-5). pap. 5.95 (978-1-4795-6557-3(1), 128547, Picture Window Bks.) Capstone.

Diller, Kevin & Lowe, Justin. Hello, My Name Is Octicorn. Talib, Binny, illus. 2016. (ENG.). 48p. (J). (gr. -1-3). 17.99 (978-0-06-238793-6(6), Balzer & Bray) HarperCollins Pubs.

DK. Pop-Up Peekaboo! Unicorn. 2019. (Pop-Up Peekaboo! Ser.). (ENG., Illus.). 12p. (J). (— 1). bds. 12.99 (978-1-4654-8331-7(4), DK Children) Dorling Kindersley Publishing, Inc.

Drouhard, Brianne. Billie the Unicorn. 2011. (ENG., Illus.). 36p. (J). (gr. -1-3). 15.95 (978-1-59702-024-4(9)) Immedium.

Duey, Kathleen. Castle Avamir. Rayyan, Omar, illus. 2004. (Unicorn's Secret Ser.). 73p. (gr. 2-5). 15.00 (978-0-7569-3357-9(9)) Perfection Learning Corp.

—The Journey Home. Rayyan, Omar, illus. 2003. (Unicorn's Secret Ser.: 8). (ENG.). 80p. (J). (gr. 2-5). pap. 5.99 (978-0-689-85374-6(2), Aladdin) Simon & Schuster Children's Publishing.

—The Mountains of the Moon. Rayyan, Omar, illus. 2005. 76p. (J). lib. bdg. 15.00 (978-1-59054-907-0(4)) Fitzgerald Bks.

—The Silver Bracelet. Rayyan, Omar, illus. 2005. 90p. (J). lib. bdg. 15.00 (978-1-59054-917-9(1)) Fitzgerald Bks.

—True Heart. Rayyan, Omar, illus. 2004. (Unicorn's Secret Ser.). 75p. (gr. 2-5). 15.00 (978-0-7569-3385-2(4)) Perfection Learning Corp.

Duncan, Jasmin. The Unicorn Legacy. 2013. 100p. pap. (978-1-909402-11-9(7)); pap. (978-1-909402-12-6(5)) Vamptasy Publishing.

Durant, Sybrina, et al. Legend of the Blue Unicorn: Return of the Dragons, 3 vols. Johnson, Britt, ed. l.t. ed. 2003. (ENG., Illus.). 25p. (J). (gr. k-5). spiral bd. 8.99 (978-1-929063-93-2(8), 331) Moons & Stars Publishing For Children.

Dyckman, Ame. You Don't Want a Unicorn! Climo, Liz, illus. (ENG.). (J). (gr. -1 — 1). 2019. 24p. bds. 7.99 (978-0-316-48886-0(0)) 2017. 40p. 18.99 (978-0-316-34347-3(1)) Little, Brown Bks. for Young Readers.

Dynyel. Windy the Winged Unicorn. 2004. 140p. 24.95 (978-1-4184-8615-0(9)) AuthorHouse.

Fabrizio, T. L. Natalie Bean. 2011. 28p. pap. 24.95 (978-1-4626-0645-0(8)) America Star Bks.

Fei, Kanara. Kalani's Wish. 2009. 44p. pap. 16.99 (978-1-4389-8118-5(X)) AuthorHouse.

Franklin, Cathy. Pinta & Polly Go to the Moon, 1 vol. Poole, Tracy, illus. 2009. 27p. pap. 24.95 (978-1-60813-861-6(5)) America Star Bks.

George, Joshua & Imagine That. Scratch & Draw Horses & Unicorns. Green, Barry, illus. 2017. (Scratch & Draw Ser.). (ENG.). 56p. (J). (gr. k-2). 12.99 (978-1-78700-073-5(7)) Top That! Publishing PLC GBR. Dist: Independent Pubs. Group.

Green with Envy. 2014. (Unicorn Magic Ser.: 3). (ENG., Illus.). 144p. (J). (gr. 1-4). pap. 6.99 (978-1-4424-9826-6(9), Aladdin) Simon & Schuster Children's Publishing.

Grove, Malachai. Malachai Grove Plunt Solinatry: The Song of Malachai. 2010. 24p. 14.99 (978-1-4520-6441-3(5)) AuthorHouse.

Haesche, Richard, Sr. The Legend of the Unicorn. 2007. (ENG.). 61p. (J). 8.99 (978-0-9798536-9-2(9)) Kreative X-Pressions Pubns.

Hale, Shannon. Itty-Bitty Kitty-Corn. Pham, LeUyen, illus. 2021. (J). (978-1-4197-5092-2(5), Abrams Bks. for Young Readers); (ENG.). 48p. (gr. -1-3). 18.99 (978-1-4197-5091-5(7), 1713701) Abrams, Inc.

—Pretty Perfect Kitty-Corn. Pham, LeUyen, illus. 2022. (Kitty-Corn Ser.). (ENG.). 48p. (J). (gr. -1-3). 18.99 (978-1-4197-5093-9(3), 1713801) Abrams, Inc.

Hale, Shannon & Hale, Dean. The Princess in Black & the Hungry Bunny Horde. Pham, LeUyen, illus. 2016. (Princess in Black Ser.: 3). (ENG.). 96p. (J). (gr. k-3). pap. 6.99 (978-0-7636-9089-2(9)); 15.99 (978-0-7636-6513-5(4)) Candlewick Pr.

—The Princess in Black & the Hungry Bunny Horde. Pham, LeUyen, illus. 2016. (Princess in Black Ser.: 3). (ENG.). 85p. (J). (gr. k-3). 17.20 (978-0-606-39109-2(6)) Turtleback.

Harrison, Paula. The Sky Unicorn. Williams, Sophy, illus. 2017. (Secret Rescuers Ser.: 2). (ENG.). 112p. (J). (gr. 2-5). pap. 6.99 (978-1-4814-7610-2(6), Simon & Schuster/Paula Wiseman Bks.) Simon & Schuster/Paula Wiseman Bks.

—The Storm Dragon. Williams, Sophy, illus. 2017. (Secret Rescuers Ser.: 1). (ENG.). 128p. (J). (gr. 2-5). pap. 6.99 (978-1-4814-7607-2(6), Simon & Schuster/Paula Wiseman Bks.) Simon & Schuster/Paula Wiseman Bks.

Hecker, Vera, illus. A Home for Rainbow. 2007. 32p. (J). (978-0-9799729-0-4(6)) Banta, Sandra.

Hegerhorst, Bethany. The Baseball Princess: Samantha's Summer & the Unicorn Flu. Abbott, Kristin, illus. 2012. 32p. (J). (978-0-9871281-5-7(9)) Murray Bks.

Hello!Lucky & Moyle, Sabrina. My Mom Is Magical! (a Hello!Lucky Book) Moyle, Eunice, illus. 2018. (Hello!Lucky Book Ser.). (ENG.). 24p. (J). (gr. -1 — 1). bds. 7.99 (978-1-4197-2962-1(4), 1212110) Abrams, Inc.

Hendrix, E. B. Angel & Evie: Catching a Unicorn. 2013. (Illus.). 42p. 19.99 (978-0-9857367-9-8(8)) Advanced Publishing LLC.

Hennessy, B. G. Claire & the Unicorn Happy Ever After. Mitchell, Susan, illus. 2006. (ENG.). 32p. (J). (gr. -1-3). 19.99 (978-1-4169-0815-9(3), Simon & Schuster Bks. For Young Readers) Simon & Schuster Bks. For Young Readers.

Heyman, Alissa. Twelve Dancing Unicorns. Gerard, Justin, illus. 2014. (ENG.). 32p. (J). (gr. -1-2). 14.95 (978-1-4027-8732-4(4)) Sterling Publishing Co., Inc.

Hicks, Angie, illus. Moonlight & the Mermaid. 2012. (ENG.). 24p. (J). 9.95 (978-1-84135-833-8(9)) Award Pubns. Ltd. GBR. Dist: Parkwest Pubns., Inc.

Holmes, Mary-Denese. Rhonda the Unicorn. 2018. (ENG., Illus.). 24p. (J). (gr. -1-3). (978-1-5289-2374-3(X)); pap. (978-1-5289-2375-0(8)) Austin Macauley Pubs. Ltd.

Hood, Morag. Sophie Johnson, Unicorn Expert. Okstad, Ella, illus. 2018. (Sophie Johnson, Unicorn Expert Ser.). (ENG.). 32p. (J). (gr. -1-3). 17.99 (978-1-5344-3161-4(6), Aladdin) Simon & Schuster Children's Publishing.

Howard, Cheryl L. Mikhael the Mighty: Be True to Who You Are & You Can Never Go Wrong. 2009. 52p. pap. 18.50 (978-1-60860-760-0(7), Strategic Bk. Publishing) Strategic Book Publishing & Rights Agency (SBPRA).

Hughes, Carol. The Princess & the Unicorn. 2009. (ENG.). 288p. (J). (gr. 4-6). lib. bdg. 22.44 (978-0-375-95562-4(3), Yearling) Random Hse. Children's Bks.

Ireland, Justina. Zach Lopez vs. the Unicorns of Doom. Champion, Tyler, illus. 2017. (Devils' Pass Ser.). (ENG.). 128p. (J). (gr. 4-8). lib. bdg. 25.99 (978-1-4965-4989-1(9), 135881, Stone Arch Bks.) Capstone.

Johnson, Sandi, et al. Legend of the Blue Unicorn: Land of OSM. Johnson, Britt, ed. Krittendon, Kim & Johnson, Jim, illus. 2014. (Little Choo-Choo Bks.). (ENG.). 40p. (J). (gr. -1-6). 14.99 (978-1-929063-09-3(1), 109) Moons & Stars Publishing For Children.

Julius, Nicholas. The Mythfitz: Unee the Unicorn. 2012. (ENG., Illus.). 62p. 28.95 (978-1-4327-9868-0(5)); pap. 23.95 (978-1-4327-9365-4(9)) Outskirts Pr., Inc.

Kann, Victoria. Goldilicious. Kann, Victoria, illus. 2009. (ENG., Illus.). 40p. (J). (gr. k-3). 19.99 (978-0-06-124408-7(2)); lib. bdg. 18.89 (978-0-06-124409-4(0)) HarperCollins Pubs. (HarperCollins).

—Pinkalicious at the Fair. 2018. (I Can Read Ser.). (ENG.). 32p. (J). (gr. -1-k). 13.89 (978-1-64310-216-0(8)) Penworthy Co., LLC, The.

—Soccer Star. 2012. (Pinkalicious I Can Read Ser.). (J). lib. bdg. 13.55 (978-0-606-26280-4(6)) Turtleback.

Kann, Victoria, illus. Pinkalicious at the Fair. 2018. 32p. (J). (978-1-5182-5372-0(5)) Harper & Row Ltd.

Kent, Jaden. Ella & Owen 7: Twin Trouble. Bodnaruk, Iryna, illus. 2018. (Ella & Owen Ser.: 7). (ENG.). 112p. (J). (gr. k-3). 16.99 (978-1-4998-0611-3(6)); pap. 5.99 (978-1-4998-0610-6(8)) Little Bee Books Inc.

—Ella & Owen 8: the Worst Pet. Bodnaruk, Iryna, illus. 2018. (Ella & Owen Ser.: 8). (ENG.). 112p. (J). (gr. k-3). 16.99 (978-1-4998-0613-7(2)); pap. 5.99 (978-1-4998-0612-0(4)) Little Bee Books Inc.

King, Karen. Unicorn Magic. Hicks, Angie, illus. 2012. (ENG.). 24p. 9.95 (978-1-84135-832-1(0)) Award Pubns. Ltd. GBR. Dist: Parkwest Pubns., Inc.

K.M. Mohr, John Kelley and. Waking Dalifi. 2005. 72p. pap. 9.95 (978-1-4116-6364-0(0)) Lulu Pr., Inc.

Koch, Claus. The Three Little Wolves & the Big Bad Boar. 2011. 68p. pap. 9.99 (978-1-4520-5321-9(9)) AuthorHouse.

Kurtz, John. Unicorn Fun Coloring Book. 2014. (Dover Fantasy Coloring Bks.). (ENG., Illus.). 32p. (J). (gr. k-5). pap. 3.99 (978-0-486-78196-9(8), 781968) Dover Pubns., Inc.

LaFevers, R. L. The Unicorn's Tale. Murphy, Kelly, illus. 2012. (Nathaniel Fludd, Beastologist Ser.: 4). (ENG.). 160p. (J). (gr. 1-4). pap. 6.99 (978-0-547-85079-5(4), 1501039, Clarion Bks.) HarperCollins Pubs.

Lee, Tanith. Black Unicorn. 2005. (ENG., Illus.). 144p. (J). (gr. -1-12). per. 12.00 (978-1-59687-162-5(8)) IBks., Inc.

LeGette, M. L. The Unicorn Girl. 2008. (ENG.). 416p. pap. 10.00 (978-1-4196-8696-2(8)) CreateSpace Independent Publishing Platform.

Lincoln, Jerri. The Little Unicorn Who Could Coloring Book. 2012. 34p. pap. 7.77 (978-1-938322-00-6(2)) Ralston Store Publishing.

Lincoln, Jerri Kay. Dancing with Unicorns. 2013. 254p. pap. 14.99 (978-1-938322-21-1(5)) Ralston Store Publishing.

Loehr, Mallory. I'm a Unicorn. Chou, Joey, illus. 2018. (Little Golden Book Ser.). 24p. (J). (-k). 5.99 (978-1-5247-1512-0(3), Golden Bks.) Random Hse. Children's Bks.

—Unicorn Wings. Silin-Palmer, Pamela, illus. 2006. (Step into Reading Ser.: Vol. 1). 32p. (J). (gr. -1-1). per. 4.99 (978-0-375-83117-1(7), Random Hse. Bks. for Young Readers) Random Hse. Children's Bks.

Loman, Sam. The Magical Unicorn Activity Book. Loman, Sam, illus. 2019. (ENG., Illus.). 176p. (J). pap. 16.99 (978-1-78950-829-1(0), d39a6a67-509e-4b02-804f-ad3b61056380) Arcturus Publishing GBR. Dist: Baker & Taylor Publisher Services (BTPS).

—The Magical Unicorn Activity Book. 2018. (ENG.). 96p. (J). pap. 9.99 (978-1-78828-715-9(0), acfc23f5-38d6-4207-8211-870d8e1a26cb) Arcturus

Publishing GBR. Dist: Baker & Taylor Publisher Services (BTPS).
MacLean, Heather. The Moonicorn Fairies. 2011. 40p. pap. *(978-1-77067-687-9(2))* FriesenPress.
—The Mousecat & the Moonicorns on Halloween Night. 2013. 40p. pap. 16.95 *(978-1-4525-7617-6(3),* Balboa Pr.) Author Solutions, LLC.
Magyarody, Katherine. The Changeling of Fenlen Forest. 2019. (ENG.). 208p. (YA). pap. 11.95 *(978-1-77337-019-4(7),* Yellow Dog) Great Plains Pubns. CAN. Dist: Independent Pubs. Group.
Manning, Matthew K. Magic Smells Awful. Ellis, Joey, illus. 2018. (Xander & the Rainbow-Barfing Unicorns Ser.). (ENG.). 128p. (J). (gr. 3-5). pap. 7.95 *(978-1-4965-5719-3(0),* 136708, Stone Arch Bks.) Capstone.
—Return to Pegasia. Ellis, Joey, illus. 2018. (Xander & the Rainbow-Barfing Unicorns Ser.). (ENG.). 128p. (J). (gr. 3-5). pap. 7.95 *(978-1-4965-5718-6(2),* 136707); lib. bdg. 22.65 *(978-1-4965-5714-8(X),* 136703) Capstone. (Stone Arch Bks.).
—Revenge of the One-Trick Pony. Ellis, Joey, illus. 2018. (Xander & the Rainbow-Barfing Unicorns Ser.). (ENG.). 128p. (J). (gr. 3-5). pap. 7.95 *(978-1-4965-5716-2(6),* 136705, Stone Arch Bks.) Capstone.
—The Search for Stalor. Ellis, Joey, illus. 2018. (Xander & the Rainbow-Barfing Unicorns Ser.). (ENG.). 128p. (J). (gr. 3-5). pap. 7.95 *(978-1-4965-5717-9(4),* 136706); lib. bdg. 22.65 *(978-1-4965-5713-1(1),* 136702) Capstone. (Stone Arch Bks.).
Marx, Jonny. Where's the Unicorn? A Magical Search-And-Find Book. Moran, Paul, illus. 2018. (Remarkable Animals Search Book Ser.: 1). (ENG.). 48p. (J). (gr. 3). pap. 10.99 *(978-1-4549-3166-9(3))* Sterling Publishing Co., Inc.
McCarthy, Meghan. My Little Pony: Twilight's Kingdom. 2017. (MLP Episode Adaptations Ser.). (Illus.). 144p. (J). (gr. 1-3). pap. 7.99 *(978-1-68405-064-2(2))* Idea & Design Works, LLC.
McDonald, Ann-Eve. The Tale of the Black Square. 2004. (J). *(978-0-9770158-2-5(3))* BeachWalk Bks. Inc.
Meadows, Daisy. Leona the Unicorn Fairy. 2012. (Illus.). 65p. (J). *(978-0-545-42601-5(4))* Scholastic, Inc.
Miller, J. Cris. Stories to Read to Children: The Pony & the Unicorn & 3 other Stories, 8 vols., Vol. 1. 2007. (Illus.). 80p. (J). 19.95 *(978-0-9725308-2-8(7))* Miller, J. Cris & Assocs.
Miller, Victoria, illus. Dora & the Unicorn King. 2011. (Dora the Explorer Ser.). (ENG.). 24p. (J). pap. 3.99 *(978-1-4424-1312-2(3),* Simon Spotlight/Nickelodeon) Simon Spotlight/Nickelodeon.
—Flowers for Mami Unicorn! 2010. (Dora the Explorer Ser.). (ENG.). 24p. (J). (gr. -1-2). pap. 3.99 *(978-1-4169-9064-2(X),* Simon Spotlight/Nickelodeon) Simon Spotlight/Nickelodeon.
Monsef, Kiyash. Once There Was. 2023. (Once There Was Ser.). (ENG., Illus.). 416p. (J). (gr. 5). 18.99 *(978-1-6659-2850-2(6),* Simon & Schuster Bks. For Young Readers) Simon & Schuster Bks. For Young Readers.
Morehouse, Toni B. Junie's Unicorn Horn. 2012. 30p. pap. 19.99 *(978-1-4772-9894-7(0))* AuthorHouse.
Murguia, Bethanie Deeney. Do You Believe in Unicorns? Murguia, Bethanie Deeney, illus. 2018. (ENG., Illus.). 32p. (J). (gr. -1-2). 14.99 *(978-0-7636-9468-5(1))* Candlewick Pr.
Nelson-Schmidt, Michelle. Bob Is a Unicorn. 2014. (ENG., Illus.). 28p. (J). 14.99 *(978-1-61067-155-2(4))* Kane Miller.
North, Poppy. The Ruby Stone. 2013. 52p. pap. 15.99 *(978-1-4797-6920-9(7))* Xlibris Corp.
Oceanak, Karla. Goodnight Unicorn: A Magical Parody. Spanjer, Kendra, illus. 2016. 32p. (gr. -1-3). 16.95 *(978-1-934649-63-3(5))* Bailiwick Pr.
O'connor, Jane. Fancy Nancy & the Quest for the Unicorn. 2018. (Fancy Nancy Picture Bks.). (J). lib. bdg. 14.75 *(978-0-606-41395-4(2))* Turtleback.
O'Connor, Jane. Fancy Nancy & the Quest for the Unicorn: Includes over 30 Stickers! Glasser, Robin Preiss, illus. 2018. (Fancy Nancy Ser.). (ENG.). 24p. (J). (gr. -1-3). pap. 5.99 *(978-0-06-237794-4(9),* HarperFestival) HarperCollins Pubs.
Ogburn, Jacqueline. The Unicorn in the Barn. Green, Rebecca, illus. (ENG.). 304p. (J). (gr. 3-7). 2019. pap. 7.99 *(978-1-328-59585-0(4),* 1730758) 2017. 16.99 *(978-0-544-76112-4(X),* 1634613) HarperCollins Pubs. (Clarion Bks.).
Once upon a Time- Lost Unicorn. 2005. (J). bds. *(978-1-4194-0097-1(5))* Paradise Pr., Inc.
Osborne, Mary Pope. Blizzard of the Blue Moon. Murdocca, Sal, illus. 2007. (Magic Tree House (R) Merlin Mission Ser.: 8). 144p. (J). (gr. 2-5). 5.99 *(978-0-375-83038-9(3),* Random Hse. Bks. for Young Readers) Random Hse. Children's Bks.
Osborne, Mary Pope, et al. Tormenta de Nieve en Luna Azul. Murdocca, Sal, illus. 2016. (SPA.). (J). (gr. 2-4). pap. 6.99 *(978-1-63245-646-5(X))* Lectorum Pubns., Inc.
Perelman, Helen. A Valentine's Surprise, 7. Waters, Erica-Jane, illus. 2011. (Candy Fairies Ser.: 7). (ENG.). 128p. (J). (gr. 2-5). pap. 5.99 *(978-1-4424-2215-5(7),* Aladdin) Simon & Schuster Children's Publishing.
Peterfreund, Diana. Ascendant. 2012. (Killer Unicorns Ser.: 2). (ENG.). 416p. (YA). (gr. 9). pap. 8.99 *(978-0-06-149005-7(9),* HarperTeen) HarperCollins Pubs.
Phipps, Selwyn E. The Magical Unicorn Society Official Handbook. Dardik, Helen & Goldhawk, Harry, illus. 2018. (Magical Unicorn Society Ser.: 1). (ENG.). 128p. (J). 12.99 *(978-1-250-20619-0(7),* 900201438) Feiwel & Friends.
Pierce, Meredith Ann. Birth of the Firebringer, Vol. 1. 2003. 208p. (YA). (gr. 7-18). pap. 7.99 *(978-0-14-250053-8(4),* Firebird) Penguin Young Readers Group.
—Dark Moon. 2003. 256p. (YA). (gr. 7-11). 7.99 *(978-0-14-250057-6(7),* Firebird) Penguin Young Readers Group.
—The Son of Summer Stars, Vol. 3. 2003. 256p. (YA). (gr. 7-7). 7.99 *(978-0-14-250074-3(7),* Firebird) Penguin Young Readers Group.
Pigg, Theresa. Sunshine, the Golden Unicorn. Roberts, Rebecca, illus. 2011. 20p. pap. 24.95 *(978-1-4626-0733-4(0))* America Star Bks.
Pilkey, Dav. Ricky Ricotta's Mighty Robot vs. the Uranium Unicorns from Uranus (Ricky Ricotta's Mighty Robot #7). Bk. 7. 2015. (Ricky Ricotta's Mighty Robot Ser.: 7). (ENG., Illus.). 128p. (J). (gr. -1-3). pap. 5.99 *(978-0-545-63015-3(0))* Scholastic, Inc.
Rednose, Skiddles. Tale of the Land of Umble. 2013. 126p. pap. 18.99 *(978-1-938487-14-9(1))* Big Country Publishing, LLC.
Rizzo, Cynthia Marie. Julie & the Unicorn. 2003. 49p. pap. 16.95 *(978-1-4137-0785-4(8))* PublishAmerica, Inc.
Rose, Robin. Sweet Little Unicorn. Cottage Door Press, ed. Uno, Kat, illus. 2017. (ENG.). 12p. (J). (gr. -1-k). bds. 10.99 *(978-1-68052-158-0(6),* 1001560) Cottage Door Pr.
Rosenthal, Amy Krouse. Uni the Unicorn. Barrager, Brigette, illus. (Uni the Unicorn Ser.). (ENG.). (J). 2017. 36p. (— 1). bds. 8.99 *(978-1-5247-6616-0(X))* 2014. 48p. (gr. -1-3). 17.99 *(978-0-385-37555-9(7))* Random Hse. Children's Bks.
—Uni the Unicorn & the Dream Come True. Barrager, Brigette, illus. (Uni the Unicorn Ser.). (J). 2019. 36p. (— 1). bds. 8.99 *(978-1-9848-4821-5(6))* 2017. 40p. (gr. -1-2). 17.99 *(978-1-101-93659-7(2))* Random Hse. Children's Bks. (Random Hse. Bks. for Young Readers).
Ryder, Chloe. Princess Ponies 4: a Unicorn Adventure! 2014. (Princess Ponies Ser.). (ENG., Illus.). 128p. (J). (gr. 2-4). pap. 6.99 *(978-1-61963-294-3(2),* 900132055, Bloomsbury USA Childrens) Bloomsbury Publishing USA.
Saveley, Barb. Dusky: The Lost Unicorn. 2008. 24p. pap. 24.95 *(978-1-60441-909-2(1))* America Star Bks.
Scalawag: (A Kathy Dubetz Production). Unicorns in the Mist: Books One & Two. 2011. 100p. pap. 19.95 *(978-1-4560-5655-1(7))* America Star Bks.
Schemery, Beau. The Unlikely Hero [Library Edition]. 2013. 160p. pap. 14.99 *(978-1-62380-920-1(7),* Harmony Ink Pr.) Dreamspinner Pr.
Selfors, Suzanne. The Order of the Unicorn. Santat, Dan, illus. 2014. (ENG.). 208p. (J). E-Book *(978-0-316-32339-0(X))* Little Brown & Co.
—The Order of the Unicorn. Santat, Dan, illus. 2014. (Imaginary Veterinary Ser.: 4). (ENG.). 208p. (J). (gr. 2-7). 29.99 *(978-0-316-36406-5(1))* Little, Brown Bks. for Young Readers.
Sharma, Radhika. The Princess & the Unicorn Prince. 2007. (ENG.). 48p. pap. 19.96 *(978-1-4357-0072-7(4))* Lulu Pr., Inc.
Shea, Bob. Unicorn Thinks He's Pretty Great. Shea, Bob, illus. 2013. (ENG., Illus.). 40p. (J). (gr. -1-k). 18.99 *(978-1-4231-5952-0(7))* Hyperion Pr.
Sima, Jessie. Not Quite Narwhal. Sima, Jessie, illus. 2017. (Not Quite Narwhal & Friends Ser.). (ENG., Illus.). 40p. (J). (gr. -1-3). 17.99 *(978-1-4814-6909-8(6),* Simon & Schuster Bks. For Young Readers) Simon & Schuster Bks. For Young Readers.
—Perfectly Pegasus. Sima, Jessie, illus. 2022. (Not Quite Narwhal & Friends Ser.). (ENG., Illus.). 48p. (J). (gr. -1-3). 17.99 *(978-1-5344-9717-7(X),* Simon & Schuster Bks. For Young Readers) Simon & Schuster Bks. For Young Readers.
Simpson, Dana. The Big Sparkly Box of Unicorn Magic: Phoebe & Her Unicorn Box Set Volume 1-4, 4 vols., Box set. 2017. (Phoebe & Her Unicorn Ser.). (ENG.). (J). pap. 45.00 *(978-1-4494-9324-0(6))* Andrews McMeel Publishing.
—Ozy & Millie. 2018. (ENG., Illus.). (J). 176p. pap. 9.99 *(978-1-4494-9595-4(8)),* 178p. (gr. 3-6). 35.99 *(978-1-4494-9943-3(0))* Andrews McMeel Publishing.
—Phoebe & Her Unicorn. 2014. (Phoebe & Her Unicorn Ser.: 1). (ENG., Illus.). 224p. (J). 9.99 *(978-1-4494-4620-8(5))* Andrews McMeel Publishing.
—Phoebe & Her Unicorn: A Heavenly Nostrils Chronicle. 2015. (ENG., Illus.). 226p. (J). (gr. 4-7). 29.99 *(978-1-4494-7379-2(2))* Andrews McMeel Publishing.
—Phoebe & Her Unicorn: A Heavenly Nostrils Chronicle. 2014. (Phoebe & Her Unicorn Ser.: 1). (Illus.). 222p. (J). lib. bdg. 20.85 *(978-0-606-36144-6(8))* Turtleback.
—Phoebe & Her Unicorn in the Magic Storm. 2017. (Phoebe & Her Unicorn Ser.: Vol. 6). (ENG., Illus.). 157p. (J). (gr. 3-6). 33.99 *(978-1-4494-9450-6(1))* Andrews McMeel Publishing.
—Phoebe & Her Unicorn in the Magic Storm. 2017. (Phoebe & Her Unicorn Ser.: 6). lib. bdg. 20.85 *(978-0-606-40512-6(7))* Turtleback.
—Phoebe & Her Unicorn in Unicorn Theater: Phoebe & Her Unicorn Series Book 8. 2018. (Phoebe & Her Unicorn Ser.: Vol. 8). (ENG., Illus.). 154p. (J). (gr. 3-6). 33.99 *(978-1-4494-9944-0(9))* Andrews McMeel Publishing.
—Razzle Dazzle Unicorn: Another Phoebe & Her Unicorn Adventure, Volume 4. 2016. (Phoebe & Her Unicorn Ser.: 4). (ENG., Illus.). 184p. (J). pap. 11.99 *(978-1-4494-7791-2(7))* Andrews McMeel Publishing.
—Unicorn Bowling: Another Phoebe & Her Unicorn Adventure. 2019. (Phoebe & Her Unicorn Ser.: Vol. 9). (ENG., Illus.). (J). 178p. (gr. 3-6). 45.99 *(978-1-5248-5132-3(9));*Volume 9. 176p. pap. 9.99 *(978-1-4494-9938-9(4))* Andrews McMeel Publishing.
—Unicorn Crossing. 2017. (Phoebe & Her Unicorn Ser.: 5). (Illus.). 175p. (J). lib. bdg. 20.85 *(978-0-606-39767-4(1))* Turtleback.
—Unicorn Crossing: Another Phoebe & Her Unicorn Adventure. (Phoebe & Her Unicorn Ser.: Vol. 5). (ENG., Illus.). (J). 2016. 175p. (gr. 3-6). 33.99 *(978-1-4494-8613-6(4))*Volume 5. 2017. 176p. pap. 9.99 *(978-1-4494-8357-9(7))* Andrews McMeel Publishing.
—Unicorn of Many Hats (Phoebe & Her Unicorn Series Book 7) 2018. (Phoebe & Her Unicorn Ser.: Vol. 7). (ENG., Illus.). 178p. (J). (gr. 3-6). 34.99 *(978-1-4494-9506-0(0))* Andrews McMeel Publishing.
—Unicorn on a Roll. 2016. (Phoebe & Her Unicorn Ser.: 2). (ENG.). 224p. (J). 13.99 *(978-1-4494-8349-4(6))* Andrews McMeel Publishing.
—Unicorn on a Roll. 2015. (Phoebe & Her Unicorn Ser.: 2). lib. bdg. 20.85 *(978-0-606-36985-5(6))* Turtleback.
—Unicorn on a Roll: Another Phoebe & Her Unicorn Adventure. 2015. (Phoebe & Her Unicorn Ser.: 2). (ENG., Illus.). 224p. (J). pap. 9.99 *(978-1-4494-7076-0(9))* Andrews McMeel Publishing.
Simpson, Dana, illus. Phoebe & Her Unicorn in the Magic Storm. 2017. 157p. (J). *(978-1-5182-5085-9(8))* Andrews McMeel Publishing.
Smith, Cleveland W. Billabongo. 2008. 172p. pap. *(978-1-84923-100-8(1))* YouWriteOn.
Smith, Sindy. Indy the Unicorn Prince. Smith, Sindy, illus. 2012. (Illus.). 46p. 29.95 *(978-1-4626-9864-6(6))* America Star Bks.
—Indy the Unicorn Prince. 2012. 48p. pap. 24.95 *(978-1-4626-7519-7(0))* America Star Bks.
Steadman, A. F. Skandar & the Phantom Rider. 2023. (Illus.). (J). x, 484p. ***(978-1-6659-1277-8(4))***; (Skandar Ser.: 2). (ENG., 496p. (gr. 3-7). 18.99 *(978-1-6659-1276-1(6))* Simon & Schuster Bks. For Young Readers. (Simon & Schuster Bks. For Young Readers).
Steadman, A. F. Skandar & the Unicorn Thief. 2022. (Skandar Ser.: 1). (ENG., Illus.). 448p. (J). (gr. 3-7). 18.99 *(978-1-6659-1273-0(1),* Simon & Schuster Bks. For Young Readers) Simon & Schuster Bks. For Young Readers.
Sykes, Julie. Unicorn Academy #1: Sophia & Rainbow. Truman, Lucy, illus. 2019. (Unicorn Academy Ser.: 1). (ENG.). 128p. (J). (gr. 1-4). 5.99 *(978-1-9848-5082-9(2),* Random Hse. Bks. for Young Readers) Random Hse. Children's Bks.
—Unicorn Academy #2: Scarlett & Blaze. Truman, Lucy, illus. 2019. (Unicorn Academy Ser.: 2). (ENG.). 128p. (J). (gr. 1-4). 5.99 *(978-1-9848-5085-0(7),* Random Hse. Bks. for Young Readers) Random Hse. Children's Bks.
—Unicorn Academy #3: Ava & Star. Truman, Lucy, illus. 2019. (Unicorn Academy Ser.: 3). (ENG.). 128p. (J). (gr. 1-4). pap. 5.99 *(978-1-9848-5088-1(1),* Random Hse. Bks. for Young Readers) Random Hse. Children's Bks.
—Unicorn Academy #4: Isabel & Cloud. Truman, Lucy, illus. 2019. (Unicorn Academy Ser.: 4). (ENG.). 128p. (J). (gr. 1-4). pap. 5.99 *(978-1-9848-5091-1(1),* Random Hse. Bks. for Young Readers) Random Hse. Children's Bks.
—Unicorn Academy #5: Layla & Dancer. Truman, Lucy, illus. 2019. (Unicorn Academy Ser.: 5). (ENG.). 128p. (J). (gr. 1-4). 12.99 *(978-1-9848-5168-0(3),* Random Hse. Bks. for Young Readers) Random Hse. Children's Bks.
—Unicorn Academy #6: Olivia & Snowflake. Truman, Lucy, illus. 2019. (Unicorn Academy Ser.: 6). (ENG.). 128p. (J). (gr. 1-4). 12.99 *(978-1-9848-5171-0(3),* Random Hse. Bks. for Young Readers) Random Hse. Children's Bks.
The Strode Family. The Magical Land of Far, Far Away. 2011. 16p. pap. *(978-1-4269-5570-9(7))* Trafford Publishing (UK) Ltd.
Vevers, Rachel. Quest for the Unicorn. 2012. 222p. pap. *(978-1-78176-316-2(X))* FeedARead.com.
Viknesh, R. My Fantasy Your Treat. 2012. 32p. pap. 28.55 *(978-1-4669-2733-9(X))* Trafford Publishing.
von Innerebner, Jessika. Kevin the Unicorn: It's Not All Rainbows. von Innerebner, Jessika, illus. 2019. (Kevin the Unicorn Ser.). (ENG., Illus.). 32p. (J). (gr. -1-2). 17.99 *(978-1-9848-1430-2(3),* Dial Bks) Penguin Young Readers Group.
Wallace, Adam. How to Catch a Unicorn. Elkerton, Andy, illus. 2019. (How to Catch Ser.: 0). (ENG.). 40p. (J). (gr. k-6). 10.99 *(978-1-4926-6973-9(3))* Sourcebooks, Inc.
Walsh, Sandy E. Gift of the Monkey Pajamas. Schubbe, Matt, illus. l.t. ed. 2015. (ENG.). 52p. (J). (gr. -1-4). pap. 12.95 *(978-1-68189-000-5(3),* THEAQ Publishing) THEAQ LLC.
Wan, Joyce. You Are My Magical Unicorn. Wan, Joyce, illus. 2018. (ENG., Illus.). 14p. (J). (gr. -1-k). bds. 6.99 *(978-1-338-33410-4(7),* Cartwheel Bks.) Scholastic, Inc.
Warren, Cindy. The Unicorn's Horn. 2011. 98p. pap. 19.95 *(978-1-4560-6987-2(X))* America Star Bks.
Watt, Fiona. That's Not My Unicorn. 2017. (Touchy-Feely Board Bks.). (ENG.). 10p. (J). 9.99 *(978-0-7945-4102-6(X),* Usborne) EDC Publishing.
Welch, Sheila Kelly. The Shadowed Unicorn. 2011. 192p. (gr. -1). pap. 12.95 *(978-1-4502-6991-9(5))* iUniverse, Inc.
Yolen, Jane. A Plague of Unicorns, 1 vol. (ENG.). 192p. (J). 2016. pap. 7.99 *(978-0-310-74611-9(6))* 2014. E-Book 4.19 *(978-0-310-74610-2(8),* 9780310746102) Zonderkidz.
—Where Have the Unicorns Gone? Sanderson, Ruth, illus. 2003. (ENG.). 32p. (J). (gr. -1-3). 9.99 *(978-0-689-86359-2(4),* Simon & Schuster/Paula Wiseman Bks.) Simon & Schuster Bks. For Young Readers.
Young, Amy. A New Friend for Sparkle. 2017. (Unicorn Named Sparkle Ser.). (ENG., Illus.). 40p. (J). 18.99 *(978-0-374-30553-6(6),* 900163984, Farrar, Straus & Giroux (BYR)) Farrar, Straus & Giroux.
—A Unicorn Named Sparkle. Young, Amy, illus. 2018. (Unicorn Named Sparkle Ser.: 1). (ENG., Illus.). 32p. (J). bds. 9.99 *(978-0-374-30872-8(1),* 900187523, Farrar, Straus & Giroux (BYR)) Farrar, Straus & Giroux.
—A Unicorn Named Sparkle: A Picture Book. Young, Amy, illus. 2016. (Unicorn Named Sparkle Ser.: 1). (ENG., Illus.). 40p. (J). 16.99 *(978-0-374-30185-9(9),* 900140948, Farrar, Straus & Giroux (BYR)) Farrar, Straus & Giroux.
Zahler, Thom & Anderson, Ted. My Little Pony: Friendship Is Magic Volume 11, Vol. 11. Fleecs, Tony & Garbowska, Agnes, illus. 2017. (My Little Pony Ser.: 11). 120p. (J). (gr. 4-7). pap. 19.99 *(978-1-63140-815-1(1),* 9781631408151) Idea & Design Works, LLC.

UNIDENTIFIED FLYING OBJECTS

Aliens & UFOs: Famous UFO Sightings & Incidents. (Critical Reading Ser.). (YA). (gr. 6-12). pap. *(978-0-8092-1104-3(1))* Jamestown.
Borgert-Spaniol, Megan. UFOs: Are Alien Aircraft Overhead? 2018. (Science Fact or Science Fiction? Ser.). (ENG., Illus.). 32p. (J). (gr. 3-6). lib. bdg. 32.79 *(978-1-5321-1542-4(3),* 28938, Checkerboard Library) ABDO Publishing Co.
Boutland, Craig. The Roswell UFO Mystery. 2019. (Unexplained (Alternator Books (r)) Ser.). (ENG., Illus.). 32p. (J). (gr. 3-6). 30.65 *(978-1-5415-6282-0(8),* 89438128-c923-468e-a27f-032ea728c8d9, Lerner Pubns.) Lerner Publishing Group.
Bowman, Chris. The Betty & Barney Hill Alien Abduction. 2019. (Paranormal Mysteries Ser.). (ENG., Illus.). 24p. (J). (gr. 3-8). pap. 8.99 *(978-1-61891-731-7(5),* 12333, Black Sheep) Bellwether Media.
—The Betty & Barney Hill Alien Abduction. Brady, D., illus. 2019. (Paranormal Mysteries Ser.). (ENG.). 24p. (J). (gr. 3-8). lib. bdg. 29.95 *(978-1-64487-093-8(2),* Black Sheep) Bellwether Media.
Bringle, Jennifer. Alien Sightings in America, 1 vol. 2011. (America's Supernatural Secrets Ser.). (ENG.). 48p. (YA). (gr. 5-5). pap. 12.75 *(978-1-4488-5578-0(0),* aa448f5a-61f2-4392-8b2b-bc1fc4730586); lib. bdg. 34.47 *(978-1-4488-5530-8(6),* e6fdbf61-f883-46cf-82df-d809f1b51b15) Rosen Publishing Group, Inc., The.
Burns, Jan. UFOs, 1 vol. 2008. (Mysterious Encounters Ser.). (ENG., Illus.). 48p. (gr. 4-8). lib. bdg. 30.38 *(978-0-7377-4048-6(5),* 916d4d04-d8c8-45f1-8f77-74f6457930e3, KidHaven Publishing) Greenhaven Publishing LLC.
Carey, Thomas J. & Schmitt, Donald R. Confessions of the Children of Roswell: Preserving the Story of America's Most Infamous UFO Incident, 1 vol. 2017. (Alien Encounters Ser.). (ENG.). 256p. (YA). (gr. 8-8). 41.47 *(978-1-5081-7630-5(2),* 98c850c5-bd58-4e80-b214-b6c370413824, Rosen Young Adult) Rosen Publishing Group, Inc., The.
Chanez, Katie. UFO Sightings. 2019. (Aliens Ser.). (ENG., Illus.). 32p. (J). (gr. 4-6). 28.65 *(978-1-5435-7109-7(3),* 140401) Capstone.
—Would We Survive an Alien Invasion? 2019. (Aliens Ser.). (ENG., Illus.). 32p. (J). (gr. 4-6). pap. 7.95 *(978-1-5435-7497-5(1),* 141013) Capstone.
Cheatham, Mark. Aliens!, 1 vol. 2012. (Jr. Graphic Monster Stories Ser.). (ENG., Illus.). 24p. (J). (gr. 2-3). pap. 11.60 *(978-1-4488-6403-4(8),* ed51a721-ade7-4356-b613-1544acfd07a5); lib. bdg. 28.93 *(978-1-4488-6222-1(1),* 7d690a89-5f16-448d-a1a5-1e6a05da1e20) Rosen Publishing Group, Inc., The. (PowerKids Pr.).
Coddington, Andrew. Aliens, 1 vol. 2016. (Creatures of Fantasy Ser.). (ENG., Illus.). 64p. (gr. 6-6). 35.93 *(978-1-5026-1862-7(1),* f7c33507-c5a1-4d65-b96c-72e537701c7e) Cavendish Square Publishing LLC.
Dailey, Kirsten. Encounters with Ufos & Extraterrestrial Life, 1 vol. Pye, Michael, ed. 2012. (Mysteries Uncovered, Secrets Declassified Ser.). (ENG., Illus.). 264p. (YA). (gr. 7-7). 42.47 *(978-1-4488-9252-5(X),* 6fa15b57-1bf5-4732-af8a-abba73cbe6c8) Rosen Publishing Group, Inc., The.
DeMolay, Jack. Ovnis: El Caso Roswell, 1 vol. Obregón, José María, tr. 2008. (Historietas Juveniles: Misterios (Jr. Graphic Mysteries) Ser.). (SPA., Illus.). 24p. (J). (gr. 2-3). lib. bdg. 28.93 *(978-1-4358-2539-0(X),* e886f791-ad7e-41a6-8ea3-d30606fff3be) Rosen Publishing Group, Inc., The.
—Ovnis: El caso Roswell (UFO: the Roswell Incidents) 2009. (Historietas Juveniles: Misterios (Jr. Graphic Mysteries) Ser.). (SPA.). 24p. (gr. 2-3). 47.90 *(978-1-61513-349-9(6),* Editorial Buenas Letras) Rosen Publishing Group, Inc., The.
—UFOs: The Roswell Incident. (Jr. Graphic Mysteries Ser.). (ENG.). 24p. (gr. 2-3). 2009. (J). 47.90 *(978-1-61513-852-4(8),* PowerKids Pr.) 2006. (Illus.). (J). lib. bdg. 28.93 *(978-1-4042-3403-1(9),* 60e4da8d-0bd5-473e-a525-40f4aded4a5e) 2006. (Illus.). pap. 10.60 *(978-1-4042-2156-7(5),* 301840d1-a278-4fb7-8ea6-87d033a36e18, PowerKids Pr.) Rosen Publishing Group, Inc., The.
Dicker, Katie. Visitors from Space. 2015. (Mystery! Ser.). (ENG., Illus.). 24p. (J). (gr. 2-5). 28.50 *(978-1-62588-206-6(8),* 17363) Black Rabbit Bks.
Diker, Katie. Visitors from Space. 2015. (ENG., Illus.). 24p. (J). pap. 8.95 *(978-1-77092-237-2(7))* RiverStream Publishing.
Dolan, Richard M. & Zabel, Bryce. Project Disclosure: Revealing Government Secrets & Breaking the Truth Embargo, 1 vol. 2014. (Conspiracies & Cover-Ups Ser.). (ENG.). 341p. (YA). (gr. 8-8). 41.47 *(978-1-4777-8155-5(2),* 14fbdb07-8aaf-4c0e-910c-afddada9ea24, Rosen Young Adult) Rosen Publishing Group, Inc., The.
Duncan, John. UFOs, 1 vol. 2005. (Unexplained Ser.). (ENG., Illus.). 36p. (gr. 4-6). lib. bdg. 28.67 *(978-0-8368-6268-3(6),* f8f55d41-06ae-4503-8002-3a23d9b421fe, Gareth Stevens Learning Library) Stevens, Gareth Publishing LLLP.
Earth Cosmology: The Effects of the Giant Destroyer Comet. 2004. (UFO Fact Bks.). (YA). cd-rom 15.00 *(978-0-934269-41-4(6))* UFO Photo Archives.
Erickson, Justin. Alien Abductions. 2011. (Unexplained Ser.). (ENG., Illus.). 24p. (J). (gr. 3-7). lib. bdg. 26.95 *(978-1-60014-582-7(5),* Torque Bks.) Bellwether Media.
Friedman, Stanton T. & Marden, Kathleen. The UFO Cover-Up: What World Governments Don't Want You to Know, 1 vol. 2017. (Alien Encounters Ser.). (ENG., Illus.). 288p. (J). (gr. 8-8). 41.47 *(978-1-5081-7699-2(X),* a280f60b-4a25-4545-9d7c-9fc40aba8576, Rosen Young Adult) Rosen Publishing Group, Inc., The.
Grace, N. B. UFO Lands in USA! Was a Spacecraft Crash Covered Up? 2011. (J). pap. *(978-0-545-32947-7(7))* Scholastic, Inc.
—UFOs (24/7: Science Behind the Scenes: Mystery Files) 2008. (24/7: Science Behind the Scenes Ser.). (ENG., Illus.). 64p. (J). (gr. 8-12). pap. 7.95 *(978-0-531-18741-8(1),* Watts, Franklin) Scholastic Library Publishing.
Hagler, Gina. American Aliens, 1 vol. 2019. (Creatures of the Paranormal Ser.). (ENG.). 48p. (J). (gr. 5-5). 29.60 *(978-1-9785-1354-9(2),* 3df33771-97ee-4783-841c-0c541f3f20e8) Enslow Publishing, LLC.
Halls, Kelly Milner. Alien Investigation: Searching for the Truth about UFOs & Aliens. Spears, Rick. C., illus. 2015. (ENG.). 64p. (J). (gr. 5-12). E-Book 53.32 *(978-1-4677-5987-8(2),* 9781467759878, Lerner Digital) Lerner Publishing Group.
Haney, Jill. Area 51. 2015. (Red Rhino Nonfiction Ser.). (J). lib. bdg. 20.80 *(978-0-606-37198-8(2))* Turtleback.
Hantula, Richard & Asimov, Isaac. UFOs, 1 vol. 2004. (Isaac Asimov's 21st Century Library of the Universe: Fact & Fantasy Ser.). (ENG., Illus.). 32p. (gr. 3-5). lib. bdg. 28.67 *(978-0-8368-3954-8(4),* 1f9bd9f5-381b-487a-bf5c-e4a3b7d33e30) Stevens, Gareth Publishing LLLP.
Harrison, Benjamin. Aliens, Sasquatches, Flowers, & Plants. 2011. 56p. (gr. -1). pap. 15.99 *(978-1-4634-6011-2(2))* AuthorHouse.
—Aliens, Sasquatches, Flowers, & Plants: Volume I. 2011. 56p. (gr. -1). pap. 15.99 *(978-1-4634-6009-9(0))* AuthorHouse.
Hawkins, John. Aliens & UFOs, 1 vol. 2012. (Mystery Hunters Ser.). (ENG., Illus.). 32p. (J). (gr. 4-5). pap. 11.60 *(978-1-4488-6437-9(2),* cb229f11-aa93-40ff-9f57-69357340fec4); lib. bdg. 28.93 *(978-1-4488-6427-0(5),* 3cf328f9-73c2-456e-8ea4-25f83cc4a4a2) Rosen Publishing Group, Inc., The. (PowerKids Pr.).

TUV

Henderson, Bonnie. UFOS: Out of the Black. 2004. (Illus.). 240p. pap. 15.95 *(978-0-910042-90-1(X))* Allegheny Pr.
Herbst, Judith. UFOs. (Unexplained Ser.). (ENG., Illus.). 48p. (gr. 5-12). 2005. pap. 8.95 *(978-0-8225-2409-0(0)*, Lerner Pubns.) 2004. lib. bdg. 26.60 *(978-0-8225-0961-5(X))* Lerner Publishing Group.
Higgins, Nadia. Area 51. 2014. (Unexplained Mysteries Ser.). (ENG., Illus.). 24p. (J). (gr. 3-7). lib. bdg. 26.95 *(978-1-62617-101-5(7)*, Epic Bks.) Bellwether Media.
—UFOs. 2014. (Unexplained Mysteries Ser.). (ENG., Illus.). 24p. (J). (gr. 3-7). lib. bdg. 26.95 *(978-1-62617-107-7(6)*, Epic Bks.) Bellwether Media.
Hile, Lori. Aliens & UFOS. King, Chris, illus. 2013. (Solving Mysteries with Science Ser.). (ENG.). 48p. (J). (gr. 3-6). pap. 9.95 *(978-1-4109-5504-3(4)*, 123432, Raintree) Capstone.
—Aliens & UFOs: Myth or Reality? 2018. (Investigating Unsolved Mysteries Ser.). (ENG., Illus.). 32p. (J). (gr. 3-9). lib. bdg. 28.65 *(978-1-5435-3570-9(4)*, 138911, Capstone Pr.) Capstone.
Hodge, Susie & Mason, Paul. Investigating UFOs & Aliens. 2010. (Extreme! Ser.). (ENG.). 32p. (gr. 3-4). pap. 47.70 *(978-1-4296-5115-8(6)*, Capstone Pr.) Capstone.
Hoena, Blake. The Roswell UFO Incident. Yotter, Tate, illus. 2019. (Paranormal Mysteries Ser.). (ENG.). 24p. (J). (gr. 3-8). lib. bdg. 29.95 *(978-1-64487-097-6(5)*, Black Sheep) Bellwether Media.
Jeffrey, Gary. UFOs, 1 vol. 2006. (Graphic Mysteries Ser.). (ENG., Illus.). 48p. (gr. 5-5). pap. 14.05 *(978-1-4042-0808-7(9)*, f9e319f1-610c-427e-8822-24c4976d0264) Rosen Publishing Group, Inc., The.
—UFOs: Alien Abduction & Close Encounters. (Graphic Mysteries Ser.). (ENG.). 48p. (gr. 5-5). 2009. (YA). 58.50 *(978-1-61512-973-7(1)*, Rosen Reference) 2006. (Illus.). (J). lib. bdg. 37.13 *(978-1-4042-0797-4(X)*, 5105307c-7e8d-46e9-9a27-0524bab04a48) Rosen Publishing Group, Inc., The.
Karst, Ken. Alien Abductions. 2018. (Enduring Mysteries Ser.). (ENG.). 48p. (J). (gr. 4-7). pap. 12.00 *(978-1-62832-556-0(9)*, 19753, Creative Paperbacks) Creative Co., The.
—Area 51. 2014. (Enduring Mysteries Ser.). (ENG.). 48p. (J). (gr. 5-8). pap. 12.00 *(978-1-62832-070-1(2)*, 21319, Creative Paperbacks) Creative Co., The.
—Area 51: Enduring Mysteries. 2014. (Illus.). 48p. (J). pap. *(978-1-60818-399-9(8))* Creative Co., The.
Kellerman, Megan & Silverstein, Janna. Tracking Alien Encounters, 1 vol. 2018. (Paranormal Seekers Ser.). (ENG.). 64p. (J). (gr. 5-8). pap. 13.95 *(978-1-5081-8558-1(1)*, 4b8aa4ee-75fa-490a-bdb8-642285ba09cf, Rosen Reference) Rosen Publishing Group, Inc., The.
Kelly, Dave & Coddington, Andrew. Aliens, UFOs, & Unexplained Encounters, 1 vol. 2017. (Paranormal Investigations Ser.). (ENG.). 64p. (gr. 6-6). 35.93 *(978-1-5026-2845-9(7)*, 19ee3e24-8ead-49da-b2aa-b93608779b37) Cavendish Square Publishing LLC.
Kenney, Karen Latchana. Mysterious UFOs & Aliens. 2017. (Searchlight Books (tm) — Fear Fest Ser.). (ENG., Illus.). 32p. (J). (gr. 3-5). 30.65 *(978-1-5124-3406-4(X)*, 1dd723e0-2272-46f8-9cf6-f108bee62f18, Lerner Pubns.); pap. 9.99 *(978-1-5124-5606-6(3)*, 549fe709-732d-4e9f-b3b5-17b18fd2d54d) Lerner Publishing Group.
Kincade, Chris. Encountering Aliens: Eyewitness Accounts, 1 vol. Mallea, Cristian, illus. 2014. (Eyewitness to the Unexplained Ser.). (ENG.). 32p. (J). (gr. 3-9). 31.32 *(978-1-4914-0244-3(X)*, 125804, Capstone Pr.) Capstone.
King, Sharon. Junior Alien Zone: Creative Experiences for Hands of All Ages! 2009. (Illus.). 51p. pap. 14.95 *(978-1-4327-1162-7(8))* Outskirts Pr., Inc.
Levete, Sarah. Aliens & UFOs, 1 vol. 2016. (Mystery Hunters Ser.). (ENG.). 48p. (J). (gr. 5-5). pap. 15.05 *(978-1-4824-5992-0(2)*, ef5f6e57-b22d-4a47-bceb-35897525d253) Stevens, Gareth Publishing LLLP.
Levy, Janey. UFOs, 1 vol. 2005. (Content-Area Literacy Collections). (ENG.). 24p. (gr. 3-4). pap. 8.85 *(978-1-4042-5671-2(7)*, dd2022ac-87fa-4a1d-b269-db2a8ae2957a) Rosen Publishing Group, Inc., The.
Linde, Barbara M. What Happened at Area 51?, 1 vol. 2014. (History's Mysteries Ser.). (ENG., Illus.). 32p. (J). (gr. 4-5). pap. 11.50 *(978-1-4824-2102-6(X)*, 51d26442-184d-4b30-aab3-931487150fc8) Stevens, Gareth Publishing LLLP.
Loh-Hagan, Virginia. Roswell. 2017. (Urban Legends: Don't Read Alone! Ser.). (ENG., Illus.). 32p. (J). (gr. 4-8). lib. bdg. 32.07 *(978-1-63472-898-0(X)*, 210018, 45th Parallel Press) Cherry Lake Publishing.
Manzanero, Paula K. Where Is Area 51? 2019. (Who HQ Ser.). (ENG.). 112p. (J). (gr. 2-4). 16.36 *(978-1-64310-812-4(3))* Penworthy Co., LLC, The.
Manzanero, Paula K. & Who HQ. Where Is Area 51? Foley, Tim, illus. 2018. (Where Is? Ser.). 112p. (J). (gr. 3-7). 5.99 *(978-1-5247-8641-0(1)*, Penguin Workshop) Penguin Young Readers Group.
Marden, Kathleen & Stoner, Denise. Making Contact: Alien Abduction Case Studies, 1 vol. 2014. (Conspiracies & Cover-Ups Ser.). (ENG., Illus.). 263p. (J). (gr. 8-8). 41.47 *(978-1-4777-8159-3(5)*, da836d16-034b-4400-93a6-74292987333b, Rosen Young Adult) Rosen Publishing Group, Inc., The.
McClellan, Ray. Alien Abductions. 2014. (Unexplained Mysteries Ser.). (ENG., Illus.). 24p. (J). (gr. 3-7). lib. bdg. 26.95 *(978-1-62617-100-8(9)*, Epic Bks.) Bellwether Media.
McCollum, Sean. Handbook to UFOs, Crop Circles, & Alien Encounters. 2016. (Paranormal Handbooks Ser.). (ENG., Illus.). 32p. (J). (gr. 3-9). lib. bdg. 28.65 *(978-1-5157-1309-8(1)*, 132356, Capstone Pr.) Capstone.
McEvoy, Paul. The Alien Files. 2003. (Real Deal Ser.). (Illus.). 32p. (J). pap. *(978-0-7608-6691-7(0))* Sundance/Newbridge Educational Publishing.
Meachen Rau, Dana. Aliens, 1 vol. 2011. (For Real? Ser.). (ENG.). 24p. (gr. 3-3). 25.50 *(978-0-7614-4861-7(6)*, a60bbfc4-5d94-4026-adbc-690229028b78) Cavendish Square Publishing LLC.
Messages from the Pleiades Vol. 1: The Contact Notes of Eduard Billy Meier. 2004. (UFO Fact Bks.). (YA). cd-rom 15.00 *(978-0-934269-49-0(1))* UFO Photo Archives.
Morey, Allan. Alien Invasion. 2019. (It's the End of the World! Ser.). (ENG., Illus.). 24p. (J). (gr. 3-7). lib. bdg. 26.95 *(978-1-64487-078-5(9)*, Torque Bks.) Bellwether Media.
The Mormon Gold Plates: Au Unusual Account. 2004. (YA). cd-rom 15.00 *(978-0-934269-57-5(2))* UFO Photo Archives.
Netzley, Patricia D. Alien Encounters. 2011. (Extraterrestrial Life Ser.). 80p. (YA). (gr. 7-12). lib. bdg. 43.93 *(978-1-60152-169-9(3))* ReferencePoint Pr., Inc.
Noll, Elizabeth. UFOs. 2016. (Strange ... but True? Ser.). (ENG.). 32p. (J). (gr. 4-6). pap. 9.99 *(978-1-64466-161-1(6)*, 10346); (Illus.). 31.35 *(978-1-68072-027-3(9)*, 10345) Black Rabbit Bks. (Bolt).
Oachs, Emily Rose. UFOs. 2018. (Investigating the Unexplained Ser.). (ENG., Illus.). 32p. (J). (gr. 3-8). lib. bdg. 27.95 *(978-1-62617-856-4(9)*, Blastoff! Discovery) Bellwether Media.
O'Neill, Terry, ed. UFOs. 2003. (Opposing Viewpoints Ser.). (Illus.). 160p. (J). 27.45 *(978-0-7377-1070-0(5)*, Greenhaven Pr., Inc.) Cengage Gale.
Orme David, David. UFOs. 2007. (Trailblazers Ser.). (ENG., Illus.). 36p. pap. *(978-1-84167-423-0(0))* Ransom Publishing Ltd.
Owings, Lisa. Alien Abductions. 2018. (Investigating the Unexplained Ser.). (ENG., Illus.). 32p. (J). (gr. 3-8). lib. bdg. 27.95 *(978-1-62617-851-9(8)*, Blastoff! Discovery) Bellwether Media.
Parks, Peggy J. Aliens, 1 vol. 2006. (Mysterious Encounters Ser.). (ENG., Illus.). 48p. (gr. 4-8). lib. bdg. 29.13 *(978-0-7377-3518-5(X)*, 38b3bf8e-38a0-468b-bf70-d63131c7b628, KidHaven Publishing) Greenhaven Publishing LLC.
Perish, Patrick. Are UFOs Real? 2013. (Unexplained: What's the Evidence? Ser.). (ENG.). 32p. (J). (gr. 2-5). lib. bdg. 28.50 *(978-1-60753-386-3(3)*, 16363) Amicus.
Portman, Michael. Are UFOs Real?, 1 vol. 2013. (Space Mysteries Ser.). (ENG., Illus.). 32p. (gr. 2-3). 29.27 *(978-1-4339-8262-0(5)*, 119db4e4-6774-40bf-ba13-11a05c3c5c7b); pap. 11.50 *(978-1-4339-8263-7(3)*, 14446fba-6f46-473c-9235-9b6516a8f9f6) Stevens, Gareth Publishing LLLP. (Gareth Stevens Learning Library).
Redfern, Nick. True Stories of Space Exploration Conspiracies, 1 vol. 2014. (Off the Record! Ser.). (ENG.). 248p. (YA). (gr. 7-7). 41.47 *(978-1-4777-7833-3(0)*, 51f7c5d4-2961-4920-9bc1-f1e3cdf2c294) Rosen Publishing Group, Inc., The.
—True Stories of the Real Men in Black, 1 vol. 2014. (Off the Record! Ser.). (ENG., Illus.). 264p. (J). (gr. 7-7). 41.47 *(978-1-4777-7837-1(3)*, f470fa10-c2b3-4081-bd88-965e99925ad5) Rosen Publishing Group, Inc., The.
Reed, Ellis M. Alien Conspiracy Theories. 2019. (Aliens Ser.). (ENG., Illus.). 32p. (J). (gr. 4-6). pap. 7.95 *(978-1-5435-7491-3(2)*, 141007); lib. bdg. 30.65 *(978-1-5435-7104-2(2)*, 140396) Capstone.
—Roswell. 2019. (Aliens Ser.). (ENG., Illus.). 32p. (J). (gr. 4-6). 28.65 *(978-1-5435-7107-3(7)*, 140399) Capstone.
Richards, Dillon H. & Stirling, Janet. Searching for UFOs, 1 vol. 2011. (Mystery Explorers Ser.). (ENG.). 64p. (J). (gr. 5-5). pap. 13.95 *(978-1-4488-4766-2(4)*, 87539c32-cfa2-4cb2-aa11-2c94d0236136); lib. bdg. 37.13 *(978-1-4488-4765-5(6)*, b89a690c-4c04-46f6-a5d2-f036a64d9617) Rosen Publishing Group, Inc., The. (Rosen Reference).
Rivkin, Jennifer. Searching for UFOs, 1 vol. 2014. (Mysterious Monsters Ser.). (ENG.). 32p. (J). (gr. 4-5). lib. bdg. 27.93 *(978-1-4777-7109-9(3)*, 3f9e43a1-aaa9-46d9-b574-0814c076bb8b, PowerKids Pr.) Rosen Publishing Group, Inc., The.
Roberts, Steven. UFOs!, 1 vol., 1. 2013. (Jr. Graphic Monster Stories Ser.). (ENG.). 24p. (J). (gr. 2-3). 28.93 *(978-1-4777-6203-5(5)*, 385d9ced-d691-4dee-af32-416f517e2698, PowerKids Pr.) Rosen Publishing Group, Inc., The.
Roleff, Tamara L., ed. Alien Abductions. 2003. (Illus.). 160p. (J). lib. bdg. 32.45 *(978-0-7377-1589-7(8)*, Greenhaven Pr., Inc.) Cengage Gale.
Rooney, Anne. UFOs & Aliens. 2010. (Amazing Mysteries Ser.). (YA). (gr. 3-6). 28.50 *(978-1-59920-368-3(5))* Black Rabbit Bks.
Rudolph, Jessica. Alien Landing Sites. 2017. (Tiptoe into Scary Places Ser.). (ENG.). 24p. (J). (gr. k-3). lib. bdg. 26.99 *(978-1-68402-268-7(1))* Bearport Publishing Co., Inc.
—Sitios de Aterrizaje de Extraterrestres. 2018. (De Puntillas en Lugares Escalofriantes/Tiptoe into Scary Places Ser.). (SPA.). 24p. (J). (gr. k-3). 18.95 *(978-1-68402-617-3(2))* Bearport Publishing Co., Inc.
Rutkowski, Chris A. I Saw It Too! Real UFO Sightings. 2009. (ENG., Illus.). 184p. (YA). (gr. 7-18). pap. 14.99 *(978-1-55488-448-3(9))* Dundurn Pr. CAN. Dist: Publishers Group West (PGW).
Salas, Robert. Inside the UFO Archives, 1 vol. 2017. (Alien Encounters Ser.). (ENG., Illus.). 248p. (J). (gr. 8-8). 41.47 *(978-1-5383-8010-9(2)*, 97c8ae2e-88e8-4f5a-b646-858b0faf6f8c, Rosen Young Adult) Rosen Publishing Group, Inc., The.
Searching for Close Encounters with Aliens, 14 vols. 2011. (Mystery Explorers Ser.). (ENG.). (J). (gr. 5-5). 259.91 *(978-1-4488-4862-1(8)*, 93c6ee5d-24a1-4e7c-8126-8fd66633854f, Rosen Reference) Rosen Publishing Group, Inc., The.
Shea, Therese. Investigating UFOs & Aliens, 1 vol. 2014. (Understanding the Paranormal Ser.). (ENG.). 48p. (YA). (gr. 5-5). 28.41 *(978-1-62275-849-4(8)*, 9534e090-1770-4835-a58f-ea1de99f1b67, Britannica Educational Publishing) Rosen Publishing Group, Inc., The.
Sievert, Terri. The Unsolved Mystery of UFOs. 2013. (Unexplained Mysteries Ser.). (ENG.). 24p. (J). (gr. 1-2). pap. 47.70 *(978-1-62065-813-0(5)*, 19392); pap. 7.95 *(978-1-62065-812-3(7)*, 121765); lib. bdg. 27.99 *(978-1-62065-135-3(1)*, 120826) Capstone. (Capstone Pr.).
Steinkraus, Kyla. Area 51. 2017. (Strange ... but True? Ser.). (ENG., Illus.). 32p. (J). (gr. 4-6). lib. bdg. *(978-1-68072-180-5(1)*, 10544, Bolt) Black Rabbit Bks.
Summers, Portia & Meachen Rau, Dana. Are Aliens Real?, 1 vol. 2016. (I Want to Know Ser.). (ENG.). 32p. (gr. 3-3). pap. 11.52 *(978-0-7660-8228-1(8)*, c871c5d7-33e6-41ac-8b25-ac74293265bd) Enslow Publishing, LLC.
Terrell, Brandon. 12 Frightening Tales of Alien Encounters. 2017. (Scary & Spooky Ser.). (ENG., Illus.). 32p. (J). (gr. 3-6). 32.80 *(978-1-63235-293-4(1)*, 11777, 12-Story Library) Bookstaves, LLC.
Tieck, Sarah. Aliens, 1 vol. 2015. (Creepy Creatures Ser.). (ENG., Illus.). 32p. (J). (gr. 2-5). 34.21 *(978-1-62403-763-4(1)*, 17828, Big Buddy Bks.) ABDO Publishing Co.
UFO Abduction at Botucatu: A Preliminary Report. 2004. (UFO Fact Bks.). (YA). cd-rom 15.00 *(978-0-934269-36-0(X))* UFO Photo Archives.
UFO... Art: In Full Color. 2004. (UFO Fact Bks.). (YA). cd-rom 25.00 *(978-0-934269-54-4(8))* UFO Photo Archives.
UFO Capture of two f-14 Jets: Lost Navy Aircraft. 2004. (YA). cd-rom *(978-0-934269-56-8(4))* UFO Photo Archives.
UFO contact from beyond Rigel: A cherokee girl's Oddesy. 2004. (UFO Fact Bks.). (YA). cd-rom 15.00 *(978-0-934269-50-6(5))* UFO Photo Archives.
UFO Contact from COMA Berenesis. 2005. (YA). cd-rom *(978-0-934269-62-9(9))* UFO Photo Archives.
UFO Contact from Planet Itibi-RA. 2003. (UFO Fact Bks.). (YA). cd-rom 15.00 *(978-0-934269-30-8(0))* UFO Photo Archives.
UFO Contact from Planet Acart: From Utopia to Reality. 2003. (UFO Fact Bks.). (YA). cd-rom 15.00 *(978-0-934269-32-2(7))* UFO Photo Archives.
UFO Contact from Planet Alcyone: Falling Bodies Theory. 2004. (UFO Fact Bks.). (YA). cd-rom 15.00 *(978-0-934269-47-6(5))* UFO Photo Archives.
UFO Contact from Planet Apu: 100 Hours with Extraterrestrials. 2004. (UFO Fact Bks.). (YA). cd-rom 15.00 *(978-0-934269-38-4(6))* UFO Photo Archives.
UFO Contact from Planet ARIAN. 2004. (YA). cd-rom 15.00 *(978-0-934269-33-9(5))* UFO Photo Archives.
UFO Contact from Planet Baavi: Proxima Centauri Group. 2004. (UFO Fact Bks.). (YA). cd-rom 15.00 *(978-0-934269-46-9(7))* UFO Photo Archives.
UFO Contact from Planet Klermer: Possibilities of the Infinite. 2004. (UFO Fact Bks.). (YA). cd-rom 15.00 *(978-0-934269-34-6(3))* UFO Photo Archives.
UFO Contact from Planet Korendor Vol. 1: Another Advanced Society. 2004. (YA). cd-rom 15.00 *(978-0-934269-63-6(7))* UFO Photo Archives.
UFO Contact from Planet Korendor, Vol. 2. 2005. (YA). cd-rom 15.00 *(978-0-934269-64-3(5))* UFO Photo Archives.
UFO Contact from Planet Nep-4: Earth Development. 2004. (UFO Fact Bks.). (YA). cd-rom 15.00 *(978-0-934269-40-7(8))* UFO Photo Archives.
UFO Contact from Planet Norca: The Shocking Truth. 2004. Orig. Title: The Shocking Truth. (YA). cd-rom 15.00 *(978-0-934269-59-9(9))* UFO Photo Archives.
UFO Contact from Planet Ummo, Vol. 3, Sesma: Daily Life on Ummo. 2004. (YA). cd-rom 15.00 *(978-0-934269-28-5(9))* UFO Photo Archives.
UFO Contact from Planet Venus: We Are Not Alone. 2004. (YA). cd-rom 15.00 *(978-0-934269-55-1(6))* UFO Photo Archives.
UFO Contact from Planet Zeti: Going Home? 2004. (UFO Fact Bks.). (YA). cd-rom 15.00 *(978-0-934269-39-1(4))* UFO Photo Archives.
UFO contact from the DAL Universe: With asket of the timmers Society. 2004. (UFO Fact Bks.). (YA). cd-rom 15.00 *(978-0-934269-48-3(3))* UFO Photo Archives.
UFO Contact of an Erotic Kind: The Assignment. 2003. (UFO Fact Bks.). (YA). cd-rom 15.00 *(978-0-934269-29-2(7))* UFO Photo Archives.
UFO Photographs Around the World, Vol. 3 of Series, Vol. 3. 2003. (UFO Fact Bks.). (YA). cd-rom 15.00 *(978-0-934269-35-3(1))* UFO Photo Archives.
UFO Photographs Around the World, Vol. 4 in Series, Vol. 4. 2003. (YA). cd-rom 15.00 *(978-0-934269-37-7(8))* UFO Photo Archives.
UFO, the DULCE Story: An Incredible Deception. 2004. (UFO Fact Bks.). (YA). cd-rom 15.00 *(978-0-934269-52-0(1))* UFO Photo Archives.
UmmoCat: The ummo Documents. 2004. (UFO Fact Bks.). (YA). cd-rom 25.00 *(978-0-934269-53-7(X))* UFO Photo Archives.
Vale, Jenna & Stirling, Janet. Tracking UFOs, 1 vol. 2018. (Paranormal Seekers Ser.). (ENG.). 64p. (J). (gr. 5-8). 36.13 *(978-1-5081-8576-5(X)*, 940b671d-d1ee-4e2d-944c-ff5370e18eb6) Rosen Publishing Group, Inc., The.
Webb, Stuart. UFOs, 1 vol. 2012. (Paranormal Files Ser.). (ENG., Illus.). 80p. (YA). (gr. 7-7). 38.47 *(978-1-4488-7176-6(X)*, 7a1bed57-3f11-4e6d-bd60-2f1326d2acfc) Rosen Publishing Group, Inc., The.
Wencel, Dave. UFOs. 2010. (Unexplained Ser.). (ENG., Illus.). 24p. (J). (gr. 3-7). lib. bdg. 26.95 *(978-1-60014-504-9(3)*, Torque Bks.) Bellwether Media.
Williams, Dinah. UFO Crash Sites. 2015. (Scary Places Ser.). (ENG.). 32p. (J). (gr. 4-8). lib. bdg. 28.50 *(978-1-62724-518-0(9))* Bearport Publishing Co., Inc.
Zalewski, Aubrey. Area 51 Alien & UFO Mysteries. 2019. (Aliens Ser.). (ENG., Illus.). 32p. (J). (gr. 4-6). 28.65 *(978-1-5435-7106-6(9)*, 140398) Capstone.
63 Photographs in Color, Meier Vol. 5: The Meier Variation V. Photos. 2004. (UFO Fact Bks.). (YA). cd-rom 25.00 *(978-0-934269-51-3(3))* UFO Photo Archives.
76 UFO Photographs in Color, Vol 3: Clower Collection. 2004. (UFO Fact Bks.). (YA). cd-rom 25.00 *(978-0-934269-44-5(0))* UFO Photo Archives.
100 UFO Photographs in Color Vol, 2 Vol. 2 Series: Series in Sequence. 2004. (UFO Fact Bks.). (YA). cd-rom 25.00 *(978-0-934269-43-8(2))* UFO Photo Archives.
100 UFO Photographs in Color, Vol.1 Vol. 1: The Best of the Best. 2004. (UFO Fact Bks.). (YA). cd-rom 25.00 *(978-0-934269-42-1(4))* UFO Photo Archives.
135 UFO Photographs in Color, Vol. 4: Best of Meier Early UFO Photos. 2004. (UFO Fact Bks.). (YA). cd-rom 25.00 *(978-0-934269-45-2(9))* UFO Photo Archives.

UNIDENTIFIED FLYING OBJECTS—FICTION

Adler, David A. Cam Jansen: the Mystery of the U. F. O. #2, 2 vols. Natti, Susanna, illus. 2004. (Cam Jansen Ser.: 2). (ENG.). 64p. (J). (gr. 2-5). 5.99 *(978-0-14-240011-1(4)*, Puffin Books) Penguin Young Readers Group.
Bramlett, Timothy A. A Visit to Skytropolis. 2012. 24p. pap. 17.99 *(978-1-4772-1173-1(X))* AuthorHouse.
Daly, Joseph M. Strange Town Volume One: The Woods Behind Trevor Malone's House. 2007. 265p. (YA). pap. 9.99 net. *(978-0-9779921-0-2(1))* Wolfs Corner Publishing.
Fontes, Justine & Fontes, Ron. Casebook: UFOs and/or Alien Encounter, 1 vol. 2009. (Top Secret Graphica Mysteries Ser.). (ENG., Illus.). 48p. (YA). (gr. 4-4). 33.93 *(978-1-60754-603-0(5)*, 54a778e6-0a9b-4887-9b2d-4d2f9b27c3c6); pap. 12.75 *(978-1-60754-604-7(3)*, aa110e88-94a4-4b4f-a6bc-576eb7411a96) Rosen Publishing Group, Inc., The. (Windmill Bks.).
Gutman, Dan. Mr. Cooper Is Super! Paillot, Jim, illus. 2015. (My Weirdest School Ser.: 1). (J). lib. bdg. 14.75 *(978-0-606-36482-9(X))* Turtleback.
—My Weirdest School #1: Mr. Cooper Is Super! Paillot, Jim, illus. 2015. (My Weirdest School Ser.: 1). (ENG.). 112p. (J). (gr. 1-5). pap. 4.99 *(978-0-06-228421-1(5)*, HarperCollins) HarperCollins Pubs.
Higgins, B. T. The Master of Disaster. 2005. 103p. pap. 10.00 *(978-1-4116-3121-2(8))* Lulu Pr., Inc.
Ladbrooke, Sheree. Big Alien School. 2011. (Illus.). 20p. pap. 12.52 *(978-1-4567-8779-0(9))* AuthorHouse.
Lancaster, J. A. Joe Parker's Prophecy of Zargala. 2010. 392p. pap. 21.18 *(978-0-557-26685-2(8))* Lulu Pr., Inc.
Larsen, Kirsten. Whoa! Ufo! 2009. pap. 34.95 *(978-0-8225-4797-6(X))* Lerner Publishing Group.
Long, Melinda & Wyrick, Monica. Art Smart, Science Detective: The Case of the Sliding Spaceship. 2018. (Young Palmetto Bks.). (ENG., Illus.). 64p. pap. 12.99 *(978-1-61117-935-4(1)*, P599510) Univ. of South Carolina Pr.
Lysiak, Hilde & Lysiak, Matthew. UFO Spotted!: a Branches Book (Hilde Cracks the Case #4) Lew-Vriethoff, Joanne, illus. 2018. (Hilde Cracks the Case Ser.: 4). (ENG.). 96p. (J). (gr. 1-3). pap. 5.99 *(978-1-338-14164-1(3))* Scholastic, Inc.
—UFO Spotted!: a Branches Book (Hilde Cracks the Case #4) (Library Edition) Lew-Vriethoff, Joanne, illus. 2018. (Hilde Cracks the Case Ser.: 4). (ENG.). 96p. (J). (gr. 1-3). lib. bdg. 24.99 *(978-1-338-14165-8(1))* Scholastic, Inc.
Magnin, Joyce. Jelly Bean Summer. 272p. (J). (gr. 3-7). 2018. pap. 7.99 *(978-1-4926-6084-2(1))* 2017. (ENG.). 16.99 *(978-1-4926-4672-3(5))* Sourcebooks, Inc.
Marsh, Carole. The Mystery at Area 51. Friedlander, Randolyn, illus. 2011. (Carole Marsh Mysteries Ser.). 32p. pap. 7.99 *(978-0-635-07961-9(5)*, Marsh, Carole Mysteries) Gallopade International.
Montgomery, R. A. Project UFO. Semionov, Vladimir & Cannella, Marco, illus. 2008. (ENG.). 144p. (J). (gr. 4-8). pap. 7.99 *(978-1-933390-27-7(1))* Chooseco LLC.
Passen, Lisa. The Attack of the 50-Foot Teacher. 2005. (Illus.). 28p. (J). (gr. k-4). reprint ed. 16.00 *(978-0-7567-9665-5(2))* DIANE Publishing Co.
Pike, Christopher, pseud. Aliens in the Sky. 2014. (Spooksville Ser.: 4). (ENG., Illus.). 128p. (J). (gr. 3-7). pap. 7.99 *(978-1-4814-1058-8(X)*, Aladdin) Simon & Schuster Children's Publishing.
Pilger, Seamus. Fart Squad #3: Unidentified Farting Objects. Gilpin, Stephen, illus. 2016. (Fart Squad Ser.: 3). (ENG.). 112p. (J). (gr. 1-5). pap. 4.99 *(978-0-06-229049-6(5)*, HarperCollins) HarperCollins Pubs.
Santillo, LuAnn. The UFO. Santillo, LuAnn, ed. 2003. (Half-Pint Kids Readers Ser.). (Illus.). 7p. (J). (gr. -1-1). pap. 1.00 *(978-1-59256-045-5(8))* Half-Pint Kids, Inc.
Sutton, Laurie S. The Secret of the Flying Saucer. Neely, Scott, illus. 2015. (You Choose Stories: Scooby-Doo Ser.). (ENG.). 112p. (J). (gr. 2-6). lib. bdg. 32.65 *(978-1-4965-0478-4(X)*, 128504, Stone Arch Bks.) Capstone.
Walker, Kathryn. Unsolved! 2008. (J). (gr. 4-7). *(978-0-7787-4140-4(0))* Crabtree Publishing Co.
Ward, Ian. Bobby Blah Blah & the Mystery of the U F O in Sniggery Woods. 2009. (Illus.). 84p. pap. 10.49 *(978-1-4389-7963-2(0))* AuthorHouse.
Wells, Robison. Dark Energy. 2016. (ENG.). 288p. (YA). (gr. 8). 17.99 *(978-0-06-227505-9(4)*, HarperTeen) HarperCollins Pubs.
Williams, Suzanna. Ninety-Five Percent Human. 2013. 270p. pap. *(978-0-9574662-2-7(6))* Beresford Publishing Hse.

UNIFORMS

see also Military Uniforms

Havemeyer, Janie. Should Kids Wear School Uniforms? 2018. (Shape Your Opinion Ser.). (ENG., Illus.). 48p. (J). (gr. 1-3). 26.60 *(978-1-59953-929-4(2))* Norwood Hse. Pr.
Kawa, Katie. Are School Uniforms Good for Students?, 1 vol. 2017. (Points of View Ser.). (ENG.). 24p. (gr. 3-3). pap. 9.25 *(978-1-5345-2340-1(5)*, 4e8a0b49-aa48-4c06-8408-93dc8c48e825); lib. bdg. 26.23 *(978-1-5345-2342-5(1)*, 0be83a28-cf39-4052-b0e5-96b0552fb663) Greenhaven Publishing LLC.
Macdonald, Fiona. Uniforms Through History, 1 vol. 2006. (Why Do We Wear? Ser.). (ENG., Illus.). 32p. (gr. 3-5). lib. bdg. 28.67 *(978-0-8368-6858-6(7)*, e311df34-6e73-45aa-b746-0a9904ba1c35, Gareth Stevens Learning Library) Stevens, Gareth Publishing LLLP.
McNab, Chris. Everyday Dress. 2004. (Twentieth-Century Developments in Fashion & Costume Ser.). (Illus.). 64p. (YA). (gr. 7-18). lib. bdg. 19.95 *(978-1-59084-427-4(0))* Mason Crest.

UNIFORMS, MILITARY

see Military Uniforms

UNIFORMS, NAVAL

see Military Uniforms

UNION OF SOUTH AFRICA

see South Africa

UNION PACIFIC RAILROAD COMPANY

Crewe, Sabrina & Uschan, Michael V. The Transcontinental Railroad, 1 vol. 2004. (Events That Shaped America Ser.). (ENG., Illus.). 32p. (gr. 3-5). lib. bdg. 28.67 *(978-0-8368-3401-7(1)*,

70444a3d-cb94-4de8-bc09-9003d3471b2f, Gareth Stevens Learning Library) Stevens, Gareth Publishing LLLP.

National Geographic Learning. Reading Expeditions (Social Studies: Seeds of Change in American History): Building the Transcontinental Railroad. 2007. (ENG., Illus.). 40p. (J). pap. 21.95 *(978-0-7922-8690-5(1))* CENGAGE Learning.

Rajczak, Michael. The Transcontinental Railroad, 1 vol., Vol. 1. 2013. (What You Didn't Know about History Ser.). (ENG., Illus.). 24p. (J). (gr. 2-3). 25.27 *(978-1-4824-0600-9(4),* 7acf73a1-4ad9-461e-a523-2d300a808728); pap. 9.15 *(978-1-4824-0599-6(7),* d7bf741a-57a6-4e5d-bf04-42184db23724) Stevens, Gareth Publishing LLLP.

Sandler, Martin W. Iron Rails, Iron Men, & the Race to Link the Nation: the Story of the Transcontinental Railroad. 2015. (ENG., Illus.). 224p. (J). (gr. 5). 24.99 *(978-0-7636-6527-2(4))* Candlewick Pr.

Shea, Therese. The Transcontinental Railroad: Using Proportions to Solve Problems, 1 vol. (Math for the REAL World Ser.). 32p. (gr. 5-5). 2009. (ENG., Illus.). pap. 10.00 *(978-1-4042-6075-7(7),* 785d186d-7453-4085-8f38-992063e03aac) 2009. 47.90 *(978-1-60851-370-3(X),* PowerKids Pr.) 2006. (ENG., Illus.). (YA). lib. bdg. 28.93 *(978-1-4042-3361-4(X),* 7d4994a5-4462-4fc6-b218-453874e356dc) Rosen Publishing Group, Inc., The.

UNIONS, LABOR

see Labor Unions

UNITARIANISM

Baxter, Pam. A Cup of Light: All about the Flaming Chalice. 2010. (J). pap. 5.00 *(978-1-55896-575-1(0),* Skinner Hse. Bks.) Unitarian Universalist Assn.

Dant, Jennifer. Everybody Is Important: A Kids' Guide to Our Seven Principles. 2010. (J). pap. 6.00 *(978-1-55896-564-5(5),* Skinner Hse. Bks.) Unitarian Universalist Assn.

—Unitarian Universalism Is a Really Long Name. Carter, Anne, illus. 2008. (ENG.). 32p. (J). (gr. 3-7). 12.00 *(978-1-55896-508-9(4),* Skinner Hse. Bks.) Unitarian Universalist Assn.

UNITED KINGDOM

see Great Britain

UNITED NATIONS

Aldridge, Rebecca. Ban Ki-Moon: United Nations Secretary-General. 2009. (Modern World Leaders Ser.). (ENG.). 128p. (gr. 7-12). 30.00 *(978-1-60413-070-6(9),* P167308, Facts On File) Infobase Holdings, Inc.

Byman, Jeremy. Madam Secretary: The Story of Madeleine Albright. rev. exp. ed. 2004. (Notable Americans Ser.). (Illus.). 128p. (YA). (gr. 6-12). 23.95 *(978-1-931798-34-1(6))* Reynolds, Morgan Inc.

Connolly, Sean. The United Nations. 2009. (Global Organizations Ser.). (ENG., Illus.). 48p. (J). (gr. 4-7). pap. *(978-1-897563-38-0(8))* Saunders Bk. Co.

Docalavich, Heather. Antiterrorism Policy & Fighting Fear, Vol. 10. Russett, Bruce, ed. 2015. (United Nations: Leadership & Challenges in a Global World Ser.). (Illus.). 88p. (J). (gr. 7). lib. bdg. 24.95 *(978-1-4222-3428-0(2))* Mason Crest.

—Economic Globalization & Sustainable Development, Vol. 10. Russett, Bruce, ed. 2015. (United Nations: Leadership & Challenges in a Global World Ser.). (Illus.). 88p. (J). (gr. 7). lib. bdg. 24.95 *(978-1-4222-3431-0(2))* Mason Crest.

—The History, Structure, & Reach of the Un, Vol. 10. Russett, Bruce, ed. 2015. (United Nations: Leadership & Challenges in a Global World Ser.). (Illus.). 88p. (J). (gr. 7). lib. bdg. 24.95 *(978-1-4222-3435-8(5))* Mason Crest.

Finley, Toiya Kristen. Russell Simmons. 2007. (Sharing the American Dream Ser.). 64p. (YA). (gr. 7-18). pap. 9.95 *(978-1-4222-0762-8(5))* Mason Crest.

Galè. Junior Worldmark Encyclopedia of the Nations, 10 vols. 6th ed. 2012. (Junior Worldmark Encyclopedia of the Nations Ser.). (ENG., Illus.). 3266p. lib. bdg. 995.00 *(978-1-4144-6313-1(8),* UXL) Cengage Gale.

Gunderson, Cory Gideon. U. N. Weapons Inspectors. 2003. (World in Conflict-the Middle East Ser.). 32p. (gr. 4-8). 27.07 *(978-1-59197-414-7(3),* Abdo & Daughters) ABDO Publishing Co.

Nelson, Sheila. The Birth of the un, Decolonization & Building Strong Nations, Vol. 10. Russett, Bruce, ed. 2015. (United Nations: Leadership & Challenges in a Global World Ser.). (Illus.). 88p. (J). (gr. 7). lib. bdg. 24.95 *(978-1-4222-3430-3(4))* Mason Crest.

—Decolonization: Dismantling Empires & Building Independence. 2008. (United Nations Ser.). (Illus.). 88p. (YA). (gr. 5-18). lib. bdg. 21.95 *(978-1-4222-0066-7(3))* Mason Crest.

—International Law & Playing by the Rules, Vol. 10. Russett, Bruce, ed. 2015. (United Nations: Leadership & Challenges in a Global World Ser.). (Illus.). 88p. (J). (gr. 7). lib. bdg. 24.95 *(978-1-4222-3433-4(9))* Mason Crest.

O'Kelley, Jeff. A Visit to the United Nations. 2006. (Early Explorers Ser.). (J). pap. *(978-1-4108-6126-9(0))* Benchmark Education Co.

Rice, Liz. Bill Richardson. (Sharing the American Dream Ser.). (Illus.). 64p. (J). (gr. 7-12). 2009. 22.95 *(978-1-4222-0589-1(4))* 2007. pap. 9.95 *(978-1-4222-0761-1(7))* Mason Crest.

Smith, Roger. Human Rights & Protecting Individuals, Vol. 10. Russett, Bruce, ed. 2015. (United Nations: Leadership & Challenges in a Global World Ser.). (Illus.). 88p. (J). (gr. 7). lib. bdg. 24.95 *(978-1-4222-3437-2(1))* Mason Crest.

—Humanitarian Relief & Lending a Hand, Vol. 10. Russett, Bruce, ed. 2015. (United Nations: Leadership & Challenges in a Global World Ser.). (Illus.). 88p. (J). (gr. 7). lib. bdg. 24.95 *(978-1-4222-3432-7(0))* Mason Crest.

Tor, Regina, et al. Growing Toward Peace. 2011. 90p. 38.95 *(978-1-258-02528-1(0))* Literary Licensing, LLC.

The United Nations: Global Leadership, 10 vols., Set. Incl. Decolonization: Dismantling Empires & Building Independence. Nelson, Sheila. (YA). lib. bdg. 21.95 *(978-1-4222-0066-7(3));* Humanitarian Relief Operations: Lending a Helping Hand. Smith, Roger. (YA). lib. bdg. 21.95 *(978-1-4222-0070-4(1));* un & the Global Marketplace: Economic Developments. Docalavich, Heather. (J). lib. bdg. 21.95 *(978-1-4222-0074-2(4),* 1260876); UNICEF & Other Human Rights Efforts: Protecting Individuals. Smith, Roger. (YA). lib. bdg. 21.95 *(978-1-4222-0069-8(8));* (gr. 5-18). 2008. (United Nations — Global Leadership Ser.). (Illus.). 88p. 2006. Set lib. bdg. 219.50 *(978-1-4222-0065-0(5),* 1260876) Mason Crest.

Walker, Ida. The un Security Council & the Center of Power, Vol. 10. Russett, Bruce, ed. 2015. (United Nations: Leadership & Challenges in a Global World Ser.). 88p. (J). (gr. 7). lib. bdg. 24.95 *(978-1-4222-3436-5(3))* Mason Crest.

UNITED NATIONS—ARMED FORCES

Beller, Susan Provost. Battling in the Pacific: Soldiering in World War II. 2007. (Soldiers on the Battlefront Ser.). (ENG., Illus.). 112p. (gr. 6-8). lib. bdg. 33.26 *(978-0-8225-6381-5(9))* Lerner Publishing Group.

UNITED NATIONS—CHILDREN'S FUND

see UNICEF

UNITED NATIONS—FICTION

Birmajer, Marcelo. Una Vida Más: Noticias Extranas IV. 2004. (SPA.). 111p. (J). pap. 9.95 *(978-958-04-7081-6(2))* Norma S.A. COL. Dist: Lectorum Pubns., Inc.

Bowen, Anne. How Did You Grow So Big, So Soon? Backer, Marni, illus. 2003. 32p. (J). (gr. -1-1). 15.95 *(978-0-87614-024-6(X),* Carolrhoda Bks.) Lerner Publishing Group.

Fidler, Mark. Blaze of the Great Cliff. 2003. 196p. pap. 14.95 *(978-0-595-28748-2(4))* iUniverse, Inc.

Zerfing, Robert A. The Silencer: A U. N. Conspiracy Novel. 2nd ed. 2003. 326p. (YA). per. 14.95 *(978-0-9747881-0-4(4))* Clawfoot Publishing.

UNITED NATIONS INTERNATIONAL CHILDREN'S EMERGENCY FUND

see UNICEF

UNITED STATES

see also names of regions of the U. S. and groups of states e.g. Atlantic States; Middle West; Mississippi valley; Northwest, Old; Northwest, Pacific; Southern States; Southwest, New; Southwest, Old; The West

Alabama to Wyoming: State Fact Cards. 2003rd ed. 2003. (Illus.). 105p. (J). ring bd. 39.00 *(978-1-884925-66-5(9))* Toucan Valley Pubns., Inc.

America the Beautiful. (Color & Learn Ser.). 36p. (J). (gr. 1-5). pap. *(978-1-882210-12-1(3))* Action Publishing, Inc.

America's 50 States. 2014. (Illus.). (J). *(978-1-4351-5773-6(7))* Barnes & Noble, Inc.

Anness Punlishing. My First Book of the 50 States of America: With Maps, Dates & Fun Facts! 2015. (ENG., Illus.). 54p. (J). (gr. -1-4). bds. 9.99 *(978-1-86147-628-9(0),* Armadillo) Anness Publishing GBR. Dist: National Bk. Network.

Balkan, Gabrielle. The 50 States: Activity Book - Custom: Maps of the 50 States of the USA. Linero, Sol, illus. 2016. (ENG.). (J). (gr. 3-6). pap. 9.99 *(978-1-84780-997-1(9),* Wide Eyed Editions) Quarto Publishing Group UK GBR. Dist: Hachette Bk. Group.

Barlowe, Dot. America the Beautiful to Paint or Color. 2006. (Dover Nature Coloring Book Ser.). (ENG., Illus.). 48p. (gr. 3-8). per. 5.99 *(978-0-486-44811-4(8),* 448118) Dover Pubns., Inc.

Benchmark Education Company, LLC Staff, compiled by. Regions of the U. S. 2006. spiral bd. 330.00 *(978-1-4108-7006-3(5))* 2005. (J). spiral bd. 265.00 *(978-1-4108-5769-9(7))* Benchmark Education Co.

—Regions of the U. S. Theme Set. 2006. (J). 259.00 *(978-1-4108-7111-4(8))* Benchmark Education Co.

—Social Studies Theme: Regions of the U. S. 2005. spiral bd. 115.00 *(978-1-4108-5330-1(6))* Benchmark Education Co.

Betances, Abigail. American Holidays, 1 vol. 2008. (Real Life Readers Ser.). (ENG.). 12p. (gr. 1-2). pap. 5.90 *(978-1-4042-7911-7(3),* 6bb16889-54a5-49a0-ac42-49f37574ccf4, Rosen Classroom) Rosen Publishing Group, Inc., The.

Boyd, Nicole. America's Many Regions, 1 vol. 2008. (Real Life Readers Ser.). (ENG.). 12p. (gr. 1-2). pap. 5.90 *(978-1-4042-7931-5(8),* be4a01a4-5e8d-41fb-b383-b9e620c581e8, Rosen Classroom) Rosen Publishing Group, Inc., The.

Carr, Aaron. The Great Seal. 2013. (J). *(978-1-62127-204-5(4));* pap. *(978-1-62127-208-3(7))* Weigl Pubs., Inc.

Celebrate Freedom: Songs, Symbols, & Sayings of the United States. 2003. (Scott Foresman Social Study Ser.). (Illus.). 32p. (gr. k-2). *(978-0-328-03672-1(2));* 48p. (gr. 3-6). *(978-0-328-03674-5(9))* Addison-Wesley Educational Pubs., Inc. (Scott Foresman).

Celebrate the States - Group 5, 10 vols., Set. 2nd ed. Incl. Minnesota. Schwabacher, Martin & Kummer, Patricia K. lib. bdg. 39.79 *(978-0-7614-2716-2(3),* 9daa6308-da8b-4f23-a60a-de71b989ce87); Ohio. Sherrow, Victoria. lib. bdg. 39.79 *(978-0-7614-2558-8(6),* 27bd0007-e74c-4e9a-82c9-7f3cbbf2db2e); Rhode Island. Klein, Ted. lib. bdg. 39.79 *(978-0-7614-2560-1(8),* 69dd7142-6f70-43e4-a302-e5f83652cfdc); Washington. Stefoff, Rebecca. lib. bdg. 39.79 *(978-0-7614-2561-8(6),* 05d27159-fa4c-4f86-a326-1ecfbaec0c3d); West Virginia. Hoffman, Nancy & Hart, Joyce. lib. bdg. 39.79 *(978-0-7614-2562-5(4),* efe44c3f-7b8a-43b3-b895-df0252139f7c); 144p. (gr. 6-6). (Celebrate the States (Second Edition) Ser.). (ENG.). 2008. Set lib. bdg. 198.95 *(978-0-7614-2557-1(8),* 4120130f-859e-4777-ac3a-67a1a0336bcf, Cavendish Square) Cavendish Square Publishing LLC.

Celebrate the States - Group 6, 10 vols., Set. 2nd rev. ed. Incl. Kentucky. Barrett, Tracy. lib. bdg. 39.79 *(978-0-7614-2715-5(5),* ecb4eb9a-b8c2-4c34-bbec-fa4d7c2a0d91); Mississippi. Shirley, David & Kummer, Patricia K. lib. bdg. 39.79 *(978-0-7614-2717-9(1),* 90a00d0c-5b41-4180-b968-7fbeef5d17f0); New Hampshire. Otfinoski, Steven. lib. bdg. 39.79 *(978-0-7614-2718-6(X),* d4b8d275-783a-437d-847e-8c8889d4f813); New Mexico. Mcdaniel, Melissa. lib. bdg. 39.79 *(978-0-7614-2719-3(8),* 7a72205b-adec-4f29-a429-fa58f8b9a73f); Wyoming. Baldwin, Guy & Hart, Joyce. lib. bdg. 39.79 *(978-0-7614-2563-2(2),* db5b7f01-ec60-4570-b18a-9fe0aa702a14); (gr. 6-6). (Celebrate the States (Second Edition) Ser.). (ENG.). 144p. 2008. Set lib. bdg. 198.95 *(978-0-7614-2714-8(7),* 2f63b384-70a7-4e4e-8aa6-a70a501a818a, Cavendish Square) Cavendish Square Publishing LLC.

Celebrate the States Group 3, 10 vols., Set. 2nd rev. ed. Incl. Alaska. Stefoff, Rebecca. lib. bdg. 39.79 *(978-0-7614-2153-5(X),* eb91c713-61e2-43d8-9c64-9fc5a1bf4ecf); Connecticut. Sherrow, Victoria. lib. bdg. 39.79 *(978-0-7614-2155-9(6),* bb79359a-bfcc-43e7-bea6-09b2d05d98a8); South Dakota. Mcdaniel, Melissa. lib. bdg. 39.79 *(978-0-7614-2156-6(4),* 18d64417-4340-4aa6-9df5-d3765b159ba4); Tennessee. Barrett, Tracy. lib. bdg. 39.79 *(978-0-7614-2151-1(3),* d1e4aa04-d839-47c6-b608-025245be4d52); Wisconsin. Zeinert, Karen & Hart, Joyce. lib. bdg. 39.79 *(978-0-7614-2157-3(2),* 017a0ad0-b23c-42a0-980e-f8c756700f3d); (Illus.). (gr. 6-6). (Celebrate the States (Second Edition) Ser.). (ENG.). 144p. 2007. Set lib. bdg. 198.95 *(978-0-7614-2150-4(5),* 6ba5e786-9f8b-4ae7-ae03-24707887e38c, Cavendish Square) Cavendish Square Publishing LLC.

Celebrate the States Group 4, 10 vols., Set. 2nd rev. ed. Incl. Florida. Chang, Perry & Hart, Joyce. lib. bdg. 39.79 *(978-0-7614-2348-5(6),* 69f44607-8a2b-46ee-a933-69daaddbfde3); Hawaii. Goldberg, Jake & Hart, Joyce. lib. bdg. 39.79 *(978-0-7614-2349-2(4),* c0f4ae0a-4cc9-4a64-80c0-09f5363ceb32); Iowa. Morrice, Polly Alison & Hart, Joyce. lib. bdg. 39.79 *(978-0-7614-2350-8(8),* f05f5962-92fa-430a-8306-2930eff9b612); Michigan. Targ Brill, Marlene. lib. bdg. 39.79 *(978-0-7614-2351-5(6),* d7634b0a-ead6-456c-836c-fdc4df8c9986); Washington, D. C. Elish, Dan. lib. bdg. 39.79 *(978-0-7614-2352-2(4),* 263a3d6a-e664-4694-a069-92bce1a8f41b); (Illus.). (gr. 6-6). (Celebrate the States (Second Edition) Ser.). (ENG.). 144p. 2007. Set lib. bdg. 198.95 *(978-0-7614-2347-8(8),* affd6324-e4c0-414f-8a2b-6468c782aff2, Cavendish Square) Cavendish Square Publishing LLC.

Cohen, Stephanie. The Northeast: Text Pairs. 2008. (Bridges/Navigators Ser.). (J). (gr. 4). 89.00 *(978-1-4108-8394-0(9))* Benchmark Education Co.

Colonial America Complete Unit. (gr. 2-5). 286.95 *(978-0-7368-4487-1(2),* Red Brick Learning) Capstone.

Coloring Fun of the U. S. States Images & Facts. 2003. (Illus.). 40p. (J). 3.95 *(978-0-9729026-3-2(5))* Midwest Cylinder Management, Inc.

CultureGrams 2005 World Edition - the Americas. 2004. (YA). per. 39.99 *(978-1-931694-89-6(3))* ProQuest LLC.

Davis, Kenneth C. Don't Know Much about the 50 States. Andriani, Renée, illus. 2004. (ENG.). 64p. (J). (gr. 1-4). pap. 11.99 *(978-0-06-446227-3(7),* HarperCollins) HarperCollins Pubs.

DePietro, Frank. Latino American Cuisine. 2012. (Illus.). 64p. (J). pap. *(978-1-4222-2337-6(X))* Mason Crest.

—Latino American Cuisine. Limón, José E., ed. 2012. (Hispanic Americans: Major Minority Ser.). (Illus.). 64p. (J). (gr. 4). 22.95 *(978-1-4222-2320-8(5))* Mason Crest.

Dickmann, Nancy. The Complete Guide to the 50 States. 2016. (Illus.). 144p. (J). *(978-1-4351-6358-4(3))* Barnes & Noble, Inc.

Dyan, Penelope. A Step in Time — A Kid's Guide to Ephesus, Turkey. Weigand, John D., photos by. 2011. (Illus.). 40p. pap. 12.95 *(978-1-935630-57-9(1))* Bellissima Publishing, LLC.

Eldridge, Alison & Eldridge, Stephen. The Bald Eagle: An American Symbol, 1 vol. 2012. (All about American Symbols Ser.). (ENG.). 24p. (gr. -1-1). 25.27 *(978-0-7660-4058-8(5),* bdb3943a-3270-4779-8304-cb07dd5f2921, Enslow Publishing) Enslow Publishing, LLC.

Espejo, Roman, ed. Custody & Divorce, 1 vol. 2013. (Teen Rights & Freedoms Ser.). (ENG., Illus.). 144p. (gr. 10-12). lib. bdg. 43.63 *(978-0-7377-6400-0(7),* dd89d64e-09b7-46d6-b577-8fa80245548f, Greenhaven Publishing) Greenhaven Publishing LLC.

Estigarribia, Diana. Smithsonian National Zoological Park. 2009. (Great Zoos of the United States Ser.). 24p. (gr. 3-4). 42.50 *(978-1-61513-225-6(2),* PowerKids Pr.) Rosen Publishing Group, Inc., The.

Farseth, Erik. American Rock: Guitar Heroes, Punks, & Metalheads. 2012. (American Music Milestones Ser.). (ENG., Illus.). 64p. (J). (gr. 5-12). lib. bdg. 30.65 *(978-0-7613-4503-9(5),* 869b1f13-0bf3-4c72-a14d-100a04c6b14c, Twenty-First Century Bks.) Lerner Publishing Group.

Fink, Sam & Jefferson, Thomas. Declaration of Independence: The Words That Made America. Fink, Sam, illus. 2007. (ENG., Illus.). 160p. (J). (gr. 3-6). pap. 29.94 *(978-0-439-70315-4(8))* Scholastic, Inc.

Franchino, Vicky. It's Cool to Learn about the United States Northeast. 2011. (Explorer Library: Social Studies Explorer Ser.). (ENG.). 48p. (gr. 4-8). pap. 15.64 *(978-1-61080-305-2(1),* 201201) Cherry Lake Publishing.

Gall, Timothy L. & Gall, Susan B. Junior Worldmark Encyclopedia of the States. 5th ed. 2007. (J). *(978-1-4144-1108-8(1)); (978-1-4144-1107-1(3)); (978-1-4144-1109-5(X)); (978-1-4144-1110-1(3));*Set. (ENG.). 307.00 *(978-1-4144-1106-4(5),* UXL) Cengage Gale.

Garrington, Sally. Focus on the United States, 1 vol. 2006. (World in Focus Ser.). (ENG., Illus.). 64p. (gr. 5-8). pap. 15.05 *(978-0-8368-6732-9(7),* f52594f7-1320-44b3-bf47-0ac9034f32cc); lib. bdg. 36.67 *(978-0-8368-6725-1(4),* ff4cf06-3b83-405e-8b3a-362a1849000e) Stevens, Gareth Publishing LLLP. (Gareth Stevens Secondary Library).

Gillard, Arthur, ed. Drug Abuse, 1 vol. 2013. (Issues That Concern You Ser.). (ENG., Illus.). 208p. (gr. 7-10). lib. bdg. 43.63 *(978-0-7377-6290-7(X),* 656a8762-bd56-4a74-b751-14c75666d155, Greenhaven Publishing) Greenhaven Publishing LLC.

Golden, Nancy. Exploring the United States with the Five Themes of Geography, 1 vol. 2004. (Library of the Western Hemisphere Ser.). (ENG., Illus.). 24p. (gr. 3-4). (J). lib. bdg. 26.27 *(978-1-4042-2670-8(2),* 626510cf-c28a-4122-b623-631279380822, PowerKids Pr.); pap. 8.25 *(978-0-8239-4630-3(4),* 1d700805-0a95-427b-855a-00abe5fdf7a8) Rosen Publishing Group, Inc., The.

Goodman, Susan E. Ultimate Field Trip #5: Blasting off to Space Academy. Doolittle, Michael J., illus. 2011. (ENG.). 48p. (J). (gr. 3-7). pap. 19.99 *(978-1-4424-4345-7(6),* Atheneum Bks. for Young Readers) Simon & Schuster Children's Publishing.

Gray, Leon. Horrible Jobs of the Industrial Revolution, 1 vol., Vol. 1. 2013. (History's Most Horrible Jobs Ser.). (ENG.). 48p. (J). (gr. 5-6). 34.61 *(978-1-4824-0343-5(9),* f7ddfa05-4ca1-4625-8a92-25f41a49422c) Stevens, Gareth Publishing LLLP.

Grayson, Robert. United States, 1 vol. 2013. (Countries of the World Set 2 Ser.). (ENG.). 144p. (YA). (gr. 6-12). lib. bdg. 42.79 *(978-1-61783-640-4(0),* 4904, Essential Library) ABDO Publishing Co.

Hetrick, Hans. Baseball's Record Breakers. 2017. (Record Breakers Ser.). (ENG., Illus.). 32p. (J). (gr. 3-9). pap. 8.95 *(978-1-5157-3764-3(0),* 133697, Capstone Pr.) Capstone.

Hill, Z. B. Tupac. 2012. (J). pap. *(978-1-4222-2556-1(9))* Mason Crest.

—Usher. 2012. (J). pap. *(978-1-4222-2557-8(7));* (Illus.). 48p. (gr. 3-4). 19.95 *(978-1-4222-2531-8(3))* Mason Crest.

Holden, Henry M. Danger in Space: Surviving the Apollo 13 Disaster, 1 vol. 2012. (American Space Missions: Astronauts, Exploration, & Discovery Ser.). (ENG., Illus.). 48p. (gr. 5-7). 27.93 *(978-0-7660-4072-4(0),* b1131eae-0299-4004-a3b1-7739ee074086) Enslow Publishing, LLC.

Italia, Bob. The United States. 2003. (Countries Set 4 Ser.). 40p. (gr. k-6). 27.07 *(978-1-57765-845-0(0),* Checkerboard Library) ABDO Publishing Co.

It's My State!, 36 vols., Set. 2nd rev. ed. Incl. California. Burgan, Michael & McGeveran, William. lib. bdg. 34.07 *(978-1-60870-045-5(3),* 01b9dc44-0ad7-4b7e-92ed-cc9018a042f6); Colorado. Jacobs Altman, Linda & Fitzgerald, Stephanie. lib. bdg. 34.07 *(978-1-60870-046-2(1),* f98f5fdb-441b-4d6a-8fd7-7b9f8e59c7e9); Connecticut. Burgan, Michael & Fitzgerald, Stephanie. lib. bdg. 34.07 *(978-1-60870-047-9(X),* 2e560650-23a9-4f2e-9d4e-88e60034a979); Delaware. King, David C. & Fitzgerald, Brian. lib. bdg. 34.07 *(978-1-60870-048-6(8),* 29dd62a4-b660-460a-a145-8ec2f62171fe); Florida. Hess, Debra & Wiesenfeld, Lori P. lib. bdg. 34.07 *(978-1-60870-049-3(6),* cac47481-858e-4d6b-b1e0-d9da7df06be8); Illinois. Price-Groff, Claire & Kaplan, Elizabeth. lib. bdg. 34.07 *(978-1-60870-050-9(X),* 184bd5e0-e61f-45a1-8b61-69dae92d87c4); Louisiana. Bjorklund, Ruth & Steinitz, Andy. lib. bdg. 34.07 *(978-1-60870-051-6(8),* a756c5c7-d344-4cbd-8312-f2cdb2e92728); Maryland. Otfinoski, Steven & Steinitz, Andy. lib. bdg. 34.07 *(978-1-60870-052-3(6),* 973de8b9-fdb9-46d2-a87d-64f6b7f4beae); Massachusetts. Bjorklund, Ruth & Fitzgerald, Stephanie. lib. bdg. 34.07 *(978-1-60870-053-0(4),* 237a2166-2825-40ef-b466-a8155ccf2bab); Minnesota. Targ Brill, Marlene & Kaplan, Elizabeth. lib. bdg. 34.07 *(978-1-60870-054-7(2),* 8ad030f8-87fd-42ed-9ab2-a05d8c3ecfe5); New Jersey. King, David C. & McGeveran, William. lib. bdg. 34.07 *(978-1-60870-055-4(0),* 7ed34966-1ff2-4a8a-9359-a61ffd712fa1); New York. Elish, Dan & Fitzgerald, Stephanie. lib. bdg. 34.07 *(978-1-60870-056-1(9),* 09295635-a487-47bb-b479-872716533eef); North Carolina. Steinitz, Andy & Graham Gaines, Ann. lib. bdg. 34.07 *(978-1-60870-057-8(7),* ff33e2dd-3df2-459d-aabc-42904fd41252); Pennsylvania. Hart, Joyce & Hantula, Richard. lib. bdg. 34.07 *(978-1-60870-058-5(5),* 9547320c-641d-4b01-bfa3-9d2c0391d89d); Texas. Jacobs Altman, Linda & Benduhn, Tea. lib. bdg. 34.07 *(978-1-60870-059-2(3),* 4e440bc3-cef2-49ef-b843-c744ceb3790c); Virginia. King, David C. & Fitzgerald, Stephanie. lib. bdg. 34.07 *(978-1-60870-060-8(7),* 60e30ab9-13b1-45d9-a151-c846a39a4f7b); Washington. Otfinoski, Steven & Benduhn, Tea. lib. bdg. 34.07 *(978-1-60870-061-5(5),* 2f85ab4b-6161-404e-97e2-b9ed868a1385); Wisconsin. Dornfeld, Margaret & Hantula, Richard. lib. bdg. 34.07 *(978-1-60870-062-2(3),* 38ebdd80-c72f-4b9a-b477-30e86af04a96); 80p. (gr. 4-4). (It's My State! (Second Edition)(r) Ser.). (ENG.). 2011. Set lib. bdg. 613.26 *(978-1-60870-044-8(5),* b63891e8-1cf4-4e50-a747-67feb4902eaf, Cavendish Square) Cavendish Square Publishing LLC.

It's My State! (First Edition, Group 1)(r), 12 vols., Set. 2003. (It's My State! (First Edition)(r) Ser.). (ENG.). (gr. 4-4). 204.42 *(978-0-7614-1417-9(7),* 81d3bed4-77b0-4daf-9812-9940855f7bcd, Cavendish Square) Cavendish Square Publishing LLC.

Kaplan, Arie. American Pop: Hit Makers, Superstars, & Dance Revolutionaries. 2012. (American Music Milestones Ser.). (ENG., Illus.). 64p. (J). (gr. 5-12). lib. bdg. 30.65 *(978-0-7613-4504-6(3),* 342882fa-0554-4fce-b27a-ba6e82bdfdfc, Twenty-First Century Bks.) Lerner Publishing Group.

Kerrigan, Michael. Citizen Soldiers: The National Guard. 2017. (Illus.). 80p. (J). *(978-1-4222-3760-1(5))* Mason Crest.

Kiesbye, Stefan, ed. Can Busy Teens Succeed Academically?, 1 vol. 2009. (At Issue Ser.). (ENG., Illus.). 96p. (gr. 10-12). pap. 28.80 *(978-0-7377-4285-5(2),* e9b54081-0652-41e2-89b9-9637f28bebf1, Greenhaven Publishing) Greenhaven Publishing LLC.

Lange, Donna. On the Edge of Disaster: Youth in the Juvenile Court System. 2003. (Youth with Special Needs Ser.). (Illus.). 127p. (YA). (gr. 7). pap. 14.95 *(978-1-4222-0428-3(6))* Mason Crest.

Latta, Sara L. The Woman Who Invented Windshield Wipers: Mary Anderson & Her Wonderful Invention, 1 vol. 2014. (Inventors at Work! Ser.). (ENG.). 48p. (gr. 3-3). 27.93 *(978-0-7660-4203-2(0),* 0da13019-a9c2-4202-9ff6-d15ebf66bb0d) Enslow Publishing, LLC.

T U V

Lindeen, Mary. Welcome to North America, 1 vol. 2011. (Wonder Readers Fluent Level Ser.). (ENG.). 16p. (J). (gr. -1-2). pap. 6.25 *(978-1-4296-7974-9(3)*, 118306, Capstone Pr.) Capstone.

MacRae, Sloan. David Wright, 1 vol. 2012. (Sports Heroes Ser.). (ENG.). 24p. (J). (gr. 2-3). pap. 9.25 *(978-1-4488-6286-3(8)*, b8f76746-07da-4699-86ba-106b69061496); lib. bdg. 26.27 *(978-1-4488-6164-4(0)*, 694b4a9f-00e9-4a36-b448-dc82a301e23b) Rosen Publishing Group, Inc., The. (PowerKids Pr.).

—Evan Longoria, 1 vol. 2012. (Sports Heroes Ser.). (ENG.). 24p. (J). (gr. 2-3). pap. 9.25 *(978-1-4488-6284-9(1)*, d634e8d3-70b5-4d42-867a-54863ad1e4de); lib. bdg. 26.27 *(978-1-4488-6163-7(2)*, 896fc20b-797e-4f96-8202-78caf53c7bb3) Rosen Publishing Group, Inc., The. (PowerKids Pr.).

Marsico, Katie. It's Cool to Learn about Countries: United States. 2010. (Explorer Library: Social Studies Explorer Ser.). (ENG., Illus.). 48p. (gr. 4-8). lib. bdg. 34.93 *(978-1-60279-825-0(7)*, 200516) Cherry Lake Publishing.

Miller, Reagan & Hyde, Natalie. What's in the Southeast? 2011. (ENG.). 32p. (J). lib. bdg. *(978-0-7787-1825-3(5))*; (All Around the U.S. Ser.: No. 3). (gr. 3-6). pap. *(978-0-7787-1831-4(X))* Crabtree Publishing Co.

Miller, Reagan & Peppas, Lynn. What's in the Southwest? 2011. (ENG.). 32p. (J). *(978-0-7787-1826-0(3))* Crabtree Publishing Co.

Murphy, Maggie. Shia Labeouf, 1 vol. 2011. (Movie Superstars Ser.). (ENG., Illus.). 32p. (J). (gr. 4-4). 28.93 *(978-1-4488-2563-9(6)*, 8cde57c8-3759-4311-952a-c2f52264abfc, PowerKids Pr.) Rosen Publishing Group, Inc., The.

My World of Neighbors. (YA). 22.00 *(978-1-931555-46-3(X))* Our Lady of Victory Schl.

National Geographic Learning. Reading Expeditions (Social Studies: Travels Across America's Past): the Northeast: Its History & People. 2007. (ENG., Illus.). 32p. (J). pap. 18.95 *(978-0-7922-8611-0(1))* CENGAGE Learning.

—Reading Expeditions (Social Studies: Travels Across America's Past): the Southwest: Its History & People. 2007. (Avenues Ser.). (ENG., Illus.). 32p. (J). pap. 18.95 *(978-0-7922-8619-6(7))* CENGAGE Learning.

Newman-D'Amico, Fran. All about America: Facts & Fun. 2008. (Dover Little Activity Bks.). (ENG., Illus.). 64p. (J). (gr. 1-4). pap. 2.50 *(978-0-486-46573-9(X)*, 46573X) Dover Pubns., Inc.

Orr, Tamra B. It's Cool to Learn about the United States Southwest. 2011. (Explorer Library: Social Studies Explorer Ser.). (ENG.). 48p. (gr. 4-8). pap. 15.64 *(978-1-61080-304-5(3)*, 201200) Cherry Lake Publishing.

Pearl, Norman. The Great Seal of the United States. Skeens, Matthew, illus. 2006. (American Symbols Ser.). (ENG.). 24p. (J). (gr. 1-3). lib. bdg. 27.32 *(978-1-4048-2214-6(3)*, 92415, Picture Window Bks.) Capstone.

Peppas, Lynn. What's in the Northeast? Crabtree Publishing Staff, ed. 2011. (All Around the U.S. Ser.: No. 2). (ENG.). 32p. (J). pap. *(978-0-7787-1830-7(1))* Crabtree Publishing Co.

Popper, Garry. Billy Joe in the U. S. A. Johnson, Andi, illus. 2004. 36p. (gr. -1-7). 4.00 *(978-1-84161-053-5(4))* Ravette Publishing, Ltd. GBR. Dist: Parkwest Pubns., Inc.

Publishing, Ferguson. Professional Sports Organizations. 2012. (Career Launcher Ser.). (ENG.). 130p. (gr. 9). 34.95 *(978-0-8160-7964-3(1)*, P179133, Ferguson Publishing Company) Infobase Holdings, Inc.

Rappaport, Doreen. In the Promised Land: Lives of Jewish Americans. Van Wright, Cornelius, illus. 2005. 32p. (J). (gr. k-4). lib. bdg. 16.89 *(978-0-06-059395-7(4))* HarperCollins Pubs.

Ray, Liz. Coming to the United States, 6 vols., Set. 2004. (Phonics Readers Books 37-72 Ser.). (ENG.). 8p. (gr. k-1). pap. 35.70 *(978-0-7368-4078-1(8))* Capstone.

Reid, Stephanie. My Country. rev. ed. 2011. (Early Literacy Ser.). (ENG.). 16p. (gr. -1-1). 19.99 *(978-1-4333-2361-4(3))*; 6.99 *(978-1-4333-2360-7(5))* Teacher Created Materials, Inc.

Reynolds, Jeff E. & Reynolds, Jeff. United States of America. 2004. (to Z Ser.). (ENG., Illus.). 40p. (J). (gr. 3-6). 21.19 *(978-0-516-23659-9(8))* Scholastic Library Publishing.

Rossi, Ann. The Southeast: Text Pairs. 2008. (Bridges/Navigators Ser.). (J). (gr. 4). 89.00 *(978-1-4108-8396-4(5))* Benchmark Education Co.

Rottman, Gordon L. The Most Daring Raid of the Civil War: The Great Locomotive Chase, 1 vol. 2011. (Most Daring Raids in History Ser.). (ENG., Illus.). 64p. (YA). (gr. 7-7). 37.13 *(978-1-4488-1870-9(2)*, 39516277-a6d8-4cc8-a833-62e9509030a5) Rosen Publishing Group, Inc., The.

Santoro, Christopher, illus. It's My State Group 8, 12 vols., Set. Incl. Alabama. Hart, Joyce. lib. bdg. 34.07 *(978-0-7614-1925-9(X)*, e1f911a7-a685-4f84-b96d-74698a515b1c); Hawaii. Bredeson, Carmen & Graham Gaines, Ann. lib. bdg. 34.07 *(978-0-7614-1926-6(8)*, 6e86b3a8-59f2-4dfa-860e-b0512d1fab27); Indiana. Derzipilski, Kathleen. lib. bdg. 34.07 *(978-0-7614-1927-3(6)*, 657bce5d-d09d-457c-8868-e0819ddc2c42); Iowa. King, David C. lib. bdg. 34.07 *(978-0-7614-1928-0(4)*, 35ae66ac-e0d7-4380-a106-2c2e7b720da9); Washington, D. C. Hicks, Terry Allan. lib. bdg. 34.07 *(978-0-7614-1929-7(2)*, 5d74eef8-f9a1-4fba-b36d-90a794674429); Wyoming. Petreycik, Rick. lib. bdg. 34.07 *(978-0-7614-1930-3(6)*, 25ee087a-c9a1-4c2f-ac20-ddadacc99001); (Illus.). 80p. (gr. 4-4). (It's My State! (First Edition)(r) Ser.). (ENG.). 2007. Set lib. bdg. 204.42 *(978-0-7614-1924-2(1)*, 41543b62-0268-4139-89f5-dcff5f032701, Cavendish Square) Cavendish Square Publishing LLC.

Schuh, Mari. The Bald Eagle. 2018. (Symbols of American Freedom Ser.). (ENG., Illus.). 24p. (J). (gr. k-3). lib. bdg. 26.95 *(978-1-62617-883-0(6)*, Blastoff! Readers) Bellwether Media.

Sherman, Patrice. John James Audubon. 2011. (ENG., Illus.). 152p. (gr. 6-12). 35.00 *(978-1-60413-953-2(6)*, P189964, Facts On File) Infobase Holdings, Inc.

Sirota, Lyn. Pink, 1 vol. 2011. (Megastars Ser.). (ENG., Illus.). 48p. (YA). (gr. 5-5). 34.47 *(978-1-4358-3577-1(8)*, d65a001e-d585-441a-ab57-3087a5179d18); pap. 12.75 *(978-1-4488-2263-8(7)*, ddf4f35a-ae50-4788-abad-3b29dc06bc1c) Rosen Publishing Group, Inc., The. (Rosen Reference).

Sís, Peter. The Train of States. Sís, Peter, illus. 2004. (Illus.). 64p. (J). (gr. 1-18). 17.99 *(978-0-06-057838-1(6))* HarperCollins Pubs.

Sis, Peter. The Train of States. Sis, Peter, illus. 2007. (ENG., Illus.). 64p. (J). (gr. k-5). pap. 8.99 *(978-0-06-057840-4(8)*, Greenwillow Bks.) HarperCollins Pubs.

Sleeping Bear Press. Diary of an American Kid. Moore, Cyd, illus. 2011. (Country Journal Ser.). (ENG.). 128p. (J). (gr. 4-8). pap. 9.95 *(978-1-58536-171-7(2)*, 202262) Sleeping Bear Pr.

Troupe, Thomas Kingsley. Harriet Tubman's Escape: a Fly on the Wall History. Tejido, Jomike, illus. 2017. (Fly on the Wall History Ser.). (ENG.). 32p. (J). (gr. 1-3). lib. bdg. 27.99 *(978-1-4795-9788-8(0)*, 133417, Picture Window Bks.) Capstone.

Visca, Curt. How to Draw Cartoon Symbols of the United States. 2009. (Kid's Guide to Drawing Ser.). 24p. (gr. 3-3). 47.90 *(978-1-61511-020-9(8)*, PowerKids Pr.) Rosen Publishing Group, Inc., The.

Wallace, Elise. Geographic Features. rev. ed. 2018. (Social Studies: Informational Text Ser.). (ENG., Illus.). 32p. (J). (gr. 3-4). pap. 10.99 *(978-1-4258-2519-5(2))* Teacher Created Materials, Inc.

Wargin, Kathy-jo. The American Reader. Darnell, K. L., illus. 2006. (State/Country Readers Ser.). (ENG.). 96p. (J). (gr. 1-4). 12.95 *(978-1-58536-095-6(3)*, 201975) Sleeping Bear Pr.

Weatherford, Carole Boston. Dorothea Lange. 2018. (2019 Av2 Fiction Ser.). (ENG.). 32p. (J). lib. bdg. 34.28 *(978-1-4896-8255-0(4)*, AV2 by Weigl) Weigl Pubs., Inc.

Wiseman, Blaine. The Northeast. 2016. (Illus.). 48p. (J). *(978-1-5105-1138-5(5))* SmartBook Media, Inc.

Zocchi, Judy. In the United States. Brodie, Neale, illus. 2005. (Global Adventures II Ser.). 32p. (J). per. 9.95 *(978-1-59646-173-4(X))* Dingles & Co.

—In the United States/en los Estados Unidos. Brodie, Neale, illus. 2005. (Global Adventures II Ser.).Tr. of En los Estados Unidos. (ENG & SPA.). 32p. (J). per. 10.95 *(978-1-59646-175-8(6))* Dingles & Co.

UNITED STATES—AIR FORCE

Abdo, Kenny. United States Air Force. 2018. (US Armed Forces Ser.). (ENG., Illus.). 24p. (J). (gr. 2-8). lib. bdg. 31.36 *(978-1-5321-2550-8(X)*, 30109, Abdo Zoom-Fly) ABDO Publishing Co.

Bozzo, Linda. U. S. Air Force. 2019. (Serving in the Military Ser.). (ENG.). 32p. (J). (gr. 2-5). lib. bdg. 28.50 *(978-1-60753-391-7(X)*, 14521) Amicus.

Braulick, Carrie A. U. S. Air Force Spy Planes [Scholastic]. 2011. (Military Vehicles Ser.). 32p. pap. 1.00 *(978-1-4296-6482-0(7)*, Capstone Pr.) Capstone.

—The U. S. Air Force Thunderbirds. 2005. (U. S. Armed Forces Ser.). (ENG., Illus.). 32p. (J). (gr. 1-2). 25.99 *(978-0-7368-4392-8(2)*, Capstone Pr.) Capstone.

Burgan, Michael. Today's U. S. Air Force, 1 vol. 2013. (U. S. Armed Forces Ser.). (ENG.). 48p. (J). (gr. 5-9). pap. 9.10 *(978-0-7565-4633-5(8)*, 121834); lib. bdg. 29.99 *(978-0-7565-4620-5(6)*, 120649) Capstone. (Compass Point Bks.).

Camelo, Wilson & Rice, Earle, Jr. Careers in the U. S. Air Force, 1 vol. 2015. (Careers in the U. S. Armed Forces Ser.). (ENG., Illus.). 128p. (gr. 6-7). 38.93 *(978-0-7660-6941-1(9)*, 432838b8-c11b-4d3f-97ef-c41bc7c13e81) Enslow Publishing, LLC.

Caulkins, Sam. My Uncle Is in the Air Force, 1 vol., 1. 2015. (Military Families Ser.). (ENG., Illus.). 24p. (J). (gr. 3-4). pap. 9.25 *(978-1-5081-4455-7(9)*, f8a4e3fc-8d33-468a-b66e-1164cf79ae75, PowerKids Pr.) Rosen Publishing Group, Inc., The.

David, Jack. Air Force Air Commandos. 2009. (Armed Forces Ser.). (ENG., Illus.). 24p. (J). (gr. 3-7). lib. bdg. 26.95 *(978-1-60014-262-8(1))* Bellwether Media.

—B-1B Lancers. 2009. (Military Machines Ser.). (ENG., Illus.). 24p. (J). (gr. 3-7). lib. bdg. 26.95 *(978-1-60014-258-1(3))* Bellwether Media.

—B-52 Stratofortresses. 2009. (Military Machines Ser.). (ENG., Illus.). 24p. (J). (gr. 3-7). lib. bdg. 26.95 *(978-1-60014-259-8(1))* Bellwether Media.

Doeden, Matt. Tuskegee Airmen. 2018. (Heroes of World War II (Alternator Books (r)) Ser.). (ENG., Illus.). 32p. (J). (gr. 3-6). 30.65 *(978-1-5415-2149-0(8)*, f1f7cb2d-9a30-4d6e-9751-c268493b806e, Lerner Pubns.) Lerner Publishing Group.

—The U. S. Air Force. rev. ed. 2017. (U. S. Military Branches Ser.). (ENG., Illus.). 24p. (J). (gr. -1-2). lib. bdg. 27.32 *(978-1-5157-6754-1(X)*, 135292, Capstone Pr.) Capstone.

—The U. S. Air Force [Scholastic]. 2010. (Military Branches Ser.). pap. 0.52 *(978-1-4296-5069-4(9)*, Capstone Pr.) Capstone.

Dolan, Edward F. Military Service, 10 vols., Set. Incl. Careers in the U. S. Air Force. 38.36 *(978-0-7614-4205-9(7)*, e4fae1b0-9c27-4222-a7e4-9bfe2018acfe); Careers in the U. S. Army. 38.36 *(978-0-7614-4206-6(5)*, a0a5c8e1-5fba-4400-800a-65381ebde5ea); Careers in the U. S. Coast Guard. 38.36 *(978-0-7614-4207-3(3)*, 7ef3c6d4-eff7-4b91-b515-6d4ff161c981); Careers in the U. S. Marine Corps. 38.36 *(978-0-7614-4209-7(X)*, b4ad4186-88cc-46f5-89ce-17b13d9c32d4); Careers in the U. S. Navy. 38.36 *(978-0-7614-4210-3(3)*, e95d1809-a3a4-48fb-8427-1c59e5c740fd); (Illus.). 80p. (YA). (gr. 7-7). (Military Service Ser.). (ENG.). 2010. Set lib. bdg. 191.80 *(978-0-7614-4203-5(0)*, 1fe14f46-9e52-44d0-bb2d-9295775cd6ab, Cavendish Square) Cavendish Square Publishing LLC.

Donovan, Sandy. The U. S. Air Force. 2005. (U. S. Armed Forces Ser.). (Illus.). 64p. (J). (gr. 4-7). lib. bdg. 26.60 *(978-0-8225-1436-7(2))* Lerner Publishing Group.

Dougherty, Martin J. Air Warfare, 1 vol. 2010. (Modern Warfare Ser.). (ENG.). 32p. (YA). (gr. 3-5). lib. bdg. 28.67 *(978-1-4339-2720-1(9)*, c61a8608-6393-475a-a093-ec2060aa1814) Stevens, Gareth Publishing LLLP.

Freedman, Jeri. Special Ops: Air Commandos, 1 vol. 2014. (Inside Special Forces Ser.). (ENG.). 64p. (YA). (gr. 6-6). 36.13 *(978-1-4777-7993-4(0)*, f75a4f6d-0103-47cd-821d-15ae13e0c2e6, Rosen Reference) Rosen Publishing Group, Inc., The.

—Your Career in the Air Force, 1 vol. 2011. (Call of Duty: Careers in the Armed Forces Ser.). (ENG.). 128p. (YA). (gr. 7-7). lib. bdg. 39.80 *(978-1-4488-5513-1(6)*, 9d01d67c-814d-4cd5-8640-3935fa48ef6d) Rosen Publishing Group, Inc., The.

Garstecki, Julia. Tuskegee Airmen. (All-American Fighting Forces Ser.). (ENG., 32p. 2017. Illus.). (gr. 2-7). pap. 9.95 *(978-1-68072-288-8(3))* 2016. (J). (gr. 4-6). pap. 9.99 *(978-1-64466-154-3(3)*, 10318) Black Rabbit Bks. (Bolt).

Goldish, Meish. Air Force: Civilian to Airman. 2010. (Becoming a Soldier Ser.). 24p. (YA). (gr. 3-6). lib. bdg. 26.99 *(978-1-936088-10-2(X))* Bearport Publishing Co., Inc.

Gordon, Nick. Air Force Air Commandos. 2013. (U. S. Military Ser.). (ENG., Illus.). 24p. (J). (gr. 3-7). lib. bdg. 26.95 *(978-1-60014-873-6(5)*, Epic Bks.) Bellwether Media.

—U. S. Air Force. 2012. (U. S. Military Ser.). (ENG., Illus.). 24p. (J). (gr. 3-7). lib. bdg. 26.95 *(978-1-60014-826-2(3)*, Epic Bks.) Bellwether Media.

Greene, Meg. Careers in the National Guards' Search & Rescue Units. 2009. (Careers in Search & Rescue Operations Ser.). 64p. (gr. 5-8). 58.50 *(978-1-61511-812-0(8)*, Rosen Reference) Rosen Publishing Group, Inc., The.

Gregory, Josh. Avionics Technician. 2012. (21st Century Skills Library: Cool Military Careers Ser.). (ENG.). 32p. (gr. 4-8). pap. 14.21 *(978-1-61080-619-0(0)*, 202229); (Illus.). 32.07 *(978-1-61080-445-5(7)*, 202055) Cherry Lake Publishing.

Hand, Carol. Special Ops: Search & Rescue Operations, 1 vol. 2014. (Inside Special Forces Ser.). (ENG.). 64p. (J). (gr. 6-6). 36.13 *(978-1-4777-7997-2(3)*, 085e888f-272d-49fa-b873-346ac8277a48, Rosen Reference) Rosen Publishing Group, Inc., The.

Harasymiw, Mark J. Pararescuemen, 1 vol. 2012. (U. S. Special Forces Ser.). (ENG., Illus.). 32p. (J). (gr. 3-4). pap. 11.50 *(978-1-4339-6571-5(2)*, e1caeac4-d4b7-4ac0-b69e-ac86616c0ec9); lib. bdg. 29.27 *(978-1-4339-6569-2(0)*, 09b57886-b9e9-4d81-b6b8-a87747d34428) Stevens, Gareth Publishing LLLP. (Gareth Stevens Learning Library).

Head, Tom. Air Commandos. 2018. (Elite Warriors Ser.). (ENG.). 32p. (gr. 2-7). 9.95 *(978-1-68072-719-7(2))*; (J). (gr. 4-6). pap. 9.99 *(978-1-64466-272-4(8)*, 12341); (J). (gr. 4-6). lib. bdg. *(978-1-68072-425-7(8)*, 12340) Black Rabbit Bks. (Bolt).

Jordan, David. The U. S. Air Force, 1 vol. 2004. (America's Armed Forces Ser.). (ENG., Illus.). 48p. (gr. 5-8). lib. bdg. 33.67 *(978-0-8368-5679-8(1)*, 07bb968a-fc5c-491e-8f45-632d05d23b4b, Gareth Stevens Secondary Library) Stevens, Gareth Publishing LLLP.

Keeter, Hunter. American Air Forces in the Vietnam War, 1 vol. 2004. (American Experience in Vietnam Ser.). (ENG., Illus.). 48p. (gr. 5-8). lib. bdg. 33.67 *(978-0-8368-5773-3(9)*, b004b61e-1b4d-4fa7-a497-ae16c061d514, Gareth Stevens Secondary Library) Stevens, Gareth Publishing LLLP.

Linde, Barbara M. Heroes of the U. S. Air Force, 1 vol. 2012. (Heroes of the U. S. Military Ser.). (ENG., Illus.). 32p. (gr. 3-4). 29.27 *(978-1-4339-7232-4(8)*, deae6624-763e-4d5b-9a79-f8858d4a84e8); pap. 11.50 *(978-1-4339-7233-1(6)*, 90e63f7d-1b76-4888-aecb-0f6d4a303eb2) Stevens, Gareth Publishing LLLP. (Gareth Stevens Learning Library).

Loria, Laura. Air Force, 1 vol. 2011. (U. S. Military Forces Ser.). (ENG.). 32p. (gr. 3-4). (J). pap. 11.50 *(978-1-4339-5844-1(9)*, 4c297145-47cd-43f6-b363-c6692c614d31, Gareth Stevens Learning Library); (YA). lib. bdg. 29.27 *(978-1-4339-5842-7(2)*, 56432eb0-0ce8-4bbe-adbc-88583359ed04) Stevens, Gareth Publishing LLLP.

Loveless, Antony. Air War. 2008. (ENG., Illus.). 32p. (J). (gr. 6-10). lib. bdg. *(978-0-7787-3812-1(4))* Crabtree Publishing Co.

Marx, Mandy R. Amazing U. S. Air Force Facts. 2016. (Amazing Military Facts Ser.). (ENG., Illus.). 24p. (J). (gr. -1-2). lib. bdg. 27.32 *(978-1-5157-0951-0(5)*, 132275, Capstone Pr.) Capstone.

Masters, Nancy Robinson. Pararescue Jumper. 2012. (21st Century Skills Library: Cool Military Careers Ser.). (ENG.). 32p. (gr. 4-8). pap. 14.21 *(978-1-61080-625-1(5)*, 202235); (Illus.). 32.07 *(978-1-61080-451-6(1)*, 202061) Cherry Lake Publishing.

McNab, Chris. The Air Force. 2017. (Illus.). 80p. (J). *(978-1-4222-3764-9(8))* Mason Crest.

—Protecting the Nation with the U. S. Air Force. 2004. (Rescue & Prevention Ser.). (Illus.). 96p. (YA). (gr. 7-18). lib. bdg. 22.95 *(978-1-59084-416-8(5))* Mason Crest.

—Surviving Captivity. Carney, John, ed. 2014. (Extreme Survival in the Military Ser.: 12). 64p. (J). (gr. 7-18). lib. bdg. 23.95 *(978-1-4222-3089-3(9))* Mason Crest.

Mitchell, P. P. Join the Air Force. 2017. (U. S. Armed Forces Ser.). 32p. (J). (gr. 1-2). pap. 63.00 *(978-1-5382-0540-2(8))* Stevens, Gareth Publishing LLLP.

Murray, Julie. United States Air Force, 1 vol. 2014. (U. S. Armed Forces Ser.). (ENG.). 24p. (J). (gr. -1-2). lib. bdg. 32.79 *(978-1-62970-093-9(2)*, 1710, Abdo Kids) ABDO Publishing Co.

Nardo, Don. Special Operations: Search & Rescue: Search & Rescue. 2012. (YA). 27.45 *(978-1-59935-362-3(8))* Reynolds, Morgan Inc.

Perritano, John. Going after Sparky! Pararescue Jumpers Bring Vietnam War Pilot Home, Vol. 8. 2018. (Special Forces Stories Ser.). 64p. (J). (gr. 7). 31.93 *(978-1-4222-4079-3(7))* Mason Crest.

Petruccio, Steven James. Air Force One Coloring Book. 2018. (Dover American History Coloring Bks.). (ENG.). 32p. (J). (gr. 3-7). pap. 3.99 *(978-0-486-82284-6(2)*, 822842) Dover Pubns., Inc.

Porterfield, Jason. USAF Special Tactics Teams. (Inside Special Operations Ser.). 64p. (gr. 6-6). 2009. 58.50 *(978-1-61513-558-5(8)*, Rosen Reference) 2008. (ENG., Illus.). (J). lib. bdg. 37.13 *(978-1-4042-1753-9(3)*, e1f18262-3c27-4679-a508-869870dac242) 2008. (ENG., Illus.). pap. 12.95 *(978-1-4358-5131-3(5)*, 708d7262-fc75-4a00-ba6a-823c5f7aaf4e, Rosen Classroom) Rosen Publishing Group, Inc., The.

Ray, Michael. The History of Air Forces Around the World, 1 vol., 1. Saxena, Shalini, ed. 2013. (World's Armed Forces Ser.). (ENG.). 144p. (YA). (gr. 8-8). 38.84 *(978-1-62275-145-7(0)*, 20f7502d-3b5c-45f9-a97d-24133a29b2e1) Rosen Publishing Group, Inc., The.

Roberts, Jeremy. U. S. Air Force Special Operations. 2004. (U. S. Armed Forces Ser.). (ENG., Illus.). 64p. (gr. 4-8). lib. bdg. 26.60 *(978-0-8225-1644-6(6))* Lerner Publishing Group.

Rose, Simon. Air Force. 2012. (J). *(978-1-61913-292-4(3))*; pap. *(978-1-61913-295-5(8))* Weigl Pubs., Inc.

—Air Force Special Operations. 2014. (Illus.). 24p. (J). *(978-1-62127-448-3(9))* Weigl Pubs., Inc.

Ryan, Peter K. Black Ops & Other Special Missions of the U. S. Air Force Combat Control Team, 1 vol. 2012. (Inside Special Forces Ser.). (ENG., Illus.). 64p. (YA). (gr. 6-6). pap. 13.95 *(978-1-4488-8389-9(X)*, e3302ab9-3620-4090-95ee-4f577a96fa4d); lib. bdg. 37.13 *(978-1-4488-8382-0(2)*, d023eb72-324b-4bfa-9e61-5271671c23d2) Rosen Publishing Group, Inc., The.

Sandler, Michael. Pararescuemen in Action. 2008. (Special Ops Ser.). (Illus.). 32p. (J). (gr. 3-6). lib. bdg. 28.50 *(978-1-59716-633-1(2))* Bearport Publishing Co., Inc.

Settle, Jimmy & Rearden, Don. Never Quit: How I Became a Special Ops Pararescue Jumper. 2018. (Illus.). viii, 293p. (J). pap. *(978-1-250-31752-0(5))* St. Martin's Pr.

Simons, Lisa M. Bolt. Airmen of the U. S. Air Force [Scholastic]. 2010. (People of the U. S. Armed Forces Ser.). (ENG.). 24p. pap. 0.49 *(978-1-4296-5804-1(5)*, Capstone Pr.) Capstone.

—U. S. Air Force by the Numbers, 1 vol. 2014. (Military by the Numbers Ser.). (ENG., Illus.). 32p. (J). (gr. 3-9). lib. bdg. 28.65 *(978-1-4765-3920-1(0)*, 123919, Capstone Pr.) Capstone.

Terrell, Brandon. Guarding Air Force One. 2016. (Highly Guarded Places Ser.). (ENG.). 24p. (J). (gr. 2-5). 32.79 *(978-1-5038-0808-9(4)*, 210643) Child's World, Inc, The.

Townsend, John. Air Force. 2016. (Action Force: World War II Ser.). 32p. (gr. 3-7). 31.35 *(978-1-59920-985-2(3)*, Smart Apple Media) Black Rabbit Bks.

Tunnell, Michael O. Candy Bomber: The Story of the Berlin Airlift's Chocolate Pilot. 2010. (ENG., Illus.). 120p. (J). (gr. 4-7). pap. 9.95 *(978-1-58089-337-4(6))* Charlesbridge Publishing, Inc.

U. S. Air Force. 2019. (Serving Our Country Ser.). (ENG.). 24p. (J). (gr. 1-4). lib. bdg. *(978-1-68151-560-1(1)*, 17592) Amicus.

Vanderhoof, Gabrielle. Air Force. 2010. (Special Forces Ser.). 64p. (YA). (gr. 7-18). lib. bdg. 22.95 *(978-1-4222-1837-2(6))* Mason Crest.

Whiting, Jim. Air Force Special Operations Command. 2014. (U. S. Special Forces Ser.). (ENG.). 48p. (J). (gr. 5-8). *(978-1-60818-460-6(9)*, 21424, Creative Education); pap. 12.00 *(978-1-62832-046-6(X)*, 21425, Creative Paperbacks) Creative Co., The.

Williams, Heather DiLorenzo & Rylands, Warren. Air Force. 2019. (Illus.). 24p. (J). *(978-1-4896-8025-9(X)*, AV2 by Weigl) Weigl Pubs., Inc.

Wood, Alix. Serving in the Air Force, 1 vol. 2013. (Protecting Our Country Ser.). 32p. (J). (gr. 3-4). (ENG.). pap. 11.00 *(978-1-4777-1400-3(6)*, 462092f9-b95d-462e-a186-29861f8dff88); (ENG.). lib. bdg. 28.93 *(978-1-4777-1297-9(6)*, 5c6667cf-1cfc-458b-bc12-364cc3dcb50f); pap. 60.00 *(978-1-4777-1401-0(4))* Rosen Publishing Group, Inc., The. (PowerKids Pr.).

Zobel, Derek. United States Air Force. 2008. (Armed Forces Ser.). (ENG., Illus.). 24p. (J). (gr. 3-7). lib. bdg. 26.95 *(978-1-60014-161-4(7))* Bellwether Media.

UNITED STATES—AIR FORCE—BIOGRAPHY

Aronin, Miriam & Pushies, Fred J. Today's Air Force Heroes. 2012. (Acts of Courage: Inside America's Military Ser.). (Illus.). 32p. (J). (gr. 2-7). lib. bdg. 28.50 *(978-1-61772-447-3(5))* Bearport Publishing Co., Inc.

Fleischman, John. Black & White Airmen: Their True History. 2007. (ENG., Illus.). 160p. (gr. 5-12). 28.80 *(978-1-4287-3953-6(X)*, Follettbound) Follett School Solutions.

Rice, Dona. Saving the World: The Chocolate Pilot. rev. ed. 2019. (Social Studies: Informational Text Ser.: 2). (ENG., Illus.). 32p. (J). (gr. 4-8). pap. 11.99 *(978-1-64491-004-7(7))* Teacher Created Materials, Inc.

Rice, Earle. Claire Chennault. 2003. (Famous Flyers Ser.). (ENG., Illus.). 112p. (gr. 6-12). 30.00 *(978-0-7910-7217-2(7)*, P113746, Facts On File) Infobase Holdings, Inc.

Settle, Jimmy & Rearden, Don. Never Quit: How I Became a Special Ops Pararescue Jumper. 2018. (ENG., Illus.). 304p. (YA). 18.99 *(978-1-250-13961-0(9)*, 900179410, St. Martin's Griffin) St. Martin's Pr.

UNITED STATES—ANTIQUITIES

see also Indians of North America—Antiquities

Benson, Sonia & Baker, Deborah J. Almanac, Early Civilizations, 2 vols. 2005. (Early Civilizations in the Americas Ser.: 1). (ENG., Illus.). 336p. (J). lib. bdg. 129.00 *(978-0-7876-7679-7(9)*, UXL) Cengage Gale.

—Primary Sources, Early Americas, 2 vols. 2005. (Early Civilizations in the Americas Ser.: 2). (ENG., Illus.). 368p. (J). lib. bdg. 129.00 *(978-0-7876-7681-0(0)*, UXL) Cengage Gale.

Hansen, Joyce & McGowan, Gary. Freedom Roads: Searching for the Underground Railroad. Ransome, James, illus. 2003. (ENG.). 166p. (J). (gr. 5-9). 18.95 *(978-0-8126-2673-5(7))* Cricket Bks.

Hawk, Fran. The Story of the H. L. Hunley & Queenie's Coin. Nance, Dan, illus. 2004. (ENG.). 40p. (J). (gr. 1-4). 16.95 *(978-1-58536-218-9(2)*, 202048) Sleeping Bear Pr.

Holliday, Diane & Malone, Bobbie. Digging & Discovery, Teachers Guide & Student Materials, 2nd Edition, on CD: Wisconsin Archaeology. 2011. (New Badger History Ser.). (ENG.). (J). cd-rom 49.95 *(978-0-87020-480-7(7))* Wisconsin Historical Society.

Linde, Barbara. Artifacts Throughout American History, 1 vol. 2019. (Journey to the Past: Investigating Primary Sources Ser.). (ENG.). 32p. (gr. 4-5). pap. 11.50 *(978-1-5382-4030-4(0)*,

099dc8a7-78c0-4c4d-be48-beb852b7f25f) Stevens, Gareth Publishing LLLP.

Manis, Shirley & Manis, Shirley. In a Scoop of Dirt: How Digging a Pond Changed North America's Prehistory. l.t. ed. 2011. (ENG., Illus.). 38p. pap. 17.95 (978-0-9839286-0-7(6)) Manis, Shirley.

Walker, Sally M. Written in Bone: Buried Lives of Jamestown & Colonial Maryland. 2009. (ENG., Illus.). 144p. (J). (gr. 5-8). lib. bdg. 22.99 (978-0-8225-7135-3(8), 663c9811-1a81-4b41-aae7-5eeb06e0e935, Carolrhoda Bks.) Lerner Publishing Group.

Ward, Jill. Georgia's First People. 2010. (J). (978-1-935077-74-9(0)); pap. (978-1-935077-81-7(3)) State Standards Publishing, LLC.

UNITED STATES—ARMED FORCES

see also official names of branches of the Armed Forces, e.g. U. S. Army; U. S. Navy

ABDO Publishing Company Staff & Murray, Julie. U. S. Armed Forces, 6 vols. 2014. (U. S. Armed Forces Ser.: 6). (ENG.). 24p. (J). (gr. -1-2). lib. bdg. 196.74 (978-1-62970-091-5(6), 1708, Abdo Kids) ABDO Publishing Co.

Alpert, Barbara. U. S. Military Robots, 1 vol. 2012. (U. S. Military Technology Ser.). (ENG., Illus.). 32p. (J). (gr. 3-9). lib. bdg. 27.32 (978-1-4296-8438-5(0), 118510, Capstone Pr.) Capstone.

America's Armed Forces, 12 vols. 2004. (America's Armed Forces Ser.). (ENG.). 48p. (gr. 5-8). lib. bdg. 202.02 (978-0-8368-5678-1(3), 7abe852d-cf54-4062-b40b-820c10c4e230, Gareth Stevens Secondary Library) Stevens, Gareth Publishing LLLP.

Bailey, Diane. Rescue from an ISIS Prison! Delta Force in Iraq During the War on Terror, Vol. 8. 2018. (Special Forces Stories Ser.). 64p. (J). (gr. 7). lib. bdg. 31.93 (978-1-4222-4080-9(0)) Mason Crest.

Baxter, Roberta. Work in the Military. 2019. (Career Finder Ser.). (ENG.). 80p. (YA). (gr. 6-12). 41.27 (978-1-68282-729-1(1), BrightPoint Pr.) ReferencePoint Pr., Inc.

Blackford, Cheryl. This Book Is Top Secret: A Collection of Awesome Military Trivia, 1 vol. 2012. (Super Trivia Collection). (ENG., Illus.). 32p. (J). (gr. 3-9). lib. bdg. 28.65 (978-1-4296-8591-7(3), 118603, Capstone Pr.) Capstone.

Bowman, Chris. Special Forces Operator. 2014. (Dangerous Jobs Ser.). (ENG., Illus.). 24p. (J). (gr. 3-7). lib. bdg. 26.95 (978-1-62617-114-5(9), Torque Bks.) Bellwether Media.

Campbell, Geoffrey A. Weapons of War. 2004. (American War Library). (Illus.). 112p. (J). (gr. 7-10). 30.85 (978-1-59018-544-5(7), Lucent Bks.) Cengage Gale.

Careers in the U. S. Armed Forces, 10 vols. 2015. (Careers in the U. S. Armed Forces Ser.). (ENG.). 128p. (J). (gr. 6-7). lib. bdg. 194.65 (978-0-7660-6694-6(0), a5570bea-d8fa-4c4a-83ee-fa91f4c5c538) Enslow Publishing, LLC.

Conkling, Winifred. Heroism Begins with Her: Inspiring Stories of Bold, Brave, & Gutsy Women in the U. S. Military. Kuo, Julia, illus. 2019. (ENG.). 240p. (J). (gr. 3-7). 18.99 (978-0-06-284741-6(4), HarperCollins) HarperCollins Pubs.

David, Jack. M2A2 Bradleys. 2009. (Military Machines Ser.). (ENG., Illus.). 24p. (J). (gr. 3-7). lib. bdg. 26.95 (978-1-60014-261-1(3)) Bellwether Media.

Dell, Pamela & Raatma, Lucia. The Science of Soldiers, 1 vol. 2012. (Science of War Ser.). (ENG.). 48p. (J). (gr. 6-9). lib. bdg. 34.65 (978-0-7565-4460-7(2), 115723, Compass Point Bks.) Capstone.

Demarest, Chris L. Alpha Bravo Charlie: The Military Alphabet. Demarest, Chris L., illus. 2005. (ENG., Illus.). 40p. (J). (gr. 1-5). 19.99 (978-0-689-86928-0(2), McElderry, Margaret K. Bks.) McElderry, Margaret K. Bks.

Dolan, Edward F. Military Service, 10 vols., Set. Incl. Careers in the U. S. Air Force. 38.36 (978-0-7614-4205-9(7), e4fae1b0-9c27-4222-a7e4-9bfe2018acfe); Careers in the U. S. Army. 38.36 (978-0-7614-4206-6(5), a0a5c8e1-5fba-4400-800a-65381ebde5ea); Careers in the U. S. Coast Guard. 38.36 (978-0-7614-4207-3(3), 7ef3c6d4-eff7-4b91-b515-6d4ff161c981); Careers in the U. S. Marine Corps. 38.36 (978-0-7614-4209-7(X), b4ad4186-88cc-46f5-89ce-17b13d9c32d4); Careers in the U. S. Navy. 38.36 (978-0-7614-4210-3(3), e95d1809-a3a4-48fb-8427-1c59e5c740fd); (Illus.). 80p. (YA). (gr. 7-7). (Military Service Ser.). (ENG.). 2010. Set lib. bdg. 191.80 (978-0-7614-4203-5(0), 1fe14f46-9e52-44d0-bb2d-9295775cd6ab, Cavendish Square) Cavendish Square Publishing LLC.

Donovan, Sandy. Protecting America: A Look at the People Who Keep Our Country Safe. 2003. (How Government Works). (ENG., Illus.). 56p. (gr. 4-8). lib. bdg. 25.26 (978-0-8225-1345-2(5)) Lerner Publishing Group.

Fishkin, Rebecca Love. Vehicles of the Iraq War, 1 vol. 2013. (War Vehicles Ser.). (ENG.). 32p. (J). (gr. 3-9). 28.65 (978-1-4296-9914-3(0), 120627, Capstone Pr.) Capstone.

Gonzalez, Lissette. The U. S. Military: Defending the Nation. (Dangerous Jobs Ser.). 24p. (gr. 2-3). 2009. 42.50 (978-1-61512-137-3(4), PowerKids Pr.) 2007. (ENG., Illus.). (J). lib. bdg. 26.27 (978-1-4042-3777-3(1), 1824257e-f710-4fc7-b56c-43f1b2c32996) Rosen Publishing Group, Inc., The.

Gregory, Josh. Aircraft Pilot. 2012. (21st Century Skills Library: Cool Military Careers Ser.). (ENG.). 32p. (gr. 4-8). pap. 14.21 (978-1-61080-618-3(2), 202228); (Illus.). 32.07 (978-1-61080-444-8(9), 202054) Cherry Lake Publishing.

—Avionics Technician. 2012. (21st Century Skills Library: Cool Military Careers Ser.). (ENG.). 32p. (gr. 4-8). pap. 14.21 (978-1-61080-619-0(0), 202229); (Illus.). 32.07 (978-1-61080-445-5(7), 202055) Cherry Lake Publishing.

—Information Systems Technician. 2012. (21st Century Skills Library: Cool Military Careers Ser.). (ENG.). 32p. (gr. 4-8). pap. 14.21 (978-1-61080-621-3(2), 202231); (Illus.). 32.07 (978-1-61080-447-9(3), 202057) Cherry Lake Publishing.

—Special Ops. 2012. (21st Century Skills Library: Cool Military Careers Ser.). (ENG.). 32p. (gr. 4-8). pap. 14.21 (978-1-61080-620-6(4), 202230); (Illus.). 32.07 (978-1-61080-446-2(5), 202056) Cherry Lake Publishing.

Hamilton, John. America's Military. 2004. (War in Iraq Ser.). (Illus.). 48p. (gr. 4-8). lib. bdg. 27.07 (978-1-59197-492-5(5), Abdo & Daughters) ABDO Publishing Co.

—Weapons of the 21st Century. 2004. (War in Iraq Ser.). (Illus.). 48p. (gr. 4-8). lib. bdg. 27.07 (978-1-59197-501-4(8), Abdo & Daughters) ABDO Publishing Co.

Hart, Joyce. Frequently Asked Questions about Being Part of a Military Family, 1 vol. 2009. (FAQ: Teen Life Ser.). (ENG., Illus.). 64p. (J). (gr. 5-6). lib. bdg. 37.13 (978-1-4358-5328-7(8), 55819231-6297-4ce2-aa7b-669164ab6757) Rosen Publishing Group, Inc., The.

King, Margaret. World War II in the Pacific. rev. ed. 2019. (Social Studies: Informational Text Ser.). (ENG., Illus.). 32p. (J). (gr. 4-8). pap. 11.99 (978-1-4258-5071-5(5)) Teacher Created Materials, Inc.

Lewis, Daniel. Armed Forces, Vol. 10. 2018. (Careers in Demand for High School Graduates Ser.). 112p. (J). (gr. 7). 34.60 (978-1-4222-4133-2(5)) Mason Crest.

Libal, Joyce. Military & Elite Forces Officer. Riggs, Ernestine G. & Gholar, Cheryl, eds. 2013. (Careers with Character Ser.: 18). 96p. (J). (gr. 7-18). 22.95 (978-1-4222-2760-2(X)) Mason Crest.

Lusted, Marcia Amidon. African Americans in the Military. 2012. (J). pap. (978-1-4222-2392-5(2)) Mason Crest.

—African Americans in the Military. Hill, Marc Lamont, ed. 2012. (Major Black Contributions from Emancipation to Civil Rights Ser.). 64p. (J). (gr. 5). 22.95 (978-1-4222-2379-6(5)) Mason Crest.

Mara, Wil. Helicopter Crew Chief. 2012. (21st Century Skills Library: Cool Military Careers Ser.). (ENG.). 32p. (gr. 4-8). pap. 14.21 (978-1-61080-623-7(9), 202233); (Illus.). 32.07 (978-1-61080-449-3(X), 202059) Cherry Lake Publishing.

—Motor Transport Operator. 2012. (21st Century Skills Library: Cool Military Careers Ser.). (ENG.). 32p. (gr. 4-8). pap. 14.21 (978-1-61080-624-4(7), 202234); (Illus.). 32.07 (978-1-61080-450-9(3), 202060) Cherry Lake Publishing.

Masters, Nancy Robinson. Drone Pilot. 2012. (21st Century Skills Library: Cool Military Careers Ser.). (ENG.). 32p. (gr. 4-8). pap. 14.21 (978-1-61080-622-0(0), 202232); (Illus.). 32.07 (978-1-61080-448-6(1), 202058) Cherry Lake Publishing.

Maxwell, Shannon. Our Daddy Is Invincible! Biggers, Liza, illus. 40p. (J). 2011. 15.95 (978-1-61751-003-8(3)) 2010. pap. 9.95 (978-1-61751-002-1(5)) Kurdyla, E L Publishing LLC. (4th Division Pr.).

McIntosh, J. S. Elite Forces Selection. 2010. (Special Forces Ser.). 64p. (YA). (gr. 7-18). lib. bdg. 22.95 (978-1-4222-1839-6(2)) Mason Crest.

Mikaelian, Allen & Wallace, Mike. Medal of Honor: Profiles of America's Military Heroes from the Civil War to the Present. 2003. (ENG.). 336p. (gr. 8-17). pap. 21.99 (978-0-7868-8576-3(9), Hachette Bks.) Hachette Bks.

Miller, Adam, et al. Courage under Fire: True Stories of Bravery from the U. S. Army, Navy, Air Force, & Marines, 1 vol. 2014. (Courage under Fire Ser.). (ENG., Illus.). 112p. (J). (gr. 3-9). pap., pap., pap. 9.95 (978-1-4914-1065-3(5), 126702, Capstone Pr.) Capstone.

Montana, Jack. Parachute Regiment. 2010. (Special Forces Ser.). 64p. (YA). (gr. 7-18). lib. bdg. 22.95 (978-1-4222-1845-7(7)) Mason Crest.

Morrison, Jessica. Military. 2016. (Illus.). 48p. (J). (978-1-5105-1160-6(1)) SmartBook Media, Inc.

—Military. 2011. (J). (gr. 5-8). pap. 14.95 (978-1-61690-665-8(0), AV2 by Weigl); (Illus.). 48p. (YA). (gr. 1-4). 29.99 (978-1-61690-661-0(8)) Weigl Pubs., Inc.

Page, Andrea. The Sioux Code Talkers of World War II, 1 vol. 2017. (ENG., Illus.). 136p. (J). (gr. 3-7). 14.95 (978-1-4556-2243-6(5), Pelican Publishing) Arcadia Publishing.

Poole, H. W. Military Families, Vol. 12. 2016. (Families Today Ser.). (Illus.). 48p. (J). (gr. 5). 20.95 (978-1-4222-3620-8(X)) Mason Crest.

Raum, Elizabeth, et al. True War Stories: Personal Accounts of History's Greatest Conflicts. Kinsella, Pat et al, illus. 2017. (J). (978-1-4914-1965-6(2)) Capstone.

—U. S. Military by the Numbers, 1 vol. 2014. (ENG., Illus.). 112p. (J). (gr. 3-9). pap., pap., pap. 9.95 (978-1-62370-061-4(2), 124571, Capstone Young Readers) Capstone.

Reeves, Diane Lindsey. Choose a Career Adventure in the Military. 2016. (Bright Futures Press: Choose a Career Adventure Ser.). (ENG., Illus.). 32p. (J). (gr. 4-6). 32.07 (978-1-63471-912-4(3), 208969) Cherry Lake Publishing.

Roza, Greg. Choosing a Career in the Military. 2009. (World of Work Ser.). 64p. (gr. 5-5). 58.50 (978-1-60854-338-0(2)) Rosen Publishing Group, Inc., The.

Rudolph, Jessica. CIA Paramilitary Operatives in Action. 2013. (Special Ops II Ser.). 32p. (J). (gr. 2-7). lib. bdg. 28.50 (978-1-61772-892-1(6)) Bearport Publishing Co., Inc.

Scillian, Devin. H Is for Honor: A Military Family Alphabet. Juhasz, Victor, illus. 2006. (ENG.). 40p. (J). (gr. 1-4). 18.99 (978-1-58536-292-9(1), 202103) Sleeping Bear Pr.

Sheen, Barbara. Cutting Edge Military Technology. 2016. (ENG.). 80p. (J). (gr. 5-12). (978-1-68282-044-5(0)) ReferencePoint Pr., Inc.

Shoup, Kate. Coding Careers in the Military, 1 vol. 2019. (Coding Careers for Tomorrow Ser.). (ENG.). 80p. (gr. 8-8). pap. 18.64 (978-1-5026-4587-6(4), 54a996b4-9fb8-4c54-a537-39253db37629) Cavendish Square Publishing LLC.

Simons, Lisa M. Bolt. The U. S. WASP: Trailblazing Women Pilots of World War II. 2017. (Women & War Ser.). (ENG., Illus.). 32p. (J). (gr. 3-9). pap. 8.19 (978-1-5157-7944-5(0), 136039, Capstone Pr.) Capstone.

—Women in Combat: Bringing the Fight to the Front Lines. 2017. (Women & War Ser.). (ENG., Illus.). 32p. (J). (gr. 3-9). lib. bdg. 28.65 (978-1-5157-7934-6(3), 136028, Capstone Pr.) Capstone.

A Soldier Comes Home. 2011. (ENG., Illus.). 32p. (J). pap. 9.99 (978-0-578-06838-1(9)) Yari Publishing.

Stein, R. Conrad. World War II in the Pacific: From Pearl Harbor to Nagasaki, 1 vol. 2011. (United States at War Ser.). (ENG., Illus.). 128p. (gr. 5-6). lib. bdg. 35.93 (978-0-7660-3640-6(5), 471c3ce0-e74c-439d-bf93-7548fa85145e) Enslow Publishing, LLC.

Stout, Glenn. Soldier Athletes. 2011. (Good Sports Ser.). (ENG.). 112p. (J). (gr. 5-7). pap. 6.99 (978-0-547-41729-5(2), 1430259, Clarion Bks.) HarperCollins Pubs.

Sutherland, Adam. Armed Services. 2012. (On the Radar: Defend & Protect Ser.). (ENG., Illus.). 32p. (gr. 4-8). lib. bdg. 26.60 (978-0-7613-7771-9(9), Lerner Pubns.) Lerner Publishing Group.

Townsend, Chris. What Does a Member of the Armed Forces Do?, 1 vol. 2018. (What Does a Citizen Do? Ser.). (ENG.). 48p. (gr. 5-5). 30.93 (978-0-7660-9866-4(4), 10e248cc-1aa4-4472-99e9-ab6f8506dee9) Enslow Publishing, LLC.

U. S. Armed Forces. 2017. (U. S. Armed Forces Ser.). 32p. (gr. 1-2). pap. 63.00 (978-1-5382-0493-1(2)); (ENG.). lib. bdg. 169.62 (978-1-5382-0479-5(7), 2490138f-81bf-4f65-8c27-f09f2dab5ef0) Stevens, Gareth Publishing LLLP.

U. S. Armed Forces Pack [Scholastic]. 2010. (People of the U. S. Armed Forces Ser.). 24p. pap. 1.96 (978-1-4296-5808-9(8), Capstone Pr.) Capstone.

Ulh, Xina M. Using Computer Science in Military Service, 1 vol. 2018. (Coding Your Passion Ser.). (ENG.). 80p. (gr. 7-7). 37.47 (978-1-5081-8399-0(6), 696c4298-acd1-46e1-bbd8-d216409267d6, Rosen Young Adult) Rosen Publishing Group, Inc., The.

Whiting, Jim. Green Berets. 2014. (U. S. Special Forces Ser.). (ENG., Illus.). 48p. (J). (gr. 5-8). lib. bdg. 35.65 (978-1-60818-463-7(3), 21433, Creative Education) Creative Co., The.

Wolny, Philip. American Troops in Afghanistan: Building a New Nation. (Frontline Coverage of Current Events Ser.). 48p. (gr. 5-5). 2009. 53.00 (978-1-61512-653-8(8)) 2004. (ENG., Illus.). (J). lib. bdg. 34.47 (978-1-4042-0343-3(5), fa9a56c2-4f53-4ba5-be0c-2e2591073d16) Rosen Publishing Group, Inc., The.

Yomtov, Nel. Patrolling. 2016. (Military Missions Ser.). (ENG., Illus.). 24p. (J). (gr. 3-7). 26.95 (978-1-62617-435-1(0), Epic Bks.) Bellwether Media.

—Rescue. 2016. (Military Missions Ser.). (ENG., Illus.). 24p. (J). (gr. 3-7). 26.95 (978-1-62617-438-2(5), Epic Bks.) Bellwether Media.

Zullo, Allan. World War I Heroes. 2014. 162p. (J). pap. (978-0-545-67533-8(2)) Scholastic, Inc.

UNITED STATES—ARMED FORCES—FICTION

Andersen, C. B. The Secret Mission. 2008. (J). (978-1-59038-906-5(9)) Deseret Bk. Co.

Cummings, Mary. And the Baker's Boy Went to Sea. 2006. (Illus.). 195p. (YA). 16.95 (978-0-9774855-0-5(1)) Sparkling Pr.

Dowell, Frances O'Roark. Shooting the Moon. 2009. (ENG.). 192p. (J). (gr. 5-9). pap. 7.99 (978-1-4169-7986-9(7), Atheneum Bks. for Young Readers) Simon & Schuster Children's Publishing.

Ganzer, Diane & Swanson, Christopher. Called to Serve. 2008. 116p. pap. 9.99 (978-1-935105-10-7(8)) Avid Readers Publishing Group.

Karr, Kathleen. Exiled: Memoirs of a Camel, 0 vols. 2012. (ENG.). 242p. (J). (gr. 4-6). pap. 9.99 (978-0-7614-5291-1(5), 9780761452911, Two Lions) Amazon Publishing.

London, C. Alexander. Semper Fido, Bk. 1. 2013. (Dog Tags Ser.: 1). (ENG.). 224p. (J). (gr. 5-9). pap. 6.99 (978-0-545-47704-8(2)) Scholastic, Inc.

Mazer, Harry. Heroes Don't Run. 2007. (Aladdin Historical Fiction Ser.). 113p. (gr. 3-7). 16.00 (978-0-7569-8111-2(5)) Perfection Learning Corp.

McRaven, William H. Make Your Bed with Skipper the Seal. McWilliam, Howard, illus. 2021. (ENG.). 48p. (J). (gr. -1-3). 18.99 (978-0-316-59235-2(8)) Little, Brown Bks. for Young Readers.

Myers, Walter Dean. Invasion. (ENG.). 224p. (YA). 2015. (gr. 7). pap. 12.99 (978-0-545-38429-2(X)) 2013. E-Book (978-0-545-57659-8(8)) Scholastic, Inc. (Scholastic Pr.).

Polacco, Patricia. Remembering Vera. Polacco, Patricia, illus. 2017. (ENG., Illus.). 32p. (J). (gr. -1-3). 18.99 (978-1-4814-4227-5(9), Simon & Schuster/Paula Wiseman Bks.) Simon & Schuster/Paula Wiseman Bks.

Romoulous. Katalambano: 187 Warriors Killers. 2007. 15.00 (978-0-9773064-4-2(5), Romoulous) MIROGLYPHICS.

—Katalambano: The Strong Survive. 2005. 15.00 (978-0-9773064-3-5(7)) MIROGLYPHICS.

Sherman, M. Zachary. Blood Brotherhood, 1 vol. Casas, Fritz, illus. 2011. (Bloodlines Ser.). (ENG.). 88p. (J). (gr. 4-8). pap. 6.95 (978-1-4342-3098-0(8), 114738, Stone Arch Bks.) Capstone.

—Emergency Ops, 1 vol. Bermudez, Raymund, illus. 2012. (Bloodlines Ser.). (ENG.). 88p. (J). (gr. 4-8). lib. bdg. 27.32 (978-1-4342-3766-8(4), 117027, Stone Arch Bks.) Capstone.

—Heart of War. Casas, Fritz et al, illus. 2013. (Bloodlines Ser.). (ENG.). 240p. (J). (gr. 4-8). pap., pap., pap. 7.95 (978-1-62370-002-7(7), 122308, Capstone Young Readers) Capstone.

—A Time for War, 1 vol. Casas, Fritz, illus. 2011. (Bloodlines Ser.). (ENG.). 88p. (J). (gr. 4-8). 27.32 (978-1-4342-2558-0(5), 113616, Stone Arch Bks.) Capstone.

Willink, Jocko. Way of the Warrior Kid: From Wimpy to Warrior the Navy SEAL Way. Bozak, Jon, illus. 2017. (Way of the Warrior Kid Ser.: 1). (ENG.). 192p. (J). 14.99 (978-1-250-15107-0(4), 900182685) Feiwel & Friends.

Zima, Marjorie H. Meghan's Military Family. 2008. 23p. pap. 24.95 (978-1-60563-437-1(9)) America Star Bks.

UNITED STATES—ARMED FORCES—WOMEN

Coleman, Miriam. Women in the Military, 1 vol. 2015. (Women Groundbreakers Ser.). (ENG.). 32p. (J). (gr. 4-5). pap. 11.00 (978-1-4994-1052-5(2), 03b6bd8a-34e7-4b3b-9ec4-f6f3fb5cfe5f, PowerKids Pr.) Rosen Publishing Group, Inc., The.

Ferguson, Amanda. American Women of the Vietnam War. (American Women at War Ser.). 112p. (gr. 8-8). 2009. 63.90 (978-1-61511-395-8(9)) 2004. (ENG., Illus.). (YA). lib. bdg. 39.80 (978-0-8239-4448-4(4), 1e969f8c-b989-41bb-a39e-09010cf3e2b8) Rosen Publishing Group, Inc., The.

Goldsmith, Connie. Women in the Military: From Drill Sergeants to Fighter Pilots. 2019. (ENG., Illus.). 120p. (YA). (gr. 6-12). 37.32 (978-1-5415-2812-3(3), 926b05ea-eead-4685-b89f-468374efd7d4, Twenty-First Century Bks.) Lerner Publishing Group.

Zeinert, Karen & Miller, Mary. The Brave Women of the Gulf Wars: Operation Desert Storm & Operation Iraqi Freedom. 2005. (Women at War Ser.). (ENG., Illus.). 96p. (J). (gr. 7-12). 30.60 (978-0-7613-2705-9(3), Millbrook Pr.) Lerner Publishing Group.

UNITED STATES—ARMY

Abdo, Kenny. United States Army. 2018. (US Armed Forces Ser.). (ENG., Illus.). 24p. (J). (gr. 2-8). lib. bdg. 31.36 (978-1-5321-2551-5(8), 30111, Abdo Zoom-Fly) ABDO Publishing Co.

Adams, Dorothy. Cavalry Hero: Casimir Pulaski. Lorentowicz, Irena, illus. 2018. 195p. (J). (gr. 8-18). pap. 14.95 (978-1-932350-74-6(8)) Bethlehem Bks.

Alberti, Enigma. Spy on History: Victor Dowd & the World War II Ghost Army. Wegener, Scott, illus. 2018. (Spy on History Ser.). (ENG.). 96p. (J). (gr. 3-9). 12.95 (978-0-7611-9326-5(X), 19326) Workman Publishing Co., Inc.

Allen, Roger MacBride & Allen, Thomas B. Mr. Lincoln's High-Tech War: How the North Used the Telegraph, Railroads, Surveillance Balloons, Ironclads, High-Powered Weapons, & More to Win the Civil War. 2009. (Illus.). 144p. (J). (gr. 5-9). 18.95 (978-1-4263-0379-1(3), National Geographic Kids) Disney Publishing Worldwide.

Aller, Susan Bivin. Ulysses S. Grant. 2006. (History Maker Bios Ser.). (Illus.). 48p. (J). (gr. 3-7). lib. bdg. 26.60 (978-0-8225-2438-0(4), Lerner Pubns.) Lerner Publishing Group.

Alvarez, Carlos. Army Delta Force. 2009. (Armed Forces Ser.). (ENG., Illus.). 24p. (J). (gr. 3-7). lib. bdg. 26.95 (978-1-60014-290-1(7)) Bellwether Media.

—Army Night Stalkers. 2009. (Armed Forces Ser.). (ENG., Illus.). 24p. (J). (gr. 3-7). lib. bdg. 26.95 (978-1-60014-280-2(X)) Bellwether Media.

—Army Rangers. 2009. (Armed Forces Ser.). (ENG., Illus.). 24p. (J). (gr. 3-7). lib. bdg. 26.95 (978-1-60014-274-1(5)) Bellwether Media.

Anderson, Dale. Soldiers & Sailors in the American Revolution, 1 vol. 2005. (World Almanac(r) Library of the American Revolution Ser.). (ENG.). 48p. (gr. 5-8). pap. 15.05 (978-0-8368-5938-6(3), fefcb9af-19a9-4101-b561-c76c583fb122); lib. bdg. 33.67 (978-0-8368-5929-4(4), 29863a8e-4cf7-476a-957d-381f6117ed23) Stevens, Gareth Publishing LLLP. (Gareth Stevens Secondary Library).

Anderson, Jane. My Name Is Deborah Samson. 2005. (J). pap. (978-1-4108-4225-1(8)) Benchmark Education Co.

Andrews Henningfeld, Diane, ed. Should Women Be Allowed to Serve in Combat in the U. S. Armed Forces?, 1 vol. 2007. (At Issue Ser.). (ENG., Illus.). 120p. (gr. 10-12). pap. 28.80 (978-0-7377-3939-8(8), 9da6ac82-283a-4d5b-a38f-2840fc18b8ee); lib. bdg. 41.03 (978-0-7377-3938-1(X), 4ca8de6e-1a60-4ec2-8685-ceef046ae2bf) Greenhaven Publishing LLC. (Greenhaven Publishing).

Archer, Jules. A House Divided: The Lives of Ulysses S. Grant & Robert E. Lee. rev. ed. 2015. (Jules Archer History for Young Readers Ser.). (ENG., Illus.). 176p. (J). (gr. 6-6). 16.99 (978-1-63220-604-6(8), Sky Pony Pr.) Skyhorse Publishing Co., Inc.

Aronson, Billy. Ulysses S. Grant, 1 vol. 2008. (Presidents & Their Times Ser.). (ENG., Illus.). 96p. (gr. 6-6). lib. bdg. 36.93 (978-0-7614-2430-7(X), 0d48df73-e370-4f52-aced-ea6cd56d6e16) Cavendish Square Publishing LLC.

Avett, Harper. I See the Bald Eagle, 1 vol. 2016. (Symbols of Our Country Ser.). (ENG., Illus.). 24p. (J). (gr. 1-1). pap. 9.25 (978-1-4994-2763-9(8), ab19a3b5-7a21-46bf-886e-e3eaadee3ee8, PowerKids Pr.) Rosen Publishing Group, Inc., The.

Bailey, Diane. General George Thomas: The Rock of Chickamauga. 2011. (J). (978-1-59556-045-2(9)); pap. (978-1-59556-051-3(3)) OTTN Publishing.

—Rescue from an ISIS Prison! Delta Force in Iraq During the War on Terror, Vol. 8. 2018. (Special Forces Stories Ser.). 64p. (J). (gr. 7). lib. bdg. 31.93 (978-1-4222-4080-9(0)) Mason Crest.

Baker, Brynn. Buffalo Soldiers: Heroes of the American West. 2015. (Military Heroes Ser.). (ENG., Illus.). 32p. (J). (gr. 3-6). lib. bdg. 27.99 (978-1-4914-4838-0(5), 128723, Capstone Pr.) Capstone.

—Roosevelt's Rough Riders: Fearless Cavalry of the Spanish-American War. 2015. (Military Heroes Ser.). (ENG., Illus.). 32p. (J). (gr. 3-6). lib. bdg. 27.99 (978-1-4914-4840-3(7), 128725, Capstone Pr.) Capstone.

Barbier, Mary. The U. S. Army, 1 vol. 2004. (America's Armed Forces Ser.). (ENG., Illus.). 48p. (gr. 5-8). lib. bdg. 33.67 (978-0-8368-5680-4(5), b92d035a-bc68-442f-94b9-d59eed1bd085, Gareth Stevens Secondary Library) Stevens, Gareth Publishing LLLP.

Barnes, Pete. Richard Bong: World War II Flying Ace. 2009. (Badger Biographies Ser.). (ENG., Illus.). 128p. (J). (gr. 2-7). pap. 12.95 (978-0-87020-434-0(3)) Wisconsin Historical Society.

Baumann, Susan K. Black Civil War Soldiers: The 54th Massachusetts Regiment, 1 vol. 2013. (Jr. Graphic African American History Ser.). (ENG., Illus.). 24p. (J). (gr. 2-3). pap. 11.60 (978-1-4777-1457-7(X), cce11ddf-e6cf-4be4-9485-d39747c793ea); lib. bdg. 28.93 (978-1-4777-1316-7(6), 93ee6db9-c457-4fe1-a49c-d10e16218f92) Rosen Publishing Group, Inc., The. (PowerKids Pr.).

Beller, Susan Provost. Billy Yank & Johnny Reb: Soldiering in the Civil War. rev. ed. 2007. (Soldiers on the Battlefront Ser.). (ENG., Illus.). 112p. (gr. 6-8). lib. bdg. 33.26 (978-0-8225-6803-2(9)) Lerner Publishing Group.

Benge, Janet & Benge, Geoff. Heroes of History - Douglas MacArthur: What Greater Honor. 2005. (ENG., Illus.). 205p. (YA). pap. 11.99 (978-1-932096-15-6(9)) Emerald Bks.

Benson, Michael. The U. S. Army. 2005. (U. S. Armed Forces Ser.). (Illus.). 64p. (J). (gr. 4-7). lib. bdg. 26.60 (978-0-8225-1645-3(4)) Lerner Publishing Group.

Besel, Jennifer M. The Army Rangers, 1 vol. 2010. (Elite Military Forces Ser.). (ENG.). 24p. (J). (gr. 1-3). lib. bdg. 25.99 (978-1-4296-5381-7(7), 113808, Capstone Pr.) Capstone.

—The Green Berets, 1 vol. 2010. (Elite Military Forces Ser.). (ENG.). 24p. (J). (gr. 1-3). lib. bdg. 25.99 (978-1-4296-5379-4(5), 113806, Capstone Pr.) Capstone.

Bircher, William. Diary of William Bircher: A Civil War Drummer, 1 vol. 2014. (First-Person Histories Ser.). (ENG., Illus.). 32p. (J). (gr. 3-6). lib. bdg. 27.99 *(978-1-4765-4195-2(7)*, 124302, Capstone Pr.) Capstone.

Black Civil War Soldiers: The 54th Massachusetts Regiment. 2013. (Jr. Graphic African American History Ser.). 24p. (J). (gr. 3-6). pap. 63.60 *(978-1-4777-1458-4(8)*, PowerKids Pr.) Rosen Publishing Group, Inc., The.

Bodie, Idella. Light-Horse Harry. 2004. (Illus.). 86p. (J). pap. 6.95 *(978-0-87844-172-3(7))* Sandlapper Publishing Co., Inc.

Boothroyd, Jennifer. Inside the US Air Force. 2017. (Lightning Bolt Books (r) — US Armed Forces Ser.). (ENG., Illus.). 24p. (J). (gr. 1-3). lib. bdg. 29.32 *(978-1-5124-3392-0(6)*, 8b0bc4ec-8c37-4bf4-b9c0-0dfc7c1090a6, Lerner Pubns.) Lerner Publishing Group.

—Inside the US Army. 2017. (Lightning Bolt Books (r) — US Armed Forces Ser.). (ENG., Illus.). 24p. (J). (gr. 1-3). 29.32 *(978-1-5124-3391-3(8)*, dd253bf8-0419-42b4-8f84-4daf51430d71, Lerner Pubns.); pap. 9.99 *(978-1-5124-5600-4(4)*, b9b4fd27-443a-4c9f-af4f-7d6a6a486755) Lerner Publishing Group.

Bozzo, Linda. Army Rangers. 2015. (Serving in the Military Ser.). (Illus.). 32p. (J). 28.50 *(978-1-60753-490-7(8))* Amicus Learning.

—Delta Force. 2015. (Serving in the Military Ser.). (Illus.). 32p. (J). 28.50 *(978-1-60753-491-4(6))* Amicus Learning.

—Green Berets. 2014. (Serving in the Military Ser.). (ENG., Illus.). 32p. (J). (gr. 2-5). lib. bdg. 28.50 *(978-1-60753-492-1(4)*, 16032) Amicus.

Braun, Eric. Trapped Behind Enemy Lines: The Story of the U. S. Army Air Force 807th Medical Evacuation Squadron. 2016. (Encounter: Narrative Nonfiction Stories Ser.). (ENG., Illus.). 224p. (J). (gr. 4-5). lib. bdg. 33.32 *(978-1-4914-8042-7(4)*, 130545, Capstone Young Readers) Capstone.

—Trapped Behind Nazi Lines: The Story of the U. S. Army Air Force 807th Medical Evacuation Squadron. 2016. (Encounter: Narrative Nonfiction Stories Ser.). (ENG., Illus.). 224p. (J). (gr. 4-5). 14.95 *(978-1-62370-605-0(X)*, 130547, Capstone Young Readers) Capstone.

Brook, Henry. Special Forces. Frith, Alex, ed. Johnson, Staz, illus. 2014. (ENG.). 80p. (J). pap. 8.99 *(978-0-7945-3337-3(X)*, Usborne) EDC Publishing.

Burgan, Michael. Benedict Arnold: American Hero & Traitor, 1 vol. Beatty, Terry, illus. 2007. (Graphic Biographies Ser.). (ENG.). 32p. (J). (gr. 3-9). per. 8.10 *(978-0-7368-7906-4(4)*, 93903, Capstone Pr.) Capstone.

Burnett, Betty. Delta Force: Counterterrorism Unit of the U. S. Army. 2009. (Inside Special Operations Ser.). 64p. (gr. 6-6). 58.50 *(978-1-61513-554-7(5)*, Rosen Reference) Rosen Publishing Group, Inc., The.

Burns, Heidi A., contrib. by. U. S. Army True Stories: Tales of Bravery. 2014. (Courage under Fire Ser.). (ENG.). 32p. (J). (gr. 3-9). lib. bdg. 28.65 *(978-1-4765-9938-0(6)*, 125756, Capstone Pr.) Capstone.

Caper, William. The U. S. Army Rangers: The Missions, 1 vol. 2012. (American Special Ops Ser.). (ENG., Illus.). 48p. (J). (gr. 5-9). lib. bdg. 32.65 *(978-1-4296-8659-4(6)*, 118996) Capstone.

Collins, Kathleen. El Marques de Lafayette: Heroe Frances de la Guerra de Independencia, 1 vol. 2003. (Grandes Personajes en la Historia de Los Estados Unidos (Famous People in American History) Ser.). (SPA.). 32p. (gr. 3-4). pap. 10.00 *(978-0-8239-4233-6(3)*, 611571c8-b964-4b87-9954-e1eb2363af67, Rosen Classroom) Rosen Publishing Group, Inc., The.

—Marquis de Lafayette: French Hero of the American Revolution. (Primary Sources of Famous People in American History Ser.). 32p. (gr. 2-3). 2009. 47.90 *(978-1-60851-703-9(9))* 2003. (ENG & SPA., Illus.). lib. bdg. 29.13 *(978-0-8239-4163-6(9)*, 22b96b9a-22f4-4124-a502-dda13c946bf7, Editorial Buenas Letras) Rosen Publishing Group, Inc., The.

—Marquis de Lafayette / el Marques de Lafayette: French Hero of the American Revolution / Héroe francés de la Revolución Estadounidense. 2009. (Famous People in American History/Grandes personajes en la historia de los Estados Unidos Ser.). (ENG & SPA.). 32p. (gr. 2-3). 47.90 *(978-1-61512-550-0(7)*, Editorial Buenas Letras) Rosen Publishing Group, Inc., The.

Conklin, Wendy. Civil War Leaders, 1 vol. rev. ed. 2005. (Social Studies: Informational Text Ser.). (ENG.). 24p. (gr. 4-8). pap. 10.99 *(978-0-7439-8917-6(1))* Teacher Created Materials, Inc.

Cooke, Tim. US Airborne Forces, 1 vol. 2012. (Ultimate Special Forces Ser.). (ENG., Illus.). 48p. (J). (gr. 4-5). 31.60 *(978-1-4488-7882-6(9)*, 679b3263-d9e7-41a8-ae57-81bf7db92459); pap. 12.75 *(978-1-4488-7959-5(0)*, ee7604c0-d8c8-440b-a7db-05ae6788c0ae) Rosen Publishing Group, Inc., The. (PowerKids Pr.).

—US Army Rangers, 1 vol. 2012. (Ultimate Special Forces Ser.). (ENG., Illus.). 48p. (J). (gr. 4-5). 31.60 *(978-1-4488-7879-6(9)*, a776910f-3bcb-4bb3-a8b2-533307479982); pap. 12.75 *(978-1-4488-7956-4(6)*, df1e1dff-77eb-46dc-9d4f-cfd929f7b2ae) Rosen Publishing Group, Inc., The. (PowerKids Pr.).

—US Army Special Forces, 1 vol. 2012. (Ultimate Special Forces Ser.). (ENG., Illus.). 48p. (J). (gr. 4-5). 31.60 *(978-1-4488-7878-9(0)*, bf7bcdd9-841b-4601-9aff-7344627b1f8e); pap. 12.75 *(978-1-4488-7955-7(8)*, c15d319a-4971-420b-a87b-1414adad925d) Rosen Publishing Group, Inc., The. (PowerKids Pr.).

—Weapons & Tactics, 1 vol. 2012. (American Civil War: the Right Answer Ser.). (ENG., Illus.). 48p. (J). (gr. 6-8). 34.60 *(978-1-4339-7551-6(3)*, 09c9b101-829c-47e5-9d35-f71c5059ba7e); pap. 15.05 *(978-1-4339-7552-3(1)*, d242f462-ea19-4922-933f-27b3c4f4d312) Stevens, Gareth Publishing LLLP. (Gareth Stevens Secondary Library).

Corrigan, Jim. General George G. Meade: Victor at Gettysburg. 2011. (J). *(978-1-59556-044-5(0))*; pap. *(978-1-59556-050-6(5))* OTTN Publishing.

Cox, Clinton. Undying Glory: The Story of the Massachusetts 54th Regiment. 2007. 196p. (YA). (gr. 4-7). per. 15.95 *(978-0-595-45116-6(0)*, Backinprint.com) iUniverse, Inc.

Crotzer Kimmel, Allison. The Eternal Soldier: The True Story of How a Dog Became a Civil War Hero. Teplow, Rotem, illus. 2019. (ENG.). 40p. (J). (gr. k-4). 18.99 *(978-1-4998-0863-6(1))* Little Bee Books Inc.

Daniel Fernandez Memorial Center Projec. Man of Honor: The Story of Daniel Fernandez. 2009. 32p. pap. 15.49 *(978-1-4389-8338-7(7))* AuthorHouse.

Darby, Jean. Dwight D. Eisenhower. 2004. (Presidential Leaders Ser.). (Illus.). 112p. (J). (gr. 6-12). lib. bdg. 29.27 *(978-0-8225-0813-7(3))* Lerner Publishing Group.

David, Jack. Army Green Berets. 2009. (Armed Forces Ser.). (ENG., Illus.). 24p. (J). (gr. 3-7). lib. bdg. 26.95 *(978-1-60014-263-5(X))* Bellwether Media.

—Humvees. 2009. (Military Machines Ser.). (ENG., Illus.). 24p. (J). (gr. 3-7). lib. bdg. 26.95 *(978-1-60014-260-4(5)*, 10283, Torque Bks.) Bellwether Media.

—United States Army. 2008. (Armed Forces Ser.). (ENG., Illus.). 24p. (J). (gr. 3-7). lib. bdg. 26.95 *(978-1-60014-162-1(5))* Bellwether Media.

Dell, Pamela. Memoir of Susie King Taylor: A Civil War Nurse. 2017. (First-Person Histories Ser.). (ENG., Illus.). 32p. (J). (gr. 3-6). lib. bdg. 27.99 *(978-1-5157-3354-6(8)*, 133346, Capstone Pr.) Capstone.

Delmar, Pete. U. S. Army Green Berets: The Missions. 2013. (American Special Ops Ser.). (ENG.). 48p. (J). (gr. 5-9). 32.65 *(978-1-4765-0113-0(0)*, 122178) Capstone.

Doeden, Matt. The U. S. Army [Scholastic]. 2009. (Military Branches Ser.). (ENG.). 24p. pap. 0.52 *(978-1-4296-5070-0(2)*, Capstone Pr.) Capstone.

—The U.S. Army. rev. ed. 2017. (U. S. Military Branches Ser.). (ENG., Illus.). 24p. (J). (gr. -1-2). lib. bdg. 27.32 *(978-1-5157-6773-2(6)*, 135300, Capstone Pr.) Capstone.

—Weapons of the Revolutionary War. rev. ed. 2017. (Weapons of War Ser.). (ENG., Illus.). 32p. (J). (gr. 3-9). lib. bdg. 27.32 *(978-1-5157-7908-7(4)*, 136023, Capstone Pr.) Capstone.

Doeden, Matt & Reed, Jennifer. The U. S. Military Branches. rev. ed. 2017. (U. S. Military Branches Ser.). (ENG.). 24p. (J). (gr. -1-2). 117.28 *(978-1-5157-6795-4(7)*, 26553, Capstone Pr.) Capstone.

Dolan, Edward F. Military Service, 10 vols., Set. Incl. Careers in the U. S. Air Force. 38.36 *(978-0-7614-4205-9(7)*, e4fae1b0-9c27-4222-a7e4-9bfe2018acfe); Careers in the U. S. Army. 38.36 *(978-0-7614-4206-6(5)*, a0a5c8e1-5fba-4400-800a-65381ebde5ea); Careers in the U. S. Coast Guard. 38.36 *(978-0-7614-4207-3(3)*, 7ef3c6d4-eff7-4b91-b515-6d4ff161c981); Careers in the U. S. Marine Corps. 38.36 *(978-0-7614-4209-7(X)*, b4ad4186-88cc-46f5-89ce-17b13d9c32d4); Careers in the U. S. Navy. 38.36 *(978-0-7614-4210-3(3)*, e95d1809-a3a4-48fb-8427-1c59e5c740fd); (Illus.). 80p. (YA). (gr. 7-7). (Military Service Ser.). (ENG.). 2010. Set lib. bdg. 191.80 *(978-0-7614-4203-5(0)*, 1fe14f46-9e52-44d0-bb2d-9295775cd6ab, Cavendish Square) Cavendish Square Publishing LLC.

Dreyer, Ellen. A Band of Brave Men: The Story of the 54th Massachusetts Regiment. 2004. (ENG., Illus.). 31p. (J). (gr. 5-5). pap. 12.00 net. *(978-0-7652-5247-0(3))* Celebration Pr.

Dugan, Christine. Marquis de Lafayette & the French (Alexander Hamilton) rev. ed. 2017. (Social Studies: Informational Text Ser.). (ENG., Illus.). 32p. (gr. 4-8). pap. 11.99 *(978-1-4258-6353-1(1))* Teacher Created Materials, Inc.

Earl, C. F. Green Berets. 2010. (Special Forces Ser.). 64p. (YA). (gr. 7-18). lib. bdg. 22.95 *(978-1-4222-1841-9(4))* Mason Crest.

Edwards, Roberta. Who Was George Washington? 2009. (Who Was... ? Ser.). lib. bdg. 16.00 *(978-0-606-04042-6(0))* Turtleback.

Edwards, Roberta & Who HQ. Who Was George Washington? Kelley, True, illus. 2009. (Who Was? Ser.). 112p. (J). (gr. 3-7). pap. 5.99 *(978-0-448-44892-3(0)*, Penguin Workshop) Penguin Young Readers Group.

Etinde-Crompton, Charlotte & Crompton, Samuel Willard. Horace Pippin: Painter & Decorated Soldier, 1 vol. 2019. (Celebrating Black Artists Ser.). (ENG.). 104p. (gr. 7-7). 38.93 *(978-1-9785-0360-1(1)*, f4497f18-7ea9-485e-9743-077c011da8ee) Enslow Publishing, LLC.

Farrell, Mary Cronk. Standing up Against Hate: How Black Women in the Army Helped Change the Course of WWII. 2019. (ENG., Illus.). 208p. (J). (gr. 5-9). 17.99 *(978-1-4197-3160-0(2)*, 1151301, Abrams Bks. for Young Readers) Abrams, Inc.

Feinstein, Stephen. Colin Powell, 1 vol. 2008. (African-American Heroes Ser.). (ENG., Illus.). 24p. (gr. k-2). lib. bdg. 25.27 *(978-0-7660-2761-9(9)*, 0a493614-833f-471e-bd26-4f9998b1c6b1, Enslow Elementary) Enslow Publishing, LLC.

Fleischman, John. Black & White Airmen: Their True History. 2007. (ENG., Illus.). 160p. (J). (gr. 3-7). 20.00 *(978-0-618-56297-8(4)*, 585704, Clarion Bks.) HarperCollins Pubs.

Garnett, Sammie & Pallotta, Jerry. U. S. Army Alphabet Book. 2012. (ENG., Illus.). (J). pap. 7.95 *(978-0-9852032-2-1(6))* Who Would Win?

Garstecki, Julia. Buffalo Soldiers. 2016. (All-American Fighting Forces Ser.). (ENG.). 32p. (J). (gr. 4-6). pap. 9.99 *(978-1-64466-151-2(9)*, 10306); (Illus.). 31.35 *(978-1-68072-000-6(7)*, 10305) Black Rabbit Bks. (Bolt).

—Delta Force. 2018. (Elite Warriors Ser.). (ENG.). 32p. (gr. 2-7). 9.95 *(978-1-68072-721-0(4))*; (J). (gr. 4-6). pap. 9.99 *(978-1-64466-274-8(4)*, 12349); (J). (gr. 4-6). lib. bdg. *(978-1-68072-427-1(4)*, 12348) Black Rabbit Bks. (Bolt).

—Go for Broke Regiment. 2016. (All-American Fighting Forces Ser.). (ENG.). 32p. (J). (gr. 4-6). pap. 9.99 *(978-1-64466-152-9(7)*, 10310); (Illus.). 31.35 *(978-1-68072-001-3(5)*, 10309) Black Rabbit Bks. (Bolt).

—Harlem Hellfighters. 2016. (All-American Fighting Forces Ser.). (ENG.). 32p. (J). (gr. 4-6). pap. 9.99 *(978-1-64466-153-6(5)*, 10314); (Illus.). 31.35 *(978-1-68072-002-0(3)*, 10313) Black Rabbit Bks. (Bolt).

Gigliotti, Jim. World War II Prison Breakout! Army Rangers Make Their Mark, Vol. 8. 2018. (Special Forces Stories Ser.). 64p. (J). (gr. 7). 31.93 *(978-1-4222-4085-4(1))* Mason Crest.

Gimpel, Lee. Fighting Wars, Planning for Peace: The Story of George C. Marshall. 2005. (World Leaders Ser.). (Illus.). 176p. (J). (gr. 6-12). lib. bdg. 26.95 *(978-1-931798-66-2(4))* Reynolds, Morgan Inc.

Gitlin, Martin. Green Berets. 2013. (Great Warriors Ser.). (ENG., Illus.). 48p. (J). (gr. 4-8). pap. 18.50 *(978-1-61783-773-9(3)*, 10805) ABDO Publishing Co.

Gordon, Nick. Army Delta Force. 2012. (U. S. Military Ser.). (ENG., Illus.). 24p. (J). (gr. 3-7). lib. bdg. 26.95 *(978-1-60014-822-4(0)*, Epic Bks.) Bellwether Media.

—Army Green Berets. 2012. (U. S. Military Ser.). (ENG., Illus.). 24p. (J). (gr. 3-7). lib. bdg. 26.95 *(978-1-60014-823-1(9)*, Epic Bks.) Bellwether Media.

—Army Night Stalkers. 2013. (U. S. Military Ser.). (ENG., Illus.). 24p. (J). (gr. 3-7). lib. bdg. 26.95 *(978-1-60014-874-3(3)*, Epic Bks.) Bellwether Media.

—Army Rangers. 2012. (U. S. Military Ser.). (ENG., Illus.). 24p. (J). (gr. 3-7). lib. bdg. 26.95 *(978-1-60014-824-8(7)*, Epic Bks.) Bellwether Media.

—U. S. Army. 2012. (U. S. Military Ser.). (ENG., Illus.). 24p. (J). (gr. 3-7). lib. bdg. 26.95 *(978-1-60014-827-9(1)*, Epic Bks.) Bellwether Media.

Green, Michael. The United States Army, 1 vol. 2013. (U. S. Military Forces Ser.). (ENG.). 24p. (J). (gr. 1-3). lib. bdg. 27.99 *(978-1-4765-0069-0(X)*, 122128, Capstone Pr.) Capstone.

Greene, Meg. Careers in the National Guards' Search & Rescue Units. 2009. (Careers in Search & Rescue Operations Ser.). 64p. (gr. 5-8). 58.50 *(978-1-61511-812-0(8)*, Rosen Reference) Rosen Publishing Group, Inc., The.

—The Hunt for Osama Bin Laden, 1 vol. 2004. (Frontline Coverage of Current Events Ser.). (ENG., Illus.). 48p. (J). (gr. 5-5). lib. bdg. 34.47 *(978-1-4042-0279-5(X)*, d2166811-bc0b-4e23-9c0b-f09e66634134) Rosen Publishing Group, Inc., The.

—The Hunt for Osama bin Laden. 2009. (Frontline Coverage of Current Events Ser.). 48p. (gr. 5-5). 53.00 *(978-1-61512-657-6(0))* Rosen Publishing Group, Inc., The.

Grove, Tim & National Air and Space Museum. First Flight Around the World: The Adventures of the American Fliers Who Won the Race. 2015. (ENG., Illus.). 96p. (J). (gr. 3-9). 21.95 *(978-1-4197-1482-5(1)*, 1087101) Abrams, Inc.

Gunderson, Jessica. Benedict Arnold: Battlefield Hero or Selfish Traitor?, 1 vol. 2013. (Perspectives on History Ser.). (ENG.). 32p. (J). (gr. 3-6). 27.99 *(978-1-4765-0243-4(9)*, 122297); pap. 7.95 *(978-1-4765-3407-7(1)*, 123538) Capstone.

Hale, Sarah Elder, ed. Ulysses S. Grant: Confident Leader & Hero. 2005. (ENG., Illus.). 48p. (J). (gr. 3-9). 17.95 *(978-0-8126-7906-9(7))* Cobblestone Pr.

Harasymiw, Mark. Before Ulysses S. Grant Was President, 1 vol. 2018. (Before They Were President Ser.). (ENG.). 24p. (gr. 2-3). lib. bdg. 24.27 *(978-1-5382-2914-9(5)*, 6482cc46-acdc-411d-b1c5-bfdd5c37de70) Stevens, Gareth Publishing LLLP.

Harasymiw, Mark J. Army, 1 vol. 2011. (U. S. Military Forces Ser.). (ENG.). 32p. (gr. 3-4). pap. 11.50 *(978-1-4339-5848-9(1)*, ea5627c1-1742-44b9-8784-e649547212ad, Gareth Stevens Learning Library); (YA). lib. bdg. 29.27 *(978-1-4339-5846-5(5)*, 8e9a1b88-6739-47ff-9f03-50385ef2def9) Stevens, Gareth Publishing LLLP.

—Rangers, 1 vol. 2012. (U. S. Special Forces Ser.). (ENG., Illus.). 32p. (J). (gr. 3-4). pap. 11.50 *(978-1-4339-6575-3(5)*, c5976298-b5bd-48ca-bb60-7ddefddd7931); lib. bdg. 29.27 *(978-1-4339-6573-9(9)*, 3ac87b81-6907-4269-a2a3-a494370fc67c) Stevens, Gareth Publishing LLLP. (Gareth Stevens Learning Library).

Head, Tom. Green Berets. 2018. (Elite Warriors Ser.). (ENG.). 32p. (gr. 2-7). 9.95 *(978-1-68072-722-7(2))*; (J). (gr. 4-6). pap. 9.99 *(978-1-64466-275-5(2)*, 12353); (J). (gr. 4-6). lib. bdg. *(978-1-68072-428-8(2)*, 12352) Black Rabbit Bks. (Bolt).

Himler, Ronald, illus. Why Did Daddy Have to Leave? 2018. (J). 17.95 *(978-0-9885295-9-5(9))* Blue Marlin Pubns.

Honders, Christine. Buffalo Soldiers, 1 vol. 2015. (Heroes of Black History Ser.). (ENG., Illus.). 32p. (J). (gr. 3-4). pap. 11.50 *(978-1-4824-2900-8(4)*, a7c2de3c-668f-4489-9767-3188a6dd0741) Stevens, Gareth Publishing LLLP.

Hoogenboom, Lynn. William Tecumseh Sherman: The Fight to Preserve the Union. 2009. (Library of American Lives & Times Ser.). 112p. (gr. 5-5). 69.20 *(978-1-60853-511-8(8))* Rosen Publishing Group, Inc., The.

Howse, Jennifer. The Civil War. 2008. (African American History Ser.). (Illus.). 48p. (YA). (gr. 5-8). pap. 10.95 *(978-1-59036-877-0(0))*; lib. bdg. 29.05 *(978-1-59036-876-3(2))* Weigl Pubs., Inc.

—Civil War. 2013. (J). *(978-1-62127-191-8(9))*; pap. *(978-1-62127-197-0(8))* Weigl Pubs., Inc.

Kajencki, AnnMarie Francis. Count Casimir Pulaski: From Poland to America, a Hero's Fight for Liberty. 2009. (Library of American Lives & Times Ser.). 112p. (gr. 5-5). 69.20 *(978-1-60853-475-3(8))* Rosen Publishing Group, Inc., The.

Knapp, Ron. Fighting U. S. Generals of World War II, 1 vol. 2013. (Inspiring Collective Biographies Ser.). (ENG.). 112p. (gr. 5-6). 35.93 *(978-0-7660-4164-6(6)*, d509e7a7-1d86-408e-91fd-74f28a8d5305); pap. 13.88 *(978-1-4644-0249-4(3)*, 57e9f019-1c57-4cd8-9d85-c53e736bef72) Enslow Publishing, LLC.

Koestler-Grack, Rachel A. William Tecumseh Sherman. 2009. (ENG., Illus.). 149p. (gr. 6-12). 35.00 *(978-1-60413-300-4(7)*, P162096, Facts On File) Infobase Holdings, Inc.

Kohl, Peter. My Dad Is in the Army, 1 vol., 1. 2015. (Military Families Ser.). (ENG., Illus.). 24p. (J). (gr. 3-4). pap. 9.25 *(978-1-5081-4434-2(6)*, 12d64cc3-617d-4733-ab90-7d2386fba3aa, PowerKids Pr.) Rosen Publishing Group, Inc., The.

Levete, Sarah. The Army, 1 vol. 2015. (Defend & Protect Ser.). (ENG.). 48p. (J). (gr. 4-5). pap. 15.05 *(978-1-4824-4119-2(5)*, 14bd9108-2d4e-4e5d-a0e0-94c5df9689cc) Stevens, Gareth Publishing LLLP.

Lewis, J. Patrick. Harlem Hellfighters. Kelley, Gary, illus. 2014. (ENG.). 32p. (J). (gr. 4-7). 27.99 *(978-1-56846-246-2(8)*, 21309, Creative Editions) Creative Co., The.

Linde, Barbara M. Heroes of the U. S. Army, 1 vol. 2012. (Heroes of the U. S. Military Ser.). (ENG., Illus.). 32p. (J). (gr. 3-4). pap. 11.50 *(978-1-4339-7237-9(9)*, 6dfcf812-3593-438f-8ea8-dfe303031833); lib. bdg. 29.27 *(978-1-4339-7236-2(0)*, 76711755-28cb-4350-81c2-f249f5c3fa80) Stevens, Gareth Publishing LLLP.

Link, Theodore. George Armstrong Custer: General de la caballeria Estadounidense, 1 vol. 2003. (Grandes Personajes en la Historia de Los Estados Unidos (Famous People in American History) Ser.). (SPA.). 32p. (gr. 3-4). pap. 10.00 *(978-0-8239-4228-2(7)*, a3d5578c-4708-4b0e-aa8f-8828084500a9, Rosen Classroom) Rosen Publishing Group, Inc., The.

—George Armstrong Custer: General de la caballería estadounidense (George Armstrong Custer: General of the U. S. Cavalry) 2009. (Grandes personajes en la historia de los Estados Unidos (Famous People in American History) Ser.). (SPA.). 32p. (gr. 2-3). 47.90 *(978-1-61512-799-3(2)*, Editorial Buenas Letras) Rosen Publishing Group, Inc., The.

—George Armstrong Custer: General of the U. S. Cavalry. (Primary Sources of Famous People in American History Ser.).Tr. of George Armstrong Custer: General de la Caballeria Estadounidense. 32p. (gr. 2-3). 2009. 47.90 *(978-1-60851-680-3(6))* 2003. (ENG & SPA., Illus.). lib. bdg. 29.13 *(978-0-8239-4158-2(2)*, e97ac072-83b4-46f2-a0fc-b11714411c70, Editorial Buenas Letras) Rosen Publishing Group, Inc., The.

—George Armstrong Custer: General of the U. S. Cavalry / General de la caballería Estadounidense. 2009. (Famous People in American History/Grandes personajes en la historia de los Estados Unidos Ser.). (ENG & SPA.). 32p. (gr. 2-3). 47.90 *(978-1-61512-545-6(0)*, Editorial Buenas Letras) Rosen Publishing Group, Inc., The.

Loveless, Antony. Apache Helicoper Pilot, 1 vol. 2009. (World's Most Dangerous Jobs Ser.). (ENG., Illus.). 32p. (J). (gr. 3-6). pap. *(978-0-7787-5112-0(0))* Crabtree Publishing Co.

—Apache Helicoper Pilots. 2009. (World's Most Dangerous Jobs Ser.). (ENG., Illus.). 32p. (J). (gr. 3-6). lib. bdg. *(978-0-7787-5098-7(1))* Crabtree Publishing Co.

Lowe, Julian. My Aunt Is in the Army Reserve, 1 vol., 1. 2015. (Military Families Ser.). (ENG., Illus.). 24p. (J). (gr. 3-4). pap. 9.25 *(978-1-5081-4426-7(5)*, 51e41183-8716-49d0-8401-2efff55d41a8, PowerKids Pr.) Rosen Publishing Group, Inc., The.

Lusted, Marcia Amidon. Army Delta Force: Elite Operations. 2013. (Military Special Ops Ser.). (ENG., Illus.). 32p. (J). (gr. 3-8). lib. bdg. 26.65 *(978-0-7613-9077-0(4)*, aad4f3ac-5bed-48b4-aecd-39128c3c3685, Lerner Pubns.) Lerner Publishing Group.

Margulies, Phillip. A Timeline of the Continental Army. 2009. (Timelines of American History Ser.). 32p. (gr. 4-4). 47.90 *(978-1-60854-383-0(8)*, Rosen Reference) Rosen Publishing Group, Inc., The.

Markovics, Joyce L. & Pushies, Fred J. Today's Army Heroes. 2012. (Acts of Courage: Inside America's Military Ser.). 32p. (J). (gr. 2-7). lib. bdg. 28.50 *(978-1-61772-445-9(9))* Bearport Publishing Co., Inc.

Marx, Mandy R. Amazing U. S. Army Facts. 2016. (Amazing Military Facts Ser.). (ENG., Illus.). 24p. (J). (gr. -1-2). lib. bdg. 27.32 *(978-1-5157-0953-4(1)*, 132277, Capstone Pr.) Capstone.

McCallum Staats, Ann. Women Heroes of the US Army: Remarkable Soldiers from the American Revolution to Today. 2019. (Women of Action Ser.: 23). (ENG., Illus.). 240p. (YA). (gr. 7). 19.99 *(978-0-914091-24-0(7))* Chicago Review Pr., Inc.

McNab, Chris. Defending the Ground: The Army. 2017. (Illus.). 80p. (J). *(978-1-4222-3762-5(1))* Mason Crest.

—Protecting the Nation with the U. S. Army. 2004. (Rescue & Prevention Ser.). (Illus.). 96p. (YA). (gr. 7-18). lib. bdg. 22.95 *(978-1-59084-414-4(9))* Mason Crest.

McPherson, Stephanie Sammartino. Douglas MacArthur. 2005. (History Maker Bios Ser.). (Illus.). 48p. (J). 26.60 *(978-0-8225-2434-2(1))* Lerner Publishing Group.

Micklos, John, Jr. Harlem Hellfighters: African-American Heroes of World War I. 2017. (Military Heroes Ser.). (ENG., Illus.). 32p. (J). (gr. 3-6). lib. bdg. 27.99 *(978-1-5157-3348-5(3)*, 133345, Capstone Pr.) Capstone.

Micklos, John & Micklos, John, Jr. Washington's Crossing the Delaware & the Winter at Valley Forge: Through Primary Sources, 1 vol. 2013. (American Revolution Through Primary Sources Ser.). (ENG., Illus.). 48p. (J). (gr. 4-6). 27.93 *(978-0-7660-4132-5(8)*, 22bf5158-e47c-42c7-9d03-25ec224712b2) Enslow Publishing, LLC.

—Why We Won the American Revolution: Through Primary Sources, 1 vol. 2013. (American Revolution Through Primary Sources Ser.). (ENG., Illus.). 48p. (J). (gr. 4-6). 27.93 *(978-0-7660-4134-9(4)*, 1427223b-d0b5-47ed-ad69-7c1c441a1350) Enslow Publishing, LLC.

Miller, Derek. Minority Soldiers Fighting in the Korean War, 1 vol. 2017. (Fighting for Their Country: Minorities at War Ser.). (ENG.). 112p. (YA). (gr. 8-8). 44.50 *(978-1-5026-2665-3(9)*, 4c864aac-c5d2-42be-9702-de415ff53155) Cavendish Square Publishing LLC.

Miller, Reagan & Arthur, Martin. Great Leaders of the Civil War. 2011. (ENG.). 48p. (J). pap. *(978-0-7787-5359-9(X))*; lib. bdg. *(978-0-7787-5342-1(5))* Crabtree Publishing Co.

Miller, Reagan & Claus, J. Matteson. Life on a Civil War Battlefield. 2011. (ENG.). 48p. (J). pap. *(978-0-7787-5357-5(3))*; lib. bdg. *(978-0-7787-5340-7(9))* Crabtree Publishing Co.

Miller, Roger G. Billy Mitchell: Evangelist of Airpower. 2007. (Illus.). 152p. (J). (gr. 10-18). lib. bdg. 25.95 *(978-1-59556-025-4(4))* OTTN Publishing.

Mitchell, P. P. Join the Army, 1 vol. 2017. (U. S. Armed Forces Ser.). (ENG., Illus.). 32p. (J). (gr. 1-2). 28.27 *(978-1-5382-0536-5(X)*, e1804b40-7613-4542-b30b-bcac8f82b508) Stevens, Gareth Publishing LLLP.

Murphy, Jim. The Crossing: How George Washington Saved the American Revolution. 2016. (ENG.). 96p. (J). (gr. 4-7). pap. 14.99 (978-0-439-69187-1(7)) Scholastic, Inc.

Murray, Julie. United States Army, 1 vol. 2014. (U. S. Armed Forces Ser.). (ENG.). 24p. (J). (gr. -1-2). lib. bdg. 32.79 (978-1-62970-094-6(0), 1711, Abdo Kids) ABDO Publishing Co.

Murray, Stuart A. P. John Trumbull: Painter of the Revolutionary War: Painter of the Revolutionary War. 2008. (ENG., Illus.). 83p. (C). (gr. 6-18). lib. bdg. 180.00 (978-0-7656-8150-8(1), Y182501) Routledge.

Myers, Walter Dean & Miles, Bill. The Harlem Hellfighters: When Pride Met Courage. 2014. (ENG.). 160p. (J). (gr. 3-7). pap. 9.99 (978-0-06-001138-3(6), Amistad) HarperCollins Pubs.

Myers, Walter Dean & William Miles. The Harlem Hellfighters: When Pride Met Courage. 2014. (J). lib. bdg. 20.85 (978-0-606-35507-0(3)) Turtleback.

Nagle, Jeanne. Delta Force, 1 vol. 2012. (U. S. Special Forces Ser.). (ENG.). 32p. (J). (gr. 3-4). pap. 11.50 (978-1-4339-6555-5(0), bd764a1c-9748-41ab-9f44-d792167f6046); lib. bdg. 29.27 (978-1-4339-6553-1(4), f4332f93-205a-4474-b4cc-99340baf711d) Stevens, Gareth Publishing LLLP. (Gareth Stevens Learning Library).

Nardo, Don. The Civil War, 1 vol. 2008. (American History Ser.). (ENG.). 104p. (gr. 7-7). pap. 29.30 (978-1-4205-0302-9(2), c76d53a8-1719-4d90-9a47-3a5eb761f337, Lucent Pr.) Greenhaven Publishing LLC.

Nelson, Drew. Green Berets, 1 vol. 2012. (U. S. Special Forces Ser.). (ENG.). 32p. (J). (gr. 3-4). pap. 11.50 (978-1-4339-6559-3(3), c6f74ec8-9756-42d1-98de-f12a170b7535); lib. bdg. 29.27 (978-1-4339-6557-9(7), 9afb9b05-57d5-4b05-afb2-9aae1070dc24) Stevens, Gareth Publishing LLLP. (Gareth Stevens Learning Library).

Nobleman, Marc Tyler. Green Berets in Action. 2008. (Special Ops Ser.). (Illus.). 32p. (J). (gr. 3-6). lib. bdg. 28.50 (978-1-59716-631-7(6)) Bearport Publishing Co., Inc.

Norfolk, Sherry & Norfolk, Bobby. The Virginia Giant: The True Story of Peter Francisco. Brennan, Cait, illus. 2014. (ENG.). 160p. (J). (gr. 4-7). 16.99 (978-1-62619-117-4(4), History Pr., The) Arcadia Publishing.

Olesen, Andrew. George Washington: The First President of the United States, 1 vol. 2015. (Spotlight on American History Ser.). (ENG., Illus.). 24p. (J). (gr. 4-6). pap. 11.00 (978-1-4994-1751-7(9), 4fbc47f3-6d10-49d7-bbac-8141eaab4641, PowerKids Pr.) Rosen Publishing Group, Inc., The.

Orr, Tamra. What's So Great about the Buffalo Soldiers. 2009. (What's So Great About... ? Ser.). 32p. (J). (gr. 2-4). lib. bdg. 25.70 (978-1-58415-831-8(X)) Mitchell Lane Pubs.

—What's So Great about the Tuskegee Airmen. 2009. (What's So Great About... ? Ser.). 32p. (J). (gr. 2-4). lib. bdg. 25.70 (978-1-58415-832-5(8)) Mitchell Lane Pubs.

Otfinoski, Steven. Pilots in Peril! The Untold Story of U. S. Pilots Who Braved the Hump in World War II. 2016. (Encounter: Narrative Nonfiction Stories Ser.). (ENG., Illus.). 232p. (J). (gr. 3-6). pap. 9.95 (978-1-4914-5166-3(1), 128780, Capstone Pr.) Capstone.

Pallotta, Jerry & Garnett, Sammie. U. S. Army Alphabet Book. 2012. (ENG., Illus.). 32p. (J). 16.95 (978-0-9852032-3-8(4)) Who Would Win?

Perritano, John. A Terrorist Goes Down! Delta Forces in Syria Take Out an ISIS Leader, Vol. 8. 2018. (Special Forces Stories Ser.). 64p. (J). (gr. 7). 31.93 (978-1-4222-4084-7(3)) Mason Crest.

Person, Stephen. Army Night Stalkers in Action. 2013. (Special Ops II Ser.). (Illus.). 32p. (J). (gr. 2-7). lib. bdg. 28.50 (978-1-61772-889-1(6)) Bearport Publishing Co., Inc.

Pimm, Nancy Roe. Smoky, the Dog That Saved My Life: The Bill Wynne Story. 2019. (Biographies for Young Readers Ser.). (ENG., Illus.). 168p. (J). 32.95 (978-0-8214-2356-1(8)); pap. 15.95 (978-0-8214-2357-8(6)) Ohio Univ. Pr.

Poolos, J. Army Rangers: Surveillance & Reconnaissance for the U. S. Army. 2009. (Inside Special Operations Ser.). 64p. (gr. 6-6). 58.50 (978-1-61513-549-3(9), Rosen Reference) Rosen Publishing Group, Inc., The.

Porterfield, Jason. Your Career in the Army, 1 vol. 2011. (Call of Duty: Careers in the Armed Forces Ser.). (ENG.). 128p. (YA). (gr. 7-7). lib. bdg. 39.80 (978-1-4488-5510-0(1), 2cc2c0d3-5a56-42c6-b5ec-b35267b084f9) Rosen Publishing Group, Inc., The.

Powell, Walter L. Benedict Arnold: Revolutionary War Hero & Traitor. (Library of American Lives & Timestm Ser.). 112p. (Illus.). (J). (gr. 4-8). lib. bdg. 31.95 (978-1-4042-6627-8(5)); 2009. (gr. 5-5). 69.20 (978-1-60853-471-5(5)) Rosen Publishing Group, Inc., The.

Raabe, Emily. Buffalo Soldiers & the Western Frontier. 2009. (Westward Ho! Ser.). 24p. (gr. 2-3). 42.50 (978-1-60854-759-3(0), PowerKids Pr.) Rosen Publishing Group, Inc., The.

Randolph, Joanne. The Call of Liberty: Marquis de Lafayette & the American Revolution. 2009. (Great Moments in American History Ser.). 32p. (gr. 3-3). 47.90 (978-1-61513-152-5(3)) Rosen Publishing Group, Inc., The.

Ratliff, Thamas. Do You Want to Be a Revolutionary War Soldier? 2015. (Do You Want to Be... Ser.). (Illus.). 32p. (gr. 3-6). 28.50 (978-1-909645-37-0(0)) Book Hse. GBR. Dist: Black Rabbit Bks.

Ratliff, Thomas. You Wouldn't Want to Be a Civil War Soldier! A War You'd Rather Not Fight. Antram, David, illus. 2013. (You Wouldn't Want to... Ser.). (ENG.). 32p. (J). 29.00 (978-0-531-25947-4(1), Watts, Franklin) Scholastic Library Publishing.

Rice, Earle, Jr. Robert E. Lee: First Soldier of the Confederacy. 2005. (Civil War Leaders Ser.). (Illus.). 176p. (J). (gr. 6-12). 28.95 (978-1-931798-47-1(8)) Reynolds, Morgan Inc.

Rice, Earle. Careers in the U. S. Army, 1 vol. 2015. (Careers in the U. S. Armed Forces Ser.). (ENG., Illus.). 128p. (gr. 6-7). 38.93 (978-0-7660-6943-5(5), 62b910ec-4a73-4711-bda6-17a0a86c24d5) Enslow Publishing, LLC.

—The Life & Times of the Brothers Custer: Galloping to Glory. 2008. (Profiles in American History Ser.). (Illus.). 48p. (J). (gr. 4-8). lib. bdg. 29.95 (978-1-58415-665-9(1)) Mitchell Lane Pubs.

Riley, Gail Blasser. Delta Force in Action. 2008. (Special Ops Ser.). (Illus.). 32p. (YA). (gr. 3-6). lib. bdg. 28.50 (978-1-59716-635-5(9)) Bearport Publishing Co., Inc.

Roberts, Jeremy. U. S. Army Special Operations Forces. 2004. (U. S. Armed Forces Ser.). (ENG., Illus.). 64p. (gr. 4-8). lib. bdg. 26.60 (978-0-8225-1646-0(2)) Lerner Publishing Group.

Rose, Simon. Army. 2012. (J). (978-1-61913-291-7(5)); pap. (978-1-61913-296-2(6)) Weigl Pubs., Inc.

—Army Rangers. 2013. (J). (978-1-62127-449-0(7)); pap. (978-1-62127-455-1(1)) Weigl Pubs., Inc.

—Delta Force. 2013. (J). (978-1-62127-450-6(0)); pap. (978-1-62127-456-8(X)) Weigl Pubs., Inc.

—Green Berets. 2013. (J). (978-1-62127-451-3(9)); pap. (978-1-62127-457-5(8)) Weigl Pubs., Inc.

Sandler, Michael. Army Rangers in Action. 2008. (Special Ops Ser.). (Illus.). 32p. (YA). (gr. 3-6). lib. bdg. 28.50 (978-1-59716-632-4(4)) Bearport Publishing Co., Inc.

Sapp, Richard. Ulysses S. Grant & the Road to Appomattox, 1 vol. 2005. (In the Footsteps of American Heroes Ser.). (ENG., Illus.). 64p. (gr. 5-8). lib. bdg. 36.67 (978-0-8368-6431-1(X), 81ecb342-56b5-4c29-a54b-d3a5183272b9, Gareth Stevens Secondary Library) Stevens, Gareth Publishing LLLP.

Shea, John M. The Tuskegee Airmen, 1 vol. 2015. (Heroes of Black History Ser.). (ENG., Illus.). 32p. (J). (gr. 3-4). 28.27 (978-1-4824-2918-3(7), 32dec262-dcb5-454b-80bd-9bab13a8f86c) Stevens, Gareth Publishing LLLP.

Shea, Therese. Black Ops & Other Special Missions of the U. S. Army Green Berets, 1 vol. 2012. (Inside Special Forces Ser.). (ENG., Illus.). 64p. (YA). (gr. 6-6). pap. 13.95 (978-1-4488-8387-5(3), 719ab3d4-2751-4199-9b5b-4e5271c0a19f); lib. bdg. 37.13 (978-1-4488-8381-3(4), e71b2aac-e7d6-427b-8ffa-4c8647af1c38) Rosen Publishing Group, Inc., The.

Sheinkin, Steve. The Notorious Benedict Arnold: A True Story of Adventure, Heroism & Treachery. 2013. (ENG., Illus.). 368p. (J). (gr. 6-8). pap. 12.99 (978-1-250-02460-2(9), 900097286) Square Fish.

Shepard, Ray Anthony. Now or Never! Fifty-Fourth Massachusetts Infantry's War to End Slavery. 2017. (ENG., Illus.). 144p. (J). (gr. 5-12). 17.95 (978-1-62979-340-5(X), Calkins Creek) Highlights Pr., c/o Highlights for Children, Inc.

Sherman, Jill. Eyewitness to the Harlem Hellfighters. 2018. (Eyewitness to World War I Ser.). (ENG.). 32p. (J). (gr. 4-7). lib. bdg. 35.64 (978-1-5038-1604-6(4), 211162) Child's World, Inc, The.

Simons, Lisa M. Bolt. Soldiers of the U. S. Army [Scholastic]. 2010. (People of the U. S. Armed Forces Ser.). (ENG.). 24p. pap. 0.49 (978-1-4296-5807-2(X), Capstone Pr.) Capstone.

—Special Ops Mission Timelines. 2016. (Special Ops Mission Timelines Ser.). (ENG.). 32p. (J). (gr. 3-9). 117.28 (978-1-4914-8709-9(7), 24376, Capstone Pr.) Capstone.

—U. S. Army by the Numbers, 1 vol. 2014. (Military by the Numbers Ser.). (ENG., Illus.). 32p. (J). (gr. 3-9). lib. bdg. 28.65 (978-1-4765-3917-1(0), 123916, Capstone Pr.) Capstone.

—U. S. Army Green Beret Missions: A Timeline. 2016. (Special Ops Mission Timelines Ser.). (ENG., Illus.). 32p. (J). (gr. 3-9). lib. bdg. 27.32 (978-1-4914-8702-0(X), 131421, Capstone Pr.) Capstone.

—U. S. Army Ranger Missions: A Timeline. 2016. (Special Ops Mission Timelines Ser.). (ENG., Illus.). 32p. (J). (gr. 3-9). lib. bdg. 27.32 (978-1-4914-8701-3(1), 131420, Capstone Pr.) Capstone.

Small, Cathleen. Strategic Inventions of the Korean War, 1 vol. 2016. (Tech in the Trenches Ser.). (ENG., Illus.). 112p. (YA). (gr. 9-9). 44.50 (978-1-5026-2345-4(5), 12a6e201-fa7a-481d-b720-d560c44d31ed) Cavendish Square Publishing LLC.

Smith, Sherri L. Who Were the Tuskegee Airmen? 2019. (Who HQ Ser.). (ENG.). 108p. (J). (gr. 2-3). 16.36 (978-1-64310-860-5(3)) Penworthy Co., LLC, The.

Smith, Sherri L. & Who HQ. Who Were the Tuskegee Airmen? Murray, Jake, illus. 2018. (Who Was? Ser.). 112p. (J). (gr. 3-7). 5.99 (978-0-399-54194-0(2), Penguin Workshop) Penguin Young Readers Group.

Sonneborn, Liz. Benedict Arnold: Hero & Traitor. 2005. (Leaders of the American Revolution Ser.). (ENG., Illus.). 136p. (gr. 5-8). lib. bdg. 30.00 (978-0-7910-8617-9(8), P114333, Facts On File) Infobase Holdings, Inc.

Spradlin, Michael P. Jack Montgomery: World War II: Gallantry at Anzio. 2019. (Medal of Honor Ser.: 1). (ENG., Illus.). 112p. (J). pap. 8.99 (978-1-250-15707-2(2), 900185139, Farrar, Straus & Giroux (BYR)) Farrar, Straus & Giroux.

—Ryan Pitts: Afghanistan: a Firefight in the Mountains of Wanat. 2019. (Medal of Honor Ser.: 2). (ENG., Illus.). 112p. (J). pap. 8.99 (978-1-250-15710-2(2), 900185142, Farrar, Straus & Giroux (BYR)) Farrar, Straus & Giroux.

Stanley, George E. George S. Patton: War Hero. Henderson, Meryl, illus. 2007. (Childhood of Famous Americans Ser.). (ENG.). 192p. (J). (gr. 3-7). pap. 7.99 (978-1-4169-1547-8(8), Simon & Schuster/Paula Wiseman Bks.) Simon & Schuster/Paula Wiseman Bks.

Stewart, Gail B. Life of a Soldier in Washington's Army. 2003. (American War Library). (ENG., Illus.). 112p. (J). 30.85 (978-1-59018-215-4(4), Lucent Bks.) Cengage Gale.

Stilwell, Alexander. Army Rangers. 2015. (J). lib. bdg. (978-1-62713-457-6(3)) Cavendish Square Publishing LLC.

—Army Rangers: What It Takes to Join the Elite, 1 vol. 2014. (Military Jobs Ser.). (ENG.). 48p. (YA). (gr. 7-7). 33.07 (978-1-5026-0166-7(4), f2bc21c0-3065-4355-93e8-c7bfd288a55f) Cavendish Square Publishing LLC.

Stine, Megan & Who HQ. Who Was Ulysses S. Grant? Geyer, Mark Edward, illus. 2014. (Who Was? Ser.). 112p. (J). (gr. 3-7). 6.99 (978-0-448-47894-4(3), Penguin Workshop) Penguin Young Readers Group.

Stokes, Betty Southard. Postcards from George, 1763-1781: George Rogers Clark Writes Home to Virginia from the Kentucky Wilderness. Cable, Annette, illus. 2010. (J). (978-1-935497-12-7(X)) Butler Bks.

Stone, Tanya Lee. Courage Has No Color, the True Story of the Triple Nickles: America's First Black Paratroopers. 2013. (ENG., Illus.). 160p. (J). (gr. 5). pap. 17.99 (978-0-7636-6548-7(7)); 24.99 (978-0-7636-5117-6(6)) Candlewick Pr.

Stotts, Stuart. Lucius Fairchild: Civil War Hero. 2011. (Badger Biographies Ser.). (ENG., Illus.). 112p. (J). pap. 12.95 (978-0-87020-460-9(2)) Wisconsin Historical Society.

Sullivan, Laura L. Life As an Ambulance Driver in World War I, 1 vol. 2017. (Life As... Ser.). (ENG.). 32p. (gr. 3-3). pap. 11.58 (978-1-5026-3055-1(9), a1609210-1da1-4a95-a6ef-af704127826e) Cavendish Square Publishing LLC.

Sutcliffe, Jane. George S. Patton JR. 2006. (History Maker Bios Ser.). (Illus.). 48p. (J). (gr. 3-7). lib. bdg. 26.60 (978-0-8225-2436-6(8), Lerner Pubns.) Lerner Publishing Group.

Tonatiuh, Duncan. Soldier for Equality: José de la Luz Sáenz & the Great War. 2019. (ENG., Illus.). 40p. (J). (gr. 1-3). 19.99 (978-1-4197-3682-7(5), 1193001, Abrams Bks. for Young Readers) Abrams, Inc.

Townsend, John. Army. 2016. (Action Force: World War II Ser.). 32p. (gr. 3-7). 31.35 (978-1-59920-982-1(9), Smart Apple Media) Black Rabbit Bks.

Troupe, Thomas Kingsley. The Tuskegee Airmen's Mission to Berlin: A Fly on the Wall History. Tejido, Jomike, illus. 2018. (Fly on the Wall History Ser.). (ENG.). 32p. (J). (gr. 1-3). lib. bdg. 27.99 (978-1-5158-1600-3(1), 136253, Picture Window Bks.) Capstone.

A True Book: the U. S Army in World War II (Library Edition) 2014. (ENG.). 48p. (J). lib. bdg. 29.00 (978-0-531-20496-2(0)) Scholastic Library Publishing.

U. S. Army. 2019. (Serving Our Country Ser.). (ENG.). 24p. (J). (gr. 1-4). lib. bdg. (978-1-68151-561-8(X), 17593) Amicus.

Venezia, Mike. Ulysses S. Grant. Venezia, Mike, illus. 2005. (Getting to Know the U. S. Presidents Ser.). (ENG., Illus.). 32p. (J). (gr. 3-7). lib. bdg. 28.00 (978-0-516-22623-1(1), Children's Pr.) Scholastic Library Publishing.

Vierow, Wendy. The Assault on Fort Wagner: Black Union Soldiers Make a Stand in South Carolina Battle. 2009. (Headlines from History Ser.). 24p. (gr. 3-3). 42.50 (978-1-61513-240-9(6), PowerKids Pr.) Rosen Publishing Group, Inc., The.

Walker, Sally M. Deadly Aim: The Civil War Story of Michigan's Anishinaabe Sharpshooters. 2019. (ENG., Illus.). 304p. (J). 19.99 (978-1-250-12525-5(1), 900174731, Holt, Henry & Co. Bks. For Young Readers) Holt, Henry & Co.

Waxman, Laura Hamilton. Colin Powell. 2005. (History Maker Bios Ser.). 48p. (J). pap. 8.95 (978-0-8225-5463-9(1)); (ENG., Illus.). (gr. 3-6). lib. bdg. 27.93 (978-0-8225-2433-5(3), Lerner Pubns.) Lerner Publishing Group.

Welch, Catherine A. George C. Marshall. (History Maker Bios Ser.). 48p. (J). 2006. (Illus.). (gr. 3-7). lib. bdg. 26.60 (978-0-8225-2435-9(X), Lerner Pubns.) 2005. pap. 8.95 (978-0-8225-5460-8(7)) Lerner Publishing Group.

Whiting, Jim. Army Rangers. 2018. (U. S. Special Forces Ser.). (ENG.). 48p. (J). (gr. 3-6). (978-1-60818-983-0(X), 19983, Creative Education) Creative Co., The.

—Delta Force. 2014. (U. S. Special Forces Ser.). (ENG.). 48p. (J). (gr. 5-8). (978-1-60818-461-3(7), 21427, Creative Education); pap. 12.00 (978-1-62832-047-3(8), 21428, Creative Paperbacks) Creative Co., The.

—Green Berets. 2014. (U. S. Special Forces Ser.). (ENG.). 48p. (J). (gr. 5-8). pap. 12.00 (978-1-62832-049-7(4), 21434, Creative Paperbacks) Creative Co., The.

—Night Stalkers. 2018. (U. S. Special Forces Ser.). (ENG.). 48p. (J). (gr. 3-6). (978-1-60818-985-4(6), 19985, Creative Education); pap. 12.00 (978-1-62832-612-3(3), 19989, Creative Paperbacks) Creative Co., The.

Wilson, Patrick. Survival Equipment. Carney, John, ed. 2014. (Extreme Survival in the Military Ser.: 12). 64p. (J). (gr. 7-18). lib. bdg. 23.95 (978-1-4222-3085-5(6)) Mason Crest.

Wood, Alix. Serving in the Army, 1 vol. 2013. (Protecting Our Country Ser.). 32p. (J). (gr. 3-4). (ENG.). 28.93 (978-1-4777-1294-8(1), 67d3c39f-2cf0-4c92-b07c-70311be6d6d3); pap. 60.00 (978-1-4777-1395-2(6)); (ENG., Illus.). pap. 11.00 (978-1-4777-1394-5(8), 2c38ffa2-5b31-439b-93fa-f4e1604f1966) Rosen Publishing Group, Inc., The. (PowerKids Pr.).

Yomtov, Nel. Civil War Weapons. 2016. (Essential Library of the Civil War Ser.). (ENG., Illus.). 112p. (J). (gr. 8-12). 59.93 (978-1-68077-467-2(0), 22358, Essential Library) ABDO Publishing Co.

—Combat. 2016. (Military Missions Ser.). (ENG., Illus.). 24p. (J). (gr. 3-7). 26.95 (978-1-62617-433-7(4), Epic Bks.) Bellwether Media.

—U. S. Ghost Army: The Master Illusionists of World War II. Valdrighi, Alessandro, illus. 2019. (Amazing World War II Stories Ser.). (ENG.). 32p. (J). (gr. 3-9). pap. 7.95 (978-1-5435-7551-4(X), 141083); lib. bdg. 34.65 (978-1-5435-7316-9(9), 140621) Capstone.

Young, Jeff C. Dwight D. Eisenhower: Soldier & President. 2004. (Notable Americans Ser.). (Illus.). 128p. (YA). (gr. 6-12). 23.95 (978-1-883846-76-3(5), First Biographies) Reynolds, Morgan Inc.

Zaloga, Steven J. The Most Daring Raid of World War II: D-Day — Pointe-Du-Hoc, 1 vol. 2011. (Most Daring Raids in History Ser.). (ENG., Illus.). 64p. (YA). (gr. 7-7). lib. bdg. 37.13 (978-1-4488-1867-9(2), 3ef3ba30-ecb1-412b-bdd2-8540d49e07d0) Rosen Publishing Group, Inc., The.

UNITED STATES—ARMY—MILITARY LIFE

Anderson, Dale. A Soldier's Life in the Civil War, 1 vol. 2004. (World Almanac(r) Library of the Civil War Ser.). (ENG., Illus.). 48p. (gr. 5-8). pap. 15.05 (978-0-8368-5595-1(7), 644f6601-6cb3-4513-a5bb-f0753119da8b, Gareth Stevens Secondary Library) Stevens, Gareth Publishing LLLP.

Beller, Susan Provost. Yankee Doodle & the Redcoats: Soldiering in the Revolutionary War. rev. ed. 2007. (Soldiers on the Battlefront Ser.). (ENG., Illus.). 112p. (gr. 6-8). lib. bdg. 33.26 (978-0-8225-6655-7(9)) Lerner Publishing Group.

Freedman, Russell. Washington at Valley Forge. 2020. (Illus.). 112p. (J). (gr. 5). pap. 14.99 (978-0-8234-4508-0(9)) Holiday Hse., Inc.

Frontline Families. 2015. (Frontline Families Ser.). (ENG.). 48p. (J). (gr. 5-6). pap., pap., pap. 505.80 (978-1-4824-3471-2(7)) Stevens, Gareth Publishing LLLP.

Goldish, Meish. Army: Civilian to Soldier. 2010. (Becoming a Soldier Ser.). 24p. (YA). (gr. 3-6). lib. bdg. 26.99 (978-1-936088-11-9(8)) Bearport Publishing Co., Inc.

—Baghdad Pups. 2011. (Dog Heroes Ser.). (Illus.). 32p. (J). (gr. 2-5). lib. bdg. 28.50 (978-1-61772-150-2(6), 1321528) Bearport Publishing Co., Inc.

Hooker, Forrestine Cooper. Child of the Fighting Tenth: On the Frontier with the Buffalo Soldiers. Wilson, Steve, ed. 2011. (ENG., Illus.). 296p. pap. 21.95 (978-0-8061-4080-3(1), P643251) Univ. of Oklahoma Pr.

Miller, Reagan & Claus, J. Matteson. Life on a Civil War Battlefield. 2011. (ENG.). 48p. (J). pap. (978-0-7787-5357-5(3)); lib. bdg. (978-0-7787-5340-7(9)) Crabtree Publishing Co.

Raum, Elizabeth. At Battle in the Revolutionary War: An Interactive Battlefield Adventure. 2015. (You Choose: Battlefields Ser.). (ENG., Illus.). 112p. (J). (gr. 3-7). pap. 6.95 (978-1-4914-2392-9(7), 127800, Capstone Pr.) Capstone.

Russo, Kristen J. Surprising Facts about Being an Army Soldier. 2017. (What You Didn't Know about the U. S. Military Life Ser.). (ENG., Illus.). 32p. (J). (gr. 3-9). lib. bdg. 28.65 (978-1-5157-7429-7(5), 135788, Capstone Pr.) Capstone.

Shoup, Kate. Life As a Soldier in the Civil War, 1 vol. 2015. (Life As... Ser.). (ENG., Illus.). 32p. (gr. 3-3). pap. 11.58 (978-1-5026-1083-6(3), 5dc3d5b6-a27f-4e0c-9e90-74c7d6dd040a) Cavendish Square Publishing LLC.

Spender, Nick. George Washington & the Winter at Valley Forge, 1 vol. 2011. (Graphic Heroes of the American Revolution Ser.). (ENG.). 24p. (J). (gr. 3-3). pap. 9.15 (978-1-4339-6014-7(1), 212546e8-51ff-4148-864f-6777e830450c, Gareth Stevens Learning Library); (Illus.). lib. bdg. 26.60 (978-1-4339-6174-8(1), a7d37558-8404-4d5a-9b25-9d6db992cc36) Stevens, Gareth Publishing LLLP.

UNITED STATES—ARMY—UNIFORMS

Langellier, John P. U. S. Army Headgear 1812-1872, 1 vol. 2003. (ENG., Illus.). 160p. (gr. 10-13). 69.95 (978-0-7643-1672-2(9), 3144, Schiffer Military History) Schiffer Publishing, Ltd.

UNITED STATES—ARTISTS

see Artists, American

UNITED STATES—AUTHORS

see Authors, American

UNITED STATES—BIOGRAPHY

Abdo, Kenny. Braun Strowman: Monster among Men. 2019. (Wrestling Biographies Ser.). (ENG., Illus.). 24p. (J). (gr. 2-8). lib. bdg. 31.36 (978-1-5321-2752-6(9), 31711, Abdo Zoom-Fly) ABDO Publishing Co.

—Chris Pratt. 2018. (Star Biographies Ser.). (ENG., Illus.). 24p. (J). (gr. 2-8). lib. bdg. 31.36 (978-1-5321-2543-0(7), 30095, Abdo Zoom-Fly) ABDO Publishing Co.

—Randy Orton: the Viper. 2019. (Wrestling Biographies Ser.). (ENG., Illus.). 24p. (J). (gr. 2-8). lib. bdg. 31.36 (978-1-5321-2753-3(7), 31713, Abdo Zoom-Fly) ABDO Publishing Co.

—Ronda Rousey: Baddest Woman on the Planet. 2019. (Wrestling Biographies Ser.). (ENG., Illus.). 24p. (J). (gr. 2-8). lib. bdg. 31.36 (978-1-5321-2754-0(5), 31715, Abdo Zoom-Fly) ABDO Publishing Co.

—Seth Rollins: the Architect. 2019. (Wrestling Biographies Ser.). (ENG., Illus.). 24p. (J). (gr. 2-8). lib. bdg. 31.36 (978-1-5321-2755-7(3), 31717, Abdo Zoom-Fly) ABDO Publishing Co.

—The Undertaker: Rest in Peace. 2019. (Wrestling Biographies Ser.). (ENG., Illus.). 24p. (J). (gr. 2-8). lib. bdg. 31.36 (978-1-5321-2756-4(1), 31719, Abdo Zoom-Fly) ABDO Publishing Co.

ABDO Publishing Company Staff. Heroes of America. 2005. (Heroes of America Ser.). (gr. 3-8). lib. bdg. 216.56 (978-1-59679-254-8(X), Abdo & Daughters) ABDO Publishing Co.

Abnett, Dan. Abraham Lincoln y la Guerra Civil, 1 vol. 2009. (Historietas Juveniles: Biografías (Jr. Graphic Biographies) Ser.). (SPA., Illus.). 24p. (gr. 2-3). (J). 28.93 (978-1-4358-8561-5(9), 7466c29f-c43f-4229-a2b0-ce29cbcf5047); pap. 10.60 (978-1-4358-3316-6(3), 6881a164-d615-429e-aaaf-9ff20b30d04e) Rosen Publishing Group, Inc., The.

—George Washington y la Guerra de Independencia, 1 vol. 2009. (Historietas Juveniles: Biografías (Jr. Graphic Biographies) Ser.). (SPA., Illus.). 24p. (gr. 2-3). pap. 10.60 (978-1-4358-3322-7(8), a38fe106-c9b7-4c5c-9508-fd86a6c2150a); (YA). 28.93 (978-1-4358-8564-6(3), 97102909-4df6-44a2-b6ce-f4870ffe0e02) Rosen Publishing Group, Inc., The.

Adams, Ashely. Standing in the Attorney General's Shoes, 1 vol. 2017. (My Government Ser.). (ENG.). 32p. (gr. 3-3). 30.21 (978-1-5026-3360-6(4), fb6470e3-3b5a-433e-a1d3-826a091ab416) Cavendish Square Publishing LLC.

Adams, Colleen. Jake Gyllenhaal, 1 vol. 2006. (Stars in the Spotlight Ser.). (ENG., Illus.). 32p. (YA). (gr. 4-4). lib. bdg. 28.93 (978-1-4042-3514-4(0), f50c4cfd-371f-4dce-886f-0898fc74e2de) Rosen Publishing Group, Inc., The.

—Johnny Depp, 1 vol. 2005. (Content-Area Literacy Collections). (ENG.). 24p. (gr. 3-4). pap. 8.85 (978-1-4042-5667-5(9), af047bd4-0a78-4c8f-b447-784beddcebdc) Rosen Publishing Group, Inc., The.

Adams, Michelle. Cliff Lee. 2011. (Robbie Reader Ser.). (Illus.). 32p. (J). (gr. 2-5). lib. bdg. 25.70 (978-1-61228-065-3(X)) Mitchell Lane Pubs.

—Katy Perry. 2011. (Blue Banner Biography Ser.). (Illus.). 32p. (YA). (gr. 4-7). lib. bdg. 25.70 (978-1-61228-051-6(X)) Mitchell Lane Pubs.

Adler, David A. A Picture Book of Benjamin Franklin. Wallner, John & Wallner, Alexandra, illus. 2018. (Picture Book Biography Ser.). 32p. (J). (gr. -1-3). pap. 7.99 (978-0-8234-4057-3(5)) Holiday Hse., Inc.

—A Picture Book of Benjamin Franklin. 2008. (J). (gr. k-3). pap. 39.95 incl. audio compact disk *(978-1-4301-0341-7(8))* Live Oak Media.

Adler, Jack. Chinese Americans. (Successful Americans Ser.). 64p. (YA). 2009. (Illus.). (gr. 9-12). 22.95 *(978-1-4222-0520-4(7))* 2007. (gr. 7-18). pap. 9.95 *(978-1-4222-0855-7(9))* Mason Crest.

Aiwei, Daniel B. CM Punk: Pro Wrestling Superstar, 1 vol. 2014. (Pro Wrestling Superstars Ser.). (ENG., Illus.). 24p. (J). (gr. 1-3). lib. bdg. 27.99 *(978-1-4765-4210-2(4)*, 124311, Capstone Pr.) Capstone.

—John Cena: Pro Wrestling Superstar, 1 vol. 2014. (Pro Wrestling Superstars Ser.). (ENG., Illus.). 24p. (J). (gr. 1-3). lib. bdg. 27.99 *(978-1-4765-4207-2(4)*, 124308, Capstone Pr.) Capstone.

Alagna, Magdalena. Billie Holiday. 2009. (Rock & Roll Hall of Famers Ser.). 112p. (gr. 5-8). 63.90 *(978-1-60852-468-6(X)*, Rosen Reference) Rosen Publishing Group, Inc., The.

—Wyatt Earp: Lawman of the American West. 2009. (Primary Sources of Famous People in American History Ser.). 32p. (gr. 2-3). 47.90 *(978-1-60851-747-3(0))* Rosen Publishing Group, Inc., The.

—Wyatt Earp: Lawman of the American West / Sheriff del oeste Americano. 2009. (Famous People in American History/Grandes personajes en la historia de los Estados Unidos Ser.). (ENG & SPA.). 32p. (gr. 2-3). 47.90 *(978-1-61512-558-6(2)*, Editorial Buenas Letras) Rosen Publishing Group, Inc., The.

—Wyatt Earp: Sheriff del legano Oeste, 1 vol. 2003. (Grandes Personajes en la Historia de Los Estados Unidos (Famous People in American History) Ser.). (SPA.). 32p. (gr. 3-4). pap. 10.00 *(978-0-8239-4241-1(4)*, cec92c20-e77a-4cdd-b99f-4a49f2f0a46e, Rosen Classroom) Rosen Publishing Group, Inc., The.

—Wyatt Earp: Sheriff del oeste americano (Wyatt Earp: Lawman of the American West) 2009. (Grandes personajes en la historia de los Estados Unidos (Famous People in American History) Ser.). (SPA.). 32p. (gr. 2-3). 47.90 *(978-1-61512-811-2(5)*, Editorial Buenas Letras) Rosen Publishing Group, Inc., The.

Aldridge, Rebecca. Apolo Anton Ohno. 2009. (Asian Americans of Achievement Ser.). (ENG., Illus.). 128p. (gr. 7-12). 35.00 *(978-1-60413-565-7(4)*, P171248, Facts On File) Infobase Holdings, Inc.

Aldrin, Buzz. Reaching for the Moon. Minor, Wendell, illus. (ENG.). 40p. (J). (gr. 1-4). 2008. 8.99 *(978-0-06-055447-7(9))* 2005. 17.99 *(978-0-06-055445-3(2))* HarperCollins Pubs. (HarperCollins).

—Reaching for the Moon. Minor, Wendell, illus. unabr. ed. 2005. (Picture Book Readalong Ser.). (gr. k-4). 28.95 incl. audio compact disk *(978-1-59519-582-1(3))* Live Oak Media.

Alexander, Lauren. Mad for Miley: An Unauthorized Biography. 2007. (Unauthorized Biographies Ser.). (ENG., Illus.). 128p. (J). (gr. 5-8). 17.44 *(978-0-8431-2684-6(1))* Penguin Young Readers Group.

Alkire, Jessie. Buzz Aldrin: Pioneer Moon Explorer. 2018. (Space Crusaders Ser.). (ENG., Illus.). 32p. (J). (gr. 3-6). lib. bdg. 32.79 *(978-1-5321-1701-5(9)*, 30690, Checkerboard Library) ABDO Publishing Co.

—Hot Wheels Developer: Elliot Handler. 2018. (Toy Trailblazers Ser.). (ENG., Illus.). 32p. (J). (gr. 3-6). lib. bdg. 32.79 *(978-1-5321-1708-4(6)*, 30704, Checkerboard Library) ABDO Publishing Co.

All-Star Players, 12 vols., Sets 1-2. Incl. All-Star Players: Set 1. 2006. lib. bdg. 115.72 *(978-1-4042-3601-1(5)*, ee6f4b42-d882-4d9d-89a6-a982e7b38577); All-Star Players: Set 2. 2008. lib. bdg. 86.79 *(978-1-4358-2564-2(0)*, f8cacf69-255e-445a-9789-a59ccc4a8526, PowerKids Pr.); (J). (gr. 4-5). 2008. Set lib. bdg. 287.40 *(978-1-4358-2669-4(8))* Rosen Publishing Group, Inc., The.

Allen, Kathy. Drew Brees. 2013. (Football Stars up Close Ser.). 24p. (J). (gr. k-5). lib. bdg. 26.99 *(978-1-61772-716-0(4))* Bearport Publishing Co., Inc.

—Tom Brady. 2013. (Football Stars up Close Ser.). 24p. (J). (gr. k-5). lib. bdg. 26.99 *(978-1-61772-717-7(2))* Bearport Publishing Co., Inc.

—Tony Romo. 2013. (Football Stars up Close Ser.). 24p. (J). (gr. k-5). lib. bdg. 26.99 *(978-1-61772-719-1(9))* Bearport Publishing Co., Inc.

Allen, Kenny. Kurt Busch, 1 vol. 2006. (NASCAR Champions Ser.). (ENG., Illus.). 24p. (J). (gr. 1-2). lib. bdg. 26.27 *(978-1-4042-3457-4(8)*, 47b756fa-9a3b-4524-92b8-90e70ca45a52) Rosen Publishing Group, Inc., The.

Allyson, Jackie. Chris Jesus Ferguson. 2007. (Superstars of Poker Ser.). (Illus.). 64p. (YA). pap. 7.95 *(978-1-4222-0371-2(9))* Mason Crest.

—Doyle Texas Dolly Brunson. 2007. (Superstars of Poker Ser.). (Illus.). 64p. (YA). pap. 7.95 *(978-1-4222-0368-2(9))* Mason Crest.

—Gus the Great Dane Hansen. 2007. (Superstars of Poker Ser.). (Illus.). 64p. (YA). pap. 7.95 *(978-1-4222-0372-9(7))* Mason Crest.

—Howard the Professor Lederer. 2009. (Superstars of Poker Ser.). (Illus.). 64p. (YA). (gr. 3-7). lib. bdg. 22.95 *(978-1-4222-0223-4(2))* Mason Crest.

—Phil Unabomber Laak. (Superstars of Poker Ser.). (Illus.). 64p. (YA). 2009. (gr. 3-7). lib. bdg. 22.95 *(978-1-4222-0222-7(4))* 2007. pap. 7.95 *(978-1-4222-0376-7(X))* Mason Crest.

Alter, Judy. Martin de Leon: Tejano Empresario. 2007. (Stars of Texas Ser.: 4). (ENG., Illus.). 72p. (J). (gr. 4-7). 14.95 *(978-1-933337-08-1(7)*, P121287) State Hse. Pr.

Alyson, Jackie. Howard the Professor Lederer. 2007. (Superstars of Poker: Texas Hold'em Ser.). (Illus.). 64p. (YA). (gr. 3-7). pap. 7.95 *(978-1-4222-0377-4(8))* Mason Crest.

Ambrosek, Renee. Shawn Fanning: The Founder of Napster. (Internet Career Biographies Ser.). 112p. (gr. 8-8). 2009. 63.90 *(978-1-61513-600-1(2))* 2006. (ENG., Illus.). (YA). lib. bdg. 39.80 *(978-1-4042-0720-2(1)*, ebe36c69-b4cf-482a-bd7c-c7f3324ae510) Rosen Publishing Group, Inc., The.

American Graphic. 2011. (American Graphic Ser.). (ENG.). 32p. (gr. 3-4). pap. 381.60 *(978-1-4296-7344-0(3)*, Capstone Pr.) Capstone.

American Graphic, 8 vols., Set. Incl. Bambino: The Story of Babe Ruth's Legendary 1927 Season. Yomtov, Nel. Foley, Tim, illus. 2010. lib. bdg. 31.32 *(978-1-4296-5473-9(2)*, 113873); Sarah Palin: Political Rebel. Yomtov, Nelson. D'Ottavi, Francesca, illus. 2011. lib. bdg. 31.32 *(978-1-4296-6018-1(X)*, 114955, Capstone Pr.); (J). (gr. 3-9). (American Graphic Ser.). (ENG.). 32p. 2011. 219.24 o.p. *(978-1-4296-6585-8(8)*, 171241, Capstone Pr.) Capstone.

American Heroes, Group 2, 12 vols., Set. Incl. Booker T. Washington: Getting into the Schoolhouse. Brimner, Larry Dane. lib. bdg. 32.64 *(978-0-7614-3063-6(6)*, 03eab1a3-95bb-48ec-8714-ed0c9c2df0d3); Chief Crazy Horse: Following a Vision. Brimner, Larry Dane. lib. bdg. 32.64 *(978-0-7614-3061-2(X)*, 748a9f2d-7e49-4e8f-9cf1-18b087238068); Eleanor Roosevelt: Making the World a Better Place. Collard, Sneed B., III. lib. bdg. 32.64 *(978-0-7614-3069-8(5)*, 1b05b04c-6b03-4112-934f-2eeace2a1983); John Glenn: Hooked on Flying. Collard, Sneed B., III. (Illus.). lib. bdg. 32.64 *(978-0-7614-3066-7(0)*, 0802b8b4-5c46-44f3-bfaf-f60b33b36ace); Pocahontas: Bridging Two Worlds. Brimner, Larry Dane. lib. bdg. 32.64 *(978-0-7614-3065-0(2)*, c65e5cb1-d030-467f-884c-63fc62bac5d7); Thomas Jefferson: Let Freedom Ring! Collard, Sneed B., III. lib. bdg. 32.64 *(978-0-7614-3067-4(9)*, 8eac1ebf-a575-4a39-a66b-9e82fcc32ff5); 48p. (gr. 3-3). (American Heroes Ser.). (ENG.). 2009. Set lib. bdg. 195.84 *(978-0-7614-3060-5(1)*, 44be042a-8327-4e50-b149-20c5b61d07c8, Cavendish Square) Cavendish Square Publishing LLC.

Anderson, Dale. Al Gore: A Wake-Up Call to Global Warming. 2009. (Voices for Green Choices Ser.). (ENG., Illus.). 48p. (J). (gr. 5-9). lib. bdg. *(978-0-7787-4666-9(6))* Crabtree Publishing Co.

—Leaders of the American Revolution, 1 vol. 2005. (World Almanac(r) Library of the American Revolution Ser.). (ENG.). 48p. (gr. 5-8). lib. bdg. 33.67 *(978-0-8368-5931-7(6)*, 5670f581-1e2e-4ddf-81e4-ea8e89f67c26, Gareth Stevens Secondary Library) Stevens, Gareth Publishing LLLP.

Anderson, Dale & Crewe, Sabrina. The Seneca Falls Women's Rights Convention, 1 vol. 2004. (Events That Shaped America Ser.). (ENG., Illus.). 32p. (J). (gr. 3-5). lib. bdg. 28.67 *(978-0-8368-3408-6(9)*, c4ccc77c-a091-449d-aa31-a0b003f98e5d, Gareth Stevens Learning Library) Stevens, Gareth Publishing LLLP.

Anderson, Michael. Biographies of the New World Power: Rutherford B. Hayes, Thomas Alva Edison, Margaret Sanger, & More, 1 vol. 2012. (Impact on America: Collective Biographies Ser.). (ENG., Illus.). 160p. (J). (gr. 8-8). 38.82 *(978-1-61530-691-6(9)*, 7eedc09b-3a58-4f4b-9a0e-ed82ec747c57) Rosen Publishing Group, Inc., The.

Anderson, Michael, ed. Biographies of the New World: Leif Eriksson, Henry Hudson, Charles Darwin, & More, 4 vols. 2012. (Impact on America: Collective Biographies Ser.). (ENG., Illus.). 136p. (YA). (gr. 8-8). 77.64 *(978-1-61530-803-3(2)*, 005cbbc3-ab18-4ff2-9e09-9bf8ab0b143f) Rosen Publishing Group, Inc., The.

—Biographies of the New World Power: Rutherford B. Hayes, Thomas Alva Edison, Margaret Sanger, & More, 4 vols. 2012. (Impact on America: Collective Biographies Ser.). (ENG., Illus.). 160p. (YA). (gr. 8-8). 77.64 *(978-1-61530-765-4(6)*, 5be9eeb4-4d17-4c14-8668-1c8580293696) Rosen Publishing Group, Inc., The.

Anderson, Sheila. America Ferrera: Latina Superstar, 1 vol. 2009. (Hot Celebrity Biographies Ser.). (ENG., Illus.). 48p. (gr. 5-7). lib. bdg. 27.93 *(978-0-7660-3210-1(8)*, d90811ee-4b34-4d8d-be15-c7dfbbc4c94d) Enslow Publishing, LLC.

Anderson, Wayne A. Jay-Z. 2008. (ENG., Illus.). 112p. (gr. 6-12). per. 12.95 *(978-0-7910-9729-8(3)*, P142885, Facts On File) Infobase Holdings, Inc.

—Tony Stewart: NASCAR Driver, 1 vol. 2007. (Behind the Wheel Ser.). (ENG., Illus.). 48p. (YA). (gr. 5-5). lib. bdg. 34.47 *(978-1-4042-0984-8(0)*, 33365667-6742-4c9d-87d5-d6900614fe43) Rosen Publishing Group, Inc., The.

Andre Norton. 2010. (ENG., Illus.). 128p. (gr. 6-12). 35.00 *(978-1-60413-682-1(0)*, P178901, Facts On File) Infobase Holdings, Inc.

Angel, Ann. Janis Joplin: Rise up Singing. 2010. (ENG., Illus.). 120p. (YA). (gr. 8-17). 24.95 *(978-0-8109-8349-6(4)*, 641601, Amulet Bks.) Abrams, Inc.

Angst, Frank. Chad Johnson. 2009. (Superstars of Pro Football Ser.). (Illus.). 64p. (YA). (gr. 5-18). lib. bdg. 22.95 *(978-1-4222-0556-3(8))* Mason Crest.

Arato, Rona. Working for Freedom: The Story of Josiah Henson. 2009. (Stories of Canada Ser.: 13). (ENG., Illus.). 88p. (J). (gr. 4-18). 18.95 *(978-1-894917-50-6(2)*, Napoleon & Co.) Dundurn Pr. CAN. Dist: Publishers Group West (PGW).

Aretha, David. Aaron Rodgers: Champion Football Star, 1 vol. 2017. (Sports Star Champions Ser.). (ENG.). 48p. (gr. 5-6). lib. bdg. 29.60 *(978-0-7660-8716-3(6)*, 8a93cff0-03e9-459c-95ff-da509f7d5f69) Enslow Publishing, LLC.

—José Altuve: Champion Baseball Star, 1 vol. 2017. (Sports Star Champions Ser.). (ENG.). 48p. (gr. 5-6). lib. bdg. 29.60 *(978-0-7660-8690-6(9)*, 57be6a8f-93dd-4d06-bece-997975b68931) Enslow Publishing, LLC.

Armstrong, Jesse. Randy Orton. 2015. (Wrestling Superstars Ser.). (ENG., Illus.). 24p. (J). (gr. 3-7). lib. bdg. 26.95 *(978-1-62617-182-4(3)*, Epic Bks.) Bellwether Media.

—Triple H. 2015. (Wrestling Superstars Ser.). (ENG., Illus.). 24p. (J). (gr. 3-7). lib. bdg. 26.95 *(978-1-62617-183-1(1)*, Epic Bks.) Bellwether Media.

Armstrong, Linda. Henry Ford. 2009. pap. 13.25 *(978-1-60559-062-2(2))* Hameray Publishing Group, Inc.

Auster, Michael A. They Led the Way. 2005. (Yellow Umbrella Fluent Level Ser.). (ENG.). 16p. (gr. k-1). pap. 35.70 *(978-0-7368-5315-6(4)*, Capstone Pr.) Capstone.

Azzarelli, Ally. Selena Gomez: Latina TV & Music Star, 1 vol. 2012. (Hot Celebrity Biographies Ser.). (ENG., Illus.). 48p. (gr. 5-7). lib. bdg. 27.93 *(978-0-7660-3875-2(0)*, 23a2c6b5-e3f8-4efa-9c20-8486ed97b133) Enslow Publishing, LLC.

—Taylor Lautner: Film Superstar, 1 vol. 2012. (Hot Celebrity Biographies Ser.). (ENG., Illus.). 48p. (gr. 5-7). lib. bdg. 27.93 *(978-0-7660-3874-5(2)*, 181bb8e3-438b-49f3-8ae4-8ecd7be07280) Enslow Publishing, LLC.

Bader, Bonnie & Who HQ. Who Was Alexander Graham Bell? Groff, David, illus. 2013. (Who Was? Ser.). 112p. (J). (gr. 3-7). 5.99 *(978-0-448-46460-2(8)*, Penguin Workshop) Penguin Young Readers Group.

Bahadur, Gaiutra. Family Ties. 2011. (J). pap. *(978-0-531-22554-7(2))* Scholastic, Inc.

Bailey, Diane. Miley Cyrus, 1 vol. 2011. (Megastars Ser.). (ENG., Illus.). 48p. (J). (gr. 5-5). pap. 12.75 *(978-1-4488-2259-1(9)*, 93bdb6a4-9231-406f-8d4f-321d32390320); lib. bdg. 34.47 *(978-1-4358-3573-3(5)*, 89cb6f5f-7cc9-47c7-89df-91d4b8cfb96c) Rosen Publishing Group, Inc., The. (Rosen Reference).

Bailey, Tom. Jennifer Chandler: Olympic Champion Diver. 2005. (Alabama Roots Biography Ser.). (Illus.). 112p. (J). pap. *(978-1-59421-014-3(4))* Seacoast Publishing, Inc.

Bair, Diane. Western Legends & Leyendas del Oeste: 6 English, 6 Spanish Adaptations. 2011. (ENG & SPA.). (J). 101.00 net. *(978-1-4108-5735-4(2))* Benchmark Education Co.

Bair, Diane & Wright, Pamela. Western Legends: Set Of 6. 2011. (Navigators Ser.). (J). pap. 50.00 net. *(978-1-4108-2577-3(9))* Benchmark Education Co.

Baldwin, James. Four Great Americans. 2006. pap. *(978-1-4065-0509-2(9))* Dodo Pr.

Banting, Erinn. Angelina Jolie. 2008. (Remarkable People Ser.). (Illus.). 24p. (J). (gr. 4-6). pap. 8.95 *(978-1-59036-987-6(4))*; lib. bdg. 24.45 *(978-1-59036-986-9(6))* Weigl Pubs., Inc.

—Katie Couric. 2007. (Remarkable People Ser.). (Illus.). 24p. (J). (gr. 4-6). pap. 8.95 *(978-1-59036-644-8(1))*; lib. bdg. 24.45 *(978-1-59036-643-1(3))* Weigl Pubs., Inc.

Baptiste, Tracey. Jerry Spinelli. 2009. (ENG., Illus.). 128p. (gr. 6-12). 35.00 *(978-0-7910-9572-0(X)*, P161831, Facts On File) Infobase Holdings, Inc.

—Madeleine L'Engle. 2009. (ENG., Illus.). 128p. (gr. 6-12). 35.00 *(978-0-7910-9573-7(8)*, P163841, Facts On File) Infobase Holdings, Inc.

Barber, Tiki. Tiki: My Life in the Game & Beyond. 2008. (ENG.). 240p. pap. 15.99 *(978-1-4169-5564-1(X)*, Gallery Bks.) Gallery Bks.

Baughan, Brian. Cesar Chavez. 2009. (Sharing the American Dream Ser.). (Illus.). 64p. (YA). (gr. 7-12). 22.95 *(978-1-4222-0582-2(7))* Mason Crest.

Bedell, J. M. & Greenhead, Bill. Superheroes of the Constitution: Action & Adventure Stories about Real-Life Heroes. 2017. (ENG., Illus.). 112p. (J). pap. 9.99 *(978-1-63158-233-2(X)*, Racehorse Publishing) Skyhorse Publishing Co., Inc.

Bednar, Chuck. Beyoncé. 2010. (Transcending Race in America Ser.). 64p. (YA). (gr. 4-8). lib. bdg. 22.95 *(978-1-4222-1607-1(1))* Mason Crest.

—David Blaine: Illusionist & Endurance Artist. (Transcending Race in America: Biographies of Biracial Achievers Ser.). (Illus.). 64p. (YA). (gr. 5-18). 2010. lib. bdg. 22.95 *(978-1-4222-1609-5(8))* 2009. pap. 9.95 *(978-1-4222-1623-1(3))* Mason Crest.

—Kris Allen. 2009. (Dream Big: American Idol Superstars Ser.). (Illus.). 64p. (J). (gr. 5-18). pap. 9.95 *(978-1-4222-1596-8(2))*; lib. bdg. 22.95 *(978-1-4222-1515-9(6))* Mason Crest.

—Tim Duncan. 2007. (Role Model Athletes Ser.). (Illus.). 64p. (YA). pap. 9.95 *(978-1-4222-0768-0(4))* Mason Crest.

Benchmark Education Company. Western Legends (Teacher Guide) 2004. *(978-1-4108-2592-6(2))* Benchmark Education Co.

Benge, Janet & Benge, Geoff. D. L. Moody: Bringing Souls to Christ. 2011. (ENG.). (YA). pap. 11.99 *(978-1-57658-552-8(2))* YWAM Publishing.

—Heroes of History - Daniel Boone: Frontiersman. 2004. (ENG.). 224p. (YA). pap. 11.99 *(978-1-932096-09-5(4))* Emerald Bks.

—Heroes of History - Davy Crockett: Ever Westward. 2011. (ENG.). 192p. (YA). pap. 11.99 *(978-1-932096-67-5(1))* Emerald Bks.

—Heroes of History - Ronald Reagan: Destiny at His Side. 2010. (ENG.). 224p. (YA). pap. 11.99 *(978-1-932096-65-1(5))* Emerald Bks.

Bennett, Doraine & Scott, Clark C. Benjamin Franklin. 2012. (Illus.). 24p. (J). *(978-1-935884-38-5(7))*; pap. *(978-1-935884-47-7(6))* State Standards Publishing, LLC.

Berman, Ron. Future Stars of America. 2006. (Future Stars Ser.). (Illus.). 90p. (gr. 3-8). pap. 9.95 *(978-0-9741997-4-0(5))* Scobre Pr. Corp.

Berne, Emma Carlson. Paris & Nicky Hilton. 2007. (Popular Culture: A View from the Paparazzi Ser.). (Illus.). 64p. (YA). (gr. 3-7). pap. 7.95 *(978-1-4222-0358-3(1))* Mason Crest.

Berne, Stanley. Empire Sweets: How I Learned to Live & Love in the Greatest Empire on Earth. 2003. 160p. (YA). pap. 40.00 *(978-0-913844-26-7(8))* Rising Tide Pr.

Bernstein, Ross. Shaquille o'Neal, 2nd Edition. 2nd rev. ed. 2009. (Amazing Athletes Ser.). (ENG., Illus.). 32p. (J). (gr. 2-5). pap. 7.95 *(978-0-7613-4489-6(6)*, 6a27e0dd-9780-40ef-b7f7-3d474cd6ceb0) Lerner Publishing Group.

Bezdecheck, Bethany. Missy Elliott. 2009. (Library of Hip-Hop Biographies Ser.). 48p. (gr. 5-5). 53.00 *(978-1-60853-697-9(1))* Rosen Publishing Group, Inc., The.

Bjornlund, Lydia D. Angelina Jolie. 2010. (Modern Role Models Ser.). (Illus.). 64p. (YA). (gr. 7-12). 22.95 *(978-1-4222-0504-4(5))* Mason Crest.

Blohm, Craig E. Great Cartoonists. 2016. (ENG.). 80p. (J). (gr. 5-12). *(978-1-60152-996-1(1))* ReferencePoint Pr., Inc.

Bodden, Valerie & Gehry, Frank O. Frank Gehry. 2008. (Xtraordinary Artists Ser.). (ENG.). 48p. (J). (gr. 5-8). lib. bdg. 22.95 *(978-1-58341-662-4(5)*, 22317, Creative Education) Creative Co., The.

Bodie, Idella. Heroes & Heroines of the American Revolution. 2004. (Illus.). 48p. (J). pap., instr.'s gde. ed. *(978-0-87844-173-0(5))* Sandlapper Publishing Co., Inc.

Boehme, Gerry. Drew Brees: Record-Breaking Quarterback, 1 vol. 2019. (At the Top of Their Game Ser.). (ENG.). 112p. (gr. 9-9). pap. 20.99 *(978-1-5026-5120-4(3)*, 51e8a5d8-11ec-48d8-a11f-49463923fe82) Cavendish Square Publishing LLC.

Bolden, Tonya. The Champ: the Story of Muhammad Ali. Christie, R. Gregory, illus. 2007. (ENG.). 40p. (J). (gr. 1-4). pap. 7.99 *(978-0-440-41782-8(1)*, Dragonfly Bks.) Random Hse. Children's Bks.

Boomhower, Ray E. The Soldier's Friend: A Life of Ernie Pyle. 2006. (Illus.). 134p. 17.95 *(978-0-87195-200-4(9))* Indiana Historical Society.

Boone, Mary. Corbin Bleu. 2008. (Blue Banner Biography Ser.). (Illus.). 32p. (J). (gr. 4-7). lib. bdg. 25.70 *(978-1-58415-674-1(0))* Mitchell Lane Pubs.

—David Wright. 2010. (Blue Banner Biography Ser.). (Illus.). 32p. (YA). (gr. 4-7). lib. bdg. 25.70 *(978-1-58415-910-0(3))* Mitchell Lane Pubs.

—Pink. 2009. (Blue Banner Biography Ser.). (Illus.). 32p. (YA). (gr. 4-7). lib. bdg. 25.70 *(978-1-58415-767-0(4))* Mitchell Lane Pubs.

—Sue Bird. 2011. (Robbie Reader Ser.). (Illus.). 32p. (J). (gr. 2-5). lib. bdg. 25.70 *(978-1-61228-062-2(5))* Mitchell Lane Pubs.

—Tim Lincecum. 2011. (Robbie Reader Ser.). (Illus.). 32p. (J). (gr. 2-5). lib. bdg. 25.70 *(978-1-61228-058-5(7))* Mitchell Lane Pubs.

—Vanessa Anne Hudgens. 2008. (Blue Banner Biography Ser.). (Illus.). 32p. (YA). (gr. 4-7). lib. bdg. 25.70 *(978-1-58415-672-7(4))* Mitchell Lane Pubs.

Boothroyd, Jennifer. Lou Gehrig. 2008. pap. 40.95 *(978-0-8225-9473-4(0))* Lerner Publishing Group.

—Robert Fulton: A Life of Innovation. 2007. (Pull Ahead Bks.). (Illus.). 32p. (J). (gr. 3-7). lib. bdg. 22.60 *(978-0-8225-6458-4(0)*, Lerner Pubns.) Lerner Publishing Group.

Borgert-Spaniol, Megan. Lincoln Logs Creator: John Lloyd Wright. 2018. (Toy Trailblazers Ser.). (ENG., Illus.). 32p. (J). (gr. 3-6). lib. bdg. 32.79 *(978-1-5321-1709-1(4)*, 30706, Checkerboard Library) ABDO Publishing Co.

—My Little Pony Pioneer. 2018. (Toy Trailblazers Ser.). (ENG.). 32p. (J). (gr. 3-6). lib. bdg. 32.79 *(978-1-5321-1710-7(8)*, 30708, Checkerboard Library) ABDO Publishing Co.

Bortz, Fred. The Big Bang Theory: Edwin Hubble & the Origins of the Universe, 1 vol. 2013. (Revolutionary Discoveries of Scientific Pioneers Ser.). (ENG., Illus.). 80p. (J). (gr. 6-6). 38.41 *(978-1-4777-1803-2(6)*, ea7bcd12-0733-48fc-baec-114fbf20adf6) Rosen Publishing Group, Inc., The.

Bowe, Brian J. The Ramones: American Punk Rock Band, 1 vol. 2011. (Rebels of Rock Ser.). (ENG., Illus.). 128p. (gr. 5-6). pap. 13.88 *(978-1-59845-213-6(4)*, 9bde1a09-784c-43d9-acaf-023915c18d66) Enslow Publishing, LLC.

Bradley, Michael. Pro Football's Underdogs: Players & Teams Who Shocked the Football World. 2017. (Sports Shockers! Ser.). (ENG., Illus.). 32p. (J). (gr. 3-9). lib. bdg. 28.65 *(978-1-5157-8048-9(1)*, 136067, Capstone Pr.) Capstone.

Braidich, Victoria. Dale Earnhardt, 1 vol. 2006. (NASCAR Champions Ser.). (ENG., Illus.). 24p. (J). (gr. 1-2). lib. bdg. 26.27 *(978-1-4042-3512-0(4)*, df9c863f-22be-41c0-a9c6-cc85d8d526fc) Rosen Publishing Group, Inc., The.

Branscomb, Leslie Wolf. Earl Warren. 2011. (Supreme Court Justices Ser.). (Illus.). 112p. 28.95 *(978-1-59935-158-2(7))* Reynolds, Morgan Inc.

—Marc Jacobs. 2011. (Profiles in Fashion Ser.). (Illus.). 112p. 28.95 *(978-1-59935-153-7(6)*, 1320457) Reynolds, Morgan Inc.

Braun, Eric. Pro Baseball's Underdogs: Players & Teams Who Shocked the Baseball World. 2017. (Sports Shockers! Ser.). (ENG., Illus.). 32p. (J). (gr. 3-9). lib. bdg. 28.65 *(978-1-5157-8047-2(3)*, 136066, Capstone Pr.) Capstone.

—Pro Basketball's Underdogs: Players & Teams Who Shocked the Basketball World. 2017. (Sports Shockers! Ser.). (ENG., Illus.). 32p. (J). (gr. 3-9). lib. bdg. 28.65 *(978-1-5157-8046-5(5)*, 136065, Capstone Pr.) Capstone.

Braun, Marta. Muybridge & the Riddle of Locomotion. 2013. (ENG., Illus.). 24p. (J). (gr. 4-12). 19.95 *(978-1-77085-229-7(8)*, 73ced1c6-a6aa-444c-af06-f8079265a71d) Firefly Bks., Ltd.

Brennan, Kristine. Danica Patrick. 2010. (Role Model Athletes Ser.). (Illus.). 64p. (YA). (gr. 7-12). 22.95 *(978-1-4222-0487-0(1))* Mason Crest.

—Indian Americans. (Successful Americans Ser.). 64p. (YA). 2009. (gr. 9-12). 22.95 *(978-1-4222-0521-1(5))* 2007. (gr. 7-18). pap. 9.95 *(978-1-4222-0862-5(1))* Mason Crest.

Brickweg, Jason. Christian. 2013. (Pro Wrestling Champions Ser.). (ENG., Illus.). 24p. (J). (gr. 3-7). lib. bdg. 26.95 *(978-1-60014-903-0(0)*, Torque Bks.) Bellwether Media.

—Zack Ryder. 2013. (Pro Wrestling Champions Ser.). (ENG., Illus.). 24p. (J). (gr. 3-7). lib. bdg. 26.95 *(978-1-60014-905-4(7)*, Torque Bks.) Bellwether Media.

Briggs, John. Pete Seeger the People's Singer. 2015. (ENG., Illus.). 112p. (J). pap. 6.99 *(978-0-9905160-7-1(5))* Atombank Bks.

Brill, Marlene Targ. Michelle Obama. 2009. (Illus.). 48p. (J). pap. 8.95 *(978-0-7613-5053-8(5))* Lerner Publishing Group.

—Michelle Obama: From Chicago's South Side to the White House. 2009. (Gateway Biographies Ser.). (ENG., Illus.). 48p. (gr. 4-8). 26.60 *(978-0-7613-5033-0(0))* Lerner Publishing Group.

Brooks, Aaron & Brown, Greg. Aaron Brooks: Rise Above. 2004. (Illus.). 48p. (J). 15.95 *(978-0-9634650-9-2(0))* Positively for Kids, Inc.

Brown, Jonatha A. Steven Spielberg, 1 vol. 2004. (Gente Que Hay Que Conocer (People We Should Know) Ser.). (SPA.). 24p. (gr. 2-4). lib. bdg. 24.67 *(978-0-8368-4585-3(4)*, 3d84b2cc-727e-4137-8f4b-a9cf9bc2fd8e, Weekly Reader Leveled Readers) Stevens, Gareth Publishing LLLP.

Brown, Risa. Day by Day with Carrie Underwood. 2014. (ENG., Illus.). 32p. (J). (gr. -1-2). 25.70 *(978-1-61228-631-0(3))* Mitchell Lane Pubs.

Brown, Terrell. Reverend Run (Run-D. M. C.) 2008. (Hip-Hop Ser.). (Illus.). 64p. (YA). (gr. 7-12). lib. bdg. 22.95 *(978-1-4222-0127-5(9))* Mason Crest.

Bryant, Jen. A River of Words: The Story of William Carlos Williams. Sweet, Melissa, illus. 2008. (ENG.). 34p. (J). (gr. 4-7). 17.50 *(978-0-8028-5302-8(1)*, Eerdmans Bks For Young Readers) Eerdmans, William B. Publishing Co.

Buckley, James. Who Were the Wright Brothers? 2014. (Who Was...? Ser.). lib. bdg. 16.00 *(978-0-606-35692-3(4))* Turtleback.

Burcaw, Shane. Not So Different: What You Really Want to Ask about Having a Disability. Carr, Matt, illus. 2017. (ENG.). 40p. (J). 19.99 *(978-1-62672-771-7(6)*, 900172893) Roaring Brook Pr.

Burgan, Michael. James Buchanan, 1 vol. 2011. (Presidents & Their Times Ser.). (ENG.). 96p. (gr. 6-6). 36.93 *(978-0-7614-4810-5(1)*, d50287da-903e-4eee-ba4d-c7d01410e0fc) Cavendish Square Publishing LLC.

Burgan, Michael & Who HQ. Who Was H. J. Heinz? Marchesi, Stephen, illus. 2019. (Who Was? Ser.). 112p. (J). (gr. 3-7). 5.99 *(978-0-448-48865-3(5))*; lib. bdg. 15.99 *(978-1-5247-9095-0(8))* Penguin Young Readers Group. (Penguin Workshop).

Burlingame, Jeff. Jennifer! Film Star Jennifer Lawrence, 1 vol. 2013. (Sizzling Celebrities Ser.). (ENG.). 48p. (gr. 4-6). pap. 11.53 *(978-1-4644-0279-1(5)*, bd5cea91-245d-4656-b418-86777670b7f7) Enslow Publishing, LLC.

—Jesse Owens: I Always Loved Running, 1 vol. 2008. (African-American Biography Library). (ENG., Illus.). 128p. (gr. 6-7). lib. bdg. 35.93 *(978-0-7660-3497-6(6)*, c6efb6b4-5e32-43da-8578-9363fa4e2314) Enslow Publishing, LLC.

—Malcolm X: I Believe in the Brotherhood of Man, All Men, 1 vol. 2010. (American Rebels Ser.). (ENG.). 160p. (gr. 9-10). 38.60 *(978-0-7660-3384-9(8)*, eb5e0065-c688-4ee6-a24b-d4a63dae6600) Enslow Publishing, LLC.

—Taylor Swift: Music Superstar, 1 vol. 2012. (Hot Celebrity Biographies Ser.). (ENG., Illus.). 48p. (gr. 5-7). lib. bdg. 27.93 *(978-0-7660-3870-7(X)*, c037aea0-2249-4265-80c6-d52d3ec5f273) Enslow Publishing, LLC.

Burns, Kylie. Carrie Underwood. 2013. (ENG., Illus.). 32p. (J). *(978-0-7787-0024-1(0))*; pap. *(978-0-7787-0043-2(7))* Crabtree Publishing Co.

Business Leaders Set, vols. 13, vol. 13. Incl. Faces Behind Beauty. Langley, Wanda. (Illus.). 160p. lib. bdg. 28.95 *(978-1-59935-097-4(1))*; Michael Dell. Friedman, Lauri S. 128p. lib. bdg. 28.95 *(978-1-59935-083-7(1))*; Oprah Winfrey. Hasday, Judy L. (Illus.). 128p. lib. bdg. 28.95 *(978-1-59935-096-7(3))*; Ralph Lauren. Weatherly, Myra. 112p. lib. bdg. 28.95 *(978-1-59935-084-4(X))*; Russell Simmons. Baughan, Brain. 112p. lib. bdg. 28.95 *(978-1-59935-075-2(0))*; Steve Jobs. Corrigan, Jim. 128p. lib. bdg. 27.95 *(978-1-59935-076-9(9))*; Warren Buffett. Johnson, Anne Janette. 128p. lib. bdg. 28.95 *(978-1-59935-080-6(7))*; (YA). (gr. 7-12). 2008. 2008. Set lib. bdg. 376.35 *(978-1-59935-094-3(7))* Reynolds, Morgan Inc.

Butts, Ellen R. & Schwartz, Joyce R. Carl Sagan. 2005. (Biography Ser.). (Illus.). 112p. (gr. 6-12). lib. bdg. 27.93 *(978-0-8225-4986-4(7))* Lerner Publishing Group.

Callery, Sean. Victor Wouk: The Father of the Hybrid Car, 1 vol. 2009. (Voices for Green Choices Ser.). (ENG., Illus.). 48p. (J). (gr. 5-9). pap. *(978-0-7787-4677-5(1))*; lib. bdg. *(978-0-7787-4664-5(X))* Crabtree Publishing Co.

Calvert, Patricia. Zebulon Pike: Lost in the Rockies, 1 vol. 2006. (Great Explorations Ser.). (ENG.). 80p. (gr. 6-6). 36.93 *(978-0-7614-1612-8(9)*, 4d70d369-f267-4e75-96e0-c7ced87675ca) Cavendish Square Publishing LLC.

Capua, Sarah De. Andrew Carnegie. 2007. (21st Century Skills Library: Life Skills Biographies Ser.). (ENG., Illus.). 48p. (gr. 4-8). lib. bdg. 34.93 *(978-1-60279-067-4(1)*, 200038) Cherry Lake Publishing.

Caravantes, Peggy. Writing Is My Business: The Story of O. Henry. 2006. (World Writers Ser.). (Illus.). 160p. (J). (gr. 3-7). lib. bdg. 27.95 *(978-1-59935-031-8(9))* Reynolds, Morgan Inc.

Carlson-Berne, Emma. Snoop Dogg. 2008. (Hip-Hop Ser.). (Illus.). 64p. (J). (gr. 7-12). lib. bdg. 22.95 *(978-1-4222-0129-9(5))* Mason Crest.

Carlson, Cheryl. Dr. Seuss [Scholastic]. 2011. (First Biographies - Writers, Artists, & Athletes Ser.). 24p. pap. 0.50 *(978-1-4296-6317-5(0)*, Pebble) Capstone.

Carole Marsh. Patriotic Biographies. 2004. (Patriotic Favorites Ser.). lib. bdg. 29.95 *(978-0-635-02225-7(7))*; 32p. (gr. 3-8). pap. 7.95 *(978-0-635-02224-0(9))* Gallopade International.

Carson, Mary Kay. Who Invented Home Video Games? Ralph Baer, 1 vol. 2012. (I Like Inventors! Ser.). (ENG., Illus.). 24p. (gr. k-2). 25.27 *(978-0-7660-3975-9(7)*, 498e6c21-f855-43d4-af28-1eaef6cd0409, Enslow Elementary) Enslow Publishing, LLC.

—Who Invented Television? Philo Farnsworth, 1 vol. 2012. (I Like Inventors! Ser.). (ENG.). 24p. (gr. k-2). 25.27 *(978-0-7660-3974-2(9)*, 39a14224-889a-4a53-a99a-869610cca7bb, Enslow Elementary) Enslow Publishing, LLC.

Casanova, Karen. Danica Patrick. 2010. (USA TODAY Lifeline Biographies Ser.). (ENG.). 112p. (gr. 6-12). lib. bdg. 34.60 *(978-0-7613-5222-8(8))* Lerner Publishing Group.

Casapulla, Louise. Ashlee Simpson. 2005. (Pop People Ser.). (Illus.). 137p. (J). *(978-0-439-76581-7(1))* Scholastic, Inc.

Casil, Amy Sterling. Tony Hawk: Skateboard Mogul, 1 vol. 2009. (Super Skateboarding Ser.). (ENG., Illus.). 48p. (gr. 5-8). (J). pap. 12.75 *(978-1-4358-5391-1(1)*, e4090b1b-10d9-47cd-9321-8950e192cf35); (YA). lib. bdg. 34.47 *(978-1-4358-5047-7(5)*, 16515748-a265-4496-9a7b-b8cd335e5797) Rosen Publishing Group, Inc., The.

Cefrey, Holly. From Slave to Cowboy: The Nat Love Story. 2009. (Great Moments in American History Ser.). 32p. (gr. 3-3). 47.90 *(978-1-61513-142-6(6))* Rosen Publishing Group, Inc., The.

—The Inventions of Alexander Graham Bell: The Telephone. 2009. (19th Century American Inventors Ser.). 24p. (gr. 2-3). 42.50 *(978-1-60854-949-8(6)*, PowerKids Pr.) Rosen Publishing Group, Inc., The.

—The Inventions of Eli Whitney: The Cotton Gin. 2009. (19th Century American Inventors Ser.). 24p. (gr. 2-3). 42.50 *(978-1-60854-951-1(8)*, PowerKids Pr.) Rosen Publishing Group, Inc., The.

—The Inventions of Granville Woods: The Railroad Telegraph System & the Third Rail. 2009. (19th Century American Inventors Ser.). 24p. (gr. 2-3). 42.50 *(978-1-60854-952-8(6)*, PowerKids Pr.) Rosen Publishing Group, Inc., The.

—The Inventions of Thomas Alva Edison: Father of the Light Bulb & the Motion Picture Camera. 2009. (19th Century American Inventors Ser.). 24p. (gr. 2-3). 42.50 *(978-1-60854-954-2(2)*, PowerKids Pr.) Rosen Publishing Group, Inc., The.

Cham, Stephanie. Yo Yo Ma. 2018. (Great Asian Americans Ser.). (ENG., Illus.). 24p. (J). (gr. -1-2). lib. bdg. 27.32 *(978-1-5157-9957-3(3)*, 136955, Capstone Pr.) Capstone.

Chatlien, Michael. Donovan McNabb. (Superstars of Pro Football Ser.). (Illus.). 64p. (YA). 2009. (gr. 7-12). lib. bdg. 22.95 *(978-1-4222-0559-4(2))* 2007. (gr. 5-18). pap. 9.95 *(978-1-4222-0829-8(X))* Mason Crest.

Christopher, Matt. Dale Earnhardt Sr. Matt Christopher Legends in Sports. 2007. (ENG., Illus.). 128p. (J). (gr. 3-7). per. 8.99 *(978-0-316-01114-3(2))* Little, Brown Bks. for Young Readers.

—On the Court with... Dwight Howard. 2010. (ENG., Illus.). 144p. (J). (gr. 3-7). pap. 10.99 *(978-0-316-08480-2(8))* Little, Brown Bks. for Young Readers.

—On the Court with... LeBron James. 2008. (ENG., Illus.). 176p. (J). (gr. 3-7). pap. 6.99 *(978-0-316-01630-8(6))* Little, Brown Bks. for Young Readers.

—On the Field with... Peyton & Eli Manning. 2008. (ENG.). 144p. (J). (gr. 3-7). pap. 10.99 *(978-0-316-03696-2(X))* Little, Brown Bks. for Young Readers.

Clark, Travis. Alex Rodriguez. 2010. (Role Model Athletes Ser.). (Illus.). 64p. (YA). (gr. 7-12). 22.95 *(978-1-4222-0488-7(X))* Mason Crest.

Cline-Ransome, Lesa. Benny Goodman & Teddy Wilson: Taking the Stage As the First Black-And-White Jazz Band in History. Ransome, James E., illus. 2014. (ENG.). 32p. (J). (gr. 3-7). 18.99 *(978-0-8234-2362-0(X))* Holiday Hse., Inc.

Cohon, Rhody & Deutsch, Stacia. Hot Pursuit: Murder in Mississippi. Orback, Craig, illus. 2010. (ENG.). 40p. (J). (gr. 3-5). pap. 7.95 *(978-0-7613-3956-4(6)*, 77cdd621-0509-4a81-bddf-ae8d265cd44d, Kar-Ben Publishing) Lerner Publishing Group.

Collard, Sneed B., III. David Crockett: Fearless Frontiersman, 1 vol. 2007. (American Heroes Ser.). (ENG., Illus.). 48p. (gr. 3-3). lib. bdg. 32.64 *(978-0-7614-2160-3(2)*, 2038e960-fec3-45e4-bd5d-bcb5eb5fba37) Cavendish Square Publishing LLC.

Collier Hillstrom, Laurie. Dale Earnhardt Jr, 1 vol. 2008. (People in the News Ser.). (ENG., Illus.). 104p. (gr. 7-7). lib. bdg. 41.03 *(978-1-4205-0088-2(0)*, 43f7f4b7-2d48-4de0-8faf-f7f67e0fd737, Lucent Pr.) Greenhaven Publishing LLC.

—Jay-Z, 1 vol. 2009. (People in the News Ser.). (ENG., Illus.). 96p. (gr. 7-7). 41.03 *(978-1-4205-0158-2(5)*, 2e0e1f79-fcbc-4297-ba70-22fd7a7cd7e1, Lucent Pr.) Greenhaven Publishing LLC.

Collins, Kathleen. Jesse James: Legendario Bandido del Oeste Americano, 1 vol. 2003. (Grandes Personajes en la Historia de Los Estados Unidos (Famous People in American History) Ser.). (SPA., Illus.). 32p. (gr. 3-4). lib. bdg. 29.13 *(978-0-8239-4136-0(1)*, ba04e6c3-aaa3-4019-8265-115cda3cdf68, Editorial Buenas Letras) Rosen Publishing Group, Inc., The.

—Marquis de Lafayette: French Hero of the American Revolution, 1 vol. 2003. (Famous People in American History / Grandes Personajes en la Historia de Los Estados Unidos Ser.). (ENG & SPA., Illus.). 32p. (gr. 2-3). lib. bdg. 29.13 *(978-0-8239-4163-6(9)*, 22b96b9a-22f4-4124-a502-dda13c946bf7, Editorial Buenas Letras) Rosen Publishing Group, Inc., The.

Conklin, Wendy. Robert E. Lee, 1 vol. rev. ed. 2005. (Social Studies: Informational Text Ser.). (ENG.). 24p. (gr. 4-8). pap. 10.99 *(978-0-7439-8918-3(X))* Teacher Created Materials, Inc.

Contro, Arturo. Landon Donovan, 1 vol. Benson, Megan, tr. 2008. (World Soccer Stars / Estrellas Del Fútbol Mundial Ser.). (SPA & ENG., Illus.). 24p. (J). (gr. 2-2). lib. bdg. 26.27 *(978-1-4042-7666-6(1)*, afb00a3b-138e-462c-bc34-f2d6500b3bbd) Rosen Publishing Group, Inc., The.

Cooper, Meghan. The Women's Suffrage Movement, 1 vol. 2017. (Interwar Years Ser.). (ENG., Illus.). 128p. (YA). (gr. 9-9). 47.36 *(978-1-5026-2711-7(6)*, 9fba2995-9bb5-4c20-8af0-ef0382acad3f) Cavendish Square Publishing LLC.

Corbett, Sue. Jeff Kinney, 1 vol. 2013. (Spotlight on Children's Authors Ser.). (ENG.). 48p. (gr. 4-4). 32.64 *(978-1-60870-932-8(9)*, 251aea30-2bca-4d41-ab75-488ef080d7b4) Cavendish Square Publishing LLC.

Corrick, James A. Dwayne "The Rock" Johnson. 2012. (Role Model Entertainers Ser.). 64p. (J). (gr. 7). 22.95 *(978-1-4222-2716-9(2))* Mason Crest.

Corrigan, Jim. John Marshall: The Story of John Marshall. 2011. (Supreme Court Justices Ser.). (Illus.). 112p. (J). 28.95 *(978-1-59935-159-6(5))* Reynolds, Morgan Inc.

Cotts, Nat. Daddy Yankee. 2009. (Hip-Hop 2 Ser.). (Illus.). 64p. (YA). (gr. 7-12). lib. bdg. 22.95 *(978-1-4222-0288-3(7))* Mason Crest.

—Don Omar. 2009. (Hip-Hop 2 Ser.). (Illus.). 64p. (YA). (gr. 7-12). lib. bdg. 22.95 *(978-1-4222-0290-6(9))* Mason Crest.

—Pitbull. 2009. (Hip-Hop 2 Ser.). (Illus.). 64p. (YA). (gr. 7-12). lib. bdg. 22.95 *(978-1-4222-0302-6(6))* Mason Crest.

—Young Jeezy. 2009. (Hip-Hop 2 Ser.). (Illus.). 64p. (YA). (gr. 7-12). lib. bdg. 22.95 *(978-1-4222-0306-4(9))* Mason Crest.

Crain, Cynthia D. & Lee, Dwight R. Milton Friedman. 2009. (Profiles in Economics Ser.). (Illus.). 144p. (YA). lib. bdg. 28.95 *(978-1-59935-108-7(0))* Reynolds, Morgan Inc.

Crayton, Lisa A. Collective Biographies of Slave Resistance Heroes, 1 vol. 2016. (Slavery & Slave Resistance Ser.). (ENG.). 128p. (gr. 6-6). 38.93 *(978-0-7660-7555-9(9)*, 8418be6d-0420-4e1e-8764-50d03426f104) Enslow Publishing, LLC.

Crompton, Samuel Willard. Barry Sanders. 2008. (Football Superstars Ser.). (ENG., Illus.). 120p. (gr. 7-12). 30.00 *(978-0-7910-9667-3(X)*, P159121, Facts On File) Infobase Holdings, Inc.

—100 Famous Americans Who Changed American History, 1 vol. 2005. (People Who Changed American History Ser.). (ENG., Illus.). 112p. (J). (gr. 5-8). lib. bdg. 33.67 *(978-0-8368-5768-9(2)*, 4dfb4b59-7a8a-4160-af79-0cebd53fe010, World Almanac Library) Stevens, Gareth Publishing LLLP.

Crum, Anna-Maria. Trackers of Dynamic Earth & Rastreadores de nuestra dinámica Tierra: 6 English, 6 Spanish Adaptations. 2011. (ENG & SPA.). (J). 97.00 net. *(978-1-4108-5718-7(2))* Benchmark Education Co.

Cuesta, Vivian. It Can Be Done: The Life & Legacy of César Chávez. 2003. (ENG., Illus.). 32p. (J). (gr. 6-8). pap. 9.00 net. *(978-0-7652-3271-7(5))* Celebration Pr.

Dakers, Diane. Calvin Klein: Fashion Design Superstar. 2010. (Crabtree Groundbreaker Biographies Ser.). (ENG., Illus.). 112p. (J). (gr. 5-8). lib. bdg. *(978-0-7787-2534-3(0))* Crabtree Publishing Co.

Daniel Fernandez Memorial Center Projec. Man of Honor: The Story of Daniel Fernandez. 2009. 32p. pap. 15.49 *(978-1-4389-8338-7(7))* AuthorHouse.

Dann, Sarah. Beyonce, 1 vol. 2013. (ENG., Illus.). 32p. (J). pap. *(978-0-7787-0039-5(9))* Crabtree Publishing Co.

—Lindsey Vonn. 2013. (ENG., Illus.). 32p. (J). *(978-0-7787-0025-8(9))*; pap. *(978-0-7787-0067-8(4))* Crabtree Publishing Co.

Darraj, Susan Muaddi. Amy Tan. 2007. (ENG.). 112p. (gr. 7-12). lib. bdg. 35.00 *(978-0-7910-9269-9(0)*, P124651, Facts On File) Infobase Holdings, Inc.

De Medeiros, James. Justin Timberlake. 2008. (Remarkable People Ser.). (Illus.). 24p. (J). (gr. 4-6). pap. 8.95 *(978-1-59036-983-8(1))*; lib. bdg. 24.45 *(978-1-59036-982-1(3))* Weigl Pubs., Inc.

de Mille, Agnes. Dance to the Piper. 2015. (Illus.). 368p. pap. 17.95 *(978-1-59017-908-6(0)*, NYRB Classics) New York Review of Bks., Inc., The.

DeCarolis, Lisa. Alexander Hamilton: Federalist & Founding Father. 2009. (Library of American Lives & Times Ser.). 112p. (gr. 5-5). 69.20 *(978-1-60853-470-8(7))* Rosen Publishing Group, Inc., The.

DeGraw, Aleine. Alexander Hamilton: American Statesman. 2009. (Primary Sources of Famous People in American History Ser.). 32p. (gr. 2-3). 47.90 *(978-1-60851-646-9(6))* Rosen Publishing Group, Inc., The.

—Alexander Hamilton: American Statesman / Estadista Estadounidense. 2009. (Famous People in American History/Grandes personajes en la historia de los Estados Unidos Ser.). (SPA.). 32p. (gr. 2-3). 47.90 *(978-1-61512-536-4(1)*, Editorial Buenas Letras) Rosen Publishing Group, Inc., The.

—Alexander Hamilton: Estadista estadounidense (Alexander Hamilton: American Statesman) 2009. (Grandes personajes en la historia de los Estados Unidos (Famous People in American History) Ser.). 32p. (gr. 2-3). 47.90 *(978-1-61512-788-7(7)*, Editorial Buenas Letras) Rosen Publishing Group, Inc., The.

Denenberg, Dennis & Roscoe, Lorraine. 50 American Heroes Every Kid Should Meet, 3rd Edition. 2nd rev. ed. 2016. (ENG., Illus.). 120p. (YA). (gr. 6-12). E-Book 54.65 *(978-1-5124-1329-8(1)*, Millbrook Pr.) Lerner Publishing Group.

—50 American Heroes Every Kid Should Meet (Revised Edition) rev. ed. 2005. (ENG., Illus.). 128p. (gr. 6-12). per. 14.95 *(978-0-7613-9548-5(2)*, First Avenue Editions) Lerner Publishing Group.

dePaola, Tomie. I'm Still Scared. 2007. (26 Fairmount Avenue Bks.). (Illus.). 83p. (gr. 2-5). 17.00 *(978-0-7569-8150-1(6))* Perfection Learning Corp.

—Things Will Never Be the Same. dePaola, Tomie, illus. 2004. (26 Fairmount Avenue Bks.). (Illus.). 69p. (J). (gr. 3-7). 13.65 *(978-0-7569-2951-0(2))* Perfection Learning Corp.

—What a Year. A 26 Fairmount Avenue Book, Vol. 4. 2004. (26 Fairmount Avenue Ser.). 75p. (J). (gr. 2-5). pap. 17.00 incl. audio *(978-0-8072-0657-7(1)*, Listening Library) Random Hse. Audio Publishing Group.

DePrince, Michaela & Deprince, Elaine. Ballerina Dreams: from Orphan to Dancer (Step into Reading, Step 4) Morrison, Frank, illus. 2014. (Step into Reading Ser.). (ENG.). 48p. (J). (gr. 2-4). 5.99 *(978-0-385-75515-3(5)*, Random Hse. Bks. for Young Readers) Random Hse. Children's Bks.

Deutsch, Stacia & Cohon, Rhody. Carlos Mencia. 2009. (Sharing the American Dream Ser.). 64p. (YA). (gr. 7-12). 22.95 *(978-1-4222-0578-5(9))* Mason Crest.

—Jermaine Dupri. (Sharing the American Dream Ser.). 64p. (YA). (gr. 7-12). 2009. 22.95 *(978-1-4222-0581-5(9))* 2007. pap. 9.95 *(978-1-4222-0744-4(7))* Mason Crest.

—Samuel L. Jackson. 2009. (Sharing the American Dream Ser.). (Illus.). 64p. (YA). (gr. 7-12). 22.95 *(978-1-4222-0580-8(0))* Mason Crest.

Devera, Czeena. John Muir. Bane, Jeff, illus. 2017. (My Early Library: My Itty-Bitty Bio Ser.). (ENG.). 24p. (J). (gr. k-1). lib. bdg. 30.64 *(978-1-63472-814-0(9)*, 209682) Cherry Lake Publishing.

DiConsiglio, John. Young Americans: Tales of Teenage Immigrants. 2005. (Illus.). 43p. *(978-0-439-12405-8(0))* Scholastic, Inc.

DiPrimio, Pete. Drew Brees. 2010. (Blue Banner Biography Ser.). (Illus.). 32p. (YA). (gr. 4-7). lib. bdg. 25.70 *(978-1-58415-911-7(1))* Mitchell Lane Pubs.

—Dwyane Wade. 2011. (Robbie Reader Ser.). 32p. (J). (gr. 2-5). lib. bdg. 25.70 *(978-1-61228-063-9(3))* Mitchell Lane Pubs.

—Tom Brady. 2008. (Robbie Reader Ser.). (Illus.). 32p. (YA). (gr. 2-5). lib. bdg. 25.70 *(978-1-58415-718-2(6))* Mitchell Lane Pubs.

Ditchfield, Christin. Condoleezza Rice: America's Leading Stateswoman. 2006. (Great Life Stories Ser.). (ENG., Illus.). 112p. (J). (gr. 6-8). lib. bdg. 30.50 *(978-0-531-13874-8(7)*, Watts, Franklin) Scholastic Library Publishing.

Dixon-Engel, Tara & Jackson, Mike. Neil Armstrong: One Giant Leap for Mankind. 2008. (Sterling Biographies(r) Ser.). (ENG., Illus.). 128p. (J). (gr. 5). pap. 5.95 *(978-1-4027-4496-9(X))* Sterling Publishing Co., Inc.

DK. DK Readers L3: Real-Life Heroes. 2017. (DK Readers Level 3 Ser.). (ENG., Illus.). 64p. (J). (gr. 2-4). pap. 3.99 *(978-1-4654-6244-2(9)*, DK Children) Dorling Kindersley Publishing, Inc.

Doak, Robin S. Barack Obama. 2013. (True Book(tm), A — Biographies Ser.). (ENG., Illus.). 48p. (J). lib. bdg. 31.00 *(978-0-531-21904-1(6))*; pap. 6.95 *(978-0-531-23875-2(X))* Scholastic Library Publishing.

Dodson Wade, Mary. Amazing Champion of the Earth Rachel Carson, 1 vol. 2009. (Amazing Americans Ser.). (ENG., Illus.). 24p. (gr. k-2). lib. bdg. 25.27 *(978-0-7660-3283-5(3)*, a572f869-c821-4721-af77-544ea995ee79) Enslow Publishing, LLC.

—Amazing Olympic Athlete Wilma Rudolph, 1 vol. 2009. (Amazing Americans Ser.). (ENG., Illus.). 24p. (gr. k-2). lib. bdg. 25.27 *(978-0-7660-3282-8(5)*, 34b5dfbd-0b67-4e34-97fe-24c1037bcaa6) Enslow Publishing, LLC.

Doeden, Matt. Lance Armstrong. 2006. (Sports Heroes & Legends Ser.). (ENG., Illus.). 120p. (gr. 5-12). lib. bdg. 30.60 *(978-0-8225-5959-7(5))* Lerner Publishing Group.

—Miguel Cabrera: Baseball Superstar, 1 vol. 2014. (Superstar Athletes Ser.). (ENG.). 24p. (J). (gr. 1-3). lib. bdg. 27.99 *(978-1-4765-8602-1(0)*, 125252) Capstone.

—Peyton Manning. 2008. (Sports Heroes & Legends Ser.). (YA). (gr. 7-12). lib. bdg. 30.60 *(978-0-8225-9041-5(7))* Twenty First Century Bks.

—Phil Kessel. 2015. (Hockey Superstars Ser.). (ENG., Illus.). 32p. (J). (gr. 3-4). pap. 7.95 *(978-1-4914-9022-8(5)*, 131545); lib. bdg. 28.65 *(978-1-4296-8278-7(7)*, 118478) Capstone.

—Shaun White. 2006. (Amazing Athletes Ser.). (Illus.). 32p. (J). (gr. 2-5). pap. 6.95 *(978-0-8225-6841-4(1)*, First Avenue Editions); lib. bdg. 23.93 *(978-0-8225-6840-7(3)*, Lerner Pubns.) Lerner Publishing Group.

—Surviving a World War II Prison Camp: Louis Zamperini. 2019. (They Survived (Alternator Books (r)) Ser.). (ENG., Illus.). 32p. (J). (gr. 3-6). 29.32 *(978-1-5415-2354-8(7)*, 7bdb1ea4-c7dc-400a-952c-f0e87a35174b, Lerner Pubns.) Lerner Publishing Group.

—Will Smith. 2007. (Just the Facts Biographies Ser.). (ENG., Illus.). 112p. (gr. 5-12). lib. bdg. 27.93 *(978-0-8225-6608-3(7)*, Lerner Pubns.) Lerner Publishing Group.

Doeden, Matt & Savage, Jeff. Eli Manning. 2009. (Sports Heroes & Legends Ser.). (ENG.). (gr. 5-12). pap. 56.72 *(978-0-7613-4808-5(5))* Lerner Publishing Group.

Doeden, Matt & Stewart, Mark. Peyton Manning. 2009. (Sports Heroes & Legends Ser.). (ENG.). (gr. 5-12). pap. 56.72 *(978-0-7613-4809-2(3))* Lerner Publishing Group.

Domblewski, Carol. Citizens Who Made a Difference: Text Pairs. 2008. (Bridges/Navigators Ser.). (J). (gr. 3). 81.00 *(978-1-4108-8354-4(X))* Benchmark Education Co.

Dougherty, Terri. Ben Stiller, 1 vol. 2007. (People in the News Ser.). (ENG., Illus.). 104p. (gr. 7-7). lib. bdg. 41.03 *(978-1-59018-723-4(7)*, 72207efe-c2b1-438d-a7e8-610f8d5842a3, Lucent Pr.) Greenhaven Publishing LLC.

—Tobey Maguire. 2010. (Modern Role Models Ser.). (Illus.). 64p. (J). (gr. 7-12). 22.95 *(978-1-4222-0505-1(3))* Mason Crest.

Down, Susan. Theodore Weld: Architect of Abolitionism. 2013. (ENG., Illus.). 64p. (J). *(978-0-7787-1062-2(9))*; pap. *(978-0-7787-1065-3(3))* Crabtree Publishing Co.

Doyle, Abby Badach. Diaries & Autobiographies Throughout American History. 2019. (Journey to the Past: Investigating Primary Sources Ser.). (ENG.). 32p. (gr. 4-5). 63.00 *(978-1-5382-4035-9(1))* Stevens, Gareth Publishing LLLP.

Doyle, Bill H. Behind Enemy Lines. 2009. 135p. (J). pap. *(978-0-545-14705-7(0))* Scholastic, Inc.

Driscoll, Laura. Hillary Clinton: An American Journey. Wood, Judith V., illus. 2008. (ENG.). 48p. (J). (gr. 3-6). 16.19 *(978-0-448-44787-2(8))* Penguin Young Readers Group.

—Presidential Pets. Slade, Christian, illus. 2009. (ENG.). 64p. (J). (gr. 1-3). 17.44 *(978-0-448-45250-0(2)*, Grosset & Dunlap) Penguin Publishing Group.

Duling, Kaitlyn. Benjamin Franklin: Inventor & Founding Father, 1 vol. 2019. (Great American Entrepreneurs Ser.). (ENG.). 128p. (gr. 9-9). pap. 22.16 *(978-1-5026-4536-4(X)*, 466b4ac5-f5a1-400d-bd8d-c6e4a33af683) Cavendish Square Publishing LLC.

—Stephen Curry: NBA Sharpshooter, 1 vol. 2019. (At the Top of Their Game Ser.). (ENG.). 112p. (gr. 9-9). pap. 20.99 *(978-1-5026-5112-9(2)*, ad2ca8a9-a1f1-49bf-a4c3-039f75b9df3d) Cavendish Square Publishing LLC.

Edge, Laura B. Hilary Duff: Celebrity with Heart, 1 vol. 2010. (Celebrities with Heart Ser.). (ENG., Illus.). 128p. (gr. 6-7). pap. 13.88 *(978-1-59845-205-1(3)*, d3a9e6ab-9378-42bb-b233-7e7ef8557987) Enslow Publishing, LLC.

Edgers, Geoff. Who Is Stan Lee? 2014. (Who Is...? Ser.). lib. bdg. 16.00 *(978-0-606-36175-0(8))* Turtleback.

Edwards, Ethan. All-Star Players: Set 2, 6 vols. Incl. Meet Derek Jeter: Captain of the New York Yankees. lib. bdg. 28.93 *(978-1-4042-4488-7(3)*, 24d1ceed-b96f-4658-9d25-85ded96adc7f); Meet Kevin Garnett: Basketball's Big Ticket. lib. bdg. 28.93 *(978-1-4042-4490-0(5)*, 84b490fb-50de-4512-b8dd-aef5080f8b2a); Meet LaDainian Tomlinson: Football's Fastest Running Back. lib. bdg. 28.93 *(978-1-4042-4491-7(3)*, ebe26808-364d-40ec-8670-44cc1f5490a6); (Illus.). 32p. (YA). (gr. 4-5). 2008. (All-Star Players Ser.). (ENG.). 2008. Set lib. bdg. 86.79 *(978-1-4358-2564-2(0)*, f8cacf69-255e-445a-9789-a59ccc4a8526, PowerKids Pr.) Rosen Publishing Group, Inc., The.

Edwards, Karen. Christopher Reeve: A Real-Life Superhero. 2005. (Illus.). 32p. (J). *(978-0-669-51411-7(X))* Great Source Education Group, Inc.

Egan, Jill. Hillary Rodham Clinton, 1 vol. 2009. (People We Should Know (Second Series) Ser.). (ENG., Illus.). 48p. (J). (gr. 3-5). pap. 11.50 *(978-1-4339-2193-3(6)*, 3ddc1eb3-4b6e-4c00-bd8c-5357bfae7b05); lib. bdg. 33.67 *(978-1-4339-2188-9(X)*, 42b88186-030f-4473-842e-b1101580a9ad) Stevens, Gareth Publishing LLLP. (Gareth Stevens Learning Library).

TUV

Egan, Tracie. Francisca Alvarez: El Angel de Goliad, 1 vol. 2003. (Grandes Personajes en la Historia de Los Estados Unidos (Famous People in American History) Ser.). (SPA., Illus.). 32p. (gr. 3-4). lib. bdg. 29.13 *(978-0-8239-4133-9(7),* c1861354-ecb1-43de-923c-4a38ac8ba1d3, Editorial Buenas Letras) Rosen Publishing Group, Inc., The.

Eggleston, Edward. Stories of Great Americans for Little Americans. 2017. (ENG., Illus.). (J). 22.95 *(978-1-374-87406-0(X));* pap. 12.95 *(978-1-374-87405-3(1))* Capitol Communications, Inc.

—Stories of Great Americans for Little Americans. 2015. (ENG., Illus.). (J). 23.95 *(978-1-298-74009-0(6));* 23.95 *(978-1-298-60320-3(X))* Creative Media Partners, LLC.

—Stories of Great Americans for Little Americans. 2007. 120p. per. *(978-1-4065-1784-2(4))* Dodo Pr.

—Stories of Great Americans for Little Americans. 2010. 162p. pap. 14.95 *(978-1-60444-104-8(6))* IndoEuropeanPublishing.com.

—Stories of Great Americans for Little Americans. 2004. reprint ed. pap. 1.99 *(978-1-4192-4958-7(4));* pap. 15.95 *(978-1-4191-4958-0(X))* Kessinger Publishing, LLC.

—Stories of Great Americans for Little Americans (Yesterday's Classics) 2007. (ENG.). 172p. (J). per. 9.95 *(978-1-59915-084-0(0))* Yesterday's Classics.

El Nabli, Dina. Danica Patrick, 1 vol. 2009. (People We Should Know (Second Series) Ser.). (ENG.). 32p. (J). (gr. 3-5). pap. 11.50 *(978-1-4339-0158-4(7),* 7fe94665-8b6a-400d-9586-1ddf46deb4be); lib. bdg. 33.67 *(978-1-4339-0018-1(1),* b0dc56d2-d453-4ca7-a6e3-72f0fd89b90e) Stevens, Gareth Publishing LLLP. (Gareth Stevens Learning Library).

Eldridge, Stephen. Logan! Rising Star Logan Lerman, 1 vol. 2013. (Sizzling Celebrities Ser.). (ENG.). 48p. (gr. 4-6). pap. 11.53 *(978-1-4644-0281-4(7),* 4a16c724-95dc-4a06-b18a-303a9b9dc39d) Enslow Publishing, LLC.

Eli Manning. 2009. (Amazing Athletes Ser.). (gr. 2-5). pap. 6.95 *(978-0-7613-4137-6(4),* First Avenue Editions) Lerner Publishing Group.

Elliot, Henry. Frederick Douglass: From Slavery to Statesman, 1 vol. 2009. (Voices for Freedom Ser.). (ENG., Illus.). 64p. (J). (gr. 5-8). pap. *(978-0-7787-4836-6(7));* lib. bdg. *(978-0-7787-4820-5(0))* Crabtree Publishing Co.

—John Muir: Protecting & Preserving the Environment. 2009. (Voices for Green Choices Ser.). (ENG., Illus.). 48p. (J). (gr. 5-9). pap. *(978-0-7787-4681-2(X));* lib. bdg. *(978-0-7787-4668-3(2))* Crabtree Publishing Co.

Esty, Amos. The Liberator: The Story of William Lloyd Garrison. 2011. (Civil Rights Leaders Ser.). 144p. 28.95 *(978-1-59935-137-7(4))* Reynolds, Morgan Inc.

Etingoff, Kim. Jennifer Aniston. 2012. (Illus.). 64p. (J). pap. *(978-1-4222-2483-0(X))* Mason Crest.

—Jennifer Aniston: From Friends to Films. 2012. (Extraordinary Success with a High School Diploma or Less Ser.). (Illus.). 64p. (J). (gr. 7-8). 22.95 *(978-1-4222-2480-9(5))* Mason Crest.

—T. I. 2009. (Hip-Hop 2 Ser.). (Illus.). 64p. (YA). (gr. 7-12). lib. bdg. 22.95 *(978-1-4222-0303-3(4))* Mason Crest.

Fandel, Jennifer. George Eastman & the Kodak Camera, 1 vol. Purcell, Gordon, illus. 2007. (Inventions & Discovery Ser.). (ENG.). 32p. (J). (gr. 3-9). 31.32 *(978-0-7368-6848-8(8),* 87929, Capstone Pr.) Capstone.

Fedorko, Jamie. Charles Barkley. (Sharing the American Dream Ser.). 64p. (YA). (gr. 7-12). 2009. 22.95 *(978-1-4222-0576-1(2))* 2007. pap. 9.95 *(978-1-4222-0737-6(4))* Mason Crest.

Fein, Eric. High Noon: Wild Bill Hickok & the Code of the Old West. 2009. (Great Moments in American History Ser.). 32p. (gr. 3-3). 47.90 *(978-1-61513-145-7(0))* Rosen Publishing Group, Inc., The.

Feinstein, Stephen. Muhammad Ali, 1 vol. 2008. (African-American Heroes Ser.). (ENG., Illus.). 24p. (gr. k-2). lib. bdg. 25.27 *(978-0-7660-2763-3(5),* cfc47266-0b5e-4d60-aa69-abcaa7b98243, Enslow Elementary) Enslow Publishing, LLC.

Felix, Rebecca. Carl Sagan: Celebrated Cosmos Scholar. 2018. (Space Crusaders Ser.). (ENG., Illus.). 32p. (J). (gr. 3-6). lib. bdg. 32.79 *(978-1-5321-1705-3(1),* 30698, Checkerboard Library) ABDO Publishing Co.

Ferris, Jeri Chase. Noah Webster & His Words. Kirsch, Vincent X., illus. 2015. (ENG.). 32p. (J). (gr. 1-4). 7.99 *(978-0-544-58242-2(X),* 1613671, Clarion Bks.) HarperCollins Pubs.

Fighting the Monster. 2004. (YA). ring bd. 59.95 *(978-0-9661256-2-7(2))* Youth Communication - New York Center.

Figley, Marty Rhodes. Prisoner for Liberty. Orback, Craig, illus. 2009. (On My Own History Ser.). (ENG.). 48p. (J). (gr. 2-4). pap. 8.99 *(978-0-8225-9022-4(0),* 71b3881b-9399-4d9c-a66b-0223c579b66b, First Avenue Editions) Lerner Publishing Group.

Finley, Toiya Kristen. Russell Simmons. 2009. (Sharing the American Dream Ser.). (Illus.). 64p. (YA). (gr. 7-12). 22.95 *(978-1-4222-0584-6(3))* Mason Crest.

Fisher, Doris. Jackson Sundown: Native American Bronco Buster, 1 vol. Cotton, Sarah, illus. 2018. (ENG.). 32p. (gr. -1-3). 16.99 *(978-1-4556-2361-7(X),* Pelican Publishing) Arcadia Publishing.

Fishman, Jon M. Jose Altuve. 2017. (Sports All-Stars (Lerner (tm) Sports) Ser.). (ENG., Illus.). 32p. (J). (gr. 2-5). pap. 9.99 *(978-1-5124-5615-8(2),* 01d63f78-d430-4686-9f1a-0c448ca6a6de); lib. bdg. 29.32 *(978-1-5124-3923-6(1),* 9a542d7f-68c0-430d-8184-fea00d309e87, Lerner Pubns.) Lerner Publishing Group.

—Kawhi Leonard. 2018. (Sports All-Stars (Lerner (tm) Sports) Ser.). (ENG., Illus.). 32p. (J). (gr. 2-5). pap. 9.99 *(978-1-5415-1203-0(0),* 83f6f79d-f1fd-43c5-80ed-56693dc5050e) Lerner Publishing Group.

—Miguel Cabrera. 2013. (Amazing Athletes Ser.). (ENG., Illus.). 32p. (J). (gr. 2-5). lib. bdg. 26.65 *(978-1-4677-1558-4(1),* 173e8988-79c3-4885-9a51-3bd8340a1fdd, Lerner Pubns.) Lerner Publishing Group.

—Rob Gronkowski. 2017. (Sports All-Stars (Lerner (tm) Sports) Ser.). (ENG., Illus.). 32p. (J). (gr. 2-5). pap. 9.99 *(978-1-5124-5619-6(5),* 02cff713-65af-423e-bd1f-9743181f1780); lib. bdg. 29.32 *(978-1-5124-3924-3(X),* 6ead3047-e6ca-4b1e-a625-3d08a87a4162, Lerner Pubns.) Lerner Publishing Group.

—Ronda Rousey. 2016. (Amazing Athletes Ser.). (ENG., Illus.). 32p. (J). (gr. 2-5). 26.65 *(978-1-5124-1333-5(X),* c558c02e-c55c-4334-afb5-be33a0b09be8, Lerner Pubns.) Lerner Publishing Group.

Fleischman, Sid. Escape! The Story of the Great Houdini. 2006. (Illus.). (J). (ENG.). 224p. (gr. 3-7). 19.99 *(978-0-06-085094-4(9),* Greenwillow Bks.); 210p. (gr. 4-8). lib. bdg. 19.89 *(978-0-06-085095-1(7))* HarperCollins Pubs.

Fleming, Candace. The Great & Only Barnum: the Tremendous, Stupendous Life of Showman P. T. Barnum. Fenwick, Ray, illus. 2009. 160p. (J). (gr. 3-7). 19.99 *(978-0-375-84197-2(0),* Schwartz & Wade Bks.) Random Hse. Children's Bks.

Flynn, Jean. Henry B. Gonzalez: Rebel with a Cause. 2004. (Illus.). 140p. (J). (gr. 3-7). per. 16.95 *(978-1-57168-846-0(3))* Eakin Pr.

Foran, Jill. Annie Oakley. 2018. (J). *(978-1-4896-9568-0(0),* AV2 by Weigl) Weigl Pubs., Inc.

Franke, Amim. Miranda Lambert, 1 vol. 2010. (Country Music Stars Ser.). (ENG.). 32p. (J). (gr. 1-1). pap. 11.50 *(978-1-4339-3936-5(3),* 1ac6038a-53ca-4aca-aa55-3f7b554a8f05); lib. bdg. 27.93 *(978-1-4339-3935-8(5),* 22afc16e-ef22-4cc4-9739-21c0b2c61a8f) Stevens, Gareth Publishing LLLP.

Franke, Livia. Kathleen Battle: American Soprano, 1 vol. 2010. (Inspiring Lives Ser.). (ENG., Illus.). 32p. (J). (gr. 1-1). pap. 11.50 *(978-1-4339-3635-7(6),* e2a04fd1-a147-4a8e-bd94-b77e16bef2f3); lib. bdg. 27.93 *(978-1-4339-3634-0(8),* f4a249ea-94dd-43a0-a7bc-1ae15f054f04) Stevens, Gareth Publishing LLLP.

Franks, Katie. Ashley Tisdale. 2009. (Kid Stars! Ser.). 24p. (gr. 2-3). 42.50 *(978-1-61513-876-0(5),* PowerKids Pr.) Rosen Publishing Group, Inc., The.

—Drake Bell & Josh Peck. (Kid Stars! Ser.). 24p. (gr. 2-3). 2009. 42.50 *(978-1-61513-879-1(X),* PowerKids Pr.) 2008. (ENG.). pap. 10.40 *(978-1-4042-4534-1(0),* d273d9f4-588c-412a-9fd9-58dc964a7ec9, Rosen Classroom) Rosen Publishing Group, Inc., The.

—Kid Stars! Set 1, 12 vols. Incl. Ashley Tisdale. lib. bdg. 26.27 *(978-1-4042-4468-9(9),* d5c6f82f-662d-4ccb-a434-8155a57f2c22); Drake Bell & Josh Peck. lib. bdg. 26.27 *(978-1-4042-4463-4(8),* c49f09da-1624-48b8-aa53-61c2b3e4917a); Dylan & Cole Sprouse. lib. bdg. 26.27 *(978-1-4042-4464-1(6),* 017490d4-eee6-45fa-be2f-f45e3488c2d3); Miley Cyrus. lib. bdg. 26.27 *(978-1-4042-4467-2(0),* 900ab84a-0891-4fb7-8f15-64814bbe5ace); Miranda Cosgrove. lib. bdg. 26.27 *(978-1-4042-4466-5(2),* b8ed3d55-a4f3-48ac-be20-811bfd7545fd); Zac Efron. lib. bdg. 26.27 *(978-1-4042-4465-8(4),* 39c1ef4d-2e95-4600-a758-a785ac40a6d4); (Illus.). 24p. (J). (gr. 2-3). (Kid Stars! Ser.). (ENG.). 2008. Set lib. bdg. 157.62 *(978-1-4358-2550-5(0),* 647c8190-858c-44b4-8387-8da6e0d955c7, PowerKids Pr.) Rosen Publishing Group, Inc., The.

—Zac Efron, 1 vol. 2008. (Kid Stars! Ser.). (ENG., Illus.). 24p. (J). (gr. 2-3). lib. bdg. 26.27 *(978-1-4042-4465-8(4),* 39c1ef4d-2e95-4600-a758-a785ac40a6d4, PowerKids Pr.) Rosen Publishing Group, Inc., The.

Frederick, Shane. John Tavares. 2015. (Hockey Superstars Ser.). (ENG., Illus.). 32p. (J). (gr. 3-4). pap. 7.95 *(978-1-4914-9025-9(X),* 131548); lib. bdg. 28.65 *(978-1-62065-158-2(0),* 120859) Capstone.

Friesen, Helen Lepp. Uncle Sam with Code. 2012. (AV2 American Icons Ser.). (ENG., Illus.). 24p. (J). (gr. -1-3). pap. 12.95 *(978-1-61913-304-4(0),* AV2 by Weigl) Weigl Pubs., Inc.

Frisch, Aaron. Jesse James. 2005. (Legends of the West (Creative Education) Ser.) (Illus.). 48p. (J). (gr. 5-9). lib. bdg. 21.95 *(978-1-58341-338-8(3),* Creative Education) Creative Co., The.

Fry, Erin. Arthur Ashe Against the Odds. 2005. (Voices Reading Ser.). (Illus.). 16p. (J). *(978-0-7367-2915-4(1))* Zaner-Bloser, Inc.

Furgang, Adam. Famous Immigrant Artists, 1 vol. 2017. (Making America Great: Immigrant Success Stories Ser.). (ENG.). 112p. (gr. 7-7). 38.93 *(978-0-7660-9245-7(3),* 2884c951-c7d4-49d0-9f20-ba7a81df150e) Enslow Publishing, LLC.

Furgang, Kathy. Jeff Kinney: Children's Book Author & Cartoonist, 1 vol. 2017. (Junior Biographies Ser.). (ENG.). 24p. (J). (gr. 3-4). pap. 10.35 *(978-0-7660-9061-3(2),* 4e2421ca-6474-4575-8ee0-2492cefba734) Enslow Publishing, LLC.

Gagne, Tammy. Darius Rucker. 2014. (Illus.). 32p. (J). (gr. 1-4). 25.70 *(978-1-61228-639-6(9))* Mitchell Lane Pubs.

—Day by Day with Calvin Johnson. 2014. (Illus.). 32p. (J). (gr. -1-2). 25.70 *(978-1-61228-633-4(X))* Mitchell Lane Pubs.

—Day by Day with Elena Delle Donne. 2014. (Illus.). 32p. (J). (gr. -1-2). 25.70 *(978-1-61228-634-1(8))* Mitchell Lane Pubs.

—Day by Day with Shaun White. 2011. (Day by Day with... Ser.). (Illus.). 32p. (J). (gr. -1-2). lib. bdg. 25.70 *(978-1-58415-986-5(3))* Mitchell Lane Pubs.

—Derek Hough. 2017. lib. bdg. 25.70 *(978-1-68020-118-5(2))* Mitchell Lane Pubs.

—Hope Solo. 2014. (Illus.). 32p. (J). 25.70 *(978-1-61228-642-6(9))* Mitchell Lane Pubs.

—Kesha. 2011. (Blue Banner Biography Ser.). (Illus.). 32p. (YA). (gr. 4-7). lib. bdg. 25.70 *(978-1-61228-052-3(8))* Mitchell Lane Pubs.

—Roy Halladay. 2011. (Robbie Reader Ser.). (Illus.). 32p. (J). (gr. 2-5). lib. bdg. 25.70 *(978-1-61228-061-5(7))* Mitchell Lane Pubs.

—What It's Like to Be America Ferrara. de la Vega, Eida, tr. from ENG. 2010. (What It's Like to Be/Que se Siente al Ser Ser.). (ENG & SPA., Illus.). 32p. (J). (gr. -1-2). lib. bdg. 25.70 *(978-1-58415-854-7(9))* Mitchell Lane Pubs.

—What It's Like to Be Oscar de la Hoya. 2012. (Illus.). 32p. (J). lib. bdg. 25.70 *(978-1-61228-322-7(5))* Mitchell Lane Pubs.

—What Its Like to Be Sonia Sotomayor. de la Vega, Eida, tr. from SPA. 2010. (What It's Like to Be/Que Se Siente al Ser Ser.). (ENG & SPA., Illus.). 32p. (J). (gr. -1-2). lib. bdg. 25.70 *(978-1-58415-853-0(0))* Mitchell Lane Pubs.

Gaines, Alison. Mary Edwards Walker: The Only Female Medal of Honor Recipient, 1 vol. 2017. (Fearless Female Soldiers, Explorers, & Aviators Ser.). (ENG.). 128p. (YA). (gr. 9-9). 47.36 *(978-1-5026-2745-2(0),* 4f3af724-2a96-4315-a3da-8590d2a2d372) Cavendish Square Publishing LLC.

Gallagher, Jim. Daniel Morgan: Fighting Frontiersman. 2006. (J). pap. *(978-1-59556-020-9(3));* (Illus.). 88p. (gr. 5-11). lib. bdg. 23.95 *(978-1-59556-015-5(7))* OTTN Publishing.

Garcia, Tracy J. Eli Whitney, 1 vol. 2013. (Jr. Graphic American Inventors Ser.). (ENG., Illus.). 24p. (J). (gr. 2-3). lib. bdg. 28.93 *(978-1-4777-0075-4(7),* b6538853-61ed-4ace-97a8-8ab78d25319a, PowerKids Pr.) Rosen Publishing Group, Inc., The.

—Thomas Edison, 1 vol. 2013. (Jr. Graphic American Inventors Ser.). (ENG., Illus.). 24p. (J). (gr. 2-3). pap. 11.60 *(978-1-4777-0137-9(0),* 74060090-11f8-4642-b468-299d14d4a649); lib. bdg. 28.93 *(978-1-4777-0076-1(5),* 19353677-59b5-4c3f-8d32-3635b9246a0e) Rosen Publishing Group, Inc., The. (PowerKids Pr.).

Gaskill, Rachel. Agnes Demille, 1 vol. 2005. (Library of American Choreographers Ser.). (ENG., Illus.). 48p. (J). (gr. 5-8). lib. bdg. 34.47 *(978-1-4042-0444-7(X),* 8518c328-94a6-48f4-89d9-7baaecf64f9a) Rosen Publishing Group, Inc., The.

Gaspar, Joe. Dustin Pedroia, 1 vol. 2010. (Baseball's MVPs Ser.). (ENG., Illus.). 24p. (J). (gr. 1-2). pap. 9.85 *(978-1-4488-1784-9(6),* 5e508f40-a3af-4fa3-8f4b-53f6be8040cd, PowerKids Pr.) Rosen Publishing Group, Inc., The.

—Jimmy Rollins, 1 vol. 2010. (Baseball's MVPs Ser.). (ENG., Illus.). 24p. (J). (gr. 1-2). pap. 9.85 *(978-1-4488-1786-3(2),* ebc8f4c9-1a1f-4469-95da-7a145007a10b, PowerKids Pr.) Rosen Publishing Group, Inc., The.

—Ryan Howard, 1 vol. 2010. (Baseball's MVPs Ser.). (ENG.). 24p. (J). (gr. 1-2). lib. bdg. 26.27 *(978-1-4488-0632-4(1),* b87e1d85-f13f-4581-9467-71bcc3bbbb24) Rosen Publishing Group, Inc., The.

Gateway Biographies: Spring 2012 New Releases. 2012. (Gateway Biographies Ser.). 48p. (gr. 4-8). lib. bdg. 53.20 *(978-0-8225-8564-0(2),* Lerner Pubns.) Lerner Publishing Group.

Gatto, Kimberly. Kevin Garnett: A Basketball Star Who Cares, 1 vol. 2011. (Sports Stars Who Care Ser.). (ENG., Illus.). 48p. (gr. 3-3). lib. bdg. 27.93 *(978-0-7660-3772-4(X),* 8c789e33-b710-485d-b11f-7d7a0bb7f539) Enslow Publishing, LLC.

Gazlay, Suzy. David Suzuki: Doing Battle with Climate Change, 1 vol. 2009. (Voices for Green Choices Ser.). (ENG., Illus.). 48p. (J). (gr. 5-9). pap. *(978-0-7787-4678-2(X));* lib. bdg. *(978-0-7787-4665-2(8))* Crabtree Publishing Co.

Gibson, Karen. Adrian Peterson. 2011. (Robbie Reader Ser.). (Illus.). 32p. (J). (gr. 2-5). lib. bdg. 25.70 *(978-1-61228-060-8(9))* Mitchell Lane Pubs.

Giff, Patricia Reilly. Dias Sombrios.Tr. of Purple Climbing Days. (SPA.). (J). 3.95 *(978-0-922852-50-5(2))* AIMS International Bks., Inc.

Gigliotti, Jim. All about Linebackers, 1 vol. 2009. (Game Day: Football Ser.). (ENG.). 48p. (YA). (gr. 3-3). lib. bdg. 33.67 *(978-1-4339-1959-6(1),* 358e522c-b0ff-42a5-82fe-72d971345462) Stevens, Gareth Publishing LLLP.

—All about Linemen, 1 vol. 2009. (Game Day: Football Ser.). (ENG.). 48p. (YA). (gr. 3-3). lib. bdg. 33.67 *(978-1-4339-1960-2(5),* 060ae728-80d1-4f68-bb12-1575003d8b0b) Stevens, Gareth Publishing LLLP.

Gigliotti, Jim & Who HQ. Who Was Nikola Tesla? Hinderliter, John, illus. 2018. (Who Was? Ser.). 112p. (J). (gr. 3-7). 5.99 *(978-0-448-48859-2(0),* Penguin Workshop) Penguin Young Readers Group.

Gilbert, Sara. Annie Oakley. 2005. (Legends of the West (Creative Education) Ser.). (Illus.). 48p. (J). (gr. 5-9). lib. bdg. 21.95 *(978-1-58341-334-0(0),* Creative Education) Creative Co., The.

Gilbreth, Frank B., Jr. & Carey, Ernestine Gilbreth. Cheaper by the Dozen. 188p. (YA). (gr. 7-18). reprint ed. lib. bdg. 24.95 *(978-0-88411-289-1(6))* Amereon Ltd.

—Cheaper by the Dozen. 180p. (YA). (gr. 7-18). pap. 5.50 *(978-0-8072-8308-0(8));* 2004. (J). (gr. 4-7). pap. 38.00 incl. audio *(978-0-8072-8307-3(X),* YA157SP) Random Hse. Audio Publishing Group. (Listening Library).

Gilbreth, Frank B., Jr., et al. Cheaper by the Dozen. 2019. (ENG.). 224p. (gr. 7-18). pap. 16.99 *(978-0-06-008460-8(X),* Harper Perennial Modern Classics) HarperCollins Pubs.

Gill, Shelley. Gabe: A Story of Me, My Dog, & The 1970s. Scheff, Marc, illus. 2016. 64p. (J). (gr. 3-7). lib. bdg. 12.95 *(978-1-57091-354-9(4))* Charlesbridge Publishing, Inc.

Gillam, Scott. Andrew Carnegie: Industrial Giant & Philanthropist, 1 vol. 2009. (Essential Lives Set 3 Ser.). (ENG., Illus.). 112p. (YA). (gr. 6-12). lib. bdg. 41.36 *(978-1-60453-521-1(0),* 6671, Essential Library) ABDO Publishing Co.

Gimpel, Lee. Fighting Wars, Planning for Peace: The Story of George C. Marshall. 2005. (World Leaders Ser.). (Illus.). 176p. (J). (gr. 6-12). lib. bdg. 26.95 *(978-1-931798-66-2(4))* Reynolds, Morgan Inc.

Gitenstein, Judy. Alvin Ailey. 2009. (Library of American Choreographers Ser.). 48p. (gr. 5-8). 53.00 *(978-1-60853-455-5(3),* Rosen Reference) Rosen Publishing Group, Inc., The.

Gitlin, Martin. Ed Reed. 2009. (Superstars of Pro Football Ser.). (Illus.). 64p. (YA). (gr. 7-12). lib. bdg. 22.95 *(978-1-4222-0558-7(4))* Mason Crest.

—Walt Disney: Entertainment Visionary, 1 vol. 2009. (Essential Lives Set 4 Ser.). (ENG., Illus.). 112p. (YA). (gr. 6-12). lib. bdg. 41.36 *(978-1-60453-700-0(0),* 6691, Essential Library) ABDO Publishing Co.

Glaser, Jason. Tim Lincecum, 1 vol. 2011. (Today's Sports Greats Ser.). (ENG., Illus.). 32p. (gr. 4-5). (J). pap. 11.50 *(978-1-4339-5880-9(5),* 5cfba1d6-41a2-4a6d-bcd4-0e4df3f4ab1a, Gareth Stevens Learning Library); (YA). lib. bdg. 29.27 *(978-1-4339-5878-6(3),* cb883806-1e75-4ffe-ae98-f45c60dedb6c) Stevens, Gareth Publishing LLLP.

—Tom Brady, 1 vol. 2011. (Today's Sports Greats Ser.). (ENG., Illus.). 32p. (gr. 4-5). (J). pap. 11.50 *(978-1-4339-5884-7(8),* 6dc017dc-c86e-4bbf-8a81-d0bbefd7b8d0, Gareth Stevens Learning Library); (YA). 29.27 *(978-1-4339-5882-3(1),* 2322c3be-8f90-4bc8-95b2-2eb8861fc368) Stevens, Gareth Publishing LLLP.

Gnojewski, Carol. Madonna: Fighting for Self-Expression, 1 vol. 2017. (Rebels with a Cause Ser.). (ENG.). 128p. (gr. 8-8). 38.93 *(978-0-7660-9255-6(0),* 8361f07d-bca5-4de3-b8d4-edc5249c8e78) Enslow Publishing, LLC.

Going, K. L. The Shape of the World: A Portrait of Frank Lloyd Wright. Stringer, Lauren, illus. 2017. (ENG.). 40p. (J). (gr. k-5). 18.99 *(978-1-4424-7821-3(7))* Beach Lane Bks.

Goldberg, Jan. Hernando de Soto: Trailblazer of the American Southeast. 2009. (Library of Explorers & Exploration Ser.). 112p. (gr. 5-8). 66.50 *(978-1-60853-607-8(6),* Rosen Reference) Rosen Publishing Group, Inc., The.

Goldsworthy, Steve. Mark Zuckerberg. 2012. (J). *(978-1-61913-872-8(7));* pap. *(978-1-61913-873-5(5))* Weigl Pubs., Inc.

Golus, Carrie. Biography Russell Simmons. 2007. (Biography Ser.). (Illus.). 112p. (J). (gr. -1). lib. bdg. *(978-0-8225-7158-2(7))* Twenty First Century Bks.

Gondosch, Linda. Where Did Sacagawea Join the Corps of Discovery? And Other Questions about the Lewis & Clark Expedition. 2011. (Six Questions of American History Ser.). (ENG., Illus.). 48p. (J). (gr. 4-6). lib. bdg. 30.65 *(978-0-7613-5226-6(0),* fd798483-1f32-4a50-af83-88af79191609, Lerner Pubns.) Lerner Publishing Group.

Goodman, Michael E. Buffalo Bill. 2005. (Legends of the West (Creative Education) Ser.). (Illus.). 48p. (J). (gr. 5-9). lib. bdg. 21.95 *(978-1-58341-336-4(7),* Creative Education) Creative Co., The.

Gordon, Nick. Dolph Ziggler. 2012. (Pro Wrestling Champions Ser.). (ENG., Illus.). 24p. (J). (gr. 3-7). lib. bdg. 26.95 *(978-1-60014-783-8(6),* Torque Bks.) Bellwether Media.

Gordon, Sherri Mabry. Josh! Leading Man Josh Hutcherson, 1 vol. 2013. (Sizzling Celebrities Ser.). (ENG.). 48p. (gr. 4-6). pap. 11.53 *(978-1-4644-0343-9(0),* 5aad21df-7231-4ab0-b438-c03d74924ffa) Enslow Publishing, LLC.

Gosman, Gillian. Benjamin Franklin, 1 vol. 2011. (Life Stories Ser.). (ENG., Illus.). 24p. (J). (gr. 3-3). pap. 9.25 *(978-1-4488-2759-6(0),* d96f395d-ae34-43c9-9680-8de06d8c53e6); lib. bdg. 26.27 *(978-1-4488-2585-1(7),* 0ce2f8ab-182f-4f36-8495-052334f7703d) Rosen Publishing Group, Inc., The. (PowerKids Pr.).

—Jaden Smith, 1 vol. 2012. (Kid Stars! Ser.). (ENG., Illus.). 24p. (J). (gr. 2-3). pap. 10.40 *(978-1-4488-6341-9(4),* eef78583-812a-4ab3-adc6-1891c8d706a5); lib. bdg. 26.27 *(978-1-4488-6191-0(8),* be360c34-39a8-4c6e-bfc9-c340f48e9878) Rosen Publishing Group, Inc., The. (PowerKids Pr.).

Gotsch, Patrice. Cesar Chavez: Changing Lives. Arreola, Gil, illus. 2006. 19p. pap. 6.30 *(978-1-55501-780-4(0))* Ballard & Tighe Pubs.

Gould, Jane H. Benjamin Franklin, 1 vol. 2012. (Jr. Graphic Founding Fathers Ser.). (ENG., Illus.). 24p. (J). (gr. 2-3). pap. 11.60 *(978-1-4488-7990-8(6),* c2607bf3-41ea-46f1-90c5-06cc7b530046); lib. bdg. 28.93 *(978-1-4488-7896-3(9),* 4e9506b1-7138-494a-9292-34a30a1d094c) Rosen Publishing Group, Inc., The. (PowerKids Pr.).

—Steve Jobs, 1 vol. 2013. (Jr. Graphic American Inventors Ser.). (ENG., Illus.). 24p. (J). (gr. 2-3). pap. 11.60 *(978-1-4777-0145-4(1),* f98a1be3-cdcf-472f-9d96-1d0f59bc9c61); lib. bdg. 28.93 *(978-1-4777-0080-8(3),* 730827ec-80e6-4264-bf85-33b2c30888e9) Rosen Publishing Group, Inc., The. (PowerKids Pr.).

Grabowski, John F. Americans of Central American Heritage. (Successful Americans Ser.). 64p. (YA). 2009. (gr. 9-12). 22.95 *(978-1-4222-0525-9(8))* 2007. (gr. 7-18). pap. 9.95 *(978-1-4222-0859-5(1))* Mason Crest.

—Johnny Depp, 1 vol. 2011. (People in the News Ser.). (ENG., Illus.). 104p. (gr. 7-7). 41.03 *(978-1-4205-0292-3(1),* ef632e0c-c4cf-467b-97c6-ad276542bcda, Lucent Pr.) Greenhaven Publishing LLC.

—Vietnamese Americans. (Successful Americans Ser.). 64p. (YA). 2009. (gr. 9-12). 22.95 *(978-1-4222-0522-8(3))* 2007. (gr. 7-18). pap. 9.95 *(978-1-4222-0869-4(9))* Mason Crest.

Graves, Will. Best Hockey Players of All Time, 1 vol. 2015. (Sports' Best Ever Ser.). (ENG.). 64p. (J). (gr. 3-6). lib. bdg. 35.64 *(978-1-62403-620-0(1),* 17317, SportsZone) ABDO Publishing Co.

Gray, Peter Winslow. Who Was Who in America: Their Childhood Years, Vol. III. 2003. (Illus.). 54p. (J). spiral bd. 10.95 *(978-1-889639-07-9(9))* AMSC, Adventures in Math & Social Studies for Children.

—Who Was Who in America Volume II: Their Childhood Years. 2003. (Illus.). (J). spiral bd. 10.95 *(978-1-889639-02-4(8))* AMSC, Adventures in Math & Social Studies for Children.

Grayson, Robert. Ed Begley, Jr. Living Green. 2009. (Voices for Green Choices Ser.). (ENG., Illus.). 48p. (J). (gr. 5-9). pap. *(978-0-7787-4680-5(1))* Crabtree Publishing Co.

—John Cena. 2012. (Role Model Entertainers Ser.). 64p. (J). (gr. 7). 22.95 *(978-1-4222-2717-6(0))* Mason Crest.

—Plaxico Burress. 2009. (Superstars of Pro Football Ser.). (Illus.). 64p. (YA). (gr. 7-12). lib. bdg. 22.95 *(978-1-4222-0552-5(5))* Mason Crest.

Graziano, Jim. Johnny Depp. 2008. (Pop Culture Ser.). (Illus.). 64p. (YA). (gr. 3-7). lib. bdg. 22.95 *(978-1-4222-0200-5(3))* Mason Crest.

Great American Thinkers, 12 vols. 2016. (Great American Thinkers Ser.). (ENG.). 128p. (gr. 9-9). lib. bdg. 284.16 *(978-1-5026-1997-6(0),* c6f399d6-8280-4a39-b260-fad171a628a4, Cavendish Square) Cavendish Square Publishing LLC.

Green, Bobby. I Sing Because... (Autobiography) the Bobby Green Story. 2009. (ENG.). 190p. pap. 19.99 *(978-1-4415-1677-0(8))* Xlibris Corp.

Green, Carl R. & Sanford, William R. Jesse James, 1 vol. rev. ed. 2008. (Outlaws & Lawmen of the Wild West Ser.). (ENG., Illus.). 48p. (J). (gr. 5-7). lib. bdg. 27.93 *(978-0-7660-3172-2(1),* 5f7068a6-2645-490d-aac7-944c447c791f) Enslow Publishing, LLC.

Green, Sara. Elon Musk. 2014. (Tech Icons Ser.). (ENG., Illus.). 24p. (J). (gr. 3-8). lib. bdg. 27.95 *(978-1-60014-988-7(X),* Pilot Bks.) Bellwether Media.

Greenberger, Robert. Gus Grissom, 1 vol. 2003. (Library of Astronaut Biographies Ser.). (ENG., Illus.). 112p. (gr. 5-8). lib. bdg. 39.80 *(978-0-8239-4458-3(1),* 27e867eb-5dff-494f-92bb-a044f76c031a, Rosen Reference) Rosen Publishing Group, Inc., The.

—Will Eisner. 2009. (Library of Graphic Novelists Ser.). 112p. (gr. 7-12). 63.90 *(978-1-60853-656-6(4))* Rosen Publishing Group, Inc., The.

—Wilt Chamberlain. 2009. (Basketball Hall of Famers Ser.). 112p. (gr. 5-8). 63.90 *(978-1-61511-536-5(6),* Rosen Reference) Rosen Publishing Group, Inc., The.

Gregory, Josh. Bill & Melinda Gates. 2013. (True Book(tm), A — Biographies Ser.). (ENG., Illus.). 48p. (J). lib. bdg. 31.00 *(978-0-531-21905-8(4));* pap. 6.95 *(978-0-531-23876-9(8))* Scholastic Library Publishing.

—Steve Jobs. 2013. (Cornerstones of Freedom™, Third Ser.). (ENG., Illus.). 64p. (J). pap. 8.95 *(978-0-531-21964-5(X))* Scholastic Library Publishing.

—Steve Jobs (a True Book: Biographies) 2013. (True Book (Relaunch) Ser.). (ENG., Illus.). 48p. (J). (gr. 3-5). pap. 6.95 *(978-0-531-23878-3(4),* Children's Pr.) Scholastic Library Publishing.

—A True Book - Biographies: Steve Jobs. 2013. (True Book: Biographies Ser.). (ENG., Illus.). 48p. (J). (gr. 3-5). lib. bdg. 21.19 *(978-0-531-21907-2(0),* Children's Pr.) Scholastic Library Publishing.

Grossi, Craig. Craig & Fred Young Readers' Edition: A Marine, a Stray Dog, & How They Rescued Each Other. 2017. (ENG., Illus.). 256p. (J). (gr. 3). 16.99 *(978-0-06-269335-8(2),* HarperCollins) HarperCollins Pubs.

Habeeb, William Mark. Arab Americans. (Successful Americans Ser.). 64p. (YA). 2009. (Illus.). (gr. 9-12). 22.95 *(978-1-4222-0514-3(2))* 2007. (gr. 7-18). pap. 9.95 *(978-1-4222-0854-0(0))* Mason Crest.

Halfmann, Janet. Seven Miles to Freedom: The Robert Smalls Story. Smith, Duane, illus. 2008. 40p. (J). (gr. 1-6). 17.95 *(978-1-60060-232-0(0))* Lee & Low Bks., Inc.

Hamilton, Toby G. Dmx. 2009. (Hip Hop (Mason Crest Paperback) Ser.). (Illus.). 64p. (YA). (gr. 4-7). pap. 7.95 *(978-1-4222-0340-8(9));* (gr. 7-12). lib. bdg. 22.95 *(978-1-4222-0289-0(5))* Mason Crest.

—Fat Joe. 2009. (Hip-Hop 2 Ser.). (Illus.). 64p. (YA). (gr. 7-12). lib. bdg. 22.95 *(978-1-4222-0291-3(7))* Mason Crest.

—Ice Cube. 2009. (Hip-Hop 2 Ser.). (Illus.). 64p. (YA). (gr. 7-12). lib. bdg. 22.95 *(978-1-4222-0294-4(1))* Mason Crest.

Hampton, Wilborn. Elvis Presley: A Twentieth Century Life. 2007. (ENG., Illus.). 192p. (YA). (gr. 7). 26.16 *(978-1-4287-4879-8(2))* Follett School Solutions.

Hannigan, Kate. A Lady Has the Floor: Belva Lockwood Speaks Out for Women's Rights. Jay, Alison, illus. 2018. 32p. (J). (gr. 2-5). 17.95 *(978-1-62979-453-2(8),* Calkins Creek) Highlights Pr., c/o Highlights for Children, Inc.

Harbo, Christopher L. Bill Gates, 1 vol. 2014. (Business Leaders Ser.). (ENG.). 24p. (J). (gr. -1-2). lib. bdg. 24.65 *(978-1-4765-9641-9(7),* 125432, Pebble) Capstone.

Hardin, Travis. Called to Serve. 2007. (Young Writers Ser.). 95p. (YA). (gr. 8-14). per. 5.99 *(978-1-58158-108-9(4))* McDougal Publishing Co.

Harkins, Susan Sales & Harkins, William H. The Life & Times of Clara Barton. 2008. (Profiles in American History Ser.). (Illus.). 48p. (J). (gr. 4-8). lib. bdg. 29.95 *(978-1-58415-667-3(8))* Mitchell Lane Pubs.

—The Life & Times of Father Jacques Marquette. 2008. (Profiles in American History Ser.). (Illus.). 48p. (J). (gr. 4-8). lib. bdg. 29.95 *(978-1-58415-528-7(0))* Mitchell Lane Pubs.

Harmon, Daniel E. Al Gore & Global Warming. 2009. (Celebrity Activists Ser.). 112p. (gr. 8-8). 66.50 *(978-1-61511-826-7(8))* Rosen Publishing Group, Inc., The.

Harness, Cheryl. The Tragic Tale of Narcissa Whitman & a Faithful History of the Oregon Trail (Direct Mail Edition) 2006. (Cheryl Harness Histories Ser.). (Illus.). 144p. (J). (gr. 5-9). 16.95 *(978-0-7922-5920-6(3),* National Geographic Kids) Disney Publishing Worldwide.

Harris, Laurie Lanzen. Presidents of the Uited States. 3rd ed. 2009. (J). lib. bdg. 55.00 *(978-1-931360-45-6(6))* Favorable Impressions.

Harrison, Kat. Lin-Manuel Miranda: Composer, Actor, & Creator of Hamilton, 1 vol. 2017. (Influential Lives Ser.). (ENG.). 128p. (gr. 7-7). lib. bdg. 40.27 *(978-0-7660-8505-3(8),* 489f042d-d509-48d1-8457-f5680c09e729) Enslow Publishing, LLC.

Hasday, Judy & Hasday, Judy L. Americans of Eastern European Heritage. 2007. (Successful Americans Ser.). (Illus.). 64p. (YA). (gr. 5-18). pap. 9.95 *(978-1-4222-0860-1(5))* Mason Crest.

Hasday, Judy L. Americans of Eastern European Heritage. 2009. (Successful Americans Ser.). (Illus.). 64p. (YA). (gr. 9-12). 22.95 *(978-1-4222-0528-0(2))* Mason Crest.

—Japanese Americans. (Successful Americans Ser.). 64p. (YA). 2009. (gr. 9-12). 22.95 *(978-1-4222-0519-8(3))* 2007. (gr. 7-18). pap. 9.95 *(978-1-4222-0863-2(X))* Mason Crest.

Haugen, Brenda. Johnathan Toews. 2015. (Hockey Superstars Ser.). (ENG., Illus.). 32p. (J). (gr. 3-4). lib. bdg. 28.65 *(978-1-62065-157-5(2),* 120858) Capstone.

—Jonathan Toews. 2015. (Hockey Superstars Ser.). (ENG.). 32p. (J). (gr. 3-4). pap. 7.95 *(978-1-4914-9024-2(1),* 131546) Capstone.

Hayes, Amy. Tim Cook: Industrial Engineer & CEO of Apple, 1 vol. 2017. (Breakout Biographies Ser.). (ENG.). 32p. (gr. 4-5). pap. 11.00 *(978-1-5081-6074-8(0),* b71acfdf-22f3-41e0-823f-a44dd06244d6, PowerKids Pr.) Rosen Publishing Group, Inc., The.

Heitkamp, Kristina Lyn. Rachel Carson: Pioneering Environmental Activist. 2017. (Spotlight on Civic Courage: Heroes of Conscience Ser.). (Illus.). 48p. (J). (gr. 10-15). 70.50 *(978-1-5383-8075-8(7));* (ENG., (gr. 6-6). pap. 12.75 *(978-1-5383-8074-1(9),* 119b7370-d960-44cd-9967-4d11a6da74e4) Rosen Publishing Group, Inc., The.

Heits, Rudolph T. DeMarcus Ware. 2010. (Superstars of Pro Football Ser.). 64p. (YA). (gr. 5-18). lib. bdg. 22.95 *(978-1-4222-1665-1(9))* Mason Crest.

Helenthal, Janet. Helen Keller. 2005. (Illus.). 16p. (J). *(978-0-7367-2853-9(8))* Zaner-Bloser, Inc.

Hemingway, Albert. Barack Obama. 2007. (Sharing the American Dream Ser.). (Illus.). 64p. (J). (gr. 7-18). pap. 9.95 *(978-1-4222-0759-8(5))* Mason Crest.

—Chuck Norris. 2009. (Sharing the American Dream Ser.). 64p. (YA). (gr. 7-12). 22.95 *(978-1-4222-0591-4(6))* Mason Crest.

Henigson, Jeff. Warhead: The True Story of One Teen Who Almost Saved the World. 2019. (Illus.). 352p. (J). (gr. 7). 17.99 *(978-0-525-64790-4(2),* Delacorte Pr.) Random Hse. Children's Bks.

Henry, Nathan L. Good Behavior. 2011. 256p. pap. 9.99 *(978-1-59990-470-2(5),* Bloomsbury USA Childrens) Bloomsbury Publishing USA.

Heos, Bridget. Jay-Z, 1 vol. 2009. (Library of Hip-Hop Biographies Ser.). (ENG., Illus.). 48p. (J). (gr. 5-5). pap. 12.75 *(978-1-4358-5438-3(1),* 02aaa371-03cc-4081-baae-00a436d0948f) Rosen Publishing Group, Inc., The.

—Kofi Kingston: Champ of Smackdown, 1 vol. 2011. (Slam! Stars of Wrestling Ser.). (ENG.). 48p. (YA). (gr. 5-5). pap. 12.75 *(978-1-4488-5595-7(0),* d222fca9-6f08-4b36-a0b6-5bb01786e8ae); lib. bdg. 34.47 *(978-1-4488-5535-3(7),* 1effa783-6849-4767-b3fc-c8495ad259d6) Rosen Publishing Group, Inc., The.

—Lady Gaga, 1 vol. 2011. (Megastars Ser.). (ENG.). 48p. (YA). (gr. 5-5). pap. 12.75 *(978-1-4488-2260-7(2),* b3a02271-ccfc-4dd4-9957-47e990308885); (Illus.). lib. bdg. 34.47 *(978-1-4358-3574-0(3),* ac5215f1-d02d-4c52-9c46-dd59e686674f) Rosen Publishing Group, Inc., The.

—Rey Mysterio: Giant Killer, 1 vol. 2011. (Slam! Stars of Wrestling Ser.). (ENG.). 48p. (YA). (gr. 5-5). pap. 12.75 *(978-1-4488-5601-5(9),* b0985025-f84c-49c5-b9f0-ae929db99866); lib. bdg. 34.47 *(978-1-4488-5538-4(1),* d2244eeb-ea72-49c4-b8ce-c1d5c106f3ab) Rosen Publishing Group, Inc., The.

—Ronde & Tiki Barber: Football Stars, 1 vol. 2010. (Sports Families Ser.). (ENG., Illus.). 48p. (gr. 5-5). (J). pap. 12.75 *(978-1-4358-8510-3(4),* b0a5e562-5af2-467b-81b0-abf38001290f, Rosen Reference); (YA). lib. bdg. 34.47 *(978-1-4358-3553-5(0),* b9ec456e-ca02-425a-b1b6-55110faea611) Rosen Publishing Group, Inc., The.

Herman, Gail & Who HQ. Who Was Davy Crockett? Squier, Robert, illus. 2013. (Who Was? Ser.). (ENG.). 112p. (J). (gr. 3-7). 5.99 *(978-0-448-46704-7(6),* Penguin Workshop) Penguin Young Readers Group.

Hermsen, Sarah, et al. American Reference Library. 2004. (Crime & Punishment in America Ser.). (ENG.). 39p. (J). 5.00 *(978-0-7876-9174-5(7),* UXL) Cengage Gale.

Hernandez, Daniel. They Call Me a Hero: A Memoir of My Youth. 2013. (ENG., Illus.). 240p. (YA). (gr. 7). 17.99 *(978-1-4424-6228-1(0),* Simon & Schuster Bks. For Young Readers) Simon & Schuster Bks. For Young Readers.

Herrera, Juan Felipe. El Canto de las Palomas/Calling the Doves. 2004. (Illus.). (J). (gr. 3-6). spiral bd. *(978-0-616-14607-1(8))* Canadian National Institute for the Blind/Institut National Canadien pour les Aveugles.

Herringshaw, DeAnn. Dorothy Dandridge: Singer & Actress, 1 vol. 2011. (Essential Lives Set 6 Ser.). (ENG., Illus.). 112p. (J). (gr. 6-12). lib. bdg. 41.36 *(978-1-61714-779-1(6),* 6723, Essential Library) ABDO Publishing Co.

Herweck, Don. Making It Go: The Life & Work of Robert Fulton, 1 vol. rev. ed. 2007. (Science: Informational Text Ser.). (ENG.). 32p. (gr. 3-6). pap. 12.99 *(978-0-7439-0578-7(4))* Teacher Created Materials, Inc.

Hicks, Kyra E. Martha Ann's Quilt for Queen Victoria. Fodi, Lee Edward, illus. 2006. 28p. (J). (gr. -1-3). 16.95 *(978-1-933285-59-7(1))* Brown Books Publishing Group.

Hicks, Peter. Lance Armstrong - Racing Hero, 1 vol. 2011. (Famous Lives Ser.). (ENG., Illus.). 32p. (YA). (gr. 3-4). lib. bdg. 30.27 *(978-1-4488-3289-7(6),* 97ea2dae-0ba0-4a58-b614-a243dbe6b188) Rosen Publishing Group, Inc., The.

Hicks, Terry Allan. Uncle Sam, 1 vol. (Symbols of America Ser.). (ENG., Illus.). 40p. (gr. 3-3). 2008. pap. 9.23 *(978-0-7614-3379-8(1),* 36ed5508-6ab2-4d17-b3bd-5437c8515901, Cavendish Square) 2007. lib. bdg. 32.64 *(978-0-7614-2137-5(8),* e6f9da10-1cd5-4edb-8cd5-0e9e233d21ec) Cavendish Square Publishing LLC.

Hill, Anne E. Sasha Cohen. 2007. (Sports Heroes & Legends Ser.). (Illus.). 106p. (YA). (gr. 7-12). lib. bdg. 30.60 *(978-0-8225-7164-3(1))* Twenty First Century Bks.

Hill, Z. B. Tupac. 2012. (Superstars of Hip-Hop Ser.). (Illus.). 48p. (J). (gr. 3-4). 19.95 *(978-1-4222-2530-1(5))* Mason Crest.

Hiller, Sandra J. Annie Oakley, 1 vol. 2014. (Jr. Graphic American Legends Ser.). (ENG.). 24p. (J). (gr. 2-3). lib. bdg. 28.93 *(978-1-4777-7185-3(9),* f8e96c68-e1fa-4372-8a16-1f4a8e3d2ba2, PowerKids Pr.) Rosen Publishing Group, Inc., The.

Hinman, Bonnie. John Legend. 2009. (Blue Banner Biography Ser.). (Illus.). 32p. (YA). (gr. 4-7). lib. bdg. 25.70 *(978-1-58415-774-8(7))* Mitchell Lane Pubs.

Historical American Biographies, 53 bks., Set. (Illus.). (YA). (gr. 6-12). lib. bdg. 1111.35 *(978-0-89490-911-5(8))* Enslow Publishing, LLC.

Hoffman, Mary Ann. Alex Rodriguez: Baseball Star. 2009. (Sports Superstars Ser.). 24p. (gr. 1-1). 42.50 *(978-1-60853-173-8(2),* PowerKids Pr.) Rosen Publishing Group, Inc., The.

—Alex Rodriguez: Baseball Star/Estrella del Beisbol. 2009. (Amazing Athletes/Atletas increíbles Ser.). (SPA.). 24p. (gr. 1-2). 42.50 *(978-1-61511-303-3(7),* Editorial Buenas Letras) Rosen Publishing Group, Inc., The.

—Dwayne Wade: Basketball Star, 1 vol. 2006. (Superstars of Sports Ser.). (ENG., Illus.). 24p. (J). (gr. 1-1). lib. bdg. 26.27 *(978-1-4042-3536-6(1),* c8eb63df-8fcd-4d86-b413-bcca193ca559) Rosen Publishing Group, Inc., The.

—Kyle Busch, 1 vol. 2010. (Superstars of NASCAR Ser.). (ENG.). 32p. (J). (gr. 1-1). pap. 11.50 *(978-1-4339-3963-1(0),* e2a6e012-b858-4a93-acfd-ccae60419042); lib. bdg. 27.93 *(978-1-4339-3962-4(2),* a1708a7a-3946-4b9b-82c8-b35dc682029c) Stevens, Gareth Publishing LLLP.

—Lebron James: Basketball Star, 1 vol. 2006. (Superstars of Sports Ser.). (ENG., Illus.). 24p. (J). (gr. 1-1). lib. bdg. 26.27 *(978-1-4042-3535-9(3),* 2da1ada3-7740-4fd8-83bf-83ad67abf6db) Rosen Publishing Group, Inc., The.

—Peyton Manning: Football Star, 1 vol. 2006. (Superstars of Sports Ser.). (ENG., Illus.). 24p. (J). (gr. 1-1). lib. bdg. 26.27 *(978-1-4042-3531-1(0),* d0173e6e-74e8-4aee-aa05-8ea10e5e28cd) Rosen Publishing Group, Inc., The.

—Scott Joplin, 1 vol. 2010. (Inspiring Lives Ser.). (ENG., Illus.). 32p. (J). (gr. 1-1). pap. 11.50 *(978-1-4339-3632-6(1),* 1c4b9b7c-c9e3-4061-911f-ac2ba6397eb8); lib. bdg. 27.93 *(978-1-4339-3631-9(3),* 9f7ad6b9-e6cf-4e50-9104-257ffeefb58e) Stevens, Gareth Publishing LLLP.

—Shaun Alexander: Football Star. (Sports Superstars Ser.). 24p. (gr. 1-1). 2009. 42.50 *(978-1-60853-182-0(1),* PowerKids Pr.) 2006. (ENG., Illus.). (J). lib. bdg. 26.27 *(978-1-4042-3532-8(9),* ba92020e-3367-4afe-9f8b-0a80d4ad96ae) Rosen Publishing Group, Inc., The.

—Shaun Alexander: Football Star/Estrella del futbol Americano. 2009. (Amazing Athletes/Atletas increíbles Ser.). 24p. (gr. 1-2). 42.50 *(978-1-61511-308-8(8),* Editorial Buenas Letras) Rosen Publishing Group, Inc., The.

Hollow, Michele C. The Grateful Dead, 1 vol. 2018. (Bands That Rock! Ser.). (ENG.). 112p. (YA). (gr. 7-7). 38.93 *(978-1-9785-0348-9(2),* 279e4bb7-03cd-40ad-96d8-2337f4f3fa12) Enslow Publishing, LLC.

—Grateful Dead: What a Long, Strange Trip It's Been, 1 vol. 2009. (Rebels of Rock Ser.). (ENG., Illus.). 104p. (gr. 5-6). pap. 13.88 *(978-0-7660-3620-8(0),* 051c6d59-07e4-4c68-b3bb-52ba1002e61b) Enslow Publishing, LLC.

Hoogenboom, Lynn. William Tecumseh Sherman: The Fight to Preserve the Union. 2009. (Library of American Lives & Times Ser.). 112p. (gr. 5-5). 69.20 *(978-1-60853-511-8(8))* Rosen Publishing Group, Inc., The.

Horn, Geoffrey M. Adam Sandler, 1 vol. 2005. (Today's Superstars Ser.). (ENG., Illus.). 32p. (gr. 3-3). lib. bdg. 34.60 *(978-0-8368-4234-0(0),* 133469fb-00d8-4be9-9761-550fb03e5a2c) Stevens, Gareth Publishing LLLP.

—Alicia Keys, 1 vol. 2005. (Today's Superstars Ser.). (ENG., Illus.). 32p. (gr. 3-3). lib. bdg. 34.60 *(978-0-8368-4233-3(2),* ec78531a4-e1ef-41a3-913d-364f4032e29d) Stevens, Gareth Publishing LLLP.

—Beyoncé, 1 vol. 2005. (Today's Superstars Ser.). (ENG., Illus.). 32p. (gr. 3-3). lib. bdg. 34.60 *(978-0-8368-4230-2(8),* 3f390ece-6d0d-4f70-992b-80b0dad45fb9) Stevens, Gareth Publishing LLLP.

—Cameron Diaz, 1 vol. 2005. (Today's Superstars Ser.). (ENG., Illus.). 32p. (gr. 3-3). lib. bdg. 34.60 *(978-0-8368-4231-9(6),* bc69a1df-67a5-4b5e-bfbb-2dbf625b1559) Stevens, Gareth Publishing LLLP.

—Jamie Foxx, 1 vol. 2005. (Today's Superstars Ser.). (ENG., Illus.). 32p. (gr. 3-3). lib. bdg. 34.60 *(978-0-8368-4232-6(4),* 89ebd883-f264-4bad-ae23-320d708a98c5) Stevens, Gareth Publishing LLLP.

Horn, Geoffrey Michael. John Brown: Putting Actions above Words. 2009. (Voices for Freedom Ser.). (ENG., Illus.). 64p. (J). (gr. 5-8). pap. *(978-0-7787-4839-7(1));* lib. bdg. *(978-0-7787-4823-6(5))* Crabtree Publishing Co.

Houle, Michelle E. Lindsey Williams: Gardening for Impoverished Families, 1 vol. 2007. (Young Heroes Ser.). (ENG., Illus.). 48p. (gr. 4-8). lib. bdg. 30.38 *(978-0-7377-3867-4(7),* fd01ea0c-813c-4ff0-b23b-0d81530eeeda, KidHaven Publishing) Greenhaven Publishing LLC.

Houts, Amy. Rachel Maddow, 1 vol. 2014. (Remarkable LGBTQ Lives Ser.). (ENG.). 112p. (YA). (gr. 7-7). 38.80 *(978-1-4777-7891-3(8),* 65a517ea-6f6b-4ffc-b140-a09c18e05dfb, Rosen Young Adult) Rosen Publishing Group, Inc., The.

Howse, Jennifer. Miley Cyrus. 2008. (Remarkable People Ser.). (Illus.). 24p. (J). (gr. 4-6). pap. 8.95 *(978-1-59036-985-2(8));* lib. bdg. 24.45 *(978-1-59036-984-5(X))* Weigl Pubs., Inc.

Hudak, Heather C. Oprah Winfrey. 2005. (Great African American Women for Kids Ser.). (Illus.). 24p. (J). (gr. 2-3). lib. bdg. 24.45 *(978-1-59036-335-5(3));* (gr. 3-7). per. 8.95 *(978-1-59036-341-6(8))* Weigl Pubs., Inc.

Hudson, Amanda. Michelle Obama, 1 vol. 2009. (People We Should Know (Second Series) Ser.). (ENG.). 48p. (J). (gr. 3-5). pap. 11.50 *(978-1-4339-2192-6(8),* 52e0e14d-5612-4f8c-b7d3-6032009fc9db); lib. bdg. 33.67 *(978-1-4339-2187-2(1),* 39091c59-0022-40d8-9376-30ac82a88229) Stevens, Gareth Publishing LLLP. (Gareth Stevens Learning Library).

Hurtig, Jennifer. Maurice Sendak. (My Favorite Writer Ser.). (Illus.). 32p. 2007. (YA). (gr. 5-18). pap. 9.95 *(978-1-59036-485-7(6))* 2006. (J). (gr. 3-7). lib. bdg. 9.95 *(978-1-59036-484-0(8))* Weigl Pubs., Inc.

Hyman, Trina Schart. Self-Portrait: Trina Schart Hyman. (ENG.). 100p. 12.95 *(978-0-201-09308-7(1))* HarperCollins Pubs.

Indovino, Shaina Carmel. Kobe Bryant. 2014. (Superstars in the World of Basketball Ser.: 10). (Illus.). 48p. (J). (gr. 5-18). 20.95 *(978-1-4222-3108-1(9))* Mason Crest.

Isbell, Hannah. Jim Henson: Puppeteer & Producer, 1 vol. 2017. (Junior Biographies Ser.). (ENG.). 24p. (gr. 3-4). pap. 10.35 *(978-0-7660-9053-8(1),* dec1e1b1-a3d9-4057-96d4-29112bf6ffd9) Enslow Publishing, LLC.

Jacoby, Randolph. Al Sharpton, Vol. 9. 2018. (Civil Rights Leaders Ser.). 128p. (J). (gr. 7). lib. bdg. 35.93 *(978-1-4222-4003-8(7))* Mason Crest.

James, Lincoln. Dale Jarrett, 1 vol. 2006. (NASCAR Champions Ser.). (ENG., Illus.). 24p. (J). (gr. 1-2). lib. bdg. 26.27 *(978-1-4042-3459-8(4),* 1440773b-f59d-48a4-acd3-50259a076845) Rosen Publishing Group, Inc., The.

Janic, Susan. Living the Dream: Hannah Montana & Miley Cyrus - The Unofficial Story. 2008. (ENG., Illus.). 144p. (J). (gr. 4-7). pap. 14.95 *(978-1-55022-848-9(X),* 18c76be9-2214-4b48-b6dc-44687670240b) ECW Pr. CAN. Dist: Baker & Taylor Publisher Services (BTPS).

Janic, Susan & Thomas, Scott. Jonas Brothers Forever: The Unofficial Story of Kevin, Joe & Nick. 2009. (ENG., Illus.). 158p. (J). (gr. 4-7). pap. 14.95 *(978-1-55022-851-9(X),* 58085575-3f03-4566-a4d1-2abb5f8b42b6) ECW Pr. CAN. Dist: Baker & Taylor Publisher Services (BTPS).

Jarrow, Gail. The Amazing Harry Kellar: Great American Magician. 2012. (ENG., Illus.). 96p. (J). (gr. 3-7). 17.95 *(978-1-59078-865-3(6),* Calkins Creek) Highlights Pr., c/o Highlights for Children, Inc.

—Robert H. Jackson: New Deal Lawyer, Supreme Court Justice, Nuremberg Prosecutor. 2008. (ENG., Illus.). 128p. (J). (gr. 4-7). 22.99 *(978-1-59078-511-9(8),* Calkins Creek) Highlights Pr., c/o Highlights for Children, Inc.

Jeffery, Marika. Carrie Underwood. (Sharing the American Dream Ser.). 2009. 64p. (YA). (gr. 7-12). 22.95 *(978-1-4222-0599-0(1))* 2008. (J). pap. 9.95 *(978-1-4222-0764-2(1))* Mason Crest.

Jesse Owens. 2004. (Illus.). 112p. pap. 9.95 *(978-0-8225-5318-2(X))* Lerner Publishing Group.

Johns, Linda. A Rocket Boy Grows Up. 2005. (Illus.). 16p. (J). *(978-0-7367-2904-8(6))* Zaner-Bloser, Inc.

Johns, Michael-Anne. Hangin' with Lindsay Lohan. 2004. (Illus.). 48p. (J). *(978-0-439-72512-5(7))* Scholastic, Inc.

Jones, Natalya. George Washington Carver: Peanut Scientist, 1 vol. 2008. (Real Life Readers Ser.). (ENG.). 16p. (gr. 2-3). pap. 7.05 *(978-1-4358-0085-4(0),* d9e0ba11-a4b2-4fd0-a9b4-5d19057f9926, Rosen Classroom) Rosen Publishing Group, Inc., The.

Jurmain, Suzanne Tripp. George Did It. Day, Larry, illus. 2007. (gr. -1-3). 17.00 *(978-0-7569-8161-7(1))* Perfection Learning Corp.

Kallen, Stuart A. Elon Musk & Tesla. 2015. (ENG., Illus.). 80p. (J). lib. bdg. *(978-1-60152-870-4(1))* ReferencePoint Pr., Inc.

Kate Shelley & the Midnight Express. 9.95 *(978-1-59112-169-5(8))* Live Oak Media.

Keedle, Jayne. Jonas Brothers, 1 vol. 2009. (Today's Superstars Ser.). (ENG.). 48p. (J). (gr. 3-3). pap. 15.05 *(978-1-4339-2163-6(4),* f7ea20a1-27a4-499c-bc3c-bbc790feacf1); lib. bdg. 34.60 *(978-1-4339-1970-1(2),* 2bf2ddd2-0209-4fc1-890a-56281f589188) Stevens, Gareth Publishing LLLP.

—Rachael Ray, 1 vol. 2009. (People We Should Know (Second Series) Ser.). (ENG., Illus.). 48p. (J). (gr. 3-5). pap. 11.50 *(978-1-4339-2149-0(9),* 5237bfe9-ed6e-44bb-b888-790467e4b19d); lib. bdg. 33.67 *(978-1-4339-2189-6(8),* 007fb7b9-0d10-4901-a7fd-6bacdddafccc) Stevens, Gareth Publishing LLLP. (Gareth Stevens Learning Library).

—Zac Efron, 1 vol. 2008. (Today's Superstars Ser.). (ENG., Illus.). 32p. (J). (gr. 3-3). lib. bdg. 34.60 *(978-0-8368-9239-0(9),* cd8b6358-e475-4bdc-8a45-e06aeb2d73d2) Stevens, Gareth Publishing LLLP.

Keenan, Sheila. Outstanding Americans. 2003. (ENG.). 256p. (J). 19.95 *(978-0-439-28358-8(2),* Scholastic Reference) Scholastic, Inc.

Keep the Lights Burning. 9.95 *(978-1-59112-293-7(7))* Live Oak Media.

Keller, Susanna. Alexander Hamilton: America's First Treasury Secretary, 1 vol. 2017. (Britannica Beginner Bios Ser.). (ENG., Illus.). 32p. (J). (gr. 2-3). pap. 13.90 *(978-1-68048-808-1(2),* eab0f6a1-72cf-4eb2-a5eb-53313f8b7c28); lib. bdg. 26.06 *(978-1-68048-809-8(0),* 2896e138-b801-4476-9722-6e478e5423ba) Rosen Publishing Group, Inc., The. (Britannica Educational Publishing).

Kelley, K. C. All about Running Backs, 1 vol. 2009. (Game Day: Football Ser.). (ENG.). 48p. (J). (gr. 3-3). lib. bdg. 33.67 *(978-1-4339-1963-3(X),* 404ce31e-f7f5-4c87-a65d-ae4a304ddb98) Stevens, Gareth Publishing LLLP.

Kelly, Scott. My Journey to the Stars. Ceolin, André, illus. 2017. (ENG.). 48p. (J). (gr. k-3). 17.99 *(978-1-5247-6377-0(2),* Crown Books For Young Readers) Random Hse. Children's Bks.

Kelly Slater. 2008. (Xtreme Athletes Ser.). (Illus.). 112p. (YA). (gr. 7-12). lib. bdg. 27.95 *(978-1-59935-078-3(5))* Reynolds, Morgan Inc.

Kennedy, Mike. Shaun White, 1 vol. 2009. (Today's Superstars Ser.). (ENG.). 48p. (J). (gr. 3-3). pap. 15.05 *(978-1-4339-2161-2(8),* 01a42eed-0da3-4739-97d5-a574479f2d90); lib. bdg. 34.60 *(978-1-4339-1968-8(0),* dcff15b6-57d1-4950-ab8d-614c1b378bfe) Stevens, Gareth Publishing LLLP.

Kennelly, Sean & Carpenter, Dan. Great Americans: American Collection. 2014. (ENG., Illus.). 48p. (J). (gr. 4). 8.99 *(978-1-4867-0257-2(0))* Flowerpot Children's Pr. Inc. CAN. Dist: Cardinal Pubs. Group.

Kent, Zachary A. Andrew Carnegie: Industrialist & Philanthropist, 1 vol. 2014. (Legendary American Biographies Ser.). (ENG.). 96p. (gr. 6-6). 29.60 *(978-0-7660-6435-5(2),* 83cad165-d751-4ea5-9e03-e842c95bc454) Enslow Publishing, LLC.

Kerns, Ann. Martha Stewart. 2006. (Biography Ser.). (Illus.). 111p. (J). (gr. 3-7). lib. bdg. 29.27 *(978-0-8225-6613-7(3),* Twenty-First Century Bks.) Lerner Publishing Group.

TUV

Kiely Miller, Barbara. John Muir, 1 vol. 2007. (Grandes Personajes (Great Americans) Ser.). 24p. (gr. 2-4). (SPA.). pap. 9.15 *(978-0-8368-8339-8(X),* 027deba2-1d65-4f22-afdd-b25c74e7ca0c); (ENG.). lib. bdg. 24.67 *(978-0-8368-8318-3(7),* 86d24b9e-cde3-4ee8-a2b1-a311970c63af); (SPA.). lib. bdg. 24.67 *(978-0-8368-8332-9(2),* fc2fd432-5fd4-462b-87ac-0011ba6ede2f) Stevens, Gareth Publishing LLLP. (Weekly Reader Leveled Readers).

Killcoyne, Hope Lourie. Key Figures of the Vietnam War, 1 vol. 2015. (Biographies of War Ser.). (ENG., Illus.). 112p. (J). (gr. 7-8). 35.47 *(978-1-68048-063-4(4),* c16e184b-2f63-49d1-9e79-fb42d670f16b4, Britannica Educational Publishing) Rosen Publishing Group, Inc., The.

Kimmich, Ian. Antonio Gates. 2009. (Superstars of Pro Football Ser.). (Illus.). 64p. (YA). (gr. 7-12). lib. bdg. 22.95 *(978-1-4222-0553-2(3))* Mason Crest.

King Farris, Christine. My Brother Martin: A Sister Remembers Growing up with the Rev. Dr. Martin Luther King Jr. Soentpiet, Chris K., illus. 2005. 35p. (J). (gr. 4-7). 15.65 *(978-0-7569-6552-5(7))* Perfection Learning Corp.

Kingsbury, Robert. The Assassination of James A. Garfield. 2009. (Library of Political Assassinations Ser.). 64p. (gr. 5-5). 58.50 *(978-1-60853-825-6(7))* Rosen Publishing Group, Inc., The.

Kirkpatrick, Rob. Alexi Lalas: Sensación del Fútbol Soccer (Soccer Sensation) 2009. (Grandes Idolos (Hot Shots) Ser.). 24p. (gr. 1-1). 42.50 *(978-1-61512-733-7(X),* Editorial Buenas Letras) Rosen Publishing Group, Inc., The.

—Alexi Lalas: Soccer Sensation / Sensación del Fútbol Soccer. 2009. (Hot Shots/Grandes ídolos Ser.). (SPA.). 24p. (gr. 1-1). 42.50 *(978-1-61513-411-3(5),* Editorial Buenas Letras) Rosen Publishing Group, Inc., The.

—Evander Holyfield: Campeón de los Pesos Pesados (Heavyweight Champion) 2009. (Grandes Idolos (Hot Shots) Ser.). (SPA.). 24p. (gr. 1-1). 42.50 *(978-1-61512-736-8(4),* Editorial Buenas Letras) Rosen Publishing Group, Inc., The.

—Evander Holyfield: Heavyweight Champion / Campeón de los Pesos Pesados. 2009. (Hot Shots/Grandes ídolos Ser.). (ENG & SPA.). 24p. (gr. 1-1). 42.50 *(978-1-61513-414-4(X),* Editorial Buenas Letras) Rosen Publishing Group, Inc., The.

—Terrell Davis: Corredor de Superbowl (Super Bowl Running Back) 2009. (Deportistas de Poder (Power Players) Ser.). 24p. (gr. 1-1). 42.50 *(978-1-61512-161-8(7),* Editorial Buenas Letras) Rosen Publishing Group, Inc., The.

Klein, Adria F. Arnold Schwarzenegger. 2009. pap. 13.25 *(978-1-60559-054-7(1))* Hameray Publishing Group, Inc.

Klein, Dvora. Eleanor Roosevelt. 2009. pap. 13.25 *(978-1-60559-059-2(2))* Hameray Publishing Group, Inc.

Klimo, Kate. Walt Disney's Magic. Ivanov, O. & Ivanov, A., illus. 2017. (J). pap. *(978-0-399-55534-3(X))* Random Hse., Inc.

Koestler-Grack, Rachel A. William Tecumseh Sherman. 2009. (ENG., Illus.). 149p. (gr. 6-12). 35.00 *(978-1-60413-300-4(7),* P162096, Facts On File) Infobase Holdings, Inc.

Kortemeier, Todd. Unsung Heroes of US History. 2017. (Unsung Heroes Ser.). (ENG., Illus.). 32p. (J). (gr. 3-6). 32.80 *(978-1-63235-312-2(1),* 11832, 12-Story Library) Bookstaves, LLC.

Kramer, Barbara. Lin-Manuel Miranda: Award-Winning Musical Writer. 2017. (Newsmakers Set 2 Ser.). (ENG., Illus.). 48p. (J). (gr. 4-8). lib. bdg. 35.64 *(978-1-5321-1183-9(5),* 25942) ABDO Publishing Co.

Kramer, S. A. & Who HQ. Who Was Daniel Boone? Ulrich, George, illus. 2006. (Who Was? Ser.). 112p. (J). (gr. 3-7). pap. 5.99 *(978-0-448-43902-0(6),* Penguin Workshop) Penguin Young Readers Group.

Krasner, Barbara. Famous Immigrant Entrepreneurs, 1 vol. 2017. (Making America Great: Immigrant Success Stories Ser.). (ENG.). 112p. (gr. 7-7). 38.93 *(978-0-7660-9241-9(0),* 5aceebd3-8ef6-4dac-af83-1d2f57840ba7) Enslow Publishing, LLC.

Kreger-Boaz, Claire. Lady Gaga, 1 vol. 2011. (People in the News Ser.). (ENG.). 104p. (gr. 7-7). lib. bdg. 41.03 *(978-1-4205-0426-2(6),* bba85bf0-e97c-4b5e-ae3e-82c371ed9865, Lucent Pr.) Greenhaven Publishing LLC.

Krensky, Stephen. Casey Jones. Schroder, Mark, illus. (On My Own Folklore Ser.). (ENG.). 48p. (J). (gr. 2-4). 2007. per. 8.99 *(978-0-8225-6476-8(9),* 0dfdc648-eccb-4701-b06c-befe82835c17, First Avenue Editions) 2006. lib. bdg. 25.26 *(978-1-57505-890-0(1),* Millbrook Pr.) Lerner Publishing Group.

Krohn, Katherine. Biography Gwen Stefani. 2007. (Biography Ser.). (Illus.). 112p. (J). (gr. -1). lib. bdg. *(978-0-8225-7157-5(9))* Twenty First Century Bks.

Krull, Kathleen. The Boy on Fairfield Street: How Ted Geisel Grew up to Become Dr. Seuss. Johnson, Steve & Fancher, Lou, illus. 2010. (ENG.). 48p. (J). (gr. k-4). pap. 7.99 *(978-0-375-85550-4(5),* Dragonfly Bks.) Random Hse. Children's Bks.

—The Boy on Fairfield Street: How Ted Geisel Grew up to Become Dr. Seuss. 2010. lib. bdg. 18.40 *(978-0-606-12416-4(0))* Turtleback.

—The Boy Who Invented TV: The Story of Philo Farnsworth. Couch, Greg, illus. 2014. 40p. (J). (gr. 1-4). 8.99 *(978-0-385-75557-3(0),* Dragonfly Bks.) Random Hse. Children's Bks.

Krumenauer, Heidi. Flo-Rida. 2010. (Blue Banner Biography Ser.). (Illus.). 32p. (YA). (gr. 4-7). lib. bdg. 25.70 *(978-1-58415-906-3(5))* Mitchell Lane Pubs.

—Jimmie Johnson. 2009. (Robbie Reader Ser.). (Illus.). 32p. (YA). (gr. 2-5). lib. bdg. 25.70 *(978-1-58415-756-4(9))* Mitchell Lane Pubs.

—Joe Flacco. 2009. (Blue Banner Biography Ser.). (Illus.). 32p. (YA). (gr. 4-7). lib. bdg. 25.70 *(978-1-58415-771-7(2))* Mitchell Lane Pubs.

—Lady Gaga. 2010. (Blue Banner Biography Ser.). (Illus.). 32p. (YA). (gr. 4-7). lib. bdg. 25.70 *(978-1-58415-904-9(9))* Mitchell Lane Pubs.

—Sean Kingston. 2008. (Blue Banner Biography Ser.). (Illus.). 32p. (YA). (gr. 4-7). lib. bdg. 25.70 *(978-1-58415-679-6(1))* Mitchell Lane Pubs.

Kudlinski, Kathleen. Dr. Seuss: Young Author & Artist. Henderson, Meryl, illus. 2005. (Childhood of Famous Americans Ser.). (ENG.). 192p. (J). (gr. 3-7). pap. 7.99 *(978-0-689-87347-8(6),* Simon & Schuster/Paula Wiseman Bks.) Simon & Schuster/Paula Wiseman Bks.

Kudlinski, Kathleen V. & Kudlinski, Kathleen. Christopher Reeve: Young Actor. Henderson, Meryl, illus. 2007. (Childhood of Famous Americans Ser.). (ENG.). 200p. (J). (gr. 4-6). 18.69 *(978-1-4169-1544-7(3))* Simon & Schuster, Inc.

Kulling, Monica. In the Bag! Margaret Knight Wraps It Up. Parkins, David, illus. 2013. (Great Idea Ser.: 3). 32p. (J). (gr. k-3). pap. 7.95 *(978-1-77049-515-9(0),* Tundra Bks.) Tundra Bks. CAN. Dist: Penguin Random Hse. LLC.

—It's a Snap! George Eastman's First Photograph. Slavin, Bill, illus. 2013. (Great Idea Ser.: 1). 32p. (J). (gr. k-3). pap. 7.95 *(978-1-77049-513-5(4),* Tundra Bks.) Tundra Bks. CAN. Dist: Penguin Random Hse. LLC.

—Spic-And-Span! Lillian Gilbreth's Wonder Kitchen. Parkins, David, illus. 2014. (Great Idea Ser.: 6). 32p. (J). (gr. k-3). 17.99 *(978-1-77049-380-3(8),* Tundra Bks.) Tundra Bks. CAN. Dist: Penguin Random Hse. LLC.

Kundiger, Marion S. Izzie of Fergus Falls: A Minnesota Childhood in The 1880s. Kundiger, Marion S., illus. 2008. (ENG., Illus.). 56p. (J). 29.95 *(978-0-9659712-8-7(7))* Ravenstone Pr.

Kupperberg, Paul. Jerry Yang. 2009. (Asian Americans of Achievement Ser.). (ENG., Illus.). 128p. (gr. 7-12). 35.00 *(978-1-60413-569-5(7),* P171271, Facts On File) Infobase Holdings, Inc.

Kurtz, Jane. Jane Kurtz & YOU, 1 vol. 2007. (Author & YOU Ser.: No. 8). (ENG., Illus.). 204p. per. 40.00 *(978-1-59158-295-3(4),* 900310521, Libraries Unlimited) ABC-CLIO, LLC.

La Bella, Laura. Kanye West, 1 vol. 2009. (Library of Hip-Hop Biographies Ser.). (ENG., Illus.). 48p. (J). (gr. 5-5). pap. 12.75 *(978-1-4358-5439-0(X),* 71b141b2-8604-4a7e-bf09-5a048556ec82) Rosen Publishing Group, Inc., The.

Labrecque, Ellen. Gertrude B. Elion & Pharmacology. 2017. (21st Century Junior Library: Women Innovators Ser.). (ENG., Illus.). 24p. (J). (gr. 2-5). pap. 12.79 *(978-1-63472-314-5(7),* 209301) Cherry Lake Publishing.

—Magic Johnson. 2007. (21st Century Skills Library: Life Skills Biographies Ser.). (ENG., Illus.). 48p. (gr. 4-8). lib. bdg. 34.93 *(978-1-60279-071-1(X),* 200044) Cherry Lake Publishing.

Labrecque, Ellen & Who HQ. Who Was Frank Lloyd Wright? Copeland, Gregory, illus. 2015. (Who Was? Ser.). 112p. (J). (gr. 3-7). 6.99 *(978-0-448-48313-9(0),* Penguin Workshop) Penguin Young Readers Group.

Lace, William W. Benjamin Franklin. 2010. (ENG., Illus.). 120p. (gr. 5-8). 35.00 *(978-1-60413-737-8(1),* P210466, Facts On File) Infobase Holdings, Inc.

—Nolan Ryan: Hall of Fame Baseball Superstar, 1 vol. 2013. (Hall of Fame Sports Greats Ser.). (ENG.). 64p. (gr. 4-6). 30.60 *(978-1-62285-025-9(4),* 625b4b00-a3ad-4fbc-916c-de8ddc417c3c) Enslow Publishing, LLC.

Ladewski, Paul. Stars on the Court. 2009. (NBA Readers Ser.). (ENG.). 32p. (J). (gr. 3-5). 16.19 *(978-0-545-09415-3(1))* Scholastic, Inc.

Lajiness, Katie. Blake Shelton. 2017. (Big Buddy Pop Biographies Set 2 Ser.). (ENG., Illus.). 32p. (J). (gr. 2-5). lib. bdg. 34.21 *(978-1-5321-1063-4(4),* 25702, Big Buddy Bks.) ABDO Publishing Co.

—Carrie Underwood. 2017. (Big Buddy Pop Biographies Set 2 Ser.). (ENG., Illus.). 32p. (J). (gr. 2-5). lib. bdg. 34.21 *(978-1-5321-1064-1(2),* 25704, Big Buddy Bks.) ABDO Publishing Co.

—Cole Sprouse. 2018. (Big Buddy Pop Biographies Ser.). (ENG., Illus.). 32p. (J). (gr. 2-5). lib. bdg. 34.21 *(978-1-5321-1803-6(1),* 30652, Big Buddy Bks.) ABDO Publishing Co.

—Justin Bieber. 2017. (Big Buddy Pop Biographies Set 2 Ser.). (ENG., Illus.). 32p. (J). (gr. 2-5). lib. bdg. 34.21 *(978-1-5321-1059-7(6),* 25694, Big Buddy Bks.) ABDO Publishing Co.

—Lady Gaga. 2017. (Big Buddy Pop Biographies Set 2 Ser.). (ENG., Illus.). 32p. (J). (gr. 2-5). lib. bdg. 34.21 *(978-1-5321-1061-0(8),* 25698, Big Buddy Bks.) ABDO Publishing Co.

Laks Gorman, Jacqueline. Chris Rock, 1 vol. 2008. (Today's Superstars Ser.). (ENG.). 32p. (YA). (gr. 3-3). lib. bdg. 34.60 *(978-0-8368-9235-2(6),* 2769f19e-0510-42d1-b59e-19e0d363f433) Stevens, Gareth Publishing LLLP.

Landau, Jennifer. Jeff Bezos & Amazon, 1 vol. 2012. (Internet Biographies Ser.). (ENG., Illus.). 128p. (J). (gr. 7-7). lib. bdg. 39.80 *(978-1-4488-6914-5(5),* 757135ed-0273-4d4f-9336-d797bf19cb19) Rosen Publishing Group, Inc., The.

Langston-George, Rebecca. The Booth Brothers: Drama, Fame, & the Death of President Lincoln. 2017. (Encounter: Narrative Nonfiction Stories Ser.). (ENG., Illus.). 112p. (J). (gr. 3-7). lib. bdg. 31.32 *(978-1-5157-7338-2(8),* 135667, Capstone Pr.) Capstone.

Lantier, Patricia. Rachel Carson: Fighting Pesticides & Other Chemical Pollutants, 1 vol. 2009. (Voices for Green Choices Ser.). (ENG., Illus.). 48p. (J). (gr. 5-9). pap. *(978-0-7787-4676-8(3));* lib. bdg. *(978-0-7787-4663-8(1))* Crabtree Publishing Co.

Latta, Sara L. Who Invented the Ferris Wheel? George Ferris, 1 vol. 2012. (I Like Inventors! Ser.). (ENG., Illus.). 24p. (gr. k-2). 25.27 *(978-0-7660-3964-3(1),* 195a988d-2f0b-40fb-b178-ddd146aa4764, Enslow Elementary) Enslow Publishing, LLC.

Lauren, Jill. That's Like Me!, 1 vol. 2009. (ENG.). 32p. (J). (gr. k-3). pap. 7.95 *(978-1-59572-208-9(4))* Star Bright Bks., Inc.

Leavitt, Amie. Miley Cyrus. 2007. (Robbie Reader Ser.). (Illus.). 32p. (J). (gr. 2-5). lib. bdg. 25.70 *(978-1-58415-590-4(6))* Mitchell Lane Pubs.

—Raven-Symone. 2007. (Robbie Reader Ser.). (Illus.). 32p. (YA). (gr. 2-5). lib. bdg. 25.70 *(978-1-58415-593-5(0))* Mitchell Lane Pubs.

Leavitt, Amie Jane. Abigail Breslin. 2009. (Robbie Reader Ser.). (Illus.). 32p. (YA). (gr. 2-5). lib. bdg. 25.70 *(978-1-58415-759-5(3))* Mitchell Lane Pubs.

—Day by Day with Miley Cyrus. 2010. (Randy's Corner Ser.). (Illus.). 32p. (J). (gr. -1-2). lib. bdg. 25.70 *(978-1-58415-856-1(5))* Mitchell Lane Pubs.

—Dylan & Cole Sprouse. 2007. (Robbie Reader Ser.). (Illus.). 32p. (YA). (gr. 2-5). lib. bdg. 25.70 *(978-1-58415-591-1(4))* Mitchell Lane Pubs.

—Miranda Cosgrove. 2008. (Robbie Reader Ser.). (Illus.). 32p. (YA). (gr. 2-5). lib. bdg. 25.70 *(978-1-58415-720-5(8))* Mitchell Lane Pubs.

—Taylor Lautner. 2010. (Robbie Reader Ser.). (Illus.). 32p. (YA). (gr. 2-5). lib. bdg. 25.70 *(978-1-58415-897-4(2))* Mitchell Lane Pubs.

Lee, Sally. Martha Washington, 1 vol. 2010. (First Ladies Ser.). (ENG.). 24p. (J). (gr. -1-2). lib. bdg. 27.32 *(978-1-4296-5011-3(7),* 112960, Capstone Pr.) Capstone.

Lee, T. S. The Lincoln Story: The Boy Who Embraced a Nation. 4th ed. 2010. (Great Heroes Ser.). 184p. (J). pap. 14.95 *(978-0-9819542-3-3(5))* DASANBOOKS.

Lemmens, Mary Jo. Christina Aguilera. 2009. (Hip-Hop 2 Ser.). 64p. (YA). (gr. 7-12). lib. bdg. 22.95 *(978-1-4222-0285-2(2))* Mason Crest.

—Cypress Hill. 2009. (Hip Hop (Mason Crest Paperback) Ser.). (Illus.). 64p. (YA). (gr. 4-7). pap. 7.95 *(978-1-4222-0345-3(X))* Mason Crest.

Lemmens, Maryjo. Cypress Hill. 2009. (Hip-Hop 2 Ser.). (Illus.). 64p. (YA). (gr. 7-12). lib. bdg. 22.95 *(978-1-4222-0287-6(9))* Mason Crest.

—Jennifer Lopez. 2009. (Hip-Hop 2 Ser.). (Illus.). 64p. (J). (gr. 7-12). lib. bdg. 22.95 *(978-1-4222-0296-8(8))* Mason Crest.

—Xzibit. 2009. (Hip-Hop 2 Ser.). (Illus.). 64p. (YA). (gr. 7-12). lib. bdg. 22.95 *(978-1-4222-0305-7(0))* Mason Crest.

Lesinski, Jeanne M. Bill Gates. 2007. (Illus.). 112p. (J). (gr. 6-9). per. 7.95 *(978-0-8225-7027-1(0),* Lerner Pubns.); lib. bdg. 29.27 *(978-0-8225-7363-0(6),* Twenty-First Century Bks.) Lerner Publishing Group.

—USA Today Lifeline Biographies, 8 vols., Set. Incl. Bill Gates: Entrepreneur & Philanthropist. (ENG.). 112p. (YA). (gr. 7-12). 2008. lib. bdg. 33.26 *(978-1-58013-570-2(6));* (USA TODAY Lifeline Biographies Ser.). (ENG.). 2008. Set lib. bdg. 934.20 *(978-1-58013-568-9(4),* Twenty-First Century Bks.) Lerner Publishing Group.

LeTourneau, Anthony Alex, illus. Hanni & Beth: Safe & Sound. 2007. (J). (gr. k-3). 17.95 *(978-0-9792918-0-7(1))* Blue Marlin Pubns.

Leventhal, Josh. Linebackers. 2016. (Football's All-Time Greats Ser.). (ENG.). 32p. (J). (gr. 4-6). pap. 9.99 *(978-1-64466-164-2(0),* 10358); (Illus.). 31.35 *(978-1-68072-040-2(6),* 10357) Black Rabbit Bks. (Bolt).

—Running Backs. 2016. (Football's All-Time Greats Ser.). (ENG.). 32p. (J). (gr. 4-6). pap. 9.99 *(978-1-64466-167-3(5),* 10370); (Illus.). 31.35 *(978-1-68072-043-3(0),* 10369) Black Rabbit Bks. (Bolt).

Levin, Judith. Ichiro Suzuki. 2009. (Baseball Superstars Ser.). (ENG., Illus.). 144p. (gr. 6-12). pap. 11.95 *(978-0-7910-9849-3(4),* P147497, Checkmark Bks.) Infobase Holdings, Inc.

Levy, Janey. Inside the Environmental Movement, 1 vol. 2017. (Eyewitness to History Ser.). (ENG.). 32p. (J). (gr. 4-5). pap. 11.50 *(978-1-5382-1157-1(2),* fdf454d7-cb45-4d4a-88e9-a942c6fc5c76) Stevens, Gareth Publishing LLLP.

—Motocross Superstars. (Motocross Ser.). 32p. (gr. 4-5). 2009. 47.90 *(978-1-61514-667-3(9))* 2007. (ENG., Illus.). (J). lib. bdg. 28.93 *(978-1-4042-3695-0(3),* 43b92e34-7cbf-4509-b5da-cfc400a95363) Rosen Publishing Group, Inc., The. (PowerKids Pr.).

—William Penn: Shaping a Nation. 2009. (American History Milestones Ser.). 32p. (gr. 5-5). 47.90 *(978-1-61511-376-7(2),* PowerKids Pr.) Rosen Publishing Group, Inc., The.

Lies, Anne. Oprah Winfrey: Media Mogul, 1 vol. 2011. (Essential Lives Set 6 Ser.). (ENG., Illus.). 112p. (J). (gr. 6-12). lib. bdg. 41.36 *(978-1-61714-786-9(9),* 6737, Essential Library) ABDO Publishing Co.

Link, Theodore. George Armstrong Custer: General of the U. S. Cavalry, 1 vol. 2003. (Famous People in American History / Grandes Personajes en la Historia de Los Estados Unidos Ser.). Tr. of George Armstrong Custer: General de la Caballería Estadounidense. (ENG & SPA., Illus.). 32p. (gr. 2-3). lib. bdg. 29.13 *(978-0-8239-4158-2(2),* e97ac072-83b4-46f2-a0fc-b11714411c70, Editorial Buenas Letras) Rosen Publishing Group, Inc., The.

Llanas, Sheila Griffin. Ettore Boiardi: Chef Boyardee Manufacturer. 2014. (Food Dudes Ser.). (ENG.). 32p. (J). (gr. 3-6). lib. bdg. 32.79 *(978-1-62403-314-8(8),* 1390, Checkerboard Library) ABDO Publishing Co.

Lobb, Nancy. 16 Extraordinary Young Americans. 2nd ed. 2007. (16 Extraordinary Ser.). (Illus.). 127p. (gr. 6-12). tchr. ed., per. 25.00 *(978-0-8251-6283-1(1))* Walch Education.

Lord, Raymond. Usher. 2008. (Hip-Hop Ser.). (Illus.). 64p. (YA). (gr. 7-12). lib. bdg. 22.95 *(978-1-4222-0131-2(7))* Mason Crest.

Louie, Ai-Ling. Vera Wang Queen of Fashion; Amazing Chinese American: Biographies of Amazing Asian Americans. 2007. (Biographies of Amazing Asian Americans Ser.). (ENG., Illus.). 48p. (J). pap. 12.99 *(978-0-9787465-3-7(8))* Dragoneagle Pr.

Lupo, Tamar. Warren Buffett. 2007. (Remarkable People Ser.). (Illus.). 24p. (J). (gr. 4-7). pap. 8.95 *(978-1-59036-652-3(2));* lib. bdg. 24.45 *(978-1-59036-651-6(4))* Weigl Pubs., Inc.

Lusted, Marcia Amidon. Mark Zuckerberg: Facebook Creator, 1 vol. 2011. (Essential Lives Set 7 Ser.). (ENG., Illus.). 112p. (YA). (gr. 6-12). lib. bdg. 41.36 *(978-1-61783-008-2(9),* 6755, Essential Library) ABDO Publishing Co.

Lynch, Kelly Ann. He Said Yes: The Story of Father Mychal Judge. Oatman, M. Scott, illus. 2007. (ENG.). 32p. (J). (gr. -1-3). 12.95 *(978-0-8091-6740-1(2),* 6740-1) Paulist Pr.

Lynette, Rachel. Ashley Shuyler: Founder of AfricAid, 1 vol. 2007. (Young Heroes Ser.). (ENG., Illus.). 48p. (gr. 4-8). lib. bdg. 29.88 *(978-0-7377-3669-4(0),* 1601dd62-8b6e-4feb-9a6a-c8394f05da12, KidHaven Publishing) Greenhaven Publishing LLC.

—Jennifer Aniston, 1 vol. 2010. (People in the News Ser.). (ENG., Illus.). 96p. (gr. 7-7). 41.03 *(978-1-4205-0235-0(2),* 9aa43648-5d0a-40fe-9a9e-0e4909d32896, Lucent Pr.) Greenhaven Publishing LLC.

MacCarry, Noel & Who HQ. Who Was Pete Seeger? Marchesi, Stephen, illus. 2017. (Who Was? Ser.). 112p. (J). (gr. 3-7). 5.99 *(978-0-448-48475-4(7),* Penguin Workshop) Penguin Young Readers Group.

Macdonald, James. Dale Earnhardt, Jr. Racing's Living Legacy, 1 vol. 2008. (Heroes of Racing Ser.). (ENG., Illus.). 128p. (gr. 5-6). lib. bdg. 35.93 *(978-0-7660-2996-5(4),* 53b50301-0a3e-4f0c-849e-d98a58897d41) Enslow Publishing, LLC.

—Dale Earnhardt, Sr. The Intimidator, 1 vol. 2009. (Heroes of Racing Ser.). (ENG., Illus.). 128p. (gr. 5-6). lib. bdg. 35.93 *(978-0-7660-3297-2(3),* c48b8efb-f6db-4411-8961-12c7bf9be0ab) Enslow Publishing, LLC.

MacLeod, Elizabeth. Harry Houdini. Mantha, John, illus. 2009. (Kids Can Read Ser.). 32p. (J). (gr. 1-3). 14.95 *(978-1-55453-298-8(1))* Kids Can Pr., Ltd. CAN. Dist: Hachette Bk. Group.

—Thomas Edison. Krystoforski, Andrej, illus. 2008. 32p. (J). (gr. 1-3). 14.95 *(978-1-55453-057-1(1))* Kids Can Pr., Ltd. CAN. Dist: Hachette Bk. Group.

Macy, Sue. The Book Rescuer: How a Mensch from Massachusetts Saved Yiddish Literature for Generations to Come. Innerst, Stacy, illus. 2019. (ENG.). 48p. (J). (gr. k-3). 17.99 *(978-1-4814-7220-3(8))* Simon & Schuster.

Madison, Taylor. Boys We Love: Today's Top 30 Hottest Stars. 2005. (Illus.). (J). *(978-0-439-74864-3(X))* Scholastic, Inc.

Magid, Jennifer. Angelina Jolie, 1 vol. 2008. (Today's Superstars Ser.). (ENG.). 32p. (YA). (gr. 3-3). lib. bdg. 34.60 *(978-0-8368-9234-5(8),* ba7517f1-566f-4076-8a1b-bba28c1aeeb3) Stevens, Gareth Publishing LLLP.

Mahaney, Ian F. Dave Mirra: Bicycle Stunt Champ, 1 vol. 2004. (Extreme Sports Biographies Ser.). (ENG., Illus.). 64p. (J). (gr. 5-8). 26.27 *(978-1-4042-2744-6(X),* 9647969a-d24d-4c2d-aabc-870d9f86fea6) Rosen Publishing Group, Inc., The.

Mara, Wil. Dwight Eisenhower, 1 vol. 2011. (Presidents & Their Times Ser.). (ENG.). 96p. (gr. 6-6). 36.93 *(978-0-7614-4812-9(8),* fbe0cc09-90ad-4c1b-8501-498b0c193ab9) Cavendish Square Publishing LLC.

—Martin Luther King Jr. 2013. (Rookie Biographies(r) Ser.). (ENG.). 32p. (J). pap. 5.95 *(978-0-531-24704-4(X));* (gr. 1-2). lib. bdg. 18.69 *(978-0-531-24738-9(4),* Children's Pr.) Scholastic Library Publishing.

—Rookie Biographies: Harriet Tubman. 2013. (Rookie Biographies(r) Ser.). (ENG., Illus.). 32p. (J). lib. bdg. 23.00 *(978-0-531-24737-2(6))* Scholastic Library Publishing.

Marchesani, Laura. Brett Favre: The All-Time Leader. 2008. (ENG.). 48p. (J). (gr. k-3). 16.19 *(978-0-448-44978-4(1))* Penguin Young Readers Group.

Marcovitz, Hal. Chris Daughtry. 2009. (Dream Big: American Idol Superstars Ser.). 64p. (YA). (gr. 5-18). 22.95 *(978-1-4222-1508-1(3));* pap. 9.95 *(978-1-4222-1595-1(4))* Mason Crest.

—Cuban Americans. (Successful Americans Ser.). (Illus.). 64p. (J). 2009. (gr. 9-12). 22.95 *(978-1-4222-0523-5(1))* 2007. (gr. 7-18). pap. 9.95 *(978-1-4222-0856-4(7))* Mason Crest.

—Derek Jeter. 2010. (Modern Role Models Ser.). (Illus.). 64p. (YA). (gr. 7-12). lib. bdg. 22.95 *(978-1-4222-0482-5(0))* Mason Crest.

—Elliott Yamin. 2009. (Dream Big: American Idol Superstars Ser.). 64p. (YA). (gr. 5-18). 22.95 *(978-1-4222-1513-5(X));* pap. 9.95 *(978-1-4222-1599-9(7))* Mason Crest.

—Kellie Pickler. 2009. (Dream Big: American Idol Superstars Ser.). 64p. (YA). (gr. 5-18). pap. 9.95 *(978-1-4222-1603-3(9));* lib. bdg. 22.95 *(978-1-4222-1510-4(5))* Mason Crest.

—Michelle. 2007. (Obamas Ser.). 64p. (YA). (gr. 3-6). pap. 9.95 *(978-1-4222-1485-5(0));* (gr. 4-7). lib. bdg. 19.95 *(978-1-4222-1478-7(8))* Mason Crest.

—Russian Americans. (Major American Immigration Ser.). (Illus.). 64p. (YA). (gr. 9-12). 2010. 22.95 *(978-1-4222-0617-1(3))* 2009. 22.95 *(978-1-4222-0513-6(4))* Mason Crest.

—Uncle Sam: International Symbol of America. Moreno, Barry, ed. 2014. (Patriotic Symbols of America Ser.: 20). 48p. (J). (gr. 4-18). lib. bdg. 20.95 *(978-1-4222-3135-7(6))* Mason Crest.

Marsh, Carole. Dick Cheney: U. S. Vice President. 2004. (1000 Readers Ser.). (Illus.). 14p. (J). (gr. k-4). pap. 2.95 *(978-0-635-02670-5(8))* Gallopade International.

—Jefferson Davis, Civil War Hero. 2004. 12p. (gr. k-4). 2.95 *(978-0-635-02366-7(0))* Gallopade International.

—Jimmy Carter. 2003. 12p. (gr. k-4). 2.95 *(978-0-635-02126-7(9))* Gallopade International.

—John C. Fremont. 2004. 12p. (gr. k-4). 2.95 *(978-0-635-02380-3(6))* Gallopade International.

—John Edwards: Vice Presidential Hopeful. 2004. (Did You Know... ? Ser.). (Illus.). 12p. (J). (gr. k-4). pap. 2.95 *(978-0-635-02671-2(6))* Gallopade International.

—John F. Kennedy. 2003. 12p. (gr. k-4). 2.95 *(978-0-635-02127-4(7))* Gallopade International.

—Jonas Salk. 2004. 12p. (gr. k-4). 2.95 *(978-0-635-02377-3(6))* Gallopade International.

—Meriwether Lewis & William Clark: Explorers of the Uncharted West: Explorers of the Uncharted West. 2003. 12p. (gr. k-4). 2.95 *(978-0-635-02133-5(1))* Gallopade International.

—Roberto Clemente: Baseball Hero & Humanitarian: Baseball Hero & Humanitarian. 2003. 12p. (gr. k-4). 2.95 *(978-0-635-02140-3(4))* Gallopade International.

—Samuel Adams. 2003. 12p. (gr. k-4). 2.95 *(978-0-635-02367-4(9))* Gallopade International.

Marsico, Katie. Ronald Reagan, 1 vol. 2011. (Presidents & Their Times Ser.). (ENG.). 96p. (gr. 6-6). 36.93 *(978-0-7614-4814-3(4),* a120eb10-6f7c-4e8f-ab7d-8a44a1d07704) Cavendish Square Publishing LLC.

—Zora Neale Hurston, 1 vol. 2008. (Essential Lives Set 2 Ser.). (ENG., Illus.). 112p. (YA). (gr. 6-12). lib. bdg. 41.36 *(978-1-60453-036-0(7),* 6653, Essential Library) ABDO Publishing Co.

Martin Luther King Jr. (Illus.). 112p. pap. 9.95 *(978-0-8225-5316-8(3))* Lerner Publishing Group.

Marvis, Barbara. Day by Day with Beyonce. 2010. (Randy's Corner Ser.). (Illus.). 32p. (J). (gr. -1-2). lib. bdg. 25.70 *(978-1-58415-859-2(X))* Mitchell Lane Pubs.

—Day by Day with Lebron James. 2010. (Randy's Corner Ser.). (Illus.). 32p. (YA). (gr. -1-2). lib. bdg. 25.70 (978-1-58415-858-5(1)) Mitchell Lane Pubs.

Mason, Paul. Extreme Sports Stars, 1 vol. 2012. (Celebrity Secrets Ser.). (ENG., Illus.). 24p. (J). (gr. 5-6). pap. 9.25 (978-1-4488-7080-6(1), 8e4bce59-9b94-4285-91a7-592d17473edd); lib. bdg. 26.27 (978-1-4488-7035-6(6), 792f96a1-441e-4805-a73f-4f730d0a4e20) Rosen Publishing Group, Inc., The. (PowerKids Pr.).

Masters, Nancy Robinson. Extraordinary People: Extraordinary Patriots of the United States of America. 2005. (Extraordinary People Ser.). (ENG., Illus.). 288p. (J). (gr. 4-7). 40.00 (978-0-516-24404-4(3), Children's Pr.) Scholastic Library Publishing.

Mattern, Joanne. Barack Obama. 2013. (Rookie Biographies(r) Ser.). (ENG.). 32p. (J). pap. 5.95 (978-0-531-24701-3(5)); lib. bdg. 23.00 (978-0-531-24735-8(X)) Scholastic Library Publishing.

—Blake Lively. 2010. (Blue Banner Biography Ser.). (Illus.). 32p. (YA). (gr. 4-7). lib. bdg. 25.70 (978-1-58415-909-4(X)) Mitchell Lane Pubs.

—Dak Prescott. 2017. lib. bdg. 25.70 (978-1-68020-127-7(1)) Mitchell Lane Pubs.

—Dakota Fanning. 2006. (Robbie Reader Ser.). (Illus.). 32p. (J). (gr. 2-5). lib. bdg. 25.70 (978-1-58415-519-5(1)) Mitchell Lane Pubs.

—Day by Day with Adam Jones. 2014. (Illus.). 32p. (J). (gr. -1-2). 25.70 (978-1-61228-632-7(1)) Mitchell Lane Pubs.

—Jaden Smith. 2009. (Robbie Reader Ser.). (Illus.). 32p. (YA). (gr. 2-5). lib. bdg. 25.70 (978-1-58415-757-1(7)) Mitchell Lane Pubs.

—James Harden. 2017. lib. bdg. 25.70 (978-1-68020-122-2(0)) Mitchell Lane Pubs.

—Ludacris. 2011. (Blue Banner Biography Ser.). (Illus.). 32p. (YA). (gr. 4-7). lib. bdg. 25.70 (978-1-61228-055-4(2)) Mitchell Lane Pubs.

—Rookie Biographies: Steve Jobs. 2013. (Rookie Biographies(r) Ser.). (ENG., Illus.). 32p. (J). lib. bdg. 23.00 (978-0-531-24739-6(2)) Scholastic Library Publishing.

—Steve Jobs (Rookie Biographies) 2013. (Rookie Biographies Ser.). (ENG., Illus.). 32p. (J). (gr. 1-2). pap. 5.95 (978-0-531-24705-1(8), Children's Pr.) Scholastic Library Publishing.

Maurer, Tracy Nelson. Noah Webster's Fighting Words. Catusanu, Mircea, illus. 2017. (ENG.). 40p. (J). (gr. 2-5). E-Book 30.65 (978-1-5124-2839-1(6), Millbrook Pr.) Lerner Publishing Group.

—Samuel Morse, That's Who! The Story of the Telegraph & Morse Code. Ramón, El Primo, illus. 2019. (ENG.). 40p. (J). 19.99 (978-1-62779-130-4(2), 900136046, Holt, Henry & Co. Bks. For Young Readers) Holt, Henry & Co.

McCarthy, Meghan. Strong Man: The Story of Charles Atlas. 2015. (Illus.). 40p. (J). (gr. k-3). 7.99 (978-0-553-11354-9(2), Dragonfly Bks.) Random Hse. Children's Bks.

McCarthy, Rose. Paul Revere: Jinete de la guerra de Independencia, 1 vol. 2003. (Grandes Personajes en la Historia de Los Estados Unidos (Famous People in American History) Ser.). (SPA.). 32p. (gr. 3-4). pap. 10.00 (978-0-8239-4236-7(8), 7a9dae9c-1087-4ed3-af54-9ea70e742eec, Rosen Classroom) Rosen Publishing Group, Inc., The.

McCully, Emily Arnold. Ida M. Tarbell: The Woman Who Challenged Big Business — And Won! 2014. (ENG., Illus.). 288p. (YA). (gr. 7). 18.99 (978-0-547-29092-8(6), 1412369, Clarion Bks.) HarperCollins Pubs.

McDonnell, Peter. A Soldier in Disguise. Tormey, Carlotta, illus. 2005. 16p. (J). pap. (978-0-7367-2909-3(7)) Zaner-Bloser, Inc.

McElroy, Lisa Tucker. Nancy Pelosi: First Woman Speaker of the House. 2007. (Gateway Biographies Ser.). (ENG., Illus.). 48p. (J). (gr. 4-8). lib. bdg. 26.60 (978-0-8225-8685-2(1), Lerner Pubns.) Lerner Publishing Group.

—Ted Kennedy: A Remarkable Life in the Senate. 2009. (Gateway Biographies Ser.). (ENG., Illus.). 48p. (J). (gr. 4-8). 26.60 (978-0-7613-4457-5(8)) Lerner Publishing Group.

McGowan, Joseph. Will Smith, 1 vol. 2009. (Today's Superstars Ser.). (ENG.). 48p. (J). (gr. 3-3). pap. 15.05 (978-1-4339-2376-0(9), 75b5b50c-9b22-479e-bdc0-5a8aafd2bab3); lib. bdg. 34.60 (978-1-4339-2380-7(7), 2f2ba5db-d6fb-41e8-8001-c91a25d8fac6) Stevens, Gareth Publishing LLLP.

McKinley, Fred B. Chinqua Where? The Spirit of Rural America, 1947-1955. Blassingame, Calvin, illus. 2003. 319p. 24.95 (978-0-9729655-0-7(5)) Willow Creel Publishing Co.

Mckissack, Patricia & Mckissack, Fredrick. Frederick Douglass: Fighter Against Slavery, 1 vol. 2013. (Famous African Americans Ser.). (ENG.). 24p. (gr. k-2). pap. 10.35 (978-1-4644-0196-1(9), dcc5b08d-3be4-4932-b752-9c1b8c1a042b, Enslow Elementary) Enslow Publishing, LLC.

—Marian Anderson: Amazing Opera Singer, 1 vol. 2013. (Famous African Americans Ser.). (ENG., Illus.). 24p. (gr. k-2). pap. 10.35 (978-1-4644-0202-9(7), 2a8cea21-2a90-4567-bf40-8b52cfc07aa4, Enslow Elementary) Enslow Publishing, LLC.

—Paul Robeson: A Voice for Change, 1 vol. 2013. (Famous African Americans Ser.). (ENG.). 24p. (gr. k-2). pap. 10.35 (978-1-4644-0205-0(1), dc893b8a-0788-4dfc-ad53-35b11b21d047); (Illus.). 25.27 (978-0-7660-4107-3(7), 07716234-1468-4642-8459-5686579373a7) Enslow Publishing, LLC. (Enslow Elementary).

McLeese, Don. Jonas Salk. 2005. (Rourke Discovery Library). (Illus.). 24p. (J). (gr. 2-5). lib. bdg. (978-1-59515-436-1(1)) Rourke Educational Media.

—Robert Fulton. 2005. (Rourke Discovery Library). (Illus.). 24p. (J). (gr. 2-5). lib. bdg. (978-1-59515-434-7(5), 1244323) Rourke Educational Media.

McNeese, Tim. New Amsterdam. 2007. (ENG., Illus.). 109p. (gr. 5-9). lib. bdg. 30.00 (978-0-7910-9334-4(4), P124708, Facts On File) Infobase Holdings, Inc.

McNeill, Allison & Hanes, Richard Clay. American Home Front in World War II Reference Library Cumulative Index. 2004. (American Homefront in World War II Reference Library). (ENG.). 32p. 5.00 (978-0-7876-9125-7(9), UXL) Cengage Gale.

McPherson, Stephanie Sammartino. Bill Clinton. 2008. (History Maker Biographies Ser.). (ENG.). 48p. (gr. 3-6). 27.93 (978-0-8225-7986-1(3), Lerner Pubns.) Lerner Publishing Group.

—Levi Strauss. 2007. (History Maker Bios Ser.). (Illus.). 48p. (J). (gr. 3-7). lib. bdg. 26.60 (978-0-8225-6581-9(1), Lerner Pubns.) Lerner Publishing Group.

—Susan B. Anthony. 2006. (History Maker Bios Ser.). (Illus.). 48p. (J). (gr. 3-7). lib. bdg. 26.60 (978-0-8225-5938-2(2), Lerner Pubns.) Lerner Publishing Group.

McVey, James. Martha Maxwell: Natural History Pioneer. 2005. (Now You Know Bio Ser.: 4). (Illus.). 84p. (J). pap. (978-0-86541-075-6(5)) Filter Pr., LLC.

Mead, Wendy. William H. Taft, 1 vol. 2012. (Presidents & Their Times Ser.). (ENG.). 96p. (gr. 6-6). 36.93 (978-1-60870-186-5(7), c3f6f76c-90ed-45ce-9fab-680c514e816d) Cavendish Square Publishing LLC.

Meet NASA Inventor Masahiro Ono & His Team's Asteroid-Harpooning Hitcher. 2017. (J). (978-0-7166-6161-0(6)) World Bk., Inc.

Meet NASA Inventor Robert Hoyt & His Team's Web-Spinning Space Spiders. 2017. (J). (978-0-7166-6157-3(8)) World Bk., Inc.

Mello, Tara Baukus. Mark Martin. rev. ed. 2007. (Race Car Legends: Collector's Edition Ser.). (ENG., Illus.). 72p. (gr. 5-9). lib. bdg. 25.00 (978-0-7910-8664-3(X), P129221, Facts On File) Infobase Holdings, Inc.

—Tony Stewart. rev. collector's ed. 2005. (Race Car Legends: Collector's Edition Ser.). (ENG., Illus.). 64p. (gr. 5-9). lib. bdg. 25.00 (978-0-7910-8670-4(4), P114376, Facts On File) Infobase Holdings, Inc.

Meltzer, Milton. Henry David Thoreau: A Biography. 2007. (Literary Greats Ser.). (ENG., Illus.). 160p. (gr. 7-12). lib. bdg. 33.26 (978-0-8225-5893-4(9), Twenty-First Century Bks.) Lerner Publishing Group.

Mentyka, Sharon. Think Smart, Be Fearless: A Biography of Bill Gates. Mildenberger, Vivien, illus. 2019. (Growing to Greatness Ser.). 48p. (J). (gr. k-4). 18.99 (978-1-63217-176-4(7), Little Bigfoot) Sasquatch Bks.

Merwin, E. & Roshell, Starshine. Lady Gaga. 2018. (Amazing Americans: Pop Music Stars Ser.). (ENG.). 24p. (J). (gr. -1-3). lib. bdg. 26.99 (978-1-68402-677-7(6)) Bearport Publishing Co., Inc.

Meyer, Susan. Jimmy Wales & Wikipedia, 1 vol. 2012. (Internet Biographies Ser.). (ENG.). 120p. (YA). (gr. 7-7). lib. bdg. 39.80 (978-1-4488-6912-1(9), fe8f98f5-7491-426f-9f2b-d3407ebe6dfc) Rosen Publishing Group, Inc., The.

Mickle, Shelley Fraser. Barbaro: America's Horse. 2007. (ENG., Illus.). 160p. (J). (gr. 3-7). pap. 9.99 (978-1-4169-4865-0(1), Simon & Schuster/Paula Wiseman Bks.) Simon & Schuster/Paula Wiseman Bks.

Micklos, John & Micklos, John, Jr. Muhammad Ali: Fighting As a Conscientious Objector, 1 vol. 2017. (Rebels with a Cause Ser.). (ENG.). 128p. (J). (gr. 8-8). 38.93 (978-0-7660-9256-3(9), c883e37b-5b0e-4b95-8a73-7ee3bcf15da2); pap. 20.95 (978-0-7660-9553-3(3), 0316448b-6e5d-4a61-a006-aefc5e29980b) Enslow Publishing, LLC.

Miklowitz, Gloria. Cesar Chavez. 2009. pap. 13.25 (978-1-60559-056-1(8)) Hameray Publishing Group, Inc.

Miller, Adam, et al. Courage under Fire: True Stories of Bravery from the U. S. Army, Navy, Air Force, & Marines, 1 vol. 2014. (Courage under Fire Ser.). (ENG., Illus.). 112p. (J). (gr. 3-9). pap., pap., pap. 9.95 (978-1-4914-1065-3(5), 126702, Capstone Pr.) Capstone.

Miller, Brandon Marie. Women of the Frontier: 16 Tales of Trailblazing Homesteaders, Entrepreneurs, & Rabble-Rousers. 2013. (Women of Action Ser.: 3). (ENG., Illus.). 256p. (J). (gr. 7). 19.95 (978-1-883052-97-3(1)) Chicago Review Pr., Inc.

Miller, Calvin Craig. Roy Wilkins: Leader of the NAACP. 2005. (Civil Rights Leaders Ser.). (Illus.). 176p. (YA). (gr. 6-12). 26.95 (978-1-931798-49-5(4)) Reynolds, Morgan Inc.

Miller, Kat. I Love Kristen Stewart, 1 vol. 2010. (Fan Club Ser.). (ENG.). 24p. (gr. 2-3). lib. bdg. 27.27 (978-1-61533-060-7(7), c6c37a06-aa01-41c0-93d9-7ddaea0f678a); (Illus.). (J). pap. 9.15 (978-1-61533-061-4(5), 6ad300f3-2517-46b4-a0e8-db3f96f0554d) Rosen Publishing Group, Inc., The. (Windmill Bks.).

—I Love Miley Cyrus, 1 vol. 2010. (Fan Club Ser.). (ENG.). 24p. (J). (gr. 2-3). lib. bdg. 27.27 (978-1-61533-045-4(3), 92f3a020-cdfc-4f80-8536-1edf60b81606); (Illus.). pap. 9.15 (978-1-61533-046-1(1), 89b171ca-5617-441d-a14a-edc942640002) Rosen Publishing Group, Inc., The. (Windmill Bks.).

—I Love the Jonas Brothers, 1 vol. 2010. (Fan Club Ser.). (ENG.). 24p. (J). (gr. 2-3). lib. bdg. 27.27 (978-1-61533-048-5(8), 53b5250a-83d0-440e-adc6-967ffac16fb0); (Illus.). pap. 9.15 (978-1-61533-049-2(6), d03d3ae6-628e-4d5a-82dc-2c493062d86a) Rosen Publishing Group, Inc., The. (Windmill Bks.).

Miller, Raymond H. Matt Groening. 2005. (Inventors & Creators Ser.). (ENG., Illus.). 48p. (gr. 4-8). 27.00 (978-0-7377-3158-3(3), Greenhaven Pr., Inc.) Cengage Gale.

Miller, Reagan & Arthur, Martin. Great Leaders of the Civil War. 2011. (ENG.). 48p. (J). pap. (978-0-7787-5359-9(X)); lib. bdg. (978-0-7787-5342-1(5)) Crabtree Publishing Co.

Mills, Cliff. Clayton Kershaw. 2014. (Illus.). 32p. (J). (gr. 1-4). 25.70 (978-1-61228-636-5(4)) Mitchell Lane Pubs.

Mills, J. Elizabeth. Ken Griffey Sr. & Ken Griffey Jr. Baseball Heroes, 1 vol. 2010. (Sports Families Ser.). (ENG., Illus.). 48p. (YA). (gr. 5-5). lib. bdg. 34.47 (978-1-4358-3554-2(9), b57b0b5e-b5df-412c-926a-b58a2182958d) Rosen Publishing Group, Inc., The.

Mintzer, Richard. Latino Americans in Sports, Film, Music & Government: Trailblazers. 2007. (Hispanic Heritage Ser.). (Illus.). 112p. (YA). (gr. 4-7). lib. bdg. 22.95 (978-1-59084-936-1(1)) Mason Crest.

Mis, Melody S. Civil Rights Leaders, 12 vols., Set. Incl. Meet Al Sharpton. lib. bdg. 26.27 (978-1-4042-4213-5(9), 98a6ed84-b3cf-4724-8502-4b7661d70999); Meet Coretta Scott King. lib. bdg. 26.27 (978-1-4042-4211-1(2), 6665c8c6-5932-449a-ba9d-55d71f765f26); Meet Jesse Jackson. lib. bdg. 26.27 (978-1-4042-4212-8(0), 7f13a688-1352-4455-9287-50c573805ee0); Meet Malcolm X. lib. bdg. 26.27 (978-1-4042-4214-2(7), 46796c58-721e-437d-97d9-595c2e45b237); Meet Martin Luther King Jr. lib. bdg. 26.27 (978-1-4042-4209-8(0), a4ce3b17-20e4-45f2-82ea-b24cbcab11c3); Meet Rosa Parks. lib. bdg. 26.27 (978-1-4042-4210-4(4), 4b44a5af-168d-44aa-9566-8c251e274076); (Illus.). 24p. (YA). (gr. 2-3). (Civil Rights Leaders Ser.). (ENG.). 2007. Set lib. bdg. 157.62 (978-1-4042-4240-1(6), f1458a8f-0a9c-4d59-9db6-e380deaeb82f) Rosen Publishing Group, Inc., The.

—Meet Al Sharpton, 1 vol. 2007. (Civil Rights Leaders Ser.). (ENG., Illus.). 24p. (YA). (gr. 2-3). lib. bdg. 26.27 (978-1-4042-4213-5(9), 98a6ed84-b3cf-4724-8502-4b7661d70999) Rosen Publishing Group, Inc., The.

Mitchell Lane Publishers Inc. Staff. Profiles in American History. 2007. (YA). lib. bdg. 460.90 (978-1-58415-532-4(9)) Mitchell Lane Pubs.

Mitchell, Susan. Will Smith, 1 vol. 2007. (Today's Superstars Ser.). (ENG., Illus.). 32p. (gr. 3-3). lib. bdg. 34.60 (978-0-8368-7653-6(9), f9976550-7f7f-41e2-8dfa-9db5734ecf1f) Stevens, Gareth Publishing LLLP.

Mitchells, Brett. The Dixie Chicks, 1 vol. 2008. (Contemporary Musicians & Their Music Ser.). (ENG., Illus.). 48p. (J). (gr. 6-6). lib. bdg. 34.47 (978-1-4042-1817-8(3), 9f3ce705-6314-489a-885b-db8eeac89120) Rosen Publishing Group, Inc., The.

—Dixie Chicks. (Contemporary Musicians & Their Music Ser.). 48p. (gr. 6-6). 2009. 53.00 (978-1-61511-932-5(9)) 2008. (ENG., Illus.). pap. 12.75 (978-1-4358-5125-2(0), 311a4104-afec-4cd1-96d3-ed1986a7ebb2, Rosen Classroom) Rosen Publishing Group, Inc., The.

Monroe, Tyler. Uncle Sam, 1 vol. 2013. (U. S. Symbols Ser.). (ENG.). 24p. (J). (gr. -1-2). 27.32 (978-1-4765-3086-4(6), 123063); pap. 7.95 (978-1-4765-3535-7(3), 123581) Capstone.

Montgomery, Sy. The Tarantula Scientist. Bishop, Nic, photos by. 2007. (Scientists in the Field Ser.). (ENG., Illus.). 80p. (J). (gr. 5-7). pap. 9.99 (978-0-618-91577-4(X), 1014892, Clarion Bks.) HarperCollins Pubs.

Monumental Milestones: Great Events of Modern Times, 16 vols., Set. 2006. (J). (gr. 4-8). lib. bdg. 319.20 (978-1-58415-292-7(3)) Mitchell Lane Pubs.

Mooney, Carla. Asante Samuel. 2009. (Superstars of Pro Football Ser.). (Illus.). 64p. (YA). (gr. 7-12). lib. bdg. 22.95 (978-1-4222-0542-6(8)) Mason Crest.

—Jonas Brothers, 1 vol. 2009. (People in the News Ser.). (ENG., Illus.). 96p. (gr. 7-7). 41.03 (978-1-4205-0236-7(0), 9e06352f-b3c8-44ef-8691-b262cd85bdf1, Lucent Pr.) Greenhaven Publishing LLC.

—Vanessa Hudgens. 2007. (Sharing the American Dream Ser.). 64p. (YA). (gr. 7-18). pap. 9.95 (978-1-4222-0749-9(8)) Mason Crest.

—Vanessa Hudgens/Carla Mooney. 2009. (Sharing the American Dream Ser.). 64p. (YA). (gr. 7-12). 22.95 (978-1-4222-0583-9(5)) Mason Crest.

Moore, Barbara R. Sojourner Truth. 2005. (Illus.). 16p. (J). (978-0-618-56039-4(4)) Houghton Mifflin Harcourt Publishing Co.

Moore, Cathy. Ellen Craft's Escape from Slavery. Braught, Mark, illus. 2010. (History Speaks: Picture Books Plus Reader's Theater Ser.). (ENG.). 48p. (gr. 2-4). (J). lib. bdg. 27.93 (978-0-7613-5875-6(7), Millbrook Pr.); pap. 9.95 (978-0-7613-6672-0(5)) Lerner Publishing Group.

Morganelli, Adrianna. Bruno Mars. 2013. (ENG., Illus.). 32p. (J). pap. (978-0-7787-0041-8(0)) Crabtree Publishing Co.

Morretta, Alison. John Brown: Armed Abolitionist, 1 vol. 2018. (Hero or Villain? Claims & Counterclaims Ser.). (ENG.). 112p. (YA). (gr. 8-8). lib. bdg. 45.93 (978-1-5026-3520-4(8), 974225df-4747-47c6-848c-ef5bfe691eff) Cavendish Square Publishing LLC.

Morrison, Jessica. Hank Aaron: Home Run Hero. 2010. (Crabtree Groundbreaker Biographies Ser.). (ENG., Illus.). 112p. (J). (gr. 5-8). lib. bdg. (978-0-7787-2538-1(3)) Crabtree Publishing Co.

Moss, Marissa. The Eye That Never Sleeps: How Detective Pinkerton Saved President Lincoln. Holmes, Jeremy, illus. 2018. (ENG.). 48p. (J). (gr. 1-4). 17.99 (978-1-4197-3064-1(9), 1137601, Abrams Bks. for Young Readers) Abrams, Inc.

Moua, Mayhoua, et al. Mayhoua Moua: A Real-Life Story from a Hmong Story Cloth. 2014. (Text Connections Ser.). (J). (gr. 3). (978-1-4509-9647-1(7)) Benchmark Education Co.

Mour, Stanley I. Innovators of American Jazz, 1 vol. 2013. (Inspiring Collective Biographies Ser.). (ENG.). 112p. (gr. 5-6). pap. 13.88 (978-1-4644-0271-5(X), be0b49d6-18d3-40a0-a1ac-31f5d32dc3ae) Enslow Publishing, LLC.

Mulhall, Jill K. James Madison, 1 vol. rev. ed. 2005. (Social Studies: Informational Text Ser.). (ENG.). 24p. (gr. 4-8). pap. 10.99 (978-0-7439-8908-4(2)) Teacher Created Materials, Inc.

—Thomas Jefferson, 1 vol. rev. ed. 2004. (Social Studies: Informational Text Ser.). (ENG.). 24p. (gr. 4-8). pap. 10.99 (978-0-7439-8747-9(0)) Teacher Created Materials, Inc.

Murphy, Maggie. The Jonas Brothers: Rock Stars, 1 vol. 2010. (Young & Famous Ser.). (ENG.). 24p. (J). (gr. 1-2). lib. bdg. 26.27 (978-1-4488-0646-1(1), 93b62d02-4549-46ad-9a6e-462e2c331f77) Rosen Publishing Group, Inc., The.

—Kristen Stewart: Twilight Star, 1 vol. 2010. (Young & Famous Ser.). (ENG., Illus.). 24p. (J). (gr. 1-2). pap. 9.85 (978-1-4488-1795-5(1), 6623a177-30c5-40cb-982f-a151ae1c1a1b, PowerKids Pr.) Rosen Publishing Group, Inc., The.

—Miley Cyrus: Rock Star, 1 vol. 2010. (Young & Famous Ser.). (ENG., Illus.). 24p. (J). (gr. 1-2). 26.27 (978-1-4488-0643-0(7), 956473f8-e7ee-43d7-9aeb-b0c0e055fe7c); pap. 9.85 (978-1-4488-1799-3(4), f0e8ec27-d6b2-42ac-a676-611f61c40f46, PowerKids Pr.) Rosen Publishing Group, Inc., The.

—Taylor Lautner: Twilight Star, 1 vol. 2010. (Young & Famous Ser.). (ENG., Illus.). 24p. (J). (gr. 1-2). lib. bdg. 26.27 (978-1-4488-0642-3(9), deee5c59-5f44-49d4-9407-71f3cdc90493) Rosen Publishing Group, Inc., The.

—Taylor Swift: Country Music Star, 1 vol. 2010. (Young & Famous Ser.). (ENG.). 24p. (J). (gr. 1-2). lib. bdg. 26.27 (978-1-4488-0645-4(3), f185df64-b096-47f3-b628-aabee44fa0f3) Rosen Publishing Group, Inc., The.

—Zac Efron: Movie Star, 1 vol. 2010. (Young & Famous Ser.). (ENG., Illus.). 24p. (J). (gr. 1-2). pap. 9.85 (978-1-4488-1801-3(X), 7bda6960-c922-45bf-865b-1ac5d1d8427b, PowerKids Pr.) Rosen Publishing Group, Inc., The.

Nagelhout, Ryan. Michael Phelps: Greatest Swimmer of All Time, 1 vol. 2017. (Breakout Biographies Ser.). (ENG.). 32p. (J). (gr. 4-5). pap. 11.00 (978-1-5081-6066-3(X), 259e5eaa-0b6e-4931-9277-78a8f6e5c59e, PowerKids Pr.) Rosen Publishing Group, Inc., The.

—Odell Beckham Jr: Pro Bowl Wide Receiver, 1 vol. 2018. (Living Legends of Sports Ser.). (ENG.). 48p. (gr. 5-6). pap. 15.05 (978-1-5383-0209-5(8), 9d26d803-9636-4b77-8c92-980fe7d90303, Britannica Educational Publishing) Rosen Publishing Group, Inc., The.

—Peyton Manning, 1 vol., Vol. 1. 2013. (Today's Great Quarterbacks Ser.). (ENG.). 32p. (J). (gr. 1-1). pap. 11.50 (978-1-4824-0480-7(X), ee443181-a70c-47a3-8e61-23cbe74c1e85) Stevens, Gareth Publishing LLLP.

Nardo, Don. Bernie Madoff, 1 vol. 2011. (People in the News Ser.). (ENG.). 96p. (gr. 7-7). lib. bdg. 41.03 (978-1-4205-0353-1(7), 34cd4de1-4839-46ca-805d-433844f0e6e0, Lucent Pr.) Greenhaven Publishing LLC.

—Mathew Brady: The Camera Is the Eye of History, 1 vol. 2008. (Americans: the Spirit of a Nation Ser.). (ENG., Illus.). 128p. (gr. 5-6). lib. bdg. 35.93 (978-0-7660-3023-7(7), 4d1b9ae1-c55c-413b-81b3-7343482ad868) Enslow Publishing, LLC.

Nash, Eric Peter. Frank Lloyd Wright: Force of Nature, Vol. 8. 2018. (American Artists Ser.). 80p. (J). (gr. 7). 33.27 (978-1-4222-4158-5(0)) Mason Crest.

Nault, Jennifer. The Insightful World of Judy Blume. 2016. (J). (978-1-5105-1953-4(X)) SmartBook Media, Inc.

Neimark, Anne. There Ain't Nobody That Can Sing Like Me: The Life of Woody Guthrie. 2017. (ENG., Illus.). 128p. (J). (gr. 5-9). pap. 13.99 (978-1-5344-0950-7(5), Atheneum Bks. for Young Readers) Simon & Schuster Children's Publishing.

Nelson, Maria. The Life of Paul Revere, 1 vol. 2012. (Famous Lives Ser.). (ENG.). 24p. (J). (gr. 1-2). pap. 9.15 (978-1-4339-6355-1(8), 28f1d255-6234-4269-a325-eee483bc787f); lib. bdg. 25.27 (978-1-4339-6353-7(1), 94adfa60-b92a-4642-bf87-ccb0fbd3bbd7) Stevens, Gareth Publishing LLLP.

Nelson, Robin. George Washington Carver: A Life of Devotion. 2006. (Pull Ahead Bks.). (Illus.). 32p. (J). (gr. 3-7). lib. bdg. 22.60 (978-0-8225-6461-4(0), Lerner Pubns.) Lerner Publishing Group.

Nichols, Kaitlyn. Davey Crockett. 2009. pap. 13.25 (978-1-60559-057-8(6)) Hameray Publishing Group, Inc.

—Martin Luther King. 2009. pap. 13.25 (978-1-60559-065-3(7)) Hameray Publishing Group, Inc.

Nichols, Susan. Famous Immigrant Politicians, 1 vol. 2017. (Making America Great: Immigrant Success Stories Ser.). (ENG.). 112p. (gr. 7-7). 38.93 (978-0-7660-9242-6(9), ee579d74-0ecd-42ba-8a74-c5ee8cdf1b9e) Enslow Publishing, LLC.

Noah, Trevor. It's Trevor Noah: Born a Crime: Stories from a South African Childhood (Adapted for Young Readers) 2019. (ENG.). 304p. (J). (gr. 5). 17.99 (978-0-525-58216-8(9), Delacorte Bks. for Young Readers) Random House Publishing Group.

—It's Trevor Noah: Born a Crime: Stories from a South African Childhood (Adapted for Young Readers) 2019. (ENG.). 304p. (J). (gr. 5). lib. bdg. 20.99 (978-0-525-58217-5(7), Delacorte Bks. for Young Readers) Random Hse. Children's Bks.

Northrup, Mary. Pioneering American Computer Geniuses, 1 vol. 2013. (Inspiring Collective Biographies Ser.). (ENG.). 112p. (gr. 5-6). pap. 13.88 (978-1-4644-0273-9(6), 0831b4e1-a218-4e41-81e9-1d642823c01b) Enslow Publishing, LLC.

Norwich, Grace. Zac Attack: An Unauthorized Biography. 2006. (Unauthorized Biographies Ser.). (ENG., Illus.). 128p. (J). (gr. 5-8). 17.44 (978-0-8431-2496-5(2)) Penguin Young Readers Group.

Noyes, Deborah. The Magician & the Spirits. 2017. (Illus.). 160p. (J). (gr. 5). 18.99 (978-0-8037-4018-1(2), Viking Books for Young Readers) Penguin Young Readers Group.

Obama, Barack. Of Thee I Sing: A Letter to My Daughters. Long, Loren, illus. 2010. (ENG.). 40p. (J). (gr. -1-3). 17.99 (978-0-375-83527-8(X), Knopf Bks. for Young Readers) Random Hse. Children's Bks.

O'Donnell, Jessica. Leontyne Price, 1 vol. 2010. (Inspiring Lives Ser.). (ENG.). 32p. (J). (gr. 1-1). lib. bdg. 27.93 (978-1-4339-3628-9(3), c7bfff22-3a05-4192-90f7-c55d145aa57b) Stevens, Gareth Publishing LLLP.

Offutt, Jason. J. C. Penney: The Man with a Thousand Partners. 2017. (ENG., Illus.). 48p. (J). lib. bdg. 27.00 (978-1-61248-208-8(2)) Truman State Univ. Pr.

O'Keefe, Sherry. Spin: The Story of Michael Jackson. 2011. (Modern Music Masters Ser.). (Illus.). 144p. (YA). (gr. 6-9). 28.95 (978-1-59935-134-6(X)) Reynolds, Morgan Inc.

Oliver-Miles, Zelda. Amelia Gayle Gorgas: First Woman of Position. 2005. (Alabama Roots Biography Ser.). (Illus.). 100p. (J). pap. (978-1-59421-017-4(9)) Seacoast Publishing, Inc.

Olson, Greg. George Caleb Bingham: Frontier Artist, Missouri Politician. 2017. (ENG., Illus.). 48p. (J). lib. bdg. 27.00 (978-1-61248-206-4(6)) Truman State Univ. Pr.

O'Neal, Claire. Cole Hamels. 2009. (Blue Banner Biography Ser.). (Illus.). 32p. (YA). (gr. 4-7). lib. bdg. 25.70 (978-1-58415-776-2(3)) Mitchell Lane Pubs.

—T. I. 2009. (Blue Banner Biography Ser.). (Illus.). 32p. (YA). (gr. 4-7). lib. bdg. 25.70 (978-1-58415-769-4(0)) Mitchell Lane Pubs.

Onobun, Fendi. Transition: One Kid's Bank Shot to the NFL. 2017. (ENG.). 248p. (YA). 22.95 (978-1-942945-51-2(5), 3fad2d37-4855-4582-8b79-032f67e38281) Night Heron Media.

Oprah Winfrey. 2004. (Illus.). 112p. pap. 9.95 (978-0-8225-5320-5(1)) Lerner Publishing Group.

Orr, Tamara. Emily Osment. 2009. (Robbie Reader Ser.). (Illus.). 32p. (YA). (gr. 2-5). lib. bdg. 25.70 (978-1-58415-755-7(0)) Mitchell Lane Pubs.

Orr, Tamra. Alan Shepard: The First American in Space. 2009. (Library of Astronaut Biographies Ser.). 112p. (gr. 5-8). 63.90 (978-1-60853-518-7(5), Rosen Reference) Rosen Publishing Group, Inc., The.

—AnnaSophia Robb. 2010. (Robbie Reader Ser.). (Illus.). 32p. (YA). (gr. 2-5). lib. bdg. 25.70 (978-1-58415-898-1(0)) Mitchell Lane Pubs.

—Chris Johnson. 2011. (Robbie Reader Ser.). (Illus.). 32p. (J). (gr. 2-5). lib. bdg. 25.70 (978-1-61228-064-6(1)) Mitchell Lane Pubs.

—Day by Day with Selena Gomez. 2011. (Day by Day with... Ser.). (Illus.). 32p. (J). (gr. -1-2). lib. bdg. 25.70 (978-1-58415-987-2(1)) Mitchell Lane Pubs.

—Kristen Stewart. 2009. (Blue Banner Biography Ser.). (Illus.). 32p. (YA). (gr. 4-7). lib. bdg. 25.70 (978-1-58415-773-1(9)) Mitchell Lane Pubs.

—Shia Labeouf. 2010. (Blue Banner Biography Ser.). (Illus.). 32p. (YA). (gr. 4-7). lib. bdg. 25.70 (978-1-58415-908-7(1)) Mitchell Lane Pubs.

—Stephanie Meyer. 2010. (Blue Banner Biography Ser.). (Illus.). 32p. (YA). (gr. 4-7). lib. bdg. 25.70 (978-1-58415-907-0(3)) Mitchell Lane Pubs.

Orr, Tamra B. The Life & Times of Susan B. Anthony. 2006. (Profiles in American History Ser.). (Illus.). 48p. (J). (gr. 3-7). lib. bdg. 29.95 (978-1-58415-445-7(4)) Mitchell Lane Pubs.

Osborne, Mary Pope & Boyce, Natalie Pope. Abraham Lincoln: A Nonfiction Companion to Magic Tree House Merlin Mission #19: Abe Lincoln at Last. Murdocca, Sal, illus. 2011. (Magic Tree House (R) Fact Tracker Ser.: 25). 128p. (J). (gr. 2-5). 6.99 (978-0-375-87024-8(5), Random Hse. Bks. for Young Readers) Random Hse. Children's Bks.

—Benjamin Franklin: A Nonfiction Companion to Magic Tree House #32: to the Future, Ben Franklin! 2019. (Magic Tree House (R) Fact Tracker Ser.: 41). (Illus.). 128p. (J). (gr. 2-5). pap. 6.99 (978-1-9848-9317-8(3), Random Hse. Bks. for Young Readers) Random Hse. Children's Bks.

Osier, Dan. Dirk Nowitzki, 1 vol. 2011. (Basketball's MVPs Ser.). (ENG.). 24p. (J). (gr. 1-2). pap. 9.85 (978-1-4488-2632-2(2), 2d39a9e1-304d-4fa8-b6a9-91653b682ca1); (Illus.). lib. bdg. 26.27 (978-1-4488-2524-0(5), 9aef8bd6-941f-4e92-9248-f01bab0c3991) Rosen Publishing Group, Inc., The. (PowerKids Pr.).

Otfinoski, Steven. Grover Cleveland, 1 vol. 2011. (Presidents & Their Times Ser.). (ENG.). 96p. (gr. 6-6). 36.93 (978-0-7614-4811-2(X), 5b89a4d8-b2d1-48b8-b613-51b12e079d94) Cavendish Square Publishing LLC.

Owens, Jim. The Survivorship Net: A Parable for the Family, Friends, & Caregivers of People with Cancer. Cass, Bill, illus. 2010. (ENG.). 48p. (J). (gr. 2). 14.95 (978-1-60443-018-9(4)) American Cancer Society, Inc.

Parker, Christi E. Abraham Lincoln, 1 vol. rev. ed. 2005. (Social Studies: Informational Text Ser.). (ENG.). 24p. (gr. 4-8). pap. 10.99 (978-0-7439-8916-9(3)) Teacher Created Materials, Inc.

Patrick, Joseph. Robert Johnson, 1 vol. 2010. (Inspiring Lives Ser.). (ENG.). 32p. (J). (gr. 1-1). lib. bdg. 27.93 (978-1-4339-3619-7(4), d02ef22f-d331-49b3-9bab-402b4c6c5120); (Illus.). pap. 11.50 (978-1-4339-3620-3(8), 463257ef-4ac7-4a7d-b227-2ea187424359) Stevens, Gareth Publishing LLLP.

Paulsen, Gary. Puppies, Dogs, & Blue Northers: Reflections on Being Raised by a Pack of Sled Dogs. 2007. (ENG., Illus.). 80p. (J). (gr. 5-7). pap. 7.99 (978-0-15-206103-6(7), 1198332, Clarion Bks.) HarperCollins Pubs.

—Woodsong. 2007. (ENG., Illus.). 144p. (J). (gr. 5-9). pap. 7.99 (978-1-4169-3939-9(3), Simon & Schuster Bks. For Young Readers) Simon & Schuster Bks. For Young Readers.

Pawlak, Debra Ann. Bruce Lee. 2009. (Sharing the American Dream Ser.). 64p. (YA). (gr. 7-12). 22.95 (978-1-4222-0586-0(X)) Mason Crest.

Payan, Michael. In the Ring with Bret Hart. 2009. (World of Wrestling Ser.). 24p. (gr. 1-1). 42.50 (978-1-60854-342-7(0), PowerKids Pr.) Rosen Publishing Group, Inc., The.

—In the Ring with Diamond Dallas Page. 2009. (World of Wrestling Ser.). 24p. (gr. 1-1). 42.50 (978-1-60854-343-4(9), PowerKids Pr.) Rosen Publishing Group, Inc., The.

—In the Ring with Goldberg. 2009. (World of Wrestling Ser.). 24p. (gr. 1-1). 42.50 (978-1-60854-346-5(3), PowerKids Pr.) Rosen Publishing Group, Inc., The.

—In the Ring with Kevin Nash. 2009. (World of Wrestling Ser.). 24p. (gr. 1-1). 42.50 (978-1-60854-347-2(1), PowerKids Pr.) Rosen Publishing Group, Inc., The.

—In the Ring with Scott Steiner. 2009. (World of Wrestling Ser.). 24p. (gr. 1-1). 42.50 (978-1-60854-348-9(X), PowerKids Pr.) Rosen Publishing Group, Inc., The.

—In the Ring with Sting. 2009. (World of Wrestling Ser.). 24p. (gr. 1-1). 42.50 (978-1-60854-349-6(8), PowerKids Pr.) Rosen Publishing Group, Inc., The.

PC Treasures Staff, ed. Tony Stewart. 2009. (Nascar Drivers Coloring Book Ser.). (ENG., Illus.). 96p. (J). pap. 2.99 (978-1-60072-160-1(5)) PC Treasures, Inc.

Peacock, L. A. The Truth (and Myths) about American Heroes. Davis, Jon, illus. 2016. 96p. (J). (978-0-545-83027-0(3)) Scholastic, Inc.

Peak, Doris-Jean. Wernher Von Braun: Alabama's Rocket Scientist. 2009. (Alabama Roots Biography Ser.). (Illus.). 112p. (J). (978-1-59421-044-0(6)) Seacoast Publishing, Inc.

Pearce, Q. L. Given Kachepa: Advocate for Human Trafficking Victims, 1 vol. 2007. (Young Heroes Ser.). (ENG., Illus.). 48p. (gr. 4-8). lib. bdg. 37.33 (978-0-7377-3668-7(2), dfb81306-01be-4abb-b38b-3ab790d1a238, KidHaven Publishing) Greenhaven Publishing LLC.

—Hannah Taylor: Helping the Homeless, 1 vol. 2008. (Young Heroes Ser.). (ENG., Illus.). 48p. (gr. 4-8). 37.33 (978-0-7377-4051-6(5), b4abafb8-9560-45e5-9982-1b5511ef2c19, KidHaven Publishing) Greenhaven Publishing LLC.

—James Quadrino: Wildlife Protector, 1 vol. 2006. (Young Heroes Ser.). (ENG., Illus.). 48p. (gr. 4-8). lib. bdg. 30.38 (978-0-7377-3612-0(7), 7865790a-81d8-4756-b15a-9a85ce0a9ddb, KidHaven Publishing) Greenhaven Publishing LLC.

Peckham, Howard Henry. William Henry Harrison, Young Tippecanoe: Childhood of Famous Americans Series. Laune, Paul, illus. 2011. 190p. 42.95 (978-1-258-07766-2(3)) Literary Licensing, LLC.

Peerson, Marie Graham. Joseph Wheeler: The Fearless 'Fightin' Joe' 2003. (Alabama Roots Biography Ser.). (Illus.). 120p. (J). (978-1-878561-40-4(5)) Seacoast Publishing, Inc.

Pelleschi, Andrea. Samuel de Champlain, 1 vol. 2013. (Jr. Graphic Famous Explorers Ser.). (ENG., Illus.). 24p. (J). (gr. 2-3). pap. 11.60 (978-1-4777-0133-1(8), 63013173-ce2d-48ef-82f4-25039d8b171a); lib. bdg. 28.93 (978-1-4777-0074-7(9), 3565da74-294b-44a7-b799-51883285f1a4) Rosen Publishing Group, Inc., The. (PowerKids Pr.).

Petrillo, Lisa. Isaac Mizrahi. 2011. (Profiles in Fashion Ser.). (Illus.). 111p. 28.95 (978-1-59935-152-0(8)) Reynolds, Morgan Inc.

Pfeffer, Wendy. Many Ways to Be a Soldier. Verstraete, Elaine, illus. 2008. (On My Own History Ser.). (ENG.). 48p. (gr. 2-4). lib. bdg. 25.26 (978-0-8225-7279-4(6), Millbrook Pr.) Lerner Publishing Group.

Pflueger, Lynda. Stonewall Jackson: General of the Confederate Army. 2015. (J). (978-0-7660-6495-9(6)) Enslow Publishing, LLC.

Phillips, Larissa. Wild Bill Hickok: Legend of the American Wild West, 1 vol. 2003. (Famous People in American History / Grandes Personajes en la Historia de Los Estados Unidos Ser.). (ENG & SPA., Illus.). 32p. (gr. 2-3). lib. bdg. 29.13 (978-0-8239-4170-4(1), 1320d7dc-508d-4207-bcad-b7e733e160e1, Editorial Buenas Letras) Rosen Publishing Group, Inc., The.

—Wild Bill Hickok: Leyenda del Oeste Americano, 1 vol. 2003. (Grandes Personajes en la Historia de Los Estados Unidos (Famous People in American History) Ser.). (SPA., Illus.). 32p. (gr. 3-4). lib. bdg. 29.13 (978-0-8239-4146-9(9), 3d433166-01dd-4318-aa97-de55b691c007, Editorial Buenas Letras) Rosen Publishing Group, Inc., The.

—Wild Bill Hickok: Legend of the American Wild West / Leyenda del oeste Americano. 2009. (Famous People in American History/Grandes personajes en la historia de los Estados Unidos Ser.). (ENG & SPA.). 32p. (gr. 2-3). 47.90 (978-1-61512-557-9(4), Editorial Buenas Letras) Rosen Publishing Group, Inc., The.

—Wild Bill Hickok: Legend of the Wild West. 2009. (Primary Sources of Famous People in American History Ser.). 32p. (gr. 2-3). 47.90 (978-1-60851-740-4(3)) Rosen Publishing Group, Inc., The.

—Wild Bill Hickok: Leyenda del oeste Americano, 1 vol. 2003. (Grandes Personajes en la Historia de Los Estados Unidos (Famous People in American History) Ser.). (SPA.). 32p. (gr. 3-4). pap. 10.00 (978-0-8239-4240-4(6), b1983696-f766-4736-9255-454712ca7641, Rosen Classroom) Rosen Publishing Group, Inc., The.

—Wild Bill Hickok: Leyenda del oeste americano (Wild Bill Hickok: Legend of the American Wild West) 2009. (Grandes personajes en la historia de los Estados Unidos (Famous People in American History) Ser.). (SPA.). 32p. (gr. 2-3). 47.90 (978-1-61512-810-5(7), Editorial Buenas Letras) Rosen Publishing Group, Inc., The.

A Pocketful of Passage. 2007. (Great Lakes Books Ser.). (ENG., Illus.). 96p. (gr. 3-7). cd-rom 12.95 (978-0-8143-3341-9(9), P120523) Wayne State Univ. Pr.

Polinsky, Paige V. Yo-Yo Maker: Pedro Flores. 2017. (Toy Trailblazers Set 2 Ser.). (ENG., Illus.). 32p. (J). (gr. 3-6). lib. bdg. 32.79 (978-1-5321-1099-3(5), 25774, Checkerboard Library) ABDO Publishing Co.

Pollack, Pam, et al. Who Was Lucille Ball? Copeland, Gregory, illus. 2017. (Who Was? Ser.). 112p. (J). (gr. 3-7). 6.99 (978-0-448-48303-0(3), Penguin Workshop) Penguin Young Readers Group.

Pollack, Pamela & Belviso, Meg. Who Was Steve Jobs? 2012. (Who Was... ? Ser.). lib. bdg. 16.00 (978-0-606-26649-9(6)) Turtleback.

Poole, Rebecca. Jimi Hendrix. 2006. (Just the Facts Biographies Ser.). (Illus.). 112p. (J). (gr. 3-7). pap. 9.95 (978-0-8225-5994-8(3), Lerner Pubns.) Lerner Publishing Group.

Porterfield, Jason. Calvin Hill & Grant Hill: One Family's Legacy in Football & Basketball. 2010. (Sports Families Ser.). 48p. (YA). (gr. 5-8). lib. bdg., E-Book 53.00 (978-1-4488-0087-2(0)) Rosen Publishing Group, Inc., The.

—Frederick Douglass: Abolitionist & Fighter for Equality. 2017. (Britannica Beginner Bios Ser.). 32p. (J). (gr. 6-10). 77.40 (978-1-5383-0019-0(2), Britannica Educational Publishing) Rosen Publishing Group, Inc., The.

Powell, Walter L. Benedict Arnold: Revolutionary War Hero & Traitor. 2009. (Library of American Lives & Times Ser.). 112p. (gr. 5-5). 69.20 (978-1-60853-471-5(5)) Rosen Publishing Group, Inc., The.

Pratt, Mary K. Michael Jackson: King of Pop. 2011. (Lives Cut Short Ser.). (YA). (gr. 7-12). 71.36 (978-1-61641-447-4(2), Essential Library) ABDO Publishing Co.

Pristash, Nicole. Dale Earnhardt Jr, 1 vol. 2008. (NASCAR Champions Ser.). (ENG., Illus.). 24p. (gr. 1-2). pap. 8.25 (978-1-4042-4541-9(3), 24760a98-4f36-48ad-81d6-4c3a31048e31, Rosen Classroom) Rosen Publishing Group, Inc., The.

—Jeff Gordon, 1 vol. 2008. (NASCAR Champions Ser.). (ENG., Illus.). 24p. (gr. 1-2). pap. 8.25 (978-1-4042-4542-6(1), ff94b0ec-e310-45db-861f-c927ceff07d8, PowerKids Pr.) Rosen Publishing Group, Inc., The.

—Jimmie Johnson, 1 vol. 2008. (NASCAR Champions Ser.). (ENG., Illus.). 24p. (gr. 1-2). pap. 8.25 (978-1-4042-4543-3(X), 3601325e-1957-4c25-b012-37ea68f7de8e, PowerKids Pr.) Rosen Publishing Group, Inc., The.

—Kevin Harvick, 1 vol. 2008. (NASCAR Champions Ser.). (ENG., Illus.). 24p. (J). (gr. 1-2). pap. 8.25 (978-1-4042-4544-0(8), 13527a9f-ac9f-4529-8ea6-cd5ee28646b4) Rosen Publishing Group, Inc., The.

Profiles in American History, 18 vols., Set. Incl. Benjamin Franklin. Whiting, Jim. (gr. 3-7). 2006. lib. bdg. 29.95 (978-1-58415-435-8(7)); Betsy Ross. Harkins, Susan Sales & Harkins, William H. (gr. 3-7). 2006. lib. bdg. 29.95 (978-1-58415-446-4(2)); Eli Whitney. Gibson, Karen Bush. (gr. 3-7). 2006. lib. bdg. 29.95 (978-1-58415-434-1(9)); John Cabot. Rice, Earle, Jr. (gr. 3-7). 2006. lib. bdg. 29.95 (978-1-58415-451-8(9)); John Hancock. Kjelle, Marylou Morano. (gr. 3-7). 2006. lib. bdg. 29.95 (978-1-58415-443-3(8)); John Peter Zenger. Gibson, Karen Bush. (gr. 3-7). 2006. lib. bdg. 29.95 (978-1-58415-437-2(3)); Life & Times of Alexander Hamilton. Roberts, Russell. (gr. 3-7). 2006. lib. bdg. 29.95 (978-1-58415-436-5(5)); Life & Times of George Rogers Clark. Roberts, Russell. (gr. 3-7). 2006. lib. bdg. 29.95 (978-1-58415-448-8(9)); Life & Times of Hernando Cortes. Whiting, Jim. (gr. 3-7). 2006. lib. bdg. 29.95 (978-1-58415-449-5(7)); Life & Times of John Adams. Whiting, Jim. (gr. 3-7). 2006. lib. bdg. 29.95 (978-1-58415-442-6(X)); Life & Times of Patrick Henry. Harkins, Susan & Harkins, William H. (gr. 4-8). 2006. lib. bdg. 29.95 (978-1-58415-438-9(1)); Life & Times of Paul Revere. Whiting, Jim. (gr. 3-7). 2006. lib. bdg. 29.95 (978-1-58415-441-9(1)); Life & Times of Sir Walter Raleigh. Rice, Earle, Jr. (gr. 3-7). 2006. lib. bdg. 29.95 (978-1-58415-452-5(7)); Life & Times of Susan B. Anthony. Orr, Tamra B. (gr. 3-7). 2006. lib. bdg. 29.95 (978-1-58415-445-7(4)); Life & Times of William Penn. Hinman, Bonnie. (gr. 4-8). 2006. lib. bdg. 29.95 (978-1-58415-433-4(0), 1259521); Nathan Hale. Tracy, Kathleen. (gr. 3-7). 2006. lib. bdg. 29.95 (978-1-58415-447-1(0)); Samuel Adams. Gibson, Karen Bush. (gr. 3-7). 2006. lib. bdg. 20.95 (978-1-58415-440-2(3)); Thomas Jefferson: The Life & Times Of. Roberts, Russell. (gr. 3-7). 2007. lib. bdg. 29.95 (978-1-58415-439-6(X)); (Illus.). 48p. (J). 2006. Set lib. bdg. 359.10 (978-1-58415-287-3(7)) Mitchell Lane Pubs.

Pulditor, Seth H. DeSean Jackson. 2010. (Superstars of Pro Football Ser.). 64p. (YA). (gr. 5-18). lib. bdg. 22.95 (978-1-4222-1663-7(2)) Mason Crest.

—Drew Brees. 2013. (J). (978-1-4222-2720-6(0)) Mason Crest.

Rajczak Nelson, Kristen. Demi Lovato, 1 vol. 2011. (Rising Stars Ser.). (ENG., Illus.). 32p. (J). (gr. 1-1). pap. 11.50 (978-1-4339-5888-5(0), 8bb931d7-0305-4281-9345-eea788a4db0f); lib. bdg. 27.93 (978-1-4339-5886-1(4), 46045e94-9748-45e7-a751-2e16e8b50896) Stevens, Gareth Publishing LLLP.

—Melania Trump: First Lady of the United States, 1 vol. 2018. (Junior Biographies Ser.). (ENG.). 24p. (gr. 3-4). 24.27 (978-0-7660-9739-1(0), bff3ff1b-52c5-4c7a-b8b5-034c18ce9ca5) Enslow Publishing, LLC.

Randolph, Ryan. Betsy Ross: The American Flag, & Life in a Young America. 2009. (Library of American Lives & Times Ser.). 112p. (gr. 5-5). 69.20 (978-1-60853-473-9(1)) Rosen Publishing Group, Inc., The.

Randolph, Ryan P. Wild West Lawmen & Outlaws. 2009. (Library of the Westward Expansion Ser.). 24p. (gr. 3-4). 42.50 (978-1-60853-944-4(X), PowerKids Pr.) Rosen Publishing Group, Inc., The.

Ransom, Candice. Daniel Boone. 2005. (History Maker Biographies Ser.). (ENG., Illus.). 48p. (gr. 3-6). lib. bdg. 27.93 (978-0-8225-2941-5(6), Lerner Pubns.) Lerner Publishing Group.

—Willie Mclean & the Civil War Surrender. Reeves, Jeni, illus. 2004. (On My Own History Ser.). (ENG.). 48p. (J). (gr. 2-4). pap. 8.99 (978-1-57505-698-2(4), 89edad43-6a3a-40ef-aa5e-51fc2307aa25, First Avenue Editions) Lerner Publishing Group.

Rappoport, Ken. Basketball's Top 10 Slam Dunkers, 1 vol. 2011. (Top 10 Sports Stars Ser.). (ENG., Illus.). 48p. (gr. 5-7). 27.93 (978-0-7660-3467-9(4), b18f2611-5da4-4da7-9fbf-f89bf392e7d7) Enslow Publishing, LLC.

—Dale Earnhardt, Jr: A Car Racer Who Cares, 1 vol. 2011. (Sports Stars Who Care Ser.). (ENG., Illus.). 48p. (gr. 3-3). lib. bdg. 27.93 (978-0-7660-3777-9(0), b854be65-d423-40f6-a010-24d9cca3be80) Enslow Publishing, LLC.

—Derek Jeter: Champion Baseball Star, 1 vol. 2012. (Sports Star Champions Ser.). (ENG., Illus.). 48p. (gr. 5-7). 29.60 (978-0-7660-4025-0(9), e17af628-ea2c-4892-97f5-a81fcbcd36f3) Enslow Publishing, LLC.

—Tim Tebow: A Football Star Who Cares, 1 vol. 2014. (Sports Stars Who Care Ser.). (ENG.). 48p. (gr. 3-3). 27.93 (978-0-7660-4297-1(9), 56df16b4-4196-41a7-a585-5e6aa2b5597a) Enslow Publishing, LLC.

Rau, Dana Meachen. Bill & Melinda Gates. 2007. (21st Century Skills Library: Life Skills Biographies Ser.). (ENG., Illus.). 48p. (gr. 4-8). lib. bdg. 34.93 (978-1-60279-068-1(X), 200039) Cherry Lake Publishing.

Rauf, Don. Thomas Paine: Author of Common Sense, 1 vol. 2017. (Spotlight on Civic Courage: Heroes of Conscience Ser.). (ENG., Illus.). 48p. (J). (gr. 6-6). 33.47 (978-1-5383-8100-7(1), 82c374e6-6b8f-4c4a-a82d-9d449ee2c3ad); pap. 12.75 (978-1-5383-8097-0(8), 870356b7-d649-44d9-a836-aaf70ed6a868) Rosen Publishing Group, Inc., The.

Raum, Elizabeth. Cam Newton. 2017. (Pro Sports Biographies Ser.). (ENG.). 24p. (J). (gr. 1-4). lib. bdg. 20.95 (978-1-68151-137-5(1), 14676) Amicus.

Rausch, Monica. Benjamin Franklin, 1 vol. 2007. (Great Americans Ser.). (ENG., Illus.). 24p. (gr. 2-4). pap. 9.15 (978-0-8368-7689-5(X), f9d7d902-1989-4c9f-a6ea-a5c5f1ef3960); lib. bdg. 24.67 (978-0-8368-7682-6(2), e5fe2671-81d7-496f-bd45-9a1d7ab28aad) Stevens, Gareth Publishing LLLP. (Weekly Reader Leveled Readers).

—Los Hermanos Wright y el Avión (the Wright Brothers & the Airplane), 1 vol. 2007. (Inventores y Sus Descubrimientos (Inventors & Their Discoveries) Ser.). (SPA., Illus.). 24p. (gr. 2-4). pap. 9.15 (978-0-8368-8001-4(3), 0089d5b8-895b-4339-9379-2bb018ad6d59, Weekly Reader Leveled Readers) Stevens, Gareth Publishing LLLP.

—Thomas Edison y la Bombilla eléctrica (Thomas Edison & the Lightbulb), 1 vol. 2007. (Inventores y Sus Descubrimientos (Inventors & Their Discoveries) Ser.). (SPA., Illus.). 24p. (gr. 2-4). pap. 9.15 (978-0-8368-8002-1(1), 93a04327-9138-4fd2-aac5-2b1d900a6bea); lib. bdg. 24.67 (978-0-8368-7997-1(X), 3bd68065-ced9-43d6-a9a3-9883450b4aab) Stevens, Gareth Publishing LLLP. (Weekly Reader Leveled Readers).

Rawson, Katherine. Abigail Breslin, 1 vol. 2009. (Kid Stars! Ser.). (ENG.). 24p. (J). (gr. 2-3). pap. 10.40 (978-1-4358-3412-5(7), 12aeb05b-516d-4b2e-857e-2548f20389f8); (Illus.). lib. bdg. 26.27 (978-1-4042-8146-2(0), 783ee48e-3680-41bd-8c46-855fe08b82bc) Rosen Publishing Group, Inc., The. (PowerKids Pr.).

—The Jonas Brothers, 1 vol. 2009. (Kid Stars! Ser.). (ENG.). 24p. (J). (gr. 2-3). pap. 10.40 (978-1-4358-3402-6(X), c9e9a18c-fbd2-4b5b-a945-38ab7f2f73b2); (Illus.). lib. bdg. 26.27 (978-1-4042-8134-9(7), a7294132-466b-4350-819f-0e4c457b934b) Rosen Publishing Group, Inc., The.

—Taylor Swift, 1 vol. 2009. (Kid Stars! Ser.). (ENG.). 24p. (J). (gr. 2-3). pap. 10.40 (978-1-4358-3410-1(0), 9f7a4f22-9409-42e8-aedf-302381f7a233); (Illus.). lib. bdg. 26.27 (978-1-4042-8138-7(X), 2921c389-8394-49cb-ba64-07cf5324fe10) Rosen Publishing Group, Inc., The. (PowerKids Pr.).

Regis, Frankye. A Voice from the Civil Rights Era, 1 vol. 2004. (Voices of Twentieth-Century Conflict Ser.). (ENG., Illus.). 184p. (C). 47.00 (978-0-313-32998-2(2), 900297270, Bloomsbury Academic) Bloomsbury Publishing Plc GBR. Dist: Macmillan.

Reusser, Kayleen. Leona Lewis. 2009. (Blue Banner Biography Ser.). (Illus.). 32p. (YA). (gr. 4-7). lib. bdg. 25.70 (978-1-58415-775-5(5)) Mitchell Lane Pubs.

—Selena Gomez. 2009. (Robbie Reader Ser.). (Illus.). 32p. (YA). (gr. 2-5). lib. bdg. 25.70 (978-1-58415-752-6(6)) Mitchell Lane Pubs.

Rhodes-Courter, Ashley. Three Little Words: A Memoir. 2009. (ENG.). 336p. (YA). (gr. 9). pap. 12.99 (978-1-4169-4807-0(4), Atheneum Bks. for Young Readers) Simon & Schuster Children's Publishing.

Rice, Condoleezza. Condoleezza Rice: a Memoir of My Extraordinary, Ordinary Family & Me. 2012. (ENG.). 336p. (J). (gr. 5). pap. 11.99 (978-0-385-73880-4(3), Ember) Random Hse. Children's Bks.

Rice, Dona. 20th Century Superstar: Disney. 2017. (J). pap. (978-1-4938-3632-1(3)) Teacher Created Materials, Inc.

Rice, Liz. Bill Richardson. 2009. (Sharing the American Dream Ser.). (Illus.). 64p. (J). (gr. 7-12). 22.95 (978-1-4222-0589-1(4)) Mason Crest.

Riddle, Sharon Kay & Sanders, Nancy/Ida. Tony Loved to Learn. Mendoza, Megan Elizabeth, illus. 2007. 32p. (J). pap. 15.00 (978-0-9761583-6-3(1)) Olive Leaf Pubns.

Ring, Susan. Elok. 2009. (J). (978-1-60596-660-1(6)); (978-1-60596-659-5(2)) Weigl Pubs., Inc.

Rivera, Sheila. Rachel Carson: A Life of Responsibility. 2007. (Pull Ahead Bks.). (Illus.). 32p. (J). (gr. 3-7). lib. bdg. 22.60 (978-0-8225-6462-1(9), Lerner Pubns.) Lerner Publishing Group.

Robbins, Trina. Hedy Lamarr & a Secret Communication System, 1 vol. Martin, Cynthia, illus. 2006. (Inventions & Discovery Ser.). (ENG.). 32p. (J). (gr. 3-9). 31.32 (978-0-7368-6479-4(2), 91515, Capstone Pr.) Capstone.

Roberts, Russell. C. C. Sabathia. 2011. (Blue Banner Biography Ser.). (Illus.). 32p. (YA). (gr. 4-7). lib. bdg. 25.70 (978-1-61228-053-0(6)) Mitchell Lane Pubs.

—Larry Fitzgerald. 2010. (Robbie Reader Ser.). (Illus.). 32p. (J). (gr. 2-5). lib. bdg. 25.70 (978-1-58415-899-8(9)) Mitchell Lane Pubs.

Roberts, Steven. Francisco Vasquez de Coronado, 1 vol. 2013. (Jr. Graphic Famous Explorers Ser.). (ENG., Illus.). 24p. (J). (gr. 2-3). pap. 11.60 (978-1-4777-0125-6(7), 77a4e6c9-2632-45f0-958b-8dc67e5aab63); lib. bdg. 28.93 (978-1-4777-0070-9(6), 423b48d7-28a6-4797-8302-25088c166fa5) Rosen Publishing Group, Inc., The. (PowerKids Pr.).

—Henry Ford, 1 vol. 2013. (Jr. Graphic American Inventors Ser.). (ENG., Illus.). 24p. (J). (gr. 2-3). pap. 11.60 (978-1-4777-0143-0(5), c43c6213-2bb3-4f40-baed-e2d5a2b3c200); lib. bdg. 28.93 (978-1-4777-0079-2(X), 52b2b704-20e1-4afb-aa49-887c77634935) Rosen Publishing Group, Inc., The. (PowerKids Pr.).

—John Cabot, 1 vol. 2013. (Jr. Graphic Famous Explorers Ser.). (ENG., Illus.). 24p. (J). (gr. 2-3). pap. 11.60 (978-1-4777-0129-4(X), 30d89349-ceda-4a3f-bc24-cfb99c4f302a); lib. bdg. 28.93 (978-1-4777-0072-3(2), 47235fe9-5b3b-4291-b7fa-7209b8bb76f6) Rosen Publishing Group, Inc., The. (PowerKids Pr.).

—Robert Fulton, 1 vol. 2013. (Jr. Graphic American Inventors Ser.). (ENG., Illus.). 24p. (J). (gr. 2-3). pap. 11.60 (978-1-4777-0139-3(7), c5dd61cb-9649-4ec8-9047-81ab9ae446ea); lib. bdg. 28.93 (978-1-4777-0077-8(3), 159a243a-5a03-4063-8f8a-03f2562d666b) Rosen Publishing Group, Inc., The. (PowerKids Pr.).

Robinson, Sharon. Jackie Robinson: American Hero. 2013. (ENG.). 48p. (J). (gr. 1-3). pap. 4.99 (978-0-545-54006-3(2), Scholastic Paperbacks) Scholastic, Inc.

Robinson, Tom. Ben Roethlisberger: Gifted & Giving Football Star, 1 vol. 2010. (Sports Stars Who Give Back Ser.). (ENG., Illus.). 128p. (gr. 5-6). lib. bdg. 35.93 (978-0-7660-3590-4(5),

36739868-90b7-4937-adf6-368d2576a931) Enslow Publishing, LLC.

Robison, Ken. Apolo Ohno. 2012. (Xtreme Athletes Ser.). (Illus.). 112p. (J). (gr. 7-12). 28.95 *(978-1-59935-186-5(2))* Reynolds, Morgan Inc.

Robson, David. Chris Rock. 2010. (Modern Role Models Ser.). (Illus.). 64p. (YA). (gr. 7-12). 22.95 *(978-1-4222-0506-8(1))* Mason Crest.

—Miley Cyrus. 2010. (Role Model Entertainers Ser.). (Illus.). 64p. (YA). (gr. 7-12). 22.95 *(978-1-4222-0501-3(0))* Mason Crest.

Robson, David W. Brian Westbrook. 2009. (Superstars of Pro Football Ser.). (Illus.). 64p. (J). (gr. 7-12). lib. bdg. 22.95 *(978-1-4222-0547-1(9))* Mason Crest.

Rockworth, Janice. Juelz Santana. 2009. (Hip-Hop 2 Ser.). (Illus.). 64p. (YA). (gr. 7-12). lib. bdg. 22.95 *(978-1-4222-0297-5(6))* Mason Crest.

—Nas. 2009. (Hip-Hop 2 Ser.). (Illus.). 64p. (YA). (gr. 7-12). lib. bdg. 22.95 *(978-1-4222-0300-2(X))* Mason Crest.

—Wu-Tang Clan. 2009. (Hip-Hop 2 Ser.). (Illus.). 64p. (YA). (gr. 7-12). lib. bdg. 22.95 *(978-1-4222-0304-0(2))* Mason Crest.

Rookie Biographies(r). 2013. (Rookie Biographies(r) Ser.). (J). 138.00 *(978-0-531-25114-0(4),* Children's Pr.) Scholastic Library Publishing.

Ross, Harriet. Great American Heroes. (J). (gr. 4-9). lib. bdg. 12.95 *(978-0-87460-182-4(7))* Lion Bks.

Roycroft, Mitch. Chris Moneymaker. 2007. (Superstars of Poker Ser.). (Illus.). 64p. (YA). pap. 7.95 *(978-1-4222-0378-1(6))* Mason Crest.

—Jennifer Harman. 2007. (Superstars of Poker Ser.). (Illus.). 64p. (YA). pap. 7.95 *(978-1-4222-0373-6(5))* Mason Crest.

—Johnny Orient Express Chan. (Superstars of Poker Ser.). (Illus.). 64p. (YA). 2009. (gr. 4-7). lib. bdg. 22.95 *(978-1-4222-0224-1(0))* 2007. pap. 7.95 *(978-1-4222-0369-9(7))* Mason Crest.

—Phil the Poker Brat Hellmuth. (Superstars of Poker Ser.). 64p. (YA). 2009. (Illus.). (gr. 4-7). lib. bdg. 22.95 *(978-1-4222-0220-3(8))* 2007. pap. 7.95 *(978-1-4222-0374-3(3))* Mason Crest.

—Phil Tiger Woods of Poker Ivey. (Superstars of Poker Ser.). (Illus.). 64p. (YA). 2009. (gr. 4-7). lib. bdg. 22.95 *(978-1-4222-0221-0(6))* 2007. pap. 7.95 *(978-1-4222-0375-0(1))* Mason Crest.

Roza, Greg. Henry Ford: Pioneer of Modern Industry, 1 vol. 2008. (Real Life Readers Ser.). (ENG.). 24p. (gr. 3-4). pap. 8.25 *(978-1-4358-0137-0(7),* d2bd773a-37a2-4dcf-8ac7-031a91d29177, Rosen Classroom) Rosen Publishing Group, Inc., The.

—Kevin Harvick: NASCAR Driver, 1 vol. 2009. (Behind the Wheel Ser.). (ENG., Illus.). 48p. (J). (gr. 5-5). pap. 12.75 *(978-1-4358-5406-2(3),* 7dee0173-5985-4c50-8c6c-d387d8ece1e6) Rosen Publishing Group, Inc., The.

—Terry Labonte. (NASCAR Champions Ser.). 24p. (gr. 1-2). 2009. 42.50 *(978-1-61514-787-8(X),* PowerKids Pr.) 2006. (ENG., Illus.). (J). lib. bdg. 26.27 *(978-1-4042-3501-4(9),* d9e9f932-7a5a-4423-9777-f24cec6c6348) Rosen Publishing Group, Inc., The.

—Venus & Serena Williams: The Sisters of Tennis, 1 vol. 2005. (Content-Area Literacy Collections). (ENG.). 24p. (gr. 3-4). pap. 8.85 *(978-1-4042-5537-1(0),* 44f3d653-ae53-4481-a480-842bc236f82f) Rosen Publishing Group, Inc., The.

Roza, Greg & Roza, Autumn. Miranda Cosgrove, 1 vol. 2010. (Today's Superstars Ser.). (ENG.). 48p. (J). (gr. 3-3). pap. 15.05 *(978-1-4339-3999-0(1),* 56806f7f-adae-4ca1-8acd-6f8c150a005e); lib. bdg. 34.60 *(978-1-4339-3998-3(3),* 95d7d5fd-4b07-459f-8e58-e304beaf70ec) Stevens, Gareth Publishing LLLP.

Rudnicki, Richard. Cyrus Eaton: Champion for Peace, 1 vol. 2016. (ENG., Illus.). 40p. (J). (gr. 4-7). 19.95 *(978-1-77108-396-6(4),* 58ea3f49-484b-485c-9629-9bfa5eade9db) Nimbus Publishing, Ltd. CAN. Dist: Baker & Taylor Publisher Services (BTPS).

Ruffin, David C. The Duties & Responsibilities of the Secretary of State, 1 vol. 2004. (Your Government in Action Ser.). (ENG., Illus.). 32p. (J). (gr. 3-3). lib. bdg. 27.60 *(978-1-4042-2688-3(5),* 108a761c-5dcc-4c65-aa4f-1c29535ef894, PowerKids Pr.) Rosen Publishing Group, Inc., The.

Ruiz, Rachel. When Hillary Rodham Clinton Played Ice Hockey. Doneva, Steliyana, illus. 2017. (Leaders Doing Headstands Ser.). (ENG.). 32p. (J). (gr. 1-4). lib. bdg. 28.65 *(978-1-5158-1573-0(0),* 136243, Picture Window Bks.) Capstone.

Rusch, Elizabeth. Gidget the Surfing Dog: Catching Waves with a Small but Mighty Pug. 2020. (Illus.). 48p. (J). (gr. 2-5). 18.99 *(978-1-63217-271-6(2),* Little Bigfoot) Sasquatch Bks.

Rusch, Elizabeth & Francis, Guy. The Planet Hunter: The Story Behind What Happened to Pluto. 2007. (ENG., Illus.). 32p. (J). (gr. -1-3). 15.95 *(978-0-87358-926-0(2))* Cooper Square Publishing Llc.

Rusick, Jessica. Kylie Jenner: Contemporary Cosmetics Mogul. 2019. (Fashion Figures Ser.). (ENG., Illus.). 32p. (J). (gr. 3-6). lib. bdg. 32.79 *(978-1-5321-1952-1(6),* 32489, Checkerboard Library) ABDO Publishing Co.

Russo, Kristin J. Viewpoints on the Boston Tea Party. 2018. (Perspectives Library: Viewpoints & Perspectives Ser.). (ENG., Illus.). 48p. (J). (gr. 5-8). lib. bdg. 39.21 *(978-1-5341-2966-5(9),* 211908) Cherry Lake Publishing.

Ryals, Lexi. More Jammin' with the Jonas Brothers: An Unauthorized Biography. 2009. (Unauthorized Biographies Ser.). (ENG.). 192p. (J). (gr. 5-8). 17.44 *(978-0-8431-8929-2(0))* Penguin Young Readers Group.

Sabin, Louis & Macken, JoAnn Early. Thomas Edison: Incredible Inventor. 2006. (Illus.). 52p. (J). *(978-0-439-88006-0(8))* Scholastic, Inc.

Saddleback Educational Publishing Staff. Pharrell Williams. 2015. (Hip-Hop Biographies (Saddleback Publishing) Ser.). (YA). lib. bdg. 23.25 *(978-0-606-36616-8(4))* Turtleback.

Saddleback Educational Publishing Staff, ed. Amelia Earhart, 1 vol. unabr. ed. 2007. (Graphic Biographies Ser.). (ENG., Illus.). 25p. (YA). (gr. 4-12). pap. 9.75 *(978-1-59905-214-4(8))* Saddleback Educational Publishing, Inc.

—Babe Ruth, 1 vol. unabr. ed. 2007. (Graphic Biographies Ser.). (ENG., Illus.). 25p. (YA). (gr. 4-12). pap. 9.75 *(978-1-59905-215-1(6))* Saddleback Educational Publishing, Inc.

—Benjamin Franklin, 1 vol. unabr. ed. 2007. (Graphic Biographies Ser.). (ENG., Illus.). 25p. (YA). (gr. 4-12). pap. 9.75 *(978-1-59905-217-5(2))* Saddleback Educational Publishing, Inc.

Sammons, Sandra. Henry Flagler, Builder of Florida. 2010. (Pineapple Press Biography Ser.). (ENG.). 70p. (J). (gr. -1-12). pap. 8.95 *(978-1-56164-467-4(6))* Pineapple Pr., Inc.

—Marjory Stoneman Douglas & the Florida Everglades. 2010. (Pineapple Press Biography Ser.). (ENG.). 70p. (J). (gr. -1-12). pap. 14.95 *(978-1-56164-471-1(4))* Pineapple Pr., Inc.

Sandford, Chester M. Modern Americans: A Biographical School. 2005. reprint ed. pap. 26.95 *(978-1-4179-9549-3(1))* Kessinger Publishing, LLC.

Sandler, Michael. Bethany Hamilton: Follow Your Dreams! 2006. (Defining Moments Ser.). (Illus.). 32p. (J). (gr. 2-5). lib. bdg. 28.50 *(978-1-59716-270-8(1))* Bearport Publishing Co., Inc.

—Jean Driscoll: Dream Big, Work Hard! 2006. (Defining Moments Ser.). (Illus.). 32p. (J). (gr. 2-5). lib. bdg. 25.27 *(978-1-59716-268-5(X))* Bearport Publishing Co., Inc.

—Mark Sanchez. 2011. (Football Heroes Making a Difference Ser.). 24p. (YA). (gr. 2-5). lib. bdg. 26.99 *(978-1-61772-310-0(X))* Bearport Publishing Co., Inc.

Sandra Day O'Connor. 2005. 12p. (gr. k-4). 2.95 *(978-0-635-02621-7(X))* Gallopade International.

Sanford, William R. & Green, Carl R. Bill Pickett: Courageous African-American Cowboy, 1 vol. 2013. (Courageous Heroes of the American West Ser.). (ENG., Illus.). 48p. (J). (gr. 5-7). 25.27 *(978-0-7660-4001-4(1),* c9d15464-f7c9-41fa-bd21-8bf27ee9da30) Enslow Publishing, LLC.

—Buffalo Bill Cody: Courageous Wild West Showman, 1 vol. 2013. (Courageous Heroes of the American West Ser.). (ENG., Illus.). 48p. (J). (gr. 5-7). 25.27 *(978-0-7660-4007-6(0),* acf6986c-0ec4-4e0c-8a8d-fd517137bc3d); pap. 11.53 *(978-1-4644-0090-2(3),* ca598850-b688-4425-8bbf-58bbc7301998) Enslow Publishing, LLC.

—Calamity Jane: Courageous Wild West Woman, 1 vol. 2013. (Courageous Heroes of the American West Ser.). (ENG., Illus.). 48p. (J). (gr. 5-7). 25.27 *(978-0-7660-4010-6(0),* 0ba4a326-e3fc-4036-9427-c886719c4386); pap. 11.53 *(978-1-4644-0093-3(8),* 3294d813-6625-4898-b0e3-ec98e86bcdec) Enslow Publishing, LLC.

—Davy Crockett: Courageous Hero of the Alamo, 1 vol. 2013. (Courageous Heroes of the American West Ser.). (ENG., Illus.). 48p. (J). (gr. 5-7). 25.27 *(978-0-7660-4005-2(4),* 6a5cf7d7-f8de-4af4-b900-46401c5edaf1) Enslow Publishing, LLC.

—John C. Frémont: Courageous Pathfinder of the Wild West, 1 vol. 2013. (Courageous Heroes of the American West Ser.). (ENG., Illus.). 48p. (J). (gr. 5-7). pap. 11.53 *(978-1-4644-0091-9(1),* 0b0ce869-27bc-40b4-9a6a-2b911812425a) Enslow Publishing, LLC.

Sanna, E. J. Lloyd Banks. 2009. (Hip-Hop 2 Ser.). (Illus.). 64p. (YA). (gr. 7-12). lib. bdg. 22.95 *(978-1-4222-0299-9(2))* Mason Crest.

Sanna, Lindsey. The Game. 2009. (Hip-Hop 2 Ser.). (Illus.). 64p. (YA). (gr. 7-12). lib. bdg. 22.95 *(978-1-4222-0292-0(5))* Mason Crest.

Santos, Rita. Donald Trump: Businessman & President, 1 vol. 2017. (Junior Biographies Ser.). (ENG.). 24p. (gr. 3-4). lib. bdg. 24.27 *(978-0-7660-8666-1(6),* 7385afec-7721-4292-9a52-5bf2e66ecba6) Enslow Publishing, LLC.

Sapet, Kerrily. Jeff Gordon. 2012. (Role Model Athletes Ser.). 64p. (J). (gr. 7). 22.95 *(978-1-4222-2710-7(3))* Mason Crest.

—Mariah Carey: Singer, Songwriter, Record Producer, Actress. 2009. (Transcending Race in America: Biographies of Biracial Achievers Ser.). 64p. (YA). (gr. 5-18). pap. 9.95 *(978-1-4222-1627-9(6))* Mason Crest.

Savage, Jeff. Adrian Peterson. 2010. pap. 39.62 *(978-0-7613-6964-6(3))* Lerner Publishing Group.

—Brett Favre. 2010. (Amazing Athletes Ser.). (ENG., Illus.). 32p. (J). (gr. 2-5). 26.65 *(978-0-7613-6651-5(2),* d9ea3486-8661-4212-810d-795b419603c3, Lerner Pubns.); pap. 39.62 *(978-0-7613-6965-3(1))* Lerner Publishing Group.

—Brian Urlacher. 2009. (Amazing Athletes Ser.). (ENG.). 32p. (gr. 2-5). 25.26 *(978-0-8225-9991-3(0))* Lerner Publishing Group.

—Dave Mirra. 2007. (Amazing Athletes Ser.). (ENG., Illus.). 32p. (J). (gr. 2-5). 25.26 *(978-0-8225-6593-2(5))* Lerner Publishing Group.

—Drew Brees. 2010. (Amazing Athletes Ser.). 32p. (J). (gr. 2-5). 25.26 *(978-0-7613-6652-2(0))* Lerner Publishing Group.

—Dwight Howard. 2010. pap. 39.62 *(978-0-7613-6968-4(6))* Lerner Publishing Group.

—Dwyane Wade. 2006. (Amazing Athletes Ser.). (Illus.). 32p. (J). (gr. 4). pap. 6.95 *(978-0-8225-6013-5(5),* First Avenue Editions) Lerner Publishing Group.

—Eli Manning, 2nd Edition. 2nd rev. ed. 2012. (Amazing Athletes Ser.). (ENG., Illus.). 32p. (J). (gr. 2-5). lib. bdg. 26.65 *(978-1-4677-0873-9(9),* 76df9308-cdf0-440c-8f7f-569f41f33430, Lerner Pubns.) Lerner Publishing Group.

—Jeff Gordon. 2007. (Amazing Athletes Ser.). (J). pap. 6.95 *(978-0-8225-6802-5(0),* Lerner Pubns.) Lerner Publishing Group.

—Josh Hamilton. 2009. pap. 40.95 *(978-0-7613-4782-8(8))* Lerner Publishing Group.

—Kobe Bryant (Revised Edition) 2010. pap. 39.62 *(978-0-7613-6970-7(8))* Lerner Publishing Group.

—Tiger Woods. 2007. (Amazing Athletes Ser.). (J). 23.93 *(978-0-8225-6889-6(6),* Lerner Pubns.) Lerner Publishing Group.

—Tony Romo. 2010. (Amazing Athletes Ser.). (ENG., Illus.). 32p. (J). (gr. 2-5). pap. 7.95 *(978-0-7613-5754-4(8),* 10816470-530a-4513-9d97-34564b21abbe); pap. 39.62 *(978-0-7613-6971-4(6))* Lerner Publishing Group.

Scally, Robert. Jeff Bezos: Founder of Amazon & the Kindle. 2012. (Business Leaders Ser.). 112p. (YA). (gr. 7-12). 28.95 *(978-1-59935-178-0(1))* Reynolds, Morgan Inc.

Schanzer, Rosalyn. George vs. George: The Revolutionary War As Seen by Both Sides. 2004. (Illus.). 64p. (J). (gr. 3-7). 16.95 *(978-0-7922-7349-3(4),* National Geographic Children's Bks.) Disney Publishing Worldwide.

Scher, Linda. The Texas City Disaster. 2007. (Code Red Ser.). (Illus.). 32p. (YA). (gr. 2-5). lib. bdg. 28.50 *(978-1-59716-363-7(5))* Bearport Publishing Co., Inc.

Scherer, Glenn & Fletcher, Marty. Who on Earth Is Aldo Leopold? Father of Wildlife Ecology, 1 vol. 2009. (Scientists Saving the Earth Ser.). (ENG., Illus.). 112p. (gr. 5-6). lib. bdg. 35.93 *(978-1-59845-115-3(4),* d94c3cd6-503b-455f-8f75-cd2f8eed3d1c) Enslow Publishing, LLC.

Schilling, Vincent. Native Athletes in Action: Sports Stars Past & Present. 2007. (Native Trailblazers Ser.). (ENG., Illus.). 128p. (YA). (gr. 3-11). pap. 9.95 *(978-0-9779183-0-0(0),* 7th Generation) BPC.

Scholl, Elizabeth. David Archuleta. 2009. (Robbie Reader Ser.). (Illus.). 32p. (YA). (gr. 2-5). lib. bdg. 25.70 *(978-1-58415-758-8(5))* Mitchell Lane Pubs.

Schubert, Barbara. George Washington. 2009. pap. 13.25 *(978-1-60559-060-8(6))* Hameray Publishing Group, Inc.

Schuette, Sarah L. Milton Hershey, 1 vol. 2014. (Business Leaders Ser.). (ENG.). 24p. (J). (gr. -1-2). lib. bdg. 24.65 *(978-1-4765-9640-2(9),* 125430) Capstone.

Schuh, Mari. Stars of Stock Car Racing, 1 vol. 2014. (Sports Stars Ser.). (ENG.). 24p. (J). (gr. -1-2). 27.32 *(978-1-4914-0593-2(7),* 125931, Capstone Pr.) Capstone.

—Troy Polamalu. 2013. (Football Stars up Close Ser.). 24p. (J). (gr. k-5). lib. bdg. 26.99 *(978-1-61772-715-3(6))* Bearport Publishing Co., Inc.

Schulte, Mary. The Dover Demon, 1 vol. 2009. (Mysterious Encounters Ser.). (ENG., Illus.). 48p. (gr. 4-8). 35.23 *(978-0-7377-4570-2(3),* 662c62b6-291d-489d-861b-7a8c091f651f, KidHaven Publishing) Greenhaven Publishing LLC.

—Eva Longoria. (Sharing the American Dream Ser.). (Illus.). 64p. (J). (gr. 7-12). 2009. 22.95 *(978-1-4222-0595-2(9))* 2007. pap. 9.95 *(978-1-4222-0754-3(4))* Mason Crest.

Schumacher, Cassandra. Cornelius Vanderbilt: Railroad Tycoon, 1 vol. 2019. (Great American Entrepreneurs Ser.). (ENG.). 128p. (gr. 9-9). lib. bdg. 47.36 *(978-1-5026-4540-1(8),* 1b23f369-9dfd-4836-aa24-44b958aa9c09) Cavendish Square Publishing LLC.

Schuman, Michael A. Bob Dylan: Singer, Songwriter, & Music Icon, 1 vol. 2018. (Influential Lives Ser.). (ENG.). 128p. (gr. 7-7). 40.27 *(978-0-7660-9206-8(2),* 2ae90c4b-9d85-4d39-9b1e-913435f4f042) Enslow Publishing, LLC.

—Charles Schulz: Cartoonist & Writer, 1 vol. 2018. (Influential Lives Ser.). (ENG.). 128p. (gr. 7-7). 40.27 *(978-0-7660-9209-9(7),* 1dd0314c-bf50-45f0-9e54-9dfca036eaed) Enslow Publishing, LLC.

—Emma! Amazing Actress Emma Stone, 1 vol. 2013. (Sizzling Celebrities Ser.). (ENG.). 48p. (gr. 4-6). pap. 11.53 *(978-1-4644-0175-6(6),* 69e385f9-0a58-4937-b22d-b3fbe3f694ec) Enslow Publishing, LLC.

Schwartz, Heather E. JoJo Siwa: Fan Favorite. 2020. (Boss Lady Bios (Alternator Books (r)) Ser.). (ENG., Illus.). 32p. (J). (gr. 3-6). 30.65 *(978-1-5415-9710-5(9),* e8e014b2-1960-467d-bd38-d64aa5659332, Lerner Pubns.) Lerner Publishing Group.

—Kylie Jenner: Makeup Mogul. 2020. (Boss Lady Bios (Alternator Books (r)) Ser.). (ENG., Illus.). 32p. (J). (gr. 3-6). 30.65 *(978-1-5415-9709-9(5),* 37b561bb-19f8-44bc-9278-877d6f21f587, Lerner Pubns.) Lerner Publishing Group.

—Science Educator & Advocate Bill Nye. 2018. (STEM Trailblazer Bios Ser.). (ENG., Illus.). 32p. (J). (gr. 2-5). pap. 8.99 *(978-1-5415-1214-6(6),* bf86ac08-f2f5-4989-907d-2e6422d700d7) Lerner Publishing Group.

Schweitzer, Karen. Americans of South American Heritage. (Successful Americans Ser.). 64p. (YA). 2009. (gr. 9-12). 22.95 *(978-1-4222-0526-6(6))* 2007. (gr. 7-18). pap. 9.95 *(978-1-4222-0861-8(3))* Mason Crest.

—Shaun White. 2010. (Modern Role Models Ser.). (Illus.). 64p. (YA). (gr. 7-12). lib. bdg. 22.95 *(978-1-4222-0493-1(6))* Mason Crest.

—Soulja Boy Tell 'Em. (Role Model Entertainers Ser.). (Illus.). 64p. (YA). 2010. (gr. 7-12). 22.95 *(978-1-4222-0509-9(6))* 2007. pap. 9.95 *(978-1-4222-0796-3(X))* Mason Crest.

Scirri, Kaitlin. Ruth Bader Ginsburg: Supreme Court Justice, 1 vol. 2019. (Barrier-Breaker Bios Ser.). (ENG.). 32p. (gr. 2-2). pap. 11.58 *(978-1-5026-4964-5(0),* 36468a8a-5b1d-423f-a4ee-eab76a22d5d6) Cavendish Square Publishing LLC.

Scott, Celicia. Mariah Carey. 2008. (Hip-Hop Ser.). (ENG., Illus.). 64p. (YA). (gr. 4-7). per. 7.95 *(978-1-4222-0265-4(8))* Mason Crest.

Seibert, Brian. George Balanchine, 1 vol. 2005. (Library of American Choreographers Ser.). (ENG., Illus.). 48p. (gr. 5-8). (J). lib. bdg. 34.47 *(978-1-4042-0447-8(4),* c7843ffc-c198-4a65-ad8c-865f5dc04b27); pap. 12.75 *(978-1-4042-0641-0(8),* 5c047294-42fd-49e1-b13a-75913e6ba4ab, Rosen Reference) Rosen Publishing Group, Inc., The.

—Jerome Robbins. 2009. (Library of American Choreographers Ser.). 48p. (gr. 5-8). 53.00 *(978-1-60853-458-6(8),* Rosen Reference) Rosen Publishing Group, Inc., The.

Seigerman, David. Becky Sauerbrunn. 2017. (Real Sports Content Network Presents Ser.). (ENG.). 128p. (J). (gr. 3-7). 17.99 *(978-1-4814-8217-2(3));* (Illus.). pap. 7.99 *(978-1-4814-8216-5(5))* Simon & Schuster Children's Publishing. (Aladdin).

—Tamba Hali. 2017. (Real Sports Content Network Presents Ser.). (ENG., Illus.). 144p. (J). (gr. 3-7). pap. 7.99 *(978-1-4814-8219-6(X),* Aladdin) Simon & Schuster Children's Publishing.

Seiple, Samantha. Lincoln's Spymaster: Allan Pinkerton, America's First Private Eye. 2015. (Illus.). 211p. (J). *(978-0-545-90821-4(3))* Scholastic, Inc.

Sharp, Katie. Ellen Degeneres, 1 vol. 2009. (People in the News Ser.). (ENG., Illus.). 96p. (gr. 7-7). 41.03 *(978-1-4205-0234-3(4),* c527eb92-6c26-4105-b591-8d4770d02ce0, Lucent Pr.) Greenhaven Publishing LLC.

Shea, Abigail. Victoria Justice, 1 vol. 2013. (Rising Stars Ser.). (ENG.). 32p. (J). (gr. 1-1). pap. 11.50 *(978-1-4339-8990-2(5),* 7e012e0b-e99b-4ab4-970b-4e5536f44e9e); (Illus.). lib. bdg. 27.93 *(978-1-4339-8989-6(1),* 5b26cdce-6209-4f57-aa9f-cf7a6ff2fc51) Stevens, Gareth Publishing LLLP.

Shea, Pegi Deitz. Noah Webster: Weaver of Words. Vachula, Monica, illus. 2009. (ENG.). 40p. (J). (gr. 2-5). 18.99 *(978-1-59078-441-9(3),* Calkins Creek) Highlights Pr., c/o Highlights for Children, Inc.

Shea, Therese M. Alexander Hamilton: Founding Father & Treasury Secretary, 1 vol. 2017. (Junior Biographies Ser.). (ENG.). 24p. (gr. 3-4). pap. 10.35 *(978-0-7660-9045-3(0),* c04e79f6-c80e-4ab8-974e-5cbba0de0d73) Enslow Publishing, LLC.

—John Lee Hooker, 1 vol. 2010. (Inspiring Lives Ser.). (ENG.). 32p. (J). (gr. 1-1). lib. bdg. 27.93 *(978-1-4339-3625-8(9),* 931a8baf-a146-4de5-96b6-4fb5c5340c41); (Illus.). pap. 11.50 *(978-1-4339-3626-5(7),* 31dd1041-73ae-444a-addd-441cfa8d13b2) Stevens, Gareth Publishing LLLP.

Sherman, Patrice & Murica, Rebecca Thatcher. What It's Like to Be Ryan Howard: Como Es Ser Ryan Howard. de la Vega, Eida, tr. from ENG. Rasemas, Joe, illus. 2009. (What It's Like to Be Ser.). (SPA & ENG.). 32p. (J). (gr. -1-2). 25.70 *(978-1-58415-845-5(X))* Mitchell Lane Pubs.

Sherrard, Valerie. Vanessa Hudgens. 2010. (Superstars! Ser.). (ENG., Illus.). 32p. (J). (gr. 3-6). lib. bdg. *(978-0-7787-7253-8(5))* Crabtree Publishing Co.

Shichtman, Sandra H. Michael Bloomberg. 2010. (Political Profiles Ser.). 112p. (J). 28.95 *(978-1-59935-135-3(8))* Reynolds, Morgan Inc.

—Sonia Sotomayor. 2011. (Supreme Court Justices Ser.). (Illus.). 111p. 28.95 *(978-1-59935-156-8(0))* Reynolds, Morgan Inc.

Shone, Rob. Muhammad Ali: The Life of a Boxing Hero. 2009. (Graphic Nonfiction Biographies Ser.). (ENG.). 48p. (YA). (gr. 4-5). 58.50 *(978-1-61513-022-1(5),* Rosen Reference) Rosen Publishing Group, Inc., The.

—Rosa Parks: The Life of a Civil Rights Heroine, 1 vol. Spender, Nik, illus. 2006. (Graphic Nonfiction Biographies Ser.). (ENG.). 48p. (gr. 4-5). pap. 14.05 *(978-1-4042-0927-5(1),* c2923d67-40d0-41b6-a57f-742175328325) Rosen Publishing Group, Inc., The.

Signature Lives - Reformation Era. 2006. (Signature Lives: Reformation Era Ser.). (ENG., Illus.). 112p. (gr. 6-7). 70.64 *(978-0-7565-1712-0(5),* Compass Point Bks.) Capstone.

Signature Lives - Revolutionary War Era, 13 bks. 2006. (Signature Lives: Revolutionary War Era Ser.). (ENG., Illus.). 112p. (gr. 6-7). 176.60 *(978-0-7565-1711-3(7),* Compass Point Bks.) Capstone.

Signature Lives: Colonial America. 2006. (Signature Lives: Colonial America Ser.). (ENG., Illus.). 112p. (gr. 6-7). 70.64 *(978-0-7565-1710-6(9),* Compass Point Bks.) Capstone.

Silate, Jennifer. The Calhoun-Randolph Debate on the Eve of the War of 1812: A Primary Source Investigation, 1 vol. 2004. (Great Historic Debates & Speeches Ser.). (ENG., Illus.). 64p. (YA). (gr. 5-8). lib. bdg. 37.13 *(978-1-4042-0150-7(5),* b416568f-5db1-4b00-bf4b-5f8362e684ce) Rosen Publishing Group, Inc., The.

—The Calhoun-Randolph Debate on the Eve of the War Of 1812: A Primary Source Investigation. 2009. (Great Historic Debates & Speeches Ser.). 64p. (gr. 5-8). 58.50 *(978-1-61513-124-2(8))* Rosen Publishing Group, Inc., The.

Simone, Jacquelyn. Ciara. 2009. (Hip-Hop Ser.). (Illus.). 64p. (YA). pap. 7.95 *(978-1-4222-0334-7(4));* (gr. 7-12). lib. bdg. 22.95 *(978-1-4222-0286-9(0))* Mason Crest.

—Outkast. 2009. (Hip-Hop 2 Ser.). (Illus.). 64p. (YA). (gr. 7-12). lib. bdg. 22.95 *(978-1-4222-0301-9(8))* Mason Crest.

Simons, Rae. Bruce Springsteen. 2008. (Pop Rock Ser.). (Illus.). 64p. (YA). (gr. 4-7). lib. bdg. 22.95 *(978-1-4222-0187-9(2))* Mason Crest.

Singer, Flora M. Flora - I Was but A Child. 2007. 180p. (J). pap. 26.50 *(978-0-9760739-8-7(6))* Yad Vashem Pubns. ISR. Dist: Coronet Bks.

Sís, Peter. The Wall: Growing up Behind the Iron Curtain. Sis, Peter, illus. 2007. (ENG., Illus.). 56p. (J). (gr. 3-7). 21.99 *(978-0-374-34701-7(8),* 900029246, Farrar, Straus & Giroux (BYR)) Farrar, Straus & Giroux.

Skelton, Renee. A Woman of Courage. 2005. (Time for Kids Ser.). (ENG., Illus.). 48p. (J). (gr. 2-4). pap. 3.99 *(978-0-06-057607-3(3))* HarperCollins Pubs.

Skelton, Renee & Time for Kids Editors. Time for Kids: A Woman of Courage. 2005. (Time for Kids Ser.). (ENG., Illus.). 48p. (J). 16.99 *(978-0-06-057608-0(1))* HarperCollins Pubs.

Slavicek, Louise Chipley. I. M. Pei. 2009. (Asian Americans of Achievement Ser.). (ENG., Illus.). 120p. (gr. 7-12). 35.00 *(978-1-60413-567-1(0),* P171270, Facts On File) Infobase Holdings, Inc.

Sloate, Susan. Ray Charles: Find Another Way! 2006. (Defining Moments Ser.). (Illus.). 32p. (J). (gr. 2-5). lib. bdg. 28.50 *(978-1-59716-267-8(1))* Bearport Publishing Co., Inc.

Sloter, James. Uphill All the Way: Memoir of a Depression Era Family, Their Trials, Tribulations & Triumphs. 2004. (Illus.). 170p. per. 12.95 *(978-0-9748333-0-9(4))* Goldenrod Pr.

Small, Cathleen. Chelsea Clinton: Democratic Campaigner & Advocate, 1 vol. 2017. (Leading Women Ser.). (ENG.). 112p. (YA). (gr. 7-7). 41.64 *(978-1-5026-3172-5(5),* da57d652-8999-4cc1-a3e4-d7d243f5444f); pap. 20.99 *(978-1-5026-3411-5(2),* d2b58a0e-2005-44eb-8811-d4a34f20115b) Cavendish Square Publishing LLC.

—Melinda Gates: Philanthropist & Education Advocate, 1 vol. 2017. (Leading Women Ser.). (ENG.). 112p. (YA). (gr. 7-7).

T U V

41.64 *(978-1-5026-2707-0(8),* a4b2b610-dab1-4807-adfd-e693276b757a) Cavendish Square Publishing LLC.

Smith, Emily R. & Conklin, Wendy. Phillis Wheatley. 2020. (Social Studies: Informational Text Ser.). (SPA., Illus.). 32p. (J). (gr. 3-5). pap. 11.99 *(978-0-7439-1362-1(0))* Teacher Created Materials, Inc.

Smith, Pohla. Shaquille O'Neal: Superhero at Center. 2009. (Sports Illustrated for Kids Bks). 176p. (gr. 7-12). 63.90 *(978-1-60853-153-0(8))* Rosen Publishing Group, Inc., The.

Smith, Terri Smith. Tony Hawk: Flying High. 2003. (J). pap. *(978-1-932724-01-1(X),* Bios for Kids) Panda Publishing, L.L.C.

Sneed, Dani. The Man Who Invented the Ferris Wheel: The Genius of George Ferris, 1 vol. 2013. (Genius Inventors & Their Great Ideas Ser.). (ENG., Illus.). 48p. (gr. 3-3). 27.93 *(978-0-7660-4136-3(0),* a77a0e44-0c69-46c5-a704-d8f7f6de7996) Enslow Publishing, LLC.

Snyder, Gail. Filipino Americans. (Successful Americans Ser.). 64p. (YA). 2009. (Illus.). (gr. 9-12). 22.95 *(978-1-4222-0524-2(X))* 2007. (gr. 5-18). pap. 9.95 *(978-1-4222-0857-1(5))* Mason Crest.

—Kelly Clarkson. 2009. (Dream Big: American Idol Superstars Ser.). 64p. (YA). (gr. 5-18). pap. 9.95 *(978-1-4222-1604-0(7));* lib. bdg. 22.95 *(978-1-4222-1506-7(7))* Mason Crest.

—Queen Latifah. 2008. (Hip-Hop Ser.). (Illus.). 64p. (YA). (ENG.). (gr. 3-7). per. 7.95 *(978-1-4222-0276-0(3));* (gr. 7-12). lib. bdg. 22.95 *(978-1-4222-0126-8(0))* Mason Crest.

Solomon, Sharon. Lewis Tewanima: Born to Run, 1 vol. Fields, Lisa, illus. 2014. (ENG.). 32p. (J). (gr. k-3). 16.99 *(978-1-4556-1941-2(8),* Pelican Publishing) Arcadia Publishing.

Sonneborn, Liz. Benedict Arnold: Hero & Traitor. 2005. (Leaders of the American Revolution Ser.). (ENG., Illus.). 136p. (gr. 5-8). lib. bdg. 30.00 *(978-0-7910-8617-9(8),* P114333, Facts On File) Infobase Holdings, Inc.

Sooner, Jeffrey. Rascal Flatts, 1 vol. 2010. (Country Music Stars Ser.). (ENG., Illus.). 32p. (J). (gr. 1-1). pap. 11.50 *(978-1-4339-3617-3(8),* 428c8905-e347-4574-85ab-a1269ba154b3); lib. bdg. 27.93 *(978-1-4339-3616-6(X),* 1f2d9b52-fcbd-4fcb-8bb9-e4827e63c664) Stevens, Gareth Publishing LLLP.

Southwell, David. Unsolved Political Mysteries. 2009. (Mysteries & Conspiracies Ser.). 80p. (gr. 10-10). 61.20 *(978-1-61514-747-2(0))* Rosen Publishing Group, Inc., The.

Spencer, Eve. Stories of America, 25 bks., Set. (J). (gr. 1-8). lib. bdg. 483.50 *(978-0-7398-3295-0(6))* Heinemann-Raintree.

Spencer, Liv. Taylor Swift: Every Day Is a Fairytale - The Unofficial Story. 2010. (ENG., Illus.). 155p. (YA). (gr. 7-18). pap. 14.95 *(978-1-55022-931-8(1),* a74e0eb1-f39d-41b8-99fe-5a351074977a) ECW Pr. CAN. Dist: Baker & Taylor Publisher Services (BTPS).

Stanley, George E. Mr. Rogers: Young Friend & Neighbor. Henderson, Meryl, illus. 2004. (Childhood of Famous Americans Ser.). (ENG.). 208p. (J). (gr. 3-7). mass mkt. 7.99 *(978-0-689-87186-3(4),* Simon & Schuster/Paula Wiseman Bks.) Simon & Schuster/Paula Wiseman Bks.

Stansfield, John. Enos Mills: Rocky Mountain Naturalist. 2005. (Now You Know Bio Ser.). (Illus.). 103p. (J). pap. 8.95 *(978-0-86541-072-5(0))* Filter Pr., LLC.

Star Biographies. 2010. (Star Biographies Ser.). 32p. lib. bdg. 213.20 *(978-1-4296-5883-6(5),* Capstone Pr.) Capstone.

Stefoff, Rebecca. Al Gore: Fighting for a Greener Planet. rev. ed. 2008. (Gateway Biographies Ser.). (ENG.). 48p. (gr. 4-8). 26.60 *(978-1-57505-948-8(7))* Lerner Publishing Group.

Stefoff, Rebecca & Bredeson, Carmen. Stephen King, 1 vol. 2011. (Today's Writers & Their Works). (ENG.). 128p. (YA). (gr. 7-7). 45.50 *(978-0-7614-4122-9(0),* 0bbafd2c-d211-414c-a09a-503ea25e71eb) Cavendish Square Publishing LLC.

Steinberg, Arnold. Whiplash! From JFK to Donald Trump, a Political Odyssey. 2017. (Illus.). x, 630p. (J). *(978-0-89803-180-5(X))* Jameson Bks., Inc.

Stewart, Gail B. Larry Page & Sergey Brin: The Google Guys, 1 vol. 2007. (Innovators Ser.). (ENG., Illus.). 48p. (gr. 4-8). lib. bdg. 31.23 *(978-0-7377-3863-6(4),* 15768c82-de25-4771-b0ef-7e487663cbe5, KidHaven Publishing) Greenhaven Publishing LLC.

Stewart, Whitney. Who Was Walt Disney? 2009. (Who Was... ? Ser.). lib. bdg. 16.00 *(978-0-606-04160-7(5))* Turtleback.

Stewart, Whitney & Who HQ. Who Was Walt Disney? Harrison, Nancy, illus. 2009. (Who Was? Ser.). 112p. (J). (gr. 3-7). pap. 5.99 *(978-0-448-45052-0(6),* Penguin Workshop) Penguin Young Readers Group.

Stine, Megan & Who HQ. Who Is Sonia Sotomayor? Putra, Dede, illus. 2017. (Who Was? Ser.). 112p. (J). (gr. 3-7). 6.99 *(978-0-399-54192-6(6),* Penguin Workshop) Penguin Young Readers Group.

—Who Was Sally Ride? Hammond, Ted, illus. 2013. (Who Was? Ser.). 112p. (J). (gr. 3-7). pap. 6.99 *(978-0-448-46687-3(2),* Penguin Workshop) Penguin Young Readers Group.

Stokes, Betty Southard. Postcards from George, 1763-1781: George Rogers Clark Writes Home to Virginia from the Kentucky Wilderness. Cable, Annette, illus. 2010. (J). *(978-1-935497-12-7(X))* Butler Bks.

Stoltman, Joan. Cesar Chavez, 1 vol. 2017. (Little Biographies of Big People Ser.). (ENG.). 24p. (J). (gr. 1-2). pap. 9.15 *(978-1-5382-0919-6(5),* a98adc72-6756-45de-8966-b5f3f57f927a); lib. bdg. 24.27 *(978-1-5382-0921-9(7),* 2e81a573-8a97-4a3f-83e4-2e9ff53d32de) Stevens, Gareth Publishing LLLP.

Stone, Adam. The Big Show. 2011. (Pro Wrestling Champions Ser.). (ENG., Illus.). 24p. (J). (gr. 3-7). lib. bdg. 26.95 *(978-1-60014-634-3(1),* Torque Bks.) Bellwether Media.

—John Cena. 2011. (Pro Wrestling Champions Ser.). (ENG., Illus.). 24p. (J). (gr. 3-7). lib. bdg. 26.95 *(978-1-60014-636-7(8),* Torque Bks.) Bellwether Media.

Stone, Amy M. Jim Carrey, 1 vol. 2007. (Today's Superstars Ser.). (ENG., Illus.). 32p. (gr. 3-3). lib. bdg. 34.60 *(978-0-8368-8197-4(4),* b2bdc58a-0929-4e4d-803e-b856d13c1149) Stevens, Gareth Publishing LLLP.

Stone, Tanya Lee. Elizabeth Leads the Way: Elizabeth Cady Stanton & the Right to Vote. Gibbon, Rebecca, illus. 2010. (ENG.). 32p. (J). (gr. 1-5). pap. 8.99 *(978-0-312-60236-9(7),* 900064232) Square Fish.

Stories of Great Americans for Little Americans. 2006. 164p. pap. 14.45 *(978-1-59462-414-8(3),* 450, Bk. Jungle) Standard Publications, Inc.

Stotts, Stuart. Lucius Fairchild: Civil War Hero. 2011. (Badger Biographies Ser.). (ENG., Illus.). 112p. (J). pap. 12.95 *(978-0-87020-460-9(2))* Wisconsin Historical Society.

Streissguth, Tom. Wilma Rudolph. 2007. (Illus.). 110p. (YA). pap. 9.95 *(978-0-8225-6693-9(1))* Lerner Publishing Group.

Strom, Laura Layton. Shockwave: Racing on the Wind: Steve Fossett. 2007. (Shockwave: Life Stories Ser.). (ENG., Illus.). 36p. (J). (gr. 3-5). 25.00 *(978-0-531-17774-7(2),* Children's Pr.) Scholastic Library Publishing.

Sullivan, Kevin & DK. DK Reader Level 2: WWE John Cena Second Edition. 2nd rev. ed. 2014. (DK Readers Level 2 Ser.). (ENG.). 32p. (J). (gr. 1-3). pap. 4.99 *(978-1-4654-2088-6(6),* DK) DK Games.

Susi, Geraldine Lee. For My People: The Jennie Dean Story, 1. 2003. (Illus.). 128p. (J). per. 11.95 *(978-1-886826-08-3(0))* Manassas Museum, The.

Sutcliffe, Jane. Barack Obama. 2010. (History Maker Biographies Ser.). (ENG.). 48p. (gr. 3-6). lib. bdg. 27.93 *(978-0-7613-5205-1(8),* Lerner Pubns.) Lerner Publishing Group.

—John Deere. 2006. (History Maker Biographies Ser.). (Illus.). 48p. (J). (gr. 3-7). lib. bdg. 26.60 *(978-0-8225-6579-6(X),* Lerner Pubns.) Lerner Publishing Group.

Swain, Gwenyth. Wanda Gag: Storybook Artist. 2005. (Illus.). 112p. (J). (gr. 3-7). 22.95 *(978-0-87351-545-0(5));* (ENG., per. 12.95 *(978-0-87351-544-3(7))* Minnesota Historical Society Pr. (Borealis Bk.).

Tappan, Eva March. Heroes of Progress: Stories of Successful Americans. 2007. 240p. per. 11.95 *(978-0-9790876-4-6(3))* Living Bks. Pr.

Taylor, Marion. Harriet Tubman. 2004. (Black Americans of Achievement Legacy Edition Ser.). (ENG., Illus.). 112p. (J). (gr. 6-12). 35.00 *(978-0-7910-8166-2(4),* P114170, Facts On File) Infobase Holdings, Inc.

Thatcher Murcia, Rebecca. Thomas Edison: Great Inventor. 2004. (Uncharted, Unexplored, & Unexplained Ser.). (Illus.). 48p. (J). (gr. 4-8). lib. bdg. 29.95 *(978-1-58415-306-1(7))* Mitchell Lane Pubs.

The Library of American Lives & Times: Set 4, 22 vols. 2004. (Library of American Lives & Times Ser.). (ENG., Illus.). 112p. (gr. 5-5). lib. bdg. 420.97 *(978-0-8239-7680-5(7),* f88013d9-08e3-4e0d-a1ca-3921526dc1f5) Rosen Publishing Group, Inc., The.

Thomas, Paul. Olaudah Equiano: from Slavery to Freedom: Band 15/Emerald (Collins Big Cat) Ambrus, Victor, illus. 2007. (Collins Big Cat Ser.). (ENG.). 48p. (J). (gr. 3-4). pap. 11.99 *(978-0-00-723096-9(6))* HarperCollins Pubs. Ltd. GBR. Dist: Independent Pubs. Group.

Thomas, Rachael L. Nerf Genius. 2018. (Toy Trailblazers Ser.). (ENG., Illus.). 32p. (J). (gr. 3-6). lib. bdg. 32.79 *(978-1-5321-1711-4(6),* 30710, Checkerboard Library) ABDO Publishing Co.

Thornley, Stew. Kevin Garnett: Champion Basketball Star, 1 vol. 2012. (Sports Star Champions Ser.). (ENG., Illus.). 48p. (gr. 5-7). 29.60 *(978-0-7660-4028-1(3),* 658e93a1-0626-4b4c-aca8-46dd8519c8f7) Enslow Publishing, LLC.

Tihe Bookazines Staff. Sports Illustrated: Brett Favre: The Tribute. 2008. (YA). pap. 14.95 *(978-1-60320-549-8(7))* Time Inc. Bks.

Time for Kids Editors. Benjamin Franklin - A Man of Many Talents. 2005. (Time for Kids Ser.). (ENG., Illus.). 48p. (J). (gr. 2-4). pap. 3.99 *(978-0-06-057609-7(X))* HarperCollins Pubs.

Timer: An American Story. 2003. 291p. (YA). per. *(978-0-9740774-0-6(2))* J L Publishing Co.

Topinka, Joseph Baar. Just Judy: A Citizen & Leader for Illinois. 2017. (ENG.). (J). pap. 16.95 *(978-0-9983282-2-5(7))* Hilton Publishing Co.

Torres, John. Usher. 2005. (Blue Banner Biography Ser.). (Illus.). 32p. (J). (gr. 4-8). lib. bdg. 25.70 *(978-1-58415-379-5(2))* Mitchell Lane Pubs.

Torres, John A. Dwight Howard: A Basketball Star Who Cares, 1 vol. 2014. (Sports Stars Who Care Ser.). (ENG.). 48p. (gr. 3-3). 27.93 *(978-0-7660-4294-0(4),* f60c9673-62c4-49fb-b3d7-3e5ce9a1d7a7) Enslow Publishing, LLC.

—Lil Wayne. 2009. (Blue Banner Biography Ser.). (Illus.). 32p. (YA). (gr. 4-7). lib. bdg. 25.70 *(978-1-58415-768-7(2))* Mitchell Lane Pubs.

—Shaun White: A Snowboarder & Skateboarder Who Cares, 1 vol. 2014. (Sports Stars Who Care Ser.). (ENG.). 48p. (gr. 3-3). pap. 11.53 *(978-1-4644-0535-8(2),* f6a156ac-e19d-4d94-a5e6-73fe0c308035); lib. bdg. 27.93 *(978-0-7660-4295-7(2),* 59117e52-bea6-4351-9be7-d013097c7ace) Enslow Publishing, LLC. (Enslow Elementary).

Torres, John Albert. Clay Aiken. 2004. (Blue Banner Biography Ser.). (Illus.). 32p. (J). (gr. 3-8). lib. bdg. 25.70 *(978-1-58415-316-0(4))* Mitchell Lane Pubs.

Towle, Mike. Walter Payton: Football's Sweetest Superstar. 2005. (Great American Sports Legends Ser.). (ENG., Illus.). 225p. (J). (gr. 3-7). per. 12.95 *(978-0-58182-476-6(9),* 1249190, Cumberland Hse.) Sourcebooks, Inc.

Tracy, Kathleen. Carrie Underwood. 2005. (Blue Banner Biography Ser.). (Illus.). 32p. (J). (gr. 4-8). lib. bdg. 25.70 *(978-1-58415-425-9(X))* Mitchell Lane Pubs.

—Demi Lovato. 2009. (Robbie Reader Ser.). (Illus.). 32p. (YA). (gr. 2-5). lib. bdg. 25.70 *(978-1-58415-754-0(2))* Mitchell Lane Pubs.

—Matt Christopher. 2008. (Classic Storytellers Ser.). (Illus.). 48p. (J). (gr. 4-7). lib. bdg. 29.95 *(978-1-58415-535-5(3))* Mitchell Lane Pubs.

—Megan Fox. 2010. (Blue Banner Biography Ser.). (Illus.). 32p. (YA). (gr. 4-7). lib. bdg. 25.70 *(978-1-58415-912-4(X))* Mitchell Lane Pubs.

Transcending Race in America: Biographies of Biracial Achievers, 13 vols., Set. Incl. Beyoncé. Bednar, Chuck. (YA). (gr. 4-8). lib. bdg. 22.95 *(978-1-4222-1607-1(1));* Booker T. Washington. Whiting, Jim. (Illus.). (YA). (gr. 4-8). lib. bdg. 22.95 *(978-1-4222-1608-8(X));* David Blaine: Illusionist & Endurance Artist. Bednar, Chuck. (Illus.). (YA). (gr. 5-18). lib. bdg. 22.95 *(978-1-4222-1609-5(8));* Frederick Douglass. Whiting, Jim. (Illus.). (YA). (gr. 5-18). lib. bdg. 22.95 *(978-1-4222-1611-8(X));* Halle Berry. Sapet, Kerrily. (Illus.). (J). (gr. 4-8). 22.95 *(978-1-4222-1612-5(8));* Prince: Singer-Songwriter, Musician, & Record Producer. Robson, David. (Illus.). (YA). (gr. 4-8). lib. bdg. 22.95 *(978-1-4222-1614-9(4));* Rosa Parks. Bednar, Chuck. (Illus.). (YA). (gr. 5-18). lib. bdg. 22.95 *(978-1-4222-1615-6(2));* Salma Hayek. Sapet, Kerrily. (Illus.). (YA). (gr. 5-18). lib. bdg. 22.95 *(978-1-4222-1616-3(0));* Soledad O'Brien. Robson, David. (Illus.). (J). (gr. 5-18). lib. bdg. 22.95 *(978-1-4222-1617-0(9));* 64p. (Illus.). 2010. 298.35 *(978-1-4222-1605-7(5))* Mason Crest.

Trent, Tererai. The Girl Who Buried Her Dreams in a Can: A True Story. Gilchrist, Jan Spivey, illus. 2015. 40p. (J). (gr. 1-3). 18.99 *(978-0-670-01654-9(3),* Viking Books for Young Readers) Penguin Young Readers Group.

Tukan, Jaytoe Anthony, Sr. John Reid Edwards: The People's Senator. 2003. per. 19.95 *(978-0-9665909-4-4(5))* Kalawantis Publishing Services, Inc.

Urban, William. Wyatt Earp: The O. K. Corral & the Law of the American West. 2009. (Library of American Lives & Times Ser.). 112p. (gr. 5-5). 69.20 *(978-1-60853-512-5(6))* Rosen Publishing Group, Inc., The.

USA TODAY(r) Health Reports: Diseases & Disorders: Spring 2012 New Releases. 2012. (USA TODAY Lifeline Biographies Ser.). 112p. (gr. 6-12). lib. bdg. 138.40 *(978-0-7613-8912-5(1),* Twenty-First Century Bks.) Lerner Publishing Group.

USA Today Lifeline Biographies, 4 vols., Set. Incl. Beatles: Music Revolutionaries. Roberts, Jeremy. (Illus.). lib. bdg. 34.60 *(978-0-7613-6421-4(8));* Derek Jeter: Spectacular Shortstop. Greenberg, Keith Elliot. 34.60 *(978-0-7613-6422-1(6));* 112p. (gr. 6-12). 2011. 2011. Set lib. bdg. 133.04 *(978-0-7613-7472-5(8))* Lerner Publishing Group.

Uschan, Michael V. Brian Urlacher. (Superstars of Pro Football Ser.). 64p. (YA). (gr. 7-12). 2009. (Illus.). lib. bdg. 22.95 *(978-1-4222-0555-6(X))* 2007. pap. 9.95 *(978-1-4222-0838-0(9))* Mason Crest.

—Tyler Perry, 1 vol. 2010. (People in the News Ser.). (ENG.). 96p. (gr. 7-7). 41.03 *(978-1-4205-0309-8(X),* 8f0a4aa0-35ed-4241-9d42-57b3b698e2d5, Lucent Pr.) Greenhaven Publishing LLC.

—50 Cent, 1 vol. 2007. (People in the News Ser.). (ENG., Illus.). 104p. (gr. 7-7). lib. bdg. 41.03 *(978-1-4205-0011-0(2),* 9216b9a9-cdc8-44b9-9151-1579177a9ca5, Lucent Pr.) Greenhaven Publishing LLC.

Vallaly, Barbara Dean, compiled by. Life on East 76th Street: Stories of an American Family 2004. (Illus.). 194p. per. 18.50 *(978-0-9755822-0-6(8))* Woodland Pr.

Van Steenwyk, Elizabeth. First Dog Fala, 1 vol. Montgomery, Michael G., illus. 2008. 32p. (J). (gr. -1-3). 16.95 *(978-1-56145-411-2(7))* Peachtree Publishing Co. Inc.

Van Tol, Alex. Sonia Sotomayor: U. S. Supreme Court Justice. 2010. (Crabtree Groundbreaker Biographies Ser.). (ENG., Illus.). 112p. (J). (gr. 5-8). lib. bdg. *(978-0-7787-2537-4(5))* Crabtree Publishing Co.

Venezia, Mike. Benjamin Harrison, 23. Venezia, Mike, illus. 2006. (Getting to Know the U. S. Presidents Ser.). (ENG., Illus.). 32p. (J). (gr. 3-6). lib. bdg. 22.44 *(978-0-516-22628-6(2))* Scholastic Library Publishing.

—Chester A. Arthur. Venezia, Mike, illus. 2006. (Getting to Know the U. S. Presidents Ser.). (ENG., Illus.). 32p. (J). (gr. 3-7). lib. bdg. 28.00 *(978-0-516-22626-2(6),* Children's Pr.) Scholastic Library Publishing.

—Grover Cleveland: Twenty-Second & Twenty-Fourth President, 1885-1889, 1893-1897. Venezia, Mike, illus. 2006. (Getting to Know the U. S. Presidents Ser.). (ENG., Illus.). 32p. (J). (gr. 3-7). lib. bdg. 28.00 *(978-0-516-22627-9(4),* Children's Pr.) Scholastic Library Publishing.

—James A. Garfield. Venezia, Mike, illus. 2006. (Getting to Know the U. S. Presidents Ser.). (ENG., Illus.). 32p. (J). (gr. 3-7). lib. bdg. 28.00 *(978-0-516-22625-5(8),* Children's Pr.) Scholastic Library Publishing.

—John F. Kennedy: Thirty-Fifth President 1961-1963, 32. Venezia, Mike, illus. 2007. (Getting to Know the U. S. Presidents Ser.). (ENG., Illus.). 32p. (J). (gr. 3-6). 22.44 *(978-0-516-22639-2(8))* Scholastic Library Publishing.

—Lyndon B. Johnson: Thirty-Sixth President, 1963-1969. Venezia, Mike, illus. 2007. (Getting to Know the U. S. Presidents Ser.). (Illus.). 32p. (J). (gr. 3-4). 28.00 *(978-0-516-22640-8(1),* Children's Pr.) Scholastic Library Publishing.

—Richard M. Nixon: Thirty-Seventh President, 1969-1974. Venezia, Mike, illus. 2007. (Getting to Know the U. S. Presidents Ser.). (Illus.). 32p. (J). (gr. 3-4). 28.00 *(978-0-516-22641-5(X),* Children's Pr.) Scholastic Library Publishing.

Vernick, Audrey. Brothers at Bat: The True Story of an Amazing All-Brother Baseball Team. Salerno, Steven, illus. 2012. (ENG.). 40p. (J). (gr. -1-3). 18.99 *(978-0-547-38557-0(9),* 1425838, Clarion Bks.) HarperCollins Pubs.

Victoria Justice. 2013. (Rising Stars Ser.). 32p. (J). (gr. 3-6). pap. 63.00 *(978-1-4339-8991-9(3))* Stevens, Gareth Publishing LLLP.

Viegas, Jennifer. Pierre Omidyar: The Founder of Ebay, 1 vol. 2006. (Internet Career Biographies Ser.). (ENG., Illus.). 112p. (YA). (gr. 8-8). lib. bdg. 39.80 *(978-1-4042-0715-8(5),* fd0765ec-bed6-4232-abd0-8d2e3fbd01dc) Rosen Publishing Group, Inc., The.

—William James: American Philosopher, Psychologist, & Theologian. 2009. (Library of American Thinkers Ser.). 112p. (gr. 6-6). 66.50 *(978-1-60853-517-0(7),* Rosen Reference) Rosen Publishing Group, Inc., The.

Vizzini, Ned. Teen Angst? Naaah ... 2010. 272p. (YA). (gr. 7-12). 9.99 *(978-0-385-73945-0(1),* Delacorte Pr.) Random Hse. Children's Bks.

Wachtel, Alan. The FBI's Most Wanted. 2009. (FBI Story Ser.). 64p. (J). (gr. 4-7). lib. bdg. 22.95 *(978-1-4222-0562-4(2))* Mason Crest.

Waldman, Neil. A Land of Big Dreamers: Voices of Courage in America. Waldman, Neil, illus. 2011. (Single Titles Ser.). (ENG., Illus.). 32p. (gr. 3-5). lib. bdg. 16.95 *(978-0-8225-6810-0(1))* Lerner Publishing Group.

Wallmark, Laurie. Grace Hopper: Queen of Computer Code. Wu, Katy, illus. 2017. (People Who Shaped Our World Ser.: 1). 48p. (J). (gr. k). 17.99 *(978-1-4549-2000-7(9))* Sterling Publishing Co., Inc.

Waters, Rosa. Ashanti. 2008. (Hip-Hop Ser.). (Illus.). 64p. (YA). (gr. 3-7). per. 7.95 *(978-1-4222-0263-0(1))* Mason Crest.

—Yung Joc. 2009. (Hip-Hop 2 Ser.). (Illus.). 64p. (YA). (gr. 7-12). lib. bdg. 22.95 *(978-1-4222-0307-1(7))* Mason Crest.

Watson, Stephanie. Prince: Musical Icon. 2016. (Lives Cut Short Ser.). (ENG., Illus.). 112p. (J). (gr. 6-12). lib. bdg. 41.36 *(978-1-68078-364-3(5),* 23216, Essential Library) ABDO Publishing Co.

Waxman, Laura Hamilton. Gerald R. Ford. 2008. (History Maker Biographies Ser.). (ENG.). 48p. (gr. 3-6). 27.93 *(978-0-8225-7985-4(5),* Lerner Pubns.) Lerner Publishing Group.

—W. K. Kellogg. 2006. (History Maker Biographies Ser.). (Illus.). 48p. (J). (gr. 3-7). lib. bdg. 26.60 *(978-0-8225-6578-9(1),* Lerner Pubns.) Lerner Publishing Group.

Weakland, Mark. When Neil Armstrong Built a Wind Tunnel. Lozano, Luciano, illus. 2017. (Leaders Doing Headstands Ser.). (ENG.). 32p. (J). (gr. 1-4). lib. bdg. 28.65 *(978-1-5158-1575-4(7),* 136245, Picture Window Bks.) Capstone.

—When Walt Disney Rode a Pig. Pino, Pablo, illus. 2017. (Leaders Doing Headstands Ser.). (ENG.). 32p. (J). (gr. 1-4). lib. bdg. 28.65 *(978-1-5158-1576-1(5),* 136246, Picture Window Bks.) Capstone.

Wearing, Judy. Abraham Lincoln. 2010. (My Life Ser.). 24p. (J). (gr. 2-4). lib. bdg. 25.70 *(978-1-61690-056-4(3))* Weigl Pubs., Inc.

—Abraham Lincoln: My Life. 2010. pap. 9.95 *(978-1-61690-057-1(1))* Weigl Pubs., Inc.

Wearing, Judy & Yasuda, Anita. Lebron James. 2011. (J). (gr. 4-6). pap. 12.95 *(978-1-61690-674-0(X),* AV2 by Weigl); (Illus.). 24p. (YA). (gr. 3-6). 27.13 *(978-1-61690-669-6(3))* Weigl Pubs., Inc.

Weber, Terri Smith. Hilary Duff: Branching Out. 2003. (J). pap. *(978-1-932724-03-5(6));* lib. bdg. *(978-1-932724-02-8(8),* Bios for Kids) Panda Publishing, L.L.C.

—Jeff Gordon: Racing to Win. 2003. (J). pap. *(978-0-9740180-2-7(3));* lib. bdg. *(978-0-9740180-0-3(7))* Panda Publishing, L.L.C. (Bios for Kids).

—Tony Hawk: Flying High. 2003. (J). lib. bdg. *(978-1-932724-00-4(1),* Bios for Kids) Panda Publishing, L.L.C.

Weintraub, Aileen. Jean Lafitte: Pirate Hero of the War Of 1812. 2009. (Library of Pirates Ser.). 24p. (gr. 3-3). 42.50 *(978-1-60853-813-3(3),* PowerKids Pr.) Rosen Publishing Group, Inc., The.

Welch, Catherine A. Eli Whitney: History Maker Bios Set. 2008. pap. 52.95 *(978-0-8225-9388-1(2))* Lerner Publishing Group.

—Farmland Innovator: A Story about Cyrus Mccormick. Jones, Jan Naimo, illus. 2007. (Creative Minds Biographies Ser.). (ENG.). 64p. (gr. 4-8). lib. bdg. 22.60 *(978-0-8225-5988-7(9))* Lerner Publishing Group.

—George H. W. Bush. 2008. (History Maker Biographies Ser.). (ENG., Illus.). 48p. (J). (gr. 3-6). 27.93 *(978-0-8225-8895-5(1),* Lerner Pubns.) Lerner Publishing Group.

Westen, Robin. Oprah Winfrey: A Biography of a Billionaire Talk Show Host, 1 vol. 2013. (African-American Icons Ser.). (ENG.). 104p. (gr. 6-7). pap. 13.88 *(978-1-59845-394-2(7),* 99e8a3c3-1b4f-4e69-b81f-cc51601d4701) Enslow Publishing, LLC.

Weston, Michael R. Jerry Yang & David Filo: The Founders of Yahoo!, 1 vol. 2006. (Internet Career Biographies Ser.). (ENG., Illus.). 112p. (YA). (gr. 8-8). lib. bdg. 39.80 *(978-1-4042-0718-9(X),* 07612a6b-c6bc-4dbc-a375-8cdf71931386) Rosen Publishing Group, Inc., The.

What It's Like to Be (Que Se Siente Al Ser), 8 vols., Set. Incl. What It's Like to Be America Ferrara. Gagne, Tammy. de la Vega, Eida, tr. 2010. lib. bdg. 25.70 *(978-1-58415-854-7(9));* What Its Like to Be Marta Vieira. Thatcher Murcia, Rebecca. de la Vega, Eida, tr. 2010. lib. bdg. 25.70 *(978-1-58415-852-3(2));* What It's Like to Be Miley Cyrus. Leavitt, Amie Jane. Vega, Eida de la, tr. 2009. lib. bdg. 25.70 *(978-1-58415-841-7(7));* What It's Like to Be President Barack Obama? Sherman, Patrice. Vega, Eida de la, tr. 2009. 25.70 *(978-1-58415-843-1(3));* What It's Like to Be Ryan Howard: Como Es Ser Ryan Howard. Sherman, Patrice & Murica, Rebecca Thatcher. de la Vega, Eida, tr. Rasemas, Joe, illus. 2009. 25.70 *(978-1-58415-845-5(X));* What It's Like to Be Shakira. Thatcher Murcia, Rebecca. de la Vega, Eida, tr. 2010. lib. bdg. 25.70 *(978-1-58415-851-6(4));* What Its Like to Be Sonia Sotomayor. Gagne, Tammy. de la Vega, Eida, tr. 2010. lib. bdg. 25.70 *(978-1-58415-853-0(0));* What It's Like to Be the Jonas Brothers: Que Se Siente Al Ser Los Hermanos Jonas. Leavitt, Amie Jane. Vega, Eida de la, tr. 2009. 25.70 *(978-1-58415-842-4(5));* (Illus.). 32p. (J). (gr. -1-2). 2010. Set lib. bdg. 205.60 *(978-1-58415-855-4(7))* Mitchell Lane Pubs.

What's So Great About... ?, 10 vols., Set. 2006. (J). (gr. 1-4). lib. bdg. 169.50 *(978-1-58415-297-2(4))* Mitchell Lane Pubs.

Wheeler, Jill C. Andy Roddick. 2007. (Awesome Athletes Set 4 Ser.). (Illus.). 32p. (gr. 3-7). 27.07 *(978-1-59928-307-4(7),* Checkerboard Library) ABDO Publishing Co.

White, Arisa & Atkins, Laura. Biddy Mason Speaks Up. Freeman, Laura, illus. 2019. (Fighting for Justice Ser.: 2). (ENG.). 112p. (J). 18.00 *(978-1-59714-403-2(7))* Heyday.

White, Joseph C. Forged in a Country Crucible. 2003. (Illus.). 278p. per. 19.95 *(978-0-9726095-1-7(2),* FCC2003) Crossing Trails Pubns.

Whitehurst, Susan. William Bradford & Plymouth: A Colony Grows. 2009. (Library of the Pilgrims Ser.). 24p. (gr. 3-4). 42.50 *(978-1-60853-916-1(4),* PowerKids Pr.) Rosen Publishing Group, Inc., The.

Whiting, Jim. Jim Beckwourth: The Man Who Opened the West. 2007. (Illus.). 144p. (YA). (gr. 6-18). lib. bdg. 25.95 *(978-1-59556-027-8(0))* OTTN Publishing.

—The Maryland Colony: Lord Baltimore. 2007. (Building America Ser.). (Illus.). 48p. (J). (gr. 4-8). lib. bdg. 29.95 *(978-1-58415-547-8(7))* Mitchell Lane Pubs.

—Russell Westbrook. 2017. (J). lib. bdg. 25.70 *(978-1-68020-133-8(6))* Mitchell Lane Pubs.

Who Wrote That? Incl. Beatrix Potter. Yuan, Margaret Speaker. 120p. lib. bdg. 35.00 *(978-0-7910-8655-1(0)*, P114366); Charles Dickens. Dailey, Donna. 112p. lib. bdg. 35.00 *(978-0-7910-8233-1(4)*, P114217); (Illus.). (gr. 6-12). 2005. (Who Wrote That? Ser.). 2005. 660.00 o.p. *(978-0-7910-9155-5(4)*, Facts On File) Infobase Holdings, Inc.

Wilcoxson, Billy. The CB Cowboys: The Sage of the Legendary Christensen Family. 2003. (Illus.). 217p. pap. 26.95 *(978-1-57168-823-1(4))* Eakin Pr.

Willett, Edward. Jimi Hendrix: Kiss the Sky, 1 vol. 2010. (American Rebels Ser.). (ENG., Illus.). 160p. (gr. 9-10). lib. bdg. 38.60 *(978-0-7660-2449-6(0)*, 707a1bd2-198f-443c-a2a8-daa8c888d782) Enslow Publishing, LLC.

William Dawes. 2006. (J). lib. bdg. *(978-1-58415-444-0(6))* Mitchell Lane Pubs.

Williams, Mary E. Mark Zuckerberg, 1 vol. 2012. (People in the News Ser.). (ENG., Illus.). 104p. (gr. 7-7). lib. bdg. 41.03 *(978-1-4205-0758-4(3)*, 8b26811b-18ec-483d-935a-ee1f93e4a770, Lucent Pr.) Greenhaven Publishing LLC.

Williams, Mel. Taylor Lautner: Overnight Sizzlin' Sensation. 2009. (ENG.). 48p. (YA). pap. 9.99 *(978-1-4424-0368-0(3)*, Simon Pulse) Simon Pulse.

Williams, Zella. America Ferrera: Award-Winning Actress, 1 vol. 2010. (Hispanic Headliners Ser.). (ENG.). 24p. (J). (gr. 2-3). pap. 9.25 *(978-1-4488-1478-7(2)*, ff6c0e22-5517-49ae-a74e-3b69a9db86f4); lib. bdg. 26.27 *(978-1-4488-1473-2(1)*, d224c6d3-1e05-42b0-a23d-5d46fe6c8bab) Rosen Publishing Group, Inc., The. (PowerKids Pr.).

—America Ferrera: Award-Winning Actress = Estrella de la Pantalla, 1 vol. 2010. (Hispanic Headliners / Hispanos en Las Noticias Ser.). (ENG & SPA.). 24p. (J). (gr. 2-3). lib. bdg. 26.27 *(978-1-4488-0713-0(1)*, 605a7225-0fe8-4700-99b7-5af412eef8fd) Rosen Publishing Group, Inc., The.

—Mark Sanchez: Quarterback on the Rise - Mariscal de Campo en Ascenso, 1 vol. 2010. (Hispanic Headliners / Hispanos en Las Noticias Ser.). (ENG & SPA.). 24p. (J). (gr. 2-3). 26.27 *(978-1-4488-1171-7(6)*, 819ae8ad-ff7b-415b-8d18-4335f2781f47) Rosen Publishing Group, Inc., The.

Wilner, Barry. Football's Top 10 Quarterbacks, 1 vol. 2011. (Top 10 Sports Stars Ser.). (ENG., Illus.). 48p. (gr. 5-7). 27.93 *(978-0-7660-3469-3(0)*, db629e6e-d21f-4a64-8b20-f64cf966fbbf) Enslow Publishing, LLC.

—Football's Top 10 Running Backs, 1 vol. 2011. (Top 10 Sports Stars Ser.). (ENG., Illus.). 48p. (gr. 5-7). 27.93 *(978-0-7660-3468-6(2)*, e64434c7-5a71-48c9-a71e-6d0858c19c85) Enslow Publishing, LLC.

—Peyton Manning: A Football Star Who Cares, 1 vol. 2011. (Sports Stars Who Care Ser.). (ENG., Illus.). 48p. (gr. 3-3). lib. bdg. 27.93 *(978-0-7660-3774-8(6)*, 904203d0-a579-49e7-b708-5ede16594e7f) Enslow Publishing, LLC.

Wilson, Rosie. Kenny Chesney, 1 vol. 2010. (Country Music Stars Ser.). (ENG., Illus.). 32p. (J). (gr. 1-1). pap. 11.50 *(978-1-4339-3608-1(9)*, f554fced-6d02-451b-9b5e-28a2ce0a7c4f); lib. bdg. 27.93 *(978-1-4339-3607-4(0)*, 0c18087d-6a08-4a61-b389-2e6201cf95d3) Stevens, Gareth Publishing LLLP.

Winter, Jonah. Dizzy. Qualls, Sean, illus. 2006. (J). 16.99 *(978-0-439-50736-3(7)*, Levine, Arthur A. Bks.) Scholastic, Inc.

—Sonia Sotomayor: A Judge Grows in the Bronx/la Juez Que Creció en el Bronx. Rodriguez, Edel, illus. 2009. (SPA & ENG.). 40p. (J). (gr. -1-3). 18.99 *(978-1-4424-0303-1(9)*, Atheneum Bks. for Young Readers) Simon & Schuster Children's Publishing.

Winters, Kay. John Appleseed: A Trail of Trees. Pullen, Zachary, illus. 2007. (J). *(978-1-4263-0101-8(4))* National Geographic Society.

Wise, Bill. Louis Sockalexis: Native American Baseball Pioneer, 1 vol. Farnsworth, Bill, illus. 2007. (ENG.). 32p. (J). (gr. 1-7). 16.95 *(978-1-58430-269-8(0))* Lee & Low Bks., Inc.

Wittekind, Erika. Gloria Steinem: Women's Liberation Leader, 1 vol. 2011. (Essential Lives Set 7 Ser.). (ENG., Illus.). 112p. (YA). (gr. 6-12). lib. bdg. 41.36 *(978-1-61783-007-5(0)*, 6753, Essential Library) ABDO Publishing Co.

Wong, Angi Ma. Barack Obama: Historymaker. 2009. (Illus.). 104p. (J). *(978-1-928753-86-5(8))* Pacific Heritage Bks.

Wong, Angi Ma, illus. Meet President Obama: America's 44th President. 2009. 32p. (J). *(978-1-928753-28-5(0))* Pacific Heritage Bks.

Woog, Adam. Pierre M. Omidyar: Creator of Ebay, 1 vol. 2007. (Innovators Ser.). (ENG., Illus.). 48p. (gr. 4-8). lib. bdg. 36.23 *(978-0-7377-3864-3(2)*, 7b23a092-2134-40da-953c-a9b71ca913fd, KidHaven Publishing) Greenhaven Publishing LLC.

Wooldridge, Connie N. & Wooldridge, Connie Nordhielm. Thank You Very Much, Captain Ericsson! Glass, Andrew, photos by. 2004. (ENG., Illus.). 32p. (J). (gr. k-3). tchr. ed. 16.95 *(978-0-8234-1626-4(7))* Holiday Hse., Inc.

Wright, David K. The Life of Paul Robeson: Actor, Singer, Political Activist, 1 vol. 2014. (Legendary African Americans Ser.). (ENG.). 96p. (gr. 6-7). 31.61 *(978-0-7660-6157-6(4)*, 6f8e9895-253b-47ce-b998-cc41b66e00f4) Enslow Publishing, LLC.

Wright, Susan. Georgia O'Keefe: An Eternal Spirit, Vol. 8. 2018. (American Artists Ser.). 128p. (J). (gr. 7). lib. bdg. 35.93 *(978-1-4222-4159-2(9))* Mason Crest.

Wyborny, Sheila. Frederick W. Smith: Founder of FedEx, 1 vol. 2007. (Innovators Ser.). (ENG., Illus.). 48p. (gr. 4-8). lib. bdg. 30.38 *(978-0-7377-3861-2(8)*, e079b006-b9a5-42cb-8328-72c83ae6416c, KidHaven Publishing) Greenhaven Publishing LLC.

Wyckoff, Edwin Brit. The African-American Heart Surgery Pioneer: The Genius of Vivien Thomas, 1 vol. 2013. (Genius Inventors & Their Great Ideas Ser.). (ENG., Illus.). 48p. (gr. 3-3). 27.93 *(978-0-7660-4140-0(9)*, 29aa2b19-9222-4a9d-a7af-cb14c12bc2ff, Enslow Elementary) Enslow Publishing, LLC.

—The Man Who Invented Television: The Genius of Philo T. Farnsworth, 1 vol. 2013. (Genius Inventors & Their Great Ideas Ser.). (ENG., Illus.). 48p. (gr. 3-3). 27.93 *(978-0-7660-4139-4(5)*, 7cd4f4da-c2dd-4295-ae8d-f5aff61b059c, Enslow Elementary) Enslow Publishing, LLC.

—The Man Who Invented the Electric Guitar: The Genius of les Paul, 1 vol. 2013. (Genius Inventors & Their Great Ideas Ser.). (ENG., Illus.). 48p. (gr. 3-3). 27.93 *(978-0-7660-4137-0(9)*, a1488d31-b620-40ad-abd7-502cbab2829d) Enslow Publishing, LLC.

—The Man Who Invented the Laser: The Genius of Theodore H. Maiman, 1 vol. 2013. (Genius Inventors & Their Great Ideas Ser.). (ENG., Illus.). 48p. (gr. 3-3). 27.93 *(978-0-7660-4138-7(7)*, 101a9735-0fa2-47eb-928c-e7705772b974, Enslow Elementary) Enslow Publishing, LLC.

—Sign Language Man: Thomas H. Gallaudet & His Incredible Work, 1 vol. 2010. (Genius at Work! Great Inventor Biographies Ser.). (ENG., Illus.). 32p. (gr. 3-3). lib. bdg. 26.60 *(978-0-7660-3447-1(X)*, 2ce6028a-0fed-4805-8569-cb8f5cab6e58) Enslow Publishing, LLC.

—The Woman Who Invented the Thread That Stops Bullets: The Genius of Stephanie Kwolek, 1 vol. 2013. (Genius Inventors & Their Great Ideas Ser.). (ENG., Illus.). 48p. (gr. 3-3). 27.93 *(978-0-7660-4141-7(7)*, 24c27399-4f45-4030-9d60-c3f00e51f0fa) Enslow Publishing, LLC.

Yancey, Diane. The Case of the Green River Killer, 1 vol. 2007. (Crime Scene Investigations Ser.). (ENG., Illus.). 104p. (gr. 7-7). lib. bdg. 42.03 *(978-1-59018-955-9(8)*, 41999a9a-8977-42a6-910e-eb0281183eee, Lucent Pr.) Greenhaven Publishing LLC.

Yasuda, Anita. Kristen Stewart. 2010. (Remarkable People Ser.). (Illus.). 24p. (J). (gr. 4-6). pap. 11.95 *(978-1-61690-164-6(0))*; lib. bdg. 25.70 *(978-1-61690-163-9(2))* Weigl Pubs., Inc.

—Miranda Cosgrove. 2011. (J). (gr. 4-6). pap. 12.95 *(978-1-61690-673-3(1)*, AV2 by Weigl); (Illus.). 24p. (YA). (gr. 3-6). 27.13 *(978-1-61690-668-9(5))* Weigl Pubs., Inc.

—Taylor Lautner. 2010. (Remarkable People Ser.). (Illus.). 24p. (J). (gr. 4-6). pap. 11.95 *(978-1-61690-161-5(6))*; lib. bdg. 25.70 *(978-1-61690-160-8(8))* Weigl Pubs., Inc.

Young, Jeff C. Albert Pujols: A Baseball Star Who Cares, 1 vol. 2014. (Sports Stars Who Care Ser.). (ENG.). 48p. (gr. 3-3). lib. bdg. 27.93 *(978-0-7660-4228-5(6)*, 8f9d1ead-0083-4a87-b109-cbde192830d0) Enslow Publishing, LLC.

—Dwyane Wade. 2012. (Role Model Athletes Ser.). 64p. (J). (gr. 7). 22.95 *(978-1-4222-2709-1(X))* Mason Crest.

Zaunders, Bo. The Great Bridge-Building Contest. Munro, Roxie, illus. 2006. 30p. (J). (gr. 4-8). reprint ed. 17.00 *(978-1-4223-5239-7(0))* DIANE Publishing Co.

Zepke, Terrance. Pirates of the Carolinas for Kids. 2009. (Carolinas for Kids Ser.). (ENG.). 72p. (J). (gr. -1-12). pap. 12.95 *(978-1-56164-459-9(5))* Pineapple Pr., Inc.

Zuehlke, Jeffrey. Ben Roethlisberger. 2007. (Amazing Athletes Ser.). (ENG., Illus.). 32p. (gr. 2-5). lib. bdg. 25.26 *(978-0-8225-7660-0(0))* Lerner Publishing Group.

—Joe Mauer, 2nd Edition. rev. ed. 2011. (ENG., Illus.). 32p. E-Book 25.26 *(978-0-7613-7204-2(0))* Lerner Publishing Group.

—Joe Mauer (Revised Edition) 2011. (Amazing Athletes Ser.). 32p. (J). pap. 45.32 *(978-0-7613-7653-8(4))* Lerner Publishing Group.

—Kevin Garnett (Revised Edition) 2010. pap. 39.62 *(978-0-7613-6969-1(4))* Lerner Publishing Group.

Zumbusch, Amelie von. Michelle Obama: Our First Lady, 1 vol. 2010. (Making History: the Obamas Ser.). (ENG., Illus.). 24p. (J). (gr. 2-3). pap. 9.25 *(978-1-4358-9868-4(0)*, 468c9a7f-e11e-4215-9610-71d2c13860bd); lib. bdg. 26.27 *(978-1-4358-9388-7(3)*, 62b0413a-3e96-4376-9e00-b445bdcb7d73) Rosen Publishing Group, Inc., The. (PowerKids Pr.).

UNITED STATES—BIOGRAPHY—DICTIONARIES

Founding Fathers. (J). tchr. ed. 41.95 *(978-0-382-40882-3(9))* Cobblestone Publishing Co.

Grandes Personajes en la Historia de los Estados Unidos (Famous People in American History) Set 1, 48 vols. 2003. (Grandes Personajes en la Historia de Los Estados Unidos (Famous People in American History) Ser.). (SPA., Illus.). 32p. (gr. 2-3). lib. bdg. 699.12 *(978-0-8239-6921-0(5)*, c8e6bbb0-a829-4769-b409-e03f5def00d3, Editorial Buenas Letras) Rosen Publishing Group, Inc., The.

Rudin, Ronald. Founding Fathers: The Celebration of Champlain & Laval in the Streets of Quebec, 1878-1908. 2003. (ENG., Illus.). 304p. *(978-0-8020-3645-2(7))*; pap. *(978-0-8020-8479-8(6))* Univ. of Toronto Pr.

Wilson, Hoyt R. They Never Gave Up. 2006. (Illus.). 112p. (J). (gr. 4-7). pap. 7.95 *(978-0-9706429-0-5(3))* Resource Publishing.

UNITED STATES—BIOGRAPHY—POETRY

Grady, Cynthia. I Lay My Stitches Down: Poems of American Slavery. Wood, Michele, illus. 2012. (ENG.). 34p. (YA). 17.00 *(978-0-8028-5386-8(2)*, Eerdmans Bks For Young Readers) Eerdmans, William B. Publishing Co.

UNITED STATES—BUREAU OF CUSTOMS

Kerrigan, Michael. Customs & Border Protection. 2017. 80p. (J). *(978-1-4222-3761-8(3))* Mason Crest.

UNITED STATES—CENSUS

Wilson, Natashya. The Census & America's People: Analyzing Data Using Line Graphs & Tables, 1 vol. (Math for the REAL World Ser.). (ENG., 32p. (gr. 4-5). 2010. Illus.). pap. 10.00 *(978-0-8239-8903-4(8)*, 5f6c0764-ecdb-44c5-b338-d62a8d91bff0, PowerKids Pr.) 2004. 47.50 *(978-0-8239-7647-8(5))* Rosen Publishing Group, Inc., The.

UNITED STATES—CENTRAL INTELLIGENCE AGENCY

Clapper, Kathryn N., et al. CIA Agents. 2018. (U. S. Federal Agents Ser.). (ENG., Illus.). 32p. (J). (gr. 3-9). lib. bdg. 27.32 *(978-1-5435-0142-1(7)*, 137079, Capstone Pr.) Capstone.

Cobb, Allan B. How the US Security Agencies Work. 2015. (How the US Government Works). (ENG., Illus.). 48p. (J). (gr. 4-8). lib. bdg. 35.64 *(978-1-62403-638-5(4)*, 17051) ABDO Publishing Co.

Goodman, Michael E. The CIA & Other American Spies. (Spies Around the World Ser.). (ENG., Illus.). 48p. (J). (gr. 5-9). 2013. pap. 12.00 *(978-0-89812-969-4(9)*, 21964, Creative Paperbacks) 2012. 23.95 *(978-1-60818-226-8(6)*, 21960) Creative Co., The.

—Modern Spies. (Wartime Spies Ser.). (ENG., Illus.). 48p. (J). (gr. 4-7). 2016. pap. 12.00 *(978-1-62832-205-7(5)*, 21085, Creative Paperbacks) 2015. *(978-1-60818-600-6(8)*, 21084, Creative Education) Creative Co., The.

Heing, Bridey. Inside the CIA, 1 vol. 2019. (Inside Law Enforcement Ser.). (ENG.). 48p. (gr. 5-5). 29.60 *(978-1-9785-0738-8(0)*, 539bfb1d-56b8-4ea0-abfb-152b4bc1475f) Enslow Publishing, LLC.

Hines, Janet. Inside America's CIA: The Central Intelligence Agency. 2009. (Inside the World's Most Famous Intelligence Agencies Ser.). 64p. (gr. 5-5). 58.50 *(978-1-61513-567-7(7))* Rosen Publishing Group, Inc., The.

Murray, Laura K. Spies in the CIA. 2016. (I Spy Ser.). (ENG.). 24p. (J). (gr. 1-4). *(978-1-60818-616-7(4)*, 20468, Creative Education) Creative Co., The.

Okonowski, Anne. Standing in the CIA Director's Shoes, 1 vol. 2017. (My Government Ser.). (ENG.). 32p. (gr. 3-3). pap. 11.58 *(978-1-5026-3062-9(1)*, 0b0e1db7-9744-4d26-9c31-ca61e2ad093a) Cavendish Square Publishing LLC.

Streissguth, Tom. The Security Agencies of the United States: How the CIA, FBI, NSA, & Homeland Security Keep Us Safe, 1 vol. 2013. (Constitution & the United States Government Ser.). (ENG., Illus.). 104p. (gr. 5-6). 35.93 *(978-0-7660-4064-9(X)*, 3e4b285d-d68a-47f7-a469-2d442178525a) Enslow Publishing, LLC.

Wright, John D. Counterterrorist Forces with the CIA. 2004. (Rescue & Prevention Ser.). (Illus.). 96p. (YA). (gr. 7-18). lib. bdg. 22.95 *(978-1-59084-407-6(6))* Mason Crest.

UNITED STATES—CHURCH HISTORY

Kent, Deborah. Dark Days in Salem: The Witchcraft Trials. 2019. (J). pap. *(978-1-9785-1521-5(9))* Enslow Publishing, LLC.

UNITED STATES—CIVIL AIR PATROL

Feinstein, Stephen. The 1980s, 1 vol. 2015. (Decades of the 20th & 21st Centuries Ser.). (ENG., Illus.). 96p. (gr. 7-7). 36.27 *(978-0-7660-6935-0(4)*, 8ec4cd9c-3b6c-4f21-b7b9-b1615c5e1974) Enslow Publishing, LLC.

UNITED STATES—CIVILIZATION

Benchmark Education Co., LLC. The Middle Colonies. 2014. (PRIME Ser.). (J). (gr. 6-8). pap. *(978-1-4509-9487-3(3))* Benchmark Education Co.

Blohm, Craig E. How the Automobile Changed the World. 2018. (How Science Changed the World Ser.). (ENG.). 80p. (YA). (gr. 6-12). 39.93 *(978-1-68282-407-8(1))* ReferencePoint Pr., Inc.

Brill, Marlene Targ. America in the 1990s. 2009. (Decades of Twentieth-Century America Ser.). (ENG.). 144p. (gr. 5-12). lib. bdg. 38.60 *(978-0-8225-7603-7(1))* Lerner Publishing Group.

Ciment, James. Postwar America: An Encyclopedia of Social, Political, Cultural, & Economic History, 4 vols., Set. 2006. (ENG., Illus.). 2008p. (C). (gr. 7-18). 450.00 *(978-0-7656-8067-9(X)*, Y183409) Routledge.

Combs, Maggie. Postwar United States. 2011. (Explorer Library: Language Arts Explorer Ser.). (ENG.). 32p. (gr. 4-8). pap. 14.21 *(978-1-61080-284-0(5)*, 201207); (Illus.). lib. bdg. 32.07 *(978-1-61080-196-6(2)*, 201168) Cherry Lake Publishing.

Craats, Rennay. Trends. 2008. (USA Past Present Future Ser.). (Illus.). 48p. (J). (gr. 4-6). pap. 10.95 *(978-1-59036-977-7(7))*; lib. bdg. 29.05 *(978-1-59036-976-0(9))* Weigl Pubs., Inc.

Dustman, Jeanne. American Culture. rev. ed. 2014. (Social Studies: Informational Text Ser.). (ENG., Illus.). 32p. (gr. 3-4). pap. 11.99 *(978-1-4333-7360-2(2))* Teacher Created Materials, Inc.

Feinstein, Stephen. The 1900s, 1 vol. 2015. (Decades of the 20th & 21st Centuries Ser.). (ENG., Illus.). 96p. (gr. 7-7). 36.27 *(978-0-7660-6920-6(6)*, 17ed0d4e-94cf-4a2d-bc50-c5320b091514) Enslow Publishing, LLC.

—The 1910s, 1 vol. 2015. (Decades of the 20th & 21st Centuries Ser.). (ENG., Illus.). 96p. (gr. 7-7). 36.27 *(978-0-7660-6922-0(2)*, 161bc14c-1811-4c5a-99bb-14b501507e19) Enslow Publishing, LLC.

—The 1920s, 1 vol. 2015. (Decades of the 20th & 21st Centuries Ser.). (ENG., Illus.). 96p. (gr. 7-7). 36.27 *(978-0-7660-6924-4(9)*, 9b95625d-a7a3-4daf-ab40-edee602319d4) Enslow Publishing, LLC.

—The 1930s, 1 vol. 2015. (Decades of the 20th & 21st Centuries Ser.). (ENG., Illus.). 96p. (gr. 7-7). 36.27 *(978-0-7660-6926-8(5)*, 00aff18c-e313-4a57-8ec9-42cefac23f78) Enslow Publishing, LLC.

—The 1940s, 1 vol. 2015. (Decades of the 20th & 21st Centuries Ser.). (ENG., Illus.). 96p. (gr. 7-7). 36.27 *(978-0-7660-6928-2(1)*, 95a248c9-faa5-4dc6-a901-504cc4a36d8a) Enslow Publishing, LLC.

—The 1950s, 1 vol. 2015. (Decades of the 20th & 21st Centuries Ser.). (ENG., Illus.). 96p. (gr. 7-7). 36.27 *(978-0-7660-6930-5(3)*, e466562d-5b5f-43c3-a081-dc805f4f5a70) Enslow Publishing, LLC.

—The 1950s from the Korean War to Elvis, 1 vol. rev. ed. 2006. (Decades of the 20th Century in Color Ser.). (ENG., Illus.). 64p. (gr. 5-6). lib. bdg. 31.93 *(978-0-7660-2635-3(3)*, 3911c77f-5407-45e0-b78a-3a933d57872e) Enslow Publishing, LLC.

—The 1960s, 1 vol. 2015. (Decades of the 20th & 21st Centuries Ser.). (ENG., Illus.). 96p. (gr. 7-7). 36.27 *(978-0-7660-6932-9(X)*, a0b9f181-938f-4187-b6f8-3868ecbc3a00) Enslow Publishing, LLC.

—The 1960s from the Vietnam War to Flower Power, 1 vol. rev. ed. 2006. (Decades of the 20th Century in Color Ser.). (ENG., Illus.). 64p. (gr. 5-6). lib. bdg. 31.93 *(978-0-7660-2636-0(1)*, 7b7625c7-2ef2-4700-83fe-d3d5cbc79d1a) Enslow Publishing, LLC.

—The 1970s, 1 vol. 2015. (Decades of the 20th & 21st Centuries Ser.). (ENG., Illus.). 96p. (gr. 7-7). 36.27 *(978-0-7660-6934-3(6)*, 9d3e8c2f-6eaa-46c4-bc2a-7ca07e6bc163) Enslow Publishing, LLC.

—The 1990s, 1 vol. 2015. (Decades of the 20th & 21st Centuries Ser.). (ENG., Illus.). 96p. (gr. 7-7). 36.27 *(978-0-7660-6937-4(0)*, e151a8f2-e40e-4550-a278-e3dc25c77986) Enslow Publishing, LLC.

—The 1990s from the Persian Gulf War to Y2K, 1 vol. rev. ed. 2006. (Decades of the 20th Century in Color Ser.). (ENG., Illus.). 64p. (gr. 5-6). lib. bdg. 31.93 *(978-0-7660-2639-1(6)*, 6cb13053-2baf-4a23-846a-26a103713550) Enslow Publishing, LLC.

—The 2000s, 1 vol. 2015. (Decades of the 20th & 21st Centuries Ser.). (ENG., Illus.). 96p. (gr. 7-7). 36.27 *(978-0-7660-6939-8(7)*, c1638775-2fc4-4b72-9a9a-10a5cd58f558) Enslow Publishing, LLC.

Galé. Bwlng Btnks Bell Btms 2, 6 vols. 2nd ed. 2012. (Bowling, Beatniks, & Bell-Bottoms Ser.). (ENG., Illus.). 1651p. lib. bdg. 634.00 *(978-1-4144-1165-1(0)*, UXL) Cengage Gale.

George, Enzo. America in the Fifties, 1 vol. 2015. (Primary Sources in U. S. History Ser.). (ENG., Illus.). 48p. (gr. 4-4). 33.07 *(978-1-5026-0494-1(9)*, 777faed1-27e4-4d4a-9ff0-468d6e560d44) Cavendish Square Publishing LLC.

Grolier Educational Staff, contrib. by. USA 1950s, 6 vols., Set. 2005. (Illus.). (J). (gr. 9-12). lib. bdg. 479.00 *(978-0-7172-6082-9(8)*, Grolier) Scholastic Library Publishing.

Hardyman, Robyn. United States. 2009. (Celebrate! (Chelsea Clubhouse) Ser.). (ENG.). 32p. (gr. 4-6). 28.00 *(978-1-60413-264-9(7)*, P169966, Chelsea Clubhse.) Infobase Holdings, Inc.

Hidden History. 2016. (Hidden History Ser.). 00032p. (J). pap. 63.00 *(978-1-4824-5838-1(1))* Stevens, Gareth Publishing LLLP.

Johnson, Cynthia & Baker, Lawrence W. Bowling, Beatniks, & Bell-Bottoms: Pop Culture of 20th- & 21st-Century America, 6 vols. 2nd ed. 2012. (Illus.). (J). *(978-1-4144-1171-2(5))*; *(978-1-4144-1170-5(7))*; *(978-1-4144-1169-9(3))*; *(978-1-4144-1168-2(5))*; *(978-1-4144-1167-5(7))*; *(978-1-4144-1166-8(9))* Cengage Gale. (UXL).

Kingston, Anna. Respecting the Contributions of African Americans, 1 vol. 2012. (Stop Bullying Now! Ser.). (ENG., Illus.). 24p. (J). (gr. 2-3). 26.27 *(978-1-4488-7448-4(3)*, 0076f467-615f-4c0f-b3f6-f4bd8cd235dd); pap. 9.25 *(978-1-4488-7521-4(8)*, ae93b8f5-2b78-4cac-bbd1-f2415f2adada) Rosen Publishing Group, Inc., The. (PowerKids Pr.).

Lindop, Edmund & DeCapua, Sarah. America in the 1950s. 2009. (Decades of Twentieth-Century America Ser.). (ENG.). 144p. (gr. 5-12). lib. bdg. 38.60 *(978-0-8225-7642-6(2))* Lerner Publishing Group.

Mellors, Julie. U-X-L American Decades 2000-09 Cumulative Index. 2012. (U-X-L American Decades Ser.). (ENG.). pap. 5.00 *(978-1-4144-9723-5(7)*, UXL) Cengage Gale.

Nelson, Kadir. Heart & Soul: The Story of America & African Americans. Nelson, Kadir, illus. (ENG., Illus.). (J). (gr. 1-5). 2013. 112p. pap. 9.99 *(978-0-06-173079-5(3))* 2011. 108p. 21.99 *(978-0-06-173074-0(2))* HarperCollins Pubs. (Balzer & Bray).

—Heart & Soul: The Story of America & African Americans. 2013. (J). lib. bdg. 19.65 *(978-0-606-35050-1(0))* Turtleback.

Puigdevall, Federico & Cañagueral, Albert. The Secrets of Early American Civilizations: The Decline of the Mayas & the Lost Cities of the Amazon, 1 vol. 2017. (Secrets of History Ser.). (ENG.). 96p. (YA). (gr. 8-8). pap. 20.99 *(978-1-5026-3440-5(6)*, e37d2538-9ad4-4ce4-abf8-3914ae5f11df); lib. bdg. 44.50 *(978-1-5026-3267-8(5)*, 3052b58d-614f-44e2-9e52-ed114e07ee54) Cavendish Square Publishing LLC.

Schwartz, Eric. What Makes America America? 2006. (How America Became America Ser.). (Illus.). 96p. (YA). lib. bdg. 22.95 *(978-1-59084-913-2(2))* Mason Crest.

Shoup, Kate. American Culture & Society, 1 vol. 2018. (Discovering America: an Exceptional Nation Ser.). (ENG.). 112p. (gr. 7-7). 44.50 *(978-1-5026-4267-7(0)*, 70a78153-f28b-45d7-82af-75ee0d272eb1) Cavendish Square Publishing LLC.

Stefoff, Rebecca. The New Republic, 1783-1830, 1 vol. 2006. (American Voices From Ser.). (ENG.). 160p. (gr. 6-6). 41.21 *(978-0-7614-1695-1(1)*, 06c7fb95-d435-4501-a58f-55f01615b5c2) Cavendish Square Publishing LLC.

Stone, Amy M. Jewish Americans, 1 vol. 2006. (World Almanac(r) Library of American Immigration Ser.). (ENG., Illus.). 48p. (gr. 5-8). pap. 15.05 *(978-0-8368-7327-6(0)*, e3f89159-d969-406e-9348-c4ad54e49520); lib. bdg. 33.67 *(978-0-8368-7314-6(9)*, b9e6cfa9-f253-4ca8-b5a0-48647b4cd37e) Stevens, Gareth Publishing LLLP. (Gareth Stevens Secondary Library).

Wirkner, Linda. Learning about Life in the New American Nation with Graphic Organizers. (Graphic Organizers in Social Studies). 24p. 2009. (gr. 3-4). 42.50 *(978-1-61513-082-5(9)*, PowerKids Pr.) 2005. (ENG.). (gr. 4-5). pap. 8.25 *(978-1-4042-5050-5(6)*, 6db573f1-ac3a-4318-81da-7b890351eed3, Rosen Classroom) 2004. (ENG., Illus.). (J). (gr. 4-5). lib. bdg. 26.27 *(978-1-4042-2810-8(1)*, d813325a-c1b5-48f2-8395-8fd44333b46a, PowerKids Pr.) Rosen Publishing Group, Inc., The.

For book reviews, descriptive annotations, tables of contents, cover images, author biographies & additional information, updated daily, subscribe to **www.booksinprint.com**

UNITED STATES—COAST GUARD

Benson, Michael. The U. S. Coast Guard. 2004. (U. S. Armed Forces Ser.). (ENG., Illus.). 64p. (gr. 4-8). lib. bdg. 26.60 *(978-0-8225-1647-7(0))* Lerner Publishing Group.

Bergaust, Erik & Foss, William O. Coast Guard in Action. 2012. 96p. 38.95 *(978-1-258-25246-5(5))*; pap. 23.95 *(978-1-258-25728-6(9))* Literary Licensing, LLC.

Best, B. J. Coast Guard Boats. 2017. (Riding to the Rescue! Ser.). (Illus.). 24p. (J). (gr. 1-1). pap. 49.32 *(978-1-5026-2556-4(3))* Cavendish Square Publishing LLC.

David, Jack. United States Coast Guard. 2008. (Armed Forces Ser.). (ENG., Illus.). 24p. (J). (gr. 3-7). lib. bdg. 26.95 *(978-1-60014-163-8(3))* Bellwether Media.

Demarest, Chris L. Mayday! Mayday! A Coast Guard Rescue. Demarest, Chris L., illus. 2004. (ENG., Illus.). 40p. (J). (gr. -1-5). 19.99 *(978-0-689-85161-2(8)*, McElderry, Margaret K. Bks.) McElderry, Margaret K. Bks.

Dolan, Edward F. Military Service, 10 vols., Set. Incl. Careers in the U. S. Air Force. 38.36 *(978-0-7614-4205-9(7)*, e4fae1b0-9c27-4222-a7e4-9bfe2018acfe); Careers in the U. S. Army. 38.36 *(978-0-7614-4206-6(5)*, a0a5c8e1-5fba-4400-800a-65381ebde5ea); Careers in the U. S. Coast Guard. 38.36 *(978-0-7614-4207-3(3)*, 7ef3c6d4-eff7-4b91-b515-6d4ff161c981); Careers in the U. S. Marine Corps. 38.36 *(978-0-7614-4209-7(X)*, b4ad4186-88cc-46f5-89ce-17b13d9c32d4); Careers in the U. S. Navy. 38.36 *(978-0-7614-4210-3(3)*, e95d1809-a3a4-48fb-8427-1c59e5c740fd); (Illus.). 80p. (YA). (gr. 7-7). (Military Service Ser.). (ENG.). 2010. Set lib. bdg. 191.80 *(978-0-7614-4203-5(0)*, 1fe14f46-9e52-44d0-bb2d-9295775cd6ab, Cavendish Square) Cavendish Square Publishing LLC.

Goldish, Meish. Coast Guard: Civilian to Guardian. 2010. (Becoming a Soldier Ser.). 24p. (YA). (gr. 3-6). lib. bdg. 26.99 *(978-1-936088-12-6(6))* Bearport Publishing Co., Inc.

Gordon, Nick. Coast Guard Rescue Swimmer. 2012. (Dangerous Jobs Ser.). (ENG., Illus.). 24p. (J). (gr. 3-7). lib. bdg. 26.95 *(978-1-60014-778-4(X)*, Torque Bks.) Bellwether Media.

—U. S. Coast Guard. 2012. (U. S. Military Ser.). (ENG., Illus.). 24p. (J). (gr. 3-7). lib. bdg. 26.95 *(978-1-60014-828-6(X)*, Epic Bks.) Bellwether Media.

Kiland, Taylor Baldwin & Silverstein Gray, Judy. Careers in the U. S. Coast Guard, 1 vol. 2015. (Careers in the U. S. Armed Forces Ser.). (ENG., Illus.). 128p. (gr. 6-7). 38.93 *(978-0-7660-6945-9(1)*, 25b3cfc6-7d87-4705-89ee-f4c2dd8e5ed3) Enslow Publishing, LLC.

Lyons, Lewis. Rescue at Sea with the U. S. & Canadian Coast Guards. 2004. (Rescue & Prevention Ser.). (Illus.). 96p. (YA). (gr. 7-18). lib. bdg. 22.95 *(978-1-59084-405-2(X))* Mason Crest.

Markovics, Joyce L. Today's Coast Guard Heroes. 2012. (Acts of Courage: Inside America's Military Ser.). 32p. (J). (gr. 2-7). lib. bdg. 28.50 *(978-1-61772-448-0(3))* Bearport Publishing Co., Inc.

Mitchell, P. P. Join the Coast Guard, 1 vol. 2017. (U. S. Armed Forces Ser.). (ENG.). 32p. (gr. 1-2). pap. 11.50 *(978-1-5382-0538-9(6)*, b71e2da8-f111-491f-ab24-2b835bc4eff0) Stevens, Gareth Publishing LLLP.

Murray, Julie. United States Coast Guard, 1 vol. 2014. (U. S. Armed Forces Ser.). (ENG.). 24p. (J). (gr. -1-2). lib. bdg. 32.79 *(978-1-62970-095-3(9)*, 1712, Abdo Kids) ABDO Publishing Co.

Noble, Dennis. The U. S. Coast Guard, 1 vol. 2004. (America's Armed Forces Ser.). (ENG., Illus.). 48p. (gr. 5-8). lib. bdg. 33.67 *(978-0-8368-5681-1(3)*, 5c999056-fde4-4f69-9880-5067d91bf80c, Gareth Stevens Secondary Library) Stevens, Gareth Publishing LLLP.

Orr, Tamra. Your Career in the Coast Guard, 1 vol. 2011. (Call of Duty: Careers in the Armed Forces Ser.). (ENG.). 128p. (YA). (gr. 7-7). lib. bdg. 39.80 *(978-1-4488-5514-8(4)*, 33e9900f-805e-4065-b927-47896ee1ec75) Rosen Publishing Group, Inc., The.

Randolph, Joanne. Coast Guard Boats. (To the Rescue! Ser.). 24p. (gr. 1-1). 2009. 42.50 *(978-1-60854-395-3(1))* 2008. (ENG., Illus.). (J). lib. bdg. 26.27 *(978-1-4042-4152-7(3)*, 5524f7c7-d6d4-459e-9ab7-9d74e42072b4) Rosen Publishing Group, Inc., The. (PowerKids Pr.).

—Coastguard Boats/Lanchas Guardacostas. 2009. (To the Rescue! / ¡Al rescate! Ser.). (ENG & SPA.). 24p. (gr. 1-1). 42.50 *(978-1-60854-401-1(X)*, Editorial Buenas Letras) Rosen Publishing Group, Inc., The.

Rose, Simon. Coast Guard. 2012. (J). *(978-1-61913-630-4(9))*; pap. *(978-1-61913-631-1(7))* Weigl Pubs., Inc.

Roza, Greg. Careers in the Coast Guard's Search & Rescue Units. 2009. (Careers in Search & Rescue Operations Ser.). 64p. (gr. 5-8). 58.50 *(978-1-61511-808-3(X)*, Rosen Reference) Rosen Publishing Group, Inc., The.

Shea, John M. Heroes of the U. S. Coast Guard, 1 vol. 2012. (Heroes of the U. S. Military Ser.). (ENG.). 32p. (J). (gr. 3-4). pap. 11.50 *(978-1-4339-7241-6(7)*, 8993ff60-91f8-4d75-997f-1f80d99dc4aa); lib. bdg. 29.27 *(978-1-4339-7240-9(9)*, 0d4219b5-4895-44db-af63-0dce74deff28) Stevens, Gareth Publishing LLLP.

Toth, Vince. My Sister Is in the Coast Guard, 1 vol., 1. 2015. (Military Families Ser.). (ENG., Illus.). 24p. (J). (gr. 3-4). pap. 9.25 *(978-1-5081-4442-7(7)*, f04064a0-76b6-4e7d-98b3-5dc86b3aa34b, PowerKids Pr.) Rosen Publishing Group, Inc., The.

U. S. Coast Guard. 2019. (Serving Our Country Ser.). (ENG.). 24p. (J). (gr. 1-4). lib. bdg. *(978-1-68151-562-5(8)*, 17594) Amicus.

Wood, Alix. Serving in the Coast Guard. 2013. (Protecting Our Country Ser.). 32p. (J). (gr. 3-6). pap. 60.00 *(978-1-4777-1403-4(0))*; (ENG., Illus.). pap. 11.00 *(978-1-4777-1402-7(2)*, 795c4aa2-e4a3-4596-8b64-0805a35f2e91); (ENG., Illus.). lib. bdg. 28.93 *(978-1-4777-1298-6(4)*, 1b41e6f8-8d2f-4aad-8da4-731f774ae23c) Rosen Publishing Group, Inc., The. (PowerKids Pr.).

UNITED STATES—COLONIES

see United States—Territories and Possessions

UNITED STATES—COMMERCE

Currie, Stephen. Outsourcing America. 2007. (Ripped from the Headlines Ser.). 64p. (J). (gr. 7-12). 23.95 *(978-1-60217-008-7(8))* Erickson Pr.

Egendorf, Laura K., ed. Should the U. S. Do Business with China?, 1 vol. 2008. (At Issue Ser.). (ENG., Illus.). 128p. (gr. 10-12). pap. 28.80 *(978-0-7377-4113-1(9)*, e446a508-c685-49a2-8d22-37e6094e3689, Greenhaven Publishing) Greenhaven Publishing LLC.

—Should the U. S. Do Business with China?, 1 vol. 2008. (At Issue Ser.). (ENG., Illus.). 128p. (gr. 10-12). 41.03 *(978-0-7377-4112-4(0)*, d47d5c35-7870-44b7-baf6-89d9133f4734, Greenhaven Publishing) Greenhaven Publishing LLC.

Francis, Amy, ed. The U. S. Policy on Cuba, 1 vol. 2008. (At Issue Ser.). (ENG., Illus.). 136p. (gr. 10-12). 41.03 *(978-0-7377-4108-7(2)*, fff89a06-f667-48d9-84e0-719ed60cc6f8); pap. 28.80 *(978-0-7377-4109-4(0)*, 31970e5b-b6b7-46c2-a4d7-31691973a5e3) Greenhaven Publishing LLC. (Greenhaven Publishing).

Goldberg, Jan. The Department of Commerce, 1 vol. 2005. (This Is Your Government Ser.). (ENG., Illus.). 64p. (J). (gr. 4-6). lib. bdg. 37.13 *(978-1-4042-0207-8(2)*, 0910e505-f224-4bf3-ba26-409af9a8b43b) Rosen Publishing Group, Inc., The.

Krueger, Lisa, ed. Does Outsourcing Harm America?, 1 vol. 2010. (At Issue Ser.). (ENG., Illus.). 120p. (gr. 10-12). 41.03 *(978-0-7377-4673-0(4)*, c7bb8054-6a8d-4ba7-8ccb-a7781af3aa74); pap. 28.80 *(978-0-7377-4674-7(2)*, 221048e5-4541-4649-a6f5-579c72a938fd) Greenhaven Publishing LLC. (Greenhaven Publishing).

Reynolds, Donna. Is It Important to Buy American Goods?, 1 vol. 2020. (Points of View Ser.). (ENG.). 24p. (J). (gr. 3-3). pap. 9.25 *(978-1-5345-3432-2(6)*, 253c1442-59ea-463d-ae72-c32505c1722c, KidHaven Publishing) Greenhaven Publishing LLC.

UNITED STATES—COMMERCIAL POLICY

Goldberg, Jan. The Department of Commerce. (This Is Your Government Ser.). 64p. 2009. (gr. 5-6). 58.50 *(978-1-60854-365-6(X)*, Rosen Reference) 2005. (ENG., Illus.). (gr. 4-6). per. 12.95 *(978-1-4042-0660-1(4)*, df411235-2cfc-44c7-8b6d-c21e709889bc) Rosen Publishing Group, Inc., The.

Peters, Jennifer. Inside the Department of Commerce, 1 vol. 2018. (Understanding the Executive Branch Ser.). (ENG.). 48p. (gr. 5-5). 29.60 *(978-0-7660-9887-9(7)*, c4ec719d-01b8-4e3b-8e34-781c2c7af4dc) Enslow Publishing, LLC.

UNITED STATES—CONGRESS

Allen, Charles F. David Crockett: Scout, Small Boy, Pilgrim, Mountaineer, Soldier, Bear-Hunter, & Congressman, Defender of the Alamo. (Illus.). 308p. reprint ed. lib. bdg. 98.00 *(978-0-7222-4856-0(3))* Library Reprints, Inc.

Bow, James. What Is the Legislative Branch? 2013. (ENG.). 32p. (J). *(978-0-7787-0879-7(9))*; pap. *(978-0-7787-0905-3(1))* Crabtree Publishing Co.

Brexel, Bernadette. Congress. 2009. (Primary Source Library of American Citizenship Ser.). 32p. (gr. 5-5). 47.90 *(978-1-61511-218-0(9)*, Rosen Reference) Rosen Publishing Group, Inc., The.

Cane, Ella. The U. S. House of Representatives, 1 vol. 2014. (Our Government Ser.). (ENG., Illus.). 24p. (J). (gr. 1-3). lib. bdg. 27.99 *(978-1-4765-4201-0(5)*, 124305) Capstone.

—The U. S. Senate, 1 vol. 2014. (Our Government Ser.). (ENG., Illus.). 24p. (J). (gr. 1-3). lib. bdg. 27.99 *(978-1-4765-4202-7(3)*, 124306) Capstone.

Cefrey, Holly. Congress, 1 vol. 2003. (Primary Source Library of American Citizenship Ser.). (ENG., Illus.). 32p. (YA). (gr. 5-5). lib. bdg. 29.13 *(978-0-8239-4470-5(0)*, d875e169-eb95-4947-abb2-c260ce266c91) Rosen Publishing Group, Inc., The.

Chambers, Veronica. Shirley Chisholm Is a Verb. Baker, Rachelle, illus. 2020. 40p. (J). (gr. -1-3). 18.99 *(978-0-8037-3089-2(6)*, Dial Bks) Penguin Young Readers Group.

Connors, Kathleen. What Does Congress Do?, 1 vol. 2017. (Look at Your Government Ser.). (ENG.). 32p. (J). (gr. 2-2). pap. 11.50 *(978-1-4824-6047-6(5)*, 2eb4fabc-249e-4d8c-b604-a634fee6cbf4) Stevens, Gareth Publishing LLLP.

Crawford, Ann Fears. Barbara Jordan: Breaking the Barriers. 2003. (Illus.). 90p. (J). (gr. 7-9). lib. bdg. 19.95 *(978-1-931823-11-1(1))* Halcyon Pr., Ltd.

Cummings, Matthew. What Is the Legislative Branch?, 1 vol. 2015. (Let's Find Out! Government Ser.). (ENG., Illus.). 32p. (J). (gr. 2-3). 26.06 *(978-1-62275-956-9(7)*, c5c494a8-6aa4-4c64-9fb9-fe3ad53cc695, Britannica Educational Publishing) Rosen Publishing Group, Inc., The.

Dodge, Andrew. Exploring Capitol Hill: A Kid's Guide to the U. S. Capitol & Congress. Wasniewski, Matthew, ed. Gibson, Barbara, illus. 12p. (J). pap. 1.95 *(978-0-916200-25-1(6))* U. S. Capitol Historical Society.

Doeden, Matt. Michele Bachmann: Tea Party Champion. 2011. (Gateway Biographies Ser.). (YA). (gr. 4-7). lib. bdg. 26.60 *(978-0-7613-9074-9(X))* Lerner Publishing Group.

Donovan, Sandy & Nelson, Robin. The Congress: A Look at the Legislative Branch. 2012. (Searchlight Books (tm) — How Does Government Work? Ser.). (ENG., Illus.). 40p. (J). (gr. 3-5). pap. 9.99 *(978-0-7613-8559-2(2)*, 2bac2e9d-909a-4122-ae23-70fbcaf76ca0) Lerner Publishing Group.

Driscoll, Laura. Hillary Clinton: An American Journey. Wood, Judith V., illus. 2008. (ENG.). 48p. (J). (gr. 3-6). 16.19 *(978-0-448-44787-2(8))* Penguin Young Readers Group.

Duignan, Brian & DeCarlo, Carolyn, eds. The Legislative Branch: Making Laws, 1 vol. 2018. (Checks & Balances in the U. S. Government Ser.). (ENG.). 128p. (gr. 10-10). lib. bdg. 39.00 *(978-1-5383-0170-8(9)*, af8a6128-331c-4572-85cd-e258771c0692, Britannica Educational Publishing) Rosen Publishing Group, Inc., The.

Duling, Kaitlyn. Standing in the Speaker of the House's Shoes, 1 vol. 2017. (My Government Ser.). (ENG.). 32p. (gr. 3-3). pap. 11.58 *(978-1-5026-3078-0(8)*, 57176e12-2fc8-46e7-bd8e-35cbf31cc21f); lib. bdg. 30.21 *(978-1-5026-3080-3(X)*, 550a6813-e4e4-4dc8-80f4-5db6fd7c1034) Cavendish Square Publishing LLC.

Egan, Tracie. How a Bill Becomes a Law. (Primary Source Library of American Citizenship Ser.). 32p. (gr. 5-5). 2009. 47.90 *(978-1-61511-219-7(7))* 2003. (ENG., Illus.). lib. bdg. 29.13 *(978-0-8239-4471-2(9)*, 70c063f9-adca-438a-9685-e0e96dd533c8) Rosen Publishing Group, Inc., The. (Rosen Reference).

Feldman, Ruth Tenzer. How Congress Works: A Look at the Legislative Branch. 2003. (How Government Works). (ENG., Illus.). 56p. (gr. 4-8). lib. bdg. 25.26 *(978-0-8225-1347-6(1))* Lerner Publishing Group.

Finley, Toiya Kristen. Russell Simmons. 2007. (Sharing the American Dream Ser.). 64p. (YA). (gr. 7-18). pap. 9.95 *(978-1-4222-0762-8(5))* Mason Crest.

Furgang, Kathy. The Declaration of Independence & Roger Sherman of Connecticut. 2009. (Framers of the Declaration of Independence Ser.). 24p. (gr. 3-3). 42.50 *(978-1-61512-632-3(5)*, PowerKids Pr.) Rosen Publishing Group, Inc., The.

Gabriel, Dani. John McCain: Get to Know the Brave POW & Senator. 2019. (People You Should Know Ser.). (ENG., Illus.). 32p. (J). (gr. 3-6). pap. 7.95 *(978-1-5435-7466-1(1)*, 140906); lib. bdg. 27.99 *(978-1-5435-7184-4(0)*, 140435) Capstone.

Goldsworthy, Kaite. Gabrielle Giffords. 2012. (J). *(978-1-61913-535-2(3))*; pap. *(978-1-61913-590-1(6))* Weigl Pubs., Inc.

Gutner, Howard. The Speaker of the House. 2003. (America's Leaders Ser.). (Illus.). 32p. (J). 23.70 *(978-1-56711-964-0(6)*, Blackbirch Pr., Inc.) Cengage Gale.

Haldy, Emma E. Davy Crockett. Bane, Jeff, illus. 2017. (My Early Library: My Itty-Bitty Bio Ser.). (ENG.). 24p. (J). (gr. k-1). lib. bdg. 30.64 *(978-1-63472-151-6(9)*, 209176) Cherry Lake Publishing.

Haskins, Jim & Benson, Kathleen. John Lewis in the Lead: A Story of the Civil Rights Movement, 1 vol. Andrews, Benny, illus. 2006. (ENG.). 40p. (gr. 2-7). 17.95 *(978-1-58430-250-6(X))*; (J). (gr. 3-8). pap. 12.95 *(978-1-60060-849-0(3)*, leelowbooks) Lee & Low Bks., Inc.

Hillard, Stephane. The U. S. Capitol: The History of U. S. Congress, 1 vol. 2017. (Landmarks of Democracy: American Institutions Ser.). (ENG.). 24p. (J). (gr. 3-3). pap. 9.25 *(978-1-5081-6097-7(X)*, 89e41327-12c8-4faa-8033-50eafa003834, PowerKids Pr.) Rosen Publishing Group, Inc., The.

Horn, Geoffrey M. Nancy Pelosi, 1 vol. 2009. (People We Should Know (Second Series) Ser.). (ENG.). 32p. (J). (gr. 3-5). pap. 11.50 *(978-1-4339-0162-1(5)*, cc982ed7-636a-43f2-8bf3-727da0c3c27f); lib. bdg. 33.67 *(978-1-4339-0021-1(1)*, 89210acd-7b88-4f6a-a1f2-f17328b75db2) Stevens, Gareth Publishing LLLP. (Gareth Stevens Learning Library).

Jakubiak, David J. What Does a Congressional Representative Do? 2010. (How Our Government Works Ser.). 24p. (J). (gr. 3-6). lib. bdg., E-Book 42.50 *(978-1-4488-0033-9(1))* Rosen Publishing Group, Inc., The.

Jarnow, Jesse. Davy Crockett: Defensor de la frontera (Davy Crockett: Frontier Hero) 2009. (Grandes personajes en la historia de los Estados Unidos (Famous People in American History) Ser.). (SPA.). 32p. (gr. 2-3). 47.90 *(978-1-61512-797-9(6)*, Editorial Buenas Letras) Rosen Publishing Group, Inc., The.

—Davy Crockett: Frontier Hero / Defensor de la Frontera. 2009. (Famous People in American History/Grandes personajes en la historia de los Estados Unidos Ser.). (ENG & SPA.). 32p. (gr. 2-3). 47.90 *(978-1-61512-543-2(4)*, Editorial Buenas Letras) Rosen Publishing Group, Inc., The.

Johnston, Marianne. Davy Crockett. 2009. (American Legends Ser.). 24p. (gr. 3-3). 42.50 *(978-1-61511-381-1(9)*, PowerKids Pr.) Rosen Publishing Group, Inc., The.

Jopp, Kelsey. Kamala Harris. 2020. (Groundbreaking Women in Politics Ser.). (ENG., Illus.). 48p. (J). (gr. 5-6). pap. 11.95 *(978-1-64493-167-7(2)*, 1644931672); lib. bdg. 34.21 *(978-1-64493-088-5(9)*, 1644930889) North Star Editions. (Focus Readers).

—Tammy Duckworth. 2020. (Groundbreaking Women in Politics Ser.). (ENG., Illus.). 48p. (J). (gr. 5-6). pap. 11.95 *(978-1-64493-166-0(4)*, 1644931664); lib. bdg. 34.21 *(978-1-64493-087-8(0)*, 1644930870) North Star Editions. (Focus Readers).

Kaiser, Emma. Alexandria Ocasio-Cortez. 2020. (Groundbreaking Women in Politics Ser.). (ENG., Illus.). 48p. (J). (gr. 5-6). pap. 11.95 *(978-1-64493-168-4(0))*; lib. bdg. 34.21 *(978-1-64493-089-2(7)*, 1644930897) North Star Editions. (Focus Readers).

Kennedy, Edward M. My Senator & Me: A Dog's-Eye View of Washington, D. C. Small, David, illus. 2011. (J). (gr. 2-5). 29.95 *(978-0-545-04379-3(4))* Weston Woods Studios, Inc.

Koestler-Grack, Rachel A. The House of Representatives. 2nd rev. ed. 2007. (U. Government: How It Works). (ENG.). 112p. (gr. 5-9). 30.00 *(978-0-7910-9285-9(2)*, P125639, Facts On File) Infobase Holdings, Inc.

Laks Gorman, Jacqueline. Member of Congress, 1 vol. 2009. (Know Your Government Ser.). (ENG.). 24p. (J). (gr. 3-3). pap. 9.15 *(978-1-4339-0122-5(6)*, a8f5d767-0414-4dd2-ae32-18152928b16e); lib. bdg. 24.67 *(978-1-4339-0094-5(7)*, 2ff26ad8-8cbd-4683-b732-3009679d7942) Stevens, Gareth Publishing LLLP. (Weekly Reader Leveled Readers).

—Miembro Del Congreso (Member of Congress), 1 vol. 2009. (Conoce Tu Gobierno (Know Your Government) Ser.). (SPA.). 24p. (gr. 3-3). (J). lib. bdg. 24.67 *(978-1-4339-0101-0(3)*, 1d70021d-068b-4a0e-afde-55dfa720a3a0); pap. 9.15 *(978-1-4339-0129-4(3)*, a8fedf7b-e2a4-4a2e-bb40-d1ff20ddbc96) Stevens, Gareth Publishing LLLP. (Weekly Reader Leveled Readers).

Leavitt, Amie Jane. Nancy Pelosi. 2007. (Blue Banner Biography Ser.). (Illus.). 32p. (YA). (gr. 4-7). lib. bdg. 25.70 *(978-1-58415-613-0(9))* Mitchell Lane Pubs.

Lee, Georgia. Tour the U. S. Capitol, 1 vol. 2013. (InfoMax Readers Ser.). (ENG.). 24p. (J). (gr. 3-3). pap. 8.25 *(978-1-4777-2769-0(8)*, e8215663-f418-478c-bb2c-9833ffa87403); pap. 49.50 *(978-1-4777-2574-0(1))* Rosen Publishing Group, Inc., The. (Rosen Classroom).

Leigh, Anna. Alexandria Ocasio-Cortez: Political Headliner. 2020. (Gateway Biographies Ser.). (ENG., Illus.). 48p. (J). (gr. 4-8). pap. 11.99 *(978-1-5415-8887-5(8)*, 4c9370a0-46fb-4703-a708-f4b25f51427b); lib. bdg. 31.99 *(978-1-5415-7747-3(7)*, 9d524870-e3ff-4ed2-81fb-53c71f64c3bd) Lerner Publishing Group. (Lerner Pubns.).

—Nancy Pelosi: Political Powerhouse. 2020. (Gateway Biographies Ser.). (ENG., Illus.). 48p. (J). (gr. 4-8). pap. 11.99 *(978-1-5415-8889-9(4)*, 71ecdbfb-6ecb-45d4-817d-86bb18fb8795); lib. bdg. 31.99 *(978-1-5415-7746-6(9)*, 3d6a23df-da43-4277-ab99-14602397f693) Lerner Publishing Group. (Lerner Pubns.).

LeVert, Suzanne. The Congress, 1 vol. 2003. (Kaleidoscope: Government Ser.). (ENG., Illus.). 48p. (gr. 4-4). 32.64 *(978-0-7614-1451-3(7)*, 07638463-faba-4ace-b0ed-c8e2e230b438) Cavendish Square Publishing LLC.

Marcovitz, Hal. Nancy Pelosi: Politician. 2009. (Women of Achievement Ser.). (ENG., Illus.). 160p. (gr. 6-12). 35.00 *(978-1-60413-075-1(X)*, P161420, Facts On File) Infobase Holdings, Inc.

Marie Ford, Jeanne. Ilhan Omar. 2020. (Groundbreaking Women in Politics Ser.). (ENG., Illus.). 48p. (J). (gr. 5-6). pap. 11.95 *(978-1-64493-169-1(9)*, 1644931699); lib. bdg. 34.21 *(978-1-64493-090-8(0)*, 1644930900) North Star Editions. (Focus Readers).

McAuliffe, Bill. The U. S. House of Representatives. 2016. (By the People Ser.). (ENG., Illus.). 48p. (J). (gr. 4-7). pap. 12.00 *(978-1-62832-271-2(3)*, 20573, Creative Paperbacks) Creative Co., The.

—The U.S. House of Representatives. 2016. (By the People Ser.). (ENG., Illus.). 48p. (J). (gr. 4-7). 39.95 *(978-1-60818-675-4(X)*, 20575, Creative Education) Creative Co., The.

McDaniel, Melissa. The U. S. Congress: Why It Matters to You (a True Book: Why It Matters) (Library Edition) 2019. (True Book (Relaunch) Ser.). (ENG., Illus.). 48p. (J). (gr. 3-5). lib. bdg. 31.00 *(978-0-531-23182-1(8)*, Children's Pr.) Scholastic Library Publishing.

McElroy, Lisa Tucker. Nancy Pelosi. 2008. pap. 52.95 *(978-0-8225-9477-2(3))* Lerner Publishing Group.

—Nancy Pelosi: First Woman Speaker of the House. 2007. (Gateway Biographies Ser.). (ENG., Illus.). 48p. (J). (gr. 4-8). lib. bdg. 26.60 *(978-0-8225-8685-2(1)*, Lerner Pubns.) Lerner Publishing Group.

Modifica, Lisa. A Timeline of Congress. (Timelines of American History Ser.). 32p. (gr. 4-4). 2009. 47.90 *(978-1-60854-380-9(3))* 2004. (ENG., Illus.). lib. bdg. 29.13 *(978-0-8239-4534-4(0)*, 4740c1bb-7f39-4535-9926-368abf823701) Rosen Publishing Group, Inc., The. (Rosen Reference).

Moriarty, J. T. Davy Crockett: Defensor de la Frontera, 1 vol. 2003. (Grandes Personajes en la Historia de Los Estados Unidos (Famous People in American History) Ser.). (SPA.). 32p. (gr. 3-4). pap. 10.00 *(978-0-8239-4226-8(0)*, d788d920-5fb2-4495-ad81-34d87f3a6a4c, Rosen Classroom) Rosen Publishing Group, Inc., The.

—Davy Crockett: Frontier Hero. 2009. (Primary Sources of Famous People in American History Ser.). 32p. (gr. 2-3). 47.90 *(978-1-60851-670-4(9))* Rosen Publishing Group, Inc., The.

—Davy Crockett: Frontier Hero = Defensor de la Frontera, 1 vol. 2003. (Famous People in American History / Grandes Personajes en la Historia de Los Estados Unidos Ser.). (ENG & SPA., Illus.). 32p. (J). (gr. 2-3). lib. bdg. 29.13 *(978-0-8239-4156-8(6)*, 053f4de4-9a56-4d3b-81e2-66f81220ca56) Rosen Publishing Group, Inc., The.

Morretta, Alison. John Lewis: Civil Rights Champion & Congressman, 1 vol. 2019. (African American Trailblazers Ser.). (ENG.). 128p. (gr. 9-9). pap. 22.16 *(978-1-5026-4548-7(3)*, eec318ac-b171-4d0d-a4cc-1624eff3acc4) Cavendish Square Publishing LLC.

Murcia, Rebecca Thatcher. The Legislative Branch. 2011. (My Guide to the Constitution Ser.). (Illus.). 48p. (J). (gr. 3-6). lib. bdg. 29.95 *(978-1-58415-942-1(1))* Mitchell Lane Pubs.

Murray, Julie. US Congress. 2017. (My Government Ser.). (ENG., Illus.). 24p. (J). (gr. -1-2). lib. bdg. 31.36 *(978-1-5321-0401-5(4)*, 26527, Abdo Kids) ABDO Publishing Co.

Nelson, Maria. Becoming a House Representative, 1 vol. 2015. (Who's Your Candidate? Choosing Government Leaders Ser.). (ENG., Illus.). 32p. (J). (gr. 3-4). pap. 11.50 *(978-1-4824-4035-5(0)*, 1ddbf9ea-45e1-4e16-897c-b7f50c2c6eb6) Stevens, Gareth Publishing LLLP.

Nelson, Robin & Donovan, Sandy. The Congress: A Look at the Legislative Branch. 2012. (Searchlight Books How Does Government Work Ser.). (ENG., Illus.). 40p. (gr. 3-5). pap. 51.01 *(978-0-7613-9230-9(0))* Lerner Publishing Group.

Nichols, Kaitlyn. Davey Crockett. 2009. pap. 13.25 *(978-1-60559-057-8(6))* Hameray Publishing Group, Inc.

Omoth, Tyler. Establishing the Legislative Branch. 2017. (Foundations of Our Nation Ser.). (ENG., Illus.). 32p. (J). (gr. 3-5). pap. 9.95 *(978-1-63517-312-3(4)*, 1635173124); lib. bdg. 31.35 *(978-1-63517-247-8(0)*, 1635172470) North Star Editions. (Focus Readers).

Pulditor, Seth H. The House of Representatives Today. 2016. (Illus.). 64p. (J). *(978-1-61900-089-6(X))* Eldorado Ink.

Raatma, Lucia. Barbara Jordan, 1 vol. 2013. (Leading Women Ser.). (ENG.). 96p. (YA). (gr. 7-7). 42.64 *(978-0-7614-4956-0(6)*, bbcd5f27-0fcc-47f5-88e7-57e8052fa895); pap. 20.99 *(978-1-62712-114-9(5)*, c1f7fc2d-5916-43ad-b6a4-acdad06e7612) Cavendish Square Publishing LLC.

—Shirley Chisholm, 1 vol. 2011. (Leading Women Ser.). (ENG., Illus.). 96p. (YA). (gr. 7-7). 42.64 *(978-0-7614-4953-9(1)*, 76e44034-3809-4585-b09c-6019d0e95e1c) Cavendish Square Publishing LLC.

Radomski, Kassandra Kathleen. So You Want to Be a U. S. Representative. 2019. (Being in Government Ser.). (ENG., Illus.). 32p. (J). (gr. 3-6). pap. 7.95 *(978-1-5435-7528-6(5)*,

141058); lib. bdg. 27.99 *(978-1-5435-7196-7(4)*, 140441) Capstone.

Really Big Coloring Books. Ted Cruz to the Future - Comic Coloring Activity Book. 2013. (ENG., Illus.). 24p. (J). *(978-1-61953-095-9(3))* Really Big Coloring Bks., Inc.

Reis, Ronald A. The US Congress for Kids: Over 200 Years of Lawmaking, Deal-Breaking, & Compromising, with 21 Activities. 2014. (For Kids Ser.: 55). (ENG., Illus.). 144p. (J). (gr. 5). pap. 16.95 *(978-1-61374-977-7(5))* Chicago Review Pr., Inc.

Rice, Liz. Bill Richardson. 2007. (Sharing the American Dream Ser.). (Illus.). 64p. (J). (gr. 7-18). pap. 9.95 *(978-1-4222-0761-1(7))* Mason Crest.

Rose, Simon. The House of Representatives. 2014. (J). *(978-1-4896-1938-9(0))* Weigl Pubs., Inc.

—House of Representatives. 2016. (Illus.). 32p. (J). *(978-1-5105-2245-9(X))* SmartBook Media, Inc.

Sanford, William R. & Green, Carl R. Davy Crockett: Courageous Hero of the Alamo, 1 vol. 2013. (Courageous Heroes of the American West Ser.). (ENG., Illus.). 48p. (J). (gr. 5-7). pap. 11.53 *(978-1-4644-0086-5(5)*, 5b090086-0a64-4b32-80db-f849a4ed5b0f) Enslow Publishing, LLC.

Sapet, Kerrily. John Lewis. 2009. (Political Profiles Ser.). 100p. (YA). (gr. 5-9). 28.95 *(978-1-59935-130-8(7))* Reynolds, Morgan Inc.

Schuh, Mari C. The U. S. House of Representatives, 1 vol. 2012. (U. S. Government Ser.). (ENG.). 24p. (J). (gr. -1-2). lib. bdg. 27.32 *(978-1-4296-7565-9(9)*, 117163, Capstone Pr.) Capstone.

Shea, Therese M. Meet the House of Representatives, 1 vol. 2012. (Guide to Your Government Ser.). (ENG., Illus.). 32p. (J). (gr. 4-5). 29.27 *(978-1-4339-7252-2(2)*, d03b9a91-3b2c-4ed3-bb24-823328c6b05c); pap. 11.50 *(978-1-4339-7253-9(0)*, 49fe7bfa-8b45-4768-8785-a19832acaedd) Stevens, Gareth Publishing LLLP. (Gareth Stevens Learning Library).

Shichtman, Sandra H. Nancy Pelosi. 2008. (Political Profiles Ser.). (Illus.). 112p. (YA). (gr. 5-9). lib. bdg. 27.95 *(978-1-59935-049-3(1))* Reynolds, Morgan Inc.

Smith, Andrea P. Davy Crockett. (Illus.). 24p. (J). 2012. 63.60 *(978-1-4488-5223-9(4))* 2011. (ENG., (gr. 2-3). pap. 11.60 *(978-1-4488-5222-2(6)*, f86cea71-ff29-4c80-9b17-a3d7ed457f3a) 2011. (ENG., (gr. 2-3). lib. bdg. 28.93 *(978-1-4488-5192-8(0)*, bedb43e6-ebca-415a-b6a2-fe06de680194) Rosen Publishing Group, Inc., The. (PowerKids Pr.).

Smith-Llera, Danielle. Exploring the Legislative Branch. 2019. (Searchlight Books (tm) — Getting into Government Ser.). (ENG., Illus.). 32p. (J). (gr. 3-5). pap. 9.99 *(978-1-5415-7480-9(X)*, d78367e6-108e-4ae3-bdff-9b3c215366d6); lib. bdg. 30.65 *(978-1-5415-5587-7(2)*, dc731c7d-8730-4f90-b41c-74a22b4f7cf1) Lerner Publishing Group. (Lerner Pubns.).

Spalding, Maddie. How the Legislative Branch Works. 2016. (How America Works). (ENG.). 24p. (J). (gr. 3-6). 32.79 *(978-1-5038-0906-2(4)*, 210663) Child's World, Inc, The.

Spath, Carolyn E. W. Standing in the Shoes of a Member of the House of Representatives, 1 vol. 2015. (My Government Ser.). (ENG., Illus.). 32p. (gr. 4-4). lib. bdg. 30.21 *(978-1-5026-0470-5(1)*, b6a485c0-11da-449a-acab-a9e7d39cb20c) Cavendish Square Publishing LLC.

Stoltman, Joan. 20 Fun Facts about Congress, 1 vol. 2018. (Fun Fact File: U. S. History! Ser.). (ENG.). 32p. (gr. 2-3). pap. 11.50 *(978-1-5382-1899-0(2)*, 913059c1-35db-498a-bd5a-4a13d83f65a9) Stevens, Gareth Publishing LLLP.

Taylor-Butler, Christine. The Congress of the United States. 2008. (True Book: American History, Revised Ser.). (ENG., Illus.). 48p. (J). (gr. 3-5). lib. bdg. 21.19 *(978-0-531-12628-8(5)*, Children's Pr.) Scholastic Library Publishing.

—The Congress of the United States (a True Book: American History) 2008. (True Book (Relaunch) Ser.). (ENG., Illus.). 48p. (J). (gr. 3-5). pap. 6.95 *(978-0-531-14778-8(9)*, Children's Pr.) Scholastic Library Publishing.

Winders, Richard Bruce. Davy Crockett: The Legend of the Wild Frontier. 2009. (Library of American Lives & Times Ser.). 112p. (gr. 5-5). 69.20 *(978-1-60853-476-0(6))* Rosen Publishing Group, Inc., The.

Zurlo, Tony. The United States Congress & the Legislative Branch: How the Senate & House of Representatives Create Our Laws, 1 vol. 2013. (Constitution & the United States Government Ser.). (ENG.). 104p. (gr. 5-6). 35.93 *(978-0-7660-4066-3(6)*, 226886de-d3dc-44c6-a3e4-8c73ebaf6df7) Enslow Publishing, LLC.

UNITED STATES—CONGRESS—FICTION

Law, Janice. Capitol Cat & Watch Dog Unite Lady Freedoms. Eckhardt, Jason C., illus. 2008. 64p. (J). *(978-1-934645-71-0(0)*, Eakin Pr.) Eakin Pr.

Santrey, Laurence & Macken, JoAnn Early. Davy Crockett: Young Pioneer. Livingston, Francis, illus. 2008. 55p. (J). pap. *(978-0-439-02048-0(4))* Scholastic, Inc.

Van Dyne, Edith. Aunt Jane's Nieces at Work. 2005. 204p. pap. 12.95 *(978-1-4218-1523-7(0)*, 1st World Library - Literary Society) 1st World Publishing, Inc.

—Aunt Jane's Nieces at Work. 2017. (ENG., Illus.). (J). 23.95 *(978-1-374-94773-3(3))*; pap. 13.95 *(978-1-374-94772-6(5))* Capital Communications, Inc.

UNITED STATES—CONGRESS—SENATE

Anderson, Janet. The Senate. 2007. (U. Government: How It Works). (ENG.). 112p. (gr. 5-9). 30.00 *(978-0-7910-9291-0(7)*, P125640, Facts On File) Infobase Holdings, Inc.

Brill, Marlene Targ. Barack Obama: Working to Make a Difference. 2006. (Gateway Biography Ser.). (Illus.). 48p. (J). 23.93 *(978-0-8225-3417-4(7))* Lerner Publishing Group.

Cohen, Sheila & Terman Cohen, Sheila. Gaylord Nelson: Champion for Our Earth. 2010. (Badger Biographies Ser.). (ENG., Illus.). 120p. (J). pap. 12.95 *(978-0-87020-443-2(2))* Wisconsin Historical Society.

Glaser, Jason. Meet the Senate, 1 vol. 2012. (Guide to Your Government Ser.). (ENG., Illus.). 32p. (J). (gr. 4-5). 29.27 *(978-1-4339-7267-6(0)*, c2f47060-2a75-4b77-aa93-2f87ded82682); pap. 11.50 *(978-1-4339-7264-5(6)*, ae81a677-9b70-4135-896d-7b5bb5f48a69) Stevens, Gareth Publishing LLLP. (Gareth Stevens Learning Library).

Grimes, Nikki. Barack Obama: Son of Promise, Child of Hope. Collier, Bryan, illus. 2012. (ENG.). 48p. (J). (gr. k-3). 9.99 *(978-1-4424-4092-0(9)*, Simon & Schuster Bks. For Young Readers) Simon & Schuster Bks. For Young Readers.

Jakubiak, David J. What Does a Senator Do? 2010. (How Our Government Works Ser.). 24p. (J). (gr. 3-6). lib. bdg., E-Book 42.50 *(978-1-4488-0029-2(3))*; (ENG., Illus.). pap. 9.25 *(978-1-4358-9816-5(8)*, f8b66662-3a5d-4737-a336-fbdfc51c4804, PowerKids Pr.); (ENG., Illus.). lib. bdg. 26.27 *(978-1-4358-9360-3(3)*, 72d2509e-ccb7-41e4-aee2-aeabeb327ae7, PowerKids Pr.) Rosen Publishing Group, Inc., The.

Mapua, Jeff. Hillary Clinton, 1 vol. 2014. (Britannica Beginner Bios Ser.). (ENG., Illus.). 32p. (J). (gr. 2-3). 26.06 *(978-1-62275-689-6(4)*, c6a1ac5c-edfc-4d9f-8b71-fe87854a49f1, Britannica Educational Publishing) Rosen Publishing Group, Inc., The.

McAuliffe, Bill. The U. S. Senate. 2016. (By the People Ser.). (ENG., Illus.). 48p. (J). (gr. 4-7). pap. 12.00 *(978-1-62832-273-6(X)*, 20579, Creative Paperbacks) Creative Co., The.

—The U.S. Senate. 2016. (By the People Ser.). (ENG., Illus.). 48p. (J). (gr. 4-7). 39.95 *(978-1-60818-677-8(6)*, 20581, Creative Education) Creative Co., The.

Nagelhout, Ryan. Standing in a Senator's Shoes, 1 vol. 2015. (My Government Ser.). (ENG.). 32p. (gr. 4-4). pap. 11.58 *(978-1-5026-0472-9(8)*, 574090e3-f63e-42c0-9613-59ed9de6ad6d) Cavendish Square Publishing LLC.

Nelson, Maria. Becoming a Senator, 1 vol. 2015. (Who's Your Candidate? Choosing Government Leaders Ser.). (ENG., Illus.). 32p. (J). (gr. 3-4). pap. 11.50 *(978-1-4824-4043-0(1)*, 5e429fa5-efe3-4d4a-b6a5-0fd6f14b972f) Stevens, Gareth Publishing LLLP.

Radomski, Kassandra Kathleen. So You Want to Be a U. S. Senator. 2019. (Being in Government Ser.). (ENG., Illus.). 32p. (J). (gr. 3-6). pap. 7.95 *(978-1-5435-7529-3(3)*, 141060); lib. bdg. 27.99 *(978-1-5435-7195-0(6)*, 140440) Capstone.

Rose, Simon. Senate. 2016. (Illus.). 32p. (J). *(978-1-5105-2249-7(2))* SmartBook Media, Inc.

Schuh, Mari C. The U. S. Senate, 1 vol. 2012. (U. S. Government Ser.). (ENG., Illus.). 24p. (J). (gr. -1-2). lib. bdg. 27.32 *(978-1-4296-7567-3(5)*, 117164, Capstone Pr.) Capstone.

Shepherd, Jodie. Hillary Clinton. 2015. (Rookie Biographies(r) Ser.). (ENG., Illus.). 32p. (J). lib. bdg. 23.00 *(978-0-531-20592-1(4))* Scholastic Library Publishing.

Sherman, Jill. Donald Trump: Outspoken Personality & President. 2017. (Gateway Biographies Ser.). (ENG., Illus.). 48p. (J). (gr. 4-8). lib. bdg. 31.99 *(978-1-5124-2596-3(6)*, 73ddd6e7-9543-41d2-9c95-2b6efefcc36c, Lerner Pubns.) Lerner Publishing Group.

Susienka, Kristen. Kamala Harris. 2019. (African American Leaders of Courage Ser.). (ENG.). 24p. (gr. 1-2). 49.50 *(978-1-7253-1107-7(0))*; 25.27 *(978-1-7253-1108-4(9)*, 4e2109a4-d349-47c8-a8b5-44023ed065f5); pap. 9.25 *(978-1-7253-1106-0(2)*, ee39cad4-ad14-4571-a791-f352a4c007b4) Rosen Publishing Group, Inc., The. (PowerKids Pr.).

Wood, Susan. Elizabeth Warren: Nevertheless, She Persisted. Green, Sarah, illus. 2018. (ENG.). 48p. (J). (gr. 1-4). 18.99 *(978-1-4197-3162-4(9)*, 1210001, Abrams Bks. for Young Readers) Abrams, Inc.

Ziff, John. The United States Senate. 2016. 64p. (J). *(978-1-61900-096-4(2))* Eldorado Ink.

UNITED STATES—CONGRESS—SENATE—BIOGRAPHY

Anderson, Dale. Al Gore: A Wake-Up Call to Global Warming. 2009. (Voices for Green Choices Ser.). (ENG., Illus.). 48p. (J). (gr. 5-9). pap. *(978-0-7787-4679-9(8))*; lib. bdg. *(978-0-7787-4666-9(6))* Crabtree Publishing Co.

Barack Obama. 2007. (Political Profiles Ser.). (Illus.). 128p. (YA). (gr. 5-9). lib. bdg. 27.95 *(978-1-59935-045-5(9))* Reynolds, Morgan Inc.

Barton, Chris. The Amazing Age of John Roy Lynch. Tate, Don, illus. 2015. (ENG.). 50p. (J). 17.00 *(978-0-8028-5379-0(X)*, Eerdmans Bks For Young Readers) Eerdmans, William B. Publishing Co.

—What Do You Do with a Voice Like That? The Story of Extraordinary Congresswoman Barbara Jordan. Holmes, Ekua, illus. 2018. (ENG.). 48p. (J). (gr. -1-3). 18.99 *(978-1-4814-6561-8(9)*, Beach Lane Bks.) Beach Lane Bks.

Biden, Jill. Joey: The Story of Joe Biden. Bates, Amy June, illus. 2020. (ENG.). 48p. (J). (gr. -1-3). 19.99 *(978-1-5344-8053-7(6)*, Simon & Schuster/Paula Wiseman Bks.) Simon & Schuster/Paula Wiseman Bks.

Blashfield, Jean F. Hillary Clinton, 1 vol. 2011. (Leading Women Ser.). (ENG.). 96p. (YA). (gr. 7-7). 42.64 *(978-0-7614-4954-6(X)*, e653b8cd-2fce-4ce2-be4a-065c33d4a87f) Cavendish Square Publishing LLC.

Blohm, Craig E. Hillary Clinton. 2016. (ENG.). 80p. (J). 38.60 *(978-1-60152-950-3(3))* ReferencePoint Pr., Inc.

Bodden, Valerie. Hillary Clinton: Historic Leader. 2009. (Essential Lives Set 4 Ser.). (ENG., Illus.). 112p. (YA). (gr. 6-12). lib. bdg. 41.36 *(978-1-60453-699-7(3)*, 6689, Essential Library) ABDO Publishing Co.

Bourcier, Cammy S. Barack Obama. 2009. (Sharing the American Dream Ser.). (Illus.). 64p. (J). (gr. 7-12). 22.95 *(978-1-4222-0574-7(6))* Mason Crest.

Brager, Bruce L. John Kerry: Senator from Massachusetts. 2005. (Twentieth Century Leaders Ser.). (Illus.). 128p. (J). (gr. 6-12). lib. bdg. 23.95 *(978-1-931798-64-8(8))* Reynolds, Morgan Inc.

Brill, Marlene Targ. Barack Obama: Working to Make a Difference. 2006. (J). pap. 6.95 *(978-0-8225-6056-2(9)*, First Avenue Editions) Lerner Publishing Group.

—Barack Obama (Revised Edition) 2009. pap. 52.95 *(978-0-7613-5031-6(4))* Lerner Publishing Group.

Caravantes, Peggy. American in Texas: The Story of Sam Houston. 2004. (Notable Americans Ser.). (Illus.). 144p. (YA). (gr. 6-12). 23.95 *(978-1-931798-19-8(2))* Reynolds, Morgan Inc.

Cham, Stephanie. Patsy Mink. 2018. (Great Asian Americans Ser.). (ENG., Illus.). 24p. (J). (gr. -1-2). lib. bdg. 27.32 *(978-1-5157-9954-2(9)*, 136952, Capstone Pr.) Capstone.

—Tammy Duckworth. 2018. (Great Asian Americans Ser.). (ENG., Illus.). 24p. (J). (gr. -1-2). lib. bdg. 27.32 *(978-1-5157-9955-9(7)*, 136953, Capstone Pr.) Capstone.

Coddington, Andrew. Davy Crockett: Frontiersman, 1 vol. Lapegüe, Matías, illus. 2016. (American Legends & Folktales Ser.). (ENG.). 32p. (gr. 3-3). 30.21 *(978-1-5026-2193-1(2)*, 9b7823f4-3a30-481b-a7ce-fac9d0a1a2a1) Cavendish Square Publishing LLC.

Cohen, Sheila & Terman Cohen, Sheila. Gaylord Nelson: Champion for Our Earth. 2010. (Badger Biographies Ser.). (ENG., Illus.). 120p. (J). pap. 12.95 *(978-0-87020-443-2(2))* Wisconsin Historical Society.

Collard, Sneed B., III. John Glenn: Hooked on Flying, 1 vol. 2009. (American Heroes Ser.). (ENG., Illus.). 48p. (gr. 3-3). lib. bdg. 32.64 *(978-0-7614-3066-7(0)*, 0802b8b4-5c46-44f3-bfaf-f60b33b36ace) Cavendish Square Publishing LLC.

Collier Hillstrom, Laurie. Al Gore, 1 vol. 2008. (People in the News Ser.). (ENG., Illus.). 112p. (gr. 7-7). lib. bdg. 41.03 *(978-1-4205-0086-8(4)*, 0b1655b8-69b1-4fa8-b474-e619552cd947, Lucent Pr.) Greenhaven Publishing LLC.

Coy, Cissie. Dennis Chávez: The First Hispanic US Senator / Dennis Chávez: el Primer Senador Hispano de Los Estados Unidos. 2017. (SPA & ENG., Illus.). 64p. (J). (gr. 4-8). pap. 9.95 *(978-1-55885-852-7(0)*, Piñata Books) Arte Publico Pr.

Davis, William Michael. Barack Obama: The Politics of Hope. 2007. (Illus.). 168p. (J). (gr. 10-18). lib. bdg. 25.95 *(978-1-59556-024-7(6)*, 1291988); (gr. 8-18). pap. 16.99 *(978-1-59556-032-2(7)*, 1291988) OTTN Publishing.

De Medeiros, James. Al Gore. 2008. (Remarkable People Ser.). (Illus.). 24p. (J). (gr. 4-6). pap. 8.95 *(978-1-59036-993-7(9))*; lib. bdg. 24.45 *(978-1-59036-992-0(0))* Weigl Pubs., Inc.

De Medeiros, Michael. Barack Obama. (J). 2013. *(978-1-62127-388-2(1))* 2008. (Illus.). 24p. (gr. 4-6). pap. 8.95 *(978-1-59036-989-0(0))* 2008. (Illus.). 24p. (gr. 4-6). lib. bdg. 24.45 *(978-1-59036-988-3(2))* Weigl Pubs., Inc.

Doak, Robin S. Hillary Clinton. 2013. (True Book: Biographies Ser.). (ENG., Illus.). 48p. (J). (gr. 3-5). lib. bdg. 21.19 *(978-0-531-21906-5(2)*, Children's Pr.); pap. 6.95 *(978-0-531-23877-6(6))* Scholastic Library Publishing.

Doeden, Matt. John Lewis: Courage in Action. 2018. (Gateway Biographies Ser.). (ENG., Illus.). 48p. (J). (gr. 4-8). 31.99 *(978-1-5415-1238-2(3)*, c3bd6e6c-7a71-4a92-a1fb-b9894d102410, Lerner Pubns.) Lerner Publishing Group.

D'Orio, Wayner. Carol Moseley-Braun. 2003. (African American Leaders Ser.). (ENG., Illus.). 112p. (gr. 6-12). 30.00 *(978-0-7910-7684-2(9)*, P113973, Facts On File) Infobase Holdings, Inc.

Egan, Jill. Hillary Rodham Clinton, 1 vol. 2009. (People We Should Know (Second Series) Ser.). (ENG., Illus.). 48p. (J). (gr. 3-5). pap. 11.50 *(978-1-4339-2193-3(6)*, 3ddc1eb3-4b6e-4c00-bd8c-5357bfae7b05); lib. bdg. 33.67 *(978-1-4339-2188-9(X)*, 42b88186-030f-4473-842e-b1101580a9ad) Stevens, Gareth Publishing LLLP. (Gareth Stevens Learning Library).

Epstein, Brad M. Barack Obama 101. Lt. ed. 2009. (My First Presidential Board Book Ser.). (Illus.). 28p. (J). (gr. -1-1). bds. *(978-1-60730-044-1(3)*, 101 Bk.) Michaelson Entertainment.

Epstein, Dwayne. Hillary Clinton, 1 vol. 2009. (People in the News Ser.). (ENG., Illus.). 128p. (gr. 7-7). 41.03 *(978-1-4205-0268-8(9)*, d39b223e-42d3-45d4-a896-84157b4a51bf, Lucent Pr.) Greenhaven Publishing LLC.

Falk, Laine. Meet President Barack Obama. 2009. (Scholastic News Nonfiction Readers Ser.). (ENG., Illus.). 24p. (J). (gr. k-3). 21.19 *(978-0-531-23403-7(7)*, Children's Pr.) Scholastic Library Publishing.

—Meet President John McCain. 2009. (J). *(978-0-531-23650-5(1))* Children's Pr., Ltd.

Feinstein, Stephen. Barack Obama, 1 vol. 2008. (African-American Heroes Ser.). (ENG., Illus.). 24p. (gr. k-2). lib. bdg. 25.27 *(978-0-7660-2893-7(3)*, 69df780e-533b-4c3f-82e5-c16548d680f1, Enslow Elementary) Enslow Publishing, LLC.

Freedman, Jeri. Elizabeth Warren: Democratic Senator from Massachusetts, 1 vol. 2017. (Leading Women Ser.). (ENG., Illus.). 112p. (YA). (gr. 7-7). 41.64 *(978-1-5026-2699-8(3)*, fd6cd751-fce0-41ed-92f6-f460528a8cbf) Cavendish Square Publishing LLC.

—Hillary Rodham Clinton: Profile of a Leading Democrat. 2009. (Career Profiles Ser.). 112p. (gr. 9-10). 63.90 *(978-1-61511-794-9(6))* Rosen Publishing Group, Inc., The.

Giblin, James Cross. The Rise & Fall of Senator Joe McCarthy. 2009. (ENG., Illus.). 304p. (YA). (gr. 7-18). 22.00 *(978-0-618-61058-7(8)*, 100444, Clarion Bks.) HarperCollins Pubs.

Gibson, Karen Bush. The Historic Fight for the 2008 Democratic Presidential Nomination: The Obama View. 2009. (Monumental Milestones Ser.). (Illus.). 48p. (YA). (gr. 4-7). lib. bdg. 29.95 *(978-1-58415-732-8(1))* Mitchell Lane Pubs.

Goldsworthy, Steve. Edward Kennedy. 2010. (Remarkable People Ser.). (Illus.). 24p. (J). (gr. 4-6). pap. 11.95 *(978-1-61690-170-7(5))*; lib. bdg. 25.70 *(978-1-61690-169-1(1))* Weigl Pubs., Inc.

Gormley, Beatrice. John Mccain: An American Hero. 2018. (ENG.). 224p. (J). (gr. 3-7). 17.99 *(978-1-5344-4386-0(X))*; (Illus.). pap. 7.99 *(978-1-5344-4385-3(1))* Simon & Schuster Children's Publishing. (Aladdin).

Grimes, Nikki. Barack Obama: Son of Promise, Child of Hope. Collier, Bryan, illus. 2008. (ENG.). 48p. (J). (gr. k-3). pap. 19.99 *(978-1-4169-7144-3(0)*, Simon & Schuster Bks. For Young Readers) Simon & Schuster Bks. For Young Readers.

—Kamala Harris: Rooted in Justice. Freeman, Laura, illus. 2020. (ENG.). 40p. (J). (gr. -1-3). 17.99 *(978-1-5344-6267-0(8)*, Atheneum Bks. for Young Readers) Simon & Schuster Children's Publishing.

Guernsey, JoAnn B. Hillary Rodham Clinton. 2005. (Biography Ser.). (Illus.). 112p. (J). (gr. 6-18). pap. 7.95 *(978-0-8225-9613-4(X))* Lerner Publishing Group.

Guernsey, Joann Bren. Hillary Rodham Clinton. 2005. (Biography Ser.). (Illus.). 112p. (J). (gr. 3-7). lib. bdg. 29.27 *(978-0-8225-2372-7(8)*, Lerner Pubns.) Lerner Publishing Group.

Harmon, Daniel E. Al Gore & Global Warming. 2009. (Celebrity Activists Ser.). 112p. (gr. 8-8). 66.50 *(978-1-61511-826-7(8))* Rosen Publishing Group, Inc., The.

Harris, Kamala. Los Superhéroes Están en Todas Partes. Roe, Mechal Renee, illus. 2019. (SPA.). 40p. (J). (gr. -1-2). 17.99 *(978-0-593-11332-5(2)*, Philomel Bks.) Penguin Young Readers Group.

—The Truths We Hold: An American Journey (Young Readers Edition) (ENG., Illus.). 304p. (gr. 7). 2020. (J). pap. 10.99 *(978-0-593-11317-2(9)*, Penguin Books) 2019. (YA). 17.99 *(978-1-9848-3706-6(0)*, Philomel Bks.) Penguin Young Readers Group.

Hiram Bingham & the Dream of Gold. 2014. (ENG.). 192p. (J). (gr. 3-7). pap. 13.95 *(978-1-59077-350-5(0))* Evans, M. & Co., Inc.

Hoe, Susan. Rosa Parks. 2007. (Sharing the American Dream Ser.). 64p. (YA). (gr. 7-18). pap. 9.95 *(978-1-4222-0760-4(9))* Mason Crest.

Horn, Geoffrey M. John Mccain, 1 vol. 2009. (People We Should Know (Second Series) Ser.). (ENG., Illus.). 32p. (J). (gr. 3-5). pap. 11.50 *(978-1-4339-0160-7(9)*, fbdf5273-8ceb-4a6e-93dd-e54d3db41f8f); lib. bdg. 33.67 *(978-1-4339-0020-4(3)*, 9a51add1-6bb7-4cac-bcd4-e17aafea87d6) Stevens, Gareth Publishing LLLP. (Gareth Stevens Learning Library).

Immell, Myra, ed. The Mccarthy Era, 1 vol. 2011. (Perspectives on Modern World History Ser.). (ENG.). 184p. (gr. 10-12). lib. bdg. 49.43 *(978-0-7377-5260-1(2)*, 9f2a225c-bbae-4f14-8e0c-b4f9b0d5cbd1, Greenhaven Publishing) Greenhaven Publishing LLC.

Iorio, Nicole. Joe Biden, 1 vol. 2009. (People We Should Know (Second Series) Ser.). (ENG.). 48p. (J). (gr. 3-5). pap. 11.50 *(978-1-4339-2148-3(0)*, 8df0f9b1-ac05-4d34-89b8-7c5ed05ff358); lib. bdg. 33.67 *(978-1-4339-1949-7(4)*, 3e91239f-da97-4d2b-b7a2-40f7ce2dd22c) Stevens, Gareth Publishing LLLP. (Gareth Stevens Learning Library).

Kann, Bob. Belle & Bob la Follette: Partners in Politics. 2008. (Badger Biographies Ser.). (ENG., Illus.). 144p. (J). (gr. 3-7). pap. 12.95 *(978-0-87020-407-4(6))* Wisconsin Historical Society.

Kawa, Katie. Alexandria Ocasio-Cortez: Making a Difference in Politics, 1 vol. 2020. (People Who Make a Difference Ser.). (ENG.). 24p. (gr. 3-3). pap. 9.25 *(978-1-5345-3468-1(7)*, ad2e3bae-0197-4318-ac69-caeccb29798b, KidHaven Publishing) Greenhaven Publishing LLC.

Kiely Miller, Barbara. Sam Houston, 1 vol. 2007. (Grandes Personajes (Great Americans) Ser.). 24p. (gr. 2-4). (SPA.). pap. 9.15 *(978-0-8368-8336-7(5)*, c6ff82ce-7527-4a48-acc7-8db99cbe62ff); (ENG.). pap. 9.15 *(978-0-8368-8323-7(3)*, 181dab52-3918-43bb-b2a9-666f98196091); (ENG.). lib. bdg. 24.67 *(978-0-8368-8316-9(0)*, c0d85d45-374f-44a0-82b7-fe4611ee39a8); (SPA., Illus.). lib. bdg. 24.67 *(978-0-8368-8329-9(2)*, 468581b2-c389-4f19-87a2-91fb6d86c83c) Stevens, Gareth Publishing LLLP. (Weekly Reader Leveled Readers).

Klein, Adria F. Barack Obama. 2009. pap. 13.25 *(978-1-60559-055-4(X))* Hameray Publishing Group, Inc.

Krull, Kathleen. The Brothers Kennedy: John, Robert, Edward. Bates, Amy June, illus. 2010. (ENG.). 40p. (J). (gr. -1-3). 16.99 *(978-1-4169-9158-8(1)*, Simon & Schuster Bks. For Young Readers) Simon & Schuster Bks. For Young Readers.

Lawson, Lela. A Career As a Senator: Understanding Government, 1 vol. 2018. (Civics for the Real World Ser.). (ENG.). 16p. (gr. 2-3). pap. 8.25 *(978-1-5383-6515-1(4)*, d537219a-8fb2-4388-a2a4-8405f739e37a, Rosen Classroom) Rosen Publishing Group, Inc., The.

Lee, Sally. Hillary Clinton, 1 vol. 2010. (First Ladies Ser.). (ENG.). 24p. (J). (gr. -1-2). lib. bdg. 27.32 *(978-1-4296-5327-5(2)*, 113736, Capstone Pr.) Capstone.

Levy, Janey. Shirley Chisholm, 1 vol. 2020. (Heroes of Black History Ser.). (ENG.). 32p. (gr. 3-4). pap. 11.50 *(978-1-5382-5798-2(X)*, 414f5e2f-acf0-470d-aa1b-7d2d9baeaccd) Stevens, Gareth Publishing LLLP.

Marcovitz, Hal. Barack. 2007. (Obamas Ser.). (Illus.). 64p. (YA). (gr. 3-6). pap. 9.95 *(978-1-4222-1484-8(2))*; (gr. 4-7). lib. bdg. 19.95 *(978-1-4222-1477-0(X))* Mason Crest.

Markel, Michelle. Hillary Rodham Clinton: Some Girls Are Born to Lead. Pham, LeUyen, illus. 2016. (ENG.). 40p. (J). (gr. -1-3). 17.99 *(978-0-06-238122-4(9)*, Balzer & Bray) HarperCollins Pubs.

Marsh, Carole. John Kerry: Successful Senator & 2004 Presidential Candidate. 2004. (J). 24p. pap. 5.95 *(978-0-635-02537-1(X))*; 24.95 *(978-0-635-02542-5(6))* Gallopade International.

McDonnell, Julia. Before Barack Obama Was President, 1 vol. 2018. (Before They Were President Ser.). (ENG.). 24p. (gr. 2-3). 24.27 *(978-1-5382-2909-5(9)*, 4cbd92b9-440c-41b5-8bd3-7af73085d418) Stevens, Gareth Publishing LLLP.

McGowan, Joseph. Al Gore, 1 vol. 2009. (People We Should Know (Second Series) Ser.). (ENG.). 48p. (J). (gr. 3-5). pap. 11.50 *(978-1-4339-2146-9(4)*, d085d240-5610-4f6c-a156-448650d8b212); lib. bdg. 33.67 *(978-1-4339-1947-3(8)*, 30467b93-158a-4097-996b-f59ce266e739) Stevens, Gareth Publishing LLLP. (Gareth Stevens Learning Library).

Mendell, David & Thomson, Sarah L. Obama: A Promise of Change. 2008. (ENG., Illus.). 192p. (J). (gr. 3-7). pap. 6.99 *(978-0-06-169700-5(1)*, Amistad) HarperCollins Pubs.

Peppas, Lynn. Why Sam Houston Matters to Texas, 1 vol. 2013. (Texas Perspectives Ser.). (ENG., Illus.). 32p. (J). (gr. 4-4). lib. bdg. 28.93 *(978-1-4777-0912-2(6)*, 60e60101-a7ab-4741-8c21-e08fda6394f0) Rosen Publishing Group, Inc., The.

Riddolls, Tom & Wearing, Judy. Hillary Clinton. 2009. (Remarkable People Ser.). (Illus.). 24p. (J). (gr. 4-6). pap.

TUV

8.95 (978-1-60596-621-2(5)); lib. bdg. 24.45 (978-1-60596-620-5(7)) Weigl Pubs., Inc.

Robinson, Tom. Barack Obama: 44th U. S. President. 2009. (J). lib. bdg. 32.79 (978-1-60453-528-0(8), Essential Library) ABDO Publishing Co.

Saddleback Educational Publishing Staff, ed. Davy Crockett, 1 vol. unabr. ed. 2007. (Graphic Biographies Ser.). (ENG., Illus.). 25p. (YA). (gr. 4-12). pap. 9.75 (978-1-59905-220-5(2)) Saddleback Educational Publishing, Inc.

Sanford, William R. & Green, Carl R. Sam Houston: Courageous Texas Hero, 1 vol. 2013. (Courageous Heroes of the American West Ser.). (ENG., Illus.). 48p. (J). (gr. 5-7). pap. 11.53 (978-1-4644-0092-6(X), 82c855d2-5888-4c8e-acf5-64777f78ae2a); lib. bdg. 25.27 (978-0-7660-4009-0(7), 49b9d718-c81f-4cc1-81fd-c8181672b4fc) Enslow Publishing, LLC.

Sapet, Kerrily. Al Gore. 2007. (Political Profiles Ser.). (Illus.). 112p. (YA). (gr. 5-9). lib. bdg. 27.95 (978-1-59935-070-7(X)) Reynolds, Morgan Inc.

Sarantou, Katlin. Tammy Duckworth. Bane, Jeff, illus. 2019. (My Early Library: My Itty-Bitty Bio Ser.). (ENG.). 24p. (J). (gr. k-1). pap. 12.79 (978-1-5341-4990-8(2), 213267); lib. bdg. 30.64 (978-1-5341-4704-1(7), 213266) Cherry Lake Publishing.

Schuman, Michael A. Barack Obama: We Are One People, 1 vol. rev. ed. 2008. (African-American Biography Library). (ENG., Illus.). 160p. (gr. 6-7). lib. bdg. 35.93 (978-0-7660-3649-9(9), 38ae7d97-e2eb-4050-b3ef-e12048222213) Enslow Publishing, LLC.

Schwartz, Heather E. John Mccain: The Courage of Conviction. 2018. (Gateway Biographies Ser.). (ENG., Illus.). 48p. (J). (gr. 4-8). lib. bdg. 31.99 (978-1-5415-3839-9(0), 1189939d-de06-4a0c-a070-19dbd43e5cbf, Lerner Pubns.) Lerner Publishing Group.

Stanley, George Edward. Davy Crockett: Frontier Legend. 2008. (Sterling Biographies Ser.). (ENG., Illus.). 123p. (J). (gr. 6-8). 18.69 (978-1-4027-6057-0(4)) Sterling Publishing Co., Inc.

Stefoff, Rebecca. Al Gore: Fighting for a Greener Planet. rev. ed. 2008. (Gateway Biographies Ser.). (ENG.). 48p. (gr. 4-8). 26.60 (978-1-57505-948-8(7)) Lerner Publishing Group.

Stoltman, Joan. Hillary Clinton, 1 vol. 2017. (Little Biographies of Big People Ser.). (ENG.). 24p. (J). (gr. 1-2). pap. 9.15 (978-1-5382-0927-1(6), 45d15419-e1ba-485e-aecd-492bac53ea80) Stevens, Gareth Publishing LLLP.

—Hillary Clinton, 1 vol. Garcia, Ana Maria, tr. 2017. (Pequeñas Biografías de Grandes Personajes (Little Biographies of Big People) Ser.). (SPA.). 24p. (J). (gr. 1-2). pap. 9.15 (978-1-5382-1558-6(6), 223ef883-505a-47a7-9806-85242aebbfaf); lib. bdg. 24.27 (978-1-5382-1531-9(4), c288e1b0-b83a-4715-865d-2d96d21028a1) Stevens, Gareth Publishing LLLP.

Streissguth, Tom. John Glenn. 2004. (Just the Facts Biographies Ser.). (ENG., Illus.). 112p. (J). (gr. 5-12). lib. bdg. 27.93 (978-0-8225-2274-4(8)) Lerner Publishing Group.

Ted Kennedy. 2009. (Political Profiles Ser.). 144p. (YA). (gr. 5-9). 28.95 (978-1-59935-089-9(0)) Reynolds, Morgan Inc.

Tracy, Kathleen. The Historic Fight for the 2008 Democratic Presidential Nomination: The Clinton View. 2009. (Monumental Milestones Ser.). (Illus.). 48p. (YA). (gr. 4-7). lib. bdg. 29.95 (978-1-58415-731-1(3)) Mitchell Lane Pubs.

—The McCarthy Era. 2008. (Monumental Milestones Ser.). (Illus.). 48p. (YA). (gr. 4-7). lib. bdg. 29.95 (978-1-58415-694-9(5)) Mitchell Lane Pubs.

Turner, Carolyn. Sam Houston. 2010. pap. 9.95 (978-1-61690-066-3(0)); 24p. (J). (gr. 2-4). lib. bdg. 25.70 (978-1-61690-065-6(2)) Weigl Pubs., Inc.

Uschan, Michael V. Joe Biden, 1 vol. 2010. (People in the News Ser.). (ENG., Illus.). 104p. (J). (gr. 7-7). 41.03 (978-1-4205-0260-2(3), 13a915de-0998-448b-a8be-f4c4cdd76705, Lucent Pr.) Greenhaven Publishing LLC.

Uschan, Michael V. & Devaney, Sherri. Barack Obama, 1 vol. 2009. (People in the News Ser.). (ENG.). 104p. (gr. 7-7). lib. bdg. 41.03 (978-1-4205-0206-0(9), 0f599642-cdf7-4910-bdbf-993a8537a06a, Lucent Pr.) Greenhaven Publishing LLC.

Wagner, Heather Lehr. Barack Obama. 2008. (Black Americans of Achievement Legacy Edition Ser.). 104p. (gr. 6-12). pap. 11.95 (978-1-60413-324-0(4), Checkmark Bks.) Infobase Holdings, Inc.

Watson, Marilyn Myrick. Barry Goldwater: State Greats Arizona. 2007. (Acacia Biographies Ser.). (Illus.). 28p. (J). (gr. 4-7). per. 6.95 (978-0-9790826-0-3(9)) Acacia Publishing, Inc.

—Bary Goldwater: State Greats Arizona. 2007. (Acacia Biographies Ser.). (Illus.). 28p. (J). (gr. 3-7). lib. bdg. 16.95 (978-0-9788283-4-9(8)) Acacia Publishing, Inc.

Wells, Catherine. Hillary Clinton. 2007. (Political Profiles Ser.). (Illus.). 112p. (YA). (gr. 5-9). lib. bdg. 27.95 (978-1-59935-047-9(5)) Reynolds, Morgan Inc.

—John McCain. 2008. (Political Profiles Ser.). (Illus.). 112p. (YA). (gr. 5-9). lib. bdg. 27.95 (978-1-59935-046-2(7)) Reynolds, Morgan Inc.

Winget, Mary Mueller. Gerald R. Ford. 2007. (Presidential Leaders Ser.). (Illus.). 112p. (J). (gr. 3-7). lib. bdg. 29.27 (978-0-8225-1509-8(1), Twenty-First Century Bks.) Lerner Publishing Group.

Winter, Jonah. Barack. Ford, A. G., illus. 32p. (J). (gr. -1-2). 2010. (ENG.). pap. 8.99 (978-0-06-170396-6(6), Tegen, Katherine Bks) 2008. lib. bdg. 18.89 (978-0-06-170393-5(1)) HarperCollins Pubs.

—Barack, 2 vols. 2009. (J). 38.75 (978-1-4407-3624-7(3)); 38.75 (978-1-4407-3620-9(0)); 40.75 (978-1-4407-3618-6(9)); 40.75 (978-1-4407-3622-3(7)); 222.75 (978-1-4407-3619-3(7)); 1.25 (978-1-4407-3625-4(1)) Recorded Bks., Inc.

—Hillary. ón, Raul, illus. 2016. 40p. (J). (gr. -1-3). 17.99 (978-0-553-53388-0(6), Schwartz & Wade Bks.) Random Hse. Children's Bks.

Woodward, Mac. Sam Houston: For Texas & the Union. 2009. (Library of American Lives & Times Ser.). 112p. (gr. 5-5). 69.20 (978-1-60853-504-0(5)) Rosen Publishing Group, Inc., The.

Young, Jeff C. Joe Biden. 2009. (Political Profiles Ser.). (Illus.). 100p. (J). (gr. 5-9). 28.95 (978-1-59935-131-5(5)) Reynolds, Morgan Inc.

UNITED STATES—CONSTITUTION

Allen, Kathy. The U. S. Constitution. rev. ed. 2016. (Pebble Plus Ser.). (ENG.). 24p. (J). (gr. -1-2). pap. 7.29 (978-1-5157-5967-6(9), 134838) Capstone.

Aloian, Molly. Constitution Day. 2008. (Celebrations in My World Ser.). (ENG., Illus.). 32p. (J). (gr. k-3). pap. (978-0-7787-4304-0(7)) Crabtree Publishing Co.

Baxter, Roberta. The Creation of the U. S. Constitution: A History Perspectives Book. 2014. (Perspectives Library). (ENG., Illus.). 32p. (J). (gr. 4-8). 32.07 (978-1-63137-616-0(0), 205247) Cherry Lake Publishing.

Beckett, Leslie & Dunn, John M. The Story of the Constitution: Creating the U. S. Government, 1 vol. 2016. (American History Ser.). (ENG.). 104p. (J). (gr. 7-7). lib. bdg. 41.03 (978-1-5345-6044-4(0), e074c482-d899-498d-8d44-399b0a0fc539, Lucent Pr.) Greenhaven Publishing LLC.

Benchmark Education Company, LLC Staff, compiled by. Freedom's Trail & U. S. Constitution. 2005. spiral bd. 75.00 (978-1-4108-5826-9(X)) Benchmark Education Co.

Bowers, Matt. Writing the Bill of Rights. 2019. (Sequence American Government Ser.). (ENG.). 32p. (J). (gr. 2-5). lib. bdg. (978-1-68151-671-4(3), 10803) Amicus.

—Writing the U. S. Constitution. 2019. (Sequence American Government Ser.). (ENG.). 32p. (J). (gr. 2-5). lib. bdg. (978-1-68151-675-2(6), 10807) Amicus.

Bradley, B. J. We the People- the 27 Amendments of the United States Constitution. 2012. 34p. pap. 15.95 (978-0-578-10413-3(X)) Winding Road Pubs.

Brezina, Corona. Fifth Amendment: Double Jeopardy, Self-Incrimination, & Due Process of Law, 1 vol. 2011. (Amendments to the United States Constitution: the Bill of Rights Ser.). (ENG., Illus.). 64p. (J). (gr. 6-6). pap. 13.95 (978-1-4488-2306-2(4), 31ab4f0a-8147-4cf5-91fe-d25977bc9d36, Rosen Reference) Rosen Publishing Group, Inc., The.

—The Fifth Amendment: Double Jeopardy, Self-Incrimination, & Due Process of Law, 1 vol. 2011. (Amendments to the United States Constitution: the Bill of Rights Ser.). (ENG., Illus.). 64p. (YA). (gr. 6-6). lib. bdg. 37.13 (978-1-4488-1260-8(7), dbfcb6b8-14a8-4122-ab31-711be13ea33a) Rosen Publishing Group, Inc., The.

Brindell Fradin, Dennis. The U. S. Constitution, 1 vol. 2008. (Turning Points in U. S. History Ser.). (ENG., Illus.). 48p. (gr. 4-4). lib. bdg. 34.07 (978-0-7614-2036-1(3), 65dbeac2-0fe3-4a71-ac1b-9eb49eb8bd4f) Cavendish Square Publishing LLC.

Brinkman, Patricia. Discover Writing the Constitution. 2006. (J). pap. (978-1-4108-6453-6(7)) Benchmark Education Co.

Buchanan, Shelly. The U. S. Constitution & You. rev. ed. 2014. (Social Studies: Informational Text Ser.). (ENG., Illus.). 32p. (J). (gr. 3-4). pap. 11.99 (978-1-4333-7364-0(5)) Teacher Created Materials, Inc.

Burgan, Michael. The Creation of the U. S. Constitution. Purcell, Gordon & Beatty, Terry, illus. 2006. (Graphic History Ser.). (ENG.). 32p. (J). (gr. 3-9). pap. 8.10 (978-0-7368-9653-5(8), 93366, Capstone Pr.) Capstone.

—The U.S. Constitution/By Michael Burgan. 2011. (Cornerstones of Freedom, Third Ser.). (Illus.). 64p. (J). lib. bdg. 30.00 (978-0-531-25042-6(3), Children's Pr.) Scholastic Library Publishing.

Carson, Brian & Ramen, Catherine. Understanding Your Right to Freedom from Searches, 1 vol. 2011. (Personal Freedom & Civic Duty Ser.). (ENG., Illus.). 160p. (YA). (gr. 7-7). lib. bdg. 39.80 (978-1-4488-4670-2(6), 5b7c2e9d-6099-49c5-b920-ff4952c87b82) Rosen Publishing Group, Inc., The.

Catrow, David. We the Kids: The Preamble of the Constitution of the United States. Catrow, David, illus. 2004. (Illus.). (J). (gr. k-5). 27.90 incl. audio (978-0-8045-6914-9(2)) Spoken Arts, Inc.

Cefrey, Holly. The United States Constitution & Early State Constitutions: Law & Order in the New Nation & States. (Life in the New American Nation Ser.). 32p. (gr. 4-4). 2009. 47.90 (978-1-61514-287-3(8)) 2003. (ENG., Illus.). lib. bdg. 29.13 (978-0-8239-4042-4(X), be159b32-cdd6-4e6e-afcb-04f05a0b0e7d, Rosen Reference) Rosen Publishing Group, Inc., The.

Cheney, Lynne. We the People: The Story of Our Constitution. Harlin, Greg, illus. (ENG.). 40p. (J). (gr. k-4). 2012. 9.99 (978-1-4424-4422-5(3)) 2008. 19.99 (978-1-4169-5418-7(X)) Simon & Schuster/Paula Wiseman Bks. (Simon & Schuster/Paula Wiseman Bks.).

Clay, Kathryn. The U. S. Constitution: Introducing Primary Sources. 2016. (Introducing Primary Sources Ser.). (ENG., Illus.). 32p. (J). (gr. -1-2). lib. bdg. 28.65 (978-1-4914-8225-4(7), 130687, Capstone Pr.) Capstone.

Demuth, Patricia Brennan & Who HQ. What Is the Constitution? Foley, Tim, illus. 2018. (What Was? Ser.). 112p. (J). (gr. 3-7). 5.99 (978-1-5247-8609-0(8)); lib. bdg. 15.99 (978-1-5247-8611-3(X)) Penguin Young Readers Group. (Penguin Workshop).

Donnelly, Karen. The Bill of Rights. 2009. (Primary Source Library of American Citizenship Ser.). 32p. (gr. 5-5). 47.90 (978-1-61511-221-0(9), Rosen Reference) Rosen Publishing Group, Inc., The.

Duignan, Brian & DeCarlo, Carolyn, eds. The U.S. Constitution & the Separation of Powers, 1 vol. 2018. (Checks & Balances in the U. S. Government Ser.). (ENG.). 128p. (gr. 10-10). lib. bdg. 39.00 (978-1-5383-0173-9(3), 7dbae470-a899-4903-b77c-5541c196286a, Britannica Educational Publishing) Rosen Publishing Group, Inc., The.

Eck, Kristin. Drafting the Constitution: Weighing Evidence to Draw Sound Conclusions, 1 vol. 2005. (Critical Thinking in American History Ser.). (ENG., Illus.). 48p. (YA). (gr. 5-8). lib. bdg. 34.47 (978-1-4042-0412-6(1), 3f43f11d-709d-490b-b2bf-8ac65cb3eb29) Rosen Publishing Group, Inc., The.

The Evolution of the Bill of Rights (NCHS) (YA). (gr. 8-12). spiral bd., tchr.'s planning gde. ed. 13.50 (978-0-382-40938-7(8)) Cobblestone Publishing Co.

Furgang, Kathy. The Ninth Amendment: Rights Retained by the People, 1 vol. 2011. (Amendments to the United States Constitution: the Bill of Rights Ser.). (ENG., Illus.). 64p. (YA). (gr. 6-6). lib. bdg. 37.13 (978-1-4488-1264-6(X), 0371a522-9b7d-4de2-a920-f46de664bb2c) Rosen Publishing Group, Inc., The.

Ganchy, Sally & Isler, Claudia. Understanding Your Right to Free Speech, 1 vol. 2011. (Personal Freedom & Civic Duty Ser.). (ENG., Illus.). 152p. (YA). (gr. 7-7). lib. bdg. 39.80 (978-1-4488-4667-2(6), 5fc1c559-f796-46f4-a6d2-b94a90cd7ceb) Rosen Publishing Group, Inc., The.

Griffin, Maave. Constitution Day. 2009. (Explore Citizenship Ser.). 24p. (gr. 3-3). 42.50 (978-1-61512-340-7(7), PowerKids Pr.) Rosen Publishing Group, Inc., The.

Griffin, Maeve. Constitution Day, 1 vol. (Explore Citizenship Ser.). (ENG.). 24p. (gr. 3-3). 2009. (J). 26.27 (978-1-4358-2978-7(6), c9d089c8-9cb7-4aa5-bbc5-cbf9e37a771a, PowerKids Pr.) 2008. pap. 8.25 (978-1-4358-0139-4(3), b2ef757f-6820-4254-a698-95cc69e4b159, Rosen Classroom) Rosen Publishing Group, Inc., The.

Harris, Duchess. Freedom of Religion. 2017. (American Values & Freedoms Ser.). (ENG., Illus.). 112p. (J). (gr. 6-12). lib. bdg. 41.36 (978-1-5321-1299-7(8), 27507, Essential Library) ABDO Publishing Co.

Harris, Duchess & Cornell, Kari A. Freedom of the Press. 2017. (American Values & Freedoms Ser.). (ENG., Illus.). 112p. (J). (gr. 6-12). lib. bdg. 41.36 (978-1-5321-1300-0(5), 27508, Essential Library) ABDO Publishing Co.

Harris, Nancy. What's the U. S. Constitution? rev. ed. 2016. (First Guide to Government Ser.). (ENG.). 32p. (J). (gr. 1-3). pap. 8.29 (978-1-4846-3690-9(2), 134102, Heinemann) Capstone.

Hofer, Charles. The Right to Bear Arms: A Look at the Second Amendment, 1 vol. 2018. (Our Bill of Rights Ser.). (ENG.). 32p. (gr. 5-5). pap. 11.00 (978-1-5383-4292-3(8), 87b85584-357a-4398-ab55-718c3de6611f, PowerKids Pr.) Rosen Publishing Group, Inc., The.

Hurt, Avery Elizabeth. The United States Constitution, 1 vol. 2018. (America's Most Important Documents: Inquiry into Historical Sources Ser.). (ENG.). 64p. (gr. 6-6). lib. bdg. 37.36 (978-1-5026-3610-2(7), fdfdc88b-c2c4-4faa-8c5e-413e112519eb) Cavendish Square Publishing LLC.

Hurt, Avery Elizabeth, ed. Interpreting the Bill of Rights, 1 vol. 2018. (Opposing Viewpoints Ser.). (ENG.). 200p. (gr. 10-12). 50.43 (978-1-5345-0293-2(9), b69ed8e4-3ec4-4eab-bcf6-6c9ddb0058b3) Greenhaven Publishing LLC.

Isaacs, Sally & Bedeksy, Baron. Understanding the US Constitution. 2008. (Documenting Early America Ser.). (ENG.). 32p. (J). (gr. 3-6). pap. (978-0-7787-4378-1(0)) Crabtree Publishing Co.

Isaacs, Sally Senzell. Understanding the U. S. Constitution. 2008. (Documenting Early America Ser.). (ENG.). 32p. (J). (gr. 1-4). 19.75 (978-1-5311-7652-5(6)) Perfection Learning Corp.

Jacobson, Bray. The U. S. Constitution, 1 vol. 2017. (Look at U. S. History Ser.). (ENG.). 32p. (J). (gr. 2-2). pap. 11.50 (978-1-4824-6043-8(2), 5e7d2eea-ba7b-4bc8-b57b-ce39edf999d5) Stevens, Gareth Publishing LLLP.

Jones, Molly. First Amendment: Freedom of Speech, the Press, & Religion, 1 vol. 2011. (Amendments to the United States Constitution: the Bill of Rights Ser.). (ENG., Illus.). 64p. (YA). (gr. 6-6). pap. 13.95 (978-1-4488-2302-4(1), 5b7b3657-36f7-48c4-897e-83474ff114f2, Rosen Reference) Rosen Publishing Group, Inc., The.

—The First Amendment: Freedom of Speech, the Press, & Religion, 1 vol. 2011. (Amendments to the United States Constitution: the Bill of Rights Ser.). (ENG., Illus.). 64p. (YA). (gr. 6-6). lib. bdg. 37.13 (978-1-4488-1252-3(6), 7e5d7718-35e6-4dfc-afd7-f05311afccf3) Rosen Publishing Group, Inc., The.

Kawa, Katie. Bill of Rights, 1 vol. 2016. (Documents of American Democracy Ser.). (ENG., Illus.). 32p. (J). (gr. 5-5). pap. 11.00 (978-1-4994-2073-9(0), 56b52929-ef46-44d7-bd38-ea101c14b022, PowerKids Pr.) Rosen Publishing Group, Inc., The.

Keegan, Anna. The United States Constitution & the Bill of Rights: The Law of the Land, 1 vol. 2015. (Spotlight on American History Ser.). (ENG., Illus.). 24p. (J). (gr. 4-6). pap. 11.00 (978-1-4994-1773-9(X), bc9d0df9-8a8d-4cbd-aa0f-50f01c90af2b, PowerKids Pr.) Rosen Publishing Group, Inc., The.

Krull, Kathleen. A Kids' Guide to America's Bill of Rights: Revised Edition. DiVito, Anna, illus. 2015. (ENG.). 240p. (J). (gr. 3-7). pap. 7.99 (978-0-06-235230-9(X), HarperCollins) HarperCollins Pubs.

Larson, Kirsten W., et al. Cause & Effect: the Bill of Rights. 2017. (Cause & Effect: the Bill of Rights Ser.). (ENG., Illus.). 32p. (J). (gr. 3-6). pap., pap., pap. 31.80 (978-1-5157-7193-7(8), 26682, Capstone Pr.) Capstone.

Leavitt, Amie. Understanding the Line of Succession, 1 vol. 2017. (What's up with Your Government? Ser.). (ENG., Illus.). 32p. (J). (gr. 4-5). 27.93 (978-1-5383-2232-1(3), 16972d6b-673f-4848-8ae0-60b4fc3dbabf); pap. 11.00 (978-1-5383-2328-1(1), c4792241-8036-47f7-8940-12be9211d929) Rosen Publishing Group, Inc., The. (PowerKids Pr.).

Leavitt, Amie Jane. The Bill of Rights in Translation: What It Really Means. rev. ed. (Kids' Translations Ser.). (ENG., Illus.). 32p. (J). (gr. 3-6). 2017. lib. bdg. 27.99 (978-1-5157-9138-6(6), 136572, Capstone Pr.) 2016. pap. 8.10 (978-1-5157-4218-0(0), 133981) Capstone.

LeVert, Suzanne. The Constitution, 1 vol. 2003. (Kaleidoscope: Government Ser.). (ENG., Illus.). 48p. (gr. 4-4). 32.64 (978-0-7614-1452-0(5), 96e641c8-3da3-42ca-9340-85363104716e) Cavendish Square Publishing LLC.

Lusted, Marcia Amidon. The U. S. Constitution. 2016. (How America Works). (ENG.). 24p. (J). (gr. 3-6). 32.79 (978-1-5038-0907-9(2), 210664) Child's World, Inc, The.

Machajewski, Sarah. Analyzing Sources of Information about the U. S. Constitution, 1 vol. 2018. (Project Learning Through American History Ser.). (ENG.). 32p. (J). (gr. 4-5). 27.93 (978-1-5383-3051-7(2), df15087e-f547-4e3c-aa22-e2cde8753ef4, PowerKids Pr.) Rosen Publishing Group, Inc., The.

Maestro, Betsy. A More Perfect Union: The Story of Our Constitution. Maestro, Giulio, illus. 2008. (ENG.). 48p. (J). (gr. 2-7). pap. 11.99 (978-0-688-10192-3(5), HarperCollins) HarperCollins Pubs.

Manger, Katherine. The U.S. Constitution, 4 vols. 2016. (Let's Find Out! Primary Sources Ser.). (ENG., Illus.). 32p. (J). (gr. 2-3). 52.12 (978-1-5081-0455-1(7), ea1f6d81-8ed7-4cf1-8fed-1613a2c0c212) Rosen Publishing Group, Inc., The.

Mara, Wil. Creating the Constitution. 2017. (Foundations of Our Nation Ser.). (ENG., Illus.). 32p. (J). (gr. 3-5). pap. 9.95 (978-1-63517-308-6(6), 1635173086); lib. bdg. 31.35 (978-1-63517-243-0(8), 1635172438) North Star Editions. (Focus Readers).

Marsh, Carole. The Counterfeit Constitution Mystery. 2009. (Real Kids, Real Places Ser.). (Illus.). 144p. (J). lib. bdg. 18.99 (978-0-635-07043-2(X), Marsh, Carole Mysteries) Gallopade International.

—I'm Reading about the U. S. Constitution. 2016. (I'm Reading About Ser.). (ENG., Illus.). (J). lib. bdg. 24.99 (978-0-635-12219-3(7)); pap. 7.99 (978-0-635-12220-9(0)) Gallopade International.

—The U. S. Constitution. Beard, Chad, ed. 2004. (American Milestones Ser.). (Illus.). 28p. (J). (gr. 4-12). pap. 5.95 (978-0-635-02696-5(1)) Gallopade International.

Metz, Lorijo. La Constitucin de los Estados Unidos y la Carta de Derechos / the United States Constitution & the Bill of Rights, 1 vol. Beullens-Maoui, Nathalie, ed. 2013. (¡Celebremos la Libertad! / Let's Celebrate Freedom! Ser.). (SPA & ENG.). 24p. (J). (gr. 3-3). 26.27 (978-1-4777-3247-2(0), 16931135-b11b-448a-b0b6-21c56e5b69ac, PowerKids Pr.) Rosen Publishing Group, Inc., The.

—The United States Constitution & the Bill of Rights, 1 vol., 1. 2013. (Let's Celebrate Freedom! Ser.). (ENG.). 24p. (J). (gr. 3-3). 26.27 (978-1-4777-2895-6(3), 341d165f-941a-4c56-812a-034700cc26b7, PowerKids Pr.) Rosen Publishing Group, Inc., The.

Micklos, John & Micklos, John, Jr. From Thirteen Colonies to One Nation, 1 vol. 2008. (Revolutionary War Library). (ENG., Illus.). 48p. (J). (gr. 3-3). lib. bdg. 27.93 (978-0-7660-3015-2(6), c96af7cf-f967-42c2-80d4-67636f4de9d3, Enslow Elementary) Enslow Publishing, LLC.

—The Making of the United States from Thirteen Colonies: Through Primary Sources, 1 vol. 2013. (American Revolution Through Primary Sources Ser.). (ENG.). 48p. (gr. 4-6). pap. 11.53 (978-1-4644-0191-6(8), 34f4b0d8-053b-4331-ab55-77e8baf3d2c8); (Illus.). (J). 27.93 (978-0-7660-4133-2(6), 451c891d-fc74-4e1d-a855-d24b94dd42cd) Enslow Publishing, LLC.

Mooney, Carla. U. S. Constitution: Discover How Democracy Works. Casteel, Tom, illus. 2016. (Build It Yourself Ser.). (ENG.). 128p. (J). (gr. 3-7). pap. 17.95 (978-1-61930-445-1(7), fa6e3b31-534c-45c1-a1fc-19450ee406bd) Nomad Pr.

—The U. S. Constitution: Discover How Democracy Works. Casteel, Tom, illus. 2016. (Build It Yourself Ser.). (ENG.). 128p. (J). (gr. 3-7). 22.95 (978-1-61930-441-3(4), 57a1d103-39ec-4abf-a59a-e8f471b7f695) Nomad Pr.

Morris, Rebecca & Harris, Duchess. The Right to Bear Arms. 2017. (American Values & Freedoms Ser.). (ENG., Illus.). 112p. (J). (gr. 6-12). lib. bdg. 41.36 (978-1-5321-1302-4(1), 27510, Essential Library) ABDO Publishing Co.

Murray, Hallie. The Right to Bear Arms: The Second Amendment, 1 vol. 2017. (Bill of Rights Ser.). (ENG., Illus.). 48p. (gr. 5-6). lib. bdg. 29.60 (978-0-7660-8551-0(1), 4ca7f522-c621-4210-a74a-06bfdfc6bf51) Enslow Publishing, LLC.

—Unreasonable Search & Seizure: The Fourth Amendment, 1 vol. 2017. (Bill of Rights Ser.). (ENG., Illus.). 48p. (gr. 5-6). lib. bdg. 29.60 (978-0-7660-8555-8(4), aa3d275f-c18b-4d7b-9eda-e7779d82bb88) Enslow Publishing, LLC.

Murray, Julie. US Constitution. 2019. (US Symbols (AK) Ser.). (ENG., Illus.). 24p. (J). (gr. -1-2). lib. bdg. 31.36 (978-1-5321-8539-7(1), 31416, Abdo Kids) ABDO Publishing Co.

Murray, Laura K. The U. S. Constitution. 2019. (Shaping the United States of America Ser.). (ENG., Illus.). 24p. (J). (gr. 1-3). pap. 7.95 (978-1-9771-1010-7(X), 140953); lib. bdg. 25.99 (978-1-9771-0841-8(5), 140460) Capstone. (Pebble).

National Geographic Learning. Reading Expeditions (Social Studies: Documents of Freedom): the Bill of Rights. 2007. (ENG., Illus.). 32p. (J). pap. 18.95 (978-0-7922-4552-0(0)) CENGAGE Learning.

Nelson, Robin. Constitution Day. 2009. (First Step Nonfiction - American Holidays Ser.). (ENG.). 24p. (gr. k-2). 23.93 (978-0-7613-4930-3(8)) Lerner Publishing Group.

Orr, Tamra. The Story of the Constitution. 2011. (My Guide to the Constitution Ser.). 48p. (J). (gr. 3-6). pap. 16.50 (978-1-61228-188-9(5)); (Illus.). lib. bdg. 29.95 (978-1-58415-946-9(4)) Mitchell Lane Pubs.

Pearl, Norman. The U. S. Constitution, 1 vol. Skeens, Matthew, illus. 2006. (American Symbols Ser.). (ENG.). 24p. (J). (gr. 1-3). 9.95 (978-1-4048-2646-5(7), 86577, Picture Window Bks.) Capstone.

Pearson, Yvonne. Celebrate Constitution Day. 2019. (U. S. Holidays Ser.). (ENG., Illus.). 24p. (J). (gr. 1-3). lib. bdg. 25.99 (978-1-9771-0268-3(9), 139268, Capstone Pr.) Capstone.

Porterfield, Jason. The Third Amendment: The Right to Privacy in the Home, 1 vol. 2011. (Amendments to the United States Constitution: the Bill of Rights Ser.). (ENG., Illus.). 64p. (YA). (gr. 6-6). lib. bdg. 37.13 (978-1-4488-1256-1(9), c65b7d1b-4a76-4763-a116-93973e0541c2) Rosen Publishing Group, Inc., The.

—Third Amendment: Upholding the Right to Privacy, 1 vol. 2011. (Amendments to the United States Constitution: the Bill of Rights Ser.). (ENG.). 64p. (YA). (gr. 6-6). pap. 13.95 (978-1-4488-2304-8(8), f030c4a2-1fe0-422e-9906-b883ae76e358, Rosen Reference) Rosen Publishing Group, Inc., The.

Rajczak Nelson, Kristen. U.S. Constitution, 1 vol. 2016. (Documents of American Democracy Ser.). (ENG., Illus.). 32p. (J). (gr. 5-5). pap. 11.00 (978-1-4994-2089-0(7), 3053fc90-183f-49b3-950c-1079e92476c2, PowerKids Pr.) Rosen Publishing Group, Inc., The.

Ransom, Candice. George Washington & the Story of the U. S. Constitution. Reeves, Jeni, illus. 2011. (History Speaks: Picture Books Plus Reader's Theater Ser.). 48p. pap. 56.72 (978-0-7613-7632-3(1)); (ENG.). (gr. 2-4). 27.93 (978-0-7613-5877-0(3), Millbrook Pr.); (ENG.). (gr. 2-4). pap. 9.95 (978-0-7613-7116-8(8)) Lerner Publishing Group.

—Who Wrote the U. S. Constitution? And Other Questions about the Constitutional Convention of 1787. 2010. (Six Questions of American History Ser.). (ENG.). (gr. 4-6). pap. 56.72 (978-0-7613-6949-3(X)) Lerner Publishing Group.

Richmond, Benjamin. What Are the Three Branches of the Government? And Other Questions about the U. S. Constitution. 2015. (Good Question! Ser.). (ENG., Illus.). 32p. (J). (gr. 2). pap. 5.95 (978-1-4549-1244-6(8)) Sterling Publishing Co., Inc.

Rokutani, John. Freedom of Speech, the Press, & Religion: The First Amendment, 1 vol. 2017. (Bill of Rights Ser.). (ENG., Illus.). 48p. (gr. 5-6). 29.60 (978-0-7660-8549-7(X), d3768a18-f12a-48d5-91c9-ddbbd74ea038) Enslow Publishing, LLC.

Schmidt, Maegan. Us Constitution & Bill of Rights, 1 vol. 2013. (Foundations of Our Nation Ser.). (ENG.). 48p. (J). (gr. 4-8). lib. bdg. 35.64 (978-1-61783-713-5(X), 7824) ABDO Publishing Co.

—US Constitution & Bill of Rights. 2013. (Foundations of Our Nation Ser.). (ENG., Illus.). 48p. (J). (gr. 4-8). pap. 18.50 (978-1-61783-763-0(6), 8754) ABDO Publishing Co.

Schuh, Mari. The United States Constitution. 2018. (Symbols of American Freedom Ser.). (ENG., Illus.). 24p. (J). (gr. k-3). pap. 7.99 (978-1-61891-474-3(X), 12127); lib. bdg. 26.95 (978-1-62617-888-5(7)) Bellwether Media. (Blastoff! Readers).

Shamir, Ruby. What's the Big Deal about Freedom. Faulkner, Matt, illus. 2017. (What's the Big Deal About Ser.: 2). 32p. (J). (gr. -1-3). 17.99 (978-0-399-54728-7(2), Philomel Bks.) Penguin Young Readers Group.

Shea, Therese. 20 Fun Facts about the US Constitution. 2013. (Fun Fact File: US History! Ser.). 32p. (J). (gr. 3-6). pap. 63.00 (978-1-4339-9200-1(0)) Stevens, Gareth Publishing LLLP.

Shea, Therese M. The United States Constitution, 1 vol. 2013. (Documents That Shaped America Ser.). (ENG., Illus.). 32p. (J). (gr. 4-5). lib. bdg. 29.27 (978-1-4339-9009-0(1), 2b0b1f26-8a58-4436-a1b9-06129de40f05) Stevens, Gareth Publishing LLLP.

—20 Fun Facts about the U. S. Constitution, 1 vol. 2013. (Fun Fact File: U. S. History! Ser.). (ENG.). 32p. (J). (gr. 2-3). 27.93 (978-1-4339-9198-1(5), e9905891-3bcd-42ec-a9af-21dce0743851); pap. 11.50 (978-1-4339-9199-8(3), 254b30c8-f37b-411a-8dfa-4083b09b8a40) Stevens, Gareth Publishing LLLP.

Sonneborn, Liz. The United States Constitution, 1 vol. 2012. (Documenting U. S. History Ser.). (ENG.). 48p. (gr. 3-6). pap. 9.95 (978-1-4329-6761-1(4), 119391, Heinemann) Capstone.

SparkNotes. The U. S. Constitution & Other Important American Documents. 2018. (No Fear Ser.: 4). (ENG.). 160p. (J). (gr. 9). pap. 7.95 (978-1-4549-2808-9(5), Spark Notes) Sterling Publishing Co., Inc.

Swain, Gwenyth. Documents of Freedom: A Look at the Declaration of Independence, the Bill of Rights, & the U. S. Constitution. 2012. (Searchlight Books How Does Government Work Ser.). (ENG., Illus.). 40p. (gr. 3-5). pap. 51.01 (978-0-7613-9231-6(9)); (J). pap. 9.99 (978-0-7613-8560-8(6), 325b05e7-6bd3-4841-b748-21d113dc82bc) Lerner Publishing Group.

Taylor-Butler, Christine. The Constitution of the United States (a True Book: American History) 2008. (True Book (Relaunch) Ser.). (ENG., Illus.). 48p. (J). (gr. 3-5). pap. 6.95 (978-0-531-14779-5(7), Children's Pr.) Scholastic Library Publishing.

Thomas, William David. ¿Qué Es una Constitución? (What Is a Constitution?), 1 vol. 2008. (Mi Gobierno de Estados Unidos (My American Government) Ser.). (SPA., Illus.). 32p. (J). (gr. 4-6). pap. 11.50 (978-0-8368-8878-2(2), 517e57e3-65f2-4b22-9207-069be5c3e776); lib. bdg. 28.67 (978-0-8368-8873-7(1), 904f865e-4a17-40e8-9e37-79f4d0fd4478) Stevens, Gareth Publishing LLLP. (Gareth Stevens Learning Library).

—What Is a Constitution?, 1 vol. 2008. (My American Government Ser.). (ENG.). 32p. (gr. 4-6). pap. 11.50 (978-0-8368-8868-3(5), cdf00799-73d9-424e-87d4-44244d6a981b); (Illus.). lib. bdg. 28.67 (978-0-8368-8863-8(4), 52c724a2-3838-4b82-91ae-b3883562c9fc) Stevens, Gareth Publishing LLLP. (Gareth Stevens Learning Library).

—What Is a Constitution? 2008. (My American Government Ser.). (ENG.). 32p. (J). (gr. 3-6). 21.30 (978-1-5311-8674-6(2)) Perfection Learning Corp.

Thompson, Gare. Shaping the Constitution: Text Pairs. 2008. (Bridges/Navigators Ser.). (J). (gr. 5). 89.00 (978-1-4108-8422-0(8)) Benchmark Education Co.

Travis, Cathy. Constitution Translated for Kids. 3rd ed. 2008. (ENG.). 112p. (J). (gr. 5-17). pap. 11.95 (978-0-9814534-1-5(4)) Ovation Bks.

—Constitution Translated for Kids / la Constitución traducida para Niños. 2008. (SPA & ENG., Illus.). 176p. (J). (gr. 3-7). pap. 12.95 (978-0-9814534-2-2(2)) Ovation Bks.

Understanding the United States Constitution, 14 vols. 2014. (Understanding the United States Constitution Ser.). (ENG.). 112p. (YA). (gr. 7-7). 271.60 (978-1-4777-7503-5(X), 7a6a6a5b-1f17-4607-b85f-83afcf3bd5ba) Rosen Publishing Group, Inc., The.

The United States Constitution Student Workbook. 2nd ed. 2003. pap. (978-0-9635364-8-8(6)) Academic Solutions, Inc.

Webster, Christine. The Pledge of Allegiance. 2003. (Cornerstones of Freedom Ser.). (ENG., Illus.). 48p. (J). (gr. 4-6). 26.00 (978-0-516-22674-3(6), Children's Pr.) Scholastic Library Publishing.

Wolfe, James & Stair, Nancy L. Understanding the Bill of Rights, 1 vol. 2015. (Primary Sources of American Political Documents Ser.). (ENG., Illus.). 112p. (gr. 7-7). 38.93 (978-0-7660-6882-7(X), f81d8cde-8aea-4bb3-b56d-e68ea5c378c8) Enslow Publishing, LLC.

Zimet, Susan & Hasak-Lowy, Todd. Roses & Radicals: The Epic Story of How American Women Won the Right to Vote. 2020. 176p. (J). (gr. 5). pap. 9.99 (978-0-425-29146-7(4), Puffin Books) Penguin Young Readers Group.

UNITED STATES—CONSTITUTION—AMENDMENTS

see Constitutional Amendments—United States

UNITED STATES—CONSTITUTIONAL CONVENTION (1787)

Conklin, Wendy. Early Congresses, 1 vol. rev. ed. 2004. (Social Studies: Informational Text Ser.). (ENG.). 24p. (gr. 4-8). pap. 10.99 (978-0-7439-8750-9(0)) Teacher Created Materials, Inc.

Giddens, Sandra. A Timeline of the Constitutional Convention. 2009. (Timelines of American History Ser.). 32p. (gr. 4-4). 47.90 (978-1-60854-382-3(X), Rosen Reference) Rosen Publishing Group, Inc., The.

Giddens, Sandra & Giddens, Owen. A Timeline of the Constitutional Convention, 1 vol. 2004. (Timelines of American History Ser.). (ENG., Illus.). 32p. (gr. 4-4). lib. bdg. 29.13 (978-0-8239-4535-1(9), 7b1ba4ac-cff3-4642-b86f-ac3b637b2247, Rosen Reference) Rosen Publishing Group, Inc., The.

Hughes, Chris. The Constitutional Convention. 2005. (People at the Center of Ser.). (Illus.). 48p. (J). (gr. -1-7). lib. bdg. 24.95 (978-1-56711-918-3(2), Blackbirch Pr., Inc.) Cengage Gale.

Maestro, Betsy & Maestro, Giulio. A More Perfect Union: The Story of Our Constitution. 2008. (Illus.). 48p. (J). (gr. -1-3). 18.40 (978-0-8335-6055-1(7)) Turtleback.

Ransom, Candice. George Washington & the Story of the U. S. Constitution. Reeves, Jeni, illus. 2011. (History Speaks: Picture Books Plus Reader's Theater Ser.). 48p. pap. 56.72 (978-0-7613-7632-3(1)); (ENG.). (gr. 2-4). 27.93 (978-0-7613-5877-0(3), Millbrook Pr.); (ENG.). (gr. 2-4). pap. 9.95 (978-0-7613-7116-8(8)) Lerner Publishing Group.

—Who Wrote the U. S. Constitution? And Other Questions about the Constitutional Convention of 1787. 2010. (Six Questions of American History Ser.). (ENG.). (gr. 4-6). pap. 56.72 (978-0-7613-6949-3(X)) Lerner Publishing Group.

Sherman, Josepha. The Constitution, 1 vol. 2003. (Primary Source Library of American Citizenship Ser.). (ENG., Illus.). 32p. (YA). (gr. 5-5). lib. bdg. 29.13 (978-0-8239-4473-6(5), 683e2fed-ae8e-4c26-9e7e-c099609c8708, Rosen Reference) Rosen Publishing Group, Inc., The.

Weston Woods Staff, creator. Shh! We're Writing the Constitution. 2011. 38.75 (978-0-439-72886-7(X)) 2004. 29.95 (978-1-55592-682-3(7)) 2004. 18.95 (978-1-55592-681-6(9)) Weston Woods Studios, Inc.

UNITED STATES—CONSTITUTIONAL HISTORY

see Constitutional History—United States

UNITED STATES—CONSTITUTIONAL LAW

see Constitutional Law—United States

UNITED STATES—CONSULAR SERVICE

see United States—Diplomatic and Consular Service

UNITED STATES—CONTINENTAL CONGRESS

Betti, Matthew. The Declaration of Independence & the Continental Congress, 1 vol. 2015. (Spotlight on American History Ser.). (ENG., Illus.). 24p. (J). (gr. 4-6). pap. 11.00 (978-1-4994-1728-9(4), c9cf0bf8-0ea7-45af-8224-7d85b123b743, PowerKids Pr.) Rosen Publishing Group, Inc., The.

Conklin, Wendy. Early Congresses, 1 vol. rev. ed. 2004. (Social Studies: Informational Text Ser.). (ENG.). 24p. (gr. 4-8). pap. 10.99 (978-0-7439-8750-9(0)) Teacher Created Materials, Inc.

Jarnow, Jesse. Patrick Henry's Liberty or Death Speech: A Primary Source Investigation. (Great Historic Debates & Speeches Ser.). 64p. (gr. 5-8). 2009. 58.50 (978-1-61513-120-4(5)) 2004. (ENG., Illus.). (J). lib. bdg. 37.13 (978-1-4042-0152-1(1), 33578fa0-39bc-431d-85a9-66a4ee0c1715) Rosen Publishing Group, Inc., The.

Morlock, Jeremy. Problem-Solving Methods of the Continental Congress, 1 vol. 2018. (Project Learning Through American History Ser.). (ENG.). 32p. (gr. 4-5). 27.93 (978-1-5383-3071-5(7), d0e28d22-98b0-410a-bee5-d3ef709cfccb, PowerKids Pr.) Rosen Publishing Group, Inc., The.

Ransom, Candice. John Hancock. 2005. (History Maker Bios Ser.). (Illus.). 48p. (J). (gr. 3-4). 26.60 (978-0-8225-1547-0(4), Lerner Pubns.) Lerner Publishing Group.

—What Was the Continental Congress? And Other Questions about the Declaration of Independence. 2011. (Six Questions of American History Ser.). (ENG.). 48p. (gr. 4-6). pap. 56.72 (978-0-7613-7642-2(9)); (Illus.). (J). pap. 11.99 (978-0-7613-7135-9(4), d59ab588-4cbc-4420-8266-4b49034cb9a8) Lerner Publishing Group.

Rosaler, Maxine. A Timeline of the First Continental Congress. 2009. (Timelines of American History Ser.). 32p. (gr. 4-4). 47.90 (978-1-60854-384-7(6), Rosen Reference) Rosen Publishing Group, Inc., The.

Uhl, Xina M. & Burnett, Betty. A Primary Source Investigation of the Continental Congress, 1 vol. 2018. (Uncovering American History Ser.). (ENG.). 64p. (gr. 6-6). pap. 13.95 (978-1-5081-8411-9(9), 7bba41c1-bb3f-42af-bb76-00ac3094bf1b, Rosen Reference) Rosen Publishing Group, Inc., The.

Welch, Catherine A. Patrick Henry. 2006. (History Maker Bios Ser.). (Illus.). 48p. (J). (gr. 3-6). lib. bdg. 26.60 (978-0-8225-5941-2(2), Lerner Pubns.) Lerner Publishing Group.

UNITED STATES—DEBTS, PUBLIC

see Debts, Public

UNITED STATES—DECLARATION OF INDEPENDENCE

Armentrout, David & Armentrout, Patricia. La Declaration de Independencia. 2005. (Documentos Que Formaron la Nacion Ser.). (Illus.). 48p. (J). (gr. 3-7). lib. bdg. 31.36 (978-1-59515-644-0(5)) Rourke Educational Media.

Betti, Matthew. The Declaration of Independence & the Continental Congress, 1 vol. 2015. (Spotlight on American History Ser.). (ENG., Illus.). 24p. (J). (gr. 4-6). pap. 11.00 (978-1-4994-1728-9(4), c9cf0bf8-0ea7-45af-8224-7d85b123b743, PowerKids Pr.) Rosen Publishing Group, Inc., The.

Bodden, Valerie. The Declaration of American Independence. 2009. (Days of Change Ser.). (ENG., Illus.). 48p. (J). (gr. 5-8). 22.95 (978-1-58341-733-1(8), 22144) Creative Co., The.

Bowers, Matt. Writing the Declaration of Independence. 2019. (Sequence American Government Ser.). (ENG.). 32p. (J). (gr. 2-5). lib. bdg. (978-1-68151-673-8(X), 10805) Amicus.

Brindell Fradin, Dennis. The Declaration of Independence, 1 vol. 2007. (Turning Points in U. S. History Ser.). (ENG., Illus.). 48p. (gr. 4-4). lib. bdg. 34.07 (978-0-7614-2129-0(7), f86eb692-5344-44c0-90b0-233796d33085) Cavendish Square Publishing LLC.

Castellano, Peter. The Declaration of Independence, 1 vol. 2017. (Look at U. S. History Ser.). (ENG.). 32p. (gr. 2-2). pap. 11.50 (978-1-4824-6031-5(9), 716a7df3-10c5-438a-9bf2-8bde1ee1eecc) Stevens, Gareth Publishing LLLP.

Clark, Willow. The True Story of the Declaration of Independence, 1 vol. 2013. (What Really Happened? Ser.). (ENG., Illus.). 24p. (J). (gr. 2-3). pap. 9.25 (978-1-4488-9840-4(4), 94101ea9-a09e-4507-ad08-82250005ab11); lib. bdg. 26.27 (978-1-4488-9691-2(6), 091fe756-fd1e-4072-9aaf-9a4ac3be666b) Rosen Publishing Group, Inc., The. (PowerKids Pr.).

Clay, Kathryn. The Declaration of Independence: Introducing Primary Sources. 2017. (Introducing Primary Sources Ser.). (ENG., Illus.). 32p. (J). (gr. -1-2). lib. bdg. 28.65 (978-1-5157-6355-0(2), 135114, Capstone Pr.) Capstone.

Coddington, Andrew. Thomas Jefferson: Architect of the Declaration of Independence, 1 vol. 2016. (Great American Thinkers Ser.). (ENG., Illus.). 128p. (YA). (gr. 9-9). 47.36 (978-1-5026-1924-2(5), 75a7aea4-6e46-499f-8c25-a7a46fbc5d49) Cavendish Square Publishing LLC.

Fingeroth, Danny. Democracy's Signature: Benjamin Franklin & the Declaration of Independence. 2009. (Great Moments in American History Ser.). 32p. (gr. 3-3). 47.90 (978-1-61513-141-9(8)) Rosen Publishing Group, Inc., The.

Fink, Sam. The Declaration of Independence: The Words That Made America. Fink, Sam, illus. 2007. (Illus.). 160p. (YA). (gr. 7). 19.65 (978-0-7569-8187-7(5)) Perfection Learning Corp.

Fradin, Dennis Brindell. The Signers: The 56 Stories Behind the Declaration of Independence. McCurdy, Michael, illus. 2003. (ENG.). 176p. (J). (gr. 5-18). 24.99 (978-0-8027-8849-8(1), 900032845, Bloomsbury USA Childrens) Bloomsbury Publishing USA.

Furgang, Kathy. The Declaration of Independence & Benjamin Franklin of Pennsylvania. 2009. (Framers of the Declaration of Independence Ser.). 24p. (gr. 3-3). 42.50 (978-1-61512-629-3(5), PowerKids Pr.) Rosen Publishing Group, Inc., The.

—The Declaration of Independence & Richard Henry Lee of Virginia. 2009. (Framers of the Declaration of Independence Ser.). 24p. (gr. 3-3). 42.50 (978-1-61512-630-9(9), PowerKids Pr.) Rosen Publishing Group, Inc., The.

—The Declaration of Independence & Robert Livingston of New York. 2009. (Framers of the Declaration of Independence Ser.). 24p. (gr. 3-3). 42.50 (978-1-61512-631-6(7), PowerKids Pr.) Rosen Publishing Group, Inc., The.

—The Declaration of Independence & Roger Sherman of Connecticut. 2009. (Framers of the Declaration of Independence Ser.). 24p. (gr. 3-3). 42.50 (978-1-61512-632-3(5), PowerKids Pr.) Rosen Publishing Group, Inc., The.

—The Declaration of Independence & Thomas Jefferson of Virginia. 2009. (Framers of the Declaration of Independence Ser.). 24p. (gr. 3-3). 42.50 (978-1-61512-633-0(3), PowerKids Pr.) Rosen Publishing Group, Inc., The.

Gagne, Tammy. Who Were the Signers of the Declaration of Independence? 2017. (Young America Ser.). (Illus.). 47p. (J). (gr. 3-6). 29.95 (978-1-61228-983-0(5)) Mitchell Lane Pubs.

Graves, Kerry A. The Declaration of Independence: The Story Behind America's Founding Document. 2003. (America in Words & Song Ser.). (Illus.). 32p. (gr. 4-6). 23.00 (978-0-7910-7334-6(3), Facts On File) Infobase Holdings, Inc.

Harris, Michael C. & Who HQ. What Is the Declaration of Independence? Hoare, Jerry, illus. 2016. (What Was? Ser.). 112p. (J). (gr. 3-7). lib. bdg. 15.99 (978-0-399-54230-5(2), Penguin Workshop) Penguin Young Readers Group.

Hicks, Terry Allan. The Declaration of Independence, 1 vol. 2007. (Symbols of America Ser.). (ENG., Illus.). 40p. (gr. 3-3). lib. bdg. 32.64 (978-0-7614-2135-1(1), b672c79b-ebcf-460a-bf6f-c79934c3be91) Cavendish Square Publishing LLC.

Hurt, Avery Elizabeth. The Declaration of Independence, 1 vol. 2018. (America's Most Important Documents: Inquiry into Historical Sources Ser.). (ENG.). 64p. (gr. 6-6). lib. bdg. 37.36 (978-1-5026-3604-1(2), 772ba093-e206-4454-a3fb-f6f8e0106590) Cavendish Square Publishing LLC.

Isaacs, Sally. Understanding the Declaration of Independence. 2008. (Documenting Early America Ser.). (ENG.). 32p. (J). (gr. 3-6). lib. bdg. (978-0-7787-4371-2(3)) Crabtree Publishing Co.

Isaacs, Sally & Bedeksy, Baron. Understanding the Declaration of Independence. 2008. (Documenting Early America Ser.). (ENG.). 32p. (J). (gr. 3-6). pap. (978-0-7787-4376-7(4)) Crabtree Publishing Co.

Jeffrey, Gary. Thomas Jefferson & the Declaration of Independence, 1 vol. 2011. (Graphic Heroes of the American Revolution Ser.). (ENG., Illus.). 24p. (J). (gr. 3-3). 26.60 (978-1-4339-6025-3(7), b3ad44c5-2d19-400f-8ba3-6b2e6bef69a2); pap. 9.15 (978-1-4339-6026-0(5), 6bfbc259-f45e-48b1-85a7-4b2b3c1cce56, Gareth Stevens Learning Library) Stevens, Gareth Publishing LLLP.

Kawa, Katie. The Declaration of Independence Wasn't Signed on July 4th: Exposing Myths about Independence Day, 1 vol. 2016. (Exposed! Myths about Early American History Ser.). (ENG.). 32p. (J). (gr. 2-3). pap. 11.50 (978-1-4824-5720-9(2), 5941bc90-1743-4f19-a9c2-e9fb846f6d55) Stevens, Gareth Publishing LLLP.

Keppeler, Jill. Team Time Machine Drafts the Declaration of Independence, 1 vol. 2019. (Team Time Machine: American Revolution Ser.). (ENG.). 32p. (J). (gr. 2-3). pap. 11.50 (978-1-5382-4678-8(3), a83e060e-5247-41dc-b12e-cb1fa334a4da) Stevens, Gareth Publishing LLLP.

Kerley, Barbara. Those Rebels, John & Tom. Fotheringham, Edwin, illus. 2012. (ENG.). 48p. (J). (gr. 2-5). 17.99 (978-0-545-22268-6(0), Scholastic Pr.) Scholastic, Inc.

Landau, Elaine. The Declaration of Independence (a True Book: American History) 2008. (True Book (Relaunch) Ser.). (ENG., Illus.). 48p. (J). (gr. 3-5). pap. 6.95 (978-0-531-14780-1(0), Children's Pr.) Scholastic Library Publishing.

—True Books: the Declaration of Independence. 2008. (True Book: American History, Revised Ser.). (ENG., Illus.). 48p. (J). (gr. 3-5). lib. bdg. 21.19 (978-0-531-12630-1(7), Children's Pr.) Scholastic Library Publishing.

Leavitt, Amie Jane. The Declaration of Independence in Translation: What It Really Means. rev. ed. (Kids' Translations Ser.). (ENG., 32p. (J). (gr. 3-6). 2017. Illus.). lib. bdg. 27.99 (978-1-5157-9137-9(8), 136571) 2016. pap. 8.10 (978-1-5157-6250-8(5), 135065) Capstone. (Capstone Pr.).

Leavitt, Amie Jane, et al. Kids' Translations. rev. ed. 2017. (Kids' Translations Ser.). (ENG.). 32p. (J). (gr. 3-6). 149.95 (978-1-5157-9144-7(0), 27305, Capstone Pr.) Capstone.

Machajewski, Sarah. Declaration of Independence, 1 vol. 2016. (Documents of American Democracy Ser.). (ENG., Illus.). 32p. (J). (gr. 5-5). pap. 11.00 (978-1-4994-2077-7(3), ead7d548-1ad2-41e1-89bc-771d375c0dea, PowerKids Pr.) Rosen Publishing Group, Inc., The.

Manger, Katherine. The Declaration of Independence, 1 vol. 2016. (Let's Find Out! Primary Sources Ser.). (ENG., Illus.). 32p. (J). (gr. 2-3). lib. bdg. 26.06 (978-1-5081-0395-0(X), 635e6a1d-75b7-47fd-bf76-74ea76aea88c) Rosen Publishing Group, Inc., The.

Mara, Wil. Writing the Declaration of Independence. 2017. (Foundations of Our Nation Ser.). (ENG., Illus.). 32p. (J). (gr. 3-5). pap. 9.95 (978-1-63517-314-7(0), 1635173140); lib. bdg. 31.35 (978-1-63517-249-2(7), 1635172497) North Star Editions. (Focus Readers).

Marcovitz, Hal. The Declaration of Independence. 2014. (Understanding American History). (ENG., Illus.). 96p. (J). lib. bdg. (978-1-60152-736-3(5)) ReferencePoint Pr., Inc.

—The Declaration of Independence: Forming a New Nation. Moreno, Barry, ed. 2014. (Patriotic Symbols of America Ser.: 20). 48p. (J). (gr. 4-18). lib. bdg. 20.95 (978-1-4222-3122-7(4)) Mason Crest.

McDaniel, Melissa. The Declaration of Independence. 2011. (Cornerstones of Freedom, Third Ser.). (ENG., Illus.). 64p. (J). pap. 8.95 (978-0-531-26555-0(2), Children's Pr.) Scholastic Library Publishing.

Meinking, Mary. The Declaration of Independence. 2016. (How America Works). (ENG.). 24p. (J). (gr. 3-6). 32.79 (978-1-5038-0901-7(3), 210666) Child's World, Inc, The.

Metz, Lorijo. La Declaracin de Independencia / the Declaration of Independence, 1 vol., 1. Beullens-Maoui, Nathalie, ed. 2014. (¡Celebremos la Libertad! / Let's Celebrate Freedom! Ser.). (SPA & ENG., Illus.). 24p. (J). (gr. 3-3). 26.27 (978-1-4777-3246-5(2), 423f1183-3272-4a57-b597-711401b5f8eb, PowerKids Pr.) Rosen Publishing Group, Inc., The.

—The Declaration of Independence, 1 vol., 1. 2014. (Let's Celebrate Freedom! Ser.). (ENG.). 24p. (J). (gr. 3-3). 26.27 (978-1-4777-2894-9(5), 9894c926-1070-4cf1-a679-be7f4e9231cd, PowerKids Pr.) Rosen Publishing Group, Inc., The.

Micklos, John & Micklos, John, Jr. From Thirteen Colonies to One Nation, 1 vol. 2008. (Revolutionary War Library). (ENG., Illus.). 48p. (J). (gr. 3-3). lib. bdg. 27.93 (978-0-7660-3015-2(6), c96af7cf-f967-42c2-80d4-67636f4de9d3, Enslow Elementary) Enslow Publishing, LLC.

—The Making of the United States from Thirteen Colonies: Through Primary Sources, 1 vol. 2013. (American Revolution Through Primary Sources Ser.). (ENG.). 48p. (gr. 4-6). pap. 11.53 (978-1-4644-0191-6(8), 34f4b0d8-053b-4331-ab55-77e8baf3d2c8); (Illus.). (J). 27.93 (978-0-7660-4133-2(6), 451c891d-fc74-4e1d-a855-d24b94dd42cd) Enslow Publishing, LLC.

Miller, Mirella S. 12 Questions about the Declaration of Independence. 2017. (Examining Primary Sources Ser.). (ENG., Illus.). 32p. (J). (gr. 3-6). 32.80 (978-1-63235-283-5(4), 11752, 12-Story Library) Bookstaves, LLC.

Moore Niver, Heather. 20 Fun Facts about the Declaration of Independence, 1 vol. 2013. (Fun Fact File: U. S. History! Ser.). (ENG.). 32p. (J). (gr. 2-3). 27.93 (978-1-4339-9183-7(7), d92c53c0-6e7e-4634-818d-a159d82b7e0d); pap. 11.50 (978-1-4339-9184-4(5), 7916e053-821d-4c95-9c38-b3b46b24f905) Stevens, Gareth Publishing LLLP.

Morey, Allan. A Timeline History of the Declaration of Independence. 2014. (Timeline Trackers: America's Beginnings Ser.). (ENG., Illus.). 48p. (J). (gr. 5-8). lib. bdg. 30.65 (978-1-4677-3640-4(6), c8655b74-edb1-4c15-9eff-1e713837deab, Lerner Pubns.) Lerner Publishing Group.

Mortensen, Lori. The Declaration of Independence, 1 vol. Skeens, Matthew, illus. 2009. (American Symbols Ser.). (ENG.). 24p. (J). (gr. 1-3). lib. bdg. 27.32 (978-1-4048-5165-8(8), 95494, Picture Window Bks.) Capstone.

Mulhall, Jill K. Declaration of Independence, 1 vol. rev. ed. 2004. (Social Studies: Informational Text Ser.). (ENG.). 24p. (gr. 4-8). pap. 10.99 (978-0-7439-8746-2(2)) Teacher Created Materials, Inc.

Murray, Laura K. The Declaration of Independence. 2019. (Shaping the United States of America Ser.). (ENG., Illus.). 24p. (J). (gr. 1-3). pap. 7.95 (978-1-9771-1011-4(8), 140954);

lib. bdg. 25.99 *(978-1-9771-0842-5(3)*, 140461) Capstone. (Pebble).

Nardo, Don. The Declaration of Independence. 2003. (World History Ser.). (ENG., Illus.). 112p. (J). 34.95 *(978-1-59018-293-2(6)*, Lucent Bks.) Cengage Gale.

—The Declaration of Independence. 2006. (Illus.). 48p. (J). (gr. 4-8). reprint ed. 17.80 *(978-1-4223-5323-3(0))* DIANE Publishing Co.

National Geographic Learning. Reading Expeditions (Social Studies: Documents of Freedom): the Declaration of Independence. 2007. (ENG., Illus.). 32p. (J). pap. 18.95 *(978-0-7922-4554-4(7))* CENGAGE Learning.

Niver, Heather Moore. 20 Fun Facts about the Declaration of Independence. 2013. (Fun Fact File: US History! Ser.). 32p. (J). (gr. 3-6). pap. 63.00 *(978-1-4339-9185-1(3))* Stevens, Gareth Publishing LLLP.

Osornio, Catherine L. The Declaration of Independence from A to Z, 1 vol. Johnson, Layne, illus. 2010. (ABC Ser.). (ENG.). 32p. (J). (gr. 1-7). 16.99 *(978-1-58980-676-4(X)*, Pelican Publishing) Arcadia Publishing.

Ransom, Candice. What Was the Continental Congress? And Other Questions about the Declaration of Independence. 2011. (Six Questions of American History Ser.). (ENG.). 48p. (gr. 4-6). pap. 56.72 *(978-0-7613-7642-2(9))*; (Illus.). (J). pap. 11.99 *(978-0-7613-7135-9(4)*, d59ab588-4cbc-4420-8266-4b49034cb9a8) Lerner Publishing Group.

Raum, Elizabeth. The Declaration of Independence, 1 vol. 2012. (Documenting U. S. History Ser.). (ENG.). 48p. (gr. 3-6). pap. 9.95 *(978-1-4329-6762-8(2)*, 119392, Heinemann) Capstone.

Rissman, Rebecca. Declaration of Independence, 1 vol. 2013. (Foundations of Our Nation Ser.). (ENG.). 48p. (J). (gr. 4-8). lib. bdg. 35.64 *(978-1-61783-708-1(3)*, 7814); (Illus.). pap. 18.50 *(978-1-61783-758-6(X)*, 8749) ABDO Publishing Co.

Sargent, Dave & Sargent, Pat. Duke: (Dappled Palomino) Good Behavior, 30 vols., Vol. 23. Lenoir, Jane, illus. 2003. (Saddle up Ser.: Vol. 23). 42p. (J). pap. 10.95 *(978-1-56763-682-6(9))*; lib. bdg. 23.60 *(978-1-56763-681-9(0))* Ozark Publishing.

St. George, Judith. The Journey of the One & Only Declaration of Independence. Hillenbrand, Will, illus. 2014. 48p. (J). (gr. 2-5). 8.99 *(978-0-14-751164-5(X)*, Puffin Books) Penguin Young Readers Group.

—The Journey of the One & Only Declaration of Independence. Hillenbrand, Will, illus. 2011. (J). (gr. 1-7). 29.95 *(978-0-439-02760-1(8)*, WHCD806) Weston Woods Studios, Inc.

St George, Judith. Journey of the One & Only Declaration of Independence. Hillenbrand, Will, illus. 2014. (ENG.). 48p. (J). (gr. 2-5). 19.80 *(978-1-5311-8647-0(5))* Perfection Learning Corp.

Stanton, Terence M. The Declaration of Independence. (American History Flashpoints! Ser.). 2009. 32p. (gr. 4-4). 47.90 *(978-1-61511-371-2(1)*, PowerKids Pr.) 2009. (J). pap. 60.00 *(978-1-4358-0164-6(4)*, PowerKids Pr.) 2009. (ENG.). 32p. (J). (gr. 4-4). lib. bdg. 28.93 *(978-1-4358-2990-9(5)*, d224e74b-af0e-403c-8609-39f6f1c593be, PowerKids Pr.) 2008. (ENG.). 32p. (gr. 4-4). pap. 10.00 *(978-1-4358-0163-9(6)*, 9d213c15-58ea-42dc-b648-4a4be770e6cc, Rosen Classroom) Rosen Publishing Group, Inc., The.

Steiner, Howard. The Declaration of Independence. 2012. 54p. pap. 14.95 *(978-1-105-24573-2(X))* Lulu Pr., Inc.

Swain, Gwenyth. Declaring Freedom: A Look at the Declaration of Independence, the Bill of Rights, & the Constitution. 2003. (How Government Works). (ENG., Illus.). 56p. (gr. 4-8). lib. bdg. 25.26 *(978-0-8225-1348-3(X))* Lerner Publishing Group.

—Documents of Freedom: A Look at the Declaration of Independence, the Bill of Rights, & the U. S. Constitution. 2012. (Searchlight Books How Does Government Work Ser.). (ENG., Illus.). 40p. (gr. 3-5). pap. 51.01 *(978-0-7613-9231-6(9))*; (J). pap. 9.99 *(978-0-7613-8560-8(6)*, 325b05e7-6bd3-4841-b748-21d113dc82bc) Lerner Publishing Group.

Wolfe, James & Viegas, Jennifer. Understanding the Declaration of Independence, 1 vol. 2015. (Primary Sources of American Political Documents Ser.). (ENG., Illus.). 112p. (gr. 7-7). 38.93 *(978-0-7660-6874-2(9)*, 7bbd1d8a-7b1f-41aa-9c4b-acb9776583e8) Enslow Publishing, LLC.

UNITED STATES—DEFENSES

Beyer, Mark. Nuclear Weapons & the Cold War. 2009. (Library of Weapons of Mass Destruction Ser.). 64p. (gr. 5-5). 58.50 *(978-1-60853-953-6(9))* Rosen Publishing Group, Inc., The.

Campbell, Geoffrey A. A Vulnerable America: An Overview of National Security. 2007. (Lucent Library of Homeland Security). (ENG., Illus.). 112p. (J). 30.85 *(978-1-59018-383-0(5)*, Lucent Bks.) Cengage Gale.

Keeter, Hunter. The U. S. Homeland Security Forces, 1 vol. 2004. (America's Armed Forces Ser.). (ENG., Illus.). 48p. (gr. 5-8). lib. bdg. 33.67 *(978-0-8368-5682-8(1)*, b7c9a2ce-1c39-4fd3-8173-a658ff1f4996, Gareth Stevens Secondary Library) Stevens, Gareth Publishing LLLP.

Meyer, Jared. Working in a War Zone: Military Contractors, 1 vol. 2007. (Extreme Careers Ser.). (ENG., Illus.). 64p. (J). (gr. 5-5). lib. bdg. 37.13 *(978-1-4042-0959-6(X)*, 579b800a-d325-4845-83e2-959efa60b94c) Rosen Publishing Group, Inc., The.

Schuler, Harold H. Fort Sisseton. 2012. (Prairie Plains Ser.: No. 5). (Illus.). 283p. (Orig.). reprint ed. pap. 22.95 *(978-0-931170-62-1(1))* Ctr. for Western Studies.

UNITED STATES—DEPARTMENT OF AGRICULTURE

Peters, Jennifer. Inside the Department of Agriculture, 1 vol. 2018. (Understanding the Executive Branch Ser.). (ENG.). 48p. (gr. 5-5). 29.60 *(978-0-7660-9884-8(2)*, b35baefa-80cd-4560-8596-6cbab2a7722e) Enslow Publishing, LLC.

Rosaler, Maxine. The Department of Agriculture. (This Is Your Government Ser.). 64p. 2009. (gr. 5-6). 58.50 *(978-1-60854-362-5(5)*, Rosen Reference) 2005. (ENG., Illus.). (J). (gr. 4-6). lib. bdg. 37.13 *(978-1-4042-0206-1(4)*, 7522f436-0447-4264-a1b3-f074b133318a) 2005. (ENG., Illus.). (gr. 4-6). per. 12.95 *(978-1-4042-0659-5(0)*, 26fedea0-11ad-4c7b-9fc5-95238c14098f) Rosen Publishing Group, Inc., The.

UNITED STATES—DEPARTMENT OF COMMERCE

Goldberg, Jan. The Department of Commerce. (This Is Your Government Ser.). 64p. 2009. (gr. 5-6). 58.50 *(978-1-60854-365-6(X)*, Rosen Reference) 2005. (ENG., Illus.). (J). (gr. 4-6). lib. bdg. 37.13 *(978-1-4042-0207-8(2)*, 0910e505-f224-4bf3-ba26-409af9a8b43b) 2005. (ENG., Illus.). (gr. 4-6). per. 12.95 *(978-1-4042-0660-1(4)*, df411235-2cfc-44c7-8b6d-c21e709889bc) Rosen Publishing Group, Inc., The.

Peters, Jennifer. Inside the Department of Commerce, 1 vol. 2018. (Understanding the Executive Branch Ser.). (ENG.). 48p. (gr. 5-5). 29.60 *(978-0-7660-9887-9(7)*, c4ec719d-01b8-4e3b-8e34-781c2c7af4dc) Enslow Publishing, LLC.

UNITED STATES—DEPARTMENT OF DEFENSE

Ruffin, David C. The Duties & Responsibilities of the Secretary of Defense. (Your Government in Action Ser.). 32p. (gr. 3-3). 2009. 43.90 *(978-1-60854-915-3(1))* 2004. (ENG., Illus.). (J). lib. bdg. 27.60 *(978-1-4042-2689-0(3)*, a4f17946-daea-4d73-ace2-91389d4dea2e) Rosen Publishing Group, Inc., The. (PowerKids Pr.).

UNITED STATES—DEPARTMENT OF HEALTH, EDUCATION, AND WELFARE

Ruffin, David C. The Duties & Responsibilities of the Secretary of Education. 2009. (Your Government in Action Ser.). 32p. (gr. 3-3). 43.90 *(978-1-60854-916-0(X)*, PowerKids Pr.) Rosen Publishing Group, Inc., The.

UNITED STATES—DEPARTMENT OF JUSTICE

Mattern, Joanne. Attorney General. 2003. (America's Leaders Ser.). (Illus.). 32p. (J). 24.94 *(978-1-56711-278-8(1)*, Blackbirch Pr., Inc.) Cengage Gale.

McElroy, Lisa Tucker. Alberto Gonzales: Attorney General. 2006. (Gateway Biographies Ser.). (Illus.). 48p. (J). (gr. 4-8). lib. bdg. 23.93 *(978-0-8225-3418-1(5))* Lerner Publishing Group.

UNITED STATES—DEPARTMENT OF LABOR

Casil, Amy Sterling. The Department of Labor. (This Is Your Government Ser.). 64p. 2009. (gr. 5-6). 58.50 *(978-1-60854-374-8(9)*, Rosen Reference) 2005. (ENG., Illus.). (J). (gr. 4-6). lib. bdg. 37.13 *(978-1-4042-0210-8(2)*, 61c352ef-04f8-434f-bb98-46ed77407c41) 2005. (ENG., Illus.). (gr. 4-6). per. 12.95 *(978-1-4042-0663-2(9)*, b0f547f1-6fdc-4da4-86c0-b1df61398173) Rosen Publishing Group, Inc., The.

Peters, Jennifer. Inside the Department of Labor, 1 vol. 2018. (Understanding the Executive Branch Ser.). (ENG.). 48p. (gr. 5-5). 29.60 *(978-0-7660-9896-1(6)*, 709e2d00-87e4-4abf-b0c7-86b2e1355650) Enslow Publishing, LLC.

UNITED STATES—DEPARTMENT OF STATE

Markel, Michelle. Hillary Rodham Clinton: Some Girls Are Born to Lead. Pham, LeUyen, illus. 2016. (ENG.). 40p. (J). (gr. -1-3). 17.99 *(978-0-06-238122-4(9)*, Balzer & Bray) HarperCollins Pubs.

Ruffin, David C. The Duties & Responsibilities of the Secretary of State. (Your Government in Action Ser.). 32p. (gr. 3-3). 2009. 43.90 *(978-1-60854-919-1(4))* 2004. (ENG., Illus.). (J). lib. bdg. 27.60 *(978-1-4042-2688-3(5)*, 108a761c-5dcc-4c65-aa4f-1c29535ef894) Rosen Publishing Group, Inc., The. (PowerKids Pr.).

Sherman, Jill. Donald Trump: Outspoken Personality & President. 2017. (Gateway Biographies Ser.). (ENG., Illus.). 48p. (J). (gr. 4-8). lib. bdg. 31.99 *(978-1-5124-2596-3(6)*, 73ddd6e7-9543-41d2-9c95-2b6efefcc36c, Lerner Pubns.) Lerner Publishing Group.

Winter, Jonah. Hillary. ón, Raúl, illus. 2016. 40p. (J). (gr. -1-3). 17.99 *(978-0-553-53388-0(6)*, Schwartz & Wade Bks.) Random Hse. Children's Bks.

UNITED STATES—DEPARTMENT OF THE TREASURY

Ruffin, David C. The Duties & Responsibilities of the Secretary of the Treasury. (Your Government in Action Ser.). 32p. (gr. 3-3). 2009. 43.90 *(978-1-60854-920-7(8))* 2004. (ENG., Illus.). (J). lib. bdg. 27.60 *(978-1-4042-2690-6(7)*, 7cc003e4-5470-49d3-a748-0886f77d8cd5) Rosen Publishing Group, Inc., The. (PowerKids Pr.).

UNITED STATES—DESCRIPTION AND TRAVEL

ABC Travel Guides for Kids-Philadelphia. 2004. (J). per. 12.95 *(978-0-9760047-0-7(4))* Rosenberger, Matthew.

Allen, Nancy. Northeast & Metropolitan Regions. 2014. (United States Regions Ser.). (ENG.). 32p. (gr. 4-8). 32.79 *(978-1-62717-673-6(X)*, 9781627176736) Rourke Educational Media.

America the Beautiful, Third Series (Revised Edition) (Fall 2014 Set Of 26) 2014. (America the Beautiful, Third Ser. (Revised Edition) Ser.). (J). lib. bdg. 1040.00 *(978-0-531-27324-1(5))* Scholastic Library Publishing.

Andrews, Barbara. The Southeast Region. 2006. (J). pap. *(978-1-4108-6432-1(4))* Benchmark Education Co.

Barter, James. San Francisco in the 1960s. 2003. (Travel Guide To Ser.). (ENG., Illus.). 96p. (J). 30.85 *(978-1-59018-359-5(2)*, Lucent Bks.) Cengage Gale.

Beken, Robert A. Tijuana River Estuary & Border Field State Park: Land of diversity, land of Hope. I.t. ed. 2004. (Illus.). 260p. spiral bd. 34.95 *(978-0-9761726-0-4(7))* Tritium Pr.

Benchmark Education Company. The Northeast Region (Teacher Guide) 2005. *(978-1-4108-4660-0(1))* Benchmark Education Co.

Blashfield, Jean F., et al. Landmarks in U. S. History. 2017. (Landmarks in U. S. History Ser.). (ENG., Illus.). 32p. (J). (gr. 3-6). 119.96 *(978-1-5157-7156-2(3)*, 26674, Capstone Pr.) Capstone.

Books, Applewood. Love (Pictorial America) Vintage Images of America's Living Past. Lantos, James, ed. 2010. (Pictorial America Ser.). (ENG.). 56p. (J). pap. 9.95 *(978-1-60889-008-8(2))* Applewood Bks.

Cain, Marie Mowery. America the Beautiful. 2013. (Big Books, Red Ser.). (ENG & SPA., Illus.). 16p. pap. 33.00 *(978-1-59246-225-4(1))* Big Books, by George!

Carole Marsh. Atlanta Coloring. 2004. (City Bks.). 24p. (gr. k-5). pap., act. bk. ed. 3.95 *(978-0-635-02230-1(3))* Gallopade International.

Clawson, Calvin C. A Ride to the Infernal Regions: Yellowstone's First Tourists. Silliman, Lee, ed. 2003. per. 19.95 *(978-1-931832-18-2(8)*, 8667872363) Riverbend Publishing.

Cohen, Stephanie. The Northeast: Set Of 6. 2011. (Navigators Ser.). (J). pap. 48.00 net. *(978-1-4108-5102-4(8))* Benchmark Education Co.

Colorado Coloring Book. 2003. (J). *(978-0-9726022-0-4(8))* Mountain States Specialties.

Colorado Pocket Guide. 2003. (Illus.). 32p. (YA). 1.75 net. *(978-0-9726022-5-9(9))* Mountain States Specialties.

Columbia in Pictures. 2004. (Illus.). lib. bdg. 27.93 *(978-0-8225-1996-6(8))* Lerner Publishing Group.

Corrigan, Jim. The 1930s Decade in Photos: Depression & Hope, 1 vol. 2010. (Amazing Decades in Photos Ser.). (ENG., Illus.). 64p. (gr. 5-6). lib. bdg. 31.93 *(978-0-7660-3132-6(2)*, 4c7df277-4a32-4387-9bdd-7f703b46ff6c) Enslow Publishing, LLC.

—The 1940s Decade in Photos: A World at War, 1 vol. 2010. (Amazing Decades in Photos Ser.). (ENG., Illus.). 64p. (gr. 5-6). lib. bdg. 31.93 *(978-0-7660-3133-3(0)*, 91d10492-f80a-4e9b-998a-1417ae2b3a5c) Enslow Publishing, LLC.

—The 1950s Decade in Photos: The American Decade, 1 vol. 2010. (Amazing Decades in Photos Ser.). (ENG., Illus.). 64p. (gr. 5-6). lib. bdg. 31.93 *(978-0-7660-3134-0(9)*, bec97985-d23f-4689-8a9f-c5753ca194cd) Enslow Publishing, LLC.

—The 1970s Decade in Photos: Protest & Change, 1 vol. 2010. (Amazing Decades in Photos Ser.). (ENG., Illus.). 64p. (gr. 5-6). lib. bdg. 31.93 *(978-0-7660-3136-4(5)*, d039b223-4fb2-40c7-b8fd-b4f25164cd7d) Enslow Publishing, LLC.

—The 1980s Decade in Photos: The Triumph of Democracy, 1 vol. 2010. (Amazing Decades in Photos Ser.). (ENG., Illus.). 64p. (gr. 5-6). lib. bdg. 31.93 *(978-0-7660-3137-1(3)*, 56541840-ebde-47f4-8f8e-cd2c606fb27d) Enslow Publishing, LLC.

—The 1990s Decade in Photos: The Rise of Technology, 1 vol. 2010. (Amazing Decades in Photos Ser.). (ENG., Illus.). 64p. (J). (gr. 5-6). lib. bdg. 31.93 *(978-0-7660-3138-8(1)*, 720edcd3-4ebe-42c2-89d7-67e7e5161c97) Enslow Publishing, LLC.

—The 2000s Decade in Photos: A New Millennium, 1 vol. 2010. (Amazing Decades in Photos Ser.). (ENG., Illus.). 64p. (gr. 5-6). lib. bdg. 31.93 *(978-0-7660-3139-5(X)*, 73e773aa-d5a7-4233-a994-b885f3b94432) Enslow Publishing, LLC.

Crabtree Publishing Company Staff & Greil, Marlene. United States: The Land. 2012. (ENG.). 32p. (J). *(978-0-7787-9835-4(6))*; pap. *(978-0-7787-9838-5(0))* Crabtree Publishing Co.

Ditchfield, Christin. The Lewis & Clark Expedition. 2006. (True Bks.). (ENG., Illus.). 48p. (J). (gr. 3-7). pap. 6.95 *(978-0-516-25222-3(4)*, Children's Pr.) Scholastic Library Publishing.

Egginton, Jane. Pick Your Brains about the USA. Williams, Caspar, illus. 2005. (Pick Your Brains - Cadogan Ser.). (ENG.). 128p. pap. 9.95 *(978-1-86011-222-5(6))* Cadogan Guides GBR. Dist: Globe Pequot Pr., The.

Fox, Michael D. & Fox, Suzanne G. Meriwether Lewis & William Clark: The Corps of Discovery & the Exploration of the American Frontier, 1 vol. 2004. (Library of American Lives & Times Ser.). (ENG., Illus.). 112p. (J). (gr. 5-5). lib. bdg. 38.27 *(978-1-4042-2650-0(8)*, 96e27260-6d09-4b7f-888a-42a5dd16e882) Rosen Publishing Group, Inc., The.

Gallardo, Yuri Caravaca & Gallardo, Yuri Caravaca, eds. Houses & Apartments under 1000 Square Feet. 2013. (ENG., Illus.). 256p. pap. 24.95 *(978-1-77085-214-3(X)*, 8883b036-2577-479d-bfb8-e1e6da76f691) Firefly Bks., Ltd.

Gamble, Adam. Good Night America. Chan, Suwin, illus. 2006. (Good Night Our World Ser.). (ENG.). 28p. (J). (gr. k — 1). bds. 9.95 *(978-0-9777979-0-5(2))* Good Night Bks.

Gamble, Adam & Jasper, Mark. Count to Sleep America. Veno, Joe, illus. 2015. (Count to Sleep Ser.). (ENG.). 20p. (J). (— 1). bds. 9.95 *(978-1-60219-231-7(6))* Good Night Bks.

—Good Night Illinois. 2013. (Good Night Our World Ser.). (ENG., Illus.). 20p. (J). (— 1). bds. 9.95 *(978-1-60219-086-3(0))* Good Night Bks.

Gondosch, Linda. Where Did Sacagawea Join the Corps of Discovery? And Other Questions about the Lewis & Clark Expedition. 2011. (Six Questions of American History Ser.). (ENG., Illus.). 48p. (J). (gr. 4-6). lib. bdg. 30.65 *(978-0-7613-5226-6(0)*, fd798483-1f32-4a50-af83-88af79191609, Lerner Pubns.) Lerner Publishing Group.

Group/McGraw-Hill, Wright. The United States Coast to Coast, 6 vols. (Book2WebTM Ser.). (gr. 4-8). 36.50 *(978-0-322-04443-2(X))* Wright Group/McGraw-Hill.

Hall, Hannah. God Bless Our Country, 1 vol. Whitlow, Steve, illus. 2016. (God Bless Book Ser.). (ENG.). 20p. (J). bds. 9.99 *(978-0-7180-4017-8(1)*, Tommy Nelson) Nelson, Thomas Inc.

Heinrichs, Ann. Alabama. Kania, Matt, illus. 2017. (U. S. A. Travel Guides). (ENG.). 40p. (J). (gr. 2-5). lib. bdg. 38.50 *(978-1-5038-1941-2(8)*, 211578) Child's World, Inc, The.

Horowitz, Joseph. Dvoerak in America. 2003. (Illus.). x, 158p. (J). pap. 8.95 *(978-0-8126-2692-6(3))* Cricket Bks.

—Dvorak in America: In Search of the New World. 2003. (ENG., Illus.). 160p. (YA). 17.95 *(978-0-8126-2681-0(8))* Cricket Bks.

Houghton, Raymond C. A Revolutionary War Road Trip on US Route 202: Spend a Revolutionary Day along One of America's Most Historic Routes. 2004. (Illus.). 154p. per. 12.99 *(978-1-931373-13-5(2))* Cyber Haus.

—A Revolutionary War Road Trip on US Route 7: Spend a Revolutionary Day along One of America's Most Historic Routes. 2004. (Illus.). 150p. per. 12.99 *(978-1-931373-10-4(8))* Cyber Haus.

—A Revolutionary War Road Trip on US Route 9W: Spend a Revolutionary Day along One of America's Most Historic Routes. 2004. (Illus.). 174p. per. 12.99 *(978-1-931373-11-1(6))* Cyber Haus.

It's My State: Group 2, 12 vols. 2003. (It's My State! (First Edition)(r) Ser.). (ENG.). (YA). (gr. 4-4). lib. bdg. 204.42 *(978-0-7614-1521-3(1)*, 129556d1-d8ff-4522-ad62-ee4afc09281b, Cavendish Square) Cavendish Square Publishing LLC.

It's My State 5, 12 vols. 2nd rev. ed. 2013. (It's My State! (Second Edition)(r) Ser.). (ENG.). (J). (gr. 4-4). 215.58 *(978-0-7614-7997-0(X)*, 0a498e2c-35f8-4828-bb11-4d68ccc164ea, Cavendish Square) Cavendish Square Publishing LLC.

Jackson, Elaine. America. 2004. (QEB Travel Through Ser.). (Illus.). 32p. (J). lib. bdg. 18.95 *(978-1-59566-057-2(7))* QEB Publishing Inc.

Jackson, Robert B. The Remarkable Ride of the Abernathy Boys. 2003. (Land We Belong to Is Grand Ser.). (Illus.). 69p. (J). pap. *(978-1-57168-798-2(X)*, Eakin Pr.) Eakin Pr.

Keller, Susanna. The True Story of Lewis & Clark, 1 vol. 2013. (What Really Happened? Ser.). (ENG., Illus.). 24p. (J). (gr. 2-3). pap. 9.25 *(978-1-4488-9846-6(3)*, e0a93e44-5e16-4d0a-8805-6b38d2ae6877); lib. bdg. 26.27 *(978-1-4488-9694-3(0)*, 45b0e550-b940-425e-969e-33f6fe3bf16f) Rosen Publishing Group, Inc., The. (PowerKids Pr.).

Kopp, Megan. United States. 2018. (J). *(978-1-5105-3572-5(1))* SmartBook Media, Inc.

Leonardo, Victoria. The Northeast Region. 2005. (J). pap. *(978-1-4108-4612-9(1))* Benchmark Education Co.

Levy, Janey & Thompson, Benjamin. Spanish Explorers of North America, 1 vol. 2008. (Real Life Readers Ser.). (ENG.). 32p. (gr. 4-5). pap. 10.00 *(978-1-4358-0171-4(7)*, e67413d3-349f-4276-8a92-a0d8edb02736, Rosen Classroom) Rosen Publishing Group, Inc., The.

Linde, Barbara M. Traveling Around the United States: Learning to Add 2 Three-Digit Numbers Without Regrouping, 1 vol. 2010. (Math for the REAL World Ser.). (ENG.). 16p. (gr. 2-3). pap. 7.05 *(978-0-8239-8899-0(6)*, a78fca04-82a4-43b6-a8df-4432f84a334f, Rosen Classroom) Rosen Publishing Group, Inc., The.

Matrishon, Maible. Island Experiences - Adventures in Bocas Del Toro, on the Caribbean Coast of Panama. 2013. 40p. pap. *(978-0-9808653-9-4(5)*, Matrishon Media) Wider Vision Publishing.

Meachen Rau, Dana. Travel in American History, 1 vol. 2006. (How People Lived in America Ser.). (ENG., Illus.). 24p. (gr. 2-4). pap. 9.15 *(978-0-8368-7217-0(7)*, d105dd4f-b179-4164-8e04-27a969131b5e, Weekly Reader Leveled Readers) Stevens, Gareth Publishing LLLP.

Morley, Jacqueline. You Wouldn't Want to... Be an American Pioneer! Antram, David, illus. rev. ed. 2012. (ENG.). 32p. (J). lib. bdg. 29.00 *(978-0-531-27500-9(0))* Scholastic Library Publishing.

Murphy, Jim. Across America on an Emigrant Train. 2003. (ENG., Illus.). 168p. (J). (gr. 5-7). pap. 10.95 *(978-0-395-76483-1(1)*, 111826, Clarion Bks.) HarperCollins Pubs.

Nelson, Ray & Nelson, Douglas. Greetings from America: Postcards from Donovan Willoughby. Tronslin, Andrea, ed. Nelson, Ray & Nelson, Douglas, illus. 2nd ed. (Illus.). 48p. (J). (gr. k-5). 14.95 *(978-1-56977-409-0(9))* Flying Rhinoceros, Inc.

Nikola-Lisa, W. America (Lee & Low): a Book of Opposites/un Libro de Contrarios (English & Spanish Edition), 1 vol. 2013. (ENG., Illus.). 24p. (J). (gr. k-4). bds. 9.95 *(978-1-58430-028-1(0)*, leelowbooks) Lee & Low Bks., Inc.

Ray, Liz. Famous U. S. Landmarks, 6 vols., Set. 2004. (Phonics Readers Books 37-72 Ser.). (ENG.). 8p. (gr. k-1). pap. 35.70 *(978-0-7368-4067-5(2))* Capstone.

Redmond, Shirley Raye. Lewis & Clark: A Prairie Dog for the President. Manders, John, illus. 2003. (Step into Reading Ser.). 48p. 14.00 *(978-0-7569-1697-8(6))* Perfection Learning Corp.

—Lewis & Clark: A Prairie Dog for the President. Manders, John, illus. 2003. (Step into Reading Ser.: No. 3). 48p. (J). (gr. k-3). pap. 5.99 *(978-0-375-81120-3(6)*, Random Hse. Bks. for Young Readers) Random Hse. Children's Bks.

Road Trip: Exploring America's Regions, 12 vols. 2013. (Road Trip: Exploring America's Regions Ser.). 24p. (J). (gr. 2-3). (ENG.). 151.62 *(978-1-4339-9675-7(8)*, 2bd7aa28-c5d2-4f63-a15d-b9ff251358a9); pap. 48.90 *(978-1-4339-9743-3(6))*; pap. 293.40 *(978-1-4339-9744-0(4))* Stevens, Gareth Publishing LLLP.

Rosart, Sharyn. I Spy the 50 States. 2018. (J). lib. bdg. 29.40 *(978-0-606-41513-2(0))* Turtleback.

Rossi, Ann. The Southeast: Set Of 6. 2011. (Navigators Ser.). (J). pap. 48.00 net. *(978-1-4108-5103-1(6))* Benchmark Education Co.

Rowland, Wickie. Good Morning Piscataqua. 2014. (Illus.). 48p. (J). pap. 12.95 *(978-0-9603896-3-6(6))* Strawbery Banke Museum.

Sabuda, Robert, illus. America the Beautiful: America the Beautiful. 2004. (ENG.). 16p. (J). (gr. -1-3). 39.99 *(978-0-689-84744-8(0)*, Little Simon) Little Simon.

Saddleback Educational Publishing Staff, ed. Daniel Boone, 1 vol. unabr. ed. 2007. (Graphic Biographies Ser.). (ENG., Illus.). 25p. (YA). (gr. 4-12). pap. 9.75 *(978-1-59905-219-9(9))* Saddleback Educational Publishing, Inc.

Sasek, Miroslav. This Is America: A National Treasury. 2016. (This Is ... Ser.). (ENG., Illus.). 80p. (J). (gr. 5). 19.95 *(978-0-7893-3258-5(2))* Universe Publishing.

Streissguth, Thomas. United States in Pictures. 2007. (Visual Geography (Lerner) Ser.). (Illus.). 80p. (YA). (gr. 7-12). lib. bdg. 31.93 *(978-0-8225-8567-1(7))* Twenty First Century Bks.

Suen, Anastasia. Mountain Region. 2014. (United States Regions Ser.). (ENG., Illus.). 32p. (gr. 4-8). 32.79 *(978-1-62717-669-9(1)*, 9781627176699) Rourke Educational Media.

Sylvester, Alden W. Five Minutes in America a Voyage in Life. 2012. (ENG.). (J). pap. 13.95 *(978-1-4675-2936-5(2))* Independent Pub.

Teacher Created Resources Staff. America: Come on a Journey of Discovery. 2008. (Qeb Travel Through Ser.). (ENG., Illus.). 32p. (gr. 4-7). pap. 7.99 *(978-1-4206-8277-9(6))* Teacher Created Resources, Inc.

Toufexis, George. U. S. A. Facts & Fun Activity Book. 2017. (Dover Kids Activity Books: U. S. A. Ser.). (ENG.). 48p. (J). (gr. 3-6). pap. 4.99 *(978-0-486-81379-0(7)*, 813797) Dover Pubns., Inc.

Wilder, Laura Ingalls. A Little House Traveler: Writings from Laura Ingalls Wilder's Journeys Across America. 2011. (Little House Nonfiction Ser.). (ENG., Illus.). 368p. (J). (gr. 5). pap. 7.99 *(978-0-06-072492-4(7)*, HarperCollins) HarperCollins Pubs.

Woodcock, John, illus. Color & Doodle Your Way Across the USA. 2013. 108p. *(978-1-78157-023-4(X)*, Ilex Pr.) Octopus Publishing Group.

Zschock, Martha. Hello, America! 2012. (Hello Ser.). (ENG., Illus.). 16p. (J). (gr. -1-k). bds. 9.99 *(978-1-933212-88-3(8)*, Commonwealth Editions) Applewood Bks.

UNITED STATES—DESCRIPTION AND TRAVEL—MAPS

see United States—Maps

UNITED STATES—DIPLOMATIC AND CONSULAR SERVICE

Broderick, Kevin Joyce. The JipiJapa Hat. 2007. 124p. per. 12.95 *(978-0-595-45071-8(7))* iUniverse, Inc.

UNITED STATES—DISCOVERY AND EXPLORATION

see America—Discovery and Exploration; United States—Exploring Expeditions

UNITED STATES—ECONOMIC CONDITIONS

Amidon Lusted, Marcia. The Great Depression: Experience the 1930s from the Dust Bowl to the New Deal. Casteel, Tom, illus. 2016. (Inquire & Investigate Ser.). (ENG.). 128p. (J). (gr. 6-10). 22.95 *(978-1-61930-336-2(1)*, 25f2b5db-fb04-4b75-85cd-8cd865e5abb5) Nomad Pr.

—The Great Depression: Experience the 1930's from the Dust Bowl to the New Deal. Casteel, Tom, illus. 2016. (Inquire & Investigate Ser.). (ENG.). 128p. (J). (gr. 6-10). pap. 17.95 *(978-1-61930-340-9(X)*, ce2d6583-b839-4faf-a77d-dd176911c683) Nomad Pr.

Bair, Sheila. The Bullies of Wall Street: This Is How Greed Messed up Our Economy. (ENG.). (YA). (gr. 7). 2016. 288p. pap. 12.99 *(978-1-4814-0086-2(X))* 2015. (Illus.). 272p. 17.99 *(978-1-4814-0085-5(1))* Simon & Schuster Bks. For Young Readers. (Simon & Schuster Bks. For Young Readers).

Bezdecheck, Bethany. Bailout! Government Intervention in Business, 1 vol. 2010. (In the News Ser.). (ENG.). 64p. (YA). (gr. 6-6). pap. 13.95 *(978-1-4488-1681-1(5)*, 0fba3626-42a1-4e38-83dc-07a29b7e9752); lib. bdg. 37.13 *(978-1-4358-9449-5(9)*, ae1575d9-0933-48fe-9ed4-a17468b5d8ae) Rosen Publishing Group, Inc., The.

Brezina, Corona. America's Recession: The Effects of the Economic Downturn, 1 vol. 2011. (Headlines! Ser.). (ENG.). 64p. (YA). (gr. 6-6). lib. bdg. 37.13 *(978-1-4488-1296-7(8)*, b7067ab9-4598-4b7b-8396-3930d51910a9) Rosen Publishing Group, Inc., The.

—The Industrial Revolution in America: A Primary Source History of America's Transformation into an Industrial Society. 2009. (Primary Sources in American History Ser.). 64p. (gr. 5-8). 58.50 *(978-1-60851-497-7(8))* Rosen Publishing Group, Inc., The.

Burgan, Michael. The Great Depression: An Interactive History Adventure. 2010. (You Choose: Historical Eras Ser.). (ENG.). 112p. (J). (gr. 3-4). pap. 41.70 *(978-1-4296-6740-1(0)*, 16458); pap. 6.95 *(978-1-4296-6276-5(X)*, 115421); (Illus.). 32.65 *(978-1-4296-5480-7(5)*, 113880) Capstone. (Capstone Pr.).

Burling, Alexis. Real-World Projects to Explore the New Deal, 1 vol. 2018. (Project-Based Learning in Social Studies). (ENG.). 64p. (gr. 5-5). 37.47 *(978-1-5081-8222-1(1)*, c6d5b955-caf2-4b04-bbfa-e3a46c4bc153) Rosen Publishing Group, Inc., The.

Cornerstones of Freedom & Trade 2013, Set. 2013. (Cornerstones of Freedom™, Third Ser.). (J). 300.00 *(978-0-531-23848-6(2)*, Children's Pr.) Scholastic Library Publishing.

Craats, Rennay. Economy. 2008. (USA Past Present Future Ser.). (Illus.). 48p. (J). (gr. 4-6). pap. 10.95 *(978-1-59036-981-4(5))*; lib. bdg. 29.05 *(978-1-59036-980-7(7))* Weigl Pubs., Inc.

Crayton, Lisa A. & Nagle, Jeanne. Recession: What It Is & How It Works, 1 vol. 2015. (Economics in the 21st Century Ser.). (ENG., Illus.). 96p. (gr. 8-8). lib. bdg. 36.27 *(978-0-7660-7356-2(4)*, c457106e-a13c-4432-a6fe-ebafeb656cf9) Enslow Publishing, LLC.

Davies, Monika. Entendamos la Economía. rev. ed. 2019. (Social Studies: Informational Text Ser.). (SPA., Illus.). 32p. (J). (gr. 3-5). pap. 11.99 *(978-1-64290-119-1(9))* Teacher Created Materials, Inc.

Desenfants, Millie. Long Ago Sally. 2011. 28p. pap. 15.99 *(978-1-4628-7305-0(7))* Xlibris Corp.

Engdahl, Kirsten, ed. Are Chain Stores Ruining America?, 1 vol. 2006. (At Issue Ser.). (ENG.). 88p. (gr. 10-12). pap. 28.80 *(978-0-7377-3096-8(X)*, a139ed5f-0ccd-4c35-af0b-1b9498ebf2aa); (Illus.). lib. bdg. 41.03 *(978-0-7377-3095-1(1)*, ebe1b4c3-0c34-43ad-a2bb-b0b8c4bc7585) Greenhaven Publishing LLC. (Greenhaven Publishing).

Frazer, Coral Celeste. Economic Inequality: The American Dream under Siege. 2018. (ENG., Illus.). 128p. (YA). (gr. 6-12). lib. bdg. 37.32 *(978-1-5124-3107-0(9)*, 1df8e5fe-2f84-4f9e-b2a7-d1561a2e7642, Twenty-First Century Bks.) Lerner Publishing Group.

Freedman, Jeri. The U.S. Auto Industry: American Carmakers & the Economic Crisis, 1 vol. 2010. (In the News Ser.). (ENG.). 64p. (YA). (gr. 6-6). pap. 13.95 *(978-1-4488-1680-4(7)*, be06593e-985a-4e6b-bdc3-edbfef9a1244); lib. bdg. 37.13 *(978-1-4358-9448-8(0)*, 6c14abc1-bcd0-4938-9ec8-eb897050bcaf) Rosen Publishing Group, Inc., The.

Fremon, David K. The Great Depression in United States History, 1 vol. 2014. (In United States History Ser.). (ENG.). 96p. (gr. 5-6). 31.61 *(978-0-7660-6087-6(X)*, cf88ec4e-8ffd-4534-a38f-8942c4f84d9c); (Illus.). (J). pap. 13.88 *(978-0-7660-6088-3(8)*, bbc8ca57-d558-489b-a477-5ecbf2bc2bbc) Enslow Publishing, LLC.

Garstecki, Julia. Life During the Industrial Revolution, 1 vol. 2015. (Daily Life in US History Ser.). (ENG.). 48p. (J). (gr. 4-8). lib. bdg. 35.64 *(978-1-62403-627-9(9)*, 16894) ABDO Publishing Co.

Gedney, Mona K. The Story of the Great Depression. 2005. (Monumental Milestones Ser.). (Illus.). 48p. (YA). (gr. 4-7). lib. bdg. 29.95 *(978-1-58415-403-7(9))* Mitchell Lane Pubs.

George, Linda & George, Charles. The Great Depression. 2013. (Illus.). 96p. (J). lib. bdg. *(978-1-60152-492-8(7))* ReferencePoint Pr., Inc.

Grant, R. G. The Great Depression, 1 vol. 2005. (How Did It Happen? Ser.). (ENG., Illus.). 48p. (gr. 4-8). lib. bdg. 38.33 *(978-1-59018-606-0(0)*, b0781d0e-ddeb-475e-a2ae-da9e894e3a0b, Lucent Pr.) Greenhaven Publishing LLC.

—Why Did the Great Depression Happen?, 1 vol. 2010. (Moments in History Ser.). (ENG., Illus.). 48p. (YA). (gr. 6-8). pap. 15.05 *(978-1-4339-4170-2(8)*, ba126829-abf9-4869-a334-3e5a8993bc0a, Gareth Stevens Secondary Library); lib. bdg. 34.60 *(978-1-4339-4169-6(4)*, 2cef96c8-83ef-49c1-9b92-65399e65e0dc) Stevens, Gareth Publishing LLLP.

Gregory, Joy. The Great Depression. 2016. (Illus.). 48p. (J). *(978-1-5105-1286-3(1))* SmartBook Media, Inc.

Hakim, Joy. A History of US: an Age of Extremes: 1880-1917 a History of US Book Eight. 3rd rev. ed. 2007. (History of US Ser.: Vol. 8). (ENG., Illus.). 228p. (gr. 4-7). per. 15.95 *(978-0-19-532722-9(5))* Oxford Univ. Pr., Inc.

Hamilton, Jill, ed. The U. S. Economy, 1 vol. 2010. (Introducing Issues with Opposing Viewpoints Ser.). (ENG.). 144p. (gr. 7-10). 43.63 *(978-0-7377-4945-8(8)*, 92335147-89bf-4968-bdd9-38d59ba24ca3, Greenhaven Publishing) Greenhaven Publishing LLC.

Haugen, David M., et al, eds. The Great Depression, 1 vol. 2010. (Perspectives on Modern World History Ser.). (ENG., Illus.). 240p. (gr. 10-12). 49.43 *(978-0-7377-4795-9(1)*, 240a855b-bc7c-468a-a879-8e0cc974f8bb, Greenhaven Publishing) Greenhaven Publishing LLC.

Haugen, David M. & Musser, Susan, eds. Should the U. S. Reduce Its Consumption?, 1 vol. 2010. (At Issue Ser.). (ENG.). 120p. (gr. 10-12). 41.03 *(978-0-7377-4894-9(X)*, 1a8d24a5-52d1-4146-924a-3fd63cca268b); pap. 28.80 *(978-0-7377-4895-6(8)*, 6597b98b-ac5c-492b-bc7f-9ccd6d1eb16e) Greenhaven Publishing LLC. (Greenhaven Publishing).

Hurt, Avery Elizabeth. The Great Depression, 1 vol. 2017. (Interwar Years Ser.). (ENG., Illus.). 128p. (YA). (gr. 9-9). 47.36 *(978-1-5026-2713-1(2)*, 98487ccd-d96e-49c4-abb1-5be7fa9b27d7) Cavendish Square Publishing LLC.

Industrialism. 2010. (ENG., Illus.). 128p. (gr. 6-12). 45.00 *(978-1-60413-222-9(1)*, P179249, Facts On File) Infobase Holdings, Inc.

Ingram, Scott. The Stock Market Crash Of 1929, 1 vol. 2004. (Landmark Events in American History Ser.). (ENG., Illus.). 48p. (gr. 5-8). pap. 15.05 *(978-0-8368-5425-1(X)*, 6e01ff38-f6fc-4247-8464-817c4a13cd62, Gareth Stevens Secondary Library) Stevens, Gareth Publishing LLLP.

—Stock Market Crash Of 1929. 2004. (Landmark Events in American History Ser.). (ENG.). 48p. (J). (gr. 3-6). 24.85 *(978-1-5311-8646-3(7))* Perfection Learning Corp.

Jd, Duchess Harris & Yomtov, Nel. Being Poor in America. 2018. (Class in America Ser.). (ENG., Illus.). 112p. (J). (gr. 6-12). lib. bdg. 41.36 *(978-1-5321-1404-5(4)*, 28790, Essential Library) ABDO Publishing Co.

Kleinmartin, Hex. The Erie Canal, 1 vol. 2015. (Expanding America Ser.). (ENG., Illus.). 96p. (YA). (gr. 8-8). lib. bdg. 44.50 *(978-1-5026-0966-3(5)*, 8ac33cb1-287b-4eff-b152-2573187de8a6) Cavendish Square Publishing LLC.

Krueger, Lisa, ed. Does Outsourcing Harm America?, 1 vol. 2010. (At Issue Ser.). (ENG., Illus.). 120p. (gr. 10-12). 41.03 *(978-0-7377-4673-0(4)*, c7bb8054-6a8d-4ba7-8ccb-a7781af3aa74); pap. 28.80 *(978-0-7377-4674-7(2)*, 221048e5-4541-4649-a6f5-579c72a938fd) Greenhaven Publishing LLC. (Greenhaven Publishing).

Lanier, Wendy H. Life During the Great Depression, 1 vol. 2015. (Daily Life in US History Ser.). (ENG., Illus.). 48p. (J). (gr. 4-8). lib. bdg. 35.64 *(978-1-62403-626-2(0)*, 16892) ABDO Publishing Co.

Lankford, Ronald D., Jr., ed. What Is the Future of the U. S. Economy?, 1 vol. 2012. (At Issue Ser.). (ENG.). 152p. (gr. 10-12). pap. 28.80 *(978-0-7377-6214-3(4)*, f458a87b-7777-46f6-8d82-13b27745e1d4); lib. bdg. 41.03 *(978-0-7377-6213-6(6)*, 65e52fb5-f94e-453f-a431-4f8f28d9dfb4) Greenhaven Publishing LLC. (Greenhaven Publishing).

Lawrence, Katherine. Labor Legislation: The Struggle to Gain Rights for America's Workforce. 2009. (Progressive Movement 1900-1920: Efforts to Reform America's New Industrial Society Ser.). 32p. (gr. 3-4). 47.90 *(978-1-60854-166-9(5))* Rosen Publishing Group, Inc., The.

Lynch, Seth. The Industrial Revolution, 1 vol. 2018. (Look at U. S. History Ser.). (ENG.). 32p. (gr. 2-2). 28.27 *(978-1-5382-2127-3(6)*, 1ecd8fa1-314d-442a-9e7b-21b76733adea) Stevens, Gareth Publishing LLLP.

Mahoney, Emily. The Industrial Revolution: The Birth of Modern America, 1 vol. 2017. (American History Ser.). (ENG.). 104p. (gr. 7-7). lib. bdg. 41.03 *(978-1-5345-6133-5(1)*, 614f7d58-9e93-4a2e-bcbd-6b880ed31008, Lucent Pr.) Greenhaven Publishing LLC.

Marsh, Carole. Industrial Revolution from Muscles to Machines! 2004. (American Milestones Ser.). (Illus.). 28p. (J). (gr. 4-12). pap. 5.95 *(978-0-635-02694-1(5))* Gallopade International.

—Industrial Revolution Reproducible Activity Book (HC) 2004. 28p. (gr. 4-12). 29.95 *(978-0-635-02695-8(3))* Gallopade International.

Mattern, Joanne. Florida's Economy: From the Mouse to the Moon. rev. ed. 2016. (Social Studies: Informational Text Ser.). (ENG., Illus.). 32p. (J). (gr. 3-8). pap. 11.99 *(978-1-4938-3548-5(3))* Teacher Created Materials, Inc.

McCormick, Anita Louise. The Industrial Revolution in United States History, 1 vol. 2014. (In United States History Ser.). (ENG., Illus.). 96p. (gr. 5-6). (J). pap. 13.88 *(978-0-7660-6103-3(5)*, 9a4a441b-43d1-4918-8e3e-31650b51b555); 31.61 *(978-0-7660-6102-6(7)*, cf54944c-3cc1-4513-a54a-66b56c3f06c8) Enslow Publishing, LLC.

McNeilly, Linden K. Perspectives on the Great Depression. 2018. (Perspectives on US History Ser.). (ENG., Illus.). 32p. (J). (gr. 3-6). 32.80 *(978-1-63235-401-3(2)*, 13723, 12-Story Library) Bookstaves, LLC.

Miller, Debra A., ed. The U. S. Economy, 1 vol. 2010. (Current Controversies Ser.). (ENG., Illus.). 192p. (gr. 10-12). 48.03 *(978-0-7377-4711-9(0)*, 83a7fe6b-f68a-4663-af9d-3e1db2551706, Greenhaven Publishing) Greenhaven Publishing LLC.

Mooney, Carla. Perspectives on the Industrial Revolution. 2018. (Perspectives on US History Ser.). (ENG., Illus.). 32p. (J). (gr. 3-6). 32.80 *(978-1-63235-402-0(0)*, 13724, 12-Story Library) Bookstaves, LLC.

Moriarty, J. T. The Rise of American Capitalism: The Growth of American Banks, 1 vol. 2003. (America's Industrial Society in the 19th Century Ser.). (ENG., Illus.). 32p. (gr. 4-5). lib. bdg. 29.13 *(978-0-8239-4022-6(5)*, 67146d07-e35e-42b0-82b4-657f394a2c3b, Rosen Reference) Rosen Publishing Group, Inc., The.

National Geographic Learning. Reading Expeditions (Social Studies: Seeds of Change in American History): the Industrial Revolution. 2006. (Nonfiction Reading & Writing Workshops Ser.). (ENG., Illus.). 40p. (J). pap. 21.95 *(978-0-7922-8685-1(5))* CENGAGE Learning.

Otfinoski, Steven. The Great Depression (a Step into History) (Library Edition) 2018. (Step into History Ser.). (ENG., Illus.). 144p. (J). (gr. 5-8). lib. bdg. 36.00 *(978-0-531-22690-2(5)*, Children's Pr.) Scholastic Library Publishing.

Peterson, Sheryl. The Great Depression & World War II. 2011. (Explorer Library: Language Arts Explorer Ser.). (ENG.). 32p. (gr. 4-8). pap. 14.21 *(978-1-61080-287-1(X)*, 201210); (Illus.). lib. bdg. 32.07 *(978-1-61080-199-7(7)*, 201174) Cherry Lake Publishing.

Prince, Jennifer S. The Life & Times of Asheville's Thomas Wolfe. 2016. (True Tales for Young Readers Ser.). (ENG., Illus.). 116p. (YA). pap. 17.00 *(978-0-86526-484-7(8)*, 01OSPS) Univ. of North Carolina Pr.

Quinby, Michelle. Connecting the 21st Century to the Past: What Makes America America, 2000-The Present. 2013. (Illus.). 48p. (J). pap. *(978-1-4222-2423-6(6))* Mason Crest.

—Connecting the 21st Century to the Past: What Makes America America, 2000-The Present. Rakove, Jack N., ed. 2012. (How America Became America Ser.). (Illus.). 48p. (J). (gr. 3-4). 19.95 *(978-1-4222-2409-0(0))* Mason Crest.

Riggs, Kate. The Great Recession. 2016. (Turning Points Ser.). (ENG.). 48p. (J). (gr. 4-7). *(978-1-60818-749-2(7)*, 20813, Creative Education) Creative Co., The.

Ripped from the Headlines, 10 bks., Set. Incl. Downloading Music. Allman, Toney. (J). 23.95 *(978-1-60217-006-3(1))*; Fat in America. Stewart, Gail. (J). 23.95 *(978-1-60217-002-5(9))*; Gas Crisis. Kallan, Stuart A. (YA). 23.95 *(978-1-60217-001-8(0))*; Illegal Immigration. Stewart, Gail. (Illus.). (J). 23.95 *(978-1-60217-003-2(7))*; Internet Predators. Allman, Toney. (J). 23.95 *(978-1-60217-000-1(2))*; Nuclear Weapons. Sheen, Barbara. (YA). 23.95 *(978-1-60217-004-9(5))*; Outsourcing America. Currie, Stephen. (J). 23.95 *(978-1-60217-008-7(8))*; Reality TV. Woog, Adam. (YA). 23.95 *(978-1-60217-005-6(3))*; Street Crime. Parks, Peggy. (Illus.). (YA). 23.95 *(978-1-60217-007-0(X))*; Your Sexuality. Hirschmann, Kris. (YA). 23.95 *(978-1-60217-009-4(6))*; 64p. (gr. 7-12). 2007. 214.95 *(978-1-60217-010-0(X))* Erickson Pr.

Robinson, Tom. The Development of the Industrial United States: 1870-1900. 2007. (Presidents of the United States Ser.). (Illus.). 48p. (J). (gr. 4-7). lib. bdg. 29.05 *(978-1-59036-745-2(6))* Weigl Pubs., Inc.

—Development of the Industrial United States: 1870-1900. 2007. (Presidents of the United States Ser.). (Illus.). 48p. (J). (gr. 4-7). per. 10.95 *(978-1-59036-746-9(4))* Weigl Pubs., Inc.

Roza, Greg. America's Transition from Agriculture to Industry: Drawing Inferences & Conclusions. (Critical Thinking in American History Ser.). 48p. (gr. 5-8). 2009. 53.00 *(978-1-61512-087-1(4)*, Rosen Reference) 2005. (ENG., Illus.). (J). lib. bdg. 34.47 *(978-1-4042-0410-2(5)*, efd9a021-9dec-489f-ad29-99732f70097c) Rosen Publishing Group, Inc., The.

Ruggiero, Adriane. The Great Depression, 1 vol. 2006. (American Voices From Ser.). (ENG., Illus.). 160p. (gr. 6-6). lib. bdg. 41.21 *(978-0-7614-1696-8(X)*, 589ebcab-94a9-4be4-878f-c6e6d48f57b0) Cavendish Square Publishing LLC.

Schumacher, Cassandra. Work, Exchange, & Technology in the United States, 1 vol. 2018. (Discovering America: an Exceptional Nation Ser.). (ENG.). 112p. (gr. 7-7). lib. bdg. 44.50 *(978-1-5026-4262-2(X)*, 68c43089-e510-4788-8d68-a2e259efe030) Cavendish Square Publishing LLC.

Smith, Robert W. Spotlight on America: Industrial Revolution. 2006. (ENG., Illus.). 48p. pap. 9.99 *(978-1-4206-3220-0(5))* Teacher Created Resources, Inc.

South, Victor. America in the 20th Century (1913-1999) 2013. (Illus.). 48p. (J). *(978-1-4222-2410-6(4))*; *(978-1-4222-2396-3(5))* Mason Crest.

Uhl, Xina M. & Brezina, Corona. A Primary Source Investigation of the Industrial Revolution, 1 vol. 2018. (Uncovering American History Ser.). (ENG.). 64p. (gr. 6-6). pap. 13.95 *(978-1-5081-8414-0(3)*, 83f51806-715a-4ad5-9d54-a97e6e84186a) Rosen Publishing Group, Inc., The.

Wolfe, James. The Industrial Revolution: Steam & Steel, 1 vol. 2015. (Age of Revolution Ser.). (ENG., Illus.). 184p. (J). (gr. 9-10). 37.82 *(978-1-68048-026-9(X)*, 97c81415-6af6-43ec-b00f-25d78064eb73, Britannica Educational Publishing) Rosen Publishing Group, Inc., The.

World Book, Inc. Staff, contrib. by. The Great Depression. 2010. (J). *(978-0-7166-1505-7(3))* World Bk., Inc.

UNITED STATES—ECONOMIC POLICY

Brezina, Corona. America's Recession: The Effects of the Economic Downturn, 1 vol. 2011. (Headlines! Ser.). (ENG.). 64p. (YA). (gr. 6-6). lib. bdg. 37.13 *(978-1-4488-1296-7(8)*, b7067ab9-4598-4b7b-8396-3930d51910a9) Rosen Publishing Group, Inc., The.

—How Stimulus Plans Work, 1 vol. 2010. (Real World Economics Ser.). (ENG., Illus.). 80p. (YA). (gr. 6-6). lib. bdg. 38.47 *(978-1-4358-9464-8(2)*, 6e1af4d0-2dba-4d5f-a2f8-c276576b2d28) Rosen Publishing Group, Inc., The.

Crayton, Lisa A. & Nagle, Jeanne. Recession: What It Is & How It Works, 1 vol. 2015. (Economics in the 21st Century Ser.). (ENG., Illus.). 96p. (gr. 8-8). lib. bdg. 36.27 *(978-0-7660-7356-2(4)*, c457106e-a13c-4432-a6fe-ebafeb656cf9) Enslow Publishing, LLC.

Frazer, Coral Celeste. Economic Inequality: The American Dream under Siege. 2018. (ENG., Illus.). 128p. (YA). (gr. 6-12). lib. bdg. 37.32 *(978-1-5124-3107-0(9)*, 1df8e5fe-2f84-4f9e-b2a7-d1561a2e7642, Twenty-First Century Bks.) Lerner Publishing Group.

Hamilton, Jill, ed. The U. S. Economy, 1 vol. 2010. (Introducing Issues with Opposing Viewpoints Ser.). (ENG.). 144p. (gr. 7-10). 43.63 *(978-0-7377-4945-8(8)*, 92335147-89bf-4968-bdd9-38d59ba24ca3, Greenhaven Publishing) Greenhaven Publishing LLC.

Haugen, David M., ed. Should the Federal Government Bail Out Private Industry?, 1 vol. 2009. (At Issue Ser.). (ENG., Illus.). 120p. (gr. 10-12). 41.03 *(978-0-7377-4656-3(4)*, 4ce095d2-6009-435d-980e-7cdc4c7a1eec); pap. 28.80 *(978-0-7377-4657-0(2)*, 29e464f4-eb7a-4c79-93eb-170e22abeb4f) Greenhaven Publishing LLC. (Greenhaven Publishing).

Hunnicutt, Susan C., ed. The Federal Budget Deficit, 1 vol. 2010. (At Issue Ser.). (ENG., Illus.). 104p. (gr. 10-12). pap. 28.80 *(978-0-7377-4686-0(6)*, 5961e9e8-625a-4566-8d04-07531f0e066e, Greenhaven Publishing) Greenhaven Publishing LLC.

Miller, Debra A., ed. The U. S. Economy, 1 vol. 2010. (Current Controversies Ser.). (ENG., Illus.). 192p. (gr. 10-12). pap. 33.00 *(978-0-7377-4712-6(9)*, cd52f3de-37c7-4626-97fc-d2934104c4f6, Greenhaven Publishing) Greenhaven Publishing LLC.

Moriarty, J. T. The Rise of American Capitalism: The Growth of American Banks. 2009. (America's Industrial Society in the 19th Century Ser.). 32p. (gr. 4-4). 47.90 *(978-1-61511-346-0(0))* Rosen Publishing Group, Inc., The.

Randolph, Ryan. Alexander Hamilton's Economic Plan: Solving Problems in America's New Economy. 2009. (Life in the New American Nation Ser.). 32p. (gr. 4-4). 47.90 *(978-1-61514-276-7(2))* Rosen Publishing Group, Inc., The.

Schumacher, Cassandra. Work, Exchange, & Technology in the United States, 1 vol. 2018. (Discovering America: an Exceptional Nation Ser.). (ENG.). 112p. (gr. 7-7). lib. bdg. 44.50 *(978-1-5026-4262-2(X)*, 68c43089-e510-4788-8d68-a2e259efe030) Cavendish Square Publishing LLC.

UNITED STATES—EMIGRATION AND IMMIGRATION

Abramovitz, Melissa. Debates on 20th-Century Immigration. 2018. (Debating History Ser.). (ENG.). 80p. (YA). (gr. 6-12). 39.93 *(978-1-68282-369-9(5))* ReferencePoint Pr., Inc.

Ada, Alma Flor & Campoy, F. Isabel. Yes! We Are Latinos: Poems & Prose about the Latino Experience. Diaz, David, illus. 2016. 96p. (J). (gr. 5). pap. 9.95 *(978-1-58089-549-1(2))* Charlesbridge Publishing, Inc.

Allport, Alan & Ferguson, John E. Immigration Policy. 2nd rev. ed. 2009. (Point/Counterpoint: Issues in Contemporary American Society Ser.). (ENG., Illus.). 152p. (gr. 9-18). 35.00 *(978-1-60413-126-0(8)*, P161422, Facts On File) Infobase Holdings, Inc.

Alva, Alfredo & Mills, Deborah. La Frontera. Navarro, Claudia, illus. 2018. (ENG.). 48p. (J). (gr. k-3). pap. 10.99 *(978-1-78285-392-3(8))*; 17.99 *(978-1-78285-388-6(X))* Barefoot Bks., Inc.

Alvarez, Pilar. New Jobs, New Opportunities: British Immigrants Arrive in America (1830s-1890s), 1 vol., 1. 2015. (Spotlight on Immigration & Migration Ser.). (ENG., Illus.). 24p. (J). (gr. 4-5). pap. 11.00 *(978-1-5081-4090-0(1)*, eb60d18d-449c-4478-bf7f-96774736908a, PowerKids Pr.) Rosen Publishing Group, Inc., The.

Ambrosek, Renee. America Debates United States Policy on Immigration. (America Debates Ser.). 64p. (gr. 5-6). 2009. 58.50 *(978-1-61511-335-4(5)*, Rosen Reference) 2007. (ENG., Illus.). (YA). lib. bdg. 37.13 *(978-1-4042-1924-3(2)*, f0cb50ae-84e2-4ebc-b1bd-6c1f343be16c) Rosen Publishing Group, Inc., The.

The American Mosaic: Immigration Today. 2014. (American Mosaic: Immigration Today Ser.). 24p. (J). (gr. 3-6). pap. 49.50 *(978-1-4777-7248-5(0)*, PowerKids Pr.) Rosen Publishing Group, Inc., The.

American Voices (Group 1), 10 vols., Set. 2003. (American Voices From Ser.). (ENG.). (gr. 6-6). 247.26 *(978-0-7614-1200-7(X)*, db1d9781-5a26-4827-8257-0a02ca9a1822, Cavendish Square) Cavendish Square Publishing LLC.

Amidon Lusted, Marcia, ed. Sanctuary Cities, 1 vol. 2018. (Opposing Viewpoints Ser.). (ENG.). 200p. (J). (gr. 10-12). 50.43 *(978-1-5345-0299-4(8)*, eb469db0-2a4d-4d4f-b4a0-6d16bd998ae1) Greenhaven Publishing LLC.

Anderson, Dale. Chinese Americans, 1 vol. 2006. (World Almanac(r) Library of American Immigration Ser.). (ENG., Illus.). 48p. (gr. 5-8). pap. 15.05 *(978-0-8368-7321-4(1)*, 0ef9c18c-82a1-4319-b8c1-6e629f084409); lib. bdg. 33.67 *(978-0-8368-7308-5(4)*, f0c7df90-7d9f-4743-9dc5-8372d491438c) Stevens, Gareth Publishing LLLP. (Gareth Stevens Secondary Library).

—Cuban Americans, 1 vol. 2006. (World Almanac(r) Library of American Immigration Ser.). (ENG., Illus.). 48p. (gr. 5-8). pap. 15.05 *(978-0-8368-7322-1(X)*, 4e492dff-e6e3-440b-81b4-8e1eddb2ced2); lib. bdg. 33.67 *(978-0-8368-7309-2(2)*, 4c3a5a58-9e38-46b0-968e-81d8a8682045) Stevens, Gareth Publishing LLLP. (Gareth Stevens Secondary Library).

—Italian Americans, 1 vol. 2006. (World Almanac(r) Library of American Immigration Ser.). (ENG.). 48p. (gr. 5-8). pap. 15.05 *(978-0-8368-7325-2(4)*, ff851c5b-f987-46fa-b281-a195b067092a); (Illus.). lib. bdg. 33.67 *(978-0-8368-7312-2(2)*, be362480-62af-4ca1-ac93-6e77feffe91b) Stevens, Gareth Publishing LLLP. (Gareth Stevens Secondary Library).

—Japanese Americans, 1 vol. 2006. (World Almanac(r) Library of American Immigration Ser.). (ENG., Illus.). 48p. (gr. 5-8). pap. 15.05 *(978-0-8368-7326-9(2)*, c3bed7bf-7f23-46f4-beb0-af9e54a3db86); lib. bdg. 33.67 *(978-0-8368-7313-9(0),* 2a4e375d-d010-4e4c-89f2-0d3f9baf9185) Stevens, Gareth Publishing LLLP. (Gareth Stevens Secondary Library).

—Polish Americans, 1 vol. 2006. (World Almanac(r) Library of American Immigration Ser.). (ENG., Illus.). 48p. (gr. 5-8). pap. 15.05 *(978-0-8368-7330-6(0),* 054bfccb-8f9e-435c-abec-2ea4ff185456); lib. bdg. 33.67 *(978-0-8368-7317-7(3),* 2426dbf8-898d-490d-aed2-d3c12b595460) Stevens, Gareth Publishing LLLP. (Gareth Stevens Secondary Library).

Anderson, Marilyn. Arab Americans, 1 vol. 2006. (World Almanac(r) Library of American Immigration Ser.). (ENG., Illus.). 48p. (gr. 5-8). pap. 15.05 *(978-0-8368-7320-7(3),* 1db781f8-aab1-4fc7-9495-d653d8064c92); lib. bdg. 33.67 *(978-0-8368-7307-8(6),* cd444ecb-c2bd-4ee2-8554-9fc83be1d707) Stevens, Gareth Publishing LLLP. (Gareth Stevens Secondary Library).

Anderson, Stuart, ed. The Changing Face of America: Immigration Since 1965, 16 vols., Set. 2003. (Illus.). 112p. (YA). lib. bdg. *(978-1-59084-679-7(6))* Mason Crest.

Arnéz, Lynda. My Journey Through Ellis Island, 1 vol. 2015. (My Place in History Ser.). (ENG., Illus.). 24p. (J). (gr. 2-3). 24.27 *(978-1-4824-4000-3(8),* 7e8cdeef-4b14-4e5e-aaa5-5b5f0663efe9) Stevens, Gareth Publishing LLLP.

Aykroyd, Clarissa. Refugees. 2005. (Changing Face of North America Ser.). (Illus.). 112p. (YA). lib. bdg. 24.95 *(978-1-59084-692-6(3))* Mason Crest.

Bailey, Diane. The African Family Table, Vol. 11. 2018. (Connecting Cultures Through Family & Food Ser.). (Illus.). 64p. (J). (gr. 7). 31.93 *(978-1-4222-4042-7(8))* Mason Crest.

—The Greek Family Table, Vol. 11. 2018. (Connecting Cultures Through Family & Food Ser.). (Illus.). 64p. (J). (gr. 7). 31.93 *(978-1-4222-4044-1(4))* Mason Crest.

—The Italian Family Table, Vol. 11. 2018. (Connecting Cultures Through Family & Food Ser.). (Illus.). 64p. (J). (gr. 7). 31.93 *(978-1-4222-4046-5(0))* Mason Crest.

Baker, Brynn. Life in America: Comparing Immigrant Experiences. 2015. (U. S. Immigration in The 1900s Ser.). (ENG., Illus.). 48p. (J). (gr. 3-6). pap. 8.95 *(978-1-4914-4174-9(7),* 128663, Capstone Pr.) Capstone.

Baker, Brynn & Kravitz, Danny. U. S. Immigration in The 1900s. 2015. (U. S. Immigration in The 1900s Ser.). (ENG.). 48p. (J). (gr. 3-4). 123.29 *(978-1-4914-6658-2(8),* 22902, Stone Arch Bks.) Capstone.

Barnett, Tracy. Immigration from South America. 2005. (Changing Face of North America Ser.). (Illus.). 112p. (J). lib. bdg. 24.95 *(978-1-59084-687-2(7))* Mason Crest.

Benoit, Peter. Cornerstones of Freedom, Third Series: Immigration. 2012. (Cornerstones of Freedom, Third Ser.). (ENG., Illus.). 64p. (J). (gr. 4-6). lib. bdg. 30.00 *(978-0-531-23057-2(0),* Children's Pr.) Scholastic Library Publishing.

Benson, Sonia. U. S. Immigration & Migration: Almanac, 2.0. 2004. (US Immigration & Migration Reference Library). (ENG., Illus.). 685p. (J). 191.00 *(978-0-7876-7732-9(9),* UXL) Cengage Gale.

—U.S. Immigration & Migration Almanac, 2 vols. 2004. (U. S. Immigration & Migration Reference Library). (Illus.). (J). *(978-0-7876-7566-0(0)); (978-0-7876-7567-7(9))* Cengage Gale. (UXL).

Bernay, Emma & Berne, Emma Carlson. Immigrants from Mexico & Central America. 2018. (Immigration Today Ser.). (ENG., Illus.). 32p. (J). (gr. 3-6). pap. 7.95 *(978-1-5435-1387-5(5),* 137792); lib. bdg. 27.99 *(978-1-5435-1383-7(2),* 137788) Capstone. (Capstone Pr.).

Bjorklund, Ruth. Immigration, 1 vol. 2012. (Debating the Issues Ser.). (ENG.). 64p. (gr. 6-6). 35.50 *(978-0-7614-4973-7(6),* 2880ba49-195a-4798-946d-7004d07cd62c) Cavendish Square Publishing LLC.

Bliss, John. Nineteenth Century Migration to America, 1 vol. 2011. (Children's True Stories: Migration Ser.). (ENG.). 32p. (J). (gr. 3-5). pap. 8.29 *(978-1-4109-4080-3(2),* 114618, Raintree) Capstone.

Broida, Marian. Projects about Nineteenth-Century European Immigrants, 1 vol. 2007. (Hands-On History Ser.). (ENG., Illus.). 48p. (gr. 3-3). lib. bdg. 34.07 *(978-0-7614-1980-8(2),* d27dec08-f4be-42aa-a850-1c326d5708f6) Cavendish Square Publishing LLC.

Bryan, Nichol. Greek Americans, 1 vol. 2004. (One Nation Set 2 Ser.). (ENG.). 32p. (gr. k-6). 27.07 *(978-1-59197-527-4(1),* Checkerboard Library) ABDO Publishing Co.

—Japanese Americans, 1 vol. 2004. (One Nation Set 2 Ser.). (ENG.). 32p. (gr. k-6). 27.07 *(978-1-59197-529-8(8),* Checkerboard Library) ABDO Publishing Co.

Budhos, Marina. Remix: Conversations with Immigrant Teenagers. 2007. (ENG., Illus.). 158p. (gr. 9-12). pap. 22.00 *(978-1-55635-610-0(2),* Resource Pubns.(OR)) Wipf & Stock Pubs.

Burgan, Michael. Ellis Island: An Interactive History Adventure, 1 vol. 2013. (You Choose: History Ser.). (ENG.). 112p. (J). (gr. 3-7). pap. 6.95 *(978-1-4765-3606-4(6),* 123612); (Illus.). 32.65 *(978-1-4765-0253-3(6),* 122323) Capstone.

Byers, Ann. Immigration: Interpreting the Constitution, 1 vol. 2014. (Understanding the United States Constitution Ser.). (ENG.). 112p. (YA). (gr. 7-7). 38.80 *(978-1-4777-7512-7(9),* 9923eb4a-70b3-4cfc-8322-494d357b3bb7) Rosen Publishing Group, Inc., The.

Campbell, Wallis. Angel Island. 2006. (Illus.). 48p. (J). pap. *(978-1-59034-808-6(7))* Mondo Publishing.

Carser, A. R. US Immigration Policy. 2017. (Special Reports Set 3 Ser.). (ENG.). 112p. (J). (gr. 6-12). lib. bdg. 41.36 *(978-1-5321-1337-6(4),* 27545, Essential Library) ABDO Publishing Co.

Cherenfant, Sabine. How Vietnamese Immigrants Made America Home, 1 vol. 2018. (Coming to America: the History of Immigration to the United States Ser.). (ENG.). 80p. (gr. 6-6). 38.80 *(978-1-5081-8138-5(1),* 4adae765-75b5-4f62-9976-3fb3d914a9e7) Rosen Publishing Group, Inc., The.

Cheung, Shu Pui, et al. Walking on Solid Ground. Wei, Deborah & Kodish, Debora, eds. Chau, Ming, photos by. 2004. (ENG & CHI., Illus.). 64p. (J). pap. 12.95 *(978-0-9644937-4-2(8),* 09644937-4-8) Philadelphia Folklore Project.

Ciongoli, A. Kenneth & Parini, Jay. Passage to Liberty: The Story of Italian Immigration & the Rebirth of America. 2003. (Illus.). 32p. (YA). (gr. 9-12). 30.00 *(978-0-7567-6841-6(1))* DIANE Publishing Co.

Conley, Kate A. The Puerto Rican Americans. 2003. (Immigrants in America Ser.). (ENG., Illus.). 112p. (J). (gr. 4-7). lib. bdg. 30.85 *(978-1-59018-432-5(7),* Lucent Bks.) Cengage Gale.

Coy, John. Their Great Gift: Courage, Sacrifice, & Hope in a New Land. Huie, Wing Young, photos by. 2016. (ENG., Illus.). 32p. (J). (gr. k-3). 19.99 *(978-1-4677-8054-4(5),* 1fba5c09-db9b-4e2d-a555-f3d28b919e24); E-Book 30.65 *(978-1-4677-9756-6(1))* Lerner Publishing Group. (Carolrhoda Bks.).

Cunningham, Anne, Vll & Cunningham, Anne, eds. Deporting Immigrants, 1 vol. 2017. (Current Controversies Ser.). (ENG.). 200p. (J). (gr. 10-12). 48.03 *(978-1-5345-0234-5(3),* 4ee65ac5-ae85-4744-a9aa-804c86344b3d) Greenhaven Publishing LLC.

Currie, Stephen. Undocumented Immigrant Youth. 2016. (ENG.). 80p. (J). (gr. 5-12). lib. bdg. *(978-1-60152-980-0(5))* ReferencePoint Pr., Inc.

D'Alessandro, Cathy. La Historia de la Inmigración de EE. UU: Datos (the History of U. S. Immigration: Data) (Spanish Version) (Grade 2) rev. ed. 2018. (Mathematics in the Real World Ser.). (SPA., Illus.). 32p. (J). (gr. 2-3). pap. 10.99 *(978-1-4258-2873-8(6))* Teacher Created Materials, Inc.

—The History of U. S. Immigration: Data (Grade 2) 2018. (Mathematics in the Real World Ser.). (ENG., Illus.). 32p. (J). (gr. 2-3). pap. 10.99 *(978-1-4258-5756-1(6))* Teacher Created Materials, Inc.

Dávila, Lourdes. How Puerto Ricans Made the US Mainland Home, 1 vol. 2018. (Coming to America: the History of Immigration to the United States Ser.). (ENG.). 80p. (gr. 6-6). 38.80 *(978-1-5081-8135-4(7),* e32362a9-f271-4eaf-96ce-c1cc56402619); pap. 16.88 *(978-1-5081-8136-1(5),* 8686813d-d482-4b3b-b30c-811e601cf537) Rosen Publishing Group, Inc., The. (Rosen Central).

Demuth, Patricia Brennan. What Was Ellis Island? 2014. (What Was... Ser.). lib. bdg. 16.00 *(978-0-606-34156-1(0))* Turtleback.

Denton, Michelle. Immigration Issues in America, 1 vol. 2017. (Hot Topics Ser.). (ENG.). 112p. (J). (gr. 7-7). lib. bdg. 41.03 *(978-1-5345-6151-9(X),* 9a17cac2-4cd8-4589-933f-d74db3cfe7c6, Lucent Pr.) Greenhaven Publishing LLC.

DePietro, Frank. Latino Americans & Immigration Laws. 2013. (Illus.). 64p. pap. *(978-1-4222-2338-3(8))* Mason Crest.

—Latino Americans & Immigration Laws. Limón, José E., ed. 2012. (Hispanic Americans: Major Minority Ser.). (Illus.). 64p. (J). (gr. 4). 22.95 *(978-1-4222-2321-5(3))* Mason Crest.

—South American Immigrants. 2013. (Illus.). 64p. (J). pap. *(978-1-4222-2346-8(9))* Mason Crest.

—South American Immigrants. Limón, José E., ed. 2012. (Hispanic Americans: Major Minority Ser.). (Illus.). 64p. (J). (gr. 4). 22.95 *(978-1-4222-2329-1(9))* Mason Crest.

DiConsiglio, John. Young Americans: Tales of Teenage Immigrants. 2005. (Illus.). 43p. *(978-0-439-12405-8(0))* Scholastic, Inc.

Doak, Robin Santos. Indian Americans. 2007. (American Immigrants Ser.). (Illus.). 48p. (J). (gr. 4-6). lib. bdg. *(978-1-60044-612-2(4))* Rourke Educational Media.

Eboch, M. M., ed. Immigration & Travel Restrictions, 1 vol. 2018. (Introducing Issues with Opposing Viewpoints Ser.). (ENG.). 120p. (gr. 7-10). lib. bdg. 43.63 *(978-1-5345-0423-3(0),* adb38db6-c1ae-4586-b416-aad005da478a, Greenhaven Publishing) Greenhaven Publishing LLC.

Egendorf, Laura K. Immigration. (History of Issues Ser.). 192-240p. (gr. 10-12). pap. 23.70 *(978-0-7377-2872-9(8),* Greenhaven Pr., Inc.) Cengage Gale.

Ferry, Joseph. Vietnamese Immigration. 2005. (Changing Face of North America Ser.). (Illus.). 112p. (YA). lib. bdg. 24.95 *(978-1-59084-682-7(6))* Mason Crest.

Fields, Julianna. First-Generation Immigrant Families. 2010. (Changing Face of Modern Families Ser.). (Illus.). 64p. (YA). (gr. 6-18). lib. bdg. 22.95 *(978-1-4222-1499-2(0))* Mason Crest.

Figorito, Marcus. Ellis Island: Welcome to America. (Reading Room Collection 1 Ser.). 16p. (gr. 2-3). 2009. 37.50 *(978-1-60851-943-9(0),* PowerKids Pr.) 2005. (ENG., Illus.). (J). lib. bdg. 22.27 *(978-1-4042-3347-8(4),* 64e18ac2-8219-4099-87a9-31e17daba597) Rosen Publishing Group, Inc., The.

Freedman, Russell. Angel Island: Gateway to Gold Mountain. 2016. lib. bdg. 22.10 *(978-0-606-39677-6(2))* Turtleback.

—Immigrant Kids. 2014. (ENG.). 80p. (J). (gr. k-3). 13.24 *(978-1-63245-247-4(2))* Lectorum Pubns., Inc.

Gaines, Jena. Haitian Immigration. 2003. (Changing Face of North America Ser.). (Illus.). 112p. (J). lib. bdg. *(978-1-59084-691-9(5))* Mason Crest.

Gallagher, Jim. Refugees & Asylum. 2020. (ENG.). 80p. (YA). (gr. 6-12). 41.27 *(978-1-68282-767-3(4))* ReferencePoint Pr., Inc.

Gallegos, Yuliana. Mi Sueno de America/My American Dream. Baeza, Georgina, tr. 2009. (ENG & SPA., Illus.). 55p. (J). (gr. 4-7). pap. 9.95 *(978-1-55885-534-2(3),* Piñata Books) Arte Publico Pr.

Gelletly, LeeAnne. Mexican Immigration. 2005. (Changing Face of North America Ser.). (Illus.). 112p. (YA). lib. bdg. 24.95 *(978-1-59084-680-3(X))* Mason Crest.

Gerdes, Louise I., ed. Should the U. S. Close Its Borders?, 1 vol. 2014. (At Issue Ser.). (ENG., Illus.). 152p. (gr. 10-12). pap. 28.80 *(978-0-7377-4690-7(4),* 7ea8647a-c7e4-48e2-beac-c61bb9d493b2, Greenhaven Publishing) Greenhaven Publishing LLC.

Gitlin, Martin, ed. The Border Wall with Mexico, 1 vol. 2017. (Current Controversies Ser.). (ENG.). 144p. (J). (gr. 10-12). pap. 33.00 *(978-1-5345-0090-7(1),* 401111fd-516f-4e7e-b978-8802fb4b0645); lib. bdg. 48.03 *(978-1-5345-0085-3(5),* 73c9cd1f-24fe-49d4-8804-70f4d202ce1b) Greenhaven Publishing LLC.

Green, Robert. Immigration. 2008. (21st Century Skills Library: Global Perspectives Ser.). (ENG., Illus.). 32p. (gr. 4-8). lib. bdg. 32.07 *(978-1-60279-128-2(7),* 200101) Cherry Lake Publishing.

Griffin, Brett. American Migration & Settlement, 1 vol. 2018. (Discovering America: an Exceptional Nation Ser.). (ENG.). 112p. (gr. 7-7). lib. bdg. 44.50 *(978-1-5026-4265-3(4),* 12165498-85f1-4377-9ff8-b318aa021305) Cavendish Square Publishing LLC.

Gunderson, Jessica, et al. Immigration Today. 2018. (Immigration Today Ser.). (ENG.). 32p. (J). (gr. 3-6). 119.96 *(978-1-5435-1401-8(4),* 27977, Capstone Pr.) Capstone.

Heaney, Shane. The Scotch-Irish Immigration to America: Economic Hardship in Ireland (1603-1775), 1 vol., 1. 2015. (Spotlight on Immigration & Migration Ser.). (ENG., Illus.). 24p. (J). (gr. 4-5). pap. 11.00 *(978-1-5081-4095-5(2),* d7652452-6ade-44de-81c0-6ea0fecae497, PowerKids Pr.) Rosen Publishing Group, Inc., The.

Heckt, Jackie. Immigration to Colonial America. 2016. (Spotlight on Immigration & Migration Ser.). (ENG.). 24p. (J). (gr. 4-7). 21.80 *(978-1-5311-8873-3(7))* Perfection Learning Corp.

—Immigration to Colonial America, 1 vol., 1. 2015. (Spotlight on Immigration & Migration Ser.). (ENG., Illus.). 24p. (J). (gr. 4-5). pap. 11.00 *(978-1-5081-4081-8(2),* d165bbd7-be03-4b72-b3bb-054d7b4c213c, PowerKids Pr.) Rosen Publishing Group, Inc., The.

Henzel, Cynthia Kennedy. Mexican Immigrants: In Their Shoes. 2017. (Immigrant Experiences Ser.). (ENG.). 32p. (J). (gr. 3-6). lib. bdg. 35.64 *(978-1-5038-2030-2(0),* 211850) Child's World, Inc, The.

—Vietnamese Immigrants: In Their Shoes. 2017. (Immigrant Experiences Ser.). (ENG.). 32p. (J). (gr. 3-6). lib. bdg. 35.64 *(978-1-5038-2032-6(7),* 211852) Child's World, Inc, The.

Hernandez, Roger E. Immigration. 2008. (Gallup Major Trends & Events Ser.). (Illus.). 120p. (YA). (gr. 7-18). lib. bdg. 22.95 *(978-1-59084-965-1(5))* Mason Crest.

Hernandez, Romel. Immigration from Central America. 2005. (Changing Face of North America Ser.). (Illus.). 112p. (YA). lib. bdg. 24.95 *(978-1-59084-688-9(5))* Mason Crest.

Hicks, Terry Allan. Ellis Island, 1 vol. (Symbols of America Ser.). (ENG., Illus.). 40p. (gr. 3-3). 2008. pap. 9.23 *(978-0-7614-3377-4(5),* 4339dc1b-d00a-43f2-8859-40a65a5abe8d, Cavendish Square) 2007. lib. bdg. 32.64 *(978-0-7614-2134-4(3),* eadd5cdd-45bd-4dab-99b1-a60a5a76c2ba) Cavendish Square Publishing LLC.

Holt, Amy. Should the United States Have Open Borders?, 1 vol. 2020. (Points of View Ser.). (ENG.). 24p. (gr. 3-3). pap. 9.25 *(978-1-5345-3428-5(8),* e865d565-cc6f-4e5c-96b4-0284afffa403, KidHaven Publishing) Greenhaven Publishing LLC.

Honovich, Nancy. Immigration from the Former Yugoslavia. 2005. (Changing Face of North America Ser.). (Illus.). 112p. (YA). lib. bdg. 24.95 *(978-1-59084-690-2(7))* Mason Crest.

Hossell, Karen Price. The Irish Americans. 2003. (Immigrants in America Ser.). (ENG., Illus.). 112p. (J). 30.85 *(978-1-56006-752-8(7),* Lucent Bks.) Cengage Gale.

Houghton, Gillian. Ellis Island: A Primary Source History of an Immigrant's Arrival in America. (Primary Sources in American History Ser.). 64p. (gr. 5-8). 2009. 58.50 *(978-1-60851-489-2(7))* 2004. (ENG., Illus.). (YA). lib. bdg. 37.13 *(978-0-8239-4003-5(9),* 588f893f-b7ee-49db-ada7-000d79072549, Rosen Reference) Rosen Publishing Group, Inc., The.

Howell, Sara. Famous Immigrants & Their Stories. 2014. (American Mosaic: Immigration Today Ser.). 24p. (J). (gr. 3-6). pap. 49.50 *(978-1-4777-6652-1(9))* Rosen Publishing Group, Inc., The.

—First-Generation Americans. 2014. (American Mosaic: Immigration Today Ser.). (Illus.). 24p. (J). (gr. 3-6). pap. 49.50 *(978-1-4777-6651-4(0),* PowerKids Pr.) Rosen Publishing Group, Inc., The.

—Immigrants' Rights, Citizens' Rights. 2014. (American Mosaic: Immigration Today Ser.). 24p. (J). (gr. 3-6). pap. 49.50 *(978-1-4777-6647-7(2),* PowerKids Pr.) Rosen Publishing Group, Inc., The.

—Inmigrantes Famosos y Sus Historias, 1 vol. 2014. (Mosaico Americano: la Inmigración Hoy en día (the American Mosaic: Immigration Today) Ser.). (SPA., Illus.). 24p. (J). (gr. 2-3). lib. bdg. 25.27 *(978-1-4777-6803-7(3),* 35d72ae4-9280-43d9-a82b-0c4316077526, PowerKids Pr.) Rosen Publishing Group, Inc., The.

—Los Derechos de Los Inmigrantes, Los Derechos de Los Ciudadanos, 1 vol. 2014. (Mosaico Americano: la Inmigración Hoy en día (the American Mosaic: Immigration Today) Ser.). (SPA., Illus.). 24p. (J). (gr. 2-3). lib. bdg. 25.27 *(978-1-4777-6819-8(X),* 17a43118-2698-4e14-a621-18a99be21637, PowerKids Pr.) Rosen Publishing Group, Inc., The.

—Los Inmigrantes Indocumentados. 2014. (Mosaico Americano: la Inmigración Hoy en día (the American Mosaic: Immigration Today) Ser.). (SPA., Illus.). 24p. (J). (gr. 3-6). pap. 49.50 *(978-1-4777-6811-2(4),* PowerKids Pr.) Rosen Publishing Group, Inc., The.

—Los Refugiados, 1 vol. 2014. (Mosaico Americano: la Inmigración Hoy en día (the American Mosaic: Immigration Today) Ser.). (SPA., Illus.). 24p. (J). (gr. 2-3). pap. 9.25 *(978-1-4777-6817-4(3),* c17f5b0b-3a11-4297-8652-738269250597, PowerKids Pr.) Rosen Publishing Group, Inc., The.

—Primera Generación de Estadounidenses, 1 vol. 2014. (Mosaico Americano: la Inmigración Hoy en día (the American Mosaic: Immigration Today) Ser.). (SPA., Illus.). 24p. (J). (gr. 2-3). lib. bdg. 25.27 *(978-1-4777-6807-5(6),* 0ea0b13b-2bcd-4d43-ba25-fd010ab65d5c, PowerKids Pr.) Rosen Publishing Group, Inc., The.

—Refugees. 2014. (American Mosaic: Immigration Today Ser.). (Illus.). 24p. (J). (gr. 3-6). pap. 49.50 *(978-1-4777-6649-1(9),* PowerKids Pr.) Rosen Publishing Group, Inc., The.

—Undocumented Immigrants, 1 vol. 2014. (American Mosaic: Immigration Today Ser.). (Illus.). 24p. (J). (ENG.). (gr. 2-3). pap. 9.25 *(978-1-4777-6745-0(2),* bd602d04-bc73-461b-8e8f-43b0fd512283); (ENG., (gr. 2-3). lib. bdg. 25.27 *(978-1-4777-6744-3(4),* f94a61d1-752c-4f82-8a14-741be1c814c0); (gr. 3-6). pap. 49.50 *(978-1-4777-6650-7(2))* Rosen Publishing Group, Inc., The. (PowerKids Pr.).

Huddleston, Emma. Exploring Ellis Island. 2019. (Travel America's Landmarks Ser.). (ENG., Illus.). 32p. (J). (gr. 2-3). pap. 9.95 *(978-1-64185-851-9(6),* 1641858516, Focus Readers) North Star Editions.

Hulick, Kathryn. The Chinese Family Table, Vol. 11. 2018. (Connecting Cultures Through Family & Food Ser.). (Illus.). 64p. (J). (gr. 7). 31.93 *(978-1-4222-4043-4(6))* Mason Crest.

—The South American Family Table, Vol. 11. 2018. (Connecting Cultures Through Family & Food Ser.). (Illus.). 64p. (J). (gr. 7). 31.93 *(978-1-4222-4051-9(7))* Mason Crest.

Hutchison, Patricia. Somali Immigrants: In Their Shoes. 2017. (Immigrant Experiences Ser.). (ENG.). 32p. (J). (gr. 3-6). lib. bdg. 35.64 *(978-1-5038-2031-9(9),* 211851) Child's World, Inc, The.

Imery-Garcia, Ash. How Mexican Immigrants Made America Home, 1 vol. 2018. (Coming to America: the History of Immigration to the United States Ser.). (ENG., Illus.). 80p. (gr. 6-6). 38.80 *(978-1-5081-8132-3(2),* c9dcf589-ac41-4b34-b47d-9465179c9906, Rosen Reference) Rosen Publishing Group, Inc., The.

Ingram, Scott. Korean Americans, 1 vol. 2006. (World Almanac(r) Library of American Immigration Ser.). (ENG., Illus.). 48p. (gr. 5-8). pap. 15.05 *(978-0-8368-7328-3(9),* 949799b3-5bae-4eff-a35c-320c545fcf59); lib. bdg. 33.67 *(978-0-8368-7315-3(7),* 7cecba9a-484f-44d3-9be6-b91d8d57c354) Stevens, Gareth Publishing LLLP. (Gareth Stevens Secondary Library).

—Mexican Americans, 1 vol. 2006. (World Almanac(r) Library of American Immigration Ser.). (ENG., Illus.). 48p. (gr. 5-8). pap. 15.05 *(978-0-8368-7329-0(7),* d40b2e85-ab11-4281-aa0d-a22c10ac7b7a); lib. bdg. 33.67 *(978-0-8368-7316-0(5),* 0f6605b8-5111-41ba-b996-6c08c8917a7e) Stevens, Gareth Publishing LLLP. (Gareth Stevens Secondary Library).

—South Asian Americans, 1 vol. 2006. (World Almanac(r) Library of American Immigration Ser.). (ENG., Illus.). 48p. (gr. 5-8). pap. 15.05 *(978-0-8368-7331-3(9),* 38d1f389-eae9-4b2e-b568-2269b4a1090b); lib. bdg. 33.67 *(978-0-8368-7318-4(1),* b5047827-4f85-4426-a9d5-c3ce59559227) Stevens, Gareth Publishing LLLP. (Gareth Stevens Secondary Library).

Johnson, Cyree Jarelle. How Greek Immigrants Made America Home, 1 vol. 2018. (Coming to America: the History of Immigration to the United States Ser.). (ENG.). 80p. (gr. 6-6). 38.80 *(978-1-5081-8120-0(9),* 2a4b9041-1e81-471b-bb79-08e7690af017, Rosen Reference) Rosen Publishing Group, Inc., The.

Kallen, Stuart A. Twentieth-Century Immigration to the United States, 1 vol. 2007. (American History Ser.). (ENG.). 104p. (gr. 7-7). pap. 29.30 *(978-1-4205-0299-2(9),* 28582e36-f8d7-4902-b757-347575404fe3); (Illus.). lib. bdg. 41.03 *(978-1-59018-186-7(7),* 9336ed02-4fca-457d-bf11-8a7875c7769e) Greenhaven Publishing LLC. (Lucent Pr.).

Kallio, Jamie. Angel Island Immigration: A History Perspectives Book. 2014. (Perspectives Library). (ENG., Illus.). 32p. (J). (gr. 4-8). 32.07 *(978-1-63137-614-6(4),* 205239) Cherry Lake Publishing.

Kaur, Paramjot. How Indian Immigrants Made America Home, 1 vol. 2018. (Coming to America: the History of Immigration to the United States Ser.). (ENG.). 80p. (gr. 6-6). 38.80 *(978-1-5081-8123-1(3),* 45b581e6-de24-4fb5-b8d4-596949e597cd, Rosen Reference) Rosen Publishing Group, Inc., The.

Keedle, Jayne. West African Americans, 1 vol. 2010. (New Americans Ser.). (ENG., Illus.). 80p. (gr. 5-5). 38.36 *(978-0-7614-4313-1(4),* b668a8dd-906e-4423-9c2e-6805722b305a) Cavendish Square Publishing LLC.

Kim, Patti. Here I Am, 1 vol. Sánchez, Sonia, illus. 2014. (Na Ser.). (ENG.). 40p. (J). (gr. k-5). pap. 7.95 *(978-1-4795-1931-6(6),* 123634, Picture Window Bks.) Capstone.

Knight, Margy Burns. Who Belongs Here? An American Story. O'Brien, Anne Sibley, illus. 2004. 32p. 19.45 *(978-0-7569-2426-3(X))* Perfection Learning Corp.

Knight, Margy Burns, et al. Who Belongs Here? An American Story. 2nd ed. 2004. (Illus.). 40p. (gr. 3-8). 16.95 *(978-0-88448-110-2(7))* Tilbury Hse. Pubs.

Krasner, Barbara, ed. Human Migration, 1 vol. 2019. (Opposing Viewpoints Ser.). (ENG.). 200p. (gr. 10-12). pap. 34.80 *(978-1-5345-0598-8(9),* 8e749bf2-f41f-48f5-aa28-2df975360f13) Greenhaven Publishing LLC.

Kravitz, Danny. In the Shadow of Lady Liberty: Immigrant Stories from Ellis Island. 2015. (U. S. Immigration in The 1900s Ser.). (ENG., Illus.). 48p. (J). (gr. 3-6). pap. 8.95 *(978-1-4914-4173-2(9),* 128662, Capstone Pr.) Capstone.

—Journey to America: A Chronology of Immigration in the 1900s. 2015. (U. S. Immigration in The 1900s Ser.). (ENG., Illus.). 48p. (J). (gr. 3-6). pap. 8.95 *(978-1-4914-4172-5(0),* 128661) Capstone.

Kroll, Steven. Ellis Island: Doorway to Freedom. 2009. (ENG.). 31p. (J). 18.00 *(978-1-4379-6699-2(3))* DIANE Publishing Co.

Kuklin, Susan. We Are Here to Stay: Voices of Undocumented Young Adults. Kuklin, Susan, illus. 2019. (ENG., Illus.). 192p. (YA). (gr. 9). 21.99 *(978-0-7636-7884-5(8))* Candlewick Pr.

Kule, Elaine A. Beginning Again: Immigrating to America. Thermes, Jennifer, illus. 2006. 40p. *(978-1-59137-473-2(1))* Options Publishing.

La Bella, Laura. How Italian Immigrants Made America Home, 1 vol. 2018. (Coming to America: the History of Immigration to the United States Ser.). (ENG.). 80p. (gr. 6-6). 38.80 *(978-1-5081-8129-3(2),* 94167a54-d865-4db2-8433-f52f3143eee9) Rosen Publishing Group, Inc., The.

Landau, Elaine. Ellis Island (a True Book: American History) 2008. (True Book (Relaunch) Ser.). (ENG., Illus.). 48p. (J). (gr. 3-5). pap. 6.95 *(978-0-531-14781-8(9),* Children's Pr.) Scholastic Library Publishing.

Larson, Kirsten W. U. S. Border Patrol. 2016. (Protecting Our People Ser.). (ENG., Illus.). 32p. (J). (gr. 2-5). lib. bdg. 20.95 *(978-1-60753-986-5(1),* 15777) Amicus.

Lawrence, Riley. Who Are Immigrants?, 1 vol. 2018. (What's the Issue? Ser.). (ENG.). 24p. (gr. 3-3). 26.23 *(978-1-5345-2579-5(3),*

1d393064-3f6a-4f64-9f73-74037738cfac, KidHaven Publishing) Greenhaven Publishing LLC.

Lemke, Donald B. The Schoolchildren's Blizzard. 2007. (Disasters in History Ser.). (ENG., Illus.). 32p. (J). (gr. 3-9). 31.32 (978-1-4296-0157-3(4), 94140, Capstone Pr.) Capstone.

Levy, Janey. Illegal Immigration & Amnesty: Open Borders & National Security, 1 vol. 2010. (In the News Ser.). (ENG., Illus.). 64p. (YA). (gr. 6-6). lib. bdg. 37.13 (978-1-4358-3583-2(2), abfac7e0-03a2-401d-a399-95b132c4f399) Rosen Publishing Group, Inc., The.

Life as a Syrian American: Set, 12 vols. 2017. (One Nation for All: Immigrants in the United States Ser.). (ENG.). (J). (gr. 4-5). lib. bdg. 167.58 (978-1-5081-6260-5(3), e6316e9a-ce05-4fc5-991b-81a6823579bd, PowerKids Pr.) Rosen Publishing Group, Inc., The.

Lingen, Marissa. Chinese Immigration. 2005. (Changing Face of North America Ser.). (Illus.). 112p. (YA). lib. bdg. 24.95 (978-1-59084-694-0(X)) Mason Crest.

Lu, Georgina W. S. How Chinese Immigrants Made America Home, 1 vol. 2018. (Coming to America: the History of Immigration to the United States Ser.). (ENG.). 80p. (gr. 6-6). 38.80 (978-1-5081-8117-0(9), e63fbb1f-2e3a-405b-a836-dc2bf25d9ace, Rosen Reference) Rosen Publishing Group, Inc., The.

MacCarald, Clara. Irish Immigrants: In Their Shoes. 2017. (Immigrant Experiences Ser.). (ENG.). 32p. (J). (gr. 3-6). lib. bdg. 35.64 (978-1-5038-2028-9(9), 211847) Child's World, Inc, The.

—Japanese Immigrants: In Their Shoes. 2017. (Immigrant Experiences Ser.). (ENG.). 32p. (J). (gr. 3-6). lib. bdg. 35.64 (978-1-5038-2027-2(0), 211849) Child's World, Inc, The.

Maestro, Betsy. Coming to America. Ryan, Susannah, illus. 2015. 40p. pap. 9.00 (978-1-61003-543-9(7)) Center for the Collaborative Classroom.

Marcovitz, Hal. Ellis Island: The Story of a Gateway to America. Moreno, Barry, ed. 2014. (Patriotic Symbols of America Ser.: 20). 48p. (J). (gr. 4-18). lib. bdg. 20.95 (978-1-4222-3123-4(2)) Mason Crest.

Markham, Lauren. The Far Away Brothers (Adapted for Young Adults) Two Teenage Immigrants Making a Life in America. 2019. (ENG.). 288p. (YA). (gr. 7). 17.99 (978-1-9848-2977-1(7), Delacorte Pr.) Random Hse. Children's Bks.

Marroquin, Feliciano. The American Dream Journey. 2008. 96p. pap. 28.95 (978-1-59754-342-2(X)) Editorial Libros en Red.

Martin, Jennifer C. The Korean Americans. 2003. (Immigrants in America Ser.). (ENG., Illus.). 112p. (J). (gr. 4-7). lib. bdg. 30.85 (978-1-59018-079-2(8), Lucent Bks.) Cengage Gale.

Maury, Rob. Citizenship: Rights & Responsibilities. (Major American Immigration Ser.). (YA). 2010. (Illus.). 64p. (gr. 9-12). lib. bdg. 22.95 (978-1-4222-0618-8(1)) 2007. pap. 9.95 (978-1-4222-0685-0(8)) Mason Crest.

—Immigration from the Middle East. 2005. (Changing Face of North America Ser.). (Illus.). 112p. (YA). lib. bdg. 24.95 (978-1-59084-695-7(8)) Mason Crest.

McCoy, Erin L. & Perl, Lila. Immigration: Welcome or Not?, 1 vol. 2018. (Today's Debates Ser.). (ENG.). 144p. (gr. 7-7). pap. 22.16 (978-1-5026-4331-5(6), 3eb38cf9-f8c0-4cce-bfbc-4afd83997c5a) Cavendish Square Publishing LLC.

McDaniel, Jan. Indian Immigration. 2005. (Changing Face of North America Ser.). (Illus.). 112p. (YA). lib. bdg. 24.95 (978-1-59084-683-4(4)) Mason Crest.

McDaniel, Melissa. Ellis Island (Cornerstones of Freedom: Third Series) 3rd ed. 2011. (Cornerstones of Freedom. Third Ser.). (ENG., Illus.). 64p. (J). (gr. 4-6). pap. 8.95 (978-0-531-26556-7(0), Children's Pr.) Scholastic Library Publishing.

Merino, Noël, ed. Illegal Immigration, 1 vol. 2015. (Opposing Viewpoints Ser.). (ENG., Illus.). 216p. (J). (gr. 10-12). pap. 34.80 (978-0-7377-7273-9(5), 39415c0f-0be3-4dd2-aaf2-6e6b4c90d23a, Greenhaven Publishing) Greenhaven Publishing LLC.

—Illegal Immigration, 1 vol. 2015. (Opposing Viewpoints Ser.). (ENG., Illus.). 216p. (J). (gr. 10-12). lib. bdg. 50.43 (978-0-7377-7272-2(7), 02556da2-5040-4471-aff3-af986f9f2d7e, Greenhaven Publishing) Greenhaven Publishing LLC.

Merrick, Caitlin & Houghton, Gillian. A Primary Source Investigation of Ellis Island, 1 vol. 2015. (Uncovering American History Ser.). (ENG., Illus.). 64p. (J). (gr. 5-6). 36.13 (978-1-4994-3505-4(3), 844ef954-4392-4f62-9e3f-fb0d9ef80875, Rosen Central) Rosen Publishing Group, Inc., The.

Metz, Lorijo. Una Nacin de Inmigrantes / a Nation of Immigrants, 1 vol., 1. Beullens-Maoui, Nathalie, ed. 2013. (¡Celebremos la Libertad! / Let's Celebrate Freedom! Ser.). (SPA & ENG.). 24p. (J). (gr. 3-3). 26.27 (978-1-4777-3251-9(9), 9af4c21c-46e2-4002-afd5-a9b374639210, PowerKids Pr.) Rosen Publishing Group, Inc., The.

—A Nation of Immigrants, 1 vol., 1. 2013. (Let's Celebrate Freedom! Ser.). (ENG.). 24p. (J). (gr. 3-3). 26.27 (978-1-4777-2899-4(6), 068aae2f-3b9e-4ea9-9cff-20430a1581a0, PowerKids Pr.) Rosen Publishing Group, Inc., The.

Meyer, Jared. Frequently Asked Questions about Being an Immigrant Teen. 2009. (FAQ: Teen Life Ser.). 64p. (gr. 5-6). 58.50 (978-1-61512-565-4(5)) Rosen Publishing Group, Inc., The.

Miller, Debra A. Illegal Immigration. 2007. (Compact Research Ser.). (Illus.). 110p. (YA). (gr. 7-12). lib. bdg. 43.93 (978-1-60152-009-8(3)) ReferencePoint Pr., Inc.

Miller, Debra A., ed. Immigration, 1 vol. 2014. (Current Controversies Ser.). (ENG., Illus.). 184p. (gr. 10-12). lib. bdg. 48.03 (978-0-7377-6874-9(6), 8d3fbe16-dc84-43ff-9fd7-eb6f7b571a68, Greenhaven Publishing) Greenhaven Publishing LLC.

Monnig, Alex. German Immigrants: In Their Shoes. 2017. (Immigrant Experiences Ser.). (ENG.). 32p. (J). (gr. 3-6). lib. bdg. 35.64 (978-1-5038-2026-5(2), 211846) Child's World, Inc, The.

Moreno, Barry. The Chinese Americans. 2007. (Major American Immigration Ser.). (YA). pap. 9.95 (978-1-4222-0672-0(6)) Mason Crest.

—The Cuban Americans. (Major American Immigration Ser.). (YA). 2010. (Illus.). 64p. (gr. 9-12). 22.95 (978-1-4222-0606-5(8)) 2007. pap. 9.95 (978-1-4222-0673-7(4)) Mason Crest.

—The German Americans. 2007. (Major American Immigration Ser.). (YA). pap. 9.95 (978-1-4222-0674-4(2)) Mason Crest.

—History of American Immigration. (Major American Immigration Ser.). (YA). 2010. (Illus.). 64p. (gr. 9-12). lib. bdg. 22.95 (978-1-4222-0613-3(0)) 2007. pap. 9.95 (978-1-4222-0680-5(7)) Mason Crest.

—The Irish Americans. 2007. (Major American Immigration Ser.). (YA). pap. 9.95 (978-1-4222-0675-1(0)) Mason Crest.

—The Italian Americans. 2007. (Major American Immigration Ser.). (YA). pap. 9.95 (978-1-4222-0676-8(9)) Mason Crest.

—The Japanese Americans. (Major American Immigration Ser.). (YA). 2010. (Illus.). 64p. (gr. 9-12). 22.95 (978-1-4222-0610-2(6)) 2007. pap. 9.95 (978-1-4222-0677-5(7)) Mason Crest.

—The Jewish Americans. (Major American Immigration Ser.). (YA). 2010. (Illus.). 64p. (gr. 9-12). 22.95 (978-1-4222-0611-9(4)) 2007. pap. 9.95 (978-1-4222-0678-2(5)) Mason Crest.

—The Korean Americans. (Major American Immigration Ser.). (YA). 2010. (Illus.). 64p. (gr. 9-12). 22.95 (978-1-4222-0612-6(2)) 2007. pap. 9.95 (978-1-4222-0679-9(3)) Mason Crest.

—The Mexican Americans. (Major American Immigration Ser.). (YA). 2010. (Illus.). 64p. (gr. 9-12). 22.95 (978-1-4222-0614-0(9)) 2007. pap. 9.95 (978-1-4222-0681-2(5)) Mason Crest.

—The Polish Americans. (Major American Immigration Ser.). (YA). 2010. (Illus.). 64p. (gr. 9-12). 22.95 (978-1-4222-0616-4(5)) 2007. pap. 9.95 (978-1-4222-0683-6(1)) Mason Crest.

—The Russian Americans. 2007. (Major American Immigration Ser.). (YA). pap. 9.95 (978-1-4222-0684-3(X)) Mason Crest.

Moreno, Barry & Ashbrock, Peg. The German Americans. 2010. (Major American Immigration Ser.). (Illus.). 64p. (YA). (gr. 9-12). 22.95 (978-1-4222-0607-2(6)) Mason Crest.

Moreno, Barry & Bowen, Richard A. The Italian Americans. 2010. (Major American Immigration Ser.). (Illus.). 64p. (YA). (gr. 9-12). 22.95 (978-1-4222-0609-6(2)) Mason Crest.

Moreno, Barry & Haugen, Brenda. The Irish Americans. 2010. (Major American Immigration Ser.). (Illus.). 64p. (YA). (gr. 9-12). 22.95 (978-1-4222-0608-9(4)) Mason Crest.

Moreno, Barry & Lingen, Marissa. The Chinese Americans. 2010. (Major American Immigration Ser.). (Illus.). 64p. (YA). (gr. 9-12). 22.95 (978-1-4222-0605-8(X)) Mason Crest.

Moynihan, Daniel Patrick, intro. Immigrants in America. 2005. (Immigrants in America Ser.). (Illus.). 112p. (gr. 6-12). 180.00 (978-0-7910-7125-0(1), Facts On File) Infobase Holdings, Inc.

Nagle, Jeanne. Coping with the Threat of Deportation, 1 vol. 2018. (Coping (2017-2020) Ser.). (ENG.). 112p. (J). (gr. 7-7). 40.13 (978-1-5081-7911-5(5), e36b4fc5-98b9-4a93-ae4b-ae32777e5feb); pap. 19.24 (978-1-5081-7910-8(7), f93ca581-2af3-4a46-986c-40ffb67f1f06) Rosen Publishing Group, Inc., The. (Rosen Young Adult).

Nazario, Sonia. La Travesía de Enrique. 2015. (SPA.). 304p. (YA). (gr. 7). pap. 9.99 (978-0-553-53554-9(4), Ember) Random Hse. Children's Bks.

Nichol, Bryan. Irish Americans, 1 vol. 2004. (One Nation Set 2 Ser.). (ENG.). 32p. (gr. k-6). 27.07 (978-1-59197-528-1(X), Checkerboard Library) ABDO Publishing Co.

Noonan, Sheila Smith. Korean Immigration. 2005. (Changing Face of North America Ser.). (Illus.). 112p. (YA). lib. bdg. 24.95 (978-1-59084-693-3(1)) Mason Crest.

O'Donnell, Liam. U. S. Immigration. Barnett, Charles, illus. 2008. (Cartoon Nation Ser.). (ENG.). 32p. (J). (gr. 3-9). 31.32 (978-1-4296-1983-7(X), 94894, Capstone Pr.) Capstone.

O'Donoghue, Sean. The Disaster of the Irish Potato Famine: Irish Immigrants Arrive in America (1845-1850), 1 vol., 1. 2015. (Spotlight on Immigration & Migration Ser.). (ENG., Illus.). 24p. (J). (gr. 4-5). pap. 11.00 (978-1-5081-4066-5(9), 5f509c61-cf73-41b0-8b0b-a43e9bb72629, PowerKids Pr.) Rosen Publishing Group, Inc., The.

Omoth, Tyler. Cuban Immigrants: In Their Shoes. 2017. (Immigrant Experiences Ser.). (ENG.). 32p. (J). (gr. 3-6). lib. bdg. 35.64 (978-1-5038-2025-8(4), 211845) Child's World, Inc, The.

—Italian Immigrants: In Their Shoes. 2017. (Immigrant Experiences Ser.). (ENG.). 32p. (J). (gr. 3-6). lib. bdg. 35.64 (978-1-5038-2029-6(7), 211848) Child's World, Inc, The.

Osborne, Linda Barrett. This Land Is Our Land: A History of American Immigration. 2016. (ENG., Illus.). 128p. (J). (gr. 8-17). 24.95 (978-1-4197-1660-7(3), 1077301, Abrams Bks. for Young Readers) Abrams, Inc.

Otfinoski, Steven. The 1990s To 2010, 1 vol. 2010. (Hispanic America Ser.). (ENG.). 80p. (gr. 5-5). 36.93 (978-0-7614-4180-9(8), b13393c9-faa0-4f43-b885-c5804ffb0006) Cavendish Square Publishing LLC.

Outman, James L. & Baker, Lawrence W. U. S. Immigration & Migration: Primary Sources. 2004. (US Immigration & Migration Reference Library). (ENG., Illus.). 272p. (J). 106.00 (978-0-7876-7669-8(1), UXL) Cengage Gale.

Outman, James L., et al. U. S. Immigration & Migration: Biographies, 2.0. 2004. (US Immigration & Migration Reference Library). (ENG., Illus.). 410p. (J). 191.00 (978-0-7876-7733-6(7), UXL) Cengage Gale.

—U.S. Immigration & Migration, 2 vols. 2004. ([U.S. Immigration & Migration Reference Library]). (Illus.). (J). 110.00 (978-0-7876-7568-4(7)); (978-0-7876-7668-1(3)) Cengage Gale. (UXL).

Parker, Lewis K. Why German Immigrants Came to America. 2009. (Coming to America Ser.). 24p. (gr. 2-3). 42.50 (978-1-61511-883-0(7), PowerKids Pr.) Rosen Publishing Group, Inc., The.

—Why Irish Immigrants Came to America. 2009. (Coming to America Ser.). 24p. (gr. 2-3). 42.50 (978-1-61511-884-7(5), PowerKids Pr.) Rosen Publishing Group, Inc., The.

—Why Italian Immigrants Came to America. 2009. (Coming to America Ser.). 24p. (gr. 2-3). 42.50 (978-1-61511-885-4(3), PowerKids Pr.) Rosen Publishing Group, Inc., The.

—Why Japanese Immigrants Came to America. 2009. (Coming to America Ser.). 24p. (gr. 2-3). 42.50 (978-1-61511-886-1(1), PowerKids Pr.) Rosen Publishing Group, Inc., The.

—Why Mexican Immigrants Came to America. 2009. (Coming to America Ser.). 24p. (gr. 2-3). 42.50 (978-1-61511-887-8(X), PowerKids Pr.) Rosen Publishing Group, Inc., The.

—Why Vietnamese Immigrants Came to America. 2009. (Coming to America Ser.). 24p. (gr. 2-3). 42.50 (978-1-61511-888-5(8), PowerKids Pr.) Rosen Publishing Group, Inc., The.

Perl, Lila. Immigration: This Land Is Whose Land?, 1 vol. 2010. (Controversy! Ser.). (ENG.). 112p. (YA). (gr. 8-8). lib. bdg. 39.79 (978-0-7614-4232-5(4), 149eaee5-3e71-4afd-af12-e079f00bce57) Cavendish Square Publishing LLC.

—To the Golden Mountain: The Story of the Chinese Who Built the Transcontinental Railroad, 1 vol. 2003. (Great Journeys Ser.). (ENG., Illus.). 112p. (gr. 6-6). 39.79 (978-0-7614-1324-0(3), 4b2da634-4509-427c-aa77-5794e2850953) Cavendish Square Publishing LLC.

Poole, H. W. The Thai Family Table, Vol. 11. 2018. (Connecting Cultures Through Family & Food Ser.). (Illus.). 64p. (J). (gr. 7). lib. bdg. 31.93 (978-1-4222-4052-6(5)) Mason Crest.

Poole, Hilary W. The Mexican Family Table, Vol. 11. 2018. (Connecting Cultures Through Family & Food Ser.). (Illus.). 64p. (J). (gr. 7). 31.93 (978-1-4222-4048-9(7)) Mason Crest.

Poole, Hilary W. & Rich, Mari. The Thai Family Table, Vol. 11. 2018. (Connecting Cultures Through Family & Food Ser.). (Illus.). 64p. (J). (gr. 7). 31.93 (978-1-4222-4047-2(9)) Mason Crest.

Prado, Emilly. Examining Assimilation, 1 vol. 2018. (Racial Literacy Ser.). (ENG.). 80p. (gr. 7-7). 37.60 (978-1-9785-0469-1(1), d5bc07b4-1e63-49e8-98c3-d656bf708907) Enslow Publishing, LLC.

Primary Sources of Immigration & Migration. 2004. (Primary Source Big Bookstm Ser.). (ENG.). 24p. (gr. 4-8). 43.95 (978-0-8239-4594-8(4)) Rosen Publishing Group, Inc., The.

Rich, Mari. The Indian Family Table, Vol. 11. 2018. (Connecting Cultures Through Family & Food Ser.). (Illus.). 64p. (J). (gr. 7). 31.93 (978-1-4222-4045-8(2)) Mason Crest.

Rinker, Kimberly. Immigration from the Dominican Republic. 2005. (Changing Face of North America Ser.). (Illus.). 112p. (YA). lib. bdg. 24.95 (978-1-59084-689-6(3)) Mason Crest.

RJF Publishing Staff & Staton, Hilarie. Ellis Island. 2009. (Symbols of American Freedom Ser.). 48p. (gr. 4-6). 30.00 (978-1-60413-519-0(0), Chelsea Clubhse.) Infobase Holdings, Inc.

Rosen Classroom, creator. Map Activities for Primary Sources of Immigration & Migration in America: Reproducible Blackline Masters. 2011. (Illus.). 15p. (J). pap. 15.99 (978-0-8239-4597-9(9), Rosen Classroom) Rosen Publishing Group, Inc., The.

Roza, Greg. Immigration & Migration, 1 vol. 2011. (Story of America Ser.). (ENG., Illus.). 32p. (J). (gr. 4-5). lib. bdg. 29.27 (978-1-4339-4768-1(4), 6d1e2199-93ca-40f7-ba9d-c0f75bbcf9c5, Gareth Stevens Learning Library) Stevens, Gareth Publishing LLLP.

Ruffin, Frances E. Ellis Island, 1 vol. 2005. (Places in American History Ser.). (ENG., Illus.). 24p. (gr. 2-4). pap. 9.15 (978-0-8368-6415-1(8), db547480-6a78-4c88-9a75-f549eb2f7187); lib. bdg. 24.67 (978-0-8368-6408-3(5), e15543f3-c794-4c89-9244-7a3ee27da489) Stevens, Gareth Publishing LLLP. (Weekly Reader Leveled Readers).

Sampathkumar, Mythili. Inside ICE, 1 vol. 2019. (Inside Law Enforcement Ser.). (ENG.). 48p. (J). (gr. 5-5). 29.60 (978-1-9785-0737-1(2), 445210dc-5825-48de-b11e-b311c7c4e9d5) Enslow Publishing, LLC.

Sánchez, Sonia, illus. Here I Am. 2014. (J). (978-1-4795-1932-3(4), Picture Window Bks.) Capstone.

Santos, Edward J. Everything You Need to Know If You & Your Parents are New Americans. 2009. (Need to Know Library). 64p. (gr. 5-5). 58.50 (978-1-60854-099-0(5)) Rosen Publishing Group, Inc., The.

Saxon-Ford, Stephanie. The Czech Americans: The Immigrant Experience. 2006. (Illus.). 111p. (J). (gr. 4-8). reprint ed. 20.00 (978-1-4223-5547-3(0)) DIANE Publishing Co.

Schmermund, Elizabeth, ed. Immigration Bans, 1 vol. 2017. (Opposing Viewpoints Ser.). (ENG.). 232p. (gr. 10-12). pap. 34.80 (978-1-5345-0057-0(X), 07f3751a-74d7-40a9-a291-9a9de511c603) Greenhaven Publishing LLC.

Schroeder, Michael J. Mexican Americans. Johnston, Robert D., ed. 2006. (ENG., Illus.). 150p. (gr. 6-12). lib. bdg. 30.00 (978-0-7910-8785-5(9), P114408, Facts On File) Infobase Holdings, Inc.

Sebree, Chet'la & Stefoff, Rebecca. Historical Sources on Immigration to the United States, 1820-1924, 1 vol. 2019. (America's Story Ser.). (ENG.). 144p. (gr. 8-8). pap. 22.16 (978-1-5026-4080-2(5), d94f2737-6e8f-4123-8ffe-995073e8ec4e) Cavendish Square Publishing LLC.

Seymour, Isobel. I am Mexican American. 2009. (Our American Family Ser.). 24p. (gr. 2-3). 42.50 (978-1-60851-149-5(9), PowerKids Pr.) Rosen Publishing Group, Inc., The.

Shea, Therese. Immigration to America: Identifying Different Points of View about an Issue. 2009. (Critical Thinking in American History Ser.). 48p. (gr. 5-8). 53.00 (978-1-61512-093-2(9), Rosen Reference) Rosen Publishing Group, Inc., The.

—Immigration to America: Identifying Different Points of View About an Issue, 1 vol. 2005. (Critical Thinking in American History Ser.). (ENG., Illus.). 48p. (J). (gr. 5-8). lib. bdg. 34.47 (978-1-4042-0414-0(8), 2820893c-8117-4c48-bedb-9e9b3100e347) Rosen Publishing Group, Inc., The.

Sioux, Tracee. Immigrants & the Westward Expansion. 2009. (Primary Sources of Immigration & Migration in America Ser.). 24p. (gr. 3-4). 42.50 (978-1-60851-776-3(4), PowerKids Pr.) Rosen Publishing Group, Inc., The.

—Immigrants, Migration, & the Growth of the American City. 2009. (Primary Sources of Immigration & Migration in America Ser.). 24p. (gr. 3-4). 42.50 (978-1-60851-778-7(0), PowerKids Pr.) Rosen Publishing Group, Inc., The.

—Immigrants, Migration, & the Industrial Revolution. 2009. (Primary Sources of Immigration & Migration in America Ser.). 24p. (gr. 3-4). 42.50 (978-1-60851-779-4(9), PowerKids Pr.) Rosen Publishing Group, Inc., The.

—Immigration, Migration, & the Industrial Revolution, 1 vol. 2003. (Primary Sources of Immigration & Migration in America Ser.). (ENG., Illus.). 24p. (gr. 3-4). pap. 9.40 (978-0-8239-8998-0(4), 7136c3ff-b4ea-41db-a705-449a93f6e243, PowerKids Pr.) Rosen Publishing Group, Inc., The.

Staley, Erin. I'm an Undocumented Immigrant, Now What?, 1 vol. 2016. (Teen Life 411 Ser.). (ENG.). 112p. (J). (gr. 7-7). 38.80 (978-1-5081-7193-5(9), 6e0f878d-ab84-4f7c-bba7-586fa312bc13) Rosen Publishing Group, Inc., The.

Stefoff, Rebecca. A Century of Immigration: 1820-1924, 1 vol. 2007. (American Voices From Ser.). (ENG., Illus.). 160p. (gr. 6-6). lib. bdg. 41.21 (978-0-7614-2172-6(6), 5ed6ed0e-95d2-451c-9def-b5203ae1bf88) Cavendish Square Publishing LLC.

Stewart, Gail. Illegal Immigration. 2007. (Ripped from the Headlines Ser.). (Illus.). 64p. (J). (gr. 7-12). 23.95 (978-1-60217-003-2(7)) Erickson Pr.

Streissguth, Tom. Welcome to America? A Pro / con Debate over Immigration, 1 vol. 2009. (Issues in Focus Today Ser.). (ENG., Illus.). 112p. (J). (gr. 6-7). lib. bdg. 35.93 (978-0-7660-2912-5(3), 75d964a8-0d22-43c4-bd11-775ff4a48d53) Enslow Publishing, LLC.

The American Mosaic: Immigration Today, 12 vols. 2014. (American Mosaic: Immigration Today Ser.). (ENG.). 24p. (J). (gr. 2-3). 151.62 (978-1-4777-6653-8(7), 6aabddc0-37eb-4657-84f3-b3526bcdaa8c, PowerKids Pr.) Rosen Publishing Group, Inc., The.

Thomas, William David. Korean Americans, 1 vol. 2010. (New Americans Ser.). (ENG.). 80p. (gr. 5-5). 38.36 (978-0-7614-4306-3(1), ad720f6d-7d20-484b-8775-6914bd396756) Cavendish Square Publishing LLC.

Thornton, Jeremy. Hard Times in Ireland: The Scotch-Irish Come to America (1603-1775) (Primary Sources of Immigration & Migration in America Ser.). 24p. (gr. 3-4). 2009. 42.50 (978-1-60851-775-6(6)) 2003. (ENG., Illus.). (J). lib. bdg. 26.27 (978-0-8239-6830-5(8), dcf78e74-4785-4379-97c0-a774e171296a) Rosen Publishing Group, Inc., The. (PowerKids Pr.).

—Hard Times in Ireland: The Scotch-Irish Come to America, 1603-1775, 1 vol. 2003. (Primary Sources of Immigration & Migration in America Ser.). (ENG., Illus.). 24p. (gr. 3-4). pap. 9.40 (978-0-8239-8956-0(9), 2fe305cf-beb6-4e18-a22c-b8fa8cfe2c72, PowerKids Pr.) Rosen Publishing Group, Inc., The.

—New Industries, New Jobs: British Immigrants Come to America (1830s-1890s), 1 vol. 2003. (Primary Sources of Immigration & Migration in America Ser.). (ENG., Illus.). 24p. (gr. 3-4). pap. 9.40 (978-0-8239-8958-4(5), 9f8ceb2d-8feb-41e4-9ead-c81419d3f529, Rosen Classroom); (J). lib. bdg. 26.27 (978-0-8239-6832-9(4), 9d129012-bccc-4824-90f1-3990a13173c0, PowerKids Pr.) Rosen Publishing Group, Inc., The.

—New Industries, New Jobs: British Immigrants Come to America(1830s-1890s) 2009. (Primary Sources of Immigration & Migration in America Ser.). 24p. (gr. 3-4). 42.50 (978-1-60851-782-4(9), PowerKids Pr.) Rosen Publishing Group, Inc., The.

—Religious Intolerance: Jewish Immigrants Come to America (1881-1914) 2009. (Primary Sources of Immigration & Migration in America Ser.). 24p. (gr. 3-4). 42.50 (978-1-60851-783-1(7), PowerKids Pr.) Rosen Publishing Group, Inc., The.

Toole, Spencer. Let's Study Immigration: Collecting Data, 1 vol. 2017. (Computer Science for the Real World Ser.). (ENG.). 24p. (J). (gr. 3-4). pap. (978-1-5383-5316-5(4), f72ee4df-4f88-4c23-ac10-7e8d2407cae8, Rosen Classroom); (Illus.). 25.27 (978-1-5383-2407-3(5), 02eb6ae4-ec40-4af0-99fc-bb21865a6d92, PowerKids Pr.) Rosen Publishing Group, Inc., The.

Townsend, Dana E. Ellis Island. (Illus.). 32p. (J). (978-0-7367-2944-4(5)) Zaner-Bloser, Inc.

U. S. Immigration & Migration, 5.0. Incl. U. S. Immigration & Migration: Almanac. Benson, Sonia. 685p. 191.00 (978-0-7876-7732-9(9)); U. S. Immigration & Migration: Biographies. Outman, James L., et al. 410p. 191.00 (978-0-7876-7733-6(7)); U. S. Immigration & Migration: Primary Sources. Outman, James L. & Baker, Lawrence W. 272p. 106.00 (978-0-7876-7669-8(1)); (Illus.). (J). (US Immigration & Migration Reference Library). (ENG.). 1,327p. 2004. 458.00 (978-0-7876-7565-3(2), UXL) Cengage Gale.

Uschan, Michael V. German Americans, 1 vol. 2006. (World Almanac(r) Library of American Immigration Ser.). (ENG., Illus.). 48p. (gr. 5-8). pap. 15.05 (978-0-8368-7323-8(8), 4b784fb3-ff5c-4742-9a24-9aff45d78e9e); lib. bdg. 33.67 (978-0-8368-7310-8(6), 20760419-bc46-4073-9fc9-af599f68c1e4) Stevens, Gareth Publishing LLLP. (Gareth Stevens Secondary Library).

—Irish Americans, 1 vol. 2006. (World Almanac(r) Library of American Immigration Ser.). (ENG., Illus.). 48p. (gr. 5-8). pap. 15.05 (978-0-8368-7324-5(6), b4bde5df-4264-4207-a4a7-4510ebf8515c); lib. bdg. 33.67 (978-0-8368-7311-5(4), 8aedb73e-7fca-4369-8010-890e867db89f) Stevens, Gareth Publishing LLLP. (Gareth Stevens Secondary Library).

Weber, Valerie J. I Come from Afghanistan, 1 vol. 2006. (This Is My Story Ser.). (ENG., Illus.). 24p. (gr. 2-4). pap. 9.15 (978-0-8368-7240-8(1), f4c337c5-1679-4bde-b638-5220a9089a6c); lib. bdg. 24.67 (978-0-8368-7233-0(9), c17f0a10-45c7-455e-a5a4-b860e29cb9b3) Stevens, Gareth Publishing LLLP. (Weekly Reader Leveled Readers).

—I Come from Chile, 1 vol. 2006. (This Is My Story Ser.). (ENG., Illus.). 24p. (gr. 2-4). lib. bdg. 24.67 *(978-0-8368-7234-7(7),* abe02570-1005-4386-b7e0-d9ae87a928d1, Weekly Reader Leveled Readers) Stevens, Gareth Publishing LLLP.

—I Come from Chile, 1 vol. 2006. (This Is My Story Ser.). (ENG., Illus.). 24p. (gr. 2-4). pap. 9.15 *(978-0-8368-7241-5(X),* d36c6c3d-ce13-45d2-b3f3-4a2a203cdb61, Weekly Reader Leveled Readers) Stevens, Gareth Publishing LLLP.

—I Come from India, 1 vol. 2006. (This Is My Story Ser.). (ENG., Illus.). 24p. (gr. 2-4). pap. 9.15 *(978-0-8368-7242-2(8),* b6882f35-58d7-448f-ab13-43e8adfa319a); lib. bdg. 24.67 *(978-0-8368-7235-4(5),* c9976f69-1f4d-46b7-ab75-0aa34bd3d9f8) Stevens, Gareth Publishing LLLP. (Weekly Reader Leveled Readers).

—I Come from Ivory Coast, 1 vol. 2006. (This Is My Story Ser.). (ENG., Illus.). 24p. (gr. 2-4). pap. 9.15 *(978-0-8368-7243-9(6),* 4ef53f23-b985-4b76-96eb-20ad8eb5a24c); lib. bdg. 24.67 *(978-0-8368-7236-1(3),* 693981c6-e162-4df9-9237-55339ab4864c) Stevens, Gareth Publishing LLLP. (Weekly Reader Leveled Readers).

—I Come from South Korea, 1 vol. 2006. (This Is My Story Ser.). (ENG., Illus.). 24p. (gr. 2-4). lib. bdg. 24.67 *(978-0-8368-7237-8(1),* 639a1b20-a602-44db-960b-a99720757f5a, Weekly Reader Leveled Readers) Stevens, Gareth Publishing LLLP.

—I Come from Ukraine, 1 vol. 2006. (This Is My Story Ser.). (ENG., Illus.). 24p. (gr. 2-4). pap. 9.15 *(978-0-8368-7245-3(2),* e99cfde8-c255-43ce-8568-f40c710999ce, Weekly Reader Leveled Readers) Stevens, Gareth Publishing LLLP.

—I Come from Ukraine, 1 vol. 2006. (This Is My Story Ser.). (ENG., Illus.). 24p. (gr. 2-4). lib. bdg. 24.67 *(978-0-8368-7238-5(X),* 645c9201-c314-4ca6-bb39-fa7a1c408d74, Weekly Reader Leveled Readers) Stevens, Gareth Publishing LLLP.

Weber, Valerie J. & Weber, Valerie J. I Come from South Korea, 1 vol. 2006. (This Is My Story Ser.). (ENG., Illus.). 24p. (gr. 2-4). pap. 9.15 *(978-0-8368-7244-6(4),* 4d5e8a06-bf89-487e-ba44-32eaeb2f1df6, Weekly Reader Leveled Readers) Stevens, Gareth Publishing LLLP.

Whitman, Sylvia. Immigrant Children. 2005. (Picture the American Past Ser.). (Illus.). 48p. (gr. 2-5). lib. bdg. 22.60 *(978-1-57505-395-0(0))* Lerner Publishing Group.

World Book, Inc. Staff, contrib. by. The World Book of America's Multicultural Heritage, 2 vols. 2003. (Illus.). 384p. (gr. 4-12). 86.99 *(978-0-7166-7303-3(7))* World Bk., Inc.

Young, Robert. A Personal Tour of Ellis Island. 64p. (J). (gr. 3-6). 6.95 *(978-1-58013-154-4(9));* 2003. (Illus.). 18.95 *(978-1-58013-079-0(8))* Lerner Publishing Group. (Kar-Ben Publishing).

UNITED STATES—EMPLOYEES

see United States—Officials and Employees

UNITED STATES—EXECUTIVE POWER

see Executive Power

UNITED STATES—EXPLORING EXPEDITIONS

Here are entered works on exploration within the United States and for explorations in other countries which are sponsored by the United States. Works on early exploration in territory which became a part of the United States are entered under America—Discovery and Exploration.

see also names of expeditions, e.g. Lewis and Clark expedition

Benge, Janet & Benge, Geoff. Heroes of History - Daniel Boone: Frontiersman. 2004. (ENG.). 224p. (YA). pap. 11.99 *(978-1-932096-09-5(4))* Emerald Bks.

Levy, Janey. Mapping America's Westward Expansion: Applying Geographic Tools & Interpreting Maps, 1 vol. 2005. (Critical Thinking in American History Ser.). (ENG., Illus.). 48p. (J). (gr. 5-8). lib. bdg. 34.47 *(978-1-4042-0416-4(4),* afbb4417-0d6b-44f0-a05a-3cec0bcb1c53) Rosen Publishing Group, Inc., The.

Lyne, William Rayford. Galisteo: Thothmes III's Colony in America, C. 1626 B. C.: the Tanoan-Egyptian Djed Festival Stone. Lyne, William Rayford, illus. 2011. (ENG., Illus.). 250p. pap. 25.00 *(978-0-9637467-3-3(1))* Creatopia Productions - Lamy, New Mexico.

Redmond, Shirley Raye. Lewis & Clark: A Prairie Dog for the President. Manders, John, illus. 2003. (Step into Reading Ser.: No. 3). 48p. (J). (gr. k-3). pap. 5.99 *(978-0-375-81120-3(6),* Random Hse. Bks. for Young Readers) Random Hse. Children's Bks.

UNITED STATES—FEDERAL BUREAU OF INVESTIGATION

Anderson, Dale. The FBI & Civil Rights. 2009. (FBI Story Ser.). 64p. (J). (gr. 4-7). lib. bdg. 22.95 *(978-1-4222-0569-3(X))* Mason Crest.

—The FBI & Organized Crime. 2009. (FBI Story Ser.). 64p. (J). (gr. 4-7). lib. bdg. 22.95 *(978-1-4222-0565-5(7))* Mason Crest.

—The FBI & White-Collar Crime. 2009. (FBI Story Ser.). 64p. (J). (gr. 4-7). lib. bdg. 22.95 *(978-1-4222-0566-2(5))* Mason Crest.

—The FBI Files: Successful Investigations. 2009. (FBI Story Ser.). 64p. (J). (gr. 4-7). lib. bdg. 22.95 *(978-1-4222-0561-7(4))* Mason Crest.

Aronson, Marc. Master of Deceit: J. Edgar Hoover & America in the Age of Lies. (ENG.). 240p. (gr. 9). 2019. (J). pap. 14.99 *(978-1-5362-0630-2(X))* 2012. (Illus.). (YA). 25.99 *(978-0-7636-5025-4(0))* Candlewick Pr.

Clapper, Kathryn N., et al. FBI Agents. 2018. (U. S. Federal Agents Ser.). (ENG., Illus.). 32p. (J). (gr. 3-9). lib. bdg. 27.32 *(978-1-5435-0141-4(9),* 137078, Capstone Pr.) Capstone.

Crewe, Sabrina. The FBI & Crimes Against Children. 2009. (FBI Story Ser.). 64p. (J). (gr. 4-7). lib. bdg. 22.95 *(978-1-4222-0570-9(3))* Mason Crest.

—A History of the FBI. 2009. (FBI Story Ser.). 64p. (J). (gr. 4-7). lib. bdg. 22.95 *(978-1-4222-0563-1(0))* Mason Crest.

Faust, Daniel R. A Career As an FBI Special Agent, 1 vol. 2015. (Federal Forces: Careers As Federal Agents Ser.). (ENG., Illus.). 32p. (J). (gr. 4-5). pap. 11.00 *(978-1-4994-1060-0(3),* 5cf71f27-3a59-4c46-8a6c-6f6c68e3dbd5, PowerKids Pr.) Rosen Publishing Group, Inc., The.

The FBI Story, 12 vols., Set. Incl. FBI & Civil Rights. Anderson, Dale. lib. bdg. 22.95 *(978-1-4222-0569-3(X));* FBI & Crimes Against Children. Crewe, Sabrina. lib. bdg. 22.95 *(978-1-4222-0570-9(3));* FBI & Cyber Crimes. Grayson, Robert. lib. bdg. 22.95 *(978-1-4222-0568-6(1));* FBI & National Security. Grayson, Robert. lib. bdg. 22.95 *(978-1-4222-0564-8(9));* FBI & Organized Crime. Anderson, Dale. lib. bdg. 22.95 *(978-1-4222-0565-5(7));* FBI & Public Corruption. Grayson, Robert. lib. bdg. 22.95 *(978-1-4222-0567-9(3));* FBI & White-Collar Crime. Anderson, Dale. lib. bdg. 22.95 *(978-1-4222-0566-2(5));* FBI Files: Successful Investigations. Anderson, Dale. lib. bdg. 22.95 *(978-1-4222-0561-7(4));* FBI's Most Wanted. Wachtel, Alan. lib. bdg. 22.95 *(978-1-4222-0562-4(2));* History of the FBI. Crewe, Sabrina. lib. bdg. 22.95 *(978-1-4222-0563-1(0));* How to Become an FBI Agent. Thomas, William David. lib. bdg. 22.95 *(978-1-4222-0571-6(1));* Investigative Techniques of the FBI. Wachtel, Alan. (Illus.). lib. bdg. 22.95 *(978-1-4222-0572-3(X));* 64p. (J). (gr. 4-7). 2009. 2010. Set lib. bdg. 275.40 *(978-1-4222-0560-0(6))* Mason Crest.

Federal Forces: Careers As Federal Agents. 2015. (Federal Forces: Careers As Federal Agents Ser.). (ENG.). 32p. (J). (gr. 4-5). pap., pap., pap. 360.00 *(978-1-4994-1291-8(6),* PowerKids Pr.) Rosen Publishing Group, Inc., The.

Federal Forces: Careers As Federal Agents Set, 12 vols. 2015. (Federal Forces: Careers As Federal Agents Ser.). (ENG.). 32p. (J). (gr. 4-5). lib. bdg. 167.58 *(978-1-4994-0772-3(6),* eb0df0a9-f388-45ce-8222-a041ddf75735, PowerKids Pr.) Rosen Publishing Group, Inc., The.

Grayson, Robert. The FBI & Cyber Crimes. 2009. (FBI Story Ser.). 64p. (J). (gr. 4-7). lib. bdg. 22.95 *(978-1-4222-0568-6(1))* Mason Crest.

—The FBI & National Security. 2009. (FBI Story Ser.). 64p. (J). (gr. 4-7). lib. bdg. 22.95 *(978-1-4222-0564-8(9))* Mason Crest.

—The FBI & Public Corruption. 2009. (FBI Story Ser.). 64p. (J). (gr. 4-7). lib. bdg. 22.95 *(978-1-4222-0567-9(3))* Mason Crest.

Horn, Geoffrey M. FBI Agent, 1 vol. 2008. (Cool Careers: Helping Careers Ser.). (ENG.). 32p. (gr. 3-3). pap. 11.50 *(978-0-8368-9326-7(3),* 5b9331d7-1253-4631-8fb8-79b0e181710d); lib. bdg. 28.67 *(978-0-8368-9193-5(7),* d56e76cd-9208-452f-9922-7c4fd17a6164) Stevens, Gareth Publishing LLLP.

Lewis, Brenda Ralph. Hostage Rescue with the FBI. 2004. (Rescue & Prevention Ser.). (Illus.). 96p. (YA). (gr. 7-18). lib. bdg. 22.95 *(978-1-59084-403-8(3))* Mason Crest.

—Rescuing Hostages: The FBI. 2017. (Illus.). 80p. (J). *(978-1-4222-3770-0(2))* Mason Crest.

Mara, Wil. FBI Special Agent. 2015. (21st Century Skills Library: Cool STEAM Careers Ser.). (ENG., Illus.). 32p. (J). (gr. 4-7). pap. 14.21 *(978-1-63362-648-5(2),* 1391909) Cherry Lake Publishing.

Mitchell, Megan. Standing in the FBI Director's Shoes, 1 vol. 2017. (My Government Ser.). (ENG.). 32p. (gr. 3-3). pap. 11.58 *(978-1-5026-3066-7(4),* 85d268e7-de6d-4682-9cb4-570f0a62e1e3); lib. bdg. 30.21 *(978-1-5026-3068-1(0),* 7f743e96-af9e-4abe-b84e-7431744475ab) Cavendish Square Publishing LLC.

Newcomb, Tim. FBI Agent, Vol. 12. 2015. (On a Mission Ser.). 48p. (J). (gr. 5). 20.95 *(978-1-4222-3394-8(4))* Mason Crest.

Poolos, Jamie. Hostage Rescuers. (Extreme Careers Ser.). 64p. (gr. 5-5). 2009. 58.50 *(978-1-61512-399-5(7),* Rosen Reference) 2007. (ENG., Illus.). lib. bdg. 37.13 *(978-1-4042-0941-1(7),* 8fdbb894-9a6f-4d83-8a1f-c316f0c58f69) Rosen Publishing Group, Inc., The.

Prentzas, G. S. FBI Special Agent. 2008. (21st Century Skills Library: Cool Careers Ser.). (ENG., Illus.). 32p. (gr. 4-8). lib. bdg. 32.07 *(978-1-60279-304-0(2),* 200143) Cherry Lake Publishing.

Sampathkumar, Mythili. Inside the FBI, 1 vol. 2019. (Inside Law Enforcement Ser.). (ENG.). 48p. (gr. 5-5). lib. bdg. 29.60 *(978-1-9785-0735-7(6),* 1474c731-ad6b-4779-8be2-6e10c8b590bd) Enslow Publishing, LLC.

Streissguth, Tom. The Security Agencies of the United States: How the CIA, FBI, NSA, & Homeland Security Keep Us Safe, 1 vol. 2013. (Constitution & the United States Government Ser.). (ENG., Illus.). 104p. (gr. 5-6). 35.93 *(978-0-7660-4064-9(X),* 3e4b285d-d68a-47f7-a469-2d442178525a) Enslow Publishing, LLC.

Thomas, William David. How to Become an FBI Agent. 2009. (FBI Story Ser.). 64p. (J). (gr. 4-7). lib. bdg. 22.95 *(978-1-4222-0571-6(1))* Mason Crest.

Wachtel, Alan. The FBI's Most Wanted. 2009. (FBI Story Ser.). 64p. (J). (gr. 4-7). lib. bdg. 22.95 *(978-1-4222-0562-4(2))* Mason Crest.

—Investigative Techniques of the FBI. 2009. (FBI Story Ser.). (Illus.). 64p. (J). (gr. 4-7). lib. bdg. 22.95 *(978-1-4222-0572-3(X))* Mason Crest.

Whiting, Jim. FBI Hostage Rescue & Swat Teams. 2014. (U. S. Special Forces Ser.). (ENG., Illus.). 48p. (J). (gr. 5-8). lib. bdg. 35.65 *(978-1-60818-462-0(5),* 21430, Creative Education) Creative Co., The.

—FBI Hostage Rescue & SWAT Teams. 2014. (U. S. Special Forces Ser.). (ENG.). 48p. (J). (gr. 5-8). pap. 12.00 *(978-1-62832-048-0(6),* 21431, Creative Paperbacks) Creative Co., The.

Wimmer, Teresa. Federal Bureau of Investigation. 2016. (Agents of Government Ser.). (ENG.). 48p. (J). (gr. 4-7). pap. 12.00 *(978-1-62832-146-3(6),* 20838, Creative Paperbacks) Creative Co., The.

Woog, Adam. Careers in the FBI, 1 vol. 2014. (Law & Order Jobs Ser.). (ENG.). 112p. (gr. 6-6). 42.63 *(978-1-62712-431-7(4),* 182c2a21-a77d-4db3-8838-a6d5d7a966c3) Cavendish Square Publishing LLC.

—Careers in the FBI. 2013. (J). *(978-1-60870-957-1(4))* Marshall Cavendish.

UNITED STATES—FICTION

Aaron, Chester. Alex, Who Won His War. 2014. 225p. (YA). *(978-1-936144-26-6(3))* Zumaya Pubns. LLC.

Adams, Nick K. The Uncivil War: Battle in the Classroom. 2010. 84p. pap. 9.99 *(978-1-60911-711-5(5),* Eloquent Bks.) Strategic Book Publishing & Rights Agency (SBPRA).

Alexander, Lyndi. Windmills. 2013. 248p. (J). pap. 14.99 *(978-1-61271-226-0(6))* Zumaya Pubns. LLC.

Ali, S. K. Saints & Misfits. 2017. (Saints & Misfits Ser.). (ENG., Illus.). 336p. (YA). (gr. 9). 18.99 *(978-1-4814-9924-8(6),* Salaam Reads) Simon & Schuster Bks. For Young Readers.

Alsaid, Adi. North of Happy. 2019. (ENG.). 320p. (YA). pap. 10.99 *(978-1-335-65999-6(4))* Harlequin Enterprises ULC CAN. Dist: HarperCollins Pubs.

Alvarez, Julia. How the Garcia Girls Lost Their Accents. 2011. 13.46 *(978-0-7848-3532-6(2),* Everbind) Marco Bk. Co.

—Return to Sender. 2010. (ENG.). 352p. (J). (gr. 3-7). 8.99 *(978-0-375-85123-0(2),* Yearling) Random Hse. Children's Bks.

American Girl Magazine: Jan/Feb 2004. (J). 19.75 *(978-1-58485-925-3(3))* American Girl Publishing, Inc.

American Girl Magazine: July/Aug 2004 Jumbo Issue. (J). 24.75 *(978-1-58485-928-4(8))* American Girl Publishing, Inc.

American Girl Magazine: March/April 2004. (J). 19.75 *(978-1-58485-926-0(1))* American Girl Publishing, Inc.

American Girl Magazine: May/June 2004. (J). 19.75 *(978-1-58485-927-7(X))* American Girl Publishing, Inc.

American Girl Magazine: Sept/Oct 2004. (J). 19.75 *(978-1-58485-929-1(6))* American Girl Publishing, Inc.

Anderson, Matt & Hutchins, Eric. White Picket Fences: Double Feature One-shot. 2008. (Illus.). 52p. (YA). pap. 6.95 *(978-0-9801314-9-9(9))* Ape Entertainment.

Anholt, Laurence. The Hypnotist. 2016. 352p. (YA). (gr. 7). 13.99 *(978-0-552-57345-0(0))* Transworld Publishers Ltd. GBR. Dist: Independent Pubs. Group.

Avi. Don't You Know There's a War On? 2nd ed. 2003. 208p. (J). pap. *(978-0-439-53096-5(2),* HarperCollins) HarperCollins Pubs.

—Don't You Know There's a War On? 2003. 193p. (gr. 3-7). 18.00 *(978-0-7569-1383-0(7))* Perfection Learning Corp.

Ballard, John. The Shining Thing, 1 vol. Hume, Jeff, illus. 2009. 35p. pap. 19.95 *(978-1-61546-655-9(X))* PublishAmerica, Inc.

Bandy, Michael S. & Stein, Eric. White Water. Stickland, Shadra, illus. 2015. (ENG.). 40p. (J). (gr. k-3). 8.99 *(978-0-7636-7945-3(3))* Candlewick Pr.

Barnes, Jennifer Lynn. Bad Blood. 2016. (Naturals Ser.: 4). (ENG.). 384p. (YA). (gr. 7-12). 36.99 *(978-1-4847-5732-1(7))* Hyperion Bks. for Children.

Barnes, Peter W. Little Miss Patriot. Barnes, Cheryl Shaw, illus. 2007. 32p. (J). lib. bdg. 17.95 *(978-1-893622-20-3(7),* VSP Bks.) Vacation Spot Publishing.

—Marshall, the Courthouse Mouse: A Tail of the U. S. Supreme Court. Barnes, Cheryl Shaw, illus. 2012. (ENG.). 40p. (J). (gr. k). 18.99 *(978-1-59698-789-0(8),* Little Patriot Pr.) Regnery Publishing.

Bart, Kathleen. Town Teddy & Country Bear Tour the USA. Bart, Kathleen, illus. 2008. (ENG., Illus.). 32p. (J). (gr. -1-3). pap. 16.95 *(978-1-932485-50-9(3))* Reverie Publishing Co.

Baucom, Ian. Through the Skylight. Gerard, Justin, illus. 2013. (ENG.). 400p. (J). (gr. 4-8). 17.99 *(978-1-4169-1777-9(2),* Atheneum Bks. for Young Readers) Simon & Schuster Children's Publishing.

Bauld, Jane Scoggins. Hector Saves the Moon, Vol. 2. Laronde, Gary, illus. 2003. (Hector's Escapades Ser.). 34p. (J). (gr. -1-3). per. 7.95 *(978-1-57168-312-0(7))* Eakin Pr.

Bennett, Virginia. The Pigeon Tale. Hardy, E. Stuart, illus. 2007. 48p. per. *(978-1-4065-4810-5(3))* Dodo Pr.

Bilbrey, Heather. The Cookie Man. Green, Megan, illus. 2008. 20p. pap. 24.95 *(978-1-60703-328-8(3))* America Star Bks.

Billingsley, ReShonda Tate. Drama Queens. 2010. (Good Girlz Ser.: 8). (ENG., Illus.). 244p. pap. 16.99 *(978-1-4391-5687-2(5),* Gallery Bks.) Gallery Bks.

Binder, John. The Girl Who Applied Everywhere. 2011. 160p. (YA). 17.99 *(978-1-936679-02-7(7))* Wicker Park Pr., Ltd.

Bishop, Barbara L. Children Today Around the U S A. Bishop, Barbara L., illus. 2008. (Illus.). 40p. pap. 13.95 *(978-1-934246-25-2(5))* Peppertree Pr., The.

Blaine, Dalton. Tim Pays Sales Tax: Understanding Citizenship, 1 vol. 2018. (Civics for the Real World Ser.). (ENG.). 16p. (gr. 2-3). pap. *(978-1-5383-6544-1(8),* 24da7a95-4c19-48dc-aa00-c093f1eec473, Rosen Classroom) Rosen Publishing Group, Inc., The.

Blessing, Charlotte. New Old Shoes. Phillips, Gary R., illus. 2009. (ENG.). 32p. (J). (gr. k-3). 16.95 *(978-0-9792035-6-5(2))* Pleasant St. Pr.

Blitt, Natalie. The Truth about Leaving. 2019. (ENG.). 304p. (YA). pap. 12.99 *(978-1-948705-09-7(5))* Amberjack Publishing Co.

Boeve, Eunice. The Summer of the Crow. 2013. 306p. pap. 14.95 *(978-1-939054-06-7(0))* Rowe Publishing.

Bourgeois, Paulette. Postal Workers. LaFave, Kim, illus. 2005. 32p. (J). lib. bdg. 15.38 *(978-1-4242-1192-0(1))* Fitzgerald Bks.

Bowen, Carl. Dragon Teeth. Tortosa, Wilson, illus. 2015. (Shadow Squadron Ser.). (ENG.). 112p. (J). (gr. 4-8). lib. bdg. 27.32 *(978-1-4965-0383-1(X),* 128362, Stone Arch Bks.) Capstone.

—Firestormers: Elite Firefighting Crew. Lee, Marc, illus. 2016. (ENG.). 224p. (J). (gr. 4-8). pap., pap., pap. 8.95 *(978-1-62370-756-9(0),* 132450, Capstone Young Readers) Capstone.

—Shadow Squadron: Rogue Agent. Tortosa, Wilson, illus. 2015. (Shadow Squadron Ser.). (ENG.). 224p. (J). (gr. 4-8). pap., pap., pap. 8.95 *(978-1-62370-296-0(8),* 128369, Capstone Young Readers) Capstone.

Bowlby, Linda S. Nasaria's Family/la Familia de Nasaria. Helms, Dana, illus. 2008. 45p. (J). (gr. -1-3). pap. 10.95 *(978-0-9779993-9-2(4))* Red Earth Publishing.

Boyd, Bentley. Moving & Grooving. 2009. (Chester Comix Ser.). (Illus.). 24p. pap. 6.95 *(978-1-933122-36-6(6))* Chester Comix, LLC.

—Reconstruction Junction. 2010. (Chester Comix Ser.). (Illus.). 24p. pap. *(978-1-933122-43-4(9))* Chester Comix, LLC.

Bray, Diane E. B. First Generation: The Story of Annie. 2008. 53p. pap. 16.95 *(978-1-60563-516-3(2))* America Star Bks.

Bridwell, Norman. Clifford Sees America. 2012. (Clifford: Scholastic Readers Level 1 Ser.). lib. bdg. 13.55 *(978-0-606-23908-0(1))* Turtleback.

Bruchac, Joseph. Brothers of the Buffalo: A Novel of the Red River War. 2016. (ENG.). 392p. (YA). (gr. 7). pap. 25.95 *(978-1-938486-92-0(7))* Fulcrum Publishing.

—Crazy Horse's Vision. Nelson, S. D., illus. 2006. (gr. 1-4). 20.45 *(978-0-7569-6691-1(4))* Perfection Learning Corp.

Buckey, Sarah Masters. The Light in the Cellar: A Molly Mystery. 2003. (American Girl Mysteries Ser.). (ENG., Illus.). 176p. (gr. 4-7). 10.95 *(978-1-59369-159-2(9))* American Girl Publishing, Inc.

Bunting, Eve. My Red Balloon. Life, Kay, illus. 2005. (ENG.). 32p. (J). (gr. k-2). 15.99 *(978-1-59078-263-7(1),* Astra Young Readers) Astra Publishing Hse.

Burg, Ann & Burg, Ann E. Unbound. 2018. (ENG.). 352p. (J). (gr. 3-7). pap. 8.99 *(978-1-338-28208-5(5),* Scholastic Pr.) Scholastic, Inc.

Burg, Ann E. Rebekkah's Journey: A World War II Refugee Story. Iskowitz, Joel, illus. 2006. (Tales of Young Americans Ser.). (ENG.). 48p. (J). (gr. 1-4). 17.95 *(978-1-58536-275-2(1),* 202086) Sleeping Bear Pr.

Burgan, Michael & Leavitt, Amie Jane. U. S. Special Ops. 2016. (U. S. Special Ops Ser.). (ENG.). 48p. (J). (gr. 3-6). 123.29 *(978-1-5157-1865-9(4),* 24996, Stone Arch Bks.) Capstone.

Burton, Jesse. True Colors! the Story of Crayola: Ready-To-Read Level 3. Burroughs, Scott, illus. 2018. (History of Fun Stuff Ser.). (ENG.). 40p. (J). (gr. 1-3). 17.99 *(978-1-5344-2567-5(5));* pap. 4.99 *(978-1-5344-2566-8(7))* Simon Spotlight. (Simon Spotlight).

Butler, Ethel And Steven, creator. Callie the Kangie Traveling America. 2012. 32p. pap. 15.99 *(978-1-4685-6197-5(9))* AuthorHouse.

Campos-Duffy, Rachel. Paloma Wants to Be Lady Freedom. 2019. (ENG., Illus.). 40p. (J). (gr. -1-3). 18.99 *(978-1-62157-970-0(0),* Regnery Kids) Regnery Publishing.

Carol Muller-Funk. Proxmire & the Exodus of Prairieville. 2009. 400p. pap. 17.99 *(978-1-4389-4013-7(0))* AuthorHouse.

Choat, Beth. Soccerland, 0 vols. 2012. (International Sports Academy Ser.: 0). (ENG., Illus.). 242p. (YA). (gr. 7-12). pap. 8.99 *(978-0-7614-6249-1(X),* 9780761462491, Skyscape) Amazon Publishing.

Clack, Cynthia. Doodles the American Hero. 2007. (ENG., Illus.). 60p. (J). lib. bdg. 20.95 *(978-0-9787533-0-6(5))* Tiger Tale Publishing Co.

Clenott, Peter. Devolution. 2013. 280p. pap. *(978-1-927792-14-8(2))* Imajin Bks.

Cole, Lisa. Chessie of the Chesapeake Bay. Cole, Lisa, illus. 2011. (Illus.). 110p. pap. 9.95 *(978-1-936343-94-2(0))* Peppertree Pr., The.

Collier, Kevin Scott. Journeys of Hope, Pearl of Wisdom. Collier, Kevin Scott, illus. 2006. (Illus.). 28p. (J). E-Book 9.95 incl. cd-rom *(978-1-933090-31-3(6))* Guardian Angel Publishing, Inc.

Cox, Stephen Angus. The Dare Boys of 1776. 2004. reprint ed. pap. 15.95 *(978-1-4191-5856-8(2));* pap. 1.99 *(978-1-4192-5856-5(7))* Kessinger Publishing, LLC.

Crabtree, Zona Mae. The Travelers. 2004. (Corn Cave Ser.: 2). (Illus.). 155p. (YA). per. 8.00 *(978-0-9726826-1-9(9))* Owl Hollow Publishing.

Crocker, Nancy. Billie Standish Was Here. 2007. (ENG.). 288p. (YA). (gr. 9-12). 16.99 *(978-1-4169-2423-4(X),* Simon & Schuster Bks. For Young Readers) Simon & Schuster Bks. For Young Readers.

Crowley, Kieran Mark. Colm & the Lazarus Key. 2009. (ENG., Illus.). 224p. (J). pap. 14.95 *(978-1-85635-646-6(9))* Mercier Pr., Ltd., The IRL. Dist: Dufour Editions, Inc.

Cusick, John M. Cherry Money Baby. 2013. (ENG.). 400p. (YA). (gr. 9). 16.99 *(978-0-7636-5557-0(0))* Candlewick Pr.

Czekaj, Jef. Austin, Lost in America: A Geography Adventure. Czekaj, Jef, illus. 2015. (ENG., Illus.). 40p. (J). (gr. -1-3). 17.99 *(978-0-06-228017-6(1),* Balzer & Bray) HarperCollins Pubs.

Daffern, Brian. Prince Albert in a Can, Bk. 1. 2004. 256p. (YA). per. 13.95 *(978-0-9709104-5-5(2))* Hickory Tales Publishing.

Dalhaimer Bartkowski, Anna. Maggie Visits Grandpa: A Coloring Adventure. Dalhaimer Bartkowski, Anna, illus. 2007. (Illus.). 32p. pap. 8.99 *(978-0-9790720-1-7(8))* Infinite Adventure.

Dallas, Sandra. Red Berries, White Clouds, Blue Sky. 2015. (ENG., Illus.). 216p. (J). (gr. 3-6). pap. 9.99 *(978-1-58536-907-2(1),* 203820) Sleeping Bear Pr.

David Iii, Paul. Brave Americans. 2013. 28p. pap. 15.95 *(978-0-7414-9638-6(0))* Infinity Publishing.

Davies, Jacqueline. Where the Ground Meets the Sky, 0 vols. unabr. ed. 2012. (ENG.). 224p. (YA). (gr. 7-12). pap. 9.99 *(978-0-7614-5187-7(0),* 9780761451877, Skyscape) Amazon Publishing.

Daviess, Maria Thompson. The Golden Bird. 2007. 92p. per. *(978-1-4068-1853-6(4))* Echo Library.

Day, Williamson. The Pretorius Stories. 2011. 96p. pap. 9.99 *(978-1-4634-7430-0(X))* AuthorHouse.

Deering, Leta. Patriotic Samáand the Mendez Twins at the Alamo. 2008. 112p. pap. 19.95 *(978-1-60610-689-1(9))* America Star Bks.

Dennett, Kathleen. The 4 Corners Mystery. 2008. 32p. pap. 24.95 *(978-1-4137-2603-9(8))* America Star Bks.

Deutsch, Stacia & Cohon, Rhody. Bell's Breakthrough. Wenzel, David, illus. 2013. (Blast to the Past Ser.: 3). (ENG.). 128p. (J). (gr. 2-5). pap. 6.99 *(978-1-4424-9536-4(7),* Simon & Schuster/Paula Wiseman Bks.) Simon & Schuster/Paula Wiseman Bks.

—Betsy Ross's Star. Francis, Guy, illus. 2015. (Blast to the Past Ser.: 8). (ENG.). 128p. (J). (gr. 2-5). pap. 6.99 *(978-1-4424-9541-8(3),* Simon & Schuster/Paula Wiseman Bks.) Simon & Schuster/Paula Wiseman Bks.

Diggs, Dylan. The Palladium. 2006. 112p. (YA). mass mkt. 3.80 *(978-1-886366-12-1(8),* 10,000) Sights Productions.

Doherty, Ellen. William's Journal. 2011. (Early Connections Ser.). (J). *(978-1-61672-680-5(6))* Benchmark Education Co.

Don, Lari. The Hungry Wolf: A Story from North America. Williamson, Melanie, illus. 2013. (Animal Stories Ser.). 48p. (J). (gr. 1-4). pap. 8.99 *(978-1-84686-872-6(6))* Barefoot Bks., Inc.

Douglas, Alan. Afloat: Or Adventures on Watery Trails. 2007. 120p. pap. 18.99 *(978-1-4346-6016-9(8));* (ENG.). 134p.

pap. 19.99 *(978-1-4346-6017-6(6))* Creative Media Partners, LLC.

—Afloat; or, Adventures on Watery Trails. 2017. (ENG., Illus.). (J). pap. *(978-0-649-50753-5(3))* Trieste Publishing Pty Ltd.

—Afloat, or, Adventures on Watery Trails. 2016. (ENG., Illus.). (J). 23.95 *(978-1-359-00992-0(2))*; 23.95 *(978-1-359-67077-9(7))* Creative Media Partners, LLC.

Down, Heather. A Deadly Distance. 2005. (Illus.). 128p. (YA). pap. *(978-0-88878-455-1(4)*, Sandcastle Bks.) Dundurn Pr.

Doyle McQuerry, Maureen. Between Before & After, 1 vol. 2019. (ENG., Illus.). 304p. (YA). 17.99 *(978-0-310-76738-1(5))* Blink.

Dunn, Matthew. Spy Trade: A Spycatcher Novella. 2015. (ENG.). 208p. mass mkt. 6.99 *(978-0-06-244142-3(6)*, William Morrow Paperbacks) HarperCollins Pubs.

Durbin, William. Until the Last Spike: The Journal of Sean Sullivan, a Transcontinental Railroad Worker, Nebraska & Points West 1867. 2013. (My Name Is America Ser.). lib. bdg. 17.20 *(978-0-606-32342-0(2))* Turtleback.

Dyan, Penelope. Even More of My Life As I Know It. 2011. 100p. pap. 8.95 *(978-1-935630-50-0(4))* Bellissima Publishing, LLC.

Elkeles, Simone. How to Ruin My Teenage Life. 2007. (How to Ruin a Summer Vacation Novel Ser.: 2). (ENG.). 288p. (YA). (gr. 9-12). per. 11.99 *(978-0-7387-1019-8(9)*, 0738710199, Flux) North Star Editions.

English, Karen. Nadia's Hands. Weiner, Jonathan, illus. 2009. (ENG.). 32p. (J). (gr. k-2). pap. 9.99 *(978-1-59078-784-7(6)*, Astra Young Readers) Astra Publishing Hse.

Epstein, Estelle Pottern. I Heard My Father's Voice. 2007. 124p. pap. 11.95 *(978-0-7414-4053-2(9))* Infinity Publishing.

Erdrich, Louise. Chickadee. Erdrich, Louise, illus. 2012. (Birchbark House Ser.: 4). (ENG., Illus.). 208p. (J). (gr. 3-7). 16.99 *(978-0-06-057790-2(8)*, HarperCollins) HarperCollins Pubs.

Eyre, David. Sacred Awa Piercing Spears. Kalahele, Imaikalani, illus. 2009. 31p. 14.95 *(978-0-87336-217-7(9))* Kamehameha Publishing.

Farnsworth, Frances. Cubby in Wonderland. 2005. pap. 20.95 *(978-1-4179-8778-8(2))* Kessinger Publishing, LLC.

Faruqi, Saadia. Meet Yasmin! Aly, Hatem, illus. 2018. (Yasmin Ser.). (ENG.). 96p. (J). (gr. k-2). pap., pap., pap. 5.95 *(978-1-68436-022-2(6)*, 137937, Picture Window Bks.) Capstone.

—Yasmin, la Guardiana Del Zoo. Aparicio Publishing LLC, Aparicio Publishing, tr. from ENG. Aly, Hatem, illus. 2020. (Yasmin en Español Ser.).Tr. of Yasmin the Zookeeper. (SPA.). 32p. (J). (gr. k-2). pap. 5.95 *(978-1-5158-5735-8(2)*, 142100); lib. bdg. 20.65 *(978-1-5158-5731-0(X)*, 142096) Capstone. (Picture Window Bks.).

—Yasmin the Fashionista. Aly, Hatem, illus. 2018. (Yasmin Ser.). (ENG.). 32p. (J). (gr. k-2). 22.65 *(978-1-5158-3103-7(5)*, 138807, Picture Window Bks.) Capstone.

—Yasmin the Painter. Aly, Hatem, illus. 2018. (Yasmin Ser.). (ENG.). 32p. (J). (gr. k-2). 22.65 *(978-1-5158-2728-3(3)*, 137932, Picture Window Bks.) Capstone.

—Yasmin the Zookeeper. Aly, Hatem, illus. 2019. (Yasmin Ser.). (ENG.). 32p. (J). (gr. k-2). pap. 5.95 *(978-1-5158-4581-2(8)*, 141181); lib. bdg. 22.65 *(978-1-5158-3785-5(8)*, 139367) Capstone. (Picture Window Bks.).

Fidler, Mark. Blaze of the Great Cliff. 2003. 196p. 24.95 *(978-0-595-65847-3(4))* iUniverse, Inc.

Fleury, Mike Stevenson. Natural Disaster 2222. 2003. (ENG.). 112p. 19.95 *(978-0-595-65436-9(3))*; 108p. (YA). pap. 9.95 *(978-0-595-25921-2(9))* iUniverse, Inc. (Writers Club Pr.).

Flint, Ann. Charlotte's Curtain Call. 2011. 190p. pap. *(978-1-908105-51-6(8))* Grosvenor Hse. Publishing Ltd.

Flower, Graham Jessie. Grace Harlowe's Overland Riders on the Great American Desert. 2007. (ENG.). 132p. pap. 18.99 *(978-1-4264-1676-7(8))* Creative Media Partners, LLC.

—Grace Harlowe's Overland Riders on the Great American Desert. 2004. reprint ed. pap. 20.95 *(978-1-4191-2221-7(5))*; pap. 1.99 *(978-1-4192-2221-4(X))* Kessinger Publishing, LLC.

Floyd, Belinda D. Going to America. 2005. 28p. per. 25.49 *(978-1-4208-8693-1(2))* AuthorHouse.

Forest, Heather. The Baker's Dozen: A Colonial American Tale. Gaber, Susan, illus. 2013. (ENG.). 32p. (J). (gr. -1-3). 8.95 *(978-1-939160-70-6(7))* August Hse. Pubs., Inc.

Francis, Peter, illus. God Bless America, 1 vol. 2016. (Land That I Love Book Ser.). (ENG.). 18p. (J). bds. 9.99 *(978-0-310-75347-6(3))* Zonderkidz.

Furman, A. L., ed. Pioneer Stories: Young Readers. Geer, Charles, illus. 2011. 190p. 42.95 *(978-1-258-09907-7(1))* Literary Licensing, LLC.

Gardner, Sheldon. Converso Legacy. 2005. 264p. (J). pap. 12.95 *(978-1-932687-19-4(X)*, Devora Publishing) Simcha Media Group.

Gildea, Kathy. The Adventures of Baylee Beagle — Greenville. 2005. (Illus.). 20p. (J). 7.95 *(978-0-9767096-0-2(0))* Maxim Pr.

Gingrich, Callista. Christmas in America. Arciero, Susan, illus. 2015. (Ellis the Elephant Ser.: 5). (ENG.). 40p. (J). (gr. -1-3). 16.99 *(978-1-62157-345-6(1)*, Regnery Kids) Regnery Publishing.

—Remember the Ladies. Arciero, Susan, illus. 2017. (Ellis the Elephant Ser.: 7). (ENG.). 40p. (J). (gr. -1-4). 16.99 *(978-1-62157-480-4(6))* Regnery Publishing.

Glick, Susan. Jemma's Got the Travel Bug, 1 vol. 2010. (ENG., Illus.). 32p. (J). (gr. -1-3). 14.99 *(978-0-7643-3632-4(0)*, 3968) Schiffer Publishing, Ltd.

Goelman, Ari. The Path of Names. 2013. (Illus.). 339p. (J). pap. *(978-0-545-47431-3(0)*, Levine, Arthur A. Bks.) Scholastic, Inc.

Goring, Ruth. Adriana's Angels. Meza, Erika, illus. 2017. (J). 16.99 *(978-1-5064-1832-2(5)*, Sparkhouse Family) 1517 Media.

Grant, Rick S. When I Grow Up. Alfonso, Anabel, illus. 2017. (J). pap. *(978-1-934370-67-4(3))* Editorial Campana.

Green, Tim. Deep Zone. 2012. (Football Genius Ser.: 5). (ENG.). 304p. (J). (gr. 3-7). pap. 7.99 *(978-0-06-201245-6(2)*, HarperCollins) HarperCollins Pubs.

—Perfect Season. 2013. (Football Genius Ser.: 6). (ENG.). 400p. (J). (gr. 3-7). 16.99 *(978-0-06-220869-9(1)*, HarperCollins) HarperCollins Pubs.

Greenwell, Ivo. The Ancestor. 2003. 264p. (YA). pap. 16.95 *(978-0-595-29494-7(4))* iUniverse, Inc.

Hahn, Mary Downing. One for Sorrow: A Ghost Story. 2018. (ENG.). 320p. (J). (gr. 5-7). pap. 7.99 *(978-1-328-49798-7(4)*, 1717853, Clarion Bks.) HarperCollins Pubs.

Hale, Edward Everett. Margaret Percival in America; a Tale Ed by a New England Minister, a B Being a Sequel to Margaret Percival a Tale Ed by Rev William Sewell, B. 2006. 288p. per. 23.99 *(978-1-4255-2654-2(3))* Michigan Publishing.

Hall, Annalisa. Tak & Lolly: Santa Clause at Church. 2009. 51p. pap. 6.99 *(978-0-557-04923-3(7))* Lulu Pr., Inc.

Hall, Donald. Lucy's Christmas. McCurdy, Michael, illus. 2007. 40p. (J). (gr. 1). pap. 14.95 *(978-1-56792-342-1(9))* Godine, David R. Pub.

Hampstead, Tom. The Kingdom of the Two Great Houses. 2011. 86p. pap. 10.95 *(978-1-60911-895-2(2)*, Strategic Bk. Publishing) Strategic Book Publishing & Rights Agency (SBPRA).

Hancock, H. Irving. Dave Darrin at Vera Cruz. 2007. 180p. per. *(978-1-4065-1973-0(1))* Dodo Pr.

Hannigan, Kate. Cape. Spaziante, Patrick, illus. 2019. (League of Secret Heroes Ser.: 1). (ENG.). 336p. (J). (gr. 3-7). 17.99 *(978-1-5344-3911-5(0)*, Simon & Schuster/Paula Wiseman Bks.) Simon & Schuster/Paula Wiseman Bks.

Harper, Chris. The Dogges of Barkshire - the Grand Kennel. Harper, Chris, illus. 2013. (Illus.). 26p. (J). pap. *(978-1-78222-086-2(0))* Paragon Publishing, Rothersthorpe.

Harper, Ken. Mystery in Mansfield. 2008. 60p. pap. 19.95 *(978-1-60441-055-6(8))* America Star Bks.

Harris, Joel Chandler. Told by Uncle Remus: New Stories of the. 2006. (Illus.). pap. 31.95 *(978-1-4254-9964-8(3))* Kessinger Publishing, LLC.

Harstad, Johan. 172 Hours on the Moon. 2012. (ENG.). 368p. (YA). (gr. 7-17). 36.99 *(978-0-316-18288-1(5))* Little, Brown Bks. for Young Readers.

Hartman, Bob. The Littlest Camel. Hudson, Brett, illus. 2004. (Lion Storyteller Ser.). (ENG.). 64p. (J). (gr. k-4). pap. 6.99 *(978-0-7459-4825-6(1)*, 9630f7c5-9623-4c3a-9153-b77f3f910277, Lion Books) Lion Hudson PLC GBR. Dist: Baker & Taylor Publisher Services (BTPS).

Hashimi, Nadia. The Sky at Our Feet. (ENG.). (J). (gr. 3-7). 2019. 320p. pap. 9.99 *(978-0-06-242194-4(8))* 2018. 304p. 16.99 *(978-0-06-242193-7(X))* HarperCollins Pubs. (HarperCollins).

Havran, Melissa. George Washington. 2013. 32p. pap. 19.99 *(978-1-4817-0157-0(6))* AuthorHouse.

Hearne, Betsy. Seven Brave Women. Andersen, Bethanne, illus. 2006. (gr. -1-3). 17.00 *(978-0-7569-6669-0(8))* Perfection Learning Corp.

Henson, S. F. Devils Within. 2017. (ENG.). 404p. (J). (gr. 8-8). 17.99 *(978-1-5107-1456-4(1)*, Sky Pony Pr.) Skyhorse Publishing Co., Inc.

Hergé. America. Orig. Title: Tintin en Amerique. (Illus.). 62p. (J). 24.95 *(978-0-8288-5000-1(3))* French & European Pubns., Inc.

—Tintin en Amerique. Orig. Title: Tintin in America. (Illus.). 62p. (J). (SPA.). 24.95 *(978-0-8288-5094-0(1))*; (FRE., 24.95 *(978-0-8288-5093-3(3))* French & European Pubns., Inc.

Herman, Debbie. Rosie Saves the World. Lyon, Tammie, illus. 2017. (ENG.). 32p. (J). (gr. -1-2). 17.99 *(978-1-5124-2085-2(9)*, 1a26aeae-930a-429d-807d-fd9e48a3eb2b, Kar-Ben Publishing) Lerner Publishing Group.

Herring, M. L. Ellie's Strand: Exploring the Edge of the Pacific. 2018. (ENG., Illus.). 112p. (J). (gr. 3-5). pap. 17.95 *(978-0-87071-941-7(6))* Oregon State Univ. Pr.

Hinton, S. E. Rumble Fish. 2013. 144p. (YA). (gr. 7). pap. 10.99 *(978-0-385-37568-9(9)*, Delacorte Pr.) Random Hse. Children's Bks.

Hobbs, Will. Beardance. 2004. (ENG., Illus.). 208p. (J). (gr. 5-9). pap. 7.99 *(978-0-689-87072-9(8)*, Simon & Schuster/Paula Wiseman Bks.) Simon & Schuster Children's Publishing.

—Crossing the Wire. 2007. (Illus.). 216p. (gr. 5-9). 17.00 *(978-0-7569-8053-5(4))* Perfection Learning Corp.

Holt, Kimberly Willis. Piper Reed, Campfire Girl. Davenier, Christine, illus. 2011. (Piper Reed Ser.: 4). (ENG.). 176p. (J). (gr. 3-6). pap. 18.99 *(978-0-312-67482-3(1)*, 900072895) Square Fish.

—Piper Reed, Clubhouse Queen. Davenier, Christine, illus. 2011. (Piper Reed Ser.: 2). (ENG.). 176p. (J). (gr. 3-6). pap. 9.99 *(978-0-312-61676-2(7)*, 900076846) Square Fish.

—Piper Reed, Forever Friend, 6. Davenier, Christine, illus. 2012. (Piper Reed Ser.: 6). (ENG.). 160p. (J). (gr. 3-6). 18.69 *(978-0-8050-9008-6(8)*, 900058970, Holt, Henry & Co.) Holt, Henry & Co.

—Piper Reed, Forever Friend. Davenier, Christine, illus. 2013. (Piper Reed Ser.: 6). (ENG.). 176p. (J). (gr. 3-6). pap. 8.99 *(978-1-250-02725-2(X)*, 900098296) Square Fish.

—Piper Reed, Navy Brat. Davenier, Christine, illus. 2011. (Piper Reed Ser.: 1). (ENG.). 176p. (J). (gr. 3-6). pap. 9.99 *(978-0-312-62548-1(0)*, 900077153) Square Fish.

—Piper Reed, Party Planner. Davenier, Christine, illus. 2011. (Piper Reed Ser.: 3). (ENG.). 176p. (J). (gr. 3-6). pap. 9.99 *(978-0-312-61677-9(5)*, 900076848) Square Fish.

Hossfeld, Harald. Rapacious Kings Sagacious Kids. 2010. 186p. pap. *(978-3-8391-4994-2(0))* Books on Demand GmbH.

Howe, Kim, illus. American Life Series: Family, Teacher, Friend, 3 books. 2006. 80p. 19.95 *(978-1-59971-554-4(6))* Aardvark Global Publishing.

Hu, Jennifer. Dodo's Story: Journey in America. 2010. 40p. 16.99 *(978-1-4520-6095-8(9))* AuthorHouse.

Hubbard, Crystal. Catching the Moon: The Story of a Young Girl's Baseball Dream, 1 vol. 2005. (ENG., Illus.). 32p. (J). (gr. 1-5). pap. 11.95 *(978-1-60060-572-7(9)*, leelowbooks) Lee & Low Bks., Inc.

Hubbard, Jenny. Paper Covers Rock. 2012. (ENG.). 192p. (YA). (gr. 9). pap. 7.99 *(978-0-385-74056-2(5)*, Ember) Random Hse. Children's Bks.

Huber, Morgan. Nanite. 2013. 140p. pap. 19.95 *(978-1-63004-633-0(7))* America Star Bks.

Huber, Randolph. Monsters from the ID. 2007. 48p. per. 16.95 *(978-1-4241-4682-6(8))* PublishAmerica, Inc.

Hughes, Dean. Four-Four-Two. 2016. (ENG., Illus.). 272p. (YA). (gr. 7). 18.99 *(978-1-4814-6252-5(0)*, Atheneum Bks. for Young Readers) Simon & Schuster Children's Publishing.

Hughes, Virginia. Peggy Finds the Theater. Leone, Sergio, illus. 2011. 186p. 42.95 *(978-1-258-10513-6(6))* Literary Licensing, LLC.

Husain, Aliya. Neither This nor That. 2010. 260p. pap. 19.99 *(978-0-557-22302-2(4))* Lulu Pr., Inc.

Johnson, Terry Lynn. Dust Storm! Orban, Jani, illus. 2018. (Survivor Diaries). (ENG.). 128p. (J). (gr. 1-5). 9.99 *(978-0-544-97098-4(5)*, 1662531, Clarion Bks.) HarperCollins Pubs.

Johnston, Annie Fellows. The Little Colonel. 2004. reprint ed. pap. 1.99 *(978-1-4192-7020-8(6))* Kessinger Publishing, LLC.

Jones, Marcia Thornton. Woodford Brave. Whipple, Kevin, illus. 2015. (ENG.). 200p. (J). (gr. 4-7). 16.95 *(978-1-62979-305-4(1)*, Calkins Creek) Highlights Pr., c/o Highlights for Children, Inc.

Jordan-Tegtmeier. Jennifer. The Small Shady Tree. 2008. 16p. pap. 8.49 *(978-1-4343-7382-3(7))* AuthorHouse.

Judybee. Danny Strikes Out in Americ: A R. E. A. d Book. Kecskés, Anna, illus. 2013. 32p. pap. *(978-1-78092-335-2(X))* MX Publishing, Ltd.

Kay, Susan. Abby & Gabby Tales. 2009. 16p. pap. 9.99 *(978-1-4389-6467-6(6))* AuthorHouse.

Keller, Laurie. The Scrambled States of America. 2011. (J). (gr. k-4). 29.95 *(978-0-545-19702-1(3))* Weston Woods Studios, Inc.

—The Scrambled States of America Talent Show. Keller, Laurie, illus. 2010. (ENG., Illus.). 40p. (J). (gr. 2-5). pap. 8.99 *(978-0-312-62824-6(2)*, 900066819) Square Fish.

Kelly, Cheryl. Adam the Adventurous Ant. 2011. 24p. pap. 15.99 *(978-1-4568-6366-1(5))* Xlibris Corp.

Kent, Elizabeth. The Enchanted Adventures of the Caroline Kemps. 2007. 148p. pap. 24.95 *(978-1-4241-9915-0(8))* America Star Bks.

Keppeler, Jill. Remi's Rights & Responsibilities: Understanding Citizenship, 1 vol. 2018. (Civics for the Real World Ser.). (ENG.). 16p. (gr. 2-3). pap. *(978-1-5081-3944-7(X)*, 800f91a4-c9fc-4ceb-a4f8-150b59013920, Rosen Classroom) Rosen Publishing Group, Inc., The.

Ketchum, Liza. The Life Fantastic: A Novel in Three Acts. 2017. (ENG.). 256p. (YA). 17.99 *(978-1-4405-9876-0(2)*, Simon Pulse) Simon Pulse.

Kiem, Elizabeth. Dancer, Daughter, Traitor, Spy. 2014. (Bolshoi Saga Ser.: 1). (Illus.). 304p. (YA). (gr. 9). pap. 10.99 *(978-1-61695-422-2(1)*, Soho Teen) Soho Pr., Inc.

Kimpton, Paul & Kimpton, Ann Kaczkowski. Starting Early: A Boy & His Bugle in America During WWII. 2011. (Adventures with Music Ser.: 1). (ENG., Illus.). 204p. (J). (gr. 4-7). pap. 8.95 *(978-1-57999-805-9(4))* G I A Pubns., Inc.

King, Emiliya. Tori Goes to Town Hall: Understanding Government, 1 vol. 2018. (Civics for the Real World Ser.). (ENG.). 12p. (gr. 1-2). pap. *(978-1-5383-6433-8(6)*, 34b18084-c7c0-427b-97df-cdb832828724, Rosen Classroom) Rosen Publishing Group, Inc., The.

Knapp, Jodi. The Adventures of Kelly & Lucky: The Beginning. 2010. 76p. pap. 20.99 *(978-1-60976-090-8(5)*, Eloquent Bks.) Strategic Book Publishing & Rights Agency (SBPRA).

Konigsburg, E. L. The Outcasts of 19 Schuyler Place. 2005. 296p. (J). (gr. 5). 13.65 *(978-0-7569-6307-1(9))* Perfection Learning Corp.

Kravitz, Danny. Tommy Mcknight & the Great Election. 2016. (Presidential Politics Ser.). (ENG., Illus.). 96p. (J). (gr. 3-6). lib. bdg. 26.65 *(978-1-4965-2585-7(X)*, 130712, Stone Arch Bks.) Capstone.

Krensky, Stephen. John Henry. Oldroyd, Mark, illus. 2007. (On My Own Folklore Ser.). (ENG.). 48p. (J). (gr. 2-4). per. 8.99 *(978-0-8225-6477-5(7)*, a768119c-8334-4843-953d-e0ea2784d85b, First Avenue Editions) Lerner Publishing Group.

Kurchinski, Alessandra. Disney Story. 2010. 36p. pap. 17.30 *(978-0-557-25447-7(7))* Lulu Pr., Inc.

Lachtman, Ofelia Dumas. The Truth about las Mariposas. 2007. 144p. (J). (gr. 6-18). pap. 9.95 *(978-1-55885-494-9(0)*, Piñata Books) Arte Publico Pr.

Landon, Lucinda. Meg Mackintosh Solves Seven American History Mysteries - Title #9: A Solve-It-Yourself Mystery. 2008. (Meg Mackintosh Mystery Ser.: 9). (ENG.). 96p. (J). (gr. 2-4). pap. 8.95 *(978-1-888695-12-0(9))* Secret Passage Pr.

Lang, Sheri. Seth Meets His Senator: Understanding Government, 1 vol. 2018. (Civics for the Real World Ser.). (ENG.). 16p. (gr. 2-3). pap. *(978-1-5383-6512-0(X)*, fea4f1c6-705c-4144-a7d7-768084e2bd77, Rosen Classroom) Rosen Publishing Group, Inc., The.

Langridge, Roger. The Muppet Show Comic Book: The Treasure of Peg-Leg Wilson. Langridge, Roger, illus. 2010. (Muppet Show Ser.). (ENG., Illus.). 112p. (J). 24.99 *(978-1-60886-530-7(4))*; (gr. 4-7). pap. 9.99 *(978-1-60886-504-8(5))* BOOM! Studios.

Larson, Kirby. Duke (Dogs of World War II) 2015. (Dogs of World War II Ser.). (ENG.). 240p. (J). (gr. 3-7). pap. 8.99 *(978-0-545-41638-2(8)*, Scholastic Paperbacks) Scholastic, Inc.

Lawlor, Laurie. He Will Go Fearless. 2012. (ENG.). 224p. (J). (gr. 5-9). pap. 10.99 *(978-0-689-86580-0(5)*, Simon & Schuster Bks. For Young Readers) Simon & Schuster Bks. For Young Readers.

Lazo Gilmore, Dorina K. Cora Cooks Pancit. Valiant, Kristi, illus. 2014. (ENG.). 32p. (J). (gr. -1-3). 17.95 *(978-1-885008-35-0(X)*, Shen's Bks.) Lee & Low Bks., Inc.

Lehrer, Ruth. Being Fishkill. 2017. (ENG.). 320p. (YA). (gr. 9). 17.99 *(978-0-7636-8442-6(2))* Candlewick Pr.

Leipold, Judith. Destiny's Wild Ride, a Tall Tale of the Legendary Hub Hubbell. White, David, illus. 2013. 32p. 24.95 *(978-1-61493-168-3(2))*; pap. 14.95 *(978-1-61493-167-6(4))* Peppertree Pr., The.

Lems-Tardif, Gina. Pilgrim Children Had Many Chores. 2017. (Learn-To-Read Ser.). (ENG., Illus.). (J). pap. 3.49 *(978-1-68310-238-0(X))* Pacific Learning, Inc.

Lester, James D. Corn Flower on the Great Plains. 2019. 110p. (J). pap. *(978-1-63293-250-1(4))* Sunstone Pr.

Lester, Julius. Day of Tears (Coretta Scott King Author Honor Title) 2007. (ENG., Illus.). 192p. (J). (gr. 5-9). pap. 9.99 *(978-1-4231-0409-4(9))* Little, Brown Bks. for Young Readers.

Levitin, Sonia. Junkman's Daughter. Porfirio, Guy, illus. rev. ed. 2007. (Tales of Young Americans Ser.). (ENG.). 32p. (J). (gr. 1-4). 17.95 *(978-1-58536-315-5(4)*, 202119) Sleeping Bear Pr.

Lewis, Fiona. Dreaming in Color. 2011. (ENG.). 304p. (J). (gr. 7). pap. 16.95 *(978-0-9845318-5-1(8))* Tiny Stachel Pr.

Lieurance, Suzanne. The Lucky Baseball: My Story in a Japanese-American Internment Camp, 1 vol. 2010. (Historical Fiction Adventures Ser.). (ENG., Illus.). 160p. (J). (gr. 3-5). lib. bdg. 31.93 *(978-0-7660-3311-5(2)*, de535228-7abe-4f5d-92ff-dfd0e351cb79) Enslow Publishing, LLC.

Littman, Sarah Darer. Anything but Okay. 2019. (ENG.). 352p. (YA). (gr. 7-7). pap. 9.99 *(978-1-338-17758-9(3)*, Scholastic Paperbacks) Scholastic, Inc.

Lockard, Donna Lee. Sasha the Tortoise's Summer Vacation. 2013. (ENG.). 36p. (J). pap. 19.95 *(978-1-4787-0938-1(3))* Outskirts Pr., Inc.

Loeper, John J. Galloping Gertrude: By Motorcar In 1908. Chironna, Ronald, illus. 2011. 80p. (J). lib. bdg. 19.95 *(978-0-9727940-1-5(8))* Hieropub LLC.

Loiske, Jennifer. Black Diamond. 2013. (ENG.). 246p. (J). pap. *(978-1-291-30145-8(3))* Lulu Pr., Inc.

Lombardo, Constance. Mr. Puffball: Stunt Cat Across America. Lombardo, Constance, illus. 2016. (Mr. Puffball Ser.: 2). (ENG., Illus.). 240p. (J). (gr. 3-7). 12.99 *(978-0-06-232068-1(8)*, HarperCollins) HarperCollins Pubs.

London, C. Alexander. Endurance. 2015. 199p. (J). *(978-0-545-80081-5(1))* Scholastic, Inc.

—Enemy Lines. 2015. 210p. (J). *(978-0-545-80076-1(5))* Scholastic, Inc.

Long, Loren & Bildner, Phil. Horsin' Around. Long, Loren, illus. 2009. (Sluggers Ser.: 2). (ENG., Illus.). 224p. (J). (gr. 3-7). pap. 8.99 *(978-1-4169-1888-2(4)*, Simon & Schuster Bks. For Young Readers) Simon & Schuster Bks. For Young Readers.

Lowry, Lois. Crow Call. Ibatoulline, Bagram, illus. 2009. (ENG.). 32p. (J). (gr. 4-7). 17.99 *(978-0-545-03035-9(8)*, Scholastic Pr.) Scholastic, Inc.

—Gooney Bird on the Map. Thomas, Middy, illus. (Gooney Bird Greene Ser.: 5). (ENG.). 128p. (J). (gr. 1-4). 2013. pap. 7.99 *(978-0-547-85088-7(3)*, 1501066) 2011. 16.99 *(978-0-547-55622-2(5)*, 1452833) HarperCollins Pubs. (Clarion Bks.).

Lucan, Dawn. My Challenge Memories. 2011. (ENG.). 106p. pap. 8.95 *(978-1-4583-4714-5(1))* Lulu Pr., Inc.

Lucas, Lexie. The Adventures of Little Boy Brown. 2011. (Illus.). 40p. pap. 16.59 *(978-1-4567-4035-1(0))* AuthorHouse.

Lyford, Cabot. Arthur the Moose. Lyford, Cabot, illus. l.t. ed. 2004. (Illus.). 32p. (J). lib. bdg. *(978-0-9748145-0-6(4))* Castlebay, Inc.

Lynch, Chris. Casualties of War. 2013. (Vietnam Ser.: 4). lib. bdg. 18.40 *(978-0-606-31964-5(6))* Turtleback.

—Free-Fire Zone. 2012. 183p. (J). *(978-0-545-49427-4(3)*, Scholastic Pr.) Scholastic, Inc.

—Free-Fire Zone. 2013. (Vietnam Ser.: 3). lib. bdg. 18.40 *(978-0-606-31963-8(8))* Turtleback.

—I Pledge Allegiance. 2011. 183p. (YA). *(978-0-545-38415-5(X))* Scholastic, Inc.

—I Pledge Allegiance. 2013. (Vietnam Ser.: 1). lib. bdg. 17.20 *(978-0-606-31961-4(1))* Turtleback.

Mabry, Samantha. All the Wind in the World. 2018. (ENG.). 272p. (gr. 9-12). pap. 13.99 *(978-1-61620-855-4(4)*, 73855) Algonquin Young Readers.

MacDonald, Jerry. Red Eyes & Crazy Jake. 2009. 24p. pap. 15.95 *(978-1-4389-2706-0(1))* AuthorHouse.

Mackall, Dandi Daley, et al. Troubled Times: the Great Depression: The Great Depression. Porfirio, Guy & Ellison, Chris, illus. 2014. (American Adventures Ser.). (ENG.). 80p. (J). (gr. 3-6). 6.99 *(978-1-58536-903-4(9)*, 203552) Sleeping Bear Pr.

MacKenzie-Krysko, Claudia & Krysko, Kenneth L. The Adventures of Granville, Coming to America. Cotton, Sue Lynn, illus. 2013. 24p. pap. 12.95 *(978-1-61493-227-7(1))* Peppertree Pr., The.

Maclachlan, Patricia. More Perfect Than the Moon. 2005. 16.00 *(978-0-7569-5437-6(1))* Perfection Learning Corp.

—Nora's Chicks. Brown, Kathryn, illus. 2013. (ENG.). 40p. (J). (gr. -1-2). 16.99 *(978-0-7636-4753-7(5))* Candlewick Pr.

Maddox, Jake. Strange Boarders. Muñiz, Berenice, illus. 2018. (Jake Maddox Graphic Novels Ser.). (ENG.). 72p. (J). (gr. 3-8). pap. 6.95 *(978-1-4965-6050-6(7)*, 137431); lib. bdg. 27.99 *(978-1-4965-6046-9(9)*, 137427) Capstone. (Stone Arch Bks.).

Madison, Ron. Ned & the General: A Lesson about Deployment. Covolo, David, illus. 2004. 26p. (J). (gr. -1-3). *(978-1-887206-25-9(6))* Ned's Head Productions.

Magenta, Emma. Orlando on a Thursday. Magenta, Emma, illus. 2010. (ENG., Illus.). 32p. (J). (gr. -1-2). 15.99 *(978-0-7636-4560-1(5))* Candlewick Pr.

Marsh, Carole. The Counterfeit Constitution Mystery. 2008. (Real Kids, Real Places Ser.). (Illus.). 144p. (J). (gr. 3-5). 14.95 *(978-0-635-06517-9(7))*; per. 5.95 *(978-0-635-06512-4(6))* Gallopade International.

Martinez, Manuel. Ana Is a Citizen! Digital Citizenship, 1 vol. 2017. (Computer Science for the Real World Ser.). (ENG.). 16p. (gr. 2-3). pap. *(978-1-5383-5216-8(8)*, 652772e9-7054-403c-a0cd-01e695cf2438, Rosen Classroom) Rosen Publishing Group, Inc., The.

—Sofia's Stop Sign Campaign: Taking Civic Action, 1 vol. 2018. (Civics for the Real World Ser.). (ENG.). 16p. (gr. 2-3). pap. *(978-1-5383-6566-3(9)*, f37eb158-d951-4a50-98f4-8a4c72a2f8b6, Rosen Classroom) Rosen Publishing Group, Inc., The.

Matagrano, Joseph F. Forever Brothers. 2007. 396p. 26.95 *(978-1-4327-0963-1(1))*; per. 16.95 *(978-1-4327-1524-3(0))* Outskirts Pr., Inc.

Mayhar, Ardath. Medicine Walk. 2007. (ENG.). 96p. (YA). (gr. 9). pap. 7.95 *(978-1-4169-6846-7(6)*, Simon Pulse) Simon Pulse.

McCaffrey, Debra. Fly...Ball: Illustrated by 2nd Grade Students of Mrs. Young's 2KY at Mohansic Elementary School. 2007. pap. 20.00 *(978-0-8059-8781-2(9))* Dorrance Publishing Co., Inc.

McCully, Emily Arnold. My Heart Glow: Alice Cogswell, Thomas Gallaudet, & the Birth of American Sign Language. McCully, Emily Arnold, illus. 2008. (ENG., Illus.). 40p. (gr. 1-4). 15.99 *(978-1-4231-0028-7(X))* Hyperion Pr.

McGovern, DeeDee Jean. The Heartland of Home: Tight Quarters in the City. 2008. 58p. pap. 16.95 *(978-1-60610-058-5(0))* America Star Bks.

McMann, Lisa. The Trap Door. 2015. (Infinity Ring Ser.: 3). lib. bdg. 17.20 *(978-0-606-37788-1(3))* Turtleback.

McSpadden, Judy. Heart for Thunder. 2010. 148p. 22.95 *(978-1-4401-9487-0(4))*; pap. 12.95 *(978-1-4401-9489-4(0))* iUniverse, Inc.

Meehan, Thomas. Annie. 2013. (Annie Book Ser.). (ENG.). 272p. (J). (gr. 5). pap. 8.99 *(978-0-14-751114-0(3)*, Puffin Books) Penguin Young Readers Group.

Merry Christmas USA. 2007. (J). bds. 21.95 *(978-0-9745191-3-5(8))* Lynn Tyner Mitchum & James Rogers.

Mochizuki, Ken. Baseball Saved Us. 97th rev. ed. 2014. (ENG.). 30p. (J). (gr. k-12). 15.65 *(978-1-63245-249-8(9))* Lectorum Pubns., Inc.

Moller, Sharon Chickering. Jeep: The Coyote Who Flew in World War II. Cranford, Darren, illus. 2014. 59p. (J). pap. 9.95 *(978-0-9860799-0-0(1))* Chickering-Moller Project.

Montgomery, R. A. Blood on the Handle. Michel, Jean, illus. 2010. (ENG.). 144p. (J). (gr. 4-8). pap. 7.99 *(978-1-933390-33-8(6))* Chooseco LLC.

—Smoke Jumpers. Peguy, Laurence, illus. 2009. (ENG.). 144p. (J). (gr. 4-8). pap. 7.99 *(978-1-933390-29-1(8))* Chooseco LLC.

Moreland, Janet & Webb, Shirley G. Dance in the Rain. 2005. (Howell Women Saga: Bk. II). 209p. (YA). pap. 14.95 *(978-0-595-34022-4(9))* iUniverse, Inc.

Moser, Fiadhnait. The Serendipity of Flightless Things. 2019. (ENG.). 320p. (J). (gr. 4-9). 16.99 *(978-1-4998-0843-8(7)*, Yellow Jacket) Bonnier Publishing USA.

Musilli Whitesell, Marjorie. I Have Four Parents. 2009. (Illus.). 20p. pap. 10.95 *(978-1-60860-448-7(9)*, Eloquent Bks.) Strategic Book Publishing & Rights Agency (SBPRA).

The Mystery of the Tiny Key. 2008. 32p. pap. 4.99 *(978-0-8341-2351-9(7)*, 083-412-3517) Beacon Hill Pr. of Kansas City.

Naberhaus, Sarvinder. Blue Sky White Stars. Nelson, Kadir, illus. 2017. 40p. (J). (gr. -1-3). 18.99 *(978-0-8037-3700-6(9)*, Dial Bks) Penguin Young Readers Group.

Nagai, Mariko. Dust of Eden. 2018. (ENG.). 144p. (J). (gr. 3-7). pap. 9.99 *(978-0-8075-1738-3(0)*, 807517380) Whitman, Albert & Co.

Nextext, creator. Tales of O. Henry. 2006. (Classic Retelling Ser.). (Illus.). 144p. (YA). (gr. 8-12). lib. bdg. *(978-0-618-08596-5(3)*, 2-00189) Holt McDougal.

North, Julian. Fate of Order: Age of Order Saga Book 3. 2017. (ENG.). 278p. (YA). pap. *(978-0-9992658-1-9(4))* Plebeian Media.

Norton, Andre. The Time Traders. 2009. 148p. pap. 5.95 *(978-1-60386-204-2(8)*, Merchant Bks.) Rough Draft Printing.

Olivas, John D. Endeavour's Long Journey/la Larga Travesía de Endeavour. Roski, Gayle G., illus. 2016. (SPA.). 40p. (J). 19.95 *(978-0-9973947-2-6(2))* East West Discovery Pr.

Orback, Craig, illus. Paul Bunyan. 2006. (On My Own Folklore Ser.). 48p. (J). (gr. -1-3). lib. bdg. 25.26 *(978-1-57505-888-7(X)*, Millbrook Pr.) Lerner Publishing Group.

Ortiz Cofer, Judith. An Island Like You: Stories of the Barrio. 2009. (ENG.). 256p. (J). (gr. 7-12). pap. 21.19 *(978-0-545-13133-9(2))* Scholastic, Inc.

Osa, Nancy. Cuba 15. 2005. 304p. (YA). (gr. 7). reprint ed. pap. 9.99 *(978-0-385-73233-8(3)*, Ember) Random Hse. Children's Bks.

Osborne, Mary Pope. Magic Tree House Books 21-24 Boxed Set: American History Quartet, 4 vols. Murdocca, Sal, illus. 2014. (Magic Tree House (R) Ser.). 96p. (J). (gr. 1-4). 27.96 *(978-0-385-38957-0(4)*, Random Hse. Bks. for Young Readers) Random Hse. Children's Bks.

Otter, Isabel. My Daddy Is a Hero. 2018. *(978-1-61067-720-2(X))* Kane Miller.

Pacileo, Janis. A Shrimp Called Pee Wee. 2012. 24p. pap. 12.45 *(978-1-4624-0135-2(X)*, Inspiring Voices) Author Solutions, LLC.

Parkinson, Curtis. Death in Kingsport. 2007. 224p. (YA). (gr. 7-9). per. 11.95 *(978-0-88776-827-9(X)*, Tundra Bks.) Tundra Bks. CAN. Dist: Penguin Random Hse. LLC.

Parry, Rosanne. Heart of a Shepherd. 2010. (ENG.). 176p. (J). (gr. 4-6). lib. bdg. 22.44 *(978-0-375-94802-2(3))* Random House Publishing Group.

—Heart of a Shepherd. 2010. 176p. (J). (gr. 3-7). pap. 7.99 *(978-0-375-84803-2(7)*, Yearling) Random Hse. Children's Bks.

Paulsen, Gary. The Quilt. 2005. 83p. (gr. 3-7). 16.00 *(978-0-7569-4781-1(2))* Perfection Learning Corp.

Payne, Sandy. Find Your Magic. Goodpaster, Nancy, illus. 2013. 50p. pap. 12.95 *(978-1-937508-16-6(1))* Bearhead Publishing, LLC.

Payson, Howard. The Boy Scouts under Sealed Orders. 2005. (Illus.). pap. 30.95 *(978-1-885529-57-2(0))* Stevens Publishing.

Pedersen, Elsa. Alaska Harvest. Werth, Kurt, illus. 2012. 194p. 42.95 *(978-1-258-23211-5(1))*; pap. 27.95 *(978-1-258-23973-2(6))* Literary Licensing, LLC.

Peirce, Lincoln. I Can't Take It! 2013. (Big Nate Graphic Novels Ser.). lib. bdg. 20.85 *(978-0-606-32313-0(9))* Turtleback.

Penner, Stephen. Professor Barrister's Dinosaur Mysteries #2: The Case of the Armored Allosaurus. 2010. 54p. pap. 19.60 *(978-1-60888-018-8(4))* Nimble Bks. LLC.

Perkins, Mitali. The Not-So-Star-Spangled Life of Sunita Sen. 2nd rev. ed. 2005. (ENG.). 192p. (J). (gr. 3-7). reprint ed. pap. 12.99 *(978-0-316-73453-0(5))* Little, Brown Bks. for Young Readers.

Petersen, Jean. Moose Shoes. Morrow, E., illus. 2007. 52p. per. 24.95 *(978-1-4241-8399-9(5))* America Star Bks.

Peterson, Esther Allen. The House That Cared. 2010. (J). pap. *(978-0-88092-505-1(1))* Royal Fireworks Publishing Co.

Phanton, Rick. Boston & the Bean. 2012. 112p. pap. 19.95 *(978-1-4626-4809-2(6))* America Star Bks.

Phillips, Dee. A Dream of America: The Story of an Immigrant. 2015. (Yesterday's Voices Ser.). (YA). lib. bdg. 19.60 *(978-0-606-36672-4(5))* Turtleback.

Pickett, Anola. Callahan Crossroads. 2015. (ENG.). 192p. (J). pap. 12.99 *(978-1-4621-1715-4(5)*, Sweetwater Bks.) Cedar Fort, Inc./CFI Distribution.

Pinkney, Andrea Davis. Bird in a Box. 2012. (ENG., Illus.). 288p. (J). (gr. 3-7). pap. 8.99 *(978-0-316-07402-5(0))* Little, Brown Bks. for Young Readers.

Pintozzi, Nick. Bentley & the Cactus Rustlers. Pintozzi, Nick & Pintozzi, Connie, illus. 2006. per. 11.00 *(978-0-9749465-4-2(0))* BentDaiSha.

Ponti, James. Framed! 2017. (Framed! Ser.: 1). (ENG., Illus.). 320p. (J). (gr. 3-7). pap. 8.99 *(978-1-4814-3631-1(7)*, Aladdin) Simon & Schuster Children's Publishing.

—Trapped! 2018. (Framed! Ser.: 3). (ENG., Illus.). 384p. (J). (gr. 3-7). 19.99 *(978-1-5344-0891-3(6)*, Aladdin) Simon & Schuster Children's Publishing.

Preston, Robert. The Auction: The Five Cousins Series. 2007. (ENG.). 34p. pap. 15.99 *(978-1-4257-5742-7(1))* Xlibris Corp.

Priceman, Marjorie. How to Make a Cherry Pie & See the U. S. A. 2013. lib. bdg. 18.40 *(978-0-606-32190-7(X))* Turtleback.

Prinz, Yvonne. All You Get Is Me. 2010. (ENG.). 288p. (YA). (gr. 9-18). 16.99 *(978-0-06-171580-8(8))* HarperCollins Pubs.

Pynn Taylor, Susan. Jelly Bean Row, 1 vol. Pratt, Lizz, illus. 2011. (ENG.). 32p. (J). (gr. k-5). pap. *(978-1-897174-80-7(2))* Breakwater Bks., Ltd.

Ralphson, G. Harvey. Boy Scouts in a Submarine. 2018. (ENG., Illus.). 146p. (YA). (gr. 7-12). pap. *(978-93-5297-275-3(9))* Alpha Editions.

—Boy Scouts in a Submarine. 2007. 104p. per. *(978-1-4068-3726-1(1))* Echo Library.

—Boy Scouts in an Airship. 2007. 104p. per. *(978-1-4068-3727-8(X))* Echo Library.

—Boy Scouts in Southern Waters. 2018. (ENG., Illus.). 158p. (YA). (gr. 7-12). pap. *(978-93-5297-277-7(5))* Alpha Editions.

—Boy Scouts in Southern Waters. 2007. 128p. (gr. -1-7). per. *(978-1-4068-3730-8(X))* Echo Library.

Remi, Georges. Tintín en América (rústica) (Tintin Ser.). (SPA.). 64p. (J). 14.95 *(978-84-261-1400-6(8))* Juventud, Editorial ESP. Dist: Distribooks, Inc.

Rexroth, Sharon. America from the Sky. 2006. (J). 9.95 *(978-1-57166-429-7(7))*; per. 22.95 *(978-1-57166-430-3(0))* Quixote Pr.

Riazi, Karuna. The Battle. 2019. (ENG., Illus.). 304p. (J). (gr. 3-7). 17.99 *(978-1-5344-2872-0(0)*, Salaam Reads) Simon & Schuster Bks. For Young Readers.

RIGBY. Now We Live in the USA! Third Grade Big Books. 2009. (Rigby on Our Way to English Ser.). (ENG.). 24p. (gr. 3-3). pap. 50.70 *(978-0-7578-4207-8(0))* Rigby Education.

Robbins, Dean. Two Friends: Susan B. Anthony & Frederick Douglass. Qualls, Sean & Alko, Selina, illus. 2016. (ENG.). 32p. (J). (gr. -1-3). 17.99 *(978-0-545-39996-8(3)*, Orchard Bks.) Scholastic, Inc.

Robertson, Tammy. Konnichiwa & Hello: Celebrating Diversity. Mash, Brittany, illus. 2014. (J). 19.99 *(978-1-945384-07-3(7))* Hawaii Way Publishing.

Rocklin, Joanne. Fleabrain Loves Franny. 2015. (ENG.). 281p. (J). (gr. 3-7). pap. 8.95 *(978-1-4197-1676-8(X)*, 1073803, Amulet Bks.) Abrams, Inc.

Rockwood, Roy. Dave Dashaway & His Hydroplane. 2009. 128p. 23.95 *(978-1-60664-625-0(7))*; pap. 10.95 *(978-1-60664-364-8(9))* Rodgers, Alan Bks.

Rosenberg, Aaron. 42 - The Official Movie Novel. 2013. (ENG.). 160p. (J). (gr. 4-6). 18.69 *(978-0-545-53753-7(3))* Scholastic, Inc.

Rotenberg, Yael. Heldishkeyt Inem Goldenem Land. Tovahleh, illus. 2018. (YID.). 37p. (J). *(978-1-68091-255-5(0))* Kinder Shpiel USA, Inc.

Roy, Ron. Capital Mysteries #9: a Thief at the National Zoo. Bush, Timothy, illus. 2007. (Capital Mysteries Ser.: 9). 96p. (J). (gr. 1-4). per. 5.99 *(978-0-375-84804-9(5)*, Random Hse. Bks. for Young Readers) Random Hse. Children's Bks.

—A Thief at the National Zoo. 9. Bush, Timothy, illus. 2007. (Capital Mysteries Ser.: No. 9). (ENG.). 87p. (J). (gr. 2-4). lib. bdg. 17.44 *(978-0-375-94804-6(X))* Random House Publishing Group.

Sanders, Nancy I. The Very Oldest Pear Tree. Imamura, Yas, illus. 2020. (ENG.). 32p. (J). (gr. -1-3). 16.99 *(978-0-8075-6681-7(0)*, 807566810) Whitman, Albert & Co.

Santacroce, John P. Running Across the Moon. 2013. 146p. pap. 14.98 *(978-0-615-76887-8(3))* Santacroce, John.

Saunders, Jami Lynn. Rabid: Book II of the Werecat Saga. 2012. 94p. (YA). pap. 4.99 *(978-1-936307-16-6(2)*, 711Press) Vendera Publishing.

Savage, Doug. Disco Fever. 2017. (Illus.). 142p. (J). *(978-1-5379-7394-4(0))* Andrews McMeel Publishing.

Say, Allen. Grandfather's Journey. 2008. (ENG.). 32p. (J). (gr. -1-3). pap. 7.99 *(978-0-547-14178-7(5)*, Sandpiper) Houghton Mifflin Harcourt Trade & Reference Pubs.

—Grandfather's Journey. 2011. (J). (gr. k-5). 29.95 *(978-0-545-10696-2(6))*; 18.95 *(978-0-545-12708-0(4))* Weston Woods Studios, Inc.

—Grandfather's Journey: A Caldecott Award Winner. Say, Allen, illus. 2008. (ENG., Illus.). 32p. (J). (gr. -1-3). 7.99 *(978-0-547-07680-5(0)*, 1042044, Clarion Bks.) HarperCollins Pubs.

Schorr, Titus. The Stars & Stripes, 1 vol., 1. 2015. (Rosen REAL Readers: Social Studies Nonfiction / Fiction: Myself, My Community, My World Ser.). (ENG.). 12p. (J). (gr. k-1). pap. 6.33 *(978-1-5081-1958-6(9)*, a1e64b30-83b9-4f31-b695-a5a9db0a19cf, Rosen Classroom) Rosen Publishing Group, Inc., The.

Schraff, Anne. Wildflower, 1 vol. unabr. ed. 2010. (Urban Underground Ser.). (ENG.). 183p. (YA). (gr. 9-12). pap. 11.95 *(978-1-61651-009-1(9))* Saddleback Educational Publishing, Inc.

Schuette, Leslie Elaine. Little Autumn's Adventure in the Smoky Mountains. 2013. 30p. 24.95 *(978-1-63004-952-2(2))* America Star Bks.

Seeger, K R. Asa-Birdie Corn. 2007. 244p. 26.95 *(978-0-595-69522-5(1))*; per. 16.95 *(978-0-595-45553-9(0))* iUniverse, Inc.

Seerattan, Tanya. Uncle Noel's Journey to Americ. 2011. 28p. pap. 15.99 *(978-1-4568-3065-6(1))* Xlibris Corp.

Sepahban, Lois. Paper Wishes. 2017. (ENG.). 192p. (J). pap. 8.99 *(978-1-250-10414-4(9)*, 900163680) Square Fish.

Shea, Therese. A Trip to the White House, 1 vol. 2006. (Neighborhood Readers Ser.). (ENG.). 16p. (gr. 1-2). pap. 6.50 *(978-1-4042-7204-0(6)*, e45cdfbc-8f15-4bce-b753-7d66fa6cae83, Rosen Classroom) Rosen Publishing Group, Inc., The.

Sheinkin, Steve. Abigail Adams, Pirate of the Caribbean. Swaab, Neil, illus. 2019. (Time Twisters Ser.). (ENG.). 176p. (J). pap. 6.99 *(978-1-250-20788-3(6)*, 900201776) Roaring Brook Pr.

—Lincoln's Grave Robbers (Scholastic Focus) 2018. (ENG.). 224p. (J). (gr. 4-7). pap. 9.99 *(978-1-338-29013-4(4))* Scholastic, Inc.

Shepherd, David & Plummer, William K. We Were There at the Driving of the Golden Spike. 2013. (ENG., Illus.). 192p. (J). (gr. 3-8). pap. 7.99 *(978-0-486-49259-9(1)*, 492591) Dover Pubns., Inc.

Sherman, M. Zachary. Control under Fire, 1 vol. Casas, Fritz, illus. 2011. (Bloodlines Ser.). (ENG.). 88p. (J). (gr. 4-8). pap. 6.95 *(978-1-4342-3100-0(3)*, 114739); lib. bdg. 27.32 *(978-1-4342-2561-0(5)*, 113620) Capstone. (Stone Arch Bks.).

—Damage Control, 1 vol. Cage, Josef, illus. 2012. (Bloodlines Ser.). (ENG.). 88p. (J). (gr. 4-8). lib. bdg. 27.32 *(978-1-4342-3765-1(6)*, 117026, Stone Arch Bks.) Capstone.

Shore, Diane Z. This Is the Feast. Lloyd, Megan, illus. 2011. (ENG.). 32p. (J). (gr. -1-3). pap. 8.99 *(978-0-06-443850-6(3)*, HarperCollins) HarperCollins Pubs.

Shotz, Jennifer Li. Scout: Storm Dog. 2019. (Scout Ser.: 3). (ENG.). 192p. (J). (gr. 3-7). pap. 7.99 *(978-0-06-280264-4(X)*, HarperCollins) HarperCollins Pubs.

Siegelson, Kim L. In the Time of Drums, 1 vol. Pinkney, Brian, illus. 2016. (ENG.). 32p. (J). (gr. 1-5). pap. 11.95 *(978-1-62014-309-4(7)*, leelowbooks) Lee & Low Bks., Inc.

Simmons, John M. Katya's Prayer. 2006. 15p. 4.95 *(978-0-9725916-2-1(1)*, 21206) White Knight Printing and Publishing.

Sisco, K. B. Jackpot's Tail. 2008. (ENG.). 32p. pap. 15.99 *(978-1-4196-4475-7(0))* CreateSpace Independent Publishing Platform.

Slanina, Anne. Annie Mouse's Route 66 Family Vacation. Collins, Kelsey, illus. 2014. (Adventures of Annie Mouse Ser.). (ENG.). 150p. (J). pap. 9.99 *(978-0-9914094-1-9(8))* Annie Mouse Bks.

Smith, Sherri L. Flygirl. 2010. 304p. (YA). (gr. 7-18). 11.99 *(978-0-14-241725-6(4)*, Penguin Books) Penguin Young Readers Group.

Soban Biniashvili, Freidele Galya. There Is a Reason Why. Zimmer, Glenn, illus. 2016. (ENG.). 38p. (J). 13.99 *(978-1-929628-90-2(0))* Hachai Publishing.

Stamper, Phil. The Gravity of Us. 2020. (ENG.). 320p. (YA). 17.99 *(978-1-5476-0014-4(4)*, 900195006, Bloomsbury Young Adult) Bloomsbury Publishing USA.

Stanley, George E. Teddy Kennedy: Lion of the Senate. Fancy, Patrick, illus. 2010. (Childhood of Famous Americans Ser.). (ENG.). 224p. (J). (gr. 3-7). pap. 5.99 *(978-1-4169-9041-3(0)*, Simon & Schuster/Paula Wiseman Bks.) Simon & Schuster/Paula Wiseman Bks.

Stilton, Gerónimo. The Race Across America. 2009. (Geronimo Stilton Ser.: 37). lib. bdg. 18.40 *(978-0-606-00228-8(6))* Turtleback.

Stockton, Frank Richard. John Gayther's Garden & the Stories Told Therein. 2008. 220p. 26.95 *(978-1-60664-746-2(6))* Rodgers, Alan Bks.

Stone, Judith. Billie the Buffalo Goes to Great Sand Dunes National Park. 2009. 24p. pap. 15.95 *(978-1-4490-1495-7(X))* AuthorHouse.

Stowe, Harriet. Uncle Toms Cabin Young Folks Edition III. 2006. pap. *(978-1-4065-1077-5(7))* Dodo Pr.

Stratton, Allan. Borderline. 2012. (ENG.). 320p. (YA). (gr. 8). pap. 10.99 *(978-0-06-145113-3(4)*, HarperTeen) HarperCollins Pubs.

Straub-Martin, Susan M. Legends, Loves & Great Lakes. 2013. 28p. pap. 15.00 *(978-0-9830321-6-8(5))* Strauberry Studios.

Sully, Katherine. Night-Night America. Poole, Helen, illus. 2017. (Night-Night Ser.). (ENG.). 20p. (J). (gr. -1-1). bds. 9.99 *(978-1-4926-5019-5(6)*, 9781492650195, Hometown World) Sourcebooks, Inc.

Taylor, Richard B. Chispita Service Dog Extraordinaire: Volume 5. Indian Country. 2010. 60p. pap. 21.99 *(978-1-4490-5617-9(2))* AuthorHouse.

Taylor, Theodore & Taylor, Theodore. The Bomb. 2007. (ENG., Illus.). 208p. (YA). (gr. 7-12). pap. 9.99 *(978-0-15-206165-4(7)*, 1198508, Clarion Bks.) HarperCollins Pubs.

Thompson, Lisa. The Wreck of the Atocha. 2007. (Illus.). 52p. (J). pap. *(978-1-4207-0719-9(1))* Sundance/Newbridge Educational Publishing.

To Keep Me SAFE! A Story for Children Affected by Military Deployments. 2003. (J). 12.00 *(978-0-9740289-0-3(8))* State of Growth Publishing Co.

Tocher, Timothy. Chief Sunrise, John McGraw, & Me. 2004. (ENG.). 168p. (J). (gr. 4-8). 16.95 *(978-0-8126-2711-4(3))* Cricket Bks.

Tong, Paul, illus. Pecos Bill. 2006. (On My Own Folklore Ser.). 48p. (J). (gr. -1-3). lib. bdg. 25.26 *(978-1-57505-889-4(8)*, Millbrook Pr.) Lerner Publishing Group.

Tucker, Zekita. Don't Call Me N!gga. 2007. per. 0.01 net. *(978-1-60402-249-0(3))* Independent Pub.

Van Hamme, Jean. The Strange Encounter, Vol. 5. 2009. (Blake & Mortimer Ser.: 5). (Illus.). 66p. pap. 15.95 *(978-1-905460-75-5(9))* CineBook GBR. Dist: National Bk. Network.

Van Riper, Guernsey, Jr. Will Rogers, Young Cowboy. 2011. 196p. 42.95 *(978-1-258-06291-0(7))* Literary Licensing, LLC.

Viva, Frank. A Trip to the Bottom of the World with Mouse. 2018. (Toon Books Level 1 Ser.). lib. bdg. 17.20 *(978-0-606-41222-3(0))* Turtleback.

Waldman, Alan/A. Erica from America & the Start of the Gang of Four. Scobie, Andrea, illus. 2013. 44p. pap. *(978-0-9840514-2-7(2))* Roxby Media Ltd.

Wallace, Elise. The Presidential Masters of Prehistory Volume 1: Discover America's Prehistoric Forefathers. Isik, Semur, illus. 2018. (Jurassic Classics Ser.). (ENG.). 32p. (J). (gr. 4-7). lib. bdg. 26.65 *(978-1-942875-51-2(7)*, 17859ffc-b4eb-44ce-b4ff-64c705f74bcd, Walter Foster Jr) Quarto Publishing Group USA.

—The Presidential Masters of Prehistory Volume 2: Discover America's Prehistoric Forefathers. Isik, Semur, illus. 2018. (Jurassic Classics Ser.). (ENG.). 32p. (J). (gr. 4-7). lib. bdg. 26.65 *(978-1-942875-52-9(5)*, 5740b880-31ac-4362-b991-6415c8e46fbf, Walter Foster Jr) Quarto Publishing Group USA.

Walsh, Alice. A Long Way from Home, 1 vol. 2012. (ENG.). 188p. (J). (gr. 4-8). 11.95 *(978-1-926920-79-5(1))* Second Story Pr. CAN. Dist: Orca Bk. Pubs. USA.

Walsh, Patrick M., Jr. Who Says Timmy Can't Play: The Derby: A Timmy Wallings Story. McGriff, Aaron, ed. WFM Services, illus. 2011. 135p. (J). *(978-0-9842929-3-6(4))* Daddy Bean Bks.

Walters, Eric. We All Fall Down. 2006. (We All Fall Down Ser.: 1). (ENG.). 192p. (J). (gr. 5). pap. 9.99 *(978-0-385-66192-8(4))* Doubleday Canada, Ltd. CAN. Dist: Penguin Random Hse. LLC.

Warner, Charles Dudley. Being A Boy. 2005. 26.95 *(978-1-4218-0314-2(3))*; 124p. pap. 10.95 *(978-1-4218-0414-9(X))* 1st World Publishing, Inc. (1st World Library - Literary Society).

—Being A Boy. 2004. reprint ed. pap. 15.95 *(978-1-4191-0953-9(7))*; pap. 1.99 *(978-1-4192-0953-6(1))* Kessinger Publishing, LLC.

Warner, Susan & Wetherell, Elizabeth. Queechy. 2008. 328p. per. 16.95 *(978-1-60312-446-1(2))* Aegypan.

Watkins, Steve. Sink or Swim: a Novel of World War II. 2017. (ENG.). 272p. (J). (gr. 3-7). 16.99 *(978-1-338-05790-4(1)*, Scholastic Pr.) Scholastic, Inc.

Watson, Michael. Search, Secrets, & Spies. 2011. 32p. pap. 13.00 *(978-1-61204-357-9(7)*, Strategic Bk. Publishing) Strategic Book Publishing & Rights Agency (SBPRA).

Webb, Brandon & Feldman, Thea. Navy SEALs: Mission at the Caves. 2018. (Special Operations Files Ser.: 1). (ENG., Illus.). 128p. (J). pap. 12.99 *(978-1-250-19427-5(X)*, 900171489, Holt, Henry & Co. Bks. For Young Readers) Holt, Henry & Co.

Webster, Frank V. The Boy Scouts of Lenox: Or, the Hike over Big Bear Mountain. 2017. (ENG., Illus.). (J). 22.95 *(978-1-374-91252-6(2))*; pap. 12.95 *(978-1-374-91251-9(4))* Capital Communications, Inc.

Weeks, Sarah & Varadarajan, Gita. Save Me a Seat (Scholastic Gold) 2016. (ENG.). 240p. (J). (gr. 3-7). 17.99 *(978-0-545-84660-8(9)*, Scholastic Pr.) Scholastic, Inc.

Weston Woods Staff, creator. Grandfather's Journey. 2011. 38.75 *(978-0-545-12710-3(6))* Weston Woods Studios, Inc.

—Scrambled States of America Talent Show. 2011. 18.95 *(978-0-545-34618-4(5))*; 38.75 *(978-0-545-34954-3(0))* Weston Woods Studios, Inc.

Whyman, Matt. Goldstrike: A Thriller. 2010. (ENG.). 272p. (YA). (gr. 7-18). 16.99 *(978-1-4169-9510-4(2)*, Atheneum Bks. for Young Readers) Simon & Schuster Children's Publishing.

Wiederblank. Save Our School. 2006. 144p. (J). 14.99 *(978-1-56871-392-2(4))* Targum Pr., Inc.

Wiesner, Leona Shew. Lundy: Adventures of A Little Boy in Early America. 2007. 72p. per. 8.95 *(978-0-595-47200-0(1))* iUniverse, Inc.

Wiggin, Kate Douglas. New Chronicles of Rebecc. 2008. 152p. (gr. 4-7). pap. 12.95 *(978-1-60664-257-3(X))* Rodgers, Alan Bks.

Wilbur, Helen L. Lily's Victory Garden. Steele, Robert Gantt, illus. 2010. (Tales of Young Americans Ser.). (ENG.). 32p. (J). (gr. 1-4). 16.95 *(978-1-58536-450-3(9)*, 202175) Sleeping Bear Pr.

Wilder, Laura Ingalls. Little House on the Prairie. 2007. (Little House Ser.). 336p. (J). (gr. 3-7). pap. 6.99 *(978-0-06-088539-7(4)*, Harper Trophy) HarperCollins Pubs.

Willink, Jocko. Marc's Mission: Way of the Warrior Kid. Bozak, Jon, illus. 2018. (Way of the Warrior Kid Ser.: 2). (ENG.). 224p. (J). 14.99 *(978-1-250-15679-2(3)*, 900185103) Feiwel & Friends.

Wolf, Joan M. Runs with Courage. 2017. (ENG.). 224p. (J). (gr. 4-7). pap. 9.99 *(978-1-58536-985-0(3)*, 204116) Sleeping Bear Pr.

Wyatt, Ellen. Sheriff Buzzy Bullet & the Bank Robbers. 2009. 28p. pap. 12.25 *(978-1-60860-391-6(1)*, Eloquent Bks.) Strategic Book Publishing & Rights Agency (SBPRA).

Yates, Donnalyn. Let's Memorize States & Capitals Using Pictures & Stories. 2011. 128p. pap. 14.95 *(978-1-257-07566-9(7))* Lulu Pr., Inc.

Yunisa. Schoolaholic Princess 3: Simfoni Cinta. 2008. 220p. pap. 14.88 *(978-1-4357-6045-5(X))* Lulu Pr., Inc.

Yusuf. Butterfly & Bumble Bee: Adventure in Yellow Stone National Park. 2010. 16p. 8.49 *(978-1-4520-4022-6(2))* AuthorHouse.

Zamor, Nehemie Djose. The Adventures of Naomi. 2011. 34p. pap. 14.99 *(978-1-61379-327-5(8))* Salem Author Services.

Zamora, Peter. A Story about Kandie Cole. 2010. 28p. pap. 13.99 *(978-1-4520-5632-6(3))* AuthorHouse.

Zoboi, Ibi, et al. Black Enough: Stories of Being Young & Black in America. (ENG.). 416p. (YA). (gr. 8). 2020. pap. 12.99 *(978-0-06-269873-5(7))* 2019. 18.99 *(978-0-06-269872-8(9))* HarperCollins Pubs. (Balzer & Bray).

UNITED STATES—FINANCE

see Finance—United States

UNITED STATES—FOOD AND DRUG ADMINISTRATION

Esherick, Joan. The FDA & Psychiatric Drugs: How a Drug Is Approved. McDonnell, Mary Ann & Esherick, Donald, eds. 2013. (State of Mental Illness & Its Therapy Ser.: 19). 128p. (J). (gr. 7-18). 24.95 *(978-1-4222-2826-5(6))* Mason Crest.

—The FDA & Psychiatric Drugs: How a Drug Is Approved. 2004. (Encyclopedia of Psychiatric Drugs & Their Disorders Ser.). (Illus.). 128p. (YA). lib. bdg. 24.95 *(978-1-59084-578-3(1))* Mason Crest.

—How a Drug Is Approved: The FDA & Psychiatric Drugs. 2003. (Psychiatric Disorders: Drugs & Psychology for the Mind & Bod Ser.). (Illus.). 124p. (YA). (gr. 7). pap. 14.95 *(978-1-4222-0402-3(2))* Mason Crest.

Jarrow, Gail. The Poison Eaters: Fighting Danger & Fraud in Our Food & Drugs. 2019. (Illus.). 160p. (J). (gr. 5-12). 18.99 *(978-1-62979-438-9(4)*, Calkins Creek) Highlights Pr., c/o Highlights for Children, Inc.

UNITED STATES—FOREIGN POLICY
see United States—Foreign Relations

UNITED STATES—FOREIGN POPULATION
see Immigrants; Minorities
also Italians—United States; and similar headings

UNITED STATES—FOREIGN PUBLIC OPINION

Berlatsky, Noah, ed. Does the World Hate the U. S. ?, 1 vol. 2012. (At Issue Ser.). (ENG.). 104p. (gr. 10-12). pap. 28.80 *(978-0-7377-6172-6(5),* beec111d-5e74-48c3-8718-59a4ae5dc579); lib. bdg. 41.03 *(978-0-7377-6171-9(7),* 3ec794be-520f-49a2-9c0a-af5693fd451a) Greenhaven Publishing LLC. (Greenhaven Publishing).

UNITED STATES—FOREIGN RELATIONS
see also Monroe Doctrine

Alagna, Magdalena. The Monroe Doctrine: An End to European Colonies in America. (Life in the New American Nation Ser.). 32p. (gr. 4-4). 2009. 47.90 *(978-1-61514-285-9(1))* 2003. (ENG., Illus.). pap. 10.00 *(978-0-8239-4258-9(9),* 535cb124-e574-4a58-801d-68b74cb78869) 2003. (ENG., Illus.). lib. bdg. 29.13 *(978-0-8239-4040-0(3),* 32f11f4a-81eb-4781-80aa-51b11ca1edb2, Rosen Reference) Rosen Publishing Group, Inc., The.

America Debates, 10 vols., Set. Incl. America Debates Civil Liberties & Terrorism. Freedman, Jeri. lib. bdg. 37.13 *(978-1-4042-1927-4(7),* fde63664-951f-4dfc-ab55-ae6531a981b7); America Debates Global Warming: Crisis or Myth? Robinson, Matthew. lib. bdg. 37.13 *(978-1-4042-1925-0(0),* c5bbec49-cbcc-419d-9683-5edb38f138b6); America Debates Privacy Versus Security. Freedman, Jeri. lib. bdg. 37.13 *(978-1-4042-1929-8(3),* 2eb69dee-61d6-4b38-aa54-f78f558adcd3); America Debates Stem Cell Research. Freedman, Jeri. lib. bdg. 37.13 *(978-1-4042-1928-1(5),* c346cbf7-3ff5-4b79-b664-a38d8b1a3d0f); America Debates United States Policy on Immigration. Ambrosek, Renee. lib. bdg. 37.13 *(978-1-4042-1924-3(2),* f0cb50ae-84e2-4ebc-b1bd-6c1f343be16c); (Illus.). 64p. (YA). (gr. 5-6). 2007. (America Debates Ser.). (ENG.). 2007. Set lib. bdg. 185.65 *(978-1-4042-1100-1(4),* c31750e3-e23f-42c2-8c58-d334a0c8a2ef) Rosen Publishing Group, Inc., The.

American Presidents in World History: [5 Volumes], 5 vols., Vol. 1. 2003. (ENG., Illus.). 144p. (C). (gr. 6-8). 254.00 *(978-0-313-32564-9(2),* 900297228, Bloomsbury Academic) Bloomsbury Publishing Plc GBR. Dist: Macmillan.

Baier, Bret & Whitney, Catherine. Three Days in Moscow Young Readers' Edition: Ronald Reagan & the Fall of the Soviet Empire. 2018. (ENG., Illus.). 240p. (J). (gr. 3-7). 17.99 *(978-0-06-286445-1(9),* HarperCollins) HarperCollins Pubs.

Baker, Lawrence W. Cold War Reference Library Cumulative Index. 2003. (Cold War Reference Library). (ENG.). 85p. (J). 5.00 *(978-0-7876-7667-4(5),* UXL) Cengage Gale.

—Immigration & Migration Reference. 2004. (US Immigration & Migration Reference Library). (ENG.). (J). 5.00 *(978-0-7876-7734-3(5),* UXL) Cengage Gale.

Berlatsky, Noah, ed. Syria, 1 vol. 2014. (Opposing Viewpoints Ser.). (ENG., Illus.). 232p. (gr. 10-12). lib. bdg. 50.43 *(978-0-7377-7006-3(6),* eda4c9e0-e7fb-483c-b4f6-b9e3ae642f8a, Greenhaven Publishing) Greenhaven Publishing LLC.

Blumberg, Rhoda. Commodore Perry in the Land of the Shogun. 2003. (Illus.). 144p. (gr. 3-7). 20.00 *(978-0-7569-1440-0(X))* Perfection Learning Corp.

—Commodore Perry in the Land of the Shogun: A Newbery Honor Award Winner. 2003. (ENG., Illus.). 144p. (J). (gr. 3-18). pap. 9.99 *(978-0-06-008625-1(4),* HarperCollins) HarperCollins Pubs.

Burgan, Michael. The Attack on Pearl Harbor: U. S. Entry into World War II, 1 vol. 2012. (Perspectives On Ser.). (ENG., Illus.). 112p. (YA). (gr. 8-8). 42.64 *(978-1-60870-448-4(3),* 8295e9d5-7add-4634-94de-b5f45c295476) Cavendish Square Publishing LLC.

—The Vietnam War, 1 vol. 2006. (Wars That Changed American History Ser.). (ENG., Illus.). 48p. (gr. 5-8). pap. 15.05 *(978-0-8368-7304-7(1),* cd889bbf-30c1-45e2-b81d-85f132c658ba); lib. bdg. 33.67 *(978-0-8368-7295-8(9),* 96d1820a-22b8-4b03-baf7-976de1636759) Stevens, Gareth Publishing LLLP. (Gareth Stevens Secondary Library).

Burnett, Betty. The Attack on the USS Cole in Yemen on October 12 2000. 2009. (Terrorist Attacks Ser.). 64p. (gr. 5-5). 58.50 *(978-1-60853-311-4(5))* Rosen Publishing Group, Inc., The.

Capaccio, George. The Marshall Plan & the Truman Doctrine, 1 vol. 2017. (Cold War Chronicles Ser.). (ENG.). 112p. (YA). (gr. 9-9). lib. bdg. 44.50 *(978-1-5026-2731-5(0),* 955a3398-c13b-423c-a3b1-9fc1d9870bdc) Cavendish Square Publishing LLC.

Cefrey, Holly. The Pinckney Treaty: America Wins the Right to Travel the Mississippi River. 2009. (Life in the New American Nation Ser.). 32p. (gr. 4-4). 47.90 *(978-1-61514-286-6(X))* Rosen Publishing Group, Inc., The.

The Cold War & Postwar: 1946-1963. 2010. (ENG., Illus.). 136p. (gr. 5-8). 35.00 *(978-1-60413-360-8(0),* P178890, Facts On File) Infobase Holdings, Inc.

Corona, Laurel. War Within a War: Vietnam & the Cold War. 2004. (Lucent Library of Historical Eras). (ENG., Illus.). 112p. (J). 33.45 *(978-1-59018-389-2(4),* Lucent Bks.) Cengage Gale.

Craats, Rennay. Foreign Affairs. 2008. (USA Past Present Future Ser.). (Illus.). 48p. (J). (gr. 4-6). pap. 10.95 *(978-1-59036-979-1(3));* lib. bdg. 29.05 *(978-1-59036-978-4(5))* Weigl Pubs., Inc.

Deedy, Carmen Agra. 14 Cows for America, 1 vol. Gonzalez, Thomas, illus. 36p. (J). (gr. 2-5). 2016. pap. 8.99 *(978-1-56145-961-2(5))* 2009. 17.99 *(978-1-56145-490-7(7))* Peachtree Publishing Co. Inc.

—14 Cows for America. Gonzalez, Thomas, illus. 2016. (ENG.). 36p. (J). (gr. -1-3). lib. bdg. 19.60 *(978-0-606-39065-1(0))* Turtleback.

Dougherty, Steve. Attack on Pearl Harbor: World War II Strikes Home in the USA. 2011. (J). pap. *(978-0-545-32930-9(2))* Scholastic, Inc.

Dudley, William, ed. How Should the U. S. Proceed in Iraq?, 1 vol. 2008. (At Issue Ser.). (ENG., Illus.). 120p. (gr. 10-12). 41.03 *(978-0-7377-4056-1(6),* 25f1b328-0652-4c68-9e52-c3872cbfebbc); pap. 28.80 *(978-0-7377-4057-8(4),* f978dad4-b8ed-4f57-b3a5-e1a81f6103e6) Greenhaven Publishing LLC. (Greenhaven Publishing).

Edwards, Sue Bradford. Bombing of Pearl Harbor, 1 vol. 2015. (Essential Library of World War II Ser.). (ENG.). 112p. (YA). (gr. 6-12). 41.36 *(978-1-62403-791-7(7),* 17780, Essential Library) ABDO Publishing Co.

Egendorf, Laura K., ed. Should the U. S. Do Business with China?, 1 vol. 2008. (At Issue Ser.). (ENG., Illus.). 128p. (gr. 10-12). pap. 28.80 *(978-0-7377-4113-1(9),* e446a508-c685-49a2-8d22-37e6094e3689, Greenhaven Publishing) Greenhaven Publishing LLC.

—Should the U. S. Do Business with China?, 1 vol. 2008. (At Issue Ser.). (ENG., Illus.). 128p. (gr. 10-12). 41.03 *(978-0-7377-4112-4(0),* d47d5c35-7870-44b7-baf6-89d9133f4734, Greenhaven Publishing) Greenhaven Publishing LLC.

Favreau, Marc. Spies: The Secret Showdown Between America & Russia. 2019. (ENG., Illus.). 320p. (YA). (gr. 7-17). 19.99 *(978-0-316-54592-1(9))* Little, Brown Bks. for Young Readers.

Feldman, Ruth Tenzer. World War I. 2004. (Chronicle of America's Wars Ser.). (Illus.). 88p. (gr. 5-12). lib. bdg. 27.93 *(978-0-8225-0148-0(1))* Lerner Publishing Group.

Greene, Meg. The Transcontinental Treaty 1819: A Primary Source Examination of the Treaty Between the United States & Spain over the American West, 1 vol. 2005. (Primary Sources of American Treaties Ser.). (ENG., Illus.). 64p. (J). (gr. 5-8). lib. bdg. 37.13 *(978-1-4042-0439-3(3),* b6d892eb-9f77-4d3a-9466-87b58369515b) Rosen Publishing Group, Inc., The.

Hanes, Sharon M., et al. Cold War: Almanac, 2 vols. 2003. (U-X-L Cold War Reference Library). (Illus.). (J). *(978-0-7876-9087-8(2));* 200p. 55.00 *(978-0-7876-7662-9(4));* (ENG., 376p. lib. bdg. 233.00 *(978-0-7876-9089-2(9))* Cengage Gale. (UXL).

Haugen, David M., et al, eds. Iraq, 1 vol. 2009. (Opposing Viewpoints Ser.). (ENG., Illus.). 192p. (gr. 10-12). pap. 34.80 *(978-0-7377-4525-2(8),* 722b2966-c9c2-49cb-b811-f845bdbe4269);No. 9. lib. bdg. 50.43 *(978-0-7377-4524-5(X),* c2c737cd-a425-40a8-8f6f-150e90beb9e4) Greenhaven Publishing LLC. (Greenhaven Publishing).

Hurt, Avery Elizabeth. Superpower Rivalries & Proxy Warfare, 1 vol. 2017. (Cold War Chronicles Ser.). (ENG.). 112p. (YA). (gr. 9-9). lib. bdg. 44.50 *(978-1-5026-2729-2(9),* ea03d290-a7a9-4ca9-ae78-5843b274a9c7) Cavendish Square Publishing LLC.

Hurt, Avery Elizabeth, ed. U. S. -Iran Relations, 1 vol. 2017. (Viewpoints on Modern World History Ser.). (ENG.). 160p. (YA). (gr. 10-12). 49.43 *(978-1-5345-0135-5(5),* 8fbf92f9-29e1-4955-a0ee-422a526130db) Greenhaven Publishing LLC.

Johnson, Robin. Pearl Harbor. 2014. (Crabtree Chrome Ser.). (ENG., Illus.). 48p. (J). (gr. 2-2). *(978-0-7787-1367-8(9))* Crabtree Publishing Co.

Kallen, Stuart A. Primary Sources. 2003. (American War Library). (ENG., Illus.). 112p. (J). 30.85 *(978-1-59018-243-7(X),* Lucent Bks.) Cengage Gale.

Keeley, Jennifer. Containing the Communists: America's Foreign Entanglements. 2003. (American War Library). (ENG., Illus.). 112p. (J). 30.85 *(978-1-59018-225-3(1),* Lucent Bks.) Cengage Gale.

Kiesbye, Stefan, ed. How Should the U. S. Proceed in Afghanistan?, 1 vol. 2009. (At Issue Ser.). (ENG., Illus.). 96p. (gr. 10-12). 41.03 *(978-0-7377-4424-8(3),* 9d8c3c8f-a329-410a-862c-64df381ca90e); pap. 28.80 *(978-0-7377-4425-5(1),* 4138f1b8-6246-4f23-b7b8-666ae7482a98) Greenhaven Publishing LLC. (Greenhaven Publishing).

Laxer, James. Empire, 1 vol. 2006. (Groundwork Guides: 2). (ENG., Illus.). 144p. (YA). (gr. 9-12). pap. 9.95 *(978-0-88899-707-4(8))* Groundwood Bks. CAN. Dist: Publishers Group West (PGW).

McAneney, Caitie. Standing in the Secretary of State's Shoes, 1 vol. 2015. (My Government Ser.). (ENG., Illus.). 32p. (gr. 4-4). pap. 11.58 *(978-1-5026-0466-8(3),* b1138928-af85-4943-abf4-fbb6b6c530b1) Cavendish Square Publishing LLC.

McNeese, Tim. The Perry Expedition & the Opening of Japan. 2012. (J). 35.00 *(978-1-60413-924-2(2),* Facts On File) Infobase Holdings, Inc.

Meyer, Edith Patterson. The Friendly Frontier: The Story of the Canadian-American Border. Mars, W. T., illus. 2011. 304p. 48.95 *(978-1-258-09384-6(7))* Literary Licensing, LLC.

Miller, Debra A., ed. Iran, 1 vol. 2011. (Current Controversies Ser.). (ENG.). 224p. (gr. 10-12). 48.03 *(978-0-7377-5181-9(9),* 3667ee4a-7722-492f-90f9-e9a6a17cb2b5); pap. 33.00 *(978-0-7377-5182-6(7),* 2d117263-1536-470e-a8cd-b3fccf952282) Greenhaven Publishing LLC. (Greenhaven Publishing).

Miller, Derek. The United States' Role in the World, 1 vol. 2018. (Discovering America: an Exceptional Nation Ser.). (ENG.). 112p. (gr. 7-7). 44.50 *(978-1-5026-4264-6(6),* ddd21d46-4c64-4145-93c6-5ae743910485) Cavendish Square Publishing LLC.

Murdico, Suzanne J. Osama bin Laden. 2009. (Middle East Leaders Ser.). 112p. (gr. 5-8). 66.50 *(978-1-61514-647-5(4),* Rosen Reference) Rosen Publishing Group, Inc., The.

Otfinoski, Steven. The Split History of the Attack on Pearl Harbor: A Perspectives Flip Book. 2018. (Perspectives Flip Books: Famous Battles Ser.). (ENG., Illus.). 64p. (J). (gr. 5-9). lib. bdg. 34.65 *(978-0-7565-5691-4(0),* 137036, Compass Point Bks.) Capstone.

—A Step into History: the Cold War (Library Edition) 2018. (Step into History Ser.). (ENG., Illus.). 144p. (J). lib. bdg. 36.00 *(978-0-531-22691-9(3),* Children's Pr.) Scholastic Library Publishing.

Piddock, Charles. The Cold War. 2016. (Illus.). 48p. (J). *(978-1-5105-1282-5(9))* SmartBook Media, Inc.

Porterfield, Jason. How Lyndon B. Johnson Fought the Vietnam War, 1 vol. 2017. (Presidents at War Ser.). (ENG.). 128p. (gr. 8-8). lib. bdg. 38.93 *(978-0-7660-8531-2(7),* d7431810-368e-46b2-bba1-293a64d0532) Enslow Publishing, LLC.

Rauf, Don. How George W. Bush Fought the Wars in Iraq & Afghanistan, 1 vol. 2017. (Presidents at War Ser.). (ENG.). 128p. (gr. 8-8). lib. bdg. 38.93 *(978-0-7660-8533-6(3),* 40b4d225-2e43-482d-85bb-1eca9904a760) Enslow Publishing, LLC.

Ross, Stewart & Woodward, Joe. Pearl Harbor. 2011. (Place in History Ser.). (Illus.). 48p. (YA). (gr. 5-9). lib. bdg. 34.25 *(978-1-84837-676-2(6))* Arcturus Publishing GBR. Dist: Black Rabbit Bks.

Roxburgh, Ellis. John F. Kennedy vs. Nikita Khrushchev: Cold War Adversaries, 1 vol. 2014. (History's Greatest Rivals Ser.). (ENG., Illus.). 48p. (J). (gr. 6-8). lib. bdg. 33.60 *(978-1-4824-2221-4(2),* bfc1cb51-8eeb-416d-af93-4cb9dbc51ac4) Stevens, Gareth Publishing LLLP.

Ruffin, David C. The Duties & Responsibilities of the Secretary of State. (Your Government in Action Ser.). 32p. (gr. 3-3). 2009. 43.90 *(978-1-60854-919-1(4))* 2004. (ENG., Illus.). (J). lib. bdg. 27.60 *(978-1-4042-2688-3(5),* 108a761c-5dcc-4c65-aa4f-1c29535ef894) Rosen Publishing Group, Inc., The. (PowerKids Pr.).

Samuels, Charlie. The Attack on Pearl Harbor, 1 vol., Vol. 1. 2013. (Turning Points in U. S. Military History Ser.). (ENG.). 48p. (J). (gr. 5-6). 34.61 *(978-1-4824-0409-8(5),* 24a85a65-96ca-4173-b00a-66c7a0e08511) Stevens, Gareth Publishing LLLP.

Sarantou, Katlin. Madeleine Albright. Bane, Jeff, illus. 2019. (My Early Library: My Itty-Bitty Bio Ser.). (ENG.). 24p. (J). (gr. k-1). pap. 12.79 *(978-1-5341-4986-1(4),* 213251); lib. bdg. 30.64 *(978-1-5341-4700-3(4),* 213250) Cherry Lake Publishing.

Schwartz, Eric. A World Contender. 2006. (How America Became America Ser.). (Illus.). 96p. (YA). lib. bdg. 22.95 *(978-1-59084-911-8(6))* Mason Crest.

Sebree, Chet'la. Historical Sources on the New Republic, 1783-1830, 1 vol. 2019. (America's Story Ser.). (ENG.). 144p. (gr. 8-8). pap. 22.16 *(978-1-5026-5213-3(7),* e1037242-52c1-44dc-8792-246b6b652f81); lib. bdg. 47.36 *(978-1-5026-5214-0(5),* f0797024-dab0-4526-98df-8d0518481634) Cavendish Square Publishing LLC.

Sharp, Constance. Beyond Our Shores: America Extends Its Reach,1890-1899. 2013. (Illus.). 48p. (J). pap. *(978-1-4222-2420-5(1))* Mason Crest.

—Beyond Our Shores: America Extends Its Reach,1890-1899. Rakove, Jack N., ed. 2012. (How America Became America Ser.). (Illus.). 48p. (J). (gr. 3-4). 19.95 *(978-1-4222-2406-9(6))* Mason Crest.

—Beyond Our Shores (1890/1899) 2018. (J). *(978-1-5105-3606-7(X))* SmartBook Media, Inc.

Sonneborn, Liz. The Acquisition of Florida: America's Twenty-Seventh State. 2009. (ENG., Illus.). 120p. (gr. 6-12). 35.00 *(978-1-60413-054-6(7),* P161432, Facts On File) Infobase Holdings, Inc.

South, Victor. America in the 20th Century (1913-1999) 2013. (Illus.). 48p. (J). pap. *(978-1-4222-2422-9(8))* Mason Crest.

—America in the 20th Century (1913-1999) Rakove, Jack N., ed. 2012. (How America Became America Ser.). (Illus.). 48p. (J). (gr. 3-4). 19.95 *(978-1-4222-2408-3(2))* Mason Crest.

—America in the 20th Century (1913/1999) 2018. (J). *(978-1-5105-3610-4(8))* SmartBook Media, Inc.

—A Shifting Role: America & the World, 1900-1912. 2013. 48p. (J). pap. *(978-1-4222-2421-2(X))* Mason Crest.

—A Shifting Role: America & the World, 1900-1912. Rakove, Jack N., ed. 2012. (How America Became America Ser.). 48p. (J). (gr. 3-4). 19.95 *(978-1-4222-2407-6(4))* Mason Crest.

—A Shifting Role (1900/1912) 2018. (J). *(978-1-5105-3608-1(6))* SmartBook Media, Inc.

Stanley, George E. America in Today's World (1969-2004), 1 vol. 2004. (Primary Source History of the United States Ser.). (ENG., Illus.). 48p. (gr. 5-8). lib. bdg. 33.67 *(978-0-8368-5831-0(X),* f90bbe7b-9042-429d-92c4-ea9b82b2d8d3, Gareth Stevens Secondary Library) Stevens, Gareth Publishing LLLP.

—An Emerging World Power (1900-1929), 1 vol. 2004. (Primary Source History of the United States Ser.). (ENG., Illus.). 48p. (gr. 5-8). pap. 15.05 *(978-0-8368-5837-2(9),* 324523d2-5e90-424c-bfff-97e703f50d4c); lib. bdg. 33.67 *(978-0-8368-5828-0(X),* 1d569960-8f8b-4d2e-81b1-983ee7fe4527) Stevens, Gareth Publishing LLLP. (Gareth Stevens Secondary Library).

Swanson, Jennifer & Larson, Kirby. Pearl Harbor. McMorris, Kelley, illus. 2018. 106p. (J). *(978-1-5444-0721-0(1))* Scholastic, Inc.

Wallenfeldt, Jeff, ed. A New World Power: America from 1920 To 1945, 4 vols. 2012. (Documenting America: the Primary Source Documents of a Nation Ser.). (ENG., Illus.). 168p. (YA). (gr. 10-10). 89.42 *(978-1-61530-784-5(2),* 06045b1f-3f45-492d-a2c0-1e7c79a7221d) Rosen Publishing Group, Inc., The.

Wiener, Gary. The United States & Russia: A Cold & Complex History, 1 vol. 2017. (World History Ser.). (ENG.). 104p. (YA). (gr. 7-7). 41.53 *(978-1-5345-6245-5(1),* af371576-2aaf-41b0-9a55-1f5f37f01755); pap. 20.99 *(978-1-5345-6311-7(3),* 93f27ef5-9b03-4420-972e-7f197abc7ec0) Greenhaven Publishing LLC. (Lucent Pr.).

Wood, Douglas. Franklin & Winston: A Christmas That Changed the World. Moser, Barry, illus. 2011. (ENG.). 40p. (J). (gr. 1-4). 16.99 *(978-0-7636-3383-7(6))* Candlewick Pr.

Yomtov, Nel. The Attack on Pearl Harbor: December 7 1941, 1 vol. Campidelli, Maurizio, illus. 2014. (24-Hour History Ser.). (ENG.). 48p. (J). (gr. 3-9). pap. 8.95 *(978-1-4329-9299-6(6),* 124615); lib. bdg. 33.99 *(978-1-4329-9293-4(7),* 124610) Capstone. (Heinemann).

Yomtov, Nel. The United States & Mexico. 2013. (Cornerstones of Freedom™, Third Ser.). (ENG., Illus.). 64p. (J). pap. 8.95 *(978-0-531-21963-8(1))* Scholastic Library Publishing.

Zimmerman, Andrea. Eliza's Cherry Trees: Japan's Gift to America, 1 vol. Chen, Ju-Hong, illus. 2011. (ENG.). 32p. (J). (gr. k-3). 16.99 *(978-1-58980-954-3(8),* Pelican Publishing) Arcadia Publishing.

UNITED STATES—FOREIGN RELATIONS—TREATIES

Greene, Meg. The Transcontinental Treaty 1819: A Primary Source Examination of the Treaty Between the United States & Spain over the American West. 2009. (Primary Sources of American Treaties Ser.). 64p. (gr. 5-8). 58.50 *(978-1-60851-514-1(1))* Rosen Publishing Group, Inc., The.

Primary Sources of American Treaties, 10 vols. 2005. (Primary Sources of American Treaties Ser.). (ENG., Illus.). (YA). (gr. 5-8). 185.65 *(978-1-4042-0626-7(4),* b466c81c-79b2-4509-af83-89043f071b60) Rosen Publishing Group, Inc., The.

UNITED STATES—FOREST SERVICE—FICTION

Rolt-Wheeler, Francis. The Boy with the U. S. Foresters. 2017. (ENG., Illus.). (J). 24.95 *(978-1-374-97205-6(3))* Capital Communications, Inc.

—The Boy with the U S Foresters. 2007. 128p. per. *(978-1-4068-4018-6(1))* Echo Library.

UNITED STATES—GOVERNMENT
see United States—Politics and Government

UNITED STATES—GOVERNMENT EMPLOYEES
see United States—Officials and Employees

UNITED STATES—HISTORY

Aaseng, Nathan. Michael Jordan: Hall of Fame Basketball Superstar, 1 vol. 2013. (Hall of Fame Sports Greats Ser.). (ENG.). 64p. (gr. 4-6). 30.60 *(978-1-62285-035-8(1),* 85d629ce-2903-4f99-aaf5-c8e372608e71) Enslow Publishing, LLC.

Akyroyd, Clarissa. Native American Horsemanship. Johnson, Troy, ed. 2013. (Native American Life Ser.: 15). 64p. (J). (gr. 5-18). 19.95 *(978-1-4222-2971-2(8))* Mason Crest.

All the People: A History of the Us Book 10. 2011. 14.78 *(978-0-7848-3647-7(7),* Everbind) Marco Bk. Co.

Allman, Toney. The Enlightenment. 2014. (Understanding World History Ser.). (Illus.). 96p. (J). lib. bdg. *(978-1-60152-740-0(3))* ReferencePoint Pr., Inc.

Aloian, Molly. The Mojave Desert. 2012. (ENG.). 32p. (J). *(978-0-7787-0713-4(X));* (Illus.). pap. *(978-0-7787-0721-9(0))* Crabtree Publishing Co.

American Graphic. 2011. (American Graphic Ser.). (ENG.). 32p. (gr. 3-4). pap. 286.20 *(978-1-4296-6439-4(8),* Capstone Pr.) Capstone.

American History. (YA). 20.00 *(978-1-931555-47-0(8))* Our Lady of Victory Schl.

American History Playing Card Deck. 2004. (History Channel Ser.). (Illus.). 120p. pap. 12.00 *(978-1-57281-440-0(3),* AMH55) U.S. Games Systems, Inc.

American Voices Group 3, 10 vols., Set. Incl. Century of Immigration: 1820-1924. Stefoff, Rebecca. lib. bdg. 41.21 *(978-0-7614-2172-6(6),* 5ed6ed0e-95d2-451c-9def-b5203ae1bf88); Time of Slavery. Sirimarco, Elizabeth. lib. bdg. 41.21 *(978-0-7614-2169-6(6),* 807c3378-871d-4140-afb9-5d2454c00e63); Wild West. Stefoff, Rebecca. lib. bdg. 41.21 *(978-0-7614-2170-2(X),* d98d8496-a771-43e2-9b03-98c032965b89); Women's Movement. Schomp, Virginia. lib. bdg. 41.21 *(978-0-7614-2171-9(8),* 423501d2-b7a9-41e0-81d6-44c29393c44c); (Illus.). 160p. (gr. 6-6). (American Voices From Ser.). (ENG.). 2007. Set lib. bdg. 206.05 *(978-0-7614-2167-2(X),* af391110-fc6d-49dd-bdf2-acffe66661bf, Cavendish Square) Cavendish Square Publishing LLC.

The Americans. 2005. (gr. 6-12). *(978-0-618-17618-2(7),* 2-37951); *(978-0-618-17568-0(7),* 2-37933); tchr. ed. *(978-0-618-16260-4(7),* 2-37912) Holt McDougal.

Ancient Americas DBA. 2003. spiral bd. 16.95 *(978-1-56004-156-6(0))* Social Studies Schl. Service.

Anderson, Dale. The Aftermath of the Civil War, 1 vol. 2004. (World Almanac(r) Library of the Civil War Ser.). (ENG., Illus.). 48p. (gr. 5-8). pap. 15.05 *(978-0-8368-5597-5(3),* ad27f227-78f5-47db-a4a4-11d6eaec8003); lib. bdg. 33.67 *(978-0-8368-5588-3(4),* c777ffc3-916f-4e09-bf81-5fbda0f6625d) Stevens, Gareth Publishing LLLP. (Gareth Stevens Secondary Library).

—The Atom Bomb Project, 1 vol. 2004. (Landmark Events in American History Ser.). (ENG., Illus.). 48p. (gr. 5-8). lib. bdg. 33.67 *(978-0-8368-5385-8(7),* 26b427fd-961b-44dd-a323-504c7a45cd5e, Gareth Stevens Secondary Library) Stevens, Gareth Publishing LLLP.

—World Almanac Library of the Civil War, 10 vols. Incl. Aftermath of the Civil War. lib. bdg. 33.67 *(978-0-8368-5588-3(4),* c777ffc3-916f-4e09-bf81-5fbda0f6625d); Causes of the Civil War. lib. bdg. 33.67 *(978-0-8368-5581-4(7),* 88052b64-ee89-4168-9b03-c8645b27670f); Civil War at Sea. lib. bdg. 33.67 *(978-0-8368-5585-2(X),* abaa704c-54ab-437b-a508-a47da1d3dc87); Civil War in the East (1861-July 1863) lib. bdg. 33.67 *(978-0-8368-5582-1(5),* ea65b134-2894-4b4a-b659-255a776186b0); Civil War in the West (1861-July 1863) lib. bdg. 33.67 *(978-0-8368-5583-8(3),* a497de3e-669b-4027-92d0-df03b0280971); Home Fronts in the Civil War. lib. bdg. 33.67 *(978-0-8368-5587-6(6),* f82d4d42-0c19-4e83-844b-321427333a72); Union Victory (July 1863 - 1865) lib. bdg. 33.67 *(978-0-8368-5584-5(1),* e28734b4-0c65-4c17-9779-244cfe64b88f); (gr. 5-8). (World Almanac(r) Library of the Civil War Ser.). (ENG., Illus.). 48p. 2004. Set lib. bdg. 168.35 *(978-0-8368-5580-7(9),* 6d23f6f8-b267-4c3a-8417-931f1aeca97a, Gareth Stevens Secondary Library) Stevens, Gareth Publishing LLLP.

Anderson, Dale & Crewe, Sabrina. The Atom Bomb Project, 1 vol. 2004. (Events That Shaped America Ser.). (ENG., Illus.). 32p. (gr. 3-5). lib. bdg. 28.67 *(978-0-8368-3404-8(6),* 036d894a-d5f7-4fe5-b31c-1ed09d16835e, Gareth Stevens Learning Library) Stevens, Gareth Publishing LLLP.

—The Seneca Falls Women's Rights Convention, 1 vol. 2004. (Events That Shaped America Ser.). (ENG., Illus.). 32p. (J). (gr. 3-5). lib. bdg. 28.67 *(978-0-8368-3408-6(9),* c4ccc77c-a091-449d-aa31-a0b003f98e5d, Gareth Stevens Learning Library) Stevens, Gareth Publishing LLLP.

Anderson, Jameson. Lebron James, 1 vol. 2014. (Awesome Athletes Ser.). (ENG.). 32p. (J). (gr. 3-6). 32.79

TUV

(978-1-62403-330-8(X), 1203, Checkerboard Library) ABDO Publishing Co.

Anderson, Michael. Biographies of the New World Power: Rutherford B. Hayes, Thomas Alva Edison, Margaret Sanger, & More, 1 vol. 2012. (Impact on America: Collective Biographies Ser.). (ENG., Illus.). 160p. (J). (gr. 8-8). 38.82 *(978-1-61530-691-6(9)*, 7eedc09b-3a58-4f4b-9a0e-ed82ec747c57) Rosen Publishing Group, Inc., The.

Anderson, Michael, ed. Biographies of the New World: Leif Eriksson, Henry Hudson, Charles Darwin, & More, 4 vols. 2012. (Impact on America: Collective Biographies Ser.). (ENG., Illus.). 136p. (YA). (gr. 8-8). 77.64 *(978-1-61530-803-3(2)*, 005cbbc3-ab18-4ff2-9e09-9bf8ab0b143f) Rosen Publishing Group, Inc., The.

Andrews, Barbara. Discover the Southwest Region. 2006. (J). pap. *(978-1-4108-6436-9(7))* Benchmark Education Co.

Animals Animals - Group 4, 12 vols. 2005. (Animals, Animals Ser.). (ENG., Illus.). 48p. (gr. 5-5). lib. bdg. 195.84 *(978-0-7614-1613-5(7)*, 3047c945-6747-4fd2-ae98-023fa263665b, Cavendish Square) Cavendish Square Publishing LLC.

Appleby, Joyce, et al. The American Vision. 2nd ed. 2004. (United States History (hs) Ser.). (ENG., Illus.). 1138p. (gr. 9-12). stu. ed. 119.32 *(978-0-07-860719-6(1)*, 0078607191) McGraw-Hill Higher Education.

—La Republica Estadounidense Hasta 1877. 2nd ed. 2005.Tr. of American Republic to 1877. (SPA., Illus.). 670p. (C). (gr. 4-7). 101.28 *(978-0-07-867372-6(0)*, 0078673720) McGraw-Hill Higher Education.

Archer, Jules. Extremists: Gadflies of American Society. 2017. (Jules Archer History for Young Readers Ser.). (ENG., Illus.). 208p. (J). (gr. 6-6). 16.99 *(978-1-63450-164-4(0)*, Sky Pony Pr.) Skyhorse Publishing Co., Inc.

Aretha, David. Sabotage, Sedition, & Sundry Acts of Rebellion. 2014. (J). *(978-1-59935-406-4(3))* Reynolds, Morgan Inc.

Army JROTC: Leadership Education & Training, Cadet Reference. 2nd ed. 2003. (Illus.). vi, 56p. (J). *(978-0-536-74189-9(1)*, Dept. of the Army) United States Government Printing Office.

Ashabranner, Brent. Great American Memorials, 5 vols. Incl. No Better Hope: What the Lincoln Memorial Means to America. Ashabranner, Jennifer. (J). 2001. lib. bdg. 25.90 *(978-0-7613-1523-0(3))*; Remembering Korea: Korean War. Ashabranner, Jennifer, photos by. 2001. lib. bdg. 25.90 *(978-0-7613-2156-9(X))*; Their Names to Live: What the Vietnam Veterans Memorial Means to America. Ashabranner, Jennifer, photos by. (J). 1998. lib. bdg. 24.90 *(978-0-7613-3235-0(9))*; Washington Monument: A Beacon for America. Ashabranner, Jennifer, photos by. (J). 2002. lib. bdg. 25.90 *(978-0-7613-1524-7(1))*; 64p. (gr. 4-8). (Illus.). 2004. 155.40 o.p. *(978-0-7613-3142-1(5)*, Twenty-First Century Bks.) Lerner Publishing Group.

Bailey, Martha. New Mexico: Uno de muchos, de muchos Uno, 1. Bailey, Martha, illus. l.t. ed. 2006. (SPA., Illus.). 96p. (J). per. *(978-0-9786448-0-2(8))* Bailey, Martha.

Baker, et al. Nueva Historia de los Estados Unidos. (SPA.). 350p. (J). 32.95 *(978-0-8056-0124-4(4)*, MI010) Minerva Bks., Ltd.

Balkan, Gabrielle. The 50 States: Explore the U. S. A. with 50 Fact-Filled Maps!, Volume 1. Linero, Sol, illus. 2015. (50 States Ser.: 1). (ENG.). 112p. (J). (gr. 2-5). 30.00 *(978-1-84780-711-3(9)*, 315236, Wide Eyed Editions) Quarto Publishing Group UK GBR. Dist: Hachette UK Distribution.

Ball, Lea. The Federalist — Anti-Federalist Debate over States' Rights: A Primary Source Investigation, 1 vol. 2004. (Great Historic Debates & Speeches Ser.). (ENG., Illus.). 64p. (J). (gr. 5-8). lib. bdg. 37.13 *(978-1-4042-0149-1(1)*, ee785929-9b2d-443f-9e90-7fc511b31aed) Rosen Publishing Group, Inc., The.

Bartley, Niccole. The Southwest. 2014. (Land That I Love: Regions of the United States Ser.). (Illus.). 32p. (J). (gr. 3-6). pap. 60.00 *(978-1-4777-6638-5(3)*, PowerKids Pr.) Rosen Publishing Group, Inc., The.

Battista, Brianna. Questions & Answers about the Trail of Tears, 1 vol. 2018. (Eye on Historical Sources Ser.). (ENG.). 32p. (gr. 4-4). 27.93 *(978-1-5383-4127-8(1)*, b51d6e33-371f-465d-b2eb-04c7aa6ed393, PowerKids Pr.) Rosen Publishing Group, Inc., The.

Beard, Daniel C. American Boy's Handy Book. 2014. (ENG., Illus.). 320p. (J). (gr. 5-12). pap. 12.95 *(978-0-8048-4403-1(8))* Tuttle Publishing.

Benchmark Education Company, LLC Staff. Coming to America: Immigration from 1840 to 1930 Teacher's Guide. 2004. *(978-1-4108-2580-3(9))* Benchmark Education Co.

Benchmark Education Company, LLC Staff, compiled by. U. S. History. 2006. (J). 173.00 *(978-1-4108-7113-8(4))* Benchmark Education Co.

—United States History: Theme Set. 2006. (J). 173.00 *(978-1-4108-7128-2(2))* Benchmark Education Co.

Benoit, Peter. Cornerstones of Freedom, Third Series: Immigration. 2012. (Cornerstones of Freedom, Third Ser.). (ENG., Illus.). 64p. (J). (gr. 4-6). lib. bdg. 30.00 *(978-0-531-23057-2(0)*, Children's Pr.) Scholastic Library Publishing.

—The Trail of Tears (Cornerstones of Freedom: Third Series) 2012. (Cornerstones of Freedom, Third Ser.). (ENG.). 64p. (J). (gr. 4-6). pap. 8.95 *(978-0-531-28167-3(1)*, Children's Pr.) Scholastic Library Publishing.

Benson, Sonia, et al. UXL Encyclopedia of U.S. History. 2008. (J). *(978-1-4144-3050-8(7))*; *(978-1-4144-3051-5(5))*; *(978-1-4144-3049-2(3))*; *(978-1-4144-3048-5(5))*; *(978-1-4144-3045-4(0))*; *(978-1-4144-3046-1(9))*; *(978-1-4144-3047-8(7))*; *(978-1-4144-3044-7(2))* Cengage Gale. (UXL).

Berg, Elizabeth & Frank, Nicole. Welcome to the United States, 1 vol. 2011. (Welcome to My Country Ser.). (ENG.). 48p. (gr. 3-3). 31.21 *(978-1-60870-160-5(3)*, 5eedc942-84f6-4aee-b36b-8130388bb584) Cavendish Square Publishing LLC.

Bernstein, Vivian. America's Story. 2005. (America's Story Ser.). (ENG., Illus.). 400p. (gr. 5-10). 51.00 *(978-0-7398-9716-4(0))* Houghton Mifflin Harcourt Publishing Co.

Bloody History of America, 8 vols. 2017. (Bloody History of America Ser.). (ENG., Illus.). (J). (gr. 8-8). lib. bdg. 150.40 *(978-0-7660-9181-8(3)*, ebc9dfbd-0c01-4b1c-a906-6eae13f854f5) Enslow Publishing, LLC.

Boardworks Learning Centers: Across the U. S. A. 2006. (J). bds. *(978-0-9755252-5-8(5))* Evergreen Pr. of Brainerd, LLC.

Bockenhauer, Mark H. National Geographic Our Fifty States. 2004. (Illus.). 240p. (J). (gr. 5-9). 24.95 *(978-0-7922-6402-6(9)*, National Geographic Kids) Disney Publishing Worldwide.

Boerst, William J. Marching in Birmingham. 2007. (Civil Rights Movement Ser.). (Illus.). 112p. (J). (gr. 3-7). lib. bdg. 27.95 *(978-1-59935-055-4(6))* Reynolds, Morgan Inc.

Bonner, John. A Child's History of the United States, 2 vol., set. reprint ed. 250.00 *(978-0-7222-7249-7(9))* Library Reprints, Inc.

Boorstin, Daniel J., et al. A History of the United States. 6th ed. 2005. (Illus.). (YA). (gr. 9-12). 85.20 *(978-0-13-181542-1(3))* Prentice Hall Pr.

Borden, Louise. America Is... Schuett, Stacey, illus. 2005. (ENG.). 40p. (J). (gr. 1-4). 9.99 *(978-1-4169-0286-7(4)*, McElderry, Margaret K. Bks.) McElderry, Margaret K. Bks.

Boyd, Bentley. George Washington Leads the Way. 2011. (Mount Vernon Comix Ser.). (Illus.). 24p. (J). (gr. 3-9). pap. 6.95 *(978-1-933122-44-1(7))* Chester Comix, LLC.

Boyer, Paul S. Holt American Nation: Online Edition Plus. 3rd ed. 2003. 17.26 *(978-0-03-037432-6(4))* Holt McDougal.

Boyer, Rick & Boyer, Marilyn. America's Struggle to Become a Nation: Understanding the Foundations of Freedom. 2015. (ENG.). 384p. pap. 34.99 *(978-0-89051-910-3(2)*, Master Books) New Leaf Publishing Group.

Boyer's Staff. The American Nation: Modern Era: Online Edition. 5th ed. 2004. (gr. 1) 17.26 *(978-0-03-038831-6(7))*; (gr. 6). 77.26 *(978-0-03-038832-3(5))* Holt McDougal.

Brannon, Barbara. Discover the Northeast Region. 2005. (J). pap. *(978-1-4108-5152-9(4))* Benchmark Education Co.

Braun, Eric, et al. America: 50 Years of Change. 2018. (America: 50 Years of Change Ser.). (ENG.). 64p. (J). (gr. 5-9). 146.60 *(978-1-5435-0417-0(5)*, 27650, Capstone Pr.) Capstone.

Brezina, Corona. The Industrial Revolution in America: A Primary Source History of America's Transformation into an Industrial Society. 2009. (Primary Sources in American History Ser.). 64p. (gr. 5-8). 58.50 *(978-1-60851-497-7(8))* Rosen Publishing Group, Inc., The.

Brindell Fradin, Dennis. Turning Points in History, 12 vols., Group 4. Incl. First Lunar Landing. 34.07 *(978-0-7614-4256-1(1)*, 2a64a349-32a7-41c4-9b47-d4ecef34bf16); Hurricane Katrina. Bloom Fradin, Judith. 34.07 *(978-0-7614-4261-5(8)*, 516d2f6d-7f79-4ec9-b419-2220b5bdeb93); Louisiana Purchase. 34.07 *(978-0-7614-4257-8(X)*, 53cdb14d-b8e2-418d-8921-ceb098a75c1e); Montgomery Bus Boycott. 34.07 *(978-0-7614-4258-5(8)*, 0d3787c1-13eb-4d62-aab1-b3d95ad87102); Stamp Act Of 1765. (Illus.). 34.07 *(978-0-7614-4260-8(X)*, ebda7934-06c6-4918-bac9-93a066b6efcd); 9/11/01. 34.07 *(978-0-7614-4259-2(6)*, 75002057-d3bf-4e16-9278-148fda1efa7d); 48p. (gr. 4-4). (Turning Points in U. S. History Ser.). (ENG.). 2010. Set lib. bdg. 204.42 *(978-0-7614-4255-4(3)*, 1c6e051b-4576-4b2a-9335-6d08323f0a30, Cavendish Square) Cavendish Square Publishing LLC.

—Turning Points in U. S. History, 12 vols., Set. Incl. Alamo. lib. bdg. 34.07 *(978-0-7614-2127-6(0)*, a890134e-b43a-4bc9-b810-370f9e8fdba1); Assassination of Abraham Lincoln. lib. bdg. 34.07 *(978-0-7614-2123-8(8)*, 12dd41a1-36d5-4e0e-a468-d45f3b974e88); Custer's Last Stand. lib. bdg. 34.07 *(978-0-7614-2124-5(6)*, 2df4829d-0a02-4a0d-aafb-98abc97067cb); Declaration of Independence. lib. bdg. 34.07 *(978-0-7614-2129-0(7)*, f86eb692-5344-44c0-90b0-233796d33085); Jamestown, Virginia. lib. bdg. 34.07 *(978-0-7614-2122-1(X)*, f90b4dfc-7667-449b-a030-3715f19e4a4f); Mayflower Compact. lib. bdg. 34.07 *(978-0-7614-2125-2(4)*, 047805e0-f50c-4cca-90d8-3562f332da95); (Illus.). 48p. (gr. 4-4). (Turning Points in U. S. History Ser.). (ENG.). 2007. Set lib. bdg. 204.42 *(978-0-7614-2121-4(1)*, e36d9e35-b00a-4735-a07e-e3d2be072d39, Cavendish Square) Cavendish Square Publishing LLC.

—Turning Points in U. S. History - Group 3, 12 vols., Set. Incl. Battle of Yorktown. lib. bdg. 34.07 *(978-0-7614-3008-7(3)*, 4430d16e-dea9-44f7-8f10-3baa94868afb); Bill of Rights. lib. bdg. 34.07 *(978-0-7614-3009-4(1)*, 24222299-d242-45b7-856f-e0aee33783d1); Boston Massacre. lib. bdg. 34.07 *(978-0-7614-3010-0(5)*, 6b4c9e64-1a1c-4750-9a34-9b6e36ad80c6); California Gold Rush. lib. bdg. 34.07 *(978-0-7614-3012-4(1)*, c3441373-627f-4735-bc6b-3171a836b1ce); Salem Witch Trials. Bloom Fradin, Judith. lib. bdg. 34.07 *(978-0-7614-3013-1(X)*, b2c5e336-94b8-47b6-be36-ca80b68e06c0); Underground Railroad. lib. bdg. 34.07 *(978-0-7614-3014-8(8)*, 9dc92785-4a3d-4835-bf07-5679dd35196f); 48p. (gr. 4-4). (Turning Points in U. S. History Ser.). (ENG.). 2009. Set lib. bdg. 204.42 *(978-0-7614-3007-0(5)*, 4218620e-1ec5-4ba6-b2c5-dea410268927, Cavendish Square) Cavendish Square Publishing LLC.

Brinkley, Alan. The Unfinished Nation with PowerWeb. 4th rev. ed. 2003. (Unfinished Nation Ser.). (J). (gr. 6-12). (Illus.). pap., pap. 70.31 *(978-0-07-293522-6(7)*, 9780072935226); Vol. 2. pap., pap. 67.19 *(978-0-07-293525-7(1)*, 9780072935257) Glencoe/McGraw-Hill.

Broida, Marian. Projects about Nineteenth-Century Chinese Immigrants, 1 vol. 2007. (Hands-On History Ser.). (ENG., Illus.). 48p. (gr. 3-3). lib. bdg. 34.07 *(978-0-7614-1978-5(0)*, b08f1fd7-21d5-46c5-8de6-13bf50870de3) Cavendish Square Publishing LLC.

Brook, Henry. True Stories of D-Day. 2006. (Illus.). 160p. (J). per. 4.99 *(978-0-7945-1161-6(9)*, Usborne) EDC Publishing.

Brown, Carron. Maravillas de Los EE. UU: Shine-A-light. Robbins, Wesley, illus. 2019.Tr. of Wonders of the USA. (SPA.). (J). 12.99 *(978-1-61067-916-9(4))* Kane Miller.

—Wonders of the USA: Shine-A-light. 2017. (ENG., Illus.). 36p. (J). 12.99 *(978-1-61067-543-7(6))* Kane Miller.

Brown, Fannie T. Where Are the Children? 2011. 114p. pap. 11.95 *(978-1-4269-6661-3(X))* Trafford Publishing.

Buell, Tonya. Slavery in America: A Primary Source History of the Intolerable Practice of Slavery. 2009. (Primary Sources in American History Ser.). 64p. (gr. 5-8). 58.50 *(978-1-60851-491-5(9))* Rosen Publishing Group, Inc., The.

Building America, 11 vols., Set. Incl. Colonial Virginia. Harkins, Susan Sales & Harkins, William H. (gr. 4-8). 2007. lib. bdg. 29.95 *(978-1-58415-548-5(5))*; Georgia: The Debtors Colony. Harkins, Susan Sales & Harkins, William H. (gr. 3-7). 2006. lib. bdg. 29.95 *(978-1-58415-465-5(9))*; Holidays & Celebrations in Colonial America. Roberts, Russell. (gr. 3-7). 2006. lib. bdg. 29.95 *(978-1-58415-467-9(5))*; Jamestown: The First Colony. Harkins, William H. & Harkins, Susan Sales. (gr. 3-7). 2006. lib. bdg. 29.95 *(978-1-58415-458-7(6))*; Life in Colonial America. Roberts, Russell. (gr. 4-8). 2007. lib. bdg. 29.95 *(978-1-58415-549-2(3))*; Maryland Colony: Lord Baltimore. Whiting, Jim. (gr. 4-8). 2007. lib. bdg. 29.95 *(978-1-58415-547-8(7))*; Massachusetts Bay Colony: The Puritans Arrive from England. Hinman, Bonnie. (gr. 3-7). 2006. lib. bdg. 29.95 *(978-1-58415-460-0(8))*; New Netherland: The Dutch Settle the Hudson Valley. Gibson, Karen Bush. (gr. 3-7). 2006. lib. bdg. 29.95 *(978-1-58415-461-7(6))*; Pennsylvania: William Penn & the City of Brotherly Love. Hinman, Bonnie. (gr. 3-7). 2006. lib. bdg. 29.95 *(978-1-58415-463-1(2))*; Plymouth Colony: The Pilgrims Settle in New England. Tracy, Kathleen. (gr. 3-7). 2006. lib. bdg. 29.95 *(978-1-58415-459-4(4))*; Texas Joins the United States. Roberts, Russell. (gr. 4-8). 2007. lib. bdg. 29.95 *(978-1-58415-550-8(7))*; (Illus.). 48p. (J). (Building America Ser.). 2007. Set lib. bdg. 329.45 *(978-1-58415-551-5(5))* Mitchell Lane Pubs.

Buller, Jon, et al. Smart about the Fifty States: A Class Report. 2003. (Smart about History Ser.). (Illus.). 64p. (J). (gr. k-4). mass mkt. 8.99 *(978-0-448-43131-4(9)*, Grosset & Dunlap) Penguin Young Readers Group.

Burgan, Michael. The Great Depression: An Interactive History Adventure, 1 vol. 2010. (You Choose: Historical Eras Ser.). (ENG.). 112p. (J). (gr. 3-7). pap. 6.95 *(978-1-4296-6276-5(X)*, 115421); (Illus.). 32.65 *(978-1-4296-5480-7(5)*, 113880) Capstone. (Capstone Pr.).

Burleigh, Robert. The Adventures of Mark Twain by Huckleberry Finn. Blitt, Barry, illus. 2011. (ENG.). 48p. (J). (gr. 2-5). 19.99 *(978-0-689-83041-9(6)*, Atheneum Bks. for Young Readers) Simon & Schuster Children's Publishing.

Burlingame, Jeff. Demi! Latina Star Demi Lovato, 1 vol. 2013. (Sizzling Celebrities Ser.). (ENG.). 48p. (gr. 4-6). pap. 11.53 *(978-1-4644-0277-7(9)*, 003aad0f-ed44-496e-9ef9-3803fb52ee68) Enslow Publishing, LLC.

Cain, Marie Mowery. American Symbols. 2013. (Big Books, Blue Ser.). (ENG & SPA., Illus.). 16p. pap. 33.00 *(978-1-59246-014-4(3))* Big Books, by George!

Campbell, Wallis. Angel Island. 2006. (Illus.). 48p. (J). pap. *(978-1-59034-808-6(7))* Mondo Publishing.

Cane, Ella. States in My World, 1 vol. 2013. (My World Ser.). (ENG.). 24p. (J). (gr. -1-2). pap. 6.95 *(978-1-4765-3463-3(2)*, 123562) Capstone.

Capriola, Arlene & Swensen, Rigmor. US History 8: Reconstruction to the Present. 2005. (Taking the High Road to Social Studies Ser.). 5.95 *(978-0-7915-1672-0(5))*; 24.95 *(978-0-7915-1666-9(0))* Phoenix Learning Resources, LLC.

Carpenter, Dan & Kennelly, Sean. Amazing America: an Adventure into American History: American Collection. Gilman, Thomas W., ed. 2014. (ENG., Illus.). 48p. (J). (gr. 4). 8.99 *(978-1-4867-0255-8(4))* Flowerpot Children's Pr. Inc. CAN. Dist: Cardinal Pubs. Group.

Cassells, E. Steve. Tracing the Past: Archaeology along the Rocky Mountain Expansion Loop Pipeline, 1. 2003. (Illus.). 40p. 6.95 *(978-0-9743137-0-2(X))* Alpine Archaeological Consultants, Inc.

Cayton, Andrew & Prentice-Hall Staff. America: Pathways to the Present. 2004. (ENG.). (YA). (gr. 11-12). 88.00 *(978-0-13-181545-2(8)*, Prentice Hall) Savvas Learning Co.

—America: Pathways to the Present, Modern American History. 2004. (ENG.). (YA). (gr. 11-12). 85.90 *(978-0-13-181547-6(4)*, Prentice Hall) Savvas Learning Co.

Celebrate the States - Group 7, 10 vols., Set. 2nd rev. ed. Incl. Arkansas. Jacobs Altman, Linda. lib. bdg. 39.79 *(978-0-7614-3001-8(6)*, 6d5caadc-3287-4bd3-9334-b55c8548c5c1); Idaho. Stefoff, Rebecca. lib. bdg. 39.79 *(978-0-7614-3003-2(2)*, 621169b5-395d-4e53-afe4-633d74831354); Maryland. Pietrzyk, Leslie & Kneib, Martha. lib. bdg. 39.79 *(978-0-7614-3004-9(0)*, 14d2469d-638c-46e1-97f4-9b6577a17792); Massachusetts. LeVert, Suzanne & Orr, Tamra B. lib. bdg. 39.79 *(978-0-7614-3005-6(9)*, 35891fa0-4a8f-492e-be4a-874fd890fc94); New Jersey. Moragne, Wendy. lib. bdg. 39.79 *(978-0-7614-3006-3(7)*, 9e599e6f-f25f-48d3-965e-92c07a7f7d35); (gr. 6-6). (Celebrate the States (Second Edition) Ser.). (ENG.). 144p. 2009. Set lib. bdg. 198.95 *(978-0-7614-3000-1(8)*, f6e5327b-8709-4965-adf3-fa68667217ee, Cavendish Square) Cavendish Square Publishing LLC.

Celebrate the States (First Edition, Group 11), 8 vols. 2003. (Celebrate the States (First Edition) Ser.). (ENG.). (gr. 6-6). 159.16 *(978-0-7614-1310-3(3)*, 7a74eeb3-ede9-4021-ac9d-4b091b3907d8, Cavendish Square) Cavendish Square Publishing LLC.

Center for Learning Network Staff. U. S. History & Geography 2 Bk. 2: Curriculum Unit, 2 vols. 2003. (Social Studies Ser.). 210p. tchr. ed., spiral bd. 29.95 *(978-1-56077-655-0(2))* Center for Learning, The.

Center for Learning Staff. The Age of Imperialism: 1895-1930 — - Elementary U. S. History Series, 11 vols. 2003. (Social Studies Ser.). (Illus.). 143p. (J). tchr. ed., spiral bd. 29.95 *(978-1-56077-748-9(6))* Center for Learning, The.

—Using Literature to Teach U. S. History: Elementary U. S. History Series, 12 vols. 2003. (Social Studies Ser.). (Illus.). 227p. (J). tchr. ed., spiral bd. 37.95 *(978-1-56077-736-6(2))* Center for Learning, The.

Cheney, Lynne. A Is for Abigail: An Almanac of Amazing American Women. 2003. (ENG., Illus.). 48p. (J). (gr. 1-7). 19.99 *(978-0-689-85819-2(1)*, Simon & Schuster Bks. For Young Readers) Simon & Schuster Bks. For Young Readers.

—Our 50 States: A Family Adventure Across America. Glasser, Robin Preiss, illus. 2006. (ENG.). 74p. (J). (gr. 2-5). 21.99 *(978-0-689-86717-0(4)*, Simon & Schuster/Paula Wiseman Bks.) Simon & Schuster/Paula Wiseman Bks.

—A Time for Freedom: What Happened When in America. 2005. (ENG., Illus.). 304p. (J). (gr. 5-9). 19.99 *(978-1-4169-0925-5(7)*, Simon & Schuster/Paula Wiseman Bks.) Simon & Schuster/Paula Wiseman Bks.

Child, Hamilton. Gazetteer & Business Directory of Sullivan County For 1872-73: Republished on CD-ROM by Between the Lakes Group 2003. (Illus.). 380p. cd-rom 20.00 *(978-0-9727403-4-0(1)*, EJ03-03C) Between the Lakes Group, LLC.

Choi, John & McGowen, Tom. Reaching for the Moon: The Cold War Space Race. 2019. (J). *(978-1-9785-1530-7(8))* Enslow Publishing, LLC.

Churchill, E. Richard & Churchill, Linda R. Short Lessons in U. S. History. 4th ed. 2008. (ENG., Illus.). 231p. (YA). (gr. 8-12). pap. 29.00 *(978-0-8251-6464-4(8))* Walch Education.

Clark, Katie. The Lincoln Memorial: Myths, Legends, & Facts, 1 vol. 2014. (Monumental History Ser.). (ENG.). 32p. (J). (gr. 3-6). 27.99 *(978-1-4914-0205-4(9)*, 125788, Capstone Pr.) Capstone.

Clickard, Carrie. Thomas Jefferson & the Mammoth Hunt: The True Story of the Quest for America's Biggest Bones. Carpenter, Nancy, illus. 2019. (ENG.). 40p. (J). (gr. -1-3). 17.99 *(978-1-4814-4268-8(6)*, Beach Lane Bks.) Beach Lane Bks.

Coletti, Sharon. Everything You Need to Supplement U. S. & State Studies. 2005. (YA). Pt. 1. ring bd. 249.95 *(978-1-933558-08-0(3))*Pt. 2. ring bd. 249.95 *(978-1-933558-09-7(1))* InspirEd Educators.

Collins, Kathleen. Marques de Lafayette: Heroe Frances de la Revolucion Estadounidense, 1 vol. 2003. (Grandes Personajes en la Historia de Los Estados Unidos (Famous People in American History) Ser.). (SPA., Illus.). 32p. (gr. 3-4). lib. bdg. 29.13 *(978-0-8239-4139-1(6)*, a74adad7-370c-4ffc-9b68-cf8170ec0101, Editorial Buenas Letras) Rosen Publishing Group, Inc., The.

Collins, Terry. Liberty, 1 vol. Bascle, Brian, illus. 2009. (Cartoon Nation Ser.). (ENG.). 32p. (J). (gr. 3-9). lib. bdg. 31.32 *(978-1-4296-2340-7(3)*, 95068, Capstone Pr.) Capstone.

Color All About: America: A Giant Coloring Book about the Birth of a Nation. 2004. (Illus.). (J). *(978-0-9763307-3-8(3))* Food Marketing Consultants, Inc.

Connolly, Kieron. America's Bloody History from Columbus to the Gold Rush, 1 vol. 2017. (Bloody History of America Ser.). (ENG.). 88p. (gr. 8-8). 37.60 *(978-0-7660-9177-1(5)*, 618bafd2-4108-420b-8da9-c09752e50a0e); pap. 20.95 *(978-0-7660-9554-0(1)*, a6ba4963-2187-45fb-9817-3c86421f98da) Enslow Publishing, LLC.

—America's Bloody History from the Civil War to the Great Depression, 1 vol. 2017. (Bloody History of America Ser.). (ENG.). 88p. (gr. 8-8). 37.60 *(978-0-7660-9178-8(3)*, 2eccc640-a875-4b93-be57-f45939ce32e2) Enslow Publishing, LLC.

—America's Bloody History from Vietnam to the War on Terror, 1 vol. 2017. (Bloody History of America Ser.). (ENG.). 88p. (gr. 8-8). 37.60 *(978-0-7660-9180-1(5)*, a92bb720-3a4b-4034-aa1a-44302d2dd1cb); pap. 20.95 *(978-0-7660-9556-4(8)*, 2aaa20cd-f1a2-4bce-a811-26f2f83462ab) Enslow Publishing, LLC.

—America's Bloody History from World War II to the Civil Rights Movement, 1 vol. 2017. (Bloody History of America Ser.). (ENG.). 88p. (gr. 8-8). 37.60 *(978-0-7660-9179-5(1)*, ce7f5754-d0d1-49f5-8ebd-935f815267bb) Enslow Publishing, LLC.

Connors, Kathleen. Let's Explore the Northeast, 1 vol. 2013. (Road Trip: Exploring America's Regions Ser.). (ENG.). 24p. (J). (gr. 2-3). 25.27 *(978-1-4339-9134-9(9)*, 15d49b6a-92d1-4b23-adb8-c8f5f9bf5718); pap. 9.15 *(978-1-4339-9135-6(7)*, 2e97713e-0cd5-4e96-ac71-ac25da5c408c) Stevens, Gareth Publishing LLLP.

Cornerstones of Freedom, Second Series, 4 bks., Set. Incl. Cornerstones of Freedom: Building the New York Subway. Santella, Andrew. 26.00 *(978-0-516-23638-4(5))*; Gilded Age. Morrow, Ann. 26.00 *(978-0-516-23641-4(5))*; Manhattan Project. Elish, Dan. 26.00 *(978-0-516-23299-7(1))*; U. S. Supreme Court. Elish, Dan. 26.00 *(978-0-516-23637-7(7))*; (Illus.). 48p. (J). (gr. 4-6). 2007. 104.00 o.p. *(978-0-531-17731-0(9)*, Children's Pr.) Scholastic Library Publishing.

Cornerstones of Freedom, Third Series Spring 2012 Set Of 10. 2012. (Cornerstones of Freedom, Third Ser.). 300.00 *(978-0-531-25834-7(3)*, Children's Pr.) Scholastic Library Publishing.

Cosson, M. J. America: Three Worlds Meet. 2011. (Explorer Library: Language Arts Explorer Ser.). (ENG., Illus.). 32p. (gr. 4-8). lib. bdg. 32.07 *(978-1-61080-193-5(8)*, 201162) Cherry Lake Publishing.

Crabtree Publishing Company Staff & Morss, Martha. United States: The People. 2012. (ENG.). 32p. (J). pap. *(978-0-7787-9839-2(9))* Crabtree Publishing Co.

Creating America: A History of the United States: Creating America Workbook Answer Key. 2005. (gr. 6-12). *(978-0-618-15629-0(1)*, 2-01341) Holt McDougal.

Creating America: A History of the United States: EEdition Plus Online. 2005. (gr. 6-12). *(978-0-618-42734-5(1)*, 2-00718) Holt McDougal.

Creating America: A History of the United States: EEdition Plus Online with purchase of print Pupil'sYear. 2005. (gr. 6-12). *(978-0-618-42727-7(9)*, 2-00711) Holt McDougal.

Creating America: A History of the United States: ETest Plus Online-1 year (per Student) 2005. (gr. 6-12). *(978-0-618-28361-3(7)*, 2-90117) Holt McDougal.

Creating America: A History of the United States: ETest Plus Online-6 year (per Student) 2005. (gr. 6-12). *(978-0-618-28382-8(X)*, 2-90122) Holt McDougal.

Creating America: A History of the United States: GeoQuest. 2005. (gr. 6-12). cd-rom *(978-0-618-03712-4(8)*, 2-81168) Holt McDougal.

Creating America: A History of the United States: Primary Source Explorer. 2005. (gr. 6-12). cd-rom *(978-0-618-03708-7(X)*, 2-81164) Holt McDougal.

Creating America: Beginnings through Reconstruction: Creating America: Beginnings through Reconstruction Workbook. 2005. (gr. 6-12). (978-0-618-19420-9(7), 2-70061) Holt McDougal.

Creating America: Beginnings Through Reconstruction: EEdition Plus Online. 2005. (gr. 6-12). (978-0-618-19411-7(8), 2-70053) Holt McDougal.

Creating America: Beginnings Through Reconstruction: EEdition Plus Online with purchase of print Pupil's Year. 2005. (gr. 6-12). (978-0-618-18720-1(0), 2-70030) Holt McDougal.

Creating America: Beginnings Through World War I. 2005. (gr. 6-12). (978-0-618-16522-3(3), 2-81245) Holt McDougal.

Creating America: Beginnings Through World War I: EEdition Plus Online. 2005. (gr. 6-12). (978-0-618-42758-1(9), 2-00742) Holt McDougal.

Creating America: Beginnings Through World War I: EEdition Plus Online with purchase of print Pupil's Year. 2005. (gr. 6-12). (978-0-618-42751-2(1), 2-00735) Holt McDougal.

Critical Anthologies of Nonfiction Writing: Set 1, 8 vols. 2004. (Critical Anthologies of Nonfiction Writing Ser.). (ENG.). (gr. 8-8). lib. bdg. 169.88 (978-1-4042-0354-9(0), c2b9ede0-c7c2-47f0-bc69-88663b53f1a7) Rosen Publishing Group, Inc., The.

Cudeyro, Erica M. American History for Young Minds - Volume 1, Looking Towards the Sky, Book 1, the First Airplane. Butler, Lindsay L., illus. 2008. 20p. pap. 11.95 (978-1-934925-34-8(9), Eloquent Bks.) Strategic Book Publishing & Rights Agency (SBPRA).

Cunningham, Kevin. Contemporary United States. 2011. (Explorer Library: Language Arts Explorer Ser.). (ENG.). 32p. (gr. 4-8). pap. 14.21 (978-1-61080-283-3(7), 201206); (Illus.). lib. bdg. 32.07 (978-1-61080-195-9(4), 201166) Cherry Lake Publishing.

Currie, Stephen. Environmentalism in America, 1 vol. 2010. (American History Ser.). (ENG., Illus.). 96p. (gr. 7-7). 41.03 (978-1-4205-0210-7(7), 0f824362-1d4b-4103-b368-982203c574b3, Lucent Pr.) Greenhaven Publishing LLC.

—The Quest for Freedom: The Abolitionist Movement. 2005. (Lucent Library of Black History). (ENG., Illus.). 112p. (YA). (gr. 7-10). lib. bdg. 33.45 (978-1-59018-703-6(2), Lucent Bks.) Cengage Gale.

Daily Life in US History, 8 vols. 2015. (Daily Life in US History Ser.: 8). (ENG.). 48p. (J). (gr. 4-8). lib. bdg. 285.12 (978-1-62403-623-1(6), 16886) ABDO Publishing Co.

D'Amico, Joan & Drumond, Karen Eich. The US History Cook Book: Delicious Recipes & Exciting Events from the Past. 2006. (Illus.). 180p. (J). (gr. 4-8). reprint ed. pap. 15.00 (978-1-4223-5809-2(7)) DIANE Publishing Co.

D'Amico, Karen E. & Drummond, Karen E. The U. S. History Cookbook: Delicious Recipes & Exciting Events from the Past. 2003. (ENG., Illus.). 192p. (J). (gr. 3-7). pap. 20.00 (978-0-471-13602-6(6), Jossey-Bass) Wiley, John & Sons, Inc.

David Haugen. Colonists. 2004. (Voices from the Revolution Ser.). lib. bdg. 22.45 (978-1-4103-0413-1(2)) Cengage Gale.

—Leaders. 2004. lib. bdg. 22.45 (978-1-56711-958-9(1), Blackbirch Pr., Inc.) Cengage Gale.

Davies, Gill. The Thirteen Colonies 1584 - 1776. 2005. (National Geographic Timelines Ser.). (Illus.). 64p. (J). 27.90 (978-0-7922-4171-3(1)) CENGAGE Learning.

Davis, Kenneth C. Don't Know Much about American History. Faulkner, Matt, illus. 2003. (ENG.). 224p. (J). (gr. 3-7). pap. 7.99 (978-0-06-440836-3(1), HarperCollins) HarperCollins Pubs.

—Don't Know Much About American History. 2004. (Don't Know Much about Ser.). 224p. (J). (gr. 4-7). pap. 40.00 incl. audio (978-0-8072-2092-4(2), Listening Library) Random Hse. Audio Publishing Group.

Day, Reed B. Two Families: A History of the Lives & Times of the Families of Isaac Newton Day & Lucilla Caroline Blachly 1640-1940. 2004. (Illus.). 296p. per. 29.95 (978-0-9760563-1-7(3), 7796) Mechling Bookbindery.

DBQ Practice U. S. History. 2003. spiral bd. 19.95 (978-1-56004-144-3(7)) Social Studies Schl. Service.

Diesen, Deborah. Equality's Call: The Story of Voting Rights in America. Mora, Magdalena, illus. 2020. (ENG.). 48p. (J). (gr. -1-3). 17.99 (978-1-5344-3958-0(7), Beach Lane Bks.) Beach Lane Bks.

Discover America State by State (Set), 51 vols., Set. 2005. (Discover America State by State Ser.). (ENG., Illus.). (J). (gr. 1-3). 941.45 (978-1-58536-294-3(8), 202286) Sleeping Bear Pr.

Disgusting History. (Disgusting History Ser.). 32p. 2010. lib. bdg. 103.96 (978-1-4296-5851-5(7)) 2009. (ENG.). (gr. 3-4). lib. bdg. 55.98 (978-1-4296-4443-3(5)) Capstone. (Capstone Pr.).

Documents That Shaped America, 12 vols. 2013. (Documents That Shaped America Ser.). 32p. (J). (gr. 4-5). (ENG.). 175.62 (978-1-4339-9678-8(2), ec593b91-3c35-4654-9b2c-1730d4fe32ac); pap. 63.00 (978-1-4339-9745-7(2)); pap. 378.00 (978-1-4339-9746-4(0)) Stevens, Gareth Publishing LLLP.

Donner, Candie. American Girl: Assembled: Meet Kaya Lapbook. Kinney, Cyndi, ed. 2013. (J). pap. 35.99 (978-1-61625-515-2(3)) Knowledge Box Central.

—American Girl: Meet Kaya Lapbook. Kinney, Cyndi, ed. 2013. (J). pap. 25.99 (978-1-61625-513-8(7)); cd-rom 19.99 (978-1-61625-512-1(9)) Knowledge Box Central.

Duby, Marjorie. From Caravels to the Constitution: Puzzles Trageting Historical Themes That Reinforce Logic & Problem-Solving Skills. Armstrong, Bev, illus. 2006. (Learning Works). 112p. (J). (gr. 5-8). per. 13.99 (978-0-88160-385-9(6), LW405, Learning Works, The) Creative Teaching Pr., Inc.

Dudley, William, ed. Volume 1: from Colonial Times to Reconstruction, 1 vol., Vol. 1. 2006. (Opposing Viewpoints in American History Ser.: Vol. 1). (ENG.). 200p. (gr. 10-12). pap. 52.40 (978-0-7377-3185-9(0), 72709137-320c-4acd-bcb8-e6bd12e11e63); lib. bdg. 69.08 (978-0-7377-3184-2(2), c6c45344-0190-44e1-9f63-bc5608c8868d) Greenhaven Publishing LLC. (Greenhaven Publishing).

—Volume 2: from Reconstruction to the Present, 1 vol., Vol. 2. 2006. (Opposing Viewpoints in American History Ser.: Vol. 2). (ENG.). 240p. (gr. 10-12). pap. 52.40 (978-0-7377-3187-3(7), aede3b11-ce90-438c-8748-2efee02d2d9f); lib. bdg. 67.13 (978-0-7377-3186-6(9), cc371089-1f64-4036-9358-c1f703ac1531) Greenhaven Publishing LLC. (Greenhaven Publishing).

Due Process DBA. 2003. spiral bd. 16.95 (978-1-56004-148-1(X)) Social Studies Schl. Service.

Dunn, Joeming W. The Pony Express, 1 vol. Martin, Cynthia, illus. 2008. (Graphic History Ser.). (ENG.). 32p. (J). (gr. 3-8). 32.79 (978-1-60270-184-7(9), 9060, Graphic Planet - Fiction) Magic Wagon.

Editors of Brain Quest. Brain Quest America: 850 Questions & Answers to Challenge the Mind. Teacher-Approved! 4th rev. ed. 2013. (Brain Quest Smart Cards Ser.). (ENG.). 152p. (J). (gr. 4-7). 11.95 (978-0-7611-7239-0(4), 17239) Workman Publishing Co., Inc.

The Elements - Group 6, 8 vols. 2005. (Elements Ser.). (ENG., Illus.). 32p. (gr. 4-4). lib. bdg. 124.84 (978-0-7614-1547-3(5), 324ab765-ec0d-47ab-8818-97da6af028c4, Cavendish Square) Cavendish Square Publishing LLC.

Encyclopaedia Britannica, Inc. Staff, compiled by. Views of the Americas. 2003. (Illus.). 64p. 14.95 (978-1-59339-043-3(2)) Encyclopaedia Britannica, Inc.

Encyclopedia Britannica's Annals of America 2003, 22 vols. 2003. 13000p. (YA). (gr. 5-18). 529.00 (978-0-85229-960-9(5)) Encyclopaedia Britannica, Inc.

Ervin, Robert Edgar. The John Hunt Morgan Raid of 1863. 2003. (Illus.). 306p. lib. bdg. 29.95 net. (978-0-9746189-0-6(X)) Ervin, Robert E.

Esty, Amos. The Liberator: The Story of William Lloyd Garrison. 2011. (Civil Rights Leaders Ser.). 144p. 28.95 (978-1-59935-137-7(4)) Reynolds, Morgan Inc.

Evan-Moor Educational Publishers. U. S. Facts & Fun Grades 1-3. 2005. (U. S. Facts & Fun Ser.). (ENG., Illus.). 192p. (J). (gr. 1-3). pap., tchr. ed. 21.99 (978-1-59673-002-1(1), EMC 6305) Evan-Moor Educational Pubs.

—U. S. Facts & Fun Grades 4-6. 2005. (U. S. Facts & Fun Ser.). (ENG., Illus.). 192p. (J). (gr. 4-6). pap., tchr. ed. 21.99 (978-1-59673-003-8(X), EMC 6306) Evan-Moor Educational Pubs.

Exposed! Myths about Early American History. 2016. (Exposed! Myths about Early American History Ser.). 00032p. (J). pap. 63.00 (978-1-4824-5845-9(4)) Stevens, Gareth Publishing LLLP.

Eyewitness to History: Set 2, 12 vols. 2014. (Eyewitness to History Ser.). (ENG.). 32p. (J). (gr. 4-5). 175.62 (978-1-4824-1172-0(5), 2a19a745-cb20-4501-9034-6baa864efcff) Stevens, Gareth Publishing LLLP.

Eyewitness to History: Sets 1-2. 2014. (Eyewitness to History Ser.). 32p. (J). (gr. 4-6). 319.20 (978-1-4824-1450-9(3)) Stevens, Gareth Publishing LLLP.

First Americans, 12 vols., Set. Incl. Apache. Casey, Carolyn. lib. bdg. 34.07 (978-0-7614-1894-8(6), 8f7dd179-6889-41f0-9d5e-bb15ace56c4d); Cherokee. De Capua, Sarah. lib. bdg. 34.07 (978-0-7614-1895-5(4), 922df5b9-a7dd-449e-a54b-636977d32dd4); Iroquois. De Capua, Sarah. lib. bdg. 34.07 (978-0-7614-1896-2(2), 97e8e22f-c7b7-4c5c-8800-f34ee329fe2b); Navajo. King, David C. lib. bdg. 34.07 (978-0-7614-1897-9(0), 0fd85569-8237-4f17-a202-425c92b0ddb1); Pueblo. Broida, Marian. lib. bdg. 34.07 (978-0-7614-1898-6(9), 11f43db1-1385-4b28-bb44-8fa46432859f); Sioux. King, David C. lib. bdg. 34.07 (978-0-7614-1899-3(7), 29b2f9c7-5125-45db-900f-d39ae63b08f8); (Illus.). 48p. (gr. 3-3). (First Americans Ser.). (ENG.). 2007. 204.42 (978-0-7614-1893-1(8), f5642165-9e14-4afb-9797-46c53e8e0436, Cavendish Square) Cavendish Square Publishing LLC.

Fisher, Douglas & McGraw-Hill Staff. The American Republic since 1877: Active Reading Note-Taking Guide. 2nd ed. 2004. (U. S. History - the Modern Era Ser.). (ENG., Illus.). 544p. (gr. 8-10). stu. ed., per. 13.60 (978-0-07-867995-7(8), 0078679958) McGraw-Hill Higher Education.

—The American Vision Active Reading Note-Taking Guide: Student Workbook. 2nd ed. 2004. (United States History (hs) Ser.). (ENG., Illus.). 584p. (gr. 9-12). stu. ed., per. 13.60 (978-0-07-868002-1(6), 0078680026) McGraw-Hill Higher Education.

Forest, Christopher. This Book Is History: A Collection of Cool U. S. History Trivia, 1 vol. 2012. (Super Trivia Collection). (ENG.). 32p. (J). (gr. 3-9). lib. bdg. 28.65 (978-1-4296-8419-4(4), 118492, Capstone Pr.) Capstone.

Foundations of Our Nation, 8 vols. 2013. (Foundations of Our Nation Ser.: 8). (ENG.). 48p. (J). (gr. 3-6). lib. bdg. 285.12 (978-1-61783-705-0(9), 7808) ABDO Publishing Co.

Franchino, Vicky. It's Cool to Learn about the United States: Northeast. 2011. (Explorer Library: Social Studies Explorer Ser.). (ENG., Illus.). 48p. (gr. 4-8). lib. bdg. 34.93 (978-1-61080-180-5(6), 201154) Cherry Lake Publishing.

Franck, Irene M. & Brownstone, David M. Frontier America, 10 vols. 2004. (Illus.). (J). 369.00 (978-0-7172-5990-8(0), Grolier) Scholastic Library Publishing.

Frank, Sarah. Filipinos in America. 2005. (In America Ser.). (ENG., Illus.). 72p. (gr. 5-8). lib. bdg. 27.93 (978-0-8225-4873-7(9), Lerner Pubns.) Lerner Publishing Group.

Freedman, Jeri. Careers in Child Care, 1 vol. 2014. (Essential Careers Ser.). (ENG.). 80p. (J). (gr. 6-6). 37.47 (978-1-4777-7884-5(5), fd38af77-7074-4324-936d-85dd11df456f, Rosen Young Adult) Rosen Publishing Group, Inc., The.

Fridell, Ron. Prisoners of War, 1 vol. 2008. (Open for Debate Ser.). (ENG., Illus.). 144p. (YA). (gr. 8-8). lib. bdg. 45.50 (978-0-7614-2577-9(2), 0e870abe-ea61-490b-8c1a-bb3149021202) Cavendish Square Publishing LLC.

Friedman-Brunt, Elyse. Conflict Resolution in American History, Gr. 8: Lessons from the Past, Lessons for Today. Chandler, Terrence, illus. 2003. 48p. (YA). pap., wbk. ed. 19.95 (978-1-878227-89-8(0)) Peace Education Foundation.

—Conflict Resolution in American History, Grade 8: Lessons from the Past, Lessons for Today. Chandler, Terrence, illus. 2003. 200p. pap., instr.'s training gde. ed. 29.95 (978-1-878227-88-1(2)) Peace Education Foundation.

Frisch, Aaron. Aaron Rodgers. 2013. (Big Time Ser.). (ENG., Illus.). 24p. (J). (gr. 1-4). 25.65 (978-1-60818-334-0(3), 21795, Creative Education) Creative Co., The.

—Adrian Peterson. 2013. (Big Time Ser.). (ENG., Illus.). 24p. (J). (gr. 1-4). 25.65 (978-1-60818-335-7(1), 21799, Creative Education) Creative Co., The.

—Katy Perry. 2013. (Big Time Ser.). (ENG., Illus.). 24p. (J). (gr. 1-4). 25.65 (978-1-60818-331-9(9), 21808, Creative Education) Creative Co., The.

—Lady Gaga. 2013. (Big Time Ser.). (ENG., Illus.). 24p. (J). (gr. 1-4). 25.65 (978-1-60818-332-6(7), 21811, Creative Education) Creative Co., The.

Frisch-Schmoll, Joy. Let's Look at the United States of America. 2019. (Let's Look at Countries Ser.). (ENG., Illus.). 24p. (J). (gr. -1-2). lib. bdg. 27.32 (978-1-9771-0382-6(0), 139353, Capstone Pr.) Capstone.

Fun Fact File. 2013. (Fun Fact File Ser.). 32p. (J). (gr. 3-6). 606.00 (978-1-4339-9734-1(7)); pap. 252.00 (978-1-4339-9826-3(2)); pap. 1512.00 (978-1-4339-9827-0(0)) Stevens, Gareth Publishing LLLP.

Fun Fact File: Complete Set. 2017. (Fun Fact File Ser.). 32p. (gr. 2-3). lib. bdg. 1515.00 (978-1-5382-0470-2(3)) Stevens, Gareth Publishing LLLP.

Fun Fact File: Founding Fathers. 2017. (Fun Fact File: Founding Fathers Ser.). 32p. (gr. 2-3). pap. 63.00 (978-1-5382-0484-9(3)) Stevens, Gareth Publishing LLLP.

Fun Fact File: US History!, 12 vols. 2013. (Fun Fact File: U. S. History! Ser.). 32p. (J). (ENG.). (gr. 2-3). 167.58 (978-1-4339-9698-6(7), c766386b-b634-4cf7-8920-aa4e038edfba); (gr. 3-6). pap. 378.00 (978-1-4339-9805-8(X)); (gr. 3-6). pap. 63.00 (978-1-4339-9804-1(1)) Stevens, Gareth Publishing LLLP.

Fun Fact File: U. S. History!: Set 2, 12 vols. 2018. (Fun Fact File: U. S. History! Ser.). (ENG.). 32p. (gr. 2-3). lib. bdg. 167.58 (978-1-5382-2182-2(9), d5ece321-ac8b-4595-8287-58204eb008a1) Stevens, Gareth Publishing LLLP.

Gabriel, Alisha. The Triangle Shirtwaist Fire Triggers Reform. 2018. (Events That Changed America Ser.). (ENG.). 32p. (J). (gr. 3-6). lib. bdg. 35.64 (978-1-5038-2524-6(8), 212331, MOMENTUM) Child's World, Inc, The.

Gale Editor, ed. Junior Worldmark Encyclopedia of the States: 4 Volume Set, 4 vols. 6th ed. 2013. (Junior Worldmark Encyclopedia of the States Ser.). (ENG., Illus.). 454.00 (978-1-4144-9859-1(4), UXL) Cengage Gale.

Garbe, Suzanne. Fantasmas de Gettysburg y Otros Lugares Embrujados Del Este. Aparicio Publishing LLC, Aparicio Publishing, tr. 2020. (América Embrujada Ser.).Tr. of Ghosts of Gettysburg & Other Hauntings of the East. (SPA., Illus.). 32p. (J). (gr. 3-9). lib. bdg. 30.65 (978-1-4966-8513-1(X), 200619, Capstone Pr.) Capstone.

—Ghosts of Gettysburg & Other Hauntings of the East, 1 vol. 2014. (Haunted America Ser.). (ENG., Illus.). 32p. (J). (gr. 3-9). lib. bdg. 28.65 (978-1-4765-3916-4(2), 123915, Capstone Pr.) Capstone.

Garcia, Jesús, et al. Creating America: A History of the United States. 2006. (Illus.). 890p. (gr. 6-12). stu. ed. (978-0-395-92899-8(0), 2-88557) Holt McDougal.

—Creating America: A History of the United States: Beginnings Through Reconstruction, 2 vols. l.t. ed. 2003. (McDougal Littell Creating America Ser.). (ENG., Illus.). 816p. (gr. 8-8). stu. ed. 111.95 (978-0-618-37698-8(4), 2-00479) Great Source Education Group, Inc.

—Creating America: A History of the United States: with Atlas by Rand Mcnally. l.t. ed. 2006. (Illus.). 917p. (gr. 7-9). stu. ed. 78.64 (978-0-618-37690-2(9), 2-00471) Holt McDougal.

—Creating America: Beginnings Through World War I. 2006. (Illus.). 751p. (gr. 6-12). stu. ed. (978-0-618-16252-9(6), 2-81241) Holt McDougal.

—Creating America: Beginnings Through World War I: A History of the United States. l.t. ed. 2005. (Illus.). 757p. (gr. 7-9). (978-0-618-37708-4(5), 2-00489) Holt McDougal.

—McDougal Littell Creating America: A History of the United States, 2 vols. l.t. ed. 2003. (McDougal Littell Creating America Ser.). (ENG., Illus.). 704p. (gr. 8-8). stu. ed. 111.95 (978-0-618-37684-1(4), 2-00465) Great Source Education Group, Inc.

Gave, Marc. La historia de los Estados Unidos en Suma. 2011. (SPA.). 32p. (J). pap. 49.00 net. (978-1-4108-2342-7(3), A23423) Benchmark Education Co.

Gilbert, Sara. The Story of Amazon. com. 2013. (Built for Success Ser.). (ENG.). 48p. (J). (gr. 5-9). pap. 12.00 (978-0-89812-759-1(9), 21875, Creative Paperbacks) Creative Co., The.

—The Story of CNN. 2013. (Built for Success Ser.). (ENG.). 48p. (J). (gr. 5-9). pap. 12.00 (978-0-89812-760-7(2), 21876, Creative Paperbacks) Creative Co., The.

The GILDED AGE & PROGRESSIVISM: 1891-1913. 2010. (ENG., Illus.). 136p. (gr. 5-8). 35.00 (978-1-60413-355-4(4), P178886, Facts On File) Infobase Holdings, Inc.

Glencoe McGraw-Hill Staff. The American Vision: Modern Times, Spanish Reading Essentials & Note-Taking Guide. 2007. (United States History (hs) Ser.). (SPA.). 280p. (gr. 9-12). pap. 12.84 (978-0-07-878520-7(0), 0078785200) McGraw-Hill Higher Education.

Glencoe McGraw-Hill Staff, creator. The American Republic since 1877 Spanish Reading Essentials & Study Guide. 2nd ed. 2004. (U. S. History - the Modern Era Ser.). (SPA., Illus.). 488p. (gr. 8-10). stu. ed., per. 8.04 (978-0-07-865407-7(6), 0078654076) McGraw-Hill Higher Education.

—The American Vision Reading Essentials & Study Guide Student Workbook. 2nd ed. 2004. (United States History (hs) Ser.). (ENG., Illus.). 534p. (gr. 9-12). per. 8.52 (978-0-07-865439-8(4), 0078654394) McGraw-Hill Higher Education.

Glencoe McGraw-Hill Staff & McGraw-Hill Education Staff. The American Vision: Modern Times. 2007. (United States History (hs) Ser.). (ENG., Illus.). 280p. (gr. 9-12). per. 12.84 (978-0-07-878518-4(9), 0078785189) McGraw-Hill Higher Education.

GLOBE. Globe Fearon American History Vol. 2: Civil War to the Present. 2003. (ENG.). 524p. (YA). (gr. 6-12). 50.95 (978-0-13-024411-6(2), GLOBE) Savvas Learning Co.

Globe Fearon American History Vol. 1: Prehistory Through Reconstruction. 2003. (American History Ser.). 542p. (YA). (gr. 6-12). 50.95 (978-0-13-024400-0(7)) Globe Fearon Educational Publishing.

Goldish, Meish. Animal Control Officers to the Rescue. 2013. (Work of Heroes: First Responders in Action Ser.). 32p. (J). (gr. 1-6). lib. bdg. 28.50 (978-1-61772-747-4(4)) Bearport Publishing Co., Inc.

Goldsmith, Marcia. Important Years: The 1980s. 2005. (Illus.). 16p. (J). (978-0-618-56043-1(2)) Houghton Mifflin Harcourt Publishing Co.

Goldsworthy, Kaite. Bald Eagle with Code. 2012. (AV2 American Icons Ser.). (ENG., Illus.). 24p. (J). pap. 12.95 (978-1-61913-300-6(8)); lib. bdg. 27.13 (978-1-61913-077-7(7)) Weigl Pubs., Inc. (AV2 by Weigl).

Gonzales, Doreen. The Secret of the Manhattan Project: Stories in American History, 1 vol. 2012. (Stories in American History Ser.). (ENG., Illus.). 128p. (gr. 5-6). 35.93 (978-0-7660-3954-4(4), 234fa205-bde3-44fa-a535-c85a73274122) Enslow Publishing, LLC.

Gonzalez, Libia. Geografia e Historia de los Estados Unidos. (SPA.). 376p. (J). pap. 52.50 (978-958-04-3011-7(X), NOR011) Norma S.A. COL. Dist: AIMS International Bks., Inc.

Goodall, Barry, Jr. Glory Gone Forgotten: The Untold Story of the 12th Kentucky Cavalry. Embry, Eugene, ed. Brown, Stevi, illus. 2nd rev. ed. 2005. 182p. (978-0-9763932-1-4(2), 500) Goodall, Barry.

Goodrich, Charles Augustus. A Child's History of the United States. 2013. (Notable American Authors Ser.). 425p. reprint ed. lthr. 79.00 (978-0-7812-2935-7(9)) Reprint Services Corp.

Goodrich, Samuel G. A Child's History of the United States. reprint ed. 150.00 (978-0-7222-7251-0(0)) Library Reprints, Inc.

Goodrich, Samuel Griswol. Peter Parleys Tales about America & Au. 2006. pap. (978-1-4068-3320-1(7)) Echo Library.

Gordon, Minette, et al. Understanding Women's Rights, 1 vol. 2011. (Personal Freedom & Civic Duty Ser.). (ENG.). 168p. (J). (gr. 7-7). lib. bdg. 39.80 (978-1-4488-4671-9(4), 81dd51a7-d7a7-43a8-b882-0d39b6f9f2f7) Rosen Publishing Group, Inc., The.

Gordon, Sharon. United States, 1 vol. 2015. (Exploring World Cultures (First Edition) Ser.). (ENG., Illus.). 32p. (gr. 3-3). pap. 12.16 (978-1-5026-0576-4(7), 5d7c5ede-b7d3-4687-97a5-9d94a3fd3a19) Cavendish Square Publishing LLC.

Gosman, Gillian. Franklin D. Roosevelt, 1 vol. 2011. (Life Stories Ser.). (ENG., Illus.). 24p. (J). (gr. 3-3). pap. 9.25 (978-1-4488-3182-1(2), 4c99ad0e-7380-4e41-8192-3dcff322e2bf, PowerKids Pr.); lib. bdg. 26.27 (978-1-4488-3222-4(5), 96acf089-22e2-4d2e-a6e6-8a4da767b5e9); lib. bdg. 26.27 (978-1-4488-3179-1(2), 3f0b1701-e059-4701-bc74-6783a09d3a80, PowerKids Pr.) Rosen Publishing Group, Inc., The.

—Life Stories, 16 vols., Set. Incl. Abraham Lincoln. lib. bdg. 26.27 (978-1-4488-2582-0(2), 07f83246-a876-470e-b803-905a492eb466); Benjamin Franklin. lib. bdg. 26.27 (978-1-4488-2585-1(7), 0ce2f8ab-182f-4f36-8495-052334f7703d); Franklin D. Roosevelt. lib. bdg. 26.27 (978-1-4488-3179-1(2), 3f0b1701-e059-4701-bc74-6783a09d3a80); George Washington. lib. bdg. 26.27 (978-1-4488-2581-3(4), 44b4d329-a6e9-4b5e-88ff-2844598ba48b); Harriet Tubman. lib. bdg. 26.27 (978-1-4488-2586-8(5), 2b2679ea-cfb1-4eca-836c-8a5dfb5868f9); Martin Luther King, Jr. lib. bdg. 26.27 (978-1-4488-2583-7(0), 9b332699-9ed0-4c81-9b0e-9bbd8bc2f68c); Rosa Parks. lib. bdg. 26.27 (978-1-4488-2584-4(9), 3797e45e-a80c-45ae-b424-7a783c9d915d); Thomas Jefferson. lib. bdg. 26.27 (978-1-4488-3178-4(4), 6e7e2cdf-68fc-42f2-98e4-ec91f3c5b148); (J). (gr. 3-3). (Life Stories Ser.). (ENG., Illus.). 24p. 2011. Set lib. bdg. 210.16 (978-1-4488-2793-0(0), 3840f588-7d47-45c9-b412-e016b1c4aa7a, PowerKids Pr.) Rosen Publishing Group, Inc., The.

Grace, Catherine O'Neill. 1621: A New Look at Thanksgiving. 2004. (Illus.). 48p. (J). (gr. 3-7). pap. 7.95 (978-0-7922-6139-1(9), National Geographic Kids) Disney Publishing Worldwide.

Grandes personajes (Great Americans), 14 vols. 2006. (Grandes Personajes (Great Americans) Ser.). (SPA.). 24p. (gr. 2-4). lib. bdg. 172.02 (978-0-8368-8373-2(X), 65f0abf4-6ac9-4a66-991e-9fb2f571fb93) Stevens, Gareth Publishing LLLP.

Grant, R. G. The Great Depression, 1 vol. 2005. (How Did It Happen? Ser.). (ENG., Illus.). 48p. (gr. 4-8). lib. bdg. 38.33 (978-1-59018-606-0(0), b0781d0e-ddeb-475e-a2ae-da9e894e3a0b, Lucent Pr.) Greenhaven Publishing LLC.

Graphic Organizers in Social Studies, 4 vols. 2004. (Graphic Organizers in Social Studies). (ENG., Illus.). (J). (gr. 3-4). 52.54 (978-1-4042-2956-3(6), 0ca9321d-754f-4af0-afff-ad11509e2f3e) Rosen Publishing Group, Inc., The.

Graves, Karen M. & Swanson Sateren, Shelley. It's Back to School ... Way Back! 2016. (It's Back to School ... Way Back! Ser.). (ENG.). 32p. (J). (gr. 3-6). 119.96 (978-1-5157-2116-1(7), 25061, Capstone Pr.) Capstone.

Great Americans, 22 vols. 2006. (Great Americans Ser.). (ENG.). 24p. (gr. 2-4). lib. bdg. 269.36 (978-0-8368-8371-8(3), 459f479a-7235-471e-adce-81c347320f50, Weekly Reader Leveled Readers) Stevens, Gareth Publishing LLLP.

Gregory, Josh. Bill & Melinda Gates. 2013. (True Book(tm), A — Biographies Ser.). (ENG., Illus.). 48p. (J). lib. bdg. 31.00 (978-0-531-21905-8(4)); pap. 6.95 (978-0-531-23876-9(8)) Scholastic Library Publishing.

Grodin, Elissa D. Everyone Counts: A Citizens' Number Book. Juhasz, Victor, illus. rev. ed. 2006. (America by the Numbers Ser.). (ENG.). 40p. (J). (gr. 1-3). 17.95 (978-1-58536-295-0(6), 202105) Sleeping Bear Pr.

Gutman, Dan. My Weird School Fast Facts: Explorers, Presidents, & Toilets. Paillot, Jim, illus. 2017. (My Weird School Fast Facts Ser.). (ENG.). 192p. (J). (gr. 1-5). pap. 5.99 (978-0-06-230623-4(5), HarperCollins) HarperCollins Pubs.

Hakim, Joy. A History of Us, 10 vols. 3rd ed. 2003. (Illus.). 186p. (J). 199.50 *(978-0-19-515259-3(X))* Oxford Univ. Pr., Inc.
—A History of US: an Age of Extremes: 1880-1917 a History of US Book Eight. 3rd rev. ed. 2007. (History of US Ser.: Vol. 8). (ENG., Illus.). 228p. (gr. 4-7). per. 15.95 *(978-0-19-532722-9(5))* Oxford Univ. Pr., Inc.
—A History of US: Sourcebook & Index: A History of US Book Eleven. 3rd rev. ed. 2006. (History of US Ser.: 11). (ENG., Illus.). 160p. (gr. 4-7). 24.95 *(978-0-19-518903-2(5))* Oxford Univ. Pr., Inc.
—A History of US: Ten-Volume Set, 10 vols. 3rd rev. ed. 2006. (History of US Ser.). (ENG., Illus.). 249.50 *(978-0-19-531491-5(3))* Oxford Univ. Pr., Inc.
Hale, Sarah Elder, ed. Antietam: Day of Courage & Sacrifice. 2005. (ENG., Illus.). 48p. (J). (gr. 3-9). 17.95 *(978-0-8126-7904-5(0))* Cobblestone Pr.
Hallett, R. B. The 10 Most Decisive Battles on American Soil. 2008. 14.99 *(978-1-55448-538-3(X))* Scholastic Library Publishing.
Hamilton, John. The United States of America, 52 vols. 2016. (United States of America Ser.). (ENG.). 48p. (J). (gr. 5-9). 1779.44 *(978-1-68078-302-5(5)*, 21589, Abdo & Daughters) ABDO Publishing Co.
Hammond World Atlas Corporation Staff. American History Through Maps. 2004. (Atlas Ser.). (Illus.). 48p. (gr. 5). 8.95 *(978-0-8437-7435-1(5)*, 774355) Hammond World Atlas Corp.
Harasymiw, Mark J. Life on a Submarine, 1 vol. 2013. (Extreme Jobs in Extreme Places Ser.). (ENG., Illus.). 32p. (gr. 3-4). pap. 11.50 *(978-1-4339-8503-4(9)*, f9317cea-c990-418a-815e-a516039cf994); lib. bdg. 29.27 *(978-1-4339-8502-7(0)*, 403feb4e-ae9e-497e-8be9-c63103ab983b) Stevens, Gareth Publishing LLLP.
Harcourt School Publishers Staff. Harcourt School Publishers Horizons Vol. 1: Us History 2003. 3rd ed. 2003. (Harcourt School Publishers Horizons Ser.). (ENG.). 780p. (gr. 5-5). tchr. ed. 202.15 *(978-0-15-320189-9(4))* Harcourt Schl. Pubs.
—Horizons. 3rd ed. 2003. (Harcourt Horizons Ser.). (ENG.). 336p. (gr. 1-1). stu. ed. 58.00 *(978-0-15-339615-1(6))*; (ENG.). 390p. (gr. 2-2). stu. ed. 58.00 *(978-0-15-339616-8(4))*; (ENG.). 520p. (gr. 3-3). 79.75 *(978-0-15-339617-5(2))*; Vol. 1. tchr. ed. 104.40 *(978-0-15-339626-7(1))*; Vol. 2. tchr. ed. 104.40 *(978-0-15-339627-4(X))* Harcourt Schl. Pubs.
—Horizons: Time for Kids Readers: US History. 3rd ed. 2003. (Harcourt Horizons Ser.). (gr. k-7). tchr. ed. 57.40 *(978-0-15-334654-5(X))* Harcourt Schl. Pubs.
—Horizons Big Book. 3rd ed. 2003. (Harcourt Horizons Ser.). (ENG.). 100p. (gr. k-k). spiral bd. 312.10 *(978-0-15-339673-1(3))* Harcourt Schl. Pubs.
—Horizons, Grade 1. 3rd ed. 2003. Vol. 1. tchr. ed. 98.30 *(978-0-15-339624-3(5))* Vol. 2. tchr. ed. 98.30 *(978-0-15-339625-0(3))* Harcourt Schl. Pubs.
—Horizons, Grade 3. 3rd ed. 2003. (Harcourt Horizons Ser.). (ENG.). (gr. 3-3). Vol. 1. 492p. tchr. ed., spiral bd. 153.45 *(978-0-15-339628-1(8))* Vol. 2. 540p. tchr. ed., spiral bd. 153.45 *(978-0-15-339629-8(6))* Harcourt Schl. Pubs.
—Horizons, Grade K. 3rd ed. 2003. tchr. ed. 113.40 *(978-0-15-339623-6(7))* Harcourt Schl. Pubs.
—Horizontes: US History. 3rd ed. 2003. (Harcourt Horizontes Ser.). (SPA., (gr. k-6). Illus.). act. bk. ed. 11.80 *(978-0-15-324555-8(7))*; Vol. 1. tchr. ed. 133.80 *(978-0-15-321981-8(5))*; Vol. 2. tchr. ed. 133.80 *(978-0-15-321982-5(3))* Harcourt Schl. Pubs.
—Social Studies: Stories in Time: Library Book Collection. 2003. (Harcourt Brace Social Studies). (Illus.). (gr. k-7). 130.90 *(978-0-15-308394-5(8))* Harcourt Schl. Pubs.
—U. S. History. 3rd ed. 2003. (Harcourt Horizons Ser.). (ENG.). 808p. (gr. 4-5). stu. ed. 89.15 *(978-0-15-339619-9(9))* Harcourt Schl. Pubs.
—United States History 2003, Vol. 1. 3rd ed. 2003. (Harcourt School Publishers Horizons Ser.). (ENG., Illus.). 464p. (gr. 4-6). 86.80 *(978-0-15-339681-6(4))* Harcourt Schl. Pubs.
—US History. 3rd ed. 2003. (Horizontes (Social Studies) Ser.). (SPA., Illus.). (gr. k-6). pupil's gde. ed. 71.90 *(978-0-15-324536-7(0))* Harcourt Schl. Pubs.
—US History - Beginning to the Civil War. 3rd ed. 2003. (Harcourt Electronic Test Ser.). pap., tchr. ed. 10.70 *(978-0-15-340792-5(1))* Harcourt Schl. Pubs.
—US History - Civil War to the Present. 3rd ed. 2003. (Harcourt Electronic Test Ser.). pap., tchr. ed. 10.70 *(978-0-15-340790-1(5))* Harcourt Schl. Pubs.
Hardyman, Robyn. United States. 2009. (Celebrate! (Chelsea Clubhouse) Ser.). (ENG.). 32p. (gr. 4-6). 28.00 *(978-1-60413-264-9(7)*, P169966, Chelsea Clubhse.) Infobase Holdings, Inc.
Harker, John B. Betsy Ross's Five Pointed Star: Elizabeth Claypoole, Quaker Flag Maker: A Historical Perspective. 2004. (Illus.). 166p. per. 20.00 *(978-1-887774-15-4(7))* Canmore Pr.
Hazen, Walter A. Everyday Life: Reform in America. 2004. (Illus.). iv, 100p. pap. 12.95 *(978-0-673-58898-2(X))* Good Year Bks.
Heeg, Berg Heeg. Voyage to Victory: The Voice of a Sailor in the Pacific 1943-1945. 2004. (YA). per. 9.95 *(978-0-938682-79-0(2)*, 682-79-2) River Road Pubns., Inc.
Hein, Connie L. Toliver in Time: For a Fourth of July Celebration. Theobald, Denise, illus. 2003. 40p. (J). lib. bdg. 19.95 *(978-0-9740855-8-6(8))*; per. 12.95 *(978-0-9740855-9-3(6))* Still Water Publishing.
Henretta, James A. America's History: High School Edition. 5th ed. 2004. 74.50 *(978-0-312-44303-0(X))* Bedford/Saint Martin's.
Hernandez, Roger E. Teens & Relationships. Developed in Association with the Gallup Organization Staff, ed. 2013. (Gallup Youth Survey: Major Issues & Trends Ser.: 14). 112p. (J). (gr. 7-18). 24.95 *(978-1-4222-2956-9(4))* Mason Crest.
Herweck, Dona. Susan B. Anthony, 1 vol. 2nd rev. ed. 2014. (TIME for KIDS(r): Informational Text Ser.). (ENG., Illus.). 28p. (J). (gr. 2-3). lib. bdg. 23.96 *(978-1-4807-1063-4(6))* Teacher Created Materials, Inc.
Herwick Rice, Dona & Bradley, Kathleen. Reconstruction: After the Civil War, 1 vol. rev. ed. 2009. (Reader's Theater Ser.). (ENG.). 32p. (J). (gr. 3-8). pap. 11.99 *(978-1-4333-0547-4(X))* Teacher Created Materials, Inc.
Hicks, Terry Allan. The Bald Eagle, 1 vol. 2007. (Symbols of America Ser.). (ENG., Illus.). 40p. (gr. 3-3). lib. bdg. 32.64 *(978-0-7614-2133-7(5)*, 4cc77ac4-353f-4135-8229-fee1fad1bf3b) Cavendish Square Publishing LLC.
Higgins, Melissa. We All Come from Different Cultures, 1 vol. 2012. (Celebrating Differences Ser.). (ENG.). 24p. (J). (gr. -1-2). pap. 7.29 *(978-1-4296-7887-2(9)*, 118219) Capstone.
Higginson, Thomas W. Young Folks' History of the United States. 2013. (Notable American Authors Ser.). (Illus.). 425p. reprint ed. lthr. 79.00 *(978-0-7812-3113-8(2))* Reprint Services Corp.
Hinman, Bonnie. Fascinating History. 2018. (Unbelievable Ser.). (ENG., Illus.). 32p. (J). (gr. 3-6). 32.80 *(978-1-63235-420-4(9)*, 13768, 12-Story Library) Bookstaves, LLC.
Hirsch, E. D., Jr., ed. The Age of Exploration, Level 5. 2003. tchr. ed. 9.95 *(978-0-7690-5077-5(8))*; stu. ed. 49.95 *(978-0-7690-2852-1(7))* Pearson Learning.
—Americans Move West. 2003. tchr. ed. 9.95 *(978-0-7690-5050-8(6))*; stu. ed. 49.95 *(978-0-7690-2955-9(8))* Pearson Learning.
—From Colonies to Independence. 2003. tchr. ed. 9.95 *(978-0-7690-5042-3(5))* Pearson Learning.
—Geography of the United States, Level 5. tchr. ed. 9.95 *(978-0-7690-5084-3(0))* Pearson Learning.
—Industrialization & Urbanization in America, Level 6. tchr. ed. 9.95 *(978-0-7690-5092-8(1))*; stu. ed. 49.95 *(978-0-7690-2857-6(8))* Pearson Learning.
—Westward Expansion after the Civil War, Level 5. tchr. ed. 9.95 *(978-0-7690-5082-9(4))*; stu. ed. 49.95 *(978-0-7690-2851-4(9))* Pearson Learning.
—Westward Expansion Before the Civil War, Level 5. tchr. ed. 9.95 *(978-0-7690-5080-5(8))*; 2003. stu. ed. 49.95 *(978-0-7690-2850-7(0))* Pearson Learning.
Hirschmann, Kris & Herndon, Ryan. Test Your Smarts! 2009. (Illus.). 80p. (J). *(978-0-545-12042-5(X))* Scholastic, Inc.
Hispanic America, 10 vols., Set. Incl. Civil War, 1840s-1890s. Hernández, Roger E. & Hernández, Roger E. lib. bdg. 36.93 *(978-0-7614-2939-5(5)*, cc454e86-45da-4258-b12d-fad641b1dcec); Early Explorations, The 1500s. Hernández, Roger E. & Hernández, Roger E. lib. bdg. 36.93 *(978-0-7614-2937-1(9)*, b16d1ad5-064e-49b4-aaa7-c60082b1692b); New Republic, 1760-1840s. Otfinoski, Steven. lib. bdg. 36.93 *(978-0-7614-2938-8(7)*, 89e70445-11b9-4386-82d9-c0b4f2c580f3); New Spain, 1600-1760s. Hernández, Roger E. & Hernández, Roger E. lib. bdg. 36.93 *(978-0-7614-2936-4(0)*, 1d602b32-4ed1-4db3-a48a-67d577fddf03); Texas War of Independence: The 1800s. Worth, Richard. lib. bdg. 36.93 *(978-0-7614-2934-0(4)*, 15e26fa2-4c55-418b-9cdd-d43ad323078b); 80p. (gr. 5-5). (Hispanic America Ser.). (ENG.). 2009. Set lib. bdg. 184.65 *(978-0-7614-2933-3(6)*, 53394993-550c-4b18-9448-5f3fc60fee67, Cavendish Square) Cavendish Square Publishing LLC.
Historia y Geografia de America. (SPA.). (J). 45.00 *(978-958-04-5985-9(1))*; (Illus.). wbk. ed. 15.00 *(978-958-04-5986-6(X))* Norma S.A. COL. Dist: Distribuidora Norma, Inc.
Historias Graficas (Graphic Histories), 10 vols. 2007. (Historias Gráficas (Graphic Histories) Ser.). (SPA.). 32p. (gr. 3-3). lib. bdg. 148.35 *(978-0-8368-7891-2(4)*, a60af979-5932-472d-a1eb-dc3ce899acb5) Stevens, Gareth Publishing LLLP.
History Through Sources, 5 bks., Set. (YA). (gr. 6-8). lib. bdg. 128.20 *(978-1-57572-222-1(4))* Heinemann-Raintree.
Hoena, Blake, et al. You Choose: Founding the United States. 2018. (You Choose: Founding the United States Ser.). (ENG.). 112p. (J). (gr. 3-7). 138.60 *(978-1-5435-1554-1(1)*, 28039, Capstone Pr.) Capstone.
Holmes, Parker. Amazing Snakes of the Southwest & West Coast, 1 vol. 2014. (Amazing Snakes Ser.). (ENG., Illus.). 24p. (J). (gr. 3-3). pap. 9.25 *(978-1-4777-6503-6(4)*, 3c2b5392-5c7e-4477-8d62-456b0b82e1ce, PowerKids Pr.) Rosen Publishing Group, Inc., The.
—Texas vs. Oklahoma. 2013. (J). *(978-1-4777-1162-0(7))*; (ENG.). 24p. (gr. 3-3). pap. 11.60 *(978-1-4777-1161-3(9)*, bbe7bd79-6e21-4f20-b128-9545edd43b8c); (ENG.). 24p. (gr. 3-3). lib. bdg. 27.60 *(978-1-4777-1157-6(0)*, 8219f75b-3b81-4a04-a3ce-38da56c0823e) Rosen Publishing Group, Inc., The. (PowerKids Pr.).
How Our Nation Began. (YA). 15.00 *(978-1-931555-45-6(1))* Our Lady of Victory Schl.
Howell, Brian. US Growth & Change in the 19th Century. 2011. (Explorer Library: Language Arts Explorer Ser.). (ENG., Illus.). 32p. (gr. 4-8). lib. bdg. 32.07 *(978-1-61080-202-4(0)*, 201180) Cherry Lake Publishing.
Huey, Lois Miner. Ick! Yuck! Eew! Our Gross American History. (ENG., Illus.). 48p. (J). (gr. 4-6). 2015. E-Book 53.32 *(978-1-4677-5989-2(9)*, 9781467759892, Lerner Digital) 2013. E-Book 43.99 *(978-1-4677-1710-6(X)*, Millbrook Pr.) Lerner Publishing Group.
Hults, Alaska, ed. American History Reader's Theater Vol. 2244: Develop Reading Fluency & Text Comprehension Skills. Hillam, Corbin & Vangsgard, Amy, illus. 2004. 96p. (J). pap. 14.99 *(978-1-59198-039-1(9)*, 2244) Creative Teaching Pr., Inc.
Hunter, Nick. Talking about the Past, 1 vol. 2014. (History at Home Ser.). (ENG., Illus.). 32p. (J). (gr. 1-3). pap. 7.99 *(978-1-4846-0236-2(6)*, 126291, Heinemann) Capstone.
Ichord, Loretta Frances & Millbrook Press. Skillet Bread, Sourdough, & Vinegar Days: Cooking in Pioneer Days. Ellis, Jan Davey, illus. 2005. 64p. (J). (gr. 4-8). per. 8.95 *(978-0-7613-9521-8(0)*, First Avenue Editions) Lerner Publishing Group.
In American History, 56 bks., Set. (Illus.). (YA). (gr. 5-12). lib. bdg. 1215.10 *(978-0-89490-972-6(X))* Enslow Publishing, LLC.
In My Own Words - Group 2, 8 vols. 2005. (In My Own Words Ser.). (ENG., Illus.). 64-96p. (gr. 6-6). lib. bdg. 136.28 *(978-0-7614-1644-9(7)*, 3eb54072-6f93-4bdf-856b-b8442fec4f32, Cavendish Square) Cavendish Square Publishing LLC.
In the Early Days: Southern Humboldt History 1853-1920. 1. 5th ed. 2006. (Illus.). 141p. per. 20.95 *(978-0-9672162-3-2(0))* Hawk Mountaintop Publishing.
It's Cool to Learn about the United States (Set), 5 vols., Set. Incl. It's Cool to Learn about the United States: Midwest. Orr, Tamra B. lib. bdg. 34.93 *(978-1-61080-179-9(2)*, 201152); It's Cool to Learn about the United States: Northeast. Franchino, Vicky. lib. bdg. 34.93 *(978-1-61080-180-5(6)*, 201154); It's Cool to Learn about the United States: Southeast. Marsico, Katie. lib. bdg. 34.93 *(978-1-61080-181-2(4)*, 201156); It's Cool to Learn about the United States: Southwest. Orr, Tamra B. lib. bdg. 34.93 *(978-1-61080-183-6(0)*, 201160); It's Cool to Learn about the United States: West. Somervill, Barbara A. lib. bdg. 34.93 *(978-1-61080-182-9(2)*, 201158); (gr. 4-8). (Explorer Library: Social Studies Explorer Ser.). (ENG., Illus.). 48p. 2011. 174.65 *(978-1-61080-191-1(1)*, 201012) Cherry Lake Publishing.
It's My State - Group 3, 12 vols. 2005. (It's My State! (First Edition)(r) Ser.). (ENG., Illus.). 80p. (gr. 4-4). lib. bdg. 204.42 *(978-0-7614-1528-2(9)*, a17ae491-0e0e-4895-8888-78be24de5459, Cavendish Square) Cavendish Square Publishing LLC.
It's My State! - Group 4, 12 vols. 2004. (It's My State! (First Edition)(r) Ser.). (ENG., Illus.). 80p. (gr. 4-4). lib. bdg. 204.42 *(978-0-7614-1685-2(4)*, 88f05534-92a6-40c4-a920-0e3dbda10032, Cavendish Square) Cavendish Square Publishing LLC.
It's My State: Group 5, 12 vols., Set. 2006. (It's My State! (First Edition)(r) Ser.). (ENG.). (J). (gr. 4-4). 204.42 *(978-0-7614-1821-4(0)*, 7b5fd454-42f2-42ab-8e0e-cf5d6fcfb43d, Cavendish Square) Cavendish Square Publishing LLC.
James, Helen Foster. Little America. Brett, Jeannie et al, illus. 2011. (Little Country Ser.). (ENG.). 20p. (J). (gr. -1-1). bds. 8.99 *(978-1-58536-179-3(8)*, 202235) Sleeping Bear Pr.
Jeffrey, Laura S. Amazing American Inventors of the 20th Century, 1 vol. 2013. (Inspiring Collective Biographies Ser.). (ENG.). 112p. (gr. 5-6). pap. 13.88 *(978-1-4644-0245-6(0)*, aee183f6-6427-4740-b462-d11190b7ada1) Enslow Publishing, LLC.
Johnson, Drew, et al. Junior Worldmark Encyclopedia of the States, 4 vols. 6th ed. 2013. (Illus.). (J). *(978-1-4144-9860-7(8))* Cengage Gale.
Jones, Stephen A. So What Did the People Find? 2009. 24p. pap. 11.50 *(978-1-4389-2736-7(3))* AuthorHouse.
Jones, Stephen Anderton. America Is Good. 2008. 60p. (gr. -1). pap. 22.50 *(978-1-4343-6321-3(X))* AuthorHouse.
Joseph, Frank. Ancient America's Lost History, 1 vol. 2017. (Discovering Ancient America Ser.). (ENG., Illus.). 200p. (gr. 9-9). 42.41 *(978-1-4994-6677-5(3)*, 8fcfb928-9965-4aa8-8b1a-075fa4ce0ce8, Rosen Young Adult) Rosen Publishing Group, Inc., The.
Jr. Graphic African American History, 12 vols. 2013. (Jr. Graphic African American History Ser.). 24p. (J). (ENG.). (gr. 2-3). 173.58 *(978-1-4777-1547-5(9)*, 9c8994b7-ac83-4a96-bca1-8916780d78cd); (gr. 3-6). pap. 381.60 *(978-1-4777-2672-3(1))*; (gr. 3-6). pap. 63.60 *(978-1-4777-2671-6(3))* Rosen Publishing Group, Inc., The. (PowerKids Pr.).
Juarez, Christine. The United States of America. 2013. (Countries Ser.). (ENG.). 24p. (J). (gr. -1-2). pap. 6.95 *(978-1-4765-3514-2(0)*, 123565, Pebble) Capstone.
Kahn, Robert, et al. Bobby & Mandee's Too Solid for Suicide. 2017. (ENG., Illus.). (YA). pap. 9.95 *(978-1-947825-28-4(3))* Yorkshire Publishing Group.
Kaleidoscope: American History (Group 2), 8 vols., Set. 2003. (Kaleidoscope: American History Ser.). (ENG.). (gr. 4-4). 130.56 *(978-0-7614-1459-9(2)*, dc853814-1f72-40be-9969-356a53ea9cbf, Cavendish Square) Cavendish Square Publishing LLC.
Kalman, Bobbie & Walker, Niki. Conoce los Estados Unidos de América. 2009. (SPA.). 32p. (J). *(978-0-7787-8196-7(8))*; (gr. 2-5). pap. *(978-0-7787-8216-2(6))* Crabtree Publishing Co.
—Spotlight on the United States of America, 1 vol. 2007. (Spotlight on My Country Ser.). (ENG., Illus.). 32p. (J). (gr. 2-5). pap. *(978-0-7787-3478-9(1))* Crabtree Publishing Co.
Kamma, Anne. If You Lived When There Was Slavery in America. Johnson, Pamela, illus. 2004. (If You... Ser.). (ENG.). 64p. (J). (gr. 2-5). pap. 6.99 *(978-0-439-56706-0(8))* Scholastic, Inc.
Kanefield, Teri. Andrew Jackson: The Making of America #2. 2019. (ENG., Illus.). 256p. (J). (gr. 5-9). pap. 7.99 *(978-1-4197-3421-2(0)*, 1197903, Abrams Bks. for Young Readers) Abrams, Inc.
Karapetian, Marjam. Bilingual Content Dictionary: English to Spanish: Social Studies - American History Through 1776. 2004. (SPA & ENG.). 14.95 *(978-0-9764829-3-2(2))* WizdomInc.
Kaserman & Haberkern, E. The United States of America, 50 vols. 2nd ed. 2003. (Illus.). 46p. (J). cd-rom *(978-0-9714299-1-8(X))* I Save A Tree.
Keesee, Timothy & Sidwell, Mark. United States History. 2012. (Illus.). 658p. (J). *(978-1-60682-005-6(2))* BJU Pr.
Kennelly, Sean. All Around America: American Collection. 2014. (ENG., Illus.). 48p. (J). (gr. 4). 8.99 *(978-1-4867-0256-5(2))* Flowerpot Children's Pr. Inc. CAN. Dist: Cardinal Pubs. Group.
Kennelly, Sean & Carpenter, Dan. Amazing America. Flowerpot Press, ed. 2012. (Illus.). 48p. (J). *(978-1-926988-94-8(9))* Flowerpot Children's Pr. Inc.
—Great Americans. Flowerpot Press, ed. 2012. (Illus.). 48p. (J). *(978-1-926988-93-1(0))* Flowerpot Children's Pr. Inc.
Kenney, Karen Latchana. US History Through Infographics. Westlund, Laura K., illus. 2014. (Super Social Studies Infographics Ser.). (ENG.). 32p. (J). (gr. 3-5). pap. 8.99 *(978-1-4677-4568-0(5)*, d75792bc-a15f-4d6d-b169-58328a716d46); lib. bdg. 26.65 *(978-1-4677-3459-2(4)*, c747001c-3c04-43ae-b1c6-ab7d11e6a7ea, Lerner Pubns.) Lerner Publishing Group.
Kennon, Caroline. Battling Terrorism in the United States, 1 vol. 2017. (American History Ser.). (ENG.). 104p. (gr. 7-7). lib. bdg. 41.03 *(978-1-5345-6141-0(2)*, c5c41274-cf46-4769-9de2-9c472e50c79c, Lucent Pr.) Greenhaven Publishing LLC.
Keppeler, Jill. Betsy Ross Didn't Create the American Flag: Exposing Myths about U. S. Symbols, 1 vol. 2016. (Exposed! Myths about Early American History Ser.). (ENG., Illus.). 32p. (J). (gr. 2-3). pap. 11.50 *(978-1-4824-5717-9(2)*, cf9181ec-aaf5-45d6-9da4-23975869c3a7) Stevens, Gareth Publishing LLLP.
—Inside the Women's Rights Movement, 1 vol. 2017. (Eyewitness to History Ser.). (ENG.). 32p. (J). (gr. 4-5). pap. 11.50 *(978-1-5382-1169-4(6)*, 923a5efe-30ca-42b2-9031-35ce9e051895) Stevens, Gareth Publishing LLLP.
Kids, National Geographic. Weird but True! USA. 2019. (Weird but True Ser.). (Illus.). 208p. (J). (gr. 3-7). pap. 8.99 *(978-1-4263-3371-2(4))*; (ENG., lib. bdg. 18.90 *(978-1-4263-3372-9(2))* Disney Publishing Worldwide. (National Geographic Kids).
Kiely Miller, Barbara. Grandes Personajes (Great Americans), 6 vols., Set. Incl. Anne Hutchinson. (Illus.). lib. bdg. 24.67 *(978-0-8368-8330-5(6)*, 14749122-7836-4305-8205-4305cf766f9f); Frederick Douglass. (Illus.). (J). lib. bdg. 24.67 *(978-0-8368-8328-2(4)*, a9c1cfc5-b917-49ea-99fb-b321f4985ef6); George Washington Carver. (Illus.). lib. bdg. 24.67 *(978-0-8368-8327-5(6)*, 59dbb862-0e49-4a09-b746-d71445de6b64); Jefe Joseph (Chief Joseph) lib. bdg. 24.67 *(978-0-8368-8331-2(4)*, 2bdc2c31-5a7c-4345-a2bb-d8df4d35901a); John Muir. lib. bdg. 24.67 *(978-0-8368-8332-9(2)*, fc2fd432-5fd4-462b-87ac-0011ba6ede2f); Sam Houston. (Illus.). lib. bdg. 24.67 *(978-0-8368-8329-9(2)*, 468581b2-c389-4f19-87a2-91fb6d86c83c); 24p. (gr. 2-4). 2007., Weekly Reader Leveled Readers (SPA.). 2007. Set lib. bdg. 119.58 o.p. *(978-0-8368-8326-8(8))*; Set pap. 35.70 o.p. *(978-0-8368-8333-6(0))* Stevens, Gareth Publishing LLLP.
—Great Americans, 6 vols., Set. Incl. Anne Hutchinson. (Illus.). lib. bdg. 24.67 *(978-0-8368-8317-6(9)*, 349e5929-1415-4b48-9fa4-586b925a16be); Chief Joseph. lib. bdg. 24.67 *(978-0-8368-8314-5(4)*, 7059abea-3114-45b1-afbb-d8e0deb55224); Frederick Douglass. (Illus.). (J). lib. bdg. 24.67 *(978-0-8368-8315-2(2)*, 6766fb17-e159-4d91-8538-2492f4a05b78); George Washington Carver. lib. bdg. 24.67 *(978-0-8368-8313-8(6)*, b323bce2-0796-497d-a3e5-22f7fc7bb709); John Muir. lib. bdg. 24.67 *(978-0-8368-8318-3(7)*, 86d24b9e-cde3-4ee8-a2b1-a311970c63af); Sam Houston. lib. bdg. 24.67 *(978-0-8368-8316-9(0)*, c0d85d45-374f-44a0-82b7-fe4611ee39a8); 24p. (gr. 2-4). 2007., Weekly Reader Leveled Readers 2007. Set lib. bdg. 119.58 o.p. *(978-0-8368-8312-1(8))* Stevens, Gareth Publishing LLLP.
Kinney, Cyndi & Trout, Judy. State History for ALL 50 States - 100 Lapbooks & Lapbook Journals & Study Guides. 2013. (YA). cd-rom 99.00 *(978-1-61625-540-4(4))* Knowledge Box Central.
Kirkman, Marissa. Life & Times. 2016. (Life & Times Ser.). (ENG.). 24p. (J). (gr. 1-3). 111.96 *(978-1-5157-2498-8(0)*, 25152, Capstone Pr.) Capstone.
Klobuchar, Lisa. USA in Our World. 2011. (Countries in Our World Ser.). 32p. (YA). (gr. 4-7). lib. bdg. 28.50 *(978-1-59920-436-9(3))* Black Rabbit Bks.
Knox, Barbara J. Hearst Castle: An American Palace. 2005. (Castles, Palaces, & Tombs Ser.). (Illus.). 32p. (J). lib. bdg. 28.50 *(978-1-59716-069-8(5))* Bearport Publishing Co., Inc.
Kopp, Megan. United States. 2013. (J). *(978-1-62127-255-7(9))*; pap. *(978-1-62127-261-8(3))* Weigl Pubs., Inc.
Kowalski, Kathiann M. Salvadorans in America. 2005. (In America Ser.). (Illus.). 80p. (J). (gr. 4-7). lib. bdg. 27.93 *(978-0-8225-2424-3(4)*, Lerner Pubns.) Lerner Publishing Group.
LaClair, Teresa. The Northern Colonies: Freedom to Worship (1600-1770) 2012. (Illus.). 48p. (J). pap. *(978-1-4222-2411-3(2))* Mason Crest.
Land That I Love: Regions of the United States, 12 vols. 2014. (Land That I Love: Regions of the United States Ser.). (ENG.). 32p. (J). (gr. 3-3). 167.58 *(978-1-4777-6639-2(1)*, 8d5554df-807a-4f82-9831-9017550174ce, PowerKids Pr.) Rosen Publishing Group, Inc., The.
Landau, Elaine. The Wounded Knee Massacre. 2004. (Cornerstones of Freedom Ser.). (ENG., Illus.). 48p. (YA). (gr. 4-7). 26.00 *(978-0-516-24244-6(X))* Scholastic Library Publishing.
Lanser, Amanda. America at War by the Numbers. 2015. (America at War by the Numbers Ser.). (ENG.). 32p. (J). (gr. 3-4). 122.60 *(978-1-4914-6661-2(8)*, 22904, Capstone Pr.) Capstone.
Lassieur, Allison. The Dust Bowl: An Interactive History Adventure. rev. ed. 2016. (You Choose: History Ser.). (ENG., Illus.). 112p. (J). (gr. 3-7). pap. 6.95 *(978-1-5157-4262-3(8)*, 134016, Capstone Pr.) Capstone.
Latham, Donna. Hurricane! The 1900 Galveston Night of Terror. 2005. (X-Treme Disasters That Changed America Ser.). (Illus.). 32p. (J). (gr. 3-7). lib. bdg. 28.50 *(978-1-59716-071-1(7))* Bearport Publishing Co., Inc.
Leacock, Elspeth & Buckley, Susan. Places in Time: A New Atlas of American History. Jones, Randy, illus. 2006. 48p. (J). (gr. 4-8). reprint ed. 15.00 *(978-1-4223-5555-8(1))* DIANE Publishing Co.
Lerner Publishing Group Staff. History Speaks: Picture Books Plus Reader's Theater, 6 vols., Set. 2011. (J). (gr. 2-4). lib. bdg. 167.58 *(978-0-7613-7483-1(3))* Lerner Publishing Group.
LernerClassroom Editors. On My Own History Teaching Guide. 2009. pap. 7.95 *(978-0-8225-5321-2(X))* Lerner Publishing Group.
LernerClassroom Editors, ed. Teaching Guide for Six Questions of American History. 2010. pap. 5.95 *(978-0-7613-6685-0(7))* Lerner Publishing Group.
Let's Explore the Northeast. 2013. (Road Trip: Exploring America's Regions Ser.). 24p. (J). (gr. 2-5). pap. 48.90 *(978-1-4339-9136-3(5))* Stevens, Gareth Publishing LLLP.
Levin, Judy. A Timeline of the Abolitionist Movement, 1 vol. 2004. (Timelines of American History Ser.). (ENG., Illus.). 32p. (J). (gr. 4-4). lib. bdg. 29.13 *(978-0-8239-4537-5(5)*, 0cb0a0cb-2bb0-4cc2-a53f-cd87d0c86654, Rosen Reference) Rosen Publishing Group, Inc., The.
Liberman, Sherri. A Historical Atlas of the Industrial Age & the Growth of America's Cities, 1 vol. 2004. (United States:

Historical Atlases of the Growth of a New Nation Ser.). (ENG., Illus.). 64p. (J). (gr. 5-5). lib. bdg. 37.13 *(978-1-4042-0205-4(6),* 477bb628-5dcf-4a84-ab56-f18cb6d9a1f2) Rosen Publishing Group, Inc., The.

Life in the New American Nation: Set 2, 10 vols. 2003. (Life in the New American Nation Ser.). (ENG., Illus.). 32p. (gr. 4-4). lib. bdg. 145.65 *(978-0-8239-7699-7(8),* cd36285c-4bc8-4676-a057-f9ef49c19ef4, Rosen Reference) Rosen Publishing Group, Inc., The.

Life in the New American Nation Set, 12 vols., Set. 2003. (Life in the New American Nation Ser.). (ENG., Illus.). 32p. (gr. 4-4). lib. bdg. 174.78 *(978-0-8239-7698-0(X),* d7d86853-c0c7-4d39-bad8-0398bdcafa52, Rosen Reference) Rosen Publishing Group, Inc., The.

Life in the Renaissance, 8 vols. 2005. (Life in the Renaissance Ser.). (ENG., Illus.). 80-96p. (gr. 6-6). lib. bdg. 147.72 *(978-0-7614-1675-3(7),* 63f04e85-c919-4eba-93e9-2b6ad99819e3, Cavendish Square) Cavendish Square Publishing LLC.

Lifeways - Group 6, 8 vols. 2005. (Lifeways Ser.). (ENG., Illus.). 128p. (gr. 6-6). lib. bdg. 164.84 *(978-0-7614-1680-7(3),* 6fa74c0a-a0fb-4cac-8c9e-b38956c0cc87, Cavendish Square) Cavendish Square Publishing LLC.

Linde, Barbara. Artifacts Throughout American History, 1 vol. 2019. (Journey to the Past: Investigating Primary Sources Ser.). (ENG.). 32p. (gr. 4-5). pap. 11.50 *(978-1-5382-4030-4(0),* 099dc8a7-78c0-4c4d-be48-beb852b7f25f) Stevens, Gareth Publishing LLLP.

Linde, Barbara M. Uncle Sam, 1 vol. 2018. (Symbols of America Ser.). (ENG.). 24p. (gr. 1-2). 24.27 *(978-1-5382-2902-6(1),* b37a5e97-5115-4e2c-bfc0-b53b71b84e7a) Stevens, Gareth Publishing LLLP.

Lindeen, Mary. Welcome to North America. 2011. (Wonder Readers Fluent Level Ser.). (ENG.). 16p. (gr. -1-2). pap. 35.94 *(978-1-4296-8204-6(3),* Capstone Pr.) Capstone.

Litmanovich, Ellina. Real-World Projects to Explore the Industrial Revolution, 1 vol. 2018. (Project-Based Learning in Social Studies). (ENG.). 64p. (gr. 5-5). 37.47 *(978-1-5081-8219-1(1),* 41e1fc54-3cf1-4062-9bb3-8607ce02a293, Rosen Reference) Rosen Publishing Group, Inc., The.

Lloyd, Jon. A View of America's Future by America's. 2005. 51p. pap. 16.95 *(978-1-4137-9110-5(7))* PublishAmerica, Inc.

Loewen, James W. Lies My Teacher Told Me: Young Readers' Edition: Everything American History Textbooks Get Wrong. adapted ed. 2019. (ENG., Illus.). 256p. (J). (gr. 7-12). 19.99 *(978-1-62097-469-8(X))* New Pr., The.

Logiudice, Carolyn. US History Reading Comrehension Book. 2003. (Illus.). 167p. (J). per. 37.95 *(978-0-7606-0449-6(5))* LinguiSystems, Inc.

A Look at U. S. History. 2017. (Look at U. S. History Ser.). 32p. (gr. 2-2). pap. 63.00 *(978-1-4824-6286-9(9));* (ENG.). lib. bdg. 169.62 *(978-1-4824-6284-5(2),* 229a462a-e2d4-4df8-ad72-64cd2906f123) Stevens, Gareth Publishing LLLP.

A Look at U. S. History: Set 2, 12 vols. 2018. (Look at U. S. History Ser.). (ENG.). 32p. (gr. 2-2). lib. bdg. 169.62 *(978-1-5382-2174-7(8),* 3f9dd6ae-9bda-42b5-be31-596e032f9858) Stevens, Gareth Publishing LLLP.

Machajewski, Sarah. Our Country's Symbols, 1 vol. 2012. (InfoMax Readers Ser.). (ENG., Illus.). 24p. (J). (gr. 1-1). pap. 8.25 *(978-1-4488-8980-8(4),* 4096fabd-54b7-4f3a-a45b-bf7d62a5cb87, Rosen Classroom) Rosen Publishing Group, Inc., The.

MacRae, Sloan. Rajon Rondo, 1 vol. 2012. (Sports Heroes Ser.). (ENG.). 24p. (J). (gr. 2-3). pap. 9.25 *(978-1-4488-6288-7(4),* 0777c52b-056c-4651-8d60-5c162dfb818f, PowerKids Pr.) Rosen Publishing Group, Inc., The.

Mahoney, Emily. The Industrial Revolution: The Birth of Modern America, 1 vol. 2017. (American History Ser.). (ENG.). 104p. (gr. 7-7). lib. bdg. 41.03 *(978-1-5345-6133-5(1),* 614f7d58-9e93-4a2e-bcbd-6b880ed31008, Lucent Pr.) Greenhaven Publishing LLC.

Making America Great: Immigrant Success Stories, 12 vols. 2017. (Making America Great: Immigrant Success Stories Ser.). (ENG.). (J). (gr. 7-7). lib. bdg. 233.58 *(978-0-7660-9247-1(X),* 729f7c45-a1a4-48b3-abc8-7a65d2e428e3) Enslow Publishing, LLC.

Mara, Wil. The Gunsmith, 1 vol. 2013. (Colonial People Ser.). (ENG.). 48p. (gr. 4-4). 34.07 *(978-1-60870-414-9(9),* 41700ab7-35ad-4c15-b465-d8c823d08968) Cavendish Square Publishing LLC.

Marcovitz, Hal. Teens & Career Choices. Developed in Association with the Gallup Organization Staff, ed. 2013. (Gallup Youth Survey: Major Issues & Trends Ser.: 14). 112p. (J). (gr. 7-18). 24.95 *(978-1-4222-2950-7(5))* Mason Crest.

—Teens & Family Issues. Developed in Association with the Gallup Organization Staff, ed. 2013. (Gallup Youth Survey: Major Issues & Trends Ser.: 14). 112p. (J). (gr. 7-18). 24.95 *(978-1-4222-2952-1(1))* Mason Crest.

—Teens & LGBT Issues. Developed in Association with the Gallup Organization Staff, ed. 2013. (Gallup Youth Survey: Major Issues & Trends Ser.: 14). 112p. (J). (gr. 7-18). 24.95 *(978-1-4222-2953-8(X))* Mason Crest.

—Teens & Suicide. Developed in Association with the Gallup Organization Staff, ed. 2013. (Gallup Youth Survey: Major Issues & Trends Ser.: 14). 112p. (J). (gr. 7-18). 24.95 *(978-1-4222-2958-3(0))* Mason Crest.

Marsh, Carole. Quit Bossing Us Around! The Declaration of Independence. 2004. (American Milestones Ser.). (Illus.). 28p. (J). (gr. 4-12). pap. 5.95 *(978-0-635-02680-4(5))* Gallopade International.

—The Young Patriot's Book of Puzzles, Games, Riddles, Stories, Poems, & Activities. 2004. (Patriotic Favorites Ser.). 48p. (gr. 1-4). pap. 5.95 *(978-0-635-01032-2(1))* Gallopade International.

Marshall, H. E. This Country of Ours. 2007. 500p. per. 17.95 *(978-1-60206-874-2(7))* Cosimo, Inc.

—This Country of Ours (Yesterday's Classics) 2006. (Illus.). 636p. (J). per. 19.95 *(978-1-59915-010-9(7))* Yesterday's Classics.

Marshall, Henrietta Elizabeth. This Country of Ours. 2017. (ENG., Illus.). (J). 30.95 *(978-1-374-99241-2(0))* Capital Communications, Inc.

Marx, Trish. Jeannette Rankin: First Lady of Congress. Andreasen, Dan, illus. 2006. (ENG.). 48p. (J). (gr. 3-7). 18.95 *(978-0-689-86290-8(3),* McElderry, Margaret K. Bks.) McElderry, Margaret K. Bks.

McDougal-Littell Publishing Staff, creator. Creating America Workbook: A History of the United States. 2006. (Illus.). 120p. (gr. 6-12). pap. *(978-0-618-16521-6(5),* 2-81244) Holt McDougal.

McGraw Hill. American History Ink Taming Horses on the Great Plains. 2007. (Jt Am Hist Graph Novel Ser.). (ENG.). 24p. (gr. 6-12). spiral bd. 15.08 *(978-0-07-878023-3(3),* 0078780233) McGraw-Hill Education.

—The American Journey, Active Reading Note-Taking Guide, Student Edition. 2nd ed. 2004. (American Journey (survey) Ser.). (ENG.). 536p. (gr. 6-9). pap. 15.20 *(978-0-07-867397-9(6),* 0078673976) McGraw-Hill Education.

—The American Journey Early Years, Student Edition. 2008. (American Journey (survey) Ser.). (ENG., Illus.). 720p. (gr. 6-8). 142.40 *(978-0-07-877715-8(1),* 0078777151) McGraw-Hill Education.

—The American Journey, Interactive Tutor Self Assessment CD-ROM. 5th ed. 2005. (American Journey (survey) Ser.). (ENG.). (gr. 6-9). 120.64 *(978-0-07-867794-6(7),* 0078677947) McGraw-Hill Education.

—The American Journey, Modern Times, Reading Essentials & Note-Taking Guide. 2nd ed. 2008. (American Journey (survey) Ser.). (ENG., Illus.). 216p. (gr. 6-8). per. 13.20 *(978-0-07-880638-4(0),* 0078806380) McGraw-Hill Education.

—The American Journey: Modern Times, Student Edition. 2nd ed. 2008. (American Journey (survey) Ser.). (ENG.). 784p. (gr. 6-8). 142.40 *(978-0-07-877718-9(6),* 0078777186) McGraw-Hill Education.

—The American Journey, Modern Times, StudentWorks Plus CD-ROM. 2nd ed. 2008. (American Journey (survey) Ser.). (ENG.). (gr. 6-8). cd-rom 181.04 *(978-0-07-880651-3(8),* 0078806518) McGraw-Hill Education.

—The American Journey, Reconstruction to the Present, Spanish Student Edition. 2005. (Amer Journey Recon/present Ser.). Tr. of American Journey, Reconstruction to the Present, Spanish Student Edition. (SPA., Illus.). 1044p. (gr. 6-9). 138.00 *(978-0-07-868134-9(0),* 0078681340) McGraw-Hill Education.

—The American Journey, Standardized Test Practice Workbook. 7th ed. 2008. (American Journey (survey) Ser.). (ENG., Illus.). 72p. (gr. 6-8). spiral bd., wbk. ed. 7.92 *(978-0-07-880612-4(7),* 0078806127) McGraw-Hill Education.

—The American Republic since 1877, StudentWorks Plus CD-ROM. 2nd ed. 2005. (U. S. History - the Modern Era Ser.). (ENG.). (gr. 8-10). stu. ed. 171.20 *(978-0-07-865416-9(5),* 0078654165) McGraw-Hill Education.

—The American Republic to 1877, Active Note-Taking Guide, Student Edition. 2nd ed. 2004. (U. S. History - the Early Years Ser.). (ENG., Illus.). 328p. (gr. 6-9). stu. ed., per. 15.20 *(978-0-07-866250-8(8),* 0078662508) McGraw-Hill Education.

—The American Republic to 1877, StudentWorks Plus CD-ROM. 2nd ed. 2005. (U. S. History - the Early Years Ser.). (ENG.). (gr. 6-9). stu. ed. 166.84 *(978-0-07-866248-5(6),* 0078662486) McGraw-Hill Education.

—The American Vision, Modern Times, Active Reading & Note-Taking Guide, Student Workbook. 2005. (American Vision: Mod Times Ser.). (ENG., Illus.). 360p. (gr. 9-12). stu. ed., per., wbk. ed. 14.04 *(978-0-07-872764-1(2),* 0078727642) McGraw-Hill Higher Education.

—The American Vision, Modern Times, Reading Essentials & Study Guide, Workbook. 2005. (American Vision: Mod Times Ser.). (ENG., Illus.). 360p. (gr. 9-12). stu. ed., per., wbk. ed. 7.00 *(978-0-07-872768-9(5),* 0078727685) McGraw-Hill Higher Education.

—The American Vision: Modern Times, Standardized Test Practice Workbook. 2007. (United States History (hs) Ser.). (ENG., Illus.). 72p. (gr. 9-12). spiral bd. 4.44 *(978-0-07-878510-8(3),* 0078785103) McGraw-Hill Higher Education.

—The American Vision: Modern Times, Student Edition. 2007. (United States History (hs) Ser.). (ENG.). 1024p. (gr. 9-12). stu. ed. 71.20 *(978-0-07-874523-2(3),* 0078745233) McGraw-Hill Higher Education.

—The American Vision, Standardized Test Practice, Student Edition. 2007. (United States History (hs) Ser.). (ENG., Illus.). 88p. (gr. 9-12). spiral bd. 4.44 *(978-0-07-878431-6(X),* 007878431X) McGraw-Hill Higher Education.

—The American Vision, StudentWorks Plus CD-ROM. 2nd ed. 2005. (United States History (hs) Ser.). (ENG.). (gr. 9-12). 166.44 *(978-0-07-865456-5(4),* 0078654564) McGraw-Hill Education.

—Civics Today, Reading Essentials & Study Guide, Student Edition. 2003. (GEOGRAPHY: WORLD & ITS PEOPLE Ser.). (ENG., Illus.). 312p. (gr. 6-9). stu. ed., per. 7.60 *(978-0-07-860531-4(8),* 0078605318) McGraw-Hill Higher Education.

McGraw Hill, creator. The American Journey & the American Journey Reconstruction to the Present, Reading Essentials Study & Guide, Workbook. 2nd ed. 2004. (American Journey (survey) Ser.). (ENG., Illus.). 456p. (gr. 6-9). stu. ed., per., wbk. ed. 7.60 *(978-0-07-865550-0(1),* 0078655501) McGraw-Hill Education.

—The American Journey, Spanish Reading Essentials & Note-Taking Guide Workbook. 7th ed. 2008. (American Journey (survey) Ser.). (SPA., Illus.). 368p. (gr. 6-8). per., wbk. ed. 7.16 *(978-0-07-880618-6(6),* 0078806186) McGraw-Hill Education.

—The American Journey, StudentWorks Plus CD-ROM. 5th ed. 2005. (American Journey (survey) Ser.). (ENG.). (gr. 6-9). 174.36 *(978-0-07-866280-5(X),* 007866280X) McGraw-Hill Education.

McGraw-Hill Education Editors. The American Vision: Modern Times, StudentWorks Plus. 2005. (American Vision: Mod Times Ser.). (ENG.). (gr. 9-12). cd-rom 85.96 *(978-0-07-872733-7(2),* 0078727332) McGraw-Hill Higher Education.

—American Vision, Spanish Reading Essentials & Study Guide, Student Edition. 2nd ed. 2004. (United States History (hs) Ser.). (SPA.). 544p. (gr. 9-12). pap. 8.52 *(978-0-07-865441-1(6),* 0078654416) McGraw-Hill Higher Education.

McGraw-Hill Education Staff. The American Vision: Modern Times, Interactive Tutor Self-Assessment. 2007. (United States History (hs) Ser.). (ENG.). (gr. 9-12). cd-rom 113.68 *(978-0-07-878527-6(8),* 0078785278) McGraw-Hill Higher Education.

—The American Vision, Interactive Tutor. 2007. (United States History (hs) Ser.). (ENG.). (gr. 9-12). cd-rom 113.68 *(978-0-07-878450-7(6),* 0078784506) McGraw-Hill Higher Education.

McGraw-Hill Staff. The American Journey. 4th ed. 2004. (American Journey (survey) Ser.). (ENG.). (gr. 6-9). stu. ed. 115.60 *(978-0-07-860980-0(1),* 0078609801) McGraw-Hill Higher Education.

—The American Republic since 1877, Reading Essentials & Study Guide, Student Edition. 2nd ed. 2004. (U. S. History - the Modern Era Ser.). (ENG.). 488p. (gr. 8-10). pap. 8.04 *(978-0-07-865405-3(X),* 007865405X) McGraw-Hill Higher Education.

Mckissack, Patricia & Mckissack, Fredrick. Booker T. Washington: African-American Leader, 1 vol. 2013. (Famous African Americans Ser.). (ENG.). 24p. (gr. k-2). pap. 10.35 *(978-1-4644-0194-7(2),* 1d182b7d-f75f-4ef5-9aa4-31409abd86db); (Illus.). lib. bdg. 25.27 *(978-0-7660-4100-4(X),* 9bdb3866-8eb0-4af7-8822-47fe7ad84434) Enslow Publishing, LLC. (Enslow Elementary).

—Carter G. Woodson: Black History Pioneer, 1 vol. 2013. (Famous African Americans Ser.). (ENG.). 24p. (gr. k-2). pap. 10.35 *(978-1-4644-0195-4(0),* 95b9c3c7-6c85-48b9-8055-2bd45d164715, Enslow Elementary) Enslow Publishing, LLC.

—Jesse Owens: Legendary Track Star, 1 vol. 2013. (Famous African Americans Ser.). (ENG., Illus.). 24p. (gr. k-2). 25.27 *(978-0-7660-4104-2(2),* 99a92186-6ddf-45a7-a2b6-3866e32768d3) Enslow Publishing, LLC.

—Madam C. J. Walker: Inventor & Millionaire, 1 vol. 2013. (Famous African Americans Ser.). (ENG.). 24p. (gr. k-2). pap. 10.35 *(978-1-4644-0201-2(9),* f8417da7-de13-404b-9ab5-94627c21acf5, Enslow Elementary) Enslow Publishing, LLC.

McLeese, Don. Robert Fulton. 2005. (Rourke Discovery Library). (Illus.). 24p. (J). (gr. 2-5). lib. bdg. *(978-1-59515-434-7(5),* 1244323) Rourke Educational Media.

McMeans, Julia. Uncle Sam: An American Icon, 1 vol. William, Loma, illus. 2018. (American Legends & Folktales Ser.). (ENG.). 32p. (gr. 3-3). 30.21 *(978-1-5026-3697-3(2),* a9ca341a-643d-403d-8ff8-48dfa30f1838) Cavendish Square Publishing LLC.

McNeese, Tim. Plessy V. Ferguson. 2006. (ENG., Illus.). 136p. (gr. 5-9). lib. bdg. 32.95 *(978-0-7910-9237-8(2),* P114571, Facts On File) Infobase Holdings, Inc.

McNeese, Tim, ed. Rivers in American Life & Times. (Illus.). (gr. 9-13). pap. *(978-0-7910-8059-7(5),* Facts On File) Infobase Holdings, Inc.

McPherson, Stephanie Sammartino. Biography Coretta Scott King. 2007. (Biography Ser.). (Illus.). 112p. (YA). (gr. 7-12). lib. bdg. 29.27 *(978-0-8225-7156-8(0))* Twenty First Century Bks.

Meinking, Mary. Cash Crop to Cash Cow: The History of Tobacco & Smoking in America. 2007. (Tobacco: the Deadly Drug Ser.). (Illus.). 112p. (YA). pap. 12.95 *(978-1-4222-0811-3(7))* Mason Crest.

Melbo, Irving Robert. Our Americ: A Textbook for Elementary School History & Social Studies. 2011. 414p. 54.95 *(978-1-258-07894-2(5))* Literary Licensing, LLC.

Miers, Earl Schenck. A Child's First Book of American History. Daugherty, James, illus. 2013. 320p. (J). *(978-1-893103-41-2(2))* Beautiful Feet Bks.

Mikoley, Kate. George Washington Wasn't the First President: Exposing Myths about US Presidents. 2019. (Exposed! More Myths about American History Ser.). (ENG.). 32p. (gr. 2-3). 63.00 *(978-1-5382-3751-9(2))* Stevens, Gareth Publishing LLLP.

Miner Huey, Lois. American Archaeology Uncovers the Westward Movement, 1 vol. 2010. (American Archaeology Ser.). (ENG., Illus.). 64p. (gr. 5-5). 34.07 *(978-0-7614-4265-3(0),* 72ab4b13-65ff-4df0-9ad9-f0412472b74d) Cavendish Square Publishing LLC.

Mitchell Lane Publishers Inc. Staff. Profiles in American History. 2007. (YA). lib. bdg. 460.90 *(978-1-58415-532-4(9))* Mitchell Lane Pubs.

Mitcheltree, Frani B. Liberty Blue. 2013. (ENG.). 34p. pap. 16.95 *(978-1-4497-8113-2(6),* WestBow Pr.) Author Solutions, LLC.

Mitten, Ellen. Appalachian Region. 2014. (United States Regions Ser.). (ENG.). 32p. (gr. 4-8). 32.79 *(978-1-62717-674-3(8),* 9781627176743) Rourke Educational Media.

Monteverde, Matthew. Michigan vs. Ohio State. 2013. (J). *(978-1-4777-1166-8(X));* (ENG.). 24p. (gr. 3-3). pap. 11.60 *(978-1-4777-1165-1(1),* dd7a7873-8b4b-4a7e-9f70-a7684455de32); (ENG.). 24p. (gr. 3-3). lib. bdg. 27.60 *(978-1-4777-1159-0(7),* abe2b711-8105-46cd-bfa2-2c4ee07de677) Rosen Publishing Group, Inc., The. (PowerKids Pr.).

Monumental Milestones: Great Events of Modern Times, 16 vols., Set. 2006. (J). (gr. 4-8). lib. bdg. 319.20 *(978-1-58415-292-7(3))* Mitchell Lane Pubs.

Moran, Margaret. Coming to America Immigration from 1840 To 1930: Set Of 6. 2011. (Navigators Ser.). (J). pap. 50.00 net. *(978-1-4108-2565-0(5))* Benchmark Education Co.

Moreno, Barry. The Arab Americans. 2007. (Major American Immigration Ser.). (YA). pap. 9.95 *(978-1-4222-0671-3(8))* Mason Crest.

—History of American Immigration. (Major American Immigration Ser.). (YA). 2010. (Illus.). 64p. (gr. 9-12). lib. bdg. 22.95 *(978-1-4222-0613-3(0))* 2007. pap. 9.95 *(978-1-4222-0680-5(7))* Mason Crest.

Moreno, Barry & Temple, Bob. The Arab Americans. 2010. (Major American Immigration Ser.). (Illus.). 64p. (YA). (gr. 9-12). 22.95 *(978-1-4222-0604-1(1))* Mason Crest.

Morrow, Ann. The Gilded Age. 2007. (Cornerstones of Freedom Ser.). (Illus.). 48p. (J). (gr. 4-6). 26.00 *(978-0-516-23641-4(5),* Children's Pr.) Scholastic Library Publishing.

Mulhall, Jill K. Lewis & Clark, 1 vol. rev. ed. 2005. (Social Studies: Informational Text Ser.). (ENG.). 24p. (J). (gr. 4-8). pap. 10.99 *(978-0-7439-8906-0(6))* Teacher Created Materials, Inc.

Murray, Julie. United States, 1 vol. 2015. (Explore the Countries Ser.). (ENG., Illus.). 40p. (J). (gr. 2-5). 35.64 *(978-1-68078-072-7(7),* 19182, Big Buddy Bks.) ABDO Publishing Co.

My Place in History: Set 2. 2017. (My Place in History Ser.). 24p. (gr. 2-3). pap. 48.90 *(978-1-5382-0486-3(X));* (ENG.). lib. bdg. 145.62 *(978-1-5382-0472-6(X),* b636a25d-b81e-423d-a1d8-9bd4e1fc6938) Stevens, Gareth Publishing LLLP.

Nagara, Innosanto. A Is for Activist. 2013. (Illus.). 32p. (J). (gr. -1-2). 11.95 *(978-1-60980-539-5(9),* Triangle Square) Seven Stories Pr.

Nagelhout, Ryan. CM Punk, 1 vol. 2013. (Superstars of Wrestling Ser.). (ENG., Illus.). 32p. (J). (gr. 1-1). pap. 11.50 *(978-1-4339-8523-2(3),* 402a2c8b-2e05-445e-9217-88e198c6332d); lib. bdg. 28.27 *(978-1-4339-8522-5(5),* 36246568-119f-4dbb-a5ef-c5cb7e5f1186) Stevens, Gareth Publishing LLLP.

Nardo, Don. Early Native North Americans, 1 vol. 2008. (American History Ser.). (ENG., Illus.). 104p. (gr. 7-7). 41.03 *(978-1-4205-0034-9(1),* b2a4d369-7562-4865-baa5-d90cbedf0ca2, Lucent Pr.) Greenhaven Publishing LLC.

—The Rise of Industrial America. 2016. (Illus.). 48p. (J). *(978-1-5105-1290-0(X))* SmartBook Media, Inc.

Nathan, Amy. Round & Round Together: Taking a Merry-Go-Round Ride into the Civil Rights Movement. 2011. (Nautilus Ser.). (ENG., Illus.). 250p. (YA). (gr. 7-12). pap. 14.95 *(978-1-58988-071-9(4),* 1325047) Dry, Paul Bks., Inc.

National Geographic Learning. Reading Expeditions (Social Studies: Readings about America): the Northeast Today. 2007. (ENG., Illus.). 32p. (J). pap. 18.95 *(978-0-7922-4532-2(6))* National Geographic School Publishing, Inc.

—Reading Expeditions (Social Studies: World Explorers): Expeditions in the Americas 1492-1700. 2007. (Nonfiction Reading & Writing Workshops Ser.). (ENG., Illus.). 32p. (J). pap. 18.95 *(978-0-7922-4544-5(X))* CENGAGE Learning.

Nelson, Sheila. Thomas Jefferson's America: The Louisiana Purchase (1800-1811) 2006. (How America Became America Ser.). (Illus.). 96p. (YA). lib. bdg. 22.95 *(978-1-59084-904-0(3))* Mason Crest.

Obama, Barack. Of Thee I Sing: A Letter to My Daughters. Long, Loren, illus. 2010. (ENG.). 40p. (J). (gr. -1-3). 17.99 *(978-0-375-83527-8(X),* Knopf Bks. for Young Readers) Random Hse. Children's Bks.

Obiols, Anna. United States, 1 vol. 2018. (On the Way to School Ser.). (ENG.). 32p. (gr. 3-3). 28.93 *(978-1-5081-9643-3(5),* 35c6959d-9a7b-4afc-bb08-2a44e855e2e3); pap. 11.00 *(978-1-5081-9644-0(3),* 737c4530-ba5c-472c-8ce3-d28b493f09f6) Rosen Publishing Group, Inc., The. (Windmill Bks.).

O'Dell, Angela. America's Story. 2017. (Illus.). (J). *(978-1-68344-058-1(7),* Master Books) New Leaf Publishing Group.

Open for Debate Group 3, 10 vols., Set. Incl. Affirmative Action. Kowalski, Kathiann M. (YA). lib. bdg. 45.50 *(978-0-7614-2300-3(1),* 773bbfe3-b5cd-4f69-9425-a2cf3e5856e8); Arab-Israeli Conflict. Worth, Richard. (YA). lib. bdg. 45.50 *(978-0-7614-2295-2(1),* e14c2d8a-17b5-4b74-951a-83ea46e46dbd); Marriage. Stefoff, Rebecca. (YA). lib. bdg. 45.50 *(978-0-7614-2299-0(4),* 1ce73b16-a21f-433b-bde3-9c4ff015f9fb); Media Bias. Wood, Marilyn & Streissguth, Tom. (YA). lib. bdg. 45.50 *(978-0-7614-2296-9(X),* d6e71a1b-dcad-4df1-8cd2-f43e8755ad1e); Racial Profiling. Kops, Deborah. (J). lib. bdg. 45.50 *(978-0-7614-2298-3(6),* a4b030ae-e8ea-4a9d-96bc-d9a129f8229e); (Illus.). 144p. (gr. 8-8). (Open for Debate Ser.). (ENG.). 2007. Set lib. bdg. 227.50 *(978-0-7614-2294-5(3),* 6380fda5-7101-4d08-9266-87783f4bdff3, Cavendish Square) Cavendish Square Publishing LLC.

Orr, Tamra B. It's Cool to Learn about the United States: Southwest. 2011. (Explorer Library: Social Studies Explorer Ser.). (ENG., Illus.). 48p. (gr. 4-8). lib. bdg. 34.93 *(978-1-61080-183-6(0),* 201160) Cherry Lake Publishing.

Otfinoski, Steven. Immigration & America. 2018. (ENG., Illus.). 144p. (J). lib. bdg. *(978-0-531-22689-6(1))* Children's Pr., Ltd.

—Major Disasters in U.S. History. 2005. (Illus.). 48p. (J). *(978-0-669-51416-2(0))* Great Source Education Group, Inc.

Pack, Linda Hager. Appalachian Toys & Games from a to Z. Banks, Pat, illus. 2013. (ENG.). 56p. 19.95 *(978-0-8131-4104-6(4),* 978-0-8131-4104-6) Univ. Pr. of Kentucky.

Paises del Mundo. Tr. of Lands & People. (SPA., Illus.). (YA). (gr. 5-8). 38.95 *(978-84-241-9401-7(2))* Everest Editora ESP. Dist: Lectorum Pubns., Inc.

Palazzo-Craig, Janet. The Making of the American Flag: Betsy Ross & George Washington, 1 vol. 2003. (Great Moments in American History Ser.). (ENG., Illus.). 32p. (gr. 3-4). lib. bdg. 29.13 *(978-0-8239-4335-7(6),* fd35f551-dd6a-40c6-8672-b3c4c53e6e50, Rosen Reference) Rosen Publishing Group, Inc., The.

Penton, ed. United States Flipper. 2003. (Smart Kids Flippers Ser.). (ENG.). (J). pap. 14.95 *(978-1-59125-250-4(4))* Penton Overseas, Inc.

T U V

Perrin, Pat. Getting Started-America's Melting Pot. 2004. (Illus.). (J). *(978-1-932663-04-4(5))* History Compass, LLC.
—Getting Started-Our 50 United States. 2004. (Illus.). (J). *(978-1-932663-03-7(7))* History Compass, LLC.
—Getting Started-Our Government. 2004. (Illus.). (J). *(978-1-932663-02-0(9))* History Compass, LLC.
Petersen, Christine. The Surveyor, 1 vol. 2011. (Colonial People Ser.). (ENG.). 48p. (gr. 4-4). 34.07 *(978-0-7614-4805-1(5),* f1d2b84e-a0e8-4249-b423-ef731729c885) Cavendish Square Publishing LLC.
Pinborough, Jan. Miss Moore Thought Otherwise: How Anne Carroll Moore Created Libraries for Children. Atwell, Debby, illus. 2013. (ENG.). 40p. (J). (gr. 1-4). 18.99 *(978-0-547-47105-1(X),* 1437999, Clarion Bks.) HarperCollins Pubs.
Pinkney, Andrea Davis. Martin & Mahalia: His Words, Her Song. 2013. (ENG., Illus.). 40p. (J). (gr. 1-17). 18.99 *(978-0-316-07013-3(0))* Little, Brown Bks. for Young Readers.
Platt, D. D. & Conkling, Philip, eds. Island Journal: An Annual Publication of the Island Institute, 20. Ralston, Peter, photos by. 20th ed. 2003. (Island Journals: 20). (Illus.). 96p. pap. 9.95 *(978-0-942719-33-8(6))* Island Institute.
Plummer, Barbara. Kids in the Backyard. 2007. 60p. per. 16.95 *(978-1-4241-9064-5(9))* America Star Bks.
Pofahl, Jane. Westward Movement: United States History. (Time Traveler Ser.). (Illus.). 32p. (gr. 3-6). 6.99 *(978-0-513-02222-5(8),* TSD22228) Denison, T. S. & Co., Inc.
Pohl, Kathleen. Descubramos Estados Unidos (Looking at the United States), 1 vol. 2008. (Descubramos Países Del Mundo (Looking at Countries) Ser.). (SPA., Illus.). 32p. (gr. 2-4). (J). lib. bdg. 28.67 *(978-0-8368-9072-3(8),* 2048a42a-54ba-4c1c-91d8-54c8446612c1); pap. 11.50 *(978-0-8368-9073-0(6),* 467cf5c4-e33f-4c67-8fed-36ebf845f0d9, Gareth Stevens Learning Library) Stevens, Gareth Publishing LLLP.
—Looking at the United States, 1 vol. 2008. (Looking at Countries Ser.). (ENG., Illus.). 32p. (gr. 2-4). pap. 11.50 *(978-0-8368-9071-6(X),* 24ccfeff-fa84-4fa0-a4d1-baf2c052eaf5, Gareth Stevens Learning Library) Stevens, Gareth Publishing LLLP.
Powerkids Readers: American Symbols. 2013. (PowerKids Readers: American Symbols Ser.). 24p. (J). (gr. k-2). pap. 297.00 *(978-1-4777-2674-7(8));* pap. 49.50 *(978-1-4777-2673-0(X))* Rosen Publishing Group, Inc., The. (PowerKids Pr.).
Powerkids Readers: American Symbols / SMbolos de Amrica. 12 vols. 2013. (PowerKids Readers: Símbolos de América / American Symbols Ser.). (ENG & SPA.). 24p. (J). (gr. k-k). 157.62 *(978-1-4777-1237-5(2),* b7046ecf-9027-427f-a745-0da87cb50e7e, PowerKids Pr.) Rosen Publishing Group, Inc., The.
Pratt, Mara L. American History Stories, Volume I - with Original Illustrations. 2011. (Illus.). 212p. *(978-1-84902-412-9(X))* Benediction Classics.
—American History Stories, Volume II - with Original Illustrations. 2011. 218p. *(978-1-84902-410-5(3))* Benediction Classics.
—American History Stories, Volume III - with Original Illustrations. 2011. 208p. *(978-1-84902-409-9(X))* Benediction Classics.
—American History Stories, Volume Iv - with Original Illustrations. 2011. 246p. *(978-1-84902-407-5(3))* Benediction Classics.
A Primary Source History of the United States, 16 vols., Set. 2004. (Primary Source History of the United States Ser.). (ENG.). 48p. (gr. 5-8). lib. bdg. 269.36 *(978-0-8368-5823-5(9),* 6db1d64d-6bff-4e8f-96e5-ace2560e8a54, Gareth Stevens Secondary Library) Stevens, Gareth Publishing LLLP.
Primary Sources in U. S. History, 10 vols. 2014. (Primary Sources in U. S. History Ser.). (ENG.). 48p. (J). (gr. 4-4). lib. bdg. 165.35 *(978-1-5026-0312-8(8),* f47cd3ec-8913-4d13-948e-5d04cbf6c952, Cavendish Square) Cavendish Square Publishing LLC.
Primary Sources of American Wars. 6 vols. 2005. (Primary Sources of American Wars Ser.). (ENG.). (J). (gr. 3-4). 78.81 *(978-1-4042-3304-1(0),* e37ab949-9a23-4413-8f92-ca7ad0ff44ab) Rosen Publishing Group, Inc., The.
Publications International Ltd. Staff, ed. Electronic Time for Learning: States. 2010. 120p. 18.98 *(978-1-4127-9853-2(1),* PIL Kids) Publications International, Ltd.
Rajczak, Michael. How Did the Liberty Bell Get Its Crack? And Other FAQs about History, 1 vol. 2016. (Q & a: Life's Mysteries Solved! Ser.). (ENG., Illus.). 32p. (J). (gr. 3-4). pap. 11.50 *(978-1-4824-4737-8(1),* 6cf5c9e8-c551-4ad2-9f4e-78dd011f1a8a) Stevens, Gareth Publishing LLLP.
Rakes, Celeste W. All American History Student Reader Vol. 1: The Explorers to the Jacksonians. 2005. (All American History Ser.). (Illus.). 442p. 44.95 *(978-1-892427-12-0(5))* Bright Ideas! Educational Resources.
Randolph, Ryan. Alexander Hamilton's Economic Plan: Solving Problems in America's New Economy. 2009. (Life in the New American Nation Ser.). 32p. (gr. 4-4). 47.90 *(978-1-61514-276-7(2))* Rosen Publishing Group, Inc., The.
Rau, Dana Meachen. The Northeast. 2012. (True Book Ser.). (ENG., Illus.). 48p. (J). (gr. 3-5). 29.00 *(978-0-531-24851-5(8),* Children's Pr.) Scholastic Library Publishing.
—The Southwest (a True Book: the U. S. Regions) 2012. (True Book (Relaunch) Ser.). (ENG., Illus.). 48p. (J). (gr. 3-5). pap. 6.95 *(978-0-531-28328-8(3),* Children's Pr.) Scholastic Library Publishing.
—A True Book: the Southwest. 2012. (True Book Ser.). (ENG., Illus.). 48p. (J). (gr. 3-5). lib. bdg. 29.00 *(978-0-531-24853-9(4),* Children's Pr.) Scholastic Library Publishing.
—A True Book: U. S. Landforms. 2012. (True Book Ser.). (ENG., Illus.). 48p. (J). lib. bdg. 29.00 *(978-0-531-24854-6(2),* Children's Pr.) Scholastic Library Publishing.
Rebellions, Revolts, & Uprisings. 2017. (Rebellions, Revolts, & Uprisings Ser.). 48p. (gr. 5-5). pap. 84.30 *(978-1-5382-0838-0(5));* (ENG.). lib. bdg. 201.60 *(978-1-5382-0837-3(7),* 62e5d376-af8d-4cbe-91d8-4ec5e0262312) Stevens, Gareth Publishing LLLP.
Remembering Medicine Creek: The Story of the First Treaty Signed in Washington. 2005. (YA). pap. 10.00 *(978-0-9772528-0-0(9))* Fireweed Pr.
Research American History Series: Series Set. 2004. (Researching American History Ser.). (Illus.). (J). *(978-1-932663-05-1(3))* History Compass, LLC.
Rice, Dona Herweck. Grand Old Flag (Foundations) 2nd rev. ed. 2015. (TIME for KIDS(r): Informational Text Ser.). (ENG., Illus.). 12p. (gr. -1-k). 7.99 *(978-1-4938-2055-9(9))* Teacher Created Materials, Inc.
Road Trip: Exploring America's Regions, 12 vols. 2013. (Road Trip: Exploring America's Regions Ser.). 24p. (J). (gr. 2-3). (ENG.). 151.62 *(978-1-4339-9675-7(8),* 2bd7aa28-c5d2-4f63-a15d-b9ff251358a9); pap. 48.90 *(978-1-4339-9743-3(6));* pap. 293.40 *(978-1-4339-9744-0(4))* Stevens, Gareth Publishing LLLP.
Robinson, Tom. The Development of the Industrial United States: 1870-1900. 2007. (Presidents of the United States Ser.). (Illus.). 48p. (J). (gr. 4-7). lib. bdg. 29.05 *(978-1-59036-745-2(6))* Weigl Pubs., Inc.
—Development of the Industrial United States: 1870-1900. 2007. (Presidents of the United States Ser.). (Illus.). 48p. (J). (gr. 4-7). per. 10.95 *(978-1-59036-746-9(4))* Weigl Pubs., Inc.
Roop, Peter & Roop, Connie. Louisiana Purchase. Comport, Sally Wern, illus. 2004. (Ready-For-Chapters Ser.). (ENG.). 80p. (J). (gr. 2-5). pap. 6.99 *(978-0-689-86443-8(4),* Simon & Schuster/Paula Wiseman Bks.) Simon & Schuster/Paula Wiseman Bks.
—Manten Las Luces Encendidas, Abbie. Hanson, Peter E., illus. 2005. (Yo Solo Biografías Ser.). (SPA.). 40p. (J). (gr. 2-5). per. 6.95 *(978-0-8225-3099-2(6))* Lerner Publishing Group.
Rosen, Daniel. New Beginnings (Direct Mail Edition) Jamestown & the Virginia Colony 1607-1699. 2005. (Crossroads America Ser.). (ENG.). 40p. (J). (gr. 5-9). 12.95 *(978-0-7922-8277-8(9))* National Geographic Society.
Rossi, Ann. Created Equal (Direct Mail Edition) Women Campaign for the Right to Vote 1840 - 1920. 2005. (Crossroads America Ser.). (ENG., Illus.). 40p. (J). (gr. 5-9). 12.95 *(978-0-7922-8275-4(2))* National Geographic Society.
Rous, Sheri, ed. United States History. 2004. (Illus.). 32p. (J). pap. 10.99 *(978-1-59198-053-7(4),* CTP 2797) Creative Teaching Pr., Inc.
Rowell, Rebecca. Parkland Students Challenge the National Rifle Association. 2019. (Taking a Stand Ser.). (ENG., Illus.). 48p. (J). (gr. 5-6). pap. 11.95 *(978-1-64185-415-3(4),* 1641854154); lib. bdg. 34.21 *(978-1-64185-357-6(3),* 1641853573) North Star Editions. (Focus Readers).
Rulers & Their Times (Group 3), 8 vols. 2003. (Rulers & Their Times Ser.). (ENG.). (gr. 6-6). 147.72 *(978-0-7614-1486-5(X),* d224756e-418b-421d-95fe-194566fc1d8c, Cavendish Square) Cavendish Square Publishing LLC.
Sakolsky, Josh. Critical Perspectives on the Industrial Revolution, 1 vol. 2004. (Critical Anthologies of Nonfiction Writing Ser.). (ENG., Illus.). 176p. (YA). (gr. 8-8). lib. bdg. 42.47 *(978-1-4042-0062-3(2),* 5fc18b24-7abf-43b6-afd3-b23c2701233b) Rosen Publishing Group, Inc., The.
Sanders, Doug. Superstorm Sandy. 2013. (Code Red Ser.). 32p. (J). (gr. 2-7). lib. bdg. 28.50 *(978-1-61772-898-3(5))* Bearport Publishing Co., Inc.
Sandler, Martin W. America's Great Disasters. Sandler, Martin W., illus. 2003. (Illus.). 96p. (J). (gr. 3-18). 17.99 *(978-0-06-029107-5(9))* HarperCollins Pubs.
Savitz, Harriet May. Dear Daughters & Sons: Three Essays on the American Spirit... a Tribute. 2003. 40p. per. 4.95 *(978-0-9639838-9-3(X))* Little Treasure Bks.
Saxena, Shalini. Paul Revere Didn't Say the British Are Coming! Exposing Myths about the American Revolution, 1 vol. 2016. (Exposed! Myths about Early American History Ser.). (ENG., Illus.). 32p. (J). (gr. 2-3). pap. 11.50 *(978-1-4824-5727-8(X),* ca11231e-c5dc-420c-a790-4373b30df43e) Stevens, Gareth Publishing LLLP.
Scholastic Library Publishing. Cornerstones of Freedom. 2012. (Third Ser.). (J). 300.00 *(978-0-531-22774-9(X),* Children's Pr.) Scholastic Library Publishing.
—Cornerstones of Freedom, Third Series. 2011. (Third Ser.). (J). 1200.00 *(978-0-531-27644-0(9),* Children's Pr.) Scholastic Library Publishing.
—A True Book-the U. S. Regions. 2012. (True Book Ser.). (J). 174.00 *(978-0-531-26024-1(0),* Children's Pr.) Scholastic Library Publishing.
Schraff, Anne. Daredevil American Heroes of Exploration & Flight, 1 vol. 2013. (Inspiring Collective Biographies Ser.). (ENG.). 112p. (gr. 5-6). pap. 13.88 *(978-1-4644-0247-0(7),* db18b208-dedd-41af-990a-ecd78f3fcae9); (Illus.). 35.93 *(978-0-7660-4163-9(8),* bdaaaf79-84cf-4cd1-af93-6695ed60793f) Enslow Publishing, LLC.
Schuh, Mari. The Bald Eagle. 2018. (Symbols of American Freedom Ser.). (ENG., Illus.). 24p. (J). (gr. k-3). pap. 7.99 *(978-1-61891-469-9(3),* 12122, Blastoff! Readers) Bellwether Media.
Scillian, Devin. One Nation: America by the Numbers. Carroll, Pam, illus. 2004. (ENG.). 40p. (J). (gr. 1-4). pap. 7.95 *(978-1-58536-249-3(2),* 202282) Sleeping Bear Pr.
Scirri, Kaitlin. Thomas Edison: Inventor & Innovator, 1 vol. 2019. (Great American Entrepreneurs Ser.). (ENG.). 128p. (J). (gr. 9-9). pap. 22.16 *(978-1-5026-4530-2(0),* a5732cd6-80d0-4368-bd81-51116e9c1ba4) Cavendish Square Publishing LLC.
Sebree, Chet'la & Schomp, Virginia. Historical Sources on Women's Rights, 1 vol. 2019. (America's Story Ser.). (ENG.). 144p. (gr. 8-8). pap. 22.16 *(978-1-5026-4098-7(8),* 1bafb10e-fa36-4d23-b0f2-a2b36223dac6) Cavendish Square Publishing LLC.
Selzer, Adam. The Smart Aleck's Guide to American History. 2009. (Illus.). 336p. (J). (gr. 4-7). pap. 13.99 *(978-0-385-73650-3(9),* Delacorte Bks. for Young Readers) Random Hse. Children's Bks.
Seneca Falls, Grades 4-9: Achieving Women's Rights. (Teaching with Primary Sources Ser.). (J). tchr. ed. 32.95 *(978-0-382-40975-2(2))* Cobblestone Publishing Co.
Serber, Michael & Peiser, Andrew. U. S. History & Government. rev. ed. 2005. 688p. (gr. 10-12). *(978-0-87720-882-2(4),* R036H) AMSCO Schl. Pubns., Inc.
Sets 1, 2, 3 & 4, 28 vols. 2004. (Primary Sources in American History Ser.). (ENG., Illus.). 64p. (gr. 5-8). lib. bdg. 519.82 *(978-1-4042-0352-5(4),* 83d10239-6175-4361-a1a2-3649826106d3) Rosen Publishing Group, Inc., The.
Sharp, Constance. Thomas Jefferson & the Growing United States (1800-1811) 2012. (J). pap. *(978-1-4222-2414-4(7))* Mason Crest.
Shea, Therese. The Statue of Liberty Wasn't Made to Welcome Immigrants: Exposing Myths about U.S. Landmarks. 2019. (Exposed! More Myths about American History Ser.). (ENG.). 32p. (gr. 2-3). 63.00 *(978-1-5382-3759-5(8))* Stevens, Gareth Publishing LLLP.
Show Me America, 5 vols., Set. Incl. Dorothea Lange: Photographer of the People: Photographer of the People. King, David C. 88p. (C). 2009. lib. bdg. 180.00 *(978-0-7656-8154-6(4),* Y181941); George Catlin: Painter of Indian Life: Painter of Indian Life. Worth, Richard. 80p. (C). 2009. lib. bdg. 180.00 *(978-0-7656-8152-2(8),* Y182314); John Trumbull: Painter of the Revolutionary War: Painter of the Revolutionary War. Murray, Stuart A. P. 83p. (C). 2008. lib. bdg. 180.00 *(978-0-7656-8150-8(1),* Y182501); Lewis Hine: Photographer of Americans at Work: Photographer of Americans at Work. Worth, Richard. 80p. (C). 2009. lib. bdg. 180.00 *(978-0-7656-8153-9(6),* Y182862); Mathew Brady: Photographer of Our Nation: Photographer of Our Nation. Murray, Stuart A. P. 83p. 2009. lib. bdg. 180.00 *(978-0-7656-8151-5(X),* Y182957); (Illus.). (gr. 6-18). (ENG.). 2009. Set lib. bdg. 165.00 *(978-0-7656-8149-2(8),* Y183560) Routledge.
Shuh, Mari. Adrian Peterson. 2013. (Football Stars up Close Ser.). 24p. (J). (gr. k-5). lib. bdg. 26.99 *(978-1-61772-718-4(0))* Bearport Publishing Co., Inc.
Shukin, Barbara. Renaissance History Portfolio: A History of Europe & the Americas from the 14th -18th Centuries. 2004. (J). ring bd. 29.95 *(978-0-9762918-2-4(7))* Homeschool Journey.
Siebert, Anne & Clark, Raymond C. All Around America: The Time Traveler's Talk Show. 2004. (gr. 6-12). pap., wbk. ed. 39.00 incl. cd-rom *(978-0-86647-186-2(3))* Pro Lingua Assocs., Inc.
—All Around America Activities: The Time Traveler's Talk Show. 2004. 76p. (gr. 6-12). pap., stu. ed., wbk. ed. 16.50 *(978-0-86647-184-8(7))* Pro Lingua Assocs., Inc.
Sikora, Frank & Batcheler, Michelle. Frank M. Johnson, Jr. Courageous Judge. 2009. (Illus.). 104p. *(978-1-59421-045-7(4))* Seacoast Publishing, Inc.
Silbert, Jack. Honest Abe's Funny Money Book. 2012. (Illus.). 32p. *(978-0-545-36740-0(9))* Scholastic, Inc.
Six Questions of American History. 2012. (Six Questions of American History Ser.). (ENG.). 48p. (gr. 4-6). Set III. pap. 56.72 *(978-0-7613-9243-9(2))*Set III, Pack. pap. 340.29 *(978-0-7613-9244-6(0))* Lerner Publishing Group.
Six Questions of American History: Spring 2012 New Releases. 2012. (Six Questions of American History Ser.). 48p. (gr. 4-6). lib. bdg. 183.60 *(978-0-7613-8909-5(1),* Lerner Pubns.) Lerner Publishing Group.
Smith, A. G. Historic American Landmarks. 2005. (Dover American History Coloring Bks.). (ENG., Illus.). 32p. (J). (gr. 3-5). 3.99 *(978-0-486-44489-5(9),* 444899) Dover Pubns., Inc.
Smith, Ruth J. Divine Providence: A Child's History of the United States. Mikler, Lisa M., illus. 2005. 224p. (J). per. 19.95 net. *(978-0-9705618-5-5(7))* Bradford Pr., Inc.
—Liberty & Justice for All: A Child's History of the United States of America. Mikler, Lisa M., illus. 2003. 208p. (J). per. 19.95 *(978-0-9705618-3-1(0))* Bradford Pr., Inc.
—Liberty & Justice for All Teacher's Guide: Liberty & Justice for All. 2003. (J). tchr. ed., per. 34.95 *(978-0-9705618-4-8(9))* Bradford Pr., Inc.
Smith, Tamara. The Story of Ulysses S. Grant. Britt, Stephanie, illus. 2005. 26p. (J). bds. 7.69 *(978-0-8249-6565-5(5),* Ideals Pubns.) Worthy Publishing.
South, Victor. Connecting the 21st Century to the Past (2000-The Present) 2018. (J). *(978-1-5105-3612-8(4))* SmartBook Media, Inc.
Spotlight on American History. 2015. (Spotlight on American History Ser.). (ENG.). 24p. (J). (gr. 4-6). pap., pap., pap. 720.00 *(978-1-4994-1836-1(1),* PowerKids Pr.) Rosen Publishing Group, Inc., The.
Spotlight on American History: Set 2, 24 vols. 2016. (Spotlight on American History Ser.). 24p. (ENG.). (gr. 4-6). 335.16 *(978-1-4994-1894-1(9),* 68defb1f-2539-496f-a3d2-3c22a645e0ac); (gr. 6-4). pap. 120.00 *(978-1-4994-2480-5(9))* Rosen Publishing Group, Inc., The. (PowerKids Pr.).
Stanley, George E. The Great Depression & World War II (1929-1949), 1 vol. 2004. (Primary Source History of the United States Ser.). (ENG., Illus.). 48p. (gr. 5-8). pap. 15.05 *(978-0-8368-5838-9(7),* 74309cec-dea3-4336-90c7-755935bcc71d); lib. bdg. 33.67 *(978-0-8368-5829-7(8),* 6d6672ea-ba5d-4813-ae64-d37a93bc2126) Stevens, Gareth Publishing LLLP. (Gareth Stevens Secondary Library).
The Star-Spangled State Book: Have Fun Learning about All 50 States. 2006. (YA). per. *(978-0-9787820-0-9(3))* King, Joel.
States. 2005. (Illus.). 96p. 12.98 *(978-0-7853-9600-0(4),* 7127301) Phoenix International Publications, Inc.
Stckvagn. Americas Story Complete Book S. 2005. pap. *(978-0-7398-9717-1(9))* Harcourt Schl. Pubs.
Steck-Vaughn Staff. Social Studies Level E: History of Our Country. 2005. (Steck-Vaughn Social Studies). (ENG., Illus.). 208p. (gr. 5-5). pap. 37.65 *(978-0-7398-9222-0(3))* Houghton Mifflin Harcourt Publishing Co.
Steele, Philip. Iran & the West, 1 vol. 2012. (Our World Divided Ser.). (ENG., Illus.). 48p. (J). (gr. 5-5). 34.47 *(978-1-4488-6031-9(8),* 46d866d9-560c-42cb-baaa-4b56e29caba2, Rosen Reference) Rosen Publishing Group, Inc., The.
Stephens, Edna Cucksey. Rock U. S. A. & the American Way! A Freedom Handbook. Herrick, Mark J., illus. 2004. (Connect-It Ser.). 124p. (J). (gr. -1-3). pap. 29.95 *(978-0-9749412-1-9(2))* EDCO Publishing, Inc.
Stewart, Mark. The United States & Canada. rev. ed. 2016. (Regions of the World Ser.). (ENG.). 64p. (J). (gr. 6-9). pap. 9.99 *(978-1-4846-3814-9(X),* 134698, Heinemann) Capstone.
Stille, Darlene R. The Emergence of Modern America: 1890-1930. 2007. (Presidents of the United States Ser.). (Illus.). 48p. (J). (gr. 4-7). lib. bdg. 29.05 *(978-1-59036-747-6(2));* per. 10.95 *(978-1-59036-748-3(0))* Weigl Pubs., Inc.
Stoltman, Joan. Protests & Riots That Changed America, 1 vol. 2018. (American History Ser.). (ENG.). 104p. (gr. 7-7). 41.03 *(978-1-5345-6415-2(2),* 301966b9-2510-40cc-acec-e9abd325953f, Lucent Pr.) Greenhaven Publishing LLC.
Stone, Oliver & Kuznick, Peter. The Untold History of the United States Vol. 1: Young Readers Edition, 1898-1963. 2015. lib. bdg. 24.50 *(978-0-606-37853-6(7))* Turtleback.
—The Untold History of the United States, Volume 1: Young Readers Edition, 1898-1945, Vol. 1. 2015. (ENG., Illus.). 400p. (J). (gr. 5). pap. 12.99 *(978-1-4814-2174-4(3),* Atheneum Bks. for Young Readers) Simon & Schuster Children's Publishing.
Stone, Tanya Lee. A Is for America: A Patriotic Alphabet Book. Kelley, Gerald, illus. 2011. 24p. (J). (gr. -1-k). mass mkt. 6.99 *(978-0-8431-9877-5(X),* Price Stern Sloan) Penguin Young Readers Group.
Streissguth, Thomas. United States in Pictures. 2007. (Visual Geography (Lerner) Ser.). (Illus.). 80p. (YA). (gr. 7-12). lib. bdg. 31.93 *(978-0-8225-8567-1(7))* Twenty First Century Bks.
Sundance/Newbridge LLC Staff. It's on the Map. 2004. (Reading PowerWorks Ser.). (gr. 1-3). 37.50 *(978-0-7608-7823-1(4));* pap. 6.10 *(978-0-7608-7824-8(2))* Sundance/Newbridge Educational Publishing.
Sutton, Lynn Parrish. Americanly. Greenberg, Melanie Hope, illus. 2018. (ENG.). 30p. (J). 11.99 *(978-1-61067-511-6(8))* Kane Miller.
Swanson Sateren, Shelley, et al. It's Back to School ... Way Back! 2016. (It's Back to School ... Way Back! Ser.). (ENG.). 32p. (J). (gr. 3-6). pap., pap., pap. 31.80 *(978-1-5157-2117-8(5),* 25062, Capstone Pr.) Capstone.
Symbols of America, 12 vols. 2005. (Symbols of America Ser.). (ENG., Illus.). 40p. (gr. 3-3). lib. bdg. 195.84 *(978-0-7614-1708-8(7),* 63e01e30-c22a-4541-a116-033c356cbe49, Cavendish Square) Cavendish Square Publishing LLC.
Tate, Suzanne. Color with the Wright Brothers: See How They Made History. Melvin, James, illus. 2003. (Suzanne Tate's History Ser.). 32p. (J). pap. 2.95 *(978-1-878405-41-8(1))* Nags Head Art, Inc.
Teacher Created Materials. Early America, Set. rev. ed. 2009. (Book Collection). (ENG., Illus.). (J). (gr. 4-6). 55.92 *(978-1-4333-1895-5(4))* Teacher Created Materials, Inc.
Teaching Hello U.S.A. 2004. (Illus.). lib. bdg., tchr. ed. 7.95 *(978-0-8225-3748-9(6))* Lerner Publishing Group.
The Library of American Lives & Times: Set 3, 14 vols. 2003. (Library of American Lives & Times Ser.). (ENG., Illus.). (gr. 5-5). lib. bdg. 267.89 *(978-0-8239-6657-8(7),* 37356dcf-9537-486b-9de8-72f0dd06e028) Rosen Publishing Group, Inc., The.
The Library of American Lives & Times: Set 4, 22 vols. 2004. (Library of American Lives & Times Ser.). (ENG., Illus.). 112p. (gr. 5-5). lib. bdg. 420.97 *(978-0-8239-7680-5(7),* f88013d9-08e3-4e0d-a1ca-3921526dc1f5) Rosen Publishing Group, Inc., The.
The United States: Historical Atlases of the Growth of a New Nation, 12 vols. 2004. (United States: Historical Atlases of the Growth of a New Nation Ser.). (ENG., Illus.). (gr. 5-5). lib. bdg. 222.78 *(978-1-4042-0357-0(5),* 1fd866f1-ac73-43ef-86b0-174f3d7ee3c4) Rosen Publishing Group, Inc., The.
The White House: PowerKids Readers: American Symbols, 12 vols. 2013. (PowerKids Readers: American Symbols Ser.). (ENG.). 24p. (J). (gr. k-k). 157.62 *(978-1-4777-1138-5(4),* 66327de1-8bf9-454a-a6ce-fb577ef8928a, PowerKids Pr.) Rosen Publishing Group, Inc., The.
Theresine, Mary. Challenge to Freedom. O'Leary, Timothy F. & Veronica, M., eds. 2011. 322p. 50.95 *(978-1-258-07535-4(0))* Literary Licensing, LLC.
Thompson, Carol & Thompson, Carol. America the Good: Stories of Goodwill by Good Americans. 2003. (Illus.). 95p. bds. 15.95 *(978-0-9744111-0-1(8))* Wren's Nest Publishing, Inc.
Thompson, Jerry D., contrib. by. Symbols of American Freedom Set, 10-Volumes. 2009. (Symbols of American Freedom Ser.). (gr. 4-6). 300.00 *(978-1-60413-830-6(0),* Chelsea Clubhse.) Infobase Holdings, Inc.
Timelines of American History: Set 2, 8 vols. 2003. (Timelines of American History Ser.). (ENG., Illus.). 32p. (gr. 4-4). lib. bdg. 116.52 *(978-1-4042-0140-8(8),* e27820bc-c9e5-409e-b4eb-fbc365bedc90) Rosen Publishing Group, Inc., The.
Timelines of American History Set 1, 10 vols. 2003. (Timelines of American History Ser.). (ENG., Illus.). 32p. (gr. 4-4). lib. bdg. 145.65 *(978-1-4042-0139-2(4),* cbb74d72-0685-4b43-9cca-953f776162af) Rosen Publishing Group, Inc., The.
Tiner, John. The Story of the Pledge of Allegiance: Discovering Our Nations Heritage. 2003. (Discovering Our Nation's Heritage Ser.). (Illus.). 48p. (J). 6.99 *(978-0-89051-393-4(7),* Master Books) New Leaf Publishing Group.
Todd, Francine E. The Todds in America: 1741-2005: An American History/Genealogy Curriculum for Grades 3-5. 2006. (ENG., Illus.). 68p. per. 17.75 *(978-1-4120-7834-4(2))* Trafford Publishing.
Townsend, Dana E. Ellis Island. (Illus.). 32p. (J). *(978-0-7367-2944-4(5))* Zaner-Bloser, Inc.
Tracy, Kathleen. Top Secret: The Story of the Manhattan Project. 2005. (Monumental Milestones Ser.). (Illus.). 48p. (YA). (gr. 4-7). lib. bdg. 29.95 *(978-1-58415-399-3(7))* Mitchell Lane Pubs.

The check digit for ISBN-10 appears in parentheses after the full ISBN-13

Uhlig, Elizabeth. I See America! Uhlig, Elizabeth, illus. 2009. (Illus.). (J). pap. 12.95 *(978-0-9815345-7-2(0))* Marble Hse. Editions.

United States History, 3 vols. 2004. (Pacemaker United States History Ser.). 738p. (YA). (gr. 6-12). 43.95 *(978-0-13-024410-9(4))* Globe Fearon Educational Publishing.

The United States Past & Present. (J). (gr. 5). *(978-0-669-11398-3(0))*; suppl. ed. *(978-0-669-11382-2(4))* Houghton Mifflin Harcourt School Pubs.

The United States Past to Present: Heath Social Studies. Incl. United States Past & Present. suppl. ed. *(978-0-669-11382-2(4))*; United States Past & Present. *(978-0-669-11398-3(0))*; The United States Past to Present. suppl. ed. *(978-0-669-11424-9(3))*; The United States Past to Present. pap., wbk. ed. *(978-0-669-11404-1(9))*; The United States Past to Present. tchr. ed., wbk. ed. *(978-0-669-11409-6(X))*; The United States Past to Present. suppl. ed. *(978-0-669-11430-0(8))*; The United States Past to Present. suppl. ed. *(978-0-669-11725-7(0))*; The United States Past to Present. suppl. ed. (J). (gr. 5-6). *(978-0-669-11390-7(5))* Houghton Mifflin Harcourt School Pubs.

Uschan, Michael V. Reconstruction, 1 vol. 2007. (Lucent Library of Black History Ser.). (ENG., Illus.). 104p. (gr. 7-7). lib. bdg. 41.03 *(978-1-4205-0009-7(0))*, 96dfe74c-6aad-4f3a-809b-feec28722e98, Lucent Pr.) Greenhaven Publishing LLC.

Vescia, Monique. Battle Reenactments, 1 vol., 1. 2015. (Role-Playing for Fun & Profit Ser.). (ENG.). 48p. (J). (gr. 5-5). pap. 12.75 *(978-1-4994-3728-7(5))*, 2af37c0b-0c46-43a6-aa7d-23dab1ffa953, Rosen Central) Rosen Publishing Group, Inc., The.

Victor, Rae Anna. George Washington's Revolutionary Marshals. 2004. (Illus.). 62p. (J). pap. 9.95 *(978-0-7414-2302-3(2))* Infinity Publishing.

Wacholtz, Anthony. Joe Mauer: Baseball Superstar, 1 vol. 2012. (Superstar Athletes Ser.). (ENG.). 24p. (J). (gr. 1-3). pap. 7.29 *(978-1-4296-8003-5(2))*, 118335); lib. bdg. 25.99 *(978-1-4296-7683-0(3))*, 117280) Capstone.

Waldman, Neil. A Land of Big Dreamers: Voices of Courage in America. Waldman, Neil, illus. 2011. (Single Titles Ser.). (ENG., Illus.). 32p. (gr. 3-5). lib. bdg. 16.95 *(978-0-8225-6810-0(1))* Lerner Publishing Group.

Walker, Paul Robert. American Indians. 2012. (All about America Ser.). (ENG., Illus.). 32p. (J). (gr. 4-7). 26.19 *(978-0-7534-6694-0(5))*, 9780753466940) Kingfisher Publications, plc GBR. Dist: Children's Plus, Inc.

Wallace, Elise. Características Geográficas. rev. ed. 2019. (Social Studies: Informational Text Ser.). (SPA., Illus.). 32p. (J). (gr. 3-4). pap. 11.99 *(978-1-64290-117-7(2))* Teacher Created Materials, Inc.

Warner, Roxie & Warner, Christian. Land of the Free, A to Z. Schartup, Adam, illus. 2014. (J). *(978-1-62086-801-0(6))* Amplify Publishing Group.

Waxman, Laura Hamilton. Why Did the Pilgrims Come to the New World? & Other Questions about the Plymouth Colony. 2010. (Six Questions of American History Ser.). 48p. (J). pap. 9.95 *(978-0-7613-6123-7(5))* Lerner Publishing Group.

Weber, Jennifer L. Key Concepts in American History, 10 vols., Set. 2010. (Key Concepts in American History Ser.). (gr. 6-12). 450.00 *(978-1-60413-961-7(7))*, Facts On File) Infobase Holdings, Inc.

Weintraub, Aileen. The Library of Pirates, 6 bks. Incl. Barbarossa Brothers: 16th-Century Pirates of the Barbary Coast. 2001. lib. bdg. 26.27 *(978-0-8239-5799-6(3))*, e8d1e5c3-d453-4177-a48a-9ec7fb9e5133); Captain Kidd: 17th-Century Pirate of the Indian Ocean & African Coast. 2005. lib. bdg. 26.27 *(978-0-8239-5797-2(7))*, 9c5dfa96-1096-456b-a6f9-50a8f7c69632); 24p. (YA). (gr. 3-4). (Illus.). 49.20 o.p. *(978-0-8239-7133-6(3))*, PowerKids Pr.) Rosen Publishing Group, Inc., The.

What Really Happened?, 6 vols., Set. Incl. True Story of Pocahontas. Adams, Colleen. (J). lib. bdg. 26.27 *(978-1-4042-4475-7(1))*, f0084636-13eb-497c-aee5-c454b0859aa2); True Story of the American Flag. Zumbusch, Amelie von. (YA). lib. bdg. 26.27 *(978-1-4042-4478-8(6))*, 03781aac-0c2f-4d15-adae-0eecc80d27d9); True Story of the Battle of Lexington & Concord. Von Zumbusch, Amelie. (YA). lib. bdg. 26.27 *(978-1-4042-4480-1(8))*, 8b6f76cd-3217-4d31-b183-3e675c3d528c); True Story of the Battle of the Alamo. Adams, Colleen. (YA). lib. bdg. 26.27 *(978-1-4042-4477-1(8))*, b8e46ea5-0ce4-45a0-833c-b85a41b14fc0); True Story of the First Thanksgiving. Adams, Colleen. (YA). lib. bdg. 26.27 *(978-1-4042-4476-4(X))*, 75e4ee5b-1790-44d7-9f9b-f53612dfdaf3); True Story of the Salem Witch Hunts. Von Zumbusch, Amelie. (YA). lib. bdg. 26.27 *(978-1-4042-4479-5(4))*, 6552d211-1cea-4aee-af1b-9bf964e4da5b); (Illus.). 24p. (gr. 2-3). 2008. 2008. Set lib. bdg. 73.80 o.p. *(978-1-4358-2540-6(3))*, PowerKids Pr.) Rosen Publishing Group, Inc., The.

Whitehurst, Susan. The Library of the Thirteen Colonies & the Lost Colony, 14 bks. Incl. Colony of New Hampshire. (YA). lib. bdg. 26.27 *(978-0-8239-5477-3(3))*, 844434d6-9da7-4509-aee0-b16f7b44c54f); Colony of Rhode Island. (J). lib. bdg. 26.27 *(978-0-8239-5476-6(5))*, 4265ab6e-9584-4fcc-a72a-df9bdd8a0442); 24p. (gr. 3-3). 1999. (Illus.). Set lib. bdg. 49.20 o.p. *(978-0-8239-7005-6(1))*, PowerKids Pr.) Rosen Publishing Group, Inc., The.

Williams, Colleen. Native American Family Life. Johnson, Troy, ed. 2013. (Native American Life Ser.: 15). 64p. (J). (gr. 5-18). 19.95 *(978-1-4222-2969-9(6))* Mason Crest.

Williams, Dinah. Terrible but True: Awful Events in American History. 2016. (ENG., Illus.). 192p. (J). (gr. 7-12). 26.19 *(978-1-4844-9747-0(3))* Scholastic, Inc.

Willis, Carrie (Hunter) & Saunders, Lucy S. Those Who Dared: Stories of Early Days in Our Country. 2011. 322p. 50.95 *(978-1-258-05701-5(8))* Literary Licensing, LLC.

Wilson, Samuel Troy. America ABC Board Book. Chan, Irene, illus. 2019. (ENG.). 32p. (J). (gr. -1 — 1). bds. 10.99 *(978-0-06-279527-4(9))*, HarperCollins) HarperCollins Pubs.

Wingate, Katherine. Political Reforms: American Citizens Gain More Control over Their Government, 1 vol. 2006. (Progressive Movement 1900 - 1920: Efforts to Reform America's New Industrial Society Ser.). (ENG., Illus.). 32p. (YA). (gr. 3-4). lib. bdg. 30.47 *(978-1-4042-0192-7(0))*, bdc4b573-f804-407b-bd4c-e4ea48be198e) Rosen Publishing Group, Inc., The.

Winter, Jonah. The Founding Fathers! Those Horse-Ridin', Fiddle-Playin', Book-Readin', Gun-Totin' Gentlemen Who Started America. Blitt, Barry, illus. 2015. (ENG.). 48p. (J). (gr. k-3). 19.99 *(978-1-4424-4274-0(3))* Simon & Schuster Children's Publishing.

Winters, Kay. Voices from the Underground Railroad. Day, Larry, illus. 2018. 48p. (J). (gr. 2-4). 18.99 *(978-0-8037-4092-1(1))*, Dial Bks) Penguin Young Readers Group.

Wiseman, Blaine. Baseball. 2010. (Record Breakers Ser.). (Illus.). 24p. (YA). (gr. 3-6). lib. bdg. 27.13 *(978-1-61690-109-7(8))*; (J). (gr. 4-6). pap. 12.95 *(978-1-61690-110-3(1))* Weigl Pubs., Inc.

Wolfson, Evelyn. Wayland A-Z: A Dictionary of Then & Now. Wolfson, Evelyn, ed. 2004. per. 15.00 *(978-0-9762756-0-2(0))* Wayland Historical Society.

Woods, Bob. Smokin' Muscle Cars, 1 vol. 2013. (Fast Wheels! Ser.). (ENG.). 48p. (gr. 4-6). 30.60 *(978-1-62285-090-7(4))*, 47275a78-b32d-486a-a3ad-e52286a28859) Enslow Publishing, LLC.

Wooster, Patricia. Show Me the United States: My First Picture Encyclopedia, 1 vol. 2013. (My First Picture Encyclopedias Ser.). (ENG.). 32p. (J). (gr. -1-2). 27.99 *(978-1-4765-0117-8(3))* A+ Bk. Publishing.

Working Americans 1880-1999, 5 vols., 5. 2003. 675.00 *(978-1-59237-034-4(9))* Grey Hse. Publishing.

World Almanac Puzzler Deck for Kids: U. S. History (BoMC) World Almanac U. S. History, 9-11. 2007. 9.95 *(978-0-8118-6241-7(0))* Chronicle Bks. LLC.

Young, Jeff C. Albert Pujols: A Baseball Star Who Cares, 1 vol. 2014. (Sports Stars Who Care Ser.). (ENG.). 48p. (gr. 3-3). pap. 11.53 *(978-1-4644-0399-6(6))*, a026f57a-8b4f-46b7-9be3-ca1d12bf398a, Enslow Elementary) Enslow Publishing, LLC.

Zehnder, Christopher. From Sea to Shining Sea: The Story of America. 2003. (ENG., Illus.). 360p. (J). (gr. 4-11). 65.00 *(978-0-89870-961-2(X))* Ignatius Pr.

Zeman, Anne & Kelly, Kate. Everything You Need to Know about American History Homework. 2011. (Illus.). 152p. (J). pap. *(978-0-545-37471-2(5))* Scholastic, Inc.

Ziefert, Harriet. Use Isbn 1593541627. 2006. (J). 15.95 *(978-1-59354-094-4(9))* Blue Apple Bks.

Zinn, Howard. A Young People's History of the United States, Volume 1 Vol. 1: Columbus to the Spanish-American War. 2007. (Illus.). 224p. (YA). (gr. 5-10). 16.95 *(978-1-58322-759-6(8))*, Triangle Square) Seven Stories Pr.

—A Young People's History of the United States, Volume 2: Class Struggle to the War on Terror. 2. 2007. (Illus.). 240p. (YA). (gr. 5-10). 17.95 *(978-1-58322-760-2(1))*, Triangle Square) Seven Stories Pr.

Zocchi, Judy. In the United States. Brodie, Neale, illus. 2005. (Global Adventures II Ser.). 32p. (J). pap. 10.95 *(978-1-59646-172-7(1))*; lib. bdg. 21.65 *(978-1-59646-085-0(7))* Dingles & Co.

—In the United States/en los Estados Unidos. Brodie, Neale, illus. 2005. (Global Adventures II Ser.).Tr. of En los Estados Unidos. (ENG & SPA.). 32p. (J). pap. 10.95 *(978-1-59646-174-1(8))*; lib. bdg. 21.65 *(978-1-59646-086-7(5))* Dingles & Co.

Zschock, Martha. Hello, America! 2012. (Hello Ser.). (ENG., Illus.). 16p. (J). (gr. -1-k). bds. 9.99 *(978-1-933212-88-3(8))*, Commonwealth Editions) Applewood Bks.

4-book Set - Group 2, 8 vols. 2005. (Kaleidoscope: Government Ser.). (ENG., Illus.). 48p. (gr. 4-4). lib. bdg. 130.56 *(978-0-7614-1597-8(1))*, f3fabefb-18f8-46c5-9e62-59c4aa82456a, Cavendish Square) Cavendish Square Publishing LLC.

5-book Set, 10 vols. 2005. (Hands-On History Ser.). (ENG., Illus.). 48p. (gr. 3-3). lib. bdg. 170.35 *(978-0-7614-1600-5(5))*, a0a19a9e-8223-4a71-a829-fbc453956ff4, Cavendish Square) Cavendish Square Publishing LLC.

The 50 States. Date not set. (Illus.). 32p. (J). 3.98 *(978-0-7525-9870-3(8))* Parragon, Inc.

UNITED STATES—HISTORY—CHRONOLOGY

Englar, Mary. An Illustrated Timeline of U. S. Presidents, 1 vol. Epstein, Len, illus. 2012. (Visual Timelines in History Ser.). (ENG.). 32p. (J). (gr. 2-4). pap. 7.49 *(978-1-4048-7254-7(X))*, 118199); lib. bdg. 29.32 *(978-1-4048-7161-8(6))*, 117156) Capstone. (Picture Window Bks.).

Time Chart of American History: A Chronological History of the United States. 2014. (Illus.). (J). *(978-1-4351-5393-6(6))* Metro Bks.

Wooster, Patricia. An Illustrated Timeline of U. S. States, 1 vol. Morgan, Rick, illus. 2011. (Visual Timelines in History Ser.). (ENG.). 32p. (J). (gr. 2-4). pap. 7.49 *(978-1-4048-7020-8(2))*, 116800, Picture Window Bks.) Capstone.

UNITED STATES—HISTORY—DICTIONARIES

Gale Cengage Learning Staff, ed. Junior Worldmark Encyclopedia of the States: 4 Volume Set, 4 vols. 6th ed. 2013. (ENG.). 1260p. E-Book, E-Book 307.00 *(978-1-4144-9864-5(0))* Cengage Gale.

Gale Encyclopedia US Hist: Bus, 2 Vol. 2007. 220.00 *(978-1-4144-3126-0(0))* Cengage Gale.

Gale Encyclopedia US Hist: Fam, 2 Vol. 2007. 220.00 *(978-1-4144-3122-2(8))* Cengage Gale.

Gale Encyclopedia US Hist: Sci Tech, 2 Vol. 2007. 220.00 *(978-1-4144-3110-9(4))* Cengage Gale.

Hermsen, Sarah & Benson, Sonia. U-X-L Encyclopedia of U. S. History, 8 vols., Vol. 10. Baker, Lawrence W., ed. rev. ed. 2008. (U-X-L Encyclopedia of U. S. History Ser.). (ENG.). 1871p. (YA). (gr. 6-8). 807.00 *(978-1-4144-3043-0(4))*, UXL) Cengage Gale.

National Geographic Kids. United States Encyclopedia: America's People, Places, & Events. 2015. (Illus.). 272p. (J). (gr. 3-7). 24.99 *(978-1-4263-2092-7(2))*, National Geographic Kids) Disney Publishing Worldwide.

UNITED STATES—HISTORY—DRAMA

Fredericks, Anthony D. American Folklore, Legends, & Tall Tales for Readers Theatre, 1 vol. 2008. (Readers Theatre Ser.). (ENG.). 156p. pap. 45.00 *(978-1-59158-734-7(4))*, 900308612, Libraries Unlimited) ABC-CLIO, LLC.

GLOBE. Eight Plays of U.S. History. 2012. (ENG., Illus.). vi, 201p. (J). (gr. 6-12). pap. 15.50 *(978-0-8359-1374-4(0))*, GLOBE) Savvas Learning Co.

Twain, Mark, pseud. Huckleberry Finn, 1 vol. 2009. (Foundation Classics Ser.). (ENG., Illus.). 56p. (J). (gr. 5-5). lib. bdg. 32.60 *(978-1-60754-541-5(1))*, 4d4dddd6-7cff-441f-ab0a-6c6f08972d2a, Windmill Bks.) Rosen Publishing Group, Inc., The.

UNITED STATES—HISTORY, ECONOMIC

see United States—Economic Conditions

UNITED STATES—HISTORY—FICTION

Adler, David A. Mama Played Baseball. O'Leary, Chris, illus. 2003. (ENG.). 32p. (J). (gr. -1-3). 16.00 *(978-0-15-202196-2(5))*, 1192100, Clarion Bks.) HarperCollins Pubs.

Atamer, Billie. Banjo Billy & the River Rat Kids. 2009. 130p. pap. 7.99 *(978-1-61667-004-7(5))* Raider Publishing International.

Babson, Jane F. A Story of Us: The Dolls' History of People of the United States. Babson, Jane F., illus. 2003. (Illus.). 56p. (J). (gr. 4-5). 10.95 *(978-0-940787-03-2(2))* Winstead Pr., Ltd.

Bain, Michelle. The Adventures of Thumbs up Johnnie Thumbs up to Red, White & Blue! Thumbs up to Red, White & Blue! Lizana, Lorenzo, illus. 2007. 48p. (J). 14.95 *(978-0-9795832-2-3(5))* Pixie Stuff LLC.

Barone, Michelle. Out of the Ordinary. 2004. (Adventures in History Ser.). (Illus.). 120p. (J). pap. *(978-1-932663-08-2(8))* History Compass, LLC.

Bartelme, Elizabeth. Simon Brute & the Western Adventure. 2012. 132p. pap. 12.95 *(978-0-9831800-8-1(3))* Hillside Education.

Birtha, Becky. Lucky Beans. Tadgell, Nicole, illus. 2012. (J). 34.28 *(978-1-61913-129-3(3))* Weigl Pubs., Inc.

Blos, Joan W. Letters from the Corrugated Castle: A Novel of Gold Rush California, 1850-1852. 2007. (ENG., Illus.). 320p. (J). (gr. 5-9). 17.99 *(978-0-689-87077-4(9))* Simon & Schuster, Inc.

Buckey, Sarah. Marie-Grace & the Orphans, 3. Kornacki, Christine, illus. 2011. (American Girl Mysteries Ser.). (ENG.). 104p. (J). (gr. 2-4). pap. 21.19 *(978-1-59369-654-2(X))* American Girl Publishing, Inc.

Call me. 2003. (J). pap. 2.25 *(978-0-590-33766-3(1))* Scholastic, Inc.

Clark, Betsy Huhn. Lizzie's Extraordinary Adventure. 2006. (Illus.). 24p. (J). 9.99 *(978-1-4276-0116-2(X))* Aardvark Global Publishing.

Columbia River Stories. 2007. (J). per. 15.00 *(978-0-9792207-0-8(X))* Earth Arts NW.

Connors, Faith Raymond. Love, Midgie. Connors, Tracy D., ed. 2008. (ENG., Illus.). 308p. pap. 12.95 *(978-0-9640138-1-0(9))*, 9780964013810) BelleAire Pr.

Cooney, Caroline B. The Ransom of Mercy Carter. 2011. (ENG.). 256p. (YA). (gr. 7-7). 8.99 *(978-0-385-74046-3(8))*, Ember) Random Hse. Children's Bks.

Davies, Jacqueline. Tricking the Tallyman. Schindler, S. D., illus. 2014. 40p. (J). (gr. k-3). 7.99 *(978-0-385-75519-1(8))*, Dragonfly Bks.) Random Hse. Children's Bks.

Deutsch, Stacia & Cohon, Rhody. Sacagawea's Strength. Wenzel, David, illus. 2006. (Blast to the Past Ser.: 5). (ENG.). 128p. (J). (gr. 2-5). pap. 6.99 *(978-1-4169-1270-5(3))*, Simon & Schuster/Paula Wiseman Bks.) Simon & Schuster/Paula Wiseman Bks.

Doyle, Bill. Betrayed! The 1977 Journal of Zeke Moorie. 4th ed. 2006. (Crime Through Time Ser.: 4). (ENG., Illus.). 144p. (J). (gr. 3-7). per. 10.99 *(978-0-316-05741-7(X))* Little, Brown Bks. for Young Readers.

—Trapped! The 2031 Journal of Otis Fitzmorgan. 6th ed. 2006. (Crime Through Time Ser.: 6). (ENG., Illus.). 144p. (J). (gr. 3-7). per. 10.99 *(978-0-316-05754-7(1))* Little, Brown Bks. for Young Readers.

Ernst, Kathleen. Caroline Takes a Chance, 6. 2012. (American Girls Collection: Caroline Stories Ser.). (ENG., Illus.). 104p. (J). (gr. 2-4). pap. 21.19 *(978-1-59369-888-1(7))* American Girl Publishing, Inc.

Flaherty, Mildred. The Great Saint Patrick's Day Flood. 2004. (Illus.). 104p. (J). pap. *(978-0-9711835-8-2(9))* Local History Co., The.

Fleming, Candace. Imogene's Last Stand. Carpenter, Nancy, illus. 2014. 40p. (J). (gr. -1-3). 7.99 *(978-0-385-38654-8(0))*, Dragonfly Bks.) Random Hse. Children's Bks.

Forbes, Esther Hoskins. Johnny Tremain: A Newbery Award Winner. 2011. (ENG., Illus.). 320p. (J). (gr. 3-7). pap. 8.99 *(978-0-547-61432-8(2))*, 1464852, Clarion Bks.) HarperCollins Pubs.

Furtney, Charles S. Tryconnel: An Antebellum Adventure along the C & O Canal. 2004. (Illus.). iii, 156p. (J). pap. *(978-0-9711835-3-7(8))* Local History Co., The.

Gaillard, Frye. Go South to Freedom. Rush, Anne Kent, illus. 2016. (ENG.). 72p. (J). 17.95 *(978-1-58838-316-7(4))*, 8799, NewSouth Bks.) NewSouth, Inc.

Gratz, Alan M. The Brooklyn Nine. 2010. 320p. (J). (gr. 3-7). 8.99 *(978-0-14-241544-3(8))*, Puffin Books) Penguin Young Readers Group.

Gunderson, Jessica & Collins, Terry. American Graphic. Kinsella, Pat & Byers, Michael, illus. 2012. (American Graphic Ser.). (ENG.). 32p. (gr. 3-4). pap. 477.00 *(978-1-4296-8478-1(X))*, Capstone Pr.) Capstone.

Haislip, Phyllis Hall. Divided Loyalties: A Revolutionary War Fifer's Story. 2005. (Illus.). 212p. (J). (gr. 4-7). per. 7.95 *(978-1-57249-369-8(0))*, White Mane Kids) White Mane Publishing Co., Inc.

Hancock, H. Irving. Uncle Sam's Boys with Pershing's Troops. 2006. 27.95 *(978-1-4218-2944-9(4))*; pap. 12.95 *(978-1-4218-3044-5(2))* 1st World Publishing, Inc.

Hannah-Jones, Nikole & Watson, Renée. The 1619 Project: Born on the Water. Smith, Nikkolas, illus. 2021. 48p. (J). (gr. 2-5). 18.99 *(978-0-593-30735-9(6))*, Kokila) Penguin Young Readers Group.

Hayhurst, James L. The Adventures of Mercury Lane: Bad Commandments, Book No. 1. 2008. (Illus.). 212p. (YA). pap. 13.95 *(978-0-9729380-1-3(X))*, Parascension Pr.) Parascension, Inc.

Hayhurst/Parascension Press, James/Lyle. The Adventures of Mercury Lane: Bad Commandments, Book No.1. 2008. (Illus.). 212p. (YA). lib. bdg. 21.95 *(978-0-615-18212-4(7))*, Parascension Pr.) Parascension, Inc.

Hedstrom-Page, Deborah. From Settlement to City with Benjamin Franklin. Martinez, Sergio, illus. 2007. (My American Journey Ser.). 84p. (J). (gr. 3-9). 9.99 *(978-0-8054-3267-1(1))* B&H Publishing Group.

Heibel, Dorothy. Message for a Spy. 2004. (Illus.). 94p. (J). pap. *(978-1-932663-07-5(X))* History Compass, LLC.

Hernandez, Natalie Nelson. Mapmakers of the Western Trails: Adventures with John Chrles Fremont, 3 bks. 2003. (Illus.). 130p. (J). per. 10.95 *(978-1-885852-31-1(2))* James Stevenson Pub.

Hill, Joyce. A Penny in My Pocket. 2007. 220p. 27.95 *(978-0-9795818-0-9(X))*; pap. 14.95 *(978-0-9795818-1-6(8))* Mushgush Pr.

History Speaks: Picture Books Plus Reader's Theater, 12 vols., Set. Incl. Ellen Craft's Escape from Slavery. Moore, Cathy. Braught, Mark, illus. (J). 2010. lib. bdg. 27.93 *(978-0-7613-5875-6(7))*; George Washington & the Story of the U. S. Constitution. Ransom, Candice. Reeves, Jeni, illus. 2011. 27.93 *(978-0-7613-5877-0(3))*; Little Rock Nine Stand up for Their Rights. Lucas, Eileen. Gustavson, Adam, illus. 2011. lib. bdg. 27.93 *(978-0-7613-5874-9(9))*; 48p. (gr. 2-4)., Millbrook Pr. 2011. Set lib. bdg. 335.16 *(978-0-7613-5100-9(0))* Lerner Publishing Group.

Hoobler, Dorothy & Hoobler, Thomas. The Century Kids, 10 vols. Hoffman, Robin, illus. Incl. 1940s: Secrets. (J). 2001. lib. bdg. 22.90 *(978-0-7613-1604-6(3))*; 1950's: Music. (J). 2001. lib. bdg. 22.90 *(978-0-7613-1605-3(1))*; 1960's: Rebels. (J). 2001. lib. bdg. 22.90 *(978-0-7613-1606-0(X))*; 1970's: Arguments. 2002. lib. bdg. 22.90 *(978-0-7613-1607-7(8))*; 1980s: Earthsong. 2002. lib. bdg. 22.90 *(978-0-7613-1608-4(6))*; 1990s: Families. 2002. lib. bdg. 22.90 *(978-0-7613-1609-1(4))*; 160p. (gr. 5-8). (Illus.). 2004. 229.00 *(978-0-7613-2985-5(4))*, Twenty-First Century Bks.) Lerner Publishing Group.

Hughes, Barbara. Then & Now. (Livewire Ser.). 192p. (YA). (gr. 6-9). pap. 8.95 *(978-0-7043-4930-8(2))* Women's Pr., Ltd., The GBR. Dist: Trafalgar Square Publishing.

Hunt, Wayne. Zack & the Validators: Good As Gold. 2011. 138p. pap. 19.99 *(978-1-4653-5816-5(1))* Xlibris Corp.

Igneri, David S. The Boy & Girl Who Hated History. Wigley, Audrey Watson, illus. 2009. 44p. pap. 24.95 *(978-1-61546-828-7(5))* America Star Bks.

Ingold, Jeanette. Hitch. 2006. (ENG., Illus.). 288p. (YA). (gr. 7-12). pap. 9.99 *(978-0-15-205619-3(X))*, 1196901, Clarion Bks.) HarperCollins Pubs.

Kennedy Center, The. Chasing George Washington. Hoyt, Ard, illus. 2011. (ENG.). 80p. (J). (gr. 2-5). pap. 5.99 *(978-1-4169-4861-2(9))*, Simon & Schuster Bks. For Young Readers) Simon & Schuster Bks. For Young Readers.

Kinsey, Natalie. Gifts from the Sea. Pederson, Judy, illus. 2005. 128p. (J). (gr. 3-7). 5.99 *(978-0-440-41970-9(0))*, Yearling) Random Hse. Children's Bks.

Krull, Kathleen. Hillary Rodham Clinton: Dreams Taking Flight. Bates, Amy June, illus. 2015. (ENG.). 48p. (J). (gr. k-5). 17.99 *(978-1-4814-5113-0(8))*, Simon & Schuster Bks. For Young Readers) Simon & Schuster Bks. For Young Readers.

LaFaye, A. Walking Home to Rosie Lee, 1 vol. Shepherd, Keith D., illus. 2019. (ENG.). 32p. (J). (gr. 1-6). pap. 11.95 *(978-1-941026-57-1(5))*, 23353382, Cinco Puntos Press) Lee & Low Bks., Inc.

Lefevre-Garros. The Wright Brothers. 2009. (ENG., Illus.). 48p. pap. 11.95 *(978-1-905460-73-1(2))* CineBook GBR. Dist: National Bk. Network.

Maccoll, Michaela. The Lost Ones. 2016. (Hidden Histories Ser.). (ENG.). 256p. (J). (gr. 4-7). 17.95 *(978-1-62091-625-4(8))*, Calkins Creek) Highlights Pr., c/o Highlights for Children, Inc.

Marlow, Susan K. Andi under the Big Top, 1 vol. 2017. (Circle C Stepping Stones Ser.: 2). (Illus.). 105p. (J). pap. 7.99 *(978-0-8254-4431-9(4))* Kregel Pubns.

Maxson, H. A. & Young, Claudia H. Tea Party at Chestertown. Kosits, Andrew, illus. 2003. (Magical History Tours Ser.). 55p. (J). per. 8.95 *(978-0-9741713-0-2(1))* Bay Oak Pubs., Ltd.

Minor, Wendell. How Big Could Your Pumpkin Grow? Minor, Wendell, illus. 2013. (Illus.). 32p. (J). (gr. -1-k). 16.99 *(978-0-399-24684-5(3))*, Nancy Paulsen Books) Penguin Young Readers Group.

Morse, William A. and & Morse, William A. And Dana Jo. Kurkle Kids: Spirit of America. 2009. 44p. pap. 16.99 *(978-1-4490-1009-6(1))* AuthorHouse.

N.C.B.L.A., creator. Our White House: Looking In, Looking Out. 2008. (ENG., Illus.). 256p. (J). (gr. 5). 29.99 *(978-0-7636-2067-7(X))* Candlewick Pr.

Nicodemus, Laura Konger. Growing up on the Farm in The 1930s' 2011. 60p. pap. 24.20 *(978-1-4269-3201-4(4))* Trafford Publishing.

Nolen, Jerdine. Calico Girl. 2019. (Penworthy Picks Middle School Ser.). (ENG.). 164p. (J). (gr. 4-5). 20.36 *(978-1-64310-939-8(1))* Penworthy Co., LLC, The.

—Calico Girl. 2018. lib. bdg. 18.40 *(978-0-606-40837-0(1))* Turtleback.

Parton, Paula. Room 17 Where History Comes Alive Book I—Indians. Parton, Paula, illus. 2007. (Illus.). 128p. per. 8.95 *(978-0-9794815-0-5(3))* Bellissima Publishing, LLC.

—Room 17 Where History Comes Alive! Book I-Indians. Parton, Paua, illus. 2007. 128p. 19.95 *(978-0-9794815-2-9(X))* Bellissima Publishing, LLC.

Pearsall, Shelley. Jump into the Sky. 2013. 352p. (J). (gr. 4-7). pap. 8.99 *(978-0-440-42140-5(3))*, Yearling) Random Hse. Children's Bks.

Pinkney, Andrea. Sojourner Truth's Step-Stomp Stride. Pinkney, Brian, illus. 2009. (ENG.). 32p. (J). (gr. 1-3). 18.99 *(978-0-7868-0767-3(9))*, Jump at the Sun) Hyperion Bks. for Children.

Polisar, Barry Louis. Stolen Man: The Story of the Amistad Rebellion. Clark, David, illus. 2007. (ENG.). 32p. (J). (gr. 2-6). per. 7.95 *(978-0-938663-50-8(X))*, a59aafb4-6286-4277-bbda-93dd15fe3126) Rainbow Morning Music Alternatives.

Rack, Charlene. The Adventures of Delaware Bear & Young George Washington. 2011. 24p. (gr. 1-2). pap. 12.79 *(978-1-4567-5681-9(8))* AuthorHouse.

Richards, J. Stuart. Hard Coal Times, Volume Two: Mules, Drivers & Spraggers, 2. 2003. (Illus.). 44p. (YA). 5.95 *(978-0-9709630-3-1(3))* Coal Hole Productions.

TUV

Riley, D. H. The Mysterians, 1 vol. 2009. 54p. pap. 16.95 *(978-1-60836-374-2(0))* America Star Bks.

Rubay, Donnell. Emma & the Oyster Pirate. 2011. 172p. pap. 13.95 *(978-1-885852-52-6(5))* James Stevenson Pub.

Sargent, Dave & Sargent, Pat. Freckles: (Flea-bitten Grey) Be Proud of Old Glory. 30 vols., Vol. 26. Lenoir, Jane, illus. 2003. (Saddle up Ser.: Vol. 26). 42p. (J). pap. 10.95 *(978-1-56763-810-3(4))*; lib. bdg. 23.60 *(978-1-56763-809-7(0))* Ozark Publishing.

Slanina, Anne Maro. Annie Mouse's Route 66 Adventure: A Photo Journal, vols. 6, vol. 5. Collins, Kelsey, illus. 2011. (ENG.). 48p. (J). pap. 14.99 *(978-0-9793379-6-3(8))* Annie Mouse Bks.

Stockton, Frank Richard. John Gayther's Garden & the Stories Told Therein. 2008. 220p. pap. 15.95 *(978-1-60664-247-4(2))* Rodgers, Alan Bks.

Sun Edit and Book Design, ed. Abraham Lincoln & the Forest of Little Pigeon Creek. 2007. (Illus.). 56p. (J). 19.95 *(978-0-9798739-0-4(8))* AmeriTales Entertainment, LLC.

Uchilla, Canchi. 1532: A Test of Courage. 2008. 108p. pap. 10.00 *(978-0-9769989-5-2(5))* Edit et Cetera Ltd.

Vail, Emily Blake. The Search for Ole Ben's Treasure. 2011. 82p. 24.99 *(978-1-4568-9874-8(4))*; pap. 15.99 *(978-1-4568-9873-1(6))* Xlibris Corp.

Varonka, Steve. Hard Coal Times: Pennsylvania Anthracite Stories, Vol. 1. 2003. (Illus.). 40p. (J). 4.72 *(978-0-9709630-2-4(5))* Coal Hole Productions.

Walters, Scott. Woman Too Young of Panther Cave. 2007. 20.95 *(978-1-934248-14-0(2))* Salem Author Services.

Watkins, Steve. On Blood Road (a Vietnam War Novel) 2018. (ENG.). 288p. (YA). (gr. 7-7). 18.99 *(978-1-338-19701-3(0),* Scholastic Pr.) Scholastic, Inc.

Weigman, Matthew. Liberty's Journey: The Story of Our Freedom. Eve, Lealand, illus. 2004. 31p. (J). 16.95 *(978-0-9747981-0-3(X))* Fahnestock Pr.

Whitby, Adele. Kay's Story 1934. 2015. (Secrets of the Manor Ser.: 6). lib. bdg. 17.20 *(978-0-606-36305-1(X))* Turtleback.

Wiggin, Kate Douglas. New Chronicles of Rebecc. 2008. 152p. (gr. 4-7). 24.95 *(978-1-60664-756-1(3))* Rodgers, Alan Bks.

Winfield, Arthur M. Rover Boys at School. 2006. pap. *(978-1-4068-3129-0(8))* Echo Library.

UNITED STATES—HISTORY, LOCAL

Benchmark Education Company, LLC Staff, compiled by. This State Is Mine & State HIST. 2005. spiral bd. 110.00 *(978-1-4108-5817-7(0))* Benchmark Education Co.

Gillis, Jennifer Blizin. Restored Villages. 2007. (Field Trips Ser.). (Illus.). 24p. (J). (gr. 2-5). lib. bdg. 27.07 *(978-1-60044-563-7(2))* Rourke Educational Media.

Herman, Debbie. From Pie Town to Yum Yum: Weird & Wacky Place Names Across the United States. Goldman, Linda Sarah, illus. 2011. (ENG.). 120p. (J). pap. 10.99 *(978-1-935279-79-2(3))* Kane Miller.

Hurtig, Jennifer. Capitals. 2008. (U. S. Sites & Symbols Ser.). (Illus.). 48p. (J). (gr. 3-5). lib. bdg. 29.05 *(978-1-59036-896-1(7))*; (gr. 4-6). pap. 10.95 *(978-1-59036-897-8(5))* Weigl Pubs., Inc.

Prior, Jennifer Overend. America's Man-Made Landmarks. rev. ed. 2014. (Social Studies: Informational Text Ser.). (ENG., Illus.). 32p. (gr. 2-4). pap. 11.99 *(978-1-4333-7370-1(X))* Teacher Created Materials, Inc.

Putnam, Jeff. National Monuments: Events & Times. 2004. (ZB Reads Trio Books). (Illus.). iii, 75p. (gr. 4-6). pap. 5.00 *(978-0-7367-1787-8(0))* Zaner-Bloser, Inc.

Stuckey, Rachel. Women in the West, 1 vol. 2015. (True History of the Wild West Ser.). (ENG., Illus.). 32p. (J). (gr. 5-5). pap. 11.00 *(978-1-4994-1181-2(2),* c3bc25fb-efc8-491d-80f8-243148908db9, PowerKids Pr.) Rosen Publishing Group, Inc., The.

UNITED STATES—HISTORY, MILITARY

America at War, 10 vols., Set. Incl. American Civil War & Reconstruction: People, Politics, & Power. Wallenfeldt, Jeffrey H., ed. 264p. (YA). lib. bdg. 52.59 *(978-1-61530-007-5(4),* caabe591-854b-4c24-a3a4-5428b6cccf32); American Revolutionary War & the War of 1812: People, Politics, & Power. Wallenfeldt, Jeffrey H. 240p. (YA). lib. bdg. 52.59 *(978-1-61530-022-8(8),* 561f6941-5903-417e-b7a2-91ced313eedc); Korean War & the Vietnam War: People, Politics, & Power. Hosch, William L. 232p. (J). lib. bdg. 52.59 *(978-1-61530-011-2(2),* ac3dd829-b1e0-46de-a740-8d1cb2c3f3af); World War I: People, Politics, & Power. Hosch, William L., ed. 240p. (YA). lib. bdg. 52.59 *(978-1-61530-013-6(9),* 2a9225aa-addc-419c-b6e7-c1a9f093d455); World War II: People, Politics, & Power. Hosch, William L. 264p. (YA). lib. bdg. 52.59 *(978-1-61530-008-2(2),* 6f99d295-8a87-4a02-be51-5ac1aca6dec4); (gr. 10-10). (America at War Ser.). (ENG., Illus.). 264p. 2010. Set lib. bdg. 262.95 *(978-1-61530-030-3(9),* 9e18dd47-8482-4795-90cf-6192d9a8499a) Rosen Publishing Group, Inc., The.

Anderson, Dale. The Civil War in the East (1861-July 1863). 1 vol. 2004. (World Almanac(r) Library of the Civil War Ser.). (ENG., Illus.). 48p. (gr. 5-8). pap. 15.05 *(978-0-8368-5591-3(4),* a8679fe7-8a42-464b-929d-fbb5c4e0806a); lib. bdg. 33.67 *(978-0-8368-5582-1(5),* ea65b134-2894-4b4a-b659-255a776186b0) Stevens, Gareth Publishing LLLP. (Gareth Stevens Secondary Library).

Asselin, Kristine Carlson. The Real Story on the Weapons & Battles of Colonial America. 2012. (Life in the American Colonies Ser.). (ENG.). 32p. (gr. 3-4). pap. 47.70 *(978-1-4296-8462-0(3),* Capstone Pr.); (J). 27.99 *(978-1-4296-6491-2(6),* 115612); (J). pap. 8.10 *(978-1-4296-7985-5(9),* 118317) Capstone.

Benge, Janet & Benge, Geoff. Heroes of History - Douglas MacArthur: What Greater Honor. 2005. (ENG., Illus.). 205p. (YA). pap. 11.99 *(978-1-932096-15-6(9))* Emerald Bks.

Braun, Eric & Doeden, Matt. You Choose: American Battles. 2018. (You Choose: American Battles Ser.). (ENG.). 112p. (J). (gr. 3-7). 138.60 *(978-1-5435-0308-1(X),* 27614, Capstone Pr.) Capstone.

Burgan, Michael. The Battle of Bunker Hill: An Interactive History Adventure. rev. ed. 2016. (You Choose: History Ser.). (ENG., Illus.). 112p. (J). (gr. 3-7). pap. 6.95 *(978-1-5157-3387-4(4),* 133374, Capstone Pr.) Capstone.

Cheatham, Mark. The Life of a Colonial Soldier, 1 vol. 2013. (Jr. Graphic Colonial America Ser.). (ENG., Illus.). 24p. (J). (gr. 2-3). pap. 11.60 *(978-1-4777-1439-3(1),* 856a9e2a-d842-4008-9543-7caf6bd62692); lib. bdg. 28.93 *(978-1-4777-1310-5(7),* f24ac1b8-8ed4-4c67-bb3c-083387a6d554) Rosen Publishing Group, Inc., The. (PowerKids Pr.).

Daniel Fernandez Memorial Center Projec. Man of Honor: The Story of Daniel Fernandez. 2009. 32p. pap. 15.49 *(978-1-4389-8338-7(7))* AuthorHouse.

Donelly, Karen. American Women Pilots of World War II, 1 vol. 2004. (American Women at War Ser.). (ENG.). 112p. (YA). (gr. 8-8). pap. 13.95 *(978-1-4358-3274-9(4),* 5d9f859d-ebd7-4c4b-9c01-4e9010f10a6f) Rosen Publishing Group, Inc., The.

Gallagher, Jim. US-Led Wars in Iraq, 1991-Present, Vol. 11. Musteen, Jason R., ed. 2015. (Major U. S. Historical Wars Ser.). (Illus.). 64p. (J). (gr. 7). lib. bdg. 23.95 *(978-1-4222-3358-0(8))* Mason Crest.

Gonzales, Doreen. The Secret of the Manhattan Project: Stories in American History, 1 vol. 2012. (Stories in American History Ser.). (ENG., Illus.). 128p. (gr. 5-6). pap. 13.88 *(978-1-4644-0024-7(5),* ff461dec-c88b-420a-be68-b2862902b529) Enslow Publishing, LLC.

Hogue, Richard, Sr. We Were the Third Herd. 2003. per. 17.95 *(978-0-9722264-0-0(0))* Richlyn Publishing.

Honders, Christine. Buffalo Soldiers, 1 vol. 2015. (Heroes of Black History Ser.). (ENG., Illus.). 32p. (J). (gr. 3-4). pap. 11.50 *(978-1-4824-2900-8(4),* a7c2de3c-668f-4489-9767-3188a6dd0741) Stevens, Gareth Publishing LLLP.

Janeczko, Paul B. The Dark Game: True Spy Stories from Invisible Ink to CIA Moles. 2012. (ENG.). 256p. (YA). (gr. 5-9). pap. 11.99 *(978-0-7636-6066-6(3))* Candlewick Pr.

Krick, Robert K. The Civil War: Gettysburg & Other Eastern Battles, 1863-1865, 1 vol. 2010. (Civil War: Essential Histories Ser.). (ENG.). 96p. (YA). (gr. 10-10). lib. bdg. 38.47 *(978-1-4488-0388-0(8),* 765b2e17-95e9-42c7-af02-68b565dec5a7) Rosen Publishing Group, Inc., The.

The Life of a Colonial Soldier. 2013. (Jr. Graphic Colonial America Ser.). 24p. (J). (gr. 3-6). pap. 63.60 *(978-1-4777-1440-9(5),* PowerKids Pr.) Rosen Publishing Group, Inc., The.

Looney, Michael. Battle of the Bulge Vol. III: The Untold Story of Hofen. 2005. 179p. 29.95 *(978-0-9700567-4-0(5))* Victory WW 2 Publishing Ltd.

Lusted, Marcia Amidon. African Americans in the Military. 2012. (J). pap. *(978-1-4222-2392-5(2))* Mason Crest.

—African Americans in the Military. Hill, Marc Lamont, ed. 2012. (Major Black Contributions from Emancipation to Civil Rights Ser.). 64p. (J). (gr. 5). 22.95 *(978-1-4222-2379-6(5))* Mason Crest.

Margulies, Philip. A Timeline of the Continental Army, 1 vol. 2004. (Timelines of American History Ser.). (ENG., Illus.). 32p. (gr. 4-4). lib. bdg. 29.13 *(978-0-8239-4544-3(8),* 2befd372-f645-4098-b89e-8b0badbc4a6e, Rosen Reference) Rosen Publishing Group, Inc., The.

McCallum Staats, Ann. Women Heroes of the US Army: Remarkable Soldiers from the American Revolution to Today. 2019. (Women of Action Ser.: 23). (ENG., Illus.). 240p. (YA). (gr. 7). 19.99 *(978-0-914091-24-0(7))* Chicago Review Pr., Inc.

McPherson, Stephanie Sammartino. Douglas MacArthur. 2005. (History Maker Bios Ser.). (Illus.). 48p. (J). 26.60 *(978-0-8225-2434-2(1))* Lerner Publishing Group.

Micklos, John & Micklos, John, Jr. Washington's Crossing the Delaware & the Winter at Valley Forge: Through Primary Sources, 1 vol. 2013. (American Revolution Through Primary Sources Ser.). (ENG., Illus.). 48p. (J). (gr. 4-6). 27.93 *(978-0-7660-4132-5(8),* 22bf5158-e47c-42c7-9d03-25ec224712b2) Enslow Publishing, LLC.

O'Maley, Elizabeth. Bones on the Ground. 2014. (J). *(978-0-87195-362-9(5))* Indiana Historical Society.

O'Neill, Robert John & Gallagher, Gary W. The Civil War: Bull Run & Other Eastern Battles, 1861-May 1863, 1 vol. 2010. (Civil War: Essential Histories Ser.). (ENG.). 96p. (YA). (gr. 10-10). lib. bdg. 38.47 *(978-1-4488-0387-3(X),* 79b08efd-49fb-4aa5-9c67-3924169a04bb) Rosen Publishing Group, Inc., The.

Orozco, Mike. The War-Time Paragons. 2011. (ENG.). 74p. pap. 15.99 *(978-1-4535-8533-7(8))* Xlibris Corp.

Perritano, John. Medal of Honor. 2018. (Red Rhino Nonfiction Ser.). lib. bdg. 20.80 *(978-0-606-41253-7(0))* Turtleback.

Pugh, Harry F. & PERKOWSKI, Gary. U. S. Special Forces Group Insignia (Post 1975) 2004. (Elite Insignia Guides Ser.). (YA). pap. *(978-0-9633231-8-7(0))* C&D Enterprises.

Raum, Elizabeth, et al. True War Stories: Personal Accounts of History's Greatest Conflicts. Kinsella, Pat et al, illus. 2017. (J). *(978-1-4914-1965-6(2))* Capstone.

Ross, Thomas A. Privileges of War: A Good Story of American Service in South Vietnam. 2004. (Illus.). 356p. 24.95 *(978-0-9754859-0-3(3),* 9005710) American Heritage Publishing.

Sabin, Edwin L. Boys' Book of Border Battles: The True Tales Behind America's Greatest Battles of the 18th & 19th Centuries. 2013. (ENG., Illus.). 352p. pap. 14.95 *(978-1-62087-158-4(0),* 620158) Skyhorse Publishing Co., Inc.

Snyder, Sally. Hold the Fort. Snyder, Sally, illus. 2003. (Illus.). 45p. (J). 20.00 *(978-1-882203-99-4(2))* Orange Frazer Pr.

Sorrels, Roy. The Legend of the Alamo: Stories in American History, 1 vol. 2012. (Stories in American History Ser.). (ENG., Illus.). 128p. (gr. 5-6). pap. 13.88 *(978-1-4644-0022-3(9),* 7f84d713-c7c3-4352-828d-9022f51a1bee) Enslow Publishing, LLC.

South, Victor. America in the 20th Century (1913/1999) 2018. (J). *(978-1-5105-3610-4(8))* SmartBook Media, Inc.

Stanley, George E. George S. Patton: War Hero. Henderson, Meryl, illus. 2007. (Childhood of Famous Americans Ser.). (ENG.). 192p. (J). (gr. 3-7). pap. 7.99 *(978-1-4169-1547-8(8),* Simon & Schuster/Paula Wiseman Bks.) Simon & Schuster/Paula Wiseman Bks.

Stewart, Gail B. Fighting for Freedom: Blacks in the American Military, 1 vol. 2006. (Lucent Library of Black History Ser.). (ENG., Illus.). 104p. (gr. 7-7). lib. bdg. 36.43 *(978-1-59018-952-8(3),* f3669212-867e-4515-80d6-d2b72a3b9351, Lucent Pr.) Greenhaven Publishing LLC.

Strange, Matthew. America at War: Military Conflicts, Home & Abroad in the 1800s. 2009. (Daily Life in America in the 1800s Ser.). 64p. (YA). (gr. 7-18). lib. bdg. 22.95 *(978-1-4222-1778-8(7))* Mason Crest.

Streissguth, Tom. The Battle of Antietam, 1 vol. 2016. (Essential Library of the Civil War Ser.). (ENG., Illus.). 112p. (J). (gr. 8-12). lib. bdg. 41.36 *(978-1-68078-272-1(X),* 21699, Essential Library) ABDO Publishing Co.

Sutcliffe, Jane. George S. Patton JR. 2006. (History Maker Bios Ser.). (Illus.). 48p. (J). (gr. 3-7). lib. bdg. 26.60 *(978-0-8225-2436-6(8),* Lerner Pubns.) Lerner Publishing Group.

U. S. Military [Scholastic]. 2010. (Military Branches Ser.). pap. 2.08 *(978-1-4296-5073-1(7),* Capstone Pr.) Capstone.

The United States at War, 12 vols. 2016. (United States at War Ser.). (ENG.). 128p. (gr. 6-6). lib. bdg. 233.58 *(978-0-7660-7501-6(X),* 5928305f-f6d7-4212-b804-105374b805d4) Enslow Publishing, LLC.

Welch, Catherine A. George C. Marshall. (History Maker Bios Ser.). 48p. (J). 2006. (Illus.). (gr. 3-7). lib. bdg. 26.60 *(978-0-8225-2435-9(X),* Lerner Pubns.) 2005. pap. 8.95 *(978-0-8225-5460-8(7))* Lerner Publishing Group.

Wilson, Patrick. Survival First Aid. Carney, John, ed. 2014. (Extreme Survival in the Military Ser.: 12). (Illus.). 64p. (J). (gr. 7-18). lib. bdg. 23.95 *(978-1-4222-3086-2(4))* Mason Crest.

Yasuda, Anita. The 12 Most Amazing American Battles. 2015. (Amazing America Ser.). (ENG., Illus.). 32p. (J). (gr. 3-6). 32.80 *(978-1-63235-006-0(8),* 11545, 12-Story Library) Bookstaves, LLC.

UNITED STATES—HISTORY, NAVAL

Baum, L. Frank. Navy Alphabet Book. 2004. (Applewood Bks.). (ENG., Illus.). 60p. (gr. -1-3). per. 14.95 *(978-1-55709-570-1(1))* Applewood Bks.

Blumberg, Rhoda. Commodore Perry in the Land of the Shogun. 2003. (Illus.). 144p. (gr. 3-7). 20.00 *(978-0-7569-1440-0(X))* Perfection Learning Corp.

—Commodore Perry in the Land of the Shogun: A Newbery Honor Award Winner. 2003. (ENG., Illus.). 144p. (J). (gr. 3-18). pap. 9.99 *(978-0-06-008625-1(4),* HarperCollins) HarperCollins Pubs.

Hobbs, Richard R. Naval Science 2 2: Maritime History, Leadership & Nautical Sciences for the NJROTC Student. 2nd ed. 2006. (ENG., Illus.). 360p. 36.95 *(978-1-59114-366-6(7),* P221125) Naval Institute Pr.

Kevin, McDonald. Tin Can Sailors Save the Day. 2015. (Illus.). 86p. (J). pap. 10.95 *(978-1-55571-786-5(1),* Paloma Bks.) L & R Publishing, LLC.

Thornton, Jeremy. The Birth of the American Navy. 2009. (Building America's Democracy Ser.). 24p. (gr. 3-3). 42.50 *(978-1-61511-765-9(2),* PowerKids Pr.) Rosen Publishing Group, Inc., The.

Wittner, David G. Commodore Matthew Perry & the Perry Expedition to Japan. 2009. (Library of American Lives & Times Ser.). 112p. (gr. 5-5). 69.20 *(978-1-60853-474-6(X))* Rosen Publishing Group, Inc., The.

UNITED STATES—HISTORY—POETRY

Dyan, Penelope. Gold Rush! a Kid's Guide to Techatticup Gold Mine, Eldorado Canyon, Nevad. Weigand, John D., photos by. 2010. (Illus.). 48p. pap. 11.95 *(978-1-935630-11-1(3))* Bellissima Publishing, LLC.

—Happy Birthday Usa! Dyan, Penelope, illus. 2010. (Illus.). 32p. pap. 11.95 *(978-1-935630-15-9(6))* Bellissima Publishing, LLC.

Grady, Cynthia. I Lay My Stitches Down: Poems of American Slavery. Wood, Michele, illus. 2012. (ENG.). 34p. (YA). 17.00 *(978-0-8028-5386-8(2),* Eerdmans Bks For Young Readers) Eerdmans, William B. Publishing Co.

Hopkins, Lee Bennett, ed. America at War: Poems Selected by Lee Bennett Hopkins. Alcorn, Stephen, illus. 2008. (ENG.). 96p. (J). (gr. 3-7). 24.99 *(978-1-4169-1832-5(9),* McElderry, Margaret K. Bks.) McElderry, Margaret K. Bks.

Longfellow, Henry. Paul Revere's Ride: The Landlord's Tale. Santore, Charles, illus. 2003. 40p. (J). lib. bdg. 17.89 *(978-0-06-623747-3(5))* HarperCollins Pubs.

Longfellow, Henry Wadsworth. Paul Revere's Ride. 2011. (ENG., Illus.). 32p. (gr. 3-6). 26.19 *(978-1-56397-799-2(0))* Highlights Pr., c/o Highlights for Children, Inc.

Minor, Wendell. America the Beautiful. Minor, Wendell, illus. 2020. (Illus.). 48p. (J). (gr. -1-2). 18.99 *(978-1-62354-121-7(2))* Charlesbridge Publishing, Inc.

Voorhees, Sue. I'm Your Very Own Flag. 2006. (J). per. 12.50 *(978-0-9764167-4-6(3))* Old Soldier Publishing.

UNITED STATES—HISTORY, POLITICAL

see United States—Politics and Government

UNITED STATES—HISTORY—SOURCES

American Voices - Group 2, 10 vols., Set. 2006. (American Voices From Ser.). (ENG.). (J). (gr. 6-6). 206.05 *(978-0-7614-1692-0(7),* b3f9dec7-c65b-4be0-b296-da87bf3767f2, Cavendish Square) Cavendish Square Publishing LLC.

Clay, Kathryn. Introducing Primary Sources. 2017. (Introducing Primary Sources Ser.). (ENG., Illus.). 32p. (J). (gr. -1-2). 275.85 *(978-1-5157-6357-4(9),* 26459, Capstone Pr.) Capstone.

Colonial Life, 5 bks., Set. Incl. Cities & Towns. Stefoff, Rebecca. 96p. lib. bdg. 165.00 *(978-0-7656-8109-6(9),* Y181735); Daily Living. Hinds, Kathryn. 96p. lib. bdg. 180.00 *(978-0-7656-8110-2(2),* Y181908); Exploration & Settlement. Stefoff, Rebecca. 96p. lib. bdg. 180.00 *(978-0-7656-8108-9(0),* Y182272); Government. Kelly, Martin & Kelly, Melissa. 96p. lib. bdg. 180.00 *(978-0-7656-8112-6(9),* Y182476); Trade & Commerce. Altman, Linda Jacobs. 98p. lib. bdg. 200.00 *(978-0-7656-8111-9(0),* Y184849); (C). (gr. 6-18). (ENG., Illus.). 96p. 2007. Set lib. bdg. 165.00 *(978-0-7656-8107-2(2),* Y181691) Routledge.

Doyle, Abby Badach. Diaries & Autobiographies Throughout American History. 2019. (Journey to the Past: Investigating Primary Sources Ser.). (ENG.). 32p. (gr. 4-5). 63.00 *(978-1-5382-4035-9(1))* Stevens, Gareth Publishing LLLP.

Flanagan, Timothy. Reconstruction: A Primary Source History of the Struggle to Unite the North & South after the Civil War, 1 vol. 2004. (Primary Sources in American History Ser.). (ENG., Illus.). 64p. (J). (gr. 5-8). lib. bdg. 37.13 *(978-1-4042-0177-4(7),* 154ba385-b204-43ac-81c4-6fc934a58a2e) Rosen Publishing Group, Inc., The.

Hakim, Joy. A History of US: Sourcebook & Index: A History of US Book Eleven. 2nd rev. ed. 2007. (History of US Ser.: 11). (ENG., Illus.). 352p. (gr. 4-7). per. 15.95 *(978-0-19-532725-0(X))* Oxford Univ. Pr., Inc.

Keenan, Sheila. O, Say Can You See? America's Symbols, Landmarks, & Important Words. Boyajian, Ann, illus. 2007. (ENG.). 64p. (J). (gr. -1-3). pap. 7.99 *(978-0-439-59360-1(3),* Scholastic Nonfiction) Scholastic, Inc.

Primary Sources of Life in the New American Nation. 2004. (Primary Source Big Bookstm Ser.). (ENG.). 24p. (gr. 4-8). 43.95 *(978-0-8239-4602-0(9))* Rosen Publishing Group, Inc., The.

Stefoff, Rebecca. Colonial Life, 1 vol. Kubinyi, Laszlo, illus. 2003. (American Voices From Ser.). (ENG.). 160p. (gr. 6-6). 41.21 *(978-0-7614-1205-2(0),* 23e5579e-62bb-4199-9af2-3fe85a1892ab) Cavendish Square Publishing LLC.

Stites, Bill. Democracy: A Primary Source Analysis, 1 vol. 2004. (Primary Sources of Political Systems Ser.). (ENG., Illus.). 64p. (YA). (gr. 5-8). lib. bdg. 37.13 *(978-0-8239-4518-4(9),* 8434ef5f-7a20-4e91-9d32-c046d6203e48) Rosen Publishing Group, Inc., The.

Tait, Leia. Primary Sources. 2007. (Social Studies Essential Skills Ser.). (Illus.). 24p. (J). lib. bdg. 24.45 *(978-1-59036-763-6(4))*; (gr. 4-7). per. 8.95 *(978-1-59036-764-3(2))* Weigl Pubs., Inc.

UNITED STATES—HISTORY—COLONIAL PERIOD, CA. 1600-1775

see also Pilgrims (New Plymouth Colony); United States—History—French and Indian War, 1755-1763

Abbott, Simon, illus. 100 Questions about Colonial America: And All the Answers Too! 2018. (100 Questions Ser.). (ENG.). 48p. (J). 7.99 *(978-1-4413-2616-4(2),* bc12b992-f6ed-4bb7-a845-5c51d3fed4e5) Peter Pauper Pr. Inc.

Alexander, richard. The Colony of Connecticut, 1 vol. 2015. (Spotlight on the 13 Colonies: Birth of a Nation Ser.). (ENG., Illus.). 24p. (J). (gr. 4-6). pap. 11.00 *(978-1-4994-0314-5(3),* 00fe6ecb-bab1-4348-8820-511cd95eec3d, PowerKids Pr.) Rosen Publishing Group, Inc., The.

Altman, Linda Jacobs. Trade & Commerce. 2007. (ENG., Illus.). 98p. (C). (gr. 6-18). lib. bdg. 200.00 *(978-0-7656-8111-9(0),* Y184849) Routledge.

Archaeology of Early Colonial Life: Grades 4-9. (Teaching with Primary Sources Ser.). (J). tchr. ed., ring bd. 28.95 *(978-0-382-44366-4(7))* Cobblestone Publishing Co.

Améz, Lynda & Améz, Lynda. My Life in the American Colonies, 1 vol. 2015. (My Place in History Ser.). (ENG., Illus.). 24p. (J). (gr. 2-3). pap. 9.15 *(978-1-4824-3992-2(1),* efda26ef-8d22-429d-85bf-8b676995b8cc) Stevens, Gareth Publishing LLLP.

Aronson, Marc. Witch-Hunt: Mysteries of the Salem Witch Trials. Anderson, Stephanie, illus. 2005. (ENG.). 288p. (YA). (gr. 7). reprint ed. pap. 12.99 *(978-1-4169-0315-4(1),* Atheneum Bks. for Young Readers) Simon & Schuster Children's Publishing.

Asselin, Kristine Carlson. The Real Story on the Weapons & Battles of Colonial America. 2012. (Life in the American Colonies Ser.). (ENG.). 32p. (gr. 3-4). pap. 47.70 *(978-1-4296-8462-0(3),* Capstone Pr.); (J). 27.99 *(978-1-4296-6491-2(6),* 115612); (J). pap. 8.10 *(978-1-4296-7985-5(9),* 118317) Capstone.

Athan, Polly, et al. Felicity's Cooking Studio. Mahal, Susan, illus. 2007. (American Girl Ser.). 55p. (J). (gr. 3-7). 15.95 *(978-1-59369-266-7(8))* American Girl Publishing, Inc.

Axelrod-Contrada, Joan. A Historical Atlas of Colonial America. (United States: Historical Atlases of the Growth of a New Nation Ser.). 64p. (gr. 5-5). 2009. 61.20 *(978-1-60854-251-2(3))* 2004. (ENG., Illus.). (J). lib. bdg. 37.13 *(978-1-4042-0200-9(5),* 7dc1731e-e46e-489c-9ea4-6420a2474347) Rosen Publishing Group, Inc., The.

—A Primary Source History of the Colony of Rhode Island, 1 vol. 2005. (Primary Sources of the Thirteen Colonies & the Lost Colony Ser.). (ENG., Illus.). 64p. (YA). (gr. 4-6). lib. bdg. 37.13 *(978-1-4042-0434-8(2),* a6eba2fa-5b70-485b-b662-f3e93f24e0a9) Rosen Publishing Group, Inc., The.

Beck, Glenn. Book of American Heroes. Ajhar, Brian, illus. 2011. (ENG.). 276p. (J). 19.99 *(978-1-4424-2332-9(3),* Simon & Schuster/Paula Wiseman Bks.) Simon & Schuster/Paula Wiseman Bks.

Benchmark Education Company. The Thirteen Colonies (Teacher Guide) 2005. *(978-1-4108-4667-9(9))* Benchmark Education Co.

Benoit, Peter. The British Colonies in North America. 2013. (Cornerstones of Freedom™, Third Ser.). (ENG., Illus.). 64p. (J). pap. 8.95 *(978-0-531-21960-7(7))* Scholastic Library Publishing.

Bjornlund, Lydia. Children in Colonial America. 2018. (Children in History Ser.). (ENG., Illus.). 48p. (J). (gr. 5-6). pap. 11.95 *(978-1-63517-975-0(0),* 1635179750); lib. bdg. 34.21 *(978-1-63517-874-6(6),* 1635178746) North Star Editions. (Focus Readers).

Bjornlund, Lydia D. Women in Colonial America. 2003. (Women in History Ser.). (ENG., Illus.). 112p. (J). 33.45 *(978-1-59018-470-7(X),* Lucent Bks.) Cengage Gale.

Bodden, Valerie. The Declaration of American Independence. 2009. (Days of Change Ser.). (ENG., Illus.). 48p. (J). (gr. 5-8). 22.95 *(978-1-58341-733-1(8),* 22144) Creative Co., The.

Bordessa, Kris. Great Colonial America Projects: You Can Build Yourself! 2006. (Build It Yourself Ser.). (ENG., Illus.). 128p. (J). (gr. 3-7). pap. 15.95 *(978-0-9771294-0-9(3),* 967a9c99-beb0-4d2e-b3e0-4d6952cc28e0) Nomad Pr.

Brannon, Barbara. Discover the Thirteen Colonies. 2005. (J). pap. *(978-1-4108-5156-7(7))* Benchmark Education Co.

Branse, J. L. A Day in the Life of a Colonial Sea Captain. 2009. (Library of Living & Working in Colonial Times Ser.). 24p. (gr. 3-3). 42.50 *(978-1-60853-737-2(4)*, PowerKids Pr.) Rosen Publishing Group, Inc., The.

Broyles, Janell. A Timeline of the Jamestown Colony, 1 vol. 2004. (Timelines of American History Ser.). (ENG., Illus.). 32p. (gr. 4-4). lib. bdg. 29.13 *(978-0-8239-4536-8(7)*, 340643bf-8e58-4b9f-9b41-c3d1f91e22f6, Rosen Reference) Rosen Publishing Group, Inc., The.

Buckley, James, Jr. & Who HQ. Who Was Blackbeard? Qiu, Joseph J. M., illus. 2015. (Who Was? Ser.). 112p. (J). (gr. 3-7). 6.99 *(978-0-448-48308-5(4)*, Penguin Workshop) Penguin Young Readers Group.

Buckley, James. Who Was Blackbeard? 2015. (Who Was... ? Ser.). lib. bdg. 16.00 *(978-0-606-37556-6(2))* Turtleback.

Burgan, Michael. The Carpenter, 1 vol. 2013. (Colonial People Ser.). (ENG.). 48p. (gr. 4-4). 34.07 *(978-1-60870-411-8(4)*, 136afbb8-30a6-4b01-9f27-76dc55766922) Cavendish Square Publishing LLC.

Capaccio, George. The Countryside in Colonial America, 1 vol. 2014. (Life in Colonial America Ser.). (ENG., Illus.). 80p. (gr. 6-6). lib. bdg. 37.36 *(978-1-62712-885-8(9)*, 12a41f3a-1a3c-4e90-b35f-cddbf2339b88) Cavendish Square Publishing LLC.

Carlisle, Rodney P. & Golson, J. Geoffrey, eds. Turning Points — Actual & Alternate Histories: Colonial America from Settlement to the Revolution, 1 vol. 2006. (Turning Points — Actual & Alternate Histories Ser.). (ENG., Illus.). 288p. (C). 103.00 *(978-1-85109-827-9(5)*, 900322364) ABC-CLIO, LLC.

Clark, Willow. The True Story of the Declaration of Independence, 1 vol. 2013. (What Really Happened? Ser.). (ENG., Illus.). 24p. (J). (gr. 2-3). pap. 9.25 *(978-1-4488-9840-4(4)*, 94101ea9-a09e-4507-ad08-82250005ab11); lib. bdg. 26.27 *(978-1-4488-9691-2(6)*, 091fe756-fd1e-4072-9aaf-9a4ac3be666b) Rosen Publishing Group, Inc., The. (PowerKids Pr.).

Colligan, L. H. The City. 2014. (J). pap. *(978-1-62712-883-4(2))* Cavendish Square Publishing LLC.

Colligan, Louise. The City in Colonial America, 1 vol. 2014. (Life in Colonial America Ser.). (ENG.). 80p. (gr. 6-6). lib. bdg. 37.36 *(978-1-62712-882-7(4)*, 54fbe2d3-b14a-48df-83bb-88026f3ae8d0) Cavendish Square Publishing LLC.

Colonial Life, 5 bks., Set. Incl. Cities & Towns. Stefoff, Rebecca. 96p. lib. bdg. 165.00 *(978-0-7656-8109-6(9)*, Y181735); Daily Living. Hinds, Kathryn. 96p. lib. bdg. 180.00 *(978-0-7656-8110-2(2)*, Y181908); Exploration & Settlement. Stefoff, Rebecca. 96p. lib. bdg. 180.00 *(978-0-7656-8108-9(0)*, Y182272); Government. Kelly, Martin & Kelly, Melissa. 96p. lib. bdg. 180.00 *(978-0-7656-8112-6(9)*, Y182476); Trade & Commerce. Altman, Linda Jacobs. 98p. lib. bdg. 200.00 *(978-0-7656-8111-9(0)*, Y184849); (C). (gr. 6-18). (ENG., Illus.). 96p. 2007. Set lib. bdg. 165.00 *(978-0-7656-8107-2(2)*, Y181691) Routledge.

Cooke, Tim. Blackbeard: A Notorious Pirate in the Caribbean, 1 vol. 2015. (Wanted! Famous Outlaws Ser.). (ENG., Illus.). 48p. (J). (gr. 6-8). pap. 15.05 *(978-1-4824-4247-2(7)*, 8f808262-5a79-4559-b632-e546660fb970) Stevens, Gareth Publishing LLLP.

Cunningham, Kevin. The Delaware Colony. 2011. (True Book-the Thirteen Colonies Ser.). (ENG., Illus.). 48p. (J). lib. bdg. 29.00 *(978-0-531-25388-5(0)*, Children's Pr.) Scholastic Library Publishing.

—The Georgia Colony. 2011. (True Book-the Thirteen Colonies Ser.). (ENG., Illus.). 48p. (J). lib. bdg. 29.00 *(978-0-531-25389-2(9)*, Children's Pr.) Scholastic Library Publishing.

Dimartino, Catherine. Early American Alliances. 2005. (ENG., Illus.). 16p. (J). (gr. 5-5). pap. 9.97 net. *(978-0-328-14893-6(8)*, Scott Foresman) Savvas Learning Co.

Dosier, Susan. Colonial Cooking. 2016. (Exploring History Through Food Ser.). (ENG., Illus.). 32p. (J). (gr. 3-6). lib. bdg. 27.99 *(978-1-5157-2356-1(9)*, 132790, Capstone Pr.) Capstone.

Evan-Moor Educational Publishers. Colonial America Grade 4-6+ 2003. (History Pockets Ser.). (ENG., Illus.). 96p. (J). (gr. 4-6). pap., tchr. ed., suppl. ed. 17.99 *(978-1-55799-906-1(6)*, EMC 3709) Evan-Moor Educational Pubs.

Explore Colonial America, 12 vols. 2016. (Explore Colonial America Ser.). 48p. (ENG.). (J). (gr. 4-5). lib. bdg. 177.60 *(978-0-7660-7498-9(6)*, a7991fa7-88b8-4595-8af3-3fe91218542e); (gr. 5-4). pap. 70.20 *(978-0-7660-7986-1(4))* Enslow Publishing, LLC.

Fajardo, Anika. The Dish on Food & Farming in Colonial America. (Life in the American Colonies Ser.). (ENG.). 32p. (gr. 3-4). 2011. pap. 47.70 *(978-1-4296-7218-4(8)*, Capstone Pr.) 2017. (J). pap. 8.10 *(978-1-5157-9748-7(1)*, 136865) Capstone.

Fisher, Verna. Colonial Farms. 2011. (Colonial Quest Ser.). (ENG.). 32p. (J). (gr. 2-5). 21.19 *(978-1-936313-58-7(8))* Nomad Pr.

—Explore Colonial America! 25 Great Projects, Activities, Experiments. Stone, Bryan, illus. 2009. (Explore Your World Ser.). (ENG.). 96p. (J). (gr. k-4). pap. 12.95 *(978-1-934670-37-8(5)*, bfa636d5-34f8-4952-bc10-af6976bc8446) Nomad Pr.

Forest, Christopher. The Rebellious Colonists & the Causes of the American Revolution. 2012. (Story of the American Revolution Ser.). (ENG.). 32p. (J). (gr. 3-4). pap. 48.60 *(978-1-4296-9291-5(X)*, 18525, Capstone Pr.) Capstone.

Fremon, David K. The Salem Witchcraft Trials in United States History, 1 vol. 2014. (In United States History Ser.). (ENG.). 96p. (gr. 5-5). 31.61 *(978-0-7660-6340-2(2)*, 84da000c-3b46-4045-a734-89409036475a) Enslow Publishing, LLC.

Fritz, Jean. The Lost Colony of Roanoke. Talbott, Hudson, illus. 2004. (ENG.). 64p. (J). (gr. 2-5). 18.99 *(978-0-399-24027-0(6)*, G.P. Putnam's Sons Books for Young Readers) Penguin Young Readers Group.

Garstecki, Julia. Life in Colonial America, 1 vol. 2015. (Daily Life in US History Ser.). (ENG., Illus.). 48p. (J). (gr. 4-8). lib. bdg. 35.64 *(978-1-62403-630-9(9)*, 16900) ABDO Publishing Co.

George, Enzo. Colonial America. 2015. (J). lib. bdg. *(978-1-62713-485-9(9))* 2014. (ENG.). 48p. (gr. 4-4). lib. bdg. 33.07 *(978-1-5026-0256-5(3)*, 5a65edbb-f7c6-4d4b-acdc-379f7dc09f0e) Cavendish Square Publishing LLC.

George, Lynn. What Do You Know about Colonial America? 2009. (20 Questions: History Ser.). 24p. (gr. 2-3). 42.50 *(978-1-60854-955-9(0)*, PowerKids Pr.) Rosen Publishing Group, Inc., The.

Goddu, Krystyna Poray. A Primary Source History of U. S. Independence. 2015. (Primary Source History Ser.). (ENG., Illus.). 32p. (J). (gr. 3-6). pap. 7.95 *(978-1-4914-1846-8(X)*, 127284, Capstone Pr.) Capstone.

Hakim, Joy. A History of US: from Colonies to Country: 1735-1791 a History of US Book Three. (History of US Ser.: 3). (ENG., Illus.). 224p. (gr. 4-7). 2nd rev. ed. 2007. per. 15.95 *(978-0-19-532717-5(9))* 3rd rev. ed. 2006. 24.95 *(978-0-19-518896-7(9))* Oxford Univ. Pr., Inc.

—A History of US: Making Thirteen Colonies: 1600-1740 a History of US Book Two. (History of US Ser.: 2). (ENG., Illus.). 192p. (gr. 4-7). 2nd rev. ed. 2007. per. 15.95 *(978-0-19-532716-8(0))* 3rd rev. ed. 2006. 24.95 *(978-0-19-518895-0(0))* Oxford Univ. Pr., Inc.

Hamen, Susan E. Thirteen Colonies, 1 vol. 2013. (Foundations of Our Nation Ser.). (ENG.). 48p. (J). (gr. 4-8). lib. bdg. 35.64 *(978-1-61783-712-8(1)*, 7822) ABDO Publishing Co.

Harasymiw, Mark J. The British Colonies, 1 vol. 2011. (Story of America Ser.). (ENG., Illus.). 32p. (J). (gr. 4-5). pap. 11.50 *(978-1-4339-4765-0(X)*, f7cb1ec4-408c-4a84-ae83-ba02cb40e3e7); lib. bdg. 29.27 *(978-1-4339-4764-3(1)*, 3b537cb5-1331-4cb4-be74-8064b6752cf5) Stevens, Gareth Publishing LLLP. (Gareth Stevens Learning Library).

Harris, Laurie Lanzen. Colonial America & the Revolutionary War: The Story of the People of the Colonies, from Early Settlers to Revolutionary Leaders. 2009. 399p. (J). (gr. 5-7). lib. bdg. 49.00 *(978-1-931360-34-0(0))* Favorable Impressions.

Hartwiger, Heidi. Tricom Trivia: Colonial Facts & Fun for Kids. 2007. 5.00 *(978-1-59712-065-4(0))* Catawba Publishing Co.

Heckt, Jackie. The Colony of Virginia, 1 vol. 2015. (Spotlight on the 13 Colonies: Birth of a Nation Ser.). (ENG., Illus.). 24p. (J). (gr. 4-6). pap. 11.00 *(978-1-4994-0587-3(1)*, 28fbf870-df94-40a3-8454-3eed3665c83b, PowerKids Pr.) Rosen Publishing Group, Inc., The.

—Immigration to Colonial America. 2016. (Spotlight on Immigration & Migration Ser.). (ENG.). 24p. (J). (gr. 4-7). 21.80 *(978-1-5311-8873-3(7))* Perfection Learning Corp.

—Immigration to Colonial America, 1 vol., 1. 2015. (Spotlight on Immigration & Migration Ser.). (ENG., Illus.). 24p. (J). (gr. 4-5). pap. 11.00 *(978-1-5081-4081-8(2)*, d165bbd7-be03-4b72-b3bb-054d7b4c213c, PowerKids Pr.) Rosen Publishing Group, Inc., The.

Heinrichs, Ann. The Barber, 1 vol. 2011. (Colonial People Ser.). (ENG.). 48p. (gr. 4-4). 34.07 *(978-0-7614-4800-6(4)*, 0ccb54d3-082a-48eb-b652-90f68b2fc8c4) Cavendish Square Publishing LLC.

—The Shipbuilder, 1 vol. 2013. (Colonial People Ser.). (ENG.). 48p. (gr. 4-4). 34.07 *(978-0-7614-0005-9(2)*, b7bd16c4-cc1f-4847-850b-5417894fcd33) Cavendish Square Publishing LLC.

—The Shoemaker, 1 vol. 2011. (Colonial People Ser.). (ENG.). 48p. (gr. 4-4). 34.07 *(978-0-7614-4798-6(9)*, fed9550a-1bb6-4923-be20-62feac6eac51) Cavendish Square Publishing LLC.

Hollar, Sherman. Biographies of Colonial America: From Sir Walter Raleigh to Phillis Wheatley, 1 vol. 2012. (Impact on America: Collective Biographies Ser.). (ENG., Illus.). 168p. (J). (gr. 8-8). lib. bdg. 38.82 *(978-1-61530-683-1(8)*, ccdf33a7-2d27-4565-92eb-8764fb430454) Rosen Publishing Group, Inc., The.

Hollar, Sherman, ed. Biographies of Colonial America: Sir Walter Raleigh, Powhatan, Phillis Wheatley, & More, 4 vols. 2012. (Impact on America: Collective Biographies Ser.). (ENG., Illus.). 168p. (YA). (gr. 8-8). 77.64 *(978-1-61530-763-0(X)*, fd7fc43d-01c1-4264-9923-817e353acbe0) Rosen Publishing Group, Inc., The.

Holt, Rinehart and Winston Staff. Call to Freedom: Beginning 1877 - Texas Online Edition. 2003. cd-rom 77.60 *(978-0-03-073346-8(4))* Holt McDougal.

Isaacs, Sally. Understanding the Declaration of Independence. 2008. (Documenting Early America Ser.). (ENG.). 32p. (J). (gr. 3-6). lib. bdg. *(978-0-7787-4371-2(3))* Crabtree Publishing Co.

Jacobson, Bray. The Thirteen Colonies, 1 vol. 2017. (Look at U. S. History Ser.). (ENG.). 32p. (gr. 2-2). pap. 11.50 *(978-1-4824-6039-1(4)*, 9745221c-2b1c-42dc-9920-f38ef6c97370) Stevens, Gareth Publishing LLLP.

Jedson, Lee. The Treaty of Paris 1783: A Primary Source Examination of the Treaty That Recognized American Independence. (Primary Sources of American Treaties Ser.). 64p. (gr. 5-8). 2009. 58.50 *(978-1-60851-517-2(6))* 2005. (ENG., Illus.). (J). lib. bdg. 37.13 *(978-1-4042-0441-6(5)*, c04803f4-66cf-4fd5-b3d6-b3710f6f6e1e) Rosen Publishing Group, Inc., The.

Jeffries, Joyce. The Colony of North Carolina, 1 vol. 2015. (Spotlight on the 13 Colonies: Birth of a Nation Ser.). (ENG., Illus.). 24p. (J). (gr. 4-6). pap. 11.00 *(978-1-4994-0554-5(5)*, f5f16c38-b867-4e64-8775-66881c07a017, PowerKids Pr.) Rosen Publishing Group, Inc., The.

—The Colony of South Carolina, 1 vol. 2015. (Spotlight on the 13 Colonies: Birth of a Nation Ser.). (ENG., Illus.). 24p. (J). (gr. 4-6). pap. 11.00 *(978-1-4994-0582-8(0)*, 5481a901-89b0-454f-9d8c-9043801b07c7, PowerKids Pr.) Rosen Publishing Group, Inc., The.

—Recipes of the Thirteen Colonies. (Cooking Your Way Through American History Ser.). (J). (gr. 3-3). 2017. pap. 63.60 *(978-1-5345-2109-4(7))* 2016. (ENG.). 24p. pap. 11.60 *(978-1-5345-2108-7(9)*, 6c230dcf-e7d6-4b85-b780-d44b31208591) 2016. (ENG.). 24p. lib. bdg. 28.88 *(978-1-5345-2110-0(0)*, 0c40c1bd-0749-4a69-af5a-eb3ae6570fcb) Greenhaven Publishing LLC. (KidHaven Publishing).

Jobes, Cecily. The Colony of Maryland, 1 vol. 2015. (Spotlight on the 13 Colonies: Birth of a Nation Ser.). (ENG., Illus.). 24p. (J). (gr. 4-6). pap. 11.00 *(978-1-4994-0504-0(9)*, c3b5fb22-abf6-4410-bbe1-f7d99afae484, PowerKids Pr.) Rosen Publishing Group, Inc., The.

Jr. Graphic Colonial America: Set 2, 12 vols. 2013. (Jr. Graphic Colonial America Ser.). (ENG.). 24p. (J). (gr. 2-3). 173.58 *(978-1-4777-1546-8(0)*, 0bb5857e-8ba0-4b45-840d-65c47698826e, PowerKids Pr.) Rosen Publishing Group, Inc., The.

Jr. Graphic Colonial America: Sets 1 - 2, 24 vols. 2013. (Jr. Graphic Colonial America Ser.). 24p. (J). (ENG.). (gr. 2-3). 347.16 *(978-1-4777-1553-6(3)*, 8026d46a-bc72-414d-b7d1-323adea1dceb); (gr. 3-6). pap. 127.20 *(978-1-4777-2730-0(2))*; (gr. 3-6). pap. 763.20 *(978-1-4777-2731-7(0))* Rosen Publishing Group, Inc., The. (PowerKids Pr.).

Kalman, Bobbie. A Visual Dictionary of a Colonial Community. 2007. (Visual Dictionaries Ser.). (ENG., Illus.). 32p. (J). (gr. 4-7). pap. *(978-0-7787-3522-9(2))* Crabtree Publishing Co.

Kalman, Maira. Thomas Jefferson: Life, Liberty & the Pursuit of Everything. Kalman, Maira, illus. 2014. (ENG., Illus.). 40p. (J). (gr. k-3). 17.99 *(978-0-399-24040-9(3)*, Nancy Paulsen Books) Penguin Young Readers Group.

Katz, Vladimir. A Timeline of the Life of George Washington. (Timelines of American History Ser.). 32p. (gr. 4-4). 2009. 47.90 *(978-1-60854-388-5(9))* 2004. (ENG., Illus.). lib. bdg. 29.13 *(978-0-8239-4538-2(3)*, 2fa8f672-9994-452f-b005-cfc1b954837f) Rosen Publishing Group, Inc., The. (Rosen Reference).

King, David C. AmericanHeritage, American Voices: Colonies & Revolution. 2003. (American Heritage, American Voices Ser.). (ENG.). 144p. (J). (gr. 5-9). pap. 22.95 *(978-1-119-10345-5(2))* Wiley, John & Sons, Inc.

Kit, Oscar. A Timeline of the Life of Thomas Jefferson. (Timelines of American History Ser.). 32p. (gr. 4-4). 2009. 47.90 *(978-1-60854-389-2(7))* 2004. (ENG., Illus.). lib. bdg. 29.13 *(978-0-8239-4539-9(1)*, 47a2bcaf-4d4e-4142-9348-ee6f4d4c961c) Rosen Publishing Group, Inc., The. (Rosen Reference).

Konstam, Angus. America Speaks, 10 vols. 2005. (Illus.). (J). *(978-0-7172-6028-7(3))*; *(978-0-7172-6029-4(1))*; *(978-0-7172-6027-0(5))*; *(978-0-7172-6026-3(7))*; *(978-0-7172-6025-6(9))*; *(978-0-7172-6024-9(0))*; *(978-0-7172-6023-2(2))*; *(978-0-7172-6022-5(4))*; *(978-0-7172-6020-1(8))*; *(978-0-7172-6021-8(6))* Grolier, Ltd.

—America Speaks, 10 vols., Set. 2005. (Illus.). (J). (gr. 5-10). lib. bdg. 269.00 *(978-0-7172-6030-0(5)*, Grolier) Scholastic Library Publishing.

Krebs, Laurie. A Day in the Life of a Colonial Shipwright. 2009. (Library of Living & Working in Colonial Times Ser.). 24p. (gr. 3-3). 42.50 *(978-1-60853-738-9(2)*, PowerKids Pr.) Rosen Publishing Group, Inc., The.

LaClair, Teresa. The Northern Colonies: Freedom to Worship (1600-1770) Rakove, Jack N., ed. 2012. (How America Became America Ser.). (Illus.). 48p. (J). (gr. 3-4). 19.95 *(978-1-4222-2397-0(3))* Mason Crest.

Landau, Elaine. The Declaration of Independence (a True Book: American History) 2008. (True Book (Relaunch) Ser.). (ENG., Illus.). 48p. (J). (gr. 3-5). pap. 6.95 *(978-0-531-14780-1(0)*, Children's Pr.) Scholastic Library Publishing.

—True Books: the Declaration of Independence. 2008. (True Book: American History, Revised Ser.). (ENG., Illus.). 48p. (J). (gr. 3-5). lib. bdg. 21.19 *(978-0-531-12630-1(7)*, Children's Pr.) Scholastic Library Publishing.

Lassieur, Allison. Colonial America: An Interactive History Adventure. 2010. (You Choose: Historical Eras Ser.). (ENG.). 112p. (J). (gr. 3-4). pap. 42.70 *(978-1-4296-6739-5(7)*, 16457); pap. 6.95 *(978-1-4296-6277-2(8)*, 115422); (Illus.). 32.65 *(978-1-4296-5481-4(3)*, 113881) Capstone. (Capstone Pr.).

Lee, David. The Colony of Delaware, 1 vol. 2015. (Spotlight on the 13 Colonies: Birth of a Nation Ser.). (ENG., Illus.). 24p. (J). (gr. 4-6). pap. 11.00 *(978-1-4994-0351-0(8)*, 4748a297-da9e-4494-be16-056b98d9c5a2, PowerKids Pr.) Rosen Publishing Group, Inc., The.

Levy, Janey. William Penn: Shaping a Nation. 2009. (Illus.). 32p. (J). 60.00 *(978-1-4358-0196-7(2)*, 1291824, PowerKids Pr.) Rosen Publishing Group, Inc., The.

Life in Colonial America, 12 vols. 2014. (Life in Colonial America Ser.). (ENG.). 80p. (YA). (gr. 6-6). 224.16 *(978-1-62713-128-5(0)*, 4b96389a-eb95-44a5-80d4-e73a2c6c1e38, Cavendish Square) Cavendish Square Publishing LLC.

The Life of a Colonial Innkeeper. 2013. (Jr. Graphic Colonial America Ser.). 24p. (J). (gr. 3-6). pap. 63.60 *(978-1-4777-1436-2(7)*, PowerKids Pr.) Rosen Publishing Group, Inc., The.

Linde, Barbara M. Slavery in Early America, 1 vol. 2011. (Story of America Ser.). (ENG., Illus.). 32p. (J). (gr. 4-5). lib. bdg. 29.27 *(978-1-4339-4776-6(5)*, cd1c573c-1c64-42b1-b3ea-2a3c83e1ba4d, Gareth Stevens Learning Library) Stevens, Gareth Publishing LLLP.

Lusted, Marcia Amidon. America's Colonization & Settlement. 2011. (Explorer Library: Language Arts Explorer Ser.). (ENG.). 32p. (gr. 4-8). pap. 14.21 *(978-1-61080-282-6(9)*, 201205); (Illus.). lib. bdg. 32.07 *(978-1-61080-194-2(6)*, 201164) Cherry Lake Publishing.

MacCarald, Clara. Perspectives on European Colonization of America. 2018. (Perspectives on US History Ser.). (ENG., Illus.). 32p. (J). (gr. 3-6). 32.80 *(978-1-63235-400-6(4)*, 13722, 12-Story Library) Bookstaves, LLC.

Machajewski, Sarah. The Colony of Georgia, 1 vol. 2015. (Spotlight on the 13 Colonies: Birth of a Nation Ser.). (ENG., Illus.). 24p. (J). (gr. 4-6). pap. 11.00 *(978-1-4994-0493-7(X)*, 2860dbc9-6f95-415e-ae1f-c64d82091390, PowerKids Pr.) Rosen Publishing Group, Inc., The.

—Interpreting Data about the Thirteen Colonies, 1 vol. 2018. (Project Learning Through American History Ser.). (ENG.). 32p. (gr. 4-5). 27.93 *(978-1-5383-3067-8(9)*, c9e55879-4df6-4aa3-87ac-f7c284624232); pap. 11.00 *(978-1-5383-3068-5(7)*, 232307c5-08d9-454e-a7eb-709c824eb45a) Rosen Publishing Group, Inc., The. (PowerKids Pr.).

—A Kid's Life in Colonial America, 1 vol. 2014. (How Kids Lived Ser.). (ENG., Illus.). 24p. (J). (gr. 3-3). lib. bdg. 25.27 *(978-1-4994-0006-9(3)*, 91b2014c-ab09-40d2-85a6-43e31ea6c73b, PowerKids Pr.) Rosen Publishing Group, Inc., The.

Malaspina, Ann. A Primary Source History of the Colony of Connecticut, 1 vol. 2005. (Primary Sources of the Thirteen Colonies & the Lost Colony Ser.). (ENG., Illus.). 64p. (YA). (gr. 4-6). lib. bdg. 37.13 *(978-1-4042-0424-9(5)*, 15326e12-e6e2-4449-abf7-a90ed37c71c8) Rosen Publishing Group, Inc., The.

Maloof, Torrey. James Oglethorpe: Not for Self, but for Others. rev. ed. 2016. (Social Studies: Informational Text Ser.). (ENG., Illus.). 32p. (gr. 2-4). pap. 10.99 *(978-1-4938-2555-4(0))* Teacher Created Materials, Inc.

Mara, Wil. The Innkeeper, 1 vol. 2011. (Colonial People Ser.). (ENG.). 48p. (gr. 4-4). 34.07 *(978-0-7614-4796-2(2)*, 0e3cdbb5-6f2b-4e19-8d12-925ab7f2aa81) Cavendish Square Publishing LLC.

—The Schoolmaster, 1 vol. 2011. (Colonial People Ser.). (ENG.). 48p. (gr. 4-4). 34.07 *(978-0-7614-4801-3(2)*, a4a1cebd-de00-4ad7-8468-880c7ef3dc47) Cavendish Square Publishing LLC.

—The Silversmith, 1 vol. 2011. (Colonial People Ser.). (ENG.). 48p. (gr. 4-4). 34.07 *(978-0-7614-4804-4(7)*, b281651d-0b8b-491e-94d1-f1b43f638296) Cavendish Square Publishing LLC.

Marciniak, Kristin. 12 Incredible Facts about the Boston Tea Party. 2016. (Turning Points in US History Ser.). (ENG., Illus.). 32p. (J). (gr. 3-6). 32.80 *(978-1-63235-126-5(9)*, 11998, 12-Story Library) Bookstaves, LLC.

Marsh, Carole. Colonial America - Common Core Lessons & Activities. 2015. (Common Core Ser.). (ENG.). (J). pap. 4.99 *(978-0-635-11984-1(6))* Gallopade International.

—Roger Williams. 2003. 12p. (gr. k-4). 2.95 *(978-0-635-02361-2(X))* Gallopade International.

Marsico, Katie. The Doctor, 1 vol. 2012. (Colonial People Ser.). (ENG.). 48p. (gr. 4-4). 34.07 *(978-0-7614-4796-2(2)*, 0e3cdbb5-6f2b-4e19-8d12-925ab7f2aa81) Cavendish Square Publishing LLC.

Martin, David. The Colony of Pennsylvania, 1 vol. 2015. (Spotlight on the 13 Colonies: Birth of a Nation Ser.). (ENG., Illus.). 24p. (J). (gr. 4-6). pap. 11.00 *(978-1-4994-0572-9(3)*, 1e60ed25-5bf4-4685-afad-6d51911bd1a7, PowerKids Pr.) Rosen Publishing Group, Inc., The.

Masters, Nancy Robinson. Extraordinary People: Extraordinary Patriots of the United States of America. 2005. (Extraordinary People Ser.). (ENG., Illus.). 288p. (J). (gr. 4-7). 40.00 *(978-0-516-24404-4(3)*, Children's Pr.) Scholastic Library Publishing.

Mattern, Joanne. Historic Williamsburg: A Revolutionary City. 2017. (Core Content Social Studies — Let's Celebrate America Ser.). (ENG., Illus.). 32p. (J). (gr. 2-5). pap. 8.99 *(978-1-63440-229-3(4)*, 99e20e4a-31a1-4a48-a7b9-14f319e76fb9) Red Chair Pr.

McAneney, Caitlin. Uncovering the Jamestown Colony, 1 vol. 2016. (Hidden History Ser.). (ENG., Illus.). 32p. (J). (gr. 4-5). pap. 11.50 *(978-1-4824-5806-0(3)*, 50cd09a8-84db-4827-be1a-a6381d7f1e4c) Stevens, Gareth Publishing LLLP.

McCallum, Ann. Eat Your U. S. History Homework: Recipes for Revolutionary Minds. Hernandez, Leeza, illus. 2015. (Eat Your Homework Ser.: 3). 48p. (J). (gr. 2-5). lib. bdg. 15.95 *(978-1-57091-923-7(2))* Charlesbridge Publishing, Inc.

McDonnell, Julia. The Pilgrims Didn't Celebrate the First Thanksgiving: Exposing Myths about Colonial History, 1 vol. 2016. (Exposed! Myths about Early American History Ser.). (ENG., Illus.). 32p. (J). (gr. 2-3). pap. 11.50 *(978-1-4824-5731-5(8)*, cd8d2895-d393-4286-983d-f53454f70b3c) Stevens, Gareth Publishing LLLP.

McGraw Hill. The American Republic to 1877, Reading Essentials & Study Guide, Student Edition. 2nd ed. 2004. (U. S. History - the Early Years Ser.). (ENG., Illus.). 264p. (gr. 6-9). stu. ed., per. 7.00 *(978-0-07-865487-9(4)*, 0078654874) McGraw-Hill Higher Education.

McKissack, Patricia C. & McKissack, Fredrick L., Jr. Hard Labor: The First African Americans 1619. Fiedler, Joseph Daniel, illus. 2004. (Milestone Ser.). (ENG.). 64p. (J). (gr. 2-5). pap. 6.99 *(978-0-689-86149-9(4)*, Simon & Schuster/Paula Wiseman Bks.) Simon & Schuster/Paula Wiseman Bks.

McLeese, Don. Phillis Wheatley. 2004. (Heroes of the American Revolution Ser.). (Illus.). 32p. (J). (gr. -1 — 1). pap. 5.95 *(978-1-59515-320-3(9))* Rourke Educational Media.

Merrill, Amy French. A Day in the Life of a Colonial Cabinetmaker. 2009. (Library of Living & Working in Colonial Times Ser.). 24p. (gr. 3-3). 42.50 *(978-1-60853-729-7(3)*, PowerKids Pr.) Rosen Publishing Group, Inc., The.

—A Day in the Life of a Colonial Dressmaker. 2009. (Library of Living & Working in Colonial Times Ser.). 24p. (gr. 3-3). 42.50 *(978-1-60853-730-3(7)*, PowerKids Pr.) Rosen Publishing Group, Inc., The.

—A Day in the Life of a Colonial Surveyor. 2009. (Library of Living & Working in Colonial Times Ser.). 24p. (gr. 3-3). 42.50 *(978-1-60853-740-2(4)*, PowerKids Pr.) Rosen Publishing Group, Inc., The.

Miller, Brandon Marie. Growing up in Revolution & the New Nation, 1775 to 1800. 2003. (Our America Ser.). (Illus.). 64p. (J). (gr. 4-7). lib. bdg. 26.60 *(978-0-8225-0078-0(7))* Lerner Publishing Group.

—Women of Colonial America: 13 Stories of Courage & Survival in the New World. 2016. (Women of Action Ser.: 14). (ENG., Illus.). 256p. (YA). (gr. 7). 19.95 *(978-1-55652-487-5(0))* Chicago Review Pr., Inc.

Misztal, Maggie. The Colony of New Jersey, 1 vol. 2015. (Spotlight on the 13 Colonies: Birth of a Nation Ser.). (ENG., Illus.). 24p. (J). (gr. 4-6). pap. 11.00 *(978-1-4994-0531-6(6)*, 39d3faf6-9332-4139-919c-d528b3280543, PowerKids Pr.) Rosen Publishing Group, Inc., The.

Morley, Jacqueline. You Wouldn't Want to Be an American Colonist! A Settlement You'd Rather Not Start. Antram, David, illus. 2013. (You Wouldn't Want to... Ser.). (ENG.). 32p. (J). 29.00 *(978-0-531-25946-7(3)*, Watts, Franklin) Scholastic Library Publishing.

Muhall, Jill K. & Alarcon, Jill. Causes of the Revolution, 1 vol. rev. ed. 2004. (Social Studies: Informational Text Ser.). (ENG., Illus.). 24p. (J). (gr. 4-8). pap. 10.99 *(978-0-7439-8785-1(3))* Teacher Created Materials, Inc.

TUV

Nardo, Don. Daily Life in Colonial America, 1 vol. 2010. (Lucent Library of Historical Eras Ser.). (ENG.). 96p. (gr. 7-10). 41.03 *(978-1-4205-0264-0(6),* db7999b3-b80c-4cf5-85ba-01c804b27a89, Lucent Pr.) Greenhaven Publishing LLC.

—The Establishment of the Thirteen Colonies, 1 vol. 2010. (Lucent Library of Historical Eras Ser.). (ENG., Illus.). 96p. (gr. 7-10). 41.03 *(978-1-4205-0267-1(0),* 23108ae8-a282-4de3-a3d5-1a99dee8490a, Lucent Pr.) Greenhaven Publishing LLC.

National Geographic Learning. Language, Literacy & Vocabulary - Reading Expeditions (U. S. History & Life): the Thirteen Colonies. 2006. (ENG., Illus.). 36p. (J). pap. 20.95 *(978-0-7922-5453-9(8))* CENGAGE Learning.

—Reading Expeditions (Social Studies: Voices from America's Past): Colonial Life. 2007. (Avenues Ser.). (ENG., Illus.). 40p. (J). pap. 21.95 *(978-0-7922-8678-3(2))* CENGAGE Learning.

Nelson, Sheila. The Original United States of America. 2006. (How America Became America Ser.). (Illus.). 96p. (YA). lib. bdg. 22.95 *(978-1-59084-903-3(5))* Mason Crest.

Omoth, Tyler. Establishing the American Colonies. 2017. (Foundations of Our Nation Ser.). (ENG., Illus.). 32p. (J). (gr. 3-5). pap. 9.95 *(978-1-63517-310-9(8),* 1635173108); lib. bdg. 31.35 *(978-1-63517-245-4(4),* 1635172454) North Star Editions. (Focus Readers).

Oney, Yannick. First American Colonies. 2004. (World Discovery History Readers Ser.). (Illus.). 32p. (J). pap. *(978-0-439-66555-1(8))* Scholastic, Inc.

Osborne, Mary Pope & Boyce, Natalie Pope. American Revolution: A Nonfiction Companion to Magic Tree House #22: Revolutionary War on Wednesday. Murdocca, Sal, illus. 2004. (Magic Tree House (R) Fact Tracker Ser.: 11). 128p. (J). (gr. 2-5). pap. 6.99 *(978-0-375-82379-4(4),* Random Hse. Bks. for Young Readers) Random Hse. Children's Bks.

Parker, Lewis K. Dutch Colonies in the Americas. 2009. (European Colonies in the Americas Ser.). 24p. (gr. 2-2). 42.50 *(978-1-61512-316-2(4),* PowerKids Pr.) Rosen Publishing Group, Inc., The.

—English Colonies in the Americas. 2009. (European Colonies in the Americas Ser.). 24p. (gr. 2-2). 42.50 *(978-1-61512-317-9(2),* PowerKids Pr.) Rosen Publishing Group, Inc., The.

—French Colonies in the Americas. 2009. (European Colonies in the Americas Ser.). 24p. (gr. 2-2). 42.50 *(978-1-61512-318-6(0),* PowerKids Pr.) Rosen Publishing Group, Inc., The.

—Russian Colonies in the Americas. 2009. (European Colonies in the Americas Ser.). 24p. (gr. 2-2). 42.50 *(978-1-61512-319-3(9),* PowerKids Pr.) Rosen Publishing Group, Inc., The.

—Spanish Colonies in the Americas. 2009. (European Colonies in the Americas Ser.). 24p. (gr. 2-2). 42.50 *(978-1-61512-320-9(2),* PowerKids Pr.) Rosen Publishing Group, Inc., The.

Pelleschi, Andrea. The Life of a Colonial Innkeeper, 1 vol. 2013. (Jr. Graphic Colonial America Ser.). (ENG.). 24p. (J). (gr. 2-3). 28.93 *(978-1-4777-1309-9(3),* 8718f95d-1bae-43b9-9fba-2f81dc3b8f62); pap. 11.60 *(978-1-4777-1435-5(9),* 88f89634-3149-413e-aebb-13fdcc77ed10) Rosen Publishing Group, Inc., The. (PowerKids Pr.).

Perritano, John. Colonization & Settlement. 2016. (Illus.). 48p. (J). *(978-1-5105-1284-9(5))* SmartBook Media, Inc.

Petersen, Christine. The Apothecary, 1 vol. 2011. (Colonial People Ser.). (ENG.). 48p. (gr. 4-4). 34.07 *(978-0-7614-4795-5(4),* 9545d33a-8fc6-403a-9486-7c9ba1589dbf) Cavendish Square Publishing LLC.

—The Blacksmith, 1 vol. 2011. (Colonial People Ser.). (ENG.). 48p. (gr. 4-4). 34.07 *(978-0-7614-4799-3(7),* 5550975a-2157-40e4-956e-eb1c4cc25d4a) Cavendish Square Publishing LLC.

—The Miller, 1 vol. 2012. (Colonial People Ser.). (ENG.). 48p. (gr. 4-4). 34.07 *(978-1-60870-416-3(5),* 5a4a9dd5-c528-4be2-9d6d-6430c2b3e8d3) Cavendish Square Publishing LLC.

—The Printer, 1 vol. 2011. (Colonial People Ser.). (ENG.). 48p. (gr. 4-4). 34.07 *(978-0-7614-4802-0(0),* d3054ccc-85a8-4324-a018-f21131a51dd9) Cavendish Square Publishing LLC.

—The Tailor, 1 vol. 2012. (Colonial People Ser.). (ENG.). 48p. (gr. 4-4). 34.07 *(978-1-60870-417-0(3),* 1af62c56-8259-4630-bcb2-11ab51657959) Cavendish Square Publishing LLC.

—The Tanner, 1 vol. 2012. (Colonial People Ser.). (ENG., Illus.). 48p. (gr. 4-4). 34.07 *(978-1-60870-418-7(1),* da15bb21-f227-4bed-83da-d2d0b0a016c7) Cavendish Square Publishing LLC.

Pratt, Mary K. A Timeline History of the Thirteen Colonies. 2014. (Timeline Trackers: America's Beginnings Ser.). (ENG., Illus.). 48p. (J). (gr. 5-8). lib. bdg. 30.65 *(978-1-4677-3639-8(2),* 218d5470-a8f9-4f88-ad38-c053f77be1e0, Lerner Pubns.) Lerner Publishing Group.

Primary Sources of Colonial America, 12 vols. 2017. (Primary Sources of Colonial America Ser.). (ENG.). (J). (gr. 6-6). lib. bdg. 215.58 *(978-1-5026-3228-9(4),* b251d2d4-4d6c-420b-bbaf-38e2099077d3) Cavendish Square Publishing LLC.

The Puritans, Algonkians & Roger Williams (NCHS) (J). (gr. 5-8). spiral bd., tchr.'s planning gde. ed. 13.50 *(978-0-382-44447-0(7))* Cobblestone Publishing Co.

The Puritans, Algonkians & Roger Williams (NCHS) Grades 5-8. (J). tchr. ed. 18.00 *(978-0-382-44537-8(6))* Cobblestone Publishing Co.

Randolph, Joanne. The Call of Liberty: Marquis de Lafayette & the American Revolution, 1 vol. 2003. (Great Moments in American History Ser.). (ENG., Illus.). 32p. (YA). (gr. 3-4). lib. bdg. 29.13 *(978-0-8239-4368-5(2),* ae5f27e2-ceda-436e-8b56-08666465528a) Rosen Publishing Group, Inc., The.

Raum, Elizabeth. The Cold, Hard Facts about Science & Medicine in Colonial America. 2011. (Life in the American Colonies Ser.). (ENG.). 32p. (J). (gr. 3-4). pap. 48.60 *(978-1-4296-7216-0(1),* 16775, Capstone Pr.); pap. 8.10 *(978-1-4296-7215-3(3),* 116825) Capstone.

Rausch, Monica. Crispus Attucks, 1 vol. 2007. (Great Americans Ser.). (ENG., Illus.). 24p. (gr. 2-4). lib. bdg. 24.67 *(978-0-8368-7681-9(4),* ff45ff1f-3c77-4316-a6e9-60d4fafb41fe, Weekly Reader Leveled Readers) Stevens, Gareth Publishing LLLP.

Raymond, Aaron. A Primary Source History of the Colony of Delaware, 1 vol. 2005. (Primary Sources of the Thirteen Colonies & the Lost Colony Ser.). (ENG., Illus.). 64p. (YA). (gr. 4-6). lib. bdg. 37.13 *(978-1-4042-0425-6(3),* 13fa6af7-a07b-4f3e-a426-6e2b89c853ef) Rosen Publishing Group, Inc., The.

Roberts, Russell. Holidays & Celebrations in Colonial America. 2006. (Building America Ser.). (Illus.). 48p. (J). (gr. 3-7). lib. bdg. 29.95 *(978-1-58415-467-9(5))* Mitchell Lane Pubs.

—Life in Colonial America. 2007. (Building America Ser.). (Illus.). 48p. (J). (gr. 4-8). lib. bdg. 29.95 *(978-1-58415-549-2(3))* Mitchell Lane Pubs.

Robson, David. Colonial America. 2012. (Illus.). 96p. (YA). lib. bdg. 43.93 *(978-1-60152-246-7(0))* ReferencePoint Pr., Inc.

Rodgers, Kelly. The Middle Colonies: Breadbasket of the New World. rev. ed. 2016. (Social Studies: Informational Text Ser.). (ENG., Illus.). 32p. (gr. 4-8). pap. 11.99 *(978-1-4938-3076-3(7))* Teacher Created Materials, Inc.

—The New England Colonies: A Place for Puritans. rev. ed. 2016. (Social Studies: Informational Text Ser.). (ENG., Illus.). 32p. (gr. 4-8). pap. 11.99 *(978-1-4938-3075-6(9))* Teacher Created Materials, Inc.

—The Southern Colonies: First & Last of 13. rev. ed. 2016. (Social Studies: Informational Text Ser.). (ENG., Illus.). 32p. (gr. 4-8). pap. 11.99 *(978-1-4938-3077-0(5))* Teacher Created Materials, Inc.

Rosaler, Maxine. A Timeline of the First Continental Congress, 1 vol. 2004. (Timelines of American History Ser.). (ENG., Illus.). 32p. (gr. 4-4). lib. bdg. 29.13 *(978-0-8239-4545-0(6),* a97b185d-7667-4b69-9358-e4319be7a2c9, Rosen Reference) Rosen Publishing Group, Inc., The.

Roza, Greg. Analyzing the Boston Tea Party: Establishing Cause-and-Effect Relationships, 1 vol. 2005. (Critical Thinking in American History Ser.). (ENG., Illus.). 48p. (J). (gr. 5-8). lib. bdg. 34.47 *(978-1-4042-0411-9(3),* e06b1fea-7392-4e68-8d58-ec82950c19bf) Rosen Publishing Group, Inc., The.

—The Colony of New York, 1 vol. 2015. (Spotlight on the 13 Colonies: Birth of a Nation Ser.). (ENG., Illus.). 24p. (J). (gr. 4-6). pap. 11.00 *(978-1-4994-0537-8(5),* 32234a4a-48df-4521-b4d6-3e1796ad51f4, PowerKids Pr.) Rosen Publishing Group, Inc., The.

—The Colony of Rhode Island, 1 vol. 2015. (Spotlight on the 13 Colonies: Birth of a Nation Ser.). (ENG.). 24p. (J). (gr. 4-6). pap. 11.00 *(978-1-4994-0577-4(4),* 703bb669-be99-4262-bc6f-169328be74f9, PowerKids Pr.) Rosen Publishing Group, Inc., The.

Ruffin, Frances E. Molly Pitcher. 2009. (American Legends Ser.). 24p. (gr. 3-3). 42.50 *(978-1-61511-384-2(3),* PowerKids Pr.) Rosen Publishing Group, Inc., The.

Schanzer, Rosalyn. George vs. George. 2007. (ENG.). 64p. (J). (gr. 4-7). 17.75 *(978-1-5311-7657-0(7))* Perfection Learning Corp.

—George vs. George: The American Revolution As Seen from Both Sides. 2007. (Illus.). 64p. (J). (gr. 3-7). per. 6.95 *(978-1-4263-0042-4(5),* National Geographic Kids) Disney Publishing Worldwide.

—George vs. George: The Revolutionary War As Seen by Both Sides. 2004. (Illus.). 64p. (J). (gr. 3-7). 16.95 *(978-0-7922-7349-3(4),* National Geographic Children's Bks.) Disney Publishing Worldwide.

Sebree, Chet'la & Stefoff, Rebecca. Historical Sources on Colonial Life, 1 vol. 2019. (America's Story Ser.). (ENG.). 144p. (J). (gr. 8-8). pap. 22.16 *(978-1-5026-4077-2(5),* 08f22958-c18e-4600-b9ea-e5d66cb813b4) Cavendish Square Publishing LLC.

Sioux, Tracee. Immigrants in Colonial America. (Primary Sources of Immigration & Migration in America Ser.). 24p. (gr. 3-4). 2009. 42.50 *(978-1-60851-777-0(2))* 2003. (ENG., Illus.). pap. 9.40 *(978-0-8239-8949-2(6),* cc1148aa-fca4-4fd7-8dbf-d52f71afc1ba) 2003. (ENG., Illus.). (J). lib. bdg. 26.27 *(978-0-8239-6823-7(5),* be18e62a-e5f6-404c-b0a5-011a018cb30c) Rosen Publishing Group, Inc., The. (PowerKids Pr.).

Smith, Emily R. Life in the Colonies, 1 vol. rev. ed. 2004. (Social Studies: Informational Text Ser.). (ENG.). 24p. (gr. 4-8). pap. 10.99 *(978-0-7439-8742-4(X))* Teacher Created Materials, Inc.

Spotlight on the 13 Colonies. 2015. (Spotlight on the 13 Colonies Ser.). (ENG.). 24p. (J). (gr. 4-5). pap., pap., pap. 693.00 *(978-1-4994-1313-7(0),* PowerKids Pr.) Rosen Publishing Group, Inc., The.

Stanley, George E. The New Republic (1763-1815), 1 vol. 2004. (Primary Source History of the United States Ser.). (ENG., Illus.). 48p. (gr. 5-8). lib. bdg. 33.67 *(978-0-8368-5825-9(5),* 89d397eb-c154-4e36-a7ed-ed2afca5dd56, Gareth Stevens Secondary Library) Stevens, Gareth Publishing LLLP.

Stefoff, Rebecca. Cities & Towns. 2007. (ENG., Illus.). 96p. (C). (gr. 6-18). lib. bdg. 165.00 *(978-0-7656-8109-6(9),* Y181735) Routledge.

—Colonial Life, 1 vol. Kubinyi, Laszlo, illus. 2003. (American Voices From Ser.). (ENG.). 160p. (gr. 6-6). 41.21 *(978-0-7614-1205-2(0),* 23e5579e-62bb-4199-9af2-3fe85a1892ab) Cavendish Square Publishing LLC.

—Exploration & Settlement. 2007. (ENG., Illus.). 96p. (C). (gr. 6-18). lib. bdg. 180.00 *(978-0-7656-8108-9(0),* Y182272) Routledge.

Stoltman, Joan. 20 Fun Facts about the 13 Colonies, 1 vol. 2018. (Fun Fact File: U. S. History! Ser.). (ENG.). 32p. (gr. 2-3). pap. 11.50 *(978-1-5382-1903-4(4),* 7adc5f9b-4d17-4912-9bf2-b9b0810cddde) Stevens, Gareth Publishing LLLP.

Sullivan, Laura. The Colonial Slave Family, 1 vol. 2015. (Colonial People Ser.). (ENG., Illus.). 48p. (gr. 4-4). 34.07 *(978-1-5026-0486-6(8),* 27404ad0-e6b7-49b2-9a9a-3dd69d10d871) Cavendish Square Publishing LLC.

—The Colonial Woodworker, 1 vol. 2015. (Colonial People Ser.). (ENG.). 48p. (gr. 4-4). 34.07 *(978-1-5026-0484-2(1),* 386ffcf4-89db-431c-95a0-e161e8b61c6a) Cavendish Square Publishing LLC.

Sullivan, Laura L. Blackbeard. 2015. (J). lib. bdg. *(978-1-62713-525-2(1))* Cavendish Square Publishing LLC.

Swanson Sateren, Shelley. School in Colonial America. 2016. (It's Back to School ... Way Back! Ser.). (ENG., Illus.). 32p. (J). (gr. 3-6). lib. bdg. 27.99 *(978-1-5157-2097-3(7),* 132702) Capstone.

Uschan, Michael V. The Salem Witch Trials, 1 vol. 2004. (Landmark Events in American History Ser.). (ENG., Illus.). 48p. (gr. 5-8). pap. 15.05 *(978-0-8368-5415-2(2),* c80ebd89-e501-4720-8818-457470b372e2); lib. bdg. 33.67 *(978-0-8368-5387-2(3),* ec56240d-e910-4b70-991f-b0a25161bb6b) Stevens, Gareth Publishing LLLP. (Gareth Stevens Secondary Library).

Wachter, Joanne. The Thirteen Colonies. 2005. (J). pap. *(978-1-4108-4619-8(9))* Benchmark Education Co.

Walker, Sally M. Ghost Walls: The Story of a 17th-Century Colonial Homestead. 2014. (ENG., Illus.). 136p. (J). (gr. 5-8). lib. bdg. 20.95 *(978-0-7613-5408-6(5),* 6238a30f-4da2-4abe-8468-663f92628278, Carolrhoda Bks.) Lerner Publishing Group.

Wells-Cole, Catherine. Slavery & the Forging of Early America. 2014. (J). *(978-1-59935-410-1(1))* Reynolds, Morgan Inc.

Whitman Publishing, creator. Discover the American Revolution: History Project Toolkit. 2011. pap. 19.95 *(978-0-7948-3590-3(2))* Whitman Publishing LLC.

Wiener. The 13 Colonies, 13 vols. 2004. (Illus.). *(978-0-7398-6890-4(X))* Harcourt Schl. Pubs.

Wirkner, Linda. Learning about America's Colonial Period with Graphic Organizers. (Graphic Organizers in Social Studies). 24p. 2009. (gr. 3-4). 42.50 *(978-1-61513-078-8(0),* PowerKids Pr.) 2005. (ENG.). (gr. 4-5). pap. 8.25 *(978-1-4042-5052-9(2),* 8a4f0f2f-c95b-4008-b0d1-c9d03a0e23b0, Rosen Classroom) 2004. (ENG., Illus.). (J). (gr. 4-5). lib. bdg. 26.27 *(978-1-4042-2811-5(X),* 99d1e06b-dec3-48a2-81d1-60023cba163f, PowerKids Pr.) Rosen Publishing Group, Inc., The.

—Learning about America's Industrial Growth & Expansion with Graphic Organizers. 2009. (Graphic Organizers in Social Studies). 24p. (gr. 3-4). 42.50 *(978-1-61513-081-8(0),* PowerKids Pr.) Rosen Publishing Group, Inc., The.

Wolfe, James. The Colonial Period, 1 vol., 1. 2015. (Early American History Ser.). (ENG., Illus.). 80p. (J). (gr. 8-8). 35.47 *(978-1-68048-268-3(8),* 56015db9-1499-4785-91d3-394381608487, Britannica Educational Publishing) Rosen Publishing Group, Inc., The.

Yale, Dallas. The Colony of New Hampshire, 1 vol. 2015. (Spotlight on the 13 Colonies: Birth of a Nation Ser.). (ENG., Illus.). 24p. (J). (gr. 4-6). pap. 11.00 *(978-1-4994-0526-2(X),* b189d1f9-50c7-4a67-9b3b-cad20f1b8d34, PowerKids Pr.) Rosen Publishing Group, Inc., The.

Yasuda, Anita. Disgusting Jobs in Colonial America: The down & Dirty Details. 2018. (Disgusting Jobs in History Ser.). (ENG., Illus.). 32p. (J). (gr. 3-6). lib. bdg. 27.99 *(978-1-5435-0369-2(1),* 137209, Capstone Pr.) Capstone.

Yero, Judith & Yero, Judith Lloyd. American Documents: the Declaration of Independence (Direct Mail Edition) 2006. (American Documents Ser.). (ENG., Illus.). 40p. (J). (gr. 5-9). 15.95 *(978-0-7922-5397-6(3))* National Geographic Society.

Yero, Judith Lloyd & Yero, Judith. American Documents: the Bill of Rights (Direct Mail Edition) 2006. (American Documents Ser.). (ENG., Illus.). 40p. (J). (gr. 5-9). 15.95 *(978-0-7922-5395-2(7))* National Geographic Society.

—American Documents: the Mayflower Compact (Direct Mail Edition) 2006. (American Documents Ser.). (ENG., Illus.). 40p. (J). (gr. 5-9). 15.95 *(978-0-7922-5891-9(6))* National Geographic Society.

UNITED STATES—HISTORY—COLONIAL PERIOD, CA. 1600-1775—FICTION

Alsheimer, Jeanette E. & Friedle, Patricia J. Path to Punishment. 2008. 220p. (J). (gr. 8-12). per. 18.95 *(978-1-57197-482-2(2),* Ivy House Publishing Group) Pentland Pr., Inc.

Ayers, Linda. The Time Bridge Travelers & the Time Travel Station, 3 bks., Bk. 3. Ayers, Ryan, illus. l.t. ed. 2007. (Time Bridge Travelers Ser.: 3). 140p. (J). lib. bdg. 16.95 *(978-0-9786302-8-7(9));* per. 7.95 *(978-0-9786302-7-0(0))* Blue Thistle Pr.

Bailey, Carolyn Sherwin. Boys & Girls of Colonial Days. 2008. (Illus.). 152p. pap. 8.95 *(978-1-59915-246-2(0))* Yesterday's Classics.

Bulla, Clyde Robert. A Lion to Guard Us. Chessare, Michele, illus. 2018. (ENG.). 128p. (J). (gr. 3-7). pap. 9.99 *(978-0-06-440333-7(5),* HarperCollins) HarperCollins Pubs.

Butters, Dorothy Gilman, pseud. The Bells of Freedom. Wilde, Carol, illus. 2008. (J). (gr. 4-6). 21.00 *(978-0-8446-6162-9(7))* Smith, Peter Pub., Inc.

Colonial People, 10 vols., Set. Incl. Apothecary. Petersen, Christine. 34.07 *(978-0-7614-4795-5(4),* 9545d33a-8fc6-403a-9486-7c9ba1589dbf); Barber. Heinrichs, Ann. 34.07 *(978-0-7614-4800-6(4),* 0ccb54d3-082a-48eb-b652-90f68b2fc8c4); Blacksmith. Petersen, Christine. 34.07 *(978-0-7614-4799-3(7),* 5550975a-2157-40e4-956e-eb1c4cc25d4a); Farmer. Mara, Wil. 34.07 *(978-0-7614-4797-9(0),* b4e76fee-661c-4aae-848f-8e178426336f); Innkeeper. Mara, Wil. 34.07 *(978-0-7614-4796-2(2),* 0e3cdbb5-6f2b-4e19-8d12-925ab7f2aa81); Printer. Petersen, Christine. 34.07 *(978-0-7614-4802-0(0),* d3054ccc-85a8-4324-a018-f21131a51dd9); Schoolmaster. Mara, Wil. 34.07 *(978-0-7614-4801-3(2),* a4a1cebd-de00-4ad7-8468-880c7ef3dc47); Shoemaker. Heinrichs, Ann. 34.07 *(978-0-7614-4798-6(9),* fed9550a-1bb6-4923-be20-62fea6eac51); Silversmith. Mara, Wil. 34.07 *(978-0-7614-4804-4(7),* b281651d-0b8b-491e-94d1-f1b43f638296); Surveyor. Petersen, Christine. 34.07 *(978-0-7614-4805-1(5),* f1d2b84e-a0e8-4249-b423-ef731729c885); 48p. (gr. 4-4). 2011. (Colonial People Ser.). 2010. Set lib. bdg. 299.30 o.p. *(978-0-7614-4794-8(6),* Cavendish Square) Cavendish Square Publishing LLC.

Cornelia Meigs. Master Simon's Garden. 2010. (Illus.). 244p. pap. 6.95 *(978-1-60386-299-8(4),* Watchmaker Publishing) Wexford College Pr.

Curtis, Alice. Little Maid of Newport. 2006. (Little Maid Ser.). (ENG., Illus.). 212p. (gr. 4-7). pap. 12.95 *(978-1-55709-339-4(3))* Applewood Bks.

de Angeli, Marguerite. Elin's Amerika. 3rd ed. 2007. (Illus.). 98p. (J). pap. 15.99 *(978-0-9800761-0-3(2))* American Swedish Historical Museum.

Deutsch, Stacia & Cohon, Rhody. Betsy Ross's Star, 8. Francis, Guy, illus. 2006. (Blast to the Past Ser.: 8). (ENG.). 121p. (J). (gr. 3-6). 16.19 *(978-1-4169-3388-5(3))* Simon & Schuster, Inc.

Draper, Sharon M. Copper Sun. 2006. (ENG.). 320p. (YA). (gr. 8-18). 19.99 *(978-0-689-82181-3(6),* Atheneum Bks. for Young Readers) Simon & Schuster Children's Publishing.

Frazier, Jan. Catch the Watercolored Wind: Jamestown 1617. 2015. (Illus.). ii, 191p. (YA). pap. 14.95 *(978-1-55571-788-9(8),* Paloma Bks.) L & R Publishing, LLC.

Gibbs, Gretchen. The Book of Maggie Bradstreet. 2012. (Bradstreet Chronicles). (ENG.). 183p. (YA). pap. 9.99 *(978-0-9852948-0-9(9))* Glenmere Pr.

Gilberstadt, Debra Pack. Unmarked Grave: Remembering an American Patriot. 2005. (YA). lib. bdg. 29.95 *(978-0-9763033-0-5(2))* Eslinger Hse. Publishing.

Hopkins, K. C. The Night the Spirits Danced. 2008. 115p. pap. 15.00 *(978-0-615-23929-3(3))* Hopkins, KC.

Kastner, Janet. The Snake Fence: A Novel. 2012. 235p. (J). pap. 14.95 *(978-1-937768-13-3(9))* QuakerPress.

Kientz, Chris & Hockensmith, Steve. It's Treason, by George! Nielsen, Lee, illus. 2017. (Secret Smithsonian Adventures Ser.: 3). 64p. (gr. 3-7). pap. 10.95 *(978-1-58834-586-8(6),* Smithsonian Bks.) Smithsonian Institution Scholarly Pr.

Leatherman, Diane. Abigail Before the Revolution. 2005. (Illus.). 64p. (J). *(978-0-9665861-2-1(3))* Bounty Project, The.

Limbaugh, Rush. Rush Revere & the First Patriots: Time-Travel Adventures with Exceptional Americans. 2014. (Rush Revere Ser.: 2). (ENG., Illus.). 256p. 21.00 *(978-1-4767-5588-5(4),* Threshold Editions) Threshold Editions.

McCall, Edith S. Adventures of the American Colonies. Rogers, Carol, illus. 2011. 126p. 40.95 *(978-1-258-06470-9(7))* Literary Licensing, LLC.

Nixon, Joan Lowery. Ann's Story, 1747. 2004. (J). *(978-0-87935-198-4(5))* Colonial Williamsburg Foundation.

—Caesar's Story, 1759. 2004. (J). *(978-0-87935-199-1(3))* Colonial Williamsburg Foundation.

—Maria's Story, 1773. 2004. (J). *(978-0-87935-227-1(2))* Colonial Williamsburg Foundation.

—Nancy's Story, 1765. 2004. (J). *(978-0-87935-225-7(6))* Colonial Williamsburg Foundation.

—Will's Story, 1771. 2004. (J). *(978-0-87935-226-4(4))* Colonial Williamsburg Foundation.

Otis, James. Neal, the Miller: A Son of Liberty. 2007. 48p. per. *(978-1-4068-4368-2(7))* Echo Library.

Prescott, Della R. Day in a Colonial Home. 2006. (Applewood Bks.). (ENG.). 96p. (gr. 4-7). per. 12.95 *(978-1-55709-374-5(1))* Applewood Bks.

Richter, Conrad. The Light in the Forest. (YA). (gr. 7-18). 21.95 *(978-0-89190-333-8(X))* Amereon Ltd.

Rinaldi, Ann. The Fifth of March: A Story of the Boston Massacre. 2004. (Great Episodes Ser.). (ENG.). 352p. (J). (gr. 5-7). pap. 8.99 *(978-0-15-205078-8(7),* 1195337, Clarion Bks.) HarperCollins Pubs.

Smith, Mary P. Wells. The Young Puritans in King Philip's War. Bridgman, L. J., illus. 2011. 396p. 54.95 *(978-1-258-05550-9(3))* Literary Licensing, LLC.

Stowe, Harriet. The First Christmas of New England & O. 2006. 108p. per. 9.95 *(978-1-59818-758-8(9))* Aegypan.

UNITED STATES—HISTORY—FRENCH AND INDIAN WAR, 1755-1763

Boehme, Gerry. The French & Indian War, 1 vol. 2017. (Primary Sources of Colonial America Ser.). (ENG.). 64p. (gr. 6-6). 35.93 *(978-1-5026-3144-2(X),* a97a77d3-5aa4-4870-b111-7ee1191006a1); pap. 16.28 *(978-1-5026-3459-7(7),* 5619c005-8624-4e07-bd14-ce54d545ce01) Cavendish Square Publishing LLC.

Caravantes, Peggy. French & Indian War. 2013. (Foundations of Our Nation Ser.). (ENG.). 48p. (J). (gr. 4-8). pap. 18.50 *(978-1-61783-759-3(8),* 8750); lib. bdg. 35.64 *(978-1-61783-709-8(1),* 7816) ABDO Publishing Co.

Cheatham, Mark. The Life of a Colonial Soldier, 1 vol. 2013. (Jr. Graphic Colonial America Ser.). (ENG., Illus.). 24p. (J). (gr. 2-3). pap. 11.60 *(978-1-4777-1439-3(1),* 856a9e2a-d842-4008-9543-7caf6bd62692); lib. bdg. 28.93 *(978-1-4777-1310-5(7),* f24ac1b8-8ed4-4c67-bb3c-083387a6d554) Rosen Publishing Group, Inc., The. (PowerKids Pr.).

Dipiazza, Francesca. When Did George Washington Fight His First Military Battle? And Other Questions about the French & Indian War. 2011. (Six Questions of American History Ser.). (ENG.). 48p. (gr. 4-6). pap. 56.72 *(978-0-7613-7643-9(7))* Lerner Publishing Group.

Gard, Carolyn. The French & Indian War: A Primary Source History of the Fight for Territory in North America. 2009. (Primary Sources in American History Ser.). 64p. (gr. 5-8). 58.50 *(978-1-60851-495-3(1))* Rosen Publishing Group, Inc., The.

Hillstrom, Laurie Collier, et al, eds. French & Indian War. 2003. (French & Indian War Ser.). (ENG., Illus.). 240p. (J). lib. bdg. 129.00 *(978-0-7876-6560-9(6),* UXL) Cengage Gale.

The Life of a Colonial Soldier. 2013. (Jr. Graphic Colonial America Ser.). 24p. (J). (gr. 3-6). pap. 63.60 *(978-1-4777-1440-9(5),* PowerKids Pr.) Rosen Publishing Group, Inc., The.

Lynch, Seth. The French & Indian War, 1 vol. 2018. (Look at U. S. History Ser.). (ENG.). 32p. (gr. 2-2). 28.27 *(978-1-5382-2123-5(3),* 9b478ca2-74e0-40f9-9ff8-32d54779c296) Stevens, Gareth Publishing LLLP.

Maynard, Charles W. Fort Ticonderoga. 2009. (Famous Forts Throughout American History Ser.). 24p. (gr. 3-4). 42.50 *(978-1-61512-521-0(3),* PowerKids Pr.) Rosen Publishing Group, Inc., The.

Quasha, Jennifer. Robert Rogers: Rogers' Rangers, & the French & Indian War. 2009. (Library of American Lives & Times Ser.). 112p. (gr. 5-5). 69.20 *(978-1-60853-503-3(7))* Rosen Publishing Group, Inc., The.

Santella, Andrew. The French & Indian War. 2011. (Cornerstones of Freedom, Third Ser.). 64p. (J). lib. bdg. 30.00 *(978-0-531-25033-4(4)*, Children's Pr.) Scholastic Library Publishing.

Small, Cathleen. Colonial Interactions with Native Americans, 1 vol. 2017. (Primary Sources of Colonial America Ser.). (ENG.). 64p. (gr. 6-6). pap. 16.28 *(978-1-5026-3461-0(9)*, 2c3c1415-09a6-4725-9c69-e6df43f51fe4); lib. bdg. 35.93 *(978-1-5026-3134-3(2)*, fa37527d-f22f-4280-8745-757bc8e57b62) Cavendish Square Publishing LLC.

Thornton, Jeremy. The French & Indian War. 2009. (Building America's Democracy Ser.). 24p. (gr. 3-3). 42.50 *(978-1-61511-766-6(0)*, PowerKids Pr.) Rosen Publishing Group, Inc., The.

UNITED STATES—HISTORY—FRENCH AND INDIAN WAR, 1755-1763—FICTION

Altsheler, Joseph A. The French & Indian War Novels: The Hunters of the Hills & The Shadow of the North, Vol. 1. 2008. 464p. (J). *(978-1-84677-586-4(8))*; pap. *(978-1-84677-585-7(X))* Leonaur Ltd.

—The French & Indian War Novels: The Lords of the Wild & The Sun of Quebec, Vol. 3. 2008. (J). reprint ed. 428p. *(978-1-84677-590-1(6))*; 424p. pap. *(978-1-84677-589-5(2))* Leonaur Ltd.

—The French & Indian War Novels: The Rulers of the Lakes & The Masters of the Peaks, Vol. 2. 2008. 416p. (J). reprint ed. *(978-1-84677-588-8(4))*; pap. *(978-1-84677-587-1(6))* Leonaur Ltd.

—The Hunters of the Hills: A Story of the Great French & Indian War. rev. ed. 2006. (French & Indian War Ser.). 316p. (J). 29.95 *(978-1-4218-2334-8(9))*; pap. 14.95 *(978-1-4218-2434-5(5))* 1st World Publishing, Inc. (1st World Library - Literary Society).

—The Hunters of the Hills: A Story of the Great French & Indian War. (French & Indian War Ser.: Vol. 1). (J). reprint ed. 26.95 *(978-0-8488-0904-1(1))* Amereon Ltd.

—The Hunters of the Hills: A Story of the Great French & Indian War. 2009. (French & Indian War Ser.: Vol. 1). 200p. (J). reprint ed. pap. *(978-0-217-62835-8(4))* Books LLC.

—The Hunters of the Hills: A Story of the Great French & Indian War. 2012. 392p. reprint ed. pap. 33.75 *(978-1-277-16849-5(0))* Creative Media Partners, LLC.

—The Hunters of the Hills: A Story of the Great French & Indian War. 2006. (French & Indian War Ser.). (J). pap. *(978-1-4065-0815-4(2))* Dodo Pr.

—The Hunters of the Hills: A Story of the Great French & Indian War. 2007. (French & Indian War Ser.). 188p. (J). per. *(978-1-4068-1680-8(9))* Echo Library.

—The Hunters of the Hills: A Story of the Great French & Indian War. 2010. (French & Indian War Ser.: Vol. 1). (Illus.). 168p. (J). (gr. 4-7). reprint ed. pap. 19.99 *(978-1-153-70670-4(9))* General Bks. LLC.

—The Hunters of the Hills: A Story of the Great French & Indian War. (French & Indian War Ser.: Vol. 1). (J). reprint ed. 2011. 372p. (gr. 4-7). 48.95 *(978-1-169-83864-2(2))* 2010. 372p. (gr. 4-7). 39.16 *(978-1-163-20015-5(8))* 2010. 372p. (gr. 4-7). pap. 27.16 *(978-1-162-64218-5(1))* 2004. pap. 33.95 *(978-1-4179-1500-2(5))* Kessinger Publishing, LLC.

—The Hunters of the Hills: A Story of the Great French & Indian War. 2011. (French & Indian War Ser.: Vol. 1). 284p. (J). (gr. 4-7). reprint ed. pap. *(978-3-8424-7700-1(7))* tredition Verlag.

—The Lords of the Wild: A Story of the Old New York Border. rev. ed. 2006. (French & Indian War Ser.). 264p. (J). 28.95 *(978-1-4218-2335-5(7))*; pap. 13.95 *(978-1-4218-2435-2(3))* 1st World Publishing, Inc. (1st World Library - Literary Society).

—The Lords of the Wild: A Story of the Old New York Border. (French & Indian War Ser.: Vol. 1). (J). reprint ed. 24.95 *(978-0-8488-0905-8(X))* Amereon Ltd.

—The Lords of the Wild: A Story of the Old New York Border. 2006. (French & Indian War Ser.). (J). pap. *(978-1-4065-0816-1(0))* Dodo Pr.

—The Lords of the Wild: A Story of the Old New York Border. 2007. (French & Indian War Ser.). 156p. (J). per. *(978-1-4068-1681-5(7))* Echo Library.

—The Lords of the Wild: A Story of the Old New York Border. 2010. (French & Indian War Ser.: Vol. 5). (Illus.). 138p. (J). (gr. 4-7). reprint ed. pap. 19.99 *(978-1-153-71020-6(X))* General Bks. LLC.

—The Lords of the Wild: A Story of the Old New York Border. (French & Indian War Ser.: Vol. 5). (J). reprint ed. 2010. 208p. (gr. 4-7). 31.96 *(978-1-169-28834-8(0))* 2010. 208p. (gr. 4-7). pap. 19.96 *(978-1-162-70072-4(6))* 2010. 39.95 *(978-1-161-46937-0(0))* 2004. pap. 1.99 *(978-1-4192-7070-3(2))* 2004. pap. 24.95 *(978-1-4191-7070-6(8))* Kessinger Publishing, LLC.

—The Lords of the Wild: A Story of the Old New York Border. 2011. (French & Indian War Ser.: Vol. 5). 236p. (J). reprint ed. pap. *(978-3-8424-4395-2(1))* tredition Verlag.

—The Masters of the Peaks: A Story of the Great North Woods. 2017. (ENG., Illus.). (J). 24.95 *(978-1-374-89896-7(1))* Capital Communications, Inc.

—The Rulers of the Lakes: A Story of George & Champlain. 2006. (French & Indian War Ser.: Vol. 3). 300p. (J). reprint ed. 29.95 *(978-1-4218-1778-1(0))*; pap. 14.95 *(978-1-4218-1878-8(7))* 1st World Publishing, Inc. (1st World Library - Literary Society).

—The Rulers of the Lakes: A Story of George & Champlain. (French & Indian War Ser.: Vol. 3). (J). reprint ed. 25.95 *(978-0-8488-0906-5(8))* Amereon Ltd.

—The Rulers of the Lakes: A Story of George & Champlain. (French & Indian War Ser.: Vol. 3). (J). 2008. 272p. 25.99 *(978-0-554-34451-5(3))* 2010. (ENG.). 370p. (gr. 4-7). reprint ed. pap. 32.75 *(978-1-177-56810-4(1))* Creative Media Partners, LLC.

—The Rulers of the Lakes: A Story of George & Champlain. 2006. (French & Indian War Ser.: Vol. 3). (J). reprint ed. pap. *(978-1-4065-0819-2(5))* Dodo Pr.

—The Rulers of the Lakes: A Story of George & Champlain. 2010. 166p. pap. 24.67 *(978-1-152-80290-2(9))*; (French & Indian War Ser.: Vol. 3). (Illus.). 160p. (J). (gr. 4-7). reprint ed. pap. 19.99 *(978-1-153-71979-7(7))* General Bks. LLC.

—The Rulers of the Lakes: A Story of George & Champlain. reprint ed. 2010. 366p. 39.16 *(978-1-163-74095-8(0))* 2010. 366p. pap. 27.16 *(978-1-163-71977-0(3))* 2007. (French & Indian War Ser.: Vol. 3). 368p. (J). 48.95 *(978-0-548-43205-1(8))* 2007. (French & Indian War Ser.: Vol. 3). 368p. (J). pap. 33.95 *(978-0-548-40955-8(2))* Kessinger Publishing, LLC.

—The Rulers of the Lakes: A Story of George & Champlain. 2011. (French & Indian War Ser.: Vol. 3). 272p. (J). (gr. 4-7). reprint ed. pap. *(978-3-8424-7701-8(5))* tredition Verlag.

—The Shadow of the North: A Story of Old New York & a Lost Campaign. 2010. (French & Indian War Ser.: Vol. 2). (ENG.). 378p. (J). (gr. 4-7). reprint ed. pap. 33.75 *(978-1-176-98060-0(2))* Creative Media Partners, LLC.

—The Shadow of the North: A Story of Old New York & a Lost Campaign. 2006. (French & Indian War Ser.: Vol. 2). (J). reprint ed. pap. *(978-1-4065-0823-9(3))* Dodo Pr.

—The Shadow of the North: A Story of Old New York & a Lost Campaign. 2007. (French & Indian War Ser.: Vol. 2). 188p. (J). reprint ed. per. *(978-1-4068-1687-7(6))* Echo Library.

—The Shadow of the North: A Story of Old New York & a Lost Campaign. 2010. (French & Indian War Ser.: Vol. 2). (Illus.). 170p. (J). (gr. 4-7). reprint ed. pap. 19.99 *(978-1-153-72063-2(9))* General Bks. LLC.

—The Shadow of the North: A Story of Old New York & a Lost Campaign. (French & Indian War Ser.: Vol. 2). (J). reprint ed. 2010. 256p. (gr. 4-7). 34.36 *(978-1-169-30396-6(X))* 2010. 256p. (gr. 4-7). pap. 22.36 *(978-1-162-70813-3(1))* 2010. 42.95 *(978-1-161-47677-4(6))* 2004. pap. 1.99 *(978-1-4192-8225-6(5))* 2004. pap. 27.95 *(978-1-4191-8225-9(0))* Kessinger Publishing, LLC.

—The Shadow of the North: A Story of Old New York & a Lost Campaign. 2011. (French & Indian War Ser.: Vol. 2). 286p. (J). reprint ed. pap. *(978-3-8424-4397-6(8))* tredition Verlag.

—The Sun of Quebec: A Story of a Great Crisis. 2006. (French & Indian War Ser.: Vol. 6). 324p. (J). reprint ed. 29.95 *(978-1-4218-2337-9(3))*; pap. 14.95 *(978-1-4218-2437-6(X))* 1st World Publishing, Inc. (1st World Library - Literary Society).

—The Sun of Quebec: A Story of a Great Crisis. (French & Indian War Ser.: Vol. 6). (J). reprint ed. 25.95 *(978-0-8488-0907-2(6))* Amereon Ltd.

—The Sun of Quebec: A Story of a Great Crisis. 2007. (French & Indian War Ser.: Vol. 6). 280p. (J). reprint ed. per. *(978-1-4065-6552-2(0))* Dodo Pr.

—The Sun of Quebec: A Story of a Great Crisis. 2007. (French & Indian War Ser.: Vol. 6). 196p. (J). reprint ed. per. *(978-1-4068-1689-1(2))* Echo Library.

—The Sun of Quebec: A Story of a Great Crisis. 2010. (French & Indian War Ser.: Vol. 6). (Illus.). 176p. (J). (gr. 4-7). reprint ed. pap. 19.99 *(978-1-153-72258-2(5))* General Bks. LLC.

—The Sun of Quebec: A Story of a Great Crisis. 2011. (French & Indian War Ser.: Vol. 6). (J). (gr. 4-7). reprint ed. *(978-1-164-50609-6(9))* Kessinger Publishing, LLC.

—The Sun of Quebec: A Story of a Great Crisis. Wrenn, Charles L., illus. (French & Indian War Ser.: Vol. 6). 356p. (J). reprint ed. 2010. (gr. 4-7). pap. 25.56 *(978-1-163-19471-3(9))* 2008. 46.95 *(978-1-4366-7287-0(2))* 2007. per. 31.95 *(978-1-4325-9779-5(5))* Kessinger Publishing, LLC.

—The Sun of Quebec: A Story of a Great Crisis. 2012. (French & Indian War Ser.: Vol. 6). 276p. (J). (gr. 4-7). reprint ed. pap. *(978-3-8472-3211-7(8))* tredition Verlag.

Altsheler, Joseph A., ed. The Masters of the Peaks: A Story of the Great North Woods. (French & Indian War Ser.: Vol. 4). 311p. (J). reprint ed. lib. bdg. 24.95 *(978-0-88411-938-8(6))* Amereon Ltd.

—The Masters of the Peaks: A Story of the Great North Woods. 2010. (French & Indian War Ser.: Vol. 4). (Illus.). 144p. (J). (gr. 4-7). reprint ed. pap. *(978-1-4432-2285-3(2))* Books LLC.

—The Masters of the Peaks: A Story of the Great North Woods. reprint ed. 2012. 182p. pap. 22.75 *(978-1-276-49474-8(2))* 2010. (French & Indian War Ser.: Vol. 4). 320p. (J). pap. 30.75 *(978-1-142-51783-0(7))* Creative Media Partners, LLC.

—The Masters of the Peaks: A Story of the Great North Woods. 2006. (French & Indian War Ser.: Vol. 4). (J). reprint ed. pap. *(978-1-4065-0817-8(9))* Dodo Pr.

—The Masters of the Peaks: A Story of the Great North Woods. 2006. (French & Indian War Ser.: Vol. 4). (J). reprint ed. pap. *(978-1-4068-0762-2(1))* Echo Library.

—The Masters of the Peaks: A Story of the Great North Woods. 2009. (French & Indian War Ser.: Vol. 4). 162p. (J). reprint ed. pap. 8.85 *(978-1-150-40712-3(3))* General Bks. LLC.

—The Masters of the Peaks: A Story of the Great North Woods. (French & Indian War Ser.: Vol. 4). (J). reprint ed. 2010. 220p. (gr. 4-7). 31.96 *(978-1-169-29283-3(6))* 2010. 220p. (gr. 4-7). pap. 19.96 *(978-1-162-70171-4(4))* 2010. 39.95 *(978-1-161-47035-2(2))* 2004. pap. 1.99 *(978-1-4192-7205-9(5))* 2004. pap. 24.95 *(978-1-4191-7205-2(0))* Kessinger Publishing, LLC.

—The Masters of the Peaks: A Story of the Great North Woods. 2011. (French & Indian War Ser.: Vol. 4). 228p. (J). reprint ed. pap. *(978-3-8424-4394-5(3))* tredition Verlag.

Cooper, James Fenimore. The Last of the Mohicans. Wyeth, N. C., illus. 2013. (Scribner Classics Ser.). (ENG.). 368p. (J). (gr. 5). 24.99 *(978-1-4424-8130-5(7))*, Atheneum Bks. for Young Readers) Simon & Schuster Children's Publishing.

Fenimore Cooper, James. Last of the Mohicans, 1 vol. VanArsdale, Anthony, illus. 2010. (Calico Illustrated Classics Ser.: No. 1). (ENG.). 112p. (J). (gr. 2-5). 38.50 *(978-1-60270-708-5(1)*, 3969, Calico Chapter Bks.) ABDO Publishing Co.

Hemphill, Kris. Ambush in the Wilderness. 2003. (Adventures in America Ser.). (Illus.). 90p. (gr. 4). 14.95 *(978-1-893110-34-2(6))* Silver Moon Pr.

Henty, George. With Wolfe in Canad: The Winning of a Continent. 2011. 378p. pap. 19.95 *(978-1-61179-149-5(9))* Fireship Pr.

—With Wolfe in Canada: The Winning of a Continent. 2006. per. 8.95 *(978-1-57646-980-4(8))* Quiet Vision Publishing.

Kastner, Janet. The Snake Fence: A Novel. 2012. 235p. (J). pap. 14.95 *(978-1-937768-13-3(9))* QuakerPress.

UNITED STATES—HISTORY—REVOLUTION, 1775-1783

Abnett, Dan. George Washington & the American Revolution. (Jr. Graphic Biographies Ser.). (ENG.). 24p. (gr. 2-3). 2009. (J). 47.90 *(978-1-61513-813-5(7)*, PowerKids Pr.) 2006. (Illus.). (J). lib. bdg. 28.93 *(978-1-4042-3395-9(4)*, f5ebb962-806c-4e30-beef-2ed75efa306a) 2006. (Illus.). pap. 10.60 *(978-1-4042-2148-2(4)*, 27420dd3-e201-4cdf-8332-ff4d4b4b3df1, PowerKids Pr.) Rosen Publishing Group, Inc., The.

—George Washington y la Guerra de Independencia, 1 vol. 2009. (Historietas Juveniles: Biografías (Jr. Graphic Biographies) Ser.). (SPA., Illus.). 24p. (YA). (gr. 2-3). 28.93 *(978-1-4358-8564-6(3)*, 97102909-4df6-44a2-b6ce-f4870ffe0e02) Rosen Publishing Group, Inc., The.

Adams, Colleen. Results of the American Revolution: Summarizing Information. (Critical Thinking in American History Ser.). 48p. (gr. 5-8). 2009. 53.00 *(978-1-61512-096-3(3)*, Rosen Reference) 2005. (ENG., Illus.). (J). lib. bdg. 34.47 *(978-1-4042-0417-1(2)*, 32c98299-36a6-42e1-b354-0081fb5dad78) Rosen Publishing Group, Inc., The.

Adamson, Thomas K. The American Revolution. 2017. (J). *(978-1-5105-3500-8(4))* SmartBook Media, Inc.

Adler, David A. Heroes of the Revolution. Smith, Donald A., illus. 2006. (ENG.). 32p. (J). (gr. 1-4). 8.99 *(978-0-8234-2017-9(5))* Holiday Hse., Inc.

Allen, Thomas B. George Washington, Spymaster: How the Americans Outspied the British & Won the Revolutionary War. 2007. (Illus.). 192p. (J). (gr. 5-9). per. 7.95 *(978-1-4263-0041-7(7)*, National Geographic Kids) Disney Publishing Worldwide.

The American Revolution Complete Program. (gr. 2-5). 430.95 *(978-0-7368-4502-1(X)*, Red Brick Learning) Capstone.

Amler, Jane Frances. Haym Salomon: Patriot Banker of the American Revolution. 2009. (Library of American Lives & Times Ser.). 112p. (gr. 5-5). 69.20 *(978-1-60853-487-6(1))* Rosen Publishing Group, Inc., The.

Anderson, Dale. The American Colonies Declare Independence, 1 vol. 2005. (World Almanac(r) Library of the American Revolution Ser.). (ENG.). 48p. (gr. 5-8). pap. 15.05 *(978-0-8368-5935-5(9)*, 47adbbb4-4b38-4d75-9f76-2f76847e8ddc); (Illus.). lib. bdg. 33.67 *(978-0-8368-5926-3(X)*, 9381c4d2-0e2d-4fc5-87ec-be147d2b03c9) Stevens, Gareth Publishing LLLP. (Gareth Stevens Secondary Library).

—The American Revolution: Events & Outcomes. 2006. (Illus.). 78p. (YA). (gr. 5-9). reprint ed. 17.00 *(978-1-4223-5441-4(5))* DIANE Publishing Co.

—The Causes of the American Revolution, 1 vol. 2005. (World Almanac(r) Library of the American Revolution Ser.). (ENG.). 48p. (gr. 5-8). pap. 15.05 *(978-0-8368-5934-8(0)*, df7b3055-2918-415a-a679-9590b0e5d839); (Illus.). lib. bdg. 33.67 *(978-0-8368-5925-6(1)*, 79c307f1-6a22-4a84-8887-44d3a73f1473) Stevens, Gareth Publishing LLLP. (Gareth Stevens Secondary Library).

—Daily Life During the American Revolution, 1 vol. 2005. (World Almanac(r) Library of the American Revolution Ser.). (ENG.). 48p. (gr. 5-8). pap. 15.05 *(978-0-8368-5939-3(1)*, d0fdedfe-aa31-4b55-9332-5dac1f9258d2); lib. bdg. 33.67 *(978-0-8368-5930-0(8)*, 2214c6b0-c1d8-4d64-b3a9-e2e8ef41d2ea) Stevens, Gareth Publishing LLLP. (Gareth Stevens Secondary Library).

—Leaders of the American Revolution, 1 vol. 2005. (World Almanac(r) Library of the American Revolution Ser.). (ENG.). 48p. (gr. 5-8). lib. bdg. 33.67 *(978-0-8368-5931-7(6)*, 5670f581-1e2e-4ddf-81e4-ea8e89f67c26, Gareth Stevens Secondary Library) Stevens, Gareth Publishing LLLP.

—Soldiers & Sailors in the American Revolution, 1 vol. 2005. (World Almanac(r) Library of the American Revolution Ser.). (ENG.). 48p. (gr. 5-8). pap. 15.05 *(978-0-8368-5938-6(3)*, fefcb9af-19a9-4101-b561-c76c583fb122); lib. bdg. 33.67 *(978-0-8368-5929-4(4)*, 29863a8e-4cf7-476a-957d-381f6117ed23) Stevens, Gareth Publishing LLLP. (Gareth Stevens Secondary Library).

Anderson, Floyd. Father of the American Navy: John Barry. Orban, Paul, illus. 2011. 188p. 42.95 *(978-1-258-07454-8(0))* Literary Licensing, LLC.

Aronson, Marc. The Real Revolution: The Global Story of American Independence. 2005. (ENG., Illus.). 256p. (YA). (gr. 7-12). 22.00 *(978-0-618-18179-7(2)*, 111143, Clarion Bks.) HarperCollins Pubs.

Axelrod, Alan. The Revolutionary War: 1775-1783. Künstler, Mort, illus. 2016. (ENG.). 48p. (J). (gr. 2-7). 13.95 *(978-0-7892-1253-5(6)*, 791253, Abbeville Kids) Abbeville Pr., Inc.

Beasley, Ava. The American Revolution up Close! Showing Events & Processes, 1 vol. 2017. (Computer Kids: Powered by Computational Thinking Ser.). (ENG.). 24p. (J). (gr. 4-5). 25.27 *(978-1-5383-2432-5(6)*, 358d2c7c-7829-4563-94a5-7a157a158857, PowerKids Pr.); pap. *(978-1-5081-3759-7(5)*, 0373d979-cf6d-4ff0-9c36-09c39f9bd2bc, Rosen Classroom) Rosen Publishing Group, Inc., The.

Beller, Susan Provost. Yankee Doodle & the Redcoats: Soldiering in the Revolutionary War. rev. ed. 2007. (Soldiers on the Battlefront Ser.). (ENG., Illus.). 112p. (gr. 6-8). lib. bdg. 33.26 *(978-0-8225-6655-7(9))* Lerner Publishing Group.

Benchmark Education Co., LLC. The Causes of the American Revolution. 2014. (PRIME Ser.). (J). (gr. 6-8). pap. *(978-1-4509-9489-7(X))* Benchmark Education Co.

—The Faces of the American Revolution. 2014. (PRIME Ser.). (J). (gr. 6-8). pap. *(978-1-4509-9491-0(1))* Benchmark Education Co.

Benchmark Education Company. George Washington & the American Revolution (Teacher Guide) 2005. *(978-1-4108-4681-5(4))* Benchmark Education Co.

Benchmark Education Company, LLC Staff, compiled by. The AMER Revolution. 2006. spiral bd. 330.00 *(978-1-4108-7010-0(3))* Benchmark Education Co.

—The American Revolution. 2005. (English Explorers Ser.). (J). spiral bd. 265.00 *(978-1-4108-5771-2(9))* Benchmark Education Co.

—The American Revolution: Theme Set. 2006. (J). 131.00 *(978-1-4108-7125-1(8))* Benchmark Education Co.

—Freedom's Trail & AMER Revolution. 2005. spiral bd. 225.00 *(978-1-4108-5825-2(1))* Benchmark Education Co.

—Social Studies Theme: The AMER Revolution. 2005. spiral bd. 115.00 *(978-1-4108-5326-4(8))* Benchmark Education Co.

Bober, Natalie S. Countdown to Independence. 2007. (ENG.). 368p. (YA). (gr. 7). pap. 19.95 *(978-1-4169-6392-9(8)*, Atheneum Bks. for Young Readers) Simon & Schuster Children's Publishing.

Bobrick, Benson. Fight for Freedom: The American Revolutionary War. 2004. (ENG., Illus.). 96p. (J). 24.99 *(978-0-689-86422-3(1)*, Atheneum Bks. for Young Readers) Simon & Schuster Children's Publishing.

Bodden, Valerie. The Declaration of American Independence. 2009. (Days of Change Ser.). (ENG., Illus.). 48p. (J). (gr. 5-8). 22.95 *(978-1-58341-733-1(8)*, 22144) Creative Co., The.

Botones para el General Washington (Buttons for General Washington) 2006. (J). pap. 6.95 *(978-0-8225-6617-5(6)*, Ediciones Lerner) Lerner Publishing Group.

Brennan, Linda. The Black Regiment of the American Revolution. Noll, Cheryl Kirk, illus. 2005. 32p. (J). (gr. 4-7). per. 8.95 *(978-1-931659-18-5(4))* Moon Mountain Publishing, Inc.

Brennan, Linda Crotta. The Birth of the United States. 2011. (Explorer Library: Language Arts Explorer Ser.). (ENG.). 32p. (gr. 4-8). pap. 14.21 *(978-1-61080-285-7(3)*, 201208); (Illus.). lib. bdg. 32.07 *(978-1-61080-197-3(0)*, 201170) Cherry Lake Publishing.

Brindell Fradin, Dennis. The Stamp Act Of 1765, 1 vol. 2010. (Turning Points in U. S. History Ser.). (ENG., Illus.). 48p. (gr. 4-4). 34.07 *(978-0-7614-4260-8(X)*, ebda7934-06c6-4918-bac9-93a066b6efcd) Cavendish Square Publishing LLC.

Britton, Tamara L. Independence Hall. 2003. (Symbols, Landmarks & Monuments Set 1 Ser.). 32p. (gr. k-6). 27.07 *(978-1-57765-853-5(1)*, Checkerboard Library) ABDO Publishing Co.

Broida, Marian. Projects about the American Revolution, 1 vol. 2007. (Hands-On History Ser.). (ENG., Illus.). 48p. (gr. 3-3). lib. bdg. 34.07 *(978-0-7614-1981-5(0)*, 9accd3af-7002-4ce8-8212-853be6e77e08) Cavendish Square Publishing LLC.

Brooks, Philip. King George III (a Wicked History) 2009. (Wicked History Ser.). (ENG.). 128p. (J). (gr. 6-12). pap. 5.95 *(978-0-531-20739-0(0)*, Watts, Franklin) Scholastic Library Publishing.

Burgan, Michael. The Battle of Bunker Hill: An Interactive History Adventure. rev. ed. 2016. (You Choose: History Ser.). (ENG., Illus.). 112p. (J). (gr. 3-7). lib. bdg. 32.65 *(978-1-5157-3384-3(X)*, 133371, Capstone Pr.) Capstone.

—Benedict Arnold: American Hero & Traitor, 1 vol. Beatty, Terry, illus. 2007. (Graphic Biographies Ser.). (ENG.). 32p. (J). (gr. 3-9). per. 8.10 *(978-0-7368-7906-4(4)*, 93903, Capstone Pr.) Capstone.

—The Split History of the American Revolution: A Perspectives Flip Book, 1 vol. 2012. (Perspectives Flip Bks.). (ENG.). 64p. (J). (gr. 5-9). pap. 8.95 *(978-0-7565-4592-5(7)*, 120436, Compass Point Bks.) Capstone.

Butcher, Andrew & Toohey, Vincent. Analysing the American Revolution, 1 vol. 2nd rev. ed. 2015. (ENG.). pap., E-Book *(978-1-107-50647-3(6))* Cambridge Univ. Pr.

Caravantes, Peggy. The American Revolution: 12 Things to Know. 2017. (America at War Ser.). (ENG., Illus.). 32p. (J). (gr. 3-6). 32.80 *(978-1-63235-264-4(8)*, 11703, 12-Story Library) Bookstaves, LLC.

Carole Marsh. How Our Nation Was Born: the American Revolution. 2004. (American Milestones Ser.). 32p. (gr. 3-8). pap. 5.95 *(978-0-635-02348-3(2))*; (gr. 4-12). 29.95 *(978-0-635-02349-0(0))* Gallopade International.

Carr, Joaquin. The American Revolution: Set Of 6. 2011. (Navigators Ser.). (J). pap. 48.00 net. *(978-1-4108-5108-6(7))* Benchmark Education Co.

—The American Revolution: Text Pairs. 2008. (Bridges/Navigators Ser.). (J). (gr. 5). 89.00 *(978-1-4108-8403-9(1))* Benchmark Education Co.

Carson, Mary Kay. Did It All Start with a Snowball Fight? And Other Questions about... The American Revolution. Elliott, Mark & Hunt, Robert, illus. 2012. (Good Question! Ser.). (ENG.). 32p. (J). pap. 5.95 *(978-1-4027-8734-8(0))* Sterling Publishing Co., Inc.

Casey, Susan. Women Heroes of the American Revolution: 20 Stories of Espionage, Sabotage, Defiance, & Rescue. 2017. (Women of Action Ser.). (ENG., Illus.). 240p. (YA). (gr. 7). pap. 14.99 *(978-1-61373-831-3(5))* Chicago Review Pr., Inc.

Castellano, Peter. The American Revolution, 1 vol. 2017. (Look at U. S. History Ser.). (ENG., Illus.). 32p. (J). (gr. 2-2). pap. 11.50 *(978-1-4824-6023-0(8)*, 610cbae6-95b5-4d77-856e-a65234d4a018) Stevens, Gareth Publishing LLLP.

Castrovilla, Selene. Revolutionary Friends: General George Washington & the Marquis de Lafayette. Kozjan, Drazen, illus. 2013. (ENG.). 40p. (J). (gr. 2-5). 16.99 *(978-1-59078-880-6(X)*, Calkins Creek) Highlights Pr., c/o Highlights for Children, Inc.

—Revolutionary Rogues: John André & Benedict Arnold. O'Brien, John, illus. 2017. (ENG.). 48p. (J). (gr. 2-5). 17.95 *(978-1-62979-341-2(8)*, Calkins Creek) Highlights Pr., c/o Highlights for Children, Inc.

Causes of the American Revolution (NCHS) Grades 7-9. (J). tchr. ed., spiral bd. 13.50 *(978-0-382-44448-7(5))* Cobblestone Publishing Co.

Cefrey, Holly. One Life to Lose for My Country: The Arrest & Execution of Nathan Hale. (Great Moments in American History Ser.). 32p. (gr. 3-3). 2009. 47.90 *(978-1-61513-135-8(3))* 2003. (ENG., Illus.). lib. bdg. 29.13 *(978-0-8239-4371-5(2)*, ffc71398-7cd2-4bd6-9226-931d0ff47e52, Rosen Reference) Rosen Publishing Group, Inc., The.

Cheatham, Mark. The Life of a Colonial Soldier, 1 vol. 2013. (Jr. Graphic Colonial America Ser.). (ENG., Illus.). 24p. (J). (gr. 2-3). pap. 11.60 *(978-1-4777-1439-3(1)*, 856a9e2a-d842-4008-9543-7caf6bd62692); lib. bdg. 28.93 *(978-1-4777-1310-5(7)*, f24ac1b8-8ed4-4c67-bb3c-083387a6d554) Rosen Publishing Group, Inc., The. (PowerKids Pr.).

Clark, Willow. The True Story of the Declaration of Independence, 1 vol. 2013. (What Really Happened? Ser.). (ENG., Illus.). 24p. (J). (gr. 2-3). pap. 9.25 *(978-1-4488-9840-4(4)*, 94101ea9-a09e-4507-ad08-82250005ab11); lib. bdg. 26.27 *(978-1-4488-9691-2(6)*, 091fe756-fd1e-4072-9aaf-9a4ac3be666b) Rosen Publishing Group, Inc., The. (PowerKids Pr.).

TUV

Collins, Kathleen. El Marques de Lafayette: Heroe Frances de la Guerra de Independencia, 1 vol. 2003. (Grandes Personajes en la Historia de Los Estados Unidos (Famous People in American History) Ser.). (SPA.). 32p. (gr. 3-4). pap. 10.00 *(978-0-8239-4233-6(3),* 611571c8-b964-4b87-9954-e1eb2363af67, Rosen Classroom) Rosen Publishing Group, Inc., The.

—Marquis de Lafayette: French Hero of the American Revolution. (Primary Sources of Famous People in American History Ser.). 32p. (gr. 2-3). 2009. 47.90 *(978-1-60851-703-9(9))* 2003. (ENG & SPA., Illus.). lib. bdg. 29.13 *(978-0-8239-4163-6(9),* 22b96b9a-22f4-4124-a502-dda13c946bf7, Editorial Buenas Letras) Rosen Publishing Group, Inc., The.

—Marquis de Lafayette / el Marques de Lafayette: French Hero of the American Revolution / Héroe francés de la Revolución Estadounidense. 2009. (Famous People in American History/Grandes personajes en la historia de los Estados Unidos Ser.). (ENG & SPA.). 32p. (gr. 2-3). 47.90 *(978-1-61512-550-0(7),* Editorial Buenas Letras) Rosen Publishing Group, Inc., The.

Collins, Terry, et al. Stories of War. 2012. (Stories of War Ser.). (ENG.). 32p. (J). (gr. 3-9). 133.28 *(978-1-4296-9164-2(6),* 18453, Capstone Pr.) Capstone.

Conklin, Wendy. Benjamin Franklin, 1 vol. rev. ed. 2004. (Social Studies: Informational Text Ser.). (ENG.). 24p. (gr. 4-8). pap. 10.99 *(978-0-7439-8755-4(1))* Teacher Created Materials, Inc.

Corporate Contibutor & Perritano, John. The Causes of the American Revolution. 2012. (ENG.). 48p. (J). *(978-0-7787-0804-9(7))* Crabtree Publishing Co.

—The Outcome of the American Revolution. 2012. (ENG.). 48p. (J). *(978-0-7787-0805-6(5))* Crabtree Publishing Co.

Corporate Contibutor Staff & Clarke, Gordon. Significant Battles of the American Revolution. 2012. (ENG.). 48p. (J). *(978-0-7787-0806-3(3))* Crabtree Publishing Co.

Corporate Contibutor Staff & Mason, Helen. Life on the Homefront During the American Revolution. 2012. (ENG.). 48p. (J). *(978-0-7787-0801-8(2));* pap. *(978-0-7787-0812-4(8))* Crabtree Publishing Co.

Cotton, Jacqueline S. Betsy Ross. 2019. (Illus.). 24p. (J). *(978-1-4896-9554-3(0),* AV2 by Weigl) Weigl Pubs., Inc.

Cox, Vicki. Betsy Ross: A Flag for a New Nation. 2005. (Leaders of the American Revolution Ser.). (ENG., Illus.). 100p. (gr. 5-8). lib. bdg. 30.00 *(978-0-7910-8618-6(6),* P114334, Facts On File) Infobase Holdings, Inc.

Crabtree Staff & Perritano, John. The Outcome of the American Revolution. 2012. (ENG., Illus.). 48p. (J). pap. *(978-0-7787-0816-2(0))* Crabtree Publishing Co.

Crawford, Laura. The American Revolution from a to Z, 1 vol. Hierstein, Judith, illus. 2009. (ABC Ser.). (ENG.). 32p. (J). (gr. k-3). 19.99 *(978-1-58980-515-6(1),* Pelican Publishing) Arcadia Publishing.

Crompton, Samuel Willard. Thomas Paine: Fighting for American Independence, 1 vol. 2017. (Rebels with a Cause Ser.). (ENG.). 128p. (gr. 8-8). lib. bdg. 38.93 *(978-0-7660-8515-2(5),* 9bbb932c-af6f-4b5e-9b36-0aa7fa6f6bff) Enslow Publishing, LLC.

Davenport, John. The American Revolution, 1 vol. 2007. (American History Ser.). (ENG.). 104p. (gr. 7-7). pap. 29.30 *(978-1-4205-0300-5(6),* 934f270b-6271-4ad9-ae90-0da5134a8988); (Illus.). lib. bdg. 41.03 *(978-1-59018-939-9(6),* 207b98cf-3065-43cd-b472-cdac059f7ea6) Greenhaven Publishing LLC. (Lucent Pr.).

Davies, Monika. True Life: Alexander Hamilton. 2nd rev. ed. 2016. (TIME(r): Informational Text Ser.). (ENG., Illus.). 48p. (gr. 6-8). pap. 13.99 *(978-1-4938-3633-8(1))* Teacher Created Materials, Inc.

DeFord, Debra. The American Revolution, 1 vol. 2006. (Wars That Changed American History Ser.). (ENG., Illus.). 48p. (gr. 5-8). pap. 15.05 *(978-0-8368-7298-9(3),* f35b7908-1d11-4a1b-be49-d88a4385e3da); lib. bdg. 33.67 *(978-0-8368-7289-7(4),* f55ab805-6056-465a-b1e5-1078ad71d0ff) Stevens, Gareth Publishing LLLP. (Gareth Stevens Secondary Library).

Derr, Aaron. Benedict Arnold: Hero or Enemy Spy? Brooks, Scott R., illus. 2018. (Hidden History — Spies Ser.). (ENG.). 32p. (J). (gr. 2-5). pap. 8.99 *(978-1-63440-293-4(6),* 2a403f3a-520f-4990-b238-6df35a52cbfe); lib. bdg. 26.65 *(978-1-63440-279-8(0),* 6a2568e9-210c-4247-a276-ddbee47fd7b9) Red Chair Pr.

—Nathan Hale: America's First Spy. Wicinas, Tami, illus. 2018. (Hidden History — Spies Ser.). (ENG.). 32p. (J). (gr. 2-5). pap. 8.99 *(978-1-63440-296-5(0),* 8a2a9e91-5332-4f0e-8e8a-8e1d098cc8a6) Red Chair Pr.

Dodge Cummings, Judy. The American Revolution: Experience the Battle for Independence. Casteel, Tom, illus. 2015. (Build It Yourself Ser.). (ENG.). 128p. (J). (gr. 3-7). 22.95 *(978-1-61930-255-6(1),* cd4935db-cfe6-409d-ba6d-dd782716a7a4); pap. 17.95 *(978-1-61930-246-4(2),* 9da0a8ed-a227-4405-acf8-5b4d3232bef3) Nomad Pr.

Doeden, Matt. The Colonists Revolt: An Interactive American Revolution Adventure. 2018. (You Choose: Founding the United States Ser.). (ENG., Illus.). 112p. (J). (gr. 3-7). pap. 6.95 *(978-1-5435-1549-7(5),* 137917); lib. bdg. 32.65 *(978-1-5435-1542-8(8),* 137910) Capstone. (Capstone Pr.).

—Weapons of the Revolutionary War. rev. ed. 2017. (Weapons of War Ser.). (ENG., Illus.). 32p. (J). (gr. 3-9). lib. bdg. 27.32 *(978-1-5157-7908-7(4),* 136023, Capstone Pr.) Capstone.

Dorais, Katherine M. The Revolutionary War & a Few Things More. 2011. 32p. (gr. -1). pap. 15.50 *(978-1-4567-1193-1(8))* AuthorHouse.

Draper, Allison Stark. The Boston Tea Party: Angry Colonists Dump British Tea. 2009. (Headlines from History Ser.). 24p. (gr. 3-3). 42.50 *(978-1-61513-244-7(9),* PowerKids Pr.) Rosen Publishing Group, Inc., The.

—What People Wore During the American Revolution. 2009. (Clothing, Costumes, & Uniforms Throughout American History Ser.). 24p. (gr. 3-3). 42.50 *(978-1-61511-875-5(6),* PowerKids Pr.) Rosen Publishing Group, Inc., The.

Early American Wars, 8 vols., Set. Incl. American Revolutionary War. Marston, Daniel & O'Neill, Robert John. lib. bdg. 38.47 *(978-1-4488-1331-5(X),* 97fdd7f5-b6c0-4a56-9c61-1c0f72d38d88); Texas War of Independence. Huffines, Alan C. & O'Neill, Robert. lib. bdg. 38.47 *(978-1-4488-1332-2(8),* 36cb7ba9-dc13-4896-8a71-3cada86c271c); War of 1812: The Fight for American Trade Rights. Benn, Carl & O'Neill, Robert. lib. bdg. 38.47 *(978-1-4488-1333-9(6),* d72506c9-ca2b-4440-b2de-85ad9710d12d); (YA). (gr. 10-10). 2011. (Early American Wars Ser.). (ENG., Illus.). 96p. 2010. Set lib. bdg. 153.88 *(978-1-4488-1387-2(5),* 2707729f-2e44-4276-a727-6c417d4c68f7) Rosen Publishing Group, Inc., The.

Espinosa, Rod. American Revolution, 1 vol. 2008. (Graphic History Ser.). (ENG., Illus.). 32p. (J). (gr. 3-8). 32.79 *(978-1-60270-179-3(2),* 9050, Graphic Planet - Fiction) Magic Wagon.

Farshtey, Greg. The American Revolution. 2003. (Daily Life Ser.). (Illus.). 48p. (J). (gr. 3-5). 26.20 *(978-0-7377-1402-9(6),* Kidhaven) Cengage Gale.

Figley, Marty Rhodes. John Greenwood's Journey to Bunker Hill. 2010. pap. 56.72 *(978-0-7613-6927-1(9))* Lerner Publishing Group.

—Prisoner for Liberty. Orback, Craig, illus. (On My Own History Ser.). (ENG.). 48p. (gr. 2-4). 2009. (J). pap. 8.99 *(978-0-8225-9022-4(0),* 71b3881b-9399-4d9c-a66b-0223c579b66b, First Avenue Editions) 2008. lib. bdg. 25.26 *(978-0-8225-7280-0(X),* Millbrook Pr.) Lerner Publishing Group.

—Salvar a la Campana de la Libertad. Lepp, Kevin, illus. 2005. (Yo Solo Biografías Ser.). (SPA.). 48p. (J). (gr. 2-5). per. 6.95 *(978-0-8225-3095-4(3))* Lerner Publishing Group.

—Salvar a la Campana de la Libertad; Saving the Liberty Bell. 2008. pap. 40.95 *(978-0-7613-3933-5(7))* Lerner Publishing Group.

—Saving the Liberty Bell. Lepp, Kevin, illus. 2004. (On My Own History Ser.). (ENG.). 48p. (J). (gr. 2-4). pap. 8.99 *(978-1-57505-696-8(8),* 910d2276-4910-411d-bd61-133c42e06133, First Avenue Editions) Lerner Publishing Group.

Figley, Mary Rhodes. Prisoner for Liberty. 2009. pap. 40.95 *(978-0-7613-4796-5(8))* Lerner Publishing Group.

Finch, Fletcher C. Considering Different Opinions Surrounding the American Revolutionary War, 1 vol. 2018. (Project Learning Through American History Ser.). (ENG.). 32p. (J). (gr. 4-5). 27.93 *(978-1-5383-3055-5(5),* 8b58f124-8cd4-4fc7-a1f5-bd3d5b2d5815); pap. 11.00 *(978-1-5383-3056-2(3),* e5feb0a6-64dc-42ec-8809-b836dc3899cc) Rosen Publishing Group, Inc., The. (PowerKids Pr.).

Ford, Barbara. Paul Revere: American Patriot, 1 vol. 2014. (Legendary American Biographies Ser.). (ENG.). 96p. (gr. 6-6). 29.60 *(978-0-7660-6485-0(9),* 71b83a69-4129-48f5-bc63-b49d99ff4350) Enslow Publishing, LLC.

Forest, Christopher. The Rebellious Colonists & the Causes of the American Revolution, 1 vol. 2012. (Story of the American Revolution Ser.). (ENG., Illus.). 32p. (J). (gr. 3-6). pap. 8.10 *(978-1-4296-9290-8(1),* 120352); lib. bdg. 27.99 *(978-1-4296-8428-6(3),* 118501) Capstone. (Capstone Pr.).

—The Rebellious Colonists & the Causes of the American Revolution. 2012. (Story of the American Revolution Ser.). (ENG.). 32p. (J). (gr. 3-4). pap. 48.60 *(978-1-4296-9291-5(X),* 18525, Capstone Pr.) Capstone.

Founding Fathers. (J). tchr. ed. 41.95 *(978-0-382-40882-3(9))* Cobblestone Publishing Co.

Friddell, Claudia. George Washington's Spies (Totally True Adventures) 2016. (Totally True Adventures Ser.). (Illus.). 112p. (J). (gr. 2-5). pap. 5.99 *(978-0-399-55077-5(1),* Random Hse. Bks. for Young Readers) Random Hse. Children's Bks.

Fritz, Jean. Alexander Hamilton: the Outsider. 2012. (ENG.). 144p. (J). (gr. 3-7). 8.99 *(978-0-14-241986-1(9),* Puffin Books) Penguin Young Readers Group.

Garstecki, Julia. The Complete Guide to the Revolutionary War. 2016. (Illus.). 144p. (J). *(978-1-4351-6359-1(1))* Barnes & Noble, Inc.

George, Lynn. What Do You Know about the American Revolution? (20 Questions: History Ser.). 24p. (gr. 2-3). 2009. 42.50 *(978-1-60854-957-3(7),* PowerKids Pr.) 2007. (ENG., Illus.). (J). lib. bdg. 26.27 *(978-1-4042-4186-2(8),* ccb2f8ed-9200-4177-8f4d-46934cb5def3) Rosen Publishing Group, Inc., The.

Goodman, Michael E. Revolutionary War Spies. (Wartime Spies Ser.). (ENG.). 48p. (J). (gr. 4-7). 2016. pap. 12.00 *(978-1-62832-206-4(3),* 21088, Creative Paperbacks) 2015. (Illus.). *(978-1-60818-601-3(6),* 21087, Creative Education) Creative Co., The.

Grayson, Robert. Revolutionary War, 1 vol. 2013. (Essential Library of American Wars Ser.). (ENG.). 112p. (YA). (gr. 6-12). lib. bdg. 41.36 *(978-1-61783-879-8(9),* 6607, Essential Library) ABDO Publishing Co.

Gregory, Josh. The Revolutionary War. 2011. (Cornerstones of Freedom, Third Ser.). 64p. (J). lib. bdg. 30.00 *(978-0-531-25039-6(3),* Children's Pr.) Scholastic Library Publishing.

—The Revolutionary War (Cornerstones of Freedom: Third Series) 2011. (Cornerstones of Freedom. Third Ser.). (ENG.). 64p. (J). (gr. 4-6). pap. 8.95 *(978-0-531-26564-2(1),* Children's Pr.) Scholastic Library Publishing.

Group/McGraw-Hill, Wright. History: Revolutionary War, 6 vols. (Book2WebTM Ser.). (gr. 4-8). 36.50 *(978-0-322-04450-0(2))* Wright Group/McGraw-Hill.

Gunderson, Jessica. Benedict Arnold: Battlefield Hero or Selfish Traitor?, 1 vol. 2013. (Perspectives on History Ser.). (ENG.). 32p. (J). (gr. 3-6). 27.99 *(978-1-4765-0243-4(9),* 122297); pap. 7.95 *(978-1-4765-3407-7(1),* 123538) Capstone.

Hakim, Joy. A History of US: from Colonies to Country: 1735-1791 a History of US Book Three. (History of US Ser.: 3). (ENG., Illus.). 224p. (gr. 4-7). 2nd rev. ed. 2007. per. 15.95 *(978-0-19-532717-5(9))* 3rd rev. ed. 2006. 24.95 *(978-0-19-518896-7(9))* Oxford Univ. Pr., Inc.

Hall, Brianna. Great Women of the American Revolution. 2012. (Story of the American Revolution Ser.). (ENG.). 32p. (J). (gr. 3-4). pap. 48.60 *(978-1-4296-9285-4(5),* 18522, Capstone Pr.) Capstone.

Hall, Brianna, et al. The Story of the American Revolution. 2012. (Story of the American Revolution Ser.). (ENG.). 32p. (J). (gr. 3-6). pap., pap., pap. 32.40 *(978-1-4296-9294-6(4),* 18527, Capstone Pr.) Capstone.

—The Story of the American Revolution Classroom Collection. 2012. (Story of the American Revolution Ser.). (ENG.). 32p. (J). (gr. 3-4). pap. 223.20 *(978-1-4296-9295-3(2),* 18528, Capstone Pr.) Capstone.

Hamilton, John. American Revolution, 2 vols. 2013. (American Revolution Ser.: 6). (ENG.). 32p. (J). (gr. 5-9). lib. bdg. 65.58 *(978-1-61783-677-0(X),* 2471, Abdo & Daughters) ABDO Publishing Co.

Hamilton, Robert M. Recipes of the American Revolution. (Cooking Your Way Through American History Ser.). 24p. (J). (gr. 3-3). 2017. pap. 63.60 *(978-1-5345-2105-6(4))* 2016. (ENG.). 28.88 *(978-1-5345-2106-3(2),* 8c32c95e-38c4-4378-a318-727859724edc) 2016. (ENG.). pap. 11.60 *(978-1-5345-2104-9(6),* e8b33e76-8555-4027-bfc4-b426e4501828) Greenhaven Publishing LLC. (KidHaven Publishing).

Hargrove, Julia. Bostons Trail to Freedom. 2003. (Historic Monuments Ser.). (Illus.). 48p. (J). (gr. 4-8). pap. 6.95 *(978-1-57310-403-6(5))* Teaching & Learning Co.

Harris, Duchess. Boston Tea Party. 2017. (Protest Movements Ser.). (ENG., Illus.). 48p. (J). (gr. 4-8). lib. bdg. 35.64 *(978-1-5321-1395-6(1),* 27693) ABDO Publishing Co.

Haugen, Brenda. The Split History of the Battles of Lexington & Concord: A Perspectives Flip Book. 2018. (Perspectives Flip Books: Famous Battles Ser.). (ENG., Illus.). 64p. (J). (gr. 5-9). lib. bdg. 34.65 *(978-0-7565-5692-1(9),* 137037, Compass Point Bks.) Capstone.

Hazen, Walter A. Everyday Life: Revolutionary War. 2004. (Illus.). 104p. (J). pap. 13.50 *(978-0-673-58899-9(8))* Good Year Bks.

Heims, Neil. Reading Johnny Tremain. 2005. (Engaged Reader Ser.). (ENG., Illus.). 96p. (gr. 5-8). lib. bdg. 25.00 *(978-0-7910-8831-9(6),* P114443, Facts On File) Infobase Holdings, Inc.

Henrickson, Beth. The Marquis de Lafayette & Other International Champions of the American Revolution, 1 vol. 2015. (Spotlight on American History Ser.). (ENG., Illus.). 24p. (J). (gr. 4-6). pap. 11.00 *(978-1-4994-1745-6(4),* 6fd49d9d-45b0-422a-832d-c0f0b5b867d7, PowerKids Pr.) Rosen Publishing Group, Inc., The.

Hinman, Bonnie. Life During the Revolutionary War, 1 vol. 2015. (Daily Life in US History Ser.). (ENG., Illus.). 48p. (J). (gr. 4-8). lib. bdg. 35.64 *(978-1-62403-628-6(7),* 16896) ABDO Publishing Co.

—The Second Continental Congress. 2017. (Young America Ser.). (Illus.). 47p. (J). 29.95 *(978-1-61228-979-3(7))* Mitchell Lane Pubs.

Hirsch, E. D., Jr., ed. The American Revolution, Level 4. 2003. stu. ed. 9.95 *(978-0-7690-5101-7(4));* stu. ed. 49.95 *(978-0-7690-2845-3(4));* tchr. ed. 9.95 *(978-0-7690-5068-3(9))* Pearson Learning.

Hoena, Blake. Fighting for Independence: An Interactive American Revolution Adventure. 2018. (You Choose: Founding the United States Ser.). (ENG., Illus.). 112p. (J). (gr. 3-7). lib. bdg. 32.65 *(978-1-5435-1540-4(1),* 137908, Capstone Pr.) Capstone.

Houghton, Raymond C. A Revolutionary War Road Trip on US Route 4: Spend a Revolutionary Day along One of America's Most Historic Routes 2004. (Illus.). 162p. per. 12.99 *(978-1-931373-09-8(4))* Cyber Haus.

—A Revolutionary War Road Trip on US Route 9: Spend a Revolutionary Day along One of America's Most Historic Routes. 2004. (Illus.). 166p. per. 12.99 *(978-1-931373-12-8(4))* Cyber Haus.

Howell, Sara. The American Revolution: Frontline Soldiers & Their Families, 1 vol. 2015. (Frontline Families Ser.). (ENG., Illus.). 48p. (J). (gr. 5-6). pap. 15.05 *(978-1-4824-3053-0(3),* fa0a6013-beff-4aa8-86d0-12280e4f4a51) Stevens, Gareth Publishing LLLP.

—What Caused the American Revolution? 2016. (Why War Happened Ser.). (ENG.). 48p. (J). (gr. 6-9). 24.85 *(978-1-5311-8767-5(6))* Perfection Learning Corp.

Huey, Lois Miner. Voices of the American Revolution: Stories from the Battlefields, 1 vol. 2010. (Voices of War Ser.). (ENG., Illus.). 32p. (J). (gr. 3-9). pap. 8.29 *(978-1-4296-5628-3(X),* 114119, Capstone Pr.) Capstone.

Ingram, Scott. The Battle of Valcour Bay. 2003. (Triangle Histories of the American Revolution Ser.). (Illus.). 32p. (J). 22.45 *(978-1-56711-778-3(3),* Blackbirch Pr., Inc.) Cengage Gale.

Isaacs, Sally. Understanding the Declaration of Independence. 2008. (Documenting Early America Ser.). (ENG.). 32p. (J). (gr. 3-6). lib. bdg. *(978-0-7787-4371-2(3))* Crabtree Publishing Co.

Isaacs, Sally & Bedeksy, Baron. Understanding the Declaration of Independence. 2008. (Documenting Early America Ser.). (ENG.). 32p. (J). (gr. 3-6). pap. *(978-0-7787-4376-7(4))* Crabtree Publishing Co.

Jedson, Lee. The Treaty of Paris 1783: A Primary Source Examination of the Treaty That Recognized American Independence. (Primary Sources of American Treaties Ser.). 64p. (gr. 5-8). 2009. 58.50 *(978-1-60851-517-2(6))* 2005. (ENG., Illus.). (J). lib. bdg. 37.13 *(978-1-4042-0441-6(5),* c04803f4-66cf-4fd5-b3d6-b3710f6f6e1e) Rosen Publishing Group, Inc., The.

Jeffries, Joyce. The Colony of North Carolina, 1 vol. 2015. (Spotlight on the 13 Colonies: Birth of a Nation Ser.). (ENG., Illus.). 24p. (J). (gr. 4-6). pap. 11.00 *(978-1-4994-0554-5(5),* f5f16c38-b867-4e64-8775-66881c07a017, PowerKids Pr.) Rosen Publishing Group, Inc., The.

—The Colony of South Carolina, 1 vol. 2015. (Spotlight on the 13 Colonies: Birth of a Nation Ser.). (ENG., Illus.). 24p. (J). (gr. 4-6). pap. 11.00 *(978-1-4994-0582-8(0),* 5481a901-89b0-454f-9d8c-9043801b07c7, PowerKids Pr.) Rosen Publishing Group, Inc., The.

Jensen, Ann. The World Turned Upside Down: Children Of 1776, 1 vol. 2009. (ENG., Illus.). 80p. (gr. 3-6). pap. 9.95 *(978-0-87033-534-1(0),* 3745, Cornell Maritime Pr./Tidewater Pubs.) Schiffer Publishing, Ltd.

Kajencki, AnnMarie Francis. Count Casimir Pulaski: From Poland to America, a Hero's Fight for Liberty. 2009. (Library of American Lives & Times Ser.). 112p. (gr. 5-5). 69.20 *(978-1-60853-475-3(8))* Rosen Publishing Group, Inc., The.

Kalman, Maira. Thomas Jefferson: Life, Liberty & the Pursuit of Everything. Kalman, Maira, illus. 2014. (ENG., Illus.). 40p. (J). (gr. k-3). 17.99 *(978-0-399-24040-9(3),* Nancy Paulsen Books) Penguin Young Readers Group.

Katz, Vladimir. A Timeline of the Life of George Washington. (Timelines of American History Ser.). 32p. (gr. 4-4). 2009. 47.90 *(978-1-60854-388-5(9))* 2004. (ENG., Illus.). lib. bdg. 29.13 *(978-0-8239-4538-2(3),* 2fa8f672-9994-452f-b005-cfc1b954837f) Rosen Publishing Group, Inc., The. (Rosen Reference).

Kelley, True. Who Was Abigail Adams? 2014. (Who Was... ? Ser.). lib. bdg. 16.00 *(978-0-606-34166-0(8))* Turtleback.

Kelley, True & Who HQ. Who Was Abigail Adams? O'Brien, John, illus. 2014. (Who Was? Ser.). 112p. (J). (gr. 3-7). 6.99 *(978-0-448-47890-6(0),* Penguin Workshop) Penguin Young Readers Group.

Kent, Deborah. The American Revolution: From Bunker Hill to Yorktown, 1 vol. 2011. (United States at War Ser.). (ENG., Illus.). 128p. (gr. 5-6). lib. bdg. 35.93 *(978-0-7660-3642-0(1),* 75ebec30-d6d2-4a5d-b914-0b95cd1bb4ca) Enslow Publishing, LLC.

Kent, Jacqueline C. Molly Pitcher. 2003. (Women of the Revolution Ser.). (J). pap. *(978-1-58417-088-4(3));* lib. bdg. *(978-1-58417-025-9(5))* Lake Street Pubs.

Keppeler, Jill. Team Time Machine Drafts the Declaration of Independence, 1 vol. 2019. (Team Time Machine: American Revolution Ser.). (ENG.). 32p. (J). (gr. 2-3). pap. 11.50 *(978-1-5382-4678-8(3),* a83e060e-5247-41dc-b12e-cb1fa334a4da) Stevens, Gareth Publishing LLLP.

Kilmeade, Brian & Yaeger, Don. George Washington's Secret Six (Young Readers Adaptation) The Spies Who Saved America. 2020. (Illus.). 176p. (J). (gr. 5). pap. 9.99 *(978-0-425-28901-3(X),* Puffin Books) Penguin Young Readers Group.

Kit, Oscar. A Timeline of the Life of Thomas Jefferson. (Timelines of American History Ser.). 32p. (gr. 4-4). 2009. 47.90 *(978-1-60854-389-2(7))* 2004. (ENG., Illus.). lib. bdg. 29.13 *(978-0-8239-4539-9(1),* 47a2bcaf-4d4e-4142-9348-ee6f4d4c961c) Rosen Publishing Group, Inc., The. (Rosen Reference).

Kjelle, Marylou. The First Continental Congress. 2017. (Young America Ser.). (Illus.). 47p. (J). (gr. 3-6). 29.95 *(978-1-61228-977-9(0))* Mitchell Lane Pubs.

Klepeis, Alicia. Stamp Act Congress. 2017. (Young America Ser.). (gr. 3-6). 29.95 *(978-1-61228-991-5(6))* Mitchell Lane Pubs.

Klepeis, Alicia Z. Nathan Hale: Revolutionary War Hero, 1 vol. William, Lorna, illus. 2018. (American Legends & Folktales Ser.). (ENG.). 32p. (gr. 3-3). 30.21 *(978-1-5026-3689-8(1),* dda8da1d-d3e0-4133-a44f-cbe0b3153926) Cavendish Square Publishing LLC.

Kneib, Martha. A Historical Atlas of the American Revolution. (United States: Historical Atlases of the Growth of a New Nation Ser.). 64p. (gr. 5-5). 2009. 61.20 *(978-1-60854-253-6(X))* 2004. (ENG., Illus.). (J). lib. bdg. 37.13 *(978-1-4042-0204-7(8),* 0de3598a-1d39-4305-ac03-a7cac42a2e59) Rosen Publishing Group, Inc., The.

Konstam, Angus. America Speaks, 10 vols. 2005. (Illus.). (J). *(978-0-7172-6029-4(1)); (978-0-7172-6028-7(3)); (978-0-7172-6027-0(5)); (978-0-7172-6026-3(7)); (978-0-7172-6025-6(9)); (978-0-7172-6024-9(0)); (978-0-7172-6023-2(2)); (978-0-7172-6022-5(4)); (978-0-7172-6021-8(6)); (978-0-7172-6020-1(8))* Grolier, Ltd.

—America Speaks, 10 vols., Set. 2005. (Illus.). (J). (gr. 5-10). lib. bdg. 269.00 *(978-0-7172-6030-0(5),* Grolier) Scholastic Library Publishing.

Krull, Kathleen. A Kids' Guide to the American Revolution. DiVito, Anna, illus. 2018. (Kids' Guide to American History Ser.: 2). (ENG.). 224p. (J). (gr. 3-7). 16.99 *(978-0-06-238110-1(5));* pap. 6.99 *(978-0-06-238109-5(1))* HarperCollins Pubs. (HarperCollins).

—What Was the Boston Tea Party? 2013. (What Was... Ser.). lib. bdg. 16.00 *(978-0-606-29971-8(8))* Turtleback.

Krull, Kathleen & Who HQ. What Was the Boston Tea Party? Mortimer, Lauren, illus. 2013. (What Was? Ser.). 112p. (J). (gr. 3-7). pap. 7.99 *(978-0-448-46288-2(5),* Penguin Workshop) Penguin Young Readers Group.

Lakin, Patricia. Abigail Adams: First Lady of the American Revolution. Bandelin, Debra & Dacey, Bob, illus. 2006. 48p. (J). lib. bdg. 15.00 *(978-1-4242-1560-7(9))* Fitzgerald Bks.

—Abigail Adams: First Lady of the American Revolution (Ready-To-Read Level 3) Dacey, Bob & Bandelin, Debra, illus. 2006. (Ready-To-Read Stories of Famous Americans Ser.). (ENG.). 48p. (J). (gr. 1-3). pap. 4.99 *(978-0-689-87032-3(9),* Simon Spotlight) Simon Spotlight.

Landau, Elaine. The Declaration of Independence (a True Book: American History) 2008. (True Book (Relaunch) Ser.). (ENG., Illus.). 48p. (J). (gr. 3-5). pap. 6.95 *(978-0-531-14780-1(0),* Children's Pr.) Scholastic Library Publishing.

—General Washington Crosses the Delaware: Would You Join the American Revolution?, 1 vol. 2014. (What Would You Do? Ser.). (ENG.). 48p. (gr. 3-4). pap. 11.53 *(978-0-7660-6316-7(X),* a3e7fa61-2614-4da4-b415-b0c379dc668d, Enslow Elementary) Enslow Publishing, LLC.

—The Revolutionary War Begins: Would You Join the Fight?, 1 vol. 2009. (What Would You Do? Ser.). (ENG., Illus.). 48p. (gr. 3-3). pap. 11.53 *(978-1-59845-197-9(9),* 245915a4-042e-4cea-87d6-fd25c464f145); lib. bdg. 27.93 *(978-0-7660-2900-2(X),* 5df936a5-b891-4227-9d73-817995342765) Enslow Publishing, LLC. (Enslow Elementary).

—The Start of the Revolutionary War: Would You Fight for Independence?, 1 vol. 2014. (What Would You Do? Ser.). (ENG.). 48p. (gr. 3-4). 27.93 *(978-0-7660-6310-5(0),* 56b7f4db-8771-4e19-834a-e54a6bc48c26); pap. 11.53 *(978-0-7660-6311-2(9),* 35195ee0-a060-4c85-82a7-d1b06c990f08, Enslow Elementary) Enslow Publishing, LLC.

—True Books: the Declaration of Independence. 2008. (True Book: American History, Revised Ser.). (ENG., Illus.). 48p. (J). (gr. 3-5). lib. bdg. 21.19 *(978-0-531-12630-1(7),* Children's Pr.) Scholastic Library Publishing.

Lanser, Amanda. The American Revolution by the Numbers. 2015. (America at War by the Numbers Ser.). (ENG., Illus.).

32p. (J). (gr. 3-9). lib. bdg. 28.65 *(978-1-4914-4294-4(8)*, 128689, Capstone Pr.) Capstone.

Santos, Jeff. Why Longfellow Lied: The Truth about Paul Revere's Midnight Ride. 2021. (Illus.). 160p. (J). (gr. 3-7). lib. bdg. 18.99 *(978-1-58089-933-8(1))* Charlesbridge Publishing, Inc.

Lassieur, Allison. Building a New Nation: An Interactive American Revolution Adventure. 2018. (You Choose: Founding the United States Ser.). (ENG., Illus.). 112p. (J). (gr. 3-7). pap. 6.95 *(978-1-5435-1543-5(6)*, 137911); lib. bdg. 32.65 *(978-1-5435-1539-8(8)*, 137907) Capstone. (Capstone Pr.).

Lee, David. The Colony of Delaware, 1 vol. 2015. (Spotlight on the 13 Colonies: Birth of a Nation Ser.). (ENG., Illus.). 24p. (J). (gr. 4-6). pap. 11.00 *(978-1-4994-0351-0(8)*, 4748a297-da9e-4494-be16-056b98d9c5a2, PowerKids Pr.) Rosen Publishing Group, Inc., The.

Libertson, Jody. Nathan Hale: Hero of the American Revolution. 2009. (Primary Sources of Famous People in American History Ser.). 32p. (gr. 2-3). 47.90 *(978-1-60851-709-1(8))* Rosen Publishing Group, Inc., The.

—Nathan Hale: Heroe de la guerra de Independencia, 1 vol. 2003. (Grandes Personajes en la Historia de Los Estados Unidos (Famous People in American History) Ser.). (SPA.). 32p. (gr. 3-4). pap. 10.00 *(978-0-8239-4235-0(X)*, 6a95018e-f493-428b-81c2-a4423aaa0918, Rosen Classroom) Rosen Publishing Group, Inc., The.

—Nathan Hale: Héroe revolucionario / Hero of the American Revolution. 2009. (Famous People in American History/Grandes personajes en la historia de los Estados Unidos Ser.). (ENG & SPA.). 32p. (gr. 2-3). 47.90 *(978-1-61512-552-4(3)*, Editorial Buenas Letras) Rosen Publishing Group, Inc., The.

—Nathan Hale: Héroe revolucionario (Nathan Hale: Hero of the American Revolution) 2009. (Grandes personajes en la historia de los Estados Unidos (Famous People in American History) Ser.). (SPA.). 32p. (gr. 2-3). 47.90 *(978-1-61512-805-1(0)*, Editorial Buenas Letras) Rosen Publishing Group, Inc., The.

The Life of a Colonial Soldier. 2013. (Jr. Graphic Colonial America Ser.). 24p. (J). (gr. 3-6). pap. 63.60 *(978-1-4777-1440-9(5)*, PowerKids Pr.) Rosen Publishing Group, Inc., The.

Linde, Barbara M. Slavery in Early America, 1 vol. 2011. (Story of America Ser.). (ENG., Illus.). 32p. (J). (gr. 4-5). lib. bdg. 29.27 *(978-1-4339-4776-6(5)*, cd1c573c-1c64-42b1-b3ea-2a3c83e1ba4d, Gareth Stevens Learning Library) Stevens, Gareth Publishing LLLP.

Loh-Hagan, Virginia. Fighting the Monarchy: Battle of Bunker Hill. 2019. (Behind the Curtain Ser.). (ENG., Illus.). 32p. (J). (gr. 4-8). pap. 14.21 *(978-1-5341-3993-0(1)*, 212801); lib. bdg. 32.07 *(978-1-5341-4337-1(8)*, 212800) Cherry Lake Publishing. (45th Parallel Press).

Lowery, Zoe. The American Revolution, 1 vol., 1. 2015. (Early American History Ser.). (ENG., Illus.). 80p. (J). (gr. 8-8). 35.47 *(978-1-68048-269-0(6)*, a7146299-2b01-4b84-aa50-8985f363314f, Britannica Educational Publishing) Rosen Publishing Group, Inc., The.

—The American Revolution: Life, Liberty, & the Pursuit of Happiness, 1 vol. 2015. (Age of Revolution Ser.). (ENG., Illus.). 168p. (J). (gr. 9-10). 37.82 *(978-1-68048-020-7(0)*, 3649a096-b624-4d35-9c65-90fadbd6f9d5, Britannica Educational Publishing) Rosen Publishing Group, Inc., The.

Lowery, Zoe, ed. The American Revolution, 4 vols. 2015. (Age of Revolution Ser.). (ENG.). 168p. (YA). (gr. 9-10). 75.64 *(978-1-68048-021-4(9)*, 90aae60e-026a-4517-8808-d85e36f0bed2, Britannica Educational Publishing) Rosen Publishing Group, Inc., The.

Lusted, Marcia Amidon. Revolution & the New Nation: 1750-Early 1800s. 2007. (Presidents of the United States Ser.). (Illus.). 48p. (J). (gr. 4-7). lib. bdg. 29.05 *(978-1-59036-739-1(1))*; per. 10.95 *(978-1-59036-740-7(5))* Weigl Pubs., Inc.

MacCarald, Clara. The American Revolution. 2017. (Foundations of Our Nation Ser.). (ENG., Illus.). 32p. (J). (gr. 3-5). pap. 9.95 *(978-1-63517-307-9(8)*, 1635173078); lib. bdg. 31.35 *(978-1-63517-242-3(X)*, 163517242X) North Star Editions. (Focus Readers).

—Living Through the Revolutionary War. 2018. (American Culture & Conflict Ser.). (ENG., Illus.). 48p. (gr. 4-8). lib. bdg. 35.64 *(978-1-64156-414-4(8)*, 9781641564144) Rourke Educational Media.

Maestro, Betsy. Liberty or Death: The American Revolution: 1763-1783. Maestro, Giulio, illus. 2005. 64p. (J). lib. bdg. 17.89 *(978-0-688-08803-3(1))*; (ENG.). (gr. 2-7). 18.99 *(978-0-688-08802-6(3)*, HarperCollins) HarperCollins Pubs.

Maloof, Torrey. Abigail Adams & the Women Who Shaped America. rev. ed. 2016. (Social Studies: Informational Text Ser.). (ENG., Illus.). 32p. (gr. 4-8). pap. 11.99 *(978-1-4938-3080-0(5))* Teacher Created Materials, Inc.

—The American Revolution: Fighting for Freedom. rev. ed. 2016. (Social Studies: Informational Text Ser.). (ENG., Illus.). 32p. (gr. 4-8). pap. 11.99 *(978-1-4938-3079-4(1))* Teacher Created Materials, Inc.

Marcovitz, Hal. Cause & Effect the American Revolution: The American Revolution. 2015. (ENG., Illus.). 80p. (J). lib. bdg. *(978-1-60152-790-5(X))* ReferencePoint Pr., Inc.

Margulies, Phillip. A Timeline of the Continental Army. 2009. (Timelines of American History Ser.). 32p. (gr. 4-4). 47.90 *(978-1-60854-383-0(8)*, Rosen Reference) Rosen Publishing Group, Inc., The.

Marsh, Carole. Samuel Adams. 2003. 12p. (gr. k-4). 2.95 *(978-0-635-02367-4(9))* Gallopade International.

Marston, Daniel & O'Neill, Robert John. The American Revolutionary War, 1 vol. 2011. (Early American Wars Ser.). (ENG., Illus.). 96p. (YA). (gr. 10-10). lib. bdg. 38.47 *(978-1-4488-1331-5(X)*, 97fdd7f5-b6c0-4a56-b0f72d38d88) Rosen Publishing Group, Inc., The.

Martin, David. The Colony of Pennsylvania, 1 vol. 2015. (Spotlight on the 13 Colonies: Birth of a Nation Ser.). (ENG., Illus.). 24p. (J). (gr. 4-6). pap. 11.00 *(978-1-4994-0572-9(3)*, 1e60ed25-5bf4-4685-afad-6d51911bd1a7, PowerKids Pr.) Rosen Publishing Group, Inc., The.

Mayr, Diane & Sisters, Write. Women of the Constitution State: 25 Connecticut Women You Should Know. Greenleaf, Lisa, illus. 2012. 136p. (J). pap. 16.00 *(978-0-9842549-1-0(9))* Apprentice Shop Bks., LLC.

McCallum, Ann. Eat Your U. S. History Homework: Recipes for Revolutionary Minds. Hernandez, Leeza, illus. 2015. (Eat Your Homework Ser.: 3). 48p. (J). (gr. 2-5). lib. bdg. 15.95 *(978-1-57091-923-7(2))* Charlesbridge Publishing, Inc.

McDonnell, Peter. A Soldier in Disguise. Tormey, Carlotta, illus. 2005. 16p. (J). pap. *(978-0-7367-2909-3(7))* Zaner-Bloser, Inc.

McGraw Hill. The American Republic to 1877, Reading Essentials & Study Guide, Student Edition. 2nd ed. 2004. (U. S. History - the Early Years Ser.). (ENG., Illus.). 264p. (gr. 6-9). stu. ed., per. 7.00 *(978-0-07-865487-9(4)*, 0078654874) McGraw-Hill Higher Education.

McIlroy, Michelle. Bernardo de Gálvez: Spanish Revolutionary War Hero, 1 vol. 2019. (Our Voices: Spanish & Latino Figures of American History Ser.). (ENG.). 48p. (gr. 6-6). pap. 12.75 *(978-1-5081-8435-5(6)*, 8ce6ceb5-a8cb-4b1b-b496-34d90bb3c113) Rosen Publishing Group, Inc., The.

McKissack, Patricia C. & McKissack, Fredrick L., Jr. Hard Labor: The First African Americans 1619. Fiedler, Joseph Daniel, illus. 2004. (Milestone Ser.). (ENG.). 64p. (J). (gr. 2-5). pap. 6.99 *(978-0-689-86149-9(4)*, Simon & Schuster/Paula Wiseman Bks.) Simon & Schuster/Paula Wiseman Bks.

McLeese, Don. Alexander Hamilton. 2004. (Heroes of the American Revolution Ser.). (Illus.). 32p. (gr. 2-5). lib. bdg. *(978-1-59515-219-0(9))* Rourke Educational Media.

McNeil, Niki, et al. HOCPP 1061 American Revolution. 2006. spiral bd. 24.00 *(978-1-60308-061-3(9))* In the Hands of a Child.

McPherson, Stephanie. My Dear Husband: Important Letters of Abigail Adams. 2009. (Great Moments in American History Ser.). 32p. (gr. 3-3). 47.90 *(978-1-61513-134-1(5))* Rosen Publishing Group, Inc., The.

Meltzer, Brad. Soy George Washington. Eliopoulos, Christopher, illus. 2023.Tr. of I Am George Washington. (SPA.). 40p. (J). (gr. k-3). pap. 14.99 ***(978-1-5433-8605-9(9))*** Vista Higher Learning, Inc.

Metz, Lorijo. The American Revolution, 1 vol., 1. 2014. (Let's Celebrate Freedom! Ser.). (ENG.). 24p. (J). (gr. 3-3). 26.27 *(978-1-4777-2896-3(1)*, f0cab1a4-e786-4d7e-925b-783fd5ba7689, PowerKids Pr.) Rosen Publishing Group, Inc., The.

—La Revolución Americana / the American Revolution, 1 vol., 1. Beullens-Maoui, Nathalie, ed. 2014. (¡Celebremos la Libertad! / Let's Celebrate Freedom! Ser.). (SPA & ENG.). 24p. (J). (gr. 3-3). 26.27 *(978-1-4777-3248-9(9)*, dd80d7b1-ca3a-4685-abee-c5f04ed3a21d, PowerKids Pr.) Rosen Publishing Group, Inc., The.

Micklos, John & Micklos, John, Jr. American Indians & African Americans of the American Revolution: Through Primary Sources, 1 vol. 2013. (American Revolution Through Primary Sources Ser.). (ENG.). 48p. (gr. 4-6). pap. 11.53 *(978-1-4644-0188-6(8)*, ce04c5fc-8efd-4be0-9346-16016124239a); (Illus.). (J). lib. bdg. 27.93 *(978-0-7660-4130-1(1)*, bd09943b-293f-4026-ab57-41ba6f7d2c3e) Enslow Publishing, LLC.

—Courageous Children & Women of the American Revolution: Through Primary Sources, 1 vol. 2013. (American Revolution Through Primary Sources Ser.). (ENG.). 48p. (gr. 4-6). pap. 11.53 *(978-1-4644-0189-3(6)*, 42461525-e520-4293-88f4-cf7617457ce6); (Illus.). (J). 27.93 *(978-0-7660-4131-8(X)*, 40dceef4-2d11-43ca-8481-3586da810fef) Enslow Publishing, LLC.

—The Making of the United States from Thirteen Colonies: Through Primary Sources, 1 vol. 2013. (American Revolution Through Primary Sources Ser.). (ENG.). 48p. (gr. 4-6). pap. 11.53 *(978-1-4644-0191-6(8)*, 34f4b0d8-053b-4331-ab55-77e8baf3d2c8); (Illus.). (J). 27.93 *(978-0-7660-4133-2(6)*, 451c891d-fc74-4e1d-a855-d24b94dd42cd) Enslow Publishing, LLC.

—An Overview of the American Revolution: Through Primary Sources, 1 vol. 2013. (American Revolution Through Primary Sources Ser.). (ENG.). 48p. (gr. 4-6). pap. 11.53 *(978-1-4644-0193-0(4)*, db613d53-c9b8-4ded-a431-7397726c2819); (Illus.). (J). lib. bdg. 27.93 *(978-0-7660-4135-6(2)*, b262916c-a1e9-4ff7-92cd-4a6b514b4be2) Enslow Publishing, LLC.

Mierka, Gregg A. Nathanael Greene: The General Who Saved the Revolution. 2006. (J). pap. *(978-1-59556-017-9(3))*; (Illus.). 88p. (gr. 5-11). lib. bdg. 23.95 *(978-1-59556-012-4(2))* OTTN Publishing.

Miller, Brandon Marie. Declaring Independence: Life During the American Revolution. 2005. (People's History Ser.). (ENG., Illus.). 96p. (gr. 5-12). 33.26 *(978-0-8225-1275-2(0))* Lerner Publishing Group.

Miloszewski, Nathan. Patriots & Loyalists, 1 vol. 2019. (Opponents in American History Ser.). (ENG.). 32p. (gr. 4-5). 27.93 *(978-1-5383-4369-2(X)*, 80d53fe7-7e4a-4966-b9c2-d09253d8ffc1, PowerKids Pr.) Rosen Publishing Group, Inc., The.

Misztal, Maggie. The Colony of New Jersey, 1 vol. 2015. (Spotlight on the 13 Colonies: Birth of a Nation Ser.). (ENG., Illus.). 24p. (J). (gr. 4-6). pap. 11.00 *(978-1-4994-0531-6(6)*, 39d3faf6-9332-4139-919c-d528b3280543, PowerKids Pr.) Rosen Publishing Group, Inc., The.

Morey, Allan. A Timeline History of the Early American Republic. 2014. (Timeline Trackers: America's Beginnings Ser.). (ENG., Illus.). 48p. (J). (gr. 5-8). lib. bdg. 30.65 *(978-1-4677-3641-1(4)*, 8aa7f37e-56d7-4aa1-831a-a70e93c39c0b, Lerner Pubns.) Lerner Publishing Group.

Morlock, Jeremy. The Most Powerful Words of the American Revolution, 1 vol. 2019. (Words That Shaped America Ser.). (ENG.). 32p. (gr. 4-5). pap. 11.50 *(978-1-5382-4811-9(5)*, 5ac89f6f-5745-4677-8139-d26985c38545) Stevens, Gareth Publishing LLLP.

Morlock, Rachael. The Real Story Behind the Founding Fathers, 1 vol. 2019. (Real Story: Debunking History Ser.). (ENG.). 32p. (J). (gr. 4-5). 27.93 *(978-1-5383-4343-2(6)*, 6ec448ac-7bf0-4f25-b8fc-f0f924a2bfa4, PowerKids Pr.) Rosen Publishing Group, Inc., The.

Moss, Marissa. America's Tea Parties: Not One but Four! Boston, Charleston, New York, Philadelphia. 2016. (ENG., Illus.). 48p. (J). (gr. 3-7). 19.95 *(978-1-4197-1874-8(6)*, 1102801, Abrams Bks. for Young Readers) Abrams, Inc.

Muhall, Jill K. & Alarcon, Jill. Causes of the Revolution, 1 vol. rev. ed. 2004. (Social Studies: Informational Text Ser.). (ENG., Illus.). 24p. (J). (gr. 4-8). pap. 10.99 *(978-0-7439-8785-1(3))* Teacher Created Materials, Inc.

Mulhall, Jill K. Abigail Adams, 1 vol. rev. ed. 2004. (Social Studies: Informational Text Ser.). (ENG.). 24p. (gr. 4-8). pap. 10.99 *(978-0-7439-8786-8(1))* Teacher Created Materials, Inc.

Murphy, Jim. The Real Benedict Arnold. 2007. (ENG., Illus.). 272p. (J). (gr. 5-7). 20.00 *(978-0-395-77609-4(0)*, 111937, Clarion Bks.) HarperCollins Pubs.

Murray, Hallie. The Role of Women in the American Revolution, 1 vol. 2019. (Warrior Women in American History Ser.). (ENG.). 104p. (gr. 7-7). pap. 21.00 *(978-1-5026-5555-4(1)*, 391d24c0-0d3e-4b52-8f48-fc26af3bab05); lib. bdg. 44.50 *(978-1-5026-5556-1(X)*, 9e8a71d5-535d-4d0e-9216-705d6441800b) Cavendish Square Publishing LLC.

—The Role of Women in the American Revolution. 2019. (J). pap. *(978-1-9785-1419-5(0))* Enslow Publishing, LLC.

Murray, Katlin. Was the American Revolution Revolutionary?, 1 vol. 2018. (Key Questions in American History Ser.). (ENG.). 32p. (gr. 4-5). 29.27 *(978-1-5081-6762-4(1)*, b2acfb39-ddd9-4e7f-ab07-4fe393bb67f9, PowerKids Pr.) Rosen Publishing Group, Inc., The.

Nagle, Jeanne. How George Washington Fought the Revolutionary War, 1 vol. 2017. (Presidents at War Ser.). (ENG.). 128p. (gr. 8-8). lib. bdg. 38.93 *(978-0-7660-8523-7(6)*, 525f9128-4e87-4008-8471-cda23af7b720) Enslow Publishing, LLC.

Nardo, Don. The American Revolution. 2003. (History of Weapons & Warfare Ser.). (ENG., Illus.). 112p. (J). 32.10 *(978-1-59018-326-7(6))* Cengage Gale.

National Geographic Learning. Reading Expeditions (Social Studies: Voices from America's Past): Colonial Life. 2007. (Avenues Ser.). (ENG., Illus.). 40p. (J). pap. 21.95 *(978-0-7922-8678-3(2))* CENGAGE Learning.

Nelson, Sheila. The Original United States of America. 2006. (How America Became America Ser.). (Illus.). 96p. (YA). lib. bdg. 22.95 *(978-1-59084-903-3(5))* Mason Crest.

Ohlin, Nancy. The American Revolution. Larkum, Adam, illus. 2016. (Blast Back! Ser.). (ENG.). 112p. (J). (gr. 2-5). pap. 5.99 *(978-1-4998-0122-4(X))* Little Bee Books Inc.

Olson, Nathan & Glaser, Jason. Nathan Hale: Revolutionary Spy, 1 vol. Martin, Cynthia & Schoonover, Brent, illus. 2006. (Graphic Biographies Ser.). (ENG.). 32p. (J). (gr. 3-9). per. 8.10 *(978-0-7368-6199-1(8)*, 87898, Capstone Pr.) Capstone.

Omoth, Tyler. Secrets of the American Revolution. 2017. (Top Secret Files Ser.). (ENG.). 32p. (J). (gr. 3-9). pap. 7.95 *(978-1-5157-4141-1(9)*, 133949); (Illus.). lib. bdg. 28.65 *(978-1-5157-4137-4(0)*, 133945) Capstone. (Capstone Pr.).

Osborne, Mary Pope & Boyce, Natalie Pope. American Revolution: A Nonfiction Companion to Magic Tree House #22: Revolutionary War on Wednesday. Murdocca, Sal, illus. 2004. (Magic Tree House (R) Fact Tracker Ser.: 11). 128p. (J). (gr. 2-5). pap. 6.99 *(978-0-375-82379-4(4)*, Random Hse. Bks. for Young Readers) Random Hse. Children's Bks.

Otfinoski, Steven. People of the American Revolution: Text Pairs. 2008. (Bridges/Navigators Ser.). (J). (gr. 5). 89.00 *(978-1-4108-8421-3(X))* Benchmark Education Co.

Palazzo-Craig, Janet. The Making of the American Flag: Betsy Ross & George Washington. 2009. (Great Moments in American History Ser.). 32p. (gr. 3-3). 47.90 *(978-1-61513-155-6(8))* Rosen Publishing Group, Inc., The.

Paley, Caitlyn. Strategic Inventions of the Revolutionary War, 1 vol. 2015. (Tech in the Trenches Ser.). (ENG., Illus.). 112p. (YA). (gr. 9-9). lib. bdg. 44.50 *(978-1-5026-1028-7(0)*, dfdfd520-1a3e-48aa-af45-9ceba531f4f7) Cavendish Square Publishing LLC.

Palmer, Kate Salley. Almost Invisible Blk Patriots. Palmer, Kate Salley, illus. 2008. (ENG., Illus.). 56p. (J). pap. 11.95 *(978-0-9667114-6-2(7))* Warbranch Pr., Inc.

Paris, Stephanie. Forming a New Government (America's Early Years) rev. ed. 2016. (Social Studies: Informational Text Ser.). (ENG., Illus.). 32p. (gr. 4-8). pap. 11.99 *(978-1-4938-3083-1(X))* Teacher Created Materials, Inc.

Parker, Christi E. American Revolution, 1 vol. rev. ed. 2004. (Social Studies: Informational Text Ser.). (ENG.). 24p. (gr. 4-8). pap. 10.99 *(978-0-7439-8748-6(9))* Teacher Created Materials, Inc.

Pfeffer, Wendy. Many Ways to Be a Soldier. Verstraete, Elaine, illus. 2008. (On My Own History Ser.). (ENG.). 48p. (gr. 2-4). lib. bdg. 25.26 *(978-0-8225-7279-4(6)*, Millbrook Pr.) Lerner Publishing Group.

Powell, Walter L. Benedict Arnold: Revolutionary War Hero & Traitor. (Library of American Lives & Timestm Ser.). 112p. (Illus.). (J). (gr. 4-8). lib. bdg. 31.95 *(978-1-4042-6627-8(5))*; 2009. (gr. 5-5). 69.20 *(978-1-60853-471-5(5))* Rosen Publishing Group, Inc., The.

Prior, Jennifer Overend. Reasons for a Revolution. rev. ed. 2016. (Social Studies: Informational Text Ser.). (ENG., Illus.). 32p. (gr. 4-8). pap. 11.99 *(978-1-4938-3078-7(3))* Teacher Created Materials, Inc.

Provost Beller, Susan. The Revolutionary War, 1 vol. Kubinyi, Laszlo, illus. 2003. (American Voices From Ser.). (ENG.). 160p. (gr. 6-6). 41.21 *(978-0-7614-1202-1(6)*, a1d88906-2389-46fb-adc8-ee2817436433) Cavendish Square Publishing LLC.

Purcell, Martha Sias. Spies of the American Revolution. 2003. (Reading Essentials in Social Studies). (Illus.). 48p. pap. 9.00 *(978-0-7891-5854-3(X))* Perfection Learning Corp.

Radomski, Kassandra. Battle for a New Nation: Causes & Effects of the Revolutionary War. 2015. (Revolutionary War Ser.). (ENG., Illus.). 48p. (J). (gr. 3-6). pap. 8.95 *(978-1-4914-2159-8(2)*, 127710, Capstone Pr.) Capstone.

Randolph, Ryan. Betsy Ross: The American Flag, & Life in a Young America. 2009. (Library of American Lives & Times Ser.). 112p. (gr. 5-5). 69.20 *(978-1-60853-473-9(1))* Rosen Publishing Group, Inc., The.

Ransom, Candice. John Hancock. 2005. (History Maker Bios Ser.). (Illus.). 48p. (J). (gr. 3-4). 26.60 *(978-0-8225-1547-0(4)*, Lerner Pubns.) Lerner Publishing Group.

Ratliff, Thomas. Do You Want to Be a Revolutionary War Soldier? 2015. (Do You Want to Be... Ser.). (Illus.). 32p. (gr. 3-6). 28.50 *(978-1-909645-37-0(0))* Book Hse. GBR. Dist: Black Rabbit Bks.

Rauf, Don. Thomas Paine: Author of Common Sense, 1 vol. 2017. (Spotlight on Civic Courage: Heroes of Conscience Ser.). (ENG., Illus.). 48p. (J). (gr. 6-6). 33.47 *(978-1-5383-8100-7(1)*, 82c374e6-6b8f-4c4a-a82d-9d449ee2c3ad); pap. 12.75 *(978-1-5383-8097-0(8)*, 870356b7-d649-44d9-a836-aaf70ed6a868) Rosen Publishing Group, Inc., The.

Raum, Elizabeth. At Battle in the Revolutionary War: An Interactive Battlefield Adventure. 2015. (You Choose: Battlefields Ser.). (ENG., Illus.). 112p. (J). (gr. 3-7). pap. 6.95 *(978-1-4914-2392-9(7)*, 127800, Capstone Pr.) Capstone.

—Resisting British Rule: An Interactive American Revolution Adventure. 2018. (You Choose: Founding the United States Ser.). (ENG., Illus.). 112p. (J). (gr. 3-7). pap. 6.95 *(978-1-5435-1548-0(7)*, 137916); lib. bdg. 32.65 *(978-1-5435-1541-1(X)*, 137909) Capstone. (Capstone Pr.).

—The Revolutionary War: An Interactive History Adventure. rev. ed. 2016. (You Choose: History Ser.). (ENG., Illus.). 112p. (J). (gr. 3-7). pap. 6.95 *(978-1-5157-4264-7(4)*, 134018, Capstone Pr.) Capstone.

—A Revolutionary War Timeline, 1 vol. 2014. (War Timelines Ser.). (ENG., Illus.). 48p. (J). (gr. 4-7). lib. bdg. 35.32 *(978-1-4765-4157-0(4)*, 124262, Capstone Pr.) Capstone.

—Spies of the American Revolution: An Interactive Espionage Adventure. 2015. (You Choose: Spies Ser.). (ENG., Illus.). 112p. (J). (gr. 3-7). lib. bdg. 32.65 *(978-1-4914-5858-7(5)*, 128821, Capstone Pr.) Capstone.

Raum, Elizabeth & Burgan, Michael. The Revolutionary War Experience: An Interactive History Adventure. 2014. (Illus.). 327p. (J). *(978-1-4914-1712-6(9))* Capstone.

Reeder, Eric. Minority Soldiers Fighting in the American Revolution, 1 vol. 2017. (Fighting for Their Country: Minorities at War Ser.). (ENG.). 112p. (YA). (gr. 8-8). 44.50 *(978-1-5026-2661-5(6)*, 8607d64b-bdd7-47ce-a266-d05c26c6518d) Cavendish Square Publishing LLC.

Renehan, Edward J., Jr. & Renehan, Edward J. The Treaty of Paris. 2007. (ENG., Illus.). 121p. (gr. 7-12). lib. bdg. 35.00 *(978-0-7910-9352-8(2)*, P124638, Facts On File) Infobase Holdings, Inc.

Rife, Douglas M. & Capaldi, Gina. The American Revolution. Lyall, Dennis, illus. 2009. (ENG.). 44p. (J). (gr. 3-17). 19.99 *(978-1-58476-612-4(3))* Innovative Kids.

Rissman, Rebecca. Declaration of Independence, 1 vol. 2013. (Foundations of Our Nation Ser.). (ENG.). 48p. (J). (gr. 4-8). lib. bdg. 35.64 *(978-1-61783-708-1(3)*, 7814); (Illus.). pap. 18.50 *(978-1-61783-758-6(X)*, 8749) ABDO Publishing Co.

Roberts, Cokie. Founding Mothers: Remembering the Ladies. Goode, Diane, illus. 2014. (ENG.). 40p. (J). (gr. 1-5). 17.99 *(978-0-06-078002-9(9)*, HarperCollins) HarperCollins Pubs.

Rogers, Amy B. & Davenport, John. The American Revolution: Fighting for Independence, 1 vol. 2016. (American History Ser.). (ENG.). 104p. (J). (gr. 7-7). 41.03 *(978-1-5345-6041-3(6)*, 4750de29-4801-477f-bcb2-7d1a9159bbf5, Lucent Pr.) Greenhaven Publishing LLC.

Roop, Peter & Roop, Connie. Botones Para el General Washington. Hanson, Peter E., illus. 2006. (Yo Solo - Historia (on My Own - History) Ser.).Tr. of Buttons for General Washington. (SPA.). 48p. (gr. 2-4). lib. bdg. 25.26 *(978-0-8225-6261-0(8))* Lerner Publishing Group.

—Let's Ride, Paul Revere! 2004. (Before I Made History Ser.). (Illus.). 60p. (J). pap. *(978-0-439-67623-6(1))* Scholastic, Inc.

—Who Cracked the Liberty Bell? And Other Questions about the American Revolution. 2007. (Chapters in History Ser.). (Illus.). 44p. (J). *(978-0-439-02523-2(0))* Scholastic, Inc.

Rose, Simon. American Revolutionary War. 2014. 49p. (J). *(978-1-4896-0512-2(6))* Weigl Pubs., Inc.

Rosen, Daniel. Independence Now (Direct Mail Edition) The American Revolution 1763-1783. 2004. (Crossroads America Ser.). (ENG., Illus.). 40p. (J). (gr. 5-9). 12.95 *(978-0-7922-6766-9(4))* National Geographic Society.

Roxburgh, Ellis. The Founding Fathers vs. King George III: The Fight for a New Nation, 1 vol. 2014. (History's Greatest Rivals Ser.). (ENG., Illus.). 48p. (J). (gr. 6-8). lib. bdg. 33.60 *(978-1-4824-2217-7(4)*, dcbc28e8-5ce7-4011-b569-40c6a352c012) Stevens, Gareth Publishing LLLP.

Roza, Greg. The Colony of New York, 1 vol. 2015. (Spotlight on the 13 Colonies: Birth of a Nation Ser.). (ENG., Illus.). 24p. (J). (gr. 4-6). pap. 11.00 *(978-1-4994-0537-8(5)*, 32234a4a-48df-4521-b4d6-3e1796ad51f4, PowerKids Pr.) Rosen Publishing Group, Inc., The.

Rudin, Ronald. Founding Fathers: The Celebration of Champlain & Laval in the Streets of Quebec, 1878-1908. 2003. (ENG., Illus.). 304p. *(978-0-8020-3645-2(7))*; pap. *(978-0-8020-8479-8(6))* Univ. of Toronto Pr.

Rushworth, Victoria. Battles of the American Revolution: Saratoga: Text Pairs. 2008. (Bridges/Navigators Ser.). (J). (gr. 5). 81.00 *(978-1-4108-8404-6(X))* Benchmark Education Co.

Samuels, Charlie. Timeline of the Revolutionary War. 2011. (Americans at War Ser.). (ENG.). 48p. (J). (gr. 6-9). 24.85 *(978-1-5311-8638-8(6))* Perfection Learning Corp.

—Timeline of the Revolutionary War, 1 vol. 2011. (Americans at War: a Gareth Stevens Timeline Ser.). (ENG., Illus.). 48p. (J). (gr. 6-8). 34.60 *(978-1-4339-5914-1(3)*, f0a3e844-4eb1-421f-9c67-0e9d97c263e3); pap. 15.05 *(978-1-4339-5916-5(X)*, 957ad4f3-2fe3-4d4f-8d96-0e0422d3d942) Stevens, Gareth Publishing LLLP. (Gareth Stevens Secondary Library).

Schanzer, Rosalyn. George vs. George. 2007. (ENG.). 64p. (J). (gr. 4-7). 17.75 *(978-1-5311-7657-0(7))* Perfection Learning Corp.

—George vs. George: The American Revolution As Seen from Both Sides. 2007. (Illus.). 64p. (J). (gr. 3-7). per. 6.95

TUV

(978-1-4263-0042-4(5), National Geographic Kids) Disney Publishing Worldwide.

—George vs. George: The Revolutionary War As Seen by Both Sides. 2004. (Illus.). 64p. (J). (gr. 3-7). 16.95 *(978-0-7922-7349-3(4)*, National Geographic Children's Bks.) Disney Publishing Worldwide.

Schiffman, Jessica, illus. Sybil Ludington: Freedom's Brave Rider. 2005. 32p. (J). pap. *(978-0-7367-2931-4(3))* Zaner-Bloser, Inc.

Schomp, Virginia. The Revolutionary War, 1 vol. 2005. (Letters from the Battlefront Ser.). (ENG., Illus.). 96p. (gr. 6-6). lib. bdg. 36.93 *(978-0-7614-1659-3(5)*, 814092ad-87d5-4b6d-97da-937b25a10b13) Cavendish Square Publishing LLC.

Schumacher, Cassandra. Code Breakers & Spies of the American Revolution, 1 vol. 2018. (Code Breakers & Spies Ser.). (ENG.). 80p. (J). (gr. 8-8). 38.79 *(978-1-5026-3844-1(4)*, 015f9852-f119-411b-beea-21221643f68d) Cavendish Square Publishing LLC.

Schwartz, Heather E. Alexander Hamilton: The Story of a Statesman. 2020. (Gateway Biographies Ser.). (ENG., Illus.). 48p. (J). (gr. 4-8). pap. 11.99 *(978-1-5415-8886-8(X)*, 53c57c54-581f-4c89-9d64-f13c6a4b348c); lib. bdg. 31.99 *(978-1-5415-7748-0(5)*, c9c12720-d8a7-4416-8f8b-af90f397aacf) Lerner Publishing Group. (Lerner Pubns.).

Sebree, Chet'la. Historical Sources on the Revolutionary War, 1 vol. 2019. (America's Story Ser.). (ENG.). 144p. (gr. 8-8). pap. 22.16 *(978-1-5026-5210-2(2)*, 56cd9c69-9cfe-40e3-bbf4-ea1b6997f364); lib. bdg. 47.36 *(978-1-5026-5211-9(0)*, 1f402bd0-7df5-4875-b7cb-39bd6379dbb9) Cavendish Square Publishing LLC.

Shea, Nicole. The American Revolution, 1 vol. 2011. (Story of America Ser.). (ENG., Illus.). 32p. (J). (gr. 4-5). pap. 11.50 *(978-1-4339-4761-2(7)*, e433e412-c3af-416d-a9fd-dceb2067af77); lib. bdg. 29.27 *(978-1-4339-4760-5(9)*, bd1371be-ee7e-4d86-90f1-3864acfab0b7) Stevens, Gareth Publishing LLLP. (Gareth Stevens Learning Library).

Shea, Therese M. The Boston Massacre, 1 vol., Vol. 1. 2014. (What You Didn't Know about History Ser.). (ENG.). 24p. (J). (gr. 2-3). 25.27 *(978-1-4824-0580-4(6)*, 401d50b2-d2ce-442f-960f-82efce892bef); pap. 9.15 *(978-1-4824-3328-9(1)*, c2537e01-8573-4e86-848f-0585e13b1797) Stevens, Gareth Publishing LLLP.

Sheinkin, Steve. King George: What Was His Problem? 2015. (YA). lib. bdg. 20.85 *(978-0-606-37587-0(2))* Turtleback.

—The Notorious Benedict Arnold: A True Story of Adventure, Heroism & Treachery. 2013. (ENG., Illus.). 368p. (J). (gr. 6-8). pap. 12.99 *(978-1-250-02460-2(9)*, 900097286) Square Fish.

—Storyteller's History: The American Revolution. 2005. (Storyteller's History Ser.). (Illus.). 144p. (J). (gr. 4-8). per. 10.95 *(978-0-9766367-0-0(0))* Summer Street Pr.

Siddons, Brian. Crispus Attucks & African American Patriots of the American Revolution, 1 vol. 2015. (Spotlight on American History Ser.). (ENG., Illus.). 24p. (J). (gr. 4-6). pap. 11.00 *(978-1-4994-1739-5(X)*, 36a9b1bb-9134-4ab4-8115-56689f89d55d, PowerKids Pr.) Rosen Publishing Group, Inc., The.

Silate, Jennifer. Betsy Ross: Creadora de la bandera Estadounidense, 1 vol. 2003. (Grandes Personajes en la Historia de Los Estados Unidos (Famous People in American History) Ser.). (SPA.). 32p. (gr. 3-4). pap. 10.00 *(978-0-8239-4222-0(8)*, b34d9aab-1916-4ad0-86a3-3cbffcb1dc18, Rosen Classroom) Rosen Publishing Group, Inc., The.

—Betsy Ross: Creadora de la bandera estadounidense (Betsy Ross: Creator of the American Flag) 2009. (Grandes personajes en la historia de los Estados Unidos (Famous People in American History) Ser.). (SPA.). 32p. (gr. 2-3). 47.90 *(978-1-61512-791-7(7)*, Editorial Buenas Letras) Rosen Publishing Group, Inc., The.

—Betsy Ross: Creator of the American Flag. 2009. (Primary Sources of Famous People in American History Ser.). 32p. (gr. 2-3). 47.90 *(978-1-60851-657-5(1))* Rosen Publishing Group, Inc., The.

—Betsy Ross: Creator of the American Flag / Creadora de la bandera Estadounidense. 2009. (Famous People in American History/Grandes personajes en la historia de los Estados Unidos Ser.). (ENG & SPA.). 32p. (gr. 2-3). 47.90 *(978-1-61512-539-5(6)*, Editorial Buenas Letras) Rosen Publishing Group, Inc., The.

Smith-Llera, Danielle. The Revoutionary War: A Chronology of America's Fight for Independence. 2015. (Revolutionary War Ser.). (ENG., Illus.). 48p. (J). (gr. 3-6). pap. 8.95 *(978-1-4914-2160-4(6)*, 127711, Capstone Pr.) Capstone.

Smith, Robert. American Revolution. 2004. (Spotlight on America Ser.). (ENG., Illus.). 80p. (gr. 4-8). pap. 12.99 *(978-0-7439-3212-7(9))* Teacher Created Resources, Inc.

Somervill, Barbara A. The Life & Times of James Madison. 2008. (Profiles in American History Ser.). (Illus.). 48p. (J). (gr. 4-7). lib. bdg. 29.95 *(978-1-58415-530-0(2))* Mitchell Lane Pubs.

Sonneborn, Liz. Benedict Arnold: Hero & Traitor. 2005. (Leaders of the American Revolution Ser.). (ENG., Illus.). 136p. (gr. 5-8). lib. bdg. 30.00 *(978-0-7910-8617-9(8)*, P114333, Facts On File) Infobase Holdings, Inc.

South, Victor. Remember the Alamo: Americans Fight for Texas, 1820-1845. 2012. (Illus.). 48p. (J). pap. *(978-1-4222-2416-8(3))* Mason Crest.

—Remember the Alamo: Americans Fight for Texas, 1820-1845. Rakove, Jack N., ed. 2012. (How America Became America Ser.). (Illus.). 48p. (J). (gr. 3-4). 19.95 *(978-1-4222-2402-1(3))* Mason Crest.

Spender, Nick. George Washington & the Winter at Valley Forge, 1 vol. 2011. (Graphic Heroes of the American Revolution Ser.). (ENG.). 24p. (J). (gr. 3-3). pap. 9.15 *(978-1-4339-6014-7(1)*, 212546e8-51ff-4148-864f-6777e830450c, Gareth Stevens Learning Library); (Illus.). lib. bdg. 26.60 *(978-1-4339-6174-8(1)*, a7d37558-8404-4d5a-9b25-9d6db992cc36) Stevens, Gareth Publishing LLLP.

Stanley, George E. The New Republic (1763-1815), 1 vol. 2004. (Primary Source History of the United States Ser.). (ENG., Illus.). 48p. (gr. 5-8). lib. bdg. 33.67 *(978-0-8368-5825-9(5)*, 89d397eb-c154-4e36-a7ed-ed2afca5dd56, Gareth Stevens Secondary Library) Stevens, Gareth Publishing LLLP.

Stewart, Gail B. Life of a Soldier in Washington's Army. 2003. (American War Library). (ENG., Illus.). 112p. (J). 30.85 *(978-1-59018-215-4(4)*, Lucent Bks.) Cengage Gale.

Stokes, Betty Southard. Postcards from George, 1763-1781: George Rogers Clark Writes Home to Virginia from the Kentucky Wilderness. Cable, Annette, illus. 2010. (J). *(978-1-935497-12-7(X))* Butler Bks.

Stokes, Jonathan W. The Thrifty Guide to the American Revolution: A Handbook for Time Travelers. Sossella, David, illus. 2019. (Thrifty Guides: 2). 160p. (J). (gr. 3-7). pap. 8.99 *(978-1-101-99813-7(X)*, Puffin Books) Penguin Young Readers Group.

Strum, Richard M. Causes of the American Revolution. 2005. (Road to War Ser.). (Illus.). 64p. (J). pap. 12.95 *(978-1-59556-005-6(X))*; (gr. 4-18). lib. bdg. 22.95 *(978-1-59556-001-8(7))* OTTN Publishing.

Sullivan, Laura. Life As a Spy in the American Revolution, 1 vol. 2015. (Life As... Ser.). (ENG., Illus.). 32p. (gr. 3-3). 30.21 *(978-1-5026-1081-2(7)*, 5d4dacd8-8e62-4603-84c8-63bd892ca5df) Cavendish Square Publishing LLC.

Thompson, Ben. Guts & Glory: the American Revolution. 2019. (Guts & Glory Ser.: 4). (ENG., Illus.). 336p. (J). (gr. 3-7). pap. 8.99 *(978-0-316-31207-3(X))* Little, Brown Bks. for Young Readers.

Thompson, Gare. Main Idea & Details/Determine Importance - Forward, March! 2010. (Connect to Literacy Ser.). 8p. pap. *(978-1-4334-0543-3(1))* Millmark Education.

Thompson, Gare & Peratt, Karen. Seeking the American Revolution - History Comes Alive! 2010. (Connect to Literacy Ser.). 8p. pap. *(978-1-4334-0544-0(X))* Millmark Education.

Thompson, Gare & West, Elizabeth. Main Idea & Details/Determine Importance: Symbols of Freedom. 2010. (Connect to Literacy Ser.). 8p. pap. *(978-1-4334-0515-0(6))* Millmark Education.

Tracy, Kathleen. Nathan Hale. 2006. (Profiles in American History Ser.). (Illus.). 48p. (J). (gr. 3-7). lib. bdg. 29.95 *(978-1-58415-447-1(0))* Mitchell Lane Pubs.

Urwin, Kirsten. Betsy Ross & the Creation of the American Flag, 1 vol. 2015. (Spotlight on American History Ser.). (ENG., Illus.). 24p. (J). (gr. 4-6). pap. 11.00 *(978-1-4994-1789-0(6)*, 8ebf0f7d-ef7a-4c92-9bae-8a6cdde1e911, PowerKids Pr.) Rosen Publishing Group, Inc., The.

Vink, Amanda. Team Time Machine Crosses the Delaware, 1 vol. 2019. (Team Time Machine: American Revolution Ser.). (ENG.). 32p. (J). (gr. 2-3). pap. 11.50 *(978-1-5382-4674-0(0)*, 385e0c0c-047a-4f25-858c-63faaee3cbb2) Stevens, Gareth Publishing LLLP.

Wachter, Joanne. George Washington & the American Revolution. 2005. (J). pap. *(978-1-4108-4633-4(4))* Benchmark Education Co.

Walker, Robert. Flag Day. 2012. (ENG.). 32p. (J). *(978-0-7787-4087-2(0))*; pap. *(978-0-7787-4092-6(7))* Crabtree Publishing Co.

Washburne, Sophie. The American Revolution, 1 vol. 2020. (Turning Points Ser.). (ENG.). 104p. (J). (gr. 7-7). pap. 20.99 *(978-1-5026-5759-6(7)*, d0e1190c-4eaa-401e-9296-01a8bfd0bf58) Cavendish Square Publishing LLC.

Webb, Sarah Powers. The American Revolution. 2016. (Primary Source History Ser.). (ENG., Illus.). 32p. (J). (gr. 3-6). lib. bdg. 27.99 *(978-1-4914-8487-6(X)*, 130944, Capstone Pr.) Capstone.

Wells-Cole, Catherine. Slavery & the Forging of Early America. 2014. (J). *(978-1-59935-410-1(1))* Reynolds, Morgan Inc.

What Was the Revolutionary War All About?, 1 vol. 2008. (Revolutionary War Library). (ENG., Illus.). 48p. (J). (gr. 3-3). lib. bdg. 27.93 *(978-0-7660-3014-5(8)*, dd1377c1-49ed-448e-af2f-787cc960042b, Enslow Elementary) Enslow Publishing, LLC.

Whig Against Tory or the Military Advent. 2004. reprint ed. pap. 15.95 *(978-1-4191-9382-8(1))* Kessinger Publishing, LLC.

White, Becky. Betsy Ross. Lloyd, Megan, illus. 2019. (I Like to Read Ser.). 32p. (J). (gr. -1-3). pap. 7.99 *(978-0-8234-4523-3(2))* Holiday Hse., Inc.

Whiting, Jim. The Life & Times of Abigail Adams. 2007. (Profiles in American History Ser.). (Illus.). 48p. (J). (gr. 4-7). lib. bdg. 29.95 *(978-1-58415-527-0(2))* Mitchell Lane Pubs.

Whitman Blair, Margaret. Liberty or Death: The Surprising Story of Runaway Slaves Who Sided with the British During the American Revolution (Large Print 16pt) l.t. ed. 2013. 122p. pap. *(978-1-4596-6716-7(6))* ReadHowYouWant.com, Ltd.

Winter, Jonah. Paul Revere & the Bell Ringers: Ready-To-Read Level 2. Dodson, Bert, illus. 2003. (Ready-To-Read Childhood of Famous Americans Ser.). (ENG.). 32p. (J). (gr. k-2). pap. 4.99 *(978-0-689-85635-8(0)*, Simon Spotlight) Simon Spotlight.

Winters, Kay. Colonial Voices: Hear Them Speak: The Outbreak of the Boston Tea Party Told from Multiple Points-Of-View! Day, Larry, illus. 2015. 48p. (J). (gr. 4-7). 9.99 *(978-0-14-751162-1(3)*, Puffin Books) Penguin Young Readers Group.

Wirkner, Linda. Learning about the American Revolution with Graphic Organizers. (Graphic Organizers in Social Studies). 24p. 2009. (gr. 3-4). 42.50 *(978-1-61513-083-2(7)*, PowerKids Pr.) 2005. (ENG.). (gr. 4-5). pap. 8.25 *(978-1-4042-5055-0(7)*, 998779bb-5f9c-4abc-9cea-3d0bf36de4f0, Rosen Classroom) Rosen Publishing Group, Inc., The.

—Learning about the American Revolutionary War with Graphic Organizers, 1 vol. 2004. (Graphic Organizers in Social Studies). (ENG., Illus.). 24p. (J). (gr. 4-5). lib. bdg. 26.27 *(978-1-4042-2813-9(6)*, b30e4025-6020-476a-92e5-382b44538787, PowerKids Pr.) Rosen Publishing Group, Inc., The.

Wister, Sally. Diary of Sally Wister: A Colonial Quaker Girl, 1 vol. 2014. (First-Person Histories Ser.). (ENG., Illus.). 32p. (J). (gr. 3-6). lib. bdg. 27.99 *(978-1-4765-4191-4(4)*, 124298, Capstone Pr.) Capstone.

Woelfle, Gretchen. Answering the Cry for Freedom: Stories of African Americans & the American Revolution. Christie, R. Gregory, illus. 2016. (ENG.). 240p. (J). (gr. 4-7). 19.99 *(978-1-62979-306-1(X)*, Calkins Creek) Highlights Pr., c/o Highlights for Children, Inc.

World Almanac Library of the American Revolution, 16 vols. 2005. (World Almanac(r) Library of the American Revolution Ser.). (ENG.). 48p. (gr. 5-8). lib. bdg. 269.36 *(978-0-8368-5924-9(3)*, 3561b4d7-fa39-4e08-8267-41dfe693b249, Gareth Stevens Secondary Library) Stevens, Gareth Publishing LLLP.

Yasuda, Anita. The American Revolutionary War. 2016. (Illus.). 48p. (J). *(978-1-5105-1278-8(0))* SmartBook Media, Inc.

Yero, Judith Lloyd & Yero, Judith. American Documents: the Mayflower Compact (Direct Mail Edition) 2006. (American Documents Ser.). (ENG., Illus.). 40p. (J). (gr. 5-9). 15.95 *(978-0-7922-5891-9(6))* National Geographic Society.

Ziff, John. The American Revolution, Vol. 11. Musteen, Jason R., ed. 2015. (Major U. S. Historical Wars Ser.). (Illus.). 64p. (J). (gr. 7). lib. bdg. 23.95 *(978-1-4222-3353-5(7))* Mason Crest.

UNITED STATES—HISTORY—REVOLUTION, 1775-1783—BIOGRAPHY

Ades, Audrey. Ethan Allen & the Green Mountain Boys. 2017. (Illus.). 32p. (J). 25.70 *(978-1-61228-952-6(5))* Mitchell Lane Pubs.

Amler, Jane Frances. Haym Salomon: Patriot Banker of the American Revolution. 2009. (Library of American Lives & Times Ser.). 112p. (gr. 5-5). 69.20 *(978-1-60853-487-6(1))* Rosen Publishing Group, Inc., The.

Anderson, Dale. The Patriots Win the American Revolution, 1 vol. 2005. (World Almanac(r) Library of the American Revolution Ser.). (ENG.). 48p. (gr. 5-8). pap. 15.05 *(978-0-8368-5937-9(5)*, 6495745e-a617-48b0-bde0-337b5317f886); lib. bdg. 33.67 *(978-0-8368-5928-7(6)*, 2bd279bf-9af4-4c5b-bc54-0df5d2bb1222) Stevens, Gareth Publishing LLLP. (Gareth Stevens Secondary Library).

Anderson, Laurie Halse. Independent Dames: What You Never Knew about the Women & Girls of the American Revolution. Faulkner, Matt, illus. 2008. (ENG.). 40p. (J). (gr. 1-5). 18.99 *(978-0-689-85808-6(6)*, Simon & Schuster Bks. For Young Readers) Simon & Schuster Bks. For Young Readers.

Anderson, Michael. Biographies of the American Revolution: Benjamin Franklin to John Paul Jones, 1 vol. 2012. (Impact on America: Collective Biographies Ser.). (ENG., Illus.). 152p. (J). (gr. 8-8). lib. bdg. 38.82 *(978-1-61530-685-5(4)*, a636d494-ad58-416b-a2ca-7192b9b545a1) Rosen Publishing Group, Inc., The.

Anderson, Michael, ed. Biographies of the American Revolution: Benjamin Franklin, John Adams, John Paul Jones, & More, 4 vols. 2012. (Impact on America: Collective Biographies Ser.). (ENG., Illus.). 152p. (YA). (gr. 8-8). 77.64 *(978-1-61530-764-7(8)*, 234b8e3b-8381-448f-b6b6-c30e256c7026) Rosen Publishing Group, Inc., The.

Archer, Jules. They Made a Revolution: The Sons & Daughters of the American Revolution. 2016. (Jules Archer History for Young Readers Ser.). (ENG.). 170p. (J). (gr. 6-6). 16.99 *(978-1-63450-195-8(0)*, Sky Pony Pr.) Skyhorse Publishing Co., Inc.

Beller, Susan Provost. Yankee Doodle & the Redcoats: Soldiering in the Revolutionary War. Day, Larry, illus. 2003. (Single Titles Ser.). (ENG.). 96p. (gr. 5-8). lib. bdg. 26.60 *(978-0-7613-2612-0(X)*, Twenty-First Century Bks.) Lerner Publishing Group.

Bodie, Idella. Heroes & Heroines of the American Revolution. 2004. (Illus.). 48p. (J). pap., instr.'s gde. ed. *(978-0-87844-173-0(5))* Sandlapper Publishing Co., Inc.

—Heroines of the American Revolution. 2003. (Illus.). 99p. (J). pap. 6.95 *(978-0-87844-170-9(0))* Sandlapper Publishing Co., Inc.

Boyer, Marilyn & Tumas, Grace. Profiles of Valor: Character Studies from the War of Independence. 2013. (Illus.). 352p. (J). *(978-0-9777685-9-2(7))* Learning Parent, The.

Braun, Eric Mark. The Real Aaron Burr: The Truth Behind the Legend. 2019. (Real Revolutionaries Ser.). (ENG., Illus.). 64p. (J). (gr. 5-9). lib. bdg. 34.65 *(978-0-7565-6250-2(3)*, 141182, Compass Point Bks.) Capstone.

Castrovilla, Selene. By the Sword. Farnsworth, Bill, illus. 2007. (ENG.). 40p. (J). (gr. 1-4). 17.95 *(978-1-59078-427-3(8)*, Calkins Creek) Highlights Pr., c/o Highlights for Children, Inc.

Crannell, Karl. John Stark: Live Free or Die. 2006. (Forgotten Heroes of the American Revolution Ser.). (Illus.). 80p. (J). (gr. 5-11). lib. bdg. 23.95 *(978-1-59556-016-2(5))* OTTN Publishing.

—John Stark: Live Free or Die! 2006. (J). pap. *(978-1-59556-021-6(1))* OTTN Publishing.

Cunningham, Mark. Molly Pitcher: the Woman Who Fought the War, 1 vol. 2014. (American Legends & Folktales Ser.). (ENG., Illus.). 32p. (gr. 3-3). 31.21 *(978-1-62712-289-4(3)*, 3a036d5c-37f1-41f4-98ea-ea33df19cf4e); pap. 11.58 *(978-1-62712-290-0(7)*, a7abaea5-f3b6-4a63-959e-3871fead1783) Cavendish Square Publishing LLC.

Draper, Allison Stark. The Start of the American Revolutionary War: Paul Revere Rides at Midnight. 2009. (Headlines from History Ser.). 24p. (gr. 3-3). 42.50 *(978-1-61513-247-8(3)*, PowerKids Pr.) Rosen Publishing Group, Inc., The.

Erlic, Lily. Paul Revere. 2019. (Illus.). 24p. (J). *(978-1-4896-9550-5(8)*, AV2 by Weigl) Weigl Pubs., Inc.

Fedyszyn, Kirra. Molly Pitcher, 1 vol. 2014. (Jr. Graphic American Legends Ser.). (ENG.). 24p. (J). (gr. 2-3). lib. bdg. 28.93 *(978-1-4777-7205-8(7)*, 2ed331ae-074b-4148-a378-66f7467ec97b, PowerKids Pr.) Rosen Publishing Group, Inc., The.

Gagne, Tammy. Who Were the Signers of the Declaration of Independence? 2017. (Young America Ser.). (Illus.). 47p. (J). (gr. 3-6). 29.95 *(978-1-61228-983-0(5))* Mitchell Lane Pubs.

Green, Joanne. An American Hero. 2008. (Illus.). 56p. per. *(978-1-897512-04-3(X))* Saga Bks.

Hale, Nathan. Nathan Hale's Hazardous Tales: One Dead Spy. 2012. (Nathan Hale's Hazardous Tales Ser.). (ENG., Illus.). 128p. (J). (gr. 3-7). 14.99 *(978-1-4197-0396-6(X)*, 1000101) Abrams, Inc.

Hall, Brianna. Great Women of the American Revolution, 1 vol. 2012. (Story of the American Revolution Ser.). (ENG., Illus.). 32p. (J). (gr. 3-6). pap. 8.10 *(978-1-4296-9284-7(7)*, 120343); lib. bdg. 27.99 *(978-1-4296-8451-4(8)*, 118514) Capstone. (Capstone Pr.).

Harris, Laurie Lanzen. Colonial America & the Revolutionary War: The Story of the People of the Colonies, from Early Settlers to Revolutionary Leaders. 2009. 399p. (J). (gr. 5-7). lib. bdg. 49.00 *(978-1-931360-34-0(0))* Favorable Impressions.

Hollar, Sherman. Biographies of Colonial America: From Sir Walter Raleigh to Phillis Wheatley, 1 vol. 2012. (Impact on America: Collective Biographies Ser.). (ENG., Illus.). 168p. (J). (gr. 8-8). lib. bdg. 38.82 *(978-1-61530-683-1(8)*, ccdf33a7-2d27-4565-92eb-8764fb430454) Rosen Publishing Group, Inc., The.

Hollar, Sherman, ed. Biographies of Colonial America: Sir Walter Raleigh, Powhatan, Phillis Wheatley, & More, 4 vols. 2012. (Impact on America: Collective Biographies Ser.). (ENG., Illus.). 168p. (YA). (gr. 8-8). 77.64 *(978-1-61530-763-0(X)*, fd7fc43d-01c1-4264-9923-817e353acbe0) Rosen Publishing Group, Inc., The.

Huey, Lois Miner. Voices of the American Revolution. 2010. (Voices of War Ser.). (ENG.). 32p. (J). (gr. 3-4). pap. 49.74 *(978-1-4296-5699-3(9)*, 15488, Capstone Pr.) Capstone.

—Voices of the American Revolution: Stories from the Battlefields, 1 vol. 2010. (Voices of War Ser.). (ENG.). 32p. (J). (gr. 3-9). lib. bdg. 28.65 *(978-1-4296-4739-7(6)*, 103280, Capstone Pr.) Capstone.

Jeffrey, Gary. Paul Revere & His Midnight Ride, 1 vol. 2011. (Graphic Heroes of the American Revolution Ser.). (ENG.). 24p. (J). (gr. 3-3). pap. 9.15 *(978-1-4339-6020-8(6)*, 0981fe11-ad56-49bb-ba3e-6601372ad8b3, Gareth Stevens Learning Library); lib. bdg. 26.60 *(978-1-4339-6019-2(2)*, c3cd73f3-b213-499a-b80e-d68ebc2109bb) Stevens, Gareth Publishing LLLP.

—Thomas Jefferson & the Declaration of Independence, 1 vol. 2011. (Graphic Heroes of the American Revolution Ser.). (ENG., Illus.). 24p. (J). (gr. 3-3). 26.60 *(978-1-4339-6025-3(7)*, b3ad44c5-2d19-400f-8ba3-6b2e6bef69a2); pap. 9.15 *(978-1-4339-6026-0(5)*, 6bfbc259-f45e-48b1-85a7-4b2b3c1cce56, Gareth Stevens Learning Library) Stevens, Gareth Publishing LLLP.

Kauffman, Scott. Francis Marion: Swamp Fox of South Carolina. 2006. (Forgotten Heroes of the American Revolution Ser.). (Illus.). 88p. (YA). (gr. 5-11). lib. bdg. 23.95 *(978-1-59556-014-8(9))* OTTN Publishing.

Kudlinski, Kathleen V. Rebel with a Cause: The Daring Adventure of Dicey Langston, Girl Spy of the American Revolution. Faber, Rudy, illus. 2015. (Encounter: Narrative Nonfiction Picture Bks.). (ENG.). 40p. (J). (gr. 3-6). lib. bdg. 29.32 *(978-1-4914-6073-3(3)*, 128973, Capstone Young Readers) Capstone.

The Legend of Jocko: Hero of the American Revolution. 2003. (YA). pap. 9.95 *(978-0-9761778-0-7(3))* Lefall & Co., Inc.

Lewis, Noah & Graham, Loretta. Edward Ned Hector. 2005. (ENG., Illus.). 36p. per. 19.99 *(978-1-4208-6817-3(9))* AuthorHouse.

Libertson, Jody. Nathan Hale: Hero of the American Revolution, 1 vol. 2003. (Primary Sources of Famous People in American History Ser.). (ENG., Illus.). 32p. (gr. 3-4). pap. 10.00 *(978-0-8239-4189-6(2)*, 22d23725-2467-4f07-94a5-866661b41ee6); lib. bdg. 29.13 *(978-0-8239-4117-9(5)*, 63522eaa-0eb2-4695-ba53-02a3b3819817, Rosen Reference) Rosen Publishing Group, Inc., The.

Maloof, Torrey. George Washington & the Men Who Shaped America. rev. ed. 2016. (Social Studies: Informational Text Ser.). (ENG., Illus.). 32p. (gr. 4-8). pap. 11.99 *(978-1-4938-3081-7(3))* Teacher Created Materials, Inc.

Marsico, Katie. Sybil Ludington's Revolutionary War Story. Girard, Thomas, illus. 2018. (Narrative Nonfiction: Kids in War Ser.). (ENG.). 32p. (J). (gr. 2-4). pap. 9.99 *(978-1-5415-1194-1(8)*, cec45b0f-080d-4da3-ab6d-0c870f19cc2b); lib. bdg. 27.99 *(978-1-5124-5676-9(4)*, 5eb11b74-cf07-4032-890a-7cd3011602d0, Lerner Pubns.) Lerner Publishing Group.

Masters, Nancy Robinson. Extraordinary People: Extraordinary Patriots of the United States of America. 2005. (Extraordinary People Ser.). (ENG., Illus.). 288p. (J). (gr. 4-7). 40.00 *(978-0-516-24404-4(3)*, Children's Pr.) Scholastic Library Publishing.

Murray, Stuart A. P. John Trumbull: Painter of the Revolutionary War: Painter of the Revolutionary War. 2008. (ENG., Illus.). 83p. (C). (gr. 6-18). lib. bdg. 180.00 *(978-0-7656-8150-8(1)*, Y182501) Routledge.

National Geographic Learning. Reading Expeditions (Social Studies: People Who Changed America): Fight for Freedom. 2007. (Reading Expeditions Social Studies). (ENG., Illus.). 40p. (J). pap. 21.95 *(978-0-7922-8620-2(0))* CENGAGE Learning.

Newton, Michael E. Alexander Hamilton: The Formative Years. 2015. (ENG., Illus.). 774p. 40.00 *(978-0-9826040-3-8(3))* Eleftheria Publishing.

Otfinoski, Steven. Patriots & Redcoats: Stories of American Revolutionary War Leaders. 2015. (Revolutionary War Ser.). (ENG., Illus.). 48p. (J). (gr. 3-6). pap. 8.95 *(978-1-4914-2158-1(4)*, 127709, Capstone Pr.) Capstone.

—People of the American Revolution: Set Of 6. 2011. (Navigators Ser.). (J). pap. 48.00 net. *(978-1-4108-5110-9(9))* Benchmark Education Co.

Parker, Christi E. George Washington, 1 vol. rev. ed. 2004. (Social Studies: Informational Text Ser.). (ENG.). 24p. (gr. 4-8). pap. 10.99 *(978-0-7439-8749-3(7))* Teacher Created Materials, Inc.

Pfeffer, Wendy. Many Ways to Be A Soldier. 2009. pap. 40.95 *(978-0-7613-4795-8(X))* Lerner Publishing Group.

Raum, Elizabeth. True Stories of the Revolutionary War, 1 vol. Kinsella, Patrick, illus. 2012. (Stories of War Ser.). (ENG.). 32p. (J). (gr. 3-9). 31.32 *(978-1-4296-8674-7(X)*, 119068); pap. 8.10 *(978-1-4296-9342-4(8)*, 120378) Capstone. (Capstone Pr.).

—True Stories of the Revolutionary War. Kinsella, Patrick, illus. 2012. (Stories of War Ser.). (ENG.). 32p. (J). (gr. 3-4). pap.

48.60 *(978-1-4296-9343-1(6)*, 18564, Capstone Pr.) Capstone.

Raum, Elizabeth, et al. Stories of War Classroom Collection. 2012. (Stories of War Ser.). (ENG.). 32p. (J). (gr. 3-4). pap., pap. 195.40 *(978-1-4296-9349-3(5)*, 18568, Capstone Pr.) Capstone.

Revolutionary War Leaders. 2005. (Revolutionary War Leaders Ser.). (gr. 5-8). 440.00 *(978-0-7910-9157-9(0)*, Facts On File) Infobase Holdings, Inc.

Riley, John B. John Paul Jones: A Photo Biography. l.t. ed. 2004. (First Biographies Ser.). (Illus.). 24p. (YA). (gr. 5-18). 16.95 *(978-1-883846-63-3(3)*, First Biographies) Reynolds, Morgan Inc.

Rockwell, Anne. A Spy Called James: The True Story of James Lafayette, Revolutionary War Double Agent. Cooper, Floyd, illus. 2016. (ENG.). 32p. (J). (gr. 2-5). lib. bdg. 19.99 *(978-1-4677-4933-6(8)*, 2dc8d93e-186e-4737-9f52-c724b0f2aff9); E-Book 29.32 *(978-1-4677-6178-9(8))* Lerner Publishing Group. (Carolrhoda Bks.).

Ruffin, Frances E. Molly Pitcher. 2009. (American Legends Ser.). 24p. (gr. 3-3). 42.50 *(978-1-61511-384-2(3)*, PowerKids Pr.) Rosen Publishing Group, Inc., The.

Scarbrough, Mary Hertz. Heroes of the American Revolution, 1 vol. 2012. (Story of the American Revolution Ser.). (ENG., Illus.). 32p. (J). (gr. 3-6). pap. 8.10 *(978-1-4296-9286-1(3)*, 120345); lib. bdg. 27.99 *(978-1-4296-8590-0(5)*, 118601) Capstone.

—Heroes of the American Revolution. 2012. (Story of the American Revolution Ser.). (ENG.). 32p. (J). (gr. 3-4). pap. 49.60 *(978-1-4296-9287-8(1)*, 18523, Capstone Pr.) Capstone.

Silate, Jennifer. Betsy Ross, 1 vol. 2003. (Primary Sources of Famous People in American History Ser.). (ENG., Illus.). 32p. (gr. 3-4). pap. 10.00 *(978-0-8239-4176-6(0)*, b47dfab6-bcb3-478d-8ebd-fb24e811eb35) Rosen Publishing Group, Inc., The.

—Betsy Ross: Creator of the American Flag, 1 vol. 2003. (Primary Sources of Famous People in American History Ser.). (ENG., Illus.). 32p. (J). (gr. 3-4). lib. bdg. 29.13 *(978-0-8239-4104-9(3)*, 89ed74c8-2280-4e97-bcb9-a5df86386585) Rosen Publishing Group, Inc., The.

Stewart, Gail B. The Revolutionary War. 2003. (People at the Center of Ser.). (Illus.). 48p. (J). 26.20 *(978-1-56711-769-1(4)*, Blackbirch Pr., Inc.) Cengage Gale.

Thornton, Jeremy. Famous Women of the American Revolution. 2009. (Building America's Democracy Ser.). 24p. (gr. 3-3). 42.50 *(978-1-61511-763-5(6)*, PowerKids Pr.) Rosen Publishing Group, Inc., The.

—Tories & Patriots: Neighbors at War. 2009. (Building America's Democracy Ser.). 24p. (gr. 3-3). 42.50 *(978-1-61511-768-0(7)*, PowerKids Pr.) Rosen Publishing Group, Inc., The.

Wales, Dirk. Twice a Hero: Polish American Heroes of the American Revolutuion. Peterson, Lynn Ihsen, illus. 2007. 31p. (J). (gr. 4-9). 18.95 incl. audio compact disk *(978-0-9632459-4-6(5))* Great Plains Pr.

Walsh, Francis. Daring Women of the American Revolution. (American History Flashpoints! Ser.). 32p. (gr. 4-4). 2009. 47.90 *(978-1-61511-367-5(3)*, PowerKids Pr.) 2009. (ENG.). (J). lib. bdg. 28.93 *(978-1-4358-2994-7(8)*, f170b92c-cc04-4a89-9f0b-79d32475f4d2, PowerKids Pr.) 2008. (ENG.). pap. 10.00 *(978-1-4358-0177-6(6)*, 9279eae1-ee95-43d8-97ca-f35d83aceba0, Rosen Classroom) Rosen Publishing Group, Inc., The.

Weston Woods Staff, creator. And Then What Happened, Paul Revere? 2011. 29.95 *(978-0-439-73467-7(3))*; 38.75 *(978-0-439-72663-4(8))*; 18.95 *(978-0-439-72661-0(1))* Weston Woods Studios, Inc.

Women of the American Revolution (NCHS) (YA). (gr. 5-8). spiral bd., tchr.'s planning gde. ed. 11.50 *(978-0-382-40933-2(7))* Cobblestone Publishing Co.

Women of the American Revolution (NCHS) Grades 5-8. 58p. (J). tchr. ed. 29.45 *(978-0-382-40934-9(5))* Cobblestone Publishing Co.

Yomtov, Nel, et al. Stories of War. 2012. (Stories of War Ser.). (ENG.). 32p. (J). (gr. 3-9). pap., pap., pap. 31.80 *(978-1-4296-9348-6(7)*, 18567, Capstone Pr.) Capstone.

UNITED STATES—HISTORY—REVOLUTION, 1775-1783—CAMPAIGNS

see also Yorktown (Va.)—History—Siege, 1781

Abnett, Dan. George Washington y la Guerra de Independencia, 1 vol. 2009. (Historietas Juveniles: Biografías (Jr. Graphic Biographies) Ser.). (SPA., Illus.). 24p. (gr. 2-3). pap. 10.60 *(978-1-4358-3322-7(8)*, a38fe106-c9b7-4c5c-9508-fd86a6c2150a) Rosen Publishing Group, Inc., The.

Anderson, Dale. Key Battles of the American Revolution 1776-1778, 1 vol. 2005. (World Almanac(r) Library of the American Revolution Ser.). (ENG.). 48p. (gr. 5-8). pap. 15.05 *(978-0-8368-5936-2(7)*, 2ce612e7-9792-4959-9833-e124e2925489); lib. bdg. 33.67 *(978-0-8368-5927-0(8)*, 9fc991b3-dbca-4338-865d-430f1ce0d1b9) Stevens, Gareth Publishing LLLP. (Gareth Stevens Secondary Library).

—The Patriots Win the American Revolution, 1 vol. 2005. (World Almanac(r) Library of the American Revolution Ser.). (ENG.). 48p. (gr. 5-8). pap. 15.05 *(978-0-8368-5937-9(5)*, 6495745e-a617-48b0-bde0-337b5317f886); lib. bdg. 33.67 *(978-0-8368-5928-7(6)*, 2bd279bf-9af4-4c5b-bc54-0df5d2bb1222) Stevens, Gareth Publishing LLLP. (Gareth Stevens Secondary Library).

Benchmark Education Co., LLC. The Battles of the American Revolution. 2014. (PRIME Ser.). (J). (gr. 6-8). pap. *(978-1-4509-9490-3(3))* Benchmark Education Co.

Bodie, Idella. Light-Horse Harry. 2004. (Illus.). 86p. (J). pap. 6.95 *(978-0-87844-172-3(7))* Sandlapper Publishing Co., Inc.

Cheney, Lynne. When Washington Crossed the Delaware: A Wintertime Story for Young Patriots. Fiore, Peter M., illus. 2012. (ENG.). 40p. (J). (gr. k-4). 7.99 *(978-1-4424-4423-2(1)*, Simon & Schuster/Paula Wiseman Bks.) Simon & Schuster/Paula Wiseman Bks.

—When Washington Crossed the Delaware: When Washington Crossed the Delaware. 2004. (ENG., Illus.). 32p. (J). (gr. k-4). 19.99 *(978-0-689-87043-9(4)*, Simon & Schuster/Paula Wiseman Bks.) Simon & Schuster/Paula Wiseman Bks.

Corporate Contibutor Staff & Roberts, Steve. King George Iii: England's Struggle to Keep America. 2012. (ENG.). 48p. (J). *(978-0-7787-0800-1(4))* Crabtree Publishing Co.

Crabtree Staff & Clarke, Gordon. Significant Battles of the American Revolution, 1 vol. 2012. (ENG., Illus.). 48p. (J). pap. *(978-0-7787-0817-9(9))* Crabtree Publishing Co.

Crabtree Staff & Perritano, John. The Causes of the American Revolution. 2012. (ENG., Illus.). 48p. (J). pap. *(978-0-7787-0815-5(2))* Crabtree Publishing Co.

Crannell, Karl. John Stark: Live Free or Die. 2006. (Forgotten Heroes of the American Revolution Ser.). (Illus.). 80p. (J). (gr. 5-11). lib. bdg. 23.95 *(978-1-59556-016-2(5))* OTTN Publishing.

—John Stark: Live Free or Die! 2006. (J). pap. *(978-1-59556-021-6(1))* OTTN Publishing.

Crewe, Sabrina & Uschan, Michael V. Lexington & Concord, 1 vol. 2004. (Events That Shaped America Ser.). (ENG., Illus.). 32p. (J). (gr. 3-5). lib. bdg. 28.67 *(978-0-8368-3398-0(8)*, 30937a1f-fc4b-47f4-8c23-50802b4fda0b, Gareth Stevens Learning Library) Stevens, Gareth Publishing LLLP.

Dean, Arlan. Crossing the Delaware: George Washington & the Battle of Trenton. (Great Moments in American History Ser.). 32p. (gr. 3-3). 2009. 47.90 *(978-1-61513-140-2(X))* 2003. (ENG., Illus.). (J). lib. bdg. 29.13 *(978-0-8239-4356-2(9)*, 556c34ba-e623-45de-aa7b-709c9fadce66) Rosen Publishing Group, Inc., The.

Forest, Christopher. The Biggest Battles of the Revolutionary War, 1 vol. 2012. (Story of the American Revolution Ser.). (ENG.). 32p. (J). (gr. 3-6). pap. 8.10 *(978-1-4296-9282-3(0)*, 120342, Capstone Pr.) Capstone.

—The Biggest Battles of the Revolutionary War. 2012. (Story of the American Revolution Ser.). (ENG.). 32p. (J). (gr. 3-4). pap. 49.60 *(978-1-4296-9283-0(9)*, 18521, Capstone Pr.) Capstone.

Gallagher, Jim. Daniel Morgan: Fighting Frontiersman. 2006. (J). pap. *(978-1-59556-020-9(3))*; (Illus.). 88p. (gr. 5-11). lib. bdg. 23.95 *(978-1-59556-015-5(7))* OTTN Publishing.

Kravitz, Danny. The Untold Story of Washington's Surprise Attack: The Daring Crossing of the Delaware River. 2015. (What You Didn't Know about the American Revolution Ser.). (ENG.). 64p. (J). (gr. 5-9). 35.32 *(978-0-7565-4973-2(6)*, 127219, Compass Point Bks.) Capstone.

Landau, Elaine. George Washington Crosses the Delaware: Would You Risk the Revolution?, 1 vol. 2009. (What Would You Do? Ser.). (ENG., Illus.). 48p. (gr. 3-3). pap. 11.53 *(978-1-59845-195-5(2)*, 98c4ac0a-48e3-4485-a5d1-eb75e1358676, Enslow Elementary) Enslow Publishing, LLC.

Levin, Jack E. & Levin, Mark R. George Washington: the Crossing. 2013. (ENG., Illus.). 64p. 18.00 *(978-1-4767-3193-3(4)*, Threshold Editions) Threshold Editions.

Micklos, John & Micklos, John, Jr. Washington's Crossing the Delaware & the Winter at Valley Forge: Through Primary Sources, 1 vol. 2013. (American Revolution Through Primary Sources Ser.). (ENG., Illus.). 48p. (J). (gr. 4-6). 27.93 *(978-0-7660-4132-5(8)*, 22bf5158-e47c-42c7-9d03-25ec224712b2); pap. 11.53 *(978-1-4644-0190-9(X)*, c759c386-064d-4048-9796-e54bc92199cf) Enslow Publishing, LLC.

—Why We Won the American Revolution: Through Primary Sources, 1 vol. 2013. (American Revolution Through Primary Sources Ser.). (ENG.). 48p. (gr. 4-6). pap. 11.53 *(978-1-4644-0192-3(6)*, 5895a7f8-08c5-4a37-9a5e-45c01416fbb5); (Illus.). (J). 27.93 *(978-0-7660-4134-9(4)*, 1427223b-d0b5-47ed-ad69-7c1c441a1350) Enslow Publishing, LLC.

Randolph, Joanne. The Call of Liberty: Marquis de Lafayette & the American Revolution. 2009. (Great Moments in American History Ser.). 32p. (gr. 3-3). 47.90 *(978-1-61513-152-5(3))* Rosen Publishing Group, Inc., The.

Rushworth, Victoria. Battles of the American Revolution: Set of 6: Saratoga. 2011. (Navigators Ser.). (J). pap. 48.00 net. *(978-1-4108-5109-3(5))* Benchmark Education Co.

Strum, Richard. Henry Knox: Washington's Artilleryman. 2006. (Forgotten Heroes of the American Revolution Ser.). (Illus.). 88p. (J). (gr. 5-11). lib. bdg. 23.95 *(978-1-59556-013-1(0))* OTTN Publishing.

Strum, Richard M. Henry Knox: Washington's Artilleryman. 2006. (J). pap. *(978-1-59556-018-6(1))* OTTN Publishing.

Thornton, Jeremy. Foreign-Born Champions of the American Revolution. 2009. (Building America's Democracy Ser.). 24p. (gr. 3-3). 42.50 *(978-1-61511-764-2(4)*, PowerKids Pr.) Rosen Publishing Group, Inc., The.

Uschan, Michael V. Lexington & Concord, 1 vol. 2003. (Landmark Events in American History Ser.). (ENG., Illus.). 48p. (gr. 5-8). pap. 15.05 *(978-0-8368-5407-7(1)*, d10b398e-21b3-430b-8266-1825f5179b5d); lib. bdg. 33.67 *(978-0-8368-5379-7(2)*, 0daf71ea-32e5-4ef1-97b4-f03ad1b845b4) Stevens, Gareth Publishing LLLP. (Gareth Stevens Secondary Library).

Vierow, Wendy. The Battle of Saratoga. 2009. (Atlas of Famous Battles of the American Revolution Ser.). 24p. (gr. 3-3). 42.50 *(978-1-60853-330-5(1)*, PowerKids Pr.) Rosen Publishing Group, Inc., The.

—The Battle of Trenton. 2009. (Atlas of Famous Battles of the American Revolution Ser.). 24p. (gr. 3-3). 42.50 *(978-1-60853-331-2(X)*, PowerKids Pr.) Rosen Publishing Group, Inc., The.

—The Battle of Yorktown. 2009. (Atlas of Famous Battles of the American Revolution Ser.). 24p. (gr. 3-3). 42.50 *(978-1-60853-332-9(8)*, PowerKids Pr.) Rosen Publishing Group, Inc., The.

Waldman, Scott P. The Battle of Lexington & Concord. 2009. (Atlas of Famous Battles of the American Revolution Ser.). 24p. (gr. 3-3). 42.50 *(978-1-60853-328-2(X)*, PowerKids Pr.) Rosen Publishing Group, Inc., The.

—The Battle of Monmouth. 2009. (Atlas of Famous Battles of the American Revolution Ser.). 24p. (gr. 3-3). 42.50 *(978-1-60853-329-9(8)*, PowerKids Pr.) Rosen Publishing Group, Inc., The.

Whitelaw, Nancy. The Shot Heard Round the World: The Battles of Lexington & Concord. 2004. (First Battles Ser.). (Illus.). 112p. (J). (gr. 6-12). 23.95 *(978-1-883846-75-6(7)*, First Biographies) Reynolds, Morgan Inc.

UNITED STATES—HISTORY—REVOLUTION, 1775-1783—DRAMA

McCaslin, Nellie. Brave New Banner. 2003. (Players Press Nellie McCaslin Ser.). (Illus.). 20p. (YA). (gr. 6-12). pap. 5.00 *(978-0-88734-436-7(4))* Players Pr., Inc.

UNITED STATES—HISTORY—REVOLUTION, 1775-1783—FICTION

Amstel, Marsha. The Horse-Riding Adventure of Sybil Ludington, Revolutionary War Messenger. Hammond, Ted & Carbajal, Richard Pimentel, illus. 2011. (History's Kid Heroes Set III Ser.). pap. 51.02 *(978-0-7613-7636-1(4)*, Graphic Universe™) Lerner Publishing Group.

—The Horse-Riding Adventure of Sybil Ludington, Revolutionary War Messenger. Carbajal, Richard & Hammond, Ted, illus. 2011. (History's Kid Heroes Ser.). (ENG.). 32p. (J). (gr. 3-5). pap. 8.99 *(978-0-7613-7073-4(0)*, 569b9769-c9a2-4f2e-ab68-5b432b193716, Graphic Universe™) Lerner Publishing Group.

Anderson, Laurie Halse. Ashes. (Seeds of America Trilogy Ser.: Bk. 3). (ENG., Illus.). (J). (gr. 5). 2017. 320p. pap. 8.99 *(978-1-4169-6147-5(X))* 2016. 304p. 19.99 *(978-1-4169-6146-8(1)*, Atheneum/Caitlyn Dlouhy Books) Simon & Schuster Children's Publishing.

—Chains. (Seeds of America Trilogy Ser.). (ENG., Illus.). (J). (gr. 5-9). 2010. 336p. pap. 8.99 *(978-1-4169-0586-8(3))* 2008. 320p. 19.99 *(978-1-4169-0585-1(5))* Simon & Schuster Children's Publishing. (Atheneum Bks. for Young Readers).

—Forge. (Seeds of America Trilogy Ser.). (ENG., Illus.). (J). (gr. 5-9). 2012. 320p. pap. 8.99 *(978-1-4169-6145-1(3))* 2010. 304p. 19.99 *(978-1-4169-6144-4(5))* Simon & Schuster Children's Publishing. (Atheneum Bks. for Young Readers).

Anderson, M. T. The Astonishing Life of Octavian Nothing, Traitor to the Nation, Volume I: The Pox Party, Vol. 1. 2008. (ENG., Illus.). 384p. (YA). (gr. 9-12). pap. 13.99 *(978-0-7636-3679-1(7))* Candlewick Pr.

Anderson, Matthew. The Astonishing Life of Octavian Nothing, Traitor to the Nation, Volume I: The Pox Party. 2009. (Astonishing Life of Octavian Nothing, Traitor to the Nation Ser.: Vol. 1). 11.94 *(978-0-7848-1900-5(9)*, Everbind) Marco Bk. Co.

—The Astonishing Life of Octavian Nothing, Traitor to the Nation, Volume I: The Pox Party. 2011. 22.00 *(978-1-60686-925-3(6))* Perfection Learning Corp.

—The Astonishing Life of Octavian Nothing, Traitor to the Nation, Volume I: The Pox Party. l.t. ed. 2020. (ENG.). pap. 15.99 *(978-1-4328-7401-8(2))* Thorndike Pr.

—The Astonishing Life of Octavian Nothing, Traitor to the Nation, Volume II: The Kingdom on the Waves. 2009. (ENG., Illus.). 592p. (YA). (gr. 9). pap. 12.99 *(978-0-7636-4626-4(1))* Candlewick Pr.

—The Astonishing Life of Octavian Nothing, Traitor to the Nation, Volume II: The Kingdom on the Waves. 2011. 24.00 *(978-1-60686-926-0(4))* Perfection Learning Corp.

Avi. The Fighting Ground. 25th anniv. ed. 2009. (ENG.). 160p. (J). (gr. 3-7). reprint ed. pap. 7.99 *(978-0-06-440185-2(5)*, HarperCollins) HarperCollins Pubs.

—The Fighting Ground. 2009. 157p. (J). (gr. 4-7). 17.20 *(978-0-8085-9452-9(4))* Turtleback.

—Fighting Ground. 25th rev. ed. 2014. (Trophy Bk Ser.). (ENG.). 160p. (J). (gr. 3-7). 10.24 *(978-1-63245-315-0(0))* Lectorum Pubns., Inc.

—Sophia's War: A Tale of the Revolution. 2012. (ENG., Illus.). 320p. (J). (gr. 3-7). 19.99 *(978-1-4424-1441-9(3)*, Beach Lane Bks.) Beach Lane Bks.

—Sophia's War: A Tale of the Revolution. 2013. (ENG., Illus.). 336p. (J). (gr. 3-7). pap. 8.99 *(978-1-4424-1442-6(1))* Simon & Schuster Children's Publishing.

Barnes, Peter W. Liberty Lee's Tail of Independence. Barnes, Cheryl Shaw, illus. 2012. (ENG.). 36p. (J). (gr. k-3). 16.95 *(978-1-59698-792-0(8)*, Little Patriot Pr.) Regnery Publishing.

Baxter, Jean Rae. Freedom Bound. 2012. (ENG., Illus.). 246p. pap. 11.95 *(978-1-55380-143-6(1))* Ronsdale Pr. CAN. Dist: SPD-Small Pr. Distribution.

Berleth, Richard. Samuel's Choice. Watling, James, illus. 2012. (ENG.). 40p. (J). (gr. -1-3). pap. 8.99 *(978-0-8075-7219-1(5)*, 807572195) Whitman, Albert & Co.

Blackwood, Gary. Year of the Hangman. 2004. 272p. (YA). (gr. 9-18). 7.99 *(978-0-14-240078-4(5)*, Speak) Penguin Young Readers Group.

—The Year of the Hangman. 2004. 261p. (YA). (gr. 8-12). 14.65 *(978-0-7569-4274-8(8))* Perfection Learning Corp.

Bond, Douglas. Guns of Providence. 2010. (J). pap. *(978-1-59638-156-8(6))* P & R Publishing.

Carlson, Drew. Attack of the Turtle. Johnson, David A., illus. 2008. (ENG.). 157p. (YA). (gr. 4-6). pap. 22.44 *(978-0-8028-5338-7(2)*, Eerdmans Bks For Young Readers) Eerdmans, William B. Publishing Co.

Carson, Jana. We Both Read-The Boy Who Carried the Flag. Westerman, Johanna, illus. 2010. (We Both Read Ser.). 44p. (J). (gr. 2-5). 9.95 *(978-1-60115-247-3(7))*; pap. 5.99 *(978-1-60115-248-0(5))* Treasure Bay, Inc.

Clark, Eleanor. Victoria Grace: Courageous Patriot. 2007. (Eleanor Ser.: Bk. 2). 209p. (J). (gr. 4-7). 14.99 *(978-0-9753036-8-9(6))* HonorNet.

Collier, James Lincoln & Collier, Christopher. My Brother Sam Is Dead (Scholastic Gold) 2005. (ENG.). 240p. (J). (gr. 7-7). per. 8.99 *(978-0-439-78360-6(7)*, Scholastic Paperbacks) Scholastic, Inc.

de la Cruz, Melissa. Alex & Eliza. (Alex & Eliza Trilogy Ser.: 1). (ENG.). (YA). (gr. 7). 2020. 400p. pap. 11.99 *(978-1-5247-3964-5(2)*, Penguin Books) 2017. 368p. 18.99 *(978-1-5247-3962-1(6)*, G.P. Putnam's Sons Books for Young Readers) Penguin Young Readers Group.

De la Cruz, Melissa. Alex & Eliza: A Love Story. l.t. ed. 2017. (ENG.). 444p. 22.99 *(978-1-4328-4051-8(7))* Cengage Gale.

de la Cruz, Melissa. Love & War. 2018. (Alex & Eliza Trilogy Ser.: 2). 384p. (YA). (gr. 7). 18.99 *(978-1-5247-3965-2(0)*, G.P. Putnam's Sons Books for Young Readers) Penguin Young Readers Group.

DeMitchell, Terri A. The Portsmouth Alarm. 2013. 161p. pap. 16.95 *(978-1-932278-92-7(3))* Mayhaven Publishing, Inc.

Deutsch, Stacia & Cohon, Rhody. Washington's War. Francis, Guy, illus. 2015. (Blast to the Past Ser.: 7). (ENG.). 128p. (J). (gr. 2-5). pap. 6.99 *(978-1-4424-9540-1(5)*, Simon & Schuster/Paula Wiseman Bks.) Simon & Schuster/Paula Wiseman Bks.

Elliott, L. M. Give Me Liberty. 2008. (ENG., Illus.). 384p. (J). (gr. 4-8). pap. 7.99 *(978-0-06-074423-6(5)*, Tegen, Katherine Bks) HarperCollins Pubs.

Ellis, Edward S. The Boy Patriot. 2007. (Illus.). 88p. per. *(978-1-4065-3449-8(8))* Dodo Pr.

Evan, Frances Y. The Forgotten Flag: Revolutionary Struggle in Connecticut. 2003. (Illus.). 92p. (J). 5.95 *(978-1-57249-338-4(0)*, White Mane Kids) White Mane Publishing Co., Inc.

Falk, Elizabeth Sullivan. Freedom's Fire. Wang, Qi Z., illus. 2004. (J). *(978-1-59336-321-5(4))*; pap. *(978-1-59336-322-2(2))* Mondo Publishing.

Figley, Marty Rhodes. The Prison-Ship Adventure of James Forten, Revolutionary War Captive. Hammond, Ted & Carbajal, Richard, illus. 2011. (History's Kid Heroes Ser.). 32p. pap. 51.02 *(978-0-7613-7637-8(2)*, Graphic Universe™) Lerner Publishing Group.

—The Prison-Ship Adventure of James Forten, Revolutionary War Captive. Carbajal, Richard & Hammond, Ted, illus. 2011. (History's Kid Heroes Ser.). (ENG.). 32p. (J). (gr. 3-5). pap. 9.99 *(978-0-7613-7075-8(7)*, 27614239-05d0-467e-96a3-323cf7fd7f91, Graphic Universe™) Lerner Publishing Group.

Forbes, Esther. Johnny Tremain. McCurdy, Michael, illus. l.t. ed. 2005. (ENG.). 440p. (gr. 5-8). pap. 15.99 *(978-0-7862-7178-8(7))* Cengage Gale.

—Johnny Tremain. 2003. (EMC Masterpiece Series Access Editions). (Illus.). xvi, 308p. (J). 13.99 *(978-0-8219-2408-2(7))* EMC/Paradigm Publishing.

Forbes, Esther Hoskins. Johnny Tremain. Ward, Lynd, illus. 2011. (Newbery Medal Ser.). (ENG.). 288p. (YA). (gr. 6-8). tchr. ed. 21.19 *(978-0-395-06766-6(9))* Houghton Mifflin Harcourt Publishing Co.

—Johnny Tremain: A Newbery Award Winner. 2018. (ENG.). 320p. (J). (gr. 3-7). 14.99 *(978-1-328-48916-6(7)*, 1716454, Clarion Bks.) HarperCollins Pubs.

—Johnny Tremain: Illustrated American Classics. Date not set. (J). lib. bdg. 22.95 *(978-0-8488-1318-5(9))* Amereon Ltd.

—Johnny Tremain: Illustrated American Classics. Random House Publishing Group.

—Johnny Tremain Set: Illustrated American Classics, 2 vols., l.t. ed. (J). reprint ed. *(978-0-89064-029-6(7))* National Assn. for Visually Handicapped.

Giff, Patricia Reilly. Storyteller. 2011. (ENG.). 176p. (J). (gr. 3-7). pap. 7.99 *(978-0-440-42175-7(6)*, Yearling) Random Hse. Children's Bks.

Gregory, Kristiana. The Winter of Red Snow (Dear America) 2010. (Dear America Ser.). (ENG.). 192p. (J). (gr. 3-9). 12.99 *(978-0-545-23802-1(1)*, Scholastic Pr.) Scholastic, Inc.

Griffin, Kitty. The Ride: The Legend of Betsy Dowdy. Priceman, Marjorie, illus. 2010. (ENG.). 40p. (J). (gr. -1-3). 17.99 *(978-1-4169-2816-4(2)*, Atheneum Bks. for Young Readers) Simon & Schuster Children's Publishing.

Gunderson, J. Secret Weapons: A Tale of the Revolutionary War, 1 vol. Aburto, Jesus, illus. 2008. (Historical Fiction Ser.). (ENG.). 56p. (J). (gr. 3-6). pap. 6.25 *(978-1-4342-0848-4(6)*, 95209, Stone Arch Bks.) Capstone.

Gunderson, Jessica. A Rebel among Redcoats: A Revolutionary War Novel. 2015. (Revolutionary War Ser.). (ENG., Illus.). 96p. (J). (gr. 3-5). lib. bdg. 26.65 *(978-1-4342-9701-3(2)*, 127020, Stone Arch Bks.) Capstone.

Guzman, Lila & Guzman, Rick. Lorenzo & the Turncoat. 2006. 183p. (J). (gr. 5). per. 9.95 *(978-1-55885-471-0(1)*, Piñata Books) Arte Publico Pr.

—Lorenzo's Revolutionary Quest. 2003. 176p. (J). pap. 9.95 *(978-1-55885-392-8(8)*, Piñata Books) Arte Publico Pr.

—Lorenzo's Secret Mission. 2005. 153p. (gr. 4-7). 19.95 *(978-0-7569-5599-1(8))* Perfection Learning Corp.

Haislip, Phyllis Hall. Between the Lines: A Revolutionary War Slave's Journey to Freedom. 2012. (ENG., Illus.). 190p. (J). pap. 8.95 *(978-1-57249-409-1(3)*, White Mane Kids) White Mane Publishing Co., Inc.

Halse Anderson, Laurie. Ashes. l.t. ed. 2017. (Seeds of America Ser.: 3). (ENG.). 410p. 22.99 *(978-1-4104-9607-2(4))* Cengage Gale.

—Chains. l.t. ed. 2017. (Seeds of America Ser.). (ENG.). 442p. 22.99 *(978-1-4104-9917-2(0))* Cengage Gale.

—Chains. 2014. (Seeds of America Trilogy). (ENG.). 336p. (J). 12.24 *(978-1-63245-094-4(1))* Lectorum Pubns., Inc.

—Chains. 2009. 9.00 *(978-0-7848-3678-1(7)*, Everbind) Marco Bk. Co.

—Chains. l.t. ed. 2009. (ENG.). 390p. (YA). 23.95 *(978-1-4104-1425-0(6))* Thorndike Pr.

—Chains. 2010. (Seeds of America Trilogy Ser.: 1). lib. bdg. 19.65 *(978-0-606-14520-6(6))* Turtleback.

—Forge. 2012. 18.00 *(978-1-61383-316-2(4))* Perfection Learning Corp.

—Forge. 2012. (Seeds of America Trilogy Ser.: 2). lib. bdg. 18.40 *(978-0-606-23680-5(5))* Turtleback.

Hardman, Ron & Hardman, Jessica. Shadow Fox: Sons of Liberty. Barnecut, Suzanne, ed. Harrigan, Mike, illus. 2010. (Shadow Fox Ser.). 186p. (J). (gr. 4-8). 22.99 *(978-0-9819607-1-5(5))* Fox Run Pr., LLC.

—Shadow Fox: Sons of Liberty. Barnecut, Suzanne, ed. Harrigan, Mike, illus. 2010. (Shadow Fox Ser.). 186p. (J). (gr. 4-8). pap. 11.99 *(978-0-9819607-0-8(7))* Fox Run Pr., LLC.

—Shadow Fox: Sons of Liberty Teacher's Edition. Barnecutt, Suzanne, ed. Harrigan, Mike, illus. 2010. (Shadow Fox Ser.: 1). 186p. (J). 34.99 *(978-0-9819607-2-2(3))* Fox Run Pr., LLC.

Harlow, Joan Hiatt. Midnight Rider. 2006. (ENG.). 384p. (J). (gr. 4-9). pap. 8.99 *(978-0-689-87010-1(8)*, McElderry, Margaret K. Bks.) McElderry, Margaret K. Bks.

Hedstrom-Page, Deborah. From Colonies to Country with George Washington. Martinez, Sergio, illus. 2007. (My American Journey Ser.). 82p. (J). (gr. 3-9). 9.99 *(978-0-8054-3265-7(5))* B&H Publishing Group.

Henty, George. True to the Old Flag: A Novel of the Loyalists in the American War of Independence. 2011. 344p. pap. 19.95 *(978-1-61179-114-3(6))* Fireship Pr.

T U V

Hering, Marianne & Sanders, Nancy I. Captured on the High Seas. 2014. (AIO Imagination Station Bks.: 14). (ENG.). 144p. (J). pap. 5.99 *(978-1-58997-775-4(0),* 4609675) Focus on the Family Publishing.

Hogan, Stephen. Johnny Lynch: Patriot Drummerboy. rev. ed. 2007. (J). *(978-0-9795474-0-9(7))* KAM Publishing.

—Johnny Lynch: Road to Camden. 2007. (J). *(978-0-9795474-1-6(5))* KAM Publishing.

Hughes, Pat. Five 4ths of July. 2013. (ENG.). 304p. (YA). (gr. 7-12). 24.94 *(978-0-670-01207-7(6),* Viking) Penguin Publishing Group.

Hunter, John P. Red Thunder: Secrets, Spies, & Scoundrels at Yorktown. 2006. 234p. (J). (gr. 6-8). 7.95 *(978-0-87935-231-8(0))* Colonial Williamsburg Foundation.

Ingle, Sheila. Courageous Kate: A Daughter of the American Revolution. 2006. (ENG.). 130p. pap. 11.95 *(978-1-891885-52-5(9))* Hub City Pr.

Kelley, Lauren E. Tuggie the Patriot Pup. 2014. (ENG., Illus.). 35p. (J). pap. 12.95 *(978-0-9903030-0-8(4))* Puppy Tale, LLC.

Klimo, Kate. Dog Diaries #6: Sweetie. Jessell, Tim, illus. 2015. (Dog Diaries: 6). 160p. (J). (gr. 2-5). pap. 7.99 *(978-0-385-39240-2(0),* Random Hse. Bks. for Young Readers) Random Hse. Children's Bks.

Lane, Marion T. Patriots of African Descent in the Revolutionary War: Part 1. 2011. 56p. 30.00 *(978-1-60976-517-0(6),* Eloquent Bks.) Strategic Book Publishing & Rights Agency (SBPRA).

Lavender, William. Just Jane: A Daughter of England Caught in the Struggle of the American Revolution. 2005. (Great Episodes Ser.). (ENG.). 336p. (YA). (gr. 7-12). pap. 15.95 *(978-0-15-205472-4(3),* 1196465, Clarion Bks.) HarperCollins Pubs.

Limbaugh, Rush & Adams Limbaugh, Kathryn. Rush Revere & the American Revolution: Time-Travel Adventures with Exceptional Americans. 2014. (Rush Revere Ser.: 3). (ENG.). 256p. 21.00 *(978-1-4767-8987-3(8),* Threshold Editions) Threshold Editions.

Limbaugh, Rush H., III & Limbaugh, Kathryn Adams. Rush Revere & the American Revolution. Hiers, Christopher, illus. 2014. 244p. (J). pap. *(978-1-4767-8989-7(4),* Threshold Editions) Threshold Editions.

Marshall, Peter, et al. Nate Donovan: Revolutionary Spy. 2007. 208p. (J). pap. 9.99 *(978-0-8054-4394-3(0),* B&H Bks.) B&H Publishing Group.

McIntyre, John T. Fighting King George. 2006. (Illus.). pap. 33.95 *(978-1-4286-1853-4(8))* Kessinger Publishing, LLC.

Messner, Kate. Spitfire. 2007. (ENG.). (J). pap. *(978-1-59531-018-7(5))* North Country Bks., Inc.

Moore, Ruth Nulton. The Christmas Surprise. Eitzen, Allan, illus. 2007. (ENG.). 160p. (gr. 4-7). pap. 22.00 *(978-1-55635-418-2(5),* Resource Pubns.(OR)) Wipf & Stock Pubs.

Morgan, Helen L. Liberty Maid: The Story of Abigail Adams. 2011. 252p. 46.95 *(978-1-258-03202-9(3))* Literary Licensing, LLC.

Moss, Marissa. Emma's Journal. 2004. (Young American Voice Bks.). (Illus.). (gr. 3-7). 17.00 *(978-0-7569-4110-9(5))* Perfection Learning Corp.

Nixon, Joan Lowery. John's Story, 1775. 2004. (J). *(978-0-87935-228-8(0))* Colonial Williamsburg Foundation.

Noble, Trinka Hakes. The Scarlet Stockings Spy. Papp, Robert, illus. 2004. (Tales of Young Americans Ser.). (ENG.). 48p. (J). (gr. 1-4). 16.95 *(978-1-58536-230-1(1),* 202055) Sleeping Bear Pr.

Noble, Trinka Hakes & Papp, Lisa. The Battles. Papp, Robert, illus. 2013. (American Adventures Ser.). (ENG.). 88p. (J). (gr. 3-6). pap. 9.99 *(978-1-58536-861-7(X),* 202368) Sleeping Bear Pr.

Olasky, Susan. Annie Henry: Adventures in the American Revolution. 2005. (Illus.). 528p. (J). pap. 16.99 *(978-1-58134-521-6(6),* Crossway Bibles) Crossway.

—Annie Henry & the Birth of Liberty. 2011. (J). pap. *(978-1-59638-375-3(5))* P & R Publishing.

—Annie Henry & the Redcoats. 2011. (J). pap. *(978-1-59638-377-7(1))* P & R Publishing.

Orgill, Roxane. Siege: How General Washington Kicked the British Out of Boston & Launched a Revolution. 2018. (ENG., Illus.). 240p. (J). (gr. 5). 17.99 *(978-0-7636-8851-6(7))* Candlewick Pr.

Osborne, Mary Pope. Revolutionary War on Wednesday. unabr. ed. 2004. (Magic Tree House Ser.: No. 22). 69p. (J). (gr. k-3). pap. 17.00 incl. audio *(978-0-8072-0931-8(7),* S FTR 254 SP, Listening Library) Random Hse. Audio Publishing Group.

Otis, James. The Minute Boys of Mohawk Valley. 2005. 29.95 *(978-1-4218-0059-2(4),* 1st World Library - Literary Society) 1st World Publishing, Inc.

—Under the Liberty Tree, a Story of the Boston Massacre. 2011. 84p. pap. 9.99 *(978-1-61203-273-3(7))* Bottom of the Hill Publishing.

Paulsen, Gary. The Rifle. 2006. (ENG.). 112p. (YA). (gr. 7-12). pap. 10.99 *(978-0-15-205839-5(7),* 253006, Clarion Bks.) HarperCollins Pubs.

—Woods Runner. 2011. (ENG.). 176p. (YA). (gr. 7). pap. 9.99 *(978-0-375-85908-3(X),* Lamb, Wendy Bks.) Random Hse. Children's Bks.

Perkins, Lucy. The American Twins of the Revolution. Perkins, Lucy, illus. 2007. (Illus.). 232p. per. 12.95 *(978-0-9776786-7-9(9))* Salem Ridge Press LLC.

Perkins, Lucy Fitch. The American Twins of the Revolution. Perkins, Lucy Fitch, illus. 2008. (Illus.). 240p. 22.95 *(978-1-934671-19-1(3))* Salem Ridge Press LLC.

Pettinato, Laura. Thirteen Americas: American Revolution & Constitution. Tiwari, Saral, illus. 2004. (J). 18.95 *(978-0-9742502-7-4(9))* Gossamer Bks., LLC.

—Thirteen Americas: The Declaration of Independence. Tiwari, Saral, illus. 2nd ed. 2004. (J). lib. bdg. *(978-0-9742502-6-7(0))* Gossamer Bks., LLC.

Pfaff, Eugene E. Guns at Guilford Court House. 2008. 132p. (YA). (gr. 6-9). pap. 14.95 *(978-0-936389-97-4(4))* Tudor Pubs., Inc.

Philbrick, Nathaniel. Ben's Revolution: Benjamin Russell & the Battle of Bunker Hill. Minor, Wendell, illus. 2017. 64p. (J). (gr. 2-4). 17.99 *(978-0-399-16674-7(2),* Nancy Paulsen Books) Penguin Young Readers Group.

Pierpoint, Eric. The Secret Mission of William Tuck. 2015. (ENG.). 320p. (J). (gr. 4-7). pap. 11.99 *(978-1-4022-8174-7(9),* 9781402281747) Sourcebooks, Inc.

Poe, Marshall. Sons of Liberty. Purvis, Leland, illus. 2008. (Turning Points Ser.). (ENG.). 128p. (J). (gr. 3-7). pap. 8.99 *(978-1-4169-5067-7(2))* Simon & Schuster, Inc.

Prentice-Hall Staff. J. Tremain. 2nd ed. (J). stu. ed. *(978-0-13-717174-3(9))* Prentice Hall (Schl. Div.).

Pryor, Bonnie. Captain Hannah Pritchard: The Hunt for Pirate Gold, 1 vol. 2012. (Historical Fiction Adventures Ser.). (ENG., Illus.). 160p. (J). (gr. 3-5). pap. 13.88 *(978-1-59845-283-9(5),* 249245aa-07ef-41ea-a6ac-68d5be3db404); lib. bdg. 31.93 *(978-0-7660-3817-2(3),* d1bf7ad2-c916-402c-ba83-61c0f084aac6) Enslow Publishing, LLC.

—Hannah Pritchard: Pirate of the Revolution, 1 vol. 2008. (Historical Fiction Adventures Ser.). (ENG., Illus.). 160p. (J). (gr. 3-5). lib. bdg. 31.93 *(978-0-7660-2851-7(8),* 26121413-8628-47dc-9a2d-81661c6d5db1) Enslow Publishing, LLC.

—Pirate Hannah Pritchard: Captured!, 1 vol. 2010. (Historical Fiction Adventures Ser.). (ENG., Illus.). 160p. (J). (gr. 3-5). lib. bdg. 31.93 *(978-0-7660-3310-8(4),* 03ee45a8-be09-4257-aaca-0cd2071fb5cf) Enslow Publishing, LLC.

Rice, Dona Herwick & Bradley, Kathleen. Molly Pitcher, 1 vol. rev. ed. 2009. (Reader's Theater Ser.). (ENG., Illus.). 24p. (gr. 2-4). pap. 8.99 *(978-1-4333-0993-9(9))* Teacher Created Materials, Inc.

Rinaldi, Ann. The Family Greene. 2011. (ENG.). 256p. (YA). (gr. 7). pap. 14.95 *(978-0-547-57723-4(0),* 1458519, Clarion Bks.) HarperCollins Pubs.

—Finishing Becca: A Story about Peggy Shippen & Benedict Arnold. 2004. (Great Episodes Ser.). (ENG.). 384p. (YA). (gr. 7-8). pap. 17.95 *(978-0-15-205079-5(5),* 1195340, Clarion Bks.) HarperCollins Pubs.

—Or Give Me Death. 2004. (Great Episodes Ser.). 226p. (gr. 5-9). 17.00 *(978-0-7569-3462-0(1))* Perfection Learning Corp.

—A Ride into Morning: The Story of Tempe Wick. 2003. (Great Episodes Ser.). (ENG.). 368p. (YA). (gr. 5-7). pap. 21.95 *(978-0-15-204683-5(6),* Clarion Bks.) HarperCollins Pubs.

—The Secret of Sarah Revere. 2003. (Great Episodes Ser.). (ENG.). 336p. (J). (gr. 5-7). pap. 9.99 *(978-0-15-204684-2(4),* 1194115, Clarion Bks.) HarperCollins Pubs.

Roop, Connie & Roop, Peter. The Top-Secret Adventure of John Darragh, Revolutionary War Spy. Trover, Zachary, illus. 2010. (History's Kid Heroes Ser.). (ENG.). 32p. (J). (gr. 3-5). pap. 8.99 *(978-0-7613-6193-0(6),* 7fa9c0ff-4a83-43e8-9a63-91b40b6156a7, Graphic Universe™) Lerner Publishing Group.

Roop, Peter & Roop, Connie. An Eye for an Eye. 2004. 168p. (J). lib. bdg. 16.92 *(978-1-4242-0772-5(X))* Fitzgerald Bks.

—The Top-Secret Adventure of John Darragh, Revolutionary War Spy. 2010. pap. 51.02 *(978-0-7613-6923-3(6))* Lerner Publishing Group.

—The Top-Secret Adventure of John Darragh, Revolutionary War Spy. Trover, Zachary, illus. 2010. (History's Kid Heroes Ser.). (ENG.). 32p. (gr. 3-5). lib. bdg. 26.60 *(978-0-7613-6174-9(X))* Lerner Publishing Group.

Scieszka, Jon. Oh Say, I Can't See #15, No. 15. McCauley, Adam, illus. 2007. (Time Warp Trio Ser.: 15). 80p. (J). (gr. 2-4). 5.99 *(978-0-14-240808-7(5),* Puffin Books) Penguin Young Readers Group.

Singmaster, Elsie. Rifles for Washington. 2005. pap. 30.95 *(978-1-4191-0108-3(0))* Kessinger Publishing, LLC.

Skead, Robert A. Patriots Redcoats & Spies, 1 vol. 2015. (American Revolutionary War Adventures Ser.). (ENG.). 192p. (J). 14.99 *(978-0-310-74841-0(0))* Zonderkidz.

Skead, Robert A. & Skead, Robert J. Submarines, Secrets & a Daring Rescue, 1 vol. 2015. (American Revolutionary War Adventures Ser.). (ENG., Illus.). 208p. (J). 14.99 *(978-0-310-74747-5(3))* Zonderkidz.

Skinner, Constance Lindsay. Becky Landers: Frontier Warrior. 2006. (Living History Library). (ENG.). 198p. (J). (gr. 4-6). per. 12.95 *(978-1-932350-06-7(3))* Ignatius Pr.

Smith, Donna Campbell. An Independent Spirit: The Tale of Betsy Dowdy & Black Bess. 2006. (Illus.). 182p. (J). per. 11.95 *(978-0-9779889-0-7(2))* Faithful Publishing.

Smith, Lane. John, Paul, George & Ben. Smith, Lane, illus. 2006. (ENG., Illus.). 40p. (J). (gr. -1-3). 18.99 *(978-0-7868-4893-5(6))* Little, Brown Bks. for Young Readers.

—John, Paul, George & Ben. 2011. (J). (gr. 2-5). 29.95 *(978-0-439-02754-0(3),* WHCD807) Weston Woods Studios, Inc.

Stratemeyer, Edward. Marching on Niagara: The Soldier Boys of the Old Frontier. 2011. 191p. (YA). pap. *(978-0-9843717-2-3(9))* Gask Castle Pr.

—With Washington in the West: A Soldier Boy's Battles in the Wilderness. 2011. 198p. (J). pap. *(978-0-9843717-1-6(0))* Gask Castle Pr.

Tarshis, Lauren. I Survived the American Revolution, 1776 (I Survived #15), Vol. 15. 2017. (I Survived Ser.: 15). (ENG., Illus.). 144p. (J). (gr. 2-5). pap. 4.99 *(978-0-545-91973-9(8),* Scholastic Paperbacks) Scholastic, Inc.

Tripp, Valerie. Felicity Story Collection. Andreasen, Dan, illus. 2008. (ENG.). 404p. (J). 29.95 *(978-1-59369-452-4(0))* American Girl Publishing, Inc.

Turner, Ann Warren. When Mr. Jefferson Came to Philadelphia: What I Learned of Freedom 1776. Hess, Mark, illus. 2004. 32p. (J). (gr. -1-3). 15.99 *(978-0-06-027579-2(0))* HarperCollins Pubs.

VanRiper, Justin & VanRiper, Gary. The Fall of Fort Ticonderoga. 2011. (Adirondack Kids Ser.: Vol. 11). 96p. (J). (gr. 2-7). pap. 9.95 *(978-0-9826250-1-9(4))* Adirondack Kids Pr.

Washington, Ida H. Brave Enough: The Story of Rob Sanford, Vermont Pioneer Boy. Smoak, I. W. & Washington, C. E., illus. 2003. vii, 128p. (J). (gr. 4-6). pap. 12.95 *(978-0-9666832-7-1(7))* Cherry Tree Bks.

Weston Woods Staff, creator. Will You Sign Here, John Hancock? 2011. 38.75 *(978-0-439-76748-4(2));* 18.95 *(978-0-439-76741-5(5))* Weston Woods Studios, Inc.

Wibberley, Leonard. John Treegate's Musket. 2007. (Living History Library). (ENG.). 173p. (J). (gr. 10-12). pap. 12.95 *(978-1-932350-16-6(0))* Ignatius Pr.

—Peter Treegate's War. 2009. (ENG.). 134p. (J). (gr. 10-12). pap. 12.95 *(978-1-932350-21-0(7))* Ignatius Pr.

—Treegate's Raiders. 2011. (ENG.). 186p. (YA). pap. 12.95 *(978-1-932350-48-7(9))* Bethlehem Bks.

Winnick, Karen B. Sybil's Night Ride. 2009. (ENG., Illus.). 32p. (J). (gr. k-2). pap. 10.99 *(978-1-59078-771-7(4),* Astra Young Readers) Astra Publishing Hse.

UNITED STATES—HISTORY—REVOLUTION, 1775-1783—NAVAL OPERATIONS

Abbot, Willis J. Blue Jackets of 1876: A History of the Naval Battles of the American Revolution Together with a Narrative of the War with Tripoli. 2006. (Illus.). pap. 30.95 *(978-1-4286-1609-7(8))* Kessinger Publishing, LLC.

Alphin, Elaine Marie & Alphin, Arthur B. I Have Not Yet Begun to Fight: A Story about John Paul Jones. Casale, Paul, tr. Casale, Paul, illus. 2004. (Creative Minds Biography Ser.). 64p. (J). 22.60 *(978-1-57505-601-2(1),* Carolrhoda Bks.) Lerner Publishing Group.

Brager, Bruce L. John Paul Jones: America's Sailor. 2006. (Founders of the Republic Ser.). (Illus.). 160p. (J). (gr. 6-12). lib. bdg. 26.95 *(978-1-931798-84-6(2))* Reynolds, Morgan Inc.

Crickard, Sarah. John Paul Jones & the Birth of the American Navy, 1 vol. 2015. (Spotlight on American History Ser.). (ENG., Illus.). 24p. (J). (gr. 4-6). pap. 11.00 *(978-1-4994-1759-3(4),* 124776b9-9541-49f4-8833-1044127807af, PowerKids Pr.) Rosen Publishing Group, Inc., The.

Harkins, Susan Sales & Harkins, William H. The Life & Times of John Paul Jones. 2007. (Profiles in American History Ser.). (Illus.). 48p. (J). (gr. 4-8). lib. bdg. 29.95 *(978-1-58415-529-4(9))* Mitchell Lane Pubs.

Micklos, John & Micklos, John, Jr. Why We Won the American Revolution: Through Primary Sources, 1 vol. 2013. (American Revolution Through Primary Sources Ser.). (ENG.). 48p. (gr. 4-6). pap. 11.53 *(978-1-4644-0192-3(6),* 5895a7f8-08c5-4a37-9a5e-45c01416fbb5) Enslow Publishing, LLC.

Riley, John B. John Paul Jones: A Photo Biography. I.t. ed. 2004. (First Biographies Ser.). (Illus.). 24p. (YA). (gr. 5-18). 16.95 *(978-1-883846-63-3(3),* First Biographies) Reynolds, Morgan Inc.

Sperry, Armstrong. John Paul Jones: The Pirate Patriot. 2017. (Great Leaders & Events Ser.). (ENG.). (J). (gr. 4-8). lib. bdg. 35.99 *(978-1-942875-42-0(8))* Quarto Publishing Group USA.

UNITED STATES—HISTORY—1783-1815

see also Constitutional History—United States; Lewis and Clark Expedition (1804-1806); Louisiana Purchase

Beyer, Mark. The Election of 1800: Congress Helps Settle a Three-Way Vote, 1 vol. 2003. (Primary Sources of Life in the New American Nation Ser.). (ENG., Illus.). 32p. (gr. 4-5). pap. 10.00 *(978-0-8239-4255-8(4),* fe1b84cf-fcb7-471d-8dbe-062a4f707a3d) Rosen Publishing Group, Inc., The.

—The Election Of 1800: Congress Helps Settle a Three-Way Vote. 2009. (Life in the New American Nation Ser.). 32p. (gr. 4-4). 47.90 *(978-1-61514-282-8(7))* Rosen Publishing Group, Inc., The.

Brezina, Corona. America's Political Scandals in the Late 1800s: Boss Tweed & Tammany Hall, 1 vol. 2003. (America's Industrial Society in the 19th Century Ser.). (ENG., Illus.). 32p. (J). (gr. 4-5). lib. bdg. 29.13 *(978-0-8239-4021-9(7),* 72f2eb4b-3fa6-4f0f-981a-14c5238df7a8) Rosen Publishing Group, Inc., The.

Brown, Don. Aaron & Alexander: The Most Famous Duel in American History. 2015. (ENG., Illus.). 32p. (J). (gr. k-4). 19.99 *(978-1-59643-998-6(X),* 900129293) Roaring Brook Pr.

Clifton, Chuck & Clifton, Joyce. A Daily Walk with Lewis & Clark - 1805. 2003. 390p. (J). spiral bd. 14.95 *(978-0-9669760-4-5(5))* Maple Canyon Co.

—A Daily Walk with Lewis & Clark - 1806. 2003. 292p. (J). spiral bd. 14.95 *(978-0-9669760-5-2(3))* Maple Canyon Co.

Kalman, Maira. Thomas Jefferson: Life, Liberty & the Pursuit of Everything. Kalman, Maira, illus. 2014. (ENG., Illus.). 40p. (J). (gr. k-3). 17.99 *(978-0-399-24040-9(3),* Nancy Paulsen Books) Penguin Young Readers Group.

Konstam, Angus. America Speaks, 10 vols. 2005. (Illus.). (J). *(978-0-7172-6020-1(8)); (978-0-7172-6028-7(3)); (978-0-7172-6029-4(1)); (978-0-7172-6021-8(6)); (978-0-7172-6022-5(4)); (978-0-7172-6023-2(2)); (978-0-7172-6024-9(0)); (978-0-7172-6025-6(9)); (978-0-7172-6026-3(7)); (978-0-7172-6027-0(5))* Grolier, Ltd.

—America Speaks, 10 vols., Set. 2005. (Illus.). (J). (gr. 5-10). lib. bdg. 269.00 *(978-0-7172-6030-0(5),* Grolier) Scholastic Library Publishing.

Lynch, Seth. The Louisiana Purchase, 1 vol. 2018. (Look at U. S. History Ser.). (ENG.). 32p. (gr. 2-2). 28.27 *(978-1-5382-2131-0(4),* 6a875d97-be5b-480b-a71b-9c467ad9da6c) Stevens, Gareth Publishing LLLP.

Lynette, Rachel. The Louisiana Purchase, 1 vol. 2013. (Pioneer Spirit: the Westward Expansion Ser.). (Illus.). 24p. (J). (ENG.). (gr. 2-3). pap. 9.25 *(978-1-4777-0895-8(2),* a62ea59e-dc6c-4758-a467-b78fe89be66c); (ENG., (gr. 2-3). lib. bdg. 26.27 *(978-1-4777-0781-4(6),* acb9c5a6-da9b-41af-a96d-5cc2e728ce70); (gr. 3-6). pap. 49.50 *(978-1-4777-0896-5(0))* Rosen Publishing Group, Inc., The. (PowerKids Pr.).

Marsh, Carole. Louisiana Purchase. 2003. 12p. (gr. k-4). 2.95 *(978-0-635-02132-8(3))* Gallopade International.

Micklos, John & Micklos, John, Jr. The Making of the United States from Thirteen Colonies: Through Primary Sources, 1 vol. 2013. (American Revolution Through Primary Sources Ser.). (ENG., Illus.). 48p. (J). (gr. 4-6). 27.93 *(978-0-7660-4133-2(6),* 451c891d-fc74-4e1d-a855-d24b94dd42cd) Enslow Publishing, LLC.

Mooney, Carla. Perspectives on the Industrial Revolution. 2018. (Perspectives on US History Ser.). (ENG., Illus.). 32p. (J). (gr. 3-6). 32.80 *(978-1-63235-402-0(0),* 13724, 12-Story Library) Bookstaves, LLC.

National Geographic Learning. Reading Expeditions (Social Studies: Voices from America's Past): the Spirit of a New Nation. 2007. (Avenues Ser.). (ENG., Illus.). 40p. (J). pap. 21.95 *(978-0-7922-8684-4(7))* CENGAGE Learning.

Yasuda, Anita. 12 Incredible Facts about the Louisiana Purchase. 2016. (Turning Points in US History Ser.). (ENG., Illus.). 32p. (J). (gr. 3-6). 32.80 *(978-1-63235-131-9(5),* 12003, 12-Story Library) Bookstaves, LLC.

UNITED STATES—HISTORY—1783-1815—FICTION

de la Cruz, Melissa. All for One. 2019. (Alex & Eliza Trilogy Ser.: 3). 400p. (YA). (gr. 7). 17.99 *(978-0-525-51588-3(7),* G.P. Putnam's Sons Books for Young Readers) Penguin Young Readers Group.

Jensen, Dorothea. A Buss from Lafayette. 2016. (ENG.). 266p. (YA). (gr. 7-12). pap. 16.95 *(978-1-939371-90-4(2))* Boutique of Quality Books Publishing Co., Inc.

Limbaugh, Rush & Adams Limbaugh, Kathryn. Rush Revere & the Presidency. 2016. (Rush Revere Ser.: 5). (ENG., Illus.). 272p. (gr. 4-7). 21.00 *(978-1-5011-5689-2(6),* Threshold Editions) Threshold Editions.

UNITED STATES—HISTORY—1783-1865

Hakim, Joy. A History of US: the New Nation: 1789-1850 a History of US Book Four. (History of US Ser.: 4). (ENG., Illus.). 208p. (gr. 4-7). 3rd rev. ed. 2006. 24.95 *(978-0-19-518897-4(7))*Bk. 4. 2nd rev. ed. 2007. per. 15.95 *(978-0-19-532718-2(7))* Oxford Univ. Pr., Inc.

Hanes, Richard Clay, et al. Shaping of America, 1783-1815, Reference Library, 5 vols. 2005. (Illus.). (J). *(978-1-4144-0184-3(1)); (978-1-4144-0185-0(X))* Cengage Gale. (UXL).

Hollar, Sherman. Biographies of Colonial America: From Sir Walter Raleigh to Phillis Wheatley, 1 vol. 2012. (Impact on America: Collective Biographies Ser.). (ENG., Illus.). 168p. (J). (gr. 8-8). lib. bdg. 38.82 *(978-1-61530-683-1(8),* ccdf33a7-2d27-4565-92eb-8764fb430454) Rosen Publishing Group, Inc., The.

Lusted, Marcia Amidon. Revolution & the New Nation: 1750-Early 1800s. 2007. (Presidents of the United States Ser.). (Illus.). 48p. (J). (gr. 4-7). lib. bdg. 29.05 *(978-1-59036-739-1(1));* per. 10.95 *(978-1-59036-740-7(5))* Weigl Pubs., Inc.

Marsh, Carole. The U. S. Constitution. Beard, Chad, ed. 2004. (American Milestones Ser.). (Illus.). 28p. (J). (gr. 4-12). pap. 5.95 *(978-0-635-02696-5(1))* Gallopade International.

McNamara, Margaret. Eliza: the Story of Elizabeth Schuyler Hamilton: With an Afterword by Phillipa Soo, the Original Eliza from Hamilton: an American Musical. Shapiro, Esmé, illus. 2018. 48p. (J). (gr. -1-3). 17.99 *(978-1-5247-6588-0(0),* Schwartz & Wade Bks.) Random Hse. Children's Bks.

Morey, Allan. A Timeline History of the Early American Republic. 2014. (Timeline Trackers: America's Beginnings Ser.). (ENG., Illus.). 48p. (J). (gr. 5-8). lib. bdg. 30.65 *(978-1-4677-3641-1(4),* 8aa7f37e-56d7-4aa1-831a-a70e93c39c0b, Lerner Pubns.) Lerner Publishing Group.

Porterfield, Jason. The Lincoln-Douglas Senatorial Debates of 1858: A Primary Source Investigation, 1 vol. 2004. (Great Historic Debates & Speeches Ser.). (ENG., Illus.). 64p. (YA). (gr. 5-8). lib. bdg. 37.13 *(978-1-4042-0153-8(X),* 4e73e7f0-7984-4000-b09f-46efd13e52ab) Rosen Publishing Group, Inc., The.

Quinby, Michelle. How America Became America: Wars at Home (1812/1820) 2018. (J). *(978-1-5105-3596-1(9))* SmartBook Media, Inc.

Roberts, Cokie. Founding Mothers: Remembering the Ladies. Goode, Diane, illus. 2014. (ENG.). 40p. (J). (gr. 1-5). 17.99 *(978-0-06-078002-9(9),* HarperCollins) HarperCollins Pubs.

Sebree, Chet'la. Historical Sources on the New Republic, 1783-1830, 1 vol. 2019. (America's Story Ser.). (ENG.). 144p. (gr. 8-8). pap. 22.16 *(978-1-5026-5213-3(7),* e1037242-52c1-44dc-8792-246b6b652f81); lib. bdg. 47.36 *(978-1-5026-5214-0(5),* f0797024-dab0-4526-98df-8d0518481634) Cavendish Square Publishing LLC.

Stanley, George E. The New Republic (1763-1815), 1 vol. 2004. (Primary Source History of the United States Ser.). (ENG., Illus.). 48p. (gr. 5-8). lib. bdg. 33.67 *(978-0-8368-5825-9(5),* 89d397eb-c154-4e36-a7ed-ed2afca5dd56, Gareth Stevens Secondary Library) Stevens, Gareth Publishing LLLP.

Wolny, Philip, ed. The New Nation, 1 vol., 1. 2015. (Early American History Ser.). (ENG., Illus.). 80p. (J). (gr. 8-8). 35.47 *(978-1-68048-270-6(X),* 1cba0d5b-a94f-4605-a6d9-1780f7135aa8, Britannica Educational Publishing) Rosen Publishing Group, Inc., The.

UNITED STATES—HISTORY—1783-1865—BIOGRAPHY

Hollar, Sherman. Biographies of the New American Nation: From George Washington to Frederick Douglass, 1 vol. 2012. (Impact on America: Collective Biographies Ser.). (ENG., Illus.). 152p. (J). (gr. 8-8). lib. bdg. 38.82 *(978-1-61530-686-2(2),* 06a9b7e5-1f49-47d2-85be-bd8dcc7f2d86) Rosen Publishing Group, Inc., The.

—Biographies of the New American Nation: George Washington, Thomas Jefferson, Frederick Douglass, & More, 4 vols. 2012. (Impact on America: Collective Biographies Ser.). (ENG., Illus.). 152p. (YA). (gr. 8-8). 77.64 *(978-1-61530-802-6(4),* 4fe77bf0-d259-4223-9877-e0ef4b0e460a) Rosen Publishing Group, Inc., The.

Hollar, Sherman, ed. Biographies of Colonial America: Sir Walter Raleigh, Powhatan, Phillis Wheatley, & More, 4 vols. 2012. (Impact on America: Collective Biographies Ser.). (ENG., Illus.). 168p. (YA). (gr. 8-8). 77.64 *(978-1-61530-763-0(X),* fd7fc43d-01c1-4264-9923-817e353acbe0) Rosen Publishing Group, Inc., The.

Masters, Nancy Robinson. Extraordinary People: Extraordinary Patriots of the United States of America. 2005. (Extraordinary People Ser.). (ENG., Illus.). 288p. (J). (gr. 4-7). 40.00 *(978-0-516-24404-4(3),* Children's Pr.) Scholastic Library Publishing.

UNITED STATES—HISTORY—1783-1865—FICTION

Hopkinson, Deborah. Independence Cake: A Revolutionary Confection Inspired by Amelia Simmons, Whose True History Is Unfortunately Unknown. Potter, Giselle, illus. 2017.

44p. (J). (gr. -1-3). 17.99 *(978-0-385-39017-0(3)*, Schwartz & Wade Bks.) Random Hse. Children's Bks.
—Under the Quilt of Night. Ransome, James E., illus. 2005. (ENG.). 40p. (J). (gr. k-5). reprint ed. 7.99 *(978-0-689-87700-1(5)*, Aladdin) Simon & Schuster Children's Publishing.
Lyons, Mary E. The Poison Place. 2007. (ENG.). 160p. (YA). (gr. 7). pap. 9.99 *(978-1-4169-6842-9(3)*, Simon & Schuster/Paula Wiseman Bks.) Simon & Schuster/Paula Wiseman Bks.
Mosley, Walter. 47. 2006. (ENG., Illus.). 272p. (J). (gr. 7-17). reprint ed. per. 11.99 *(978-0-316-01635-3(7))* Little, Brown Bks. for Young Readers.
Turner, Diane D. My Name Is Oney Judge. Massey, Cal, illus. 2010. (J). pap. *(978-0-88378-321-4(5))* Third World Press.

UNITED STATES—HISTORY—19TH CENTURY

Alarcon, Roben. American Indians in the 1800s, 1 vol. rev. ed. 2005. (Social Studies: Informational Text Ser.). (ENG., Illus.). 24p. (J). (gr. 4-8). pap. 10.99 *(978-0-7439-8913-8(9))* Teacher Created Materials, Inc.
Anderson, Dale. A Soldier's Life in the Civil War, 1 vol. 2004. (World Almanac(r) Library of the Civil War Ser.). (ENG., Illus.). 48p. (gr. 5-8). pap. 15.05 *(978-0-8368-5595-1(7)*, 644f6601-6cb3-4513-a5bb-f0753119da8b, Gareth Stevens Secondary Library) Stevens, Gareth Publishing LLLP.
Brannon, Cecelia H. Zoom in on the National Anthem, 1 vol. 2016. (Zoom in on American Symbols Ser.). (ENG., Illus.). 24p. (gr. 2-2). pap. 10.95 *(978-0-7660-8446-9(9)*, 70dcf44c-43c7-46a5-872f-c8dd7f1a1c43) Enslow Publishing, LLC.
Bussey, Jennifer. 1820-1840 (Events That Changed the World) 2004. (gr. 10-12). 22.45 *(978-0-7377-2032-7(8)*, Greenhaven Pr., Inc.) Cengage Gale.
Carosella, Melissa. Frederick Douglass: Líder Del Movimiento Abolicionista. rev. ed. 2019. (Social Studies: Informational Text Ser.). (SPA., Illus.). 32p. (J). (gr. 4-8). pap. 11.99 *(978-1-64290-120-7(2))* Teacher Created Materials, Inc.
Carson, Mary Kay. The Underground Railroad for Kids: From Slavery to Freedom with 21 Activities. 2005. (For Kids Ser.: 3). (ENG., Illus.). 176p. (J). (gr. 4). pap. 19.99 *(978-1-55652-554-4(0))* Chicago Review Pr., Inc.
Chastain, Zachary. Scandals & Glory: Politics in the 1800s. 2009. (Daily Life in America in the 1800s Ser.). 64p. (YA). (gr. 7-18). lib. bdg. 22.95 *(978-1-4222-1787-0(6))* Mason Crest.
—Scandals & Glory: Politics in The 1800s. 2009. (Daily Life in America in the 1800s Ser.). 64p. (YA). (gr. 7-18). pap. 9.95 *(978-1-4222-1860-0(0))* Mason Crest.
Connell, Kate. Servant to Abigail Adams: The Early Colonial Adventures of Hannah Cooper. 2003. (I Am American Ser.). (ENG., Illus.). 40p. (J). (gr. 3-7). pap. 6.99 *(978-0-7922-5828-5(2)*, National Geographic Children's Bks.) National Geographic Society.
Depew, Lanette. A Bridge Spanning Time. 2003. (ENG.). 128p. (J). pap. 9.95 *(978-1-57072-236-3(6))* Overmountain Pr.
Down, Susan. Theodore Weld: Architect of Abolitionism. 2013. (ENG., Illus.). 64p. (J). *(978-0-7787-1062-2(9))*; pap. *(978-0-7787-1065-3(3))* Crabtree Publishing Co.
Doyle, Kelly. 1880-1900 (Events That Changed the World) 2004. (Illus.). (gr. 10-12). 22.45 *(978-0-7377-2036-5(0)*, Greenhaven Pr., Inc.) Cengage Gale.
Fisanick, Christina. 1800-1820 (Events That Changed the World) 2004. (gr. 10-12). 22.45 *(978-0-7377-2030-3(1)*, Greenhaven Pr., Inc.) Cengage Gale.
Howell, Brian. U.S. Growth & Change in the 19th Century. 2011. (Explorer Library: Language Arts Explorer Ser.). (ENG.). 32p. (gr. 4-8). pap. 14.21 *(978-1-61080-290-1(X)*, 201213) Cherry Lake Publishing.
Kawa, Katie. Recipes of the Westward Expansion. (Cooking Your Way Through American History Ser.). (J). (gr. 3-3). 2017. pap. 63.60 *(978-1-5345-2101-8(1))* 2016. (ENG.). 24p. pap. 11.60 *(978-1-5345-2100-1(3)*, dfd4e24d-8bbd-4cfd-8531-ab751f9c1ad3) 2016. (ENG.). 24p. lib. bdg. 28.88 *(978-1-5345-2102-5(X)*, 6fac664a-f60a-4f4d-a6c1-76e3f53c023d) Greenhaven Publishing LLC. (KidHaven Publishing).
Krull, Kathleen & Brewer, Paul. Lincoln Tells a Joke: How Laughter Saved the President (and the Country) Innerst, Stacy, illus. 2010. (ENG.). 40p. (J). (gr. 1-4). 17.99 *(978-0-15-206639-0(X)*, 1199695, Clarion Bks.) HarperCollins Pubs.
Malaspina, Ann. Heart on Fire: Susan B. Anthony Votes for President. James, Steve, illus. 2012. (ENG.). 32p. (J). (gr. 1-3). 17.99 *(978-0-8075-3188-4(X)*, 080753188X) Whitman, Albert & Co.
Mckissack, Patricia & Mckissack, Fredrick. Frederick Douglass: Fighter Against Slavery, 1 vol. 2013. (Famous African Americans Ser.). (ENG., Illus.). 24p. (gr. k-2). 25.27 *(978-0-7660-4098-4(4)*, 119432c1-b3c2-4bd9-a960-5bce9bdb12f1, Enslow Elementary) Enslow Publishing, LLC.
Miller, Reagan & Claus, J. Matteson. Life on a Civil War Battlefield. 2011. (ENG.). 48p. (J). pap. *(978-0-7787-5357-5(3))*; lib. bdg. *(978-0-7787-5340-7(9))* Crabtree Publishing Co.
Ochiltree, Dianne. Molly, by Golly! The Legend of Molly Williams, America's First Female Firefighter. Kemly, Kathleen, illus. 2012. (ENG.). 32p. (J). (gr. 2-5). 17.99 *(978-1-59078-721-2(8)*, Calkins Creek) Highlights Pr., c/o Highlights for Children, Inc.
Primary Sources of America's Industrial Society in the 19th Century. 2004. (Primary Source Big Bookstm Ser.). (ENG.). 24p. (gr. 4-8). 43.95 *(978-0-8239-4598-6(7))* Rosen Publishing Group, Inc., The.
Raum, Elizabeth. Expanding a Nation: Causes & Effects of the Louisiana Purchase, 1 vol. 2013. (Cause & Effect Ser.). (ENG.). 32p. (J). (gr. 3-6). 27.99 *(978-1-4765-0236-6(6)*, 122290); pap. 8.95 *(978-1-4765-3402-2(0)*, 123533) Capstone.
Seguin, Marilyn. Young & Courageous: American Girls Who Made History. 2012. (J). pap. *(978-0-8283-2463-2(8))* Branden Bks.
Sharp, Constance. Thomas Jefferson & the Growing United States (1800-1811) Rakove, Jack N., ed. 2012. (How America Became America Ser.). 48p. (J). (gr. 3-4). 19.95 *(978-1-4222-2400-7(7))* Mason Crest.
Zdrok, Jodie L. 1840-1860 (Events That Changed the World) 2004. (Events That Changed the World Ser.). (Illus.). 175p. (gr. 10-12). 22.45 *(978-0-7377-2034-1(4)*, Greenhaven Pr., Inc.) Cengage Gale.

UNITED STATES—HISTORY—19TH CENTURY—FICTION

Alexander, Kwame. The Door of No Return. I.t. ed. 2023. (ENG.). (J). lib. bdg. 22.99 Cengage Gale.
—The Door of No Return. 2022. (ENG., Illus.). 432p. (J). (gr. 5-17). 17.99 *(978-0-316-44186-5(4))* Little, Brown Bks. for Young Readers.
Alger, Horatio. The Young Musician. reprint ed. pap. 79.00 *(978-1-4047-3629-0(8))* Classic Textbooks.
—The Young Musician. 2006. pap. *(978-1-4068-0673-1(0))* Echo Library.
Edinger, Monica. Africa Is My Home: A Child of the Amistad. Byrd, Robert, illus. 2015. (ENG.). 64p. (J). (gr. 5). pap. 9.99 *(978-0-7636-7647-6(0))* Candlewick Pr.
Fletcher, Susan. Walk Across the Sea. 2003. (ENG., Illus.). 224p. (J). (gr. 4-8). pap. 11.95 *(978-0-689-85707-2(1)*, Atheneum Bks. for Young Readers) Simon & Schuster Children's Publishing.
Hart, Alison. Fires of Jubilee. 2003. (ENG., Illus.). 192p. (J). (gr. 3-7). pap. 9.99 *(978-0-689-85528-3(1)*, Simon & Schuster/Paula Wiseman Bks.) Simon & Schuster/Paula Wiseman Bks.
Hedstrom-Page, Deborah. From Log Cabin to White House with Abraham Lincoln. Martinez, Sergio, illus. 2007. (My American Journey Ser.). 82p. (J). (gr. 3-9). 9.99 *(978-0-8054-3269-5(8))* B&H Publishing Group.
Howard, Elizabeth Fitzgerald. Virgie Goes to School with Us Boys. Lewis, E. B., illus. 2005. (gr. k-3). 18.00 *(978-0-7569-5088-0(0))* Perfection Learning Corp.
Hughes, Lynn Gordon. To Live a Truer Life: A Story of the Hopedale Community. Lindro, illus. 2003. 32p. (J). 10.00 *(978-0-9725017-2-9(X))* Blackstone Editions.
Kirkle, Diane Luise. Rachel Serves a Stew. Batson, Susann, illus. 2009. 28p. pap. 10.95 *(978-1-935137-59-7(X))* Guardian Angel Publishing, Inc.
Lee, Stacey. The Downstairs Girl. 2019. (ENG.). 384p. (YA). (gr. 7). 18.99 *(978-1-5247-4095-5(0)*, G.P. Putnam's Sons Books for Young Readers) Penguin Young Readers Group.
LeZotte, Ann Clare. Show Me a Sign (Show Me a Sign, Book 1), 1 vol., Vol. 1. (Show Me a Sign Ser.). (ENG.). (J). (gr. 3-7). 2021. 304p. pap. 8.99 *(978-1-338-25582-9(7))* 2020. 288p. 18.99 *(978-1-338-25581-2(9)*, Scholastic Pr.) Scholastic, Inc.
Morpurgo, Michael. Twist of Gold. 2nd ed. 2007. (ENG.). 304p. (J). (gr. 4-7). pap. 7.99 *(978-1-4052-2928-9(4))* Farshore GBR. Dist: HarperCollins Pubs.
Reed, Wilfred. Andy & Mark & the Time Machine: Custer's Last Stand. 2003. 240p. (YA). pap. 15.95 *(978-0-595-26496-4(4)*, Writers Club Pr.) iUniverse, Inc.
Rinaldi, Ann. An Unlikely Friendship: A Novel of Mary Todd Lincoln & Elizabeth Keckley. 2008. (Great Episodes Ser.). (ENG., Illus.). 256p. (J). (gr. 5-7). pap. 7.99 *(978-0-15-206398-6(6)*, 1199153, Clarion Bks.) HarperCollins Pubs.
Stratemeyer, Edward. The Rover Boys at College: The Right Road & the Wrong. I.t. ed. 2007. (ENG.). 180p. pap. 19.99 *(978-1-4264-4042-7(1))* Creative Media Partners, LLC.
Sutherland, Robert. The Schooner's Revenge. 2008. (ENG.). 176p. (J). pap. 11.99 *(978-0-00-200853-2(X)*, Harper Trophy) HarperCollins Pubs.
Winfield, Arthur M. Rover Boys at College or the Right Road. 2006. pap. 30.95 *(978-1-4286-4106-8(8))* Kessinger Publishing, LLC.
Wright, Barbara. Crow. 2013. (ENG.). 320p. (J). (gr. 6-8). lib. bdg. 22.44 *(978-0-375-96928-7(4))* Random Hse. Bks. for Young Readers.

UNITED STATES—HISTORY—TRIPOLITAN WAR, 1801-1805

Abbot, Willis J. Blue Jackets of 1876: A History of the Naval Battles of the American Revolution Together with a Narrative of the War with Tripoli. 2006. (Illus.). pap. 30.95 *(978-1-4286-1609-7(8))* Kessinger Publishing, LLC.
January, Brendan. The Aftermath of the Wars Against the Barbary Pirates. 2009. (Aftermath of History Ser.). (ENG.). 160p. (gr. 9-12). 38.60 *(978-0-8225-9094-1(8))* Lerner Publishing Group.

UNITED STATES—HISTORY—WAR OF 1812

Adams, Simon. The War of 1812. 2018. (Uncovering the Past: Analyzing Primary Sources Ser.). (Illus.). 48p. (J). (gr. 5-6). *(978-0-7787-4800-7(6))* Crabtree Publishing Co.
Alvarez, Pilar F. The War of 1812: New Challenges for a New Nation, 1 vol. 2016. (Spotlight on American History Ser.). (ENG., Illus.). 24p. (J). (gr. 4-6). 27.93 *(978-1-5081-4947-7(X)*, 8f199c8b-8103-4efe-9d50-6d4584bca238, PowerKids Pr.) Rosen Publishing Group, Inc., The.
Barile, Mary. Alphonso Wetmore: Soldier, Adventurer, & Writer. 2015. (ENG., Illus.). 48p. (J). 24.00 *(978-1-61248-147-0(7))* Truman State Univ. Pr.
Benn, Carl & O'Neill, Robert. The War of 1812: The Fight for American Trade Rights, 1 vol. 2011. (Early American Wars Ser.). (ENG., Illus.). 96p. (YA). (gr. 10-10). lib. bdg. 38.47 *(978-1-4488-1333-9(6)*, d72506c9-ca2b-4440-b2de-85ad9710d12d) Rosen Publishing Group, Inc., The.
Beyer, Mark. The War of 1812: The New American Nation Goes to War with England. (Life in the New American Nation Ser.). 32p. (gr. 4-4). 2009. 47.90 *(978-1-61514-288-0(6))* 2003. (ENG., Illus.). pap. 10.00 *(978-0-8239-4261-9(9))*, c76f1b45-09ec-413c-9b2d-eb626b723280) 2003. (ENG., Illus.). lib. bdg. 29.13 *(978-0-8239-4043-1(8)*, 8ab33f82-a5ca-4457-8eb3-b2558e7887bc, Rosen Reference) Rosen Publishing Group, Inc., The.
Chang, Kirsten. The Star-Spangled Banner. 2018. (Symbols of American Freedom Ser.). (ENG., Illus.). 24p. (J). (gr. k-3). lib. bdg. 26.95 *(978-1-62617-886-1(0)*, Blastoff! Readers) Bellwether Media.
Childress, Diana. The War of 1812. 2004. (Chronicle of America's Wars Ser.). (ENG., Illus.). 96p. (gr. 5-12). 27.93 *(978-0-8225-0800-7(1))* Lerner Publishing Group.
Clemens Warrick, Karen. The War Of 1812, 1 vol. 2016. (United States at War Ser.). (ENG., Illus.). 128p. (gr. 6-6). 38.93 *(978-0-7660-7671-6(7)*, 10508926-bd4b-4c37-81e2-5a13986a45ed) Enslow Publishing, LLC.
Crewe, Sabrina & Ingram, Scott. The Writing of the Star-Spangled Banner, 1 vol. 2004. (Events That Shaped America Ser.). (ENG., Illus.). 32p. (J). (gr. 3-5). lib. bdg. 28.67 *(978-0-8368-3409-3(7)*, a54f622d-575c-4918-8132-a69cb08e8a37, Gareth Stevens Learning Library) Stevens, Gareth Publishing LLLP.
Crump, Jennifer. Canada on Fire: The War Of 1812. 2011. (Canadians at War Ser.: 4). (ENG., Illus.). 208p. (YA). (gr. 6). pap. 19.99 *(978-1-55488-753-8(4))* Dundurn Pr. CAN. Dist: Publishers Group West (PGW).
Cunningham, Alvin Robert. Washington Is Burning! The War of 1812. 2003. (Reading Essentials in Social Studies). (Illus.). 48p. (J). 9.00 *(978-0-7891-5896-3(5))* Perfection Learning Corp.
Cunningham, Kevin. The War Of 1812. 2018. (Expansion of Our Nation Ser.). (ENG., Illus.). 32p. (J). (gr. 3-5). pap. 9.95 *(978-1-63517-989-7(0)*, 1635179890); lib. bdg. 31.35 *(978-1-63517-888-3(6)*, 1635178886) North Star Editions. (Focus Readers).
—The War of 1812. 2018. (Illus.). 32p. (J). pap. *(978-1-4896-9895-7(7)*, AV2 by Weigl) Weigl Pubs., Inc.
Figley, Marty Rhodes. Washington Is Burning. Orback, Craig, illus. (On My Own History Ser.). 48p. (J). (gr. 2-4). 2007. (ENG.). per. 8.99 *(978-0-8225-6050-0(X)*, 220511bf-9018-498f-8ff3-a73d591dfbeb, First Avenue Editions) 2006. lib. bdg. 25.26 *(978-1-57505-875-7(8))* Lerner Publishing Group.
Flatt, Lizann. The Legacy of the War of 1812. 2011. (ENG.). 48p. (J). pap. *(978-0-7787-7966-7(1))*; (gr. 5-9). lib. bdg. *(978-0-7787-7961-2(0))* Crabtree Publishing Co.
Fulton, Kristen. Long May She Wave: The True Story of Caroline Pickersgill & Her Star-Spangled Creation. Berry, Holly, illus. 2017. (ENG.). 40p. (J). (gr. -1-3). 17.99 *(978-1-4814-6096-5(X)*, McElderry, Margaret K. Bks.) McElderry, Margaret K. Bks.
Gaspar, Joe. The National Anthem, 1 vol. 2013. (PowerKids Readers: American Symbols Ser.). (ENG.). 24p. (J). (gr. k-k). 26.27 *(978-1-4777-0740-1(9)*, ff65aee1-5513-4b6a-9de3-34effc7028c1); (Illus.). pap. 9.25 *(978-1-4777-0821-7(9)*, 57794ebc-a538-4a97-b2ed-62d887a777bf) Rosen Publishing Group, Inc., The. (PowerKids Pr.).
—The National Anthem / el Himno Nacional, 1 vol. Alamn, Eduardo, ed. 2013. (PowerKids Readers: Símbolos de América / American Symbols Ser.). (ENG & SPA.). 24p. (J). (gr. k-k). 26.27 *(978-1-4777-1208-5(9)*, e37a3c7f-a2f3-44a0-86e6-47c33e70d673, PowerKids Pr.) Rosen Publishing Group, Inc., The.
Giddens, Sandra. A Timeline of the War of 1812. 2009. (Timelines of American History Ser.). 32p. (gr. 4-4). 47.90 *(978-1-60854-392-2(7)*, Rosen Reference) Rosen Publishing Group, Inc., The.
Giddens, Sandra & Giddens, Owen. A Timeline of the War of 1812, 1 vol. 2004. (Timelines of American History Ser.). (ENG., Illus.). 32p. (gr. 4-4). lib. bdg. 29.13 *(978-0-8239-4542-9(1)*, 5278eaa4-1049-48df-98af-6a00dc4ab77b, Rosen Reference) Rosen Publishing Group, Inc., The.
Grove, Tim. Star-Spangled: The Story of a Flag, a Battle, & the American Anthem. 2020. (ENG., Illus.). 176p. (J). (gr. 5-9). 19.99 *(978-1-4197-4102-9(0)*, 1211801, Abrams Bks. for Young Readers) Abrams, Inc.
Hess, Debra. The Star Spangled Banner, 1 vol. 2005. (Symbols of America Ser.). (ENG., Illus.). 40p. (gr. 3-3). lib. bdg. 32.64 *(978-0-7614-1710-1(9)*, 78ac45ea-2a1f-4af8-a561-fdddb72608b4) Cavendish Square Publishing LLC.
—The Star-Spangled Banner, 1 vol. 2008. (Symbols of America Ser.). (ENG.). 40p. (gr. 3-3). pap. 9.23 *(978-0-7614-3392-7(9)*, 80f9c4eb-419a-487b-9908-119fa761e234) Cavendish Square Publishing LLC.
Hinman, Bonnie. The War of 1812: 12 Things to Know. 2017. (America at War Ser.). (ENG., Illus.). 32p. (J). (gr. 3-6). 32.80 *(978-1-63235-269-9(9)*, 11708, 12-Story Library) Bookstaves, LLC.
Ingram, Scott. The Writing of the Star-Spangled Banner, 1 vol. 2004. (Landmark Events in American History Ser.). (ENG., Illus.). 48p. (gr. 5-8). pap. 15.05 *(978-0-8368-5418-3(7)*, e93295b0-1af5-42c3-842e-4db0ec8fced3); lib. bdg. 33.67 *(978-0-8368-5390-2(3)*, 5058ce85-66a6-4f57-9bab-0adc8a80c538) Stevens, Gareth Publishing LLLP. (Gareth Stevens Secondary Library).
Isaacs, Sally Senzell. What Caused the War of 1812? 2011. (ENG.). 48p. (J). pap. *(978-0-7787-7967-4(X))* Crabtree Publishing Co.
Jacobson, Ryan. The Story of the Star-Spangled Banner, 1 vol. Martin, Cynthia & Beatty, Terry, illus. 2006. (Graphic History Ser.). (ENG.). 32p. (J). (gr. 3-9). 31.32 *(978-0-7368-5493-1(2)*, 90154) Capstone.
Johnson, Robin. Famous People of the War of 1812. 2011. (ENG.). 48p. (J). pap. *(978-0-7787-7964-3(5))*; (gr. 5-9). lib. bdg. *(978-0-7787-7959-9(9))* Crabtree Publishing Co.
Kissock, Heather. The Star-Spangled Banner. 2017. (Illus.). 24p. (J). *(978-1-5105-0605-3(5))* SmartBook Media, Inc.
Kjelle, Marylou Morano. Francis Scott Key. 2006. (What's So Great About...? Ser.). (Illus.). 32p. (YA). (gr. 2-4). lib. bdg. 25.70 *(978-1-58415-474-7(8))* Mitchell Lane Pubs.
Kulling, Monica. Francis Scott Key's Star-Spangled Banner. Walz, Richard, illus. 2012. (Step into Reading Ser.). (ENG.). 48p. (J). (gr. k-3). pap. 3.99 *(978-0-375-86725-5(2)*, Random Hse. Bks. for Young Readers) Random Hse. Children's Bks.
—Francis Scott Key's Star-Spangled Banner. 2012. (Step into Reading Level 3 Ser.). lib. bdg. 13.55 *(978-0-606-23857-1(3))* Turtleback.
Lowitz, Sadyebeth & Lowitz, Anson. Mr Key's Song: The Star Spangled Banner. 2011. 58p. 36.95 *(978-1-258-10511-2(X))* Literary Licensing, LLC.
Lusted, Marcia Amidon. The Star-Spangled Banner. 2019. (Shaping the United States of America Ser.). (ENG., Illus.). 24p. (J). (gr. 1-3). pap. 7.95 *(978-1-9771-1013-8(4)*, 140956); lib. bdg. 25.99 *(978-1-9771-0844-9(X)*, 140463) Capstone. (Pebble).
Mattern, Joanne. Fort McHenry: Our Flag Was Still There. 2017. (Core Content Social Studies — Let's Celebrate America Ser.). (ENG., Illus.). 32p. (J). (gr. 2-5). pap. 8.99 *(978-1-63440-233-0(2)*, efcfd31a-c91d-4ec1-a1c8-d49346369427); lib. bdg. 26.65 *(978-1-63440-223-1(5)*, 825f81e0-0df1-4472-8ea2-2e72a1d80fc7) Red Chair Pr.
Maynard, Charles W. Fort McHenry. 2009. (Famous Forts Throughout American History Ser.). 24p. (gr. 3-4). 42.50 *(978-1-61512-519-7(1)*, PowerKids Pr.) Rosen Publishing Group, Inc., The.
Micklos, John, Jr. Primary Source History of the War of 1812. 2016. (Primary Source History Ser.). (ENG., Illus.). 32p. (J). (gr. 3-6). lib. bdg. 27.99 *(978-1-4914-8488-3(8)*, 130946, Capstone Pr.) Capstone.
Mulhall, Jill K. The War of 1812, 1 vol. rev. ed. 2005. (Social Studies: Informational Text Ser.). (ENG.). 24p. (J). (gr. 4-8). pap. 10.99 *(978-0-7439-8907-7(4))* Teacher Created Materials, Inc.
The National Anthem. 2013. (PowerKids Readers: American Symbols Ser.). 24p. (J). (gr. k-2). pap. 49.50 *(978-1-4777-0822-4(7)*, PowerKids Pr.) Rosen Publishing Group, Inc., The.
Nelson, Maria. The National Anthem, 1 vol. 2014. (Symbols of America Ser.). (ENG.). 24p. (J). (gr. 1-2). 24.27 *(978-1-4824-1874-3(6)*, a7320d58-b460-4703-b4bc-1febd8bd6cf2) Stevens, Gareth Publishing LLLP.
Orr, Tamra B. The Star-Spangled Banner: Introducing Primary Sources. 2016. (Introducing Primary Sources Ser.). (ENG., Illus.). 32p. (J). (gr. -1-2). lib. bdg. 28.65 *(978-1-4914-8226-1(5)*, 130688, Capstone Pr.) Capstone.
Owens, Tom. The Star-Spangled Banner: The Flag & Its Anthem. 2003. (Illus.). 48p. (J). pap. *(978-0-7891-5890-1(6))* Perfection Learning Corp.
Poulakidas, Georgene. The War of 1812. (Primary Sources of American Wars Ser.). 24p. (gr. 3-4). 2009. 42.50 *(978-1-60851-529-5(X)*, PowerKids Pr.) 2005. (ENG., Illus.). (YA). lib. bdg. 26.27 *(978-1-4042-2681-4(8)*, c2fbdb6a-f271-4ebf-a699-760ba2c3be98) Rosen Publishing Group, Inc., The.
Quinby, Michelle. How America Became America: Wars at Home (1812/1820) 2018. (J). *(978-1-5105-3596-1(9))* SmartBook Media, Inc.
—Wars at Home: America Forms an Identity (1812-1820) 2012. (J). pap. *(978-1-4222-2415-1(5))* Mason Crest.
—Wars at Home: America Forms an Identity (1812-1820) Rakove, Jack N., ed. 2012. (How America Became America Ser.). 48p. (J). (gr. 3-4). 19.95 *(978-1-4222-2401-4(5))* Mason Crest.
Radomski, Kassandra. Mr. Madison's War: Causes & Effects of the War Of 1812. 2013. (Cause & Effect Ser.). (ENG.). 32p. (J). (gr. 3-6). pap. 8.95 *(978-1-4765-3405-3(5)*, 123536) Capstone.
RJF Publishing Staff & Burgan, Michael. Fort McHenry. 2009. (Symbols of American Freedom Ser.). 48p. (gr. 4-6). 30.00 *(978-1-60413-520-6(4)*, Chelsea Clubhse.) Infobase Holdings, Inc.
Schwaeber, Barbie. The Star-Spangled Banner. 2006. (American Favorites Ser.). (ENG., Illus.). 32p. (J). (gr. 3-7). 9.85 *(978-1-59249-652-5(0))* Soundprints.
Schwartz, Heather E. The War of 1812: By the Dawn's Early Light. rev. ed. 2017. (Social Studies: Informational Text Ser.). (ENG., Illus.). 32p. (gr. 4-8). pap. 11.99 *(978-1-4938-3794-6(X))* Teacher Created Materials, Inc.
Silate, Jennifer. The Calhoun-Randolph Debate on the Eve of the War of 1812: A Primary Source Investigation, 1 vol. 2004. (Great Historic Debates & Speeches Ser.). (ENG., Illus.). 64p. (YA). (gr. 5-8). lib. bdg. 37.13 *(978-1-4042-0150-7(5)*, b416568f-5db1-4b00-bf4b-5f8362e684ce) Rosen Publishing Group, Inc., The.
—The Calhoun-Randolph Debate on the Eve of the War Of 1812: A Primary Source Investigation. 2009. (Great Historic Debates & Speeches Ser.). 64p. (gr. 5-8). 58.50 *(978-1-61513-124-2(8))* Rosen Publishing Group, Inc., The.
Sonneborn, Liz. The War of 1812, 1 vol. 2004. (Primary Sources in American History Ser.). (ENG., Illus.). 64p. (gr. 5-8). lib. bdg. 37.13 *(978-0-8239-4515-3(4)*, d236dbfc-8edc-4c9f-a6b1-b6baead13fc4, Rosen Reference) Rosen Publishing Group, Inc., The.
—The War of 1812: A Primary Source History of America's Second War with Britain. 2009. (Primary Sources in American History Ser.). 64p. (gr. 5-8). 58.50 *(978-1-60851-506-6(0))* Rosen Publishing Group, Inc., The.
Toler, Pamela. The War Of 1812, Vol. 11. Musteen, Jason R., ed. 2015. (Major U. S. Historical Wars Ser.). (Illus.). 64p. (J). (gr. 7). lib. bdg. 23.95 *(978-1-4222-3361-0(8))* Mason Crest.
Toler, Pamela D. Causes of the War of 1812. 2009. (J). lib. bdg. *(978-1-59556-036-0(X))* OTTN Publishing.
Troupe, Thomas Kingsley. Birth of the Star-Spangled Banner: A Fly on the Wall History. Tejido, Jomike, illus. 2018. (Fly on the Wall History Ser.). (ENG.). 32p. (J). (gr. 1-3). lib. bdg. 27.99 *(978-1-5158-1601-0(X)*, 136254, Picture Window Bks.) Capstone.
Welch, Catherine A. La Bandera de Estrellas Centelleantes; the Star-Spangled Banner. 2008. pap. 40.95 *(978-0-7613-3867-3(5))* Lerner Publishing Group.
—The Star-Spangled Banner. Warwick, Carrie, illus. 2004. (On My Own History Ser.). 48p. (J). (gr. 1-3). pap. 6.95 *(978-1-57505-697-5(6))*; (ENG.). (gr. 2-4). 25.26 *(978-1-57505-590-9(2))* Lerner Publishing Group.
Zee, Amy Van. The War Of 1812: A History Perspectives Book. 2013. (Perspectives Library). (ENG., Illus.). 32p. (J). (gr. 4-8). 32.07 *(978-1-62431-424-7(4)*, 202816); pap. 14.21 *(978-1-62431-500-8(3)*, 202818) Cherry Lake Publishing.

UNITED STATES—HISTORY—WAR OF 1812—CAMPAIGNS

see also New Orleans, Battle of, New Orleans, La., 1815
Clarke, Gordon. Major Battles of the War of 1812. 2011. (ENG.). 48p. (J). pap. *(978-0-7787-7965-0(3))*; (gr. 5-9). lib. bdg. *(978-0-7787-7960-5(2))* Crabtree Publishing Co.
Crump, Jennifer. The War of 1812 Against the States (JR) Heroes of a Great Canadian Victory. 2007. (Amazing Stories Ser.). (ENG.). 96p. (J). pap. 9.95 *(978-1-55439-711-2(1)*, 711) James Lorimer & Co. Ltd., Pubs. CAN. Dist: Formac Lorimer Bks. Ltd.
Gordon, Irene. Tecumseh: Diplomat & Warrior in the War Of 1812. 2009. (Amazing Stories Ser.). (ENG., Illus.). 128p. (J). (gr. 6-12). pap. 9.95 *(978-1-55277-430-4(9)*, 430) James

TUV

Lorimer & Co. Ltd., Pubs. CAN. Dist: Formac Lorimer Bks. Ltd.
Monroe, Tyler. The Star-Spangled Banner. 2013. (U. S. Symbols Ser.). (ENG.). 24p. (J). (gr. -1-2). 27.32 *(978-1-4765-3087-1(4),* 123064); pap. 7.95 *(978-1-4765-3536-4(1),* 123582) Capstone. (Capstone Pr.).

UNITED STATES—HISTORY—WAR OF 1812—FICTION

Ades, Audrey. Judah Touro Didn't Want to Be Famous. Mildenberger, Vivien, illus. 2020. (ENG.). 32p. (J). (gr. k-3). 17.99 *(978-1-5415-4561-8(3),* 35256b85-1e87-4c96-b654-f9cca58b6dcc, Kar-Ben Publishing) Lerner Publishing Group.
Cook, Kajsa C. The Untold Story: About the War of 1812. 2011. 84p. pap. 12.99 *(978-1-4520-6557-1(8))* AuthorHouse.
Ernst, Kathleen. Meet Caroline, 1. 2012. (American Girls Collection: Caroline Stories Ser.). (ENG., Illus.). 104p. (J). (gr. 2-4). pap. 18.69 *(978-1-59369-882-9(8))* American Girl Publishing, Inc.
Guyatt, Ben. Billy Green Saves the Day. 2009. (ENG.). 160p. (J). (gr. 7-18). pap. 10.99 *(978-1-55488-041-6(6))* Dundurn Pr. CAN. Dist: Publishers Group West (PGW).
Hall, Marjory. The Gold-Lined Box. 2003. 224p. 11.95 *(978-0-9714612-6-0(0))* Green Mansion Pr. LLC.
Kramer, Alan & Kramer, Candice. The Star-Spangled Banner Story. 2005. (J). pap. *(978-1-4108-4203-9(7))* Benchmark Education Co.
Milford, Kate. The Left-Handed Fate. Wheeler, Eliza, illus. 2017. (ENG.). 384p. (J). pap. 13.99 *(978-1-250-12183-7(3),* 900157594) Square Fish.
Noble, Trinka Hakes & Papp, Lisa. The Battles. Papp, Robert, illus. 2013. (American Adventures Ser.). (ENG.). 88p. (J). (gr. 3-6). pap. 9.99 *(978-1-58536-861-7(X),* 202368) Sleeping Bear Pr.
Papp, Lisa. The Town That Fooled the British: A War of 1812 Story. Papp, Lisa, illus. 2011. (Tales of Young Americans Ser.). (ENG., Illus.). 32p. (J). (gr. 1-4). 18.99 *(978-1-58536-484-8(3),* 202192) Sleeping Bear Pr.
Perkins, Lucy Fitch. American Twins of 1812. (J). (gr. 2-5). 20.95 *(978-0-89190-473-1(5))* Amereon Ltd.
—The American Twins of 1812. 2009. (Illus.). 112p. (J). pap. 13.95 *(978-1-934610-17-6(8))* Bluewater Pubns.
Peterson, Mike. Freehand: A Young Boy's Adventures in the War Of 1812. Baldwin, Christopher, illus. 2012. (ENG.). 44p. (J). pap. 6.95 *(978-1-938384-03-5(2))* Baldwin, Christopher John.
Scheffler, Stephanie. Elizabeth & the War of 1812. 2010. 292p. (YA). 28.95 *(978-1-4502-3539-6(5));* (ENG.). pap. 18.95 *(978-1-4502-3540-2(9))* iUniverse, Inc.
Sutherland, Robert. Son of the Hounds, 1 vol. 2004. (ENG.). 128p. (J). (gr. 4-6). pap. 7.95 *(978-1-55041-906-1(4),* 77bf8d6c-0c3e-4248-be0c-2679e5a404c7) Trifolium Bks., Inc. CAN. Dist: Firefly Bks., Ltd.
Tomlinson, Everett T. The War of 1812. 2010. 204p. reprint ed. pap. 24.75 *(978-1-146-39267-9(2))* Creative Media Partners, LLC.
—The War of 1812. 2009. 112p. reprint ed. pap. 14.14 *(978-0-217-61361-3(6))* General Bks. LLC.
Wiley, Melissa. Little House by Boston Bay. 2007. (Little House Prequel Ser.). (ENG.). 160p. (J). (gr. 3-7). pap. 7.99 *(978-0-06-114828-6(8),* HarperCollins) HarperCollins Pubs.
Winstead, Amy. The Star-Spangled Banner. Dacey, Bob & Bandelin, Debra, illus. 2003. (ENG.). 32p. (J). 18.65 *(978-0-8249-5462-8(9),* Ideals Pubns.) Worthy Publishing.

UNITED STATES—HISTORY—1815-1861

The Antebellum Women's Movement, 1820-1860. (YA). (gr. 6-9). spiral bd., tchr.'s planning gde. ed. 12.00 *(978-0-382-44465-4(5))* Cobblestone Publishing Co.
Blumberg, Rhoda. Commodore Perry in the Land of the Shogun. 2003. (Illus.). 144p. (gr. 3-7). 20.00 *(978-0-7569-1440-0(X))* Perfection Learning Corp.
—Commodore Perry in the Land of the Shogun: A Newbery Honor Award Winner. 2003. (ENG., Illus.). 144p. (J). (gr. 3-18). pap. 9.99 *(978-0-06-008625-1(4),* HarperCollins) HarperCollins Pubs.
Casciato, Daniel. Expansion & Reform: (Early 1800s-1861) 2007. (Presidents of the United States Ser.). (Illus.). 48p. (J). (gr. 4-7). lib. bdg. 29.05 *(978-1-59036-741-4(3))* Weigl Pubs., Inc.
—Expansion & Reform: Early 1800s-1861. 2007. (Presidents of the United States Ser.). (Illus.). 48p. (J). (gr. 4-7). per. 11.95 *(978-1-59036-742-1(1))* Weigl Pubs., Inc.
Hakim, Joy. A History of US: Liberty for All? 1820-1860 a History of US Book Five. 3rd rev. ed. 2006. (History of US Ser.: 5). (ENG., Illus.). 224p. (gr. 4-7). 24.95 *(978-0-19-518898-1(5))* Oxford Univ. Pr., Inc.
Lanier, Wendy & Nelson, Robin. What Was the Missouri Compromise? And Other Questions about the Struggle over Slavery. 2012. (Start to Finish, Second Series: Nature's Cycles Ser.). (ENG.). 48p. (gr. k-3). pap. 39.62 *(978-0-7613-9293-4(9))* Lerner Publishing Group.
Lanier, Wendy Hinote. What Was the Missouri Compromise? And Other Questions about the Struggle over Slavery. 2012. (Six Questions of American History Ser.). (ENG., Illus.). 48p. (J). (gr. 4-6). pap. 11.99 *(978-0-7613-8565-3(7),* 33f0adec-f615-4d33-a027-8dd0fb8b729f) Lerner Publishing Group.
Larkin, Tanya. What Was Cooking in Julia Grant's White House? 2009. (Cooking Throughout American History Ser.). 24p. (gr. 3-3). 42.50 *(978-1-61511-952-3(3),* PowerKids Pr.) Rosen Publishing Group, Inc., The.
McDougal-Littell Publishing Staff, contrib. by. A Nation Dividing 1800-1860. 2004. (Stories in History Ser.). (Illus.). 176p. (gr. 6-12). 13.32 *(978-0-618-14222-4(3),* 2-00242) Holt McDougal.
Quinby, Michelle. Wars at Home: America Forms an Identity (1812-1820) 2012. (J). pap. *(978-1-4222-2415-1(5))* Mason Crest.
—Wars at Home: America Forms an Identity (1812-1820) Rakove, Jack N., ed. 2012. (How America Became America Ser.). 48p. (J). (gr. 3-4). 19.95 *(978-1-4222-2401-4(5))* Mason Crest.

UNITED STATES—HISTORY—1815-1861—FICTION

Brill, Marlene Targ. Allen Jay & the Undergound Railroad, 4 bks., Set. Porter, Janice Lee, illus. 2007. (Readalongs for Beginning Readers Ser.). (J). (gr. 1-3). pap. 37.95 incl. audio *(978-1-59519-947-8(0))* Live Oak Media.
Broyles, Anne. Priscilla & the Hollyhocks. Alter, Anna, illus. 2019. 32p. (J). (gr. 1-4). pap. 7.99 *(978-1-57091-676-2(4))* Charlesbridge Publishing, Inc.
Crawford, Neil. The Journeyers. 2006. (ENG.). 248p. (J). per. *(978-0-9778205-4-2(8))* Helm Publishing.
Porter, Janice Lee, illus. Allen Jay & the Underground Railroad, 4 bks., Set. 2006. (Readalongs for Beginning Readers Ser.). (J). (gr. 2-5). pap. 39.95 incl. audio compact disk *(978-1-59519-951-5(9))* Live Oak Media.
Wilson, Diane Lee. Black Storm Comin' 2006. (ENG.). 240p. (J). (gr. 5-9). pap. 8.99 *(978-0-689-87138-2(4),* McElderry, Margaret K. Bks.) McElderry, Margaret K. Bks.
—Black Storm Comin' 2006. (Illus.). 291p. (gr. 5-9). 17.00 *(978-0-7569-6908-0(5))* Perfection Learning Corp.

UNITED STATES—HISTORY—WAR WITH MEXICO, 1845-1848

see Mexican War, 1846-1848

UNITED STATES—HISTORY—CIVIL WAR, 1861-1865

see also Slavery—United States

Ablard, Michelle. The Civil War: Brother Against Brother. rev. ed. 2017. (Social Studies: Informational Text Ser.). (ENG., Illus.). 32p. (gr. 4-8). pap. 11.99 *(978-1-4938-3804-2(0))* Teacher Created Materials, Inc.
Abnett, Dan. Abraham Lincoln & the Civil War. (Jr. Graphic Biographies Ser.). (ENG.). 24p. (gr. 2-3). 2009. (J). 47.90 *(978-1-61513-807-4(2),* PowerKids Pr.) 2006. (Illus.). (J). lib. bdg. 28.93 *(978-1-4042-3392-8(X),* 92e3c8e5-f3e2-4a55-954a-8ef3b235e069) 2006. (Illus.). pap. 10.60 *(978-1-4042-2145-1(X),* 0586a643-99bf-4e0d-bd7a-2e7c219dab67, PowerKids Pr.) Rosen Publishing Group, Inc., The.
—Abraham Lincoln y la Guerra Civil, 1 vol. 2009. (Historietas Juveniles: Biografías (Jr. Graphic Biographies) Ser.). (SPA., Illus.). 24p. (gr. 2-3). (J). 28.93 *(978-1-4358-8561-5(9),* 7466c29f-c43f-4229-a2b0-ce29cbcf5047); pap. 10.60 *(978-1-4358-3316-6(3),* 6881a164-d615-429e-aaaf-9ff20b30d04e) Rosen Publishing Group, Inc., The.
—The Monitor versus the Merrimac: Ironclads at War. 2009. (Graphic Civil War Battles Ser.). (ENG.). 48p. (YA). (gr. 4-5). 58.50 *(978-1-61512-902-7(2),* Rosen Reference) Rosen Publishing Group, Inc., The.
—The Monitor vs. the Merrimack: Ironclads at War!, 1 vol. 2006. (Graphic Battles of the Civil War Ser.). (ENG., Illus.). 48p. (gr. 4-5). pap. 14.05 *(978-1-4042-6480-9(9),* 77da9482-1619-48c9-9f4a-f12ffcbdd265, Rosen Classroom) Rosen Publishing Group, Inc., The.
Adamson, Deanna. The Other Side of the Lines: Southern Heroes of the US Civil War. 2011. 88p. pap. 10.95 *(978-1-4327-7194-2(9))* Outskirts Pr., Inc.
Adamson, Thomas K. The Civil War. 2017. (J). *(978-1-5105-3502-2(0))* SmartBook Media, Inc.
Allen, Roger MacBride & Allen, Thomas B. Mr. Lincoln's High-Tech War: How the North Used the Telegraph, Railroads, Surveillance Balloons, Ironclads, High-Powered Weapons, & More to Win the Civil War. 2009. (Illus.). 144p. (J). (gr. 5-9). 18.95 *(978-1-4263-0379-1(3),* National Geographic Kids) Disney Publishing Worldwide.
Aloian, Molly. Emancipation. 2013. (ENG., Illus.). 48p. (J). *(978-0-7787-1100-1(5));* pap. *(978-0-7787-1120-9(X))* Crabtree Publishing Co.
Anderson, Dale. The Aftermath of the Civil War, 1 vol. 2004. (World Almanac(r) Library of the Civil War Ser.). (ENG., Illus.). 48p. (gr. 5-8). pap. 15.05 *(978-0-8368-5597-5(3),* ad27f227-78f5-47db-a4a4-11d6eaec8003); lib. bdg. 33.67 *(978-0-8368-5588-3(4),* c777ffc3-916f-4e09-bf81-5fbda0f6625d) Stevens, Gareth Publishing LLLP. (Gareth Stevens Secondary Library).
—The Causes of the Civil War, 1 vol. 2004. (World Almanac(r) Library of the Civil War Ser.). (ENG., Illus.). 48p. (gr. 5-8). pap. 15.05 *(978-0-8368-5590-6(6),* ae885cb8-42d8-49e0-b9ca-32f9a28d4d37); lib. bdg. 33.67 *(978-0-8368-5581-4(7),* 88052b64-ee89-4168-9b03-c8645b27670f) Stevens, Gareth Publishing LLLP. (Gareth Stevens Secondary Library).
—The Civil War in the West (1861-July 1863), 1 vol. 2004. (World Almanac(r) Library of the Civil War Ser.). (ENG., Illus.). 48p. (gr. 5-8). pap. 15.05 *(978-0-8368-5592-0(2),* f1a73c48-7757-40ac-bab0-b107533729d6); lib. bdg. 33.67 *(978-0-8368-5583-8(3),* a497de3e-669b-4027-92d0-df03b0280971) Stevens, Gareth Publishing LLLP. (Gareth Stevens Secondary Library).
—The Home Fronts in the Civil War, 1 vol. 2004. (World Almanac(r) Library of the Civil War Ser.). (ENG., Illus.). 48p. (gr. 5-8). lib. bdg. 33.67 *(978-0-8368-5587-6(6),* f82d4d42-0c19-4e83-844b-321427333a72, Gareth Stevens Secondary Library) Stevens, Gareth Publishing LLLP.
—A Soldier's Life in the Civil War, 1 vol. 2004. (World Almanac(r) Library of the Civil War Ser.). (ENG., Illus.). 48p. (gr. 5-8). pap. 15.05 *(978-0-8368-5595-1(7),* 644f6601-6cb3-4513-a5bb-f0753119da8b, Gareth Stevens Secondary Library) Stevens, Gareth Publishing LLLP.
—World Almanac Library of the Civil War, 10 vols. Incl. Aftermath of the Civil War. lib. bdg. 33.67 *(978-0-8368-5588-3(4),* c777ffc3-916f-4e09-bf81-5fbda0f6625d); Causes of the Civil War. lib. bdg. 33.67 *(978-0-8368-5581-4(7),* 88052b64-ee89-4168-9b03-c8645b27670f); Civil War at Sea. lib. bdg. 33.67 *(978-0-8368-5585-2(X),* abaa704c-54ab-437b-a508-a47da1d3dc87); Civil War in the East (1861-July 1863) lib. bdg. 33.67 *(978-0-8368-5582-1(5),* ea65b134-2894-4b4a-b659-255a776186b0); Civil War in the West (1861-July 1863) lib. bdg. 33.67 *(978-0-8368-5583-8(3),* a497de3e-669b-4027-92d0-df03b0280971); Home Fronts in the Civil War. lib. bdg. 33.67 *(978-0-8368-5587-6(6),* f82d4d42-0c19-4e83-844b-321427333a72); Union Victory (July 1863 - 1865) lib. bdg. 33.67 *(978-0-8368-5584-5(1),* e28734b4-0c65-4c17-9779-244cfe64b88f); (gr. 5-8). (World Almanac(r) Library of the Civil War Ser.). (ENG., Illus.). 48p. 2004. Set lib. bdg. 168.35 *(978-0-8368-5580-7(9),* 6d23f6f8-b267-4c3a-8417-931f1aeca97a, Gareth Stevens Secondary Library) Stevens, Gareth Publishing LLLP.
—World Almanac Library of the Civil War, 8 bks. Incl. Aftermath of the Civil War. pap. 15.05 *(978-0-8368-5597-5(3),* ad27f227-78f5-47db-a4a4-11d6eaec8003); Causes of the Civil War. pap. 15.05 *(978-0-8368-5590-6(6),* ae885cb8-42d8-49e0-b9ca-32f9a28d4d37); Civil War in the East (1861-July 1863) pap. 15.05 *(978-0-8368-5591-3(4),* a8679fe7-8a42-464b-929d-fbb5c4e0806a); Civil War in the West (1861-July 1863) pap. 15.05 *(978-0-8368-5592-0(2),* f1a73c48-7757-40ac-bab0-b107533729d6); Soldier's Life in the Civil War. pap. 15.05 *(978-0-8368-5595-1(7),* 644f6601-6cb3-4513-a5bb-f0753119da8b); Union Victory (July 1863 - 1865) pap. 15.05 *(978-0-8368-5593-7(0),* ce8cac87-1d6e-4de0-9561-7135bd10ad50); (gr. 5-8)., Gareth Stevens Secondary Library (World Almanac Library of the Civil War). (Illus.). 48p. 2004. Set pap. 95.60 o.p. *(978-0-8368-5589-0(2),* World Almanac Library) Stevens, Gareth Publishing LLLP.
Anderson, Maxine. Great Civil War Projects: You Can Build Yourself. 2nd ed. 2012. (Build It Yourself Ser.). (ENG.). 128p. (J). (gr. 3-7). 21.95 *(978-1-936749-46-1(7),* ae9f055a-9ca4-4f17-993d-78ccafdd80af); pap. 15.95 *(978-1-936749-45-4(9),* 1cc6a3fd-463c-4b56-9a9f-a4f84c7e6b5a) Nomad Pr.
Anderson, Michael, contrib. by. Abraham Lincoln, 1 vol. 2012. (Pivotal Presidents: Profiles in Leadership Ser.). (ENG., Illus.). 80p. (gr. 8-8). (J). lib. bdg. 36.47 *(978-1-61530-942-9(X),* 3e79c9e2-6cf7-49e1-8a7e-6f531fd252d5); (YA). 72.94 *(978-1-61530-953-5(5),* fe64ec48-46cf-4b6d-afb3-c461b9174bea) Rosen Publishing Group, Inc., The.
Archer, Jules. A House Divided: The Lives of Ulysses S. Grant & Robert E. Lee. rev. ed. 2015. (Jules Archer History for Young Readers Ser.). (ENG., Illus.). 176p. (J). (gr. 6-6). 16.99 *(978-1-63220-604-6(8),* Sky Pony Pr.) Skyhorse Publishing Co., Inc.
Armentrout, David, et al. The Gettysburg Address. 2005. (Documents that Shaped the Nation Ser.). (Illus.). 48p. (gr. 4-6). 20.95 *(978-1-59515-232-9(6))* Rourke Educational Media.
Armstrong, Jennifer. Photo by Brady: A Picture of the Civil War. 2013. (ENG., Illus.). 128p. (J). pap. 11.95 *(978-0-689-85786-7(1),* Simon & Schuster/Paula Wiseman Bks.) Simon & Schuster/Paula Wiseman Bks.
Arnold, James R. The Civil War. 2005. (Chronicle of America's Wars Ser.). (Illus.). 96p. (J). (gr. 5-12). 27.93 *(978-0-8225-0140-4(6))* Lerner Publishing Group.
Arnold, James R. & Wiener, Roberta. Life Goes On: The Civil War at Home, 1861-1865. 2005. (Civil War Ser.). (Illus.). 72p. (gr. 5-12). lib. bdg. 25.26 *(978-0-8225-2315-4(9))* Lerner Publishing Group.
Aronson, Billy. Abraham Lincoln, 1 vol. 2009. (Presidents & Their Times Ser.). (ENG.). 96p. (gr. 6-6). lib. bdg. 36.93 *(978-0-7614-2839-8(9),* a404bef1-3923-404a-bd06-75978e2cbebe) Cavendish Square Publishing LLC.
Bader, Bonnie & Who HQ. Who Was Robert E. Lee? O'Brien, John, illus. 2014. (Who Was? Ser.). 112p. (J). (gr. 3-7). 5.99 *(978-0-448-47909-5(5),* Penguin Workshop) Penguin Young Readers Group.
Baptiste, Tracey. The Civil War & Reconstruction Eras, 1 vol. 2015. (African American Experience: from Slavery to the Presidency Ser.). (ENG., Illus.). 80p. (J). (gr. 7-8). 35.47 *(978-1-68048-039-9(1),* e7f0de6d-1523-408b-9831-b566bcc6c36c, Britannica Educational Publishing) Rosen Publishing Group, Inc., The.
Baptiste, Tracey, ed. The Civil War & Reconstruction Eras, 4 vols. 2015. (African American Experience: from Slavery to the Presidency Ser.). (ENG.). 80p. (YA). (gr. 7-8). 70.94 *(978-1-68048-040-5(5),* 5493c455-171a-4df2-9371-9f612b36021a, Britannica Educational Publishing) Rosen Publishing Group, Inc., The.
Bauer, Patricia. B Is for Battle Cry: A Civil War Alphabet. Geister, David, illus. 2009. (History Ser.). (ENG.). 40p. (J). (gr. 1-4). 17.95 *(978-1-58536-356-8(1),* 202142) Sleeping Bear Pr.
Baumann, Susan K. Black Civil War Soldiers: The 54th Massachusetts Regiment, 1 vol. 2013. (Jr. Graphic African American History Ser.). (ENG., Illus.). 24p. (J). (gr. 2-3). pap. 11.60 *(978-1-4777-1457-7(X),* cce11ddf-e6cf-4be4-9485-d39747c793ea); lib. bdg. 28.93 *(978-1-4777-1316-7(6),* 93ee6db9-c457-4fe1-a49c-d10e16218f92) Rosen Publishing Group, Inc., The. (PowerKids Pr.).
Baxter, Kathleen & McConnell, Robert L., contrib. by. Civil War Witness: Mathew Brady's Photos Reveal the Horrors of War, 1 vol. 2013. (Captured History Ser.). (ENG., Illus.). 64p. (J). (gr. 5-9). 35.32 *(978-0-7565-4693-9(1),* 123110, Compass Point Bks.) Capstone.
Baxter, Roberta. The Southern Home Front of the Civil War, 1 vol. 2011. (Why We Fought: the Civil War Ser.). (ENG.). 48p. (J). (gr. 3-6). pap. 9.95 *(978-1-4329-3918-2(1),* 112832, Heinemann) Capstone.
Bednarz, Robert, et al. Horizons: Us History - Civil War-Present. 3rd ed. 2003. (Harcourt School Publishers Horizons Ser.). (ENG., Illus.). 680p. (gr. 5-6). pupil's gde. ed. 93.85 *(978-0-15-321350-2(7))* Harcourt Schl. Pubs.
Beller, Susan Provost. Billy Yank & Johnny Reb: Soldiering in the Civil War. rev. ed. 2007. (Soldiers on the Battlefront Ser.). (ENG., Illus.). 112p. (gr. 6-8). lib. bdg. 33.26 *(978-0-8225-6803-2(9))* Lerner Publishing Group.
Benchmark Education Company, LLC Staff, compiled by. The Civil War: Theme Set. 2006. (J). 173.00 *(978-1-4108-7127-5(4))* Benchmark Education Co.
Benoit, Peter. The Confederate States of America. 2011. (True Bk Ser.). (ENG.). 48p. (J). pap. 6.95 *(978-0-531-26623-6(0),* Children's Pr.) Scholastic Library Publishing.
—The Surrender at Appomattox. 2012. (Cornerstones of Freedom, Third Ser.). (ENG.). 64p. (J). (gr. 4-6). lib. bdg. 24.94 *(978-0-531-25041-9(5))* Scholastic Library Publishing.
Benson, Alana. Great Exit Projects on the Civil War & Reconstruction, 1 vol. 2019. (Great Social Studies Exit Projects Ser.). (ENG.). 64p. (gr. 5-5). 36.13 *(978-1-4994-4033-1(2),* 217db278-5ca4-4b7a-99f0-9c6d8d765678, Rosen Young Adult) Rosen Publishing Group, Inc., The.
Berry, Carrie. Diary of Carrie Berry: A Confederate Girl, 1 vol. 2014. (First-Person Histories Ser.). (ENG., Illus.). 32p. (J). (gr. 3-6). lib. bdg. 27.99 *(978-1-4765-4192-1(2),* 124299, Capstone Pr.) Capstone.
Bickerstaff, Linda. The Red Badge of Courage & the Civil War. 2009. (Looking at Literature Through Primary Sources Ser.). 64p. (gr. 5-8). 58.50 *(978-1-61514-307-8(6))* Rosen Publishing Group, Inc., The.
Bircher, William. Diary of William Bircher: A Civil War Drummer, 1 vol. 2014. (First-Person Histories Ser.). (ENG., Illus.). 32p. (J). (gr. 3-6). lib. bdg. 27.99 *(978-1-4765-4195-2(7),* 124302, Capstone Pr.) Capstone.
Black Civil War Soldiers: The 54th Massachusetts Regiment. 2013. (Jr. Graphic African American History Ser.). 24p. (J). (gr. 3-6). pap. 63.60 *(978-1-4777-1458-4(8),* PowerKids Pr.) Rosen Publishing Group, Inc., The.
Borges, Antonion. Cocoa & Company: A Civil War Classic. 2007. (ENG.). 124p. per. 19.95 *(978-1-4241-4829-5(4))* America Star Bks.
Brocker, Susan. Voices from the Civil War & Voces de la Guerra Civil: 6 English, 6 Spanish Adaptations. 2011. (ENG & SPA.). (J). 97.00 net. *(978-1-4108-5714-9(X))* Benchmark Education Co.
Brown Bear Books. Politics. 2011. (Civil War Ser.). (ENG.). 112p. (J). (gr. 9-12). 42.80 *(978-1-936333-48-6(1),* 16458) Brown Bear Bks.
—Weapons, Tactics, & Strategy. 2011. (Civil War Ser.). (ENG.). 112p. (J). (gr. 9-12). 42.80 *(978-1-936333-46-2(5),* 16459) Brown Bear Bks.
Brown, Susan Taylor. Robert Smalls Sails to Freedom. Marshall, Felicia, illus. 2006. (On My Own History Ser.). 48p. (J). (gr. 3-7). pap. 6.95 *(978-0-8225-6051-7(8),* First Avenue Editions); (ENG.). (gr. 2-4). lib. bdg. 25.26 *(978-1-57505-872-6(3))* Lerner Publishing Group.
Brownell, Richard. The Civil War: The Fall of the Confederacy & the End of Slavery. 2005. (History's Great Defeats Ser.). (ENG., Illus.). 109p. (YA). (gr. 7-10). lib. bdg. 30.85 *(978-1-59018-429-5(7),* Lucent Bks.) Cengage Gale.
Budd, Anitra. Disgusting Jobs During the Civil War: The down & Dirty Details. 2018. (Disgusting Jobs in History Ser.). (ENG., Illus.). 32p. (J). (gr. 3-6). lib. bdg. 27.99 *(978-1-5435-0367-8(5),* 137207, Capstone Pr.) Capstone.
Burgan, Michael. Spies of the Civil War: An Interactive History Adventure. 2015. (You Choose: Spies Ser.). (ENG., Illus.). 112p. (J). (gr. 3-7). pap. 6.95 *(978-1-4914-5932-4(8),* 128852, Capstone Pr.) Capstone.
Burleigh, Robert. O Captain, My Captain: Walt Whitman, Abraham Lincoln, & the Civil War. Hundley, Sterling, illus. 2019. (ENG.). 64p. (J). (gr. 5-17). 19.99 *(978-1-4197-3358-1(3),* 1120101, Abrams Bks. for Young Readers) Abrams, Inc.
Burton, Melissa. Divided They Stood. 2014. 42p. pap. 14.95 *(978-1-934898-46-8(5))* McClanahan Publishing Hse., Inc.
Byers, Ann. Strategic Inventions of the Civil War, 1 vol. 2015. (Tech in the Trenches Ser.). (ENG., Illus.). 112p. (YA). (gr. 9-9). lib. bdg. 44.50 *(978-1-5026-1030-0(2),* 4e1aa84d-c159-48a7-979f-475635875d0d) Cavendish Square Publishing LLC.
Calkins, Chris. Auto Tour of Civil War Petersburg: 1861-1865, 1 vol. 2003. (Illus.). 80p. per. 7.66 *(978-0-9744824-0-8(4))* Petersburg Museums, The.
Capek, Michael. The Battle over Slavery: Causes & Effects of the U.S. Civil War. 2015. (Civil War Ser.). (ENG., Illus.). 48p. (J). (gr. 3-6). lib. bdg. 29.99 *(978-1-4914-2009-6(X),* 127484, Capstone Pr.) Capstone.
—Civil War Causes, 1 vol. 2016. (Essential Library of the Civil War Ser.). (ENG., Illus.). 112p. (J). (gr. 8-12). lib. bdg. 41.36 *(978-1-68078-275-2(4),* 21705, Essential Library) ABDO Publishing Co.
Caravantes, Peggy. Petticoat Spies: Six Women Spies of the US Civil War. 2004. (Notable Americans Ser.). (Illus.). 112p. (YA). (gr. 6-12). 23.95 *(978-1-883846-88-6(9),* First Biographies) Reynolds, Morgan Inc.
Carole Marsh. When Brother Fought Brother: the American Civil War. 2004. (American Milestones Ser.). 32p. (gr. 3-8). pap. 5.95 *(978-0-635-02346-9(6));* (gr. 4-12). 29.95 *(978-0-635-02347-6(4))* Gallopade International.
Castellano, Peter. The Civil War, 1 vol. 2017. (Look at U. S. History Ser.). (ENG., Illus.). 32p. (J). (gr. 2-2). pap. 11.50 *(978-1-4824-6027-8(0),* 114f911a-3013-4bce-a422-d6e974440f03) Stevens, Gareth Publishing LLLP.
Civil War. (Color & Learn Ser.). 36p. (J). (gr. 1-5). pap. *(978-1-882210-07-7(7))* Action Publishing, Inc.
The Civil War: The American Civil War 1861-1865. 2007. (Illus.). 33p. (J). (gr. 4-7). per. 6.95 *(978-0-9795887-1-6(5))* EZ Comics.
The Civil War Instructional Guide. 2009. (Grade 8: Social Studies Exit Project Kits Ser.). spiral bd. *(978-1-4042-4027-8(6),* Rosen Classroom) Rosen Publishing Group, Inc., The.
The Civil War Kids 150: Fifty Fun Things to Do, See, Make, & Find. 150th anniv. ed. 2012. (Illus.). 80p. pap. 12.95 *(978-0-7627-8205-5(6),* Lyons Pr.) Globe Pequot Pr., The.
Civil War Tales of the Tennessee Valley 2003. (Illus.). 241p. per. 17.95 *(978-0-9719946-7-6(6))* Bluewater Pubns.
Clark, Willow. The True Story of the Civil War, 1 vol. 2013. (What Really Happened? Ser.). (ENG., Illus.). 24p. (J). (gr. 2-3). pap. 9.25 *(978-1-4488-9844-2(7),* 81eeb54c-c0ce-4cbb-97d5-fca8085ef25f); lib. bdg. 26.27 *(978-1-4488-9693-6(2),* ca43a71d-99a8-4a9f-9214-23b2a5cdf14f) Rosen Publishing Group, Inc., The. (PowerKids Pr.).
—The True Story of the Emancipation Proclamation, 1 vol. 2013. (What Really Happened? Ser.). (ENG., Illus.). 24p. (J). (gr. 2-3). 26.27 *(978-1-4488-9695-0(9),* ed9c49fd-1083-41ae-b071-1a993beabfb5); pap. 9.25 *(978-1-4488-9848-0(X),* f7848aa6-8a09-463b-b38a-5f880afeb521) Rosen Publishing Group, Inc., The. (PowerKids Pr.).
Coddington, Andrew. Code Breakers & Spies of the Civil War, 1 vol. 2018. (Code Breakers & Spies Ser.). (ENG.). 80p. (YA). (gr. 8-8). 38.79 *(978-1-5026-3847-2(9),* c7cda8cb-7fe6-498b-95b0-4c1d964379a7) Cavendish Square Publishing LLC.
Colbert, Nancy A. The Firing on Fort Sumter: A Splintered Nation Goes to War. 2004. (First Battles Ser.). (Illus.). 112p. (J). (gr. 6-12). 23.95 *(978-1-883846-51-0(X),* First Biographies) Reynolds, Morgan Inc.

Cole, Tayler. Fact or Fiction? Researching the Causes of the American Civil War, 1 vol. 2018. (Project Learning Through American History Ser.). (ENG.). 32p. (gr. 4-5). 27.93 (978-1-5383-3059-3(8), 3f7f278c-2ac0-4a6c-8ecc-4463632d5923, PowerKids Pr.) Rosen Publishing Group, Inc., The.

Conklin, Wendy. Battles of the Civil War, 1 vol. rev. ed. 2005. (Social Studies: Informational Text Ser.). (ENG., Illus.). 24p. (gr. 4-8). pap. 10.99 (978-0-7439-8919-0(8)) Teacher Created Materials, Inc.

—Civil War Leaders. rev. ed. 2017. (Social Studies: Informational Text Ser.). (ENG., Illus.). 32p. (gr. 4-8). pap. 11.99 (978-1-4938-3887-5(3)) Teacher Created Materials, Inc.

—Robert E. Lee, 1 vol. rev. ed. 2005. (Social Studies: Informational Text Ser.). (ENG.). 24p. (gr. 4-8). pap. 10.99 (978-0-7439-8918-3(X)) Teacher Created Materials, Inc.

Connolly, Kieron. America's Bloody History from the Civil War to the Great Depression, 1 vol. 2017. (Bloody History of America Ser.). (ENG.). 88p. (gr. 8-8). 37.60 (978-0-7660-9178-8(3), 2eccc640-a875-4b93-be57-f45939ce32e2) Enslow Publishing, LLC.

Cooke, Tim. After the War, 1 vol. 2012. (American Civil War: the Right Answer Ser.). (ENG., Illus.). 48p. (J). (gr. 6-8). 34.60 (978-1-4339-7531-8(9), 4f59dc6e-b471-48da-9930-9fb5ab4b06ab); pap. 15.05 (978-1-4339-7532-5(7), f32f003b-b9ac-451e-aa04-226618ca243c) Stevens, Gareth Publishing LLLP. (Gareth Stevens Secondary Library).

—Causes of the War, 1 vol. 2012. (American Civil War: the Right Answer Ser.). (ENG., Illus.). 48p. (J). (gr. 6-8). pap. 15.05 (978-1-4339-7536-3(X), 824013a5-fd98-4be7-821d-1e0bb4a86e23); lib. bdg. 34.60 (978-1-4339-7535-6(1), 35413caa-60d4-4e41-aea4-43d818cb473d) Stevens, Gareth Publishing LLLP.

—Causes of the War: 1860-1861. 2012. (Civil War Highlights Ser.). (Illus.). 48p. (gr. 5-12). lib. bdg. 37.10 (978-1-59920-813-8(X)) Black Rabbit Bks.

—The Home Front, 1 vol. 2012. (American Civil War: the Right Answer Ser.). (ENG., Illus.). 48p. (J). (gr. 6-8). 34.60 (978-1-4339-7543-1(2), a7e960c1-c997-42ce-a9cd-5adf23a981e3); pap. 15.05 (978-1-4339-7544-8(0), 9e570b5e-4625-431c-b3e6-10daacbf2272) Stevens, Gareth Publishing LLLP. (Gareth Stevens Secondary Library).

—Home Front, 1861-1865. 2012. (Civil War Highlights Ser.). (Illus.). 48p. (gr. 5-12). 37.10 (978-1-59920-817-6(2)) Black Rabbit Bks.

—Politics of the War: 1861-1865. 2012. (Civil War Highlights Ser.). (Illus.). 48p. (gr. 5-12). lib. bdg. 37.10 (978-1-59920-818-3(0)) Black Rabbit Bks.

—Weapons & Tactics, 1 vol. 2012. (American Civil War: the Right Answer Ser.). (ENG., Illus.). 48p. (J). (gr. 6-8). 34.60 (978-1-4339-7551-6(3), 09c9b101-829c-47e5-9d35-f71c5059ba7e); pap. 15.05 (978-1-4339-7552-3(1), d242f462-ea19-4922-933f-27b3c4f4d312) Stevens, Gareth Publishing LLLP. (Gareth Stevens Secondary Library).

Cordell, M. R. Courageous Women of the Civil War: Soldiers, Spies, Medics, & More. 2016. (Women of Action Ser.: 17). (ENG., Illus.). 256p. (YA). (gr. 7). 19.99 (978-1-61373-200-7(7)) Chicago Review Pr., Inc.

Cornell, Kari A. African Americans in the Civil War, 1 vol. 2016. (Essential Library of the Civil War Ser.). (ENG., Illus.). 112p. (J). (gr. 8-12). lib. bdg. 41.36 (978-1-68078-271-4(1), 21697, Essential Library) ABDO Publishing Co.

—Women in the Civil War, 1 vol. 2016. (Essential Library of the Civil War Ser.). (ENG., Illus.). 112p. (J). (gr. 8-12). lib. bdg. 41.36 (978-1-68078-280-6(0), 21715, Essential Library) ABDO Publishing Co.

Corrick, James A. The Civil War & Emancipation, 1 vol. 2007. (Lucent Library of Black History Ser.). (ENG., Illus.). 104p. (J). (gr. 7-7). lib. bdg. 41.03 (978-1-4205-0008-0(2), e49d4f5d-f292-4497-87e1-8cd18b6c3b79, Lucent Pr.) Greenhaven Publishing LLC.

Cosson, Jody. Civil War & Reconstruction: 1850-1877. 2007. (Presidents of the United States Ser.). (Illus.). (J). (gr. 4-7). 47p. lib. bdg. 29.05 (978-1-59036-743-8(X)); 48p. per. 10.95 (978-1-59036-744-5(8)) Weigl Pubs., Inc.

Crewe, Sabrina & Uschan, Michael V. Fort Sumter: the Civil War Begins, 1 vol. 2004. (Events That Shaped America Ser.). (ENG., Illus.). 32p. (gr. 3-5). lib. bdg. 28.67 (978-0-8368-3414-7(3), 496f2773-44ea-4736-aa2d-ede3d36b4e03, Gareth Stevens Learning Library) Stevens, Gareth Publishing LLLP.

Crompton, Samuel W. The Civil War, Vol. 11. Musteen, Jason R., ed. 2015. (Major U. S. Historical Wars Ser.). (Illus.). 64p. (J). (gr. 7). lib. bdg. 23.95 (978-1-4222-3354-2(5)) Mason Crest.

Crozier, A. J. Technology & the Civil War: Set Of 6. 2011. (Navigators Ser.). (J). pap. 48.00 net. (978-1-4108-6260-0(7)) Benchmark Education Co.

—Technology & the Civil War: Text Pairs. 2008. (Bridges/Navigators Ser.). (J). (gr. 5). 89.00 (978-1-4108-8423-7(6)) Benchmark Education Co.

Cummings, Judy Dodge. Civil War, 1 vol. 2013. (Essential Library of American Wars Ser.). (ENG.). 112p. (YA). (gr. 6-12). lib. bdg. 41.36 (978-1-61783-877-4(2), 6603, Essential Library) ABDO Publishing Co.

—Civil War Leaders, 1 vol. 2016. (Essential Library of the Civil War Ser.). (ENG., Illus.). 112p. (J). (gr. 8-12). lib. bdg. 41.36 (978-1-68078-276-9(2), 21707, Essential Library) ABDO Publishing Co.

—The Emancipation Proclamation, 1 vol. 2016. (Essential Library of the Civil War Ser.). (ENG., Illus.). 112p. (J). (gr. 8-12). lib. bdg. 41.36 (978-1-68078-279-0(7), 21713, Essential Library) ABDO Publishing Co.

Cunningham, Anne C., ed. Reparations, 1 vol. 2016. (Opposing Viewpoints Ser.). (ENG.). 200p. (YA). (gr. 10-12). pap. 34.80 (978-1-5345-0031-0(6), 16909227-432e-40be-aa13-1ea79da07a14); lib. bdg. 50.43 (978-1-5345-0025-9(1), d6134639-a1ad-4a13-b7ef-2c003946c3a4) Greenhaven Publishing LLC. (Greenhaven Publishing).

Day, Nancy. Your Travel Guide to Civil War America. 2005. (Passport to History Ser.). (Illus.). 96p. (gr. 5-8). lib. bdg. 26.50 (978-0-8225-3078-7(3)) Lerner Publishing Group.

DeFord, Debra. The Civil War, 1 vol. 2006. (Wars That Changed American History Ser.). (ENG.). 48p. (gr. 5-8). pap. 15.05 (978-0-8368-7300-9(9), b3b13f69-75a5-4826-936b-37830cc6452a); (Illus.). lib. bdg. 33.67 (978-0-8368-7291-0(6), f9d9b7d5-f7ad-4824-b5b2-bede0c61961c) Stevens, Gareth Publishing LLLP. (Gareth Stevens Secondary Library).

Delmar, Pete. Vehicles of the Civil War, 1 vol. 2013. (War Vehicles Ser.). (ENG.). 32p. (J). (gr. 3-9). 28.65 (978-1-4296-9912-9(4), 120625, Capstone Pr.) Capstone.

Devereaux Jordan, Anne & Schomp, Virginia. The Civil War, 1 vol. 2007. (Drama of African-American History Ser.). (ENG., Illus.). 80p. (gr. 6-6). lib. bdg. 38.36 (978-0-7614-2179-5(3), 146ebe8a-4308-4cb1-abfc-dedf6c7f07df) Cavendish Square Publishing LLC.

Dodge Cummings, Judy. The Civil War: The Conflict Between the States. Carbaugh, Sam, illus. 2017. (Inquire & Investigate Ser.). (ENG.). 128p. (J). (gr. 7-9). 22.95 (978-1-61930-602-8(6), fdce0859-eb76-426c-a9ca-dc8165603816); pap. 17.95 (978-1-61930-606-6(9), 921d03bb-1aa0-46e4-aef2-d39c1f4fe06f) Nomad Pr.

Doeden, Matt. The Civil War: An Interactive History Adventure. rev. ed. 2016. (You Choose: History Ser.). (ENG., Illus.). 112p. (J). (gr. 3-7). pap. 6.95 (978-1-5157-3389-8(0), 133376); lib. bdg. 32.65 (978-1-5157-3386-7(6), 133373) Capstone. (Capstone Pr.).

—The Civil War [Scholastic]: An Interactive History Adventure. 2010. (You Choose: History Ser.). 112p. pap. 0.90 (978-1-4296-5977-2(7), Capstone Pr.) Capstone.

—Weapons of the Civil War. rev. ed. 2017. (Weapons of War Ser.). (ENG., Illus.). 32p. (J). (gr. 3-9). lib. bdg. 27.32 (978-1-5157-7909-4(2), 136024, Capstone Pr.) Capstone.

—Weapons of War. rev. ed. 2017. (Weapons of War Ser.). (ENG.). 32p. (J). (gr. 3-9). 117.28 (978-1-5157-7936-0(X), 26953, Capstone Pr.) Capstone.

Dosier, Susan. Civil War Cooking: The Confederacy. 2016. (Exploring History Through Food Ser.). (ENG., Illus.). 32p. (J). (gr. 3-6). lib. bdg. 27.99 (978-1-5157-2354-7(2), 132788, Capstone Pr.) Capstone.

—Civil War Cooking: The Union. 2016. (Exploring History Through Food Ser.). (ENG., Illus.). 32p. (J). (gr. 3-6). lib. bdg. 27.99 (978-1-5157-2353-0(4), 132787, Capstone Pr.) Capstone.

Downey, Fairfax. Famous Horses of the Civil War. Chapman, Frederick T., illus. 2011. 128p. 40.95 (978-1-258-00351-7(1)) Literary Licensing, LLC.

Drama of African-American History, 5 bks., Set. Incl. Africa: A Look Back. Haskins, James & Benson Haskins, Kathleen. (J). lib. bdg. 38.36 (978-0-7614-2148-1(3), 1c1cd1b9-2063-462a-943d-5d55457363e9); Civil War. Devereaux Jordan, Anne & Schomp, Virginia. lib. bdg. 38.36 (978-0-7614-2179-5(3), 146ebe8a-4308-4cb1-abfc-dedf6c7f07df); Reconstruction Era. Stroud, Bettye & Schomp, Virginia. lib. bdg. 38.36 (978-0-7614-2181-8(5), 563d4ded-5401-44f3-8d44-514783079efe); Slave Trade & the Middle Passage. Sharp, S. Pearl & Schomp, Virginia. lib. bdg. 38.36 (978-0-7614-2176-4(9), 54b03cf0-3993-459b-8d39-1da98298bb58); Slavery & Resistance. Devereaux Jordan, Anne & Schomp, Virginia. (J). lib. bdg. 38.36 (978-0-7614-2178-8(5), 4fb9f4af-0981-4ebf-ae63-bf2b8438c5bc); (Illus.). 80p. (gr. 6-6). 2007. lib. bdg. (978-0-7614-2174-0(2), Cavendish Square) Cavendish Square Publishing LLC.

Draper, Allison Stark. What People Wore During the Civil War. 2009. (Clothing, Costumes, & Uniforms Throughout American History Ser.). 24p. (gr. 3-3). 42.50 (978-1-61511-876-2(4), PowerKids Pr.) Rosen Publishing Group, Inc., The.

Dreyer, Ellen. A Band of Brave Men: The Story of the 54th Massachusetts Regiment. 2004. (ENG., Illus.). 31p. (J). (gr. 5-5). pap. 12.00 net. (978-0-7652-5247-0(3)) Celebration Pr.

Elliot, Henry. Harriet Beecher Stowe: The Voice of Humanity in White America, 1 vol. 2009. (Voices for Freedom Ser.). (ENG., Illus.). 64p. (J). (gr. 5-8). pap. (978-0-7787-4837-3(5)); lib. bdg. (978-0-7787-4821-2(9)) Crabtree Publishing Co.

Epperson, James F. Causes of the Civil War. 2005. (Road to War Ser.). (Illus.). 64p. (J). pap. 12.95 (978-1-59556-006-3(8)); (gr. 4-18). lib. bdg. 22.95 (978-1-59556-002-5(5)) OTTN Publishing.

Essential Library of the Civil War, 10 vols. 2016. (Essential Library of the Civil War Ser.). (ENG.). 112p. (J). (gr. 8-12). lib. bdg. 413.60 (978-1-68078-270-7(3), 21695, Essential Library) ABDO Publishing Co.

Ferry, Joseph. The Star-Spangled Banner: Story of Our National Anthem. Moreno, Barry, ed. 2014. (Patriotic Symbols of America Ser.: 20). 48p. (J). (gr. 4-18). 20.95 (978-1-4222-3132-6(1)) Mason Crest.

Fetter-Vorm, Jonathan & Kelman, Ari. Battle Lines: A Graphic History of the Civil War. Fetter-Vorm, Jonathan, illus. 2015. (ENG., Illus.). 224p. 35.00 (978-0-8090-9474-5(6), 900076226, Hill & Wang) Farrar, Straus & Giroux.

Figley, Marty Rhodes. President Lincoln, Willie Kettles, & the Telegraph Machine. 2010. pap. 56.72 (978-0-7613-6929-5(5)) Lerner Publishing Group.

Fiore, C. A. Young Heros of the Civil War. (J). pap. 9.99 (978-0-88092-486-3(1)) Royal Fireworks Publishing Co.

Fiore, Carmen Anthony. Young Heroes of the Civil War. 2006. (J). pap. (978-0-88092-639-3(2)); lib. bdg. (978-0-88092-638-6(4)) Royal Fireworks Publishing Co.

Fitzgerald, Stephanie. A Civil War Timeline, 1 vol. 2014. (War Timelines Ser.). (ENG., Illus.). 48p. (J). (gr. 4-7). lib. bdg. 35.32 (978-1-4765-4156-3(6), 124260, Capstone Pr.) Capstone.

Fitzgerald, Stephanie, et al. War Timelines, 1 vol. 2014. (War Timelines Ser.). (ENG.). 48p. (J). (gr. 4-7). 149.28 (978-1-4765-6962-8(2), 20636) Capstone.

Fluharty, Linda Cunningham. Civil War - West Virginia: Union Lives Lost. 2004. (Illus.). 175p. lib. bdg. 35.00 (978-0-9759097-1-3(1)) Fluharty, Linda Cunningham.

Ford, Carin T. The Civil War's African-American Soldiers Through Primary Sources, 1 vol. 2013. (Civil War Through Primary Sources Ser.). (ENG.). 48p. (gr. 4-6). 27.93 (978-0-7660-4125-7(5), 915d7238-d55d-464b-8277-85e0d474ba77); pap. 11.53 (978-1-4644-0183-1(7), 0ff0bfa0-13e7-4d9f-9071-ebe5a4ccbad2) Enslow Publishing, LLC.

—An Overview of the American Civil War Through Primary Sources, 1 vol. 2013. (Civil War Through Primary Sources Ser.). (ENG.). 48p. (gr. 4-6). pap. 11.53 (978-1-4644-0182-4(9), 9d39fd21-b8df-44cb-92e3-8fdb6f2aba7b); lib. bdg. 27.93 (978-0-7660-4124-0(7), 6d8918d2-d504-4c86-8fb0-4cfd22ee2927) Enslow Publishing, LLC.

—Women of the Civil War Through Primary Sources, 1 vol. 2013. (Civil War Through Primary Sources Ser.). (ENG.). 48p. (gr. 4-6). pap. 11.53 (978-1-4644-0186-2(1), 04c72a75-5e99-4115-84a9-94fead775983); lib. bdg. 27.93 (978-0-7660-4128-8(X), 5f41f4c4-2882-4499-923e-169e4305d44f) Enslow Publishing, LLC.

Fox, Arthur B. Pittsburgh During the American Civil War 1860-1865. 2004. (Illus.). 236p. pap. 29.95 (978-0-9760563-0-0(5), 7526S) Mechling Bookbindery.

Furbee, Mary Rodd. Outrageous Women of Civil War Times. 2003. (Outrageous Women Ser.: 7). (ENG., Illus.). 132p. (J). (gr. 5-9). pap. 14.95 (978-0-471-22926-1(1), Jossey-Bass) Wiley, John & Sons, Inc.

Gagne, Tammy. Civil War Technology. 2017. (War Technology Ser.). (ENG., Illus.). 48p. (J). (gr. 4-8). lib. bdg. 35.64 (978-1-5321-1189-1(4), 25954) ABDO Publishing Co.

George, Enzo. The Civil War. 2015. (J). lib. bdg. (978-1-62713-491-0(3)) 2014. (ENG.). 48p. (gr. 4-4). 33.07 (978-1-5026-0251-0(2), 09cc4971-d722-4bc0-b1ec-a7284cd8b80d) Cavendish Square Publishing LLC.

—The Civil War: The War Between Brothers, 1 vol. 2014. (Voices of War Ser.). (ENG.). 48p. (gr. 4-4). lib. bdg. 33.07 (978-1-62712-858-2(1), 7263f0d3-c53a-4b07-a347-1380025493f3) Cavendish Square Publishing LLC.

George, Lynn. What Do You Know about the Civil War? 2009. (20 Questions: History Ser.). 24p. (gr. 2-3). 42.50 (978-1-60854-958-0(5), PowerKids Pr.) Rosen Publishing Group, Inc., The.

Glaser, Jason. The Most Powerful Words of the Civil War, 1 vol. 2019. (Words That Shaped America Ser.). (ENG.). 32p. (gr. 4-5). pap. 11.50 (978-1-5382-4815-7(8), a3bf0336-ddc4-440e-a6af-ff448d698198) Stevens, Gareth Publishing LLLP.

Goodman, Michael E. Civil War Spies. (Wartime Spies Ser.). (ENG.). 48p. (J). (gr. 4-7). 2016. pap. 12.00 (978-1-62832-203-3(9), 21079, Creative Paperbacks) 2015. (Illus.). (978-1-60818-598-6(2), 21078, Creative Education) Creative Co., The.

Goodman, Susan E. Robert Henry Hendershot. Ettlinger, Doris, illus. 2003. (Brave Kids Ser.). (ENG.). 64p. (J). (gr. 1-4). pap. 6.99 (978-0-689-84980-0(X), Simon & Schuster/Paula Wiseman Bks.) Simon & Schuster/Paula Wiseman Bks.

Grayson, Robert. Civil War Spies, 1 vol. 2016. (Essential Library of the Civil War Ser.). (ENG., Illus.). 112p. (J). (gr. 8-12). lib. bdg. 41.36 (978-1-68078-277-6(0), 21709, Essential Library) ABDO Publishing Co.

—12 Incredible Facts about the US Civil War. 2015. (Turning Points in US History Ser.). (ENG., Illus.). 32p. (J). (gr. 3-5). 32.80 (978-1-63235-133-3(1), 12-Story Library) Bookstaves, LLC.

Gregory, Josh. The Gettysburg Address. 2013. (ENG.). 64p. (J). pap. 8.95 (978-0-531-27669-3(4)) Scholastic Library Publishing.

Griskey, Michele. Harriet Beecher Stowe. 2005. (Classic Storytellers Ser.). (Illus.). 48p. (J). (gr. 4-8). lib. bdg. 29.95 (978-1-58415-375-7(X)) Mitchell Lane Pubs.

Grolier Educational Staff, contrib. by. The Civil War, 10 Vols. 2004. (Illus.). (J). 339.00 (978-0-7172-5883-3(1), Grolier) Scholastic Library Publishing.

Hakim, Joy. A History of US: War, Terrible War: 1855-1865 a History of US Book Six. (History of US Ser.: 6). (ENG., Illus.). 176p. (gr. 4-7). 3rd rev. ed. 2006. 24.95 (978-0-19-518899-8(3))Bk. 6. 2nd rev. ed. 2007. per. 15.95 (978-0-19-532720-5(9)) Oxford Univ. Pr., Inc.

Hale, Nathan. Nathan Hale's Hazardous Tales: Big Bad Ironclad! 2012. (Nathan Hale's Hazardous Tales Ser.). (ENG., Illus.). 128p. (J). (gr. 3-7). 14.99 (978-1-4197-0395-9(1), 1000001, Amulet Bks.) Abrams, Inc.

—The Underground Abductor. 2017. (Nathan Hale's Hazardous Tales Ser.). (J). lib. bdg. 24.45 (978-0-606-40708-3(1)) Turtleback.

—The Underground Abductor (Nathan Hale's Hazardous Tales #5) An Abolitionist Tale about Harriet Tubman. 2015. (Nathan Hale's Hazardous Tales Ser.). (ENG., Illus.). 128p. (J). (gr. 3-9). 14.99 (978-1-4197-1536-5(4), 1103801) Abrams, Inc.

Hale, Sarah Elder, ed. Abraham Lincoln: Defender of the Union. 2005. (ENG., Illus.). 48p. (J). (gr. 3-9). 17.95 (978-0-8126-7902-1(4)) Cobblestone Pr.

—Nation at War: Soldiers, Saints, & Spies. 2005. (ENG., Illus.). 48p. (J). (gr. 3-9). 17.95 (978-0-8126-7900-7(8)) Cobblestone Pr.

—Robert E. Lee: Duty & Honor. 2005. (ENG., Illus.). 48p. (J). (gr. 3-9). 17.95 (978-0-8126-7905-2(9)) Cobblestone Pr.

—Ulysses S. Grant: Confident Leader & Hero. 2005. (ENG., Illus.). 48p. (J). (gr. 3-9). 17.95 (978-0-8126-7906-9(7)) Cobblestone Pr.

—Young Heroes of the North & South. 2005. (ENG., Illus.). 48p. (J). (gr. 3-9). 17.95 (978-0-8126-7901-4(6)) Cobblestone Pr.

Halfmann, Janet. Seven Miles to Freedom: The Robert Smalls Story, 1 vol. Smith, Duane, illus. 2008. 40p. (J). (gr. 1-6). (ENG.). pap. 12.95 (978-1-60060-986-2(4), leelowbooks); 17.95 (978-1-60060-232-0(0)) Lee & Low Bks., Inc.

Halls, Kelly Milner. Life During the Civil War, 1 vol. 2015. (Daily Life in US History Ser.). (ENG., Illus.). 48p. (J). (gr. 4-8). lib. bdg. 35.64 (978-1-62403-625-5(2), 16890) ABDO Publishing Co.

Hamen, Susan E. Civil War Aftermath & Reconstruction, 1 vol. 2016. (Essential Library of the Civil War Ser.). (ENG., Illus.). 112p. (J). (gr. 8-12). lib. bdg. 41.36 (978-1-68078-274-5(6), 21703, Essential Library) ABDO Publishing Co.

Harris, Duchess. The Grand Contraband Camp. 2018. (Freedom's Promise Ser.). (ENG., Illus.). 48p. (J). (gr. 4-8). lib. bdg. 35.64 (978-1-5321-1769-5(8), 30826) ABDO Publishing Co.

Hazen, Walter A. The Civil War. 2007. (Everyday Life (Good Year Books) Ser.). (Illus.). 92p. (J). (gr. 5-12). per. 12.95 (978-1-59647-199-3(9)) Good Year Bks.

Helweg, Laura. How Abraham Lincoln Fought the Civil War, 1 vol. 2017. (Presidents at War Ser.). (ENG.). 128p. (gr. 8-8). lib. bdg. 38.93 (978-0-7660-8525-1(2), 32e10f4d-cea7-4f45-af17-c9cffae4f869) Enslow Publishing, LLC.

Hernández, Roger E. & Hernández, Roger E. The Civil War, 1840s-1890s, 1 vol. 2009. (Hispanic America Ser.). (ENG.). 80p. (gr. 5-5). lib. bdg. 36.93 (978-0-7614-2939-5(5), cc454e86-45da-4258-b12d-fad641b1dcec) Cavendish Square Publishing LLC.

Herschbach, Elisabeth. Black Soldiers in the Civil War. 2020. (Civil War Ser.). (ENG., Illus.). 48p. (J). (gr. 5-6). pap. 11.95 (978-1-64493-157-8(5), 1644931575); lib. bdg. 34.21 (978-1-64493-078-6(1), 1644930781) North Star Editions. (Focus Readers).

Herwick Rice, Dona & Conklin, Wendy. Causes of the Civil War, 1 vol. rev. ed. 2009. (Reader's Theater Ser.). (ENG.). 32p. (J). (gr. 3-8). pap. 11.99 (978-1-4333-0545-0(3)) Teacher Created Materials, Inc.

Hirsch, E. D., Jr., ed. The Civil War, Level 5. tchr. ed. 9.95 (978-0-7690-5081-2(6)); stu. ed. 49.95 (978-0-7690-2848-4(9)) Pearson Learning.

Hoogenboom, Lynn. William Tecumseh Sherman: The Fight to Preserve the Union. 2009. (Library of American Lives & Times Ser.). 112p. (gr. 5-5). 69.20 (978-1-60853-511-8(8)) Rosen Publishing Group, Inc., The.

Howell, Brian. The US Civil War & Reconstruction. 2011. (Explorer Library: Language Arts Explorer Ser.). (ENG., Illus.). 32p. (gr. 4-8). lib. bdg. 32.07 (978-1-61080-201-7(2), 201178) Cherry Lake Publishing.

—The U.S. Civil War & Reconstruction. 2011. (Explorer Library: Language Arts Explorer Ser.). (ENG.). 32p. (gr. 4-8). pap. 14.21 (978-1-61080-289-5(6), 201212) Cherry Lake Publishing.

Howell, Sara. The Civil War: Frontline Soldiers & Their Families, 1 vol. 2015. (Frontline Families Ser.). (ENG., Illus.). 48p. (J). (gr. 5-6). pap. 15.05 (978-1-4824-3057-8(6), f4d6d2d2-92b3-443e-ad7c-2f201db3da9a) Stevens, Gareth Publishing LLLP.

Howse, Jennifer. The Civil War. 2008. (African American History Ser.). (Illus.). 48p. (YA). (gr. 5-8). pap. 10.95 (978-1-59036-877-0(0)); lib. bdg. 29.05 (978-1-59036-876-3(2)) Weigl Pubs., Inc.

—Civil War. 2013. (J). (978-1-62127-191-8(9)); pap. (978-1-62127-197-0(8)) Weigl Pubs., Inc.

Hutchison, Patricia. The Civil War: 12 Things to Know. 2017. (America at War Ser.). (ENG., Illus.). 32p. (J). (gr. 3-6). 32.80 (978-1-63235-265-1(6), 11704, 12-Story Library) Bookstaves, LLC.

Idzikowski, Lisa. The Real Story Behind the Civil War, 1 vol. 2019. (Real Story: Debunking History Ser.). (ENG.). 32p. (gr. 4-5). 27.93 (978-1-5383-4344-9(4), 0b220f88-dfd8-4d38-b294-33f49bef9112, PowerKids Pr.) Rosen Publishing Group, Inc., The.

Imery-Garcia, Ash. Loreta Janeta Velázquez: Cuban Confederate Soldier, 1 vol. 2019. (Our Voices: Spanish & Latino Figures of American History Ser.). (ENG.). 48p. (gr. 6-6). pap. 12.75 (978-1-5081-8516-1(6), 7d47c243-edc0-427a-99f4-b4b7b25f082e, Rosen Reference) Rosen Publishing Group, Inc., The.

Junyk, Myra. The 10 Most Defining Moments of the Civil War. 2008. (J). 14.99 (978-1-55448-518-5(5)) Scholastic Library Publishing.

Kalman, Maira. Looking at Lincoln. Kalman, Maira, illus. 2017. (ENG., Illus.). 48p. (J). (gr. k-3). pap. 8.99 (978-0-14-751798-2(2), Puffin Books) Penguin Young Readers Group.

Kanefield, Teri. Abraham Lincoln: The Making of America #3. 2018. (Making of America Ser.). (ENG., Illus.). 240p. (J). (gr. 5-9). 16.99 (978-1-4197-3159-4(9), 1198001, Abrams Bks. for Young Readers) Abrams, Inc.

Kantor, MacKinlay. Lee & Grant at Appomattox. 2015. (ENG.). 144p. pap. 9.95 (978-0-9904604-0-4(1)) Flying Point Pr.

Kawa, Katie. Slavery Wasn't Only in the South: Exposing Myths about the Civil War, 1 vol. 2019. (Exposed! More Myths about American History Ser.). (ENG.). 32p. (gr. 2-3). pap. 11.50 (978-1-5382-3754-0(7), 85774fa5-adde-4413-acf7-8701cefd0381) Stevens, Gareth Publishing LLLP.

Kay, Betty Carlson. The Civil War from A to Z: Two Points of View. 2010. 144p. pap. 11.70 (978-1-4520-9451-9(9)) AuthorHouse.

Kent, Deborah. The Great Civil War Draft Riots. 2005. (Cornerstones of Freedom Ser.). (ENG., Illus.). 48p. (YA). (gr. 4-7). lib. bdg. 26.00 (978-0-516-23632-2(6)) Scholastic Library Publishing.

Kent, Zachary A. The Civil War: From Fort Sumter to Appomattox, 1 vol. 2011. (United States at War Ser.). (ENG., Illus.). 128p. (gr. 5-6). lib. bdg. 35.93 (978-0-7660-3638-3(3), 20e864cb-77c9-4177-a1b5-fa80d19b5236) Enslow Publishing, LLC.

Kerley, Barbara. Walt Whitman: Words for America, 1 vol. Selznick, Brian, illus. 2004. (ENG.). 56p. (gr. 2-5). 19.99 (978-0-439-35791-3(8), Scholastic Pr.) Scholastic, Inc.

Kirkman, Marissa. The Life & Times of Abraham Lincoln & the U. S. Civil War. 2016. (Life & Times Ser.). (ENG., Illus.). 24p. (J). (gr. 1-3). lib. bdg. 27.99 (978-1-5157-2474-2(3), 132846, Capstone Pr.) Capstone.

Kissock, Heather. Civil War & Reconstruction. 2016. (Illus.). 48p. (J). (978-1-5105-1280-1(2)) SmartBook Media, Inc.

Kolpin, Amanda & Kolpin, Molly. The Story of the Civil War, 1 vol. 2014. (Story of the Civil War Ser.). (ENG.). 32p. (J). (gr. 3-6). pap., pap., pap. 31.80 (978-1-4914-0738-7(7), 21510, Capstone Pr.) Capstone.

Kolpin, Molly & Kolpin, Amanda. The Story of the Civil War, 1 vol. 2014. (Story of the Civil War Ser.). (ENG.). 32p. (J). (gr.

TUV

3-6). 119.96 (978-1-4914-0737-0(9), 21509, Capstone Pr.) Capstone.
Kopp, Megan. The Civil War. 2018. (Uncovering the Past: Analyzing Primary Sources Ser.). (Illus.). 48p. (J). (gr. 5-6). (978-0-7787-4814-4(6)) Crabtree Publishing Co.
Krull, Kathleen & Brewer, Paul. Lincoln Tells a Joke: How Laughter Saved the President (and the Country) Innerst, Stacy, illus. 2010. (ENG.). 40p. (J). (gr. 1-4). 17.99 (978-0-15-206639-0(X), 1199695, Clarion Bks.) HarperCollins Pubs.
Lanser, Amanda. The Civil War by the Numbers. 2015. (America at War by the Numbers Ser.). (ENG., Illus.). 32p. (J). (gr. 3-9). lib. bdg. 28.65 (978-1-4914-4295-1(6), 128690, Capstone Pr.) Capstone.
Lassieur, Allison. At Battle in the Civil War: An Interactive Battlefield Adventure. 2015. (You Choose: Battlefields Ser.). (ENG., Illus.). 112p. (J). (gr. 3-4). pap. 32.65 (978-1-4914-2149-9(5), 127630, Capstone Pr.) Capstone.
Levy, Debbie. Soldier Song: A True Story of the Civil War. Ford, Gilbert, illus. 2017. (ENG.). 80p. (J). (gr. 3-7). 18.99 (978-1-4847-2598-6(0)) Disney Pr.
MacCarald, Clara. Children During the Civil War. 2018. (Children in History Ser.). (ENG., Illus.). 48p. (J). (gr. 5-6). pap. 11.95 (978-1-63517-973-6(4), 1635179734); lib. bdg. 34.21 (978-1-63517-872-2(X), 163517872X) North Star Editions. (Focus Readers).
Machajewski, Sarah. A Kid's Life During the American Civil War, 1 vol. 2014. (How Kids Lived Ser.). (ENG., Illus.). 24p. (J). (gr. 3-3). lib. bdg. 25.27 (978-1-4994-0004-5(7), 627cc90f-865e-42c7-8729-8fb29da6fff2, PowerKids Pr.) Rosen Publishing Group, Inc., The.
Marcovitz, Hal. Confederate Flag: Controversial Symbol of the South. Moreno, Barry, ed. 2014. (Patriotic Symbols of America Ser.: 20). 48p. (J). (gr. 4-18). 20.95 (978-1-4222-3121-0(6)) Mason Crest.
Marsh, Carole. What Was the Civil War All about Anyway? 2010. (Student's Civil War, 150th Anniversary: 1861-1865 Ser.). (Illus.). 36p. (J). pap. 9.99 (978-0-635-07640-3(3)) Gallopade International.
—When Did It Happen in the Civil War? 2010. (Civil War Ser.). (Illus.). 36p. (J). pap. 9.99 (978-0-635-07641-0(1)) Gallopade International.
—Where Did the Civil War Happen? 2010. (Student's Civil War, 150th Anniversary: 1861-1865 Ser.). (Illus.). 36p. (J). pap. 9.99 (978-0-635-07642-7(X)) Gallopade International.
—Who Were the Key Players in the Civil War? 2010. (Student's Civil War, 150th Anniversary: 1861-1865 Ser.). (Illus.). 36p. (J). pap. 9.99 (978-0-635-07639-7(X)) Gallopade International.
Martin, Iain C. Gettysburg: The True Account of Two Young Heroes in the Greatest Battle of the Civil War. (ENG., Illus.). 208p. (gr. 6-6). 2015. (J). pap. 16.99 (978-1-63220-438-7(X)) 2013. (YA). 16.95 (978-1-62087-532-2(2), 620532) Skyhorse Publishing Co., Inc. (Sky Pony Pr.).
Martinez, Manuel. Bloodiest Civil War Battles: Looking at Data, 1 vol. 2017. (Computer Kids: Powered by Computational Thinking Ser.). (ENG.). 24p. (J). (gr. 3-4). 25.27 (978-1-5383-2389-2(3), 07fa736b-828d-4906-a097-a259bb30d5d4, PowerKids Pr.); pap. (978-1-5081-3780-1(3), 6405af4d-60cd-454f-9bc4-76fbe774eeab, Rosen Classroom) Rosen Publishing Group, Inc., The.
McNamara, Margaret. Discover the North & the South. 2006. (J). pap. (978-1-4108-6447-5(2)) Benchmark Education Co.
—The North & the South. 2006. (J). pap. (978-1-4108-6444-4(8)) Benchmark Education Co.
McNeese, Tim. Robert E. Lee. 2009. (Leaders of the Civil War Era Ser.). (ENG., Illus.). 152p. (gr. 6-12). lib. bdg. 35.00 (978-1-60413-304-2(X), P162088, Facts On File) Infobase Holdings, Inc.
Meacham, Margaret. Oyster Moon, 1 vol. 2009. (ENG., Illus.). 112p. (J). (gr. 8-18). pap. 9.95 (978-0-87033-459-7(X), 9780870334597, Cornell Maritime Pr./Tidewater Pubs.) Schiffer Publishing, Ltd.
Meltzer, Brad. I Am Abraham Lincoln. Eliopoulos, Christopher, illus. 2014. (Ordinary People Change the World Ser.). 40p. (J). (gr. k-4). 15.99 (978-0-8037-4083-9(2), Dial Bks) Penguin Young Readers Group.
Meltzer, Brad. Soy Abraham Lincoln. Eliopoulos, Christopher, illus. 2023.Tr. of I Am Abraham Lincoln. (SPA.). (J). (gr. k-3). pap. 14.99 **(978-1-5433-8602-8(4))** Vista Higher Learning, Inc.
Meriwether, Louise & Green, Jonathan. The Freedom Ship of Robert Smalls. 2018. (Young Palmetto Bks.). (ENG., Illus.). 32p. (J). 19.99 (978-1-61117-855-5(X), P568005) Univ. of South Carolina Pr.
Micklos Jr., John. A Primary Source History of the US Civil War. 2016. (Primary Source History Ser.). (ENG., Illus.). 32p. (J). (gr. 3-6). lib. bdg. 27.99 (978-1-4914-8489-0(6), 130947, Capstone Pr.) Capstone.
Miller, Mirella S. 12 Questions about the Gettysburg Address. 2017. (Examining Primary Sources Ser.). (ENG., Illus.). 32p. (J). (gr. 3-6). 32.80 (978-1-63235-284-2(2), 11753, 12-Story Library) Bookstaves, LLC.
Miller, Reagan & Claus, J. Matteson. Life on a Civil War Battlefield. 2011. (ENG.). 48p. (J). pap. (978-0-7787-5357-5(3)); lib. bdg. (978-0-7787-5340-7(9)) Crabtree Publishing Co.
Miller, Reagan & Cocca, Lisa Colozza. Reconstruction & the Aftermath of the Civil War. 2011. (ENG.). 48p. (J). pap. (978-0-7787-5358-2(1)); lib. bdg. (978-0-7787-5341-4(7)) Crabtree Publishing Co.
Miller, Reagan & Doak, Melissa J. Life on the Homefront During the Civil War. 2011. (ENG.). 48p. (J). pap. (978-0-7787-5361-2(1)); lib. bdg. (978-0-7787-5344-5(1)) Crabtree Publishing Co.
Miller, Reagan & Gould, Jane H. The Civil War Begins. 2011. (ENG.). 48p. (J). pap. (978-0-7787-5355-1(7)); lib. bdg. (978-0-7787-5338-4(7)) Crabtree Publishing Co.
Miller, Reagan & Putnam, Jeff. A Nation Divided: Causes of the Civil War. 2011. (ENG.). 48p. (J). pap. (978-0-7787-5354-4(9)); lib. bdg. (978-0-7787-5337-7(9)) Crabtree Publishing Co.
Morris, Rob & Marcello, Paul. The Civil War Close Up, 1 vol. 2015. (War Chronicles Ser.). (ENG., Illus.). 72p. (YA). (gr. 9-9). 36.13 (978-1-4994-6160-2(7), 4d8a1dc1-c175-43be-8df8-7f7ed6cea179, Rosen Young Adult) Rosen Publishing Group, Inc., The.
Morrison, Taylor. Civil War Artist. 2004. (ENG., Illus.). 32p. (J). (gr. -1-3). pap. 5.95 (978-0-618-49538-2(X), 499080, Clarion Bks.) HarperCollins Pubs.
Moss, Marissa. Nurse, Soldier, Spy: The Story of Sarah Edmonds, a Civil War Hero. 2016. (ENG., Illus.). 48p. (J). (gr. 1-4). pap. 9.95 (978-1-4197-2065-9(1), 658703, Abrams Bks. for Young Readers) Abrams, Inc.
—Nurse, Soldier, Spy: The Story of Sarah Edmonds, a Civil War Hero. Hendrix, John, illus. 2011. (ENG.). 48p. (J). (gr. 3-7). 19.95 (978-0-8109-9735-6(5), 658701, Abrams Bks. for Young Readers) Abrams, Inc.
Mountjoy, Shane. Causes of the Civil War: The Differences Between the North & South. 2009. (Civil War: a Nation Divided Ser.). (ENG., Illus.). 144p. (gr. 6-12). 35.00 (978-1-60413-036-2(9), P165050, Facts On File) Infobase Holdings, Inc.
Murray, Hallie. The Role of Female Doctors & Nurses in the Civil War, 1 vol. 2019. (Warrior Women in American History Ser.). (ENG.). 104p. (gr. 7-7). pap. 21.00 (978-1-5026-5543-1(8), 1d4603e4-36a5-404a-8032-14ce1cb0311f); lib. bdg. 44.50 (978-1-5026-5544-8(6), a5c3b949-3c8d-40e5-8e7a-8277fd0a565b) Cavendish Square Publishing LLC.
—The Role of Female Doctors & Nurses in the Civil War. 2019. pap. (978-1-9785-1407-2(7)) Enslow Publishing, LLC.
Murray, Stuart A. P. Mathew Brady: Photographer of Our Nation: Photographer of Our Nation. 2009. (ENG., Illus.). 83p. (gr. 6-18). lib. bdg. 180.00 (978-0-7656-8151-5(X), Y182957) Routledge.
Nardo, Don. Bull Run to Gettysburg: Early Battles of the Civil War, 1 vol. 2010. (Civil War Ser.). (ENG.). 64p. (J). (gr. 5-9). lib. bdg. 34.65 (978-0-7565-4368-6(1), 103325, Compass Point Bks.) Capstone.
—The Civil War, 1 vol. 2008. (American History Ser.). (ENG.). 104p. (gr. 7-7). pap. 29.30 (978-1-4205-0302-9(2), c76d53a8-1719-4d90-9a47-3a5eb761f337); (Illus.). 41.03 (978-1-4205-0065-3(1), 8e960008-977b-42a5-ad59-9737d4bc2924) Greenhaven Publishing LLC. (Lucent Pr.).
Nelson, Sheila. Americans Divided: The Civil War. 2006. (How America Became America Ser.). (Illus.). 96p. (YA). lib. bdg. 22.95 (978-1-59084-908-8(6)) Mason Crest.
Nemeth, Jason. Voices of the Civil War: Stories from the Battlefields, 1 vol. 2010. (Voices of War Ser.). (ENG., Illus.). 32p. (J). (gr. 3-9). pap. 8.29 (978-1-4296-5625-2(5), 114116) Capstone.
Newsome, Joel. Minority Soldiers Fighting in the Civil War, 1 vol. 2017. (Fighting for Their Country: Minorities at War Ser.). (ENG.). 112p. (YA). (gr. 8-8). 44.50 (978-1-5026-2662-2(4), 2f6e3120-31f9-40f3-9b08-8640b8a8d70a) Cavendish Square Publishing LLC.
Nextext, creator. The Civil War: 1860-1865. 2004. (Stories in History Ser.). (Illus.). 205p. (J). (gr. 3-7). 13.32 (978-0-618-14214-9(2), 2-00234) Holt McDougal.
Ohlin, Nancy. The Civil War. Larkum, Adam, illus. 2016. (Blast Back! Ser.). (ENG.). 112p. (J). (gr. 2-5). pap. 5.99 (978-1-4998-0120-0(3)) Little Bee Books Inc.
Olson, Kay Melchisedech. The Terrible, Awful Civil War: The Disgusting Details about Life During America's. 2010. (Disgusting History Ser.). (ENG.). 32p. (J). (gr. 3-4). pap. 49.60 (978-1-4296-6480-6(0), 16232, Capstone Pr.) Capstone.
—The Terrible, Awful Civil War: The Disgusting Details about Life During America's Bloodiest War. 2010. (Disgusting History Ser.). (ENG.). 32p. (J). (gr. 3-6). pap. 8.10 (978-1-4296-6349-6(9), 115546); lib. bdg. 27.99 (978-1-4296-3960-6(1), 102570) Capstone.
Olson, Steve. Lincoln's Gettysburg Address: A Primary Source Investigation, 1 vol. 2004. (Great Historic Debates & Speeches Ser.). (ENG.). 64p. (YA). (gr. 5-8). pap. 13.95 (978-1-4358-3275-6(2), 0f4bd463-1b63-4906-8041-7269a5e59f9a) Rosen Publishing Group, Inc., The.
Olson, Steven P. Lincoln's Gettysburg Address: A Primary Source Investigation. 2009. (Great Historic Debates & Speeches Ser.). 64p. (gr. 5-8). 58.50 (978-1-61513-115-0(9)) Rosen Publishing Group, Inc., The.
O'Muhr, G. Causes & Effects of the American Civil War. 2009. (American History Milestones Ser.). 32p. (gr. 5-5). 47.90 (978-1-61511-373-6(8)); (ENG.). (J). lib. bdg. 28.93 (978-1-4358-3013-4(X), 4a3d23ff-223f-4ead-996a-2182c870852e) Rosen Publishing Group, Inc., The. (PowerKids Pr.).
O'Muhr, G. & Flynn, Claire E. Causes & Effects of the American Civil War, 1 vol. 2008. (Real Life Readers Ser.). (ENG., Illus.). 32p. (J). (gr. 5-5). pap. 10.00 (978-1-4358-0203-2(9), 52e8972d-a02c-44f8-b29c-a9052a4c5a0d, PowerKids Pr.) Rosen Publishing Group, Inc., The.
Orr, Tamra. The Railroad & the Civil War (1860s) 2012. (J). lib. bdg. 29.95 (978-1-61228-289-3(X)) Mitchell Lane Pubs.
Otfinoski, Steven. The Split History of the Battle of Fort Sumter: A Perspectives Flip Book. 2018. (Perspectives Flip Books: Famous Battles Ser.). (ENG., Illus.). 64p. (J). (gr. 5-9). lib. bdg. 34.65 (978-0-7565-5689-1(9), 137034, Compass Point Bks.) Capstone.
Page, Thomas Nelson. A Captured Santa Claus. reprint ed. pap. 28.00 (978-1-4047-4699-2(4)) Classic Textbooks.
—A Captured Santa Claus. 2013. (Notable American Authors Ser.). reprint ed. lthr. 79.00 (978-0-7812-4699-6(7)) Reprint Services Corp.
Parker, Christi E. Abraham Lincoln, 1 vol. rev. ed. 2005. (Social Studies: Informational Text Ser.). (ENG.). 24p. (gr. 4-8). pap. 10.99 (978-0-7439-8916-9(3)) Teacher Created Materials, Inc.
—Civil War Is Coming, 1 vol. rev. ed. 2005. (Social Studies: Informational Text Ser.). (ENG.). 24p. (gr. 4-8). pap. 10.99 (978-0-7439-8915-2(5)) Teacher Created Materials, Inc.
Perritano, John. The Ghosts of Civil War Soldiers, 1 vol. 2014. (Jr. Graphic Ghost Stories Ser.). (ENG.). 24p. (J). (gr. 2-3). lib. bdg. 28.93 (978-1-4777-7133-4(6), b9afdcaf-bcd7-45eb-ab30-e3830907b0c0, PowerKids Pr.) Rosen Publishing Group, Inc., The.
Phillips, Larissa. Women Civil War Spies of the Confederacy, 1 vol. 2004. (American Women at War Ser.). (ENG., Illus.). 112p. (gr. 8-8). lib. bdg. 39.80 (978-0-8239-4451-4(4), 0e231b97-a361-4988-a631-9ba03b3bf6f3) Rosen Publishing Group, Inc., The.
Pierre, Yvette. Living Through the Civil War. 2018. (American Culture & Conflict Ser.). (ENG., Illus.). 48p. (gr. 4-8). lib. bdg. 35.64 (978-1-64156-415-1(6), 9781641564151) Rourke Educational Media.
Pingry, Patricia A. Meet Robert E. Lee. Johnson, Meredith, illus. 2004. (J). 9.95 (978-0-8249-5465-9(3), Ideals Pubns.) Worthy Publishing.
—Story of Star Spangled Banner. 2014. (ENG., Illus.). 24p. (J). (gr. -1-1). bds. 6.99 (978-0-8249-1930-6(0), Ideals Pubns.) Worthy Publishing.
Poulakidas, Georgene. The Civil War, 1 vol. 2005. (Primary Sources of American Wars Ser.). (ENG., Illus.). 24p. (J). (gr. 3-4). pap. 9.25 (978-1-4358-3276-3(0), 903a62b5-7560-4a7f-a74a-99f21cc820f5, PowerKids Pr.) Rosen Publishing Group, Inc., The.
Provost Beller, Susan. The Civil War, 1 vol. 2003. (American Voices From Ser.). (ENG., Illus.). 160p. (gr. 6-6). 41.21 (978-0-7614-1204-5(2), c96d484e-8d5c-4e83-981e-fcf57a4e5279) Cavendish Square Publishing LLC.
Publishers, Chelsea House, creator. The Civil War: A Nation Divided Set. 2009. (Civil War: a Nation Divided Ser.). (ENG.). (gr. 6-12). 280.00 (978-1-60413-653-1(7), P166847, Facts On File) Infobase Holdings, Inc.
Randolph, Jennifer & Benchmark Education Co. Staff. Women of the Civil War. 2014. (Text Connections Ser.). (J). (gr. 5). (978-1-4900-1377-0(6)) Benchmark Education Co.
Randolph, Joanne, ed. The Cavalry in the Civil War, 1 vol. 2018. (Civil War & Reconstruction: Rebellion & Rebuilding Ser.). (ENG., Illus.). 32p. (J). (gr. 4-5). 27.93 (978-1-5383-4085-1(2), a4607f6b-d1f5-4748-ab82-51fa38bd3270, PowerKids Pr.) Rosen Publishing Group, Inc., The.
Ransom, Candice. Willie Mclean & the Civil War Surrender. Reeves, Jeni, illus. 2004. (On My Own History Ser.). (ENG.). 48p. (J). (gr. 2-4). pap. 8.99 (978-1-57505-698-2(4), 89edad43-6a3a-40ef-aa5e-51fc2307aa25, First Avenue Editions) Lerner Publishing Group.
Rappaport, Doreen & Verniero, Joan C. United No More! Stories of the Civil War. Reeves, Rick, illus. 2006. 144p. (J). (gr. 3-7). lib. bdg. 17.89 (978-0-06-050600-1(8)) HarperCollins Pubs.
Ratliff, Thomas. You Wouldn't Want to Be a Civil War Soldier! A War You'd Rather Not Fight. Antram, David, illus. 2013. (You Wouldn't Want to... Ser.). (ENG.). 32p. (J). 29.00 (978-0-531-25947-4(1), Watts, Franklin) Scholastic Library Publishing.
Reynolds, Donna. The Civil War, 1 vol. 2020. (Turning Points Ser.). (ENG.). 104p. (J). (gr. 7-7). pap. 20.99 (978-1-5026-5762-6(7), db20a2d6-63fa-4e08-91d7-d4bfb2938472) Cavendish Square Publishing LLC.
Rice, Earle. The Life & Times of the Brothers Custer: Galloping to Glory. 2008. (Profiles in American History Ser.). (Illus.). 48p. (J). (gr. 4-8). lib. bdg. 29.95 (978-1-58415-665-9(1)) Mitchell Lane Pubs.
Rife, Douglas M. & Capaldi, Gina. Letters for Freedom: the Civil War. Lyall, Dennis, illus. 2011. (ENG.). 44p. (J). (gr. 3-17). 19.99 (978-1-60169-018-0(5)) Innovative Kids.
Roberts, Russell. The Formation of the Confederacy. 2020. (Civil War Ser.). (ENG., Illus.). 48p. (J). (gr. 5-6). pap. 11.95 (978-1-64493-160-8(5), 1644931605); lib. bdg. 34.21 (978-1-64493-081-6(1), 1644930811) North Star Editions. (Focus Readers).
Rodgers, Kelly. Civil War & Reconstruction in Florida. rev. ed. 2016. (Social Studies: Informational Text Ser.). (ENG.). 32p. (gr. 3-8). pap. 11.99 (978-1-4938-3539-3(4)) Teacher Created Materials, Inc.
Rogers, Amy B. Recipes of the Civil War, 1 vol. 2016. (Cooking Your Way Through American History Ser.). (ENG.). 24p. (J). (gr. 3-3). pap. 11.60 (978-1-5345-2088-2(0), d46016a6-1dbc-4c51-9731-e95f441b9d95, KidHaven Publishing) Greenhaven Publishing LLC.
Rose, Simon. Civil War. 2014. (Illus.). 48p. (J). (978-1-4896-1554-1(7)) Weigl Pubs., Inc.
—The War of 1812. 2014. (Illus.). 48p. (J). (978-1-4896-0516-0(9)) Weigl Pubs., Inc.
Roxburgh, Ellis. Abraham Lincoln vs. Jefferson Davis: Presidents of a Divided Nation, 1 vol. 2015. (History's Greatest Rivals Ser.). (ENG., Illus.). 48p. (J). (gr. 6-8). pap. 15.05 (978-1-4824-4219-9(1), b135bb93-4357-466b-a1e4-3a9fd5bddc79) Stevens, Gareth Publishing LLLP.
—Ulysses S. Grant vs. Robert E. Lee: Civil War Rivals, 1 vol. 2014. (History's Greatest Rivals Ser.). (ENG.). 48p. (J). (gr. 6-8). lib. bdg. 33.60 (978-1-4824-2225-2(5), f75f3b37-f111-445a-8d6e-ee259f66309f) Stevens, Gareth Publishing LLLP.
Ruffin, Frances E. Clara Barton. 2009. (American Legends Ser.). 24p. (gr. 3-3). 42.50 (978-1-61511-379-8(7), PowerKids Pr.) Rosen Publishing Group, Inc., The.
Sakany, Lois. Women Civil War Spies of the Union, 1 vol. 2004. (American Women at War Ser.). (ENG., Illus.). 112p. (gr. 8-8). lib. bdg. 39.80 (978-0-8239-4450-7(6), badfd22d-70f2-4115-bb75-98ffbe423da6) Rosen Publishing Group, Inc., The.
Samuels, Charlie. Attack on Fort Sumter. 2014. (Turning Points in US Military History Ser.). (ENG.). 48p. (J). (gr. 5-8). 24.85 (978-1-5311-8637-1(8)) Perfection Learning Corp.
—The Attack on Fort Sumter, 1 vol., Vol. 1. 2013. (Turning Points in U. S. Military History Ser.). (ENG.). 48p. (J). (gr. 5-6). 34.61 (978-1-4824-0401-2(X), 3799e427-27f7-45ec-8bd2-3a1bc08c368e) Stevens, Gareth Publishing LLLP.
Sandler, Martin W. Civil War. 2014. (ENG., Illus.). 96p. (J). (gr. 3-18). pap. 12.99 (978-0-06-446264-8(1), HarperCollins) HarperCollins Pubs.
—What Was America's Deadliest War? And Other Questions about the Civil War. Hunt, Robert, illus. 2014. (Good Question! Ser.). (ENG.). 32p. (J). pap. 6.99 (978-1-4027-9046-1(5)) Sterling Publishing Co., Inc.
Scholastic Library Publishing. A True Book-the Civil War. 2011. (True Book-the Civil War Ser.). (J). 116.00 (978-0-531-24922-2(0), Children's Pr.) Scholastic Library Publishing.
Schomp, Virginia. The Civil War, 1 vol. 2005. (Letters from the Battlefront Ser.). (ENG., Illus.). 96p. (gr. 6-6). lib. bdg. 36.93 (978-0-7614-1660-9(9), 0daee61d-1f45-4e9f-b43d-4cda5e432351) Cavendish Square Publishing LLC.
Schroeder-Lein, Glenna R. The Encyclopedia of Civil War Medicine. 2008. (ENG., Illus.). 457p. (C). 180.00 (978-0-7656-1171-0(6), Y184328) Routledge.
Schwartz, Heather E. Causes of the Civil War: A House Divided. rev. ed. 2017. (Social Studies: Informational Text Ser.). (ENG., Illus.). 32p. (gr. 4-8). pap. 11.99 (978-1-4938-3803-5(2)) Teacher Created Materials, Inc.
Seabrook, Lochlainn. Honest Jeff & Dishonest Abe: A Southern Children's Guide to the Civil War. 2012. 318p. pap. 24.95 (978-0-9838185-9-5(2)) Sea Raven Pr.
—The Quotable Nathan Bedford Forrest: Selections from the Writings & Speeches of the Confederacy's Most Brilliant Cavalryman. 2012. (Illus.). 130p. pap. 12.95 (978-0-9838185-5-7(X)) Sea Raven Pr.
Sebree, Chet'la & Provost Beller, Susan. Historical Sources on the Civil War, 1 vol. 2019. (America's Story Ser.). (ENG.). 144p. (J). (gr. 8-8). pap. 22.16 (978-1-5026-4092-5(9), cd52cc71-9ec6-4bcd-ba65-fdc0526755ba) Cavendish Square Publishing LLC.
Senior, Kathryn. You Wouldn't Want to Be a Nurse During the American Civil War! A Job That's Not for the Squeamish. 2010. (You Wouldn't Want to... Ser.). 32p. (J). 29.00 (978-0-531-20506-8(1), Watts, Franklin) Scholastic Library Publishing.
Shattuck, Jason. The Civil War, 1 vol., 1. 2015. (Early American History Ser.). (ENG., Illus.). 80p. (J). (gr. 8-8). 35.47 (978-1-68048-272-0(6), d8dbbf81-4525-4170-805c-84f6fa27be06, Britannica Educational Publishing) Rosen Publishing Group, Inc., The.
Shea, Therese. Interpreting America's Civil War: Organizing & Interpreting Information in Outlines, Graphs, Timelines, Maps, & Charts. 2009. (Critical Thinking in American History Ser.). 48p. (gr. 5-8). 53.00 (978-1-61512-094-9(7), Rosen Reference) Rosen Publishing Group, Inc., The.
Sheffield, Sarah. Life During the American Civil War. 2009. (Reading Room Collection 2 Ser.). 24p. (gr. 3-4). 42.50 (978-1-60851-978-1(3), PowerKids Pr.) Rosen Publishing Group, Inc., The.
Shoup, Kate. Life As a Soldier in the Civil War, 1 vol. 2015. (Life As... Ser.). (ENG., Illus.). 32p. (gr. 3-3). pap. 11.58 (978-1-5026-1083-6(3), 5dc3d5b6-a27f-4e0c-9e90-74c7d6dd040a) Cavendish Square Publishing LLC.
Sjonger, Rebecca. Abraham Lincoln: The Gettysburg Address. 2019. (Deconstructing Powerful Speeches Ser.). 48p. (J). (gr. 6-6). pap. (978-0-7787-5253-0(4)) Crabtree Publishing Co.
Smith, Debra. Young Heroes of the Confederacy, 1 vol. 2012. (ENG., Illus.). 128p. (J). (gr. 3-7). pap. 12.95 (978-1-4556-1684-8(2), Pelican Publishing) Arcadia Publishing.
Sodaro, Craig. Civil War Spies. 2013. 48p. pap. 9.95 (978-1-4765-3590-6(6)) Capstone.
Spitz, Michael. Life As a Doctor in the Civil War, 1 vol. 2017. (Life As... Ser.). (ENG.). 32p. (gr. 3-3). pap. 11.58 (978-1-5026-3035-3(4), e11411b3-38c4-4f65-a99a-a2e86b7df7dd) Cavendish Square Publishing LLC.
Stanley, George E. The Crisis of the Union (1815-1865), 1 vol. 2004. (Primary Source History of the United States Ser.). (ENG., Illus.). 48p. (gr. 5-8). pap. 15.05 (978-0-8368-5835-8(2), 452e7b11-2a34-4839-b274-bb66ff248c3b); lib. bdg. 33.67 (978-0-8368-5826-6(3), 6147e996-e6b7-46a9-a707-c5808e70afc4) Stevens, Gareth Publishing LLLP. (Gareth Stevens Secondary Library).
Steele, Philip. Did Anything Good Come Out of the Civil War?, 1 vol., 1. 2015. (Innovation Through Adversity Ser.). (ENG.). 48p. (J). (gr. 6-7). 33.47 (978-1-5081-7074-7(6), e1e6116b-932c-4e91-b2ab-ce5159bd6a13, Rosen Young Adult) Rosen Publishing Group, Inc., The.
Stefoff, Rebecca. The Civil War, 1861-1863, 1 vol. 2003. (North American Historical Atlases Ser.). (ENG., Illus.). 48p. (gr. 5-5). 32.64 (978-0-7614-1346-2(4), 7a732198-d893-4465-a19f-e1968738d330) Cavendish Square Publishing LLC.
—The Civil War & Reconstruction, 1863-1877, 1 vol. 2003. (North American Historical Atlases Ser.). (ENG., Illus.). 48p. (gr. 5-5). 32.64 (978-0-7614-1347-9(2), 2e3d0af5-5fd6-47eb-aef0-579b0aaea21c) Cavendish Square Publishing LLC.
Stewart, Whitney. Mr. Lincoln's Gift: A Civil War Story. Dunham Akiyama, Laine, illus. 2008. 32p. (J). 19.95 (978-0-9754917-4-4(1)) Friends of Hildene, Inc.
Stotts, Stuart. Lucius Fairchild: Civil War Hero. 2011. (Badger Biographies Ser.). (ENG., Illus.). 112p. (J). pap. 12.95 (978-0-87020-460-9(2)) Wisconsin Historical Society.
Streissguth, Tom. Sherman's March to the Sea. 2020. (Civil War Ser.). (ENG., Illus.). 48p. (J). (gr. 5-6). lib. bdg. 34.21 (978-1-64493-084-7(6), 1644930846, Focus Readers) North Star Editions.
—Sherman's March to the Sea. 2020. (Civil War Ser.). (ENG., Illus.). 48p. (J). (gr. 5-6). pap. 11.95 (978-1-64493-163-9(X), 164493163X, Focus Readers) North Star Editions.
Sutherland, Jonathan. Civil War Victory & the Costly Aftermath. 2017. (Civil War Ser.: Vol. 5). (ENG., Illus.). 79p. (YA). (gr. 7-12). 24.95 (978-1-4222-3886-8(5)) Mason Crest.
—The Origins of the Civil War. 2017. (Civil War Ser.: Vol. 5). (ENG., Illus.). 79p. (YA). (gr. 7-12). 24.95 (978-1-4222-3882-0(2)) Mason Crest.
—The Politics of the Civil War. 2017. (Civil War Ser.: Vol. 5). (ENG., Illus.). 79p. (J). (gr. 7-12). 24.95 (978-1-4222-3885-1(7)) Mason Crest.
—Slavery & the Abolition Movement. 2017. (Civil War Ser.: Vol. 5). (ENG., Illus.). 79p. (J). (gr. 7-12). 24.95 (978-1-4222-3883-7(0)) Mason Crest.
Thompson, Ben. Guts & Glory: the American Civil War. Butzer, C. M., illus. 2015. (Guts & Glory Ser.: 1). (ENG.). 352p. (J).

(gr. 3-7). pap. 8.99 *(978-0-316-32051-1(X))* Little, Brown Bks. for Young Readers.

Thompson, Michael D. Working on the Dock of the Bay: Labor & Enterprise in an Antebellum Southern Port. 2018. (ENG., Illus.). 296p. (J). pap. 31.99 *(978-1-61117-857-9(6),* P568034) Univ. of South Carolina Pr.

Trumbauer, Lisa. Abraham Lincoln & the Civil War. rev. ed. 2016. (Life in the Time Of Ser.). (ENG.). 32p. (J). (gr. 1-3). pap. 8.29 *(978-1-4846-3822-4(0),* 134722, Heinemann) Capstone.

Turner, Thomas. 101 Things You Didn't Know about the Civil War: The People, Battles, & Events That Defined the War Between the States. 2018. (101 Things Ser.). (ENG., Illus.). 240p. pap. 14.99 *(978-1-5072-0926-4(6))* Adams Media Corp.

Uschan, Michael V. Fort Sumter: the Civil War Begins, 1 vol. 2004. (Landmark Events in American History Ser.). (ENG., Illus.). 48p. (gr. 5-8). pap. 15.05 *(978-0-8368-5423-7(3),* f2072275-921f-4e0a-8f62-626cfa436310); lib. bdg. 33.67 *(978-0-8368-5395-7(4),* 73887cc9-c06e-4302-8f18-3120ba2f7f2c) Stevens, Gareth Publishing LLLP. (Gareth Stevens Secondary Library).

Vierow, Wendy. The Assault on Fort Wagner: Black Union Soldiers Make a Stand in South Carolina Battle. (Headlines from History Ser.). 24p. (gr. 3-3). 2009. 42.50 *(978-1-61513-240-9(6),* PowerKids Pr.) 2004. (ENG., Illus.). (YA). lib. bdg. 26.27 *(978-0-8239-6223-5(7),* ed030bee-610d-49db-bef8-b95145c9aa14) Rosen Publishing Group, Inc., The.

—Shots Fired at Fort Sumter, 1 vol. 2004. (Headlines from History Ser.). (ENG., Illus.). 24p. (J). (gr. 3-3). lib. bdg. 26.27 *(978-0-8239-6220-4(2),* c8c172c2-feda-4992-8986-3145f785292d) Rosen Publishing Group, Inc., The.

—Shots Fired at Fort Sumter: Civil War Breaks Out! 2009. (Headlines from History Ser.). 24p. (gr. 3-3). 42.50 *(978-1-61513-238-6(4),* PowerKids Pr.) Rosen Publishing Group, Inc., The.

Vonne, Mira. Gross Facts about the American Civil War. 2017. (Gross History Ser.). (ENG., Illus.). 32p. (J). (gr. 3-9). lib. bdg. 27.32 *(978-1-5157-4155-8(9),* 133955, Capstone Pr.) Capstone.

Walker, Sally M. Deadly Aim: The Civil War Story of Michigan's Anishinaabe Sharpshooters. 2019. (ENG., Illus.). 304p. (J). 19.99 *(978-1-250-12525-5(1),* 900174731, Holt, Henry & Co. Bks. For Young Readers) Holt, Henry & Co.

—Shipwreck Search: Discovery of the H. L. Hunley. Verstraete, Elaine, illus. 2007. (On My Own Science Ser.). (ENG.). 48p. (J). (gr. 2-4). per. 7.99 *(978-0-8225-6449-2(1),* c091eaf0-8595-4cc4-81dd-f04fe879a8c7, First Avenue Editions) Lerner Publishing Group.

Watkins, Samuel R. & Zeinert, Karen. The Diary of Sam Watkins, a Confederate Soldier, 1 vol. Kubinyi, Laszlo, illus. 2005. (In My Own Words Ser.). (ENG.). 64p. (gr. 6-6). lib. bdg. 34.07 *(978-0-7614-1646-3(3),* a1c27a5b-dfd0-4957-ab36-8a191680fbdd) Cavendish Square Publishing LLC.

We the People: Civil War Era. 2011. (We the People: Civil War Era Ser.). (ENG.). 48p. (gr. 5-6). pap. 79.50 *(978-0-7565-4538-3(2));* pap. 477.00 *(978-0-7565-4539-0(0))* Capstone. (Compass Point Bks.).

Westwell, Ian. The Civil War. 2008. (Wars Day by Day Ser.). (ENG.). 48p. (J). (gr. 5-8). 37.10 *(978-1-933834-38-2(2),* 16820) Brown Bear Bks.

Whitman Publishing, creator. Discover the Civil War: History Project Toolkit. 2011. pap. 19.95 *(978-0-7948-3587-3(2))* Whitman Publishing LLC.

Why We Fought: the Civil War Set, 5 vols. Incl. Battles of the Civil War. Fay, Gail. pap. 9.95 *(978-1-4329-3916-8(5),* 112828); Southern Home Front of the Civil War. Baxter, Roberta. pap. 9.95 *(978-1-4329-3918-2(1),* 112832); (J). (gr. 3-6). (Why We Fought: the Civil War Ser.). (ENG.). 48p. 2011. pap., pap., pap. 29.85 o.p. *(978-1-4329-3921-2(1),* 14906, Heinemann) Capstone.

Wilson, Camilla. Civil War Spies: Behind Enemy Lines. 2010. vii, 104p. (J). pap. *(978-0-545-13002-8(6))* Scholastic, Inc.

Windsor, Wesley. The Civil War: America Torn Apart, 1860-1865. 2012. (J). pap. *(978-1-4222-2418-2(X))* Mason Crest.

—The Civil War: America Torn Apart, 1860-1865. Rakove, Jack N., ed. 2012. (How America Became America Ser.). 48p. (J). (gr. 3-4). 19.95 *(978-1-4222-2404-5(X))* Mason Crest.

—The Civil War (1860/1865) 2018. (J). *(978-1-5105-3602-9(7))* SmartBook Media, Inc.

Wood, Ira. Fort Sumter: Where the Civil War Began. 2009. (Reading Room Collection 1 Ser.). 16p. (gr. 2-3). 37.50 *(978-1-60851-944-6(9),* PowerKids Pr.) Rosen Publishing Group, Inc., The.

World Book, Inc. Staff. Documenting History, 12 vols., Set. 2010. 768p. (YA). 329.00 *(978-0-7166-1498-2(7))* World Bk., Inc.

Yomtov, Nel. Civil War Weapons. 2016. (Essential Library of the Civil War Ser.). (ENG., Illus.). 112p. (J). (gr. 8-12). 59.93 *(978-1-68077-467-2(0),* 22358); lib. bdg. 41.36 *(978-1-68078-278-3(9),* 21711) ABDO Publishing Co. (Essential Library).

UNITED STATES—HISTORY—CIVIL WAR, 1861-1865—BIOGRAPHY

Anderson, Paul C. George Armstrong Custer: The Indian Wars & the Battle of the Little Bighorn. 2009. (Library of American Lives & Times Ser.). 112p. (gr. 5-5). 69.20 *(978-1-60853-483-8(9))* Rosen Publishing Group, Inc., The.

Bailey, Diane. General George Thomas: The Rock of Chickamauga. 2011. (J). *(978-1-59556-045-2(9));* pap. *(978-1-59556-051-3(3))* OTTN Publishing.

Brown Bear Books. People. 2011. (Civil War Ser.). (ENG.). 112p. (J). (gr. 9-12). 42.80 *(978-1-936333-47-9(3),* 16457) Brown Bear Bks.

Capstone Press. Voices of War. 2010. (Voices of War Ser.). (ENG.). 32p. lib. bdg. 106.60 *(978-1-4296-5905-5(X),* Capstone Pr.) Capstone.

Collins, Terry, et al. Stories of War. 2012. (Stories of War Ser.). (ENG.). 32p. (J). (gr. 3-9). 133.28 *(978-1-4296-9164-2(6),* 18453, Capstone Pr.) Capstone.

Conklin, Wendy. Civil War Leaders. rev. ed. (Social Studies: Informational Text Ser.). (ENG., (gr. 4-8). 2017. Illus.). 32p. pap. 11.99 *(978-1-4938-3887-5(3))* 2005. 24p. pap. 10.99 *(978-0-7439-8917-6(1))* Teacher Created Materials, Inc.

Cooke, Tim. Key Figures, 1 vol. 2012. (American Civil War: the Right Answer Ser.). (ENG., Illus.). 48p. (J). (gr. 6-8). 34.60 *(978-1-4339-7547-9(5),* 1cf96379-2a91-47f0-8720-88f41800bced); pap. 15.05 *(978-1-4339-7548-6(3),* 190e8121-c520-4988-ba42-3dd7662036a7) Stevens, Gareth Publishing LLLP. (Gareth Stevens Secondary Library).

Corrigan, Jim. General George G. Meade: Victor at Gettysburg. 2011. (J). *(978-1-59556-044-5(0));* pap. *(978-1-59556-050-6(5))* OTTN Publishing.

—General James Longstreet: Lee's "Old War Horse" 2012. (J). *(978-1-59556-043-8(2));* pap. *(978-1-59556-049-0(1))* OTTN Publishing.

Dell, Pamela. Memoir of Susie King Taylor: A Civil War Nurse. 2017. (First-Person Histories Ser.). (ENG.). 32p. (J). (gr. 3-6). pap. 8.95 *(978-1-5157-3356-0(4),* 133348); (Illus.). lib. bdg. 27.99 *(978-1-5157-3354-6(8),* 133346) Capstone. (Capstone Pr.).

Dougherty, Terri. Admiral David Farragut: "Full Speed Ahead!" 2011. (J). *(978-1-59556-041-4(6));* pap. *(978-1-59556-047-6(5))* OTTN Publishing.

Favor, Lesli J. Women Doctors & Nurses of the Civil War. 2009. (American Women at War Ser.). 112p. (gr. 8-8). 63.90 *(978-1-61511-404-7(1))* Rosen Publishing Group, Inc., The.

Favor, Leslie. Women Doctors & Nurses of the Civil War, 1 vol. 2004. (American Women at War Ser.). (ENG.). 112p. (YA). (gr. 8-8). pap. 13.95 *(978-1-4358-3273-2(6),* d5d1a2e9-429e-42e8-b242-5f13ee7d9c16) Rosen Publishing Group, Inc., The.

Fiore, Carmen Anthony. Young Heroes of the Civil War. 2006. (J). pap. *(978-0-88092-639-3(2));* lib. bdg. *(978-0-88092-638-6(4))* Royal Fireworks Publishing Co.

Friedman, Robin. The Silent Witness. Nivola, Claire A., illus. 2008. (ENG.). 32p. (J). (gr. -1-3). pap. 7.99 *(978-0-547-01436-4(8),* 1030951, Clarion Bks.) HarperCollins Pubs.

Gaines, Alison. Robert E. Lee: Commander of the Confederate Army, 1 vol. 2018. (Hero or Villain? Claims & Counterclaims Ser.). (ENG.). 112p. (YA). (gr. 8-8). lib. bdg. 45.93 *(978-1-5026-3529-7(1),* 51372946-9a07-4231-b080-f8ec6d117800) Cavendish Square Publishing LLC.

Haines, J. D. Put the Boys In: The Story of the Virginia Military Institute Cadets at the Battle of New Market. 2003. (Illus.). 69p. per. *(978-1-57168-816-3(1))* Eakin Pr.

Hale, Sarah Elder, ed. Nation at War: Soldiers, Saints, & Spies. 2005. (ENG., Illus.). 48p. (J). (gr. 3-9). 17.95 *(978-0-8126-7900-7(8))* Cobblestone Pr.

—Young Heroes of the North & South. 2005. (ENG., Illus.). 48p. (J). (gr. 3-9). 17.95 *(978-0-8126-7901-4(6))* Cobblestone Pr.

Harasymiw, Mark. Before Ulysses S. Grant Was President, 1 vol. 2018. (Before They Were President Ser.). (ENG.). 24p. (gr. 2-3). lib. bdg. 24.27 *(978-1-5382-2914-9(5),* 6482cc46-acdc-411d-b1c5-bfdd5c37de70) Stevens, Gareth Publishing LLLP.

Haskins, Jim. Black Stars of Civil War Times. 2003. (Black Stars Ser.: 2). (ENG., Illus.). 132p. (J). (gr. 5-9). pap. 12.95 *(978-0-471-22069-5(8))* Wiley, John & Sons, Inc.

Hughes, Christopher. The Civil War. 2003. (People at the Center of Ser.). (Illus.). 48p. (J). 24.95 *(978-1-56711-764-6(3),* Blackbirch Pr., Inc.) Cengage Gale.

Jones-Radgowski, Jehan. The Escape of Robert Smalls: A Daring Voyage Out of Slavery. Kang, Poppy, illus. 2019. (ENG.). 40p. (J). (gr. 3-6). 18.95 *(978-1-5435-1281-6(X),* 137747, Capstone Editions) Capstone.

King Taylor, Susie. The Diary of Susie King Taylor, Civil War Nurse, 1 vol. Kubinyi, Laszlo, illus. 2005. (In My Own Words Ser.). (ENG.). 64p. (gr. 6-6). lib. bdg. 34.07 *(978-0-7614-1648-7(X),* 48248ecd-081e-4457-96e8-f6e61b278e2f) Cavendish Square Publishing LLC.

Kolpin, Molly. Great Women of the Civil War, 1 vol. 2014. (Story of the Civil War Ser.). (ENG.). 32p. (J). (gr. 3-6). lib. bdg. 27.99 *(978-1-4914-0719-6(0),* 125972, Capstone Pr.) Capstone.

Lakin, Patricia. Clara Barton: Spirit of the American Red Cross (Ready-To-Read Level 3) Sullivan, Simon, illus. 2004. (Ready-To-Read Stories of Famous Americans Ser.). (ENG.). 48p. (J). (gr. 1-3). pap. 4.99 *(978-0-689-86513-8(9),* Simon Spotlight) Simon Spotlight.

Link, Theodore. George Armstrong Custer: General de la caballería Estadounidense, 1 vol. 2003. (Grandes Personajes en la Historia de los Estados Unidos (Famous People in American History) Ser.). (SPA.). 32p. (gr. 3-4). pap. 10.00 *(978-0-8239-4228-2(7),* a3d5578c-4708-4b0e-aa8f-8828084500a9, Rosen Classroom) Rosen Publishing Group, Inc., The.

—George Armstrong Custer: General of the U. S. Cavalry. (Primary Sources of Famous People in American History Ser.).Tr. of George Armstrong Custer: General de la Caballería Estadounidense. 32p. (gr. 2-3). 2009. 47.90 *(978-1-60851-680-3(6))* 2003. (ENG & SPA., Illus.). lib. bdg. 29.13 *(978-0-8239-4158-2(2),* e97ac072-83b4-46f2-a0fc-b11714411c70, Editorial Buenas Letras) Rosen Publishing Group, Inc., The.

Marsico, Katie. John Cook's Civil War Story. Belmonte, David, illus. 2018. (Narrative Nonfiction: Kids in War Ser.). (ENG.). 32p. (J). (gr. 2-4). 27.99 *(978-1-5124-5680-6(2),* 5f6f9e26-2fd6-4442-9c13-4ea16f171ba8, Lerner Pubns.); pap. 9.99 *(978-1-5415-1191-0(3),* 22ac3d17-499b-4ec8-b3fc-10cf1dced47f) Lerner Publishing Group.

Miller, Brandon Marie. Robert E. Lee: The Man, the Soldier, the Myth. 2019. (Illus.). 304p. (J). (gr. 5-12). 19.95 *(978-1-62979-910-0(6),* Calkins Creek) Highlights Pr., c/o Highlights for Children, Inc.

Miller, Reagan & Arthur, Martin. Great Leaders of the Civil War. 2011. (ENG.). 48p. (J). pap. *(978-0-7787-5359-9(X));* lib. bdg. *(978-0-7787-5342-1(5))* Crabtree Publishing Co.

Murray, Hallie. The Role of Female Confederate Spies in the Civil War, 1 vol. 2019. (Warrior Women in American History Ser.). (ENG.). 104p. (gr. 7-7). pap. 21.00 *(978-1-5026-5540-0(3),* eaa72ffe-9b57-4ea3-8b26-a98d4ac093e2); lib. bdg. 44.50 *(978-1-5026-5541-7(1),* 813ee375-f83d-4738-8a94-3357dd568210) Cavendish Square Publishing LLC.

—The Role of Female Confederate Spies in the Civil War. 2019. (J). pap. *(978-1-9785-1404-1(2))* Enslow Publishing, LLC.

—The Role of Female Union Spies in the Civil War, 1 vol. 2019. (Warrior Women in American History Ser.). (ENG.). 104p. (gr. 7-7). pap. 21.00 *(978-1-5026-5552-3(7),* 40c157e3-a9ba-4c9a-b76e-20fdbcf1acbe); lib. bdg. 44.50 *(978-1-5026-5553-0(5),* 5447ba82-d148-40f6-aebd-ab6b1462b113) Cavendish Square Publishing LLC.

—The Role of Female Union Spies in the Civil War. 2020. (J). pap. *(978-1-9785-1416-4(6))* Enslow Publishing, LLC.

Nemeth, Jason. Voices of the Civil War. 2010. (Voices of War Ser.). (ENG.). 32p. (J). (gr. 3-4). pap. 50.74 *(978-1-4296-5700-6(6),* 15489, Capstone Pr.) Capstone.

—Voices of the Civil War: Stories from the Battlefields, 1 vol. 2010. (Voices of War Ser.). (ENG.). 32p. (J). (gr. 3-9). lib. bdg. 28.65 *(978-1-4296-4736-6(1),* 103277) Capstone.

Nichols, Joan Kane. Civil War Heroines. 2005. (ENG., Illus.). 16p. (J). (gr. 5-5). pap. 9.97 net. *(978-0-328-14901-8(2),* Scott Foresman) Savvas Learning Co.

—The Civil War Sisterhood: Women Who Made a Difference. 2005. (ENG., Illus.). 16p. (J). (gr. 5-5). pap. 9.97 net. *(978-0-328-14902-5(0),* Scott Foresman) Savvas Learning Co.

—Women of the Civil War. 2005. (ENG., Illus.). 16p. (J). (gr. 5-5). pap. 9.97 net. *(978-0-328-14900-1(4),* Scott Foresman) Savvas Learning Co.

Phillips, Larissa. Women Civil War Spies of the Confederacy. (American Women at War Ser.). 112p. (gr. 8-8). 2009. 63.90 *(978-1-61511-402-3(5))* 2004. (ENG., Illus.). lib. bdg. 39.80 *(978-0-8239-4451-4(4),* 0e231b97-a361-4988-a631-9ba03b3bf6f3) Rosen Publishing Group, Inc., The.

Raum, Elizabeth, et al. Stories of War Classroom Collection. 2012. (Stories of War Ser.). (ENG.). 32p. (J). (gr. 3-4). pap., pap. 195.40 *(978-1-4296-9349-3(5),* 18568, Capstone Pr.) Capstone.

Rice, Dona Herwick & Housel, Debra. Civil War Hero of Marye's Heights, 1 vol. rev. ed. 2009. (Reader's Theater Ser.). (ENG., Illus.). 32p. (J). (gr. 3-8). pap. 11.99 *(978-1-4333-0546-7(1))* Teacher Created Materials, Inc.

Roppelt, Donna J. & DeAngelis, Therese. General A.P. Hill: Light Division Leader. 2011. (J). *(978-1-59556-042-1(4));* pap. *(978-1-59556-048-3(3))* OTTN Publishing.

Sakany, Lois. Women Civil War Spies of the Union. (American Women at War Ser.). 112p. (gr. 8-8). 2009. 63.90 *(978-1-61511-403-0(3))* 2004. (ENG., Illus.). lib. bdg. 39.80 *(978-0-8239-4450-7(6),* badfd22d-70f2-4115-bb75-98ffbe423da6) Rosen Publishing Group, Inc., The.

Wittman, Susan S. Heroes of the Civil War, 1 vol. 2014. (Story of the Civil War Ser.). (ENG., Illus.). 32p. (J). (gr. 3-6). lib. bdg. 27.99 *(978-1-4914-0720-2(4),* 125973, Capstone Pr.) Capstone.

A Woman Officer in the Confederate Army. (J). pap. 9.95 *(978-0-88388-211-5(6))* Bellerophon Bks.

Yomtov, Nel. True Stories of the Civil War. Molinari, Carlo, illus. 2012. (Stories of War Ser.). (ENG.). 32p. (J). (gr. 3-4). pap. 49.60 *(978-1-4296-9341-7(X),* 18563); pap. 8.10 *(978-1-4296-9340-0(1),* 120377); lib. bdg. 31.32 *(978-1-4296-8624-2(3),* 118645) Capstone. (Capstone Pr.).

Yomtov, Nel, et al. Stories of War. 2012. (Stories of War Ser.). (ENG.). 32p. (J). (gr. 3-9). pap., pap., pap. 31.80 *(978-1-4296-9348-6(7),* 18567, Capstone Pr.) Capstone.

UNITED STATES—HISTORY—CIVIL WAR, 1861-1865—CAMPAIGNS

see also Bull Run, 1st Battle of, Va., 1861; Gettysburg, Battle of, Gettysburg, Pa., 1863; Sherman's March to the Sea

Abnett, Dan. The Battle of the Wilderness: Deadly Inferno. 2009. (Graphic Civil War Battles Ser.). (ENG.). 48p. (YA). (gr. 4-5). 58.50 *(978-1-61512-901-0(4),* Rosen Reference) Rosen Publishing Group, Inc., The.

—The Battle of the Wilderness: Deadly Inferno, 1 vol. Verma, Dheeraj, illus. 2006. (Graphic Battles of the Civil War Ser.). (ENG.). 48p. (YA). (gr. 4-5). lib. bdg. 37.13 *(978-1-4042-0780-6(5),* 5e568da3-4ef5-4ddd-85d9-85dca2aa8b66) Rosen Publishing Group, Inc., The.

—The Battle of the Wilderness: Deadly Inferno, 1 vol. 2006. (Graphic Battles of the Civil War Ser.). (ENG., Illus.). 48p. (gr. 4-5). pap. 14.05 *(978-1-4042-6479-3(5),* 539d8da0-40fb-4031-8c14-137df6480c03, Rosen Classroom) Rosen Publishing Group, Inc., The.

Anderson, Dale. The Civil War in the East (1861-July 1863), 1 vol. 2004. (World Almanac(r) Library of the Civil War Ser.). (ENG., Illus.). 48p. (gr. 5-8). pap. 15.05 *(978-0-8368-5591-3(4),* a8679fe7-8a42-464b-929d-fbb5c4e0806a); lib. bdg. 33.67 *(978-0-8368-5582-1(5),* ea65b134-2894-4b4a-b659-255a776186b0) Stevens, Gareth Publishing LLLP. (Gareth Stevens Secondary Library).

—The Union Victory (July 1863 - 1865), 1 vol. 2004. (World Almanac(r) Library of the Civil War Ser.). (ENG., Illus.). 48p. (gr. 5-8). pap. 15.05 *(978-0-8368-5593-7(0),* ce8cac87-1d6e-4de0-9561-7135bd10ad50); lib. bdg. 33.67 *(978-0-8368-5584-5(1),* e28734b4-0c65-4c17-9779-244cfe64b88f) Stevens, Gareth Publishing LLLP. (Gareth Stevens Secondary Library).

Anderson, Paul Christopher. Robert E. Lee: Legendary Commander of the Confederacy. 2009. (Library of American Lives & Times Ser.). 112p. (gr. 5-5). 69.20 *(978-1-60853-501-9(0))* Rosen Publishing Group, Inc., The.

Bailey, Diane. General George Thomas: The Rock of Chickamauga. 2011. (J). *(978-1-59556-045-2(9));* pap. *(978-1-59556-051-3(3))* OTTN Publishing.

Brager, Bruce L. There He Stands: The Story of Stonewall Jackson. 2005. (Civil War Leaders Ser.). (Illus.). 176p. (J). (gr. 6-12). 26.95 *(978-1-931798-44-0(3))* Reynolds, Morgan Inc.

Brown Bear Books. Battles & Campaigns. 2011. (Civil War Ser.). (ENG.). 112p. (J). (gr. 9-12). lib. bdg. 42.80 *(978-1-936333-43-1(0),* 16454) Brown Bear Bks.

Christianson, Gregory. Gettysburg: Kids Who Did the Impossible. 2019. (ENG., Illus.). 144p. (J). pap. 19.95 *(978-1-61121-399-7(1))* Savas Beatie.

Cooke, Tim. The Confederacy on the Advance: 1861-1862. 2012. (Civil War Highlights Ser.). (Illus.). 48p. (gr. 5-12). lib. bdg. 37.10 *(978-1-59920-814-5(8))* Black Rabbit Bks.

—Triumph of the Union: 1864-1865. 2012. (Civil War Highlights Ser.). (Illus.). 48p. (gr. 5-12). 37.10 *(978-1-59920-816-9(4))* Black Rabbit Bks.

—The Turning Point, 1863. 2012. (Civil War Highlights Ser.). (Illus.). 48p. (gr. 5-12). 37.10 *(978-1-59920-815-2(6))* Black Rabbit Bks.

Corrigan, Jim. Civil War in the West. 2004. (History of the Old West Ser.). (Illus.). 64p. (YA). (gr. 5-18). lib. bdg. 19.95 *(978-1-59084-067-2(4))* Mason Crest.

—General George G. Meade: Victor at Gettysburg. 2011. (J). *(978-1-59556-044-5(0));* pap. *(978-1-59556-050-6(5))* OTTN Publishing.

Doeden, Matt. At the Battle of Antietam: An Interactive Battlefield Adventure. 2018. (You Choose: American Battles Ser.). (ENG., Illus.). 112p. (J). (gr. 3-7). lib. bdg. 32.65 *(978-1-5435-0288-6(1),* 137158, Capstone Pr.) Capstone.

—At the Battle of the Ironclads: An Interactive Battlefield Adventure. 2018. (You Choose: American Battles Ser.). (ENG., Illus.). 112p. (J). (gr. 3-7). lib. bdg. 32.65 *(978-1-5435-0290-9(3),* 137159, Capstone Pr.) Capstone.

Dupuy, Trevor Nevitt. The Military History of Civil War Land Battles. Fisher, Leonard Everett, illus. 2011. 98p. 38.95 *(978-1-258-07607-8(1));* 38.95 *(978-1-258-01405-6(X))* Literary Licensing, LLC.

Engle, Stephen Douglas. The Civil War: The Siege of Vicksburg & Other Western Battles, 1861-July 1863, 1 vol. O'Neill, Robert, ed. 2010. (Civil War: Essential Histories Ser.). (ENG.). 96p. (YA). (gr. 10-10). lib. bdg. 38.47 *(978-1-4488-0390-3(X),* d25be999-12c6-4c0b-a8e7-928196cdb50d) Rosen Publishing Group, Inc., The.

Fay, Gail. Battles of the Civil War, 1 vol. (Why We Fought: the Civil War Ser.). (ENG.). 48p. (J). (gr. 3-6). 2011. pap. 9.95 *(978-1-4329-3916-8(5),* 112828) 2010. 35.99 *(978-1-4329-3910-6(6),* 112809) Capstone. (Heinemann).

Ford, Carin T. The Battle of Gettysburg & Lincoln's Gettysburg Address, 1 vol. 2004. (Civil War Library). (ENG., Illus.). 48p. (gr. 3-3). lib. bdg. 27.93 *(978-0-7660-2253-9(6),* a6bd528d-8814-4bf0-92d6-163b2d6e27dc) Enslow Publishing, LLC.

Hale, Sarah Elder, ed. Stonewall Jackson: Spirit of the South. 2005. (ENG., Illus.). 48p. (J). (gr. 3-9). 17.95 *(978-0-8126-7907-6(5))* Cobblestone Pr.

Hama, Larry. The Battle of First Bull Run: The Civil War Begins. 2009. (Graphic Civil War Battles Ser.). (ENG.). 48p. (YA). (gr. 4-5). 58.50 *(978-1-61512-898-3(0),* Rosen Reference) Rosen Publishing Group, Inc., The.

January, Brendan. Gettysburg: July 1-3 1863, 1 vol. 2006. (American Battlefields Ser.). (ENG., Illus.). 32p. (gr. 4-4). 26.93 *(978-1-59270-025-7(X),* 0a9a5d62-ad80-4d62-bdd2-4bc25a4fef60) Cavendish Square Publishing LLC.

Jopp, Kelsey. Early Battles of the Civil War. 2020. (Civil War Ser.). (ENG., Illus.). 48p. (J). (gr. 5-6). pap. 11.95 *(978-1-64493-158-5(3),* 1644931583); lib. bdg. 34.21 *(978-1-64493-079-3(X),* 164493079X) North Star Editions. (Focus Readers).

Koestler-Grack, Rachel A. William Tecumseh Sherman. 2009. (ENG., Illus.). 149p. (gr. 6-12). 35.00 *(978-1-60413-300-4(7),* P162096, Facts On File) Infobase Holdings, Inc.

Kolpin, Molly. The Biggest Battles of the Civil War, 1 vol. 2014. (Story of the Civil War Ser.). (ENG.). 32p. (J). (gr. 3-6). lib. bdg. 27.99 *(978-1-4914-0718-9(2),* 125971) Capstone.

Krick, Robert K. The Civil War: Gettysburg & Other Eastern Battles, 1863-1865, 1 vol. 2010. (Civil War: Essential Histories Ser.). (ENG.). 96p. (YA). (gr. 10-10). lib. bdg. 38.47 *(978-1-4488-0388-0(8),* 765b2e17-95e9-42c7-af02-68b565dec5a7) Rosen Publishing Group, Inc., The.

Landau, Elaine. The Battle of Gettysburg: Would You Lead the Fight?, 1 vol. 2009. (What Would You Do? Ser.). (ENG., Illus.). 48p. (gr. 3-3). pap. 11.53 *(978-1-59845-192-4(8),* b42e7fe9-07aa-4c93-a046-4eaf27c59486, Enslow Elementary) Enslow Publishing, LLC.

—The Great Battle of Gettysburg: Would You Stand & Fight?, 1 vol. 2014. (What Would You Do? Ser.). (ENG.). 48p. (gr. 3-4). 27.93 *(978-0-7660-6295-5(3),* 91e65b0f-0320-4cb1-82f3-1759b75503e6); pap. 11.53 *(978-0-7660-6296-2(1),* b6c59ea6-a5ac-4dd8-bb8f-da91d35bb489, Enslow Elementary) Enslow Publishing, LLC.

Loh-Hagan, Virginia. Union Triumph: Battle of Gettysburg. 2019. (Behind the Curtain Ser.). (ENG., Illus.). 32p. (J). (gr. 4-8). pap. 14.21 *(978-1-5341-3999-2(0),* 212825); lib. bdg. 32.07 *(978-1-5341-4343-2(2),* 212824) Cherry Lake Publishing. (45th Parallel Press).

Marrin, Albert. Virginia's General: Robert E. Lee & the Civil War. 2003. (Illus.). 201p. (YA). pap. 14.95 *(978-1-893103-14-6(5))* Beautiful Feet Bks.

McLeese, Don. Stonewall Jackson. 2005. (Civil War Military Leaders Ser.). (Illus.). 32p. (J). (gr. 3-6). lib. bdg. 19.95 *(978-1-59515-477-4(9))* Rourke Educational Media.

McNeese, Tim. Civil War Battles. 2009. (ENG., Illus.). 144p. (gr. 6-12). 35.00 *(978-1-60413-034-8(2),* P163833, Facts On File) Infobase Holdings, Inc.

Miller, Reagan & Hiller, Sandi J. Turning Point Battles of the Civil War. 2011. (ENG.). 48p. (J). pap. *(978-0-7787-5360-5(3));* lib. bdg. *(978-0-7787-5343-8(3))* Crabtree Publishing Co.

Miller, Reagan & Stowell, Cinci. Final Campaigns of the Civil War. 2011. (ENG.). 48p. (J). pap. *(978-0-7787-5356-8(5));* lib. bdg. *(978-0-7787-5339-1(5))* Crabtree Publishing Co.

O'Neill, Robert John & Gallagher, Gary W. The Civil War: Bull Run & Other Eastern Battles, 1861-May 1863, 1 vol. 2010. (Civil War: Essential Histories Ser.). (ENG.). 96p. (YA). (gr. 10-10). lib. bdg. 38.47 *(978-1-4488-0387-3(X),*

TUV

79b08efd-49fb-4aa5-9c67-3924169a04bb) Rosen Publishing Group, Inc., The.

O'Neill, Robert John & Glatthaar, Joseph T. The Civil War: Sherman's Capture of Atlanta & Other Western Battles, 1863-1865, 1 vol. 2010. (Civil War: Essential Histories Ser.). (ENG.). 96p. (YA). (gr. 10-10). lib. bdg. 38.47 *(978-1-4488-0389-7(6)*, e8238cfa-f9a6-4398-b6df-9d64c756955d) Rosen Publishing Group, Inc., The.

Pingry, Patricia A. The Story of Gettysburg. Britt, Stephanie, illus. 2003. (ENG.). 26p. (J). (gr. -1-k). bds. 7.69 *(978-0-8249-6503-7(5)*, Ideals Pubns.) Worthy Publishing.

Power, J. Tracey. Stonewall Jackson: Hero of the Confederacy. 2009. (Library of American Lives & Times Ser.). 112p. (gr. 5-5). 69.20 *(978-1-60853-507-1(X))* Rosen Publishing Group, Inc., The.

Rice, Earle, Jr. Robert E. Lee: First Soldier of the Confederacy. 2005. (Civil War Leaders Ser.). (Illus.). 176p. (J). (gr. 6-12). 28.95 *(978-1-931798-47-1(8))* Reynolds, Morgan Inc.

Roberts, Russell. Turning Points of the Civil War. 2020. (Civil War Ser.). (ENG., Illus.). 48p. (J). (gr. 5-6). pap. 11.95 *(978-1-64493-164-6(8)*, 1644931648); lib. bdg. 34.21 *(978-1-64493-085-4(4)*, 1644930854) North Star Editions. (Focus Readers).

Robertson, James I., Jr. Robert E. Lee: Virginian Soldier, American Citizen. 2005. (ENG., Illus.). 176p. (YA). (gr. 7-12). 29.99 *(978-0-689-85731-7(4)*, Atheneum Bks. for Young Readers) Simon & Schuster Children's Publishing.

Roppelt, Donna J. & DeAngelis, Therese. General A.P. Hill: Light Division Leader. 2011. (J). *(978-1-59556-042-1(4))*; pap. *(978-1-59556-048-3(3))* OTTN Publishing.

Rosen, Daniel. Battles of the Civil War: Set of 6: Antietam. 2011. (Navigators Ser.). (J). pap. 48.00 net. *(978-1-4108-6259-4(3))* Benchmark Education Co.

—Battles of the Civil War: Antietam: Text Pairs. 2008. (Bridges/Navigators Ser.). (J). (gr. 5). 89.00 *(978-1-4108-8405-3(8))* Benchmark Education Co.

Samuels, Charlie. Timeline of the Civil War, 1 vol. 2011. (Americans at War: a Gareth Stevens Timeline Ser.). (ENG.). 48p. (J). (gr. 6-8). pap. 15.05 *(978-1-4339-5912-7(7)*, a1efaff1-b661-4bf0-82b8-e6adafa3506e); lib. bdg. 34.60 *(978-1-4339-5910-3(0)*, f688d1ee-2ae7-44bb-b032-a1b2fbedfd6e) Stevens, Gareth Publishing LLLP. (Gareth Stevens Secondary Library).

Tanaka, Shelley. Gettysburg: The Legendary Battle & the Address That Inspired a Nation. Craig, David, illus. 2003. (Day That Changed America Ser.). (ENG.). 48p. 16.99 *(978-0-7868-1922-5(7))* Hyperion Pr.

Vierow, Wendy. The Battle of Bull Run, 1 vol. 2004. (Headlines from History Ser.). (ENG., Illus.). 24p. (YA). (gr. 3-3). lib. bdg. 26.27 *(978-0-8239-6221-1(0)*, e0f665fe-566e-427c-ab3b-77b063f40379) Rosen Publishing Group, Inc., The.

—The Battle of Bull Run: Confederate Forces Overwhelm Union Troops. 2009. (Headlines from History Ser.). 24p. (gr. 3-3). 42.50 *(978-1-61513-241-6(4)*, PowerKids Pr.) Rosen Publishing Group, Inc., The.

—The Battle of Gettysburg: The Civil War's Biggest Battle. 2009. (Headlines from History Ser.). 24p. (gr. 3-3). 42.50 *(978-1-61513-242-3(2)*, PowerKids Pr.) Rosen Publishing Group, Inc., The.

—The Capture of New Orleans: Union Fleet Takes Control of the Lower Mississippi. 2009. (Headlines from History Ser.). 24p. (gr. 3-3). 42.50 *(978-1-61513-245-4(7)*, PowerKids Pr.) Rosen Publishing Group, Inc., The.

—The Capture of New Orleans: Union Fleet Takes Control of the Lower Mississippi River, 1 vol. 2004. (Headlines from History Ser.). (ENG., Illus.). 24p. (YA). (gr. 3-3). lib. bdg. 26.27 *(978-0-8239-6222-8(9)*, 775c6083-abd6-4be8-90fc-56df6867eda4) Rosen Publishing Group, Inc., The.

Waldman, Scott P. The Battle of Bunker Hill. 2009. (Atlas of Famous Battles of the American Revolution Ser.). 24p. (gr. 3-3). 42.50 *(978-1-60853-327-5(1)*, PowerKids Pr.) Rosen Publishing Group, Inc., The.

UNITED STATES—HISTORY—CIVIL WAR, 1861-1865—FICTION

Alcorn, Anita C. Caught in the Crossfire: A Boy's View of the Battle of Mill Springs, KY. 2006. 48p. pap. 8.95 *(978-0-7414-3581-1(0))* Infinity Publishing.

Alger, Horatio. Frank's Campaign: Or, The Farm & the Camp. 2006. (ENG.). 196p. pap. 19.99 *(978-1-4264-0484-9(0))*; 188p. pap. 21.99 *(978-1-4264-0527-3(8))* Creative Media Partners, LLC.

—Frank's Campaign: Or, The Farm & the Camp. 2006. pap. *(978-1-4065-0705-8(9))* Dodo Pr.

Alger Jr. Horatio Staff. Frank's Campaign. rev. ed. 2006. 300p. 29.95 *(978-1-4218-1761-3(6))*; pap. 14.95 *(978-1-4218-1861-0(2))* 1st World Publishing, Inc. (1st World Library - Literary Society).

Altsheler, Joseph A. The Guns of Bull Run: A Story of the Civil War's Eve. 2006. (Civil War Ser.: Vol. 1). 300p. (J). reprint ed. 29.95 *(978-1-4218-1777-4(2))*; pap. 14.95 *(978-1-4218-1877-1(9))* 1st World Publishing, Inc. (1st World Library - Literary Society).

—The Guns of Bull Run: A Story of the Civil War's Eve. 2009. 278p. reprint ed. pap. 14.99 *(978-1-60512-409-4(5))*; (Civil War Ser.: Vol. 1). (J). 27.99 *(978-1-60512-309-7(9))* Akasha Publishing, LLC. (Akasha Classics).

—The Guns of Bull Run: A Story of the Civil War's Eve. 2007. (Civil War Ser.: Vol. 1). (ENG.). 238p. (J). reprint ed. per. 20.99 *(978-1-4346-7678-8(1))* Creative Media Partners, LLC.

—The Guns of Bull Run: A Story of the Civil War's Eve. 2006. (Civil War Ser.: Vol. 1). (J). reprint ed. pap. *(978-1-4065-0812-3(8))* Dodo Pr.

—The Guns of Bull Run: A Story of the Civil War's Eve. 2007. (Civil War Ser.: Vol. 1). 176p. (J). reprint ed. per. *(978-1-4068-1678-5(7))* Echo Library.

—The Guns of Bull Run: A Story of the Civil War's Eve. 2010. (Civil War Ser.: Vol. 1). (Illus.). 162p. (J). (gr. 4-7). reprint ed. pap. 19.99 *(978-1-153-70504-2(4))* General Bks. LLC.

—The Guns of Bull Run: A Story of the Civil War's Eve. (Civil War Ser.: Vol. 1). (J). reprint ed. 2010. 238p. (gr. 4-7). 33.56 *(978-1-169-29842-2(7))* 2010. 238p. (gr. 4-7). pap. 21.56 *(978-1-162-69670-6(2))* 2010. 41.95 *(978-1-161-46535-8(9))* 2004. pap. 1.99 *(978-1-4192-6519-8(9))* 2004. pap. 26.95 *(978-1-4191-6519-1(4))* Kessinger Publishing, LLC.

—The Guns of Bull Run: A Story of the Civil War's Eve. 2009. (Civil War Ser.: Vol. 1). (YA). (gr. 4-7). reprint ed. pap. 16.95 *(978-1-933573-82-3(1))* Zeezok Publishing, LLC.

—The Guns of Bull Run: A Story of the Civil War's Eve. 2011. (Civil War Ser.: Vol. 1). 256p. (J). (gr. 4-7). reprint ed. pap. *(978-3-8424-5271-8(3))* tredition Verlag.

—The Guns of Bull Run (Webster's French Thesaurus Edition) 2008. (Civil War Ser.: Vol. 1). (ENG & FRE.). 306p. reprint ed. pap. 28.95 *(978-0-497-97879-2(2))* Icon Group International, Inc.

—The Guns of Bull Run (Webster's Spanish Thesaurus Edition) 2008. (Civil War Ser.: Vol. 1). (ENG & SPA.). 313p. pap. 28.95 *(978-0-497-99968-1(4))* Icon Group International, Inc.

—The Guns of Shiloh. 2006. (Civil War Ser.: Vol. 2). 292p. (J). reprint ed. 28.95 *(978-1-4218-1774-3(8))*; pap. 13.95 *(978-1-4218-1874-0(4))* 1st World Publishing, Inc. (1st World Library - Literary Society).

—The Guns of Shiloh. 2010. (Civil War Ser.: Vol. 2). (ENG.). 356p. (J). (gr. 4-7). reprint ed. pap. 32.75 *(978-1-177-56053-5(4))* Creative Media Partners, LLC.

—The Guns of Shiloh. 2006. (Civil War Ser.: Vol. 2). (J). reprint ed. pap. *(978-1-4065-0813-0(6))* Dodo Pr.

—The Guns of Shiloh. 2006. (Civil War Ser.: Vol. 2). (J). reprint ed. pap. *(978-1-4068-0745-5(1))* Echo Library.

—The Guns of Shiloh. 2010. 156p. pap. 24.39 *(978-1-152-46676-0(3))*; (Civil War Ser.: Vol. 2). (Illus.). (J). (gr. 4-7). reprint ed. pap. 19.99 *(978-1-153-70505-9(2))* General Bks. LLC.

—The Guns of Shiloh. (Civil War Ser.: Vol. 2). (J). 2010. 216p. pap. *(978-1-4076-3068-7(7))* 2012. 362p. reprint ed. pap. *(978-1-290-02433-4(2))* HardPr.

—The Guns of Shiloh. 2003. (Civil War Ser.: Vol. 2). 232p. (J). reprint ed. pap. 36.99 *(978-1-4043-5087-8(X))* IndyPublish.com.

—The Guns of Shiloh. (Civil War Ser.: Vol. 2). (J). reprint ed. 2010. 226p. (gr. 4-7). 31.96 *(978-1-169-29437-0(5))* 2010. 226p. (gr. 4-7). pap. 19.96 *(978-1-162-69671-3(0))* 2010. 39.95 *(978-1-161-46536-5(7))* 2004. pap. 1.99 *(978-1-4192-6520-4(2))* 2004. pap. 24.95 *(978-1-4191-6520-7(8))* Kessinger Publishing, LLC.

—The Guns of Shiloh. (Civil War Ser.: Vol. 2). reprint ed. 2008. 228p. (J). pap. 14.45 *(978-1-60597-269-5(X))* 2007. 232p. per. 12.45 *(978-1-60424-259-1(0))* Standard Publications, Inc. (Bk. Jungle).

—The Guns of Shiloh. 2009. (Civil War Ser.: Vol. 2). 278p. (J). (gr. 4-7). reprint ed. pap. 16.95 *(978-1-933573-83-0(X))* Zeezok Publishing, LLC.

—The Guns of Shiloh. 2011. (Civil War Ser.: Vol. 2). 260p. (J). (gr. 4-7). reprint ed. pap. *(978-3-8424-2812-6(X))* tredition Verlag.

—The Rock of Chickamauga: A Story of the Western Crisis. 2006. (Civil War Ser.: Vol. 6). 292p. (J). reprint ed. 28.95 *(978-1-4218-1775-0(6))*; pap. 13.95 *(978-1-4218-1875-7(2))* 1st World Publishing, Inc. (1st World Library - Literary Society).

—The Rock of Chickamauga: A Story of the Western Crisis. (Civil War Ser.: Vol. 6). (J). reprint ed. 25.95 *(978-0-8488-0071-0(0))* Amereon Ltd.

—The Rock of Chickamauga: A Story of the Western Crisis. 2010. (Civil War Ser.: Vol. 6). (J). reprint ed. 360p. (gr. 4-7). pap. 32.75 *(978-1-177-86302-5(2))*; 356p. pap. 32.75 *(978-1-142-78423-2(1))* Creative Media Partners, LLC.

—The Rock of Chickamauga: A Story of the Western Crisis. 2006. (Civil War Ser.: Vol. 6). (J). reprint ed. pap. *(978-1-4065-0818-5(7))* Dodo Pr.

—The Rock of Chickamauga: A Story of the Western Crisis. 2007. (Civil War Ser.: Vol. 6). 176p. (J). reprint ed. per. *(978-1-4068-1682-2(5))* Echo Library.

—The Rock of Chickamauga: A Story of the Western Crisis. 2010. (Civil War Ser.: Vol. 6). (Illus.). 154p. (J). (gr. 4-7). reprint ed. pap. 19.99 *(978-1-153-71942-1(8))* General Bks. LLC.

—The Rock of Chickamauga: A Story of the Western Crisis. 2010. (Civil War Ser.: Vol. 6). 220p. (J). pap. *(978-1-4076-5409-6(8))* HardPr.

—The Rock of Chickamauga: A Story of the Western Crisis. (Civil War Ser.: Vol. 6). (J). 2010. 236p. (gr. 4-7). pap. 21.56 *(978-1-162-70708-2(9))* 2010. 236p. (gr. 4-7). reprint ed. 33.56 *(978-1-169-29814-9(1))* 2010. reprint ed. 41.95 *(978-1-161-47572-2(9))* 2004. reprint ed. pap. 1.99 *(978-1-4192-8082-5(1))* 2004. reprint ed. pap. 26.95 *(978-1-4191-8082-8(7))* Kessinger Publishing, LLC.

—The Rock of Chickamauga: A Story of the Western Crisis. 2011. (Civil War Ser.: Vol. 6). 260p. (J). (gr. 4-7). reprint ed. pap. *(978-3-8424-7218-1(8))* tredition Verlag.

—The Scouts of Stonewall: The Story of the Great Valley Campaign. 2006. (Civil War Ser.: Vol. 3). 312p. (J). reprint ed. 29.95 *(978-1-4218-1779-8(9))*; pap. 14.95 *(978-1-4218-1879-5(5))* 1st World Publishing, Inc. (1st World Library - Literary Society).

—The Scouts of Stonewall: The Story of the Great Valley Campaign. l.t. ed. (Civil War Ser.: Vol. 3). (J). reprint ed. 2007. (ENG.). 240p. pap. 22.99 *(978-1-4264-1531-9(1))* 2011. 370p. (gr. 4-7). pap. 32.75 *(978-1-245-65787-7(9))* 2008. 244p. 24.99 *(978-0-554-31333-7(2))* 2008. 244p. 27.99 *(978-0-554-22030-7(X))* 2006. 250p. pap. 20.99 *(978-1-4264-1498-5(6))* Creative Media Partners, LLC.

—The Scouts of Stonewall: The Story of the Great Valley Campaign. 2006. (Civil War Ser.: Vol. 3). (J). reprint ed. pap. *(978-1-4065-0820-8(9))* Dodo Pr.

—The Scouts of Stonewall: The Story of the Great Valley Campaign. 2007. (Civil War Ser.: Vol. 3). 184p. (J). reprint ed. per. *(978-1-4068-1684-6(1))* Echo Library.

—The Scouts of Stonewall: The Story of the Great Valley Campaign. 2010. (Civil War Ser.: Vol. 3). (Illus.). 166p. (J). (gr. 4-7). reprint ed. pap. 19.99 *(978-1-153-72009-0(4))* General Bks. LLC.

—The Scouts of Stonewall: The Story of the Great Valley Campaign. reprint ed. 2010. (Civil War Ser.: Vol. 3). 252p. (J). (gr. 4-7). 33.56 *(978-1-169-30265-5(3))* 2010. (Civil War Ser.: Vol. 3). 252p. (J). (gr. 4-7). pap. 21.56 *(978-1-162-70768-6(2))* 2010. (Civil War Ser.: Vol. 3). 252p. (J). 41.95 *(978-1-161-47632-3(6))* 2004. pap. 26.95 *(978-1-4191-8162-7(9))* 2004. (Civil War Ser.: Vol. 3). (J). pap. 1.99 *(978-1-4192-8162-4(3))* Kessinger Publishing, LLC.

—The Scouts of Stonewall: The Story of the Great Valley Campaign. 2011. (Civil War Ser.: Vol. 3). 278p. (J). (gr. 4-7). reprint ed. pap. *(978-3-8424-6100-0(3))* tredition Verlag.

—The Shades of the Wilderness: A Story of Lee's Great Stand. 2006. (Civil War Ser.: Vol. 7). 308p. (J). reprint ed. 29.95 *(978-1-4218-2336-2(5))*; pap. 14.95 *(978-1-4218-2436-9(1))* 1st World Publishing, Inc. (1st World Library - Literary Society).

—The Shades of the Wilderness: A Story of Lee's Great Stand. (Civil War Ser.: Vol. 7). 312p. (J). reprint ed. lib. bdg. 25.95 *(978-0-88411-940-1(8))* Amereon Ltd.

—The Shades of the Wilderness: A Story of Lee's Great Stand. 2008. (Civil War Ser.: Vol. 7). 280p. (J). reprint ed. 25.99 *(978-0-554-33603-9(0))* Creative Media Partners, LLC.

—The Shades of the Wilderness: A Story of Lee's Great Stand. 2006. (Civil War Ser.: Vol. 7). (J). reprint ed. pap. *(978-1-4065-0822-2(5))* Dodo Pr.

—The Shades of the Wilderness: A Story of Lee's Great Stand. 2007. (Civil War Ser.: Vol. 7). 180p. (J). reprint ed. per. *(978-1-4068-1686-0(8))* Echo Library.

—The Shades of the Wilderness: A Story of Lee's Great Stand. 2010. (Civil War Ser.: Vol. 7). (Illus.). 162p. (J). (gr. 4-7). reprint ed. pap. 19.99 *(978-1-153-72059-5(0))* General Bks. LLC.

—The Shades of the Wilderness: A Story of Lee's Great Stand. (Civil War Ser.: Vol. 7). (J). reprint ed. 2011. (gr. 4-7). *(978-1-164-50265-4(4))* 2010. 324p. (gr. 4-7). pap. 24.76 *(978-1-163-19558-1(8))* 2008. 324p. 45.95 *(978-1-4366-8424-8(2))* 2007. 324p. per. 30.95 *(978-1-4325-9861-7(9))* Kessinger Publishing, LLC.

—The Shades of the Wilderness: A Story of Lee's Great Stand. 2007. (Civil War Ser.: Vol. 7). 308p. reprint ed. per. 16.45 *(978-1-60424-029-0(6)*, Bk. Jungle) Standard Publications, Inc.

—The Shades of the Wilderness: A Story of Lee's Great Stand. 2011. (Civil War Ser.: Vol. 7). 280p. (J). reprint ed. pap. *(978-3-8424-4396-9(X))* tredition Verlag.

—The Star of Gettysburg: A Story of Southern High Tide. 2006. (Civil War Ser.: Vol. 5). 324p. (J). reprint ed. 29.95 *(978-1-4218-1780-4(2))*; pap. 14.95 *(978-1-4218-1880-1(9))* 1st World Publishing, Inc. (1st World Library - Literary Society).

—The Star of Gettysburg: A Story of Southern High Tide. 2006. (Civil War Ser.: Vol. 5). (J). reprint ed. pap. *(978-1-4065-0824-6(1))* Dodo Pr.

—The Star of Gettysburg: A Story of Southern High Tide. 2007. (Civil War Ser.: Vol. 5). 192p. (J). reprint ed. per. *(978-1-4068-1688-4(4))* Echo Library.

—The Star of Gettysburg: A Story of Southern High Tide. 2010. (Civil War Ser.: Vol. 5). 174p. (J). (gr. 4-7). reprint ed. pap. 19.99 *(978-1-153-72161-5(9))* General Bks. LLC.

—The Star of Gettysburg: A Story of Southern High Tide. (Civil War Ser.: Vol. 5). (J). reprint ed. 2010. 262p. (gr. 4-7). 34.36 *(978-1-169-30586-1(5))* 2010. 262p. (gr. 4-7). pap. 22.36 *(978-1-162-70899-7(9))* 2010. 42.95 *(978-1-161-47763-4(2))* 2004. pap. 1.99 *(978-1-4192-8344-4(8))* 2004. pap. 27.95 *(978-1-4191-8344-7(3))* Kessinger Publishing, LLC.

—The Star of Gettysburg: A Story of Southern High Tide. 2011. (Civil War Ser.: Vol. 5). 280p. (J). (gr. 4-7). reprint ed. pap. *(978-3-8424-5317-3(5))* tredition Verlag.

—The Star of Gettysburg (Webster's Korean Thesaurus Edition) 2008. (Civil War Ser.: Vol. 5). (Illus.). 340p. (C). pap. 28.95 *(978-0-546-50036-3(6))* Icon Group International, Inc.

—The Sword of Antietam: A Story of the Nation's Crisis. 2006. (Civil War Ser.: Vol. 4). 296p. (J). reprint ed. 28.95 *(978-1-4218-1776-7(4))*; pap. 13.95 *(978-1-4218-1876-4(0))* 1st World Publishing, Inc. (1st World Library - Literary Society).

—The Sword of Antietam: A Story of the Nation's Crisis. l.t. ed. (Civil War Ser.: Vol. 4). (J). reprint ed. 2006. 262p. pap. 23.99 *(978-1-4264-2714-5(X))* 2011. 358p. (gr. 4-7). pap. 32.75 *(978-1-245-13385-2(3))* 2008. 264p. 25.99 *(978-0-554-31885-1(7))* 2008. 264p. 28.99 *(978-0-554-22582-1(4))* 2007. (ENG.). 242p. pap. 20.99 *(978-1-4264-2657-5(7))* Creative Media Partners, LLC.

—The Sword of Antietam: A Story of the Nation's Crisis. 2006. (Civil War Ser.: Vol. 4). (J). reprint ed. pap. *(978-1-4065-0825-3(X))* Dodo Pr.

—The Sword of Antietam: A Story of the Nation's Crisis. 2007. (Civil War Ser.: Vol. 4). 176p. (J). reprint ed. per. *(978-1-4068-1690-7(6))* Echo Library.

—The Sword of Antietam: A Story of the Nation's Crisis. 2010. (Civil War Ser.: Vol. 4). (Illus.). 160p. (J). (gr. 4-7). reprint ed. pap. 19.99 *(978-1-153-72276-6(3))* General Bks. LLC.

—The Sword of Antietam: A Story of the Nation's Crisis. 2010. (Civil War Ser.: Vol. 4). 224p. (J). reprint ed. pap. *(978-1-4076-4642-8(7))* HardPr.

—The Sword of Antietam: A Story of the Nation's Crisis. (Civil War Ser.: Vol. 4). (J). reprint ed. 2011. 352p. (gr. 4-7). 46.95 *(978-1-169-87969-0(1))* 2010. 352p. (gr. 4-7). 37.56 *(978-1-163-20537-2(0))* 2010. 352p. (gr. 4-7). pap. 25.56 *(978-1-162-77564-7(5))* 2005. 352p. 46.95 *(978-1-4326-1485-0(1))* 2005. pap. 31.95 *(978-0-7661-9405-2(1))* 2004. pap. 1.99 *(978-1-4192-8469-4(X))* Kessinger Publishing, LLC.

—The Sword of Antietam: A Story of the Nation's Crisis. 2009. (Civil War Ser.: Vol. 4). (J). reprint ed. pap. 16.95 *(978-1-933573-85-4(6))* Zeezok Publishing, LLC.

—The Sword of Antietam: A Story of the Nation's Crisis. 2011. (Civil War Ser.: Vol. 4). 264p. (J). (gr. 4-7). reprint ed. pap. *(978-3-8424-3211-6(9))* tredition Verlag.

—The Sword of Antietam (Webster's French Thesaurus Edition) 2008. (ENG & FRE.). 299p. (C). reprint ed. pap. 28.95 *(978-0-497-97890-7(3))* Icon Group International, Inc.

—The Tree of Appomattox: A Story of the Civil War's Close. 2006. (Civil War Ser.: Vol. 8). 324p. (J). reprint ed. 29.95 *(978-1-4218-2338-6(1))*; pap. 14.95 *(978-1-4218-2438-3(8))* 1st World Publishing, Inc. (1st World Library - Literary Society).

—The Tree of Appomattox: A Story of the Civil War's Close. 2007. (Civil War Ser.: Vol. 8). (ENG.). 266p. (J). reprint ed. pap. 21.99 *(978-1-4346-1190-1(6))* Creative Media Partners, LLC.

—The Tree of Appomattox: A Story of the Civil War's Close. 2006. (Civil War Ser.: Vol. 8). (J). reprint ed. pap. *(978-1-4065-0828-4(4))* Dodo Pr.

—The Tree of Appomattox: A Story of the Civil War's Close. 2007. (Civil War Ser.: Vol. 8). 192p. (J). reprint ed. per. *(978-1-4068-1693-8(0))* Echo Library.

—The Tree of Appomattox: A Story of the Civil War's Close. 2010. (Civil War Ser.: Vol. 8). (Illus.). 174p. (J). (gr. 4-7). reprint ed. pap. 19.99 *(978-1-153-72402-9(2))* General Bks. LLC.

—The Tree of Appomattox: A Story of the Civil War's Close. Wrenn, Charles L., illus. (Civil War Ser.: Vol. 8). 332p. (J). (gr. 4-7). reprint ed. 2011. 45.95 *(978-1-169-88135-8(1))* 2010. 36.76 *(978-1-163-21361-2(6))* 2010. pap. 24.76 *(978-1-162-78752-7(X))* Kessinger Publishing, LLC.

—The Tree of Appomattox: A Story of the Civil War's Close. 2005. (Civil War Ser.: Vol. 8). (J). reprint ed. pap. 30.95 *(978-1-4179-2071-6(8))* Kessinger Publishing, LLC.

—The Tree of Appomattox: A Story of the Civil War's Close. Wrenn, Charles L., illus. 2005. (Civil War Ser.: Vol. 8). 332p. (J). reprint ed. 45.95 *(978-1-4326-1333-4(2))* Kessinger Publishing, LLC.

—The Tree of Appomattox: A Story of the Civil War's Close. 2011. (Civil War Ser.: Vol. 8). 294p. (J). (gr. 4-7). reprint ed. pap. *(978-3-8424-8485-6(2))* tredition Verlag.

Angleberger, Tom & Hemphill, Michael. Stonewall Hinkleman & the Battle of Bull Run. 2014. 192p. (J). (gr. 3-7). pap. 7.99 *(978-0-14-751182-9(8)*, Puffin Books) Penguin Young Readers Group.

Ballard, Allen. Where Im Bound. 2006. pap. 18.95 *(978-0-595-39856-0(1)*, Backinprint.com) iUniverse, Inc.

Barnhart, Aaron. Firebrand. 2015. (ENG., Illus.). 168p. (J). 19.95 *(978-0-9669258-6-9(6))* Quindaro Pr.

Bearden, Romare. Li'l Dan, the Drummer Boy: A Civil War Story. Bearden, Romare, illus. 2003. (ENG., Illus.). 40p. (J). (gr. -1-3). 24.99 *(978-0-689-86237-3(7)*, Simon & Schuster Bks. For Young Readers) Simon & Schuster Bks. For Young Readers.

Beddor, Frank & Cavalier, Liz. Hatter M: Mad with Wonder: Mad with Wonder, Vol. 2. 2009. (ENG., Illus.). 208p. (gr. 7). pap. 14.95 *(978-0-9818737-2-5(3))* Automatic Pictures Publishing.

—Mad with Wonder: Volume 2. 2009. (ENG., Illus.). 208p. (gr. 7). 24.99 *(978-0-9818737-1-8(5))* Automatic Pictures Publishing.

Bierce, Ambrose. An Occurrence at Owl Creek Bridge. 2010. (Creative Short Stories Ser.). (ENG.). 48p. (J). (gr. 5-8). 19.95 *(978-1-58341-922-9(5)*, 22124, Creative Education) Creative Co., The.

Blackwood, Gary. Second Sight. 2007. (ENG.). 288p. (J). (gr. 5-18). 8.99 *(978-0-14-240747-9(X)*, Puffin Books) Penguin Young Readers Group.

Blackwood, Gary L. Second Sight. 2007. (Illus.). 279p. (J). (gr. 5-9). 14.65 *(978-0-7569-8132-7(8))* Perfection Learning Corp.

Blaine, John. The Blue Ghost Mystery: A Rick Brant Science Adventure Story. 2011. 188p. 42.95 *(978-1-258-09526-0(2))* Literary Licensing, LLC.

Blair, Margaret Whitman. The Sand Castle: Blockade Running & the Battle of Fort Fisher. 2005. (White Mane Kids Ser.: 17). (Illus.). 187p. (J). (gr. 4-7). per. 8.95 *(978-1-57249-346-9(1)*, White Mane Kids) White Mane Publishing Co., Inc.

Bonner, Anne. Secrets at Pine Haven: Civil War Comes to Florida. 2006. (Illus.). 180p. (J). per. 12.95 *(978-1-878398-75-8(X)*, Blue Note Bks.) Blue Note Pubns.

Brill, Marlene Targ. Diary of a Drummer Boy. Garland, Michael, illus. 2018. (ENG.). 50p. (J). (gr. 4-6). pap. 9.99 *(978-1-7320276-4-0(1))* Golden Alley Pr.

Bruchac, Joseph. March Toward the Thunder. 2009. 320p. (YA). (gr. 7-18). 11.99 *(978-0-14-241446-0(8)*, Speak) Penguin Young Readers Group.

Carolyn, Reeder. Shades of Gray. 2014. (ENG.). 160p. (J). (gr. 5-12). 11.24 *(978-1-63245-242-9(1))* Lectorum Pubns., Inc.

Cauvin, Raoul. Bluecoats - Greenhorn, Vol. 4. Lambil, Willy, illus. 4th ed. 2011. (Bluecoats Ser.: 4). 48p. (J). (gr. -1-12). pap. 11.95 *(978-1-84918-066-5(0))* CineBook GBR. Dist: National Bk. Network.

—The Blues in the Mud. Lambil, Willy, illus. 2014. (Bluecoats Ser.: 7). 48p. (J). (gr. -1-12). pap. 11.95 *(978-1-84918-183-9(7))* CineBook GBR. Dist: National Bk. Network.

—Bronco Benny. Lambil, Willy, illus. 2013. (Bluecoats Ser.: 6). 48p. (J). (gr. -1-12). pap. 11.95 *(978-1-84918-146-4(2))* CineBook GBR. Dist: National Bk. Network.

—The Navy Blues. Lambil, Willy, illus. 2009. (Bluecoats Ser.: 2). 46p. (J). (gr. 4-7). pap. 11.95 *(978-1-905460-82-3(1))* CineBook GBR. Dist: National Bk. Network.

—Robertsonville Prison, Volume 1. Lambil, Willy, illus. 2009. (Bluecoats Ser.: 1). 46p. (J). (gr. -1-17). pap. 11.95 *(978-1-905460-71-7(6))* CineBook GBR. Dist: National Bk. Network.

—Rumberley. Lambil, Willy, illus. 2012. (Bluecoats Ser.: 5). 48p. (J). (gr. 3-8). pap. 11.95 *(978-1-84918-108-2(X))* CineBook GBR. Dist: National Bk. Network.

Chickasaw Adventures: The Civil War. 2005. (J). *(978-1-4265-0000-8(9))* Layne Morgan Media, Inc.

Connell, Kate. Yankee Blue or Rebel Gray? The Civil War Adventures of Sam Shaw. 2003. (I Am American Ser.). (Illus.). 40p. (J). (gr. 3-7). pap. 6.99 *(978-0-7922-5179-8(2)*, National Geographic Children's Bks.) Disney Publishing Worldwide.

Cook, Kajsa. Discoveries in the Shriver Family Attic: How a Woman & Her Children Dealt with the Battle of Gettysburg. 2009. (Illus.). 122p. (J). (gr. 4-8). pap. 8.95 *(978-1-57249-398-8(4)*, White Mane Kids) White Mane Publishing Co., Inc.

Crane, Stephen. The Red Badge of Courage. 2004. (Dover Children's Evergreen Classics Ser.). (ENG.). 160p. (YA). (gr. 3-8). pap. 5.99 *(978-0-486-43422-3(2)*, 434222) Dover Pubns., Inc.

—The Red Badge of Courage. 2008. (Bring the Classics to Life Ser.). (ENG., Illus.). 72p. (gr. 3-12). pap., act. bk. ed. 10.95 *(978-0-931334-42-9(X)*, EDCTR-302B) EDCON Publishing Group.

—The Red Badge of Courage. (EMC Masterpiece Series Access Editions). (J). 11.99 *(978-0-8219-1981-1(4))* EMC/Paradigm Publishing.

—The Red Badge of Courage. 2005. (Illus.). 175p. (gr. 3-7). 21.00 *(978-0-7569-5810-7(5))* Perfection Learning Corp.
—The Red Badge of Courage. 2005. (Aladdin Classics Ser.). (ENG.). 256p. (J). (gr. 5-9). pap. 6.99 *(978-0-689-87835-0(4),* Aladdin) Simon & Schuster Children's Publishing.
—The Red Badge of Courage. 2008. (ENG.). 160p. pap. 11.45 *(978-1-60597-411-8(0),* Bk. Jungle) Standard Publications, Inc.
—The Red Badge of Courage: With a Discussion of Self-Esteem. Clift, Eva, illus. 2003. (Values in Action Illustrated Classics Ser.). 190p. (J). *(978-1-59203-034-7(3))* Learning Challenge, Inc.
Cregar, Elyse M. Hanna's Courage: A Story of Love & Betrayal at the Battle of Gettysburg. 2012. 212p. pap. 8.99 *(978-0-9621292-2-3(4))* Tamerac Publishing.
Crist-Evans, Craig. Moon over Tennessee: A Boy's Civil War Journal. Christensen, Bonnie, illus. 2003. (ENG.). 64p. (J). (gr. 5-7). pap. 8.95 *(978-0-618-31107-1(6),* 460020, Clarion Bks.) HarperCollins Pubs.
Curtis, Alice Turner. A Yankee Girl at Fort Sumter. 2005. 26.95 *(978-1-4218-0301-2(1),* 1st World Library - Literary Society) 1st World Publishing, Inc.
—Yankee Girl at Fort Sumter. 2004. reprint ed. pap. 19.95 *(978-1-4191-9516-7(6));* pap. 1.99 *(978-1-4192-9516-4(0))* Kessinger Publishing, LLC.
Dixon, Chuck & Kwapisz, Gary. Civil War Adventure: Book One. 2015. (Dover Graphic Novels Ser.). (ENG., Illus.). 144p. pap. 10.95 *(978-0-486-79509-6(8),* 795098) Dover Pubns., Inc.
Dunsky, Martha & Wyrick, Monica. Fire & Forgiveness: A Nun's Truce with General Sherman. 2019. (Young Palmetto Bks.). (ENG., Illus.). 48p. (J). 18.99 *(978-1-61117-985-9(8),* P601132) Univ. of South Carolina Pr.
Elkberg, Nancy. What Kind of War Was It, Anyhow? Reynolds, Rhonda, tr. Reynolds, Rhonda, illus. 2003. 45p. (J). pap. 8.95 *(978-1-58838-085-2(8),* Junebug Bks.) NewSouth, Inc.
Elliott, L. M. Annie, Between the States. 2006. (ENG.). 544p. (YA). (gr. 8-12). per. 10.99 *(978-0-06-001213-7(7),* Tegen, Katherine Bks) 2004. (Illus.). 496p. (J). (gr. 7-18). 16.99 *(978-0-06-001211-3(0))* HarperCollins Pubs.
Ernst, Kathleen. Ghosts of Vicksburg. 2003. (White Main Kids Ser.: 13). (Illus.). 180p. (J). pap. 8.95 *(978-1-57249-322-3(4),* White Mane Kids) White Mane Publishing Co., Inc.
—Retreat from Gettysburg. 2010. (White Mane Kids Ser.). (Illus.). 145p. (YA). pap. *(978-1-57249-403-9(4),* White Mane Kids) White Mane Publishing Co., Inc.
Fireside, Bryna J. Private Joel & the Sewell Mountain Seder. Costello, Shawn, illus. 2008. (Passover Ser.). 47p. (J). (gr. 3-6). lib. bdg. 16.95 *(978-0-8225-7240-4(0),* Kar-Ben Publishing) Lerner Publishing Group.
Fletcher, Susan. Dadblamed Union Army Cow. Root, Kimberly Bulcken, illus. 2016. (ENG.). 32p. (J). (gr. k-3). 7.99 *(978-0-7636-8770-0(7))* Candlewick Pr.
Frazier, Jan. Prairie Points:: a Civil War Sanctuary. 2017. (ENG., Illus.). (J). pap. 12.95 *(978-1-55571-864-0(7),* Hellgate Pr.) L & R Publishing, LLC.
Garcia, Kami & Stohl, Margaret. Beautiful Creatures. 2010. (Beautiful Creatures Ser.: 1). (ENG.). 592p. (YA). (gr. 7-17). pap. 16.99 *(978-0-316-07703-3(8))* Little, Brown Bks. for Young Readers.
García, Kami & Stohl, Margaret. Beautiful Creatures. 2010. (Beautiful Creatures Ser.: 1). (YA). lib. bdg. 23.30 *(978-0-606-26699-4(2))* Turtleback.
Garland, Sherry. Voices of Gettysburg, 1 vol. Hierstein, Judith, illus. 2010. (Voices of History Ser.). (ENG.). 40p. (J). (gr. 3-3). 17.99 *(978-1-58980-653-5(0),* Pelican Publishing) Arcadia Publishing.
Gutman, Dan. Abner & Me. 2007. (Baseball Card Adventures Ser.). (ENG., Illus.). 176p. (J). (gr. 5-9). pap. 7.99 *(978-0-06-053445-5(1),* HarperCollins) HarperCollins Pubs.
—Abner & Me. 2007. (Baseball Card Adventures Ser.). (Illus.). 166p. (gr. 5-9). 16.00 *(978-0-7569-7920-1(X))* Perfection Learning Corp.
Hahn, Mary Downing. Hear the Wind Blow. 2017. (ENG.). 288p. (J). (gr. 5-7). pap. 7.99 *(978-1-328-74092-2(7),* 1677135, Clarion Bks.) HarperCollins Pubs.
—Promises to the Dead. 2009. (ENG.). 208p. (J). (gr. 5-7). pap. 7.99 *(978-0-547-25838-6(0),* 1402071, Clarion Bks.) HarperCollins Pubs.
Haislip, Phyllis Hall. Anybody's Hero: The Battle of Old Men & Young Boys. 2004. (Illus.). 220p. (J). pap. 8.95 *(978-1-57249-343-8(7),* White Mane Kids) White Mane Publishing Co., Inc.
—Lili's Gift: A Civil War Healer's Story. 2008. (ENG., Illus.). 204p. (J). pap. 8.95 *(978-1-57249-392-6(5),* White Mane Kids) White Mane Publishing Co., Inc.
—Lottie's Courage: A Contraband Slave's Story. 2003. (Illus.). 120p. (J). pap. 7.95 *(978-1-57249-311-7(9),* White Mane Kids) White Mane Publishing Co., Inc.
Harness, Cheryl. Ghosts of the Civil War. Harness, Cheryl, illus. 2004. (ENG., Illus.). 48p. (J). (gr. 2-5). 8.99 *(978-0-689-86992-1(4),* Simon & Schuster Bks. For Young Readers) Simon & Schuster Bks. For Young Readers.
Harris, Dorthy. Taylor's Dream Ends Summer School Nightm. 2006. 95p. pap. 16.95 *(978-1-4241-3574-5(5))* PublishAmerica, Inc.
Hart, Alison. Gabriel's Journey, 1 vol. 2011. (Racing to Freedom Ser.: 2). 160p. (J). (gr. 3-7). pap. 4.99 *(978-1-56145-530-0(X))* Peachtree Publishing Co. Inc.
Haynes, Betsy. Cowslip. 2008. (J). (gr. 4-7). 22.50 *(978-0-8446-6244-2(5))* Smith, Peter Pub., Inc.
Henty, George. With Lee in Virgini. 2007. 392p. 39.95 *(978-1-4344-8351-5(7));* per. 24.95 *(978-1-4344-8350-8(9))* Wildside Pr., LLC.
—With Lee in Virginia: A Story of the American Civil War. 2011. 404p. pap. 19.95 *(978-1-61179-178-5(2))* Fireship Pr.
Hopkinson, Deborah. Billy & the Rebel: Based on a True Civil War Story. Floca, Brian, illus. 2005. 44p. (J). lib. bdg. 15.00 *(978-1-4242-1148-7(4))* Fitzgerald Bks.
—Billy & the Rebel: Based on a True Civil War Story. Floca, Brian, illus. 2006. (Ready-to-Read Ser.). 44p. (gr. 1-3). 14.00 *(978-0-7569-6390-3(7))* Perfection Learning Corp.
—Billy & the Rebel: Based on a True Civil War Story (Ready-To-Read Level 3) Floca, Brian, illus. (Ready-To-Read Ser.). (ENG.). 48p. (J). (gr. 1-3). 2006. pap. 4.99 *(978-0-689-83396-0(2))* 2005. 17.99 *(978-0-689-83964-1(2))* Simon Spotlight. (Simon Spotlight).
—From Slave to Soldier: Based on a True Civil War Story (Ready-To-Read Level 3) Floca, Brian, illus. 2007. (Ready-To-Read Ser.). (ENG.). 48p. (J). (gr. 1-3). pap. 4.99 *(978-0-689-83966-5(9),* Simon Spotlight) Simon Spotlight.
Hubbs, M. E. The Secret of Wattensaw Bayou. Lyndon, Tracy S., illus. 2013. 170p. pap. 12.95 *(978-1-934610-76-3(3))* Bluewater Pubns.
Immel, Mary Blair. Captured! A Boy Trapped in the Civil War. 2005. (Illus.). xi, 153p. (J). *(978-0-87195-184-7(3));* pap. 6.95 *(978-0-87195-188-5(6))* Indiana Historical Society.
Johnson, Nancy. A Sweet-Sounding Place: A Civil War Story. 2008. (ENG.). 128p. (J). (gr. 3-7). pap. 10.95 *(978-0-89272-770-4(5))* Down East Bks.
Johnston, Annie Fell. The Little Colonel. 2006. (Illus.). pap. *(978-1-4065-1132-1(3))* Dodo Pr.
—The Little Colonel. 2005. reprint ed. pap. 21.95 *(978-0-7661-9402-1(7))* Kessinger Publishing, LLC.
—The Little Colonel's Chum: Mary Ware (il. 2006. (Illus.). pap. *(978-1-4065-1125-3(0))* Dodo Pr.
Johnston, Annie Fellows. The Little Colonel. 2018. (ENG., Illus.). 72p. (YA). (gr. 7-12). pap. *(978-93-5297-426-9(3))* Alpha Editions.
—The Little Colonel. 2018. (ENG., Illus.). 74p. (YA). (gr. 7-12). pap. *(978-3-7326-9515-7(8))* Outlook Verlagsgesellschaft mbH.
—The Little Colonel's Chum: Mary Ware. 2018. (ENG., Illus.). 182p. (YA). (gr. 7-12). pap. *(978-93-5297-428-3(X))* Alpha Editions.
Johnston, K. E. M. The Witness Tree & the Shadow of the Noose: Mystery, Lies, & Spies in Manassas. 2009. 111p. (J). (gr. 5-7). pap. 8.95 *(978-1-57249-397-1(6),* White Mane Kids) White Mane Publishing Co., Inc.
Joyce, Alexandria. Trail of the Caribou: A Tale of Dire Wolves in the Time of the Ice Age. 2011. 216p. (gr. 4-6). pap. 15.95 *(978-1-4620-5066-6(2))* iUniverse, Inc.
Kantorek, Keith A. A Soldier's Choice. 2009. (ENG.). 108p. 24.50 *(978-0-557-10928-9(0));* pap. 9.50 *(978-0-557-10764-3(4))* Lulu Pr., Inc.
Kay, Alan. Breaking the Rules. 2007. (Young Heroes of History Ser.: 7). 149p. (J). pap. 7.95 *(978-1-57249-389-6(5),* White Mane Kids) White Mane Publishing Co., Inc.
Kay, Alan N. Crossroads at Gettysburg. 2005. (Young Heroes of History Ser.: 6). (Illus.). 166p. (J). (gr. 3-7). per. 7.95 *(978-1-57249-359-9(3),* White Mane Kids) White Mane Publishing Co., Inc.
—No Girls Allowed. 2003. (Young Heroes of History Ser.: Vol. 5). (Illus.). 140p. (J). pap. 6.95 *(978-1-57249-324-7(0),* White Mane Kids) White Mane Publishing Co., Inc.
Kendall, Jane. Horse Diaries #9: Tennessee Rose. Sheckels, Astrid, illus. 2012. (Horse Diaries: 9). (ENG.). 160p. (J). (gr. 3-7). pap. 7.99 *(978-0-375-87006-4(7),* Random Hse. Bks. for Young Readers) Random Hse. Children's Bks.
Kirkland, Joseph. The Captain of Company K. (Americans in Fiction Ser.). (Illus.). (J). reprint ed. lib. bdg. 27.00 *(978-0-8398-1057-5(1))* Irvington Pubs.
—The Captain of Company K. 2013. (Collected Works of Joseph Kirkland). 351p. reprint ed. lthr. 79.00 *(978-0-7812-1319-6(3))* Reprint Services Corp.
Klingel, Deanna K. Avery's Battlefield. 2011. (J). *(978-1-60682-171-8(7))* BJU Pr.
—Avery's Crossroad. 2011. (J). *(978-1-60682-193-0(8))* BJU Pr.
Lambil, Willy & Raoul, Cauvin. The Blues in Black & White. 2004. (Blue Tunics Ser.: Vol. 1). (Illus.). (J). 12.45 *(978-0-9752688-0-3(5))* Reney Editions, Inc.
Landis, Matthew. The Not So Boring Letters of Private Nobody. 2019. (ENG.). 320p. (J). (gr. 5-9). 8.99 *(978-0-7352-2799-6(3),* Puffin Books) Penguin Young Readers Group.
Law, Preston E. Drummer Boy for the Bonnie Blue: Marching Through Maryland, Virginia, & Pennsylvania with Robert E. Lee's Army. 2012. (J). pap. *(978-1-57249-410-7(7),* White Mane Kids) White Mane Publishing Co., Inc.
Lawlor, Laurie. Wind on the River. 2004. 156p. (J). lib. bdg. 16.92 *(978-1-4242-0771-8(1))* Fitzgerald Bks.
Lyons, Kelly Starling. Hope's Gift. Tate, Don, illus. 2012. 32p. (J). (gr. 1-3). 17.99 *(978-0-399-16001-1(9),* G.P. Putnam's Sons Books for Young Readers) Penguin Young Readers Group.
Malkus, Alida Sims. We Were There at the Battle of Gettysburg. Vosburgh, Leonard, illus. 2013. (ENG.). 192p. (J). (gr. 3-8). pap. 6.99 *(978-0-486-49261-2(3),* 492613) Dover Pubns., Inc.
Marsh, Carole. The Mystery at Fort Sumter. Friedlander, Randolyn, illus. 2010. (Real Kids, Real Places Ser.). 32p. (J). pap. 7.99 *(978-0-635-07432-4(X),* Marsh, Carole Mysteries) Gallopade International.
—The Mystery at Fort Sumter: First Shot Fired in the Civil War! 2010. (Real Kids, Real Places Ser.). (Illus.). 158p. (J). 18.99 *(978-0-635-07430-0(3),* Marsh, Carole Mysteries) Gallopade International.
Marvel Editors. Genuine Sweet. 2016. (J). lib. bdg. 14.75 *(978-0-606-38314-1(X))* Turtleback.
—Marvel's Captain America Civil War Junior Novel. 2016. (J). lib. bdg. 17.20 *(978-0-606-38313-4(1))* Turtleback.
Masters, Susan Rowan. Night Journey to Vicksburg. Kilcoyne, Hope L., ed. Smith, Duane A., illus. 2003. (Adventures in America Ser.). 74p. (J). (gr. 4). 14.95 *(978-1-893110-30-4(3))* Silver Moon Pr.
McDivitt, Barry. The Youngest Spy. 2007. (ENG.). 176p. (YA). (gr. 3-9). per. 12.95 *(978-1-897235-17-1(8))* Thistledown Pr., Ltd. CAN. Dist: Univ. of Toronto Pr.
McGee, Anne Loader. Anni's Attic. 2012. 326p. (-18). pap. 12.99 *(978-1-936307-24-1(3))* Vendera Publishing.
McGowen, Tom. Jesse Bowman: A Union Boy's War Story, 1 vol. 2008. (Historical Fiction Adventures Ser.). (ENG., Illus.). 160p. (J). (gr. 3-5). lib. bdg. 31.93 *(978-0-7660-2929-3(8),* 3446d244-af18-4b4d-a21f-884845f15e61) Enslow Publishing, LLC.
McMullan, Margaret. How I Found the Strong. 2006. (ENG.). 144p. (YA). (gr. 7-12). reprint ed. mass mkt. 6.99 *(978-0-553-49492-1(9),* Laurel Leaf) Random Hse. Children's Bks.
Meehan, William. Fife. 2006. (ENG.). 180p. (YA). (gr. 4-6). per. 12.95 *(978-0-595-39223-0(7))* iUniverse, Inc.
Meloy, Alice McFeely. As the Crow Flies: Preface to Gettysburg: the Enemy Is Here! 2012. 106p. (J). pap. 8.95 *(978-1-57249-411-4(5),* White Mane Kids) White Mane Publishing Co., Inc.
Michael R. Zomber. Sweet Betsy That's Me: A child of the Civil War. 2009. 116p. pap. 10.95 *(978-1-4401-6323-4(5))* iUniverse, Inc.
Mickles Sr., Robert T. S. Blood Kin, a Savannah Story. 2007. 108p. per. 9.95 *(978-0-595-45129-6(2))* iUniverse, Inc.
Miller, Bobbi. The Girls of Gettysburg. 2014. (ENG.). 160p. (J). (gr. 3-7). 16.95 *(978-0-8234-3163-2(0))* Holiday Hse., Inc.
Montgomery, R. A. House of Danger. 2005. (Choose Your Own Adventure Ser.). (Illus.). 108p. (gr. 4-8). pap. 5.50 *(978-0-7608-9694-5(1))* Sundance/Newbridge Educational Publishing.
—House of Danger. Sundaravej, Sittisan, illus. 2006. (ENG.). 144p. (J). (gr. 4-8). per. 7.99 *(978-1-933390-06-2(9),* CHCL06) Chooseco LLC.
Morris, Gilbert. Drummer Boy at Bull Run. 2011. (Bonnets & Bugles Ser.: 1). (ENG.). 192p. (J). (gr. 4-4). pap. 7.99 *(978-0-8024-0911-9(3),* 566) Moody Pubs.
Myers, Anna. Assassin. 2007. (ENG.). 224p. (YA). (gr. 7). per. 10.99 *(978-0-8027-9643-1(5),* 900044867, Bloomsbury USA Childrens) Bloomsbury Publishing USA.
—Assassin. 2011. (ENG.). 192p. (YA). (gr. 4-6). 22.44 *(978-0-8027-8989-1(7),* 9780802789891) 2005. (J). *(978-978-080-278-3(9))* Walker & Co.
Nix, Josef. My Mama's War. 2009. 104p. pap. 9.99 *(978-1-60860-666-5(X),* Strategic Bk. Publishing) Strategic Book Publishing & Rights Agency (SBPRA).
Noble, Trinka Hakes. The Last Brother: A Civil War Tale. Papp, Robert, illus. 2006. (Tales of Young Americans Ser.). (ENG.). 48p. (J). (gr. 1-4). 17.95 *(978-1-58536-253-0(0),* 202069) Sleeping Bear Pr.
Noble, Trinka Hakes & Papp, Lisa. The Battles. Papp, Robert, illus. 2013. (American Adventures Ser.). (ENG.). 88p. (J). (gr. 3-6). pap. 9.99 *(978-1-58536-861-7(X),* 202368) Sleeping Bear Pr.
Nolen, Jerdine. Calico Girl. (ENG.). (J). (gr. 3-7). 2018. 208p. pap. 8.99 *(978-1-4814-5982-2(1))* 2017. (Illus.). 192p. 18.99 *(978-1-4814-5981-5(3))* Simon & Schuster/Paula Wiseman Bks. (Simon & Schuster/Paula Wiseman Bks.).
Novel Units. Rifles for Watie Novel Units Teacher Guide. 2019. (ENG.). (YA). pap. 12.99 *(978-1-56137-598-1(5),* Novel Units, Inc.) Classroom Library Co.
Older, Daniel José. Dactyl Hill Squad (Dactyl Hill Squad #1) (Dactyl Hill Squad Ser.: 1). (ENG.). (J). (gr. 3-7). 2019. 288p. pap. 6.99 *(978-1-338-26882-9(1))* 2018. (Illus.). 272p. 16.99 *(978-1-338-26881-2(3))* Scholastic, Inc. (Levine, Arthur A. Bks.).
—Freedom Fire (Dactyl Hill Squad #2) 2020. (Dactyl Hill Squad Ser.: 2). (ENG., Illus.). 320p. (J). (gr. 3-7). pap. 6.99 *(978-1-338-26885-0(6))* Scholastic, Inc.
Optic, Oliver, pseud. Fighting for the Right. 2007. 136p. per. *(978-1-4068-3635-6(4))* Echo Library.
—The Soldier Boy: Or, Tom Somers in the Army. 2017. (ENG., Illus.). (J). 24.95 *(978-1-374-95847-0(6));* pap. 14.95 *(978-1-374-95846-3(8))* Capital Communications, Inc.
—The Soldier Boy; or, Tom Somers in the Army. 2007. 156p. per. *(978-1-4068-4347-7(4))* Echo Library.
—Stand by the Union. 2007. 140p. (gr. 4-7). per. *(978-1-4068-4345-3(8))* Echo Library.
—Taken by the Enemy. 2007. 132p. (gr. 4-7). per. *(978-1-4068-4346-0(6))* Echo Library.
—Within the Enemy's Lines. 2007. 132p. (gr. 4-7). per. *(978-1-4068-4348-4(2))* Echo Library.
Orzechowski, Shawneen. Sarah's Secret: Civil War Deserter at Fredericksburg. 2011. 104p. (J). pap. 8.95 *(978-1-57249-400-8(X),* White Mane Kids) White Mane Publishing Co., Inc.
Osborne, Mary Pope. Civil War on Sunday. unabr. ed. 2004. (Magic Tree House Ser.: No. 21). 76p. (J). (gr. k-3). pap. 17.00 incl. audio *(978-0-8072-0930-1(9),* S FTR 253 SP, Listening Library) Random Hse. Audio Publishing Group.
Parsons, Bruce. Siah Carter & the Ship Monitor. 2009. 36p. pap. 16.99 *(978-1-4490-3435-1(7))* AuthorHouse.
Peck, Richard. The River Between Us. 2003. (ENG.). 164p. (J). (gr. 7-7). 21.19 *(978-0-8037-2735-9(6),* Dial) Penguin Publishing Group.
—The River Between Us. 2005. (ENG.). 176p. (J). (gr. 3-7). reprint ed. pap. 8.99 *(978-0-14-240310-5(5),* Puffin Books) Penguin Young Readers Group.
Perez, Norah. The Slopes of War. 2008. (ENG., Illus.). 224p. (YA). (gr. 7-12). pap. 11.99 *(978-0-547-01614-6(X),* 1031432, Clarion Bks.) HarperCollins Pubs.
Philbrick, Rodman. The Mostly True Adventures of Homer P. Figg (Scholastic Gold) 2011. (ENG.). 240p. (J). (gr. 4-7). pap. 8.99 *(978-0-439-66821-7(2),* Scholastic Paperbacks) Scholastic, Inc.
Poe, Marshall. A House Divided. Purvis, Leland, illus. 2009. (Turning Points Ser.). (ENG.). 128p. (J). (gr. 3-7). pap. 8.99 *(978-1-4169-5057-8(5),* Simon & Schuster/Paula Wiseman Bks.) Simon & Schuster/Paula Wiseman Bks.
Polacco, Patricia. Just in Time Abraham Lincoln. 2012. 29.95 *(978-0-8045-4240-1(6))* Spoken Arts, Inc.
—Pink & Say. 2003. (Illus.). (J). (gr. 3-4). pap. 9.99 net. *(978-1-930332-54-6(8))* Lectorum Pubns., Inc.
Rimer, David & Robertson, William P. The Bucktails' Antietam Trials. 2005. (White Mane Kids Ser.: No. 14). (Illus.). 175p. (J). (gr. 4-7). per. 7.95 *(978-1-57249-337-7(2),* White Mane Kids) White Mane Publishing Co., Inc.
Rinaldi, Ann. An Acquaintance with Darkness. 2005. (Great Episodes Ser.). (ENG.). 384p. (YA). (gr. 7-8). pap. 9.99 *(978-0-15-205387-1(5),* 1196220, Clarion Bks.) HarperCollins Pubs.
—Juliet's Moon. 2010. (ENG., Illus.). 256p. (YA). (gr. 7). pap. 14.99 *(978-0-547-25874-4(7),* 1402328, Clarion Bks.) HarperCollins Pubs.
—Leigh Ann's Civil War. 2011. (Great Episodes Ser.). (ENG.). 320p. (YA). (gr. 7). pap. 17.99 *(978-0-547-54999-6(7),* 1450168, Clarion Bks.) HarperCollins Pubs.
—My Vicksburg. 2011. (ENG.). 160p. (YA). (gr. 7). pap. 11.95 *(978-0-547-55000-8(6),* 1450172, Clarion Bks.) HarperCollins Pubs.
—Sarah's Ground. (ENG.). 192p. (YA). 2012. (gr. 7). pap. 9.99 *(978-1-4424-8107-7(2))* 2004. (Illus.). 15.95 *(978-0-689-85924-3(4))* Simon & Schuster Bks. For Young Readers. (Simon & Schuster Bks. For Young Readers).
Robertson, William P. & Rimer, David. The Battling Bucktails at Fredericksburg. 2005. (WM Kids Ser.: Vol. 16). (Illus.). 154p. (J). (gr. 4-7). per. 7.95 *(978-1-57249-345-2(3),* White Mane Kids) White Mane Publishing Co., Inc.
Savage, Bridgette Z. Fly Like the Wind. Savage, Charles J., ed. Savage, Bridgette Z., illus. Savage, Charles J., photos by. 2005. (ENG., Illus.). 112p. (YA). (gr. 5). per. 16.99 *(978-0-9771494-0-7(4))* Buckbeech Studios.
Schraff, Anne. The Burning of the Valley. 2008. (Passages to History Ser.). 115p. (J). (gr. 4-6). lib. bdg. 13.95 *(978-0-7569-8400-7(9))* Perfection Learning Corp.
Schwabach, Karen. The Storm Before Atlanta. 2011. 320p. (J). (gr. 3-7). pap. 7.99 *(978-0-375-85867-3(9),* Yearling) Random Hse. Children's Bks.
Scott, Kathy. Beacon Hill. 2005. 85p. pap. 16.95 *(978-1-4137-8423-7(2))* PublishAmerica, Inc.
Shoulders, Michael. Crossing the Deadline: Stephen's Journey Through the Civil War. 2016. (ENG.). 384p. (YA). (gr. 4-7). 16.99 *(978-1-58536-951-5(9),* 204098) Sleeping Bear Pr.
Spain, Susan Rosson. The Deep Cut, 0 vols. 2014. (ENG.). 228p. (J). (gr. 5-7). pap. 9.99 *(978-1-4778-4768-8(5),* 9781477847688, Two Lions) Amazon Publishing.
—The Deep Cut, 1 vol. 2006. (ENG., Illus.). 224p. (J). (gr. 5-9). 16.99 *(978-0-7614-5316-1(4))* Marshall Cavendish Corp.
Spier, Peter. The Star-Spangled Banner. 2004. (J). (gr. -1-6). 18.95 *(978-1-55592-143-9(4))* Weston Woods Studios, Inc.
Steele, William O. The Perilous Road: A Newbery Honor Award Winner. 2004. (ENG., Illus.). 176p. (J). (gr. 3-7). 17.00 *(978-0-15-205203-4(8),* 1195690); pap. 9.99 *(978-0-15-205204-1(6),* 1195693) HarperCollins Pubs. (Clarion Bks.).
Sybesma, Lila Jeanne Elliot. Yours: The Civil War, a Love Triangle, & the Steamboat Sultana. 2019. (Illus.). xiii, 307p. (YA). pap. *(978-0-87195-431-2(1))* Indiana Historical Society.
Sykes, Shelley & Szymanski, Lois. A Whisper of War. 2003. (J). 5.95 *(978-1-57249-327-8(5),* White Mane Kids) White Mane Publishing Co., Inc.
Trout, Robert J. Drumbeat: The Story of a Civil War Drummer Boy. 2007. 190p. (J). (gr. 4-9). pap. 12.95 *(978-1-57249-390-2(9),* White Mane Kids) White Mane Publishing Co., Inc.
Verne, Jules. The Secret of the Island. Kingston, W. H. G., tr. 2008. 160p. 24.95 *(978-1-60664-753-0(9))* Rodgers, Alan Bks.
Wargin, Kathy-jo. The Legend of Old Abe. Caple, Laurie, illus. 2006. (Myths, Legends, Fairy & Folktales Ser.). (ENG.). 40p. (J). (gr. 2-5). 17.95 *(978-1-58536-232-5(8),* 202057) Sleeping Bear Pr.
Warner, Susan. Daisy in the Field. 2017. (ENG., Illus.). (J). 26.95 *(978-1-374-97071-7(9))* Capital Communications, Inc.
Warner, Susan & Wetherell, Elizabeth. Daisy in the Field. 2011. 272p. 29.95 *(978-1-4638-9964-6(5));* pap. 16.95 *(978-1-4638-0163-2(7))* Rodgers, Alan Bks.
Wells, Rosemary. Red Moon at Sharpsburg. 2008. (ENG.). 256p. (YA). (gr. 7-18). 9.99 *(978-0-14-241205-3(8),* Speak) Penguin Young Readers Group.
Wiechman, Kathy Cannon. Like a River: A Civil War Novel. (ENG.). 336p. (J). (gr. 4-7). 2015. 18.99 *(978-1-62979-209-5(8))* 2012. (Illus.). E-Book *(978-1-62979-061-9(3))* Highlights Pr., c/o Highlights for Children, Inc. (Calkins Creek).
Wilson, John. Battle Scars. 2005. (Illus.). 168p. (J). (gr. 5-9). 6.95 *(978-1-55337-703-0(6))* Kids Can Pr., Ltd. CAN. Dist: Hachette Bk. Group.
—Battle Scars: The American Civil War, Part Two. 2016. (Fields of Conflict Ser.). (ENG.). 192p. (YA). (gr. 8-12). pap. 12.95 *(978-1-77203-093-8(7),* Wandering Fox) Heritage Hse. CAN. Dist: Orca Bk. Pubs. USA.
—The Flags of War. 2004. 168p. (J). (gr. 5-9). 6.95 *(978-1-55337-568-5(8))* Kids Can Pr., Ltd. CAN. Dist: Hachette Bk. Group.
—The Flags of War: The American Civil War, Part One. 2015. (Fields of Conflict Ser.). (ENG.). 192p. (YA). (gr. 8-12). pap. 12.95 *(978-1-77203-070-9(8),* Wandering Fox) Heritage Hse. CAN. Dist: Orca Bk. Pubs. USA.
Wincik, Stephanie. The Journey: A Northern Lights Adventure. 2007. 111p. (J). per. 9.99 *(978-0-9725650-4-2(3))* One Horse Pr.

UNITED STATES—HISTORY—CIVIL WAR, 1861-1865—NAVAL OPERATIONS

Abnett, Dan. The Monitor Versus the Merrimac: Ironclads at War, 1 vol. Verma, Dheeraj, illus. 2006. (Graphic Battles of the Civil War Ser.). (ENG.). 48p. (J). (gr. 4-5). lib. bdg. 37.13 *(978-1-4042-0778-3(3),* c1104d37-0229-4941-a9a3-6bd0f959a40e) Rosen Publishing Group, Inc., The.
Anderson, Dale. The Civil War at Sea, 1 vol. 2004. (World Almanac(r) Library of the Civil War Ser.). (ENG., Illus.). 48p. (gr. 5-8). lib. bdg. 33.67 *(978-0-8368-5585-2(X),* abaa704c-54ab-437b-a508-a47da1d3dc87, Gareth Stevens Secondary Library) Stevens, Gareth Publishing LLLP.
Bailey, Tom. Raphael Semmes: Commander of the Alabama. 2011. (Illus.). 120p. (J). *(978-1-59421-062-4(4))* Seacoast Publishing, Inc.
Brager, Bruce. The Monitor Versus the Merrimack. 2003. (Great Battles Thru the Ages Ser.). (ENG., Illus.). 112p. (gr. 6-12). 30.00 *(978-0-7910-7439-8(0),* P113829, Facts On File) Infobase Holdings, Inc.
Dougherty, Terri. Admiral David Farragut: "Full Speed Ahead!" 2011. (J). *(978-1-59556-041-4(6));* pap. *(978-1-59556-047-6(5))* OTTN Publishing.
Hawk, Fran. The Story of the H. L. Hunley & Queenie's Coin. Nance, Dan, illus. 2004. (ENG.). 40p. (J). (gr. 1-4). 16.95 *(978-1-58536-218-9(2),* 202048) Sleeping Bear Pr.
O'Brien, Patrick. Duel of the Ironclads: The Monitor vs. the Virginia. 2003. (Illus.). 40p. (J). (gr. 1-5). 18.85 *(978-0-8027-8843-6(2))* Walker & Co.
Thompson, Gare. The Monitor: The Iron Warship That Changed the World. Day, Larry, illus. 2003. (All Aboard Reading: Station Stop 3 Ser.). (ENG.). 48p. (J). (gr. 2-4). 16.19 *(978-0-448-43283-0(8))* Penguin Young Readers Group.
Walker, Sally M. Shipwreck Search: Discovery of the H. L. Hunley. Verstraete, Elaine, illus. 2006. (On My Own Science Ser.). (ENG.). 48p. (gr. 2-4). lib. bdg. 25.26

TUV

(978-1-57505-878-8(2), Millbrook Pr.) Lerner Publishing Group.

UNITED STATES—HISTORY—1865-1898

see also Reconstruction (U.S. History, 1865-1877)

Anderson, Michael, ed. Biographies of the New World Power: Rutherford B. Hayes, Thomas Alva Edison, Margaret Sanger, & More, 4 vols. 2012. (Impact on America: Collective Biographies Ser.). (ENG., Illus.). 160p. (YA). (gr. 8-8). 77.64 *(978-1-61530-765-4(6)*, 5be9eeb4-4d17-4c14-8668-1c8580293696) Rosen Publishing Group, Inc., The.

Cooke, Tim. After the War, 1 vol. 2012. (American Civil War: the Right Answer Ser.). (ENG., Illus.). 48p. (J). (gr. 6-8). 34.60 *(978-1-4339-7531-8(9)*, 4f59dc6e-b471-48da-9930-9fb5ab4b06ab); pap. 15.05 *(978-1-4339-7532-5(7)*, f32f003b-b9ac-451e-aa04-226618ca243c) Stevens, Gareth Publishing LLLP. (Gareth Stevens Secondary Library).

Flanagan, Timothy. Reconstruction: A Primary Source History of the Struggle to Unite the North & South after the Civil War, 1 vol. 2004. (Primary Sources in American History Ser.). (ENG., Illus.). 64p. (J). (gr. 5-8). lib. bdg. 37.13 *(978-1-4042-0177-4(7)*, 154ba385-b204-43ac-81c4-6fc934a58a2e) Rosen Publishing Group, Inc., The.

Hakim, Joy. A History of US: Reconstructing America: 1865-1890 a History of US Book Seven. (History of US Ser.: 7). (ENG., Illus.). 208p. (gr. 4-7). 3rd rev. ed. 2006. 24.95 *(978-0-19-518900-1(0))*Bk. 7. 2nd rev. ed. 2007. per. 15.95 *(978-0-19-532721-2(7))* Oxford Univ. Pr., Inc.

Hale, Sarah Elder, ed. Rebuilding a Nation: Picking up the Pieces. 2005. (ENG., Illus.). 48p. (J). (gr. 3-9). 17.95 *(978-0-8126-7909-0(1))* Cobblestone Pr.

Herringshaw, DeAnn. The United States Enters the 20th Century. 2011. (Explorer Library: Language Arts Explorer Ser.). (ENG.). 32p. (gr. 4-8). pap. 14.21 *(978-1-61080-288-8(8)*, 201211); (Illus.). lib. bdg. 32.07 *(978-1-61080-200-0(4)*, 201176) Cherry Lake Publishing.

Kenison, Misti. Where's Your Hat, Abe Lincoln? 2017. (Young Historians Ser.: 0). (Illus.). 28p. (J). (gr. -1-k). bds. 9.99 *(978-1-4926-5250-2(4))* Sourcebooks, Inc.

Miller, Reagan & Colozza, Lisa Colozza. Reconstruction & the Aftermath of the Civil War. 2011. (ENG.). 48p. (J). lib. bdg. *(978-0-7787-5341-4(7))* Crabtree Publishing Co.

Mooney, Carla. Perspectives on the Industrial Revolution. 2018. (Perspectives on US History Ser.). (ENG., Illus.). 32p. (J). (gr. 3-6). 32.80 *(978-1-63235-402-0(0)*, 13724, 12-Story Library) Bookstaves, LLC.

The New South & the Old West: 1866-1890. 2010. (ENG., Illus.). 136p. (gr. 5-8). 35.00 *(978-1-60413-354-7(6)*, P178885, Facts On File) Infobase Holdings, Inc.

Stanley, George E. The Era of Reconstruction & Expansion (1865-1900), 1 vol. 2004. (Primary Source History of the United States Ser.). (ENG., Illus.). 48p. (gr. 5-8). pap. 15.05 *(978-0-8368-5836-5(0)*, 08655e3b-d220-4d45-b204-59fc8821bfcf); lib. bdg. 33.67 *(978-0-8368-5827-3(1)*, 5503fe38-8350-45ea-ba88-0d82f7941d3a) Stevens, Gareth Publishing LLLP. (Gareth Stevens Secondary Library).

Stuckey. Call to Freedom: 1877-Present: Online Edition Plus. 3rd ed. 2003. 17.26 *(978-0-03-037427-2(8))*; 17.26 *(978-0-03-037431-9(6))* Holt McDougal.

—Call to Freedom: Beginning-1877: Online Edition Plus. 3rd ed. 2003. 17.26 *(978-0-03-037429-6(4))*; 17.26 *(978-0-03-037428-9(6))* Holt McDougal.

UNITED STATES—HISTORY—1865-1898—FICTION

Abnett, Dan. Dragon Frontier. 2015. (Dragon Frontier Ser.). (ENG., Illus.). 336p. (J). (gr. 4). pap. 12.99 *(978-0-14-134296-2(X))* Penguin Bks., Ltd. GBR. Dist: Independent Pubs. Group.

Bradbury, Bianca. Flight into Spring. 2005. (ENG.). 190p. (gr. 7). per. 11.95 *(978-1-932350-01-2(2))* Ignatius Pr.

Cast, P. C. & Cast, Kristin. Neferet's Curse: A House of Night Novella. 2013. (House of Night Novellas Ser.: 3). (ENG., Illus.). 160p. (YA). (gr. 7). 14.99 *(978-1-250-00025-5(4)*, 900078258, St. Martin's Griffin) St. Martin's Pr.

Hannigan, Kate. The Detective's Assistant. 2016. (ENG.). 368p. (J). (gr. 3-7). pap. 7.99 *(978-0-316-40349-8(0))* Little, Brown Bks. for Young Readers.

Lawlor, Laurie. He Will Go Fearless. 2006. (ENG.). 224p. (J). (gr. 5). 15.95 *(978-0-689-86579-4(1)*, Simon & Schuster Bks. For Young Readers) Simon & Schuster Bks. For Young Readers.

Park, Linda Sue. Prairie Lotus. 2020. (ENG.). 272p. (J). (gr. 5-7). 16.99 *(978-1-328-78150-5(X)*, 1685061, Clarion Bks.) HarperCollins Pubs.

—Prairie Lotus Signed Edition. 2020. (ENG.). 272p. (J). (gr. 5-7). 16.99 *(978-0-358-36014-8(5)*, Clarion Bks.) HarperCollins Pubs.

Platt, Randall. Professor Renoir's Collection of Oddities, Curiosities, & Delights. 2019. (ENG.). 416p. (J). (gr. 3). 16.99 *(978-0-06-264334-6(7)*, HarperCollins) HarperCollins Pubs.

Walsh, Alice. Pomiuk, Prince of the North. 2006. (ENG., Illus.). 64p. (J). (gr. 3). pap., tchr. ed. 6.95 *(978-0-88878-447-6(3))* Dundurn Pr. CAN. Dist: Publishers Group West (PGW).

UNITED STATES—HISTORY—1898-

Boyer, Paul. Holt American Nation: Modern Era: Online Edition Plus. 3rd ed. 2003. 17.26 *(978-0-03-037433-3(2))* Holt McDougal.

Stuckey. Call to Freedom: 1877-Present: Online Edition Plus. 3rd ed. 2003. 17.26 *(978-0-03-037427-2(8))*; 17.26 *(978-0-03-037431-9(6))* Holt McDougal.

—Call to Freedom: Beginning-1877: Online Edition Plus. 3rd ed. 2003. 17.26 *(978-0-03-037429-6(4))*; 17.26 *(978-0-03-037428-9(6))* Holt McDougal.

UNITED STATES—HISTORY—1898-1919

Brill, Marlene Targ. America in the 1900s. 2009. (Decades of Twentieth-Century America Ser.). (ENG.). 144p. (gr. 5-12). lib. bdg. 38.60 *(978-0-8225-3436-5(3))* Lerner Publishing Group.

Brill, Marlene Targ & Richards, Marlee. America in the 1910s. 2009. (Decades of Twentieth-Century America Ser.). (ENG.). 144p. (gr. 5-12). lib. bdg. 38.60 *(978-0-8225-3437-2(1))* Lerner Publishing Group.

Corrigan, Jim. The 1900s Decade in Photos: A Decade of Discovery, 1 vol. 2010. (Amazing Decades in Photos Ser.). (ENG., Illus.). 64p. (gr. 5-6). lib. bdg. 31.93 *(978-0-7660-3129-6(2)*, d80c8ada-dc2d-4dc4-af5b-4f0485af5688) Enslow Publishing, LLC.

UNITED STATES—HISTORY—WAR OF 1898

see Spanish-American War, 1898

UNITED STATES—HISTORY—20TH CENTURY

Amidon Lusted, Marcia. The Roaring Twenties: Discover the Era of Prohibition, Flappers, & Jazz. Keller, Jennifer, illus. 2014. (Inquire & Investigate Ser.). (ENG.). 128p. (J). (gr. 6-10). 22.95 *(978-1-61930-260-0(8)*, 3fbac5e6-72fa-49c6-bfc5-f8a5e498939a) Nomad Pr.

Anderson, Michael, ed. Biographies of the New World Power: Rutherford B. Hayes, Thomas Alva Edison, Margaret Sanger, & More, 4 vols. 2012. (Impact on America: Collective Biographies Ser.). (ENG., Illus.). 160p. (YA). (gr. 8-8). 77.64 *(978-1-61530-765-4(6)*, 5be9eeb4-4d17-4c14-8668-1c8580293696) Rosen Publishing Group, Inc., The.

Archer, Jules. The Incredible '60s: The Stormy Years That Changed America. rev. ed. 2015. (Jules Archer History for Young Readers Ser.). (ENG., Illus.). 288p. (J). (gr. 6-6). 16.99 *(978-1-63220-605-3(6)*, Sky Pony Pr.) Skyhorse Publishing Co., Inc.

Aronson, Marc. Master of Deceit: J. Edgar Hoover & America in the Age of Lies. (ENG.). 240p. (gr. 9). 2019. (J). pap. 14.99 *(978-1-5362-0630-2(X))* 2012. (Illus.). (YA). 25.99 *(978-0-7636-5025-4(0))* Candlewick Pr.

Baier, Bret & Whitney, Catherine. Three Days in January: Young Readers' Edition: Dwight Eisenhower's Final Mission. 2019. (ENG., Illus.). 256p. (J). (gr. 3-7). 17.99 *(978-0-06-291534-4(7)*, HarperCollins) HarperCollins Pubs.

Bartoletti, Susan Campbell, adapted by. The Untold History of the United States, Volume 1: Young Readers Edition, 1898-1945, Vol. 1. 2014. (ENG., Illus.). 400p. (J). (gr. 5-9). 19.99 *(978-1-4814-2173-7(5)*, Atheneum Bks. for Young Readers) Simon & Schuster Children's Publishing.

Brill, Marlene Targ. America in the 1980s. 2009. (Decades of Twentieth-Century America Ser.). (ENG.). 144p. (gr. 5-12). lib. bdg. 38.60 *(978-0-8225-7602-0(3))* Lerner Publishing Group.

—America in the 1990s. 2009. (Decades of Twentieth-Century America Ser.). (ENG.). 144p. (gr. 5-12). lib. bdg. 38.60 *(978-0-8225-7603-7(1))* Lerner Publishing Group.

—Annie Shapiro & the Clothing Workers' Strike. Akib, Jamel, illus. 2010. (History Speaks: Picture Books Plus Reader's Theater Ser.). (ENG.). 48p. (gr. 2-4). pap. 9.95 *(978-0-7613-6132-9(4))* Lerner Publishing Group.

Brown, Jonatha A., et al. César Chávez, 1 vol. 2007. (Biografías Gráficas (Graphic Biographies) Ser.). (SPA.). 32p. (gr. 3-3). pap. 11.50 *(978-0-8368-7886-8(8)*, 800d35ed-e1f9-4913-90fe-28c87f958399); (Illus.). lib. bdg. 29.67 *(978-0-8368-7879-0(5)*, 08774358-75bd-4346-a4e3-766b518a332f) Stevens, Gareth Publishing LLLP.

Coates, Tim. The Shooting of John F. Kennedy 1963: The Warren Commission. 2003. (Moments of History Ser.). (Illus.). 320p. *(978-1-84381-025-4(5))* Coates, Tim.

Cohon, Rhody & Deutsch, Stacia. Hot Pursuit: Murder in Mississippi. Orback, Craig, illus. 2010. (ENG.). 40p. (J). (gr. 3-5). pap. 7.95 *(978-0-7613-3956-4(6)*, 77cdd621-0509-4a81-bddf-ae8d265cd44d, Kar-Ben Publishing) Lerner Publishing Group.

The Cold War & Postwar: 1946-1963. 2010. (ENG., Illus.). 136p. (gr. 5-8). 35.00 *(978-1-60413-360-8(0)*, P178890, Facts On File) Infobase Holdings, Inc.

Combs, Maggie. Postwar United States. 2011. (Explorer Library: Language Arts Explorer Ser.). (ENG.). 32p. (gr. 4-8). pap. 14.21 *(978-1-61080-284-0(5)*, 201207); (Illus.). lib. bdg. 32.07 *(978-1-61080-196-6(2)*, 201168) Cherry Lake Publishing.

Coy, Cissie. Dennis Chávez: The First Hispanic US Senator / Dennis Chávez: el Primer Senador Hispano de Los Estados Unidos. 2017. (SPA & ENG., Illus.). 64p. (J). (gr. 4-8). pap. 9.95 *(978-1-55885-852-7(0)*, Piñata Books) Arte Publico Pr.

The Decades of Twentieth-Century America, 10 vols., Set. Incl. America in the 1900s. Brill, Marlene Targ. lib. bdg. 38.60 *(978-0-8225-3436-5(3))*; America in the 1910s. Brill, Marlene Targ & Richards, Marlee. lib. bdg. 38.60 *(978-0-8225-3437-2(1))*; America in the 1920s. Lindop, Edmund & Goldstein, Margaret. (Illus.). lib. bdg. 38.60 *(978-0-7613-2831-5(9))*; America in the 1930s. Lindop, Edmund & Goldstein, Margaret. lib. bdg. 38.60 *(978-0-7613-2832-2(7))*; America in the 1940s. Lindop, Edmund & Goldstein, Margaret. lib. bdg. 38.60 *(978-0-7613-2945-9(5))*; America in the 1950s. Lindop, Edmund & DeCapua, Sarah. lib. bdg. 38.60 *(978-0-8225-7642-6(2))*; America in the 1960s. Lindop, Edmund & Goldstein, Margaret. lib. bdg. 38.60 *(978-0-7613-3453-8(X))*; America in the 1970s. Brill, Marlene Targ & Richards, Marlee. lib. bdg. 38.60 *(978-0-8225-3438-9(X))*; America in the 1980s. Brill, Marlene Targ. lib. bdg. 38.60 *(978-0-8225-7602-0(3))*; America in the 1990s. Brill, Marlene Targ. lib. bdg. 38.60 *(978-0-8225-7603-7(1))*; 144p. (gr. 5-12). 2009. (Decades of Twentieth-Century America Ser.). (ENG.). 2010. Set lib. bdg. 386.00 *(978-0-8225-8172-7(8)*, Twenty-First Century Bks.) Lerner Publishing Group.

Fandel, Jennifer. Martin Luther King, Jr. 2005. (Genius Ser.). (Illus.). 48p. (J). (gr. 5-9). lib. bdg. 21.95 *(978-1-58341-329-6(4)*, Creative Education) Creative Co., The.

Fiorelli, June Estep. Fannie Lou Hamer: A Voice for Freedom. 2004. (Avisson Young Adult Ser.). (Illus.). 117p. (J). pap. 19.95 *(978-1-888105-62-9(3))* Avisson Pr., Inc.

Gaines, Jena. Haitian Immigration. 2003. (Changing Face of North America Ser.). (Illus.). 112p. (J). lib. bdg. *(978-1-59084-691-9(5))* Mason Crest.

Ganeri, Anita. I Have a Dream: Martin Luther King, Jr. & the Fight for Equal Rights. 2013. (Turning Points in History Ser.). (Illus.). 48p. (gr. 5-12). 37.10 *(978-1-59920-972-2(1))* Black Rabbit Bks.

Gershenson, Harold P. America the Musical 1900-2000: A Nation's History Through Music. Chesworth, Michael, illus. 2006. (J). *(978-1-58987-201-1(0))* Kindermusik International.

Goodman, Susan E. Hazelle Boxberg. Ettlinger, Doris, illus. 2004. (Brave Kids Ser.). (ENG.). 64p. (J). (gr. 1-4). pap. 5.99 *(978-0-689-84982-4(6)*, Simon & Schuster/Paula Wiseman Bks.) Simon & Schuster/Paula Wiseman Bks.

Hakim, Joy. A History of US: All the People Bk. 10: Since 1945 a History of US Book Ten. 4th ed. 2010. (History of US Ser.: 10). (ENG., Illus.). 304p. (YA). (gr. 5-18). 24.95 *(978-0-19-973502-0(6))* Oxford Univ. Pr., Inc.

—A History of US: War, Peace, & All That Jazz: 1918-1945 a History of US Book Nine. 3rd rev. ed. 2006. (History of US Ser.: 9). (ENG., Illus.). 224p. (gr. 4-7). 24.95 *(978-0-19-530738-2(0))* Oxford Univ. Pr., Inc.

Hardy, Sheila Jackson & Hardy, P. Stephen. Extraordinary People: Extraordinary People Civil Rights Movement. 2006. (Extraordinary People Ser.). (ENG., Illus.). 288p. (J). (gr. 6-18). lib. bdg. 40.00 *(978-0-516-25461-6(8)*, Children's Pr.) Scholastic Library Publishing.

Hillstrom, Kevin. The Progressive Era, 1 vol. 2008. (American History Ser.). (ENG., Illus.). 104p. (gr. 7-7). 41.03 *(978-1-4205-0067-7(8)*, 855b3f02-1134-463a-b161-4c4f6fa73d56, Lucent Pr.) Greenhaven Publishing LLC.

Hinton, Kerry. The Black Power Movement & Civil Unrest, 1 vol. 2017. (Spotlight on the Civil Rights Movement Ser.). (ENG., Illus.). 48p. (J). (gr. 6-6). pap. 12.75 *(978-1-5383-8016-1(1)*, 4bdedc04-7722-49e7-b025-982ca62992fc) Rosen Publishing Group, Inc., The.

Honovich, Nancy. Immigration from the Former Yugoslavia. 2005. (Changing Face of North America Ser.). (Illus.). 112p. (YA). lib. bdg. 24.95 *(978-1-59084-690-2(7))* Mason Crest.

Hudak, Heather C. McCarthyism & the Red Scare. 2017. (Uncovering the Past: Analyzing Primary Sources Ser.). 48p. (J). (gr. 5-6). *(978-0-7787-3939-5(2))* Crabtree Publishing Co.

Jackson, Robert B. The Remarkable Ride of the Abernathy Boys. 2003. (Land We Belong to Is Grand Ser.). (Illus.). 69p. (J). pap. *(978-1-57168-798-2(X)*, Eakin Pr.) Eakin Pr.

Jarrow, Gail. Red Madness: How a Medical Mystery Changed What We Eat. 2014. (Deadly Diseases Ser.). (ENG., Illus.). 192p. (J). (gr. 5). 18.99 *(978-1-59078-732-8(3)*, Calkins Creek) Highlights Pr., c/o Highlights for Children, Inc.

Kops, Deborah. Racial Profiling, 1 vol. 2007. (Open for Debate Ser.). (ENG., Illus.). 144p. (J). (gr. 8-8). lib. bdg. 45.50 *(978-0-7614-2298-3(6)*, a4b030ae-e8ea-4a9d-96bc-d9a129f8229e) Cavendish Square Publishing LLC.

Lüsted, Marcia Amidon. Lyndon B. Johnson & the Civil Rights ACT, 1 vol. 2017. (Spotlight on the Civil Rights Movement Ser.). (ENG., Illus.). 48p. (J). (gr. 6-6). 33.47 *(978-1-5383-8048-2(X)*, 7e6c6e30-9ee8-43e5-9413-0bf6bf097a92) Rosen Publishing Group, Inc., The.

Lynne, Douglas. Contemporary United States: 1968 to the Present. 2007. (Presidents of the United States Ser.). (Illus.). 48p. (J). (gr. 4-7). lib. bdg. 29.05 *(978-1-59036-753-7(7))*; per. 10.95 *(978-1-59036-754-4(5))* Weigl Pubs., Inc.

Mellors, Julie. U-X-L American Decades 2000-09 Cumulative Index. 2012. (U-X-L American Decades Ser.). (ENG.). pap. 5.00 *(978-1-4144-9723-5(7)*, UXL) Cengage Gale.

Mikiowitz, Gloria D. Bill Gates. 2004. (ENG., Illus.). 37p. (J). (gr. 2-5). pap. 7.33 *(978-0-7685-1214-4(X)*, Dominie Elementary) Savvas Learning Co.

National Geographic Learning. Reading Expeditions (Social Studies: People Who Changed America): the Civil Rights Movement. 2006. (Nonfiction Reading & Writing Workshops Ser.). (ENG., Illus.). 40p. (J). pap. 21.95 *(978-0-7922-8628-8(6))* CENGAGE Learning.

Noonan, Sheila Smith. Korean Immigration. 2005. (Changing Face of North America Ser.). (Illus.). 112p. (YA). lib. bdg. 24.95 *(978-1-59084-693-3(1))* Mason Crest.

Pendergast, Tom & Pendergast, Sara, eds. The Sixties in America, 4 vols. 2004. (Sixties in America Reference Library). (ENG.). 701p. 348.00 *(978-0-7876-9249-0(2)*, UXL) Cengage Gale.

Potter, Tony, prod. Plantation Home Model. 2005. 3p. (J). pap. 19.95 *(978-1-58980-274-2(8)*, Pelican Publishing) Arcadia Publishing.

Rice, Dona Herwick & Isecke, Harriet. Civil Rights: Freedom Riders, 1 vol. rev. ed. 2009. (Reader's Theater Ser.). (ENG., Illus.). 32p. (gr. 3-8). pap. 11.99 *(978-1-4333-0554-2(2))* Teacher Created Materials, Inc.

Smith-Llera, Danielle. Lunch Counter Sit-Ins: How Photographs Helped Foster Peaceful Civil Rights Protests. 2018. (Captured History Ser.). (ENG., Illus.). 64p. (J). (gr. 5-9). lib. bdg. 35.32 *(978-0-7565-5878-9(6)*, 138646, Compass Point Bks.) Capstone.

Smith, Robert W. 20th Century Wars. Hoffman, Nancy, ed. McCarthy, Kevin, illus. 2006. (Spotlight on America Ser.). (ENG.). 96p. (gr. 5-9). pap. 13.99 *(978-1-4206-3219-4(1))* Teacher Created Resources, Inc.

South, Victor. America in the 20th Century (1913-1999) 2013. (Illus.). 48p. (J). pap. *(978-1-4222-2422-9(8))* Mason Crest.

—America in the 20th Century (1913-1999) Rakove, Jack N., ed. 2012. (How America Became America Ser.). (Illus.). 48p. (J). (gr. 3-4). 19.95 *(978-1-4222-2408-3(2))* Mason Crest.

—America in the 20th Century (1913/1999) 2018. (J). *(978-1-5105-3610-4(8))* SmartBook Media, Inc.

Southwell, David. Unsolved Political Mysteries. 2009. (Mysteries & Conspiracies Ser.). 80p. (gr. 10-10). 61.20 *(978-1-61514-747-2(0))* Rosen Publishing Group, Inc., The.

Southwell, David & Twist, Sean. Unsolved Political Mysteries, 1 vol. 2007. (Mysteries & Conspiracies Ser.). (ENG., Illus.). 80p. (YA). (gr. 10-10). lib. bdg. 38.47 *(978-1-4042-1083-7(0)*, 22459ed0-c097-42d8-b4df-4471a5b1fe0b) Rosen Publishing Group, Inc., The.

Stone, Oliver & Kuznick, Peter. The Untold History of the United States, Volume 2: Young Readers Edition, 1945-1962. 2020. (ENG., Illus.). 320p. (J). (gr. 5). pap. 12.99 *(978-1-4814-2177-5(8))* Simon & Schuster Children's Publishing.

Vietze, Andrew. The Life & Death of Martin Luther King Jr, 1 vol. 2017. (Spotlight on the Civil Rights Movement Ser.). (ENG., Illus.). 48p. (J). (gr. 6-6). pap. 12.75 *(978-1-5383-8039-0(0)*, 119383a8-59e0-43b8-81f6-bb0064f5f386) Rosen Publishing Group, Inc., The.

Woog, Adam. The Fight Renewed: The Civil Rights Movement. 2005. (Lucent Library of Black History). (ENG., Illus.). 112p. (YA). (gr. 7-10). lib. bdg. 33.45 *(978-1-59018-701-2(6)*, Lucent Bks.) Cengage Gale.

Wright, John & Waugh, Steven. The USA, 1929-1980. 2005. (ENG., Illus.). 144p. pap. 38.50 *(978-0-340-88903-9(9)*, Hodder Education) Hodder Education Group GBR. Dist: Trans-Atlantic Pubns., Inc.

UNITED STATES—HISTORY—20TH CENTURY—FICTION

Blakemore, Megan Frazer. The Spy Catchers of Maple Hill. 2014. (ENG.). 320p. (J). (gr. 3-6). 16.99 *(978-1-61963-348-3(5)*, 900134200, Bloomsbury USA Childrens) Bloomsbury Publishing USA.

Bruchac, Joseph. Two Roads. 320p. (J). (gr. 5). 2019. 8.99 *(978-0-7352-2887-0(6)*, Puffin Books) 2018. 17.99 *(978-0-7352-2886-3(8)*, Dial Bks) Penguin Young Readers Group.

Chaconas, Dori. Pennies in a Jar, 1 vol. Lewin, Ted, illus. 2007. 36p. (J). (gr. 1-4). 16.95 *(978-1-56145-422-8(2))* Peachtree Publishing Co. Inc.

Cho, John. Troublemaker. (ENG.). 224p. (J). (gr. 3-7). 2023. pap. 7.99 *(978-0-7595-5446-7(3))* 2022. 16.99 *(978-0-7595-5447-4(1))* Little, Brown Bks. for Young Readers.

Crenshaw, Mills. The Christmas of 45. 2010. 176p. pap. 11.99 *(978-1-59955-455-6(0))* Cedar Fort, Inc./CFI Distribution.

Crowe, Chris. Death Coming up the Hill. 2018. (ENG.). 208p. (YA). (gr. 9). pap. 15.99 *(978-1-328-90410-2(5)*, 1700750, Clarion Bks.) HarperCollins Pubs.

Easton, Kelly. Walking on Air. 2010. (ENG.). 240p. (YA). (gr. 7). pap. 11.99 *(978-1-4424-1437-2(5)*, McElderry, Margaret K. Bks.) McElderry, Margaret K. Bks.

Greenwood, Diana. Insight, 1 vol. 2012. (ENG.). 224p. (YA). pap. 7.99 *(978-0-310-72315-8(9))* Zondervan.

Gwaltney, Doris. Homefront. 2006. (ENG.). 320p. (J). (gr. 6-8). 21.19 *(978-0-689-86842-9(1))* Simon & Schuster, Inc.

Hartry, Nancy. Watching Jimmy. 2012. (Illus.). 160p. (J). (gr. 4-7). pap. 9.95 *(978-1-77049-360-5(3)*, Tundra Bks.) Tundra Bks. CAN. Dist: Penguin Random Hse. LLC.

Holm, Jennifer L. Full of Beans. 2018. 224p. (J). (gr. 3-7). 8.99 *(978-0-553-51038-6(X)*, Yearling) Random Hse. Children's Bks.

Johnson, Angela. A Sweet Smell of Roses. Velasquez, Eric, illus. 2007. (ENG.). 32p. (J). (gr. k-3). 8.99 *(978-1-4169-5361-6(2)*, Simon & Schuster Bks. For Young Readers) Simon & Schuster Bks. For Young Readers.

Kidd, Ronald. The Year of the Bomb. 2009. (ENG.). 208p. (YA). (gr. 7). pap. 5.99 *(978-1-4169-9625-5(7))*; 16.99 *(978-1-4169-5892-5(4))* Simon & Schuster Bks. For Young Readers. (Simon & Schuster Bks. For Young Readers).

Larson, Kirby. The Friendship Doll. 2012. (ENG.). 208p. (J). (gr. 4-7). 7.99 *(978-0-375-85089-9(9)*, Yearling) Random Hse. Children's Bks.

Magoon, Kekla. The Rock & the River. (ENG.). 304p. (J). (gr. 5-9). 2010. pap. 8.99 *(978-1-4169-7803-9(8))*1. 2009. 19.99 *(978-1-4169-7582-3(9))* Simon & Schuster Children's Publishing. (Aladdin).

Matti, Truus. Mister Orange. 2013. (ENG., Illus.). 156p. (J). (gr. 3). 16.95 *(978-1-59270-123-0(X))* Enchanted Lion Bks., LLC.

Mitchell, Margaree King. When Grandmama Sings. Ransome, James, illus. 2012. (ENG.). 40p. (J). (gr. k-4). 16.99 *(978-0-688-17563-4(5)*, HarperCollins) HarperCollins Pubs.

Myers, Edward. Duck & Cover. 2004. 200p. (J). per. 11.95 *(978-0-9674477-8-0(X))* Montemayor Pr.

Myers, Walter Dean. Patrol: An American Soldier in Vietnam. Grifalconi, Ann, illus. 2005. (ENG.). 40p. (J). (gr. 3-7). pap. 7.99 *(978-0-06-073159-5(1)*, HarperCollins) HarperCollins Pubs.

Schlitz, Laura Amy. The Hired Girl. 2017. (ENG.). 400p. (J). (gr. 5-9). pap. 11.99 *(978-0-7636-9450-0(9))* Candlewick Pr.

—The Hired Girl. l.t. ed. 2020. (ENG.). pap. 15.99 *(978-1-4328-7417-9(9))* Thorndike Pr.

—The Hired Girl. 2018. lib. bdg. 22.10 *(978-0-606-40389-4(2))* Turtleback.

Schwabach, Karen. The Hope Chest. 2010. 288p. (J). (gr. 3-7). 8.99 *(978-0-375-84096-8(6)*, Yearling) Random Hse. Children's Bks.

Shaw, Deirdre. Fair Play. 2005. (American Dreams Ser.: 5). (ENG.). 176p. (YA). mass mkt. 5.99 *(978-0-689-87850-3(8))* Pocket Books.

Smith, Montez Roller. Growing Pains. 2007. (Illus.). 226p. (J). (gr. 4-7). pap. 14.95 *(978-0-9795826-2-8(1))* House Upon A Hill Bks.

—Growing Tall. 2007. (Illus.). 199p. (J). (gr. 4-7). pap. 14.95 *(978-0-9795826-0-8(1))* House Upon A Hill Bks.

Stentiford, Tyler Michael. A Darker Secret. 2009. (ENG.). 128p. (YA). pap. 9.99 *(978-1-60138-315-0(0))* Atlantic Publishing Group, Inc.

Stevenson, Robin. Record Breaker, 1 vol. 2013. (ENG.). 152p. (J). (gr. 4-7). pap. 9.95 *(978-1-55469-959-9(2))* Orca Bk. Pubs. USA.

Trimble, Tonya. Curiosity, with a Capital S. Enik, Ted, illus. 2011. 144p. (J). pap. 9.95 *(978-0-9816453-9-1(9))*; 16.95 *(978-0-9829421-5-4(X))* Tell Me Pr., LLC.

Watts, Jeri. Kizzy Ann Stamps. 2013. (ENG., Illus.). 192p. (J). (gr. 4-7). pap. 8.99 *(978-0-7636-6976-8(8))* Candlewick Pr.

Wheeler, Eliza. Home in the Woods. Wheeler, Eliza, illus. 2019. (Illus.). 40p. (J). (gr. k-3). 18.99 *(978-0-399-16290-9(9)*, Nancy Paulsen Books) Penguin Young Readers Group.

Williams-Garcia, Rita. One Crazy Summer. 2009. (KOR.). 272p. (J). pap. *(978-89-7199-494-8(0))* Dolbegae Publishing Co.

—One Crazy Summer. 2011. (ENG.). 240p. (J). (gr. 3-7). pap. 9.99 *(978-0-06-076090-8(7)*, Quill Tree Bks.) HarperCollins Pubs.

—One Crazy Summer. (J). 2011. 1.25 *(978-1-4498-2201-9(0))* 2010. 69.75 *(978-1-4498-2197-5(9))* 2010. 67.75 *(978-1-4498-2199-9(5))* Recorded Bks., Inc.

—One Crazy Summer. 2011. (J). lib. bdg. 17.20 *(978-0-606-23555-6(8))* Turtleback.

—One Crazy Summer: A Newbery Honor Award Winner. 2010. (ENG.). 224p. (J). (gr. 3-7). 18.99 *(978-0-06-076088-5(5))*; lib. bdg. 16.89 *(978-0-06-076089-2(3))* HarperCollins Pubs. (Quill Tree Bks.).

Volk, Lauren. Echo Mountain. 2020. (ENG.). 368p. (J). (gr. 5). 17.99 *(978-0-525-55556-8(0)*, Dutton Books for Young Readers) Penguin Young Readers Group.

UNITED STATES—HISTORY—1919-1933

Baxter, Roberta. The Great Depression: A History Perspectives Book. 2014. (Perspectives Library). (ENG., Illus.). 32p. (J). (gr. 4-8). 32.07 *(978-1-63137-618-4(7)*, 205255) Cherry Lake Publishing.

Beyer, Mark. Temperance & Prohibition: The Movement to Pass Anti-Liquor Laws in America, 1 vol. 2005. (Primary Sources of the Progressive Movement Ser.). (ENG., Illus.). 32p. (gr. 3-4). pap. 10.00 *(978-1-4042-0861-2(5)*, 4aaa1a18-e46a-48ec-95e1-aff662d7c87c) Rosen Publishing Group, Inc., The.

—Temperance & Prohibition: The Movement to Pass Anti-liquor Laws in America. 2009. (Progressive Movement 1900-1920: Efforts to Reform America's New Industrial Society Ser.). 32p. (gr. 3-4). 47.90 *(978-1-60854-171-3(1))* Rosen Publishing Group, Inc., The.

Blumenthal, Karen. Bootleg: Murder, Moonshine, & the Lawless Years of Prohibition. 2013. (ENG., Illus.). 176p. (YA). (gr. 7-12). pap. 14.99 *(978-1-250-03427-4(2)*, 900120600) Square Fish.

Burgan, Michael. The Great Depression: An Interactive History Adventure. 2010. (You Choose: Historical Eras Ser.). (ENG.). 112p. (J). (gr. 3-4). pap. 41.70 *(978-1-4296-6740-1(0)*, 16458, Capstone Pr.) Capstone.

Cooper, Michael L. Dust to Eat: Drought & Depression in The 1930s. 2004. (ENG., Illus.). 96p. (YA). (gr. 7-9). tchr. ed. 17.00 *(978-0-618-15449-4(3)*, 111116, Clarion Bks.) HarperCollins Pubs.

Corrigan, Jim. The 1920s Decade in Photos: The Roaring Twenties, 1 vol. 2010. (Amazing Decades in Photos Ser.). (ENG., Illus.). 64p. (gr. 5-6). lib. bdg. 31.93 *(978-0-7660-3131-9(4)*, 294d20a6-0b4f-44c2-8328-924e58cfe8b3) Enslow Publishing, LLC.

—The 1930s Decade in Photos: Depression & Hope, 1 vol. 2010. (Amazing Decades in Photos Ser.). (ENG., Illus.). 64p. (gr. 5-6). lib. bdg. 31.93 *(978-0-7660-3132-6(2)*, 4c7df277-4a32-4387-9bdd-7f703b46ff6c) Enslow Publishing, LLC.

Gedney, Mona K. The Story of the Great Depression. 2005. (Monumental Milestones Ser.). (Illus.). 48p. (YA). (gr. 4-7). lib. bdg. 29.95 *(978-1-58415-403-7(9))* Mitchell Lane Pubs.

George, Enzo. The Jazz Age & the Great Depression, 1 vol. 2015. (Primary Sources in U. S. History Ser.). (ENG., Illus.). 48p. (gr. 4-4). 33.07 *(978-1-5026-0490-3(6)*, bd691883-11ba-4a62-b2ef-e67818332d46) Cavendish Square Publishing LLC.

Gregory, Joy. The Great Depression. 2016. (Illus.). 48p. (J). *(978-1-5105-1286-3(1))* SmartBook Media, Inc.

Haugen, David M., et al, eds. The Great Depression, 1 vol. 2010. (Perspectives on Modern World History Ser.). (ENG., Illus.). 240p. (gr. 10-12). 49.43 *(978-0-7377-4795-9(1)*, 240a855b-bc7c-468a-a879-8e0cc974f8bb, Greenhaven Publishing) Greenhaven Publishing LLC.

Herringshaw, DeAnn. The United States Enters the 20th Century. 2011. (Explorer Library: Language Arts Explorer Ser.). (ENG.). 32p. (gr. 4-8). pap. 14.21 *(978-1-61080-288-8(8)*, 201211); (Illus.). lib. bdg. 32.07 *(978-1-61080-200-0(4)*, 201176) Cherry Lake Publishing.

Howes, Kelly King & Carnagie, Julie L. The Roaring Twenties Almanac & Primary Sources. 2005. (Roaring 20's Reference Library). (ENG., Illus.). 352p. (J). (gr. 3-7). 129.00 *(978-1-4144-0212-3(0)*, UXL) Cengage Gale.

—The Roaring Twenties Biographies. 2005. (Roaring 20's Reference Library). (ENG., Illus.). 304p. (J). (gr. 3-7). 129.00 *(978-1-4144-0211-6(2)*, UXL) Cengage Gale.

Hurt, Avery Elizabeth. The Great Depression, 1 vol. 2017. (Interwar Years Ser.). (ENG., Illus.). 128p. (YA). (gr. 9-9). 47.36 *(978-1-5026-2713-1(2)*, 98487ccd-d96e-49c4-abb1-5be7fa9b27d7) Cavendish Square Publishing LLC.

Kupperberg, Paul. Critical Perspectives on the Great Depression, 1 vol. 2004. (Critical Anthologies of Nonfiction Writing Ser.). (ENG.). 176p. (YA). (gr. 8-8). lib. bdg. 42.47 *(978-1-4042-0061-6(4)*, 503c641a-9115-4515-a449-cb6051917877) Rosen Publishing Group, Inc., The.

Kupperberg, Paul, ed. Critical Perspectives on the Great Depression. 2009. (Critical Anthologies of Nonfiction Writing Ser.). 176p. (gr. 8-8). 63.90 *(978-1-61512-081-9(5))* Rosen Publishing Group, Inc., The.

Lindop, Edmund & Goldstein, Margaret. America in the 1920s. 2009. (Decades of Twentieth-Century America Ser.). (ENG., Illus.). 144p. (gr. 5-12). lib. bdg. 38.60 *(978-0-7613-2831-5(9))* Lerner Publishing Group.

Loh-Hagan, Virginia. Famine & Dust: Dust Bowl. 2019. (Behind the Curtain Ser.). (ENG., Illus.). 32p. (J). (gr. 4-8). pap. 14.21 *(978-1-5341-4000-4(X)*, 212829); lib. bdg. 32.07 *(978-1-5341-4344-9(0)*, 212828) Cherry Lake Publishing. (45th Parallel Press).

McDaniel, Melissa. Cornerstones of Freedom, Third Series: the Great Depression. 2012. (ENG., Illus.). 64p. (J). (gr. 4-6). lib. bdg. 30.00 *(978-0-531-23056-5(2))* Scholastic Library Publishing.

—The Great Depression (Cornerstones of Freedom: Third Series) 2012. (Cornerstones of Freedom. Third Ser.). (ENG., Illus.). 64p. (J). (gr. 4-6). pap. 8.95 *(978-0-531-28156-7(6)*, Children's Pr.) Scholastic Library Publishing.

Mortlock, Michele & Who HQ. What Were the Roaring Twenties? Murray, Jake, illus. 2018. (What Was? Ser.). 112p. (J). (gr. 3-7). 5.99 *(978-1-5247-8638-0(1))*; lib. bdg. 15.99 *(978-1-5247-8639-7(X))* Penguin Young Readers Group. (Penguin Workshop).

Mullenbach, Cheryl. The Great Depression for Kids: Hardship & Hope in 1930s America, with 21 Activities. 2015. (For Kids Ser.: 59). (ENG., Illus.). 144p. (J). (gr. 4). pap. 16.95 *(978-1-61373-051-5(9))* Chicago Review Pr., Inc.

Nardo, Don. Migrant Mother: How a Photograph Defined the Great Depression, 1 vol. 2010. (Captured History Ser.). (ENG., Illus.). 64p. (J). (gr. 5-7). pap. 8.95 *(978-0-7565-4448-5(3)*, 115529); lib. bdg. 35.32 *(978-0-7565-4397-6(5)*, 113896) Capstone. (Compass Point Bks.).

National Geographic Learning. Reading Expeditions (Social Studies: Voices from America's Past): the Roaring 20s. 2007. (ENG., Illus.). 40p. (J). pap. 21.95 *(978-0-7922-4551-3(2))* National Geographic School Publishing, Inc.

Niver, Heather Moore. Real-World Projects to Explore World War I & the Roaring '20s, 1 vol. 2018. (Project-Based Learning in Social Studies). (ENG., Illus.). 64p. (J). (gr. 5-5). 37.47 *(978-1-5081-8225-2(6)*, 2271897a-73bd-4150-a216-d87b9d43c70a) Rosen Publishing Group, Inc., The.

O'Mara, John. The Great Depression, 1 vol. 2019. (Look at U. S. History Ser.). (ENG.). 32p. (gr. 2-2). pap. 11.50 *(978-1-5382-4875-1(1)*, bb8529a0-100d-4cb8-a4f8-202c8254a6da) Stevens, Gareth Publishing LLLP.

Otfinoski, Steven. The Great Depression (a Step into History) (Library Edition) 2018. (Step into History Ser.). (ENG., Illus.). 144p. (J). (gr. 5-8). lib. bdg. 36.00 *(978-0-531-22690-2(5)*, Children's Pr.) Scholastic Library Publishing.

Pascal, Janet. What Was the Great Depression? 2015. (What Was... Ser.). lib. bdg. 16.00 *(978-0-606-37550-4(3))* Turtleback.

Pascal, Janet B. & Who HQ. What Was the Great Depression? Putra, Dede, illus. 2015. (What Was? Ser.). 112p. (J). (gr. 3-7). 5.99 *(978-0-448-48427-3(7)*, Penguin Workshop) Penguin Young Readers Group.

Peterson, Sheryl. The Great Depression & World War II. 2011. (Explorer Library: Language Arts Explorer Ser.). (ENG.). 32p. (gr. 4-8). pap. 14.21 *(978-1-61080-287-1(X)*, 201210); (Illus.). lib. bdg. 32.07 *(978-1-61080-199-7(7)*, 201174) Cherry Lake Publishing.

Ruggiero, Adriane. The Great Depression, 1 vol. 2006. (American Voices From Ser.). (ENG., Illus.). 160p. (gr. 6-6). lib. bdg. 41.21 *(978-0-7614-1696-8(X)*, 589ebcab-94a9-4be4-878f-c6e6d48f57b0) Cavendish Square Publishing LLC.

Ruth, Amy. Growing up in the Great Depression, 1929 to 1941. 2003. (Our America Ser.). (Illus.). 64p. (J). (gr. 4-7). lib. bdg. 26.60 *(978-0-8225-0655-3(6))* Lerner Publishing Group.

Saidian, Siyavush. The Great Depression: Worldwide Economic Crisis, 1 vol. 2017. (American History Ser.). (ENG.). 104p. (gr. 7-7). lib. bdg. 41.03 *(978-1-5345-6131-1(5)*, 05906c5b-6889-4ea0-85eb-f2215c73dd73, Lucent Pr.) Greenhaven Publishing LLC.

Sebree, Chet'la & Ruggiero, Adriane. Historical Sources on the Great Depression, 1 vol. 2019. (America's Story Ser.). (ENG.). 144p. (J). (gr. 8-8). pap. 22.16 *(978-1-5026-4095-6(3)*, 00e3f499-0250-4850-b046-4586ce9a507a) Cavendish Square Publishing LLC.

Wallenfeldt, Jeff, ed. A New World Power: America from 1920 To 1945, 4 vols. 2012. (Documenting America: the Primary Source Documents of a Nation Ser.). (ENG., Illus.). 168p. (YA). (gr. 10-10). 89.42 *(978-1-61530-784-5(2)*, 06045b1f-3f45-492d-a2c0-1e7c79a7221d) Rosen Publishing Group, Inc., The.

Wallenfeldt, Jeffrey H. A New World Power: America from 1920 to 1945, 1 vol. 2012. (Documenting America: the Primary Source Documents of a Nation Ser.). (ENG., Illus.). 168p. (J). (gr. 10-10). lib. bdg. 44.71 *(978-1-61530-694-7(3)*, 464203e0-e791-4a10-b121-3bccef65d268) Rosen Publishing Group, Inc., The.

World Book, Inc. Staff, contrib. by. The Great Depression. 2010. (J). *(978-0-7166-1505-7(3))* World Bk., Inc.

Worth, Richard. Prohibition: The Rise & Fall of the Temperance Movement. 2019. (J). pap. *(978-1-9785-1539-0(1))* Enslow Publishing, LLC.

UNITED STATES—HISTORY—1933-1945

Amidon Lusted, Marcia. The Great Depression: Experience the 1930s from the Dust Bowl to the New Deal. Casteel, Tom, illus. 2016. (Inquire & Investigate Ser.). (ENG.). 128p. (J). (gr. 6-10). 22.95 *(978-1-61930-336-2(1)*, 25f2b5db-fb04-4b75-85cd-8cd865e5abb5) Nomad Pr.

—The Great Depression: Experience the 1930's from the Dust Bowl to the New Deal. Casteel, Tom, illus. 2016. (Inquire & Investigate Ser.). (ENG.). 128p. (J). (gr. 6-10). pap. 17.95 *(978-1-61930-340-9(X)*, ce2d6583-b839-4faf-a77d-dd176911c683) Nomad Pr.

Baxter, Roberta. The Great Depression. 2014. (Perspectives Library). (ENG., Illus.). 32p. (J). (gr. 4-8). pap. 14.21 *(978-1-63137-663-4(2)*, 205256) Cherry Lake Publishing.

—The Great Depression: A History Perspectives Book. 2014. (Perspectives Library). (ENG., Illus.). 32p. (J). (gr. 4-8). 32.07 *(978-1-63137-618-4(7)*, 205255) Cherry Lake Publishing.

Brown, Don. The Great American Dust Bowl. (ENG., Illus.). 80p. (J). (gr. 7). 2017. pap. 9.99 *(978-1-328-74087-8(0)*, 1677125) 2013. 18.99 *(978-0-547-81550-3(6)*, 1496217) HarperCollins Pubs. (Clarion Bks.).

Burgan, Michael. The Great Depression: An Interactive History Adventure. 2010. (You Choose: Historical Eras Ser.). (ENG.). 112p. (J). (gr. 3-4). pap. 41.70 *(978-1-4296-6740-1(0)*, 16458, Capstone Pr.) Capstone.

Cooper, Michael L. Dust to Eat: Drought & Depression in The 1930s. 2004. (ENG., Illus.). 96p. (YA). (gr. 7-9). tchr. ed. 17.00 *(978-0-618-15449-4(3)*, 111116, Clarion Bks.) HarperCollins Pubs.

Corrigan, Jim. The 1940s Decade in Photos: A World at War, 1 vol. 2010. (Amazing Decades in Photos Ser.). (ENG., Illus.). 64p. (gr. 5-6). lib. bdg. 31.93 *(978-0-7660-3133-3(0)*, 91d10492-f80a-4e9b-998a-1417ae2b3a5c) Enslow Publishing, LLC.

George, Linda & George, Charles. The Great Depression. 2013. (Illus.). 96p. (J). lib. bdg. *(978-1-60152-492-8(7))* ReferencePoint Pr., Inc.

Gitlin, Martin. The Great Depression & World War II: 1929-1945. 2007. (Presidents of the United States Ser.). (Illus.). 48p. (J). (gr. 4-7). lib. bdg. 29.05 *(978-1-59036-749-0(9))*; per. 10.95 *(978-1-59036-750-6(2))* Weigl Pubs., Inc.

Graves, Kerry A. School in the Great Depression. 2016. (It's Back to School ... Way Back! Ser.). (ENG., Illus.). 32p. (J). (gr. 3-6). lib. bdg. 27.99 *(978-1-5157-2098-0(5)*, 132703, Capstone Pr.) Capstone.

Gregory, Joy. The Great Depression. 2016. (Illus.). 48p. (J). *(978-1-5105-1286-3(1))* SmartBook Media, Inc.

Haugen, David M., et al, eds. The Great Depression, 1 vol. 2010. (Perspectives on Modern World History Ser.). (ENG., Illus.). 240p. (gr. 10-12). 49.43 *(978-0-7377-4795-9(1)*, 240a855b-bc7c-468a-a879-8e0cc974f8bb, Greenhaven Publishing) Greenhaven Publishing LLC.

Hurt, Avery Elizabeth. The Great Depression, 1 vol. 2017. (Interwar Years Ser.). (ENG., Illus.). 128p. (YA). (gr. 9-9). 47.36 *(978-1-5026-2713-1(2)*, 98487ccd-d96e-49c4-abb1-5be7fa9b27d7) Cavendish Square Publishing LLC.

Immell, Myra, ed. The Mccarthy Era, 1 vol. 2011. (Perspectives on Modern World History Ser.). (ENG.). 184p. (gr. 10-12). lib. bdg. 49.43 *(978-0-7377-5260-1(2)*, 9f2a225c-bbae-4f14-8e0c-b4f9b0d5cbd1, Greenhaven Publishing) Greenhaven Publishing LLC.

Kimmelman, Leslie. Hot Dog! Eleanor Roosevelt Throws a Picnic. Juhasz, Victor, illus. 2014. (ENG.). 40p. (J). (gr. 3-6). 16.99 *(978-1-58536-830-3(X)*, 203013) Sleeping Bear Pr.

Kupperberg, Paul. Critical Perspectives on the Great Depression, 1 vol. 2004. (Critical Anthologies of Nonfiction Writing Ser.). (ENG.). 176p. (YA). (gr. 8-8). lib. bdg. 42.47 *(978-1-4042-0061-6(4)*, 503c641a-9115-4515-a449-cb6051917877) Rosen Publishing Group, Inc., The.

Kupperberg, Paul, ed. Critical Perspectives on the Great Depression. 2009. (Critical Anthologies of Nonfiction Writing Ser.). 176p. (gr. 8-8). 63.90 *(978-1-61512-081-9(5))* Rosen Publishing Group, Inc., The.

Lindop, Edmund & Goldstein, Margaret. America in the 1940s. 2009. (Decades of Twentieth-Century America Ser.). (ENG.). 144p. (gr. 5-12). lib. bdg. 38.60 *(978-0-7613-2945-9(5))* Lerner Publishing Group.

Loh-Hagan, Virginia. Famine & Dust: Dust Bowl. 2019. (Behind the Curtain Ser.). (ENG., Illus.). 32p. (J). (gr. 4-8). pap. 14.21 *(978-1-5341-4000-4(X)*, 212829); lib. bdg. 32.07 *(978-1-5341-4344-9(0)*, 212828) Cherry Lake Publishing. (45th Parallel Press).

Marriott, Emma. Did Anything Good Come Out of the Great Depression?, 1 vol., 1. 2015. (Innovation Through Adversity Ser.). (ENG.). 48p. (J). (gr. 6-7). 33.47 *(978-1-5081-7072-3(X)*, 2d15bf62-3340-4325-b7dd-5c36f1ace30c, Rosen Young Adult) Rosen Publishing Group, Inc., The.

McCarthy, Meghan. Aliens Are Coming! The True Account of the 1938 War of the Worlds Radio Broadcast. 2009. 40p. (J). (gr. -1-2). pap. 8.99 *(978-0-385-73678-7(9)*, Dragonfly Bks.) Random Hse. Children's Bks.

McDaniel, Melissa. Cornerstones of Freedom, Third Series: the Great Depression. 2012. (ENG., Illus.). 64p. (J). (gr. 4-6). lib. bdg. 30.00 *(978-0-531-23056-5(2))* Scholastic Library Publishing.

—The Great Depression (Cornerstones of Freedom: Third Series) 2012. (Cornerstones of Freedom. Third Ser.). (ENG., Illus.). 64p. (J). (gr. 4-6). pap. 8.95 *(978-0-531-28156-7(6)*, Children's Pr.) Scholastic Library Publishing.

McNeill, Allison & Hanes, Richard Clay. American Home Front in World War II Reference Library Cumulative Index. 2004. (American Homefront in World War II Reference Library). (ENG.). 32p. 5.00 *(978-0-7876-9125-7(9)*, UXL) Cengage Gale.

McNeilly, Linden K. Perspectives on the Great Depression. 2018. (Perspectives on US History Ser.). (ENG., Illus.). 32p. (J). (gr. 3-6). 32.80 *(978-1-63235-401-3(2)*, 13723, 12-Story Library) Bookstaves, LLC.

Mullenbach, Cheryl. The Great Depression for Kids: Hardship & Hope in 1930s America, with 21 Activities. 2015. (For Kids Ser.: 59). (ENG., Illus.). 144p. (J). (gr. 4). pap. 16.95 *(978-1-61373-051-5(9))* Chicago Review Pr., Inc.

Nardo, Don. Migrant Mother: How a Photograph Defined the Great Depression, 1 vol. 2010. (Captured History Ser.). (ENG., Illus.). 64p. (J). (gr. 5-7). pap. 8.95 *(978-0-7565-4448-5(3)*, 115529); lib. bdg. 35.32 *(978-0-7565-4397-6(5)*, 113896) Capstone. (Compass Point Bks.).

National Geographic Learning. Reading Expeditions (Social Studies: Seeds of Change in American History): the Home Front During World War II. 2007. (Nonfiction Reading & Writing Workshops Ser.). (ENG., Illus.). 40p. pap. 21.95 *(978-0-7922-4558-2(X))* CENGAGE Learning.

O'Mara, John. The Great Depression, 1 vol. 2019. (Look at U. S. History Ser.). (ENG.). 32p. (gr. 2-2). pap. 11.50 *(978-1-5382-4875-1(1)*, bb8529a0-100d-4cb8-a4f8-202c8254a6da) Stevens, Gareth Publishing LLLP.

Otfinoski, Steven. The Great Depression (a Step into History) (Library Edition) 2018. (Step into History Ser.). (ENG., Illus.). 144p. (J). (gr. 5-8). lib. bdg. 36.00 *(978-0-531-22690-2(5)*, Children's Pr.) Scholastic Library Publishing.

Pascal, Janet. What Was the Great Depression? 2015. (What Was... Ser.). lib. bdg. 16.00 *(978-0-606-37550-4(3))* Turtleback.

Pascal, Janet B. & Who HQ. What Was the Great Depression? Putra, Dede, illus. 2015. (What Was? Ser.). 112p. (J). (gr. 3-7). 5.99 *(978-0-448-48427-3(7)*, Penguin Workshop) Penguin Young Readers Group.

Peterson, Sheryl. The Great Depression & World War II. 2011. (Explorer Library: Language Arts Explorer Ser.). (ENG.). 32p. (gr. 4-8). pap. 14.21 *(978-1-61080-287-1(X)*, 201210); (Illus.). lib. bdg. 32.07 *(978-1-61080-199-7(7)*, 201174) Cherry Lake Publishing.

Ruggiero, Adriane. The Great Depression, 1 vol. 2006. (American Voices From Ser.). (ENG., Illus.). 160p. (gr. 6-6). lib. bdg. 41.21 *(978-0-7614-1696-8(X)*, 589ebcab-94a9-4be4-878f-c6e6d48f57b0) Cavendish Square Publishing LLC.

Ruth, Amy. Growing up in the Great Depression, 1929 to 1941. 2003. (Our America Ser.). (Illus.). 64p. (J). (gr. 4-7). lib. bdg. 26.60 *(978-0-8225-0655-3(6))* Lerner Publishing Group.

Sebree, Chet'la & Ruggiero, Adriane. Historical Sources on the Great Depression, 1 vol. 2019. (America's Story Ser.). (ENG.). 144p. (J). (gr. 8-8). pap. 22.16 *(978-1-5026-4095-6(3)*, 00e3f499-0250-4850-b046-4586ce9a507a) Cavendish Square Publishing LLC.

Wallenfeldt, Jeff, ed. A New World Power: America from 1920 To 1945, 4 vols. 2012. (Documenting America: the Primary Source Documents of a Nation Ser.). (ENG., Illus.). 168p. (YA). (gr. 10-10). 89.42 *(978-1-61530-784-5(2)*, 06045b1f-3f45-492d-a2c0-1e7c79a7221d) Rosen Publishing Group, Inc., The.

World Book, Inc. Staff, contrib. by. The Great Depression. 2010. (J). *(978-0-7166-1505-7(3))* World Bk., Inc.

UNITED STATES—HISTORY—WORLD WAR, 1939-1945

see World War, 1939-1945—United States

UNITED STATES—HISTORY—1945-1953

Corrigan, Jim. The 1950s Decade in Photos: The American Decade, 1 vol. 2010. (Amazing Decades in Photos Ser.). (ENG., Illus.). 64p. (gr. 5-6). lib. bdg. 31.93 *(978-0-7660-3134-0(9)*, bec97985-d23f-4689-8a9f-c5753ca194cd) Enslow Publishing, LLC.

Cunningham, Jesse G., ed. The McCarthy Hearings. 2003. (At Issue in History Ser.). (Illus.). 144p. (YA). (gr. 7-10). pap. 18.70 *(978-0-7377-1347-3(X)*, Greenhaven Pr., Inc.) Cengage Gale.

Gitlin, Martin. Post-War United States: 1945-Early 1970s. 2007. (Presidents of the United States Ser.). (Illus.). 48p. (J). (gr. 4-7). lib. bdg. 29.05 *(978-1-59036-751-3(0))*; per. 10.95 *(978-1-59036-752-0(9))* Weigl Pubs., Inc.

Immell, Myra, ed. The Mccarthy Era, 1 vol. 2011. (Perspectives on Modern World History Ser.). (ENG.). 184p. (gr. 10-12). lib. bdg. 49.43 *(978-0-7377-5260-1(2)*, 9f2a225c-bbae-4f14-8e0c-b4f9b0d5cbd1, Greenhaven Publishing) Greenhaven Publishing LLC.

Lindop, Edmund & DeCapua, Sarah. America in the 1950s. 2009. (Decades of Twentieth-Century America Ser.). (ENG.). 144p. (gr. 5-12). lib. bdg. 38.60 *(978-0-8225-7642-6(2))* Lerner Publishing Group.

Lindop, Edmund & Goldstein, Margaret. America in the 1940s. 2009. (Decades of Twentieth-Century America Ser.). (ENG.). 144p. (gr. 5-12). lib. bdg. 38.60 *(978-0-7613-2945-9(5))* Lerner Publishing Group.

Stanley, George E. America & the Cold War (1949-1969), 1 vol. 2004. (Primary Source History of the United States Ser.). (ENG., Illus.). 48p. (gr. 5-8). pap. 15.05 *(978-0-8368-5839-6(5)*, 9a4c7a15-acb6-4b2c-9a63-95b3969a77c5); lib. bdg. 33.67 *(978-0-8368-5830-3(1)*, 7157e3a7-bf9d-4f4e-91ca-910d7325a14c) Stevens, Gareth Publishing LLLP. (Gareth Stevens Secondary Library).

Tracy, Kathleen. The McCarthy Era. 2008. (Monumental Milestones Ser.). (Illus.). 48p. (YA). (gr. 4-7). lib. bdg. 29.95 *(978-1-58415-694-9(5))* Mitchell Lane Pubs.

UNITED STATES—HISTORY—1961-

ABDO Publishing Company Staff, et al. United We Stand, Set. 2003. (United We Stand Ser.: 4). (Illus.). (J). (gr. k-3). lib. bdg. 96.84 *(978-1-57765-876-4(0)*, SandCastle) ABDO Publishing Co.

Braun, Eric. Protest Movements: Then & Now. 2018. (America: 50 Years of Change Ser.). (ENG., Illus.). 64p. (J). (gr. 5-9). lib. bdg. 34.65 *(978-1-5435-0385-2(3)*, 137210, Capstone Pr.) Capstone.

Brill, Marlene Targ & Richards, Marlee. America in the 1970s. 2009. (Decades of Twentieth-Century America Ser.). (ENG.). 144p. (gr. 5-12). lib. bdg. 38.60 *(978-0-8225-3438-9(X))* Lerner Publishing Group.

Corrigan, Jim. The 1960s Decade in Photos: Love, Freedom, & Flower Power, 1 vol. 2010. (Amazing Decades in Photos Ser.). (ENG., Illus.). 64p. (gr. 5-6). lib. bdg. 31.93 *(978-0-7660-3135-7(7)*, 40dfcd6e-e072-4f11-bda0-1cf46956b5a1) Enslow Publishing, LLC.

—The 1970s Decade in Photos: Protest & Change, 1 vol. 2010. (Amazing Decades in Photos Ser.). (ENG., Illus.). 64p. (gr. 5-6). lib. bdg. 31.93 *(978-0-7660-3136-4(5)*, d039b223-4fb2-40c7-b8fd-b4f25164cf2d) Enslow Publishing, LLC.

—The 1980s Decade in Photos: The Triumph of Democracy, 1 vol. 2010. (Amazing Decades in Photos Ser.). (ENG., Illus.). 64p. (gr. 5-6). lib. bdg. 31.93 *(978-0-7660-3137-1(3)*, 56541840-ebde-47f4-8f8e-cd2c606fb27d) Enslow Publishing, LLC.

—The 1990s Decade in Photos: The Rise of Technology, 1 vol. 2010. (Amazing Decades in Photos Ser.). (ENG., Illus.). 64p. (J). (gr. 5-6). lib. bdg. 31.93 *(978-0-7660-3138-8(1)*, 720edcd3-4ebe-42c2-89d7-67e7e5161c97) Enslow Publishing, LLC.

Hibbert, Clare. A Day That Changed History: The Assassination of John F Kennedy. 2013. (Turning Points in History Ser.). 48p. (gr. 5-12). 37.10 *(978-1-59920-971-5(3))* Black Rabbit Bks.

Kelley, Tracey. Assassination of John F. Kennedy. 2013. (Turning Points in History Ser.). 48p. (gr. 5-9). 24.95 *(978-1-59920-771-1(0))* Black Rabbit Bks.

Levy, Debbie. The Vietnam War. 2004. (Chronicle of America's Wars Ser.). (Illus.). 96p. (J). (gr. 5-12). 27.93 *(978-0-8225-0421-4(9))* Lerner Publishing Group.

Lindop, Edmund & Goldstein, Margaret. America in the 1960s. 2009. (Decades of Twentieth-Century America Ser.). (ENG.). 144p. (gr. 5-12). lib. bdg. 38.60 *(978-0-7613-3453-8(X))* Lerner Publishing Group.

Marcovitz, Hal & marcovitz, hal. The 1960s: Part of the Understanding American History Series. 2013. (Illus.). 96p. (YA). lib. bdg. *(978-1-60152-494-2(3))* ReferencePoint Pr., Inc.

O'Connor, Jim & Who HQ. What Was the Vietnam War? Foley, Tim, illus. 2019. (What Was? Ser.). 112p. (J). (gr. 3-7). 5.99 *(978-1-5247-8977-0(1)*, Penguin Workshop) Penguin Young Readers Group.

Pendergast, Tom, et al, eds. Primary Sources, Sixties in America. 2004. (Sixties in America Reference Library). (ENG., Illus.). 304p. (J). lib. bdg. 129.00 *(978-0-7876-9248-3(4)*, UXL) Cengage Gale.

Schomp, Virginia. The Vietnam Era, 1 vol. 2006. (American Voices From Ser.). (ENG., Illus.). 160p. (gr. 6-6). 41.21 *(978-0-7614-1693-7(5)*, 9f6ec0da-6102-44c7-923e-ac157479f65e) Cavendish Square Publishing LLC.

UNITED STATES—HISTORY—21ST CENTURY

Bartoletti, Susan Campbell, adapted by. The Untold History of the United States, Volume 1: Young Readers Edition, 1898-1945, Vol. 1. 2014. (ENG., Illus.). 400p. (J). (gr. 5-9).

19.99 *(978-1-4814-2173-7(5)*, Atheneum Bks. for Young Readers) Simon & Schuster Children's Publishing.
Corrigan, Jim. The 2000s Decade in Photos: A New Millennium, 1 vol. 2010. (Amazing Decades in Photos Ser.). (ENG., Illus.). 64p. (gr. 5-6). lib. bdg. 31.93 *(978-0-7660-3139-5(X)*, 73e773aa-d5a7-4233-a994-b885f3b94432) Enslow Publishing, LLC.
Stone, Oliver & Kuznick, Peter. The Untold History of the United States, Volume 2: Young Readers Edition, 1945-1962. (ENG., Illus.). 320p. (J). (gr. 5). 2020. pap. 12.99 *(978-1-4814-2177-5(8))* Vol. 2. 2019. 19.99 *(978-1-4814-2176-8(X)*, Atheneum Bks. for Young Readers) Simon & Schuster Children's Publishing.
TIME Annual 2009. 2009. (Time Inc. Home Entertainment Library-Bound Titles Ser.). (gr. 5-12). 39.93 *(978-0-7613-4232-8(X)*, Twenty-First Century Bks.) Lerner Publishing Group.
Time Inc. Home Entertainment Library-Bound Titles, 9 vols., Set. Incl. GOLF Magazine: The Best Instruction Guide Ever. 144p. (YA). (gr. 5-12). 2008. lib. bdg. 39.93 *(978-0-8225-7278-7(8)*, Twenty-First Century Bks.); Life Nature's Fury. 144p. (gr. 5-12). 2008. lib. bdg. 39.93 *(978-0-7613-4051-5(3)*, Twenty-First Century Bks.); Life Remembering Martin Luther King, Jr. His Life & Crusade in Pictures. Johnson, Charles & Adelman, Bob. 144p. (gr. 5-12). 2008. lib. bdg. 39.93 *(978-0-7613-4178-9(1)*, Twenty-First Century Bks.); Life Strange but True. 128p. (gr. 5-12). 2009. 39.93 *(978-0-7613-4231-1(1)*, Twenty-First Century Bks.); Time: The Year in Review. Twenty-First Century Books, creator. (Illus.). 122p. (YA). (gr. 7-12). 2008. lib. bdg. 33.27 *(978-1-57505-972-3(X))*; TIME for Kids Almanac 2009. 256p. (YA). (gr. 5-12). 2008. lib. bdg. 39.93 *(978-0-7613-4052-2(1)*, Twenty-First Century Bks.); Time Living Wonders: The Marvels & Mysteries of Life on Earth. 128p. (gr. 5-12). 2009. 39.93 *(978-0-7613-4229-8(X)*, Twenty-First Century Bks.); Time Nature's Wonders: The Science & Splendor of Earth's Most Fascinating Places. Lerner Publishing Group Staff, ed. 128p. (gr. 5-12). 2008. lib. bdg. 39.93 *(978-0-7613-4228-1(1)*, Twenty-First Century Bks.); 2008. Set lib. bdg. 389.97 *(978-0-8225-7275-6(3)*, Twenty-First Century Bks.) Lerner Publishing Group.
Twenty-First Century Books, creator. Time: The Year in Review. 2008. (Time Inc. Home Entertainment Library-Bound Titles Ser.). (Illus.). 122p. (YA). (gr. 7-12). lib. bdg. 33.27 *(978-1-57505-972-3(X))* Lerner Publishing Group.

UNITED STATES—INSULAR POSSESSIONS
see United States—Territories and Possessions

UNITED STATES—LABOR AND LABORING CLASSES
see Labor—United States

UNITED STATES—LAW
see Law—United States

UNITED STATES—MAIL
see Postal Service

UNITED STATES—MANNERS AND CUSTOMS
see United States—Social Life and Customs

UNITED STATES—MANUFACTURES
see Industries—United States

UNITED STATES—MAPS
Attainment Company, prod. Geography Reader: 96 Lessons Focus on USA Destinations. 2005. 203p. (YA). (gr. 7-12). spiral bd. 39.00 incl. audio compact disk *(978-1-57861-547-6(X)*, IEP Resources) Attainment Co., Inc.
Balkan, Gabrielle. The 50 States: Activity Book: Maps of the 50 States of the USA, Volume 2. Linero, Sol, illus. 2016. (50 States Ser.: 2). (ENG.). 32p. (J). (gr. 3-6). pap., act. bk. ed. 11.99 *(978-1-84780-862-2(X)*, 311627, Wide Eyed Editions) Quarto Publishing Group UK GBR. Dist: Hachette UK Distribution.
Chadow, Alysa. US States. 2003. pap. 14.00 *(978-0-8059-6054-9(6))* Dorrance Publishing Co., Inc.
Emerald Books, creator. Heroes of History - Maps of the United States Workbook: A Reproducible Workbook & Curriculum Guide. 2005. (Heroes of History Ser.). (ENG., Illus.). 127p. (gr. 5-9). per. 19.99 *(978-1-932096-26-2(4))* Emerald Bks.
Equipo Staff. Atlas Enciclopedico Paises de America. (SPA., Illus.). 224p. (YA). (gr. 5-8). *(978-84-241-2522-6(3)*, EV5866) Everest Editora ESP. Dist: Lectorum Pubns., Inc.
Evan-Moor Educational Publishers. Maps of the Usa. 2004. (World & U. S. Maps Ser.). (ENG., Illus.). 128p. (J). (gr. 1-6). pap., tchr. ed. 21.99 *(978-1-55799-955-9(4)*, EMC 3721) Evan-Moor Educational Pubs.
In the United States. (J). (gr. 4). 3.80 *(978-0-8374-1453-9(9)*, 404) Weekly Reader Corp.
Map - United States. 2004. (Wall Charts Ser.). (J). 4.99 *(978-1-85997-987-7(4))* Byeway Bks.
Rajczak, Michael. Maps Throughout American History, 1 vol. 2019. (Journey to the Past: Investigating Primary Sources Ser.). (ENG.). 32p. (gr. 4-5). pap. 11.50 *(978-1-5382-4042-7(4)*, 7e62c4e6-d1cc-4184-b31f-9c97c2f98f22) Stevens, Gareth Publishing LLLP.
Rand McNally Staff. Atlas Schoolhouse Illustrated United States Atlas. 2005. 112p. (J). 9.95 *(978-0-528-93459-9(7))* Rand McNally.
—Kids' Road Atlas. (Backseat Bks.). 80p. (J). pap. 3.95 *(978-0-528-96544-9(1))* Rand McNally.
State by State Sticker Book. 2012. (J). 5.95 *(978-0-8437-0985-8(5))* Hammond World Atlas Corp.
Thermes, Jennifer. Manhattan: Mapping the Story of an Island. 2019. (ENG., Illus.). 64p. (J). (gr. 3-7). 19.99 *(978-1-4197-3655-1(8)*, 1219101, Abrams Bks. for Young Readers) Abrams, Inc.
Treasure Maps of Clarion County. 2004. per. 19.95 *(978-0-9743881-1-3(4))* Hufnagel Software.
U. S. A. History Map. 2004. (J). *(978-0-9759433-3-5(2))* Maps For Kids Inc.
U. S. A. History Notebook Map. 2004. (J). *(978-0-9759433-5-9(9))* Maps For Kids Inc.
U. S. A. History Poster Map. 2004. (J). *(978-0-9759433-4-2(0))* Maps For Kids Inc.

UNITED STATES—MARINE CORPS
Abdo, Kenny. United States Marine Corps. 2018. (US Armed Forces Ser.). (ENG., Illus.). 24p. (J). (gr. 2-8). lib. bdg. 31.36 *(978-1-5321-2554-6(2)*, 30117, Abdo Zoom-Fly) ABDO Publishing Co.
Baker, Brynn. Navajo Code Talkers: Secret American Indian Heroes of World War II. 2015. (Military Heroes Ser.). (ENG., Illus.). 32p. (J). (gr. 3-6). lib. bdg. 27.99 *(978-1-4914-4837-3(7)*, 128722, Capstone Pr.) Capstone.
Benson, Michael. The U. S. Marine Corps. 2004. (U. S. Armed Forces Ser.). (ENG., Illus.). 64p. (gr. 4-8). lib. bdg. 26.60 *(978-0-8225-1648-4(9))* Lerner Publishing Group.
Boothroyd, Jennifer. Inside the US Marine Corps. 2017. (Lightning Bolt Books (r) — US Armed Forces Ser.). (ENG., Illus.). 24p. (J). (gr. 1-3). 29.32 *(978-1-5124-3393-7(4)*, ee93620b-5e11-4add-aaba-5c03ca62d11a, Lerner Pubns.) Lerner Publishing Group.
Bozzo, Linda. Marine Expeditionary Units. 2014. (Serving in the Military Ser.). (ENG., Illus.). 32p. (J). (gr. 2-5). lib. bdg. 28.50 *(978-1-60753-493-8(2)*, 16033) Amicus.
—U. S. Marines. 2018. (Serving in the Military Ser.). (ENG.). 32p. (J). (gr. 2-5). lib. bdg. 28.50 *(978-1-60753-392-4(8)*, 14524) Amicus.
Broyles, Janell. Chemical Biological Incident Response Force. (Inside Special Operations Ser.). 64p. (gr. 6-6). 2009. 58.50 *(978-1-61513-551-6(0)*, Rosen Reference) 2008. (ENG., Illus.). (J). lib. bdg. 37.13 *(978-1-4042-1751-5(7)*, fc902811-3dad-40c9-9f30-8c61f23fd82c) 2008. (ENG., Illus.). pap. 12.95 *(978-1-4358-5129-0(3)*, 3ab1c13e-d79e-4df0-bd1a-ead9dfb3b84e, Rosen Classroom) Rosen Publishing Group, Inc., The.
Cook, Colleen Ryckert. Your Career in the Marines, 1 vol. 2011. (Call of Duty: Careers in the Armed Forces Ser.). (ENG.). 128p. (YA). (gr. 7-7). lib. bdg. 39.80 *(978-1-4488-5512-4(8)*, f4648796-544a-4dcc-8841-fe06d558eaf5) Rosen Publishing Group, Inc., The.
Cooke, Tim. US Marine Corps, 1 vol. 2012. (Ultimate Special Forces Ser.). (ENG., Illus.). 48p. (J). (gr. 4-5). 31.60 *(978-1-4488-7880-2(2)*, 4cb178e3-2cff-4dd6-ba04-0cb85c2e6488); pap. 12.75 *(978-1-4488-7957-1(4)*, dab06b82-78d8-4ebf-90c0-0ff39b253450) Rosen Publishing Group, Inc., The. (PowerKids Pr.).
David, Jack. Marine Corps Force Recon. 2009. (Armed Forces Ser.). (ENG., Illus.). 24p. (J). (gr. 3-7). lib. bdg. 26.95 *(978-1-60014-264-2(8))* Bellwether Media.
—United States Marine Corps. 2008. (Armed Forces Ser.). (ENG., Illus.). 24p. (J). (gr. 3-7). lib. bdg. 26.95 *(978-1-60014-164-5(1))* Bellwether Media.
Garstecki, Julia. Marine Raiders Regiment. 2018. (Elite Warriors Ser.). (ENG.). 32p. (gr. 2-7). 9.95 *(978-1-68072-723-4(0))*; (J). (gr. 4-6). pap. 9.99 *(978-1-64466-276-2(0)*, 12357); (J). (gr. 4-6). lib. bdg. *(978-1-68072-429-5(0)*, 12356) Black Rabbit Bks. (Bolt).
Goldish, Meish. Marine Corps: Civilian to Marine. 2010. (Becoming a Soldier Ser.). 24p. (YA). (gr. 3-6). lib. bdg. 26.99 *(978-1-936088-13-3(4))* Bearport Publishing Co., Inc.
Goldish, Meish & Parkhurst, Anthony. Horses, Donkeys, & Mules in the Marines. 2012. (America's Animal Soldiers Ser.). 24p. (J). (gr. 1-6). lib. bdg. 26.99 *(978-1-61772-453-4(X))* Bearport Publishing Co., Inc.
Gordon, Nick. Marine Corps Force Recon. 2013. (U. S. Military Ser.). (ENG., Illus.). 24p. (J). (gr. 3-7). lib. bdg. 26.95 *(978-1-60014-875-0(1)*, Epic Bks.) Bellwether Media.
—U. S. Marine Corps. 2012. (U. S. Military Ser.). (ENG., Illus.). 24p. (J). (gr. 3-7). lib. bdg. 26.95 *(978-1-60014-829-3(8)*, Epic Bks.) Bellwether Media.
Green, Michael. The United States Marines, 1 vol. 2013. (U. S. Military Forces Ser.). (ENG.). 24p. (J). (gr. 1-3). lib. bdg. 27.99 *(978-1-4765-0072-6(X)*, 122131, Capstone Pr.) Capstone.
Gutner, Howard. America's Secret Weapon: The Navajo Code Talkers of World War II. 2003. (ENG., Illus.). 32p. (J). (gr. 6-8). pap. 7.97 net. *(978-0-7652-3266-3(9)*, Celebration Pr.) Savvas Learning Co.
Higgins, Melissa. Sgt. Reckless - The War Horse: Korean War Hero. Iglesias, Alvaro, illus. 2014. (Animal Heroes Ser.). (ENG.). 32p. (J). (gr. k-2). 29.32 *(978-1-4795-5462-1(6)*, 126111, Picture Window Bks.) Capstone.
Hoena, Blake. Navajo Code Talkers: Top Secret Messengers of World War II. Massegu, Marcel P., illus. 2019. (Amazing World War II Stories Ser.). (ENG.). 32p. (J). (gr. 3-9). pap. 7.95 *(978-1-5435-7549-1(8)*, 141081); lib. bdg. 34.65 *(978-1-5435-7314-5(2)*, 140619) Capstone.
Jones, Keisha. My Brother Is in the Marine Corps, 1 vol., 1. 2015. (Military Families Ser.). (ENG., Illus.). 24p. (J). (gr. 3-4). pap. 9.25 *(978-1-5081-4430-4(3)*, dc427b0d-b0f1-4a4c-8bff-21f89c7045bd, PowerKids Pr.) Rosen Publishing Group, Inc., The.
Kallen, Stuart A. Navajo Code Talkers. 2018. (Heroes of World War II (Alternator Books (r)) Ser.). (ENG., Illus.). 32p. (J). (gr. 3-6). 30.65 *(978-1-5124-8644-5(2)*, b22bb522-0710-477b-9a82-187c62ea0db1, Lerner Pubns.) Lerner Publishing Group.
Keeter, Hunter. The U. S. Marine Corps, 1 vol. 2004. (America's Armed Forces Ser.). (ENG., Illus.). 48p. (J). (gr. 5-8). lib. bdg. 33.67 *(978-0-8368-5683-5(X)*, 914db4b0-64e5-4d3c-be0a-e8a8014c1222, Gareth Stevens Secondary Library) Stevens, Gareth Publishing LLLP.
Kissock, Heather. Great Seal. 2017. (Illus.). 24p. (J). *(978-1-5105-0599-5(7))* SmartBook Media, Inc.
Loria, Laura. Marine Force Recon, 1 vol. 2012. (U. S. Special Forces Ser.). (ENG.). 32p. (J). (gr. 3-4). pap. 11.50 *(978-1-4339-6563-0(1)*, d559fd7a-7d5c-4735-8c51-222f0b1f19d9); lib. bdg. 29.27 *(978-1-4339-6561-6(5)*, 75aa237d-0793-4c7e-94c9-2192cc9422af) Stevens, Gareth Publishing LLLP. (Gareth Stevens Learning Library).
Marinaro, Stacy. If I Became a U. S. Marine. 2009. 46p. 24.95 *(978-0-615-21988-2(8))* Marinaro, Stacy.
Marx, Mandy R. Amazing U. S. Marine Facts. 2016. (Amazing Military Facts Ser.). (ENG., Illus.). 24p. (J). (gr. -1-2). lib. bdg. 27.32 *(978-1-5157-0954-1(X)*, 132278, Capstone Pr.) Capstone.
Miller, Adam. U. S. Marines True Stories: Tales of Bravery. 2014. (Courage under Fire Ser.). (ENG.). 32p. (J). (gr. 3-9). lib. bdg. 28.65 *(978-1-4765-9935-9(1)*, 125755, Capstone Pr.) Capstone.
Mitchell, P. P. Join the Marines, 1 vol. 2017. (U. S. Armed Forces Ser.). (ENG.). 32p. (gr. 1-2). pap. 11.50 *(978-1-5382-0544-0(0)*, 684280e3-cd3f-4653-a6ce-ea3d7935a6e6) Stevens, Gareth Publishing LLLP.
Montana, Jack. Marines. 2010. (Special Forces Ser.). 64p. (YA). (gr. 7-18). lib. bdg. 22.95 *(978-1-4222-1842-6(2))* Mason Crest.
Murray, Julie. United States Marine Corps, 1 vol. 2014. (U. S. Armed Forces Ser.). (ENG.). 24p. (J). (gr. -1-2). lib. bdg. 32.79 *(978-1-62970-096-0(7)*, 1713, Abdo Kids) ABDO Publishing Co.
Nelson, Maria. Heroes of the U. S. Marines, 1 vol. 2012. (Heroes of the U. S. Military Ser.). (ENG., Illus.). 32p. (J). (gr. 3-4). pap. 11.50 *(978-1-4339-7245-4(X)*, ca91776c-2df9-4551-ad35-df97133d4f27); lib. bdg. 29.27 *(978-1-4339-7244-7(1)*, 4a95d087-4d3a-40bc-b749-2154696f2f7d) Stevens, Gareth Publishing LLLP.
Orr, Tamra B. USMC Special Reaction Teams, 1 vol. 2008. (Inside Special Operations Ser.). (ENG., Illus.). 64p. (gr. 6-6). pap. 12.95 *(978-1-4358-5130-6(7)*, a38b48b0-f178-4f01-848c-75afaebc9cce, Rosen Classroom) Rosen Publishing Group, Inc., The.
Portman, Michael. Marine Corps, 1 vol. 2011. (U. S. Military Forces Ser.). (ENG., Illus.). 32p. (gr. 3-4). (J). pap. 11.50 *(978-1-4339-5856-4(2)*, 2e4dd5a3-992e-497e-9d88-99aed8a1b076, Gareth Stevens Learning Library); (YA). lib. bdg. 29.27 *(978-1-4339-5854-0(6)*, ddc53ccf-5738-4c68-9b7c-276eb56c0655) Stevens, Gareth Publishing LLLP.
Raum, Elizabeth. U. S. Marines by the Numbers, 1 vol. 2014. (Military by the Numbers Ser.). (ENG., Illus.). 32p. (J). (gr. 3-9). lib. bdg. 28.65 *(978-1-4765-3919-5(7)*, 123918, Capstone Pr.) Capstone.
Reed, Jennifer. Marines of the U. S. Marine Corps [Scholastic]. 2010. (People of the U. S. Armed Forces Ser.). (ENG.). 24p. pap. 0.49 *(978-1-4296-5805-8(3)*, Capstone Pr.) Capstone.
—The U. S. Marine Corps. rev. ed. 2017. (U. S. Military Branches Ser.). (ENG., Illus.). 24p. (J). (gr. -1-2). lib. bdg. 27.32 *(978-1-5157-6772-5(8)*, 135298, Capstone Pr.) Capstone.
—The U. S. Marine Corps [Scholastic]. 2010. (Military Branches Ser.). (ENG.). 24p. pap. 0.52 *(978-1-4296-5072-4(9)*, Capstone Pr.) Capstone.
Rose, Simon. Marine Corps. 2012. (J). *(978-1-61913-294-8(X))*; pap. *(978-1-61913-298-6(2))* Weigl Pubs., Inc.
—Marine Corps Special Operations. 2013. (J). 27.13 *(978-1-62127-452-0(7))*; pap. *(978-1-62127-458-2(6))* Weigl Pubs., Inc.
Rudolph, Jessica & Pushies, Fred J. Marine Scout Snipers in Action. 2013. (Special Ops II Ser.). 32p. (J). (gr. 2-7). lib. bdg. 28.50 *(978-1-61772-891-4(8))* Bearport Publishing Co., Inc.
Russo, Kristen J. Surprising Facts about Being a Marine. 2017. (What You Didn't Know about the U. S. Military Life Ser.). (ENG., Illus.). 32p. (J). (gr. 3-9). lib. bdg. 28.65 *(978-1-5157-7427-3(9)*, 135786, Capstone Pr.) Capstone.
Sandler, Michael. Marine Force Recon in Action. 2008. (Special Ops Ser.). (Illus.). 32p. (J). (gr. 3-6). lib. bdg. 28.50 *(978-1-59716-634-8(0))* Bearport Publishing Co., Inc.
Saxena, Shalini, ed. The History of Marines Around the World, 1 vol., 1. 2013. (World's Armed Forces Ser.). (ENG.). 120p. (YA). (gr. 8-8). 38.84 *(978-1-62275-148-8(5)*, 8d4c62e5-7873-4cdd-a713-a14cbb02abef) Rosen Publishing Group, Inc., The.
Shoup, Kate. Life As a Navajo Code Talker in World War II, 1 vol. 2017. (Life As... Ser.). (ENG.). 32p. (gr. 3-3). pap. 11.58 *(978-1-5026-3051-3(6)*, 8c5232e5-8cb4-44af-b319-3a757917e174) Cavendish Square Publishing LLC.
Simons, Lisa M. Bolt. U. S. Marine Raider Missions: A Timeline. 2016. (Special Ops Mission Timelines Ser.). (ENG., Illus.). 32p. (J). (gr. 3-9). lib. bdg. 27.32 *(978-1-4914-8704-4(6)*, 131423, Capstone Pr.) Capstone.
Sodaro, Craig. The U. S. Marines Special Operations Regiment: The Missions. 2012. (American Special Ops Ser.). (ENG., Illus.). 48p. (J). (gr. 5-9). 32.65 *(978-1-4296-8658-7(8)*, 118995) Capstone.
U. S. Marines. 2019. (Serving Our Country Ser.). (ENG.). 24p. (J). (gr. 1-4). lib. bdg. *(978-1-68151-563-2(6)*, 17595) Amicus.
Whiting, Jim. Marine Corps Forces Special Operations Command. 2014. (U. S. Special Forces Ser.). (ENG.). 48p. (J). (gr. 5-8). *(978-1-60818-464-4(1)*, 21436, Creative Education); pap. 12.00 *(978-1-62832-050-3(8)*, 21437, Creative Paperbacks) Creative Co., The.
—Marine Force Recon. 2018. (U. S. Special Forces Ser.). (ENG.). 48p. (J). (gr. 3-6). *(978-1-60818-984-7(8)*, 19984, Creative Education) Creative Co., The.
Wood, Alix. Serving in the Marine Corps, 1 vol. 2013. (Protecting Our Country Ser.). 32p. (J). (gr. 3-4). (ENG.). pap. 11.00 *(978-1-4777-1398-3(0)*, 6830c8a6-384c-48c0-86d0-c7f1e0de846c); (ENG.). lib. bdg. 28.93 *(978-1-4777-1296-2(8)*, 48edb559-27f8-4296-a4ec-6484f8252b49); pap. 60.00 *(978-1-4777-1399-0(9))* Rosen Publishing Group, Inc., The. (PowerKids Pr.).
Yomtov, Nel. Recon. 2016. (Military Missions Ser.). (ENG., Illus.). 24p. (J). (gr. 3-7). 26.95 *(978-1-62617-437-5(7)*, Epic Bks.) Bellwether Media.

UNITED STATES—MARINE CORPS—BIOGRAPHY
Bradley, James & Powers, Ron. Flags of Our Fathers: A Young People's Edition. 2005. (Illus.). 224p. (YA). (gr. 4-7). mass mkt. 7.99 *(978-0-440-22920-9(0)*, Laurel Leaf) Random Hse. Children's Bks.
—Flags of Our Fathers: Heroes of Iwo Jima. 2003. (ENG., Illus.). 240p. (YA). (gr. 4-7). reprint ed. pap. 8.99 *(978-0-385-73064-8(0)*, Delacorte Bks. for Young Readers) Random Hse. Children's Bks.
Grossi, Craig. Craig & Fred Young Readers' Edition: A Marine, a Stray Dog, & How They Rescued Each Other. 2018. (ENG.). 256p. (J). (gr. 3). pap. 7.99 *(978-0-06-269336-5(0)*, HarperCollins) HarperCollins Pubs.
Sandler, Michael & Pushies, Fred J. Today's Marine Heroes. 2012. (Acts of Courage: Inside America's Military Ser.). (Illus.). 32p. (J). (gr. 2-7). lib. bdg. 28.50 *(978-1-61772-444-2(0))* Bearport Publishing Co., Inc.

UNITED STATES—MARINE CORPS—VOCATIONAL GUIDANCE
Dolan, Edward F. Military Service, 10 vols., Set. Incl. Careers in the U. S. Air Force. 38.36 *(978-0-7614-4205-9(7)*, e4fae1b0-9c27-4222-a7e4-9bfe2018acfe); Careers in the U. S. Army. 38.36 *(978-0-7614-4206-6(5)*, a0a5c8e1-5fba-4400-800a-65381ebde5ea); Careers in the U. S. Coast Guard. 38.36 *(978-0-7614-4207-3(3)*, 7ef3c6d4-eff7-4b91-b515-6d4ff161c981); Careers in the U. S. Marine Corps. 38.36 *(978-0-7614-4209-7(X)*, b4ad4186-88cc-46f5-89ce-17b13d9c32d4); Careers in the U. S. Navy. 38.36 *(978-0-7614-4210-3(3)*, e95d1809-a3a4-48fb-8427-1c59e5c740fd); (Illus.). 80p. (YA). (gr. 7-7). (Military Service Ser.). (ENG.). 2010. Set lib. bdg. 191.80 *(978-0-7614-4203-5(0)*, 1fe14f46-9e52-44d0-bb2d-9295775cd6ab, Cavendish Square) Cavendish Square Publishing LLC.
Kiland, Taylor Baldwin & Stein, R. Conrad. Careers in the U. S. Marine Corps, 1 vol. 2015. (Careers in the U. S. Armed Forces Ser.). (ENG., Illus.). 128p. (gr. 6-7). 38.93 *(978-0-7660-6947-3(8)*, 82a0c94d-245c-4f7f-b14f-6937f82f2319) Enslow Publishing, LLC.
McNab, Chris. Learning Mental Endurance for Survival. Carney, John, ed. 2014. (Extreme Survival in the Military Ser.: 12). 64p. (J). (gr. 7-18). lib. bdg. 23.95 *(978-1-4222-3082-4(1))* Mason Crest.

UNITED STATES MARSHALS
Alagna, Magdalena. Wyatt Earp: Lawman of the American West. 2009. (Primary Sources of Famous People in American History Ser.). 32p. (gr. 2-3). 47.90 *(978-1-60851-747-3(0))* Rosen Publishing Group, Inc., The.
—Wyatt Earp: Lawman of the American West / Sheriff del oeste Americano. 2009. (Famous People in American History/Grandes personajes en la historia de los Estados Unidos Ser.). (ENG & SPA.). 32p. (gr. 2-3). 47.90 *(978-1-61512-558-6(2)*, Editorial Buenas Letras) Rosen Publishing Group, Inc., The.
—Wyatt Earp: Sheriff del legano Oeste, 1 vol. 2003. (Grandes Personajes en la Historia de Los Estados Unidos (Famous People in American History) Ser.). (SPA.). 32p. (gr. 3-4). pap. 10.00 *(978-0-8239-4241-1(4)*, cec92c20-e77a-4cdd-b99f-4a49f2f0a46e, Rosen Classroom) Rosen Publishing Group, Inc., The.
—Wyatt Earp: Sheriff del oeste americano (Wyatt Earp: Lawman of the American West) 2009. (Grandes personajes en la historia de los Estados Unidos (Famous People in American History) Ser.). (SPA.). 32p. (gr. 2-3). 47.90 *(978-1-61512-811-2(5)*, Editorial Buenas Letras) Rosen Publishing Group, Inc., The.
Clapper, Kathryn N., et al. U. S. Marshals. 2018. (U. S. Federal Agents Ser.). (ENG., Illus.). 32p. (J). (gr. 3-9). lib. bdg. 27.32 *(978-1-5435-0140-7(0)*, 137077, Capstone Pr.) Capstone.
Goodman, Michael E. Wyatt Earp. 2005. (Legends of the West Ser.). (Illus.). 48p. (J). (gr. 5-9). lib. bdg. 21.95 *(978-1-58341-339-5(1)*, Creative Education) Creative Co., The.
Nelson, Vaunda Micheaux. Bad News for Outlaws: The Remarkable Life of Bass Reeves, Deputy U. S. Marshal. Christie, R. Gregory, illus. 2009. (ENG.). 40p. (J). (gr. 3-6). lib. bdg. 19.99 *(978-0-8225-6764-6(4)*, 8c280ef7-9537-47d5-9cb7-1dc0fc1aa019, Carolrhoda Bks.) Lerner Publishing Group.
Rogers, Kate. Air Marshals, 1 vol., 1. 2015. (Careers for Heroes Ser.). (ENG., Illus.). 24p. (J). (gr. 3-4). pap. 9.25 *(978-1-5081-4387-1(0)*, 39ac8020-8f6f-4a41-a63a-d1e5c0599095, PowerKids Pr.) Rosen Publishing Group, Inc., The.
Urban, William. Wyatt Earp: The O. K. Corral & the Law of the American West. 2009. (Library of American Lives & Times Ser.). 112p. (gr. 5-5). 69.20 *(978-1-60853-512-5(6))* Rosen Publishing Group, Inc., The.

UNITED STATES MILITARY ACADEMY
Coulson, Art. Unstoppable: How Jim Thorpe & the Carlisle Indian School Football Team Defeated Army. Hardcastle, Nick, illus. 2018. (Encounter: Narrative Nonfiction Picture Bks.). (ENG.). 40p. (J). (gr. 1-5). 15.95 *(978-1-5435-0406-4(X)*, 137233, Capstone Editions) Capstone.
Epstein, Brad M. Army 101: My First Text-Board-Book. I.t. ed. 2007. (101 — My First Text-Board Books). (Illus.). 20p. (J). bds. *(978-1-932530-42-1(8)*, 101 Bk.) Michaelson Entertainment.
Kimmel, Heidi. Cornerstones of Freedom: West Point. 2008. (Cornerstones of Freedom Ser.). (ENG.). 48p. (J). pap. 5.95 *(978-0-531-21109-0(6)*, Children's Pr.) Scholastic Library Publishing.

UNITED STATES MILITARY ACADEMY—FICTION
Efaw, Amy. Battle Dress. 2003. 400p. (J). (gr. 7-18). pap. 6.99 *(978-0-06-053520-9(2))* HarperCollins Pubs.
—Battle Dress. 2010. (ENG.). 304p. (YA). (gr. 7-18). 8.99 *(978-0-14-241397-5(6)*, Speak) Penguin Young Readers Group.
Hancock, H. Irving. Dick Prescott's First Year at West Point. 2007. 144p. per. *(978-1-4065-1978-5(2))* Dodo Pr.
—Dick Prescott's Fourth Year at West Point. rev. ed. 2006. 208p. 27.95 *(978-1-4218-1735-4(7))*; pap. 12.95 *(978-1-4218-1835-1(3))* 1st World Publishing, Inc. (1st World Library - Literary Society).
—Dick Prescott's Fourth Year at West Point. 2007. 176p. per. *(978-1-4065-1981-5(2))* Dodo Pr.
—Dick Prescott's Second Year at West Point. rev. ed. 2006. 208p. 27.95 *(978-1-4218-1736-1(5))*; pap. 12.95 *(978-1-4218-1836-8(1))* 1st World Publishing, Inc. (1st World Library - Literary Society).
—Dick Prescott's Second Year at West Point. 2007. 176p. per. *(978-1-4065-1979-2(0))* Dodo Pr.
—Dick Prescott's Third Year at West Point. rev. ed. 2006. 208p. 27.95 *(978-1-4218-1737-8(3))*; pap. 12.95 *(978-1-4218-1837-5(X))* 1st World Publishing, Inc. (1st World Library - Literary Society).

—Dick Prescott's Third Year at West Point. 2007. 176p. per. (978-1-4065-1980-8(4)) Dodo Pr.

UNITED STATES—MILITARY HISTORY

see United States—History, Military

UNITED STATES—MILITARY POLICY

Cunningham, Anne C., ed. Drones, Surveillance, & Targeted Killings, 1 vol. 2016. (Current Controversies Ser.). (ENG.). 168p. (J). (gr. 10-12). pap. 33.00 (978-1-5345-0036-5(7), b449b6a2-128d-4f99-aef4-79e1ba527ce5); lib. bdg. 48.03 (978-1-5345-0020-4(0), b535a98d-51c0-4849-82b0-bb226a3e126a) Greenhaven Publishing LLC. (Greenhaven Publishing).

Egan, Tracie. Weapons of Mass Destruction & North Korea. (Library of Weapons of Mass Destruction Ser.). 64p. (gr. 5-5). 2009. 58.50 (978-1-60853-961-1(X)) 2004. (ENG., Illus.). (J). lib. bdg. 37.13 (978-1-4042-0296-2(X), 92b49345-de0d-4fe7-9fdc-4f194164ad58) Rosen Publishing Group, Inc., The.

Laxer, James. Empire, 1 vol. 2006. (Groundwork Guides: 2). (ENG., Illus.). 144p. (YA). (gr. 9-12). pap. 9.95 (978-0-88899-707-4(8)) Groundwood Bks. CAN. Dist: Publishers Group West (PGW).

UNITED STATES—MORAL CONDITIONS

Haugen, David M. & Musser, Susan, eds. American Values, 1 vol. 2014. (Opposing Viewpoints Ser.). (ENG., Illus.). 208p. (gr. 10-12). lib. bdg. 50.43 (978-0-7377-6945-6(9), 9f99754e-4f1a-477e-8b57-0376ea91f313, Greenhaven Publishing) Greenhaven Publishing LLC.

UNITED STATES—NATIONAL AERONAUTICS AND SPACE ADMINISTRATION

Amstutz, Lisa J. NASA & the Astronauts. 2018. (Destination Space Ser.). (ENG., Illus.). 48p. (J). (gr. 5-6). pap. 11.95 (978-1-63517-569-1(0), 1635175690); lib. bdg. 34.21 (978-1-63517-497-7(X), 163517497X) North Star Editions. (Focus Readers).

Anderson, Rane. Stem: Mission to Mars: Problem Solving (Grade 3) 2017. (Mathematics in the Real World Ser.). (ENG., Illus.). 32p. (J). (gr. 3-4). pap. 11.99 (978-1-4807-5801-8(9)) Teacher Created Materials, Inc.

Avera, Randy. The Truth about Challenger. 2003. (Illus.). 344p. 34.00 (978-1-932258-00-4(0), SAN # 254-9522) Randolph Publishing.

Becker, Helaine. Counting on Katherine: How Katherine Johnson Saved Apollo 13. Phumiruk, Dow, illus. 2018. (ENG.). 40p. (J). 18.99 (978-1-250-13752-4(7), 900178843, Holt, Henry & Co. Bks. For Young Readers) Holt, Henry & Co.

Borgert-Spaniol, Megan. Katherine Johnson: Guiding Spacecraft. 2017. (STEM Superstar Women Ser.). (ENG., Illus.). 32p. (J). (gr. 3-6). lib. bdg. 32.79 (978-1-5321-1281-2(5), 27605, Checkerboard Library) ABDO Publishing Co.

Brinkley, Douglas. American Moonshot Young Readers' Edition: John F. Kennedy & the Great Space Race. 2019. (ENG., Illus.). 272p. (J). (gr. 3-7). 16.99 (978-0-06-266028-2(4), HarperCollins) HarperCollins Pubs.

Britton, Tamara L. NASA. 2005. (Symbols, Landmarks, & Monuments Set 3 Ser.: Set III). (Illus.). 32p. (gr. k-6). 27.07 (978-1-59197-836-7(X), Checkerboard Library) ABDO Publishing Co.

Cassutt, Michael. The Astronaut Maker: How One Mysterious Engineer Ran Human Spaceflight for a Generation. 2018. (ENG., Illus.). 480p. 30.00 (978-1-61373-700-2(9)) Chicago Review Pr., Inc.

Cline-Ransome, Lesa. Counting the Stars: The Story of Katherine Johnson, NASA Mathematician. ón, Raúl, illus. 2019. (ENG.). 32p. (J). (gr. -1-3). 17.99 (978-1-5344-0475-5(9), Simon & Schuster Bks. For Young Readers) Simon & Schuster Bks. For Young Readers.

Elish, Dan. NASA, 1 vol. 2007. (Kaleidoscope: Space Ser.). (ENG., Illus.). 48p. (gr. 4-4). lib. bdg. 32.64 (978-0-7614-2046-0(0), 7d2c4392-852c-4109-8304-40daa8b73ba5) Cavendish Square Publishing LLC.

Fabiny, Sarah & Who HQ. What Is NASA? Hammond, Ted, illus. 2019. (What Was? Ser.). 112p. (J). (gr. 3-7). 5.99 (978-1-5247-8603-8(9)); 15.99 (978-1-5247-8605-2(5)) Penguin Young Readers Group. (Penguin Workshop).

Feldman, Thea. Katherine Johnson. 2019. (Ready-To-Read Ser.). (ENG.). 47p. (J). (gr. 2-3). 13.89 (978-1-64310-883-4(2)) Penworthy Co., LLC, The.

—Katherine Johnson. Petersen, Alyssa, illus. 2017. 47p. (J). (978-1-5182-5284-6(2), Simon Spotlight) Simon Spotlight.

—Katherine Johnson: Ready-To-Read Level 3. Petersen, Alyssa, illus. 2017. (You Should Meet Ser.). (ENG.). 48p. (J). (gr. 1-3). 17.99 (978-1-5344-0341-3(8)); pap. 4.99 (978-1-5344-0340-6(X)) Simon Spotlight. (Simon Spotlight).

Gehl, Laura. Always Looking Up: Nancy Grace Roman, Astronomer. Pigott, Louise & Oxton, Alex, illus. 2019. (She Made History Ser.). (ENG.). 32p. (J). (gr. -1-3). 17.99 (978-0-8075-0296-9(0), 807502960) Whitman, Albert & Co.

Goldstein, Margaret J. Astronaut & Physicist Sally Ride. 2018. (STEM Trailblazer Bios Ser.). (ENG., Illus.). 32p. (J). (gr. 2-5). 26.65 (978-1-5415-0009-9(1), 0a678350-1fa6-471a-80d7-c4b325e81ef4, Lerner Pubns.) Lerner Publishing Group.

Greve, Tom. Thanks, Nasa! 2012. (Let's Explore Science Ser.). (ENG.). 48p. (gr. 4-6). pap. 10.95 (978-1-61810-253-9(2), 9781618102539) Rourke Educational Media.

Harris, Duchess & Rowell, Rebecca. Hidden Heroes: The Human Computers of NASA. 2018. (Freedom's Promise Ser.). (ENG.). 48p. (J). (gr. 4-8). lib. bdg. 35.64 (978-1-5321-1770-1(1), 30828) ABDO Publishing Co.

Johnson, Katherine. Reaching for the Moon: The Autobiography of NASA Mathematician Katherine Johnson. (ENG., Illus.). (J). (gr. 5). 2020. 272p. pap. 8.99 (978-1-5344-4084-5(4)) 2019. 256p. 17.99 (978-1-5344-4083-8(6)) Simon & Schuster Children's Publishing. (Atheneum Bks. for Young Readers).

Laser-Sailing Starships: Meet NASA Inventor Philip Lubin & His Team's. 2017. (J). (978-0-7166-6159-7(4)) World Bk., Inc.

Loh-Hagan, Virginia. Dorothy Vaughan. Bane, Jeff, illus. 2018. (Mi Mini Biografía (My Itty-Bitty Bio): My Early Library). (ENG.). 24p. (J). (gr. k-1). pap. 12.79 (978-1-5341-0810-3(6), 210604); lib. bdg. 30.64 (978-1-5341-0711-3(8), 210603) Cherry Lake Publishing.

—Katherine Johnson. Bane, Jeff, illus. 2018. (Mi Mini Biografía (My Itty-Bitty Bio): My Early Library). (ENG.). 24p. (J). (gr. k-1). pap. 12.79 (978-1-5341-0809-7(2), 210600); lib. bdg. 30.64 (978-1-5341-0710-6(X), 210599) Cherry Lake Publishing.

—Mary Jackson. Bane, Jeff, illus. 2018. (Mi Mini Biografía (My Itty-Bitty Bio): My Early Library). (ENG.). 24p. (J). (gr. k-1). pap. 12.79 (978-1-5341-0811-0(4), 210608); lib. bdg. 30.64 (978-1-5341-0712-0(6), 210607) Cherry Lake Publishing.

—Sally Ride. Bane, Jeff, illus. 2018. (Mi Mini Biografía (My Itty-Bitty Bio): My Early Library). (ENG.). 24p. (J). (gr. k-1). pap. 12.79 (978-1-5341-0808-0(4), 210596); lib. bdg. 30.64 (978-1-5341-0709-0(6), 210595) Cherry Lake Publishing.

Meet NASA Inventor Kendra Short & Her Printable Probes & Cosmic Confetti. 2017. (J). (978-0-7166-6158-0(6)) World Bk., Inc.

Meet NASA Inventor Masahiro Ono & His Team's Asteroid-Harpooning Hitcher. 2017. (J). (978-0-7166-6161-0(6)) World Bk., Inc.

Meet NASA Inventor Robert Hoyt & His Team's Web-Spinning Space Spiders. 2017. (J). (978-0-7166-6157-3(8)) World Bk., Inc.

Rauf, Don. Choose a Career Adventure at NASA. 2016. (Bright Futures Press: Choose a Career Adventure Ser.). (ENG., Illus.). 32p. (J). (gr. 4-6). 32.07 (978-1-63471-913-1(1), 208973) Cherry Lake Publishing.

Redfern, Nick. True Stories of Space Exploration Conspiracies, 1 vol. 2014. (Off the Record! Ser.). (ENG.). 248p. (YA). (gr. 7-7). 41.47 (978-1-4777-7833-3(0), 51f7c5d4-2961-4920-9bc1-f1e3cdf2c294) Rosen Publishing Group, Inc., The.

Riddolls, Tom. Sally Ride: The First American Woman in Space. 2010. (Crabtree Groundbreaker Biographies Ser.). (ENG., Illus.). 112p. (J). pap. (978-0-7787-2550-3(2)); (gr. 5-8). lib. bdg. (978-0-7787-2541-1(3)) Crabtree Publishing Co.

Rissman, Rebecca. Hidden Women: The African-American Mathematicians of NASA Who Helped America Win the Space Race. 2018. (Encounter: Narrative Nonfiction Stories Ser.). (ENG., Illus.). 112p. (J). (gr. 3-7). pap. 9.95 (978-1-5157-9963-4(8), 136958, Capstone Pr.) Capstone.

Rustad, Martha E. H. NASA. 2012. (Exploring Space Ser.). (ENG.). 24p. (gr. k-1). pap. 41.70 (978-1-4296-8329-6(5), Capstone Pr.) Capstone.

—NASA, 1 vol. 2012. (Exploring Space Ser.). (ENG.). 24p. (J). (gr. -1-2). lib. bdg. 27.32 (978-1-4296-7581-9(0), 117178, Capstone Pr.) Capstone.

Schwartz, Heather E. NASA Astronomer Nancy Grace Roman. 2018. (STEM Trailblazer Bios Ser.). (ENG., Illus.). 32p. (J). (gr. 2-5). 26.65 (978-1-5124-9979-7(X), f9d26d58-4169-4b0f-8e65-837456b8c53a, Lerner Pubns.) Lerner Publishing Group.

Slade, Suzanne. A Computer Called Katherine: How Katherine Johnson Helped Put America on the Moon. Miller Jamison, Veronica, illus. 2019. (ENG.). 40p. (J). (gr. -1-3). 18.99 (978-0-316-43517-8(1)) Little, Brown Bks. for Young Readers.

Wilkins, Ebony Joy. DK Life Stories: Katherine Johnson. Ager, Charlotte, illus. 2019. (DK Life Stories Ser.). (ENG.). 128p. (J). (gr. 3-7). pap. 5.99 (978-1-4654-7912-9(0), DK Children) Dorling Kindersley Publishing, Inc.

Wimmer, Teresa. National Aeronautics & Space Administration. (Agents of Government Ser.). (ENG.). 48p. (J). (gr. 4-7). 2016. pap. 12.00 (978-1-62832-148-7(2), 20844, Creative Paperbacks) 2015. (Illus.). (978-1-60818-547-4(8), 20843, Creative Education) Creative Co., The.

Zobel, Derek. NASA. 2010. (Exploring Space Ser.). (ENG., Illus.). 24p. (J). (gr. k-3). lib. bdg. 26.95 (978-1-60014-293-2(1), Blastoff! Readers) Bellwether Media.

UNITED STATES—NATIONAL GUARD

Greene, Meg. Careers in the National Guards' Search & Rescue Units. 2009. (Careers in Search & Rescue Operations Ser.). 64p. (gr. 5-8). 58.50 (978-1-61511-812-0(8), Rosen Reference) Rosen Publishing Group, Inc., The.

Kerrigan, Michael. The National Guard. 2004. (Rescue & Prevention Ser.). (Illus.). 96p. (J). (gr. 7-18). lib. bdg. 22.95 (978-1-59084-410-6(6)) Mason Crest.

Mitchell, P. P. Join the National Guard. 2017. (U. S. Armed Forces Ser.). 32p. (gr. 1-2). pap. 63.00 (978-1-5382-0552-5(1)) Stevens, Gareth Publishing LLLP.

Thompson, Jim. My Cousin Is in the National Guard, 1 vol., 1. 2015. (Military Families Ser.). (ENG., Illus.). 24p. (J). (gr. 3-4). 25.27 (978-1-5081-4448-9(6), 450e33a0-c3d5-4813-ace4-d764ec15e874, PowerKids Pr.) Rosen Publishing Group, Inc., The.

UNITED STATES—NATIONAL PARK SERVICE

Duling, Kaitlyn. The Formation of the National Park Service, 1 vol. 2017. (History of Conservation: Preserving Our Planet Ser.). (ENG.). 112p. (YA). (gr. 9-9). 44.50 (978-1-5026-3130-5(X), 79b9e6e9-e9a8-43b9-806c-329b3016e99e) Cavendish Square Publishing LLC.

Pimentel, Annette Bay. Mountain Chef: How One Man Lost His Groceries, Changed His Plans, & Helped Cook up the National Park Service. Lo, Rich, illus. 40p. (J). (gr. 1-4). 2019. pap. 7.99 (978-1-58089-985-7(4)) 2016. (ENG.). 16.95 (978-1-58089-711-2(8)) Charlesbridge Publishing, Inc.

Tornio, Stacy & Keffer, Ken. The National Parks! 2016. (Ranger Rick's Travels Ser.). (Illus.). 144p. (J). (gr. 2-6). pap. 16.95 (978-1-63076-230-8(X)) Muddy Boots Pr.

—Ranger Rick Goes to the National Parks! 2016. (Illus.). 138p. (J). (978-1-5182-3207-7(8)) Muddy Bks.

UNITED STATES—NATIONAL PARKS AND RESERVES

see National Parks and Reserves—United States

UNITED STATES—NATURAL HISTORY

see Natural History—United States

UNITED STATES—NATURAL MONUMENTS

see Natural Monuments

UNITED STATES—NATURAL RESOURCES

see Natural Resources—United States; United States—Economic Conditions

UNITED STATES NAVAL ACADEMY—FICTION

Hancock, H. Irving. Dave Darrin's First Year at Annapolis. rev. ed. 2006. 212p. 27.95 (978-1-4218-1739-2(X)); pap. 12.95 (978-1-4218-1839-9(6)) 1st World Publishing, Inc. (1st World Library - Literary Society).

—Dave Darrin's First Year at Annapolis. 2018. (ENG., Illus.). 168p. (YA). (gr. 7-12). pap. (978-93-5297-335-4(6)) Alpha Editions.

—Dave Darrin's First Year at Annapolis. 2017. (ENG., Illus.). (J). 23.95 (978-1-374-94527-2(7)) Capital Communications, Inc.

—Dave Darrin's First Year at Annapolis. 2007. 160p. pap. 19.99 (978-1-4264-6408-9(8)) Creative Media Partners, LLC.

—Dave Darrin's First Year at Annapolis. 2007. 180p. per. (978-1-4065-1974-7(X)) Dodo Pr.

—Dave Darrin's Fourth Year at Annapolis. rev. ed. 2006. 216p. 27.95 (978-1-4218-1746-0(2)); pap. 12.95 (978-1-4218-1846-7(9)) 1st World Publishing, Inc. (1st World Library - Literary Society).

—Dave Darrin's Fourth Year at Annapolis. 2018. (ENG., Illus.). 174p. (YA). (gr. 7-12). pap. (978-93-5297-338-5(0)) Alpha Editions.

—Dave Darrin's Second Year at Annapolis. rev. ed. 2006. 184p. 26.95 (978-1-4218-1734-7(9)); pap. 11.95 (978-1-4218-1834-4(5)) 1st World Publishing, Inc. (1st World Library - Literary Society).

—Dave Darrin's Second Year at Annapolis. 2018. (ENG., Illus.). 144p. (YA). (gr. 7-12). pap. (978-93-5297-336-1(4)) Alpha Editions.

—Dave Darrin's Second Year at Annapolis. 2007. 152p. per. (978-1-4065-1976-1(6)) Dodo Pr.

—Dave Darrin's Second Year at Annapolis: Or, Two Midshipmen As Naval Academy Youngsters. 2017. (ENG., Illus.). (J). 22.95 (978-1-374-88974-3(1)); pap. 12.95 (978-1-374-88973-6(3)) Capital Communications, Inc.

—Dave Darrin's Third Year at Annapolis. rev. ed. 2006. 216p. 27.95 (978-1-4218-1747-7(0)); pap. 12.95 (978-1-4218-1847-4(7)) 1st World Publishing, Inc. (1st World Library - Literary Society).

—Dave Darrin's Third Year at Annapolis. 2007. 184p. per. (978-1-4065-1977-8(4)) Dodo Pr.

Sherman, M. Zachary. Heart of the Enemy, 1 vol. Cage, Josef, illus. 2012. (Bloodlines Ser.). (ENG.). 88p. (J). (gr. 4-8). lib. bdg. 27.32 (978-1-4342-3767-5(2), 117028, Stone Arch Bks.) Capstone.

UNITED STATES—NAVY

Abdo, Kenny. Navy SEALs. 2018. (US Armed Forces Ser.). (ENG.). 24p. (J). (gr. 2-8). lib. bdg. 31.36 (978-1-5321-2549-2(6), 30107, Abdo Zoom-Fly) ABDO Publishing Co.

—United States Navy. 2018. (US Armed Forces Ser.). (ENG., Illus.). 24p. (J). (gr. 2-8). lib. bdg. 31.36 (978-1-5321-2553-9(4), 30115, Abdo Zoom-Fly) ABDO Publishing Co.

Albright, Rosie. Military Dolphins, 1 vol. 2012. (Animal Detectives Ser.). (ENG., Illus.). 24p. (J). (gr. 1-1). pap. 9.25 (978-1-4488-6258-0(2), 9c0e6fa6-8a35-405b-81e7-025a14458c89); lib. bdg. 26.27 (978-1-4488-6153-8(5), 1008b099-7df5-4879-b0f4-b1739b8bfea6) Rosen Publishing Group, Inc., The. (PowerKids Pr.).

—Military Dolphins: Delfines Del Ejército, 1 vol. Alamán, Eduardo, tr. 2012. (Animal Detectives / Detectives Del Reino Animal Ser.). (SPA & ENG., Illus.). 24p. (J). (gr. 1-1). lib. bdg. 26.27 (978-1-4488-6716-5(9), 1056389d-9e30-4450-b259-450bb1a861dc) Rosen Publishing Group, Inc., The.

Alvarez, Carlos. MH-53E Sea Dragons. 2010. (Military Machines Ser.). (ENG., Illus.). 24p. (J). (gr. 3-7). lib. bdg. 26.95 (978-1-60014-495-0(0), Torque Bks.) Bellwether Media.

Anderson, Dale. Soldiers & Sailors in the American Revolution, 1 vol. 2005. (World Almanac(r) Library of the American Revolution Ser.). (ENG.). 48p. (gr. 5-8). pap. 15.05 (978-0-8368-5938-6(3), fefcb9af-19a9-4101-b561-c76c583fb122); lib. bdg. 33.67 (978-0-8368-5929-4(4), 29863a8e-4cf7-476a-957d-381f6117ed23) Stevens, Gareth Publishing LLLP. (Gareth Stevens Secondary Library).

Besel, Jennifer M. The U. S. Navy SEALs: The Missions, 1 vol. 2012. (American Special Ops Ser.). (ENG.). 48p. (J). (gr. 5-9). lib. bdg. 32.65 (978-1-4296-8715-7(0), 119508) Capstone.

Boothroyd, Jennifer. Inside the US Navy. 2017. (Lightning Bolt Books (r) — US Armed Forces Ser.). (ENG., Illus.). 24p. (J). (gr. 1-3). pap. 9.99 (978-1-5124-5602-8(0), 75bcb9e4-abb2-4a7a-8517-65f50560f3c4); lib. bdg. 29.32 (978-1-5124-3394-4(2), fd1f5a79-43f3-4e75-833d-90c22703fb72, Lerner Pubns.) Lerner Publishing Group.

Bow, James. Navy Seals. 2012. (ENG.). 48p. (J). (978-0-7787-7926-1(2)); pap. (978-0-7787-7935-3(1)) Crabtree Publishing Co.

Bozzo, Linda. Navy SEALs. 2015. (Serving in the Military Ser.). (Illus.). 32p. (J). 28.50 (978-1-60753-494-5(0)) Amicus Learning.

Cooke, Tim. US Navy SEALs, 1 vol. 2012. (Ultimate Special Forces Ser.). (ENG., Illus.). 48p. (J). (gr. 4-5). 31.60 (978-1-4488-7881-9(0), 7b4771f0-26db-4be8-a823-2b1c31161b06); pap. 12.75 (978-1-4488-7958-8(2), 71981c3d-16a0-4e02-8bc9-0018557ffeb8) Rosen Publishing Group, Inc., The. (PowerKids Pr.).

David, Jack. United States Navy. 2008. (Armed Forces Ser.). (ENG., Illus.). 24p. (J). (gr. 3-7). lib. bdg. 26.95 (978-1-60014-165-2(X)) Bellwether Media.

Dolan, Edward F. Careers in the U. S. Navy, 1 vol. 2010. (Military Service Ser.). (ENG., Illus.). 80p. (YA). (gr. 7-7). 38.36 (978-0-7614-4210-3(3), e95d1809-a3a4-48fb-8427-1c59e5c740fd) Cavendish Square Publishing LLC.

—Military Service, 10 vols., Set. Incl. Careers in the U. S. Air Force. 38.36 (978-0-7614-4205-9(7), e4fae1b0-9c27-4222-a7e4-9bfe2018acfe); Careers in the U. S. Army. 38.36 (978-0-7614-4206-6(5), a0a5c8e1-5fba-4400-800a-65381ebde5ea); Careers in the U. S. Coast Guard. 38.36 (978-0-7614-4207-3(3), 7ef3c6d4-eff7-4b91-b515-6d4ff161c981); Careers in the U. S. Marine Corps. 38.36 (978-0-7614-4209-7(X), b4ad4186-88cc-46f5-89ce-17b13d9c32d4); Careers in the U. S. Navy. 38.36 (978-0-7614-4210-3(3), e95d1809-a3a4-48fb-8427-1c59e5c740fd); (Illus.). 80p. (YA). (gr. 7-7). (Military Service Ser.). (ENG.). 2010. Set lib. bdg. 191.80 (978-0-7614-4203-5(0), 1fe14f46-9e52-44d0-bb2d-9295775cd6ab, Cavendish Square) Cavendish Square Publishing LLC.

Donovan, Sandy. U. S. Naval Special Warfare Forces. 2004. (U. S. Armed Forces Ser.). (ENG., Illus.). 64p. (gr. 4-8). lib. bdg. 26.60 (978-0-8225-1650-7(0)) Lerner Publishing Group.

Foster, Linda. United States Naval Academy: Annapolis. Miller, Roger, photos by. 2006. (Illus.). 168p. 39.95 (978-0-911897-49-4(6)) Image Publishing, Ltd.

Garstecki, Julia. SEALs. 2018. (Elite Warriors Ser.). (ENG.). 32p. (J). (gr. 4-6). pap. 9.99 (978-1-64466-277-9(9), 12361); lib. bdg. (978-1-68072-430-1(4), 12360) Black Rabbit Bks. (Bolt).

—Seals. 2018. (Elite Warriors Ser.). (ENG.). 32p. (gr. 2-7). 9.95 (978-1-68072-724-1(9), Bolt) Black Rabbit Bks.

Goldish, Meish. Navy: Civilian to Sailor. 2010. (Becoming a Soldier Ser.). 24p. (YA). (gr. 3-6). lib. bdg. 26.99 (978-1-936088-14-0(2)) Bearport Publishing Co., Inc.

Gordon, Nick. Navy SEALs. 2012. (U. S. Military Ser.). (ENG., Illus.). 24p. (J). (gr. 3-7). lib. bdg. 26.95 (978-1-60014-825-5(5), Epic Bks.) Bellwether Media.

—U. S. Navy. 2012. (U. S. Military Ser.). (ENG., Illus.). 24p. (J). (gr. 3-7). lib. bdg. 26.95 (978-1-60014-830-9(1), Epic Bks.) Bellwether Media.

Gregory, Josh. Avionics Technician. 2012. (21st Century Skills Library: Cool Military Careers Ser.). (ENG.). 32p. (gr. 4-8). pap. 14.21 (978-1-61080-619-0(0), 202229); (Illus.). 32.07 (978-1-61080-445-5(7), 202055) Cherry Lake Publishing.

—The Hunt for Bin Laden: Operation Neptune Spear. 2013. (ENG.). 64p. (J). pap. 8.95 (978-0-531-27674-7(0)) Scholastic Library Publishing.

Gunderson, Jessica. U. S. Navy True Stories: Tales of Bravery. 2014. (Courage under Fire Ser.). (ENG.). 32p. (J). (gr. 3-9). lib. bdg. 28.65 (978-1-4765-9937-3(8), 125758, Capstone Pr.) Capstone.

Hodges, Tammy. Breakfast with the Blues. l.t. ed. 2006. (Illus.). 32p. (J). (978-1-934035-00-9(9)) Trent's Prints.

Jackson, Kay. Navy Ships in Action. 2009. (Amazing Military Vehicles Ser.). 24p. (gr. 3-3). 42.50 (978-1-61511-321-7(5), PowerKids Pr.); (ENG.). (YA). lib. bdg. 26.27 (978-1-4358-2750-9(3), 523d6f08-b4d1-43dc-99e5-2bb597717ec3); (ENG., Illus.). (J). pap. 9.25 (978-1-4358-3160-5(8), 5d5e7e6c-4d00-4310-94b9-fa0d804c174b, PowerKids Pr.) Rosen Publishing Group, Inc., The.

—Navy Submarines in Action. 2009. (Amazing Military Vehicles Ser.). 24p. (gr. 3-3). 42.50 (978-1-61511-324-8(X), PowerKids Pr.); (ENG.). (J). pap. 9.25 (978-1-4358-3161-2(6), 5719c62c-48fa-4d6a-81e6-92de9c55a180, PowerKids Pr.); (ENG.). (YA). lib. bdg. 26.27 (978-1-4358-2751-6(1), e22fa1c6-a616-4a79-a880-93c3e08bdaa7) Rosen Publishing Group, Inc., The.

Jordan, David. The U. S. Navy, 1 vol. 2004. (America's Armed Forces Ser.). (ENG., Illus.). 48p. (gr. 5-8). lib. bdg. 33.67 (978-0-8368-5684-2(8), 0fba2fe8-19b2-432b-a411-41286ab90318, Gareth Stevens Secondary Library) Stevens, Gareth Publishing LLLP.

Kiland, Taylor Baldwin. Careers in the U. S. Navy, 1 vol. 2015. (Careers in the U. S. Armed Forces Ser.). (ENG., Illus.). 128p. (gr. 6-7). 38.93 (978-0-7660-6949-7(4), bc19356f-74c7-4b93-8224-7660f1194e4d) Enslow Publishing, LLC.

Kiland, Taylor Baldwin & Teitelbaum, Michael. Military Submarines: Sea Power, 1 vol. 2015. (Military Engineering in Action Ser.). (ENG., Illus.). 48p. (gr. 6-6). 29.60 (978-0-7660-6918-3(4), 399bfcaa-0f0c-45cf-b446-0caa09228e4a); pap. 12.70 (978-0-7660-7069-1(7), 587a4539-b0d8-4781-8601-b0015f58a2e7) Enslow Publishing, LLC.

Leavitt, Amie Jane. U. S. Navy by the Numbers, 1 vol. 2014. (Military by the Numbers Ser.). (ENG., Illus.). 32p. (J). (gr. 3-9). lib. bdg. 28.65 (978-1-4765-3918-8(9), 123917, Capstone Pr.) Capstone.

Loh-Hagan, Virginia. Immortals vs. Navy SEALs. 2019. (Battle Royale: Lethal Warriors Ser.). (ENG., Illus.). 32p. (J). (gr. 4-8). pap. 14.21 (978-1-5341-5053-9(6), 213519); lib. bdg. 32.07 (978-1-5341-4767-6(5), 213518) Cherry Lake Publishing. (45th Parallel Press).

Lunis, Natalie & Pushies, Fred J. The Takedown of Osama Bin Laden. 2012. (Special Ops Ser.). 32p. (J). (gr. 2-7). lib. bdg. 28.50 (978-1-61772-459-6(9)) Bearport Publishing Co., Inc.

Marciniak, Kristin. Navy SEALs. 2013. (Great Warriors Ser.). (ENG., Illus.). 48p. (J). (gr. 4-8). pap. 18.50 (978-1-61783-775-3(X), 10807) ABDO Publishing Co.

Marini, Matthew. Special Forces, Vol. 12. 2015. (On a Mission Ser.). (Illus.). 48p. (J). (gr. 5). 20.95 (978-1-4222-3401-3(0)) Mason Crest.

Marsico, Katie. Calvin Graham's World War II Story. Hill, Dave, illus. 2018. (Narrative Nonfiction: Kids in War Ser.). (ENG.). 32p. (J). (gr. 2-4). lib. bdg. 27.99 (978-1-5124-5681-3(0), 804aec63-24d9-46d5-80b8-cfeb552b88d1, Lerner Pubns.) Lerner Publishing Group.

Marx, Mandy R. Amazing U. S. Navy Facts. 2016. (Amazing Military Facts Ser.). (ENG., Illus.). 24p. (J). (gr. -1-2). lib. bdg. 27.32 (978-1-5157-0952-7(3), 132276, Capstone Pr.) Capstone.

McNab, Chris. Survival at Sea. Carney, John, ed. 2014. (Extreme Survival in the Military Ser.: 12). 64p. (J). (gr. 7-18). lib. bdg. 23.95 (978-1-4222-3084-8(8)) Mason Crest.

McNeil, Niki, et al. HOCPP 1106 the United States Navy. 2006. spiral bd. 23.50 (978-1-60308-106-1(2)) In the Hands of a Child.

Miller, Nancy. My Mom Is in the Navy, 1 vol., 1. 2015. (Military Families Ser.). (ENG., Illus.). 24p. (J). (gr. 3-4). pap. 9.25 (978-1-5081-4438-0(9), 45b897c6-e7bd-428e-a515-9a898922be32, PowerKids Pr.) Rosen Publishing Group, Inc., The.

Mitchell, P. P. Join the Navy, 1 vol. 2017. (U. S. Armed Forces Ser.). (ENG.). 32p. (gr. 1-2). pap. 11.50 *(978-1-5382-0548-8(3),* e4976ae0-082a-48a6-a877-74f352372433) Stevens, Gareth Publishing LLLP.

Montana, Jack. Navy SEALs. 2010. (Special Forces Ser.). 64p. (YA). (gr. 7-18). lib. bdg. 22.95 *(978-1-4222-1843-3(0))* Mason Crest.

Murray, Julie. Navy SEALs, 1 vol. 2014. (U. S. Armed Forces Ser.). (ENG.). 24p. (J). (gr. -1-2). lib. bdg. 32.79 *(978-1-62970-092-2(4),* 1709, Abdo Kids) ABDO Publishing Co.

Nardo, Don. In the Water: Frogmen & Commandos. 2015. (J). *(978-1-59935-462-0(4))* Reynolds, Morgan Inc.

Nelson, Drew. Navy SEALs, 1 vol. 2012. (U. S. Special Forces Ser.). (ENG., Illus.). 32p. (J). (gr. 3-4). pap. 11.50 *(978-1-4339-6567-8(4),* a2437764-440b-4a38-a314-7c04afde67df); lib. bdg. 29.27 *(978-1-4339-6565-4(8),* e170ef28-4f1e-4199-85ed-a9dcc150ce65) Stevens, Gareth Publishing LLLP. (Gareth Stevens Learning Library).

Orr, Tamra. Your Career in the Navy, 1 vol. 2011. (Call of Duty: Careers in the Armed Forces Ser.). (ENG.). 128p. (YA). (gr. 7-7). lib. bdg. 39.80 *(978-1-4488-5511-7(X),* 02c198b6-e85a-4e72-ba0e-b64d488d3830) Rosen Publishing Group, Inc., The.

Payment, Simone. Black Ops & Other Special Missions of the U. S. Navy Seals, 1 vol. 2012. (Inside Special Forces Ser.). (ENG., Illus.). 64p. (YA). (gr. 6-6). pap. 13.95 *(978-1-4488-8385-1(7),* 75594c52-3fc2-4ae3-b9cd-d4a4e36a2dd3); lib. bdg. 37.13 *(978-1-4488-8380-6(6),* 173e6cd6-4db7-43ad-9fb6-667c43e8fc22) Rosen Publishing Group, Inc., The.

—Navy Seals: Special Operations for the U. S. Navy. (Inside Special Operations Ser.). 64p. (gr. 6-6). 2009. 58.50 *(978-1-61513-556-1(1))* 2008. (ENG., Illus.). (J). lib. bdg. 37.13 *(978-1-4042-0874-2(7),* 0927f958-a981-48dd-8574-5082d6913ec0) Rosen Publishing Group, Inc., The. (Rosen Reference).

Perritano, John. Storming the Somali Pirates! Navy Seals Save Hostages!, Vol. 8. 2018. (Special Forces Stories Ser.). 64p. (J). (gr. 7). 31.93 *(978-1-4222-4082-3(7))* Mason Crest.

Person, Stephen. Navy SEAL Team Six in Action. 2013. (Special Ops II Ser.). (Illus.). 32p. (J). (gr. 2-7). lib. bdg. 28.50 *(978-1-61772-890-7(X))* Bearport Publishing Co., Inc.

Reed, Jennifer. Marineros de la Armada de EE. UU. 2010. (Gente de Las Fuerzas Armadas de EE. UU. /People of the Armed Forces Ser.).Tr. of Sailors of the U. S. Navy. (MUL.). 24p. (J). (gr. -1-2). lib. bdg. 27.32 *(978-1-4296-6117-1(8),* 115145) Capstone.

—Sailors of the U. S. Navy [Scholastic]. 2010. (People of the U. S. Armed Forces Ser.). (ENG.). 24p. pap. 0.49 *(978-1-4296-5806-5(1),* Capstone Pr.) Capstone.

—The U. S. Navy [Scholastic]. 2010. (Military Branches Ser.). (ENG.). 24p. pap. 0.52 *(978-1-4296-5071-7(0),* Capstone Pr.) Capstone.

—The U.S. Navy. rev. ed. 2017. (U. S. Military Branches Ser.). (ENG., Illus.). 24p. (J). (gr. -1-2). lib. bdg. 27.32 *(978-1-5157-6755-8(8),* 135297, Capstone Pr.) Capstone.

Richards, Tracy. My Navy Dad. 2010. 20p. pap. 14.95 *(978-1-4490-3217-3(6))* AuthorHouse.

Rose, Simon. Navy SEALs. 2013. (J). *(978-1-62127-453-7(5));* pap. *(978-1-62127-459-9(4))* Weigl Pubs., Inc.

Simons, Lisa M. Bolt. U. S. Navy SEAL Missions: A Timeline. 2016. (Special Ops Mission Timelines Ser.). (ENG., Illus.). 32p. (J). (gr. 3-9). lib. bdg. 27.32 *(978-1-4914-8703-7(8),* 131422, Capstone Pr.) Capstone.

Snedden, Robert. The Navy, 1 vol. 2015. (Defend & Protect Ser.). (ENG.). 48p. (J). (gr. 4-5). pap. 15.05 *(978-1-4824-4123-9(3),* e3a6717b-6435-4df3-83d6-66e99f6d7a84) Stevens, Gareth Publishing LLLP.

Stillwell, Alexander. Military Jobs: Navy SEALs. 2015. (J). lib. bdg. *(978-1-62713-465-1(4))* Cavendish Square Publishing LLC.

Stilwell, Alexander. Navy SEALs: What It Takes to Join the Elite, 1 vol. 2014. (Military Jobs Ser.). (ENG.). 48p. (YA). (gr. 7-7). 33.07 *(978-1-5026-0226-8(1),* aabf56fa-732c-4347-a3dd-e32648dade6f) Cavendish Square Publishing LLC.

Streissguth, Tom. The U. S. Navy. 2004. (U. S. Armed Forces Ser.). (ENG., Illus.). 64p. (gr. 4-8). lib. bdg. 26.60 *(978-0-8225-1649-1(7))* Lerner Publishing Group.

Townsend, John. Navy. 2016. (Action Force: World War II Ser.). 32p. (gr. 3-7). 31.35 *(978-1-59920-984-5(5),* Smart Apple Media) Black Rabbit Bks.

U. S. Navy. 2019. (Serving Our Country Ser.). (ENG.). 24p. (J). (gr. 1-4). lib. bdg. *(978-1-68151-564-9(4),* 17596) Amicus.

White, Steve. Naval Warship: FSF-1 Sea Fighter. 2007. (High-Tech Military Weapons Ser.). (ENG., Illus.). 48p. (J). (gr. 4-7). pap. 6.95 *(978-0-531-18707-4(1))* Scholastic Library Publishing.

White, Steve D. Naval Warship FSF-1: Sea Fighter. 2007. (High Interest Books: High-Tech Military Weapons Ser.). (ENG., Illus.). 48p. (J). (gr. 7-9). lib. bdg. 21.19 *(978-0-531-12091-0(0),* Children's Pr.) Scholastic Library Publishing.

Whiting, Jim. Navy SEALs. 2014. (U. S. Special Forces Ser.). (ENG.). 48p. (J). (gr. 5-8). *(978-1-60818-465-1(X),* 21439, Creative Education); pap. 12.00 *(978-1-62832-051-0(6),* 21440, Creative Paperbacks) Creative Co., The.

—SEAL Team Six. 2018. (U. S. Special Forces Ser.). (ENG.). 48p. (J). (gr. 3-6). pap. 12.00 *(978-1-62832-613-0(1),* 19990, Creative Paperbacks) Creative Co., The.

Wood, Alix. Serving in the Navy, 1 vol. 2013. (Protecting Our Country Ser.). 32p. (J). (gr. 3-4). (ENG.). 28.93 *(978-1-4777-1295-5(X),* 988dae8f-9f68-430b-848f-844d14032b9e); pap. 60.00 *(978-1-4777-1397-6(2))* Rosen Publishing Group, Inc., The. (PowerKids Pr.).

Yomtov, Nel. Navy Seals in Action. 2008. (Special Ops Ser.). (Illus.). 32p. (J). (gr. 3-6). lib. bdg. 28.50 *(978-1-59716-630-0(8))* Bearport Publishing Co., Inc.

UNITED STATES—NAVY—BIOGRAPHY

Abdo Publishing. Chris Kyle, 1 vol. 2015. (Essential Lives Set 9 Ser.). (ENG., Illus.). 112p. (YA). (gr. 6-12). 41.36 *(978-1-62403-893-8(X),* 17818, Essential Library) ABDO Publishing Co.

Alphin, Elaine Marie & Alphin, Arthur B. I Have Not Yet Begun to Fight: A Story about John Paul Jones. Casale, Paul, tr. Casale, Paul, illus. 2004. (Creative Minds Biography Ser.). 64p. (J). 22.60 *(978-1-57505-601-2(1),* Carolrhoda Bks.) Lerner Publishing Group.

Bradford, James C. John Paul Jones & the American Navy. 2009. (Library of American Lives & Times Ser.). 112p. (gr. 5-5). 69.20 *(978-1-60853-490-6(1))* Rosen Publishing Group, Inc., The.

Brager, Bruce L. John Paul Jones: America's Sailor. 2006. (Founders of the Republic Ser.). (Illus.). 160p. (J). (gr. 6-12). lib. bdg. 26.95 *(978-1-931798-84-6(2))* Reynolds, Morgan Inc.

Crickard, Sarah. John Paul Jones & the Birth of the American Navy, 1 vol. 2015. (Spotlight on American History Ser.). (ENG., Illus.). 24p. (J). (gr. 4-6). pap. 11.00 *(978-1-4994-1759-3(4),* 124776b9-9541-49f4-8833-1044127807af, PowerKids Pr.) Rosen Publishing Group, Inc., The.

Dougherty, Terri. Admiral David Farragut: "Full Speed Ahead!" 2011. (J). *(978-1-59556-041-4(6));* pap. *(978-1-59556-047-6(5))* OTTN Publishing.

Egan, Tracie. John Paul Jones: Héroe de la marina estadounidense (John Paul Jones: American Naval Hero) 2009. (Grandes personajes en la historia de los Estados Unidos (Famous People in American History) Ser.). (SPA.). 32p. (gr. 2-3). 47.90 *(978-1-61512-802-0(6),* Editorial Buenas Letras) Rosen Publishing Group, Inc., The.

Harasymiw, Mark J. Heroes of the U. S. Navy, 1 vol. 2012. (Heroes of the U. S. Military Ser.). (ENG., Illus.). 32p. (J). (gr. 3-4). 29.27 *(978-1-4339-7248-5(4),* 19a3f101-0cda-4614-8b31-a6a91706bfb7); pap. 11.50 *(978-1-4339-7249-2(2),* 9c9ee6d5-724a-49a9-b415-2792077c3947) Stevens, Gareth Publishing LLLP.

Harkins, Susan Sales & Harkins, William H. The Life & Times of John Paul Jones. 2007. (Profiles in American History Ser.). (Illus.). 48p. (J). (gr. 4-8). lib. bdg. 29.95 *(978-1-58415-529-4(9))* Mitchell Lane Pubs.

Makos, Adam. Devotion (Adapted for Young Adults) An Epic Story of Heroism & Friendship. 2022. (Illus.). 368p. (YA). (gr. 7). 18.99 *(978-0-593-48145-5(3));* (ENG., lib. bdg. 21.99 *(978-0-593-48146-2(1))* Random Hse. Children's Bks. (Delacorte Pr.).

—Devotion (Young Readers Edition) An Epic Story of Heroism & Friendship. 2022. (ENG.). 368p. (YA). (gr. 7). pap. 12.99 *(978-0-593-48148-6(8),* Ember) Random Hse. Children's Bks.

McDoniel, Estelle. Registered Nurse to Rear Admiral: A First for Navy Women. 2003. (Illus.). viii, 81p. (J). 16.95 *(978-1-57168-766-1(1),* Eakin Pr.) Eakin Pr.

Micklos, John, Jr. SEAL Team Six: Battling Terrorism Worldwide. 2017. (Military Heroes Ser.). (ENG., Illus.). 32p. (J). (gr. 3-6). lib. bdg. 27.99 *(978-1-5157-3347-8(5),* 133344, Capstone Pr.) Capstone.

Moening, Kate. Michelle Howard: Four-Star Admiral. 2020. (Women Leading the Way Ser.). (ENG., Illus.). 24p. (J). (gr. k-3). pap. 7.99 *(978-1-61891-798-0(6),* 12583, Blastoff! Readers) Bellwether Media.

Moore Niver, Heather. Grace Hopper: Computer Scientist & Navy Admiral, 1 vol. 2018. (Junior Biographies Ser.). (ENG.). 24p. (gr. 3-4). 24.27 *(978-1-9785-0204-8(4),* bbdc89c2-eae3-43ea-a912-80fcb61f1050) Enslow Publishing, LLC.

A Navy Medical Corpsman's Journey. 2003. 37p. (YA). lib. bdg. 20.00 net. *(978-0-9747035-1-0(6))* Strickland, Wilton.

Rudolph, Jessica & Pushies, Fred J. Today's Navy Heroes. 2012. (Acts of Courage: Inside America's Military Ser.). 32p. (J). (gr. 2-7). lib. bdg. 28.50 *(978-1-61772-446-6(7))* Bearport Publishing Co., Inc.

Russo, Kristen J. Surprising Facts about Being a Navy Sailor. 2017. (What You Didn't Know about the U. S. Military Life Ser.). (ENG., Illus.). 32p. (J). (gr. 3-9). lib. bdg. 28.65 *(978-1-5157-7430-3(9),* 135789, Capstone Pr.) Capstone.

Sperry, Armstrong. John Paul Jones: The Pirate Patriot. 2017. (Great Leaders & Events Ser.). (ENG.). (J). (gr. 4-8). lib. bdg. 35.99 *(978-1-942875-42-0(8))* Quarto Publishing Group USA.

Sutcliffe, Jane & Kodera, Craig. Chester Nimitz & the Sea, 1 vol. 2013. (ENG., Illus.). 32p. (J). (gr. k-3). 16.99 *(978-1-4556-1796-8(2),* Pelican Publishing) Arcadia Publishing.

Wasdin, Howard E. & Templin, Stephen. I Am a Seal Team Six Warrior. 2012. (YA). lib. bdg. 19.65 *(978-0-606-26244-6(X))* Turtleback.

—I Am a SEAL Team Six Warrior: Memoirs of an American Soldier. 2012. (ENG., Illus.). 192p. (YA). (gr. 6). pap. 10.99 *(978-1-250-01643-0(6),* 900086904, St. Martin's Griffin) St. Martin's Pr.

Wittner, David G. Commodore Matthew Perry & the Perry Expedition to Japan. 2009. (Library of American Lives & Times Ser.). 112p. (gr. 5-5). 69.20 *(978-1-60853-474-6(X))* Rosen Publishing Group, Inc., The.

UNITED STATES—NAVY—HISTORY

Abbot, Willis J. Blue Jackets of 1876: A History of the Naval Battles of the American Revolution Together with a Narrative of the War with Tripoli. 2006. (Illus.). pap. 30.95 *(978-1-4286-1609-7(8))* Kessinger Publishing, LLC.

Elish, Dan. Inside the Situation Room: How a Photograph Showed America Defeating Osama Bin Laden. 2018. (Captured History Ser.). (ENG., Illus.). 64p. (J). (gr. 5-9). pap. 8.95 *(978-0-7565-5881-9(6),* 138649, Compass Point Bks.) Capstone.

Goldish, Meish. Sea Lions in the Navy. 2012. (America's Animal Soldiers Ser.). 24p. (J). (gr. 1-6). lib. bdg. 26.99 *(978-1-61772-450-3(5))* Bearport Publishing Co., Inc.

Goldish, Meish & Ridgway, Sam H. Bottlenose Dolphins in the Navy. 2012. (America's Animal Soldiers Ser.). 24p. (J). (gr. 1-6). lib. bdg. 26.99 *(978-1-61772-451-0(3))* Bearport Publishing Co., Inc.

Gomez-Centurion, Carlos. Armada Invencible. (SPA.). 96p. (J). *(978-84-207-3813-0(1))* Grupo Anaya, S.A.

Green, Michael. The United States Navy, 1 vol. 2013. (U. S. Military Forces Ser.). (ENG., Illus.). 24p. (J). (gr. 1-3). lib. bdg. 27.99 *(978-1-4765-0070-6(3),* 122129, Capstone Pr.) Capstone.

Hemingway, Al. American Naval Forces in the Vietnam War, 1 vol. 2004. (American Experience in Vietnam Ser.). (ENG., Illus.). 48p. (gr. 5-8). lib. bdg. 33.67 *(978-0-8368-5776-4(3),* dcff3fb0-f816-413c-9826-9a9528fd873c, Gareth Stevens Secondary Library) Stevens, Gareth Publishing LLLP.

Micklos, John & Micklos, John, Jr. Why We Won the American Revolution: Through Primary Sources, 1 vol. 2013. (American Revolution Through Primary Sources Ser.). (ENG.). 48p. (gr. 4-6). pap. 11.53 *(978-1-4644-0192-3(6),* 5895a7f8-08c5-4a37-9a5e-45c01416fbb5); (Illus.). (J). 27.93 *(978-0-7660-4134-9(4),* 1427223b-d0b5-47ed-ad69-7c1c441a1350) Enslow Publishing, LLC.

Murray, Julie. United States Navy, 1 vol. 2014. (U. S. Armed Forces Ser.). (ENG.). 24p. (J). (gr. -1-2). lib. bdg. 32.79 *(978-1-62970-097-7(5),* 1714, Abdo Kids) ABDO Publishing Co.

Nagle, Jeanne. Navy, 1 vol. 2011. (U. S. Military Forces Ser.). (ENG., Illus.). 32p. (gr. 3-4). (J). pap. 11.50 *(978-1-4339-5860-1(0),* 34da941c-9820-42b6-9718-1856703ceaef, Gareth Stevens Learning Library); (YA). 29.27 *(978-1-4339-5858-8(9),* 8c1cd65a-8471-47fa-a5f5-934c2ce0087c) Stevens, Gareth Publishing LLLP.

Rose, Simon. Navy. 2012. (J). *(978-1-61913-293-1(1));* pap. *(978-1-61913-297-9(4))* Weigl Pubs., Inc.

Rutherford, David B. A Navy SEAL's Guide for Helping Kids Get Squared Away: Field Manuals for Kids, Vol. 1. 2007. (ENG.). 118p. (J). per. 15.00 *(978-0-9801464-0-0(2))* Leadline Publishing.

Sheinkin, Steve. The Port Chicago 50: Disaster, Mutiny, & the Fight for Civil Rights. 2014. (ENG., Illus.). 208p. (J). (gr. 5-9). 21.99 *(978-1-59643-796-8(0),* 900083654) Roaring Brook Pr.

Stein, R. Conrad. Cornerstones of Freedom: Annapolis. 2009. (Cornerstones of Freedom Ser.). (ENG.). 48p. (J). (gr. 4-6). pap. 5.95 *(978-0-531-21100-7(2),* Children's Pr.) Scholastic Library Publishing.

Thornton, Jeremy. The Birth of the American Navy. 2009. (Building America's Democracy Ser.). 24p. (gr. 3-3). 42.50 *(978-1-61511-765-9(2),* PowerKids Pr.) Rosen Publishing Group, Inc., The.

A True Book: the U. S. Navy in World War II (Library Edition) 2014. (True Book, a — World at War Ser.). (ENG.). 48p. (J). lib. bdg. 31.00 *(978-0-531-20497-9(9))* Scholastic Library Publishing.

USS Wisconsin: Hampton Roads Naval Historical Foundation Photo Museum Guide. 2003. per. 12.95 *(978-1-930127-05-0(7))* Oxford Museum Pr.

Waldman, Scott. Victory at Sea: John Paul Jones & the Continental Navy. 2009. (Great Moments in American History Ser.). 32p. (gr. 3-3). 47.90 *(978-1-61513-156-3(6))* Rosen Publishing Group, Inc., The.

UNITED STATES—OFFICIALS AND EMPLOYEES

Cuesta, Vivian. It Can Be Done: The Life & Legacy of César Chávez. 2003. (ENG., Illus.). 32p. (J). (gr. 6-8). pap. 9.00 net. *(978-0-7652-3271-7(5))* Celebration Pr.

Faust, Daniel R. A Career As an FBI Special Agent, 1 vol. 2015. (Federal Forces: Careers As Federal Agents Ser.). (ENG., Illus.). 32p. (J). (gr. 4-5). pap. 11.00 *(978-1-4994-1060-0(3),* 5cf71f27-3a59-4c46-8a6c-6f6c68e3dbd5, PowerKids Pr.) Rosen Publishing Group, Inc., The.

Jakubiak, David J. What Does a Supreme Court Justice Do? 2010. (How Our Government Works Ser.). 24p. (J). (gr. 3-6). lib. bdg., E-Book 42.50 *(978-1-4488-0031-5(5))* Rosen Publishing Group, Inc., The.

Kolpin, Amanda. Understanding Presidential Appointments, 1 vol. 2017. (What's up with Your Government? Ser.). (ENG., Illus.). 32p. (J). (gr. 4-5). 27.93 *(978-1-5383-2234-5(X),* 774b3ad9-50e9-45da-bd03-fba2a63c297a); pap. 11.00 *(978-1-5383-2330-4(3),* 46ed3155-da78-4792-aee3-99a5f8ba9948) Rosen Publishing Group, Inc., The. (PowerKids Pr.).

Side by Side/Lado a Lado. 2010.Tr. of Side by Side - The Story of Dolores Huerta & Cesar Chavez. (ENG., Illus.). 32p. (J). (gr. -1-3). 17.99 *(978-0-06-122781-3(1))* HarperCollins Español.

Slade, Suzanne. A Computer Called Katherine: How Katherine Johnson Helped Put America on the Moon. Miller Jamison, Veronica, illus. 2019. (ENG.). 40p. (J). (gr. -1-3). 18.99 *(978-0-316-43517-8(1))* Little, Brown Bks. for Young Readers.

Sotomayor, Sonia. Pasando Páginas: La Historia de Mi Vida. Delacre, Lulu, illus. 2018. 40p. (J). (gr. -1-3). 18.99 *(978-0-525-51549-4(6),* Philomel Bks.) Penguin Young Readers Group.

Stevens, Stewart, Sr. The White House Chandeliers: My Experiences While Working for Seven U. S. Presidents. 2016. (ENG., Illus.). xi, 127p. (gr. 6-17). pap. 25.00 *(978-0-9974925-0-7(3))* Lightning Fast Bk. Publishing.

Storrs, Landon R. Y. The Second Red Scare & the Unmaking of the New Deal Left. 2012. (Politics & Society in Modern America Ser.: 88). (ENG., Illus.). 424p. (C). 63.00 *(978-0-691-15396-4(5),* 33193) Princeton Univ. Pr.

Topinka, Joseph Baar. Just Judy: A Citizen & Leader for Illinois. 2017. (ENG.). (J). pap. 16.95 *(978-0-9983282-2-5(7))* Hilton Publishing Co.

Townsend, Chris. What Does an Officeholder Do?, 1 vol. 2018. (What Does a Citizen Do? Ser.). (ENG.). 48p. (gr. 5-5). 30.93 *(978-0-7660-9881-7(8),* a410a0f6-47e6-4eac-a1a4-b603bd73cc52) Enslow Publishing, LLC.

Woog, Adam. Careers in Homeland Security, 1 vol. 2014. (Law & Order Jobs Ser.). (ENG.). 112p. (gr. 6-6). 42.63 *(978-1-62712-422-5(5),* e7e4dcb8-2a4c-4fc8-a8b1-049529cdcc4c) Cavendish Square Publishing LLC.

—Careers in Homeland Security. 2013. (J). 34.21 *(978-1-60870-959-5(0))* Marshall Cavendish Corp.

UNITED STATES—PAINTERS

see Painters—United States

UNITED STATES—POETRY

Adams, Michelle Medlock. Ha! Ha! Halloween. Johnson, Meredith, illus. 2005. 30p. (J). (gr. 3-7). 12.95 *(978-0-8249-5508-3(0),* Ideals Pubns.) Worthy Publishing.

Bates, Katharine Lee. My America, the Beautiful: A Little Patriot's Celebration. Melrose, Katie, illus. 2018. (ENG.). 20p. (J). (gr. -1-3). bds. 12.99 *(978-1-64170-019-1(X),* 550019) Familius LLC.

Blanco, Richard. One Today. Pilkey, Dav, illus. 2015. (ENG.). 40p. (J). (gr. -1-3). 18.00 *(978-0-316-37144-5(0))* Little, Brown Bks. for Young Readers.

Dyan, Penelope. An Apple a Day! a Kid's Guide to Julian, Californ. Weigand, John D., photos by. 2010. (Illus.). 48p. pap. 11.95 *(978-1-935630-12-8(1))* Bellissima Publishing, LLC.

—One Big Hole in the Ground, a Kid's Guide to Grand Canyon, Us. Weigand, John D., photos by. 2010. (Illus.). 50p. pap. 11.95 *(978-1-935630-02-9(4))* Bellissima Publishing, LLC.

—Take a Dam Tour! a Kid's Guide to Hoover Dam, Nevad. Weigand, John D., photos by. 2010. (Illus.). 50p. pap. 11.95 *(978-1-935630-05-0(9))* Bellissima Publishing, LLC.

—What Happens in Vegas a Kid's Guide to Las Vegas, Nevad. Weigand, John D., photos by. 2010. (Illus.). 48p. pap. 11.95 *(978-1-935630-06-7(7))* Bellissima Publishing, LLC.

Landry, Cornell P. Goodnight Nola: An Endearing Bedtime Book for All Ages. Schmitt, Louis J., illus. 2009. (ENG.). 36p. (J). 16.95 *(978-0-9818126-4-9(3))* Ampersand, Inc.

Lee Bates, Katharine & Gamwell, Calvert. America the Beautiful: A Pop-up Book about the Famous Song by Katharine Lee Bates. Jordan, Carrie, illus. 2006. 16p. (J). (gr. 4-8). reprint ed. 17.00 *(978-1-4223-5447-6(4))* DIANE Publishing Co.

Myers, Walter Dean. We Are America. 2015. (J). lib. bdg. 17.20 *(978-0-606-36963-3(5))* Turtleback.

—We Are America: A Tribute from the Heart. Myers, Christopher, illus. (ENG.). 40p. (J). (gr. 1-5). 2015. pap. 7.99 *(978-0-06-052310-7(7))* 2011. 16.99 *(978-0-06-052308-4(5))* HarperCollins Pubs. (HarperCollins).

Myers, Walter Dean & Myers, Christopher. We Are America: A Tribute from the Heart. 2012. (ENG.). (J). (gr. 3-6). 29.95 incl. audio compact disk *(978-1-4301-1112-2(7))* Live Oak Media.

Perdomo, Willie. Visiting Langston. Collier, Bryan, illus. 2005. (ENG.). 32p. (J). (gr. -1-3). reprint ed. pap. 10.99 *(978-0-8050-7881-7(9),* 900030908) Square Fish.

Sardelli, Darren. Galaxy Pizza & Meteor Pie. 2009. 12.95 *(978-0-615-28469-9(8))* Laugh-A-Lot Bks.

Soto, Gary. A Fire in My Hands: Revised & Expanded Edition. exp. rev. ed. 2013. (ENG.). 96p. (YA). (gr. 7-12). pap. 7.99 *(978-0-544-10482-2(X),* 1540791, Clarion Bks.) HarperCollins Pubs.

Testa, Maria. Something about America. 2007. (ENG., Illus.). 96p. (YA). (gr. 7-18). pap. 7.99 *(978-0-7636-3415-5(8))* Candlewick Pr.

Yanique, Tiphanie & Djeli, Moses. I Am the Virgin Islands. 2012. *(978-1-934370-30-8(4))* Editorial Campana.

UNITED STATES—POLITICS AND GOVERNMENT

Adler, David A. A Picture Book of Alexander Hamilton. Collins, Matt, illus. 2019. (Picture Book Biography Ser.). 32p. (J). (gr. -1-3). 17.99 *(978-0-8234-3961-4(5))* Holiday Hse., Inc.

Albee, Sarah. Alexander Hamilton: A Plan for America. Ko, Chin, illus. 2018. (I Can Read Level 2 Ser.). (ENG.). 32p. (J). (gr. -1-3). pap. 4.99 *(978-0-06-243290-2(7),* HarperCollins) HarperCollins Pubs.

—Alexander Hamilton: a Plan for America. Ko, Chin, illus. 2018. (I Can Read Level 2 Ser.). (ENG.). 32p. (J). (gr. -1-3). 16.99 *(978-0-06-243291-9(5),* HarperCollins) HarperCollins Pubs.

Aldritt, Jeremy. Thomas Paine & the Power of Common Sense, 1 vol. 2015. (Spotlight on American History Ser.). (ENG., Illus.). 24p. (J). (gr. 4-6). pap. 11.00 *(978-1-4994-1765-4(9),* 6d93e3a5-db18-41c4-af43-5de9b1569455, PowerKids Pr.) Rosen Publishing Group, Inc., The.

Allen, John. The Trump Presidency. 2020. (ENG.). 80p. (J). (gr. 6-12). 41.27 *(978-1-68282-759-8(3))* ReferencePoint Pr., Inc.

Aloian, Molly. Constitution Day. 2008. (Celebrations in My World Ser.). (ENG., Illus.). 32p. (J). (gr. k-3). pap. *(978-0-7787-4304-0(7))* Crabtree Publishing Co.

American Presidents in World History: [5 Volumes], 5 vols., Vol. 1. 2003. (ENG., Illus.). 144p. (C). (gr. 6-8). 254.00 *(978-0-313-32564-9(2),* 900297228, Bloomsbury Academic) Bloomsbury Publishing Plc GBR. Dist: Macmillan.

Amidon Lusted, Marcia, ed. States' Rights & the Role of the Federal Government, 1 vol. 2018. (Current Controversies Ser.). (ENG.). 200p. (gr. 10-12). 48.03 *(978-1-5345-0313-7(7),* 7aa40abf-605d-4ce9-8b77-b47990a32144) Greenhaven Publishing LLC.

Anderson, Dale. The Aftermath of the Civil War, 1 vol. 2004. (World Almanac(r) Library of the Civil War Ser.). (ENG., Illus.). 48p. (gr. 5-8). pap. 15.05 *(978-0-8368-5597-5(3),* ad27f227-78f5-47db-a4a4-11d6eaec8003); lib. bdg. 33.67 *(978-0-8368-5588-3(4),* c777ffc3-916f-4e09-bf81-5fbda0f6625d) Stevens, Gareth Publishing LLLP. (Gareth Stevens Secondary Library).

—The American Colonies Declare Independence, 1 vol. 2005. (World Almanac(r) Library of the American Revolution Ser.). (ENG.). 48p. (gr. 5-8). pap. 15.05 *(978-0-8368-5935-5(9),* 47adbbb4-4b38-4d75-9f76-2f76847e8ddc); (Illus.). lib. bdg. 33.67 *(978-0-8368-5926-3(X),* 9381c4d2-0e2d-4fc5-87ec-be147d2b03c9) Stevens, Gareth Publishing LLLP. (Gareth Stevens Secondary Library).

—The Causes of the Civil War, 1 vol. 2004. (World Almanac(r) Library of the Civil War Ser.). (ENG., Illus.). 48p. (gr. 5-8). pap. 15.05 *(978-0-8368-5590-6(6),* ae885cb8-42d8-49e0-b9ca-32f9a28d4d37); lib. bdg. 33.67 *(978-0-8368-5581-4(7),* 88052b64-ee89-4168-9b03-c8645b27670f) Stevens, Gareth Publishing LLLP. (Gareth Stevens Secondary Library).

—Forming a New American Government, 1 vol. 2005. (World Almanac(r) Library of the American Revolution Ser.). (ENG.). 48p. (gr. 5-8). pap. 15.05 *(978-0-8368-5941-6(3),* cacc52f7-acbc-453e-8984-be38d2ab926d); (Illus.). lib. bdg. 33.67 *(978-0-8368-5932-4(4),* e141d36e-df11-4ebc-b48a-79acd8ea9a89) Stevens, Gareth Publishing LLLP. (Gareth Stevens Secondary Library).

—The Home Fronts in the Civil War, 1 vol. 2004. (World Almanac(r) Library of the Civil War Ser.). (ENG., Illus.). 48p. (gr. 5-8). lib. bdg. 33.67 (978-0-8368-5587-6(6), f82d4d42-0c19-4e83-844b-321427333a72, Gareth Stevens Secondary Library) Stevens, Gareth Publishing LLLP.

—Leaders of the American Revolution, 1 vol. 2005. (World Almanac(r) Library of the American Revolution Ser.). (ENG.). 48p. (gr. 5-8). lib. bdg. 33.67 (978-0-8368-5931-7(6), 5670f581-1e2e-4ddf-81e4-ea8e89f67c26, Gareth Stevens Secondary Library) Stevens, Gareth Publishing LLLP.

—World Almanac Library of the Civil War, 10 vols. Incl. Aftermath of the Civil War. lib. bdg. 33.67 (978-0-8368-5588-3(4), c777ffc3-916f-4e09-bf81-5fbda0f6625d); Causes of the Civil War. lib. bdg. 33.67 (978-0-8368-5581-4(7), 88052b64-ee89-4168-9b03-c8645b27670f); Civil War at Sea. lib. bdg. 33.67 (978-0-8368-5585-2(X), abaa704c-54ab-437b-a508-a47da1d3dc87); Civil War in the East (1861-July 1863) lib. bdg. 33.67 (978-0-8368-5582-1(5), ea65b134-2894-4b4a-b659-255a776186b0); Civil War in the West (1861-July 1863) lib. bdg. 33.67 (978-0-8368-5583-8(3), a497de3e-669b-4027-92d0-df03b0280971); Home Fronts in the Civil War. lib. bdg. 33.67 (978-0-8368-5587-6(6), f82d4d42-0c19-4e83-844b-321427333a72); Union Victory (July 1863 - 1865) lib. bdg. 33.67 (978-0-8368-5584-5(1), e28734b4-0c65-4c17-9779-244cfe64b88f); (gr. 5-8). (World Almanac(r) Library of the Civil War Ser.). (ENG., Illus.). 48p. 2004. Set lib. bdg. 168.35 (978-0-8368-5580-7(9), 6d23f6f8-b267-4c3a-8417-931f1aeca97a, Gareth Stevens Secondary Library) Stevens, Gareth Publishing LLLP.

Anderson, Michael, contrib. by. Abraham Lincoln, 1 vol. 2012. (Pivotal Presidents: Profiles in Leadership Ser.). (ENG., Illus.). 80p. (gr. 8-8). (J). lib. bdg. 36.47 (978-1-61530-942-9(X), 3e79c9e2-6cf7-49e1-8a7e-6f531fd252d5); (YA). 72.94 (978-1-61530-953-5(5), fe64ec48-46cf-4b6d-afb3-c461b9174bea) Rosen Publishing Group, Inc., The.

—Ronald Reagan, 4 vols. 2012. (Pivotal Presidents: Profiles in Leadership Ser.). (ENG., Illus.). 80p. (YA). (gr. 8-8). 72.94 (978-1-61530-958-0(6), dd617cf5-f55d-4034-bafa-3b0e589d19a9) Rosen Publishing Group, Inc., The.

Anderson, Nancy. I Am a Citizen of the United States, 1 vol. 2016. (Rosen REAL Readers: Social Studies Nonfiction / Fiction: Myself, My Community, My World Ser.). (ENG.). 12p. (gr. k-1). pap. 6.33 (978-1-5081-2323-1(3), b2c7de0a-2e30-4ac0-a832-8abb0dc926a8, Rosen Classroom) Rosen Publishing Group, Inc., The.

Anderson, Wayne. Fighting Racial Discrimination: Treating All Americans Fairly under the Law. 2009. (Progressive Movement 1900-1920: Efforts to Reform America's New Industrial Society Ser.). 32p. (gr. 3-4). 47.90 (978-1-60854-164-5(9)) Rosen Publishing Group, Inc., The.

Andronik, Catherine M. & Kenney, Karen Latchana. Abraham Lincoln's Presidency. 2016. (Presidential Powerhouses Ser.). (ENG., Illus.). 104p. (YA). (gr. 6-12). 35.99 (978-1-4677-7925-8(3), 9e967ebf-e20b-4c3c-82d8-9a5d2ae0b0db); E-Book 54.65 (978-1-4677-8547-1(4)) Lerner Publishing Group. (Lerner Pubns.).

Anthony, David. The Progressive Era: Activists Change America, 1 vol. 2017. (American History Ser.). (ENG.). 104p. (gr. 7-7). lib. bdg. 41.03 (978-1-5345-6139-7(0), c568f833-c9a7-40f2-ae90-b287a0d737ca, Lucent Pr.) Greenhaven Publishing LLC.

Apel, Melani. The Federal Reserve Act: Making the American Banking System Stronger. 2009. (Progressive Movement 1900-1920: Efforts to Reform America's New Industrial Society Ser.). 32p. (gr. 3-4). 47.90 (978-1-60854-172-0(X)) Rosen Publishing Group, Inc., The.

Apel, Melanie Ann. The Federal Reserve Act: Making the American Banking System Stronger, 1 vol. 2006. (Progressive Movement 1900 - 1920: Efforts to Reform America's New Industrial Society Ser.). (ENG., Illus.). 32p. (J). (gr. 4-5). lib. bdg. 30.47 (978-1-4042-0196-5(3), 817bd687-879e-4b4d-a2ec-0ce42a71142a) Rosen Publishing Group, Inc., The.

Armentrout, David & Armentrout, Patricia. The Emancipation Proclamation. 2005. (Documents that Shaped the Nation Ser.). (Illus.). 48p. (J). (gr. 4-6). 20.95 (978-1-59515-233-6(4)) Rourke Educational Media.

Aronin, Miriam. Dwight D. Eisenhower. 2016. (First Look at America's Presidents Ser.). (ENG., Illus.). 24p. (J). (gr. -1-3). 26.99 (978-1-943553-31-0(9)) Bearport Publishing Co., Inc.

—Woodrow Wilson. 2016. (First Look at America's Presidents Ser.). (ENG., Illus.). 24p. (J). (gr. -1-3). 26.99 (978-1-943553-30-3(0)) Bearport Publishing Co., Inc.

Aronson, Billy. Richard M. Nixon, 1 vol. 2008. (Presidents & Their Times Ser.). (ENG., Illus.). 96p. (gr. 6-6). lib. bdg. 36.93 (978-0-7614-2428-4(8), 7d1fb918-7384-47cb-80e3-91d437f81f88) Cavendish Square Publishing LLC.

Aronson, Marc. The Real Revolution: The Global Story of American Independence. 2005. (ENG., Illus.). 256p. (YA). (gr. 7-12). 22.00 (978-0-618-18179-7(2), 111143, Clarion Bks.) HarperCollins Pubs.

Asselin, Kristine Carlson. The Real Story about Government & Politics in Colonial America. rev. ed. 2017. (Life in the American Colonies Ser.). (ENG.). 32p. (J). (gr. 3-6). pap. 8.10 (978-1-5157-9747-0(3), 136864) Capstone.

Baier, Bret & Whitney, Catherine. Three Days in January: Young Readers' Edition: Dwight Eisenhower's Final Mission. 2019. (ENG., Illus.). 256p. (J). (gr. 3-7). 17.99 (978-0-06-291534-4(7), HarperCollins) HarperCollins Pubs.

Ball, Lea. The Federalist — Anti-Federalist Debate over States' Rights: A Primary Source Investigation, 1 vol. 2004. (Great Historic Debates & Speeches Ser.). (ENG., Illus.). 64p. (J). (gr. 5-8). lib. bdg. 37.13 (978-1-4042-0149-1(1), ee785929-9b2d-443f-9e90-7fc511b31aed) Rosen Publishing Group, Inc., The.

—The Federalist-Anti-Federalist Debate over States' Rights: A Primary Source Investigation. 2009. (Great Historic Debates & Speeches Ser.). 64p. (gr. 5-8). 58.50 (978-1-61513-125-9(6)) Rosen Publishing Group, Inc., The.

Bamaton, Paul. Elections: Choosing Our Leaders, 1 vol. 2009. (Explore Citizenship Ser.). (ENG.). 24p. (J). (gr. 3-3). 26.27 (978-1-4358-2979-4(4), 2c4c92c7-cac0-4a89-a9ff-68b689473790, PowerKids Pr.) Rosen Publishing Group, Inc., The.

Banigan, Melissa. Developing a Strategy for a Political Campaign, 1 vol. 2019. (Be the Change! Political Participation in Your Community Ser.). (ENG.). 64p. (gr. 7-7). pap. 13.95 (978-1-7253-4074-9(7), 971277c5-4cd4-4f87-8719-7e40caa5fdb1) Rosen Publishing Group, Inc., The.

Bard, Mariel & Bard, Jonathan. Republicans & Democrats, 1 vol. 2019. (Opponents in American History Ser.). (ENG.). 32p. (gr. 4-5). pap. 11.00 (978-1-5383-4546-7(3), 1871e2df-6d9e-4cd4-913c-a91c5adb662d, PowerKids Pr.) Rosen Publishing Group, Inc., The.

Bari, Ellen. Our Government: Text Pairs. 2008. (Bridges/Navigators Ser.). (J). (gr. 3). 89.00 (978-1-4108-8368-1(X)) Benchmark Education Co.

Bartoletti, Susan Campbell, adapted by. The Untold History of the United States, Volume 1: Young Readers Edition, 1898-1945, Vol. 1. 2014. (ENG., Illus.). 400p. (J). (gr. 5-9). 19.99 (978-1-4814-2173-7(5), Atheneum Bks. for Young Readers) Simon & Schuster Children's Publishing.

Barton, Chris. The Amazing Age of John Roy Lynch. Tate, Don, illus. 2015. (ENG.). 50p. (J). 17.00 (978-0-8028-5379-0(X), Eerdmans Bks For Young Readers) Eerdmans, William B. Publishing Co.

Bauder, Julia, ed. Is the Political Divide Harming America?, 1 vol. 2006. (At Issue Ser.). (ENG., Illus.). 88p. (gr. 10-12). 41.03 (978-0-7377-3521-5(X), ff6f7036-52fb-45d6-8876-b290a850f124); pap. 28.80 (978-0-7377-3522-2(8), ea0347c7-c594-4c56-b9f0-d89e31068550) Greenhaven Publishing LLC. (Greenhaven Publishing).

Beasley, Ava. What Is Equality? Civic Virtues, 1 vol. 2018. (Civics for the Real World Ser.). (ENG.). 8p. (gr. k-1). pap. (978-1-5383-6323-2(2), 1507fc6c-6bb5-4078-9687-35d5832ca0d6, Rosen Classroom) Rosen Publishing Group, Inc., The.

Beckett, Leslie. Does Voting Matter?, 1 vol. 2017. (Points of View Ser.). (ENG.). 24p. (J). (gr. 3-3). pap. 9.25 (978-1-5345-2491-0(6), 3c167fc8-abe6-4e79-962a-e5cd11b7532b); lib. bdg. 26.23 (978-1-5345-2429-3(0), 7e6935ae-5017-472f-8dd2-388100e7ae28) Greenhaven Publishing LLC.

Beier, Anne. The Importance of Being an Active Citizen, 1 vol. 2003. (Primary Source Library of American Citizenship Ser.). (ENG., Illus.). 32p. (YA). (gr. 5-5). lib. bdg. 29.13 (978-0-8239-4475-0(1), f04cfc64-de2b-4e63-bea9-b6a7176ec4ad, Rosen Reference) Rosen Publishing Group, Inc., The.

Belton, Blair. The Articles of Confederation, 1 vol. 2013. (Documents That Shaped America Ser.). 32p. (J). (gr. 4-5). (ENG.). 29.27 (978-1-4339-8993-3(X), 4cd6bcb5-3dc8-4d16-9910-98f8ce19d907); (ENG.). pap. 11.50 (978-1-4339-8994-0(8), b318040e-43a4-4945-b295-4437b4b1303d); pap. 63.00 (978-1-4339-8995-7(6)) Stevens, Gareth Publishing LLLP.

Benchmark Education Company. The United States Government (Teacher Guide) 2005. (978-1-4108-4640-2(7)) Benchmark Education Co.

Benchmark Education Company, LLC Staff, compiled by. Government & Citizenship. 2005. (English Explorers Ser.). (J). spiral bd. 265.00 (978-1-4108-5767-5(0)) Benchmark Education Co.

—Government & Citizenship: Theme Set. 2006. (J). 121.00 (978-1-4108-7096-4(0)) Benchmark Education Co.

—GOVT & Citizenship. 2006. spiral bd. 330.00 (978-1-4108-7007-0(3)) Benchmark Education Co.

Benoit, Peter. Cornerstones of Freedom, Third Series: Immigration. 2012. (Cornerstones of Freedom, Third Ser.). (ENG., Illus.). 64p. (J). (gr. 4-6). lib. bdg. 30.00 (978-0-531-23057-2(0), Children's Pr.) Scholastic Library Publishing.

Berlatsky, Noah, ed. The Republican Party, 1 vol. 2015. (Opposing Viewpoints Ser.). (ENG.). 224p. (gr. 10-12). pap. 34.80 (978-0-7377-7285-2(9), 868a72fe-cfcf-432e-8e67-a8d9d3b4ccf1, Greenhaven Publishing) Greenhaven Publishing LLC.

—Voting Rights, 1 vol. 2015. (Opposing Viewpoints Ser.). (ENG.). 248p. (gr. 10-12). pap. 34.80 (978-0-7377-7301-9(4), 1b57b9d6-c45b-442a-b2e1-397dc60fb40b, Greenhaven Publishing) Greenhaven Publishing LLC.

Best, B. J. Abraham Lincoln, the Emancipation Proclamation, & the 13th Amendment, 1 vol. 2015. (Primary Sources of the Abolitionist Movement Ser.). (ENG., Illus.). 64p. (gr. 6-6). lib. bdg. 35.93 (978-1-5026-0530-6(9), 5c51cbc4-3e82-49b1-ae18-5508c4cc5f81) Cavendish Square Publishing LLC.

Betti, Matthew. The Declaration of Independence & the Continental Congress, 1 vol. 2015. (Spotlight on American History Ser.). (ENG., Illus.). 24p. (J). (gr. 4-6). pap. 11.00 (978-1-4994-1728-9(4), c9cf0bf8-0ea7-45af-8224-7d85b123b743, PowerKids Pr.) Rosen Publishing Group, Inc., The.

Beyer, Mark. The Election of 1800: Congress Helps Settle a Three-Way Vote, 1 vol. 2003. (Primary Sources of Life in the New American Nation Ser.). (ENG., Illus.). 32p. (gr. 4-5). pap. 10.00 (978-0-8239-4255-8(4), fe1b84cf-fcb7-471d-8dbe-062a4f707a3d) Rosen Publishing Group, Inc., The.

—The Election Of 1800: Congress Helps Settle a Three-Way Vote. 2009. (Life in the New American Nation Ser.). 32p. (gr. 4-4). 47.90 (978-1-61514-282-8(7)) Rosen Publishing Group, Inc., The.

Bishirjian, Richard J. The American Political Tradition & the Nature of Public Philosophy. 2004. (C). per. 12.50 (978-1-58152-339-3(4), Copley Publishing Group) Copley Custom Textbooks.

Blake, Kevin. Harry S. Truman: The 33rd President. 2016. (First Look at America's Presidents Ser.). (ENG., Illus.). 24p. (J). (gr. -1-3). 26.99 (978-1-943553-29-7(7)) Bearport Publishing Co., Inc.

—Lyndon B. Johnson. 2016. (First Look at America's Presidents Ser.). (ENG., Illus.). 24p. (J). (gr. -1-3). 26.99 (978-1-943553-32-7(7)) Bearport Publishing Co., Inc.

Bober, Natalie S. Countdown to Independence. 2007. (ENG.). 368p. (YA). (gr. 7). pap. 19.95 (978-1-4169-6392-9(8), Atheneum Bks. for Young Readers) Simon & Schuster Children's Publishing.

—Thomas Jefferson: Draftsman of a Nation. 2008. (ENG., Illus.). 376p. per. 16.95 (978-0-8139-2732-9(3), P144204) University of Virginia Pr.

Bodden, Valerie. The Declaration of American Independence. 2009. (Days of Change Ser.). (ENG., Illus.). 48p. (J). (gr. 5-8). 22.95 (978-1-58341-733-1(8), 22144) Creative Co., The.

Boehme, Gerry. Edward Snowden: Heroic Whistleblower or Traitorous Spy?, 1 vol. 2017. (Spying, Surveillance, & Privacy in the 21st Century Ser.). (ENG.). 112p. (YA). (gr. 8-8). 44.50 (978-1-5026-2673-8(X), b9725b3f-13e6-4b1a-bd59-0e9e54544ef9) Cavendish Square Publishing LLC.

Bolden, Tonya. Emancipation Proclamation: Lincoln & the Dawn of Liberty. 2013. (ENG., Illus.). 128p. (J). (gr. 5-9). 24.95 (978-1-4197-0390-4(0), 672401, Abrams Bks. for Young Readers) Abrams, Inc.

Booker, Dwayne. Why Do I Have Chores? Taking Civic Action, 1 vol. 2018. (Civics for the Real World Ser.). (ENG.). 8p. (gr. k-1). pap. (978-1-5383-6394-2(1), 1f86971a-b246-4a23-a5d4-950d3c23daab, Rosen Classroom) Rosen Publishing Group, Inc., The.

Boshier, Rosa. Ronald Reagan: 40th US President, 1 vol. 2013. (Essential Lives Set 8 Ser.). (ENG.). 112p. (YA). (gr. 6-12). lib. bdg. 41.36 (978-1-61783-895-8(0), 6767, Essential Library) ABDO Publishing Co.

Bougie, Matt. Who Are Progressives & What Do They Believe In?, 1 vol. 2019. (Politics Today Ser.). (ENG.). 64p. (gr. 7-7). pap. 16.28 (978-1-5026-4521-0(1), dc381d4b-eb38-452f-90b1-cad0ab3a1f43) Cavendish Square Publishing LLC.

Bowers, Matt. Writing the Declaration of Independence. 2019. (Sequence American Government Ser.). (ENG.). 32p. (J). (gr. 2-5). lib. bdg. (978-1-68151-673-8(X), 10805) Amicus.

—Writing the U. S. Constitution. 2019. (Sequence American Government Ser.). (ENG.). 32p. (J). (gr. 2-5). lib. bdg. (978-1-68151-675-2(6), 10807) Amicus.

Boyd, Bentley. Government. 2nd ed. 2010. (Chester the Crab's Comix with Content Ser.). (Illus.). 24p. pap. 6.95 (978-1-933122-38-0(2)) Chester Comix, LLC.

Brannon, Barbara. Discover the United States Government. 2005. (J). pap. (978-1-4108-5146-8(X)) Benchmark Education Co.

Braxton, Simone. Working Together in the Classroom: Civic Virtues, 1 vol. 2018. (Civics for the Real World Ser.). (ENG.). 12p. (gr. 1-2). pap. (978-1-5383-6412-3(3), d7e7e881-b8ca-4c88-a89a-00cc2b49cf44, Rosen Classroom) Rosen Publishing Group, Inc., The.

Brennan, Linda Crotta. Franklin D. Roosevelt's Presidency. 2016. (Presidential Powerhouses Ser.). (ENG., Illus.). 104p. (YA). (gr. 6-12). 35.99 (978-1-4677-7928-9(8), ab64e692-1d98-4b8b-ae25-219dbb29d6c0); E-Book 54.65 (978-1-4677-8549-5(0)) Lerner Publishing Group. (Lerner Pubns.).

Brexel, Bernadette. The Populist Party: A Voice for the Farmers in an Industrial Society. 2009. (America's Industrial Society in the 19th Century Ser.). 32p. (gr. 4-4). 47.90 (978-1-61511-344-6(4)) Rosen Publishing Group, Inc., The.

—The Populist Party: A Voice for the Farmers in the Industrialized Society, 1 vol. 2003. (Primary Sources of America's Industrial Society in the 19th Century Ser.). (ENG., Illus.). 32p. (gr. 4-5). pap. 10.00 (978-0-8239-4284-8(8), 9512a6c0-88be-4c92-b6cc-31c3d0a8a398); lib. bdg. 29.13 (978-0-8239-4029-5(2), e5331fa0-9bce-418d-bb2d-dabead132b0b, Rosen Reference) Rosen Publishing Group, Inc., The.

—Prosecuting Trusts: The Courts Break up Monopolies in America. (Progressive Movement 1900-1920: Efforts to Reform America's New Industrial Society Ser.). 32p. (gr. 3-4). 2009. 47.90 (978-1-60854-169-0(X)) 2006. (ENG., Illus.). (YA). lib. bdg. 30.47 (978-1-4042-0188-0(2), 8ce92136-10c1-4925-9965-7478ef257117) Rosen Publishing Group, Inc., The.

Brezina, Corona. Financing & Conducting a Political Campaign, 1 vol. 2019. (Be the Change! Political Participation in Your Community Ser.). (ENG.). 64p. (gr. 7-7). pap. 13.95 (978-1-7253-4080-0(1), f7c59003-19c9-46e7-83f9-db114d8f6cbe) Rosen Publishing Group, Inc., The.

Bright-Moore, Susan & Bedesky, Baron. How Is a Government Elected? 2008. (Your Guide to Government Ser.). (ENG.). 32p. (J). (gr. k-5). lib. bdg. (978-0-7787-4325-5(X)); (Illus.). pap. (978-0-7787-4330-9(6)) Crabtree Publishing Co.

Brindell Fradin, Dennis. The Declaration of Independence, 1 vol. 2007. (Turning Points in U. S. History Ser.). (ENG., Illus.). 48p. (gr. 4-4). lib. bdg. 34.07 (978-0-7614-2129-0(7), f86eb692-5344-44c0-90b0-233796d33085) Cavendish Square Publishing LLC.

—The Emancipation Proclamation, 1 vol. 2008. (Turning Points in U. S. History Ser.). (ENG., Illus.). 48p. (J). (gr. 4-4). lib. bdg. 34.07 (978-0-7614-2038-5(X), e0c254de-5d25-4baf-bfe6-f3f40a5f3650) Cavendish Square Publishing LLC.

—The U. S. Constitution, 1 vol. 2008. (Turning Points in U. S. History Ser.). (ENG., Illus.). 48p. (gr. 4-4). lib. bdg. 34.07 (978-0-7614-2036-1(3), 65dbeac2-0fe3-4a71-ac1b-9eb49eb8bd4f) Cavendish Square Publishing LLC.

—9/11/01, 1 vol. 2010. (Turning Points in U. S. History Ser.). (ENG.). 48p. (gr. 4-4). 34.07 (978-0-7614-4259-2(6), 75002057-d3bf-4e16-9278-148fda1efa7d) Cavendish Square Publishing LLC.

Brockenbrough, Martha. Alexander Hamilton, Revolutionary. 2019. (ENG.). 384p. (YA). pap. 12.99 (978-1-250-21170-5(0), 900174028) Square Fish.

Brown Bear Books. Politics. 2011. (Civil War Ser.). (ENG.). 112p. (J). (gr. 9-12). 42.80 (978-1-936333-48-6(1), 16458) Brown Bear Bks.

Brown, Liz. Civics. 2007. (Social Studies Essential Skills Ser.). (Illus.). 24p. (J). (gr. 4-7). lib. bdg. 24.45 (978-1-59036-765-0(0)); per. 8.95 (978-1-59036-766-7(9)) Weigl Pubs., Inc.

Brownell, Richard. The Civil War: The Fall of the Confederacy & the End of Slavery. 2005. (History's Great Defeats Ser.). (ENG., Illus.). 109p. (YA). (gr. 7-10). lib. bdg. 30.85 (978-1-59018-429-5(7), Lucent Bks.) Cengage Gale.

Bryan, Bethany. The Federalist Papers, 1 vol. 2018. (America's Most Important Documents: Inquiry into Historical Sources Ser.). (ENG.). 64p. (gr. 6-6). lib. bdg. 37.36 (978-1-5026-3607-2(7), c88b02cd-1d98-4816-8be4-f0a1764b27e8) Cavendish Square Publishing LLC.

Bryfonski, Dedria, ed. Deregulation, 1 vol. 2010. (Opposing Viewpoints Ser.). (ENG., Illus.). 280p. (gr. 10-12). 50.43 (978-0-7377-5108-6(8), 57798edf-01f0-437d-8908-719b41291c6e); pap. 34.80 (978-0-7377-5109-3(6), eb4c69ab-9368-4d06-8b3f-e5bf7298ea63) Greenhaven Publishing LLC. (Greenhaven Publishing).

Buchanan, Shelly. Our Government: The Three Branches, 1 vol. rev. ed. 2014. (Social Studies: Informational Text Ser.). (ENG., Illus.). 32p. (gr. 3-4). pap. 11.99 (978-1-4333-7365-7(3)) Teacher Created Materials, Inc.

Burgan, Michael. The Branches of U. S. Government. 2011. (Cornerstones of Freedom, Third Ser.). (Illus.). 64p. (J). lib. bdg. 30.00 (978-0-531-25028-0(8), Children's Pr.) Scholastic Library Publishing.

—The Creation of the U. S. Constitution, 1 vol. Purcell, Gordon & Beatty, Terry, illus. 2006. (Graphic History Ser.). (ENG.). 32p. (J). (gr. 3-9). 31.32 (978-0-7368-6491-6(1), 91818); pap. 8.10 (978-0-7368-9653-5(8), 93366) Capstone. (Capstone Pr.).

—TV Shapes Presidential Politics in the Kennedy-Nixon Debates: 4D an Augmented Reading Experience. 2018. (Captured Television History 4D Ser.). (ENG., Illus.). 64p. (J). (gr. 5-9). pap. 8.99 (978-0-7565-5827-7(1), 138352, Compass Point Bks.) Capstone.

—The U.S. Constitution/By Michael Burgan. 2011. (Cornerstones of Freedom, Third Ser.). (Illus.). 64p. (J). lib. bdg. 30.00 (978-0-531-25042-6(3), Children's Pr.) Scholastic Library Publishing.

—The Voting Rights Act Of 1965: An Interactive History Adventure. 2015. (You Choose: History Ser.). (ENG., Illus.). 112p. (J). (gr. 3-7). pap. 6.95 (978-1-4914-1805-5(2), 127252, Capstone Pr.) Capstone.

Burling, Alexis. Real-World Projects to Explore the New Deal, 1 vol. 2018. (Project-Based Learning in Social Studies). (ENG.). 64p. (gr. 5-5). 37.47 (978-1-5081-8222-1(1), c6d5b955-caf2-4b04-bbfa-e3a46c4bc153) Rosen Publishing Group, Inc., The.

Burnett, Iris & Greager, Clay. So You Think You Can Be President? 200 Questions to Determine If You Are Right (or Left) Enough to Be the Next Commander-In-Chief. 2008. (ENG.). 240p. pap. 12.95 (978-1-60239-202-1(1)) Skyhorse Publishing Co., Inc.

Byers, Ann. The Emancipation Proclamation, 1 vol. 2018. (America's Most Important Documents: Inquiry into Historical Sources Ser.). (ENG.). 64p. (J). (gr. 6-6). lib. bdg. 37.36 (978-1-5026-3598-3(4), 7f22fdda-24b7-47c9-8648-ab69c99a32a1) Cavendish Square Publishing LLC.

Carlson-Berne, Emma. The Three Branches of Government: Working As a Team, 1 vol. 2017. (Computer Kids: Powered by Computational Thinking Ser.). (ENG., Illus.). 24p. (J). (gr. 4-5). 25.27 (978-1-5383-2436-3(9), e9c3c1a6-1d5e-4560-b65d-9f0b6f4ba3de, PowerKids Pr.) Rosen Publishing Group, Inc., The.

Carlson Berne, Emma. The Three Branches of Government: Working As a Team, 1 vol. 2017. (Computer Science for the Real World Ser.). (ENG.). 24p. (J). (gr. 4-5). pap. (978-1-5383-5306-6(7), a5d11292-2b0b-4492-941c-3efcff296594, Rosen Classroom) Rosen Publishing Group, Inc., The.

Casciato, Daniel. Expansion & Reform: (Early 1800s-1861) 2007. (Presidents of the United States Ser.). (Illus.). 48p. (J). (gr. 4-7). lib. bdg. 29.05 (978-1-59036-741-4(3)) Weigl Pubs., Inc.

—Expansion & Reform: Early 1800s-1861. 2007. (Presidents of the United States Ser.). (Illus.). 48p. (J). (gr. 4-7). per. 11.95 (978-1-59036-742-1(1)) Weigl Pubs., Inc.

Cefrey, Holly. The Interstate Commerce Act: The Government Takes Control of Trade Between States. 2009. (America's Industrial Society in the 19th Century Ser.). 32p. (gr. 4-4). 47.90 (978-1-61511-342-2(8)) Rosen Publishing Group, Inc., The.

—The United States Constitution & Early State Constitutions: Law & Order in the New Nation & States. (Life in the New American Nation Ser.). 32p. (gr. 4-4). 2009. 47.90 (978-1-61514-287-3(8)) 2003. (ENG., Illus.). lib. bdg. 29.13 (978-0-8239-4042-4(X), be159b32-cdd6-4e6e-afcb-04f05a0b0e7d, Rosen Reference) Rosen Publishing Group, Inc., The.

Chang, Kirsten. The Pledge of Allegiance. 2018. (Symbols of American Freedom Ser.). (ENG., Illus.). 24p. (J). (gr. k-3). pap. 7.99 (978-1-61891-471-2(5), 12124, Blastoff! Readers) Bellwether Media.

Chastain, Zachary. Scandals & Glory: Politics in the 1800s. 2009. (Daily Life in America in the 1800s Ser.). 64p. (YA). (gr. 7-18). lib. bdg. 22.95 (978-1-4222-1787-0(6)) Mason Crest.

—Scandals & Glory: Politics in The 1800s. 2009. (Daily Life in America in the 1800s Ser.). 64p. (YA). (gr. 7-18). pap. 9.95 (978-1-4222-1860-0(0)) Mason Crest.

Cheney, Lynne. We the People: The Story of Our Constitution. Harlin, Greg, illus. (ENG.). 40p. (J). (gr. k-4). 2012. 9.99 (978-1-4424-4422-5(3)) 2008. 19.99 (978-1-4169-5418-7(X)) Simon & Schuster/Paula Wiseman Bks. (Simon & Schuster/Paula Wiseman Bks.).

Clark, Willow. The True Story of the Declaration of Independence, 1 vol. 2013. (What Really Happened? Ser.). (ENG., Illus.). 24p. (J). (gr. 2-3). pap. 9.25 (978-1-4488-9840-4(4), 94101ea9-a09e-4507-ad08-82250005ab11); lib. bdg. 26.27 (978-1-4488-9691-2(6), 091fe756-fd1e-4072-9aaf-9a4ac3be666b) Rosen Publishing Group, Inc., The. (PowerKids Pr.).

—The True Story of the Emancipation Proclamation, 1 vol. 2013. (What Really Happened? Ser.). (ENG., Illus.). 24p. (J).

(gr. 2-3). 26.27 *(978-1-4488-9695-0(9),* ed9c49fd-1083-41ae-b071-1a993beabfb5); pap. 9.25 *(978-1-4488-9848-0(X),* f7848aa6-8a09-463b-b38a-5f880afeb521) Rosen Publishing Group, Inc., The. (PowerKids Pr.).

Clasky, Leonard. Victor Volunteers: Civic Virtues, 1 vol. 2018. (Civics for the Real World Ser.). (ENG.). 12p. (gr. 1-2). pap. *(978-1-5383-6415-4(8),* 27c38cf4-405b-4126-bd3f-c2a8c93e3a86, Rosen Classroom) Rosen Publishing Group, Inc., The.

Clay, Kathryn. The Declaration of Independence: Introducing Primary Sources. 2017. (Introducing Primary Sources Ser.). (ENG., Illus.). 32p. (J). (gr. -1-2). lib. bdg. 28.65 *(978-1-5157-6355-0(2),* 135114, Capstone Pr.) Capstone.

Colbert, David. Benjamin Franklin. 2008. (10 Days Ser.). (ENG.). 160p. (J). (gr. 3-8). pap. 8.99 *(978-1-4169-6446-9(0),* Simon & Schuster/Paula Wiseman Bks.) Simon & Schuster/Paula Wiseman Bks.

Colligan, Louise. Government in Colonial America, 1 vol. 2014. (Life in Colonial America Ser.). (ENG.). 80p. (gr. 6-6). lib. bdg. 37.36 *(978-1-62712-891-9(3),* 4e389e5f-27a2-41fa-8c80-5946792ef1af) Cavendish Square Publishing LLC.

Connell, Kate. Servant to Abigail Adams: The Early American Adventures of Hannah Cooper. 2004. (Illus.). 40p. (J). (gr. 4-8). pap. 7.00 *(978-0-7567-8216-0(3))* DIANE Publishing Co.

Cooke, Tim. Causes of the War, 1 vol. 2012. (American Civil War: the Right Answer Ser.). (ENG., Illus.). 48p. (J). (gr. 6-8). pap. 15.05 *(978-1-4339-7536-3(X),* 824013a5-fd98-4be7-821d-1e0bb4a86e23); lib. bdg. 34.60 *(978-1-4339-7535-6(1),* 35413caa-60d4-4e41-aea4-43d818cb473d) Stevens, Gareth Publishing LLLP.

—Politics of the War: 1861-1865. 2012. (Civil War Highlights Ser.). (Illus.). 48p. (gr. 5-12). lib. bdg. 37.10 *(978-1-59920-818-3(0))* Black Rabbit Bks.

Corey, Shana. A Time to Act: John F. Kennedy's Big Speech. Christie, R. Gregory, illus. 2017. (ENG.). 56p. (J). (gr. 3). 18.95 *(978-0-7358-4275-5(2))* North-South Bks., Inc.

Corso, Phil. The Electoral College, 1 vol. 2019. (U. S. Presidential Elections: How They Work Ser.). (ENG.). 32p. (gr. 4-5). pap. 11.60 *(978-1-7253-1074-2(0),* 312969ff-bb62-4ba6-ae0a-9f625160136f, PowerKids Pr.) Rosen Publishing Group, Inc., The.

Cosson, Jody. Civil War & Reconstruction: 1850-1877. 2007. (Presidents of the United States Ser.). (Illus.). (J). (gr. 4-7). 47p. lib. bdg. 29.05 *(978-1-59036-743-8(X));* 48p. per. 10.95 *(978-1-59036-744-5(8))* Weigl Pubs., Inc.

Cox, Vicki. The History of the Third Parties. 2007. (U. Government: How It Works). (ENG., Illus.). 125p. (gr. 5-9). lib. bdg. 30.00 *(978-0-7910-9421-1(9),* P127243, Facts On File) Infobase Holdings, Inc.

Coy, Cissie. Dennis Chávez: The First Hispanic US Senator / Dennis Chávez: el Primer Senador Hispano de Los Estados Unidos. 2017. (SPA & ENG., Illus.). 64p. (J). (gr. 4-8). pap. 9.95 *(978-1-55885-852-7(0),* Piñata Books) Arte Publico Pr.

Crompton, Samuel Willard. How Woodrow Wilson Fought World War I, 1 vol. 2017. (Presidents at War Ser.). (ENG.). 128p. (gr. 8-8). lib. bdg. 38.93 *(978-0-7660-8529-9(5),* 64acc819-1e5c-4ab3-bc93-b627f6f32da0) Enslow Publishing, LLC.

Cunningham, Kevin. The Emancipation Proclamation. 2020. (Civil War Ser.). (ENG., Illus.). 48p. (J). (gr. 5-6). pap. 11.95 *(978-1-64493-159-2(1),* 1644931591); lib. bdg. 34.21 *(978-1-64493-080-9(3),* 1644930803) North Star Editions. (Focus Readers).

Darby, Jean. Dwight D. Eisenhower. 2004. (Presidential Leaders Ser.). (Illus.). 112p. (J). (gr. 6-12). lib. bdg. 29.27 *(978-0-8225-0813-7(3))* Lerner Publishing Group.

David, Alex. Examining Give Me Liberty or Give Me Death by Patrick Henry, 1 vol. 2020. (American Debates & Speeches Ser.). (ENG.). 64p. (gr. 7-7). pap. 16.24 *(978-1-9785-1506-2(5),* 9aed1dc4-4f63-4774-9704-68285b1b5a46) Enslow Publishing, LLC.

—Examining the Federalist & Anti-Federalist Debates, 1 vol. 2020. (American Debates & Speeches Ser.). (ENG.). 64p. (gr. 7-7). pap. 16.24 *(978-1-9785-1512-3(X),* 0908abfb-26e8-4472-9dc8-f74da1aee7d0) Enslow Publishing, LLC.

Davies, Monika. True Life: Alexander Hamilton. 2nd rev. ed. 2016. (TIME(r): Informational Text Ser.). (ENG., Illus.). 48p. (gr. 6-8). pap. 13.99 *(978-1-4938-3633-8(1))* Teacher Created Materials, Inc.

Day, Meredith, ed. Lyndon B. Johnson, 1 vol. 2016. (Pivotal Presidents: Profiles in Leadership Ser.). (ENG., Illus.). 80p. (gr. 8-8). lib. bdg. 36.47 *(978-1-68048-527-1(X),* 5e555973-7621-4474-aec5-45e2fe88a7dc) Rosen Publishing Group, Inc., The.

DeCarlo, Carolyn. Great Exit Projects on the Vietnam War & the Antiwar Movement, 1 vol. 2019. (Great Social Studies Exit Projects Ser.). (ENG.). 64p. (gr. 5-5). pap. 13.95 *(978-1-4994-4048-5(0),* f65c7091-9c33-42ae-97c1-3b2e092e2eba) Rosen Publishing Group, Inc., The.

DeCarolis, Lisa. Alexander Hamilton: Federalist & Founding Father. 2009. (Library of American Lives & Times Ser.). 112p. (gr. 5-5). 69.20 *(978-1-60853-470-8(7))* Rosen Publishing Group, Inc., The.

DeGraw, Aleine. Alexander Hamilton: American Statesman. 2009. (Primary Sources of Famous People in American History Ser.). 32p. (gr. 2-3). 47.90 *(978-1-60851-646-9(6))* Rosen Publishing Group, Inc., The.

—Alexander Hamilton: American Statesman / Estadista Estadounidense. 2009. (Famous People in American History/Grandes personajes en la historia de los Estados Unidos Ser.). (SPA.). 32p. (gr. 2-3). 47.90 *(978-1-61512-536-4(1),* Editorial Buenas Letras) Rosen Publishing Group, Inc., The.

—Alexander Hamilton: Estadista Estadounidense, 1 vol. 2003. (Grandes Personajes en la Historia de Los Estados Unidos (Famous People in American History) Ser.). (SPA., Illus.). 32p. (gr. 3-4). pap. 10.00 *(978-0-8239-4219-0(8),* fddf036c-d53d-4973-8e1e-b3966f9f7021) Rosen Publishing Group, Inc., The.

—Alexander Hamilton: Estadista estadounidense (Alexander Hamilton: American Statesman) 2009. (Grandes personajes en la historia de los Estados Unidos (Famous People in American History) Ser.). 32p. (gr. 2-3). 47.90 *(978-1-61512-788-7(7),* Editorial Buenas Letras) Rosen Publishing Group, Inc., The.

Demuth, Patricia Brennan & Who HQ. What Is the Constitution? Foley, Tim, illus. 2018. (What Was? Ser.). 112p. (J). (gr. 3-7). 5.99 *(978-1-5247-8609-0(8));* lib. bdg. 15.99 *(978-1-5247-8611-3(X))* Penguin Young Readers Group. (Penguin Workshop).

Dixon, Dale. We Are Equal! Civic Virtues, 1 vol. 2018. (Civics for the Real World Ser.). (ENG.). 8p. (gr. k-1). pap. *(978-1-5383-6320-1(8),* 09dc2afc-ddc5-4ae1-9208-35373820c26d, Rosen Classroom) Rosen Publishing Group, Inc., The.

—What Is Democracy? Understanding Citizenship, 1 vol. 2018. (Civics for the Real World Ser.). (ENG.). 12p. (gr. 1-2). pap. *(978-1-5383-6469-7(7),* 8f0779b6-08c5-41f6-8447-fcc79b6d0589, Rosen Classroom) Rosen Publishing Group, Inc., The.

Doak, Robin. Conflicts in Iraq & Afghanistan, 1 vol. 2006. (Wars That Changed American History Ser.). (ENG., Illus.). 48p. (gr. 5-8). pap. 15.05 *(978-0-8368-7305-4(X),* 29fa993c-828d-482e-b2b3-25e1567f9404); lib. bdg. 33.67 *(978-0-8368-7296-5(7),* 0f3f40c3-3b0e-49e2-9c88-969478c20f60) Stevens, Gareth Publishing LLLP. (Gareth Stevens Secondary Library).

Drayton, Tiffanie. Developing Political Leadership Skills, 1 vol. 2019. (Be the Change! Political Participation in Your Community Ser.). (ENG.). 64p. (gr. 7-7). pap. 13.95 *(978-1-7253-4077-0(1),* 57e30b56-f963-43cb-b2b9-aa95d2e15156) Rosen Publishing Group, Inc., The.

[DS529] Our Government [Lakeshore]. 2010. (Our Government Ser.). 24p. pap. 27.80 *(978-1-4296-4806-6(6),* Capstone Pr.) Capstone.

Dudley Gold, Susan. The Civil Rights Act Of 1964, 1 vol. 2011. (Landmark Legislation Ser.). (ENG.). 128p. (YA). (gr. 8-8). 42.64 *(978-1-60870-040-0(2),* e28f32c0-3ceb-450e-a7b4-d51afcb1631e) Cavendish Square Publishing LLC.

—The Missouri Compromise, 1 vol. 2011. (Landmark Legislation Ser.). (ENG.). 128p. (YA). (gr. 8-8). 42.64 *(978-1-60870-041-7(0),* 183c9afd-ef50-4b45-ad79-61237b1a486d) Cavendish Square Publishing LLC.

Duignan, Brian & DeCarlo, Carolyn, eds. The Executive Branch: Carrying Out & Enforcing Laws, 1 vol. 2018. (Checks & Balances in the U. S. Government Ser.). (ENG.). 128p. (gr. 10-10). 39.00 *(978-1-5383-0164-7(4),* 1b0fb071-6f66-47ac-9a9b-1d06e5b0b739, Britannica Educational Publishing) Rosen Publishing Group, Inc., The.

Dunbar-Ortiz, Roxanne. An Indigenous Peoples' History of the United States for Young People. 2019. (ReVisioning History for Young People Ser.: 2). (ENG., Illus.). 272p. (YA). (gr. 7). pap. 18.95 *(978-0-8070-4939-6(5),* Beacon Pr.) Beacon Pr.

Eck, Kristin. Drafting the Constitution: Weighing Evidence to Draw Sound Conclusions, 1 vol. 2005. (Critical Thinking in American History Ser.). (ENG., Illus.). 48p. (YA). (gr. 5-8). lib. bdg. 34.47 *(978-1-4042-0412-6(1),* 3f43f11d-709d-490b-b2bf-3ac65cb3eb29) Rosen Publishing Group, Inc., The.

Egan, Tracie. The President & the Executive Branch. (Primary Source Library of American Citizenship Ser.). 32p. (gr. 5-5). 2009. 47.90 *(978-1-61511-229-6(4))* 2003. (ENG., Illus.). lib. bdg. 29.13 *(978-0-8239-4477-4(8),* 826a953c-71e4-40ff-a4f6-4cebcbef54a2) Rosen Publishing Group, Inc., The. (Rosen Reference).

Ehman, Ashley M. Passing a Budget, 1 vol. 2018. (How Government Works). (ENG.). 64p. (J). (gr. 5-5). pap. 16.28 *(978-1-5026-4137-3(2),* ab9182c9-5f48-4ba0-96b6-24e9bcd1650a) Cavendish Square Publishing LLC.

Elish, Dan. The Watergate Scandal. 2004. (Cornerstones of Freedom Ser.). (ENG., Illus.). 48p. (J). 26.00 *(978-0-516-24239-2(3),* Children's Pr.) Scholastic Library Publishing.

Elston, Heidi. Harry S. Truman, 1 vol. 2016. (United States Presidents *2017 Ser.). (ENG., Illus.). 40p. (J). (gr. 2-5). 35.64 *(978-1-68078-119-9(7),* 21855, Big Buddy Bks.) ABDO Publishing Co.

The Emancipation Proclamation & the End of Slavery in America, 1 vol. 2014. (Celebration of the Civil Rights Movement Ser.). (ENG., Illus.). 80p. (J). (gr. 6-6). 37.47 *(978-1-4777-7749-7(0),* 20d82c0d-2d59-4140-9fc1-adf790e79e4c) Rosen Publishing Group, Inc., The.

Encyclopaedia Britannica, ed. The American Presidency. 2009. (Illus.). 144p. (YA). (gr. 7-12). 29.95 *(978-1-59339-843-9(3))* Encyclopaedia Britannica, Inc.

Englar, Mary. An Illustrated Timeline of U. S. Presidents, 1 vol. Epstein, Len, illus. 2012. (Visual Timelines in History Ser.). (ENG.). 32p. (J). (gr. 2-4). pap. 7.49 *(978-1-4048-7254-7(X),* 118199); lib. bdg. 29.32 *(978-1-4048-7161-8(6),* 117156) Capstone. (Picture Window Bks.).

Epperson, James F. Causes of the Civil War. 2005. (Road to War Ser.). (Illus.). 64p. (J). pap. 12.95 *(978-1-59556-006-3(8));* (gr. 4-18). lib. bdg. 22.95 *(978-1-59556-002-5(5))* OTTN Publishing.

Epstein, Brad M. Barack Obama 101. Lt. ed. 2009. (My First Presidential Board Book Ser.). (Illus.). 28p. (J). (gr. -1-1). bds. *(978-1-60730-044-1(3),* 101 Bk.) Michaelson Entertainment.

Etingoff, Kim. Harry Truman: From Farmer to President. 2012. (J). pap. *(978-1-4222-2485-4(6));* 64p. (gr. 7-8). 22.95 *(978-1-4222-2482-3(1))* Mason Crest.

EZ Comics, ed. James A. Baker, III: The Authorised Comic Book Biography. 2009. (ENG., Illus.). 44p. (YA). *(978-0-9795887-3-0(1))* EZ Comics.

Federalism. 2010. (ENG., Illus.). 128p. (gr. 6-12). 45.00 *(978-1-60413-218-2(3),* P179245, Facts On File) Infobase Holdings, Inc.

Feinstein, Stephen. The 1900s, 1 vol. 2015. (Decades of the 20th & 21st Centuries Ser.). (ENG., Illus.). 96p. (gr. 7-7). 36.27 *(978-0-7660-6920-6(6),* 17ed0d4e-94cf-4a2d-bc50-c5320b091514) Enslow Publishing, LLC.

—The 1910s, 1 vol. 2015. (Decades of the 20th & 21st Centuries Ser.). (ENG., Illus.). 96p. (gr. 7-7). 36.27 *(978-0-7660-6922-0(2),* 161bc14c-1811-4c5a-99bb-14b501507e19) Enslow Publishing, LLC.

—The 1920s, 1 vol. 2015. (Decades of the 20th & 21st Centuries Ser.). (ENG., Illus.). 96p. (gr. 7-7). 36.27 *(978-0-7660-6924-4(9),* 9b95625d-a7a3-4daf-ab40-edee602319d4) Enslow Publishing, LLC.

—The 1930s, 1 vol. 2015. (Decades of the 20th & 21st Centuries Ser.). (ENG., Illus.). 96p. (gr. 7-7). 36.27 *(978-0-7660-6926-8(5),* 00aff18c-e313-4a57-8ec9-42cefac23f78) Enslow Publishing, LLC.

—The 1940s, 1 vol. 2015. (Decades of the 20th & 21st Centuries Ser.). (ENG., Illus.). 96p. (gr. 7-7). 36.27 *(978-0-7660-6928-2(1),* 95a248c9-faa5-4dc6-a901-504cc4a36d8a) Enslow Publishing, LLC.

—The 1950s, 1 vol. 2015. (Decades of the 20th & 21st Centuries Ser.). (ENG., Illus.). 96p. (gr. 7-7). 36.27 *(978-0-7660-6930-5(3),* e466562d-5b5f-43c3-a081-dc805f4f5a70) Enslow Publishing, LLC.

—The 1960s, 1 vol. 2015. (Decades of the 20th & 21st Centuries Ser.). (ENG., Illus.). 96p. (gr. 7-7). 36.27 *(978-0-7660-6932-9(X),* a0b9f181-938f-4187-b6f8-3868ecbc3a00) Enslow Publishing, LLC.

—The 1970s, 1 vol. 2015. (Decades of the 20th & 21st Centuries Ser.). (ENG., Illus.). 96p. (gr. 7-7). 36.27 *(978-0-7660-6934-3(6),* 9d3e8c2f-6eaa-46c4-bc2a-7ca07e6bc163) Enslow Publishing, LLC.

—The 1980s, 1 vol. 2015. (Decades of the 20th & 21st Centuries Ser.). (ENG., Illus.). 96p. (gr. 7-7). 36.27 *(978-0-7660-6935-0(4),* 8ec4cd9c-3b6c-4f21-b7b9-b1615c5e1974) Enslow Publishing, LLC.

—The 1990s, 1 vol. 2015. (Decades of the 20th & 21st Centuries Ser.). (ENG., Illus.). 96p. (gr. 7-7). 36.27 *(978-0-7660-6937-4(0),* e151a8f2-e40e-4550-a278-e3dc25c77986) Enslow Publishing, LLC.

—The 2000s, 1 vol. 2015. (Decades of the 20th & 21st Centuries Ser.). (ENG., Illus.). 96p. (gr. 7-7). 36.27 *(978-0-7660-6939-8(7),* c1638775-2fc4-4b72-9a9a-10a5cd58f558) Enslow Publishing, LLC.

Fingeroth, Danny. Democracy's Signature: Benjamin Franklin & the Declaration of Independence. 2009. (Great Moments in American History Ser.). 32p. (gr. 3-3). 47.90 *(978-1-61513-141-9(8))* Rosen Publishing Group, Inc., The.

Fink, Sam. The Declaration of Independence: The Words That Made America. Fink, Sam, illus. 2007. (Illus.). 160p. (YA). (gr. 7). 19.65 *(978-0-7569-8187-7(5))* Perfection Learning Corp.

Fink, Sam & Jefferson, Thomas. Declaration of Independence: The Words That Made America. Fink, Sam, illus. 2007. (ENG., Illus.). 160p. (J). (gr. 3-6). pap. 29.94 *(978-0-439-70315-4(8))* Scholastic, Inc.

Finley, Toiya Kristen. Russell Simmons. 2007. (Sharing the American Dream Ser.). 64p. (YA). (gr. 7-18). pap. 9.95 *(978-1-4222-0762-8(5))* Mason Crest.

Ford, Carin T. The Emancipation Proclamation, Lincoln, & Slavery Through Primary Sources, 1 vol. 2013. (Civil War Through Primary Sources Ser.). (ENG.). 48p. (gr. 4-6). pap. 11.53 *(978-1-4644-0187-9(X),* 39a9f8dc-63ab-4b9b-94df-bb3af9d021ae); (Illus.). (J). lib. bdg. 27.93 *(978-0-7660-4129-5(8),* b2263e7e-8ce7-4531-a353-b06b36d2fe69) Enslow Publishing, LLC.

Ford, Jeanne Marie. How the Government Works. 2016. (How America Works). (ENG.). 24p. (J). (gr. 3-6). 32.79 *(978-1-5038-0904-8(8),* 210661) Child's World, Inc, The.

Fowler, Leona. Writing Letters to Leaders: Taking Civic Action, 1 vol. 2018. (Civics for the Real World Ser.). (ENG.). 12p. (gr. 1-2). pap. *(978-1-5383-6481-9(6),* fde7fc4e-9566-4fb0-9a16-927d1327fc1b, Rosen Classroom) Rosen Publishing Group, Inc., The.

Francis, Amy, ed. The U. S. Policy on Cuba, 1 vol. 2008. (At Issue Ser.). (ENG., Illus.). 136p. (gr. 10-12). 41.03 *(978-0-7377-4108-7(2),* fff89a06-f667-48d9-84e0-719ed60cc6f8); pap. 28.80 *(978-0-7377-4109-4(0),* 31970e5b-b6b7-46c2-a4d7-31691973a5e3) Greenhaven Publishing LLC. (Greenhaven Publishing).

Freedman, Jeri. Elizabeth Warren: Democratic Senator from Massachusetts, 1 vol. 2017. (Leading Women Ser.). (ENG., Illus.). 112p. (YA). (gr. 7-7). 41.64 *(978-1-5026-2699-8(3),* fd6cd751-fce0-41ed-92f6-f460528a8cbf) Cavendish Square Publishing LLC.

Fremon, David K. The Watergate Scandal in United States History, 1 vol. 2014. (In United States History Ser.). (ENG., Illus.). 96p. (gr. 5-6). (J). pap. 13.88 *(978-0-7660-6108-8(6),* 620b45c8-e671-4b5c-b7d8-6d22b4045811); 31.61 *(978-0-7660-6107-1(8),* 7733f69b-38ff-41c5-8ffe-24a281bb7dcc) Enslow Publishing, LLC.

Friedman, Mark. The Democratic Process (Cornerstones of Freedom: Third Series) 2012. (Cornerstones of Freedom. Third Ser.). (ENG., Illus.). 64p. (J). (gr. 4-6). pap. 8.95 *(978-0-531-28155-0(8),* Children's Pr.) Scholastic Library Publishing.

Friesen, Helen Lepp. El Tío Sam. 2014. (SPA., Illus.). 24p. (J). *(978-1-62127-625-8(2))* Weigl Pubs., Inc.

Fritz, Jean. Alexander Hamilton: the Outsider. 2012. (ENG.). 144p. (J). (gr. 3-7). 8.99 *(978-0-14-241986-1(9),* Puffin Books) Penguin Young Readers Group.

Furgang, Kathy. The Declaration of Independence & Benjamin Franklin of Pennsylvania. 2009. (Framers of the Declaration of Independence Ser.). 24p. (gr. 3-3). 42.50 *(978-1-61512-629-3(5),* PowerKids Pr.) Rosen Publishing Group, Inc., The.

—The Declaration of Independence & Richard Henry Lee of Virginia. 2009. (Framers of the Declaration of Independence Ser.). 24p. (gr. 3-3). 42.50 *(978-1-61512-630-9(9),* PowerKids Pr.) Rosen Publishing Group, Inc., The.

—The Declaration of Independence & Robert Livingston of New York. 2009. (Framers of the Declaration of Independence Ser.). 24p. (gr. 3-3). 42.50 *(978-1-61512-631-6(7),* PowerKids Pr.) Rosen Publishing Group, Inc., The.

—The Declaration of Independence & Roger Sherman of Connecticut. 2009. (Framers of the Declaration of Independence Ser.). 24p. (gr. 3-3). 42.50 *(978-1-61512-632-3(5),* PowerKids Pr.) Rosen Publishing Group, Inc., The.

—The Declaration of Independence & Thomas Jefferson of Virginia. 2009. (Framers of the Declaration of Independence Ser.). 24p. (gr. 3-3). 42.50 *(978-1-61512-633-0(3),* PowerKids Pr.) Rosen Publishing Group, Inc., The.

Gagne, Tammy. The Power of the States. 2011. (My Guide to the Constitution Ser.). (Illus.). 48p. (J). (gr. 3-6). lib. bdg. 29.95 *(978-1-58415-945-2(6))* Mitchell Lane Pubs.

Gale Encyclopedia of U. S. History: Government & Politics, 2 vols. rev. ed. 2008. (Gale Encyclopedia of U. S. History Ser.). (ENG., Illus.). 900p. 339.00 *(978-1-4144-3118-5(X))* Cengage Gale.

Geller, Kevin. Harry S. Truman, 1 vol. 2017. (Pivotal Presidents: Profiles in Leadership Ser.). (ENG., Illus.). 80p. (J). (gr. 8-8). lib. bdg. 36.47 *(978-1-68048-633-9(0),* 6fbd2e3d-226b-4f14-9f06-044fc28f431d, Britannica Educational Publishing) Rosen Publishing Group, Inc., The.

Gelletly, LeeAnne. A Woman's Place in Early America. 2012. (Illus.). 64p. (J). pap. *(978-1-4222-2365-9(5))* Mason Crest.

—A Woman's Place in Early America. Harrington, A. Page, ed. 2012. (Finding a Voice: Women's Fight for Equality in U. S. Society Ser.). (Illus.). 64p. (J). (gr. 5). 22.95 *(978-1-4222-2355-0(8))* Mason Crest.

Gerdes, Louise I., ed. National Service, 1 vol. 2011. (Opposing Viewpoints Ser.). (ENG.). 248p. (gr. 10-12). pap. 34.80 *(978-0-7377-5234-2(3),* 8ca1008b-ae90-4f33-9b9d-82039a815fbb); lib. bdg. 50.43 *(978-0-7377-5233-5(5),* 6bb6047c-3918-4004-94c2-8cea7433c4e0) Greenhaven Publishing LLC. (Greenhaven Publishing).

—Super PACs, 1 vol. 2014. (At Issue Ser.). (ENG.). 112p. (gr. 10-12). pap. 28.80 *(978-0-7377-6865-7(7),* d5e768b1-8dea-4745-865b-8da9f5e2cdf4); lib. bdg. 41.03 *(978-0-7377-6864-0(9),* 5e9c8f0e-5d44-4808-80c5-4e9efb46cef3) Greenhaven Publishing LLC. (Greenhaven Publishing).

Giddens, Sandra. A Timeline of the Constitutional Convention. 2009. (Timelines of American History Ser.). 32p. (gr. 4-4). 47.90 *(978-1-60854-382-3(X),* Rosen Reference) Rosen Publishing Group, Inc., The.

Giddens, Sandra & Giddens, Owen. A Timeline of the Constitutional Convention, 1 vol. 2004. (Timelines of American History Ser.). (ENG., Illus.). 32p. (gr. 4-4). lib. bdg. 29.13 *(978-0-8239-4535-1(9),* 7b1ba4ac-cff3-4642-b86f-ac3b637b2247, Rosen Reference) Rosen Publishing Group, Inc., The.

Giesecke, Ernestine. National Government. rev. ed. 2016. (Kids' Guide to Government Ser.). (ENG.). 32p. (J). (gr. 3-5). pap. 7.99 *(978-1-4846-3812-5(3),* 134591, Heinemann) Capstone.

Gigliotti, Jim. Ronald Reagan, the 40th President. 2016. (First Look at America's Presidents Ser.). (ENG., Illus.). 24p. (J). (gr. -1-3). 26.99 *(978-1-944102-69-2(8))* Bearport Publishing Co., Inc.

The GILDED AGE & PROGRESSIVISM: 1891-1913. 2010. (ENG., Illus.). 136p. (gr. 5-8). 35.00 *(978-1-60413-355-4(4),* P178886, Facts On File) Infobase Holdings, Inc.

Gillard, Arthur, ed. Social Protest, 1 vol. 2014. (Issues That Concern You Ser.). (ENG., Illus.). 136p. (gr. 7-10). lib. bdg. 43.63 *(978-0-7377-6934-0(3),* dd806b88-940f-4d8f-95d5-5fb6e1633df1, Greenhaven Publishing) Greenhaven Publishing LLC.

Gitlin, Martin. The Great Depression & World War II: 1929-1945. 2007. (Presidents of the United States Ser.). (Illus.). 48p. (J). (gr. 4-7). lib. bdg. 29.05 *(978-1-59036-749-0(9));* per. 10.95 *(978-1-59036-750-6(2))* Weigl Pubs., Inc.

—Post-War United States: 1945-Early 1970s. 2007. (Presidents of the United States Ser.). (Illus.). 48p. (J). (gr. 4-7). lib. bdg. 29.05 *(978-1-59036-751-3(0));* per. 10.95 *(978-1-59036-752-0(9))* Weigl Pubs., Inc.

Glencoe McGraw-Hill Staff. United States Government: Democracy in Action, StudentWorks with Audio Summaries. 2007. (Government in the U. S. Ser.). (ENG.). (gr. 9-12). cd-rom 148.20 *(978-0-07-878365-4(8),* 0078783658) McGraw-Hill Higher Education.

Glencoe McGraw-Hill Staff, creator. United States Government: Democracy in Action. 2007. (Government in the U. S. Ser.). (ENG., Illus.). 320p. (gr. 9-12). per. 12.28 *(978-0-07-878125-4(6),* 0078781256) McGraw-Hill Higher Education.

Goldsmith, Marcia. Important Years: The 1980s. 2005. (Illus.). 16p. (J). *(978-0-618-56043-1(2))* Houghton Mifflin Harcourt Publishing Co.

Gormley, Beatrice. George W. Bush: Our Forty-Third President. 2015. (Real-Life Story Ser.). (ENG., Illus.). 256p. (J). (gr. 3-7). 17.99 *(978-1-4814-4645-7(2),* Aladdin) Simon & Schuster Children's Publishing.

—Joe Biden: Our 46th President. 2021. (ENG.). 256p. (J). (gr. 3-7). 17.99 *(978-1-5344-7932-6(5));* pap. 6.99 *(978-1-5344-7931-9(7))* Simon & Schuster Children's Publishing. (Aladdin).

Gosman, Gillian. Thomas Jefferson, 1 vol. 2011. (Life Stories Ser.). (Illus.). 24p. (J). (gr. 3-3). (ENG.). pap. 9.25 *(978-1-4488-3180-7(6),* aa940604-afba-402c-9f00-9fa5315e3895, PowerKids Pr.); (SPA & ENG., lib. bdg. 26.27 *(978-1-4488-3221-7(7),* e5e60a96-36ef-45db-b4dc-d760cd59aa5a); (ENG., lib. bdg. 26.27 *(978-1-4488-3178-4(4),* 6e7e2cdf-68fc-42f2-98e4-ec91f3c5b148, PowerKids Pr.) Rosen Publishing Group, Inc., The.

Gottfried, Ted. Millard Fillmore, 1 vol. 2008. (Presidents & Their Times Ser.). (ENG., Illus.). 96p. (gr. 6-6). lib. bdg. 36.93 *(978-0-7614-2431-4(8),* a45fa7df-8893-4ace-9783-fbc698df63d9) Cavendish Square Publishing LLC.

Gould, Jane H. Alexander Hamilton, 1 vol. 2012. (Jr. Graphic Founding Fathers Ser.). (ENG., Illus.). 24p. (J). (gr. 2-3). pap. 11.60 *(978-1-4488-7989-2(2),* 1d6bf400-d883-42f3-9cf5-9ec5414ffb13); lib. bdg. 28.93 *(978-1-4488-7895-6(0),* 2bbd35e0-af34-4c29-b0ab-a3eb8774959f) Rosen Publishing Group, Inc., The. (PowerKids Pr.).

Gould, Sloane. I Want to Be the President! Understanding Government, 1 vol. 2018. (Civics for the Real World Ser.). (ENG.). 16p. (gr. 2-3). pap. *(978-1-5383-6522-9(7),* 410c087e-0fba-464a-ae52-bbc9a7daff44, Rosen Classroom) Rosen Publishing Group, Inc., The.

—Speaking up in Class: Civic Virtues, 1 vol. 2018. (Civics for the Real World Ser.). (ENG.). 8p. (gr. k-1). pap. *(978-1-5081-3935-5(0),* cc0a8a4e-9074-40a0-acc7-8166d6ca1f4b, Rosen Classroom) Rosen Publishing Group, Inc., The.

Griffin, Maeve. Constitution Day. 2009. (Explore Citizenship Ser.). 24p. (gr. 3-3). 42.50 *(978-1-61512-340-7(7),* PowerKids Pr.) Rosen Publishing Group, Inc., The.

Griffin, Maeve. Constitution Day, 1 vol. (Explore Citizenship Ser.). (ENG.). 24p. (gr. 3-3). 2009. (J). 26.27 *(978-1-4358-2978-7(6),* c9d089c8-9cb7-4aa5-bbc5-cbf9e37a771a, PowerKids Pr.) 2008. pap. 8.25 *(978-1-4358-0139-4(3),* b2ef757f-6820-4254-a698-95cc69e4b159, Rosen Classroom) Rosen Publishing Group, Inc., The.

Grodin, Elissa D. D Is for Democracy: A Citizen's Alphabet. Juhasz, Victor, illus. 2004. (ENG.). 40p. (J). (gr. 1-4). 16.95 *(978-1-58536-234-9(4),* 202059) Sleeping Bear Pr.

Grolier Educational Staff, contrib. by. Flash Focus, 4 vols. 2004. (Illus.). (J). Vol. 1. *(978-0-7172-5934-2(X))* Vol. 2. *(978-0-7172-5938-0(2))* Vol. 3. *(978-0-7172-5937-3(4))* Vol. 4. *(978-0-7172-5940-3(4))* Grolier, Ltd.

Gunderson, Jessica. The Election Of 1860: A Nation Divides on the Eve of War. 2016. (Presidential Politics Ser.). (ENG.). 48p. (J). pap. 54.70 *(978-1-4914-8737-2(2),* 24425); (Illus.). (gr. 3-6). lib. bdg. 29.99 *(978-1-4914-8240-7(0),* 130711) Capstone.

—The Real Alexander Hamilton: The Truth Behind the Legend. 2019. (Real Revolutionaries Ser.). (ENG., Illus.). 64p. (J). (gr. 5-9). pap. 7.95 *(978-0-7565-6128-4(0),* 140075); lib. bdg. 34.65 *(978-0-7565-5892-5(1),* 138697) Capstone. (Compass Point Bks.).

—Understanding Your Role in Elections. 2018. (Kids' Guide to Government Ser.). (ENG., Illus.). 32p. (J). (gr. 3-6). lib. bdg. 27.99 *(978-1-5435-0318-0(7),* 137184, Capstone Pr.) Capstone.

Haerens, Margaret, ed. Government Gridlock, 1 vol. 2015. (Opposing Viewpoints Ser.). (ENG., Illus.). 232p. (gr. 10-12). 50.43 *(978-0-7377-7266-1(2),* af82fe80-85fb-4cdf-bd5c-f37969d8894f, Greenhaven Publishing) Greenhaven Publishing LLC.

Haldy, Emma E. Abraham Lincoln. Bane, Jeff, illus. 2016. (My Early Library: My Itty-Bitty Bio Ser.). (ENG.). 24p. (J). (gr. k-1). 30.64 *(978-1-63470-476-2(2),* 207635) Cherry Lake Publishing.

—Abraham Lincoln SP. Bane, Jeff, illus. 2018. (My Early Library: Mi Mini Biografía (My Itty-Bitty Bio) Ser.). (SPA.). 24p. (J). (gr. k-1). lib. bdg. 30.64 *(978-1-5341-2993-1(6),* 212020) Cherry Lake Publishing.

Hale, Sarah Elder, ed. Abraham Lincoln: Defender of the Union. 2005. (ENG., Illus.). 48p. (J). (gr. 3-9). 17.95 *(978-0-8126-7902-1(4))* Cobblestone Pr.

Harper, Leslie. How Do Laws Get Passed?, 1 vol. 2012. (Civics Q&a Ser.). (ENG., Illus.). 24p. (J). (gr. 2-3). pap. 9.25 *(978-1-4488-7509-2(9),* a0c47672-0a01-430e-9d21-3f3ce9d629e2); lib. bdg. 26.27 *(978-1-4488-7436-1(X),* 28fea57e-f00e-4756-81f7-3900ae5c76b1) Rosen Publishing Group, Inc., The. (PowerKids Pr.).

—What Are Checks & Balances?, 1 vol. 2012. (Civics Q&a Ser.). (ENG., Illus.). 24p. (J). (gr. 2-3). 26.27 *(978-1-4488-7433-0(5),* 1084f4be-dd87-4dc6-899d-cc62445afa85); pap. 9.25 *(978-1-4488-7506-1(4),* b91efaa2-93a1-4217-8c1e-346bfabd335f) Rosen Publishing Group, Inc., The. (PowerKids Pr.).

Harper, Reggie. Who Works at the U. S. Capitol? Understanding Government, 1 vol. 2018. (Civics for the Real World Ser.). (ENG.). 16p. (gr. 2-3). pap. *(978-1-5081-3940-9(7),* ca6b2a45-f736-41e5-b9b9-e4ca9611773c, Rosen Classroom) Rosen Publishing Group, Inc., The.

Harris, Duchess. Governmental Checks & Balances. 2017. (American Values & Freedoms Ser.). (ENG.). 112p. (J). (gr. 6-12). lib. bdg. 41.36 *(978-1-5321-1301-7(3),* 27509, Essential Library) ABDO Publishing Co.

Harris, Kamala. The Truths We Hold: An American Journey (Young Readers Edition) (ENG., Illus.). 304p. (gr. 7). 2020. (J). pap. 10.99 *(978-0-593-11317-2(9),* Penguin Books) 2019. (YA). 17.99 *(978-1-9848-3706-6(0),* Philomel Bks.) Penguin Young Readers Group.

Harris, Michael C. & Who HQ. What Is the Declaration of Independence? Hoare, Jerry, illus. 2016. (What Was? Ser.). 112p. (J). (gr. 3-7). lib. bdg. 15.99 *(978-0-399-54230-5(2),* Penguin Workshop) Penguin Young Readers Group.

Harris, Nancy. Mount Rushmore. rev. ed. 2016. (Patriotic Symbols Ser.). (ENG.). 24p. (J). (gr. -1-1). pap. 6.29 *(978-1-4846-3588-9(4),* 133656, Heinemann) Capstone.

Hartley, John. Holt American Civics. 5th ed. 2005. (Holt American Civics Ser.). (ENG., Illus.). 784p. (gr. 9-9). 98.35 *(978-0-03-037778-5(1))* Houghton Mifflin Harcourt Publishing Co.

Haulley, Fletcher. The Deparment of Homeland Security, 1 vol. 2005. (This Is Your Government Ser.). (ENG., Illus.). 64p. (J). (gr. 4-6). lib. bdg. 37.13 *(978-1-4042-0209-2(9),* cb6cd31a-5bf6-494c-8fe0-965b27083d84) Rosen Publishing Group, Inc., The.

—The Department of Homeland Security. 2009. (This Is Your Government Ser.). 64p. (gr. 5-6). 58.50 *(978-1-60854-371-7(4),* Rosen Reference) Rosen Publishing Group, Inc., The.

Heing, Bridey, ed. America's Urban-Rural Divide, 1 vol. 2019. (Introducing Issues with Opposing Viewpoints Ser.). (ENG.). 120p. (J). (gr. 7-10). pap. 29.30 *(978-1-5345-0660-2(8),* 3b9954bf-d1f9-4408-a474-b6e0c5d4dec0) Greenhaven Publishing LLC.

Hensley, Tana. Priya Starts a Petition: Taking Civic Action, 1 vol. 2018. (Civics for the Real World Ser.). (ENG.). 16p. (gr. 2-3). pap. *(978-1-5383-6560-1(X),* 5dd8d9c7-a69c-422a-b122-7aaabcf0ba23, Rosen Classroom) Rosen Publishing Group, Inc., The.

—We Have Different Cultures: Understanding Citizenship, 1 vol. 2018. (Civics for the Real World Ser.). (ENG.). 12p. (gr. 1-2). pap. *(978-1-5081-3938-6(5),* 4d6e4499-fd63-4ac4-928a-6a4e4b20eab4, Rosen Classroom) Rosen Publishing Group, Inc., The.

Herringshaw, DeAnn. The United States Enters the 20th Century. 2011. (Explorer Library: Language Arts Explorer Ser.). (ENG.). 32p. (gr. 4-8). pap. 14.21 *(978-1-61080-288-8(8),* 201211); (Illus.). lib. bdg. 32.07 *(978-1-61080-200-0(4),* 201176) Cherry Lake Publishing.

Herwick Rice, Dona & Conklin, Wendy. Causes of the Civil War, 1 vol. rev. ed. 2009. (Reader's Theater Ser.). (ENG.). 32p. (J). (gr. 3-8). pap. 11.99 *(978-1-4333-0545-0(3))* Teacher Created Materials, Inc.

Hiber, Amanda, ed. Is the United States Ready for a Minority President?, 1 vol. 2007. (At Issue Ser.). (ENG., Illus.). 112p. (gr. 10-12). 41.03 *(978-0-7377-3878-0(2),* 33436de7-e1be-4d9e-a059-2a6fc759e904); pap. 28.80 *(978-0-7377-3879-7(0),* 7fec2bde-69d8-47e6-af30-2de2909c8f3d) Greenhaven Publishing LLC. (Greenhaven Publishing).

Hicks, Terry Allan. The Declaration of Independence, 1 vol. 2007. (Symbols of America Ser.). (ENG., Illus.). 40p. (gr. 3-3). lib. bdg. 32.64 *(978-0-7614-2135-1(1),* b672c79b-ebcf-460a-bf6f-c79934c3be91) Cavendish Square Publishing LLC.

Higgins, Nadia. US Government Through Infographics. Sciuto, Alex, illus. 2014. (Super Social Studies Infographics Ser.). (ENG.). 32p. (J). (gr. 3-5). lib. bdg. 26.65 *(978-1-4677-3463-9(2),* 78cde239-547e-47e0-82b6-10b421eb9fea, Lerner Pubns.) Lerner Publishing Group.

Hillstrom, Kevin. The Progressive Era, 1 vol. 2008. (American History Ser.). (ENG., Illus.). 104p. (gr. 7-7). 41.03 *(978-1-4205-0067-7(8),* 855b3f02-1134-463a-b161-4c4f6fa73d56, Lucent Pr.) Greenhaven Publishing LLC.

Hinman, Bonnie. Donald Trump: 45th President of the United States. 2017. (Newsmakers Set 2 Ser.). (ENG., Illus.). 48p. (J). (gr. 4-8). 55.65 *(978-1-68078-970-6(8),* 26371) ABDO Publishing Co.

—The Second Continental Congress. 2017. (Young America Ser.). (Illus.). 47p. (J). 29.95 *(978-1-61228-979-3(7))* Mitchell Lane Pubs.

Hinton, KaaVonia. To Preserve the Union: Causes & Effects of the Missouri Compromise, 1 vol. 2013. (Cause & Effect Ser.). (ENG.). 32p. (J). (gr. 3-6). 27.99 *(978-1-4765-0238-0(2),* 122292); pap. 8.95 *(978-1-4765-3404-6(7),* 123535) Capstone.

Hobbes, Emma. Thomas More & Utopia. 2016. (J). lib. bdg. *(978-1-68048-551-6(2))* Rosen Publishing Group, Inc., The.

Hoffman, Mary Ann. I Am a Good Citizen, 1 vol. 2011. (Kids of Character Ser.). (ENG., Illus.). 24p. (J). (gr. 1-2). pap. 9.15 *(978-1-4339-4851-0(6),* ff2c96bf-58d1-4e55-8eda-e2a24f6832fb); lib. bdg. 25.27 *(978-1-4339-4850-3(8),* 330462f9-6f2c-42d1-8ef7-301b51b0f728) Stevens, Gareth Publishing LLLP.

Holt, Rinehart and Winston Staff. American Civics: Online Edition Plus. 3rd ed. 2003. 17.26 *(978-0-03-037434-0(0))* Holt McDougal.

Honders, Christine. Is the Balance of Power in Government Balanced?, 1 vol. 2018. (Key Questions in American History Ser.). (ENG.). 32p. (gr. 4-5). 29.27 *(978-1-5081-6758-7(3),* 65702597-2924-4b35-a32e-3a2db9b0e76a, PowerKids Pr.) Rosen Publishing Group, Inc., The.

—Watergate & the Resignation of President Nixon, 1 vol. 2018. (American History Ser.). (ENG.). 104p. (gr. 7-7). 41.03 *(978-1-5345-6427-5(6),* 09e66a89-585c-4750-b227-8241dc49ea84, Lucent Pr.) Greenhaven Publishing LLC.

Horn, Geoffrey M. The Cabinet & Federal Agencies, 1 vol. 2003. (World Almanac(r) Library of American Government Ser.). (ENG., Illus.). 48p. (gr. 5-8). pap. 15.05 *(978-0-8368-5481-7(0),* 4050d233-003b-4314-bdb9-f62a1a6a4ae2); lib. bdg. 33.67 *(978-0-8368-5476-3(4),* 98b2a3f7-34e4-4fb3-ba10-06f38d6f346f) Stevens, Gareth Publishing LLLP. (Gareth Stevens Secondary Library).

—The Presidency, 1 vol. 2003. (World Almanac(r) Library of American Government Ser.). (ENG., Illus.). 48p. (gr. 5-8). lib. bdg. 33.67 *(978-0-8368-5458-9(6),* 20237a60-d17b-4dc3-b116-a4b89a0da031, Gareth Stevens Secondary Library) Stevens, Gareth Publishing LLLP.

—World Almanac(r) Library of American Government, 4 vols. Incl. Cabinet & Federal Agencies. lib. bdg. 33.67 *(978-0-8368-5476-3(4),* 98b2a3f7-34e4-4fb3-ba10-06f38d6f346f); Presidency. lib. bdg. 33.67 *(978-0-8368-5458-9(6),* 20237a60-d17b-4dc3-b116-a4b89a0da031); Supreme Court. lib. bdg. 33.67 *(978-0-8368-5459-6(4),* 2d96a4ed-9b8c-4cd6-906c-983ff6becd30); (gr. 5-8). (World Almanac(r) Library of American Government Ser.). (ENG., Illus.). 48p. 2003. Set lib. bdg. 67.34 *(978-0-8368-5555-5(8),* e0274e35-dab2-49dd-9e0d-d42efc0bdcf1, Gareth Stevens Secondary Library) Stevens, Gareth Publishing LLLP.

How the US Government Works, 6 vols. 2015. (How the US Government Works: 6). (ENG.). 48p. (J). (gr. 4-8). lib. bdg. 213.84 *(978-1-62403-632-3(5),* 17039) ABDO Publishing Co.

How to Contact an Elected Official, 1 vol. 2014. (Be a Community Leader Ser.). (ENG.). 32p. (J). (gr. 5-5). lib. bdg. 27.93 *(978-1-4777-6689-7(8),* 096fb5da-0710-4444-b19c-34a0ada7a0ec, PowerKids Pr.) Rosen Publishing Group, Inc., The.

Hudak, Heather C. McCarthyism & the Red Scare. 2017. (Uncovering the Past: Analyzing Primary Sources Ser.). 48p. (J). (gr. 5-6). *(978-0-7787-3939-5(2))* Crabtree Publishing Co.

Huddle, Lorena. Woodrow Wilson, 1 vol. 2017. (Pivotal Presidents: Profiles in Leadership Ser.). (ENG., Illus.). 80p. (J). (gr. 8-8). lib. bdg. 36.47 *(978-1-68048-635-3(7),* e35b543f-74c9-482f-8d07-267b266ea228, Britannica Educational Publishing) Rosen Publishing Group, Inc., The.

Huddleston, Emma. Exploring Independence Hall. 2019. (Travel America's Landmarks Ser.). (ENG., Illus.). 32p. (J). (gr. 2-3). pap. 9.95 *(978-1-64185-853-3(2),* 1641858532); lib. bdg. 31.35 *(978-1-64185-784-0(6),* 1641857846) North Star Editions. (Focus Readers).

Huffman, Mindy. What's Best for My Class? Civic Virtues, 1 vol. 2018. (Civics for the Real World Ser.). (ENG.). 16p. (gr. 2-3). pap. *(978-1-5383-6502-1(2),* d3865ce5-b9b7-4e50-946f-e12e91e6f923, Rosen Classroom) Rosen Publishing Group, Inc., The.

Hughes, Chris. The Constitutional Convention. 2005. (People at the Center of Ser.). (Illus.). 48p. (J). (gr. -1-7). lib. bdg. 24.95 *(978-1-56711-918-3(2),* Blackbirch Pr., Inc.) Cengage Gale.

Hurt, Avery Elizabeth. The Declaration of Independence, 1 vol. 2018. (America's Most Important Documents: Inquiry into Historical Sources Ser.). (ENG.). 64p. (gr. 6-6). lib. bdg. 37.36 *(978-1-5026-3604-1(2),* 772ba093-e206-4454-a3fb-f6f8e0106590) Cavendish Square Publishing LLC.

—Thomas Paine's Common Sense, 1 vol. 2018. (America's Most Important Documents: Inquiry into Historical Sources Ser.). (ENG.). 64p. (gr. 6-6). lib. bdg. 37.36 *(978-1-5026-3601-0(8),* c05511b4-ee61-48f5-bf4c-393681f4ec9d) Cavendish Square Publishing LLC.

—The United States Constitution, 1 vol. 2018. (America's Most Important Documents: Inquiry into Historical Sources Ser.). (ENG.). 64p. (gr. 6-6). lib. bdg. 37.36 *(978-1-5026-3610-2(7),* fdfdc88b-c2c4-4faa-8c5e-413e112519eb) Cavendish Square Publishing LLC.

Isaacs, Sally. Understanding the Articles of Confederation. 2008. (Documenting Early America Ser.). (ENG., Illus.). 32p. (J). (gr. 3-6). lib. bdg. *(978-0-7787-4372-9(1))* Crabtree Publishing Co.

—Understanding the Declaration of Independence. 2008. (Documenting Early America Ser.). (ENG.). 32p. (J). (gr. 3-6). lib. bdg. *(978-0-7787-4371-2(3))* Crabtree Publishing Co.

Isaacs, Sally & Bedesky, Baron. Understanding the Declaration of Independence. 2008. (Documenting Early America Ser.). (ENG.). 32p. (J). (gr. 3-6). pap. *(978-0-7787-4376-7(4))* Crabtree Publishing Co.

—Understanding the US Constitution. 2008. (Documenting Early America Ser.). (ENG.). 32p. (J). (gr. 3-6). pap. *(978-0-7787-4378-1(0))* Crabtree Publishing Co.

Isaacs, Sally Senzell. Understanding the U. S. Constitution. 2008. (Documenting Early America Ser.). (ENG.). 32p. (J). (gr. 1-4). 19.75 *(978-1-5311-7652-5(6))* Perfection Learning Corp.

Isecke, Harriet. Lyndon B. Johnson: Un Texano en la Casa Blanca / Lyndon B. Johnson - A Texan in the White House. 2013. (Primary Source Readers Ser.). (SPA.). lib. bdg. 19.65 *(978-0-606-31873-0(9))* Turtleback.

Jain, Varun. Understanding American Politics: A Book for Teenagers. 2014. 54p. pap. 15.99 *(978-1-4931-6161-4(X))* Xlibris Corp.

Jakubiak, David J. How Our Government Works, 12 vols., Set. Incl. What Does a Congressional Representative Do? lib. bdg. 26.27 *(978-1-4358-9362-7(X),* ae02193a-85fc-4981-97d2-b8fe04442f25); What Does a Governor Do? lib. bdg. 26.27 *(978-1-4358-9358-0(1),* 99261648-5866-45a8-bd50-116464955214); What Does a Mayor Do? lib. bdg. 26.27 *(978-1-4358-9359-7(X),* ea92488c-442d-4fdf-bc36-818103f8549a); What Does a Senator Do? lib. bdg. 26.27 *(978-1-4358-9360-3(3),* 72d2509e-ccb7-41e4-aee2-aeabeb327ae7); What Does a Supreme Court Justice Do? lib. bdg. 26.27 *(978-1-4358-9361-0(1),* 0b1487b1-e8ca-474e-a67b-59e45e307f29); What Does the President Do? lib. bdg. 26.27 *(978-1-4358-9357-3(3),* 2da102a5-9dda-4280-99bb-0230c16564fe); (J). (gr. 3-3). (How Our Government Works). (ENG., Illus.). 24p. 2010. Set lib. bdg. 157.62 *(978-1-4358-9405-1(7),* 63b041c6-3aef-4a63-96da-0365b2ceebb3, PowerKids Pr.) Rosen Publishing Group, Inc., The.

—What Does a Congressional Representative Do?, 1 vol. 2010. (How Our Government Works). (ENG., Illus.). 24p. (J). (gr. 3-3). pap. 9.25 *(978-1-4358-9820-2(6),* c823ad98-d5b2-41e6-aa87-c3f0923f6b05); lib. bdg. 26.27 *(978-1-4358-9362-7(X),* ae02193a-85fc-4981-97d2-b8fe04442f25) Rosen Publishing Group, Inc., The. (PowerKids Pr.).

—What Does a Governor Do? 2010. (How Our Government Works Ser.). 24p. (J). (gr. 3-6). lib. bdg., E-Book 42.50 *(978-1-4488-0022-3(6));* (ENG., Illus.). pap. 9.25 *(978-1-4358-9812-7(5),* 2966d192-e6bd-47e0-9533-ead4af9bd606, PowerKids Pr.); (ENG., Illus.). lib. bdg. 26.27 *(978-1-4358-9358-0(1),* 99261648-5866-45a8-bd50-116464955214, PowerKids Pr.) Rosen Publishing Group, Inc., The.

—What Does a Senator Do? 2010. (How Our Government Works Ser.). 24p. (J). (gr. 3-6). lib. bdg., E-Book 42.50 *(978-1-4488-0029-2(3));* (ENG., Illus.). pap. 9.25 *(978-1-4358-9816-5(8),* f8b66662-3a5d-4737-a336-fbdfc51c4804, PowerKids Pr.); (ENG., Illus.). lib. bdg. 26.27 *(978-1-4358-9360-3(3),* 72d2509e-ccb7-41e4-aee2-aeabeb327ae7, PowerKids Pr.) Rosen Publishing Group, Inc., The.

—What Does the President Do?, 1 vol. 2010. (How Our Government Works). 24p. (J). (gr. 3-3). (ENG.). pap. 9.25 *(978-1-4358-9810-3(9),* 6a746901-36f3-476f-89ee-0b42cd5eb478, PowerKids Pr.); lib. bdg., E-Book 42.50 *(978-1-4488-0020-9(X));* (ENG., Illus.). lib. bdg. 26.27 *(978-1-4358-9357-3(3),* 2da102a5-9dda-4280-99bb-0230c16564fe, PowerKids Pr.) Rosen Publishing Group, Inc., The.

Jarnow, Jesse. Patrick Henry's Liberty or Death Speech: A Primary Source Investigation. (Great Historic Debates & Speeches Ser.). 64p. (gr. 5-8). 2009. 58.50 *(978-1-61513-120-4(5))* 2004. (ENG., Illus.). (J). lib. bdg. 37.13 *(978-1-4042-0152-1(1),* 33578fa0-39bc-431d-85a9-66a4ee0c1715) Rosen Publishing Group, Inc., The.

Jeffrey, Gary. Thomas Paine Writes Common Sense, 1 vol. 2011. (Graphic Heroes of the American Revolution Ser.). (ENG.). 24p. (gr. 3-3). (J). pap. 9.15 *(978-1-4339-6029-1(X),* 0b304be1-d0ef-44f8-8344-e85077307d9a, Gareth Stevens Learning Library); (YA). lib. bdg. 26.60 *(978-1-4339-6028-4(1),* 68e1aab1-5954-40b5-8644-751c4fa60a0d) Stevens, Gareth Publishing LLLP.

Jeffries, Joyce. What Are Political Parties?, 1 vol. 2018. (What's the Issue? Ser.). (ENG.). 24p. (gr. 3-3). pap. 9.25 *(978-1-5345-2813-0(X),* 837788f3-1e0f-4232-8855-d098cabff33c, KidHaven Publishing) Greenhaven Publishing LLC.

Jianmei, Wang. America: My Horn, Your Country. 2009. pap. 29.00 *(978-1-61584-424-1(4))* Independent Pub.

Johnson, Etta. The United States Government. 2005. (J). pap. *(978-1-4108-4592-4(3))* Benchmark Education Co.

Jones, Emma. What's Border Security?, 1 vol. 2018. (What's the Issue? Ser.). (ENG.). 24p. (gr. 3-3). pap. 9.25 *(978-1-5345-2804-8(0),* 6009dfb2-0112-4a3f-a015-cb882cb5cd1a, KidHaven Publishing) Greenhaven Publishing LLC.

Kaleidoscope - Government Series, 4 bks., Set. *(978-0-7614-1450-6(9),* Cavendish Square) Cavendish Square Publishing LLC.

Kallen, Stuart A., ed. Does Equality Exist in America?, 1 vol. 2006. (At Issue Ser.). (ENG., Illus.). 112p. (gr. 10-12). pap. 28.80 *(978-0-7377-3434-8(5),* 3bb18673-7efb-4926-a1eb-3da071dedc26); lib. bdg. 41.03 *(978-0-7377-3433-1(7),* 66bb5b16-77b8-48fe-83f4-9c404136a65c) Greenhaven Publishing LLC. (Greenhaven Publishing).

Kanefield, Teri. Abraham Lincoln: The Making of America #3. 2018. (Making of America Ser.). (ENG., Illus.). 240p. (J). (gr. 5-9). 16.99 *(978-1-4197-3159-4(9),* 1198001, Abrams Bks. for Young Readers) Abrams, Inc.

—Andrew Jackson: The Making of America #2. 2019. (ENG., Illus.). 256p. (J). (gr. 5-9). pap. 7.99 *(978-1-4197-3421-2(0),* 1197903, Abrams Bks. for Young Readers) Abrams, Inc.

Kawa, Katie. The Most Powerful Presidential Words, 1 vol. 2019. (Words That Shaped America Ser.). (ENG.). 32p. (gr. 4-5). pap. 11.50 *(978-1-5382-4795-2(X),* a7a51070-e634-4726-b426-d350f2e5ccce) Stevens, Gareth Publishing LLLP.

Keegan, Anna. The United States Constitution & the Bill of Rights: The Law of the Land, 1 vol. 2015. (Spotlight on American History Ser.). (ENG., Illus.). 24p. (J). (gr. 4-6). pap. 11.00 *(978-1-4994-1773-9(X),* bc9d0df9-8a8d-4cbd-aa0f-50f01c90af2b, PowerKids Pr.) Rosen Publishing Group, Inc., The.

Keller, Susanna. Alexander Hamilton: America's First Treasury Secretary, 1 vol. 2017. (Britannica Beginner Bios Ser.). (ENG., Illus.). 32p. (J). (gr. 2-3). pap. 13.90 *(978-1-68048-808-1(2),* eab0f6a1-72cf-4eb2-a5eb-53313f8b7c28); lib. bdg. 26.06 *(978-1-68048-809-8(0),* 2896e138-b801-4476-9722-6e478e5423ba) Rosen Publishing Group, Inc., The. (Britannica Educational Publishing).

Kelly, Martin & Kelly, Melissa. Government. 2007. (ENG., Illus.). 96p. (C). (gr. 6-18). lib. bdg. 180.00 *(978-0-7656-8112-6(9),* Y182476) Routledge.

Kenison, Misti. Where's Your Hat, Abe Lincoln? 2017. (Young Historians Ser.: 0). (Illus.). 28p. (J). (gr. -1-k). bds. 9.99 *(978-1-4926-5250-2(4))* Sourcebooks, Inc.

Keppeler, Jill. What is a Point of View? Civic Virtues, 1 vol. 2018. (Civics for the Real World Ser.). (ENG.). 16p. (gr. 2-3). pap. *(978-1-5383-6499-4(9),* 945a9f8b-fb3c-4a38-8ad8-8890f6c4f3f1, Rosen Classroom) Rosen Publishing Group, Inc., The.

—You Can Fix a Community Problem: Taking Civic Action, 1 vol. 2018. (Civics for the Real World Ser.). (ENG.). 16p. (gr. 2-3). pap. *(978-1-5383-6581-6(2),* 213c9b44-2e06-401d-9b76-8e67d9572d07, Rosen Classroom) Rosen Publishing Group, Inc., The.

Kerrigan, Michael. Homeland Security. 2017. (Illus.). 80p. (J). *(978-1-4222-3767-0(2))* Mason Crest.

King, David C. Herbert Hoover, 1 vol. 2010. (Presidents & Their Times Ser.). (ENG.). 96p. (gr. 6-6). 36.93 *(978-0-7614-3626-3(X),* 615aec33-0c81-4349-9feb-512d0ea69ed3) Cavendish Square Publishing LLC.

King, Emiliya. What Are Rights? Understanding Citizenship, 1 vol. 2018. (Civics for the Real World Ser.). (ENG.). 8p. (gr. k-1). pap. *(978-1-5383-6376-8(3),* c710fb8f-015e-4900-a661-27498866e842, Rosen Classroom) Rosen Publishing Group, Inc., The.

King, Margaret. Just Right Words: Revising the Constitution (Level 5) 2017. (TIME for KIDS(r): Informational Text Ser.). (ENG., Illus.). 48p. (J). (gr. 4-8). pap. 13.99 *(978-1-4258-4992-4(X))* Teacher Created Materials, Inc.

Kishel, Ann-Marie. Government Services. 2007. (First Step Nonfiction - Government Ser.). (ENG., Illus.). 24p. (gr. k-2). lib. bdg. 23.93 *(978-0-8225-6397-6(5),* Lerner Pubns.) Lerner Publishing Group.

Kjelle, Marylou. The First Continental Congress. 2017. (Young America Ser.). (Illus.). 47p. (J). (gr. 3-6). 29.95 *(978-1-61228-977-9(0))* Mitchell Lane Pubs.

Klein, Adria F. Barack Obama. 2009. pap. 13.25 *(978-1-60559-055-4(X))* Hameray Publishing Group, Inc.

Klepeis, Alicia. Stamp Act Congress. 2017. (Young America Ser.). (gr. 3-6). 29.95 *(978-1-61228-991-5(6))* Mitchell Lane Pubs.

Knudsen, Shannon. When Were the First Slaves Set Free During the Civil War? And Other Questions about the Emancipation Proclamation. 2010. (Six Questions of American History Ser.). (ENG.). (gr. 4-6). pap. 56.72 *(978-0-7613-6948-6(1));* (Illus.). 48p. (J). pap. 11.99 *(978-0-7613-6121-3(9),* 439921d9-9f33-4651-8e71-fe9a4cd4c225); (Illus.). 48p. (J). lib. bdg. 30.65 *(978-1-58013-670-9(2),* 5021e694-5f71-402d-8d11-6438e13df8bb, Lerner Pubns.) Lerner Publishing Group.

Kovach, John. Bob Ehrlich: His Historical Campaign for Governor & How a Young Girl Made a Difference. 2003.

T
U
V

(Illus.). 52p. (J). pap. 9.95 *(978-0-7414-1497-7(X))* Infinity Publishing.

Kowalski, Kathiann M. A Balancing Act: A Look at Checks & Balances. 2003. (How Government Works). (ENG., Illus.). 56p. (gr. 4-8). lib. bdg. 25.26 *(978-0-8225-1350-6(1))* Lerner Publishing Group.

—Checks & Balances: A Look at the Powers of Government. 2012. (Searchlight Books How Does Government Work Ser.). (ENG., Illus.). 40p. (gr. 3-5). pap. 51.01 *(978-0-7613-9229-3(7))*; (J). pap. 9.99 *(978-0-7613-8558-5(4)*, fc6d5eed-78aa-45be-bcdb-e8d68973bfba) Lerner Publishing Group.

Krasner, Barbara. Exploring Checks & Balances. 2019. (Searchlight Books (tm) — Getting into Government Ser.). (ENG., Illus.). 32p. (J). (gr. 3-5). pap. 9.99 *(978-1-5415-7476-2(1)*, 0332dd75-5cc4-4189-96c6-7ce69be6e934, Lerner Pubns.) Lerner Publishing Group.

Krasner, Barbara, ed. The Two-Party System in the United States, 1 vol. 2018. (Current Controversies Ser.). (ENG.). 200p. (gr. 10-12). 48.03 *(978-1-5345-0389-2(7)*, 6d742bf6-bee8-46f7-a2db-d0437d161e62) Greenhaven Publishing LLC.

Krick, Robert K. The Civil War: Gettysburg & Other Eastern Battles, 1863-1865, 1 vol. 2010. (Civil War: Essential Histories Ser.). (ENG.). 96p. (YA). (gr. 10-10). lib. bdg. 38.47 *(978-1-4488-0388-0(8)*, 765b2e17-95e9-42c7-af02-68b565dec5a7) Rosen Publishing Group, Inc., The.

Kulling, Monica. Alexander Hamilton: from Orphan to Founding Father. Fabbretti, Valerio, illus. 2017. (Step into Reading Ser.). 48p. (J). (gr. k-3). pap. 4.99 *(978-1-5247-1698-1(7)*, Random Hse. Bks. for Young Readers) Random Hse. Children's Bks.

Laks Gorman, Jacqueline. Conoce tu Gobierno, 4 vols., Set. Incl. ¿Cuáles Son Tus Derechos Básicos? (What Are Your Basic Rights?) lib. bdg. 24.67 *(978-0-8368-8850-8(2)*, 666cfc3c-8d68-4741-a6a1-1533472e68fb); ¿Por Qué Son Importantes Las Elecciones? (Why Are Elections Important?) lib. bdg. 24.67 *(978-0-8368-8852-2(9)*, 0792bbeb-dee3-4351-8e5d-b366ac807a12); ¿Por Qué Tenemos Leyes? (Why Do We Have Laws?) lib. bdg. 24.67 *(978-0-8368-8853-9(7)*, 77e8cec0-47e5-44c2-98f2-4c89d8f0c76f); ¿Quiénes Gobiernan Nuestro País? (Who Leads Our Country?) lib. bdg. 24.67 *(978-0-8368-8851-5(0)*, d8616f2c-6b52-4373-93f8-e10b92427a89); (Illus.). (gr. 2-4)., Weekly Reader Leveled Readers (Conoce Tu Gobierno (Know Your Government) Ser.). (SPA.). 24p. 2008. Set lib. bdg. 49.34 *(978-0-8368-8849-2(9)*, 247b0367-e5e1-4bfd-a053-c114fcf28823, Weekly Reader) Stevens, Gareth Publishing LLLP.

—Conoce Tu Gobierno (Know Your Government), 4 vols., Set. Incl. Alcalde (Mayor) lib. bdg. 24.67 *(978-1-4339-0100-3(5)*, 0d6e6ddb-74c0-4c42-9269-74da6ef30617); Gobernador (Governor) (Illus.). lib. bdg. 24.67 *(978-1-4339-0098-3(X)*, feae38e3-bb9f-43fb-99c7-df131281a778); Juez (Judge) (Illus.). lib. bdg. 24.67 *(978-1-4339-0099-0(8)*, 81ff6d81-e8fc-431f-bc43-3c99f0e1d99e); Miembro Del Congreso (Member of Congress) lib. bdg. 24.67 *(978-1-4339-0101-0(3)*, 1d70021d-068b-4a0e-afde-55dfa720a3a0); Presidente (President) (Illus.). lib. bdg. 24.67 *(978-1-4339-0102-7(1)*, e1be5049-46ae-4e25-a5bd-ec2fbf9246d1); Vicepresidente (Vice President) lib. bdg. 24.67 *(978-1-4339-0103-4(X)*, 737220dd-c644-45dd-9a9d-a8c616b7e23d); (J). (gr. 3-3). (Conoce Tu Gobierno (Know Your Government) Ser.). (SPA.). 24p. 2009. Set lib. bdg. 49.34 *(978-1-4339-0104-1(8)*, 4223b248-4880-4ee4-b14a-e738608e94f6, Weekly Reader Leveled Readers) Stevens, Gareth Publishing LLLP.

—Gobernador (Governor), 1 vol. 2009. (Conoce Tu Gobierno (Know Your Government) Ser.). (SPA., Illus.). 24p. (J). (gr. 3-3). pap. 9.15 *(978-1-4339-0126-3(9)*, eec44052-bd3b-486f-a389-10510db5abe5); lib. bdg. 24.67 *(978-1-4339-0098-3(X)*, feae38e3-bb9f-43fb-99c7-df131281a778) Stevens, Gareth Publishing LLLP. (Weekly Reader Leveled Readers).

—Know Your Government, 4 vols., Set. Incl. What Are Your Basic Rights? lib. bdg. 24.67 *(978-0-8368-8840-9(5)*, 4ec054a6-7858-4576-8ce6-5ff6ddde96de); Who Leads Our Country? lib. bdg. 24.67 *(978-0-8368-8841-6(3)*, 232ad48e-f3c0-41de-bf43-9a723b1aa950); Why Are Elections Important? lib. bdg. 24.67 *(978-0-8368-8842-3(1)*, e9297f60-1610-4f1d-9b07-6839bcaf7ac3); (Illus.). (gr. 2-4)., Weekly Reader Leveled Readers (Know Your Government Ser.). (ENG.). 24p. 2008. Set lib. bdg. 49.34 *(978-0-8368-8839-3(1)*, 68947e1a-340b-4846-b4cf-b0d021301496, Weekly Reader) Stevens, Gareth Publishing LLLP.

—Member of Congress, 1 vol. 2009. (Know Your Government Ser.). (ENG.). 24p. (J). (gr. 3-3). pap. 9.15 *(978-1-4339-0122-5(6)*, a8f5d767-0414-4dd2-ae32-18152928b16e); lib. bdg. 24.67 *(978-1-4339-0094-5(7)*, 2ff26ad8-8cbd-4683-b732-3009679d7942) Stevens, Gareth Publishing LLLP. (Weekly Reader Leveled Readers).

—¿Quiénes Gobiernan Nuestro País? (Who Leads Our Country?), 1 vol. 2008. (Conoce Tu Gobierno (Know Your Government) Ser.). (SPA.). 24p. (gr. 2-4). pap. 9.15 *(978-0-8368-8856-0(1)*, b4060846-c7a1-4172-82df-81a71c4141ca); (Illus.). lib. bdg. 24.67 *(978-0-8368-8851-5(0)*, d8616f2c-6b52-4373-93f8-e10b92427a89) Stevens, Gareth Publishing LLLP. (Weekly Reader Leveled Readers).

—Who Leads Our Country?, 1 vol. 2008. (Know Your Government Ser.). (ENG.). 24p. (gr. 2-4). pap. 9.15 *(978-0-8368-8846-1(4)*, e85f725a-b64a-4121-b207-b9126d5bb638); (Illus.). lib. bdg. 24.67 *(978-0-8368-8841-6(3)*, 232ad48e-f3c0-41de-bf43-9a723b1aa950) Stevens, Gareth Publishing LLLP. (Weekly Reader Leveled Readers).

Landau, Elaine. The Declaration of Independence (a True Book: American History) 2008. (True Book (Relaunch) Ser.). (ENG., Illus.). 48p. (J). (gr. 3-5). pap. 6.95 *(978-0-531-14780-1(0)*, Children's Pr.) Scholastic Library Publishing.

—The Emancipation Proclamation: Would You Do What Lincoln Did?, 1 vol. 2008. (What Would You Do? Ser.). (ENG., Illus.). 48p. (J). (gr. 3-3). lib. bdg. 27.93 *(978-0-7660-2899-9(2)*, 39c1ee83-f4bc-4608-8499-383b6829d109, Enslow Elementary) Enslow Publishing, LLC.

—Lincoln's Emancipation Proclamation: Would You Sign the Great Document?, 1 vol. 2014. (What Would You Do? Ser.). (ENG.). 48p. (gr. 3-4). (J). 27.93 *(978-0-7660-6290-0(2)*, 37f0154d-481d-46d8-bc19-2898c06edb7a); pap. 11.53 *(978-0-7660-6291-7(0)*, a46b69f5-a3d3-442c-86d5-136b35468973, Enslow Elementary) Enslow Publishing, LLC.

—True Books: the Declaration of Independence. 2008. (True Book: American History, Revised Ser.). (ENG., Illus.). 48p. (J). (gr. 3-5). lib. bdg. 21.19 *(978-0-531-12630-1(7)*, Children's Pr.) Scholastic Library Publishing.

Landmarks of Democracy: American Institutions, 10 vols. 2017. (Landmarks of Democracy: American Institutions Ser.). 24p. (ENG.). (gr. 3-3). 126.35 *(978-1-5081-6109-7(7)*, 9c1f02de-f721-4045-8128-4f295dac1ce8); (gr. 7-8). pap. 41.25 *(978-1-5081-6110-3(0))* Rosen Publishing Group, Inc., The. (PowerKids Pr.).

Lanier, Wendy & Nelson, Robin. What Was the Missouri Compromise? And Other Questions about the Struggle over Slavery. 2012. (Start to Finish, Second Series: Nature's Cycles Ser.). (ENG.). 48p. (gr. k-3). pap. 39.62 *(978-0-7613-9293-4(9))* Lerner Publishing Group.

Lanier, Wendy Hinote. What Was the Missouri Compromise? And Other Questions about the Struggle over Slavery. 2012. (Six Questions of American History Ser.). (ENG., Illus.). 48p. (J). (gr. 4-6). pap. 11.99 *(978-0-7613-8565-3(7)*, 33f0adec-f615-4d33-a027-8dd0fb8b729f); lib. bdg. 30.65 *(978-0-7613-5331-7(3)*, a2fb97b4-b354-4c72-a24a-4306e916a70a, Lerner Pubns.) Lerner Publishing Group.

Lansford, Tom & Watson, Robert P. George W. Bush. 2004. (gr. 10-12). 22.45 *(978-0-7377-2598-8(2)*, Greenhaven Pr., Inc.) Cengage Gale.

Larson, Kirsten W. The CIA. 2016. (Protecting Our People Ser.). (ENG., Illus.). 32p. (J). (gr. 2-5). lib. bdg. 20.95 *(978-1-60753-982-7(9)*, 15773) Amicus.

Leavitt, Amie. Understanding Checks & Balances, 1 vol. 2017. (What's up with Your Government? Ser.). (ENG., Illus.). 32p. (J). (gr. 4-5). pap. 11.00 *(978-1-5383-2322-9(2)*, a23f39ff-091e-4ebd-a867-e5fb0b3a90d7, PowerKids Pr.) Rosen Publishing Group, Inc., The.

Leavitt, Amie Jane. The Declaration of Independence in Translation: What It Really Means. rev. ed. (Kids' Translations Ser.). (ENG., 32p. (J). (gr. 3-6). 2017. Illus.). lib. bdg. 27.99 *(978-1-5157-9137-9(8)*, 136571) 2016. pap. 8.10 *(978-1-5157-6250-8(5)*, 135065) Capstone. (Capstone Pr.).

—A History of the Republican Party. 2012. (J). lib. bdg. 29.95 *(978-1-61228-261-9(X))* Mitchell Lane Pubs.

Leavitt, Amie. Understanding Checks & Balances, 1 vol. 2017. (What's up with Your Government? Ser.). (ENG., Illus.). 32p. (J). (gr. 4-5). lib. bdg. 27.93 *(978-1-5081-6265-0(4)*, 3c2d0355-187f-4316-813f-7560350ae5d3, PowerKids Pr.) Rosen Publishing Group, Inc., The.

Leonard, Barry, ed. Symbols of the US Government: Ben's Activity Book. 2005. (Illus.). 46p. (J). (gr. k-4). pap. 15.00 *(978-0-7567-4540-0(3))* DIANE Publishing Co.

Let's Find Out! Government. 2015. (Let's Find Out! Government Ser.). (ENG.). 32p. (J). (gr. 2-3). pap., pap., pap. 619.20 *(978-1-68048-148-8(7)*, Britannica Educational Publishing) Rosen Publishing Group, Inc., The.

LeVert, Suzanne. The Constitution, 1 vol. 2003. (Kaleidoscope: Government Ser.). (ENG., Illus.). 48p. (gr. 4-4). 32.64 *(978-0-7614-1452-0(5)*, 96e641c8-3da3-42ca-9340-85363104716e) Cavendish Square Publishing LLC.

—State Government, 1 vol. 2005. (Kaleidoscope: Government Ser.). (ENG., Illus.). 48p. (gr. 4-4). lib. bdg. 32.64 *(978-0-7614-1596-1(3)*, 0f003ae2-7593-4bfb-b67c-d9cdf5c8a0ef) Cavendish Square Publishing LLC.

Levinson, Cynthia & Levinson, Sanford. Fault Lines in the Constitution: The Framers, Their Fights, & the Flaws That Affect Us Today, 1 vol. rev. ed. 2019. (Illus.). 272p. (J). (gr. 5-9). 22.95 *(978-1-68263-105-8(2))*; pap. 14.99 *(978-1-68263-106-5(0))* Peachtree Publishing Co. Inc.

Liljeblad, Fredrik. Democracy at Work. 2007. (21st Century Skills Library: Citizens & Their Governments Ser.). (ENG., Illus.). 32p. (gr. 4-8). lib. bdg. 32.07 *(978-1-60279-058-2(2)*, 200003) Cherry Lake Publishing.

Linde, Barbara M. Becoming a Supreme Court Justice, 1 vol. 2015. (Who's Your Candidate? Choosing Government Leaders Ser.). (ENG., Illus.). 32p. (J). (gr. 3-4). pap. 11.50 *(978-1-4824-4051-5(2)*, d4e3a4e2-a86d-4450-ab19-9a846a8ff364) Stevens, Gareth Publishing LLLP.

—Uncle Sam, 1 vol. 2018. (Symbols of America Ser.). (ENG.). 24p. (gr. 1-2). 24.27 *(978-1-5382-2902-6(1)*, b37a5e97-5115-4e2c-bfc0-b53b71b84e7a) Stevens, Gareth Publishing LLLP.

Lloyd, Jon. A View of America's Future by America's. 2005. 51p. pap. 16.95 *(978-1-4137-9110-5(7))* PublishAmerica, Inc.

Loria, Laura. What Is Citizenship?, 1 vol. 2015. (Let's Find Out! Government Ser.). (ENG., Illus.). 32p. (J). (gr. 2-3). 26.06 *(978-1-62275-976-7(1)*, 55c0173a-198a-4284-a710-086f3a9af4dc, Britannica Educational Publishing) Rosen Publishing Group, Inc., The.

Lowell, Barbara. Alexander Hamilton: American Hero. Ermos, George, illus. 2018. (Penguin Young Readers, Level 4 Ser.). 32p. (J). (gr. 1-3). pap. 4.99 *(978-1-5247-8773-8(6)*, Penguin Young Readers) Penguin Young Readers Group.

Lukes, Bonnie L. Woodrow Wilson & the Progressive Era. 2006. (World Leaders Ser.). (Illus.). 192p. (J). (gr. 6-10). lib. bdg. 26.95 *(978-1-931798-79-2(6))* Reynolds, Morgan Inc.

Lusted, Marcia Amidon. Revolution & the New Nation: 1750-Early 1800s. 2007. (Presidents of the United States Ser.). (Illus.). 48p. (J). (gr. 4-7). lib. bdg. 29.05 *(978-1-59036-739-1(1))*; per. 10.95 *(978-1-59036-740-7(5))* Weigl Pubs., Inc.

Lynch, Seth. The Emancipation Proclamation, 1 vol. 2018. (Look at U. S. History Ser.). (ENG.). 32p. (J). (gr. 2-2). 28.27 *(978-1-5382-2119-8(5)*, 6585d053-970a-4d85-9432-f4efcb166780) Stevens, Gareth Publishing LLLP.

Lynne, Douglas. Contemporary United States: 1968 to the Present. 2007. (Presidents of the United States Ser.). (Illus.). 48p. (J). (gr. 4-7). lib. bdg. 29.05 *(978-1-59036-753-7(7))*; per. 10.95 *(978-1-59036-754-4(5))* Weigl Pubs., Inc.

Machajewski, Sarah. Declaration of Independence, 1 vol. 2016. (Documents of American Democracy Ser.). (ENG., Illus.). 32p. (J). (gr. 5-5). pap. 11.00 *(978-1-4994-2077-7(3)*, ead7d548-1ad2-41e1-89bc-771d375c0dea, PowerKids Pr.) Rosen Publishing Group, Inc., The.

Maloof, Torrey. We the People: Founding Documents (America's Early Years) rev. ed. 2016. (Social Studies: Informational Text Ser.). (ENG., Illus.). 32p. (gr. 4-8). pap. 11.99 *(978-1-4938-3084-8(8))* Teacher Created Materials, Inc.

Manger, Katherine. The Declaration of Independence, 1 vol. 2016. (Let's Find Out! Primary Sources Ser.). (ENG., Illus.). 32p. (J). (gr. 2-3). lib. bdg. 26.06 *(978-1-5081-0395-0(X)*, 635e6a1d-75b7-47fd-bf76-74ea76aea88c) Rosen Publishing Group, Inc., The.

—The U.S. Constitution, 4 vols. 2016. (Let's Find Out! Primary Sources Ser.). (ENG., Illus.). 32p. (J). (gr. 2-3). 52.12 *(978-1-5081-0455-1(7)*, ea1f6d81-8ed7-4cf1-8fed-1613a2c0c212) Rosen Publishing Group, Inc., The.

Manning, Jack. Voting in Elections, 1 vol. 2014. (Our Government Ser.). (ENG.). 24p. (J). (gr. 1-3). lib. bdg. 27.99 *(978-1-4914-0334-1(9)*, 125847) Capstone.

Mapua, Jeff. Bill & Hillary Clinton, 1 vol. 2014. (Making a Difference: Leaders Who Are Changing the World Ser.). 48p. (YA). (gr. 5-5). (ENG.). 28.41 *(978-1-62275-425-0(5)*, e10cbf68-8220-4825-b884-6f256183833c); (ENG.). pap. 15.05 *(978-1-62275-427-4(1)*, 09ac0fd0-2ff9-48a5-ad53-c10d0c1c31c3); pap. 84.30 *(978-1-62275-428-1(X))* Rosen Publishing Group, Inc., The.

Mara, Wil. Democracy at Work. 2016. (21st Century Skills Library: a Citizen's Guide Ser.). (ENG., Illus.). 32p. (J). (gr. 4-7). 32.07 *(978-1-63471-065-7(7)*, 208339) Cherry Lake Publishing.

—FBI Special Agent. 2015. (21st Century Skills Library: Cool STEAM Careers Ser.). (ENG., Illus.). 32p. (J). (gr. 4-7). pap. 14.21 *(978-1-63362-648-5(2)*, 1391909) Cherry Lake Publishing.

—Gerald Ford, 1 vol. 2010. (Presidents & Their Times Ser.). (ENG.). 96p. (gr. 6-6). 36.93 *(978-0-7614-3629-4(4)*, 40f28fc5-cbd7-405e-8248-dcf8c10a7788) Cavendish Square Publishing LLC.

—Harry Truman, 1 vol. 2012. (Presidents & Their Times Ser.). (ENG., Illus.). 96p. (gr. 6-6). 36.93 *(978-1-60870-185-8(9)*, 1e388eab-e112-43b3-81e4-33d929da8328) Cavendish Square Publishing LLC.

—John F. Kennedy, 1 vol. 2010. (Presidents & Their Times Ser.). (ENG.). 96p. (gr. 6-6). 36.93 *(978-0-7614-3628-7(6)*, 467bf370-4420-4ea1-848f-38b72f6db0e4) Cavendish Square Publishing LLC.

—Writing the Declaration of Independence. 2017. (Foundations of Our Nation Ser.). (ENG., Illus.). 32p. (J). (gr. 3-5). pap. 9.95 *(978-1-63517-314-7(0)*, 1635173140); lib. bdg. 31.35 *(978-1-63517-249-2(7)*, 1635172497) North Star Editions. (Focus Readers).

Marcovitz, Hal. The Declaration of Independence. 2014. (Understanding American History). (ENG., Illus.). 96p. (J). lib. bdg. *(978-1-60152-736-3(5))* ReferencePoint Pr., Inc.

—The Declaration of Independence: Forming a New Nation. Moreno, Barry, ed. 2014. (Patriotic Symbols of America Ser.: 20). 48p. (J). (gr. 4-18). lib. bdg. 20.95 *(978-1-4222-3122-7(4))* Mason Crest.

—Independence Hall: Birthplace of Freedom. Moreno, Barry, ed. 2014. (Patriotic Symbols of America Ser.: 20). 48p. (J). (gr. 4-18). lib. bdg. 20.95 *(978-1-4222-3124-1(0))* Mason Crest.

Margulies, Philip. The Deparatment of Energy, 1 vol. 2005. (This Is Your Government Ser.). (ENG., Illus.). 64p. (J). (gr. 4-6). lib. bdg. 37.13 *(978-1-4042-0208-5(0)*, 7ac735be-136a-44e3-bdaa-16d0f5c6653c) Rosen Publishing Group, Inc., The.

Margulies, Phillip. The Department of Energy. 2009. (This Is Your Government Ser.). 64p. (gr. 5-6). 58.50 *(978-1-60854-368-7(4)*, Rosen Reference) Rosen Publishing Group, Inc., The.

Marrin, Albert. FDR & the American Crisis. (Illus.). 336p. (YA). (gr. 7). 2016. pap. 15.99 *(978-0-385-75362-3(4)*, Ember) 2015. 24.99 *(978-0-385-75359-3(4)*, Knopf Bks. for Young Readers) Random Hse. Children's Bks.

Marsh, Carole. Barack Obama - America's 44th President. 2009. (Here & Now Ser.). 40p. (J). (gr. 2-9). 29.99 *(978-0-635-06983-2(0))* Gallopade International.

—Georgia Government: the Cornerstone of Everyday Life in Our State! The Cornerstone of Everyday Life in Our State! 2004. 28p. pap. 5.95 *(978-0-635-02682-8(1))* Gallopade International.

—The Obama Family - Life in the White House: President Barack Obama, First Lady Michelle Obama, First Children Malia & Sasha. 2008. (Here & Now Ser.). 32p. (J). (gr. 2-9). pap. 8.99 *(978-0-635-07051-7(0))* Gallopade International.

Martin, Bill, Jr. & Sampson, Michael. I Pledge Allegiance. Raschka, Chris, illus. 2004. (ENG.). 40p. (J). (gr. 1-4). reprint ed. pap. 9.99 *(978-0-7636-2527-6(2))* Candlewick Pr.

Martin, David. The Colony of Pennsylvania, 1 vol. 2015. (Spotlight on the 13 Colonies: Birth of a Nation Ser.). (ENG., Illus.). 24p. (J). (gr. 4-6). pap. 11.00 *(978-1-4994-0572-9(3)*, 1e60ed25-5bf4-4685-afad-6d51911bd1a7, PowerKids Pr.) Rosen Publishing Group, Inc., The.

Martinez, Manuel. Why Do We Have Rules? Understanding Citizenship, 1 vol. 2018. (Civics for the Real World Ser.). (ENG.). 8p. (gr. k-1). pap. *(978-1-5383-6364-5(X)*, 0994b10b-181e-4866-b1f8-4faade4a8eb4, Rosen Classroom) Rosen Publishing Group, Inc., The.

Matzke, Ann H. What Are the Branches of Democracy? 2012. (Little World Social Studies). (ENG., Illus.). 24p. (gr. k-2). pap. 9.95 *(978-1-61810-279-9(6)*, 9781618102799) Rourke Educational Media.

McCallum, Rory. We Can Share: Civic Virtues, 1 vol. 2018. (Civics for the Real World Ser.). (ENG.). 8p. (gr. k-1). pap. *(978-1-5081-3934-8(2)*, 69bd99b5-b7bc-498a-ad61-66a87b66329c, Rosen Classroom) Rosen Publishing Group, Inc., The.

—What Are Your Rights & Responsibilities? Understanding Citizenship, 1 vol. 2018. (Civics for the Real World Ser.). (ENG.). 16p. (gr. 2-3). pap. *(978-1-5383-6541-0(3)*, afdf2b3e-ec29-4e52-a602-8d8c790621c8, Rosen Classroom) Rosen Publishing Group, Inc., The.

McDaniel, Melissa. The Declaration of Independence. 2011. (Cornerstones of Freedom, Third Ser.). (ENG., Illus.). 64p. (J). pap. 8.95 *(978-0-531-26555-0(2)*, Children's Pr.) Scholastic Library Publishing.

—The U. S. Congress: Why It Matters to You (a True Book: Why It Matters) (Library Edition) 2019. (True Book (Relaunch) Ser.). (ENG., Illus.). 48p. (J). (gr. 3-5). lib. bdg. 31.00 *(978-0-531-23182-1(8)*, Children's Pr.) Scholastic Library Publishing.

McDougal, Anna. We Work Better Together: Civic Virtues, 1 vol. 2018. (Civics for the Real World Ser.). (ENG.). 12p. (gr. 1-2). pap. *(978-1-5383-6409-3(3)*, a9c4da9b-962a-4d99-bf90-6830970bfb97, Rosen Classroom) Rosen Publishing Group, Inc., The.

McElroy, Lisa Tucker. Alberto Gonzalez. 2006. (J). pap. 8.95 *(978-0-8225-6058-6(5)*, First Avenue Editions) Lerner Publishing Group.

McGraw Hill. United States Government, Democracy in Action, Spanish Reading Essentials & Study Guide, Workbook. 2nd ed. 2005. (Government in the U. S. Ser.). (SPA., Illus.). 309p. (gr. 9-12). stu. ed., per., wbk. ed. 19.68 *(978-0-07-865920-1(5)*, 0078659205) McGraw-Hill Education.

—United States Government, Democracy in Action, StudentWorks CD-ROM. 2nd ed. 2005. (Government in the U. S. Ser.). (ENG.). (gr. 9-12). 149.68 *(978-0-07-865936-2(1)*, 0078659361) McGraw-Hill Education.

McGraw-Hill Education Staff. United States Government: Democracy in Action. 2nd ed. 2005. (Government in the U. S. Ser.). (ENG., Illus.). 320p. (gr. 9-12). per., wbk. ed., pupil's gde. ed. 9.56 *(978-0-07-865918-8(3)*, 0078659183) McGraw-Hill Higher Education.

—United States Government: Democracy in Action: Spanish Reading Essentials & Study Guide. 2007. (Government in the U. S. Ser.). (SPA., Illus.). 320p. (gr. 9-12). per. 12.28 *(978-0-07-878362-3(3)*, 0078783623) McGraw-Hill Higher Education.

McKee, Rosie. What Are My Duties? Understanding Citizenship, 1 vol. 2018. (Civics for the Real World Ser.). (ENG.). 8p. (gr. k-1). pap. *(978-1-5383-6370-6(4)*, baf0bc21-82c7-4655-9d45-a7c6e66cf340, Rosen Classroom) Rosen Publishing Group, Inc., The.

McLeese, Don. Alexander Hamilton. 2004. (Heroes of the American Revolution Ser.). (Illus.). 32p. (gr. 2-5). lib. bdg. *(978-1-59515-219-0(9))* Rourke Educational Media.

McNamara, Margaret. Eliza: the Story of Elizabeth Schuyler Hamilton: With an Afterword by Phillipa Soo, the Original Eliza from Hamilton: an American Musical. Shapiro, Esmé, illus. 2018. 48p. (J). (gr. -1-3). 17.99 *(978-1-5247-6588-0(0)*, Schwartz & Wade Bks.) Random Hse. Children's Bks.

McNeil, Niki, et al. HOCPP1032 American Government. 2004. spiral bd. 20.00 *(978-1-60308-032-3(5))* In the Hands of a Child.

McPherson, Stephanie Sammartino. Liberty or Death: A Story about Patrick Henry. Debon, Nicolas, illus. 2003. (Creative Minds Biographies Ser.). (ENG.). 64p. (gr. 4-8). 22.60 *(978-1-57505-178-9(8)*, Carolrhoda Bks.) Lerner Publishing Group.

Mcpherson, Stephanie Sammartino. Martha Washington: Legendary First Lady of the United States, 1 vol. 2014. (Legendary American Biographies Ser.). (ENG.). 96p. (gr. 6-6). 29.60 *(978-0-7660-6475-1(1)*, afd97b4a-9287-4fc5-a030-e63ea9ca3b05) Enslow Publishing, LLC.

Meersman, Erika. Majority Rule vs. Individual Rights, 1 vol. 2017. (Spotlight on Civic Action Ser.). (ENG.). 32p. (J). (gr. 4-5). pap. 12.75 *(978-1-5383-2792-0(9)*, 6ba18107-9fff-442f-89aa-828f1087f2d8); lib. bdg. 27.93 *(978-1-5081-6394-7(4)*, 033ff170-40ff-4239-b75c-8b40d5f043f2) Rosen Publishing Group, Inc., The. (PowerKids Pr.).

Melton, Buckner F. Aaron Burr: The Rise & Fall of an American Politician. 2009. (Library of American Lives & Times Ser.). 112p. (gr. 5-5). 69.20 *(978-1-60853-468-5(5))* Rosen Publishing Group, Inc., The.

Meltzer, Milton. Lincoln in His Own Words. Alcorn, Stephen, illus. 2018. (ENG.). 240p. (YA). (gr. 7). pap. 12.99 *(978-1-328-89574-5(2)*, 1699521, Clarion Bks.) HarperCollins Pubs.

Metz, Lorijo. La Declaracin de Independencia / the Declaration of Independence, 1 vol., 1. Beullens-Maoui, Nathalie, ed. 2014. (¡Celebremos la Libertad! / Let's Celebrate Freedom! Ser.). (SPA & ENG., Illus.). 24p. (J). (gr. 3-3). 26.27 *(978-1-4777-3246-5(2)*, 423f1183-3272-4a57-b597-711401b5f8eb, PowerKids Pr.) Rosen Publishing Group, Inc., The.

—The Declaration of Independence, 1 vol., 1. 2014. (Let's Celebrate Freedom! Ser.). (ENG.). 24p. (J). (gr. 3-3). 26.27 *(978-1-4777-2894-9(5)*, 9894c926-1070-4cf1-a679-be7f4e9231cd, PowerKids Pr.) Rosen Publishing Group, Inc., The.

Meyer, Jared. Working in a War Zone: Military Contractors. 2009. (Extreme Careers Ser.). 64p. (gr. 5-5). 58.50 *(978-1-61512-422-0(5)*, Rosen Reference) Rosen Publishing Group, Inc., The.

Miller, Amanda. What Does the President Do? 2009. (Scholastic News Nonfiction Readers Ser.). (Illus.). 24p. (J). (gr. 1-2). 22.00 *(978-0-531-21088-8(X))* Scholastic Library Publishing.

Miller, Derek. Money in Politics, 1 vol. 2019. (Dilemmas in Democracy Ser.). (ENG.). 80p. (gr. 7-7). lib. bdg. 37.36 *(978-1-5026-4493-0(2)*, 34caaa1a-ed6a-4396-a62a-f5fcb6ad6b39) Cavendish Square Publishing LLC.

—Vetoing Bills, 1 vol. 2018. (How Government Works). (ENG.). 64p. (J). (gr. 5-5). pap. 16.28

(978-1-5026-4158-8(5), 04d86b83-32b1-4d48-ac36-79e6be07a1fa) Cavendish Square Publishing LLC.

Miller, Mirella S. 12 Questions about the Declaration of Independence. 2017. (Examining Primary Sources Ser.). (ENG., Illus.). 32p. (J). (gr. 3-6). 32.80 (978-1-63235-283-5(4), 11752, 12-Story Library) Bookstaves, LLC.

Mis, Melody S. Meet Jesse Jackson, 1 vol. 2007. (Civil Rights Leaders Ser.). (ENG., Illus.). 24p. (YA). (gr. 2-3). lib. bdg. 26.27 (978-1-4042-4212-8(0), 7f13a688-1352-4455-9287-50c573805ee0) Rosen Publishing Group, Inc., The.

Modifica, Lisa. A Timeline of Congress, 1 vol. 2004. (Timelines of American History Ser.). (ENG., Illus.). 32p. (gr. 4-4). lib. bdg. 29.13 (978-0-8239-4534-4(0), 4740c1bb-7f39-4535-9926-368abf823701, Rosen Reference) Rosen Publishing Group, Inc., The.

Moore Niver, Heather. 20 Fun Facts about the Declaration of Independence, 1 vol. 2013. (Fun Fact File: U. S. History! Ser.). (ENG.). 32p. (J). (gr. 2-3). 27.93 (978-1-4339-9183-7(7), d92c53c0-6e7e-4634-818d-a159d82b7e0d); pap. 11.50 (978-1-4339-9184-4(5), 7916e053-821d-4c95-9c38-b3b46b24f905) Stevens, Gareth Publishing LLLP.

Morey, Allan. A Timeline History of the Declaration of Independence. 2014. (Timeline Trackers: America's Beginnings Ser.). (ENG., Illus.). 48p. (J). (gr. 5-8). lib. bdg. 30.65 (978-1-4677-3640-4(6), c8655b74-edb1-4c15-9eff-1e713837deab, Lerner Pubns.) Lerner Publishing Group.

Morlock, Rachael. The Real Story Behind the Founding Fathers, 1 vol. 2019. (Real Story: Debunking History Ser.). (ENG.). 32p. (J). (gr. 4-5). 27.93 (978-1-5383-4343-2(6), 6ec448ac-7bf0-4f25-b8fc-f0f924a2bf4a, PowerKids Pr.) Rosen Publishing Group, Inc., The.

Morris-Lipsman, Arlene. Presidential Races: The Battle for Power in the United States. 2007. (People's History Ser.). (ENG., Illus.). 112p. (gr. 5-12). lib. bdg. 33.26 (978-0-8225-6783-7(0)) Lerner Publishing Group.

Mortensen, Lori. The Declaration of Independence, 1 vol. Skeens, Matthew, illus. 2009. (American Symbols Ser.). (ENG.). 24p. (J). (gr. 1-3). lib. bdg. 27.32 (978-1-4048-5165-8(8), 95494, Picture Window Bks.) Capstone.

Mountjoy, Shane. Causes of the Civil War: The Differences Between the North & South. 2009. (Civil War: a Nation Divided Ser.). (ENG., Illus.). 144p. (gr. 6-12). 35.00 (978-1-60413-036-2(9), P165050, Facts On File) Infobase Holdings, Inc.

Moxon, Kay & Magee, Eric. A2 US Government & Politics: Representation in the USA. 2009. (ENG.). 64p. pap., wbk. ed. 15.95 (978-0-340-99002-5(3)) Hodder Education Group GBR. Dist: Trans-Atlantic Pubns., Inc.

Mulhall, Jill K. James Madison, 1 vol. rev. ed. 2005. (Social Studies: Informational Text Ser.). (ENG.). 24p. (gr. 4-8). pap. 10.99 (978-0-7439-8908-4(2)) Teacher Created Materials, Inc.

—Thomas Jefferson, 1 vol. rev. ed. 2004. (Social Studies: Informational Text Ser.). (ENG.). 24p. (gr. 4-8). pap. 10.99 (978-0-7439-8747-9(0)) Teacher Created Materials, Inc.

Murcia, Rebecca Thatcher. The Legislative Branch. 2011. (My Guide to the Constitution Ser.). 48p. (J). (gr. 3-6). pap. 16.50 (978-1-61228-184-1(2)); (Illus.). lib. bdg. 29.95 (978-1-58415-942-1(1)) Mitchell Lane Pubs.

Murray, Glen L. The Dumbing down of Americ. 2009. 68p. pap. 15.99 (978-1-4415-1642-8(5)) Xlibris Corp.

Murray, Julie. Mayor. 2017. (My Government Ser.). (ENG., Illus.). 24p. (J). (gr. -1-2). lib. bdg. 31.36 (978-1-5321-0398-8(0), 26524, Abdo Kids) ABDO Publishing Co.

—US Constitution. 2019. (US Symbols (AK) Ser.). (ENG., Illus.). 24p. (J). (gr. -1-2). lib. bdg. 31.36 (978-1-5321-8539-7(1), 31416, Abdo Kids) ABDO Publishing Co.

Murray, Laura K. The Declaration of Independence. 2019. (Shaping the United States of America Ser.). (ENG., Illus.). 24p. (J). (gr. 1-3). pap. 7.95 (978-1-9771-1011-4(8), 140954); lib. bdg. 25.99 (978-1-9771-0842-5(3), 140461) Capstone. (Pebble).

—The U. S. Constitution. 2019. (Shaping the United States of America Ser.). (ENG., Illus.). 24p. (J). (gr. 1-3). pap. 7.95 (978-1-9771-1010-7(X), 140953); lib. bdg. 25.99 (978-1-9771-0841-8(5), 140460) Capstone. (Pebble).

Musser, Susan, ed. America's Global Influence. 2007. (Opposing Viewpoints Ser.). (ENG., Illus.). 223p. (J). (gr. 10-12). 27.50 (978-0-7377-3424-9(8)); (YA). (gr. 8-12). pap. 39.70 (978-0-7377-3423-2(X)) Cengage Gale. (Greenhaven Pr., Inc.).

Nagelhout, Ryan. Emancipation Proclamation, 1 vol. 2016. (Documents of American Democracy Ser.). (ENG., Illus.). 32p. (J). (gr. 5-5). pap. 11.00 (978-1-4994-2061-4(1), 515d919a-4b81-4a74-9fc0-c271ac727e37, PowerKids Pr.) Rosen Publishing Group, Inc., The.

—Thomas Paine's Common Sense, 1 vol. 2013. (Documents That Shaped America Ser.). (ENG.). 32p. (J). (gr. 4-5). 29.27 (978-1-4339-9013-7(X), 6422b8d2-5c0a-49a8-abeb-412a02746314); pap. 11.50 (978-1-4339-9014-4(8), cbade4d6-c6c0-4be1-8220-bf76bf726e50) Stevens, Gareth Publishing LLLP.

Nardo, Don. The Declaration of Independence. 2003. (World History Ser.). (ENG., Illus.). 112p. (J). 34.95 (978-1-59018-293-2(6), Lucent Bks.) Cengage Gale.

—The Declaration of Independence. 2006. (Illus.). 48p. (J). (gr. 4-8). reprint ed. 17.80 (978-1-4223-5323-3(0)) DIANE Publishing Co.

National Geographic Learning. Language, Literacy & Vocabulary - Reading Expeditions (U. S. History & Life): Government in Action. 2006. (ENG., Illus.). 36p. (J). pap. 20.95 (978-0-7922-5447-8(3)) CENGAGE Learning.

—Reading Expeditions (Social Studies: Documents of Freedom): the Declaration of Independence. 2007. (ENG., Illus.). 32p. (J). pap. 18.95 (978-0-7922-4554-4(7)) CENGAGE Learning.

—Reading Expeditions (Social Studies: People Who Changed America): the Progressives. 2006. (Nonfiction Reading & Writing Workshops Ser.). (ENG., Illus.). 40p. (J). pap. 21.95 (978-0-7922-8624-0(3)) CENGAGE Learning.

—Reading Expeditions (Social Studies: Voices from America's Past): the Spirit of a New Nation. 2007. (Avenues Ser.). (ENG., Illus.). 40p. (J). pap. 21.95 (978-0-7922-8684-4(7)) CENGAGE Learning.

Nelson, Maria. Becoming a House Representative, 1 vol. 2015. (Who's Your Candidate? Choosing Government Leaders Ser.). (ENG., Illus.). 32p. (J). (gr. 3-4). pap. 11.50 (978-1-4824-4035-5(0), 1ddbf9ea-45e1-4e16-897c-b7f50c2c6eb6) Stevens, Gareth Publishing LLLP.

—Becoming a Senator, 1 vol. 2015. (Who's Your Candidate? Choosing Government Leaders Ser.). (ENG., Illus.). 32p. (J). (gr. 3-4). pap. 11.50 (978-1-4824-4043-0(1), 5e429fa5-efe3-4d4a-b6a5-0fd6f14b972f) Stevens, Gareth Publishing LLLP.

Nelson, Sheila. The Original United States of America. 2006. (How America Became America Ser.). (Illus.). 96p. (YA). lib. bdg. 22.95 (978-1-59084-903-3(5)) Mason Crest.

Niver, Heather Moore. Articles of Confederation, 1 vol. 2016. (Documents of American Democracy Ser.). (ENG., Illus.). 32p. (J). (gr. 5-5). pap. 11.00 (978-1-4994-2069-2(2), 12884a58-d3dc-411d-add9-4f9e0cf4e1ec, PowerKids Pr.) Rosen Publishing Group, Inc., The.

—20 Fun Facts about the Declaration of Independence. 2013. (Fun Fact File: US History! Ser.). 32p. (J). (gr. 3-6). pap. 63.00 (978-1-4339-9185-1(3)) Stevens, Gareth Publishing LLLP.

Oachs, Emily Rose. Thomas Jefferson's Presidency. 2016. (Presidential Powerhouses Ser.). (ENG., Illus.). 104p. (YA). (gr. 6-12). 35.99 (978-1-4677-7923-4(7), f04c63b9-b37c-4da8-81b6-da668eacfffa); E-Book 54.65 (978-1-4677-8602-7(0)) Lerner Publishing Group. (Lerner Pubns.).

Obama, Barack. Our Enduring Spirit: President Barack Obama's First Words to America. Ruth, Greg, illus. 2009. 48p. (J). lib. bdg. 18.89 (978-0-06-183456-1(4)) HarperCollins Pubs.

Obama, Barack & Nelson, Kadir. Change Has Come: An Artist Celebrates Our American Spirit. Nelson, Kadir, illus. 2009. (ENG., Illus.). 64p. (J). (gr. 1). 12.99 (978-1-4169-8955-4(2), Simon & Schuster Bks. For Young Readers) Simon & Schuster Bks. For Young Readers.

O'Neill, Robert John & Gallagher, Gary W. The Civil War: Bull Run & Other Eastern Battles, 1861-May 1863, 1 vol. 2010. (Civil War: Essential Histories Ser.). (ENG.). 96p. (YA). (gr. 10-10). lib. bdg. 38.47 (978-1-4488-0387-3(X), 79b08efd-49fb-4aa5-9c67-3924169a04bb) Rosen Publishing Group, Inc., The.

Orr, Tamra. The Story of the Constitution. 2011. (My Guide to the Constitution Ser.). 48p. (J). (gr. 3-6). pap. 16.50 (978-1-61228-188-9(5)); (Illus.). lib. bdg. 29.95 (978-1-58415-946-9(4)) Mitchell Lane Pubs.

—Tenth Amendment: Limiting Federal Powers, 1 vol. 2011. (Amendments to the United States Constitution: the Bill of Rights Ser.). (ENG., Illus.). 64p. (YA). (gr. 6-6). pap. 13.95 (978-1-4488-2311-6(0), 8d6c2149-3bcb-4b33-a0ef-ce349342af2f) Rosen Publishing Group, Inc., The.

—The Tenth Amendment: Limiting Federal Powers, 1 vol. 2011. (Amendments to the United States Constitution: the Bill of Rights Ser.). (ENG., Illus.). 64p. (YA). (gr. 6-6). lib. bdg. 37.13 (978-1-4488-1265-3(8), 8a39852c-761a-4c0c-bbef-d25b71429744) Rosen Publishing Group, Inc., The.

Orr, Tamra B. Government at Work. 2007. (21st Century Skills Library: Citizens & Their Governments Ser.). (ENG., Illus.). 32p. (gr. 4-8). lib. bdg. 32.07 (978-1-60279-059-9(0), 200005) Cherry Lake Publishing.

Osornio, Catherine L. The Declaration of Independence from A to Z, 1 vol. Johnson, Layne, illus. 2010. (ABC Ser.). (ENG.). 32p. (J). (gr. 1-7). 16.99 (978-1-58980-676-4(X), Pelican Publishing) Arcadia Publishing.

Otfinoski, Steven. Patriots & Redcoats: Stories of American Revolutionary War Leaders. 2015. (Revolutionary War Ser.). (ENG., Illus.). 48p. (J). (gr. 3-6). pap. 8.95 (978-1-4914-2158-1(4), 127709, Capstone Pr.) Capstone.

—A Step into History: the Cold War (Library Edition) 2018. (Step into History Ser.). (ENG., Illus.). 144p. (J). lib. bdg. 36.00 (978-0-531-22691-9(3), Children's Pr.) Scholastic Library Publishing.

Panchyk, Richard. Franklin Delano Roosevelt for Kids: His Life & Times with 21 Activities. 2007. (For Kids Ser.: 24). (ENG., Illus.). 160p. (J). (gr. 4-8). pap. 14.95 (978-1-55652-657-2(1)) Chicago Review Pr., Inc.

Paris, Stephanie. Forming a New Government (America's Early Years) rev. ed. 2016. (Social Studies: Informational Text Ser.). (ENG., Illus.). 32p. (gr. 4-8). pap. 11.99 (978-1-4938-3083-1(X)) Teacher Created Materials, Inc.

Parker, Christi E. Abraham Lincoln, 1 vol. rev. ed. 2005. (Social Studies: Informational Text Ser.). (ENG.). 24p. (gr. 4-8). pap. 10.99 (978-0-7439-8916-9(3)) Teacher Created Materials, Inc.

—George Washington, 1 vol. rev. ed. 2004. (Social Studies: Informational Text Ser.). (ENG.). 24p. (gr. 4-8). pap. 10.99 (978-0-7439-8749-3(7)) Teacher Created Materials, Inc.

Paul, Michael. Pan Am 103 & State-Sponsored Terrorism, 1 vol. 2005. (Terrorism in Today's World Ser.). (ENG., Illus.). 48p. (gr. 5-8). pap. 15.05 (978-0-8368-6566-0(9), dbf6dc52-c493-4616-9877-ccf92dae8487); lib. bdg. 33.67 (978-0-8368-6559-2(6), 24dd1667-ab69-4cf6-8d84-688dc94847d3) Stevens, Gareth Publishing LLLP. (Gareth Stevens Secondary Library).

Payan, Gregory. The Federalists & Anti-Federalists: How & Why Political Parties Were Formed in Young America. 2009. (Life in the New American Nation Ser.). 32p. (gr. 4-4). 47.90 (978-1-61514-283-5(5)) Rosen Publishing Group, Inc., The.

Peppas, Lynn. The Battle of the Alamo. 2017. (Uncovering the Past: Analyzing Primary Sources Ser.). (Illus.). 48p. (J). (gr. 5-6). (978-0-7787-3940-1(6)) Crabtree Publishing Co.

Perl, Erica S. Truth or Lie: Presidents! Slack, Michael, illus. 2019. (Step into Reading Ser.). (ENG.). 48p. (J). (gr. k-3). pap. 4.99 (978-1-9848-9391-8(2), Random Hse. Bks. for Young Readers) Random Hse. Children's Bks.

Perrin, Pat. Getting Started-America's Melting Pot. 2004. (Illus.). (J). (978-1-932663-04-4(5)) History Compass, LLC.

—Getting Started-Our 50 United States. 2004. (Illus.). (J). (978-1-932663-03-7(7)) History Compass, LLC.

—Getting Started-Our Government. 2004. (Illus.). (J). (978-1-932663-02-0(9)) History Compass, LLC.

Perritano, John. Radical Republicans: The Struggle for Equality. 2008. (Graphic America Ser.). (ENG., Illus.). 32p. (J). (gr. 3-6). lib. bdg. (978-0-7787-4187-9(7)) Crabtree Publishing Co.

Petechuk, David. PACs, Super PACs, & Fundraising. 2016. (Illus.). 64p. (J). (978-1-61900-093-3(8)) Eldorado Ink.

Petersen, Christine. How the Legislative Branch Works, 1 vol. 2015. (How the US Government Works). (ENG.). 48p. (J). (gr. 4-8). lib. bdg. 35.64 (978-1-62403-637-8(6), 17049) ABDO Publishing Co.

Pettiford, Rebecca. El Capitolio. 2016. (Los Primeros Viajes Escolares (First Field Trips)).Tr. of State Capitol. (SPA.). 24p. (J). (gr. k-2). lib. bdg. 25.65 (978-1-62031-328-2(6), Bullfrog Bks.) Jump! Inc.

—State Capitol. Fretland VanVoorst, Jenny, ed. 2016. (First Field Trips). (Illus.). 24p. (J). (gr. k-2). lib. bdg. 25.65 (978-1-62031-297-1(2), Bullfrog Bks.) Jump! Inc.

Piddock, Charles. The Cold War. 2016. (Illus.). 48p. (J). (978-1-5105-1282-5(9)) SmartBook Media, Inc.

Pingry, Patricia A. The Story of Ronald Reagan. Mahan, Ben, illus. 2006. (ENG.). 26p. (J). (gr. -1-k). bds. 7.69 (978-0-8249-6621-8(X), Ideals Pubns.) Worthy Publishing.

Political Profiles Set, vols. 13, vol. 13. Incl. Al Gore. Sapet, Kerrily. (Illus.). 112p. (YA). 2007. lib. bdg. 27.95 (978-1-59935-070-7(X)); Arnold Schwarzenegger. Young, Jeff C. (Illus.). 112p. (YA). 2007. 27.95 (978-1-59935-050-9(5)); Barack Obama. (Illus.). 128p. (YA). 2007. lib. bdg. 27.95 (978-1-59935-045-5(9)); Hillary Clinton. Wells, Catherine. (Illus.). 112p. (YA). 2007. lib. bdg. 27.95 (978-1-59935-047-9(5)); Joe Biden. Young, Jeff C. (Illus.). 100p. (J). 2009. 28.95 (978-1-59935-131-5(5)); John Lewis. Sapet, Kerrily. 100p. (YA). 2009. 28.95 (978-1-59935-130-8(7)); John McCain. Wells, Catherine. (Illus.). 112p. (YA). 2008. lib. bdg. 27.95 (978-1-59935-046-2(7)); Michelle Obama. 112p. (YA). 2009. lib. bdg. 28.95 (978-1-59935-090-5(4)); Nancy Pelosi. Shichtman, Sandra H. (Illus.). 112p. (YA). 2008. lib. bdg. 27.95 (978-1-59935-049-3(1)); Rudy Giuliani. Sharp, Anna Layton. (Illus.). 128p. (YA). 2008. lib. bdg. 27.95 (978-1-59935-048-6(3)); Ted Kennedy. 144p. (YA). 2009. 28.95 (978-1-59935-089-9(0)); (gr. 5-9). 2007. Set lib. bdg. 376.35 (978-1-59935-072-1(6)) Reynolds, Morgan Inc.

Pollack, Pam, et al. Who Was Alexander Hamilton? Putra, Dede, illus. 2017. (Who Was? Ser.). 112p. (J). (gr. 3-7). 5.99 (978-0-399-54427-9(5), Penguin Workshop) Penguin Young Readers Group.

Porterfield, Jason. How Lyndon B. Johnson Fought the Vietnam War, 1 vol. 2017. (Presidents at War Ser.). (ENG.). 128p. (gr. 8-8). lib. bdg. 38.93 (978-0-7660-8531-2(7), d7431810-368e-46b2-bba1-293a64dd0532) Enslow Publishing, LLC.

—Problems & Progress in American Politics: The Growth of the Democratic Party in the Late 1800s. 2009. (America's Industrial Society in the 19th Century Ser.). 32p. (gr. 4-4). 47.90 (978-1-61511-339-2(8)) Rosen Publishing Group, Inc., The.

Prentzas, G. S. The Emancipation Proclamation. 2011. (Cornerstones of Freedom, Third Ser.). (Illus.). 64p. (J). (ENG.). pap. 8.95 (978-0-531-26557-4(9)); lib. bdg. 30.00 (978-0-531-25032-7(6)) Scholastic Library Publishing. (Children's Pr.).

Price, Sean. U. S. Presidents: Truth & Rumors. Doty, Eldon, illus. 2010. (Truth & Rumors Ser.). (ENG.). 32p. (J). (gr. 3-9). lib. bdg. 30.65 (978-1-4296-3952-1(0), 102562, Capstone Pr.) Capstone.

Primary Sources of American Political Documents, 12 vols. 2015. (Primary Sources of American Political Documents Ser.). (ENG.). 112p. (J). (gr. 7-7). lib. bdg. 233.58 (978-0-7660-6686-1(X), 3f7328c2-f510-4c18-8dbc-793f6de76d47) Enslow Publishing, LLC.

Progressivism. 2010. (ENG., Illus.). 128p. (gr. 6-12). 45.00 (978-1-60413-223-6(X), P179250, Facts On File) Infobase Holdings, Inc.

Quinby, Michelle. Connecting the 21st Century to the Past: What Makes America America, 2000-The Present. 2013. (Illus.). 48p. (J). pap. (978-1-4222-2423-6(6)) Mason Crest.

—Connecting the 21st Century to the Past: What Makes America America, 2000-The Present. Rakove, Jack N., ed. 2012. (How America Became America Ser.). (Illus.). 48p. (J). (gr. 3-4). 19.95 (978-1-4222-2409-0(0)) Mason Crest.

Raatma, Lucia. Barbara Jordan, 1 vol. 2013. (Leading Women Ser.). (ENG.). 96p. (YA). (gr. 7-7). 42.64 (978-0-7614-4956-0(6), bbcd5f27-0fcc-47f5-88e7-57e8052fa895) Cavendish Square Publishing LLC.

Rajczak, Michael. Becoming President, 1 vol. 2015. (Who's Your Candidate? Choosing Government Leaders Ser.). (ENG., Illus.). 32p. (J). (gr. 3-4). pap. 11.50 (978-1-4824-4039-3(3), bcb12e6d-e565-4fa1-9a06-5f2e58218a21) Stevens, Gareth Publishing LLLP.

Randolph, Joanne. The Iroquois League. 2009. (Reading Room Collection 2 Ser.). 24p. (gr. 3-4). 42.50 (978-1-60851-995-8(3), PowerKids Pr.) Rosen Publishing Group, Inc., The.

Ransom, Candice. George Washington & the Story of the U. S. Constitution. Reeves, Jeni, illus. 2011. (History Speaks: Picture Books Plus Reader's Theater Ser.). 48p. pap. 56.72 (978-0-7613-7632-3(1)); (ENG.). (gr. 2-4). 27.93 (978-0-7613-5877-0(3), Millbrook Pr.); (ENG.). (gr. 2-4). pap. 9.95 (978-0-7613-7116-8(8)) Lerner Publishing Group.

—What Was the Continental Congress? And Other Questions about the Declaration of Independence. 2011. (Six Questions of American History Ser.). (ENG.). 48p. (gr. 4-6). pap. 56.72 (978-0-7613-7642-2(9)); (Illus.). (J). pap. 11.99 (978-0-7613-7135-9(4), d59ab588-4cbc-4420-8266-4b49034cb9a8) Lerner Publishing Group.

—Who Wrote the U. S. Constitution? And Other Questions about the Constitutional Convention of 1787. 2010. (Six Questions of American History Ser.). (ENG.). (gr. 4-6). pap. 56.72 (978-0-7613-6949-3(X)) Lerner Publishing Group.

Rauf, Don. How George W. Bush Fought the Wars in Iraq & Afghanistan, 1 vol. 2017. (Presidents at War Ser.). (ENG.). 128p. (gr. 8-8). lib. bdg. 38.93 (978-0-7660-8533-6(3), 40b4d225-2e43-482d-85bb-1eca9904a760) Enslow Publishing, LLC.

—Washington's Farewell Address, 1 vol. 2016. (Let's Find Out! Primary Sources Ser.). (ENG., Illus.). 32p. (J). (gr. 2-3). lib. bdg. 26.06 (978-1-5081-0407-0(7), 8aea0638-2193-4c99-bb41-0151eb8a6b8a) Rosen Publishing Group, Inc., The.

Raum, Elizabeth. The Declaration of Independence, 1 vol. 2012. (Documenting U. S. History Ser.). (ENG.). 48p. (gr. 3-6). pap. 9.95 (978-1-4329-6762-8(2), 119392, Heinemann) Capstone.

Reader, Jack. Separation of Powers: The Importance of Checks & Balances, 1 vol. 2017. (Spotlight on Civic Action Ser.). (ENG.). 32p. (J). (gr. 4-5). 27.93 (978-1-5081-6399-2(5), 71bfebb3-7d64-467c-bc8c-6ec149772377, PowerKids Pr.) Rosen Publishing Group, Inc., The.

Remy, Richard C. United States Government: Democracy in Action. 2007. (Illus.). 898p. (J). 94.64 (978-0-07-874762-5(7), 9780078747625) Glencoe/McGraw-Hill.

Rice, Earle, Jr. How Franklin D. Roosevelt Fought World War II, 1 vol. 2017. (Presidents at War Ser.). (ENG.). 128p. (gr. 8-8). lib. bdg. 38.93 (978-0-7660-8527-5(9), 90068e3a-c02b-490c-960b-c2d1bf00735c) Enslow Publishing, LLC.

Rice, Earle. FDR & the New Deal. 2009. (Monumental Milestones Ser.). (Illus.). 48p. (J). (gr. 4-7). lib. bdg. 29.95 (978-1-58415-828-8(X)) Mitchell Lane Pubs.

Rice, Liz. Bill Richardson. (Sharing the American Dream Ser.). (Illus.). 64p. (J). (gr. 7-12). 2009. 22.95 (978-1-4222-0589-1(4)) 2007. pap. 9.95 (978-1-4222-0761-1(7)) Mason Crest.

Rissman, Rebecca. Declaration of Independence, 1 vol. 2013. (Foundations of Our Nation Ser.). (ENG.). 48p. (J). (gr. 4-8). lib. bdg. 35.64 (978-1-61783-708-1(3), 7814); (Illus.). pap. 18.50 (978-1-61783-758-6(X), 8749) ABDO Publishing Co.

RJF Publishing Staff & Staton, Hilarie. Independence Hall. 2009. (Symbols of American Freedom Ser.). 48p. (gr. 4-6). 30.00 (978-1-60413-521-3(2), Chelsea Clubhse.) Infobase Holdings, Inc.

Roberts, Russell. A History of the Democratic Party. 2012. 48p. (J). (gr. 3-6). lib. bdg. 29.95 (978-1-61228-259-6(8)) Mitchell Lane Pubs.

Robinson, Tom. The Development of the Industrial United States: 1870-1900. 2007. (Presidents of the United States Ser.). (Illus.). 48p. (J). (gr. 4-7). lib. bdg. 29.05 (978-1-59036-745-2(6)) Weigl Pubs., Inc.

—Development of the Industrial United States: 1870-1900. 2007. (Presidents of the United States Ser.). (Illus.). 48p. (J). (gr. 4-7). per. 10.95 (978-1-59036-746-9(4)) Weigl Pubs., Inc.

Romero, Libby. National Geographic Kids Readers: Alexander Hamilton (L3) 2018. (Readers Ser.). (Illus.). 48p. (J). (gr. 3-7). pap. 4.99 (978-1-4263-3038-4(3)); (ENG.). lib. bdg. 14.90 (978-1-4263-3039-1(1)) Disney Publishing Worldwide. (National Geographic Kids).

Roome, Hugh. Franklin D. Roosevelt: American Hero (Rookie Biographies) 2017. (Rookie Biographies Ser.). (ENG., Illus.). 32p. (J). (gr. 1-2). pap. 5.95 (978-0-531-23863-9(6), Children's Pr.) Scholastic Library Publishing.

—Franklin D. Roosevelt: American Hero (Rookie Biographies) (Library Edition) 2017. (Rookie Biographies Ser.). (ENG., Illus.). 32p. (J). (gr. 1-2). lib. bdg. 25.00 (978-0-531-23229-3(8), Children's Pr.) Scholastic Library Publishing.

Roosevelt, Eleanor. & Markel, Michelle. When You Grow up to Vote: How Our Government Works for You. Lin, Grace, illus. 2018. (ENG.). 96p. (J). 19.99 (978-1-62672-879-0(8), 900176491) Roaring Brook Pr.

Rosaler, Maxine. A Timeline of the First Continental Congress. (Timelines of American History Ser.). 32p. (gr. 4-4). 2009. 47.90 (978-1-60854-384-7(6)) 2004. (ENG., Illus.). lib. bdg. 29.13 (978-0-8239-4545-0(6), a97b185d-7667-4b69-9358-e4319be7a2c9) Rosen Publishing Group, Inc., The. (Rosen Reference).

Rowell, Rebecca. John F. Kennedy's Presidency. 2016. (Presidential Powerhouses Ser.). (ENG., Illus.). 104p. (YA). (gr. 6-12). E-Book 54.65 (978-1-4677-8600-3(4), Lerner Pubns.) Lerner Publishing Group.

Roxburgh, Ellis. Thomas Jefferson vs. John Adams: Founding Fathers & Political Rivals, 1 vol. 2015. (History's Greatest Rivals Ser.). (ENG., Illus.). 48p. (J). (gr. 6-8). pap. 15.05 (978-1-4824-4239-7(6), 349f4b41-e98f-45d4-8ece-ef7a1fda66f9) Stevens, Gareth Publishing LLLP.

Roza, Greg. Evaluating the Articles of Confederation: Determining the Validity of Information & Arguments. 2009. (Critical Thinking in American History Ser.). 48p. (gr. 5-8). 53.00 (978-1-61512-092-5(0), Rosen Reference) Rosen Publishing Group, Inc., The.

Rubin, Susan Goldman. Give Us the Vote! Over Two Hundred Years of Fighting for the Ballot. 2020. (ENG., Illus.). 128p. (J). (gr. 5). 19.99 (978-0-8234-3957-7(7)) Holiday Hse., Inc.

Ruffin, David C. The Duties & Responsibilities of the Secretary of Defense. 2009. (Your Government in Action Ser.). 32p. (gr. 3-3). 43.90 (978-1-60854-915-3(1), PowerKids Pr.) Rosen Publishing Group, Inc., The.

—The Duties & Responsibilities of the Secretary of Education. 2009. (Your Government in Action Ser.). 32p. (gr. 3-3). 43.90 (978-1-60854-916-0(X), PowerKids Pr.) Rosen Publishing Group, Inc., The.

—The Duties & Responsibilities of the Secretary of Homeland Security. 2009. (Your Government in Action Ser.). 32p. (gr. 3-3). 43.90 (978-1-60854-918-4(6), PowerKids Pr.) Rosen Publishing Group, Inc., The.

Rusch, Elizabeth. You Call This Democracy? How to Fix Our Government & Deliver Power to the People. 2020. (ENG., Illus.). 288p. (YA). (gr. 7). 19.99 (978-0-358-17692-3(1), 1758901); pap. 9.99 (978-0-358-38742-8(6), 1787374) HarperCollins Pubs. (Greenwillow Bks.).

Ruschmann, Paul. Energy Policy. 2009. (Point/Counterpoint: Issues in Contemporary American Society Ser.). (ENG.).

TUV

144p. (gr. 9-18). 35.00 *(978-1-60413-333-2(3)*, P165459, Facts On File) Infobase Holdings, Inc.

Ryckman, Tatiana. Alexander Hamilton: The First Secretary of the Treasury & an Author of the Federalist Papers, 1 vol. 2016. (Great American Thinkers Ser.). (ENG., Illus.). 128p. (J). (gr. 9-9). 47.36 *(978-1-5026-1934-1(2)*, e61e020c-0a13-45b1-95be-cb5f62d6901b) Cavendish Square Publishing LLC.

Sakany, Lois. Progressive Leaders: The Platforms & Policies of America's Reform Politicians. (Progressive Movement 1900-1920: Efforts to Reform America's New Industrial Society Ser.). 32p. (gr. 3-4). 2009. 47.90 *(978-1-60854-168-3(1))* 2006. (ENG., Illus.). (YA). lib. bdg. 30.47 *(978-1-4042-0193-4(9)*, 440d7278-674c-4b79-8c8c-36efba421ac9) Rosen Publishing Group, Inc., The.

Sales, Amanda. Mike Pence: Vice President of the United States, 1 vol. 2018. (Influential Lives Ser.). (ENG.). 128p. (J). (gr. 7-7). 40.27 *(978-1-9785-0343-4(1)*, c918029a-a9fb-4d28-b202-6de6d25fab1e) Enslow Publishing, LLC.

Samuel, Charlie. Government & Politics in Colonial America. 2009. (Primary Sources of Everyday Life in Colonial America Ser.). 24p. (gr. 3-4). 42.50 *(978-1-60851-625-4(3)*, PowerKids Pr.) Rosen Publishing Group, Inc., The.

Santoro, Christopher, illus. It's My State! - Group 6, 12 vols. Incl. Georgia. Haywood, Karen Diane. lib. bdg. 34.07 *(978-0-7614-1862-7(8)*, c387b796-fb96-4994-b1e0-943c2e5e5ae1); Louisiana. Bjorklund, Ruth. lib. bdg. 34.07 *(978-0-7614-1863-4(6)*, 793379b3-5746-4c17-a57a-166a1cb8cbd4); Michigan. Haney, Johannah. lib. bdg. 34.07 *(978-0-7614-1861-0(X)*, 2d007384-5db7-456e-915f-6a3d00fdca6d); Nevada. Hicks, Terry Allan. lib. bdg. 34.07 *(978-0-7614-1860-3(1)*, 5122d465-0b42-447f-8d17-ca24fa1547aa); Rhode Island. Petreycik, Rick. lib. bdg. 34.07 *(978-0-7614-1859-7(8)*, 2d28ca89-1f74-4420-8edc-15875fe7dbd8); Vermont. Dornfeld, Margaret. lib. bdg. 34.07 *(978-0-7614-1864-1(4)*, e164a437-fb40-4016-a37b-abd2e3cb74a0); (Illus.). 80p. (gr. 4-4). 2005. (It's My State! (First Edition)(r) Ser.). (ENG.). 2006. 204.42 *(978-0-7614-1858-0(X)*, 6c4d8f9f-020d-4c8b-aa18-960748875f89, Cavendish Square) Cavendish Square Publishing LLC.

Santos, Rita. Mike Pence: U. S. Vice President, 1 vol. 2018. (Junior Biographies Ser.). (ENG.). 24p. (gr. 3-4). 24.27 *(978-1-9785-0207-9(9)*, c3213dc1-c30b-41f3-aac6-8ac82032347b) Enslow Publishing, LLC.

Santos, Rita, ed. The Deep State, 1 vol. 2018. (At Issue Ser.). (ENG.). 128p. (gr. 10-12). pap. 28.80 *(978-1-5345-0320-5(X)*, 39371ff8-108e-4ffb-8028-6eed7195ab3f, Greenhaven Publishing) Greenhaven Publishing LLC.

Sapet, Kerrily. Al Gore. 2007. (Political Profiles Ser.). (Illus.). 112p. (YA). (gr. 5-9). lib. bdg. 27.95 *(978-1-59935-070-7(X))* Reynolds, Morgan Inc.

Scherer, Randy, ed. Political Scandals, 1 vol. 2007. (At Issue Ser.). (ENG., Illus.). 112p. (gr. 10-12). pap. 28.80 *(978-0-7377-3764-6(6)*, ab028217-28d0-4c5f-96fc-26ccb7840e8b, Greenhaven Publishing) Greenhaven Publishing LLC.

Schmermund, Elizabeth, ed. Identity Politics, 1 vol. 2017. (Opposing Viewpoints Ser.). (ENG.). 216p. (YA). (gr. 10-12). 50.43 *(978-1-5345-0174-4(6)*, d4761f36-2f8e-44eb-a112-17e8fd499adf) Greenhaven Publishing LLC.

Schmidt, Maegan. Us Constitution & Bill of Rights, 1 vol. 2013. (Foundations of Our Nation Ser.). (ENG.). 48p. (J). (gr. 4-8). lib. bdg. 35.64 *(978-1-61783-713-5(X)*, 7824) ABDO Publishing Co.

—US Constitution & Bill of Rights. 2013. (Foundations of Our Nation Ser.). (ENG., Illus.). 48p. (J). (gr. 4-8). pap. 18.50 *(978-1-61783-763-0(6)*, 8754) ABDO Publishing Co.

Schomp, Virginia. The Vietnam War, 1 vol. 2005. (Letters from the Battlefront Ser.). (ENG., Illus.). 96p. (gr. 6-6). lib. bdg. 36.93 *(978-0-7614-1663-0(3)*, 5c2a71c6-c1cc-428c-916f-7693754b0619) Cavendish Square Publishing LLC.

Schuh, Mari. The United States Constitution. 2018. (Symbols of American Freedom Ser.). (ENG., Illus.). 24p. (J). (gr. k-3). lib. bdg. 26.95 *(978-1-62617-888-5(7)*, Blastoff! Readers) Bellwether Media.

Schwartz, Eric. What Makes America America? 2006. (How America Became America Ser.). (Illus.). 96p. (YA). lib. bdg. 22.95 *(978-1-59084-913-2(2))* Mason Crest.

Schwartz, Heather E. Alexander Hamilton: The Story of a Statesman. 2020. (Gateway Biographies Ser.). (ENG., Illus.). 48p. (J). (gr. 4-8). pap. 11.99 *(978-1-5415-8886-8(X)*, 53c57c54-581f-4c89-9d64-f13c6a4b348c); lib. bdg. 31.99 *(978-1-5415-7748-0(5)*, c9c12720-d8a7-4416-8f8b-af90f397aacf) Lerner Publishing Group. (Lerner Pubns.).

—Causes of the Civil War: A House Divided. rev. ed. 2017. (Social Studies: Informational Text Ser.). (ENG., Illus.). 32p. (gr. 4-8). pap. 11.99 *(978-1-4938-3803-5(2))* Teacher Created Materials, Inc.

—Our Leaders in Government. rev. ed. 2016. (Social Studies: Informational Text Ser.). (ENG., Illus.). 32p. (gr. 2-4). pap. 10.99 *(978-1-4938-2552-3(6))* Teacher Created Materials, Inc.

—Theodore Roosevelt's Presidency. 2016. (Presidential Powerhouses Ser.). (ENG., Illus.). 104p. (YA). (gr. 6-12). E-Book 54.65 *(978-1-4677-8601-0(2)*, Lerner Pubns.) Lerner Publishing Group.

Searchlight Books - How Does Government Work? 2012. (Searchlight Books How Does Government Work Ser.). (ENG., Illus.). 40p. (gr. 3-5). lib. bdg. 167.58 *(978-0-7613-6513-6(3)*, Lerner Pubns.);Set. pap. 51.02 *(978-0-7613-9235-4(1))*;Set. Pack. pap. 306.09 *(978-0-7613-9236-1(X))* Lerner Publishing Group.

Sebree, Chet'la. Historical Sources on the New Republic, 1783-1830, 1 vol. 2019. (America's Story Ser.). (ENG.). 144p. (gr. 8-8). pap. 22.16 *(978-1-5026-5213-3(7)*, e1037242-52c1-44dc-8792-246b6b652f81); lib. bdg. 47.36 *(978-1-5026-5214-0(5)*, f0797024-dab0-4526-98df-8d0518481634) Cavendish Square Publishing LLC.

Seeley, M. H. 20 Fun Facts about Alexander Hamilton, 1 vol. 2017. (Fun Fact File: Founding Fathers Ser.). (ENG., Illus.). 32p. (J). (gr. 2-3). pap. 11.50 *(978-1-5382-0288-3(3)*, 76d79366-9bf3-4b7d-a923-d9a526bd2a69) Stevens, Gareth Publishing LLLP.

Serber, Michael & Peiser, Andrew. U. S. History & Government. rev. ed. 2005. 688p. (gr. 10-12). *(978-0-87720-882-2(4)*, R036H) AMSCO Schl. Pubns., Inc.

Sexton, Colleen A. Arnold Schwarzenegger. 2005. (A&E Biography Ser.). (Illus.). 112p. (J). (gr. 6-12). 29.27 *(978-0-8225-1634-7(9))*; (ENG & SPA., pap. 7.95 *(978-0-8225-5328-1(7))* Lerner Publishing Group.

Sharp, Constance. America Is Born, 1770-1800. 2012. (J). pap. *(978-1-4222-2413-7(9))* Mason Crest.

—America Is Born, 1770-1800. Rakove, Jack N., ed. 2012. (How America Became America Ser.). 48p. (J). (gr. 3-4). 19.95 *(978-1-4222-2399-4(X))* Mason Crest.

—America Is Born, 1770-1800. 2018. (J). *(978-1-5105-3592-3(6))* SmartBook Media, Inc.

Shattuck, Randy. Theodore Roosevelt. 2016. lib. bdg. *(978-1-68048-529-5(6))* Rosen Publishing Group, Inc., The.

Shea, John. The Declaration of Independence. 2013. (Documents That Shaped America Ser.). (ENG.). 32p. (J). (gr. 4-7). 22.30 *(978-1-5311-8875-7(3))* Perfection Learning Corp.

—The Declaration of Independence. 2013. (Documents That Shaped America Ser.). 32p. (J). (gr. 4-6). pap. 63.00 *(978-1-4339-8999-5(9))* Stevens, Gareth Publishing LLLP.

Shea, John M. The Declaration of Independence, 1 vol. 2013. (Documents That Shaped America Ser.). (ENG.). 32p. (J). (gr. 4-5). 29.27 *(978-1-4339-8997-1(2)*, a16d506c-f4fb-45f0-8a67-81ba9befd7c3); pap. 11.50 *(978-1-4339-8998-8(0)*, 7ba49be5-afb9-45aa-81da-1823c99e084f) Stevens, Gareth Publishing LLLP.

Shea, Therese M. Alexander Hamilton: Founding Father & Treasury Secretary, 1 vol. 2017. (Junior Biographies Ser.). (ENG.). 24p. (gr. 3-4). pap. 10.35 *(978-0-7660-9045-3(0)*, c04e79f6-c80e-4ab8-974e-5cbba0de0d73) Enslow Publishing, LLC.

Sherman, Jill. The American Identity. 2016. (American Citizenship Ser.). (ENG., Illus.). 48p. (J). (gr. 4-8). lib. bdg. 35.64 *(978-1-68078-239-4(8)*, 22079) ABDO Publishing Co.

Shoup, Kate. Standing in the Secretary of Homeland Security's Shoes, 1 vol. 2017. (My Government Ser.). (ENG.). 32p. (gr. 3-3). pap. 11.58 *(978-1-5026-3074-2(5)*, da1fbbef-23ca-4693-90db-4d1c1d2df6ec); lib. bdg. 30.21 *(978-1-5026-3076-6(1)*, abcf4066-97b3-41fb-bf90-dc0eed3d4a4c) Cavendish Square Publishing LLC.

Silate, Jennifer. The Calhoun-Randolph Debate on the Eve of the War of 1812: A Primary Source Investigation, 1 vol. 2004. (Great Historic Debates & Speeches Ser.). (ENG., Illus.). 64p. (YA). (gr. 5-8). lib. bdg. 37.13 *(978-1-4042-0150-7(5)*, b416568f-5db1-4b00-bf4b-5f8362e684ce) Rosen Publishing Group, Inc., The.

—The Calhoun-Randolph Debate on the Eve of the War Of 1812: A Primary Source Investigation. 2009. (Great Historic Debates & Speeches Ser.). 64p. (gr. 5-8). 58.50 *(978-1-61513-124-2(8))* Rosen Publishing Group, Inc., The.

Skahill, Carolyn M. The Socialist Party: Eugene V. Debs & the Radical Politics of the American Working Class, 1 vol. 2006. (Progressive Movement 1900 - 1920: Efforts to Reform America's New Industrial Society Ser.). (ENG., Illus.). 32p. (YA). (gr. 3-4). lib. bdg. 30.47 *(978-1-4042-0198-9(X)*, 75f47ff0-c8ac-4b28-a3b6-e6a19f5d585b) Rosen Publishing Group, Inc., The.

Slepian, Curtis. Hamilton vs. Jefferson (Alexander Hamilton) rev. ed. 2017. (Social Studies: Informational Text Ser.). (ENG., Illus.). 32p. (gr. 4-8). pap. 11.99 *(978-1-4258-6354-8(X))* Teacher Created Materials, Inc.

Smith, Adam I. P. Abraham Lincoln: President, 1 vol. 2016. (History Makers Ser.). (ENG., Illus.). 144p. (J). (gr. 9-9). 47.36 *(978-1-5026-1912-9(1)*, a00797b5-af27-4994-925c-24cf2ac38b7d) Cavendish Square Publishing LLC.

Smith-Llera, Danielle. Exploring the Legislative Branch. 2019. (Searchlight Books (tm) — Getting into Government Ser.). (ENG., Illus.). 32p. (J). (gr. 3-5). pap. 9.99 *(978-1-5415-7480-9(X)*, d78367e6-108e-4ae3-bdff-9b3c215366d6); lib. bdg. 30.65 *(978-1-5415-5587-7(2)*, dc731c7d-8730-4f90-b41c-74a22b4f7cf1) Lerner Publishing Group. (Lerner Pubns.).

Sobel, Syl. How the U. S. Government Works: ... & How It All Comes Together to Make a Nation. 3rd rev. ed. 2019. (ENG.). 48p. (J). (gr. 3-5). pap. 9.99 *(978-1-4380-1163-9(6))* Sourcebooks, Inc.

Somervill, Barbara A. The Life & Times of James Madison. 2008. (Profiles in American History Ser.). (Illus.). 48p. (J). (gr. 4-7). lib. bdg. 29.95 *(978-1-58415-530-0(2))* Mitchell Lane Pubs.

Somerville, Clive. The Drug Enforcement Administration. 2017. (Illus.). 80p. (J). *(978-1-4222-3765-6(6))* Mason Crest.

Sonneborn, Liz. The Articles of Confederation, 1 vol. 2012. (Documenting U. S. History Ser.). (ENG.). 48p. (gr. 3-6). (J). lib. bdg. 33.32 *(978-1-4329-6749-9(5)*, 119380); pap. 9.95 *(978-1-4329-6758-1(4)*, 119388) Capstone. (Heinemann).

South, Victor. America in the 20th Century (1913-1999) 2013. (Illus.). 48p. (J). *(978-1-4222-2396-3(5))*; *(978-1-4222-2410-6(4))* Mason Crest.

—Connecting the 21st Century to the Past (2000-The Present) 2018. (J). *(978-1-5105-3612-8(4))* SmartBook Media, Inc.

Southwell, David. Unsolved Political Mysteries. 2009. (Mysteries & Conspiracies Ser.). 80p. (gr. 10-10). 61.20 *(978-1-61514-747-2(0))* Rosen Publishing Group, Inc., The.

Southwell, David & Twist, Sean. Unsolved Political Mysteries, 1 vol. 2007. (Mysteries & Conspiracies Ser.). (ENG., Illus.). 80p. (YA). (gr. 10-10). lib. bdg. 38.47 *(978-1-4042-1083-7(0)*, 22459ed0-c097-42d8-b4df-4471a5b1fe0b) Rosen Publishing Group, Inc., The.

Spengler, Kremena. Understanding the Path to Citizenship. 2019. (Sequence American Government Ser.). (ENG.). 32p. (J). (gr. 2-5). pap. 9.99 *(978-1-68152-456-6(2)*, 11042) Amicus.

St. George, Judith. The Journey of the One & Only Declaration of Independence. Hillenbrand, Will, illus. 2011. (J). (gr. 1-7). 29.95 *(978-0-439-02760-1(8)*, WHCD806) Weston Woods Studios, Inc.

Stabler, David. Kid Presidents: True Tales of Childhood from America's Presidents. Horner, Doogie, illus. 2014. (Kid Legends Ser.: 1). 224p. (J). (gr. 3-7). 13.99 *(978-1-59474-731-1(8))* Quirk Bks.

Stanley, George E. America & the Cold War (1949-1969), 1 vol. 2004. (Primary Source History of the United States Ser.). (ENG., Illus.). 48p. (gr. 5-8). pap. 15.05 *(978-0-8368-5839-6(5)*, 9a4c7a15-acb6-4b2c-9a63-95b3969a77c5); lib. bdg. 33.67 *(978-0-8368-5830-3(1)*, 7157e3a7-bf9d-4f4e-91ca-910d7325a14c) Stevens, Gareth Publishing LLLP. (Gareth Stevens Secondary Library).

—America in Today's World (1969-2004), 1 vol. 2004. (Primary Source History of the United States Ser.). (ENG., Illus.). 48p. (gr. 5-8). lib. bdg. 33.67 *(978-0-8368-5831-0(X)*, f90bbe7b-9042-429d-92c4-ea9b82b2d8d3, Gareth Stevens Secondary Library) Stevens, Gareth Publishing LLLP.

—The Crisis of the Union (1815-1865), 1 vol. 2004. (Primary Source History of the United States Ser.). (ENG., Illus.). 48p. (gr. 5-8). pap. 15.05 *(978-0-8368-5835-8(2)*, 452e7b11-2a34-4839-b274-bb66ff248c3b); lib. bdg. 33.67 *(978-0-8368-5826-6(3)*, 6147e996-e6b7-46a9-a707-c5808e70afc4) Stevens, Gareth Publishing LLLP. (Gareth Stevens Secondary Library).

—An Emerging World Power (1900-1929), 1 vol. 2004. (Primary Source History of the United States Ser.). (ENG., Illus.). 48p. (gr. 5-8). pap. 15.05 *(978-0-8368-5837-2(9)*, 324523d2-5e90-424c-bfff-97e703f50d4c); lib. bdg. 33.67 *(978-0-8368-5828-0(X)*, 1d569960-8f8b-4d2e-81b1-983ee7fe4527) Stevens, Gareth Publishing LLLP. (Gareth Stevens Secondary Library).

Stanton, Terence M. The Branches of the U. S. Government, 1 vol. 2008. (Real Life Readers Ser.). (ENG.). 32p. (gr. 4-5). pap. 10.00 *(978-1-4358-0173-8(3)*, 049fe561-c253-4738-b55a-0a4b62c6eae0, Rosen Classroom) Rosen Publishing Group, Inc., The.

—The Declaration of Independence. (American History Flashpoints! Ser.). 2009. 32p. (gr. 4-4). 47.90 *(978-1-61511-371-2(1)*, PowerKids Pr.) 2009. (J). pap. 60.00 *(978-1-4358-0164-6(4)*, PowerKids Pr.) 2009. (ENG.). 32p. (J). (gr. 4-4). lib. bdg. 28.93 *(978-1-4358-2990-9(5)*, d224e74b-af0e-403c-8609-39f6f1c593be, PowerKids Pr.) 2008. (ENG.). 32p. (gr. 4-4). pap. 10.00 *(978-1-4358-0163-9(6)*, 9d213c15-58ea-42dc-b648-4a4be770e6cc, Rosen Classroom) Rosen Publishing Group, Inc., The.

Steck-Vaughn, creator. Cast Your Vote!: High School: National, State, & Local Government. 2007. (Illus.). 72p. (J). (gr. 4-7). pap. 12.99 *(978-1-4190-3637-8(8))* Steck-Vaughn.

Steck-Vaughn Staff, creator. Cast Your Vote! Grades 3-5: National, State, & Local Government. 2007. (Illus.). 72p. (J). (gr. 4-7). pap. 12.99 *(978-1-4190-3635-4(1))* Steck-Vaughn.

Stefoff, Rebecca. The New Republic, 1783-1830, 1 vol. 2006. (American Voices From Ser.). (ENG.). 160p. (gr. 6-6). 41.21 *(978-0-7614-1695-1(1)*, 06c7fb95-d435-4501-a58f-55f01615b5c2) Cavendish Square Publishing LLC.

Steinberg, Arnold. Whiplash! From JFK to Donald Trump, a Political Odyssey. 2017. (Illus.). x, 630p. (J). *(978-0-89803-180-5(X))* Jameson Bks., Inc.

Steinberg, Don. America Bowl: 44 Presidents vs. 44 Super Bowls in the Ultimate Matchup! 2010. (ENG., Illus.). 96p. (J). (gr. 5-8). 24.94 *(978-1-59643-683-1(2)*, 9781596436831) Roaring Brook Pr.

Stille, Darlene R. The Emergence of Modern America: 1890-1930. 2007. (Presidents of the United States Ser.). (Illus.). 48p. (J). (gr. 4-7). lib. bdg. 29.05 *(978-1-59036-747-6(2))*; per. 10.95 *(978-1-59036-748-3(0))* Weigl Pubs., Inc.

Stone, Oliver & Kuznick, Peter. The Untold History of the United States, Volume 2: Young Readers Edition, 1945-1962. (ENG., Illus.). 320p. (J). (gr. 5). 2020. pap. 12.99 *(978-1-4814-2177-5(8))* Vol. 2. 2019. 19.99 *(978-1-4814-2176-8(X)*, Atheneum Bks. for Young Readers) Simon & Schuster Children's Publishing.

Storrs, Landon R. Y. The Second Red Scare & the Unmaking of the New Deal Left. 2012. (Politics & Society in Modern America Ser.: 88). (ENG., Illus.). 424p. (C). 63.00 *(978-0-691-15396-4(5)*, 33193) Princeton Univ. Pr.

Strum, Richard. Henry Knox: Washington's Artilleryman. 2006. (Forgotten Heroes of the American Revolution Ser.). (Illus.). 88p. (J). (gr. 5-11). lib. bdg. 23.95 *(978-1-59556-013-1(0))* OTTN Publishing.

Strum, Richard M. Causes of the American Revolution. 2005. (Road to War Ser.). (Illus.). 64p. (J). pap. 12.95 *(978-1-59556-005-6(X))*; (gr. 4-18). lib. bdg. 22.95 *(978-1-59556-001-8(7))* OTTN Publishing.

—Henry Knox: Washington's Artilleryman. 2006. (J). pap. *(978-1-59556-018-6(1))* OTTN Publishing.

Stumpff, April D. & Messersmith, Patrick. Ann Richards: A Woman's Place Is in the Dome. 2006. (Stars of Texas Ser.: 6). (ENG., Illus.). 80p. (J). (gr. 4-7). 14.95 *(978-1-933337-12-8(5)*, P148096) State Hse. Pr.

Sundance/Newbridge LLC Staff. America Is Voting. 2004. (Reading PowerWorks Ser.). (gr. 1-3). 37.50 *(978-0-7608-9723-2(9))* Sundance/Newbridge Educational Publishing.

Swain, Gwenyth. Documents of Freedom: A Look at the Declaration of Independence, the Bill of Rights, & the U. S. Constitution. 2012. (Searchlight Books How Does Government Work Ser.). (ENG., Illus.). 40p. (gr. 3-5). pap. 51.01 *(978-0-7613-9231-6(9))*; (J). pap. 9.99 *(978-0-7613-8560-8(6)*, 325b05e7-6bd3-4841-b748-21d113dc82bc) Lerner Publishing Group.

Taylor-Butler, Christine. The Congress of the United States. 2008. (True Book: American History, Revised Ser.). (ENG., Illus.). 48p. (J). (gr. 3-5). lib. bdg. 21.19 *(978-0-531-12628-8(5)*, Children's Pr.) Scholastic Library Publishing.

—The Congress of the United States (a True Book: American History) 2008. (True Book (Relaunch) Ser.). (ENG., Illus.). 48p. (J). (gr. 3-5). pap. 6.95 *(978-0-531-14778-8(9)*, Children's Pr.) Scholastic Library Publishing.

—The Constitution. 2007. (True Book(tm), a — American History Ser.). (ENG., Illus.). 48p. (J). (gr. 3-5). lib. bdg. 31.00 *(978-0-531-12629-5(3)*, Children's Pr.) Scholastic Library Publishing.

—The Constitution of the United States (a True Book: American History) 2008. (True Book (Relaunch) Ser.). (ENG., Illus.). 48p. (J). (gr. 3-5). pap. 6.95 *(978-0-531-14779-5(7)*, Children's Pr.) Scholastic Library Publishing.

Taylor, Charlotte. Electing U. S. Leaders, 1 vol. 2020. (Being a U. S. Citizen Ser.). (ENG.). 24p. (J). (gr. 1-2). pap. 10.35 *(978-1-9785-1743-1(2)*, c4f3939f-c96a-414e-a841-f509f61e7b16) Enslow Publishing, LLC.

The Choices Program - Brown University Staff. A More Perfect Union: Shaping American Government, 2 vols. 5th ed. 2005. (Illus.). 168p. (YA). pap. 34.00 *(978-1-891306-88-4(X))* Choices Program, Brown Univ.

Thiel, Kristin. American & National Identity, 1 vol. 2018. (Discovering America: an Exceptional Nation Ser.). (ENG.). 112p. (gr. 7-7). lib. bdg. 44.50 *(978-1-5026-4263-9(8)*, ae2c7270-046d-4246-8cdc-eb25c24546f4) Cavendish Square Publishing LLC.

—Politics & Power in the United States, 1 vol. 2018. (Discovering America: an Exceptional Nation Ser.). (ENG.). 112p. (gr. 7-7). lib. bdg. 44.50 *(978-1-5026-4261-5(1)*, 933cabcc-45fc-4f99-af42-bcfad2232381) Cavendish Square Publishing LLC.

This Is Your Governement, 12 vols. 2005. (This Is Your Government Ser.). (ENG., Illus.). (YA). (gr. 5-6). 222.78 *(978-1-4042-0371-6(0)*, d3a02f99-1012-493f-ba9b-b72ad0e76e9b, Rosen Reference) Rosen Publishing Group, Inc., The.

Thomas, Garen. Yes We Can: A Biography of President Barack Obama. 2nd rev. ed. 2008. (ENG., Illus.). 256p. (J). (gr. 3-6). 12.99 *(978-0-312-58639-3(6)*, 900062157) Feiwel & Friends.

Thomas Paine's Common Sense. 2013. (Documents That Shaped America Ser.). 32p. (J). (gr. 4-6). pap. 63.00 *(978-1-4339-9015-1(6))* Stevens, Gareth Publishing LLLP.

Thomas, Ray aka The Bull Cutter. What's Wrong in America. 2008. 216p. pap. 14.95 *(978-1-4327-2531-0(9))* Outskirts Pr., Inc.

Thomas, William David. ¿Cómo Elegimos a Nuestros líderes? (How Do We Elect Our Leaders?), 1 vol. 2008. (Mi Gobierno de Estados Unidos (My American Government) Ser.). (SPA., Illus.). 32p. (gr. 4-6). lib. bdg. 28.67 *(978-0-8368-8870-6(7)*, 6329a910-fbe4-4447-987c-c931cbcd44b4, Gareth Stevens Learning Library) Stevens, Gareth Publishing LLLP.

—¿Cómo Elegimos a Nuestros líderes? (How Do We Elect Our Leaders?), 1 vol. 2008. (Mi Gobierno de Estados Unidos (My American Government) Ser.). (SPA.). 32p. (gr. 4-6). pap. 11.50 *(978-0-8368-8875-1(8)*, e44f3a0a-a6ae-4092-9579-fc5002f3aa79, Gareth Stevens Learning Library) Stevens, Gareth Publishing LLLP.

—¿Cuáles Son Las Partes Del Gobierno? (What Are the Parts of Government?), 1 vol. 2008. (Mi Gobierno de Estados Unidos (My American Government) Ser.). (SPA.). 32p. (gr. 4-6). pap. 11.50 *(978-0-8368-8877-5(4)*, d1153070-d627-4f3c-a1e8-aedea387f406, Gareth Stevens Learning Library) Stevens, Gareth Publishing LLLP.

—The Home Front in the Vietnam War, 1 vol. 2004. (American Experience in Vietnam Ser.). (ENG., Illus.). 48p. (gr. 5-8). lib. bdg. 33.67 *(978-0-8368-5775-7(5)*, 88d9c093-0192-4a50-aeaa-fa6fdaa9afa8, Gareth Stevens Secondary Library) Stevens, Gareth Publishing LLLP.

—How Do We Elect Our Leaders?, 1 vol. 2008. (My American Government Ser.). (ENG., Illus.). 32p. (gr. 4-6). pap. 11.50 *(978-0-8368-8865-2(0)*, 8de7b30c-25e3-4d8b-82fb-4b34d50ad788); lib. bdg. 28.67 *(978-0-8368-8860-7(X)*, c7d46ad2-a0ce-4f68-b056-4267636313a1) Stevens, Gareth Publishing LLLP. (Gareth Stevens Learning Library).

—My American Government, 8 vols., Set. Incl. How Do We Elect Our Leaders? lib. bdg. 28.67 *(978-0-8368-8860-7(X)*, c7d46ad2-a0ce-4f68-b056-4267636313a1); What Are Citizens' Basic Rights? lib. bdg. 28.67 *(978-0-8368-8861-4(8)*, 392aa92c-5cf0-4283-80d8-e70137bf9c0a); What Are the Parts of Government? lib. bdg. 28.67 *(978-0-8368-8862-1(6)*, 48d52e72-eb0d-409f-8498-f3e421778243); What Is a Constitution? lib. bdg. 28.67 *(978-0-8368-8863-8(4)*, 52c724a2-3838-4b82-91ae-b3883562c9fc); (Illus.). (gr. 4-6). (My American Government Ser.). (ENG.). 32p. 2008. Set lib. bdg. 114.68 *(978-0-8368-8859-1(6)*, e5a6db90-a371-42ed-955d-2eb8af0b05f2, Gareth Stevens Learning Library) Stevens, Gareth Publishing LLLP.

—What Are the Parts of Government?, 1 vol. 2008. (My American Government Ser.). (ENG.). 32p. (gr. 4-6). pap. 11.50 *(978-0-8368-8867-6(7)*, 5cd5a58e-6d1a-4b57-bdc0-91264023d74a, Gareth Stevens Learning Library) Stevens, Gareth Publishing LLLP.

—What Are the Parts of Government?, 1 vol. 2008. (My American Government Ser.). (ENG., Illus.). 32p. (gr. 4-6). lib. bdg. 28.67 *(978-0-8368-8862-1(6)*, 48d52e72-eb0d-409f-8498-f3e421778243, Gareth Stevens Learning Library) Stevens, Gareth Publishing LLLP.

Thomas, William David & Thomas, William David. Mi Gobierno de Estados Unidos, 6 vols., Set. Incl. ¿Cómo Elegimos a Nuestros líderes? (How Do We Elect Our Leaders?) lib. bdg. 28.67 *(978-0-8368-8870-6(7)*, 6329a910-fbe4-4447-987c-c931cbcd44b4); ¿Cuáles Son Las Partes Del Gobierno? (What Are the Parts of Government?) lib. bdg. 28.67 *(978-0-8368-8872-0(3)*, 74c4b834-424e-4ea2-8c97-a9f6dd9a5e9b); ¿Cuáles Son Los Derechos Básicos de Los Ciudadanos? (What Are Citizens' Basic Rights?) lib. bdg. 28.67 *(978-0-8368-8871-3(5)*, e238e556-be3c-4943-b672-dd1f73bb0fcf); ¿Qué Es una Constitución? (What Is a Constitution?) (J). lib. bdg. 28.67 *(978-0-8368-8873-7(1)*, 904f865e-4a17-40e8-9e37-79f4d0fd4478); (Illus.). (gr. 4-6). (Mi Gobierno de Estados Unidos (My American Government) Ser.). (SPA.). 32p. 2008. Set lib. bdg. 86.01

(978-0-8368-8869-0(3), 471ddade-3e7d-45b1-95ce-164b3e114554, Gareth Stevens Learning Library) Stevens, Gareth Publishing LLLP.

Thompson, Jerry D., contrib. by. Symbols of American Freedom Set, 10-Volumes. 2009. (Symbols of American Freedom Ser.). (gr. 4-6). 300.00 (978-1-60413-830-6(0), Chelsea Clubhse.) Infobase Holdings, Inc.

Thornton, Jeremy. Tories & Patriots: Neighbors at War. 2009. (Building America's Democracy Ser.). 24p. (gr. 3-3). 42.50 (978-1-61511-768-0(7), PowerKids Pr.) Rosen Publishing Group, Inc., The.

Time Magazine Editors. Alexander Hamilton: Life Stories of Extraordinary Americans. 2018. (Heroes of History Ser.: 1). (ENG., Illus.). 144p. (J). (gr. 6-17). pap. 9.99 (978-1-68330-850-8(6), Time Home Entertainment) Time Inc. Bks.

Toole, Spencer. Starting a Petition: Taking Civic Action, 1 vol. 2018. (Civics for the Real World Ser.). (ENG.). 16p. (gr. 2-3). pap. (978-1-5383-6563-2(4), e2220a33-ca81-4fec-9bd0-5b3b01d5e0ad, Rosen Classroom) Rosen Publishing Group, Inc., The.

—You Can Volunteer! Civic Virtues, 1 vol. 2018. (Civics for the Real World Ser.). (ENG.). 12p. (gr. 1-2). pap. (978-1-5383-6418-5(2), 1ef58dfb-2d1c-46e7-9730-3284e9e67ba5, Rosen Classroom) Rosen Publishing Group, Inc., The.

Torres, John A. How Barack Obama Fought the War on Terrorism, 1 vol. 2017. (Presidents at War Ser.). (ENG.). 128p. (gr. 8-8). lib. bdg. 38.93 (978-0-7660-8535-0(X), 6808ab9c-609c-4f7e-b33b-789b6476f7fb) Enslow Publishing, LLC.

Tracy, Kathleen. The McCarthy Era. 2008. (Monumental Milestones Ser.). (Illus.). 48p. (YA). (gr. 4-7). lib. bdg. 29.95 (978-1-58415-694-9(5)) Mitchell Lane Pubs.

—The Watergate Scandal. 2006. (Monumental Milestones Ser.). (Illus.). 48p. (YA). (gr. 4-7). lib. bdg. 29.95 (978-1-58415-470-9(5)) Mitchell Lane Pubs.

Trumbauer, Lisa. Abraham Lincoln & the Civil War. rev. ed. 2016. (Life in the Time Of Ser.). (ENG.). 32p. (J). (gr. 1-3). pap. 8.29 (978-1-4846-3822-4(0), 134722, Heinemann) Capstone.

Tukan, Jaytoe Anthony, Sr. John Reid Edwards: The People's Senator. 2003. per. 19.95 (978-0-9665909-4-4(5)) Kalawantis Publishing Services, Inc.

Turner, Myra Faye & Harris, Duchess. Political Resistance in the Current Age. 2017. (Protest Movements Ser.). (ENG., Illus.). 48p. (J). (gr. 4-8). lib. bdg. 35.64 (978-1-5321-1398-7(6), 27696) ABDO Publishing Co.

U. S. Government. (J). tchr. ed. 41.95 (978-0-382-40684-3(2)) Cobblestone Publishing Co.

Uhl, Xina M. & Burnett, Betty. A Primary Source Investigation of the Continental Congress, 1 vol. 2018. (Uncovering American History Ser.). (ENG.). 64p. (gr. 6-6). pap. 13.95 (978-1-5081-8411-9(9), 7bba41c1-bb3f-42af-bb76-00ac3094bf1b, Rosen Reference) Rosen Publishing Group, Inc., The.

Uhl, Xina M. & Flanagan, Timothy. A Primary Source Investigation of Reconstruction, 1 vol. 2018. (Uncovering American History Ser.). (ENG.). 64p. (gr. 6-6). pap. 13.95 (978-1-5081-8405-8(4), b6716a0c-44ee-418b-b9fc-be349d9fb5a8, Rosen Reference) Rosen Publishing Group, Inc., The.

Uschan, Michael V. Watergate, 1 vol. 2009. (American History Ser.). (ENG., Illus.). 104p. (gr. 7-7). 41.03 (978-1-4205-0135-3(6), 25c4e805-a3e4-4787-8933-293ffb81b51e, Lucent Pr.) Greenhaven Publishing LLC.

Valelly, Richard M. The Voting Rights Act, 00 vols. rev. ed. 2005. (Landmark Events in U. S. History Ser.). (ENG., Illus.). 400p. (gr. 9-18). 150.00 (978-1-56802-989-4(6)) CQ Pr.

Vaughn, Wally G. & Davis, Mattie Campbell, eds. The Selma Campaign, 1963-1965: The Decisive Battle of the Civil Rights Movement. 2006. (ENG., Illus.). 244p. pap. 19.95 (978-0-912469-44-7(7)) Majority Pr., The.

Ventura, Marne. Hillary Clinton: Historic Politician. 2017. (Newsmakers Set 2 Ser.). (ENG., Illus.). 48p. (J). (gr. 4-8). lib. bdg. 35.64 (978-1-5321-1181-5(9), 25938) ABDO Publishing Co.

—Hillary Clinton: Historic Politician. 2017. (Newsmakers Set 2 Ser.). (ENG.). 48p. (J). (gr. 4-8). 55.65 (978-1-68078-966-9(X), 26367) ABDO Publishing Co.

Vescia, Monique. The Emancipation Proclamation, 1 vol. 2016. (Let's Find Out! Primary Sources Ser.). (ENG., Illus.). 32p. (J). (gr. 2-3). lib. bdg. 26.06 (978-1-5081-0405-6(0), bf2c8f3c-c00f-498d-9c78-61f20b774f67) Rosen Publishing Group, Inc., The.

Vickers, Roy Henry. The Elders Are Watching. 5th rev. deluxe ed. 2003. (ENG., Illus.). 56p. (J). 18.95 (978-1-55192-641-4(5)) Raincoast Bk. Distribution CAN. Dist: Publishers Group West (PGW).

Vierow, Wendy. The 1864 Presidential Election: A War-Weary Nation Reelects President Abraham Lincoln. 2009. (Headlines from History Ser.). 24p. (gr. 3-3). 42.50 (978-1-61513-239-3(2), PowerKids Pr.) Rosen Publishing Group, Inc., The.

Wagner, Heather Lehr. Barack Obama. 2008. (Black Americans of Achievement Legacy Edition Ser.). 104p. (gr. 6-12). pap. 11.95 (978-1-60413-324-0(4), Checkmark Bks.) Infobase Holdings, Inc.

Wallenfeldt, Jeff, ed. A New World Power: America from 1920 To 1945, 4 vols. 2012. (Documenting America: the Primary Source Documents of a Nation Ser.). (ENG., Illus.). 168p. (YA). (gr. 10-10). 89.42 (978-1-61530-784-5(2), 06045b1f-3f45-492d-a2c0-1e7c79a7221d) Rosen Publishing Group, Inc., The.

Wallenfeldt, Jeffrey H. A New World Power: America from 1920 to 1945, 1 vol. 2012. (Documenting America: the Primary Source Documents of a Nation Ser.). (ENG., Illus.). 168p. (J). (gr. 10-10). lib. bdg. 44.71 (978-1-61530-694-7(3), 464203e0-e791-4a10-b121-3bccef65d268) Rosen Publishing Group, Inc., The.

Warren, Andrea. Enemy Child: The Story of Norman Mineta, a Boy Imprisoned in a Japanese American Internment Camp During World War II. 2019. (Illus.). 224p. (J). (gr. 5). 22.99 (978-0-8234-4151-8(2), Margaret Ferguson Books) Holiday Hse., Inc.

Waxman, Laura Hamilton. What Are the Articles of Confederation? And Other Questions about the Birth of the United States. 2012. (Six Questions of American History Ser.). (ENG.). 48p. (gr. 4-6). pap. 56.72 (978-0-7613-9238-5(6)); pap. 9.95 (978-0-7613-8564-6(9)) Lerner Publishing Group.

Welch, Catherine A. Patrick Henry. 2006. (History Maker Bios Ser.). (Illus.). 48p. (J). (gr. 3-6). lib. bdg. 26.60 (978-0-8225-5941-2(2), Lerner Pubns.) Lerner Publishing Group.

Westcott, Jim. Tea Party, Libertarian, & Other Political Parties. 2016. (Illus.). 64p. (J). (978-1-61900-095-7(4)) Eldorado Ink.

What's up with Your Government?, 12 vols. 2017. (What's up with Your Government? Ser.). (ENG.). (J). (gr. 4-5). lib. bdg. 167.58 (978-1-5081-6259-9(X), 70914c0b-e44a-45d7-a315-314fcfa7ff3f, PowerKids Pr.) Rosen Publishing Group, Inc., The.

White, Casey. John Jay: Diplomat of the American Experiment. (Library of American Thinkers Ser.). 112p. (gr. 6-6). 2009. 66.50 (978-1-60853-515-6(0), Rosen Reference) 2006. (ENG., Illus.). (YA). lib. bdg. 39.80 (978-1-4042-0507-9(1), d02aee73-ee35-409b-89c1-7c009ebf0d42) Rosen Publishing Group, Inc., The.

Williams, Robert F. & Williams, Mabel, as told by. Robert & Mabel Williams Resource Guide. 2005. (ENG., Illus.). 86p. pap. 10.00 (978-0-9727422-7-6(1)) Freedom Archives, The.

Wilson, Steve. Andrew Jackson's Presidency: Democracy in Action, 1 vol. 2016. (Spotlight on American History Ser.). (ENG., Illus.). 24p. (J). (gr. 4-6). 27.93 (978-1-5081-4938-5(0), 6649632c-035b-4121-ad0c-f1d92c5f188f, PowerKids Pr.) Rosen Publishing Group, Inc., The.

Wingate, Kate. Political Reforms: American Citizens Gain More Control over Their Government. 2009. (Progressive Movement 1900-1920: Efforts to Reform America's New Industrial Society Ser.). 32p. (gr. 3-4). 47.90 (978-1-60854-167-6(3)) Rosen Publishing Group, Inc., The.

Wingate, Katherine. Political Reforms: American Citizens Gain More Control over Their Government, 1 vol. (Progressive Movement 1900 - 1920: Efforts to Reform America's New Industrial Society Ser.). (ENG., Illus.). 32p. (gr. 3-4). 2006. (YA). lib. bdg. 30.47 (978-1-4042-0192-7(0), bdc4b573-f804-407b-bd4c-e4ea48be198e) 2005. pap. 10.00 (978-1-4042-0853-7(4), 5d495f1a-157b-4ab1-adab-5d57c3bbf602) Rosen Publishing Group, Inc., The.

Wirkner, Linda. Learning about Life in the New American Nation with Graphic Organizers. (Graphic Organizers in Social Studies). 24p. 2009. (gr. 3-4). 42.50 (978-1-61513-082-5(9), PowerKids Pr.) 2005. (ENG.). (gr. 4-5). pap. 8.25 (978-1-4042-5050-5(6), 6db573f1-ac3a-4318-81da-7b890351eed3, Rosen Classroom) 2004. (ENG., Illus.). (J). (gr. 4-5). lib. bdg. 26.27 (978-1-4042-2810-8(1), d813325a-c1b5-48f2-8395-8fd44333b46a, PowerKids Pr.) Rosen Publishing Group, Inc., The.

Wittekind, Erika. James Madison's Presidency. 2016. (Presidential Powerhouses Ser.). (ENG., Illus.). 104p. (YA). (gr. 6-12). 35.99 (978-1-4677-7929-6(6), e13b2ba0-3b43-4bfa-ba26-961be1313ce5); E-Book 54.65 (978-1-4677-8599-0(7)) Lerner Publishing Group. (Lerner Pubns.).

Wolfe, James & Callahan, Kerry P. Understanding the Articles of Confederation, 1 vol. 2015. (Primary Sources of American Political Documents Ser.). (ENG.). 128p. (gr. 7-7). 38.93 (978-0-7660-6866-7(8), 061f74f6-17b4-426b-8022-244c00b21d5f) Enslow Publishing, LLC.

Wolfe, James & Viegas, Jennifer. Understanding the Declaration of Independence, 1 vol. 2015. (Primary Sources of American Political Documents Ser.). (ENG., Illus.). 112p. (gr. 7-7). 38.93 (978-0-7660-6874-2(9), 7bbd1d8a-7b1f-41aa-9c4b-acb9776583e8) Enslow Publishing, LLC.

Wood, Alix. Visit Independence Hall, 1 vol. 2012. (Landmarks of Liberty Ser.). (ENG.). 24p. (gr. 2-3). pap. 9.15 (978-1-4339-6386-5(8), 2abc971b-72f5-4e95-8683-fa410e14b23d, Gareth Stevens Learning Library); (J). lib. bdg. 25.27 (978-1-4339-6384-1(1), 60b05e64-ba78-4f71-bed6-49779686fcba) Stevens, Gareth Publishing LLLP.

Wood, Douglas. Americans. Sayles, Elizabeth, illus. 2018. (ENG.). 40p. (J). (gr. -1-3). 17.99 (978-1-4169-2756-3(5), Simon & Schuster Bks. For Young Readers) Simon & Schuster Bks. For Young Readers.

Wood, Ethel, compiled by. The Presidency. 2004. (Historical Reader Ser.). (Illus.). 240p. (gr. 6-12). 13.32 (978-0-618-04821-2(9), 2-00153) Holt McDougal.

World Book, Inc. Staff, contrib. by. The World Book of America's Presidents, 2 vols. 2005. (Illus.). (gr. 5-12). 99.00 (978-0-7166-3698-4(0)) World Bk., Inc.

Your Government in Action, 10 vols. 2004. (Your Government in Action Ser.). (ENG., Illus.). (J). (gr. 3-3). 138.00 (978-1-4042-2966-2(3), 7f060ea2-035a-4560-ab8c-cdef50a3d72a) Rosen Publishing Group, Inc., The.

Zahensky, Kenneth. George W. Bush. 2016. (J). lib. bdg. (978-1-68048-526-4(1)) Rosen Publishing Group, Inc., The.

Zahensky, Kenneth, ed. George W. Bush, 1 vol. 2017. (Pivotal Presidents: Profiles in Leadership Ser.). (ENG., Illus.). 80p. (J). (gr. 8-8). 36.47 (978-1-68048-629-2(2), 313237e8-c2d5-4974-8ba2-eee0eb5e0ae8, Britannica Educational Publishing) Rosen Publishing Group, Inc., The.

Zamosky, Lisa. Lideres de Gobierno de Antes y de Hoy. rev. ed. 2019. (Social Studies: Informational Text Ser.). (SPA., Illus.). 32p. (J). (gr. 2-3). pap. 11.99 (978-1-64290-112-2(1)) Teacher Created Materials, Inc.

Ziff, John. The Modern Democratic Party. 2016. 64p. (J). (978-1-61900-091-9(1)) Eldorado Ink.

—The Modern Republican Party. 2016. 64p. (J). (978-1-61900-092-6(X)) Eldorado Ink.

—The United States Senate. 2016. 64p. (J). (978-1-61900-096-4(2)) Eldorado Ink.

Zimmerman, Bob. The American Challenge: Twenty-One Winning Strategies for the 21st Century. 2003. (Illus.). 303p. (gr. 8-18). bds. 25.00 (978-0-932555-04-5(7)) Uxor Pr., Inc.

Zuchora-Walske, Christine. Andrew Jackson's Presidency. 2016. (Presidential Powerhouses Ser.). (ENG., Illus.). 104p. (YA). (gr. 6-12). 35.99 (978-1-4677-7926-5(1), 78407cea-eed3-4c5d-9bd1-0b769822ca4e); E-Book 54.65 (978-1-4677-8548-8(2)) Lerner Publishing Group. (Lerner Pubns.).

UNITED STATES—POLITICS AND GOVERNMENT—FICTION

Barnes, Peter W. House Mouse, Senate Mouse. Barnes, Cheryl Shaw, illus. 2012. (ENG.). 40p. (J). (gr. k-3). 17.99 (978-1-59698-790-6(1), Little Patriot Pr.) Regnery Publishing.

Cushman, Karen. The Loud Silence of Francine Green. 2019. (ENG.). 240p. (J). (gr. 5-7). pap. 9.99 (978-1-328-49799-4(2), 1717855, Clarion Bks.) HarperCollins Pubs.

—The Loud Silence of Francine Green. 2008. (ENG.). 240p. (YA). (gr. 6-8). 21.19 (978-0-375-84117-0(2)) Random House Publishing Group.

Limbaugh, Rush & Adams Limbaugh, Kathryn. Rush Revere & the Presidency. 2016. (Rush Revere Ser.: 5). (ENG., Illus.). 272p. (gr. 4-7). 21.00 (978-1-5011-5689-2(6), Threshold Editions) Threshold Editions.

Sargent, Dave & Sargent, Pat. Duke: (Dappled Palomino) Good Behavior, 30 vols., Vol. 23. Lenoir, Jane, illus. 2003. (Saddle up Ser.: Vol. 23). 42p. (J). pap. 10.95 (978-1-56763-682-6(9)); lib. bdg. 23.60 (978-1-56763-681-9(0)) Ozark Publishing.

UNITED STATES—POST OFFICE DEPARTMENT

Wales, Dirk. A Lucky Dog: Owney, U.S. Rail Mail Mascot. Kenna, Diane, illus. 2003. 32p. (J). 15.95 (978-0-9632459-0-8(2)) Great Plains Pr.

UNITED STATES—POSTAL SERVICE

see Postal Service

UNITED STATES—PRESIDENTS

see Presidents—United States

UNITED STATES—PUBLIC DEBTS

see Debts, Public

UNITED STATES—RACE RELATIONS

Adamson, Heather. The Civil Rights Movement [Scholastic]: An Interactive History Adventure. (You Choose: History Ser.). 112p. 2010. pap. 0.86 (978-1-4296-5179-0(2)) 2009. (gr. 3-4). pap. 0.86 (978-1-4296-4047-3(2)) Capstone. (Capstone Pr.).

Adler, David A. A Picture Book of Rosa Parks. Casilla, Robert, illus. 2015. 32p. pap. 8.00 (978-1-61003-405-0(8)) Center for the Collaborative Classroom.

African American Eras. 2010. (978-1-4144-3600-5(9)); (978-1-4144-3598-5(3)); (978-1-4144-3597-8(5)); (978-1-4144-3599-2(1)) Cengage Gale. (UXL).

Anderson, Wayne. Fighting Racial Discrimination: Treating All Americans Fairly under the Law. 2009. (Progressive Movement 1900-1920: Efforts to Reform America's New Industrial Society Ser.). 32p. (gr. 3-4). 47.90 (978-1-60854-164-5(9)) Rosen Publishing Group, Inc., The.

Bailey, Diane. Ida B. Wells: Discovering History's Heroes. 2019. (Jeter Publishing Ser.). (ENG.). 160p. (J). (gr. 2-5). pap. 6.99 (978-1-5344-2484-5(9), Aladdin) Simon & Schuster Children's Publishing.

—Ida B. Wells: Discovering History's Heroes. 2019. (Jeter Publishing Ser.). (ENG.). 160p. (J). (gr. 2-5). E-Book (978-1-5344-2486-9(5)); (Illus.). 18.99 (978-1-5344-2485-2(7)) Simon & Schuster/Paula Wiseman Bks. (Simon & Schuster/Paula Wiseman Bks.).

Banting, Erinn. The Civil Rights Movement. 2008. (African American History Ser.). (Illus.). 48p. (YA). (gr. 5-8). lib. bdg. 29.05 (978-1-59036-882-4(7)); pap. 10.95 (978-1-59036-883-1(5)) Weigl Pubs., Inc.

Bartoletti, Susan Campbell. They Called Themselves the K. K. k: The Birth of an American Terrorist Group. (ENG., Illus.). 176p. (YA). (gr. 7). 2014. pap. 14.99 (978-0-544-22582-4(1), 1563371) 2010. 19.00 (978-0-618-44033-7(X), 581244) HarperCollins Pubs. (Clarion Bks.).

Bauchner, Elizabeth. Teen Minorities in Rural North America: Growing up Different. 2009. (Youth in Rural North America Ser.). (Illus.). 96p. (YA). (gr. 3-7). lib. bdg. 22.95 (978-1-4222-0014-8(0)) Mason Crest.

Bausum, Ann. The March Against Fear: The Last Great Walk of the Civil Rights Movement & the Emergence of Black Power. 2017. (Illus.). 144p. (YA). (gr. 7-12). 18.99 (978-1-4263-2665-3(3), National Geographic Kids) Disney Publishing Worldwide.

Berlatsky, Noah, ed. Interracial America, 1 vol. 2011. (Opposing Viewpoints Ser.). (ENG., Illus.). 224p. (gr. 10-12). pap. 34.80 (978-0-7377-5728-6(0), c2cc9548-14f2-49f8-9a00-0f12bd54c9fb, Greenhaven Publishing) Greenhaven Publishing LLC.

bjornlund, lydia. The Civil Rights Movement. 2012. (Illus.). 96p. (J). lib. bdg. (978-1-60152-478-2(1)) ReferencePoint Pr., Inc.

Blakemore, M. T. White Privilege. 2017. (Race in America Ser.). (ENG., Illus.). 112p. (J). (gr. 6-12). lib. bdg. 41.36 (978-1-5321-1039-9(1), 25654, Essential Library) ABDO Publishing Co.

Blohm, Craig E. The Civil Rights Movement. 2018. (Push for Social Change Ser.). (ENG.). 80p. (YA). (gr. 6-12). 39.93 (978-1-68282-419-1(5)) ReferencePoint Pr., Inc.

Bolden, Tonya. Capital Days: Michael Shiner's Journal & the Growth of Our Nation's Capital. 2015. (ENG., Illus.). 96p. (J). (gr. 5-9). 21.95 (978-1-4197-0733-9(7), 1056601, Abrams Bks. for Young Readers) Abrams, Inc.

Bridges, Ruby. Ruby Bridges Goes to School: My True Story. 2009. (Scholastic Reader Level 2 Ser.). lib. bdg. 13.55 (978-0-606-06808-6(2)) Turtleback.

Brimner, Larry Dane. Birmingham Sunday. 2010. (ENG., Illus.). 48p. (J). (gr. 7-12). 18.99 (978-1-59078-613-0(0), Calkins Creek) Highlights Pr., c/o Highlights for Children, Inc.

Burling, Alexis. Race in the Criminal Justice System. 2017. (Race in America Ser.). (ENG.). 112p. (J). (gr. 6-12). lib. bdg. 41.36 (978-1-5321-1036-8(7), 25648, Essential Library) ABDO Publishing Co.

Carlson-Berne, Emma. Face of Freedom: How the Photos of Frederick Douglass Celebrated Racial Equality. 2017. (Captured History Ser.). (ENG., Illus.). 64p. (J). (gr. 5-9). pap. 8.95 (978-0-7565-5619-8(8), 135812); lib. bdg. 35.32 (978-0-7565-5617-4(1), 135802) Capstone. (Compass Point Bks.).

Cohon, Rhody & Deutsch, Stacia. Hot Pursuit: Murder in Mississippi. Orback, Craig, illus. 2010. (ENG.). 40p. (J). (gr. 3-5). pap. 7.95 (978-0-7613-3956-4(6), 77cdd621-0509-4a81-bddf-ae8d265cd44d, Kar-Ben Publishing) Lerner Publishing Group.

Coleman, Wim & Perrin, Pat. Racism on Trial: From the Medgar Evers Murder Case to Ghosts of Mississippi, 1 vol. 2009. (Famous Court Cases That Became Movies Ser.). (ENG., Illus.). 112p. (gr. 6-7). lib. bdg. 35.93 (978-0-7660-3059-6(8), fdc7ea56-35b4-4971-bb05-2efa75ae67aa) Enslow Publishing, LLC.

Conklin, Wendy. Civil Rights Movement, 1 vol. rev. ed. 2007. (Social Studies: Informational Text Ser.). (ENG.). 32p. (J). (gr. 4-8). pap. 11.99 (978-0-7439-0670-8(5)) Teacher Created Materials, Inc.

Connolly, Sean. Racial & Ethnic Equality. 2005. (Campaigns for Change Ser.). (Illus.). 48p. (J). (gr. 6-9). lib. bdg. 29.95 (978-1-58340-516-1(X)) Black Rabbit Bks.

Coy, Cissie. Dennis Chávez: The First Hispanic US Senator / Dennis Chávez: el Primer Senador Hispano de Los Estados Unidos. 2017. (SPA & ENG., Illus.). 64p. (J). (gr. 4-8). pap. 9.95 (978-1-55885-852-7(0), Piñata Books) Arte Publico Pr.

Crayton, Lisa A. Everything You Need to Know about Confronting Racist Behavior, 1 vol. 2018. (Need to Know Library). (ENG.). 64p. (gr. 6-6). 36.13 (978-1-5081-7915-3(8), 750eab12-ea28-42ec-a862-39fd4e65f755) Rosen Publishing Group, Inc., The.

Daly, Ruth. Rosa Parks. 2014. (Illus.). 24p. (J). (978-1-4896-2452-9(X)) Weigl Pubs., Inc.

De Medeiros, James. The Migration North. (J). 2013. 29.99 (978-1-62127-193-2(5)) 2013. pap. 14.95 (978-1-62127-199-4(4)) 2008. (Illus.). 48p. (gr. 5-8). pap. 10.95 (978-1-59036-881-7(9)) 2008. (Illus.). 48p. (gr. 5-8). lib. bdg. 29.05 (978-1-59036-880-0(0)) Weigl Pubs., Inc.

Deal, Heidi. Perspectives on the Civil Rights Movement. 2018. (Perspectives on US History Ser.). (ENG., Illus.). 32p. (J). (gr. 3-6). 32.80 (978-1-63235-398-6(9), 13720, 12-Story Library) Bookstaves, LLC.

Donaldson, Madeline. Ruby Bridges. 2009. (History Maker Biographies Ser.). (ENG., Illus.). 48p. (J). (gr. 3-6). 27.93 (978-0-7613-4220-5(6), 1299456, Lerner Pubns.) Lerner Publishing Group.

Dray, Philip. Yours for Justice, Ida B. Wells: The Daring Life of a Crusading Journalist, 1 vol. Alcorn, Stephen, illus. 2008. 48p. (J). (gr. 5-9). 18.95 (978-1-56145-417-4(6)) Peachtree Publishing Co. Inc.

Dunbar-Ortiz, Roxanne. An Indigenous Peoples' History of the United States for Young People. 2019. (ReVisioning History for Young People Ser.: 2). (ENG., Illus.). 272p. (YA). (gr. 7). pap. 18.95 (978-0-8070-4939-6(5), Beacon Pr.) Beacon Pr.

Eboch, M. M. Race & Economics. 2017. (Race in America Ser.). (ENG., Illus.). 112p. (J). (gr. 6-12). lib. bdg. 41.36 (978-1-5321-1034-4(0), 25644, Essential Library) ABDO Publishing Co.

Ed, Kelly Bakshi. Roots of Racism. 2017. (Race in America Ser.). (ENG., Illus.). 112p. (J). (gr. 6-12). lib. bdg. 41.36 (978-1-5321-1037-5(5), 25650, Essential Library) ABDO Publishing Co.

Edwards, Sue Bradford. What Are Race & Racism? 2017. (Race in America Ser.). (ENG., Illus.). 112p. (J). (gr. 6-12). lib. bdg. 41.36 (978-1-5321-1038-2(3), 25652, Essential Library) ABDO Publishing Co.

Ellis, Carol. African American Activists. 2012. (J). pap. (978-1-4222-2384-0(1)) Mason Crest.

—African American Activists. Hill, Marc Lamont, ed. 2012. (Major Black Contributions from Emancipation to Civil Rights Ser.). 64p. (J). (gr. 5). 22.95 (978-1-4222-2371-0(X)) Mason Crest.

Esty, Amos. Plessy V. Ferguson. 2012. (Civil Rights Movement Ser.). (Illus.). 112p. (YA). (gr. 7-12). 28.95 (978-1-59935-182-7(X)) Reynolds, Morgan Inc.

Finegan, Jeffrey E., Sr. Colonel Washington & Me: George Washington, His Slave William Lee & Their Incredible Journey Together. Nikolopoulos, Stephanie, ed. 2012. (ENG., Illus.). 32p. (J). 16.95 (978-0-9852819-0-8(1)) Seigle Bks.

Finlayson, Reggie. We Shall Overcome: The History of the American Civil Rights Movement. 2005. (People's History Ser.). (Illus.). 96p. (gr. 6-12). lib. bdg. 26.60 (978-0-8225-0647-8(5)) Lerner Publishing Group.

Gale Research Inc. Unlocking Current Issues: Race & the Law. 2018. (Unlocking Current Issues Ser.). (ENG., Illus.). 240p. 51.00 (978-1-4103-8096-8(3)) Cengage Gale.

Gates Jr., Henry Louis & Bolden, Tonya. Dark Sky Rising: Reconstruction & the Dawn of Jim Crow (Scholastic Focus) 2019. (ENG., Illus.). 240p. (J). (gr. 4-7). 19.99 (978-1-338-26204-9(1), Scholastic Nonfiction) Scholastic, Inc.

George, Charles. Black Nationalism, 1 vol. 2009. (Lucent Library of Black History Ser.). (ENG., Illus.). 96p. (gr. 7-7). 41.03 (978-1-4205-0083-7(X), ed4146b4-9d52-4854-a51e-02d57fd644e0, Lucent Pr.) Greenhaven Publishing LLC.

George, Enzo. The Civil Rights Movement, 1 vol. 2015. (Primary Sources in U. S. History Ser.). (ENG., Illus.). 48p. (gr. 4-4). 33.07 (978-1-5026-0496-5(5), 498536a3-b514-4822-a18a-14f545378d56) Cavendish Square Publishing LLC.

Green, Meghan. Racism in America: A Long History of Hate, 1 vol. 2017. (Hot Topics Ser.). (ENG.). 112p. (gr. 7-7). 41.03 (978-1-5345-6143-4(9), e08b177d-ff77-4777-b788-7e5899c5cf77, Lucent Pr.) Greenhaven Publishing LLC.

Hamby, Rachel. Barbara Rose Johns Jump-Starts the Civil Rights Movement. 2018. (J). (978-1-64185-354-5(9), Focus Readers) North Star Editions.

Hardy, Sheila Jackson & Hardy, P. Stephen. Extraordinary People: Extraordinary People Civil Rights Movement. 2006. (Extraordinary People Ser.). (ENG., Illus.). 288p. (J). (gr. 6-18). lib. bdg. 40.00 (978-0-516-25461-6(8), Children's Pr.) Scholastic Library Publishing.

Harris, Duchess. Civil Rights Sit-Ins. 2017. (Protest Movements Ser.). (ENG., Illus.). 48p. (J). (gr. 4-8). lib. bdg. 35.64 (978-1-5321-1396-3(X), 27694) ABDO Publishing Co.

TUV

Harris, Duchess & Head, Tom. Ruby Bridges & the Desegregation of American Schools. 2018. (Freedom's Promise Ser.). (ENG., Illus.). 48p. (J). (gr. 4-8). lib. bdg. 35.64 (978-1-5321-1774-9(4), 30836) ABDO Publishing Co.

Harris, Duchess & Wheeler, Jill C. Race in Sports Media Coverage. 2018. (Race & Sports Ser.). (ENG., Illus.). 112p. (J). (gr. 6-12). lib. bdg. 41.36 (978-1-5321-1674-2(8), 30600, Essential Library) ABDO Publishing Co.

Haskins, Jim. Delivering Justice: W. W. Law & the Fight for Civil Rights. Andrews, Benny, illus. 2008. (ENG.). 32p. (J). (gr. k-3). pap. 7.99 (978-0-7636-3880-1(3)) Candlewick Pr.

Haugen, David M., ed. Interracial Relationships, 1 vol. 2006. (At Issue Ser.). (ENG.). 104p. (gr. 10-12). 41.03 (978-0-7377-2390-8(4), 9bb6786c-4df7-46c6-8239-c38cbe557fa8); pap. 28.80 (978-0-7377-2391-5(2), 9603119c-8d11-4ebe-934e-fdde1bb90b87) Greenhaven Publishing LLC. (Greenhaven Publishing).

Henneberg, Susan, ed. Race in America, 1 vol. 2016. (Opposing Viewpoints Ser.). (ENG.). 208p. (YA). (gr. 10-12). pap. 34.80 (978-1-5345-0028-0(6), aeeebecc-869f-4874-95a1-ff12564b3ed1); lib. bdg. 50.43 (978-1-5345-0022-8(7), 5aced661-562f-43e5-8463-2e697dd7f025) Greenhaven Publishing LLC. (Greenhaven Publishing).

Herda, D. J. Slavery & Citizenship: The Dred Scott Case, 1 vol. 2016. (U. S. Supreme Court Landmark Cases Ser.). (ENG., Illus.). 128p. (J). (gr. 7-7). 38.93 (978-0-7660-8426-1(4), ffcb8d36-7c36-4d76-8da3-8ca5072dc032) Enslow Publishing, LLC.

Herzog, Brad. W Is for Welcome: A Celebration of America's Diversity. Carroll, Pam et al, illus. 2018. (ENG.). 32p. (J). (gr. 1-4). 17.99 (978-1-58536-402-2(9), 204404) Sleeping Bear Pr.

Hiber, Amanda, ed. Is the United States Ready for a Minority President?, 1 vol. 2007. (At Issue Ser.). (ENG., Illus.). 112p. (gr. 10-12). 41.03 (978-0-7377-3878-0(2), 33436de7-e1be-4d9e-a059-2a6fc759e904, Greenhaven Publishing) Greenhaven Publishing LLC.

Hinman, Bonnie. Eternal Vigilance: The Story of Ida B. Wells-Barnett. 2011. (Civil Rights Leaders Ser.). 128p. (gr. 6-10). lib. bdg. 28.95 (978-1-59935-111-7(0)) Reynolds, Morgan Inc.

Hinton, Kerry. The Black Power Movement & Civil Unrest, 1 vol. 2017. (Spotlight on the Civil Rights Movement Ser.). (ENG., Illus.). 48p. (J). (gr. 6-6). pap. 12.75 (978-1-5383-8016-1(1), 4bdedc04-7722-49e7-b025-982ca62992fc) Rosen Publishing Group, Inc., The.

Hoe, Susan C. Rosa Parks. 2009. (Sharing the American Dream Ser.). 64p. (YA). (gr. 7-12). 22.95 (978-1-4222-0597-6(5)) Mason Crest.

Hoena, Blake. Colin Kaepernick: Athletes Who Made a Difference. LeDoyen, Sam, illus. 2020. (Athletes Who Made a Difference Ser.). (ENG.). 32p. (J). (gr. 3-6). 27.99 (978-1-5415-7817-3(1), 0e5549d4-a64b-4b6f-b23b-6a04cc6d117b); pap. 8.99 (978-1-7284-0293-2(X), 0b88e6ab-3fce-449c-94dd-35cc2f8646aa) Lerner Publishing Group. (Graphic Universe™).

Holliday, Laurel. Dreaming in Color Living in Black & White: Our Own Stories of Growing up Black in America. 2012. (ENG.). 208p. (YA). (gr. 7). pap. 10.99 (978-1-4424-7177-1(8), Simon Pulse) Simon Pulse.

Honders, Christine. Mexican American Rights Movement, 1 vol. 2016. (Civic Participation: Working for Civil Rights Ser.). (ENG., Illus.). 32p. (J). (gr. 5-5). pap. 11.00 (978-1-4994-2684-7(4), 7d056249-1a63-41dd-bea6-5a72cc18ca10, PowerKids Pr.) Rosen Publishing Group, Inc., The.

Hooks, Gwendolyn. If You Were a Kid During the Civil Rights Movement. 2017. (If You Were a Kid Ser.). (ENG., Illus.). 32p. (J). lib. bdg. 26.00 (978-0-531-22384-0(1), Children's Pr.) Scholastic Library Publishing.

Hopkinson, Deborah. Sweet Land of Liberty, 1 vol. Jenkins, Leonard, illus. 2019. 32p. (J). (gr. 1-4). pap. 7.95 (978-1-68263-124-9(9)) Peachtree Publishing Co. Inc.

Houtman, Jacqueline, et al. Bayard Rustin: The Invisible Activist. 2014. (J). pap. (978-1-937768-58-4(9)) QuakerPress.

—Troublemaker for Justice: The Story of Bayard Rustin, the Man Behind the March on Washington. 2019. (ENG., Illus.). 172p. (YA). (gr. 8-12). pap. 13.95 (978-0-87286-765-9(X)) City Lights Bks.

Hurt, Avery Elizabeth. The Fight for Civil Rights, 1 vol. 2019. (Activism in Action: a History Ser.). (ENG.). 112p. (gr. 8-8). pap. 18.65 (978-1-5081-8540-6(9), fdddd27d-591b-485e-bc4d-972a3b2a39c0, Rosen Young Adult) Rosen Publishing Group, Inc., The.

Jakoubek, Robert. Martin Luther King Jr. 2008. (Black Americans of Achievement Legacy Edition Ser.). 112p. (gr. 6-12). pap. 11.95 (978-1-60413-328-8(7), Checkmark Bks.) Infobase Holdings, Inc.

Jd, Duchess Harris & Mooney, Carla. The One Percent. 2018. (Class in America Ser.). (ENG., Illus.). 112p. (J). (gr. 6-12). lib. bdg. 41.36 (978-1-5321-1410-6(9), 28802, Essential Library) ABDO Publishing Co.

Jd, Duchess Harris & Murray, Laura K. Class & Race. 2018. (Class in America Ser.). (ENG., Illus.). 112p. (J). (gr. 6-12). lib. bdg. 41.36 (978-1-5321-1406-9(0), 28794, Essential Library) ABDO Publishing Co.

Jeffrey, Gary. The Little Rock Nine & the Fight for Equal Education, 1 vol. 2012. (Graphic History of the Civil Rights Movement Ser.). (ENG., Illus.). 24p. (J). (gr. 3-3). lib. bdg. 26.60 (978-1-4339-7483-0(5), f8b2bcb2-4bfd-4b07-8022-90f9173c2140) Stevens, Gareth Publishing LLLP.

—Medgar Evers & the NAACP, 1 vol. 2012. (Graphic History of the Civil Rights Movement Ser.). (ENG.). 24p. (J). (gr. 3-3). pap. 9.15 (978-1-4339-7496-0(7), ca64b1d6-fefc-4c19-abc3-26d09adc0f65); lib. bdg. 26.60 (978-1-4339-7495-3(9), ea12e35b-f103-4170-b56f-5a87e44275c6) Stevens, Gareth Publishing LLLP.

—Rosa Parks & the Montgomery Bus Boycott, 1 vol. 2012. (Graphic History of the Civil Rights Movement Ser.). (ENG., Illus.). 24p. (J). (gr. 3-3). pap. 9.15 (978-1-4339-7500-4(9), 22d1d608-8b38-4dfe-bff0-ce7560a74e4c); lib. bdg. 26.60 (978-1-4339-7499-1(1), 184f7806-e906-404a-b9c8-b12a88f7caa0) Stevens, Gareth Publishing LLLP.

Jones, Naomi E. Ida B. Wells-Barnett: Suffragette & Social Activist, 1 vol. 2019. (African American Trailblazers Ser.). (ENG.). 128p. (gr. 9-9). pap. 22.16 (978-1-5026-4560-9(2), cb519ffa-ab7a-438d-b1e0-9a25e98d89c7) Cavendish Square Publishing LLC.

Kallen, Stuart A. A History of Free Blacks in America. 2006. (Lucent Library of Black History). (ENG., Illus.). 112p. (YA). (gr. 7-10). lib. bdg. 33.45 (978-1-59018-776-0(8), Lucent Bks.) Cengage Gale.

Kanefield, Teri. The Girl from the Tar Paper School: Barbara Rose Johns & the Advent of the Civil Rights Movement. 2014. (ENG., Illus.). 56p. (J). (gr. 5-9). 19.95 (978-1-4197-0796-4(5), 1005601, Abrams Bks. for Young Readers) Abrams, Inc.

Kemp, Kristin. Amazing Americans: Rosa Parks, 1 vol. rev. ed. 2014. (Social Studies: Informational Text Ser.). (ENG., Illus.). 32p. (gr. 3-4). pap. 11.99 (978-1-4333-7375-6(0)) Teacher Created Materials, Inc.

—Amazing Americans: Thurgood Marshall, 1 vol. rev. ed. 2014. (Social Studies: Informational Text Ser.). (ENG., Illus.). 32p. (gr. 3-4). pap. 11.99 (978-1-4333-7374-9(2)) Teacher Created Materials, Inc.

King, Martin Luther, Jr. I Have a Dream. 2007. (Illus.). 40p. (J). (gr. -1-3). 14.65 (978-0-7569-8119-8(0)) Perfection Learning Corp.

Klein, Carol Swartout. Painting for Peace in Ferguson. 2nd ed. 2015. (ENG.). 54p. (J). (gr. 2-3). 25.95 (978-0-9963901-0-1(3)); pap. 15.95 (978-0-9892079-9-7(4)) TreeHse. Publishing Group.

Levinson, Cynthia. The Youngest Marcher: The Story of Audrey Faye Hendricks, a Young Civil Rights Activist. Brantley-Newton, Vanessa, illus. 2017. (ENG.). 40p. (J). (gr. k-5). 18.99 (978-1-4814-0070-1(3)) Simon & Schuster, Inc.

Linde, Barbara M. Rosa Parks, 1 vol. 2011. (Civil Rights Crusaders Ser.). (ENG., Illus.). 24p. (gr. 2-3). (J). pap. 9.15 (978-1-4339-5696-6(9), 71cefba7-22f3-4354-98bd-7e94eafa0085, Gareth Stevens Learning Library); (YA). lib. bdg. 25.27 (978-1-4339-5694-2(2), 044c3bb3-585b-4515-90cb-1919fa7f338a) Stevens, Gareth Publishing LLLP.

Lo Bosco, Maryellen. Confronting Racism, 1 vol. 2017. (Speak up! Confronting Discrimination in Your Daily Life Ser.). (ENG., Illus.). 64p. (YA). (gr. 7-7). pap. 13.95 (978-1-5383-8176-2(1), 938354d9-232e-4616-a0a8-44bf707a611a) Rosen Publishing Group, Inc., The.

Lombardo, Jennifer. Unsung Heroes: Women of the Civil Rights Movement, 1 vol. annot. ed. 2019. (Lucent Library of Black History Ser.). (ENG.). 104p. (gr. 7-7). pap. 20.99 (978-1-5345-6868-6(9), 533375c4-a5f4-4900-b701-fcb39eca4f2c); lib. bdg. 41.03 (978-1-5345-6865-5(4), c025ad44-3f0f-4f0f-acbe-0f4f23f5571d) Greenhaven Publishing LLC. (Lucent Pr.).

Lowery, Lynda Blackmon. Turning 15 on the Road to Freedom: My Story of the 1965 Selma Voting Rights March. Loughran, P. J., illus. 2015. 128p. (YA). (gr. 7). 19.99 (978-0-8037-4123-2(5), Dial Bks) Penguin Young Readers Group.

Lowery, Zoe. Barack Obama & a "Post-Racial Society", 1 vol. 2015. (African American Experience: from Slavery to the Presidency Ser.). (ENG., Illus.). 80p. (J). (gr. 7-8). 35.47 (978-1-68048-051-1(0), fb6f6c35-22fd-494d-adbf-ccbaadc135d8, Britannica Educational Publishing) Rosen Publishing Group, Inc., The.

Lowery, Zoe, ed. Barack Obama & the Idea of a Postracial Society, 4 vols. 2015. (African American Experience: from Slavery to the Presidency Ser.). (ENG.). 80p. (YA). (gr. 7-8). 70.94 (978-1-68048-052-8(9), 9ad714e7-60ff-4038-a0fe-ed102443e9a5, Britannica Educational Publishing) Rosen Publishing Group, Inc., The.

Lucas, Eileen. Cracking the Wall: The Struggles of the Little Rock Nine. Anthony, Mark, illus. 2007. pap. 39.95 incl. audio compact disk (978-1-59519-943-0(8)); pap. 37.95 incl. audio (978-1-59519-939-3(X)) Live Oak Media.

Mahoney, Emily Jankowski. American Civil Rights Movement, 1 vol. 2016. (Civic Participation: Working for Civil Rights Ser.). (ENG., Illus.). 32p. (J). (gr. 5-5). pap. 11.00 (978-1-4994-2791-2(3), 488ee833-b57f-4c13-9b92-ba8674c4fe08, PowerKids Pr.) Rosen Publishing Group, Inc., The.

Main, Mary & Thomason, Cathy. African-Americans in Law & Politics. 2012. (J). pap. (978-1-4222-2391-8(4)) Mason Crest.

—African-Americans in Law & Politics. Hill, Marc Lamont, ed. 2012. (Major Black Contributions from Emancipation to Civil Rights Ser.). 64p. (J). (gr. 5). 22.95 (978-1-4222-2378-9(7)) Mason Crest.

Mara, Wil. DK Readers L3: the Story of Civil Rights. 2018. (DK Readers Level 3 Ser.). (ENG., Illus.). 64p. (J). (gr. 2-4). pap. 4.99 (978-1-4654-6927-4(3), DK Children) Dorling Kindersley Publishing, Inc.

—Rosa Parks: Mother of the Civil Rights Movement. 2014. (Rookie Biographies(tm) Ser.). (ENG.). 32p. (J). lib. bdg. 25.00 (978-0-531-20561-7(4)) Scholastic Library Publishing.

Marcovitz, Hal. Race Relations. 2008. (Gallup Major Trends & Events Ser.). (Illus.). 127p. (YA). (gr. 7-18). lib. bdg. 22.95 (978-1-59084-968-2(X)) Mason Crest.

—Teens & Race. Developed in Association with the Gallup Organization Staff, ed. 2013. (Gallup Youth Survey: Major Issues & Trends Ser.: 14). 112p. (J). (gr. 7-18). 24.95 (978-1-4222-2955-2(6)) Mason Crest.

McClaurin, Irma & Schomp, Virginia. Facing the Future, 1 vol. 2008. (Drama of African-American History Ser.). (ENG.). 80p. (gr. 6-6). lib. bdg. 38.36 (978-0-7614-2644-8(2), cc118c82-a975-414c-b9a1-3f23353a9b9d) Cavendish Square Publishing LLC.

Mckissack, Patricia & Mckissack, Fredrick. Ida B. Wells-Barnett: Fighter for Justice, 1 vol. 2013. (Famous African Americans Ser.). (ENG.). 24p. (gr. k-2). pap. 10.35 (978-1-4644-0198-5(5), eb7e9a8e-6b17-4790-bf93-adb0f9aff98b, Enslow Elementary); (Illus.). 25.27 (978-0-7660-4108-0(5), f37a0a7c-6b05-4e1f-9f84-ee2615e0615f) Enslow Publishing, LLC.

McNeese, Tim. Plessy V. Ferguson. 2006. (ENG., Illus.). 136p. (gr. 5-9). lib. bdg. 32.95 (978-0-7910-9237-8(2), P114571, Facts On File) Infobase Holdings, Inc.

Michelson, Richard. As Good As Anybody: Martin Luther King, Jr. , & Abraham Joshua Heschel's Amazing March Toward Freedom. ón, Raul, illus. 2013. (ENG.). 40p. (J). (gr. 1-4). 8.99 (978-0-385-75387-6(X), Dragonfly Bks.) Random Hse. Children's Bks.

Miller, Derek. The African American Press, 1 vol. 2018. (Fourth Estate: Journalism in North America Ser.). (ENG.). 112p. (gr. 8-8). lib. bdg. 44.50 (978-1-5026-3479-5(1), 9fe62cd8-8829-474e-bfc5-a37f4fb3ab94) Cavendish Square Publishing LLC.

Miller, Jake. The March from Selma to Montgomery: African Americans Demand the Vote, 1 vol. 2003. (Library of the Civil Rights Movement Ser.). (ENG., Illus.). 24p. (J). (gr. 3-3). lib. bdg. 26.27 (978-0-8239-6254-9(7), 3898752a-1469-4877-9067-18fa40a1c37f, PowerKids Pr.) Rosen Publishing Group, Inc., The.

Mitchell Haugen, Hayley, ed. Race in Ralph Ellison's Invisible Man, 1 vol. 2011. (Social Issues in Literature Ser.). (ENG., Illus.). 168p. (gr. 10-12). 48.03 (978-0-7377-5811-5(2), 847eecda-dc07-4a37-869a-44d7c7028a97); pap. 33.00 (978-0-7377-5812-2(0), b8072bcf-a3a4-4612-a72f-04ad477f4070) Greenhaven Publishing LLC. (Greenhaven Publishing).

—Racism, 1 vol. 2007. (Social Issues Firsthand Ser.). (ENG.). 112p. (gr. 10-12). lib. bdg. 39.93 (978-0-7377-2901-6(5), bae3b51f-8f16-4541-a40c-3b32c091847d, Greenhaven Publishing) Greenhaven Publishing LLC.

Mooney, Carla. Confronting Discrimination Against Immigrants, 1 vol. 2017. (Speak up! Confronting Discrimination in Your Daily Life Ser.). (ENG.). 64p. (YA). (gr. 7-7). pap. 13.95 (978-1-5383-8164-9(8), 9d9f0d41-7d36-430b-9309-a1eddf8463a8, Rosen Young Adult) Rosen Publishing Group, Inc., The.

Morretta, Alison. Ida B. Wells-Barnett & the Crusade Against Lynching, 1 vol. 2016. (Primary Sources of the Civil Rights Movement Ser.). (ENG., Illus.). 64p. (gr. 6-6). 35.93 (978-1-5026-1874-0(5), 44127a2f-3bba-4d97-985b-e0917805406e) Cavendish Square Publishing LLC.

Myers, Walter Dean. Ida B. Wells: Let the Truth Be Told. Christensen, Bonnie, illus. 2008. (ENG.). 40p. (J). (gr. -1-3). 17.99 (978-0-06-027705-5(X), Amistad) HarperCollins Pubs.

Nathan, Amy. Round & Round Together: Taking a Merry-Go-Round Ride into the Civil Rights Movement. 2011. (Nautilus Ser.). (ENG., Illus.). 250p. (YA). (gr. 7-12). pap. 14.95 (978-1-58988-071-9(4), 1325047) Dry, Paul Bks., Inc.

National Geographic Learning. Reading Expeditions (Social Studies: People Who Changed America): the Civil Rights Movement. 2006. (Nonfiction Reading & Writing Workshops Ser.). (ENG., Illus.). 40p. (J). pap. 21.95 (978-0-7922-8628-8(6)) CENGAGE Learning.

Niver, Heather Moore. Real-World Projects to Explore the Civil Rights Movement, 1 vol. 2018. (Project-Based Learning in Social Studies). (ENG., Illus.). 64p. (J). (gr. 5-5). 37.47 (978-1-5081-8213-9(2), 03d6d6ab-d2bd-4a35-92d1-8c9d61a2d717) Rosen Publishing Group, Inc., The.

Ohlin, Nancy. The Civil Rights Movement. Simó, Roger, illus. 2017. (Blast Back! Ser.). (ENG.). 112p. (J). (gr. 2-5). 16.99 (978-1-4998-0455-3(5)); pap. 5.99 (978-1-4998-0454-6(7)) Little Bee Books Inc.

O'Maley, Elizabeth. Bones on the Ground. 2014. (J). (978-0-87195-362-9(5)) Indiana Historical Society.

Orr, Tamra. Coping with Racial Inequality, 1 vol. 2017. (Coping (2017-2020) Ser.). (ENG., Illus.). 112p. (J). (gr. 7-7). 40.13 (978-1-5081-7396-0(6), dd44a0c7-946c-4929-a399-f55a8518494e, Rosen Young Adult) Rosen Publishing Group, Inc., The.

Orr, Tamra B. The Civil Rights Movement: Advocating for Equality, 1 vol. 2018. (American History Ser.). (ENG.). 104p. (gr. 7-7). 41.03 (978-1-5345-6418-3(7), 424c8eec-7528-4285-ac78-2f8121be0f47, Lucent Pr.) Greenhaven Publishing LLC.

Osborne, Linda Barrett. Miles to Go for Freedom: Segregation & Civil Rights in the Jim Crow Years. 2012. (ENG., Illus.). 128p. (J). (gr. 7-17). 25.99 (978-1-4197-0020-0(0), 691901) Abrams, Inc.

Otfinoski, Steven. The 1990s To 2010, 1 vol. 2010. (Hispanic America Ser.). (ENG.). 80p. (gr. 5-5). 36.93 (978-0-7614-4180-9(8), b13393c9-faa0-4f43-b885-c5804ffb0006) Cavendish Square Publishing LLC.

Parks, Peggy J. How Prevalent Is Racism in Society? 2014. (In Controversy Ser.). (ENG., Illus.). 96p. (J). lib. bdg. (978-1-60152-716-5(0)) ReferencePoint Pr., Inc.

Partridge, Elizabeth. Marching for Freedom: Walk Together Children & Don't You Grow Weary. 2009. (ENG.). 80p. (J). (gr. 5-18). 19.99 (978-0-670-01189-6(4), Viking Books for Young Readers) Penguin Young Readers Group.

Peacock, Thomas Love & Wisuri, Marlene. To Be Free: Understanding & eliminating Racism. 2010. (ENG., illus.). 104p. (J). 24.00 (978-1-890434-80-9(9)) Afton Historical Society Pr.

Perritano, John. Free at Last! How the Freeing of the Slaves Changed American History. 2008. (Graphic America Ser.). (ENG., Illus.). 32p. (J). (gr. 3-6). pap. (978-0-7787-4212-8(1)); lib. bdg. (978-0-7787-4185-5(0)) Crabtree Publishing Co.

Perry, M. LaVora. A History of the Civil Rights Movement. 2012. (J). pap. (978-1-4222-2395-6(7)) Mason Crest.

—A History of the Civil Rights Movement. Hill, Marc Lamont, ed. 2012. (Major Black Contributions from Emancipation to Civil Rights Ser.). 64p. (J). (gr. 5). 22.95 (978-1-4222-2382-6(5)) Mason Crest.

Pferdehirt, Julia. Blue Jenkins: Working for Workers. 2011. (Badger Biographies Ser.). (ENG., Illus.). 160p. (J). pap. 12.95 (978-0-87020-427-2(0)) Wisconsin Historical Society.

Prado, Emilly. Examining Assimilation, 1 vol. 2018. (Racial Literacy Ser.). (ENG.). 80p. (gr. 7-7). 37.60 (978-1-9785-0469-1(1), d5bc07b4-1e63-49e8-98c3-d656bf708907) Enslow Publishing, LLC.

Raatma, Lucia, et al. Civil Rights Movement: Then & Now. 2018. (America: 50 Years of Change Ser.). (ENG., Illus.). 64p. (J). (gr. 5-9). lib. bdg. 34.65 (978-1-5435-0387-6(X), 137216, Capstone Pr.) Capstone.

Rajczak Nelson, Kristen. Inside the Civil Rights Movement, 1 vol. 2017. (Eyewitness to History Ser.). (ENG.). 32p. (J). (gr. 4-5). pap. 11.50 (978-1-5382-1153-3(X), 954bf577-dbde-4334-b29e-a7dbb7261ac1) Stevens, Gareth Publishing LLLP.

Rappaport, Doreen. Nobody Gonna Turn Me 'Round: Stories & Songs of the Civil Rights Movement. Evans, Shane W., illus. 2008. (ENG.). 64p. (J). (gr. 4-7). pap. 9.99 (978-0-7636-3892-4(7)) Candlewick Pr.

Rauf, Don & Fireside, Harvey. Separate but Equal: Plessy V. Ferguson, 1 vol. 2016. (U. S. Supreme Court Landmark Cases Ser.). (ENG., Illus.). 128p. (gr. 7-7). 38.93 (978-0-7660-8434-6(5), f5084a60-474b-4f82-85ef-b3531537a699) Enslow Publishing, LLC.

Raum, Elizabeth. The Life of Ruby Bridges. 2019. (Sequence Change Maker Biographies Ser.). (ENG.). 32p. (J). (gr. 2-5). lib. bdg. (978-1-68151-679-0(9), 10811) Amicus.

Regis, Frankye. A Voice from the Civil Rights Era, 1 vol. 2004. (Voices of Twentieth-Century Conflict Ser.). (ENG., Illus.). 184p. (C). 47.00 (978-0-313-32998-2(2), 900297270, Bloomsbury Academic) Bloomsbury Publishing Plc GBR. Dist: Macmillan.

Reynolds, Jason & Kendi, Ibram X. Stamped (for Kids) Racism, Antiracism, & You. Baker, Rachelle, illus. 2021. (ENG.). 176p. (J). (gr. 1-5). 15.99 (978-0-316-16758-1(4)) Little, Brown Bks. for Young Readers.

—Stamped: Racism, Antiracism, & You: A Remix of the National Book Award-Winning Stamped from the Beginning. 2020. (ENG.). 320p. (YA). (gr. 7-17). 18.99 (978-0-316-45369-1(2)) Little, Brown Bks. for Young Readers.

Rhuday-Perkovich, Olugbemisola. The Civil Rights Movement (a Step into History) (Library Edition) 2018. (Step into History Ser.). (ENG., Illus.). 144p. (J). (gr. 5-8). lib. bdg. 36.00 (978-0-531-22688-9(3), Children's Pr.) Scholastic Library Publishing.

Rissman, Rebecca. Race & Policing. 2017. (Race in America Ser.). (ENG., Illus.). 112p. (J). (gr. 6-12). lib. bdg. 41.36 (978-1-5321-1035-1(9), 25646, Essential Library) ABDO Publishing Co.

Robinson, Sharon. Promises to Keep: How Jackie Robinson Changed America: How Jackie Robinson Changed America. 2004. (ENG., Illus.). 64p. (gr. 4-7). 18.99 (978-0-439-42592-6(1)) Scholastic, Inc.

Robinson, Tom. Malcolm X: Rights Activist & Nation of Islam Leader, 1 vol. 2013. (Essential Lives Set 8 Ser.). (ENG.). 112p. (YA). (gr. 6-12). lib. bdg. 41.36 (978-1-61783-893-4(4), 6765, Essential Library) ABDO Publishing Co.

Rogers, Amy B. What's Racism?, 1 vol. 2017. (What's the Issue? Ser.). (ENG.). 24p. (J). (gr. 3-3). pap. 9.25 (978-1-5345-2505-4(X), f6926bbd-8465-405d-84e3-804755b6c128); lib. bdg. 26.23 (978-1-5345-2437-8(1), d95e1bd6-aa53-420a-9ba1-dfe2bb1256a2) Greenhaven Publishing LLC.

Rubin, Susan Goldman. Give Us the Vote! Over Two Hundred Years of Fighting for the Ballot. 2020. (ENG., Illus.). 128p. (J) (gr. 5). 19.99 (978-0-8234-3957-7(7)) Holiday Hse., Inc.

Sandeen, Del. Coping with Racial Profiling, 1 vol. 2019. (Coping (2017-2020) Ser.). (ENG., Illus.). 112p. (J). (gr. 7-7). 40.13 (978-1-5081-8740-0(1), e33673b6-5575-43da-a8ac-39fa9124719e) Rosen Publishing Group, Inc., The.

Sanna, Ellyn. Native North American Indians. 2012. (Gallup Guides for Youth Facing Persistent Prejudice Ser.). 64p. (J). (gr. 7-8). 22.95 (978-1-4222-2469-4(4)); pap. 9.95 (978-1-4222-2478-6(3)) Mason Crest.

Schuetz, Rachael Law. The Long Road to Change: An American Story of Civil Rights & Barack Obama's Journey to the White House. 2009. (Illus.). 36p. (J). 16.00 (978-0-615-27983-1(X)) NRS Enterprises.

Schwartz, Heather E. Freedom Riders: A Primary Source Exploration of the Struggle for Racial Justice. 2014. (We Shall Overcome Ser.). (ENG.). 32p. (J). (gr. 3-6). lib. bdg. 27.99 (978-1-4914-0222-1(9), 125793, Capstone Pr.) Capstone.

Sebree, Chet'la & Sirimarco, Elizabeth. Historical Sources on the Civil Rights Movement, 1 vol. 2019. (America's Story Ser.). (ENG., Illus.). 144p. (J). (gr. 8-8). pap. 22.16 (978-1-5026-4089-5(9), 34535ecb-5ee4-45c5-acf2-bd67fb582411) Cavendish Square Publishing LLC.

Shea, Therese. Rosa Parks, 1 vol. 2014. (Britannica Beginner Bios Ser.). (ENG., Illus.). 32p. (J). (gr. 2-3). 26.06 (978-1-62275-697-1(5), 620224ac-0b2f-49de-a43f-50329a4ef347, Britannica Educational Publishing) Rosen Publishing Group, Inc., The.

Shelton, Paula Young. Child of the Civil Rights Movement. ón, Raul, illus. 2013. (ENG.). 48p. (J). (gr. -1-3). 8.99 (978-0-385-37606-8(5), Dragonfly Bks.) Random Hse. Children's Bks.

Shoup, Kate. The Freedom Riders: Civil Rights Activists Fighting Segregation, 1 vol. 2017. (Peaceful Protesters Ser.). (ENG.). 112p. (YA). (gr. 9-9). 44.50 (978-1-5026-3118-3(0), 69d9e4c1-7c0f-4c7c-8bbd-391857d312a1); pap. 20.99 (978-1-5026-3399-6(X), 88255d4c-27c7-46a9-9c5d-476581ae0602) Cavendish Square Publishing LLC.

Staley, Erin. Martin Luther King Jr. & the Speech That Inspired the World, 1 vol. 2014. (Celebration of the Civil Rights Movement Ser.). (ENG.). 80p. (YA). (gr. 6-6). 37.47 (978-1-4777-7745-9(8), 8b6a61dd-ecba-4719-8f88-7e12ebc34fee) Rosen Publishing Group, Inc., The.

Staton, Hilarie. Civil Rights. 2015. (Uncovering the Past: Analyzing Primary Sources Ser.). (ENG.). 48p. (J). (gr. 6-9). 21.75 (978-1-5311-8691-3(2)) Perfection Learning Corp.

Staton, Hilarie N. Civil Rights. 2015. (Uncovering the Past: Analyzing Primary Sources Ser.). (ENG., Illus.). 48p. (J). (gr. 5-6). (978-0-7787-1549-8(3)) Crabtree Publishing Co.

Takaki, Ronald. A Different Mirror for Young People: A History of Multicultural America. 2012. (For Young People Ser.). (Illus.). 384p. (J). (gr. 5). pap. 22.95 *(978-1-60980-416-9(3),* Triangle Square) Seven Stories Pr.

Taylor, Charlotte. The United States: a Melting Pot, 1 vol. 2020. (Being a U. S. Citizen Ser.). (ENG.). 24p. (gr. 1-2). pap. 10.35 *(978-1-9785-1755-4(6),* d09067b2-7a80-40f3-bb12-79a58f1f30c9) Enslow Publishing, LLC.

Terp, Gail. Nonviolent Resistance in the Civil Rights Movement, 1 vol. 2015. (Stories of the Civil Rights Movement Ser.). (ENG., Illus.). 48p. (J). (gr. 4-8). 35.64 *(978-1-62403-882-2(4),* 18134) ABDO Publishing Co.

Tisdale, Rachel. The Little Rock Nine, 1 vol., 1. 2014. (We Shall Overcome Ser.). (ENG.). 32p. (J). (gr. 4-5). 28.93 *(978-1-4777-6057-4(1),* 4a01ffb3-b725-4d3c-8134-23788bf3affe, PowerKids Pr.) Rosen Publishing Group, Inc., The.

—The Montgomery Bus Boycott, 1 vol., 1. 2014. (We Shall Overcome Ser.). (ENG., Illus.). 32p. (J). (gr. 4-5). 28.93 *(978-1-4777-6053-6(9),* d5f8c9ba-72f0-4dd3-adfb-d3a079ad26eb, PowerKids Pr.) Rosen Publishing Group, Inc., The.

Toth, Henrietta. The Murder of Emmett Till, 1 vol. 2017. (Spotlight on the Civil Rights Movement Ser.). (ENG., Illus.). 48p. (J). (gr. 6-6). pap. 12.75 *(978-1-5383-8054-3(4),* 3b16bc12-3c08-48ab-bbe3-b39c57cdc263) Rosen Publishing Group, Inc., The.

Tougas, Shelley. Birmingham 1963: How a Photograph Rallied Civil Rights Support, 1 vol. 2010. (Captured History Ser.). (ENG., Illus.). 64p. (J). (gr. 5-7). pap. 8.95 *(978-0-7565-4446-1(7),* 115527, Compass Point Bks.) Capstone.

—Little Rock Girl 1957: How a Photograph Changed the Fight for Integration, 1 vol. 2011. (Captured History Ser.). (ENG.). 64p. (J). (gr. 5-8). lib. bdg. 35.32 *(978-0-7565-4440-9(8),* 114961); pap. 8.95 *(978-0-7565-4512-3(9),* 116901) Capstone. (Compass Point Bks.).

Tracy, Kathleen. The Life & Times of Rosa Parks. 2008. (Illus.). 48p. (J). (gr. 4-8). lib. bdg. 29.95 *(978-1-58415-666-6(X))* Mitchell Lane Pubs.

Uschan, Michael V. The Civil Rights Movement, 1 vol. 2010. (American History Ser.). (ENG.). 128p. (gr. 7-7). 41.03 *(978-1-4205-0261-9(1),* b4cb94dc-a14b-4853-9b95-77c46af42b7d, Lucent Pr.) Greenhaven Publishing LLC.

Wagner, Heather Lehr. Benjamin Hooks. 2003. (African American Leaders Ser.). (ENG., Illus.). 112p. (gr. 6-12). 30.00 *(978-0-7910-7685-9(7),* P113974, Facts On File) Infobase Holdings, Inc.

Walsh, Francis & O'Hern, Kerri. The Montgomery Bus Boycott, 1 vol. 2005. (Graphic Histories Ser.). (ENG., Illus.). 32p. (gr. 3-3). lib. bdg. 29.67 *(978-0-8368-6205-8(8),* 6acefa0e-056d-4ebf-a09f-d82cf79f9173) Stevens, Gareth Publishing LLLP.

Weatherford, Carole Boston. The Beatitudes: From Slavery to Civil Rights. Ladwig, Tim, illus. 2009. (ENG.). 36p. (J). (gr. 3-7). 17.00 *(978-0-8028-5352-3(8),* Eerdmans Bks For Young Readers) Eerdmans, William B. Publishing Co.

Welch, Catherine A. Ida B. Wells-Barnett: Powerhouse with a Pen. 2005. (Trailblazers Biographies Ser.). (Illus.). 112p. (gr. 5-9). 27.93 *(978-1-57505-352-3(7))* Lerner Publishing Group.

Wilkerson, Isabel. Caste (Adapted for Young Adults) 2022. (ENG.). 352p. (YA). (gr. 7). 18.99 *(978-0-593-42794-1(7));* lib. bdg. 21.99 *(978-0-593-42795-8(5))* Random Hse. Children's Bks. (Delacorte Pr.).

Wilkerson, Isabel, contrib. by. Caste (Adapted for Young Adults) 2023. (ENG.). 352p. (YA). (gr. 7). pap. 12.99 ***(978-0-593-42797-2(1),*** Ember) Random Hse. Children's Bks.

Winter, Max. Civil Rights Movement, 1 vol. 2014. (African-American History Ser.). (ENG.). 48p. (J). (gr. 4-8). lib. bdg. 35.64 *(978-1-62403-145-8(5),* 1171) ABDO Publishing Co.

Woog, Adam. The Fight Renewed: The Civil Rights Movement. 2005. (Lucent Library of Black History). (ENG., Illus.). 112p. (YA). (gr. 7-10). lib. bdg. 33.45 *(978-1-59018-701-2(6),* Lucent Bks.) Cengage Gale.

World Book, Inc. Staff, contrib. by. African American Civil Rights Movement. 2010. (J). *(978-0-7166-1500-2(2))* World Bk., Inc.

Worth, Richard. The 1950s To 1960s, 1 vol. 2010. (Hispanic America Ser.). (ENG.). 80p. (gr. 5-5). 36.93 *(978-0-7614-4177-9(8),* be97564a-71ed-4280-b913-1ef20a16eaaa) Cavendish Square Publishing LLC.

Zeiger, Jennifer. The Civil Rights Movement. 2011. (Cornerstones of Freedom, Third Ser.). (ABK., Illus.). 64p. (J). lib. bdg. 30.00 *(978-0-531-25029-7(6),* Children's Pr.) Scholastic Library Publishing.

—The Civil Rights Movement (Cornerstones of Freedom: Third Series) 2011. (Cornerstones of Freedom. Third Ser.). (ENG., Illus.). 64p. (J). (gr. 4-6). pap. 8.95 *(978-0-531-26554-3(4),* Children's Pr.) Scholastic Library Publishing.

UNITED STATES—RELIGION

Allen, John. Threats to Civil Liberties: Religion. 2018. (Threats to Civil Liberties Ser.). (ENG.). 80p. (J). (gr. 6-12). 39.93 *(978-1-68282-453-5(5))* ReferencePoint Pr., Inc.

Capaccio, George. Religion. 2014. (Illus.). 80p. (J). pap. *(978-1-62712-889-6(1))* Cavendish Square Publishing LLC.

—Religion in Colonial America, 1 vol. 2014. (Life in Colonial America Ser.). (ENG., Illus.). 80p. (gr. 6-6). lib. bdg. 37.36 *(978-1-62712-888-9(3),* dd434c65-c2f8-4baa-aa28-65ef529e27e6) Cavendish Square Publishing LLC.

Haugen, David M. & Musser, Susan, eds. Religion in America, 1 vol. 2010. (Opposing Viewpoints Ser.). (ENG.). 240p. (gr. 10-12). 50.43 *(978-0-7377-4988-5(1),* b7320708-da2c-4df8-aaee-5fea43dbf302); pap. 34.80 *(978-0-7377-4989-2(X),* 9251eb63-8e01-4e18-acee-445ebe80ef4b) Greenhaven Publishing LLC. (Greenhaven Publishing).

Melman, Anna. Muslims in America. 2010. (World of Islam Ser.). (Illus.). 64p. (YA). (gr. 4-7). lib. bdg. 22.95 *(978-1-4222-0535-8(5))* Mason Crest.

Nardo, Don. Religious Beliefs in Colonial America, 1 vol. 2010. (Lucent Library of Historical Eras Ser.). (ENG., Illus.). 96p. (gr. 7-10). 41.03 *(978-1-4205-0266-4(2),* 4dad8aa5-f082-425b-9308-a4e089b0bc4c, Lucent Pr.) Greenhaven Publishing LLC.

Smith-Llera, Danielle, et al. United States by Region. 2016. (United States by Region Ser.). (ENG.). 32p. (J). (gr. 3-6). pap., pap., pap. 39.75 *(978-1-5157-2466-7(2),* 25131, Capstone Pr.) Capstone.

Tiner, John. The Story of the Pledge of Allegiance: Discovering Our Nations Heritage. 2003. (Discovering Our Nation's Heritage Ser.). (Illus.). 48p. (J). 6.99 *(978-0-89051-393-4(7),* Master Books) New Leaf Publishing Group.

UNITED STATES—SOCIAL CONDITIONS

Allen, John. School Shootings & Violence (Thinking Critically) 2019. (Thinking Critically Ser.). (ENG.). 80p. (J). (gr. 6-12). 41.27 *(978-1-68282-663-8(5))* ReferencePoint Pr., Inc.

America Debates, 10 vols., Set. Incl. America Debates Civil Liberties & Terrorism. Freedman, Jeri. lib. bdg. 37.13 *(978-1-4042-1927-4(7),* fde63664-951f-4dfc-ab55-ae6531a981b7); America Debates Global Warming: Crisis or Myth? Robinson, Matthew. lib. bdg. 37.13 *(978-1-4042-1925-0(0),* c5bbec49-cbcc-419d-9683-5edb38f138b6); America Debates Privacy Versus Security. Freedman, Jeri. lib. bdg. 37.13 *(978-1-4042-1929-8(3),* 2eb69dee-61d6-4b38-aa54-f78f558adcd3); America Debates Stem Cell Research. Freedman, Jeri. lib. bdg. 37.13 *(978-1-4042-1928-1(5),* c346cbf7-3ff5-4b79-b664-a38d8b1a3d0f); America Debates United States Policy on Immigration. Ambrosek, Renee. lib. bdg. 37.13 *(978-1-4042-1924-3(2),* f0cb50ae-84e2-4ebc-b1bd-6c1f343be16c); (Illus.). 64p. (YA). (gr. 5-6). 2007. (America Debates Ser.). (ENG.). 2007. Set lib. bdg. 185.65 *(978-1-4042-1100-1(4),* c31750e3-e23f-42c2-8c58-d334a0c8a2ef) Rosen Publishing Group, Inc., The.

Amidon Lusted, Marcia. The Great Depression: Experience the 1930s from the Dust Bowl to the New Deal. Casteel, Tom, illus. 2016. (Inquire & Investigate Ser.). (ENG.). 128p. (J). (gr. 6-10). 22.95 *(978-1-61930-336-2(1),* 25f2b5db-fb04-4b75-85cd-8cd865e5abb5) Nomad Pr.

—The Great Depression: Experience the 1930's from the Dust Bowl to the New Deal. Casteel, Tom, illus. 2016. (Inquire & Investigate Ser.). (ENG.). 128p. (J). (gr. 6-10). pap. 17.95 *(978-1-61930-340-9(X),* ce2d6583-b839-4faf-a77d-dd176911c683) Nomad Pr.

—The Roaring Twenties: Discover the Era of Prohibition, Flappers, & Jazz. Keller, Jennifer, illus. 2014. (Inquire & Investigate Ser.). (ENG.). 128p. (J). (gr. 6-10). 22.95 *(978-1-61930-260-0(8),* 3fbac5e6-72fa-49c6-bfc5-f8a5e498939a) Nomad Pr.

Anderson, Dale. The Home Fronts in the Civil War, 1 vol. 2004. (World Almanac(r) Library of the Civil War Ser.). (ENG., Illus.). 48p. (gr. 5-8). lib. bdg. 33.67 *(978-0-8368-5587-6(6),* f82d4d42-0c19-4e83-844b-321427333a72, Gareth Stevens Secondary Library) Stevens, Gareth Publishing LLLP.

Anthony, David. The Progressive Era: Activists Change America, 1 vol. 2017. (American History Ser.). (ENG.). 104p. (gr. 7-7). lib. bdg. 41.03 *(978-1-5345-6139-7(0),* c568f833-c9a7-40f2-ae90-b287a0d737ca, Lucent Pr.) Greenhaven Publishing LLC.

Bauchner, Elizabeth. Teen Minorities in Rural North America: Growing up Different. 2009. (Youth in Rural North America Ser.). (Illus.). 96p. (YA). (gr. 7-18). lib. bdg. 22.95 *(978-1-4222-0014-8(0))* Mason Crest.

Bell, Samantha S. Children in the Holocaust. 2018. (Children in History Ser.). (ENG., Illus.). 48p. (J). (gr. 5-6). pap. 11.95 *(978-1-63517-977-4(7),* 1635179777); lib. bdg. 34.21 *(978-1-63517-876-0(2),* 1635178762) North Star Editions. (Focus Readers).

Benson, Kerry Elizabeth. ADA & Your Rights at School & Work, 1 vol. 2019. (Equal Access: Fighting for Disability Protections Ser.). (ENG.). 64p. (gr. 5-5). pap. 13.95 *(978-1-5081-8327-3(9),* 807f97a8-3fff-4ab9-97b4-d137896f3dfb) Rosen Publishing Group, Inc., The.

Boehm, Richard G., et al. Game Time! United States. 2003. (Harcourt Brace Social Studies). (gr. k-7). 7.80 *(978-0-15-312367-2(2))* Harcourt Schl. Pubs.

Braun, Eric. Never Again: The Parkland Shooting & the Teen Activists Leading a Movement. 2019. (Gateway Biographies Ser.). (ENG., Illus.). 48p. (J). (gr. 4-8). lib. bdg. 31.99 *(978-1-5415-5270-8(9),* 1d67ab4e-63d9-4275-93c9-da0dd22e15c6, Lerner Pubns.) Lerner Publishing Group.

—Protest Movements: Then & Now. 2018. (America: 50 Years of Change Ser.). (ENG., Illus.). 64p. (J). (gr. 5-9). lib. bdg. 34.65 *(978-1-5435-0385-2(3),* 137210, Capstone Pr.) Capstone.

Brill, Marlene Targ. America in the 1900s. 2009. (Decades of Twentieth-Century America Ser.). (ENG.). 144p. (gr. 5-12). lib. bdg. 38.60 *(978-0-8225-3436-5(3))* Lerner Publishing Group.

Brindell Fradin, Dennis. 9/11/01, 1 vol. 2010. (Turning Points in U. S. History Ser.). (ENG.). 48p. (gr. 4-4). 34.07 *(978-0-7614-4259-2(6),* 75002057-d3bf-4e16-9278-148fda1efa7d) Cavendish Square Publishing LLC.

Bringle, Jennifer. Homelessness in America Today, 1 vol. 2010. (In the News Ser.). (ENG.). 64p. (YA). (gr. 6-6). pap. 13.95 *(978-1-4488-1683-5(1),* 6241e3be-e844-4705-9a45-558e2a54ac7a); lib. bdg. 37.13 *(978-1-4358-9451-8(0),* 3eb95f88-779a-475e-9f88-7b03a108f42e) Rosen Publishing Group, Inc., The.

Brown Bear Books. The War & U. S. Society. 2013. (NAM: the Vietnam War Ser.). (ENG.). 48p. (J). (gr. 5-8). 37.10 *(978-1-78121-045-1(4),* 16765) Brown Bear Bks.

Brown, Harriet & Witowski, Teri. Kit's World: A Girl's-Eye View of the Great Depression. Rane, Walter & Hood, Philip, illus. 2008. 30p. (YA). (gr. 3-18). 24.95 *(978-1-59369-459-3(8))* American Girl Publishing, Inc.

Cartlidge, Cherese. Homeless Youth. 2016. (ENG., Illus.). 80p. (J). (gr. 5-12). *(978-1-60152-978-7(3))* ReferencePoint Pr., Inc.

Catalano, Angela. Community Plans: Making Choices about Money in Communities, 1 vol. 2004. (Exploring Community Ser.). (ENG., Illus.). 24p. (gr. 2-3). pap. 8.25 *(978-1-4042-5014-7(X),* cf7a6c2b-c08f-4a8a-8b97-d626272fc608, PowerKids Pr.) Rosen Publishing Group, Inc., The.

—Community Resources: The Land & the People in Communities, 1 vol. 2004. (Exploring Community Ser.). (ENG., Illus.). 24p. (gr. 2-3). pap. 8.25 *(978-1-4042-5016-1(6),* 8a337dc2-4913-41f0-ac19-4c867ba25828, PowerKids Pr.) Rosen Publishing Group, Inc., The.

Center for Learning Network Staff. Violence in America. 2005. (Social Studies Ser.). 83p. (YA). tchr. ed., spiral bd. 20.95 *(978-1-56077-793-9(1))* Center for Learning, The.

Chastain, Zachary. Rooting for the Home Team: Sports in The 1800s. 2009. (Daily Life in America in the 1800s Ser.). 64p. (YA). (gr. 7-18). pap. 9.95 *(978-1-4222-1859-4(7));* lib. bdg. 22.95 *(978-1-4222-1786-3(8))* Mason Crest.

Coletti, Sharon. Everything You Need to Supplement U. S. & State Studies. 2005. (YA). Pt. 1. ring bd. 249.95 *(978-1-933558-08-0(3))*Pt. 2. ring bd. 249.95 *(978-1-933558-09-7(1))* InspirEd Educators.

Combs, Maggie. Postwar United States. 2011. (Explorer Library: Language Arts Explorer Ser.). (ENG.). 32p. (gr. 4-8). pap. 14.21 *(978-1-61080-284-0(5),* 201207); (Illus.). lib. bdg. 32.07 *(978-1-61080-196-6(2),* 201168) Cherry Lake Publishing.

Corrigan, Jim. The 1990s Decade in Photos: The Rise of Technology, 1 vol. 2010. (Amazing Decades in Photos Ser.). (ENG., Illus.). 64p. (J). (gr. 5-6). lib. bdg. 31.93 *(978-0-7660-3138-8(1),* 720edcd3-4ebe-42c2-89d7-67e7e5161c97) Enslow Publishing, LLC.

—The 2000s Decade in Photos: A New Millennium, 1 vol. 2010. (Amazing Decades in Photos Ser.). (ENG., Illus.). 64p. (gr. 5-6). lib. bdg. 31.93 *(978-0-7660-3139-5(X),* 73e773aa-d5a7-4233-a994-b885f3b94432) Enslow Publishing, LLC.

Daily Life in America in the 1800s, 15 vols., Set. Incl. America at War: Military Conflicts, Home & Abroad in the 1800s. Strange, Matthew. pap. 9.95 *(978-1-4222-1851-8(1));* Bleeding, Blistering, & Purging: Health & Medicine in The 1800s. Strange, Matthew. pap. 9.95 *(978-1-4222-1848-8(1));* Buggies, Bicycles & Iron Horses: Transportation in the 1800s. McIntosh, Kenneth. pap. 9.95 *(978-1-4222-1849-5(X));* Cornmeal & Cider: Food & Drink in the 1800s. Chastain, Zachary. pap. 9.95 *(978-1-4222-1850-1(3));* From the Parlor to the Altar: Romance & Marriage in The 1800s. Chastain, Zachary. pap. 9.95 *(978-1-4222-1852-5(X));* Guardians of the Home: Women's Lives in The 1800s. Strange, Matthew. pap. 9.95 *(978-1-4222-1853-2(8));* Home Sweet Home: Around the House in the 1800s. Chastain, Zachary. pap. 9.95 *(978-1-4222-1854-9(6));* Jump Ropes, Jacks, & Endless Chores: Children's Lives in The 1800s. Strange, Matthew. pap. 9.95 *(978-1-4222-1855-6(4));* Outlaws & Lawmen: Crime & Punishment in the 1800s. McIntosh, Kenneth. pap. 9.95 *(978-1-4222-1857-0(0));* Passing the Time: Entertainment in The 1800s. Chastain, Zachary. pap. 9.95 *(978-1-4222-1858-7(9));* Reviving the Spirit, Reforming Society: Religion in The 1800s. McIntosh, Kenneth. pap. 9.95 *(978-1-4222-1856-3(2));* Rooting for the Home Team: Sports in The 1800s. Chastain, Zachary. pap. 9.95 *(978-1-4222-1859-4(7));* Saloons, Shootouts, & Spurs: The Wild West in The 1800's. McIntosh, Kenneth. pap. 9.95 *(978-1-4222-1862-4(7));* Scandals & Glory: Politics in The 1800s. Chastain, Zachary. pap. 9.95 *(978-1-4222-1860-0(0));* Sweat of Their Brow: Occupations in the 1800s. Chastain, Zachary. pap. 9.95 *(978-1-4222-1861-7(9));* (YA). (gr. 7-18). 2009. (Illus.). 64p. 2011. Set pap. 149.25 *(978-1-4222-1847-1(3,* 1317825); Set lib. bdg. 344.25 *(978-1-4222-1774-0(4),* 1317825) Mason Crest.

Deibel, Zac. Racial Segregation: Plessy V. Ferguson, 1 vol. 2018. (Courting History Ser.). (ENG.). 64p. (gr. 6-6). lib. bdg. 37.36 *(978-1-5026-3589-1(5),* dd1dbc16-d9e0-402c-90d2-04f0625ec7d1) Cavendish Square Publishing LLC.

DePietro, Frank. Central American Immigrants. 2012. (J). pap. *(978-1-4222-2334-5(5))* Mason Crest.

—Central American Immigrants. Limón, José E., ed. 2012. (Hispanic Americans: Major Minority Ser.). 64p. (J). (gr. 4). 22.95 *(978-1-4222-2317-8(5))* Mason Crest.

Desetta, Al & Wolin, Sybil, eds. The Struggle to Be Strong: True Stories by Teens about Overcoming Tough Times (Updated Edition) 2nd ed. 2019. (ENG.). 192p. (YA). pap. 18.99 *(978-1-63198-460-0(8),* 84600) Free Spirit Publishing Inc.

Dias, Marley. Marley Dias Gets It Done: & So Can You! 2018. (ENG., Illus.). 208p. (J). (gr. 5-5). pap. 14.99 *(978-1-338-13689-0(5),* Scholastic Pr.) Scholastic, Inc.

Duse Sr, Phillip M. Phil Duse Exposes Government Quack Silliness to Us Law-Abiding Citizens. 2013. 76p. pap. 9.95 *(978-1-60414-724-7(5))* Fideli Publishing, Inc.

Evans, Shira. National Geographic Readers: Helpers in Your Neighborhood (Prereader) 2018. (Readers Ser.). (ENG., Illus.). 24p. (J). (gr. -1-k). lib. bdg. 14.90 *(978-1-4263-3215-9(7),* National Geographic Kids) Disney Publishing Worldwide.

Ferguson, Amanda. The Attack Against the U. S. Embassies in Kenya & Tanzania. 2009. (Terrorist Attacks Ser.). 64p. (gr. 5-5). 58.50 *(978-1-60853-309-1(3))* Rosen Publishing Group, Inc., The.

Fighting the Monster. 2004. (YA). ring bd. 59.95 *(978-0-9661256-2-7(2))* Youth Communication - New York Center.

Freedman, Russell. Children of the Great Depression. 2010. (ENG., Illus.). 128p. (J). (gr. 5-7). pap. 10.99 *(978-0-547-48035-0(0),* 1439386, Clarion Bks.) HarperCollins Pubs.

Friedman, Lauri S. Abortion. 2008. (Compact Research Ser.). (YA). (gr. 7-12). lib. bdg. 43.93 *(978-1-60152-047-0(6))* ReferencePoint Pr., Inc.

Gallagher, Aileen. The Muckrakers: American Journalism During the Age of Reform. 2009. (Progressive Movement 1900-1920: Efforts to Reform America's New Industrial Society Ser.). 32p. (gr. 3-4). 47.90 *(978-1-60854-173-7(8))* Rosen Publishing Group, Inc., The.

The GILDED AGE & PROGRESSIVISM: 1891-1913. 2010. (ENG., Illus.). 136p. (gr. 5-8). 35.00 *(978-1-60413-355-4(4),* P178886, Facts On File) Infobase Holdings, Inc.

Gitlin, Martin. World War II U. S. Homefront: A History Perspectives Book. 2014. (Perspectives Library). (ENG., Illus.). 32p. (J). (gr. 4-8). 32.07 *(978-1-63137-621-4(7),* 205267) Cherry Lake Publishing.

Gorman, Jacqueline Laks. The Modern Feminist Movement. 2011. (ENG., Illus.). 64p. (gr. 6-12). 35.00 *(978-1-60413-935-8(8),* P189949, Facts On File) Infobase Holdings, Inc.

Hakim, Joy. A History of US: an Age of Extremes: 1880-1917 a History of US Book Eight. 3rd rev. ed. 2007. (History of US Ser.: Vol. 8). (ENG., Illus.). 228p. (gr. 4-7). per. 15.95 *(978-0-19-532722-9(5))* Oxford Univ. Pr., Inc.

—A History of US: Reconstructing America: 1865-1890 a History of US Book Seven. (History of US Ser.: 7). (ENG., Illus.). 208p. (gr. 4-7). 3rd rev. ed. 2006. 24.95 *(978-0-19-518900-1(0))*Bk. 7. 2nd rev. ed. 2007. per. 15.95 *(978-0-19-532721-2(7))* Oxford Univ. Pr., Inc.

Harrison, Geoffrey C. & Scott, Thomas F. The Fight for Freedom. Stewart, Mark & Kennedy, Mike, eds. 2014. (Great Debates Ser.). (ENG.). 48p. (J). (gr. 5-8). lib. bdg. 29.27 *(978-1-59953-588-3(2))* Norwood Hse. Pr.

Haugen, David M., et al, eds. The Great Depression, 1 vol. 2010. (Perspectives on Modern World History Ser.). (ENG., Illus.). 240p. (gr. 10-12). 49.43 *(978-0-7377-4795-9(1),* 240a855b-bc7c-468a-a879-8e0cc974f8bb, Greenhaven Publishing) Greenhaven Publishing LLC.

Hazen, Walter. Reform Movement. 2005. (Illus.). 112p. pap. 12.95 *(978-1-59647-085-9(2))* Good Year Bks.

Heitkamp, Kristina Lyn. Confronting Anti-Semitism, 1 vol. 2017. (Speak up! Confronting Discrimination in Your Daily Life Ser.). (ENG.). 64p. (YA). (gr. 7-7). 36.13 *(978-1-5081-7742-5(2),* 570e86bf-dc77-4676-8bc2-f3db94b5670b, Rosen Young Adult) Rosen Publishing Group, Inc., The.

Hyde, Natalie. Life in a Mining Community. 2009. (Learn about Rural Life Ser.). (ENG., Illus.). 32p. (J). (gr. 3-6). pap. *(978-0-7787-5087-1(6));* lib. bdg. *(978-0-7787-5074-1(4))* Crabtree Publishing Co.

Jd, Duchess Harris & Mooney, Carla. The One Percent. 2018. (Class in America Ser.). (ENG., Illus.). 112p. (J). (gr. 6-12). lib. bdg. 41.36 *(978-1-5321-1410-6(9),* 28802, Essential Library) ABDO Publishing Co.

Josephson, Judith P. Growing up in World War II, 1941-1945. 2003. (Our America Ser.). (Illus.). 64p. (J). (gr. 4-7). lib. bdg. 26.60 *(978-0-8225-0660-7(2))* Lerner Publishing Group.

Kiesbye, Stefan, ed. Can Busy Teens Succeed Academically?, 1 vol. 2009. (At Issue Ser.). (ENG.). 96p. (gr. 10-12). 41.03 *(978-0-7377-4286-2(0),* 5bc92631-14f7-4b5c-8360-9d0bd655338d, Greenhaven Publishing) Greenhaven Publishing LLC.

King, David C. AmericanHeritage, American Voices: Colonies & Revolution. 2003. (American Heritage, American Voices Ser.). (ENG.). 144p. (J). (gr. 5-9). pap. 22.95 *(978-1-119-10345-5(2))* Wiley, John & Sons, Inc.

Konstam, Angus. America Speaks, 10 vols. 2005. (Illus.). (J). *(978-0-7172-6026-3(7)); (978-0-7172-6027-0(5)); (978-0-7172-6028-7(3)); (978-0-7172-6023-2(2)); (978-0-7172-6024-9(0)); (978-0-7172-6021-8(6)); (978-0-7172-6022-5(4)); (978-0-7172-6025-6(9)); (978-0-7172-6020-1(8)); (978-0-7172-6029-4(1))* Grolier, Ltd.

—America Speaks, 10 vols., Set. 2005. (Illus.). (J). (gr. 5-10). lib. bdg. 269.00 *(978-0-7172-6030-0(5),* Grolier) Scholastic Library Publishing.

Krumsiek, Allison. Teens & Alcohol: A Dangerous Combination, 1 vol. 2018. (Hot Topics Ser.). (ENG.). 104p. (J). (gr. 7-7). pap. 20.99 *(978-1-5345-6497-8(7),* 319958d9-2eb2-463c-84aa-db2087086f47, Lucent Pr.) Greenhaven Publishing LLC.

Levy, Debbie. Slaves on a Southern Plantation. 2004. (Daily Life Ser.). (ENG., Illus.). 48p. (J). 27.50 *(978-0-7377-1827-0(7),* Greenhaven Pr., Inc.) Cengage Gale.

Libal, Joyce. Migrant Youth: Falling Between the Cracks. 2009. (Youth in Rural North America Ser.). (Illus.). 96p. (YA). (gr. 3-7). lib. bdg. 22.95 *(978-1-4222-0020-9(5))* Mason Crest.

Llanas, Sheila. Children in the Civil Rights Era. 2018. (Children in History Ser.). (ENG., Illus.). 48p. (J). (gr. 5-6). pap. 11.95 *(978-1-63517-974-3(2),* 1635179742); lib. bdg. 34.21 *(978-1-63517-873-9(8),* 1635178738) North Star Editions. (Focus Readers).

Lynch, Seth. The Industrial Revolution, 1 vol. 2018. (Look at U. S. History Ser.). (ENG.). 32p. (gr. 2-2). 28.27 *(978-1-5382-2127-3(6),* 1ecd8fa1-314d-442a-9e7b-21b76733adea) Stevens, Gareth Publishing LLLP.

Lynette, Rachel. What to Do When Your Parent Is Out of Work, 1 vol. 2010. (Let's Work It Out Ser.). (ENG.). 24p. (J). (gr. 2-3). pap. 9.25 *(978-1-4358-9764-9(1),* 85a9bef5-b51a-44f8-b8a3-d7b01466ce73, PowerKids Pr.); (Illus.). lib. bdg. 26.27 *(978-1-4358-9338-2(7),* 410da821-22a7-4fd9-b08c-462b6193cd7d) Rosen Publishing Group, Inc., The.

Mahoney, Emily. The Industrial Revolution: The Birth of Modern America, 1 vol. 2017. (American History Ser.). (ENG.). 104p. (gr. 7-7). lib. bdg. 41.03 *(978-1-5345-6133-5(1),* 614f7d58-9e93-4a2e-bcbd-6b880ed31008, Lucent Pr.) Greenhaven Publishing LLC.

Marcovitz, Hal. Race Relations. 2008. (Gallup Major Trends & Events Ser.). (Illus.). 127p. (YA). (gr. 7-18). lib. bdg. 22.95 *(978-1-59084-968-2(X))* Mason Crest.

—Teens & Volunteerism. Developed in Association with the Gallup Organization Staff, ed. 2013. (Gallup Youth Survey: Major Issues & Trends Ser.: 14). 112p. (J). (gr. 7-18). 24.95 *(978-1-4222-2960-6(2))* Mason Crest.

Marcovitz, Hal & marcovitz, hal. The 1960s: Part of the Understanding American History Series. 2013. (Illus.). 96p. (YA). lib. bdg. *(978-1-60152-494-2(3))* ReferencePoint Pr., Inc.

Martin, Iain C. Gettysburg: The True Account of Two Young Heroes in the Greatest Battle of the Civil War. 2013. (ENG.,

TUV

Illus.). 208p. (YA). (gr. 6-6). 16.95 *(978-1-62087-532-2(2),* 620532, Sky Pony Pr.) Skyhorse Publishing Co., Inc.

McAneney, Caitie. Aboard the Amistad, 1 vol. 2019. (History on the High Seas Ser.). (ENG.). 24p. (J). (gr. 2-3). pap. 9.15 *(978-1-5382-3790-8(3),* 13bfb77a-c055-44f8-aaa3-db6037088fef) Stevens, Gareth Publishing LLLP.

McIntosh, Kenneth & Livingston, Phyllis. Youth with Alcohol & Drug Addiction: Escape from Bondage. 2009. (Helping Youth with Mental, Physical, & Social Challenges Ser.). (Illus.). 128p. (YA). (gr. 7-18). lib. bdg. 24.95 *(978-1-4222-0143-5(0))* Mason Crest.

McNeill, Allison & Hanes, Richard Clay. American Home Front in World War II Reference Library Cumulative Index. 2004. (American Homefront in World War II Reference Library). (ENG.). 32p. 5.00 *(978-0-7876-9125-7(9),* UXL) Cengage Gale.

Meade, Marion. Free Woman: The Life & Times of Victoria Woodhull. 2011. 176p. pap. 15.95 *(978-1-61756-052-1(9))* Open Road Integrated Media, Inc.

Miller, Brandon Marie. Declaring Independence: Life During the American Revolution. 2005. (People's History Ser.). (ENG., Illus.). 96p. (gr. 5-12). 33.26 *(978-0-8225-1275-2(0))* Lerner Publishing Group.

Miller, Debra A. The Patriot Act, 1 vol. 2007. (Hot Topics Ser.). (ENG., Illus.). 112p. (gr. 7-7). lib. bdg. 41.03 *(978-1-59018-981-8(7),* bbc5ead7-8fa1-4ddf-b860-f44969a6dd51, Lucent Pr.) Greenhaven Publishing LLC.

Miller, Reagan & Doak, Melissa J. Life on the Homefront During the Civil War. 2011. (ENG.). 48p. (J). lib. bdg. *(978-0-7787-5344-5(1))* Crabtree Publishing Co.

Murray, Glen L. The Dumbing down of Americ. 2009. 68p. pap. 15.99 *(978-1-4415-1642-8(5))* Xlibris Corp.

Nardo, Don. The Atlantic Slave Trade, 1 vol. 2007. (Lucent Library of Black History Ser.). (ENG., Illus.). 104p. (gr. 7-7). lib. bdg. 41.03 *(978-1-4205-0007-3(4),* de99408b-5d64-48ef-8125-db14a314f232, Lucent Pr.) Greenhaven Publishing LLC.

National Geographic Learning. Reading Expeditions (Social Studies: Seeds of Change in American History): Immigrants Today. 2007. (ENG., Illus.). 40p. (J). pap. 21.95 *(978-0-7922-4560-5(1))* CENGAGE Learning.

—Reading Expeditions (Social Studies: Seeds of Change in American History): the Home Front During World War II. 2007. (Nonfiction Reading & Writing Workshops Ser.). (ENG., Illus.). 40p. pap. 21.95 *(978-0-7922-4558-2(X))* CENGAGE Learning.

Nazario, Sonia. La Travesía de Enrique. 2015. (SPA.). 304p. (YA). (gr. 7). pap. 9.99 *(978-0-553-53554-9(4),* Ember) Random Hse. Children's Bks.

Pearl, Melissa Sherman & Sherman, David A. What's Mine Is Yours: Charities Started by Kids! 2017. (Community Connections: How Do They Help? Ser.). (ENG., Illus.). 24p. (J). (gr. 2-5). lib. bdg. 29.21 *(978-1-63472-847-8(5),* 209814) Cherry Lake Publishing.

Piehl, Norah, ed. Underage Drinking, 1 vol. 2010. (Social Issues Firsthand Ser.). (ENG., Illus.). 120p. (gr. 10-12). 39.93 *(978-0-7377-4799-7(4),* c72efb66-2ddd-443e-94ac-083885a0a299, Greenhaven Publishing) Greenhaven Publishing LLC.

Prince, Jennifer S. The Life & Times of Asheville's Thomas Wolfe. 2016. (True Tales for Young Readers Ser.). (ENG., Illus.). 116p. (YA). pap. 17.00 *(978-0-86526-484-7(8),* 01OSPS) Univ. of North Carolina Pr.

Progressivism. 2010. (ENG., Illus.). 128p. (gr. 6-12). 45.00 *(978-1-60413-223-6(X),* P179250, Facts On File) Infobase Holdings, Inc.

Roberts, Russell. Children in the Industrial Revolution. 2018. (Children in History Ser.). (ENG., Illus.). 48p. (J). (gr. 5-6). pap. 11.95 *(978-1-63517-978-1(5),* 1635179785); lib. bdg. 34.21 *(978-1-63517-877-7(0),* 1635178770) North Star Editions. (Focus Readers).

Rodger, Ellen. My New Home after Iraq. 2018. (Leaving My Homeland: after the Journey Ser.). (Illus.). 32p. (J). (gr. 4-4). *(978-0-7787-4975-2(4))* Crabtree Publishing Co.

—A Refugee's Journey from Myanmar. 2017. (Leaving My Homeland Ser.). (Illus.). 32p. (J). (gr. 4-4). *(978-0-7787-3674-5(1))* Crabtree Publishing Co.

Roesser, Marie. The Dust Bowl, 1 vol. 2019. (Look at U. S. History Ser.). (ENG.). 32p. (J). (gr. 2-2). pap. 11.50 *(978-1-5382-4871-3(9),* 1b3cd4d7-a080-4cb0-b5eb-3f37f254e2d0) Stevens, Gareth Publishing LLLP.

Sakany, Lois. Progressive Leaders: The Platforms & Policies of America's Reform Politicians. (Progressive Movement 1900-1920: Efforts to Reform America's New Industrial Society Ser.). 32p. (gr. 3-4). 2009. 47.90 *(978-1-60854-168-3(1))* 2006. (ENG., Illus.). (YA). lib. bdg. 30.47 *(978-1-4042-0193-4(9),* 440d7278-674c-4b79-8c8c-36efba421ac9) Rosen Publishing Group, Inc., The.

Sandler, Martin W. 1919 the Year That Changed America. 2019. (ENG., Illus.). 192p. (J). 24.99 *(978-1-68119-801-9(0),* 900187333, Bloomsbury Children's Bks.) Bloomsbury Publishing USA.

Seeley, M. H. America's Oddest Fads, 1 vol. 2016. (Weird America Ser.). (ENG.). 32p. (J). (gr. 3-4). pap. 11.50 *(978-1-4824-5747-6(4),* fa2b01be-ffb5-4df2-bbb9-d708cc1b6958) Stevens, Gareth Publishing LLLP.

Snyder, Gail. Teens & Alcohol. Developed in Association with the Gallup Organization Staff, ed. 2013. (Gallup Youth Survey: Major Issues & Trends Ser.: 14). 112p. (J). (gr. 7-18). 24.95 *(978-1-4222-2949-1(1))* Mason Crest.

Steck-Vaughn Staff. Social Studies Level H-J: America Is... 2003. (Steck-Vaughn Shutterbug Bks.). (ENG., Illus.). 16p. (gr. 1-2). pap. 41.55 *(978-0-7398-7652-7(X))* Harcourt Schl. Pubs.

Stone, Tanya Lee. The House That Jane Built: A Story about Jane Addams. Brown, Kathryn, illus. 2015. (ENG.). 32p. (J). (gr. 1-4). 19.99 *(978-0-8050-9049-9(5),* 900060591, Holt, Henry & Co. Bks. For Young Readers) Holt, Henry & Co.

Strange, Matthew. Guardians of the Home: Women's Lives in The 1800s. 2009. (Daily Life in America in the 1800s Ser.). 64p. (YA). (gr. 7-18). pap. 9.95 *(978-1-4222-1853-2(8));* lib. bdg. 22.95 *(978-1-4222-1780-1(9))* Mason Crest.

Thomas, William David. Korean Americans, 1 vol. 2010. (New Americans Ser.). (ENG.). 80p. (gr. 5-5). 38.36 *(978-0-7614-4306-3(1),* ad720f6d-7d20-484b-8775-6914bd396756) Cavendish Square Publishing LLC.

Vonne, Mira. Gross Facts about the American Colonies. 2017. (Gross History Ser.). (ENG., Illus.). 32p. (J). (gr. 3-9). lib. bdg. 27.32 *(978-1-5157-4154-1(0),* 133954, Capstone Pr.) Capstone.

Worth, Richard. Lewis Hine: Photographer of Americans at Work: Photographer of Americans at Work. 2009. (ENG., Illus.). 80p. (C). (gr. 6-18). lib. bdg. 180.00 *(978-0-7656-8153-9(6),* Y182862) Routledge.

Yomtov, Nel. Immigrants from India & Southeast Asia. 2018. (Immigration Today Ser.). (ENG., Illus.). 32p. (J). (gr. 3-6). lib. bdg. 27.99 *(978-1-5435-1382-0(4),* 137787, Capstone Pr.) Capstone.

Zoldak, Joyce. When Danger Hits Home: Survivors of Domestic Violence. 2009. (J). pap. 24.95 *(978-1-4222-1473-2(7))* Mason Crest.

UNITED STATES—SOCIAL LIFE AND CUSTOMS

Abbott, Simon, illus. 100 Questions about Colonial America: And All the Answers Too! 2018. (100 Questions Ser.). (ENG.). 48p. (J). 7.99 *(978-1-4413-2616-4(2),* bc12b992-f6ed-4bb7-a845-5c51d3fed4e5) Peter Pauper Pr. Inc.

Aloian, Molly. Cultural Traditions in the United States. 2014. (Cultural Traditions in My World Ser.). (ENG., Illus.). 32p. (J). (gr. 2-3). *(978-0-7787-0305-1(3))* Crabtree Publishing Co.

Ancona, George. Mi Casa: My House. 2005. (Somos Latinos (We Are Latinos) Ser.). (SPA & ENG., Illus.). 32p. (J). (gr. 1-3). pap. 8.95 *(978-0-516-25065-6(5),* Children's Pr.) Scholastic Library Publishing.

Anderson, Dale. Daily Life During the American Revolution, 1 vol. 2005. (World Almanac(r) Library of the American Revolution Ser.). (ENG.). 48p. (gr. 5-8). pap. 15.05 *(978-0-8368-5939-3(1),* d0fdedfe-aa31-4b55-9332-5dac1f9258d2); lib. bdg. 33.67 *(978-0-8368-5930-0(8),* 2214c6b0-c1d8-4d64-b3a9-e2e8ef41d2ea) Stevens, Gareth Publishing LLLP. (Gareth Stevens Secondary Library).

Anderson, Laurie Halse. Thank You, Sarah: The Woman Who Saved Thanksgiving. Faulkner, Matt, illus. 2005. (ENG.). 40p. (J). (gr. k-3). 7.99 *(978-0-689-85143-8(X),* Simon & Schuster Bks. For Young Readers) Simon & Schuster Bks. For Young Readers.

Barter, James. San Francisco in the 1960s. 2003. (Travel Guide To Ser.). (ENG., Illus.). 96p. (J). 30.85 *(978-1-59018-359-5(2),* Lucent Bks.) Cengage Gale.

Berg, Elizabeth. Festivals of the World: the United States, 1 vol. 2011. (Festivals of the World Ser.). (ENG.). 32p. (gr. 4-4). 31.21 *(978-1-60870-106-3(9),* 5c3d7bfe-7a79-4ff2-a5a1-222e29a03a6c) Cavendish Square Publishing LLC.

Braun, Eric. If I Were a Cowboy, 1 vol. Reid, Mick, illus. 2010. (Dream Big! Ser.). (ENG.). 24p. (J). (gr. k-3). lib. bdg. 27.32 *(978-1-4048-5531-1(9),* 96023, Picture Window Bks.) Capstone.

Brill, Marlene Targ. America in the 1980s. 2009. (Decades of Twentieth-Century America Ser.). (ENG.). 144p. (gr. 5-12). lib. bdg. 38.60 *(978-0-8225-7602-0(3))* Lerner Publishing Group.

Broida, Marian. Projects about the American Revolution, 1 vol. 2007. (Hands-On History Ser.). (ENG., Illus.). 48p. (gr. 3-3). lib. bdg. 34.07 *(978-0-7614-1981-5(0),* 9accd3af-7002-4ce8-8212-853be6e77e08) Cavendish Square Publishing LLC.

Brown, Harriet & Witowski, Teri. Kit's World: A Girl's-Eye View of the Great Depression. Rane, Walter & Hood, Philip, illus. 2008. 30p. (YA). (gr. 3-18). 24.95 *(978-1-59369-459-3(8))* American Girl Publishing, Inc.

Bryfonski, Dedria, ed. Deregulation, 1 vol. 2010. (Opposing Viewpoints Ser.). (ENG., Illus.). 280p. (gr. 10-12). 50.43 *(978-0-7377-5108-6(8),* 57798edf-01f0-437d-8908-719b41291c6e); pap. 34.80 *(978-0-7377-5109-3(6),* eb4c69ab-9368-4d06-8b3f-e5bf7298ea63) Greenhaven Publishing LLC. (Greenhaven Publishing).

Bullard, Lisa. Chelsea's Chinese New Year. Saunders, Katie, illus. 2012. (Cloverleaf Books (tm) — Holidays & Special Days Ser.). 24p. (J). (gr. k-2). (ENG.). pap. 8.99 *(978-0-7613-8579-0(7),* 6d2e5b1b-e9b4-4293-9afa-0c34ee933125); pap. 39.62 *(978-0-7613-9247-7(5))* Lerner Publishing Group. (Millbrook Pr.).

Center for Learning Network Staff. Catch-22: Curriculum Unit. 2005. (Novel Ser.). 76p. (YA). tchr. ed., spiral bd. 19.95 *(978-1-56077-792-2(3))* Center for Learning, The.

Chastain, Zachary. From the Parlor to the Altar: Romance & Marriage in The 1800s. 2009. (Daily Life in America in the 1800s Ser.). 64p. (YA). (gr. 7-18). pap. 9.95 *(978-1-4222-1852-5(X));* lib. bdg. 22.95 *(978-1-4222-1779-5(5))* Mason Crest.

—Home Sweet Home: Around the House in the 1800s. 2009. (Daily Life in America in the 1800s Ser.). 64p. (YA). (gr. 7-18). pap. 9.95 *(978-1-4222-1854-9(6));* lib. bdg. 22.95 *(978-1-4222-1781-8(7))* Mason Crest.

—Passing the Time: Entertainment in The 1800s. 2009. (Daily Life in America in the 1800s Ser.). 64p. (YA). (gr. 7-18). pap. 9.95 *(978-1-4222-1858-7(9));* lib. bdg. 22.95 *(978-1-4222-1785-6(X))* Mason Crest.

Colligan, L. H. The City. 2014. (J). pap. *(978-1-62712-883-4(2))* Cavendish Square Publishing LLC.

Colligan, Louise. The City in Colonial America, 1 vol. 2014. (Life in Colonial America Ser.). (ENG.). 80p. (gr. 6-6). lib. bdg. 37.36 *(978-1-62712-882-7(4),* 54fbe2d3-b14a-48df-83bb-88026f3ae8d0) Cavendish Square Publishing LLC.

Colman, Penny. Thanksgiving: The True Story. 2008. (ENG., Illus.). 160p. (YA). (gr. 5-11). 30.99 *(978-0-8050-8229-6(8),* 900041217, Holt, Henry & Co. Bks. For Young Readers) Holt, Henry & Co.

Colonial Life, 5 bks., Set. Incl. Cities & Towns. Stefoff, Rebecca. 96p. lib. bdg. 165.00 *(978-0-7656-8109-6(9),* Y181735); Daily Living. Hinds, Kathryn. 96p. lib. bdg. 180.00 *(978-0-7656-8110-2(2),* Y181908); Exploration & Settlement. Stefoff, Rebecca. 96p. lib. bdg. 180.00 *(978-0-7656-8108-9(0),* Y182272); Government. Kelly, Martin & Kelly, Melissa. 96p. lib. bdg. 180.00 *(978-0-7656-8112-6(9),* Y182476); Trade & Commerce. Altman, Linda Jacobs. 98p. lib. bdg. 200.00 *(978-0-7656-8111-9(0),* Y184849); (C). (gr. 6-18). (ENG., Illus.). 96p. 2007. Set lib. bdg. 165.00 *(978-0-7656-8107-2(2),* Y181691) Routledge.

Combs, Maggie. Postwar United States. 2011. (Explorer Library: Language Arts Explorer Ser.). (ENG.). 32p. (gr. 4-8). pap. 14.21 *(978-1-61080-284-0(5),* 201207); (Illus.). lib. bdg. 32.07 *(978-1-61080-196-6(2),* 201168) Cherry Lake Publishing.

Connell, Kate. Servant to Abigail Adams: The Early American Adventures of Hannah Cooper. 2004. (Illus.). 40p. (J). (gr. 4-8). pap. 7.00 *(978-0-7567-8216-0(3))* DIANE Publishing Co.

Crabtree Publishing Company Staff & Morss, Martha. United States: The People. 2012. (ENG.). 32p. (J). *(978-0-7787-9836-1(4))* Crabtree Publishing Co.

Crabtree Publishing Company Staff & Weiss, Lynne. United States: The Culture. 2012. (ENG.). 32p. (J). pap. *(978-0-7787-9837-8(2))* Crabtree Publishing Co.

Dawson, Emily C. Holidays & Celebrations. 2010. (Special Days Ser.). (ENG.). 24p. (J). (gr. k-2). lib. bdg. 25.65 *(978-1-60753-030-5(9),* 17190) Amicus.

Day, Nancy. Your Travel Guide to Civil War America. 2005. (Passport to History Ser.). (Illus.). 96p. (gr. 5-8). lib. bdg. 26.50 *(978-0-8225-3078-7(3))* Lerner Publishing Group.

—Your Travel Guide to Colonial America. 2005. (Passport to History Ser.). (Illus.). 96p. (gr. 5-8). lib. bdg. 26.50 *(978-0-8225-3079-4(1))* Lerner Publishing Group.

dePaola, Tomie. Things Will Never Be the Same. dePaola, Tomie, illus. 2004. (26 Fairmount Avenue Bks.). (Illus.). 69p. (J). (gr. 3-7). 13.65 *(978-0-7569-2951-0(2))* Perfection Learning Corp.

Domnauer, Teresa. Life in the West (a True Book: Westward Expansion) 2010. (True Book (Relaunch) Ser.). (ENG., Illus.). 48p. (J). (gr. 3-5). pap. 6.95 *(978-0-531-21246-2(7),* Children's Pr.) Scholastic Library Publishing.

Donovan, Sandra. The Middle Eastern American Experience. 2010. (USA TODAY Cultural Mosaic Ser.). (ENG., Illus.). 80p. (gr. 6-8). lib. bdg. 33.26 *(978-0-7613-4087-4(4))* Lerner Publishing Group.

Draper, Allison Stark. What People Wore During the American Revolution. 2009. (Clothing, Costumes, & Uniforms Throughout American History Ser.). 24p. (gr. 3-3). 42.50 *(978-1-61511-875-5(6),* PowerKids Pr.) Rosen Publishing Group, Inc., The.

—What People Wore During the Civil War. 2009. (Clothing, Costumes, & Uniforms Throughout American History Ser.). 24p. (gr. 3-3). 42.50 *(978-1-61511-876-2(4),* PowerKids Pr.) Rosen Publishing Group, Inc., The.

—What People Wore in Early America. 2009. (Clothing, Costumes, & Uniforms Throughout American History Ser.). 24p. (gr. 3-3). 42.50 *(978-1-61511-881-6(0),* PowerKids Pr.) Rosen Publishing Group, Inc., The.

—What People Wore on Southern Plantations. 2009. (Clothing, Costumes, & Uniforms Throughout American History Ser.). 24p. (gr. 3-3). 42.50 *(978-1-61511-882-3(9),* PowerKids Pr.) Rosen Publishing Group, Inc., The.

Dustman, Jeanne. American Culture. rev. ed. 2014. (Social Studies: Informational Text Ser.). (ENG., Illus.). 32p. (gr. 3-4). pap. 11.99 *(978-1-4333-7360-2(2))* Teacher Created Materials, Inc.

Ehrlich, Amy. When I Was Your Age Vols. I & II: Original Stories about Growing Up. 2012. lib. bdg. 26.95 *(978-0-606-23806-9(9))* Turtleback.

Ehrlich, Amy, ed. When I Was Your Age Vol. 2: Original Stories about Growing Up. 2006. (Illus.). 187p. (YA). (gr. 8-11). reprint ed. 17.00 *(978-1-4223-5199-4(8))* DIANE Publishing Co.

Engdahl, Sylvia, ed. Free Press, 1 vol. 2011. (Teen Rights & Freedoms Ser.). (ENG., Illus.). 184p. (gr. 10-12). 43.63 *(978-0-7377-5827-6(9),* d9784d40-9b05-483a-92d1-105d1463f01e, Greenhaven Publishing) Greenhaven Publishing LLC.

Fajardo, Anika. The Dish on Food & Farming in Colonial America. 2011. (Life in the American Colonies Ser.). (ENG.). 32p. (gr. 3-4). pap. 47.70 *(978-1-4296-7218-4(8),* Capstone Pr.) Capstone.

Fisher, Verna. Colonial Homes. 2010. (Colonial Quest Ser.). (ENG.). 32p. (J). (gr. 2-5). 21.19 *(978-1-934670-98-9(7))* Nomad Pr.

Friedman, Hannah. Everything Sucks: Losing My Mind & Finding Myself in a High School Quest for Cool. 2009. (ENG.). 264p. (YA). (gr. 8-12). pap. 12.95 *(978-0-7573-0775-1(2),* HCI Teens) Health Communications, Inc.

Gelletly, LeeAnne. A Woman's Place in Early America. 2012. (Illus.). 64p. (J). pap. *(978-1-4222-2365-9(5))* Mason Crest.

—A Woman's Place in Early America. Harrington, A. Page, ed. 2012. (Finding a Voice: Women's Fight for Equality in U. S. Society Ser.). (Illus.). 64p. (J). (gr. 5). 22.95 *(978-1-4222-2355-0(8))* Mason Crest.

George, Enzo. America in the Fifties, 1 vol. 2015. (Primary Sources in U. S. History Ser.). (ENG., Illus.). 48p. (gr. 4-4). 33.07 *(978-1-5026-0494-1(9),* 777faed1-27e4-4d4a-9ff0-468d6e560d44) Cavendish Square Publishing LLC.

Gerber, Larry. Torture, 1 vol. 2011. (Headlines! Ser.). (ENG.). 64p. (YA). (gr. 6-6). lib. bdg. 37.13 *(978-1-4488-1291-2(7),* 4434ca90-d452-4e1a-ab45-aecd7505cd50) Rosen Publishing Group, Inc., The.

Gillis, Jennifer Blizin. Restored Villages. 2007. (Field Trips Ser.). (Illus.). 24p. (J). (gr. 2-5). lib. bdg. 27.07 *(978-1-60044-563-7(2))* Rourke Educational Media.

Glasser, Debbie, et al. New Kid, New Scene: A Guide to Moving & Switching Schools. 2011. (Illus.). 112p. (J). 14.95 *(978-1-4338-1039-8(5),* Magination Pr.) American Psychological Assn.

Gogerly, Liz. Costume Around the World: United States. 2008. (Costume Around the World Ser.). (ENG., Illus.). 32p. (gr. 4-6). 28.00 *(978-0-7910-9774-8(9),* P459461, Chelsea Clubhse.) Infobase Holdings, Inc.

Hanauer, Jodi. A Child of the 80's Looks Back. 2004. 60p. pap. 19.95 *(978-1-4137-2461-5(2))* America Star Bks.

Harasymiw, Teppo. Customs & Celebrations Across America, 1 vol. 2008. (Real Life Readers Ser.). (ENG.). 12p. (gr. 2-3). pap. 5.90 *(978-1-4042-7954-4(7),* 3aed4213-b886-428e-a695-c4ebd5f631f1, Rosen Classroom) Rosen Publishing Group, Inc., The.

Hardyman, Robyn. United States. 2009. (Celebrate! (Chelsea Clubhouse) Ser.). (ENG.). 32p. (gr. 4-6). 28.00 *(978-1-60413-264-9(7),* P169966, Chelsea Clubhse.) Infobase Holdings, Inc.

Harness, Cheryl. Our Colonial Year. 2005. (ENG., Illus.). 40p. (J). (gr. -1-3). 19.99 *(978-0-689-83479-0(9),* Simon & Schuster Bks. For Young Readers) Simon & Schuster Bks. For Young Readers.

Hazen, Walter A. Colonial Times: With Cross-Curricular Activities in Each Chapter: Colonial Times. 2008. (ENG., Illus.). 96p. (J). pap. 12.95 *(978-1-59647-266-2(9))* Good Year Bks.

—The Frontier: With Cross-Curricular Activities in Each Chapter: the Frontier. 2008. (Illus.). 96p. (J). pap. 12.95 *(978-1-59647-268-6(5))* Good Year Bks.

Heinz, Brian J. Nathan of Yesteryear & Michael of Today. Friar, Joanne, illus. 2006. (Exceptional Social Studies Titles for Intermediate Grades). (ENG.). 32p. (J). (gr. 3-6). lib. bdg. 22.60 *(978-0-7613-2893-3(9),* Millbrook Pr.) Lerner Publishing Group.

Hernández, Roger E. & Hernández, Roger E. The Civil War, 1840s-1890s, 1 vol. 2009. (Hispanic America Ser.). (ENG.). 80p. (gr. 5-5). lib. bdg. 36.93 *(978-0-7614-2939-5(5),* cc454e86-45da-4258-b12d-fad641b1dcec) Cavendish Square Publishing LLC.

Herrera, Juan Felipe. El Canto de las Palomas/Calling the Doves. 2004. (Illus.). (J). (gr. 3-6). spiral bd. *(978-0-616-14607-1(8))* Canadian National Institute for the Blind/Institut National Canadien pour les Aveugles.

Higgins, Nadia. US Culture Through Infographics. Kulihin, Vic, illus. 2014. (Super Social Studies Infographics Ser.). (ENG.). 32p. (J). (gr. 3-5). pap. 8.99 *(978-1-4677-4565-9(0),* 86018c5c-45f0-4d58-a01c-cc9acf73988b); lib. bdg. 26.65 *(978-1-4677-3464-6(0),* 9ef82bb0-a499-420d-83c5-a8d2940529fb, Lerner Pubns.) Lerner Publishing Group.

—US Government Through Infographics. Sciuto, Alex, illus. 2014. (Super Social Studies Infographics Ser.). (ENG.). 32p. (J). (gr. 3-5). pap. 8.99 *(978-1-4677-4567-3(7),* e065736e-6a07-4d1c-a1d1-50f7bbf2b909) Lerner Publishing Group.

Hinds, Kathryn. Daily Living. 2007. (ENG., Illus.). 96p. (C). (gr. 6-18). lib. bdg. 180.00 *(978-0-7656-8110-2(2),* Y181908) Routledge.

Hooks, Earnest. Let's go see Mother Wilkerson's Farm. 2011. 72p. pap. 27.08 *(978-1-4389-5072-3(1))* AuthorHouse.

Jessup, Dylan. We're All Americans, 1 vol. 2012. (InfoMax Readers Ser.). (ENG., Illus.). 24p. (J). (gr. 1-1). pap. 8.25 *(978-1-4488-9079-8(9),* 2ca6782d-ecb1-4883-b0b0-e3995b082381, Rosen Classroom) Rosen Publishing Group, Inc., The.

Kalman, Bobbie. A Visual Dictionary of Victorian Life. 2010. (Crabtree Visual Dictionaries Ser.). (ENG.). 32p. (J). (gr. 1-7). lib. bdg. *(978-0-7787-3507-6(9))* Crabtree Publishing Co.

Kocienda, Genevieve. Only in America Low Intermediate Book with Online Access, 1 vol. 2014. (ENG., Illus.). 28p. (J). pap., E-Book, E-Book 9.50 *(978-1-107-63700-9(7))* Cambridge Univ. Pr.

Lanier, Wendy H. Life During the Great Depression, 1 vol. 2015. (Daily Life in US History Ser.). (ENG., Illus.). 48p. (J). (gr. 4-8). lib. bdg. 35.64 *(978-1-62403-626-2(0),* 16892) ABDO Publishing Co.

Lassieur, Allison. Colonial America: An Interactive History Adventure. 2010. (You Choose: Historical Eras Ser.). (ENG.). 112p. (J). (gr. 3-4). pap. 42.70 *(978-1-4296-6739-5(7),* 16457); pap. 6.95 *(978-1-4296-6277-2(8),* 115422); (Illus.). 32.65 *(978-1-4296-5481-4(3),* 113881) Capstone. (Capstone Pr.).

The Life of a Colonial Innkeeper. 2013. (Jr. Graphic Colonial America Ser.). 24p. (J). (gr. 3-6). pap. 63.60 *(978-1-4777-1436-2(7),* PowerKids Pr.) Rosen Publishing Group, Inc., The.

The Life of a Colonial Schoolteacher. 2013. (Jr. Graphic Colonial America Ser.). 24p. (J). (gr. 3-6). pap. 63.60 *(978-1-4777-1428-7(6),* PowerKids Pr.) Rosen Publishing Group, Inc., The.

Linde, Barbara. Artifacts Throughout American History, 1 vol. 2019. (Journey to the Past: Investigating Primary Sources Ser.). (ENG.). 32p. (gr. 4-5). pap. 11.50 *(978-1-5382-4030-4(0),* 099dc8a7-78c0-4c4d-be48-beb852b7f25f) Stevens, Gareth Publishing LLLP.

Lindop, Edmund & Goldstein, Margaret. America in the 1930s. 2009. (Decades of Twentieth-Century America Ser.). (ENG.). 144p. (gr. 5-12). lib. bdg. 38.60 *(978-0-7613-2832-2(7))* Lerner Publishing Group.

Loh-Hagan, Virginia. PoPo's Lucky Chinese New Year. Benoit, Renné, illus. 2016. (ENG.). 32p. (J). (gr. 1-4). 16.99 *(978-1-58536-978-2(0),* 204113) Sleeping Bear Pr.

Lowery, Linda. El Día de los Muertos. Knutson, Barbara, illus. 2005. (Yo Solo Festividades Ser.).Tr. of Day of the Dead. (SPA.). 48p. (J). (gr. 2-4). per. 5.95 *(978-0-8225-3123-4(2))* Lerner Publishing Group.

—El Día de los Muertos. Translations.com Staff, tr. Knutson, Barbara, illus. 2005. (Yo Solo - Festividades (on My Own - Holidays) Ser.).Tr. of Day of the Dead. (SPA & ENG.). 48p. (gr. 2-4). lib. bdg. 25.26 *(978-0-8225-3122-7(4))* Lerner Publishing Group.

Lusted, Marcia Amidon. America's Colonization & Settlement. 2011. (Explorer Library: Language Arts Explorer Ser.). (ENG.). 32p. (gr. 4-8). pap. 14.21 *(978-1-61080-282-6(9),* 201205); (Illus.). lib. bdg. 32.07 *(978-1-61080-194-2(6),* 201164) Cherry Lake Publishing.

MacElroy, Mary H. Work & Play in Colonial Days. reprint ed. 150.00 *(978-0-7222-6600-7(6))* Library Reprints, Inc.

Machajewski, Sarah. A Kid's Life in Colonial America, 1 vol. 2014. (How Kids Lived Ser.). (ENG., Illus.). 24p. (J). (gr. 3-3). lib. bdg. 25.27 *(978-1-4994-0006-9(3),* 91b2014c-ab09-40d2-85a6-43e31ea6c73b, PowerKids Pr.) Rosen Publishing Group, Inc., The.

Mara, Wil. The Farmer, 1 vol. 2011. (Colonial People Ser.). (ENG.). 48p. (gr. 4-4). 34.07 *(978-0-7614-4797-9(0),* b4e76fee-661c-4aae-848f-8e178426336f) Cavendish Square Publishing LLC.

Marcovitz, Hal. Teens, Religion & Values. Developed in Association with the Gallup Organization Staff. ed. 2013. (Gallup Youth Survey: Major Issues & Trends Ser.: 14). 112p. (J). (gr. 7-18). 24.95 *(978-1-4222-2962-0(9))* Mason Crest.

Marcovitz, Hal & marcovitz, hal. The 1960s: Part of the Understanding American History Series. 2013. (Illus.). 96p. (YA). lib. bdg. *(978-1-60152-494-2(3))* ReferencePoint Pr., Inc.

Meachen Rau, Dana. Clothing in American History, 1 vol. 2006. (How People Lived in America Ser.). (ENG., Illus.). 24p. (gr. 2-4). pap. 9.15 *(978-0-8368-7212-5(6),* a37ae113-8e62-47bc-8b1d-d0e5aea50218, Weekly Reader Leveled Readers) Stevens, Gareth Publishing LLLP.

Meachen Rau, Dana & Meachen Rau, Dana. Clothing in American History, 1 vol. 2006. (How People Lived in America Ser.). (ENG., Illus.). 24p. (gr. 2-4). lib. bdg. 24.67 *(978-0-8368-7205-7(3),* e403abf5-c964-42fa-8252-164c39c63993, Weekly Reader Leveled Readers) Stevens, Gareth Publishing LLLP.

Michaels, Vanessa Lynn & Harrow, Jeremy. Frequently Asked Questions about Family Violence, 1 vol. 2011. (FAQ: Teen Life Ser.). (ENG.). 64p. (gr. 5-6). lib. bdg. 37.13 *(978-1-4488-4628-3(5),* 8d874e20-8eda-4aa0-9f84-330b02f17a81) Rosen Publishing Group, Inc., The.

Miller, Brandon Marie. Good Women of a Well-Blessed Land: Women's Lives in Colonial America. 2003. (People's History Ser.). (Illus.). 96p. (J). 29.27 *(978-0-8225-0032-2(9))* Lerner Publishing Group.

—Women of Colonial America: 13 Stories of Courage & Survival in the New World. 2016. (Women of Action Ser.: 14). (ENG., Illus.). 256p. (YA). (gr. 7). 19.95 *(978-1-55652-487-5(0))* Chicago Review Pr., Inc.

Moriarty, J. T. Manifest Destiny: A Primary Source History of America's Territorial Expansion in the 19th Century. 2009. (Primary Sources in American History Ser.). 64p. (gr. 5-8). 58.50 *(978-1-60851-490-8(0))* Rosen Publishing Group, Inc., The.

Mortlock, Michele & Who HQ. What Were the Roaring Twenties? Murray, Jake, illus. 2018. (What Was? Ser.). 112p. (J). (gr. 3-7). 5.99 *(978-1-5247-8638-0(1));* lib. bdg. 15.99 *(978-1-5247-8639-7(X))* Penguin Young Readers Group. (Penguin Workshop).

Murray, Julie. Chinese New Year. 2018. (Holidays (Abdo Kids Junior) Ser.). (ENG., Illus.). 24p. (J). (gr. -1-2). lib. bdg. 31.36 *(978-1-5321-8170-2(1),* 29813, Abdo Kids) ABDO Publishing Co.

Nardo, Don. Daily Life in Colonial America, 1 vol. 2010. (Lucent Library of Historical Eras Ser.). (ENG.). 96p. (gr. 7-10). 41.03 *(978-1-4205-0264-0(6),* db7999b3-b80c-4cf5-85ba-01c804b27a89, Lucent Pr.) Greenhaven Publishing LLC.

National Geographic Learning. Reading Expeditions (Social Studies: Voices from America's Past): the Roaring 20s. 2007. (ENG., Illus.). 40p. (J). pap. 21.95 *(978-0-7922-4551-3(2))* National Geographic School Publishing, Inc.

Olson, Kay Melchisedech. The Terrible, Awful Civil War: The Disgusting Details about Life During America's. 2010. (Disgusting History Ser.). (ENG.). 32p. (J). (gr. 3-4). pap. 49.60 *(978-1-4296-6480-6(0),* 16232, Capstone Pr.) Capstone.

—The Terrible, Awful Civil War: The Disgusting Details about Life During America's Bloodiest War. 2010. (Disgusting History Ser.). (ENG.). 32p. (J). (gr. 3-6). pap. 8.10 *(978-1-4296-6349-6(9),* 115546); lib. bdg. 27.99 *(978-1-4296-3960-6(1),* 102570) Capstone.

Parks, Peggy J. Teenage Suicide. 2011. (Compact Research Ser.). 96p. (YA). (gr. 7-12). lib. bdg. 43.93 *(978-1-60152-156-9(1))* ReferencePoint Pr., Inc.

Pelleschi, Andrea. The Life of a Colonial Innkeeper, 1 vol. 2013. (Jr. Graphic Colonial America Ser.). (ENG.). 24p. (J). (gr. 2-3). 28.93 *(978-1-4777-1309-9(3),* 8718f95d-1bae-43b9-9fba-2f81dc3b8f62); pap. 11.60 *(978-1-4777-1435-5(9),* 88f89634-3149-413e-aebb-13fdcc77ed10) Rosen Publishing Group, Inc., The. (PowerKids Pr.).

—The Life of a Colonial Schoolteacher, 1 vol. 2013. (Jr. Graphic Colonial America Ser.). (ENG.). 24p. (J). (gr. 2-3). 28.93 *(978-1-4777-1305-1(0),* 7f9127e6-d10b-4fe7-875a-68fcb987506f); pap. 11.60 *(978-1-4777-1427-0(8),* 2979a0f2-71df-42aa-befa-f6bdd7f7243a) Rosen Publishing Group, Inc., The. (PowerKids Pr.).

Penne, Barbra & Renehan, Patrick. Your Rights As an LGBTQ+ Teen, 1 vol. 2017. (LGBTQ+ Guide to Beating Bullying Ser.). (ENG., Illus.). 64p. (J). (gr. 6-6). 36.13 *(978-1-5081-7439-4(3),* 7f5511ac-a4e9-4874-9f82-82d288f98fbf, Rosen Young Adult) Rosen Publishing Group, Inc., The.

Pierre, Yvette. Living Through the Civil War. 2018. (American Culture & Conflict Ser.). (ENG., Illus.). 48p. (gr. 4-8). lib. bdg. 35.64 *(978-1-64156-415-1(6),* 9781641564151) Rourke Educational Media.

Ponto, Joanna. Mardi Gras. (Illus.). 32p. 2016. (J). pap. *(978-0-7660-7472-5(0))* 2015. (ENG., (gr. 3-3). 26.93 *(978-0-7660-7460-6(9),* 9c009fcb-c32d-4628-b58c-91ca00ccf427) Enslow Publishing, LLC.

Rajczak Nelson, Kristen. Life in the American Colonies, 1 vol. 2013. (What You Didn't Know about History Ser.). (ENG., Illus.). 24p. (J). (gr. 2-3). pap. 9.15 *(978-1-4339-8435-8(0),* 568d4140-47a3-41b4-8917-92ac64cacа96); lib. bdg. 25.27 *(978-1-4339-8434-1(2),* 7631b24d-6084-4437-a4c6-c868ac91a99a) Stevens, Gareth Publishing LLLP.

—Life on a Wagon Train, 1 vol. 2013. (What You Didn't Know about History Ser.). (ENG., Illus.). 24p. (J). (gr. 2-3). pap. 9.15 *(978-1-4339-8445-7(8),* 9b458fc3-3d4c-4a1d-a23f-1647e3661dab); lib. bdg. 25.27 *(978-1-4339-8444-0(X),* cd79e9b1-b73f-4f37-9a43-5ef18bc1fd78) Stevens, Gareth Publishing LLLP.

Raum, Elizabeth. The Dreadful, Smelly Colonies: The Disgusting Details about Life in Colonial Amer. 2010. (Disgusting History Ser.). (ENG.). 32p. (J). (gr. 3-4). pap. 48.60 *(978-1-4296-6477-6(0),* 16229, Capstone Pr.) Capstone.

—The Dreadful, Smelly Colonies: The Disgusting Details about Life in Colonial America, 1 vol. 2010. (Disgusting History Ser.). (ENG.). 32p. (J). (gr. 3-6). pap. 8.10 *(978-1-4296-6351-9(0),* 115548) Capstone.

—The Scoop on Clothes, Homes, & Daily Life in Colonial America. 2011. (Life in the American Colonies Ser.). (ENG.). 32p. (gr. 3-4). pap. 47.70 *(978-1-4296-7214-6(5),* Capstone Pr.) Capstone.

Rice, Dona Herweck. America Then & Now. rev. ed. 2018. (Social Studies: Informational Text Ser.). (ENG., Illus.). 24p. (J). (gr. 1-3). pap. 10.99 *(978-1-4258-2514-0(1))* Teacher Created Materials, Inc.

—Estados Unidos Entonces y Ahora. rev. ed. 2019. (Social Studies: Informational Text Ser.). (SPA., Illus.). 24p. (J). (gr. 1-3). pap. 10.99 *(978-1-64290-111-5(3))* Teacher Created Materials, Inc.

Riney-Kehrberg, Pamela. Always Plenty to Do: Growing up on a Farm in the Long Ago. 2011. (ENG., Illus.). 144p. (J). (gr. 4-7). 21.95 *(978-0-89672-692-5(4),* P193196) Texas Tech Univ. Pr.

Roberts, Russell. Holidays & Celebrations in Colonial America. 2006. (Building America Ser.). (Illus.). 48p. (J). (gr. 3-7). lib. bdg. 29.95 *(978-1-58415-467-9(5))* Mitchell Lane Pubs.

—Life in Colonial America. 2007. (Building America Ser.). (Illus.). 48p. (J). (gr. 4-8). lib. bdg. 29.95 *(978-1-58415-549-2(3))* Mitchell Lane Pubs.

Robins, Maureen Picard. One Land, Many Cultures. 2012. (Little World Social Studies). (ENG.). 24p. (gr. k-2). pap. 9.95 *(978-1-61810-276-8(1),* 9781618102768) Rourke Educational Media.

Robinson, Fay. Celebrating Chinese New Year, 1 vol. 2012. (Celebrating Holidays Ser.). (ENG., Illus.). 48p. (gr. 3-3). pap. 11.53 *(978-1-59845-398-0(X),* 6e659187-5601-4703-a9a6-830eb7b4ed81); lib. bdg. 27.93 *(978-0-7660-4031-1(3),* 57aadf6e-b63e-4b04-8815-e89fa6a330cb) Enslow Publishing, LLC. (Enslow Elementary).

Robinson, Fay & Ponto, Joanna. Chinese New Year, 1 vol. 2016. (Story of Our Holidays Ser.). (ENG., Illus.). 32p. (gr. 3-3). pap. 11.52 *(978-0-7660-8324-0(1),* a6a654db-902b-4288-b6a8-d7315840049c) Enslow Publishing, LLC.

Sebree, Chet'la & Stefoff, Rebecca. Historical Sources on Colonial Life, 1 vol. 2019. (America's Story Ser.). (ENG.). 144p. (J). (gr. 8-8). pap. 22.16 *(978-1-5026-4077-2(5),* 08f22958-c18e-4600-b9ea-e5d66cb813b4) Cavendish Square Publishing LLC.

Sheffield, Sarah. Life During the American Civil War. 2009. (Reading Room Collection 2 Ser.). 24p. (gr. 3-4). 42.50 *(978-1-60851-978-1(3),* PowerKids Pr.) Rosen Publishing Group, Inc., The.

Sirvaitis, Karen. The European American Experience. 2010. (USA TODAY Cultural Mosaic Ser.). (ENG.). 80p. (gr. 6-8). lib. bdg. 33.26 *(978-0-7613-4088-1(2))* Lerner Publishing Group.

Small, Cathleen. American Life & Communication from the Telephone to Twitter, 1 vol. 2016. (Pop Culture Ser.). (ENG.). 112p. (J). (gr. 7-7). 41.64 *(978-1-5026-1977-8(6),* facc0764-e0e2-4c74-99cc-64a9d2834f15) Cavendish Square Publishing LLC.

Spilsbury, Louise. Horrible Jobs in Colonial Times, 1 vol., Vol. 1. 2014. (History's Most Horrible Jobs Ser.). (ENG.). 48p. (J). (gr. 5-6). 34.61 *(978-1-4824-0330-5(7),* 4464af6e-1660-4ba5-87ed-1714369c375d) Stevens, Gareth Publishing LLLP.

Steer, Deirdre Clancy. The 80s And 90s. 2009. (ENG., Illus.). 32p. (gr. 6-12). 35.00 *(978-1-60413-386-8(4),* P161429, Facts On File) Infobase Holdings, Inc.

Stefoff, Rebecca. Colonial Life, 1 vol. Kubinyi, Laszlo, illus. 2003. (American Voices From Ser.). (ENG.). 160p. (gr. 6-6). 41.21 *(978-0-7614-1205-2(0),* 23e5579e-62bb-4199-9af2-3fe85a1892ab) Cavendish Square Publishing LLC.

Sterngass, Jon. Same-Sex Marriage, 1 vol. 2012. (Controversy! Ser.). (ENG.). 112p. (YA). (gr. 8-8). 39.79 *(978-1-60870-490-3(4),* e6911bc9-12d4-4b1d-ad20-64cbe273650d) Cavendish Square Publishing LLC.

Stewart, Gail B. Missing Persons, 1 vol. 2011. (Crime Scene Investigations Ser.). (ENG.). 96p. (gr. 7-7). lib. bdg. 42.03 *(978-1-4205-0534-4(3),* 7c5d8685-46bf-4c2b-81f0-e1fb4a9ba04c, Lucent Pr.) Greenhaven Publishing LLC.

Sullivan, Laura. The Colonial Wigmaker, 1 vol. 2015. (Colonial People Ser.). (ENG.). 48p. (gr. 4-4). 34.07 *(978-1-5026-0480-4(9),* 353e7018-3711-49c1-95c9-e4d18934ccb3) Cavendish Square Publishing LLC.

—The Colonial Woodworker, 1 vol. 2015. (Colonial People Ser.). (ENG.). 48p. (gr. 4-4). 34.07 *(978-1-5026-0484-2(1),* 386ffd4-89db-431c-95a0-e161e8b61c6a) Cavendish Square Publishing LLC.

Summers, Jacque. Disgusting Jobs in Modern America: The down & Dirty Details. 2018. (Disgusting Jobs in History Ser.). (ENG., Illus.). 32p. (J). (gr. 3-6). lib. bdg. 27.99 *(978-1-5435-0366-1(7),* 137199, Capstone Pr.) Capstone.

Tabor, Nancy Maria Grande. Celebraciones / Celebrations: Dias Feriados de Los Estados Unidos y Mexico. Tabor, Nancy Maria Grande, illus. 2004. (Charlesbridge Bilingual Bks.).Tr. of Celebrations (Bilingual). (Illus.). 32p. (J). (gr. -1-2). pap. 7.95 *(978-1-57091-550-5(4))* Charlesbridge Publishing, Inc.

Teacher Created Resources Staff. America: Come on a Journey of Discovery. 2008. (Qeb Travel Through Ser.). (ENG., Illus.). 32p. (J). (gr. 4-7). pap. 7.99 *(978-1-4206-8277-9(6))* Teacher Created Resources, Inc.

Troupe, Thomas Kingsley. Your Life as a Settler in Colonial America. Canga, C. B., illus. 2012. (Way It Was Ser.). (ENG.). 32p. (J). (gr. 2-5). pap. 8.95 *(978-1-4048-7251-6(5),* 118194, Picture Window Bks.) Capstone.

Uhlig, Elizabeth. I See America! Uhlig, Elizabeth, illus. 2009. (Illus.). (J). pap. 12.95 *(978-0-9815345-7-2(0))* Marble Hse. Editions.

Weber, Valerie J. I Come from Afghanistan, 1 vol. 2006. (This Is My Story Ser.). (ENG., Illus.). 24p. (gr. 2-4). pap. 9.15 *(978-0-8368-7240-8(1),* f4c337c5-1679-4bde-b638-5220a9089a6c); lib. bdg. 24.67 *(978-0-8368-7233-0(9),* c17f0a10-45c7-455e-a5a4-b860e29cb9b3) Stevens, Gareth Publishing LLLP. (Weekly Reader Leveled Readers).

—I Come from Chile, 1 vol. 2006. (This Is My Story Ser.). (ENG., Illus.). 24p. (gr. 2-4). lib. bdg. 24.67 *(978-0-8368-7234-7(7),* abe02570-1005-4386-b7e0-d9ae87a928d1, Weekly Reader Leveled Readers) Stevens, Gareth Publishing LLLP.

—I Come from Chile, 1 vol. 2006. (This Is My Story Ser.). (ENG., Illus.). 24p. (gr. 2-4). pap. 9.15 *(978-0-8368-7241-5(X),* d36c6c3d-ce13-45d2-b3f3-4a2a203cdb61, Weekly Reader Leveled Readers) Stevens, Gareth Publishing LLLP.

—I Come from India, 1 vol. 2006. (This Is My Story Ser.). (ENG., Illus.). 24p. (gr. 2-4). pap. 9.15 *(978-0-8368-7242-2(8),* b6882f35-58d7-448f-ab13-43e8adfa319a); lib. bdg. 24.67 *(978-0-8368-7235-4(5),* c9976f69-1f4d-46b7-ab75-0aa34bd3d9f8) Stevens, Gareth Publishing LLLP. (Weekly Reader Leveled Readers).

—I Come from Ivory Coast, 1 vol. 2006. (This Is My Story Ser.). (ENG., Illus.). 24p. (gr. 2-4). pap. 9.15 *(978-0-8368-7243-9(6),* 4ef53f23-b985-4b76-96eb-20ad8eb5a24c); lib. bdg. 24.67 *(978-0-8368-7236-1(3),* 693981c6-e162-4df9-9237-55339ab4864c) Stevens, Gareth Publishing LLLP. (Weekly Reader Leveled Readers).

—I Come from South Korea, 1 vol. 2006. (This Is My Story Ser.). (ENG., Illus.). 24p. (gr. 2-4). lib. bdg. 24.67 *(978-0-8368-7237-8(1),* 639a1b20-a602-44db-960b-a99720757f5a, Weekly Reader Leveled Readers) Stevens, Gareth Publishing LLLP.

—I Come from Ukraine, 1 vol. 2006. (This Is My Story Ser.). (ENG., Illus.). 24p. (gr. 2-4). pap. 9.15 *(978-0-8368-7245-3(2),* e99cfde8-c255-43ce-8568-f40c710999ce, Weekly Reader Leveled Readers) Stevens, Gareth Publishing LLLP.

—I Come from Ukraine, 1 vol. 2006. (This Is My Story Ser.). (ENG., Illus.). 24p. (gr. 2-4). lib. bdg. 24.67 *(978-0-8368-7238-5(X),* 645c9201-c314-4ca6-bb39-fa7a1c408d74, Weekly Reader Leveled Readers) Stevens, Gareth Publishing LLLP.

Weber, Valerie J. & Weber, Valerie J. I Come from South Korea, 1 vol. 2006. (This Is My Story Ser.). (ENG., Illus.). 24p. (gr. 2-4). pap. 9.15 *(978-0-8368-7244-6(4),* 4d5e8a06-bf89-487e-ba44-32eaeb2f1df6, Weekly Reader Leveled Readers) Stevens, Gareth Publishing LLLP.

Whitman, Sylvia. Children of the World War II Home Front. 2005. (Picture the American Past Ser.). (Illus.). 48p. (J). (gr. 2-5). lib. bdg. 22.60 *(978-1-57505-484-1(1))* Lerner Publishing Group.

Whitney, Louise Doak & Whitney, Gleaves. B Is for Buckaroo: A Cowboy Alphabet. Guy, Susan, illus. rev. ed. 2003. (Sports Ser.). (ENG.). 40p. (J). (gr. 1-4). 17.95 *(978-1-58536-139-7(9),* 202000) Sleeping Bear Pr.

Wilder, Laura Ingalls. A Little House Traveler: Writings from Laura Ingalls Wilder's Journeys Across America. 2011. (Little House Nonfiction Ser.). (ENG., Illus.). 368p. (J). (gr. 5). pap. 7.99 *(978-0-06-072492-4(7),* HarperCollins) HarperCollins Pubs.

World Book, Inc. Staff, contrib. by. Christmas Memories in America, 1900 to Now. 2019. (Illus.). 80p. (J). *(978-0-7166-0838-7(3))* World Bk., Inc.

Worth, Richard. The 1970s to The 1980s, 1 vol. 2010. (Hispanic America Ser.). (ENG.). 80p. (gr. 5-5). 36.93 *(978-0-7614-4178-6(6),* 96cd516d-96be-4c76-9718-5b4584d99fae) Cavendish Square Publishing LLC.

Yasuda, Anita. Disgusting Jobs on the American Frontier: The down & Dirty Details. 2018. (Disgusting Jobs in History Ser.). (ENG., Illus.). 32p. (J). (gr. 3-6). lib. bdg. 27.99 *(978-1-5435-0368-5(3),* 137208, Capstone Pr.) Capstone.

Zocchi, Judy. In the United States. Brodie, Neale, illus. 2005. (Global Adventures II Ser.). 32p. (J). pap. 10.95 *(978-1-59646-172-7(1));* lib. bdg. 21.65 *(978-1-59646-065-0(7))* Dingles & Co.

—In the United States/en los Estados Unidos. Brodie, Neale, illus. 2005. (Global Adventures II Ser.).Tr. of En los Estados Unidos. (ENG & SPA.). 32p. (J). pap. 10.95 *(978-1-59646-174-1(8));* lib. bdg. 21.65 *(978-1-59646-066-7(5))* Dingles & Co.

UNITED STATES—SOCIAL LIFE AND CUSTOMS—COLONIAL PERIOD, CA. 1600-1775

Barter, James. Colonial New York. 2003. (Travel Guide To Ser.). (ENG., Illus.). 112p. (J). 30.85 *(978-1-59018-250-5(2),* Lucent Bks.) Cengage Gale.

Broida, Marian. Projects about Colonial Life, 1 vol. Prato, Rodica, illus. 2005. (Hands-On History Ser.). (ENG.). 48p. (gr. 3-3). lib. bdg. 34.07 *(978-0-7614-1603-6(X),* ae6a310f-78fc-4385-9ed2-e8ff31bd42ac) Cavendish Square Publishing LLC.

Burgan, Michael. The Carpenter, 1 vol. 2013. (Colonial People Ser.). (ENG.). 48p. (gr. 4-4). 34.07 *(978-1-60870-411-8(4),* 136afbb8-30a6-4b01-9f27-76dc55766922); pap. 13.93 *(978-1-62712-045-6(9),* b23c84c1-3a77-4c4b-8529-98cec50e325c) Cavendish Square Publishing LLC.

Colonial Life. (J). tchr. ed. 41.95 *(978-0-382-40663-8(X))* Cobblestone Publishing Co.

Colonial Life, 5 bks., Set. Incl. Cities & Towns. Stefoff, Rebecca. 96p. lib. bdg. 165.00 *(978-0-7656-8109-6(9),* Y181735); Daily Living. Hinds, Kathryn. 96p. lib. bdg. 180.00 *(978-0-7656-8110-2(2),* Y181908); Exploration & Settlement. Stefoff, Rebecca. 96p. lib. bdg. 180.00 *(978-0-7656-8108-9(0),* Y182272); Government. Kelly, Martin & Kelly, Melissa. 96p. lib. bdg. 180.00 *(978-0-7656-8112-6(9),* Y182476); Trade & Commerce. Altman, Linda Jacobs. 98p. lib. bdg. 200.00 *(978-0-7656-8111-9(0),* Y184849); (C). (gr. 6-18). (ENG., Illus.). 96p. 2007. Set lib. bdg. 165.00 *(978-0-7656-8107-2(2),* Y181691) Routledge.

Fisher, Verna. Colonial Towns. 2011. (Colonial Quest Ser.). (ENG.). 32p. (J). (gr. 2-5). 21.19 *(978-1-936313-60-0(X))* Nomad Pr.

Heinrichs, Ann. The Shipbuilder, 1 vol. 2013. (Colonial People Ser.). (ENG.). 48p. (gr. 4-4). pap. 13.93 *(978-1-62712-048-7(3),* d51ce8f1-e09a-4a09-b755-73bb6e5b92f0) Cavendish Square Publishing LLC.

Hinman, Bonnie. The Scoop on School & Work in Colonial America. 2012. (Life in the American Colonies Ser.). (ENG.). 32p. (gr. 3-4). pap. 47.70 *(978-1-4296-8461-3(5),* Capstone Pr.); (J). pap. 8.10 *(978-1-4296-7986-2(7),* 118318) Capstone.

Krebs, Laurie. A Day in the Life of a Colonial Shipwright. 2009. (Library of Living & Working in Colonial Times Ser.). 24p. (gr. 3-3). 42.50 *(978-1-60853-738-9(2),* PowerKids Pr.) Rosen Publishing Group, Inc., The.

Maestro, Betsy. The New Americans: Colonial Times: 1620-1689. Maestro, Giulio, illus. 2004. (ENG.). 48p. (J). (gr. 2-7). pap. 11.99 *(978-0-06-057572-4(7),* HarperCollins) HarperCollins Pubs.

Mara, Wil. The Gunsmith, 1 vol. 2013. (Colonial People Ser.). (ENG.). 48p. (gr. 4-4). 34.07 *(978-1-60870-414-9(9),* 41700ab7-35ad-4c15-b465-d8c823d08968); pap. 13.93 *(978-1-62712-046-3(7),* 579f8b88-f353-434a-ae3d-8bfe60213555) Cavendish Square Publishing LLC.

Mead, Wendy. The Merchant, 1 vol. 2013. (Colonial People Ser.). (ENG.). 48p. (gr. 4-4). 34.07 *(978-1-60870-415-6(7),* f18c8cad-bf17-4dc2-972b-b264fb47ea42); pap. 13.93 *(978-1-62712-047-0(5),* 6a3babb9-af96-4e31-a45f-9ce34247d589) Cavendish Square Publishing LLC.

Petersen, Christine. The Wheelwright, 1 vol. 2013. (Colonial People Ser.). (ENG.). 48p. (gr. 4-4). 34.07 *(978-1-60870-419-4(X),* 9b3fa622-cc05-404d-a730-415b9514b035); pap. 13.93 *(978-1-62712-049-4(1),* bdf2b57d-e06b-4052-a881-9886cdfa4cde) Cavendish Square Publishing LLC.

Sherman, Patrice. Colonial America. 2009. (How'd They Do That? Ser.). (Illus.). 64p. (J). (gr. 4-8). lib. bdg. 33.95 *(978-1-58415-817-2(4))* Mitchell Lane Pubs.

Stefoff, Rebecca. Colonial Life, 1 vol. Kubinyi, Laszlo, illus. 2003. (American Voices From Ser.). (ENG.). 160p. (gr. 6-6). 41.21 *(978-0-7614-1205-2(0),* 23e5579e-62bb-4199-9af2-3fe85a1892ab) Cavendish Square Publishing LLC.

Vonne, Mira. Gross Facts about the American Colonies. 2017. (Gross History Ser.). (ENG., Illus.). 32p. (J). (gr. 3-9). lib. bdg. 27.32 *(978-1-5157-4154-1(0),* 133954, Capstone Pr.) Capstone.

Yasuda, Anita. Disgusting Jobs in Colonial America: The down & Dirty Details. 2018. (Disgusting Jobs in History Ser.). (ENG., Illus.). 32p. (J). (gr. 3-6). lib. bdg. 27.99 *(978-1-5435-0369-2(1),* 137209, Capstone Pr.) Capstone.

UNITED STATES—SOCIAL POLICY

Burlingame, Jeff. Government Entitlements, 1 vol. 2012. (Controversy! Ser.). (ENG.). 112p. (YA). (gr. 8-8). 39.79 *(978-1-60870-491-0(2),* 95f7f406-2e9b-475c-bc7b-5d1e037bc6b7) Cavendish Square Publishing LLC.

Heitkamp, Kristina Lyn, ed. Learned Helplessness, Welfare, & the Poverty Cycle, 1 vol. 2018. (Current Controversies Ser.). (ENG.). 176p. (gr. 10-12). 48.03 *(978-1-5345-0388-5(9),* aa5eed77-34c7-42a4-99bd-8f85ad49ce98) Greenhaven Publishing LLC.

UNITED STATES—SOLDIERS

see Soldiers—United States

UNITED STATES—STATE GOVERNMENTS

see State Governments

UNITED STATES—STATISTICS

TIME for Kids Almanac 2009. 2008. (Time Inc. Home Entertainment Library-Bound Titles Ser.). 256p. (YA). (gr. 5-12). lib. bdg. 39.93 *(978-0-7613-4052-2(1),* Twenty-First Century Bks.) Lerner Publishing Group.

UNITED STATES—SUPREME COURT

Aldred, Lisa. Thurgood Marshall. 2004. (Black Americans of Achievement Legacy Edition Ser.). (ENG., Illus.). 112p. (gr. 6-12). 35.00 *(978-0-7910-8163-1(X),* P114167, Facts On File) Infobase Holdings, Inc.

Barrington, Richard. Sonia Sotomayor, 1 vol. 2014. (Making a Difference: Leaders Who Are Changing the World Ser.). (ENG.). 48p. (YA). (gr. 5-5). 28.41 *(978-1-62275-435-9(2),* 643eba7b-a816-4c8e-9c3d-1b628b35c60a) Rosen Publishing Group, Inc., The.

Beier, Anne. The Supreme Court & the Judicial Branch. (Primary Source Library of American Citizenship Ser.). 32p. (gr. 5-5). 2009. 47.90 *(978-1-61511-230-2(8))* 2003. (ENG., Illus.). lib. bdg. 29.13 *(978-0-8239-4478-1(6),* 8d29fc15-bd1e-40ae-bd8e-3adeb26adac8) Rosen Publishing Group, Inc., The. (Rosen Reference).

Benson, Michael. William H. Taft. 2004. (Presidential Leaders Ser.). (ENG., Illus.). 112p. (gr. 6-12). 29.27 *(978-0-8225-0849-6(4),* Lerner Pubns.) Lerner Publishing Group.

Boerst, William J. Galileo Galilei & the Science of Motion. 2004. (Profiles in Science Ser.). (Illus.). 144p. (YA). (gr. 6-12). lib. bdg. 26.95 *(978-1-931798-00-6(1))* Reynolds, Morgan Inc.

Brannen, Daniel E., et al. Supreme Court Drama: Cases That Changed America. 2nd ed. 2011. *(978-1-4144-8668-0(5)); (978-1-4144-8660-4(X)); (978-1-4144-8659-8(6)); (978-1-4144-8658-1(8)); (978-1-4144-8657-4(X))*;Set. (ENG.). 1630p. 557.00 *(978-1-4144-8656-7(1))* Cengage Gale. (UXL).

Branscomb, Leslie Wolf. Earl Warren. 2011. (Supreme Court Justices Ser.). (Illus.). 112p. 28.95 *(978-1-59935-158-2(7))* Reynolds, Morgan Inc.

Burton, Dolores T. & Marcellino, Patricia Ann. A Story of Courage: Supreme Court Justice Sonia Sotomayor. 2017. (ENG.). 146p. (J). (gr. 4-7). pap. 10.00 *(978-0-9974421-2-0(3))* Breaklight Pubns.

TUV

Byers, Ann. Clarence Thomas: Conservative Supreme Court Justice, 1 vol. 2019. (African American Trailblazers Ser.). (ENG.). 128p. (gr. 9-9). pap. 22.16 *(978-1-5026-4554-8(8)*, ea5122e5-b0a0-4a2b-863b-4b3f321e20c8) Cavendish Square Publishing LLC.

Cane, Ella. The U. S. Supreme Court, 1 vol. 2014. (Our Government Ser.). (ENG., Illus.). 24p. (J). (gr. 1-3). lib. bdg. 27.99 *(978-1-4765-4203-4(1)*, 124307) Capstone.

Carey Rohan, Rebecca. Thurgood Marshall: The First African-American Supreme Court Justice, 1 vol. 2016. (Great American Thinkers Ser.). (ENG.). 128p. (J). (gr. 9-9). 47.36 *(978-1-5026-1932-7(6)*, 756c9265-9225-4c4f-8b5b-6445c19afc2c) Cavendish Square Publishing LLC.

Carmon, Irin. Notorious RGB Young Readers' Edition: The Life & Times of Ruth Bader Ginsburg. 2017. (ENG., Illus.). 208p. (J). (gr. 3-7). 17.99 *(978-0-06-274853-9(X)*, HarperCollins) HarperCollins Pubs.

Colins, Luke. Thurgood Marshall, 1 vol. 2014. (Great African-Americans Ser.). (ENG., Illus.). 24p. (J). (gr. -1-2). lib. bdg. 24.65 *(978-1-4765-3956-0(1)*, 123955, Capstone Pr.) Capstone.

Corrigan, Jim. John Marshall: The Story of John Marshall. 2011. (Supreme Court Justices Ser.). (Illus.). 112p. (J). 28.95 *(978-1-59935-159-9(5))* Reynolds, Morgan Inc.

Cox, Vicki. Clarence Thomas: Supreme Court Justice. 2008. (Black Americans of Achievement Ser.). (ENG., Illus.). 120p. (gr. 7-12). 35.00 *(978-1-60413-048-5(2)*, P159423, Facts On File) Infobase Holdings, Inc.

De Capua, Sarah. Sandra Day O'Connor, 1 vol. 2013. (Leading Women Ser.). (ENG.). 96p. (YA). (gr. 7-7). 42.64 *(978-0-7614-4961-4(2)*, e5bd4eec-f5ac-4615-923a-b14ad1304d8e); pap. 20.99 *(978-1-62712-117-0(X)*, d5c45fcc-aabe-4f9c-84d2-ea7d6e642c32) Cavendish Square Publishing LLC.

DiPrimio, Pete. The Judicial Branch. 2011. (My Guide to the Constitution Ser.). (Illus.). 48p. (J). (gr. 3-6). lib. bdg. 29.95 *(978-1-58415-944-5(8))* Mitchell Lane Pubs.

Elish, Dan. The U. S. Supreme Court. 2007. (Cornerstones of Freedom Ser.). (Illus.). 48p. (J). (gr. 4-6). 26.00 *(978-0-516-23637-7(7)*, Children's Pr.) Scholastic Library Publishing.

Fowler, Leona. Making Decisions on the Supreme Court: Understanding Government, 1 vol. 2018. (Civics for the Real World Ser.). (ENG.). 16p. (gr. 2-3). pap. *(978-1-5383-6519-9(7)*, 7b67ec02-0eeb-4d90-9af8-ecb17041a4b0, Rosen Classroom) Rosen Publishing Group, Inc., The.

Fridell, Ron. Gideon V. Wainwright: The Right to Free Counsel, 1 vol. 2007. (Supreme Court Milestones Ser.). (ENG., Illus.). 128p. (YA). (gr. 8-8). lib. bdg. 45.50 *(978-0-7614-2146-7(7)*, 9f2f00fa-e6c0-4232-8f92-24e278c9bb2a) Cavendish Square Publishing LLC.

Furgang, Kathy. Ruth Bader Ginsburg: Supreme Court Justice, 1 vol. 2019. (Junior Biographies Ser.). (ENG.). 24p. (gr. 3-4). 24.27 *(978-1-9785-0790-6(9)*, dbce21c1-e875-4a4c-861e-c30ec5685b1a) Enslow Publishing, LLC.

Goldstone, Lawrence. Unpunished Murder: Massacre at Colfax & the Quest for Justice (Scholastic Focus) (ENG.). 288p. (gr. 7). 2020. (YA). pap. 9.99 *(978-1-338-23946-1(5))* 2018. (Illus.). (J). 17.99 *(978-1-338-23945-4(7)*, Scholastic Nonfiction) Scholastic, Inc.

Horn, Geoffrey M. The Supreme Court, 1 vol. 2003. (World Almanac(r) Library of American Government Ser.). (ENG., Illus.). 48p. (gr. 5-8). lib. bdg. 33.67 *(978-0-8368-5459-6(4)*, 2d96a4ed-9b8c-4cd6-906c-983ff6becd30, Gareth Stevens Secondary Library) Stevens, Gareth Publishing LLLP.

—Thurgood Marshall, 1 vol. 2004. (Trailblazers of the Modern World Ser.). (ENG., Illus.). 48p. (gr. 5-8). pap. 15.05 *(978-0-8368-5258-5(3)*, 0eaf0b52-0726-4be3-b1fa-870937b22719); lib. bdg. 33.67 *(978-0-8368-5098-7(X)*, 243d2da1-a59e-4bd5-a401-db59905c50c5) Stevens, Gareth Publishing LLLP. (Gareth Stevens Secondary Library).

Howse, Jennifer. Sandra Day O'Connor. 2007. (Remarkable People Ser.). (Illus.). 24p. (J). (gr. 3-7). pap. 8.95 *(978-1-59036-648-6(4))*; lib. bdg. 24.45 *(978-1-59036-647-9(6))* Weigl Pubs., Inc.

Hunt, Santana. What Does the U. S. Supreme Court Do?, 1 vol. 2017. (Look at Your Government Ser.). (ENG., Illus.). 32p. (J). (gr. 2-2). pap. 11.50 *(978-1-4824-6059-9(9)*, 6354a8ef-1595-42f3-a749-8674351e06a2) Stevens, Gareth Publishing LLLP.

Isle, Mick. A Timeline of the Supreme Court. 2009. (Timelines of American History Ser.). 32p. (gr. 4-4). 47.90 *(978-1-60854-391-5(9)*, Rosen Reference) Rosen Publishing Group, Inc., The.

Jakubiak, David J. What Does a Supreme Court Justice Do? 2010. (How Our Government Works Ser.). 24p. (J). (gr. 3-6). lib. bdg., E-Book 42.50 *(978-1-4488-0031-5(5))*; (ENG., Illus.). pap. 9.25 *(978-1-4358-9818-9(4)*, e1b03e4f-966f-44ef-b010-eb814dc79290, PowerKids Pr.); (ENG., Illus.). lib. bdg. 26.27 *(978-1-4358-9361-0(1)*, 0b1487b1-e8ca-474e-a67b-59e45e307f29, PowerKids Pr.) Rosen Publishing Group, Inc., The.

Jarrow, Gail. Robert H. Jackson: New Deal Lawyer, Supreme Court Justice, Nuremberg Prosecutor. 2008. (ENG., Illus.). 128p. (J). (gr. 4-7). 22.99 *(978-1-59078-511-9(8)*, Calkins Creek) Highlights Pr., c/o Highlights for Children, Inc.

Jones, Brenn. Learning about Equal Rights from the Life of Ruth Bader Ginsburg. 2009. (Character Building Book Ser.). 24p. (gr. 2-3). 42.50 *(978-1-61511-000-1(3)*, PowerKids Pr.) Rosen Publishing Group, Inc., The.

Kanefield, Teri. Thurgood Marshall: The Making of America #6. 2020. (Making of America Ser.). (ENG., Illus.). 256p. (J). (gr. 5-9). 16.99 *(978-1-4197-4104-3(7)*, 1264101, Abrams Bks. for Young Readers) Abrams, Inc.

Kemp, Kristin. Amazing Americans: Thurgood Marshall, 1 vol. rev. ed. 2014. (Social Studies: Informational Text Ser.). (ENG., Illus.). 32p. (gr. 3-4). pap. 11.99 *(978-1-4333-7374-9(2))* Teacher Created Materials, Inc.

Kolpin, Amanda. Understanding Supreme Court Cases. 2018. (What's up with Your Government? Ser.). (ENG.). 32p. (J). (gr. 4-7). 20.80 *(978-1-5311-8618-0(1))* Perfection Learning Corp.

—Understanding Supreme Court Cases, 1 vol. 2017. (What's up with Your Government? Ser.). (ENG., Illus.). 32p. (J). (gr. 4-5). 27.93 *(978-1-5383-2236-9(6)*, 6d20cc53-4d76-419d-8fa5-7a0c5d3c5af7); pap. 11.00 *(978-1-5383-2332-8(X)*, b0c1d349-79bb-4b3d-a43b-31ae4b82f64d) Rosen Publishing Group, Inc., The. (PowerKids Pr.).

Kramer, Barbara. National Geographic Readers: Sonia Sotomayor. 2016. (Readers Bios Ser.). (Illus.). 48p. (J). (gr. 1-3). pap. 5.99 *(978-1-4263-2289-1(5)*, National Geographic Kids) Disney Publishing Worldwide.

LeVert, Suzanne. The Supreme Court, 1 vol. 2003. (Kaleidoscope: Government Ser.). (ENG., Illus.). 48p. (gr. 4-4). 32.64 *(978-0-7614-1453-7(3)*, dd23a85d-6bcc-40a6-aa4c-db817489aaed) Cavendish Square Publishing LLC.

Levy, Debbie. I Dissent: Ruth Bader Ginsburg Makes Her Mark. Baddeley, Elizabeth, illus. 2016. (ENG.). 40p. (J). (gr. -1-3). 18.99 *(978-1-4814-6559-5(7)*, Simon & Schuster Bks. For Young Readers) Simon & Schuster Bks. For Young Readers.

Linde, Barbara M. Becoming a Supreme Court Justice, 1 vol. 2015. (Who's Your Candidate? Choosing Government Leaders Ser.). (ENG., Illus.). 32p. (J). (gr. 3-4). pap. 11.50 *(978-1-4824-4051-5(2)*, d4e3a4e2-a86d-4450-ab19-9a846a8ff364) Stevens, Gareth Publishing LLLP.

—Thurgood Marshall, 1 vol. 2011. (Civil Rights Crusaders Ser.). (ENG., Illus.). 24p. (gr. 2-3). (J). pap. 9.15 *(978-1-4339-5700-0(0)*, a763392e-f931-40e5-a06b-9318b2a8cb6e, Gareth Stevens Learning Library); (YA). 25.27 *(978-1-4339-5698-0(5)*, d09a8987-29e0-4a37-8c3b-77d76a0f9247) Stevens, Gareth Publishing LLLP.

Littlefield, Sophie. Oliver Wendell Holmes Jr: The Supreme Court & American Legal Thought. 2009. (Library of American Lives & Times Ser.). 112p. (gr. 5-5). 69.20 *(978-1-60853-496-8(0))* Rosen Publishing Group, Inc., The.

Madani, Hamed. The Supreme Court & the Judicial Branch: How the Federal Courts Interpret Our Laws, 1 vol. 2013. (Constitution & the United States Government Ser.). (ENG., Illus.). 104p. (gr. 5-6). 35.93 *(978-0-7660-4065-6(8)*, e7b7c827-a140-4248-89e4-33714c7cbfa8) Enslow Publishing, LLC.

McElroy, Lisa Tucker. John G. Roberts, Jr: Chief Justice. 2006. (Gateway Biographies Ser.). (ENG., Illus.). 48p. (J). (gr. 4-8). lib. bdg. 26.60 *(978-0-8225-6389-1(4)*, Lerner Pubns.) Lerner Publishing Group.

McNeese, Tim, ed. Great Supreme Court Decisions Set. 2007. (Great Supreme Court Decisions Ser.). (ENG.). (gr. 5-8). 395.40 *(978-0-7910-9679-6(3)*, P179176, Facts On File) Infobase Holdings, Inc.

Mead, Wendy. William H. Taft, 1 vol. 2012. (Presidents & Their Times Ser.). (ENG.). 96p. (gr. 6-6). 36.93 *(978-1-60870-186-5(7)*, c3f6f76c-90ed-45ce-9fab-680c514e816d) Cavendish Square Publishing LLC.

Meltzer, Brad. I Am Sonia Sotomayor. Eliopoulos, Christopher, illus. 2018. (Ordinary People Change the World Ser.). 40p. (J). (gr. k-4). 15.99 *(978-0-7352-2873-3(6)*, Dial Bks) Penguin Young Readers Group.

Micklos Jr., John. Ruth Bader Ginsburg: Get to Know the Justice Who Speaks Her Mind. 2019. (People You Should Know Ser.). (ENG., Illus.). 32p. (J). (gr. 3-6). pap. 7.95 *(978-1-5435-5926-2(3)*, 139904, Capstone Pr.) Capstone.

Murray, Julie. Supreme Court. 2017. (My Government Ser.). (ENG., Illus.). 24p. (J). (gr. -1-2). lib. bdg. 31.36 *(978-1-5321-0400-8(6)*, 26526, Abdo Kids) ABDO Publishing Co.

Naden, Corinne & Flum Galvin, Irene. Marbury V. Madison: The Court's Foundation, 1 vol. 2006. (Supreme Court Milestones Ser.). (ENG., Illus.). 128p. (YA). (gr. 8-8). 45.50 *(978-0-7614-1840-5(7)*, 76516cd7-d560-4af1-a357-98dc26318a2e) Cavendish Square Publishing LLC.

Nelson, Drew. Meet the Supreme Court, 1 vol. 2012. (Guide to Your Government Ser.). (ENG., Illus.). 32p. (J). (gr. 4-5). 29.27 *(978-1-4339-7268-3(9)*, 25f37c43-417a-4b98-8f77-51de66ad2af8); pap. 11.50 *(978-1-4339-7269-0(7)*, 29ed6014-f216-45fa-96b9-0674a2acddb0) Stevens, Gareth Publishing LLLP. (Gareth Stevens Learning Library).

Panchyk, Richard. Our Supreme Court: A History with 14 Activities. 2006. (For Kids Ser.: 20). (ENG., Illus.). 208p. (J). (gr. 5-7). pap. 18.95 *(978-1-55652-607-7(5))* Chicago Review Pr., Inc.

Patrick, John J. The Supreme Court of the United States: A Student Companion. 3rd rev. ed. 2006. (Illus.). 416p. (YA). (gr. 6-18). pap. 71.00 *(978-0-19-530925-6(1))* Oxford Univ. Pr., Inc.

Polinsky, Paige. Sonia Sotomayor: Supreme Court Justice. 2019. (Women Leading the Way Ser.). (ENG., Illus.). 24p. (J). (gr. k-3). pap. 7.99 *(978-1-61891-506-1(1)*, 12156, Blastoff! Readers) Bellwether Media.

Polinsky, Paige V. Sonia Sotomayor: Supreme Court Justice. 2019. (Women Leading the Way Ser.). (ENG., Illus.). 24p. (J). (gr. k-3). lib. bdg. 26.95 *(978-1-62617-945-5(X)*, Blastoff! Readers) Bellwether Media.

Randolph, Ryan P. How to Draw the Life & Times of William Howard Taft, 1 vol. 2005. (Kid's Guide to Drawing the Presidents of the United States of America Ser.). (ENG., Illus.). 32p. (YA). (gr. 4-4). 30.27 *(978-1-4042-3003-3(3)*, 04d8ccfb-589a-48c8-833e-ad21ebc569b3) Rosen Publishing Group, Inc., The.

Roland, James. Ruth Bader Ginsburg: Iconic Supreme Court Justice. 2016. (Gateway Biographies Ser.). (ENG., Illus.). 48p. (J). (gr. 4-8). E-Book 47.99 *(978-1-5124-0597-2(3)*, Lerner Pubns.) Lerner Publishing Group.

Rose, Simon. Supreme Court. 2016. (Illus.). 32p. (J). *(978-1-5105-2251-0(4))* SmartBook Media, Inc.

Rosen, Daniel. Dred Scott & the Supreme Court: Text Pairs. 2008. (Bridges/Navigators Ser.). (J). (gr. 5). 94.00 *(978-1-4108-8413-8(9))* Benchmark Education Co.

Sandra Day O'Connor. 2005. 12p. (gr. k-4). 2.95 *(978-0-635-02621-7(X))* Gallopade International.

Scirri, Kaitlin. Ruth Bader Ginsburg: Supreme Court Justice, 1 vol. 2019. (Barrier-Breaker Bios Ser.). (ENG.). 32p. (gr. 2-2). pap. 11.58 *(978-1-5026-4964-5(0)*, 36468a8a-5b1d-423f-a4ee-eab76a22d5d6) Cavendish Square Publishing LLC.

Shichtman, Sandra H. Sonia Sotomayor. 2011. (Supreme Court Justices Ser.). (Illus.). 111p. 28.95 *(978-1-59935-156-8(0))* Reynolds, Morgan Inc.

Sommers, Michael A. A Timeline of the Supreme Court, 1 vol. 2004. (Timelines of American History Ser.). (ENG., Illus.). 32p. (gr. 4-4). lib. bdg. 29.13 *(978-0-8239-4541-2(3)*, de6a6a6c-6ee8-4a0c-aa97-19e64a51d5ff, Rosen Reference) Rosen Publishing Group, Inc., The.

Sotomayor, Sonia. Pasando Páginas: La Historia de Mi Vida. Delacre, Lulu, illus. 2018. 40p. (J). (gr. -1-3). 18.99 *(978-0-525-51549-4(6)*, Philomel Bks.) Penguin Young Readers Group.

—Turning Pages: My Life Story. Delacre, Lulu, illus. 2018. 40p. (J). (gr. -1-3). 17.99 *(978-0-525-51408-4(2)*, Philomel Bks.) Penguin Young Readers Group.

Spiller, Sara. Ruth Bader Ginsburg. Bane, Jeff, illus. 2019. (My Early Library: My Itty-Bitty Bio Ser.). (ENG.). 24p. (J). (gr. k-1). pap. 12.79 *(978-1-5341-3925-1(7)*, 212529); lib. bdg. 30.64 *(978-1-5341-4269-5(X)*, 212528) Cherry Lake Publishing.

Stoltman, Joan. Thurgood Marshall, 1 vol. 2018. (Heroes of Black History Ser.). (ENG.). 32p. (gr. 3-4). 28.27 *(978-1-5382-3021-3(6)*, 9e41f34f-bc53-4ad9-9b23-60da96338bda) Stevens, Gareth Publishing LLLP.

—20 Fun Facts about the Supreme Court, 1 vol. 2018. (Fun Fact File: U. S. History! Ser.). (ENG.). 32p. (gr. 2-3). pap. 11.50 *(978-1-5382-1915-7(8)*, ed22f6a9-6206-4600-9d12-50bde1615fb7) Stevens, Gareth Publishing LLLP.

Suen, Anastasia. The U. S. Supreme Court, 1 vol. Skeens, Matthew, illus. 2008. (American Symbols Ser.). (ENG.). 24p. (J). (gr. 1-3). 27.32 *(978-1-4048-4707-1(3)*, 95118, Picture Window Bks.) Capstone.

Supreme Court DBQs: Exploring the Cases that Changed History. 2007. (YA). spiral bd. 29.95 *(978-1-932785-28-9(0))* Bill of Rights Institute, The.

Supreme Court Milestones - Group 5, 10 vols., Set. Incl. Plessy V. Ferguson: Separate but Unequal. Axelrod-Contrada, Joan. lib. bdg. 45.50 *(978-0-7614-2951-7(4)*, a3e6613e-d3f8-4e02-8703-fc09a859b6ce); Roberts V. Jaycees: Women's Rights. Dudley Gold, Susan. lib. bdg. 45.50 *(978-0-7614-2952-4(2)*, 04f9ffbc-33ce-4da1-a392-41abaff897a0); U. S. V. Eichman: Flag Burning & Free Speech. Fridell, Ron. lib. bdg. 45.50 *(978-0-7614-2953-1(0)*, 7f038b36-3bb1-4f21-a39a-5bf77dfbfc17); U. S. V. Nixon: The Limits of Presidential Privilege. Stefoff, Rebecca. lib. bdg. 45.50 *(978-0-7614-2955-5(7)*, 4db6aa1a-1655-4841-87db-dd1d01e53f02); Worcester V. Georgia: American Indian Rights. Dudley Gold, Susan. lib. bdg. 45.50 *(978-0-7614-2956-2(5)*, 6c168d5f-1554-4a47-b5c9-55ffb19b2600); 128p. (YA). (gr. 8-8). (Supreme Court Milestones Ser.). (ENG.). 2009. Set lib. bdg. 227.50 *(978-0-7614-2949-4(2)*, 1e58a2e6-2c2b-45a6-9776-aeb6675e200c, Cavendish Square) Cavendish Square Publishing LLC.

Supreme Court Milestones Group 3, 10 vols., Set. Incl. Gideon V. Wainwright: The Right to Free Counsel. Fridell, Ron. (YA). lib. bdg. 45.50 *(978-0-7614-2146-7(7)*, 9f2f00fa-e6c0-4232-8f92-24e278c9bb2a); New York Times Co. V. Sullivan: Freedom of the Press or Libel? Dudley Gold, Susan. (YA). lib. bdg. 45.50 *(978-0-7614-2145-0(9)*, 53fb67e0-7ad8-4d30-bcc8-bfdf67d3b98a); Reno V. Aclu: Internet Censorship. Axelrod-Contrada, Joan. (YA). lib. bdg. 45.50 *(978-0-7614-2144-3(0)*, b8cb54ba-eff9-4bc1-a337-1ce93d2d0e3b); Tinker V. des Moines: Free Speech for Students. Dudley Gold, Susan. (YA). lib. bdg. 45.50 *(978-0-7614-2142-9(4)*, 50a15397-ed35-4b8d-b27b-01c21a7b756d); United States V. Amistad: Slave Ship Mutiny. Dudley Gold, Susan. (J). lib. bdg. 45.50 *(978-0-7614-2143-6(2)*, 37ed5658-e209-4386-81f8-e545b2d42868); (Illus.). 128p. (gr. 8-8). (Supreme Court Milestones Ser.). (ENG.). 2007. Set lib. bdg. 227.50 *(978-0-7614-2140-5(8)*, 08b86cd9-1c4b-4ebc-b604-8260ce171a32, Cavendish Square) Cavendish Square Publishing LLC.

Taylor-Butler, Christine. The Supreme Court. 2008. (True Book: American History, Revised Ser.). (ENG., Illus.). 48p. (J). (gr. 3-5). 21.19 *(978-0-531-12636-3(6)*, Children's Pr.) Scholastic Library Publishing.

Torres, John A. Sonia Sotomayor: First Latina Supreme Court Justice, 1 vol. 2015. (Influential Latinos Ser.). (ENG., Illus.). 128p. (gr. 7-7). 38.93 *(978-0-7660-7001-1(8)*, 651b4c34-0dcb-4d08-b8bc-f31f9a85801e) Enslow Publishing, LLC.

Tyner, Artika R. So You Want to Be a Supreme Court Justice. 2019. (Being in Government Ser.). (ENG., Illus.). 32p. (J). (gr. 3-6). pap. 7.95 *(978-1-5435-7527-9(7)*, 141057); lib. bdg. 27.99 *(978-1-5435-7197-4(2)*, 140442) Capstone.

US Supreme Court Landmark Cases, 16 vols. 2016. (U. S. Supreme Court Landmark Cases Ser.). (ENG.). 128p. (J). (gr. 7-7). lib. bdg. 311.44 *(978-0-7660-8418-6(3)*, d29fb48f-d56c-42b4-b87e-c00a3618fd57) Enslow Publishing, LLC.

Wagner, Heather Lehr. The Supreme Court. 2nd rev. ed. 2007. (U. Government: How It Works). (ENG., Illus.). 104p. (gr. 5-9). lib. bdg. 30.00 *(978-0-7910-9283-5(6)*, P125641, Facts On File) Infobase Holdings, Inc.

Weakland, Mark. When Bill Gates Memorized the Encyclopedia. Volpari, Daniela, illus. 2018. (Leaders Doing Headstands Ser.). (ENG.). 32p. (J). (gr. 1-4). pap. 7.95 *(978-1-5158-3048-1(9)*, 138683, Picture Window Bks.) Capstone.

—When Ruth Bader Ginsburg - Chewed 100 Sticks of Gum. Volpari, Daniela, illus. 2018. (Leaders Doing Headstands Ser.). (ENG.). 32p. (J). (gr. 1-4). lib. bdg. 28.65 *(978-1-5158-3039-9(X)*, 138676, Picture Window Bks.) Capstone.

Wetterer, Charles M. & Wetterer, Margaret K. Chief Justice. Walters, Kurt K. C., illus. 2005. 32p. (J). *(978-1-59336-306-2(0))*; pap. *(978-1-59336-307-9(9))* Mondo Publishing.

Wheeler, Jill C. Thurgood Marshall. 2003. (Breaking Barriers Ser.). 64p. (gr. 3-8). lib. bdg. 27.07 *(978-1-57765-907-5(4)*, Abdo & Daughters) ABDO Publishing Co.

Whitelaw, Nancy. Mr. Civil Rights: The Story of Thurgood Marshall. 2nd rev. exp. ed. 2004. (Notable Americans Ser.). (Illus.). 144p. (YA). (gr. 6-12). 23.95 *(978-1-931798-02-0(8))* Reynolds, Morgan Inc.

—Thurgood Marshall. 2011. (Supreme Court Justices Ser.). (Illus.). 128p. 28.95 *(978-1-59935-157-5(9))* Reynolds, Morgan Inc.

Wilson, Natashya. How to Draw the Life & Times of William Howard Taft. 2009. (Kid's Guide to Drawing the Presidents of the United States of America Ser.). 32p. (gr. 4-4). 50.50 *(978-1-61511-165-7(4)*, PowerKids Pr.) Rosen Publishing Group, Inc., The.

Winter, Jonah. Ruth Bader Ginsburg: The Case of R. B. G. vs. Inequality. Innerst, Stacy, illus. 2017. (ENG.). 48p. (J). (gr. 1-4). 18.95 *(978-1-4197-2559-3(9)*, 1163401, Abrams Bks. for Young Readers) Abrams, Inc.

—Sonia Sotomayor. Rodriguez, Edel, illus. 2015. 40p. pap. 8.00 *(978-1-61003-616-0(6))* Center for the Collaborative Classroom.

—Sonia Sotomayor: A Judge Grows in the Bronx/la Juez Que Creció en el Bronx. Rodriguez, Edel, illus. 2009. (SPA & ENG.). 40p. (J). (gr. -1-3). 18.99 *(978-1-4424-0303-1(9)*, Atheneum Bks. for Young Readers) Simon & Schuster Children's Publishing.

—Thurgood. Collier, Bryan, illus. 2019. 40p. (J). (gr. k-4). 17.99 *(978-1-5247-6533-0(3)*, Schwartz & Wade Bks.) Random Hse. Children's Bks.

Wroble, Lisa A. The Right to Counsel: From Gideon V. Wainwright to Gideon's Trumpet, 1 vol. 2009. (Famous Court Cases That Became Movies Ser.). (ENG., Illus.). 104p. (gr. 6-7). lib. bdg. 35.93 *(978-0-7660-3057-2(1)*, 54eadea1-20f9-4133-ad4c-186d5574f8dc) Enslow Publishing, LLC.

Zimmerman, W. Frederick. The Nine Current Supreme Court Justices: Colorful Info for Curious Minds #3. 2007. 36p. per. 17.81 *(978-1-934840-01-6(7))* Nimble Bks. LLC.

UNITED STATES—TAXATION

see Taxation—United States

UNITED STATES—TERRITORIAL EXPANSION

Alagna, Magdalena. The Louisiana Purchase: Expanding America's Boundaries. 2009. (Life in the New American Nation Ser.). 32p. (gr. 4-4). 47.90 *(978-1-61514-284-2(3))* Rosen Publishing Group, Inc., The.

Burgan, Michael. The Louisiana Purchase. rev. ed. 2016. (Making a New Nation Ser.). (ENG., Illus.). 48p. (J). (gr. 3-5). pap. 8.99 *(978-1-4846-3596-4(5)*, 133674, Heinemann) Capstone.

Casciato, Daniel. Expansion & Reform: (Early 1800s-1861) 2007. (Presidents of the United States Ser.). (Illus.). 48p. (J). (gr. 4-7). lib. bdg. 29.05 *(978-1-59036-741-4(3))* Weigl Pubs., Inc.

—Expansion & Reform: Early 1800s-1861. 2007. (Presidents of the United States Ser.). (Illus.). 48p. (J). (gr. 4-7). per. 11.95 *(978-1-59036-742-1(1))* Weigl Pubs., Inc.

Chastain, Zachary. Scandals & Glory: Politics in the 1800s. 2009. (Daily Life in America in the 1800s Ser.). 64p. (YA). (gr. 7-18). lib. bdg. 22.95 *(978-1-4222-1787-0(6))* Mason Crest.

—Scandals & Glory: Politics in The 1800s. 2009. (Daily Life in America in the 1800s Ser.). 64p. (YA). (gr. 7-18). pap. 9.95 *(978-1-4222-1860-0(0))* Mason Crest.

Christopher, Nick. The Dream of Manifest Destiny: Immigrants & the Westward Expansion, 1 vol., 1. 2015. (Spotlight on Immigration & Migration Ser.). (ENG., Illus.). 24p. (J). (gr. 4-5). pap. 11.00 *(978-1-5081-4071-9(5)*, c3c88689-d9f8-432c-a97c-a01dd9104c81, PowerKids Pr.) Rosen Publishing Group, Inc., The.

Clinton, Greg. The Louisiana Purchase, 1 vol. 2015. (Expanding America Ser.). (ENG., Illus.). 96p. (YA). (gr. 8-8). lib. bdg. 44.50 *(978-1-5026-0962-5(2)*, f35c0639-c860-46a9-9a7f-2ff61ac97757) Cavendish Square Publishing LLC.

Collins, Terry. Into the West: Causes & Effects of U. S. Westward Expansion, 1 vol. 2013. (Cause & Effect Ser.). (ENG.). 32p. (J). (gr. 3-6). 27.99 *(978-1-4765-0237-3(4)*, 122291); pap. 8.95 *(978-1-4765-3403-9(9)*, 123534) Capstone.

Deibel, Zachary. Manifest Destiny & the Mexican-American War, 1 vol. 2017. (Primary Sources of Westward Expansion Ser.). (ENG.). 64p. (gr. 6-6). lib. bdg. 35.93 *(978-1-5026-2643-1(8)*, a4378558-bf98-40fa-baa8-802b89a94b03) Cavendish Square Publishing LLC.

—Native American Resistance, 1 vol. 2017. (Primary Sources of Westward Expansion Ser.). (ENG.). 64p. (gr. 6-6). 35.93 *(978-1-5026-2644-8(6)*, 62d493ea-ce19-4add-8527-f48beddb405e) Cavendish Square Publishing LLC.

Domnauer, Teresa. True Books: Westward Expansion. 2010. (True Book Ser.). (ENG., Illus.). 48p. (J). (gr. 2-5). 29.00 *(978-0-531-20586-0(X))* Scholastic Library Publishing.

Expansionism. 2010. (Extraordinary Jobs Ser.). (ENG., Illus.). 128p. (gr. 6-12). 45.00 *(978-1-60413-221-2(3)*, P179248, Facts On File) Infobase Holdings, Inc.

Faber, Harold. John Charles Frémont: Pathfinder to the West, 1 vol. 2003. (Great Explorations Ser.). (ENG., Illus.). 80p. (gr. 6-6). 36.93 *(978-0-7614-1481-0(9)*, 3e4bbf2f-84e0-4ea8-a1d0-512b8d5cf8c6) Cavendish Square Publishing LLC.

Favor, Lesli J. A Historical Atlas of America's Manifest Destiny. (United States: Historical Atlases of the Growth of a New Nation Ser.). 64p. (gr. 5-5). 2009. 61.20 *(978-1-60854-250-5(5))* 2004. (ENG., Illus.). (J). lib. bdg. 37.13 *(978-1-4042-0201-6(3)*, 7e0d0682-29df-4e8b-ad8c-c06cddc7ee7f) Rosen Publishing Group, Inc., The.

George, Enzo. The Expanding Frontier. 2015. (J). lib. bdg. *(978-1-62713-489-7(1))* 2014. (ENG.). 48p. (gr. 4-4). lib. bdg. 33.07 *(978-1-5026-0248-0(2)*, fba6921a-3a7b-4c53-9a95-475306e8cf70) Cavendish Square Publishing LLC.

George, Lynn. What Do You Know about Westward Expansion? 2009. (20 Questions: History Ser.). 24p. (gr.

2-3). 42.50 *(978-1-60854-960-3(7),* PowerKids Pr.) Rosen Publishing Group, Inc., The.

Greathouse, Lisa. Crossing a Continent (California) rev. ed. 2017. (Social Studies: Informational Text Ser.). (ENG., Illus.). 32p. (J). (gr. 3-5). pap. 11.99 *(978-1-4258-3241-4(5))* Teacher Created Materials, Inc.

Hamby, Rachel. Children on the American Frontier. 2018. (Children in History Ser.). (ENG., Illus.). 48p. (J). (gr. 5-6). pap. 11.95 *(978-1-63517-979-8(3),* 1635179793); lib. bdg. 34.21 *(978-1-63517-878-4(9),* 1635178789) North Star Editions. (Focus Readers).

Howell, Brian. U.S. Growth & Change in the 19th Century. 2011. (Explorer Library: Language Arts Explorer Ser.). (ENG.). 32p. (gr. 4-8). pap. 14.21 *(978-1-61080-290-1(X),* 201213) Cherry Lake Publishing.

—US Growth & Change in the 19th Century. 2011. (Explorer Library: Language Arts Explorer Ser.). (ENG., Illus.). 32p. (gr. 4-8). lib. bdg. 32.07 *(978-1-61080-202-4(0),* 201180) Cherry Lake Publishing.

Jarnow, Jesse. Manifest Destiny: A Primary Source History of the Settlement of the American Heartland in the Late 19th Century, 1 vol. 2004. (Primary Sources in American History Ser.). (ENG., Illus.). 64p. (J). (gr. 5-8). lib. bdg. 37.13 *(978-1-4042-0176-7(9),* 559b8bf3-0c24-4a9a-982b-31b17d92ca81) Rosen Publishing Group, Inc., The.

Klar, Jeremy. The Louisiana Purchase & Westward Expansion, 1 vol., 1. 2015. (Early American History Ser.). (ENG., Illus.). 80p. (J). (gr. 8-8). lib. bdg. 35.47 *(978-1-68048-271-3(8),* 8edb574c-c4f3-43ba-b586-ea3500ead70c, Britannica Educational Publishing) Rosen Publishing Group, Inc., The.

Kleinmartin, Hex. The Erie Canal, 1 vol. 2015. (Expanding America Ser.). (ENG., Illus.). 96p. (YA). (gr. 8-8). lib. bdg. 44.50 *(978-1-5026-0966-3(5),* 8ac33cb1-287b-4eff-b152-2573187de8a6) Cavendish Square Publishing LLC.

Landau, Elaine. Jefferson's Louisiana Purchase: Would You Make the Deal of the Century?, 1 vol. 2014. (What Would You Do? Ser.). (ENG.). 48p. (gr. 3-4). 27.93 *(978-0-7660-6305-1(4),* 4a599c69-5c92-4682-95d0-9a93f9891693); pap. 11.53 *(978-0-7660-6306-8(2),* 0c240e39-3a16-4732-bbd2-78d7c4c61d18, Enslow Elementary) Enslow Publishing, LLC.

—The Louisiana Purchase: Would You Close the Deal?, 1 vol. 2008. (What Would You Do? Ser.). (ENG., Illus.). 48p. (gr. 3-3). pap. 11.53 *(978-1-59845-196-2(0),* ba81a5a3-263e-4e3c-99e1-1f0721932655); lib. bdg. 27.93 *(978-0-7660-2902-6(6),* ab076af9-e6df-4809-afdd-7ab429047f40) Enslow Publishing, LLC. (Enslow Elementary).

Lassieur, Allison. Westward Expansion: An Interactive History Adventure. rev. ed. 2016. (You Choose: History Ser.). (ENG., Illus.). 112p. (J). (gr. 3-7). pap. 6.95 *(978-1-5157-4259-3(8),* 134014, Capstone Pr.) Capstone.

Lawrence, Blythe. The Louisiana Purchase. 2018. (Expansion of Our Nation Ser.). (ENG., Illus.). 32p. (J). (gr. 3-5). pap. 9.95 *(978-1-63517-984-2(X),* 163517984X); lib. bdg. 31.35 *(978-1-63517-883-8(5),* 1635178835) North Star Editions. (Focus Readers).

—The Louisiana Purchase. 2018. (Illus.). 32p. (J). *(978-1-4896-9874-2(4),* AV2 by Weigl) Weigl Pubs., Inc.

Levy, Janey. Mapping America's Westward Expansion: Applying Geographic Tools & Interpreting Maps. 2009. (Critical Thinking in American History Ser.). 48p. (gr. 5-8). 53.00 *(978-1-61512-095-6(5),* Rosen Reference) Rosen Publishing Group, Inc., The.

Loh-Hagan, Virginia. Heading West: Oregon Trail & Westward Expansion. 2019. (Behind the Curtain Ser.). (ENG.). 32p. (J). (gr. 4-8). pap. 14.21 *(978-1-5341-3995-4(8),* 212809); (Illus.). lib. bdg. 32.07 *(978-1-5341-4339-5(4),* 212808) Cherry Lake Publishing. (45th Parallel Press).

Lynch, Seth. The Louisiana Purchase, 1 vol. 2018. (Look at U. S. History Ser.). (ENG.). 32p. (gr. 2-2). 28.27 *(978-1-5382-2131-0(4),* 6a875d97-be5b-480b-a71b-9c467ad9da6c) Stevens, Gareth Publishing LLLP.

Lynette, Rachel. The Louisiana Purchase, 1 vol. 2013. (Pioneer Spirit: the Westward Expansion Ser.). (Illus.). 24p. (J). (ENG.). (gr. 2-3). pap. 9.25 *(978-1-4777-0895-8(2),* a62ea59e-dc6c-4758-a467-b78fe89be66c); (ENG., (gr. 2-3). lib. bdg. 26.27 *(978-1-4777-0781-4(6),* acb9c5a6-da9b-41af-a96d-5cc2e728ce70); (gr. 3-6). pap. 49.50 *(978-1-4777-0896-5(0))* Rosen Publishing Group, Inc., The. (PowerKids Pr.).

—The Oregon Trail, 1 vol. 2013. (Pioneer Spirit: the Westward Expansion Ser.). (ENG.). 24p. (J). (gr. 2-3). 26.27 *(978-1-4777-0786-9(7),* 85daa1aa-68ff-435a-9f1f-19327c89708a); (Illus.). pap. 9.25 *(978-1-4777-0905-4(3),* ab0ff1dd-2296-4d9a-9b10-8084ed8aad2a) Rosen Publishing Group, Inc., The. (PowerKids Pr.).

Marsh, Carole. John C. Fremont. 2004. 12p. (gr. k-4). 2.95 *(978-0-635-02380-3(6))* Gallopade International.

—What a Deal! The Louisiana Purchase. 2003. 32p. (J). (gr. 3-8). pap. 5.95 *(978-0-635-02123-6(4))* Gallopade International.

Mattern, Joanne. The Gateway Arch: Celebrating Western Expansion. 2017. (Core Content Social Studies — Let's Celebrate America Ser.). (ENG., Illus.). 32p. (J). (gr. 2-5). pap. 8.99 *(978-1-63440-238-5(3),* a460910d-62ac-482a-b5c1-70a8fc8929b4); lib. bdg. 26.65 *(978-1-63440-228-6(6),* 87a0f930-7e15-4ac0-9985-faabb8adeab8) Red Chair Pr.

Maynard, Charles W. John Charles Fremont: The Pathfinder. 2009. (Famous Explorers of the American West Ser.). 24p. (gr. 3-4). 42.50 *(978-1-61512-503-6(5),* PowerKids Pr.) Rosen Publishing Group, Inc., The.

Miner Huey, Lois. American Archaeology Uncovers the Westward Movement, 1 vol. 2010. (American Archaeology Ser.). (ENG., Illus.). 64p. (gr. 5-5). 34.07 *(978-0-7614-4265-3(0),* 72ab4b13-65ff-4df0-9ad9-f0412472b74d) Cavendish Square Publishing LLC.

Moriarty, J. T. Manifest Destiny: A Primary Source History of America's Territorial Expansion in the 19th Century. 2009. (Primary Sources in American History Ser.). 64p. (gr. 5-8). 58.50 *(978-1-60851-490-8(0))* Rosen Publishing Group, Inc., The.

Mulhall, Jill K. Expanding the Nation, 1 vol. rev. ed. 2005. (Social Studies: Informational Text Ser.). (ENG.). 24p. (gr. 4-8). pap. 10.99 *(978-0-7439-8905-3(8))* Teacher Created Materials, Inc.

Musolf, Nell. The Split History of Westward Expansion in the United States: A Perspectives Flip Book, 1 vol. 2012. (Perspectives Flip Bks.). (ENG.). 64p. (J). (gr. 5-9). pap. 8.95 *(978-0-7565-4596-3(X),* 120438, Compass Point Bks.) Capstone.

Nelson, Sheila. From Sea to Shining Sea: Americans Move West, 13 vols. 2005. (How America Became America Ser.). (Illus.). 96p. (J). lib. bdg. *(978-1-59084-900-2(0))* Mason Crest.

—Thomas Jefferson's America: The Louisiana Purchase (1800-1811) 2006. (How America Became America Ser.). (Illus.). 96p. (YA). lib. bdg. 22.95 *(978-1-59084-904-0(3))* Mason Crest.

O'Donoghue, Sean. Thomas Jefferson & the Louisiana Purchase, 1 vol. 2016. (Spotlight on American History Ser.). (ENG., Illus.). 24p. (J). (gr. 4-6). 27.93 *(978-1-5081-4948-4(8),* 05df1466-a916-4843-9a6b-54ecd33a7ede, PowerKids Pr.) Rosen Publishing Group, Inc., The.

Olson, Steven. The Oregon Trail: A Primary Source History of the Route to the American West. 2009. (Primary Sources in American History Ser.). 64p. (gr. 5-8). 58.50 *(978-1-60851-501-1(X))* Rosen Publishing Group, Inc., The.

The Oregon Trail. 2013. (Pioneer Spirit: the Westward Expansion Ser.). 24p. (J). (gr. 3-6). pap. 49.50 *(978-1-4777-0906-1(1),* PowerKids Pr.) Rosen Publishing Group, Inc., The.

Otfinoski, Steven. A Primary Source History of Westward Expansion. 2015. (Primary Source History Ser.). (ENG., Illus.). 32p. (J). (gr. 3-6). lib. bdg. 27.99 *(978-1-4914-1841-3(9),* 127277, Capstone Pr.) Capstone.

Primary Sources of Westward Expansion, 12 vols. 2017. (Primary Sources of Westward Expansion Ser.). (ENG.). 64p. (gr. 6-6). lib. bdg. 215.58 *(978-1-5026-2646-2(2),* bf5577d4-f518-4906-9728-c9abc40b0b4f, Cavendish Square) Cavendish Square Publishing LLC.

Raabe, Emily. Thomas Jefferson & the Louisiana Purchase. 2009. (Westward Ho! Ser.). 24p. (gr. 2-3). 42.50 *(978-1-60854-763-0(9),* PowerKids Pr.) Rosen Publishing Group, Inc., The.

Rajczak Nelson, Kristen. Life As a Pioneer, 1 vol. 2013. (What You Didn't Know about History Ser.). (ENG., Illus.). 24p. (J). (gr. 2-3). pap. 9.15 *(978-1-4339-8420-4(2),* 2236198f-8a63-4d4f-ab46-7a6833211d41); lib. bdg. 25.27 *(978-1-4339-8419-8(9),* 70ffdfd8-94ae-4044-9740-bc2cc0ae94ad) Stevens, Gareth Publishing LLLP.

Randolph, Ryan P. Following the Great Herds: The Plains Indians & the American Buffalo. 2009. (Library of the Westward Expansion Ser.). 24p. (gr. 3-4). 42.50 *(978-1-60853-934-5(2),* PowerKids Pr.) Rosen Publishing Group, Inc., The.

Raum, Elizabeth. Cutting a Path: Daniel Boone & the Cumberland Gap. 2015. (Adventures on the American Frontier Ser.). (ENG., Illus.). 32p. (J). (gr. 3-6). pap. 7.95 *(978-1-4914-4909-7(8),* 128744) Capstone.

—Expanding a Nation: Causes & Effects of the Louisiana Purchase, 1 vol. 2013. (Cause & Effect Ser.). (ENG.). 32p. (J). (gr. 3-6). 27.99 *(978-1-4765-0236-6(6),* 122290); pap. 8.95 *(978-1-4765-3402-2(0),* 123533) Capstone.

Rice, Katelyn. The Great Leap Westward. rev. ed. 2017. (Social Studies: Informational Text Ser.). (ENG., Illus.). 32p. (gr. 4-8). pap. 11.99 *(978-1-4938-3791-5(5))* Teacher Created Materials, Inc.

RJF Publishing Staff & Hankins, Chelsey. The Gateway Arch. 2009. (Symbols of American Freedom Ser.). 48p. (gr. 4-6). 30.00 *(978-1-60413-513-8(1),* Chelsea Clubhse.) Infobase Holdings, Inc.

Roberts, Russell. The Railroad Fuels Westward Expansion (1870s) 2012. (Illus.). 47p. (J). lib. bdg. 29.95 *(978-1-61228-290-9(3))* Mitchell Lane Pubs.

Romano, Amy. A Historical Atlas of the United States & Its Territories. 2009. (United States: Historical Atlases of the Growth of a New Nation Ser.). 64p. (gr. 5-5). 61.20 *(978-1-60854-255-0(6))* Rosen Publishing Group, Inc., The.

Roza, Greg. Westward Expansion, 1 vol. 2011. (Story of America Ser.). (ENG., Illus.). 32p. (J). (gr. 4-5). pap. 11.50 *(978-1-4339-4781-0(1),* a461c41e-ac53-4d94-b48f-966439839c9a); lib. bdg. 29.27 *(978-1-4339-4780-3(3),* 22526696-52e7-4d1f-8437-511ab40fc7a0) Stevens, Gareth Publishing LLLP. (Gareth Stevens Learning Library).

Sechrist, Darren. Westward, Ho!, 1 vol. 2008. (ENG., Illus.). 32p. (J). pap. *(978-0-7787-4217-3(2))* Crabtree Publishing Co.

Sharp, Constance. Beyond Our Shores: America Extends Its Reach,1890-1899. 2013. (Illus.). 48p. (J). pap. *(978-1-4222-2420-5(1))* Mason Crest.

—Beyond Our Shores: America Extends Its Reach,1890-1899. Rakove, Jack N., ed. 2012. (How America Became America Ser.). (Illus.). 48p. (J). (gr. 3-4). 19.95 *(978-1-4222-2406-9(6))* Mason Crest.

—Beyond Our Shores (1890/1899) 2018. (J). *(978-1-5105-3606-7(X))* SmartBook Media, Inc.

Smith, Robert W. & Smith, Robert. Westward Movement. 2006. (Spotlight on America Ser.). (ENG., Illus.). 96p. (gr. 5-9). pap. 13.99 *(978-1-4206-3216-3(7))* Teacher Created Resources, Inc.

Steele, Christy. California & the Southwest Join the United States, 1 vol. 2004. (America's Westward Expansion Ser.). (ENG., Illus.). 48p. (gr. 5-8). lib. bdg. 33.67 *(978-0-8368-5786-3(0),* 12bac90f-b38b-4e68-9457-aecac44c0b39, Gareth Stevens Secondary Library) Stevens, Gareth Publishing LLLP.

—Pioneer Life in the American West, 1 vol. 2004. (America's Westward Expansion Ser.). (ENG., Illus.). 48p. (gr. 5-8). pap. 15.05 *(978-0-8368-5797-9(6),* 1e313d11-4bc8-4653-8fba-dbedc6dc962e); lib. bdg. 33.67 *(978-0-8368-5790-0(9),* fe0283bd-a406-4492-b189-30c5021396a2) Stevens, Gareth Publishing LLLP. (Gareth Stevens Secondary Library).

—Texas Joins the United States, 1 vol. 2004. (America's Westward Expansion Ser.). (ENG., Illus.). 48p. (gr. 5-8). lib. bdg. 33.67 *(978-0-8368-5791-7(7),* 5bbe3e00-4e06-4bfe-b879-5ee9087bba68, Gareth Stevens Secondary Library) Stevens, Gareth Publishing LLLP.

Stefoff, Rebecca. Opening of the West, 1 vol. 2003. (American Voices From Ser.). (ENG., Illus.). 160p. (gr. 6-6). 41.21 *(978-0-7614-1201-4(8),* 80e9629c-104d-4ab6-89f2-29c5a462eded) Cavendish Square Publishing LLC.

—Texas & the Far West, 1 vol. 2003. (North American Historical Atlases Ser.). (ENG., Illus.). 48p. (gr. 5-5). 32.64 *(978-0-7614-1345-5(6),* 0ac39afa-f94c-43f2-bb35-12911614d67a) Cavendish Square Publishing LLC.

Stoltman, Joan. 20 Fun Facts about Westward Expansion, 1 vol. 2018. (Fun Fact File: U. S. History! Ser.). (ENG.). 32p. (gr. 2-3). pap. 11.50 *(978-1-5382-1919-5(0),* 5a247029-dcc4-48e0-b42c-9d50f95dca60); lib. bdg. 27.93 *(978-1-5382-1921-8(2),* 6fc1b9f0-d70b-4b5a-91f9-771df24f3eb9) Stevens, Gareth Publishing LLLP.

Streissguth, Tom. Perspectives on Westward Expansion. 2018. (Perspectives on US History Ser.). (ENG., Illus.). 32p. (J). (gr. 3-6). 32.80 *(978-1-63235-404-4(7),* 13726, 12-Story Library) Bookstaves, LLC.

Torr, James D., ed. Westward Expansion. 2003. (Interpreting American History Through Primary Documents Ser.x). (Illus.). 208p. (J). 32.45 *(978-0-7377-1134-9(5),* Greenhaven Pr., Inc.) Cengage Gale.

Uhl, Xina M. Settlers, Traders, & Trails. 2017. (Westward Expansion: America's Push to the Pacific Ser.). 48p. (J). (gr. 10-14). 84.30 *(978-1-5383-0017-6(6),* Britannica Educational Publishing) Rosen Publishing Group, Inc., The.

Whitman Publishing, creator. Discover Westward Expansion History Project Toolkit. 2011. (Illus.). 19.95 *(978-0-7948-3589-7(9))* Whitman Publishing LLC.

Wolny, Philip. Native American Treatment & Resistance. 2017. (Westward Expansion: America's Push to the Pacific Ser.). (Illus.). 48p. (J). (gr. 10-14). 84.30 *(978-1-5383-0015-2(X),* Britannica Educational Publishing) Rosen Publishing Group, Inc., The.

UNITED STATES—TERRITORIES AND POSSESSIONS

Benchmark Education Co., LLC. The New England Colonies. 2014. (PRIME Ser.). (J). (gr. 6-8). pap. *(978-1-4509-9486-6(5))* Benchmark Education Co.

—The Southern Colonies. 2014. (PRIME Ser.). (J). (gr. 6-8). pap. *(978-1-4509-9488-0(1))* Benchmark Education Co.

Bradley, Jada. U. S. Territories & Possessions, Vol. 19. 2015. (Let's Explore the States Ser.). (Illus.). 64p. (J). (gr. 5). 23.95 *(978-1-4222-3335-1(9))* Mason Crest.

Brown, Jonatha A. Puerto Rico & Other Outlying Areas, 1 vol. 2005. (Portraits of the States Ser.). (ENG., Illus.). 32p. (gr. 3-5). pap. 11.50 *(978-0-8368-4693-5(1),* aa09b7de-2b3f-4da8-a978-e8d97adbf717); lib. bdg. 28.67 *(978-0-8368-4674-4(5),* 5b3552ea-07ba-476b-bae7-dbf87cb924cc) Stevens, Gareth Publishing LLLP. (Gareth Stevens Learning Library).

Romano, Amy. A Historical Atlas of the United States & Its Territories. 2009. (United States: Historical Atlases of the Growth of a New Nation Ser.). 64p. (gr. 5-5). 61.20 *(978-1-60854-255-0(6))* Rosen Publishing Group, Inc., The.

Scholastic Library Publishing. A True Book-the Thirteen Colonies. 2011. (True Book-the Thirteen Colonies Ser.). (J). (gr. 3-5). 377.00 *(978-0-531-22149-5(0),* Children's Pr.) Scholastic Library Publishing.

UNITED STATES—TREATIES

see United States—Foreign Relations—Treaties

UNITED STATES—VICE-PRESIDENTS

see Vice-presidents—United States

UNITED STATES—WOMEN

see Women—United States

UNITED STATES—WORLD WAR, 1939-1945

see World War, 1939-1945—United States

UNITED STATES CAPITOL (WASHINGTON, D.C.)

Campodonica, Carol A. How Congress Works. Miller, Bondell, ed. Anderson, Bill, illus. Uni Photo Picture Agency Staff, photos by. Date not set. (J). (gr. 4-5). pap. *(978-0-9648488-9-4(9))* Buzzard Pr. International.

Carr, Aaron. Capitol Building. 2014. (J). *(978-1-4896-2890-9(8))* Weigl Pubs., Inc.

Clay, Kathryn. The U. S. Capitol: Introducing Primary Sources. 2017. (Introducing Primary Sources Ser.). (ENG., Illus.). 32p. (J). (gr. -1-2). lib. bdg. 28.65 *(978-1-5157-6354-3(4),* 135113, Capstone Pr.) Capstone.

Hicks, Terry Allan. The Capitol, 1 vol. (Symbols of America Ser.). (ENG., Illus.). 40p. (gr. 3-3). 2008. pap. 9.23 *(978-0-7614-3374-3(0),* aa2adf09-17ca-4671-a5dc-1ba298124c1d, Cavendish Square) 2007. lib. bdg. 32.64 *(978-0-7614-2132-0(7),* 983498dc-4064-4d9b-a5fd-9541490d6e2c) Cavendish Square Publishing LLC.

Hillard, Stephane. The U. S. Capitol: The History of U. S. Congress, 1 vol. 2017. (Landmarks of Democracy: American Institutions Ser.). (ENG.). 24p. (J). (gr. 3-3). pap. 9.25 *(978-1-5081-6097-7(X),* 89e41327-12c8-4faa-8033-50eafa003834, PowerKids Pr.) Rosen Publishing Group, Inc., The.

Lee, Georgia. Tour the U. S. Capitol, 1 vol. 2013. (InfoMax Readers Ser.). (ENG.). 24p. (J). (gr. 3-3). pap. 8.25 *(978-1-4777-2769-0(8),* e8215663-f418-478c-bb2c-9833ffa87403); pap. 49.50 *(978-1-4777-2574-0(1))* Rosen Publishing Group, Inc., The. (Rosen Classroom).

McDougal, Anna. Kate Visits the U. S. Capitol! Understanding Government, 1 vol. 2018. (Civics for the Real World Ser.). (ENG.). 16p. (gr. 2-3). pap. *(978-1-5081-3939-3(3),* ef44d662-df3c-4d87-ba1d-82b06c3e46c8, Rosen Classroom) Rosen Publishing Group, Inc., The.

Murray, Julie. United States Capitol. 2016. (US Landmarks Ser.). (ENG., Illus.). 24p. (J). (gr. -1-2). lib. bdg. 31.36 *(978-1-68080-915-2(6),* 23305, Abdo Kids) ABDO Publishing Co.

Silate, Jennifer. The United States Capitol. (Primary Sources of American Symbols Ser.). 24p. (gr. 3-3). 2009. 42.50 *(978-1-60851-511-0(7),* PowerKids Pr.) 2005. (ENG., Illus.). (J). lib. bdg. 26.27 *(978-1-4042-2694-4(X),* 5bb4d991-6590-4bff-88bb-72dc94d90bf4) Rosen Publishing Group, Inc., The.

Sirota, Lyn & Sirota, Lyn A. Capitol. 2013. (Illus.). 24p. (J). *(978-1-62127-460-5(8))* Weigl Pubs., Inc.

Sirota, Lyn A. Capitol. 2013. (Illus.). 24p. (J). pap. *(978-1-62127-466-7(7))* Weigl Pubs., Inc.

UNITED STATES PEACE CORPS

see Peace Corps (U.S.)

UNITED STATES VIRGIN ISLANDS

Burgan, Michael. Puerto Rico y Otras Áreas Periféricas (Puerto Rico & Other Outlying Areas), 1 vol. 2003. (World Almanac(r) Biblioteca de Los Estados (World Almanac(r) Library of the States) Ser.). (SPA.). 48p. (gr. 4-6). lib. bdg. 33.67 *(978-0-8368-5726-9(7),* 143e99dc-fbff-4a14-8c25-211ce284c1ac, Gareth Stevens Learning Library) Stevens, Gareth Publishing LLLP.

UNITED STATES VIRGIN ISLANDS—FICTION

Callender, Kacen. Hurricane Child (Scholastic Gold) (ENG.). (J). (gr. 3-7). 2019. 240p. pap. 8.99 *(978-1-338-12931-1(7))* 2018. 224p. 17.99 *(978-1-338-12930-4(9))* Scholastic, Inc. (Scholastic Pr.).

Lewis-Brown, Alscess. Mosquito Get in Trouble Too. Hatfield, Cynthia, illus. 2009. (J). *(978-1-934370-09-4(6))* Editorial Campana.

Sewer, Anecia. Why Transfer Day, Anyway? Samuel, Karen, illus. 2007. 16p. (J). 15.99 *(978-0-9752986-0-2(7))* Research Institute Pr., The.

Skurzynski, Gloria. Mysteries in Our National Parks: Escape from Fear: A Mystery in Virgin Islands National Park. 2008. (Mysteries in Our National Park Ser.). (Illus.). 160p. (J). (gr. 3-7). mass mkt. 4.99 *(978-1-4263-0181-0(2),* National Geographic Kids) Disney Publishing Worldwide.

UNIVERSAL HISTORY

see World History

UNIVERSE

Alex, Joanne DeFilipp. I Wonder What's Out There: A Vision of the Universe for Primary Classes. 2003. (Illus.). 64p. (J). spiral bd. *(978-0-939195-32-9(1))* Parent Child Pr., Inc.

Altman, Peter. Life & the Universe: Answerable & Unanswerable Questions, 1 vol. 2017. (Big Questions Ser.). (ENG.). 232p. (YA). (gr. 9-9). lib. bdg. 49.50 *(978-1-5026-2812-1(0),* eaf97bb8-4305-4941-85f8-4ef6c6e9050b) Cavendish Square Publishing LLC.

Ansdell, Megan. The Big Bang Explained, 1 vol. 2018. (Mysteries of Space Ser.). (ENG.). 80p. (gr. 7-7). 38.93 *(978-0-7660-9956-2(3),* e3c19f7d-5009-4ede-8c06-812ec0ff0ad7) Enslow Publishing, LLC.

Bal, Floor. It Started with a Big Bang: The Origin of Earth, You & Everything Else. Doninck, Sebastiaan Van, illus. 2019. (ENG.). 34p. (J). (gr. k-3). 18.99 *(978-1-5253-0255-8(8))* Kids Can Pr., Ltd. CAN. Dist: Hachette Bk. Group.

Becklake, Sue & Kelly, Miles. Space. Kelly, Richard, ed. 2017. (ENG., Illus.). 48p. (J). pap. 9.95 *(978-1-84810-911-7(3))* Miles Kelly Publishing, Ltd. GBR. Dist: Parkwest Pubns., Inc.

Benchmark Education Company, LLC Staff, compiled by. The Universe: Theme Set. 2006. (J). 135.00 *(978-1-4108-7149-7(5))* Benchmark Education Co.

Bennett, Jeffrey. I, Humanity. 2016. (ENG., Illus.). 32p. (J). (gr. 2-4). 15.00 *(978-1-937548-52-0(X))* Big Kid Science.

Blumenthal, Kelly. Cosmic Inflation Explained, 1 vol. 2018. (Mysteries of Space Ser.). (ENG.). 80p. (gr. 7-7). 38.93 *(978-0-7660-9953-1(9),* 3cece186-2538-4690-a407-cfe243e693cd) Enslow Publishing, LLC.

Bortz, Fred. Beyond Jupiter: The Story of Planetary Astronomer Heidi Hammel. 2006. (ENG., Illus.). 128p. (gr. 7-9). per. 19.95 *(978-0-309-09552-5(2),* Joseph Henry Pr.) National Academies Pr.

—The Big Bang Theory: Edwin Hubble & the Origins of the Universe, 1 vol. 2013. (Revolutionary Discoveries of Scientific Pioneers Ser.). (ENG., Illus.). 80p. (J). (gr. 6-6). 38.41 *(978-1-4777-1803-2(6),* ea7bcd12-0733-48fc-baec-114fbf20adf6) Rosen Publishing Group, Inc., The.

Briggs, Andrew, et al. Hunt with Newton: What Are the Secrets of the Universe? Hudson, Brett, illus. 2018. (Curious Science Quest Ser.). (ENG.). 112p. (J). (gr. 4-7). pap. 9.99 *(978-0-7459-7753-9(7),* ee1a0055-339f-430c-9580-68819015c4f1, Lion Children's) Lion Hudson PLC GBR. Dist: Baker & Taylor Publisher Services (BTPS).

Burbank, Shirley Ann. Where Did I Come From? 2010. 40p. pap. 21.32 *(978-1-4535-3304-8(4))* Xlibris Corp.

Butt, Kyle. God Made the World. 2006. (ENG., Illus.). (J). (gr. -1-3). 3.00 *(978-0-932859-69-3(0))* Apologetics Pr., Inc.

Chin, Jason. Your Place in the Universe. 2020. (Illus.). 40p. (J). (gr. 3-7). 18.99 *(978-0-8234-4623-0(9),* Neal Porter Bks) Holiday Hse., Inc.

Clark, Stuart. Discovering the Universe. 2012. (ENG., Illus.). 48p. (J). 15.00 *(978-1-899762-77-4(9))* Award Pubns. Ltd. GBR. Dist: Parkwest Pubns., Inc.

Cornell, Kari. Theoretical Physicist Stephen Hawking. 2016. (STEM Trailblazer Bios Ser.). (ENG., Illus.). 32p. (J). (gr. 2-5). 26.65 *(978-1-4677-9528-9(3),* 73d57c91-05df-4980-82c7-559911b3b49e, Lerner Pubns.) Lerner Publishing Group.

El Cosmos. (SPA.). (YA). (gr. 5-8). pap. *(978-84-7131-925-8(X))* Editex, Editorial S.A. ESP. Dist: Lectorum Pubns., Inc.

Culp, Jennifer. Neil DeGrasse Tyson, 1 vol. 2014. (Great Science Writers Ser.). (ENG., Illus.). 112p. (J). (gr. 7-7). 38.80 *(978-1-4777-7691-9(5),* be204f99-ab43-4c05-8351-d4966a76b067) Rosen Publishing Group, Inc., The.

DeCristofano, Carolyn Cinami. Big Bang! The Tongue-Tickling Tale of a Speck That Became Spectacular. Carroll, Michael, illus. 2005. 32p. (J). (gr. k-3). pap. 7.95 *(978-1-57091-619-9(5))* Charlesbridge Publishing, Inc.

DeSantis, Andrea, illus. Space Kids: An Introduction for Young Explorers. 2018. (ENG.). 40p. (J). (gr. 2). 24.95 *(978-3-89955-795-4(6))* Die Gestalten Verlag DEU. Dist: Ingram Publisher Services.

TUV

DK. DK Braille: It Can't Be True: Incredible Tactile Comparisons. 2016. (DK Braille Bks.). (ENG.). 72p. (J). (gr. 4-7). 29.99 *(978-1-4654-4406-6(8),* DK Children) Dorling Kindersley Publishing, Inc.

—DKfindout! Universe. 2018. (DK Findout! Ser.). (ENG., Illus.). 64p. (J). (gr. 1-4). pap. 10.99 *(978-1-4654-7092-8(1),* DK Children) Dorling Kindersley Publishing, Inc.

Earth Cosmology: The Destroyer Comet. 2004. (YA). cd-rom 15.00 *(978-0-934269-61-2(0))* UFO Photo Archives.

Earth Cosmology: The Effects of the Giant Destroyer Comet. 2004. (UFO Fact Bks.). (YA). cd-rom 15.00 *(978-0-934269-41-4(6))* UFO Photo Archives.

Encyclopaedia Britannica, Inc. Staff. Britannica Illustrated Science Library Series (18 Title Series), 18 vols. 2010. 599.00 *(978-1-61535-423-8(9))* Encyclopaedia Britannica, Inc.

Encyclopaedia Britannica, Inc. Staff, compiled by. Britannica Illustrated Science Library: Universe, 16 vols. 2008. (Illus.). (J). 29.95 *(978-1-59339-399-1(7))* Encyclopaedia Britannica, Inc.

Encyclopedia Britannica Staff, creator. Universe. 2011. (Britannica Illustrated Science Library Ser.). 104p. (J). 37.44 *(978-1-61535-457-3(3))* Encyclopaedia Britannica, Inc.

Farber, Ryan Jeffrey. Parallel Universes Explained, 1 vol. 2018. (Mysteries of Space Ser.). (ENG.). 80p. (gr. 7-7). 38.93 *(978-1-9785-0457-8(8),* 043308e0-27d3-44f6-aebc-cd2c3e180d32) Enslow Publishing, LLC.

Ferrie, Chris. There Was a Black Hole That Swallowed the Universe. Batori, Susan, illus. 2019. 40p. (J). (gr. -1-3). 17.99 *(978-1-4926-8077-2(X))* Sourcebooks, Inc.

Fleisher, Paul. The Big Bang. 2005. (Great Ideas of Science Ser.). (Illus.). 80p. (YA). (gr. 9-12). lib. bdg. 27.93 *(978-0-8225-2133-4(4))* Lerner Publishing Group.

Ford, Harry & Barnham, Kay. Outer Space. 2003. (Knowledge Masters Ser.). (Illus.). 32p. (YA). pap. incl. cd-rom *(978-1-903954-09-6(6),* Pavilion Children's Books) Pavilion Bks.

Gallagher, Belinda & Camilla, De La Bedoyere. Space: Identify & Record Your Sightings. Kelly, Richard, ed. 2017. (Illus.). 96p. (J). pap., instr.'s hndbk. ed. 9.95 *(978-1-78209-166-0(1))* Miles Kelly Publishing, Ltd. GBR. Dist: Parkwest Pubns., Inc.

Garcia, Gloria. El Universo. (SPA.). 8p. 9.95 *(978-84-272-7277-4(4))* Molino, Editorial ESP. Dist: Distribooks, Inc.

Garlick, Mark A. Atlas of the Universe. 2008. (Insiders Ser.). (ENG., Illus.). 128p. (J). (gr. 4-9). 24.99 *(978-1-4169-5558-0(5),* Simon & Schuster Bks. For Young Readers) Simon & Schuster Bks. For Young Readers.

Gaughan, Richard. Antimatter Explained, 1 vol. 2018. (Mysteries of Space Ser.). (ENG.). 80p. (gr. 7-7). 38.93 *(978-1-9785-0453-0(5),* b23c6896-570c-44cb-afdb-5c426251a5fd) Enslow Publishing, LLC.

—Wormholes Explained, 1 vol. 2018. (Mysteries of Space Ser.). (ENG.). 80p. (gr. 7-7). 38.93 *(978-0-7660-9965-4(2),* 50898e31-3da7-4939-83fc-32809f8340db) Enslow Publishing, LLC.

Gernadnik, Mary. How Do We Know the Age of the Universe? 2009. (Great Scientific Questions & the Scientists Who Answered Them Ser.). 112p. (gr. 7-12). 63.90 *(978-1-61513-197-6(3))* Rosen Publishing Group, Inc., The.

Gifford, Clive. The Universe, Black Holes, & the Big Bang. 2015. (Watch This Space! Ser.). (ENG., Illus.). 32p. (J). (gr. 4-5). lib. bdg. *(978-0-7787-2024-9(1))* Crabtree Publishing Co.

Goldberg, Marc. If You Had to Draw a Universe for Me ... 50 Questions About the Universe, Matter & Scientists. 2018. (ENG., Illus.). ix, 112p. (J). pap. *(978-981-327-721-2(1))* World Scientific Publishing Co. Pte Ltd.

Hagler, Gina. Dark Energy Explained, 1 vol. 2018. (Mysteries of Space Ser.). (ENG.). 80p. (gr. 7-7). 38.93 *(978-1-9785-0454-7(3),* 12c0262c-d19d-411a-95f0-70e11e93c25d) Enslow Publishing, LLC.

Hansen, Grace. The Milky Way. 2017. (Our Galaxy Ser.). (ENG., Illus.). 24p. (J). (gr. -1-2). lib. bdg. 32.79 *(978-1-5321-0052-9(3),* 25178, Abdo Kids) ABDO Publishing Co.

Hantula, Richard & Asimov, Isaac. The Birth of Our Universe, 1 vol. 2004. (Isaac Asimov's 21st Century Library of the Universe: near & Far Ser.). (ENG., Illus.). 32p. (gr. 3-5). lib. bdg. 28.67 *(978-0-8368-3964-7(1),* 773f71ca-766d-411d-9708-95641aec1357) Stevens, Gareth Publishing LLLP.

—Black Holes, Pulsars, & Quasars, 1 vol. 2004. (Isaac Asimov's 21st Century Library of the Universe: near & Far Ser.). (ENG., Illus.). 32p. (gr. 3-5). lib. bdg. 28.67 *(978-0-8368-3965-4(X),* 565ba30c-0089-4db9-aafb-c623953c1985) Stevens, Gareth Publishing LLLP.

—Is There Life in Outer Space?, 1 vol. 2004. (Isaac Asimov's 21st Century Library of the Universe: Fact & Fantasy Ser.). (ENG., Illus.). 32p. (gr. 3-5). lib. bdg. 28.67 *(978-0-8368-3950-0(1),* 1853261a-58ea-4fc4-aa2b-0f7b2f7b76f2) Stevens, Gareth Publishing LLLP.

—Isaac Asimov's Biblioteca Del Universo Del Siglo XXI (Isaac Asimov's 21st Century Library of the Universe), 24 vols., Set. Incl. Asteroides (Asteroids) lib. bdg. 28.67 *(978-0-8368-3853-4(X),* e7081b8a-3755-4cd1-a05e-618a7dc0d3be); Júpiter (Jupiter) lib. bdg. 28.67 *(978-0-8368-3854-1(8),* f7ba75eb-ea29-476f-90e2-126821ed266e); Luna (the Moon) lib. bdg. 28.67 *(978-0-8368-3855-8(6),* e186285f-763c-407c-b6e7-c647e44523d1); Marte (Mars) lib. bdg. 28.67 *(978-0-8368-3856-5(4),* e4c4282c-98b2-4093-a7fb-af1ed9e982f0); Mercurio (Mercury) lib. bdg. 28.67 *(978-0-8368-3857-2(2),* 08ce5c1c-4855-4a1b-a429-f6b6072454a7); Neptuno (Neptune) lib. bdg. 28.67 *(978-0-8368-3858-9(0),* c23dcb68-cd60-4e2d-b4f2-f06c3c7f3c3e); Plutón y Caronte (Pluto & Charon) lib. bdg. 28.67 *(978-0-8368-3859-6(9),* 3ae2196b-697f-47c9-b87e-33d46b0492ac); Saturno (Saturn) lib. bdg. 28.67 *(978-0-8368-3860-2(2),* 7cabdd3e-00cc-44df-a42c-237e34e0fb1c); Sol (the Sun) lib. bdg. 28.67 *(978-0-8368-3861-9(0),* 9f699839-5c2c-4a78-add1-2139c0ea36ea); Tierra (Earth) lib. bdg. 28.67 *(978-0-8368-3862-6(9),* e4466647-832c-4d71-bc0e-015bd32caceb); Urano (Uranus) lib. bdg. 28.67 *(978-0-8368-3863-3(7),* 0961b1a9-ec0c-484d-912c-d85c5b782d39); Venus (Venus) lib. bdg. 28.67 *(978-0-8368-3864-0(5),* a8d10885-563a-47ee-a670-50eedf2e8c38); (gr. 3-5). (Isaac Asimov's Biblioteca Del Universo Del Siglo XXI (Isaac Asimov's 21st Century Library of the Universe) Ser.). (SPA., Illus.). 32p. 2003. Set lib. bdg. 344.04 *(978-0-8368-3852-7(1),* a67ac4cc-33bb-4103-bfdb-560d38317a0b, Gareth Stevens Learning Library) Stevens, Gareth Publishing LLLP.

Hasan, Heather, ed. How Mathematical Models, Computer Simulations, & Exploration Can Be Used to Study the Universe: An Anthology of Current Thought. 2009. (Contemporary Discourse in the Field of Astronomy Ser.). 240p. (gr. 10-10). 63.90 *(978-1-61511-904-2(3))* Rosen Publishing Group, Inc., The.

Hersey, John, illus. Amazing Space: Go on a Journey to the Edge of the Universe. 2019. (ENG.). 48p. (J). (gr. 2-7). 19.99 *(978-1-78312-393-3(1))* Carlton Bks., Ltd. GBR. Dist: Two Rivers Distribution.

Hixson, Bryce. Galactic Cookie Dough. Hixson, Bryce, illus. 2003. (Illus.). (J). per. 14.95 *(978-1-931801-06-5(1))* Loose In The Lab.

Holden, Barry. The Milky Way BIG BOOK Edition, 1 vol. 2014. (ENG.). 16p. (gr. 2-2). pap. *(978-1-77654-100-3(6),* Red Rocket Readers) Flying Start Bks.

Holt, Rinehart and Winston Staff. Holt Science & Technology Chapter 18: Earth Science: Studying Space. 5th ed. 2004. (Illus.). pap. 12.86 *(978-0-03-030331-9(1))* Holt McDougal.

Hutmacher, Kimberly M. The Universe Began with a Bang & Other Cool Space Facts. 2019. (Mind-Blowing Science Facts Ser.). (ENG., Illus.). 32p. (J). (gr. 4-6). lib. bdg. 28.65 *(978-1-5435-5769-5(4),* 139725) Capstone.

Institute for Creation Research Staff, contrib. by. Guide to the Universe. 2016. (Illus.). 115p. (J). *(978-1-935587-82-8(X))* Institute for Creation Research.

Jackson, Tom. The Universe: An Illustrated History of Astronomy. 2012. (Illus.). 144p. (J). *(978-0-9853230-2-8(7))* Shelter Harbor Pr.

James, Muirden. El Universo Tr. of Universe. (SPA.). 96p. (YA). (gr. 5-8). 18.36 *(978-84-241-1993-5(2))* Everest Editora ESP. Dist: Lectorum Pubns., Inc.

Jankowski, Matt. How Big Is the Universe?, 1 vol. 2018. (Space Mysteries Ser.). (ENG.). 32p. (gr. 2-3). 29.27 *(978-1-5382-1947-8(5),* 55097357-5fae-40e8-8804-4fb717e63206) Stevens, Gareth Publishing LLLP.

Jedicke, Peter. Cosmology: Exploring the Universe. 2003. (Hot Science Ser.). (Illus.). 48p. (J). lib. bdg. 28.50 *(978-1-58340-366-2(3))* Black Rabbit Bks.

Keranen, Rachel. The Big Bang Theory, 1 vol. 2017. (Great Discoveries in Science Ser.). (ENG.). 128p. (YA). (gr. 9-9). 47.36 *(978-1-5026-2770-4(1),* 626384c9-0575-4084-b811-38c459afdf2e) Cavendish Square Publishing LLC.

—The Big Bang Theory & Light Spectra, 1 vol. 2016. (Space Systems Ser.). (ENG., Illus.). 112p. (J). (gr. 8-8). lib. bdg. 44.50 *(978-1-5026-2295-2(5),* a65f561b-ae97-4098-8171-fb224d9c8181) Cavendish Square Publishing LLC.

—The Composition of the Universe: the Evolution of Stars & Galaxies, 1 vol. 2016. (Space Systems Ser.). (ENG., Illus.). 112p. (J). (gr. 8-8). 44.50 *(978-1-5026-2285-3(8),* 229b7660-80d5-4658-892a-6813bc61ff8f) Cavendish Square Publishing LLC.

Kook, Ima. Big Bang Theory: The Bang That Created Our Universe. 2008. (As Dreamed by Itsy Ser.). (Illus.). 24p. (J). pap. 12.00 *(978-1-892298-21-8(X))* Abique Pub.

Kukla, Lauren. The Amazing Universe. 2016. (Exploring Our Universe Ser.). (ENG., Illus.). 32p. (J). (gr. 3-6). lib. bdg. 32.79 *(978-1-68078-402-2(1),* 23663, Checkerboard Library) ABDO Publishing Co.

May, Brian, et al. Exploring the Mysteries of the Universe, 1 vol. 2016. (STEM Guide to the Universe Ser.). (ENG.). 200p. (J). (gr. 9-9). lib. bdg. 47.80 *(978-1-4994-6407-8(X),* 234730b3-6281-4f61-92ad-8e9d041ae185) Rosen Publishing Group, Inc., The.

McMahon, Michael. Why Do the Stars Shine? Level 4 Factbook. 2010. (Cambridge Young Readers Ser.). (ENG., Illus.). 16p. pap. 6.00 *(978-0-521-13723-2(3))* Cambridge Univ. Pr.

Media, Cont. The Cosmos. 2008. 96p. (YA). 17.99 *(978-1-931703-01-7(9))* Creative Publishing Consultants.

Miotto, Enrico. El Universo Tr. of Universe. (SPA.). 40p. (YA). (gr. 5-8). 10.36 *(978-84-207-5192-4(8))* Grupo Anaya, S.A. ESP. Dist: Lectorum Pubns., Inc.

Morgan, Jennifer. Born with a Bang: The Universe Tells Our Cosmic Story. Andersen, Dana Lynne, illus. 2011. 48p. (J). (gr. 2-5). pap. 12.99 *(978-1-58469-032-0(1),* Dawn Pubns.) Sourcebooks, Inc.

—Born with a Bang: The Universe Tells Our Cosmic Story. Andersen, Dana Lynne, illus. 2004. (Sharing Nature with Children Book Ser.). 48p. (J). (gr. 2-18). 19.95 *(978-1-58469-033-7(X))* Take Heart Pubns.

Murphy, Pat & Klutz Editors. Guide to the Galaxy. 2011. (ENG.). 50p. (J). (gr. 3-3). 19.99 *(978-1-59174-920-2(4))* Klutz.

Negus, James. Black Holes Explained, 1 vol. 2018. (Mysteries of Space Ser.). (ENG.). 80p. (gr. 7-7). 38.93 *(978-0-7660-9962-3(8),* 7783bd0d-c360-49db-975e-bc5d98f8de31); pap. 19.17 *(978-0-7660-9963-0(6),* 58f89145-c5de-4492-8846-4e4e116650df) Enslow Publishing, LLC.

—Supernovas Explained, 1 vol. 2018. (Mysteries of Space Ser.). (ENG.). 80p. (gr. 7-7). 38.93 *(978-1-9785-0458-5(6),* eb4ffc53-63c2-4889-9cbf-d8119157e5e4) Enslow Publishing, LLC.

Our Universe. 2004. (Illus.). lib. bdg. 7.95 *(978-0-8225-4790-7(2))* Lerner Publishing Group.

Oxtra, Cristina. Stephen Hawking: Get to Know the Man Behind the Theory. 2019. (People You Should Know Ser.). (ENG., Illus.). 32p. (J). (gr. 3-6). pap. 7.95 *(978-1-5435-7468-5(8),* 140908); lib. bdg. 27.99 *(978-1-5435-7186-8(7),* 140437) Capstone.

Pamplona, Alberto Hernández. A Visual Guide to the Universe, 1 vol. 2017. (Visual Exploration of Science Ser.). (ENG.). 104p. (J). (gr. 8-8). 38.80 *(978-1-5081-7585-8(3),* 84f6d373-825b-4bd3-8716-7be994ea572d, Rosen Young Adult) Rosen Publishing Group, Inc., The.

Pissanos, Paul. From Aristotle to Hawking. 2012. (Illus.). 272p. pap. 73.23 *(978-1-4678-8506-5(1))* AuthorHouse.

Priddy, Roger. Smart Kids: Space: For Kids Who Really Love Space! 2012. (Smart Kids Ser.). (ENG., Illus.). 32p. (J). (gr. -1-2). 10.99 *(978-0-312-51459-4(X),* 900085038) St. Martin's Pr.

—The Sun. 2011. (ENG., Illus.). 30p. (J). *(978-1-84915-726-1(X),* Priddy Bks.) St. Martin's Pr.

Pulliam, Christine & Daniels, Patricia. Space Encyclopedia: A Tour of Our Solar System & Beyond. Aguilar, David A., illus. 2013. 191p. (J). *(978-1-4263-1629-6(1))* National Geographic Society.

Rice, Dona Herweck. We Are Here. 2015. (Science: Informational Text Ser.). (ENG., Illus.). 32p. (J). (gr. 3-5). pap. 11.99 *(978-1-4807-4687-9(8))* Teacher Created Materials, Inc.

Richards, Jon & Simkins, Ed. Our Universe, 1 vol. 2017. (Infographics: How It Works). (ENG.). 32p. (J). (gr. 4-5). pap. 11.50 *(978-1-5382-1360-5(5),* e3ead7c6-0612-4a86-84d4-1067348234dc); lib. bdg. 28.27 *(978-1-5382-1362-9(1),* d6c35060-9886-4d26-b0f1-7c74b957ccfd) Stevens, Gareth Publishing LLLP.

Rubino, Michael. Bang! How We Came to Be. 2011. (Illus.). 69p. (J). (gr. -1-12). pap. 17.00 *(978-1-61614-472-2(6))* Prometheus Bks., Pubs.

Sanders, Ella Frances. Eating the Sun: Small Musings on a Vast Universe. 2019. (ENG., Illus.). 160p. 20.00 *(978-0-14-313316-2(0),* Penguin Bks.) Penguin Publishing Group.

Schmermund, Elizabeth. New Frontiers in Astronomy, 1 vol. 2016. (Great Discoveries in Science Ser.). (ENG., Illus.). 128p. (J). (gr. 9-9). 47.36 *(978-1-5026-1959-4(8),* eb6c16d1-0d7f-4978-ac03-12cc72472779) Cavendish Square Publishing LLC.

Schomp, Virginia. The Ancient Maya, 1 vol. 2010. (Myths of the World Ser.). (ENG.). 96p. (gr. 6-6). 36.93 *(978-0-7614-4217-2(0),* 1367a57a-3a02-4180-9b7b-770dd65be176) Cavendish Square Publishing LLC.

Scientific American Staff. Extreme Physics. 2009. (Scientific American Cutting-Edge Science Ser.). 176p. (gr. 9-9). 63.90 *(978-1-60853-076-2(0))* Rosen Publishing Group, Inc., The.

Senker, Cath. Stephen Hawking. 2015. (Against the Odds Biographies Ser.). (ENG., Illus.). 48p. (J). (gr. 3-6). 35.99 *(978-1-4846-2466-1(1),* 129624, Heinemann) Capstone.

Silverstein, Alvin, et al. The Universe. 2003. (Science Concepts Ser.). (ENG., Illus.). 64p. (J). (gr. 5-9). lib. bdg. 26.60 *(978-0-7613-2255-9(8),* Twenty-First Century Bks.) Lerner Publishing Group.

Simon, Seymour. The Universe. 2006. (ENG., Illus.). 32p. (J). (gr. k-4). pap. 7.99 *(978-0-06-087725-5(1),* HarperCollins) HarperCollins Pubs.

Solway, Andrew. The Universe. 2010. (21st Century Science Ser.). (ENG.). 112p. (YA). (gr. 9-12). 42.80 *(978-1-933834-76-4(5),* 16387) Brown Bear Bks.

Sparrow, Giles. Discovering the Universe, 1 vol. 2017. (Space Explorers Ser.). (ENG.). 32p. (gr. 2-2). 26.93 *(978-0-7660-9264-8(X),* 1c59f5fd-312a-4147-864e-ce72a1a56cbc) Enslow Publishing, LLC.

—Our Universe, 1 vol. 2017. (Space Explorers Ser.). (ENG.). 32p. (gr. 2-2). 26.93 *(978-0-7660-9263-1(1),* a4989e50-e5dd-4f68-98c0-37421c2a223f) Enslow Publishing, LLC.

—Probing Deep Space, 1 vol. 2006. (Secrets of the Universe Ser.). (ENG., Illus.). 48p. (gr. 6-8). lib. bdg. 33.67 *(978-0-8368-7279-8(7),* 1fc28e8c-561b-4afa-a044-60d80f56400a, Gareth Stevens Secondary Library) Stevens, Gareth Publishing LLLP.

Sparrow, Giles & Stone, Jerry. Universe. 2018. (Illus.). 64p. (J). *(978-1-5444-1092-0(1))* Dorling Kindersley Publishing, Inc.

Sparrow, Giles, et al. How the Universe Works, 1 vol. 2015. (Discoveries in Space Science Ser.). (ENG., Illus.). 80p. (YA). (gr. 9-9). lib. bdg. 37.36 *(978-1-5026-1014-0(0),* 77d174fb-694c-48ed-ac15-4906335b5575) Cavendish Square Publishing LLC.

Teacher Created Resources Staff. Space Guides - Discovering the Universe: A Galaxy of Mind-Expanding Information! 2008. (ENG., Illus.). 32p. (gr. 4-13). pap. 7.99 *(978-1-4206-8268-7(7))* Teacher Created Resources, Inc.

Terp, Gail. The Milky Way & Other Galaxies. 2018. (Deep Space Discovery Ser.). (ENG.). 32p. (gr. 2-7). 9.95 *(978-1-68072-714-2(1));* (J). (gr. 4-6). pap. 9.99 *(978-1-64466-267-0(1),* 12321); (Illus.). (J). (gr. 4-6). lib. bdg. *(978-1-68072-420-2(7),* 12320) Black Rabbit Bks. (Bolt).

—La Vía láctea y Otras Galaxias. 2018. (Descubrimiento Del Espacio Profundo Ser.). (SPA.). 32p. (J). (gr. 4-6). lib. bdg. *(978-1-68072-970-2(5),* 12447, Bolt) Black Rabbit Bks.

Thompson, Ian, et al, illus. The Awesome Book of the Universe: Awesome. 2013. (ENG.). 32p. (J). (gr. 3-7). 7.99 *(978-1-77093-779-6(X))* Flowerpot Pr.

Tyson, Neil deGrasse & Mone, Gregory. Astrophysics for Young People in a Hurry. 2019. (ENG., Illus.). (J). (gr. 3-7). 192p. 17.95 *(978-1-324-00328-1(6),* 340328); 176p. pap. 11.95 *(978-0-393-35650-2(7),* 35650) Norton, W. W. & Co., Inc. (Norton Young Readers).

The Universe. (Jump Ser.). 36p. (J). (gr. 2-7). pap. *(978-1-882210-21-3(2))* Action Publishing, Inc.

Venezia, Mike. Stephen Hawking: Cosmologist Who Gets a Big Bang Out of the Universe. Venezia, Mike, illus. 2009. (Getting to Know the World's Greatest Inventors & Scientists Ser.). (ENG., Illus.). 32p. (J). (gr. 2-5). 28.00 *(978-0-531-23728-1(1))* Scholastic Library Publishing.

Ventura, Marne. Astrophysicist & Space Advocate Neil DeGrasse Tyson. 2014. (STEM Trailblazer Bios Ser.). (ENG., Illus.). 32p. (J). (gr. 2-5). lib. bdg. 26.65 *(978-1-4677-2461-6(0),* a21f9ee4-73a5-4f2e-acaf-10b786644cae, Lerner Pubns.) Lerner Publishing Group.

Whitt, Stephen. The Turtle & the Universe. Hernandez, Stephanie, illus. 2008. 86p. (J). (gr. 3-7). pap. 14.99 *(978-1-59102-626-6(1))* Prometheus Bks., Pubs.

Williams, Brian. The Universe. 2010. (What About... Ser.). (Illus.). 40p. (J). (gr. 6-8). lib. bdg. 19.95 *(978-1-4222-1566-1(0))* Mason Crest.

—Universe: Biggest & Best. 2004. (Biggest & Best Ser.). (Illus.). 40p. (J). pap. 7.95 *(978-1-84236-025-5(6))* Miles Kelly Publishing, Ltd. GBR. Dist: Independent Pubs. Group.

—What about the Universe. 2008. 40p. pap. *(978-1-84810-075-6(2))* Miles Kelly Publishing, Ltd.

World Book, Inc. Staff, contrib. by. The Universe — Mysteries & Marvels. 2010. (Illus.). 64p. (J). *(978-0-7166-9546-2(4))* World Bk., Inc.

—The Universe — A Cosmic Tour. 2010. (Illus.). 64p. (J). *(978-0-7166-9545-5(6))* World Bk., Inc.

Zuchora-Walske, Christine. We're the Center of the Universe! Science's Biggest Mistakes about Astronomy & Physics. 2014. (Science Gets It Wrong Ser.). (ENG., Illus.). 32p. (J). (gr. 4-6). lib. bdg. 26.65 *(978-1-4677-3663-3(5),* 5ba1d614-30d8-4032-bed1-0faf23fb880e, Lerner Pubns.) Lerner Publishing Group.

UNIVERSITIES AND COLLEGES

see also Education, Higher; Scholarships; Students also headings beginning with the word College and names of individual institutions

Allshouse, Sara & Burns, Adam. University of San Francisco College Prowler off the Record. 2005. (College Prowler off the Record Guides: Vol. 181). 160p. (YA). (gr. 12-18). pap., stu. ed. 14.95 *(978-1-59658-180-7(8))* College Prowler, Inc.

Alter, Austin & Lyon, Abby. Rhode Island School of Design College Prowler off the Record. 2005. (College Prowler off the Record Guides: Vol. 106). 160p. (YA). (gr. 12-18). pap., stu. ed. 14.95 *(978-1-59658-105-0(0))* College Prowler, Inc.

Amboba, Ethan & Lyon, Abby. Occidental College College Prowler off the Record. 2nd ed. 2005. (College Prowler off the Record Guides: Vol. 94). 160p. (YA). (gr. 12-18). pap., stu. ed. 14.95 *(978-1-59658-093-0(3))* College Prowler, Inc.

Amidon Lusted, Marcia, ed. The College Admissions Process, 1 vol. 2017. (Issues That Concern You Ser.). (ENG.). 112p. (YA). (gr. 7-10). 43.63 *(978-1-5345-0223-9(8),* 5f7168f7-49b8-45d3-a342-2cb933483082) Greenhaven Publishing LLC.

Amodeo, Jessica & Pecsenye, Jessica. University of Colorado College Prowler off the Record. 2nd ed. 2005. (College Prowler off the Record Guides: Vol. 151). 160p. (YA). (gr. 12-18). pap., stu. ed. 14.95 *(978-1-59658-150-0(6))* College Prowler, Inc.

Andrew, Stacy & Davis, Cristine. Morehouse College College Prowler off the Record. 2005. (College Prowler off the Record Guides: Vol. 86). 160p. (YA). (gr. 12-18). pap., stu. ed. 14.95 *(978-1-59658-085-5(2),* Off The Record) College Prowler, Inc.

Ascani, Kristi & Stuart, Leinora. UW Huskies from a to Z. Morden, Naphtali & Moss, Stephan, illus. 2013. (ENG.). 56p. (J). 21.95 *(978-1-937499-06-8(5))* Green Beanie Bks.

Ayala, Anikka & Nash, Kevin. University of Notre Dame College Prowler off the Record. 2nd ed. 2005. (College Prowler off the Record Guides: Vol. 171). 160p. (YA). (gr. 12-18). pap., stu. ed. 14.95 *(978-1-59658-170-8(0))* College Prowler, Inc.

Baier, Ellen & Skindzier, Jon. Franklin & Marshall College College Prowler off the Record. 2005. (College Prowler off the Record Guides: Vol. 52). 160p. (YA). (gr. 12-18). pap., stu. ed. 14.95 *(978-1-59658-051-0(8))* College Prowler, Inc.

Bailey, Diane. Kansas Basketball, 1 vol. 2013. (America's Most Winning Teams Ser.). (ENG.). 48p. (J). (gr. 5-5). 34.41 *(978-1-4488-9405-5(0),* 84486018-65e8-45c8-942d-7d30db4af72e); pap. 12.75 *(978-1-4488-9429-1(8),* 6db8e256-cdfe-4f48-95a5-431e73a95af3) Rosen Publishing Group, Inc., The.

Ballow, Jonah & Gray, Kevan. University of Kansas College Prowler off the Record. 2nd ed. 2005. (College Prowler off the Record Guides: Vol. 159). 160p. (YA). (gr. 12-18). pap., stu. ed. 14.95 *(978-1-59658-158-6(1))* College Prowler, Inc.

Barrish, Lily & Pecsenye, Jessica. University of Central Florida College Prowler off the Record. 2005. (College Prowler off the Record Guides: Vol. 149). 160p. (YA). (gr. 12-18). pap., stu. ed. 14.95 *(978-1-59658-148-7(4))* College Prowler, Inc.

Beane, Abbie, et al. Middlebury College College Prowler off the Record. 2005. (College Prowler off the Record Guides: Vol. 85). 160p. (YA). (gr. 12-18). pap., stu. ed. 14.95 *(978-1-59658-084-8(4))* College Prowler, Inc.

Bender, Abby & Weisgerber, Amy. Purdue University College Prowler off the Record. 2005. (College Prowler off the Record Guides: Vol. 103). 160p. (YA). (gr. 12-18). pap., stu. ed. 14.95 *(978-1-59658-102-9(6))* College Prowler, Inc.

Benson, Elisa & Gohari, Omid. Colgate University College Prowler off the Record. 2005. (College Prowler off the Record Guides: Vol. 29). 160p. (YA). (gr. 12-18). pap., stu. ed. 14.95 *(978-1-59658-028-2(3))* College Prowler, Inc.

Biggers, Nikki & Mason, Chris. Cal Poly College Prowler off the Record: Inside California Polytechnic State University. 2005 (College Prowler off the Record Guides: Vol. 21). 160p. (YA). (gr. 12-18). pap., stu. ed. 14.95 *(978-1-59658-020-6(8))* College Prowler, Inc.

Bist, Richard & Skindzier, Jon. Florida State University College Prowler off the Record. 2005. (College Prowler off the Record Guides: Vol. 50). 160p. (YA). (gr. 12-18). pap., stu. ed. 14.95 *(978-1-59658-049-7(6))* College Prowler, Inc.

Bohler, Victoria & Gray, Kevan. Loyola College in Maryland College Prowler off the Record. 2005. (College Prowler off the Record Guides: Vol. 76). 160p. (YA). (gr. 12-18). pap., stu. ed. 14.95 *(978-1-59658-075-6(5))* College Prowler, Inc.

Brennan, Genevieve. Wellesley College College Prowler off the Record. 2005. (College Prowler off the Record Guides: Vol. 200). 160p. (YA). (gr. 12-18). pap., stu. ed. 14.95 *(978-1-59658-199-9(9))* College Prowler, Inc.

Bretzius Matthew. West Virginia University College Prowler off the Record. 2005. (College Prowler off the Record Guides: Vol. 203). 160p. (YA). (gr. 12-18). pap., stu. ed. 14.95 *(978-1-59658-202-6(2))* College Prowler, Inc.

Brown, Antoinette & Skindzier, Jon. St John's University NY College Prowler off the Record: Inside Saint Johns New York. 2nd ed. 2005. (College Prowler off the Record Guides:

Vol. 122). 160p. (YA). (gr. 12-18). pap., stu. ed. 14.95 *(978-1-59658-121-0(2))* College Prowler, Inc.
Durgan, Michael. Death at Kent State: How a Photograph Brought the Vietnam War Home to America. 2016. (Captured History Ser.). (ENG., Illus.). 64p. (J). (gr. 5-9). lib. bdg. 35.32 *(978-0-7565-5424-8(1),* 132560, Compass Point Bks.) Capstone.
Byers, Ann. Ohio State Football, 1 vol. 2013. (America's Most Winning Teams Ser.). 48p. (J). (gr. 5-5). (ENG.). 34.41 *(978-1-4488-9401-7(8),* dbf0bb59-c599-4e4b-b42d-c310ba80d35a); (ENG.). pap. 12.75 *(978-1-4488-9438-3(7),* b422e00c-276d-4c89-ba94-076bc8e6a167); pap. 70.50 *(978-1-4488-9439-0(5))* Rosen Publishing Group, Inc., The.
C. Ridley, Joi & Gray, Kevan. Howard University College Prowler off the Record. 2nd ed. 2005. (College Prowler off the Record Guides: Vol. 66). 160p. (YA). (gr. 12-18). pap., stu. ed. 14.95 *(978-1-59658-065-7(8),* Off The Record) College Prowler, Inc.
Campbell, Margaret & Gohari, Omid. Duke University College Prowler off the Record. 2nd ed. 2005. (College Prowler off the Record Guides: Vol. 45). 160p. (YA). (gr. 12-18). pap., stu. ed. 14.95 *(978-1-59658-044-2(5))* College Prowler, Inc.
Carlin, Daniel. Washington University in St Louis College Prowler off the Record. 2nd ed. 2005. (College Prowler off the Record Guides: Vol. 199). 160p. (YA). (gr. 12-18). pap., stu. ed. 14.95 *(978-1-59658-198-2(0))* College Prowler, Inc.
Chadderdon, Andrea & Nash, Kevin. University of Oklahoma College Prowler off the Record. 2nd ed. 2005. (College Prowler off the Record Guides: Vol. 172). 160p. (YA). (gr. 12-18). pap., stu. ed. 14.95 *(978-1-59658-171-5(9))* College Prowler, Inc.
Chang, Tristen & Pecsenye, Jessica. UC Davis College Prowler off the Record: Inside University of California Davis. 2nd ed. 2005. (College Prowler off the Record Guides: Vol. 142). 160p. (YA). (gr. 12-18). pap., stu. ed. 14.95 *(978-1-59658-141-8(7))* College Prowler, Inc.
Chasan, Emily & Gray, Kevan. Tufts University College Prowler off the Record. 2nd ed. 2005. (College Prowler off the Record Guides: Vol. 136). 160p. (YA). (gr. 12-18). pap., stu. ed. 14.95 *(978-1-59658-135-7(2))* College Prowler, Inc.
C.Laird, Elizabeth & Skindzier, Jon. Guilford College College Prowler off the Record. 2005. (College Prowler off the Record Guides: Vol. 59). 160p. (YA). (gr. 12-18). pap., stu. ed. 14.95 *(978-1-59658-058-9(5))* College Prowler, Inc.
Clapp, Sarah & Varacalli, Lauren. Denison University College Prowler off the Record. 2005. (College Prowler off the Record Guides: Vol. 41). 160p. (YA). (gr. 12-18). pap., stu. ed. 14.95 *(978-1-59658-040-4(2))* College Prowler, Inc.
Cloud, Megan & Nash, Kevin. Barnard College College Prowler off the Record. 2005. (College Prowler off the Record Guides: Vol. 8). 160p. (YA). (gr. 12-18). pap., stu. ed. 14.95 *(978-1-59658-007-7(0))* College Prowler, Inc.
Cole, Kristin & Burns, Adam. Loyola Marymount University College Prowler off the Record. 2005. (College Prowler off the Record Guides: Vol. 77). 160p. (YA). (gr. 12-18). pap., stu. ed. 14.95 *(978-1-59658-076-3(3))* College Prowler, Inc.
Coleman, Andrew & Mason, Chris. Clemson University College Prowler off the Record. 2nd ed. 2005. (College Prowler off the Record Guides: Vol. 27). 160p. (YA). (gr. 12-18). pap., stu. ed. 14.95 *(978-1-59658-026-8(7))* College Prowler, Inc.
Coleman, Miriam. Plan It: Conducting Short-Term & Long-Term Research, 1 vol. 2012. (Core Skills Ser.). (ENG., Illus.). 32p. (J). (gr. 4-5). pap. 11.00 *(978-1-4488-7523-8(4),* f262eeec-b2b1-43a8-933e-443dcab505cc); lib. bdg. 28.93 *(978-1-4488-7450-7(5),* ca15013c-7335-48eb-a6fb-f73d9c71aa09) Rosen Publishing Group, Inc., The. (PowerKids Pr.).
Collins, Anna. Should Student-Athletes Be Paid?, 1 vol. 2020. (Points of View Ser.). (ENG.). 24p. (gr. 3-3). pap. 9.25 *(978-1-5345-3420-9(2),* a1a6ee93-b21e-4232-a6bf-bb0b1ffc53f9, KidHaven Publishing) Greenhaven Publishing LLC.
Collins, Elizabeth & Lyon, Abby. Swarthmore College College Prowler off the Record. 2nd ed. 2005. (College Prowler off the Record Guides: Vol. 129). 160p. (YA). (gr. 12-18). pap., stu. ed. 14.95 *(978-1-59658-128-9(X))* College Prowler, Inc.
Connell, Sarah & Nash, Kevin. Bates College College Prowler off the Record. 2005. (College Prowler off the Record Guides: Vol. 9). 160p. (YA). (gr. 12-18). pap., stu. ed. 14.95 *(978-1-59658-008-4(9))* College Prowler, Inc.
Cook, Jane Hampton. B Is for Baylor. Connally, Erin, illus. 2010. (Big Bear Bks.). (ENG.). 64p. (gr. 17). 29.95 *(978-1-60258-270-5(X))* Baylor Univ. Pr.
Cook, Peter & Nash, Kevin. Pomona College College Prowler off the Record. 2nd ed. 2005. (College Prowler off the Record Guides: Vol. 100). 160p. (YA). (gr. 12-18). pap., stu. ed. 14.95 *(978-1-59658-099-2(2))* College Prowler, Inc.
Cooper, Amy & Keller, Carolyn. Rochester Institute of Technology College Prowler off the Record: Inside RIT. 2005. (College Prowler off the Record Guides: Vol. 109). 160p. (YA). (gr. 12-18). pap., stu. ed. 14.95 *(978-1-59658-108-1(5))* College Prowler, Inc.
Core, Sarah & Varacalli, Lauren. College of Wooster College Prowler off the Record. 2005. (College Prowler off the Record Guides: Vol. 33). 160p. (YA). (gr. 12-18). pap., stu. ed. 14.95 *(978-1-59658-032-9(1))* College Prowler, Inc.
Cruttenden, Jamie & Pecsenye, Jessica. University of Pittsburgh College Prowler off the Record. 2nd ed. 2005. (College Prowler off the Record Guides: Vol. 175). 160p. (YA). (gr. 12-18). pap., stu. ed. 14.95 *(978-1-59658-174-6(3))* College Prowler, Inc.
Cusick, John. Wesleyan University College Prowler off the Record. 2005. (College Prowler off the Record Guides: Vol. 201). 160p. (YA). (gr. 12-18). pap., stu. ed. 14.95 *(978-1-59658-200-2(6))* College Prowler, Inc.
Cyr, Jessica & Keller, Carolyn. Ohio University College Prowler off the Record. 2nd ed. 2005. (College Prowler off the Record Guides: Vol. 96). 160p. (YA). (gr. 12-18). pap., stu. ed. 14.95 *(978-1-59658-095-4(X))* College Prowler, Inc.
Davis, Amy & Mandelbaum, Jolie. Michigan State University College Prowler off the Record. 2nd ed. 2005. (College Prowler off the Record Guides: Vol. 84). 160p. (YA). (gr. 12-18). pap., stu. ed. 14.95 *(978-1-59658-083-1(6))* College Prowler, Inc.
Davis, Jenny & Skindzier, Jon. Indiana University College Prowler off the Record. 2nd ed. 2005. (College Prowler off the Record Guides: Vol. 67). 160p. (YA). (gr. 12-18). pap., stu. ed. 14.95 *(978-1-59658-066-4(6))* College Prowler, Inc.
Davis, Lauren & Varacalli, Lauren. Bucknell University College Prowler off the Record. 2005. (College Prowler off the Record Guides: Vol. 20). 160p. (YA). (gr. 12-18). pap., stu. ed. 14.95 *(978-1-59658-019-0(4))* College Prowler, Inc.
Dearing, Kate & Lyon, Abby. Tulane University College Prowler off the Record. 2nd ed. 2005. (College Prowler off the Record Guides: Vol. 137). 160p. (YA). (gr. 12-18). pap., stu. ed. 14.95 *(978-1-59658-136-4(0))* College Prowler, Inc.
Dickson, Kristin & Pecsenye, Jessica. Trinity University Texas College Prowler off the Record. 2005. (College Prowler off the Record Guides: Vol. 135). 160p. (YA). (gr. 12-18). pap., stu. ed. 14.95 *(978-1-59658-134-0(4))* College Prowler, Inc.
Doctorick, Jonathan & Gohari, Omid. Duquesne University College Prowler off the Record. 2005. (College Prowler off the Record Guides: Vol. 46). 160p. (YA). (gr. 12-18). pap., stu. ed. 14.95 *(978-1-59658-045-9(3))* College Prowler, Inc.
Doscher, Melissa. Yale University College Prowler off the Record. 2nd ed. 2005. (College Prowler off the Record Guides: Vol. 208). 160p. (YA). (gr. 12-18). pap., stu. ed. 14.95 *(978-1-59658-207-1(3))* College Prowler, Inc.
DuPree, Ben & Skindzier, Jon. Reed College College Prowler off the Record. 2nd ed. 2005. (College Prowler off the Record Guides: Vol. 104). 160p. (YA). (gr. 12-18). pap., stu. ed. 14.95 *(978-1-59658-103-6(4))* College Prowler, Inc.
Dutt, Arjun & Varacalli, Lauren. Claremont Mckenna College College Prowler off the Record. 2005. (College Prowler off the Record Guides: Vol. 26). 160p. (YA). (gr. 12-18). pap., stu. ed. 14.95 *(978-1-59658-025-1(9),* Off The Record) College Prowler, Inc.
Eagan, Colin & Varacalli, Lauren. Davidson College College Prowler off the Record. 2005. (College Prowler off the Record Guides: Vol. 40). 160p. (YA). (gr. 12-18). pap., stu. ed. 14.95 *(978-1-59658-039-8(9))* College Prowler, Inc.
Earl, Archie William, Sr. The Inside Scoop on American Colleges & Universities. 2004. (YA). pap. 6.99 *(978-1-884169-32-8(5))* International Educational Improvement Ctr. Pr.
Easley, Michael F. Look Out, College, Here I Come! 2007. (J). *(978-0-8106-2037-7(5));* pap. *(978-0-8106-2038-4(3))* National Education Assn.
Epstein, Brad M. Arizona State University 101: My First Text-Board-Book. I.t. ed. 2003. (101 — My First Text-Board Books). (Illus.). 20p. (J). bds. *(978-0-9727702-3-1(2),* 101 Bk.) Michaelson Entertainment.
—Clemson University 101: My First Text-Board-Book. I.t. ed. 2004. (101 — My First Text-Board Books). (ENG., Illus.). 20p. (J). bds. *(978-1-932530-06-3(1),* 101 Bk.) Michaelson Entertainment.
—Kansas State Univ 101: My First Text-Board-Book. I.t. ed. 2007. (101 — My First Text-Board Books). (Illus.). 20p. (J). bds. *(978-1-932530-57-5(6),* 101 Bk.) Michaelson Entertainment.
—Louisiana State University 101: My First Text-Board-Book. I.t. ed. 2004. (My First Text Board Bks.). (Illus.). 20p. (J). bds. *(978-1-932530-09-4(6))* Michaelson Entertainment.
—Ohio State 101. 2013. (My First Text-Board-Book Ser.). (ENG., Illus.). 24p. (J). bds. *(978-1-60730-064-9(8),* 101 Bk.) Michaelson Entertainment.
—Purdue University 101: My First Text-Board-Book. I.t. ed. 2004. (101 — My First Text-Board Books). (ENG., Illus.). 20p. (J). bds. *(978-1-932530-11-7(8),* 101 Bk.) Michaelson Entertainment.
—Stanford 101. 2013. (My First Text-Board-Book Ser.). (ENG., Illus.). 20p. (J). (gr. -1). bds. *(978-1-60730-066-3(4),* 101 Bk.) Michaelson Entertainment.
—UCLA 101: My First Text-Board-Book. I.t. ed. 2004. (My First Text Board Bks.). (Illus.). 20p. (J). bds. *(978-1-932530-15-5(0,* 101 Bk.) Michaelson Entertainment.
—University of Florida 101: My First Text-Board-Book. I.t. ed. 2004. (101 — My First Text-Board Books). (Illus.). 20p. (J). bds. *(978-1-932530-21-6(5),* 101 Bk.) Michaelson Entertainment.
—University of Georgia 101: My First Text-Board-Book. I.t. ed. 2004. (101 — My First Text-Board Books). (ENG., Illus.). 20p. (J). bds. *(978-1-932530-08-7(8),* 101 Bk.) Michaelson Entertainment.
—University of Illinois 101: My First Text-Board-Book. I.t. ed. 2004. (101 — My First Text-Board Books). (ENG., Illus.). 20p. (J). bds. *(978-1-932530-17-9(7),* 101 Bk.) Michaelson Entertainment.
—University of Kansas 101: My First Text-Board-Book. 2006. (101 — My First Text-Board Books). (ENG., Illus.). 20p. (J). bds. *(978-1-932530-40-7(1),* 101 Bk.) Michaelson Entertainment.
—University of Nebraska 101: My First Text-Board-book. 2013. (My First Text-Board-Book Ser.). (ENG., Illus.). 20p. (J). bds. *(978-1-60730-063-2(X))* Michaelson Entertainment.
—University of Washington 101. 2013. (My First Text-Board-Book Ser.). (ENG., Illus.). 20p. (J). (gr. -1). bds. *(978-1-60730-068-7(0),* 101 Bk.) Michaelson Entertainment.
—Usc 101: My First Text-Board-Book. I.t. ed. 2004. (101 — My First Text-Board Books). (ENG., Illus.). 20p. (J). bds. *(978-0-9727702-0-0(8),* 101 Bk.) Michaelson Entertainment.
Eske, Aaron & Nash, Kevin. University of Nebraska College Prowler off the Record. 2nd ed. 2005. (College Prowler off the Record Guides: Vol. 168). 160p. (YA). (gr. 12-18). pap., stu. ed. 14.95 *(978-1-59658-167-8(0))* College Prowler, Inc.
Evans, Mcana & Pecsenye, Jessica. Harvey Mudd College College Prowler off the Record. 2005. (College Prowler off the Record Guides: Vol. 63). 160p. (YA). (gr. 12-18). pap., stu. ed. 14.95 *(978-1-59658-062-6(3))* College Prowler, Inc.
Ewing, Drew & Burns, Adam. St Louis University College Prowler off the Record: Inside Saint Louis. 2nd ed. 2005. (College Prowler off the Record Guides: Vol. 123). 160p. (YA). (gr. 12-18). pap., stu. ed. 14.95 *(978-1-59658-122-7(0))* College Prowler, Inc.
Fackrell, Caitlin & Lyon, Abby. Lewis & Clark College College Prowler off the Record. 2005. (College Prowler off the Record Guides: Vol. 75). 160p. (YA). (gr. 12-18). pap., stu. ed. 14.95 *(978-1-59658-074-9(7))* College Prowler, Inc.
Fassio, Dan & Burns, Adam. Washington & Lee University College Prowler off the Record. 2005. (College Prowler off the Record Guides: Vol. 198). 160p. (YA). (gr. 12-18). pap., stu. ed. 14.95 *(978-1-59658-197-5(2))* College Prowler, Inc.
Fitzgerald, Brendan & Burns, Adam. Hofstra University College Prowler off the Record. 2005. (College Prowler off the Record Guides: Vol. 65). 160p. (YA). (gr. 12-18). pap., stu. ed. 14.95 *(978-1-59658-064-0(X))* College Prowler, Inc.
Flegal, Eric & Pecsenye, Jessica. UCLA College Prowler off the Record: Inside University of California Los Angeles. 2nd ed. 2005. (College Prowler off the Record Guides: Vol. 144). 160p. (YA). (gr. 12-18). pap., stu. ed. 14.95 *(978-1-59658-143-2(3))* College Prowler, Inc.
Fleming, Jessica & Burns, Adam. Texas Christian University College Prowler off the Record. 2005. (College Prowler off the Record Guides: Vol. 133). 160p. (YA). (gr. 12-18). pap., stu. ed. 14.95 *(978-1-59658-132-6(8))* College Prowler, Inc.
Florence, Sylvia & Keller, Carolyn. James Madison University College Prowler off the Record. 2nd ed. 2005. (College Prowler off the Record Guides: Vol. 70). 160p. (YA). (gr. 12-18). pap., stu. ed. 14.95 *(978-1-59658-069-5(0))* College Prowler, Inc.
Foster, Jessica & Pecsenye, Jessica. University of South Carolina College Prowler off the Record. 2nd ed. 2005. (College Prowler off the Record Guides: Vol. 182). 160p. (YA). (gr. 12-18). pap., stu. ed. 14.95 *(978-1-59658-181-4(6))* College Prowler, Inc.
Fosyth, Rebekah & Burns, Adam. Rose-Hulman Institute of Technology College Prowler off the Record. 2005. (College Prowler off the Record Guides: Vol. 111). 160p. (YA). (gr. 12-18). pap., stu. ed. 14.95 *(978-1-59658-110-4(7),* Off The Record) College Prowler, Inc.
Fraser, Alison & Lyon, Abby. Princeton University College Prowler off the Record. 2005. (College Prowler off the Record Guides: Vol. 101). 160p. (YA). (gr. 12-18). pap., stu. ed. 14.95 *(978-1-59658-100-5(X))* College Prowler, Inc.
Fried, Alyssa & Seaman, Jim. Penn State College Prowler off the Record: Inside Pennsylvania State University. 2nd ed. 2005. (College Prowler off the Record Guides: Vol. 97). 160p. (YA). (gr. 12-18). pap., stu. ed. 14.95 *(978-1-59658-096-1(8))* College Prowler, Inc.
Friedman, Sarah & Gohari, Omid. Bryn Mawr College College Prowler off the Record. 2005. (College Prowler off the Record Guides: Vol. 19). 160p. (YA). (gr. 12-18). pap., stu. ed. 14.95 *(978-1-59658-018-3(6))* College Prowler, Inc.
G. de la Parra, John & Rahimi, Joey. The Cooper Union College Prowler off the Record. 2nd ed. 2005. (College Prowler off the Record Guides: Vol. 37). 160p. (YA). (gr. 12-18). pap., stu. ed. 14.95 *(978-1-59658-036-7(4),* Off The Record) College Prowler, Inc.
Garrett, Tiffany & Seaman, Jim. Miami University of Ohio College Prowler off the Record. 2005. (College Prowler off the Record Guides: Vol. 83). 160p. (YA). (gr. 12-18). pap., stu. ed. 14.95 *(978-1-59658-082-4(8))* College Prowler, Inc.
Gatker, Anna & Varacalli, Lauren. Babson College College Prowler off the Record. 2005. (College Prowler off the Record Guides: Vol. 6). 160p. (YA). (gr. 12-18). pap., stu. ed. 14.95 *(978-1-59658-005-3(4))* College Prowler, Inc.
Gilbert, Heather & Nash, Kevin. Virginia Tech College Prowler off the Record: Inside Virginia Polytechnic Institute. 2nd ed. 2005. (College Prowler off the Record Guides: Vol. 196). 160p. (YA). (gr. 12-18). pap., stu. ed. 14.95 *(978-1-59658-195-1(6))* College Prowler, Inc.
Gilmore, David. Xavier University College Prowler off the Record. 2005. (College Prowler off the Record Guides: Vol. 207). 160p. (YA). (gr. 12-18). pap., stu. ed. 14.95 *(978-1-59658-206-4(5))* College Prowler, Inc.
Glabe, Scott & Rahimi, Joey. Dartmouth College College Prowler off the Record. 2nd ed. 2005. (College Prowler off the Record Guides: Vol. 39). 160p. (YA). (gr. 12-18). pap., stu. ed. 14.95 *(978-1-59658-038-1(0))* College Prowler, Inc.
Goldsmith, Emily & Nash, Kevin. Vassar College College Prowler off the Record. 2005. (College Prowler off the Record Guides: Vol. 194). 160p. (YA). (gr. 12-18). pap., stu. ed. 14.95 *(978-1-59658-193-7(X))* College Prowler, Inc.
Gordon, Josh & Pecsenye, Jessica. Pitzer College College Prowler off the Record. 2005. (College Prowler off the Record Guides: Vol. 99). 160p. (YA). (gr. 12-18). pap., stu. ed. 14.95 *(978-1-59658-098-5(4))* College Prowler, Inc.
Gordon, Julie & Skindzier, Jon. George Washington University College Prowler off the Record. 2nd ed. 2005. (College Prowler off the Record Guides: Vol. 54). 160p. (YA). (gr. 12-18). pap., stu. ed. 14.95 *(978-1-59658-053-4(4))* College Prowler, Inc.
Gordon, Lily & Nash, Kevin. Union College College Prowler off the Record. 2nd ed. 2005. (College Prowler off the Record Guides: Vol. 138). 160p. (YA). (gr. 12-18). pap., stu. ed. 14.95 *(978-1-59658-137-1(9))* College Prowler, Inc.
Goss, Nicole, et al. University of Georgia College Prowler off the Record. 2nd ed. 2005. (College Prowler off the Record Guides: Vol. 156). 160p. (YA). (gr. 12-18). pap., stu. ed. 14.95 *(978-1-59658-155-5(7))* College Prowler, Inc.
Gossett, Kelley & Nash, Kevin. Boston College College Prowler off the Record. 2nd ed. 2005. (College Prowler off the Record Guides: Vol. 13). 160p. (YA). (gr. 12-18). pap., stu. ed. 14.95 *(978-1-59658-012-1(7))* College Prowler, Inc.
Granberry, Debra & Skindzier, Jon. Furman University College Prowler off the Record. 2nd ed. 2005. (College Prowler off the Record Guides: Vol. 53). 160p. (YA). (gr. 12-18). pap., stu. ed. 14.95 *(978-1-59658-052-7(6))* College Prowler, Inc.
Grashkina, Alexandra. Williams College College Prowler off the Record. 2005. (College Prowler off the Record Guides: Vol. 206). 160p. (YA). (gr. 12-18). pap., stu. ed. 14.95 *(978-1-59658-205-7(7))* College Prowler, Inc.
Gray, Kevan. Spelman College College Prowler off the Record. 2005. (College Prowler off the Record Guides: Vol. 121). 160p. (YA). (gr. 12-18). pap., stu. ed. 14.95 *(978-1-59658-120-3(4),* Off The Record) College Prowler, Inc.
Greenfeld, Barbara & Weinstein, Robert A. The Kids' College Almanac Fourth Edition: A First Look at College. 4th ed. 2010. (ENG., Illus.). 352p. pap. 16.95 *(978-1-59357-736-0(2),* JIST Works) JIST Publishing.
Gunderman, Shelby & Burns, Adam. UC San Diego College Prowler off the Record: Inside University of California San Diego. 2005. (College Prowler off the Record Guides: Vol. 146). 160p. (YA). (gr. 12-18). pap., stu. ed. 14.95 *(978-1-59658-145-6(X))* College Prowler, Inc.
Hall, Erin & Skindzier, Jon. University of Texas College Prowler off the Record. 2nd ed. 2005. (College Prowler off the Record Guides: Vol. 186). 160p. (YA). (gr. 12-18). pap., stu. ed. 14.95 *(978-1-59658-185-2(9))* College Prowler, Inc.
Hansen, Peter & Skindzier, Jon. University of Richmond College Prowler off the Record. 2005. (College Prowler off the Record Guides: Vol. 178). 160p. (YA). (gr. 12-18). pap., stu. ed. 14.95 *(978-1-59658-177-7(8))* College Prowler, Inc.
Harmon, Daniel E. Notre Dame Football, 1 vol. 2013. (America's Most Winning Teams Ser.). 48p. (J). (gr. 5-5). (ENG.). 34.41 *(978-1-4488-9399-7(2),* e85fc847-842d-4d26-9e29-30d5476ccd1d); (ENG.). pap. 12.75 *(978-1-4488-9436-9(0),* 3cca3830-0c99-4449-8037-df2e1214257e); pap. 70.50 *(978-1-4488-9437-6(9))* Rosen Publishing Group, Inc., The.
Hassiebeck, Kellie & Gohari, Omid. Depauw University College Prowler off the Record. 2005. (College Prowler off the Record Guides: Vol. 42). 160p. (YA). (gr. 12-18). pap., stu. ed. 14.95 *(978-1-59658-041-1(0))* College Prowler, Inc.
Hein, Michelle & Skindzier, Jon. Muhlenberg College College Prowler off the Record. 2005. (College Prowler off the Record Guides: Vol. 88). 160p. (YA). (gr. 12-18). pap., stu. ed. 14.95 *(978-1-59658-087-9(9))* College Prowler, Inc.
Heing, Bridey & Baldino, Greg. Critical Perspectives on the College Admissions Process, 1 vol. 2017. (Analyzing the Issues Ser.). (ENG.). 208p. (gr. 8-8). lib. bdg. 50.93 *(978-0-7660-8479-7(5),* 91e8a741-e087-44d8-a60f-8e1d80c3be85) Enslow Publishing, LLC.
Helmer, Jay & Skindzier, Jon. Kenyon College College Prowler off the Record. 2005. (College Prowler off the Record Guides: Vol. 72). 160p. (YA). (gr. 12-18). pap., stu. ed. 14.95 *(978-1-59658-071-8(2))* College Prowler, Inc.
Hofius, Sarah & Skindzier, Jon. Ithaca College College Prowler off the Record. 2005. (College Prowler off the Record Guides: Vol. 69). 160p. (YA). (gr. 12-18). pap., stu. ed. 14.95 *(978-1-59658-068-8(2))* College Prowler, Inc.
Hondorp, Michael & Nash, Kevin. University of Michigan College Prowler off the Record. 2nd ed. 2005. (College Prowler off the Record Guides: Vol. 164). 160p. (YA). (gr. 12-18). pap., stu. ed. 14.95 *(978-1-59658-163-0(8))* College Prowler, Inc.
Hood, Dominic & Skindzier, Jon. Harvard University College Prowler off the Record. 2005. (College Prowler off the Record Guides: Vol. 62). 160p. (YA). (gr. 12-18). pap., stu. ed. 14.95 *(978-1-59658-061-9(5))* College Prowler, Inc.
Hopkins, Adrianna & Lyon, Abby. University of North Carolina College Prowler off the Record. 2nd ed. 2005. (College Prowler off the Record Guides: Vol. 170). 160p. (YA). (gr. 12-18). pap., stu. ed. 14.95 *(978-1-59658-169-2(7))* College Prowler, Inc.
Huang, Christine & Nash, Kevin. UC Berkeley College Prowler off the Record: Inside University of California Berkeley. 2nd ed. 2005. (College Prowler off the Record Guides: Vol. 141). 160p. (YA). (gr. 12-18). pap., stu. ed. 14.95 *(978-1-59658-140-1(9))* College Prowler, Inc.
Intravia, Emily & Swope, Gretchen. Fordham University College Prowler off the Record. 2005. (College Prowler off the Record Guides: Vol. 51). 160p. (YA). (gr. 12-18). pap., stu. ed. 14.95 *(978-1-59658-050-3(X))* College Prowler, Inc.
Jade, Torea, et al. Northwestern University College Prowler off the Record. 2005. (College Prowler off the Record Guides: Vol. 92). 160p. (YA). (gr. 12-18). pap., stu. ed. 14.95 *(978-1-59658-091-6(7))* College Prowler, Inc.
Jardy, Adam & Pecsenye, Jessica. Ohio State University College Prowler off the Record. 2005. (College Prowler off the Record Guides: Vol. 95). 160p. (YA). (gr. 12-18). pap., stu. ed. 14.95 *(978-1-59658-094-7(1))* College Prowler, Inc.
Jendrey, Julie. San Diego State University College Prowler off the Record. 2005. (College Prowler off the Record Guides: Vol. 113). 160p. (YA). (gr. 12-18). pap., stu. ed. 14.95 *(978-1-59658-112-8(3))* College Prowler, Inc.
Johnston, Cathy & Pecsenye, Jessica. Hamilton College College Prowler off the Record. 2005. (College Prowler off the Record Guides: Vol. 60). 160p. (YA). (gr. 12-18). pap., stu. ed. 14.95 *(978-1-59658-059-6(3))* College Prowler, Inc.
Jordan, Keith. Don't Stress the Process: The College Plan. 2005. (J). lib. bdg. 18.95 *(978-0-9761218-0-0(8))* Knowledge College Planning.
Joseph, Jessica, et al. Suny Albany College Prowler off the Record: Inside State University of New York. 2005. (College Prowler off the Record Guides: Vol. 126). 160p. (YA). (gr. 12-18). pap., stu. ed. 14.95 *(978-1-59658-125-8(5))* College Prowler, Inc.
Joseph, Tiffani & Keller, Carolyn. Temple University College Prowler off the Record. 2nd ed. 2005. (College Prowler off the Record Guides: Vol. 131). 160p. (YA). (gr. 12-18). pap., stu. ed. 14.95 *(978-1-59658-130-2(1))* College Prowler, Inc.
Kamberg, Mary-Lane. North Carolina Basketball, 1 vol. 2013. (America's Most Winning Teams Ser.). 48p. (J). (gr. 5-5). (ENG.). 34.41 *(978-1-4488-9404-8(2),* 1b7cad76-541f-4dd4-9342-b450ce04d24d); (ENG.). pap. 12.75 *(978-1-4488-9435-2(2),* 716f09be-6a83-4b37-9a94-4e7d6dd4e93c); pap. 70.50 *(978-1-4488-9444-4(1))* Rosen Publishing Group, Inc., The.
Katz, Andrew & Gohari, Omid. Brandeis University College Prowler off the Record. 2nd ed. 2005. (College Prowler off the Record Guides: Vol. 16). 160p. (YA). (gr. 12-18). pap., stu. ed. 14.95 *(978-1-59658-015-2(1))* College Prowler, Inc.
Keller, Carolyn & Seaman, Jim. Allegheny College College Prowler off the Record. 2005. (College Prowler off the Record Guides: Vol. 1). 160p. (YA). (gr. 12-18). pap., stu. ed. 14.95 *(978-1-59658-000-8(3))* College Prowler, Inc.
Kennedy, Lauren, et al. Arizona State University College Prowler off the Record. 2005. (College Prowler off the Record Guides: Vol. 4). 160p. (YA). (gr. 12-18). pap., stu. ed. 14.95 *(978-1-59658-003-9(8))* College Prowler, Inc.
Killeen, Jared & Nash, Kevin. Bard College College Prowler off the Record. 2005. (College Prowler off the Record Guides: Vol. 7). 160p. (YA). (gr. 12-18). pap., stu. ed. 14.95 *(978-1-59658-006-0(2))* College Prowler, Inc.
Kittay, Matthew & Mason, Chris. Brown University College Prowler off the Record. 2nd ed. 2005. (College Prowler off the Record Guides: Vol. 18). 160p. (YA). (gr. 12-18). pap., stu. ed. 14.95 *(978-1-59658-017-6(8))* College Prowler, Inc.
Klein, Jennifer & Gray, Kevan. University of Pennsylvania College Prowler off the Record. 2nd ed. 2005. (College

TUV

Prowler off the Record Guides: Vol. 174). 160p. (YA). (gr. 12-18). pap., stu. ed. 14.95 *(978-1-59658-173-9(5))* College Prowler, Inc.

Klein, Nadav & Varacalli, Lauren. Amherst College College Prowler off the Record. 2005. (College Prowler off the Record Guides: Vol. 3). 160p. (YA). (gr. 12-18). pap., stu. ed. 14.95 *(978-1-59658-002-2(X))* College Prowler, Inc.

Knight, Russell & Williams, Tim. University of Puget Sound College Prowler off the Record. 2005. (College Prowler off the Record Guides: Vol. 176). 160p. (YA). (gr. 12-18). pap., stu. ed. 14.95 *(978-1-59658-175-3(1))* College Prowler, Inc.

Koestler, Larry & Scheff, William. Lehigh University College Prowler off the Record. 2005. (College Prowler off the Record Guides: Vol. 74). 160p. (YA). (gr. 12-18). pap., stu. ed. 14.95 *(978-1-59658-073-2(9))* College Prowler, Inc.

Krakauer, Steve & Skindzier, Jon. Syracuse University College Prowler off the Record. 2005. (College Prowler off the Record Guides: Vol. 130). 160p. (YA). (gr. 12-18). pap., stu. ed. 14.95 *(978-1-59658-129-6(8))* College Prowler, Inc.

Kutscher, Scott & Lyon, Abby. Suny Binghamton College Prowler off the Record: Inside State University of New York. 2005. (College Prowler off the Record Guides: Vol. 125). 160p. (YA). (gr. 12-18). pap., stu. ed. 14.95 *(978-1-59658-124-1(7))* College Prowler, Inc.

L, Jessica & Skindzier, Jon. Grove City College College Prowler off the Record. 2005. (College Prowler off the Record Guides: Vol. 58). 160p. (YA). (gr. 12-18). pap., stu. ed. 14.95 *(978-1-59658-057-2(7))* College Prowler, Inc.

L. Wright, Sean & Nash, Kevin. Villanova University College Prowler off the Record. 2005. (College Prowler off the Record Guides: Vol. 195). 160p. (YA). (gr. 12-18). pap., stu. ed. 14.95 *(978-1-59658-194-4(8))* College Prowler, Inc.

Lang, Alex & Burns, Adam. University of Iowa College Prowler off the Record. 2nd ed. 2005. (College Prowler off the Record Guides: Vol. 158). 160p. (YA). (gr. 12-18). pap., stu. ed. 14.95 *(978-1-59658-157-9(3))* College Prowler, Inc.

Langlieb, David & Burns, Adam. Haverford College College Prowler off the Record. 2005. (College Prowler off the Record Guides: Vol. 64). 160p. (YA). (gr. 12-18). pap., stu. ed. 14.95 *(978-1-59658-063-3(1))* College Prowler, Inc.

Langston, Mandy & Nash, Kevin. University of Kentucky College Prowler off the Record. 2nd ed. 2005. (College Prowler off the Record Guides: Vol. 160). 160p. (YA). (gr. 12-18). pap., stu. ed. 14.95 *(978-1-59658-159-3(X))* College Prowler, Inc.

Langwith, Jacqueline, ed. College, 1 vol. 2009. (Introducing Issues with Opposing Viewpoints Ser.). (ENG.). 152p. (gr. 7-10). 43.63 *(978-0-7377-4336-4(0),* 99487ef7-5312-4495-8ee7-39d92642ad83, Greenhaven Publishing) Greenhaven Publishing LLC.

Latina, Paul A. The Places You'll Go: While at the University of Florida. 2012. 20p. pap. 16.50 *(978-1-61204-831-4(5),* Strategic Bk. Publishing) Strategic Book Publishing & Rights Agency (SBPRA).

Leanoard, James & Nash, Kevin. University of San Diego College Prowler off the Record. 2nd ed. 2005. (College Prowler off the Record Guides: Vol. 180). 160p. (YA). (gr. 12-18). pap., stu. ed. 14.95 *(978-1-59658-179-1(4))* College Prowler, Inc.

LeBaron, Sarah & Dawson, Kai. Oberlin College College Prowler off the Record. 2005. (College Prowler off the Record Guides: Vol. 93). 160p. (YA). (gr. 12-18). pap., stu. ed. 14.95 *(978-1-59658-092-3(5))* College Prowler, Inc.

Lee, Brittany. Rollins College. Moore, Kim & Burns, Adam, eds. 2005. (College Prowler off the Record Guides: Vol. 110). (Illus.). 150p. (gr. 12-18). pap., stu. ed. 14.95 *(978-1-59658-109-8(3))* College Prowler, Inc.

Lee, Danielle. JumpStart Your Future: A Guide for the College-Bound Christian. 2006. (Illus.). iii, 123p. (YA). per. 12.99 *(978-0-9769298-9-5(9))* Olive Pr., The.

Lee, Susie & Skindzier, Jon. MIT College Prowler off the Record: Inside Massachusetts Institute of Technology. 2nd ed. 2005. (College Prowler off the Record Guides: Vol. 82). 160p. (YA). (gr. 12-18). pap., stu. ed. 14.95 *(978-1-59658-081-7(X))* College Prowler, Inc.

Leitikow, Greg & Varacalli, Lauren. Colorado College College Prowler off the Record. 2005. (College Prowler off the Record Guides: Vol. 34). 160p. (YA). (gr. 12-18). pap., stu. ed. 14.95 *(978-1-59658-033-6(X))* College Prowler, Inc.

Lenfest, Kevyn & Mandelbaum, Jolie. University of Vermont College Prowler off the Record. 2nd ed. 2005. (College Prowler off the Record Guides: Vol. 188). 160p. (YA). (gr. 12-18). pap., stu. ed. 14.95 *(978-1-59658-187-6(5))* College Prowler, Inc.

Lewis, Brooke & Varacalli, Lauren. Dickinson College College Prowler off the Record. 2005. (College Prowler off the Record Guides: Vol. 43). 160p. (YA). (gr. 12-18). pap., stu. ed. 14.95 *(978-1-59658-042-8(9))* College Prowler, Inc.

Lewis, Jeff & Burns, Adam. University of New Hampshire College Prowler off the Record. 2nd ed. 2005. (College Prowler off the Record Guides: Vol. 169). 160p. (YA). (gr. 12-18). pap., stu. ed. 14.95 *(978-1-59658-168-5(9))* College Prowler, Inc.

Lewis, Jennifer & Williams, Tim. Mount Holyoke College College Prowler off the Record. 2005. (College Prowler off the Record Guides: Vol. 87). 160p. (YA). (gr. 12-18). pap., stu. ed. 14.95 *(978-1-59658-086-2(0))* College Prowler, Inc.

Lexa, Katrina & Skindzier, Jon. Hampton University College Prowler off the Record. 2nd ed. 2005. (College Prowler off the Record Guides: Vol. 61). 160p. (YA). (gr. 12-18). pap., stu. ed. 14.95 *(978-1-59658-060-2(7))* College Prowler, Inc.

Lieberman, Dan & Rahimi, Joey. Carnegie Mellon University College Prowler off the Record. 2nd ed. 2005. (College Prowler off the Record Guides: Vol. 24). 160p. (YA). (gr. 12-18). pap., stu. ed. 14.95 *(978-1-59658-023-7(2))* College Prowler, Inc.

Lindin, Kerri & Pecsenye, Jessica. University of Rochester College Prowler off the Record. 2nd ed. 2005. (College Prowler off the Record Guides: Vol. 179). 160p. (YA). (gr. 12-18). pap., stu. ed. 14.95 *(978-1-59658-178-4(6))* College Prowler, Inc.

Low, Jessica & Nash, Kevin. Bentley College College Prowler off the Record. 2005. (College Prowler off the Record Guides: Vol. 12). 160p. (YA). (gr. 12-18). pap., stu. ed. 14.95 *(978-1-59658-011-4(9))* College Prowler, Inc.

Lunis, Natalie. Spooky Schools. 2013. (Scary Places Ser.). 32p. (J). (gr. 4-8). lib. bdg. 25.27 *(978-1-61772-750-4(4))* Bearport Publishing Co., Inc.

Lynn Sauthoff, Taryn & Williams, Tim. Rutgers New Brunswick College Prowler off the Record. 2005. (College Prowler off the Record Guides: Vol. 112). 160p. (YA). (gr. 12-18). pap., stu. ed. 14.95 *(978-1-59658-111-1(5))* College Prowler, Inc.

Maehl, Sarah & Nash, Kevin. Beloit College College Prowler off the Record. 2005. (College Prowler off the Record Guides: Vol. 11). 160p. (YA). (gr. 12-18). pap., stu. ed. 14.95 *(978-1-59658-010-7(0))* College Prowler, Inc.

Mahon, Amy & Gohari, Omid. Elon University College Prowler off the Record. 2005. (College Prowler off the Record Guides: Vol. 47). 160p. (YA). (gr. 12-18). pap., stu. ed. 14.95 *(978-1-59658-046-6(1))* College Prowler, Inc.

Marshall, Ashley & Keller, Carolyn. Texas a & M University College Prowler off the Record. 2nd ed. 2005. (College Prowler off the Record Guides: Vol. 132). 160p. (YA). (gr. 12-18). pap., stu. ed. 14.95 *(978-1-59658-131-9(X))* College Prowler, Inc.

Mass, Aaron & Burns, Adam. Wake Forest University College Prowler off the Record. 2nd ed. 2005. (College Prowler off the Record Guides: Vol. 197). 160p. (YA). (gr. 12-18). pap., stu. ed. 14.95 *(978-1-59658-196-8(4))* College Prowler, Inc.

McRobert, Megan & Skindzier, Jon. Smith College College Prowler off the Record. 2005. (College Prowler off the Record Guides: Vol. 119). 160p. (YA). (gr. 12-18). pap., stu. ed. 14.95 *(978-1-59658-118-0(2))* College Prowler, Inc.

Meers, Whitney & Nash, Kevin. University of South Florida College Prowler off the Record. 2005. (College Prowler off the Record Guides: Vol. 183). 160p. (YA). (gr. 12-18). pap., stu. ed. 14.95 *(978-1-59658-182-1(4))* College Prowler, Inc.

Megill, Colin & Davis, Cristine. University of Connecticut College Prowler off the Record. 2nd ed. 2005. (College Prowler off the Record Guides: Vol. 152). 160p. (YA). (gr. 12-18). pap., stu. ed. 14.95 *(978-1-59658-151-7(4))* College Prowler, Inc.

Meyer, Jared & Jolis, Annie. University of Maryland College Prowler off the Record. 2nd ed. 2005. (College Prowler off the Record Guides: Vol. 161). 160p. (YA). (gr. 12-18). pap., stu. ed. 14.95 *(978-1-59658-160-9(3))* College Prowler, Inc.

Miller, Kirystan & Burns, Adam. Iowa State University College Prowler off the Record. 2005. (College Prowler off the Record Guides: Vol. 68). 160p. (YA). (gr. 12-18). pap., stu. ed. 14.95 *(978-1-59658-067-1(4))* College Prowler, Inc.

Mitchell, Kyra & Varacalli, Lauren. Baylor University College Prowler off the Record. 2005. (College Prowler off the Record Guides: Vol. 10). 160p. (YA). (gr. 12-18). pap., stu. ed. 14.95 *(978-1-59658-009-1(7))* College Prowler, Inc.

Monroe-Daley, J. S. A Is for Arizona. 2009. (Illus.). (J). 14.95 *(978-1-934878-65-1(0))* Amplify Publishing Group.

Mooney, Carla. Duke Basketball, 1 vol. 2013. (America's Most Winning Teams Ser.). 48p. (J). (gr. 5-5). (ENG.). 34.41 *(978-1-4488-9406-2(9),* 8b14f98c-46a4-4565-bb2b-9c6a2e9b894a); (ENG.). pap. 12.75 *(978-1-4488-9427-7(1),* 157c9381-dda7-4523-a5bb-7dc85f79fb98); pap. 70.50 *(978-1-4488-9428-4(X))* Rosen Publishing Group, Inc., The.

—Nebraska Football, 1 vol. 2013. (America's Most Winning Teams Ser.). 48p. (J). (gr. 5-5). (ENG.). 34.41 *(978-1-4488-9400-0(X),* cca64b1f-1af8-4dc7-a296-62101847e950); (ENG.). pap. 12.75 *(978-1-4488-9433-8(6),* 007edbc3-6fe8-44e2-a24a-8ac595b212ec); pap. 70.50 *(978-1-4488-9434-5(4))* Rosen Publishing Group, Inc., The.

—Teen Guide to Paying for College. 2016. (ENG.). 64p. (J). (gr. 5-12). lib. bdg. *(978-1-68282-084-1(X))* ReferencePoint Pr., Inc.

Murphy, Ryan & Varacalli, Lauren. Drexel University College Prowler off the Record. 2nd ed. 2005. (College Prowler off the Record Guides: Vol. 44). 160p. (YA). (gr. 12-18). pap., stu. ed. 14.95 *(978-1-59658-043-5(7))* College Prowler, Inc.

Murray, Melanie & Varacalli, Lauren. College of Charleston College Prowler off the Record. 2005. (College Prowler off the Record Guides: Vol. 30). 160p. (YA). (gr. 12-18). pap., stu. ed. 14.95 *(978-1-59658-029-9(1))* College Prowler, Inc.

Nash, Kevin. Suny Stony Brook College Prowler off the Record: Inside State University of New York. 2005. (College Prowler off the Record Guides: Vol. 128). 160p. (YA). (gr. 12-18). pap., stu. ed. 14.95 *(978-1-59658-127-2(1))* College Prowler, Inc.

—Valparaiso University College Prowler off the Record. 2005. (College Prowler off the Record Guides: Vol. 192). 160p. (YA). (gr. 12-18). pap., stu. ed. 14.95 *(978-1-59658-191-3(3))* College Prowler, Inc.

Nicklin, Miriam & Pecsenye, Jessica. University of Virginia College Prowler off the Record. 2nd ed. 2005. (College Prowler off the Record Guides: Vol. 189). 160p. (YA). (gr. 12-18). pap., stu. ed. 14.95 *(978-1-59658-188-3(3))* College Prowler, Inc.

Nicole, Bridget & Gray, Kevan. University of Illinois College Prowler off the Record. 2nd ed. 2005. (College Prowler off the Record Guides: Vol. 157). 160p. (YA). (gr. 12-18). pap., stu. ed. 14.95 *(978-1-59658-156-2(5))* College Prowler, Inc.

Niekerk, Katie & Seaman, Jim. University of Denver College Prowler off the Record. 2nd ed. 2005. (College Prowler off the Record Guides: Vol. 154). 160p. (YA). (gr. 12-18). pap., stu. ed. 14.95 *(978-1-59658-153-1(0))* College Prowler, Inc.

Nolan, Lindsey & Varacalli, Lauren. Auburn University College Prowler off the Record. 2nd ed. 2005. (College Prowler off the Record Guides: Vol. 5). 160p. (YA). (gr. 12-18). pap., stu. ed. 14.95 *(978-1-59658-004-6(6))* College Prowler, Inc.

Olson, Remy & Mason, Chris. Case Western Reserve University College Prowler off the Record. 2nd ed. 2005. (College Prowler off the Record Guides: Vol. 25). 160p. (YA). (gr. 12-18). pap., stu. ed. 14.95 *(978-1-59658-024-4(0))* College Prowler, Inc.

Paley, Briyah. Northeastern University. Belinsky, Robin et al, eds. 2nd ed. 2005. (College Prowler off the Record Guides: Vol. 91). (Illus.). 154p. (gr. 12-18). pap., stu. ed. 14.95 *(978-1-59658-090-9(9))* College Prowler, Inc.

Palmer, Amy & Keller, Carolyn. University of Minnesota College Prowler off the Record. 2nd ed. 2005. (College Prowler off the Record Guides: Vol. 165). 160p. (YA). (gr. 12-18). pap., stu. ed. 14.95 *(978-1-59658-164-7(6))* College Prowler, Inc.

Pattinson, Darcy. Kentucky Basketball. 2013. (America's Most Winning Teams Ser.). (Illus.). 48p. (J). (gr. 5-8). pap. 70.50 *(978-1-4488-9432-1(8))* Rosen Publishing Group, Inc., The.

Pattison, Darcy. Kentucky Basketball, 1 vol. 2013. (America's Most Winning Teams Ser.). (ENG., Illus.). 48p. (J). (gr. 5-5). 34.41 *(978-1-4488-9403-1(4),* 7f0413be-4f21-4edd-96a4-fe2f8f8bd0ce); pap. 12.75 *(978-1-4488-9431-4(X),* 7b0cc04a-b7ef-4d66-bebd-68a654adb3d2) Rosen Publishing Group, Inc., The.

Peckyno, Ryan. West Point Military Academy College Prowler off the Record. 2005. (College Prowler off the Record Guides: Vol. 202). 160p. (YA). (gr. 12-18). pap., stu. ed. 14.95 *(978-1-59658-201-9(4))* College Prowler, Inc.

Piehl, Norah, ed. Choosing a College, 1 vol. 2012. (Issues That Concern You Ser.). (ENG., Illus.). 128p. (gr. 7-10). lib. bdg. 43.63 *(978-0-7377-5691-3(8),* 005f961e-df7f-4a46-bcc3-2823e6f257e5, Greenhaven Publishing) Greenhaven Publishing LLC.

Pinkerton, Steve & Pecsenye, Jessica. Pepperdine University College Prowler off the Record. 2005. (College Prowler off the Record Guides: Vol. 98). 160p. (YA). (gr. 12-18). pap., stu. ed. 14.95 *(978-1-59658-097-8(6))* College Prowler, Inc.

Pommer, Christina & Skindzier, Jon. Johns Hopkins University College Prowler off the Record. 2005. (College Prowler off the Record Guides: Vol. 71). 160p. (YA). (gr. 12-18). pap., stu. ed. 14.95 *(978-1-59658-070-1(4))* College Prowler, Inc.

Pope-Roush, Jordan & Skindzier, Jon. Emory University College Prowler off the Record. 2nd ed. 2005. (College Prowler off the Record Guides: Vol. 49). 160p. (YA). (gr. 12-18). pap., stu. ed. 14.95 *(978-1-59658-048-0(8))* College Prowler, Inc.

Pouliot, Seth & Nash, Kevin. University of Massachusetts College Prowler off the Record. 2nd ed. 2005. (College Prowler off the Record Guides: Vol. 162). 160p. (YA). (gr. 12-18). pap., stu. ed. 14.95 *(978-1-59658-161-6(1))* College Prowler, Inc.

R., Ben & Nash, Kevin. Suny Buffalo College Prowler off the Record: Inside State University of New York. 2005. (College Prowler off the Record Guides: Vol. 127). 160p. (YA). (gr. 12-18). pap., stu. ed. 14.95 *(978-1-59658-126-5(3))* College Prowler, Inc.

R, Sarah & Seaman, Jim. Rhodes College College Prowler off the Record. 2nd ed. 2005. (College Prowler off the Record Guides: Vol. 107). 160p. (YA). (gr. 12-18). pap., stu. ed. 14.95 *(978-1-59658-106-7(9))* College Prowler, Inc.

Rakovic, Robert & Pecsenye, Jessica. Seton Hall University College Prowler off the Record. 2005. (College Prowler off the Record Guides: Vol. 117). 160p. (YA). (gr. 12-18). pap., stu. ed. 14.95 *(978-1-59658-116-6(6))* College Prowler, Inc.

Renick, Ricki & Swope, Gretchen. University of Mississippi College Prowler off the Record. 2005. (College Prowler off the Record Guides: Vol. 166). 160p. (YA). (gr. 12-18). pap., stu. ed. 14.95 *(978-1-59658-165-4(4))* College Prowler, Inc.

Richmond, Derek & Skindzier, Jon. Georgetown University College Prowler off the Record. 2nd ed. 2005. (College Prowler off the Record Guides: Vol. 55). 160p. (YA). (gr. 12-18). pap., stu. ed. 14.95 *(978-1-59658-054-1(2))* College Prowler, Inc.

Robinson, Hadley & Seaman, Jim. UC Santa Cruz College Prowler off the Record: Inside University of California Santa Cruz. 2nd ed. 2005. (College Prowler off the Record Guides: Vol. 148). 160p. (YA). (gr. 12-18). pap., stu. ed. 14.95 *(978-1-59658-147-0(6))* College Prowler, Inc.

Rosario, Nicole & Williams, Tim. University of Wisconsin College Prowler off the Record. 2nd ed. 2005. (College Prowler off the Record Guides: Vol. 191). 160p. (YA). (gr. 12-18). pap., stu. ed. 14.95 *(978-1-59658-190-6(5))* College Prowler, Inc.

Rosenbaum, Jason & Weisgerber, Amy. University of Missouri College Prowler off the Record. 2nd ed. 2005. (College Prowler off the Record Guides: Vol. 167). 160p. (YA). (gr. 12-18). pap., stu. ed. 14.95 *(978-1-59658-166-1(2))* College Prowler, Inc.

Ross, Jordan & Gohari, Omid. Emerson College College Prowler off the Record. 2nd ed. 2005. (College Prowler off the Record Guides: Vol. 48). 160p. (YA). (gr. 12-18). pap., stu. ed. 14.95 *(978-1-59658-047-3(X))* College Prowler, Inc.

Rossi, Regine & Dawson, Kai. Rensselaer Polytechnic Institute College Prowler off the Record: Inside RPI. 2005. (College Prowler off the Record Guides: Vol. 105). 160p. (YA). (gr. 12-18). pap., stu. ed. 14.95 *(978-1-59658-104-3(2))* College Prowler, Inc.

Rossi, Regine & Nash, Kevin. University of Florida College Prowler off the Record. 2nd ed. 2005. (College Prowler off the Record Guides: Vol. 155). 160p. (YA). (gr. 12-18). pap., stu. ed. 14.95 *(978-1-59658-154-8(9))* College Prowler, Inc.

Roth, Pam & Williams, Tim. Lafayette College College Prowler off the Record. 2nd ed. 2005. (College Prowler off the Record Guides: Vol. 73). 160p. (YA). (gr. 12-18). pap., stu. ed. 14.95 *(978-1-59658-072-5(0))* College Prowler, Inc.

Rudolph, Allyson & Gohari, Omid. Colby College College Prowler off the Record. 2005. (College Prowler off the Record Guides: Vol. 28). 160p. (YA). (gr. 12-18). pap., stu. ed. 14.95 *(978-1-59658-027-5(5))* College Prowler, Inc.

Rugg, Frederick E. Rugg's Recommendations on the Colleges. 20th rev. ed. 2003. 220p. (YA). (gr. 10-12). pap. 22.95 *(978-1-883062-48-4(9))* Rugg's Recommendations.

—Twenty More Tips on the Colleges. 6p. (YA). 9th rev. ed. 2003. (gr. 10-12). pap. 8.95 *(978-1-883062-49-1(7))* 10th rev. ed. 2004. pap. 8.95 *(978-1-883062-54-5(3))* 11th rev. ed. 2005. pap. 8.95 *(978-1-883062-59-0(4))* Rugg's Recommendations.

S. Wong, Derrick & Varacalli, Lauren. Bowdoin College College Prowler off the Record. 2005. (College Prowler off the Record Guides: Vol. 15). 160p. (YA). (gr. 12-18). pap., stu. ed. 14.95 *(978-1-59658-014-5(3))* College Prowler, Inc.

Salaver, Jillianne & Williams, Tim. UC Irvine College Prowler off the Record: Inside University of California Irvine. 2nd ed. 2005. (College Prowler off the Record Guides: Vol. 143). 160p. (YA). (gr. 12-18). pap., stu. ed. 14.95 *(978-1-59658-142-5(5))* College Prowler, Inc.

Sanders, Carly. Whitman College College Prowler off the Record. 2005. (College Prowler off the Record Guides: Vol. 205). 160p. (YA). (gr. 12-18). pap., stu. ed. 14.95 *(978-1-59658-204-0(9))* College Prowler, Inc.

Sandoval, Kate & Keller, Carolyn. UC Santa Barbara College Prowler off the Record: Inside University of California Santa Barbara. 2nd ed. 2005. (College Prowler off the Record Guides: Vol. 147). 160p. (YA). (gr. 12-18). pap., stu. ed. 14.95 *(978-1-59658-146-3(8))* College Prowler, Inc.

Schubach, Alanna & Pecsenye, Jessica. American University College Prowler off the Record. 2nd ed. 2005. (College Prowler off the Record Guides: Vol. 2). 160p. (YA). (gr. 12-18). pap., stu. ed. 14.95 *(978-1-59658-001-5(1))* College Prowler, Inc.

Schuvent, Julia & Skindzier, Jon. Rice University College Prowler off the Record. 2005. (College Prowler off the Record Guides: Vol. 108). 160p. (YA). (gr. 12-18). pap., stu. ed. 14.95 *(978-1-59658-107-4(7))* College Prowler, Inc.

Sendrowski, Brian, Jr. & Gohari, Omid. Connecticut College College Prowler off the Record. 2005. (College Prowler off the Record Guides: Vol. 36). 160p. (YA). (gr. 12-18). pap., stu. ed. 14.95 *(978-1-59658-035-0(6))* College Prowler, Inc.

Shaw, Katie & Nash, Kevin. University of Washington College Prowler off the Record. 2nd ed. 2005. (College Prowler off the Record Guides: Vol. 190). 160p. (YA). (gr. 12-18). pap., stu. ed. 14.95 *(978-1-59658-189-0(1))* College Prowler, Inc.

Sheik, Mayra & Varacalli, Lauren. Caltech College Prowler off the Record: Inside California Institute of Technology. 2nd ed. 2005. (College Prowler off the Record Guides: Vol. 22). 160p. (YA). (gr. 12-18). pap., stu. ed. 14.95 *(978-1-59658-021-3(6))* College Prowler, Inc.

Singer, Jenny & Scheff, William. Marquette University College Prowler off the Record. 2nd ed. 2005. (College Prowler off the Record Guides: Vol. 81). 160p. (YA). (gr. 12-18). pap., stu. ed. 14.95 *(978-1-59658-080-0(1))* College Prowler, Inc.

Skindzier, Jon. Southern Methodist University College Prowler off the Record. 2005. (College Prowler off the Record Guides: Vol. 120). 160p. (YA). (gr. 12-18). pap., stu. ed. 14.95 *(978-1-59658-119-7(0))* College Prowler, Inc.

Smith, Stacy & Davis, Cristine. University of Rhode Island College Prowler off the Record. 2005. (College Prowler off the Record Guides: Vol. 177). 160p. (YA). (gr. 12-18). pap., stu. ed. 14.95 *(978-1-59658-176-0(X))* College Prowler, Inc.

Spiro, Ian & Jendrey, Julie. Stanford University College Prowler off the Record. 2nd ed. 2005. (College Prowler off the Record Guides: Vol. 124). 160p. (YA). (gr. 12-18). pap., stu. ed. 14.95 *(978-1-59658-123-4(9))* College Prowler, Inc.

Standifer, Lauren, et al. Grinnell College College Prowler off the Record. 2005. (College Prowler off the Record Guides: Vol. 57). 160p. (YA). (gr. 12-18). pap., stu. ed. 14.95 *(978-1-59658-056-5(9))* College Prowler, Inc.

Steinman, Joshua & Nash, Kevin. University of Chicago College Prowler off the Record. 2nd ed. 2005. (College Prowler off the Record Guides: Vol. 150). 160p. (YA). (gr. 12-18). pap., stu. ed. 14.95 *(978-1-59658-149-4(2))* College Prowler, Inc.

Stephens, Kate. College, Quicker: 24 Practical Ways to Save Money & Get Your Degree Faster. 2015. (ENG., Illus.). 288p. (C). (gr. 9-13). pap. 14.99 *(978-1-4926-1338-1(X))* Sourcebooks, Inc.

Stewart, Nicolette & Nash, Kevin. Skidmore College College Prowler off the Record. 2005. (College Prowler off the Record Guides: Vol. 118). 160p. (YA). (gr. 12-18). pap., stu. ed. 14.95 *(978-1-59658-117-3(4))* College Prowler, Inc.

Striker, Oliver & Varacalli, Lauren. Cornell University College Prowler off the Record. 2005. (College Prowler off the Record Guides: Vol. 38). 160p. (YA). (gr. 12-18). pap., stu. ed. 14.95 *(978-1-59658-037-4(2))* College Prowler, Inc.

Tafoya, Nathan & Nash, Kevin. University of Arizona College Prowler off the Record. 2nd ed. 2005. (College Prowler off the Record Guides: Vol. 140). 160p. (YA). (gr. 12-18). pap., stu. ed. 14.95 *(978-1-59658-139-5(5))* College Prowler, Inc.

Thomas, Jesse & Keller, Carolyn. University of Oregon College Prowler off the Record. 2nd ed. 2005. (College Prowler off the Record Guides: Vol. 173). 160p. (YA). (gr. 12-18). pap., stu. ed. 14.95 *(978-1-59658-172-2(7))* College Prowler, Inc.

Todd, Danielle & Keller, Carolyn. University of Delaware College Prowler off the Record. 2nd ed. 2005. (College Prowler off the Record Guides: Vol. 153). 160p. (YA). (gr. 12-18). pap., stu. ed. 14.95 *(978-1-59658-152-4(2))* College Prowler, Inc.

Tompkins, Michelle & Rahimi, Joey. Columbia University College Prowler off the Record. 2nd ed. 2005. (College Prowler off the Record Guides: Vol. 35). 160p. (YA). (gr. 12-18). pap., stu. ed. 14.95 *(978-1-59658-034-3(8))* College Prowler, Inc.

Tran, Christine & Nash, Kevin. Scripps College College Prowler off the Record. 2005. (College Prowler off the Record Guides: Vol. 115). 160p. (YA). (gr. 12-18). pap., stu. ed. 14.95 *(978-1-59658-114-2(X))* College Prowler, Inc.

Treadway, Kathryn & Seaman, Jim. Providence College College Prowler off the Record. 2nd ed. 2005. (College Prowler off the Record Guides: Vol. 102). 160p. (YA). (gr. 12-18). pap., stu. ed. 14.95 *(978-1-59658-101-2(8))* College Prowler, Inc.

Trousdale, Jonathan & Skindzier, Jon. Georgia Tech College Prowler off the Record: Inside Georgia Institute of Technology. 2005. (College Prowler off the Record Guides: Vol. 56). 160p. (YA). (gr. 12-18). pap., stu. ed. 14.95 *(978-1-59658-055-8(0))* College Prowler, Inc.

Turley, Meredith & Burns, Adam. New York University College Prowler off the Record: Inside NYU. 2005. (College Prowler off the Record Guides: Vol. 90). 160p. (YA). (gr. 12-18). pap., stu. ed. 14.95 *(978-1-59658-089-3(5))* College Prowler, Inc.

Tylevich, Katherine & Skindzier, Jon. Macalester College College Prowler off the Record. 2nd ed. 2005. (College Prowler off the Record Guides: Vol. 80). 160p. (YA). (gr. 12-18). pap., stu. ed. 14.95 *(978-1-59658-079-4(8))* College Prowler, Inc.

Ucla Basketball. 2013. (America's Most Winning Teams Ser.). 48p. (J). (gr. 5-8). pap. 70.50 *(978-1-4488-9446-8(8))* Rosen Publishing Group, Inc., The.

Ugarte, Julia & Jendrey, Julie. Seattle University College Prowler off the Record. 2nd ed. 2005. (College Prowler off the Record Guides: Vol. 116). 160p. (YA). (gr. 12-18). pap., stu. ed. 14.95 *(978-1-59658-115-9(8))* College Prowler, Inc.

Unkovic, Rachel & Burns, Adam. Trinity College Connecticut College Prowler off the Record. 2005. (College Prowler off the Record Guides: Vol. 134). 160p. (YA). (gr. 12-18). pap., stu. ed. 14.95 *(978-1-59658-133-3(6))* College Prowler, Inc.

Valhouli, Alex & Skindzier, Jon. University of Southern California College Prowler off the Record. 2nd ed. 2005. (College Prowler off the Record Guides: Vol. 184). 160p. (YA). (gr. 12-18). pap., stu. ed. 14.95 *(978-1-59658-183-8(2))* College Prowler, Inc.
Vance, Ashley & Gohari, Omid. Brigham Young University College Prowler off the Record: Inside BYU. 2nd ed. 2005. (College Prowler off the Record Guides: Vol. 17). 160p. (YA). (gr. 12-18). pap., stu. ed. 14.95 *(978-1-59658-016-9(X))* College Prowler, Inc.
Wade McCormick, Lisa. Ucla Basketball, 1 vol. 2013. (America's Most Winning Teams Ser.). (ENG.). 48p. (J). (gr. 5-5). 34.41 *(978-1-4488-9408-6(5),* cb31b573-aa89-4774-8735-6b664d832bea); pap. 12.75 *(978-1-4488-9443-7(3),* 6c67f157-20a7-45b1-80e2-8d2cc1d4622a) Rosen Publishing Group, Inc., The.
Walker, Caren & Varacalli, Lauren. Boston University College Prowler off the Record. 2nd ed. 2005. (College Prowler off the Record Guides: Vol. 14). 160p. (YA). (gr. 12-18). pap., stu. ed. 14.95 *(978-1-59658-013-8(5))* College Prowler, Inc.
Watkins, Boyce. Everything You Ever Wanted to Know about College: A Guide for Minority Students. 2004. xiii, 330p. (YA). per. 25.00 *(978-0-9742632-0-5(6))* Blue Boy Publishing Co.
Webb, Anne Aldridge. Appalachian State, A to Z. Bostian, Laurie, illus. 2010. (J). 18.95 *(978-1-933251-69-1(7))* Parkway Pubs., Inc.
Whitley, Jared & Mandelbaum, Jolie. University of Utah College Prowler off the Record. 2nd ed. 2005. (College Prowler off the Record Guides: Vol. 187). 160p. (YA). (gr. 12-18). pap., stu. ed. 14.95 *(978-1-59658-186-9(7))* College Prowler, Inc.
Wiedrich, Merrick & Scheff, William. University of Alabama College Prowler off the Record. 2nd ed. 2005. (College Prowler off the Record Guides: Vol. 139). 160p. (YA). (gr. 12-18). pap., stu. ed. 14.95 *(978-1-59658-138-8(7))* College Prowler, Inc.
Wild, Cynthia & Nash, Kevin. UC Riverside College Prowler off the Record: Inside University of California Riverside. 2nd ed. 2005. (College Prowler off the Record Guides: Vol. 145). 160p. (YA). (gr. 12-18). pap., stu. ed. 14.95 *(978-1-59658-144-9(1))* College Prowler, Inc.
Williams, Jacob & Burns, Adam. University of Tennessee College Prowler off the Record. 2nd ed. 2005. (College Prowler off the Record Guides: Vol. 185). 160p. (YA). (gr. 12-18). pap., stu. ed. 14.95 *(978-1-59658-184-5(0))* College Prowler, Inc.
Williams, Rozalia. College FAQ Book: Over 5,000 Not Frequently Asked Questions about College! 2005. (Illus.). 494p. (YA). per. 24.95 *(978-0-9755103-0-8(4))* Hidden Curriculum Education.
Williams, Tim. New School University College Prowler off the Record. 2nd ed. 2005. (College Prowler off the Record Guides: Vol. 89). 160p. (YA). (gr. 12-18). pap., stu. ed. 14.95 *(978-1-59658-088-6(7),* Off The Record) College Prowler, Inc.
Wines, Shawn & Pecsenye, Jessica. University of Miami College Prowler off the Record. 2nd ed. 2005. (College Prowler off the Record Guides: Vol. 163). 160p. (YA). (gr. 12-18). pap., stu. ed. 14.95 *(978-1-59658-162-3(X))* College Prowler, Inc.
Woolsey, Matthew & Keller, Carolyn. Vanderbilt University College Prowler off the Record. 2nd ed. 2005. (College Prowler off the Record Guides: Vol. 193). 160p. (YA). (gr. 12-18). pap., stu. ed. 14.95 *(978-1-59658-192-0(1))* College Prowler, Inc.
Zang, Adam & Varacalli, Lauren. Carleton College College Prowler off the Record. 2005. (College Prowler off the Record Guides: Vol. 23). 160p. (YA). (gr. 12-18). pap., stu. ed. 14.95 *(978-1-59658-022-0(4))* College Prowler, Inc.

UNIVERSITIES AND COLLEGES—DIRECTORIES

Kwapong, Ohene. 12 Steps to Getting Admitted into Colleges & Universities in the United States. 2003. 79p. (YA). pap. 10.95 *(978-0-595-29647-7(5))* iUniverse, Inc.
Rugg, Frederick E. Thirty Questions & Answers on the Colleges. (YA). 9th rev. ed. 2003. 20p. pap. 9.95 *(978-1-883062-52-1(7))* 10th rev. ed. 2004. 20p. pap. 9.95 *(978-1-883062-56-9(X))* 11th rev. ed. 2005. 21p. pap. 9.95 *(978-1-883062-61-3(6))* Rugg's Recommendations.

UNIVERSITIES AND COLLEGES—FICTION

see also Schools—Fiction

Ahmad, M. I. Aldebaram. 2009. (ENG.). 95p. pap. 13.00 *(978-0-557-08323-7(0))* Lulu Pr., Inc.
Beck, Lynn G. & Sesa. Powercat, the Pacific Tiger. 2012. (J). 14.95 *(978-1-937406-00-4(8))* Amplify Publishing Group.
Bee, Clair. Buzzer Basket: A Chip Hilton Sports Story. 2011. 184p. (gr. 4-7). 42.95 *(978-1-258-06936-0(9))* Literary Licensing, LLC.
—Freshman Quarterback: Chip Hilton Sports Story No. 9. 2011. 222p. (gr. 8-12). 44.95 *(978-1-258-07328-2(5))* Literary Licensing, LLC.
—Hardcourt Upset: A Chip Hilton Sports Story. 2011. 190p. (gr. 3-8). 42.95 *(978-1-258-08011-2(7))* Literary Licensing, LLC.
—Pay-off Pitch: A Chip Hilton Sports Story. 2011. 192p. (gr. 3-8). 42.95 *(978-1-258-09970-1(5))* Literary Licensing, LLC.
Binder, John. The Girl Who Applied Everywhere. 2011. 160p. (YA). 17.99 *(978-1-936679-02-7(7))* Wicker Park Pr., Ltd.
Blumenthal, Bliss. Wiley's Way: El Camino de Wiley. 2004. (ENG & SPA., Illus.). 96p. (J). (gr. 4-6). mass mkt. 9.95 *(978-0-292-70615-6(4))* Univ. of Texas Pr.
Butler, Dori H. Campus Attack, Sabotage! 2011. (Readers' & Writers' Genre Workshop Ser.). (YA). pap. *(978-1-4509-3018-5(2))* Benchmark Education Co.
Caine, Rachel, pseud. Bite Club: The Morganville Vampires, 10 vols. 2011. (Morganville Vampires Ser.: 10). (ENG.). 368p. (YA). (gr. 9). pap. 9.99 *(978-0-451-23468-1(5),* Berkley) Penguin Publishing Group.
—Black Dawn: The Morganville Vampires. 2012. (Morganville Vampires Ser.: 12). (ENG.). 400p. (YA). (gr. 9). pap. 9.99 *(978-0-451-23793-4(5),* Berkley) Penguin Publishing Group.
—Ghost Town: The Morganville Vampires, 9 vols. 2011. (Morganville Vampires Ser.: 9). (ENG.). 368p. (YA). (gr. 9-18). 9.99 *(978-0-451-23291-5(7),* Berkley) Penguin Publishing Group.
—Last Breath: The Morganville Vampires, 11 vols. 2012. (Morganville Vampires Ser.: 11). (ENG.). 368p. (YA). (gr. 9). 9.99 *(978-0-451-23580-0(0),* Berkley) Penguin Publishing Group.
—Lord of Misrule. 2009. (Morganville Vampires Ser.: Bk. 5). 352p. (YA). lib. bdg. 20.00 *(978-1-4242-4704-2(7))* Fitzgerald Bks.
—Lord of Misrule: The Morganville Vampires, Book 5. 2009. (Morganville Vampires Ser.: 5). (ENG.). 256p. (YA). (gr. 9-18). mass mkt. 7.99 *(978-0-451-22572-6(4),* Berkley) Penguin Publishing Group.
—Midnight Alley. 2007. (Morganville Vampires Ser.: Bk. 3). 256p. (YA). lib. bdg. 20.00 *(978-1-4242-4705-9(5))* Fitzgerald Bks.
—Midnight Alley: The Morganville Vampires, Book III. 2007. (Morganville Vampires Ser.: 3). (ENG.). 256p. (YA). (gr. 9-18). mass mkt. 7.99 *(978-0-451-22238-1(5),* Berkley) Penguin Publishing Group.
—The Morganville Vampires, Volume 4, Vol. 4. 2011. (Morganville Vampires Ser.: Bks. 7-8). (ENG.). 464p. (YA). (gr. 9-18). 12.99 *(978-0-451-23426-1(X),* Berkley) Penguin Publishing Group.
Charbonneau, Joelle. Independent Study. 2015. (Testing Ser.: 2). lib. bdg. 20.85 *(978-0-606-36832-2(9))* Turtleback.
—Independent Study: The Testing, Book 2. (Testing Ser.: 2). (ENG.). (YA). (gr. 7). 2015. 336p. pap. 15.99 *(978-0-544-43945-0(7),* 1596844) 2014. 320p. 17.99 *(978-0-547-95920-7(6),* 1520240) HarperCollins Pubs. (Clarion Bks.).
—The Testing. 2015. (Testing Ser.: 1). (ENG.). 352p. (YA). (gr. 7). pap. 15.99 *(978-0-544-33623-0(2),* 1584169, Clarion Bks.) HarperCollins Pubs.
Choi, Mary H. K. Emergency Contact. (ENG.). (YA). (gr. 9). 2019. 416p. pap. 12.99 *(978-1-5344-0897-5(5))* 2018. (Illus.). 400p. 17.99 *(978-1-5344-0896-8(7))* Simon & Schuster Bks. For Young Readers. (Simon & Schuster Bks. For Young Readers).
Condie, Ally. First Day. 2007. 304p. (YA). pap. 15.95 *(978-1-59038-775-7(9))* Deseret Bk. Co.
—Reunion. 2008. 288p. (YA). pap. 15.95 *(978-1-59038-989-8(1))* Deseret Bk. Co.
Davis, Catherine Jennings & Thompson, Traci Shirley. Goodnight Cavaliers. 2013. (J). 17.95 *(978-1-62086-038-0(4))* Amplify Publishing Group.
Durst, Sarah Beth. Enchanted Ivy. (ENG.). (YA). (gr. 7). 2011. 336p. pap. 9.99 *(978-1-4169-8646-1(4))* 2010. 320p. 16.99 *(978-1-4169-8645-4(6))* McElderry, Margaret K. Bks. (McElderry, Margaret K. Bks.).
Ellen, Tom & Ivison, Lucy. Freshmen. 2019. (ENG.). 368p. (YA). (gr. 9). pap. 11.99 *(978-1-5247-0181-9(5),* Ember) Random Hse. Children's Bks.
Flower, Graham Jessie. Grace Harlowe's Second Year at Overton College. 2004. reprint ed. pap. 20.95 *(978-1-4191-2223-1(1))* Kessinger Publishing, LLC.
Grant, Vicki. 36 Questions That Changed My Mind about You. 2017. (ENG., Illus.). 288p. (YA). (gr. 8-17). 17.99 *(978-0-7624-6318-3(X),* Running Pr. Kids) Running Pr.
Hazuka, Tom. Last Chance for First. 2008. 296p. (YA). (gr. 9-18). pap. 8.95 *(978-0-9798824-0-1(0))* Brown Barn Bks.
Johnson-Choong, Shelly. A Light to Come Home By. 2nd unabr. ed. 2004. 212p. (C). reprint ed. pap. 12.95 *(978-1-932280-52-4(9),* 80529) Granite Publishing & Distribution.
Kade, Stacey. Finding Felicity. 2018. (ENG., Illus.). 304p. (YA). (gr. 9). 17.99 *(978-1-4814-6425-3(6),* Simon & Schuster Bks. For Young Readers) Simon & Schuster Bks. For Young Readers.
Karras, Kim. Accidentally Me. 2016. (ENG.). 245p. (YA). pap. 15.99 *(978-1-4621-1867-0(4),* Sweetwater Bks.) Cedar Fort, Inc./CFI Distribution.
Kearney, Meg. When You Never Said Goodbye: An Adoptee's Search for Her Birth Mother: a Novel in Poems & Journal Entries. 2017. (ENG.). 224p. (YA). (gr. 9-17). 17.95 *(978-0-89255-479-9(7),* 255479) Persea Bks., Inc.
Korman, Gordon. Son of the Mob. rev. ed. 2017. (ENG.). 240p. (J). (gr. 7-17). pap. 13.99 *(978-1-4847-9845-4(7))* Little, Brown Bks. for Young Readers.
Kropp, Paul. Home Run. 2006. (Running the Bases Ser.: 2). (ENG.). 208p. (YA). (gr. 7). pap. 11.95 *(978-0-385-66148-5(7))* Doubleday Canada, Ltd. CAN. Dist: Penguin Random Hse. LLC.
Kunze, Lauren & Onur, Rina. The Ivy. 2010. (Ivy Ser.: 1). (ENG.). 320p. (YA). (gr. 9-18). 16.99 *(978-0-06-196045-1(4),* Greenwillow Bks.) HarperCollins Pubs.
—The Ivy: Secrets. 2011. (Ivy Ser.: 2). (ENG.). 320p. (YA). (gr. 9-18). 16.99 *(978-0-06-196047-5(0),* Greenwillow Bks.) HarperCollins Pubs.
LaCour, Nina. We Are Okay. (ENG.). (YA). (gr. 9). 2019. 256p. pap. 11.99 *(978-0-14-242293-9(2),* Penguin Books) 2017. 240p. 17.99 *(978-0-525-42589-2(6),* Dutton Books for Young Readers) Penguin Young Readers Group.
LaZebnik, Claire. The Trouble with Flirting. 2013. (ENG.). 336p. (YA). (gr. 8). pap. 9.99 *(978-0-06-192127-8(0),* HarperTeen) HarperCollins Pubs.
Lithgow, John. Mahalia Mouse Goes to College: Book & CD. Oleynikov, Igor, illus. 2007. (ENG.). 40p. (J). (gr. -1-3). 19.99 *(978-1-4169-2715-0(8),* Simon & Schuster Bks. For Young Readers) Simon & Schuster Bks. For Young Readers.
Mc Daniel, Jessica & Morgan, Amanda. Goodnight Tigers. 2010. 32p. (J). 17.95 *(978-1-4507-0621-6(5))* Independent Pub.
McDonald, Megan. Judy Moody Goes to College. Reynolds, Peter H., illus. 2018. (Judy Moody Ser.: 8). (ENG.). 176p. (J). (gr. 1-4). pap. 5.99 *(978-1-5362-0078-2(6))* Candlewick Pr.
Mcdonald, Megan. Judy Moody Goes to College. (Judy Moody Ser.: 8). 2010. lib. bdg. 16.00 *(978-0-606-12352-5(0))* 2009. lib. bdg. 16.00 *(978-0-606-01313-0(X))* Turtleback.
McDonald, Megan. Judy Moody Goes to College, Bk. 8. Reynolds, Peter H., illus. 2010. (Judy Moody Ser.: 8). (ENG.). 144p. (J). (gr. 1-4). 16.99 *(978-0-7636-4856-5(6))* Candlewick Pr.
Miller, Lauren. Parallel. 2013. (ENG.). 432p. (YA). (gr. 8). 17.99 *(978-0-06-219977-5(3),* HarperTeen) HarperCollins Pubs.
Montgomery, L. M. Anne of the Island. 2018. (ENG., Illus.). 240p. (J). (gr. 2-5). pap. *(978-93-5297-102-2(7))* Alpha Editions.
—Anne of the Island. 2017. (ENG., Illus.). (J). 28.99 *(978-1-366-55836-7(7))* Blurb, Inc.
—Anne of the Island. 2017. (ENG., Illus.). (J). 25.95 *(978-1-374-89884-4(8))*; pap. 15.95 *(978-1-374-89883-7(X))* Capital Communications, Inc.
—Anne of the Island. (ENG., Illus.). (J). 2017. pap. 15.90 *(978-1-375-53109-2(3))* 2015. 26.95 *(978-1-297-59159-4(3))* Creative Media Partners, LLC.
—Anne of the Island. 2008. (Anne of Green Gables Ser.). (ENG.). 272p. (J). (gr. 4-7). pap. 9.95 *(978-0-9782552-8-2(3))* Davenport Pr. CAN. Dist: Independent Pubs. Group.
—Anne of the Island. 2006. (ENG.). pap. *(978-1-4068-2171-0(3))* Echo Library.
—Anne of the Island. 2010. (Puffin Classics Ser.). (ENG.). 368p. (J). (gr. 5-7). pap. 7.99 *(978-0-14-132736-5(7),* Puffin Books) Penguin Young Readers Group.
—Anne of the Island. 2018. (Anne of Green Gables: the Complete Collection: 3). (ENG.). 312p. (J). (gr. 6-12). 8.99 *(978-1-78226-445-3(0),* 6a902ad3-6883-4c7e-8532-21673815d7a9) Sweet Cherry Publishing GBR. Dist: Baker & Taylor Publisher Services (BTPS).
—Anne of the Island. 2018. (ENG., Illus.). 258p. (YA). 24.99 *(978-1-5287-0650-6(1),* Classic Bks. Library) The Editorium, LLC.
—Anne of the Island. 2019. (ENG.). 250p. (J). pap. 11.89 *(978-1-7278-8584-2(8))* CreateSpace Independent Publishing Platform.
—Anne of the Island. (ENG.). (J). 2019. 252p. pap. 11.99 *(978-1-7018-6205-0(0))* 2019. 352p. pap. 19.99 *(978-1-0899-1090-9(8))* 2019. 740p. pap. 43.99 *(978-1-0776-6557-6(1))* 2019. 466p. pap. 32.99 *(978-1-0799-0876-3(5))* 2019. 788p. pap. 45.99 *(978-1-0804-7520-9(6))* 2019. 498p. pap. 33.99 *(978-1-0825-6062-0(6))* 2019. 788p. pap. 45.99 *(978-1-0828-3158-4(1))* 2019. 352p. pap. 19.99 *(978-1-0726-8332-2(6))* 2019. 498p. pap. 31.99 *(978-1-0753-6839-4(1))* 2019. 342p. pap. 19.99 *(978-1-0968-7543-7(8))* 2019. 526p. pap. 29.99 *(978-1-0985-3618-3(5))* 2019. 252p. pap. 17.99 *(978-1-0705-9734-8(1))* 2019. 500p. pap. 29.99 *(978-1-0707-5185-6(5))* 2019. 498p. pap. 32.99 *(978-1-0916-4685-8(6))* 2019. 462p. pap. 25.99 *(978-1-7965-5869-2(9))* 2019. 136p. pap. 8.60 *(978-1-7953-3769-4(9))* 2018. (Illus.). 224p. pap. 14.99 *(978-1-7919-1456-1(X))* Independently Published.
—Anne of the Island. 2019. (ENG.). 232p. (J). pap. 27.99 *(978-1-7077-7514-9(1))* Independently Published.
—Anne of the Island. 2012. (World Classics Ser.). (ENG.). 212p. pap. 19.99 *(978-1-909438-92-7(8),* Sovereign) Bollinger, Max GBR. Dist: Lightning Source UK, Ltd.
—Anne of the Island. l.t. ed. 2006. (ENG.). pap. *(978-1-4068-3175-7(1))* Echo Library.
—Anne of the Island. 2004. reprint ed. pap. 1.99 *(978-1-4192-0718-1(0))*; pap. 30.95 *(978-1-4179-0885-1(8))* Kessinger Publishing, LLC.
—Anne of the Island. l.t. ed. 2004. 396p. 26.00 *(978-1-58287-640-5(1))* North Bks.
Montgomery, Lucy Maud. Anne of the Island. 2019. (ENG.). (J). (gr. 2-5). 276p. pap. 12.95 *(978-0-368-79656-2(6))*; 94p. pap. 12.55 *(978-0-368-28130-3(2))* Blurb, Inc.
—Anne of the Island. 2018. (ENG.). 328p. (J). (gr. 2-5). 44.95 *(978-0-343-91137-9(X))*; pap. 27.95 *(978-0-343-91136-2(1))* Creative Media Partners, LLC.
—Anne of the Island. 2019. (ENG.). (J). (gr. 2-5). 734p. pap. 46.99 *(978-1-6881-5126-0(5))*; 736p. pap. 43.99 *(978-1-0968-8163-6(2))*; 448p. pap. 25.99 *(978-1-0932-8992-3(9))* Independently Published.
Oelke, Lianne. Nice Try, Jane Sinner. (ENG.). 432p. (YA). (gr. 9). 2019. pap. 9.99 *(978-0-358-09756-3(8),* 1747620) 2018. 17.99 *(978-0-544-86785-7(8),* 1648799) HarperCollins Pubs. (Clarion Bks.).
Olsen, Kaki. Swan & Shadow: A Swan Lake Story. 2016. (ENG.). 299p. (YA). pap. 18.99 *(978-1-4621-1814-4(3),* Sweetwater Bks.) Cedar Fort, Inc./CFI Distribution.
Padian, Maria. Wrecked. 2017. (ENG.). 368p. (YA). (gr. 9-12). pap. 12.99 *(978-1-61620-745-8(0),* 73745) Algonquin Young Readers.
Pascal, Francine. Libertad Incondicional.Tr. of Love, Lies & Jessica Wakefield. (SPA.). 224p. (J). 8.95 *(978-84-272-3162-7(8))* Molino, Editorial ESP. Dist: AIMS International Bks., Inc.
—Otra Oportunidad.Tr. of Love of Her Life. (SPA.). 200p. (J). 8.95 *(978-84-272-3166-5(0))* Molino, Editorial ESP. Dist: AIMS International Bks., Inc.
Perry, Jolene. The Next Door Boys. 2011. 266p. (YA). *(978-1-59955-910-0(2),* Bonneville Bks.) Cedar Fort, Inc./CFI Distribution.
Pratt, Non & BOOM! Studios. Giant Days. 2018. (ENG.). 288p. (gr. 9-17). 18.99 *(978-1-4197-3126-6(2),* 1220701, Amulet Bks.) Abrams, Inc.
Reynolds Naylor, Phyllis. Now I'll Tell You Everything. 2013. (Alice Ser.: 25). (ENG., Illus.). 528p. (YA). (gr. 9). 17.99 *(978-1-4424-4590-1(4))* Simon & Schuster Children's Publishing.
Roux, Madeleine. Asylum. (Asylum Ser.: 1). (ENG.). (YA). (gr. 9). 2014. 336p. pap. 15.99 *(978-0-06-222097-4(7))* 2013. (Illus.). 320p. 17.99 *(978-0-06-222096-7(9))* HarperCollins Pubs. (HarperCollins).
—Asylum. 2015. (SPA.). 320p. (YA). (gr. 9-12). pap. 20.99 *(978-987-612-778-3(0))* V&R Editoras.
—Sanctum. 2014. (Illus.). 343p. (YA). *(978-0-06-235182-1(6))* Harper & Row Ltd.
—Sanctum. 2014. (Asylum Ser.: 2). (ENG., Illus.). 352p. (YA). (gr. 9). 17.99 *(978-0-06-222099-8(3),* HarperCollins) HarperCollins Pubs.
Shine, Joe. I Become Shadow. 2015. (ENG.). 336p. (YA). (gr. 9). pap. 10.99 *(978-1-61695-537-3(6),* Soho Teen) Soho Pr., Inc.
Soto, Gary. Jesse. 2006. (ENG., Illus.). 192p. (YA). (gr. 7-12). pap. 7.99 *(978-0-15-205425-0(1),* 253005, Clarion Bks.) HarperCollins Pubs.
—Jesse. 2006. 166p. (gr. 7-12). 16.95 *(978-0-7569-6688-1(4))* Perfection Learning Corp.
Stolarz, Laurie Faria. Red Is for Remembrance. l.t. ed. 2008. (Blue Is for Nightmares Ser.: Bk. 4). 385p. (YA). (gr. 7). 22.95 *(978-1-4104-0339-1(4))* Thorndike Pr.
Thompson, Alicia. Psych Major Syndrome. 2010. (ENG.). 336p. pap. 8.99 *(978-1-4231-1549-6(X))* Disney Pr.
Warner, Gertrude Chandler, creator. The Mystery of the Grinning Gargoyle. 2014. (Boxcar Children Mysteries Ser.: 137). (ENG., Illus.). 128p. (J). (gr. 2-5). pap. 5.99 *(978-0-8075-0893-0(4),* 807508934, Random Hse. Bks. for Young Readers) Random Hse. Children's Bks.

UNIVERSITY OF NOTRE DAME

Monteverde, Matthew. Notre Dame vs. USC. 2013. (J). *(978-1-4777-1164-4(3))*; (ENG.). 24p. (gr. 3-3). pap. 11.60 *(978-1-4777-1163-7(5),* 8ae3da7e-0453-4d9c-894a-26d2e514041a); (ENG.). 24p. (gr. 3-3). lib. bdg. 27.60 *(978-1-4777-1158-3(9),* 859b9a3b-6326-46f3-8ab6-9d3439855ffc) Rosen Publishing Group, Inc., The. (PowerKids Pr.).

UNMARRIED MOTHERS—FICTION

Dessen, Sarah. Someone Like You. 2011. 10.36 *(978-0-7848-3539-5(X),* Everbind) Marco Bk. Co.
—Someone Like You. 2004. (ENG.). 304p. (YA). (gr. 7-7). 10.99 *(978-0-14-240177-4(3),* Speak) Penguin Young Readers Group.
—Someone Like You. 2004. 281p. (YA). (gr. 7). 16.65 *(978-0-7569-4967-9(X))* Perfection Learning Corp.
—Someone Like You. 2004. 281p. (gr. 7). lib. bdg. 22.10 *(978-1-4176-2674-8(7))* Turtleback.
Millward, Carol. Star in the Middle. 2009. 304p. (YA). (gr. 9-12). 16.95 *(978-1-934813-13-3(3))* Westside Bks.
Woodson, Jacqueline. The Dear One. 2010. (ENG.). 176p. (YA). (gr. 7-18). 8.99 *(978-0-14-241705-8(X),* Puffin Books) Penguin Young Readers Group.
Wright, Julie. My Not-So-Fairytale Life. 2005. 256p. (YA). pap. 15.95 *(978-1-59038-476-3(8))* Deseret Bk. Co.

UPPER ATMOSPHERE

see Atmosphere, Upper

UPPER CLASS—FICTION

MacLean, Sarah. The Season. (ENG.). 352p. (J). (gr. 7). 2010. 8.99 *(978-0-545-04887-3(7))* 2009. 17.99 *(978-0-545-04886-6(9))* Scholastic, Inc. (Orchard Bks.).
Smedley, Frank E. Frank Fairlegh. 2008. 244p. pap. 15.95 *(978-1-60664-178-1(6))*; 224p. pap. 15.95 *(978-1-60664-179-8(4))* Aegypan.
—Frank Fairlegh: Scenes from the Life of a Private Pupil. 2017. (ENG., Illus.). (J). 31.95 *(978-1-374-91360-8(X))* Capital Communications, Inc.
Van Dyne, Edith. Aunt Jane's Nieces in Society. 2005. 28.95 *(978-1-4218-1424-7(2))*; 276p. pap. 13.95 *(978-1-4218-1524-4(9))* 1st World Publishing, Inc. (1st World Library - Literary Society).
—Aunt Jane's Nieces in Society. 2004. reprint ed. pap. 1.99 *(978-1-4192-0824-9(1))*; pap. 20.95 *(978-1-4191-0824-2(7))* Kessinger Publishing, LLC.

URANIUM

Gardner, Jane P. Uranium. 2017. (Chemistry of Everyday Elements Ser.: Vol. 10). (ENG., Illus.). 64p. (J). (gr. 7-12). 23.95 *(978-1-4222-3847-9(4))* Mason Crest.
Mineo, Tyrone. Uranium, 1 vol., Vol. 1. 2013. (Rare & Precious Metals Ser.). (ENG.). 24p. (J). (gr. 2-3). 25.27 *(978-1-4824-0531-6(8),* ca632550-30ad-4fac-a0e0-58263071fb2b) Stevens, Gareth Publishing LLLP.
Perritano, John. Uranium, Vol. 12. 2015. (North American Natural Resources Ser.). (Illus.). 64p. (J). (gr. 7). 23.95 *(978-1-4222-3390-0(1))* Mason Crest.
Tiner, John Hudson. Uranium & Plutonium Make Nuclear Power. 2003. (From Resource to Energy Source Ser.). (J). *(978-1-58417-288-8(6))*; pap. *(978-1-58417-289-5(4))* Lake Street Pubs.

URANIUM—FICTION

Friend, Gaythel & Miller, Dalton. The Mystery of the Green Box. 2006. 88p. per. 8.95 *(978-1-59824-147-1(8))* E-BookTime LLC.
Gilligan, Shannon. Struggle down Under. Semionov, Vladimir, illus. 2007. (ENG.). 144p. (J). (gr. 4-8). pap. 7.99 *(978-1-933390-21-5(2))* Chooseco LLC.

URANUS (PLANET)

Adamson, Thomas K. The Secrets of Uranus. 2015. (Planets Ser.). (ENG., Illus.). 32p. (J). (gr. 2-4). lib. bdg. 32.65 *(978-1-4914-5869-3(0),* 128832) Capstone.
—Uranus [Scholastic]: Revised Edition. 2010. (Exploring the Galaxy Ser.). (ENG.). 24p. pap. 0.49 *(978-1-4296-5815-7(0),* Capstone Pr.) Capstone.
Beth, Georgia. Discover Uranus. 2018. (Searchlight Books (tm) — Discover Planets Ser.). (ENG., Illus.). 32p. (J). (gr. 3-5). 30.65 *(978-1-5415-2342-5(3),* 25ce55cf-a470-485b-878b-5d9b160c24ad, Lerner Pubns.) Lerner Publishing Group.
Bloom, J. P. Urano (Uranus), 1 vol. 2016. (Planetas (Planets) Ser.). (SPA., Illus.). 24p. (J). (gr. -1-2). lib. bdg. 32.79 *(978-1-68080-758-5(7),* 22678, Abdo Kids) ABDO Publishing Co.
—Uranus, 1 vol. 2015. (Planets Ser.). (ENG.). 24p. (J). (gr. -1-2). lib. bdg. 32.79 *(978-1-62970-721-1(X),* 17241, Abdo Kids) ABDO Publishing Co.
—Uranus. 2017. (Planets Ser.). (ENG.). 24p. (J). (gr. -1-2). pap. 7.95 *(978-1-4966-1286-1(8),* 135018, Capstone Classroom) Capstone.
Carson, Mary Kay. Far-Out Guide to Uranus, 1 vol. 2010. (Far-Out Guide to the Solar System Ser.). (ENG., Illus.). 48p. (gr. 4-6). 27.93 *(978-0-7660-3185-2(3),* c4f8ee8d-959a-4c90-9bb3-c86e9dfa2bf1); pap. 11.53 *(978-1-59845-188-7(X),* 29076029-53d5-438d-8fe2-7ae24254afca, Enslow Elementary) Enslow Publishing, LLC.
Dittmer, Lori. Uranus. 2018. (Seedlings Ser.). (Illus.). 24p. (J). (ENG.). (gr. -1-1). pap. 7.99 *(978-1-62832-535-5(6),* 19664, Creative Paperbacks); (FRE., *(978-1-77092-411-6(6),* 19700); (ENG., (gr. -1-k). *(978-1-60818-919-9(8),* 19666, Creative Education) Creative Co., The.
Glaser, Chaya. Urano: Frío y Azul. 2015. (Fuera de Este Mundo Ser.). (SPA., Illus.). 24p. (J). (gr. -1-3). lib. bdg. 26.99 *(978-1-62724-598-2(7))* Bearport Publishing Co., Inc.
—Uranus: Cold & Blue. 2015. (Out of This World Ser.). (ENG.). 24p. (J). (gr. -1-3). lib. bdg. 26.99 *(978-1-62724-567-8(7))* Bearport Publishing Co., Inc.

TUV

Goldstein, Margaret J. Uranus. 2005. (Pull Ahead Bks.). (Illus.). 32p. (gr. 2-4). lib. bdg. 22.60 *(978-0-8225-4654-2(X))* Lerner Publishing Group.

Hantula, Richard & Asimov, Isaac. Urano (Uranus), 1 vol. 2003. (Isaac Asimov's Biblioteca Del Universo Del Siglo XXI (Isaac Asimov's 21st Century Library of the Universe) Ser.).Tr. of Uranus: The Sideways Planet. (SPA., Illus.). 32p. (gr. 3-5). lib. bdg. 28.67 *(978-0-8368-3863-3(7),* 0961b1a9-ec0c-484d-912c-d85c5b782d39, Gareth Stevens Learning Library) Stevens, Gareth Publishing LLLP.

Hunter, Valerie. Journey to Uranus, 1 vol. 2014. (Spotlight on Space Science Ser.). (ENG.). 32p. (J). (gr. 5-5). pap. 12.75 *(978-1-4994-0379-4(8),* 0fac9ed2-6a7a-4d7b-8f36-636d0dd8bc65, PowerKids Pr.) Rosen Publishing Group, Inc., The.

Jefferis, David. Gas Giants: Huge Far off Worlds. 2008. (ENG., Illus.). 32p. (J). (gr. 3-7). pap. *(978-0-7787-3750-6(0))* Crabtree Publishing Co.

Kazunas, Ariel. Uranus. 2011. (21st Century Junior Library: Solar System Ser.). (ENG., Illus.). 24p. (gr. 2-5). lib. bdg. 29.21 *(978-1-61080-084-6(2),* 201078) Cherry Lake Publishing.

Keiser, Cody. Exploring Uranus. 2017. (Journey Through Our Solar System Ser.). 24p. (gr. 1-2). 49.50 *(978-1-5345-2253-4(0),* KidHaven Publishing); (ENG.). pap. 9.25 *(978-1-5345-2289-3(1),* 1f4b99e1-69c6-4e0a-be0b-444667c46c2c); (ENG.). lib. bdg. 26.23 *(978-1-5345-2281-7(6),* 3953ed88-aac1-416d-a509-2b8a28a8c7e5) Greenhaven Publishing LLC.

Murray, Julie. Uranus. 2018. (Planets (Dash!) Ser.). (ENG., Illus.). 24p. (J). (gr. k-4). lib. bdg. 31.36 *(978-1-5321-2532-4(1),* 30073, Abdo Zoom-Dash) ABDO Publishing Co.

Orme, Helen & Orme, David. Let's Explore Uranus, 1 vol. 2007. (Space Launch! Ser.). (ENG., Illus.). 24p. (J). (gr. 2-4). lib. bdg. 25.67 *(978-0-8368-7949-0(X),* 57156fc1-321a-4b64-b18e-2dc1b60398d4, Gareth Stevens Learning Library) Stevens, Gareth Publishing LLLP.

Owen, Ruth. Uranus, 1 vol. 2013. (Explore Outer Space Ser.). (ENG.). 32p. (J). (gr. 2-3). 29.93 *(978-1-61533-728-6(8),* 69316a79-b6fe-43d8-93fb-ac7834cbdca5, PowerKids Pr.); pap. 11.00 *(978-1-61533-773-6(3),* 4a69f5f1-3019-49e6-a262-af00487ed1e8, Windmill Bks.) Rosen Publishing Group, Inc., The.

—Uranus. 2013. (Explore Outer Space Ser.). 32p. (J). (gr. 3-6). pap. 60.00 *(978-1-61533-774-3(1))* Windmill Bks.

Ring, Susan. Uranus. (J). 2013. 27.13 *(978-1-62127-269-4(9))* 2013. pap. 12.95 *(978-1-62127-278-6(8))* 2004. (Illus.). pap. 8.95 *(978-1-59036-224-2(1))* 2004. (Illus.). 24p. (gr. 4-7). lib. bdg. 24.45 *(978-1-59036-097-2(4))* Weigl Pubs., Inc.

Ring, Susan & Roumanis, Alexis. Uranus. 2016. (Illus.). 24p. (J). *(978-1-5105-0992-4(5))* SmartBook Media, Inc.

Roumanis, Alexis. Uranus. 2016. (J). *(978-1-5105-2057-8(0))* SmartBook Media, Inc.

—Uranus. 2015. (J). *(978-1-4896-3304-0(9))* Weigl Pubs., Inc.

Sexton, Colleen. Uranus. 2010. (Exploring Space Ser.). (ENG., Illus.). 24p. (J). (gr. k-3). lib. bdg. 26.95 *(978-1-60014-408-0(X),* Blastoff! Readers) Bellwether Media.

Sherman, Josepha. Uranus, 1 vol. 2010. (Space! Ser.). (ENG.). 64p. (gr. 5-5). lib. bdg. 35.50 *(978-0-7614-4248-6(0),* 70c8f133-407c-4c01-a3ba-2773ba84606a) Cavendish Square Publishing LLC.

Slade, Suzanne. A Look at Uranus. (Astronomy Now! Ser.). 24p. (gr. 2-3). 2009. 42.50 *(978-1-61511-474-0(2),* PowerKids Pr.) 2007. (ENG., Illus.). (J). lib. bdg. 26.27 *(978-1-4042-3831-2(X),* 1e40ce88-fc15-4ea2-8cb8-7770358167c5) Rosen Publishing Group, Inc., The.

Sommer, Nathan. Uranus. 2019. (Space Science Ser.). (ENG., Illus.). 24p. (J). (gr. 3-7). lib. bdg. 26.95 *(978-1-62617-979-0(4),* Torque Bks.) Bellwether Media.

Sparrow, Giles. Destination Uranus, Neptune, & Pluto, 1 vol. 2009. (Destination Solar System Ser.). (ENG., Illus.). 32p. (J). (gr. 3-4). 28.93 *(978-1-4358-3446-0(1),* 05e1d277-a173-4544-8294-068018bd164f); pap. 11.00 *(978-1-4358-3463-7(1),* da375e81-83d8-47ac-b022-097405e0edbb) Rosen Publishing Group, Inc., The. (PowerKids Pr.).

Stefoff, Rebecca. Uranus, 1 vol. 2003. (Blastoff! Ser.). (ENG., Illus.). 64p. (gr. 5-5). 34.07 *(978-0-7614-1401-8(0),* 78e4018b-0950-425e-8a72-71e7df2df75c) Cavendish Square Publishing LLC.

Taylor-Butler, Christine. Planet Uranus (a True Book: Space) (Library Edition) 2014. (True Book (Relaunch) Ser.). (ENG.). 48p. (J). (gr. 3-5). lib. bdg. 31.00 *(978-0-531-21158-8(4),* Children's Pr.) Scholastic Library Publishing.

—Uranus. 2007. (Scholastic News Nonfiction Readers Ser.). (ENG., Illus.). 24p. (J). (gr. 1-2). 22.00 *(978-0-531-14754-2(1))* Scholastic Library Publishing.

Uranus. 2nd rev. ed. 2009. (New Solar System Ser.). (ENG.). 32p. (gr. 3-6). 23.00 *(978-1-60413-214-4(0),* P166422, Facts On File) Infobase Holdings, Inc.

Viegas, Jennifer. Uranus. (Library of Planets Ser.). 48p. (gr. 5-8). 2009. 55.90 *(978-1-60853-322-5(2),* Rosen Reference) 2008. (ENG., Illus.). (YA). lib. bdg. 34.47 *(978-1-4042-1428-6(3),* ab137445-9875-4658-aaf0-f04b50e6c63b) Rosen Publishing Group, Inc., The.

Vogt, Gregory. Uranus. 2009. (Early Bird Astronomy Ser.). (ENG.). 48p. (gr. 2-5). lib. bdg. 26.60 *(978-0-7613-4156-7(0))* Lerner Publishing Group.

Wimmer, Teresa. Uranus. 2007. (My First Look at: Planets Ser.). (Illus.). 24p. (J). (gr. -1-3). lib. bdg. 24.25 *(978-1-58341-523-8(8),* Creative Education) Creative Co., The.

World Book, Inc. Staff, contrib. by. Saturn & Uranus. (J). 2010. *(978-0-7166-9535-6(9))* 2006. (Illus.). 63p. *(978-0-7166-9506-6(5))* 2nd ed. 2006. (Illus.). 64p. *(978-0-7166-9519-6(7))* World Bk., Inc.

URBAN RENEWAL

see also City Planning; Sociology, Urban

Amidon Lusted, Marcia, ed. Gentrification & the Housing Crisis, 1 vol. 2018. (Opposing Viewpoints Ser.). (ENG.). 200p. (gr. 10-12). 50.43 *(978-1-5345-0412-7(5),* e8c71111-d332-4d12-8405-58d0db1ddc4f) Greenhaven Publishing LLC.

WalkerTheo. THE CITY EXPERIMENT: REBUILDING GREENSBURG, KANSAS LOW INTERMEDIATE BOOK WITH ONLINE ACCESS, 1 vol. 2014. (ENG., Illus.). 24p. (J). pap., E-Book 9.50 *(978-1-107-62256-2(5))* Cambridge Univ. Pr.

URBAN RENEWAL—FICTION

Simonet, Evan, illus. Jake & the Sailing Tree. 2009. (J). *(978-1-60108-019-6(0))* Red Cygnet Pr.

Thornton, D. S. Scrap City. Bowater, Charlie, illus. 2015. (Middle-Grade Novels Ser.). (ENG.). 352p. (J). (gr. 4-8). lib. bdg. 27.99 *(978-1-4965-0475-3(5),* 128500, Stone Arch Bks.) Capstone.

Zoboi, Ibi. Pride: A Pride & Prejudice Remix. (ENG.). 304p. (YA). (gr. 8). 2019. pap. 11.99 *(978-0-06-256405-4(6))* 2018. 17.99 *(978-0-06-256404-7(8))* 2018. E-Book *(978-0-06-256407-8(2),* 9780062564078) HarperCollins Pubs. (Balzer & Bray).

URBAN SOCIOLOGY

see Sociology, Urban

URUGUAY

Behnke, Alison. Uruguay in Pictures. 2009. (Visual Geography Series, Second Ser.). (ENG.). 80p. (gr. 5-12). 31.93 *(978-1-57505-961-7(4),* Twenty-First Century Bks.) Lerner Publishing Group.

Jermyn, Leslie & Wong, Winnie. Uruguay, 1 vol. 2nd rev. ed. 2010. (Cultures of the World (Second Edition)(r) Ser.). (ENG.). 144p. (gr. 5-5). 49.79 *(978-0-7614-4482-4(3),* f59c08f8-1055-46b0-aeaa-19dd4dd85acf) Cavendish Square Publishing LLC.

Nevins, Deb, et al. Uruguay, 1 vol. 2018. (Cultures of the World (Third Edition)(r) Ser.). (ENG.). 144p. (gr. 5-5). lib. bdg. 48.79 *(978-1-5026-3644-7(1),* 42931d0a-2bf1-46c9-b377-5d916a24b4bd) Cavendish Square Publishing LLC.

Oachs, Emily Rose. Uruguay. 2016. (Exploring Countries Ser.). (ENG., Illus.). 32p. (J). (gr. 3-7). 27.95 *(978-1-62617-406-1(7),* Blastoff! Readers) Bellwether Media.

Oldfield, Matt & Oldfield, Tom. Luis Suarez: el Pistolero. 2016. (ENG., Illus.). 160p. (J). (gr. 4-7). pap. 8.99 *(978-1-78606-012-9(4))* Blake, John Publishing, Ltd. GBR. Dist: Independent Pubs. Group.

Shields, Charles J. Uruguay. (South America Today Ser.). 2009. (Illus.). 63p. (J). (gr. 4-7). 21.95 *(978-1-4222-0642-3(4))* 2007. 64p. (YA). (gr. 7-18). pap. 9.95 *(978-1-4222-0709-3(9))* Mason Crest.

—Uruguay, Vol. 13. Henderson, James D., ed. 2015. (Discovering South America: History, Politics, & Culture Ser.). (Illus.). 64p. (J). (gr. 7). lib. bdg. 22.95 *(978-1-4222-3305-4(7))* Mason Crest.

Yoshimi, Kusaba, ed. The World's Poorest President Speaks Out. Wong, Andrew, tr. Gaku, Nakagawa, illus. 2020. 40p. (J). 16.95 *(978-1-59270-289-3(9))* Enchanted Lion Bks., LLC.

USEFUL ARTS

see Technology

UTAH

Brown, Jonatha A. Utah, 1 vol. 2006. (Portraits of the States Ser.). (ENG.). 32p. (gr. 3-5). pap. 11.50 *(978-0-8368-4726-0(1),* 64f9482c-7acb-4c8d-bc65-006be4a16db7); (Illus.). lib. bdg. 28.67 *(978-0-8368-4709-3(1),* febed6c1-2a95-4543-8c83-f6ce8eb10448) Stevens, Gareth Publishing LLLP. (Gareth Stevens Learning Library).

Fein, E. How to Draw Utah's Sights & Symbols. 2009. (Kid's Guide to Drawing America Ser.). 32p. (gr. k-k). 50.50 *(978-1-61511-100-8(X),* PowerKids Pr.) Rosen Publishing Group, Inc., The.

Gregory, Josh. Utah (a True Book: My United States) (Library Edition) 2018. (True Book (Relaunch) Ser.). (ENG., Illus.). 48p. (J). (gr. 3-5). 31.00 *(978-0-531-23582-9(3),* Children's Pr.) Scholastic Library Publishing.

Hall, Becky. A Is for Arches: A Utah Alphabet. Larson, Katherine, illus. 2003. (Discover America State by State Ser.). (ENG.). 40p. (J). (gr. 1-3). 18.99 *(978-1-58536-096-3(1),* 201976) Sleeping Bear Pr.

Heinrichs, Ann. Utah. Kania, Matt, illus. 2017. (U. S. A. Travel Guides). (ENG.). 40p. (J). (gr. 2-5). lib. bdg. 38.50 *(978-1-5038-1984-9(1),* 211621) Child's World, Inc, The.

Hirschmann, Kris. Utah, 1 vol. 2003. (World Almanac(r) Library of the States Ser.). (ENG., Illus.). 48p. (gr. 4-6). pap. 15.05 *(978-0-8368-5332-2(6),* 6a586503-0538-42fd-8a73-25255a0b93ee); lib. bdg. 33.67 *(978-0-8368-5161-8(7),* 935128be-8624-4d6f-8017-7dc9decfabf0) Stevens, Gareth Publishing LLLP. (Gareth Stevens Learning Library).

Marsh, Carole. Utah Current Events Projects: 30 Cool, Activities, Crafts, Experiments & More for Kids to Do to Learn about Your State! 2003. (Utah Experience Ser.). 32p. (gr. k-5). pap. 5.95 *(978-0-635-02063-5(7),* Marsh, Carole Bks.) Gallopade International.

—Utah Geography Projects: 30 Cool, Activities, Crafts, Experiments & More for Kids to Do to Learn about Your State! 2003. (Utah Experience Ser.). 32p. (gr. k-5). pap. 5.95 *(978-0-635-01862-5(4),* Marsh, Carole Bks.) Gallopade International.

—Utah Government Projects: 30 Cool, Activities, Crafts, Experiments & More for Kids to Do to Learn about Your State! 2003. (Utah Experience Ser.). 32p. (gr. k-5). pap. 5.95 *(978-0-635-01963-9(9),* Marsh, Carole Bks.) Gallopade International.

—Utah Symbols & Facts Projects: 30 Cool, Activities, Crafts, Experiments & More for Kids to Do to Learn about Your State! 2003. (Utah Experience Ser.). 32p. (gr. k-5). pap. 5.95 *(978-0-635-01913-4(2),* Marsh, Carole Bks.) Gallopade International.

Murray, Julie. Utah, 1 vol. 2006. (United States Ser.). (ENG., Illus.). 32p. (gr. 2-4). 27.07 *(978-1-59197-703-2(7),* Buddy Bks.) ABDO Publishing Co.

Obregon, Jose Maria. Utah, 1 vol. Brusca, Maria Cristina, tr. 2005. (Bilingual Library of the United States of America Ser.: Set 2). (ENG & SPA., Illus.). 32p. (J). (gr. 2-2). lib. bdg. 28.93 *(978-1-4042-3110-8(2),* 25ca503c-0e60-4cfa-9dd1-c35172347eae) Rosen Publishing Group, Inc., The.

Obregón, José María. Utah. 2009. (Bilingual Library of the United States of America Ser.). (ENG & SPA.). 32p. (gr. 2-2). 47.90 *(978-1-60853-388-6(3),* Editorial Buenas Letras) Rosen Publishing Group, Inc., The.

Orr, Tamra B. Zion (a True Book: National Parks) (Library Edition) 2017. (True Book (Relaunch) Ser.). (ENG., Illus.). 48p. (J). (gr. 3-5). lib. bdg. 31.00 *(978-0-531-23397-9(9),* Children's Pr.) Scholastic Library Publishing.

Sanders, Doug. Utah, 1 vol. Santoro, Christopher, illus. 2005. (It's My State! (First Edition)(r) Ser.). (ENG.). 80p. (gr. 4-4). lib. bdg. 34.07 *(978-0-7614-1530-5(0),* ed449a64-dbf7-471c-b5d4-98125ff26f4b) Cavendish Square Publishing LLC.

Stefoff, Rebecca & Mead, Wendy. Utah, 1 vol. 2nd rev. ed. 2010. (Celebrate the States (Second Edition) Ser.). (ENG.). 144p. (gr. 6-6). 39.79 *(978-0-7614-4035-2(6),* f1f563bd-1f76-4c9f-8333-0390596e9d15) Cavendish Square Publishing LLC.

Trueit, Trudi Strain. Utah. 2007. (Rookie Read-About Geography: States Ser.). (ENG., Illus.). 32p. (J). (gr. 1-2). 18.69 *(978-0-531-12574-8(2),* Children's Pr.) Scholastic Library Publishing.

UTAH—FICTION

Amato, Carol J. The Lost Treasure of the Golden Sun. 2005. 172p. (J). *(978-0-9713756-3-5(1))* Stargazer Publishing Co.

Beaty, Janice J. & Beaty, Lillian C., illus. Jarod & the Mystery of the Utah Arches: A National Park Adventure Series Book. 2016. 118p. (J). pap. *(978-1-63293-122-1(2))* Sunstone Pr.

Crane, Cheri J. Moment of Truth: A Novel. 2005. 238p. (YA). *(978-1-59156-727-1(0))* Covenant Communications.

Evans, Richard Paul. If Only. 2015. (ENG., Illus.). 288p. (YA). (gr. 9). pap. 12.99 *(978-1-4814-4853-6(6),* Simon Pulse) Simon Pulse.

Fitzgerald, John. Great Brain. 2006. 20.75 *(978-0-8446-7293-9(9))* Smith, Peter Pub., Inc.

Fitzgerald, John D. More Adventures of the Great Brain. Mayer, Mercer, illus. 2004. (Great Brain Ser.: 2). (ENG.). 176p. (J). (gr. 3-7). pap. 8.99 *(978-0-14-240065-4(3),* Puffin Books) Penguin Young Readers Group.

—More Adventures of the Great Brain. 2004. (Great Brain Ser.). 142p. (J). (gr. 3-7). pap., tchr.'s training gde. ed. 36.00 incl. audio *(978-0-8072-0860-1(4),* Listening Library) Random Hse. Audio Publishing Group.

Fogg, K. L. Diamondback Cave: A Novel. 2008. 377p. (J). *(978-1-59811-512-3(X))* Covenant Communications.

Greene, Michele Dominguez. Keep Sweet. 2011. (ENG.). 224p. (YA). (gr. 9). pap. 9.99 *(978-1-4424-0977-4(0),* Simon Pulse) Simon Pulse.

Hall, Susan Liberty. Scented Adventures of the Bouquet Sisters in Fairyland. Josephine, Wall, illus. 2011. 85p. (YA). pap. 21.50 *(978-0-9833247-6-8(X))* Inkwell Books LLC.

Hulet, Debra. Independence Rock. 2011. 208p. pap. 13.99 *(978-1-59955-441-9(0),* Bonneville Bks.) Cedar Fort, Inc./CFI Distribution.

Hurley, Jeanette Clinger. The Crystal Prince: Love Is the Only Way. 2010. (Illus.). 77p. pap. 32.95 *(978-0-578-03963-3(X))* Outskirts Pr., Inc.

Jacobs, Lily. The Littlest Bunny in Utah: An Easter Adventure. Dunn, Robert, illus. 2015. (Littlest Bunny Ser.). (ENG.). 32p. (J). (gr. -1-3). 9.99 *(978-1-4926-1219-3(7),* Hometown World) Sourcebooks, Inc.

James, Eric. Santa's Sleigh Is on Its Way to Utah: A Christmas Adventure. Dunn, Robert, illus. 2016. (Santa's Sleigh Is on Its Way Ser.). (ENG.). 32p. (J). (gr. k-2). 12.99 *(978-1-4926-4360-9(2),* 9781492643609, Hometown World) Sourcebooks, Inc.

—The Spooky Express Utah. Piwowarski, Marcin, illus. 2017. (Spooky Express Ser.). (ENG.). 32p. (J). (gr. k-6). 9.99 *(978-1-4926-5405-6(1),* Hometown World) Sourcebooks, Inc.

—Tiny the Utah Easter Bunny. 2018. (Tiny the Easter Bunny Ser.). (ENG.). 40p. (J). (gr. k-3). 9.99 *(978-1-4926-5971-6(1),* Hometown World) Sourcebooks, Inc.

Jasper, Mark. Good Night Utah. Hart, Jason, illus. 2012. (Good Night Our World Ser.). (ENG.). 20p. (J). (gr. -1 — 1). bds. 9.95 *(978-1-60219-059-7(3))* Good Night Bks.

Johnson, Annabel & Johnson, Edgar. Wilderness Bride. 2003. 232p. (J). 12.95 *(978-0-9714612-7-7(9))* Green Mansion Pr. LLC.

Kearns, Ann. Dell's Discovery. 2006. 108p. (YA). per. 9.95 *(978-0-9710696-6-4(2))* Jorlan Publishing, Inc.

Lauren, Christina. Autoboyography. 2017. (ENG., Illus.). 416p. (YA). (gr. 9). 19.99 *(978-1-4814-8168-7(1),* Simon & Schuster Bks. For Young Readers) Simon & Schuster Bks. For Young Readers.

London, Jonathan. Desolation Canyon. London, Sean, illus. 2015. (Aaron's Wilderness Ser.: 1). (ENG.). 168p. (J). (gr. 3-5). pap. 12.99 *(978-1-941821-29-9(4),* West Winds Pr.) West Margin Pr.

Mangum, Kay Lynn. A Love Like Lilly. 2006. 336p. (YA). pap. 15.95 *(978-1-59038-580-7(2))* Deseret Bk. Co.

Nichols, Walter H. The Measure of a Boy. 2005. (Illus.). pap. 28.95 *(978-1-885529-73-2(2))* Stevens Publishing.

Nielsen, Gwyn English. Torey the Turkey Goes Skiing. 2003. (Illus.). 24p. (Orig.). (gr. -1-4). pap. 5.99 *(978-0-9660726-0-0(X))* C.G.S. Pr.

Norton, Charles. The Perfect Plan & the Four Brother's Pact. 2012. 24p. pap. 15.99 *(978-1-4691-6503-5(1))* Xlibris Corp.

O'Neill, Elizabeth. Alfred Visits Utah. 2009. 24p. (J). pap. 12.00 *(978-0-9822288-3-8(X))* Funny Bone Bks.

Pearson, Carol Lynn. Summer of Truth. 2007. 104p. per. 9.99 *(978-1-59955-046-6(6))* Cedar Fort, Inc./CFI Distribution.

Perry, Jolene. The Next Door Boys. 2011. 266p. (YA). *(978-1-59955-910-0(2),* Bonneville Bks.) Cedar Fort, Inc./CFI Distribution.

Raleigh, Michael H. Ted & Jimmy, 1 vol. 2010. 99p. pap. 19.95 *(978-1-4489-6225-9(0))* America Star Bks.

Sargent, Dave & Sargent, Pat. Bashful: (Dusty Dun) Be Brave. Lenoir, Jane, illus. 2003. (Saddle up Ser.: Vol. 1). 42p. (J). pap. 10.95 *(978-1-56763-684-0(5))*; lib. bdg. 23.60 *(978-1-56763-683-3(7))* Ozark Publishing.

Stanley, Brenda. I Am Nuchu. 2010. 334p. (YA). (gr. 9-18). 16.95 *(978-1-934813-47-8(8))* Westside Bks.

Stilton, Geronimo. Geronimo Stilton Graphic Novels #13: The Fastest Train in the West, Vol. 13. 2013. (Geronimo Stilton Graphic Novels Ser.: 13). (ENG., Illus.). 56p. (J). (gr. 2-6). 9.99 *(978-1-59707-448-3(9),* 900123335, Papercutz) Mad Cave Studios.

Sully, Katherine. Night-Night Utah. Poole, Helen, illus. 2017. (Night-Night Ser.). (ENG.). 20p. (J). (gr. -1-1). bds. 9.99 *(978-1-4926-5476-6(0),* Hometown World) Sourcebooks, Inc.

Sumner Johnson, Janet. The Last Great Adventure of the PB & J Society. 2016. (Middle-Grade Novels Ser.). (ENG., Illus.). 256p. (J). (gr. 4-8). lib. bdg. 26.65 *(978-1-4965-2695-3(3),* 131275, Stone Arch Bks.) Capstone.

Tipton, R. Kent. Kid Posse & the Phantom Robber. 2003. (ENG., Illus.). (J). pap. 14.95 *(978-1-878044-89-1(3))* Mayhaven Publishing, Inc.

Van Draanen, Wendelin. Wild Bird. 2019. (ENG.). 336p. (YA). (gr. 7). pap. 10.99 *(978-1-101-94047-1(6),* Ember) Random Hse. Children's Bks.

Williams, Sarah DeFord. Palace Beautiful. 2011. (ENG.). (J). 224p. (gr. 6-8). 21.19 *(978-0-399-25298-3(3))*; 240p. (gr. 5-18). 6.99 *(978-0-14-241745-4(9),* Puffin Books) Penguin Young Readers Group.

Young, Judy. Danger at the Dinosaur Stomping Grounds. 2017. (Wild World of Buck Bray Ser.). (ENG., Illus.). 240p. (J). (gr. 3-6). 16.99 *(978-1-58536-368-1(5),* 204321); pap. 9.99 *(978-1-58536-369-8(3),* 204334) Sleeping Bear Pr.

UTAH—HISTORY

Alvarez, Carlos & Finn, Denny Von. Salt Flat Racers. 2010. (World's Fastest Ser.). (ENG., Illus.). 24p. (J). (gr. 3-7). lib. bdg. 26.95 *(978-1-60014-334-2(2))* Bellwether Media.

Banting, Erinn. Zion. 2020. (J). *(978-1-7911-1604-0(3),* AV2 by Weigl) Weigl Pubs., Inc.

Ching, Jacqueline. Utah: Past & Present, 1 vol. 2010. (United States: Past & Present Ser.). (ENG.). 48p. (YA). (gr. 5-5). pap. 12.75 *(978-1-4358-9524-9(X),* 117410f9-cf5d-47c5-9d54-78c07a6fe2e2); lib. bdg. 34.47 *(978-1-4358-9497-6(9),* 273ad4d5-8d36-4b92-a5c7-d03a78b3d27d) Rosen Publishing Group, Inc., The. (Rosen Reference).

Felix, Rebecca. What's Great about Utah? 2015. (Our Great States Ser.). (ENG., Illus.). 32p. (J). (gr. 2-5). pap. 7.95 *(978-1-4677-6088-1(9),* 220f57ce-d516-45e9-a4e0-585bd28c1076) Lerner Publishing Group.

Gish, Melissa. Utah. 2009. (This Land Called America Ser.). (Illus.). 32p. (YA). (gr. 3-6). 19.95 *(978-1-58341-797-3(4))* Creative Co., The.

Hall, Carol S. & Hansen, T. J. This Is Utah. 257p. (J). (gr. 1-6). pap. 39.95 *(978-1-56861-048-1(3))* Swift Learning Resources.

Hamilton, John. Utah, 1 vol. 2016. (United States of America Ser.). (ENG., Illus.). 48p. (J). (gr. 5-9). 34.21 *(978-1-68078-347-6(5),* 21679, Abdo & Daughters) ABDO Publishing Co.

Harvey, Dan. Rocky Mountain: Colorado, Utah, Wyoming, Vol. 19. 2015. (Let's Explore the States Ser.). (Illus.). 64p. (J). (gr. 5). 23.95 *(978-1-4222-3332-0(4))* Mason Crest.

Jerome, Kate B. Lucky to Live in Utah. 2017. (Arcadia Kids Ser.). (ENG., Illus.). 32p. (J). 16.99 *(978-0-7385-2793-2(9))* Arcadia Publishing.

—The Wise Animal Handbook Utah. 2017. (Arcadia Kids Ser.). (ENG., Illus.). 32p. (J). 16.99 *(978-0-7385-2846-5(3))* Arcadia Publishing.

Kent, Deborah. America the Beautiful: Utah (Revised Edition) 2014. (America the Beautiful, Third Ser. (Revised Edition) Ser.). (ENG.). 144p. (J). lib. bdg. 40.00 *(978-0-531-28295-3(3))* Scholastic Library Publishing.

LeBoutillier, Nate. The Story of the Utah Jazz. 2010. (NBA — A History of Hoops Ser.). 48p. (YA). (gr. 5-18). 23.95 *(978-1-58341-964-9(0),* Creative Education) Creative Co., The.

Lusted, Marcia Amidon. Utah: The Beehive State, 1 vol. 2010. (Our Amazing States Ser.). (ENG.). 24p. (J). (gr. 3-3). pap. 9.25 *(978-1-4488-0752-9(2),* f3e2529c-8c9d-4fac-b21c-41e01d7778d6, PowerKids Pr.) Rosen Publishing Group, Inc., The.

Marsh, Carole. Exploring Utah Through Project-Based Learning: Geography, History, Government, Economics & More. 2016. (Utah Experience Ser.). (ENG.). (J). pap. 9.99 *(978-0-635-12368-8(1))* Gallopade International.

—I'm Reading about Utah. 2014. (Utah Experience Ser.). (ENG., Illus.). (J). pap., pap. 8.99 *(978-0-635-11319-1(8))* Gallopade International.

—Utah History Projects: 30 Cool, Activities, Crafts, Experiments & More for Kids to Do to Learn about Your State! 2003. (Utah Experience Ser.). 32p. (gr. k-5). pap. 5.95 *(978-0-635-01813-7(6),* Marsh, Carole Bks.) Gallopade International.

Parker, Janice. Utah. 2011. (Illus.). 48p. (J). *(978-1-61690-493-7(3))* Weigl Pubs., Inc.

—Utah: The Beehive State. 2016. (J). *(978-1-4896-4950-8(6))* Weigl Pubs., Inc.

Rodriguez, Cindy. Utah: The Beehive State. 2012. (Illus.). 24p. (J). 27.13 *(978-1-61913-409-6(8))* Weigl Pubs., Inc.

Sanders, Doug & Herrington, Lisa M. Utah, 1 vol. 2nd rev. ed. 2012. (It's My State! (Second Edition)(r) Ser.). (ENG.). 80p. (gr. 4-4). 34.07 *(978-1-60870-659-4(1),* fd884228-0b5b-4168-b831-3dd69a63fff1) Cavendish Square Publishing LLC.

Sanders, Doug, et al. Utah, 1 vol. 3rd rev. ed. 2015. (It's My State! (Third Edition)(r) Ser.). (ENG., Illus.). 80p. (J). (gr. 4-4). 35.93 *(978-1-62713-178-0(7),* 17e23f21-c126-4234-b923-5dcf9f4fd357) Cavendish Square Publishing LLC.

Skogen, J. M. On the Hardwood: Utah Jazz. 2013. (On the Hardwood Ser.). (ENG., Illus.). 48p. (gr. 3-8). pap. 8.95 *(978-1-61570-833-8(2))* Scobre Pr. Corp.

The Utah Journey Program Kit: All program components for the Utah Journey, 1 vol. 2009. 129.95 *(978-1-4236-0733-5(3))* Gibbs Smith, Publisher.

UTENSILS, KITCHEN

see Household Equipment and Supplies

UTILITIES, PUBLIC

see Public Utilities

UTOPIAS—FICTION

Blakemore, Megan Frazer. The Daybreak Bond. 2018. (ENG.). 336p. (J). pap. 9.99 *(978-1-68119-896-5(7),* 900191672, Bloomsbury Children's Bks.) Bloomsbury Publishing USA.

Looraem, Ellen. The Unnameables. 2011. (ENG., Illus.). 336p. (J). (gr. 5-7). pap. 18.99 *(978-0-547-55213-2(0),* 1450658, Clarion Bks.) HarperCollins Pubs.
DeStefano, Lauren. Perfect Ruin. 2013. (Internment Chronicles Ser.: 1). (ENG., Illus.). 368p. (YA). (gr. 7). 18.99 *(978-1-4424-8061-2(0),* Simon & Schuster Bks. For Young Readers) Simon & Schuster Bks. For Young Readers.
Fiedler, Lisa. Hopper's Destiny. To, Vivienne, illus. 2016. (Mouseheart Ser.: 2). (ENG.). 368p. (J). (gr. 3-7). pap. 8.99 *(978-1-4814-2090-7(9),* McElderry, Margaret K. Bks.) McElderry, Margaret K. Bks.
—Mouseheart. To, Vivienne, illus. 2015. (Mouseheart Ser.: 1). (ENG.). 336p. (J). (gr. 3-7). pap. 8.99 *(978-1-4424-8783-3(6),* McElderry, Margaret K. Bks.) McElderry, Margaret K. Bks.
Grant, Michael. Bzrk. (Bzrk Ser.). (ENG.). 400p. (YA). (gr. 9-12). 2013. pap. 9.99 *(978-1-60684-418-2(0),* be48eae0-186e-42f3-9a8f-7a9a80661ce8) 2012. 17.99 *(978-1-60684-312-3(5),* ba9d46d5-5aa2-4bc4-bb35-da33ac28de6c) Lerner Publishing Group. (Carolrhoda Lab™).
—BZRK Reloaded. 2013. (Bzrk Ser.). (ENG.). 432p. (YA). (gr. 9-12). 18.99 *(978-1-60684-394-9(X),* 20fe8bbb-63fa-40af-8c0e-54890e077fe3, Carolrhoda Lab™) Lerner Publishing Group.
Hawk, Delores. The Edge of Finali. 2012. 350p. pap. 14.25 *(978-0-9859522-0-4(2))* Asimow, Dyanne.
Hinchliffe, Stuart Jarod. Princess Tiffany Arabella & the Time of Dreams. 2009. 196p. 24.50 *(978-1-60860-627-6(9),* Strategic Bk. Publishing) Strategic Book Publishing & Rights Agency (SBPRA).
Hirsch, Jeff. The Darkest Path. 2013. (YA). pap. *(978-0-545-51224-4(7),* Scholastic, Inc.) Scholastic, Inc.
Hourlier, Sylvaine. Blacky & the Enchanted Mountain, 1 vol. 2010. 48p. pap. 16.95 *(978-1-4512-1140-5(6))* America Star Bks.
Lois, Lowry. Son. 2014. (Giver Quartet Ser.: 4). lib. bdg. 20.85 *(978-0-606-35979-5(6))* Turtleback.
Lowry, Lois. Messenger. (Giver Quartet Ser.: 3). (ENG.). 192p. (YA). (gr. 7). 2018. pap. 10.99 *(978-1-328-46620-4(5),* 1713613) 2012. 17.99 *(978-0-547-99567-0(9),* 1525433) HarperCollins Pubs. (Clarion Bks.).
Metzger, Joanna. The Space Program. Elizalde, Marcelo, illus. 2006. 142p. (J). *(978-1-59336-695-7(7))* Mondo Publishing.
Nelson, O. T. (Terry). The Girl Who Owned a City: The Graphic Novel. Jones, Joëlle, illus. 2012. (ENG.). 128p. (YA). (gr. 5-12). pap. 12.99 *(978-0-7613-5634-9(7),* 843782ee-ab46-4a65-a48f-1b0107ddcfa7, Graphic Universe™) Lerner Publishing Group.
Simmons, Kristen. Article 5. 2013. (Article 5 Ser.: 1). (ENG.). 384p. (YA). (gr. 8-12). pap. 10.99 *(978-0-7653-2961-5(1),* 900075746, Tor Teen) Doherty, Tom Assocs., LLC.
Thomas, John Ira. Zoo Force: Dear Eniko. Smith, Jeremy, illus. 2003. 68p. per. 6.95 *(978-0-9743147-1-6(4))* Candle Light Pr.
White, Ruth. You'll Like It Here (Everybody Does) 2012. 272p. (J). (gr. 4-7). 7.99 *(978-0-375-86596-1(9),* Yearling) Random Hse. Children's Bks.

V

VACATIONS

Adamson, Heather. Family Vacations. 2010. (Special Days Ser.). (ENG.). 24p. (J). (gr. k-2). lib. bdg. 25.65 *(978-1-60753-029-9(5),* 17189) Amicus.
Allen, Francesca, illus. Vacation. 2006. (Usborne Look & Say Ser.). 10p. (J). (gr. -1-k). bds. 7.99 *(978-0-7945-1315-3(8),* Usborne) EDC Publishing.
Auld, Mary. Going on Vacation. 2011. (My Family & Me Ser.). (Illus.). 24p. (J). lib. bdg. 24.25 *(978-1-59771-230-9(2))* Sea-To-Sea Pubns.
Bernardo, Kat. Stem: The Science of Travel: Multiplication (Grade 3) 2017. (Mathematics in the Real World Ser.). (ENG., Illus.). 32p. (J). (gr. 3-4). pap. 11.99 *(978-1-4807-5797-4(7))* Teacher Created Materials, Inc.
Brode, Robyn. August, 1 vol. 2nd rev. ed. 2009. (Months of the Year (Second Edition) Ser.). (ENG.). 24p. (J). (gr. 1-1). pap. 9.15 *(978-1-4339-2101-8(4),* 015f85e0-a7b6-4cb8-843d-828d84578e73); lib. bdg. 24.67 *(978-1-4339-1924-4(9),* 638b22d0-feb3-41e3-acf2-920df1dcaf80) Stevens, Gareth Publishing LLLP. (Weekly Reader Leveled Readers).
—August / Agosto, 1 vol. 2009. (Months of the Year / Meses Del Ano Ser.). (ENG & SPA.). 24p. (J). (gr. 1-1). pap. 9.15 *(978-1-4339-2113-1(8),* d36b8b35-00b4-4af4-b447-613d09d265d7); lib. bdg. 24.67 *(978-1-4339-1936-7(2),* 08c615d4-1b6c-43c9-8fb5-bd85c05faaa7) Stevens, Gareth Publishing LLLP. (Weekly Reader Leveled Readers).
—July, 1 vol. 2nd rev. ed. 2009. (Months of the Year (Second Edition) Ser.). (ENG.). 24p. (J). (gr. 1-1). pap. 9.15 *(978-1-4339-2100-1(6),* 999cfeb5-7ef8-4978-bcf5-819f6475df27); lib. bdg. 24.67 *(978-1-4339-1923-7(0),* 7de8a18b-0bee-4b00-af54-422c26607453) Stevens, Gareth Publishing LLLP. (Weekly Reader Leveled Readers).
—July / Julio, 1 vol. 2009. (Months of the Year / Meses Del Ano Ser.). (ENG & SPA.). 24p. (J). (gr. 1-1). pap. 9.15 *(978-1-4339-2112-4(X),* 1ee4ff40-6e00-42d8-8a61-dcdefff29e49); lib. bdg. 24.67 *(978-1-4339-1935-0(4),* d0545bf3-4d53-4a8e-a1bb-119ee57a2ee6) Stevens, Gareth Publishing LLLP. (Weekly Reader Leveled Readers).
—June, 1 vol. 2nd rev. ed. 2009. (Months of the Year (Second Edition) Ser.). (ENG.). 24p. (J). (gr. 1-1). pap. 9.15 *(978-1-4339-2099-8(9),* 27670c9b-e702-4961-b8e3-1196acfb07ba); lib. bdg. 24.67 *(978-1-4339-1922-0(2),* 3ef7b3c4-0a78-4148-a18f-c5ff8636a5c) Stevens, Gareth Publishing LLLP. (Weekly Reader Leveled Readers).
—June / Junio, 1 vol. 2009. (Months of the Year / Meses Del Ano Ser.). (ENG & SPA.). 24p. (J). (gr. 1-1). pap. 9.15 *(978-1-4339-2111-7(1),* a8158983-22af-48a8-85b7-9219e41ee6c5); lib. bdg. 24.67 *(978-1-4339-1934-3(6),* 542b9c05-bb20-4ea6-bfd9-6f1cf22a59c7) Stevens, Gareth Publishing LLLP. (Weekly Reader Leveled Readers).
Color All About: A Giant Coloring Book about Summer Vacation: Summer Vacation. 2004. (Illus.). 36p. (J). *(978-1-59949-006-9(4))* Food Marketing Consultants, Inc.
Day, Amelia. Olivia's Ocean Adventure, 1 vol. 2013. (Core Math Skills: Numbers & Operations in Base 10 Ser.). (ENG.). 24p. (J). (gr. 1-1). 26.27 *(978-1-4777-2222-0(X),* 9cd40fa0-788a-48a7-a127-f99db4a6fc4b, Rosen Classroom) Rosen Publishing Group, Inc., The.
—Olivia's Ocean Adventure: Understand Place Value, 1 vol. 2013. (Rosen Math Readers Ser.). (ENG.). 24p. (J). (gr. 1-1). pap. 8.25 *(978-1-4777-2037-0(5),* f8c1f145-b20c-4523-8f1e-f66a833f86c0); pap. 49.50 *(978-1-4777-2038-7(3))* Rosen Publishing Group, Inc., The. (Rosen Classroom).
EventoSusan. YOUR DREAM VACATION HIGH BEGINNING BOOK WITH ONLINE ACCESS, 1 vol. 2014. (ENG., Illus.). 24p. (J). pap., E-Book, E-Book 9.50 *(978-1-107-69043-1(9))* Cambridge Univ. Pr.
Eystad, Janet Lynn. What I Got into Last Summer. 2012. 28p. 24.95 *(978-1-4626-5316-4(2))* America Star Bks.
Gibson, Ray. Little book of vacation Activities. 2005. (ENG.). 96p. (J). 7.95 *(978-0-7945-1171-5(6),* Usborne) EDC Publishing.
Gilpin, Rebecca. Travel Activity Book. 2013. (Doodle Bks). 96p. (J). pap. 12.99 *(978-0-7945-3287-1(X),* Usborne) EDC Publishing.
Hankinson, Kim. Lonely Planet Kids My Vacation Scrapbook 1. Hankinson, Kim, illus. 2018. (Lonely Planet Kids Ser.). (ENG., Illus.). 48p. (J). (gr. 1-3). pap. 9.99 *(978-1-78701-319-3(7),* 5735) Lonely Planet Global Ltd. IRL. Dist: Hachette Bk. Group.
Harper, Suzanne & Sheppard, Bonnie. The 10 Most Extreme Vacations. 2008. (J). 14.99 *(978-1-55448-534-5(7))* Scholastic Library Publishing.
Heos, Bridget. Manners on Vacation. Longhi, Katya, illus. 2015. (Monstrous Manners Ser.). (ENG.). 24p. (J). (gr. 1-4). lib. bdg. 19.95 *(978-1-60753-747-2(8),* 15277) Amicus.
Hibbert, Clare. Beside the Seaside: Seaside Holidays Then & Now. 2018. (Beside the Seaside Ser.). (ENG., Illus.). 24p. (J). (gr. 1-3). pap. 12.99 *(978-1-4451-3758-2(5),* Franklin Watts) Hachette Children's Group GBR. Dist: Hachette Bk. Group.
The Land & the People. 2016. (Land & the People Ser.). 48p. (gr. 5-5). pap. 84.30 *(978-1-4824-5327-0(4));* (ENG.). lib. bdg. 201.60 *(978-1-4824-4975-4(7),* cdb47273-4520-4f8a-95c8-ef4dc77aba76) Stevens, Gareth Publishing LLLP.
Laval, Thierry. Mini Look & Find on Vacation (Mini Look & Find) Laval, Thierry, illus. 2017. (Mini Look & Find Ser.). (ENG., Illus.). 14p. (J). (gr. -1-k). 9.95 *(978-0-531-23083-1(X),* Children's Pr.) Scholastic Library Publishing.
Maskel, Hazel. 1001 Things to Spot on Vacation. 2011. (1001 Things to Spot Ser.). 32p. (J). ring bd. 9.99 *(978-0-7945-3087-7(7),* Usborne) EDC Publishing.
McNeill, Suzanne. Vacation Crafting: 150+ Summer Camp Projects for Boys & Girls to Make. 2018. (ENG., Illus.). 160p. (J). pap. 16.99 *(978-1-64124-017-8(2),* 0178) Fox Chapel Publishing Co., Inc.
Mercado, Nancy E. Boredom Busters! Activities to Do for Kids Like You! 2003. (Illus.). 38p. (J). *(978-0-439-52312-7(5))* Scholastic, Inc.
Phillips, Clifton. Waterworld Wonderways. 2007. 36p. 9.99 *(978-0-9797106-2-9(6))* Avid Readers Publishing Group.
Richards, Jon. Vacations & Holidays. 2005. (How Things Have Changed Ser.). (Illus.). 32p. (J). (gr. 3-7). lib. bdg. 27.10 *(978-1-59389-197-8(0))* Chrysalis Education.
Robson, Kirsteen. Wipe-Clean Vacation Activities. 2015. (Wipe-Clean Bks.). (ENG.). 22p. (J). (gr. k-5). pap. 7.99 *(978-0-7945-3480-6(5),* Usborne) EDC Publishing.
Ross, Stewart. Seaside Holidays. 2013. (Start-Up Connections Ser.). (ENG., Illus.). 32p. (J). pap. 12.99 *(978-0-237-54421-8(0))* Evans Brothers, Ltd. GBR. Dist: Independent Pubs. Group.
Rowe, Brooke. What's Your Perfect Vacation? 2015. (Best Quiz Ever Ser.). (ENG., Illus.). 32p. (J). (gr. 4-8). 32.07 *(978-1-63470-037-5(6),* 206816) Cherry Lake Publishing.
Ticktock Media, Ltd. Staff. Summer Vacation. 2009. (Busy Tots Ser.). (ENG.). 10p. (J). (gr. -1-k). bds. 6.95 *(978-1-84696-800-6(3),* TickTock Books) Octopus Publishing Group GBR. Dist: Independent Pubs. Group.
Tocquigny, Rick. Life Lessons from Family Vacations. 2015. (Illus.). 224p. 14.95 *(978-1-63076-081-6(1))* Taylor Trade Publishing.
Ward, Ellie. Vacation Doodles. 2010. (Y Ser.). (ENG., Illus.). 96p. (J). (gr. 3). pap. 7.95 *(978-1-84732-652-2(8))* Carlton Bks., Ltd. GBR. Dist: Two Rivers Distribution.

VACATIONS—FICTION

Adams, Sherred Willcox. Five Little Friends. 2006. pap. 15.95 *(978-1-4304-4149-6(6))* Kessinger Publishing, LLC.
Alpine, Rachele. You Throw Like a Girl. 2017. (Mix Ser.). (ENG., Illus.). 272p. (J). (gr. 4-8). pap. 8.99 *(978-1-4814-5984-6(8),* Simon & Schuster/Paula Wiseman Bks.) Simon & Schuster/Paula Wiseman Bks.
Altreche, Jeanine. Talula Goes to New York. 2007. 32p. per. 12.95 *(978-1-4327-0538-1(5))* Outskirts Pr., Inc.
Ambrose, Adrianne. We're with the Band. 2011. (XOXO, Betty & Veronica Ser.). (ENG.). 192p. (J). (gr. 4-7). 17.44 *(978-0-448-45577-8(3),* Grosset & Dunlap) Penguin Publishing Group.
Ameen, Judith. Harold & the Magic Books. 2005. 40p. pap. 8.95 *(978-1-933265-42-1(6))* Wasteland Pr.
Andersen, C. B. The Forgotten Treasure. 2004. 215p. (J). pap. *(978-1-59038-314-8(1))* Deseret Bk. Co.
Applegate, Katherine. Spring Break. 2010. (Summer Ser.). (ENG., Illus.). 240p. (YA). (gr. 9-18). pap. 8.99 *(978-1-4169-9094-9(1),* Simon Pulse) Simon Pulse.
Arena, Jen. Lady Liberty's Holiday. Hunt, Matt, illus. 2016. (ENG.). 40p. (J). (gr. k-3). 17.99 *(978-0-553-52067-5(9),* Knopf Bks. for Young Readers) Random Hse. Children's Bks.
Azurmendi, Mattie. Sock Vacation. 2011. 20p. pap. 14.95 *(978-1-257-64550-3(1))* Lulu Pr., Inc.
Bader, Arlys Elaine. The Adventures of Garth & Cloey. 2008. 40p. pap. 16.99 *(978-1-4389-2472-4(0))* AuthorHouse.
Baer, Julien. The Book in the Book in the Book. Bailly, Simon, illus. 2019. 56p. (J). (gr. -1-3). 18.99 *(978-0-8234-4243-0(8))* Holiday Hse., Inc.
Bailey, Ethel M. T. Lily Pond Village, 1 vol. 2009. 57p. pap. 16.95 *(978-1-60703-379-0(8))* America Star Bks.
Banks, Kate. Dillon Dillon. 2005. 149p. (gr. 3-7). 18.00 *(978-0-7569-5767-4(2))* Perfection Learning Corp.
Barks, Carl, et al. Walt Disney's Vacation Parade Volume 5. Clark, John, ed. 2008. (ENG., Illus.). 80p. pap. 9.95 *(978-1-60360-031-6(0),* 9781603600316) Gemstone Publishing, Inc.
—Walt Disney's Vacation Parade Volume 6. 2009. 80p. pap. 9.99 *(978-1-60360-096-5(5))* Gemstone Publishing, Inc.
Barnett, Angela. Mystic Grove. 2006. pap. 10.00 *(978-1-4257-1912-8(0))* Xlibris Corp.
Battiste, Alyse. Super Sally's Fantastic Fun Day. 2007. (Illus.). 68p. (J). pap. 15.97 *(978-0-9798217-1-4(1))* Candalyse Publishing.
Beachy, Elaine. Biff & Becka's Stupendous Vacation. 2013. 156p. (J). 30.95 *(978-1-4497-9069-1(0));* pap. 13.95 *(978-1-4497-9070-7(4))* Author Solutions, LLC. (WestBow Pr.).
Bentley, Sue. A Forest Charm #6, 6 vols. Swan, Angela, illus. 2010. (Magic Puppy Ser.: 6). (ENG.). 128p. (J). (gr. 1-3). pap. 5.99 *(978-0-448-45065-0(8),* Grosset & Dunlap) Penguin Young Readers Group.
—Sunshine Shimmers. 2014. (Magic Puppy Ser.: 12). lib. bdg. 14.75 *(978-0-606-34141-7(2))* Turtleback.
—Sunshine Shimmers #12. Swan, Angela, illus. 2014. (Magic Puppy Ser.: 12). (ENG.). 128p. (J). (gr. 1-3). 5.99 *(978-0-448-46791-7(7),* Grosset & Dunlap) Penguin Young Readers Group.
—Vacation Dreams. 2013. (Magic Bunny Ser.: 2). lib. bdg. 16.00 *(978-0-606-31676-7(0))* Turtleback.
—Vacation Dreams #2. Swan, Angela, illus. 2013. (Magic Bunny Ser.: 2). (ENG.). 128p. (J). (gr. 1-3). pap. 6.99 *(978-0-448-46728-3(3),* Grosset & Dunlap) Penguin Young Readers Group.
—Winter Wonderland #5. Swan, Angela, illus. 2013. (Magic Ponies Ser.: 5). (ENG.). 128p. (J). (gr. 1-3). 6.99 *(978-0-448-46786-3(0),* Grosset & Dunlap) Penguin Young Readers Group.
Berenstain, Jan. Berenstain Bears Go on Vacation. 2010. (Berenstain Bears Ser.). (ENG., Illus.). 32p. (J). (gr. -1-3). pap. 7.99 *(978-0-06-057433-8(X),* HarperCollins) HarperCollins Pubs.
Berenstain, Jan & Berenstain, Stan. The Berenstain Bears Out West. Berenstain, Jan, illus. 2006. (I Can Read Level 1 Ser.). (ENG., Illus.). 32p. (J). (gr. k-3). pap. 4.99 *(978-0-06-058354-5(1),* HarperCollins) HarperCollins Pubs.
Bevin, Teresa. Tina Springs into Summer/Tina Se Lanza Al Verano. Rodriguez, Perfecto, illus. 2005. (ENG & SPA.). 114p. (J). pap. 21.00 *(978-1-928589-28-0(6))* Gival Pr., LLC.
Beyers, Kathryn. Babe's Vacation. 2012. 32p. pap. 17.49 *(978-1-4771-5671-1(2))* Xlibris Corp.
Bickford, Janette. Vern's Vacation. 2012. 16p. pap. 12.68 *(978-1-4669-2311-9(3))* Trafford Publishing.
Birdsall, Jeanne. The Penderwicks: A Summer Tale of Four Sisters, Two Rabbits, & a Very Interesting Boy. (Penderwicks Ser.: 1). (ENG.). (J). (gr. 3-7). 2007. 288p. 8.99 *(978-0-440-42047-7(4),* Yearling) 2005. 272p. 17.99 *(978-0-375-83143-0(6),* Knopf Bks. for Young Readers) Random Hse. Children's Bks.
—The Penderwicks: A Summer Tale of Four Sisters, Two Rabbits & a Very Interesting Boy. 2007. (Penderwicks (Hardback) Ser.). 262p. (gr. 3-7). 18.00 *(978-0-7569-7798-6(3))* Perfection Learning Corp.
—The Penderwicks: A Summer Tale of Four Sisters, Two Rabbits, & a Very Interesting Boy. 2007. (Penderwicks Ser.: 1). (Illus.). 262p. (gr. 4-7). lib. bdg. 18.40 *(978-1-4177-7275-9(1))* Turtleback.
—The Penderwicks: A Summer Tale of Four Sisters, Two Rabbits & a Very Interesting Boy. 2009. 8.80 *(978-0-7848-2826-7(1),* Everbind) Marco Bk. Co.
—The Penderwicks: A Summer Tale of Four Sisters, Two Rabbits & a Very Interesting Boy. l.t. ed. 2006. (Penderwick Ser.). 304p. (J). (gr. 3-7). 23.95 *(978-0-7862-8897-7(3))* Thorndike Pr.
—The Penderwicks at Point Mouette. 2011. (Playaway Children Ser.). (J). (gr. k). 44.99 *(978-1-61707-434-9(9))* Findaway World, LLC.
—The Penderwicks at Point Mouette. (Penderwicks Ser.: 3). (ENG.). (J). (gr. 3-7). 2012. 320p. 8.99 *(978-0-375-85135-3(6),* Yearling) 2011. 304p. 16.99 *(978-0-375-85851-2(2),* Knopf Bks. for Young Readers) Random Hse. Children's Bks.
Blackstone, Stella. Bear Takes a Trip. Harter, Debbie, illus. 2012. (Bear Ser.). (ENG.). 24p. (J). (gr. -1-1). bds. 8.99 *(978-1-84686-757-6(6))* Barefoot Bks., Inc.
Blackstone, Stella & Harter, Debbie. Bear Takes a Trip. 2012. (Illus.). 24p. (J). (gr. -1-1). pap. 6.99 *(978-1-84686-756-9(8))* Barefoot Bks., Inc.
Blackstone, Stella & Parker, Elizabeth. L'Ours Fait un Voyage. Harter, Debbie, illus. 2013.Tr. of Bear Takes a Trip. (FRE & ENG.). 24p. (J). (gr. k-1). pap. 6.99 *(978-1-84686-946-4(3))* Barefoot Bks., Inc.
Blume, Judy. Fudge-A-Mania. 2007. (ENG.). 176p. (J). (gr. 3-7). 8.99 *(978-0-14-240877-3(8),* Puffin Books) Penguin Young Readers Group.
—Otherwise Known As Sheila the Great. 2004. (ENG.). 160p. (J). (gr. 3-7). 6.99 *(978-0-425-19380-8(2),* Berkley) Penguin Publishing Group.
—Otherwise Known As Sheila the Great. 2007. (ENG.). 176p. (J). (gr. 3-7). 8.99 *(978-0-14-240879-7(4),* Puffin Books) Penguin Young Readers Group.
—Otherwise Known as Sheila the Great. 2007. 154p. (gr. 4-7). 16.00 *(978-0-7569-7915-7(3))* Perfection Learning Corp.
—Otherwise Known as Sheila the Great. 2007. (Fudge Bks.: 2). 138p. (gr. 4-7). lib. bdg. 18.40 *(978-1-4177-8370-0(2))* Turtleback.
Bond, Michael. Paddington Abroad. Fortnum, Peggy, illus. 2015. (Paddington Ser.). (ENG.). 176p. (J). (gr. 3-7). 9.99 *(978-0-06-231222-8(7),* HarperCollins) HarperCollins Pubs.
Bowman, Lucy. Sticker Dolly Dressing on Vacation (Revised Cover) 2015. (Sticker Dolly Dressing Ser.). (ENG.). 24+p. (J). (gr. k-5). pap. 8.99 *(978-0-7945-3555-1(0),* Usborne) EDC Publishing.
Bracken- Murphy, Julie. Sammy's Summer Vacation. 2007. 52p. per. 13.95 *(978-1-4327-0615-9(2))* Outskirts Pr., Inc.
Brauner, Susan. The Adventures of Sohi: Mystery of Moon Island. 2011. 207p. 28.95 *(978-1-4327-6752-5(6));* pap. 15.95 *(978-1-4327-6536-1(1))* Outskirts Pr., Inc.
Brege, K. B. Champ... A Wave of Terror! Five Ways to Finish. 2006. (Mick Morris Myth Solver Ser.: No. 3). (J). mass mkt. 6.99 *(978-0-9774119-2-4(3))* Team B Creative LLC.
Bridgman, C. A. Santa's Hawaiian Vacation. (J). 14.95 *(978-0-681-32827-3(4))* Booklines Hawaii, Ltd.
Bridwell, Norman. Clifford Sees America. 2012. (Clifford: Scholastic Readers Level 1 Ser.). lib. bdg. 13.55 *(978-0-606-23908-0(1))* Turtleback.
Brown, Jeff. Flat Stanley's Worldwide Adventures #1: the Mount Rushmore Calamity. Pamintuan, Macky, illus. 2009. (Flat Stanley's Worldwide Adventures Ser.: 1). (ENG.). 96p. (J). (gr. 2-5). 15.99 *(978-0-06-142991-0(0));* pap. 4.99 *(978-0-06-142990-3(2),* 91be4692-a157-4cdf-bf09-64fa0741a507) HarperCollins Pubs. (HarperCollins).
—Flat Stanley's Worldwide Adventures #10: Showdown at the Alamo. Pamintuan, Macky, illus. 2013. (Flat Stanley's Worldwide Adventures Ser.: 10). (ENG.). 112p. (J). (gr. 1-5). 15.99 *(978-0-06-218988-2(3));* pap. 4.99 *(978-0-06-218987-5(5))* HarperCollins Pubs. (HarperCollins).
—Showdown at the Alamo. 2013. (Flat Stanley's Worldwide Adventures Ser.: 10). (J). lib. bdg. 14.75 *(978-0-606-35046-4(2))* Turtleback.
Brown, Marc. Arthur & the School Pet. 2005. (Step into Reading Sticker Bks.). (Illus.). 24p. 14.00 *(978-0-7569-5571-7(8))* Perfection Learning Corp.
—Arthur & the School Pet. 2003. (Step into Reading Ser.). (ENG., Illus.). 24p. (J). (gr. k-3). pap. 5.99 *(978-0-375-81001-5(3),* Random Hse. Bks. for Young Readers) Random Hse. Children's Bks.
—Arthur & the School Pet. 2003. (Arthur Step into Reading Ser.). (gr. -1-2). lib. bdg. 13.55 *(978-0-613-57492-1(3))* Turtleback.
—Arthur in New York. 2008. (Step into Reading Ser.). (ENG., Illus.). 24p. (J). (gr. k-3). pap. 5.99 *(978-0-375-82976-5(8),* Random Hse. Bks. for Young Readers) Random Hse. Children's Bks.
—Arthur's Classroom Fib. 2007. (Arthur Step into Reading Ser.). lib. bdg. 13.55 *(978-1-4177-7281-0(6))* Turtleback.
Brown, Monica. Lola Levine & the Vacation Dream. 2017. (Lola Levine Ser.: 5). (J). lib. bdg. 16.00 *(978-0-606-40222-4(5))* Turtleback.
Brown, Ruth Alberta. Tabitha's Vacation. 2005. reprint ed. pap. 27.95 *(978-1-4191-1538-7(3))* Kessinger Publishing, LLC.
Buffie, Margaret. Who Is Frances Rain? 20th ed. 2017. 184p. (J). (gr. 7-9). 7.95 *(978-1-55453-209-4(4))* Kids Can Pr., Ltd. CAN. Dist: Hachette Bk. Group.
Burn, Michael. Childhood at Oriol. 2005. (ENG., Illus.). 360p. pap. 16.95 *(978-1-885586-32-2(9))* Turtle Point Pr.
Burshek, Edward & Burshek, Tonja. Explorers of the Word: Episode 1: the Creation. Peterson, Melanie, illus. 2007. (ENG.). 76p. per. 19.95 *(978-1-4241-6691-6(8))* America Star Bks.
Bush, Laura. Our Great Big Backyard. Rogers, Jacqueline, illus. 2018. (ENG.). 40p. (J). (gr. -1-3). pap. 8.99 *(978-0-06-246841-3(3),* HarperCollins) HarperCollins Pubs.
Bush, Laura & Hager, Jenna Bush. Our Great Big Backyard. Rogers, Jacqueline, illus. 2016. (ENG.). 40p. (J). (gr. -1-3). 18.99 *(978-0-06-246835-2(9),* HarperCollins) HarperCollins Pubs.
Buske, Jody. Wilderness Awakening. 2006. 108p. pap. 19.95 *(978-1-4241-2685-9(1))* PublishAmerica, Inc.
Cali, Davide & Chaud, Benjamin. The Truth about My Unbelievable Summer ... 2016. (ENG., Illus.). 44p. (J). (gr. 1-4). 12.99 *(978-1-4521-4483-2(4))* Chronicle Bks. LLC.
Candlewick Press. Peppa Pig & the Great Vacation. 2014. (Peppa Pig Ser.). (ENG.). 32p. (J). (-k). 14.99 *(978-0-7636-6986-7(5),* Candlewick Entertainment) Candlewick Pr.
Candlewick Press Editors. Peppa Pig & the Great Vacation. 2015. (Peppa Pig Ser.). lib. bdg. 16.00 *(978-0-606-36857-5(4))* Turtleback.
Capucilli, Alyssa Satin. Biscuit's First Trip. 2010. (Biscuit 8x8 Ser.). (J). lib. bdg. 13.55 *(978-0-606-10115-8(2))* Turtleback.
Carey, Rosa Nouchette. Uncle Max. 2007. pap. *(978-1-4065-1269-4(9))* Dodo Pr.
Carr, Annie Roe. Nan Sherwoods Winter Holidays or Rescuin. 2007. pap. *(978-1-4065-1296-0(6))* Dodo Pr.
Carroll, D. L. Sir Licksalot & the Island Fools. 2012. 120p. pap. 19.95 *(978-1-4626-8092-4(5))* America Star Bks.
Carson, John E. & Carson, Marlene R. The Wire Forest of Peru. 2007. (Ramblin' Rose Ser.). 205p. (YA). (gr. 8-12). per. 8.99 *(978-0-9776043-9-5(X))* Aspirations Media, Inc.
Champman, Joan. Val's Vacation, 1 vol. 2006. (Neighborhood Readers Ser.). (ENG.). 16p. (gr. 1-2). pap. 6.50 *(978-1-4042-6990-3(8),* 811719e2-1d1b-4665-9465-9d71a2df88fe, Rosen Classroom) Rosen Publishing Group, Inc., The.
Chandler, Ann. Siena Summer, 1 vol. 2009. (ENG., Illus.). 142p. (YA). (gr. 8-12). pap. 12.95 *(978-1-896580-17-3(3))* Tradewind Bks. CAN. Dist: Orca Bk. Pubs. USA.
Chase, L. P. Elliot Stone & the Mystery of the Summer Vacation Sea Monster. DiRocco, Carl, illus. 2011. (ENG.). 165p. (J). pap. 8.99 *(978-0-9792918-7-6(9))* Blue Marlin Pubns.
Chittenden, Charlotte E. What Two Children Did. 2007. (ENG., Illus.). 132p. per. *(978-1-4065-1360-8(1))* Dodo Pr.
Christiansen, Rebecca. Maybe in Paris. 2017. (ENG.). 224p. (YA). (gr. 6-6). 16.99 *(978-1-5107-0880-8(4),* Sky Pony Pr.) Skyhorse Publishing Co., Inc.
Christie, Ed. The Sweet Smell of Rotten Eggs: Volume Two, the Dude Ranch Rangers. 2009. 108p. pap. 10.95 *(978-1-4401-3764-8(1))* iUniverse, Inc.
Christopherson, Keven. Adventures of the Sky Kids: Lost Treasure of Kolob Canyon. 2005. 58p. pap. 16.95 *(978-1-4137-6514-4(9))* America Star Bks.
Clover, Peter. Rescue Riders: Race Against Time. l.t. ed. 2007. 88p. per. *(978-1-905665-29-7(6))* Pollinger In Print.

TUV

Conforto, Lisa. The Very Compromising Adventures of Thumby Blackstone, 1 vol. 2010. 34p. 24.95 *(978-1-4512-0270-0(9))* PublishAmerica, Inc.
Cook, Jessica & Stephens, Michael. What If Mommy Took a Vacation? 2011. 28p. pap. 13.99 *(978-1-4634-3601-8(7))* AuthorHouse.
Corwin, Jeff. Your Backyard Is Wild: Junior Explorer Series Book 1. 2009. 96p. (J). (gr. 1-3). 4.99 *(978-0-14-241404-0(2),* Puffin Books) Penguin Young Readers Group.
Cottrell-Bentley, Lisa M. Wright on Time: Collection 1. Bauerle, Tanja, illus. 2012. 376p. pap. 19.99 *(978-1-937848-00-2(0))* Do Life Right, Inc.
—Wright on Time: Minnesota. Bauerle, Tanja, illus. 2012. 126p. pap. 12.99 *(978-1-937848-02-6(7))* Do Life Right, Inc.
Cotugno, Katie. 9 Days & 9 Nights. (ENG.). (YA). (gr. 8). 2019. 288p. pap. 9.99 *(978-0-06-267410-4(2))* 2018. 272p. 17.99 *(978-0-06-267409-8(9))* HarperCollins Pubs. (Balzer & Bray).
Couloumbis, Audrey. Lexie. Denos, Julia, illus. 2012. (ENG.). 208p. (J). (gr. 3-7). pap. 6.99 *(978-0-375-85633-4(1),* Yearling) Random Hse. Children's Bks.
Cousins, Lucy. Maisy Goes on Vacation: A Maisy First Experiences Book. Cousins, Lucy, illus. 2012. (Maisy Ser.). (ENG., Illus.). 32p. (J). (gr. -1-2). pap. 7.99 *(978-0-7636-6039-0(6))* Candlewick Pr.
Cowan, Charlotte. Moose with Loose Poops. Neal, Penelope, illus. 2008. (Dr. Hippo Ser.). (ENG.). 32p. (J). (gr. -1-2). 17.95 *(978-0-9753516-5-9(6))* Hippocratic Pr., The.
Cowdell, Nikki. The Bradshaw Vacation. 2008. 77p. pap. 12.33 *(978-1-4092-3667-2(6))* Lulu Pr., Inc.
Crane, C. H. A Christmas Quest: A Young Boy's Unexpected Christmas Vacation. 2013. 122p. (gr. 4-6). 22.33 *(978-1-4907-0807-2(3));* pap. 12.33 *(978-1-4907-0808-9(1))* Trafford Publishing.
Cross, P. C. Summer Job: A Virgil & Cy Mystery. 2008. 260p. pap. 16.95 *(978-0-595-50921-8(5))* iUniverse, Inc.
Cuillain, Adam, et al. The Pirates on Holiday. Van Wyk, Rupert, illus. 2014. (Race Ahead with Reading Ser.). (ENG.). 32p. (J). (gr. 2-2). *(978-0-7787-1311-1(3))* Crabtree Publishing Co.
Culbertson, Jan E. The Legend of Dunsmoor Manor. 2006. 88p. pap. 13.95 *(978-1-58909-348-5(8))* Bookstand Publishing.
—The Legend of the Lost Tiki. 2006. 95p. (YA). pap. 13.95 *(978-1-58909-315-7(1))* Bookstand Publishing.
Cummings, Quasheba Giri. The World's First Submarine. 2008. 20p. pap. 15.49 *(978-1-4389-1273-8(0))* AuthorHouse.
Curious George Takes a Trip (Reader Level 1) 2007. (Curious George TV Ser.). (ENG., Illus.). 24p. (J). (gr. -1-3). pap. 4.99 *(978-0-618-88403-2(3),* 491698, Clarion Bks.) HarperCollins Pubs.
Daniels, Darla. Carrie Goes Camping. 2011. 24p. pap. 16.95 *(978-1-4626-0642-9(3))* America Star Bks.
—The Magic Ring: Summer Vacation in London. 2012. 30p. 16.95 *(978-1-4626-6252-4(8))* America Star Bks.
Daniels, J. M. The Secret of the Little Dutch Doll. 2009. 68p. pap. 25.49 *(978-1-4343-9356-2(9))* AuthorHouse.
Danziger, Paula. What a Trip, Amber Brown. 2003. (Amber Brown Ser.). (Illus.). (J). (gr. -1-2). audio compact disk 28.95 *(978-1-59112-569-3(3))* Live Oak Media.
Davie, Jan. Arthur's Amulet. 2004. 86p. pap. *(978-1-84401-228-2(X))* Athena Pr.
Davies, Jacqueline. The House Takes a Vacation, 0 vols. White, Lee, illus. 2013. (ENG.). 34p. (J). (gr. k-3). pap. 9.99 *(978-1-4778-1619-6(4),* 9781477816196, Two Lions) Amazon Publishing.
Delhohne, Jean-Philippe. Visit to Another Planet. 2004. (Illus.). 31p. (J). (gr. k-4). reprint ed. *(978-0-7567-7768-5(2))* DIANE Publishing Co.
dePaola, Tomie. Strega Nona Takes a Vacation. dePaola, Tomie, illus. 2003. (Illus.). 32p. (J). (gr. -1-3). pap. 8.99 *(978-0-14-250076-7(3),* Puffin Books) Penguin Young Readers Group.
—Strega Nona Takes a Vacation. dePaola, Tomie, illus. 2003. (Illus.). (J). (gr. -1-3). 13.65 *(978-0-7569-1469-1(8))* Perfection Learning Corp.
DeSio, Delores . Up a Tree with Mary Mcphee: A Mystery for Children. 2006. 86p. pap. 16.95 *(978-1-4241-4309-2(8))* PublishAmerica, Inc.
Destiny, A. & Helms, Rhonda. Sparks in Scotland. 2015. (Flirt Ser.). (ENG.). 224p. (YA). (gr. 7). pap. 9.99 *(978-1-4814-2121-8(2),* Simon Pulse) Simon Pulse.
Deutsch, Neil. Rose & the Pelican. 2013. 32p. pap. 19.99 *(978-1-4817-0947-7(X))* AuthorHouse.
Deutsch, Stacia. Spirit Riding Free: Lucky's Diary. 2018. (ENG., Illus.). 176p. (J). (gr. 3-7). 9.99 *(978-0-316-47636-2(6))* Little, Brown Bks. for Young Readers.
Diesen, Deborah. The Pout-Pout Fish, Far, Far from Home. Hanna, Dan, illus. (Pout-Pout Fish Adventure Ser.). (ENG.). 32p. (J). 2019. bds. 8.99 *(978-0-374-31078-3(5),* 900194752) 2017. 16.99 *(978-0-374-30194-1(8),* 900141733) Farrar, Straus & Giroux. (Farrar, Straus & Giroux (BYR)).
Douglas, Ryke Leigh. The Big Wheel. 2010. (Illus.). 21p. (J). pap. 15.95 *(978-1-4327-4495-3(X))* Outskirts Pr., Inc.
Dower, Laura. Give Me a Break. 2004. 166p. (J). lib. bdg. 16.92 *(978-1-4242-0649-0(9))* Fitzgerald Bks.
Dudek, V. A. Soldiers of Fate. 2009. 94p. pap. 15.99 *(978-1-4415-2702-8(8))* Xlibris Corp.
Earls, Nick. After Summer. 2005. (ENG.). 240p. (YA). (gr. 7). pap. 13.99 *(978-0-618-45781-6(X),* 483009, Clarion Bks.) HarperCollins Pubs.
Ellen, Connie. Marvel Mansion Gang. 2012. 114p. 22.19 *(978-1-4269-6666-8(0))* Trafford Publishing.
Elliott, Rebecca. Eva at the Beach: a Branches Book (Owl Diaries #14) Elliott, Rebecca, illus. 2021. (Owl Diaries: 14). (ENG., Illus.). 80p. (J). (gr. k-2). pap. 5.99 *(978-1-338-29879-6(8))* Scholastic, Inc.
—Eva at the Beach: a Branches Book (Owl Diaries #14) (Library Edition) Elliott, Rebecca, illus. 2021. (Owl Diaries: 14). (ENG., Illus.). 80p. (J). (gr. k-2). lib. bdg. 24.99 *(978-1-338-29881-9(X))* Scholastic, Inc.
Emzer, Counselor. The Day Before Summer Vacation. 2004. 31p. pap. 24.95 *(978-1-4137-2680-0(1))* PublishAmerica, Inc.
Enchanted Lion Books. Vacation. 2018. (ENG., Illus.). 128p. (J). 24.95 *(978-1-59270-246-6(5))* Enchanted Lion Bks., LLC.
Enright, Elizabeth. Gone-Away Lake. Krush, Beth & Krush, Joe, illus. 2006. 256p. (J). (gr. 4-8). reprint ed. pap. 6.00 *(978-1-4223-5436-0(9))* DIANE Publishing Co.
Falconer, Ian. Olivia Goes to Venice. Falconer, Ian, illus. 2010. (ENG., Illus.). 48p. (J). (gr. -1-2). 19.99 *(978-1-4169-9674-3(5),* Atheneum Bks. for Young Readers) Simon & Schuster Children's Publishing.
Feldkamp, Jim And Cate. The Adventures of Tommy & Clara on Mount Catherine. 2008. 32p. pap. 14.49 *(978-1-4389-1366-7(4))* AuthorHouse.
Fenton, Geleta. Joel's Adventure at Sea. Siniard, Ricky, illus. 2013. 50p. (J). mass mkt. 9.95 *(978-0-9824433-2-3(3))* Octopus Publishing Co.
Finley, Martha. Elsie's Vacation & after Events. 2006. 27.95 *(978-1-4218-2997-5(5));* pap. 12.95 *(978-1-4218-3097-1(3))* 1st World Publishing, Inc.
—Elsie's Vacation & after Events. 2018. (ENG., Illus.). 192p. (YA). (gr. 7-12). pap. *(978-93-5297-360-6(7))* Alpha Editions.
—Elsie's Vacation & after Events. 2017. (ENG., Illus.). (J). 23.95 *(978-1-374-90322-7(1));* pap. 13.95 *(978-1-374-90321-0(3))* Capital Communications, Inc.
—Elsie's Vacation & after Events. 2018. (ENG., Illus.). 300p. (J). pap. 15.95 *(978-1-378-55558-3(9))* Creative Media Partners, LLC.
Flaggert, Candy. Ok, Said Carrie Katherine, 1 vol. Chipka, Sandy, illus. 2008. (ENG.). 25p. 24.95 *(978-1-60563-502-6(2))* America Star Bks.
Fogelin, Adrian. My Brother's Hero, 1 vol. 2005. (Neighborhood Novels Ser.: 3). 224p. (J). (gr. 3-7). reprint ed. pap. 7.95 *(978-1-56145-352-8(8))* Peachtree Publishing Co. Inc.
Frazee, Marla. A Couple of Boys Have the Best Week Ever. Frazee, Marla, illus. 2008. (ENG., Illus.). 40p. (J). (gr. 1-4). 17.99 *(978-0-15-206020-6(0),* 1198080, Clarion Bks.) HarperCollins Pubs.
Fromental, Jean-Luc. Oops! Jolivet, Joëlle, illus. 2010. (ENG.). 42p. (J). (gr. -1-3). 17.95 *(978-0-8109-8749-4(X),* 681701) Abrams, Inc.
Gallagher, Diana G. Beach Blues: The Complicated Life of Claudia Cristina Cortez, 1 vol. Garvey, Brann, illus. 2008. (Claudia Cristina Cortez Ser.). (ENG.). 88p. (J). (gr. 4-8). pap. 6.10 *(978-1-4342-0869-9(9),* 95230, Stone Arch Bks.) Capstone.
Garsee, Linmarie. Annabelle's Vacation with Grandma Hayley: A Mountain Quiltfest Adventure. 2012. 50p. pap. 21.99 *(978-1-4772-7737-9(4))* AuthorHouse.
Gateley, Edwina. God Goes on Vacation. Gateley, Edwina, illus. 2009. (ENG., Illus.). 32p. (Orig.). (J). pap. 9.95 *(978-0-8091-6747-0(6))* Paulist Pr.
Gay, Marie-Louise. Summer in the City. 2013. 148p. pap. *(978-1-4596-6493-7(0))* ReadHowYouWant.com, Ltd.
Gay, Marie-Louise & Homel, David. Travels with My Family, 1 vol. 2007. (Travels with My Family Ser.: 1). (ENG., Illus.). 120p. (J). (gr. 2-5). pap. 8.95 *(978-0-88899-833-0(3))* Groundwood Bks. CAN. Dist: Publishers Group West (PGW).
Gehrke, William & Gehrke, Dolores. Sonia's Choice. 2011. 28p. pap. 15.99 *(978-1-4634-0825-1(0))* AuthorHouse.
Geraldi, Michele J. Pennies at Piper Park. 2009. 24p. pap. 12.99 *(978-1-4389-2829-6(7))* AuthorHouse.
Germain, Kerry. Kimo's Summer Vacation. Montes, Keoni, illus. 2003. 52p. (J). 12.95 *(978-0-9705889-4-4(1))* Island Paradise Publishing.
Gillam, David. Gingertown. Gilliam, David, illus. 2012. 216p. (J). 29.99 *(978-1-60131-122-1(2))* Big Tent Bks.
Gingras, Marie Claude. Let's Spend Summer with Fred. 2012. 198p. 24.95 *(978-1-4626-4413-1(9))* America Star Bks.
Ginoschio De Osceola, Ibrahim. Enter the Corn Bunny, Vol. 1. 2007. 56p. per. 8.95 *(978-0-595-45273-6(6))* iUniverse, Inc.
Glass, June. Poker Fat: Takes a Vacation. 2005. (J). pap. 9.00 *(978-0-8059-6150-8(X))* Dorrance Publishing Co., Inc.
Glatt, Lisa, et al. Abigail Iris: The One & Only. 2009. (Abigail Iris Ser.). (ENG., Illus.). 160p. (J). (gr. 4-6). 21.19 *(978-0-8027-9782-7(2),* 9780802797827) Walker & Co.
Gonzalez, Genaro. A So-Called Vacation. 2009. 192p. (YA). (gr. 9-18). pap. 10.95 *(978-1-55885-545-8(9),* Piñata Books) Arte Publico Pr.
Goode, Suzi. The Lost Wizard Series Bk 1. 2007. pap. 11.95 *(978-1-59374-817-3(5))* Whiskey Creek Pr., LLC.
Goscinny, René. Nicholas on Vacation. Bell, Anthea, tr. Sempé, Jean-Jacques, illus. 2013. (ENG.). 136p. (J). (gr. 1-4). pap. 9.95 *(978-0-7148-6224-8(X))* Phaidon Pr., Inc.
—Nicholas on Vacation. Bell, Anthea, tr. Sempé, Jean-Jacques, illus. rev. ed. 2006. (ENG.). 132p. (gr. 8-17). 19.95 *(978-0-7148-4678-1(3))* Phaidon Pr., Inc.
Gowar, Mick. Dad's Van. 2009. (ENG., Illus.). 24p. (J). pap. *(978-0-7787-3897-8(3));* lib. bdg. *(978-0-7787-3866-4(3))* Crabtree Publishing Co.
Gram, Golden. Gail the Snail: Goes on Vacation. 2008. 20p. pap. 11.95 *(978-1-59858-860-6(5))* Dog Ear Publishing, LLC.
Grandpa Casey. Another Müsh-Mice Adventure: Florida Vacation, 1 vol. Brennan, Lisa, illus. 2009. 45p. pap. 24.95 *(978-1-60813-329-1(X))* America Star Bks.
Gray, Kes. Daisy & the Trouble with Kittens. Sharratt, Nick & Parsons, Garry, illus. 2010. (Daisy Ser.). (ENG.). 256p. (J). (gr. 2-4). pap. 11.99 *(978-1-86230-834-3(9),* Red Fox) Random House Children's Books GBR. Dist: Independent Pubs. Group.
Greene, Stephanie. Princess Posey & the Crazy, Lazy Vacation. Roth Sisson, Stephanie, illus. 2016. (Princess Posey, First Grader Ser.: 10). (ENG.). 96p. (J). (gr. k-3). 6.99 *(978-0-14-751293-2(X),* Puffin Books) Penguin Young Readers Group.
Greenwald, Lisa. Dog Beach Unleashed: The Seagate Summers Book Two. 2015. (Seagate Summers Ser.). (ENG., Illus.). 36p. (J). (gr. 5-9). 15.95 *(978-1-4197-1481-8(3),* 1072001, Amulet Bks.) Abrams, Inc.
—Dog Beach Unleashed (the Seagate Summers #2) 2016. (ENG.). 256p. (J). (gr. 3-7). pap. 7.95 *(978-1-4197-2056-7(2),* 1072003, Amulet Bks.) Abrams, Inc.
Greer, Hannah. The Lighthouse Summer Greer, Tica, illus. 2009. 156p. pap. 24.95 *(978-1-60813-493-9(8))* America Star Bks.
Grey, C. R. Flight of the King. 2016. (Animas Ser.: 2). (ENG.). 320p. (J). (gr. 3-7). pap. 7.99 *(978-1-4231-8467-6(X))* Hyperion Bks. for Children.
Gutknecht, Allison. Spring Break Mistake. 2017. (Mix Ser.). (ENG., Illus.). 240p. (J). (gr. 4-8). pap. 7.99 *(978-1-4814-7153-4(8),* Simon & Schuster/Paula Wiseman Bks.) Simon & Schuster/Paula Wiseman Bks.
Gutman, Dan. Back to School, Weird Kids Rule! 2014. (My Weird School Ser.). (J). lib. bdg. 16.00 *(978-0-606-35502-5(2))* Turtleback.
—The Get Rich Quick Club. (ENG.). 128p. (J). 2006. (gr. 3-7). pap. 6.99 *(978-0-06-053442-4(7),* HarperCollins) 2004. 15.99 *(978-0-06-053440-0(0))* HarperCollins Pubs.
Haddix, Margaret Peterson. The Summer of Broken Things. 2018. (ENG., Illus.). 400p. (YA). (gr. 7). 17.99 *(978-1-4814-1764-8(9))* Simon & Schuster Children's Publishing.
Haesche, Richard Paul, Sr. The Treasure of Pirates Cave. 2007. (ENG.). 378p. (YA). 11.99 *(978-0-9798536-7-8(2))* Kreative X-Pressions Pubns.
Hale, Shannon & Hale, Dean. The Princess in Black Takes a Vacation. Pham, LeUyen, illus. 2016. (J). (gr. k-3). (Princess in Black Ser.: 4). (ENG.). 96p. 15.99 *(978-0-7636-6512-8(6));* 87p. *(978-1-5182-4386-8(X))* Candlewick Pr.
Hall, Angela Marie. Priscilla Pennybrook: Hello World, I Have Arrived!, 1 vol. 2009. 55p. pap. 16.95 *(978-1-61582-899-9(0))* America Star Bks.
Han, Jenny. It's Not Summer Without You. (Summer I Turned Pretty Ser.). (ENG.). (YA). (gr. 7). 2011. 320p. pap. 11.99 *(978-1-4169-9556-2(0))* 2010. 288p. 19.99 *(978-1-4169-9555-5(2))* 2022. (Illus.). 320p. pap. 11.99 *(978-1-6659-3799-3(8))* Simon & Schuster Bks. For Young Readers. (Simon & Schuster Bks. For Young Readers).
—The Summer I Turned Pretty. (Summer I Turned Pretty Ser.). (ENG.). (YA). (gr. 7). 2010. 304p. pap. 11.99 *(978-1-4169-6829-0(6))* 2009. 288p. 19.99 *(978-1-4169-6823-8(7))* Simon & Schuster Bks. For Young Readers. (Simon & Schuster Bks. For Young Readers).
—The Summer I Turned Pretty. 2010. lib. bdg. 22.10 *(978-0-606-14529-9(X))* Turtleback.
—We'll Always Have Summer. 2011. (YA). 1.25 *(978-1-4640-1977-7(0))* Recorded Bks., Inc.
—We'll Always Have Summer. (Summer I Turned Pretty Ser.). (ENG., Illus.). (YA). (gr. 7). 2012. 320p. pap. 11.99 *(978-1-4169-9559-3(5))* 2011. 304p. 19.99 *(978-1-4169-9558-6(7))* Simon & Schuster Bks. For Young Readers. (Simon & Schuster Bks. For Young Readers).
Hancock, H. Irving. The High School Boys' Fishing Trip: Or, Dick & Co. 's Rivals in the Wilderness. 2017. (ENG., Illus.). (J). 23.95 *(978-1-374-93026-1(1))* Capital Communications, Inc.
—The High School Boys in Summer Camp: Or, the Dick Prescott Six Training for the Gridley Eleven. 2017. (ENG., Illus.). (J). 23.95 *(978-1-374-93028-5(8));* pap. 13.95 *(978-1-374-93027-8(X))* Capital Communications, Inc.
Hapka, Catherine, pseud. Vacation in the Wild. 2014. (I Can Read! Level 2 Ser.). (J). lib. bdg. 13.55 *(978-0-606-35064-8(0))* Turtleback.
Hargreaves, Adam. Mr. Adventure. 2016. (Mr. Men & Little Miss Ser.). (ENG., Illus.). 32p. (J). (gr. -1-2). pap. 4.99 *(978-0-451-53415-6(8),* Grosset & Dunlap) Penguin Young Readers Group.
Harvey, Jacqueline. Alice-Miranda on Vacation. 2013. (Alice-Miranda Ser.). (ENG.). 288p. (J). (gr. 2-5). 7.99 *(978-0-385-73996-2(6),* Yearling) Random Hse. Children's Bks.
Harvey, Roland. At the Beach. 2007. (ENG., Illus.). 32p. (J). (gr. -1-k). pap. 13.99 *(978-1-74114-704-9(2))* Allen & Unwin AUS. Dist: Independent Pubs. Group.
Hawthorne, Rachel. Island Girls & Boys. 2005. (ENG.). 336p. (YA). (gr. 9). pap. 8.99 *(978-0-06-075546-1(6),* HarperTeen) HarperCollins Pubs.
Hay, Angela. Grace S Incredible! Unforgettable! Summer! 2012. 38p. pap. 19.99 *(978-1-62419-562-4(8))* Salem Author Services.
Hayes, Celeste. Cacao & the Jaded Orb: A Sphinx & Trevi Adventure. 2011. (Illus.). 62p. (J). pap. 22.95 *(978-0-9785695-2-5(0))* Adam's Creations Publishing, LLC.
Henighan, Tom. Doom Lake Holiday. 2009. (ENG.). 240p. (YA). (gr. 6). pap. 12.99 *(978-1-55002-847-8(2))* Dundurn Pr. CAN. Dist: Publishers Group West (PGW).
Henning, Ann. Cow Patty Patti. 2004. 47p. pap. 24.95 *(978-1-4137-3456-0(1))* PublishAmerica, Inc.
Herman, Alison & Grossman, Lynne. Dolly Goes on Vacation. Eve, Lealand, illus. 2007. 22p. (J). 24.95 *(978-0-9746153-2-5(3))* DMH Pr., Inc.
Herring, Bruce D. The Wizard of Wonderland, 1 vol. 2010. 192p. pap. 24.95 *(978-1-4489-5844-3(X))* America Star Bks.
Hibbs, Gillian. Tilly's Staycation. Hibbs, Gillian, illus. 2014. (Child's Play Library). (ENG., Illus.). 32p. (J). *(978-1-84643-601-7(X))* Child's Play International Ltd.
Hinkelman, Carole & Rebik, Nan. The Herman Chronicles: "Herman the Horrible Trailer Mouse "Herman & the Donkeys " Herman's Midnight Trek " Herman's Vacation. 2012. 84p. (gr. 2-4). pap. 11.50 *(978-1-4669-5202-7(4))* Trafford Publishing.
Hopkins, Cathy. Mates, Dates, & Great Escapes. 2011. (Mates, Dates Ser.). (ENG.). 224p. (YA). (gr. 7). pap. 10.99 *(978-1-4424-3080-8(X),* Simon Pulse) Simon Pulse.
Hordos, Sandra. Marissa Plans a Princess Tea Party. Allen, Joshua, illus. 2010. 28p. pap. 12.49 *(978-1-4520-2557-5(6))* AuthorHouse.
Horsfall, S. J. Jodie & Lilly... & the Fake Mansion. 2009. 58p. pap. 7.50 *(978-0-557-12474-9(3))* Lulu Pr., Inc.
Horvath, Polly. The Vacation, 1 vol. (ENG.). 208p. pap. 12.95 *(978-0-88899-693-0(4))* Groundwood Bks. CAN. Dist: Publishers Group West (PGW).
Huelin, Jodi. Alvin's Easter Break. 2014. (ENG., Illus.). 24p. (J). (gr. -1-3). pap. 3.99 *(978-0-06-225222-7(4),* HarperFestival) HarperCollins Pubs.
Hueller, Andy. Dizzy Fantastic & Her Flying Bicycle. 2010. (Illus.). 155p. (J). pap. 8.99 *(978-1-59955-395-5(3))* Cedar Fort, Inc./CFI Distribution.
Ibeh, Chinwe. Tishan Worst Moment. 2010. 28p. pap. 21.99 *(978-1-4500-9385-9(X))* Xlibris Corp.
Ireland, Mary E. & Brandstaedter, German H. Vacaciones de Eric.Las. Clingan, Darrell, tr. 2011.Tr. of Eric's Vacation.
(Illus.). 237p. (YA). (gr. 11). pap. 7.25 *(978-0-7399-7766-8(0))* Rod & Staff Pubs., Inc.
Irwin, Chris. Nightmare of Shadows. 2007. 140p. pap. 18.95 *(978-0-615-15008-6(X))* Irwin, Christine.
Irwin, Inez Haynes. Maida's Little House. 2004. reprint ed. pap. 27.95 *(978-1-4179-4236-7(3))* Kessinger Publishing, LLC.
Joan, Marler. Secrets of the Wind. 2006. pap. *(978-1-888251-37-1(9))* Voice & Vision Pubns.
Joseph, Curtis M. Order of Godalming: Max Baxter, 1 vol. 2009. 64p. pap. 19.95 *(978-1-60836-525-8(5))* America Star Bks.
Jules, Jacqueline. The Beach Trip. Smith, Kim, illus. 2016. (Sofia Martinez Ser.). (ENG.). 32p. (J). (gr. k-2). lib. bdg. 21.32 *(978-1-4795-8719-3(2),* 131113, Picture Window Bks.) Capstone.
Jungle Crossing. 2011. (ENG.). 228p. (J). (gr. 5-7). pap. 13.99 *(978-0-547-55009-1(X),* 1450218, Clarion Bks.) HarperCollins Pubs.
Keast, Ellen Frances. A Rainy Week. 2011. 16p. pap. 10.00 *(978-1-60976-777-8(2),* Eloquent Bks.) Strategic Book Publishing & Rights Agency (SBPRA).
Kessler, Liz. Poppy the Pirate Dog. Phillips, Mike, illus. 2015. (Candlewick Sparks Ser.). (ENG.). 64p. (J). (gr. k-4). pap. 5.99 *(978-0-7636-7661-2(6))* Candlewick Pr.
—A Year Without Autumn. 2012. (ENG.). 304p. (J). (gr. 4-7). pap. 9.99 *(978-0-7636-6060-4(4))* Candlewick Pr.
Khalsa, Dayal Kaur. My Family Vacation. 2003. (Illus.). 24p. (J). (gr. 1-4). pap. 6.95 *(978-0-88776-629-9(3),* Tundra Bks.) Tundra Bks. CAN. Dist: Penguin Random Hse. LLC.
Kinney, Jeff. The Getaway. 2018. (Diary of a Wimpy Kid Ser.). (ENG., Illus.). 224p. (J). (gr. 3-7). pap. 7.99 *(978-1-4197-3266-9(8),* Amulet Bks.) Abrams, Inc.
—The Getaway. (Diary of a Wimpy Kid Ser.: 12). 2018. lib. bdg. 29.40 *(978-0-606-41279-7(4))* 2017. (J). lib. bdg. 25.70 *(978-0-606-40451-8(1))* Turtleback.
—The Long Haul. (CHI.). (J). 2015. 368p. (gr. 4-8). pap. *(978-986-6104-59-6(1))* 2014. *(978-986-6104-52-7(4))* DaskoviK, Izdatel'sko-torgovaja korporacija.
—The Long Haul. 2014. (JPN.). 221p. (J). *(978-4-591-14196-0(9))* Poplar Publishing.
—The Long Haul. 2013. (Diary of a Wimpy Kid Ser.: 9). (J). 43.75 *(978-1-4906-4058-7(4));* 40.75 *(978-1-4906-4383-0(4))* Recorded Bks., Inc.
—The Long Haul. 2014. (Diary of a Wimpy Kid Ser.: 9). (SWE.). (J). lib. bdg. 25.70 *(978-0-606-36074-6(3))* Turtleback.
Kirby, Stan. Captain Awesome Takes Flight. O'Connor, George, illus. 2017. (Captain Awesome Ser.: 19). (ENG.). 128p. (J). (gr. k-4). pap. 5.99 *(978-1-4814-9441-0(4),* Little Simon) Little Simon.
Kirkpatrick, Teresa. The Adventures of Four Friends on Vacation, 1 vol. 2009. 119p. pap. 19.95 *(978-1-60836-927-0(7))* America Star Bks.
Knowles, Kent. Lucius & the Storm. Knowles, Kent, illus. 2007. (Illus.). 32p. (J). (gr. -1-3). 15.95 *(978-1-60108-005-9(0))* Red Cygnet Pr.
Kondrchek, Jamie & Rasemas, Joe. What Day Is It? (Que Dia Es Hoy?) Vega, Eida de la, tr. Rasemas, Joe, illus. 2009. (Day in the Life Ser.). (SPA & ENG., Illus.). 32p. (J). (gr. -1-1). 25.70 *(978-1-58415-838-7(7))* Mitchell Lane Pubs.
Kraft, Erik P. Lenny & Mel's Summer Vacation. Kraft, Erik P., illus. 2012. (Ready-For-Chapters Ser.). (ENG., Illus.). 64p. (J). (gr. 2-5). pap. 6.99 *(978-0-689-86874-0(X),* Simon & Schuster/Paula Wiseman Bks.) Simon & Schuster/Paula Wiseman Bks.
Krulik, Nancy. Super Special: Going Overboard! John and Wendy, illus. 2012. (Katie Kazoo, Switcheroo Ser.: No. 9). 144p. (J). (gr. 2-4). pap. 6.99 *(978-0-448-45681-2(8),* Grosset & Dunlap) Penguin Young Readers Group.
LaBree Stute, Lela. Summer Pugs. 2010. (ENG.). 44p. pap. 19.99 *(978-0-557-41763-6(5))* Lulu Pr., Inc.
Langlois, Annie. L' Evasion d'Alfred le Dindon. Beaulieu, Jimmÿ, illus. 2004. (Roman Jeunesse Ser.). (FRE.). 96p. (J). (gr. 4-7). pap. *(978-2-89021-687-7(X))* Diffusion du livre Mirabel (DLM).
Leray, Merrill. The Kidnapping. 2009. 58p. pap. 15.99 *(978-1-4415-4380-6(5))* Xlibris Corp.
Lewis, Steven & Parker, Shelley. Return to Allapatria. 2006. 395p. (J). pap. *(978-0-9547092-9-7(2))* Accent Pr. Ltd.
Lloyd-Jones, Sally. Goldfish on Vacation. Espinosa, Leo, illus. 2018. (ENG.). 40p. (J). (gr. -1-3). 17.99 *(978-0-385-38611-1(7),* Schwartz & Wade Bks.) Random Hse. Children's Bks.
Logan, Dottie Colegrove. Picnic on the Beach: Nana & Me Series, Book Three. 2010. 16p. 12.99 *(978-1-4490-3689-8(9))* AuthorHouse.
London, Jonathan. Froggy Goes to Hawaii. Remkiewicz, Frank, illus. 2012. (Froggy Ser.). 32p. (J). (gr. -1-k). pap. 7.99 *(978-0-14-242119-2(7),* Puffin Books) Penguin Young Readers Group.
—Froggy Goes to Hawaii. 2012. (Froggy Ser.). lib. bdg. 17.20 *(978-0-606-26083-1(8))* Turtleback.
Lopez, Christopher P. The Absolute Truth about Lying. Racine, Victoria, illus. 2011. 36p. pap. 24.95 *(978-1-4626-3245-9(9))* America Star Bks.
Loving, Winifred "Oyoko". My Grandma Loves to Play. 2013. 28p. pap. 16.99 *(978-1-4669-7405-0(2))* Trafford Publishing.
Mackintosh, David. Waiting for Chicken Smith. Mackintosh, David, illus. 2019. (ENG., Illus.). 32p. (J). (gr. -1-2). 16.99 *(978-1-5362-0771-2(3))* Candlewick Pr.
Mackler, Carolyn. Tangled. 2011. (ENG.). 336p. (YA). (gr. 9-12). pap. 10.99 *(978-0-06-173106-8(4),* HarperTeen) HarperCollins Pubs.
Marsh, Carole. The Secret of Skullcracker Swamp. 2006. (Pretty Darn Scary Mysteries Ser.). (Illus.). 113p. (YA). (gr. 7-14). 14.95 *(978-0-635-06238-3(0));* (J). (gr. 3-5). per. 7.99 *(978-0-635-06234-5(8))* Gallopade International.
Matas, Carol. Far. 2008. (Freak Ser.). (ENG.). 152p. (J). (gr. 5-18). pap. *(978-1-55470-094-3(9))* Me to We.
McGirr, Randel W. Bible Camp. 2007. 176p. per. 13.95 *(978-0-595-44663-6(9))* iUniverse, Inc.
McKay, Hilary. Lulu & the Dog from the Sea. 2014. (Lulu Ser.: 2). (J). lib. bdg. 14.75 *(978-0-606-41567-5(X))* Turtleback.
McLean, Matthew. A Bewitching Summer, 1 vol. 2009. 100p. pap. 19.95 *(978-1-60836-686-6(3))* America Star Bks.

McPhail, David. Pig Pig Returns. McPhail, David, illus. 2011. (ENG., Illus.). 32p. (J). (gr. -1-3). 15.95 *(978-1-58089-356-5(2))* Charlesbridge Publishing, Inc.
Meadows, Daisy. Joy the Summer Vacation Fairy. Ripper, Georgie, illus. 2007. (Rainbow Magic — Special Edition Ser.). 177p. (gr. -1-3). lib. bdg. 17.20 *(978-1-4177-7081-6(3))* Turtleback.
Menefee, Angelo K. Billy's First Summer Vacation. 2007. (Illus.). (J). per. 16.95 *(978-1-60002-249-4(9))* Mountain Valley Publishing, LLC.
Menge, Dawn. Queen Vernita Visits the Blue Ice Mountains. 2009. 32p. (J). pap. 19.95 *(978-1-4327-1169-6(5))* Outskirts Pr., Inc.
Millner, Robert W. The Chicken Coop Gang. 2011. 130p. 29.99 *(978-1-4568-5517-8(4))*; pap. 19.99 *(978-1-4568-5516-1(6))* Xlibris Corp.
Mincin, Sabrina. Catching a Shooting Star. 2012. 28p. pap. 12.95 *(978-1-4575-0862-2(1))* Dog Ear Publishing, LLC.
Mitchell, Charlie. The Great M & M Caper. 2009. 82p. pap. 15.99 *(978-1-4415-2242-9(5))* Xlibris Corp.
Montague, Chester. Timmy's Vacation. 2008. 40p. pap. 24.95 *(978-1-60441-225-3(9))* America Star Bks.
Montgomery, E. j. Hailey Walker & the Mystery of the Absent Professor. 2013. 180p. pap. 13.95 *(978-1-4575-2068-6(0))* Dog Ear Publishing, LLC.
Morgan, Retta & Morgan, Kris. Love Hates. 2011. 152p. pap. 11.99 *(978-1-4567-1448-2(1))* AuthorHouse.
Moundlic, Charlotte. The Bathing Costume: Or the Worst Vacation of My Life. Tallec, Olivier, illus. 2013. (ENG.). 40p. (J). (gr. k-3). 15.95 *(978-1-59270-141-4(8))* Enchanted Lion Bks., LLC.
Mumford, Carole. Christmas Vacation in Colorado: A Magnificent Six Adventure, 1 vol. 2009. 75p. pap. 19.95 *(978-1-60749-231-3(8))* America Star Bks.
Mun-Ensor, Michelle. Aloh. 2011. 32p. pap. 24.95 *(978-1-4560-9848-3(9))* America Star Bks.
Napoli, Donna Jo & Johnston, Shelagh. Hotel Jungle. Spengler, Kenneth, tr. Spengler, Kenneth, illus. 2004. 33p. (J). 15.95 *(978-1-59336-002-3(9))*; pap. *(978-1-59336-003-0(7))* Mondo Publishing.
Nash, Tim. The Club. 2009. 112p. pap. 12.49 *(978-1-4490-2087-3(9))* AuthorHouse.
Norman, Donna Marie. Just a Swim? Widowati, Marini, illus. 2008. 29p. pap. 24.95 *(978-1-60672-182-7(8))* America Star Bks.
North, Merry. My Vacation: Picture, Play, & Tote. 2003. (Picture, Play & Tote-Book Ser.). (Illus.). 10p. (J). (gr. -1-18). bds. 5.99 *(978-1-57151-720-3(0))* Playhouse Publishing.
Oakley, Graham. Church Mice Take a Break. (ENG., Illus.). 25p. (J). 17.99 *(978-0-340-73254-0(7))* Hodder & Stoughton GBR. Dist: Trafalgar Square Publishing.
Oceanak, Karla. Artsy-Fartsy. Spanjer, Kendra, illus. 2016. (Aldo Zelnick Comic Novel Ser.: 1). (ENG.). 160p. (J). (gr. 1-8). pap. 8.95 *(978-1-934649-65-7(1))* Bailiwick Pr.
—Bogus: An Aldo Zelnick Comic Novel. Spanjer, Kendra, illus. 2016. (Aldo Zelnick Comic Novel Ser.: 2). (ENG.). 160p. (J). (gr. 3-7). pap. 8.95 *(978-1-934649-66-4(X))* Bailiwick Pr.
—Cahoots. Spanjer, Kendra, illus. 2011. (Aldo Zelnick Comic Novel Ser.: 3). (ENG.). 151p. (J). (gr. 3-7). 12.95 *(978-1-934649-08-4(2))* Bailiwick Pr.
—Cahoots: An Aldo Zelnick Comic Novel. Spanjer, Kendra, illus. 2016. (Aldo Zelnick Comic Novel Ser.: 3). (ENG.). 160p. (J). (gr. 1-8). pap. 8.95 *(978-1-934649-67-1(8))* Bailiwick Pr.
—Dumbstruck: An Aldo Zelnick Comic Novel. Spanjer, Kendra, illus. 2016. (Aldo Zelnick Comic Novel Ser.: 4). (ENG.). 160p. (J). (gr. 1-8). pap. 8.95 *(978-1-934649-68-8(6))* Bailiwick Pr.
—Egghead: An Aldo Zelnick Comic Novel. Spanjer, Kendra, illus. 2016. (Aldo Zelnick Comic Novel Ser.: 5). (ENG.). 160p. (J). (gr. 1-8). pap. 8.95 *(978-1-934649-69-5(4))* Bailiwick Pr.
—Finicky: An Aldo Zelnick Comic Novel. Spanjer, Kendra, illus. 2016. (Aldo Zelnick Comic Novel Ser.: 6). (ENG.). 160p. (J). (gr. 1-8). pap. 8.95 *(978-1-934649-70-1(8))* Bailiwick Pr.
—Hotdogger: An Aldo Zelnick Comic Novel. Spanjer, Kendra, illus. 2016. (Aldo Zelnick Comic Novel Ser.: 8). (ENG.). 160p. (J). (gr. 1-8). pap. 8.95 *(978-1-934649-72-5(4))* Bailiwick Pr.
—Ignoramus: An Aldo Zelnick Comic Novel. Spanjer, Kendra, illus. 2016. (Aldo Zelnick Comic Novel Ser.: 9). (ENG.). 160p. (J). (gr. 1-8). pap. 8.95 *(978-1-934649-73-2(2))* Bailiwick Pr.
—Logjam. Spanjer, Kendra, illus. 2016. (Aldo Zelnick Comic Novel Ser.: 12). (ENG.). 160p. (gr. 1-8). 12.95 *(978-1-934649-64-0(3))* Bailiwick Pr.
Ockler, Sarah. Twenty Boy Summer. 2010. (ENG.). 320p. (YA). (gr. 7-17). pap. 17.99 *(978-0-316-05158-3(6))* Little, Brown Bks. for Young Readers.
Odhiambo, Tori. Close to Home: The African Savannah. 2012. 32p. pap. 21.99 *(978-1-4691-9510-0(0))* Xlibris Corp.
Oh, Ellen. Spirit Hunters #2: the Island of Monsters. 2018. (Spirit Hunters Ser.: 2). (ENG.). 256p. (J). (gr. 3-7). 16.99 *(978-0-06-243011-3(4)*, HarperCollins) HarperCollins Pubs.
Olds, Laurie. Cars on Vacation. 2009. 24p. pap. 12.25 *(978-1-4490-1633-3(2))* AuthorHouse.
Oso Se Va de Viaje. 2014. (ENG & SPA., Illus.). (J). *(978-1-78285-086-5(0))* Barefoot Bks., Inc.
Papademetriou, Lisa & Minsky, Terri. A Very Lizzie Summer. 2005. (Lizzie Mcguire Super Special Ser.). (Illus.). 265p. (J). *(978-1-4155-9625-8(5))* Disney Pr.
Papell, David. Harlem Awakenings Color Edition. 2007. (ENG.). 50p. pap. *(978-0-615-17931-5(2))* Papell, David.
Parish, Herman. Amelia Bedelia Chapter Book #3: Amelia Bedelia Road Trip! (Special Edition) 2013. (ENG., Illus.). 160p. (J). *(978-0-06-227057-3(5)*, Harper Design) HarperCollins Pubs.
—Amelia Bedelia Road Trip! 2013. (Amelia Bedelia Chapter Book Ser.: 3). (J). lib. bdg. 14.75 *(978-0-606-32453-3(4))* Turtleback.
Parisi, Bettie. The Quiet. 2009. 36p. pap. 15.00 *(978-1-4269-1015-9(0))* Trafford Publishing.
Park, Barbara. Junie B., First Grader - Aloha-Ha-Ha! Brunkus, Denise, illus. 2007. (Junie B. Jones Ser.). 119p. (gr. 1-4). 15.00 *(978-0-7569-8085-6(2))* Perfection Learning Corp.
—Junie B. First Grader - Aloha-Ha-Ha! 2007. (Junie B. Jones Ser.: 26). lib. bdg. 14.75 *(978-1-4177-8157-7(2))* Turtleback.
—Junie B. Jones #26: Aloha-Ha-Ha! Brunkus, Denise, illus. 2007. (Junie B. Jones Ser.: 26). (ENG.). 128p. (J). (gr. 1-4). per. 5.99 *(978-0-375-83404-2(4)*, Random Hse. Bks. for Young Readers) Random Hse. Children's Bks.
Payne, Helen. Vacation Paws. Youngblood, Carol, illus. 2006. 50p. per. 10.00 *(978-0-9786276-6-9(0))* Mentzer Printing Ink.
Payot Karpathakis, Emmanuelle. Pixie en Vacaciones. 2013. 40p. pap. *(978-1-909193-28-4(3))* Summertime Publishing.
—Pixie's Holidays. 2013. 40p. pap. *(978-1-909193-25-3(9))* Summertime Publishing.
Peeler, Gail. Jackson's Magic Wishing Well. 2008. 25p. 35.50 *(978-1-4357-2950-6(1))* Lulu Pr., Inc.
Perez, Angela J. Zack Attack! Hazard, Andrea, illus. 2007. 36p. (J). 17.95 *(978-0-9778328-9-7(9))* His Work Christian Publishing.
Perisic, Zoran. An Alien Called Freddy. 2012. 152p. pap. 9.95 *(978-1-60594-907-9(8)*, Llumina Pr.) Aeon Publishing Inc.
Perkins, Lynne Rae. Pictures from Our Vacation. Perkins, Lynne Rae, illus. 2007. (Illus.). 32p. (J). (gr. k-3). 17.89 *(978-0-06-085098-2(1))*; (ENG.). 17.99 *(978-0-06-085097-5(3))* HarperCollins Pubs. (Greenwillow Bks.).
—Secret Sisters of the Salty Sea. Perkins, Lynne Rae, illus. 2019. (ENG., Illus.). 256p. (J). (gr. 3-7). pap. 6.99 *(978-0-06-249967-7(X)*, Greenwillow Bks.) HarperCollins Pubs.
—Secret Sisters of the Salty Sea. 2018. (ENG., Illus.). 240p. (J). (gr. 3-7). 16.99 *(978-0-06-249966-0(1)*, Greenwillow Bks.) HarperCollins Pubs.
Perry, Tristan. Cinnamon Takes a Vacation: Furry Tails #2, 1 vol. 2009. 122p. pap. 19.95 *(978-1-60836-451-0(8))* America Star Bks.
Peschke, Marci. Vacation Queen. Mourning, Tuesday, illus. 2016. (Kylie Jean Ser.). (ENG.). 112p. (J). (gr. 1-3). lib. bdg. 22.65 *(978-1-5158-0058-3(X)*, 131864, Picture Window Bks.) Capstone.
Peterson, Doug. LarryBoy, Versus the Volcano, 1 vol., 9. 2004. (Big Idea Books / LarryBoy Ser.). (ENG., Illus.). 96p. (J). pap. 4.99 *(978-0-310-70728-8(5))* Zonderkidz.
Peterson, Jim. The Summer House Kitten. 2007. 48p. pap. 16.95 *(978-1-60441-914-6(8))* America Star Bks.
Potter, Barbara L. The Fly That Went on Vacation. 2010. 16p. 8.49 *(978-1-4490-9353-2(1))* AuthorHouse.
Prime, D. De Nuevo en Vacaciones. (Serie Sara y Pablo - Sarah & Paul Ser.: No. 6).Tr. of Go on Vacation. (SPA.). (J). 2.99 *(978-0-7899-0495-9(0)*, 498900) Editorial Unilit.
Princess Protection Program Staff. The Palace of Mystery, No. 4. 2010. (Princess Protection Program Ser.). 144p. pap. 4.99 *(978-1-4231-2727-7(7))* Disney Pr.
Rabe, Tish. On the First Day of Summer Vacation. Jennings, Sarah, illus. 2019. (ENG.). 32p. (J). (gr. -1-3). 9.99 *(978-0-06-266852-3(8)*, HarperCollins) HarperCollins Pubs.
Ramirez, Terry. Growing up with Olivi: The Beguiling Blue-Haired Beauty of Boysenberry Lane. 2009. 96p. pap. 9.95 *(978-0-595-47668-8(6))* iUniverse, Inc.
Rand, Johnathan. American Chillers #22 Nuclear Jelly Fish of New Jersey. 2007. 208p. (J). pap. 5.99 *(978-1-893699-93-9(5))* AudioCraft Publishing, Inc.
Reberg, Evelyne. Vacances infernales Tom Tom. pap. 21.95 *(978-2-227-73108-0(7))* Bayard Editions FRA. Dist: Distribooks, Inc.
Reiff, Lauren & Geiser, Christina. Meows-Key Motel: A Great Vacation Spot for Hip Cats. 2009. 12p. pap. 8.95 *(978-1-4389-8801-6(X))* AuthorHouse.
Reimiller, Diane. Brayden & Ryan's Summer Vacation. Jastrzebski, Brandy, illus. 2012. 24p. pap. 24.95 *(978-1-4626-7792-4(4))* America Star Bks.
Reynolds, Evan. My Vacation. 2004. (J). 12.95 *(978-0-9759790-0-6(0))* Plant the Seed Publishing.
Richardson, Tracy. Indian Summer. 2010. (ENG.). 198p. (YA). (gr. 7). pap. 11.95 *(978-1-935462-25-5(3))* Luminis Bks., Inc.
Richens, Carol & Smith, Lori. Lori's Summer Fun with Tamara! 2009. 33p. 16.40 *(978-1-4357-1113-6(0))* Lulu Pr., Inc.
Richmond, Lori. Bunny's Staycation (Mama's Business Trip) 2018. (ENG., Illus.). 32p. (J). (gr. -1-k). 17.99 *(978-0-545-92589-1(4)*, Scholastic Pr.) Scholastic, Inc.
Rigby Education Staff. Mr. Merton's Vacation. (Sails Literacy Ser.). (Illus.). 16p. (gr. 2-3). 27.00 *(978-0-7635-9948-5(4))* Rigby Education.
Rippin, Sally. The Spotty Vacation. Fukuoka, Aki, illus. 2013. (Billie B. Brown Ser.). (ENG.). 43p. (J). *(978-1-61067-233-7(X))* Kane Miller.
—The Spotty Vacation: Billie B. Brown. 2014. (ENG., Illus.). 48p. (J). pap. 4.99 *(978-1-61067-183-5(X))* Kane Miller.
Roberts, Christa. Living the Dream. 2011. (XOXO, Betty & Veronica Ser.). (ENG.). 160p. (J). (gr. 4-6). 17.44 *(978-0-448-45578-5(1))* Penguin Young Readers Group.
Roberts, Johanna Lonsdorf. Summer at the Cabin. Shaggy Dog Press, ed. Challoner, Audrey, illus. 2007. 32p. (J). per. *(978-0-9722007-2-1(X))* Shaggy Dog Pr.
Rohan, Margaret de. Celia & Granny Meg go to Paris: A survival Guide. 2011. (ENG., Illus.). 184p. pap. *(978-1-84876-650-1(5))* Troubador Publishing Ltd.
—Celia & Granny Meg Return to Paris: The man with no Face. 2012. (ENG., Illus.). 176p. pap. *(978-1-78088-243-7(2))* Troubador Publishing Ltd.
Rooks, Elizabeth. Where Does Santa Go on Vacation after Christmas? 2012. 24p. pap. 17.99 *(978-1-4772-6535-2(X))* AuthorHouse.
Rose, Valerie. The Family Reunion Is Not A Real Vacation. 2003. 28p. (J). 9.95 *(978-0-9703489-2-0(4)*, Little Petals) Roses Are READ Productions.
Ross, Jill. The Blake Family Vacation. Pruitt, Gwendolyn, illus. 2010. (ENG.). 130p. (J). (gr. 3-7). pap. 9.95 *(978-1-59825-950-6(4))* Shenanigans Series.
Rouse, Betty Munn. The Adventures of the Phillyfab Family. 2011. 68p. pap. 12.95 *(978-1-4567-3005-5(3))* AuthorHouse.
Rutledge, Eddie. Amani's World: Amani & Friends Go to New York City. 2012. 24p. pap. 17.99 *(978-1-4772-9554-0(2))* AuthorHouse.
—Amani's World: Amani Goes to Washington D. C. Anderson, Susan, illus. 2009. 16p. pap. 8.75 *(978-1-4490-2095-8(X))* AuthorHouse.
Rylant, Cynthia. Henry & Mudge & the Tumbling Trip. Bracken, Carolyn, illus. 2006. (Henry & Mudge Ser.). 40p. (gr. k-3). 14.00 *(978-0-7569-6904-2(2))* Perfection Learning Corp.
—Henry & Mudge & the Tumbling Trip: Ready-To-Read Level 2. Bracken, Carolyn, illus. 2006. (Henry & Mudge Ser.: 27). (ENG.). 40p. (J). (gr. k-2). pap. 4.99 *(978-0-689-83452-3(7)*, Simon Spotlight) Simon Spotlight.
Sanchez, Alex. Rainbow Road. 2007. (ENG., Illus.). 266p. (YA). (gr. 7-12). pap. 12.99 *(978-1-4169-1191-3(X)*, Simon & Schuster Bks. For Young Readers) Simon & Schuster Bks. For Young Readers.
Santa Takes A Vacation. 2005. (J). 5.95 *(978-0-9769321-4-7(8))* Steingart, Nathan Publishing.
Santillo, LuAnn. At the Beach, 6 vols. Santillo, LuAnn, ed. 2003. (Half-Pint Kids Readers Ser.). (Illus.). 42p. (J). (gr. -1-1). pap. 6.95 *(978-1-59256-084-4(9))* Half-Pint Kids, Inc.
—A Fun Trip. Santillo, LuAnn, ed. 2003. (Half-Pint Kids Readers Ser.). (Illus.). 7p. (J). (gr. -1-1). pap. 1.00 *(978-1-59256-085-1(7))* Half-Pint Kids, Inc.
—The Picnic. Santillo, LuAnn, ed. 2003. (Half-Pint Kids Readers Ser.). (Illus.). 7p. (J). (gr. -1-1). pap. 1.00 *(978-1-59256-090-5(3))* Half-Pint Kids, Inc.
Scholastic. Family Trip (Peppa Pig) EOne, illus. 2018. (ENG.). 24p. (J). (gr. -1-k). pap. 4.99 *(978-1-338-22875-5(7))* Scholastic, Inc.
Sclafani, Terry. The Thompson Twins Cruise Adventure. 2007. 84p. per. 10.95 *(978-1-4327-1542-7(9))* Outskirts Pr., Inc.
Sconyers, Jennifer. John Bunny Goes on Vacation. 2010. 20p. pap. 12.99 *(978-1-4490-7774-7(9))* AuthorHouse.
Sempe, Goscinny. Las Vacaciones del Pequeno Nicolas. 2003. (SPA., Illus.). 150p. (J). (gr. 5-8). pap. 9.95 *(978-84-204-4813-8(3))* Santillana USA Publishing Co., Inc.
Shankle, Melanie. Piper & Mabel: Two Very Wild but Very Good Dogs, 1 vol. Watkins, Laura, illus. 2020. (ENG.). 32p. (J). 17.99 *(978-0-310-76086-3(0))* Zonderkidz.
Sheldon, Dyan. Sophie Pitt-Turnbull Discovers America. 2007. (ENG.). 192p. (YA). (gr. 7-12). per. 7.99 *(978-0-7636-3295-3(3))* Candlewick Pr.
Sherrard, Valerie. Driftwood, 1 vol. 2013. (ENG.). 200p. (J). (gr. 4-6). pap. 9.95 *(978-1-55455-305-1(9)*, 10d7acab-2e6a-47c1-beb3-19e3d2a87524) Trifolium Bks., Inc. CAN. Dist: Firefly Bks., Ltd.
Shortle, Stacy & Mooney, Dean J. M. A Train Ride to Grandma's (with NO Chocolate Donut!) Wulfing, Amy J., illus. 2009. 48p. (J). 18.95 *(978-0-9759850-5-2(1))* Maple Leaf Ctr.
Simmons, J. A. Hannah's First Airplane Ride. 2013. 32p. pap. 24.95 *(978-1-63004-197-7(1))* America Star Bks.
Simon, Leslie. Wish You Were Here: An Essential Guide to Your Favorite Music Scenes — From Punk to Indie & Everything in Between. 2009. (ENG., Illus.). 256p. pap. 17.99 *(978-0-06-157371-2(X)*, Dey Street Bks.) HarperCollins Pubs.
Sinha, Rhea. Latte's Vacation. Sinha, Rhea, illus. 2011. (Illus.). 20p. pap. 7.50 *(978-1-61170-045-9(0))* Robertson Publishing.
Smith, Clete Barrett. Aliens on Vacation. Slade, Christian, illus. 2012. (Intergalactic Bed & Breakfast Ser.: 1). (ENG.). 272p. (J). (gr. 3-7). pap. 6.99 *(978-1-4231-5723-6(0))* Little, Brown Bks. for Young Readers.
Smith, Emma Bland. Book 3: Saving the Alligators. Ortega, Mirelle, illus. 2019. (Gavin Mcnally's Year Off Ser.). (ENG.). 48p. (J). (gr. 3-7). lib. bdg. 34.21 *(978-1-5321-3508-8(4)*, 31935, Spellbound) Magic Wagon.
Smith, Nigel. Nathalia Buttface & the Most Epically Embarrassing Trip Ever (Nathalia Buttface) 2017. (Nathalia Buttface Ser.). (ENG.). 256p. (J). 6.99 *(978-0-00-820422-8(5)*, HarperCollins Children's Bks.) HarperCollins Pubs. Ltd. GBR. Dist: HarperCollins Pubs.
Smith, William. Frankie & Earnie Meet, 1 vol. 2009. pap. 24.95 *(978-1-60749-333-4(0))* America Star Bks.
Snider, Jesse Blaze. Toy Story: Toy Overboard. Watson, Nathan, illus. 2011. 128p. (J). pap. 9.99 *(978-1-60886-605-2(X))* BOOM! Studios.
Sprague, Howard Lee. Snowflake's Vacation. Borrajero, Judy, illus. 2011. 40p. pap. 9.95 *(978-1-881276-16-6(3))* Serey/Jones Pubs.
Sproule, Acquanetta M. Scamp. 2010. 40p. pap. 18.00 *(978-0-557-37187-7(2))* Lulu Pr., Inc.
St. Anthony, Jane. Grace above All. 2015. (Fesler-Lampert Minnesota Heritage Ser.). (ENG.). 176p. pap. 9.95 *(978-0-8166-9814-1(7))* Univ. of Minnesota Pr.
St. Antoine, Sara. Three Bird Summer. 2018. (ENG.). 256p. (J). (gr. 5). pap. 6.99 *(978-1-5362-0045-4(X))* Candlewick Pr.
St John, Patricia. Other Kitten. 2007. (Illus.). 96p. pap. *(978-1-84427-290-7(7))* Scripture Union.
Standish, Burt L. Frank Merriwell's Vacation. Rudman, Jack, ed. 2003. (Frank Merriwell Ser.). (YA). (gr. 9-18). 29.95 *(978-0-8373-9325-4(6))*; pap. 9.95 *(978-0-8373-9025-3(7)*, FM-025) Merriwell, Frank Inc.
Stanek, Robert, pseud. The Bugville Critters Go on Vacation. 2008. (ENG., Illus.). (J). 32p. per. 9.95 *(978-1-57545-148-0(4))*; 52p. per. 19.95 *(978-1-57545-125-1(5))* RP Media.
—Bugville Critters Start Summer Vacation. 2011. (Illus.). 32p. pap. 4.99 *(978-1-57545-257-9(X)*, Reagent Pr. Bks. for Young Readers) RP Media.
—The Bugville Critters Vacation Surprise: Buster Bee's School Days #3. 2008. (ENG., Illus.). 68p. (J). per. 18.95 *(978-1-57545-172-5(7))* RP Media.
—Go on Vacation. 2008. (ENG., Illus.). 32p. (J). pap. 5.59 *(978-1-57545-191-6(3))* RP Media.
—Start Summer Vacation. 2010. (Illus.). 32p. pap. 8.99 *(978-1-57545-174-9(3)*, Reagent Pr. Bks. for Young Readers) RP Media.
Staniszewski, Anna. Once upon a Cruise: a Wish Novel. 2016. (Wish Ser.). (ENG.). 256p. (J). (gr. 3-7). pap. 6.99 *(978-0-545-87966-6(8)*, Scholastic Paperbacks) Scholastic, Inc.
Steiner, Barbara. The Cry of the Loon: A Samantha Mystery. Tibbles, Jean-Paul, illus. 2006. (ENG.). 192p. (gr. 4-18). 10.95 *(978-1-59369-479-1(2))* American Girl Publishing, Inc.
Steinkraus, Kyla. The Trouble with Trading. 2011. (ENG., Illus.). (J). (gr. 2-3). pap. 7.95 *(978-1-61236-986-8(3))* Rourke Educational Media.
Stern, Jacqueline. Mystery of the Whispering Walls. 2004. (J). 148p. pap. *(978-1-57168-844-6(7))*; (Hollow Tree Mystery Ser.: Bk. 6). (Illus.). v, 142p. *(978-1-57168-850-7(1)*, Eakin Pr.) Eakin Pr.
Stephens, Sarah Hines. Spring Break-Up. 2006. (Zoey 101 Ser.). 103p. (J). *(978-1-4156-8963-9(6))* Scholastic, Inc.
Stewart, Bob. Baily Bumble Bee. Gorum, Jerry, illus. 2009. (ENG.). 32p. pap. 14.49 *(978-1-4389-7254-1(7))* AuthorHouse.
Sticker Dolly Dressing on Vacation (Revised) 2017. (Sticker Dolly Dressing Ser.). (ENG.). 1p. pap. 9.99 *(978-0-7945-3791-3(X)*, Usborne) EDC Publishing.
Stilton, Geronimo. A Fabumouse Vacation for Geronimo (Geronimo Stilton #9), Vol. 9. 2004. (Geronimo Stilton Ser.: 9). (ENG., Illus.). 128p. (J). (gr. 2-5). pap. 7.99 *(978-0-439-55971-3(5)*, Scholastic Paperbacks) Scholastic, Inc.
Stilton, Gerónimo. The Stinky Cheese Vacation. 2014. (Geronimo Stilton Ser.: 57). lib. bdg. 18.40 *(978-0-606-35843-9(9))* Turtleback.
Stinson, Kathy. Seven Clues, 1 vol. 2005. (Lorimer Streetlights Ser.). (ENG.). 104p. (J). (gr. 2-5). 7.95 *(978-1-55028-889-6(X)*, 889) James Lorimer & Co. Ltd., Pubs. CAN. Dist: Formac Lorimer Bks. Ltd.
Storm, Tallia & Courtenay, Lucy. Pop Girl. 2017. 314p. (J). *(978-1-338-16024-6(9))* Scholastic, Inc.
Tackett, Wendy. The Jefferson Wish. 2011. 124p. (gr. 4-6). 20.95 *(978-1-4620-3771-1(2))*; pap. 10.95 *(978-1-4620-3768-1(2))* iUniverse, Inc.
Tamaki, Mariko. This One Summer. Tamaki, Jillian, illus. 2014. (ENG.). 320p. (YA). (gr. 7). 22.99 *(978-1-62672-094-7(0)*, 900135617, First Second Bks.) Roaring Brook Pr.
—This One Summer. Tamaki, Jillian, illus. 2014. (ENG.). 320p. (YA). (gr. 7). pap. 18.99 *(978-1-59643-774-6(X)*, 900081621, First Second Bks.) Roaring Brook Pr.
Thrasher, Grady. Tim & Sally's Beach Adventure. Rabon, Elaine Hearn, illus. 2008. (ENG.). 48p. (J). (gr. -1-3). 18.95 *(978-1-58818-161-9(8))* Hill Street Pr., LLC.
Tremblay, Amanda. The Tornado Trial. 2010. 65p. pap. 12.00 *(978-0-557-14051-0(X))* Lulu Pr., Inc.
Trinidad Joe. Santa's Key West Vacation. 2007. (Illus.). 80p. per. 12.95 *(978-0-9799474-0-7(5))* Seastory Pr.
Tucker, Valerie Nell. The Hermit's Box. 2009. 36p. pap. 15.49 *(978-1-4490-2285-3(5))* AuthorHouse.
Tuthill, Louisa C. Hurrah for New England! or the Virginia Boy's Vacation. 2004. reprint ed. pap. 1.99 *(978-1-4192-2504-8(9))*; pap. 15.95 *(978-1-4191-2504-1(4))* Kessinger Publishing, LLC.
Udvari, Joseph G. Courage. 2012. 132p. pap. *(978-1-84961-169-5(6))* RealTime Publishing.
Vacations: Set B Individual Title Six-Packs. (Smart Start Ser.). (gr. k-1). 23.00 *(978-0-7635-0418-2(1))* Rigby Education.
Van Dyne, Edith. Aunt Jane's Nieces on Vacation. 2005. 27.95 *(978-1-4218-1027-0(1))*; 200p. pap. 12.95 *(978-1-4218-1127-7(8))* 1st World Publishing, Inc. (1st World Library - Literary Society).
—Aunt Jane's Nieces on Vacation. 2017. (ENG., Illus.). (J). pap. 13.95 *(978-1-374-83427-9(0))* Capital Communications, Inc.
—Aunt Jane's Nieces on Vacation. 2004. reprint ed. pap. 21.95 *(978-1-4191-0825-9(5))*; pap. 1.99 *(978-1-4192-0825-6(X))* Kessinger Publishing, LLC.
Vega, Danielle. The Merciless IV: Last Rites. 2019. (Merciless Ser.). (ENG.). 320p. (YA). (gr. 9). pap. 10.99 *(978-0-425-29219-8(3)*, Razorbill) Penguin Young Readers Group.
Viguié, Debbie. The Summer of Cotton Candy, 1 vol. 2008. (Sweet Seasons Novel Ser.: 1). (ENG., Illus.). 224p. (YA). (gr. 8-11). pap. 9.99 *(978-0-310-71558-0(X))* Zondervan.
Voake, Steve. Daisy Dawson at the Beach. Meserve, Jessica, illus. 2012. (Daisy Dawson Ser.: 4). (ENG.). 96p. (J). (gr. 1-4). pap. 5.99 *(978-0-7636-5946-2(0))* Candlewick Pr.
—Daisy Dawson on the Farm. Meserve, Jessica, illus. 2012. (Daisy Dawson Ser.: 5). (ENG.). 96p. (J). (gr. 1-4). 14.99 *(978-0-7636-5882-3(0))* Candlewick Pr.
Voelkel, Jon & Voelkel, Pamela. Middleworld. 2007. (Jaguar Stones Ser.: Bk. 1). (Illus.). 397p. (gr. 6-9). *(978-1-57525-561-3(8))* Smith & Kraus Pubs., Inc.
Vulliamy, Clara. The Vacation Mystery (Dotty Detective, Book 6) 2019. (Dotty Detective Ser.: 6). (ENG.). 176p. (J). 4.99 *(978-0-00-830091-3(7)*, HarperCollins Children's Bks.) HarperCollins Pubs. Ltd. GBR. Dist: HarperCollins Pubs.
Waldman, Maya, illus. To-Do List. 2007. (ENG.). 48p. (J). (gr. k). 12.95 *(978-0-9741319-5-5(4))* 4N Publishing LLC.
Walker, Anna. I Love Vacations. Walker, Anna, illus. 2011. (ENG., Illus.). 32p. (J). (gr. -1-1). 9.99 *(978-1-4169-8321-7(X)*, Simon & Schuster Bks. For Young Readers) Simon & Schuster Bks. For Young Readers.
Wallace, Sheila Ryan. Diving for the Gold. 2004. 142p. (YA). pap. 15.95 *(978-0-7414-2269-9(7))* Infinity Publishing.
Walters, Eric. Skye Above, 1 vol. Parkins, David, illus. 2014. (Orca Echoes Ser.). (ENG.). 64p. (J). (gr. 1-3). pap. 6.95 *(978-1-4598-0701-3(4))* Orca Bk. Pubs. USA.
Webb, Holly. The Secret Puppy. Williams, Sophy, illus. 2016. (Pet Rescue Adventures Ser.). (ENG.). 128p. (J). (gr. 1-4). 4.99 *(978-1-58925-483-1(X))* Tiger Tales.
—The Secret Puppy & Other Tales. Williams, Sophy, illus. 2018. (Pet Rescue Adventures Ser.). (ENG.). 384p. (J). (gr. 1-4). pap. 10.99 *(978-1-68010-414-1(4))* Tiger Tales.
Weetman, Nova. A Hot Cold Summer: Choose Your Own Ever After. 2016. (ENG.). 256p. (J). pap. 5.99 *(978-1-61067-354-9(9))* Kane Miller.
Wetherby, Mark. The Tales of Mossy Dell. 2009. (Illus.). 88p. pap. 10.49 *(978-1-4389-7726-3(3))* AuthorHouse.
Williams, Alan. Archy the Flying Dolphin & the Vampire's Curse. 2007. pap. 15.38 *(978-1-4251-3151-7(4))* Trafford Publishing.
Winter, Christopher. Henrietta the Farmer & the Long, Long, Long, Long Vacation! O'Shea, Bonnie, illus. 2012. 32p. pap. 13.95 *(978-1-60594-856-0(X))* Aeon Publishing Inc.
Wisdom, Gail Ann. Trouble with Bullies. 2013. 48p. pap. 20.45 *(978-1-4908-0026-4(3)*, WestBow Pr.) Author Solutions, LLC.
Wittlinger, Ellen. Zigzag. (ENG., Illus.). (YA). (gr. 7). 2003. 272p. 16.95 *(978-0-689-84996-1(6))* 2005. 288p. reprint ed. pap. 9.99 *(978-0-689-84998-5(2))* Simon & Schuster Bks. For Young Readers. (Simon & Schuster Bks. For Young Readers).
Wojciechowski, Susan. Beany Goes to Camp. Natti, Susanna, illus. 2005. (Beany Adventures Ser.). 104p. (J). (gr. 4-7). 13.65 *(978-0-7569-6499-3(7))* Perfection Learning Corp.
Wood, Maryrose. The Incorrigible Children of Ashton Place: Book VI: The Long-Lost Home. Wheeler, Eliza, illus. (Incorrigible Children of Ashton Place Ser.: 6). (ENG.). 448p. (J). (gr. 3-7). 2019. pap. 7.99 *(978-0-06-211045-9(4))* 2018.

15.99 *(978-0-06-211044-2(6))* HarperCollins Pubs. (Balzer & Bray).
Wright, Kiyah. Vacation Fun. 2011. 24p. pap. 14.95 *(978-1-4634-4055-8(3))* AuthorHouse.
Wright, Mary. Justice for All. 2004. 177p. pap. 24.95 *(978-1-4137-4083-7(9))* America Star Bks.
Yeager, Graham. Diablo: The Third Millersburg Novel. 2006. 145p. (YA). per. 7.99 *(978-0-9765478-4-6(8))* Stone Acres Publishing Co.
Yoon, Salina. Penguin on Vacation. (Penguin Ser.). (ENG., Illus.). (J). (gr. -1-1). 2015. 34p. bds. 7.99 *(978-0-8027-3837-0(0),* 900142737) 2013. 40p. 14.99 *(978-0-8027-3397-9(2),* 900084821) Bloomsbury Publishing USA. (Bloomsbury USA Childrens).
Zadunajsky, Donna M. Tayla Takes a Trip. Bicking, Judith, illus. 2013. (ENG.). 40p. pap. 9.99 *(978-1-938037-36-8(7))* Zadunajsky, Donna M.

VACCINATION

see also Immunity

Abramovitz, Melissa. 12 Ways to Prevent Disease. 2017. (Healthy Living Ser.). (ENG., Illus.). 32p. (J). (gr. 3-6). pap. 9.95 *(978-1-63235-388-7(1),* 11856, 12-Story Library) Bookstaves, LLC.
—12 Ways to Prevent Disease. 2017. (J). *(978-1-62143-512-9(1))* Pr. Room Editions LLC.
Alter, Judy. Vaccines. 2008. (21st Century Skills Innovation Library: Innovation in Medicine Ser.). (ENG., Illus.). 32p. (gr. 4-8). lib. bdg. 32.07 *(978-1-60279-223-4(2),* 200154) Cherry Lake Publishing.
Brown, Don. A Shot in the Arm! 2021. (J). *(978-1-4197-5010-6(0),* Amulet Bks.) Abrams, Inc.
—A Shot in the Arm! Big Ideas That Changed the World #3. 2021. (Big Ideas That Changed the World Ser.). (ENG., Illus.). 144p. (J). (gr. 3-7). 13.99 *(978-1-4197-5001-4(1),* 1711501) Abrams, Inc.
De La Bedoyere, Guy. The First Polio Vaccine, 1 vol. 2005. (Milestones in Modern Science Ser.). (ENG., Illus.). 48p. (gr. 6-8). pap. 15.05 *(978-0-8368-5862-4(X),* cdbed880-4cce-4698-bb22-8ee550daa304); lib. bdg. 33.67 *(978-0-8368-5855-6(7),* 496637c3-8ee4-403a-9989-c372f37dbb1c) Stevens, Gareth Publishing LLLP. (Gareth Stevens Secondary Library).
Ellis, Carol. Vaccines, 1 vol. 2013. (Advances in Medicine Ser.). (ENG.). 64p. (gr. 6-6). pap. 16.28 *(978-1-62712-012-8(2),* 875b5268-9433-43c5-88e9-6e6ca2b9c668); (Illus.). 36.93 *(978-1-60870-470-5(X),* 26923e57-d6d4-43a1-9ef7-9bf7d424ba7d) Cavendish Square Publishing LLC.
Espejo, Roman, ed. Should Vaccinations Be Mandatory?, 1 vol. 2014. (At Issue Ser.). (ENG.). 128p. (gr. 10-12). lib. bdg. 41.03 *(978-0-7377-6862-6(2),* bf6063c9-6103-45e4-878c-e4d34c5cda5c, Greenhaven Publishing) Greenhaven Publishing LLC.
Haelle, Tara. Vaccination Investigation: The History & Science of Vaccines. 2018. (ENG., Illus.). 120p. (YA). (gr. 6-12). 37.32 *(978-1-5124-2530-7(3),* 38bac5f7-ccd1-41a0-ad3b-3de27c914fb5, Twenty-First Century Bks.) Lerner Publishing Group.
Hantula, Richard. Jonas Salk, 1 vol. 2004. (Trailblazers of the Modern World Ser.). (ENG., Illus.). 48p. (J). (gr. 5-8). lib. bdg. 33.67 *(978-0-8368-5100-7(5),* 91b76e1b-e792-41ca-b702-2c41f73c8f78, Gareth Stevens Secondary Library) Stevens, Gareth Publishing LLLP.
Hillstrom, Kevin. Vaccines, 1 vol. 2012. (Nutrition & Health Ser.). (ENG., Illus.). 104p. (gr. 7-10). lib. bdg. 37.33 *(978-1-4205-0724-9(9),* 00b9fac8-b8c4-4a8a-b9e8-45cfeac8cd28, Lucent Pr.) Greenhaven Publishing LLC.
Hutchison, Patricia. Vaccines. 2018. (J). *(978-1-4896-9620-5(2),* AV2 by Weigl) Weigl Pubs., Inc.
Idzikowski, Lisa, ed. Vaccination, 1 vol. 2019. (At Issue Ser.). (ENG.). 128p. (gr. 10-12). pap. 28.80 *(978-1-5345-0628-2(4),* 156aefa7-47ac-4c72-b119-6f289f8202a1) Greenhaven Publishing LLC.
Jd, Duchess Harris & Hudak, Heather C. The Discovery of the Polio Vaccine. 2018. (Perspectives on American Progress Ser.). (ENG., Illus.). 48p. (J). (gr. 4-8). lib. bdg. 35.64 *(978-1-5321-1488-5(5),* 29108) ABDO Publishing Co.
Llanas, Sheila. Jonas Salk: Medical Innovator & Polio Vaccine Developer, 1 vol. 2013. (Essential Lives Set 8 Ser.). (ENG., Illus.). 112p. (YA). (gr. 6-12). lib. bdg. 41.36 *(978-1-61783-896-5(9),* 6769, Essential Library) ABDO Publishing Co.
Merino, Noël, ed. Vaccines, 1 vol. 2015. (At Issue Ser.). (ENG.). 120p. (gr. 10-12). 41.03 *(978-0-7377-7193-0(3),* b08c2312-72b5-4c6c-9b94-6e6db09c0e40, Greenhaven Publishing) Greenhaven Publishing LLC.
—Vaccines, 1 vol. 2015. (At Issue Ser.). (ENG.). 120p. (gr. 10-12). pap. 28.80 *(978-0-7377-7194-7(1),* 2a842a22-c0a1-48dc-8139-2db62ca96d24, Greenhaven Publishing) Greenhaven Publishing LLC.
Nardo, Don. How Vaccines Changed the World. 2018. (How Science Changed the World Ser.). (ENG.). 80p. (YA). (gr. 6-12). 39.93 *(978-1-68282-413-9(6))* ReferencePoint Pr., Inc.
Osborne, Naomi. Should All Children Get Vaccines?, 1 vol. 2019. (Points of View Ser.). (ENG.). 24p. (gr. 3-3). 26.23 *(978-1-5345-3191-8(2),* 0229eaa9-dc11-4123-a9ac-59ccf6851886, KidHaven Publishing) Greenhaven Publishing LLC.
Petersen, Christine. Frequently Asked Questions about Vaccines & Vaccinations, 1 vol. 2011. (FAQ: Teen Life Ser.). (ENG., Illus.). 64p. (YA). (gr. 5-6). lib. bdg. 37.13 *(978-1-4488-1328-5(X),* 2501f01a-d44e-42d6-82fa-8eb9a9f9c5cf) Rosen Publishing Group, Inc., The.
Richardson, Erik. Vaccination, 1 vol. 2017. (Great Discoveries in Science Ser.). (ENG.). 128p. (YA). (gr. 9-9). lib. bdg. 47.36 *(978-1-5026-2780-3(9),* 84291d80-7b29-4c10-a758-0f810ab8cb77) Cavendish Square Publishing LLC.
Shulman, Neil, et al. The Germ Patrol: All about Shots for Tots... & Big Kids, Too! 2004. (Illus.). 36p. (gr. -1-3). pap. 14.95 *(978-0-9639002-8-9(5))* Rx Humor.
Vaccines. 2011. (ENG., Illus.). 120p. (gr. 6-12). 35.00 *(978-1-60413-339-4(2),* P179269, Facts On File) Infobase Holdings, Inc.
Wells, Ken R., ed. Vaccines, 1 vol. 2006. (History of Drugs Ser.). (ENG., Illus.). 176p. (gr. 10-12). lib. bdg. 41.23 *(978-0-7377-2857-6(4),* fc8ebec6-e424-4b44-adcc-3cf6d6cc1c53, Greenhaven Publishing) Greenhaven Publishing LLC.

VADER, DARTH (FICTITIOUS CHARACTER)—FICTION

Aaron, Jason. Vader down: Volume 1. Deodato, Mike & Martin, Laura, illus. 2016. (Star Wars: Vader Down Ser.). (ENG.). 36p. (J). (gr. 6-12). lib. bdg. 31.36 *(978-1-61479-561-2(4),* 24395, Graphic Novels) Spotlight.
—Vader down: Volume 3. Deodato, Mike & Martin, Laura, illus. 2016. (Star Wars: Vader Down Ser.). (ENG.). 24p. (J). (gr. 6-12). lib. bdg. 31.36 *(978-1-61479-563-6(0),* 24397, Graphic Novels) Spotlight.
—Vader down: Volume 5. Deodato, Mike & Martin, Laura, illus. 2016. (Star Wars: Vader Down Ser.). (ENG.). 24p. (J). (gr. 6-12). lib. bdg. 31.36 *(978-1-61479-565-0(7),* 24399, Graphic Novels) Spotlight.
Blackman, Haden. Darth Vader & the Lost Command. Leonardi, Rick, illus. 2012. (Star Wars: Darth Vader & the Lost Command Ser.). (ENG.). 24p. (J). (gr. 6-12). 31.36 *(978-1-59961-980-4(6),* 13805, Graphic Novels) Spotlight.
—Darth Vader & the Lost Command. Leonardi, Rick et al, illus. 2012. (Star Wars: Darth Vader & the Lost Command Ser.). (ENG.). 24p. (J). (gr. 6-12). 31.36 *(978-1-59961-983-5(0),* 13808, Graphic Novels) Spotlight.
—Darth Vader & the Lost Command, Vol. 2. Leonardi, Rick, illus. 2012. (Star Wars: Darth Vader & the Lost Command Ser.). (ENG.). 24p. (J). (gr. 6-12). 31.36 *(978-1-59961-981-1(4),* 13806, Graphic Novels) Spotlight.
—Darth Vader & the Lost Command, Vol. 3. Leonardi, Rick et al, illus. 2012. (Star Wars: Darth Vader & the Lost Command Ser.). (ENG.). 24p. (J). (gr. 6-12). 31.36 *(978-1-59961-982-8(2),* 13807, Graphic Novels) Spotlight.
—Lost Command. Leonardi, Rick, illus. 2012. (Star Wars: Darth Vader & the Lost Command Ser.). (ENG.). 24p. (J). (gr. 6-12). 31.36 *(978-1-59961-984-2(9),* 13809, Graphic Novels) Spotlight.
Disney Press Editors. Star Wars: Escape from Darth Vader. 2014. (Star Wars: World of Reading Ser.). (J). lib. bdg. 13.55 *(978-0-606-35924-5(9))* Turtleback.
Gillen, Kieron. Shadows & Secrets: Volume 1. Larroca, Salvador & Delgado, Edgar, illus. 2016. (Star Wars: Darth Vader Set 2 Ser.). (ENG.). 24p. (J). (gr. 6-12). lib. bdg. 31.36 *(978-1-61479-547-6(9),* 24381, Graphic Novels) Spotlight.
—Shadows & Secrets: Volume 2. Larroca, Salvador & Delgado, Edgar, illus. 2016. (Star Wars: Darth Vader Set 2 Ser.). (ENG.). 24p. (J). (gr. 6-12). lib. bdg. 31.36 *(978-1-61479-548-3(7),* 24382, Graphic Novels) Spotlight.
—Shadows & Secrets: Volume 3. Larroca, Salvador & Delgado, Edgar, illus. 2016. (Star Wars: Darth Vader Set 2 Ser.). (ENG.). 24p. (J). (gr. 6-12). lib. bdg. 31.36 *(978-1-61479-549-0(5),* 24383, Graphic Novels) Spotlight.
—Shadows & Secrets: Volume 4. Larroca, Salvador & Delgado, Edgar, illus. 2016. (Star Wars: Darth Vader Set 2 Ser.). (ENG.). 24p. (J). (gr. 6-12). lib. bdg. 31.36 *(978-1-61479-550-6(9),* 24384, Graphic Novels) Spotlight.
—Shadows & Secrets: Volume 5. Larroca, Salvador & Delgado, Edgar, illus. 2016. (Star Wars: Darth Vader Set 2 Ser.). (ENG.). 24p. (J). (gr. 6-12). lib. bdg. 31.36 *(978-1-61479-551-3(7),* 24385, Graphic Novels) Spotlight.
—Shadows & Secrets: Volume 6. Larroca, Salvador & Delgado, Edgar, illus. 2016. (Star Wars: Darth Vader Set 2 Ser.). (ENG.). 24p. (J). (gr. 6-12). lib. bdg. 31.36 *(978-1-61479-552-0(5),* 24386, Graphic Novels) Spotlight.
—Vader down: Volume 4. Larroca, Salvador & Delgado, Edgar, illus. 2016. (Star Wars: Vader Down Ser.). (ENG.). 24p. (J). (gr. 6-12). lib. bdg. 31.36 *(978-1-61479-564-3(9),* 24398, Graphic Novels) Spotlight.
—Vader down: Volume 6. Larroca, Salvador & Delgado, Edgar, illus. 2016. (Star Wars: Vader Down Ser.). (ENG.). 24p. (J). (gr. 6-12). lib. bdg. 31.36 *(978-1-61479-566-7(5),* 24400, Graphic Novels) Spotlight.
Hibbert, Clare. DK Readers L1: Star Wars: Tatooine Adventures. 2011. (DK Readers Level 1 Ser.). (ENG.). 48p. (J). (gr. k-4). 4.99 *(978-0-7566-7128-0(0),* DK Children) Dorling Kindersley Publishing, Inc.
King, Trey. Death Star Battle. 2016. (Illus.). 30p. (J). *(978-1-4806-9628-0(5),* Disney Lucasfilm Press) Disney Publishing Worldwide.
Landers, Ace. Revenge of the Sith. White, Dave, illus. 2015. (J). *(978-1-4806-9629-7(3))* Scholastic, Inc.
—Revenge of the Sith. 2015. (LEGO Star Wars 8X8 Ser.). lib. bdg. 13.55 *(978-0-606-37767-6(0))* Turtleback.
—Vader's Secret Missions. 2015. (Illus.). 63p. (J). *(978-1-4806-8324-2(8))* Scholastic, Inc.
Lucasfilm Press, Lucasfilm. 5-Minute Star Wars Stories Strike Back. 2017. (Illus.). 20p. (J). (gr. 1-3). 12.99 *(978-1-368-00351-3(6),* Disney Lucasfilm Press) Disney Publishing Worldwide.
Nesworthy, Lauren. Darth Vader, Rebel Hunter! 2016. (Illus.). 48p. (J). *(978-1-5182-1849-1(0))* Dorling Kindersley Publishing, Inc.
Saunders, Catherine. The Jedi & the Force. 2014. (Illus.). 144p. (J). *(978-1-4351-5416-2(9))* Dorling Kindersley Publishing, Inc.
Scholastic Editors & Fry, Jason. Darth Vader. 2017. (Backstories Ser.: Vol. 6). (ENG., Illus.). 128p. (J). (gr. 3-7). 16.00 *(978-0-606-39145-0(2))* Turtleback.

VALENTINE'S DAY

Appleby, Alex. Happy Valentine's Day!, 1 vol., Vol. 1. 2013. (Happy Holidays! Ser.). (ENG., Illus.). 24p. (J). (gr. k-k). 25.27 *(978-1-4339-9951-2(X),* ea954de6-20ad-4985-9c59-fd3e4d827f20); pap. 9.15 *(978-1-4339-9953-6(6),* ff01eed0-e8ca-4d6a-ad61-e4e4e0c2d80d) Stevens, Gareth Publishing LLLP.
Bernay, Emma & Berne, Emma Carlson. Valentine's Day. Cushley, Aaron, illus. 2018. (Holidays in Rhythm & Rhyme Ser.). (ENG.). 24p. (J). (gr. k-2). lib. bdg. 33.99 *(978-1-68410-398-0(3),* 140368) Cantata Learning.
Bloomsbury USA. Carry & Play: I Love You. 2015. (ENG., Illus.). 10p. (J). (gr. -1-1). bds. 6.99 *(978-1-61963-802-0(9),* 900148901, Bloomsbury Activity Bks.) Bloomsbury Publishing USA.
Bodden, Valerie. Valentine's Day. 2005. (My First Look at Holidays Ser.). (Illus.). 24p. (J). (gr. k-3). lib. bdg. 15.95 *(978-1-58341-371-5(5),* Creative Education) Creative Co., The.
Brown, Tammy B. The Valentine's Day Cookbook. 2021. (Holiday Recipe Box Ser.). (ENG.). 24p. (J). (gr. 4-6). *(978-1-62310-313-2(4),* 13064, Hi Jinx) Black Rabbit Bks.
Farmer, Jacqueline. Valentine Be Mine. Halsey, Megan & Addy, Sean, illus. 2013. 32p. (J). (gr. k-3). pap. 7.95 *(978-1-58089-390-9(2))* Charlesbridge Publishing, Inc.
Gilpin, Rebecca. Valentine Things to Make & Do. 2006. (Usborne Activities Ser.). (Illus.). 31p. (J). *(978-0-439-78705-5(X))* Scholastic, Inc.
Gleisner, Jenna Lee. Celebrating Valentine's Day. 2018. (Welcoming the Seasons Ser.). (ENG.). 24p. (J). (gr. -1-2). lib. bdg. 32.79 *(978-1-5038-2387-7(3),* 212230) Child's World, Inc, The.
Goeller, Dorothy. Valentine's Day, 1 vol. 2010. (All about Holidays Ser.). (ENG., Illus.). 24p. (-1). pap. 10.35 *(978-1-59845-179-5(0),* 8a6de660-1dcc-4de9-ae9f-79c938dcc867); (gr. -1-1). 25.27 *(978-0-7660-3810-3(6),* bd21dd3e-da70-486b-b147-40fe5883d7bf) Enslow Publishing, LLC. (Enslow Publishing).
Golden Books. Vintage Valentines. 2005. (Press Out Book Ser.). (ENG., Illus.). 12p. (J). (gr. -1-2). pap. 4.99 *(978-0-375-87514-4(X),* Golden Bks.) Random Hse. Children's Bks.
Grack, Rachel. Valentine's Day. 2018. (Celebrating Holidays Ser.). (ENG., Illus.). 24p. (J). (gr. k-3). lib. bdg. 26.95 *(978-1-62617-755-0(4),* Blastoff! Readers) Bellwether Media.
Haley, Charly. Valentine's Day. 2019. (Holidays Ser.). (ENG.). 24p. (J). (gr. 1-1). pap. 8.95 *(978-1-64185-572-3(X),* 164185572X) North Star Editions.
—Valentine's Day. 2018. (Holidays (Cody Koala) Ser.). (ENG.). 24p. (J). (gr. k-3). lib. bdg. 31.36 *(978-1-5321-6201-5(4),* 30185, Pop! Cody Koala) Pop!
Hayes, Amy. Celebrate Valentine's Day, 1 vol. 2014. (Our Holidays Ser.). (ENG.). 24p. (J). (gr. 1-1). 25.93 *(978-1-5026-0236-7(9),* 23232875-9270-4e80-85be-2d7b48239599) Cavendish Square Publishing LLC.
—Valentine's Day. 2015. (J). *(978-1-62713-481-1(6))* Cavendish Square Publishing LLC.
Keogh, Josie. Valentine's Day, 1 vol. 2013. (PowerKids Readers: Happy Holidays! Ser.). (ENG., Illus.). 24p. (J). (gr. k-k). pap. 9.25 *(978-1-4488-9710-0(6),* fb359fa6-2aef-4ea7-89f5-bb57e6514538); lib. bdg. 26.27 *(978-1-4488-9627-1(4),* d4fb37e6-315d-4a7c-9b40-beb66c6e055d) Rosen Publishing Group, Inc., The. (PowerKids Pr.).
—Valentine's Day: Día de San Valentín, 1 vol. Alamán, Eduardo, tr. 2013. (PowerKids Readers: !Felices Fiestas! / Happy Holidays! Ser.). (ENG & SPA., Illus.). 24p. (gr. k-k). lib. bdg. 26.27 *(978-1-4488-9970-8(2),* b1db2a16-056f-426f-95a2-943b38682b74, PowerKids Pr.) Rosen Publishing Group, Inc., The.
Landau, Elaine. What Is Valentine's Day?, 1 vol. 2012. (I Like Holidays! Ser.). (ENG., Illus.). 24p. (J). (gr. k-2). pap. 10.35 *(978-1-59845-296-9(7),* 078585a5-369c-4811-9525-86824bcf918c, Enslow Elementary); lib. bdg. 25.27 *(978-0-7660-3699-4(5),* d2bb3d78-87bf-4218-9c1a-e8544255dc1d) Enslow Publishing, LLC.
Lee, Sally. A Short History of Valentine's Day. 2015. (Holiday Histories Ser.). (ENG., Illus.). 24p. (J). (gr. -1-2). lib. bdg. 27.32 *(978-1-4914-6098-6(9),* 128993, Capstone Pr.) Capstone.
Lindeen, Mary. Valentine's Day. 2018. (Beginning-To-Read Ser.). (ENG.). 32p. (J). (gr. k-2). pap. 13.26 *(978-1-68404-164-0(3));* (Illus.). (gr. -1-2). lib. bdg. 22.60 *(978-1-59953-908-9(X))* Norwood Hse. Pr.
Lynette, Rachel. Let's Throw a Valentine's Day Party!, 1 vol. 2011. (Holiday Parties Ser.). (J). (ENG.). 24p. (gr. 2-3). pap. 9.25 *(978-1-4488-2729-9(9),* 42953540-80a9-4e13-a047-4076cdb65c9f); (ENG.). 24p. (gr. 2-3). lib. bdg. 26.27 *(978-1-4488-2570-7(9),* 1199b94c-884d-4612-8703-412142f90f39); 49.50 *(978-1-4488-2730-5(2))* Rosen Publishing Group, Inc., The. (PowerKids Pr.).
Mad Libs & Stern, Leonard. Dear Valentine Letters Mad Libs: Stationery to Fill Out & Send! 2006. (Mad Libs Ser.). (Illus.). 48p. (J). (gr. 3-7). 6.99 *(978-0-8431-2088-2(6),* Mad Libs) Penguin Young Readers Group.
Markovics, Pearl. Valentine's Day. 2018. (Happy Holidays! Ser.). (ENG., Illus.). 16p. (J). (gr. -1-1). 6.99 *(978-1-64280-153-8(4))* Bearport Publishing Co., Inc.
McGee, Randel. Paper Crafts for Valentine's Day, 1 vol. 2008. (Paper Craft Fun for Holidays Ser.). (ENG., Illus.). 48p. (gr. 3-3). pap. 11.53 *(978-1-4644-0329-3(5),* 288c7207-b89c-4bb7-9ed7-df3465df3346, Enslow Elementary) Enslow Publishing, LLC.
McGrath, Barbara Barbieri. The M & M's(r) Brand Valentine Book. Tagel, Peggy, illus. 2004. 12p. (J). (gr. -1-k). bds. 6.95 *(978-1-57091-422-5(2))* Charlesbridge Publishing, Inc.
McNeil, Niki, et al. HOCPP 1033 Valentine's Day. 2005. spiral bd. 20.00 *(978-1-60308-033-0(3))* In the Hands of a Child.
—HOCPP 1145 Be My Valentine. 2007. spiral bd. 15.50 *(978-1-60308-145-0(3))* In the Hands of a Child.
Mercer, Abbie. Happy Valentine's Day. (Holiday Fun Ser.). 24p. (gr. 2-3). 2009. 42.50 *(978-1-61513-379-6(8),* PowerKids Pr.) 2007. (ENG., Illus.). (J). lib. bdg. 26.27 *(978-1-4042-3809-1(3),* f8bbd793-e32a-4545-8337-de69f15a0bea) Rosen Publishing Group, Inc., The.
Miller, Reagan. Valentine's Day, 1 vol. 2009. (Celebrations in My World Ser.). (ENG., Illus.). 32p. (J). (gr. k-2). pap. *(978-0-7787-4777-2(8));* (gr. 1-3). *(978-0-7787-4759-8(X))* Crabtree Publishing Co.
Murray, Julie. Valentine's Day. 2017. (Holidays (Abdo Kids Junior) Ser.). (ENG., Illus.). 24p. (J). (gr. -1-2). lib. bdg. 31.36 *(978-1-5321-0395-7(6),* 26521, Abdo Kids) ABDO Publishing Co.
Otto, Carolyn. Holidays Around the World: Celebrate Valentine's Day: With Love, Cards, & Candy. 2016. (Holidays Around the World Ser.). 32p. (J). (gr. 3-7). pap. 7.99 *(978-1-4263-2747-6(1),* National Geographic Kids) Disney Publishing Worldwide.
Owen, Ruth. More Valentine's Day Origami, 1 vol. 2014. (Holiday Origami Ser.). (ENG., Illus.). 32p. (J). (gr. 2-3). 30.27 *(978-1-4777-5698-0(1),* 763a2325-9a75-4449-9a32-994a9dbdfaa5, PowerKids Pr.) Rosen Publishing Group, Inc., The.
—Valentine's Day Origami, 1 vol. 2012. (Holiday Origami Ser.). (ENG., Illus.). 32p. (J). (gr. 2-3). 30.27 *(978-1-4488-7865-9(9),* 5d861dd6-ac8f-47e4-b3bd-ea0f1d195d7e); pap. 12.75 *(978-1-4488-7924-3(8),* 1465687d-e3ff-4c3d-9fee-ab16d11fd7fc) Rosen Publishing Group, Inc., The. (PowerKids Pr.).
—Valentine's Day Sweets & Treats, 1 vol. 2012. (Holiday Cooking for Kids! Ser.). (ENG., Illus.). 32p. (J). (gr. 2-3). 31.27 *(978-1-4488-8080-5(7),* b26c814f-cf8e-44af-a97a-8cd8c660d76a); pap. 12.75 *(978-1-4488-8127-7(7),* f7d0c3ab-6081-4dd2-b211-68bc4a5adedd) Rosen Publishing Group, Inc., The. (Windmill Bks.).
Pettiford, Rebecca. Día de San Valentín. 2015.Tr. of Valentine's Day. (SPA., Illus.). 24p. (J). lib. bdg. *(978-1-62031-244-5(1),* Bullfrog Bks.) Jump! Inc.
—Valentine's Day. 2015. (Illus.). 24p. (J). lib. bdg. *(978-1-62031-187-5(9),* Bullfrog Bks.) Jump! Inc.
Ponto, Joanna. Valentine's Day, 1 vol. 2015. (Story of Our Holidays Ser.). (ENG., Illus.). 32p. (gr. 3-3). 26.93 *(978-0-7660-7462-0(5),* ef41a069-9275-406c-ab16-d5c4ad0bcf98); pap. 11.52 *(978-0-7660-7474-3(9),* 841efd98-a1b8-4fb1-ad3b-9de5e57cb186) Enslow Publishing, LLC.
Ritter, Elizabeth A. Happy Valentine's Day!, 1 vol. 2016. (Celebrations Ser.). (ENG.). 24p. (J). (gr. 1-1). pap. 9.25 *(978-1-4994-2673-1(9),* 5ff003ba-a26f-4163-8877-1e11389409dc, PowerKids Pr.) Rosen Publishing Group, Inc., The.
Sebra, Richard. It's Valentine's Day! 2017. (Bumba Books (r) — It's a Holiday! Ser.). (ENG., Illus.). 24p. (J). (gr. -1-1). 26.65 *(978-1-5124-2562-8(1),* c2e0bd87-3db5-47d4-b5a6-c9e78fe6c5fe); E-Book 39.99 *(978-1-5124-2741-7(1));* E-Book 4.99 *(978-1-5124-3708-9(5),* 9781512437089); E-Book 39.99 *(978-1-5124-3707-2(7),* 9781512437072) Lerner Publishing Group. (Lerner Pubns.).
Sévigny, Eric, illus. Caillou: Mystery Valentine. 2016. (Clubhouse Ser.). (ENG.). 24p. (J). (gr. -1-1). pap. 4.99 *(978-2-89718-181-9(8))* Caillouet, Gerry.
Siewert, Pauline, illus. It's Valentine's Day! A Valentine Book & Activity Kit. 2005. 10p. (J). bds. 9.95 *(978-1-58117-377-2(6),* Intervisual/Piggy Toes) Bendon, Inc.
Strain Trueit, Trudi. Valentine's Day, 1 vol. 2011. (Holiday Fun Ser.). (ENG.). 24p. (gr. k-1). 25.50 *(978-0-7614-4889-1(6),* 09316546-9752-4aff-8dae-7559e4fc092c) Cavendish Square Publishing LLC.
Suen, Anastasia. Valentine's Day Gifts. 2017. (Craft It! Ser.). (ENG.). 24p. (gr. 2-4). pap. 9.95 *(978-1-68342-883-1(8),* 9781683428831) Rourke Educational Media.
Trueit, Trudi Strain. Rookie Read-About Holidays: Valentine's Day. 2013. (ENG.). 32p. (J). 23.00 *(978-0-531-27207-7(9));* pap. 5.95 *(978-0-531-27357-9(1))* Scholastic Library Publishing.
Williams, Colleen Madonna Flood. My Adventure on Valentine's Day. 2009. (ENG.). 44p. (J). 8.99 *(978-1-59092-558-4(0))* Blue Forge Pr.
Yasuda, Anita. Valentine's Day. 2011. (J). (gr. 3-5). pap. 12.95 *(978-1-61690-684-9(7),* AV2 by Weigl); (Illus.). 24p. (gr. 2-5). 27.13 *(978-1-61690-678-8(2))* Weigl Pubs., Inc.
Zocchi, Judy. On Valentine's Day. Wallis, Rebecca, illus. 2005. (Holiday Happenings Ser.). 32p. (J). lib. bdg. 21.65 *(978-1-891997-79-2(3));* per. 10.95 *(978-1-59646-229-8(9))* Dingles & Co.
—On Valentine's Day/el día de San Valentín. Wallis, Rebecca, illus. 2005. (Holiday Happenings Ser.).Tr. of Día de San Valentín. (ENG & SPA.). 32p. (J). pap. 10.95 *(978-1-59646-230-4(2));* lib. bdg. 21.65 *(978-1-891997-78-5(5));* per. 10.95 *(978-1-59646-231-1(0))* Dingles & Co.

VALENTINE'S DAY—FICTION

Andrews, Julie & Hamilton, Emma Walton. Valentines from the Heart. 2015. (Very Fairy Princess Ser.). (Illus.). (J). lib. bdg. 16.00 *(978-0-606-37466-8(3))* Turtleback.
Andrews, Julie & Hamilton, Emma Walton. The Very Fairy Princess Follows Her Heart. Davenier, Christine, illus. 2013. (Very Fairy Princess Ser.). (ENG.). 32p. (J). (gr. -1-3). 16.99 *(978-0-316-18559-2(0))* Little, Brown Bks. for Young Readers.
Awdry, W. A Valentine for Percy. 2015. (Thomas & Friends Step into Reading Ser.). (Illus.). 24p. lib. bdg. 14.75 *(978-0-606-38471-1(5))* Turtleback.
—A Valentine for Percy. Courtney, Richard, illus. 2015. 24p. (J). *(978-1-4806-9757-7(5))* Random Hse., Inc.
Baglio, Ben M. Corgi in the Cupcakes. Baum, Ann, illus. 2008. 142p. (J). pap. *(978-0-439-02533-1(8))* Scholastic, Inc.
—Kitty in the Candy Hearts. 2007. (Illus.). 147p. (J). pap. *(978-0-439-87119-8(0))* Scholastic, Inc.
Balian, Lorna. A Sweetheart for Valentine, 1 vol. 2005. (ENG., Illus.). 32p. (J). 15.95 *(978-1-932065-14-5(8))* Star Bright Bks., Inc.
Barkley, Callie. Ellie's Lovely Idea. Riti, Marsha, illus. 2013. (Critter Club Ser.: 6). (ENG.). 128p. (J). (gr. k-4). 17.99 *(978-1-4424-8219-7(2));* pap. 6.99 *(978-1-4424-8218-0(4))* Little Simon. (Little Simon).
—Ellie's Lovely Idea. 2013. (Critter Club Ser.: 6). (J). lib. bdg. 16.00 *(978-0-606-32321-5(X))* Turtleback.
Benton, Jim. Attack of the 50-Ft. Cupid. Benton, Jim, illus. 2004. (Franny K. Stein, Mad Scientist Ser.: 2). (ENG., Illus.). 112p. (J). (gr. 2-5). 17.99 *(978-0-689-86292-2(X),* Simon & Schuster Bks. For Young Readers) Simon & Schuster Bks. For Young Readers.
—Attack of the 50-Ft. Cupid. Benton, Jim, illus. 2011. (Franny K. Stein, Mad Scientist Ser.). (ENG., Illus.). 112p. (J). (gr. 2-6). 31.36 *(978-1-59961-818-0(4),* 7828, Chapter Bks.) Spotlight.

Berenstain, Mike. The Berenstain Bears' Valentine Love Bug. Berenstain, Mike, illus. 2014. (Berenstain Bears Ser.). (ENG., Illus.). 24p. (J). (gr. -1-3). pap. 6.99 *(978-0-06-207562-8(4)*, HarperFestival) HarperCollins Pubs.

Berger, Samantha. A Crankenstein Valentine. Santat, Dan, illus. 2014. (ENG.). 40p. (J). (gr. -1-3). 18.99 *(978-0-316-37638-9(8))* Little, Brown Bks. for Young Readers.

Berry Byrd, Holly. Babies Love Valentines. Cottage Door Press, ed. Hogan, Martina, illus. 2016. (Babies Love Ser.). (ENG.). 12p. (J). (gr. -1 — 1). bds. 7.99 *(978-1-68052-149-8(7)*, 1001430) Cottage Door Pr.

Bickel, Karla. Fishnet Valentine. Bickel, Karla, illus. l.t. ed. 2004. (Illus.). 16p. (J). (gr. -1-5). pap. 5.00 *(978-1-891452-13-0(4)*, 4) Heart Arbor Bks.

Bond, Felicia. Day It Rained Hearts. Bond, Felicia, illus. 2006. (ENG., Illus.). 36p. (J). (gr. -1-3). pap. 8.99 *(978-0-06-073123-6(0)*, HarperCollins) HarperCollins Pubs.

Boone, William Rogers & Jennings, Bonnie Boone. The Valentine Sheep. Keck, Becky Boone, illus. 2007. (ENG.). 26p. per. 13.99 *(978-1-4259-9046-6(0))* AuthorHouse.

Bunting, Eve. Mr. Goat's Valentine. Zimmer, Kevin, illus. 2016. (ENG.). 32p. (J). (gr. k-2). 16.99 *(978-1-58536-944-7(6)*, 204024) Sleeping Bear Pr.

Cabot, Meg. The Princess Diaries: Volume 7 & 3/4: Valentine Princess. 2006. (Princess Diaries: 7.75). (ENG.). 96p. (YA). (gr. 8-12). 13.99 *(978-0-06-084718-0(2)*, HarperTeen) HarperCollins Pubs.

Capucilli, Alyssa Satin. Biscuit's Valentine's Day. Schories, Pat, illus. 2019. (Biscuit Ser.). (ENG.). 20p. (J). (gr. -1-3). pap. 6.99 *(978-0-694-01222-0(X)*, HarperFestival) HarperCollins Pubs.

Carlson, Melody. Secret Admirer, 1 vol. 2016. (Faithgirlz / Girls of Harbor View Ser.). (ENG.). 272p. (J). pap. 9.99 *(978-0-310-75371-1(6))* Zonderkidz.

Carlson, Nancy. Louanne Pig in the Mysterious Valentine. rev. ed. 2004. (Carolrhoda Picture Books Ser.). (Illus.). 32p. (J). (gr. k-2). 15.95 *(978-1-57505-671-5(2))* Lerner Publishing Group.

—Louanne Pig in the Mysterious Valentine, 2nd Edition. 2nd rev. ed. 2004. (Nancy Carlson Picture Bks.). (ENG., Illus.). 32p. (J). (gr. k-2). per. 9.99 *(978-1-57505-722-4(0)*, 996de222-b558-480f-94ac-14e4e20b0b97, Carolrhoda Bks.) Lerner Publishing Group.

Carter, David A. Love Bugs: A Pop up Book. Carter, David A., illus. 2003. (ENG., Illus.). 12p. (J). (gr. 2-5). 8.99 *(978-0-689-85815-4(9)*, Little Simon) Little Simon.

Cazet, Denys, reader. Minnie & Moo: Will You Be My Valentine? 2004. (Read-Alongs for Beginning Readers Ser.). (Illus.). (J). (gr. -1-3). 25.95 incl. audio *(978-1-59112-892-2(7))*; pap. 29.95 incl. audio *(978-1-59112-893-9(5))*; pap. 31.95 incl. audio compact disk *(978-1-59112-897-7(8))* Live Oak Media.

Chand, Emlyn. Vicky Finds a Valentine: Bird Brain Books. Giffin, Noelle, illus. ed. 2013. (ENG.). 50p. (gr. k-1). pap. 10.95 *(978-1-62253-116-5(7))*; 21.95 *(978-1-62253-117-2(5))* Evolved Publishing.

Clough, Lisa & Briant, Ed. Petal & Poppy & the Mystery Valentine. 2015. (ENG., Illus.). 32p. (J). (gr. 1-4). pap. 4.99 *(978-0-544-55549-5(X)*, 1610456, Clarion Bks.) HarperCollins Pubs.

—Petal & Poppy & the Mystery Valentine. 2015. (Green Light Readers Level 2 Ser.). lib. bdg. 13.55 *(978-0-606-37452-1(3))* Turtleback.

Cohen, Miriam. Bee My Valentine, 1 vol. Himler, Ronald, illus. (ENG.). 32p. (J). (gr. k-3). 2009. pap. 5.95 *(978-1-59572-086-3(3))* 2008. 15.95 *(978-1-59572-085-6(5))* Star Bright Bks., Inc.

Cooke, Brandy. My Valentine. Wilkinson, Annie, illus. 2010. (ENG.). 12p. (J). (gr. -1 — 1). bds. 8.99 *(978-1-4424-0779-4(4)*, Little Simon) Little Simon.

Cooper, Mimi. Me Versus Cooties. 2006. 17p. 9.99 *(978-1-4116-8256-6(4))* Lulu Pr., Inc.

Cronin, Doreen. Click, Clack, Moo I Love You! Lewin, Betsy, illus. 2017. (Click Clack Book Ser.). (ENG.). 40p. (J). (gr. -1-3). 17.99 *(978-1-4814-4496-5(4)*, Atheneum/Caitlyn Dlouhy Books) Simon & Schuster Children's Publishing.

—Click, Clack, Moo I Love You! Lewin, Betsy, illus. 2020. (Doreen Cronin: Click, Clack & More Ser.). (ENG.). 36p. (J). (gr. -1-3). 31.36 *(978-1-5321-4465-3(2)*, 35155, Picture Bk.) Spotlight.

D'Andrea, Deborah, concept. Picture Me Bee My Honey. 2003. 10p. (J). (gr. -1-18). bds. 2.99 *(978-1-57151-520-9(8))* Playhouse Publishing.

Darling, Angela. Rachel's Valentine Crush. 2013. (Crush Ser.: 5). (ENG., Illus.). 160p. (J). (gr. 3-7). 15.99 *(978-1-4424-8641-6(4))*; pap. 5.99 *(978-1-4424-8640-9(6))* Simon Spotlight. (Simon Spotlight).

Davenport, Kathy. Holly's Chocolate Heart. 2011. 40p. 17.49 *(978-1-4567-1520-5(8))* AuthorHouse.

Dean, James & Dean, Kimberly. Pete the Cat: Valentine's Day Is Cool. Dean, James, illus. 2013. (Pete the Cat Ser.). (ENG., Illus.). 24p. (J). (gr. -1-3). 10.99 *(978-0-06-219865-5(3)*, HarperFestival) HarperCollins Pubs.

deGroat, Diane. Roses Are Pink, Your Feet Really Stink. deGroat, Diane, illus. 2022. (ENG., Illus.). 32p. (J). (gr. -1-3). pap. 8.99 *(978-0-688-15220-8(1)*, HarperCollins) HarperCollins Pubs.

Disney Book Group Staff & Higginson, Sheila Sweeny. Minnie: Minnie's Valentine. Disney Storybook Artists Staff, illus. 2013. 10p. 5.99 *(978-1-4231-8811-7(X))* Disney Pr.

Disney Books. Mickey Mouse Clubhouse: Minnie's Valentine. rev. ed. 2007. (ENG., Illus.). 24p. (J). (gr. -1-k). pap. 4.99 *(978-1-4231-0746-0(2)*, Disney Press Books) Disney Publishing Worldwide.

—Minnie: Be My Sparkly Valentine. 2014. (ENG., Illus.). 24p. (J). (gr. -1-k). pap. 5.99 *(978-1-4231-6414-2(8)*, Disney Press Books) Disney Publishing Worldwide.

Dougherty, Brandi. The Littlest Valentine. Todd, Michelle, illus. 2017. (J). *(978-1-338-20702-6(4))* Scholastic, Inc.

—The Valentine's Day Disaster. 2008. 204p. (J). pap. *(978-0-545-03168-4(0))* Scholastic, Inc.

Dunrea, Olivier. Ollie's Valentine. Dunrea, Olivier, illus. 2015. (Gossie & Friends Ser.). (ENG., Illus.). 14p. (J). (— 1). bds. 7.99 *(978-0-544-50269-7(8)*, 1604447, Clarion Bks.) HarperCollins Pubs.

Dyan, Penelope. Mikey & Me & the Valentines — the Continuing Story of a Girl & Her Dog. Dyan, Penelope, illus. 2010. (Illus.). 50p. pap. 14.95 *(978-1-935118-96-1(X))* Bellissima Publishing, LLC.

—My Valentines. 2011. 34p. pap. 11.95 *(978-1-935630-52-4(0))* Bellissima Publishing, LLC.

Elliott, Laura Malone. A String of Hearts. Munsinger, Lynn, illus. 2010. (ENG.). 32p. (J). (gr. -1-2). 16.99 *(978-0-06-000085-1(6)*, Tegen, Katherine Bks) HarperCollins Pubs.

Farley, Robin. Mia: the Sweetest Valentine. Ivanov, Aleksey & Ivanov, Olga, illus. 2012. (Mia Ser.). (ENG.). 24p. (J). (gr. -1-3). 4.99 *(978-0-06-210012-2(5)*, HarperFestival) HarperCollins Pubs.

Ferber, Brenda. The Yuckiest, Stinkiest, Best Valentine Ever. Arnold, Tedd, illus. 2015. (ENG.). 40p. (J). (gr. -1-2). 8.99 *(978-0-14-751709-8(5)*, Puffin Books) Penguin Young Readers Group.

Friedman, Laurie. Heart to Heart with Mallory. 2008. pap. 34.95 *(978-0-8225-9439-0(0))* Lerner Publishing Group.

—Heart to Heart with Mallory. Pollak, Barbara, illus. (Mallory Ser.: 6). (ENG.). 160p. (J). (gr. 2-5). 2007. per. 7.99 *(978-0-8225-7133-9(1)*, b2c6ea4e-9452-4902-bcd8-b84c16b1ce2f, Darby Creek) 2006. lib. bdg. 15.95 *(978-1-57505-932-7(0)*, Twenty-First Century Bks.) Lerner Publishing Group.

—Love, Ruby Valentine. Avril, Lynne, illus. 2006. (Ruby Valentine Ser.). (ENG.). 32p. (J). (gr. k-3). lib. bdg. 16.95 *(978-1-57505-899-3(5)*, 76ef85c3-9ebb-43e3-afc4-3afa1ae7878d, Carolrhoda Bks.) Lerner Publishing Group.

—Ruby Valentine & the Sweet Surprise. Avril, Lynne, illus. 2014. (Ruby Valentine Ser.). (ENG.). 32p. (J). (gr. k-3). 16.95 *(978-0-7613-8873-9(7)*, 7491b02d-c3ff-421c-a33c-6400cf28d745, Carolrhoda Bks.) Lerner Publishing Group.

—Ruby Valentine Saves the Day. Avril, Lynne, illus. 2010. (Ruby Valentine Ser.). (ENG.). 32p. (J). (gr. k-3). lib. bdg. 16.95 *(978-0-7613-4213-7(3)*, 5712cf7b-cdd0-4bc4-bb02-98aa513f9e9a, Carolrhoda Bks.) Lerner Publishing Group.

Fruchter, Jason, illus. Happy Love Day, Daniel Tiger! A Lift-The-Flap Book. 2015. (Daniel Tiger's Neighborhood Ser.). (ENG.). 14p. (J). (gr. -1-2). bds. 6.99 *(978-1-4814-4855-0(2)*, Simon Spotlight) Simon Spotlight.

Garcia, Mary. Play with Me: Togetherness Time for Your Preschooler & You: St. Valentine's Day. 2007. (J). *(978-0-9790931-1-1(2))* SMARTseeds Co., LLC, The.

Golden Books. Puppy Hugs & Kisses! (PAW Patrol) Lovett, Nate, illus. 2016. (ENG.). 64p. (J). (gr. -1-2). pap. 4.99 *(978-0-399-55878-8(0)*, Golden Bks.) Random Hse. Children's Bks.

Greene, Stephanie. Princess Posey & the First Grade Ballet. Roth Sisson, Stephanie, illus. 2014. (Princess Posey, First Grader Ser.: 9). 96p. (J). (gr. k-3). pap. 6.99 *(978-0-14-751292-5(1)*, Puffin Books) Penguin Young Readers Group.

Gutman, Dan. My Weird School #20: Mr. Louie Is Screwy! Paillot, Jim, illus. 2007. (My Weird School Ser.: 20). (ENG.). 112p. (J). (gr. 1-5). pap. 5.99 *(978-0-06-123479-8(6)*, HarperCollins) HarperCollins Pubs.

—My Weird School Special: Oh, Valentine, We've Lost Our Minds! Paillot, Jim, illus. 2014. (My Weird School Special Ser.). (ENG.). 144p. (J). (gr. 1-5). pap. 6.99 *(978-0-06-228403-7(7)*, HarperCollins) HarperCollins Pubs.

—Oh, Valentine, We've Lost Our Minds! 2014. (My Weird School Ser.). (J). lib. bdg. 16.00 *(978-0-606-36460-7(9))* Turtleback.

Happy Valentine's Day Curious George. 2011. (Curious George Ser.). (ENG., Illus.). 14p. (J). (gr. -1-3). 8.99 *(978-0-547-13107-8(0)*, 1048361, Clarion Bks.) HarperCollins Pubs.

Hill, Eric. I Love You, Spot. 2016. (Spot Ser.). (ENG., Illus.). 10p. (J). (— 1). bds. 7.99 *(978-0-14-136613-5(3)*, Warne) Penguin Young Readers Group.

Hillert, Margaret. I Love You, Dear Dragon. 2016. (BeginningtoRead Ser.). (ENG., Illus.). 32p. (J). (-2). lib. bdg. 22.60 *(978-1-59953-770-2(2))* Norwood Hse. Pr.

—Te Quiero, Querido Dragón. Pullan, Jack, illus. 2017. (BeginningtoRead Ser.). Tr. of I Love You, Dear Dragon. (ENG & SPA.). 32p. (J). (-2). 22.60 *(978-1-59953-833-4(4))*; pap. 11.94 *(978-1-68404-019-3(1))* Norwood Hse. Pr.

Hills, Tad. Duck & Goose, Goose Needs a Hug. Hills, Tad, illus. 2012. (Duck & Goose Ser.). (ENG., Illus.). 22p. (J). (-k). bds. 8.99 *(978-0-307-98293-3(9))* Random Hse. Children's Bks.

Hoff, Syd. Danny & the Dinosaur: First Valentine's Day. Hoff, Syd, illus. 2016. (ENG., Illus.). 24p. (J). (gr. -1-3). pap. 6.99 *(978-0-06-241044-3(X)*, HarperFestival) HarperCollins Pubs.

Hoien, Ruth S. Ruthie's Four Hearts. (J). pap. 3.99 *(978-0-88019-105-0(8))* Schmul Publishing Co., Inc.

Holub, Joan. Big Heart! A Valentine's Day Tale. Terry, Will, illus. 2007. (Ant Hill Ser.). (ENG.). 24p. (J). (gr. -1-k). lib. bdg. 13.89 *(978-1-4169-2562-0(7)*, Simon & Schuster/Paula Wiseman Bks.) Simon & Schuster/Paula Wiseman Bks.

—Big Heart! A Valentine's Day Tale (Ready-To-Read Pre-Level 1) Terry, Will, illus. 2007. (Ant Hill Ser.). (ENG.). 24p. (J). (gr. -1-k). pap. 4.99 *(978-1-4169-0957-6(5)*, Simon Spotlight) Simon Spotlight.

Inches, Alison. Dora Quiere Mucho a Boots. Saunders, Zina, illus. 2005. (Dora the Explorer Ser.). (SPA.). 24p. (J). (gr. -1-2). pap. 3.99 *(978-1-4169-0620-9(7)*, Libros Para Ninos) Libros Para Ninos.

Jackson, Everett E. Kimme Gets a Valentine. 2008. 28p. pap. 16.99 *(978-1-4389-0982-0(9))* AuthorHouse.

Jennings, Sharon. Batnapped. *(978-1-897039-30-4(1))* High Interest Publishing (HIP).

Kann, Victoria. Pinkalicious: Pink of Hearts. Kann, Victoria, illus. 2011. (Pinkalicious Ser.). (ENG., Illus.). 24p. (J). (gr. -1-2). pap. 6.99 *(978-0-06-198923-0(1)*, HarperFestival) HarperCollins Pubs.

Katschke, Judy. Our Funny Valentine. Elsom, Clare, illus. 2015. 32p. (J). *(978-0-545-77605-9(8))* Scholastic, Inc.

Kaye, Marilyn. Valentine's Day Surprise: The after School Club. 2014. (ENG., Illus.). 80p. (J). (gr. 3-7). pap. 13.99 *(978-1-4814-2886-6(1)*, Simon & Schuster/Paula Wiseman Bks.) Simon & Schuster/Paula Wiseman Bks.

Kelsey, Annie. Love & Chicken Nuggets. Larsen, Kate, illus. 2017. (Pippa Morgan's Diary Ser.: 2). (ENG.). 176p. (J). (gr. 3-7). pap. 9.99 *(978-1-4926-4794-2(2))* Sourcebooks, Inc.

Kent, Renee Holmes. Adventures in Misty Falls, Vol. 8. 2004. (Adventures in Misty Falls Ser.: Vol. 8). (Illus.). 100p. (gr. 4-7). pap. 4.99 *(978-1-56309-456-9(8)*, N017104) Woman's Missionary Union.

Killian, Beth. Everything She Wants. 2006. (310 Ser.). (ENG.). 240p. (YA). (gr. 8-12). pap. 15.99 *(978-1-4165-2168-6(2)*, MTV Bks.) MTV Books.

Kimmelman, Leslie. A Valentine for Frankenstein. Banks, Timothy, illus. 2018. (ENG.). 32p. (J). (gr. k-3). 17.99 *(978-1-5124-3129-2(X)*, 167d90ab-668e-49b7-9865-a741925f37aa, Carolrhoda Bks.) Lerner Publishing Group.

Kirby, Stan. Captain Awesome Gets Crushed. O'Connor, George, illus. 2013. (Captain Awesome Ser.: 9). (ENG.). 128p. (J). (gr. k-2). pap. 6.99 *(978-1-4424-8212-8(5))*; 17.99 *(978-1-4424-8213-5(3))* Little Simon. (Little Simon).

—Captain Awesome Gets Crushed. 2013. (Captain Awesome Ser.: 9). lib. bdg. 16.00 *(978-0-606-32331-4(7))* Turtleback.

Kleinberg, Naomi. My Fuzzy Valentine (Sesame Street) Moroney, Christopher, illus. 2005. (ENG.). 12p. (J). (gr. k — 1). bds. 5.99 *(978-0-375-83392-2(7)*, Random Hse. Bks. for Young Readers) Random Hse. Children's Bks.

Kline, Suzy. Horrible Harry on the Ropes. Remkiewicz, Frank, illus. 2011. (Horrible Harry Ser.: 24). 80p. (J). (gr. 2-4). 4.99 *(978-0-14-241695-2(9)*, Puffin Books) Penguin Young Readers Group.

Knudson, Mike. Raymond & Graham: Dancing Dudes. 2010. (Raymond & Graham Ser.: 2). (Illus.). 144p. (J). (gr. 3-7). 6.99 *(978-0-14-241508-5(1)*, Puffin Books) Penguin Young Readers Group.

Kroll, Steven. The Biggest Valentine Ever. Bassett, Jeni, illus. 2005. (ENG.). 32p. (J). (gr. -1-k). pap. 3.99 *(978-0-439-76419-3(X))* Scholastic, Inc.

LaFleur, John & Dubin, Shawn. Dreary & Naughty: Friday the 13th of February: Friday the 13th of February, 1 vol. 2013. (ENG., Illus.). 64p. (YA). (gr. 8-12). 14.99 *(978-0-7643-4495-4(1)*, 4929) Schiffer Publishing, Ltd.

Lang, Suzanne. Grumpy Monkey Valentine Gross-Out. Lang, Max, illus. 2022. (Grumpy Monkey Ser.). 32p. (J). (gr. -1-3). 10.99 *(978-0-593-48692-4(7))* Random Hse. Children's Bks.

Lee, Erin. Enny Penny's Valentine's Day Wish. Trivedi, Ishan, illus. 2018. (Enny Penny Ser.: 4). (ENG.). 24p. (J). (gr. k-2). pap. 9.95 *(978-0-9910907-3-0(X))* StoryBk. Genius, LLC.

Lee, Quinlan B. Valentine Surprise. Haefele, Steve, illus. 2008. (Clifford the Big Red Dog Ser.). (J). *(978-0-545-02845-5(0))* Scholastic, Inc.

Levithan, David. Marly's Ghost. Selznick, Brian, illus. 2007. (ENG.). 208p. (YA). (gr. 7-18). 7.99 *(978-0-14-240912-1(X)*, Speak) Penguin Young Readers Group.

Long, Ethan. Valensteins. (ENG., Illus.). (J). 2018. 30p. bds. 7.99 *(978-1-68119-894-1(0)*, 900191673, Bloomsbury Children's Bks.) 2017. 32p. 17.99 *(978-1-61963-433-6(3)*, 900135962, Bloomsbury USA Childrens) Bloomsbury Publishing USA.

Love-Byrd, Cheri. How Many Do I Love You? a Valentine Counting Book. Cottage Door Press, ed. Stoyva, Mei, illus. 2017. (ENG.). 13p. (J). (gr. -1-k). bds. 7.99 *(978-1-68052-274-7(4)*, 1002590) Cottage Door Pr.

Lunsford, Susie. The Magical Wishing Well Forest Series. 2006. pap. 25.32 *(978-1-4134-9491-4(9))* Xlibris Corp.

Martin, Ann M. Abby's un-Valentine (the Baby-Sitters Club #127) A Geronimo Stilton Adventure. 2011. (Thea Stilton Ser.: 127). (ENG.). 160p. (J). (gr. 2-5). E-Book 8.99 *(978-0-545-87475-5(0)*, Scholastic Paperbacks) Scholastic, Inc.

Mayer, Mercer. Just a Little Love. 2013. (Little Critter: I Can Read! Ser.). (J). lib. bdg. 13.55 *(978-0-606-32176-1(4))* Turtleback.

—Little Critter: Happy Valentine's Day, Little Critter! Mayer, Mercer, illus. 2005. (Little Critter Ser.). (ENG., Illus.). 20p. (J). (gr. -1-3). pap. 6.99 *(978-0-06-053973-3(9)*, HarperFestival) HarperCollins Pubs.

McGrath, Barbara Barbieri. Valentine's Shapes. Tagel, Peggy, illus. 2016. (First Celebrations Ser.: 4). 12p. (J). (— 1). bds. 6.95 *(978-1-58089-532-3(8))* Charlesbridge Publishing, Inc.

McNamara, Margaret. The Fairy Bell Sisters #4: Clara & the Magical Charms. Denos, Julia, illus. 2013. (Fairy Bell Sisters Ser.: 4). (ENG.). 128p. (J). (gr. 1-5). pap. 4.99 *(978-0-06-222810-9(2)*, Balzer & Bray) HarperCollins Pubs.

—Too Many Valentines: Ready-To-Read Level 1. Gordon, Mike, illus. 2003. (Robin Hill School Ser.). (ENG.). 32p. (J). (gr. -1-1). pap. 4.99 *(978-0-689-85537-5(0)*, Simon Spotlight) Simon Spotlight.

Moffitt, Debra. Girls in Charge. 2011. (Pink Locker Society Novels Ser.: 4). (ENG.). 208p. (J). (gr. 3-7). pap. 18.99 *(978-0-312-64506-9(6)*, 900068660, St. Martin's Griffin) St. Martin's Pr.

Mongredien, Sue. Be My Valentine. 2010. (Sleepover Club Ser.). (ENG.). 128p. (J). (gr. 2-6). pap. 6.99 *(978-0-00-727705-6(9))* Lion Hudson PLC GBR. Dist: Independent Pubs. Group.

My Little Love. 2003. (Illus.). 256p. (J). (gr. -1-1). pap. 14.99 *(978-0-06-051764-9(6))* HarperCollins Pubs.

Newton, A. I. The Alien Next Door 6: the Mystery Valentine. Sarkar, Anjan, illus. 2018. (Alien Next Door Ser.: 6). (ENG.). 112p. (J). (gr. k-3). 16.99 *(978-1-4998-0726-4(0))*; pap. 5.99 *(978-1-4998-0725-7(2))* Little Bee Books Inc.

—The Mystery Valentine, 6. 2019. (Alien Next Door Ch Bks). (ENG.). 95p. (J). (gr. 2-3). 15.59 *(978-0-87617-272-8(9))* Penworthy Co., LLC, The.

Numeroff, Laura. Happy Valentine's Day, Mouse! Lap Edition. Bond, Felicia, illus. 2015. (If You Give... Ser.). (ENG.). 24p. (J). (gr. -1-3). bds. 12.99 *(978-0-06-242740-3(7)*, HarperFestival) HarperCollins Pubs.

Oceanak, Karla. Ignoramus. Spanjer, Kendra, illus. 2013. (Aldo Zelnick Comic Novel Ser.: 9). (ENG.). 160p. (J). (gr. 3-7). 12.95 *(978-1-934649-41-4(4)*, 1365432) Bailiwick Pr.

O'Connor, Jane. Fancy Nancy: Nancy Clancy Seeks a Fortune. Glasser, Robin Preiss, illus. 2016. (Nancy Clancy Ser.: 7). (ENG.). 144p. (J). (gr. 1-5). 9.99 *(978-0-06-226969-0(0)*, HarperCollins) HarperCollins Pubs.

—Fancy Nancy Heart to Heart. Glasser, Robin Preiss, illus. 2009. (Fancy Nancy Ser.). (ENG.). 24p. (J). (gr. -1-3). pap. 4.99 *(978-0-06-123596-2(2)*, HarperFestival) HarperCollins Pubs.

—Fancy Nancy: Nancy Clancy, Secret Admirer. Glasser, Robin Preiss, illus. 2013. (Nancy Clancy Ser.: 2). (ENG.). (J). (gr. 1-5). 144p. pap. 5.99 *(978-0-06-208420-0(8))*; 128p. 9.99 *(978-0-06-208295-4(7))* HarperCollins Pubs. (HarperCollins).

—Fancy Nancy: Nancy Clancy's Tres Charming Chapter Book Box Set: Books 1-3, 3 vols., Set. Glasser, Robin Preiss, illus. 2013. (Nancy Clancy Ser.). (ENG.). 384p. (J). (gr. 1-5). 24.99 *(978-0-06-227793-0(6)*, HarperCollins) HarperCollins Pubs.

—Nancy Clancy, Secret Admirer. 2013. (Nancy Clancy Ser.: 2). (J). lib. bdg. 14.75 *(978-0-606-35045-7(4))* Turtleback.

Pace, Anne Marie. Groundhug Day. Denise, Christopher, illus. 2017. (ENG.). 48p. (J). (gr. -1-k). 18.99 *(978-1-4847-5356-9(9))* Little, Brown Bks. for Young Readers.

Paratore, Coleen Murtagh. Sunny Holiday. 2008. (Sunny Holiday Ser.: 1). (ENG.). 176p. (J). (gr. 2-4). 18.69 *(978-0-545-07588-6(2))* Scholastic, Inc.

Parish, Herman. Amelia Bedelia's First Valentine. Avril, Lynne, illus. (Amelia Bedelia Ser.). (ENG.). 32p. (J). (gr. -1-3). 2014. pap. 7.99 *(978-0-06-154460-6(4))* 2011. 9.99 *(978-0-06-203275-1(5))* 2009. 16.99 *(978-0-06-154458-3(2))* HarperCollins Pubs. (Greenwillow Bks.).

—Amelia Bedelia's First Valentine. 2014. (Amelia Bedelia Picture Bks.). (J). lib. bdg. 17.20 *(978-0-606-35971-9(0))* Turtleback.

Park, Barbara. Junie B. Jones & the Mushy Gushy Valentine. unabr. ed. 2004. (Junie B. Jones Ser.: No. 14). 69p. (J). (gr. k-3). pap. 17.00 incl. audio *(978-0-8072-0335-4(1)*, Listening Library) Random Hse. Audio Publishing Group.

—Junie B. My Valentime. Brunkus, Denise, illus. 2013. (Junie B. Jones Ser.). (ENG.). 12p. (gr. -1-2). pap. 5.99 *(978-0-385-37302-9(3)*, Random Hse. Bks. for Young Readers) Random Hse. Children's Bks.

Perelman, Helen. Heart to Heart. 2007. (High School Musical Stories from East High Ser.). 125p. (J). (gr. 3-7). 12.65 *(978-0-7569-8340-6(1))* Perfection Learning Corp.

Perry, Naresha. Zora's Valentine. 2005. per. 17.00 *(978-0-8059-9751-4(2))* Dorrance Publishing Co., Inc.

Petersen, David. Snowy Valentine. Petersen, David, illus. 2011. (ENG., Illus.). 32p. (J). (gr. -1-3). 14.99 *(978-0-06-146378-5(7)*, HarperCollins) HarperCollins Pubs.

Peterson, John & Slater, Teddy. The Littles Have a Happy Valentine's Day. Rogers, Jacqueline, illus. 2003. (Littles First Readers Ser.: No. 11). (ENG.). 32p. (J). (gr. k-2). pap. 3.99 *(978-0-439-42499-8(2)*, Scholastic Paperbacks) Scholastic, Inc.

Priddy, Roger. Shiny Shapes: Love You Always. 2016. (Shiny Shapes Ser.). (ENG.). 10p. (J). bds. 7.99 *(978-0-312-52053-3(0)*, 900161214) St. Martin's Pr.

Publications International Ltd. Staff, ed. Sesame Street(r) Elmo's Valentine. 2013. 12p. (J). bds. 7.98 *(978-1-4508-7410-6(X)*, 95d0f5ac-f093-4d77-bf25-5caf2a717091) Phoenix International Publications, Inc.

Reed, Melody. The Major Eights 6: the Secret Valentine. Pépin, Émilie, illus. 2020. (Major Eights Ser.: 6). (ENG.). 112p. (J). (gr. k-3). pap. 5.99 *(978-1-4998-0761-5(9))*; (gr. 2-5). 16.99 *(978-1-4998-0762-2(7))* Little Bee Books Inc.

Rey, H. A. Curious George Makes a Valentine. 2018. (Curious George TV Tie-In Early Reader Ser.). lib. bdg. 14.75 *(978-0-606-40424-2(4))* Turtleback.

Ricci, Christine. Dora's Valentine Adventure. A and J Studios Staff, illus. 2006. (Dora the Explorer Ser.). (ENG.). 14p. (J). (gr. -1-k). bds. 6.99 *(978-1-4169-1754-0(3)*, Simon Spotlight/Nickelodeon) Simon Spotlight/Nickelodeon.

Roberts, Bethany. Valentine Mice! Cushman, Doug, illus. 2016. (Green Light Readers Level 1 Ser.). (ENG.). 32p. (J). (gr. -1-3). 12.99 *(978-0-544-80897-3(5)*, 1641296, Clarion Bks.) HarperCollins Pubs.

—Valentine Mice! Board Book. Cushman, Doug, illus. 2011. (Green Light Readers Level 1 Ser.). (ENG.). 28p. (J). (gr. k — 1). bds. 5.99 *(978-0-547-37144-3(6)*, 1423785, Clarion Bks.) HarperCollins Pubs.

Rose, Nancy. The Secret Life of Squirrels: a Love Story. 2016. (ENG., Illus.). 32p. (J). (gr. -1-3). 16.99 *(978-0-316-27263-6(9))* Little, Brown Bks. for Young Readers.

Roy, Ron. Calendar Mysteries #2: February Friend. Gurney, John Steven, illus. 2009. (Calendar Mysteries Ser.: 2). 80p. (J). (gr. 1-4). 6.99 *(978-0-375-85662-4(5)*, Random Hse. Bks. for Young Readers) Random Hse. Children's Bks.

—A to Z Mysteries Super Edition #8: Secret Admirer. Gurney, John Steven, illus. 2015. (to Z Mysteries Ser.: 8). 144p. (J). (gr. 1-4). 5.99 *(978-0-553-52399-7(6)*, Random Hse. Bks. for Young Readers) Random Hse. Children's Bks.

Roza, Greg. El Día de San Valentín (Valentines for Vinnie) 2007. (Lecturas del barrio (Neighborhood Readers) Ser.). (SPA.). 12p. 33.50 *(978-1-4042-7301-6(8)*, Rosen Classroom) Rosen Publishing Group, Inc., The.

—Valentines for Vinnie. (Neighborhood Readers Ser.). (ENG.). 12p. 2007. 33.50 *(978-1-4042-7300-9(X))* 2006. (gr. 1-2). pap. 5.90 *(978-1-4042-6799-2(9)*, af158d89-bed9-49af-9c39-e9cee6966306) Rosen Publishing Group, Inc., The. (Rosen Classroom).

Ryder, Chloe. Princess Ponies 12: an Enchanted Heart. 2019. (Princess Ponies Ser.). (ENG., Illus.). 128p. (J). pap. 5.99 *(978-1-5476-0190-5(6)*, 900203169, Bloomsbury Children's Bks.) Bloomsbury Publishing USA.

Rylant, Cynthia. Henry & Mudge & Mrs. Hopper's House. Bracken, Carolyn, illus. 2004. (Ready-to-Read Ser.). 40p. (gr. k-2). 14.00 *(978-0-7569-2200-9(3))* Perfection Learning Corp.

—Henry & Mudge & Mrs. Hopper's House. Bracken, Carolyn, illus. 2004. (Henry & Mudge Ready-To-Read Ser.: 22). 40p. (gr. k-2). lib. bdg. 13.55 *(978-0-613-90376-9(5))* Turtleback.

—Henry & Mudge & Mrs. Hopper's House: Ready-To-Read Level 2. Bracken, Carolyn, illus. (Henry & Mudge Ser.: 22). (ENG.). 40p. (J). (gr. k-2). 2004. pap. 4.99 *(978-0-689-83446-2(2))* 2003. 17.99 *(978-0-689-81153-1(5))* Simon Spotlight. (Simon Spotlight).

—If You'll Be My Valentine. Kosaka, Fumi, illus. 2005. (ENG.). 32p. (J). (gr. -1-3). pap. 7.99 *(978-0-06-009271-9(8)*, HarperCollins) HarperCollins Pubs.

Schertle, Alice. Little Blue Truck's Valentine. McElmurry, Jill, illus. 2020. (ENG.). 20p. (J). (gr. -1). 13.99

T
U
V

(978-0-358-27244-1(0), 1771924, Clarion Bks.) HarperCollins Pubs.

Schulz, Charles. Be My Valentine, Charlie Brown. (J). pap. 46.80 *(978-0-590-06610-5(2))* Scholastic, Inc.

Schulz, Charles M. Buon San Valentino, Dolce Babù. pap. 19.95 *(978-88-451-2996-4(9))* Fabbri Editori - RCS Libri ITA. Dist: Distribooks, Inc.

Scollon, William. Minnie: Be My Sparkly Valentine. 2014. (Mickey Mouse 8x8 Ser.). (J). lib. bdg. 16.00 *(978-0-606-35903-0(6))* Turtleback.

Scotton, Rob. Love, Splat. Scotton, Rob, illus. (Splat the Cat Ser.). (ENG., Illus.). 40p. (J). (gr. -1-2). 2011. 9.99 *(978-0-06-207776-9(7))* 2008. 17.99 *(978-0-06-083157-8(X))* HarperCollins Pubs. (HarperCollins)

Setzer, Lee Ann. Sariah Mcduff: Book Three of the Sariah Mcduff Series: Valentine's Day Scrooge. Bonham, Bob, illus. 2005. (J). per. 5.95 *(978-1-55517-841-3(3))* Cedar Fort, Inc./CFI Distribution.

Shaw, Natalie. Olivia & the Perfect Valentine. 2013. (Olivia 8x8 Ser.). lib. bdg. 14.75 *(978-0-606-35200-0(7))* Turtleback.

Siwa, JoJo. Candy Kisses (JoJo & BowBow Book #2) 2019. (JoJo & BowBow Ser.). (ENG., Illus.). 152p. (J). (gr. 1-4). pap. 6.99 *(978-1-4197-3600-1(0)*, 1269903, Amulet Bks.) Abrams, Inc.

Smith, Jane. It's Valentine's Day, Chloe Zoe! Smith, Jane, illus. 2016. (Chloe Zoe Ser.). (ENG., Illus.). 32p. (J). (gr. -1-3). 12.99 *(978-0-8075-2462-6(X)*, 080752462X) Whitman, Albert & Co.

Star, Nancy. Case of the Kidnapped Cupid. Bernardin, James, illus. 2005. (Calendar Club Mysteries Ser.). 79p. (J). *(978-0-439-67263-4(5))* Scholastic, Inc.

Stilton, Gerónimo. Geronimo's Valentine. 2009. (Geronimo Stilton Ser.: 36). (Illus.). 103p. (J). 18.40 *(978-1-4364-5051-5(9))* Turtleback.

—Valentine's Day Disaster. Keys, Larry et al, illus. 2006. (Geronimo Stilton Ser.: No. 23). 122p. (J). lib. bdg. 18.46 *(978-1-4242-0292-8(2))* Fitzgerald Bks.

Stone Arch Books. Valentine's Day & the Lunar New Year, 1 vol. Nguyen, Dustin, illus. 2014. (Batman: Li'l Gotham Ser.). (ENG.). 32p. (J). (gr. 1-5). 22.60 *(978-1-4342-9218-6(5)*, 125724, Stone Arch Bks.) Capstone.

Sutherland, Margaret. Valentines Are for Saying I Love You. Wummer, Amy, illus. 2007. 24p. (J). (gr. -1-k). mass mkt. 4.99 *(978-0-448-44702-5(9)*, Grosset & Dunlap) Penguin Young Readers Group.

Thaler, Mike. Valentine's Day from the Black Lagoon, 1 vol. Lee, Jared, illus. 2014. (Black Lagoon Adventures Ser.). (ENG.). 64p. (J). (gr. 2-6). lib. bdg. 31.36 *(978-1-61479-209-3(7)*, 3618, Chapter Bks.) Spotlight.

Thompson, Lauren. Mouse Loves Love: Ready-To-Read Pre-Level 1. Erdogan, Buket, illus. 2018. (Mouse Ser.). (ENG.). 32p. (J). (gr. -1-k). 17.99 *(978-1-5344-2150-9(5))*; pap. 4.99 *(978-1-5344-2149-3(1))* Simon Spotlight. (Simon Spotlight).

—Mouse's First Valentine. Erdogan, Buket, illus. 2004. (Classic Board Bks.). (ENG.). 34p. (J). (gr. -1 — 1). bds. 8.99 *(978-0-689-85585-6(0)*, Little Simon) Little Simon.

Underwood, Deborah. Here Comes Valentine Cat. Rueda, Claudia, illus. 2015. 88p. (J). (-k). 17.99 *(978-0-525-42915-9(8)*, Dial Bks) Penguin Young Readers Group.

Wallace, Nancy Elizabeth. The Valentine Express, 0 vols. 2012. (ENG., Illus.). 32p. (J). (gr. -1-2). pap. 9.99 *(978-0-7614-5447-2(0)*, 9780761454472, Two Lions) Amazon Publishing.

Walstead, Alice. How to Catch a Loveosaurus. Elkerton, Andy, illus. 2022. (How to Catch Ser.). 40p. (J). (gr. -1-3). 10.99 *(978-1-7282-6878-1(8))* Sourcebooks, Inc.

Wan, Joyce. You Are My Sweetheart. Wan, Joyce, illus. 2018. (ENG., Illus.). 14p. (J). (gr. -1 — 1). bds. 6.99 *(978-1-338-04536-9(9)*, Cartwheel Bks.) Scholastic, Inc.

Weeks, Sarah. Be Mine, Be Mine, Sweet Valentine. Kosaka, Fumi, illus. 2005. (ENG.). 20p. (J). (gr. -1-k). 9.99 *(978-0-694-01514-6(8)*, HarperFestival) HarperCollins Pubs.

Weinberg, Jennifer Liberts. Princess Hearts. 2012. (Disney Princess Step into Reading Ser.). lib. bdg. 13.55 *(978-0-606-26975-9(4))* Turtleback.

Wells, Rosemary. Max's Valentine. 2003. (Max & Ruby Ser.). (ENG., Illus.). 16p. (J). (gr. -1 — 1). bds. 5.99 *(978-0-670-03668-4(4)*, Viking Books for Young Readers) Penguin Young Readers Group.

Wilhelm, Hans. I Love Valentine's Day! 2010. (Illus.). (J). pap. *(978-0-545-13475-0(7)*, Cartwheel Bks.) Scholastic, Inc.

Yee, Wong Herbert. Mouse & Mole: Secret Valentine. Yee, Wong Herbert, illus. (Mouse & Mole Story Ser.). (ENG., Illus.). 48p. (J). 2017. (gr. -1-3). 12.99 *(978-1-328-97533-1(9)*, 1708707) 2017. (gr. -1-3). pap. 4.99 *(978-1-328-74059-5(5)*, 1677035) 2013. (gr. 1-4). 15.99 *(978-0-547-88719-7(1)*, 1507662) HarperCollins Pubs. (Clarion Bks.).

Zenz, Aaron, illus. Porcupine Valentine. 2016. (J). *(978-0-545-90155-0(3))* Scholastic, Inc.

VALLEY FORGE (PA.)

Allen, Thomas B. Remember Valley Forge: Patriots, Tories, & Redcoats Tell Their Stories. 2015. (Illus.). 64p. (J). (gr. 5-9). pap. 7.99 *(978-1-4263-2250-1(X)*, National Geographic Kids) Disney Publishing Worldwide.

Micklos, John & Micklos, John, Jr. Washington's Crossing the Delaware & the Winter at Valley Forge: Through Primary Sources, 1 vol. 2013. (American Revolution Through Primary Sources Ser.). (ENG., Illus.). 48p. (J). (gr. 4-6). 27.93 *(978-0-7660-4132-5(8)*, 22bf5158-e47c-42c7-9d03-25ec224712b2) Enslow Publishing, LLC.

Spender, Nick. George Washington & the Winter at Valley Forge, 1 vol. 2011. (Graphic Heroes of the American Revolution Ser.). (ENG.). 24p. (J). (gr. 3-3). pap. 9.15 *(978-1-4339-6014-7(1)*, 212546e8-51ff-4148-864f-6777e830450c, Gareth Stevens Learning Library) Stevens, Gareth Publishing LLLP.

VALUES

see also Ethics

ABDO Publishing Company Staff. What We Stand For, 6 vols. 2014. (What We Stand For Ser.: 6). (ENG.). 24p. (J). (gr. k-4). lib. bdg. 196.74 *(978-1-62403-291-2(5)*, 1722, Super SandCastle) ABDO Publishing Co.

ABDO Publishing Company Staff & Doudna, Kelly. Character Concepts, 1 vol. 2007. (Character Concepts Ser.: 8). (ENG.). 24p. (J). (gr. k-3). lib. bdg. 193.68 *(978-1-59928-734-8(X)*, SandCastle) ABDO Publishing Co.

Aguilera, Dana, et al. Character in Motion! Real Life Stories Series 5th Grade Student Workbook. 2006. 68p. (J). per. 5.95 *(978-0-9765722-8-2(1))* Positively for Kids, Inc.

Allan, Delores. Magical Moments with Roy & Toni: Have You Ever. 2011. 24p. pap. 12.79 *(978-1-4634-2687-3(9))* AuthorHouse.

Aloian, Molly. Live It: Respect, 1 vol. 2009. (Crabtree Character Sketches Ser.). (ENG., Illus.). 32p. (J). (gr. 3-6). pap. *(978-0-7787-4912-7(6))*; lib. bdg. *(978-0-7787-4879-3(0))* Crabtree Publishing Co.

—Live It: Responsibility, 1 vol. 2009. (Crabtree Character Sketches Ser.). (ENG., Illus.). 32p. (J). (gr. 3-6). pap. *(978-0-7787-4913-4(4))*; lib. bdg. *(978-0-7787-4880-9(4))* Crabtree Publishing Co.

Amoroso, Cynthia. Patriotism. 2018. (Illus.). 24p. (J). *(978-1-4896-6075-6(5)*, AV2 by Weigl) Weigl Pubs., Inc.

Amoroso, Cynthia & Jacklin, Danielle. Generosity. 2018. (Illus.). 24p. *(978-1-4896-6066-4(6)*, AV2 by Weigl) Weigl Pubs., Inc.

Baldoni, Justin. Boys Will Be Human: A Get-Real Gut-Check Guide to Becoming the Strongest, Kindest, Bravest Person You Can Be. 2022. (ENG.). 304p. (J). (gr. 6). 14.99 *(978-0-06-306718-9(8)*, HarperCollins) HarperCollins Pubs.

Barron, T. A. The Hero's Trail: True Stories of Young People to Inspire Courage, Compassion, & Hope, Newly Revised & Updated Edition. 2007. (ENG., Illus.). 192p. (J). (gr. 3-7). 8.99 *(978-0-14-240760-8(7)*, Puffin Books) Penguin Young Readers Group.

Bell, Rob. Love Wins: For Teens. 2013. (ENG., Illus.). 160p. (YA). (gr. 8). 17.99 *(978-0-06-222187-2(6)*, HarperCollins) HarperCollins Pubs.

Bergeron, Pastor Susan "Suzy". A Preteens Mothers Best Friend. 2012. 16p. pap. 12.68 *(978-1-4669-5618-6(6))* Trafford Publishing.

Bireda, Martha. Trabue Woods Book of Values. 2006. 108p. per. *(978-4-902837-20-9(X))* Aoishima Kenkyusha.

Boykin, Timothy. Timster's World: So What Makes You So Special? 2010. 36p. pap. 16.99 *(978-1-4389-8506-0(1))* AuthorHouse.

Chang, Kirsten. I Am Generous. 2020. (Character Education Ser.). (ENG., Illus.). 24p. (J). (gr. k-3). pap. 7.99 *(978-1-61891-791-1(9)*, 12576, Blastoff! Readers) Bellwether Media.

—I Am Humble. 2020. (Character Education Ser.). (ENG., Illus.). 24p. (J). (gr. k-3). pap. 7.99 *(978-1-61891-792-8(7)*, 12577, Blastoff! Readers) Bellwether Media.

Character Values [Really Good Stuff]. 2011. (Character Values Ser.). 24p. pap. 35.70 *(978-1-4296-6086-0(4)*, Pebble) Capstone.

Clayton, Dallas. An Awesome Book of Thanks!, 0 vols. Clayton, Dallas, illus. unabr. ed. 2010. (ENG.). 86p. (J). (gr. -1-2). 17.95 *(978-1-935597-37-7(X)*, 9781935597377, Two Lions) Amazon Publishing.

Cohen, Marina. Live It: Cooperation. 2009. (Crabtree Character Sketches Ser.). (ENG., Illus.). 32p. (J). (gr. 3-6). lib. bdg. *(978-0-7787-4889-2(8))* Crabtree Publishing Co.

—Live It: Inclusiveness. 2009. (ENG., Illus.). 32p. (J). (gr. 3-6). lib. bdg. *(978-0-7787-4890-8(1))* Crabtree Publishing Co.

Colby, Jennifer. Stories of Persistence. 2018. (21st Century Skills Library: Social Emotional Library). (ENG.). 32p. (J). (gr. 4-7). pap. 14.21 *(978-1-5341-0840-0(8)*, 210724); (Illus.). lib. bdg. 32.07 *(978-1-5341-0741-0(X)*, 210723) Cherry Lake Publishing.

Dalmatian Press Staff. A Lesson In... Thankfulness: Book to Color with Stickers. 2003. (Big Idea's Veggie Tales Ser.). (ENG., Illus.). 32p. (J). pap. 2.99 *(978-1-4037-0293-7(4)*, Spirit Pr.) Bendon, Inc.

Deroche, Ed, et al. Character: A Guide for Middle Grade Students. 2004. (ENG.). 176p. pap., wbk. ed. 9.95 *(978-1-55864-152-5(1)*, JIST Life) JIST Publishing.

Donovan Guntly, Jenette. I Can Show I Care, 1 vol. 2004. (Doing the Right Thing Ser.). (ENG., Illus.). 16p. (gr. k-1). lib. bdg. 22.67 *(978-0-8368-4247-0(2)*, eb546dd0-4359-47d0-a649-48aee39e8a9f, Gareth Stevens Learning Library) Stevens, Gareth Publishing LLLP.

—I Can Show Respect, 1 vol. 2004. (Doing the Right Thing Ser.). (ENG., Illus.). 16p. (gr. k-1). lib. bdg. 22.67 *(978-0-8368-4248-7(0)*, 516c90a7-6c93-47fb-8a33-102ca12d67ab, Gareth Stevens Learning Library) Stevens, Gareth Publishing LLLP.

Dyan, Penelope. Life Is a Dream! Dyan, Penelope, illus. 2013. (Illus.). 34p. pap. 11.95 *(978-1-61477-091-6(3))* Bellissima Publishing, LLC.

—What Is Truth? Dyan, Penelope, illus. 2011. (Illus.). 34p. pap. 11.95 *(978-1-935630-96-8(2))* Bellissima Publishing, LLC.

Edgar, Kathleen J., et al. Compassion. 2003. (J). *(978-1-59203-055-2(6))* Learning Challenge, Inc.

—Courage. 2003. (J). *(978-1-59203-056-9(4))* Learning Challenge, Inc.

—Determination. 2003. (J). *(978-1-59203-057-6(2))* Learning Challenge, Inc.

—Imagination. 2003. (J). *(978-1-59203-058-3(0))* Learning Challenge, Inc.

—Responsibility. 2003. (J). *(978-1-59203-059-0(9))* Learning Challenge, Inc.

—Vision. 2003. (J). *(978-1-59203-060-6(2))* Learning Challenge, Inc.

Engelhardt, Lisa O. Making Good Choices: Just for Me Book. Fitzgerald, Anne, illus. 2012. 32p. (J). pap. 7.95 *(978-0-87029-514-0(4))* Abbey Pr.

Erroll, Mark. I Am Honest / Soy Honesto, 1 vol. 2011. (Kids of Character / Chicos con Carácter Ser.). (ENG & SPA., Illus.). 24p. (J). (gr. 1-2). 25.27 *(978-1-4339-4866-4(4)*, 7818c1ff-227c-4003-b173-4ceac6a276ee) Stevens, Gareth Publishing LLLP.

Foster-Lasser, Sage & Lasser, Jon. Grow Grateful. Lyles, Christopher, illus. 2018. 32p. (J). *(978-1-4338-2903-1(7)*, Magination Pr.) American Psychological Assn.

Geisen, Cynthia. We Are Different & Alike: A Book about Diversity. Fitzgerald, Anne, illus. 2013. 32p. (J). 7.95 *(978-0-87029-557-7(8))* Abbey Pr.

Gervais, Bernadette & Pittau, Francesco. That's Disgusting! 2004. (ENG., Illus.). 80p. (J). (gr. -1-17). bds. 9.99 *(978-1-57912-351-2(1)*, 81351, Black Dog & Leventhal Pubs. Inc.) Running Pr.

Goodman, Errol. I Am Helpful / Soy Acomedida, 1 vol. 2011. (Kids of Character / Chicos con Carácter Ser.). (ENG & SPA., Illus.). 24p. (J). (gr. 1-2). 25.27 *(978-1-4339-4860-2(5)*, 404778e7-46d8-4f67-831f-248e1e343784) Stevens, Gareth Publishing LLLP.

Greve, Meg. Integrity. 2012. (Little World Social Skills Ser.). (ENG., Illus.). 24p. (gr. k-2). pap. 9.95 *(978-1-61810-270-6(2)*, 9781618102706) Rourke Educational Media.

Guzman, Maria Del C. Sheep of Many Colors: Coloring Book. Lovell, Edith, illus. 2013. 26p. pap. 5.99 *(978-0-9855639-4-3(X))* Guzman, Maria del C.

Harbo, Christopher. Superman Is Cooperative. Schigiel, Gregg, illus. 2019. (DC Super Heroes Character Education Ser.). (ENG.). 24p. (J). (gr. k-2). lib. bdg. 27.32 *(978-1-5158-4020-6(4)*, 139808, Stone Arch Bks.) Capstone.

Harris, Duchess. Why News Matters. 2017. (News Literacy Ser.). (ENG., Illus.). 48p. (J). (gr. 4-8). lib. bdg. 35.64 *(978-1-5321-1391-8(9)*, 27689) ABDO Publishing Co.

Havergal, Frances Ridley. Little Pillows & Morning Bells: Good-Night Thoughts & Waking Thoughts for the Little Ones. 2004. 200p. (J). per. 14.95 *(978-1-932474-25-1(0))* Solid Ground Christian Bks.

Holmes, Kirsty Louise. My Beliefs. 2018. (Our Values - Level 1 Ser.). (Illus.). 24p. (J). (gr. 1-1). *(978-0-7787-4727-7(1))* Crabtree Publishing Co.

Hood, Karen Jean Matsko. Kids' Kindness: Adventures in Learning, Vol. 9. Whispering Pine Press International, ed. Artistic Design Services Staff, illus. 2015. 160p. (J). 29.95 *(978-1-59808-759-8(2))*; per. 19.95 *(978-1-59808-757-4(6))* Whispering Pine Pr. International, Inc.

It's Good 2b Good Staff & Zerner, Sandra. It's Good 2B Good: Why It's Not Bad to Be Good. 2011. (ENG., Illus.). 106p. (J). pap. 12.95 *(978-0-615-51275-4(5))* It's Good 2B Good LLC.

Jackson, Sharinese. Choices: Upper Elementary. Nyamor, Eric, illus. 2010. 112p. pap. 12.95 *(978-0-9840660-3-2(9))* Second Time Media & Communications.

James, Emily. How to Be Respectful: A Question & Answer Book about Respect. 2017. (Character Matters Ser.). (ENG., Illus.). 32p. (J). (gr. -1-2). lib. bdg. 27.99 *(978-1-5157-7200-2(4)*, 135557, Capstone Pr.) Capstone.

—How to Be Responsible: A Question & Answer Book about Responsibility. 2017. (Character Matters Ser.). (ENG., Illus.). 32p. (J). (gr. -1-2). lib. bdg. 27.99 *(978-1-5157-7201-9(2)*, 135558, Capstone Pr.) Capstone.

James, Wayan. We Honor Our Elders, 1 vol. 2016. (Rosen REAL Readers: Social Studies Nonfiction / Fiction: Myself, My Community, My World Ser.). (ENG.). 8p. (gr. k-1). pap. 5.46 *(978-1-5081-2275-3(X)*, 457f135c-c82e-4ab5-adce-2ab380b4d14b, Rosen Classroom) Rosen Publishing Group, Inc., The.

Joseph, Kurt. I Am Respectful / Soy Respetuoso, 1 vol. 2011. (Kids of Character / Chicos con Carácter Ser.). (ENG & SPA., Illus.). 24p. (J). (gr. 1-2). 25.27 *(978-1-4339-4878-7(8)*, 698e05ce-6067-4fd4-9a20-bfb7f0580ad9) Stevens, Gareth Publishing LLLP.

Kent, Susan. Learning How to Say You Are Sorry. 2009. (Violence Prevention Library). 24p. (gr. 2-3). 42.50 *(978-1-60854-267-3(X)*, PowerKids Pr.) Rosen Publishing Group, Inc., The.

Keuss, Jeff & Sloth, Lia. Character in Motion! Athlete Series. 2006. (Illus.). 136p. (YA). per. 5.95 *(978-0-9765722-0-6(6))* Positively for Kids, Inc.

Kunjufu, Jawanza. A Culture of Respect. 2007. (ENG., Illus.). 24p. (J). (gr. k-2). pap. 9.95 *(978-1-934155-06-6(3))* African American Images.

Lang, Carol, et al. Character in Motion! Real Life Stories Series 3rd Grade Student Workbook. 2006. 63p. (J). per. 5.95 *(978-0-9765722-9-9(X))* Positively for Kids, Inc.

Lasi, Cindy. A B C d Is for Down. 2013. 32p. pap. 13.95 *(978-1-4525-8235-1(1)*, Balboa Pr.) Author Solutions, LLC.

Lewis, Barbara A. What Do You Stand For? Character Building. 2006. (ENG., Illus.). 60p. (gr. 1-6). 13.99 *(978-1-57542-217-6(4)*, 1125) Free Spirit Publishing Inc.

—What Do You Stand for? a Kid's Guide ToBuilding Character. 2014. 30.00 *(978-1-63419-753-3(4))* Perfection Learning Corp.

MacKenzie, Carine. My First Book of Christian Values. rev. ed. 2008. (My First Bks.). (ENG., Illus.). 64p. (J). (gr. -1-2). pap. 3.99 *(978-1-84550-262-1(0)*, d4190bae-38cb-4c6a-a005-a0f8142739e5) Christian Focus Pubns. GBR. Dist: Baker & Taylor Publisher Services (BTPS).

Marcovitz, Hal. Teens, Religion, & Values. 2008. (Gallup Youth Survey, Major Issues & Trends Ser.). (Illus.). 112,128p. (YA). (gr. 7-9). lib. bdg. 22.95 *(978-1-59084-726-8(1))* Mason Crest.

Marshall, Shelley. Molly the Great Misses the Bus: A Book about Being on Time, 1 vol. 2010. (Character Education with Super Ben & Molly the Great Ser.). (ENG., Illus.). 24p. (J). (gr. k-2). 25.27 *(978-0-7660-3518-8(2)*, c0917edd-6bbf-419b-a49b-c47d4566593b, Enslow Elementary) Enslow Publishing, LLC.

—Molly the Great's Messy Bed: A Book about Responsibility, 1 vol. 2010. (Character Education with Super Ben & Molly the Great Ser.). (ENG., Illus.). 24p. (J). (gr. k-2). 25.27 *(978-0-7660-3517-1(4)*, 5d1d4af2-8d96-472d-8853-38c07e14e1da) Enslow Publishing, LLC.

Mead, David. Little Ben Franklin Learns a Lesson in Generosity: Generosity. Sharp, Chris, illus. 2003. (American Virtues for Kids Ser.). (J). bds. 6.95 *(978-0-9746440-2-8(1)*, Ideals Pubns.) Worthy Publishing.

Meiners, Cheri J. Making a Difference: Teaching Kindness, Character & Purpose (Kindness Book for Children, Good Manners Book for Kids, Learn to Read Ages 4-6) 2018. (ENG., Illus.). 48p. (J). 16.95 *(978-1-63353-598-5(3))* Mango Media.

Merino, Noël, ed. Ethics, 1 vol. 2015. (Opposing Viewpoints Ser.). (ENG.). 224p. (gr. 10-12). pap. 34.80 *(978-0-7377-7261-6(1)*, 340228c1-b64b-4d8f-95c9-01a33ce32d10, Greenhaven Publishing) Greenhaven Publishing LLC.

Moulton, Mark Kimball, et al. Change the World Before Bedtime, 1 vol. 2nd rev. ed. 2018. (ENG., Illus.). 40p. (J). (gr. -1-3). 16.99 *(978-0-7643-5581-3(3)*, 16191) Schiffer Publishing, Ltd.

Mundy, Michaelene. It's Great to Be Grateful! A Kid's Guide to Being Thankful. Alley, R. W., illus. 2012. 32p. (J). pap. 7.95 *(978-0-87029-512-6(8))* Abbey Pr.

Munroe, Terri, et al. Rachel's Challenge: A Columbine Legacy Student Workbook. 2006. (YA). per. 5.95 *(978-0-9765722-4-4(9))* Positively for Kids, Inc.

Murphy, Frank. Stand up for Respect. 2019. (21st Century Junior Library: Growing Character Ser.). (ENG., Illus.). 24p. (J). (gr. 2-5). pap. 12.79 *(978-1-5341-5030-0(7)*, 213427); lib. bdg. 30.64 *(978-1-5341-4744-7(6)*, 213426) Cherry Lake Publishing.

—Stand up for Responsibility. 2019. (21st Century Junior Library: Growing Character Ser.). (ENG., Illus.). 24p. (J). (gr. 2-5). pap. 12.79 *(978-1-5341-5031-7(5)*, 213431); lib. bdg. 30.64 *(978-1-5341-4745-4(4)*, 213430) Cherry Lake Publishing.

Murray, Julie. Kindness. 2017. (Character Education (Abdo Kids Junior) Ser.). (ENG., Illus.). 24p. (J). (gr. -1-2). lib. bdg. 31.36 *(978-1-5321-0010-9(8)*, 25104, Abdo Kids) ABDO Publishing Co.

Mutyala, Sita. What Is Vemana Saying? 2009. (ENG., Illus.). 32p. (J). 14.95 *(978-0-9818113-0-7(2))* WeShine Pr. Co.

Obama, Barack. Of Thee I Sing: A Letter to My Daughters. Long, Loren, illus. 2010. (ENG.). 40p. (J). (gr. -1-3). 17.99 *(978-0-375-83527-8(X)*, Knopf Bks. for Young Readers) Random Hse. Children's Bks.

Parker, Natasha. You - Are Special Like the World: (English/French/Spanish/German/Italian/Portugese/Chinese) 2012. 50p. pap. 20.95 *(978-1-4633-3940-1(2))* Palibrio.

Parr, todd. The Kindness Book. 2019. (ENG., Illus.). 32p. (J). (gr. -1-3). 18.99 *(978-0-316-42381-6(5))* Little, Brown Bks. for Young Readers.

Phelan, Thomas. 1-2-3 Magia para Niños: Ayudando a Sus Hijos a Entender las Nuevas Reglas. 2010. 112p. (J). (gr. -1). pap. 9.95 *(978-1-889140-42-1(2))* Sourcebooks, Inc.

Pryor, Kimberley Jane. Doing Your Best, 1 vol. 2011. (Values Ser.). (ENG.). 32p. (gr. 1-1). 31.21 *(978-1-60870-142-1(5)*, 24ab185f-2acc-4d7e-8717-59cc6d2b0957) Cavendish Square Publishing LLC.

—Values, 6 bks., Set. Incl. Cooperation. lib. bdg. 31.21 *(978-0-7614-3124-4(1)*, cccf9923-8a00-49c2-82a0-84bf1238b38a); Courage. lib. bdg. 31.21 *(978-0-7614-3131-2(4)*, 95af7a8c-ef12-4ebe-afd8-4258975d065b); Honesty. lib. bdg. 31.21 *(978-0-7614-3125-1(X)*, 25d02e8e-623d-4700-a41d-dc8ab055b1fb); Kindness. lib. bdg. 31.21 *(978-0-7614-3126-8(8)*, 4ef81db6-882a-497e-bd4c-285da2967b6b); Respect. lib. bdg. 31.21 *(978-0-7614-3128-2(4)*, b23d1e29-f134-41cb-b3e8-903be8fb1fcb); Tolerance. lib. bdg. 31.21 *(978-0-7614-3129-9(2)*, b0ae1e8f-51ca-446a-ae07-f89640842daf); 32p. (gr. 1-1). 2009. (Values Ser.). 2008. Set lib. bdg. 119.70 net. *(978-0-7614-3123-7(3)*, Cavendish Square) Cavendish Square Publishing LLC.

Puppet Rescue, creator. Rosie & Yellowtail Share. 2007. (Illus.). 10p. (J). 4.95 *(978-0-9799958-0-4(9))* Puppet Rescue.

Rich, Winifred. Wake Up! To All You Are. 2011. 44p. pap. 16.95 *(978-1-4525-3460-2(8))* Get Published.

Rogers, Jennifer. While the Stars Are at Play. 2013. 30p. pap. 13.99 *(978-1-4525-6681-8(X))* Balboa Pr.

Rorick, William. Society. 2008. 60p. pap. 17.95 *(978-1-4327-2481-8(9))* Outskirts Pr., Inc.

Schuette, Sarah L. Character Values Bilingual. Saunders-Smith, Gail, ed. (Pebble Ser.). (Illus.). (J). (gr. k-1). lib. bdg. 95.58 *(978-0-7368-2353-1(0))* Capstone.

Singh, Rajinder. Journey of the Phoenix. Bergen, Brenda, illus. 2011. 24p. (J). (gr. -1-3). 10.00 *(978-0-918224-83-5(7))* Radiance Pubs.

—The King's Mascot. Williams-El, Belinda Irene, illus. 2011. (ENG & ACO.). 28p. (J). (gr. -1-3). 10.00 *(978-0-918224-85-9(3))* Radiance Pubs.

Smith, Sarah. Self-Discipline & Responsibility, Vol. 7. 2018. (Leadership Skills & Character Building Ser.). 64p. (J). (gr. 7). lib. bdg. 31.93 *(978-1-4222-4000-7(2))* Mason Crest.

Stern, Robin. We Follow the Rules, 1 vol. 2012. (InfoMax Readers Ser.). (ENG., Illus.). 16p. (J). (gr. k-k). pap. 7.00 *(978-1-4488-8911-2(1)*, d6de687f-03b5-4238-89b2-beee33ff98ac, Rosen Classroom) Rosen Publishing Group, Inc., The.

Swainston, Jeani. Grandma Stuff: ... it's what love Is made Of. 2006. (J). *(978-0-9791384-0-9(X))* Rock Cliff Media.

Thomas, Pat. Everyone Matters: A First Look at Respect for Others. Harker, Lesley, illus. 2010. (First Look At... Ser.). (ENG.). 32p. (J). (gr. k-2). pap. 8.99 *(978-0-7641-4517-9(7))* Sourcebooks, Inc.

Thompson, Freida. Believe. 2010. 16p. pap. 8.49 *(978-1-4490-5128-0(6))* AuthorHouse.

Turfle, Susan. Keep Feeding Your Spark: A Collection of Children's Poems to Nurture Critical Thinking, Curiosity, Gratitude & Humor. Turfle, Susan, illus. 2021. (ENG., Illus.). 80p. 23.99 Making Ripples Publishing.

Walker, Robert. Live It: Initiative. 2009. (ENG., Illus.). 32p. (J). (gr. 3-6). lib. bdg. *(978-0-7787-4888-5(X))* Crabtree Publishing Co.

Weinstein, Bruce. Is It Still Cheating If I Don't Get Caught? Russell, Harriet, illus. 2009. (ENG.). 160p. (YA). (gr. 5-9). pap. 18.99 *(978-1-59643-306-9(X)*, 900045299) Roaring Brook Pr.

What Really Matters. 2007. (J). per. 10.00 *(978-1-930052-35-2(9))* Cherokee Bks.

Whiteside, Doug. Thank You... No, Thank You! 2009. 80p. pap. 10.49 *(978-1-4389-8173-4(2))* AuthorHouse.

VALUES—FICTION

Adame, Marie. Lemonade & Piglet in the Curse of the Rock of Musim. 2012. pap. 8.95 *(978-0-7414-7251-9(1))* Infinity Publishing.

Alam, Sarah H. Enchanting Fables. 2008. 48p. pap. 16.95 *(978-1-60441-768-5(4))* America Star Bks.

Allen-Wilson, Regina. Bobo & the Pooch. 2013. 26p. pap. 12.00 *(978-1-4575-2084-6(2))* Dog Ear Publishing, LLC.

The check digit for ISBN-10 appears in parentheses after the full ISBN-13

..na, Reverend & Binkow, Howard. Howard B. Wigglebottom on Yes or No: A Fable about Trust. Long, Taillefer, illus. 2013. (Howard B. Wigglebottom Ser.). (ENG.). 32p. (J). (gr. -1-3). 15.00 *(978-0-9826165-8-1(9),* b4fc9dd6-c62f-4d01-9859-ca9c48ca88f0, We Do Listen) We Do Listen Foundation.

Andreae, Giles. My Little World of Happy, 9 vols. 2013. (World of Happy Ser.). (ENG., Illus.). 90p. (J). (— 1). bds. 15.99 *(978-1-4052-6082-4(3))* Farshore GBR. Dist: Independent Pubs. Group.

Angelo, Tony. Go-bez Nibe: Very Clever Firefly, 1 vol. Lubitsky, Maribeth Jenkins, illus. 2010. 48p. 24.95 *(978-1-4489-5184-0(4))* PublishAmerica, Inc.

Baker, Lavayne L. The Return of the Black Dinosaur. 2009. 28p. pap. 12.49 *(978-1-4490-1723-1(1))* AuthorHouse.

Bakker, Merel. Maks & Mila on a Special Journey. Mini Pois Etc, illus. 2013. 54p. *(978-2-9700865-0-5(6))* Mila Publishing, Merel Bakker.

Barth, Kathleen E. The Amazing Adventures of Quigley D Pigley & His Friends. 2009. 16p. pap. 8.49 *(978-1-4389-8322-6(0))* AuthorHouse.

—The Amazing Adventures of Quigley D Pigley & His Friends: How to Become an Astronaut. 2009. 16p. pap. 8.49 *(978-1-4389-8606-7(8))* AuthorHouse.

Batten, Scott A. Johnny the Phoenix. 2008. 64p. pap. 23.95 *(978-1-4343-7297-0(9))* AuthorHouse.

Beauvais, Clémentine & Beauvais, Clémentine. Hello, Monster! Shearring, Maisie Paradise, illus. 2018. (ENG.). 28p. (J). (gr. k-3). 14.95 *(978-0-500-65170-4(1),* 565170) Thames & Hudson.

Benchimol, Brigitte. Jadyn & the Magic Bubble: I Met Gandhi. Adams, Mark Wayne, illus. 2008. (J). 24.95 *(978-0-9799339-7-4(8))* East West Discovery Pr.

Berry, Ron. Let Your Light Shine. 2007. (ENG., Illus.). 16p. (J). (gr. -1-k). bds. 12.99 *(978-0-8249-6723-9(2),* Ideals Pubns.) Worthy Publishing.

Biachi, Kelvin K. Tortoise the King. 2010. 74p. pap. 21.50 *(978-1-60911-875-4(8),* Eloquent Bks.) Strategic Book Publishing & Rights Agency (SBPRA).

Blitz, Shmuel & Zakon, Miriam Stark. The Search for the Stones. Lumer, Marc, illus. 2009. 96p. (J). *(978-1-4226-0934-7(0),* Shaar Pr.) Mesorah Pubns., Ltd.

Blosser, Connie S. A Bear Named Blue. 2013. 20p. pap. 24.95 *(978-1-4626-9340-5(7))* America Star Bks.

Bohlken, Robert L. Listening to the Mukies: And Their Character Building Adventures. Veasey, Michele, illus. 2003. (ENG.). (J). (gr. 4-6). pap. 10.95 *(978-0-930643-15-7(1))* Images Unlimited Publishing.

—Listening to the Mukies & Their Character Building Adventures. Veasey, Michele, illus. 2003. (ENG.). (J). (gr. 2-7). 14.95 *(978-0-930643-17-1(8))* Images Unlimited Publishing.

Bombaci, James J. The Million Dollar Dog. 2010. 32p. pap. 14.99 *(978-1-4490-4936-2(2))* AuthorHouse.

Briere, Paule. The Undesirables. Beha, Philippe, illus. 2009. (ENG.). 32p. (J). (gr. -1-3). 16.95 *(978-1-894965-88-0(4))* Simply Read Bks. CAN. Dist: Ingram Publisher Services.

Broach, Elise. Gumption! Egielski, Richard, illus. 2010. (ENG.). 40p. (J). (gr. k-3). 19.99 *(978-1-4169-1628-4(8),* Atheneum Bks. for Young Readers) Simon & Schuster Children's Publishing.

Brookover, Brian D. Neddy & Little Roy Go to Town. 2013. 40p. pap. 20.99 *(978-1-4817-1185-2(7))* AuthorHouse.

Bunny, Hull. The Hidden Treasure. Fleming, Kye, illus. 2007. (Young Masters Ser.). (J). (gr. -1). 13.95 incl. audio compact disk *(978-0-9721478-8-0(8))* BrassHeart Music.

Bush, Leanne. A Very Special Christmas with Grandm. 2008. 18p. pap. 24.95 *(978-1-4241-9777-4(5))* America Star Bks.

Calvert, Ellen Hasenecz. Nine Goldfish in David's Pond. Fleming, Diana Trucks, illus. 2013. 36p. pap. 14.99 *(978-1-936745-18-0(6))* Nuevo Bks.

Camara-Macauley, Marcella. The Candy Girl. 2008. 32p. pap. 21.99 *(978-1-4415-2957-2(8))* Xlibris Corp.

Campbell, Yma Ome. Manners & Morals in Minutes for Children. 2010. 44p. pap. 16.99 *(978-1-4520-8251-6(0))* AuthorHouse.

Chachas, George & Wojtak, James. Doolittle's Very, Very Bad Day. De Soto, Ben, illus. 2011. 26p. (J). pap. 9.95 *(978-0-9793144-2-1(9))* Doolittle Edutainment Corp.

—The Story of Doolittle: An Exceptional Young Gorilla. De Soto, Ben, illus. 2011. 32p. (J). pap. 9.95 *(978-0-9793144-0-7(2))* Doolittle Edutainment Corp.

Choi, JeongIm. Who's Coming Tonight? Gang, MinJeong, illus. rev. ed. 2014. (MySELF Bookshelf Ser.). (ENG.). 32p. (J). (gr. k-2). lib. bdg. 25.27 *(978-1-59953-653-8(6))* Norwood Hse. Pr.

Cline, Renee. Kawndra the Tiger. 2009. 28p. pap. 15.49 *(978-1-4389-6484-3(6))* AuthorHouse.

Compestine, Ying Chang. Revolution Is Not a Dinner Party. 2009. (ENG.). 272p. (J). (gr. 6-8). pap. 10.99 *(978-0-312-58149-7(1),* 900062006) Square Fish.

Cook, Julia. Cheaters Never Prosper, Volume 4. DuFalla, Anita, illus. 2016. (Responsible Me! Ser.). (ENG.). 32p. (J). (gr. k-6). pap. 10.95 *(978-1-944882-08-2(1))* Boys Town Pr.

—The Judgmental Flower, Volume 8. DuFalla, Anita, illus. 2016. (Building Relationships Ser.). (ENG.). 32p. (J). (gr. k-6). pap. 11.95 *(978-1-944882-05-1(7))* Boys Town Pr.

Cooper, Dolores Thome. Hands Are Not for Hitting. 2005. (Illus.). 32p. (J). 7.95 *(978-1-881539-39-1(3))* Tabby Hse. Bks.

Cox, Phil Roxbee. Give That Back, Jack. 2004. (Cautionary Tales Ser.). 24p. (J). pap. 7.95 *(978-0-7945-0466-3(3),* Usborne) EDC Publishing.

Curtis, Morgan. Second-hand Alligata: A Cajun Tale. 2010. 20p. 13.99 *(978-1-4520-1673-3(9))* AuthorHouse.

Dalrymple, Marilyn. Bartholomew's Buttons. 2006. 18p. (J). 9.73 *(978-1-4116-9200-8(4))* Lulu Pr., Inc.

Davis, Holly. Thankful Together. Sokolova, Valerie, illus. 2006. 36p. (J). 5.99 *(978-0-7847-1436-2(3),* 04077) Standard Publishing.

Defosse, Rosana Curiel. Santiago y el talisman de la Luz. Barradas, Leticia, illus. (Santiago Y Los Valores Ser.). (SPA.). 32p. (J). (gr. 3-5). pap. 7.95 *(978-970-29-0131-0(6))* Santillana USA Publishing Co., Inc.

—Santiago y los Dobraks. Barradas, Leticia, illus. (SPA.). 32p. (J). (gr. 3-5). pap. 7.95 *(978-970-29-0111-2(1))* Santillana USA Publishing Co., Inc.

dePaola, Tomie. The Good Samaritan & Other Parables: Gift Edition. 2017. (ENG.). 32p. (J). (gr. 1-4). 18.99 *(978-0-8234-3888-4(0))* Holiday Hse., Inc.

—Look & Be Grateful. (Illus.). (J). 2019. 24p. (— 1). bds. 7.99 *(978-0-8234-4267-6(5))* 2015. (ENG.). 32p. (gr. -1-3). 16.95 *(978-0-8234-3443-5(5))* Holiday Hse., Inc.

Dharma Publishing Staff. The Monkey King: A Story about Compassion & Leadership. 2nd ed. 2013. (Jataka Tales Ser.). (Illus.). 36p. (gr. -1-7). pap. 8.95 *(978-0-89800-495-3(0))* Dharma Publishing.

—The Spade Sage: The Story about Finding Happiness. 2nd ed. 2013. (ENG.). 36p. (gr. -1-7). pap. 8.95 *(978-0-89800-522-6(1))* Dharma Publishing.

—Three Wise Birds: A Story about Wisdom & Leadership. 3rd ed. 2013. (Jataka Tales Ser.). (Illus.). 36p. (gr. -1-7). pap. 8.95 *(978-0-89800-521-9(3))* Dharma Publishing.

Dimplechin, Lord Reginald. McKenzie Was Here. 2012. 24p. pap. 24.95 *(978-1-4626-8674-2(5))* America Star Bks.

Dober, Jim. Hickory Woods Adventures: Waiting for A Bubble. 2010. pap. 14.99 *(978-1-61579-688-5(6))* Salem Author Services.

Doll, Nancy L. Buddee the Bugger & Me: Told by Mac, 1 vol. 2009. 48p. pap. 24.95 *(978-1-60749-979-4(7))* America Star Bks.

Duncan-Pauley, Chadney. A Bull's Paradise. 2009. (ENG.). 32p. pap. 15.60 *(978-0-557-17660-1(3))* Lulu Pr., Inc.

Dunston, Marc. The Magic of Giving, 1 vol. Cantrell, Katie, illus. 2010. (ENG.). 32p. (J). (gr. k-3). 16.99 *(978-1-58980-805-8(3),* Pelican Publishing) Arcadia Publishing.

Dureke, Jottn O. Z - the Goodluck Bird. Dureke, Jottn O., tr. 2004. (Illus.). 44p. (YA). pap. 6.95 *(978-0-9701144-1-9(9))* Jahs Publishing Group.

Durrett, Marjorie Centineo. Stick People Stories. 2009. (ENG.). 24p. pap. 10.49 *(978-1-4490-2856-5(X))* AuthorHouse.

Dyan, Penelope. I Did It, & I Hid It! a Book about Taking Responsibility. Dyan, Penelope, illus. 2009. (Illus.). 44p. pap. 11.95 *(978-1-935118-68-8(4))* Bellissima Publishing, LLC.

Ebanks, Timali. A Caymanian Heritage Series: Christmas Time. 2013. 24p. pap. 12.50 *(978-1-4575-1726-6(4))* Dog Ear Publishing, LLC.

Edgeworth, Maria. The Bracelets or Amiability & Industry Rewarded. 2004. reprint ed. pap. 15.95 *(978-1-4191-5513-0(X))*; pap. 1.99 *(978-1-4192-5513-7(4))* Kessinger Publishing, LLC.

Elkins, Christy. The Seedling Heart. 2011. (ENG.). 33p. pap. 12.00 *(978-0-557-23498-1(0))* Lulu Pr., Inc.

Emory, Kb. Tyler Tales: What Is My Color/ Different Families. 2012. 36p. pap. 21.99 *(978-1-4797-2504-5(8))* Xlibris Corp.

Escalante, Travis. The Story of Rocks & Balloons. 2013. 28p. 16.99 *(978-0-9897168-5-7(6))* Mindstir Media.

Esopo. El Leon y la Zorra. 2003. (SPA.). 24p. *(978-84-246-1564-2(6),* GL0475) La Galera, S.A. Editorial ESP. Dist: Lectorum Pubns., Inc.

Ferreira, Ann Devine & Bailey. Hi I'm Bailey & I'm Getting A New Special Family. 2011. 32p. 17.95 *(978-1-4269-5303-3(8))* Trafford Publishing.

Finch, Susan M. Dino Manners: Some Prehistoric Lessons Featuring Our Friends from the Cretaceous Period. Seda, Alison, illus. 2009. 32p. pap. 16.50 *(978-1-4490-5102-0(2))* AuthorHouse.

Finkelstein, Ruth. Guess-the-Ending Mitzvah Book. Lazewnik, Sara, illus. 2004. 26p. (J). (gr. k-3). 9.95 *(978-0-9628157-4-4(8))* Finkelstein, Ruth.

Finnan, Gary. Hector: At Ground Level a Very Simple Love Story. 2013. 112p. (gr. 10-12). 28.99 *(978-1-4525-7345-8(X))*; pap. 11.99 *(978-1-4525-7343-4(3))* Author Solutions, LLC. (Balboa Pr.).

Fontaine, La. EL LEÓN Y EL RATÓN. 2003. (SPA.). 24p. *(978-84-246-1925-1(0),* GL0474) La Galera, S.A. Editorial ESP. Dist: Lectorum Pubns., Inc.

Fox, Jeannine. Feeding Penny Pig. 2009. 32p. (J). 14.95 *(978-0-9841589-1-1(X))* Mimi's Funhouse, LLC.

Frias, Miriam Rocio. Cuentos para Niños Buenos - Relatos Reafirman Valores Humanos. (SPA.). (J). 7.98 *(978-970-643-238-4(8))* Selector, S.A. de C.V. MEX. Dist: Spanish Pubs., LLC.

Fun Short Stories on Values & Morals of Life. 2003. (Illus.). 90p. (YA). per. *(978-0-9742122-0-3(2))* Aunty Ems Boutique.

Gales, Rick. Granny Puckerlips: Keepin' It Real with Kindness & Respect. 2013. 108p. (gr. 9-12). 28.95 *(978-1-4908-0438-5(2))*; pap. 11.95 *(978-1-4908-0437-8(4))* Author Solutions, LLC. (WestBow Pr.).

Garcia, Katherine. Jojo & the Tule Tree. 2013. 20p. pap. 9.95 *(978-1-935752-39-4(1))* Bryce Cullen Publishing.

Gayle, Sherri. Bubbles of Faith. 2013. 48p. pap. 11.95 *(978-1-61244-076-7(2))* Halo Publishing International.

Gentilin, Isabella. Whispers of an Angel. 2010. 32p. pap. 13.00 *(978-1-60911-778-8(6),* Eloquent Bks.) Strategic Book Publishing & Rights Agency (SBPRA).

Glover, Larry. Ser Agradable. Benton, Kimberly, ed. Hazouri, Aaron, illus. 2020.Tr. of Be Nice. (SPA.). 25p. (gr. -1-3). pap. 9.99 *(978-1-7348268-6-9(X))* Child Like Faith Children's Bks. LLC.

Goetz, Bracha. My Own Thank You Story in Rainbow Colored Land. 2012. (ENG.). (J). pap. *(978-1-4675-2407-0(7))* Independent Pub.

Goobie, Beth. Ni un Día Más, 1 vol. 2009. (Spanish Soundings Ser.). Orig. Title: Kicked Out. (SPA.). 112p. (YA). (gr. 8-12). pap. 9.95 *(978-1-55469-137-1(0))* Orca Bk. Pubs. USA.

Gordon, Jon. Thank You & Good Night. Wallace, Donald, illus. 2016. (Jon Gordon Ser.). (ENG.). 36p. (J). (gr. -1-4). 18.00 *(978-1-118-98691-2(1))* Wiley, John & Sons, Inc.

Gragg, Karla. Memphis Learns the Hard Way. Unger, Erin, illus. 2013. 28p. pap. 6.95 *(978-0-9818396-7-7(3))* True Horizon Publishing.

Grateful Steps Publishing & Tipton, Angela. Butterflies Don't Crawl. Irvine, Wii, illus. 2009. 32p. (J). 16.95 *(978-1-935130-14-7(5))* Grateful Steps.

Green, John. Terdellaline: A Free-Spirited, Energeti. 2005. 48p. pap. 16.95 *(978-1-4137-9528-8(5))* PublishAmerica, Inc.

Greene, Janice. I Spy E-Spy (Spy), 1 vol. 2017. (Pageturners Ser.). (ENG.). 76p. (YA). (gr. 9-12). 10.75 *(978-1-68021-400-0(4))* Saddleback Educational Publishing, Inc.

Griffin, Dorothy J. What Goes Around Comes Around. 2013. 20p. pap. 12.45 *(978-1-4908-1053-9(6),* WestBow Pr.) Author Solutions, LLC.

Grooms, Molly. We Are Puppies. 2005. 40p. bds. *(978-90-5843-815-7(5))* YoYo Bks.

Harris, Brian. Joe's Bedtime Stories for Boys & Girls. 2009. (Illus.). 240p. pap. 16.99 *(978-1-4389-7600-6(3))* AuthorHouse.

Harris, Rita & Long, Paul. The 19 Cats of Alabama. 2004. (ENG.). 35p. 24.95 *(978-1-4137-3006-7(X))* America Star Bks.

Hautman, Pete. Eden West. 2015. (ENG.). 320p. (YA). (gr. 9). 17.99 *(978-0-7636-7418-2(4))* Candlewick Pr.

Hawkins, Phycillia Maria. What's up Chuck? The Little Boy with ADHD. 2011. 16p. (gr. -1). pap. 9.36 *(978-1-4567-6200-1(1))* AuthorHouse.

Herman, Alison & Grossman, Lynne. Dolly Goes on Vacation. Eve, Lealand, illus. 2007. 22p. (J). 24.95 *(978-0-9746153-2-5(3))* DMH Pr., Inc.

—Dolly Goes to the Beach. Eve, Lealand, illus. 2007. 24p. (J). 24.95 *(978-0-9746153-1-8(5))* DMH Pr., Inc.

—Dolly Goes to the Supermarket. Eve, Lealand, illus. 2007. 22p. (J). 24.96 *(978-0-9746153-0-1(7))* DMH Pr., Inc.

Hermes, Patricia. Emma Dilemma & the New Nanny, 0 vols. Carter, Abby, illus. 2012. (Emma Dilemma Ser.: 1). (ENG.). 114p. (J). (gr. 3-6). pap. 6.99 *(978-0-7614-5619-3(8),* 9780761456193, Two Lions) Amazon Publishing.

—Emma Dilemma, the Nanny, & the Secret Ferret, 0 vols. 2012. (Emma Dilemma Ser.: 5). (ENG., Illus.). 146p. (J). (gr. 3-6). 15.99 *(978-0-7614-5650-6(3),* 9780761456506, Two Lions) Amazon Publishing.

Herndon, S. N. Uncle Deek's Boating Adventure. 2012. 46p. 24.95 *(978-1-4512-7187-4(5))* America Star Bks.

Hibbs, Lisa. Allie Doogledorf & the Mighty Mess. 2009. 36p. pap. 21.99 *(978-1-4500-0777-1(5))* Xlibris Corp.

Higgs, Carolyn. The Little Knight, 1 vol. 2009. 20p. pap. 24.95 *(978-1-61546-095-3(0))* America Star Bks.

Hile, Doretta. A Place for All of Us. Barnes, William, illus. 2007. 36p. per. 14.94 *(978-1-59858-421-9(9))* Dog Ear Publishing, LLC.

Hilton, Jennifer & McCurry, Kristen. Thank You, God: A Book about Thankfulness. Rimmington, Natasha, illus. 2018. (Frolic First Faith Ser.). 22p. (J). (gr. -1 — 1). bds. 6.99 *(978-1-5064-2502-3(X),* Sparkhouse Family) 1517 Media.

Hinton, Maureen. William's Troublesome Tongue. 2010. 36p. pap. 13.95 *(978-1-60911-396-4(9),* Eloquent Bks.) Strategic Book Publishing & Rights Agency (SBPRA).

Hoban, Russell. The Sorely Trying Day. Hoban, Lillian, illus. 2010. (ENG.). 48p. (J). (gr. -1-3). 14.95 *(978-1-59017-343-5(0),* NYR Children's Collection) New York Review of Bks., Inc., The.

Holiday, Michael. Clam Land: Lessons in Life. 2013. 48p. pap. *(978-1-4602-2094-8(3))* FriesenPress.

Hoose, Phillip & Hoose, Hannah. Oye, Hormiguita (Hey, Little Ant Spanish Edition) Tilley, Debbie, illus. 2004.Tr. of Hey Little Ant! 32p. (J). (gr. -1-2). pap. 8.99 *(978-1-58246-089-5(2),* Tricycle Pr.) Random Hse. Children's Bks.

Hopkins, Ellen. Burned. 2006. (ENG., Illus.). 544p. (YA). (gr. 9-12). 21.99 *(978-1-4169-0354-3(2),* McElderry, Margaret K. Bks.) McElderry, Margaret K. Bks.

Hotton, Rick. Holy Mole: Life Is What You Make It: Subtle Wisdom from an Unconventional Comic Strip. 2013. (ENG.). 96p. pap. *(978-1-62343-164-8(6))* Willow Creek Pr., Inc.

House, Brandy. Scorch the Dragon, 1 vol. 2009. 32p. pap. 24.95 *(978-1-60749-209-2(1))* America Star Bks.

Hull, Bunny. Young Masters: The Magic Eye. Fleming, Kye, illus. 2007. (Young Masters Ser.). (J). (gr. -1). 13.95 incl. audio compact disk *(978-0-9721478-7-3(X))* BrassHeart Music.

Ikegwuonu, Patricia Ryan. I Love My Hair, Too! 2013. 20p. pap. 24.95 *(978-1-4626-7556-2(5))* PublishAmerica, Inc.

Ivan, Benson. The Snow That Just Wouldn't Stop. Scott, Rosseau, illus. 2008. 24p. (J). pap. 8.95 *(978-0-9774754-4-5(1))* Spiritbuilding Pubs.

Jackson, Amani D. I'm a Big Boy Now. 2009. 16p. pap. 9.99 *(978-1-4389-2195-2(0))* AuthorHouse.

Jackson-Cox, Purusha. The Seasons of Life. 2008. (ENG.). 24p. pap. 19.95 *(978-1-4343-4030-6(9))* AuthorHouse.

Jaysree. Drama. 2004. 134p. (YA). pap. 11.95 *(978-0-595-29662-0(9))* iUniverse, Inc.

Jean-Baptiste, Marie V. Goodnight & Seeyoutomorrow. 2013. 28p. pap. 24.95 *(978-1-4626-9551-5(5))* America Star Bks.

Jeffers, Oliver. Here We Are: Notes for Living on Planet Earth. Jeffers, Oliver, illus. 2017. (ENG., Illus.). 48p. (J). (gr. -1-2). 19.99 *(978-0-399-16789-8(7),* Philomel Bks.) Penguin Young Readers Group.

Johnson, Kristin. In It Together: A Story of Fairness. Byrne, Mike, illus. 2018. (Cloverleaf Books (tm) — Stories with Character Ser.). (ENG.). 24p. (J). (gr. k-2). pap. 8.99 *(978-1-5415-1068-5(2),* 832e11af-cbe0-4049-9bde-ea470b9ad403); lib. bdg. 25.32 *(978-1-5124-8649-0(3),* 0bbe6ba7-5b99-480d-800a-bc7633614f91) Lerner Publishing Group. (Millbrook Pr.).

Johnston, Camille. A Gifted Book. Donahue, Linda, illus. 2008. 19p. pap. 24.95 *(978-1-60563-329-9(1))* America Star Bks.

Johnston, Carrie Lynn. Sir Bear Knight. 2008. 20p. per. 24.95 *(978-1-4241-9224-3(2))* America Star Bks.

Kallander, Susan & Boomgaarden, Larry. Up in Smoke. 2010. (Illus.). 24p. pap. 11.50 *(978-1-60860-934-5(0),* Eloquent Bks.) Strategic Book Publishing & Rights Agency (SBPRA).

Katz, Karen. No Hitting! A Lift-The-Flap Book. 2004. (ENG., Illus.). 14p. (J). (gr. -1-k). 7.99 *(978-0-448-43612-8(4),* Grosset & Dunlap) Penguin Young Readers Group.

Kenney, Cindy. Project Precious Paws, Bk. 3. 2009. 86p. (J). 9.95 *(978-0-9817159-5-7(8))*; pap. 5.99 *(978-0-9817159-4-0(X))* Precious Moments, Inc.

Kline, Lpc. Flutter Flies Away: A Book about Rules. 2009. 32p. pap. 14.99 *(978-1-4389-9747-6(7))* AuthorHouse.

Korman, Gordon. Slacker. 2017. (ENG.). 240p. (J). (gr. 3-7). pap. 8.99 *(978-0-545-82316-6(1),* Scholastic Pr.) Scholastic, Inc.

Lammertink, Ilona. Don't Be Afraid to Say No! Georger, Lucie, illus. 2013. (ENG.). 32p. (J). (gr. k-2). 15.95 *(978-1-60537-148-1(3))* Clavis Publishing.

Lamphere-Slaughter, Sharyn. Droopy Drawers & the Peg Leg Pirate. 2009. 24p. pap. 12.99 *(978-1-4490-6055-8(2))* AuthorHouse.

Law, Felicia. Cairo the Camel: A Tale of Responsibility, 1 vol. Danson, Lesley, illus. 2010. (Animal Fair Values Ser.). (ENG.). 32p. (J). (gr. 2-2). pap. 11.55 *(978-1-60754-911-6(5),* a78d8ec8-9646-430a-8d2a-0c75db1695aa); lib. bdg. 27.27 *(978-1-60754-903-1(4),* 5cec6e8c-a5ea-4b01-bb39-8138ce45df3b) Rosen Publishing Group, Inc., The. (Windmill Bks.).

Lee, R. Lacey Learns: Love & Beauty. 2012. 44p. pap. 21.99 *(978-1-4797-1535-0(2))* Xlibris Corp.

Lee, Spike & Lee, Tonya Lewis. Giant Steps to Change the World. Qualls, Sean, illus. 2011. (ENG.). 40p. (J). (gr. -1). 19.99 *(978-0-689-86815-3(4),* Simon & Schuster Bks. For Young Readers) Simon & Schuster Bks. For Young Readers.

Lescuyer, Moira. Little Life Reminders. 2010. 16p. 7.95 *(978-1-4525-0037-9(1))* Get Published.

Lilly, T. S. The Upgrade. 2008. 60p. pap. 16.95 *(978-1-60441-536-0(3))* America Star Bks.

Lima, Rick. Redd: The Beta Fish. 2009. 28p. pap. 12.49 *(978-1-4389-4320-6(2))* AuthorHouse.

Linseman, Daniel. Shroobear's First Swim: Book I of the Shroobear Short Stories. 2008. 36p. pap. 15.49 *(978-1-4343-8252-8(4))* AuthorHouse.

Litzenberg, Corinne M. Grandpa's Basement, 1 vol. 2007. (ENG., Illus.). 32p. (J). 14.95 *(978-0-7643-2720-9(8),* 2980) Schiffer Publishing, Ltd.

Logsted, Greg. Something Happened. 2008. (ENG.). 208p. (J). (gr. 7-9). pap. 8.99 *(978-1-4169-5078-3(8),* Simon Pulse) Simon Pulse.

Longus. The ADVENTURES of SILVANA & the MAGIC UNICORN. 2008. 48p. 18.95 *(978-1-4357-1877-7(1))* Lulu Pr., Inc.

Lorenzo, Alejandro. Mateo's Progress/Jornadas de Mateo: Tales for Children of All Ages/Cuentos para Niños de Todas las Edades. 2004. (SPA & ENG., Illus.). 96p. (J). 20.00 *(978-0-9714366-3-3(0))* Pureplay Pr.

Lowery, Marie Hayes. Beau & Friends. 2012. 20p. pap. 17.99 *(978-1-4817-0106-8(1))* AuthorHouse.

Luscier, Kim. Steven Learns about Temper Tantrums, 1 vol. 2009. 48p. pap. 16.95 *(978-1-60749-692-2(5))* America Star Bks.

Maddox, Jake. The Hunter's Code. Tiffany, Sean, illus. 2008. (Jake Maddox Sports Stories Ser.). (ENG.). 72p. (J). (gr. 3-6). 25.99 *(978-1-4342-0782-1(X),* 95187); pap. 5.95 *(978-1-4342-0878-1(8),* 95235) Capstone. (Stone Arch Bks.).

—Jake Maddox: off the Bench, 1 vol. Tiffany, Sean, illus. 2010. (Team Jake Maddox Sports Stories Ser.). (ENG.). 72p. (J). (gr. 3-6). pap. 5.95 *(978-1-4342-2278-7(0),* 103141); lib. bdg. 25.32 *(978-1-4342-1922-0(4),* 102381) Capstone. (Stone Arch Bks.).

—Win or Lose. Tiffany, Sean, illus. 2010. (Team Jake Maddox Sports Stories Ser.). (ENG.). 72p. (J). (gr. 3-6). pap. 5.95 *(978-1-4342-2281-7(0),* 103144, Stone Arch Bks.) Capstone.

Maidment, Stella & Wilde, Oscar. The Star Child. Whelan, Olwyn, tr. Whelan, Olwyn, illus. gif. ed. 2003. 40p. (YA). *(978-1-84365-012-6(6),* Pavilion Children's Books) Pavilion Bks.

Mallory, Barbara. Shantelle: Angels, Stars & Faith. 2008. pap. 16.95 *(978-1-60563-038-0(1))* America Star Bks.

Marie, Tina. Isabella Learns the Value of Money. 2011. 24p. pap. 12.95 *(978-1-4567-4537-0(9))* AuthorHouse.

Marr, Kendra Lynn. I Was Rufus. 2013. 20p. pap. 24.95 *(978-1-4626-9917-9(0))* America Star Bks.

Marro, Barbara. Smitty's Cave Adventures. 2010. 147p. pap. 12.95 *(978-1-4327-4340-6(6))* Outskirts Pr., Inc.

Matyas, Diane. The Terrible Captain Jack Visits the Museum: Or A Guide of Museum Manners for Incorrigible Pirates & the Like. 2008. (Illus.). 24p. (J). *(978-0-9623017-2-8(8))* Noble Maritime Collection, The.

Mayer, Mercer. You Go First, 1 vol. 2013. (ENG., Illus.). 24p. (J). pap. 3.99 *(978-1-4003-2245-9(6),* Tommy Nelson) Nelson, Thomas Inc.

McCann, Thomas P. "Tom". The Tree Nobody Wanted: A Christmas Story. 2007. 14.95 *(978-0-9797407-0-1(3))* Exeter Pr.

McClain M.Ed. Ncc, Ashley. Not So Perfect Polly. 2011. 40p. pap. *(978-1-4269-7126-6(5))* Trafford Publishing (UK) Ltd.

McClure, Brian D. The Ants. Plumlee, Buddy, illus. 2009. (Brian D. Mcclure Childrens Book Collection). 57p. (J). (gr. -1-3). 16.95 *(978-1-933426-10-5(1))* Universal Flag Publishing.

—The Birds & the Frogs. Plumlee, Buddy, illus. 2009. (Brian D. Mcclure Childrens Book Collection). 37p. (J). (gr. -1-3). 16.95 *(978-1-933426-13-6(6))* Universal Flag Publishing.

—The Meal. Plumlee, Buddy, illus. 2009. (Brian D. Mcclure Childrens Book Collection). 59p. (J). (gr. -1-3). 16.95 *(978-1-933426-04-4(7))* Universal Flag Publishing.

—The Up down Day. Plumlee, Buddy, illus. 2009. (Brian D. Mcclure Childrens Book Collection). 47p. (J). (gr. -1-3). 14.95 *(978-1-933426-07-5(1))* Universal Flag Publishing.

McDine, Donna M. Hockey Agony. Hammond, Julie, illus. 2013. 20p. pap. 9.95 *(978-1-61633-360-7(X))* Guardian Angel Publishing, Inc.

Mendoza, S. J. How about Me. 2012. 156p. pap. 19.99 *(978-1-4797-0704-1(X))* Xlibris Corp.

Mescall, Ron. The Adventures of Goo Goo Malou: A Parent's Guide for Teaching Values. 2009. 24p. pap. 10.96 *(978-1-4269-0836-1(9))* Trafford Publishing.

Miller, Dennis. ABCs of Character. Wallace, Sam Amber, illus. 2003. 52p. (J). lib. bdg. 15.95 *(978-0-9722259-1-5(9))* Twin Peaks Publishing, Inc.

Miller, Gary R. Taming Chaos Workbook: Leaders Discussion Guide. 2017. (ENG., Illus.). 108p. (J). (gr. 7-9). pap. 14.95 *(978-1-68350-155-8(1))* Morgan James Publishing.

Miller, Jennifer. Christmas Tails. Knight, Vanessa, illus. 2009. 56p. pap. 17.26 *(978-1-4251-8987-7(3))* Trafford Publishing.

Miller, Linda K. Ronald the Church Mouse. 2008. 96p. pap. 12.00 *(978-1-60693-063-2(X),* Eloquent Bks.) Strategic Book Publishing & Rights Agency (SBPRA).

Miner, Deb. I get Around. Miner, Deb, illus. 2007. (ENG., Illus.). 32p. (J). bds. 11.00 *(978-0-9794262-0-9(0))* do be you.

Murphy, Stuart J. Good Job, Ajay! 2010. (I See I Learn Ser.: 3). (Illus.). 32p. (J). (gr. -1-k). pap. 6.95 *(978-1-58089-455-5(0))* Charlesbridge Publishing, Inc.

Nambiar, Vinesh. Adventures in Human Values - Series 4: Strength, Bravery, Gratitude, Acceptance, Discipline, Happiness, Cooperation, Hope, Self-Control. 2007. (Illus.). (J). 9.99 *(978-0-9798986-3-1(3))* Human Values 4 Kids Foundation, The.

Neylon, Robbie. The Real Me. 2013. 24p. pap. 15.99 *(978-1-4797-5718-3(7))* Xlibris Corp.

Nighthawk, Tori. Don't Judge a Bird by Its Feathers. Nighthawk, Tori, illus. 2013. (ENG., Illus.). 60p. (J). (gr. -1-3). 17.99 *(978-0-9858811-9-1(4))* Stone, Anne Publishing.

Orr, Fran E. When Mommy Was a Soldier, 1 vol. 2008. (ENG.). 26p. 24.95 *(978-1-4241-9576-3(4))* America Star Bks.

Otoshi, Kathryn. Zero. 2010. (Illus.). 32p. (J). (gr. -1-3). 17.95 *(978-0-9723946-3-5(X))* KO Kids Bks.

Page, Shari. Little Master of Tall Tales. 2004. 17p. pap. 11.07 *(978-1-4116-1568-7(9))* Lulu Pr., Inc.

Pallone, Robert. The Adventures of Main Man: A Child's View of the World. 2010. 28p. pap. 12.95 *(978-1-4490-5598-1(2))* AuthorHouse.

Paratore, Coleen Murtagh. The Big Book about Being Big. Fennell, Clare, illus. 2019. 40p. (J). (gr. -1-2). 17.99 *(978-1-4926-9684-1(6)*, Little Pickle Pr.) Sourcebooks, Inc.

Parrish, Terry. Wiffenpoof. 2012. 28p. pap. 24.95 *(978-1-4626-7942-3(0))* America Star Bks.

Pearce, Jackson. Purity. 2013. (ENG.). 224p. (YA). (gr. 10-17). pap. 13.99 *(978-0-316-18247-8(8))* Little, Brown Bks. for Young Readers.

Pearson, Mary E. The Adoration of Jenna Fox. 2009. (Jenna Fox Chronicles Ser.: 1). (ENG.). 288p. (YA). (gr. 7-12). pap. 11.99 *(978-0-312-59441-1(0)*, 900062867) Square Fish.

Peeler, Casey. Losing Charley. 2015. (ENG.). (C). pap. 12.99 *(978-0-9961521-2-9(1))* Peeler, Casey.

Peirce, Lincoln. Big Nate — Great Minds Think Alike. 2014. (Big Nate Graphic Novels Ser.). lib. bdg. 20.85 *(978-0-606-35229-1(5))* Turtleback.

Perez, Angela J. Zack Attack! Hazard, Andrea, illus. 2007. 36p. (J). 17.95 *(978-0-9778328-9-7(9))* His Work Christian Publishing.

Price, Diane J. Tiny Story, Vol. 1. Csavas, Sally, illus. 2008. 28p. (J). 9.00 *(978-0-9789637-0-5(9))* Price, Diane Joan.

Puzzanghera, Marcia. Holly the Multi-Colored Girl. 2012. 24p. pap. 19.99 *(978-1-4685-6249-1(5))* AuthorHouse.

Quinn, Gloria W. Lemon Water. 2012. 24p. pap. 24.95 *(978-1-4626-8877-7(2))* America Star Bks.

Raghbeer, Anjali. Rescue by Design. Modak, Tejas, illus. 2012. (Art Tales from India Ser.). (ENG.). 24p. (J). 14.95 *(978-81-8328-194-2(X))* Wisdom Tree IND. Dist: SCB Distributors.

Raichert, Lance, illus. Treasury of Values for Children. 2012. 159p. (J). *(978-1-4508-3729-3(8))* Phoenix International Publications, Inc.

Raines, Jennifer. Laughs for Porcupine, 1 vol. 2009. 18p. pap. 24.95 *(978-1-60836-784-9(3))* America Star Bks.

Ramrattan Smith, Sherry & Smith, Benjamin Eric. Brothers: Best Friends Growing Up. 2010. 28p. pap. 14.95 *(978-1-4490-6339-9(X))* AuthorHouse.

Rawlings, John S. Sometimes Boxes Make the Best Forts. Espina, Vito, illus. 2006. (J). pap. 15.00 *(978-0-8059-7181-1(5))* Dorrance Publishing Co., Inc.

Rice, Clay. The Stick. 2014. (ENG., Illus.). 32p. (J). (gr. -1-k). 16.95 *(978-1-939629-28-9(4)*, 552928) Familius LLC.

Richards, Arlene. That's Bingzy! Busy Building Self-Esteem. 2007. (J). per. 15.95 *(978-0-9794323-2-3(4))* Bing Note, Inc.

Romero, Vivian. On the Lam with Lambert. 2009. 24p. pap. 12.99 *(978-1-4490-2773-5(3))* AuthorHouse.

Rosales, Irene González. Esmeralda Does Very Good Things. 2012. 46p. pap. 14.95 *(978-0-9824348-2-6(0))* Rosales, Irene.

Rosenthal, Amy Krouse. It's Not Fair! Lichtenheld, Tom, illus. 2008. (ENG.). 40p. (J). (gr. -1-3). 16.99 *(978-0-06-115257-3(9)*, HarperCollins) HarperCollins Pubs.

Rushford, Betty. Best Buddies: And the Fruit of the Spirit. 2003. 41p. pap. 24.95 *(978-1-59286-746-2(4))* America Star Bks.

Russell, Allyson. The Lizard Who Wanted to Be a Mouse. Bubp, Jennifer, illus. 2009. 28p. pap. 12.95 *(978-1-59858-938-2(5))* Dog Ear Publishing, LLC.

Sangha Mitra, Ms Janice. Golden Bear: The Story of a Flowering Heart. Sangha Mitra, Ms Janice, illus. 4th ed. 2013. (ENG., Illus.). 38p. pap. *(978-0-9805945-2-2(9))* Little Bear Values.

Sankey, Erica. Magic Dust. 2010. 32p. pap. 16.49 *(978-1-4490-0893-2(3))* AuthorHouse.

Santana, Sr. Stella. We Are the People of This World: Book One. Bear, Andrea, illus. 2011. 40p. pap. 14.95 *(978-1-61204-643-3(6)*, Eloquent Bks.) Strategic Book Publishing & Rights Agency (SBPRA).

Sapp, Brent. Teknon & the Champion Warriors. Cariello, Sergio, illus. 2003. 7.99 *(978-1-57229-219-2(9))* FamilyLife.

Schraff, Anne. The Quality of Mercy, 1 vol. unabr. ed. 2010. (Urban Underground Ser.). (ENG.). 183p. (YA). (gr. 9-12). pap. 11.95 *(978-1-61651-006-0(4))* Saddleback Educational Publishing, Inc.

—The Terrible Orchid Sky (Adventure), 1 vol. 2017. (Pageturners Ser.). (ENG.). 76p. (YA). (gr. 9-12). 10.75 *(978-1-68021-380-5(6))* Saddleback Educational Publishing, Inc.

—To Be a Man, 1 vol. unabr. ed. 2010. (Urban Underground Ser.). (ENG.). 181p. (YA). (gr. 9-12). pap. 11.95 *(978-1-61651-008-4(0))* Saddleback Educational Publishing, Inc.

Shang, Anthony. When Jack Meets Jill: A Backstory to the Nursery Rhyme. 2014. 80p. (gr. 2-2). pap. 12.17 *(978-1-4828-9675-6(3))* Partridge Pub.

Short M.S., Jeff. A Kid's World, 1 vol. 2009. (Illus.). 48p. pap. 24.95 *(978-1-60836-760-3(6))* America Star Bks.

Silberman, Dani. The Three Monkey Brothers. 2009. 28p. pap. 14.50 *(978-1-60860-366-4(0)*, Eloquent Bks.) Strategic Book Publishing & Rights Agency (SBPRA).

Simon, Jenne. A Roar of Respect. Nowowiejska, Kasia, illus. 2016. 32p. (J). pap. *(978-1-338-03341-0(7))* Scholastic, Inc.

Simon, Mary Manz. Tiger Forgives. Clearwater, Linda & Couri, Kathy, illus. 2006. (First Virtues for Toddlers Ser.). 20p. (J). 5.99 *(978-0-7847-1413-3(4)*, 04065) Standard Publishing.

Singletary, Gladys Renae. A Snowman with a Heart. 2012. 24p. pap. 17.99 *(978-1-4685-9642-7(X))* AuthorHouse.

Sinke, Grandma Janet Mary. I Wanna Go to Grandma's House. Pennington, Craig, illus. 2003. (Grandma Janet Mary Ser.). 50p. (J). *(978-0-9742732-0-4(1))* My Grandma & Me Pubs.

Skocz, Anita Joyce. Kite Tale. 2011. 40p. pap. 16.95 *(978-1-4525-3889-1(1))* Get Published.

Smith, Jennifer & Morgan, Andre. Zelza Zero. 2010. 20p. pap. 12.99 *(978-1-4490-4546-3(4))* AuthorHouse.

Smith, Sindy. Little Lucy Lou. Smith, Sindy, illus. 2012. (Illus.). 38p. 29.95 *(978-1-4489-3350-1(1))* America Star Bks.

Sommer, Carl. If Only I Were... 2003. (Another Sommer-Time Story Ser.). (Illus.). 48p. (J). (gr. k-4). lib. bdg. 23.95 incl. audio *(978-1-57537-752-0(7))* Advance Publishing, Inc.

—If Only I Were... James, Kennon, illus. 2003. (Another Sommer-Time Story Ser.). (ENG.). 48p. (J). (gr. k-4). lib. bdg. 23.95 incl. audio compact disk *(978-1-57537-702-5(0))* Advance Publishing, Inc.

—Mayor for A Day Read-along 2003. (Another Sommer-Time Story Ser.). (Illus.). 48p. (J). lib. bdg. 23.95 incl. audio *(978-1-57537-763-6(2))* Advance Publishing, Inc.

—No One Will Ever Know Read-Along. 2003. (Another Sommer-Time Story Ser.). (Illus.). 48p. (J). lib. bdg. 23.95 incl. audio *(978-1-57537-756-8(X))* Advance Publishing, Inc.

—No One Will Ever Know Read-Along, 1 bk. Westbrook, Dick, illus. 2003. (Another Sommer-Time Story Ser.). (ENG.). 48p. (J). lib. bdg. 23.95 incl. audio compact disk *(978-1-57537-706-3(3))* Advance Publishing, Inc.

—Noise! Noise! Noise! James, Kennon, illus. 2003. (Another Sommer-Time Story Ser.). (ENG.). 48p. (J). lib. bdg. 23.95 incl. audio compact disk *(978-1-57537-719-3(5))* Advance Publishing, Inc.

—Proud Rooster & Little Hen 2003. (Another Sommer-Time Story Ser.). (Illus.). 48p. (J). lib. bdg. 23.95 incl. audio *(978-1-57537-760-5(8))* Advance Publishing, Inc.

—Proud Rooster & Little Hen. Budwine, Greg, illus. 2003. (Another Great Achiever Ser.). (ENG.). 48p. (J). lib. bdg. 23.95 incl. audio compact disk *(978-1-57537-710-0(1))* Advance Publishing, Inc.

Spinelli, Eileen. Thankful, 1 vol. 2015. (ENG., Illus.). 32p. (J). 16.99 *(978-0-310-00088-4(2))* Zonderkidz.

Springstubb, Tricia. Cody & the Rules of Life. Wheeler, Eliza, illus. (Cody Ser.). (ENG.). 176p. (J). (gr. 2-5). 2018. pap. 7.99 *(978-1-5362-0054-6(9))* 2017. 14.99 *(978-0-7636-7920-0(8))* Candlewick Pr.

St. John, Patricia. Friska My Friend & the Other Kitten. 2003. (Illus.). 192p. 6.49 *(978-1-85999-312-5(5))* Scripture Union GBR. Dist: Gabriel Resources.

Standish, Burt L. Frank Merriwell's Generosity. Rudman, Jack, ed. 2003. (Frank Merriwell Ser.). 29.95 *(978-0-8373-9352-0(3))*; pap. 9.95 *(978-0-8373-9052-9(4))* Merriwell, Frank Inc.

Stein, Catherine. Madley Doesn't Want To. 2011. 24p. pap. 11.32 *(978-1-4634-2259-2(8))* AuthorHouse.

Stewart, Bob. Baily Bumble Bee. Gorum, Jerry, illus. 2009. (ENG.). 32p. pap. 14.49 *(978-1-4389-7254-1(7))* AuthorHouse.

Stripland, Rubye Weldon. Lucy Bell, Queen of the Pasture Book Four. 2009. 94p. pap. 10.96 *(978-1-4357-4742-5(9))* Lulu Pr., Inc.

Sydor, Colleen. Timmerman Was Here. Debon, Nicolas, illus. 2009. 32p. (J). (gr. -1-1). 19.95 *(978-0-88776-890-3(3)*, Tundra Bks.) Tundra Bks. CAN. Dist: Penguin Random Hse. LLC.

Tewkesbury, Alexa. Danny's Daring Days, 1 vol. 2009. (Topz Secret Diaries). (ENG., Illus.). 128p. pap. *(978-1-85345-502-5(4))* Crusade for World Revival.

Thomas, Jason. The Adventures of Bird & Gator: Best Friends. 2012. 24p. pap. 12.56 *(978-1-4669-4973-7(2))* Trafford Publishing.

Thomas, Nayomi. The Thankables: Three Little Creatures with Very Large Features. 2013. 20p. pap. 10.99 *(978-1-4908-0562-7(1)*, WestBow Pr.) Author Solutions, LLC.

Thomas The Toad. Willie the Frog Learns to Fly. 2009. 68p. pap. 27.49 *(978-1-4389-6997-8(X))* AuthorHouse.

Thrasher, Amanda M. Mischief in the Mushroom Patch. 2009. 174p. 23.75 *(978-1-60860-722-8(4)*, Strategic Bk. Publishing) Strategic Book Publishing & Rights Agency (SBPRA).

Tidwell, Deborah Swayne. Magic Eraser: And the Substitute Teacher. 2008. 24p. pap. 12.99 *(978-1-4343-8107-1(2))* AuthorHouse.

Tommy. Bubba & Cecil. 2009. 52p. pap. 16.95 *(978-1-60836-860-0(2))* America Star Bks.

Torrance-Matthews, Armer, et al. Miss Bertha, the Talking Tree: A Delightful Story of a Talking Tree. 2010. 36p. pap. 18.95 *(978-1-4269-2051-6(2))* Trafford Publishing.

Valentine, Billy. Trust Love: A Tale of Angels. 2008. 176p. (J). 23.95 *(978-0-595-48801-8(3))* iUniverse, Inc.

VanCil, Marybelle. Sadie Fourpaws & the Magic Rocking Chair. 2009. (Illus.). 57p. pap. 26.95 *(978-1-4327-3642-2(6))* Outskirts Pr., Inc.

Vertley, Barbara. Back in the Day. 2007. 52p. per. 16.95 *(978-1-4241-9549-7(7))* PublishAmerica, Inc.

Vishpriya. Tales from Indi: Character Counts! RESPECT. Ruble, Eugene, illus. 2009. 24p. pap. 10.95 *(978-1-933090-57-3(X))* Guardian Angel Publishing, Inc.

Walder, Lysa. Katie the Paramedic. 2009. (Illus.). 28p. pap. 12.49 *(978-1-4389-7134-6(6))* AuthorHouse.

Waterton, Betty. A Salmon for Simon, 1 vol. Blades, Ann, illus. 35th ed. 2013. (ENG.). 32p. (J). (gr. -1-2). 14.95 *(978-1-55498-392-6(4))* Groundwood Bks. CAN. Dist: Publishers Group West (PGW).

Weiss, Fred G. Mag-Nan-I-Mous Monkey & Gerald Giraffe. 2013. 28p. 18.99 *(978-0-9898820-5-7(5))* Mindstir Media.

Westling, Vicki Diane. Cats Keep Out: Sam & Friends. 2009. 40p. pap. 16.99 *(978-1-4490-3623-2(6))* AuthorHouse.

White, Becky. PawPrints on Your Heart. Cranford, Darren, illus. 2013. 64p. (J). 18.95 *(978-0-9860169-0-5(X))* Vision Chapters Publishing Co.

White, Jamie Nicole. How I Wish I Could Share My Nice Words. 2013. 28p. pap. 24.95 *(978-1-4626-6953-0(0))* America Star Bks.

White, Pauline. Jewel Baxter & Friends, 1 vol. 2009. 48p. pap. 16.95 *(978-1-60813-541-7(1))* America Star Bks.

Wilhelm, Kj. Grandma Coocoonutts Goes to Boston. 2009. 28p. pap. 15.99 *(978-1-4363-9933-3(5))* Xlibris Corp.

Willard, Gerald. Amy Firefly. 2009. 40p. pap. 18.50 *(978-1-60693-448-7(1)*, Eloquent Bks.) Strategic Book Publishing & Rights Agency (SBPRA).

Williams, Shannon. School Rules! Nelson, Anndria, illus. 2010. 36p. pap. 16.99 *(978-1-4520-3924-4(0))* AuthorHouse.

Wilson, Rosalee. A Mushy Mouse Tale. 2009. (ENG.). 69p. pap. 24.58 *(978-0-557-10084-2(4))* Lulu Pr., Inc.

Womack, Vernesia. What If... 2004. (J). pap. 7.00 *(978-0-8059-6383-0(9))* Dorrance Publishing Co., Inc.

Wyatt, Cherokee. The Adventures of Margaret Mouse: Harvest Carnival. I.t. ed. 2006. (Illus.). 32p. (J). 6.95 *(978-0-9761326-5-3(6))* www.margaretmouse.com publishing co.

Yang, John, Sr. You Can Eat Cheese but Don't Be Cheesy. 2003. (Illus.). 58p. (J). per. *(978-0-9743080-0-5(5))* Painting With Words.

Yasuda, Anita. I've Got the No-Skateboard Blues, 1 vol. Santillan, Jorge H., illus. 2012. (Sports Illustrated Kids Victory School Superstars Ser.). (ENG.). 56p. (J). (gr. 1-3). pap. 5.95 *(978-1-4342-3866-5(0)*, 118048); lib. bdg. 26.65 *(978-1-4342-2244-2(6)*, 103107) Capstone. (Stone Arch Bks.).

Zambak Çucok Publishing Staff, ed. Lost: Niloya 3. 2016. (J). pap. 4.99 *(978-1-4621-1864-9(X)*, Horizon Pubs.) Cedar Fort, Inc./CFI Distribution.

—The Onion: Niloya 2. 2016. (J). pap. 4.99 *(978-1-4621-1863-2(1)*, Horizon Pubs.) Cedar Fort, Inc./CFI Distribution.

—The Rainbow: Niloya 1. 2016. (J). pap. 4.99 *(978-1-4621-1862-5(3)*, Horizon Pubs.) Cedar Fort, Inc./CFI Distribution.

VAMPIRES

Altmann, Scott. Vampire Mazes. 2011. (Dover Children's Activity Bks.). (ENG., Illus.). 48p. (J). (gr. 3-4). pap. 4.99 *(978-0-486-47922-4(6)*, 479226) Dover Pubns., Inc.

Baker, Linda R. American Vampires, 1 vol. 2019. (Creatures of the Paranormal Ser.). (ENG.). 48p. (J). (gr. 5-5). pap. 12.70 *(978-1-9785-1359-4(3)*, 1e9a3549-65f7-4de3-a890-eb5cac91e80f) Enslow Publishing, LLC.

Bennett, Adelaide. Ancient Werewolves & Vampires: The Roots of the Teeth. 2010. (Making of a Monster Ser.). (Illus.). 64p. (YA). (gr. 7-18). pap. 9.95 *(978-1-4222-1955-3(0))*; lib. bdg. 22.95 *(978-1-4222-1802-0(3))* Mason Crest.

—Global Legends & Lore: Vampires & Werewolves Around the World. 2010. (Making of a Monster Ser.). 64p. (YA). (gr. 7-18). pap. 9.95 *(978-1-4222-1963-8(1))* Mason Crest.

Biskup, Agnieszka. Vampires & Cells. Cogliitore, Diego, illus. 2011. (Monster Science Ser.). (ENG.). 32p. (J). (gr. 3-4). pap. 49.60 *(978-1-4296-7332-7(X)*, 16834); pap. 8.10 *(978-1-4296-7331-0(1)*, 116879) Capstone. (Capstone Pr.).

Boutland, Craig. Bloodthirsty Vampires. 2019. (Unexplained (Alternator Books (r)) Ser.). (ENG., Illus.). 32p. (J). (gr. 3-6). pap. 10.99 *(978-1-5415-7382-6(X)*, 8b3d3089-0eb4-456c-b097-de8e1487db31); lib. bdg. 30.65 *(978-1-5415-6286-8(0)*, e4e22f2c-2f27-48da-b73e-bb51c639a97a) Lerner Publishing Group. (Lerner Pubns.).

Branzei, Sylvia. The History of Vampires & Other Real Blood Drinkers. Keely, Jack, illus. 2009. (All Aboard Reading: Station Stop 3 Ser.). (ENG.). 48p. (J). (gr. 2-4). 16.19 *(978-0-448-45032-2(1))* Penguin Young Readers Group.

Bringle, Jennifer. Vampires in Film & Television, 1 vol. 2011. (Vampires Ser.). (ENG.). 64p. (gr. 5-5). pap. 13.95 *(978-1-4488-2229-4(7)*, 74e88c1c-e073-4985-b5f0-c9824f5f43d3, Rosen Reference); (ENG.). 64p. (YA). (gr. 5-5). lib. bdg. 37.13 *(978-1-4488-1226-4(7)*, dca51e21-a3a6-4b5b-9c60-e6f87e25e9a8); 77.70 *(978-1-4488-2236-2(X)*, Rosen Reference) Rosen Publishing Group, Inc., The.

Brinker, Spencer. More or Less & a Vampire's Guess. 2015. (Illus.). 32p. (J). lib. bdg. 28.50 *(978-1-62724-330-8(5))* Bearport Publishing Co., Inc.

Cast, P. C. & Doner, Kim. The Fledgling Handbook 101. 2010. (House of Night Novels Ser.). (ENG., Illus.). 176p. (YA). (gr. 7-12). pap. 19.99 *(978-0-312-59512-8(3)*, 900062752, St. Martin's Griffin) St. Martin's Pr.

Castellano, Peter. Vampires, 1 vol. 2015. (Monsters! Ser.). (ENG.). 32p. (J). (gr. 1-2). pap. 11.50 *(978-1-4824-4095-9(4)*, e964bb7a-3e21-492d-b69c-56befc228e60) Stevens, Gareth Publishing LLLP.

Cohen, Robert Z. Transylvania: Birthplace of Vampires, 1 vol. 2011. (Vampires Ser.). (ENG.). 64p. (J). (gr. 5-5). pap. 13.95 *(978-1-4488-2231-7(9)*, d6762d3c-344b-44f3-aa1c-8e043393ee37, Rosen Reference); (ENG.). 64p. (YA). (gr. 5-5). lib. bdg. 37.13 *(978-1-4488-1228-8(3)*, 7cfa48c2-d702-4be0-b962-ec1408191d44); (J). 77.70 *(978-1-4488-2234-8(3)*, Rosen Reference) Rosen Publishing Group, Inc., The.

Creatures of Legend, 5 vols. 2014. (Creatures of Legend Ser.: 6). (ENG.). 48p. (J). (gr. 4-8). lib. bdg. 178.20 *(978-1-62403-149-6(8)*, 4932) ABDO Publishing Co.

Dutton, Michael & Roytman, Arkady. 3-D Coloring Book — Vampires & Zombies. 2011. (Dover 3-D Coloring Book Ser.). (ENG., Illus.). 32p. (J). (gr. 2-6). pap. 5.99 *(978-0-486-48415-0(7))* Dover Pubns., Inc.

Etingoff, Kim. Howling at the Moon: Vampires & Werewolves in the New World. 2010. (Making of a Monster Ser.). (Illus.). 64p. (YA). (gr. 7-18). pap. 9.95 *(978-1-4222-1958-4(5))*; lib. bdg. 22.95 *(978-1-4222-1805-1(8))* Mason Crest.

—The Science of the Beast: The Facts Behind the Fangs. 2010. (Making of a Monster Ser.). (Illus.). 64p. (YA). (gr. 7-18). pap. 9.95 *(978-1-4222-1961-4(5))*; lib. bdg. 22.95 *(978-1-4222-1808-2(2))* Mason Crest.

Frisch, Aaron. Vampires. 2013. (That's Spooky! Ser.). (ENG., Illus.). 24p. (J). (gr. 3-7). 25.65 *(978-1-60818-248-0(7)*, Creative Education) Creative Co., The.

Gale, Ryan. Vampires. 2019. (Monster Histories Ser.). (ENG., Illus.). 32p. (J). (gr. 4-6). pap. 7.95 *(978-1-5435-7503-3(X)*, 141033); lib. bdg. 30.65 *(978-1-5435-7126-4(3)*, 140408) Capstone.

Gallagher, Belinda. Vampires. Kelly, Richard, ed. 2017. (ENG., Illus.). 48p. (J). pap. 9.95 *(978-1-84810-475-4(8))* Miles Kelly Publishing, Ltd. GBR. Dist: Parkwest Pubns., Inc.

Gish, Ashley. Vampires. 2019. (X-Books: Mythical Creatures Ser.). (ENG.). 32p. (J). (gr. 3-5). pap. 9.99 *(978-1-62832-762-5(6)*, 19249, Creative Paperbacks) Creative Co., The.

Griffiths, Katie. Vampires, 1 vol. 2015. (Creatures of Fantasy Ser.). (ENG.). 64p. (gr. 6-6). 35.93 *(978-1-5026-0928-1(2)*, 1762b9ba-ac5f-4452-900c-d0ef125e6995) Cavendish Square Publishing LLC.

Guiley, Rosemary ellen. Vampires: Mysteries, Legends & Unexplained Phenomena. 2009. (ENG.). 128p. (gr. 6-12). pap. 10.95 *(978-0-7910-9895-0(8)*, P160498, Checkmark Bks.) Infobase Holdings, Inc.

Jeffrey, Gary. Vampires, 1 vol. Verma, Dheeraj, illus. 2012. (Graphic Mythical Creatures Ser.). (ENG.). 24p. (J). (gr. 3-3). pap. 9.15 *(978-1-4339-6773-3(1)*, 2c671d30-1499-419e-95e5-a3094040b6c4); lib. bdg. 26.60 *(978-1-4339-6771-9(5)*, c02f1bfe-3661-43fa-8873-b052f3dca01e) Stevens, Gareth Publishing LLLP. (Gareth Stevens Learning Library).

Kespert, Deborah. 3-D Chillers: Vampires, Zombies, & Werewolves. 2012. (3-D Chillers Ser.). (ENG.). 48p. (J). (gr. 3-7). pap. 7.99 *(978-0-545-38779-8(5)*, Scholastic Paperbacks) Scholastic, Inc.

Knudsen, Shannon. Giants, Trolls, & Ogres. 2009. (Fantasy Chronicles Ser.). (ENG., Illus.). 48p. (J). (gr. 4-7). lib. bdg. 27.93 *(978-0-8225-9985-2(6))* Lerner Publishing Group.

Loh-Hagan, Virginia. Vampires. 2016. (Magic, Myth, & Mystery Ser.). (ENG., Illus.). 32p. (J). (gr. 4-8). 32.07 *(978-1-63471-109-8(2)*, 208547, 45th Parallel Press) Cherry Lake Publishing.

Martin, Nicholas. Fighting the Fangs: A Guide to Vampires & Werewolves. 2010. (Making of a Monster Ser.). (Illus.). 64p. (YA). (gr. 7-18). pap. 9.95 *(978-1-4222-1957-7(7))*; lib. bdg. 22.95 *(978-1-4222-1804-4(X))* Mason Crest.

Marx, Mandy R. Great Vampire Legends, 1 vol. 2010. (Vampires Ser.). (ENG.). 32p. (J). (gr. 3-9). lib. bdg. 28.65 *(978-1-4296-4576-8(8)*, 103058, Capstone Pr.) Capstone.

Mason, Jennifer. Vampire Myths, 1 vol. 2017. (Myths Across the Map Ser.). (ENG.). 48p. (J). (gr. 5-6). pap. 15.05 *(978-1-5382-1447-3(4)*, 53f78906-5ef9-4058-b353-b1272f12e711); lib. bdg. 33.60 *(978-1-5382-1374-2(5)*, addb068d-85eb-4ae3-9a99-ef690d235fb4) Stevens, Gareth Publishing LLLP.

Mason, Paul & Hachette Children's Group. The Vampire Hunter's Guide. 2012. (Monster Tracker Ser.). (ENG., Illus.). 32p. (gr. 4-6). lib. bdg. 28.50 *(978-1-59771-317-7(1))* Sea-To-Sea Pubns.

McMeans, Bonnie. Vampires, 1 vol. 2006. (Mysterious Encounters Ser.). (ENG., Illus.). 48p. (gr. 4-8). lib. bdg. 35.23 *(978-0-7377-3476-8(0)*, 07dee933-589a-43d7-9dd3-1970d385f8e7, KidHaven Publishing) Greenhaven Publishing LLC.

Navarre, Sam. Vampires in America, 1 vol. 2011. (America's Supernatural Secrets Ser.). (ENG.). 48p. (YA). (gr. 5-5). pap. 12.75 *(978-1-4488-5574-2(8)*, 22365b69-3b8c-40eb-9472-51bd9c507ef3); lib. bdg. 34.47 *(978-1-4488-5528-5(4)*, 7648c750-488c-46ee-9705-5a49d008c2e9) Rosen Publishing Group, Inc., The. (Rosen Reference).

Netzley, Patricia D. Do Vampires Exist? 2015. (ENG., Illus.). 80p. (J). lib. bdg. *(978-1-60152-860-5(4))* ReferencePoint Pr., Inc.

O'Hearn, Michael. Vampires vs. Werewolves: Battle of the Bloodthirsty Beasts. Kendree, McLean, illus. 2011. (Monster Wars Ser.). (ENG.). 32p. (gr. 3-4). pap. 47.70 *(978-1-4296-7266-5(8)*, Capstone Pr.) Capstone.

Orme, David. Vampires. 2010. (Fact to Fiction Grafx Ser.). (Illus.). 36p. (J). lib. bdg. 16.95 *(978-1-60686-474-6(2))* Perfection Learning Corp.

Owen, Ruth. Vampires & Other Bloodsuckers. 2013. (Not near Normal: the Paranormal Ser.). 32p. (J). (gr. 3-8). lib. bdg. 28.50 *(978-1-61772-722-1(9))* Bearport Publishing Co., Inc.

Petechuk, David. The Undead: Vampires, Zombies, & Other Strange Monsters. 2015. (J). *(978-1-61900-070-4(9))* Eldorado Ink.

Peter Pauper Press Staff, et al. Vampires, Werewolves, Zombies: From the papers of Herr Doktor Max Sturm & Baron Ludwig Von Drang. Waldman, Bruce, illus. 2010. 168p. 9.95 *(978-1-59359-647-7(2))* Peter Pauper Pr. Inc.

Pipe, Jim. The Undead, 1 vol. 2013. (Twilight Realm Ser.). (ENG., Illus.). 32p. (J). (gr. 4-5). 29.27 *(978-1-4339-8759-5(7)*, 533a389e-da75-46b4-917c-d0a08cac3ca1); pap. 11.50 *(978-1-4339-8760-1(0)*, 861b5c5a-d78f-41be-8ca5-e1d7cdd68ebd) Stevens, Gareth Publishing LLLP. (Gareth Stevens Learning Library).

Rainey, Rich. Vampire Life, 1 vol. 2010. (Vampires Ser.). (ENG.). 32p. (J). (gr. 3-9). lib. bdg. 28.65 *(978-1-4296-4577-5(6)*, 103059, Capstone Pr.) Capstone.

Roberts, Steven. The Undead!, 1 vol., 1. 2013. (Jr. Graphic Monster Stories Ser.). (ENG.). 24p. (J). (gr. 2-3). 28.93 *(978-1-4777-6207-3(8)*, f77f5684-00c9-4c12-8d50-f1ecbddcf7ec, PowerKids Pr.) Rosen Publishing Group, Inc., The.

—Vampires!, 1 vol. 2012. (Jr. Graphic Monster Stories Ser.). (ENG., Illus.). 24p. (J). (gr. 2-3). pap. 11.60 *(978-1-4488-8006-5(8)*, 8217aba7-e2b9-4279-9079-165f83012e89); lib. bdg. 28.93 *(978-1-4488-7906-9(X)*, a6bb3ddc-1160-4030-a9ba-96b6fd9c3359) Rosen Publishing Group, Inc., The. (PowerKids Pr.).

Rooney, Anne. Vampire Castle. 2008. (Crabtree Contact Ser.). (ENG.). 32p. (J). (gr. 3-7). pap. *(978-0-7787-3788-9(8))*; (Illus.). lib. bdg. *(978-0-7787-3766-7(7))* Crabtree Publishing Co.

Sabatino, Michael. The Legend of Dracula, 1 vol. 2015. (Famous Legends Ser.). (ENG., Illus.). 32p. (J). (gr. 2-3). 26.93 *(978-1-4824-2734-9(6)*, 26121a94-c404-4f2e-bce2-e72215b454c5) Stevens, Gareth Publishing LLLP.

Sanna, Emily. Pop Monsters: The Modern-Day Craze for Vampires & Werewolves. 2010. (Making of a Monster Ser.).

64p. (YA). (gr. 7-18). pap. 9.95 *(978-1-4222-1959-1(3))* Mason Crest.

ee a Vampire? 2018. (J). *(978-0-7166-2186-7(X))* World Bk., Inc.

Seigel, Rachel. Vampires. 2018. (Mythical Creatures Ser.). (ENG., Illus.). 32p. (J). (gr. 2-3). pap. 9.95 *(978-1-64185-007-0(8)*, 164185007 8); lib. bdg. 31.35 *(978-1-63517-905-7(X)*, 163517905X) North Star Editions. (Focus Readers).

—Vampires. 2018. (Illus.). 32p. (J). *(978-1-4896-9859-9(0)*, AV2 by Weigl) Weigl Pubs., Inc.

Shaffer, Jody Jensen. Vampires & Light. 1 vol. Flocco, Gervasio, illus. 2013. (Monster Science Ser.). (ENG.). 32p. (J). (gr. 3-9). pap. 8.10 *(978-1-62065-820-8(8)*, 121776, Capstone Pr.) Capstone.

Shea, Therese M. Vampires Divide!, 1 vol. 2018. (Monsters Do Math! Ser.). (ENG.). 24p. (gr. 2-3). 24.27 *(978-1-5382-2935-4(8)*, 3e0701a7-911d-4405-8223-f685720e5eb2) Stevens, Gareth Publishing LLLP.

Spencer, Liv. Love Bites: The Unofficial Saga of Twilight. 2010. (ENG., Illus.). 203p. (YA). (gr. 7). pap. 14.95 *(978-1-55022-930-1(3)*, 5794965c-1c31-4a08-9c84-7624b5b00c5d) ECW Pr. CAN. Dist: Baker & Taylor Publisher Services (BTPS).

Stefoff, Rebecca. Vampires, Zombies, & Shape-Shifters, 1 vol. 2008. (Secrets of the Unexplained Ser.). (ENG., Illus.). 96p. (gr. 6-6). lib. bdg. 36.93 *(978-0-7614-2635-6(3)*, 8bdd50c7-d277-4665-b7a9-aadf279eaf73) Cavendish Square Publishing LLC.

Stewart, Sheila. The Psychology of Our Dark Side: Humans' Love Affair with Vampires & Werewolves. 2010. (Making of a Monster Ser.). (Illus.). 64p. (YA). (gr. 7-18). pap. 9.95 *(978-1-4222-1960-7(7))*; lib. bdg. 22.95 *(978-1-4222-1807-5(4))* Mason Crest.

Streissguth, Thomas & Streissguth, Tom. Legends of Dracula. 2003. (Biography Ser.). (Illus.). 112p. (YA). (gr. 6-18). pap. 7.95 *(978-0-8225-9682-0(2)*, Carolrhoda Bks.) Lerner Publishing Group.

Ticktock Media, Ltd. Staff. Undead: Zombies, Vampires, Werewolves. 2008. (ENG.). 96p. (J). (gr. 4-7). pap. 9.95 *(978-1-84696-797-9(X)*, TickTock Books) Octopus Publishing Group GBR. Dist: Independent Pubs. Group.

Tieck, Sarah. Vampires, 1 vol. 2015. (Creepy Creatures Ser.). (ENG., Illus.). 32p. (J). (gr. 2-5). 34.21 *(978-1-62403-767-2(4)*, 17836, Big Buddy Bks.) ABDO Publishing Co.

Troupe, Thomas Kingsley. The Legend of the Vampire, 1 vol. Kemarskaya, Oksana, illus. 2010. (Legend Has It Ser.). (ENG.). 32p. (J). (gr. 2-4). lib. bdg. 27.99 *(978-1-4048-6031-5(2)*, 102992, Picture Window Bks.) Capstone.

Tyler, Madeline. Surviving a Vampire Invasion, 1 vol. 2018. (Surviving the Impossible Ser.). (ENG.). 32p. (gr. 4-5). pap. 11.50 *(978-1-5382-3514-0(5)*, b0222e30-095b-4d27-8fe1-71e30fd2666a) Stevens, Gareth Publishing LLLP.

Uhl, Xina M. Vampires. 2017. (Strange but True Ser.). (ENG.). (J). (gr. 4-7). pap. 9.95 *(978-1-68072-481-3(9))*; 32p. pap. 9.99 *(978-1-64466-218-2(3)*, 11490); (Illus.). 32p. lib. bdg. *(978-1-68072-184-3(4)*, 10552) Black Rabbit Bks. (Bolt).

Vampires. 2009. (FACT ATLAS Ser.). 72p. (J). (gr. 3-7). pap. 13.99 *(978-0-8416-1100-9(9))* Hammond World Atlas Corp.

Weakland, Mark Andrew & Collins, Terry Lee. Truth Behind Vampires. 2016. (ENG., Illus.). 24p. (J). pap. *(978-1-4062-8895-7(0))* Capstone.

Weingarten, Ethan. Transylvania, 1 vol. 2014. (Scariest Places on Earth Ser.). (ENG.). 24p. (J). (gr. 2-3). 24.27 *(978-1-4824-1161-4(X)*, 2aa69228-7c38-446c-bc7d-cf6d272487ad) Stevens, Gareth Publishing LLLP.

West, David & Ganeri, Anita. Vampires & the Undead, 1 vol. West, David & Ganeri, Anita, illus. 2010. (Dark Side Ser.). (ENG., Illus.). 32p. (J). (gr. 4-5). pap. 11.50 *(978-1-4488-1570-8(3)*, 0ebffbf0-3642-4df7-a310-77588e9e9423); lib. bdg. 30.27 *(978-1-61531-899-5(2)*, bac4e18d-5fb6-42bd-8a9b-6d52efeaee2d) Rosen Publishing Group, Inc., The.

—Witches & Warlocks, 1 vol. West, David & Ganeri, Anita, illus. 2010. (Dark Side Ser.). (ENG., Illus.). 32p. (J). (gr. 4-5). pap. 11.50 *(978-1-4488-1574-6(6)*, 41d47ae5-fc87-4087-8acb-45f7948769b6, PowerKids Pr.) Rosen Publishing Group, Inc., The.

White, Steve & McKenzie-Ray, Mark. Hunting Vampires, 1 vol. 2016. (Monster Hunting Ser.). (ENG., Illus.). 88p. (YA). (gr. 8-8). 38.80 *(978-1-4994-6530-3(0)*, 1de1961a-4b8b-4127-8b3f-8aae17380ec4, Rosen Young Adult) Rosen Publishing Group, Inc., The.

World Book, Inc. Staff, contrib. by. Searching for the Real Dracula. 2015. (Illus.). 48p. (J). *(978-0-7166-2674-9(8))* World Bk., Inc.

VAMPIRES—FICTION

Adams, James D. Creepy Campfire Tales: Halloween Campout, Vol. 1. 2008. 132p. (J). per. 12.95 *(978-1-60404-103-3(X))* Owl Creek Media Ltd.

—Creepy Campfire Tales Vol. 1: Halloween Campout. 2008. 132p. (YA). 26.95 *(978-1-60404-104-0(8))* Owl Creek Media Ltd.

Adamson, Ged. Elsie Clarke & the Vampire Hairdresser. 2013. (ENG., Illus.). 28p. (J). (gr. -1-1). 16.95 *(978-1-62087-983-2(2)*, 620983, Sky Pony Pr.) Skyhorse Publishing Co., Inc.

Arden, Alys. The Casquette Girls: A Novel, 0 vols. 2015. (Casquette Girls Ser.: 1). (ENG., Illus.). 574p. (YA). (gr. 8-13). pap. 9.99 *(978-1-5039-4654-5(1)*, 9781503946545, Skyscape) Amazon Publishing.

—The Romeo Catchers. 2017. (Casquette Girls Ser.: 2). (ENG., Illus.). 604p. (YA). (gr. 7-12). pap. 12.95 *(978-1-5039-4000-0(4)*, 9781503940000, Skyscape) Amazon Publishing.

Atwater-Rhodes, Amelia. Persistence of Memory. 2010. (Den of Shadows Ser.: 5). (ENG.). 224p. (YA). (gr. 7). pap. 8.99 *(978-0-440-24004-4(2)*, Delacorte Pr.) Random Hse. Children's Bks.

—Poison Tree. 2013. 240p. (YA). (gr. 7). pap. 8.99 *(978-0-385-73755-5(6)*, Ember) Random Hse. Children's Bks.

AZ Books Staff & Evans, Olivia. Haunted Castle. Shumovich, Nadezhda, ed. 2012. (Terribly Funny Monsters Ser.). (ENG., Illus.). 10p. (J). bds. 15.95 *(978-1-61889-134-1(0))* AZ Bks. LLC.

Banks, Steven. Middle School Bites. Fearing, Mark, illus. 2020. (Middle School Bites Ser.: 1). 304p. (J). (gr. 3-7). 13.99 *(978-0-8234-4543-1(7))* Holiday Hse., Inc.

Bardhan-Quallen, Sudipta. Hampire! Fine, Howard, illus. 2011. (ENG.). 32p. (J). (gr. -1-3). 16.99 *(978-0-06-114239-0(5)*, HarperCollins) HarperCollins Pubs.

The Beautiful & the Damned. 2014. (ENG., Illus.). 288p. (YA). (gr. 7). pap. 11.99 *(978-1-4424-8836-6(0)*, Simon Pulse) Simon Pulse.

Becket. Key the Steampunk Vampire Girl - Book One: And the Dungeon of Despair. 2013. 242p. (J). pap. 9.99 *(978-0-9898785-2-4(X))* Becket.

Bell, Amber Dawn. Cave of Terror. 2008. 280p. pap. 12.95 *(978-0-9818550-3-5(2))* Highland Pr. Publishing.

Bently, Peter. Casketball Capers. 1. Harrison, Chris, illus. 2011. (Vampire School Ser.: 1). (ENG.). 96p. (J). (gr. 1-4). 17.44 *(978-0-8075-8462-0(2))* Whitman, Albert & Co.

Bickle, Laura. The Outside. 2014. (ENG.). 320p. (YA). (gr. 7). pap. 8.99 *(978-0-544-33635-3(6)*, 1584181, Clarion Bks.) HarperCollins Pubs.

Black, Holly. The Coldest Girl in Coldtown. 2013. 419p. (YA). *(978-0-316-27755-6(X))* Little Brown & Co.

—The Coldest Girl in Coldtown. 2014. (Coldest Girl in Coldtown Ser.). (ENG.). 448p. (YA). (gr. 10-17). pap. 12.99 *(978-0-316-21309-7(8))* Little, Brown Bks. for Young Readers.

Blackhurst, Rebecca. Count Grumpula & the Wood Witch. Errington, Rachael, illus. 2013. 18p. *(978-0-473-24899-4(9))* Cobble Creep Productions.

Blevins, Wiley. Cinderella & the Vampire Prince. Cox, Steve, illus. 2016. (Scary Tales Retold Ser.). (ENG.). 24p. (J). (gr. k-3). lib. bdg. 27.99 *(978-1-63440-090-9(9)*, 36876e97-b32f-433d-82e1-3754e7a21e9e) Red Chair Pr.

Blue, Parker. Catch Me. 2015. (ENG., Illus.). 222p. (J). pap. 14.95 *(978-1-61194-623-9(9))* BelleBks., Inc.

—Try Me. 2010. 218p. pap. 14.95 *(978-0-9843256-6-5(2)*, Bell Bridge Bks.) BelleBks., Inc.

Brambles, Lindsay. Becoming Darkness. 2015. (ENG.). 496p. (YA). (gr. 9-9). 17.95 *(978-1-63079-017-2(6)*, 128563, Switch Pr.) Capstone.

Brewer, Heather. Eighth Grade Bites #1: The Chronicles of Vladimir Tod. 2008. (Chronicles of Vladimir Tod Ser.: 1). (ENG.). 192p. (YA). (gr. 7). 10.99 *(978-0-14-241187-2(6)*, Speak) Penguin Young Readers Group.

—Eleventh Grade Burns. 4. 4th ed. 2010. (Chronicles of Vladimir Tod Ser.: 4). (ENG.). 208p. (J). (gr. 7-12). 24.94 *(978-0-525-42243-3(9))* Penguin Young Readers Group.

—Eleventh Grade Burns #4: The Chronicles of Vladimir Tod. 4 vols. 2010. (Chronicles of Vladimir Tod Ser.: 4). (ENG.). 320p. (YA). (gr. 7-18). 10.99 *(978-0-14-241647-1(9)*, Speak) Penguin Young Readers Group.

—First Kill. 2012. (Slayer Chronicles Ser.: 1). lib. bdg. 19.65 *(978-0-606-26670-3(4))* Turtleback.

—Ninth Grade Slays #2: The Chronicles of Vladimir Tod. 2 vols. 2009. (Chronicles of Vladimir Tod Ser.: 2). (ENG.). 288p. (YA). (gr. 7-18). 10.99 *(978-0-14-241342-5(9)*, Speak) Penguin Young Readers Group.

—Tenth Grade Bleeds. 2010. (Chronicles of Vladimir Tod Ser.: 03). lib. bdg. 19.65 *(978-0-606-10594-1(8))* Turtleback.

—Tenth Grade Bleeds #3: The Chronicles of Vladimir Tod. 2010. (Chronicles of Vladimir Tod Ser.: 3). (ENG.). 304p. (YA). (gr. 7-18). pap. 10.99 *(978-0-14-241560-3(X)*, Speak) Penguin Young Readers Group.

—Twelfth Grade Kills #5: The Chronicles of Vladimir Tod. 2011. (Chronicles of Vladimir Tod Ser.: 5). (ENG.). 336p. (YA). (gr. 7-18). 9.99 *(978-0-14-241752-2(1)*, Speak) Penguin Young Readers Group.

Brezenoff, Steve. Bites. 2013. (Ravens Pass Ser.). (ENG.). 96p. (J). (gr. 2-3). pap. 36.90 *(978-1-4342-6289-9(8)*, 20260, Stone Arch Bks.) Capstone.

—Bites, 1 vol. Pinelli, Amerigo, illus. 2013. (Ravens Pass Ser.). (ENG.). 96p. (J). (gr. 3-6). pap. 6.15 *(978-1-4342-6217-2(0)*, 123515); lib. bdg. 25.32 *(978-1-4342-4617-2(5)*, 120606) Capstone. (Stone Arch Bks.).

Brown, Lisa. Vampire Boy's Good Night. Brown, Lisa, illus. 2010. (ENG., Illus.). 32p. (J). (gr. -1-2). 16.99 *(978-0-06-114011-2(2)*, HarperCollins) HarperCollins Pubs.

Brown, Mick. From Round about Midnight until about Five! 2012. 60p. pap. 27.45 *(978-1-4772-2701-5(6))* AuthorHouse.

Brush Creations & Holmes, A. M. X. Robbie Virtual vs. Vlad the Vampire: Book 1. 2007. 56p. pap. 9.95 *(978-0-7414-3621-4(3))* Infinity Publishing.

Bundy, E. A. Phillip Marrow, Jr. 2013. (ENG.). 206p. (YA). pap. 10.99 *(978-1-61955-008-7(3))* Singing Winds Pr.

Burghall, Johan. The Vale of the Faeries. 2012. 274p. (-18). pap. *(978-0-9571863-3-0(9))* Burghall, Johan.

Burke, Anjalena Anita. Ghost: The Dead End Series Book 1, 1 vol. 2009. 73p. pap. 16.95 *(978-1-61582-686-5(6))* PublishAmerica, Inc.

Burns, Laura J. & Metz, Melinda. Sacrifice. 2011. (ENG.). 272p. (YA). (gr. 9). 17.99 *(978-1-4424-3900-9(9)*, Simon & Schuster Bks. For Young Readers) Simon & Schuster Bks. For Young Readers.

Caine, Rachel, pseud. Bite Club: The Morganville Vampires, 10 vols. 2011. (Morganville Vampires Ser.: 10). (ENG.). 368p. (YA). (gr. 9). pap. 9.99 *(978-0-451-23468-1(5)*, Berkley) Penguin Publishing Group.

—Bitter Blood: The Morganville Vampires. 2013. (Morganville Vampires Ser.: 13). (ENG.). 432p. (YA). (gr. 9). pap. 9.99 *(978-0-451-41424-3(1)*, Berkley) Penguin Publishing Group.

—Black Dawn: The Morganville Vampires. 2012. (Morganville Vampires Ser.: 12). (ENG.). 400p. (YA). (gr. 9). pap. 9.99 *(978-0-451-23793-4(5)*, Berkley) Penguin Publishing Group.

—Carpe Corpus: The Morganville Vampires, Book 6. 2009. (Morganville Vampires Ser.: 6). (ENG.). 256p. (YA). (gr. 9-18). mass mkt. 7.99 *(978-0-451-22719-5(0)*, Berkley) Penguin Publishing Group.

—Fade Out. 2009. (Morganville Vampires Ser.: Bk. 7). 256p. (YA). lib. bdg. 20.00 *(978-1-4242-4701-1(2))* Fitzgerald Bks.

—Fade Out: The Morganville Vampires. 2009. (Morganville Vampires Ser.: 7). (ENG.). 256p. (YA). (gr. 9-18). mass mkt. 7.99 *(978-0-451-22866-6(9)*, Berkley) Penguin Publishing Group.

—Fall of Night: The Morganville Vampires. 2013. (Morganville Vampires Ser.: 14). (ENG.). 368p. (YA). (gr. 9). pap. 9.99 *(978-0-451-41426-7(8)*, Berkley) Penguin Publishing Group.

—Feast of Fools. 2008. (Morganville Vampires Ser.: Bk. 4). 256p. (YA). lib. bdg. 20.00 *(978-1-4242-4702-8(0))* Fitzgerald Bks.

—Feast of Fools: The Morganville Vampires, Book 4. 2008. (Morganville Vampires Ser.: 4). (ENG.). 256p. (YA). (gr. 9-18). mass mkt. 7.99 *(978-0-451-22463-7(9)*, Berkley) Penguin Publishing Group.

—Ghost Town: The Morganville Vampires, 9 vols. 2011. (Morganville Vampires Ser.: 9). (ENG.). 368p. (YA). (gr. 9-18). 9.99 *(978-0-451-23291-5(7)*, Berkley) Penguin Publishing Group.

—Kiss of Death: The Morganville Vampires, 8 vols. 2010. (Morganville Vampires Ser.: 8). (ENG.). 256p. (YA). (gr. 9-18). 6.99 *(978-0-451-22973-1(8)*, Berkley) Penguin Publishing Group.

—Last Breath: The Morganville Vampires, 11 vols. 2012. (Morganville Vampires Ser.: 11). (ENG.). 368p. (YA). (gr. 9). 9.99 *(978-0-451-23580-0(0)*, Berkley) Penguin Publishing Group.

—Lord of Misrule. 2009. (Morganville Vampires Ser.: Bk. 5). 352p. (YA). lib. bdg. 20.00 *(978-1-4242-4704-2(7))* Fitzgerald Bks.

—Lord of Misrule: The Morganville Vampires, Book 5. 2009. (Morganville Vampires Ser.: 5). (ENG.). 256p. (YA). (gr. 9-18). mass mkt. 7.99 *(978-0-451-22572-6(4)*, Berkley) Penguin Publishing Group.

—Midnight Alley. 2007. (Morganville Vampires Ser.: Bk. 3). 256p. (YA). lib. bdg. 20.00 *(978-1-4242-4705-9(5))* Fitzgerald Bks.

—Midnight Alley: The Morganville Vampires, Book III. 2007. (Morganville Vampires Ser.: 3). (ENG.). 256p. (YA). (gr. 9-18). mass mkt. 7.99 *(978-0-451-22238-1(5)*, Berkley) Penguin Publishing Group.

—Midnight Bites: Stories of the Morganville Vampires. 2016. (Morganville Vampires Ser.). (ENG.). 512p. (YA). (gr. 9). pap. 12.00 *(978-1-101-98978-4(5)*, Berkley) Penguin Publishing Group.

—The Morganville Vampires, Volume 1. 2009. (Morganville Vampires Ser.: Bks. 1-2). (ENG.). 480p. (YA). (gr. 9-18). 9.99 *(978-0-451-23054-6(X)*, Berkley) Penguin Publishing Group.

—The Morganville Vampires, Volume 2, 2. 2010. (Morganville Vampires Ser.: Bks. 3-4). (ENG.). 464p. (YA). (gr. 9-12). pap. 9.99 *(978-0-451-23289-2(5)*, Berkley) Penguin Publishing Group.

—The Morganville Vampires, Volume 3, Vol. 3. 2011. (Morganville Vampires Ser.: Bks. 5-6). (ENG.). 464p. (YA). (gr. 9-18). 9.99 *(978-0-451-23355-4(7)*, Berkley) Penguin Publishing Group.

—The Morganville Vampires, Volume 4, Vol. 4. 2011. (Morganville Vampires Ser.: Bks. 7-8). (ENG.). 464p. (YA). (gr. 9-18). 12.99 *(978-0-451-23426-1(X)*, Berkley) Penguin Publishing Group.

Caine, Rachel, pseud & Vincent, Rachel. Immortal: Love Stories with Bite. Cast, P.c., ed. 2009. (Illus.). 280p. (J). (gr. 9-12). pap. 8.95 *(978-1-933771-92-2(5))* BenBella Bks.

Capstone Press. Vampires. 2010. (Vampires Ser.). (ENG.). 32p. lib. bdg. 79.95 *(978-1-4296-5906-2(8)*, Capstone Pr.) Capstone.

Carter, Rebecca. Moonlit Daydreams. 2010. (ENG.). 71p. pap. 11.99 *(978-0-557-35588-4(5))* Lulu Pr., Inc.

Cary, Kate. Bloodline. 2006. 352p. (YA). (gr. 7-12). 9.99 *(978-1-59514-078-4(6)*, Razorbill) Penguin Young Readers Group.

—Bloodline 2. 2008. (ENG.). 320p. (YA). (gr. 7-18). pap. 9.99 *(978-1-59514-179-8(0)*, Razorbill) Penguin Young Readers Group.

Cast, P. C. & Cast, Kristin. Betrayed: A House of Night Novel. 2009. (House of Night Novels Ser.: 2). (ENG.). 320p. (YA). (gr. 7-12). 21.99 *(978-0-312-59629-3(4)*, 900063091) St. Martin's Pr.

—Burned: A House of Night Novel. (House of Night Novels Ser.: 7). (ENG.). 336p. (YA). (gr. 7-12). 2011. pap. 13.00 *(978-0-312-38796-9(2)*, 900054119) 2010. 22.00 *(978-0-312-60616-9(8)*, 900059356) St. Martin's Pr. (St. Martin's Griffin).

—Chosen. 2010. (House of Night Novels (Quality) Ser.). (CHI.). 367p. pap. *(978-957-0316-42-1(X))* Locus Publishing Co.

—Chosen: A House of Night Novel. (House of Night Novels Ser.: 3). (ENG.). 320p. (YA). (gr. 8-12). 2009. 21.99 *(978-0-312-36029-0(0)*, 900039880) 2008. pap. 11.99 *(978-0-312-36030-6(4)*, 900039883, St. Martin's Griffin) St. Martin's Pr.

—Destined: A House of Night Novel. 2013. (House of Night Novels Ser.: 9). (ENG.). 336p. (YA). (gr. 7-12). pap. 12.99 *(978-0-312-38798-3(9)*, 900054121, St. Martin's Griffin) St. Martin's Pr.

—Hidden: A House of Night Novel. 2012. (House of Night Novels Ser.: 10). (ENG.). 320p. (YA). (gr. 7-12). 21.99 *(978-0-312-59442-8(9)*, 900062749, St. Martin's Griffin) St. Martin's Pr.

—Hunted. I.t. ed. 2010. (House of Night Ser.: Bk. 5). (ENG.). 548p. 23.95 *(978-1-4104-1951-4(7))* Thorndike Pr.

—Hunted: A House of Night Novel. (House of Night Novels Ser.: 5). (ENG.). 336p. (YA). (gr. 7-12). 2010. pap. 13.00 *(978-0-312-57799-5(0)*, 900061613) 2009. 21.99 *(978-0-312-37982-7(X)*, 900050335) St. Martin's Pr. (St. Martin's Griffin).

—Loved. unabr. ed. 2017. (House of Night Other World Ser.: 1). (ENG.). 352p. 18.99 *(978-1-5384-3112-2(2)*, HCahrr) Blackstone Audio, Inc.

—Marked. I.t. ed. 2008. (House of Night Ser.: No. 1). (ENG.). 442p. (YA). 23.95 *(978-1-4104-1021-4(8))* Thorndike Pr.

—Marked. 2007. (House of Night Ser.: 1). 306p. (YA). lib. bdg. 22.10 *(978-1-4178-0853-3(5))* Turtleback.

—Marked: A House of Night Novel. (House of Night Novels Ser.: 1). (ENG.). 320p. (YA). (gr. 8-12). 2009. 21.99 *(978-0-312-36025-2(8)*, 900039877) 2007. pap. 13.00 *(978-0-312-36026-9(6)*, 900039881, St. Martin's Griffin) St. Martin's Pr.

—Neferet's Curse: A House of Night Novella. 2013. (House of Night Novellas Ser.: 3). (ENG., Illus.). 160p. (YA). (gr. 7). 14.99 *(978-1-250-00025-5(4)*, 900078258, St. Martin's Griffin) St. Martin's Pr.

—Redeemed: A House of Night Novel. 2014. (YA). 310p. *(978-1-250-05952-9(6))*; (House of Night Novels Ser.: 12). (ENG.). 320p. (gr. 7-12). 21.99 *(978-0-312-59444-2(5)*, 900062751, St. Martin's Griffin) St. Martin's Pr.

—Tempted: A House of Night Novel. (House of Night Novels Ser.: 6). (ENG.). 336p. (YA). (gr. 7-12). 2011. pap. 12.99 *(978-0-312-60938-2(8)*, 900065238) 2009. 19.99 *(978-0-312-56748-4(0)*, 900059355) St. Martin's Pr. (St. Martin's Griffin).

—Untamed. I.t. ed. 2009. (House of Night Ser.: Bk. 4). (ENG.). 510p. (YA). 23.95 *(978-1-4104-1965-1(7))* Thorndike Pr.

—Untamed: A House of Night Novel. (House of Night Novels Ser.: 4). (ENG.). 352p. (YA). 2009. (gr. 7-12). 21.99 *(978-0-312-59630-9(8)*, 900063092) 2008. (gr. 8-12). pap. 11.99 *(978-0-312-37983-4(8)*, 900050334, St. Martin's Griffin) St. Martin's Pr.

Cast, P. C. & Doner, Kim. The Fledgling Handbook 101. 2010. (House of Night Novels Ser.). (ENG., Illus.). 176p. (YA). (gr. 7-12). pap. 19.99 *(978-0-312-59512-8(3)*, 900062752, St. Martin's Griffin) St. Martin's Pr.

Cast, P. C. & Kristin. Awakened. I.t. ed. 2011. (House of Night Ser.). (ENG.). 436p. 23.99 *(978-1-4104-3776-1(0))* Thorndike Pr.

—Betrayed. I.t. ed. 2008. (House of Night Ser.: No. 2). (ENG.). 472p. (YA). 23.95 *(978-1-4104-1025-2(0))* Thorndike Pr.

—Burned. I.t. ed. 2011. (House of Night Ser.). (ENG.). 552p. 23.99 *(978-1-4104-3440-1(0))* Thorndike Pr.

—Chosen. I.t. ed. 2009. (House of Night Ser.: Bk. 3). (ENG.). 406p. (YA). 23.95 *(978-1-4104-1608-7(9))* Thorndike Pr.

—Tempted. I.t. ed. 2010. (House of Night Novel Ser.). (ENG.). 552p. 23.99 *(978-1-4104-3141-7(X))* Thorndike Pr.

Cast, P.c. & Cast, Kristin. Awakened: A House of Night Novel. (House of Night Novels Ser.: 8). (ENG.). 304p. (YA). (gr. 7-12). 2012. pap. 12.99 *(978-0-312-38797-6(0)*, 900054120) 2011. 21.99 *(978-0-312-65024-7(8)*, 900059357) St. Martin's Pr. (St. Martin's Griffin).

—Betrayed: A House of Night Novel. 2007. (House of Night Novels Ser.: 2). (ENG.). 320p. (YA). (gr. 7-12). pap. 13.00 *(978-0-312-36028-3(2)*, 900039882, St. Martin's Griffin) St. Martin's Pr.

Church, Oliver. Living Dead - the Reaper's Reward. 2009. 258p. pap. 12.99 *(978-0-578-00160-9(8))* Folk Prophet Bks.

Clare, Cassandra. City of Fallen Angels. 2011. (Mortal Instruments Ser.: 4). (ENG.). 432p. (YA). (gr. 9-18). 24.99 *(978-1-4424-0354-3(3)*, McElderry, Margaret K. Bks.) McElderry, Margaret K. Bks.

—City of Fallen Angels, 11 vols. (Mortal Instruments Ser.: 4). (YA). 2012. 133.75 *(978-1-4618-0638-7(0))* 2011. 135.75 *(978-1-4618-0637-0(2))* 2011. 133.75 *(978-1-4618-0641-7(0))* 2011. 317.75 *(978-1-4618-0642-4(9))* 2011. 1.25 *(978-1-4640-2483-2(9))* Recorded Bks., Inc.

—City of Glass. (Mortal Instruments Ser.: 3). (ENG., (YA). (gr. 9). 2015. Illus.). 592p. pap. 14.99 *(978-1-4814-5598-5(2))* 2009. 560p. 24.99 *(978-1-4169-1430-3(7))* McElderry, Margaret K. Bks. (McElderry, Margaret K. Bks.).

—City of Glass. 2010. 23.00 *(978-1-60686-827-0(6))* Perfection Learning Corp.

—City of Glass. 2009. pap. *(978-1-4424-9308-7(9))* Simon & Schuster.

—City of Glass. 2015. (Mortal Instruments Ser.: Bk. 3). (Illus.). 592p. (J). lib. bdg. 25.75 *(978-0-606-37733-1(6))* Turtleback.

—City of Heavenly Fire. 2014. (Mortal Instruments Ser.: 6). (ENG., Illus.). 752p. (YA). (gr. 9). 24.99 *(978-1-4424-1689-5(0)*, McElderry, Margaret K. Bks.) McElderry, Margaret K. Bks.

—City of Lost Souls. (Mortal Instruments Ser.: 5). (ENG., (YA). (gr. 9). 2015. Illus.). 592p. pap. 14.99 *(978-1-4814-5600-5(8))* 2012. 544p. 24.99 *(978-1-4424-1686-4(6))* McElderry, Margaret K. Bks. (McElderry, Margaret K. Bks.).

—City of Lost Souls, 16 vols. 2012. (Mortal Instruments Ser.: Bk. 5). (YA). 135.75 *(978-1-4640-3948-5(8))*; 133.75 *(978-1-4640-3951-5(8))*; 317.75 *(978-1-4640-3949-2(6))*; 133.75 *(978-1-4640-3952-2(6))* Recorded Bks., Inc.

—City of Lost Souls. 2015. (Mortal Instruments Ser.: Bk. 5). 592p. (YA). lib. bdg. 25.75 *(978-0-606-37736-2(0))* Turtleback.

—City of Lost Souls. 2012. 512p. pap. *(978-1-4063-3760-0(9))* Walker Bks., Ltd.

Clare, Cassandra, et al. The Bane Chronicles. Clare, Cassandra, ed. 2014. (Bane Chronicles Ser.). (ENG., Illus.). 528p. (YA). (gr. 9). 24.99 *(978-1-4424-9599-9(5)*, McElderry, Margaret K. Bks.) McElderry, Margaret K. Bks.

—Tales from the Shadowhunter Academy. (Tales from the Shadowhunter Academy Ser.). (ENG.). (YA). (gr. 9). 2017. 704p. pap. 14.99 *(978-1-4814-4326-5(7))* 2016. (Illus.). 672p. 24.99 *(978-1-4814-4325-8(9))* McElderry, Margaret K. Bks. (McElderry, Margaret K. Bks.).

Collins, Nancy A. Vamps. 2008. (Vamps Ser.: 1). (ENG.). 256p. (YA). (gr. 9-18). pap. 8.99 *(978-0-06-134917-1(8)*, HarperTeen) HarperCollins Pubs.

Collins, Tim. Fangs a Lot: Final Notes from a Totally Lame Vampire. Pinder, Andrew, illus. 2014. (ENG.). 320p. (J). (gr. 5-9). 13.99 *(978-1-4814-2134-8(4)*, Aladdin) Simon & Schuster Children's Publishing.

—Notes from a Hairy-Not-Scary Werewolf. Pinder, Andrew, illus. 2013. (ENG.). 288p. (J). (gr. 5-9). 12.99 *(978-1-4424-8207-4(9)*, Aladdin) Simon & Schuster Children's Publishing.

—Notes from a Totally Lame Vampire: Because the Undead Have Feelings Too! Pinder, Andrew, illus. 2010. (ENG.). 336p. (J). (gr. 5-9). 12.99 *(978-1-4424-1183-8(X)*, Aladdin) Simon & Schuster Children's Publishing.

—Prince of Dorkness: More Notes from a Totally Lame Vampire. Pinder, Andrew, illus. 2011. (ENG.). 336p. (J). (gr. 5-9). 12.99 *(978-1-4424-3388-5(4)*, Aladdin) Simon & Schuster Children's Publishing.

Cook, Kristi. Eternal. (ENG., Illus.). (YA). (gr. 9). 2014. 432p. pap. 9.99 *(978-1-4424-8531-0(0))* 2013. 416p. 16.99 *(978-1-4424-8532-7(9))* Simon Pulse. (Simon Pulse).

Cooper, Helen Wendy. The Vegetarian Vampire. 2012. (ENG., Illus.). 53p. pap. 8.50 *(978-1-78035-365-4(0)*, Fastprint

TUV

Publishing) Upfront Publishing Ltd. GBR. Dist: Printondemand-worldwide.com.

—The Vegetarian Vampire: The Lost Fangs. 2013. (ENG., Illus.). 50p. pap. 8.50 *(978-1-78035-651-8(X)*, Fastprint Publishing) Upfront Publishing Ltd. GBR. Dist: Printondemand-worldwide.com.

Cosby, Sam & Metzger, Clancy. Ceruleadons: Blue dreams rain to Tears. 2008. 304p. 28.95 *(978-0-595-51125-9(2))* iUniverse, Inc.

Cover, Arthur Byron, et al. Buffy the Vampire Slayer: Coyote Moon - Night of the Living Rerun - Portal Through Time. 2010. (Buffy the Vampire Slayer Ser.: 1). (ENG.). 704p. (YA). (gr. 9-12). 26.19 *(978-1-4424-1209-5(7)*, Simon Pulse) Simon Pulse.

Cox, Michael & Smedley. Invasion of the Sausage Snatchers. 2003. (ENG., Illus.). 128p. pap. *(978-0-340-79592-7(1)*, Hodder Children's Books) Hachette Children's Group.

Crowson, Andrew. Flip Flap Spooky. Crowson, Andrew, illus. 2003. (Illus.). 12p. (J). bds. *(978-1-85602-475-4(X)*, Pavilion Children's Books) Pavilion Bks.

Cunningham, P. E. Slayer for Hire. 2013. 204p. pap. *(978-1-77130-285-2(2))* Evernight Publishing.

Datlow, Ellen & Windling, Terri. Teeth: Vampire Tales. 2011. (ENG.). 480p. (YA). (gr. 8-18). pap. 9.99 *(978-0-06-193514-5(X)*, HarperCollins) HarperCollins Pubs.

De la Cruz, Melissa. Blue Bloods. 2007. (Blue Bloods Ser.: 1). (J). lib. bdg. 20.85 *(978-1-4178-2375-8(5))* Turtleback.

de la Cruz, Melissa. Blue Bloods 3-Book Boxed Set, 3 bks., Set. 2009. (Blue Bloods Ser.). (ENG.). 944p. (J). (gr. 5-9). pap. 24.99 *(978-1-4231-2595-2(9)*, Disney-Hyperion) Disney Publishing Worldwide.

—Blue Bloods-Blue Bloods, Vol. 1. 2007. (Blue Bloods Ser.: 1). (ENG.). 336p. (J). (gr. 5-9). pap. 9.99 *(978-1-4231-0126-0(X)*, Disney-Hyperion) Disney Publishing Worldwide.

—Gates of Paradise-A Blue Bloods Novel, Book 7. 2013. (Blue Bloods Ser.: 7). (ENG.). 368p. (J). (gr. 5-9). pap. 9.99 *(978-1-4231-6110-3(6)*, Disney-Hyperion) Disney Publishing Worldwide.

DEKELB-RITTENHOUSE, Diane. Immortal Longings. 2012. (ENG.). 340p. (J). (gr. 7). pap. 14.95 *(978-0-9845318-4-4(X))* Tiny Stachel Pr.

Dent, Sue. Never Ceese: Can Two Who Were Wronged Make It Right? 2006. 336p. (YA). lib. bdg. 17.99 *(978-1-59958-017-3(9))* Journey Stone Creations, LLC.

Despeyroux, Denise. The Big Book of Vampires. Falcone, Fernando, illus. 2012. (ENG.). 112p. (J). (gr. 4-7). 17.95 *(978-1-77049-371-1(9)*, Tundra Bks.) Tundra Bks. CAN. Dist: Penguin Random Hse. LLC.

Deutsch, Stacia, adapted by. Hotel Transylvania 2: Movie Novelization. 2015. (Illus.). 141p. (J). *(978-1-4806-9404-0(5)*, Simon Spotlight) Simon Spotlight.

Diver, Lucienne. Fangtabulous. 2017. (Vamped Ser.: Vol. 4). (ENG., Illus.). (YA). pap. 14.95 *(978-1-62268-121-1(5))* Bella Rosa Bks.

—Fangtastic. 2017. (Vamped Ser.: Vol. 3). (ENG., Illus.). (YA). pap. 14.95 *(978-1-62268-119-8(3))* Bella Rosa Bks.

—Revamped. 2017. (Vamped Ser.: Vol. 2). (ENG., Illus.). (YA). (gr. 8-12). pap. 14.95 *(978-1-62268-117-4(7))* Bella Rosa Bks.

—Vamped. 2017. (ENG., Illus.). (YA). pap. 14.95 *(978-1-62268-115-0(0))* Bella Rosa Bks.

Donbavand, Tommy. Attack of the Trolls. 2012. (Scream Street Ser.: 8). lib. bdg. 16.00 *(978-0-606-31471-8(7))* Turtleback.

—Scream Street: Attack of the Trolls. 2012. (Scream Street Ser.: 8). (ENG., Illus.). 128p. (J). (gr. 3-7). pap. 5.99 *(978-0-7636-5760-4(3))* Candlewick Pr.

—Scream Street: Blood of the Witch. 2009. (Scream Street Ser.: 2). (ENG., Illus.). 128p. (J). (gr. 3-7). pap. 5.99 *(978-0-7636-4607-3(5))* Candlewick Pr.

—Scream Street: Fang of the Vampire. Cartoon Saloon, Ltd., illus. 2009. (Scream Street Ser.: 1). (ENG.). 160p. (J). (gr. 3-7). pap. 7.99 *(978-0-7636-4608-0(3))* Candlewick Pr.

—Scream Street: Invasion of the Normals. 2012. (Scream Street Ser.: 7). (ENG., Illus.). 128p. (J). (gr. 3-7). pap. 5.99 *(978-0-7636-5759-8(X))* Candlewick Pr.

—Scream Street: Skull of the Skeleton, 5. Cartoon Saloon, Ltd., illus. 2010. (Scream Street Ser.: 5). (ENG.). 128p. (J). (gr. 3-7). pap. 5.99 *(978-0-7636-4635-6(0))* Candlewick Pr.

—Terror of the Nightwatchman. 2014. (Scream Street Ser.: 9). lib. bdg. 16.00 *(978-0-606-35872-9(2))* Turtleback.

Dufaux, Jean. Rapaces. Marini, Enrico, illus. 2004. (SPA.). Vol. 1. 56p. pap. 17.95 *(978-1-59497-003-0(3))* Vol. 2. 56p. pap. 17.95 *(978-1-59497-004-7(1))* Vol. 3. 64p. pap. 17.95 *(978-1-59497-005-4(X))* Public Square Bks.

Durst, Sarah Beth. Drink, Slay, Love. (ENG., Illus.). 400p. (YA). (gr. 9). 2012. pap. 10.99 *(978-1-4424-2374-9(9))* 2011. 17.99 *(978-1-4424-2373-2(0))* McElderry, Margaret K. Bks. (McElderry, Margaret K. Bks.).

Duval, Alex. Bloodlust. 2006. (Vampire Beach Ser.: 1). (ENG.). 208p. (YA). (gr. 7-12). mass mkt. 6.99 *(978-1-4169-1166-1(9)*, Simon Pulse) Simon Pulse.

—Ritual. 2007. (Vampire Beach Ser.). (ENG.). 208p. (YA). (gr. 9-12). mass mkt. 5.99 *(978-1-4169-1168-5(5)*, Simon Pulse) Simon Pulse.

—Vampire Beach 1: Bloodlust; Initiation. 2010. (Vampire Beach Ser.: 1). (ENG.). 416p. (YA). (gr. 9). pap. 9.99 *(978-1-4424-0693-3(3)*, Simon Pulse) Simon Pulse.

—Vampire Beach 2: Ritual; Legacy. 2011. (Vampire Beach Ser.: 2). (ENG.). 448p. (YA). (gr. 9). pap. 9.99 *(978-1-4424-0694-0(1)*, Simon Pulse) Simon Pulse.

Egielski, Richard. The Sleepless Little Vampire. 2011. (J). pap. *(978-0-545-14598-5(8)*, Levine, Arthur A. Bks.) Scholastic, Inc.

Emerson, Kevin. The Demon Hunter, 4. 2009. (Oliver Nocturne Ser.: 4). (ENG.). 224p. (J). (gr. 6-8). pap. 18.69 *(978-0-545-05804-9(X))* Scholastic, Inc.

Erway, Chad Lee. An Appointment with Fear. 2019. (ENG., Illus.). 184p. (J). (gr. 2-7). pap. 9.99 *(978-1-7335610-1-3(3))* Parallel Vortex.

Fantaskey, Beth. Jessica Rules the Dark Side. 2012. (ENG.). 320p. (YA). (gr. 9). 16.99 *(978-0-547-39309-4(1)*, 1426896, Clarion Bks.) HarperCollins Pubs.

Feasey, Steve. Dark Moon: A Wereling Novel. 2011. (Wereling Ser.: 2). (ENG.). 336p. (YA). (gr. 7-18). pap. 19.99 *(978-0-312-64643-1(7)*, 900068714) Feiwel & Friends.

—Wereling. 2010. (Wereling Ser.: 1). (ENG.). 288p. (YA). (gr. 7-18). pap. 15.99 *(978-0-312-59612-5(X)*, 900062995) Feiwel & Friends.

Feder, Jane. Spooky Friends. Downing, Julie, illus. 2013. (ENG.). 40p. (J). (gr. 1-2). 16.99 *(978-0-545-47815-1(4)*, Scholastic Pr.) Scholastic, Inc.

Fisher, Rusty. Littlest Vampire's Story, 1 vol. 2014. (Story Time for Little Monsters Ser.). (ENG., Illus.). 24p. (J). (gr. -1-4). lib. bdg. 31.36 *(978-1-62402-020-9(8)*, 626, Looking Glass Library) Magic Wagon.

Fontes, Justine & Fontes, Ron. Casebook: Vampires, 1 vol. 2009. (Top Secret Graphica Mysteries Ser.). (ENG., Illus.). 48p. (YA). (gr. 4-4). 33.93 *(978-1-60754-606-1(X)*, 905f4f61-5848-4785-a4dd-b4700b07545b); pap. 12.75 *(978-1-60754-607-8(8)*, 62c74cb2-3a96-41db-8d71-ecf9c9dd2853) Rosen Publishing Group, Inc., The. (Windmill Bks.).

Forte, Lauren. The Littlest Vampire (Disney Junior Vampirina) Robinson, Bill, illus. 2018. (Little Golden Book Ser.). (ENG.). 24p. (J). (-k). 4.99 *(978-0-7364-3781-3(9)*, Golden/Disney) Random Hse. Children's Bks.

Frade, B. A. Vampire Vacation. 2017. (Tales of the Scaremaster Ser.). (J). lib. bdg. 22.10 *(978-0-606-40225-5(X))* Turtleback.

Fry, Sonali. I'm a Little Vampire. Rescek, Sanja, illus. 2014. (ENG.). 16p. (J). (gr. -1 — 1). bds. 5.99 *(978-1-4814-0504-1(7)*, Little Simon) Little Simon.

Fukuda, Andrew. The Hunt. 2012. (Hunt Trilogy Ser.: 1). (ENG.). 304p. (YA). (gr. 7). pap. 12.99 *(978-1-250-00529-8(9)*, 900080955, St. Martin's Griffin) St. Martin's Pr.

Gardner, Whitney. Fake Blood. Gardner, Whitney, illus. 2018. (ENG., Illus.). 336p. (J). (gr. 5). 21.99 *(978-1-4814-9556-1(9))*; pap. 14.99 *(978-1-4814-9557-8(7))* Simon & Schuster Bks. For Young Readers. (Simon & Schuster Bks. For Young Readers).

Gilson. Melusine Vol. 3: The Vampires' Ball. 2008. (Melusine Ser.: 3). (Illus.). 48p. (J). (gr. 4-7). pap. 11.95 *(978-1-905460-69-4(4))* CineBook GBR. Dist: National Bk. Network.

Gleason, Colleen. The Chess Queen Enigma: A Stoker & Holmes Novel. (ENG.). 360p. (YA). (gr. 7-12). 2016. pap. 9.99 *(978-1-4521-5649-1(2))* 2015. (Stoker & Holmes Ser.: 3). 17.99 *(978-1-4521-4317-0(X))* Chronicle Bks. LLC.

Golightly, Holly, creator. School Bites. 2004. 64p. (YA). per. *(978-0-9745367-2-9(5)*, SB1A) BroadSword Comics/ Jim Balent Studios.

Gow, Kailin. The Stoker Sisters. 2010. 266p. (YA). pap. *(978-1-59748-947-8(6))* Sparklesoup LLC.

Grandma. There Is a Vampire in Our Cellar: Adventures of Butterfly Nectar Meadows. 2008. 20p. pap. 24.95 *(978-1-60813-128-0(9))* America Star Bks.

Graves, Judith. Second Skin. 2011. 280p. (J). pap. 16.99 *(978-1-61603-006-3(2))* Leap Bks.

—Under My Skin. Cox, Val, illus. 2010. 328p. (YA). (gr. 8-18). pap. 16.99 *(978-1-61603-000-1(3))* Leap Bks.

Gray, Amy. How to Be a Vampire: A Fangs-On Guide for the Newly Undead. Erwert, Scott, illus. 2009. (ENG.). 144p. (YA). (gr. 7-18). 14.99 *(978-0-7636-4915-9(5))* Candlewick Pr.

Gray, Claudia. Afterlife. 2012. (Evernight Ser.: 4). (ENG.). 384p. (YA). (gr. 8). pap. 10.99 *(978-0-06-128451-9(3)*, HarperTeen) HarperCollins Pubs.

—Balthazar. 2013. (Evernight Ser.: 5). (ENG.). 400p. (YA). (gr. 8). pap. 11.99 *(978-0-06-196119-9(1)*, HarperTeen) HarperCollins Pubs.

—Evernight. 2009. (Evernight Ser.: 1). (ENG.). 352p. (YA). (gr. 8). pap. 8.99 *(978-0-06-128444-1(0)*, HarperTeen) HarperCollins Pubs.

—Hourglass. 2011. (Evernight Ser.: 3). (ENG.). 368p. (YA). (gr. 8). pap. 10.99 *(978-0-06-128448-9(3)*, HarperTeen) HarperCollins Pubs.

—Stargazer. (Evernight Ser.: 2). (ENG.). (YA). (gr. 8). 2010. 352p. pap. 9.99 *(978-0-06-128446-5(7))* 2009. 336p. 17.99 *(978-0-06-128440-3(8))* HarperCollins Pubs. (HarperTeen).

Greenburg, Dan. Don't Count on Dracula. Davis, Jack E., illus. 2004. (Zack Files Ser.). 58p. lib. bdg. 15.00 *(978-0-7569-2236-8(4))* Perfection Learning Corp.

—Secrets of Dripping Fang, Book Three: The Vampire's Curse, Bk. 3. Fischer, Scott M., illus. 2006. (Secrets of Dripping Fang Ser.: Bk. 3). (ENG.). 144p. (J). (gr. 3-7). 12.99 *(978-0-15-205469-4(3)*, 1196455, Clarion Bks.) HarperCollins Pubs.

Greenwald, Tom. My Dog Is Better Than Your Dog. Stower, Adam, illus. 2015. 198p. (J). pap. *(978-0-545-91669-1(0)*, Scholastic Pr.) Scholastic, Inc.

Griffin, Adele. The Knaveheart's Curse: A Vampire Island Book. 2009. (Vampire Island Ser.: 2). (ENG.). 160p. (J). (gr. 3-7). 6.99 *(978-0-14-241407-1(7)*, Puffin Books) Penguin Young Readers Group.

Gunter, Miles & Shannon, Kelsey. Yeti vs. Vampire. 2012. (Illus.). 96p. (YA). pap. 12.95 *(978-0-9822253-5-6(0))* Antarctic Pr., Inc.

Hahn, Mary Downing. Look for Me by Moonlight. 2008. (ENG.). 208p. (YA). (gr. 7). pap. 7.99 *(978-0-547-07616-4(9)*, 1042006, Clarion Bks.) HarperCollins Pubs.

Harper, Benjamin. The Boy Who Cried Vampire: A Graphic Novel. López, Alex, illus. 2017. (Far Out Fables Ser.). (ENG.). 40p. (J). (gr. 3-6). pap. 4.95 *(978-1-4965-5425-3(6)*, 136358); lib. bdg. 25.32 *(978-1-4965-5421-5(3)*, 136354) Capstone. (Stone Arch Bks.).

Harris, Lewis. A Taste for Red. 2010. (ENG.). 180p. (J). (gr. 5-7). pap. 12.95 *(978-0-547-39851-8(4)*, 1427650, Clarion Bks.) HarperCollins Pubs.

—A Taste for Red. 2010. (ENG.). 176p. (J). (gr. 4-6). 18.69 *(978-0-547-14462-7(8))* Houghton Mifflin Harcourt Publishing Co.

Hautman, Pete. Sweetblood. 2010. (ENG.). 208p. (YA). (gr. 7). pap. 8.99 *(978-1-4424-0755-8(7)*, Simon & Schuster Bks. For Young Readers) Simon & Schuster Bks. For Young Readers.

Havard, Amanda. The Survivors. 2011. (ENG.). (YA). 294p. 21.99 *(978-0-9833190-0-9(6))*; 300p. pap. 11.99 *(978-0-9833190-2-3(2))* Chafie Pr., LLC.

—The Survivors: Body & Blood. 2013. 458p. (YA). 23.99 *(978-0-9833190-8-5(1))* Chafie Pr., LLC.

Henderson, Jason. Alex Van Helsing: The Triumph of Death. 2012. (Alex Van Helsing Ser.: 3). (ENG.). 320p. (YA). (gr. 8). 17.99 *(978-0-06-195103-9(X)*, HarperTeen) HarperCollins Pubs.

—Alex Van Helsing: Vampire Rising. (Alex Van Helsing Ser.: 1). (ENG.). (YA). (gr. 8). 2011. 272p. pap. 8.99 *(978-0-06-195100-8(5))* 2010. 256p. 16.99 *(978-0-06-195099-5(8))* HarperCollins Pubs. (HarperTeen).

Henseleit, Jack. The Witching Hours: the Vampire Knife. 2018. (ENG.). 240p. (J). (gr. 3-7). 16.99 *(978-0-316-52466-7(2))* Little, Brown Bks. for Young Readers.

Hicks, Rebecca. Little Vampires. Hicks, Rebecca, illus. 2007. (Illus.). 56p. per. 8.95 *(978-0-9799290-0-7(8))* Lunasea Studios.

Hill, Will. Darkest Night (Department 19, Book 5) 2016. (Department 19 Ser.: 5). (ENG.). 736p. (J). pap. 9.99 *(978-0-00-815427-1(9)*, HarperCollins Children's Bks.) HarperCollins Pubs. Ltd. GBR. Dist: HarperCollins Pubs.

—Department 19: First Edition, 1. 2012. (Department Nineteen Ser.: 1). (ENG.). 544p. (YA). (gr. 9-12). pap. 9.99 *(978-1-59514-485-0(4)*, Razorbill) Penguin Young Readers Group.

Hodgman, Ann. My Babysitter Is a Vampire. Pierard, John, illus. 2018. (My Babysitter Ser.: Vol. 1). (ENG.). 104p. (YA). (gr. 7-12). pap. 11.95 *(978-1-59687-738-2(3))* ibooks, Inc.

Hoena, Blake. Beet Juice Buddies. Bardin, Dave, illus. 2018. (Monster Heroes Ser.). (ENG.). 32p. (J). (gr. k-2). lib. bdg. 21.32 *(978-1-4965-6416-0(2)*, 138263, Stone Arch Bks.) Capstone.

Hoena, Blake & Hoena, Blake A. Vampires & Veggies. Bardin, Dave, illus. 2016. (Monster Heroes Ser.). (ENG.). 32p. (J). (gr. k-2). lib. bdg. 21.32 *(978-1-4965-3755-3(6)*, 133083, Stone Arch Bks.) Capstone.

Holder, Nancy, et al. Crusade. (Crusade Ser.). (ENG.). (YA). (gr. 9). 2011. 496p. pap. 9.99 *(978-1-4169-9803-7(9))* 2010. 480p. 16.99 *(978-1-4169-9802-0(0))* Simon Pulse. (Simon Pulse).

—Damned. 2011. (Crusade Ser.). (ENG.). 544p. (YA). (gr. 9). pap. 9.99 *(978-1-4169-9805-1(5)*, Simon Pulse) Simon Pulse.

—Vanquished. 2012. (Crusade Ser.). (ENG.). 496p. (YA). (gr. 9). 16.99 *(978-1-4169-9806-8(3))*; pap. 9.99 *(978-1-4169-9807-5(1))* Simon Pulse. (Simon Pulse).

Holloway, Christopher. Gloumain Chronicles Book 1. the Aznadac Heir. 2013. 262p. (J). pap. *(978-1-78299-219-6(7))* FeedARead.com.

Hopkins, Ellen, ed. A New Dawn: Your Favorite Authors on Stephenie Meyer's Twilight Series: Completely Unauthorized. 2009. (Illus.). 200p. (J). (gr. 9-12). pap. 12.95 *(978-1-933771-93-9(3)*, SmartPop) BenBella Bks.

Howard, Kate. Hotel of Horrors. 2012. (Scooby Doo 8X8 Ser.). lib. bdg. 14.75 *(978-0-606-31559-3(4))* Turtleback.

Howe, Deborah & Howe, James. Bunnicula: A Rabbit-Tale of Mystery. Daniel, Alan, illus. 2006. (Bunnicula & Friends Ser.). (ENG.). 128p. (J). (gr. 3-7). pap. 8.99 *(978-1-4169-2817-1(0)*, Atheneum Bks. for Young Readers) Simon & Schuster Children's Publishing.

Howe, James. Bunnicula Strikes Again! 2004. (Bunnicula Ser.). 116p. (J). (gr. 3-7). pap. 29.00 incl. audio *(978-0-8072-8213-7(8)*, Listening Library) Random Hse. Audio Publishing Group.

—Bunnicula Strikes Again! Daniel, Alan, illus. 2007. (Bunnicula & Friends Ser.). (ENG.). 144p. (J). (gr. 3-7). pap. 7.99 *(978-1-4169-3968-9(7)*, Atheneum Bks. for Young Readers) Simon & Schuster Children's Publishing.

—The Celery Stalks at Midnight. unabr. ed. 2004. (Bunnicula Ser.). 111p. (J). (gr. 3-7). pap. 29.00 incl. audio *(978-0-8072-8357-8(6)*, YA173SP, Listening Library) Random Hse. Audio Publishing Group.

—The Celery Stalks at Midnight, 3. Morrill, Leslie, illus. 2006. (Bunnicula & Friends Ser.). (ENG.). 144p. (J). (gr. 3-7). pap. 7.99 *(978-1-4169-2814-0(6))* Simon & Schuster, Inc.

—Hot Fudge. Mack, Jeff, illus. 2006. (Bunnicula & Friends Ser.). 42p. (gr. k-4). 14.00 *(978-0-7569-7224-0(8))* Perfection Learning Corp.

—The Vampire Bunny. Mack, Jeff, illus. 2005. (Bunnicula & Friends Ser.). 41p. (J). (gr. 1-3). 11.65 *(978-0-7569-6832-8(1))* Perfection Learning Corp.

—The Vampire Bunny: Ready-To-Read Level 3. Mack, Jeff, illus. 2004. (Bunnicula & Friends Ser.: 1). (ENG.). 48p. (J). (gr. 1-3). 17.99 *(978-0-689-85724-9(1)*, Simon Spotlight) Simon Spotlight.

Hunter, C. C. Eternal. unabr. ed. 2014. (Shadow Falls: after Dark Ser.: 2). (ENG.). 400p. (YA). (gr. 7-12). 19.99 *(978-1-250-05630-6(6)*, 900138741, St. Martin's Griffin) St. Martin's Pr.

—Eternal: Shadow Falls: after Dark. 2014. (Shadow Falls: after Dark Ser.: 2). (ENG.). 400p. (YA). (gr. 7-12). pap. 12.99 *(978-1-250-04461-7(8)*, 900127030, St. Martin's Griffin) St. Martin's Pr.

—Reborn. 2014. (Shadow Falls: after Dark Ser.: 1). (ENG.). 400p. (YA). (gr. 7). pap. 14.99 *(978-1-250-03591-2(0)*, 900121850, St. Martin's Griffin) St. Martin's Pr.

Ireland, Justina. Jeff Allen vs. the Time Suck Vampire. Champion, Tyler, illus. 2017. (Devils' Pass Ser.). (ENG.). 128p. (J). (gr. 4-8). lib. bdg. 25.99 *(978-1-4965-4986-0(4)*, 135878, Stone Arch Bks.) Capstone.

Jefford, Nikki. Aurora Sky: Vampire Hunter, Vol. 1. 2013. 260p. pap. 10.99 *(978-1-939997-48-7(8))* Wispvine Publishing.

Jenkins, A. M. Night Road. 2010. (ENG.). 368p. (YA). (gr. 8-12). pap. 8.99 *(978-0-06-054606-9(9)*, HarperTeen) HarperCollins Pubs.

Jinks, Catherine. The Reformed Vampire Support Group. 2010. (ENG., Illus.). 368p. (YA). (gr. 7-12). 24.94 *(978-0-15-206609-3(8))* Harcourt Children's Bks.

—The Reformed Vampire Support Group. 2010. (ENG.). 384p. (YA). (gr. 7). pap. 8.99 *(978-0-547-41166-8(9)*, 1429152, Clarion Bks.) HarperCollins Pubs.

Johnson, Pete. The Vampire Fighters. 2012. (Illus.). 272p. (J). (gr. 4-7). pap. 10.99 *(978-0-440-86940-5(4))* Transworld Publishers Ltd. GBR. Dist: Independent Pubs. Group.

Jozev. Claws of Darkness. 2006. (Journal of the Vampire Hunter; Claws of Darkness Ser.). (ENG., Illus.). 64p. (YA). pap. 5.95 *(978-1-59796-090-8(X))* DrMaster Pubns. Inc.

—Journal of the Vampire Hunter Vol. 3: Claws of Darkness. Zhao, Yun, tr. 2006. (Journal of the Vampire Hunter; Claws of Darkness Ser.). (ENG., Illus.). 64p. (YA). pap. 5.95 *(978-1-59796-088-5(8))* DrMaster Pubns. Inc.

—Journal of the Vampire Hunter Vol. 4: Claws of Darkness. 2006. (Journal of the Vampire Hunter; Claws of Darkness Ser.). (ENG., Illus.). 64p. (YA). pap. 5.95 *(978-1-59796-089-2(6))* DrMaster Pubns. Inc.

Julie Shelton. World of Vampires Part 1: The Huntress. 2006. 49p. pap. 10.00 *(978-1-59926-998-6(8))* Xlibris Corp.

Jungman, Ann. Vlad the Drac. Thompson, George, illus. 2006. (Vlad the Drac Ser.). 124p. (J). (gr. 2-4). per. 6.95 *(978-1-903015-22-3(7))* Barn Owl Bks, London GBR. Dist: Independent Pubs. Group.

—Vlad the Drac Superstar. Thompson, George, illus. 2006. (Vlad the Drac Ser.). 122p. (J). (gr. 2-4). pap. 6.95 *(978-1-903015-45-2(6))* Barn Owl Bks, London GBR. Dist: Independent Pubs. Group.

Kadence, Sam. Evolution. 2013. 230p. pap. 14.99 *(978-1-62380-410-7(8)*, Harmony Ink Pr.) Dreamspinner Pr.

—Evolution [Library Edition]. 2013. 230p. pap. 14.99 *(978-1-62380-924-9(X)*, Harmony Ink Pr.) Dreamspinner Pr.

Kagawa, Julie. The Eternity Cure. 2014. (Blood of Eden Ser.: 2). (ENG.). 416p. (YA). pap. 9.99 *(978-0-373-21113-5(9)*, Harlequin Teen) Harlequin Enterprises ULC CAN. Dist: HarperCollins Pubs.

—The Immortal Rules. 2013. (Blood of Eden Ser.: 1). (ENG.). 464p. (YA). pap. 12.99 *(978-0-373-21080-0(9)*, Harlequin Teen) Harlequin Enterprises ULC CAN. Dist: HarperCollins Pubs.

—The Immortal Rules. 2013. (Blood of Eden Ser.: 1). (J). lib. bdg. 20.85 *(978-0-606-26947-6(9))* Turtleback.

Katcher, Brian. The Improbable Theory of Ana & Zak. 2016. (ENG.). 336p. (YA). (gr. 8). 20.85 *(978-0-606-39261-7(0))* Turtleback.

Kayla Taylor. Fatal Elements: Book 1. 2009. 368p. pap. 20.95 *(978-1-4401-8495-6(X))* iUniverse, Inc.

Keating, T. P. Bleeding Hearts: the Diary of a Country Vampire. 2005. 272p. (YA). pap. 12.48 *(978-1-4116-4815-9(3))* Lulu Pr., Inc.

Keeble, Helen. Fang Girl. 2012. (ENG.). 352p. (YA). (gr. 8). pap. 9.99 *(978-0-06-208225-1(6)*, HarperTeen) HarperCollins Pubs.

Klause, Annette Curtis. The Silver Kiss. 2007. (ENG.). 224p. (YA). (gr. 7). pap. 8.99 *(978-0-385-73422-6(0)*, Delacorte Bks. for Young Readers) Random Hse. Children's Bks.

Kokoro, Natsume & Natsume, Kokoro. Lovephobia Volume 2. 2012. (ENG., Illus.). 200p. (YA). pap. 12.95 *(978-1-56970-283-3(7)*, 54e5551a-cbc7-4c38-afff-8fbb524680d1) Digital Manga Publishing.

Lake, Nick. Blood Ninja. (ENG., Illus.). (YA). (gr. 7). 2010. 400p. pap. 12.99 *(978-1-4169-8628-7(6))* 2009. 384p. 16.99 *(978-1-4169-8627-0(8))* Simon & Schuster Bks. For Young Readers. (Simon & Schuster Bks. For Young Readers).

—Blood Ninja II: The Revenge of Lord Oda. (ENG., Illus.). (YA). (gr. 7). 2011. 416p. pap. 9.99 *(978-1-4169-8630-0(8))* 2010. 400p. 16.99 *(978-1-4169-8629-4(4))* Simon & Schuster Bks. For Young Readers. (Simon & Schuster Bks. For Young Readers).

—Blood Ninja III: The Betrayal of the Living. 2013. (ENG., Illus.). 368p. (YA). (gr. 9). pap. 9.99 *(978-1-4424-2680-1(2)*, Simon & Schuster Bks. For Young Readers) Simon & Schuster Bks. For Young Readers.

Lane, Travis. Redhaze: Trilogy. 2004. 192p. pap. 24.95 *(978-1-4137-6094-1(5))* PublishAmerica, Inc.

Larbalestier, Justine & Brennan, Sarah Rees. Team Human. 2012. (ENG.). 352p. (YA). (gr. 8). 17.99 *(978-0-06-208964-9(1)*, HarperTeen) HarperCollins Pubs.

Leamon, Kevin. Oh No. Not Again! 2010. 27p. 14.95 *(978-0-557-63078-3(9))* Lulu Pr., Inc.

Leblanc, Louise. Leo's Midnight Rescue. Prud'homme, Jules, illus. 2004. 62p. (J). lib. bdg. 12.00 *(978-1-4242-1217-0(0))* Fitzgerald Bks.

—Leo's Midnight Rescue, 1 vol. Cummins, Sarah, tr. Prud'homme, Jules, illus. 2004. (Formac First Novels Ser.: 53). (ENG.). 64p. (J). (gr. 2-5). 4.95 *(978-0-88780-640-7(6)*, 640); 14.95 *(978-0-88780-641-4(4)*, 641) Formac Publishing Co., Ltd. CAN. Dist: Formac Lorimer Bks. Ltd.

—Leo's Skiing Surprise. Prud'homme, Jules, illus. 2007. (Formac First Novels Ser.: 5). (ENG.). 64p. (J). (gr. 2-5). 14.95 *(978-0-88780-738-1(0)*, 738); 4.95 *(978-0-88780-736-7(4)*, 736) Formac Publishing Co., Ltd. CAN. Dist: Formac Lorimer Bks. Ltd.

Leblanc, Louise & Prud'homme, Jules. Les Vampires Sortent de L'ombre. 2003. (Premier Roman Ser.). (FRE., Illus.). 64p. (J). (gr. 1-4). pap. *(978-2-89021-609-9(8))* Diffusion du livre Mirabel (DLM).

Lockard, Lynn. Gone Batty!!! 2009. 40p. pap. 16.99 *(978-1-4389-8516-9(9))* AuthorHouse.

London, J. A. After Daybreak: A Darkness Before Dawn Novel. 2013. (Darkness Before Dawn Ser.: 3). (ENG., Illus.). 336p. (YA). (gr. 9). pap. 9.99 *(978-0-06-202067-3(6)*, HarperTeen) HarperCollins Pubs.

—Darkness Before Dawn. 2012. (Darkness Before Dawn Ser.: 1). (ENG., Illus.). 368p. (YA). (gr. 9). pap. 9.99 *(978-0-06-202065-9(X)*, HarperTeen) HarperCollins Pubs.

Lowe, E. Van. Never Slow Dance with a Zombie. 2009. (ENG.). 256p. (YA). (gr. 8-12). pap. 16.99 *(978-0-7653-2040-7(1)*, 900050608, Tor Teen) Doherty, Tom Assocs., LLC.

Maizel, Rebecca. Infinite Days: A Vampire Queen Novel. 2010. (Vampire Queen Ser.: 1). (ENG.). 336p. (YA). (gr. 7-18). pap. 16.99 *(978-0-312-64991-3(6)*, 900069066, St. Martin's Griffin) St. Martin's Pr.

—Stolen Nights: A Vampire Queen Novel. 2013. (Vampire Queen Ser.: 2). (ENG.). 320p. (YA). (gr. 7-12). pap. 16.99 *(978-0-312-64992-0(4)*, 900069067, St. Martin's Griffin) St. Martin's Pr.

Maniscalco, Kerri. Hunting Prince Dracula. (Stalking Jack the Ripper Ser.: 2). (ENG., Illus.). (YA). (gr. 10-17). 2018. 480p. pap. 12.99 *(978-0-316-55167-0(8))* 2017. 448p. 19.99 *(978-0-316-55166-3(X))* Little Brown & Co. (Jimmy Patterson).

Marini, Enrico & Dufaux, Jean. Rapaces, Vol. 4. 2005. (SPA., Illus.). 56p. pap. 17.95 *(978-1-59497-107-5(2))* Public Square Bks.

Marrone, Amanda. Devoured. 2009. (ENG.). 304p. (YA). (gr. 9-18). pap. 9.99 *(978-1-4169-7890-9(9)*, Simon Pulse) Simon Pulse.

—Slayed. 2010. (ENG., Illus.). 272p. (YA). (gr. 9-18). pap. 9.99 *(978-1-4169-9487-9(4)*, Simon Pulse) Simon Pulse.

Marsh, Carole. The Mystery at Dracula's Castle: Transylvania, Romania. (Around the World in 80 Mysteries Ser.). 133p. (J). 2009. 18.99 *(978-0-635-07039-5(1)*, Marsh, Carole Mysteries) 2008. (Illus.). (gr. 3-5). 14.95 *(978-0-635-06471-4(5))*9. 2008. (ENG., Illus.). (gr. 4-6). 18.69 *(978-0-635-06469-1(3))* Gallopade International.

Marshall, Carol. A Vampire's Story: Bella's Diary. 2009. 194p. pap. 9.99 *(978-1-61667-011-5(8))* Raider Publishing International.

McGowan, Maureen. Sleeping Beauty: Vampire Slayer. 2010. 320p. pap. 8.95 *(978-1-60747-779-2(3)*, Pickwick Pr.) Phoenix Bks., Inc.

McHeffey, Adam. Asiago, 0 vols. McHeffey, Adam, illus. 2012. (ENG., Illus.). 32p. (J). (gr. 1-3). 16.99 *(978-0-7614-6138-8(8)*, 9780761461388, Two Lions) Amazon Publishing.

McKenzie, J. Lee. Vampires Don't Believe in Mermaids. 2011. 54p. pap. 16.95 *(978-1-4560-1157-4(X))* America Star Bks.

Mead, Richelle. Blood Promise. 2010. (Vampire Academy Ser.: 4). lib. bdg. 20.85 *(978-0-606-14565-7(6))* Turtleback.

—Blood Promise: A Vampire Academy Novel. 2010. (Vampire Academy Ser.: 4). (ENG.). 528p. (YA). (gr. 7-18). pap. 13.99 *(978-1-59514-310-5(6)*, Razorbill) Penguin Young Readers Group.

—Bloodlines. 2012. (Bloodlines Ser.: 1). (ENG.). 448p. (YA). (gr. 7-18). pap. 12.99 *(978-1-59514-473-7(0)*, Razorbill) Penguin Young Readers Group.

—The Fiery Heart: A Bloodlines Novel. 2014. (Bloodlines Ser.: 4). (ENG.). 448p. (YA). (gr. 7). pap. 12.99 *(978-1-59514-631-1(8)*, Razorbill) Penguin Young Readers Group.

—Frostbite: A Vampire Academy Novel. 2008. (Vampire Academy Ser.: 2). 336p. (YA). (gr. 7-18). pap. 12.99 *(978-1-59514-175-0(8)*, Razorbill) Penguin Young Readers Group.

—The Golden Lily: A Bloodlines Novel. 2013. (Bloodlines Ser.: 2). (ENG.). 448p. (YA). (gr. 7). pap. 12.99 *(978-1-59514-602-1(4)*, Razorbill) Penguin Young Readers Group.

—The Indigo Spell: A Bloodlines Novel. 2013. (Bloodlines Ser.: 3). (ENG.). 448p. (YA). (gr. 7). pap. 12.99 *(978-1-59514-613-7(X)*, Razorbill) Penguin Young Readers Group.

—Last Sacrifice: A Vampire Academy Novel. 2011. (Vampire Academy Ser.: 6). (ENG.). 608p. (YA). (gr. 7-18). 13.99 *(978-1-59514-440-9(4)*, Razorbill) Penguin Young Readers Group.

—The Ruby Circle: A Bloodlines Novel. 2015. (Bloodlines Ser.: 6). (ENG.). 384p. (YA). (gr. 7). pap. 12.99 *(978-1-59514-633-5(4)*, Razorbill) Penguin Young Readers Group.

—Shadow Kiss. 2013. (Vampire Academy (Graphic Novels) Ser.: 3). lib. bdg. 24.50 *(978-0-606-34129-5(3))* Turtleback.

—Shadow Kiss: A Vampire Academy Novel. 2008. (Vampire Academy Ser.: 3). 448p. (YA). (gr. 7-18). pap. 12.99 *(978-1-59514-197-2(9)*, Razorbill) Penguin Young Readers Group.

—Silver Shadows: A Bloodlines Novel. 2015. (Bloodlines Ser.: 5). (ENG.). 416p. (YA). (gr. 7). pap. 12.99 *(978-1-59514-632-8(6)*, Razorbill) Penguin Young Readers Group.

—Spirit Bound: A Vampire Academy Novel. 2011. (Vampire Academy Ser.: 5). (ENG.). 512p. (YA). (gr. 7-18). 13.99 *(978-1-59514-366-2(1)*, Razorbill) Penguin Young Readers Group.

—Vampire Academy. 2007. (Vampire Academy Ser.: 1). 336p. (YA). (gr. 7-18). 11.99 *(978-1-59514-174-3(X)*, Razorbill) Penguin Young Readers Group.

—Vampire Academy: A Graphic Novel. Vieceli, Emma, illus. 2011. (Vampire Academy Ser.: 1). 144p. (YA). (gr. 7-18). pap. 12.99 *(978-1-59514-429-4(3)*, Razorbill) Penguin Young Readers Group.

—Vampire Academy 10th Anniversary Edition. 10th ed. 2016. (Vampire Academy Ser.). 512p. (YA). (gr. 7). pap. 11.99 *(978-0-448-49429-6(9)*, Razorbill) Penguin Young Readers Group.

—Vampire Academy Box Set 1-6, 6 vols. 2013. (Vampire Academy Ser.). (ENG.). 2784p. (YA). (gr. 7). pap., pap., pap. 77.94 *(978-1-59514-758-5(6)*, Razorbill) Penguin Young Readers Group.

Meehl, Brian. Suck It Up. 2009. (Suck It up Ser.). (ENG.). 336p. (YA). (gr. 7). pap. 12.99 *(978-0-440-42091-0(1)*, Delacorte Bks. for Young Readers) Random Hse. Children's Bks.

Meistle, Jarrod. Victor the Vampire. 2011. 28p. pap. 12.99 *(978-1-4628-4514-9(2))* Xlibris Corp.

—Victor the Vampire & the Bully. 2012. 28p. pap. 14.99 *(978-1-4691-3879-4(4))* Xlibris Corp.

Merasty, Marla Paul. Chuck the Different Vampire. 2012. 32p. pap. *(978-1-77067-501-8(9))* FriesenPress.

Mercer, Sienna. My Sister the Vampire #1: Switched. 2007. (My Sister the Vampire Ser.: 1). (ENG.). 208p. (J). (gr. 3-7). pap. 6.99 *(978-0-06-087113-0(X)*, HarperCollins) HarperCollins Pubs.

—My Sister the Vampire #2: Fangtastic! 2007. (My Sister the Vampire Ser.: 2). (ENG.). 208p. (J). (gr. 3-7). per. 6.99 *(978-0-06-087115-4(6)*, HarperCollins) HarperCollins Pubs.

—My Sister the Vampire #3: Re-Vamped! 2007. (My Sister the Vampire Ser.: 3). (ENG.). 208p. (J). (gr. 3-7). pap. 7.99 *(978-0-06-087118-5(0)*, HarperCollins) HarperCollins Pubs.

Meyer, Stephenie. Amanecer / Breaking Dawn. 2008. (Saga Crepusculo / the Twilight Saga Ser.: 4).Tr. of Breaking Dawn. (SPA.). 832p. (YA). (gr. 9-12). pap. 23.95 *(978-607-11-0033-7(X)*, Alfaguara) Penguin Random House Grupo Editorial ESP. Dist: Penguin Random Hse. LLC.

—Breaking Dawn. 2008. (Twilight Saga Ser.: 4). (ENG.). 768p. (YA). (gr. 7-17). 24.99 *(978-0-316-06792-8(X))* Little, Brown Bks. for Young Readers.

—Breaking Dawn. 2010. (Twilight Saga Ser.: 4). (YA). lib. bdg. 29.40 *(978-0-606-23108-4(0))* Turtleback.

—Eclipse. 2007. (Twilight Saga Ser.: 3). (ENG.). 640p. (YA). (gr. 7-17). 22.99 *(978-0-316-16020-9(2))* Little, Brown Bks. for Young Readers.

—Eclipse. 2008. 576p. *(978-1-904233-91-6(0)*, Atom Books) Little, Brown Book Group Ltd.

—Eclipse. 2011. (Twilight Saga: Bk. 3). 13.08 *(978-0-7848-3531-9(4)*, Everbind) Marco Bk. Co.

—Eclipse. 2010. (Twilight Saga: Bk. 3). 629p. (YA). (gr. 9-12). 22.10 *(978-1-60686-303-9(7))* Perfection Learning Corp.

—Eclipse. 2007. (Twilight Saga Spanish Ser.: 3). (SPA.). 637p. (gr. 7-12). lib. bdg. 28.15 *(978-1-4177-9862-9(9))* Turtleback.

—New Moon. 2008. (Twilight Saga: Bk. 2). 563p. (gr. 9-12). 21.00 *(978-1-60686-336-7(3))* Perfection Learning Corp.

—New Moon. 2006. (Twilight Saga Ser.: 2). (ENG.). 608p. (J). (gr. 7-17). 24.99 *(978-0-316-16019-3(9))* Little, Brown Bks. for Young Readers.

—New Moon. 2011. (Twilight Saga: Bk. 2). 11.72 *(978-0-7848-3535-7(7)*, Everbind) Marco Bk. Co.

—The Short Second Life of Bree Tanner: An Eclipse Novella. 2010. (Twilight Saga Ser.). (ENG.). 192p. (YA). (gr. 7-17). 17.99 *(978-0-316-12558-1(X))* Little, Brown Bks. for Young Readers.

—Twilight. 2008. (Twilight Saga: Bk. 1). (CHI.). 375p. (YA). pap. *(978-7-5448-0333-5(3))* Jieli Publishing Hse.

—Twilight. 2005. (Twilight Saga Ser.: 1). (ENG.). 544p. (YA). (gr. 7-17). 24.99 *(978-0-316-16017-9(2))* Little, Brown Bks. for Young Readers.

—Twilight. 2008. 480p. pap. *(978-1-905654-34-5(0)*, Atom Books) Little, Brown Book Group Ltd.

—Twilight. 2009. (Twilight Saga: Bk. 1). 11.72 *(978-0-7848-1934-0(3)*, Everbind) Marco Bk. Co.

—Twilight. (Twilight Saga: Bk. 1). 2010. 498p. (YA). (gr. 9-12). 20.10 *(978-1-60686-352-7(5))* 2006. 21.00 *(978-0-7569-6825-0(9))* Perfection Learning Corp.

—Twilight. (Twilight Ser.: 1). (YA). 2007. 1.25 *(978-1-4193-9974-9(8))* 2006. 87.75 *(978-1-4193-9975-6(6))* Recorded Bks., Inc.

—Twilight. 2006. (Twilight Saga Ser.: 1). (Illus.). 498p. (YA). (gr. 9-12). lib. bdg. 28.15 *(978-1-4177-5591-2(1))* Turtleback.

—The Twilight Saga Collection Set, 4 vols. 2008. (ENG.). 2560p. (YA). (gr. 7-17). 92.00 *(978-0-316-03184-4(4))* Little, Brown Bks. for Young Readers.

Mikumo, Gakuto. Strike the Blood, Vol. 6 (light Novel) Return of the Alchemist. 2017. (Strike the Blood (light Novel) Ser.: 6). (ENG., Illus.). 224p. (YA). (gr. 8-17). pap. 14.00 *(978-0-316-34558-3(X)*, Yen Pr.) Yen Pr. LLC.

Millard, Adam. Peter Crombie, Teenage Zombie. 2012. 238p. pap. *(978-0-9573999-7-6(9))* Crowded Quarantine Pubns.

Miller, Sara. Vampirina in the Fall. 2018. (Illus.). 32p. (J). *(978-1-5444-0806-4(4))* Disney Publishing Worldwide.

Mongredien, Sue. Oliver Moon's Fangtastic Sleepover. 2011. (Oliver Moon, Junior Wizard Ser.). (ENG.). 92p. (J). (gr. 2-5). 17.44 *(978-0-7945-3094-5(X))* EDC Publishing.

Mosley, Walter. When the Thrill Is Gone: A Leonid Mcgill Mystery, 3 vols. 2012. (Leonid Mcgill Mystery Ser.: 3). (ENG.). 384p. (gr. 12). 16.00 *(978-0-451-23565-7(7)*, Berkley) Penguin Publishing Group.

Moss, Marissa. Blood Diaries: Tales of a 6th-Grade Vampire. 2014. (ENG., Illus.). 136p. (J). (gr. 4-6). 13.00 *(978-1-939547-05-7(9)*, 443b9f74-42dd-4a5c-a10d-c918bb9b0e82) Creston Bks.

Mounteer, J. B. Camp (Were) Wolf. 2007. (ENG.). 24p. per. 16.99 *(978-1-4259-9185-2(8))* AuthorHouse.

Muncaster, Harriet. Isadora Moon Goes Camping. 2017. (Isadora Moon Ser.: 2). (ENG., Illus.). 128p. (J). (gr. 1-4). 6.99 *(978-0-399-55827-6(6)*, Random Hse. Bks. for Young Readers) Random Hse. Children's Bks.

—Isadora Moon Goes to School. 2017. (Isadora Moon Ser.: 1). (ENG., Illus.). 128p. (J). (gr. 1-4). 6.99 *(978-0-399-55823-8(3)*, Random Hse. Bks. for Young Readers) Random Hse. Children's Bks.

—Isadora Moon Goes to the Ballet. 2018. (Isadora Moon Ser.: 3). (ENG., Illus.). 128p. (J). (gr. 1-4). 5.99 *(978-0-399-55831-3(4)*, Random Hse. Bks. for Young Readers) Random Hse. Children's Bks.

—Isadora Moon Has a Birthday. 2018. (Isadora Moon Ser.: 4). (ENG., Illus.). 128p. (J). (gr. 1-4). 6.99 *(978-0-399-55835-1(7))*; 14.99 *(978-0-399-55833-7(0))* Random Hse. Children's Bks. (Random Hse. Bks. for Young Readers).

Mungin, Shanyece. Entwined, 1 vol. 2010. 117p. pap. 19.95 *(978-1-4489-9685-8(6))* America Star Bks.

Murphy, Lisa. Little Vampire. 2009. (ENG.). 242p. pap. 16.95 *(978-1-4092-9494-8(3))* Lulu Pr., Inc.

Nash, Susan Smith. The Good Deeds Society: Family Plot. 2008. (Illus.). 220p. (YA). pap. 18.00 *(978-0-9797573-2-7(0))* Texture Pr.

Neill, Chloe. Charmfall: A Novel of the Dark Elite. 2012. (Dark Elite Ser.: 3). (ENG.). 288p. (YA). (gr. 9). 9.99 *(978-0-451-23080-5(9)*, Berkley) Penguin Publishing Group.

Night, P. J. You Can't Come in Here!, 2. 2011. (You're Invited to a Creepover Ser.: 2). (ENG.). 160p. (J). (gr. 3-7). pap. 7.99 *(978-1-4424-2095-3(2)*, Simon Spotlight) Simon & Schuster Children's Publishing.

—You Can't Come in Here! 2018. (You're Invited to a Creepover Ser.: 2). (ENG.). 160p. (J). (gr. 3-7). 17.99 *(978-1-5344-1658-1(7)*, Simon Spotlight) Simon Spotlight.

—You Can't Come in Here!, 1 vol. 2013. (You're Invited to a Creepover Ser.). (ENG.). 160p. (J). (gr. 3-6). lib. bdg. 31.36 *(978-1-61479-066-2(3)*, 15854, Chapter Bks.) Spotlight.

Noble, Marty. Vampires Coloring Book. 2010. (Dover Horror Coloring Bks.). (ENG., Illus.). 32p. (gr. 6-8). pap. 3.99 *(978-0-486-47848-7(3)*, 478483) Dover Pubns., Inc.

O'Callaghan, G. The Eternals. 2007. 376p. per. *(978-1-84693-055-3(3))* Best Global Publishing Ltd.

Orme, David & Orme, David. Vampires. 2008. (ENG., Illus.). 36p. pap. *(978-1-84167-692-0(6))* Ransom Publishing Ltd.

O'Shea, M.J. Blood Moon. 2016. (ENG., Illus.). (J). 24.99 *(978-1-63477-941-8(X)*, Harmony Ink Pr.) Dreamspinner Pr.

—Cold Moon. 2nd ed. 2016. (ENG., Illus.). (J). 24.99 *(978-1-63477-954-8(1)*, Harmony Ink Pr.) Dreamspinner Pr.

—Cold Moon [Library Edition]. 2nd ed. 2014. 180p. pap. 14.99 *(978-1-62798-460-7(7)*, Harmony Ink Pr.) Dreamspinner Pr.

Pace, Anne Marie. Vampirina at the Beach-Vampirina Ballerina. 2017. (Vampirina Ser.: 3). (ENG., Illus.). 40p. (J). (gr. -1-k). 17.99 *(978-1-4847-7342-0(X)*, Disney-Hyperion) Disney Publishing Worldwide.

—Vampirina Ballerina-A Vampirina Ballerina Book. 2012. (Vampirina Ser.: 1). (ENG., Illus.). 40p. (J). (gr. -1-k). 16.99 *(978-1-4231-5753-3(2)*, Disney-Hyperion) Disney Publishing Worldwide.

—Vampirina in the Snow-A Vampirina Ballerina Book. 2018. (Vampirina Ser.: 4). (ENG., Illus.). 40p. (J). (gr. -1-k). 17.99 *(978-1-368-02318-4(5)*, Disney-Hyperion) Disney Publishing Worldwide.

Papineau, Lucie. Bebe-Vampire, Gloups! 2004. (FRE., Illus.). (J). (gr. k-3). spiral bd. *(978-0-616-07259-2(7))* Canadian National Institute for the Blind/Institut National Canadien pour les Aveugles.

Papp, Robert, illus. The Vampire Mystery. 2009. (Boxcar Children Mysteries Ser.: 120). (ENG.). 128p. (J). (gr. 2-5). pap. 6.99 *(978-0-8075-8461-3(4)*, 807584614, Random Hse. Bks. for Young Readers) Random Hse. Children's Bks.

Patrick, David. Nero Demare & the Legend of the Vampires. 2007. 284p. (YA). per. 17.95 *(978-0-595-42014-8(1))* iUniverse, Inc.

Pauley, Kimberly. Sucks to Be Me: The All-True Confessions of Mina Hamilton, Teen Vampire. 2008. (ENG.). 293p. (YA). (gr. 6-8). 24.94 *(978-0-7869-5028-7(5))* Wizards of the Coast.

Paulk, William. The Creatures of Vision City: Pokie's Party, Book One. 2009. 48p. pap. 10.99 *(978-1-4389-5659-6(2))* AuthorHouse.

Perry, Pete. The Secret of Bedside Manor. 2009. (Illus.). 140p. pap. 36.49 *(978-1-4389-6668-7(7))* AuthorHouse.

Phillips, Dee. The Vampire's Lair. 2016. (Cold Whispers II Ser.). (ENG., Illus.). 32p. (J). (gr. 2-6). 28.50 *(978-1-944102-30-2(2))* Bearport Publishing Co., Inc.

Pike, Christopher, pseud. Thirst (Boxed Set) Thirst No. 1; Thirst No. 2; Thirst No. 3, 3 vols. 2013. (Thirst Ser.). (ENG.). 1744p. (YA). (gr. 9). pap. 30.99 *(978-1-4424-8375-0(X)*, Simon Pulse) Simon Pulse.

—Thirst No. 1: The Last Vampire, Black Blood, Red Dice. 2009. (Thirst Ser.: 1). (ENG., Illus.). 624p. (YA). (gr. 9). pap. 14.99 *(978-1-4169-8308-8(2)*, Simon Pulse) Simon Pulse.

—Thirst No. 2 No. 2: Phantom, Evil Thirst, Creatures of Forever, Bk. 2. 2010. (Thirst Ser.: 2). (ENG.). 608p. (YA). (gr. 9). pap. 14.99 *(978-1-4169-8309-5(0)*, Simon Pulse) Simon Pulse.

—Thirst No. 3: The Eternal Dawn. 2010. (Thirst Ser.: 3). (ENG.). 512p. (YA). (gr. 9-18). pap. 14.99 *(978-1-4424-1317-7(4)*, Simon Pulse) Simon Pulse.

—Thirst No. 4: The Shadow of Death, 4. 2011. (Thirst Ser.: 4). (ENG., Illus.). 528p. (YA). (gr. 9). pap. 10.99 *(978-1-4424-1319-1(0)*, Simon Pulse) Simon Pulse.

—Thirst No. 5: The Sacred Veil. 2013. (Thirst Ser.: 5). (ENG., Illus.). 512p. (YA). (gr. 7). pap. 14.99 *(978-1-4424-6731-6(2)*, Simon Pulse) Simon Pulse.

Pinkwater, Daniel M. Vampires of Blinsh. Renier, Aaron, illus. 2020. (ENG.). 40p. (J). (gr. -1-3). 17.99 *(978-1-4197-4681-9(2)*, 1268001, Abrams Bks. for Young Readers) Abrams, Inc.

Pixie, B. R. Just a Little Human. 2011. 98p. pap. 19.95 *(978-1-4512-3551-7(8))* America Star Bks.

Poulsen, David A. The Book of Vampire. 4th rev. ed. 2007. (Salt & Pepper Chronicles). (ENG., Illus.). 160p. (J). (gr. 4-7). 6.95 *(978-1-55263-805-7(7))* Leaf Storm Pr.

—The Vampire's Visit. 2007. (Salt & Pepper Chronicles). (ENG.). 160p. (J). (gr. 4-7). 6.95 *(978-1-55263-721-0(2))* Leaf Storm Pr.

Publications International Ltd. Staff, ed. Vampires & Other Scary Creatures(Look & Find) 2010. (Illus.). 24p. (J). 7.98 *(978-1-60553-839-6(6))* Publications International, Ltd.

Rand, Johnathan. Amer Ch Double Thrillers. 2010. 256p. pap. 6.99 *(978-1-893699-26-7(9))* AudioCraft Publishing, Inc.

Ratnett, Michael. Dracula Steps Out. Goulding, June & Smyth, Iain, illus. 2005. 12p. (J). (gr. k-4). reprint ed. 16.00 *(978-0-7567-8585-7(5))* DIANE Publishing Co.

Rees, Douglas. Vampire High. 2010. (ENG.). 240p. (YA). (gr. 6-8). lib. bdg. 24.94 *(978-0-385-90143-7(7))* Random House Publishing Group.

—Vampire High. 2010. (Vampire High Ser.). 240p. (YA). (gr. 7-18). pap. 9.99 *(978-0-385-73920-7(6)*, Delacorte Bks. for Young Readers) Random Hse. Children's Bks.

Reid, Katie. Blood Driven. 2011. 370p. pap. 29.95 *(978-1-4560-5417-5(1))* PublishAmerica, Inc.

Rex, Adam. Fat Vampire: A Never Coming of Age Story. 2011. (ENG.). 336p. (YA). (gr. 9). pap. 8.99 *(978-0-06-192092-9(4)*, Balzer & Bray) HarperCollins Pubs.

Rice, Morgan. Before Dawn (Vampire, Fallen-Book 1) 2016. (ENG., Illus.). 118p. (J). pap. 6.99 *(978-1-63291-611-2(8))* Morgan Rice Bks.

Richardson, E. E. The Curse Box. 2013. (ENG.). 64p. (YA). (gr. 6-12). pap. 6.95 *(978-1-78112-176-4(1))*; lib. bdg. 22.60 *(978-1-78112-175-7(3))* Lerner Publishing Group.

Richmond, Blair. Out of Breath: The Lithia Trilogy, Book 1. 2018. (ENG.). 268p. (YA). 27.95 *(978-1-61822-077-6(2)*, Ashland Creek Pr.) Byte Level Research.

Riviello, Linda. Werewolves, Vampires & Ghosts... Oh My! 2009. (J). pap. 12.95 *(978-1-61623-088-3(6))* Independent Pub.

Robinson, A. M. Vampire Crush. 2010. (ENG.). 416p. (YA). (gr. 8-18). pap. 8.99 *(978-0-06-198971-1(1)*, HarperTeen) HarperCollins Pubs.

Rosen, Jonathan. From Sunset till Sunrise: Devin Dexter #2. 2018. (Devin & Dexter Ser.: 2). (ENG.). 314p. (J). (gr. 4-8). pap. 7.99 *(978-1-5107-3409-8(0)*, Sky Pony Pr.) Skyhorse Publishing Co., Inc.

Roy, Ron. A to Z Mysteries: the Vampire's Vacation. Gurney, John Steven, illus. 2004. (to Z Mysteries Ser.: 22). 96p. (J). (gr. 1-4). pap. 6.99 *(978-0-375-82479-1(0)*, Random Hse. Bks. for Young Readers) Random Hse. Children's Bks.

Rykken, John. Bloodwood: The Chronicles of Max Mayhem. 2011. 264p. (gr. 10-12). 26.95 *(978-1-4620-0656-4(6))*; pap. 16.95 *(978-1-4620-0657-1(4))* iUniverse, Inc.

Sage, Angie. Araminta Spookie 3: Frognapped. Pickering, Jimmy, illus. 2008. (Araminta Spookie Ser.: 3). (ENG.). 224p. (J). (gr. 2-5). pap. 6.99 *(978-0-06-077489-9(4)*, Tegen, Katherine Bks) HarperCollins Pubs.

—Araminta Spookie 4: Vampire Brat. Pickering, Jimmy, illus. 2009. (Araminta Spookie Ser.: 4). (ENG.). 224p. (J). (gr. 2-5). pap. 6.99 *(978-0-06-077492-9(4)*, Tegen, Katherine Bks) HarperCollins Pubs.

Saveley, Barb. Dusky II: Journey of Tears. 2010. 40p. 18.95 *(978-1-4389-8243-4(7))* AuthorHouse.

Sazaklis, John. Campfire Vampire. Fabicka, Patrycja, illus. 2019. (Boo Bks.). (ENG.). 32p. (J). (gr. k-2). lib. bdg. 21.32 *(978-1-5158-4485-3(4)*, 140581, Picture Window Bks.) Capstone.

Schreiber, Ellen. Kissing Coffins. 2007. (Vampire Kisses Ser.: No. 2). (ENG.). 240p. (J). pap., pap. 5.99 *(978-0-06-077624-4(2)*, HarperTeen) HarperCollins Pubs.

—Vampire Kisses. 2003. (Vampire Kisses Ser.: 1). (ENG.). 208p. (YA). (gr. 8-18). 17.99 *(978-0-06-009334-1(X)*, Tegen, Katherine Bks) HarperCollins Pubs.

—Vampire Kisses: Finstere Sehnsucht / Dunkle Ahnung / Düsteres Versprechen. 2005. (Vampire Kisses Ser.: No. 1). 272p. (YA). (gr. 7-18). reprint ed. pap. 5.99 *(978-0-06-009336-5(6)*, Harper Trophy) HarperCollins Pubs.

—Vampire Kisses: Finstere Sehnsucht / Dunkle Ahnung / Düsteres Versprechen. l.t. ed. 2008. (Vampire Kisses Ser.: No. 1). 294p. (YA). 22.95 *(978-1-4104-0727-6(6))* Thorndike Pr.

—Vampire Kisses 2: Kissing Coffins. 2005. (Vampire Kisses Ser.: 2). (ENG.). 176p. (YA). (gr. 8-18). 17.99 *(978-0-06-077622-0(6)*, Tegen, Katherine Bks) HarperCollins Pubs.

—Vampire Kisses 3: Vampireville. 2006. (Vampire Kisses Ser.: 3). (ENG.). 192p. (YA). (gr. 8-12). 17.99 *(978-0-06-077625-1(0)*, Tegen, Katherine Bks) HarperCollins Pubs.

—Vampire Kisses 4: Dance with a Vampire, 4. 2009. (Vampire Kisses Ser.: 4). (ENG.). 208p. (YA). (gr. 8-12). pap. 9.99 *(978-0-06-177898-8(2)*, Tegen, Katherine Bks) HarperCollins Pubs.

—Vampire Kisses 5: the Coffin Club. 2009. (Vampire Kisses Ser.: 5). (ENG.). 208p. (YA). (gr. 8). pap. 11.99 *(978-0-06-128886-9(1)*, Tegen, Katherine Bks) HarperCollins Pubs.

—Vampire Kisses 7: Love Bites. 2011. (Vampire Kisses Ser.: 7). (ENG.). 208p. (YA). (gr. 8). pap. 9.99 *(978-0-06-168944-4(0)*, Tegen, Katherine Bks) HarperCollins Pubs.

—Vampire Kisses 8: Cryptic Cravings. 2012. (Vampire Kisses Ser.: 8). (ENG.). 240p. (YA). (gr. 8). pap. 11.99 *(978-0-06-168947-5(5)*, Tegen, Katherine Bks) HarperCollins Pubs.

—Vampire Kisses 9: Immortal Hearts, 9. 2013. (Vampire Kisses Ser.: 9). (ENG.). 272p. (YA). (gr. 8-12). pap. 10.99 *(978-0-06-207009-8(6)*, Tegen, Katherine Bks) HarperCollins Pubs.

—Vampire Kisses: Blood Relatives, Volume II, Vol. II. rem, illus. 2008. (ENG.). 192p. (J). (gr. 8-18). pap. 9.99 *(978-0-06-134082-6(0)*, Tegen, Katherine Bks) HarperCollins Pubs.

—Vampire Kisses: Blood Relatives, Volume III, Vol. 3. Kwon, Elisa & rem, illus. 2009. (ENG.). 192p. (J). (gr. 8-18). pap. 9.99 *(978-0-06-134083-3(9)*, Tegen, Katherine Bks) HarperCollins Pubs.

—Vampire Kisses Boxed Set: Vampire Kisses; Kissing Coffins; Vampireville. 2008. (Vampire Kisses Ser.: Nos. 1-3). (J). pap. 15.99 *(978-0-06-169160-7(7)*, HarperTeen) HarperCollins Pubs.

—Vampire Kisses: Graveyard Games, No. 1. Xian Nu Studio, Xian Nu, illus. 2011. (ENG.). 192p. (YA). (gr. 8). pap. 10.99 *(978-0-06-202672-9(0)*, Tegen, Katherine Bks) HarperCollins Pubs.

—Vampire Kisses: the Beginning. 2009. (ENG.). 576p. (YA). (gr. 8). pap. 10.99 *(978-0-06-177894-0(X)*, Tegen, Katherine Bks) HarperCollins Pubs.

—Vampireville. 2007. (Vampire Kisses Ser.: No. 3). (ENG.). 208p. (YA). (gr. 7-12). pap., pap. 5.99 *(978-0-06-077627-5(7)*, HarperTeen) HarperCollins Pubs.

Serra, Louis. The Reluctant Vampire. 2006. (YA). per. 12.00 *(978-0-9769132-5-2(9))* Capri Publishing.

Shakespeare, William & Gabel, Claudia. Romeo & Juliet & Vampires. 2010. (ENG.). 256p. (YA). (gr. 9-18). pap. 9.99 *(978-0-06-197624-7(5)*, HarperTeen) HarperCollins Pubs.

Shan, Darren, pseud. Birth of a Killer. 2011. (Saga of Larten Crepsley Ser.: 1). (ENG.). 288p. (YA). (gr. 10-17). pap. 15.99 *(978-0-316-07862-7(X))* Little, Brown Bks. for Young Readers.

—Brothers to the Death. 2013. (Saga of Larten Crepsley Ser.: 4). (ENG.). 272p. (YA). (gr. 10-17). pap. 10.99 *(978-0-316-07871-9(9))* Little, Brown Bks. for Young Readers.

—Cirque du Freak: Allies of the Night. 2005. (Cirque du Freak Ser.: 8). (ENG., Illus.). 256p. (J). (gr. 7-17). pap. 13.99 *(978-0-316-11437-0(5))* Little, Brown Bks. for Young Readers.

—Cirque du Freak: Hunters of the Dusk. 2005. (Cirque du Freak Ser.: 7). (ENG., Illus.). 224p. (J). (gr. 7-17). pap. 11.99 *(978-0-316-60211-2(6))* Little, Brown Bks. for Young Readers.

—Cirque du Freak: Killers of the Dawn. 2006. (Cirque du Freak Ser.: 9). (ENG., Illus.). 224p. (J). (gr. 7-17). pap. 14.99 *(978-0-316-10654-2(2))* Little, Brown Bks. for Young Readers.

—Cirque du Freak: Lord of the Shadows. 2007. (Cirque du Freak Ser.: 11). (ENG., Illus.). 256p. (J). (gr. 7-17). pap. 14.99 *(978-0-316-01661-2(6))* Little, Brown Bks. for Young Readers.

—Cirque du Freak: Sons of Destiny. 2007. (Cirque du Freak Ser.: 12). (ENG., Illus.). 272p. (J). (gr. 7-17). pap. 15.99 *(978-0-316-01663-6(2))* Little, Brown Bks. for Young Readers.

—The Cirque du Freak: the Lake of Souls. 2006. (Cirque du Freak Ser.: 10). (ENG., Illus.). 272p. (J). (gr. 7-17). per. 15.99 *(978-0-316-01665-0(9))* Little, Brown Bks. for Young Readers.

—The Cirque du Freak: the Vampire Prince. 2004. (Cirque du Freak Ser.: 6). (ENG., Illus.). 208p. (J). (gr. 7-17). pap. 11.99 *(978-0-316-60274-7(4))* Little, Brown Bks. for Young Readers.

—Cirque du Freak: Trials of Death. 2004. (Cirque du Freak Ser.: 5). (Illus.). 224p. (J). (gr. 7-17). pap. 13.99 *(978-0-316-60395-9(3))* Little, Brown Bks. for Young Readers.

—Cirque du Freak: Tunnels of Blood. 2003. (Cirque du Freak Ser.: 3). (ENG., Illus.). 240p. (J). (gr. 7-17). pap. 11.99 *(978-0-316-60608-0(1))* Little, Brown Bks. for Young Readers.

—Cirque du Freak: Vampire Mountain. 2003. (Cirque du Freak Ser.: 4). (ENG., Illus.). 208p. (J). (gr. 7-17). pap. 11.99 *(978-0-316-60542-7(5))* Little, Brown Bks. for Young Readers.
—Hunters of the Dusk. 2005. (Cirque du Freak Ser.: 7). (J). lib. bdg. 22.10 *(978-1-4177-3731-4(X))* Turtleback.
—Killers of the Dawn, Book 9. 2004. (ENG.). 192p. *(978-0-00-713781-7(8))* HarperCollins Pubs. Australia.
—The Lake of Souls, Book 10. 2004. (Darren Shan Saga: Bk. 10). (ENG.). 192p. *(978-0-00-715919-2(6))* HarperCollins Pubs. Australia.
—Lord of the Shadows, Book 11. 2005. (Darren Shan Saga: Bk. 11). (ENG.). 192p. *(978-0-00-715920-8(X))* HarperCollins Pubs. Australia.
—Lord of the Shadows, 11. 2006. (Cirque du Freak Ser.: Bk. 11). (ENG., Illus.). 220p. (J). (gr. 6-8). 28.69 *(978-0-316-15628-8(0))* Little Brown & Co.
—Lord of the Shadows. 2007. (Cirque du Freak Ser.: 11). (J). lib. bdg. 22.10 *(978-1-4177-7441-8(X))* Turtleback.
—Ocean of Blood. 2012. (Saga of Larten Crepsley Ser.: 2). (ENG.). 272p. (YA). (gr. 10-17). pap. 15.99 *(978-0-316-07867-2(0))* Little, Brown Bks. for Young Readers.
—Palace of the Damned. 2012. (Saga of Larten Crepsley Ser.: 3). (ENG.). 272p. (YA). (gr. 10-17). pap. 15.99 *(978-0-316-07869-6(7))* Little, Brown Bks. for Young Readers.
—Sons of Destiny, Book 12. 2005. (Darren Shan Saga: Bk. 12). (ENG.). 208p. *(978-0-00-715921-5(8))* HarperCollins Pubs. Australia.
—Sons of Destiny, 12. 2006. (Cirque du Freak Ser.: bK. 12). (ENG., Illus.). 240p. (J). (gr. 6-8). 28.69 *(978-0-316-15629-5(9))* Little Brown & Co.
—Tunnels of Blood. 2003. (Cirque du Freak Ser.: 3). (J). (gr. 3-6). lib. bdg. 20.85 *(978-0-613-71782-3(1))* Turtleback.
—Vampire Destiny Trilogy: Books 10 - 12. 2005. (ENG.). 496p. pap., pap., pap. *(978-0-00-717959-6(6))* HarperCollins Pubs. Australia.
—Vampire Mountain. (Cirque du Freak Ser.: 4). 2003. (J). (gr. 5-8). lib. bdg. 22.10 *(978-0-613-71781-6(3))* Vol. 4. 2010. lib. bdg. 24.55 *(978-0-606-14433-9(1))* Turtleback.
—The Vampire Prince. 2004. (Cirque du Freak Ser.: 6). (J). lib. bdg. 19.65 *(978-1-4177-3732-1(8))* Turtleback.
—Vampire War Trilogy: Books 7 - 9. 2005. (ENG.). 496p. pap., pap., pap. *(978-0-00-717958-9(8))* HarperCollins Pubs. Australia.
—Wolf Island. 2010. (Demonata Ser.: 8). (ENG.). 216p. (J). (gr. 10-17). pap. 13.99 *(978-0-316-04881-1(X))* Little, Brown Bks. for Young Readers.

Shaw, Stephanie. Schnitzel: A Cautionary Tale for Lazy Louts. Barry, Kevin M., illus. 2016. (ENG.). 32p. (J). (gr. k-3). 17.99 *(978-1-58536-957-7(8), 204104)* Sleeping Bear Pr.
Shouoto, Aya. He's My Only Vampire, Vol. 10. 2017. (He's My Only Vampire Ser.: 10). (ENG., Illus.). 176p. (gr. 11-17). pap. 13.00 *(978-0-316-39912-8(4),* Yen Pr.) Yen Pr. LLC.
—He's My Only Vampire, Vol. 9. 2016. (He's My Only Vampire Ser.: 9). (ENG., Illus.). 160p. (gr. 11-17). pap. 13.00 *(978-0-316-34584-2(9))* Yen Pr. LLC.
Simon, Francesca. Horrid Henry & the Zombie Vampire. Ross, Tony, illus. 2012. (Horrid Henry Ser.: 0). (ENG.). 112p. (J). (gr. 2-5). pap. 7.99 *(978-1-4022-6785-7(1),* Sourcebooks Jabberwocky) Sourcebooks, Inc.
Smith, Cynthia Leitich. Blessed. 2011. (Tantalize Ser.: 3). (ENG., Illus.). 480p. (YA). (gr. 9-18). 17.99 *(978-0-7636-4326-3(2))* Candlewick Pr.
—Eternal, 2. 2009. (Tantalize Ser.: 2). (ENG., Illus.). 320p. (YA). (gr. 9-12). 17.99 *(978-0-7636-3573-2(1))* Candlewick Pr.
—Tantalize. 2008. (Tantalize Ser.: 1). (ENG., Illus.). 336p. (YA). (gr. 9). pap. 9.99 *(978-0-7636-4059-0(X))* Candlewick Pr.
Smith, L. J. The Awakening & the Struggle, 2 vols. 2007. (Vampire Diaries: 1). 492p. (YA). (gr. 7). lib. bdg. 20.85 *(978-1-4178-2599-8(5))* Turtleback.
—Daughters of Darkness. 2016. (Night World Ser.: 2). (ENG., Illus.). 256p. (YA). (gr. 9). 13.99 *(978-1-4814-7964-6(4),* Simon Pulse) Simon Pulse.
—The Fury & Dark Reunion. 2007. (Vampire Diaries: 3). (YA). lib. bdg. 20.85 *(978-0-606-07135-2(0))* Turtleback.
—Night World. 2016. (Night World Ser.: 1). (ENG., Illus.). 256p. (YA). (gr. 9). 13.99 *(978-1-4814-7962-2(8),* Simon Pulse) Simon Pulse.
—Spellbinder. 2016. (Night World Ser.: 3). (ENG., Illus.). 256p. (YA). (gr. 9). 13.99 *(978-1-4814-8681-1(0),* Simon Pulse) Simon Pulse.
—The Vampire Diaries: the Awakening & the Struggle, 2 vols. 2022. (Vampire Diaries: Nos. 1-2). (ENG.). 512p. (YA). (gr. 9). pap. 11.99 *(978-0-06-114097-6(X),* HarperTeen) HarperCollins Pubs.
—The Vampire Diaries: the Fury & Dark Reunion, 2 vols. 2007. (Vampire Diaries: Nos. 3-4). (ENG.). 528p. (YA). (gr. 8-12). pap. 12.99 *(978-0-06-114098-3(8),* HarperTeen) HarperCollins Pubs.
—The Vampire Diaries: the Hunters: Destiny Rising. 2013. (Vampire Diaries: the Hunters Ser.: 3). (ENG.). 416p. (YA). (gr. 9). pap. 10.99 *(978-0-06-201774-1(8),* HarperTeen) HarperCollins Pubs.
—The Vampire Diaries: the Hunters: Moonsong Vol. 9. 2013. (Vampire Diaries: the Hunters Ser.: 2). (ENG.). 416p. (YA). (gr. 9). pap. 10.99 *(978-0-06-201771-0(3),* HarperTeen) HarperCollins Pubs.
—The Vampire Diaries: the Hunters: Phantom. (Vampire Diaries: the Hunters Ser.: 1). (ENG.). (YA). (gr. 9). 2012. 432p. pap. 10.99 *(978-0-06-201769-7(1))* 2011. 416p. 17.99 *(978-0-06-201768-0(3))* HarperCollins Pubs. (HarperTeen).
—The Vampire Diaries: the Return: Midnight. 2012. (Vampire Diaries: the Return Ser.: 3). (ENG.). 592p. (YA). (gr. 8). pap. 10.99 *(978-0-06-172086-4(0),* HarperTeen) HarperCollins Pubs.
—The Vampire Diaries: the Return: Nightfall. 2010. (Vampire Diaries: the Return Ser.: 1). (ENG.). 608p. (YA). (gr. 8). pap. 11.99 *(978-0-06-172080-2(1),* HarperTeen) HarperCollins Pubs.
—The Vampire Diaries: the Return: Shadow Souls. 2011. (Vampire Diaries: the Return Ser.: 2). (ENG.). 624p. (YA). (gr. 8). pap. 11.99 *(978-0-06-172083-3(6),* HarperTeen) HarperCollins Pubs.
—The Vampire Diaries: the Struggle. 2010. (Vampire Diaries: 2). (ENG.). 304p. (YA). (gr. 8). mass mkt. 8.99 *(978-0-06-199076-2(0),* HarperCollins) HarperCollins Pubs.
Smith, L. J. & Clark, Aubrey. The Salvation: Unmasked. 3. 2014. (Vampire Diaries: 3). (ENG.). 310p. (YA). (gr. 7-12). pap. 9.99 *(978-1-4778-2335-4(2),* 9781477823354, 47North) Amazon Publishing.
—The Salvation: Unseen, 1. 2013. (Vampire Diaries: 1). (ENG.). 306p. (YA). (gr. 7-12). pap. 9.99 *(978-1-4778-0967-9(8),* 9781477809679, 47North) Amazon Publishing.
—The Salvation: Unspoken, 0 vols., 2. 2013. (Vampire Diaries: 2). (ENG.). 308p. (YA). (gr. 7-12). pap. 9.99 *(978-1-61218-462-3(6),* 9781612184623, 47North) Amazon Publishing.
Smith, L. J. & Kevin Williamson & Julie Plec, Kevin Williamson. The Vampire Diaries: Stefan's Diaries #1: Origins No. 5. 2010. (Vampire Diaries: Stefan's Diaries: 1). (ENG.). 256p. (YA). (gr. 9-18). pap. 11.99 *(978-0-06-200393-5(3),* HarperTeen) HarperCollins Pubs.
—The Vampire Diaries: Stefan's Diaries #4: the Ripper, 4. 2011. (Vampire Diaries: Stefan's Diaries: 4). (ENG.). 256p. (YA). (gr. 9-12). pap. 11.99 *(978-0-06-211393-1(3),* HarperTeen) HarperCollins Pubs.
—The Vampire Diaries: Stefan's Diaries #5: the Asylum. 2012. (Vampire Diaries: Stefan's Diaries: 5). (ENG.). 256p. (YA). (gr. 9). pap. 11.99 *(978-0-06-211395-5(X),* HarperTeen) HarperCollins Pubs.
—The Vampire Diaries: Stefan's Diaries #6: the Compelled. 2012. (Vampire Diaries: Stefan's Diaries: 6). (ENG.). 256p. (YA). (gr. 9). pap. 11.99 *(978-0-06-211398-6(4),* HarperTeen) HarperCollins Pubs.
Smith, L. J., et al. The Vampire Diaries: Stefan's Diaries #2: Bloodlust. 2011. (Vampire Diaries: Stefan's Diaries: 2). (ENG.). 256p. (YA). (gr. 9-18). pap. 11.99 *(978-0-06-200394-2(1),* HarperTeen) HarperCollins Pubs.
Sommer-Bodenburg, Angela. El Pequeno Vampiro. Glienke, Amelie, illus. 2003. (SPA.). 192p. (J). (gr. 3-5). pap. 11.95 *(978-968-19-0673-3(X))* Santillana USA Publishing Co., Inc.
Somper, Justin. Dead Deep. 2009. pap. 1.00 *(978-1-4074-4559-5(6))* Recorded Bks., Inc.
—Demons of the Ocean. 2006. 1.00 *(978-1-4294-1974-1(1))* Recorded Bks., Inc.
—Demons of the Ocean. 2007. (Vampirates Ser.: 1). (Illus.). 330p. (J). 19.65 *(978-1-4177-8287-1(0))* Turtleback.
—Immortal War. 2013. (Vampirates Ser.: 6). (J). lib. bdg. 22.10 *(978-0-606-26696-3(8))* Turtleback.
—Vampirates: Demons of the Ocean. 2007. (Vampirates Ser.: 1). (ENG.). 352p. (J). (gr. 3-7). per. 18.99 *(978-0-316-01444-1(3))* Little, Brown Bks. for Young Readers.
—Vampirates: Black Heart. 2010. (Vampirates Ser.: 4). (ENG.). 512p. (J). (gr. 3-7). pap. 22.99 *(978-0-316-02088-6(5))* Little, Brown Bks. for Young Readers.
—Vampirates: Blood Captain. 2009. (Vampirates Ser.: 3). (ENG.). 592p. (J). (gr. 3-7). pap. 26.99 *(978-0-316-02086-2(9))* Little, Brown Bks. for Young Readers.
—Vampirates: Empire of Night. 2011. (Vampirates Ser.: 5). (ENG.). 512p. (J). (gr. 3-7). pap. 22.99 *(978-0-316-03323-7(5))* Little, Brown Bks. for Young Readers.
—Vampirates: Immortal War. 2013. (Vampirates Ser.: 6). (ENG.). 512p. (J). (gr. 3-7). pap. 23.99 *(978-0-316-03325-1(1))* Little, Brown Bks. for Young Readers.
—Vampirates: Tide of Terror. 2008. (Vampirates Ser.: 2). (ENG.). 480p. (J). (gr. 3-7). pap. 21.99 *(978-0-316-01445-8(1))* Little, Brown Bks. for Young Readers.
Sowles, Joann I. Martin. Darkness (the Brookehaven Vampires Series #2) The Brookehaven Vampires. 2011. (YA). *(978-0-9844867-3-1(9))* Brookehaven Publishing.
Specter, Baron. Vampires Are Not Your Friends, 1 vol. Kneupper, Setch, illus. 2012. (Graveyard Diaries). (ENG.). 128p. (J). (gr. 2-5). 38.50 *(978-1-61641-902-8(4),* 9182, Calico Chapter Bks.) ABDO Publishing Co.
Speer, Cindy Lynn. Unbalanced. 2010. 241p. pap. *(978-1-934841-90-7(0))* Zumaya Pubns. LLC.
St. Crow, Lili. Betrayals, 10 vols. 2010. (Strange Angels Ser.: 2). (YA). 95.75 *(978-1-4407-7156-9(1))* Recorded Bks., Inc.
—Betrayals. 2009. (Strange Angels Ser.: 2). lib. bdg. 20.85 *(978-0-606-09020-9(7))* Turtleback.
—Betrayals: A Strange Angels Novel, 2. 2009. (Strange Angels Ser.: 2). (ENG., Illus.). 304p. (YA). (gr. 7-18). pap. 26.19 *(978-1-59514-252-8(5),* Razorbill) Penguin Young Readers Group.
—Defiance, 4. 2011. (Strange Angels Ser.: 4). (ENG.). 304p. (YA). (gr. 7-18). 26.19 *(978-1-59514-392-1(0),* Razorbill) Penguin Young Readers Group.
—Jealousy, 10 vols. 2010. (Strange Angels Ser.: 3). (J). 86.75 *(978-1-4498-2774-8(8));* 68.75 *(978-1-4498-2773-1(X));* 83.75 *(978-1-4498-2776-2(4));* 1.25 *(978-1-4498-2777-9(2));* 209.75 *(978-1-4498-2772-4(1))* Recorded Bks., Inc.
—Jealousy. 2010. (Strange Angels Ser.: 3). lib. bdg. 20.85 *(978-0-606-14566-4(4))* Turtleback.
—Jealousy: A Strange Angels Novel. 2010. (Strange Angels Ser.: 3). (ENG.). 320p. (YA). (gr. 7-18). 9.99 *(978-1-59514-290-0(8),* Razorbill) Penguin Young Readers Group.
—Strange Angels, 9 vols. 2009. (Strange Angels Ser.: 1). (J). 117.75 *(978-1-4407-6197-3(3));* 84.75 *(978-1-4407-6195-9(7));* 87.75 *(978-1-4407-6193-5(0));* 114.75 *(978-1-4407-6199-7(X));* 181.75 *(978-1-4407-6194-2(9))* Recorded Bks., Inc.
—Strange Angels. 2009. (Strange Angels Ser.: 1). lib. bdg. 20.85 *(978-0-606-08957-9(8))* Turtleback.
Steele, Michael Anthony. Vampire Zoo Hullabaloo. Jeralds, Scott, illus. 2017. (Scooby-Doo! Beginner Mysteries Ser.). (ENG.). 112p. (J). (gr. 1-3). lib. bdg. 22.65 *(978-1-4965-4770-5(5),* 135307, Stone Arch Bks.) Capstone.
Stilton, Gerónimo. Un granizado de moscas para el Conde. Wolf, Matt, illus. (SPA.). 128p. (J). (gr. 3-5). pap. 7.95 *(978-1-59437-452-4(X))* Santillana USA Publishing Co., Inc.
Stilton, Geronimo. My Name Is Stilton, Geronimo Stilton (Geronimo Stilton #19), Volume 19. 2005. (Geronimo Stilton Ser.: 19). (ENG., Illus.). 128p. (J). (gr. 2-5). pap. 7.99 *(978-0-439-69142-0(7),* Scholastic Paperbacks) Scholastic, Inc.
Stilton, Gerónimo. Return of the Vampire. 2012. (Geronimo Stilton — Creepella Von Cacklefur Ser.: 4). lib. bdg. 18.40 *(978-0-606-26180-7(X))* Turtleback.
Stine, R. L. Dangerous Girls. 2003. 256p. (J). 111.92 *(978-0-06-056909-9(3));* 111.92 *(978-0-06-056910-5(7));* (ENG., Illus.). (gr. 7-18). 13.99 *(978-0-06-053080-8(4))* HarperCollins Pubs.
—Drop Dead Gorgeous. 2019. (Return to Fear Street Ser.: 3). (ENG.). 336p. (YA). (gr. 8). pap. 10.99 *(978-0-06-269429-4(4),* HarperTeen) HarperCollins Pubs.
—How to Be a Vampire. 2011. (R. L. Stine's Ghosts of Fear Street Ser.). (ENG.). 128p. (J). (gr. 3-7). pap. 7.99 *(978-1-4424-2760-0(4),* Aladdin) Simon & Schuster Children's Publishing.
—Please Don't Feed the Vampire a Give Yourself Goosebumps Book. 2015. (Goosebumps Ser.: 32). lib. bdg. 17.20 *(978-0-606-37070-7(6))* Turtleback.
—Temptation: Goodnight Kiss; Goodnight Kiss 2; "the Vampire Club" 2012. (ENG.). 416p. (YA). (gr. 7). pap. 11.99 *(978-1-4424-5068-4(1),* Simon Pulse) Simon Pulse.
—Vampire Breath (Classic Goosebumps #21) 2011. (Classic Goosebumps Ser.: 21). (ENG.). 160p. (J). (gr. 3-7). pap. 7.99 *(978-0-545-29837-7(7),* Scholastic Paperbacks) Scholastic, Inc.
Stoker, Bram. Count Dracula. 2004. (Fast Track Classics Ser.). (Illus.). 48p. (J). pap. *(978-0-237-52401-2(5))* Evans Brothers, Ltd.
—Dracula, 1 vol. 2009. (Foundation Classics Ser.). (ENG., Illus.). 56p. (J). (gr. 5-5). lib. bdg. 32.60 *(978-1-60754-847-8(X),* 7390a06a-9533-43c0-9531-39027aa96515, Windmill Bks.) Rosen Publishing Group, Inc., The.
—Dracula, 1 vol. Simon, Ute, illus. 2011. (Calico Illustrated Classics Ser.: No. 3). (ENG.). 112p. (J). (gr. 2-5). 38.50 *(978-1-61641-101-5(5),* 4009, Calico Chapter Bks.) ABDO Publishing Co.
—Dracula. Gilbert, Anne Yvonne, illus. 2010. (ENG.). 96p. (YA). (gr. 7-18). 19.99 *(978-0-7636-4793-3(4),* Templar) Candlewick Pr.
—Dracula. Johnson, Staz, illus. 2012. 152p. (gr. 6). (ENG.). pap. 16.95 *(978-1-906332-68-6(1));* pap. 18.95 *(978-1-906332-67-9(3),* Classical Comics, Ltd.) Classical Comics GBR. Dist: Publishers Group West (PGW).
—Dracula. Kliros, Thea, illus. abr. ed. 2011. (Dover Children's Thrift Classics Ser.). (ENG.). 96p. (J). (gr. 3-8). reprint ed. pap. 4.00 *(978-0-486-29567-1(2),* 295672) Dover Pubns., Inc.
—Dracula. 2006. (Clasicos Para La Juventud). (SPA.). 126p. (YA). *(978-987-1129-52-2(1))* Grupo Visor E.A.S.A.
—Dracula. 2009. (Puffin Classics Ser.). (Illus.). 656p. (J). (gr. 5-7). 8.99 *(978-0-14-132566-8(6),* Puffin Books) Penguin Young Readers Group.
Surrisi, C. M. Vampires on the Run: A Quinnie Boyd Mystery. (Quinnie Boyd Mysteries Ser.). (ENG.). 296p. (J). (gr. 4-8). 2018. pap. 9.99 *(978-1-5415-3847-4(1),* bcffe0e1-f11d-4184-8f3a-e68d24760d2f) 2017. 16.99 *(978-1-5124-1150-8(7),* 7aed6910-020c-4ae6-a0b2-d7143911d482) 2017. E-Book 26.65 *(978-1-5124-2692-2(X))* Lerner Publishing Group. (Carolrhoda Bks.).
Sutton, Laurie S. Goldilocks & the Three Vampires: A Graphic Novel. Jennings, Christopher S., illus. 2016. (Far Out Fairy Tales Ser.). (ENG.). 40p. (J). (gr. 3-6). lib. bdg. 25.32 *(978-1-4965-3783-6(1),* 133106, Stone Arch Bks.) Capstone.
Swift, John. Tea with a Vampire. 2007. pap. 9.00 *(978-0-8059-8963-2(3))* Dorrance Publishing Co., Inc.
Taddonio, Lea. Pain in the Neck. 2019. (Shiverwood Academy Ser.). (ENG., Illus.). 48p. (J). (gr. 3-7). lib. bdg. 34.21 *(978-1-5321-3504-0(1),* 31927, Spellbound) Magic Wagon.
Taylor, Dereen. The Mystery of the Vampire Boy: Dare You Peek Through the Pop-Up Windows? Spoor, Mike, illus. 2014. 12p. (J). (gr. k-5). 16.99 *(978-1-86147-410-0(5),* Armadillo) Anness Publishing GBR. Dist: National Bk. Network.
Taylor, Drew Hayden. The Night Wanderer: A Native Gothic Novel. 5th ed. 2007. (ENG., Illus.). 228p. (YA). (gr. 7-12). pap. 12.95 *(978-1-55451-099-3(6),* 9781554510993) Annick Pr., Ltd. CAN. Dist: Publishers Group West (PGW).
Thaler, Mike. Hubie Cool: Vampire Hunter. Lee, Jared D., illus. 2015. 64p. (J). pap. *(978-0-545-85075-9(4))* Scholastic, Inc.
Thompson, Kate. Midnight's Choice. unabr. ed. 2004. (Switchers Ser.: Vol. 2). 240p. (J). (gr. 5-9). pap. 38.00 incl. audio *(978-0-8072-8769-9(5),* Listening Library) Random Hse. Audio Publishing Group.
Thomson, Sarah L. Mercy: The Last New England Vampire, 1 vol. 2011. (ENG.). 178p. (J). pap. 16.95 *(978-1-934031-36-0(4),* 53a309a3-c17e-4f20-bdd3-f4fe46e103af) Islandport Pr., Inc.
Troupe, Thomas Kingsley. The Voiceless Vampire. Gilpin, Stephen, illus. 2015. (Furry & Flo Ser.). (ENG.). 128p. (J). (gr. 2-3). lib. bdg. 25.32 *(978-1-4342-9645-0(8),* 126932, Stone Arch Bks.) Capstone.
Turner, Max. End of Days. 2010. (Night Runner Novels Ser.: 2). (ENG.). 304p. (YA). (gr. 8-12). pap. 20.99 *(978-0-312-59252-3(3),* 900062452, St. Martin's Griffin) St. Martin's Pr.
Vanholme, Virginie. The Vampire from the Marshes. Mauricet, illus. 2008. (Scared to Death Ser.: 1). 46p. pap. 11.95 *(978-1-905460-47-2(3))* CineBook GBR. Dist: National Bk. Network.
Varlow, Scarlet. Blood & Cookies. Cotroneo, Marilisa, illus. 2019. (Creature Feature Ser.). (ENG.). 112p. (J). (gr. 2-5). lib. bdg. 38.50 *(978-1-5321-3496-8(7),* 31911, Calico Chapter Bks.) ABDO Publishing Co.
Verday, Jessica. The Beautiful & the Damned. 2013. (ENG., Illus.). 272p. (YA). (gr. 7). 17.99 *(978-1-4424-8835-9(2),* Simon Pulse) Simon Pulse.
Verstraete, Majanka. Valentina & the Haunted Mansion (Valentina's Spooky Adventures - 1) Giffin, Noelle, illus. l.t. ed. 2013. (ENG.). 48p. 21.95 *(978-1-62253-057-1(8));* pap. 10.95 *(978-1-62253-056-4(X))* Evolved Publishing.
—Valentina & the Whackadoodle Witch: Valentina's Spooky Adventures. Giffin, Noelle, illus. l.t. ed. 2013. (ENG.). 46p. (gr. k-4). pap. 10.95 *(978-1-62253-059-5(4))* Evolved Publishing.
Westerfeld, Scott. Peeps. 2006. (ENG.). 288p. (YA). (gr. 9-12). 8.99 *(978-1-59514-083-8(2),* Razorbill) Penguin Young Readers Group.
Wilde, Terry Lee. The Vampire... in My Dreams. 2008. (ENG.). 244p. (YA). (gr. 7-12). pap. 13.00 *(978-1-59998-837-5(2))* Samhain Publishing, LTD.
Yancey, Rick. The Curse of the Wendigo. 2010. (Monstrumologist Ser.: 2). (ENG., Illus.). 448p. (YA). (gr. 9-18). 17.99 *(978-1-4169-8450-4(X),* Simon & Schuster Bks. For Young Readers) Simon & Schuster Bks. For Young Readers.
Zornow, Jeff. Werewolf, 1 vol. Zornow, Jeff, illus. 2007. (Graphic Horror Ser.). (ENG., Illus.). 32p. (J). (gr. 3-6). 32.79 *(978-1-60270-062-8(1),* 9078, Graphic Planet - Fiction) Magic Wagon.

VAN BUREN, MARTIN, 1782-1862

Lazo, Caroline Evensen. Martin Van Buren. 2005. (Presidential Leaders Ser.). (Illus.). 112p. (J). (gr. 3-7). lib. bdg. 29.27 *(978-0-8225-1394-0(3))* Lerner Publishing Group.
Rumsch, BreAnn. Martin Van Buren, 1 vol. 2016. (United States Presidents *2017 Ser.). (ENG., Illus.). 40p. (J). (gr. 2-5). lib. bdg. 35.64 *(978-1-68078-121-2(9),* 21859, Big Buddy Bks.) ABDO Publishing Co.
Schmidt, Roderic. How to Draw the Life & Times of Martin Van Buren. (Kid's Guide to Drawing the Presidents of the United States of America Ser.). 32p. (gr. 4-4). 2009. 50.50 *(978-1-61511-155-8(7),* PowerKids Pr.) 2005. (ENG.). (YA). 30.27 *(978-1-4042-2985-3(X),* e46db694-b581-44ce-a01a-f83a179c8a2c) Rosen Publishing Group, Inc., The.
Venezia, Mike. Martin Van Buren. Venezia, Mike, illus. 2005. (Getting to Know the U. S. Presidents Ser.). (ENG., Illus.). 32p. (J). (gr. 3-4). 28.00 *(978-0-516-22613-2(4),* Children's Pr.) Scholastic Library Publishing.

VAN DIEMAN'S LAND

see Tasmania

VAN GOGH, VINCENT, 1853-1890

see Gogh, Vincent Van, 1853-1890

VANILLA

Kamer, Julie. The Biography of Vanilla, 1 vol. 2006. (How Did That Get Here? Ser.). (ENG., Illus.). 32p. (J). (gr. 4-7). pap. *(978-0-7787-2526-8(X));* lib. bdg. *(978-0-7787-2490-2(5))* Crabtree Publishing Co.

VAN WINKLE, RIP (FICTITIOUS CHARACTER)—FICTION

Irving, Washington. & Busch, Jeffrey. Rip Van Winkle. (Classics Illustrated Ser.). (Illus.). 52p. (YA). pap. 4.95 *(978-1-57209-009-5(X))* Classics International Entertainment, Inc.

VASQUEZ DE CORONADO, FRANCISCO, 1510-1549

see Coronado, Francisco Vasquez de, 1510-1554

VASSALS

see Feudalism

VATICAN CITY

Fox, Martha Capwell. Vatican City. 2005. (Modern Nations Ser.). (ENG., Illus.). 112p. (YA). (gr. 7-10). lib. bdg. 30.85 *(978-1-59018-733-3(4),* 1244593, Lucent Bks.) Cengage Gale.
Nanji, Shenaaz. Vatican City. 2014. (J). *(978-1-4896-1158-1(4))* Weigl Pubs., Inc.
Stine, Megan & Who HQ. Where Is the Vatican? Conley, Laurie A., illus. 2019. (Where Is? Ser.). 112p. (J). (gr. 3-7). 5.99 *(978-1-5247-9259-6(4));* 15.99 *(978-1-5247-9260-2(8))* Penguin Young Readers Group. (Penguin Workshop).

VEGETABLE ANATOMY

see Plant Anatomy

VEGETABLE GARDENING

see also Vegetables

Amstutz, Lisa J. Edible Gardening: Growing Your Own Vegetables, Fruits, & More. 2016. (Gardening Guides). (ENG., Illus.). 32p. (J). (gr. 3-9). lib. bdg. 28.65 *(978-1-4914-8235-3(4),* 130701, Capstone Pr.) Capstone.
Archer, Joe & Craig, Caroline. Plant, Cook, Eat! A Children's Cookbook. 2018. (ENG., Illus.). 112p. (J). (gr. 2-5). lib. bdg. 19.99 *(978-1-58089-817-1(3))* Charlesbridge Publishing, Inc.
Bath, Louella. Growing Vegetables, 1 vol. 2015. (Garden Squad! Ser.). (ENG.). 24p. (J). (gr. 3-4). 25.27 *(978-1-4994-1014-3(X),* 2c59179f-e15e-407d-8cf6-754329e4b2ed, PowerKids Pr.) Rosen Publishing Group, Inc., The.
Berkes, Marianne. What's in the Garden?, 1 vol. Arbo, Cris, illus. 2013. (ENG.). 32p. (J). (gr. -1-4). pap. 8.99 *(978-1-58469-190-7(5),* Dawn Pubns.) Sourcebooks, Inc.
Brown, Robert L. Daddy Grows Colors, 1 vol. 2009. 28p. pap. 24.95 *(978-1-60836-124-3(1))* America Star Bks.
Burns Chong, Susan. Community Gardens, 1 vol. 2013. (Urban Gardening & Farming for Teens Ser.). (ENG.). 64p. (YA). (gr. 6-6). 38.41 *(978-1-4777-1777-6(3),* 131f5f0a-fe54-4fa0-abdf-c109c022d0a9) Rosen Publishing Group, Inc., The.
Cornell, Kari. Dig In! 12 Easy Gardening Projects Using Kitchen Scraps. Larson, Jennifer S., photos by. 2018. (ENG., Illus.). 64p. (J). (gr. 4-8). 31.99 *(978-1-5124-3065-3(X),* 93daadb8-08b4-493e-9152-2857c3f05581, Millbrook Pr.) Lerner Publishing Group.
Grant, Amanda. Grow It, Cook It with Kids. 2010. (ENG., Illus.). 128p. (J). *(978-1-84597-969-0(9))* Ryland Peters & Small.
Hengel, Katherine. Garden to Table: A Kid's Guide to Planting, Growing, & Preparing Food. 2014. (ENG., Illus.). 144p. (J). (gr. 2-7). pap. 15.95 *(978-1-938063-42-8(2),* Mighty Media Junior Readers) Mighty Media Pr.
Heos, Bridget. So You Want to Grow a Salad? Fabbri, Daniele, illus. 2015. (Grow Your Food Ser.). (ENG.). 24p. (J). (gr. 1-4). lib. bdg. 19.95 *(978-1-60753-741-0(9),* 15271) Amicus.
Hirsch, Rebecca. Save the Planet: Growing Your Own Garden. 2010. (Explorer Library: Language Arts Explorer Ser.). (ENG.). 32p. (gr. 4-8). pap. 14.21 *(978-1-60279-666-9(1),* 200913) Cherry Lake Publishing.
Kuskowski, Alex. Kitchen Gardens: A Kid's Guide to Gardening. 2015. (Super Simple Gardening Ser.). (ENG.). 32p. (J). (gr. k-4). 34.21 *(978-1-62403-525-8(6),* 17333, Super SandCastle) ABDO Publishing Co.
—Salad Gardens: A Kid's Guide to Gardening. 2015. (Super Simple Gardening Ser.). (ENG.). 32p. (J). (gr. k-4). 34.21

The check digit for ISBN-10 appears in parentheses after the full ISBN-13

(978-1-62403-526-5(4), 17335, Super SandCastle) ABDO Publishing Co.

Lanz, Helen. Grow Your Own Lettuce. 2012. (Grow Your Own Ser.). (ENG., Illus.). 32p. (gr. 3-6). lib. bdg. 28.50 *(978-1-59771-311-5(2))* Sea-To-Sea Pubns.

—Grow Your Own Potatoes. 2012. (Grow Your Own Ser.). (ENG., Illus.). 32p. (gr. 3-6). lib. bdg. 28.50 *(978-1-59771-312-2(0))* Sea-To-Sea Pubns.

—Grow Your Own Tomatoes. 2012. (Grow Your Own Ser.). (ENG., Illus.). 32p. (gr. 3-6). lib. bdg. 28.50 *(978-1-59771-314-6(7))* Sea-To-Sea Pubns.

Leavitt, Amie. A Backyard Vegetable Garden for Kids. 2008. (Gardening for Kids Ser.). 48p. (YA). (gr. 1-4). lib. bdg. 29.95 *(978-1-58415-634-5(1))* Mitchell Lane Pubs.

Liversidge, Cassie. Pasta Sauce! Grow Your Own Ingredients. 2013. (ENG., Illus.). 40p. (J). (gr. k-3). 14.95 *(978-1-62087-533-9(0)*, 620533, Sky Pony Pr.) Skyhorse Publishing Co., Inc.

Martin, Jacqueline Briggs. Farmer Will Allen & the Growing Table. Larkin, Shabazz, illus. 2013. (Food Heroes Ser.: 1). (ENG.). 32p. (J). (gr. k). 19.95 *(978-0-9836615-3-5(7))* READERS to EATERS.

McDougall, Nancy & Hendy, Jenny. 300 Step-By-Step Cooking & Gardening Projects for Kids: The Ultimate Book for Budding Gardeners & Super Chefs, with Amazing Things to Grow & Cook Yourself, Shown in over 2300 Photographs. 2015. (Illus.). 512p. (J). (gr. -1 — 1). pap. 14.99 *(978-1-86147-707-1(4)*, Armadillo) Anness Publishing GBR. Dist: National Bk. Network.

Minden, Cecilia. Gardening by the Numbers. 2007. (21st Century Skills Library: Real World Math Ser.). (ENG., Illus.). 32p. (gr. 4-8). lib. bdg. 32.07 *(978-1-60279-008-7(6)*, 200064) Cherry Lake Publishing.

Pettiford, Rebecca. Vegetables. Fretland VanVoorst, Jenny, ed. 2015. (Illus.). (J). lib. bdg. *(978-1-62031-233-9(6))* Jump! Inc.

Rigby Education Staff. The Vegetable Garden. (Chiquilibros Ser.). (Illus.). (gr. -1-1). 12.00 *(978-0-7635-8538-9(6))* Rigby Education.

Schuh, Mari. How Fruits & Vegetables Grow, 5 vols., Set. Incl. Blueberries Grow on a Bush. (ENG.). 24p. (J). (gr. -1-2). 2010. lib. bdg. 24.65 *(978-1-4296-5282-7(9)*, 113701, Pebble); (How Fruits & Vegetables Grow Ser.). (ENG.). 24p. 2010. 67.95 o.p. *(978-1-4296-5283-4(7)*, 170507, Pebble) Capstone.

Sévigny, Eric, illus. In the Garden. 2005. (Playtime Ser.). (ENG.). 24p. (J). (gr. -1-1). pap. 4.99 *(978-2-89450-383-6(0))* Caillouet, Gerry.

Stagliano, Katie, et al. Katie's Cabbage. 2014. (Young Palmetto Bks.). (ENG., Illus.). 40p. 19.99 *(978-1-61117-504-2(6)*, P450848) Univ. of South Carolina Pr.

Sundance/Newbridge LLC Staff. The Vegetable Garden. 2007. (Early Science Ser.). (gr. k-3). 18.95 *(978-1-4007-6287-3(1))*; pap. 6.10 *(978-1-4007-6283-5(9))* Sundance/Newbridge Educational Publishing.

VEGETABLE GARDENING—FICTION

Brown, Robert L. Daddy Grows Colors, 1 vol. 2010. 26p. 24.95 *(978-1-4512-1746-9(3))* PublishAmerica, Inc.

Coy, John. Two Old Potatoes & Me. Fisher, Carolyn, illus. 2013. (ENG.). (J). (gr. k-3). pap. 7.99 *(978-1-935666-46-2(0))* Nodin Pr.

Curious George the Perfect Carrot (Reader Level 1) 2010. (Curious George TV Ser.). (ENG., Illus.). 24p. (J). (gr. -1-3). pap. 4.99 *(978-0-547-24299-6(9)*, 1099423, Clarion Bks.) HarperCollins Pubs.

dePaola, Tomie. Strega Nona's Harvest. dePaola, Tomie, illus. (Illus.). 32p. (J). (gr. -1-3). 2012. (ENG.). mass mkt. 8.99 *(978-0-14-242338-7(6)*, Puffin Books) 2009. 17.99 *(978-0-399-25291-4(6)*, G.P. Putnam's Sons Books for Young Readers) Penguin Young Readers Group.

Ehlert, Lois. Growing Vegetable Soup/Sembrar Sopa de Verduras Board Book: Bilingual English-Spanish. 2012.Tr. of Growing Vegetable Soup. (ENG., Illus.). 32p. (J). (gr. -1 — 1). bds. 5.99 *(978-0-547-73497-2(2)*, 1484981, Clarion Bks.) HarperCollins Pubs.

Gibson, James E. Rico, the Mysterious Worm, 1 vol. 2009. 17p. pap. 24.95 *(978-1-60749-148-4(6))* America Star Bks.

Hillert, Margaret. Dear Dragon Grows a Garden. David Schimmell, illus. rev. ed. 2014. (Beginning-To-Read Ser.). (ENG.). 32p. (J). (gr. k-2). pap. 13.26 *(978-1-60357-414-3(X))* Norwood Hse. Pr.

—Dear Dragon Grows a Garden. Schimmell, David, illus. rev. ed. 2014. (BeginningtoRead Ser.). (ENG.). 32p. (J). (gr. k-2). lib. bdg. 22.60 *(978-1-59953-578-4(5))* Norwood Hse. Pr.

January, Rick & January, Stella. Come Out to the Garden. 2012. (ENG., Illus.). 30p. (J). 24.95 *(978-1-937084-40-0(X)*, BQB Publishing) Boutique of Quality Books Publishing Co., Inc.

Koehn, Wendel. Wendel Plants Potatoes. 2012. 24p. pap. 14.93 *(978-1-4669-5956-9(8))* Trafford Publishing.

Ode, Eric. Too Many Tomatoes. Culotta, Kent, illus. 2016. (ENG.). 32p. (J). 11.99 *(978-1-61067-400-3(6))* Kane Miller.

Peterson, Mary. Snail Has Lunch. Peterson, Mary, illus. 2016. (Pix Ser.). (ENG., Illus.). 64p. (J). (gr. 1-4). 12.99 *(978-1-4814-5302-8(5)*, Aladdin) Simon & Schuster Children's Publishing.

Picou, Lin & Moreta, Gladys. Too Much Tv! Reese, Bob, illus. 2011. (Little Birdie Readers Ser.). (ENG.). 24p. (gr. 1-2). pap. 9.95 *(978-1-61236-019-5(X)*, 9781612360195) Rourke Educational Media.

Roberts, Margiad & Owen, Carys Eurwen. Tecwyn Yn Plannu Tatws. 2005. (WEL., Illus.). 36p. pap. *(978-0-86381-408-2(5))* Gwasg Carreg Gwalch.

Square Cat ABC. 2014. (ENG., Illus.). 32p. (J). (gr. -1-3). 15.99 *(978-1-4424-9895-2(1)*, Aladdin) Simon & Schuster Children's Publishing.

Tolstoy, Alexei. Enormous Turnip. 2003. (Green Light Readers Level 2 Ser.). (gr. k-3). lib. bdg. 13.50 *(978-0-613-64495-2(6))* Turtleback.

Waddell, Barbara. Hooray, Hooray, Today's the Day. 2010. 36p. 15.49 *(978-1-4269-4477-2(2))* Trafford Publishing.

White, Gene. Billy's Big Tomato. Davis, Shelley & Davis, Betsy, illus. 2013. 24p. pap. 11.00 *(978-0-9886360-9-5(3))* Kids At Heart Publishing, LLC.

Worcester, Sue. Ernesto Nia Lakeru. 2011. 28p. pap. 28.03 *(978-1-4568-8257-0(0))* Xlibris Corp.

Young, Jessica. Room to Bloom. Sécheret, Jessica, illus. 2017. (Finley Flowers Ser.). (ENG.). 128p. (J). (gr. 1-3). lib. bdg. 25.32 *(978-1-4795-9806-9(2)*, 133581, Picture Window Bks.) Capstone.

VEGETABLE KINGDOM

see Botany; Plants

VEGETABLES

see also Vegetable Gardening; Vegetarianism

Aboff, Marcie. The Incredible Vegetable Group, 1 vol. Poling, Kyle, illus. 2011. (First Graphics: Myplate & Healthy Eating Ser.). (ENG.). 24p. (J). (gr. k-3). lib. bdg. 24.65 *(978-1-4296-6089-1(9)*, 115038) Capstone.

—The Incredible Vegetable Group. Poling, Kyle, illus. 2011. (First Graphics: Myplate & Healthy Eating Ser.). (ENG.). 24p. (J). (gr. 1-2). pap. 37.74 *(978-1-4296-7169-9(6)*, 16727) Capstone.

Adams, Julia. Vegetables, 1 vol. 2011. (Good Food Ser.). (ENG.). 24p. (J). (gr. 1-1). lib. bdg. 26.27 *(978-1-4488-3274-3(8)*, a66de0c2-ffb6-4875-8735-89da3818730e, PowerKids Pr.) Rosen Publishing Group, Inc., The.

AZ Books Staff. Fruits & Vegetables. Slusar, Julia, ed. 2012. (Pull It Out Ser.). (ENG.). 10p. (J). (— 1). 7.95 *(978-1-61889-192-1(8))* AZ Bks. LLC.

Bass, Jennifer Vogel. Edible Colours. 2016. (ENG., Illus.). 30p. (J). bds. 8.99 *(978-1-62672-284-2(6)*, 900148613) Roaring Brook Pr.

—Edible Numbers. 2016. (ENG., Illus.). 30p. (J). bds. 8.99 *(978-1-62672-285-9(4)*, 900148616) Roaring Brook Pr.

Bath, Louella. Growing Vegetables, 1 vol. 2015. (Garden Squad! Ser.). (ENG.). 24p. (J). (gr. 3-4). 25.27 *(978-1-4994-1014-3(X)*, 2c59179f-e15e-407d-8cf6-754329e4b2ed, PowerKids Pr.) Rosen Publishing Group, Inc., The.

Benduhn, Tea. Vegetables, 1 vol. 2007. (Find Out about Food Ser.). (ENG.). 24p. (gr. k-2). pap. 9.15 *(978-0-8368-8262-9(8)*, 84ac455b-6899-4dfb-8122-3ab918c7eb48); (Illus.). lib. bdg. 24.67 *(978-0-8368-8255-1(5)*, 69834f68-028f-43e4-a5af-fc69e62ecb58) Stevens, Gareth Publishing LLLP. (Weekly Reader Leveled Readers).

—Vegetables / Vegetales, 1 vol. 2007. (Find Out about Food / Conoce la Comida Ser.). (SPA & ENG.). 24p. (gr. k-2). pap. 9.15 *(978-0-8368-8466-1(3)*, a9fdbe12-d487-4d30-9678-966c86d797a7); (Illus.). lib. bdg. 24.67 *(978-0-8368-8459-3(0)*, 114a85ea-d4c0-4c30-8783-3145e150ca4a) Stevens, Gareth Publishing LLLP. (Weekly Reader Leveled Readers).

Blanch, Xavier. Hortalizas. 2003. (SPA & CAT.). (J). *(978-84-246-0693-0(0)*, GL30335) La Galera, S.A. Editorial ESP. Dist: Lectorum Pubns., Inc.

Blane, Francisco. Vegetables Are Good! Lap Book. 2009. (My First Reader's Theater Set B Ser.). (J). 28.00 *(978-1-60634-990-8(2))* Benchmark Education Co.

Bodden, Valerie. Vegetables. 2015. (Healthy Plates Ser.). (ENG.). 24p. (J). (gr. 1-4). pap. 9.99 *(978-1-62832-112-8(1)*, 21219, Creative Paperbacks); *(978-1-60818-512-2(5)*, 21218, Creative Education) Creative Co., The.

Borgert-Spaniol, Megan. Vegetable Group. 2012. (Eating Right with Myplate Ser.). (ENG., Illus.). 24p. (J). (gr. k-3). lib. bdg. 26.95 *(978-1-60014-760-9(7)*, 11402, Blastoff! Readers) Bellwether Media.

Byers, Ann. Fruits & Vegetables: From the Garden to Your Table, 1 vol. 2012. (Truth about the Food Supply Ser.). (ENG., Illus.). 48p. (J). (gr. 5-5). lib. bdg. 34.47 *(978-1-4488-6799-8(1)*, 3f574775-5fda-4a9d-8b2f-9b9691a885d2, Rosen Reference) Rosen Publishing Group, Inc., The.

Byrd, Tracy. Fruits & Vegetables & How They Grow: A to Z. 2012. 60p. pap. 24.99 *(978-1-4772-4897-3(8))* AuthorHouse.

Cardenas, Ernesto A. Vegetables for Me! 2009. 19.95 *(978-1-60698-017-0(3))*; pap. 3.95 *(978-1-60698-015-6(7))* Milo Educational Bks. & Resources.

Charney, Steve & Goldbeck, David. The ABC's of Fruits & Vegetables & Beyond: Delicious Alphabet Poems Plus Food, Facts & Fun for Everyone. Larson, Maria Burgaleta, illus. 2007. 112p. (J). (gr. -1-4). per. 16.95 *(978-1-886101-07-4(8))* Ceres Pr.

Christian, Cheryl. What's in My Garden? A Book of Colors. Ericsson, Annie Beth, illus. 2009. 16p. (J). (gr. -1). bds. 6.25 *(978-1-59572-166-2(5))* Star Bright Bks., Inc.

Cleary, Brian P. & Goneau, Martin. Green Beans, Potatoes, & Even Tomatoes: What Is in the Vegetables Group? 2011. (Food Is CATegorical Ser.). pap. 45.32 *(978-0-7613-8350-5(6)*, Millbrook Pr.) Lerner Publishing Group.

Deal, Darlene. Play with Your Food & Learn How to Eat Right: Nutritional Book about Fruits & Vegetables. 2004. (ENG & SPA., Illus.). 22p. (J). (gr. 1-4). pap. 9.95 *(978-0-9747299-0-9(6))* Deal, Darlene.

Derkazarian, Susan. Fruits & Vegetables. (Rookie Read-About Health Ser.). (ENG., Illus.). 32p. (J). (gr. k-2). 2006. pap. 5.95 *(978-0-516-25926-0(1))* 2005. lib. bdg. 20.50 *(978-0-516-23673-5(3))* Scholastic Library Publishing. (Children's Pr.).

Dilkes, D. H. Vegetables, 1 vol. 2011. (All about Good Foods We Eat Ser.). (ENG., Illus.). 24p. (gr. -1-1). pap. 10.35 *(978-1-59845-255-6(X)*, 1e461a20-b209-4b22-b299-12a70f36102b); lib. bdg. 25.27 *(978-0-7660-3926-1(9)*, 13092f11-7842-4451-8def-9d0337d22b4c) Enslow Publishing, LLC. (Enslow Publishing).

Dolbear, Emily J. How Did That Get to My Table? Salad. 2009. (Community Connections: How Did That Get to My Table? Ser.). (ENG.). 24p. (gr. 2-5). lib. bdg. 29.21 *(978-1-60279-473-3(1)*, 200262) Cherry Lake Publishing.

Duke, Nell K., et al. Munching & Crunching the ABCs. 2018. (J). pap. *(978-0-87659-821-4(1))* Gryphon Hse., Inc.

Edwards, Nicola. Vegetables, 1 vol. 2007. (See How Plants Grow Ser.). (ENG., Illus.). 24p. (J). (gr. 2-2). lib. bdg. 26.27 *(978-1-4042-3700-1(3)*, ade92f17-1644-407a-9adf-c1f5a29d5d33, PowerKids Pr.) Rosen Publishing Group, Inc., The.

Ehlert, Lois. Eating the Alphabet Lap-Sized Board Book: Fruits & Vegetables from a to Z. Ehlert, Lois, illus. alt. ed. 2006. (ENG., Illus.). 28p. (J). (gr. -1 — 1). bds. 11.99 *(978-0-15-205688-9(2)*, 1197100, Clarion Bks.) HarperCollins Pubs.

Ericsson, Annie Beth & Christian, Cheryl. ¿Que hay en mi Jardin? (Spanish/English) Un libro de colores/A Book of Colors. del Risco, Eida, tr. 2009. (ENG & SPA., Illus.). 16p. (J). bds. 6.25 *(978-1-59572-181-5(9))* Star Bright Bks., Inc.

Esperanzate-Buenafe, Norma. You Don't Have to Like It. 2011. (ENG.). 25p. (J). pap. 16.95 *(978-1-4327-7771-5(8))* Outskirts Pr., Inc.

Franklin, Jean. Get the Carrot. Grudzina, Rebecca; Franklin, ed. 2016. (Spring Forward Ser.). (ENG.). (J). (gr. 1). 6.84 net. *(978-1-4900-6014-9(6))* Benchmark Education Co.

Fruit & Vegetables I Like to Eat, 1 vol. 2015. (Our Wonderful World Ser.). 8p. (J). (gr. -1-1). pap. 9.35 *(978-1-5081-1234-1(7)*, 2621eb30-a829-4480-ac97-b7a863f8f730); pap. 9.35 *(978-1-5081-1240-2(1)*, 6b5c4d6d-a406-4ef0-94da-652300198808); pap. 9.35 *(978-1-5081-1246-4(0)*, ceb73220-c817-429a-9913-731e7be61a7b); pap. 9.35 *(978-1-5081-1258-7(4)*, b15049a8-2f47-432a-b9df-5c2a76a24a13); pap. 9.35 *(978-1-5081-1222-8(3)*, 2b8a914d-62ee-42fa-8d13-d81f9e70c551); (ENG & SPA.). pap. 9.35 *(978-1-5081-1252-5(5)*, 423c3526-f383-46c6-8edf-aac81ba7794b) Rosen Publishing Group, Inc., The. (Rosen Classroom).

Fruits & Vegetables. 2019. (Illus.). (J). *(978-1-4351-6977-7(8))* Barnes & Noble, Inc.

Fruits & Vegetables I Like to Eat - English Take Home Book. 2007. (Journeys Ser.). (J). pap. 15.00 *(978-1-4042-5462-6(5)*, Rosen Classroom) Rosen Publishing Group, Inc., The.

Fruits & Vegetables I Like to Eat - Spanish Take Home Book. 2007. (Journeys Ser.). (J). pap. 49.95 *(978-1-4042-5513-5(3)*, Rosen Classroom) Rosen Publishing Group, Inc., The.

Gibbons, Gail. The Vegetables We Eat. (ENG., Illus.). 32p. (J). (gr. -1-3). 2008. pap. 7.99 *(978-0-8234-2153-4(8))* 2007. 17.99 *(978-0-8234-2001-8(9))* Holiday Hse., Inc.

Green, Emily K. Vegetables. 2006. (Blastoff! Readers Ser.). (ENG., Illus.). 24p. (J). (gr. k-3). lib. bdg. 24.95 *(978-1-60014-002-0(5)*, Blastoff! Readers) Bellwether Media.

—Vegetables. 2011. (Blastoff! Readers Ser.). (Illus.). 24p. (J). pap. 5.95 *(978-0-531-25857-6(2)*, Children's Pr.) Scholastic Library Publishing.

Gul, Hasibe, et al. Nutritious Vegetables. 2011. (ENG., Illus.). 16p. (J). (gr. -1 — 1). pap. 3.95 *(978-1-59784-239-6(7)*, Tughra Bks.) Blue Dome, Inc.

Head, Honor. Salad. 2010. (J). 24.25 *(978-1-59920-259-4(X))* Black Rabbit Bks.

Heos, Bridget. So You Want to Grow a Salad? Fabbri, Daniele, illus. 2015. (Grow Your Food Ser.). (ENG.). 24p. (J). (gr. 1-4). lib. bdg. 19.95 *(978-1-60753-741-0(9)*, 15271) Amicus.

Herrington, Lisa M. Tomatoes to Ketchup. 2013. (Rookie Read-About Science Ser.). (ENG.). 32p. (J). (gr. k-3). lib. bdg. 18.69 *(978-0-531-24743-3(0)*, Children's Pr.) Scholastic Library Publishing.

Houbre, Gilbert. Vegetables. Houbre, Gilbert, illus. 2012. (ENG., Illus.). 36p. (J). (gr. -1-k). spiral bd. 19.99 *(978-1-85103-402-4(1))* Moonlight Publishing, Ltd. GBR. Dist: Independent Pubs. Group.

Hughes, Meredith Sayles. Green Power: Leaf & Flower Vegetables. 2005. (Plants We Eat Ser.). (Illus.). 104p. (gr. 6-9). 26.60 *(978-0-8225-2839-5(8))* Lerner Publishing Group.

Hunter, Charlotte. Fruit or Vegetable. 2018. (Plants, Animals, & People Ser.). (ENG., Illus.). 16p. (gr. -1-2). lib. bdg. 28.50 *(978-1-64156-158-7(0)*, 9781641561587) Rourke Educational Media.

James, Dawn L. Turning Tomatoes into Ketchup, 1 vol. 2014. (Step-By-Step Transformations Ser.). (ENG.). 24p. (gr. 1-1). lib. bdg. 25.93 *(978-1-62713-010-3(1)*, 52267c27-4a1a-4b24-bc0b-8a650e51acef) Cavendish Square Publishing LLC.

Kalz, Jill. Vegetables. 2003. 24p. (J). lib. bdg. 21.35 *(978-1-58340-300-6(0))* Black Rabbit Bks.

Kennedy, Pamela & Brady, Anne Kennedy. Very Veggie Devos for Little Ones. Reed, Lisa, illus. 2017. (VeggieTales Ser.). (ENG.). 32p. (J). (gr. -1-k). bds. 12.99 *(978-0-8249-1997-9(1))* Worthy Publishing.

Klepeis, Alicia Z. Fruits & Vegetables Explained, 1 vol. 2016. (Distinctions in Nature Ser.). (ENG.). 32p. (gr. 3-3). 30.21 *(978-1-5026-1744-6(7)*, e4489408-3428-40c7-946f-ea50507a4efd) Cavendish Square Publishing LLC.

Ku, Blae & Tha, Shay. Fruits & Vegetables: A Picture Book in Karen & English. 2016. (KAR & ENG., Illus.). 54p. (J). 26.00 *(978-1-4809-6685-7(1)*, RoseDog Bks.) Dorrance Publishing Co., Inc.

Kuskowski, Alex. Salad Gardens: A Kid's Guide to Gardening. 2015. (Super Simple Gardening Ser.). (ENG.). 32p. (J). (gr. k-4). 34.21 *(978-1-62403-526-5(4)*, 17335, Super SandCastle) ABDO Publishing Co.

Lanz, Helen. Grow Your Own Potatoes. 2012. (Grow Your Own Ser.). (ENG., Illus.). 32p. (gr. 3-6). lib. bdg. 28.50 *(978-1-59771-312-2(0))* Sea-To-Sea Pubns.

—Grow Your Own Tomatoes. 2012. (Grow Your Own Ser.). (ENG., Illus.). 32p. (gr. 3-6). lib. bdg. 28.50 *(978-1-59771-314-6(7))* Sea-To-Sea Pubns.

Lassieur, Allison. Vegetables. 2014. (Where Does Our Food Come From? Ser.). (ENG., Illus.). 32p. (J). (gr. 2-5). lib. bdg. 28.50 *(978-1-60753-496-9(7)*, 16050) Amicus.

Malam, John. Grow Your Own Sandwich, 1 vol. 2011. (Grow It Yourself! Ser.). (ENG.). 32p. (J). (gr. k-2). 29.99 *(978-1-4329-5108-5(4)*, 115224, Heinemann) Capstone.

Marsico, Katie. Your Healthy Plate: Vegetables. 2012. (21st Century Basic Skills Library: Your Healthy Plate Ser.). (ENG.). 24p. (gr. k-3). pap. 12.79 *(978-1-61080-399-1(X)*, 201334); (Illus.). lib. bdg. 26.35 *(978-1-61080-347-2(7)*, 201290) Cherry Lake Publishing.

Martineau, Susan & James, Hel. Fruits & Vegetables. 2012. (Healthy Eating Ser.). (Illus.). 32p. (gr. 2-6). pap. 8.95 *(978-1-59920-243-3(3))* Black Rabbit Bks.

Matthews, Colin. I Know Fruits & Vegetables, 1 vol. 2017. (What I Know Ser.). (ENG.). 24p. (J). (gr. k-k). pap. 9.15 *(978-1-4824-6293-7(1)*, 06103a6a-cd76-4b12-bc69-f59977e86454) Stevens, Gareth Publishing LLLP.

Milet Publishing. My First Bilingual Book-Vegetables (English-Portuguese), 1 vol. 2011. (My First Bilingual Book Ser.). (ENG., Illus.). 24p. (J). (gr. k — 1). bds. 7.99 *(978-1-84059-665-6(1))* Milet Publishing.

Milet Publishing Staff. My First Bilingual Book - Vegetables, 1 vol. 2011. (My First Bilingual Book Ser.). (ENG., Illus.). 24p. (J). (gr. k — 1). bds. 7.99 *(978-1-84059-669-4(4))*; bds. 8.99 *(978-1-84059-660-1(0))*; bds. 8.99 *(978-1-84059-666-3(X))*; bds. 7.99 *(978-1-84059-658-8(9))* Milet Publishing.

—My First Bilingual Book-Vegetables, 1 vol. 2011. (My First Bilingual Book Ser.). (ENG., Illus.). 24p. (J). (gr. k — 1). bds. 7.99 *(978-1-84059-663-2(5))* Milet Publishing.

—My First Bilingual Book-Vegetables (English-Arabic), 1 vol. 2011. (My First Bilingual Book Ser.). (ENG & ARA., Illus.). 24p. (J). (gr. k — 1). bds. 8.99 *(978-1-84059-656-4(2))* Milet Publishing.

—My First Bilingual Book-Vegetables (English-Farsi), 1 vol. 2011. (My First Bilingual Book Ser.). (ENG., Illus.). 24p. (J). (gr. k — 1). bds. 7.99 *(978-1-84059-659-5(7))* Milet Publishing.

—My First Bilingual Book-Vegetables (English-Spanish), 1 vol. 2011. (My First Bilingual Book Ser.). (ENG & SPA., Illus.). 24p. (J). (gr. k — 1). bds. 8.99 *(978-1-84059-668-7(6))* Milet Publishing.

—My First Bilingual Book-Vegetables (English-Urdu), 1 vol. 2011. (My First Bilingual Book Ser.). (ENG., Illus.). 24p. (J). (gr. k — 1). bds. 8.99 *(978-1-84059-670-0(8))* Milet Publishing.

—My First Bilingual Book-Vegetables (English-Vietnamese), 1 vol. 2011. (My First Bilingual Book Ser.). (ENG., Illus.). 24p. (J). (gr. k — 1). bds. 8.99 *(978-1-84059-671-7(6))* Milet Publishing.

—Vegetables, 1 vol. 2011. (My First Bilingual Book Ser.). (ENG., Illus.). 24p. (J). (gr. k — 1). bds. 7.99 *(978-1-84059-657-1(0))*; bds. 7.99 *(978-1-84059-664-9(3))*; bds. 8.99 *(978-1-84059-667-0(8))* Milet Publishing.

—Vegetables - My First Bilingual Book, 1 vol. 2011. (My First Bilingual Book Ser.). (ENG & GER., Illus.). 24p. (J). (gr. k — 1). bds. 8.99 *(978-1-84059-661-8(9))* Milet Publishing.

—Vegetables (Le Verdure), 1 vol. 2011. (My First Bilingual Book Ser.). (ENG & ITA., Illus.). 24p. (J). (gr. k — 1). bds. 8.99 *(978-1-84059-662-5(7))* Milet Publishing.

Mitchell, Melanie S. Potatoes. 2005. (First Step Nonfiction Ser.). (Illus.). 24p. (gr. k-2). lib. bdg. 17.27 *(978-0-8225-4612-2(4))* Lerner Publishing Group.

Morganelli, Adrianna. The Biography of Tomatoes. 2007. (How Did That Get Here? Ser.). (ENG., Illus.). 32p. (J). (gr. 2-9). lib. bdg. *(978-0-7787-2494-0(8))*; pap. *(978-0-7787-2530-5(8))* Crabtree Publishing Co.

Murray, Laura K. Bean. 2015. (Grow with Me Ser.). (ENG., Illus.). 32p. (J). (gr. 3-6). *(978-1-60818-560-3(5)*, 20864, Creative Education) Creative Co., The.

National Geographic Learning. Windows on Literacy Fluent (Science: Life Science): Big Red Tomatoes. 2007. (Rise & Shine Ser.). (ENG.). 24p. (C). (gr. k-2). pap. 14.95 *(978-0-7922-9221-0(9))* CENGAGE Learning.

Nelson, Robin. Tomatoes. 2009. pap. 34.95 *(978-0-7613-4124-6(2))* Lerner Publishing Group.

—Vegetables. 2003. (First Step Nonfiction - Food Groups Ser.). (ENG., Illus.). 24p. (gr. k-2). lib. bdg. 23.93 *(978-0-8225-4626-9(4))* Lerner Publishing Group.

Nugent, Samantha. Vegetables. 2015. (Let's Learn about Food Ser.). (ENG.). (J). lib. bdg. 27.13 *(978-1-4896-4003-1(7)*, AV2 by Weigl) Weigl Pubs., Inc.

Oda, Mayumi. Happy Veggies. 2018. (Illus.). 40p. (J). (gr. -1-3). 12.95 *(978-1-946764-06-5(X)*, Plum Blossom Bks.) Parallax Pr.

Owen, Ruth. Vegetables! Life on a Produce Farm, 1 vol. 2012. (Food from Farmers Ser.). (ENG., Illus.). 32p. (J). (gr. 1-2). pap. 12.75 *(978-1-61533-540-4(4)*, 7914b556-b027-41e2-aca6-867cfef68a2b); lib. bdg. 29.93 *(978-1-61533-531-2(5)*, d26b4038-01f7-45de-a747-55a2efc8135f) Rosen Publishing Group, Inc., The. (Windmill Bks.).

Pankova, Yuliya, ed. Veggies - Guess What? 2013. (Guess What? Ser.). (ENG.). 10p. (J). (— 1). bds. 5.95 *(978-1-61889-319-2(X))* AZ Bks. LLC.

Peanuckle. Mrs. Peanuckle's Vegetable Alphabet. Ford, Jessie, illus. 2017. (Mrs. Peanuckle's Alphabet Ser.: 1). 28p. (J). (— 1). bds. 8.99 *(978-1-62336-870-8(7)*, 9781623368708, Rodale Kids) Random Hse. Children's Bks.

Pettiford, Rebecca. Vegetables. Fretland VanVoorst, Jenny, ed. 2015. (Illus.). (J). lib. bdg. *(978-1-62031-233-9(6))* Jump! Inc.

Potato. 2003. 38.95 *(978-0-8136-4132-4(2))*; 36.95 *(978-0-8136-9263-0(6))* Modern Curriculum Pr.

Potatoes, Potatoes: Level J, 6 vols. (Wonder Worldtm Ser.). 16p. 29.95 *(978-0-7802-2904-4(5))* Wright Group/McGraw-Hill.

Puppet Rescue, creator. Caterpillar says Eat Your Greens. 2007. (Illus.). 10p. (J). 4.95 *(978-0-9799958-1-1(7))* Puppet Rescue.

Rajczak Nelson, Kristen. Very Tasty Vegetable Recipes, 1 vol. 2014. (Ingredients for a Healthy Life Ser.). (ENG., Illus.). 24p. (J). (gr. 2-3). 24.27 *(978-1-4824-0575-0(X)*, dc838eb0-eda5-49b0-b20b-86ba8ae57572) Stevens, Gareth Publishing LLLP.

Riggs, Kate. Tomato. (Grow with Me Ser.). (ENG.). 32p. (J). (gr. 3-6). 2013. pap. 9.99 *(978-0-89812-772-0(6)*, 21983, Creative Paperbacks) 2012. (Illus.). 19.95 *(978-1-60818-219-0(3)*, 21977, Creative Education) Creative Co., The.

Rodger, Ellen. The Biography of Potatoes. 2007. (How Did That Get Here? Ser.). (ENG., Illus.). 32p. (J). (gr. 2-9). lib. bdg. *(978-0-7787-2492-6(1))*; pap. *(978-0-7787-2528-2(6))* Crabtree Publishing Co.

Rondeau, Amanda. Vegetables Are Vital, 1 vol. 2003. (What Should I Eat? Ser.). (Illus.). 24p. (J). (gr. k-3). lib. bdg. 24.21 *(978-1-57765-835-1(3)*, SandCastle) ABDO Publishing Co.

Rosa-Mendoza, Gladys, creator. Fruits & Vegetables. 2004. (English-Spanish Foundations Ser.: Vol. 10).Tr. of Frutas y Vegetales. (SPA & ENG., Illus.). 22p. (J). bds. 6.95 *(978-1-931398-10-7(0))* Me+Mi Publishing.

Samson, Tess. We Like Vegetables. 2010. (Sight Word Readers Ser.). (J). 3.49 *(978-1-60719-615-0(8))* Newmark Learning LLC.

T
U
V

Sayre, April Pulley. Rah, Rah, Radishes! A Vegetable Chant. Sayre, April Pulley, photos by. 2014. (Classic Board Bks.). (ENG., Illus.). 34p. (J). (gr. -1 — 1). bds. 8.99 *(978-1-4424-9927-0(3)*, Little Simon) Little Simon.

Schuh, Mari. Carrots Grow Underground. 2010. (How Fruits & Vegetables Grow Ser.). (ENG.). 24p. (J). (gr. k-1). pap. 37.74 *(978-1-4296-6186-7(0)*, 16061, Pebble) Capstone.

—Vegetables on Myplate. 2012. (What's on Myplate? Ser.). (ENG.). 24p. (J). (gr. k-1). pap. 43.74 *(978-1-4296-9425-4(4)*, 18617, Capstone Pr.) Capstone.

Scott, Celicia. My Daily Diet: Vegetables. Prock, Lisa Albers, ed. 2014. (On My Plate Ser.: 6). 48p. (J). (gr. 5-18). 20.95 *(978-1-4222-3100-5(3))* Mason Crest.

Vaughn, Inés. Potatoes/Papas. 2009. (Native Foods of Latin America / Alimentos indígenas de Latino América Ser.). (ENG & SPA.). 24p. (gr. 2-3). 42.50 *(978-1-61514-798-4(5)*, Editorial Buenas Letras) Rosen Publishing Group, Inc., The.

—Squash/Calabazas. 2009. (Native Foods of Latin America / Alimentos indígenas de Latino América Ser.). (ENG & SPA.). 24p. (gr. 2-3). 42.50 *(978-1-61514-799-1(3)*, Editorial Buenas Letras) Rosen Publishing Group, Inc., The.

—Tomatoes/Tomates. 2009. (Native Foods of Latin America / Alimentos indígenas de Latino América Ser.). (ENG & SPA.). 24p. (gr. 2-3). 42.50 *(978-1-61514-800-4(0)*, Editorial Buenas Letras) Rosen Publishing Group, Inc., The.

Vaughn, Inés & Sanz, Ma Pilar. Squash: Calabazas, 1 vol. 2009. (Native Foods of Latin America / Alimentos Indígenas de Latinoamérica Ser.). (SPA & ENG., Illus.). 24p. (J). (gr. 2-3). lib. bdg. 26.27 *(978-1-4358-2727-1(9)*, 5ae2989a-35a8-4cc2-8427-a8f82880a2a0) Rosen Publishing Group, Inc., The.

—Tomatoes: Tomates, 1 vol. 2009. (Native Foods of Latin America / Alimentos Indígenas de Latinoamérica Ser.). (SPA & ENG.). 24p. (J). (gr. 2-3). lib. bdg. 26.27 *(978-1-4358-2724-0(4)*, 624a1055-ce0d-40ed-a11b-63bbf1ae778d) Rosen Publishing Group, Inc., The.

Velázquez Press, creator. Velázquez Biliteracy Program PreK Hora de la Comida Set. 2017. (SPA.). (J). *(978-1-59495-709-3(6))* Velázquez Pr.

Waters, Rosa. My Daily Diet: Dairy. 2014. (J). *(978-1-4222-3094-7(5))* Mason Crest.

Weiss, Ellen. From Eye to Potato. 2007. (Scholastic News Nonfiction Readers Ser.). (ENG., Illus.). 24p. (J). (gr. 1-2). 22.00 *(978-0-531-18535-3(4))* Scholastic Library Publishing.

Wellington, Monica. Color & Garden VEGETABLES. 2011. (Dover Kids Activity Bks.). (ENG., Illus.). 32p. (J). (gr. -1-3). pap. 4.99 *(978-0-486-47959-0(5)*, 479595) Dover Pubns., Inc.

Will Mayo, Gretchen. Frozen Vegetables, 1 vol. 2004. (Where Does Our Food Come From? Ser.). (ENG., Illus.). 24p. (gr. 2-4). (C). pap. 9.15 *(978-0-8368-4073-5(9)*, d2a5a141-acdd-4a91-97f7-b5114b784a4a); lib. bdg. 23.67 *(978-0-8368-4066-7(6)*, 170a6ba0-2d7c-4230-b42d-f97608f75aba, Weekly Reader Leveled Readers) Stevens, Gareth Publishing LLLP.

Yasuda, Anita. Eating Green. 2016. (Illus.). 32p. (J). *(978-1-5105-2213-8(1))* SmartBook Media, Inc.

Yummy Yummy Vegetables. 2004. (J). per. 15.99 *(978-0-9744205-4-7(9))* Golden Eagle Publishing Hse., Inc.

VEGETABLES—CANNING

see Canning and Preserving

VEGETABLES—FICTION

Bailey, Lori Gayle. The Dog Who Loved Cucumbers. 2009. 24p. pap. 11.95 *(978-1-4490-2457-4(2))* AuthorHouse.

Baker, Keith. LMNO Peas. Baker, Keith, illus. 2010. (Peas Ser.). (ENG., Illus.). 40p. (J). (gr. -1-3). 18.99 *(978-1-4169-9141-0(7)*, Beach Lane Bks.) Beach Lane Bks.

—LMNO Peas. Baker, Keith, illus. 2014. (Peas Ser.). (ENG., Illus.). 36p. (J). (gr. -1-k). bds. 8.99 *(978-1-4424-8978-3(2)*, Little Simon) Little Simon.

—1-2-3 Peas. Baker, Keith, illus. 2012. (Peas Ser.). (ENG., Illus.). 40p. (J). (gr. -1-3). 18.99 *(978-1-4424-4551-2(3)*, Beach Lane Bks.) Beach Lane Bks.

Barkow, Henriette. Giant Turnip - Big Book. Johnson, Richard, illus. 2004. (ENG & MAY.). 23p. (J). *(978-1-85269-896-6(9))* Mantra Lingua.

Barkow, Henriette & Johnson, Richard, illus. The Giant Turnip: Rrepa Gjigante. 2004. 24p. (J). *(978-1-85269-732-7(6))* Mantra Lingua.

Barnes, Ben. Don't Eat My Garden. Barnes, Page, illus. 2007. 28p. per. 24.95 *(978-1-4241-8964-9(0))* America Star Bks.

Bass, Jules. Herb, the Vegetarian Dragon. Harter, Debbie, illus. 2005. 32p. (J). (gr. 1-5). reprint ed. pap. 6.99 *(978-1-84148-127-2(0))* Barefoot Bks., Inc.

Benson, Sherry. Introducing Jelly Bean. 2008. 27p. pap. 24.95 *(978-1-60672-427-9(4))* America Star Bks.

Bertrand, Diane Gonzales, et al. Adelita & the Veggie Cousins / Adelita y las primas Verduritas. Rodriguez, Tina, illus. 2011. (SPA.). (J). 16.95 *(978-1-55885-699-8(4)*, Piñata Books) Arte Publico Pr.

Black, Michael Ian. I'm Bored. Ohi, Debbie Ridpath, illus. 2012. (I'm Bks.). (ENG.). 40p. (J). (gr. -1-3). 17.99 *(978-1-4424-1403-7(0)*, Simon & Schuster Bks. For Young Readers) Simon & Schuster Bks. For Young Readers.

—Qué Aburrido! 2014. (SPA.). 36p. (J). (gr. k-1). pap. 16.95 *(978-1-933032-90-0(1))* Lectorum Pubns., Inc.

Bloom, Amy Beth. Little Sweet Potato. Jones, Noah Z., illus. 2012. (ENG.). 32p. (J). (gr. -1-2). 16.99 *(978-0-06-180439-7(8)*, Tegen, Katherine Bks) HarperCollins Pubs.

Blu De Golyer. The Adventures of Captain Greenspud. 2009. 28p. pap. 13.99 *(978-1-4389-6582-6(6))* AuthorHouse.

Bookins, Daddy. Outdside with Lil Boo. Piotti, Dania, illus. 2012. 38p. pap. 13.50 *(978-0-9848019-3-0(6))* Inkwell Books LLC.

Breisacher, Cathy. Chip & Curly: The Great Potato Race. Heinsz, Joshua, illus. 2019. (ENG.). 32p. (J). (gr. k-3). 16.99 *(978-1-58536-408-4(8)*, 204660) Sleeping Bear Pr.

Brett, Jan. The Turnip. Brett, Jan, illus. 2015. (Illus.). 32p. (J). (-k). 18.99 *(978-0-399-17070-6(7)*, G.P. Putnam's Sons Books for Young Readers) Penguin Young Readers Group.

Brewer, Jo Ann. Miss Q-Cee & the Sweet Potatoes. 2011. 28p. pap. 15.99 *(978-1-4568-6245-9(6))* Xlibris Corp.

Brown, Jr. Jimmy's Alphabet Garden. 2013. 32p. pap. 13.50 *(978-1-4575-1797-6(3))* Dog Ear Publishing, LLC.

Bryant, Janine. Yucky Green Beans. l.t. ed. 2005. 12p. (J). per. 5.00 *(978-0-9703474-8-0(0))* Pinninti Pubs.

Carter, Denzel T. Pedro's Carrot, 1 vol. 2015. (Rosen REAL Readers: STEM & STEAM Collection). (ENG.). 8p. (gr. k-1). pap. 5.46 *(978-1-4994-9548-5(X)*, f66bebf0-4250-427c-85fc-41358faf2b5d, Rosen Classroom) Rosen Publishing Group, Inc., The.

Chapman, Jared. Fruits in Suits. 2017. (ENG., Illus.). 40p. (J). (gr. -1-k). 14.95 *(978-1-4197-2298-1(0)*, 1132701, Abrams Appleseed) Abrams, Inc.

—Vegetables in Holiday Underwear. 2019. (ENG., Illus.). 40p. (J). (gr. -1-2). 14.99 *(978-1-4197-3654-4(X)*, 1263101) Abrams, Inc.

—Vegetables in Underwear. 2015. (ENG., Illus.). 40p. (J). (gr. -1-k). 14.95 *(978-1-4197-1464-1(3)*, 1098701) Abrams, Inc.

Chen, Sam. A Real Meal Table Fable. Peschel, Georgia, illus. 2007. 60p. (J). *(978-0-9800764-0-0(4))* Uncle Jim's Publishing.

Christie, Jackie. Wacky WaterSlide Wipeout. 2011. 28p. (gr. -1). pap. 16.09 *(978-1-4269-5821-2(8))* Trafford Publishing.

Crabb, James Anthony. The Dinosaur & Dragon Juice Café. 2008. (Illus.). 32p. pap. 17.95 *(978-0-9556105-8-5(3))* Picnic Publishing Ltd. GBR. Dist: Trans-Atlantic Pubns., Inc.

Daynes, Katie. Enormous Turnip. Overwater, Georgien, illus. 2006. (First Reading Level 3 Ser.). 48p. (J). (gr. 1-4). 8.99 *(978-0-7945-1376-4(X)*, Usborne) EDC Publishing.

De Anda, Diane. The Patchwork Garden. Ventura, Gabriela Baeza, tr. Kemarskaya, Oksana, illus. 2013.Tr. of Pedacitos de Huerto. (ENG & SPA.). 32p. (J). 16.95 *(978-1-55885-763-6(X)*, Piñata Books) Arte Publico Pr.

De Golyer, Blu. The Adventures of Captain Greenspud. 2009. 28p. pap. 14.50 *(978-1-60860-425-8(X)*, Eloquent Bks.) Strategic Book Publishing & Rights Agency (SBPRA).

de Las Casas, Dianne. The Gigantic Sweet Potato, 1 vol. Gentry, Marita, illus. 2010. (ENG.). 32p. (J). (gr. k-3). 16.99 *(978-1-58980-755-6(3)*, Pelican Publishing) Arcadia Publishing.

DeFelice, Cynthia. One Potato, Two Potato. U'Ren, Andrea, illus. 2006. (ENG.). 32p. (J). (gr. -1-3). 19.99 *(978-0-374-35640-8(8)*, 900028331, Farrar, Straus & Giroux (BYR)) Farrar, Straus & Giroux.

dePaola, Tomie. Strega Nona & Her Tomatoes. 2017. (Simon & Schuster Ready-To-Read Level 1 Ser.). lib. bdg. 13.55 *(978-0-606-40214-9(4))* Turtleback.

Dickson, Vivian. To Be a Bean. 2nd ed. 2013. 24p. pap. *(978-0-9873438-1-9(5))* Link Spots.

Dippy Doodle's Beary Big Tomato. 2003. (J). 7.95 *(978-0-9713174-9-9(6))* Boyds Collection Ltd., The.

Doodler, Todd H. One Potato, Two Potato. Doodler, Todd H., illus. 2013. (ENG., Illus.). 32p. (J). (gr. -1-k). 14.99 *(978-1-4424-8517-4(5)*, Little Simon) Little Simon.

—Veggies with Wedgies. Doodler, Todd H., illus. 2014. (ENG., Illus.). 32p. (J). (gr. -1-k). 18.99 *(978-1-4424-9340-7(2)*, Little Simon) Little Simon.

—Veggies with Wedgies Present Doin' the Wedgie. Doodler, Todd H., illus. 2015. (ENG., Illus.). 26p. (J). (gr. -1-k). bds. 7.99 *(978-1-4424-9351-3(8)*, Little Simon) Little Simon.

Dowell, Frances O'Roark. Sam the Man & the Rutabaga Plan. Bates, Amy June, illus. (Sam the Man Ser.: 2). (ENG.). (J). (gr. 1-4). 2018. 144p. pap. 7.99 *(978-1-4814-4070-7(5)*, Atheneum Bks. for Young Readers) 2017. 128p. 16.99 *(978-1-4814-4069-1(1)*, Atheneum/Caitlyn Dlouhy Books) Simon & Schuster Children's Publishing.

Elkins, J. You Are the Pea, & I Am the Carrot. Lemaitre, Pascal, illus. 2013. (ENG.). 32p. (J). (gr. -1-2). 16.95 *(978-1-4197-0850-3(3)*, 1033201, Abrams Bks. for Young Readers) Abrams, Inc.

Falwell, Cathryn. Mystery Vine. Falwell, Cathryn, illus. 2009. (Illus.). 32p. (J). lib. bdg. 17.89 *(978-0-06-177197-2(X)*, Greenwillow Bks.) HarperCollins Pubs.

Fashion Parade: Individual Title, 6 pack. (Bookweb Ser.). 32p. (gr. 6-18). 34.00 *(978-0-7578-0890-6(5))* Rigby Education.

Fine, Karen. Veggiesaurus Lex. 2009. 24p. pap. 12.99 *(978-1-4490-0290-9(0))* AuthorHouse.

Foges Clare, Clare. Kitchen Disco. Murphy Al, Al, illus. 2017. (ENG.). 32p. (gr. -1-k). 16.95 *(978-0-571-33697-5(3))* Faber & Faber, Inc.

Foster, Lisa. 5 Little Tomatoes. 2008. 44p. pap. 17.95 *(978-1-4327-2306-4(5))* Outskirts Pr., Inc.

Ganzer, Diane & St. Croix, Sammy. Adventures of a Kitten Named Raspberry & Other Tales. 2009. 176p. pap. 9.95 *(978-1-935105-30-5(2))* Avid Readers Publishing Group.

Goodrow, Carol. The Treasure of Health & Happiness. 2006. (ENG., Illus.). 96p. (J). (gr. 4-7). 14.00 *(978-1-891369-60-5(1))* Breakaway Bks.

Grand, Robert Alan. The Cosmic Carrot: A Journey to Wellness, Clear Vision & Good Nutrition. Webb, Ros, illus. 2019. 40p. (gr. 3-7). pap. 10.95 *(978-1-64279-266-9(7))* Morgan James Publishing.

Grimly, Gris. Little Jordan Ray's Muddy Spud. Grimly, Gris, illus. 2005. (ENG., Illus.). 40p. pap. 19.95 *(978-0-9729388-6-0(9))* Last Gasp of San Francisco.

Hansen, Chance. Green Pea Makes a Flourless Cookie. 2012. 28p. pap. 13.50 *(978-1-4669-2637-0(6))* Trafford Publishing.

Harriton, Maxine. A School Trip to the Fruit Planet. 1. l.t. ed. 2006. 34p. (J). (gr. -1-1). lib. bdg. 18.95 *(978-0-9787248-0-1(1)*, 00-01-851-447X) UpTree Publishing.

Hawkins, Linda J. Alexander & the Great Vegetable Feud. Bowles, Jennifer, illus. 2004. 40p. (J). (gr. k-5). 19.99 *(978-0-9742806-1-5(5))* Heart to Heart Publishing, Inc.

Haydon, David J. The Spuds - the Windy Day. Ferns, Kevin, illus. 2010. 20p. pap. *(978-1-907611-11-7(8))* Paragon Publishing, Rothersthorpe.

HB Staff. Four Very Big Beans. 97th ed. 2003. (First-Place Reading Ser.). (gr. 1-18). pap. 16.50 *(978-0-15-308144-6(9))* Harcourt Schl. Pubs.

Hebert, J. J. Weepy the Dragon. 2012. 36p. pap. 9.99 *(978-0-9853650-7-3(2))* Mindstir Media.

Henry, Darell W. That Potato Ain't That Big. 2009. (ENG.). 30p. pap. 14.99 *(978-1-4415-8140-2(5))* Xlibris Corp.

Hensdill, Norma Mae. I'm Granny's Little Mess, Just Look at the Rest. 2009. 36p. pap. 17.99 *(978-1-4389-5054-9(3))* AuthorHouse.

Hoffmann, Mark. Fruit Bowl. 2018. (Illus.). 40p. (J). (gr. -1-2). 18.99 *(978-1-5247-1991-3(9)*, Knopf Bks. for Young Readers) Random Hse. Children's Bks.

Holt, Kimberly Willis. Piggy's Sweet Potato Pie Lesson. 2007. (Illus.). 22p. (J). per. 18.99 *(978-0-9759691-4-4(5))* Catch 22 Publishing.

Hood, Morag. Carrot & Pea: An Unlikely Friendship. Hood, Morag, illus. 2017. (ENG., Illus.). 32p. (J). (gr. -1-3). 16.99 *(978-0-544-86842-7(0)*, 1648802, Clarion Bks.) HarperCollins Pubs.

Houdek, Andi. Stop That Pudding! Collier, Kevin, illus. 2010. 16p. pap. 9.95 *(978-1-61633-079-8(1))* Guardian Angel Publishing, Inc.

Howell, Trisha Adelena. The Adventures of Melon & Turnip. Lopez, Paul, illus. 2004. 32p. 15.95 *(978-1-931210-04-1(7))* Howell Canyon Pr.

Jacqueline Juin Snow. A Potato Tale. 2009. 16p. pap. 8.49 *(978-1-4389-6360-0(2))* AuthorHouse.

Jasnoch, Dorothy. Frankie the Bunny the Fall Scramble Begins. Korzeniowski, Samson, ed. Jasnoch, Dorothy, illus. 2012. (Illus.). 28p. pap. 12.99 *(978-1-937752-04-0(6))* Owl About Bks. Pubs.

Jin, Susie Lee. Mine! Jin, Susie Lee, illus. 2016. (ENG., Illus.). 40p. (J). (gr. -1-3). 16.99 *(978-1-4814-2772-2(5)*, Simon & Schuster Bks. For Young Readers) Simon & Schuster Bks. For Young Readers.

Joeison. Oliver Mccoy - the Vegetable Boy. 2011. (ENG., Illus.). 60p. (J). 19.95 *(978-0-9830039-1-5(2))* SLM Bk. Publishing.

Jones, Christianne C. Pruebalo, 1 vol. Ruiz, Carlos, tr. Won Yi, Hye, illus. 2006. (Read-It! Readers en Español: Story Collection). (SPA.). 24p. (J). (gr. -1-3). 22.65 *(978-1-4048-1692-3(5)*, 91277, Picture Window Bks.) Capstone.

Jones, Dennis. The Adventures of the Fruitiebears: Book 2 Fruitiecars. 2011. (Illus.). 48p. pap. 19.48 *(978-1-4567-9001-1(3))* AuthorHouse.

Kann, Victoria & Kann, Elizabeth. Pinkalicious: Pinkalicious (Spanish Edition), 1 vol. Kann, Victoria, illus. 2011. (Pinkalicious Ser.). (SPA., Illus.). 40p. (J). (gr. -1-3). 18.99 *(978-0-06-179959-4(9))* HarperCollins Español.

Kaus, Cathy. The Bean Bandit, 1 vol. 2010. 24p. 24.95 *(978-1-4489-2202-4(X))* PublishAmerica, Inc.

Keller, Laurie. Potato Pants! Keller, Laurie, illus. 2018. (ENG., Illus.). 40p. (J). 18.99 *(978-1-250-10723-7(7)*, 900164825, Holt, Henry & Co. Bks. For Young Readers) Holt, Henry & Co.

Kennedy, Pamela. Good Night, Sleep Tight. 2019. (VeggieTales Ser.). (ENG., Illus.). 20p. (J). (gr. -1-1). bds. 7.99 *(978-0-8249-1691-6(3)*, Worthy Kids/Ideals) Worthy Publishing.

Kenney, Cindy. Junior Asparagus. 2004. (ENG., Illus.). 100p. (J). pap. 3.99 *(978-0-310-70722-6(6))* Zonderkidz.

—Laura Carrot. 2004. (ENG., Illus.). 100p. (J). pap. 3.99 *(978-0-310-70723-3(4))* Zonderkidz.

—Vegetables Bible Storybook, 1 vol. 2006. (Big Idea Books / VeggieTales Ser.). (ENG., Illus.). 256p. (J). (gr. -1-3). 17.99 *(978-0-310-71008-0(1))* Zonderkidz.

Kramer, Alan. The Jack & the Beanstalk Trial. 2006. (J). pap. *(978-1-4108-6181-8(3))* Benchmark Education Co.

Lacera, Jorge. Zombies Don't Eat Veggies!, 1 vol. Lacera, Megan, illus. 2019. (ENG.). 40p. (J). (gr. -1-3). 20.95 *(978-1-62014-794-8(7)*, leelowcbp, Children's Book Press) Lee & Low Bks., Inc.

Ladybird. The Enormous Turnip # Ladybird Readers Level 1, Vol. 1. 2016. (Ladybird Readers Ser.). (Illus.). 48p. (J). pap., act. bk. ed. 9.99 *(978-0-241-25408-0(6))* Penguin Bks., Ltd. GBR. Dist: Independent Pubs. Group.

Lakshmi, Padma. Tomatoes for Neela. Martinez-Neal, Juana, illus. 2021. 40p. (J). (gr. -1-2). 17.99 *(978-0-593-20270-8(8)*, Viking Books for Young Readers) Penguin Young Readers Group.

Lasky, Kathryn. My Uncle Eats Carrots on the Roof. 2008. (J). 16.99 *(978-0-374-35119-9(8)*, Farrar, Straus & Giroux (BYR)) Farrar, Straus & Giroux.

Lassiter, Erin & Garcia, Jolanda. EarTwiggle's Adventure 1: The Treasure Hunt. 2004. (Illus.). (J). 12.99 *(978-0-9762573-0-1(0))* Ear Twiggles Productions, Inc.

Lavoie, Rejean. Des Legumes Pour Frank Einstein. Begin, Jean-Guy, illus. 2004. (Des 9 Ans. Ser.: Vol. 44). (FRE.). 120p. (J). 8.95 *(978-2-89599-006-2(9))* Editions de la Paix CAN. Dist: World of Reading, Ltd.

Lea, Larry, et al. Larry Learns to Listen, 1 vol. 2003. (Big Idea Books / VeggieTales Ser.). (ENG., Illus.). 12p. (J). (gr. -1-1). bds. 4.99 *(978-0-310-70539-0(8))* Zonderkidz.

Lima Bean Dream. (J). (gr. 3-5). pap. 9.90 *(978-0-669-15612-6(4))*; pap. 9.90 *(978-0-669-15895-3(X))* Houghton Mifflin Harcourt School Pubs.

Lin, Grace. Ugly Vegetables. 2014. 16.95 *(978-1-63419-748-9(8))* Perfection Learning Corp.

Manning, Dennis & Crisalli, Joseph. The Turnip War. 2011. 120p. pap. 7.76 *(978-1-4357-1566-0(7))* Lulu Pr., Inc.

Marie, Cherry. The President Eats Vegetables & So Do I! 2012. 44p. pap. 12.00 *(978-0-9853259-0-9(9))* Professional Publishing Hse. LLC.

Marshall, Linda Elovitz. Talia & the Rude Vegetables. Assirelli, Francesca, illus. 2011. (ENG.). 24p. (J). (gr. k-3). pap. 6.95 *(978-0-7613-5218-1(X)*, 680c74b9-4069-4eeb-aba3-3e3f20cd5862, Kar-Ben Publishing) Lerner Publishing Group.

Masson, Lynne. The Vegetable Patch. 2012. (Illus.). 64p. pap. 28.99 *(978-1-4772-3859-2(X))* AuthorHouse.

Matsumoto, Reiko Odate. The Sweet Potato. 2012. 24p. pap. 17.99 *(978-1-4685-7456-2(6))* AuthorHouse.

Mattern, Joanne. The Food Pyramid Disaster. 2005. (J). pap. *(978-1-4108-4195-7(2))* Benchmark Education Co.

McCall, Val. Twelve Rabbits & a Turtle: Bilingual English French. 2012. 46p. pap. 9.95 *(978-1-938367-00-7(6))* Destinee Media.

McClements, George. Night of the Veggie Monster. McClements, George, illus. (ENG., Illus.). 32p. (J). (gr. -1-1). 2014. 7.99 *(978-1-61963-180-9(6)*, 900125204) 2008. 18.99 *(978-1-59990-061-2(0)*, 900044531) Bloomsbury Publishing USA. (Bloomsbury USA Childrens).

McCreadie, Sandi. Thistle Fables. 2013. 64p. pap. 23.99 *(978-1-4808-0313-8(8))* Archway Publishing.

McDonald, Susan. Only Just One Mushroom. 2012. 32p. pap. 32.70 *(978-1-4771-3617-1(7))* Xlibris Corp.

McTrustry, Chris. Red Goes Green, 1 vol. rev. ed. 2013. (Literary Text Ser.). (ENG., Illus.). 32p. (J). (gr. 3-4). pap. 11.99 *(978-1-4333-5641-4(4))* Teacher Created Materials, Inc.

Meyers, Dolores. Herbie's New Home. 2011. 20p. pap. 24.95 *(978-1-60749-665-6(8))* America Star Bks.

Miller, Pat Zietlow. Sophie's Squash. Wilsdorf, Anne, illus. 2013. (Sophie's Squash Ser.). (ENG.). 40p. (J). (gr. -1-2). 17.99 *(978-0-307-97896-7(6)*, Schwartz & Wade Bks.) Random Hse. Children's Bks.

Morrow. Lima Bean Dream. (J). (gr. 3-5). 75.00 *(978-0-669-13451-3(1))* Houghton Mifflin Harcourt School Pubs.

My Vegetable Garden. 2003. (J). per. *(978-1-57657-896-4(8))* Paradise Pr., Inc.

North, Laura. Jack & the Bean Pie. Phillips, Mike, illus. 2014. (Tadpoles: Fairytale Twists Ser.). (ENG.). 32p. (J). (gr. 1-2). *(978-0-7787-0441-6(6))*; pap. *(978-0-7787-0449-2(1))* Crabtree Publishing Co.

Orshoski, Paul. We Read Phonics-I Do Not Like Greens! Ebbeler, Jeffrey, illus. 2011. (We Read Phonics: Level 4 Ser.). (ENG.). 32p. (J). (gr. 1-3). 17.44 *(978-1-60115-331-9(7))* Treasure Bay, Inc.

Padua, Grace. The Travels of Chikippo. Baker, David, illus. 2012. 26p. 24.95 *(978-1-4626-9782-3(8))* America Star Bks.

Parks, Carmen. Farmers Market/Día de Mercado. Ada, Alma Flor & Campoy, F. Isabel, trs. Martinez, Edward, illus. 2010. (ENG.). 28p. (J). (gr. -1-3). pap. 5.99 *(978-0-547-36900-6(X)*, 1422975, Clarion Bks.) HarperCollins Pubs.

Peachey, Ted. The Adventures of Ryan & His Magic Carrot. 2010. 90p. pap. 9.99 *(978-1-60911-222-6(9)*, Eloquent Bks.) Strategic Book Publishing & Rights Agency (SBPRA).

Pierro, Rita. No Veggies for Me. lukel, Onur, illus. 2011. 32p. pap. 24.95 *(978-1-4626-4554-1(2))* America Star Bks.

Pisella, Donna. The Blue Goblin. 2013. (ENG.). 30p. (J). 22.95 *(978-1-4787-1269-5(4))* Outskirts Pr., Inc.

Prignano, Barbara. The Tiny Tomato & His Terrific Manners. Kalpart, illus. 2013. 32p. pap. 12.95 *(978-1-62857-080-9(6)*, Strategic Bk. Publishing) Strategic Book Publishing & Rights Agency (SBPRA).

Pryor, Katherine. Zora's Zucchini. Raff, Anna, illus. 2015. (Kids Garden Club Ser.: 2). (ENG.). 32p. (J). (gr. -1-5). 16.95 *(978-0-9836615-7-3(X))* READERS to EATERS.

—Zora's Zucchini (1 Hardcover/1 CD) 2016. (ENG.). (J). (gr. -1-2). audio compact disk 29.95 *(978-1-4301-2183-1(1))* Live Oak Media.

Ras, J. J. The Ketchup Story. 2007. 48p. pap. 19.94 *(978-1-84728-470-9(1))* Lulu Pr., Inc.

Reynolds, Aaron. Creepy Carrots! Brown, Peter, illus. 2012. (Creepy Tales! Ser.). (ENG.). 40p. (J). (gr. -1-3). 18.99 *(978-1-4424-0297-3(0)*, Simon & Schuster Bks. For Young Readers) Simon & Schuster Bks. For Young Readers.

—Las Zanahorias Maléficas. 2015.Tr. of Creepy Carrots. (SPA.). 40p. (J). (gr. k-3). 24.95 *(978-84-16117-13-0(6))* Ediciones Obelisco ESP. Dist: Spanish Pubs., LLC.

Rinaldi, Francis. Brock Lee & the Salad Kids. 2005. 20p. 7.53 *(978-1-4116-5552-2(4))* Lulu Pr., Inc.

Rivoal, Marine, creator. Three Little Peas. 2014. (Illus.). 48p. (J). (gr. -1-3). 16.95 *(978-1-59270-155-1(8))* Enchanted Lion Bks., LLC.

Robb, Jackie & Stringle, Berny. The Story of Pea Brain. Duncan, Karen & Stringle, Sam, illus. 2004. (Bang on the Door Ser.). 32p. (YA). pap. *(978-1-85602-383-2(4)*, Pavilion Children's Books) Pavilion Bks.

Robinson, Hilary. Snow White & the Enormous Turnip, 1 vol. Sanfilippo, Simona, illus. 2012. (ENG.). 32p. (J). pap. *(978-0-7787-8035-9(X))* Crabtree Publishing Co.

Sayre, April Pulley. Rah, Rah, Radishes! A Vegetable Chant. Sayre, April Pulley, photos by. 2011. (ENG., Illus.). 32p. (J). (gr. -1-3). 18.99 *(978-1-4424-2141-7(X)*, Beach Lane Bks.) Beach Lane Bks.

Scelsa, Greg. I Like Potatoes. Faulkner, Stacey, ed. Ostrom, Bob, illus. 2006. (J). pap. 2.99 *(978-1-59198-316-3(9))* Creative Teaching Pr., Inc.

Scholastic. Red Pepper, Yellow Squash: a Book of Colors (Rookie Toddler) 2014. (Rookie Toddler Ser.). (ENG.). 14p. (J). (gr. -1 — 1). bds. 6.95 *(978-0-531-20917-2(2)*, Children's Pr.) Scholastic Library Publishing.

Segal, John. Carrot Soup. Segal, John, illus. 2006. (ENG., Illus.). 32p. (J). (gr. -1-3). 19.99 *(978-0-689-87702-5(1)*, McElderry, Margaret K. Bks.) McElderry, Margaret K. Bks.

—Sopa de Zanahoria. Mlawer, Teresa, tr. from ENG. 2006. (Illus.). (gr. -1-k). 12.99 *(978-1-933032-13-9(8))* Lectorum Pubns., Inc.

Seplowitz, P'Nina. Once upon a Vegetable. 2012. 32p. pap. 14.51 *(978-1-4669-1414-8(9))* Trafford Publishing.

Sevigny, Eric, illus. Caillou: Le Jardin de Carottes. 2017. (Lis Avec Caillou Ser.). (FRE.). 32p. (J). (gr. -1-1). 4.95 *(978-2-89718-365-3(9))* Caillouet, Gerry.

—Caillou: The Carrot Patch. 2017. (Read with Caillou Ser.). (ENG.). 32p. (J). (gr. -1-1). 3.99 *(978-2-89718-367-7(5))* Caillouet, Gerry.

Sims, Janice. Grandma's Basket. Storr, Nicola, illus. 2010. 28p. pap. *(978-1-904408-68-0(0))* Bank House Bks.

Smith, Carrie. The Enormous Turnip: Classic Tales Edition. Rogers, Jacqueline, illus. 2011. (Classic Tales Ser.). (J). *(978-1-936258-70-3(6))* Benchmark Education Co.

Smith, Lesley, illus. Great Big Enormous Turnip. Smith, Lesley, 2012. (ENG.). 32p. (J). pap. 6.50 *(978-1-84135-192-6(X))* Award Pubns. Ltd. GBR. Dist: Parkwest Pubns., Inc.

Stanek, Robert, pseud. Visit Garden Box Farms. 2008. (ENG., Illus.). 28p. (J). pap. 5.29 *(978-1-57545-190-9(5))* RP Media.

Stango, Diane. Too Many Tomatoes, 1 vol. 2006. (Neighborhood Readers Ser.). (ENG.). 12p. (gr. k-1). pap. 5.90 *(978-1-4042-6718-3(2)*, cbbef832-ae95-468b-ac51-12f8d88d36b8, Rosen Classroom) Rosen Publishing Group, Inc., The.

—Vicky's Vegetables, 1 vol. 2006. (Neighborhood Readers Ser.). (ENG.). 16p. (gr. 1-2). pap. 6.50 *(978-1-4042-7156-2(2)*, 357d5fb3-9da0-4339-b007-34702d8176f4, Rosen Classroom) Rosen Publishing Group, Inc., The.

Stremanos, A. M., illus. Rosemary's Taken over My Potatoes. 2008. 20p. (J). 5.00 *(978-0-9801372-0-0(9))* Benedetti, Jef.

Stroud, David Wayne. Funny, Dust & Honey & the Giant Carrot. Nardandrea, Swannee, illus. l.t. ed. 2005. 32p. (J). 17.95 *(978-0-9762835-2-2(2))* Shooting Star Publishing.

Sunday Potatoes, Monday Potatoes. (Early Intervention Levels Ser.). 10.50 *(978-0-7362-0509-2(8))*; 63.00 *(978-0-7362-2139-9(5))* CENGAGE Learning.
Talbot Healy, John Adrian. The Flea & the Cauliflower. 2009. (Illus.). 92p. pap. 30.49 *(978-1-4490-1360-8(0))* AuthorHouse.
Tel-Or, Nava. Tristan & the Magical Vegetable Stew. 2011. (Illus.). 36p. (gr. -1). pap. 22.24 *(978-1-4567-7024-2(1))* AuthorHouse.
Tolstoy, Aleksei & Sharkey, Niamh. The Gigantic Turnip. 2006. (Illus.). 40p. (J). (gr. -1-2). 10.99 *(978-1-905236-72-5(7))* Barefoot Bks., Inc.
Tolstoy, Aleksei, et al. The Gigantic Turnip. 2009. (Illus.). (J). 16.99 *(978-1-84686-298-4(1))* Barefoot Bks., Inc.
Tone, Satoe. The Very Big Carrot. 2013. (ENG., Illus.). 26p. (J). 12.00 *(978-0-8028-5426-1(5)*, Eerdmans Bks For Young Readers) Eerdmans, William B. Publishing Co.
Toscano, Leesa. Eat Your Vegetables. Bodoff, Janet, illus. 2012. 24p. pap. 24.95 *(978-1-4626-5278-5(6))* America Star Bks.
Triplett, Annette. From the Farm to You Coloring Book. Vale, Joe, ed. Murphy, Dennis, illus. 2012. 28p. (J). *(978-0-933842-34-2(1))* Univ. of Missouri, Extension.
Van Lemon, M. Champions of the Garden Games: Winter Fun for Everyone. 2009. 48p. pap. 20.95 *(978-1-4490-3580-8(9))* AuthorHouse.
Warner, Gertrude Chandler, creator. The Mystery of the Traveling Tomatoes. 2008. (Boxcar Children Mysteries Ser.: 117). (ENG., Illus.). 128p. (J). (gr. 2-5). 14.99 *(978-0-8075-5579-8(7)*, 807555797); pap. 6.99 *(978-0-8075-5580-4(0)*, 807555800) Random Hse. Children's Bks. (Random Hse. Bks. for Young Readers).
Warren, Donna E. Colors of the Rainbow. 2011. 26p. pap. 12.00 *(978-1-61204-318-0(6)*, Eloquent Bks.) Strategic Book Publishing & Rights Agency (SBPRA).
Waszak, Madonna. Mason's Mashed Potato Tree. Johnston, Lisa Harp, illus. 2011. 34p. pap. 14.95 *(978-1-4575-0159-3(7))* Dog Ear Publishing, LLC.
Watson, M. Veg Patch Gang. 2005. (Illus.). 40p. pap. *(978-1-84401-005-9(8))* Athena Pr.
Waxman, Melanie Brown. The Little Carrot, 1 vol. Friend, Bonnie, illus. 2009. 39p. pap. 24.95 *(978-1-61546-046-5(2))* America Star Bks.
Wenger, Shaunda. The Farm Stand Mystery. 2006. (Early Explorers Ser.). (J). pap. *(978-1-4108-6121-4(X))* Benchmark Education Co.
Wilson, CeCe. Lily's Tomato, 1 vol. 2015. (Rosen REAL Readers: STEM & STEAM Collection). (ENG.). 12p. (gr. k-1). pap. 6.33 *(978-1-4994-9620-8(6)*, e45757b8-b9ad-404a-9233-cb3c2b8936b7, Rosen Classroom) Rosen Publishing Group, Inc., The.
Winningham, Barbara. The Turtle Pit. 2013. 36p. 24.95 *(978-1-62709-875-5(5))*; pap. 24.95 *(978-1-62709-493-1(8))* America Star Bks.
Yaldezian, Lisa M. 500 Presents for Penelope Potts. Seltzer, Jerry, illus. 2006. (J). 16.95 *(978-1-60131-005-7(6))* Big Tent Bks.
Yurnel, Demain. Little Yellow Pear Tomatoes. Tamarin, Nicole, illus. 2005. 32p. (J). 15.95 *(978-0-9740190-2-4(X))* Illumination Arts Publishing Co., Inc.

VEGETABLES—MARKETING

see Farm Produce—Marketing

VEGETARIANISM

Askew, Claire. Generation V: The Complete Guide to Going, Being, & Staying Vegan as a Teenager. 2011. (Tofu Hound Ser.). (ENG., Illus.). 160p. (YA). pap. 14.95 *(978-1-60486-338-3(2))* PM Pr.
Boothroyd, Jennifer. Why Doesn't Everyone Eat Meat? Vegetarianism & Special Diets. 2016. (Lightning Bolt Books (r) — Healthy Eating Ser.). (ENG., Illus.). 32p. (J). (gr. 1-3). 29.32 *(978-1-4677-9471-8(6)*, ecae22a8-b56a-40b0-a513-14d4a1fcad88, Lerner Pubns.) Lerner Publishing Group.
Brainard, Jason. Life As a Vegetarian: Eating Without Meat, 1 vol. annot. ed. 2019. (Nutrition & Health Ser.). (ENG.). 104p. (gr. 7-7). pap. 20.99 *(978-1-5345-6885-3(9)*, ba10dc38-74ea-4961-b66e-6d51f4a8f697); lib. bdg. 41.03 *(978-1-5345-6872-3(7)*, bdc158d9-bd38-4caa-b062-319a5d507de4) Greenhaven Publishing LLC. (Lucent Pr.).
Cornell, Kari. Terrific Veggies on the Side. Cohen, Brie, photos by. 2013. (You're the Chef Ser.). (ENG., Illus.). 32p. (gr. 3-5). lib. bdg. 26.60 *(978-0-7613-6640-9(7)*, Millbrook Pr.) Lerner Publishing Group.
DeMaris, Sheri-Lynn. Macro Magic for Kids & Parents: Taking the Mystery Out of Macrobiotic Cooking. (J). 2010. *(978-89-21-42450-1(4))* 2009. *(978-1-892142-45-0(7))* Cedar Tree Bks.
Francis, Amy, ed. Vegetarianism, 1 vol. 2015. (Current Controversies Ser.). (ENG.). 232p. (gr. 10-12). 48.03 *(978-0-7377-7227-2(1)*, dd3931db-8cb8-4a28-b8a7-744798d8534e, Greenhaven Publishing) Greenhaven Publishing LLC.
Gifford, Clive & Meldrum, Jacqueline. Living on the Veg: A Kids' Guide to Life Without Meat. 2019. (ENG., Illus.). 80p. (J). 19.99 *(978-1-63198-429-7(2)*, 84297) Free Spirit Publishing Inc.
Gillard, Arthur, ed. Vegetarianism, 1 vol. 2014. (Issues That Concern You Ser.). (ENG., Illus.). 104p. (gr. 7-10). lib. bdg. 43.63 *(978-0-7377-6936-4(X)*, 3af58a4c-a9be-4478-8d6f-39d943a1fc82, Greenhaven Publishing) Greenhaven Publishing LLC.
Green, Erica. An Ethical Diet, 1 vol. 2019. (Ethical Living Ser.). (ENG., Illus.). 64p. (J). (gr. 6-6). 36.13 *(978-1-5081-8052-4(0)*, 4a191024-bc67-4750-95be-a702be019922) Rosen Publishing Group, Inc., The.
Langely, Andrew. Should We Eat Animals? 2007. (What Do You Think? Ser.). (Illus.). 56p. (J). pap. 9.49 *(978-1-4329-0369-5(1))* Heinemann.
Larson, Jennifer S. Delicious Vegetarian Main Dishes. Cohen, Brie, photos by. 2013. (You're the Chef Ser.). (ENG., Illus.). 32p. (gr. 3-5). lib. bdg. 26.60 *(978-0-7613-6635-5(0)*, Millbrook Pr.) Lerner Publishing Group.
Martin, Claudia. Vegetarian Food, 1 vol. 2018. (Cooking Skills Ser.). (ENG.). 48p. (gr. 5-5). pap. 12.70 *(978-1-9785-0668-8(6)*, d7b6bad3-0f29-405d-aac8-3ca3a486ce67); lib. bdg. 29.60 *(978-1-9785-0641-1(4)*, b4a71fd2-1b53-4e4b-b1b0-65dd93aae5f5) Enslow Publishing, LLC.
Rau, Dana Meachen. Going Vegan: A Healthy Guide to Making the Switch, 1 vol. 2012. (Food Revolution Ser.). (ENG.). 64p. (J). (gr. 6-9). lib. bdg. 35.32 *(978-0-7565-4521-5(8)*, 117114, Compass Point Bks.) Capstone.
—Going Vegetarian: A Healthy Guide to Making the Switch, 1 vol. 2012. (Food Revolution Ser.). (ENG., Illus.). 64p. (J). (gr. 6-9). 35.32 *(978-0-7565-4522-2(6)*, 117115); pap. 9.10 *(978-0-7565-4530-7(7)*, 118363) Capstone. (Compass Point Bks.).
El Reino Vegetal, 6 vols., Vol. 2. (Explorers. Exploradores Nonfiction Sets Ser.). (SPA.). 32p. (gr. 3-6). 44.95 *(978-0-7699-0641-6(9))* Shortland Pubns. (U. S. A.) Inc.
Roth, Ruby. That's Why We Don't Eat Animals: A Book about Vegans, Vegetarians, & All Living Things. Roth, Ruby, illus. 2009. (Illus.). 48p. (J). (gr. 1-4). 16.95 *(978-1-55643-785-4(4))* North Atlantic Bks.
—V Is for Vegan: The ABCs of Being Kind. Roth, Ruby, illus. 2013. (Illus.). 32p. (J). (gr. -1-2). 12.95 *(978-1-58394-649-7(7))* North Atlantic Bks.
—Vegan Is Love: Having Heart & Taking Action. Roth, Ruby, illus. 2012. (Illus.). 44p. (J). (gr. 2-5). 16.95 *(978-1-58394-354-0(4))* North Atlantic Bks.

VEHICLES

Abbot, Henry. I Want to Drive a Police Car, 1 vol. 2016. (At the Wheel Ser.). (ENG.). 24p. (J). (gr. 1-1). 25.27 *(978-1-4994-2943-5(6)*, e2408962-32d0-4781-89fd-eb600d12ad55); pap. 9.25 *(978-1-4994-2664-9(X)*, 9e4649b0-0590-4d8f-8d3e-510224cce694) Rosen Publishing Group, Inc., The. (PowerKids Pr.).
Adamson, Thomas K. Garbage Trucks. 2017. (Mighty Machines in Action Ser.). (ENG., Illus.). 24p. (J). (gr. k-3). lib. bdg. 26.95 *(978-1-62617-605-8(1)*, Blastoff! Readers) Bellwether Media.
—Hot Rods. 2018. (Full Throttle Ser.). (ENG., Illus.). 24p. (J). (gr. 3-7). lib. bdg. 26.95 *(978-1-62617-872-4(0)*, Epic Bks.) Bellwether Media.
Allan, John. Let's Look at Monster Machines. 2019. (Illus.). 24p. (J). *(978-1-912108-16-9(X))*; (ENG., (gr. 1-3). lib. bdg. 26.65 *(978-1-5415-5531-0(7)*, e7a9cc92-4539-4b0e-a235-eb457f604693, Hungry Tomato (r)) Lerner Publishing Group.
Allen, Kathy. Let's Draw Vehicles with Crayola (r) ! 2018. (Let's Draw with Crayola (r) ! Ser.). (ENG., Illus.). 32p. (J). (gr. -1-3). pap. 6.99 *(978-1-5415-1169-9(7)*, 9b34d722-0197-40b7-814c-29cf726d5990, Lerner Pubns.) Lerner Publishing Group.
Amson-Bradshaw, Georgia. Vehicles. 2018. (Adventures in STEAM Ser.). (ENG., Illus.). 48p. (J). (gr. 3-6). lib. bdg. 27.99 *(978-1-5435-3289-0(6)*, 138832, Capstone Pr.) Capstone.
Andrus, Aubre. National Geographic Readers: Let's Go! (Prereader) 2019. (Readers Ser.). (Illus.). 24p. (J). (gr. -1-k). pap. 4.99 *(978-1-4263-3335-4(8))*; (ENG., lib. bdg. 14.90 *(978-1-4263-3336-1(6))* Disney Publishing Worldwide. (National Geographic Kids).
Appleby, Alex. Dinosaurs on the Go, 1 vol. 2013. (Dinosaur School Ser.). 24p. (J). (gr. k-k). (ENG.). pap. 9.15 *(978-1-4339-9062-5(8)*, ad5f4f50-705a-44c8-8b50-2b57f2abc8ad); pap. 48.90 *(978-1-4339-9063-2(6))*; (ENG., Illus.). lib. bdg. 25.27 *(978-1-4339-9061-8(X)*, fa7ee29b-2ae5-4ecd-bb99-648c3c38e0bf) Stevens, Gareth Publishing LLLP.
Armadillo. Things That Go! Tractors Trucks Trains Planes Helicopters Balloons Ships Ferries Boats Bicycles Motorcycles Cars. 2016. (Illus.). 48p. (J). (gr. -1-12). bds. 9.99 *(978-1-86147-693-7(0)*, Armadillo) Anness Publishing GBR. Dist: National Bk. Network.
Awa, Solomon. How to Build an Iglu & a Qamutiik: Inuit Tools & Techniques, 1 vol. Breithaupt, Andrew, illus. 2013. (ENG & IKU.). 32p. (J). (gr. 4-8). 12.95 *(978-1-927095-31-7(X))* Inhabit Media Inc. CAN. Dist: Consortium Bk. Sales & Distribution.
Baer, Edith. This Is the Way We Go to School. 2014. 17.00 *(978-1-63419-734-2(8))* Perfection Learning Corp.
Barlow, Amanda. Things That Go. 2004. (Baby Board Bks.). (ENG., Illus.). 1p. (J). (gr. -1-18). bds. 4.99 *(978-0-7460-4101-7(2))* EDC Publishing.
Basic Vehicles. 2005. (Transportation Ser.). (YA). (gr. k-3). 118.80 *(978-0-7368-4191-7(1)*, Pebble) Capstone.
Beck, Isabel L., et al. Trophies Kindergarten: A Big, Big Van. 2003. (Trophies Ser.). (gr. k-6). 13.80 *(978-0-15-329546-1(5))* Harcourt Schl. Pubs.
Bell, Samantha. Farm Quad. 2016. (21st Century Basic Skills Library: Welcome to the Farm Ser.). (ENG., Illus.). 24p. (J). (gr. k-3). 26.35 *(978-1-63471-040-4(1)*, 208240) Cherry Lake Publishing.
—Four-Wheel Drive Utility Tractor. 2016. (21st Century Basic Skills Library: Welcome to the Farm Ser.). (ENG., Illus.). 24p. (J). (gr. k-3). 26.35 *(978-1-63471-038-1(X)*, 208232) Cherry Lake Publishing.
Best, B. J. Ambulances. 2017. (Riding to the Rescue! Ser.). (Illus.). 24p. (J). (gr. 1-1). pap. 49.32 *(978-1-5026-2553-3(9))* Cavendish Square Publishing LLC.
—Police Cars. 2017. (Riding to the Rescue! Ser.). 24p. (gr. 1-1). pap. 49.32 *(978-1-5026-2555-7(5))* Cavendish Square Publishing LLC.
Bidder, Jane. Inventions We Use to Go Places, 1 vol. 2006. (Everyday Inventions Ser.). (ENG., Illus.). 32p. (gr. 2-4). lib. bdg. 28.67 *(978-0-8368-6901-9(X)*, cebb70a3-7b82-4bb0-9b3b-6f604dc2316e, Gareth Stevens Learning Library) Stevens, Gareth Publishing LLLP.
Biesty, Stephen. Stephen Biesty's Incredible Cross-Sections. 25th ed. 2019. (DK Stephen Biesty Cross-Sections Ser.). (ENG., Illus.). 48p. (J). (gr. 4-7). 19.99 *(978-1-4654-8389-8(6)*, DK Children) Dorling Kindersley Publishing, Inc.
Biggs, Brian. Everything Goes: Blue Bus, Red Balloon: a Book of Colors. Biggs, Brian, illus. 2013. (ENG., Illus.). 24p. (J). (gr. -1 — 1). bds. 7.99 *(978-0-06-195814-4(X)*, Balzer & Bray) HarperCollins Pubs.
Blaine, Victor. My Scooter, 1 vol. 2014. (Watch Me Go! Ser.). (ENG.). 24p. (J). (gr. 1-2). lib. bdg. 25.27 *(978-1-4994-0253-7(8)*, 7ba98b1c-4b18-4f58-875c-70b5808a0b35, PowerKids Pr.) Rosen Publishing Group, Inc., The.
—My Sled, 1 vol. 2014. (Watch Me Go! Ser.). (ENG., Illus.). 24p. (J). (gr. 1-2). lib. bdg. 25.27 *(978-1-4994-0249-0(X)*, 61d1ef7f-3ca8-4f56-a6fe-7578bb972bac, PowerKids Pr.) Rosen Publishing Group, Inc., The.
Boothroyd, Jennifer. From the Model T to Hybrid Cars: How Transportation Has Changed. 2011. (Comparing Past & Present Ser.). pap. 45.32 *(978-0-7613-8392-5(1))*; pap. 7.95 *(978-0-7613-7837-2(5))* Lerner Publishing Group.
Brooks, Felicity. Usborne Lift & Look Emergency Vehicles. Van Wyk, Hanri, illus. 2007. (Lift & Look Board Bks.). 10p. (J). (gr. -1-k). bds. 9.99 *(978-0-7945-1596-6(7)*, Usborne) EDC Publishing.
Bulleman, Curtis David & Coloring Books Staff. Car Crazy! 2011. (Dover 3-D Coloring Book Ser.). (ENG., Illus.). 32p. (J). (gr. 2-6). 5.99 *(978-0-486-48418-1(1))* Dover Pubns., Inc.
Burch, Lynda S. Wicky Wacky Things that Go! Emergency Vehicles. Burch, Lynda S., photos by. 2004. (Illus.). 30p. (J). E-Book 9.95 incl. cd-rom *(978-1-933090-13-9(8))* Guardian Angel Publishing, Inc.
Chancellor, Deborah. Fire Rescue. 2013. (Emergency Vehicles Ser.). 24p. (gr. k-3). 28.50 *(978-1-59920-889-3(X))* Black Rabbit Bks.
—Police Rescue. 2013. (Emergency Vehicles Ser.). (Illus.). 24p. (gr. k-3). lib. bdg. 28.50 *(978-1-59920-890-9(3))* Black Rabbit Bks.
Chandler, Matthew Allan. The Tech Behind off-Road Vehicles. 2019. (Tech on Wheels Ser.). (ENG., Illus.). 32p. (J). (gr. 3-9). lib. bdg. 28.65 *(978-1-5435-7422-7(X)*, 140710) Capstone.
Channing, Margot. On the Go. Claude, Jean, illus. 2017. (First Words & Pictures Ser.). (ENG.). 14p. (J). (gr. -1 — 1). bds. 9.99 *(978-1-68152-201-2(2)*, 14731) Amicus.
Child's Play. City. Cocoretto, illus. 2017. (Wheels at Work (US Edition) Ser.: 4). (ENG.). 12p. (J). bds. *(978-1-78628-081-7(7))* Child's Play International Ltd.
—Construction. Cocoretto, illus. 2017. (Wheels at Work (US Edition) Ser.: 4). (ENG.). 12p. (J). bds. *(978-1-78628-083-1(3))* Child's Play International Ltd.
—Emergency. Cocoretto, illus. alt. ed. 2017. (Wheels at Work (US Edition) Ser.: 4). (ENG.). 12p. (J). bds. *(978-1-78628-080-0(9))* Child's Play International Ltd.
—Farm. Cocoretto, illus. 2017. (Wheels at Work (US Edition) Ser.: 4). (ENG.). 12p. (J). bds. *(978-1-78628-082-4(5))* Child's Play International Ltd.
Community Vehicles. 2005. (Transportation Ser.). (YA). (gr. k-3). 118.80 *(978-0-7368-4192-4(X)*, Pebble) Capstone.
Contraire, Bastien. Vehicles: Hide & Sneak. 2017. (ENG., Illus.). 26p. (gr. -1 — 1). bds. 9.95 *(978-0-7148-7516-3(3))* Phaidon Pr., Inc.
Dale, Jay. Ways We Go to School. 2012. (Engage Literacy Green Ser.). (ENG.). 16p. (J). (gr. k-2). pap. 36.94 *(978-1-4296-9021-8(6)*, 18403, Capstone Pr.) Capstone.
Dale, Jay & Scott, Kay. Ways We Go to School, 1 vol. 2012. (Engage Literacy Green Ser.). (ENG.). 16p. (J). (gr. k-2). pap. 6.99 *(978-1-4296-9020-1(8)*, 120020, Capstone Pr.) Capstone.
David, Jack. ATVs. 2008. (Cool Rides Ser.). (ENG., Illus.). 24p. (J). (gr. 3-7). lib. bdg. 26.95 *(978-1-60014-146-1(3))* Bellwether Media.
de Seve, Karen. National Geographic Little Kids First Big Book of Things That Go. 2017. (National Geographic Little Kids First Big Bks.). (Illus.). 128p. (J). (gr. -1-k). 14.99 *(978-1-4263-2804-6(4))*; (ENG., lib. bdg. 24.90 *(978-1-4263-2805-3(2))* Disney Publishing Worldwide. (National Geographic Kids).
DeGregorio, Chieri & DeGregorio, Steve. Vehicles. 2019. (Kids' Picture Show Ser.). (Illus.). 16p. (J). (-k). bds. 7.99 *(978-1-5247-9076-9(1)*, Penguin Workshop) Penguin Young Readers Group.
Deneux, Xavier. TouchThinkLearn: Vehicles: (Board Books for Baby Learners, Touch Feel Books for Children) 2015. (Touch Think Learn Ser.). (ENG., Illus.). 22p. (J). (gr. -1 — 1). bds. 16.99 *(978-1-4521-4516-7(4))* Chronicle Bks. LLC.
Dieker, Wendy Strobel. Los Camiones de Basura. 2018. (Máquinas Poderosas Ser.). (SPA.). 16p. (J). (gr. -1-2). lib. bdg. *(978-1-68151-606-6(3)*, 15214) Amicus.
—Los Camiones de Remolque. 2018. (Máquinas Poderosas Ser.). (SPA.). 16p. (J). (gr. -1-2). *(978-1-68151-609-7(8)*, 15217) Amicus.
—Tow Trucks. 2018. (Spot Mighty Machines Ser.). (ENG.). 16p. (J). (gr. -1-2). pap. 7.99 *(978-1-68152-297-5(7)*, 14987); lib. bdg. *(978-1-68151-377-5(3)*, 14981) Amicus.
Dinmont, Kerry. Ambulancias en Acción (Ambulances on the Go) 2017. (Bumba Books (r) en Español — Máquinas en Acción (Machines That Go) Ser.). (SPA., Illus.). 24p. (J). (gr. -1-1). 26.65 *(978-1-5124-2876-6(0)*, 57c2c71a-a178-4839-807e-835d7990e97c, Ediciones Lerner) Lerner Publishing Group.
Dittmer, Lori. The Future of Transportation. 2012. (What's Next? Ser.). (Illus.). 48p. (J). (gr. 5-12). 23.95 *(978-1-60818-224-4(X)*, Creative Education) Creative Co., The.
DK. Baby Touch & Feel: Things That Go. 2009. (Baby Touch & Feel Ser.). (ENG., Illus.). 14p. (J). (gr. -1 — 1). bds. 7.99 *(978-0-7566-5841-0(1)*, DK Children) Dorling Kindersley Publishing, Inc.
—The Big Book of Things That Go. 2016. (DK Big Bks.). (ENG., Illus.). 32p. (J). (gr. k-4). 17.99 *(978-1-4654-4509-4(9)*, DK Children) Dorling Kindersley Publishing, Inc.
—Cars, Trains, Ships, & Planes: A Visual Encyclopedia of Every Vehicle. 2015. (DK Our World in Pictures Ser.). (ENG., Illus.). 256p. (J). (gr. 4-7). 24.99 *(978-1-4654-3805-8(X)*, DK Children) Dorling Kindersley Publishing, Inc.
—My First Touch & Feel Picture Cards: Things That Go. 2018. (My First Board Bks.). (ENG.). 17p. (J). (— 1). 9.99 *(978-1-4654-6812-3(9)*, DK Children) Dorling Kindersley Publishing, Inc.
Doman, Mary Kate. Rescue Vehicles, 1 vol. 2011. (All about Big Machines Ser.). (ENG., Illus.). 24p. (gr. -1-1). pap. 10.35 *(978-1-59845-244-0(4)*, d8efe931-e2d7-4553-90a1-a565d3bb8419); lib. bdg. 25.27 *(978-0-7660-3934-6(X)*, 7f3e809f-b811-4dcd-91d3-41452b961477) Enslow Publishing, LLC. (Enslow Publishing).
Dorling Kindersley Publishing Staff. Emergency Vehicles. 2009. (See How They Go! Ser.). (ENG.). 20p. (J). (gr. -1-3). 16.19 *(978-0-7566-5230-2(8))* Dorling Kindersley Publishing, Inc.
Duffield, Katy. Emergency Vehicles. 2018. (My World Ser.). (ENG., Illus.). 16p. (gr. -1-2). lib. bdg. 28.50 *(978-1-64156-200-3(5)*, 9781641562003) Rourke Educational Media.
duopress labs. Go, New York, Go! Cleland, Josh, illus. 2018. (ENG.). 22p. (J). (gr. -1-k). bds. 9.99 *(978-1-946064-97-4(1)*, 806497) Duo Pr. LLC.
—Zoom! Beep! Vroom! Busy Cities. Cleland, Josh, illus. 2018. 22p. (J). (gr. -1 — 1). bds. 9.95 *(978-1-947458-27-7(2)*, 805827) Duo Pr. LLC.
Ebel, Julia Taylor, Jr. Hansi & the Ice Man. Canter, Idalia, illus. 2014. 32p. (YA). lib. bdg. 19.95 *(978-1-933251-81-3(6))* Parkway Pubs., Inc.
Enz, Tammy. The Science Behind Batman's Ground Vehicles. Vecchio, Luciano, illus. 2016. (Science Behind Batman Ser.). (ENG.). 24p. (J). (gr. 1-3). lib. bdg. 27.99 *(978-1-5157-2034-8(9)*, 132666, Stone Arch Bks.) Capstone.
Felix, Rebecca. Heavy, Heavier, & Heaviest. 2014. (Size It Up Ser.). (ENG., Illus.). 16p. (J). (gr. k-2). lib. bdg. 25.65 *(978-1-60753-576-8(9)*, 15837) Amicus.
Fortuna, Lois. Ambulances, 1 vol. 2016. (To the Rescue! Ser.). (ENG.). 24p. (J). (gr. k-k). 24.27 *(978-1-4824-4659-3(6)*, f3f39f45-2b63-404a-ad05-e406083ab9f7) Stevens, Gareth Publishing LLLP.
—Police Cars, 1 vol. 2016. (To the Rescue! Ser.). (ENG., Illus.). 24p. (J). (gr. k-k). lib. bdg. 24.27 *(978-1-4824-4661-6(8)*, 94192ca2-a047-4c16-9c21-00438ad4a7f4) Stevens, Gareth Publishing LLLP.
—Rescue Helicopters, 1 vol. 2016. (To the Rescue! Ser.). (ENG.). 24p. (J). (gr. k-k). pap. 9.15 *(978-1-4824-4663-0(4)*, d18ab2e1-72be-44aa-80fa-03319240c075) Stevens, Gareth Publishing LLLP.
—Snowmobiles, 1 vol. 2016. (To the Rescue! Ser.). (ENG.). 24p. (J). (gr. k-k). pap. 9.15 *(978-1-4824-4665-4(0)*, 1a7182fa-3c27-450c-8509-6ec3713ab631) Stevens, Gareth Publishing LLLP.
Freeman, Marcia S. Police Cars [Scholastic]. 2009. (Community Vehicles Ser.). 24p. (gr. k-1). pap. 0.36 *(978-1-4296-4244-6(0)*, Pebble) Capstone.
Gabrielson, Curt. Kinetic Contraptions: Build a Hovercraft, Airboat, & More with a Hobby Motor. 2010. (ENG., Illus.). 192p. (J). (gr. 7-18). pap. 18.99 *(978-1-55652-957-3(0))* Chicago Review Pr., Inc.
Galvin, Laura Gates. First Look at Rescue Vehicles. Eaddy, Susan, illus. 2009. (ENG.). 16p. (J). (gr. -1-k). 6.95 *(978-1-60727-106-2(0))*; bds. 6.95 *(978-1-60727-093-5(5))* Soundprints.
Giant Vehicles, 4 vols. 2005. (Giant Vehicles Ser.). (ENG.). 24p. (gr. 2-4). lib. bdg. 51.34 *(978-0-8368-4909-7(4)*, 30c6dacc-743e-43f6-a192-74813d46331c, Gareth Stevens Learning Library) Stevens, Gareth Publishing LLLP.
Gibbons, Gail. Transportation! How People Get Around. 2019. (Illus.). 32p. (J). (gr. -1-3). pap. 8.99 *(978-0-8234-4188-4(1))* Holiday Hse., Inc.
Gordon, Sharon. Fast, Slow, 1 vol. (Just the Opposite Ser.). (ENG.). 24p. (gr. k-1). 2008. pap. 9.23 *(978-0-7614-3281-4(7)*, f218e495-952f-454b-bcd1-27ce65deb44a) 2003. (Illus.). lib. bdg. 25.50 *(978-0-7614-1570-1(X)*, 26f23ffd-f5e2-4020-8fcb-f4b5419afa79, Cavendish Square) Cavendish Square Publishing LLC.
—Rapido, Lento / Fast, Slow, 1 vol. 2008. (Exactamente lo Opuesto / Just the Opposite Ser.). (ENG & SPA., Illus.). 24p. (gr. k-1). lib. bdg. 25.50 *(978-0-7614-2447-5(4)*, c9a1db90-b7b1-4bb7-8403-86a7dd0b0861) Cavendish Square Publishing LLC.
—Rapido, Lento (Fast, Slow), 1 vol. 2008. (Exactamente lo Opuesto (Just the Opposite) Ser.). (SPA., Illus.). 24p. (gr. k-1). lib. bdg. 25.50 *(978-0-7614-2367-6(2)*, 8e3a2a49-9830-474b-97b7-88c66e82fba2) Cavendish Square Publishing LLC.
Gould, Robert. Rescue Vehicles. Gould, Robert, photos by. 2005. (Big Stuff Ser.). (ENG., Illus.). 16p. (J). bds. 7.95 *(978-1-929945-51-1(5))* Big Guy Bks., Inc.
Graham, Buck. My First Big Book of Questions & Answers: Things That Go. 2005. (Illus.). 10p. bds. 9.98 *(978-0-7853-7227-1(X)*, 7171500) Publications International, Ltd.
Graham, Ian. Emergency! 2006. (QEB Machines at Work Ser.). (Illus.). 36p. (J). lib. bdg. 16.95 *(978-1-59566-188-3(3))* QEB Publishing Inc.
Graubart, Norman D. Ambulances, 1 vol. 2014. (Giants on the Road Ser.). (ENG.). 24p. (J). (gr. 1-2). lib. bdg. 25.27 *(978-1-4994-0029-8(2)*, 748ecfdd-9c8b-410e-88f5-4f9d2ffdea5c, PowerKids Pr.) Rosen Publishing Group, Inc., The.
Green, Rod. Giant Vehicles. Biesty, Stephen, illus. 2014. (Inside Vehicles Ser.). (ENG.). 16p. (J). (gr. k-4). 15.99 *(978-0-7636-7404-5(4)*, Templar) Candlewick Pr.
Green, Sara. On-Screen Vehicles. 2019. (Movie Magic Ser.). (ENG., Illus.). 32p. (J). (gr. 3-8). lib. bdg. 27.95 *(978-1-64487-044-0(4)*, Blastoff! Discovery) Bellwether Media.
Hansen, Grace. Maquinas Asombrosas! (Machines to Thrill You!) 2016. (Ver para Creer (Seeing Is Believing) Ser.). (SPA., Illus.). 24p. (J). (gr. -1-2). lib. bdg. 32.79 *(978-1-68080-769-1(2)*, 22700, Abdo Kids) ABDO Publishing Co.
Harrison, Paul. Speed Machines. 2009. (Up Close Ser.). 24p. (gr. 3-3). 47.90 *(978-1-60854-705-0(1)*, PowerKids Pr.) Rosen Publishing Group, Inc., The.
Haughom, Lisa, illus. Things That Go! 2010. 16p. (J). *(978-1-58865-542-4(3))* Kidsbooks, LLC.
Hearst, Michael. Unconventional Vehicles: Forty-Five of the Strangest Cars, Trains, Planes, Submersibles, Dirigibles, & Rockets EVER. Jenssen, Hans, illus. 2021. (ENG.). 104p. (J). (gr. 3-7). 19.99 *(978-1-4521-7286-6(2))* Chronicle Bks. LLC.

Hinkler Books, creator. 101 First Words: Things That Go. 2011. (101 First Words Ser.). (Illus.). 16p. (J). (gr. -1). bds. 7.99 (978-1-74184-818-2(0)) Hinkler Bks. Pty, Ltd. AUS. Dist: Ideals Pubns.

Horne, Jane. Rough & Tough Emergency. 2008. 12p. (978-1-84610-414-5(9)) Make Believe Ideas.

Horsepower [Really Good Stuff]. 2010. (Horsepower Ser.). 32p. pap. 79.50 (978-1-4296-5361-9(2), Capstone Pr.) Capstone.

Imperato, Teresa. Speed Machines: A Pop-up Book with Moving Gears. Robinson, Keith, illus. 2005. 8p. (J). 14.95 (978-1-58117-323-9(7), Intervisual/Piggy Toes) Bendon, Inc.

Innovative Kids Staff, creator. Vehicles. 2012. (ENG., Illus.). 1p. (J). (gr. -1 — 1). 10.99 (978-1-60169-224-5(2)) Innovative Kids.

Ives, Rob. Amazing Origami Vehicles. 2019. (Amazing Origami Ser.). (ENG., Illus.). 32p. (J). (gr. 3-6). 27.99 (978-1-5415-0125-6(X), 1ea8c9f2-8daa-4666-ae38-6729383d770e, Hungry Tomato (r)) Lerner Publishing Group.

—Build Your Own Land Vehicles. 2018. (Makerspace Models Ser.). (ENG., Illus.). 32p. (J). (gr. 3-6). lib. bdg. 27.99 (978-1-5124-5968-5(2), 8d8e67e1-dd22-4679-bdea-3614590c5cf5, Hungry Tomato (r)) Lerner Publishing Group.

Jonath, Leslie & Nash, Josh. On the Go: A Mini AniMotion Book. 2010. (ENG., Illus.). 12p. (J). (gr. -1). 9.99 (978-0-7407-9800-9(6)) Andrews McMeel Publishing.

Joyce, Bridget & Furman, Eric. Tonka Rescue Trucks! Dean Kleven Studios & Finley, Shawn, illus. 2007. (Fold & Go Vehicles Ser.). 15.98 (978-1-4127-2981-9(5)) Publications International, Ltd.

Jugran, Jan. Hugs. Larranaga, Ana Martin, illus. 2007. (ENG.). 12p. (J). (gr. -1 — 1). 9.99 (978-1-58476-620-9(4), IKIDS) Innovative Kids.

Kalman, Bobbie. Getting from Place to Place in My Community. 2017. (My World Ser.). (Illus.). 24p. (J). (gr. 1-1). (978-0-7787-9596-4(9)); pap. (978-0-7787-9604-6(3)) Crabtree Publishing Co.

Kenney, Karen Latchana. What Makes Vehicles Safer? 2015. (Engineering Keeps Us Safe Ser.). (ENG., Illus.). 32p. (J). (gr. 4-6). E-Book 39.99 (978-1-4677-8652-2(7), Lerner Pubns.) Lerner Publishing Group.

Knight, M. J. Why Should I Walk More Often? 2009. (One Small Step Ser.). (YA). (gr. 2-5). 28.50 (978-1-59920-268-6(9)) Black Rabbit Bks.

Knight M J. Why Should I Walk More Often? 2009. (One Small Step Ser.). (ENG., Illus.). 32p. (J). (gr. -1-3). pap. (978-1-897563-50-2(7)) Saunders Bk. Co.

Kramer, Nash. What Goes Fastest? 2012. (Level B Ser.). (ENG., Illus.). 16p. (J). (gr. k-2). pap. 7.95 (978-1-927136-19-5(9), 19421) RiverStream Publishing.

Lake, Joss. The Evolution of Transportation Technology, 1 vol. 2018. (Evolving Technology Ser.). (ENG.). 64p. (gr. 6-7). lib. bdg. 34.29 (978-1-5383-0287-3(X), fe1e2690-75e4-45e2-8e0c-c82ce7519171, Britannica Educational Publishing) Rosen Publishing Group, Inc., The.

Learning Fun, Early & Priddy, Roger. Things That Go. 2010. (ENG., Illus.). 20p. (J). bds. (978-1-84915-141-2(5), Priddy Bks.) St. Martin's Pr.

Less, Emma. Mechanics. 2018. (Real-Life Superheroes Ser.). (ENG.). 16p. (J). (gr. k-2). pap. 7.99 (978-1-68152-282-1(9), 14918) Amicus.

Life in the Fast Lane, 14 vols. 2014. (Life in the Fast Lane Ser.). (ENG.). 48p. (J). (gr. 4-4). 231.49 (978-1-62713-146-9(9), 7301c78e-7001-4c1c-8efc-11d560bfba57, Cavendish Square) Cavendish Square Publishing LLC.

Lindeen, Mary. Snowplows. 2007. (Mighty Machines Ser.). (ENG., Illus.). 24p. (J). (gr. k-3). lib. bdg. 26.95 (978-1-60014-120-1(X)) Bellwether Media.

Litchfield, J. & Brooks, F. Rescue Vehicles. 2004. (ENG., Illus.). 10p. (J). bds. 4.99 (978-0-7945-0589-9(9)) EDC Publishing.

Loh-Hagan, Virginia. Parade Float Designer. 2015. (Odd Jobs Ser.). (ENG., Illus.). 32p. (J). (gr. 4-8). 32.07 (978-1-63470-027-6(9), 206764) Cherry Lake Publishing.

Machines in Motion, 12 vols. 2013. (Machines in Motion Ser.). 48p. (J). (gr. 3-3). (ENG.). 207.66 (978-1-4339-9685-6(5), 9b3e3af5-cdfa-48b4-973c-a17669d5c953); pap. 84.30 (978-1-4339-9817-1(3)); pap. 505.80 (978-1-4339-9818-8(1)) Stevens, Gareth Publishing LLLP.

MacNeill, Scott. How Things Work Vehicles - Motorcycle. 2013. (Dover Science for Kids Coloring Bks.). (ENG.). 48p. (J). (gr. 3-8). pap. 4.99 (978-0-486-49221-6(4), 492214) Dover Pubns., Inc.

Mahaney, Ian F. Extreme off-Road Vehicles, 1 vol. 2015. (Extreme Machines Ser.). (ENG.). 32p. (J). (gr. 3-4). pap. 11.00 (978-1-4994-1185-0(5), 0583d631-36ee-4ab9-a4b3-e00e1d171be6, PowerKids Pr.) Rosen Publishing Group, Inc., The.

—Extreme Snow Vehicles, 1 vol. 2015. (Extreme Machines Ser.). (ENG.). 32p. (J). (gr. 3-4). pap. 11.00 (978-1-4994-1187-4(1), bffea800-780f-46a9-ab65-b5661825c245, PowerKids Pr.) Rosen Publishing Group, Inc., The.

—Extreme Unmanned Vehicles, 1 vol. 2015. (Extreme Machines Ser.). (ENG.). 32p. (J). (gr. 3-4). pap. 11.00 (978-1-4994-1189-8(8), 0635b97c-7a59-46aa-b52a-6b8e4d9b0bab, PowerKids Pr.) Rosen Publishing Group, Inc., The.

Manolis, Kay. Police Cars. 2008. (Mighty Machines Ser.). (ENG., Illus.). 24p. (J). (gr. k-3). lib. bdg. 26.95 (978-1-60014-179-9(X)) Bellwether Media.

Marshall, Jane. Rescue Vehicles. 2013. (Wild Rides Ser.). 32p. (gr. 2-4). (978-1-84898-620-6(3), TickTock Books) Octopus Publishing Group.

Martin, Claudia. My Little Book of Rescue Vehicles. 2016. (Illus.). 64p. (J). (978-1-4351-6335-5(4)) Barnes & Noble, Inc.

Marx, Mandy R. ATVs. 2018. (Horsepower Ser.). (ENG., Illus.). 32p. (J). (gr. 3-9). pap. 7.95 (978-1-5435-2475-8(3), 137983); lib. bdg. 27.32 (978-1-5435-2467-3(2), 137975) Capstone. (Capstone Pr.).

Masters, Neil. Working Vehicles Coloring Book. 2013. (ENG.). 32p. 11.98 (978-1-62884-655-3(0), Baby Professor (Education Kids)) Speedy Publishing LLC.

Max and Sid, illus. My First Vehicles. 2016. (My First Ser.). (ENG.). 12p. (J). (gr. -1 — 1). bds. 5.99 (978-1-4998-0188-0(2)) Little Bee Books Inc.

Maynard, Chris. I Wonder Why Planes Have Wings: And Other Questions about Transportation. 2012. (I Wonder Why Ser.). (ENG., Illus.). 32p. (J). (gr. k-3). pap. 6.99 (978-0-7534-6703-9(8), 900076420, Kingfisher) Roaring Brook Pr.

McDonnell, Rory. Matemáticas con Ruedas / Math with Wheels, 1 vol. de la Vega, Eida, tr. 2016. (¡Matemáticas en Todas Partes! / Math Is Everywhere! Ser.). (ENG & SPA.). 24p. (gr. k-k). lib. bdg. 24.27 (978-1-4824-5218-1(9), 7ca60409-5b23-4987-9b1c-f3729bb494cf) Stevens, Gareth Publishing LLLP.

Meachen Rau, Dana. ¡a Conducir! (Driving), 1 vol. 2008. (En Movimiento (on the Move) Ser.). (SPA., Illus.). 32p. (gr. k-1). lib. bdg. 25.50 (978-0-7614-2422-2(9), d562d517-0bcb-4f77-9d9e-55c736a736ce) Cavendish Square Publishing LLC.

Meister, Cari. Tow Trucks. 2013. (ENG., Illus.). 24p. (J). lib. bdg. 25.65 (978-1-62031-048-9(1)) Jump! Inc.

Mighty Machines. Date not set. (Illus.). (J). 48p. 5.98 (978-1-4054-0207-1(5)); 256p. (978-1-4054-1538-5(X)) Parragon, Inc.

Mighty Machines: A Lego Adventure in the Real World. 2017. (Illus.). 32p. (J). (978-1-5182-4494-0(7)) Scholastic, Inc.

The Mighty World of Emergency Vehicles. 2016. (Illus.). 46p. (J). (978-1-68188-098-3(9)) Fog City Pr.

Milet Publishing Staff. My First Bilingual Book - Vehicles, 1 vol. 2014. (My First Bilingual Book Ser.). (ENG., Illus.). 20p. (J). (— 1). bds. 7.99 (978-1-84059-933-6(2)); bds. 8.99 (978-1-84059-937-4(5)); bds. 8.99 (978-1-84059-924-4(3)); bds. 7.99 (978-1-84059-925-1(1)); bds. 7.99 (978-1-84059-935-0(9)); bds. 7.99 (978-1-84059-929-9(4)) Milet Publishing.

—My First Bilingual Book - Vehicles (English-Russian), 1 vol. 2014. (My First Bilingual Book Ser.). (ENG., Illus.). 20p. (J). (— 1). bds. 7.99 (978-1-84059-932-9(4)) Milet Publishing.

—Vehicles, 1 vol. 2014. (My First Bilingual Book Ser.). (ENG & ITA., Illus.). 20p. (J). (— 1). bds. 7.99 (978-1-84059-928-2(6)); bds. 7.99 (978-1-84059-934-3(0)); bds. 8.99 (978-1-84059-922-0(7)) Milet Publishing.

—Vehicles - My First Bilingual Book, 1 vol. 2014. (My First Bilingual Book Ser.). (ENG & POR., Illus.). 20p. (J). (— 1). bds. 8.99 (978-1-84059-930-5(8)); bds. 7.99 (978-1-84059-923-7(5)); bds. 8.99 (978-1-84059-931-2(6)); bds. 7.99 (978-1-84059-936-7(7)); bds. 8.99 (978-1-84059-926-8(X)) Milet Publishing.

—Vehicles (English-German), 1 vol. 2014. (My First Bilingual Book Ser.). (ENG & GER., Illus.). 20p. (J). (— 1). bds. 8.99 (978-1-84059-927-5(8)) Milet Publishing.

Mitton, Tony & Parker, Ant. Amazing Machines. 2003. (Illus.). 93p. (J). (978-0-7534-5938-6(8), Kingfisher) Roaring Brook Pr.

—Cool Cars. 2014. (Amazing Machines Ser.). (ENG., Illus.). 24p. (J). (gr. -1-k). 6.99 (978-0-7534-7207-1(4), 900143118, Kingfisher) Roaring Brook Pr.

—Cool Cars. 2014. (Amazing Machines Ser.). (J). lib. bdg. 14.75 (978-0-606-36132-3(4)) Turtleback.

Morey, Allan. Police Cars. 2014. (Illus.). 24p. (J). lib. bdg. 25.65 (978-1-62031-104-2(6), Bullfrog Bks.) Jump! Inc.

Morkes, Andrew. Driverless Vehicle Developers. 2019. (Cool Careers in Science Ser.). (Illus.). 96p. (J). (gr. 12). lib. bdg. 34.60 (978-1-4222-4296-4(X)) Mason Crest.

Musgrave, Ruth A. Things That Go. 2020. (First Board Bks.). (Illus.). 26p. (J). (gr. -1 — 1). bds. 7.99 (978-1-4263-3698-0(5), National Geographic Kids) Disney Publishing Worldwide.

My Big Book of Vehicles. 2004. 12p. (J). bds. 7.99 (978-1-85854-660-5(5)) Brimax Books Ltd. GBR. Dist: Byeway Bks.

My Community: Vehicles, 6 vols. 2015. (My Community: Vehicles Ser.: 6). (ENG.). 24p. (J). (gr. -1-2). lib. bdg. 188.16 (978-1-68080-127-9(9), 19303, Abdo Kids) ABDO Publishing Co.

National Geographic Kids. National Geographic Kids Look & Learn: Things That Go. 2014. (Look & Learn Ser.). 24p. (J). (gr. -1-k). bds. 6.99 (978-1-4263-1706-4(9), National Geographic Kids) Disney Publishing Worldwide.

Newman, Lauren. Self-Driving Cars. 2017. (21st Century Skills Innovation Library: Emerging Tech Ser.). (ENG., Illus.). 32p. (J). (gr. 4-8). lib. bdg. 32.07 (978-1-63472-698-6(7), 210118) Cherry Lake Publishing.

Nishida, Masaki. Drawing Manga Vehicles. (How to Draw Manga Ser.). 24p. (gr. 3-3). 2009. 47.90 (978-1-61513-442-7(5), PowerKids Pr.) 2007. (ENG., Illus.). (J). lib. bdg. 28.93 (978-1-4042-3848-0(4), 9f47f5c1-8fcf-47da-9898-62ff2af6633e) Rosen Publishing Group, Inc., The.

Off Road Vehicles. 2004. (Mega MacHines Ser.). (Illus.). 16p. (J). (978-2-7643-0200-2(2)) Phidal Publishing, Inc./Editions Phidal, Inc.

Olivera, Ramon. ABCs on Wheels. Olivera, Ramon, illus. 2016. (ENG., Illus.). 40p. (J). (gr. -1-k). 19.99 (978-1-4814-3244-3(3), Little Simon) Little Simon.

O'Toole, Janet & Anness Publishing Staff. Vehicles: Lift the Flaps to Find Out about Vehicles! Adams, Ben, illus. 2013. 16p. (J). (gr. -1-12). bds. 6.99 (978-1-84322-728-1(2), Armadillo) Anness Publishing GBR. Dist: National Bk. Network.

Oxlade, Chris. Emergency Machines. 2018. (ENG., Illus.). 48p. (J). (gr. 1-5). pap. 6.95 (978-0-2281-0112-3(3), 92a13dd1-4926-4e72-9f0a-9c96376b6e15) Firefly Bks., Ltd.

—The History of Transportation. 2017. (History of Technology Ser.). (ENG., Illus.). 32p. (J). (gr. 2-5). lib. bdg. 29.99 (978-1-4846-4038-8(1), 135139, Heinemann) Capstone.

Parker, Steve. Emergency Vehicles. 2010. (How It Works Ser.). (Illus.). 40p. (J). (gr. 3-18). lib. bdg. 19.95 (978-1-4222-1793-1(0), 1317906) Mason Crest.

—On the Road. 2010. (J). 28.50 (978-1-59920-283-9(2)) Black Rabbit Bks.

—Speed Machines. Pang, Alex, illus. 2010. (How It Works Ser.). 40p. (J). (gr. 3-18). lib. bdg. 19.95 (978-1-4222-1800-6(7), 1317938) Mason Crest.

Parker, Steve & West, David. On Land, 1 vol. West, David, illus. 2012. (Future Transport Ser.). (ENG., Illus.). 32p. (gr. 5-5). 31.21 (978-1-60870-779-9(2), 0950fa8d-6c8c-4dd1-aa2a-6a269b69dd83) Cavendish Square Publishing LLC.

Pearson, Debora. Animachines. Hilb, Nora, illus. 2016. (ENG.). 16p. (J). (— 1). bds. 7.99 (978-1-55451-831-9(8)) Annick Pr., Ltd. CAN. Dist: Publishers Group West (PGW).

Penguin Books Staff. Vehicles. (Learners Ser.). (Illus.). 48p. (J). 3.50 (978-0-7214-1704-2(3), Dutton Juvenile) Penguin Publishing Group.

Peppas, Lynn. Atvs & Off-Roaders. 2012. (ENG.). 32p. (J). (978-0-7787-3017-0(4)); pap. (978-0-7787-3022-4(0)) Crabtree Publishing Co.

—Green Machines: Eco-Friendly Rides. 2011. (ENG., Illus.). 32p. (J). lib. bdg. (978-0-7787-2729-3(7)); (Vehicles on the Move Ser.: No. 15). pap. (978-0-7787-2736-1(X)) Crabtree Publishing Co.

Phillips, Jessica, illus. Zoom Along. 2018. (Zoom Along Ser.). (ENG.). 16p. (J). (gr. -1 — 1). bds. 15.99 (978-1-77138-797-2(1)) Kids Can Pr., Ltd. CAN. Dist: Hachette Bk. Group.

Poolos, J. ATVs/Vehículos Todo Terreno, 1 vol. Alaman, Eduardo, tr. 2007. (Wild Rides / Autos de Locura Ser.). (SPA & ENG., Illus.). 24p. (J). (gr. 2-3). lib. bdg. 26.27 (978-1-4042-7641-3(6), 9e7fd8d3-efe4-45b1-b17f-8a5865cb4bea) Rosen Publishing Group, Inc., The.

—Wild about ATVs. (Wild Rides Ser.). 24p. (gr. 2-3). 2009. 42.50 (978-1-60854-797-5(3), PowerKids Pr.) 2007. (ENG., Illus.). (J). lib. bdg. 26.27 (978-1-4042-3793-3(3), dea92cdf-ca31-4d08-9b0b-af333b9adfef) Rosen Publishing Group, Inc., The.

—Wild about ATVs/Vehículos todo Terreno. 2009. (Wild Rides/Autos de locura Ser.). 24p. (gr. 2-3). 42.50 (978-1-60854-802-6(3), Editorial Buenas Letras) Rosen Publishing Group, Inc., The.

—Wild about Lowriders. 2009. (Wild Rides Ser.). 24p. (gr. 2-3). 42.50 (978-1-60854-800-2(7), PowerKids Pr.); (SPA.). 42.50 (978-1-60854-807-1(4), Editorial Buenas Letras) Rosen Publishing Group, Inc., The.

Potts, Nikki. My First Guide to Fast Vehicles. 2017. (My First Guides). (ENG., Illus.). 24p. (J). (gr. 1-3). lib. bdg. 27.99 (978-1-5157-3594-6(X), 133593, Capstone Pr.) Capstone.

Priddy, Roger. My Big Rescue Book. 2004. (Illus.). 10p. (J). (978-1-84332-215-3(3)) St. Martin's Pr.

—Playtown: Emergency: A Lift-The-Flap Book. 2016. (Playtown Ser.). (ENG., Illus.). 14p. (J). bds. 12.99 (978-0-312-52009-0(3), 900156775) St. Martin's Pr.

Publications International Ltd. Staff, ed. Things That Go Board Book. 2014. (Illus.). 22p. (J). bds. 4.98 (978-1-4508-8581-2(0), 1450885810) Phoenix International Publications, Inc.

Randolph, Joanne. Ambulances, 1 vol. 2008. (To the Rescue! Ser.). (ENG., Illus.). 24p. (J). (gr. 1-1). lib. bdg. 26.27 (978-1-4042-4150-3(7), c89f3a78-fed6-4cda-9402-5c4e0788949a, PowerKids Pr.) Rosen Publishing Group, Inc., The.

—Ambulances/Ambulancias, 1 vol. Alaman, Eduardo, tr. 2007. (To the Rescue! / ¡Al Rescate! Ser.). (ENG & SPA., Illus.). 24p. (J). (gr. 1-1). lib. bdg. 26.27 (978-1-4042-7670-3(X), 282ab15f-d3a9-49a7-a55c-19a17b04db3c) Rosen Publishing Group, Inc., The.

—Police Cars, 1 vol. 2008. (To the Rescue! Ser.). (ENG., Illus.). 24p. (J). (gr. 1-1). lib. bdg. 26.27 (978-1-4042-4153-4(1), 2151a274-04d3-4d7f-9256-082389f7a226, PowerKids Pr.) Rosen Publishing Group, Inc., The.

—Police Cars/Patrullas, 1 vol. Alaman, Eduardo, tr. 2007. (To the Rescue! / ¡Al Rescate! Ser.). (ENG & SPA., Illus.). 24p. (J). (gr. 1-1). lib. bdg. 26.27 (978-1-4042-7674-1(2), dc70a713-bf58-45f2-9c73-57689f1f92c8) Rosen Publishing Group, Inc., The.

Reinke, Beth Bence. Garbage Trucks on the Go. 2018. (Bumba Books (r) — Machines That Go Ser.). (ENG., Illus.). 24p. (J). (gr. -1-1). 26.65 (978-1-5124-8253-9(6), 2aca02bf-a6f8-48ee-9a5e-29e500a16bbc, Lerner Pubns.) Lerner Publishing Group.

Ricciuti, Edward R. Qué Hay Dentro de un Carro de Policía? / What's Inside a Police Car?, 1 vol. 2008. (Qué Hay Dentro? / What's Inside? Ser.). (ENG & SPA., Illus.). 32p. (gr. 1-2). lib. bdg. 25.50 (978-0-7614-2475-8(X), 5ed21c50-efc2-4339-8da0-b3b93baec255) Cavendish Square Publishing LLC.

—Qué Hay Dentro de un Carro de Policía? (What's Inside a Police Car?), 1 vol. 2008. (Qué Hay Dentro? (What's Inside?) Ser.). (SPA., Illus.). 32p. (gr. 1-2). lib. bdg. 25.50 (978-0-7614-2396-6(6), 4bb7c4f5-511f-424c-aadd-296dcd1e6406) Cavendish Square Publishing LLC.

—What's Inside a Police Car, 1 vol. 2008. (What's Inside? Ser.). (ENG., Illus.). 32p. (gr. 1-2). pap. 9.23 (978-0-7614-3348-4(1), 54d163e2-0083-46a1-b508-9207c4a93d4f) Cavendish Square Publishing LLC.

Rice, Dona Herweck. En Movimiento. 2nd rev. ed. 2011. (TIME for KIDS(r): Informational Text Ser.). (SPA.). 12p. (gr. k-1). 7.99 (978-1-4333-4410-7(6)) Teacher Created Materials, Inc.

—On the Go, 1 vol. 2nd rev. ed. 2011. (TIME for KIDS(r): Informational Text Ser.). (ENG.). 12p. (gr. k-1). 7.99 (978-1-4333-3571-6(9)) Teacher Created Materials, Inc.

Riggs, Kate. To the Rescue! Williams, Nate, illus. 2016. (ENG.). 14p. (J). (gr. -1 — 1). bds. 7.99 (978-1-56846-288-2(3), 20560, Creative Editions) Creative Co., The.

Ripley Entertainment. Life in the Fast Lane. 2010. (Ripley's Believe It or Not Ser.). 36p. (YA). (gr. 3-18). lib. bdg. 19.95 (978-1-4222-1538-8(5)) Mason Crest.

Ripley's Believe It Or Not! Ripley Twists: Mighty Machines PORTRAIT EDN. 2014. (Twist Ser.). (ENG.). 48p. (J). 12.95 (978-1-893951-85-3(5)) Ripley Entertainment, Inc.

Royston, Angela. Race That Bike! Forces in Vehicles. 2015. (Feel the Force Ser.). (ENG., Illus.). 48p. (J). (gr. 3-6). 35.99 (978-1-4846-2599-6(4), 130081, Heinemann) Capstone.

Scholastic. The Wheels on the Truck Go 'Round & 'Round (Rookie Toddler) 2012. (Rookie Toddler Ser.). (ENG.). 14p. (J). (gr. -1 — 1). bds. 6.95 (978-0-531-20855-7(9), Children's Pr.) Scholastic Library Publishing.

Shaffer, Lindsay. ATVs. 2018. (Full Throttle Ser.). (ENG., Illus.). 24p. (J). (gr. 3-7). lib. bdg. 26.95 (978-1-62617-870-0(4), Epic Bks.) Bellwether Media.

Sheen, Barbara. Cutting Edge Transportation Technology. 2016. (ENG.). 80p. (J). (gr. 5-12). lib. bdg. (978-1-68282-046-9(7)) ReferencePoint Pr., Inc.

Sonnad, Haydn. Self-Driving Cars. 2019. (21st Century Skills Innovation Library: Disruptors in Tech Ser.). (ENG., Illus.). 32p. (J). (gr. 4-8). pap. 14.21 (978-1-5341-5047-8(1), 213495); lib. bdg. 32.07 (978-1-5341-4761-4(6), 213494) Cherry Lake Publishing.

Spaight, Anne J. Carros de Policía en Acción (Police Cars on the Go) 2017. (Bumba Books (r) en Español — Máquinas en Acción (Machines That Go) Ser.). (SPA., Illus.). 24p. (J). (gr. -1-1). 26.65 (978-1-5124-2880-3(9), da1bb92e-ee4c-49fa-b7ca-126fc3c8f9ed, Ediciones Lerner) Lerner Publishing Group.

Speed Machines: Set 2, 12 vols. 2013. (Speed Machines Ser.). (ENG.). 32p. (J). (gr. 4-5). 173.58 (978-1-4777-1149-1(X), f74bb01f-694f-4df5-befd-725488896566, PowerKids Pr.) Rosen Publishing Group, Inc., The.

Spengler, Kremena T. An Illustrated Timeline of Transportation, 1 vol. Doty, Eldon, illus. 2011. (Visual Timelines in History Ser.). (ENG.). 32p. (J). (gr. 2-4). pap. 7.49 (978-1-4048-7019-2(9), 116799, Picture Window Bks.) Capstone.

Sweeney, Bernadette. Monster Machines. 2007. (Steck-Vaughn BOLDPRINT Anthologies Ser.). (ENG., Illus.). 48p. (gr. 5-8). pap. 16.90 (978-1-4190-4024-5(3)) Houghton Mifflin Harcourt Publishing Co.

Tagel, Peggy, illus. On the Go. 2003. (Squishy Shapes Ser.). 10p. (J). 12.95 (978-1-57145-739-4(9), Silver Dolphin Bks.) Readerlink Distribution Services, LLC.

To the Rescue! 2016. (To the Rescue! Ser.). 24p. (gr. k-k). pap. 48.90 (978-1-4824-5346-1(0)); (ENG.). lib. bdg. 145.62 (978-1-4824-4522-0(0), cc52856c-f3b2-45d1-bc08-b68a937f69e4) Stevens, Gareth Publishing LLLP.

Tuxworth, Nicola. Things That Go. 2016. (Illus.). 20p. (J). (gr. -1-12). bds. 6.99 (978-1-84322-752-6(5), Armadillo) Anness Publishing GBR. Dist: National Bk. Network.

Vehicles. 2016. (Illus.). (J). (978-1-62885-155-7(4)) Kidsbooks, LLC.

Vehicles. 2003. (First Concepts Book Ser.). 32p. (J). 3.98 (978-0-7525-8894-0(X)) Parragon, Inc.

Vehicles. (Cute & Cushy Ser.). 10p. (J). bds. (978-2-7643-0207-1(X)) Phidal Publishing, Inc./Editions Phidal, Inc.

Vehículos Gigantes, 8 vols. 2005. (Vehículos Gigantes (Giant Vehicles) Ser.). (SPA.). 24p. (gr. 2-4). lib. bdg. 102.68 (978-0-8368-5984-3(7), a3b18b82-8bb6-45b7-951e-b0a000e91a24, Gareth Stevens Learning Library) Stevens, Gareth Publishing LLLP.

Veitch, Catherine. Big Machines Rescue!, 1 vol. 2014. (Big Machines Ser.). (ENG.). 24p. (J). (gr. -1-1). 25.99 (978-1-4846-0588-2(8), 126690, Heinemann) Capstone.

Ward, Lesley. Electric Vehicles. rev. ed. 2018. (Smithsonian: Informational Text Ser.). (ENG., Illus.). 32p. (J). (gr. 3-5). pap. 11.99 (978-1-4938-6702-8(4)) Teacher Created Materials, Inc.

Watch Me Go!, 12 vols. 2014. (Watch Me Go! Ser.). (ENG.). 24p. (J). (gr. 1-2). lib. bdg. 151.62 (978-1-4777-5729-1(5), f81bb091-ae82-4a54-b9d9-233d19e05a01, PowerKids Pr.) Rosen Publishing Group, Inc., The.

West, David. Rescue Vehicles. 2015. (Mechanic Mike's Machines Ser.). (ENG.). 24p. (J). (gr. k-3). 28.50 (978-1-62588-058-1(8), 19316, Smart Apple Media) Black Rabbit Bks.

Will, Sandra. Transportation Inventions: From Subways to Submarines. 2006. (Which Came First? Ser.). (Illus.). 32p. (YA). (gr. 3-6). lib. bdg. 28.50 (978-1-59716-133-6(0)) Bearport Publishing Co., Inc.

Wolfe, Jane. Pull the Lever: Who's in Here? Benham, Tors, illus. 2014. (ENG.). 8p. (J). (gr. -1-2). bds. 6.99 (978-1-86147-394-3(X), Armadillo) Anness Publishing GBR. Dist: National Bk. Network.

Worms, Penny. Off-Road Vehicles. 2016. (Motormania Ser.). 32p. (gr. 2-7). 31.35 (978-1-59920-995-1(0), Smart Apple Media) Black Rabbit Bks.

VEHICLES, MILITARY

Abramovitz, Melissa. Military Helicopters. 2012. (Military Machines Ser.). (ENG.). 24p. (gr. k-1). pap. 41.70 (978-1-4296-8314-2(7), Capstone Pr.) Capstone.

—Military Trucks. 2012. (Military Machines Ser.). (ENG.). 24p. (gr. k-1). pap. 41.70 (978-1-4296-8317-3(1), Capstone Pr.) Capstone.

—Military Vehicles. 2015. (Wild about Wheels Ser.). (ENG., Illus.). 24p. (J). (gr. -1-2). lib. bdg. 27.32 (978-1-4914-2116-1(9), 127599, Capstone Pr.) Capstone.

Alpert, Barbara. Military Amphibious Vehicles. 2012. (Military Machines Ser.). (ENG.). 24p. (gr. k-1). pap. 41.70 (978-1-4296-8313-5(9), Capstone Pr.) Capstone.

—Military Amphibious Vehicles, 1 vol. 2012. (Military Machines Ser.). (ENG., Illus.). 24p. (J). (gr. -1-2). lib. bdg. 27.32 (978-1-4296-7569-7(1), 117166, Capstone Pr.) Capstone.

—Military Ships. 2012. (Military Machines Ser.). (ENG.). 24p. (gr. k-1). pap. 41.70 (978-1-4296-8316-6(3), Capstone Pr.) Capstone.

Alvarez, Carlos. MH-53J Pave Lows. 2009. (Military Machines Ser.). (ENG., Illus.). 24p. (J). (gr. 3-7). lib. bdg. 26.95 (978-1-60014-281-9(8)) Bellwether Media.

—Strykers. 2010. (Military Machines Ser.). (ENG., Illus.). 24p. (J). (gr. 3-7). lib. bdg. 26.95 (978-1-60014-496-7(9), Torque Bks.) Bellwether Media.

Bodden, Valerie. Armored Vehicles. 2012. (Built for Battle Ser.). (ENG., Illus.). 24p. (J). (gr. 1-4). 25.65 (978-1-60818-123-0(5), 22102, Creative Education) Creative Co., The.

Boutland, Craig. Attack Vehicles on Land: Tanks & Armored Fighting Vehicles. 2019. (Military Machines in the War on Terrorism Ser.). (ENG., Illus.). 32p. (J). (gr. 3-9). lib. bdg. 28.65 (978-1-5435-7380-0(0), 140669) Capstone.

—New Generation Vehicles: Drones, Mine Clearance, & Bomb Disposal. 2019. (Military Machines in the War on Terrorism Ser.). (ENG., Illus.). 32p. (J). (gr. 3-9). lib. bdg. 28.65 (978-1-5435-7385-5(1), 140673) Capstone.

—Special Forces Vehicles: 4x4s, Dirt Bikes, & Rigid-Hulled Boats. 2019. (Military Machines in the War on Terrorism Ser.). (ENG., Illus.). 32p. (J). (gr. 3-9). lib. bdg. 28.65 *(978-1-5435-7384-8(3),* 140672) Capstone.
—Transport Vehicles: Cargo Planes, Helicopters, Trucks, & Jeeps. 2019. (Military Machines in the War on Terrorism Ser.). (ENG., Illus.). 32p. (J). (gr. 3-9). lib. bdg. 28.65 *(978-1-5435-7382-4(7),* 140671) Capstone.
Brody, Walt. How Military Helicopters Work. 2019. (Lightning Bolt Books (r) — Military Machines Ser.). (ENG., Illus.). 24p. (J). (gr. 1-3). 29.32 *(978-1-5415-5740-6(9),* 738f2f1e-a3a8-4701-8f91-324d276c96af); pap. 9.99 *(978-1-5415-7457-1(5),* 5af9b522-6edc-4f0f-abe1-9ecbb292e6df) Lerner Publishing Group. (Lerner Pubns.).
Burrows, Terry. Hovercrafts & Humvees: Engineering Goes to War. 2017. (STEM on the Battlefield Ser.). (ENG., Illus.). 48p. (J). (gr. 4-6). 31.99 *(978-1-5124-3929-8(0),* 0f902c5c-a4ce-415c-aaad-d99cfb90675f, Lerner Pubns.) Lerner Publishing Group.
Cain, Bill & Hama, Larry. Tank of Tomorrow. 2007. (High-Tech Military Weapons Ser.). (ENG., Illus.). 48p. (J). (gr. 4-7). pap. 6.95 *(978-0-531-18710-4(1))* Scholastic Library Publishing.
Clay, Kathryn. My First Guide to Military Vehicles. 2015. (My First Guides). (ENG., Illus.). 24p. (J). (gr. 1-3). lib. bdg. 27.99 *(978-1-4914-2050-8(2),* 127528, Capstone Pr.) Capstone.
Cohn, Jessica. Military Machines, 1 vol. 2013. (Machines in Motion Ser.). 48p. (J). (gr. 3-3). (ENG.). pap. 15.05 *(978-1-4339-9605-4(7),* be9e9466-a0fb-4133-90ce-0e6fa7147cdd); pap. 84.30 *(978-1-4339-9606-1(5))*; (ENG., Illus.). lib. bdg. 34.61 *(978-1-4339-9604-7(9),* 5d11d558-1934-40ca-a0e1-e03398e71ffc) Stevens, Gareth Publishing LLLP.
Colson, Rob Scott. Tanks & Military Vehicles, 1 vol. 2013. (Ultimate Machines Ser.). (ENG., Illus.). 24p. (J). (gr. 5-5). pap. 9.25 *(978-1-4777-0119-5(2),* 2095d0fa-a36e-4626-b302-7f178df433e9); lib. bdg. 26.27 *(978-1-4777-0067-9(6),* 87a019d5-ad03-401d-94ac-b4844a0da467) Rosen Publishing Group, Inc., The. (PowerKids Pr.).
Cornish, Geoff. Battleground Support. 2004. (Military Hardware in Action Ser.). (Illus.). 48p. (J). (gr. 4-9). lib. bdg. 25.26 *(978-0-8225-4708-2(2))* Lerner Publishing Group.
—Tanks. 2003. (Military Hardware in Action Ser.). (ENG., Illus.). 48p. (J). (gr. 5-9). lib. bdg. 25.26 *(978-0-8225-4701-3(5))* Lerner Publishing Group.
David, Jack. Humvees. 2009. (Military Machines Ser.). (ENG., Illus.). 24p. (J). (gr. 3-7). lib. bdg. 26.95 *(978-1-60014-260-4(5),* 10283, Torque Bks.) Bellwether Media.
—M2A2 Bradleys. 2009. (Military Machines Ser.). (ENG., Illus.). 24p. (J). (gr. 3-7). lib. bdg. 26.95 *(978-1-60014-261-1(3))* Bellwether Media.
—Torque: M2A2 Bradleys. 2009. (Torque Ser.). 24p. (J). (gr. 3-7). 20.00 *(978-0-531-21737-5(X),* Children's Pr.) Scholastic Library Publishing.
—Torque - Military Machines, 4 vols., Set. Incl. Torque: B-1B Lancers. 20.00 *(978-0-531-21736-8(1))*; Torque: B-52 Stratofortresses. 20.00 *(978-0-531-21735-1(3))*; Torque: Humvees. 20.00 *(978-0-531-21734-4(5))*; Torque: M2A2 Bradleys. 20.00 *(978-0-531-21737-5(X))*. 24p. (J). (gr. 3-7). 2009. 2009. Set lib. bdg. 80.00 *(978-0-531-26137-8(9),* Children's Pr.) Scholastic Library Publishing.
Dell, Pamela & Delmar, Pete. The Science of Military Vehicles, 1 vol. 2012. (Science of War Ser.). (ENG., Illus.). 48p. (J). (gr. 6-9). pap. 9.10 *(978-0-7565-4525-3(0),* 1337566, Compass Point Bks.) Capstone.
Delmar, Pete. Vehicles of the Civil War, 1 vol. 2013. (War Vehicles Ser.). (ENG.). 32p. (J). (gr. 3-9). 28.65 *(978-1-4296-9912-9(4),* 120625, Capstone Pr.) Capstone.
Doman, Mary Kate. Big Military Machines, 1 vol. 2011. (All about Big Machines Ser.). (ENG., Illus.). 24p. (gr. -1-1). pap. 10.35 *(978-1-59845-243-3(6),* 13847093-d60d-4a47-bd72-f54ea6741012, Enslow Publishing) Enslow Publishing, LLC.
Ellis, Catherine. Cars & Trucks. 2009. (Mega Military Machines Ser.). 24p. (gr. 1-1). 42.50 *(978-1-61514-634-5(2),* PowerKids Pr.) Rosen Publishing Group, Inc., The.
—Cars & Trucks/Autos y Camiones. 2009. (Mega Military Machines/Megamaquinas militares Ser.). (ENG & SPA.). 24p. (gr. 1-1). 42.50 *(978-1-61514-639-0(3),* Editorial Buenas Letras) Rosen Publishing Group, Inc., The.
—Cars & Trucks/Autos y Camiones, 1 vol. Brusca, Maria Cristina, tr. 2007. (Mega Military Machines / Megamaquinas Militares Ser.). (ENG & SPA., Illus.). 24p. (J). (gr. 1-1). lib. bdg. 26.27 *(978-1-4042-7624-6(6),* 689c5426-3605-40ed-8679-951bd7faa888) Rosen Publishing Group, Inc., The.
—Mega Military Machines, 8 vols., Set. Incl. Helicopters. lib. bdg. 26.27 *(978-1-4042-3666-0(X),* facd0f27-3462-47b5-b5a3-def9eec06576); Planes. lib. bdg. 26.27 *(978-1-4042-3667-7(8),* b1e40b2a-8cb3-469a-a164-9be2bb0d9df3); Ships. lib. bdg. 26.27 *(978-1-4042-3668-4(6),* 3dfa74f4-cc52-4ffd-a6df-b85d5b75d593); Submarines. lib. bdg. 26.27 *(978-1-4042-3665-3(1),* 4cfc3986-ff68-4e6c-88e2-e9cebe9f068d); (Illus.). 24p. (J). (gr. 1-1). (Mega Military Machines Ser.). (ENG.). 2007. Set lib. bdg. 105.08 *(978-1-4042-3606-6(6),* eb12dc79-670c-4a79-85d5-eaface832785) Rosen Publishing Group, Inc., The.
Fein, Eric. Vehicles of World War II, 1 vol. 2013. (War Vehicles Ser.). (ENG.). 32p. (J). (gr. 3-9). 28.65 *(978-1-4296-9915-0(9),* 120628, Capstone Pr.) Capstone.
Fein, Eric, et al. War Vehicles. 2013. (War Vehicles Ser.). (ENG.). 32p. (J). (gr. 3-9). 153.25 *(978-1-4296-9916-7(7),* 18833, Capstone Pr.) Capstone.
Finn, Denny Von. M-ATVs. 2013. (Military Vehicles Ser.). (ENG., Illus.). 24p. (J). (gr. 3-7). lib. bdg. 26.95 *(978-1-60014-943-6(X),* Epic Bks.) Bellwether Media.
—Strykers. 2014. (Military Vehicles Ser.). (ENG., Illus.). 24p. (J). (gr. 3-7). lib. bdg. 26.95 *(978-1-62617-082-7(7),* Epic Bks.) Bellwether Media.
Fishkin, Rebecca Love. Vehicles of the Iraq War, 1 vol. 2013. (War Vehicles Ser.). (ENG.). 32p. (J). (gr. 3-9). 28.65 *(978-1-4296-9914-3(0),* 120627, Capstone Pr.) Capstone.
Garstecki, Julia. Military Ground Vehicles. 2017. (Military Tech Ser.). (ENG., Illus.). 32p. (J). (gr. 4-6). lib. bdg. *(978-1-68072-165-2(8),* 10514, Bolt) Black Rabbit Bks.
—Vehículos Militares Terrestres. 2017. (Tecnología Militar Ser.). (SPA., Illus.). 32p. (J). (gr. 4-6). lib. bdg. *(978-1-68072-582-7(3),* 10589, Bolt) Black Rabbit Bks.
Gilpin, Daniel. Military Vehicles, 1 vol. Pang, Alex, illus. 2011. (Machines Close-Up Ser.). (ENG.). 32p. (gr. 4-4). 31.21 *(978-1-60870-109-4(3),* 14a3a8bb-2574-46e7-aa93-863cf03f9611) Cavendish Square Publishing LLC.
Goldsworthy, Steve. The Tech Behind Amphibious Vehicles. 2019. (Tech on Wheels Ser.). (ENG., Illus.). 32p. (J). (gr. 3-9). 28.65 *(978-1-5435-7306-0(1),* 140616) Capstone.
Gosman, Gillian. Simple Machines in the Military, 1 vol. 2014. (Simple Machines Everywhere Ser.). (ENG., Illus.). 24p. (J). (gr. 2-3). pap. 9.25 *(978-1-4777-6834-1(3),* e5bdae66-ccd0-4093-8cf2-8d1058b6769f, PowerKids Pr.) Rosen Publishing Group, Inc., The.
Hansen, Grace. Military Amphibious Vehicles. 2016. (Military Aircraft & Vehicles Ser.). (ENG., Illus.). 24p. (J). (gr. -1-2). lib. bdg. 32.79 *(978-1-68080-932-9(6),* 23339, Abdo Kids) ABDO Publishing Co.
—Military Tracked Vehicles. 2016. (Military Aircraft & Vehicles Ser.). (ENG., Illus.). 24p. (J). (gr. -1-2). lib. bdg. 32.79 *(978-1-68080-936-7(9),* 23347, Abdo Kids) ABDO Publishing Co.
—Military Wheeled Vehicles. 2016. (Military Aircraft & Vehicles Ser.). (ENG., Illus.). 24p. (J). (gr. -1-2). lib. bdg. 32.79 *(978-1-68080-937-4(7),* 23349, Abdo Kids) ABDO Publishing Co.
Jackson, Kay. Armored Vehicles in Action. 2009. (Amazing Military Vehicles Ser.). 24p. (gr. 3-3). 42.50 *(978-1-61511-309-5(6),* PowerKids Pr.) Rosen Publishing Group, Inc., The.
Jackson, Robert. 101 Great Tanks, 1 vol. 2010. (101 Greatest Weapons of All Times Ser.). (ENG., Illus.). 112p. (YA). (gr. 10-10). lib. bdg. 39.80 *(978-1-4358-3595-5(6),* baffb633-ab21-4909-9b67-6e2899b82c94) Rosen Publishing Group, Inc., The.
Levine, Michelle. Vehicles of the Vietnam War, 1 vol. 2013. (War Vehicles Ser.). (ENG.). 32p. (J). (gr. 3-9). 28.65 *(978-1-4296-9913-6(2),* 120626, Capstone Pr.) Capstone.
Meister, Cari. Totally Amazing Facts about Military Land Vehicles. 2017. (Mind Benders Ser.). (ENG., Illus.). 112p. (J). (gr. 3-6). lib. bdg. 23.99 *(978-1-5157-4527-3(9),* 134243, Capstone Pr.) Capstone.
Mighty Military Machines, 12 vols. 2014. (Mighty Military Machines Ser.). (ENG.). 32p. (J). (gr. 1-1). lib. bdg. 161.58 *(978-1-4824-1649-7(2),* 3b196470-0e28-407f-9aa8-79f6d010a63e) Stevens, Gareth Publishing LLLP.
Nelson, Drew. Armored Vehicles, 1 vol. 2013. (Military Machines Ser.). (ENG., Illus.). 32p. (J). (gr. 3-4). pap. 11.50 *(978-1-4339-8453-2(9),* 426b51a8-23a9-4740-9e90-6a6dafef1017); lib. bdg. 29.27 *(978-1-4339-8452-5(0),* ccb412a1-fa60-436f-a818-35a9920d953e) Stevens, Gareth Publishing LLLP.
Parker, Steve. Military Machines. 2010. (How It Works Ser.). 40p. (J). (gr. 3-18). lib. bdg. 19.95 *(978-1-4222-1797-9(3))* Mason Crest.
Peppas, Lynn. Powerful Armored Vehicles, 1 vol. 2011. (ENG.). 32p. (J). pap. *(978-0-7787-2755-2(6))* Crabtree Publishing Co.
Riggs, Kate. Armored Vehicles. 2016. (Seedlings Ser.). (ENG., Illus.). 24p. (J). (gr. -1-k). 28.50 *(978-1-60818-659-4(8),* 20517, Creative Education) Creative Co., The.
Schaub, Michelle. Vehicles of World War I, 1 vol. 2013. (War Vehicles Ser.). (ENG.). 32p. (J). (gr. 3-9). 28.65 *(978-1-4296-9911-2(6),* 120624, Capstone Pr.) Capstone.
Slingerland, Janet. Military Vehicles. 2018. (Vehicles on the Job Ser.). (ENG.). 24p. (J). (gr. 1-3). 25.27 *(978-1-59953-943-0(8))* Norwood Hse. Pr.
Souter, Gerry & Kiland, Taylor Baldwin. Armored Tanks: Battlefield Dominance, 1 vol. 2015. (Military Engineering in Action Ser.). (ENG., Illus.). 48p. (gr. 6-6). 29.60 *(978-0-7660-6908-4(7),* b87b3960-6fc1-4af6-97e2-ecacb2f14c65) Enslow Publishing, LLC.
Stark, William N. Mighty Military Land Vehicles. 2016. (Military Machines on Duty Ser.). (ENG., Illus.). 24p. (J). (gr. 1-3). lib. bdg. 27.99 *(978-1-4914-8848-5(4),* 131475, Capstone Pr.) Capstone.
Summers, Elizabeth. Weapons & Vehicles of the Iraq War. 2015. (Tools of War Ser.). (ENG., Illus.). 32p. (J). (gr. 3-9). lib. bdg. 27.32 *(978-1-4914-4081-0(3),* 128652, Capstone Pr.) Capstone.
—Weapons & Vehicles of the Vietnam War. 2015. (Tools of War Ser.). (ENG., Illus.). 32p. (J). (gr. 3-9). lib. bdg. 27.32 *(978-1-4914-4082-7(1),* 128654, Capstone Pr.) Capstone.
—Weapons & Vehicles of World War I. 2015. (Tools of War Ser.). (ENG., Illus.). 32p. (J). (gr. 3-9). lib. bdg. 27.32 *(978-1-4914-4095-7(3),* 128653, Capstone Pr.) Capstone.
—Weapons & Vehicles of World War II. 2015. (Tools of War Ser.). (ENG., Illus.). 32p. (J). (gr. 3-9). lib. bdg. 27.32 *(978-1-4914-4080-3(5),* 128651, Capstone Pr.) Capstone.
Teitelbaum, Michael & Kiland, Taylor Baldwin. Military Humvees: Armored Mobility, 1 vol. 2015. (Military Engineering in Action Ser.). (ENG.). 48p. (gr. 6-6). pap. 12.70 *(978-0-7660-7065-3(4),* 73b19f35-530d-483e-a6ef-821f015394b7) Enslow Publishing, LLC.
Turner, Tracy. Weapons of War. 2015. (Head-To-Head Ser.). (ENG., Illus.). 24p. (gr. 3-8). 28.50 *(978-1-62588-151-9(7))* Black Rabbit Bks.
West, David. Combat Helicopters. West, David, illus. 2019. (War Machines Ser.). (ENG., Illus.). 32p. (J). (gr. 5-6). pap. *(978-0-7787-6679-7(9),* 91c2879e-11ce-476c-8571-32ba4cb4f1f6); lib. bdg. *(978-0-7787-6665-0(9),* 98858c15-9e42-4909-b493-e7db24498fc7) Crabtree Publishing Co.

VELAZQUEZ, DIEGO, 1599-1660

Venezia, Mike. Diego Velázquez. Venezia, Mike, illus. 2004. (Getting to Know the World's Greatest Artists Ser.). (ENG., Illus.). 32p. (J). (gr. 3-4). pap. 6.95 *(978-0-516-26980-1(1),* Children's Pr.) Scholastic Library Publishing.

VELAZQUEZ, DIEGO, 1599-1660—FICTION

de Trevino, Elizabeth Borton. I, Juan de Pareja. 3rd ed. pap. 3.95 *(978-0-13-800129-2(4))* Prentice Hall (Schl. Div.).
—I, Juan de Pareja. I.t. ed. 2005. 244p. 20.95 *(978-0-7862-7666-0(5))* Thorndike Pr.
De Trevino, Elizabeth Borton. I, Juan de Pareja: The Story of a Great Painter & the Slave He Helped Become a Great Artist. 2008. (ENG.). 192p. (YA). (gr. 7-12). pap. 9.99 *(978-0-312-38005-2(4),* 900050528) Square Fish.
I, Juan de Pareja. 3rd ed. (J). pap., stu. ed. *(978-0-13-667452-8(6))* Prentice Hall (Schl. Div.).
Mayhew, James. Katie & the Spanish Princess. 2015. (Katie Ser.). (ENG., Illus.). 32p. (J). (gr. -1-k). pap. 11.99 *(978-1-4083-3242-9(6))* Hodder & Stoughton GBR. Dist: Hachette Bk. Group.

VELOCITY

see Speed

VENEREAL DISEASES

see Sexually Transmitted Diseases

VENEZUELA

Baguley, Kitt. Venezuela, 1 vol. 2009. (ENG., Illus.). 288p. pap. 17.99 *(978-0-7614-5569-1(8))* Marshall Cavendish Corp.
Birdoff, Ariel Factor. Venezuela. (Los Países de Donde Venimos/Countries We Come From Ser.). (Illus.). 32p. (J). (gr. k-3). 2019. (SPA.). 19.95 *(978-1-64280-233-7(6))* 2018. (ENG.). 19.95 *(978-1-68402-688-3(1))* Bearport Publishing Co., Inc.
Conley, Kate A. Venezuela. 2004. (Countries Set 5 Ser.). 40p. (gr. k-6). 27.07 *(978-1-59197-298-3(1),* Checkerboard Library) ABDO Publishing Co.
Crooker, Richard. Venezuela. 2006. (Modern World Nations Ser.). (ENG., Illus.). 114p. (gr. 6-12). lib. bdg. 35.00 *(978-0-7910-8834-0(0),* P114446, Facts On File) Infobase Holdings, Inc.
Dawson, Mike. Growing up Yanomamö: Missionary Adventures in the Amazon Rainforest. Pintor, Ruben, illus. 2009. (ENG.). 336p. (J). pap. 19.95 *(978-1-60265-009-1(8))* Exegetica Publishing.
Dillon, Doug. We Visit Venezuela. 2010. (Your Land & My Land Ser.). (Illus.). 64p. (J). (gr. 3-6). lib. bdg. 33.95 *(978-1-58415-884-4(0))* Mitchell Lane Pubs.
Doeden, Matt. Miguel Cabrera: Baseball Superstar, 1 vol. 2014. (Superstar Athletes Ser.). (ENG.). 24p. (J). (gr. 1-3). lib. bdg. 27.99 *(978-1-4765-8602-1(0),* 125252) Capstone.
Gagne, Tammy. The Evolution of Government & Politics in Venezuela. 2014. (gr. 4-8). 29.95 *(978-1-61228-582-5(1))* Mitchell Lane Pubs.
Jones, Helga. Venezuela. (Country Explorers Ser.). (Illus.). 48p. (gr. 2-4). 2008. (ENG.). lib. bdg. 29.27 *(978-0-8225-8663-0(0))* 2005. lib. bdg. 22.60 *(978-1-57505-146-8(X))* Lerner Publishing Group.
Mattern, Joanne. Cataratas Ángel, 1 vol. 2003. (Maravillas Naturales (Nature's Greatest Hits) Ser.). (SPA.). 24p. (J). (gr. 2-2). lib. bdg. 26.27 *(978-0-8239-6878-7(2),* 2dbdd809-397a-493a-9ff3-d8500ad9f12f) Rosen Publishing Group, Inc., The.
Ng, Yumi. Welcome to Venezuela, 1 vol. 2004. (Welcome to My Country Ser.). (ENG., Illus.). 48p. (gr. 2-4). lib. bdg. 29.67 *(978-0-8368-3123-8(3),* 3ff29fbb-7416-4744-a78f-9d7bdafcf2ac) Stevens, Gareth Publishing LLLP.
Orr, Tamra. Venezuelan Heritage. 2018. (21st Century Junior Library: Celebrating Diversity in My Classroom Ser.). (ENG., Illus.). 24p. (J). (gr. 2-4). lib. bdg. 30.64 *(978-1-5341-2908-5(1),* 211676) Cherry Lake Publishing.
Patterson, Irania & McElvane, Catherine. Wings & Dreams (Alas y Suenos) The Legend of Angel Falls (La Leyenda del Salto Angel) 2010. (ENG & SPA.). 40p. (J). (gr. 1-3). 19.95 *(978-0-9815192-4-1(5))* Novello Festival Pr.
Pohl, Kathleen. Looking at Venezuela, 1 vol. 2008. (Looking at Countries Ser.). (ENG., Illus.). 32p. (gr. 2-4). (J). lib. bdg. 28.67 *(978-0-8368-9074-7(4),* 6db78c9d-710b-4264-b4ad-f620f9a17ef0); pap. 11.50 *(978-0-8368-9075-4(2),* 9180a5e8-0cca-46ef-85d1-aa3b141b2000) Stevens, Gareth Publishing LLLP. (Gareth Stevens Learning Library).
Rauf, Don. Miguel Cabrera: Triple Crown Winner, 1 vol. 2015. (Living Legends of Sports Ser.). (ENG., Illus.). 48p. (J). (gr. 5-6). 28.41 *(978-1-68048-094-8(4),* 968eb844-8174-4692-9809-821e47c2b185, Britannica Educational Publishing) Rosen Publishing Group, Inc., The.
Shields, Charles J. Venezuela. (South America Today Ser.). 2009. (Illus.). 63p. (J). (gr. 4-7). 21.95 *(978-1-4222-0643-0(2))* 2007. 64p. (YA). (gr. 7-18). pap. 9.95 *(978-1-4222-0710-9(2))* Mason Crest.
Wardrope, William. Venezuela, 1 vol. 2003. (Countries of the World Ser.). (ENG., Illus.). 96p. (gr. 6-8). lib. bdg. 33.67 *(978-0-8368-2369-1(9),* ed423855-10fe-430f-86a0-ce8335fedfa8) Stevens, Gareth Publishing LLLP.
Watson, Galadriel. Angel Falls. 2005. (Natural Wonders of the U. S. A. Ser.). (Illus.). 32p. (J). (gr. 4-7). per. 9.95 *(978-1-59036-273-0(X))* Weigl Pubs., Inc.
Watson, Galadriel Findlay. Angel Falls. 2013. (J). 28.55 *(978-1-62127-472-8(1))* Weigl Pubs., Inc.
—Angel Falls: The Largest Waterfall in the World. 2004. (Illus.). 32p. (J). lib. bdg. 26.00 *(978-1-59036-267-9(5))* Weigl Pubs., Inc.
Willis, Terri. Venezuela. 2003. (Enchantment of the World Ser.). (ENG., Illus.). 144p. (YA). (gr. 5-9). 37.00 *(978-0-516-24214-9(8),* Children's Pr.) Scholastic Library Publishing.

VENEZUELA—FICTION

Carney, Lacy & Robey, Samantha. The Last Name Banks. 2012. 148p. (J). pap. 11.99 *(978-0-9856863-1-4(6))* FireFly Lights.
Cowcher, Helen. Jaguar. (J). (gr. 1-2). *(978-0-590-36037-1(X))*; (SPA., Illus.). pap. 3.96 net. *(978-0-590-87599-8(X),* SO30738, Scholastic Pr.) Scholastic, Inc.
Ficklin, Jonene H. Orinoco Intrigue. 2005. (YA). 14.95 *(978-0-9761188-1-7(5))* Victor's Crown Publishing.
L'Engle, Madeleine. Dragons in the Waters. 2011. (Polly O'Keefe Ser.: 2). (ENG.). 320p. (YA). (gr. 6-10). pap. 12.99 *(978-0-312-67442-7(2),* 900072857) Square Fish.
Spradlin, Michael P. Pararescue Corps. Karkavelas, Spiros, illus. 2019. (Pararescue Corps Ser.). (ENG.). 240p. (J). (gr. 4-8). pap., pap., pap. 9.95 *(978-1-4965-8105-1(9),* 140248, Stone Arch Bks.) Capstone.
—Viper Strike: A 4D Book. Karkavelas, Spiros, illus. 2018. (Pararescue Corps Ser.). (ENG.). 128p. (J). (gr. 4-8). lib. bdg. 27.32 *(978-1-4965-5202-0(4),* 136214, Stone Arch Bks.) Capstone.

VENEZUELA—HISTORY

Anderson, Corey. Hola, Venezuela. 2019. (Countries of the World Ser.). (ENG., Illus.). 48p. (J). (gr. 4-8). pap. 17.07 *(978-1-5341-5095-9(1),* 213687); lib. bdg. 39.21 *(978-1-5341-4809-3(4),* 213686) Cherry Lake Publishing.
Bomgraber, Elizabeth. The People & Culture of Venezuela, 1 vol. 2017. (Celebrating Hispanic Diversity Ser.). (ENG., Illus.). 32p. (J). (gr. 4-5). 27.93 *(978-1-5081-6307-7(3),* 34eda4ba-947a-4f4c-9dfa-42c7c82c2fdd, PowerKids Pr.) Rosen Publishing Group, Inc., The.
Cunill, Pedro. Venezuela II. (Biblioteca Iberoamericana Ser.). (SPA., Illus.). 128p. *(978-84-207-3096-7(3),* BI-2036) Grupo Anaya, S.A.
Gibson, Karen Bush. Venezuela. 2009. (J). *(978-1-58415-791-5(7))* Mitchell Lane Pubs.
Jones, Helga. Venezuela. 2008. pap. 40.95 *(978-0-8225-9308-9(4))* Lerner Publishing Group.
Kohen Winter, Jane & Baguley, Kitt. Venezuela, 1 vol. 3rd rev. ed. 2012. (Cultures of the World (Third Edition)(r) Ser.). (ENG.). 144p. (gr. 5-5). 48.79 *(978-1-60870-803-1(9),* ee58405c-bcaa-4a78-9a67-55a101e1ccfc) Cavendish Square Publishing LLC.
Mattern, Joanne. Angel Falls: World's Highest Waterfall. 2009. (Nature's Greatest Hits Ser.). 24p. (gr. 2-2). 42.50 *(978-1-61514-837-0(X),* PowerKids Pr.) Rosen Publishing Group, Inc., The.
—Cataratas Ángel: Las cataratas más altas del mundo (Angel Falls: World's Highest Waterfall) 2009. (Maravillas naturales (Natures Greatest Hits) Ser.). (SPA.). 24p. (gr. 2-2). 42.50 *(978-1-61514-362-7(9),* Editorial Buenas Letras) Rosen Publishing Group, Inc., The.
Murray, Julie. Venezuela. 2017. (Explore the Countries Set 4 Ser.). (ENG., Illus.). 40p. (J). (gr. 2-5). lib. bdg. 35.64 *(978-1-5321-1054-2(5),* 25684, Big Buddy Bks.) ABDO Publishing Co.
Pohl, Kathleen. Descubramos Venezuela (Looking at Venezuela), 1 vol. 2008. (Descubramos Países Del Mundo (Looking at Countries) Ser.). (SPA.). 32p. (gr. 2-4). (J). lib. bdg. 28.67 *(978-0-8368-9076-1(0),* 9a7ebab1-b51e-4b5e-bedd-c6621a4afb40); pap. 11.50 *(978-0-8368-9077-8(9),* 9f812abf-5472-4422-93aa-c9b64277824f, Gareth Stevens Learning Library) Stevens, Gareth Publishing LLLP.
Schuetz, Kari. Venezuela. 2012. (Exploring Countries Ser.). (ENG., Illus.). 32p. (J). (gr. 3-7). lib. bdg. 27.95 *(978-1-60014-735-7(6),* Blastoff! Readers) Bellwether Media.
Shields, Charles J. Venezuela, Vol. 13. Henderson, James D., ed. 2015. (Discovering South America: History, Politics, & Culture Ser.). (Illus.). 64p. (J). (gr. 7). lib. bdg. 22.95 *(978-1-4222-3306-1(5))* Mason Crest.
Sullivan, Laura L. Venezuela, 1 vol. 2019. (Exploring World Cultures (First Edition) Ser.). (ENG.). 32p. (gr. 3-3). lib. bdg. 31.64 *(978-1-5026-4716-0(8),* ae5e505b-3474-4d02-9b18-8826a55f0cf9) Cavendish Square Publishing LLC.
Watson, Galadriel Findlay. Angel Falls. 2013. (J). pap. 13.95 *(978-1-62127-478-0(0))* Weigl Pubs., Inc.

VENICE (ITALY)

Kids Go Europe: Treasure Hunt Venice. 2006. (J). spiral bd. 9.95 *(978-0-9772699-0-7(6))* Kids Go Europe, Inc.
Rossi, Renzo. Venice. 2004. (Great Cities Through the Ages Ser.). (Illus.). 44p. (J). (gr. 5). 18.95 *(978-1-59270-014-1(4))* Enchanted Lion Bks., LLC.
Sasek, M. This Is Venice. 2005. (This Is ... Ser.). (ENG., Illus.). 64p. (J). (gr. 2-12). 17.95 *(978-0-7893-1223-5(9))* Universe Publishing.

VENICE (ITALY)—FICTION

Armstrong, Alan W. Looking for Marco Polo. Jessell, Tim, illus. 2011. (ENG.). 304p. (J). (gr. 4-6). lib. bdg. 21.19 *(978-0-375-93321-9(2),* Yearling) Random Hse. Children's Bks.
Baucom, Ian. Through the Skylight. Gerard, Justin, illus. (ENG.). 400p. (J). (gr. 4-8). 2014. pap. 6.99 *(978-1-4424-8167-1(6))* 2013. 17.99 *(978-1-4169-1777-9(2))* Simon & Schuster Children's Publishing. (Atheneum Bks. for Young Readers).
Collins, Pat Lowery. Hidden Voices: The Orphan Musicians of Venice. 2009. (ENG., Illus.). 352p. (YA). (gr. 7). 17.99 *(978-0-7636-3917-4(6))* Candlewick Pr.
Cornelia, Funke. The Thief Lord. 2004. Tr. of Herr der Diebe. 376p. (J). (gr. 5-18). pap. 44.00 incl. audio *(978-0-8072-2278-2(X),* Listening Library) Random Hse. Audio Publishing Group.
—The Thief Lord. 2003. Tr. of Herr der Diebe. (gr. 3-6). 18.40 *(978-0-613-84572-4(2))* Turtleback.
Cowling, Douglas. Vivaldi's Ring of Mystery. Fernandez, Laura & Jacobson, Rick, illus. 2004. (ENG.). 44p. (J). *(978-0-439-96904-8(2),* North Winds Pr) Scholastic Canada, Ltd.
Gregory, Philippa. Fools' Gold. van Deelen, Fred, illus. 2014. (Order of Darkness Ser.: 3). (ENG.). 384p. (YA). (gr. 9). 19.99 *(978-1-4424-7690-5(7),* Simon Pulse) Simon Pulse.
Henty, George. The Lion of Saint Mark: A Story of Venice in the Fourteenth Century. 2007. (ENG.). 310p. pap. 23.99 *(978-1-4346-1158-1(2))*; 346p. pap. 24.99 *(978-1-4346-1229-8(5))* Creative Media Partners, LLC.
Higgins, Jack & Richards, Justin. Death Run. 2009. (ENG.). 288p. (YA). (gr. 7-18). 8.99 *(978-0-14-241475-0(1),* Speak) Penguin Young Readers Group.
Lovric, Michelle. The Undrowned Child, 1. 2012. (Undrowned Child Ser.). (ENG.). 464p. (J). (gr. 6-8). lib. bdg. 22.44 *(978-0-385-90814-6(8),* Delacorte Pr.) Random Hse. Children's Bks.
Marcellino, Fred. Arrivederci, Crocodile: Or See You Later, Alligator. Marcellino, Fred & Puybaret, Eric, illus. 2019. (ENG.). 40p. (J). (gr. -1-3). 17.99 *(978-1-5344-0401-4(5),* Atheneum Bks. for Young Readers) Simon & Schuster Children's Publishing.

TUV

Napoli, Donna Jo. Daughter of Venice. 2003. (ENG.). 288p. (YA). (gr. 7). mass mkt. 9.99 *(978-0-440-22928-5(6),* Laurel Leaf) Random Hse. Children's Bks.

Osborne, Mary Pope. Carnival at Candlelight, Vol. 5. Murdocca, Sal, illus. 2006. (Magic Tree House (R) Merlin Mission Ser.: 5). 144p. (J). (gr. 2-5). 6.99 *(978-0-375-83034-1(0),* Random Hse. Bks. for Young Readers) Random Hse. Children's Bks.

Osborne, Mary Pope & PLC Editors Staff. Carnival at Candlelight. Murdocca, Sal, illus. 2006. (Magic Tree House Merlin Missions Ser.: No. 5). 105p. (gr. 2-6). 15.00 *(978-0-7569-6690-4(6))* Perfection Learning Corp.

Papa Piccolo: Evaluation Guide. 2006. (J). 17.95 *(978-1-55942-419-6(2))* Witcher Productions.

Paris, Harper. The Mystery of the Mosaic. Calo, Marcos, illus. 2014. (Greetings from Somewhere Ser.: 2). (ENG.). 128p. (J). (gr. k-2). pap. 6.99 *(978-1-4424-9721-4(1),* Little Simon) Little Simon.

—The Mystery of the Mosaic. Calo, Marcos, illus. 2014. (Greetings from Somewhere Ser.: Vol. 2). (ENG.). 115p. (J). (gr. k-2). lib. bdg. 16.80 *(978-1-62765-837-9(8))* Perfection Learning Corp.

Rabley, Stephen. Easystart: Marcel & the Mona Lisa. 2nd ed. 2008. (Pearson English Graded Readers Ser.). (ENG., Illus.). 20p. pap. 11.99 *(978-1-4058-6955-3(0),* Pearson ELT) Pearson Education.

Renek, Nava. Venice Is for Cats. 2013. (Illus.). pap. 20.00 *(978-0-923389-53-6(9))* Spuyten Duyvil Publishing.

Shefelman, Janice. Anna Maria's Gift. Papp, Robert, illus. 2011. (Stepping Stone Book(TM) Ser.). 112p. (J). (gr. 2-5). pap. 4.99 *(978-0-375-85882-6(2),* Random Hse. Bks. for Young Readers) Random Hse. Children's Bks.

Shefelman, Janice Jordan. Anna Maria's Gift. Papp, Robert, illus. 2010. (Stepping Stones Chapter Book: History Ser.). (ENG.). 112p. (J). (gr. 1-4). lib. bdg. 17.44 *(978-0-375-95881-6(9))* Random House Publishing Group.

Stilton, Geronimo. Geronimo Stilton Graphic Novels #6: Who Stole the Mona Lisa?, Vol. 6. 2010. (Geronimo Stilton Graphic Novels Ser.: 6). (ENG., Illus.). 56p. (J). (gr. 2-6). 9.99 *(978-1-59707-221-2(4),* 900070133, Papercutz) Mad Cave Studios.

Stilton, Gerónimo. The Mystery in Venice. 2012. (Geronimo Stilton Ser.: 48). lib. bdg. 18.40 *(978-0-606-23729-1(1))* Turtleback.

Webb, Holly. A Magical Venice Story: the Girl of Glass: Book 4, Bk. 4. 2018. (Magical Venice Story Ser.). (ENG.). 256p. (J). (gr. 4-7). 9.99 *(978-1-4083-2768-5(6),* Orchard Bks.) Hachette Children's Group GBR. Dist: Hachette Bk. Group.

—A Magical Venice Story: the Maskmaker's Daughter: Book 3. 2018. (Magical Venice Story Ser.). (ENG.). 256p. (J). (gr. 4-7). pap. 9.99 *(978-1-4083-2766-1(X),* Orchard Bks.) Hachette Children's Group GBR. Dist: Hachette Bk. Group.

Woodford, Pamela. Lilly & Harry. 2013. (Brighter Little Minds Ser.). (ENG., Illus.). 18p. (J). 10.95 *(978-1-871305-79-1(9))* Orpen Pr. IRL. Dist: Dufour Editions, Inc.

VENICE (ITALY)—HISTORY

Candlewick Press. Venice: a 3D Keepsake Cityscape. McMenemy, Sarah, illus. 2014. (Panorama Pops Ser.). (ENG.). 20p. (J). (gr. k-4). 8.99 *(978-0-7636-7186-0(X))* Candlewick Pr.

Dyan, Penelope. Marco Polo Was Here! a Kid's Guide to Venice, Italy. Weigand, John D., photos by. 2009. (Illus.). 42p. pap. 11.95 *(978-1-935118-69-5(2))* Bellissima Publishing, LLC.

Naughton, Diane. Venice: The Floating City, 1 vol. 2014. (ENG., Illus.). 28p. (J). pap., E-Book 9.50 *(978-1-107-62163-3(1))* Cambridge Univ. Pr.

Nussbaum, Ben. Protecting a Sinking City. rev. ed. 2019. (Smithsonian: Informational Text Ser.). (ENG., Illus.). 32p. (J). (gr. 2-3). pap. 10.99 *(978-1-4938-6674-8(5))* Teacher Created Materials, Inc.

Verzov, Ella & Oirechman, Chana. Tamar of Venice. 2013. (Illus.). 54p. (J). *(978-1-61465-170-3(1))* Menucha Pubs. Inc.

VENOM

see Poisons

VENUS (PLANET)

Adamson, Thomas K. Do You Really Want to Visit Venus? Fabbri, Daniele, illus. 2013. (Do You Really Want to Visit the Solar System? Ser.). (ENG.). 24p. (J). (gr. 1-4). 27.10 *(978-1-60753-196-8(8),* 16264) Amicus.

—Venus [Scholastic]: Revised Edition. 2010. (Exploring the Galaxy Ser.). (ENG.). 24p. pap. 0.49 *(978-1-4296-5816-4(9),* Capstone Pr.) Capstone.

Beckett, Leslie. Exploring Venus. 2017. (Journey Through Our Solar System Ser.). 24p. (gr. 1-2). 49.50 *(978-1-5345-2258-9(1),* KidHaven Publishing); (ENG.). pap. 9.25 *(978-1-5345-2287-9(5),* ca107038-a229-41d7-8f9c-f661ef46f906); (ENG.). lib. bdg. 26.23 *(978-1-5345-2273-2(5),* 9ac084e3-33c8-41af-970b-f12c8ecc6c80) Greenhaven Publishing LLC.

Bjorklund, Ruth. Venus, 1 vol. 2010. (Space! Ser.). (ENG.). 64p. (gr. 5-5). lib. bdg. 35.50 *(978-0-7614-4251-6(0),* 4bbc101c-81b3-4b74-b831-547ef5dc9c4b) Cavendish Square Publishing LLC.

Bloom, J. P. Venus, 1 vol. 2015. (Planets Ser.). (ENG.). 24p. (J). (gr. -1-2). lib. bdg. 32.79 *(978-1-62970-722-8(8),* 17243, Abdo Kids) ABDO Publishing Co.

—Venus. 2017. (Planetas Ser.). 24p. (J). (gr. -1-2). (SPA.). pap. 7.95 *(978-1-4966-1305-9(8),* 135027); (ENG.). pap. 7.95 *(978-1-4966-1287-8(6),* 135019) Capstone. (Capstone Classroom).

—Venus (Venus), 1 vol. 2016. (Planetas (Planets) Ser.). (SPA., Illus.). 24p. (J). (gr. -1-2). lib. bdg. 32.79 *(978-1-68080-759-2(5),* 22680, Abdo Kids) ABDO Publishing Co.

Carlson-Berne, Emma. The Secrets of Venus. 2015. (Planets Ser.). (ENG., Illus.). 32p. (J). (gr. 2-4). lib. bdg. 32.65 *(978-1-4914-5870-9(4),* 128833, Capstone Pr.) Capstone.

Carson, Mary Kay. Far-Out Guide to Venus, 1 vol. 2010. (Far-Out Guide to the Solar System Ser.). (ENG.). 48p. (gr. 4-6). 27.93 *(978-0-7660-3181-4(0),* f16b2313-fd0a-426e-804d-3d39f93c40cd); (Illus.). pap. 11.53 *(978-1-59845-182-5(0),* 70aacc1f-a42e-41a4-9620-10a972218964, Enslow Elementary) Enslow Publishing, LLC.

Chrismer, Melanie. Venus. 2007. (Scholastic News Nonfiction Readers Ser.). (ENG., Illus.). 24p. (J). (gr. 1-2). 22.00 *(978-0-531-14755-9(X))* Scholastic Library Publishing.

Dickmann, Nancy. Exploring the Inner Planets, 1 vol. 2015. (Spectacular Space Science Ser.). (ENG., Illus.). 48p. (J). (gr. 5-6). 33.47 *(978-1-4994-3629-7(7),* ab513eb5-c984-4eb0-b82d-98012308a5f4, Rosen Central) Rosen Publishing Group, Inc., The.

Dittmer, Lori. Vénus. 2018. (Graines de Savoir Ser.). (FRE., Illus.). 24p. (J). *(978-1-77092-412-3(4),* 19701) Creative Co., The.

—Venus. 2018. (Seedlings Ser.). 24p. (J). (gr. -1-1). (ENG., Illus.). pap. 8.99 *(978-1-62832-536-2(4),* 19667, Creative Paperbacks); (SPA.). *(978-1-60818-954-0(6),* 19671, Creative Education); (ENG., Illus.). *(978-1-60818-920-5(1),* 19669, Creative Education) Creative Co., The.

Dunn, Mary R. A Look at Venus. 2009. (Astronomy Now! Ser.). 24p. (gr. 2-3). 42.50 *(978-1-61511-475-7(0),* PowerKids Pr.) Rosen Publishing Group, Inc., The.

Fleisher, Paul. Venus. 2009. (Early Bird Astronomy Ser.). (ENG.). 48p. (gr. 2-5). lib. bdg. 26.60 *(978-0-7613-4151-2(X))* Lerner Publishing Group.

Goldstein, Margaret J. Discover Venus. 2018. (Searchlight Books (tm) — Discover Planets Ser.). (ENG., Illus.). 32p. (J). (gr. 3-5). lib. bdg. 30.65 *(978-1-5415-2340-1(7),* aa367b80-46e3-4f41-80a7-4c136edb5c65, Lerner Pubns.) Lerner Publishing Group.

—Venus. 2003. (Our Universe Ser.). (ENG., Illus.). 32p. (gr. 2-4). lib. bdg. 22.60 *(978-0-8225-4649-8(3))* Lerner Publishing Group.

Hantula, Richard & Asimov, Isaac. Venus (Venus), 1 vol. 2003. (Isaac Asimov's Biblioteca Del Universo Del Siglo XXI (Isaac Asimov's 21st Century Library of the Universe) Ser.). (SPA., Illus.). 32p. (gr. 3-5). lib. bdg. 28.67 *(978-0-8368-3864-0(5),* a8d10885-563a-47ee-a670-50eedf2e8c38, Gareth Stevens Learning Library) Stevens, Gareth Publishing LLLP.

Hollar, Sherman. The Inner Planets: Mercury, Venus, & Mars, 1 vol. 2011. (Solar System Ser.). (ENG., Illus.). 96p. (J). (gr. 8-8). 35.29 *(978-1-61530-512-4(2),* d524e35f-a616-40a6-a97b-953a5b929220) Rosen Publishing Group, Inc., The.

James, Lincoln. Venus, 1 vol. 2010. (Our Solar System Ser.). (ENG.). 24p. (J). (gr. k-2). pap. 9.15 *(978-1-4339-3846-7(4),* d4470807-306b-4cc2-a0cb-a4fc2b8186b7); (Illus.). lib. bdg. 25.27 *(978-1-4339-3845-0(6),* a8ee5ab3-85b2-4e90-8fea-af7fd08418d8) Stevens, Gareth Publishing LLLP.

Jefferis, David. Hot Planets: Mercury & Venus. 2008. (ENG., Illus.). 32p. (J). (gr. 3-7). pap. *(978-0-7787-3751-3(9))* Crabtree Publishing Co.

Kazunas, Ariel. Venus. 2011. (21st Century Junior Library: Solar System Ser.). (ENG., Illus.). 24p. (gr. 2-5). lib. bdg. 29.21 *(978-1-61080-085-3(0),* 201080) Cherry Lake Publishing.

Land-Sailing Venus Rover: Meet NASA Inventor Geoffrey Landis & His Team's. 2017. (J). *(978-0-7166-6160-3(8))* World Bk., Inc.

Margaret, Amy. Venus. 2009. (Library of the Planets Ser.). 24p. (gr. 3-3). 42.50 *(978-1-60853-920-8(2),* PowerKids Pr.) Rosen Publishing Group, Inc., The.

Murray, Julie. Venus. 2018. (Planets (Dash!) Ser.). (ENG., Illus.). 24p. (J). (gr. k-4). lib. bdg. 31.36 *(978-1-5321-2533-1(X),* 30075, Abdo Zoom-Dash) ABDO Publishing Co.

Oldfield, Dawn Bluemel. Venus: Super Hot. 2015. (Out of This World Ser.). (ENG.). 24p. (J). (gr. -1-3). lib. bdg. 26.99 *(978-1-62724-562-3(6))* Bearport Publishing Co., Inc.

—Venus: Supercaliente. 2015. (Fuera de Este Mundo Ser.). (SPA., Illus.). 24p. (J). (gr. -1-3). lib. bdg. 26.99 *(978-1-62724-599-9(5))* Bearport Publishing Co., Inc.

Orme, Helen & Orme, David. Let's Explore Venus, 1 vol. 2007. (Space Launch! Ser.). (ENG., Illus.). 24p. (gr. 2-4). lib. bdg. 25.67 *(978-0-8368-7950-6(3),* 2d42fcd1-8d88-4a86-8001-d4839c23ff59, Gareth Stevens Learning Library) Stevens, Gareth Publishing LLLP.

Owen, Ruth. Venus, 1 vol. 2013. (Explore Outer Space Ser.). (ENG.). 32p. (J). (gr. 2-3). pap. 11.00 *(978-1-61533-763-7(6),* a9e7b2d9-87f4-43fa-829b-1f83f92b726e); lib. bdg. 29.93 *(978-1-61533-723-1(7),* d660c885-d8ca-4392-a864-eb1b685c28ff) Rosen Publishing Group, Inc., The. (Windmill Bks.).

—Venus. 2013. (Explore Outer Space Ser.). 32p. (J). (gr. 3-6). pap. 60.00 *(978-1-61533-764-4(4))* Windmill Bks.

Rathburn, Betsy. Venus. 2019. (Space Science Ser.). (ENG., Illus.). 24p. (J). (gr. 3-7). lib. bdg. 26.95 *(978-1-62617-980-6(8),* Torque Bks.) Bellwether Media.

Renfield, R. K. Venus. (Library of Planets Ser.). 48p. (gr. 5-8). 2009. 55.90 *(978-1-60853-823-2(0),* Rosen Reference) 2007. (ENG.). (J). 34.47 *(978-1-4042-1968-7(4),* c2cf8cd1-9bd0-4417-b807-8b9d993b00ff) Rosen Publishing Group, Inc., The.

Ring, Susan. Venus. (J). 2013. *(978-1-62127-270-0(2))* 2013. pap. *(978-1-62127-279-3(6))* 2004. (Illus.). pap. 8.95 *(978-1-59036-223-5(3))* 2004. (Illus.). 24p. (gr. 4-7). lib. bdg. 24.45 *(978-1-59036-096-5(6))* Weigl Pubs., Inc.

Ring, Susan & Roumanis, Alexis. Venus. 2016. (Illus.). 24p. (J). *(978-1-5105-0995-5(X))* SmartBook Media, Inc.

Romero, Libby. Discover Mars & Venus. 2006. (J). pap. *(978-1-4108-6507-6(X))* Benchmark Education Co.

—Mars & Venus. 2006. (J). pap. *(978-1-4108-6504-5(5))* Benchmark Education Co.

Roumanis, Alexis. Venus. 2016. (J). *(978-1-5105-2059-2(7))* SmartBook Media, Inc.

—Venus. 2015. (J). *(978-1-4896-3308-8(1))* Weigl Pubs., Inc.

Sexton, Colleen. Venus. 2010. (Exploring Space Ser.). (ENG., Illus.). 24p. (J). (gr. k-3). lib. bdg. 26.95 *(978-1-60014-403-5(9),* Blastoff! Readers) Bellwether Media.

Snyder, J. M. Journey to Venus, 1 vol. 2014. (Spotlight on Space Science Ser.). (ENG.). 32p. (J). (gr. 5-5). pap. 12.75 *(978-1-4994-0380-0(1),* 3051f65f-cac1-41e9-9758-3b68657590a1, PowerKids Pr.) Rosen Publishing Group, Inc., The.

Sparrow, Giles. Destination Venus, 1 vol. 2009. (Destination Solar System Ser.). (ENG.). 32p. (J). (gr. 3-4). lib. bdg. 28.93 *(978-1-4358-3442-2(9),* 4e6cd2e8-c95f-48d8-8f17-f0971e1b81b0); (Illus.). pap. 11.00 *(978-1-4358-3457-6(7),* ec486159-8da5-47e3-9ab7-aedb2ac56332) Rosen Publishing Group, Inc., The. (PowerKids Pr.).

Steinkraus, Kyla. Planetas Rocosos - Mercurio, Venus, la Tierra y Marte. 2017. (Inside Outer Space Ser.).Tr. of Rocky Planets - Mercury, Venus, Earth, & Mars. (SPA.). 24p. (gr. k-3). pap. 9.95 *(978-1-68342-262-4(7),* 9781683422624) Rourke Educational Media.

Stone, Tanya Lee. Venus, 1 vol. 2003. (Blastoff! Ser.). (ENG., Illus.). 64p. (gr. 5-5). 34.07 *(978-0-7614-1405-6(3),* b640cfb3-0bfa-4da9-873d-384df522d210) Cavendish Square Publishing LLC.

Teitelbaum, Michael. Mars & Venus Space Exploration: Set Of 6. 2011. (Navigators Ser.). (J). pap. 50.00 net. *(978-1-4108-6243-3(7))* Benchmark Education Co.

Wimmer, Teresa. Venus. 2007. (My First Look at: Planets Ser.). (Illus.). 24p. (J). (gr. -1-3). lib. bdg. 24.25 *(978-1-58341-524-5(6),* Creative Education) Creative Co., The.

World Book, Inc. Staff, contrib. by. Mercury & Venus. (J). 2010. *(978-0-7166-9534-9(0))* 2006. (Illus.). 63p. *(978-0-7166-9502-8(2))* 2nd ed. 2006. (Illus.). 64p. *(978-0-7166-9517-2(0))* World Bk., Inc.

VERDI, GIUSEPPE, 1813-1901

Bauer, Helen. Verdi for Kids: His Life & Music with 21 Activities. 2013. (For Kids Ser.: 48). (ENG., Illus.). 144p. (J). (gr. 4). pap. 16.95 *(978-1-61374-500-7(1))* Chicago Review Pr., Inc.

Schoell, William. Giuseppe Verdi & Italian Opera. 2007. (Classical Composers Ser.). (Illus.). 128p. (J). (gr. 3-7). lib. bdg. 27.95 *(978-1-59935-041-7(6))* Reynolds, Morgan Inc.

Snowman, Daniel. Giuseppe Verdi: Composer, 1 vol. 2016. (History Makers Ser.). (ENG., Illus.). 144p. (YA). (gr. 9-9). 47.36 *(978-1-5026-2449-9(4),* ae8d04c4-d014-480a-90e7-ece631c91f82) Cavendish Square Publishing LLC.

Whiting, Jim. The Life & Times of Guiseppe Verdi. 2004. (Masters of Music Ser.). (Illus.). 48p. (gr. 4-8). lib. bdg. 20.95 *(978-1-58415-281-1(8))* Mitchell Lane Pubs.

VERMEER, JOHANNES, 1632-1675

Mis, Melody S. Vermeer. 2009. (Meet the Artist Ser.). 24p. (gr. 2-3). 42.50 *(978-1-61514-633-8(4),* PowerKids Pr.) Rosen Publishing Group, Inc., The.

Wood, Alix. Johannes Vermeer, 1 vol. 2013. (Artists Through the Ages Ser.). (ENG., Illus.). 32p. (J). (gr. 2-3). pap. 11.00 *(978-1-61533-633-3(8),* 0b49d21b-ed88-4285-babf-044a5a73f5b9); lib. bdg. 29.93 *(978-1-61533-623-4(0),* fcf77482-fd27-4f4c-8bba-2c5d84131 85d) Rosen Publishing Group, Inc., The. (Windmill Bks.).

VERMONT

Adam, Sarah E., illus. Abby in Vermont Coloring & Activity Book. 2008. 32p. (J). 4.95 *(978-0-9793790-1-7(6))* Howard Printing, Inc.

Brown, Jonatha A. Vermont, 1 vol. 2006. (Portraits of the States Ser.). (ENG.). 32p. (gr. 3-5). pap. 11.50 *(978-0-8368-4727-7(X),* e7110bea-a372-4fa4-b7a6-a838aea97fb3); (Illus.). lib. bdg. 28.67 *(978-0-8368-4710-9(5),* 66bf443d-4239-49b0-b86c-2711b9c571fe) Stevens, Gareth Publishing LLLP. (Gareth Stevens Learning Library).

Czech, Jan M. From Sea to Shining Sea: Vermont. 2008. (ENG.). 80p. (J). pap. 7.95 *(978-0-531-20816-8(8),* Children's Pr.) Scholastic Library Publishing.

Dornfeld, Margaret. Vermont, 1 vol. Santoro, Christopher, illus. 2005. (It's My State! (First Edition)(r) Ser.). (ENG.). 80p. (gr. 4-4). lib. bdg. 34.07 *(978-0-7614-1864-1(4),* e164a437-fb40-4016-a3f5-abd2e3cb74a0) Cavendish Square Publishing LLC.

Dupeyron, Sarah, illus. The ABC's of Vermont Coloring Book. 2007. 32p. (J). 4.95 *(978-0-9793790-0-0(8))* Howard Printing, Inc.

Elish, Dan. Vermont, 1 vol. 2nd rev. ed. 2006. (Celebrate the States (Second Edition) Ser.). (ENG., Illus.). 144p. (gr. 6-6). lib. bdg. 39.79 *(978-0-7614-2018-7(5),* ce048578-480c-4251-a39c-439ecf88b990) Cavendish Square Publishing LLC.

Hackett, Jennifer. Vermont (a True Book: My United States) (Library Edition) 2018. (True Book (Relaunch) Ser.). (ENG., Illus.). 48p. (J). (gr. 3-5). lib. bdg. 31.00 *(978-0-531-23583-6(1),* Children's Pr.) Scholastic Library Publishing.

Hassig, Susan M. & Quek, Lynette. Panama, 1 vol. 2nd rev. ed. 2007. (Cultures of the World (Second Edition)(r) Ser.). (ENG., Illus.). 144p. (gr. 5-5). lib. bdg. 49.79 *(978-0-7614-2028-6(2),* ba52c295-3c5e-4f11-849f-68a1ffe4430a) Cavendish Square Publishing LLC.

Keizer, Garret, et al, contrib. by. The Twelve Seasons of Vermont: A Vermont Life Book. 2005. (Illus.). 112p. 34.95 *(978-1-931389-07-5(1))* Vermont Life Magazine.

Marsh, Carole. Vermont Current Events Projects: 30 Cool, Activities, Crafts, Experiments & More for Kids to Do to Learn about Your State! 2003. (Vermont Experience Ser.). 32p. (gr. k-5). pap. 5.95 *(978-0-635-02065-9(3),* Marsh, Carole Bks.) Gallopade International.

—Vermont Geography Projects: 30 Cool, Activities, Crafts, Experiments & More for Kids to Do to Learn about Your State! 2003. (Vermont Experience Ser.). 32p. (gr. k-5). pap. 5.95 *(978-0-635-01863-2(2),* Marsh, Carole Bks.) Gallopade International.

—Vermont Government Projects: 30 Cool, Activities, Crafts, Experiments & More for Kids to Do to Learn about Your State! 2003. (Vermont Experience Ser.). 32p. (gr. k-5). pap. 5.95 *(978-0-635-01964-6(7),* Marsh, Carole Bks.) Gallopade International.

—Vermont People Projects: 30 Cool, Activities, Crafts, Experiments & More for Kids to Do to Learn about Your State! 2003. (Vermont Experience Ser.). 32p. (gr. k-5). pap. 5.95 *(978-0-635-02014-7(9),* Marsh, Carole Bks.) Gallopade International.

—Vermont Symbols & Facts Projects: 30 Cool, Activities, Crafts, Experiments & More for Kids to Do to Learn about Your State! 2003. (Vermont Experience Ser.). 32p. (gr. k-5). pap. 5.95 *(978-0-635-01914-1(0),* Marsh, Carole Bks.) Gallopade International.

Murray, Julie. Vermont, 1 vol. 2006. (Buddy Book Ser.). (ENG., Illus.). 32p. (gr. 2-4). 27.07 *(978-1-59197-704-9(5),* Buddy Bks.) ABDO Publishing Co.

Parker, Bridget. Vermont. 2016. (States Ser.). (ENG., Illus.). 32p. (J). (gr. 3-6). lib. bdg. 27.99 *(978-1-5157-0433-1(5),* 132044, Capstone Pr.) Capstone.

Peters, S. True. How to Draw Vermont's Sights & Symbols. 2009. (Kid's Guide to Drawing America Ser.). 32p. (gr. k-k). 50.50 *(978-1-61511-101-5(8),* PowerKids Pr.) Rosen Publishing Group, Inc., The.

Taylor-Butler, Christine. Vermont. 2007. (Rookie Read-About Geography Ser.). (Illus.). 31p. (J). (gr. 1-2). 20.50 *(978-0-531-12593-9(9),* Children's Pr.) Scholastic Library Publishing.

Way, Jennifer. Vermont. 2009. (Bilingual Library of the United States of America Ser.). (ENG & SPA.). 32p. (gr. 2-2). 47.90 *(978-1-60853-389-3(1),* Editorial Buenas Letras) Rosen Publishing Group, Inc., The.

—Vermont, 1 vol. Brusca, Maria Cristina, tr. 2005. (Bilingual Library of the United States of America Ser.: Set 2). (ENG & SPA., Illus.). 32p. (J). (gr. 2-2). lib. bdg. 28.93 *(978-1-4042-3111-5(0),* b9dfcab1-6b3d-4f5f-81c7-f0c1e3792ce4) Rosen Publishing Group, Inc., The.

VERMONT—FICTION

Alvarez, Julia. De Como Tia Lola Aprendio a Ensenar (How Aunt Lola Learned to Teach Spanish Edition) 2011. (Tia Lola Stories Ser.: 2). (SPA.). 160p. (J). (gr. 3-7). 7.99 *(978-0-375-85793-5(1),* Yearling) Random Hse. Children's Bks.

—De Como Tia Lola Salvo el Verano (How Aunt Lola Saved the Summer Spanish Edition) 2012. (Tia Lola Stories Ser.: 3). (SPA.). 192p. (J). (gr. 3-7). 7.99 *(978-0-307-93023-1(8),* Yearling) Random Hse. Children's Bks.

—Devolver Al Remitente (Return to Sender Spanish Edition) 2010. (SPA.). 368p. (J). (gr. 3-7). 8.99 *(978-0-375-85124-7(0),* Yearling) Random Hse. Children's Bks.

—How Tia Lola Came to Visit Stay. 2004. 147p. (gr. 3-7). 17.00 *(978-0-7569-3641-9(1))* Perfection Learning Corp.

—How Tia Lola Ended up Starting Over. 2012. (Tia Lola Stories Ser.: 4). (ENG.). 160p. (J). (gr. 3-7). pap. 6.99 *(978-0-375-87320-1(1),* Yearling) Random Hse. Children's Bks.

—How Tia Lola Learned to Teach. 2011. (ENG.). 144p. (J). (Tia Lola Stories Ser.). (gr. 4-6). lib. bdg. 22.44 *(978-0-375-96460-2(6),* Knopf Bks. for Young Readers); (Tia Lola Stories Ser.: 2). (Illus.). (gr. 3-7). pap. 7.99 *(978-0-375-85792-8(3),* Yearling) Random Hse. Children's Bks.

—How Tia Lola Saved the Summer. 2012. (Tia Lola Stories Ser.: 3). (ENG.). 176p. (J). (gr. 3-7). 7.99 *(978-0-375-86687-6(6),* Yearling) Random Hse. Children's Bks.

Anderson, Matthew. The Game of Sunken Places. 2005. (Norumbegan Quartet: No. 1). 260p. (J). (gr. 4-7). 13.65 *(978-0-7569-5253-2(0))* Perfection Learning Corp.

Arenstam, Peter. Nicholas: a Vermont Tale. Holman, Karen Busch, illus. 2010. (Nicholas Northeastern Ser.: 4). 144p. (J). (gr. k-7). 14.95 *(978-1-58726-522-8(2),* Mitten Pr.) Ann Arbor Editions LLC.

Baughman, Sarah R. The Light in the Lake. 2019. (ENG., Illus.). 320p. (J). (gr. 3-7). 16.99 *(978-0-316-42242-0(8))* Little, Brown Bks. for Young Readers.

Beres, E. Jean. The Sugaring Season. 2008. 92p. pap. 19.95 *(978-1-60610-633-4(3))* America Star Bks.

Blakemore, Megan Frazer. The Spy Catchers of Maple Hill. 2014. (ENG.). 320p. (J). (gr. 3-6). 16.99 *(978-1-61963-348-3(5),* 900134200, Bloomsbury USA Childrens) Bloomsbury Publishing USA.

Blaushild, A. M. Angel Radio. 2016. (ENG., Illus.). (YA). 27.99 *(978-1-63477-935-7(5),* Harmony Ink Pr.) Dreamspinner Pr.

Bitt, Natalie. Snow One Like You. 2017. 258p. (J). pap. *(978-1-338-17474-8(6))* Scholastic, Inc.

Canfield, Dorothy. Understood Betsy. 2004. reprint ed. pap. 1.99 *(978-1-4192-9201-9(3));* pap. 24.95 *(978-1-4179-0955-1(2))* Kessinger Publishing, LLC.

Carlson, Melody. Viva Vermont!, 1 vol. 2014. (Carter House Girls Ser.: 4). (ENG.). 224p. (YA). pap. 9.99 *(978-0-310-74714-7(7))* Zondervan.

Chase, L. P. Elliot Stone & the Mystery of the Summer Vacation Sea Monster. DiRocco, Carl, illus. 2011. (ENG.). 165p. (J). pap. 8.99 *(978-0-9792918-7-6(9))* Blue Marlin Pubns.

Clark, Seneca & Giardi, Sandy. Frankie Goes to Fenway: The Tale of the Faithful, Red Sox-Loving Mouse. Decedue, Julie, illus. 2008. 56p. (J). 18.95 *(978-0-9767276-3-7(3))* Three Bean Pr.

Conforto, Lisa. The Very Compromising Adventures of Thumby Blackstone, 1 vol. 2010. 34p. 24.95 *(978-1-4512-0270-0(9))* PublishAmerica, Inc.

Cook, Eileen. The Education of Hailey Kendrick. 2011. (ENG.). 288p. (YA). (gr. 9). pap. 9.99 *(978-1-4424-1326-9(3),* Simon Pulse) Simon Pulse.

Edwards, Judith. At the Top of the Mountain. 2013. (Images from the Past Ser.). (ENG., Illus.). 144p. (gr. 3-7). pap. 12.95 *(978-1-884592-63-8(5))* Applewood Bks.

—Invasion on the Mountain: The Adventures of Will Ryan & the Civilian Conservation Corps, 1933, Book I. 2011. (Images from the Past Ser.). (ENG., Illus.). 90p. (J). (gr. 4-7). pap. 12.50 *(978-1-884592-55-3(4))* Applewood Bks.

—Trouble on the Mountain: The Adventures of Will Ryan & the Civilian Conservation Corps, 1934-35 Book II. 2012. (Images from the Past Ser.). (ENG., Illus.). 118p. (J). (gr. 3-7). pap. 12.50 *(978-1-884592-60-7(0))* Applewood Bks.

Fisher, Dorothy Canfield. Understood Betsy. 2018. (ENG., Illus.). 108p. (J). 12.99 *(978-1-5154-3494-8(X))* Wilder Pubns., Corp.

Gilligan, Shannon. The Lake Monster Mystery. Newton, Keith, illus. 2009. (ENG.). 80p. (J). (gr. 2-2). pap. 8.99 *(978-1-933390-60-4(3))* Chooseco LLC.

Hahn, Mary Downing. All the Lovely Bad Ones: A Ghost Story. 2009. (ENG.). 208p. (J). (gr. 3-7). pap. 7.99 *(978-0-547-24878-3(4),* 1100893, Clarion Bks.) HarperCollins Pubs.

Hart, Alison. Horse Diaries #2: Bell's Star. Sanderson, Ruth, illus. 2009. (Horse Diaries: 2). 144p. (J). (gr. 3-7). pap. 7.99

(978-0-375-85204-6(2), Random Hse. Bks. for Young Readers) Random Hse. Children's Bks.

Henry, Marguerite. Justin Morgan Had a Horse. 2011. 8.32 *(978-0-7848-3468-8(7)*, Everbind) Marco Bk. Co.

—Justin Morgan Had a Horse. Dennis, Wesley, illus. (ENG.). 176p. (J). (gr. 3-7). 2015. 21.99 *(978-1-4814-2562-9(5))* 2006. pap. 7.99 *(978-1-4169-2785-3(9))* Simon & Schuster Children's Publishing. (Aladdin).

Hesse, Karen. Witness. 2004. 168p. (J). (gr. 5-9). pap. 29.00 incl. audio *(978-0-8072-2094-8(9)*, Listening Library) Random Hse. Audio Publishing Group.

—Witness (Scholastic Gold) (ENG.). (J). (gr. 4-7). 2019. 192p. pap. 7.99 *(978-1-338-35967-1(3))* 2003. (Illus.). 176p. pap. 7.99 *(978-0-439-27200-1(9)*, Scholastic Paperbacks) Scholastic, Inc.

Hilton, Marilyn. Full Cicada Moon. 2017. lib. bdg. 19.65 *(978-0-606-39789-6(2))* Turtleback.

Jacobs, Lily. The Littlest Bunny in Vermont: An Easter Adventure. Dunn, Robert, illus. 2015. (Littlest Bunny Ser.). (ENG.). 32p. (J). (gr. -1-3). 9.99 *(978-1-4926-1225-4(1)*, Hometown World) Sourcebooks, Inc.

Jaimet, Kate. Edge of Flight, 1 vol. 2012. (Orca Sports Ser.). (ENG.). 160p. (J). (gr. 4-7). pap. 9.95 *(978-1-4598-0160-8(1))* Orca Bk. Pubs. USA.

James, Eric. Santa's Sleigh Is on Its Way to Vermont: A Christmas Adventure. Dunn, Robert, illus. 2016. (Santa's Sleigh Is on Its Way Ser.). (ENG.). 32p. (J). (gr. k-2). 12.99 *(978-1-4926-4362-3(9)*, 9781492643623, Hometown World) Sourcebooks, Inc.

—The Spooky Express Vermont. Piwowarski, Marcin, illus. 2017. (Spooky Express Ser.). (ENG.). 32p. (J). (gr. k-6). 9.99 *(978-1-4926-5407-0(8)*, Hometown World) Sourcebooks, Inc.

—Tiny the Vermont Easter Bunny. 2018. (Tiny the Easter Bunny Ser.). (ENG.). 40p. (J). (gr. k-3). 9.99 *(978-1-4926-5973-0(8)*, Hometown World) Sourcebooks, Inc.

Johnson, Maureen. Truly Devious: A Mystery. 2018. (Truly Devious Ser.: 1). (ENG., Illus.). 432p. (YA). (gr. 9). 17.99 *(978-0-06-233805-1(6)*, Tegen, Katherine Bks) HarperCollins Pubs.

—The Vanishing Stair. 2019. (Truly Devious Ser.: 2). (ENG.). (YA). (gr. 9). 400p. pap. 12.99 *(978-0-06-233809-9(9))*; 384p. 17.99 *(978-0-06-233808-2(0))*; 400p. E-Book *(978-0-06-233810-5(2)*, 9780062338105) HarperCollins Pubs. (Tegen, Katherine Bks).

Júlia, Álvarez. How Tia Lola Came to Visit Stay. 2014. (Tia Lola Stories Ser.). (ENG.). 160p. (J). (gr. 3-7). 11.24 *(978-1-63245-289-4(8))* Lectorum Pubns., Inc.

Kelley, Jane. Nature Girl. 2011. (ENG., Illus.). 256p. (J). (gr. 3-7). pap. 7.99 *(978-0-375-85635-8(8)*, Yearling) Random Hse. Children's Bks.

LaFleur, Suzanne. Love, Aubrey. 2011. (ENG.). 272p. (J). (gr. 3-7). pap. 7.99 *(978-0-375-85159-9(3)*, Yearling) Random Hse. Children's Bks.

Lasky, Kathryn. Sugaring Time. 2003. (Illus.). 21.25 *(978-0-8446-7248-9(3))* Smith, Peter Pub., Inc.

Logan, Kenneth. True Letters from a Fictional Life. 2016. (ENG.). 336p. (YA). (gr. 8). 17.99 *(978-0-06-238025-8(7)*, HarperTeen) HarperCollins Pubs.

Mademann Vaughan, Kathryn. My Day at the Zoo. Martin, Don, illus. 2004. (J). per. 19.95 *(978-0-9747447-1-1(9))* Chaser Media LLC.

McManus, Karen M. Two Can Keep a Secret. 2019. (ENG.). 352p. lib. bdg. 21.80 *(978-1-6636-2970-8(6))* Perfection Learning Corp.

—Two Can Keep a Secret. (ENG.). 352p. (YA). (gr. 9). 2021. pap. 12.99 *(978-1-5247-1471-0(2)*, Ember) 2019. 19.99 *(978-1-5247-1472-7(0)*, Delacorte Pr.) Random Hse. Children's Bks.

Messner, Kate. The Brilliant Fall of Gianna Z. 2017. (ENG.). 224p. (J). pap. 8.99 *(978-1-68119-547-6(X)*, 900177249, Bloomsbury USA Childrens) Bloomsbury Publishing USA.

—The Brilliant Fall of Gianna Z. 2017. (J). lib. bdg. 19.65 *(978-0-606-40595-9(X))* Turtleback.

—The Brilliant Fall of Gianna Z. 2010. (ENG.). 208p. (YA). (gr. 4-6). 24.94 *(978-0-8027-9842-8(X)*, 9780802798428) Walker & Co.

—Chirp. 2020. (ENG.). 240p. (J). 17.99 *(978-1-5476-0281-0(3)*, 900210016, Bloomsbury Children's Bks.) Bloomsbury Publishing USA.

Moulton, Erin E. Flutter: The Story of Four Sisters & an Incredible Journey. 2012. (ENG.). 224p. (J). (gr. 3-7). pap. 6.99 *(978-0-14-242133-8(2)*, Puffin Books) Penguin Young Readers Group.

Oneill, Elizabeth. Alfred Visits Vermont. 2008. 24p. pap. 12.00 *(978-0-9799121-9-1(9))* Funny Bone Bks.

Parent, David D. Drummers Forward! Marching with Angels: The Exciting Tale of a Drummer Boy Serving with the First Vermont Brigade & His Adventures During the Americ. 2013. 188p. pap. 13.50 *(978-1-62516-582-4(X)*, Strategic Bk. Publishing) Strategic Book Publishing & Rights Agency (SBPRA).

Parkhurst, Johanna. Here's to You, Zeb Pike [Library Edition]. 2014. 180p. pap. 14.99 *(978-1-62798-526-0(3)*, Harmony Ink Pr.) Dreamspinner Pr.

Paterson, Katherine. Preacher's Boy. 2013. (ENG.). 176p. (J). (gr. 5-7). pap. 7.99 *(978-0-544-10490-7(0)*, 1540798, Clarion Bks.) HarperCollins Pubs.

Peck, Robert Newton. A Day No Pigs Would Die. 139p. (YA). (gr. 7-18). pap. 4.99 *(978-0-8072-1384-1(5))*; pap. 4.99 *(978-0-8072-1357-5(8))* Random Hse. Audio Publishing Group. (Listening Library).

Perl, Erica S. When Life Gives You O. J. 2013. (When Life Gives You O. J. Ser.). (ENG.). (J). 208p. (gr. 4-6). 21.19 *(978-0-375-95924-0(6)*, Knopf Bks. for Young Readers); 224p. (gr. 3-7). 8.99 *(978-0-375-85902-1(0)*, Yearling) Random Hse. Children's Bks.

Porter, Eleanor. Pollyanna. 2018. (ENG., Illus.). 258p. (J). (gr. 4-7). 27.20 *(978-1-7317-0764-2(9))*; pap. 15.14 *(978-1-7317-0765-9(7))* Simon & Brown.

Porter, Eleanor H. Pollyanna. Hindley, Kate, illus. 2017. (Alma Junior Classics Ser.). (ENG.). 288p. (J). pap. 12.00 *(978-1-84749-640-9(7)*, 900184120, Alma Classics) Bloomsbury Publishing USA.

—Pollyanna. l.t. ed. 2007. (ENG.). 206p. pap. 22.99 *(978-1-4346-1071-3(3))* Creative Media Partners, LLC.

—Pollyanna. 2018. (ENG., Illus.). 120p. (J). (gr. 4-7). pap. 5.99 *(978-1-7268-3443-8(3))* Independently Published.

—Pollyanna. 2016. (J). pap. *(978-1-5124-2614-4(8))* Lerner Publishing Group.

Shankman, Ed. Champ & Me by the Maple Tree: A Vermont Tale. O'Neill, Dave, illus. 2010. (Shankman & O'Neill Ser.). (ENG.). 32p. (J). (gr. -1-3). 14.95 *(978-0-9819430-5-3(5)*, Commonwealth Editions) Applewood Bks.

Stahler, David, Jr. Gathering of Shades. 2006. (ENG.). 256p. pap. *(978-0-06-052296-4(8))* HarperCollins Canada, Ltd.

—A Gathering of Shades. 2005. (ENG.). 304p. (J). 15.99 *(978-0-06-052294-0(1)*, HarperTeen) HarperCollins Pubs.

—Spinning Out. 2011. (ENG.). 288p. (YA). (gr. 7-17). 16.99 *(978-0-8118-7780-0(9))* Chronicle Bks. LLC.

Strohm, Stephanie Kate. The Taming of the Drew. (ENG.). 304p. 2017. (YA). (gr. 7-12). pap. 9.99 *(978-1-5107-2636-9(5))* 2016. (J). (gr. 6-6). 17.99 *(978-1-5107-0215-8(6))* Skyhorse Publishing Co., Inc. (Sky Pony Pr.).

Tougias, Michael. Good Night Vermont. Stevenson, Harvey, illus. 2007. (Good Night Our World Ser.). (ENG.). 20p. (J). (gr. k — 1). bds. 9.95 *(978-1-60219-017-7(8))* Good Night Bks.

Tracy, Kristen. Hung Up. 2014. (ENG., Illus.). 288p. (YA). (gr. 9). 17.99 *(978-1-4424-6075-1(X)*, Simon Pulse) Simon Pulse.

Valentine, Nicole. A Time Traveler's Theory of Relativity. 2019. (ENG., Illus.). 352p. (J). (gr. 4-8). 17.99 *(978-1-5415-5538-9(4)*, 2b60b16e-6e91-4b27-b7dd-76c86cce49dc, Carolrhoda Bks.) Lerner Publishing Group.

Villanueva, Pedro. Chronicle of a New Kid. 2017. (Text Connections Guided Close Reading Ser.). (J). (gr. 1). *(978-1-4900-1825-6(5))* Benchmark Education Co.

Wallace, Kali. The Memory Trees. 2017. (ENG.). 432p. (YA). (gr. 9). 17.99 *(978-0-06-236623-8(8)*, Tegen, Katherine Bks) HarperCollins Pubs.

Washington, Ida H. Brave Enough: The Story of Rob Sanford, Vermont Pioneer Boy. Smoak, I. W. & Washington, C. E., illus. 2003. vii, 128p. (J). (gr. 4-6). pap. 12.95 *(978-0-9666832-7-1(7))* Cherry Tree Bks.

Winthrop, Elizabeth. Counting on Grace. 2007. (ENG., Illus.). 240p. (J). (gr. 3-7). 8.99 *(978-0-553-48783-1(3)*, Yearling) Random Hse. Children's Bks.

Wise, Anna. The Vala of Trinity: Book One Norse Series, 1 vol. 2009. 195p. pap. 24.95 *(978-1-61582-763-3(3))* America Star Bks.

Wojciechowska, Maia. A Kingdom in a Horse. 2012. (ENG.). 160p. (J). (gr. 2-7). pap. 9.95 *(978-1-61608-481-3(2)*, 608481, Sky Pony Pr.) Skyhorse Publishing Co., Inc.

Wolitzer, Meg. Belzhar. 2015. lib. bdg. 22.10 *(978-0-606-37573-3(2))* Turtleback.

Wolper, Joanna. The Man Who Could Be Santa. 2008. (Illus.). 78p. (J). pap. *(978-0-88092-765-9(8))*; lib. bdg. *(978-0-88092-764-2(X))* Royal Fireworks Publishing Co.

VERMONT—HISTORY

Ades, Audrey. Ethan Allen & the Green Mountain Boys. 2017. (Illus.). 32p. (J). 25.70 *(978-1-61228-952-6(5))* Mitchell Lane Pubs.

Carole Marsh. Vermont Indians. 2004. (Vermont Experience Ser.). 36p. (gr. 3-8). pap. 7.95 *(978-0-635-02334-6(2))*; lib. bdg. 29.95 *(978-0-635-02335-3(0))* Gallopade International.

Davies, Jean S. Neighborly Notes: From Turn of the Century Small Town Vermont 2004. (Illus.). 256p. per. 24.95 *(978-0-9749151-9-7(X))* CoZi Publishing LLC.

Domfeld, Margaret & McGeveran, William. Vermont, 1 vol. 2nd rev. ed. 2012. (It's My State! (Second Edition)(r) Ser.). (ENG.). 80p. (gr. 4-4). 34.07 *(978-1-60870-660-0(5)*, 31aa003b-11bf-4d80-bf23-e7d6b0652964) Cavendish Square Publishing LLC.

Foran, Jill. Vermont. 2011. (Guide to American States Ser.). (Illus.). 48p. (YA). (gr. 3-6). 29.99 *(978-1-61690-818-8(1))*; (J). 29.99 *(978-1-61690-494-4(1))* Weigl Pubs., Inc.

—Vermont: The Green Mountain State. 2016. (J). *(978-1-4896-4953-9(0))* Weigl Pubs., Inc.

Friesen, Helen Lepp. Vermont: The Green Mountain State. 2012. (J). *(978-1-61913-411-9(X))*; pap. *(978-1-61913-412-6(8))* Weigl Pubs., Inc.

Gilbert, Sara. Vermont. 2009. (This Land Called America Ser.). (Illus.). 32p. (YA). (gr. 3-6). 19.95 *(978-1-58341-798-0(2))* Creative Co., The.

Hamilton, John. Vermont, 1 vol. 2016. (United States of America Ser.). (ENG., Illus.). 48p. (J). (gr. 5-9). 34.21 *(978-1-68078-348-3(3)*, 21681, Abdo & Daughters) ABDO Publishing Co.

Heinrichs, Ann. America the Beautiful: Vermont (Revised Edition) 2014. (America the Beautiful, Third Ser. (Revised Edition) Ser.). (ENG.). 144p. (J). lib. bdg. 40.00 *(978-0-531-28296-0(1))* Scholastic Library Publishing.

—Vermont. Kania, Matt, illus. 2017. (U. S. A. Travel Guides). (ENG.). 40p. (J). (gr. 2-5). lib. bdg. 38.50 *(978-1-5038-1985-6(X)*, 211622) Child's World, Inc, The.

Koontz, Robin Michal. Vermont: The Green Mountain State, 1 vol. 2010. (Our Amazing States Ser.). (ENG., Illus.). 24p. (J). (gr. 3-3). pap. 9.25 *(978-1-4488-0730-7(1)*, 1406659b-8148-4014-b210-85785638963e, PowerKids Pr.) Rosen Publishing Group, Inc., The.

Marsh, Carole. Exploring Vermont Through Project-Based Learning: Geography, History, Government, Economics & More. 2016. (Vermont Experience Ser.). (ENG.). (J). pap. 9.99 *(978-0-635-12369-5(X))* Gallopade International.

—I'm Reading about Vermont. 2014. (Vermont Experience Ser.). (ENG., Illus.). (J). pap., pap. 8.99 *(978-0-635-11320-7(1))* Gallopade International.

—Vermont History Projects: 30 Cool, Activities, Crafts, Experiments & More for Kids to Do to Learn about Your State! 2003. (Vermont Experience Ser.). 32p. (gr. k-5). pap. 5.95 *(978-0-635-01814-4(4)*, Marsh, Carole Bks.) Gallopade International.

Otfinoski, Steven, et al. Vermont, 1 vol. 3rd rev. ed. 2015. (It's My State! (Third Edition)(r) Ser.). (ENG., Illus.). 80p. (gr. 4-4). 35.93 *(978-1-62713-181-0(7)*, 937420f2-5baa-454d-a8be-0dffe0134e39) Cavendish Square Publishing LLC.

Sommers, Michael. Vermont: Past & Present, 1 vol. 2010. (United States: Past & Present Ser.). (ENG.). 48p. (YA). (gr. 5-5). pap. 12.75 *(978-1-4358-9525-6(8)*, c4762d16-5589-4ca0-9a20-f573e0d95d45); lib. bdg. 34.47 *(978-1-4358-9498-3(7)*, 45c77420-6f15-4326-8788-973d5463d65a) Rosen Publishing Group, Inc., The. (Rosen Reference).

Ziff, John. Northern New England: Maine, New Hampshire, Vermont, Vol. 19. 2015. (Let's Explore the States Ser.). (Illus.). 64p. (J). (gr. 5). 23.95 *(978-1-4222-3330-6(8))* Mason Crest.

VERNE, JULES, 1828-1905

Buckley, James. Who Was Jules Verne? 2019. (Who HQ Ser.). (ENG.). 112p. (J). (gr. 2-4). 16.36 *(978-1-64310-816-2(6))* Penworthy Co., LLC, The.

—Who Was Jules Verne? 2016. (Who Was... ? Ser.). lib. bdg. 16.00 *(978-0-606-38861-0(3))* Turtleback.

Schoell, William. Remarkable Journeys: The Story of Jules Verne. 2004. (World Writers Ser.). (Illus.). 112p. (YA). (gr. 6-12). 23.95 *(978-1-883846-92-3(7)*, First Biographies) Reynolds, Morgan Inc.

VERRAZANO, GIOVANNI DA, 1485-1527

Healy, Nick. Giovanni Da Verrazano. 2003. (Explorers of the Unknown Ser.). (J). *(978-1-58417-037-2(9))*; pap. *(978-1-58417-100-3(6))* Lake Street Pubs.

VERS LIBRE

see Free Verse

VERSIFICATION

see also Poetry

Fandel, Jennifer. Rhyme, Meter, & Other Word Music. 2005. (Understanding Poetry Ser.). (Illus.). 48p. (YA). (gr. 4-7). lib. bdg. 21.95 *(978-1-58341-342-5(1))* Creative Co., The.

Roza, Greg. Patterns in Poetry: Recognizing & Analyzing Poetic Form & Meter, 1 vol. (Math for the REAL World Ser.). 32p. 2010. (ENG.). (gr. 5-6). pap. 10.00 *(978-1-4042-5146-5(4)*, 958f6876-3fb5-411e-84ee-dd3bd321fd6c) 2009. (gr. 4-5). 47.90 *(978-1-60851-415-1(3))* 2004. (ENG., Illus.). (J). (gr. 5-6). lib. bdg. 28.93 *(978-1-4042-2941-9(8)*, 8a7f09a5-770d-46ee-9aec-22a7ac2b168e) Rosen Publishing Group, Inc., The. (PowerKids Pr.).

VERTEBRATES

see also Amphibians; Birds; Fishes; Mammals; Reptiles

Boothroyd, Jennifer. On the Ground. 2006. (First Step Nonfiction — Animal Homes Ser.). (ENG., Illus.). 8p. (J). (gr. k-2). pap. 5.99 *(978-0-8225-5665-7(0)*, a56ce638-481f-4a13-9f63-f0775d25ed20) Lerner Publishing Group.

Chan, Diana/Fong. Animal Kingdom: Vertebrates, Animals with Backbones. 2015. (Illus.). 39p. (J). *(978-0-9864134-0-7(2))* Educational Adventures Publishing.

Collard III, Sneed B. Catching Air: Taking the Leap with Gliding Animals, 1 vol. 2017. (How Nature Works: 0). (ENG., Illus.). 40p. (J). (gr. 3-7). 17.95 *(978-0-88448-496-7(3)*, 884496) Tilbury Hse. Pubs.

Duke, Shirley. Vertebrates & Invertebrates Explained, 1 vol. 2016. (Distinctions in Nature Ser.). (ENG., Illus.). 32p. (gr. 3-3). pap. 11.58 *(978-1-5026-1779-8(X)*, 4084cbba-291a-4bc7-9994-73e52b847670) Cavendish Square Publishing LLC.

Johnston, Ginny & Cutchins, Judy. Ice Age Giants of the South. 2015. (Southern Fossil Discoveries Ser.). (Illus.). 48p. (J). (gr. -1-12). pap. 14.95 *(978-1-56164-793-4(4))* Pineapple Pr., Inc.

Kalman, Bobbie. What Is a Vertebrate? (ENG.). 32p. (J). 2008. *(978-0-7787-7673-4(5))* 2007. (Illus.). (gr. 1-4). lib. bdg. *(978-0-7787-3277-8(0))* 2007. (Illus.). (gr. 3-3). pap. *(978-0-7787-3297-6(5))* Crabtree Publishing Co.

—What Is a Vertibrate? 2008. (ENG.). 32p. (J). *(978-0-7787-7672-7(7))* Crabtree Publishing Co.

McNeil, Niki, et al. HOCPP 1133 Vertebrates. 2006. spiral bd. 24.00 *(978-1-60308-133-7(X))* In the Hands of a Child.

O'Hare, Ted. Vertebrates. 2005. (What Is an Animal Ser.). (Illus.). 24p. (J). (gr. 1-4). lib. bdg. 22.97 *(978-1-59515-422-4(1))* Rourke Educational Media.

Pascoe, Elaine. Animals with Backbones. 2009. (Kid's Guide to the Classification of Living Things Ser.). 32p. (gr. 3-4). 47.90 *(978-1-61511-198-5(0)*, PowerKids Pr.) Rosen Publishing Group, Inc., The.

Selsam, Millicent E. & Hunt, Joyce. First Look at Animals with Backbones & a First Look at Animals Without Backbones. 2003. 68p. pap. 14.95 *(978-0-595-29122-9(8)*, Backinprint.com) iUniverse, Inc.

Zondervan Staff. Spiders, Snakes, Bees, & Bats, 1 vol. 2010. (I Can Read! / Made by God Ser.). (ENG., Illus.). 32p. (J). (gr. -1-2). pap. 4.99 *(978-0-310-72007-2(9))* Zonderkidz.

VESPUCCI, AMERIGO, 1451-1512

Hoogenboom, Lynn. Amerigo Vespucci. 2009. (Primary Source Library of Famous Explorers Ser.). 24p. (gr. 4-4). 42.50 *(978-1-60854-118-8(5)*, PowerKids Pr.) Rosen Publishing Group, Inc., The.

Lambert, Lorene. Who in the World Was the Forgotten Explorer: The Story of Amerigo Vespucci. 2005. (Who in the World Ser.: 0). (ENG., Illus.). 48p. (J). (gr. 2-4). per. 9.50 *(978-0-9728603-8-3(X)*, 86038) Well-Trained Mind Pr.

VESSELS (SHIPS)

see Ships

VETERINARIANS

Acevedo, Gianira Candelario. Becoming a Veterinarian. 2017. (Text Connections Guided Close Reading Ser.). (J). (gr. 1). *(978-1-4900-1813-3(1))* Benchmark Education Co.

Adamson, Heather. A Day in the Life of a Veterinarian, 1 vol. 2003. (Community Helpers at Work Ser.). (ENG., Illus.). 24p. (J). (gr. 1-3). 25.99 *(978-0-7368-2287-9(9)*, 89395, Capstone Pr.) Capstone.

Ames, Michelle. Veterinarians in Our Community, 1 vol. 2009. (On the Job Ser.). (ENG., Illus.). 24p. (J). (gr. 1-1). pap. 9.25 *(978-1-4358-2457-7(1)*, 12b23776-7523-4e40-9bcd-a8791f291e6f); lib. bdg. 26.27 *(978-1-4042-8071-7(5)*, 51b90cdd-00a4-40ef-8224-c05608693786) Rosen Publishing Group, Inc., The. (PowerKids Pr.).

Ardely, Anthony. I Can Be a Veterinarian, 1 vol. 2018. (I Can Be Anything! Ser.). (ENG.). 24p. (gr. k-k). 24.27 *(978-1-5382-1772-6(4)*, e29782f0-c6ee-4858-b80d-853afb70f155) Stevens, Gareth Publishing LLLP.

Arnold, Quinn M. Les Vétérinaires. 2017. (Graines de Savoir Ser.). (FRE., Illus.). 24p. (J). (gr. -1-k). *(978-1-77092-390-4(X)*, 20430) Creative Co., The.

—Veterinarians. 2017. (Seedlings Ser.). (ENG., Illus.). 24p. (J). (gr. -1-k). *(978-1-60818-876-5(0)*, 20363, Creative Education) Creative Co., The.

Ask the Veterinarians: Fourth Grade Guided Comprehension Level O. (On Our Way to English Ser.). (gr. 4-18). 34.50 *(978-0-7578-7169-6(0))* Rigby Education.

Askew, Amanda & Crowson, Andrew. Vet. 2012. (ENG., Illus.). 24p. (gr. 1-3). pap. 7.95 *(978-1-926853-51-2(2))* Saunders Bk. Co. CAN. Dist: RiverStream Publishing.

Bell, Samantha. Veterinarian. Bane, Jeff, illus. 2017. (My Early Library: My Friendly Neighborhood Ser.). (ENG.). 24p. (J). (gr. k-1). lib. bdg. 30.64 *(978-1-63472-830-0(0)*, 209746) Cherry Lake Publishing.

Bellisario, Gina. Let's Meet a Veterinarian. Atkinson, Cale, illus. 2013. (Cloverleaf Books (tm) — Community Helpers Ser.). (ENG.). 24p. (J). (gr. k-2). pap. 8.99 *(978-1-4677-0806-7(2)*, e590f7c6-fa2e-4fe4-bd80-bf674de595ce, Millbrook Pr.) Lerner Publishing Group.

Brooks, Felicity. Vicky the Vet. Litchfield, Jo, illus. 2004. (Jobs People Do Ser.). 24p. (J). (gr. -1). lib. bdg. 14.95 *(978-1-58086-699-6(9)*, Usborne) EDC Publishing.

—Vicky the Vet Kid Kit. Litchfield, Jo, illus. 2007. (Kid Kits Ser.). 23p. (J). pap. 15.99 *(978-1-60130-008-9(5)*, Usborne) EDC Publishing.

Bruno, Nikki. Gross Jobs Working with Animals: 4D an Augmented Reading Experience. 2019. (Gross Jobs 4D Ser.). (ENG., Illus.). 32p. (J). (gr. 3-9). lib. bdg. 31.99 *(978-1-5435-5489-2(X)*, 139360, Capstone Pr.) Capstone.

Carson, J. Visiting the Vet: Learning the V Sound. 2009. (PowerPhonics Ser.). 24p. (gr. 1-1). 39.90 *(978-1-60851-476-2(5)*, PowerKids Pr.) Rosen Publishing Group, Inc., The.

Claire, Linda. En el Trabajo: Veterinarios: Comparación de Grupos. rev. ed. 2019. (Mathematics in the Real World Ser.). (SPA.). 20p. (gr. k-1). 8.99 *(978-1-4258-2822-6(1))* Teacher Created Materials, Inc.

—On the Job: Vet. 2018. (Mathematics in the Real World Ser.). (ENG., Illus.). 20p. (J). (gr. k-1). 8.99 *(978-1-4258-5615-1(2))* Teacher Created Materials, Inc.

Clendening, John. Veterinary Hospitals, 1 vol. 2014. (Animal Rescue Ser.). (ENG.). 32p. (J). (gr. 4-4). lib. bdg. 27.93 *(978-1-4777-7023-8(2)*, c21eb96c-7c46-40ba-88b9-65b1e1f682c4, PowerKids Pr.) Rosen Publishing Group, Inc., The.

Driscoll, Laura. I Want to Be a Veterinarian. Echeverri, Catalina, illus. 2018. (I Can Read Level 1 Ser.). (ENG.). 32p. (J). (gr. -1-3). 16.99 *(978-0-06-243247-6(8))*; pap. 5.99 *(978-0-06-243261-2(3))* HarperCollins Pubs. (HarperCollins).

Early Macken, JoAnn. Veterinarians, 1 vol. 2010. (People in My Community (Second Edition) Ser.). (ENG.). 24p. (J). (gr. k-2). pap. 9.15 *(978-1-4339-3813-9(8)*, df9be73c-6df6-466f-93a3-6c1af403acf5); lib. bdg. 25.27 *(978-1-4339-3812-2(X)*, a38dabe0-95be-415f-a3f3-dd223b65f6b9) Stevens, Gareth Publishing LLLP.

Facts on File, Inc. Staff. Animals. 2010. (New Discovering Careers for Your Future Ser.). (Illus.). 128p. (gr. 4-9). 24.95 *(978-0-8160-8044-1(5)*, Ferguson Publishing Company) Infobase Holdings, Inc.

Forest, Anne. Veterinarians on the Job. (Jobs in Our Community Ser.). (J). (gr. 1-1). 2017. pap. 49.50 *(978-1-5345-2150-6(X))* 2016. (ENG.). 24p. 26.23 *(978-1-5345-2151-3(8)*, ada960b6-f996-4908-aa3b-47da7fd2ef18) 2016. (ENG.). 24p. pap. 9.25 *(978-1-5345-2149-0(6)*, 0b18d51f-4efa-4744-9806-1e8e09474b27) Greenhaven Publishing LLC. (KidHaven Publishing).

Gregory, Josh. What Do They Do? Veterinarians. 2010. (Community Connections: What Do They Do? Ser.). (ENG., Illus.). 24p. (gr. 2-5). lib. bdg. 29.21 *(978-1-60279-810-6(9)*, 200510) Cherry Lake Publishing.

Honders, Christine. What's It Really Like to Be a Veterinarian?, 1 vol. 2019. (Jobs Kids Want Ser.). (ENG.). 24p. (gr. 1-2). 25.27 *(978-1-7253-0030-9(3)*, c39cce84-7c8c-4389-acc6-713093d8259c, PowerKids Pr.) Rosen Publishing Group, Inc., The.

Hutchings, Amy. What Happens at a Vet's Office?, 1 vol. 2009. (Where People Work Ser.). (ENG.). 24p. (gr. 1-1). (J). lib. bdg. 24.67 *(978-1-4339-0071-6(8)*, efdaa023-6e04-4075-bb6b-4a0a74763c63); pap. 9.15 *(978-1-4339-0135-5(8)*, 4e9c97f9-84ef-46b6-87c6-f007e888d5b7) Stevens, Gareth Publishing LLLP. (Weekly Reader Leveled Readers).

—What Happens at a Vet's Office? / ¿Qué Pasa en una Clínica Veterinaria?, 1 vol. 2009. (Where People Work / ¿dónde Trabaja la Gente? Ser.). (SPA & ENG., Illus.). 24p. (J). (gr. 1-1). pap. 9.15 *(978-1-4339-0143-0(9)*, 61ed8c1b-f3b9-423c-b2ba-c9525654dff7); lib. bdg. 24.67 *(978-1-4339-0079-2(3)*, 93d37124-4f50-4067-b1cb-bdb4130a6e23) Stevens, Gareth Publishing LLLP. (Weekly Reader Leveled Readers).

Jackson, Donna M. Er Vets. 2009. (ENG., Illus.). 96p. (J). (gr. 3-7). pap. 8.99 *(978-0-547-23758-9(8)*, 1083868, Clarion Bks.) HarperCollins Pubs.

Jeffries, Joyce. Meet the Vet, 1 vol. 2013. (People Around Town Ser.). 24p. (J). (gr. k-k). (ENG.). pap. 9.15 *(978-1-4339-9388-6(0)*, f59ac408-8990-4339-9b3f-58617ea0a318); pap. 48.90 *(978-1-4339-9389-3(9))*; (ENG., Illus.). lib. bdg. 25.27 *(978-1-4339-9387-9(2)*, e87c7398-f7be-4edb-924b-4cefc286042e) Stevens, Gareth Publishing LLLP.

—Meet the Vet / Conoce a Los Veterinarios, 1 vol. 2013. (People Around Town / Gente de Mi Ciudad Ser.). (ENG & SPA., Illus.). 24p. (J). (gr. k-k). lib. bdg. 25.27 *(978-1-4339-9474-6(7)*, e59bdd9e-b369-4042-aff3-4d80a6ca4481) Stevens, Gareth Publishing LLLP.

Kalman, Bobbie. Veterinarians Help Keep Animals Healthy, 1 vol. 2004. (My Community & Its Helpers Ser.). (ENG., Illus.). 32p. (J). pap. *(978-0-7787-2125-3(6))* Crabtree Publishing Co.

—Los Veterinarios Cuidan la Salud de los Animales. 2006. (Mi Communidad y Quienes Contribuyen a Ella Ser.). (SPA.,

Illus.). 32p. (J). (gr. 3-7). pap. *(978-0-7787-8443-2(6))*; lib. bdg. *(978-0-7787-8429-6(0))* Crabtree Publishing Co.

Leaf, Christina. Veterinarians. 2018. (Community Helpers Ser.). (ENG., Illus.). 24p. (J). (gr. k-3). lib. bdg. 26.95 *(978-1-62617-751-2(1)*, Blastoff! Readers) Bellwether Media.

Less, Emma. Veterinarians. 2018. (Real-Life Superheroes Ser.). (ENG.). 16p. (J). (gr. k-2). pap. 7.99 *(978-1-68152-283-8(7)*, 14922) Amicus.

Liebman, Dan. Je Veux Etre Veterinaire. Lior, Tsipora, tr. 2006. (Je Veux Etre Ser.). (FRE., Illus.). 24p. (J). (gr. -1-2). pap. 5.95 *(978-1-55407-105-0(4)*, 6bd90030-2417-4540-a33c-61b495514053) Firefly Bks., Ltd.

Liebman, Dan & Liebman, Dan. I Want to Be a Vet. 2nd rev. ed. 2018. (I Want to Be Ser.). (ENG., Illus.). 24p. (J). (gr. -1-2). pap. 3.99 *(978-0-2281-0156-7(5)*, 922d117e-ca88-4496-880f-2221248ae11a) Firefly Bks., Ltd.

Lindeen, Mary. A Visit to the Vet. 2018. (BeginningtoRead Ser.). (ENG.). 32p. (J). (gr. -1-2). lib. bdg. 22.60 *(978-1-59953-913-3(6))*; (gr. k-2). pap. 13.26 *(978-1-68404-169-5(4))* Norwood Hse. Pr.

McKinnon, Elaine. Pets at the Vet, 1 vol. 2016. (Community Helpers Ser.). (ENG., Illus.). 24p. (J). (gr. 1-1). pap. 9.25 *(978-1-4994-2706-6(9)*, 95a6fd10-e92d-4535-8699-7983a19c9520, PowerKids Pr.) Rosen Publishing Group, Inc., The.

Meachen Rau, Dana. Una Veterinaria (Veterinarian), 1 vol. 2008. (Trabajos en Pueblos y Ciudades (Jobs in Town) Ser.). (SPA., Illus.). 24p. (gr. k-1). lib. bdg. 25.50 *(978-0-7614-2787-2(2)*, 992e7d7f-afa6-4377-94fd-ee5bca0e7762) Cavendish Square Publishing LLC.

—Veterinarian, 1 vol. 2008. (Jobs in Town Ser.). (ENG., Illus.). 24p. (gr. k-1). lib. bdg. 25.50 *(978-0-7614-2622-6(1)*, 8cc34403-68fb-46e0-80b5-33a44f94a29e, Cavendish Square) Cavendish Square Publishing LLC.

Miller, Connie Colwell. I'll Be a Veterinarian. Baroncelli, Silvia, illus. 2016. (When I Grow Up Ser.). (ENG.). 24p. (J). (gr. 1-4). lib. bdg. 20.95 *(978-1-60753-764-9(8)*, 15576) Amicus.

—Vétérinaire. Baroncelli, Silvia, illus. 2016. (Plus Tard, Je Serai... Ser.). (FRE.). 24p. (J). (gr. 1-4). *(978-1-77092-358-4(6)*, 17621) Amicus.

Murray, Aaron R. Veterinarians Help Us, 1 vol. 2012. (All about Community Helpers Ser.). (ENG., Illus.). 24p. (gr. -1-1). 25.27 *(978-0-7660-4046-5(1)*, 6fcc0fcf-8c0f-4052-9987-f35e6d59e889, Enslow Publishing) Enslow Publishing, LLC.

Parks, Peggy J. Veterinarian. 2004. (EXPLORING CAREERS Ser.). (ENG.). (J). 27.50 *(978-0-7377-2068-6(9)*, Greenhaven Pr., Inc.) Cengage Gale.

Ready, Dee. Veterinarians Help. 2013. (Our Community Helpers Ser.). (ENG.). 24p. (J). (gr. k-1). pap. 38.74 *(978-1-62065-852-9(6)*, 19422, Pebble) Capstone.

Ready, Dee & Ready, Dee. Veterinarians Help, 1 vol. 2013. (Our Community Helpers Ser.). (ENG.). 24p. (J). (gr. -1-2). pap. 6.29 *(978-1-62065-851-2(8)*, 121790, Pebble) Capstone.

Rich, Mari. Big-Animal Vets!, Vol. 10. 2015. (Scientists in Action Ser.). (Illus.). 48p. (J). (gr. 5). 20.95 *(978-1-4222-3419-8(3))* Mason Crest.

Riggs, Kate. Seedlings: Veterinarians. 2017. (Seedlings Ser.). (ENG., Illus.). 24p. (J). (gr. -1-1). pap. 8.99 *(978-1-62832-491-4(0)*, 20364, Creative Paperbacks) Creative Co., The.

Shaw, Gina. Curious about Zoo Vets. 2015. (Smithsonian Ser.). (Illus.). 32p. (J). (gr. 1-3). bds. 4.99 *(978-0-448-48687-1(3)*, Grosset & Dunlap) Penguin Young Readers Group.

Siemens, Jared. Veterinarians. 2016. (Illus.). 24p. (J). *(978-1-5105-2113-1(5))* SmartBook Media, Inc.

—Veterinarians. 2015. (Illus.). 24p. (J). pap. *(978-1-4896-3662-1(5))* Weigl Pubs., Inc.

Somervill, Barbara A. Veterinarian. (21st Century Skills Library: Cool STEAM Careers Ser.). (ENG., Illus.). 32p. (gr. 4-7). 2015. (J). 32.07 *(978-1-63362-566-2(4)*, 206448) 2008. lib. bdg. 32.07 *(978-1-60279-301-9(8)*, 200140) Cherry Lake Publishing.

Thomas, William David. Veterinarian, 1 vol. 2008. (Cool Careers: Helping Careers Ser.). (ENG.). 32p. (gr. 3-3). pap. 11.50 *(978-0-8368-9330-4(1)*, 42d28c3c-dd40-407d-bee4-4308f662488a); lib. bdg. 28.67 *(978-0-8368-9197-3(X)*, 055ce3f6-ef46-47be-b3b0-7e3389d5a623) Stevens, Gareth Publishing LLLP.

Trueit, Trudi Strain. Animal Physical Therapist. 2014. (J). *(978-0-7614-8074-7(9))* Marshall Cavendish Corp.

—Veterinarian. 2014. (J). *(978-0-7614-8076-1(5))* Marshall Cavendish Corp.

Ventura, Marne. Veterinarian. 2019. (Jobs with Animals Ser.). (ENG., Illus.). 32p. (J). (gr. 4-6). pap. 7.95 *(978-1-5435-6043-5(1)*, 140088); lib. bdg. 28.65 *(978-1-5435-5781-7(3)*, 139737) Capstone.

Waldendorf, Kurt. Hooray for Veterinarians! 2016. (Bumba Books (r) — Hooray for Community Helpers! Ser.). (ENG., Illus.). 24p. (J). (gr. -1-1). 26.65 *(978-1-5124-1438-7(7)*, 1619444c-a943-40e2-a662-6e11f3d9ad8f, Lerner Pubns.) Lerner Publishing Group.

—¡Que Vivan Los Veterinarios! (Hooray for Veterinarians!) 2017. (Bumba Books (r) en Español — ¡Que Vivan Los Ayudantes Comunitarios! (Hooray for Community Helpers!) Ser.). (SPA., Illus.). 24p. (J). (gr. -1-1). 26.65 *(978-1-5124-4133-8(3)*, 95eeae36-0d9f-41ee-bae7-8a7c5e063245, Ediciones Lerner) Lerner Publishing Group.

VETERINARIANS—FICTION

Anderson, Laurie Halse. Acting Out, 14 vols. 2012. (Vet Volunteers Ser.: 14). (ENG.). 144p. (J). (gr. 3-7). pap. 7.99 *(978-0-14-241676-1(2)*, Puffin Books) Penguin Young Readers Group.

—End of the Race, 12 vols. 2012. (Vet Volunteers Ser.: 12). (ENG.). 160p. (J). (gr. 3-7). 7.99 *(978-0-14-241228-2(7)*, Puffin Books) Penguin Young Readers Group.

—Fight for Life. 2007. (Vet Volunteers Ser.: 1). (ENG.). 160p. (J). (gr. 3-7). 7.99 *(978-0-14-240862-9(X)*, Puffin Books) Penguin Young Readers Group.

—Helping Hands. 2013. (Vet Volunteers Ser.: 15). (ENG.). 144p. (J). (gr. 3-7). pap. 7.99 *(978-0-14-241677-8(0)*, Puffin Books) Penguin Young Readers Group.

—Homeless, 2. 2007. (Vet Volunteers Ser.: 2). (ENG.). 160p. (J). (gr. 3-7). 7.99 *(978-0-14-240863-6(8)*, Puffin) Penguin Young Readers Group.

—Masks, 11 vols. 2012. (Vet Volunteers Ser.: 11). (ENG.). 128p. (J). (gr. 3-7). 7.99 *(978-0-14-241257-2(0)*, Puffin Books) Penguin Young Readers Group.

—New Beginnings, 13 vols., 13. 2012. (Vet Volunteers Ser.: 13). (ENG.). 192p. (J). (gr. 3-7). 7.99 *(978-0-14-241675-4(4)*, Puffin) Penguin Young Readers Group.

—Say Good-Bye, No. 5. 2008. (Vet Volunteers Ser.: 5). (ENG.). 160p. (J). (gr. 3-7). 7.99 *(978-0-14-241100-1(0)*, Puffin Books) Penguin Young Readers Group.

—Storm Rescue. 2008. (Vet Volunteers Ser.: 6). (ENG.). 144p. (J). (gr. 3-7). 7.99 *(978-0-14-241101-8(9)*, Puffin Books) Penguin Young Readers Group.

—Teacher's Pet. 2009. (Vet Volunteers Ser.: 7). (ENG.). 160p. (J). (gr. 3-7). 7.99 *(978-0-14-241252-7(X)*, Puffin Books) Penguin Young Readers Group.

—Trapped. 2009. (Vet Volunteers Ser.: 8). (ENG.). 144p. (J). (gr. 3-7). 7.99 *(978-0-14-241223-7(6)*, Puffin Books) Penguin Young Readers Group.

—Trickster. 2008. (Vet Volunteers Ser.: 3). (ENG.). 160p. (J). (gr. 3-7). 7.99 *(978-0-14-241083-7(7)*, Puffin Books) Penguin Young Readers Group.

Banerjee, Anjali. Seaglass Summer. 2011. (ENG.). 176p. (J). (gr. 4-6). lib. bdg. 22.44 *(978-0-385-90555-8(6)*, Lamb, Wendy Bks.); (Illus.). (gr. 3-7). pap. 7.99 *(978-0-375-84399-0(X)*, Yearling) Random Hse. Children's Bks.

Bier, Erich & Bier, Donna. Lester the Bear. 2013. (ENG., Illus.). 22p. (J). (gr. -1-3). 14.95 *(978-1-62086-297-1(2))* Amplify Publishing Group.

Bruel, Nick. Bad Kitty Goes to the Vet (classic Black-And-white Edition) Bruel, Nick, illus. 2016. (Bad Kitty Ser.). (ENG., Illus.). 144p. (J). 15.99 *(978-1-59643-977-1(7)*, 900127754) Roaring Brook Pr.

Carris, Joan. Magic at the Bed & Biscuit. Jones, Noah Z., illus. (ENG.). (J). (gr. 1-4). 2012. 112p. pap. 5.99 *(978-0-7636-5849-6(9))* 2011. 128p. 15.99 *(978-0-7636-4306-5(8))* Candlewick Pr.

—Welcome to the Bed & Biscuit. Jones, Noah Z., illus. 2009. (Bed & Biscuit Ser.). (ENG.). 128p. (J). (gr. 2-4). 18.69 *(978-0-7636-2151-3(X))* Candlewick Pr.

Chukovsky, Kornei. Doctor Ouch. Seabaugh, Jan, tr. from RUS. Seabaugh, Jan, illus. 2004. (Children's International Ser.: 1). Orig. Title: Aibolit. 43p. (J). pap. 6.99 *(978-0-9740551-0-7(7))* Smith, Viveca Publishing.

Chwast, Seymour. Dr. Dolittle. Chwast, Seymour, illus. 2015. (ENG., Illus.). 40p. (J). (gr. 4-7). 18.99 *(978-1-56846-258-5(1)*, 20825, Creative Editions) Creative Co., The.

Clarke, Jane. Posy the Puppy (Dr. KittyCat #1) 2016. (Dr. KittyCat Ser.: 1). (ENG.). 96p. (J). (gr. 2-5). pap. 5.99 *(978-0-545-87333-8(9)*, Scholastic Paperbacks) Scholastic, Inc.

Crow, Melinda Melton. Rocky & Daisy Go to the Vet. 2013. (My Two Dogs Ser.). (ENG., Illus.). 32p. (J). (gr. 1-3). pap. 35.70 *(978-1-4342-6297-4(9)*, 20269, Stone Arch Bks.) Capstone.

—Rocky & Daisy Go to the Vet, 1 vol. Sassin, Eva, illus. 2013. (My Two Dogs Ser.). (ENG.). 32p. (J). (gr. 2-3). pap. 5.95 *(978-1-4342-6203-5(0)*, 123497); lib. bdg. 22.65 *(978-1-4342-6009-3(7)*, 123059) Capstone. (Stone Arch Bks.).

Davis, David Denton. Polly's Promise: A Story about Thriving Rather Than Simply Surviving... Turning Apparent Disability into Gifted Ability. 2013. 80p. pap. 21.95 *(978-1-4787-0275-7(3))* Outskirts Pr., Inc.

Davis, Kauline, et al. Fat Dogs & Coughing Horses. 2012. (ENG.). 61p. (J). pap. 12.95 *(978-1-932739-22-0(X)*, 20b21610-a10a-43c3-93b3-d291665aef4f) Purdue Univ. Pr.

Dempsey, Tami. We Are a Champion! 2010. (ENG.). 36p. pap. 15.49 *(978-1-4490-8102-7(9))* AuthorHouse.

Disney Book Group Staff & Miller, Sara. Doc Mcstuffins: Take Your Pet to the Vet. 2015. (World of Reading Ser.). (J). lib. bdg. 13.55 *(978-0-606-37535-1(X))* Turtleback.

Dyan, Penelope. Blake the Cat & His Very Loose Tooth! Dyan, Penelope, illus. 2011. (Illus.). 34p. pap. 10.95 *(978-1-935630-77-7(6))* Bellissima Publishing, LLC.

Fontana, Shea & Nee, Chris. Smitten with a Kitten. 2016. (Doc Mcstuffins Ser.). (ENG., Illus.). 24p. (J). (gr. -1-1). 17.44 *(978-1-4844-8806-5(7))* Disney Pr.

Garcia, Randolph. The Steamer Trunk Adventures #2: The Ghosts of Machu Picchu. 2006. (ENG.). 88p. per. 16.95 *(978-1-4241-1843-4(3))* PublishAmerica, Inc.

Gilmore, Sophie. Little Doctor & the Fearless Beast. 2019. (ENG., Illus.). 32p. (J). 17.95 *(978-1-77147-344-6(4))* Owlkids Bks. Inc. CAN. Dist: Publishers Group West (PGW).

Henry, Heather French. Pepper's Purple Heart: A Veteran's Day Story. Henry, Heather French, illus. 2004. (Claire's Holiday Adventures Ser.: Vol. 1). (Illus.). 32p. (J). (gr. k-4). pap. 8.95 *(978-0-9706341-1-5(0))* Cubbie Blue Publishing.

Hensley, Terri Anne. Henry visits the Veterinarian. 2007. (J). per. 6.95 *(978-0-9789057-2-9(5))* Huntington Ludlow Media Group.

Hillert, Margaret. Ayuda para Querido Dragón. Pullan, Jack, illus. 2017. (BeginningtoRead Ser.). Orig. Title: Help for Dear Dragon. (ENG & SPA.). 32p. (J). (-2). 22.60 *(978-1-59953-832-7(6))* Norwood Hse. Pr.

—Help for Dear Dragon. Pullan, Jack, illus. 2016. (BeginningtoRead Ser.). (ENG.). 32p. (J). (-2). lib. bdg. 22.60 *(978-1-59953-769-6(9))* Norwood Hse. Pr.

Jones, Kristy. The Adventures of Ziggy the Trucker Dog. 2010. (ENG.). 24p. pap. 15.99 *(978-1-4500-8751-3(5))* Xlibris Corp.

Jordan, Apple. I Can Be a Farm Vet (Barbie) Riley, Kellee, illus. 2016. (Step into Reading Ser.). (ENG.). 24p. (J). (gr. -1-1). 5.99 *(978-1-101-93245-2(7)*, Random Hse. Bks. for Young Readers) Random Hse. Children's Bks.

Kelly, Jacqueline. Counting Sheep: Calpurnia Tate, Girl Vet. White, Teagan & Meyer, Jennifer L., illus. 2017. (Calpurnia Tate, Girl Vet Ser.: 2). (ENG.). 128p. (J). pap. 6.99 *(978-1-250-12945-1(1)*, 900161283) Square Fish.

—The Curious World of Calpurnia Tate. 2017. (Calpurnia Tate Ser.: 2). (J). lib. bdg. 18.40 *(978-0-606-39939-5(9))* Turtleback.

—A Prickly Problem: Calpurnia Tate, Girl Vet. 2018. (Calpurnia Tate, Girl Vet Ser.: 4). (ENG., Illus.). 112p. (J). pap. 6.99 *(978-1-250-17719-3(7)*, 900161295) Square Fish.

—Skunked!: Calpurnia Tate, Girl Vet. White, Teagan & Meyer, Jennifer L., illus. 2016. (Calpurnia Tate, Girl Vet Ser.: 1). (ENG.). 112p. (J). 15.99 *(978-1-62779-868-6(4)*, 900161279, Holt, Henry & Co. Bks. For Young Readers) Holt, Henry & Co.

—Skunked!: Calpurnia Tate, Girl Vet. White, Teagan & Meyer, Jennifer L., illus. 2017. (Calpurnia Tate, Girl Vet Ser.: 1). (ENG.). 128p. (J). pap. 6.99 *(978-1-250-12944-4(3)*, 900161280) Square Fish.

—A Squirrelly Situation: Calpurnia Tate, Girl Vet. Meyer, Jennifer L., illus. 2021. (Calpurnia Tate, Girl Vet Ser.: 5). (ENG.). 112p. (J). pap. 6.99 *(978-1-250-21115-6(8)*, 900161298) Square Fish.

—Who Gives a Hoot?: Calpurnia Tate, Girl Vet. Meyer, Jennifer L., illus. 2018. (Calpurnia Tate, Girl Vet Ser.: 3). (ENG.). 128p. (J). pap. 6.99 *(978-1-250-14339-6(X)*, 900161290) Square Fish.

Leonard, Marcia & Handelman, Dorothy. The Pet Vet. Handelman, Dorothy, illus. Leonard, Marcia, photos by. 2005. (ENG & SPA., Illus.). 32p. (J). (gr. -1-1). pap. 4.99 *(978-0-8225-3299-6(9))* Lerner Publishing Group.

Lively, Deborah Dreher. Vanishing Treasure of the Virungas. 2008. 88p. pap. 11.50 *(978-1-934925-54-6(3)*, Strategic Bk. Publishing) Strategic Book Publishing & Rights Agency (SBPRA).

Lofting, Hugh. The Voyages of Doctor Dolittle. 2019. (ENG., Illus.). 320p. (gr. 3-6). pap. 14.95 *(978-0-486-83436-8(0)*, 834360) Dover Pubns., Inc.

Lynch, Chris. In a Wired Future, Animals Need Our Help. 2010. (Cyberia Ser.: 1). (ENG.). 160p. (J). (gr. 4-6). 18.69 *(978-0-545-02796-0(9))* Scholastic, Inc.

—Monkey See, Monkey Don't. 2011. (Cyberia Ser.: 2). (ENG.). 144p. (J). (gr. 4-7). pap. 5.99 *(978-0-545-02797-7(7))* Scholastic, Inc.

Mackall, Dandi Daley. Double Trouble, 1 vol. Wolf, Claudia, illus. 2011. (I Can Read! / a Horse Named Bob Ser.). (ENG.). 32p. (J). pap. 4.99 *(978-0-310-71785-0(X))* Zonderkidz.

Mitchell, Sherry. Fernando the Veterinarian. 2012. 20p. pap. 17.99 *(978-1-4685-8098-3(1))* AuthorHouse.

Moncomble, Gerard & Van den Dries, Sidonie. Half & Half-A Doctor for the Animals. Fortier, Natali & Brenier, Claire, illus. 2008. (J). 32p. pap. 4.99 *(978-1-60115-204-6(3))*; (ENG.). 29p. 17.44 *(978-1-60115-203-9(5))* Treasure Bay, Inc.

Odgers, Darrel & Odgers, Sally. Bush Rescue. Dawson, Janine, illus. 2016. 89p. (J). *(978-1-61067-563-5(0))* Kane Miller.

—Cranky Paws. Dawson, Janine, illus. 2009. (Pet Vet Ser.: 1). 96p. (J). (gr. 2-6). pap. 4.99 *(978-1-935279-01-3(7))* Kane Miller.

—The Mare's Tale. Dawson, Janine, illus. 2009. (Pet Vet Ser.: 2). 96p. (J). (gr. 2-6). pap. 4.99 *(978-1-935279-02-0(5))* Kane Miller.

Odgers, Darrel & Sally. The Pup's Tale: Pet Vet Book 6. Dawson, Janine, illus. 2015. 96p. (J). pap. 4.99 *(978-1-61067-351-8(4))* Kane Miller.

Odgers, Sally & Darrel. Bush Rescue: Pup Patrol. Dawson, Janine, illus. 2017. 96p. (J). pap. 4.99 *(978-1-61067-519-2(3))* Kane Miller.

—Storm Rescue: Pup Patrol. Dawson, Janine, illus. 2018. 89p. (J). pap. 4.99 *(978-1-61067-657-1(2))* Kane Miller.

Phillips, Matthew. Ingo Flamingo, 1 vol. 2009. 19p. pap. 24.95 *(978-1-60836-340-7(6))* America Star Bks.

Popper, Garry. The Beast of Didley Dale. Forshaw, John, illus. 2004. (Bret the Vet Ser.). 40p. 7.00 *(978-1-84161-024-5(0))* Ravette Publishing, Ltd. GBR. Dist: Parkwest Pubns., Inc.

Santillo, LuAnn. The Vet. Santillo, LuAnn, ed. 2003. (Half-Pint Kids Readers Ser.). (Illus.). 7p. (J). (gr. -1-1). pap. 1.00 *(978-1-59256-123-0(3))* Half-Pint Kids, Inc.

Schoon, Christian. Under Nameless Stars. 2014. (ENG.). 368p. (J). (gr. 9). pap. 9.99 *(978-1-908844-87-3(6)*, Strange Chemistry) Watkins Media Limited GBR. Dist: Penguin Random Hse. LLC.

Schwartz, Jean. The Snake with a Bellyache. Fisher, Todd, illus. 2007. 20p. per. 10.95 *(978-1-934246-41-2(7))* Peppertree Pr., The.

Selfors, Suzanne. The Fairy Swarm. Santat, Dan, illus. 2016. (Imaginary Veterinary Ser.: 6). (ENG.). 240p. (J). (gr. 2-7). pap. 7.99 *(978-0-316-28692-3(3))* Little, Brown Bks. for Young Readers.

—The Lonely Lake Monster. Santat, Dan, illus. 2014. (Imaginary Veterinary Ser.: 2). (ENG.). 240p. (J). (gr. 2-7). pap. 7.99 *(978-0-316-22561-8(4))* Little, Brown Bks. for Young Readers.

—The Order of the Unicorn. Santat, Dan, illus. 2014. (ENG.). 208p. (J). E-Book *(978-0-316-32339-0(X))* Little Brown & Co.

—The Order of the Unicorn. Santat, Dan, illus. 2014. (Imaginary Veterinary Ser.: 4). (ENG.). 208p. (J). (gr. 2-7). 29.99 *(978-0-316-36406-5(1))* Little, Brown Bks. for Young Readers.

—The Sasquatch Escape. Santat, Dan, illus. 2014. (Imaginary Veterinary Ser.: 1). (ENG.). 240p. (J). (gr. 2-7). pap. 8.99 *(978-0-316-22569-4(X))* Little, Brown Bks. for Young Readers.

Skafish, Brad. Red Letter Day: The Bad Cats Learn about Letters! 2012. 20p. pap. 11.95 *(978-1-62141-260-1(1))* Booklocker.com, Inc.

Smith, Maggie Caldwell. Tommy Wilson, Junior Veterinarian: The Case of the Orphaned Bobcat. Heyer, Carol & White, Charlotte L., illus. 2006. (J). per. 7.95 *(978-0-9788391-1-6(0))* Magpie Pr., Pine Mountain Club, CA.

Smith, Margaret Ann. A New Kind of Life for Eddie Eagle. 2008. 36p. pap. 24.95 *(978-1-60441-168-3(6))* America Star Bks.

Stern, A. J. Doggy Day Care, 2 vols. Marts, Doreen Mulryan, illus. 2010. (Frankly, Frannie Ser.: 2). 128p. (J). (gr. 1-3). pap. 4.99 *(978-0-448-45350-7(9)*, Grosset & Dunlap) Penguin Young Readers Group.

Stockham, Jess, illus. Vet. 2011. (First Time Ser.). 24p. (J). (gr. 2-2). pap. *(978-1-84643-337-5(1))* Child's Play International Ltd.

Travitzky, Paul Joseph & Travitzky, Brianna Marie. Brianna Marie Wants to Be... A Veterinarian. 2010. 20p. 11.00 *(978-1-4490-7701-3(3))* AuthorHouse.

Viselman, Kenn. Li'l Pet Hospital: The Great Race. 2003. 32p. pap. 3.99 *(978-0-06-054840-7(1)*, Harper Entertainment) HarperCollins Pubs.

Webb, Holly. The Missing Kitten & Other Tales. Williams, Sophy, illus. 2018. (Pet Rescue Adventures Ser.). (ENG.). 384p. (J). (gr. 1-4). pap. 10.99 *(978-1-68010-415-8(2))* Tiger Tales.

VETERINARY MEDICINE

Ames, Michelle. Veterinarians in Our Community, 1 vol. 2009. (On the Job Ser.). (ENG., Illus.). 24p. (J). (gr. 1-1). pap. 9.25 *(978-1-4358-2457-7(1)*, 12b23776-7523-4e40-9bcd-a8791f291e6f); lib. bdg. 26.27 *(978-1-4042-8071-7(5)*, 51b90cdd-00a4-40ef-8224-c05608693786) Rosen Publishing Group, Inc., The. (PowerKids Pr.).

Ardely, Anthony. I Can Be a Veterinarian, 1 vol. 2018. (I Can Be Anything! Ser.). (ENG.). 24p. (gr. k-k). 24.27 *(978-1-5382-1772-6(4)*, e29782f0-c6ee-4858-b80d-853afb70f155) Stevens, Gareth Publishing LLLP.

Arnold, Quinn M. Veterinarians. 2017. (Seedlings Ser.). (ENG., Illus.). 24p. (J). (gr. -1-k). *(978-1-60818-876-5(0)*, 20363, Creative Education) Creative Co., The.

Bellisario, Gina. Let's Meet a Veterinarian. Atkinson, Cale, illus. 2013. (Cloverleaf Books (tm) — Community Helpers Ser.). (ENG.). 24p. (J). (gr. k-2). pap. 8.99 *(978-1-4677-0806-7(2)*, e590f7c6-fa2e-4fe4-bd80-bf674de595ce, Millbrook Pr.) Lerner Publishing Group.

Brooks, Felicity. Vicky the Vet. Litchfield, Jo, illus. 2004. (Jobs People Do Ser.). 24p. (J). (gr. -1). lib. bdg. 14.95 *(978-1-58086-699-6(9)*, Usborne) EDC Publishing.

—Vicky the Vet Kid Kit. Litchfield, Jo, illus. 2007. (Kid Kits Ser.). 23p. (J). pap. 15.99 *(978-1-60130-008-9(5)*, Usborne) EDC Publishing.

Chilman-Blair, Kim. Medikidz Explain Swine Flu, 1 vol. 2010. (Superheroes on a Medical Mission Ser.). (ENG., Illus.). 40p. (YA). (gr. 5-5). pap. 12.75 *(978-1-4488-1843-3(5)*, 5e291958-d352-4e86-9bd7-b067336c5bc8); lib. bdg. 34.47 *(978-1-4358-9457-0(X)*, f78b64aa-ec32-43e2-adbf-f76ba760b037) Rosen Publishing Group, Inc., The. (Rosen Reference).

Clendening, John. Veterinary Hospitals, 1 vol. 2014. (Animal Rescue Ser.). (ENG.). 32p. (J). (gr. 4-4). lib. bdg. 27.93 *(978-1-4777-7023-8(2)*, c21eb96c-7c46-40ba-88b9-65b1e1f682c4, PowerKids Pr.) Rosen Publishing Group, Inc., The.

DiConsiglio, John. 24/7: Science Behind the Scenes: Medical Files: When Birds Get Flu & Cows Go Mad! 2007. (24/7: Science Behind the Scenes Ser.). (ENG., Illus.). 64p. (J). (gr. 8-12). 29.00 *(978-0-531-12069-9(4)*, Watts, Franklin) Scholastic Library Publishing.

Early Macken, JoAnn. Veterinarians, 1 vol. 2010. (People in My Community (Second Edition) Ser.). (ENG.). 24p. (J). (gr. k-2). pap. 9.15 *(978-1-4339-3813-9(8)*, df9be73c-6df6-466f-93a3-6c1af403acf5); lib. bdg. 25.27 *(978-1-4339-3812-2(X)*, a38dabe0-95be-415f-a3f3-dd223b65f6b9) Stevens, Gareth Publishing LLLP.

Evento, Susan & Meredith Books Staff. Vet Emergencies 24/7. 2008. (Illus.). 48p. (J). (gr. 4-7). per. 6.99 *(978-0-696-23979-3(5))* Meredith Bks.

Ewing, Susan M. Working with Animals. 2018. (Career Files Ser.). (ENG., Illus.). 32p. (J). (gr. 3-6). 32.80 *(978-1-63235-452-5(7)*, 13845, 12-Story Library) Bookstaves, LLC.

Facts on File, Inc. Staff. Animals. 2010. (New Discovering Careers for Your Future Ser.). (Illus.). 128p. (gr. 4-9). 24.95 *(978-0-8160-8044-1(5)*, Ferguson Publishing Company) Infobase Holdings, Inc.

Forest, Anne. Veterinarians on the Job. (Jobs in Our Community Ser.). (J). (gr. 1-1). 2017. pap. 49.50 *(978-1-5345-2150-6(X))* 2016. (ENG.). 24p. 26.23 *(978-1-5345-2151-3(8)*, ada960b6-f996-4908-aa3b-47da7fd2ef18) 2016. (ENG.). 24p. pap. 9.25 *(978-1-5345-2149-0(6)*, 0b18d51f-4efa-4744-9806-1e8e09474b27) Greenhaven Publishing LLC. (KidHaven Publishing).

Gregory, Josh. What Do They Do? Veterinarians. 2010. (Community Connections: What Do They Do? Ser.). (ENG., Illus.). 24p. (gr. 2-5). lib. bdg. 29.21 *(978-1-60279-810-6(9)*, 200510) Cherry Lake Publishing.

Halls, Kelly Milner. Albino Animals. 2004. (Illus.). 72p. (J). pap. 8.95 *(978-1-58196-016-7(6))* Lerner Publishing Group.

Jackson, Donna M. Er Vets. 2009. (ENG., Illus.). 96p. (J). (gr. 3-7). pap. 8.99 *(978-0-547-23758-9(8)*, 1083868, Clarion Bks.) HarperCollins Pubs.

Kalman, Bobbie. Veterinarians Help Keep Animals Healthy, 1 vol. 2004. (My Community & Its Helpers Ser.). (ENG., Illus.). 32p. (J). pap. *(978-0-7787-2125-3(6))* Crabtree Publishing Co.

Leaf, Christina. Veterinarians. 2018. (Community Helpers Ser.). (ENG., Illus.). 24p. (J). (gr. k-3). lib. bdg. 26.95 *(978-1-62617-751-2(1)*, Blastoff! Readers) Bellwether Media.

Less, Emma. Veterinarians. 2018. (Real-Life Superheroes Ser.). (ENG.). 16p. (J). (gr. k-2). pap. 7.99 *(978-1-68152-283-8(7)*, 14922) Amicus.

Lindeen, Mary. A Visit to the Vet. 2018. (BeginningtoRead Ser.). (ENG.). 32p. (J). (gr. -1-2). lib. bdg. 22.60 *(978-1-59953-913-3(6))*; (gr. k-2). pap. 13.26 *(978-1-68404-169-5(4))* Norwood Hse. Pr.

McKinnon, Elaine. Pets at the Vet, 1 vol. 2016. (Community Helpers Ser.). (ENG., Illus.). 24p. (J). (gr. 1-1). pap. 9.25 *(978-1-4994-2706-6(9)*, 95a6fd10-e92d-4535-8699-7983a19c9520, PowerKids Pr.) Rosen Publishing Group, Inc., The.

Miller, Connie Colwell. I'll Be a Veterinarian. Baroncelli, Silvia, illus. 2016. (When I Grow Up Ser.). (ENG.). 24p. (J). (gr. 1-4). lib. bdg. 20.95 *(978-1-60753-764-9(8)*, 15576) Amicus.

—Vétérinaire. Baroncelli, Silvia, illus. 2016. (Plus Tard, Je Serai... Ser.). (FRE.). 24p. (J). (gr. 1-4). *(978-1-77092-358-4(6)*, 17621) Amicus.

Murray, Aaron R. Veterinarians Help Us, 1 vol. 2012. (All about Community Helpers Ser.). (ENG., Illus.). 24p. (gr. -1-1). 25.27 *(978-0-7660-4046-5(1)*,

6fcc0fcf-8c0f-4052-9987-f35e6d59e889, Enslow Publishing) Enslow Publishing, LLC.
Margi, Lela. Karl's New Beak: 3-D Printing Builds a Bird a Better Life. Popham, Harriet, illus. 2019. (ENG.). 32p. (gr. -1-2). 17.95 *(978-1-68446-026-7(3)*, 139699, Capstone Editions) Capstone.
Orr, Tamra. Avian Flu. 2009. (Coping in a Changing World Ser.). 112p. (gr. 7-7). 63.90 *(978-1-61512-018-5(1))* Rosen Publishing Group, Inc., The.
Ready, Dee. Veterinarians Help. 2013. (Our Community Helpers Ser.). (ENG.). 24p. (J). (gr. k-1). pap. 38.74 *(978-1-62065-852-9(6)*, 19422, Pebble) Capstone.
Ready, Dee & Ready, Dee. Veterinarians Help, 1 vol. 2013. (Our Community Helpers Ser.). (ENG.). 24p. (J). (gr. -1-2). pap. 6.29 *(978-1-62065-851-2(8)*, 121790, Pebble) Capstone.
Rice, Dona & Montgomery, Anne. Helping Injured Animals. rev. ed. 2019. (Smithsonian: Informational Text Ser.). (ENG., Illus.). 24p. (J). (gr. 1-2). pap. 8.99 *(978-1-4938-6646-5(X))* Teacher Created Materials, Inc.
Rich, Mari. Big-Animal Vets!, Vol. 10. 2015. (Scientists in Action Ser.). (Illus.). 48p. (J). (gr. 5). 20.95 *(978-1-4222-3419-8(3))* Mason Crest.
Somervill, Barbara A. Veterinarian. 2008. (21st Century Skills Library: Cool Careers Ser.). (ENG., Illus.). 32p. (gr. 4-8). lib. bdg. 32.07 *(978-1-60279-301-9(8)*, 200140) Cherry Lake Publishing.
Strain Trueit, Trudi. Animal Physical Therapist, 1 vol. 2014. (Careers with Animals Ser.). (ENG., Illus.). 64p. (gr. 5-5). 36.93 *(978-1-62712-458-4(6)*, 4137b0ba-faf7-45ea-8c08-b7b0cfbbe4c0) Cavendish Square Publishing LLC.
Thomas, William David. Veterinarian, 1 vol. 2008. (Cool Careers: Helping Careers Ser.). (ENG.). 32p. (gr. 3-3). lib. bdg. 28.67 *(978-0-8368-9197-3(X)*, 055ce3f6-ef46-47be-b3b0-7e3389d5a623) Stevens, Gareth Publishing LLLP.
Worthington, Niles. A Vet's Job, 1 vol. 2015. (Community Workers Ser.). (ENG., Illus.). 24p. (gr. 1-1). pap. 9.23 *(978-1-5026-0436-1(1)*, 4a947a40-e6f5-4be0-b435-e4f819db1322) Cavendish Square Publishing LLC.
Zombie Animals: Parasites Take Control! 2015. (Zombie Animals: Parasites Take Control! Ser.). (ENG.). 24p. (J). (gr. 2-3). pap., pap., pap. 293.40 *(978-1-4824-3500-9(4))* Stevens, Gareth Publishing LLLP.

VETERINARY MEDICINE—FICTION

Ahlberg, Allan. Mrs. Vole the Vet. Chichester Clark, Emma, illus. (ENG.). 24p. (J). pap. 6.95 *(978-0-14-037880-1(4))* Penguin Bks., Ltd. GBR. Dist: Trafalgar Square Publishing.
Anderson, Laurie Halse. End of the Race. 12 vols. 2012. (Vet Volunteers Ser.: 12). (ENG.). 160p. (J). (gr. 3-7). 7.99 *(978-0-14-241228-2(7)*, Puffin Books) Penguin Young Readers Group.
—Helping Hands. 2013. (Vet Volunteers Ser.: 15). (ENG.). 144p. (J). (gr. 3-7). pap. 7.99 *(978-0-14-241677-8(0)*, Puffin Books) Penguin Young Readers Group.
Baglio, Ben M. Collie with a Card. Baum, Ann, illus. 2004. 136p. (J). pap. *(978-0-439-68760-7(8))* Scholastic, Inc.
Carpenter, Christopher, illus. Lilly's Heart: The Veterinary Clinic Cases Series. 2006. 32p. (J). per. 9.95 *(978-0-9766641-0-9(0))* Ichabod Ink.
Coe, Victoria J. Fenway & Hattie up to New Tricks. 2019. (Fenway & Hattie Ser.: 3). (ENG.). 208p. (J). (gr. 3-7). 7.99 *(978-1-5247-3785-6(2)*, Puffin Books) Penguin Young Readers Group.
Goldman, Marcia. Lola Goes to the Doctor. 2014. (Lola Ser.). (ENG., Illus.). 32p. (J). (gr. -1-k). 18.99 *(978-1-939547-11-8(3)*, 540afca5-ea5c-457e-b12c-820d972780b6) Creston Bks.
Henson, Heather. The Whole Sky. 2017. (ENG., Illus.). 256p. (J). (gr. 5-7). 16.99 *(978-1-4424-1405-1(7)*, Atheneum/Caitlyn Dlouhy Books) Simon & Schuster Children's Publishing.
Johnson, Maddie. How Tickles Saved Pickles: A True Story. Johnson, Maddie, photos by. 2018. (ENG., Illus.). 40p. (J). (gr. -1-3). 17.99 *(978-1-5344-3662-6(6)*, McElderry, Margaret K. Bks.) McElderry, Margaret K. Bks.
Kadohata, Cynthia. Checked. Zorat, Maurizio, illus. 2018. (ENG.). 416p. (J). (gr. 5-9). 17.99 *(978-1-4814-4661-7(4)*, Atheneum/Caitlyn Dlouhy Books) Simon & Schuster Children's Publishing.
Kerr, Judith. Mog & the Vet. (ENG., Illus.). 32p. (J). pap. 9.99 *(978-0-00-664620-4(4))* HarperCollins Pubs. Ltd. GBR. Dist: Trafalgar Square Publishing.
Lynn, Elizabeth B. Forget the Vet. Meyer, Ashley M., illus. 2012. 32p. 24.95 *(978-1-936688-21-0(2))* AKA:yoLa.
Monsef, Kiyash. Once There Was. 2023. (Once There Was Ser.). (ENG., Illus.). 416p. (J). (gr. 5). 18.99 *(978-1-6659-2850-2(6)*, Simon & Schuster Bks. For Young Readers) Simon & Schuster Bks. For Young Readers.
North, Sherry. Champ's Story: Dogs Get Cancer Too! (Spanish Edition) Rietz, Kathleen, illus. 2010. (SPA.). 32p. (J). (gr. -1-4). 17.95 *(978-1-60718-681-6(0))* Arbordale Publishing.
—Champ's Story: Dogs Get Cancer Too!, 1 vol. Rietz, Kathleen, illus. 2010. (ENG.). 32p. (J). (gr. -1-4). 16.95 *(978-1-60718-077-7(4))*; pap. 8.95 *(978-1-60718-088-3(X))* Arbordale Publishing.
Ries, Lori. Aggie the Brave. Dormer, Frank W., illus. (Aggie & Ben Ser.). (ENG.). 48p. (J). (gr. -1-3). 2012. pap. 5.95 *(978-1-57091-636-6(5))* 2010. 12.95 *(978-1-57091-635-9(7))* Charlesbridge Publishing, Inc.
Wilson, Diane Lee. Firehorse. (ENG.). 336p. (YA). (gr. 7). 2010. pap. 8.99 *(978-1-4424-0331-4(4))* 2006. (Illus.). 17.99 *(978-1-4169-1551-5(6))* McElderry, Margaret K. Bks. (McElderry, Margaret K. Bks.).

VETERINARY MEDICINE—VOCATIONAL GUIDANCE

Adamson, Heather. A Day in the Life of a Veterinarian, 1 vol. 2003. (Community Helpers at Work Ser.). (ENG., Illus.). 24p. (J). (gr. 1-3). 25.99 *(978-0-7368-2287-9(9)*, 89395, Capstone Pr.) Capstone.
Allman, Toney. Careers If You Like Animals. 2017. (Career Discovery Ser.). (ENG., Illus.). 80p. (YA). (gr. 5-12). *(978-1-68282-134-3(X))* ReferencePoint Pr., Inc.
Byers, Ann. Internship & Volunteer Opportunities for People Who Love Animals, 1 vol. 2012. (Foot in the Door Ser.). (ENG., Illus.). 80p. (YA). (gr. 6-6). lib. bdg. 38.47 *(978-1-4488-8293-9(1)*, ae6d55e9-ece0-4088-91a7-37780d2226b2) Rosen Publishing Group, Inc., The.
Driscoll, Laura. I Want to Be a Veterinarian. Echeverri, Catalina, illus. 2018. (I Can Read Level 1 Ser.). (ENG.). 32p. (J). (gr. -1-3). 16.99 *(978-0-06-243247-6(8))*; pap. 5.99 *(978-0-06-243261-2(3))* HarperCollins Pubs. (HarperCollins).
Hutchings, Amy. What Happens at a Vet's Office?, 1 vol. 2009. (Where People Work Ser.). (ENG.). 24p. (gr. 1-1). (J). lib. bdg. 24.67 *(978-1-4339-0071-6(8)*, efdaa023-6e04-4075-bb6b-4a0a74763c63); pap. 9.15 *(978-1-4339-0135-5(8)*, 4e9c97f9-84ef-46b6-87c6-f007e888d5b7) Stevens, Gareth Publishing LLLP. (Weekly Reader Leveled Readers).
—What Happens at a Vet's Office? / ¿Qué Pasa en una Clínica Veterinaria?, 1 vol. 2009. (Where People Work / ¿dónde Trabaja la Gente? Ser.). (SPA & ENG., Illus.). 24p. (J). (gr. 1-1). pap. 9.15 *(978-1-4339-0143-0(9)*, 61ed8c1b-f3b9-423c-b2ba-c9525654dff7); lib. bdg. 24.67 *(978-1-4339-0079-2(3)*, 93d37124-4f50-4067-b1cb-bdb4130a6e23) Stevens, Gareth Publishing LLLP. (Weekly Reader Leveled Readers).
Kalman, Bobbie. Veterinarians Help Keep Animals Healthy, 1 vol. 2004. (My Community & Its Helpers Ser.). (ENG., Illus.). 32p. (J). pap. *(978-0-7787-2125-3(6))* Crabtree Publishing Co.
Parks, Peggy J. Veterinarian. 2004. (EXPLORING CAREERS Ser.). (ENG.). (J). 27.50 *(978-0-7377-2068-6(9)*, Greenhaven Pr., Inc.) Cengage Gale.
Somervill, Barbara A. Veterinarian. 2015. (21st Century Skills Library: Cool STEAM Careers Ser.). (ENG., Illus.). 32p. (J). (gr. 4-7). 32.07 *(978-1-63362-566-2(4)*, 206448) Cherry Lake Publishing.
Strain Truit, Trudi. Veterinarian, 1 vol. 2014. (Careers with Animals Ser.). (ENG., Illus.). 64p. (gr. 5-5). 36.93 *(978-1-62712-464-5(0)*, 1b2135f1-8619-45a6-8974-d34ccf89a00a) Cavendish Square Publishing LLC.
Thomas, William David. Veterinarian, 1 vol. 2008. (Cool Careers: Helping Careers Ser.). (ENG.). 32p. (gr. 3-3). pap. 11.50 *(978-0-8368-9330-4(1)*, 42d28c3c-dd40-407d-bee4-4308f662488a) Stevens, Gareth Publishing LLLP.
Trueit, Trudi Strain. Animal Physical Therapist. 2014. (J). *(978-0-7614-8074-7(9))* Marshall Cavendish Corp.
—Veterinarian. 2014. (J). *(978-0-7614-8076-1(5))* Marshall Cavendish Corp.

VIADUCTS

see Bridges

VIANNEY, JEAN BAPTISTE, MARIE, SAINT, 1786-1859

DeDomenico, Elizabeth Marie. Saint John Vianney: A Priest for All People. Hatke, Ben, illus. 2008. (Encounter the Saints Ser.). 122p. (J). (gr. 4-7). pap. 7.95 *(978-0-8198-7115-2(X))* Pauline Bks. & Media.

VIBRATION

see also Light; Waves

McAneney, Caitlin. How Elephants & Other Animals Hear the Earth, 1 vol. 2015. (Superior Animal Senses Ser.). (ENG., Illus.). 24p. (J). (gr. 3-4). pap. 9.25 *(978-1-4994-0991-8(5)*, 70e65fe8-e3fc-4a08-9917-ae6e2a5a6cfb, PowerKids Pr.) Rosen Publishing Group, Inc., The.
Solway, Andrew. Exploring Sound, Light, & Radiation, 1 vol. 2007. (Exploring Physical Science Ser.). (ENG., Illus.). 48p. (YA). (gr. 6-6). lib. bdg. 34.47 *(978-1-4042-3746-9(1)*, 00bfa945-8d0e-4dbe-832a-882598e802ba) Rosen Publishing Group, Inc., The.

VICE-PRESIDENTS—UNITED STATES

Anderson, Dale. Al Gore: A Wake-Up Call to Global Warming. 2009. (Voices for Green Choices Ser.). (ENG., Illus.). 48p. (J). (gr. 5-9). pap. *(978-0-7787-4679-9(8))*; lib. bdg. *(978-0-7787-4666-9(6))* Crabtree Publishing Co.
Biden, Jill. Joey: The Story of Joe Biden. Bates, Amy June, illus. 2020. (ENG.). 48p. (J). (gr. -1-3). 19.99 *(978-1-5344-8053-7(6)*, Simon & Schuster/Paula Wiseman Bks.) Simon & Schuster/Paula Wiseman Bks.
Braun, Eric Mark. The Real Aaron Burr: The Truth Behind the Legend. 2019. (Real Revolutionaries Ser.). (ENG., Illus.). 64p. (J). (gr. 5-9). lib. bdg. 34.65 *(978-0-7565-6250-2(3)*, 141182, Compass Point Bks.) Capstone.
Collier Hillstrom, Laurie. Al Gore, 1 vol. 2008. (People in the News Ser.). (ENG., Illus.). 112p. (gr. 7-7). lib. bdg. 41.03 *(978-1-4205-0086-8(4)*, 0b1655b8-69b1-4fa8-b474-e619552cd947, Lucent Pr.) Greenhaven Publishing LLC.
De Medeiros, James. Al Gore. 2008. (Remarkable People Ser.). (Illus.). 24p. (J). (gr. 4-6). pap. 8.95 *(978-1-59036-993-7(9))*; lib. bdg. 24.45 *(978-1-59036-992-0(0))* Weigl Pubs., Inc.
Duling, Kaitlyn. Standing in the Vice President's Shoes, 1 vol. 2017. (My Government Ser.). (ENG.). 32p. (gr. 3-3). pap. 11.58 *(978-1-5026-3082-7(6)*, f2b119a5-3d2f-4ecd-96df-df52ae0231d8) Cavendish Square Publishing LLC.
Harmon, Daniel E. Al Gore & Global Warming. (Celebrity Activists Ser.). 112p. (gr. 8-8). 2009. 66.50 *(978-1-61511-826-7(8))* 2008. (ENG., Illus.). (YA). lib. bdg. 39.80 *(978-1-4042-1761-4(4)*, 1dd7378e-da81-4373-8d20-b638db2fbe65) Rosen Publishing Group, Inc., The.
Laks Gorman, Jacqueline. Vice President, 1 vol. 2009. (Know Your Government Ser.). (ENG.). 24p. (J). (gr. 3-3). pap. 9.15 *(978-1-4339-0124-9(2)*, 8f190b5f-566e-4ad9-9adc-733cc858317f); lib. bdg. 24.67 *(978-1-4339-0096-9(3)*, af6c4021-b770-4c03-bd5f-1423e73340a6) Stevens, Gareth Publishing LLLP. (Weekly Reader Leveled Readers).
—Vicepresidente (Vice President), 1 vol. 2009. (Conoce Tu Gobierno (Know Your Government) Ser.). (SPA.). 24p. (J). (gr. 3-3). pap. 9.15 *(978-1-4339-0131-7(5)*, d09251bd-8a3a-4261-915a-4d402ed5a037); lib. bdg. 24.67 *(978-1-4339-0103-4(X)*, 737220dd-c644-45dd-9a9d-a8c616b7e23d) Stevens, Gareth Publishing LLLP. (Weekly Reader Leveled Readers).
Marsh, Carole. Dick Cheney: U. S. Vice President. 2004. (1000 Readers Ser.). (Illus.). 14p. (J). (gr. k-4). pap. 2.95 *(978-0-635-02670-5(8))* Gallopade International.
—John Edwards: Vice Presidential Hopeful. 2004. (Did You Know... ? Ser.). (Illus.). 12p. (J). (gr. k-4). pap. 2.95 *(978-0-635-02671-2(6))* Gallopade International.
McGowan, Joseph. Al Gore, 1 vol. 2009. (People We Should Know (Second Series) Ser.). (ENG.). 48p. (J). (gr. 3-5). pap. 11.50 *(978-1-4339-2146-9(4)*, d085d240-5610-4f6c-a156-448650d8b212); lib. bdg. 33.67 *(978-1-4339-1947-3(8)*, 30467b93-158a-4097-996b-f59ce266e739) Stevens, Gareth Publishing LLLP. (Gareth Stevens Learning Library).
McGrath, Brian. Aaron Burr: More Than a Villain (Alexander Hamilton) rev. ed. 2017. (Social Studies: Informational Text Ser.). (ENG., Illus.). 32p. (gr. 4-8). pap. 11.99 *(978-1-4258-6355-5(8))* Teacher Created Materials, Inc.
Melton, Buckner F. Aaron Burr: The Rise & Fall of an American Politician. 2009. (Library of American Lives & Times Ser.). 112p. (gr. 5-5). 69.20 *(978-1-60853-468-5(5))* Rosen Publishing Group, Inc., The.
Murray, Julie. Vice President. 2017. (My Government Ser.). (ENG., Illus.). 24p. (J). (gr. -1-2). lib. bdg. 31.36 *(978-1-5321-0402-2(2)*, 26528, Abdo Kids) ABDO Publishing Co.
Nelson, Maria. Becoming Vice President, 1 vol. 2015. (Who's Your Candidate? Choosing Government Leaders Ser.). (ENG., Illus.). 32p. (J). (gr. 3-4). pap. 11.50 *(978-1-4824-4055-3(5)*, bb192cd6-1573-4156-a002-f25982c4d2bb) Stevens, Gareth Publishing LLLP.
Sales, Amanda. Mike Pence: Vice President of the United States, 1 vol. 2018. (Influential Lives Ser.). (ENG.). 128p. (J). (gr. 7-7). 40.27 *(978-1-9785-0343-4(1)*, c918029a-a9fb-4d28-b202-6de6d25fab1e) Enslow Publishing, LLC.
Sapet, Kerrily. Al Gore. 2007. (Political Profiles Ser.). (Illus.). 112p. (YA). (gr. 5-9). lib. bdg. 27.95 *(978-1-59935-070-7(X))* Reynolds, Morgan Inc.
Stefoff, Rebecca. Al Gore. rev. ed. 2009. pap. 52.95 *(978-0-7613-9899-8(6))* Lerner Publishing Group.
—Al Gore: Fighting for a Greener Planet. rev. ed. 2008. (Gateway Biographies Ser.). (ENG.). 48p. (gr. 4-8). 26.60 *(978-1-57505-948-8(7))* Lerner Publishing Group.
Uschan, Michael V. Joe Biden, 1 vol. 2010. (People in the News Ser.). (ENG., Illus.). 104p. (J). (gr. 7-7). 41.03 *(978-1-4205-0260-2(3)*, 13a915de-0998-448b-a8be-f4c4cdd76705, Lucent Pr.) Greenhaven Publishing LLC.
Winget, Mary Mueller. Gerald R. Ford. 2007. (Presidential Leaders Ser.). (Illus.). 112p. (J). (gr. 3-7). lib. bdg. 29.27 *(978-0-8225-1509-8(1)*, Twenty-First Century Bks.) Lerner Publishing Group.
Young, Jeff C. Joe Biden. 2009. (Political Profiles Ser.). (Illus.). 100p. (J). (gr. 5-9). 28.95 *(978-1-59935-131-5(5))* Reynolds, Morgan Inc.

VICTORIA, QUEEN OF GREAT BRITAIN, 1819-1901

Bailey, Gerry & Foster, Karen. Queen Victoria's Diamond. Noyes, Leighton & Radford, Karen, illus. 2008. (Stories of Great People Ser.). (ENG.). 40p. (J). (gr. 3-6). lib. bdg. *(978-0-7787-3697-4(0))*; pap. *(978-0-7787-3719-3(5))* Crabtree Publishing Co.
Gigliotti, Jim. Who Was Queen Victoria? 2014. (Who Was... ? Ser.). lib. bdg. 16.00 *(978-0-606-35697-8(5))* Turtleback.
Gigliotti, Jim & Who HQ. Who Was Queen Victoria? Hergenrother, Max, illus. 2014. (Who Was? Ser.). 112p. (J). (gr. 3-7). 6.99 *(978-0-448-48182-1(0)*, Penguin Workshop) Penguin Young Readers Group.
Guy, John. Victoria. 2004. (Illus.). 32p. (J). (gr. 4-7). pap. 5.95 *(978-1-86007-033-4(7)*, TickTock Books) Octopus Publishing Group GBR. Dist: Independent Pubs. Group.
Hicks, Kyra E. Martha Ann's Quilt for Queen Victoria. Fődi, Lee Edward, illus. 2012. 32p. (J). pap. 12.95 *(978-0-9824796-8-1(9))* Black Threads Pr.
—Martha Ann's Quilt for Queen Victoria. Fodi, Lee Edward, illus. 2006. 28p. (J). (gr. -1-3). 16.95 *(978-1-933285-59-7(1))* Brown Books Publishing Group.
Lacey, Saskia. The History of Victorian Innovations: Equivalent Fractions (Grade 3) 2017. (Mathematics in the Real World Ser.). (ENG., Illus.). 32p. (J). (gr. 3-4). pap. 11.99 *(978-1-4807-5803-2(5))* Teacher Created Materials, Inc.
Price-Groff, Claire. Queen Victoria & Nineteenth-Century England, 1 vol. 2003. (Rulers & Their Times Ser.). (ENG., Illus.). 80p. (gr. 6-6). 36.93 *(978-0-7614-1488-9(6)*, a5457368-9ea7-4c07-a900-a3c624bb17f8) Cavendish Square Publishing LLC.
Schomp, Virginia. Victoria & Her Court, 1 vol. 2011. (Life in Victorian England Ser.). (ENG.). 80p. (gr. 6-6). 36.93 *(978-1-60870-028-8(3)*, d1a1f919-bba5-4108-b4d8-76df456e41b3) Cavendish Square Publishing LLC.
Whitelaw, Nancy. Queen Victoria & the British Empire. 2004. (World Leaders Ser.). (Illus.). 160p. (YA). (gr. 6-12). lib. bdg. 26.95 *(978-1-931798-29-7(X))* Reynolds, Morgan Inc.

VIDEO GAMES

Anthropy, Anna. Make Your Own Twine Games! 2019. (Illus.). 144p. (J). (gr. 4-7). pap. 17.95 *(978-1-59327-938-7(8))* No Starch Pr., Inc.
Arbona, Alejandro. Awesome Minds: Video Game Creators: An Entertaining History about the Creation of Video Games. Educational & Entertaining. O'Mara Holeman, Chelsea, illus. 2018. 156p. (J). (gr. 3-7). 14.95 *(978-1-947458-22-2(1)*, 805822) Duo Pr. LLC.
Austic, Greg. Game Design. 2013. (21st Century Skills Innovation Library: Makers As Innovators Ser.). (ENG., Illus.). 32p. (J). (gr. 4-8). 32.07 *(978-1-62431-142-0(3)*, 202888); pap. 14.21 *(978-1-62431-274-8(8)*, 202890) Cherry Lake Publishing.
Austic, Greg & Willis, John. Game Design. 2017. (Illus.). 32p. (J). *(978-1-5105-1214-6(4))* SmartBook Media, Inc.
Barba, Rick. Assassin's Creed: A Walk Through History (1189-1868): A Visual Guide. 2016. (Illus.). 128p. (J). *(978-1-5182-3673-0(1))* Scholastic, Inc.
Bard, Jonathan & Bard, Mariel. Gamers & Streamers, 1 vol. 2019. (Digital Insiders Ser.). (ENG.). 32p. (J). (gr. 3-4). pap. 11.50 *(978-1-5382-4751-8(8)*, a02cfc59-e029-4fee-81c6-0499ce94def4) Stevens, Gareth Publishing LLLP.
Barton, Chris. Attack! Boss! Cheat Code! A Gamer's Alphabet. Spiotto, Joey, illus. 2014. (ENG.). 32p. (J). (gr. 1-4). 14.95 *(978-1-57687-701-2(9)*, powerHouse Bks.) powerHse. Bks.
Beth, Georgia. Stem: The Battle Between 2-D & 3-d: Shapes (Grade 5) 2018. (Mathematics in the Real World Ser.). (ENG., Illus.). 32p. (J). (gr. 4-8). pap. 11.99 *(978-1-4258-5823-0(6))* Teacher Created Materials, Inc.
Bjornlund, Lydia. The History of Video Games. 2014. (Video Games & Society Ser.). (ENG., Illus.). 96p. (J). lib. bdg. *(978-1-60152-746-2(2))* ReferencePoint Pr., Inc.
Bode, Heather L. E-Sports & the World of Competitive Gaming. 2019. (World of Video Games Ser.). (ENG.). 80p. (YA). (gr. 6-12). *(978-1-68282-557-0(4))* ReferencePoint Pr., Inc.
BradyGames Staff & Birlew, Dan. Monster Hunter Official Strategy Guide. 2004. (ENG., Illus.). 144p. pap. 14.99 *(978-0-7440-0362-8(8))* Pearson Education.
Burns, Jan. Shigeru Miyamoto: Nintendo Game Designer, 1 vol. 2006. (Innovators Ser.). (ENG., Illus.). 48p. (gr. 4-8). lib. bdg. 34.58 *(978-0-7377-3534-5(1)*, 08b727ff-472d-42fa-91c4-ad8dda65c780, KidHaven Publishing) Greenhaven Publishing LLC.
Carson, Mary Kay. Who Invented Home Video Games? Ralph Baer, 1 vol. 2012. (I Like Inventors! Ser.). (ENG., Illus.). 24p. (gr. k-2). pap. 10.35 *(978-1-4644-0135-0(7)*, 1a7befe1-b4e9-402b-a075-3ad3a801a7eb, Enslow Elementary) Enslow Publishing, LLC.
Castro, Rachel. Shigeru Miyamoto. 2019. (STEM Superstars Ser.). (ENG.). 24p. (J). (gr. k-2). 22.60 *(978-1-68450-921-8(1))* Norwood Hse. Pr.
Cawthon, Scott. The Freddy Files. 2017. (Illus.). 160p. (YA). *(978-1-74276-601-0(3))* Scholastic, Inc.
—The Freddy Files: An AFK Book. 2019. (ENG., Illus.). 224p. (YA). (gr. 7-7). pap. 9.99 *(978-1-338-56381-8(5))* Scholastic, Inc.
Ceceri, Kathy. Video Games: Design & Code Your Own Adventure. Crosier, Mike, illus. 2015. (Build It Yourself Ser.). (ENG.). 128p. (J). (gr. 3-7). 22.95 *(978-1-61930-291-4(8)*, 84ece263-3351-4150-b93b-fcde6572dc2c) Nomad Pr.
Cefrey, Holly. Career Building Through Machinima: Using Video Games to Make Movies. 2009. (Digital Career Building Ser.). 64p. (gr. 6-6). 58.50 *(978-1-61512-168-7(4))* Rosen Publishing Group, Inc., The.
Christopher, Nick. Are Video Games Too Violent?, 1 vol. 2017. (Points of View Ser.). (ENG.). 24p. (J). (gr. 3-3). pap. 9.25 *(978-1-5345-2487-3(8)*, 368c8041-230d-434a-8e33-bfd22c62be91); lib. bdg. 26.23 *(978-1-5345-2425-5(8)*, 3216fd34-7db3-4049-9b8d-c7ac7c62cd20) Greenhaven Publishing LLC.
Cohen, Judith Love. You Can Be A Woman Video Game Producer. lt. ed. 2005. (Illus.). 72p. (J). 17.95 *(978-1-880599-74-7(0))*; pap. 12.95 *(978-1-880599-73-0(2))* Cascade Pass, Inc.
Colby, Jennifer. Pinball to Gaming Systems. 2019. (21st Century Junior Library: Then to Now Tech Ser.). (ENG.). 24p. (J). (gr. 2-5). pap. 12.79 *(978-1-5341-5012-6(9)*, 213355); (Illus.). lib. bdg. 30.64 *(978-1-5341-4726-3(8)*, 213354) Cherry Lake Publishing.
Cornell, Kari. Nintendo Video Game Designer Shigeru Miyamoto. 2016. (STEM Trailblazer Bios Ser.). (ENG., Illus.). 32p. (J). (gr. 2-5). 26.65 *(978-1-4677-9531-9(3)*, abd1fcb9-a262-4bab-823a-aa911674c4fa, Lerner Pubns.) Lerner Publishing Group.
Corporate Contributor Staff. The Economics of a Video Game. 2013. (ENG.). 48p. (J). *(978-0-7787-7970-4(X))*; pap. *(978-0-7787-7975-9(0))* Crabtree Publishing Co.
Creative Team at Walter Foster Publishing Staff. Learn to Draw Angry Birds: Learn to Draw All of Your Favorite Angry Birds & Those Bad Piggies! 2012. (Licensed Learn to Draw Ser.). (ENG., Illus.). 64p. (J). (gr. 1-3). pap. 9.95 *(978-1-60058-306-3(7)*, 1600583067) Quarto Publishing Group USA.
Croce, Nicholas. Cool Careers Without College for People Who Love Video Games, 1 vol. 2006. (Cool Careers Without College (2002-2006) Ser.). (ENG., Illus.). 144p. (YA). (gr. 7-7). lib. bdg. 41.13 *(978-1-4042-0747-9(3)*, 894b1c7c-996b-4aa3-92c4-cf2b0580df6c) Rosen Publishing Group, Inc., The.
—Cool Careers Without College for people who love Video Games. 2009. (Cool Careers Without College Ser.). 144p. (gr. 6-6). 66.50 *(978-1-61511-982-0(5))* Rosen Publishing Group, Inc., The.
Culp, Jennifer. Call of Duty: Vince Zampella, Grant Collier, & Jason West, 1 vol. 2014. (Internet Biographies Ser.). (ENG., Illus.). 128p. (J). (gr. 7-7). 39.80 *(978-1-4777-7923-1(X)*, 0194884b-08d2-4c74-80ff-13c1166fcf70, Rosen Young Adult) Rosen Publishing Group, Inc., The.
Cunningham, Kevin. Video Game Designer. 2015. (21st Century Skills Library: Cool STEAM Careers Ser.). (ENG., Illus.). 32p. (J). (gr. 4-7). 32.07 *(978-1-63362-567-9(2)*, 206452) Cherry Lake Publishing.
—Video Games: From Concept to Consumer. 2013. (Calling All Innovators). (ENG.). 64p. (J). lib. bdg. 30.00 *(978-0-531-26523-9(4))* Scholastic Library Publishing.
Duffield, Katy S. Ken Kutaragi: PlayStation Developer, 1 vol. 2007. (Innovators Ser.). (ENG., Illus.). 48p. (gr. 4-8). lib. bdg. 34.58 *(978-0-7377-3862-9(6)*, 452f45d5-dcdd-49b9-a151-e9d1511551e1, KidHaven Publishing) Greenhaven Publishing LLC.
Egan, Jill & Stewart, Rhea A. How Video Game Designers Use Math. 2009. (Math in the Real World Ser.). 32p. (gr. 4-6). 28.00 *(978-1-60413-603-6(0)*, Chelsea Clubhse.) Infobase Holdings, Inc.
Ellenport, Craig. Esports: A Billion Eyeballs & Growing, Vol. 6. 2018. (Tech 2. 0: World-Changing Entertainment Companies Ser.). (Illus.). 64p. (J). (gr. 7). 31.93 *(978-1-4222-4054-0(1))* Mason Crest.
Falcom, Nihon. The Legend of Heroes: the Characters: The Characters. 2014. (ENG., Illus.). 272p. (YA). pap. 49.99 *(978-1-926778-90-7(1)*, b0bcedf0-25f4-4f6a-bba9-0b74f2f352c8) URON Entertainment Corp. CAN. Dist: Diamond Comic Distributors, Inc.
—The Legend of Heroes: the Illustrations: The Illustrations. 2014. (ENG., Illus.). 272p. (YA). pap. 49.99 *(978-1-926778-91-4(X)*,

TUV

c576c8e9-89d7-487d-a308-ba8ccc49deae) URON Entertainment Corp. CAN. Dist: Diamond Comic Distributors, Inc.

Farkas, Bart G. Way of the Samurai 2 Official Strategy Guide. 2004. (ENG., Illus.). 128p. pap. 14.99 *(978-0-7440-0371-0(7))* Pearson Education.

Farshtey, Greg. Lego Ninjago Official Guide. 2011. (Illus.). 128p. (J). pap. *(978-0-545-38285-4(8))* Scholastic, Inc.

Farwell, Nick. Minecraft. Burlinson, James & Cordner, Theo, illus. 2014. 79p. (J). *(978-0-545-68575-7(3))* Scholastic, Inc.

Farwell, Nick & Steer, Don. Minecraft Redstone Handbook. Burlinson, James et al, illus. 2015. 93p. (J). *(978-0-545-82320-3(X))* Scholastic, Inc.

Feldman, Thea. If You Love Video Games, You Could Be... Ready-To-Read Level 2. Kwee, Natalie, illus. 2019. (If You Love Ser.). (ENG.). 32p. (J). (gr. k-2). 17.99 *(978-1-5344-4399-0(1))*; pap. 4.99 *(978-1-5344-4398-3(3))* Simon Spotlight. (Simon Spotlight).

Furgang, Adam. For People Who Love Gaming, 1 vol. 2016. (Cool Careers Without College Ser.). (ENG., Illus.). 104p. (J). (gr. 7-7). 41.12 *(978-1-5081-7282-6(X)*, 93121f31-e029-46d3-999f-2f800ffde523) Rosen Publishing Group, Inc., The.

—Tyler "Ninja" Blevins: Twitch's Top Streamer with 11 Million Followers, 1 vol. 2019. (Top Video Gamers in the World Ser.). (ENG.). 48p. (gr. 5-5). pap. 12.75 *(978-1-7253-4600-0(1)*, 1f19cbe4-e505-41d5-bac1-636d56b896b2, Rosen Reference) Rosen Publishing Group, Inc., The.

Gimpel, Diane Marczely. Violence in Video Games. 2013. (Hot Topics in Media Ser.). (ENG.). 48p. (J). (gr. 4-8). pap. 18.50 *(978-1-61783-786-9(5)*, 10760) ABDO Publishing Co.

Gluckstern, Rachel. Playing Nice with Others in Fortnite. 2019. *(978-1-7253-4814-1(4))* Rosen Publishing Group, Inc., The.

Green, Sara. Nintendo. 2016. (Brands We Know Ser.). (ENG., Illus.). 24p. (J). (gr. 3-8). lib. bdg. 27.95 *(978-1-62617-350-7(8)*, Pilot Bks.) Bellwether Media.

Gregory, Josh. Animals in Minecraft. 2018. (21st Century Skills Innovation Library: Unofficial Guides Junior Ser.). (ENG., Illus.). 24p. (J). (gr. 2-4). lib. bdg. 30.64 *(978-1-5341-2983-2(9)*, 211976) Cherry Lake Publishing.

—Building in Minecraft. 2018. (21st Century Skills Innovation Library: Unofficial Guides Junior Ser.). (ENG., Illus.). 24p. (J). (gr. 2-4). lib. bdg. 30.64 *(978-1-5341-2984-9(7)*, 211980) Cherry Lake Publishing.

—Fortnite: Save the World. 2020. (21st Century Skills Innovation Library: Unofficial Guides). (ENG., Illus.). 32p. (J). (gr. 4-8). pap. 14.21 *(978-1-5341-6194-8(5)*, 214776); lib. bdg. 32.07 *(978-1-5341-5964-8(9)*, 214775) Cherry Lake Publishing.

—How Minecraft Was Made. 2018. (21st Century Skills Innovation Library: Unofficial Guides Junior Ser.). (ENG., Illus.). 24p. (J). (gr. 2-4). lib. bdg. 30.64 *(978-1-5341-2988-7(X)*, 211996) Cherry Lake Publishing.

—The Making of Fortnite. 2019. (21st Century Skills Innovation Library: Unofficial Guides). (ENG., Illus.). 32p. (J). (gr. 4-8). pap. 14.21 *(978-1-5341-5103-1(6)*, 213719); lib. bdg. 32.07 *(978-1-5341-4817-8(5)*, 213718) Cherry Lake Publishing.

—Minecon. 2018. (21st Century Skills Innovation Library: Unofficial Guides). (ENG., Illus.). 32p. (J). (gr. 4-8). lib. bdg. 32.07 *(978-1-5341-2992-4(8)*, 212012) Cherry Lake Publishing.

—Minecraft: Guide to Building. 2017. (21st Century Skills Innovation Library: Unofficial Guides). (ENG., Illus.). 32p. (J). (gr. 4-8). lib. bdg. 32.07 *(978-1-63472-195-0(0)*, 209352) Cherry Lake Publishing.

—Minecraft: Guide to Combat. 2017. (21st Century Skills Innovation Library: Unofficial Guides). (ENG., Illus.). 32p. (J). (gr. 4-8). lib. bdg. 32.07 *(978-1-63472-196-7(9)*, 209356) Cherry Lake Publishing.

—Minecraft: Story Mode. 2018. (21st Century Skills Innovation Library: Unofficial Guides). (ENG., Illus.). 32p. (J). (gr. 4-8). lib. bdg. 32.07 *(978-1-5341-2989-4(6)*, 212000) Cherry Lake Publishing.

—Minecraft: Virtual Reality. 2018. (21st Century Skills Innovation Library: Unofficial Guides). (ENG., Illus.). 32p. (J). (gr. 4-8). lib. bdg. 32.07 *(978-1-5341-2991-7(X)*, 212008) Cherry Lake Publishing.

—Mining & Farming in Minecraft. 2018. (21st Century Skills Innovation Library: Unofficial Guides Junior Ser.). (ENG., Illus.). 24p. (J). (gr. 2-4). lib. bdg. 30.64 *(978-1-5341-2986-3(3)*, 211988) Cherry Lake Publishing.

—Redstone & Transportation in Minecraft. 2018. (21st Century Skills Innovation Library: Unofficial Guides Junior Ser.). (ENG., Illus.). 24p. (J). (gr. 2-4). lib. bdg. 30.64 *(978-1-5341-2987-0(1)*, 211992) Cherry Lake Publishing.

—Starter Guide to Minecraft. 2018. (21st Century Skills Innovation Library: Unofficial Guides Junior Ser.). (ENG., Illus.). 24p. (J). (gr. 2-4). lib. bdg. 30.64 *(978-1-5341-2981-8(2)*, 211968) Cherry Lake Publishing.

Hackett, Jennifer. Designing a Game (a True Book: Get Ready to Code) (Library Edition) 2019. (True Book (Relaunch) Ser.). (ENG., Illus.). 48p. (J). (gr. 3-5). lib. bdg. 31.00 *(978-0-531-12733-9(8)*, Children's Pr.) Scholastic Library Publishing.

—Game Design (a True Book: Behind the Scenes) (Library Edition) 2017. (True Book (Relaunch) Ser.). (ENG., Illus.). 48p. (J). (gr. 3-5). lib. bdg. 31.00 *(978-0-531-23503-4(3)*, Children's Pr.) Scholastic Library Publishing.

Hakala, John L. Violence & Video Games. 2019. (World of Video Games Ser.). (ENG.). 80p. (YA). (gr. 6-12). *(978-1-68282-563-1(9))* ReferencePoint Pr., Inc.

Hall, Kevin. Rubén el Rubius Gundersen: Star Spanish Gamer with More Than 6 Billion+ Views, 1 vol. 2019. (Top Video Gamers in the World Ser.). (ENG.). 48p. (gr. 5-5). pap. 12.75 *(978-1-7253-4609-3(5)*, 0034a971-790d-4535-b9bd-ab979f3b57f2, Rosen Central) Rosen Publishing Group, Inc., The.

Hamilton, Jill, ed. Video Games, 1 vol. 2010. (Introducing Issues with Opposing Viewpoints Ser.). (ENG.). 136p. (gr. 7-10). 43.63 *(978-0-7377-4946-5(6)*, 6b8631c3-7592-4c7b-a1ed-dca1d1897933, Greenhaven Publishing) Greenhaven Publishing LLC.

Hamilton, Tracy Brown. Perfecting Your Dance Moves in Fortnite. 2019. (J). *(978-1-7253-4810-3(1))* Rosen Publishing Group, Inc., The.

Hartman, Ashley Strehle. Youth & Video Games. 2019. (World of Video Games Ser.). (ENG.). 80p. (YA). (gr. 6-12). *(978-1-68282-565-5(5))* ReferencePoint Pr., Inc.

Harvey, Janet. Building Structures & Collecting Resources in Fortnite. 2019. (J). pap. *(978-1-7253-4794-6(6))* Rosen Publishing Group, Inc., The.

Higgins, Nadia. Making a Video Game. 2018. (Sequence Entertainment Ser.). (ENG.). 32p. (J). (gr. 2-5). pap. 9.99 *(978-1-68152-364-4(7)*, 15204); lib. bdg. *(978-1-68151-444-4(3)*, 15198) Amicus.

Hile, Kevin. Video Games, 1 vol. 2009. (Technology 360 Ser.). (ENG., Illus.). 104p. (gr. 7-10). lib. bdg. 41.53 *(978-1-4205-0170-4(4)*, fdb80b4a-80bb-453c-8ab0-8db7726e5502, Lucent Pr.) Greenhaven Publishing LLC.

Hollinger, Elizabeth M. Star Ocean(r) Till the End of Time: Official Strategy Guide. 2004. (ENG., Illus.). 272p. (YA). pap. 15.99 *(978-0-7440-0390-1(3))* Pearson Education.

Holmes, Kirsty. Action-Adventure Games. 2019. (Game On! Ser.). (Illus.). 32p. (J). (gr. 4-4). *(978-0-7787-5260-8(7))*; pap. *(978-0-7787-5289-9(5))* Crabtree Publishing Co.

—Building Virtual Worlds. 2019. (Game On! Ser.). (Illus.). 32p. (J). (gr. 4-4). *(978-0-7787-5257-8(7))*; pap. *(978-0-7787-5270-7(4))* Crabtree Publishing Co.

—Platform Games. 2019. (Game On! Ser.). (Illus.). 32p. (J). (gr. 4-4). *(978-0-7787-5259-2(3))*; pap. *(978-0-7787-5272-1(0))* Crabtree Publishing Co.

—Speed Racers. 2019. (Game On! Ser.). (Illus.). 32p. (J). (gr. 4-4). *(978-0-7787-5261-5(5))*; pap. *(978-0-7787-5329-2(8))* Crabtree Publishing Co.

—Strategy Games. 2019. (Game On! Ser.). (Illus.). 32p. (J). (gr. 4-4). *(978-0-7787-5269-1(0))*; pap. *(978-0-7787-5330-8(1))* Crabtree Publishing Co.

Hudak, Heather C. Gifted Game Designers. 2018. (It's a Digital World! Ser.). (ENG., Illus.). 32p. (J). (gr. 3-6). lib. bdg. 32.79 *(978-1-5321-1533-2(4)*, 28920, Checkerboard Library) ABDO Publishing Co.

Hulick, Kathryn. American Life & Video Games from Pong to Minecraft(r), 1 vol. 2016. (Pop Culture Ser.). (ENG., Illus.). 112p. (J). (gr. 7-7). 41.64 *(978-1-5026-1975-4(X)*, dc1c1603-ff93-43a2-bc5b-0ad8d351e49c) Cavendish Square Publishing LLC.

Hustad, Douglas. Gaming & Professional Sports Teams. 2018. (ESports: Game On! Ser.). (ENG.). 48p. (J). (gr. 5-8). 29.27 *(978-1-59953-965-2(9))* Norwood Hse. Pr.

Hutt, Sarah. Crack the Code! Activities, Games, & Puzzles That Reveal the World of Coding. Vaughan, Brenna, illus. 2018. (Girls Who Code Ser.). 128p. (J). (gr. 3-7). pap. 12.99 *(978-0-399-54256-5(6)*, Penguin Workshop) Penguin Young Readers Group.

Jakubiak, David J. A Smart Kid's Guide to Playing Online Games, 1 vol. 2009. (Kids Online Ser.). (ENG.). 24p. (J). (gr. 2-3). pap. 9.25 *(978-1-4358-3350-0(3)*, 6d0825f1-61aa-48c1-9dbf-aa2f56d23977); (Illus.). lib. bdg. 26.27 *(978-1-4042-8115-8(0)*, c73742de-c036-4a36-a82b-ec957c365bc3) Rosen Publishing Group, Inc., The. (PowerKids Pr.).

Jankowski, Matthew. The Modern Nerd's Guide to Esports, 1 vol. 2017. (Geek Out! Ser.). (ENG.). 32p. (J). (gr. 3-4). pap. 11.50 *(978-1-5382-1205-9(6)*, ae4c972c-cdc2-4123-86b2-305856a3120e); lib. bdg. 28.27 *(978-1-5382-1207-3(2)*, e2dfcfa0-6538-4351-bc7f-b0d92b9105f1) Stevens, Gareth Publishing LLLP.

Jozefowicz, Chris. Video Game Developer, 1 vol. 2009. (Cool Careers: Cutting Edge Ser.). (ENG., Illus.). 32p. (J). (gr. 3-3). pap. 11.50 *(978-1-4339-2157-5(X)*, a1c078a2-5ff7-401b-bb58-83afe34e4598) Stevens, Gareth Publishing LLLP.

—Video Games, 1 vol. 2009. (Ultimate 10: Entertainment Ser.). (ENG.). 48p. (gr. 3-3). (J). pap. 11.50 *(978-1-4339-2215-2(0)*, 322a0c78-ccf7-4747-bc8c-0136ac2246bf); (YA). lib. bdg. 33.67 *(978-0-8368-9167-6(8)*, 5b182d67-5e95-48b9-9228-72c44a955cfb) Stevens, Gareth Publishing LLLP.

Kaplan, Arie. The Awesome Inner Workings of Video Games. 2015. (ShockZone (tm) — Games & Gamers Ser.). (ENG., Illus.). 32p. (J). (gr. 5-8). E-Book 46.65 *(978-1-4677-5994-6(5)*, 9781467759946, Lerner Digital) Lerner Publishing Group.

—The Biggest Names of Video Games. (ShockZone (tm) — Games & Gamers Ser.). (ENG., Illus.). 32p. (J). (gr. 5-8). 2013. lib. bdg. 26.65 *(978-1-4677-1253-8(1)*, 35881a19-644a-4db4-95a9-b1ee2d90c23c, Lerner Pubns.) 2015. E-Book 46.65 *(978-1-4677-5995-3(3)*, 9781467759953, Lerner Digital) Lerner Publishing Group.

—The Brain-Boosting Benefits of Gaming. (ShockZone (tm) — Games & Gamers Ser.). (ENG., Illus.). 32p. (J). (gr. 5-8). 2013. lib. bdg. 26.65 *(978-1-4677-1251-4(5)*, 543de898-20e2-4e20-b64e-8e42754e476c, Lerner Pubns.) 2015. E-Book 46.65 *(978-1-4677-5996-0(1)*, 9781467759960, Lerner Digital) Lerner Publishing Group.

—The Epic Evolution of Video Games. (ShockZone (tm) — Games & Gamers Ser.). (ENG., Illus.). 32p. (J). (gr. 5-8). 2013. pap. 8.99 *(978-1-4677-1585-6(9)*, 6d864648-a489-418c-af50-42cf59fc33ae) 2015. E-Book 46.65 *(978-1-4677-5998-4(8)*, 9781467759984, Lerner Digital) Lerner Publishing Group.

Keppeler, Jill. The Inventors of Minecraft: Markus Notch Persson & His Coding Team, 1 vol. 2017. (Breakout Biographies Ser.). (ENG.). 32p. (J). (gr. 4-5). pap. 11.00 *(978-1-5081-6062-5(7)*, 855789cf-dc7d-471c-afb0-3f6765f22789, PowerKids Pr.) Rosen Publishing Group, Inc., The.

Kids, Carlton. ESports Superstars: Get the Lowdown on the World of Pro Gaming. 2019. (Y Ser.). (ENG., Illus.). 64p. (J). (gr. 3-7). pap. 9.95 *(978-1-78312-452-7(0))* Carlton Bks., Ltd. GBR. Dist: Two Rivers Distribution.

Kids, National Geographic. Animal Jam Journal. 2017. 112p. (J). (gr. 3-7). 9.99 *(978-1-4263-3079-7(0)*, National Geographic Kids) Disney Publishing Worldwide.

Krensky, Stephen. The High Score & Lowdown on Video Games! Ready-To-Read Level 3. Burroughs, Scott, illus. 2015. (History of Fun Stuff Ser.). (ENG.). 48p. (J). (gr. 1-3). 16.99 *(978-1-4814-2916-0(7))*; pap. 4.99 *(978-1-4814-2915-3(9))* Simon Spotlight. (Simon Spotlight).

La Bella, Laura. Careers for Tech Girls in Video Game Development, 1 vol. 2015. (Tech Girls Ser.). (ENG., Illus.). 80p. (J). (gr. 7-8). 37.47 *(978-1-4994-6107-7(0)*, 84fa7211-1db3-4387-ae0b-de2a42ea6e0b, Rosen Young Adult) Rosen Publishing Group, Inc., The.

Loh-Hagan, Virginia. Sound Effects Artist. 2015. (Illus.). 32p. (J). pap. 9.95 *(978-1-63470-056-6(2))* Cherry Lake Publishing.

Lüsted, Marcia Amidon. Cheating in E-Sports. 2018. (ESports: Game On! Ser.). (ENG., Illus.). 48p. (J). (gr. 5-8). 29.27 *(978-1-59953-963-8(2))* Norwood Hse. Pr.

Majaski, Christina. The Ultimate Unofficial Guide to Robloxing: Everything You Need to Know to Build Awesome Games! 2017. 160p. (J). 17.99 *(978-1-5107-3087-8(7)*, Sky Pony Pr.) Skyhorse Publishing Co., Inc.

Maley, Michael. Video Games & Esports: The Growing World of Gamers, 1 vol. annot. ed. 2019. (Hot Topics Ser.). (ENG.). 104p. (gr. 7-7). pap. 20.99 *(978-1-5345-6819-8(0)*, 0d80c3a4-f12b-4316-b5eb-79658d08b5d3); lib. bdg. 41.03 *(978-1-5345-6820-4(4)*, ea47eabf-5970-48b2-b537-296793ab4799) Greenhaven Publishing LLC. (Lucent Pr.).

Marquardt, Meg. Inside Video Games. 2018. (Inside Technology Ser.). (ENG., Illus.). 48p. (J). (gr. 4-8). lib. bdg. 35.64 *(978-1-5321-1794-7(9)*, 30876) ABDO Publishing Co.

—Pioneers in E-Sports. 2018. (ESports: Game On! Ser.). (ENG., Illus.). 48p. (J). (gr. 5-8). 29.27 *(978-1-59953-964-5(0))* Norwood Hse. Pr.

—Women in E-Sports. 2018. (ESports: Game On! Ser.). (ENG.). 48p. (J). (gr. 5-8). 29.27 *(978-1-59953-966-9(7))* Norwood Hse. Pr.

Mauleón, Daniel Montgomery Cole. Athletic Esports: The Competitive Gaming World of Basketball, Football, Soccer, & More! 2019. (Wide World of Esports Ser.). (ENG., Illus.). 32p. (J). (gr. 3-9). pap. 7.95 *(978-1-5435-7451-7(3)*, 140891); lib. bdg. 30.65 *(978-1-5435-7352-7(5)*, 140634) Capstone.

—Online Battle Arena Esports: The Competitive Gaming World of League of Legends, Dota 2, & More! 2019. (Wide World of Esports Ser.). (ENG., Illus.). 32p. (J). (gr. 3-9). pap. 7.95 *(978-1-5435-7453-1(X)*, 140893); lib. bdg. 30.65 *(978-1-5435-7354-1(1)*, 140636) Capstone.

—Paid to Game. 2019. (Video Game Revolution Ser.). (ENG., Illus.). 32p. (J). (gr. 3-9). 30.65 *(978-1-5435-7157-8(3)*, 140424) Capstone.

—Video Games Are Good for You! 2019. (Video Game Revolution Ser.). (ENG., Illus.). 32p. (J). (gr. 3-9). lib. bdg. 30.65 *(978-1-5435-7159-2(X)*, 140426) Capstone.

Mauleón, Daniel Montgomery Cole & Mauleón, Daniel Montgomery Cole. Esports Revolution. 2019. (Video Game Revolution Ser.). (ENG., Illus.). 32p. (J). (gr. 3-9). E-Book 30.65 *(978-1-5435-7168-4(9)*, 83099) Capstone.

McCarthy, Cecilia Pinto. E-Sports Game Design. 2017. (ESports: Game On! Ser.). (ENG., Illus.). 48p. (J). (gr. 5-8). 29.27 *(978-1-59953-892-1(X))* Norwood Hse. Pr.

McCollum, Sean. Video Game Trivia: What You Never Knew about Popular Games, Design Secrets, & the Coolest Characters. (Illus.). 32p. (J). 2019. *(978-1-5435-2539-7(3))* 2018. (ENG., (gr. 3-9). lib. bdg. 28.65 *(978-1-5435-2527-4(X)*, 138023) Capstone. (Capstone Pr.).

Miko, Christopher & Romines, Garrett. The Unofficial Holy Bible for Minecrafters: New Testament: Stories from the Bible Told Block by Block. 2016. (ENG.). 320p. (J). (gr. k). pap. 19.99 *(978-1-5107-0182-3(6)*, Sky Pony Pr.) Skyhorse Publishing Co., Inc.

Miller, Megan. Hacks for Minecrafters: Command Blocks: The Unofficial Guide to Tips & Tricks That Other Guides Won't Teach You. 128p. (J). (gr. 1-7). 2019. pap. 7.99 *(978-1-5107-4107-2(0))* 2015. (ENG., Illus.). 12.99 *(978-1-63450-663-2(4))* Skyhorse Publishing Co., Inc. (Sky Pony Pr.).

—Hacks for Minecrafters: Master Builder: The Unofficial Guide to Tips & Tricks That Other Guides Won't Teach You. 128p. (J). 2019. (ENG.). (gr. 3-6). pap. 7.99 *(978-1-5107-3803-4(7))* 2014. (Illus.). (gr. 1-1). 12.99 *(978-1-63450-043-2(1))* Skyhorse Publishing Co., Inc. (Sky Pony Pr.).

—Hacks for Minecrafters: Redstone: The Unofficial Guide to Tips & Tricks That Other Guides Won't Teach You. (ENG.). 128p. (J). (gr. 1-7). 2019. pap. 7.99 *(978-1-5107-4106-5(2))* 2015. (Illus.). 12.99 *(978-1-63450-665-6(0))* Skyhorse Publishing Co., Inc. (Sky Pony Pr.).

Milton, Stephanie. Minecraft Combat Handbook. 2014. (Illus.). 79p. (J). pap. *(978-0-545-77603-5(1)*, Scholastic) Scholastic, Inc.

Milton, Stephanie & Soares, Paul. Minecraft Combat Handbook. Cordner, Theo & Bolder, Joe, illus. 2015. 95p. (J). *(978-0-545-82319-7(6))* Scholastic, Inc.

Mojang AB & The Official Minecraft Team. Minecraft: Guide Collection 4-Book Boxed Set (2018 Edition) Exploration; Creative; Redstone; the Nether & the End, 4 vols. 2018. (Minecraft Ser.). (ENG., Illus.). 368p. (gr. 3-7). pap. 39.99 *(978-1-9848-1834-8(1))* Random Hse. Worlds.

—Minecraft: Guide to Farming. 2018. (Minecraft Ser.). (ENG., Illus.). 80p. (YA). (gr. 3-7). 12.99 *(978-1-101-96642-6(4))* Random Hse. Worlds.

—Minecraft: Guide to Redstone (2017 Edition) 2017. (Minecraft Ser.). (ENG., Illus.). 96p. (gr. 3-7). 12.99 *(978-1-5247-9722-5(7))* Random Hse. Worlds.

—Minecraft: Guide to the Nether & the End. 2017. (Minecraft Ser.). (ENG., Illus.). 80p. (gr. 3-7). 12.99 *(978-1-5247-9723-2(5))* Random Hse. Worlds.

—Minecraft: Mobestiary. 2017. (Minecraft Ser.). (ENG., Illus.). 104p. (gr. 3-7). 19.99 *(978-1-5247-9716-4(2))* Random Hse. Worlds.

Mooney, Carla. Careers If You Like Video Games. 2017. (Career Discovery Ser.). (ENG.). 80p. (YA). (gr. 5-12). *(978-1-68282-144-2(7))* ReferencePoint Pr., Inc.

—Inside the e-Sports Industry. 2017. (ESports: Game On! Ser.). (ENG., Illus.). 48p. (J). (gr. 5-8). 29.27 *(978-1-59953-891-4(1))* Norwood Hse. Pr.

—Learning the Island Landscape in Fortnite. 2019. (J). *(978-1-7253-4806-6(3))* Rosen Publishing Group, Inc., The.

Morgan, Winter. Discoveries in the Overworld: Lost Minecraft Journals, Book One. 2015. (Lost Journals for Minecrafters Ser.). (ENG.). 112p. (J). (gr. 1-7). pap. 7.99 *(978-1-5107-0350-6(0)*, Sky Pony Pr.) Skyhorse Publishing Co., Inc.

Nakaya, Andrea C. Are Video Games Harmful? 2016. (ENG.). 80p. (J). (gr. 5-12). *(978-1-68282-070-4(X))* ReferencePoint Pr., Inc.

—Video Games & Youth. 2014. (Video Games & Society Ser.). (ENG., Illus.). 80p. (J). lib. bdg. *(978-1-60152-750-9(0))* ReferencePoint Pr., Inc.

Needler, Matthew & Southam, Phil. Minecraft Construction Handbook. Barker, James et al, illus. 2015. 87p. (J). *(978-0-545-82321-0(8))* Scholastic, Inc.

Netzley, Patricia. How Do Video Games Affect Society? 2014. (Video Games & Society Ser.). (ENG., Illus.). 80p. (J). lib. bdg. *(978-1-60152-748-6(9))* ReferencePoint Pr., Inc.

Netzley, Patricia D. How Does Video Game Violence Affect Society? 2013. (Illus.). 96p. (YA). lib. bdg. *(978-1-60152-490-4(0))* ReferencePoint Pr., Inc.

—Video Games, Violence & Crime. 2014. (Video Games & Society Ser.). (ENG., Illus.). 80p. (J). lib. bdg. *(978-1-60152-752-3(7))* ReferencePoint Pr., Inc.

Noll, Elizabeth. Coding in Video Games. 2018. (Coding Is Everywhere Ser.). (ENG., Illus.). 24p. (J). (gr. k-3). pap. 7.99 *(978-1-61891-480-4(4)*, 12133, Blastoff! Readers) Bellwether Media.

Owen, Ruth. The Wonderful Worlds of a Video Game Designer. 2015. (Get to Work with Science & Technology Ser.). (ENG., Illus.). 32p. (J). (gr. 2-7). lib. bdg. 29.32 *(978-1-910549-32-2(0)*, 9fc6f4ee-25a2-47db-9e76-a5d34e4cb18c) Ruby Tuesday Books Limited GBR. Dist: Lerner Publishing Group.

Owings, Lisa. Gaming's Greatest Moments. 2020. (Best of Gaming (UpDog Books (tm)) Ser.). (ENG., Illus.). 24p. (J). (gr. 3-5). 30.65 *(978-1-5415-9051-9(1)*, ce46bdda-5161-43b9-b8b0-e11c98fa6545, Lerner Pubns.) Lerner Publishing Group.

—Pro Gaming. 2020. (Best of Gaming (UpDog Books (tm)) Ser.). (ENG., Illus.). 24p. (J). (gr. 3-5). 30.65 *(978-1-5415-9047-2(3)*, a1cd63f1-9813-4c0b-8d52-71172381808b, Lerner Pubns.) Lerner Publishing Group.

—The World of Esports. 2020. (Best of Gaming (UpDog Books (tm)) Ser.). (ENG., Illus.). 24p. (J). (gr. 3-5). 30.65 *(978-1-5415-9048-9(1)*, be00b94f-005e-436a-a90d-0b0a6f4ce74a, Lerner Pubns.) Lerner Publishing Group.

Oxlade, Chris. Gaming Technology. 2011. (New Technology Ser.). 48p. (YA). (gr. 7-12). lib. bdg. 34.25 *(978-1-59920-531-1(9))* Black Rabbit Bks.

Paris, David. History of Video Games (Grade 6) 2nd rev. ed. 2016. (TIME(r): Informational Text Ser.). (ENG., Illus.). 48p. (gr. 5-8). pap. 13.99 *(978-1-4938-3594-2(7))* Teacher Created Materials, Inc.

Parker, K. J. Guardian Universe Core Fuzion. 2004. (Illus.). 228p. (YA). per. 25.00 *(978-0-9744698-0-5(7))* Dilly Green Bean Games.

parks, peggy j. Video Games. 2008. (Compact Research Ser.). (Illus.). 104p. (YA). (gr. 7-12). lib. bdg. 43.93 *(978-1-60152-053-1(0))* ReferencePoint Pr., Inc.

Peters, Diane. Gaming: Deal with It Before It Outplays You, 1 vol. Shannon, Ben, illus. 2010. (Lorimer Deal with It Ser.). (ENG.). 32p. (J). (gr. 4-9). 24.95 *(978-1-55277-490-8(2)*, ea35940a-5832-4a2c-9b95-b23dbd0e6c37) James Lorimer & Co. Ltd., Pubs. CAN. Dist: Lerner Publishing Group.

—Gaming Deal with It: Deal with It Before It Outplays You, 1 vol. Shannon, Ben, illus. 2010. (Lorimer Deal with It Ser.). (ENG.). 32p. (J). (gr. 4-9). pap. 12.95 *(978-1-55277-434-2(1)*, 9781552774342) James Lorimer & Co. Ltd., Pubs. CAN. Dist: Orca Bk. Pubs. USA.

Peterson, Tara & Hogan, Joyce W. Should We Play Video Games? A Persuasive Text. 2006. (Illus.). 30p. (J). pap. *(978-1-59336-338-3(9))* Mondo Publishing.

Polette, Nancy. Improvisation & Theatre Games with Children's Literature. 2004. (J). pap. 10.95 *(978-1-931334-41-9(2))* Pieces of Learning.

Polydoros, Lori. Awesome Video Game Competitions. 2017. (Cool Competitions Ser.). (ENG., Illus.). 32p. (J). (gr. 3-9). lib. bdg. 27.32 *(978-1-5157-7353-5(1)*, 135691, Capstone Pr.) Capstone.

Polydoros, Lori & Adamson, Thomas K. Cool Competitions. 2017. (Cool Competitions Ser.). (ENG., Illus.). 32p. (J). (gr. 3-9). 117.28 *(978-1-5157-7368-9(X)*, 26739, Capstone Pr.) Capstone.

Powell, Marie. Asking Questions about Video Games. 2015. (21st Century Skills Library: Asking Questions about Media Ser.). (ENG., Illus.). 32p. (J). (gr. 4-8). 32.07 *(978-1-63362-491-7(9)*, 206872); pap. 14.21 *(978-1-63362-507-5(9)*, 206873) Cherry Lake Publishing.

Pratchett, Rhianna & Robson, Eddie. Video Games. 2008. (ENG., Illus.). 32p. (J). (gr. 6-10). lib. bdg. *(978-0-7787-3817-6(5))* Crabtree Publishing Co.

Rhodes, Sam. STEAM Jobs for Gamers. 2018. (STEAM Jobs Ser.). (ENG., Illus.). 32p. (J). (gr. 3-9). lib. bdg. 28.65 *(978-1-5435-3093-3(1)*, 138672, Capstone Pr.) Capstone.

Ross, Michael & Ross, Christopher. Building Faith Block by Block: [an Unofficial Minecraft Guide] 60 a-To-Z (Kid Only) Survival Secrets. 2017. (ENG., Illus.). 256p. (YA). (gr. 6-13). pap. 15.99 *(978-0-7369-7085-3(1)*, 6970853) Harvest Hse. Pubs.

Rubenstein, Glenn. Sports Gamer: The Best in Sports Video Games. (J). (gr. 3-9). pap. 3.99 *(978-1-930623-22-4(4))* Sports Illustrated For Kids.

Scholastic. Ready, Set, Play!: an AFK Book. 2017. (Game On! Ser.). (ENG., Illus.). 128p. (J). (gr. k-3). pap. 7.99 *(978-1-338-18994-0(8))* Scholastic, Inc.

Scholastic, Inc. Staff. Game On! 2017: All the Best Games - Awesome Facts & Coolest Secrets. 2016. (Game On! Ser.). (ENG., Illus.). 224p. (J). (gr. 3-7). pap. 14.99 *(978-1-338-03272-7(0))* Scholastic, Inc.

—Game On! 2019: All the Best Games: Awesome Facts & Coolest Secrets. 2018. (Game On! Ser.). (ENG., Illus.). 224p. (J). (gr. 7-7). pap. 14.99 *(978-1-338-28356-3(1))* Scholastic, Inc.

Schwartz, Heather E. The Basics of Game Design. 2019. (Video Game Revolution Ser.). (ENG., Illus.). 32p. (J). (gr. 3-9). lib. bdg. 28.65 *(978-1-5435-7151-6(4)*, 140418) Capstone.

—The History of Gaming. 2019. (Video Game Revolution Ser.). (ENG., Illus.). 32p. (J). (gr. 3-9). lib. bdg. 28.65 *(978-1-5435-7156-1(5)*, 140423) Capstone.

—Video Games Save the World. 2019. (Video Game Revolution Ser.). (ENG., Illus.). 32p. (J). (gr. 3-9). lib. bdg. 28.65 *(978-1-5435-7158-5(1)*, 140425) Capstone.

Seigel, Rachel. The Debate about Playing Video Games. 2018. (Pros & Cons Ser.). (ENG., Illus.). 48p. (J). (gr. 5-6). pap. 11.95 *(978-1-63517-596-7(8)*, 1635175968); lib. bdg. 34.21 *(978-1-63517-524-0(0)*, 1635175240) North Star Editions. (Focus Readers).

Slingerland, Janet. Video Game Coding. 2019. (Coding Ser.). (ENG., Illus.). 32p. (J). (gr. 3-5). 31.35 *(978-1-64185-329-3(8)*, 1641853298, Focus Readers) North Star Editions.

Stolze, Greg. Rites of the Dragon. 2004. (Vampire, the Requiem Ser.). (Illus.). 120p. (YA). 24.99 *(978-1-58846-254-1(4))* White Wolf Publishing, Inc.

Terry, Paul. Top 10 for Kids Gaming. 2015. (ENG., Illus.). 96p. (J). (gr. 3-6). pap. 9.95 *(978-1-77085-564-9(5)*, 3ccabe8f-6166-4c63-97ed-56d2f855a14d) Firefly Bks., Ltd.

The Yogscast. Yogscast: the Diggy Diggy Book. 2016. (ENG., Illus.). 112p. (J). (gr. 3-7). pap. 8.99 *(978-0-545-95663-5(3))* Scholastic, Inc.

Thiel, Kristin. How Are Video Games Made & Sold?, 1 vol. 2019. (Where Do Goods Come From? Ser.). (ENG.). 32p. (gr. 3-3). pap. 11.58 *(978-1-5026-5040-5(1)*, de9be1e1-0de2-405b-9212-2b63a6f04735) Cavendish Square Publishing LLC.

Thomas Nelson Publishing Staff. Adventures in Odyssey & the Great Escape: The Ultimate Test of Time Awaits You Inside! 2008. cd-rom 19.95 *(978-0-9754280-2-3(0))* Nelson, Thomas Inc.

—Adventures in Odyssey & the Treasure of the Incas: The Chase Is on. Discover the Treasure. Reveal the Truth. 2008. cd-rom 19.95 *(978-0-9754280-0-9(4))* Nelson, Thomas Inc.

Triumph Books, Triumph. The Super World of Mario: The Ultimate Unofficial Guide to Super Mario(r). 2018. 96p. 11.95 *(978-1-62937-589-2(6))* Triumph Bks.

Troupe, Thomas Kingsley. Fighting Game Esports: The Competitive Gaming World of Super Smash Bros., Street Fighter, & More! 2019. (Wide World of Esports Ser.). (ENG., Illus.). 32p. (J). (gr. 3-9). pap. 7.95 *(978-1-5435-7454-8(8)*, 140894); lib. bdg. 28.65 *(978-1-5435-7355-8(X)*, 140637) Capstone.

—First-Person Action Esports: The Competitive Gaming World of Overwatch, Counter-Strike, & More! 2019. (Wide World of Esports Ser.). (ENG., Illus.). 32p. (J). (gr. 3-9). pap. 7.95 *(978-1-5435-7452-4(1)*, 140892); lib. bdg. 28.65 *(978-1-5435-7353-4(3)*, 140635) Capstone.

—Video Games vs. Reality. 2018. (Video Games vs. Reality Ser.). (ENG.). 32p. (J). (gr. 3-9). 122.60 *(978-1-5435-2585-4(7)*, 28135, Capstone Pr.) Capstone.

Trueit, Trudi Strain. Video Gaming. 2008. (21st Century Skills Innovation Library: Innovation in Entertainment Ser.). (ENG., Illus.). 32p. (gr. 4-8). lib. bdg. 32.07 *(978-1-60279-218-0(6)*, 200149) Cherry Lake Publishing.

Video Games: Career Launcher. 2010. (Ferguson Career Launcher Ser.). (ENG.). 160p. (gr. 9-18). pap. 14.95 *(978-0-8160-7982-7(X)*, P174243, Checkmark Bks.) Infobase Holdings, Inc.

Watson, Stephanie. Video Game Designer. 2017. (ENG., Illus.). 64p. (J). (gr. 5-12). *(978-1-68282-184-8(6))* ReferencePoint Pr., Inc.

Waxman, Laura Hamilton. Superstars of Gaming. 2020. (Best of Gaming (UpDog Books (tm)) Ser.). (ENG., Illus.). 24p. (J). (gr. 3-5). 30.65 *(978-1-5415-9050-2(3)*, 3b1bf71e-6eb4-4da1-b821-8060a8537d87, Lerner Pubns.) Lerner Publishing Group.

West, Tracey. Normal Pokédex. 2005. (Pokemon Ser.). 47p. *(978-0-439-72200-1(4))* Scholastic, Inc.

West, Tracey & Noll, Katherine. Psychic Pokédex. 2005. (Illus.). 47p. (J). pap. *(978-0-439-81051-7(5))* Scholastic, Inc.

West, Tracey & Nolls, Katherine. Ice & Fighting Pokédex. 2005. 47p. *(978-0-439-72194-3(6))* Scholastic, Inc.

—Official Pokémon Pokédex. 2006. (Illus.). 111p. (J). *(978-0-439-85586-0(1))* Scholastic, Inc.

Wilkinson, Colin. Gaming: Playing Safe & Playing Smart, 1 vol. 2011. (Digital & Information Literacy Ser.). (ENG., Illus.). 48p. (J). (gr. 6-6). pap. 12.75 *(978-1-4488-5611-4(6)*, 1b011366-4553-43cd-aabc-1d20b35dbea0); lib. bdg. 33.47 *(978-1-4488-5552-0(7)*, c16ba6f8-1510-4e65-8be7-faaa399f961a) Rosen Publishing Group, Inc., The. (Rosen Reference).

Williams-Noren, Carolyn. Do Kids Need Video Game Ratings? 2018. (Shape Your Opinion Ser.). (ENG., Illus.). 48p. (J). (gr. 1-3). 26.60 *(978-1-59953-932-4(2))*; pap. 13.26 *(978-1-68404-204-3(6))* Norwood Hse. Pr.

Wolny, Philip. Mark Markiplier Fischbach: Star YouTube Gamer with 10 Billion+ Views, 1 vol. 2019. (Top Video Gamers in the World Ser.). (ENG.). 48p. (gr. 5-5). pap. 12.75 *(978-1-7253-4603-1(6)*, d92ab8e7-4c84-40c0-bb94-81c04b8cc320, Rosen Reference) Rosen Publishing Group, Inc., The.

—Markiplier, 1 vol. 2019. (Top Video Gamers in the World Ser.). (ENG.). 48p. (gr. 5-5). 33.47 *(978-1-7253-4604-8(4)*, c2cc43e3-60fc-4b01-8199-35d4232d7263, Rosen Reference) Rosen Publishing Group, Inc., The.

Wood, Alix. Video Game Designer, 1 vol., 1. 2014. (World's Coolest Jobs Ser.). (ENG.). 32p. (J). (gr. 4-4). 28.93 *(978-1-4777-6015-4(6)*, 2b245d46-941d-4d0f-970d-0ff1753a3a67, PowerKids Pr.) Rosen Publishing Group, Inc., The.

Wood, John. Gaming Technology: Streaming, VR, & More, 1 vol. 2018. (STEM in Our World Ser.). (ENG.). 32p. (gr. 4-5). lib. bdg. 28.27 *(978-1-5382-2638-4(3)*, 83e47978-d96c-4323-a9d4-827b44408167) Stevens, Gareth Publishing LLLP.

World Book, Inc. Staff, contrib. by. Mammals. 2019. (Illus.). 96p. (J). *(978-0-7166-3725-7(1))* World Bk., Inc.

—Video Games. 2019. (Illus.). 96p. (J). *(978-0-7166-3735-6(9))* World Bk., Inc.

Wyckoff, Edwin Brit. The Guy Who Invented Home Video Games: Ralph Baer & His Awesome Invention, 1 vol. 2010. (Genius at Work! Great Inventor Biographies Ser.). (ENG., Illus.). 32p. (gr. 3-3). 26.60 *(978-0-7660-3450-1(X)*, 0a222df2-4958-4088-9d0c-0d61c373743b) Enslow Publishing, LLC.

Zalme, Ron, illus. How to Draw Nintendo Greatest Heroes & Villains. 2007. *(978-0-439-91324-9(1))* Scholastic, Inc.

Zeiger, James. Minecraft: Redstone & Transportation. 2016. (21st Century Skills Innovation Library: Unofficial Guides). (ENG., Illus.). 32p. (J). (gr. 4-8). 32.07 *(978-1-63470-522-6(X)*, 207819) Cherry Lake Publishing.

VIENNA (AUSTRIA)—FICTION

Clifford, Ross. The Shiddakovich Adventure. 2008. (ENG.). 122p. pap. 12.88 *(978-1-4092-3520-0(3))* Lulu Pr., Inc.

Glatshteyn, Yankev. Emil & Karl: A Novel. Shandler, Jeffrey, tr. 2008. (ENG.). 208p. (J). (gr. 4-9). per. 18.99 *(978-0-312-37387-0(2)*, 900045531) Square Fish.

Henry, Marguerite. White Stallion of Lipizza. Dennis, Wesley, illus. 2014. (ENG.). 192p. (J). (gr. 3-7). pap. 7.99 *(978-1-4814-0391-7(5)*, Aladdin) Simon & Schuster Children's Publishing.

Ibbotson, Eva. The Star of Kazan. 2006. (ENG., Illus.). 416p. (J). (gr. 3-7). reprint ed. 10.99 *(978-0-14-240582-6(5)*, Puffin Books) Penguin Young Readers Group.

Osborne, Mary Pope. Moonlight on the Magic Flute, Bk. 13. Murdocca, Sal, illus. 2010. (Magic Tree House (R) Merlin Mission Ser.: 13). 144p. (J). (gr. 2-5). pap. 5.99 *(978-0-375-85647-1(1)*, Random Hse. Bks. for Young Readers) Random Hse. Children's Bks.

Salten, Felix. The Hound of Florence. Paterson, Huntley, tr. 2014. (Bambi's Classic Animal Tales Ser.). (ENG., Illus.). 288p. (J). (gr. 3-7). pap. 6.99 *(978-1-4424-8748-2(8)*, Aladdin) Simon & Schuster Children's Publishing.

Watts, Irene N. A Telling Time, 1 vol. Shoemaker, Kathryn E., illus. 2004. (ENG.). 32p. (J). (gr. 1-3). 17.95 *(978-1-896580-39-5(4))* Tradewind Bks. CAN. Dist: Orca Bk. Pubs. USA.

Weyr, Garret. The Language of Spells: (Fantasy Middle Grade Novel, Magic & Wizard Book for Middle School Kids) Hamett, Katie, illus. 2018. (ENG.). 256p. (J). (gr. 5-9). 16.99 *(978-1-4521-5958-4(0))* Chronicle Bks. LLC.

VIENNA (AUSTRIA)—HISTORY

Allport, Alan. The Congress of Vienna. 2011. (ENG., Illus.). 126p. (gr. 9). 35.00 *(978-1-60413-497-1(6)*, P189855, Facts On File) Infobase Holdings, Inc.

Dyan, Penelope. Oh Vienna! a Kid's Guide to Vienna, Austri. Weigand, John D., photos by. 2013. (Illus.). 34p. pap. 11.95 *(978-1-61477-073-2(5))* Bellissima Publishing, LLC.

VIETNAM

Alberti, Theresa. Vietnam ABCs: A Book about the People & Places of Vietnam, 1 vol. Blanks, Natascha Alex, illus. 2007. (Country ABCs Ser.). (ENG.). 32p. (J). (gr. k-5). lib. bdg. 28.65 *(978-1-4048-2251-1(8)*, 93661, Picture Window Bks.) Capstone.

Conley, Kate A. Vietnam. 2004. (Countries Set 5 Ser.). (Illus.). 40p. (J). (gr. k-6). 27.07 *(978-1-59197-299-0(X)*, Checkerboard Library) ABDO Publishing Co.

Duling, Kaitlyn. Vietnam, 1 vol. 2018. (Exploring World Cultures (First Edition) Ser.). (ENG.). 32p. (J). (gr. 3-3). 31.64 *(978-1-5026-3822-9(3)*, 07e87a5c-9864-4ec9-91c0-fb46fa7fd76a) Cavendish Square Publishing LLC.

Gray, Shirley W. & Gray, Shirley Wimbish. Vietnam. 2003. (True Bks.). (ENG., Illus.). 48p. (J). 25.00 *(978-0-516-24211-8(3)*, Children's Pr.) Scholastic Library Publishing.

Morgan, Tom. In a Vietnamese City, 1 vol. Holmes, Jim, illus. 2003. (Child's Day Ser.). (ENG.). 32p. (gr. 2-2). 32.64 *(978-0-7614-1409-4(6)*, 862c1817-db1c-4ddd-ba3f-3e57f997ae9f) Cavendish Square Publishing LLC.

Rau, Dana Meachen. It's Cool to Learn about Countries: Vietnam. 2011. (Explorer Library: Social Studies Explorer Ser.). (ENG., Illus.). 48p. (gr. 4-8). lib. bdg. 34.93 *(978-1-61080-097-6(4)*, 201088) Cherry Lake Publishing.

Rose, Elizabeth. A Primary Source Guide to Vietnam. (Countries of the World). 24p. (gr. 2-3). 2009. 42.50 *(978-1-61512-049-9(1)*, PowerKids Pr.) 2003. (ENG., Illus.). (J). lib. bdg. 26.27 *(978-0-8239-6734-6(4)*, 747e4cc7-3c5d-4349-afb8-6cf94cd30e7c) Rosen Publishing Group, Inc., The.

Seah, Audrey & Nair, Charissa M. Vietnam, 1 vol. 2nd rev. ed. 2006. (Cultures of the World (Second Edition)(r) Ser.). (ENG., Illus.). 144p. (gr. 5-5). lib. bdg. 49.79 *(978-0-7614-1789-7(3)*, c15c9427-7951-415e-9c2a-7b8e3fa92e3b) Cavendish Square Publishing LLC.

Simmons, Pat. Vietnam. (World Focus Ser.). (Illus.). 31p. (J). (gr. 3-7). pap. 3.99 *(978-0-431-07264-7(7))* Oxfam Publishing GBR. Dist: Stylus Publishing, LLC.

Taus-Bolstad, Stacy. Vietnam in Pictures. 2003. (Visual Geography Ser.). (Illus.). 80p. (J). (gr. 5-12). 27.93 *(978-0-8225-4678-8(7))* Lerner Publishing Group.

Zocchi, Judy. In Vietnam. Brodie, Neale, illus. 2005. (Global Adventures II Ser.). 32p. (J). per. 10.95 *(978-1-59646-165-9(9))* Dingles & Co.

VIETNAM—FICTION

Choi, Na-mi. Song of the Mekong River: Vietnam. Cowley, Joy, ed. Jo, Sinae, illus. 2015. (Global Kids Storybooks Ser.). (ENG.). 32p. (gr. 1-4). 26.65 *(978-1-925246-01-8(9))*; 7.99 *(978-1-925246-53-7(1))*; 26.65 *(978-1-925246-27-8(2))* ChoiceMaker Pty. Ltd., The AUS. (Big and SMALL). Dist: Lerner Publishing Group.

Dowell, Frances O'Roark. Shooting the Moon. 2009. (ENG.). 192p. (J). (gr. 5-9). pap. 7.99 *(978-1-4169-7986-9(7)*, Atheneum Bks. for Young Readers) Simon & Schuster Children's Publishing.

Dunivan, Dennis W. Escape from Communist Heaven. 2013. (ENG., Illus.). 392p. (J). (gr. -1-12). 17.99 *(978-1-59181-229-6(1))* Sentient Pubns.

Garland, Sherry. Children of the Dragon: Selected Tales from Vietnam, 1 vol. Hyman, Trina Schart, illus. 2012. (ENG.). 32p. (J). (gr. 3-7). 16.99 *(978-1-4556-1709-8(1)*, Pelican Publishing) Arcadia Publishing.

—The Lotus Seed. Kiuchi, Tatsuro, illus. 2014. 32p. pap. 7.00 *(978-1-61003-219-3(5))* Center for the Collaborative Classroom.

Hoffmire, Baird, illus. How Tiger Got His Stripes: A Folktale from Vietnam. 2006. (Story Cove Ser.). (ENG.). 32p. (J). (gr. -1-3). pap. 4.95 *(978-0-87483-799-5(5))* August Hse. Pubs., Inc.

Hoppey, Tim. Jungle Scout: A Vietnam War Story, 1 vol. Espinoza, Ramon, illus. 2008. (Historical Fiction Ser.). (ENG.). 56p. (J). (gr. 3-6). pap. 6.25 *(978-1-4342-0846-0(X)*, 95207, Stone Arch Bks.) Capstone.

Kadohata, Cynthia. A Million Shades of Gray. 2011. (ENG., Illus.). 240p. (J). (gr. 5-9). pap. 8.99 *(978-1-4424-2919-2(4)*, Atheneum Bks. for Young Readers) Simon & Schuster Children's Publishing.

Lai, Thanhhà. Inside Out & Back Again. 2014. (ENG.). 288p. (J). (gr. 3-7). 12.24 *(978-1-63245-350-1(9))* Lectorum Pubns., Inc.

—Inside Out & Back Again. 2009. 9.68 *(978-0-7848-3887-7(9)*, Everbind) Marco Bk. Co.

—Inside Out & Back Again. 2013. 18.00 *(978-1-61383-970-6(7))* Perfection Learning Corp.

—Inside Out & Back Again. 2013. 262p. (J). lib. bdg. 18.40 *(978-0-606-27126-4(0))* Turtleback.

—Inside Out & Back Again: A Newbery Honor Award Winner. (ENG.). (J). (gr. 3-7). 2013. 288p. pap. 9.99 *(978-0-06-196279-0(1))* 2011. 272p. 16.99 *(978-0-06-196278-3(3))* HarperCollins Pubs. (HarperCollins).

—Inside Out & Back Again: a Harper Classic. 2017. (Harper Classic Ser.). (ENG.). 288p. (J). (gr. 3-7). 16.99 *(978-0-06-257402-2(7)*, HarperCollins) HarperCollins Pubs.

—Listen, Slowly. 2015. (ENG.). (J). (gr. 3-7). 288p. E-Book *(978-0-06-222920-5(6)*, 9780062229205); (Illus.). 272p. 16.99 *(978-0-06-222918-2(4)*, HarperCollins) HarperCollins Pubs.

Literature Connections English: Fallen Angels. 2004. (gr. 6-12). *(978-0-395-83360-5(4)*, 2-70783) Holt McDougal.

Lynch, Chris. Free-Fire Zone. 2012. 183p. (J). *(978-0-545-49427-4(3)*, Scholastic Pr.) Scholastic, Inc.

—I Pledge Allegiance. 2011. 183p. (YA). *(978-0-545-38415-5(X))* Scholastic, Inc.

—I Pledge Allegiance. 2013. (Vietnam Ser.: 1). lib. bdg. 17.20 *(978-0-606-31961-4(1))* Turtleback.

Marsden, Carolyn & Niem, Thay Phap. The Buddha's Diamonds. 2010. (ENG., Illus.). 112p. (J). (gr. 2-4). 18.69 *(978-0-7636-3380-6(1))* Candlewick Pr.

McAfee, Joan K. The Road to el Dorado. 2003. (Illus.). 186p. (YA). pap. 12.95 *(978-0-89745-273-1(9))* Sunflower Univ. Pr.

Meloy, Maile. The Apprentices. Schoenherr, Ian, illus. 2014. (Apothecary Ser.: 2). (ENG.). 432p. (J). (gr. 5). pap. 9.99 *(978-0-14-242598-5(2)*, Puffin Books) Penguin Young Readers Group.

Nuo, Johnny. Dinh Van Binh: Vietnamese Village Boy. 2006. (Illus.). 176p. per. 15.12 *(978-1-4120-9966-0(8))* Trafford Publishing.

Phillips, Dee. Vietnam, 1 vol., Bk. 9. 2014. (Yesterday's Voices Ser.). (ENG.). 48p. (YA). (gr. 5-12). pap. 10.75 *(978-1-62250-911-9(0))* Saddleback Educational Publishing, Inc.

Poulsen, David A. Old Man. 2013. 276p. pap. *(978-1-4596-6325-1(X))* ReadHowYouWant.com, Ltd.

Sherman, M. Zachary. Fighting Phantoms, 1 vol. Casas, Fritz, illus. 2011. (Bloodlines Ser.). (ENG.). 88p. (J). (gr. 4-8). lib. bdg. 27.32 *(978-1-4342-2560-3(7)*, 113619, Stone Arch Bks.) Capstone.

Thong, Roseanne. Fly Free. Neilan, Eujin Kim, illus. 2010. (ENG.). 32p. (J). (gr. -1-3). 17.99 *(978-1-59078-550-8(9)*, Astra Young Readers) Astra Publishing Hse.

Tran-Davies, Nhung N. A Grain of Rice, 1 vol. 2019. (ENG.). 224p. (YA). (gr. 8-12). pap. 10.95 *(978-1-926890-25-8(6))* Tradewind Bks. CAN. Dist: Orca Bk. Pubs. USA.

Tran, Truong. Going Home, Coming Home. Phong, Ann, illus. 2003. Tr. of Ve Nha Tham Que Hu'o'Ng. (ENG. & VIE.). 32p. (J). 16.95 *(978-0-89239-179-0(0))* Lee & Low Bks., Inc.

Trottier, Maxine. The Walking Stick, 1 vol. Galouchko, Annouchka Gravel, illus. 2012. (ENG.). 24p. (J). (gr. 1-2). pap. 9.95 *(978-1-55455-239-9(7)*, 247c24e0-df88-48f2-afe7-70f03f39ef55) Fitzhenry & Whiteside, Ltd. CAN. Dist: Firefly Bks., Ltd.

Vander Zee, Ruth. Always with You. Himler, Ron, illus. 2008. (ENG.). 32p. (J). (gr. -1-3). 17.00 *(978-0-8028-5295-3(5)*, Eerdmans Bks For Young Readers) Eerdmans, William B. Publishing Co.

VIETNAM—FOREIGN RELATIONS—UNITED STATES

Burgan, Michael. The Vietnam War, 1 vol. 2006. (Wars That Changed American History Ser.). (ENG., Illus.). 48p. (gr. 5-8). pap. 15.05 *(978-0-8368-7304-7(1)*, cd889bbf-30c1-45e2-b81d-85f132c658ba, Gareth Stevens Secondary Library) Stevens, Gareth Publishing LLLP.

VIETNAM—HISTORY

Bui, Nam. Fish over Diamond. 2012. 138p. 30.99 *(978-1-4691-9624-4(7))* Xlibris Corp.

Clare, John D. Vietnam, 1939-75. 2nd rev. ed. 2004. (Hodder 20th Century History Ser.). (ENG., Illus.). 48p. (YA). pap. 26.50 *(978-0-340-81476-5(4)*, Hodder Education) Hodder Education Group GBR. Dist: Trans-Atlantic Pubns., Inc.

Ho, Van & Skrypuch, Marsha. Too Young to Escape: A Vietnamese Girl Waits to Be Reunited with Her Family. 2018. (ENG., Illus.). 152p. (J). (gr. 3-7). 16.95 *(978-1-77278-066-6(9))* Pajama Pr. CAN. Dist: Publishers Group West (PGW).

Johnson, Kristin F. Ho Chi Minh: North Vietnamese President, 1 vol. 2011. (Essential Lives Set 7 Ser.). (ENG., Illus.). 112p. (YA). (gr. 6-12). lib. bdg. 41.36 *(978-1-61783-006-8(2)*, 6751, Essential Library) ABDO Publishing Co.

Kjelle, Marylou Morano. Saigon. 2009. (J). *(978-1-58415-793-9(3))* Mitchell Lane Pubs.

Labrie, Julia. Cultural Traditions in Vietnam. 2017. (Cultural Traditions in My World Ser.). 32p. (J). (gr. 2-3). *(978-0-7787-8101-1(2))* Crabtree Publishing Co.

Markovics, Joyce L. Vietnam. 2015. (Countries We Come From Ser.). (ENG., Illus.). 32p. (J). (gr. k-3). lib. bdg. 28.50 *(978-1-62724-860-0(9))* Bearport Publishing Co., Inc.

Murray, Julie. Vietnam. 2017. (Explore the Countries Set 4 Ser.). (ENG., Illus.). 40p. (J). (gr. 2-5). lib. bdg. 35.64 *(978-1-5321-1055-9(3)*, 25686, Big Buddy Bks.) ABDO Publishing Co.

Murray, Laura K. Vietnam War Technology. 2017. (War Technology Ser.). (ENG., Illus.). 48p. (J). (gr. 4-8). lib. bdg. 35.64 *(978-1-5321-1190-7(8)*, 25956) ABDO Publishing Co.

Nevins, Debbie, et al. Vietnam, 1 vol. 3rd rev. ed. 2014. (Cultures of the World (Third Edition)(r) Ser.). (ENG., Illus.). 144p. (gr. 5-5). lib. bdg. 48.79 *(978-1-5026-0080-6(3)*, 91575d7d-ff76-4875-9f0f-b5b146193146) Cavendish Square Publishing LLC.

Oachs, Emily Rose. Vietnam. 2018. (Country Profiles Ser.). (ENG., Illus.). 32p. (J). (gr. 3-8). lib. bdg. 27.95 *(978-1-62617-737-6(6)*, Blastoff! Discovery) Bellwether Media.

O'Connor, Jim & Who HQ. What Was the Vietnam War? Foley, Tim, illus. 2019. (What Was? Ser.). 112p. (J). (gr. 3-7). 5.99 *(978-1-5247-8977-0(1)*, Penguin Workshop) Penguin Young Readers Group.

O'Connor, Karen. Vietnam. 2009. pap. 52.95 *(978-0-7613-4736-1(4))* 2008. (Illus.). 48p. (J). (gr. 2-5). 27.93 *(978-0-8225-9415-4(3))* Lerner Publishing Group.

Orr, Tamra. Vietnamese Heritage. 2018. (21st Century Junior Library: Celebrating Diversity in My Classroom Ser.). (ENG., Illus.). 24p. (J). (gr. 2-4). pap. 12.79 *(978-1-5341-0838-7(6)*, 210716); lib. bdg. 30.64 *(978-1-5341-0739-7(8)*, 210715) Cherry Lake Publishing.

Parker, Lewis K. Why Vietnamese Immigrants Came to America. 2009. (Coming to America Ser.). 24p. (gr. 2-3). 42.50 *(978-1-61511-888-5(8)*, PowerKids Pr.) Rosen Publishing Group, Inc., The.

Sexton, Colleen & Simmons, Walter. Vietnam. 2010. (Exploring Countries Ser.). (ENG., Illus.). 32p. (J). (gr. 3-7). lib. bdg. 27.95 *(978-1-60014-492-9(6)*, Blastoff! Readers) Bellwether Media.

Simmons, Walter. Vietnam. 2011. (ENG., Illus.). 32p. (J). *(978-0-531-26473-7(4))* Bellwether Media.

Skrypuch, Marsha Forchuk. Last Airlift: A Vietnamese Orphan's Rescue from War   2012. (ENG., Illus.). 120p. (J). (gr. 3-7). 17.95 *(978-0-9869495-4-8(X))* Pajama Pr. CAN. Dist: Publishers Group West (PGW).

Stibbens, Steve. Knights over the Delta: An Oral History of the 114th Aviation Company in Vietnam, 1963-72. Stibbens, Steve, ed. 2003. 60.00 *(978-0-9742465-0-5(6))* 114th Aviation Co. Assn.

Taylor, Trace. Vietnam. (ICP Our World Ser.). (gr. k-1). 2011. (ENG.). 16p. (J). pap. 8.00 *(978-1-61541-075-0(9))* 2010. pap. 39.62 *(978-1-61541-093-4(7))* American Reading Co.

Taylor, Trace & SáNchez, LucIA M. Viet Nam. 2010. pap. 39.62 *(978-1-61541-123-8(2))* American Reading Co.

Taylor, Trace & Sánchez, Lucía M. Vietnam. 2014. (1Y Nuestro Mundo Ser.). (SPA.). 16p. (J). (gr. k-1). pap. 8.00 *(978-1-61541-122-1(4))* American Reading Co.

Yasuda, Anita. Vietnam. 2016. (Illus.). 32p. (J). *(978-1-4896-4615-6(9))* Weigl Pubs., Inc.

Zocchi, Judy. In Vietnam. Brodie, Neale, illus. 2005. (Global Adventures II Ser.). 32p. (J). pap. 10.95 *(978-1-59646-164-2(0))*; lib. bdg. 21.65 *(978-1-59646-081-2(4))* Dingles & Co.

—In Vietnam/en Vietnam. Brodie, N. eale, illus. 2005. (Global Adventures II Ser.). Tr. of En Vietnam. (ENG & SPA.). 32p. (J). pap. 10.95 *(978-1-59646-166-6(7))* Dingles & Co.

—In Vietnam/en Vietnam. Brodie, Neale, illus. 2005. (Global Adventures II Ser.). Tr. of En Vietnam. (ENG & SPA.). 32p. (J). lib. bdg. 21.65 *(978-1-59646-082-9(2))*; per. 10.95 *(978-1-59646-167-3(5))* Dingles & Co.

VIETNAM WAR, 1961-1975

The American Experience in Vietnam, 10 vols., Set. 2004. (American Experience in Vietnam Ser.). (ENG.). 48p. (gr. 5-8). lib. bdg. 168.35 *(978-0-8368-5771-9(2)*, f93b3903-b904-4a0e-ad8e-308f475f439c) Stevens, Gareth Publishing LLLP.

Atwood, Kathryn J. Courageous Women of the Vietnam War: Medics, Journalists, Survivors, & More. 2018. (Women of Action Ser.: 21). (ENG., Illus.). 240p. (YA). (gr. 7). 19.99 *(978-1-61373-074-4(8))* Chicago Review Pr., Inc.

Barr, Linda. Long Road to Freedom: Journey of the Hmong. 2004. (High Five Reading - Purple Ser.). (ENG., Illus.). 64p. (gr. 3-4). per. 9.00 *(978-0-7368-3852-8(X))* Capstone.

Benoit, Peter. The Vietnam War. 2013. (Cornerstones of Freedom™, Third Ser.). (ENG., Illus.). 64p. (J). pap. 8.95 *(978-0-531-21966-9(6))* Scholastic Library Publishing.

Brown Bear Books. Causes & Outbreak. 2013. (NAM: the Vietnam War Ser.). (ENG., Illus.). 48p. (J). (gr. 5-8). 37.10 *(978-1-78121-042-0(X)*, 16760) Brown Bear Bks.

—Disengagement & Defeat 1969-1975. 2013. (NAM: the Vietnam War Ser.). (ENG., Illus.). 48p. (J). (gr. 5-8). 37.10 *(978-1-78121-044-4(6)*, 16761) Brown Bear Bks.

—The Experience of War. 2013. (NAM: the Vietnam War Ser.). (ENG.). 48p. (J). (gr. 5-8). 37.10 *(978-1-78121-047-5(0)*, 16762) Brown Bear Bks.

—The International War. 2013. (NAM: the Vietnam War Ser.). (ENG.). 48p. (J). (gr. 5-8). 37.10 *(978-1-78121-046-8(2)*, 16763) Brown Bear Bks.

—The Johnson Years 1965-1968. 2013. (NAM: the Vietnam War Ser.). (ENG.). 48p. (J). (gr. 5-8). 37.10 *(978-1-78121-043-7(8)*, 16764) Brown Bear Bks.

—Vietnam War. 2010. (Modern Military History Ser.). (ENG.). 64p. (J). (gr. 8-11). 39.95 *(978-1-933834-51-1(X)*, 16527) Brown Bear Bks.

—The War & U. S. Society. 2013. (NAM: the Vietnam War Ser.). (ENG.). 48p. (J). (gr. 5-8). 37.10 *(978-1-78121-045-1(4)*, 16765) Brown Bear Bks.

Burgan, Michael. Death at Kent State: How a Photograph Brought the Vietnam War Home to America. 2016. (Captured History Ser.). (ENG., Illus.). 64p. (J). (gr. 5-9). lib. bdg. 35.32 *(978-0-7565-5424-8(1)*, 132560, Compass Point Bks.) Capstone.

—The Vietnam War, 1 vol. 2006. (Wars That Changed American History Ser.). (ENG., Illus.). 48p. (gr. 5-8). pap. 15.05 *(978-0-8368-7304-7(1)*, cd889bbf-30c1-45e2-b81d-85f132c658ba); lib. bdg. 33.67 *(978-0-8368-7295-8(9)*, 96d1820a-22b8-4b03-baf7-976de1636759) Stevens, Gareth Publishing LLLP. (Gareth Stevens Secondary Library).

—The Vietnam War: An Interactive Modern History Adventure, 1 vol. 2014. (You Choose: Modern History Ser.). (ENG., Illus.). 112p. (J). (gr. 3-7). 32.65 *(978-1-4765-4187-7(6)*, 124294, Capstone Pr.) Capstone.

Chant, Christopher. The Escalation of American Involvement in the Vietnam War. 2017. (Vietnam War Ser.: Vol. 5). (ENG., Illus.). 79p. (J). (gr. 7-12). 24.95 *(978-1-4222-3889-9(X))* Mason Crest.

—The Fall of Saigon & the End of the Vietnam War. 2017. (Vietnam War Ser.: Vol. 5). (ENG., Illus.). 80p. (J). (gr. 7-12). 24.95 *(978-1-4222-3892-9(X))* Mason Crest.

TUV

—The Origins of Conflict in the Vietnam War. 2017. (Vietnam War Ser.: Vol. 5). (ENG., Illus.). 79p. (J). (gr. 7-12). 24.95 *(978-1-4222-3888-2(1))* Mason Crest.

—Stalemate: U. S. Public Opinion of the War in Vietnam. 2017. (Vietnam War Ser.: Vol. 5). (ENG., Illus.). 80p. (J). (gr. 7-12). 24.95 *(978-1-4222-3891-2(1))* Mason Crest.

—The U. S. Ground War in Vietnam 1965 1973. 2017. (Vietnam War Ser.: Vol. 5). (ENG., Illus.). 79p. (J). (gr. 7-12). 24.95 *(978-1-4222-3890-5(3))* Mason Crest.

Clare, John D. Vietnam, 1939-75. 2nd rev. ed. 2004. (Hodder 20th Century History Ser.). (ENG., Illus.). 48p. (YA). pap. 26.50 *(978-0-340-81476-5(4)*, Hodder Education) Hodder Education Group GBR. Dist: Trans-Atlantic Pubns., Inc.

Coddington, Andrew. Code Breakers & Spies of the Vietnam War, 1 vol. 2018. (Code Breakers & Spies Ser.). (ENG.). 80p. (J). (gr. 8-8). 38.79 *(978-1-5026-3859-5(2)*, 3e16192e-bf41-42c1-893c-961a10c6934c) Cavendish Square Publishing LLC.

Connolly, Kieron. America's Bloody History from Vietnam to the War on Terror, 1 vol. 2017. (Bloody History of America Ser.). (ENG.). 88p. (gr. 8-8). 37.60 *(978-0-7660-9180-1(5)*, a92bb720-3a4b-4034-aa1a-44302c2dd1cb); pap. 20.95 *(978-0-7660-9556-4(8)*, 2aaa20cd-f1a2-4bce-a811-26f2f83462ab) Enslow Publishing, LLC.

Cooper, Candy J. P.O.W. 2011. (J). *(978-0-531-22553-0(4))* Scholastic, Inc.

Corona, Laurel. War Within a War: Vietnam & the Cold War. 2004. (Lucent Library of Historical Eras). (ENG., Illus.). 112p. (J). 33.45 *(978-1-59018-389-2(4)*, Lucent Bks.) Cengage Gale.

Cunningham, Mark E. & Zwier, Lawrence. The Aftermath of the French Defeat in Vietnam. 2009. (Aftermath of History Ser.). (ENG.). 160p. (gr. 9-12). 38.60 *(978-0-8225-9093-4(X))* Lerner Publishing Group.

Daynes, Katie. The Vietnam War. 2008. (Young Reading Series 3 Gift Books Ser.). (Illus.). 64p. (J). 8.99 *(978-0-7945-1991-9(1)*, Usborne) EDC Publishing.

DeCarlo, Carolyn. Great Exit Projects on the Vietnam War & the Antiwar Movement, 1 vol. 2019. (Great Social Studies Exit Projects Ser.). (ENG.). 64p. (gr. 5-5). pap. 13.95 *(978-1-4994-4048-5(0)*, f65c7091-9c33-42ae-97c1-3b2e092e2eba) Rosen Publishing Group, Inc., The.

Dudley Gold, Susan. The Pentagon Papers: National Security or the Right to Know, 1 vol. 2006. (Supreme Court Milestones Ser.). (ENG., Illus.). 128p. (YA). (gr. 8-8). 45.50 *(978-0-7614-1843-6(1)*, f905cf70-6773-479d-8840-68679c7e7d7a) Cavendish Square Publishing LLC.

Duffield, Katy. The Tet Offensive: Crucial Battles of the Vietnam War. 2017. (Major Battles in US History Ser.). (ENG., Illus.). 32p. (J). (gr. 3-5). pap. 9.95 *(978-1-63517-081-8(8)*, 1635170818, Focus Readers) North Star Editions.

Edison, Erin. The Vietnam Veterans Memorial: A 4D Book. 2018. (National Landmarks Ser.). (ENG., Illus.). 24p. (J). (gr. 1-3). lib. bdg. 27.99 *(978-1-5435-3132-9(6)*, 138737, Capstone Pr.) Capstone.

Feinstein, Stephen. The 1960s from the Vietnam War to Flower Power, 1 vol. rev. ed. 2006. (Decades of the 20th Century in Color Ser.). (ENG., Illus.). 64p. (gr. 5-6). lib. bdg. 31.93 *(978-0-7660-2636-0(1)*, 7b7625c7-2ef2-4700-83fe-d3d5cbc79d1a) Enslow Publishing, LLC.

Ferguson, Amanda. American Women of the Vietnam War. (American Women at War Ser.). 112p. (gr. 8-8). 2009. 63.90 *(978-1-61511-395-8(9))* 2004. (ENG., Illus.). (YA). lib. bdg. 39.80 *(978-0-8239-4448-4(4)*, 1e969f8c-b989-41bb-a39e-09010cf3e2b8) Rosen Publishing Group, Inc., The.

Ferry, Joseph. The Vietnam Veterans Memorial. 2004. (American Symbols & Their Meanings Ser.). (Illus.). 48p. (J). (gr. 4-18). lib. bdg. 19.95 *(978-1-59084-039-9(9))* Mason Crest.

Freedman, Russell. Vietnam. 2019. (ENG.). 160p. (J). (gr. 5). pap. 15.99 *(978-0-8234-4274-4(8))* Holiday Hse., Inc.

—Vietnam: A History of the War. 2016. (ENG., Illus.). 160p. (J). (gr. 5). 22.99 *(978-0-8234-3658-3(6))* Holiday Hse., Inc.

Gagne, Tammy. The Vietnam War. 2016. (Illus.). 48p. (J). *(978-1-5105-1292-4(6))* SmartBook Media, Inc.

Galt, Margot Fortunato. Stop This War! American Protest of the Conflict in Vietnam. 2005. (People's History Ser.). (Illus.). 96p. (gr. 6-12). lib. bdg. 26.60 *(978-0-8225-1740-5(X))* Lerner Publishing Group.

George, Enzo. The Vietnam Conflict: War with Communism, 1 vol. 2014. (Voices of War Ser.). (ENG.). 48p. (gr. 4-4). lib. bdg. 33.07 *(978-1-62712-873-5(5)*, 1aa8eb8f-b01c-41b4-9054-8fb0d9c94ad8) Cavendish Square Publishing LLC.

Gibson, Karen Bush. The Vietnam War. (Monumental Milestones Ser.). (J). 2007. (Illus.). 48p. (gr. 4-8). lib. bdg. 29.95 *(978-1-58415-541-6(8))* 2006. lib. bdg. *(978-1-58415-469-3(1))* Mitchell Lane Pubs.

Gifford, Clive. The Vietnam War, 1 vol. 2005. (How Did It Happen? Ser.). (ENG., Illus.). 48p. (gr. 4-8). lib. bdg. 38.33 *(978-1-59018-609-1(5)*, 2a782da3-f614-4f59-941e-305ec86ae00c, Lucent Pr.) Greenhaven Publishing LLC.

—Why Did the Vietnam War Happen?, 1 vol. 2010. (Moments in History Ser.). (ENG.). 48p. (gr. 6-8). (J). pap. 15.05 *(978-1-4339-4179-5(1)*, 4c9d017e-94e8-4df2-9b60-1503dbf1adc7, Gareth Stevens Secondary Library); (Illus.). (YA). lib. bdg. 34.60 *(978-1-4339-4178-8(3)*, 49a09c6a-e207-45a7-83ee-602b45d6bad5) Stevens, Gareth Publishing LLLP.

Gitlin, Martin. Vietnam War, 1 vol. 2013. (Essential Library of American Wars Ser.). (ENG., Illus.). 112p. (YA). (gr. 6-12). lib. bdg. 41.36 *(978-1-61783-880-4(2)*, 6609, Essential Library) ABDO Publishing Co.

Grant, R. G. The Vietnam War, 1 vol. 2004. (Atlas of Conflicts Ser.). (ENG., Illus.). 64p. (gr. 6-8). pap. 15.05 *(978-0-8368-5674-3(0)*, b1582d05-a76b-48f3-9ff8-cf39ac818db4); lib. bdg. 36.67 *(978-0-8368-5667-5(8)*, be950aaa-47f1-4bef-94a4-6dd044ad5f31) Stevens, Gareth Publishing LLLP. (Gareth Stevens Secondary Library).

Haugen, David M. & Musser, Susan, eds. The Vietnam War, 1 vol. 2011. (Perspectives on Modern World History Ser.). (ENG.). 264p. (gr. 10-12). 49.43 *(978-0-7377-5008-9(1)*, 158fbbd0-4eac-4ac2-8fba-d98b03fb8988, Greenhaven Publishing) Greenhaven Publishing LLC.

Hemingway, Al. American Naval Forces in the Vietnam War, 1 vol. 2004. (American Experience in Vietnam Ser.). (ENG., Illus.). 48p. (gr. 5-8). lib. bdg. 33.67 *(978-0-8368-5776-4(3)*, dcff3fb0-f816-413c-9826-9a9528fd873c, Gareth Stevens Secondary Library) Stevens, Gareth Publishing LLLP.

Hogue, Richard, Sr. We Were the Third Herd. 2003. per. 17.95 *(978-0-9722264-0-0(0))* Richlyn Publishing.

Horn, Geoffrey M. John Mccain, 1 vol. 2009. (People We Should Know (Second Series) Ser.). (ENG., Illus.). 32p. (J). (gr. 3-5). pap. 11.50 *(978-1-4339-0160-7(9)*, fbdf5273-8ceb-4a6e-93dd-e54d3db41f8f); lib. bdg. 33.67 *(978-1-4339-0020-4(3)*, 9a51add1-6bb7-4cac-bcd4-e17aafea87d6) Stevens, Gareth Publishing LLLP. (Gareth Stevens Learning Library).

Hosch, William L. Korean War & the Vietnam War: People, Politics, & Power, 1 vol. 2010. (America at War Ser.). (ENG., Illus.). 232p. (J). (gr. 10-10). lib. bdg. 52.59 *(978-1-61530-011-2(2)*, ac3dd829-b1e0-46de-a740-8d1cb2c3f3af) Rosen Publishing Group, Inc., The.

—The Korean War & the Vietnam War: People, Politics, & Power, 4 vols. 2010. (America at War Ser.). (ENG.). 232p. (YA). (gr. 10-10). 105.18 *(978-1-61530-088-4(0)*, 204dd3bd-432d-4c01-92e3-a9020fbb76cd) Rosen Publishing Group, Inc., The.

Jeffrey, Gary & Spender, Nik, illus. The Vietnam War. 2013. (ENG.). 48p. (J). *(978-0-7787-1236-7(2))*; pap. *(978-0-7787-1240-4(0))* Crabtree Publishing Co.

Keeter, Hunter. American Air Forces in the Vietnam War, 1 vol. 2004. (American Experience in Vietnam Ser.). (ENG., Illus.). 48p. (gr. 5-8). lib. bdg. 33.67 *(978-0-8368-5773-3(9)*, b004b61e-1b4d-4fa7-a497-ae16c061d514, Gareth Stevens Secondary Library) Stevens, Gareth Publishing LLLP.

Kenney, Karen Latchana. TV Brings Battle into the Home with the Vietnam War: 4D an Augmented Reading Experience. 2018. (Captured Television History 4D Ser.). (ENG., Illus.). 64p. (J). (gr. 5-9). lib. bdg. 39.99 *(978-0-7565-5825-3(5)*, 138350, Compass Point Bks.) Capstone.

Kent, Deborah. The Vietnam War: From Da Nang to Saigon, 1 vol. 2011. (United States at War Ser.). (ENG., Illus.). 128p. (gr. 5-6). lib. bdg. 35.93 *(978-0-7660-3637-6(5)*, 1e2d6b41-c032-4b3a-88ea-60d465d874f1) Enslow Publishing, LLC.

Killcoyne, Hope Lourie. Key Figures of the Vietnam War, 1 vol. 2015. (Biographies of War Ser.). (ENG., Illus.). 112p. (J). (gr. 7-8). 35.47 *(978-1-68048-063-4(4)*, c16e184b-2f63-49d1-9e79-fb42d67016b4, Britannica Educational Publishing) Rosen Publishing Group, Inc., The.

Kjelle, Marylou Morano. Saigon. 2009. (J). *(978-1-58415-793-9(3))* Mitchell Lane Pubs.

Levete, Sarah. The Vietnam War: Frontline Soldiers & Their Families, 1 vol. 2015. (Frontline Families Ser.). (ENG., Illus.). 48p. (J). (gr. 5-6). pap. 15.05 *(978-1-4824-3061-5(4)*, 24a48056-19d6-4112-8c82-5b18b78f7517) Stevens, Gareth Publishing LLLP.

Levine, Michelle. Vehicles of the Vietnam War, 1 vol. 2013. (War Vehicles Ser.). (ENG.). 32p. (J). (gr. 3-9). 28.65 *(978-1-4296-9913-6(2)*, 120626, Capstone Pr.) Capstone.

Levy, Debbie. The Vietnam War. 2004. (Chronicle of America's Wars Ser.). (Illus.). 96p. (J). (gr. 5-12). 27.93 *(978-0-8225-0421-4(9))* Lerner Publishing Group.

MacCaraid, Clara. Living Through the Vietnam War. 2018. (American Culture & Conflict Ser.). (ENG., Illus.). 48p. (gr. 4-8). lib. bdg. 35.64 *(978-1-64156-418-2(0)*, 9781641564182) Rourke Educational Media.

Marcovitz, Hal. The Vietnam War, 1 vol. 2007. (World History Ser.). (ENG., Illus.). 104p. (gr. 7-7). lib. bdg. 41.53 *(978-1-4205-0024-0(4)*, 61a2a5e0-a19c-47e0-b272-4ec696cca51e, Lucent Pr.) Greenhaven Publishing LLC.

McCune, Susan. Lihn Is from Vietnam, 1 vol., 1. 2015. (Rosen REAL Readers: Social Studies Nonfiction / Fiction: Myself, My Community, My World Ser.). (ENG.). 12p. (J). (gr. k-1). pap. 6.33 *(978-1-5081-1827-5(2)*, b3403b61-9d3d-4ded-8ab0-bd17831c40bb, Rosen Classroom) Rosen Publishing Group, Inc., The.

Miller, Derek. Vietnam & the Rise of Photojournalism, 1 vol. 2018. (Fourth Estate: Journalism in North America Ser.). (ENG.). 112p. (gr. 8-8). lib. bdg. 44.50 *(978-1-5026-3483-2(X)*, 04bd1665-281b-46bb-a1c6-79510fb6022c) Cavendish Square Publishing LLC.

Morales, Gilbert, ed. Critical Perspectives on the Vietnam War. 2009. (Critical Anthologies of Nonfiction Writing Ser.). 176p. (gr. 8-8). 63.90 *(978-1-61512-082-6(3))* Rosen Publishing Group, Inc., The.

Murray, Stuart. Vietnam War Battles & Leaders. 2004. (Battles & Leaders Ser.). (ENG., Illus.). 96p. (J). (gr. 5-8). 26.19 *(978-0-7566-0770-8(1))* Dorling Kindersley Publishing, Inc.

O'Connor, Jim & Who HQ. What Was the Vietnam War? Foley, Tim, illus. 2019. (What Was? Ser.). 112p. (J). (gr. 3-7). 5.99 *(978-1-5247-8977-0(1)*, Penguin Workshop) Penguin Young Readers Group.

Otfinoski, Steven. The Vietnam War (a Step into History) (Library Edition) 2017. (Step into History Ser.). (ENG., Illus.). 144p. (J). (gr. 5-8). lib. bdg. 36.00 *(978-0-531-22570-7(4)*, Children's Pr.) Scholastic Library Publishing.

Partridge, Elizabeth. Boots on the Ground: America's War in Vietnam. 2018. (Illus.). 213p. (J). pap. *(978-0-14-242375-2(0))* Penguin Bks., Ltd.

Perritano, John. Going after Sparky! Pararescue Jumpers Bring Vietnam War Pilot Home, Vol. 8. 2018. (Special Forces Stories Ser.). 64p. (J). (gr. 7). 31.93 *(978-1-4222-4079-3(7))* Mason Crest.

Porterfield, Jason. How Lyndon B. Johnson Fought the Vietnam War, 1 vol. 2017. (Presidents at War Ser.). (ENG.). 128p. (gr. 8-8). lib. bdg. 38.93 *(978-0-7660-8531-2(7)*, d7431810-368e-46b2-bba1-293a64dd0532) Enslow Publishing, LLC.

Rice, Earle, Jr. Point of No Return: Tonkin Gulf & the Vietnam War. 2004. (First Battles Ser.). (Illus.). 144p. (YA). (gr. 6-12). 23.95 *(978-1-931798-16-7(8))* Reynolds, Morgan Inc.

Rice, Earle. Causes of the Vietnam War. 2009. (J). lib. bdg. *(978-1-59556-034-6(3))* OTTN Publishing.

—The Vietnam War, Vol. 11. Musteen, Jason R., ed. 2015. (Major U. S. Historical Wars Ser.). (Illus.). 64p. (J). (gr. 7). lib. bdg. 23.95 *(978-1-4222-3359-7(6))* Mason Crest.

Rose, Simon. The Vietnam War: 1954-1975. 2014. (Illus.). 48p. (J). pap. *(978-1-62127-656-2(2))* Weigl Pubs., Inc.

Samuels, Charlie. Machines & Weaponry of the Vietnam War, 1 vol. 2013. (Machines That Won the War Ser.). (ENG., Illus.). 48p. (J). (gr. 5-6). pap. 15.05 *(978-1-4339-8600-0(0)*, c3075805-43c1-4b7a-b55a-9f3f345a9677); lib. bdg. 34.60 *(978-1-4339-8599-7(3)*, ff35beae-f162-4186-bb61-f60b8e596527) Stevens, Gareth Publishing LLLP.

—Timeline of the Vietnam War, 1 vol. 2011. (Americans at War: a Gareth Stevens Timeline Ser.). (ENG., Illus.). 48p. (J). (gr. 6-8). pap. 15.05 *(978-1-4339-5920-2(8)*, e5e15db0-6102-45e3-9c66-da15fa58049d); lib. bdg. 34.60 *(978-1-4339-5918-9(6)*, 2b851306-2bae-45bd-8752-cb99d5ebbe6f) Stevens, Gareth Publishing LLLP. (Gareth Stevens Secondary Library).

Schomp, Virginia. The Vietnam Era, 1 vol. 2006. (American Voices From Ser.). (ENG., Illus.). 160p. (gr. 6-6). 41.21 *(978-0-7614-1693-7(5)*, 9f6ec0da-6102-44c7-923e-ac157479f65e) Cavendish Square Publishing LLC.

—The Vietnam War, 1 vol. 2005. (Letters from the Battlefront Ser.). (ENG., Illus.). 96p. (gr. 6-6). lib. bdg. 36.93 *(978-0-7614-1663-0(3)*, 5c2a71c6-c1cc-428c-916f-7693754b0619) Cavendish Square Publishing LLC.

Schynert, Mark. Women of the Vietnam War. 2004. (Women in History Ser.). (ENG., Illus.). 112p. (J). (gr. 7-10). 34.80 *(978-1-59018-474-5(2)*, Lucent Bks.) Cengage Gale.

Sherman, Jill. The Vietnam War: 12 Things to Know. 2017. (America at War Ser.). (ENG., Illus.). 32p. (J). (gr. 3-6). 32.80 *(978-1-63235-267-5(2)*, 11706, 12-Story Library) Bookstaves, LLC.

Skrypuch, Marsha Forchuk. Adrift at Sea: A Vietnamese Boy's Story of Survival. Deines, Brian, illus. 2016. (ENG.). 40p. (J). (gr. 1-4). 19.95 *(978-1-77278-005-5(7))* Pajama Pr. CAN. Dist: Publishers Group West (PGW).

—Last Airlift: A Vietnamese Orphan's Rescue from War . (ENG., Illus.). 120p. (J). (gr. 3-7). 2013. pap. 12.95 *(978-0-9869495-1-7(5))* 2012. 17.95 *(978-0-9869495-4-8(X))* Pajama Pr. CAN. Dist: Publishers Group West (PGW).

—One Step at a Time: A Vietnamese Child Finds Her Way. (ENG., Illus.). 128p. (J). (gr. 3-7). 2014. pap. 12.95 *(978-1-927485-02-6(9))* 2013. 17.95 *(978-1-927485-01-9(0))* Pajama Pr. CAN. Dist: Publishers Group West (PGW).

Small, Cathleen. Strategic Inventions of the Vietnam War, 1 vol. 2015. (Tech in the Trenches Ser.). (ENG., Illus.). 112p. (YA). (gr. 9-9). lib. bdg. 44.50 *(978-1-5026-1032-4(9)*, 422c2596-c39b-40ca-ba32-d74fef944b11) Cavendish Square Publishing LLC.

Spradlin, Michael P. Leo Thorsness: Vietnam: Valor in the Sky. 2019. (Medal of Honor Ser.: 3). (ENG., Illus.). 112p. (J). 15.99 *(978-1-250-15715-7(3)*, 900185148, Farrar, Straus & Giroux (BYR)) Farrar, Straus & Giroux.

Steele, Philip. Did Anything Good Come Out of the Vietnam War?, 1 vol., 1. 2015. (Innovation Through Adversity Ser.). (ENG.). 48p. (J). (gr. 6-7). 33.47 *(978-1-5081-7076-1(2)*, 0bde0cbb-787c-4efa-992f-01bd13e051a4, Rosen Young Adult) Rosen Publishing Group, Inc., The.

Streissguth, Tom. The Vietnam War. 2017. (J). *(978-1-5105-3510-7(1))* SmartBook Media, Inc.

Summers, Elizabeth. Weapons & Vehicles of the Vietnam War. 2015. (Tools of War Ser.). (ENG., Illus.). 32p. (J). (gr. 3-9). lib. bdg. 27.32 *(978-1-4914-4082-7(1)*, 128654, Capstone Pr.) Capstone.

Sutherland, Johnathan & Canwell, Diane. American Women in the Vietnam War, 1 vol. 2004. (American Experience in Vietnam Ser.). (ENG., Illus.). 48p. (gr. 5-8). lib. bdg. 33.67 *(978-0-8368-5777-1(1)*, fe71410d-2f2b-42fa-8997-80da00054706, Gareth Stevens Secondary Library) Stevens, Gareth Publishing LLLP.

Thomas, William David. The Home Front in the Vietnam War, 1 vol. 2004. (American Experience in Vietnam Ser.). (ENG., Illus.). 48p. (gr. 5-8). lib. bdg. 33.67 *(978-0-8368-5775-7(5)*, 88d9c093-0192-4a50-aeaa-fa6fdaa9afa8, Gareth Stevens Secondary Library) Stevens, Gareth Publishing LLLP.

Townley, Alvin. Captured: an American Prisoner of War in North Vietnam (Scholastic Focus) 2019. (ENG., Illus.). 256p. (YA). (gr. 7-7). 18.99 *(978-1-338-25566-9(5)*, Scholastic Nonfiction) Scholastic, Inc.

Westwell, Ian. The Vietnam War. 2008. (Wars Day by Day Ser.). (ENG.). 48p. (J). (gr. 5-8). 37.10 *(978-1-933834-39-9(0)*, 16821) Brown Bear Bks.

Wiest, Andrew & McNab, Chris. The Vietnam War, 1 vol. 2016. (Primary Sources in World Warfare Ser.). (ENG.). 256p. (YA). (gr. 9-9). lib. bdg. 56.71 *(978-1-5026-2468-0(0)*, 47c84ec9-ab74-41b4-9ba9-8465cf79312b) Cavendish Square Publishing LLC.

Zullo, Allan. Vietnam War Heroes (10 True Tales) 2015. (10 True Tales Ser.). (ENG.). 192p. (J). (gr. 3-7). pap. 5.99 *(978-0-545-83750-7(2))* Scholastic, Inc.

VIETNAM WAR, 1961-1975—AFRICAN AMERICANS

Schmermund, Elizabeth. Minority Soldiers Fighting in the Vietnam War, 1 vol. 2017. (Fighting for Their Country: Minorities at War Ser.). (ENG.). 112p. (YA). (gr. 8-8). 44.50 *(978-1-5026-2666-0(7)*, 38a54acc-b49c-4ef6-9a08-712e5da89e9c) Cavendish Square Publishing LLC.

Sutherland, Johnathan & Canwell, Diane. African Americans in the Vietnam War, 1 vol. 2004. (American Experience in Vietnam Ser.). (ENG., Illus.). 48p. (gr. 5-8). lib. bdg. 33.67 *(978-0-8368-5772-6(0)*, 208cb630-74f5-459d-a36c-dc75d64786d4, Gareth Stevens Secondary Library) Stevens, Gareth Publishing LLLP.

VIETNAM WAR, 1961-1975—FICTION

Arnold, Tedd. Rat Life. 2009. 208p. (YA). (gr. 7-18). pap. 7.99 *(978-0-14-241431-6(X)*, Speak) Penguin Young Readers Group.

Bauer, Michael Gerard. The Running Man. 2008. 304p. (YA). (gr. 9-18). lib. bdg. 17.89 *(978-0-06-145509-4(1)*, HarperTeen) HarperCollins Pubs.

—The Running Man. 2004. 280p. (YA). pap. *(978-1-86291-575-6(X)*, Omnibus Bks.) Scholastic Australia.

Boyd, Candy Dawson. Charlie Pippin. 2011. (ENG.). 190p. (J). (gr. 4-7). pap. 9.99 *(978-1-4424-5232-9(3)*, Simon & Schuster Bks. For Young Readers) Simon & Schuster Bks. For Young Readers.

Bryant, Jen. Kaleidoscope Eyes. 2010. 272p. (J). (gr. 3-7). 7.99 *(978-0-440-42190-0(X)*, Yearling) Random Hse. Children's Bks.

Burg, Ann E. All the Broken Pieces. 2012. (ENG.). 240p. (J). (gr. 6). pap. 8.99 *(978-0-545-08093-4(2)*, Scholastic Paperbacks) Scholastic, Inc.

Cataneo, D. M. Eggplant Alley. 2013. (ENG.). 352p. (YA). (gr. 7-14). 17.95 *(978-1-59373-146-5(9))* Bunker Hill Publishing, Inc.

Collins, Suzanne. Year of the Jungle: Memories from the Home Front. Proimos, James, illus. 2013. (ENG.). 40p. (J). (gr. k-7). 18.99 *(978-0-545-42516-2(6)*, Scholastic Pr.) Scholastic, Inc.

Crowe, Chris. Death Coming up the Hill. 2018. (ENG.). 208p. (YA). (gr. 9). pap. 15.99 *(978-1-328-90410-2(5)*, 1700750, Clarion Bks.) HarperCollins Pubs.

Franklin, Kristine L. Dove Song. 2006. (ENG.). 192p. (J). (gr. 5-9). per. 5.99 *(978-0-7636-3219-9(8))* Candlewick Pr.

Hoppey, Tim. Jungle Scout: A Vietnam War Story, 1 vol. Espinoza, Ramon, illus. 2008. (Historical Fiction Ser.). (ENG.). 56p. (J). (gr. 3-6). pap. 6.25 *(978-1-4342-0846-0(X)*, 95207, Stone Arch Bks.) Capstone.

Hughes, Dean. Search & Destroy. 2005. (ENG., Illus.). 224p. (YA). 16.95 *(978-0-689-87023-1(X)*, Atheneum Bks. for Young Readers) Simon & Schuster Children's Publishing.

—Search & Destroy. 2015. (ENG., Illus.). 256p. (YA). (gr. 7). pap. 11.99 *(978-1-4814-2703-6(2)*, Atheneum Bks. for Young Readers) Simon & Schuster Children's Publishing.

Kadohata, Cynthia. Cracker! The Best Dog in Vietnam. (ENG.). (J). (gr. 5-9). 2008. 336p. pap. 8.99 *(978-1-4169-0638-4(X))* 2007. (Illus.). 320p. 19.99 *(978-1-4169-0637-7(1))* Simon & Schuster Children's Publishing. (Atheneum Bks. for Young Readers).

Keenan, Sheila. Dogs of War: a Graphic Novel. Fox, Nathan, illus. 2013. (ENG.). 208p. (J). (gr. 3-7). pap. 14.99 *(978-0-545-12888-9(9)*, Graphix) Scholastic, Inc.

Kerley, Barbara. Greetings from Planet Earth. 2010. (ENG.). 256p. (J). (gr. 4-6). 21.19 *(978-0-439-80204-8(0))* Scholastic, Inc.

Kimball, Richard. Shadows of the Men with Green Faces. 2011. 162p. 29.99 *(978-1-4653-5070-1(5))*; pap. 19.99 *(978-1-4653-5069-5(1))* Xlibris Corp.

King, A. S. Everybody Sees the Ants. 2012. (ENG.). 320p. (YA). (gr. 10-17). pap. 11.99 *(978-0-316-12927-5(5))* Little, Brown Bks. for Young Readers.

Lai, Thanhhà. Listen, Slowly. (ENG.). (J). (gr. 3-7). 2016. 288p. pap. 9.99 *(978-0-06-222919-9(2)*, HarperCollins) 2015. 288p. E-Book *(978-0-06-222920-5(6)*, 9780062229205) 2015. (Illus.). 272p. 16.99 *(978-0-06-222918-2(4)*, HarperCollins) HarperCollins Pubs.

Lai, Thanhha. Listen, Slowly. 2016. (J). lib. bdg. 17.20 *(978-0-606-38747-7(1))* Turtleback.

Lynch, Chris. Casualties of War. 2013. (Vietnam Ser.: 4). lib. bdg. 18.40 *(978-0-606-31964-5(6))* Turtleback.

—Free-Fire Zone. 2012. 183p. (J). *(978-0-545-49427-4(3)*, Scholastic Pr.) Scholastic, Inc.

—Free-Fire Zone. 2013. (Vietnam Ser.: 3). lib. bdg. 18.40 *(978-0-606-31963-8(8))* Turtleback.

—I Pledge Allegiance. 2011. (Vietnam Ser.: 1). (ENG.). 192p. (J). (gr. 5-9). 16.99 *(978-0-545-27029-8(4)*, Scholastic Pr.); 183p. (YA). *(978-0-545-38415-5(X))* Scholastic, Inc.

—I Pledge Allegiance. 2013. (Vietnam Ser.: 1). lib. bdg. 17.20 *(978-0-606-31961-4(1))* Turtleback.

—Sharpshooter. 2012. (J). *(978-0-545-43650-2(8)*, Scholastic Pr.); 2. (Vietnam Ser.: 2). (ENG.). 192p. (gr. 6-8). 22.44 *(978-0-545-27026-7(X))* Scholastic, Inc.

—Sharpshooter. 2013. (Vietnam Ser.: 2). lib. bdg. 18.40 *(978-0-606-31962-1(X))* Turtleback.

Metivier, Gary. Cody & Grandpa's Christmas Tradition, 1 vol. Van Wagoner, Traci, illus. 2016. (ENG.). 32p. (J). (gr. k-3). 16.99 *(978-1-4556-2170-5(6)*, Pelican Publishing) Arcadia Publishing.

Myers, Walter Dean. Fallen Angels. 2008. (ENG.). 336p. (J). (gr. 7). pap. 10.99 *(978-0-545-05576-5(8)*, Scholastic Paperbacks) Scholastic, Inc.

—Patrol: An American Soldier in Vietnam. Grifalconi, Ann, illus. 2005. (ENG.). 40p. (J). (gr. 3-7). pap. 7.99 *(978-0-06-073159-5(1)*, HarperCollins) HarperCollins Pubs.

—Patrol: An American Soldier in Vietnam. 2005. 17.00 *(978-0-7569-5428-4(2))* Perfection Learning Corp.

Paulsen, Gary. The Car. 2006. (ENG., Illus.). 192p. (YA). (gr. 7-12). pap. 9.99 *(978-0-15-205827-2(3)*, 253004, Clarion Bks.) HarperCollins Pubs.

—The Car. 2006. 182p. (gr. 7-12). 17.00 *(978-0-7569-6685-0(X))* Perfection Learning Corp.

Phillips, Dee. Vietnam: The Story of a Marine. 2015. (Yesterday's Voices Ser.). (YA). lib. bdg. 19.60 *(978-0-606-36677-9(6))* Turtleback.

Piner, Huston. My Life As a Myth. 2017. (ENG., Illus.). (YA). pap. 11.99 *(978-1-947139-73-2(8))* NineStar Pr.

Poulsen, David A. Old Man. 2013. (ENG.). 224p. (YA). pap. 12.99 *(978-1-4597-0547-0(5))* Dundurn Pr. CAN. Dist: Publishers Group West (PGW).

—Old Man. 2013. 276p. pap. *(978-1-4596-6325-1(X))* ReadHowYouWant.com, Ltd.

Qualey, Marsha. Come in from the Cold. 2008. (ENG.). 224p. (YA). (gr. 7). pap. 14.95 *(978-0-547-01439-5(2)*, 1030986, Clarion Bks.) HarperCollins Pubs.

Santacroce, John P. Running Across the Moon. 2013. 146p. pap. 14.98 *(978-0-615-76887-8(3))* Santacroce, John.

Sherlock, Patti. Letters from Wolfie. 2007. (ENG.). 240p. (J). (gr. 5-18). 7.99 *(978-0-14-240358-7(X)*, Puffin Books) Penguin Young Readers Group.

Sherman, M. Zachary. Emergency Ops, 1 vol. Bermudez, Raymund, illus. 2012. (Bloodlines Ser.: 1). (ENG.). 88p. (J). (gr. 4-8). lib. bdg. 27.32 *(978-1-4342-3766-8(4)*, 117027, Stone Arch Bks.) Capstone.

—Fighting Phantoms, 1 vol. Casas, Fritz, illus. 2011. (Bloodlines Ser.). (ENG.). 88p. (J). (gr. 4-8). lib. bdg. 27.32 *(978-1-4342-2560-3(7)*, 113619, Stone Arch Bks.) Capstone.

Stentiford, Tyler Michael. A Darker Secret. 2009. (ENG.). 128p. (YA). pap. 9.99 *(978-1-60138-315-0(0))* Atlantic Publishing Group, Inc.

Trip to Freedom: Six-Pack. (Greetings Ser.: Vol. 3). (gr. 3-5). 31.00 *(978-0-7635-1777-9(1))* Rigby Education.

Watkins, Steve. On Blood Road (a Vietnam War Novel) 2018. (ENG.). 288p. (YA). (gr. 7-12). 18.99 *(978-1-338-19701-3(0),* Scholastic Pr.) Scholastic, Inc.

VIETNAMESE AMERICANS

Bryan, Nichol. Vietnamese Americans, 1 vol. 2004. (One Nation Set 2 Ser.). (ENG.). 32p. (gr. k-6). 27.07 *(978-1-59197-534-2(4),* Checkerboard Library) ABDO Publishing Co.

Cherenfant, Sabine. How Vietnamese Immigrants Made America Home, 1 vol. 2018. (Coming to America: the History of Immigration to the United States Ser.). (ENG.). 80p. (gr. 6-6). 38.80 *(978-1-5081-8138-5(1),* 4adae765-75b5-4f62-9976-3fb3d914a9e7) Rosen Publishing Group, Inc., The.

Coleman, Lori. Vietnamese in America. 2005. (In America Ser.). (Illus.). 80p. (J). (gr. 5-8). lib. bdg. 27.93 *(978-0-8225-3951-3(9))* Lerner Publishing Group.

Ferry, Joseph. Vietnamese Immigration. 2005. (Changing Face of North America Ser.). (Illus.). 112p. (YA). lib. bdg. 24.95 *(978-1-59084-682-7(6))* Mason Crest.

Grabowski, John F. Vietnamese Americans. (Successful Americans Ser.). 64p. (YA). 2009. (gr. 9-12). 22.95 *(978-1-4222-0522-8(3))* 2007. (gr. 7-18). pap. 9.95 *(978-1-4222-0869-4(9))* Mason Crest.

Hall, Margaret C. Vietnamese Americans. 2003. (We Are America Ser.). (Illus.). 32p. (J). (gr. 2-4). lib. bdg. 24.22 *(978-1-4034-0738-2(X))* Heinemann-Raintree.

Henzel, Cynthia Kennedy. Vietnamese Immigrants: In Their Shoes. 2017. (Immigrant Experiences Ser.). (ENG.). 32p. (J). (gr. 3-6). lib. bdg. 35.64 *(978-1-5038-2032-6(7),* 211852) Child's World, Inc, The.

Huong's Journey: Inside the U. S. A. 2009. (Inside the USA Ser.). (Illus.). 16p. (C). pap. 14.95 *(978-0-7362-7059-5(0))* CENGAGE Learning.

Parker, Lewis K. Why Vietnamese Immigrants Came to America. 2009. (Coming to America Ser.). 24p. (gr. 2-3). 42.50 *(978-1-61511-888-5(8),* PowerKids Pr.) Rosen Publishing Group, Inc., The.

Stanek, Muriel. We Came from Vietnam. McMahon, Wm. Franklin, photos by. 2004. (Illus.). 46p. (J). (gr. k-4). reprint ed. *(978-0-7567-7795-1(X))* DIANE Publishing Co.

VIETNAMESE AMERICANS—FICTION

Burg, Ann E. All the Broken Pieces. 2012. (ENG.). 240p. (J). (gr. 6). pap. 8.99 *(978-0-545-08093-4(2),* Scholastic Paperbacks) Scholastic, Inc.

Jules, Jacqueline. Duck for Turkey Day. 2018. (ENG.). 32p. (J). (gr. -1-1). 19.49 *(978-1-64310-547-5(7))* Penworthy Co., LLC, The.

—Duck for Turkey Day. 2018. (2019 Av2 Fiction Ser.). (ENG.). 32p. (J). (gr. 1-3). lib. bdg. 34.28 *(978-1-4896-8259-8(7),* AV2 by Weigl) Weigl Pubs., Inc.

—Duck for Turkey Day. Mitter, Kathryn, illus. 2017. (ENG.). 32p. (J). (gr. -1-3). pap. 8.99 *(978-0-8075-1735-2(6),* 807517356) Whitman, Albert & Co.

Lai, Thanhhà. Butterfly Yellow. 2019. (ENG.). 304p. (YA). (gr. 8). 17.99 *(978-0-06-222921-2(4),* HarperCollins) HarperCollins Pubs.

—Inside Out & Back Again. 2014. (ENG.). 288p. (J). (gr. 3-7). 12.24 *(978-1-63245-350-1(9))* Lectorum Pubns., Inc.

—Inside Out & Back Again. 2009. 9.68 *(978-0-7848-3887-7(9),* Everbind) Marco Bk. Co.

—Inside Out & Back Again. 2013. 18.00 *(978-1-61383-970-6(7))* Perfection Learning Corp.

—Inside Out & Back Again. 2013. 262p. (J). lib. bdg. 18.40 *(978-0-606-27126-4(0))* Turtleback.

—Inside Out & Back Again: A Newbery Honor Award Winner. (ENG.). (J). (gr. 3-7). 2013. 288p. pap. 9.99 *(978-0-06-196279-0(1))* 2011. 272p. 16.99 *(978-0-06-196278-3(3))* HarperCollins Pubs. (HarperCollins).

—Inside Out & Back Again: a Harper Classic. 2017. (Harper Classic Ser.). (ENG.). 288p. (J). (gr. 3-7). 16.99 *(978-0-06-257402-2(7),* HarperCollins) HarperCollins Pubs.

Manning, Matthew K. Operation Stargazer. Douglas, Allen, illus. 2018. (Drone Academy Ser.). (ENG.). 112p. (J). (gr. 4-8). lib. bdg. 27.32 *(978-1-4965-6076-6(0),* 137498, Stone Arch Bks.) Capstone.

Mosher, Richard. Zazoo. 2004. (ENG.). 272p. (YA). (gr. 7-18). reprint ed. pap. 15.95 *(978-0-618-43904-1(8))* Houghton Mifflin Harcourt Publishing Co.

Perera, Hilda. MAI. (SPA.). 120p. (J). 7.95 *(978-84-348-1149-2(9),* SM1210) SM Ediciones ESP. Dist: AIMS International Bks., Inc., Lectorum Pubns., Inc.

Pung, Alice. Marly Walks on the Moon: Marly: Book 4. 2016. (Our Australian Girl Ser.: 4). 144p. (J). (gr. 3-7). 14.99 *(978-0-14-330852-2(1))* Penguin Random Hse. AUS. Dist: Independent Pubs. Group.

Schraff, Anne. Memories Are Forever. 2008. (Passages Ser.). 135p. lib. bdg. 13.95 *(978-0-7569-8405-2(X))* Perfection Learning Corp.

Silver, Gail. Steps & Stones: An Anh's Anger Story. Kromer, Christiane, illus. 2011. 40p. (J). (gr. -1-3). 16.95 *(978-1-935209-87-4(6),* Plum Blossom Bks.) Parallax Pr.

Sugarman, Brynn Olenberg. Rebecca's Journey Home. Shapiro, Michelle, illus. 2006. 32p. (J). (gr. -1-3). lib. bdg. 17.95 *(978-1-58013-157-5(3),* Kar-Ben Publishing) Lerner Publishing Group.

Tran, Truong. Going Home, Coming Home. Phong, Ann, illus. 2003.Tr. of Ve Nha Tham Que Hu'o'Ng. (ENG & VIE.). 32p. (J). 16.95 *(978-0-89239-179-0(0))* Lee & Low Bks., Inc.

Zepeda, Gwendolyn. Maya & Annie on Saturdays & Sundays: Los Sábados y Domingos de Maya y Annie. 2018. (ENG & SPA., Illus.). 32p. (J). (gr. 1-4). 17.95 *(978-1-55885-859-6(8))* Arte Publico Pr.

VIETNAMESE CONFLICT, 1961-1975

see Vietnam War, 1961-1975

VIETNAMESE LANGUAGE

Animals Habitats, 1 vol., 1. 2015. (Our Wonderful World Ser.). 8p. (J). (gr. 2-4). pap. 9.35 *(978-1-5081-1257-0(6),* 4ff35b18-891e-4122-a906-4f70ba4b040c, Rosen Classroom) Rosen Publishing Group, Inc., The.

Kudela, Katy R. My First Book of Vietnamese Words, 1 vol. Translations.com Staff, tr. 2010. (Bilingual Picture Dictionaries Ser.). (MUL., Illus.). 32p. (J). (gr. -1-2). pap. 8.10 *(978-1-4296-6163-8(1),* 115315, Capstone Pr.) Capstone.

—My First Book of Vietnamese Words. Translations.com, tr. 2010. (Bilingual Picture Dictionaries Ser.). (MUL.). 32p. (J). (gr. 1-2). pap. 48.60 *(978-1-4296-6164-5(X),* 16049, Capstone Pr.) Capstone.

Lanchais, Aurelie, et al. Kto A? 2005. (Who Am I? What Am I? Ser.).Tr. of Who Am I? (RUS, ENG, TUR, VIE & CHI., Illus.). 16p. (J). (gr. -1-1). 9.95 *(978-1-84059-232-0(X))* Milet Publishing.

—Who Am I? 2005. (Who Am I? What Am I? Ser.). (CHI, ENG, VIE, GUJ & RUS., Illus.). 16p. (J). (gr. -1-1). 9.95 *(978-1-84059-229-0(X))* Milet Publishing.

Milet Publishing. My First Bilingual Book-Colors (English-Vietnamese) 2011. (My First Bilingual Book Ser.). (ENG.). 24p. (J). (gr. k — 1). bds. 8.99 *(978-1-84059-606-9(6))* Milet Publishing.

Milet Publishing Staff. Animals - My First Bilingual Book, 1 vol. 2011. (My First Bilingual Book Ser.). (ENG., Illus.). 24p. (J). (gr. k — 1). bds. 8.99 *(978-1-84059-623-6(6))* Milet Publishing.

—Bilingual Visual Dictionary. 2011. (Milet Multimedia Ser.). (ENG & VIE., Illus.). 1p. (J). (gr. k-2). cd-rom 19.95 *(978-1-84059-595-6(7))* Milet Publishing.

—My Bilingual Book-Hearing (English-Vietnamese), 1 vol. 2014. (My Bilingual Book Ser.). (ENG., Illus.). 24p. (J). (gr. -1-k). 9.95 *(978-1-84059-787-5(9))* Milet Publishing.

—My Bilingual Book-Sight (English-Vietnamese), 1 vol. 2014. (My Bilingual Book Ser.). (ENG., Illus.). 24p. (J). (gr. -1-k). 9.95 *(978-1-84059-803-2(4))* Milet Publishing.

—My Bilingual Book-Smell (English-Vietnamese), 1 vol. 2014. (My Bilingual Book Ser.). (ENG., Illus.). 24p. (J). (gr. -1-k). 9.95 *(978-1-84059-819-3(0))* Milet Publishing.

—My Bilingual Book-Touch (English-Vietnamese), 1 vol. 2014. (My Bilingual Book Ser.). (ENG., Illus.). 24p. (J). (gr. -1-k). 9.95 *(978-1-84059-851-3(4))* Milet Publishing.

—My First Bilingual Book-Home (English-Vietnamese), 1 vol. 2011. (My First Bilingual Book Ser.). (ENG., Illus.). 24p. (J). (gr. k — 1). bds. 8.99 *(978-1-84059-655-7(4))* Milet Publishing.

—My First Bilingual Book-Jobs (English-Vietnamese), 1 vol. 2012. (My First Bilingual Book Ser.). (ENG., Illus.). 24p. (J). (gr. k — 1). bds. 7.99 *(978-1-84059-715-8(1))* Milet Publishing.

—My First Bilingual Book-Music (English-Vietnamese), 1 vol. 2012. (My First Bilingual Book Ser.). (ENG., Illus.). 24p. (J). (gr. k — 1). bds. 7.99 *(978-1-84059-731-8(3))* Milet Publishing.

—My First Bilingual Book-Opposites (English-Vietnamese), 1 vol. 2012. (My First Bilingual Book Ser.). (ENG., Illus.). 24p. (J). (gr. k — 1). bds. 8.99 *(978-1-84059-747-9(X))* Milet Publishing.

—My First Bilingual Book-Sports (English-Vietnamese), 1 vol. 2012. (My First Bilingual Book Ser.). (ENG., Illus.). 24p. (J). (gr. k — 1). bds. 7.99 *(978-1-84059-763-9(1))* Milet Publishing.

—My First Bilingual Book-Vegetables (English-Vietnamese), 1 vol. 2011. (My First Bilingual Book Ser.). (ENG., Illus.). 24p. (J). (gr. k — 1). bds. 8.99 *(978-1-84059-671-7(6))* Milet Publishing.

Nguyen, An Mai. Let's Learn Animals in Vietnamese. 2006. (VIE & ENG., Illus.). (J). bds. 6.95 *(978-0-9776482-3-8(0))* Viet Baby, LLC.

—Let's Learn Colors in Vietnamese. 2006. (VIE & ENG., Illus.). (J). bds. 6.95 *(978-0-9776482-1-4(4))* Viet Baby, LLC.

—Let's Learn How to Count in Vietnamese. 2006. (VIE & ENG., Illus.). (J). bds. 6.95 *(978-0-9776482-2-1(2))* Viet Baby, LLC.

—Let's Learn the Vietnamese Alphabet. 2006. (VIE & ENG., Illus.). (J). bds. 6.95 *(978-0-9776482-0-7(6))* Viet Baby, LLC.

Tran, Phuoc Thi Minh. My First Book of Vietnamese Words: An ABC Rhyming Book of Vietnamese Language & Culture. Nguyen, Dong & Nguyen, Hop Thi, illus. 2017. (My First Words Ser.). 32p. (J). (gr. -1-3). 10.95 *(978-0-8048-4907-4(2))* Tuttle Publishing.

Turhan, Sedat. New Bilingual Visual Dictionary (English-Vietnamese), 1 vol. 2nd ed. 2017. (New Bilingual Visual Dictionary Ser.). (ENG., Illus.). 148p. (J). (gr. k-2). 19.95 *(978-1-78508-896-4(3))* Milet Publishing.

VIEWS

Barlowe, Dot. Tropical Paradise Scenes to Paint or Color. 2009. (Dover Nature Coloring Book Ser.). (ENG., Illus.). 48p. (gr. 6-8). pap. 5.99 *(978-0-486-46562-3(4),* 465624) Dover Pubns., Inc.

Baxter, Nicola. Learn about Our World. Elliott, Rebecca, illus. 2013. (ENG.). 16p. (J). (gr. k-2). bds. 17.99 *(978-1-84322-985-8(4),* Armadillo) Anness Publishing GBR. Dist: National Bk. Network.

Hawkins, Emily. Atlas of Miniature Adventures: A Pocket-Sized Collection of Small-scale Wonders - Because Bigger Isn't Always Better. Letherland, Lucy, illus. 2016. (Atlas Of Ser.). (ENG.). 64p. (J). 9.99 *(978-1-84780-909-4(2),* Wide Eyed Editions) Quarto Publishing Group UK GBR. Dist: Littlehampton Bk Services, Ltd.

It's My State: Group 2, 12 vols. 2003. (It's My State! (First Edition)(r) Ser.). (ENG.). (YA). (gr. 4-4). lib. bdg. 204.42 *(978-0-7614-1521-3(1),* 129556d1-d8ff-4522-ad62-ee4afc09281b, Cavendish Square) Cavendish Square Publishing LLC.

VIKINGS

Here are entered works on the Scandinavian sea-warriors who plundered the northern and western coasts of Europe from the 8th to the 10th centuries. Works on the inhabitants of Scandinavia since the 10th century are entered under Scandinavians. Works on the inhabitants of Scandinavia prior to the 10th century are entered under Northmen.

see also Northmen

Allan, Tony. Exploring the Life, Myth, & Art of the Vikings, 1 vol. 2011. (Civilizations of the World Ser.). (ENG.). 144p. (gr. 8-8). E-Book 47.80 *(978-1-4488-4837-9(7),* 92c37f50-3df1-461c-b2a2-98cb111ebb38); (YA). lib. bdg. 47.80 *(978-1-4488-4833-1(4),* fe20b559-bf95-4076-ba34-53d6e153ad55) Rosen Publishing Group, Inc., The.

Anderson, Peter. Vikings. 2011. (History's Greatest Warriors Ser.). (ENG., Illus.). 24p. (J). (gr. 3-7). lib. bdg. 26.95 *(978-1-60014-632-9(5),* Torque Bks.) Bellwether Media.

Anderson, Scoular. How to Be a Viking: Band 12/Copper (Collins Big Cat) Anderson, Scoular, illus. 2007. (Collins Big Cat Ser.). (ENG., Illus.). 32p. (J). (gr. 2-4). pap. 10.99 *(978-0-00-723079-2(6))* HarperCollins Pubs. Ltd. GBR. Dist: Independent Pubs. Group.

Bailey, Linda. Stowing Away with the Vikings. Slavin, Bill, illus. 2018. (ENG.). 56p. (J). (gr. 3-7). pap. 11.99 *(978-1-77138-987-7(7))* Kids Can Pr., Ltd. CAN. Dist: Hachette Bk. Group.

Bedford, Kate. The Vikings. 2011. (Children in History Ser.). (Illus.). 32p. (J). (gr. 4-7). lib. bdg. 28.50 *(978-1-59771-272-9(8))* Sea-To-Sea Pubns.

Bingham, Jane. Explore!: Vikings. 2017. (Explore! Ser.). (ENG., Illus.). 32p. (J). (gr. 4-6). pap. 12.99 *(978-0-7502-9737-0(9));* 17.99 *(978-0-7502-9548-2(1))* Hachette Children's Group GBR. (Wayland). Dist: Hachette Bk. Group.

Bodden, Valerie. Vikings. 2017. (X-Books: Fighters Ser.). (ENG., Illus.). 32p. (J). (gr. 3-6). *(978-1-60818-816-1(7),* 20381, Creative Education) Creative Co., The.

—Vikings (Great Warriors) 2013. 24p. pap. *(978-1-60818-469-9(2))* Creative Co., The.

—X-Books: Vikings. 2017. (X-Bks.). (Illus.). 32p. (J). (gr. 3-7). pap. 9.99 *(978-1-62832-419-8(8),* 20382, Creative Paperbacks) Creative Co., The.

Brown Bear Books. The Vikings. 2015. (At Home With ... Ser.). (ENG., Illus.). 32p. (J). (gr. 4-6). lib. bdg. 31.35 *(978-1-78121-085-7(3),* 16441) Brown Bear Bks.

Burnett, Alan & Burnett, Allan. The Vikings & All That. Anderson, Scoular, illus. 2016. (and All That Ser.). (ENG.). 112p. (gr. 4-8). pap. 7.95 *(978-1-78027-393-8(2),* Birlinn) Birlinn, Ltd. GBR. Dist: Casemate Pubs. & Bk. Distributors, LLC.

Clements, J. M. Vikings. 2012. (Illus.). 205p. (J). *(978-1-4351-4591-7(7))* Metro Bks.

Cox, P. Roxbee. Who Were the Vikings? rev. ed. (Starting Point History Ser.). (ENG.). 1p. (J). (gr. 1-18). pap. 4.99 *(978-0-7945-0177-8(X))* EDC Publishing.

d'Aulaire, Ingri & d'Aulaire, Edgar Parin. Leif the Lucky. 2014. (Illus.). 60p. 17.95 *(978-0-8166-9545-4(8))* Univ. of Minnesota Pr.

Defries, Cheryl L. Leif Eriksson: Viking Explorer of the New World, 1 vol. 2009. (Great Explorers of the World Ser.). (ENG., Illus.). 112p. (gr. 6-7). lib. bdg. 35.93 *(978-1-59845-126-9(X),* f7aabf72-a3ae-4c0d-a7a8-53f0a6f5ea26) Enslow Publishing, LLC.

Dorling Kindersley Publishing Staff. Vikings: DKFindOut! 2018. (Illus.). 64p. (J). *(978-0-241-32302-1(9))* Dorling Kindersley Publishing, Inc.

Dougherty, Martin J. The Untold History of the Vikings, 1 vol. 2016. (History Exposed Ser.). (ENG.). 224p. (YA). (gr. 9-9). 56.71 *(978-1-5026-1902-0(4),* b4e9fa56-f2dc-46f6-9bb6-4522783a4d65) Cavendish Square Publishing LLC.

Dowling, Lucy. Why Why Why... Were Vikings So Fierce? 2010. (Why Why Why Ser.). 32p. (YA). (gr. 1-3). lib. bdg. 18.95 *(978-1-4222-1591-3(1))* Mason Crest.

Fowke, Robert. Vikings. (ENG., Illus.). 128p. (J). pap. *(978-0-340-68611-9(1))* Hodder & Stoughton.

Gandolfi, Claudine. Scratch & Sketch Vikings: An Art Activity Book for Legendary Artists & Explorers of All Ages. Zschock, Martha Day, illus. 2015. (Scratch & Sketch Ser.). (ENG.). 64p. (J). spiral bd. 12.99 *(978-1-4413-1813-8(5),* 2ef4d3c7-8369-434f-a18e-6838f73d0fdb) Peter Pauper Pr. Inc.

Ganeri, Anita. Discover Through Craft: the Vikings. 2019. (Discover Through Craft Ser.). (ENG., Illus.). 32p. (J). (gr. 2-4). pap. 10.99 *(978-1-4451-5080-2(8),* Franklin Watts) Hachette Children's Group GBR. Dist: Hachette Bk. Group.

—How to Live Like a Viking Warrior. Epelbaum, Mariano, illus. 2015. (How to Live Like ... Ser.). (ENG.). 32p. (J). (gr. 3-6). lib. bdg. 27.99 *(978-1-4677-6354-7(3),* b777eb9b-1d65-475c-8f9c-8cd0579a0a5b, Hungry Tomato (r)) Lerner Publishing Group.

Gitlin, Martin. Vikings. 2013. (Great Warriors Ser.). (ENG., Illus.). 48p. (J). (gr. 4-8). pap. 18.50 *(978-1-61783-779-1(2),* 10811) ABDO Publishing Co.

Goldsmith, Rose. How Did the Vikings Come to Canada? 2012. (Level F Ser.). (ENG., Illus.). 16p. (J). (gr. k-2). pap. 7.95 *(978-1-927136-51-5(2),* 19413) RiverStream Publishing.

Grant, Neil. Everyday Life of the Vikings. 2005. (Uncovering History Ser.). (Illus.). 46p. (J). (gr. 6-9). lib. bdg. 29.95 *(978-1-58340-706-6(5))* Black Rabbit Bks.

Greenling, Jason. The Technology of the Vikings, 1 vol. 2016. (Ancient Innovations Ser.). (ENG., Illus.). 64p. (gr. 6-6). 35.93 *(978-1-5026-2241-9(6),* 43cd570e-0050-4300-81fa-2dd9c5ee8ed5) Cavendish Square Publishing LLC.

Gunderson, Jessica. Vikings. 2012. (Fearsome Fighters Ser.). (ENG., Illus.). 48p. (J). (gr. 5-9). 23.95 *(978-1-60818-185-8(5),* 21887, Creative Education) Creative Co., The.

Higgins, Nadia. National Geographic Kids: Everything Vikings: All the Incredible Facts & Fierce Fun You Can Plunder. 2015. (National Geographic Kids Everything Ser.). (Illus.). 64p. (J). (gr. 3-7). pap. 12.99 *(978-1-4263-2076-7(0),* National Geographic Kids) Disney Publishing Worldwide.

Hinds, Kathryn. Vikings, 1 vol. 2010. (Barbarians! Ser.). (ENG.). 80p. (gr. 6-6). 38.36 *(978-0-7614-4074-1(7),* 099ce436-f8bc-407e-924a-e48d46d1f27d) Cavendish Square Publishing LLC.

Hopkins, Andrea. Viking Explorers & Settlers. 2009. (Viking Library). 24p. (gr. 3-3). 42.50 *(978-1-60854-256-7(4),* PowerKids Pr.) Rosen Publishing Group, Inc., The.

—Viking Families & Farms. 2009. (Viking Library). 24p. (gr. 3-3). 42.50 *(978-1-60854-257-4(2),* PowerKids Pr.) Rosen Publishing Group, Inc., The.

—Viking Longships. 2009. (Viking Library). 24p. (gr. 3-3). 42.50 *(978-1-60854-259-8(9),* PowerKids Pr.) Rosen Publishing Group, Inc., The.

—Viking Raiders & Traders. 2009. (Viking Library). 24p. (gr. 3-3). 42.50 *(978-1-60854-260-4(2),* PowerKids Pr.) Rosen Publishing Group, Inc., The.

—Vikings: The Norse Discovery of America. 2009. (Viking Library). 24p. (gr. 3-3). 42.50 *(978-1-60854-261-1(0),* PowerKids Pr.) Rosen Publishing Group, Inc., The.

Hubbard, Ben. Viking Warriors, 1 vol. 2016. (Conquerors & Combatants Ser.). (ENG.). 224p. (YA). (gr. 9-9). lib. bdg. 56.71 *(978-1-5026-2455-0(9),* 567b816d-9977-4493-a21c-6e156574ff4a) Cavendish Square Publishing LLC.

Hyde, Natalie. Explore with Leif Eriksson. 2014. (Travel with the Great Explorers Ser.). (ENG., Illus.). 32p. (J). (gr. 4-5). *(978-0-7787-1427-9(6))* Crabtree Publishing Co.

Hynson, Colin. How People Lived In Viking Times, 1 vol. 2008. (How People Lived Ser.). (ENG., Illus.). 32p. (gr. 4-4). (J). lib. bdg. 30.27 *(978-1-4042-4434-4(4),* d58b66ec-c4bd-4f37-8cf4-f37744bffd99, PowerKids Pr.); pap. 10.60 *(978-1-4358-2624-3(8),* c03f6996-789f-4199-a6e7-7a0dd4a58fdf, Rosen Classroom) Rosen Publishing Group, Inc., The.

Jeffrey, Gary. The Dark Ages & the Vikings. Spender, Nick, illus. 2014. (Graphic Medieval History Ser.). (ENG.). 48p. (J). (gr. 5-5). *(978-0-7787-0401-0(7))* Crabtree Publishing Co.

Knudsen, Shannon. Leif Eriksson. Oldroyd, Mark, illus. 2005. (On My Own Biography Ser.). (ENG.). 48p. (gr. 2-4). (J). pap. 7.99 *(978-1-57505-828-3(6),* 33194921-1e69-48b6-9e3e-3c60df1b5a8b, First Avenue Editions); lib. bdg. 25.26 *(978-1-57505-649-4(6),* Carolrhoda Bks.) Lerner Publishing Group.

Lassieur, Allison. Life As a Viking. 2010. (You Choose: Warriors Ser.). (ENG.). 112p. (J). (gr. 3-4). pap. 41.70 *(978-1-4296-5727-3(8),* 15503, Capstone Pr.) Capstone.

—Life as a Viking: An Interactive History Adventure. 2010. (You Choose: Warriors Ser.). (ENG., Illus.). 112p. (J). (gr. 3-7). pap. 6.95 *(978-1-4296-5639-9(5),* 114130, Capstone Pr.) Capstone.

Leonard, Kiri Ostergaard. Vikings of Legend & Lore Paper Dolls. 2013. (ENG.). 32p. (gr. 3-8). pap. 9.99 *(978-0-486-49334-3(2),* 493342) Dover Pubns., Inc.

Levy, Janey. At Sea on a Viking Ship: Solving Problems of Length & Weight Using the Four Math Operations. 2004. (Math Big Bookstm Ser.). (ENG.). 24p. (gr. 3-4). 43.95 *(978-0-8239-7642-3(4))* Rosen Publishing Group, Inc., The.

Lockyer, John. Vikings, 1 vol. 2018. (ENG., Illus.). 21p. (J). pap. *(978-1-77654-258-1(4),* Red Rocket Readers) Flying Start Bks.

Macdonald, Fiona. The Medieval Chronicles: Vikings, Knights, & Castles. Antram, David, illus. 2013. 92p. (J). *(978-1-4351-5067-6(8))* Barnes & Noble, Inc.

MacDonald, Fiona. Viking Raiders. 2009. (History Explorers Ser.). (ENG.). 24p. (J). (gr. k-2). pap. 5.95 *(978-1-84696-216-5(1),* TickTock Books) Octopus Publishing Group GBR. Dist: Independent Pubs. Group.

Macdonald, Fiona. Vikings. 2010. (Remarkable Man & Beast Ser.). (Illus.). 48p. (J). (gr. 3-18). lib. bdg. 19.95 *(978-1-4222-1977-5(1))* Mason Crest.

MacDonald, Fiona. Vikings: Dress, Eat, Write & Play Just Like the Vikings. 2008. (Hands-on History Ser.). (ENG., Illus.). 32p. (J). (gr. 3-7). pap. *(978-0-7787-4072-8(2))* Crabtree Publishing Co.

Malam, John. The Vikings, 1 vol. 2011. (Dig It: History from Objects Ser.). (ENG., Illus.). 32p. (YA). (gr. 3-4). lib. bdg. 30.27 *(978-1-4488-3286-6(1),* 3fef1162-6d62-44f3-844f-cf09c5d84419) Rosen Publishing Group, Inc., The.

Margeson, Susan. DK Eyewitness Books: Viking: Discover the Story of the Vikings — Their Ships, Weapons, Legends, & Saga of War. 2009. (DK Eyewitness Ser.). (ENG., Illus.). 72p. (J). (gr. 3-7). 16.99 *(978-0-7566-5829-8(2),* DK Children) Dorling Kindersley Publishing, Inc.

Mason Crest Publishers Staff. Vikings, Vol. 5. 2019. (Untold History of Ancient Civilizations Ser.). (Illus.). 64p. (J). (gr. 8). lib. bdg. 31.93 *(978-1-4222-3522-5(X))* Mason Crest.

McKinley, Herald. Vikings: Raiders & Explorers. 2015. (J). lib. bdg. *(978-1-62713-409-5(3))* Cavendish Square Publishing LLC.

McLeese, Don. Vikings. 2009. 32p. pap. 7.99 *(978-0-8249-1445-5(7),* Ideals Pubns.) Worthy Publishing.

McNeil, Niki, et al. HOCPP 1082 Vikings. 2006. spiral bd. 24.00 *(978-1-60308-082-8(1))* In the Hands of a Child.

McRae, Anne & Agosta, Loredana. The Vikings. Cecchi, Lorenzo et al, illus. 2008. (Back to Basics Ser.). 32p. (J). (gr. 2-5). lib. bdg. *(978-88-6098-051-9(8))* McRae Bks. Srl.

Medina, Nico & Who HQ. Who Was Leif Erikson? Putra, Dede, illus. 2018. (Who Was? Ser.). 112p. (J). (gr. 3-7). 6.99 *(978-0-448-48861-5(2),* Penguin Workshop) Penguin Young Readers Group.

Miles, John C. Discover the Vikings: Warriors, Exploration & Trade. 2018. (Discover the Vikings Ser.). (ENG., Illus.). 32p. (J). (gr. 3-6). pap. 11.99 *(978-1-4451-5369-8(6),* Franklin Watts) Hachette Children's Group GBR. Dist: Hachette Bk. Group.

Miner Huey, Lois. American Archaeology Uncovers the Vikings, 1 vol. 2010. (American Archaeology Ser.). (ENG.). 64p. (gr. 5-5). 34.07 *(978-0-7614-4270-7(7),* 8037f8b4-0c8b-4e94-831a-85cc50743cb4) Cavendish Square Publishing LLC.

Nardo, Don. The Vikings, 1 vol. 2010. (World History Ser.). (ENG.). 112p. (gr. 7-7). 41.53 *(978-1-4205-0316-6(2),* 4ff27f54-92a7-4acb-aa69-8ad20b4fdfa7, Lucent Pr.) Greenhaven Publishing LLC.

Newland, Sonya. The Genius of the Vikings. 2019. (Genius of the Ancients Ser.). (ENG.). 32p. (J). (gr. 4-5). pap. *(978-0-7787-6598-1(9),* 161fe44c-50f5-4f33-91ea-780eaba86221); lib. bdg. *(978-0-7787-6590-5(3),* a405f0bd-39fd-42df-a7c1-2d932baaa1f1) Crabtree Publishing Co.

Ohlin, Nancy. Vikings. Larkum, Adam, illus. 2017. (Blast Back! Ser.). (ENG.). 112p. (J). (gr. 2-5). 16.99 *(978-1-4998-0386-0(9))* Little Bee Books Inc.

Olson, Elsie. Vikings! Fierce & Fearless Conquerors. 2017. (History's Hotshots Ser.). (ENG., Illus.). 32p. (J). (gr. 3-6). lib. bdg. 32.79 *(978-1-5321-1276-8(9),* 27600, Checkerboard Library) ABDO Publishing Co.

TUV

Osborne, Mary Pope & Boyce, Natalie Pope. Vikings: A Nonfiction Companion to Magic Tree House 15 Viking Ships at Sunrise. 2015. (Magic Tree House Fact Tracker Ser.: 33). lib. bdg. 16.00 *(978-0-606-37707-2(7))* Turtleback.

—Vikings: A Nonfiction Companion to Magic Tree House #15: Viking Ships at Sunrise. Molinari, Carlo, illus. 2015. (Magic Tree House (R) Fact Tracker Ser.: 33). 128p. (J). (gr. 2-5). 6.99 *(978-0-385-38638-8(9))*, Random Hse. Bks. for Young Readers) Random Hse. Children's Bks.

Park, Louise & Love, Timothy. The Scandinavian Vikings, 1 vol. 2010. (Ancient & Medieval People Ser.). (ENG.). 32p. (gr. 5-5). 31.21 *(978-0-7614-4445-9(9),* 659468e5-be90-4a06-b3a4-4ee7a04c0078) Cavendish Square Publishing LLC.

Philip, Neil. Myths of the Vikings: Odin's Family & Other Tales of the Norse Gods. Foa, Maryclare, illus. 2018. 128p. (J). (gr. 3-7). 13.99 *(978-1-86147-860-3(7)*, Armadillo) Anness Publishing GBR. Dist: National Bk. Network.

Powell, Jillian. The Vikings, 1 vol. 2010. (Gruesome Truth About Ser.). (ENG.). 32p. (J). (gr. 5-5). lib. bdg. 29.93 *(978-1-61533-221-2(9),* 9d5c4ae6-ba81-4fea-b29d-c2c9b47a5ddc, Windmill Bks.) Rosen Publishing Group, Inc., The.

Raum, Elizabeth. What Did the Vikings Do for Me?, 1 vol. 2010. (Linking the Past & Present Ser.). (ENG., Illus.). 32p. (J). (gr. 3-6). 35.99 *(978-1-4329-3745-4(6)*, 102897); pap. 8.29 *(978-1-4329-3752-2(9)*, 102903) Capstone. (Heinemann).

Rice, Earle. The Life & Times of Erik the Red. 2008. (Biography from Ancient Civilizations Ser.). (Illus.). 48p. (J). (gr. 4-8). lib. bdg. 29.95 *(978-1-58415-701-4(1))* Mitchell Lane Pubs.

—The Life & Times of Leif Eriksson. 2008. (Biography from Ancient Civilizations Ser.). (Illus.). 43p. (J). (gr. 4-8). lib. bdg. 29.95 *(978-1-58415-702-1(X))* Mitchell Lane Pubs.

Richardson, Hazel. Life of the Ancient Vikings. 2005. (Peoples of the Ancient World Ser.). (ENG., Illus.). 32p. (J). (gr. -1-9). pap. *(978-0-7787-2074-4(8))*; lib. bdg. *(978-0-7787-2044-7(6))* Crabtree Publishing Co.

Ridley, Sarah. Life in Viking Times. 2015. (Everyday History Ser.). (Illus.). 32p. (J). 31.35 *(978-1-59920-952-4(7))* Black Rabbit Bks.

Romero, Libby. National Geographic Readers: Vikings (L2) 2018. (Readers Ser.). (Illus.). 32p. (J). (gr. 1-3). pap. 4.99 *(978-1-4263-3218-0(1))*; (ENG., lib. bdg. 14.90 *(978-1-4263-3219-7(X))* Disney Publishing Worldwide. (National Geographic Kids).

Scheff, Matt & Campbell, Dave. Minnesota Vikings, 1 vol. 2016. (NFL up Close Ser.). (ENG., Illus.). 32p. (J). (gr. 3-9). lib. bdg. 32.79 *(978-1-68078-223-3(1)*, 22049, SportsZone) ABDO Publishing Co.

Smith, A. G. BOOST Story of the Vikings Coloring Book. 2013. (Dover World History Coloring Bks.). (ENG.). 48p. (J). (gr. 3-5). pap. 5.99 *(978-0-486-49439-5(X)*, 49439X) Dover Pubns., Inc.

Steele, Philip. DKfindout! Vikings. 2018. (DK Findout! Ser.). (ENG., Illus.). 64p. (J). (gr. 1-4). pap. 10.99 *(978-1-4654-7120-8(0)*, DK Children) Dorling Kindersley Publishing, Inc.

—Hands-On History! Viking World: Learn about the Legendary Norse Raiders, with 15 Step-By-step Projects & More Than 350 Exciting Pictures. 2013. (Illus.). 64p. (J). (gr. 3-7). 12.99 *(978-1-84322-694-9(4))* Anness Publishing GBR. Dist: National Bk. Network.

Steele, Philip & Ljosland, Ragnhild. Vikings. 2018. (Illus.). 64p. (J). *(978-1-5444-1093-7(X))* Dorling Kindersley Publishing, Inc.

Steele, Philip & MacDonald, Fiona. The Vikings & the Celts: Ancient Warriors & Raiders. 2010. (Illus.). 128p. (J). (gr. -1-12). pap. 17.99 *(978-1-84476-878-3(3))* Anness Publishing GBR. Dist: National Bk. Network.

Strain Trueit, Trudi. The Vikings, 1 vol. 2012. (Technology of the Ancients Ser.). (ENG.). 64p. (gr. 6-6). 35.50 *(978-1-60870-769-0(5),* bfde65a9-f39b-43d0-98ff-f355d9f71ac8) Cavendish Square Publishing LLC.

Taylor, Dereen. Vikings, 1 vol. 2009. (Flashback History Ser.). (ENG., Illus.). 48p. (gr. 4-4). (J). pap. 12.75 *(978-1-4358-5502-1(7),* 1c00e04f-6dec-412a-854f-f7fdc3d0be48, PowerKids Pr.); (YA). 32.93 *(978-1-4358-5501-4(9),* 4a6b1ec0-5841-40fc-96b5-a9b4cb2ce256) Rosen Publishing Group, Inc., The.

Terp, Gail. Vikings. 2019. (History's Warriors Ser.). (ENG., Illus.). 32p. (J). (gr. 4-6). pap. 9.99 *(978-1-64466-045-4(8)*, 12769); lib. bdg. *(978-1-68072-854-5(7)*, 12768) Black Rabbit Bks. (Bolt).

Thompson, Avril & Phipps, Liza. History Showtime: Vikings. 2017. (History Showtime Ser.). (ENG., Illus.). 32p. (J). (gr. 2-4). pap. 11.99 *(978-1-4451-1487-3(9)*, Franklin Watts) Hachette Children's Group GBR. Dist: Hachette Bk. Group.

Thompson, Ben. Guts & Glory: the Vikings. 2016. (Guts & Glory Ser.: 2). (ENG., Illus.). 320p. (J). (gr. 3-7). pap. 8.99 *(978-0-316-32057-3(9))* Little, Brown Bks. for Young Readers.

Toth, Henrietta. Viking Explorers, 1 vol. 2016. (Spotlight on Explorers & Colonization Ser.). (ENG., Illus.). 48p. (J). (gr. 6-6). pap. 12.75 *(978-1-4777-8832-5(8),* 99e43bde-33d5-4e4a-91be-d92fdad36ed7) Rosen Publishing Group, Inc., The.

Troupe, Thomas Kingsley. Your Life As an Explorer on a Viking Ship. Ebbeler, Jeffrey, illus. 2012. (Way It Was Ser.). (ENG.). 32p. (J). (gr. 2-5). lib. bdg. 27.32 *(978-1-4048-7160-1(8),* 117155, Picture Window Bks.) Capstone.

—Your Life As an Explorer on a Viking Ship. Ebbeler, Jeffrey, illus. 2012. (Way It Was Ser.). (ENG.). 32p. (J). (gr. 2-5). pap. 8.95 *(978-1-4048-7252-3(3)*, 118196, Picture Window Bks.) Capstone.

Vallepur, Shalini. People Did What in the Viking Age? 2020. (Illus.). 32p. (J). *(978-0-7787-7422-8(8))* Crabtree Publishing Co.

The Vikings. 2014. (Ladybird Histories Ser.). (ENG., Illus.). 64p. (J). (gr. 2-4). 13.99 *(978-0-7232-8841-1(0))* Penguin Bks., Ltd. GBR. Dist: Independent Pubs. Group.

Vonne, Mira. Gross Facts about Vikings. 2017. (Gross History Ser.). (ENG., Illus.). 32p. (J). (gr. 3-9). lib. bdg. 27.32 *(978-1-5157-4158-9(3)*, 133958, Capstone Pr.) Capstone.

West, David. The Vikings, 1 vol. 2016. (Discovering Ancient Civilizations Ser.). (ENG.). 32p. (gr. 3-3). pap. 11.50 *(978-1-4824-5047-7(X),* 4e465ccb-bf4a-4c27-832d-2bb0f3ce8b5e) Stevens, Gareth Publishing LLLP.

Williams, Colleen Madonna Flood. My Adventure with Vikings. 2009. (ENG.). 44p. (J). 8.99 *(978-1-59092-474-7(6))* Blue Forge Pr.

Wingate, Philippa & Millard, Anne. Viking World. Wood, Gerald, illus. 2004. (Illustrated World History Ser.). 64p. (J). (gr. 6). lib. bdg. 19.95 *(978-1-58086-628-6(X)*, Usborne) EDC Publishing.

Woolf, Alex. Meet the Vikings. 2014. (Encounters with the Past Ser.). 32p. (J). (gr. 3-6). pap. 63.00 *(978-1-4824-0900-0(3))* Stevens, Gareth Publishing LLLP.

Yasuda, Anita. Explore Norse Myths! With 25 Great Projects. Stone, Bryan, illus. 2015. (Explore Your World Ser.). (ENG.). 96p. (J). (gr. 1-5). 19.95 *(978-1-61930-316-4(7),* e49fb609-39c4-4183-a5a6-eb96d5c1a30f) Nomad Pr.

Yomtov, Nel. Vikings: Scandinavia's Ferocious Sea Raiders. dB, Silvio, illus. 2019. (Graphic History: Warriors Ser.). (ENG.). 32p. (J). (gr. 3-9). pap. 7.95 *(978-1-5435-5931-6(X)*, 139909); lib. bdg. 31.32 *(978-1-5435-5506-6(3)*, 139378) Capstone.

VIKINGS—FICTION

Aptekar, Devan. How to Train Your Dragon - Befriending a Foe. 2010. (How to Train Your Dragon Ser.). 24p. (J). (gr. -1-2). pap. 3.99 *(978-0-06-156735-3(3)*, HarperFestival) HarperCollins Pubs.

Auerbach, Adam. The Three Vikings. Auerbach, Adam, illus. 2019. (ENG., Illus.). 40p. (J). 21.99 *(978-1-62779-601-9(0)*, 900156502, Holt, Henry & Co. Bks. For Young Readers) Holt, Henry & Co.

Batson, Wayne Thomas. Isle of Fire, 1 vol. 2009. (ENG.). 352p. (J). pap. 9.99 *(978-1-4003-1512-3(3)*, Tommy Nelson) Nelson, Thomas Inc.

Bowen, Carl. Thor & Loki. Smith, Tod & Lokus, Rex, illus. 2016. (Norse Myths: a Viking Graphic Novel Ser.). (ENG.). 56p. (J). (gr. 4-8). lib. bdg. 27.99 *(978-1-4965-3490-3(5)*, 132602, Stone Arch Bks.) Capstone.

Bowen, Carl, et al. Norse Myths: a Viking Graphic Novel, 4 vols. Smith, Tod & Garcia, Eduardo, illus. 2016. (Norse Myths: a Viking Graphic Novel Ser.). (ENG.). 56p. (J). (gr. 4-8). 114.60 *(978-1-4965-3519-1(7)*, 25015, Stone Arch Bks.) Capstone.

Boyd, David. Beware the Vikings. Rooth, Mike, illus. 2007. 48p. (J). lib. bdg. 23.08 *(978-1-4242-1624-6(9))* Fitzgerald Bks.

Chabert, Jack. Poptropica: Book 1: Mystery of the Map, Bk. 1. 2016. (Poptropica Ser.). (ENG., Illus.). 112p. (J). (gr. 1-4). 9.95 *(978-1-4197-2067-3(8)*, 1140201, Amulet Bks.) Abrams, Inc.

Ciddor, Anna. Wolfspell: Viking Magic Book 2. 2007. (Viking Magic Ser.). (ENG., Illus.). 192p. (J). (gr. 4-7). pap. 12.99 *(978-1-74114-013-2(7))* Allen & Unwin AUS. Dist: Independent Pubs. Group.

Cowell, Cressida. A Hero's Guide to Deadly Dragons, Bk. 6. 2010. (ENG., Illus.). 272p. (J). *(978-0-340-99913-4(6),* Hodder Children's Books) Hachette Children's Group GBR. Dist: Hachette Bk. Group.

—How to Be a Pirate. 2010. (ENG., Illus.). 240p. (J). *(978-0-340-99908-0(X)*, Hodder Children's Books) Hachette Children's Group GBR. Dist: Hachette Bk. Group.

—How to Be a Viking. 2014. (How to Train Your Dragon Ser.). (ENG.). 32p. (J). (gr. -1-3). 17.99 *(978-0-316-28635-0(4))* Little, Brown Bks. for Young Readers.

—How to Betray a Dragon's Hero. 2014. (How to Train Your Dragon Ser.: 11). (J). lib. bdg. 18.45 *(978-0-606-35943-6(5))* Turtleback.

—How to Break a Dragon's Heart, Bk. 8. 2010. (ENG., Illus.). 320p. (J). *(978-0-340-99692-8(7)*, Hodder Children's Books) Hachette Children's Group GBR. Dist: Hachette Bk. Group.

—How to Break a Dragon's Heart. 2012. (How to Train Your Dragon Ser.: 8). (J). lib. bdg. 18.45 *(978-0-606-26163-0(X))* Turtleback.

—How to Cheat a Dragon's Curse, Bk. 4. 2010. (ENG., Illus.). 256p. (J). *(978-0-340-99910-3(1)*, Hodder Children's Books) Hachette Children's Group GBR. Dist: Hachette Bk. Group.

—How to Fight a Dragon's Fury. 2016. (How to Train Your Dragon Ser.: 12). (J). lib. bdg. 18.40 *(978-0-606-39195-5(9))* Turtleback.

—How to Seize a Dragon's Jewel. 2014. (How to Train Your Dragon Ser.: 10). (J). lib. bdg. 18.45 *(978-0-606-35307-6(0))* Turtleback.

—How to Steal a Dragon's Sword. 2013. (How to Train Your Dragon Ser.: 9). (J). lib. bdg. 18.45 *(978-0-606-31742-9(2))* Turtleback.

—How to Train Your Dragon. 2010. (ENG., Illus.). (J). 240p. *(978-0-340-99907-3(1))*; 240p. pap. *(978-0-340-99716-1(8))*;No. 1. 304p. *(978-0-340-99717-8(6))* Hachette Children's Group GBR. (Hodder Children's Books). Dist: Hachette Bk. Group.

—How to Train Your Dragon. (How to Train Your Dragon Ser.: 1). (ENG., Illus.). (J). (gr. 3-7). 2004. 224p. 14.99 *(978-0-316-73737-1(2))*Bk. 1. 2010. 256p. pap. 8.99 *(978-0-316-08527-4(8))* Little, Brown Bks. for Young Readers.

—A How to Train Your Dragon: a Hero's Guide to Deadly Dragons. 2010. (How to Train Your Dragon Ser.: 6). (ENG., Illus.). 272p. (J). (gr. 3-7). pap. 8.99 *(978-0-316-08532-8(4))* Little, Brown Bks. for Young Readers.

—How to Train Your Dragon: How to Be a Pirate. 2010. (How to Train Your Dragon Ser.: 2). (ENG.). 240p. (J). (gr. 3-7). pap. 8.99 *(978-0-316-08528-1(6))* Little, Brown Bks. for Young Readers.

—How to Train Your Dragon: How to Betray a Dragon's Hero. 2014. (How to Train Your Dragon Ser.: 11). (ENG., Illus.). 416p. (J). (gr. 3-7). pap. 8.99 *(978-0-316-24411-4(2))* Little, Brown Bks. for Young Readers.

—How to Train Your Dragon: How to Cheat a Dragon's Curse. 2010. (How to Train Your Dragon Ser.: 4). (ENG.). 272p. (J). (gr. 3-7). pap. 8.99 *(978-0-316-08530-4(8))* Little, Brown Bks. for Young Readers.

—How to Train Your Dragon: How to Fight a Dragon's Fury. 2016. (How to Train Your Dragon Ser.: 12). (ENG., Illus.). 496p. (J). (gr. 3-7). pap. 8.99 *(978-0-316-36516-1(5))* Little, Brown Bks. for Young Readers.

—How to Train Your Dragon: How to Ride a Dragon's Storm. (How to Train Your Dragon Ser.: 7). (ENG., (J). (gr. 3-7). 2011. Illus.). 288p. pap. 8.99 *(978-0-316-07909-9(X))* 2010. 272p. 14.99 *(978-0-316-07916-7(2))* Little, Brown Bks. for Young Readers.

—How to Train Your Dragon: How to Ride a Dragon's Storm: Book 7, Bk. 7. 2010. (ENG., Illus.). 288p. (J). *(978-0-340-99912-7(8)*, Hodder Children's Books) Hachette Children's Group GBR. Dist: Hachette Bk. Group.

—How to Train Your Dragon: How to Seize a Dragon's Jewel. 2014. (How to Train Your Dragon Ser.: 10). (ENG., Illus.). 416p. (J). (gr. 3-7). pap. 8.99 *(978-0-316-24408-4(2))* Little, Brown Bks. for Young Readers.

—How to Train Your Dragon: How to Speak Dragonese. 2010. (How to Train Your Dragon Ser.: 3). (ENG., Illus.). 256p. (J). (gr. 3-7). pap. 8.99 *(978-0-316-08529-8(4))* Little, Brown Bks. for Young Readers.

—How to Train Your Dragon: How to Speak Dragonese: Book 3, Bk. 3. 2010. (ENG., Illus.). 256p. (J). *(978-0-340-99909-7(8)*, Hodder Children's Books) Hachette Children's Group GBR. Dist: Hachette Bk. Group.

—How to Train Your Dragon: How to Steal a Dragon's Sword. 2013. (How to Train Your Dragon Ser.: 9). (ENG.). 384p. (J). (gr. 3-7). pap. 8.99 *(978-0-316-20570-2(2))* Little, Brown Bks. for Young Readers.

—How to Train Your Dragon: How to Twist a Dragon's Tale, Bk. 5. 2010. (How to Train Your Dragon Ser.: 5). (ENG.). 272p. (J). (gr. 3-7). pap. 8.99 *(978-0-316-08531-1(6))* Little, Brown Bks. for Young Readers.

—How to Train Your Dragon Special Edition: With Brand New Short Stories! 2014. (How to Train Your Dragon Ser.: 1). (ENG., Illus.). 432p. (J). (gr. 3-7). pap. 10.00 *(978-0-316-40747-2(X))* Little, Brown Bks. for Young Readers.

—How to Train Your Dragon: the Complete Series: Paperback Gift Set. 2017. (How to Train Your Dragon Ser.). (ENG.). 3328p. (J). (gr. 3-7). pap. 108.00 *(978-0-316-34700-6(0))* Little, Brown Bks. for Young Readers.

—How to Twist a Dragon's Tale, Bk. 5. 2010. (ENG., Illus.). 272p. (J). *(978-0-340-99911-0(X)*, Hodder Children's Books) Hachette Children's Group GBR. Dist: Hachette Bk. Group.

Cross, Gillian. Brother Aelred's Feet: Band 15/Emerald (Collins Big Cat) Stevens, Tim, illus. 2007. (Collins Big Cat Ser.). (ENG.). 40p. (J). (gr. 3-4). pap. 11.99 *(978-0-00-723093-8(1))* HarperCollins Pubs. Ltd. GBR. Dist: Independent Pubs. Group.

Dahl, Lisa. Gorm the Viking: The Lost Voyage. 2013. 282p. (gr. 4-6). 26.95 *(978-1-4759-5809-6(9))*; pap. 16.95 *(978-1-4759-5807-2(2))* iUniverse, Inc.

Dahl, Michael. The Viking Claw. 2011. (Finnegan Zwake Ser.: 4). (ENG.). 192p. (YA). (gr. 7). pap. 9.99 *(978-1-4424-3101-0(6)*, Simon Pulse) Simon Pulse.

David, Erica. How to Track a Dragon. 2016. (Simon & Schuster Ready-To-Read Level 2 Ser.). lib. bdg. 13.55 *(978-0-606-38992-1(X))* Turtleback.

Davis, Mike. Land of the Lost Mammoths: A Science Adventure. 2003. (Illus.). 174p. (J). 15.95 *(978-0-9747078-0-8(5))* Perceval Pr.

Dinsdale, Christopher. Stolen Away. 2006. (ENG., Illus.). 240p. (J). per. 10.95 *(978-1-894917-20-9(0)*, Napoleon & Co.) Dundurn Pr. CAN. Dist: Publishers Group West (PGW).

Dixon, Sean. The Winter Drey. 2009. (Trilogy of the Tree Ser.: Pt. 2). (ENG., Illus.). 200p. (J). (gr. 4-9). pap. *(978-1-55470-190-2(2))* Me to We.

Elkerton, Andy. Viking Adventures: Bitra & the Witch. 2022. (Viking Adventures Ser.). (ENG., Illus.). 32p. (J). (gr. 1-3). pap. 9.99 *(978-1-4451-5841-9(8)*, Franklin Watts) Hachette Children's Group GBR. Dist: Hachette Bk. Group.

—Viking Adventures: Oolaf & the Golden Book. 2022. (Viking Adventures Ser.). (ENG., Illus.). 32p. (J). (gr. 1-3). pap. 9.99 *(978-1-4451-5842-6(6)*, Franklin Watts) Hachette Children's Group GBR. Dist: Hachette Bk. Group.

—Viking Adventures: the World to the West. 2022. (Viking Adventures Ser.). (ENG., Illus.). 32p. (J). (gr. 1-3). pap. 9.99 *(978-1-4451-5839-6(6)*, Franklin Watts) Hachette Children's Group GBR. Dist: Hachette Bk. Group.

Erich, James. Seidman [Library Edition]. 2012. 210p. pap. 14.99 *(978-1-62380-904-1(5)*, Harmony Ink Pr.) Dreamspinner Pr.

Farmer, Nancy. The Islands of the Blessed. (ENG., Illus.). 496p. (YA). (gr. 7). 2012. pap. 13.99 *(978-1-4169-0738-1(6)*, Atheneum Bks. for Young Readers) 2009. 18.99 *(978-1-4169-0737-4(8)*, Atheneum/Richard Jackson Bks.) Simon & Schuster Children's Publishing.

—The Islands of the Blessed. l.t. ed. 2010. (Sequel to the Land of the Silver Apples Ser.). (ENG.). 607p. (J). 23.95 *(978-1-4104-2253-8(4))* Thorndike Pr.

—The Sea of Trolls. (ENG., Illus.). 480p. 2006. (YA). (gr. 9-9). reprint ed. pap. 13.99 *(978-0-689-86746-0(8))*1. 2004. (J). (gr. 5-8). 21.99 *(978-0-689-86744-6(1))* Simon & Schuster Children's Publishing. (Atheneum Bks. for Young Readers).

French, Allen. The Story of Rolf: A Viking Adventure. 2005. (Dover Children's Classics Ser.). (ENG.). 154p. (J). (gr. 3-6). per. 9.95 *(978-0-486-44133-7(4)*, 441334) Dover Pubns., Inc.

—The Story of Rolf & the Viking Bow. 2008. 148p. (gr. 7-12). pap. 8.15 *(978-1-60459-522-2(1))* Wilder Pubns., Corp.

Furman, Simon. Dragons: Defenders of Berk, the Endless Night Vol. 1: Defenders of Berk. 2016. (FBI Profiler Novel Ser.: 1). (Illus.). 64p. (J). (gr. 3-7). pap. 6.99 *(978-1-78276-214-0(0))* Titan Bks. Ltd. GBR. Dist: Penguin Random Hse. LLC.

—Dragons Riders of Berk - Volume 1: Dragons down & Dangers of the Deep, Vol. 1. 2016. (Dragons: Riders of Berk Ser.: 1). (Illus.). 64p. (J). (gr. 3-7). pap. 12.99 *(978-1-78276-696-4(0))* Titan Bks. Ltd. GBR. Dist: Penguin Random Hse. LLC.

—Dragons Riders of Berk: Myths & Mysteries. Nasif, Iwan, illus. 2016. (Dragons: Riders of Berk Ser.: 3). (ENG.). 112p. (J). (gr. 1-4). pap. 12.99 *(978-1-78585-177-3(2))* Titan Bks. Ltd. GBR. Dist: Penguin Random Hse. LLC.

—Dragons Riders of Berk: the Stowaway Vol.4. 2015. (Riders of Berk Ser.). (ENG., Illus.). 64p. (J). (gr. 3-7). pap. 6.99 *(978-1-78276-079-5(2))* Titan Bks. Ltd. GBR. Dist: Penguin Random Hse. LLC.

Furman, Simon & Nazif, Iwan. Dragons - Riders of Berk: Tales from Berk, Vol. 2. 2016. (Dragons: Riders of Berk Ser.: 2). (Illus.). 112p. (J). (gr. 3-7). pap. 12.99 *(978-1-78585-176-6(4))* Titan Bks. Ltd. GBR. Dist: Penguin Random Hse. LLC.

Hall, Jennie. The Viking Tales. 2008. 88p. pap. 8.15 *(978-1-60459-529-1(9))* Wilder Pubns., Corp.

Hamme, Van. Giants. Rosinski, illus. 2013. (Thorgal Ser.: 14). 48p. pap. 11.95 *(978-1-84918-156-3(X))* CineBook GBR. Dist: National Bk. Network.

Hapka, Catherine, pseud. How to Train Your Dragon: Meet the Dragons. Grosvenor, Charles & Gerard, Justin, illus. 2010. (I Can Read Book 1 Ser.). 32p. (J). (gr. k-3). pap. 3.99 *(978-0-06-156733-9(7))* HarperCollins Pubs.

Haugaard, Erik Christian. Hakon of Rogen's Saga. Dillon, Leo & Dillon, Diane, illus. 2013. 144p. pap. 11.95 *(978-0-8166-8127-3(9))* Univ. of Minnesota Pr.

Henighan, Tom. Viking Terror. 2006. (ENG.). 180p. (J). pap. 12.99 *(978-1-55002-605-4(4))* Dundurn Pr. CAN. Dist: Publishers Group West (PGW).

Holliday, Susan. Kingsholt. 2015. (ENG., Illus.). 120p. (J). (gr. -1-12). pap. 11.95 *(978-1-78279-976-4(1)*, Our Street Bks.) Hunt, John Publishing Ltd. GBR. Dist: National Bk. Network.

Hulme-Cross, Benjamin. The Viking's Revenge. Rinaldi, Angelo, illus. 2015. (Warrior Heroes Ser.). (ENG.). 160p. (J). (gr. 6-6). *(978-0-7787-1767-6(4))* Crabtree Publishing Co.

Jacobsen, Annie. Ivar, the Short, but Brave Viking. Hanson, Susan Jo, illus. 2007. (J). lib. bdg. 16.95 *(978-0-9778276-1-9(5))* Pickled Herring Pr.

Johnson, Lois Walfrid. The Raider's Promise. 2006. (Viking Quest Ser.: 5). (ENG., Illus.). 304p. (J). (gr. 3-3). per. 10.99 *(978-0-8024-3116-5(X))* Moody Pubs.

Johnson, Vargie. Eric the Red the Fearless: What Made Them Famous? 2006. (J). per. 15.00 *(978-1-931195-94-2(3))* KiwE Publishing, Ltd.

Jones, Cath. The Magic Helmet. Gray, Dean, illus. 2021. (Early Bird Readers — Gold (Early Bird Stories (tm)) Ser.). (ENG.). 32p. (J). (gr. k-3). 30.65 *(978-1-5415-9009-0(0),* 2cb67c0e-c1b9-458b-ab34-b7f29347e3a4, Lerner Pubns.) Lerner Publishing Group.

Jorgensen, Norman. The Last Viking. Foley, James, illus. 2018. 32p. (J). (gr. -1-k). 12.95 *(978-1-925163-15-5(6))* Fremantle Pr. AUS. Dist: Independent Pubs. Group.

—Last Viking Returns. Foley, James, illus. 2018. (Last Viking Ser.). 32p. (J). (gr. -1-k). 12.95 *(978-1-925163-16-2(4))* Fremantle Pr. AUS. Dist: Independent Pubs. Group.

Judge, Chris & Wickham, Mark. Brian & the Vikings. 2014. (ENG., Illus.). 32p. (J). pap. 14.00 *(978-1-84717-687-5(9))* O'Brien Pr., Ltd., The IRL. Dist: Casemate Pubs. & Bk. Distributors, LLC.

Kurd, Tariq. Gordon the Goblin in Oh My! Is That a Pork Pie? Robertson, Laura, illus. 2012. 36p. pap. *(978-1-907762-10-9(8))* Malt Publishing.

Langrish, Katherine. Troll Blood. 2008. (ENG., Illus.). 352p. (J). (gr. 5-8). 16.99 *(978-0-06-111674-2(2)*, HarperCollins) HarperCollins Pubs.

—Troll Blood. Stevens, Tim & Wyatt, David, illus. 2008. 352p. (YA). (gr. 5-8). lib. bdg. 17.89 *(978-0-06-111675-9(0)*, Eos) HarperCollins Pubs.

—Troll Fell. 2004. (Illus.). 272p. (J). (gr. 5-18). (ENG.). 16.99 *(978-0-06-058304-0(5))*; lib. bdg. 16.89 *(978-0-06-058305-7(3))* HarperCollins Pubs.

—Troll Mill. 2008. (ENG., Illus.). 336p. (YA). (gr. 7). pap. 7.99 *(978-0-06-058309-5(6)*, Eos) HarperCollins Pubs.

Leake, Jessica. Beyond a Darkened Shore. 2018. (ENG.). 448p. (YA). (gr. 9). 17.99 *(978-0-06-266626-0(6)*, HarperTeen) HarperCollins Pubs.

Leighton-Porter, Wendy. The Shadow of the Norman Arrow. 2013. 270p. pap. *(978-1-909411-07-4(8))* Mauve Square Publishing.

MacPhail, David. Thorfinn & the Disgusting Feast, 32 vols. Morgan, Richard, illus. 2016. (Thorfinn the Nicest Viking Ser.). 136p. (J). pap. 8.95 *(978-1-78250-231-9(9)*, Kelpies) Floris Bks. GBR. Dist: Consortium Bk. Sales & Distribution.

—Thorfinn the Nicest Viking & the Rotten Scots, 32 vols. Morgan, Richard, illus. 2016. (Thorfinn the Nicest Viking Ser.). 136p. (J). pap. 8.95 *(978-1-78250-229-6(7)*, Kelpies) Floris Bks. GBR. Dist: Consortium Bk. Sales & Distribution.

Messner, Kate. Journey Through Ash & Smoke. 2017. (Ranger in Time Ser.: 5). lib. bdg. 16.00 *(978-0-606-39723-0(X))* Turtleback.

Osborne, Mary Pope. Barcos Vikingos Al Amanecer. Brovelli, Marcela, tr. from ENG. Murdocca, Sal, illus. 2007. (Casa del Arbol Ser.: 15). (SPA.). 73p. (J). per. 6.99 *(978-1-933032-21-4(9))* Lectorum Pubns., Inc.

—Viking Ships at Sunrise. unabr. ed. 2004. (Magic Tree House Ser.: No. 15). 71p. (J). (gr. k-3). pap. 17.00 incl. audio *(978-0-8072-0784-0(5)*, LFTR 243 SP, Listening Library) Random Hse. Audio Publishing Group.

Pendergrass, Daphne. Riders of Berk: A Fiery Discovery. 2015. lib. bdg. 13.55 *(978-0-606-36311-2(4))* Turtleback.

Phillips, Dee. Viking, 1 vol., Bk. 8. 2014. (Yesterday's Voices Ser.). (ENG.). 48p. (YA). (gr. 5-12). pap. 10.75 *(978-1-62250-910-2(2))* Saddleback Educational Publishing, Inc.

—Viking: The Story of a Raider. 2015. (Yesterday's Voices Ser.). (YA). lib. bdg. 19.60 *(978-0-606-36676-2(8))* Turtleback.

Rayner, Keith. Torvig's Gift. 2006. 208p. pap. 19.95 *(978-1-4241-1518-1(3))* America Star Bks.

Riel, Jörn & Chodzin, Sherab. The Raiders Vol. 2: The Inuk Quartet. Cann, Helen, illus. 2013. 128p. (J). (gr. 4-6). pap. 9.99 *(978-1-84686-744-6(4))* Barefoot Bks., Inc.

Scieszka, Jon. Viking It & Liking It. McCauley, Adam, illus. 2004. (Time Warp Trio Ser.: No. 12). 73p. (gr. 2-6). 15.00 *(978-0-7569-2589-5(4))* Perfection Learning Corp.

—Viking It & Liking It. 2004. (Time Warp Trio Ser.: 12). 16.00 *(978-1-4176-3613-6(0))* Turtleback.

—Viking It & Liking It #12. McCauley, Adam, illus. 2004. (Time Warp Trio Ser.: 12). 96p. (J). (gr. 2-4). pap. 5.99 *(978-0-14-240002-9(5)*, Puffin Books) Penguin Young Readers Group.

Simon, Francesca. Hack & Whack. Cotterill, Charlotte, illus. 2017. (ENG.). 32p. (gr. -1-k). 16.95 *(978-0-571-32871-0(7)*, Faber & Faber Children's Bks.) Faber & Faber, Inc.

Speregen, Debra Newberger. How to Train Your Dragon: A Pocket Full of Dreams. Phillipson, Andrew & Shimabukuro, Denise, illus. 2010. (Pocket Full of Dreams Ser.). (J). 9.99 *(978-1-941341-79-7(9))* DreamWorks Animation Pr.

Stilton, Geronimo. The Helmet Holdup (Geronimo Stilton Micekings #6) 2017. (Geronimo Stilton Micekings Ser.: 6). (ENG., Illus.). 128p. (J). (gr. 2-5). pap. 7.99 *(978-1-338-15921-9(6)*, Scholastic Paperbacks) Scholastic, Inc.

Stilton, Gerónimo & Clement, Emily. Attack of the Dragons. Facciotto, Giuseppe & Costa, Alessandro, illus. 2016. 115p. (J). *(978-0-605-93525-9(4))* Scholastic, Inc.

Stilton, Gerónimo & Schaffer, Andrea. The Helmet Holdup. Facciotto, Giuseppe & Costa, Alessandro, illus. 2017. 112p. (J). *(978-1-5379-5611-4(6))* Scholastic, Inc.

Stroud, Jonathan. Heroes of the Valley. 2009. (JPN., Illus.). 587p. (YA). *(978-4-652-07954-6(0))* Fukuinkan Shoten.

Sutcliff, Rosemary. Sword Song. 2005. (ENG., Illus.). 288p. (YA). (gr. 7-12). per. 13.99 *(978-0-374-46984-9(9)*, 900028277, Farrar, Straus & Giroux (BYR)) Farrar, Straus & Giroux.

Testa, Maggie. Gift of the Night Fury. 2014. lib. bdg. 13.55 *(978-0-606-36110-1(3))* Turtleback.

Titan Comics, Titan. Dragons Riders of Berk: the Legend of Ragnarok, Vol. 5. 2015. (Riders of Berk Ser.). (ENG., Illus.). 64p. (J). (gr. 3-7). pap. 6.99 *(978-1-78276-080-1(6))* Titan Bks. Ltd. GBR. Dist: Penguin Random Hse. LLC.

—Dragons Riders of Berk: Underworld, Vol. 6. 2015. (Riders of Berk Ser.). (ENG., Illus.). 64p. (J). (gr. 3-7). pap. 6.99 *(978-1-78276-081-8(4))* Titan Bks. Ltd. GBR. Dist: Penguin Random Hse. LLC.

Van Hamme, Jean. Beyond the Shadows. Rosinski, Grzegorz, illus. 2008. (Thorgal Ser.: 3). 96p. pap. 19.95 *(978-1-905460-45-8(7))* CineBook GBR. Dist: National Bk. Network.

—The Brand of the Exiles. Rosinski, Grzegorz, illus. 2013. (Thorgal Ser.: 12). 48p. (J). (gr. 7-12). pap. 11.95 *(978-1-84918-136-5(5))* CineBook GBR. Dist: National Bk. Network.

—The Cage, Vol. 15. Rosinski, Grzegorz, illus. 2014. (Thorgal Ser.: 15). 48p. pap. 11.95 *(978-1-84918-186-0(1))* CineBook GBR. Dist: National Bk. Network.

—Child of the Stars. Rosinski, Adolf, illus. 2007. (Thorgal Ser.: 1). 96p. per. 19.95 *(978-1-905460-23-6(6))* CineBook GBR. Dist: National Bk. Network.

—Ogotai's Crown. Rosinski, Grzegorz, illus. 2013. (Thorgal Ser.: 13). 48p. (J). (gr. -1-12). pap. 11.95 *(978-1-84918-142-6(X))* CineBook GBR. Dist: National Bk. Network.

van Hamme, Jean. Thorgal - City of the Lost God, Vol. 6. Rosinski, Grzegorz, illus. 2009. (Thorgal Ser.: 6). 96p. pap. 19.95 *(978-1-84918-001-6(6))* CineBook GBR. Dist: National Bk. Network.

Van Hamme, Jean. The Three Elders of Aran. Rosinski, illus. 2007. (Thorgal Ser.: 2). 96p. (J). (gr. 4-7). pap. 19.95 *(978-1-905460-31-1(7))* CineBook GBR. Dist: National Bk. Network.

Viking Sagas 9 Book Set. 2013. *(978-1-909302-99-0(6))* Abela Publishing.

Wilson, Diane Lee. Raven Speak. 2011. (ENG.). 256p. (YA). (gr. 7). pap. 11.99 *(978-1-4169-8654-6(5)*, McElderry, Margaret K. Bks.) McElderry, Margaret K. Bks.

VILLA, PANCHO, 1878-1923

Marcovitz, Hal. Pancho Villa. 2003. (Great Hispanic Heritage Ser.). (ENG., Illus.). 112p. (gr. 6-12). 30.00 *(978-0-7910-7257-8(6)*, P113774, Facts On File) Infobase Holdings, Inc.

VILLAGES

Barber, Nicola. Village Homes. 2007. (Homes Around the World Ser.). (ENG., Illus.). 32p. (J). (gr. 3-7). pap. *(978-0-7787-3558-8(3))*; lib. bdg. *(978-0-7787-3546-5(X))* Crabtree Publishing Co.

Freedman, Jeri. Historical Villages, 1 vol., 1. 2015. (Role-Playing for Fun & Profit Ser.). (ENG.). 48p. (J). (gr. 5-5). pap. 12.75 *(978-1-4994-3724-9(2)*, e6b64735-104e-4f02-bc65-33b10fee838f, Rosen Central) Rosen Publishing Group, Inc., The.

Gillis, Jennifer Blizin. Restored Villages. 2007. (Field Trips Ser.). (Illus.). 24p. (J). (gr. 2-5). lib. bdg. 27.07 *(978-1-60044-563-7(2))* Rourke Educational Media.

Huebsch, Dave. Village Assignment: True Stories of Humor, Adventure, & Drama in Guatemala's Highland Villages. 2004. (Illus.). 268p. per. 16.95 *(978-0-9741734-0-5(1))* Highlight Publishing.

Kalman, Bobbie. My Community Long Ago. 2010. (My World Ser.). (ENG.). 24p. (J). (gr. k-3). *(978-0-7787-9517-9(9))*; pap. *(978-0-7787-9542-1(X))* Crabtree Publishing Co.

Marsico, Katie. What's It Like to Live Here? Fishing Village. 2014. (Community Connections: What's It Like to Live Here? Ser.). (ENG., Illus.). 24p. (J). (gr. 2-5). 29.21 *(978-1-62431-565-7(8)*, 203248) Cherry Lake Publishing.

McDowell, Pamela. Fishing Town. 2015. (Illus.). 24p. (J). pap. *(978-1-4896-3606-5(4))* Weigl Pubs., Inc.

Padrino, Mercedes. Feudalism & Village Life in the Middle Ages, 1 vol. 2005. (World Almanac(r) Library of the Middle Ages Ser.). (ENG., Illus.). 48p. (gr. 5-8). lib. bdg. 33.67 *(978-0-8368-5894-5(8)*, a1874a76-84a9-4b6f-9bee-3a555d439846, Gareth Stevens Secondary Library) Stevens, Gareth Publishing LLLP.

Popper, Garry & Volke, Gordon. Big World Activity Sticker Book. Johnson, Andi, illus. 2004. 16p. 6.00 *(978-1-84161-082-5(8))* Ravette Publishing, Ltd. GBR. Dist: Parkwest Pubns., Inc.

Schomp, Virginia. The Countryside, 1 vol. 2011. (Life in Victorian England Ser.). (ENG.). 80p. (gr. 6-6). 36.93 *(978-1-60870-030-1(5)*, 5b990116-67f2-425a-b48c-d9de159facf7) Cavendish Square Publishing LLC.

Watson, Danielle. The Countryside in Medieval Europe, 1 vol. 2016. (Life in Medieval Europe Ser.). (ENG., Illus.). 80p. (gr. 6-6). 37.36 *(978-1-5026-1882-5(6)*, 61b54de7-dda0-4554-ba12-8ad1bdc0c6d9) Cavendish Square Publishing LLC.

VILLAGES—FICTION

Accord Publishing, Accord. The Twelve Days of Christmas. Fang, Jade, illus. 2011. (ENG.). 26p. (J). 17.99 *(978-1-4494-0361-4(1))* Andrews McMeel Publishing.

Aine, Mhari. The Little Children & the Fairies. 2008. 56p. pap. *(978-1-84748-375-1(5))* Athena Pr.

Aisha. Parsley, Sage, Rosemary & Thyme. 2012. 24p. 24.95 *(978-1-4626-5122-1(4))* America Star Bks.

Alcott, Louisa. Jack & Jill: A Village Story. 2007. 372p. per. 16.45 *(978-1-59462-863-4(7)*, Bk. Jungle) Standard Publications, Inc.

Alexander, Brad. Antiniak: A Different Kind of Village. 2011. (ENG.). 74p. pap. 15.50 *(978-1-257-10163-4(3))* Lulu Pr., Inc.

Alfaro Sifontes, Manuel Guillermo. Alboroto en un Lugar Remoto. 2005. (Illus.). 32p. (J). *(978-1-58018-052-8(3))* Cambridge BrickHouse, Inc.

Andrade, Marcia. Gust's Maze. 2010. 142p. pap. 11.50 *(978-1-60911-101-4(X)*, Eloquent Bks.) Strategic Book Publishing & Rights Agency (SBPRA).

Atinuke. No 1 Car Spotter & the Firebird. Johnson-Cadwell, Warwick, illus. 2012. (Fiction Ser.). (ENG.). 112p. (J). pap. 4.99 *(978-1-61067-052-4(3))* Kane Miller.

Balian, Lorna. A Sweetheart for Valentine, 1 vol. 2005. (ENG., Illus.). 32p. (J). 15.95 *(978-1-932065-14-5(8))* Star Bright Bks., Inc.

Barraclough, Lindsey. Long Lankin. 2014. (ENG.). 464p. (YA). (gr. 7). pap. 9.99 *(978-0-7636-6937-9(7))* Candlewick Pr.

Bertini, Anthony. From Me to You. Bentley, Jonathan, illus. 2019. (ENG.). 32p. (J). 12.99 *(978-1-61067-903-9(2))* Kane Miller.

Blanton, Edwin. Together We Can. 2012. 24p. pap. *(978-1-105-51042-7(5))* Lulu.com.

Bloom, Janice Stitziel. A Grateful Heart under My Bed. Woodcock, Marcy, illus. 2007. 36p. (J). per. 15.99 *(978-1-934643-06-8(8))* Villager Bk. Publishing.

—Wonderfully Made under My Bed. Woodcock, Marcy, illus. 2007. 36p. (J). per. 15.99 *(978-1-934643-00-6(9))* Villager Bk. Publishing.

Bolander, Sharon Miller. Hiram's Song. 2012. 20p. pap. 24.95 *(978-1-4626-6234-0(X))* America Star Bks.

Bourbeau, Julie. The Wednesdays. Beene, Jason, illus. 2013. (ENG.). 256p. (J). (gr. 2-5). pap. 7.99 *(978-0-375-87286-0(8)*, Yearling) Random Hse. Children's Bks.

Brown, Joneé M. The Corner of Rainbow. 2nd ed. 2017. (ENG.). 132p. (J). pap. 15.99 *(978-1-56229-318-5(4)*, Christian Living Books, Inc.) Pneuma Life Publishing, Inc.

Bruno Galán, Pep. The Silly Nanny Goat. 2007. (ENG., Illus.). 36p. (J). 17.95 *(978-84-96788-86-2(5))* OQO, Editora ESP. Dist: Baker & Taylor Bks.

Buckham, Derek. The Santa Stories. 2008. 81p. pap. 34.50 *(978-1-4092-4803-3(8))* Lulu Pr., Inc.

Cash, Marie Romero. The Saint Maker's Daughter: A Christmas Dream Fulfilled. 2019. (J). *(978-1-63293-261-7(X))* Sunstone Pr.

Cavill, Ian. Elle in the Village. 2010. 56p. pap. 13.49 *(978-1-4490-7822-5(2))* AuthorHouse.

Cohen, Penny L. Tapuchim & Dvash. Polsky, Beanie, illus. 2012. 36p. pap. 24.95 *(978-1-4626-6667-6(1))* PublishAmerica, Inc.

Coombs, Kate. The Secret-Keeper. Solomon, Heather M., illus. 2006. (ENG.). 32p. (J). (gr. -1-3). 17.99 *(978-0-689-83963-4(4)*, Atheneum Bks. for Young Readers) Simon & Schuster Children's Publishing.

Corlett, William. The Tunnel Behind the Waterfall. 2010. (Magician's House Quartet Ser.: 3). (ENG.). 320p. (YA). (gr. 5-8). pap. 14.99 *(978-1-4424-1413-6(8)*, Simon Pulse) Simon Pulse.

Crabtree, Zona Mae. White Dove. 2005. (Corn Cave Ser.: 3). (ENG., Illus.). (YA). per. 8.00 *(978-0-9726826-2-6(7))* Owl Hollow Publishing.

Creech, Sharon. The Unfinished Angel. 2013. (ENG.). 160p. (J). (gr. 3-7). pap. 7.99 *(978-0-06-143097-8(8)*, HarperCollins) HarperCollins Pubs.

Crook, M. J. Village on Crooked Hill. 2008. 168p. pap. 11.99 *(978-1-4389-0486-3(X))* AuthorHouse.

Cunnane, Kelly. For You Are a Kenyan Child. Juan, Ana, illus. 2006. (ENG.). 40p. (J). (gr. -1-3). 17.99 *(978-0-689-86194-9(X)*, Atheneum Bks. for Young Readers) Simon & Schuster Children's Publishing.

Deedy, Carmen Agra. The Rooster Who Would Not Be Quiet! Yelchin, Eugene, illus. 2017. (ENG.). 48p. (J). (gr. -1-3). 18.99 *(978-0-545-72288-9(8)*, Scholastic Pr.) Scholastic, Inc.

Deshpande, Shashi. 3 Novels. 2006. 379p. *(978-0-14-333511-5(1)*, Puffin) Penguin Publishing Group.

Dickens, Frances. The Giant from Nowhere. Hudspith, Peter, illus. 2018. 56p. 21.95 *(978-1-78592-535-1(0)*, 696800) Kingsley, Jessica Pubs. GBR. Dist: Hachette UK Distribution.

Doyle, Malachy & Philpot, Graham. Jack the Giant-Killer. 2009. (Hopscotch Adventures Ser.). (Illus.). 31p. (J). (gr. 1). lib. bdg. 25.65 *(978-1-59771-184-5(5))* Sea-To-Sea Pubns.

Ernestine. Town Girl. 2011. 36p. pap. 21.99 *(978-1-4628-4649-8(1))* Xlibris Corp.

Ferchaud, Steve, illus. Glen Robbie: A Scottish Fairy Tale. 2006. (J). 22.95 *(978-1-58478-013-7(4)*, Highland Children's Pr.) Heather & Highlands Publishing.

Gabriel, Elizabeth P. & Gabriel, Pamela P. Ziccah Blows Her Horn. 2008. 24p. pap. 12.99 *(978-1-4389-2447-2(X))* AuthorHouse.

Garcia Iii, Joe. Dragon Boogers. 2010. 40p. pap. 16.99 *(978-1-4490-5639-1(3))* AuthorHouse.

Gay, Marie-Louise & Homel, David. On the Road Again, 1 vol. 2011. (Travels with My Family Ser.: 2). (ENG., Illus.). 144p. (J). (gr. 2-5). pap. 8.95 *(978-1-55498-087-1(9))* Groundwood Bks. CAN. Dist: Publishers Group West (PGW).

Gilbert, Hary. Oxford Bookworms Library: the Year of Sharing: Level 2: 700-Word Vocabulary. 3rd ed. 2008. (ENG., Illus.). 64p. 11.00 *(978-0-19-479077-2(0))* Oxford Univ. Pr., Inc.

Goodman-Schneps, Oriana. The Seventh Chime. 2009. 52p. pap. 15.99 *(978-1-4415-2748-6(6))* Xlibris Corp.

Gratton, Tessa. Strange Grace. 2018. (ENG., Illus.). 400p. (YA). (gr. 7). 18.99 *(978-1-5344-0208-9(X)*, McElderry, Margaret K. Bks.) McElderry, Margaret K. Bks.

Gregory, Steven. The Lion's Drum: A Retelling of an African Folk Tale. Obata, Claudia, illus. 2007. 32p. (J). 13.95 *(978-0-615-15540-1(5))* Words & Music.

Hahn, Molly. Under the Sneep Tree: The Wamboozling of a Village. 2009. pap. *(978-1-61623-907-7(7))* Independent Pub.

Hari & Deepti, Hari &. The Seekers. 2019. (Illus.). 40p. (J). (gr. -1-3). 18.99 *(978-1-5247-0152-9(1)*, Knopf Bks. for Young Readers) Random Hse. Children's Bks.

Harvey, Sharon M. Legend of the Pumpkin Carver. 2010. 100p. pap. 22.95 *(978-1-4327-1214-3(4))* Outskirts Pr., Inc.

Higgy, M. J. Creator's Dream. 2012. (Illus.). 16p. pap. 18.30 *(978-1-4772-3862-2(X))* AuthorHouse.

Hinwood, Christine. The Returning. 2013. (ENG.). 320p. (YA). (gr. 9-12). 24.94 *(978-0-8037-3528-6(6)*, Dial) Penguin Publishing Group.

Hiss, Jill. Peppeto's Magic Jelly Bean. 2005. 19.00 *(978-0-8059-9893-1(4))* Dorrance Publishing Co., Inc.

Hoffman, Amalia. Klezmer Bunch. 2009. (ENG.). 36p. 15.95 *(978-965-229-447-0(0))* Gefen Publishing Hse., Ltd ISR. Dist: Strauss Consultants.

Holmqvist, Carin. African Tales. 2009. (ENG.). 64p. pap. 28.70 *(978-0-557-18184-1(4))* Lulu Pr., Inc.

Hudson, Bonnie Rose. The Hidden Village. 2017. (J). *(978-1-62856-311-5(7))* BJU Pr.

Iinuma, Yuuki. Itsuwaribito, Vol. 14. 2015. (ENG.). 192p. pap. 9.99 *(978-1-4215-6525-5(0))* Viz Media.

Izzo, Donna. Frilly Lilly's Candyland Express. 2011. 24p. pap. 15.99 *(978-1-4653-6159-2(6))* Xlibris Corp.

James, Ian. Why the Sky Is Far Away: A Tale from Nigeria. 2006. (J). pap. *(978-1-4108-6172-6(4))* Benchmark Education Co.

Janelle, Nicole & Cholette, Daniel. Naby Recycles. 2012. 32p. pap. 14.60 *(978-1-105-53454-6(5))* Lulu Pr., Inc.

Johnson, Carol V. Somerset Dreams. 2011. (Illus.). 112p. pap. 32.12 *(978-1-4567-9012-7(9))* AuthorHouse.

Jones, Diana Wynne. Enchanted Glass. 2011. (ENG.). 304p. (J). (gr. 3-7). pap. 7.99 *(978-0-06-186685-2(7)*, Greenwillow Bks.) HarperCollins Pubs.

Jones, T. Llew. Storïau Cwm-Pen-Llo. 2005. (WEL., Illus.). 100p. pap. *(978-0-86381-750-2(5))* Gwasg Carreg Gwalch.

Judge, Chris. The Snow Beast. Judge, Chris, illus. 2015. (ENG., Illus.). 32p. (J). (gr. -1-3). 17.99 *(978-1-4677-9313-1(2)*, a711d3a5-9c18-4a5e-a4f5-dd8ef98bb756) Lerner Publishing Group.

Kail, Leanna. The Owl Who Couldn't Whoo. Rottinger, Amy, illus. 2013. 24p. pap. 11.95 *(978-1-61244-129-0(7))* Halo Publishing International.

Kelly, Erin Entrada. Lalani of the Distant Sea. 2019. (ENG., Illus.). 400p. (J). (gr. 3-7). 16.99 *(978-0-06-274727-3(4)*, Greenwillow Bks.) HarperCollins Pubs.

Kim, JiYu. The Wise Boy. Hwang, YoSeob, illus. 2014. (MySELF Bookshelf Ser.). (ENG.). 32p. (J). (gr. k-2). pap. 11.94 *(978-1-60357-690-1(8))*; lib. bdg. 25.27 *(978-1-59953-655-2(2))* Norwood Hse. Pr.

Knight, Richard. Winter Shadow. Johnson, Richard, illus. 2011. 80p. (J). (gr. 1-5). pap. 9.99 *(978-1-84686-624-1(3))* Barefoot Bks., Inc.

Knight, Richard John & Walker, Richard. Winter Shadow. Johnson, Richard, illus. 2009. 80p. (J). (gr. 3-9). 16.99 *(978-1-84686-116-1(0))* Barefoot Bks., Inc.

Krishnaswami, Uma. Out of the Way! Out of the Way!, 1 vol. Krishnaswamy, Uma, illus. 2012. (ENG.). 28p. (J). (gr. -1-2). 17.95 *(978-1-55498-130-4(1))* Groundwood Bks. CAN. Dist: Publishers Group West (PGW).

—Out of the Way! Out of the Way!, 1 vol. Uma Krishnaswamy, illus. 2022. (ENG.). 24p. (J). (gr. k-2). pap. 11.99 ***(978-81-8146-792-8(2))*** Tulika Pubs. IND. Dist: Independent Pubs. Group.

Lange, Willem. Favor Johnson: A Christmas Story. Dodson, Bert, illus. 2009. (ENG.). 32p. (J). (gr. 1-3). 16.95 *(978-1-59373-082-6(9))* Bunker Hill Publishing, Inc.

Lederer, Ryan. The Adventures of Captain Candy. 2007. (Illus.). 48p. (J). (gr. 4-7). 15.95 *(978-0-9795852-1-0(X))* Seven Locks Pr.

Lester, Julius. The Girl Who Saved Yesterday. Angel, Carl, illus. 2016. (ENG.). 32p. (J). (gr. 2-5). 16.99 *(978-1-939547-24-8(5)*, 13dc2969-1695-493e-a2a3-10c58eaf602d) Creston Bks.

Lincoln, Dallas Ford. The Sawmill Sant. 2011. 36p. pap. 16.95 *(978-1-4626-4335-6(3))* America Star Bks.

Lord, Jennifer Fallin. Pipersville: And the troll that lost his big Toe. 2011. 32p. pap. 14.50 *(978-1-4670-3820-1(2))* AuthorHouse.

Loveridge, Pamela. The Knife of Blood. 2012. 28p. pap. 32.70 *(978-1-4797-4804-4(8))* Xlibris Corp.

MacLeod, Jennifer Tzivia. Fast Asleep in a Little Village in Israel. Beeke, Tiphanie, illus. 2018. (ENG.). 32p. (J). 17.95 *(978-1-68115-539-5(7)*, 73160a0c-1e6a-4190-81ea-4157ce5b2e5a, Apples & Honey Pr.) Behrman Hse., Inc.

Malton, H. Mel. Pioneer Poltergeist: An Alan Nearing Mystery. 2007. (Alan Nearing Mystery Ser.: 2). (ENG.). 208p. (J). pap. 8.95 *(978-1-894917-60-5(X)*, Napoleon & Co.) Dundurn Pr. CAN. Dist: Publishers Group West (PGW).

Mandla, Garden Green Hills: And Finally Ants Run the Village. 2013. 102p. pap. 15.99 *(978-1-4797-1482-7(8))* Xlibris Corp.

Maruno, Jennifer. Totem, 0 vols. 2014. (ENG.). 168p. (YA). pap. 10.99 *(978-1-4597-1934-7(4)*, 9781459719347) Dundurn Pr. CAN. Dist: Publishers Group West (PGW).

Matthews, T. J. The Village Safari. Rheburg, Judy, illus. 2005. (J). *(978-0-938978-36-7(5))* Wycliffe Bible Translators.

Mcallister, Bruce. The Village Sang to the Sea. 2013. 172p. pap. *(978-0-9534784-9-1(1))* Aeon Pr.

McDowell, Andrew. Beyond the Forest. 2007. 286p. pap. 16.95 *(978-0-7414-4238-3(8))* Infinity Publishing.

McKinlay, Meg. A Single Stone. 2017. (ENG.). 272p. (J). (gr. 5). 17.99 *(978-0-7636-8837-0(1))* Candlewick Pr.

Medina, Sylvia M. & Ballock-Dixon, Saige J. Jade Elephant. Eagle, Joy, illus. 2012. 36p. pap. 11.49 *(978-0-9836602-4-8(7))* Green Kids Club, Inc.

Mehrlich Iii, Ferdinand Paul. Splugworth Saves the Day, 1 vol. Mehrlich, Cynthia, illus. 2009. 43p. pap. 24.95 *(978-1-60836-765-8(7))* America Star Bks.

Moolenschot, Catherine. A Rough Road. 2008. (ENG.). 142p. pap. 17.96 *(978-1-4092-4153-9(X))* Lulu Pr., Inc.

Moore, Baba Evans. While the Village Sleeps. 2003. 400p. (YA). pap. 14.95 *(978-0-9709762-0-8(8))* Moore, Evans.

Mora, Pat. Dona Flor: A Tall Tale about a Giant Woman with a Great Big Heart. ön, Raul, illus. 2010. (ENG.). 32p. (J). (gr. -1-2). pap. 8.99 *(978-0-375-86144-4(0)*, Dragonfly Bks.) Random Hse. Children's Bks.

Nancy Mann Israel. The Juggler & His Wife. 2009. 24p. pap. 12.95 *(978-1-4389-5334-2(8))* AuthorHouse.

Narsimhan, Mahtab. The Third Eye: Tara Trilogy. 2007. (Tara Trilogy Ser.: 1). (ENG.). 240p. (YA). (gr. 5-7). pap. 12.99 *(978-1-55002-750-1(6)*, Boardwalk Bks.) Dundurn Pr. CAN. Dist: Ingram Publisher Services.

Nettrour, Nelani. The Dragonlands Bk. 3: The Village. Lt. ed. 2004. (Illus.). 148p. (J). pap. 19.95 *(978-1-932657-12-8(6))* Third Millennium Pubns.

Olsen, Grant Orrin. Rhino Trouble. Carpenter, Mike, illus. 2015. (J). 14.99 *(978-1-4621-1665-2(5))* Cedar Fort, Inc./CFI Distribution.

Quirk, Katie. A Girl Called Problem. 2013. (ENG., Illus.). 256p. (J). pap. 8.50 *(978-0-8028-5404-9(4)*, Eerdmans Bks For Young Readers) Eerdmans, William B. Publishing Co.

Raud, Eno. The Gothamites. Cullen, Adam, tr. Parn, Priit, illus. 2019. (ENG.). 44p. (J). (gr. k-3). 18.00 *(978-1-939810-28-1(0)*, Elsewhere Editions) Steerforth Pr.

Reardon, A. C. Galish: The adventure of Isabelle & Eva. 2011. 168p. pap. 14.69 *(978-1-4567-7818-7(8))* AuthorHouse.

Resman, Michael. Liliana Ageiraü. Cayetano, Eldred Roy, tr. Gathigo, Cyrus Ngatia, illus. 2013. 40p. pap. *(978-976-8142-50-4(2))* Producciones de la Hamaca.

Rossignol, Manon Éléonor & Lecor, Tex. Isory Poutch et le Sortilege de Cacouna. 2004. (FRE., Illus.). 398p. (J). *(978-2-9807852-1-4(0)*, Spotlight Poets) Editions le Poutchoman.

Sapre, Reshme. The Unfortunate Tale of Kachuva the Tortoise: As Told by Chukwa Sulcata. Robinson, Jayme, illus. 2012. (ENG.). 40p. 16.95 *(978-0-9829362-0-7(6))* Hathi Chiti Bks. for Kids.

Schott, Elizabeth, illus. Jake & Sam at the Empty Abbey. 2006. 96p. (J). per. 9.95 *(978-0-9724421-1-4(1))* Fountain Square Publishing.

Schwab, V. E. The near Witch. 2020. 320p. pap. 16.99 *(978-1-78909-114-4(4))* 2019. 360p. 19.99 *(978-1-78909-112-0(8))* Titan Bks. Ltd. GBR. (Titan Bks.). Dist: Penguin Random Hse. LLC.

Shah, Idries. The Clever Boy & the Terrible, Dangerous Animal. Santiago, Rose Mary, illus. 2005. 32p. (J). (gr. -1 — 1). pap. 6.99 *(978-1-883536-51-0(0)*, Hoopoe Bks.) I S H K.

—The Clever Boy & the Terrible, Dangerous Animal/el Muchachito Listo y el Terrible y Peligroso Animal. Wirkala, Rita, tr. Santiago, Rose Mary, illus. 2005. 32p. (J). (gr. -1-3). 18.00 *(978-1-883536-39-8(1))*; pap., per. 6.95 *(978-1-883536-40-4(5))* I S H K. (Hoopoe Bks.).

—The Silly Chicken. Jackson, Jeff, illus. 2005. 32p. (J). pap.; pap. 6.99 *(978-1-883536-50-3(2)*, Hoopoe Bks.) I S H K.

—The Silly Chicken/el Pollo Bobo. Wirkala, Rita, tr. Jackson, Jeff, illus. 2005. 32p. (J). (gr. -1-3). 18.00 *(978-1-883536-37-4(5)*, Hoopoe Bks.) I S H K.

Sher, Steven. Where the Shouting Began. 2008. (J). *(978-1-932727-08-1(6))* Montemayor Pr.

Shinn, Sharon. The Safe-Keeper's Secret. 2005. (ENG.). 240p. (YA). (gr. 7-7). 7.99 *(978-0-14-240357-0(1)*, Firebird) Penguin Young Readers Group.

Smith, Icy. Mystery of the Giant Mask of Sanxingdui. Roski, Gayle Garner, illus. 2015. (J). *(978-0-9913454-8-9(7))* East West Discovery Pr.

Stevens, Mitchell. The Village of Lights. Pritchett, Emily, illus. 2018. (ENG.). 32p. (J). (gr. 2-5). 14.99 *(978-1-4621-2275-2(2))* Cedar Fort, Inc./CFI Distribution.

Stiegemeyer, Julie. Under the Baobab Tree, 1 vol. Lewis, E. B., illus. 2012. (ENG.). 32p. (J). 16.99 *(978-0-310-72561-9(5))* Zonderkidz.

Suits, Patti J. Topa & the Path of the Pum. 2008. 112p. pap. 10.99 *(978-1-4343-9520-7(0))* AuthorHouse.

Swanepoel, Sharon. The Adventures of Seek & Save Volume 3: The Village. Locsinto, Lucas, illus. 2011. (J). *(978-0-9772647-6-6(9))* God's Glory Media.

Swarabi, Fatma Abdulla & El Amin, Khalid Hamid. Marim & Her Grandmother. 2010. 28p. pap. 13.99 *(978-1-4490-8156-0(8))* AuthorHouse.

Thomson, Elizabeth & Albert, Sarah. Andros: the Last Villager. 2008. (ENG.). 226p. pap. 17.04 *(978-1-4357-3557-6(9))* Lulu Pr., Inc.

Vickie A. Soman. The Sahara Desert Angel: Education & Nature Folktales 2. 2010. 208p. pap. 14.95 *(978-1-4502-1465-0(7))* iUniverse, Inc.

Vince Crandall, Vince. The Village Baker. 2011. (ENG.). 39p. pap. 16.95 *(978-1-257-16195-9(4))* Lulu Pr., Inc.

Vincent, Patti. The Village Heroes Meet the Dragon. 2008. 44p. pap. 19.95 *(978-1-4389-1764-1(3))* AuthorHouse.

Vogel-Placides, Joan Katherine. The Safe Place. Placides, Del S., illus. 2013. 58p. 13.99 *(978-0-9888718-3-0(1))* DOMINIONHOUSE Publishing & Design.

Waldman, Debby. A Sack Full of Feathers, 1 vol. Revell, Cindy, illus. 2007. (ENG.). 32p. (J). (gr. -1-k). 9.95 *(978-1-55143-863-4(1))* Orca Bk. Pubs. USA.

Wells, H. G. The Invisible Man. Fisher, Eric Scott, illus. 2011. (Calico Illustrated Classics Ser.: No. 3). (ENG.). 112p. (J). (gr. 2-5). 38.50 *(978-1-61641-103-9(1)*, 4013, Calico Chapter Bks.) ABDO Publishing Co.

White, Betty. Touring Polka-Dot Village. 2012. 24p. 24.95 *(978-1-4626-5869-5(5))* America Star Bks.

Williamson, Judithe Anne. Princess Kara in Her Village, 1 vol. 2009. 107p. pap. 19.95 *(978-1-60813-817-3(8))* America Star Bks.

Wills, Joseph. The World. 2013. 200p. pap. *(978-1-906954-76-5(3))* Live It Publishing.

Wright, Sky'asia. The Big, Blue Raspberry. 2012. 30p. pap. 5.99 *(978-0-9857095-1-8(0))* RRJ Publishing, Inc.

Yeoman, John. Sixes & Sevens. Blake, Quentin, illus. 2012. (ENG.). 32p. (J). (gr. -1-k). pap. 11.99 *(978-1-84939-308-9(7))* Andersen Pr. GBR. Dist: Independent Pubs. Group.

VILLAS

see Architecture, Domestic

VIOLENCE

Agassi, Martine. Hands Are Not for Hitting. Heinlen, Marieka, illus. rev. ed. 2009. (Best Behavior(r) Paperback Ser.). (ENG.). 40p. (J). (gr. -1-2). pap. 11.99 *(978-1-57542-308-1(1)*, 23081) Free Spirit Publishing Inc.

—Hands Are Not for Hitting / Las Manos No Son para Pegar. Heinlen, Marieka, illus. 2009. (Best Behavior(r) Board Book Ser.). (ENG.). (J). (gr. -1 — 1). 26p. bds. 9.99 *(978-1-57542-309-8(X)*, 23098); 40p. pap. 11.99 *(978-1-57542-310-4(3)*, 23104) Free Spirit Publishing Inc.

T U V

Allen, John. School Shootings & Violence (Thinking Critically) 2019. (Thinking Critically Ser.). (ENG.). 80p. (J). (gr. 6-12). 41.27 *(978-1-68282-663-8(5))* ReferencePoint Pr., Inc.

Allman, Toney. School Violence. 2016. (Matters of Opinion Ser.). (ENG., Illus.). 64p. (J). (gr. 4-6). lib. bdg. 27.93 *(978-1-59953-757-3(5))* Norwood Hse. Pr.

Andrews Henningfeld, Diane, ed. Family Violence, 1 vol. 2011. (Global Viewpoints Ser.). (ENG., Illus.). 248p. (gr. 10-12). 47.83 *(978-0-7377-5650-0(0)*, d095cd90-e3cf-4f6c-91dd-8a979a56dc5a); pap. 32.70 *(978-0-7377-5651-7(9)*, 043ab1e5-2156-4941-88b6-d6b8041a1257) Greenhaven Publishing LLC. (Greenhaven Publishing).

Andryszewski, Tricia. Terrorism in America. 2003. (Headliners Ser.). (Illus.). 64p. (J). (gr. 5-8). lib. bdg. 25.90 *(978-0-7613-2803-2(3)*, Millbrook Pr.) Lerner Publishing Group.

Apel, Lorelei. Dealing with Weapons at School & at Home. 2009. (Conflict Resolution Library). 24p. (gr. 2-3). 42.50 *(978-1-60853-411-1(1)*, PowerKids Pr.) Rosen Publishing Group, Inc., The.

Banks, Delilah & Giacobello, John. Surviving Family Violence, 1 vol., 1. 2015. (Family Issues & You Ser.). (ENG.). 48p. (J). (gr. 5-5). pap. 12.75 *(978-1-4994-3705-8(6)*, d2d70cd5-bfb2-406f-988e-ad0c085914a6, Rosen Central) Rosen Publishing Group, Inc., The.

Banks, Jewelene. Don't Give That Boy No Gun. 2010. pap. 12.00 *(978-1-61658-990-5(6))* Independent Pub.

Becnel, Barbara, ed. Gangs & Violence: Stanley Tookie Williams Street Peace Series, 8 bks., Vol. 1, Bk. 3. 2008. 24p. (J). 6.95 *(978-0-9753584-4-3(8))* Damamli Publishing Co.

—Gangs & Weapons: Stanley Tookie Williams Street Peace Series, 8 bks., Vol. 1, Bk. 3. 2008. 24p. (J). *(978-0-9753584-3-6(X))* Damamli Publishing Co.

Berry, Joy. Help Me Be Good about Fighting. 2009. (ENG.). 40p. (J). (gr. k-2). pap. 7.95 *(978-1-60577-128-1(7))* Berry, Joy Enterprises.

Bowen, Shane. Out of the Darkness. 2010. 220p. pap. 21.95 *(978-0-557-26249-6(6))* Lulu Pr., Inc.

Brezina, Corona. Deadly School & Campus Violence, 1 vol. 2008. (Violence & Society Ser.). (ENG., Illus.). 64p. (YA). (gr. 6-6). lib. bdg. 37.13 *(978-1-4042-1792-8(4)*, 2796ee01-5e1c-4616-a833-a36d1cb1df48) Rosen Publishing Group, Inc., The.

Brown, Isobel. Domestic Crime. 2004. (Crime & Detection Ser.). (Illus.). 96p. (YA). (gr. 7-18). lib. bdg. 22.95 *(978-1-59084-370-3(3))* Mason Crest.

Bryfonski, Dedria, ed. Family Violence, 1 vol. 2012. (Current Controversies Ser.). (ENG.). 224p. (gr. 10-12). pap. 33.00 *(978-0-7377-6226-6(8)*, 7f3ffd55-dd38-4c8f-9e53-b634fb634c7e); lib. bdg. 48.03 *(978-0-7377-6225-9(X)*, e11dcbc2-4017-4bb1-9c9d-25d1420750f6) Greenhaven Publishing LLC. (Greenhaven Publishing).

Byers, Ann. Frequently Asked Questions about Gangs & Urban Violence, 1 vol. 2011. (FAQ: Teen Life Ser.). (ENG.). 64p. (YA). (gr. 5-6). lib. bdg. 37.13 *(978-1-4488-1325-4(5)*, b3c32653-c932-47aa-a877-e04465a0f020) Rosen Publishing Group, Inc., The.

Cobb, Carlene. Coping with an Abusive Relationship. 2009. (Coping Ser.). 192p. (gr. 7-12). 63.90 *(978-1-61511-990-5(6))* Rosen Publishing Group, Inc., The.

Daniels, Peggy, ed. School Violence, 1 vol. 2009. (Issues That Concern You Ser.). (ENG., Illus.). 128p. (gr. 7-10). lib. bdg. 43.63 *(978-0-7377-4186-5(4)*, 24421c6f-c0cb-4f81-9528-8b8b0283f4fc, Greenhaven Publishing) Greenhaven Publishing LLC.

Donahue, Mary P. Everything You Need to Know about Domestic Violence, 1 vol. 2018. (Need to Know Library). (ENG.). 64p. (gr. 6-6). pap. 13.95 *(978-1-5081-8345-7(7)*, 00a9e9d6-4908-45f1-a553-46a2d3abaf07, Rosen Young Adult) Rosen Publishing Group, Inc., The.

Edwards, Nicola. Domestic Violence. (Illus.). 32p. (YA). (gr. 1-18). lib. bdg. 27.10 *(978-1-932333-08-4(8))* Chrysalis Education.

Emanuele, Patricia. Coping with Aggression. 2009. (Coping Ser.). 192p. (gr. 7-12). 63.90 *(978-1-61511-989-9(2))* Rosen Publishing Group, Inc., The.

Etingoff, Kim. Gunman on Campus. Stephens, Ronald, ed. 2014. (Safety First Ser.). (ENG., Illus.). 48p. (J). (gr. 5-18). lib. bdg. 20.95 *(978-1-4222-3047-3(3))* Mason Crest.

Fein, Eric. High Noon: Wild Bill Hickok & the Code of the Old West. 2009. (Great Moments in American History Ser.). 32p. (gr. 3-3). 47.90 *(978-1-61513-145-7(0))* Rosen Publishing Group, Inc., The.

Gerdes, Louise I., ed. Domestic Violence, 1 vol. 2011. (Opposing Viewpoints Ser.). (ENG., Illus.). 240p. (gr. 10-12). 50.43 *(978-0-7377-5719-4(1)*, 676de496-7c07-48fc-b4d2-17f94c17eb3c); pap. 34.80 *(978-0-7377-5720-0(5)*, 6b717245-0d8e-4651-8b97-0d81e4ab09f2) Greenhaven Publishing LLC. (Greenhaven Publishing).

—Violence, 1 vol. 2007. (Opposing Viewpoints Ser.). (ENG.). 240p. (gr. 10-12). pap. 34.80 *(978-0-7377-3365-5(9)*, 4debe204-de29-4d84-ba35-ced316044b97); (Illus.). lib. bdg. 50.43 *(978-0-7377-3364-8(0)*, 407ffb4e-b73d-4198-8e9e-882a9b9eda4d) Greenhaven Publishing LLC. (Greenhaven Publishing).

Giacabello, John. You & Violence in Your Family. 2009. (Family Matters Ser.). 48p. (gr. 5-8). 53.00 *(978-1-61512-484-8(5)*, Rosen Reference) Rosen Publishing Group, Inc., The.

Gifford, Clive. Violence on the Screen. 2010. (Voices Ser.). (Illus.). 48p. pap. *(978-0-237-54218-4(8))* Evans Brothers, Ltd.

Gitlin, Marty. Helping a Friend in an Abusive Relationship, 1 vol. 2016. (How Can I Help? Friends Helping Friends Ser.). (ENG., Illus.). 64p. (J). (gr. 6-6). pap. 13.95 *(978-1-4994-6436-8(3)*, 51f7c56f-6c2d-447f-b926-9c6212f4b749) Rosen Publishing Group, Inc., The.

Gordon, Sherri Mabry. Beyond Bruises: The Truth about Teens & Abuse, 1 vol. 2009. (Issues in Focus Today Ser.). (ENG., Illus.). 128p. (gr. 6-7). lib. bdg. 35.93 *(978-0-7660-3064-0(4)*, 5822eb56-2aec-4498-acba-f6743849a612) Enslow Publishing, LLC.

Hacker, Caryn Sabes. A Bully Grows Up: Erik Meets the Wizard: Adult Guide Edition, 1. Boureau, Silvere, illus. 2006. 34p. (J). tchr. ed. 15.95 *(978-0-9791046-0-2(2))* Caryn Solutions, LLC.

Katz, Samuel M. Global Counterstrike: International Counterterrorism. 2005. (Terrorist Dossiers Ser.). (Illus.). 72p. (J). (gr. 6-12). 26.60 *(978-0-8225-1566-1(0))* Lerner Publishing Group.

Kreiner, Anna. Todo lo que necesitas saber sobre la violencia en la escuela (Everything You Need to Know about Violence in School) 2009. (Todo lo que necesitas (the Need to Know Library) Ser.). (SPA.). 64p. (gr. 6-6). 58.50 *(978-1-60854-411-0(7)*, Editorial Buenas Letras) Rosen Publishing Group, Inc., The.

La Bella, Laura. Dating Violence, 1 vol. 2015. (Confronting Violence Against Women Ser.). (ENG.). 64p. (J). (gr. 6-7). 36.13 *(978-1-4994-6030-8(9)*, 1c57eb01-628e-4327-80ca-c28ce9863c6a, Rosen Young Adult) Rosen Publishing Group, Inc., The.

—Living in a Violent Household, 1 vol. 2015. (Confronting Violence Against Women Ser.). (ENG.). 64p. (J). (gr. 6-7). 36.13 *(978-1-4994-6034-6(1)*, d405813d-7635-4b42-9873-e08937b26e7e, Rosen Young Adult) Rosen Publishing Group, Inc., The.

Landau, Elaine. Date Violence. 2005. (Life Balance Ser.). (ENG., Illus.). 80p. (J). (gr. 5-8). pap. 6.95 *(978-0-531-16613-0(9)*, Watts, Franklin) Scholastic Library Publishing.

Langwith, Jacqueline, ed. Violence, 1 vol. 2010. (Introducing Issues with Opposing Viewpoints Ser.). (ENG., Illus.). 144p. (gr. 7-10). 43.63 *(978-0-7377-4736-2(6)*, be02e416-8ca5-4a4b-86a5-2ea51f3cf612, Greenhaven Publishing) Greenhaven Publishing LLC.

Lankford, Ronald D., Jr., ed. Gun Violence, 1 vol. 2009. (Social Issues Firsthand Ser.). (ENG., Illus.). 96p. (gr. 10-12). 39.93 *(978-0-7377-4797-3(8)*, a744d362-6a43-4d10-b6d6-86f2e0a7077c, Greenhaven Publishing) Greenhaven Publishing LLC.

Lennon, Liz. I Don't Hit. 2013. (ENG., Illus.). (J). 25.65 *(978-1-59771-411-2(9))* Sea-To-Sea Pubns.

Lentini, Rochelle, et al. Tucker the Turtle Takes Time to Tuck & Think. SanGiacomo, Scott, illus. 2016. 16p. (J). pap. *(978-0-87659-705-7(3))* Gryphon Hse., Inc.

Mara, Wil. Violence in Pop Culture. 2018. (21st Century Skills Library: Global Citizens: Modern Media Ser.). (ENG., Illus.). 32p. (J). (gr. 4-7). lib. bdg. 32.07 *(978-1-5341-2928-3(6)*, 211756) Cherry Lake Publishing.

McGee, Kathleen M. & Buddenberg, Laura J. Unmasking Sexual Con Games: Helping Teens Avoid Emotional Grooming & Dating Violence. 3rd ed. 2004. (Leader's Guide with Session Plans Ser.). (ENG., Illus.). 199p. pap. 29.95 *(978-1-889322-54-4(7)*, 25-015) Boys Town Pr.

Michaels, Vanessa Lynn & Harrow, Jeremy. Frequently Asked Questions about Family Violence, 1 vol. 2011. (FAQ: Teen Life Ser.). (ENG.). 64p. (gr. 5-6). lib. bdg. 37.13 *(978-1-4488-4628-3(5)*, 8d874e20-8eda-4aa0-9f84-330b02f17a81) Rosen Publishing Group, Inc., The.

Mintzer, Rich. Coping with Random Acts of Violence. 2009. (Coping Ser.). 196p. (gr. 7-12). 63.90 *(978-1-61512-009-3(2))* Rosen Publishing Group, Inc., The.

mooney, carla. Teen Violence. 2013. (ENG.). 96p. (YA). lib. bdg. *(978-1-60152-496-6(X))* ReferencePoint Pr., Inc.

Netzley, Patricia D. How Does Video Game Violence Affect Society? 2013. (Illus.). 96p. (YA). lib. bdg. *(978-1-60152-490-4(0))* ReferencePoint Pr., Inc.

—Video Games, Violence & Crime. 2014. (Video Games & Society Ser.). (ENG., Illus.). 80p. (J). lib. bdg. *(978-1-60152-752-3(7))* ReferencePoint Pr., Inc.

Orr, Tamra B. & Orr, Tamra. Violence in Our Schools: Halls of Hope, Halls of Fear. 2003. (Single Title: Social Studies Ser.). (ENG., Illus.). 192p. (YA). 30.50 *(978-0-531-12268-6(9)*, Watts, Franklin) Scholastic Library Publishing.

Piano, Doreen, ed. Violence, 1 vol. 2007. (Social Issues Firsthand Ser.). (ENG.). 128p. (gr. 10-12). lib. bdg. 39.93 *(978-0-7377-2909-2(0)*, 03e959a1-7f7b-42c6-a8a3-5f24a4916da8, Greenhaven Publishing) Greenhaven Publishing LLC.

Randolph, Ryan P. Wild West Lawmen & Outlaws. 2009. (Library of the Westward Expansion Ser.). 24p. (gr. 3-4). 42.50 *(978-1-60853-944-4(X)*, PowerKids Pr.) Rosen Publishing Group, Inc., The.

Roberts, Kathryn, ed. Violence Against Women, 1 vol. 2018. (Global Viewpoints Ser.). (ENG.). 200p. (gr. 10-12). 47.83 *(978-1-5345-0392-2(7)*, 93ff679c-fb75-4355-b7ab-65392a5e5d0b) Greenhaven Publishing LLC.

Roesler, Jill. Asking Questions about Violence in Popular Culture. 2015. (21st Century Skills Library: Asking Questions about Media Ser.). (ENG., Illus.). 32p. (J). (gr. 4-8). 32.07 *(978-1-63362-492-4(7)*, 206876) Cherry Lake Publishing.

Royston, Angela. Gun Crimes. 2010. (Solve It with Science Ser.). (Illus.). 48p. (YA). (gr. 5-9). lib. bdg. 34.25 *(978-1-59920-330-0(8))* Black Rabbit Bks.

Schmermund, Elizabeth, ed. Campus Sexual Violence, 1 vol. 2016. (At Issue Ser.). (ENG.). 184p. (YA). (gr. 10-12). pap. 28.80 *(978-1-5345-0037-2(5)*, 48560665-0ddd-4234-bbcb-8fe28e6cf3cb); lib. bdg. 41.03 *(978-1-5345-0018-1(9)*, c91fb451-af3c-4f31-a2b1-9dca807c2709) Greenhaven Publishing LLC. (Greenhaven Publishing).

Slavens, Elaine. Fighting Deal with It: Deal with It Without Coming to Blows, 1 vol. Murray, Steven, illus. 2nd ed. 2010. (Lorimer Deal with It Ser.). (ENG.). 32p. (J). (gr. 4-8). pap. 12.95 *(978-1-55277-517-2(8)*, 9781552775172) James Lorimer & Co. Ltd., Pubs. CAN. Dist: Orca Bk. Pubs. USA.

Smith-Llera, Danielle. TV Exposes Brutality on the Selma March: 4D an Augmented Reading Experience. 2019. (Captured Television History 4D Ser.). (ENG., Illus.). 64p. (J). (gr. 5-9). pap. 8.99 *(978-0-7565-6005-8(5)*, 139136); 39.99 *(978-0-7565-6001-0(2)*, 139132) Capstone. (Compass Point Bks.).

Sorensen McGee, Kathleen & Holmes Buddenberg, Laura. Unmasking Sexual Con Games Teen's Guide: A Teen's Guide to Avoiding Emotional Grooming & Dating Violence. 3rd ed. 2004. (Leader's Guide with Session Plans Ser.). (ENG.). 79p. pap. 5.95 *(978-1-889322-55-1(5)*, 25-016) Boys Town Pr.

Watkins, Christine, ed. How Can Gang Violence Be Prevented?, 1 vol. 2006. (At Issue Ser.). (ENG., Illus.). 104p. (J). (gr. 10-12). pap. 28.80 *(978-0-7377-2381-6(5)*, 1679ff94-2ea8-4da9-8dc7-0a5eca337108, Greenhaven Publishing) Greenhaven Publishing LLC.

Wilcox, Christine. Understanding Violent Behavior. 2017. (Understanding Psychology Ser.). (ENG.). 80p. (YA). (gr. 5-12). *(978-1-68282-283-8(4))* ReferencePoint Pr., Inc.

Wilson, Mike. Domestic Violence. 2008. (Opposing Viewpoints Ser.). (ENG., Illus.). 217p. (YA). (gr. 10-12). pap. 39.70 *(978-0-7377-4206-0(2)*, LML02109-243102, Greenhaven Pr., Inc.) Cengage Gale.

Wingate, Brian. Violence at Sports Events. (Violence & Society Ser.). 64p. (gr. 6-6). 2009. 58.50 *(978-1-60854-727-2(2))* 2008. (ENG., Illus.). (YA). lib. bdg. 37.13 *(978-1-4042-1796-6(7)*, f99384c3-3864-4210-ab14-1885f7044649) Rosen Publishing Group, Inc., The.

Wittekind, Erika. Violence as Entertainment: Why Aggression Sells. 2012. (Exploring Media Literacy Ser.). (ENG.). 80p. (J). (gr. 5-8). pap. 9.10 *(978-0-7565-4536-9(6)*, 118368); lib. bdg. 35.32 *(978-0-7565-4520-8(X)*, 117101) Capstone. (Compass Point Bks.).

Zoldak, Joyce. When Danger Hits Home: Survivors of Domestic Violence. (Survivors Ser.). 2010. 128p. (YA). (gr. 7-12). 24.95 *(978-1-4222-0460-3(X))* 2009. (J). pap. 24.95 *(978-1-4222-1473-2(7))* Mason Crest.

VIOLENCE—FICTION

Ayarbe, Heidi. Freeze Frame. 2010. (ENG.). 400p. (YA). (gr. 8). pap. 8.99 *(978-0-06-135175-4(X)*, HarperTeen) HarperCollins Pubs.

Baron, Kathi. Shattered. 2009. 262p. (J). (gr. 9-12). 16.95 *(978-1-934813-08-9(7))* Westside Bks.

Bilen, Tracy. What She Left Behind. 2012. (ENG.). 256p. (YA). (gr. 9-12). pap. 9.99 *(978-1-4424-3951-1(3)*, Simon Pulse) Simon Pulse.

Bowler, Tim. Blade: Playing Dead. 2010. (Blade Ser.: 1). (ENG.). 256p. (YA). (gr. 9-18). 7.99 *(978-0-14-241600-6(2)*, Speak) Penguin Young Readers Group.

Caletti, Deb. A Heart in a Body in the World. 2018. (ENG., Illus.). 368p. (YA). (gr. 9). 18.99 *(978-1-4814-1520-0(4)*, Simon Pulse) Simon Pulse.

Carmichael, Katrina. Back Together Again. 2008. 20p. pap. 7.95 *(978-0-9814650-5-0(6))* G Publishing LLC.

Chessen, Sherri. Gorp's Secret: An Empowering Tale in Pumpernickel Park. Bronson, Linda, illus. 2008. (ENG.). 36p. (J). 16.95 *(978-0-9724249-3-6(8))* Gorp Group Pr., The.

Cohen, Joshua C. Leverage. 2012. (ENG.). 432p. (YA). (gr. 9). pap. 8.99 *(978-0-14-242086-7(7)*, Speak) Penguin Young Readers Group.

Connor, Leslie. The Things You Kiss Goodbye. 2014. (ENG.). 368p. (YA). (gr. 9). 17.99 *(978-0-06-089091-9(6)*, Tegen, Katherine Bks) HarperCollins Pubs.

Dawson, Delilah S. Strike. 2016. (ENG., Illus.). 480p. (YA). (gr. 9). 17.99 *(978-1-4814-2342-7(8)*, Simon Pulse) Simon Pulse.

Delgado, Alvin. Spirit of the Gang. 2007. (ENG.). 192p. pap. 12.95 *(978-1-4303-1334-2(X))* Lulu Pr., Inc.

Doucet, Sharon Arms. Fiddle Fever. 2007. (ENG.). 176p. (J). (gr. 5-7). pap. 12.95 *(978-0-618-77682-5(6)*, 100543, Clarion Bks.) HarperCollins Pubs.

Dowd, Siobhan. Bog Child. 2010. (ENG.). 336p. (YA). (gr. 7). pap. 10.99 *(978-0-375-84135-4(0))* Fickling, David Bks. GBR. Dist: Penguin Random Hse. LLC.

Favole, Robert. Monday Redux. 2003. 200p. (YA). 15.99 *(978-1-930826-11-3(7))* Flywheel Publishing Co.

Flake, Sharon G. Bang! 2007. (J). 20.85 *(978-1-4177-7952-9(7))* Turtleback.

Flinn, Alex. Fade to Black. 2005. 192p. (J). (gr. 8-12). 16.99 *(978-0-06-056839-9(9)*, HarperTeen) HarperCollins Pubs.

Gabriel, Kimberly. Every Stolen Breath, 1 vol. 2019. (ENG.). 336p. (YA). 17.99 *(978-0-310-76666-7(4))* Blink.

Galante, Cecilia. Hershey Herself. 2008. (Mix Ser.). (ENG.). 336p. (J). (gr. 4-8). pap. 15.99 *(978-1-4169-5463-7(5))* Simon & Schuster, Inc.

Giles, Gail. Shattering Glass. 2004. 215p. (J). (gr. 7-18). pap. 37.00 incl. audio *(978-1-4000-9013-6(X)*, Listening Library) Random Hse. Audio Publishing Group.

Greg, Neri. Yummy: The Last Days of a Southside Shorty. 2014. (ENG.). 94p. (YA). (gr. k-3). 21.20 *(978-1-63245-250-4(2))* Lectorum Pubns., Inc.

Hassan, Michael. Crash & Burn. 2014. (ENG.). 544p. (YA). (gr. 9). pap. 9.99 *(978-0-06-211291-0(0)*, Balzer & Bray) HarperCollins Pubs.

Heneghan, James. Hit Squad, 1 vol. 2003. (Orca Soundings Ser.). (ENG.). 128p. (YA). (gr. 8-12). pap. 9.95 *(978-1-55143-269-4(2)*, 1551432692) Orca Bk. Pubs. USA.

—Hit Squad. 2004. (Orca Soundings Ser.). 106p. 19.95 *(978-0-7569-4300-4(0))* Perfection Learning Corp.

Hopkins, Ellen. People Kill People. (ENG.). (YA). (gr. 9). 2019. 464p. pap. 13.99 *(978-1-4814-4294-7(5))* 2018. (Illus.). 448p. 19.99 *(978-1-4814-4293-0(7))* McElderry, Margaret K. Bks. (McElderry, Margaret K. Bks.).

Horowitz, Anthony & Johnston, Antony. Eagle Strike: an Alex Rider Graphic Novel. Kanako & Yuzuru, illus. 2017. (Alex Rider Ser.). (ENG.). 176p. (J). (gr. 4-7). pap. 14.99 *(978-0-7636-9256-8(5))* Candlewick Pr.

Houde, Monique. Blinded by Love. 2004. (YA). pap. 14.95 *(978-0-9748689-0-5(6))* Choices For Tomorrow.

Houran, Lori Haskins. Too Many Cats. Mathieu, Joe, illus. 2009. (Step into Reading Ser.). 32p. (J). (gr. -1-1). pap. 5.99 *(978-0-375-85197-1(6)*, Random Hse. Bks. for Young Readers) Random Hse. Children's Bks.

Huggins, Peter. In the Company of Owls. Koz, Paula Goodman, illus. 2008. (ENG.). 96p. (J). 15.95 *(978-1-58838-036-4(X)*, 8845, NewSouth Bks.) NewSouth, Inc.

Jerry, Spinelli. Wringer. 2014. (ENG.). 256p. (J). (gr. 8-12). 13.24 *(978-1-63245-323-5(1))* Lectorum Pubns., Inc.

Jones, Patrick. Taking Sides. 2015. (Locked Out Ser.). (ENG.). 104p. (YA). (gr. 6-12). lib. bdg. 27.99 *(978-1-4677-5800-0(0)*, 666c07ab-a572-44f0-a456-5017c9fe1267, Darby Creek) Lerner Publishing Group.

Key, Watt. Dirt Road Home: A Novel. 2011. (Alabama Moon Ser.: 2). (ENG.). 240p. (J). (gr. 5-9). pap. 8.99 *(978-0-312-67435-9(X)*, 900072850) Square Fish.

—Fourmile, 1 vol. 2012. (ENG.). 240p. (J). (gr. 4-7). 26.99 *(978-0-374-35095-6(7)*, 900031668, Farrar, Straus & Giroux (BYR)) Farrar, Straus & Giroux.

—Fourmile. 2014. (ENG.). 256p. (J). (gr. 4-7). pap. 10.99 *(978-1-250-03995-8(9)*, 900123698) Square Fish.

King, A. S. Still Life with Tornado. 2017. (ENG.). 320p. (YA). (gr. 9). pap. 10.99 *(978-1-101-99490-0(8)*, Penguin Bks.) Penguin Young Readers Group.

Lake, Nick. In Darkness. 2014. (ENG.). 368p. (YA). (gr. 9). pap. 10.99 *(978-1-61963-122-9(9)*, 900120824, Bloomsbury USA Childrens) Bloomsbury Publishing USA.

Lester, Julius. Guardian. 2008. (ENG., Illus.). 144p. (YA). (gr. 9-18). 16.99 *(978-0-06-155890-0(7)*, Amistad) HarperCollins Pubs.

Leveen, Tom. Mercy Rule. 2018. (ENG.). 456p. (YA). (gr. 9-9). 17.99 *(978-1-5107-2698-7(5)*, Sky Pony Pr.) Skyhorse Publishing Co., Inc.

Mac, Carrie. Pain & Wastings, 1 vol. 2008. (Orca Soundings Ser.). (ENG.). 122p. (YA). (gr. 9-12). 22.44 *(978-1-55143-906-8(9))* Orca Bk. Pubs. USA.

McDaniel, Lurlene. Red Heart Tattoo. 2013. (ENG.). 224p. (YA). (gr. 7). pap. 8.99 *(978-0-440-24019-8(0)*, Ember) Random Hse. Children's Bks.

Michaels, Rune. Genesis Alpha. 2007. (ENG., Illus.). 208p. (YA). (gr. 7-12). 16.99 *(978-1-4169-1886-8(8)*, Atheneum Bks. for Young Readers) Simon & Schuster Children's Publishing.

Moore, Monica A. Everyday Heroes. 2006. (ENG.). 52p. per. 12.95 *(978-1-59800-563-9(4))* Outskirts Pr., Inc.

Mulder, Michelle. Yeny & the Children for Peace, 1 vol. 2008. (Kids' Power Book Ser.: 2). (ENG., Illus.). 118p. (J). (gr. 3-8). pap. 14.95 *(978-1-897187-45-6(9)*, 1897187459) Second Story Pr. CAN. Dist: Orca Bk. Pubs. USA.

Myers, Jason. Run the Game. 2012. (ENG.). 544p. (YA). (gr. 10). pap. 9.99 *(978-1-4424-1432-7(4)*, Simon Pulse) Simon Pulse.

Myers, Walter Dean. Shooter. 2004. (ENG.). 224p. (J). 15.99 *(978-0-06-029519-6(8)*, HarperTeen) HarperCollins Pubs.

Nijkamp, Marieke. This Is Where It Ends. (YA). (gr. 8-12). 2019. 336p. pap. 10.99 *(978-1-4926-7111-4(8))* 2016. (ENG.). 288p. 17.99 *(978-1-4926-2246-8(X)*, 9781492622468) Sourcebooks, Inc.

—This Is Where It Ends. 2016. lib. bdg. 22.10 *(978-0-606-39479-6(6))* 2017. lib. bdg. 22.10 *(978-0-606-39992-0(5))* Turtleback.

Novel Units. Wringer Novel Units Teacher Guide. 2019. (ENG.). (J). pap., tchr. ed. 12.99 *(978-1-58130-676-7(8)*, Novel Units, Inc.) Classroom Library Co.

Oates, Joyce Carol. Freaky Green Eyes. 2005. 341p. (YA). 15.65 *(978-0-7569-6308-8(7))* Perfection Learning Corp.

Ostow, Micol. Family. 2011. (ENG.). 384p. (YA). (gr. 9-12). 17.99 *(978-1-60684-155-6(6)*, 3cf413e9-28d9-4423-89bd-f642128d3c03, Carolrhoda Lab™) Lerner Publishing Group.

Paulsen, Gary. Paintings from the Cave: Three Novellas. 2012. (ENG.). 176p. (YA). (gr. 7-7). pap. 8.99 *(978-0-553-49466-2(X)*, Ember) Random Hse. Children's Bks.

Peters, Julie Anne. Rage: a Love Story. 2010. 304p. (YA). (gr. 9). pap. 9.99 *(978-0-375-84411-9(2)*, Knopf Bks. for Young Readers) Random Hse. Children's Bks.

Phillips, Dee. Fight, 1 vol. unabr. ed. 2010. (Right Now! Ser.). (ENG.). 45p. (YA). (gr. 9-12). pap. 10.75 *(978-1-61651-248-4(2))* Saddleback Educational Publishing, Inc.

Quick, Matthew. Boy21. 2013. (ENG.). 272p. (YA). (gr. 7-17). pap. 11.99 *(978-0-316-12796-7(5))* Little, Brown Bks. for Young Readers.

Quintero, Sofia. Efrain's Secret. 2011. (ENG.). 272p. (YA). (gr. 9). pap. 8.99 *(978-0-440-24062-4(X)*, Ember) Random Hse. Children's Bks.

Rodman, Sean. Firewall, 1 vol. 2017. (Orca Soundings Ser.). (ENG.). 144p. (YA). (gr. 8-12). pap. 9.95 *(978-1-4598-1453-0(3))* Orca Bk. Pubs. USA.

Scheerger, Sarah Lynn. Are You Still There. 2015. (ENG.). 288p. (YA). (gr. 8-12). 16.99 *(978-0-8075-4557-7(0)*, 807545570) Whitman, Albert & Co.

Schraff, Anne E. The Outcasts. 2012. (Urban Underground — Harriet Tubman High School Ser.: 21). (YA). lib. bdg. 20.80 *(978-0-606-23794-9(1))* Turtleback.

—See No Evil. 2012. (Urban Underground — Harriet Tubman High School Ser.: 22). (YA). lib. bdg. 20.80 *(978-0-606-23795-6(X))* Turtleback.

Simonet, Andrew. Wilder. 2021. (ENG.). 320p. (YA). pap. 10.99 *(978-1-250-21159-0(X)*, 900189992) Square Fish.

Sitomer, Alan Lawrence. Homeboyz. 2008. (ENG.). 304p. (J). (gr. 5-9). pap. 8.99 *(978-1-4231-0031-7(X)*, Jump at the Sun) Hyperion Bks. for Children.

Soto, Gary. Buried Onions. 2006. (ENG., Illus.). 176p. (YA). (gr. 7-12). pap. 10.99 *(978-0-15-206265-1(3)*, 1063436, Clarion Bks.) HarperCollins Pubs.

—Buried Onions. 2006. 149p. 16.95 *(978-0-7569-7218-9(3))* Perfection Learning Corp.

Spinelli, Jerry. Wringer. 2004. (ENG.). 256p. (J). (gr. 3-7). pap. 8.99 *(978-0-06-059282-0(6)*, HarperCollins) HarperCollins Pubs.

—Wringer: A Newbery Honor Award Winner. 2018. (ENG.). 256p. (J). (gr. 3-7). pap. 9.99 *(978-0-06-440578-2(8)*, HarperCollins) HarperCollins Pubs.

Strasser, Todd. If I Grow Up. (ENG.). 240p. (YA). (gr. 7). 2010. pap. 10.99 *(978-1-4169-9443-5(2))* 2009. 17.99 *(978-1-4169-2523-1(6))* Simon & Schuster Bks. For Young Readers. (Simon & Schuster Bks. For Young Readers).

Surviving Southside, 6 vols., Set. Incl. Benito Runs. Fontes, Justine. lib. bdg. 27.99 *(978-0-7613-6151-0(0)*, 1e02666c-1414-4f2b-9c03-e05b4294b401); Shattered Star. Simon, Charnan. lib. bdg. 27.99 *(978-0-7613-6154-1(5)*, 1a8163e0-50cc-490f-9aa9-787901e7c8fd); 104p. (YA). (gr. 6-12). (Surviving Southside Ser.). (ENG.). 2011. Set lib. bdg. 335.16 *(978-0-7613-6148-0(0)*, Darby Creek) Lerner Publishing Group.

Tullson, Diane. Lockdown, 1 vol. 2008. (Orca Soundings Ser.). (ENG.). 128p. (YA). (gr. 8-12). pap. 9.95 *(978-1-55143-916-7(6))* Orca Bk. Pubs. USA.

van Diepen, Allison. Light of Day. 2017. (ENG.). 336p. (YA). (gr. 9). pap. 9.99 *(978-0-06-230348-6(1),* HarperTeen) HarperCollins Pubs.

Walsh, Ann. By the Skin of His Teeth. 2005. (Illus.). 144p. (YA). pap., tchr. ed. 6.95 *(978-0-88878-448-3(1))* Beach Holme Pubs., Ltd. CAN. Dist: Literary Pr. Group of Canada.

Weyn, Suzanne. Beaten. 2015. (Surviving Southside Ser.). (ENG.). 104p. (YA). (gr. 6-12). E-Book 53.32 *(978-1-4677-6007-2(2),* 9781467760072, Lerner Digital) Lerner Publishing Group.

Wilde, Jerry. Peace in the Halls: Stories & Activities to Manage Anger & Prevent School Violence. 2003. 112p. (YA). (gr. 4-12). pap. 9.95 *(978-0-9657610-4-8(5))* LGR Publishing, Inc.

Zevin, Gabrielle. Because It Is My Blood: A Novel. 2013. (Birthright Ser.: 2). (ENG.). 384p. (YA). (gr. 7). pap. 19.99 *(978-1-250-03422-9(1),* 900120595) Square Fish.

—In the Age of Love & Chocolate: A Novel. 2014. (Birthright Ser.: 3). (ENG.). 320p. (YA). (gr. 7). pap. 15.99 *(978-1-250-05071-7(5),* 900134142) Square Fish.

VIOLIN

Auh, Yoonil. A Guide to Practicing Repertoire: Level 1, 11 vols. Auh, Yoonil, ed. 2003. (Illus.). 85p. (gr. k-12). pap. 135.00 *(978-1-882858-61-3(1))* Yoon-il Auh/Intrepid Pixels.

—A Guide to Practicing Repertoire: Level 2, 11 vols. Auh, Yoonil, ed. 2003. (Illus.). 85p. (gr. k-12). pap. 135.00 *(978-1-882858-62-0(X))* Yoon-il Auh/Intrepid Pixels.

—Representation Music. Auh, Yoonil, ed. 2003. (Illus.). 28p. (gr. k-12). pap., instr.'s gde. ed. 25.00 *(978-1-882858-55-2(7))* Yoon-il Auh/Intrepid Pixels.

—Representation Music: A New Approch to Creating Sound & Representing Music. Auh, Yoonil, ed. 2003. (Illus.). 45p. (gr. k-12). pap. 17.00 *(978-1-882858-54-5(9))* Yoon-il Auh/Intrepid Pixels.

—Singing Hand: Study of Vibrato. Auh, Yoonil, ed. 2003. (Illus.). (gr. k-12). 50p. pap. 16.00 *(978-1-882858-59-0(X));* 45p. pap. 16.00 *(978-1-882858-60-6(3))* Yoon-il Auh/Intrepid Pixels.

Bennett, Ned. A New Tune a Day - Performance Pieces for Violin. 2006. (ENG., Illus.). 48p. pap. 15.99 incl. audio compact disk *(978-0-8256-8217-9(7),* 14022761) Music Sales Corp.

—A New Tune a Day Perfomrance Pieces for Flute. 2006. (ENG., Illus.). 48p. pap. 12.95 incl. audio compact disk *(978-0-8256-8219-3(3),* 14022758) Music Sales Corp.

—A New Tune a Day Performace Pieces for Cello. 2006. (ENG., Illus.). 48p. pap. 12.95 incl. audio compact disk *(978-0-8256-8218-6(5),* 14022756) Music Sales Corp.

Davey, Peter. Abracadabra Violin, Bk. 1. Hussey, Christopher & Sebba, Jane, eds. Damerum, Kanako & Parks, Paul, illus. 2nd ed. 2004. (Abracadabra Strings Ser.). (ENG.). 64p. (J). pap. 10.95 *(978-0-7136-6308-2(1),* A&C Black) Bloomsbury Publishing Plc GBR. Dist: Consortium Bk. Sales & Distribution.

—Abracadabra Violin, Bk. 1. 2nd ed. 2003. (Abracadabra Strings Ser.). (ENG., Illus.). 1p. pap. 15.95 incl. audio compact disk *(978-0-7136-6309-9(X),* A&C Black) Bloomsbury Publishing Plc GBR. Dist: Consortium Bk. Sales & Distribution.

Hal Leonard Corp. Staff, creator. Disney Movie Hits for Violin Play along with a Full Symphony Orchestra! Book/Online Audio. 2003. (ENG.). 20p. pap. 14.99 *(978-0-634-00099-7(3),* 00841426) Leonard, Hal Corp.

Landau, Elaine. Is the Violin for You? 2010. (Ready to Make Music Ser.). (ENG., Illus.). 40p. (gr. 4-6). lib. bdg. 27.93 *(978-0-7613-5423-9(9),* Lerner Pubns.) Lerner Publishing Group.

Martin, Iain C., illus. Fun Factory Violin Book. 2004. (ENG.). 32p. pap. 15.99 *(978-0-85162-183-8(X),* 48011784) Leonard, Hal Corp.

McCabe, Larry. Easiest Fiddle Tunes for Children, 1 vol. 2007. (Easiest Tunes for Children Ser.). (ENG., Illus.). 32p. 14.95 *(978-0-7866-7561-6(6))* Mel Bay Pubns., Inc.

Miles, Lucinda (Cindy). Old-Time Fiddling Gospel Favorites. 2005. (Illus.). 84p. (YA). audio compact disk 19.99 *(978-0-9710446-6-1(X))* Miles Music.

Riggs, Kate. Violin. 2014. (Making Music Ser.). (ENG.). 24p. (J). (gr. 1-4). pap. 9.99 *(978-0-89812-950-2(8),* 21220, Creative Paperbacks) Creative Co., The.

Roach-Langille, Nancy & Mitchell, Francis G. Fiddle Fantasy: A Selection of Fiddle Tunes by Maritime Composers. Mitchell, Francis G., ed. Roach-Langille, Nancy, illus. 2nd ed. 2004. (ENG., Illus.). 6p. pap. *(978-1-895814-28-6(6),* NWP103) New World Publishing.

Smith, Melanie. Beginner Violin Theory for Children, Book One, 1 vol. 2005. (ENG., Illus.). 84p. pap. 19.99 *(978-0-7866-7087-1(8),* 20296) Mel Bay Pubns., Inc.

Wearing, Katie. Abracadabra Strings Beginners - Abracadabra Violin Beginner (Pupil's Book + CD), 1 vol. 2007. (Abracadabra Ser.). (ENG., Illus.). 32p. (J). pap. 11.95 *(978-0-7136-9365-2(7))* HarperCollins Pubs. Ltd. GBR. Dist: Independent Pubs. Group.

White, Cathy Finch. Anna Learns to Play the Violin. 2010. 28p. pap. 12.49 *(978-1-4520-5579-4(3))* AuthorHouse.

VIOLIN—INSTRUCTION AND STUDY

Auh, Yoon-Il. Pre-School Virtuoso, Bk. IV. (Auh School of Violin Ser.). 40p. (J). (gr. k-5). stu. ed. 10.00 *(978-1-882858-06-4(9))* Yoon-il Auh/Intrepid Pixels.

Hussey, Christopher. Abracadabra Strings - Abracadabra Christmas: Violin Showstoppers, 1 vol. 2015. (Abracadabra Ser.). (ENG.). 32p. (J). pap. 22.95 *(978-1-4729-2054-6(6))* HarperCollins Pubs. Ltd. GBR. Dist: Independent Pubs. Group.

Wohlfahrt, Franz. Easiest Elementary Method for Violin: Op. 38. (Carl Fischer Music Library: No. 1061). 56p. (J). pap. 10.95 *(978-0-8258-0053-5(6),* L1061) Fischer, Carl LLC.

VIOLINISTS

Frisch, Aaron. Dark Fiddler. Kelley, Gary, illus. 2008. (ENG.). 32p. (J). (gr. 1-3). 17.95 *(978-1-56846-200-4(X),* 22043, Creative Editions) Creative Co., The.

Herbert, Denis & Silver, Joanne. Complément éducatif: Mon Enfance Lilloise Racontée à Ma Fille: Récits D'antan (1950 à 1955) 2010. *(978-0-9819417-4-5(5))* Beach Lloyd Pubs., LLC.

Newman, Tracy. Itzhak: A Boy Who Loved the Violin. Halpin, Abigail, illus. 2020. (ENG.). 40p. (J). (gr. -1-3). 18.99 *(978-1-4197-4110-4(1),* 1214301, Abrams Bks. for Young Readers) Abrams, Inc.

Romeu, Emma. El Rey de las Octavas. Moreiro, Enrique S., illus. 2007. (SPA.). 40p. (J). (gr. 3-5). 17.99 *(978-1-933032-26-9(X))* Lectorum Pubns., Inc.

Sutryn, Barbara M. Heartstrings: A Biography of Wilmos Csehy. Lt. ed. 2004. (Illus.). 160p. (YA). 21.00 *(978-1-892135-33-9(7))* Lamp Post Publishing, Inc.

Toth, Henrietta. Lindsey Stirling: Violinist with More Than 2 Billion Views, 1 vol. 2019. (Top YouTube Stars Ser.). (ENG.). 48p. (gr. 5-5). pap. 12.75 *(978-1-7253-4627-7(3),* 223e6153-df5f-4200-87ea-40f117925ac9) Rosen Publishing Group, Inc., The.

VIPERS

see Snakes

VIRGIN ISLANDS OF THE UNITED STATES

see United States Virgin Islands

VIRGIN MARY

see Mary, Blessed Virgin, Saint

VIRGINIA

Barrett, Tracy. Virginia, 1 vol. 2nd rev. ed. 2007. (Celebrate the States (Second Edition) Ser.). (ENG., Illus.). 144p. (gr. 6-6). lib. bdg. 39.79 *(978-0-7614-1734-7(6),* e43813b7-fd8d-4972-a6d1-356d9728c0fd) Cavendish Square Publishing LLC.

Connors, Kathleen. People of the Chesapeake Bay, 1 vol. 2013. (Exploring the Chesapeake Bay Ser.). 32p. (J). (gr. 3-4). (ENG.). 29.27 *(978-1-4339-9776-1(2),* b014a0dd-f22c-4e40-b5e8-e0ba0fb7d94d); (ENG.). pap. 11.50 *(978-1-4339-9777-8(0),* ec648a77-65b4-4a69-a88d-725db1b04be8); pap. 63.00 *(978-1-4339-9778-5(9))* Stevens, Gareth Publishing LLLP.

—Plants & Animals of the Chesapeake Bay, 1 vol. 2013. (Exploring the Chesapeake Bay Ser.). 32p. (J). (gr. 3-4). (ENG.). 29.27 *(978-1-4339-9780-8(0),* c90dd9f0-6246-4367-9b8c-3b8ff12f1933); (ENG.). pap. 11.50 *(978-1-4339-9781-5(9),* e24a2ae6-ddf3-4b6f-a605-7ccff7ce0b53); pap. 63.00 *(978-1-4339-9782-2(7))* Stevens, Gareth Publishing LLLP.

Edwards, Pamela Duncan. O Is for Old Dominion: A Virginia Alphabet. Howell, Troy, illus. 2005. (Discover America State by State Ser.). (ENG.). 40p. (J). (gr. 1-3). 18.99 *(978-1-58536-161-8(5),* 202021) Sleeping Bear Pr.

Gamble, Adam. Good Night Virginia. Veno, Joe, illus. 2008. (Good Night Our World Ser.). (ENG.). 20p. (J). (gr. k — 1). bds. 9.95 *(978-1-60219-026-9(7))* Good Night Bks.

Heinrichs, Ann. Virginia. Kania, Matt, illus. 2017. (U. S. A. Travel Guides). (ENG.). 40p. (J). (gr. 2-5). lib. bdg. 38.50 *(978-1-5038-1986-3(8),* 211623) Child's World, Inc, The.

Kent, Deborah. America the Beautiful: Third Series: Virginia (Revised Edition) 2014. (America the Beautiful Ser.: 3). (ENG.). 144p. (J). lib. bdg. 40.00 *(978-0-531-24899-7(2))* Scholastic Library Publishing.

King, David C. Virginia, 1 vol. Santoro, Christopher, illus. 2006. (It's My State! (First Edition)(r) Ser.). (ENG.). 80p. (gr. 4-4). lib. bdg. 34.07 *(978-0-7614-1827-6(X),* 93c3c082-249d-4fa3-b093-108d8a664988) Cavendish Square Publishing LLC.

Mader, Jan. Virginia. 2003. (Rookie Read-About Geography Ser.). (ENG., Illus.). 32p. (J). (gr. 1-2). 20.50 *(978-0-516-22718-4(1),* Children's Pr.) Scholastic Library Publishing.

Marsh, Carole. Virginia Classic Christmas Trivia. 2005. (Illus.). 32p. (J). (gr. 4-7). pap. 6.95 *(978-0-635-03352-9(6))* Gallopade International.

—Virginia Current Events Projects: 30 Cool, Activities, Crafts, Experiments & More for Kids to Do to Learn about Your State! 2003. (Virginia Experience Ser.). 32p. (gr. k-8). pap. 5.95 *(978-0-635-02064-2(5),* Marsh, Carole Bks.) Gallopade International.

—Virginia Geography Projects: 30 Cool, Activities, Crafts, Experiments & More for Kids to Do to Learn about Your State! 2003. (Virginia Experience Ser.). 32p. (gr. k-5). pap. 5.95 *(978-0-635-01864-9(0),* Marsh, Carole Bks.) Gallopade International.

—Virginia Government Projects: 30 Cool, Activities, Crafts, Experiments & More for Kids to Do to Learn about Your State! 2003. (Virginia Experience Ser.). 32p. (gr. k-5). pap. 5.95 *(978-0-635-01965-3(5),* Marsh, Carole Bks.) Gallopade International.

—Virginia People Projects: 30 Cool, Activities, Crafts, Experiments & More for Kids to Do to Learn about Your State! 2003. (Virginia Experience Ser.). 32p. (gr. k-5). pap. 5.95 *(978-0-635-02015-4(7),* Marsh, Carole Bks.) Gallopade International.

—Virginia Symbols & Facts Projects: 30 Cool, Activities, Crafts, Experiments & More for Kids to Do to Learn about Your State! 2003. (Virginia Experience Ser.). 32p. (gr. k-5). pap. 5.95 *(978-0-635-01915-8(9),* Marsh, Carole Bks.) Gallopade International.

Melson, William G. Geology Explained: Virginia's Fort Valley & Massanutten Mountains. 2004. (Illus.). 170p. per. 15.95 *(978-0-9744173-0-1(0),* Ft. Valley Geology Study Ctr.) InterPress.

Mis, M. S. How to Draw Virginia's Sights & Symbols. 2009. (Kid's Guide to Drawing America Ser.). 32p. (gr. k-k). 50.50 *(978-1-61511-102-2(6),* PowerKids Pr.) Rosen Publishing Group, Inc., The.

Murray, Julie. Virginia, 1 vol. 2006. (Buddy Book Ser.). (ENG., Illus.). 32p. (gr. 2-4). 27.07 *(978-1-59197-705-6(3),* Buddy Bks.) ABDO Publishing Co.

Norfolk, Sherry & Norfolk, Bobby. The Virginia Giant: The True Story of Peter Francisco. Brennan, Cait, illus. 2014. (ENG.). 160p. (J). (gr. 4-7). 16.99 *(978-1-62619-117-4(4),* History Pr., The) Arcadia Publishing.

Parker, Bridget. Virginia. 2016. (States Ser.). (ENG., Illus.). 32p. (J). (gr. 3-6). lib. bdg. 27.99 *(978-1-5157-0434-8(3),* 132045, Capstone Pr.) Capstone.

Saving the Chesapeake Bay. 2013. (Exploring the Chesapeake Bay Ser.). 32p. (J). (gr. 3-6). pap. 63.00 *(978-1-4339-9786-0(X))* Stevens, Gareth Publishing LLLP.

Shepard, Betty Bruce. Virginia: An Affectionate Journey Through History. Lederman, Marsha, illus. 2007. 32p. (J). (gr. -1-3). 17.95 *(978-1-893622-14-2(2),* VSP Bks.) Vacation Spot Publishing.

Sullivan, E. J. V Is for Virginia. Eldredge, Ernie, illus. 2006. 24p. (J). lib. bdg. *(978-1-58173-526-0(X))* Sweetwater Pr.

Thompson, Gare. The Monitor: The Iron Warship That Changed the World. Day, Larry, illus. 2003. (All Aboard Reading: Station Stop 3 Ser.). (ENG.). 48p. (J). (gr. 2-4). 16.19 *(978-0-448-43283-0(8))* Penguin Young Readers Group.

Way, Jennifer. Virginia. 2009. (Bilingual Library of the United States of America Ser.). (ENG & SPA.). 32p. (gr. 2-2). 47.90 *(978-1-60853-390-9(5),* Editorial Buenas Letras) Rosen Publishing Group, Inc., The.

White-Adams, Beverly & Adams, Rusty. The Adventures of Rusty: Rusty Goes to Virginia Vol. 1. 2011. 32p. pap. *(978-1-4269-8935-3(0))* Trafford Publishing (UK) Ltd.

VIRGINIA—FICTION

Allen, Elaine Ann. Olly's Treasure, 1 vol. 2011. (ENG., Illus.). 40p. (J). (gr. -1-3). 16.99 *(978-0-7643-3772-7(6),* 4107, Schiffer Publishing Ltd) Schiffer Publishing, Ltd.

Altsheler, Joseph A. The Guns of Bull Run: A Story of the Civil War's Eve. 2006. (Civil War Ser.: Vol. 1). 300p. (J). reprint ed. 29.95 *(978-1-4218-1777-4(2));* pap. 14.95 *(978-1-4218-1877-1(9))* 1st World Publishing, Inc. (1st World Library - Literary Society).

—The Guns of Bull Run: A Story of the Civil War's Eve. 2009. 278p. reprint ed. pap. 14.99 *(978-1-60512-409-4(5));* (Civil War Ser.: Vol. 1). (J). 27.99 *(978-1-60512-309-7(9))* Akasha Publishing, LLC. (Akasha Classics).

—The Guns of Bull Run: A Story of the Civil War's Eve. 2007. (Civil War Ser.: Vol. 1). (ENG.). 238p. (J). reprint ed. per. 20.99 *(978-1-4346-7678-8(1))* Creative Media Partners, LLC.

—The Guns of Bull Run: A Story of the Civil War's Eve. 2006. (Civil War Ser.: Vol. 1). (J). reprint ed. pap. *(978-1-4065-0812-3(8))* Dodo Pr.

—The Guns of Bull Run: A Story of the Civil War's Eve. 2010. (Civil War Ser.: Vol. 1). (Illus.). 162p. (J). (gr. 4-7). reprint ed. pap. 19.99 *(978-1-153-70504-2(4))* General Bks. LLC.

—The Guns of Bull Run: A Story of the Civil War's Eve. (Civil War Ser.: Vol. 1). (J). reprint ed. 2010. 238p. (gr. 4-7). 33.56 *(978-1-169-29842-2(7))* 2010. 238p. (gr. 4-7). pap. 21.56 *(978-1-162-69670-6(2))* 2010. 41.95 *(978-1-161-46535-8(9))* 2004. pap. 1.99 *(978-1-4192-6519-8(9))* 2004. pap. 26.95 *(978-1-4191-6519-1(4))* Kessinger Publishing, LLC.

—The Guns of Bull Run: A Story of the Civil War's Eve. 2009. (Civil War Ser.: Vol. 1). (YA). (gr. 4-7). reprint ed. pap. 16.95 *(978-1-933573-82-3(1))* Zeezok Publishing, LLC.

—The Guns of Bull Run: A Story of the Civil War's Eve. 2011. (Civil War Ser.: Vol. 1). 256p. (J). (gr. 4-7). reprint ed. pap. *(978-3-8424-5271-8(3))* tredition Verlag.

—The Scouts of Stonewall: The Story of the Great Valley Campaign. 2006. (Civil War Ser.: Vol. 3). 312p. (J). reprint ed. 29.95 *(978-1-4218-1779-8(9));* pap. 14.95 *(978-1-4218-1879-5(5))* 1st World Publishing, Inc. (1st World Library - Literary Society).

—The Scouts of Stonewall: The Story of the Great Valley Campaign. Lt. ed. (Civil War Ser.: Vol. 3). (J). reprint ed. 2007. (ENG.). 240p. pap. 22.99 *(978-1-4264-1531-9(1))* 2011. 370p. (gr. 4-7). pap. 32.75 *(978-1-245-65787-7(9))* 2008. 244p. 27.99 *(978-0-554-22030-7(X))* 2008. 244p. 24.99 *(978-0-554-31333-7(2))* 2006. 250p. pap. 20.99 *(978-1-4264-1498-5(6))* Creative Media Partners, LLC.

—The Scouts of Stonewall: The Story of the Great Valley Campaign. 2006. (Civil War Ser.: Vol. 3). (J). reprint ed. pap. *(978-1-4065-0820-8(9))* Dodo Pr.

—The Scouts of Stonewall: The Story of the Great Valley Campaign. 2007. (Civil War Ser.: Vol. 3). 184p. (J). reprint ed. per. *(978-1-4068-1684-6(1))* Echo Library.

—The Scouts of Stonewall: The Story of the Great Valley Campaign. 2010. (Civil War Ser.: Vol. 3). (Illus.). 166p. (J). (gr. 4-7). reprint ed. pap. 19.99 *(978-1-153-72009-0(4))* General Bks. LLC.

—The Scouts of Stonewall: The Story of the Great Valley Campaign. reprint ed. 2010. (Civil War Ser.: Vol. 3). 252p. (J). (gr. 4-7). 33.56 *(978-1-169-30265-5(3))* 2010. (Civil War Ser.: Vol. 3). 252p. (J). (gr. 4-7). pap. 21.56 *(978-1-162-70768-6(2))* 2010. (Civil War Ser.: Vol. 3). 252p. (J). 41.95 *(978-1-161-47632-3(6))* 2004. pap. 26.95 *(978-1-4191-8162-7(9))* 2004. (Civil War Ser.: Vol. 3). (J). pap. 1.99 *(978-1-4192-8162-4(3))* Kessinger Publishing, LLC.

—The Scouts of Stonewall: The Story of the Great Valley Campaign. 2011. (Civil War Ser.: Vol. 3). 278p. (J). (gr. 4-7). reprint ed. pap. *(978-3-8424-6100-0(3))* tredition Verlag.

—The Shades of the Wilderness: A Story of Lee's Great Stand. 2006. (Civil War Ser.: Vol. 7). 308p. (J). reprint ed. 29.95 *(978-1-4218-2336-2(5));* pap. 14.95 *(978-1-4218-2436-9(1))* 1st World Publishing, Inc. (1st World Library - Literary Society).

—The Shades of the Wilderness: A Story of Lee's Great Stand. (Civil War Ser.: Vol. 7). 312p. (J). reprint ed. lib. bdg. 25.95 *(978-0-88411-940-1(8))* Amereon Ltd.

—The Shades of the Wilderness: A Story of Lee's Great Stand. 2008. (Civil War Ser.: Vol. 7). 280p. (J). reprint ed. 25.99 *(978-0-554-33603-9(0))* Creative Media Partners, LLC.

—The Shades of the Wilderness: A Story of Lee's Great Stand. 2006. (Civil War Ser.: Vol. 7). (J). reprint ed. pap. *(978-1-4065-0822-2(5))* Dodo Pr.

—The Shades of the Wilderness: A Story of Lee's Great Stand. 2007. (Civil War Ser.: Vol. 7). 180p. (J). reprint ed. per. *(978-1-4068-1686-0(8))* Echo Library.

—The Shades of the Wilderness: A Story of Lee's Great Stand. 2010. (Civil War Ser.: Vol. 7). (Illus.). 162p. (J). (gr. 4-7). reprint ed. pap. 19.99 *(978-1-153-72059-5(0))* General Bks. LLC.

—The Shades of the Wilderness: A Story of Lee's Great Stand. (Civil War Ser.: Vol. 7). (J). reprint ed. 2011. (gr. 4-7). *(978-1-164-50265-4(4))* 2010. 324p. (gr. 4-7). pap. 24.76 *(978-1-163-19558-1(8))* 2008. 324p. 45.95 *(978-1-4366-8424-8(2))* 2007. 324p. per. 30.95 *(978-1-4325-9861-7(9))* Kessinger Publishing, LLC.

—The Shades of the Wilderness: A Story of Lee's Great Stand. 2007. (Civil War Ser.: Vol. 7). 308p. reprint ed. per. 16.45 *(978-1-60424-029-0(6),* Bk. Jungle) Standard Publications, Inc.

—The Shades of the Wilderness: A Story of Lee's Great Stand. 2011. (Civil War Ser.: Vol. 7). 280p. (J). reprint ed. pap. *(978-3-8424-4396-9(X))* tredition Verlag.

—The Tree of Appomattox: A Story of the Civil War's Close. 2006. (Civil War Ser.: Vol. 8). 324p. (J). reprint ed. 29.95 *(978-1-4218-2338-6(1));* pap. 14.95 *(978-1-4218-2438-3(8))* 1st World Publishing, Inc. (1st World Library - Literary Society).

—The Tree of Appomattox: A Story of the Civil War's Close. 2007. (Civil War Ser.: Vol. 8). (ENG.). 266p. (J). reprint ed. pap. 21.99 *(978-1-4346-1190-1(6))* Creative Media Partners, LLC.

—The Tree of Appomattox: A Story of the Civil War's Close. 2006. (Civil War Ser.: Vol. 8). (J). reprint ed. pap. *(978-1-4065-0828-4(4))* Dodo Pr.

—The Tree of Appomattox: A Story of the Civil War's Close. 2007. (Civil War Ser.: Vol. 8). 192p. (J). reprint ed. per. *(978-1-4068-1693-8(0))* Echo Library.

—The Tree of Appomattox: A Story of the Civil War's Close. 2010. (Civil War Ser.: Vol. 8). (Illus.). 174p. (J). (gr. 4-7). reprint ed. pap. 19.99 *(978-1-153-72402-9(2))* General Bks. LLC.

—The Tree of Appomattox: A Story of the Civil War's Close. Wrenn, Charles L., illus. (Civil War Ser.: Vol. 8). 332p. (J). (gr. 4-7). reprint ed. 2011. 45.95 *(978-1-169-88135-8(1))* 2010. 36.76 *(978-1-163-21361-2(6))* 2010. pap. 24.76 *(978-1-162-78752-7(X))* Kessinger Publishing, LLC.

—The Tree of Appomattox: A Story of the Civil War's Close. 2005. (Civil War Ser.: Vol. 8). (J). reprint ed. pap. 30.95 *(978-1-4179-2071-6(8))* Kessinger Publishing, LLC.

—The Tree of Appomattox: A Story of the Civil War's Close. Wrenn, Charles L., illus. 2005. (Civil War Ser.: Vol. 8). 332p. (J). reprint ed. 45.95 *(978-1-4326-1333-4(2))* Kessinger Publishing, LLC.

—The Tree of Appomattox: A Story of the Civil War's Close. 2011. (Civil War Ser.: Vol. 8). 294p. (J). (gr. 4-7). reprint ed. pap. *(978-3-8424-8485-6(2))* tredition Verlag.

Amateau, Gigi. Chancey: Horses of the Maury River Stables. 2010. (Horses of the Maury River Ser.: 1). (ENG., Illus.). 256p. (J). (gr. 4-7). pap. 8.99 *(978-0-7636-4523-6(0))* Candlewick Pr.

—Macadoo: Horses of the Maury River Stables. (Horses of the Maury River Ser.: 2). (ENG.). (J). (gr. 4-7). 2015. 208p. pap. 6.99 *(978-0-7636-7670-4(5))* 2013. 192p. 15.99 *(978-0-7636-3766-8(1))* Candlewick Pr.

Armstrong, Alan. Raleigh's Page. Jessell, Tim, illus. 2009. (ENG.). 336p. (J). (gr. 3-7). 7.99 *(978-0-375-83320-5(X),* Yearling) Random Hse. Children's Bks.

Arnold, Ginger Fudge. Two Tipsy Tots, 1 vol. Crème, Aurora C., illus. 2009. 32p. pap. 24.95 *(978-1-4489-1891-1(X))* America Star Bks.

Aryal, Aimee Sutter. Hello Hokie Bird! Meadows, Sarah, illus. 2003. (J). 18.95 *(978-0-9743442-0-1(6))* Amplify Publishing Group.

Basham, Tom. Sailing Home. Calvert, Lissa, illus. 2012. 168p. *(978-1-77097-370-1(2))* FriesenPress.

Basham, Tom & Calvert, Lissa. Sailing Home. 2012. 168p. pap. *(978-1-77097-371-8(0))* FriesenPress.

Bayard, Louis. Lucky Strikes. 2016. (ENG., Illus.). 320p. (YA). 29.99 *(978-1-62779-390-2(9),* 900148815, Holt, Henry & Co. Bks. For Young Readers) Holt, Henry & Co.

—Lucky Strikes. 2017. (YA). lib. bdg. 20.85 *(978-0-606-39951-7(8))* Turtleback.

The Beach by the Bay: Tanner & Kai Go Surfing. 2007. (Illus.). 24p. (J). 15.95 *(978-0-9796039-0-7(0))* Sandbridge Sons Publishing.

Bernardin, James & Plehal, Christopher J. Yes, Virginia: There Is a Santa Claus. 2010. (ENG., Illus.). 32p. (J). (gr. -1-2). 17.99 *(978-0-06-200173-3(6),* HarperCollins) HarperCollins Pubs.

Bettino, Teresa Adele. The Adventures of Sugarbabe & Thunder. 2013. 34p. pap. 12.00 *(978-0-9742842-0-0(3))* Bettino, Teresa Adele.

Bradby, Marie. Some Friend. 2007. (ENG.). 256p. (J). (gr. 3-7). pap. 7.99 *(978-1-4169-3452-3(9),* Atheneum Bks. for Young Readers) Simon & Schuster Children's Publishing.

Briggs, Martha Wren. The Little Ferry Travels with Virginia Bk. 6: The Little Ferry Goes to Yorktown. Starbuck-McMillan, Elizabeth, illus. 2007. (The Little Ferry Travels with Virginia Ser.: Vol. 6). 30p. (YA). (gr. 5-8). pap. 6.95 *(978-0-9633240-8-5(X))* Dory Pr.

Brooke, Lauren. All or Nothing. 2007. (Chestnut Hill Ser.: No. 6). 184p. (J). lib. bdg. 15.38 *(978-1-4242-1719-9(9))* Fitzgerald Bks.

—Making Strides. 2005. (Chestnut Hill Ser.: No. 2). 219p. (J). (gr. 4-7). 12.65 *(978-0-7569-6478-8(4))* Perfection Learning Corp.

—The New Class. 2005. (Chestnut Hill Ser.: No. 1). 212p. (J). (gr. 4-7). lib. bdg. 12.65 *(978-0-7569-6479-5(2))* Perfection Learning Corp.

Brown, Cara D. Isabelle's Wish. 2013. 48p. (gr. 2-2). pap. 8.95 *(978-1-4759-7421-8(3))* iUniverse, Inc.

Bulla, Clyde Robert. A Lion to Guard Us. Chessare, Michele, illus. 2018. (ENG.). 128p. (J). (gr. 3-7). pap. 9.99 *(978-0-06-440333-7(5),* HarperCollins) HarperCollins Pubs.

Burgess, Linda, text. Mount Vernon's Magnificent Menagerie: And the Very Mysterious Guest. 2012. (ENG., Illus.). 48p. (J). 15.95 *(978-0-931917-31-8(X))* Mount Vernon Ladies' Assn. of the Union.

Burnham, Niki & Saidens, Amy. Royally Jacked. 2003. (Romantic Comedies Ser.). (ENG.). 208p. (YA). mass mkt. 6.99 *(978-0-689-86668-5(2),* Simon Pulse) Simon Pulse.

Chapman Willis, Cynthia. Dog Gone: A Picture Book. 2009. (ENG.). 240p. (J). (gr. 3-7). pap. 17.99 *(978-0-312-56113-0(X),* 900058843) Square Fish.

Crane, Stephen. The Red Badge of Courage. (EMC Masterpiece Series Access Editions). (J). 11.99 *(978-0-8219-1981-1(4))* EMC/Paradigm Publishing.

Cromwell, Daisy. Arthur, the Talking Goat. Paxton, Cameron L., illus. 2007. 52p. (J). pap. 18.99 *(978-0-9800675-1-4(0))* Mirror Publishing.

Davis, Catherine Jennings & Thompson, Traci Shirley. Goodnight Cavaliers. 2013. (J). 17.95 *(978-1-62086-038-0(4))* Amplify Publishing Group.

Dooley, Sarah. Free Verse. 2017. lib. bdg. 19.65 *(978-0-606-39788-9(4))* Turtleback.

TUV

Earhart, Kristin. Buttercup Mystery. Geddes, Serena, illus. 2015. (Marguerite Henry's Misty Inn Ser.: 2). (ENG.). 128p. (J). (gr. 2-5). pap. 6.99 *(978-1-4814-1416-6(X)*, Aladdin) Simon & Schuster Children's Publishing.

—Finding Luck. Geddes, Serena, illus. 2016. (Marguerite Henry's Misty Inn Ser.: 4). (ENG.). 128p. (J). (gr. 2-5). pap. 6.99 *(978-1-4814-1422-7(4)*, Aladdin) Simon & Schuster Children's Publishing.

—Runaway Pony. Geddes, Serena, illus. 2015. (Marguerite Henry's Misty Inn Ser.: 3). (ENG.). 128p. (J). (gr. 2-5). pap. 6.99 *(978-1-4814-1419-7(4)*, Aladdin) Simon & Schuster Children's Publishing.

—Runaway Pony. 2015. (Marguerite Henry's Misty Inn Ser.: 3). lib. bdg. 16.00 *(978-0-606-37835-2(9))* Turtleback.

—Welcome Home! Geddes, Serena, illus. 2015. (Marguerite Henry's Misty Inn Ser.: 1). (ENG.). 128p. (J). (gr. 2-5). 16.99 *(978-1-4814-1414-2(3)*, Aladdin) Simon & Schuster Children's Publishing.

—Welcome Home! 2015. (Marguerite Henry's Misty Inn Ser.: 1). lib. bdg. 16.00 *(978-0-606-37126-1(5))* Turtleback.

Elliott, L. M. Annie, Between the States. 2006. (ENG.). 544p. (YA). (gr. 8-12). per. 10.99 *(978-0-06-001213-7(7)*, Tegen, Katherine Bks) 2004. (Illus.). 496p. (J). (gr. 7-18). 16.99 *(978-0-06-001211-3(0))* HarperCollins Pubs.

Erskine, Kathryn. Mockingbird. (ENG.). (J). (gr. 5-18). 2011. 256p. 8.99 *(978-0-14-241775-1(0)*, Puffin Books) 2010. 240p. 17.99 *(978-0-399-25264-8(9)*, Philomel Bks.) Penguin Young Readers Group.

—Mockingbird. (J). 2012. 1.25 *(978-1-4407-4671-0(0))* 2010. 72.75 *(978-1-4407-4667-3(2))* 2010. 74.75 *(978-1-4407-4665-9(6))* 2010. 210.75 *(978-1-4407-4662-8(1))* 2010. (SPA.). 62.75 *(978-1-4407-4663-5(X))* 2010. 64.75 *(978-1-4407-4661-1(3))* Recorded Bks., Inc.

—Mockingbird. 2011. lib. bdg. 18.40 *(978-0-606-15356-0(X))* Turtleback.

—Seeing Red. 2013. (ENG.). 352p. (YA). E-Book *(978-0-545-57645-1(8))*; (J). (gr. 5-9). 16.99 *(978-0-545-46440-6(4))* Scholastic, Inc. (Scholastic Pr.).

Gourley, Robbin. Bring Me Some Apples & I'll Make You a Pie: A Story about Edna Lewis. 2016. (ENG., Illus.). 48p. (J). (gr. -1-3). pap. 7.99 *(978-0-544-80901-7(7)*, 1641300, Clarion Bks.) HarperCollins Pubs.

Hahn, Mary Downing. Closed for the Season. 2010. (ENG.). 192p. (J). (gr. 5-7). pap. 7.99 *(978-0-547-39853-2(0)*, 1427651, Clarion Bks.) HarperCollins Pubs.

—The Girl in the Locked Room: A Ghost Story. (ENG.). 208p. (J). (gr. 5-7). 2019. pap. 9.99 *(978-0-358-09755-6(X)*, 1747618) 2018. 18.99 *(978-1-328-85092-8(7)*, 1693448) HarperCollins Pubs. (Clarion Bks.).

Haislip, Phyllis Hall. Anybody's Hero: The Battle of Old Men & Young Boys. 2004. (Illus.). 220p. (J). pap. 8.95 *(978-1-57249-343-8(7)*, White Mane Kids) White Mane Publishing Co., Inc.

—Lili's Gift: A Civil War Healer's Story. 2008. (ENG., Illus.). 204p. (J). pap. 8.95 *(978-1-57249-392-6(5)*, White Mane Kids) White Mane Publishing Co., Inc.

—Lottie's Courage: A Contraband Slave's Story. 2003. (Illus.). 120p. (J). pap. 7.95 *(978-1-57249-311-7(9)*, White Mane Kids) White Mane Publishing Co., Inc.

Hall, Kate W. Richmond Rocks! 2009. (Illus.). (J). 14.95 *(978-1-61623-975-6(1)*, Richmondmom.com Publishing) Palari Publishing LLP.

Hall, Lucy. From England to Jamestowne: A Journey to Find My Father. 2007. (J). *(978-0-9763706-5-9(4))* Tendril Pr., LLC.

Harris, Teresa E. The Perfect Place. (ENG.). 272p. (J). (gr. 5-7). 2018. pap. 7.99 *(978-1-328-78418-6(5)*, 1683760) 2014. 17.99 *(978-0-547-25519-4(5)*, 1388242) HarperCollins Pubs. (Clarion Bks.).

—The Perfect Place. 2018. lib. bdg. 18.40 *(978-0-606-40433-4(3))* Turtleback.

Harvey, Tom. Guido, the Swan with an Attitude. 2011. 44p. (gr. -1). pap. 17.99 *(978-1-4269-6855-6(8))* Trafford Publishing.

Heald, Robin. Liberty Saves the Day! Elkerton, Andy, illus. 2017. (J). *(978-0-87935-290-5(6))* Colonial Williamsburg Foundation.

Henry, Marguerite. Cinnabar, the One o'Clock Fox. Dennis, Wesley, illus. (ENG.). 144p. (J). (gr. 3-7). 2015. 19.99 *(978-1-4814-0401-3(0))* 2014. pap. 7.99 *(978-1-4814-0400-6(8))* Simon & Schuster Children's Publishing. (Aladdin).

—Misty of Chincoteague. 2011. (CHI.). 165p. (J). (gr. 3-7). pap. *(978-7-5434-8018-6(2))* Hebei Jiaoyu Chubanshe.

—Misty of Chincoteague. Dennis, Wesley, illus. 2007. 173p. (gr. 3-7). 17.00 *(978-0-7569-8227-0(8))* Perfection Learning Corp.

—Misty of Chincoteague. Dennis, Wesley, illus. 60th ed. 2006. (ENG.). 176p. (J). (gr. 3-7). pap. 7.99 *(978-1-4169-2783-9(2)*, Aladdin) Simon & Schuster Children's Publishing.

—Sea Star: Orphan of Chincoteague. Dennis, Wesley, illus. 2007. (ENG.). 176p. (J). (gr. 3-7). pap. 7.99 *(978-1-4169-2784-6(0)*, Aladdin) Simon & Schuster Children's Publishing.

—Stormy, Misty's Foal. Dennis, Wesley, illus. (ENG.). (J). (gr. 3-7). 2015. 256p. 21.99 *(978-1-4814-2561-2(7))* 2007. 224p. pap. 7.99 *(978-1-4169-2788-4(3))* Simon & Schuster Children's Publishing. (Aladdin).

Henty, George. With Lee in Virgini. 2007. 392p. 39.95 *(978-1-4344-8351-5(7))*; per. 24.95 *(978-1-4344-8350-8(9))* Wildside Pr., LLC.

Higgins, Carter. A Rambler Steals Home. 2017. (ENG.). 224p. (J). (gr. 5-7). 16.99 *(978-0-544-60201-4(3)*, 1616648, Clarion Bks.) HarperCollins Pubs.

Hollenbeck, Kathleen M. Dancing on the Sand: A Story of an Atlantic Blue Crab. 2005. (ENG., Illus.). 32p. (J). (gr. -1-2). 8.95 *(978-1-59249-234-3(7)*, SC4017) Soundprints.

Holt, Kimberly Willis. Piper Reed, Forever Friend. 6. Davenier, Christine, illus. 2012. (Piper Reed Ser.: 6). (ENG.). 160p. (J). (gr. 3-6). 18.69 *(978-0-8050-9008-6(8)*, 900058970, Holt, Henry & Co.) Holt, Henry & Co.

—Piper Reed, Forever Friend. Davenier, Christine, illus. 2013. (Piper Reed Ser.: 6). (ENG.). 176p. (J). (gr. 3-6). pap. 8.99 *(978-1-250-02725-2(X)*, 900098296) Square Fish.

Houston, Julian. New Boy. 2007. 282p. (gr. 7-12). 18.00 *(978-0-7569-8139-6(5))* Perfection Learning Corp.

Hunter, John P. Red Thunder: Secrets, Spies, & Scoundrels at Yorktown. 2006. 234p. (J). (gr. 6-8). 7.95 *(978-0-87935-231-8(0))* Colonial Williamsburg Foundation.

Jacobs, Lily. The Littlest Bunny in Virginia: An Easter Adventure. Dunn, Robert, illus. 2015. (Littlest Bunny Ser.). (ENG.). 32p. (J). (gr. -1-3). 9.99 *(978-1-4926-1228-5(6)*, Hometown World) Sourcebooks, Inc.

James, Eric. Santa's Sleigh Is on Its Way to Virginia: A Christmas Adventure. Dunn, Robert, illus. 2015. (Santa's Sleigh Is on Its Way Ser.). (ENG.). 32p. (J). (gr. k-2). 12.99 *(978-1-4926-2754-8(2)*, Hometown World) Sourcebooks, Inc.

—The Spooky Express Virginia. Piwowarski, Marcin, illus. 2017. (Spooky Express Ser.). (ENG.). 32p. (J). (gr. k-6). 9.99 *(978-1-4926-5408-7(6)*, Hometown World) Sourcebooks, Inc.

—Tiny the Virginia Easter Bunny. 2018. (Tiny the Easter Bunny Ser.). (ENG.). 40p. (J). (gr. k-3). 9.99 *(978-1-4926-5974-7(6)*, Hometown World) Sourcebooks, Inc.

—Tiny the West Virginia Easter Bunny. 2018. (Tiny the Easter Bunny Ser.). (ENG.). 40p. (J). (gr. k-3). 9.99 *(978-1-4926-5977-8(0)*, Hometown World) Sourcebooks, Inc.

Johnson, Phyllis. Betsy Star Ballerin. 2011. 24p. 16.95 *(978-1-4575-0149-4(X))* Dog Ear Publishing, LLC.

Johnston, K. E. M. The Witness Tree & the Shadow of the Noose: Mystery, Lies, & Spies in Manassas. 2009. 111p. (J). (gr. 5-7). pap. 8.95 *(978-1-57249-397-1(6)*, White Mane Kids) White Mane Publishing Co., Inc.

Joyce, Alexandria. Trail of the Caribou: A Tale of Dire Wolves in the Time of the Ice Age. 2011. 216p. (gr. 4-6). pap. 15.95 *(978-1-4620-5066-6(2))* iUniverse, Inc.

Katschke, Judy. Home at Last. Geddes, Serena, illus. 2018. (Marguerite Henry's Misty Inn Ser.: 8). (ENG.). 144p. (J). (gr. 2-5). 17.99 *(978-1-4814-6995-1(9))*; pap. 6.99 *(978-1-4814-6994-4(0))* Simon & Schuster Children's Publishing. (Aladdin).

King, Sarah. The Great Adventures of Piggy the Peruvian Guinea Pig. 2016. (ENG., Illus.). 36p. (J). pap. 10.95 *(978-1-63047-568-0(8))* Morgan James Publishing.

Lorenzi, Natalie Dias. Flying the Dragon. 240p. (J). (gr. 4-7). 2014. (ENG.). pap. 8.95 *(978-1-58089-435-7(6))* 2012. 16.95 *(978-1-58089-434-0(8))* Charlesbridge Publishing, Inc.

Lough, Whitney. Smoke Hole Adventure. Cosner, Jeff, illus. 2013. 36p. (J). 12.00 *(978-0-87012-833-2(7))* McClain Printing Co.

Lyne, Jennifer H. Catch Rider. 2014. (ENG.). 288p. (YA). (gr. 7). pap. 8.99 *(978-0-544-30182-5(X)*, 1577488, Clarion Bks.) HarperCollins Pubs.

Marsh, Carole. The Mystery at Mount Vernon. Friedlander, Randolyn, illus. 2010. (Real Kids, Real Places Ser.). 32p. pap. 7.99 *(978-0-635-07444-7(3)*, Marsh, Carole Mysteries) Gallopade International.

—The Mystery at Mount Vernon: Home of America's First President George Washington. 2010. (Real Kids, Real Places Ser.). (Illus.). 158p. (J). 18.99 *(978-0-635-07443-0(5)*, Marsh, Carole Mysteries) Gallopade International.

—Pocahontas. (Read-Along Ser.). (J). 7.99 incl. audio *(978-1-55723-739-2(5))* Walt Disney Records.

Mathieson, Karen. Duel or Duet: Book Two of the Rosemary Ridge Trilogy. 2013. 160p. (J). pap. 7.99 *(978-1-940350-05-9(0))* Mathieson Creative Media.

—Liza, Elizabeth: Book Three of the Rosemary Ridge Trilogy. 2013. 164p. (J). pap. 7.99 *(978-1-940350-08-0(5))* Mathieson Creative Media.

McDonald, Megan. Judy Moody & Friends: Amy Namey in Ace Reporter. Madrid, Erwin, illus. 2014. (Judy Moody & Friends Ser.: 3). (ENG.). 64p. (J). (gr. -1-1). 12.99 *(978-0-7636-5715-4(8))* Candlewick Pr.

Mcdonald, Megan. Judy Moody Saves the World! Reynolds, Peter H., illus. 2004. (Judy Moody Ser.: Bk. 3). 144p. (J). (gr. 1-5). 13.65 *(978-0-7569-2588-8(6))* Perfection Learning Corp.

McDonald, Megan. Judy Moody Saves the World! Reynolds, Peter H., illus. 2010. (Judy Moody Ser.: 3). (ENG.). 160p. (J). (gr. 1-4). 16.99 *(978-0-7636-4860-2(4))* Candlewick Pr.

Mcdonald, Megan. Judy Moody Saves the World! 2010. (Judy Moody Ser.: 3). 144p. lib. bdg. 16.00 *(978-0-606-12340-2(7))* Turtleback.

—Stink & the Great Guinea Pig Express. Reynolds, Peter H., illus. 2010. (Stink Ser.: No. 4). (ENG.). 128p. (J). (gr. 1-5). 31.36 *(978-1-59961-683-4(1)*, 13830, Chapter Bks.) Spotlight.

—Stink & the Great Guinea Pig Express. 2013. (Stink Ser.: 4). lib. bdg. 14.75 *(978-0-606-31590-6(X))* Turtleback.

McDonald, Megan. Stink & the Great Guinea Pig Express, Bk. 4. Reynolds, Peter H., illus. 2013. (Stink Ser.: 4). (ENG.). 128p. (J). (gr. 1-4). 15.99 *(978-0-7636-6391-9(3))* Candlewick Pr.

McGowen, Julie. Virginia's Voyage. 2007. 48p. per. 16.95 *(978-1-4241-6672-5(1))* America Star Bks.

McMahan, Stephanie K. The Mystery of the Golden Rings. 2007. 140p. 21.95 *(978-0-595-68451-9(3))*; per. 11.95 *(978-0-595-43998-0(5))* iUniverse, Inc.

McVicker, Mary. Secret of Belle Meadow, 1 vol. 2009. (ENG., Illus.). 152p. (gr. 3-6). per. 9.95 *(978-0-87033-554-9(5)*, 3720, Cornell Maritime Pr./Tidewater Pubs.) Schiffer Publishing, Ltd.

Middleton, William. The Chipmunk Jamboree. 2013. 24p. pap. 12.45 *(978-1-4624-0669-2(6)*, Inspiring Voices) Author Solutions, LLC.

Mills, Charles. The Secret of Scarlett Cove. 2004. (Honors Club Story Ser.: Bk. 3). 127p. (J). 7.99 *(978-0-8163-1999-2(5))* Pacific Pr. Publishing Assn.

Moore, Stephanie Perry. True Friends. 1. 2005. (Carmen Browne Ser.: 1). (ENG.). 128p. (YA). (gr. 4-6). pap. 6.99 *(978-0-8024-8172-6(8))* Moody Pubs.

Mullins, Norman D. Mountain Boy: The Adventures of Orion Saddler. 2004. 104p. (YA). per. 9.95 *(978-0-9724867-4-3(7))* Woodland Pr., LLC.

Nolen, Jerdine. Calico Girl. (ENG.). (J). (gr. 3-7). 2018. 208p. pap. 8.99 *(978-1-4814-5982-2(1))* 2017. (Illus.). 192p. 18.99 *(978-1-4814-5981-5(3))* Simon & Schuster/Paula Wiseman Bks. (Simon & Schuster/Paula Wiseman Bks.).

Oladokun, Alexander. Acrux Mandor: The Prodigal's Curse (Hardcover) 2013. (ENG.). 204p. 28.50 *(978-1-300-68651-4(0))* Lulu Pr., Inc.

Olasky, Susan. Annie Henry: Adventures in the American Revolution. 2005. (Illus.). 528p. (J). pap. 16.99 *(978-1-58134-521-6(6)*, Crossway Bibles) Crossway.

—Annie Henry & the Mysterious Stranger. 2003. (Adventures of the American Revolution Ser.: Vol. 3). 144p. (YA). (gr. 3-7). pap. 5.99 *(978-0-89107-907-1(6))* Crossway.

—Annie Henry & the Mysterious Stranger. 2011. (J). pap. *(978-1-59638-376-0(3))* P & R Publishing.

O'Neill, Elizabeth. Alfred Visits Virginia. 2006. (Illus.). 24p. (J). (gr. -1-3). pap. 12.00 *(978-0-9771836-8-5(8))* Funny Bone Bks.

Otis, James. Richard of Jamestown: A story of the Virginia Colony. 2007. (Illus.). 140p. (J). per. 9.95 *(978-0-9790876-0-8(0))* Living Bks. Pr.

Paterson, Katherine. Bridge to Terabithia. Diamond, Donna, illus. l.t. ed. 2007. (Literacy Bridge Middle Reader Ser.). 187p. (J). (gr. 4-7). 23.95 *(978-0-7862-9620-0(8))* Thorndike Pr.

—Bridge to Terabithia Movie Tie-In Edition. Diamond, Donna, illus. movie tie-in ed. 2006. (ENG.). 208p. (J). (gr. 3-7). pap. 7.99 *(978-0-06-125370-6(7)*, HarperFestival) HarperCollins Pubs.

—Bridge to Terabithia Movie Tie-In Edition. Diamond, Donna, illus. movie tie-in ed. 2006. (ENG.). 176p. (J). (gr. 3-7). pap. 7.99 *(978-0-06-122728-8(5)*, HarperFestival) HarperCollins Pubs.

Pistole, Katy. Flying High. 2003. (Illus.). 126p. (J). 7.99 *(978-0-8163-1942-8(1))* Pacific Pr. Pubns.

Powell, Patricia Hruby. Loving vs. Virginia: A Documentary Novel of the Landmark Civil Rights Case (Books about Love for Kids, Civil Rights History Book) Strickland, Shadra, illus. 2017. (ENG.). 260p. (YA). (gr. 7-12). 21.99 *(978-1-4521-2590-9(2))* Chronicle Bks. LLC.

Pyle, Howard. The Story of Jack Ballister's Fortunes: Being the Narrative of the Adventures of a Young Gentleman of Good Family, Who Was Kidnapped in the Year 1719 & Carried to the Plantations of the Continent of Virginia, Where He Fell in with That Famous Pirate Captain Edward Teach, or Blackbeard; of His Escape from the Pirates & the Rescue of a Young Lady from Out Their Hands. unabr. ed. 2012. (Illus.). 436p. 49.99 *(978-1-4622-8858-8(8))* Repressed Publishing LLC.

Ransom, Candice. Finding Day's Bottom. 2006. 176p. (J). (gr. 3-7). lib. bdg. 15.95 *(978-1-57505-933-4(9)*, Carolrhoda Bks.) Lerner Publishing Group.

Readler, Blaine C. Under the Radar: The Spy Drone Adventure. 2006. (ENG.). 248p. (J). (gr. 7-12). per. *(978-1-933255-18-7(8))* DNA Pr.

Reeder, Carolyn. Moonshiner's Son. 2003. (ENG., Illus.). 208p. (J). (gr. 3-7). pap. 7.99 *(978-0-689-85550-4(8)*, Aladdin) Simon & Schuster Children's Publishing.

Reynolds, Jason. As Brave As You. (ENG.). 432p. (J). (gr. 5). 2017. pap. 8.99 *(978-1-4814-1591-0(3)*, Atheneum Bks. for Young Readers) 2016. (Illus.). 19.99 *(978-1-4814-1590-3(5)*, Atheneum/Caitlyn Dlouhy Books) Simon & Schuster Children's Publishing.

Reynolds Naylor, Phyllis. Alice on Board. 2012. (Alice Ser.: 24). (ENG., Illus.). 288p. (YA). (gr. 9). 17.99 *(978-1-4424-4588-8(2)*, Atheneum Bks. for Young Readers) Simon & Schuster Children's Publishing.

—A Shiloh Christmas. 2015. (Shiloh Quartet Ser.). (ENG., Illus.). 256p. (J). (gr. 3-7). 17.99 *(978-1-4814-4151-3(5))* Simon & Schuster Children's Publishing.

Rimer, David & Robertson, William P. The Bucktails' Antietam Trials. 2005. (White Mane Kids Ser.: No.14). (Illus.). 175p. (J). (gr. 4-7). per. 7.95 *(978-1-57249-337-7(2)*, White Mane Kids) White Mane Publishing Co., Inc.

Rinaldi, Ann. The Letter Writer. 2008. (Great Episodes Ser.). (ENG., Illus.). 224p. (YA). (gr. 7-12). 22.44 *(978-0-15-206402-0(8))* Harcourt Children's Bks.

—Or Give Me Death. 2004. (Great Episodes Ser.). 226p. (gr. 5-9). 17.00 *(978-0-7569-3462-0(1))* Perfection Learning Corp.

—Sarah's Ground. 2004. (ENG., Illus.). 192p. (YA). 15.95 *(978-0-689-85924-3(4)*, Simon & Schuster Bks. For Young Readers) Simon & Schuster Bks. For Young Readers.

Robertson, William P. & Rimer, David. The Battling Bucktails at Fredericksburg. 2005. (WM Kids Ser.: Vol. 16). (Illus.). 154p. (J). (gr. 4-7). per. 7.95 *(978-1-57249-345-2(3)*, White Mane Kids) White Mane Publishing Co., Inc.

Roop, Peter & Roop, Connie. An Eye for an Eye. 2004. 168p. (J). lib. bdg. 16.92 *(978-1-4242-0772-5(X))* Fitzgerald Bks.

Roy, Ron. Capital Mysteries #11: the Secret at Jefferson's Mansion. Bush, Timothy, illus. 2009. (Capital Mysteries Ser.: 11). (ENG.). 96p. (J). (gr. 1-4). 6.99 *(978-0-375-84533-8(X)*, Random Hse. Bks. for Young Readers) Random Hse. Children's Bks.

—A to Z Mysteries Super Edition 3: White House White-Out. Gurney, John Steven, illus. 2008. (to Z Mysteries Ser.: 3). 144p. (J). (gr. 1-4). 6.99 *(978-0-375-84721-9(9)*, Random Hse. Bks. for Young Readers) Random Hse. Children's Bks.

—White House White-Out. Gurney, John, illus. 2008. (A to Z Mysteries Ser.: No. 3). 124p. (gr. 1-4). 15.00 *(978-0-7569-8799-2(7))* Perfection Learning Corp.

Rue, Nancy N. Sophie Steps Up, 1 vol. 2009. (Faithgirlz! Ser.: No. 4). (ENG.). 128p. (J). pap. 6.99 *(978-0-310-71841-3(4))* Zonderkidz.

—Sophie's Friendship Fiasco. 2009. (Faithgirlz! Ser.: No. 7). (ENG.). 128p. (J). pap. 6.99 *(978-0-310-71842-0(2))* Zonderkidz.

Salisbury, Linda. Earthquake Surprise: A Bailey Fish Adventure. Tomatore, Carol, illus. 2012. 192p. (J). pap. 8.95 *(978-1-881539-65-0(2))* Tabby Hse. Bks.

Salisbury, Linda G. The Thief at Keswick Inn: A Bailey Fish Adventure. Grotke, Christopher A., illus. 2006. (Bailey Fish Adventures Ser.). 191p. (J). (gr. 3-7). per. 8.95 *(978-1-881539-41-4(5))* Tabby Hse. Bks.

—Trouble in Contrary Woods: A Bailey Fish Adventure. Tomatore, Carol, illus. 2009. (J). 8.85 *(978-1-881539-46-9(6))* Tabby Hse. Bks.

Sanders, Scott Loring. Gray Baby. 2009. (ENG.). 336p. (YA). (gr. 7-18). 17.00 *(978-0-547-07661-4(4)*, 1042029, Clarion Bks.) HarperCollins Pubs.

Seeley, Bonnie L. Chincoteague Daisy Chain. Lidard, Kelly & Seeley, Douglas A., illus. 2003. 32p. (J). bds. 12.95 *(978-0-9728380-0-9(7))* Seelcraft Publishing.

Sharpe, Susan. Waterman's Boy. 2007. (ENG.). 176p. (J). (gr. 3-7). pap. 11.95 *(978-1-4169-6453-7(3)*, Simon & Schuster/Paula Wiseman Bks.) Simon & Schuster/Paula Wiseman Bks.

Siwak, Brenda S. Counting on the Bay. Dodge, Barbara A., illus. 2006. (J). per. 14.95 *(978-0-9790906-0-8(1))* Pleasant Plains Pr.

Smallman, Steve. Santa Is Coming to Virginia. Dunn, Robert, illus. 2013. (ENG.). 32p. (J). (-3). 9.99 *(978-1-4022-8800-5(X)*, Sourcebooks Jabberwocky) Sourcebooks, Inc.

Smith, Eunice Geil. Treasure Hunt. 2006. 119p. (J). (gr. 3-7). per. 9.99 *(978-0-8361-9332-9(6))* Herald Pr.

Smith, L. J. The Awakening & the Struggle, 2 vols. 2007. (Vampire Diaries: 1). 492p. (YA). (gr. 7). lib. bdg. 20.85 *(978-1-4178-2599-8(5))* Turtleback.

—The Vampire Diaries: the Hunters: Moonsong Vol. 9. 2013. (Vampire Diaries: the Hunters Ser.: 2). (ENG.). 416p. (YA). (gr. 9). pap. 10.99 *(978-0-06-201771-0(3)*, HarperTeen) HarperCollins Pubs.

—The Vampire Diaries: the Hunters: Phantom. (Vampire Diaries: the Hunters Ser.: 1). (ENG.). (YA). (gr. 9). 2012. 432p. pap. 10.99 *(978-0-06-201769-7(1))* 2011. 416p. 17.99 *(978-0-06-201768-0(3))* HarperCollins Pubs. (HarperTeen).

Smith, Laverne Byrd. Pokey the Playful Whale: (who wanted to live on Land) 2010. (Illus.). 36p. pap. 25.50 *(978-1-4490-7620-7(3))* AuthorHouse.

Smith, Steven K. Summer of the Woods. 2013. 158p. pap. 7.99 *(978-0-9893414-1-7(0))* MyBoys3 Pr.

Smolik, Jane Petrlik. Currents. 2015. (Illus.). 336p. (J). (gr. 4-7). lib. bdg. 16.95 *(978-1-58089-648-1(0))* Charlesbridge Publishing, Inc.

Spain, Susan Rosson. The Deep Cut, 0 vols. 2014. (ENG.). 228p. (J). (gr. 5-7). pap. 9.99 *(978-1-4778-4768-8(5)*, 9781477847688, Two Lions) Amazon Publishing.

—The Deep Cut, 1 vol. 2006. (ENG., Illus.). 224p. (J). (gr. 5-9). 16.99 *(978-0-7614-5316-1(4))* Marshall Cavendish Corp.

Squiers, Connie. The Copper Colt. 2013. 94p. pap. 7.95 *(978-1-937829-78-0(2)*, Total Publishing & Media) Yorkshire Publishing Group.

St. Mark Kindergarten. Kindergarten Goes to Outer Space for the Day. 2009. 28p. pap. 12.49 *(978-1-4490-0587-0(X))* AuthorHouse.

Stevens, B. K. Fighting Chance. 2015. (ENG.). 336p. (YA). pap. 18.99 *(978-1-929345-14-4(3)*, Poisoned Pen Press) Sourcebooks, Inc.

Sully, Katherine. Night-Night Virginia. Poole, Helen, illus. 2017. (Night-Night Ser.). (ENG.). 20p. (J). (gr. -1-1). bds. 9.99 *(978-1-4926-4767-6(5)*, 9781492647676, Hometown World) Sourcebooks, Inc.

Szymanski, Lois. Wild Colt, 1 vol. 2012. (ENG., Illus.). 40p. (J). 16.99 *(978-0-7643-3975-2(3)*, 4445) Schiffer Publishing, Ltd.

Szymanski, Lois K. The True Story of Sea Feather, 1 vol. 2010. (ENG., Illus.). 48p. (gr. 3-6). pap. 14.99 *(978-0-7643-3609-6(6)*, 4019) Schiffer Publishing, Ltd.

Thomas, Beth. Jack & the Richmond Bubble. 2012. pap. 11.95 *(978-0-7414-7495-7(6))* Infinity Publishing.

Thompson, Kimberly. Toulouse Tangled up in Lights. Easey, Chris, illus. 2011. 64p. (J). 19.95 *(978-0-9818976-1-5(4))* Little Pigeon Bks.

Tuthill, Louisa C. Hurrah for New England! or the Virginia Boy's Vacation. 2004. reprint ed. pap. 1.99 *(978-1-4192-2504-8(9))*; pap. 15.95 *(978-1-4191-2504-1(4))* Kessinger Publishing, LLC.

Walker, Sally M. Freedom Song: The Story of Henry Box Brown. Qualls, Sean, illus. 2012. (ENG.). 40p. (J). (gr. -1-3). 18.99 *(978-0-06-058310-1(X)*, HarperCollins) HarperCollins Pubs.

Walt Disney Company Staff. Pocahontas. 2005. (WEL., Illus.). 24p. *(978-1-899877-04-1(5))* Y Ddraig Fach.

Wells, Carolyn. Patty Fairfield. 2015. (ENG., Illus.). (J). (gr. -1-7). 25.95 *(978-1-298-88381-0(4))* Creative Media Partners, LLC.

—Patty Fairfield. 2011. 166p. (gr. -1-7). 25.95 *(978-1-4638-9972-1(6))* Rodgers, Alan Bks.

Wells, Rosemary. Red Moon at Sharpsburg. 2008. (ENG.). 256p. (YA). (gr. 7-18). 9.99 *(978-0-14-241205-3(8)*, Speak) Penguin Young Readers Group.

West, Joseph, Jr. Watching the Hokies with Daddy. 2005. (Illus.). 23p. (J). 18.95 *(978-0-9770680-0-5(5))* Titan Publishing.

Westrick, Anne. Brotherhood. 2014. 384p. (J). (gr. 5). pap. 8.99 *(978-0-14-242237-3(1)*, Puffin Books) Penguin Young Readers Group.

White, Ruth. Belle Prater's Boy. unabr. ed. 2004. 196p. (J). (gr. 5-9). pap. 38.00 incl. audio *(978-0-8072-8682-1(6)*, YA234SP, Listening Library) Random Hse. Audio Publishing Group.

—The Search for Belle Prater. 2007. 169p. (J). (gr. 4-7). 14.15 *(978-0-7569-7274-5(4))* Perfection Learning Corp.

Winders, Gertrude Hecker. Jeb Stuart: Boy in the Saddle. Doremus, Robert, illus. 2011. 202p. 44.95 *(978-1-258-08155-3(5))* Literary Licensing, LLC.

Winters, Cat. The Raven's Tale. 2019. (ENG., Illus.). 368p. (gr. 7-17). 17.99 *(978-1-4197-3362-8(1)*, 1153101, Amulet Bks.) Abrams, Inc.

Wood, D. K. Nightmare at Indian Cave. 2006. pap. 10.00 *(978-1-4257-1640-0(7))* Xlibris Corp.

Wood, Michael. Villains in Virginia Beach. 2004. 100p. (YA). per. *(978-1-59196-534-3(9))* Instant Pub.

VIRGINIA—HISTORY

Abnett, Dan. The Battle of the Wilderness: Deadly Inferno. 2009. (Graphic Civil War Battles Ser.). (ENG.). 48p. (YA). (gr. 4-5). 58.50 *(978-1-61512-901-0(4)*, Rosen Reference) Rosen Publishing Group, Inc., The.

—The Battle of the Wilderness: Deadly Inferno, 1 vol. Verma, Dheeraj, illus. 2006. (Graphic Battles of the Civil War Ser.). (ENG.). 48p. (YA). (gr. 4-5). lib. bdg. 37.13 *(978-1-4042-0780-6(5)*, 5e568da3-4ef5-4ddd-85d9-85dca2aa8b66) Rosen Publishing Group, Inc., The.

—The Battle of the Wilderness: Deadly Inferno, 1 vol. 2006. (Graphic Battles of the Civil War Ser.). (ENG., Illus.). 48p. (gr. 4-5). pap. 14.05 *(978-1-4042-6479-3(5)*, 539d8da0-40fb-4031-8c14-137df6480c03, Rosen Classroom) Rosen Publishing Group, Inc., The.

—The Monitor Versus the Merrimac: Ironclads at War, 1 vol. Verma, Dheeraj, illus. 2006. (Graphic Battles of the Civil War Ser.). (ENG.). 48p. (J). (gr. 4-5). lib. bdg. 37.13 *(978-1-4042-0778-3(3),* c1104d37-0229-4941-a9a3-6bd0f959a40e) Rosen Publishing Group, Inc., The.

Abraham, Isaiah. My Great Grandmother's Memorial Service. 2013. (Illus.). 32p. pap. 14.95 *(978-1-937829-72-8(3),* Total Publishing & Media) Yorkshire Publishing Group.

Adams, Colleen. Pocahontas. 2009. (Reading Room Collection 1 Ser.). 16p. (gr. 2-3). 37.50 *(978-1-60851-949-1(X),* PowerKids Pr.) Rosen Publishing Group, Inc., The.

—Pocahontas: The Life of an Indian Princess, 1 vol. 2005. (Reading Room Collection 1 Ser.). (ENG., Illus.). 16p. (J). (gr. 2-3). lib. bdg. 22.27 *(978-1-4042-3348-5(2),* 9742d742-8b33-4c42-acaf-7741d03ed4f6) Rosen Publishing Group, Inc., The.

Bennett, Doraine. Appalachian Plateau. 2011. (Illus.). 32p. (J). *(978-1-935884-09-5(3));* pap. *(978-1-935884-14-9(X))* State Standards Publishing, LLC.

—Blue Ridge Mountains. 2011. (Illus.). 32p. (J). *(978-1-935884-10-1(7));* pap. *(978-1-935884-15-6(8))* State Standards Publishing, LLC.

—Coastal Plain (Tidewater) 2011. (Illus.). 32p. (J). *(978-1-935884-12-5(3));* pap. *(978-1-935884-17-0(4))* State Standards Publishing, LLC.

—Piedmont. 2011. (Illus.). 32p. *(978-1-935884-11-8(5));* pap. *(978-1-935884-16-3(6))* State Standards Publishing, LLC.

—Valley & Ridge. 2011. (Illus.). 32p. (J). *(978-1-935884-13-2(1));* pap. *(978-1-935884-18-7(2))* State Standards Publishing, LLC.

Bjorklund, Ruth. Jamestown & the Settlement of Virginia, 1 vol. 2017. (Primary Sources of Colonial America Ser.). (ENG.). 64p. (gr. 6-6). 35.93 *(978-1-5026-3138-1(5),* b8ff73bc-bc0e-4cf7-97b7-81316ef123cb); pap. 16.28 *(978-1-5026-3456-6(2),* 0877bab9-7963-4c03-b922-8455571ec491) Cavendish Square Publishing LLC.

Bober, Natalie S. Thomas Jefferson: Draftsman of a Nation. 2008. (ENG., Illus.). 376p. per. 16.95 *(978-0-8139-2732-9(3),* P144204) University of Virginia Pr.

Boehm Jerome, Kate. Richmond & the State of Virginia: Cool Stuff Every Kid Should Know. 2011. (Arcadia Kids Ser.). (ENG., Illus.). 48p. (J). (gr. 3-6). pap. 11.99 *(978-1-4396-0098-6(8))* Arcadia Publishing.

Brindell Fradin, Dennis. Jamestown, Virginia, 1 vol. 2007. (Turning Points in U. S. History Ser.). (ENG., Illus.). 48p. (gr. 4-4). lib. bdg. 34.07 *(978-0-7614-2122-1(X),* f90b4dfc-7667-449b-a030-3715f19e4a4f) Cavendish Square Publishing LLC.

Broyles, Janell. A Timeline of the Jamestown Colony. 2009. (Timelines of American History Ser.). 32p. (gr. 4-4). 47.90 *(978-1-60854-385-4(4),* Rosen Reference) Rosen Publishing Group, Inc., The.

Burrows, Jennifer. Arlington National Cemetery. 2009. (War Memorials Ser.). (Illus.). 32p. (YA). (gr. 3-6). lib. bdg. 29.95 *(978-1-60694-425-7(8))* Rourke Educational Media.

Carole Marsh. Virginia Indians. 2004. (Virginia Experience Ser.). 36p. (gr. 3-8). 29.95 *(978-0-635-02337-7(7));* pap. 7.95 *(978-0-635-02336-0(9))* Gallopade International.

Connors, Kathleen. Visiting the Chesapeake Bay, 1 vol. 2013. (Exploring the Chesapeake Bay Ser.). (ENG.). 32p. (J). (gr. 3-4). 29.27 *(978-1-4339-9788-4(6),* 4aa416ed-5360-4c89-8a93-881be3375abc); pap. 11.50 *(978-1-4339-9789-1(4),* 51081937-2d4f-45c8-b32e-8aed4adb132c) Stevens, Gareth Publishing LLLP.

Cunningham, Kevin. The Virginia Colony. 2011. (True Book-the Thirteen Colonies Ser.). (ENG., Illus.). 48p. (J). lib. bdg. 29.00 *(978-0-531-25399-1(6),* Children's Pr.) Scholastic Library Publishing.

—The Virginia Colony (a True Book: the Thirteen Colonies) 2011. (True Book (Relaunch) Ser.). (ENG., Illus.). 48p. (J). (gr. 3-5). pap. 6.95 *(978-0-531-26612-0(5),* Children's Pr.) Scholastic Library Publishing.

Davidson, Tish. Atlantic: North Carolina, Virginia, West Virginia, Vol. 19. 2015. (Let's Explore the States Ser.). (Illus.). 64p. (J). (gr. 5). 23.95 *(978-1-4222-3320-7(0))* Mason Crest.

Dean, Arlan. The Wilderness Trail: From the Shenandoah Valley to the Ohio River. 2009. (Famous American Trails Ser.). 24p. (gr. 3-3). 42.50 *(978-1-61512-493-0(4),* PowerKids Pr.) Rosen Publishing Group, Inc., The.

DeAngelis, Gina. Virginia. 2009. (From Sea to Shining Sea, Second Ser.). (ENG.). 80p. (J). pap. 7.95 *(978-0-531-21144-1(4),* Children's Pr.) Scholastic Library Publishing.

Ditchfield, Christin. Exploring the Virginia Colony. 2016. (Exploring the 13 Colonies Ser.). (ENG., Illus.). 48p. (J). (gr. 3-6). lib. bdg. 34.65 *(978-1-5157-2229-8(5),* 132753) Capstone.

Doeden, Matt. At the Battle of the Ironclads: An Interactive Battlefield Adventure. 2018. (You Choose: American Battles Ser.). (ENG., Illus.). 112p. (J). (gr. 3-7). pap. 6.95 *(978-1-5435-0294-7(6),* 137163, Capstone Pr.) Capstone.

Donohue, Moira Rose. Christopher Newport. 2013. (Illus.). 24p. (J). *(978-1-938813-05-4(7));* pap. *(978-1-938813-09-2(X))* State Standards Publishing, LLC.

—L. Douglas Wilder. 2012. (Illus.). 32p. (J). *(978-1-935884-63-7(8));* pap. *(978-1-935884-69-9(7))* State Standards Publishing, LLC.

—Maggie L. Walker. 2012. (Illus.). 32p. (J). *(978-1-935884-62-0(X));* pap. *(978-1-935884-68-2(9))* State Standards Publishing, LLC.

Dubois, Muriel L. Virginia, 1 vol. 2005. (Portraits of the States Ser.). (ENG., Illus.). 32p. (gr. 3-5). pap. 11.50 *(978-0-8368-4655-3(9),* b8526676-0d40-4469-b69f-159d05d0e51f, Gareth Stevens Learning Library) Stevens, Gareth Publishing LLLP.

Dudley Gold, Susan. Parody of Public Figures: Hustler Magazine V. Falwell, 1 vol. 2014. (First Amendment Cases Ser.). (ENG.). 160p. (YA). (gr. 9-9). pap. 24.51 *(978-1-62712-391-4(1),* 64e5c27f-b3f7-4f0b-a23a-d31201a04960); lib. bdg. 45.50 *(978-1-62712-390-7(3),* fca2f633-2c95-47c2-83a0-39083694e674) Cavendish Square Publishing LLC.

Exploring the Chesapeake Bay, 12 vols. 2013. (Exploring the Chesapeake Bay Ser.). 32p. (J). (gr. 3-4). (ENG.). 175.62 *(978-1-4339-9843-0(2),* 3dbf9bdb-3190-4d9b-96e4-ce1612f28569); pap. 63.00 *(978-1-4339-9844-7(0));* pap. 378.00 *(978-1-4339-9845-4(9))* Stevens, Gareth Publishing LLLP.

Feldman, Thea. A Pony with Her Writer: The Story of Marguerite Henry & Misty (Ready-To-Read Level 2) Sanson, Rachel, illus. 2019. (Tails from History Ser.). (ENG.). 32p. (J). (gr. k-2). 17.99 *(978-1-5344-5154-4(4));* pap. 4.99 *(978-1-5344-5153-7(6))* Simon Spotlight. (Simon Spotlight).

Friedman, Robin. The Silent Witness. Nivola, Claire A., illus. 2008. (ENG.). 32p. (J). (gr. -1-3). pap. 7.99 *(978-0-547-01436-4(8),* 1030951, Clarion Bks.) HarperCollins Pubs.

Gilman, Sarah. Colonial Jamestown, 1 vol. 2016. (Explore Colonial America Ser.). (ENG., Illus.). 48p. (gr. 4-5). 29.60 *(978-0-7660-7871-0(X),* 318a6c3a-3416-49c1-be51-01146e8da4cd) Enslow Publishing, LLC.

Gold, Susan Dudley. Parody of Public Figures: Hustler Magazine Inc. V. Falwell. 2013. (J). 42.79 *(978-1-60870-906-9(X))* Marshall Cavendish Corp.

Goldsworthy, Steve. Pentagon. 2012. (J). *(978-1-61913-260-3(5));* (ENG., Illus.). 24p. (gr. 4-7). lib. bdg. 27.13 *(978-1-61913-254-2(0),* AV2 by Weigl) Weigl Pubs., Inc.

Hackett, Jennifer. Virginia (a True Book: My United States) 2018. (True Book (Relaunch) Ser.). (ENG., Illus.). 48p. (J). (gr. 3-5). pap. 7.95 *(978-0-531-24722-8(8),* Children's Pr.) Scholastic Library Publishing.

—Virginia (a True Book: My United States) (Library Edition) 2018. (True Book (Relaunch) Ser.). (ENG., Illus.). 48p. (J). (gr. 3-5). 31.00 *(978-0-531-23171-5(2),* Children's Pr.) Scholastic Library Publishing.

Hamilton, John. Virginia, 1 vol. 2016. (United States of America Ser.). (ENG., Illus.). 48p. (J). (gr. 5-9). 34.21 *(978-1-68078-349-0(1),* 21683, Abdo & Daughters) ABDO Publishing Co.

Harkins, Susan Sales & Harkins, William H. Colonial Virginia. 2007. (Building America Ser.). (Illus.). 48p. (J). (gr. 4-8). lib. bdg. 29.95 *(978-1-58415-548-5(5))* Mitchell Lane Pubs.

The Hatfields & the McCoys, 1 vol. 2014. (Jr. Graphic American Legends Ser.). (ENG., Illus.). 24p. (J). (gr. 2-3). lib. bdg. 28.93 *(978-1-4777-7193-8(X),* 9a03d15c-200e-4c50-bd9b-7d0e162521d8, PowerKids Pr.) Rosen Publishing Group, Inc., The.

Higgins, Melissa. Jamestown Colony, 1 vol. 2013. (Foundations of Our Nation Ser.). (ENG.). 48p. (J). (gr. 4-8). lib. bdg. 35.64 *(978-1-61783-710-4(5),* 7818) ABDO Publishing Co.

History of the Chesapeake Bay. 2013. (Exploring the Chesapeake Bay Ser.). 32p. (J). (gr. 3-6). pap. 63.00 *(978-1-4339-9774-7(6))* Stevens, Gareth Publishing LLLP.

Jerome, Kate B. Lucky to Live in Virginia. 2017. (Arcadia Kids Ser.). (ENG., Illus.). 32p. (J). 16.99 *(978-0-7385-2775-8(0))* Arcadia Publishing.

—The Wise Animal Handbook Virginia. 2017. (Arcadia Kids Ser.). (ENG., Illus.). 32p. (J). 16.99 *(978-0-7385-2847-2(1))* Arcadia Publishing.

Johnson, Anna Maria, et al. Virginia: The Old Dominion State, 1 vol. 3rd ed. 2019. (It's My State! (Fourth Edition)(r) Ser.). (ENG.). 80p. (gr. 4-4). pap. 18.64 *(978-1-5026-4451-0(7),* bf26b507-6a06-46ba-9d17-d172c524d6a2) Cavendish Square Publishing LLC.

Kallio, Jamie. What's Great about Virginia? 2014. (Our Great States Ser.). (ENG., Illus.). 32p. (J). (gr. 2-5). lib. bdg. 26.65 *(978-1-4677-3341-0(5),* 7c2096b4-3fb6-4364-9142-c221ba4b2ddc, Lerner Pubns.) Lerner Publishing Group.

Khalid, Jinnow. Arlington National Cemetery & the Tomb of the Unknown Soldier, 1 vol. 2017. (Landmarks of Democracy: American Institutions Ser.). (ENG., Illus.). 24p. (J). (gr. 3-3). 25.27 *(978-1-5081-6095-3(3),* f5ada86b-a78d-4ffd-8370-03d6bb458796, PowerKids Pr.) Rosen Publishing Group, Inc., The.

King, David C. & Fitzgerald, Stephanie. Virginia, 1 vol. 2nd rev. ed. 2011. (It's My State! (Second Edition)(r) Ser.). (ENG.). 80p. (gr. 4-4). lib. bdg. 34.07 *(978-1-60870-060-8(7),* 60e30ab9-13b1-45d9-a151-c846a39a4f7b) Cavendish Square Publishing LLC.

King, David C., et al. Virginia, 1 vol. 3rd rev. ed. 2014. (It's My State! (Third Edition)(r) Ser.). (ENG.). 80p. (gr. 4-4). 35.93 *(978-1-5026-0019-6(6),* 5e68e215-1edb-47cc-8853-c4c42c91eb6f) Cavendish Square Publishing LLC.

Levy, Janey. Life in Jamestown Colony, 1 vol., Vol. 1. 2013. (What You Didn't Know about History Ser.). (ENG.). 24p. (J). (gr. 2-3). 25.27 *(978-1-4824-0586-6(5),* 2d53cf66-8e71-46bc-bc25-cea7b8d6a4ab) Stevens, Gareth Publishing LLLP.

—Slavery at Mount Vernon, 1 vol. 2016. (Hidden History Ser.). (ENG., Illus.). 32p. (J). (gr. 4-5). pap. 11.50 *(978-1-4824-5802-2(0),* 7c4da709-75cc-4d55-99aa-2cc697c29e15) Stevens, Gareth Publishing LLLP.

Linde, Barbara M. Arlington National Cemetery, 1 vol. 2018. (Symbols of America Ser.). (ENG.). 24p. (gr. 1-2). 24.27 *(978-1-5382-2897-5(1),* 9e7f9589-d527-472a-905a-3c6f7311413a) Stevens, Gareth Publishing LLLP.

Lusted, Marcia Amidon. The Jamestown Colony Disaster: A Cause-And-Effect Investigation. 2016. (Cause-And-Effect Disasters Ser.). (ENG., Illus.). 40p. (J). (gr. 4-6). lib. bdg. 30.65 *(978-1-5124-1116-4(7),* f85d6eae-20ea-4efb-8904-88c496b2fadb); E-Book 46.65 *(978-1-5124-1127-0(2))* Lerner Publishing Group. (Lerner Pubns.).

—Virginia: The Old Dominion, 1 vol. 2009. (Our Amazing States Ser.). (ENG., Illus.). 24p. (J). (gr. 3-3). pap. 9.25 *(978-1-4358-3372-2(4),* 04963f2f-0cc4-4b5e-b613-82e2359b88cb); lib. bdg. 26.27 *(978-1-4042-8123-3(1),* 27f91b5f-7cc2-40b8-bc3f-3cc98004b0fe) Rosen Publishing Group, Inc., The. (PowerKids Pr.).

Markovics, Joyce. Historic & Lively: What Am I? 2018. (American Place Puzzlers Ser.). (ENG.). 24p. (J). (gr. -1-3). E-Book 41.36 *(978-1-68402-540-4(0))* Bearport Publishing Co., Inc.

Marsh, Carole. Exploring Virginia Through Project-Based Learning: Geography, History, Government, Economics & More. 2016. (Virginia Experience Ser.). (ENG.). (J). pap. 9.99 *(978-0-635-12370-1(3))* Gallopade International.

—Virginia History Projects: 30 Cool, Activities, Crafts, Experiments & More for Kids to Do to Learn about Your State! 2003. (Virginia Experience Ser.). 32p. (gr. k-5). pap. 5.95 *(978-0-635-01815-1(2),* Marsh, Carole Bks.) Gallopade International.

Marsico, Katie. The Chesapeake Bay. 2013. (Explorer Library: Social Studies Explorer Ser.). (ENG.). 32p. (gr. 4-8). pap. 14.21 *(978-1-62431-037-9(0),* 202505); (Illus.). lib. bdg. 32.07 *(978-1-62431-013-3(3),* 202503) Cherry Lake Publishing.

McClafferty, Carla Killough. Buried Lives: The Enslaved People of George Washington's Mount Vernon. 2018. (ENG., Illus.). 168p. (J). (gr. 5-7). 24.99 *(978-0-8234-3697-2(7))* Holiday Hse., Inc.

McNeese, Tim. Jamestown. 2007. (ENG., Illus.). 112p. (gr. 5-9). lib. bdg. 30.00 *(978-0-7910-9335-1(2),* P124585, Facts On File) Infobase Holdings, Inc.

—Williamsburg. 2007. (ENG., Illus.). 112p. (gr. 5-9). lib. bdg. 30.00 *(978-0-7910-9333-7(6),* P124643, Facts On File) Infobase Holdings, Inc.

Miller, Jake. The Colony of Virginia: A Primary Source History. (Primary Source Library of the Thirteen Colonies & the Lost Colony Ser.). 24p. (gr. 3-4). 2009. 42.50 *(978-1-60854-162-1(2))* 2005. (ENG., Illus.). (J). lib. bdg. 26.27 *(978-1-4042-3029-3(7),* e429ed07-dbb8-4557-a745-2978c3f4a92e) Rosen Publishing Group, Inc., The. (PowerKids Pr.).

Miner Huey, Lois. American Archaeology Uncovers the Earliest English Colonies, 1 vol. 2010. (American Archaeology Ser.). (ENG.). 64p. (gr. 5-5). 34.07 *(978-0-7614-4264-6(2),* 75bbcf73-c2c4-44e6-b73f-0a8679f9611b) Cavendish Square Publishing LLC.

Moore Niver, Heather. Tributaries of the Chesapeake Bay, 1 vol. 2013. (Exploring the Chesapeake Bay Ser.). (ENG., Illus.). 32p. (J). (gr. 3-4). pap. 11.50 *(978-1-4339-9793-8(2),* 8f35a463-4c01-4bd1-be38-71cdffd395a9); lib. bdg. 29.27 *(978-1-4339-9792-1(4),* b6919ea1-67a9-4fe2-84e6-b1114a0590bf) Stevens, Gareth Publishing LLLP.

Nagelhout, Ryan. Saving the Chesapeake Bay, 1 vol. 2013. (Exploring the Chesapeake Bay Ser.). (ENG., Illus.). 32p. (J). (gr. 3-4). pap. 11.50 *(978-1-4339-9785-3(1),* 8d856c30-b5c6-4731-a3b6-785bfd7a2aea); lib. bdg. 29.27 *(978-1-4339-9784-6(3),* 49d2e09a-fd80-4a58-8dd1-de1f29a70604) Stevens, Gareth Publishing LLLP.

Nelson, Sheila. The Southern Colonies: The Quest for Prosperity. 2006. (How America Became America Ser.). (Illus.). 96p. (YA). lib. bdg. 22.95 *(978-1-59084-902-6(7))* Mason Crest.

Parker, Janice. Virginia. 2011. (Guide to American States Ser.). (Illus.). 48p. (J). (gr. 3-6). 29.99 *(978-1-61690-819-5(X));* 29.99 *(978-1-61690-495-1(X))* Weigl Pubs., Inc.

—Virginia: The Old Dominion. 2016. (J). *(978-1-4896-4956-0(5),* Berkley) Penguin Publishing Group.

—Virginia: The Old Dominion. 2016. (Illus.). 48p. (J). *(978-1-5105-2097-4(X))* SmartBook Media, Inc.

Polette, Nancy. Pocahontas. 2003. (Rookie Biographies Ser.). (ENG., Illus.). 32p. (J). (gr. 1-2). 20.50 *(978-0-516-22859-4(5),* Children's Pr.) Scholastic Library Publishing.

Porterfield, Jason. Virginia: Past & Present. 2009. 48p. (J). 70.50 *(978-1-4358-5577-9(9));* (ENG.). (gr. 5-5). pap. 12.75 *(978-1-4358-5576-2(0),* 491c6bf8-7eac-4a1d-ae22-596bbbb03eb6); (ENG., Illus.). (gr. 5-5). lib. bdg. 34.47 *(978-1-4358-5289-1(3),* b7548806-b2be-400e-94b2-ccdb5b1f30fb) Rosen Publishing Group, Inc., The. (Rosen Reference).

Pratt, Laura. Virginia: The Old Dominion State. 2012. (J). *(978-1-61913-413-3(6));* pap. *(978-1-61913-414-0(4))* Weigl Pubs., Inc.

Ruffin, Frances E. Jamestown, 1 vol. 2005. (Places in American History Ser.). (ENG., Illus.). 24p. (gr. 2-4). lib. bdg. 24.67 *(978-0-8368-6410-6(7),* 4fa0404b-c119-41de-b270-b4328057ef7b, Weekly Reader Leveled Readers) Stevens, Gareth Publishing LLLP.

Schmid, Katie Kelley. Nat Turner & Slave Life on a Southern Plantation, 1 vol. 2013. (Jr. Graphic African American History Ser.). (Illus.). 24p. (J). (ENG.). (gr. 2-3). pap. 11.60 *(978-1-4777-1453-9(7),* 8bc536b5-87fd-4812-ba81-35b2ae4fa79e); (ENG., (gr. 2-3). lib. bdg. 28.93 *(978-1-4777-1314-3(X),* 92a828d3-4636-48db-8581-fb3bf864f169); (gr. 3-6). pap. 63.60 *(978-1-4777-1454-6(5))* Rosen Publishing Group, Inc., The. (PowerKids Pr.).

Schwartz, Heather E. Pocahontas: Her Life & Legend. rev. ed 2016. (Social Studies: Informational Text Ser.). (ENG., Illus.). 32p. (gr. 4-8). pap. 11.99 *(978-1-4938-3072-5(4))* Teacher Created Materials, Inc.

Shea, Therese M. History of the Chesapeake Bay, 1 vol. 2013. (Exploring the Chesapeake Bay Ser.). (ENG.). 32p. (J). (gr. 3-4). 29.27 *(978-1-4339-9772-3(X),* 4b26b1f6-9d40-49cd-9a6c-95298f24e328); pap. 11.50 *(978-1-4339-9773-0(8),* 4f0c2f97-5c60-466c-a859-ad37cf84580e) Stevens, Gareth Publishing LLLP.

Sita, Lisa. Pocahontas: The Powhatan Culture & the Jamestown Colony, 1 vol. 2004. (Library of American Lives & Times Ser.). (ENG., Illus.). 112p. (J). (gr. 5-5). lib. bdg. 38.27 *(978-1-4042-2653-1(2),* 0630cc02-b680-457c-b3b0-922753babdca) Rosen Publishing Group, Inc., The.

Solomon, Sharon. Christopher Newport: Jamestown Explorer, 1 vol. Bridy, Dan, illus. 2013. (ENG.). 32p. (J). (gr. k-3). 19.99 *(978-1-4556-1752-4(0),* Pelican Publishing) Arcadia Publishing.

Stansberry, Don & Cluster Springs Elementary School Staff. Skipping Through the ABC's of History. Barczak, Marliss & Long, Lisa, eds. 2011. (Illus.). 31p. (J). (gr. -1-3). 16.95 *(978-0-929915-50-0(X))* Headline Bks., Inc.

Stefoff, Rebecca. John Brown & Armed Resistance to Slavery, 1 vol. 2015. (Primary Sources of the Abolitionist Movement Ser.). (ENG., Illus.). 64p. (gr. 6-6). 35.93 *(978-1-5026-0534-4(1),* e6c3336d-1bcb-4020-a1a6-45873b6f485c) Cavendish Square Publishing LLC.

Sullivan, Laura L., et al. Virginia. 2015. (J). lib. bdg. *(978-1-62712-772-1(0))* Cavendish Square Publishing LLC.

Thomas, Peggy. Farmer George Plants a Nation. Johnson, Layne, illus. 2008. (ENG.). 40p. (J). (gr. 2-5). 17.95 *(978-1-59078-460-0(X),* Calkins Creek) Highlights Pr., c/o Highlights for Children, Inc.

Tougas, Joe. Virginia. 2009. (This Land Called America Ser.). (Illus.). 32p. (YA). (gr. 3-6). 19.95 *(978-1-58341-799-7(0))* Creative Co., The.

Traylor, Waverley. Indian Legends of the Great Dismal Swamp. Traylor, Margaret, ed. Hancock, Stefanie, illus. 2004. 72p. (gr. 8-18). pap. 9.95 *(978-0-9715068-3-1(3))* Traylor, Waverley Publishing.

Tributaries of the Chesapeake Bay. 2013. (Exploring the Chesapeake Bay Ser.). 32p. (J). (gr. 3-6). pap. 63.00 *(978-1-4339-9794-5(0))* Stevens, Gareth Publishing LLLP.

Visiting the Chesapeake Bay. 2013. (Exploring the Chesapeake Bay Ser.). 32p. (J). (gr. 3-6). pap. 63.00 *(978-1-4339-9790-7(8))* Stevens, Gareth Publishing LLLP.

Walker, Frank S., Jr. Remembering: A History of Orange County, Virginia. 2004. (Illus.). 314p. 30.00 *(978-1-932547-00-9(2))* Orange County Historical Society, Inc.

Way, Jennifer. Virginia, 1 vol. Brusca, Maria Cristina, tr. 2005. (Bilingual Library of the United States of America Ser.: Set 2). (ENG & SPA., Illus.). 32p. (J). (gr. 2-2). lib. bdg. 28.93 *(978-1-4042-3112-2(9),* dcd3210f-ece2-4cb6-8228-75ef2791c467) Rosen Publishing Group, Inc., The.

Whiteknact, Sandra. A Primary Source History of the Colony of Virginia. (Primary Sources of the Thirteen Colonies & the Lost Colony Ser.). 64p. 2009. (gr. 5-8). 58.50 *(978-1-60851-890-6(6))* 2005. (ENG., Illus.). (gr. 4-6). per. 12.95 *(978-1-4042-0678-6(7),* a10281a9-c588-4722-be3d-0affce385c45) 2005. (ENG., Illus.). (YA). (gr. 4-6). lib. bdg. 37.13 *(978-1-4042-0437-9(7),* 6b15f685-fee2-4c22-9744-1be584ea32f7) Rosen Publishing Group, Inc., The.

VIRTUAL REALITY

Allen, John. Real-World Stem: Improving Virtual Reality. 2017. (Real-World Stem Ser.). (ENG.). 80p. (YA). (gr. 5-12). *(978-1-68282-237-1(0))* ReferencePoint Pr., Inc.

Beth, Georgia. Stem: The Battle Between 2-D & 3-d: Shapes (Grade 5) 2018. (Mathematics in the Real World Ser.). (ENG., Illus.). 32p. (J). (gr. 4-8). pap. 11.99 *(978-1-4258-5823-0(6))* Teacher Created Materials, Inc.

Bodden, Valerie. Virtual-Reality Headsets. 2017. (Modern Engineering Marvels Ser.). (ENG., Illus.). 32p. (J). (gr. 3-6). lib. bdg. 32.79 *(978-1-5321-1091-7(X),* 25758, Checkerboard Library) ABDO Publishing Co.

Chuirazzi, Sara. Using VR in Engineering, 1 vol. 2019. (VR on the Job: Understanding Virtual & Augmented Reality Ser.). (ENG.). 80p. (gr. 8-8). pap. 18.64 *(978-1-5026-4563-0(7),* 032af2b9-6a42-40c0-9d58-498af04170d1) Cavendish Square Publishing LLC.

Grant, Rachel. Animation & Presentation from Scratch: 4D an Augmented Reading Experience. 2018. (Code It Yourself 4D Ser.). (ENG., Illus.). 48p. (J). (gr. 3-5). lib. bdg. 33.99 *(978-1-5157-6659-9(4),* 135228, Capstone Pr.) Capstone.

Gregory, Josh. Virtual Reality & Minecraft. 2019. (21st Century Skills Innovation Library: Unofficial Guides Junior Ser.). (ENG.). 24p. (J). (gr. 2-4). pap. 12.79 *(978-1-5341-3984-8(2),* 212765); (Illus.). lib. bdg. 30.64 *(978-1-5341-4328-9(9),* 212764) Cherry Lake Publishing.

Gregory, Joshua. Careers in Virtual Reality Technology. 2018. (Bright Futures Press: Emerging Tech Careers Ser.). (ENG., Illus.). 32p. (J). (gr. 4-7). lib. bdg. 32.07 *(978-1-5341-2979-5(0),* 211960) Cherry Lake Publishing.

Halls, Kelly Milner. Virtual Reality Specialist. 2009. (21st Century Skills Library: Cool Science Careers Ser.). (ENG., Illus.). 32p. (gr. 4-8). lib. bdg. 32.07 *(978-1-60279-503-7(7),* 200307) Cherry Lake Publishing.

Henneberg, Susan, ed. Virtual Reality, 1 vol. 2016. (Opposing Viewpoints Ser.). (ENG.). 200p. (YA). (gr. 10-12). pap. 34.80 *(978-1-5345-0030-3(8),* b2d755e2-8abd-4ecb-8aad-be0bc52dac13); lib. bdg. 50.43 *(978-1-5345-0026-6(X),* 2a2ea671-2e43-41c5-8175-3ce7bfd942d2) Greenhaven Publishing LLC. (Greenhaven Publishing).

Hollander, Barbara Gottfried. Bitcoins: Navigating Open Source Currency, 1 vol. 2014. (Digital & Information Literacy Ser.). (ENG.). 48p. (YA). (gr. 5-5). 33.47 *(978-1-4777-7930-9(2),* fd16ba19-b660-4f43-a85a-bedc5ef2c89b, Rosen Reference) Rosen Publishing Group, Inc., The.

Holmes, Kirsty. Building Virtual Worlds. 2019. (Game On! Ser.). (Illus.). 32p. (J). (gr. 4-4). *(978-0-7787-5257-8(7));* pap. *(978-0-7787-5270-7(4))* Crabtree Publishing Co.

Kuromiya, Jun. The Future of Entertainment. 2020. (Searchlight Books (tm) — Future Tech Ser.). (ENG., Illus.). 32p. (J). (gr. 3-5). 30.65 *(978-1-5415-9734-1(6),* e50c9475-d602-403d-8653-5753277b8860, Lerner Pubns.) Lerner Publishing Group.

Martin, Brett S. Augmented Reality. 2017. (Tech Bytes Ser.). (ENG.). 48p. (J). (gr. 4-6). pap. 14.60 *(978-1-68404-117-6(1));* (Illus.). 26.60 *(978-1-59953-886-0(5))* Norwood Hse. Pr.

—Virtual Reality. 2017. (Tech Bytes Ser.). (ENG.). 48p. (J). (gr. 4-6). pap. 14.60 *(978-1-68404-120-6(1));* (Illus.). 26.60 *(978-1-59953-885-3(7))* Norwood Hse. Pr.

McCarthy, Cecilia Pinto. How Virtual Reality Will Impact Society. 2018. (Technology's Impact Ser.). (ENG.). 80p. (YA). (gr. 6-12). 39.93 *(978-1-68282-501-3(9))* ReferencePoint Pr., Inc.

Mooney, Carla. What Is the Future of Virtual Reality? 2016. (ENG., Illus.). 80p. (J). (gr. 5-12). lib. bdg. *(978-1-68282-094-0(7))* ReferencePoint Pr., Inc.

T U V

Morkes, Andrew. Alternative Reality Developers. 2019. (Cool Careers in Science Ser.). (Illus.). 96p. (J). (gr. 12). lib. bdg. 34.60 *(978-1-4222-4293-3(5))* Mason Crest.
Nagle, Jeanne. Getting to Know Alice, 1 vol. 2014. (Code Power: a Teen Programmer's Guide Ser.). (ENG., Illus.). 64p. (J). (gr. 6-6). 36.13 *(978-1-4777-7693-3(1),* eafff913-23d6-4c22-b449-d05a4ffb6988, Rosen Reference) Rosen Publishing Group, Inc., The.
Peterson, Christy. Cutting-Edge Augmented Reality. 2018. (Searchlight Books (tm) — Cutting-Edge STEM Ser.). (ENG., Illus.). 32p. (J). (gr. 3-5). pap. 9.99 *(978-1-5415-2774-4(7),* 7f0292f8-ede2-4e57-a6e0-928b4ef27fd5); lib. bdg. 30.65 *(978-1-5415-2343-2(1),* 8e939742-4676-4532-9e34-0a5693fd1e5a, Lerner Pubns.) Lerner Publishing Group.
—Cutting-Edge Virtual Reality. 2018. (Searchlight Books (tm) — Cutting-Edge STEM Ser.). (ENG., Illus.). 32p. (J). (gr. 3-5). pap. 9.99 *(978-1-5415-2777-5(1),* ce38e098-bab2-421a-9a82-176df8c9a5f1); lib. bdg. 30.65 *(978-1-5415-2347-0(4),* 130c2956-c6f3-46ae-9395-18c5809e8c0a, Lerner Pubns.) Lerner Publishing Group.
Rauf, Don. Virtual Reality, 1 vol., 1. 2015. (Digital & Information Literacy Ser.). (ENG.). 48p. (J). (gr. 6-6). pap. 12.75 *(978-1-4994-3781-2(1),* 0a790fe4-e09b-4e36-8ff3-05ad4b446c49, Rosen Central) Rosen Publishing Group, Inc., The.
Small, Cathleen. Using VR in Medicine, 1 vol. 2019. (VR on the Job: Understanding Virtual & Augmented Reality Ser.). (ENG.). 80p. (J). (gr. 8-8). lib. bdg. 37.36 *(978-1-5026-4570-8(X),* 64770452-8483-4128-95d6-66d446e5f6bd) Cavendish Square Publishing LLC.
Virtual Reality: Individual Title Six-Packs. (Bookweb Ser.). 32p. (gr. 6-18). 34.00 *(978-0-7578-0899-9(9))* Rigby Education.

VIRTUAL REALITY—FICTION

Anderson, Suzette. Cybertreks: Wildest West. 2004. 196p. pap. 13.95 *(978-0-595-30840-8(6))* iUniverse, Inc.
Barlow, Cassie & Norrod, Sue. Journey Through the Unified Field, 1 vol. Gantt, Amy, illus. 2019. (ENG.). 128p. (J). (gr. 3-7). pap. 9.95 *(978-1-4556-2478-2(0),* Pelican Publishing) Arcadia Publishing.
Bartel, Jen & Bartel, Tyler. Crystal Fighters. 2018. (Illus.). 144p. (J). (gr. 7). pap. 12.99 *(978-1-5067-0795-2(5),* Dark Horse Books) Dark Horse Comics.
Bond, Gwenda. Fallout. 2016. (Lois Lane Ser.). (ENG.). 304p. (YA). (gr. 9-12). pap. 9.95 *(978-1-63079-006-6(0),* 127340, Switch Pr.) Capstone.
—Triple Threat. (Lois Lane Ser.). (ENG.). 360p. (YA). (gr. 9-12). 2018. pap. 9.95 *(978-1-63079-084-4(2),* 134777) 2017. 16.95 *(978-1-63079-082-0(6),* 134776) Capstone. (Switch Pr.).
Cole, Steve. Z. Rex. (ENG.). (J). 2010. 256p. (gr. 5-18). 8.99 *(978-0-14-241712-6(2),* Puffin Books)1. 2009. 276p. (gr. 6-8). 22.44 *(978-0-399-25253-2(3))* Penguin Young Readers Group.
Dashner, James. The Eye of Minds. 2013. 310p. (YA). *(978-0-385-38370-7(3),* Delacorte Pr) Random House Publishing Group.
—The Eye of Minds (the Mortality Doctrine, Book One) 2014. (Mortality Doctrine Ser.: 1). (ENG.). 352p. (YA). (gr. 7). pap. 13.99 *(978-0-385-74140-8(5),* Ember) Random Hse. Children's Bks.
—The Rule of Thoughts (the Mortality Doctrine, Book Two), Bk. 2. 2016. (Mortality Doctrine Ser.: 2). (ENG.). 352p. (YA). (gr. 7). pap. 11.99 *(978-0-385-74142-2(1),* Ember) Random Hse. Children's Bks.
Doeden, Matt. Hansel & Gretel: An Interactive Fairy Tale Adventure. Miramon, Sabrina, illus. 2017. (You Choose: Fractured Fairy Tales Ser.). (ENG.). 112p. (J). (gr. 3-7). pap. 6.95 *(978-1-5157-6952-1(6),* 135424); lib. bdg. 32.65 *(978-1-5157-6944-6(5),* 135418) Capstone. (Capstone Pr.).
Drake, Raelyn. Realm of Mystics. 2017. (Level Up Ser.). (ENG.). 120p. (YA). (gr. 6-12). pap. 7.99 *(978-1-5124-5359-1(5),* 2db305fb-5671-42ec-b0de-48cb8df9c814); lib. bdg. 26.65 *(978-1-5124-3989-2(4),* f51a5363-838f-45b4-b9b7-c89b4fcd2ba4) Lerner Publishing Group. (Darby Creek).
Duckro, Rebecca S. Adventures of Charlie KeeperTechnobrat. 2006. 156p. per. 12.95 *(978-0-595-40498-8(7))* iUniverse, Inc.
Durango, Julia. The Leveller. 2017. (ENG.). 272p. (YA). (gr. 8). pap. 9.99 *(978-0-06-231401-7(7),* HarperTeen) HarperCollins Pubs.
Fields, Jan. The Calm Before the Storm: A Night in Sleepy Hollow, 1 vol. Altmann, Scott, illus. 2013. (Adventures in Extreme Reading Ser.). (ENG.). 112p. (J). (gr. 2-5). 38.50 *(978-1-61641-920-2(2),* 60, Calico Chapter Bks.) ABDO Publishing Co.
—Hack Attack: A Trip to Wonderland, 1 vol. Altmann, Scott, illus. 2013. (Adventures in Extreme Reading Ser.). (ENG.). 112p. (J). (gr. 2-5). 38.50 *(978-1-61641-919-6(9),* 58, Calico Chapter Bks.) ABDO Publishing Co.
—Lightning Strikes Twice: Escaping Great Expectations, 1 vol. Altmann, Scott, illus. 2013. (Adventures in Extreme Reading Ser.). (ENG.). 112p. (J). (gr. 2-5). 38.50 *(978-1-61641-922-6(9),* 64, Calico Chapter Bks.) ABDO Publishing Co.
—A Novel Nightmare: The Purloined Story, 1 vol. Altmann, Scott, illus. 2013. (Adventures in Extreme Reading Ser.). (ENG.). 112p. (J). (gr. 2-5). 38.50 *(978-1-61641-924-0(5),* 68, Calico Chapter Bks.) ABDO Publishing Co.
Freitas, Donna. The Mind Virus. 2018. (Unplugged Ser.: 3). (ENG.). 432p. (YA). (gr. 8). pap. 9.99 *(978-0-06-211867-7(6),* HarperTeen) HarperCollins Pubs.
Gabel, Claudia & Klam, Cheryl. Etherworld. 2016. (Elusion Ser.: 2). (ENG.). 352p. (YA). (gr. 9). pap. 9.99 *(978-0-06-212245-2(2),* Tegen, Katherine Bks) HarperCollins Pubs.
Harrington, Kim. Attack of the Not-So-Virtual Monsters (Gamer Squad 1) Gamer Squad #1. 2017. (Gamer Squad Ser.). 208p. (J). (gr. 3-7). pap. 6.95 *(978-1-4549-2612-2(0))* Sterling Publishing Co., Inc.
—Close Encounters of the Nerd Kind (Gamer Squad 2) Gamer Squad #2. 2017. (Gamer Squad Ser.). 208p. (J). (gr. 3-7). pap. 6.95 *(978-1-4549-2613-9(9))* Sterling Publishing Co., Inc.
Kawahara, Reki. Accel World, Vol. 2 (light Novel) The Red Storm Princess, Vol. 2. 2014. (Accel World Ser.: 2). (ENG., Illus.). 256p. (gr. 8-17). pap. 13.00 *(978-0-316-29636-6(8),* Yen Pr.) Yen Pr. LLC.
—Sword Art Online 12 (light Novel) Alicization Rising. 2017. (Sword Art Online Ser.: 12). (ENG., Illus.). 216p. (gr. 8-17). 14.00 *(978-0-316-39045-3(3),* Yen Pr.) Yen Pr. LLC.
—Sword Art Online 15 (light Novel) Alicization Invading. 2018. (Sword Art Online Ser.: 15). (ENG., Illus.). 240p. (gr. 8-17). pap. 14.00 *(978-0-316-39049-1(6),* Yen Pr.) Yen Pr. LLC.
Kawahara, Reki & Sigsawa, Keiichi. Sword Art Online Alternative Gun Gale Online, Vol. 2 (light Novel) Second Squad Jam: Start. 2018. (Sword Art Online Alternative Gun Gale Online (light Novel) Ser.: 2). (ENG., Illus.). 256p. (gr. 8-17). pap. 14.00 *(978-1-9753-5384-1(6),* 9781975353841, Yen Pr.) Yen Pr. LLC.
—Sword Art Online Alternative Gun Gale Online, Vol. 3 (light Novel) Second Squad Jam: Finish. 2019. (Sword Art Online Alternative Gun Gale Online (light Novel) Ser.: 3). (ENG., Illus.). 336p. (gr. 8-17). pap. 14.00 *(978-1-9753-5385-8(4),* 9781975353858, Yen Pr.) Yen Pr. LLC.
Keats, Israel. Alien Invasion. 2017. (Level Up Ser.). (ENG.). 120p. (YA). (gr. 6-12). pap. 7.99 *(978-1-5124-5356-0(0),* b9358e54-28d0-4870-96f3-95ea47d4215e); lib. bdg. 26.65 *(978-1-5124-3984-7(3),* 4bd61854-84ad-4b3c-a63b-159a2525f4ee) Lerner Publishing Group. (Darby Creek).
—Labyrinth. 2017. (Level Up Ser.). (ENG.). 128p. (YA). (gr. 6-12). pap. 7.99 *(978-1-5124-5357-7(9),* e7f5d859-1e75-4e25-a08a-54652805091b); 26.65 *(978-1-5124-3987-8(8),* 33c50e5e-c0e4-4b3b-8d1c-e5a349efcbe5) Lerner Publishing Group. (Darby Creek).
—The Zephyr Conspiracy. 2017. (Level Up Ser.). (ENG.). 112p. (YA). (gr. 6-12). pap. 7.99 *(978-1-5124-5361-4(7),* 7e569a6f-416c-40e8-8dfc-520ae09833c9); lib. bdg. 26.65 *(978-1-5124-3985-4(1),* 07cc3b67-9541-407e-a23c-ab2e2516b1d9) Lerner Publishing Group. (Darby Creek).
Keene, Carolyn. Identity Theft: Book Two in the Identity Mystery Trilogy. 34th ed. 2009. (Nancy Drew (All New) Girl Detective Ser.: 34). (ENG.). 176p. (J). (gr. 3-7). pap. 6.99 *(978-1-4169-6831-3(8),* Aladdin) Simon & Schuster Children's Publishing.
Kincaid, S. J. Insignia. 2013. (Insignia Ser.: 1). (ENG.). 480p. (YA). (gr. 8). pap. 10.99 *(978-0-06-209300-4(2),* Tegen, Katherine Bks) HarperCollins Pubs.
—Vortex. 2013. (Insignia Ser.: 2). (ENG.). 400p. (YA). (gr. 8). 17.99 *(978-0-06-209302-8(9),* Tegen, Katherine Bks) HarperCollins Pubs.
MacHale, D. J. Black Water. 2007. (Pendragon Ser.: 5). (ENG., Illus.). 448p. (J). (gr. 5-9). 19.99 *(978-1-4169-5779-9(0),* Aladdin) Simon & Schuster Children's Publishing.
Martin, R. T. Pod Racer. 2017. (Level Up Ser.). (ENG.). 112p. (YA). (gr. 6-12). pap. 7.99 *(978-1-5124-5358-4(7),* ca2a9320-8539-4cd2-b818-bbab252d30a7); lib. bdg. 26.65 *(978-1-5124-3988-5(6),* c051e999-497c-4d60-b57b-c3aac1520b93) Lerner Publishing Group. (Darby Creek).
—Safe Zone. 2017. (Level Up Ser.). (ENG.). 112p. (YA). (gr. 6-12). pap. 7.99 *(978-1-5124-5360-7(9),* 4b340d12-02d0-489e-a9cd-c0f80ec63dde); lib. bdg. 26.65 *(978-1-5124-3986-1(X),* 239c2cad-d57a-4415-85bc-2ab2fc7ecf43) Lerner Publishing Group. (Darby Creek).
McGrath, Robin. Livyers World. 2007. (ENG.). 150p. (J). (gr. 4-7). per. *(978-1-897174-15-9(2))* Breakwater Bks., Ltd.
Milanes, Janelle. Analee, in Real Life. (ENG.). (YA). (gr. 7). 2019. 432p. pap. 12.99 *(978-1-5344-1030-5(9))* 2018. (Illus.). 416p. 18.99 *(978-1-5344-1029-9(5))* Simon Pulse. (Simon Pulse).
Reedy, Trent. Gamer Army. 2018. (ENG.). 336p. (J). (gr. 3-7). 17.99 *(978-1-338-04529-1(6),* Levine, Arthur A. Bks.) Scholastic, Inc.
Riazi, Karuna. The Battle. 2019. (ENG., Illus.). 304p. (J). (gr. 3-7). 17.99 *(978-1-5344-2872-0(0),* Salaam Reads) Simon & Schuster Bks. For Young Readers.
Segel, Jason & Miller, Kirsten. OtherEarth. 2018. (Last Reality Ser.: 2). (ENG.). 320p. (YA). (gr. 7). 18.99 *(978-1-101-93936-9(2),* Delacorte Pr.) Random Hse. Children's Bks.
—Otherearth. 2018. 310p. (YA). *(978-0-525-70794-3(8),* Delacorte Pr) Random House Publishing Group.
—Otherworld. 2018. (Last Reality Ser.: 1). (ENG.). 384p. (YA). (gr. 7). pap. 10.99 *(978-1-101-93935-2(4),* Ember) Random Hse. Children's Bks.
Seven, John. The Terror of the Tengu, 1 vol. Hans, Stephanie, illus. 2014. (Time-Tripping Faradays Ser.). (ENG.). 192p. (J). (gr. 4-8). 26.65 *(978-1-4342-9173-8(1),* 125643, Stone Arch Bks.) Capstone.
Sharpe, Gerald. Parade of Lights. Moya, Patricia, illus. 2007. (What Lies Beneath the Bed Ser.). 487p. (J). per. 11.00 *(978-1-933894-01-0(6))* IJN Publishing, Inc.
Skurzynski, Gloria. Afterwar. 2011. (ENG., Illus.). 528p. (YA). (gr. 7). pap. 9.99 *(978-1-4424-1681-9(5),* Atheneum Bks. for Young Readers) Simon & Schuster Children's Publishing.
Strange, Jason. Realm of Ghosts, 1 vol. Parks, Phil, illus. 2011. (Jason Strange Ser.). (ENG.). 72p. (J). (gr. 3-6). 25.32 *(978-1-4342-2962-5(9),* 114195); pap. 6.25 *(978-1-4342-3096-6(1),* 114736) Capstone. (Stone Arch Bks.).
Tesler, Monica. The Forgotten Shrine. (Bounders Ser.: 3). (ENG.). (J). (gr. 5-9). 2018. 400p. pap. 8.99 *(978-1-4814-4600-6(2))* 2017. (Illus.). 384p. 17.99 *(978-1-4814-4599-3(5))* Simon & Schuster Children's Publishing. (Aladdin).
—The Heroes Return. 2018. (Bounders Ser.: 4). (ENG., Illus.). 400p. (J). (gr. 5-9). 17.99 *(978-1-5344-0247-8(0),* Aladdin) Simon & Schuster Children's Publishing.
Valentine, Stephen J. The Lazarus Game. 2015. 311p. (YA). pap. 19.99 *(978-1-4621-1554-9(3))* Cedar Fort, Inc./CFI Distribution.
Vande Velde, Vivian. Heir Apparent. 2004. (ENG., Illus.). 352p. (J). (gr. 5-7). reprint ed. pap. 8.99 *(978-0-15-205125-9(2),* 1060977, Clarion Bks.) HarperCollins Pubs.
Watson, C. G. The Absoluteness of Nothing. 2017. (ENG.). 272p. (YA). (gr. 9). pap. 10.99 *(978-1-4814-3185-9(4),* Simon Pulse) Simon Pulse.
West, Tracey, adapted by. Jack in! MegaMan! 2006. 59p. (J). *(978-0-439-76837-5(3))* Scholastic, Inc.

VIRUSES

Abramovitz, Melissa. West Nile Virus. 2003. (Diseases & Disorders Ser.). (ENG., Illus.). 96p. (J). 33.45 *(978-1-59018-343-4(6),* Lucent Bks.) Cengage Gale.
—West Nile Virus, 1 vol. 2013. (Diseases & Disorders Ser.). (ENG., Illus.). 112p. (gr. 7-7). lib. bdg. 41.53 *(978-1-4205-0936-6(5),* e4ea3479-4a9e-452d-99ec-2f49d722a144, Lucent Pr.) Greenhaven Publishing LLC.
Berger, Melvin. Germs Make Me Sick! Hafner, Marylin, illus. 2015. (Let's-Read-And-Find-Out Science 2 Ser.). (ENG.). 32p. (J). (gr. -1-3). pap. 7.99 *(978-0-06-238187-3(3),* HarperCollins) HarperCollins Pubs.
—Germs Make Me Sick! 2015. (Let's-Read-And-Find-Out Science: Stage 2 Ser.). (J). lib. bdg. 17.20 *(978-0-606-37742-3(5))* Turtleback.
Berlatsky, Noah, ed. The H1N1 Flu, 1 vol. 2010. (At Issue Ser.). (ENG.). 112p. (gr. 10-12). 41.03 *(978-0-7377-5089-8(8),* 53d29033-c732-431e-843c-b2cefbbc89db); pap. 28.80 *(978-0-7377-5090-4(1),* a896a196-def2-404e-b842-4ac8e205383e) Greenhaven Publishing LLC. (Greenhaven Publishing).
Biskup, Agnieszka. Understanding Viruses with Max Axiom, Super Scientist, 1 vol. Derington, Nick, illus. 2009. (Graphic Science Ser.). (ENG.). 32p. (J). (gr. 3-9). pap. 8.10 *(978-1-4296-3453-3(7),* 95996) Capstone.
Bringle, Jennifer. Young Women & the HPV Vaccine, 1 vol. 2011. (Girls' Health Ser.). (ENG., Illus.). 48p. (YA). (gr. 5-6). lib. bdg. 34.47 *(978-1-4488-4575-0(0),* 7bd8f5b2-ba65-4ff4-abd4-2fcf3016ccd0) Rosen Publishing Group, Inc., The.
Brunelle, Lynn & Gave, Marc. Viruses, 1 vol. 2003. (Discovery Channel School Science: Universes Large & Small Ser.). (ENG., Illus.). 32p. (gr. 5-7). lib. bdg. 28.67 *(978-0-8368-3375-1(9),* 6df3ab91-f97d-409f-a16d-39c24028e2d4, Gareth Stevens Learning Library) Stevens, Gareth Publishing LLLP.
Bueche, Shelley. The Ebola Virus. 2003. (Parasites Ser.). (ENG., Illus.). 32p. (J). 27.80 *(978-0-7377-1780-8(7),* Greenhaven Pr., Inc.) Cengage Gale.
Carter, Elizabeth. Everything You Need to Know about Human Papillomavirus. 2009. (Need to Know Library). 64p. (gr. 5-5). 58.50 *(978-1-60854-073-0(1))* Rosen Publishing Group, Inc., The.
Casil, Amy Sterling. Hantavirus, 1 vol. 2004. (Epidemics: Deadly Diseases Throughout History Ser.). (ENG., Illus.). 64p. (YA). (gr. 5-5). lib. bdg. 37.13 *(978-1-4042-0254-2(4),* c486f526-0a74-48d1-a6cd-d845420ee4d7) Rosen Publishing Group, Inc., The.
Cline-Ransome, Lesa. Germs: Fact & Fiction, Friends & Foes. Ransome, James, illus. 2017. (ENG.). 40p. (J). 18.99 *(978-0-8050-7915-9(7),* 900031507, Holt, Henry & Co. Bks. For Young Readers) Holt, Henry & Co.
Close, Edward. Germ Warfare, 1 vol., 1. 2014. (Discovery Education: How It Works). (ENG.). 32p. (gr. 4-5). pap. 11.00 *(978-1-4777-6301-8(5),* 29f44393-31b7-4127-9561-8ce18591cf69, PowerKids Pr.) Rosen Publishing Group, Inc., The.
Denton, Michelle. The Zika Virus, 1 vol. 2017. (Diseases & Disorders Ser.). (ENG.). 104p. (gr. 7-7). lib. bdg. 41.53 *(978-1-5345-6129-8(3),* 0939b17b-0e04-4bf3-93bd-c374e92cc4eb, Lucent Pr.) Greenhaven Publishing LLC.
Eaton, Louise & Rogers, Kara, eds. Examining Viruses & Bacteria, 1 vol. 2017. (Building Blocks of Life Ser.). (ENG.). 272p. (YA). (gr. 10-10). lib. bdg. 47.59 *(978-1-5383-0009-1(5),* 342cb5c0-e163-49d0-89b4-e23ddb207ae5) Rosen Publishing Group, Inc., The.
EBOLA & MARBURG VIRUS, 2ND EDITION. 2nd rev. ed. 2010. (ENG., Illus.). 104p. (gr. 9). 34.95 *(978-1-60413-252-6(3),* P179257, Facts On File) Infobase Holdings, Inc.
Edwards, Sue Bradford. The Zika Virus. 2016. (Special Reports Set 2 Ser.). (ENG., Illus.). 112p. (J). (gr. 6-12). lib. bdg. 41.36 *(978-1-68078-400-8(5),* 23565, Essential Library) ABDO Publishing Co.
Goldstein, Margaret J. Everything You Need to Know about Multiple Sclerosis. 2009. (Need to Know Library). 64p. (gr. 5-5). 58.50 *(978-1-60854-078-5(2))* Rosen Publishing Group, Inc., The.
Goldstein, Natalie. Viruses. (Germs: the Library of Disease-Causing Organisms Ser.). 48p. (gr. 5-5). 2009. 53.00 *(978-1-61512-719-1(4))* 2003. (ENG., Illus.). lib. bdg. 34.47 *(978-0-8239-4496-5(4),* faed0209-a8ce-4fa6-b1c8-9d09f1078fa8) Rosen Publishing Group, Inc., The.
Goldstein, Natalie & Baum, Margaux. Viruses, 1 vol. 2016. (Germs: Disease-Causing Organisms Ser.). (ENG.). 48p. (J). (gr. 5-5). pap. 12.75 *(978-1-4777-8855-4(7),* 3fe8e0ae-2049-457e-813f-7b30285b30e9, Rosen Reference) Rosen Publishing Group, Inc., The.
Hand, Carol. The Gross Science of Germs All Around You, 1 vol. 2018. (Way Gross Science Ser.). (ENG.). 48p. (gr. 5-5). 33.47 *(978-1-5081-8168-2(3),* ac8952df-5b68-4a53-aacb-a3245233163a, Rosen Reference) Rosen Publishing Group, Inc., The.
Holt, Rinehart and Winston Staff. Holt Science & Technology Chapter 10: Life Science: Bacteria & Viruses. 5th ed. 2004. (Illus.). pap. 12.86 *(978-0-03-030206-0(4))* Holt McDougal.
Leuenroth, Stephanie. Hantavirus Pulmonary Syndrome. 2006. (Deadly Diseases & Epidemics Ser.). (ENG., Illus.). 112p. (gr. 9-12). 34.95 *(978-0-7910-8676-6(3),* P114382, Facts On File) Infobase Holdings, Inc.
Lewis, Mark K. Ebola: How a Viral Fever Changed History. 2019. (Infected! Ser.). (ENG., Illus.). 32p. (J). (gr. 3-9). lib. bdg. 28.65 *(978-1-5435-7239-1(1),* 140585) Capstone.
Markovics, Joyce L. Tiny Invaders! Deadly Microorganisms, 1 vol. 2013. (Nature's Invaders Ser.). (ENG.). 32p. (J). (gr. 3-9). lib. bdg. 28.65 *(978-1-4765-0142-0(4),* 122219, Capstone Pr.) Capstone.
May, Suellen. Invasive Microbes. 2007. (Invasive Species Ser.). (ENG., Illus.). 100p. (gr. 6-12). lib. bdg. 30.00 *(978-0-7910-9131-9(7),* P114536, Facts On File) Infobase Holdings, Inc.
Nardo, Don. Human Papillomavirus (HPV), 1 vol. 2007. (Diseases & Disorders Ser.). (ENG., Illus.). 104p. (gr. 7-7). lib. bdg. 41.53 *(978-1-59018-998-6(1),* 4e83f290-2e56-42e5-b2ad-15ab49e60632, Lucent Pr.) Greenhaven Publishing LLC.
Plumb, Jennifer. Everything You Need to Know about Chicken Pox & Shingles. 2009. (Need to Know Library). 64p. (gr. 5-5). 58.50 *(978-1-60854-057-0(X))* Rosen Publishing Group, Inc., The.
Rake, Jody Sullivan. Why Feet Smell & Other Gross Facts about Your Body. 2012. (Gross Me Out Ser.). (ENG.). 24p. (gr. 1-2). pap. 41.70 *(978-1-4296-8377-7(5));* (J). pap. 7.29 *(978-1-4296-7955-8(7),* 118287); (J). lib. bdg. 25.99 *(978-1-4296-7610-6(8),* 117207) Capstone. (Capstone Pr.).
Romanek, Trudee. Achoo! The Most Interesting Book You'll Ever Read about Germs. Cowles, Rose, illus. 2003. (Mysterious You Ser.). (ENG.). 40p. (J). (gr. 4-9). pap. 8.95 *(978-1-55337-451-0(7))* Kids Can Pr., Ltd. CAN. Dist: Hachette Bk. Group.
Shea, John M. Combating Computer Viruses, 1 vol. 2012. (Cyberspace Survival Guide Ser.). (ENG., Illus.). 32p. (J). (gr. 3-4). 29.27 *(978-1-4339-7212-6(3),* 79f43b74-4cf6-448c-a33f-68b57b893acd); pap. 11.50 *(978-1-4339-7213-3(1),* 1ed19db0-8182-432b-a437-8c87655c1c42) Stevens, Gareth Publishing LLLP. (Gareth Stevens Learning Library).
—Viruses up Close, 1 vol. 2013. (Under the Microscope Ser.). (ENG.). 32p. (J). (gr. 4-5). 29.27 *(978-1-4339-8354-2(0),* f8d7c5b0-245d-4282-81c4-63c3fd91db37); pap. 12.70 *(978-1-4339-8355-9(9),* 3fe5c227-2766-4122-aba8-bee6d8c20666) Stevens, Gareth Publishing LLLP.
Viruses up Close. 2013. (Under the Microscope Ser.). 32p. (J). (gr. 4-6). pap. 70.20 *(978-1-4339-8356-6(7))* Stevens, Gareth Publishing LLLP.
Yount, Lisa. Luc Montagnier. 2011. (ENG.). 144p. (gr. 6-12). 35.00 *(978-1-60413-661-6(8),* P218631, Facts On File) Infobase Holdings, Inc.

VISION

see also Blind; Eye; Optical Illusions

Aloian, Molly. What Is Sight? 2013. (ENG., Illus.). 24p. (J). *(978-0-7787-0969-5(8));* (gr. 1-2). pap. *(978-0-7787-0996-1(5))* Crabtree Publishing Co.
Appleby, Alex. What I See, 1 vol. 2014. (My Five Senses Ser.). (ENG.). 24p. (J). (gr. k-k). 24.27 *(978-1-4824-0808-9(2),* 956e203e-c476-4591-a994-19b891c34901) Stevens, Gareth Publishing LLLP.
Barraclough, Sue. What Can I See? 2005. (J). *(978-1-4034-7080-5(4));* (ENG.). 32p. pap. *(978-1-4034-7086-7(3))* Steck-Vaughn.
Beaumont, Susanna. Baby Senses Sight. 2005. (Baby Senses Ser.). (Illus.). 12p. (gr. -1-k). per., bds. *(978-1-905051-48-9(4))* Make Believe Ideas.
Beckering, Analise. Sight. 2009. (World of Wonder Ser.). (Illus.). 24p. (J). (gr. 2-4). pap. 8.95 *(978-1-60596-053-1(5))* Weigl Pubs., Inc.
Bekkering, Annalise. Sight. 2009. (World of Wonder Ser.). (Illus.). 24p. (J). (gr. 2-4). lib. bdg. 24.45 *(978-1-60596-052-4(7))* Weigl Pubs., Inc.
Bellamy, Adam. What's That I See?, 1 vol. 2017. (All about My Senses Ser.). (ENG.). 24p. (gr. k-1). lib. bdg. 24.27 *(978-0-7660-8605-0(4),* bcfd0b74-ab8f-4b5e-a49f-be6c95596973) Enslow Publishing, LLC.
Biskup, Agnieszka. The Science Behind Superman's Sight. 2017. (Science Behind Superman Ser.). (ENG., Illus.). 24p. (J). (gr. 1-3). lib. bdg. 27.99 *(978-1-5157-5098-7(1),* 134628, Stone Arch Bks.) Capstone.
—Seeing Through Walls: Superman & the Science of Sight. 2016. (Superman Science Ser.). (ENG., Illus.). 32p. (J). (gr. 3-9). lib. bdg. 27.99 *(978-1-5157-0912-1(4),* 132210, Stone Arch Bks.) Capstone.
Carlson-Berne, Emma. Let's Explore the Sense of Sight. 2020. (Bumba Books (r) — Discover Your Senses Ser.). (ENG., Illus.). 24p. (J). (gr. -1-1). 26.65 *(978-1-5415-7687-2(X),* eb78e00c-322c-4f6a-a97b-7be53e7e6eed, Lerner Pubns.) Lerner Publishing Group.
Carr, Aaron. Vista. 2014. (SPA., Illus.). 24p. (J). *(978-1-62127-577-0(9))* Weigl Pubs., Inc.
Caster, Shannon. Eyes, 1 vol. 2010. (Human Body: a Closer Look Ser.). (ENG., Illus.). 24p. (J). (gr. 2-3). pap. 9.25 *(978-1-4358-9826-4(5),* f3a613b9-7582-46c5-9474-01d23bdaa9b0, PowerKids Pr.) Rosen Publishing Group, Inc., The.
Coan, Sharon. Message Received!, 1 vol. rev. ed. 2014. (Science: Informational Text Ser.). (ENG., Illus.). 24p. (gr. 1-2). pap. 9.99 *(978-1-4807-4565-0(0))* Teacher Created Materials, Inc.
Cucini, Sara. My Senses: Sight. 2017. (Eyediscover Ser.). (ENG., Illus.). 24p. (J). (gr. k-2). 28.55 *(978-1-4896-5692-6(8),* AV2 by Weigl) Weigl Pubs., Inc.
Dayton, Connor. Sight, 1 vol. 2014. (Your Five Senses & Your Sixth Sense Ser.). (ENG., 24p. (J). (gr. 1-2). Illus.). 26.27 *(978-1-4777-2850-5(3),* db51c2c0-b802-4bf9-a17f-ff5451f50319);1. pap. 9.25 *(978-1-4777-2851-2(1),* dea01b6f-f017-4b9b-852c-494dd9ae1d80) Rosen Publishing Group, Inc., The. (PowerKids Pr.).
—La Vista / Sight, 1 vol., 1. De La Vega, Eida, ed. 2014. (Tus Cinco Sentidos y Tu Sexto Sentido / Your Five Senses & Your Sixth Sense Ser.). (SPA & ENG.). 24p. (J). (gr. 1-2). 26.27 *(978-1-4777-3265-6(9),* 37c7fe3a-bfd7-4ae5-a38d-0478cd216299, PowerKids Pr.) Rosen Publishing Group, Inc., The.
Douglas, Lloyd G. My Eyes. 2004. (Wel-My Body Ser.). (J). 19.00 *(978-0-516-24060-2(9),* Children's Pr.) Scholastic Library Publishing.
Durrie, Karen. Sight. 2012. (J). *(978-1-61913-310-5(5));* pap. *(978-1-61913-315-0(6))* Weigl Pubs., Inc.
Enslow, Brian. My Eyes, 1 vol. 2010. (All about My Body Ser.). (ENG., Illus.). 24p. (-1). pap. 10.35 *(978-1-59845-169-6(3),* f5e6217a-9f0d-4360-9c6d-8b74fa389075); (gr. -1-1). 25.27 *(978-0-7660-3813-4(0),*

1207de2d-716b-4b3c-8c38-0d7c966efcb1) Enslow Publishing, LLC. (Enslow Publishing).

Ferguson, Beth. The Eyes, 1 vol. 2005. (Kaleidoscope: Human Body Ser.). (ENG., Illus.). 48p. (gr. 4-4). lib. bdg. 32.64 *(978-0-7614-1590-9(4),* f6f2592c-9c38-427e-898c-7eb04f1caf7d) Cavendish Square Publishing LLC.

Francis, Suzanne, et al. Spy by Night: Stealth & Secrets after Dark. 2007. (Illus.). 32p. (J). pap. *(978-0-545-01557-8(X))* Scholastic, Inc.

Furgang, Kathy. My Eyes. 2009. (My Body Ser.). 24p. (gr. 3-3). 42.50 *(978-1-61514-688-8(1),* PowerKids Pr.) Rosen Publishing Group, Inc., The.

Ganeri, Anita. Sight. 2013. (Senses Ser.). 24p. (gr. k-3). 28.50 *(978-1-59920-852-7(0))* Black Rabbit Bks.

Gray, Susan H. Vision. 2008. (21st Century Skills Innovation Library: Innovation in Medicine Ser.). (ENG., Illus.). 32p. (gr. 4-8). lib. bdg. 32.07 *(978-1-60279-226-5(7),* 200157) Cherry Lake Publishing.

Hall, Kirsten. Animal Sight, 1 vol. 2005. (Animals & Their Senses Ser.). (ENG., Illus.). 24p. (gr. k-2). pap. 9.15 *(978-0-8368-4809-0(8),* 8f251d5b-b471-4cb6-9da4-2c03fbfb7ba8); lib. bdg. 24.67 *(978-0-8368-4803-8(9),* 67514a68-142e-487d-8e61-b66c55a625f5) Stevens, Gareth Publishing LLLP. (Weekly Reader Leveled Readers).

—Animal Sight / la Vista en Los Animales, 1 vol. 2005. (Animals & Their Senses / Los Sentidos de Los Animales Ser.). (ENG & SPA., Illus.). 24p. (gr. k-2). pap. 9.15 *(978-0-8368-4821-2(7),* 8304dc8c-4857-47fd-8429-4847b5ac9e20); lib. bdg. 24.67 *(978-0-8368-4815-1(2),* d84c68f9-c58e-49b7-a7e3-6e79cae58e79) Stevens, Gareth Publishing LLLP. (Weekly Reader Leveled Readers).

Hamdan, Russell. Your Eyes, 1 vol. 2018. (Your Amazing Body! Ser.). (ENG.). 24p. (gr. k-k). 24.27 *(978-1-5382-1808-2(9),* dd008872-a7ea-44ea-9821-4a02dd954fed) Stevens, Gareth Publishing LLLP.

Harmon, Daniel E. Jump-Starting a Career in Optometry & Ophthalmology, 1 vol. 2018. (Health Care Careers in 2 Years Ser.). (ENG.). 80p. (gr. 7-7). pap. 16.30 *(978-1-5081-8504-8(2),* 8978eba1-0332-4a90-8108-cbb25cff9e82, Rosen Young Adult) Rosen Publishing Group, Inc., The.

Hewitt, Sally. Look Here! 2008. (Let's Start Science Ser.). (ENG.). 24p. (J). pap. *(978-0-7787-4059-9(5))* Crabtree Publishing Co.

Hidalgo, Maria. Sight. 2003. 24p. (J). lib. bdg. 21.35 *(978-1-58340-303-7(5))* Black Rabbit Bks.

Huddle, Rusty & Viegas, Jennifer. The Eye in 3D, 1 vol. 2015. (Human Body in 3D Ser.). (ENG., Illus.). 64p. (J). (gr. 5-6). 36.13 *(978-1-4994-3589-4(4),* ac4f2675-0153-4641-aae8-d2aa18b2610c, Rosen Central) Rosen Publishing Group, Inc., The.

Issa, Joanna. What Can I See?, 1 vol. 2014. (These Are My Senses Ser.). (ENG., Illus.). 24p. (J). (gr. -1-1). pap. 5.99 *(978-1-4846-0431-1(8),* 126587, Heinemann) Capstone.

Klingel, Cynthia & Noyed, Robert B. Eyes / Los Ojos, 1 vol. 2010. (Let's Read about Our Bodies / Hablemos Del Cuerpo Humano Ser.). (SPA & ENG., Illus.). 24p. (gr. k-2). pap. 9.15 *(978-1-4339-3733-0(6),* 4ab206b6-818f-481d-b48d-cc9c9d66c56d) Stevens, Gareth Publishing LLLP.

Kubler, Annie, illus. What Can I See? 2011. (Small Senses Ser.). 12p. (J). spiral bd. *(978-1-84643-378-8(9))* Child's Play International Ltd.

Llewellyn, Claire. Seeing. 2005. (I Know That! Ser.). (Illus.). 24p. (J). (gr. 1-3). lib. bdg. 22.80 *(978-1-932889-48-2(5))* Sea-To-Sea Pubns.

Loria, Laura. The Eyes in Your Body, 1 vol. 2014. (Let's Find Out! the Human Body Ser.). (ENG.). 32p. (J). (gr. 2-3). 26.06 *(978-1-62275-648-3(7),* de895084-a50a-4650-8f68-aa881106d7ec, Britannica Educational Publishing) Rosen Publishing Group, Inc., The.

Lowery, Lawrence F. Look & See. 2017. (I Wonder Why Ser.). (ENG., Illus.). 36p. (J). (gr. k-2). pap. 13.99 *(978-1-68140-355-7(2),* P531927) National Science Teachers Assn.

Mandy and Ness Staff, et al. Rosie's Room. 2005. (Senses Ser.). (URD, ENG, TUR, VIE & CHI., Illus.). 16p. (J). (gr. -1-1). pap. 9.95 *(978-1-84059-162-0(5))* Milet Publishing.

Mattern, Joanne. How Animals See, 1 vol. 2018. (Science of Senses Ser.). (ENG.). 32p. (gr. 3-3). pap. 11.58 *(978-1-5026-4204-2(2),* 6afbf8aa-971c-4d17-9cba-fc6cb6e42c4f) Cavendish Square Publishing LLC.

Meachen Rau, Dana. Look! [Scholastic]: A Book about Sight. Peterson, Rick, illus. 2010. (Amazing Body: the Five Senses Ser.). 24p. pap. 0.56 *(978-1-4048-4390-5(6),* Picture Window Bks.) Capstone.

Milet Publishing Staff. My Bilingual Book - Sight, 1 vol. 2014. (My Bilingual Book Ser.). (ENG., Illus.). 24p. (J). (gr. -1-k). 9.95 *(978-1-84059-801-8(8))* Milet Publishing.

—My Bilingual Book-Sight, 1 vol. 2014. (My Bilingual Book Ser.). (ENG., Illus.). 24p. (J). (gr. -1-k). 9.95 *(978-1-84059-795-0(X))* Milet Publishing.

—My Bilingual Book-Sight (English-Bengali), 1 vol. 2014. (My Bilingual Book Ser.). (ENG & BEN., Illus.). 24p. (J). (gr. -1-k). 9.95 *(978-1-84059-789-9(5))* Milet Publishing.

—My Bilingual Book-Sight (English-Chinese), 1 vol. 2014. (My Bilingual Book Ser.). (ENG & CHI., Illus.). 24p. (J). (gr. -1-k). 9.95 *(978-1-84059-790-5(9))* Milet Publishing.

—My Bilingual Book-Sight (English-Farsi), 1 vol. 2014. (My Bilingual Book Ser.). (ENG., Illus.). 24p. (J). (gr. -1-k). 9.95 *(978-1-84059-791-2(7))* Milet Publishing.

—My Bilingual Book-Sight (English-French), 1 vol. 2014. (My Bilingual Book Ser.). (ENG & FRE., Illus.). 24p. (J). (gr. -1-k). 9.95 *(978-1-84059-792-9(5))* Milet Publishing.

—My Bilingual Book-Sight (English-German), 1 vol. 2014. (My Bilingual Book Ser.). (ENG & GER., Illus.). 24p. (J). (gr. -1-k). 9.95 *(978-1-84059-793-6(3))* Milet Publishing.

—My Bilingual Book-Sight (English-Italian), 1 vol. 2014. (My Bilingual Book Ser.). (ENG & ITA., Illus.). 24p. (J). (gr. -1-k). 9.95 *(978-1-84059-794-3(1))* Milet Publishing.

—My Bilingual Book-Sight (English-Polish), 1 vol. 2014. (My Bilingual Book Ser.). (ENG & POR., Illus.). 24p. (J). (gr. -1-k). 9.95 *(978-1-84059-796-7(8))* Milet Publishing.

—My Bilingual Book-Sight (English-Portuguese), 1 vol. 2014. (My Bilingual Book Ser.). (ENG & POR., Illus.). 24p. (J). (gr. -1-k). 9.95 *(978-1-84059-797-4(6))* Milet Publishing.

—My Bilingual Book-Sight (English-Russian), 1 vol. 2014. (My Bilingual Book Ser.). (ENG & RUS., Illus.). 24p. (J). (gr. -1-k). 9.95 *(978-1-84059-798-1(4))* Milet Publishing.

—My Bilingual Book-Sight (English-Somali), 1 vol. 2014. (My Bilingual Book Ser.). (ENG., Illus.). 24p. (J). (gr. -1-k). 9.95 *(978-1-84059-799-8(2))* Milet Publishing.

—My Bilingual Book-Sight (English-Spanish), 1 vol. 2014. (My Bilingual Book Ser.). (ENG & SPA., Illus.). 24p. (J). (gr. -1-k). 9.95 *(978-1-84059-800-1(X))* Milet Publishing.

—My Bilingual Book-Sight (English-Urdu), 1 vol. 2014. (My Bilingual Book Ser.). (ENG., Illus.). 24p. (J). (gr. -1-k). 9.95 *(978-1-84059-802-5(6))* Milet Publishing.

—My Bilingual Book-Sight (English-Vietnamese), 1 vol. 2014. (My Bilingual Book Ser.). (ENG., Illus.). 24p. (J). (gr. -1-k). 9.95 *(978-1-84059-803-2(4))* Milet Publishing.

—Sight - English-Arabic, 1 vol. 2014. (My Bilingual Book Ser.). (ENG & ARA., Illus.). 24p. (J). (gr. -1-k). 9.95 *(978-1-84059-788-2(7))* Milet Publishing.

Mlawer, Teresa, tr. What Do I See? / ¿Qué Veo? Kubler, Annie, illus. 2015. (Small Senses Bilingual Ser.: 5). (ENG.). 12p. (J). bds. *(978-1-84643-725-0(3))* Child's Play International Ltd.

Morgan, Sally. How Sight Works. 2010. (Our Senses Ser.). 24p. (J). (gr. k-2). pap. 8.25 *(978-1-61532-559-7(X),* PowerKids Pr.) Rosen Publishing Group, Inc., The.

Morris, Kim Ely. Through the Eyes of Love. 2009. (ENG., Illus.). 24p. pap. 14.99 *(978-1-4389-6756-1(X))* AuthorHouse.

Murphy, Patricia J. True Books: Sight. 2003. (True Bks.). (ENG.). 48p. (gr. 3-5). pap. 6.95 *(978-0-516-26968-9(2),* Children's Pr.) Scholastic Library Publishing.

Murray, Julie. I Can See, 1 vol. 2015. (Senses Ser.). (ENG., Illus.). 24p. (J). (gr. -1-2). 31.36 *(978-1-62970-926-0(3),* 18310, Abdo Kids) ABDO Publishing Co.

Nelson, Robin. La Vista. Translations.com Staff, tr. from ENG. 2006. (Mi Primer Paso Al Mundo Real - Los Sentidos (First Step Nonfiction - Senses) Ser.). (SPA., Illus.). 24p. (gr. k-2). lib. bdg. 23.93 *(978-0-8225-6222-1(7),* Ediciones Lerner) Lerner Publishing Group.

—La Vista (Seeing) 2006. (Mi Primer Paso al Mundo Real Ser.). (Illus.). 23p. (J). (gr. -1-3). per. 5.95 *(978-0-8225-6545-1(5),* Ediciones Lerner) Lerner Publishing Group.

Owings, Lisa. Seeing. 2018. (Five Senses Ser.). (ENG., Illus.). 24p. (J). (gr. k-3). pap. 7.99 *(978-1-61891-297-8(6),* 12102, Blastoff! Readers) Bellwether Media.

Pryor, Kimberley Jane. Seeing. 2003. (Senses Ser.). (Illus.). 32p. (gr. 2-4). 23.00 *(978-0-7910-7555-5(9),* Facts On File) Infobase Holdings, Inc.

Randolph, Joanne, ed. The Eyes Have It, 1 vol. 2017. (Amazing Human Body Ser.). (ENG.). 48p. (gr. 6-6). pap. 12.70 *(978-0-7660-8993-8(2),* efdebb8a-deb0-4342-a286-bfe22c1d82da) Enslow Publishing, LLC.

Riley, Peter. Light & Seeing. 2007. (Essential Science/Watts Ser.). (Illus.). 32p. (J). (gr. 4-7). lib. bdg. 28.50 *(978-1-59920-028-6(7))* Black Rabbit Bks.

Rotner, Shelley. Whose Eye Am I? (Illus.). 32p. (J). (gr. -1-3). 2018. pap. 7.99 *(978-0-8234-4045-0(1))* 2016. (ENG.). 16.95 *(978-0-8234-3558-6(X))* Holiday Hse., Inc.

Ruchlis, Hyman. The Wonder of Light: A Picture Story of How & Why We See. Hirsh, Alice, illus. 2011. 160p. 41.95 *(978-1-258-09816-2(4))* Literary Licensing, LLC.

Rustad, Martha E. H. Seeing. 2014. (Illus.). 24p. (J). lib. bdg. 25.65 *(978-1-62031-116-5(X),* Bullfrog Bks.) Jump! Inc.

Schuh, Mari. The Sense of Sight. 2007. (Senses Ser.). (ENG., Illus.). 24p. (J). (gr. 2-5). lib. bdg. 26.95 *(978-1-60014-071-6(8))* Bellwether Media.

Scirri, Kaitlin. The Science of Invisibility & X-Ray Vision, 1 vol. 2018. (Science of Superpowers Ser.). (ENG.). 48p. (gr. 4-4). 33.07 *(978-1-5026-3790-1(1),* 55b850c3-c1f1-4248-89dd-6134f201f18d) Cavendish Square Publishing LLC.

Sheen, Barbara. Artificial Eyes. 2016. (Tech Bytes Ser.). (ENG., Illus.). 48p. (J). (gr. 4-6). lib. bdg. 26.60 *(978-1-59953-761-0(3))* Norwood Hse. Pr.

Sian Revision Vision & Hearing. 2004. (J). *(978-1-59242-079-7(6))* Delta Education, LLC.

Simon, Seymour. Eyes & Ears. 2005. (Illus.). (gr. k-3). 17.00 *(978-0-7569-5398-0(7))* Perfection Learning Corp.

Spilsbury, Louise. Sight, 1 vol. 2012. (Science Behind Ser.). (ENG.). 32p. (J). (gr. 2-4). pap. 8.29 *(978-1-4109-4503-7(0),* 117696, Raintree) Capstone.

Spiro, Ruth. Baby Loves the Five Senses: Sight! Chan, Irene, illus. 2019. (Baby Loves Science Ser.). 20p. (J). (— 1). bds. 8.99 *(978-1-62354-103-3(4))* Charlesbridge Publishing, Inc.

Stanley, Debbie. Coping with Vision Disorders. 2009. (Coping Ser.). 192p. (gr. 7-12). 63.90 *(978-1-61512-017-8(3))* Rosen Publishing Group, Inc., The.

Stewart, Melissa. The Eyes Have It: The Secrets of Eyes & Seeing, 1 vol. Hamlin, Janet, illus. 2010. (Gross & Goofy Body Ser.). (ENG.). 48p. (gr. 3-3). 32.64 *(978-0-7614-4167-0(0),* ef19629c-5d27-47b8-9ffc-d561c78f7247) Cavendish Square Publishing LLC.

Tekiela, Stan. Peepers & Peekers, 1 vol. 2013. (Adventure Boardbook Ser.). (ENG., Illus.). 22p. (J). (gr. -1-k). bds. 8.95 *(978-1-59193-423-3(0),* Adventure Pubns.) AdventureKEEN.

Viegas, Jennifer. The Eye: Learning How We See. 2009. (3-D Library of the Human Body Ser.). 48p. (gr. 5-8). 55.90 *(978-1-60853-321-3(2),* Rosen Reference) Rosen Publishing Group, Inc., The.

Woodward, Kay. Sight, 1 vol. 2004. (Our Senses Ser.). (ENG., Illus.). 24p. (gr. 1-3). lib. bdg. 25.67 *(978-0-8368-4407-8(6),* 9f163abc-d099-40c6-9f0f-895f27957812, Gareth Stevens Learning Library) Stevens, Gareth Publishing LLLP.

Wright, Frankie. Sight. 2016. (Illus.). 16p. (J). pap. *(978-1-338-03050-1(7))* Scholastic, Inc.

VISUAL INSTRUCTION

see Audio-Visual Education

VITAMINS

Brezina, Corona. What Are Vitamins?, 1 vol. 2018. (Let's Find Out! Good Health Ser.). (ENG.). 32p. (gr. 2-3). lib. bdg. 26.06 *(978-1-5383-0306-1(X),* da385eb7-a27b-4c8e-8f65-7aa72f5e36b9, Britannica Educational Publishing) Rosen Publishing Group, Inc., The.

Centore, Michael, contrib. by. Vitamins & Minerals. 2017. (Illus.). 64p. (J). *(978-1-4222-3745-8(1))* Mason Crest.

Cohen, Marina. Why We Need Vitamins. 2011. (Science of Nutrition Ser.). (ENG.). 48p. (J). (gr. 5-9). lib. bdg. *(978-0-7787-1690-7(2));* pap. *(978-0-7787-1697-6(X))* Crabtree Publishing Co.

Ibitokun, Bernadette O. Kids, Know Your Vitamins. 2012. (ENG.). 41p. (J). 30.95 *(978-1-4787-1950-2(8))* Outskirts Pr., Inc.

Sertori, Trisha. Vitamins & Minerals, 1 vol. 2009. (Body Fuel for Healthy Bodies Ser.). (ENG.). 32p. (gr. 4-4). lib. bdg. 21.27 *(978-0-7614-3802-1(5),* 81531297-13ee-4209-8dd5-6c30be8089c2) Cavendish Square Publishing LLC.

Vitality: Individual Title Six-Packs. (Bookweb Ser.). 32p. (gr. 6-18). 34.00 *(978-0-7578-0906-4(5))* Rigby Education.

Watson, Stephanie. Vitamins & Minerals: Getting the Nutrients Your Body Needs, 1 vol. 2010. (Healthy Habits Ser.). (ENG., Illus.). 64p. (YA). (gr. 5-5). pap. 13.95 *(978-1-4488-0613-3(5),* 83d6025c-1098-4ccd-9ff7-0cff792fc7a2); lib. bdg. 37.13 *(978-1-4358-9443-3(X),* f005eb6c-f697-40e7-9759-741c28d4e6b1) Rosen Publishing Group, Inc., The. (Rosen Reference).

Woodford, Chris. Potassium, 1 vol. 2003. (Elements Ser.). (ENG., Illus.). 32p. (gr. 4-4). 31.21 *(978-0-7614-1463-6(0),* 90676866-a560-43c7-90d7-fa01f2205f4d) Cavendish Square Publishing LLC.

VIVARIUMS

see Terrariums

VOCABULARY

Abrams, Majella. Reading Pals: Short & Long Vowels Gr. K-1. Taylor, Jennifer, ed. Sexton, Brenda, illus. 2007. (J). per. 6.99 *(978-1-59198-436-8(X))* Creative Teaching Pr., Inc.

Ace Academics, ed. English Vocabulary: A Whole Course in a Box! 2007. (Exambusters Ser.). 384p. (gr. 7-18). *(978-1-881374-85-5(8),* Exambusters) Ace Academics, Inc.

Acredolo, Linda & Goodwyn, Susan. My First Spoken Words: Babies. 2007. (My first spoken Words Ser.). (ENG., Illus.). 12p. (gr. -1-k). 12.99 *(978-0-8249-6719-2(4),* Ideals Pubns.) Worthy Publishing.

Adams, Jennifer. Around the World in 80 Days: A BabyLit(TM) Transportation Primer, 1 vol. Oliver, Alison, illus. 2018. (BabyLit Ser.). 22p. (J). (— 1). bds. 9.99 *(978-1-4236-4746-1(7))* Gibbs Smith, Publisher.

Alexander, Rilla, illus. TouchWords: Clothes. 2019. (Touch Think Learn Ser.). (ENG.). 16p. (J). (gr. -1 — 1). 16.99 *(978-1-4521-7561-4(6))* Chronicle Bks. LLC.

Allen, Margaret. Reading Pals: Rhyming Words Using Blends & Digraphs Gr. K-1. Taylor, Jennifer, ed. Sexton, Brenda, illus. 2007. (J). per. 6.99 *(978-1-59198-437-5(8))* Creative Teaching Pr., Inc.

Allen, Molly. Reading Pals: Sight Words Gr. K-1. Taylor, Jennifer, ed. Sexton, Brenda, illus. 2007. (J). per. 6.99 *(978-1-59198-438-2(6))* Creative Teaching Pr., Inc.

Allen, William H., creator. TEH Learns to Read: Primary Words. 2004. (J). 34.95 *(978-0-9745938-2-1(6))* LD Coach, LLC.

Alphasnaps & Snapphonics: Snapphonics Big Book: Eek! Squeak! A Leak! 2003. 36.95 *(978-0-673-60206-0(0))* Celebration Pr.

Alphasnaps & Snapphonics: Snapphonics Big Book: Scat the Cat. 2003. 36.95 *(978-0-673-60207-7(9))* Celebration Pr.

Amery, H. First Hundred Words. 2004. (ENG.). 32p. (J). pap. 6.95 *(978-0-7945-0002-3(1))* EDC Publishing.

—First Thousand Words. 2004. (J). (SPA.). 70p. pap. 9.99 *(978-0-7945-0463-2(9));* (FRE.). 64p. 12.99 *(978-0-7945-0283-6(0));* (HEB & ENG.). 64p. 12.99 *(978-0-7945-0029-0(3))* EDC Publishing.

—First Thousand Words in Spanish IL. rev. ed. 2004. (First Thousand Words Ser.). (SPA.). 64p. (J). lib. bdg. 20.99 *(978-1-58086-564-7(X))* EDC Publishing.

Amery, H. & Cartwright, S. First Spanish Word Book. 2004. (Treasury of Farmyard Tales Ser.). (SPA & ENG.). 48p. (J). 10.95 *(978-0-7945-0476-2(0))* EDC Publishing.

Amery, Heather. Farmyard Tales First Word Book. 2004. (Farmyard Tales Bks.). (ENG., Illus.). 1p. (J). 10.95 *(978-0-7460-4084-3(9))* EDC Publishing.

—First Hundred Words. Tyler, Jenny, ed. Cartwright, Stephen, illus. 2006. (Usborne First Hundred Words Ser.). 32p. (J). (gr. -1). lib. bdg. 14.95 *(978-1-58086-505-0(4))* EDC Publishing.

—First Hundred Words Coloring Book. 2009. (First Hundred Words Ser.). 32p. (J). (gr. k). pap. 5.99 *(978-0-7945-2485-2(0),* Usborne) EDC Publishing.

—First Thousand Words in English. Irving, Nicole, ed. Cartwright, Stephen, illus. 2003. (First Thousand Words Ser.). 63p. (J). (gr. -1). lib. bdg. 20.95 *(978-1-58086-474-9(0))* EDC Publishing.

—First Thousand Words in Italian. Cartwright, Stephen, illus. rev. ed. 2004. (First Thousand Words Ser.). (ITA & ENG.). 64p. (J). (gr. -1-6). 12.99 *(978-0-7945-0286-7(5));* lib. bdg. 20.99 *(978-1-58086-560-9(7))* EDC Publishing. (Usborne).

—First Thousand Words in Japanese. Cartwright, Stephen, illus. rev. ed. 2004. (First Thousand Words Ser.). (JPN & ENG.). 64p. (J). (gr. -1-6). 12.95 *(978-0-7945-0480-9(9));* lib. bdg. 20.95 *(978-1-58086-552-4(6))* EDC Publishing. (Usborne).

—What's Happening on the Farm? Cartwright, Stephen, illus. rev. ed. 2006. (What's Happening? Ser.). 32p. (J). (gr. -1-3). 5.99 *(978-0-7945-1288-0(7),* Usborne) EDC Publishing.

Amery, Heather & Cartwright, Stephen. First French Word Book. 2004. (Farmyard Tales First Words Ser.). (ENG & FRE., Illus.). 48p. (J). 10.95 *(978-0-7945-0295-9(4),* Usborne) EDC Publishing.

—First Thousand Words. 2004. (First Thousand Words Ser.). (ENG., Illus.). 63p. (J). 12.99 *(978-0-7945-0282-9(2),* Usborne) EDC Publishing.

Analogies 1: Grade 7-8 Quiz Book. 2004. (Analogies Ser.). pap. 8.20 *(978-0-8388-2226-5(6))* Educators Publishing Service, Inc.

Analogies & Multiple Meanings (Gr. 2-3) 2003. (J). *(978-1-58232-125-7(6))* ECS Learning Systems, Inc.

Anderson, Jill, ed. Let's Get to Work! Vamos a Trabajar! Evrard, Gaetan, illus. 2005. (Word Play/Juegos con Pala Ser.). (ENG.). 20p. (J). (gr. -1-17). bds. 6.95 *(978-1-58728-512-7(6))* Cooper Square Publishing Llc.

—Let's Go on Safari!/Vamos de Safari! Utton, Peter, illus. 2005. (Word Play/Juegos con Pala Ser.). (ENG.). 20p. (J). (gr. -1-17). bds. 6.95 *(978-1-58728-522-6(3))* Cooper Square Publishing Llc.

Animales. (Coleccion Libritos Acordeon). (SPA., Illus.). 10p. (J). pap. 5.50 *(978-950-11-0790-6(6),* SGM906) Sigmar ARG. Dist: Continental Bk. Co., Inc.

Anness Publishing. Busy Little People: Fun Pictures & Games for Babies & Toddlers! 2015. (Illus.). 48p. (J). (gr. k-1). bds. 9.99 *(978-1-86147-629-6(9),* Armadillo) Anness Publishing GBR. Dist: National Bk. Network.

Armadillo. Kittens. 2015. (Illus.). 24p. (J). (gr. -1-k). bds. 6.99 *(978-1-86147-645-6(0),* Armadillo) Anness Publishing GBR. Dist: National Bk. Network.

—Let's Learn 250 Words: A Very First Reading Book. 2016. (Illus.). 48p. (J). (gr. -1-12). bds. 9.99 *(978-1-86147-706-4(6),* Armadillo) Anness Publishing GBR. Dist: National Bk. Network.

Armadillo, Jeffrey. My First Animals: Over 200 Animals to Name & Learn About. Lewis, Jan, illus. 2015. 48p. (J). (gr. -1-12). bds. 9.99 *(978-1-86147-652-4(3),* Armadillo) Anness Publishing GBR. Dist: National Bk. Network.

Armadillo Press. Dog & Friends! A Box of Exciting Picture Books, 6 vols. 2017. (ENG., Illus.). 54p. (J). (gr. -1-12). bds. 14.99 *(978-1-86147-640-1(X),* Armadillo) Anness Publishing GBR. Dist: National Bk. Network.

Armadillo Press Staff. A Little Box of Baby Animals: Six Cute Boardbooks Packed with Pictures!, 6 vols. 2018. (Illus.). 72p. (J). (gr. -1-12). bds. 14.99 *(978-1-86147-639-5(6),* Armadillo) Anness Publishing GBR. Dist: National Bk. Network.

—My Very First Box of Books: A Set of Six Exciting Picture Books, 6 vols. 2018. (Illus.). 72p. (J). (gr. -1-12). bds. 14.99 *(978-1-86147-739-2(2),* Armadillo) Anness Publishing GBR. Dist: National Bk. Network.

Armadillo Publishing. Australian Animals. 2018. (Illus.). 24p. (J). (gr. -1-12). bds. 6.99 *(978-1-86147-703-3(1),* Armadillo) Anness Publishing GBR. Dist: National Bk. Network.

Armadillo Publishing Staff. Words - Let's Look & See. 2015. (ENG., Illus.). 24p. (J). (gr. -1-12). bds. 6.99 *(978-1-86147-485-8(7),* Armadillo) Anness Publishing GBR. Dist: National Bk. Network.

AstroWord. 2004. (Scott Foresman Reading Ser.). (gr. k-18). cd-rom 69.00 *(978-0-673-64439-8(1));* (gr. 1-18). cd-rom 69.00 *(978-0-673-62235-8(5));* (gr. 2-18). cd-rom 69.00 *(978-0-673-62236-5(3));* (gr. 3-18). cd-rom 69.00 *(978-0-673-62237-2(1));* (gr. 4-18). cd-rom 69.00 *(978-0-673-62238-9(X));* (gr. 5-18). cd-rom 69.00 *(978-0-673-62239-6(8));* (gr. 6-18). cd-rom 69.00 *(978-0-673-62240-2(1))* Addison-Wesley Educational Pubs., Inc.

Award, Anna. Bathtime: A Teach Your Toddler Tab Book. 2017. (ENG., Illus.). 8p. (J). bds. 8.00 *(978-1-909763-25-8(X))* Award Pubns. Ltd. GBR. Dist: Parkwest Pubns., Inc.

—Mealtime: Teach Your Toddler Tab Book. 2017. (ENG., Illus.). 8p. (J). bds. 8.00 *(978-1-909763-24-1(1))* Award Pubns. Ltd. GBR. Dist: Parkwest Pubns., Inc.

Baby's First Word Book. 2004. 10p. (J). bds. 4.99 *(978-1-85854-925-5(6))* Brimax Books Ltd. GBR. Dist: Byeway Bks.

Baby's First Words. 2003. (Illus.). (J). bds. 7.98 *(978-0-7525-8651-9(3))* Parragon, Inc.

Baggott, Stella. Baby's Very First Bath Book. 2011. (Baby's Very First Ser.). 10p. (J). 9.99 *(978-0-7945-2972-7(0),* Usborne) EDC Publishing.

—Baby's Very First Black & White Library. 2012. (Little Black & White Library). 10p. (J). ring bd. 6.99 *(978-0-7945-3241-3(1),* Usborne) EDC Publishing.

—Baby's Very First Touchy-Feely Animals Book. 2011. (Baby's Very First Ser.). 10p. (J). ring bd. 7.99 *(978-0-7945-2895-9(3),* Usborne) EDC Publishing.

—Baby's Very First Touchy-Feely Christmas Book. Baggott, Stella, illus. 2010. (Baby's Very First Board Bks). (Illus.). 10p. (J). bds. 6.99 *(978-0-7945-2852-2(X),* Usborne) EDC Publishing.

—Baby's Very First Touchy-Feely Lift the Flap Play Book. 2013. (Baby's Very First Board Bks). 10p. (J). ring bd. 12.99 *(978-0-7945-3386-1(8),* Usborne) EDC Publishing.

Barefoot Books, Big & Small. Teckentrup, Britta, illus. 2013. (ENG.). 16p. (J). (gr. -1-k). bds. 7.99 *(978-1-84686-951-8(X))* Barefoot Bks., Inc.

—Fast & Slow. Teckentrup, Britta, illus. 2013. (ENG.). 16p. (J). (gr. -1-k). bds. 7.99 *(978-1-84686-952-5(8))* Barefoot Bks., Inc.

—My Big Barefoot Book of Wonderful Words. Fatus, Sophie, illus. 2014. (ENG.). 48p. (J). (gr. -1-1). 19.99 *(978-1-78285-092-2(9))* Barefoot Bks., Inc.

Baxter, Nicola. My First 200 Words: Learning Is Fun with Teddy the Bear! Lacome, Susie, illus. 2016. 24p. (J). (gr. -1-12). pap. 7.99 *(978-1-86147-759-0(7),* Armadillo) Anness Publishing GBR. Dist: National Bk. Network.

—My First Words: Nature. Lacome, Susie, illus. 2016. 24p. (J). (gr. -1-12). pap. 7.99 *(978-1-86147-770-5(8),* Armadillo) Anness Publishing GBR. Dist: National Bk. Network.

—Out & About: Name 200 Things in the World Around You! Lacome, Susie, illus. 2016. 24p. (J). (gr. -1-12). pap. 7.99 *(978-1-86147-777-4(5),* Armadillo) Anness Publishing GBR. Dist: National Bk. Network.

—Teddy Bear's Fun to Learn First 1000 Words. Lacome, Susie, illus. 2013. 96p. (J). (gr. -1-k). 12.99 *(978-1-84322-955-1(2))* Anness Publishing GBR. Dist: National Bk. Network.

Baxter, Nicola & Birkinshaw, Marie. A Treasury for Little Ones: Hours of Fun for Babies & Toddlers - Stories & Rhymes, Puzzles to Solve, & Things to Make & Do. Endersby, Frank, illus. 2014. 80p. (J). (gr. -1-6). 14.99 *(978-1-86147-368-4(0),* Armadillo) Anness Publishing GBR. Dist: National Bk. Network.

Beech, Linda. 240 Vocabulary Words Kids Need to Know: Grade 3. 2012. (ENG., Illus.). 80p. (gr. 3-3). pap. 12.99 *(978-0-545-46863-3(9),* Teaching Resources) Scholastic, Inc.

Beech, Linda Ward. 240 Vocabulary Words Kids Need to Know: 24 Ready-to-Reproduce Packets That Make

TUV

Vocabulary Building Fun & Effective. 2012. (ENG.). 80p. (gr. 5-5). pap. 12.99 *(978-0-545-46865-7(5))*; (Illus.). (gr. 4-4). pap. 12.99 *(978-0-545-46864-0(7))* Scholastic, Inc. (Teaching Resources).
—240 Vocabulary Words Kids Need to Know - Grade 6: 24 Ready-to-Reproduce Packets That Make Vocabulary Building Fun & Effective. 2012. (ENG.). 80p. (gr. 6-6). pap. 12.99 *(978-0-545-46866-4(3)*, Teaching Resources) Scholastic, Inc.
Benchmark Education Company, LLC Staff, compiled by. High Frequency Word Component Set. 2005. spiral bd. 210.00 *(978-1-4108-4156-8(1))* Benchmark Education Co.
Besson, Agnès. My First 1000 Animals. Surein, Manuel, illus. 2016. (ENG.). 64p. (J). (gr. -1 — 1). 19.95 *(978-1-77085-796-4(6)*, 9818f11c-4c8b-410d-ad29-9e2040acbde0) Firefly Bks., Ltd.
Beyond the Code: Grades 2-3, Bk. 2. 2004. (Beyond the code Ser.). pap. 6.75 *(978-0-8388-2402-3(1))* Educators Publishing Service, Inc.
Bicknell, J. Buby Baby Words_Padded. 2010. (Illus.). 12p. pap. *(978-1-84879-161-9(5))* Make Believe Ideas.
Bicknell, Joanna. Cuddle Buddy: Baby Words. 2006. 10p. (gr. -1). *(978-1-84610-094-9(1))* Make Believe Ideas.
Bicknell, Joanna, ed. Baby Fun Words. 2005. 12p. *(978-1-905051-16-8(6))* Make Believe Ideas.
Black, Jessica L. & Mullican, Judy. Let's Build a Snowman: Cuddle Book. Crowell, Knox, illus. 6p. (J). (gr. -1-1). bds. 10.95 *(978-1-57332-222-5(9)*, HighReach Learning, Incorporated) Carson-Dellosa Publishing, LLC.
Black, Nessa. Canoeing. 2020. (Spot Outdoor Fun Ser.). (ENG.). 16p. (J). (gr. -1-2). *(978-1-68151-809-1(0)*, 10683) Amicus.
—Gardening. 2020. (Spot Outdoor Fun Ser.). (ENG.). 16p. (J). (gr. -1-2). lib. bdg. *(978-1-68151-811-4(2)*, 10685) Amicus.
—Hiking. 2020. (Spot Outdoor Fun Ser.). (ENG.). 16p. (J). (gr. -1-2). lib. bdg. *(978-1-68151-812-1(0)*, 10686) Amicus.
—Rock Climbing. 2020. (Spot Outdoor Fun Ser.). (ENG.). 16p. (J). (gr. -1-2). lib. bdg. *(978-1-68151-814-5(7)*, 10688) Amicus.
Blackstone, Stella & Scribens, Sunny. Baby's First Words. Engel, Christiane, illus. 2017. (ENG.). 30p. (J). (gr. -1-k). bds. 14.99 *(978-1-78285-321-3(9))* Barefoot Bks., Inc.
Blanchard, Cherie & Plant, Cherie A. Word Roots A2: Learning the Building Blocks of Better Spelling & Vocabulary. 2013. (Word Roots Ser.). 80p. (gr. 5-12). pap. 16.99 *(978-0-89455-865-8(X))* Critical Thinking Co., The.
—Word Roots B2 Bk. 2: Learning the Building Blocks of Better Spelling & Vocabulary. 2005. (Word Roots Ser.). 136p. (gr. 7-12). pap. 16.99 *(978-0-89455-866-5(8))* Critical Thinking Co., The.
Block, Cheryl. Think Analogies A1: Learning to Connect Words & Relationships. 2011. (Think Analogies Books ThinkAnalogy Puzzles Software Ser.). 56p. (gr. 3-5). pap. 11.99 *(978-0-89455-791-0(2))* Critical Thinking Co., The.
Bobby Fling, 6 vols. 8p. (gr. k-1). 21.50 *(978-0-322-02068-9(9))* Wright Group/McGraw-Hill.
Body, Wendy. Minki's Day, 4 vols. 2005. (QEB Readers). (Illus.). 24p. (J). (gr. -1-3). lib. bdg. 15.95 *(978-1-59566-106-7(9))* QEB Publishing Inc.
—Mup's Days of the Week, 4 vols. 2005. (QEB Readers). (Illus.). 24p. (J). (gr. -1-3). lib. bdg. 15.95 *(978-1-59566-104-3(2))* QEB Publishing Inc.
Boehm, Gregory A. Big Big Book of Word Search. 2005. 224p. (YA). mass mkt. *(978-1-59412-000-8(5))* Mud Puddle, Inc.
Bond, G. T. GT Bond's 24 Words Toddlers Can Read in Color. 2007. 60p. pap. 24.95 *(978-0-615-14954-7(5))* S & S Pr.
—60 Words Toddlers Can Read in Black & White. 2007. 140p. pap. 16.95 *(978-0-615-14930-1(8))* S & S Pr.
Bonnett, Rosaline. Very First Words on the Farm. 2011. (Very First Words Board Books Ser.). 12p. (J). ring bd. 6.99 *(978-0-7945-3042-6(7)*, Usborne) EDC Publishing.
Brighter Child, compiled by. First Words. 2006. (ENG., Illus.). 54p. (gr. -1-1). 2.99 *(978-0-7696-4719-7(7)*, 0769647197, Brighter Child) Carson-Dellosa Publishing, LLC.
—Sight Words. 2006. (ENG., Illus.). 54p. (gr. -1-2). 2.99 *(978-0-7696-6470-5(9)*, 0769664709, Brighter Child) Carson-Dellosa Publishing, LLC.
Brighter Minds, creator. Animal Sight Words Flashcards. 2006. (PBS Kids Ser.). (J). 9.95 *(978-1-57791-310-8(8))* Brighter Minds Children's Publishing.
Brooke, Susan Rich. World of Eric Carle: Where Do You Live? Lift-A-Flap Sound Book. 2018. (ENG., Illus.). 10p. (J). bds. 14.99 *(978-1-5037-2206-4(6)*, 2510, PI Kids) Phoenix International Publications, Inc.
Brooks, F. & Litchfield, J. Mis Primeras Palabras. 2004.Tr. of Very First Words. (SPA., Illus.). 10p. (J). 6.95 *(978-0-7460-4823-8(8))* EDC Publishing.
Brooks, Felicity. First Word Book on the Farm. 2015. (My First Word Bks.). (ENG.). 20p. (J). 9.99 *(978-0-7945-3445-5(7)*, Usborne) EDC Publishing.
—Lift-the-Flap Word Book. 2011. (Lift-the-Flap Word Book Ser.). 14p. (J). pap. 11.99 *(978-0-7945-2562-0(8)*, Usborne) EDC Publishing.
—My First 100 Words. 2018. (ENG.). 24p. (J). 15.99 *(978-0-7945-4210-8(7)*, Usborne) EDC Publishing.
—My First Word Book. Bonnet, Rosalinde, illus. 2014. (ENG.). (J). 9.99 *(978-0-7945-3381-6(7)*, Usborne) EDC Publishing.
—Very First Animals Board Book. 2010. (Very First Words Board Bks). 10p. (J). bds. 6.99 *(978-0-7945-2479-1(6)*, Usborne) EDC Publishing.
Brooks, Felicity, et al, eds. Everyday Words. rev. ed. 2006. (Everyday Words Ser.). (Illus.). 47p. (J). (gr. -1-3). pap. 9.99 *(978-0-7945-0120-4(6)*, Usborne) EDC Publishing.
Brownell, Rick. Expressive & Receptive One-Word Picture Vocabulary Tests: EOWPVT-2000 Plates. 3rd rev. ed. (ENG & SPA.). *(978-1-57128-136-4(3))* High Noon Bks.
—Expressive & Receptive One-Word Picture Vocabulary Tests: ROWPVT-2000 Plates. 2nd rev. ed. (ENG & SPA.). *(978-1-57128-140-1(1))* High Noon Bks.
Bruzzone, Catherine, et al. French-English Picture Dictionary. 2011. (First Bilingual Picture Dictionaries Ser.). (ENG., Illus.). 48p. (J). (gr. 2-4). pap. 8.99 *(978-0-7641-4660-2(2))* Sourcebooks, Inc.
Buen Viaje Pinguinos! (Coleccion Leo Con Figuras). (SPA., Illus.). 14p. (J). pap. 4.50 *(978-950-11-0929-0(1)*, SGM291) Sigmar ARG. Dist: Continental Bk. Co., Inc.
Burchers, Sam, Jr., et al. Vocabulary Classic Series: The Call of the Wild. 2004. Orig. Title: The Call of the Wild. 216p. (YA). (gr. 6-12). pap. 7.95 *(978-0-9652422-0-2(X))* New Monic Bks.
Butts, Ed. Singing Sight Words, 2 vols. 2008. (Singing Sight Words Ser.: 1). (ENG., Illus.). 48p. (J). Vol. 1. (gr. -1-3). 17.95 *(978-1-55386-088-4(8)*, 1553860888) Vol. 2. 17.95 *(978-1-55386-091-4(8)*, 1553860918) Vol. 3. 17.95 *(978-1-55386-094-5(2)*, 1553860942) Vol. 4. 17.95 *(978-1-55386-097-6(7)*, 1553860977) Jordan, Sara Publishing.
Cáccamo, Pepe. A Cazar Palabras. Fernandez, Maria Xose, illus. (SPA.). 142p. (J). (gr. k-2). *(978-84-95123-36-7(3)*, KA1393) Kalandraka Editora, S.L. ESP. Dist: Lectorum Pubns., Inc.
Cacciapuoti, Aurora. Let's Learn Spanish: First Words for Everyone (Learning Spanish for Children; Spanish for Preschooler; Spanish Learning Book) 2020. (ENG., Illus.). 48p. (J). 12.99 *(978-1-4521-6626-1(9))* Chronicle Bks. LLC.
Callella, Kim. Build-a-Skill Instant Books Short & Long Vowels. Shiotsu, Vicky & Faulkner, Stacey, eds. Campbell, Jenny & Tom, Darcy, illus. 2007. (J). 4.99 *(978-1-59198-412-2(2))* Creative Teaching Pr., Inc.
Callella, Trisha. Greek & Latin Roots: Teaching Vocabulary to Improve Reading Comprehension. Rous, Sheri, ed. Peterson, Barbara, illus. 2004. 144p. pap. 16.99 *(978-0-88160-381-1(3)*, LW-438) Creative Teaching Pr., Inc.
—More Greek & Latin Roots: Teaching Vocabulary to Improve Reading Comprehension. Faulkner, Stacey, ed. Hilliam, Corbin, illus. 2006. (J). pap. 18.99 *(978-1-59198-328-6(2))* Creative Teaching Pr., Inc.
—Prefixes & Suffixes: Teaching Vocabulary to Improve Reading Comprehension. Williams, Carolea & Rous, Sheri, eds. Peterson, Barbara, illus. 2004. 144p. pap. 16.99 *(978-0-88160-380-4(5)*, LW-437) Creative Teaching Pr., Inc.
Campanella, Marco, et al. My Day with Billy Brownmouse. 2014. (ENG., Illus.). 10p. (J). pap. 10.00 *(978-1-84135-384-5(1))* Award Pubns. Ltd. GBR. Dist: Parkwest Pubns., Inc.
Campbell, Barbara. Lets Build Something: A Story Book/Coloring Book/Workbook. 2009. 64p. pap. 14.95 *(978-0-692-00349-7(5))* Mumford Institute.
Campbell, Dorthina A. Step Forward Strategies for Struggling Readers: Student Resource Guide. 2005. 59p. (J). stu. ed., per. 8.99 *(978-0-9768208-0-2(3))* Edutech Learning Resource Ctr.
Carle, Eric. All about the Very Hungry Caterpillar. Carle, Eric, illus. 2018. (World of Eric Carle Ser.). (ENG., Illus.). 10p. (J). (gr. k-k). bds. 9.99 *(978-1-5247-8588-8(1)*, Grosset & Dunlap) Penguin Young Readers Group.
—My Very First Book of Words. Carle, Eric, illus. 2006. (ENG., Illus.). 20p. (J). (gr. -1 — 1). bds. 6.99 *(978-0-399-24510-7(3))* Penguin Young Readers Group.
—The Very Busy Spider's Favorite Words. 2007. (ENG., Illus.). 20p. (J). (gr. -1-k). bds. 5.99 *(978-0-448-44703-2(7))* Penguin Young Readers Group.
—The Very Hungry Caterpillar's Favorite Words. 2007. (World of Eric Carle Ser.). (ENG., Illus.). 20p. (J). (gr. -1-k). bds. 5.99 *(978-0-448-44704-9(5))* Penguin Young Readers Group.
Carpenter, Tad. I Say, You Say Colors! 2014. (ENG., Illus.). 18p. (J). (gr. -1 — 1). bds. 6.99 *(978-0-316-20072-1(7))* Little, Brown Bks. for Young Readers.
Cernak, Kim. Build-a-Skill Instant Books Consonant Blends & Digraphs. Shiotsu, Vicky & Faulkner, Stacey, eds. Campbell, Jenny & Tom, Darcy, illus. 2007. (J). 4.99 *(978-1-59198-410-8(6))* Creative Teaching Pr., Inc.
Cernek, Kim & Williams, Rozanne Lanczak. Build-a-Skill Instant Books Color, Shape & Number Words. Shiotsu, Vicky & Faulkner, Stacey, eds. Campbell, Jenny & Tom, Darcy, illus. 2007. (J). 4.99 *(978-1-59198-411-5(4))* Creative Teaching Pr., Inc.
Cestnik, Jay & Cestnik, Lisa. 100 Sight Word Mini-Books. 2005. (ENG.). 112p. (gr. k-2). pap. 15.99 *(978-0-439-38780-4(9)*, Teaching Resources) Scholastic, Inc.
Chanko, Pamela. Word Families: 30 Instant Centers with Reproducible Templates & Activities That Help Kids Practice Important Literacy Skills-Independently! 2006. (Shoe Box Learning Centers Ser.). (ENG.). 80p. pap. 12.99 *(978-0-439-53795-7(9)*, Teaching Resources) Scholastic, Inc.
Channing, Margot. Around Town. Claude, Jean, illus. 2018. (First Words & Pictures Ser.). (ENG.). 14p. (J). (gr. -1 — 1). bds. 9.99 *(978-1-68152-410-8(4))*, Amicus.
Chappell, Jackie. Our School Is Like A Family. 2007. (ENG., Illus.). 16p. (gr. k-2). 28.50 *(978-1-60472-110-2(3))* Rourke Educational Media.
Chedru, Delphine & Duisit, Bernard. This or That? Industrial Inspiration for Twenty-First-Century Living. 2017. (Flip Flap Pop-Up Ser.: 0). (Illus.). 16p. (J). (gr. -1-1). 14.95 *(978-0-500-65093-6(4)*, 565093) Thames & Hudson.
Choosing the Right Word (Gr. 3+) 2003. (J). *(978-1-58232-052-6(7))* ECS Learning Systems, Inc.
CICO Kidz, compiled by. My Very First 100 Words: In English, French, & Spanish. 2018. (ENG., Illus.). 12p. (J). 9.95 *(978-1-78249-454-6(5)*, 1782494545, Cico Kidz) Ryland Peters & Small GBR. Dist: WIPRO.
Clark, Isobel. My Big Book of Words. Tulip, Jenny, illus. 2009. 48p. (J). (gr. 4-7). 9.99 *(978-0-7548-1941-7(8))* Anness Publishing GBR. Dist: National Bk. Network.
Clarke, Isabel. My Big Book of Words. Tulip, Jenny, illus. 2014. 40p. (J). (gr. -1-k). 12.99 *(978-1-86147-325-7(7)*, Armadillo) Anness Publishing GBR. Dist: National Bk. Network.
Cleary, Brian P. Straight & Curvy, Meek & Nervy: More about Antonyms. Gable, Brian, illus. (Words Are CATegorical (r) Ser.). (ENG.). 32p. (gr. 2-5). 2011. (J). pap. 7.99 *(978-1-58013-939-7(6)*, 01bf4a58-3e8d-43ce-9c9b-a848235a20ad, Millbrook Pr.) 2009. 16.95 *(978-0-8225-7878-9(6))* 2008. pap. 39.62 *(978-0-7613-7605-7(4)*, Millbrook Pr.) Lerner Publishing Group.
Clink! Clink! Clink!, 6 vols. 8p. (gr. k-1). 21.50 *(978-0-322-02057-3(3))* Wright Group/McGraw-Hill.
Coat, Janik & Duisit, Bernard. What Are You Wearing Today? 2018. (Flip Flap Pop-Up Ser.: 0). (ENG., Illus.). 16p. (J). (gr. -1-3). 14.95 *(978-0-500-65143-8(4)*, 565143) Thames & Hudson.
Collins Dictionaries. Children's Dictionary: Illustrated Dictionary for Ages 7+ (Collins Children's Dictionaries) Herbert-Liew, Maria, illus. 2018. (ENG.). 472p. (J). (gr. 4). 18.99 *(978-0-00-827117-6(8))* HarperCollins Pubs. Ltd. GBR. Dist: Independent Pubs. Group.
Collins Easy Learning. First Words Flashcards: Ideal for Home Learning. 2017. (Collins Easy Learning Preschool Ser.). (ENG.). 52p. (J). (gr. -1). 8.99 *(978-0-00-820109-8(9))* HarperCollins Pubs. Ltd. GBR. Dist: Independent Pubs. Group.
Collins-Matza, Carol. The Palindrome Kids. 2010. 32p. pap. 12.95 *(978-1-60844-513-4(5))* Dog Ear Publishing, LLC.
Collins 11+. 11+ Verbal Reasoning Vocabulary Practice Workbook: For the 2023 CEM Tests. 2016. (Letts 11+ Success Ser.). (ENG.). 80p. (J). (gr. 5-6). pap. 14.95 *(978-1-84419-899-3(5))* HarperCollins Pubs. Ltd. GBR. Dist: Independent Pubs. Group.
Come on into the Rain Forest: Word Study: Plurals, Level C. 2003. ("Plaid" Phonics & Stories Libraries). (gr. 2-3). 38.50 *(978-0-8136-9152-7(4))* Modern Curriculum Pr.
Come to My House: 6 Small Books. (Greetings Ser.: Vol. 3). 24p. (gr. 2-3). 31.00 *(978-0-7635-9418-3(0))* Rigby Education.
Corrigan, Kathleen. ABC, 1 vol. 2014. (Canadian Board Bks.). (ENG & FRE.). 20p. bds. 7.99 *(978-1-62370-223-6(2)*, Capstone Young Readers) Capstone.
—123, 1 vol. 2014. (Canadian Board Bks.). (ENG & FRE.). 20p. bds. 7.99 *(978-1-62370-224-3(0)*, Capstone Young Readers) Capstone.
Cosneau, Olivia & Duisit, Bernard. How Do You Sleep? 2018. (Flip Flap Pop-Up Ser.: 0). (ENG., Illus.). 14p. (J). (gr. -1-2). 14.95 *(978-0-500-65144-5(2)*, 565144) Thames & Hudson.
—What's Up? 2017. (Flip Flap Pop-Up Ser.: 0). (ENG., Illus.). 16p. (J). (gr. -1-1). 14.95 *(978-0-500-65092-9(6)*, 565092) Thames & Hudson.
Covello, Paul. Everyday ABC. 2018. (ENG., (J). Illus.). bds. 10.99 *(978-1-4434-5613-5(6)*, HarperCollins); 30p. (gr. -1-k). bds. 10.50 *(978-1-4434-5441-4(9)*, Harper Trophy) HarperCollins Pubs.
Cox, Phil Roxbee & Cartwright, S. Fox on a Box. 2004. (Easy Words to Read Ser.). 16p. (J). (gr. 1-18). pap. 6.95 *(978-0-7945-0443-4(4))* EDC Publishing.
Cox, Phil Roxbee & Cartwright, Stephen. Frog on a Log. 2004. (Illus.). 10p. (J). 4.99 *(978-0-7945-0302-4(0)*, Usborne) EDC Publishing.
Crews, G. Ellen G Goes Fishing. marion, designs & proctor, brian, illus. 2007. 28p. pap. 4.99 *(978-0-9795236-0-1(5))* Crews Pubns., LLC.
Dale, Jay. Wonder Words. Gulliver, Amanda, illus. 2012. (Wonder Words Ser.). (ENG.). 16p. (J). (gr. k-2). pap., pap., pap. 137.77 *(978-1-4296-9575-6(7)*, 18803, Capstone Pr.) Capstone.
—Wonder Words Classroom Collection. Gulliver, Amanda, illus. 2012. (Wonder Words Ser.). (ENG.). 16p. (J). (gr. k-2). pap., pap. 785.35 *(978-1-4296-9576-3(5)*, 18804, Capstone Pr.) Capstone.
Data Notes Staff. Word Mapping for Literacy & Language. 2005. 14p. (gr. 11-12). stu. ed., wbk. ed. 25.95 *(978-0-911569-18-6(9))* Prosperity & Profits Unlimited, Distribution Services.
Davidson, Carli, photos by. Heads & Tails: (Dog Books, Books about Dogs, Dog Gifts for Dog Lovers) 2017. (ENG., Illus.). 20p. (J). bds. 8.99 *(978-1-4521-5137-3(7))* Chronicle Bks. LLC.
—Shake, Wiggle & Roll. 2017. (ENG., Illus.). 20p. (J). bds. 8.99 *(978-1-4521-5136-6(9))* Chronicle Bks. LLC.
Davis, Caroline. First Opposites. 2012. (Illus.). 10p. (J). (gr. -1-1). bds. 7.99 *(978-1-84322-844-8(0)*, Armadillo) Anness Publishing GBR. Dist: National Bk. Network.
—First Pictures. 2012. (Illus.). 196p. (J). (gr. -1-12). bds. 7.99 *(978-1-84322-774-8(6)*, Armadillo) Anness Publishing GBR. Dist: National Bk. Network.
Deneux, Xavier. TouchThinkLearn: Farm: (Childrens Books Ages 1-3, Interactive Books for Toddlers, Board Books for Toddlers) 2015. (Touch Think Learn Ser.). (ENG., Illus.). 22p. (J). (gr. -1 — 1). bds. 16.99 *(978-1-4521-4517-4(2))* Chronicle Bks. LLC.
—TouchThinkLearn: Little Critters: (Early Elementary Board Book, Interactive Children's Books) 2017. (Touch Think Learn Ser.). (ENG., Illus.). 16p. (J). (gr. -1 — 1). bds. 14.99 *(978-1-4521-6594-3(7))* Chronicle Bks. LLC.
—TouchThinkLearn: Vehicles: (Board Books for Baby Learners, Touch Feel Books for Children) 2015. (Touch Think Learn Ser.). (ENG., Illus.). 22p. (J). (gr. -1 — 1). bds. 16.99 *(978-1-4521-4516-7(4))* Chronicle Bks. LLC.
—TouchThinkLearn: Wild Animals: (Childrens Books Ages 1-3, Interactive Books for Toddlers, Board Books for Toddlers) 2017. (Touch Think Learn Ser.). (ENG., Illus.). 22p. (J). (gr. -1 — 1). bds. 15.99 *(978-1-4521-6288-1(3))* Chronicle Bks. LLC.
dePaola, Tomie. Andy, That's My Name. dePaola, Tomie, illus. 2019. (ENG., Illus.). 32p. (J). (gr. -1-3). 7.99 *(978-1-5344-3014-3(8)*, Simon & Schuster Bks. For Young Readers) Simon & Schuster Bks. For Young Readers.
Di, Editors of the American Heritage. 100 Words Every Fourth Grader Should Know. 2014. (100 Words Ser.). (ENG.). 96p. (gr. 2-5). pap. 9.99 *(978-0-544-10611-6(3)*, 1540730, Collins Reference) HarperCollins Pubs.
Diaz-Cubero, Jose H. Practicas de Ortografia: 3 Grado. (SPA & ENG.). (J). (gr. 3). 9.95 *(978-84-357-0127-3(1)*, CPR88) Ediciones y Distribuciones Codice, S.A. ESP. Dist: Continental Bk. Co., Inc.
—Practicas de Ortografia: 6 Grado. (SPA & ENG.). (J). (gr. 6). 9.95 *(978-84-357-0124-2(7)*, CPR94) Ediciones y Distribuciones Codice, S.A. ESP. Dist: Continental Bk. Co., Inc.
Diktattrainer 5. Klasse. (Duden-Schuelerhilfen Ser.). (GER.). 112p. (J). incl. cd-rom *(978-3-411-71011-9(X))* Bibliographisches Institut & F. A. Brockhaus AG DEU. Dist: International Bk. Import Service, Inc.
Diktattrainer 6. Klasse. (Duden-Schuelerhilfen Ser.). (GER.). 112p. (J). incl. cd-rom *(978-3-411-71021-8(7))* Bibliographisches Institut & F. A. Brockhaus AG DEU. Dist: International Bk. Import Service, Inc.
Disney Books. Disney Baby: 100 First Words LiftthеFlap. 2018. (ENG., Illus.). 12p. (J). (gr. -1 — 1). bds. 10.99 *(978-1-4847-1801-8(1)*, Disney Press Books) Disney Publishing Worldwide.
—Disney Baby: First Colors, Shapes, Numbers. 2018. (ENG., Illus.). 24p. (J). (gr. -1 — 1). bds. 7.99 *(978-1-368-03702-0(X)*, Disney Press Books) Disney Publishing Worldwide.
—Disney Baby: My First Words. 2016. (ENG., Illus.). 24p. (J). (gr. -1 — 1). bds. 7.99 *(978-1-4847-5261-6(9)*, Disney Press Books) Disney Publishing Worldwide.
DK. Baby: First Words! 2013. (Chunky Baby Ser.). (ENG.). 16p. (J). (gr. -1 — 1). bds. 7.99 *(978-1-4654-0168-7(7)*, DK Children) Dorling Kindersley Publishing, Inc.
—Baby Touch & Feel: First Words. 2016. (Baby Touch & Feel Ser.). (ENG., Illus.). 14p. (J). (— 1). bds. 7.99 *(978-1-4654-5471-3(3)*, DK Children) Dorling Kindersley Publishing, Inc.
—Baby Touch & Feel: Halloween. 2017. (Baby Touch & Feel Ser.). (ENG., Illus.). 14p. (J). (— 1). bds. 7.99 *(978-1-4654-6235-0(X)*, DK Children) Dorling Kindersley Publishing, Inc.
—LEGO CITY: Busy Word Book. 2018. (ENG., Illus.). 64p. (J). (gr. -1-k). 15.99 *(978-1-4654-6627-3(4)*, DK Children) Dorling Kindersley Publishing, Inc.
—My First Touch & Feel Picture Cards: First Words. 2018. (My First Board Bks.). (ENG.). 17p. (J). (— 1). 12.99 *(978-1-4654-6813-0(7)*, DK Children) Dorling Kindersley Publishing, Inc.
—My First Touch & Feel Picture Cards: Things That Go. 2018. (My First Board Bks.). (ENG.). 17p. (J). (— 1). 9.99 *(978-1-4654-6812-3(9)*, DK Children) Dorling Kindersley Publishing, Inc.
—Pop-Up Peekaboo: First Words. 2018. (Pop-Up Peekaboo! Ser.). (ENG., Illus.). 12p. (J). (— 1). bds. 12.99 *(978-1-4654-6839-0(0)*, DK Children) Dorling Kindersley Publishing, Inc.
—Sophie la Girafe: Sophie's Big First Word Book. 2016. (Sophie la Girafe Ser.). (ENG., Illus.). 18p. (J). (gr. -1 — 1). bds. 9.99 *(978-1-4654-4494-3(7)*, DK Children) Dorling Kindersley Publishing, Inc.
—1000 Useful Words: Build Vocabulary & Literacy Skills. 2018. (Vocabulary Builders Ser.). (ENG., Illus.). 64p. (J). (gr. -1-2). 14.99 *(978-1-4654-7084-3(0)*, DK Children) Dorling Kindersley Publishing, Inc.
Do you Like Rice?, 6 vols. 8p. (gr. k-1). 21.50 *(978-0-322-02058-0(1))* Wright Group/McGraw-Hill.
Dorling Kindersley Publishing Staff. Baby's First Words. 2018. (Illus.). 14p. (J). bds. *(978-0-241-30177-7(7))* Dorling Kindersley Publishing, Inc.
Doudna, Kelly. Any Day but Today! 2004. (Sight Words Ser.). (ENG., Illus.). 24p. (J). (gr. k-3). lib. bdg. 24.21 *(978-1-59197-464-2(X))* ABDO Publishing Co.
—Are Buses Big? 2005. (Illus.). 23p. (J). 48.42 *(978-1-59679-353-8(8))* ABDO Publishing Co.
—The Balloons Go up, up, up! 2005. (Illus.). 23p. (J). pap. 48.42 *(978-1-59679-355-2(4))* ABDO Publishing Co.
—Can You Fly? 2005. (Illus.). 23p. (J). pap. 48.42 *(978-1-59679-359-0(7))* ABDO Publishing Co.
—Is It a Party? 2005. (Illus.). 23p. (J). pap. 48.42 *(978-1-59679-387-3(2))* ABDO Publishing Co.
—Is the TV On? 2005. (Illus.). 23p. (J). pap. 48.42 *(978-1-59679-389-7(9))* ABDO Publishing Co.
—It Is My Hat. 2005. (Illus.). 23p. (J). pap. 48.42 *(978-1-59679-393-4(7))* ABDO Publishing Co.
—It's My Mission to Make a Definition!, 1 vol. 2007. (Science Made Simple Ser.). (Illus.). 24p. (J). (gr. k-3). lib. bdg. 24.21 *(978-1-59928-600-6(9)*, SandCastle) ABDO Publishing Co.
—Just Make Some Art! 2004. (Sight Words Ser.). (ENG., Illus.). 24p. (J). (gr. k-3). lib. bdg. 24.21 *(978-1-59197-481-9(X)*, SandCastle) ABDO Publishing Co.
—My Brother, My Sister. 2005. (Illus.). 23p. (J). 48.42 *(978-1-59679-403-0(8))* ABDO Publishing Co.
—My House Is Big! 2005. (Illus.). 23p. (J). 48.42 *(978-1-59679-405-4(4))* ABDO Publishing Co.
—There Are Ants down There! 2004. (Sight Words Ser.). (ENG., Illus.). 24p. (J). (gr. k-3). lib. bdg. 24.21 *(978-1-59197-473-4(9)*, SandCastle) ABDO Publishing Co.
—To the Camp! 2005. (Illus.). 23p. (J). pap. 48.42 *(978-1-59679-421-4(6))* ABDO Publishing Co.
—Up the Path. 2005. (Illus.). 23p. (J). pap. 48.42 *(978-1-59679-423-8(2))* ABDO Publishing Co.
—Was That Fun? 2004. (Sight Words Ser.). (ENG., Illus.). 24p. (J). (gr. k-3). lib. bdg. 24.21 *(978-1-59197-475-8(5)*, SandCastle) ABDO Publishing Co.
—We Can Jump! 2005. (Illus.). 23p. (J). pap. 48.42 *(978-1-59679-429-0(1))* ABDO Publishing Co.
—We Go to the Park. 2005. (Illus.). 23p. (J). pap. 48.42 *(978-1-59679-431-3(3))* ABDO Publishing Co.
—When Can You Play Again? 2004. (Sight Words Ser.). (ENG., Illus.). 24p. (J). (gr. k-3). lib. bdg. 24.21 *(978-1-59197-478-9(X)*, SandCastle) ABDO Publishing Co.
Dragon's Song: Word Study: Synonyms, Antonyms, Level C. 2003. ("Plaid" Phonics & Stories Libraries). (gr. 2-3). 38.50 *(978-0-8136-9155-8(9))* Modern Curriculum Pr.
Draze, Dianne. Red Hot Root Words Bk. 1: Mastering Vocabulary with Prefixes, Suffixes & Root Words. 2003. (J). pap. 16.95 *(978-1-883055-57-8(1))* Dandy Lion Pubns.
Duncan, Leonard C. Greek Roots J-Ology. Bigelow, Holly, illus. Date not set. 140p. (J). (gr. 6-12). spiral bd. 25.00 *(978-0-941414-01-2(9))* L. C. D.
Dunn, Opal. Un Deux Trois (Dual Language French/English) Aggs, Patrice, illus. 2006. (ENG.). 24p. (J). (gr. k-3). pap. 9.99 *(978-1-84507-623-8(0)*, Frances Lincoln Children's Bks.) Quarto Publishing Group UK GBR. Dist: Hachette Bk. Group.
duopress labs. Go, New York, Go! Cleland, Josh, illus. 2018. (ENG.). 22p. (J). (gr. -1-k). bds. 9.99 *(978-1-946064-97-4(1)*, 806497) Duo Pr. LLC.
—Zoom! Beep! Vroom! Busy Cities. Cleland, Josh, illus. 2018. 22p. (J). (gr. -1 — 1). bds. 9.95 *(978-1-947458-27-7(2)*, 805827) Duo Pr. LLC.
Dupuis, Lynda. Au Pied de la Lettre: Manuel de Lecture, de Vocabulaire, d'expression Orale et Ecrite. rev. ed. 2010. (ENG.). 232p. (C). pap. 77.18 *(978-0-7575-7461-0(0)*, P716410) Kendall Hunt Publishing Co.
Durber, Matt. Backyard. Litchfield, Jo, illus. 2007. (Look & Say Board Bks). 10p. (J). (gr. -1-k). bds. 7.99 *(978-0-7945-1692-5(0)*, Usborne) EDC Publishing.

Dyan, Penelope. If You Snooze! Dyan, Penelope, illus. 2012. (Illus.). 34p. pap. 11.95 *(978-1-61477-059-6(X))* Bellissima Publishing, LLC.
—In Gracie's Yard! Dyan, Penelope, illus. 2012. (Illus.). 34p. pap. 11.95 *(978-1-61477-067-1(0))* Bellissima Publishing, LLC.
—Respect! Dyan, Penelope, illus. 2012. (Illus.). 34p. pap. 11.95 *(978-1-61477-058-9(1))* Bellissima Publishing, LLC.
Dyson, Nikki, illus. 1,000 Things to Eat. 2015. (1,000 Pictures Ser.). (ENG.). 34p. (J). (gr. k-5). 14.99 *(978-0-7945-3406-6(6),* Usborne) EDC Publishing.
Eck, Kristin. Colors in My House. (Board Bks.). (gr. k-1). 2009. 16p. 23.90 *(978-1-61511-639-3(7))* 2004. (Illus.). (J). lib. bdg. 8.95 *(978-1-4042-2698-2(2))* Rosen Publishing Group, Inc., The. (PowerKids Pr.).
—Hide-and-Seek Clothes. 2004. (Hide-And-Seek Books). (Illus.). (J). lib. bdg. 21.25 *(978-1-4042-2705-7(9),* PowerKids Pr.) Rosen Publishing Group, Inc., The.
—Hide & Seek Clothes. 2009. (Tough Toddler Bks). 16p. (gr. k-k). 42.50 *(978-1-60854-569-8(5),* PowerKids Pr.) Rosen Publishing Group, Inc., The.
—Shapes in My House. 2004. (Look-And-Learn Books). (Illus.). (J). lib. bdg. 8.95 *(978-1-4042-2699-9(0),* PowerKids Pr.) Rosen Publishing Group, Inc., The.
Education Pub Staff. Code Cards. 2004. pap. 8.05 *(978-0-8388-1788-9(2))* Educators Publishing Service, Inc.
Education.com. Alphabet? Alphabet! A Workbook of Uppercase Letters & Beginning Sounds. 2015. (ENG.). 128p. (J). (gr. -1-k). pap. 7.99 *(978-0-486-80254-1(X))* Dover Pubns., Inc.
Eeles, Alex. The Boy Who Said No Yellow Band. Ortu, Davide, illus. 2017. (Cambridge Reading Adventures Ser.). (ENG.). 16p. pap. 6.15 *(978-1-108-40077-0(9))* Cambridge Univ. Pr.
Eggleton, Jill. Mrs. Mcfee. Webb, Philip, illus. 2009. 39.95 *(978-0-7664-3147-8(9))* Abrams & Co. Pubs., Inc.
Einhorn, Kama. 240 Vocabulary Words Kids Need to Know: Grade 1. 2012. (ENG.). 80p. (gr. 1-1). pap. 12.99 *(978-0-545-46050-7(6),* Teaching Resources) Scholastic, Inc.
EMC-Paradigm Publishing Staff. Discovering Literature: Vocabulary Resource. (J). (gr. 6). *(978-0-8219-2030-5(8))* EMC/Paradigm Publishing.
Enriquece tu Vocabulario: Student & Teacher Support Resources. 2003. (MacMillan/McGraw-Hill. Estudios Sociales Ser.). (ENG & SPA.). (gr. 1-18). *(978-0-02-149765-2(6));* (gr. 2-18). *(978-0-02-149766-9(4));* (gr. 3-18). *(978-0-02-149767-6(2));* (gr. 4-18). *(978-0-02-149976-2(4));* (gr. 5-18). *(978-0-02-149769-0(9))* Macmillan/McGraw-Hill Schl. Div.
Escoffier, Michaël. Have You Seen My Trumpet? Di Giacomo, Kris, illus. 2016. (ENG.). 48p. (J). (gr. -1-3). 17.95 *(978-1-59270-201-5(5))* Enchanted Lion Bks., LLC.
—Take Away the A. Di Giacomo, Kris, illus. 2014. 56p. (J). (gr. -1-3). 17.95 *(978-1-59270-156-8(6))* Enchanted Lion Bks., LLC.
—Where's the Baboon? A 2-In-1 Book Game. Di Giacomo, Kris, illus. 2015. 40p. (J). (gr. -1-3). 17.95 *(978-1-59270-189-6(2))* Enchanted Lion Bks., LLC.
Evan-Moor. Vocabulary Centers, Grades 1-2. 2006. (Take It to Your Seat Ser.). (ENG., Illus.). 192p. (J). pap. 24.99 *(978-1-59673-148-6(6),* EMC 3348) Evan-Moor Educational Pubs.
—Vocabulary Centers, Grades 2-3. 2006. (Take It to Your Seat Ser.). (ENG., Illus.). 192p. (J). pap. 24.99 *(978-1-59673-149-3(4),* EMC 3349) Evan-Moor Educational Pubs.
—Vocabulary Centers, Grades 4-5. 2006. (Take It to Your Seat Ser.). (ENG., Illus.). 192p. (J). pap. 24.99 *(978-1-59673-151-6(6),* EMC 3351) Evan-Moor Educational Pubs.
—Vocabulary Centers, Grades K-1. 2006. (Take It to Your Seat Ser.). (ENG., Illus.). 192p. (J). pap. 24.99 *(978-1-59673-147-9(8),* EMC 3347) Evan-Moor Educational Pubs.
Evan-Moor Educational Publishers. At the Park: Grades 1-3. 2005. (Look, Listen, & Speak Ser.). (ENG.). 80p. (J). (gr. k-3). cd-rom 29.99 *(978-1-55799-927-6(9),* EMC 2740) Evan-Moor Educational Pubs.
—Daily Academic Vocabulary Grade 2. 2007. (Daily Academic Vocabulary Ser.). (ENG., Illus.). 160p. (J). (gr. 2-2). pap., tchr. ed. 29.99 *(978-1-59673-201-8(6))* Evan-Moor Educational Pubs.
—Daily Academic Vocabulary Grade 3. 2007. (Daily Academic Vocabulary Ser.). (ENG., Illus.). 160p. (J). (gr. 3-3). pap., tchr. ed. 29.99 *(978-1-59673-202-5(4))* Evan-Moor Educational Pubs.
—Daily Academic Vocabulary Grade 4. 2007. (Daily Academic Vocabulary Ser.). (ENG., Illus.). 160p. (J). (gr. 4-4). pap., tchr. ed. 29.99 *(978-1-59673-203-2(2))* Evan-Moor Educational Pubs.
—Daily Academic Vocabulary Grade 6+ 2007. (Daily Academic Vocabulary Ser.). (ENG., Illus.). 160p. (J). (gr. 6-6). pap., tchr. ed. 29.99 *(978-1-59673-205-6(9))* Evan-Moor Educational Pubs.
—Daily Word Problems, Grade 3. 2019. (Daily Word Problems Math Ser.). (ENG.). 128p. (J). (gr. 3-3). pap., tchr. ed. 23.99 *(978-1-62938-857-1(2))* Evan-Moor Educational Pubs.
—Daily Word Problems, Grade 4. 2019. (Daily Word Problems Math Ser.). (ENG.). 128p. (J). (gr. 4-4). pap., tchr. ed. 23.99 *(978-1-62938-858-8(0))* Evan-Moor Educational Pubs.
—Daily Word Problems, Grade 5. 2019. (Daily Word Problems Math Ser.). (ENG.). 128p. (J). (gr. 5-5). pap., tchr. ed. 23.99 *(978-1-62938-859-5(9))* Evan-Moor Educational Pubs.
—Daily Word Problems Math: Grade 2 Teacher Edition. 2019. (Daily Word Problems Math Ser.). (ENG.). 128p. (J). (gr. 2-2). pap., tchr. ed. 23.99 *(978-1-62938-856-4(4))* Evan-Moor Educational Pubs.
Falletta, Bernadette. We Love to Read Stories Coloring Book & Word Search Puzzles. 2005. 23p. (J). 10.95 *(978-1-4116-6291-9(1))* Lulu Pr., Inc.
Farnsworth, Lauren. Clever Babies Love Art: Wild Animals. 2016. (Clever Babies Love Art Ser.). (ENG., Illus.). 14p. (J). (— 1). bds. 7.99 *(978-1-78055-397-9(8),* Buster Bks.) O'Mara, Michael Bks., Ltd. GBR. Dist: Independent Pubs. Group.
Fatus, Sophie. My Big, Barefoot Book of Wonderful Words. 2014. (Illus.). (J). pap. *(978-1-78285-168-4(2))* Barefoot Bks., Inc.
Fatus, Sophie & Paris, Mertxe. My Big Barefoot Book of Spanish & English Words. 2016. (SPA & ENG.). (J). pap. *(978-1-78285-275-9(1))* Barefoot Bks., Inc.
Feldman, Jean & Karapetkova, Holly. ABC 123. unabr. ed. 2010. (ENG.). 16p. (gr. -1-k). 12.99 *(978-1-61741-589-0(8))* Rourke Educational Media.
Fernandez, Joyce. Little Bird - Pajarito. 2010. 31p. 15.95 *(978-0-615-23709-1(6))* My Second Language Publishing, USA.
Filipek, Nina. Words. O'Toole, Jeanette, illus. 2009. (Bright Basics Ser.). 12p. (J). (gr. -1-k). bds. 11.40 *(978-1-60754-685-6(X))* Windmill Bks.
Find It, Write It, Read It: Sentences. 2004. (J). pap. 7.95 *(978-1-56911-179-6(0))* Learning Resources, Inc.
Find It, Write It, Read It: Words. 2004. (J). pap. 7.95 *(978-1-56911-178-9(2))* Learning Resources, Inc.
First 100 Words: Busy Day. (Illus.). 12p. (J). *(978-1-902272-36-8(6))* Tucker Slingsby, Ltd.
First Word Book. 2003. (J). per. *(978-1-884907-29-6(6));* (SPA & ENG.). per. *(978-1-884907-31-9(8))* Paradise Pr., Inc.
Fish, Simon. Silly Shapes. 2012. (ENG.). (J). pap. *(978-1-4675-0898-8(5))* Independent Pub.
Flip Flaps Colours. 2014. (ENG., Illus.). 36p. 10.00 *(978-1-906572-79-2(8))* Award Pubns. Ltd. GBR. Dist: Parkwest Pubns., Inc.
Flowerpot Press Staff, contrib. by. Sockheadz: First Words. 2013. (ENG., Illus.). 20p. (J). (gr. -1-k). 6.99 *(978-1-77093-595-2(9))* Flowerpot Children's Pr. Inc. CAN. Dist: Cardinal Pubs. Group.
Foley, Mark. Trivial Matters for Children. 2008. (ENG.). 123p. pap. 12.95 *(978-0-615-19609-1(8))* Foley, Mark.
Forte, Imogene. Ready to Learn: Words & Vocabulary. 2003. (Illus.). 64p. per. 7.95 *(978-0-86530-591-5(9))* Incentive Pubns., Inc.
Foundations: Early Emergent-Upper Emergent - 1 Each of 25 Student Books: Level E. 124.95 *(978-0-322-02722-0(5))* Wright Group/McGraw-Hill.
Franceschelli, Christopher. A Box of Blocks. Peski Studio, illus. 2017. (ENG.). 290p. (J). (gr. -1 — 1). bds. 50.00 *(978-1-4197-2818-1(0))* Abrams, Inc.
Frasconi, Antonio. See & Say: A Picture Book in Four Languages. 2018. (ENG., Illus.). 32p. (gr. -1-3). 16.95 *(978-0-486-81647-0(8),* 816478) Dover Pubns., Inc.
Frazier. Time Zones 1: Student Book, Vol. 1. 2010. (ENG., Illus.). 160p. (J). pap., stu. ed. *(978-1-4240-6008-5(7))* Thomson ELT.
Fried, Miriam. My Jelly Bean Book. 2005. (Illus.). (J). *(978-1-57400-049-8(7))* Data Trace Publishing, Co.
Friedland, Joyce, ed. The Hunger Games: Novel-Ties Teachers Study Guide. 2011. (ENG.). 27p. pupil's gde. ed. 16.95 *(978-0-7675-5352-0(7))* Learning Links Inc.
—Rules: Novel-Ties Study Guide. 2011. 26p. pap. 16.95 *(978-0-7675-4468-9(4))* Learning Links Inc.
Frost, Maddie, illus. Indestructibles: Busy City: Chew Proof · Rip Proof · Nontoxic · 100% Washable (Book for Babies, Newborn Books, Safe to Chew) 2018. (Indestructibles Ser.). (ENG.). 12p. (J). (gr. -1 — 1). pap. 5.95 *(978-1-5235-0468-8(4),* 100468) Workman Publishing Co., Inc.
—Indestructibles: Hello, Farm! Chew Proof · Rip Proof · Nontoxic · 100% Washable (Book for Babies, Newborn Books, Safe to Chew) 2018. (Indestructibles Ser.). (ENG.). 12p. (J). (gr. -1 — 1). pap. 5.99 *(978-1-5235-0467-1(6),* 100467) Workman Publishing Co., Inc.
—Indestructibles: My Neighborhood: Chew Proof · Rip Proof · Nontoxic · 100% Washable (Book for Babies, Newborn Books, Safe to Chew) 2018. (Indestructibles Ser.). (ENG.). 12p. (J). (gr. -1 — 1). pap. 5.99 *(978-1-5235-0469-5(2),* 100469) Workman Publishing Co., Inc.
Fujikawa, Gyo. Gyo Fujikawa's A to Z Picture Book. 2010. (Illus.). 72p. (J). (gr. -1-2). 12.95 *(978-1-4027-6818-7(4),* 1318769) Sterling Publishing Co., Inc.
Gallagher, Belinda, ed. Mix & Match: Six Fun Scenes to Search & Find. 2008. (Illus.). 14p. (J). *(978-1-84236-786-5(2))* Miles Kelly Publishing, Ltd.
Ganeri, Anita. Ancient Egypt: The Complete Homework Solution. 2010. (Study Buddies Ser.). (ENG.). 32p. (J). (gr. 4-7). pap. 6.95 *(978-1-84898-183-6(X),* TickTock Books) Octopus Publishing Group GBR. Dist: Independent Pubs. Group.
Geatches, Hazel, ed. At the Beach. 2012. (ENG., Illus.). 32p. 11.00 *(978-0-19-464628-4(9))* Oxford Univ. Pr., Inc.
—Cities. 2012. (ENG., Illus.). 40p. pap. 11.00 *(978-0-19-464682-6(3))* Oxford Univ. Pr., Inc.
—Earth. 2012. (ENG., Illus.). 40p. pap., act. bk. ed. 11.00 *(978-0-19-464679-6(3))* Oxford Univ. Pr., Inc.
Geller, Amy. My First Words Outside, 1 vol. 2013. (ENG., Illus.). 20p. (J). bds. 6.99 *(978-1-59572-332-1(3))* Star Bright Bks., Inc.
George, Joshua. Tiny Town Hide & Seek Words. Ribbon, Lemon, illus. 2018. (Tiny Town Hide & Seek Board Bks.). (ENG.). 12p. (J). (-k). bds. 6.99 *(978-1-78700-380-4(9))* Top That! Publishing PLC GBR. Dist: Independent Pubs. Group.
Giles, Sophie & Davis, Kate. My First 1000 Words. Peters, Andy & Hewett, Angela, illus. 2014. (ENG.). 125p. 17.50 *(978-1-84135-642-6(5))* Award Pubns. Ltd. GBR. Dist: Parkwest Pubns., Inc.
Gobo, creator. My Magnetic First Words Runaway Cat. 2006. (Illus.). 8p. (J). (gr. -1-3). 9.95 *(978-1-932915-17-4(6))* Sandvik Innovations, LLC.
Gold, Ethel, illus. Outdoor Things. (Picture Bks.: No. S8817-3). 28p. (J). (gr. -1). pap. 3.95 *(978-0-7214-5142-8(X),* Dutton Juvenile) Penguin Publishing Group.
—Things That Go. (Picture Bks.: No. S8817-1). 28p. (J). (gr. -1). pap. 3.95 *(978-0-7214-5140-4(3),* Dutton Juvenile) Penguin Publishing Group.
Gold, Kimberley. Outer Space. (Puzzle Shapes Ser.). (Illus.). 10p. (J). bds. *(978-2-89393-937-7(6))* Phidal Publishing, Inc./Editions Phidal, Inc.
Goodwyn, Susan. My First Spoken Words: Animals. 2007. (Smart Kids Talking Bks.). (ENG., Illus.). 12p. (gr. -1-k). bds. 12.99 *(978-0-8249-6718-5(6),* Ideals Pubns.) Worthy Publishing.
Gordon, Jo Ann. Articulation Tales: Stories for Articulation Remediation. 2006. 136p. pap. 24.00 *(978-1-57128-314-6(5))* Academic Therapy Pubns., Inc.
Got, Yves. Mi Gran Libro de Las Palabras: Las Vacaciones de Dodo. 2003. (SPA.). 28p. *(978-84-233-3271-7(3),* DS3843) Ediciones Destino ESP. Dist: Lectorum Pubns., Inc.
Grundwortschatz. (Duden-Schuelerhilfen Ser.). (GER.). 80p. (J). (gr. 3-4). *(978-3-411-06342-0(4))* Bibliographisches Institut & F. A. Brockhaus AG DEU. Dist: International Bk. Import Service, Inc.
Gunzi, Christane. My Favourite Things. 2013. (Illus.). 6p. (J). bds. 7.95 *(978-1-907604-37-9(5))* Award Pubns. Ltd. GBR. Dist: Parkwest Pubns., Inc.
—My Lovely Day. 2013. (Illus.). 6p. (J). bds. 7.95 *(978-1-907604-36-2(7))* Award Pubns. Ltd. GBR. Dist: Parkwest Pubns., Inc.
—Words. 2nd rev. ed. 2015. (Illus.). 34p. (J). bds. 7.99 *(978-1-905503-71-1(7))* Award Pubns. Ltd. GBR. Dist: Parkwest Pubns., Inc.
Gunzi, Christiane. Clothes. 2003. (My Very First Look At Ser.). (ENG., Illus.). 24p. (J). (gr. -1-k). 9.95 *(978-1-58728-672-8(6));* pap. 5.95 *(978-1-58728-686-5(6))* Cooper Square Publishing Llc.
—My Home. 2003. (My Very First Look At Ser.). (ENG., Illus.). 24p. (J). (gr. -1-k). pap. 5.95 *(978-1-58728-685-8(8));* 9.95 *(978-1-58728-671-1(8))* Cooper Square Publishing Llc.
—My Very First Look at Words. 2003. (My Very First Look At Ser.). (ENG., Illus.). 24p. (J). (gr. -1-k). 9.95 *(978-1-58728-670-4(X))* Cooper Square Publishing Llc.
Haddon, Jean. Words: A Computer Lesson. Vargo, Sharon Hawkins, illus. 2003. (Silly Millies Ser.). 32p. (J). (gr. -1-1). pap. 4.99 *(978-0-7613-1797-5(X));* lib. bdg. 17.90 *(978-0-7613-2870-4(X))* Lerner Publishing Group. (Millbrook Pr.).
Hahn, Marika, illus. Things to Wear. (Picture Bks.: No. S8817-4). 28p. (J). (gr. -1). pap. 3.95 *(978-0-7214-5143-5(8),* Dutton Juvenile) Penguin Publishing Group.
Hall, Dorothy & Daniel, Marie. Guess the Covered Word for Seasons & Holidays. 2003. (Four Blocks Ser.). 48p. pap. 25.99 *(978-0-88724-125-3(5))* Four Blocks.
Hall, Nancy. Get Set for the Code Book B. 2004. (Explode the code Ser.). pap. 5.95 *(978-0-8388-1782-7(3))* Educators Publishing Service, Inc.
—Go for the Code Book C. 2004. (Explode the code Ser.). pap. 5.95 *(978-0-8388-1784-1(X))* Educators Publishing Service, Inc.
Hambleton, Laura & Turhan, Sedat. Telling Tails: Fun with Homonyms, 1 vol. Hambleton, Laura, illus. 2007. (Milet Wordwise Ser.). (ENG., Illus.). 28p. (J). (gr. k-2). pap. 6.95 *(978-1-84059-498-0(5))* Milet Publishing.
Haney Perez, Jessica. My First 100 Words Book: A Lift-the-Flap, Pull-Tab Learning Book. March, Chloe, illus. 2005. (Learn to Read Ser.). 10p. (J). 10.95 *(978-1-58117-210-2(9),* Intervisual/Piggy Toes) Bendon, Inc.
Hanson, Anders. Can You See Me? 2005. (Illus.). 23p. (J). pap. 48.42 *(978-1-59679-361-3(9))* ABDO Publishing Co.
—Come in & Swim! 2005. (Illus.). 23p. (J). pap. 48.42 *(978-1-59679-367-5(8))* ABDO Publishing Co.
—Go for It! 2005. (Illus.). 23p. (J). pap. 48.42 *(978-1-59679-373-6(2))* ABDO Publishing Co.
—Here Comes the Sun. 2005. (Illus.). 23p. (J). pap. 48.42 *(978-1-59679-377-4(5))* ABDO Publishing Co.
—I Like My Family! 2005. (Illus.). 23p. (J). pap. 48.42 *(978-1-59679-383-5(X))* ABDO Publishing Co.
—Little Like Me. 2005. (Illus.). 23p. (J). pap. 48.42 *(978-1-59679-395-8(3))* ABDO Publishing Co.
—Seasons Come & Go. 2005. (Illus.). 23p. (J). pap. 48.42 *(978-1-59679-413-9(5))* ABDO Publishing Co.
—The Snowman's Clothes. 2005. (Illus.). 23p. (J). pap. 48.42 *(978-1-59679-417-7(8))* ABDO Publishing Co.
—We Say Hooray! 2005. (Illus.). 23p. (J). pap. 48.42 *(978-1-59679-439-9(9))* ABDO Publishing Co.
—What Do I Look Like? 2005. (Illus.). 23p. (J). pap. 48.42 *(978-1-59679-443-6(7))* ABDO Publishing Co.
—You & I Can Read! 2005. (Illus.). 23p. (J). pap. 48.42 *(978-1-59679-445-0(3))* ABDO Publishing Co.
Harcourt School Publishers Staff. Decoding & Word Recognition Assessment. 3rd ed. 2003. (Harcourt School Publishers Trophies Ser.). (ENG.). 40p. (gr. k-k). pap. 42.60 *(978-0-15-340340-8(3));* 56p. (gr. 2-2). pap. 43.05 *(978-0-15-340341-5(1))* Harcourt Schl. Pubs.
—Harcourt Language: Vocabulary Power. 2nd ed. 2003. (Harcourt Title I Reading Programs Ser.). (Illus.). (gr. 2-18). pupil's gde. ed. 5.90 *(978-0-15-320608-5(X));* (gr. 3-18). 5.90 *(978-0-15-320609-2(8));* (gr. 4-18). 5.90 *(978-0-15-320610-8(1));* (gr. 5-18). 5.90 *(978-0-15-320611-5(X))* Harcourt Schl. Pubs.
Harpster, Steve, illus. First Word Search: Fun First Words. 2011. (First Word Search Ser.). (ENG.). 64p. (J). pap. 4.95 *(978-1-4027-7807-0(4))* Sterling Publishing Co., Inc.
Harris, Valerie F. & Jones, Eula V. Shaping up for Sight Word Success. Date not set. 30p. (J). (gr. k-6). wbk. ed. *(978-1-889654-03-4(5))* Enricharamics, Inc.
Harry, Pamela. My Body & Me, 1 vol. 2010. 16p. pap. 24.95 *(978-1-4489-6155-9(6))* PublishAmerica, Inc.
Harte, May. 1, 2, 3 in My House. 2004. (Look-And-Learn Books). (Illus.). (J). lib. bdg. 8.95 *(978-1-4042-2823-8(3),* PowerKids Pr.) Rosen Publishing Group, Inc., The.
Haughom, Lisa, illus. People, Places & Things. 2010. (J). *(978-1-58865-541-7(5))* Kidsbooks, LLC.
—Things That Go! 2010. 16p. (J). *(978-1-58865-542-4(3))* Kidsbooks, LLC.
Haydon, Julie. First 1000 Words. 2004. (Illus.). 95p. (J). *(978-1-74121-402-4(5))* Hinkler Bks. Pty, Ltd.
Hayes, Larry E. My Name Starts with S (Library Version) Anderson, Airlie, illus. 2004. (My Name Starts With Ser.). 32p. (J). lib. bdg. 12.95 *(978-0-9725292-8-0(4))* Inspire Pubns.
Hazan, Maurice, creator. El Camino: Practicing Everyday Vocabulary. (SPA.). (J). 124.95 *(978-1-932770-44-5(5),* SG5) Symtalk, Inc.
Heidrich, Delana. Figuratively Speaking: Using Classic Literature to teach 40 Literary Terms, Vol. 1020. Clark, Kim, ed. Armstrong, Beverly & Grayson, Rick, illus. 2004. 136p. (J). (gr. 5-8). pap. 14.99 *(978-0-88160-317-0(1),* LW-1020) Creative Teaching Pr., Inc.
The Heinle Picture Dictionary for Children: Monkey Puppet. 2007. (C). cd-rom 19.95 *(978-1-4240-1834-5(X))* Cengage Heinle.
Helenek, Sophie. My First Book SKY WONDERS: BOOK of the YEAR 2014 for Babies & Toddlers Category by Creative Child Magazine. 2014. (My First Book Ser.). (ENG., Illus.). 16p. (J). (gr. -1 — 1). bds. 5.99 *(978-0-9894505-3-9(8))* Nursery Bks.
Henderson, Meryl. Indoor Things. (Picture Bks.: No. S8817-2). (Illus.). 28p. (J). (gr. -1). pap. 3.95 *(978-0-7214-5141-1(1),* Dutton Juvenile) Penguin Publishing Group.
Hentzell, Brittany, illus. Annie & Arnie's Arduous Afternoon. 2005. spiral bd. 12.95 *(978-0-9773550-0-6(4))* Smartypants Bks.
Herzog, Joyce. Excursion into Words: Student Activity Book. Sinclair, Angie & Sinclair, Dan, eds. 2005. (J). spiral bd. 15.00 *(978-1-887225-46-5(3))* Herzog, Joyce.
Hicks, Diana & Littlejohn, Andrew. American English Primary Colors 2 Vocabulary Cards. 2004. (ENG.). 96p. 35.00 *(978-0-521-60319-5(6))* Cambridge Univ. Pr.
Hicks, Isreal. The Alphabet Heroes: ABCs & Beyond. 2017. (ENG., Illus.). (J). *(978-0-9959297-1-5(8))* Enter Play Media.
Hiding: KinderWords Individual Title Six-Packs. (Kinderstarters Ser.). 8p. (gr. -1-1). 21.00 *(978-0-7635-8703-1(6))* Rigby Education.
Hills, Laila, illus. Animal Friends. 2017. (J). *(978-1-62885-342-1(5))* Kidsbooks, LLC.
Hinkler Books, creator. 101 First Words. 2011. (101 First Words Ser.). (Illus.). 16p. (J). (gr. -1). bds. 7.99 *(978-1-74184-816-8(4))* Hinkler Bks. Pty, Ltd. AUS. Dist: Ideals Pubns.
—101 First Words: Animals. 2011. (101 First Words Ser.). (Illus.). 16p. (J). (gr. -1). bds. 7.99 *(978-1-74184-817-5(2))* Hinkler Bks. Pty, Ltd. AUS. Dist: Ideals Pubns.
—101 First Words: At Home. 2011. (101 First Words Ser.). (Illus.). 16p. (J). (gr. -1). bds. 7.99 *(978-1-74184-819-9(9))* Hinkler Bks. Pty, Ltd. AUS. Dist: Ideals Pubns.
—101 First Words: Things That Go. 2011. (101 First Words Ser.). (Illus.). 16p. (J). bds. 7.99 *(978-1-74184-818-2(0))* Hinkler Bks. Pty, Ltd. AUS. Dist: Ideals Pubns.
Hoffmann, Sara E. Ana & the Pet Show. Strange, Katie, illus. 2013. (My Reading Neighborhood: First-Grade Sight Word Stories Ser.). (ENG.). 16p. (J). (gr. -1-1). pap. 6.99 *(978-1-4677-1170-8(5),* 9bddd68a-0c9d-49aa-aa01-5db7327d9e39) Lerner Publishing Group.
—Ben Gives a Gift. Dieterichs, Shelley, illus. 2013. (My Reading Neighborhood: Kindergarten Sight Word Stories Ser.). (ENG.). 16p. (J). (gr. -1-1). pap. 6.99 *(978-1-4677-1164-7(0),* 2f5bdf34-2085-4933-93cb-8aa9fc5ecdab) Lerner Publishing Group.
—Fall Fun for Kit. Roraback, Robin, illus. 2013. (My Reading Neighborhood: Kindergarten Sight Word Stories Ser.). (ENG.). 16p. (J). (gr. -1-1). pap. 6.99 *(978-1-4677-1165-4(9),* 84cfeb8d-f83d-491b-9de8-ac1d9388ce60) Lerner Publishing Group.
—Nan Swims. Roraback, Robin, illus. 2013. (My Reading Neighborhood: Kindergarten Sight Word Stories Ser.). (ENG.). 16p. (J). (gr. -1-1). pap. 6.99 *(978-1-4677-1166-1(7),* d4287f5f-4352-420e-9100-f2ad471fc8d2) Lerner Publishing Group.
—Nia Bakes Cookies. Strange, Katie, illus. 2013. (My Reading Neighborhood: First-Grade Sight Word Stories Ser.). (ENG.). 16p. (J). (gr. -1-1). pap. 6.99 *(978-1-4677-1172-2(1),* 54d04a36-9838-46dc-8ea2-205935d70f37) Lerner Publishing Group.
—A Picnic with Kit. Roraback, Robin, illus. 2013. (My Reading Neighborhood: Kindergarten Sight Word Stories Ser.). (ENG.). 16p. (J). (gr. -1-1). pap. 6.99 *(978-1-4677-1168-5(3),* e92f764a-4122-4d4c-898f-1b08b7dec526) Lerner Publishing Group.
—Sam Is Six. Dieterichs, Shelley, illus. 2013. (My Reading Neighborhood: Kindergarten Sight Word Stories Ser.). (ENG.). 16p. (J). (gr. -1-1). pap. 6.99 *(978-1-4677-1163-0(2),* d301adb7-bb52-4498-b077-2c2a8631b281) Lerner Publishing Group.
Holt, Rinehart and Winston Staff. Elements of Literature: Assessment: Literature, Reading & Vocabulary. 2003. 4th ed. pap. 40.20 *(978-0-03-068518-7(4))* 5th ed. pap. 40.20 *(978-0-03-068519-4(2))* 5th ed. pap. 40.20 *(978-0-03-068517-0(6))* Holt McDougal.
—Elements of Literature: Vocabulary Development. 5th ed. 2003. (Illus.). pap. 30.40 *(978-0-03-073938-5(1));* pap. 30.40 *(978-0-03-073939-2(X))* Holt McDougal.
—Vocabulary Workshop. 2003. (Elements of Language Ser.). (gr. 6-18). 19.20 *(978-0-03-056023-1(3))* Holt McDougal.
Hop, Jog, & Tap: Consonants g, h, j; Short Vowel o word families: Level A, 6 vols. (Wright Skills Ser.). 12p. (gr. k-3). 17.95 *(978-0-322-01449-7(2))* Wright Group/McGraw-Hill.
Hoppner, Gabi. Backyard Fun. 2004. (What A Series of Fun! Ser.). (Illus.). 10p. (J). bds. 3.99 *(978-1-59384-054-9(3))* Parklane Publishing.
—Fun on Wheels. 2004. (What A Series of Fun! Ser.). (Illus.). 10p. (J). bds. 3.99 *(978-1-59384-055-6(1))* Parklane Publishing.
Las Horas. (Coleccion Libritos Acordeon). (SPA., Illus.). 10p. (J). pap. 5.50 *(978-950-11-0827-9(9),* SGM279) Sigmar ARG. Dist: Continental Bk. Co., Inc.
Howard, Linda & Dockray, Tracy Arah, illus. Mi Gran Libro de Palabras Play-Doh. 2006. (SPA.). 10p. (J). (gr. -1-4). reprint ed. 10.00 *(978-1-4223-5586-2(1))* DIANE Publishing Co.
Hudson, Amanda. This Is My Ball, 1 vol. 2008. (Our Toys Ser.). (ENG., Illus.). 16p. (gr. k-1). (J). lib. bdg. 21.67 *(978-0-8368-9252-9(6),* 12235892-f7fa-4a8b-b94c-e90d57dcc184); pap. 6.30 *(978-0-8368-9351-9(4),* 46a893bc-a19e-4bbb-a4a5-fec5dcc12390) Stevens, Gareth Publishing LLLP. (Weekly Reader Leveled Readers).
—This Is My Ball / Ésta Es Mi Pelota, 1 vol. 2008. (Our Toys / Nuestros Juguetes Ser.). (SPA & ENG.). 16p. (gr. k-k). pap. 6.30 *(978-0-8368-9355-7(7),* 90b25969-7e82-4470-9892-d7cdfb7bb3a0, Weekly Reader Leveled Readers) Stevens, Gareth Publishing LLLP.
—This Is My Bear, 1 vol. 2008. (Our Toys Ser.). (ENG., Illus.). 16p. (gr. k-1). (J). lib. bdg. 21.67 *(978-0-8368-9253-6(4),*

7491166d-de9d-4985-931d-1ad8668e381f); pap. 6.30 *(978-0-8368-9352-6(2),* 4b40f611-49a9-46bc-a88d-feb5c8e85292) Stevens, Gareth Publishing LLLP. (Weekly Reader Leveled Readers).

—This Is My Bear / Éste Es Mi Oso, 1 vol. 2008. (Our Toys / Nuestros Juguetes Ser.). (SPA & ENG.). 16p. (gr. k-k). pap. 6.30 *(978-0-8368-9356-4(5),* c0f08e9a-97e6-4d05-a8ab-c3e7ee4c5936); (Illus.). (J). lib. bdg. 21.67 *(978-0-8368-9257-4(7),* f77425f0-d46b-4c49-bca2-e13c85e883ff) Stevens, Gareth Publishing LLLP. (Weekly Reader Leveled Readers).

—This Is My Book, 1 vol. 2008. (Our Toys Ser.). (ENG., Illus.). 16p. (gr. k-1). (J). lib. bdg. 21.67 *(978-0-8368-9254-3(2),* 474daae6-8958-407a-947b-ffa935e9c87b); pap. 6.30 *(978-0-8368-9353-3(0),* 2cc6adb6-3cd9-43c5-b6c5-5c008e28e13c) Stevens, Gareth Publishing LLLP. (Weekly Reader Leveled Readers).

—This Is My Book / Éste Es Mi Libro, 1 vol. 2008. (Our Toys / Nuestros Juguetes Ser.). (ENG & SPA.). 16p. (gr. k-k). pap. 6.30 *(978-0-8368-9357-1(3),* af7ed5e0-3463-4f9e-85e3-36124bf44618); (Illus.). (J). lib. bdg. 21.67 *(978-0-8368-9258-1(5),* 8b827754-3019-4493-b16b-94ac75f2d656) Stevens, Gareth Publishing LLLP. (Weekly Reader Leveled Readers).

—This Is My Truck, 1 vol. 2008. (Our Toys Ser.). (ENG., Illus.). 16p. (gr. k-1). (J). lib. bdg. 21.67 *(978-0-8368-9255-0(0),* 9a459ed5-b893-4005-941d-f51b843fa30d); pap. 6.30 *(978-0-8368-9354-0(9),* 8bc04754-a818-4aa3-93e1-1d0a2d98565a) Stevens, Gareth Publishing LLLP. (Weekly Reader Leveled Readers).

—This Is My Truck / Éste Es Mi Camión, 1 vol. 2008. (Our Toys / Nuestros Juguetes Ser.). 16p. (gr. k-k). (SPA & ENG.). pap. 6.30 *(978-0-8368-9358-8(1),* b2327768-06b6-4484-be62-c9e780c2413c); (ENG & SPA., Illus.). (J). lib. bdg. 21.67 *(978-0-8368-9259-8(3),* 14899ea7-40e8-49a1-a34b-ab1675379817) Stevens, Gareth Publishing LLLP. (Weekly Reader Leveled Readers).

Hudson, Cheryl Willis. Book of Opposites. Simpson, Howard, illus. (Afro-Bets Ser.). (J). pap. 4.95 *(978-0-940975-11-8(4))* Just Us Bks., Inc.

Hughes, Mónica & Ripley, Frances. 350 Words. 2011. (I Love Reading Book & CD-ROM Packs Ser.). (ENG., Illus.). 96p. (J). (gr. k-2). pap. 16.95 *(978-1-84898-179-9(1),* TickTock Books) Octopus Publishing Group GBR. Dist: Independent Pubs. Group.

Hughes, Susan. Bath Time. 2017. (Time To Ser.). (ENG., Illus.). 14p. (J). (gr. -1). bds. 7.99 *(978-1-55451-947-7(0))* Annick Pr., Ltd. CAN. Dist: Publishers Group West (PGW).

—Nap Time. 2017. (ENG., Illus.). 14p. (J). (gr. -1). bds. 7.99 *(978-1-55451-949-1(7))* Annick Pr., Ltd. CAN. Dist: Publishers Group West (PGW).

—Play Time. 2017. (ENG., Illus.). 14p. (J). (gr. -1). bds. 7.99 *(978-1-55451-951-4(9))* Annick Pr., Ltd. CAN. Dist: Publishers Group West (PGW).

Hunsicker, Ranelda Mack. Faerie Gold: A Guide for Teachers & Students. 2005. (Classics for Young Readers Ser.). (Illus.). 64p. (J). 6.99 *(978-0-87552-741-3(8))* P & R Publishing.

—Heidi: A Guide for Teachers & Students. 2006. (Classics for Young Readers Ser.). 51p. (J). (gr. 3). per. 6.99 *(978-0-87552-740-6(X))* P & R Publishing.

—Little Women: A Guide for Teachers & Students. 2003. (Classics for Young Readers Ser.). 64p. (J). 6.99 *(978-0-87552-737-6(X))* P & R Publishing.

HuskMitNavn, illus. The Wrong Book. 2018. (ENG.). 14p. (J). bds. 14.95 *(978-1-58423-673-3(6),* 2a00f5cc-f841-4c71-bc2d-b1df524a6413) Gingko Pr., Inc.

Hutchins, J. Spanish First Words (Primeras Palabras en Espanol) 2013. (SPA & ENG.). lib. bdg. 14.75 *(978-0-606-32400-7(3))* Turtleback.

Hynson, Colin. Ancient Rome: The Complete Homework Solution. 2010. (Study Buddies Ser.). (ENG.). 32p. (J). (gr. 4-7). pap. 6.95 *(978-1-84898-182-9(1),* TickTock Books) Octopus Publishing Group GBR. Dist: Independent Pubs. Group.

Ideals Children's Books Staff, creator. My First Words: Fun to Play Bilingual Learning Game! 2007. (Bilingual Builders Ser.). (ENG., Illus.). 10p. (J). (gr. -1-1). bds. 8.99 *(978-0-8249-6696-6(1),* Ideals Pubns.) Worthy Publishing.

Inglés Básico para niños: Edad 7-12, Basic English for Children: ¡Aprenda las 250 Palabras Más Importantes en Inglés!, Learn the 250 Most Important Words in English! 2005. 30.00 *(978-0-9769266-2-7(8))* Weapons of Mass Instruction.

Inside My World, 12 vols. 2014. (Inside My World Ser.). (ENG.). 24p. (J). (gr. k-k). lib. bdg. 145.62 *(978-1-4824-1632-9(8),* 7297feba-2dff-452f-bcf1-3395470e8ee6) Stevens, Gareth Publishing LLLP.

Iversen, Sandra. Alphabet Book Aa. 2009. (Quick60 Alphabet Bks.). (ENG., Illus.). 12p. (J). pap. *(978-1-77540-000-4(X))* Iversen Publishing Ltd.

—Alphabet Book Bb. 2009. (Quick60 Alphabet Bks.). (ENG., Illus.). 12p. (J). pap. *(978-1-77540-001-1(8))* Iversen Publishing Ltd.

—Alphabet Book Cc. 2009. (Quick60 Alphabet Bks.). (ENG., Illus.). 12p. (J). pap. *(978-1-77540-002-8(6))* Iversen Publishing Ltd.

—Alphabet Book Dd. 2009. (Quick60 Alphabet Bks.). (ENG., Illus.). 12p. (J). pap. *(978-1-77540-003-5(4))* Iversen Publishing Ltd.

—Alphabet Book Ee. 2009. (Quick60 Alphabet Bks.). (ENG., Illus.). 12p. (J). pap. *(978-1-77540-004-2(2))* Iversen Publishing Ltd.

—Alphabet Book Ff. 2009. (Quick60 Alphabet Bks.). (ENG., Illus.). 12p. (J). pap. *(978-1-77540-005-9(0))* Iversen Publishing Ltd.

—Alphabet Book Gg. 2009. (Quick60 Alphabet Bks.). (ENG., Illus.). 12p. (J). pap. *(978-1-77540-006-6(9))* Iversen Publishing Ltd.

—Alphabet Book Hh. 2009. (Quick60 Alphabet Bks.). (ENG., Illus.). 12p. (J). pap. *(978-1-77540-007-3(7))* Iversen Publishing Ltd.

—Alphabet Book Ii. 2009. (Quick60 Alphabet Bks.). (ENG., Illus.). 12p. (J). pap. *(978-1-77540-008-0(5))* Iversen Publishing Ltd.

—Alphabet Book Jj. 2009. (Quick60 Alphabet Bks.). (ENG., Illus.). 12p. (J). pap. *(978-1-77540-009-7(3))* Iversen Publishing Ltd.

—Alphabet Book Kk. 2009. (Quick60 Alphabet Bks.). (ENG., Illus.). 12p. (J). pap. *(978-1-77540-010-3(7))* Iversen Publishing Ltd.

—Alphabet Book Ll. 2009. (Quick60 Alphabet Bks.). (ENG., Illus.). 12p. (J). pap. *(978-1-77540-011-0(5))* Iversen Publishing Ltd.

—Alphabet Book Mm. 2009. (ENG., Illus.). 12p. (J). pap. *(978-1-77540-012-7(3))* Iversen Publishing Ltd.

—Alphabet Book Nn. 2009. (Quick60 Alphabet Bks.). (ENG., Illus.). 12p. (J). pap. *(978-1-77540-013-4(1))* Iversen Publishing Ltd.

—Alphabet Book Oo. 2009. (Quick60 Alphabet Bks.). (ENG., Illus.). 12p. (J). pap. *(978-1-77540-014-1(X))* Iversen Publishing Ltd.

—Alphabet Book Pp. 2009. (Quick60 Alphabet Bks.). (ENG., Illus.). 12p. (J). pap. *(978-1-77540-015-8(8))* Iversen Publishing Ltd.

—Alphabet Book Qq. 2009. (Quick60 Alphabet Bks.). (ENG., Illus.). 12p. (J). pap. *(978-1-77540-016-5(6))* Iversen Publishing Ltd.

—Alphabet Book Zz. 2009. (Quick60 Alphabet Bks.). (ENG., Illus.). 12p. (J). pap. *(978-1-77540-025-7(5))* Iversen Publishing Ltd.

James, Trisha. I Know Things That Go, 1 vol. 2017. (What I Know Ser.). (ENG.). 24p. (J). (gr. k-k). pap. 9.15 *(978-1-4824-6309-5(1),* c2580a63-e184-4ac8-b41b-65f77a4ae94c) Stevens, Gareth Publishing LLLP.

Jenkins, Emily. Small Medium Large, 1 vol. Bogacki, Tomek, illus. 2011. (ENG.). 32p. (J). 18.99 *(978-1-59572-278-2(5));* pap. 8.99 *(978-1-59572-299-7(8))* Star Bright Bks., Inc.

Johnson, Margaret. Gone! Level Starter/Beginner American English. 2010. (Cambridge Experience Readers Ser.). (ENG., Illus.). 48p. pap. 14.75 *(978-0-521-14904-4(5))* Cambridge Univ. Pr.

Johnson, Paul F. & Halfman, Patti. 50 Quick Play Vocabulary Games. 2004. (YA). per. 34.95 *(978-0-7606-0539-4(4))* LinguiSystems, Inc.

Jones, Stephanie, des. First Words Look & Say Flashcards. 2007. (Look & Say Flashcards Ser.). (Illus.). 30p. (J). (gr. -1-k). 9.99 *(978-0-7945-1497-6(9),* Usborne) EDC Publishing.

Jones, Tammy. I Am Active. 2009. (Sight Word Readers Set A Ser.). (J). *(978-1-60719-139-1(3))* Newmark Learning LLC.

—I Go! 2009. (Sight Word Readers Set A Ser.). (J). 3.49 net. *(978-1-60719-143-8(1))* Newmark Learning LLC.

—I Like the Spring! 2009. (Sight Word Readers Set A Ser.). (J). 3.49 net. *(978-1-60719-138-4(5))* Newmark Learning LLC.

—I Like to Play Sports. 2009. (Sight Word Readers Set A Ser.). (J). 3.49 net. *(978-1-60719-135-3(0))* Newmark Learning LLC.

—Jobs Around Town. 2009. (Sight Word Readers Set A Ser.). (J). 3.49 net. *(978-1-60719-158-2(X))* Newmark Learning LLC.

—Look at the Shapes. 2009. (Sight Word Readers Set A Ser.). (J). 3.49 net. *(978-1-60719-152-0(0))* Newmark Learning LLC.

Jorden, Brooke. 100 First Words for Little Geeks. Kershner, Kyle, illus. 2018. (100 First Words Ser.). (ENG.). 20p. (J). (gr. -1 — 1). bds. 9.99 *(978-1-945547-95-9(2),* 554795) Familius LLC.

Jorden, Tyler. 100 First Words for Little Geniuses, Volume 2. Kershner, Kyle, illus. 2018. (100 First Words Ser.: 2). (ENG.). 20p. (J). (gr. -1-3). bds. 9.99 *(978-1-64170-034-4(3),* 550034) Familius LLC.

Juguetes. (Coleccion Libritos Acordeon). (SPA., Illus.). 10p. (J). pap. 5.50 *(978-950-11-0825-5(2),* SGM252) Sigmar ARG. Dist: Continental Bk. Co., Inc.

Jullien, Jean. Before & After. 2017. (ENG., Illus.). 40p. (gr. -1 — 1). bds. 16.95 *(978-0-7148-7408-1(6))* Phaidon Pr., Inc.

Just the Right Word! Classroom Set. (J). (gr. k-3). 109.22 *(978-0-7362-2534-2(X))* CENGAGE Learning.

Kauffman, Dorothy. Oxford Picture Dictionary for the Content Areas English Dictionary. 2nd ed. 2010. (Oxford Picture Dictionary for the Content Areas 2e Ser.). (Illus.). 208p. pap. 30.80 *(978-0-19-452500-8(7))* Oxford Univ. Pr., Inc.

Kauffman, Dorothy & Apple, Gary. Oxford Picture Dictionary for the Content Areas English/Spanish Dictionary. 2nd ed. 2010. (Oxford Picture Dictionary for the Content Areas 2e Ser.). (ENG., Illus.). 216p. pap. 30.80 *(978-0-19-452502-2(3))* Oxford Univ. Pr., Inc.

Kauffman, Dorothy, et al. OPD for Content Areas 2e Classroom Set Pack. Set. Pack. 2nd ed. 2010. (ENG., Illus.). xiii, 196p. pap. 478.50 *(978-0-19-452526-8(0))* Oxford Univ. Pr., Inc.

Kelley, K. C. Baby Bears. 2018. (Spot Baby Animals Ser.). (ENG., Illus.). 16p. (J). (gr. -1-2). pap. 7.99 *(978-1-68152-250-0(0),* 14842) Amicus.

—Blast off to Space. 2018. (Amazing Adventures Ser.). (ENG., Illus.). 16p. (J). (gr. k-2). pap. 7.99 *(978-1-68152-271-5(3),* 14887) Amicus.

—Flowers. 2018. (Spot Awesome Nature Ser.). (ENG.). 16p. (J). (gr. -1-2). pap. 7.99 *(978-1-68152-247-0(0),* 14822) Amicus.

Kelley, Maria Felicia. Buz Words: Discovering Words in Pairs. Kelley, Maria Felicia, illus. I.t. ed. 2007. (Illus.). 29p. (J). (gr. -1-3). per. 7.95 *(978-0-9650918-2-4(1))* April Arts Press & Productions.

Kelley, Michelle. Rules, Rules, Rules. 2007. (ENG., Illus.). 16p. (gr. k-2). 28.50 *(978-1-60472-111-9(1))* Rourke Educational Media.

Kennard, Pippa & Kennard, Pippa. Bunny Island. Fukuda, Yukihiro & Fukuda, Yukihiro, photos by. 2015. (ENG., Illus.). 32p. (J). (gr. -1-1). pap. 4.99 *(978-1-77085-657-8(9),* 92e37a85-6b03-43b3-ab95-b2db0ea9539c) Firefly Bks., Ltd.

Kennst du Das? Deine Welt. (Duden Ser.). (GER., Illus.). 16p. (J). *(978-3-411-70431-6(4))* Bibliographisches Institut & F. A. Brockhaus AG DEU. Dist: International Bk. Import Service, Inc.

Kent, Lorna, illus. Baby's First Word Book. 2004. 12p. (J). bds. 7.99 *(978-1-85854-478-6(5))* Brimax Books Ltd. GBR. Dist: Byeway Bks.

—Word Magic: Magnetic Sentence Builder. 8p. (J). bds. *(978-1-58048-382-7(8))* Sandvik Publishing.

Kerrin, Jessica Scott. Martin Bridge: Ready for Takeoff! Kelly, Joseph, illus. 2005. (Martin Bridge Ser.). (ENG.). 120p. (J). (gr. 2-5). 6.95 *(978-1-55337-772-6(9))* Kids Can Pr., Ltd. CAN. Dist: Hachette Bk. Group.

Kershner, Kyle. 100 First Words for Little Artists, Volume 3. 2019. (100 First Words Ser.: 3). (ENG., Illus.). 20p. (J). (gr. -1-3). bds. 9.99 *(978-1-64170-128-0(5),* 550128) Familius LLC.

Könnecke, Ole. The Big Book of Words & Pictures. Könnecke, Ole, illus. 2012. (Gecko Press Titles Ser.). (Illus.). 22p. (J). (gr. -1-k). bds. 14.95 *(978-1-877579-05-9(X))* Gecko Pr. NZL. Dist: Lerner Publishing Group.

Kovecses, Anna. One Thousand Things. 2015. (Learn with Little Mouse Ser.). (ENG., Illus.). 80p. (J). (-k). 17.99 *(978-1-84780-607-9(4),* 313737, Wide Eyed Editions) Quarto Publishing Group UK GBR. Dist: Hachette UK Distribution.

Krause, Claudia. Word Wheels. (Orig.). (J). pap. *(978-0-9655689-0-6(3))* Krause, Claudia.

Ku, Blae & Tha, Shay. Fruits & Vegetables: A Picture Book in Karen & English. 2016. (KAR & ENG., Illus.). 54p. (J). 26.00 *(978-1-4809-6685-7(1),* RoseDog Bks.) Dorrance Publishing Co., Inc.

Ladybird. On the Farm - Read It Yourself with Ladybird Level 2. 2016. (Read It Yourself with Ladybird Ser.). (ENG., Illus.). 32p. (J). (gr. 2-4). 5.99 *(978-0-241-23731-1(9))* Penguin Bks., Ltd. GBR. Dist: Independent Pubs. Group.

LaFleur, Richard & Tillery, Brad. Ovid Vocabulary Cards for AP Selections. 2007. (ENG.). 80p. pap. 15.00 *(978-0-86516-657-8(9))* Bolchazy-Carducci Pubs.

Lakeshore Learning Materials Staff, contrib. by. The Big Surprise: A Homophone Story, Set of 6 Student Books. 2007. (J). pap. 18.95 *(978-1-59746-028-6(1))* Lakeshore Learning Materials.

—The Big Surprise: A Homophone Story Big Book. 2007. (J). pap. 19.95 *(978-1-59746-024-8(9))* Lakeshore Learning Materials.

—The Game: A Multiple Meaning Story, Set of 6 Student Books. 2007. (J). pap. 18.95 *(978-1-59746-029-3(X))* Lakeshore Learning Materials.

—The Game: A Multiple Meaning Story Big Book. 2007. (J). pap. 19.95 *(978-1-59746-025-5(7))* Lakeshore Learning Materials.

—The Great Race: A Synonym Story Big Book. 2007. (J). pap. 19.95 *(978-1-59746-022-4(2))* Lakeshore Learning Materials.

—Partner Reading Book Set. 2007. (J). pap. 39.95 *(978-1-59746-021-7(4))* Lakeshore Learning Materials.

—Spanish Alphabet Big Book. 2006. (SPA.). (J). pap. 19.95 *(978-1-59746-000-2(1))* Lakeshore Learning Materials.

—A Special Gift: An Antonym Story, Set of 6 Student Books. 2007. (J). pap. 18.95 *(978-1-59746-027-9(3))* Lakeshore Learning Materials.

—A Special Gift: An Antonym Story Big Book. 2007. (J). pap. 19.95 *(978-1-59746-023-1(0))* Lakeshore Learning Materials.

Lamb, Stacey, illus. Wipe Clean First Letters. 2011. (Wipe-Clean Bks). 20p. (J). pap. 7.99 *(978-0-7945-3100-3(8),* Usborne) EDC Publishing.

LaQuay, Kate & LoGiudice, Carolyn. Spotlight on Vocabulary Antonyms Level 1, 6 vols. 2005. (Illus.). (J). per. 11.95 *(978-0-7606-0586-8(6))* LinguiSystems, Inc.

LaQuay, Kate & Logiudice, Carolyn. Spotlight on Vocabulary Associations Level 1, 6 vols. 2005. (Illus.). per. 11.95 *(978-0-7606-0604-9(8))* LinguiSystems, Inc.

—Spotlight on Vocabulary Attributes Level 1, 6 vols. 2005. (Illus.). (J). per. 11.95 *(978-0-7606-0588-2(2))* LinguiSystems, Inc.

LaQuay, Kate & LoGiudice, Carolyn. Spotlight on Vocabulary Categories Level 1, 6 vols. 2005. (Illus.). (J). per. 11.95 *(978-0-7606-0589-9(0))* LinguiSystems, Inc.

—Spotlight on Vocabulary Concepts Level 1, 6 vols. 2005. (Illus.). (J). per. 11.95 *(978-0-7606-0590-5(4))* LinguiSystems, Inc.

L'Arronge, Lilli. Me Tall, You Small. 2017. (ENG., Illus.). 40p. (J). (gr. -1-3). 16.95 *(978-1-77147-194-7(8))* Owlkids Bks. Inc. CAN. Dist: Publishers Group West (PGW).

Lashley, Steven. E. The Buggouts: The Buggouts learning Club. Hunter, Laura E., ed. I.t. ed. 2005. (Illus.). 12p. (J). cd-rom 15.00 *(978-1-59971-244-4(X))* Aardvark Global Publishing.

Laval, Thierry. Mini Look & Find on the Farm (Mini Look & Find) Laval, Thierry, illus. 2017. (Mini Look & Find Ser.). (ENG., Illus.). 14p. (J). (gr. -1-k). 9.95 *(978-0-531-23080-0(5),* Children's Pr.) Scholastic Library Publishing.

Lazarri, Andrea. Vocabulary To Go. 2006. (J). per. 39.95 *(978-0-7606-0663-6(3))* LinguiSystems, Inc.

LD COACH. TEH Learns to Read: Action Words, Volume Five. 2004. (Illus.). 40p. (J). 34.95 *(978-0-9745938-5-2(0))* LD Coach, LLC.

—TEH Learns to Read: Basic Words, Volume Six. 2004. (Illus.). 40p. (J). 34.95 *(978-0-9745938-6-9(9))* LD Coach, LLC.

—TEH Learns to Read: Elementary Words, Volume Seven. 2004. (Illus.). 40p. (J). 34.95 *(978-0-9745938-7-6(7))* LD Coach, LLC.

—TEH Learns to Read: Mixed Sight Words — Group A, Volume Eight. 2004. (Illus.). 40p. (J). 34.95 *(978-0-9745938-8-3(5))* LD Coach, LLC.

—TEH Learns to Read: More Action Words, Volume Nine. 2004. (Illus.). 40p. (J). 34.95 *(978-0-9745938-9-0(3))* LD Coach, LLC.

Le Jars, David. Por Aqui y Por Alli. 2004. (Hablemos Ser.).Tr. of Here & There. (ENG., Illus.). 24p. (J). (gr. -1-k). 9.95 *(978-1-58728-949-1(0));* pap. 5.95 *(978-1-58728-953-8(9))* T&N Children's Publishing. (Two-Can Publishing).

Learning Company Books Staff, ed. Reader Rabbit: Rhyming Words. 2003. (Illus.). 32p. (J). pap., wbk. ed. *(978-0-7630-7578-1(7))* Magma.

Learning New Words (Gr. K-1) 2003. (J). *(978-1-58232-032-8(2))* ECS Learning Systems, Inc.

Lee, Brian, illus. A Castle. 2005. (What's Inside? Ser.). (J). *(978-0-7607-6568-5(5))* backpackbook.

Lengua Espanola: Cuarto Grado. (SPA & ENG.). (J). (gr. 4). 21.95 *(978-84-357-0027-6(5),* CPR76) Ediciones y Distribuciones Codice, S.A. ESP. Dist: Continental Bk. Co., Inc.

Lengua Espanola: Quinto Grado. (SPA & ENG.). (J). (gr. 5). 22.00 *(978-84-357-0171-6(9),* CPR78) Ediciones y Distribuciones Codice, S.A. ESP. Dist: Continental Bk. Co., Inc.

Lengua Espanola: Sexto Grado. (SPA & ENG.). (J). (gr. 6). 22.00 *(978-84-357-0170-9(0),* CPR80) Ediciones y Distribuciones Codice, S.A. ESP. Dist: Continental Bk. Co., Inc.

Let's Read — Word Building. 2003. 16p. (J). 3.79 *(978-1-58792-051-6(4))* Trend Enterprises, Inc.

Levine, Julia Pimsleur. Little Pim: Animals. 2012. (ENG.). 10p. (J). (gr. -1 — 1). bds. 8.95 *(978-1-4197-0174-0(6),* 687501) Abrams, Inc.

Levitt, Paul M., et al. The Weighty Word Book. Stevens, Janet, illus. 3rd ed. 2009. (ENG.). 96p. (J). 21.95 *(978-0-8263-4555-4(7),* P161849) Univ. of New Mexico Pr.

—Weighty Words, Too. Karcz, Katherine, illus. 2009. (ENG.). 96p. (J). (gr. 4-18). 21.95 *(978-0-8263-4558-5(1),* P161848) Univ. of New Mexico Pr.

Lewis, Jan. Farm. 2015. (Illus.). 24p. (J). (gr. -1-k). bds. 6.99 *(978-1-86147-635-7(3),* Armadillo) Anness Publishing GBR. Dist: National Bk. Network.

—My First Words. 2015. (ENG., Illus.). 24p. (J). (gr. -1 — 1). bds. 6.99 *(978-1-86147-498-8(9),* Armadillo) Anness Publishing GBR. Dist: National Bk. Network.

Lewis, Jan, illus. Animals. 2017. 14p. (J). (gr. -1-12). 11.99 *(978-1-86147-727-9(9),* Armadillo) Anness Publishing GBR. Dist: National Bk. Network.

—Animals: Turn the Wheels Find the Pictures. 2016. 10p. (J). (gr. -1-12). bds. 14.99 *(978-1-86147-713-2(9),* Armadillo) Anness Publishing GBR. Dist: National Bk. Network.

—At School. 2017. 14p. (J). (gr. -1-12). 11.99 *(978-1-86147-726-2(0),* Armadillo) Anness Publishing GBR. Dist: National Bk. Network.

—Look & Learn with Little Dino: Action Words. 2014. (ENG.). 24p. (J). (gr. k-2). bds. 6.99 *(978-1-86147-382-0(6),* Armadillo) Anness Publishing GBR. Dist: National Bk. Network.

—Look & Learn with Little Dino: Busy Day. 2014. (ENG.). 24p. (J). (gr. k-2). bds. 6.99 *(978-1-86147-379-0(6),* Armadillo) Anness Publishing GBR. Dist: National Bk. Network.

—Love from Santa, 6 vols. 2013. (ENG.). 60p. (J). (gr. -1-2). bds. 7.99 *(978-1-86147-313-4(3),* Armadillo) Anness Publishing GBR. Dist: National Bk. Network.

—My First Animals. 2014. (ENG.). 24p. (J). (gr. -1-k). bds. 6.99 *(978-1-86147-373-8(7),* Armadillo) Anness Publishing GBR. Dist: National Bk. Network.

—My First Learning Library: 3 Great Books: First Abc First 123 First Words, 3 vols. 2014. (ENG.). 72p. (J). (gr. -1-1). bds. 9.99 *(978-1-86147-387-5(7),* Armadillo) Anness Publishing GBR. Dist: National Bk. Network.

—My First Words: Over 300 Everyday Words & Pictures. 2015. 48p. (J). (gr. -1-12). bds. 9.99 *(978-1-86147-627-2(2),* Armadillo) Anness Publishing GBR. Dist: National Bk. Network.

—Santa's Christmas Box of Books: A Festive Box of Fun Picture Books. 2017. (ENG.). 1p. (J). (gr. -1-12). bds. 14.99 *(978-1-86147-738-5(4),* Armadillo) Anness Publishing GBR. Dist: National Bk. Network.

—Words: Turn the Wheels, Find the Pictures. 2015. 10p. (J). (gr. -1-12). bds. 14.99 *(978-1-86147-660-9(4),* Armadillo) Anness Publishing GBR. Dist: National Bk. Network.

Lindeen, Mary. Texture. 2018. (Beginning-To-Read Ser.). (ENG.). 32p. (J). (gr. k-2). pap. 13.26 *(978-1-68404-151-0(1));* (Illus.). (gr. -1-2). lib. bdg. 22.60 *(978-1-59953-904-1(7))* Norwood Hse. Pr.

Lindsay, Kristine. Basic Vocabulary - 1. 2005. (J). ring bd. 49.95 *(978-1-58804-385-6(1))* P C I Education.

—Basic Vocabulary 2. 2005. (J). ring bd. 49.95 *(978-1-58804-386-3(X))* P C I Education.

Lionni, Leo. What? 2014. (ENG., Illus.). 16p. (J). (— 1). bds. 6.99 *(978-0-385-75406-4(X),* Knopf Bks. for Young Readers) Random Hse. Children's Bks.

—Where? 2014. (ENG., Illus.). 16p. (J). (— 1). bds. 5.99 *(978-0-385-75407-1(8),* Knopf Bks. for Young Readers) Random Hse. Children's Bks.

—Who? 2014. (ENG., Illus.). 16p. (J). (— 1). bds. 6.99 *(978-0-385-75405-7(1),* Knopf Bks. for Young Readers) Random Hse. Children's Bks.

Litchfield & Allman. Los Animales (Animals) 2004. (First Words Board Bks.). (SPA., Illus.). 12p. (J). 4.95 *(978-0-7460-4519-0(0))* EDC Publishing.

Litchfield, Jo. At Home. 2004. (First Words Board Bks.). (SPA & ENG., Illus.). 1p. (J). (gr. -1-18). bds. 4.95 *(978-0-7460-4092-8(X))* EDC Publishing.

—Home. Litchfield, Jo & Allen, Francesca, illus. 2006. (Usborne Look & Say Ser.). 12p. (J). (gr. -1-k). bds. 7.99 *(978-0-7945-1425-9(1),* Usborne) EDC Publishing.

—Things That Move. 2004. (First Words Board Bks.). (ENG., Illus.). 1p. (J). bds. 4.95 *(978-0-7460-4149-9(7))* EDC Publishing.

—The Usborne Book of Everyday Words. Treays, Rebecca et al, eds. Allman, Howard, photos by. 2006. (Everyday Words Ser.). (Illus.). 48p. (J). (gr. -1). lib. bdg. 15.99 *(978-1-58086-964-5(5))* EDC Publishing.

—The Usborne Book of Everyday Words in French. 2006. (Everyday Words Ser.). (Illus.). 48p. (J). (gr. -1-3). per. 9.99 *(978-0-7945-0882-1(0),* Usborne) EDC Publishing.

Litchfield, Jo, illus. Baby Sister Look & Say. 2008. (Look & Say Board Bks). 12p. (J). bds. 7.99 *(978-0-7945-2102-8(9),* Usborne) EDC Publishing.

Litchfield, Jo & Brooks, Felicity. Everyday Words Sticker Book. 2004. (Everyday Words Ser.). (Illus.). 1p. (J). (gr. -1-3). (SPA & ENG.). pap. 8.95 *(978-0-7460-4236-6(1));* (FRE & ENG., pap. 8.95 *(978-0-7460-4237-3(X))* EDC Publishing.

Ljungkvist, Laura. A Line Can Be ... 2015. (ENG., Illus.). 24p. (J). (-k). bds. 12.99 *(978-1-57687-753-1(1),* powerHouse Bks.) powerHse. Bks.

Llewellyn, Claire. It's Fun to Learn about Words: A Busy Picture Book Full of Fabulous Facts & Things to Do! 2016. (Illus.). 32p. (J). (gr. -1-12). 9.99 *(978-1-86147-743-9(0),* Armadillo) Anness Publishing GBR. Dist: National Bk. Network.

Llewellyn, Claire & Holden, Arianne. It's Great to Play & Fun to Learn: A Stimulating Play-And-Learn Book with over 130

Amazing Facts, Exercises & Projects, & More Than 5000 Bright Action-Packed Photographs. 2014. (ENG., Illus.). 256p. (J). (gr. k-4). 16.99 *(978-1-84322-981-0(1)*, Armadillo) Anness Publishing GBR. Dist: National Bk. Network.

Lloyd, Sue & Wernham, Sara. Word Book. Stephen, Lib & Wade, Sarah, illus. 2003. (ENG.). 48p. (J). (gr. k-2). pap. 5.00 *(978-1-84414-028-2(8)*, Jolly Phonics) Jolly Learning, Ltd. GBR. Dist: American International Distribution Corp.

Luch, Alex A. My 1st Tablet: Baby's First 100 Plus Words. 2012. 22p. (J). bds. 7.95 *(978-1-936061-88-4(0))* WS Publishing.

Loewen, Nancy. She Sells Seashells & Other Tricky Tongue Twisters, 1 vol. Wu, Donald, illus. 2010. (Ways to Say It Ser.). (ENG.). 24p. (J). (gr. 3-5). lib. bdg. 28.65 *(978-1-4048-6273-9(0)*, 113744, Picture Window Bks.) Capstone.

LoGiudice, Carolyn & LaQuay, Kate. Spotlight on Vocabulary Antonyms Level 2, 6 vols. 2005. (Illus.). (J). per. 11.95 *(978-0-7606-0598-1(X))* LinguiSystems, Inc.

Logiudice, Carolyn & LaQuay, Kate. Spotlight on Vocabulary Associations Level 2, 5 vols. 2005. (Illus.). (J). per. 11.95 *(978-0-7606-0599-8(8))* LinguiSystems, Inc.

Lomp, Stephan. Indestructibles: Bebé, Vamos a Comer! / Baby, Let's Eat! Chew Proof · Rip Proof · Nontoxic · 100% Washable (Book for Babies, Newborn Books, Safe to Chew) 2018. (Indestructibles Ser.). (SPA., Illus.). 12p. (J). (gr. -1 — 1). pap. 5.99 *(978-1-5235-0318-6(1)*, 100318) Workman Publishing Co., Inc.

Lomp, Stephan, illus. Indestructibles: Baby, Let's Eat! Chew Proof · Rip Proof · Nontoxic · 100% Washable (Book for Babies, Newborn Books, Safe to Chew) 2018. (Indestructibles Ser.). (ENG.). 12p. (J). (gr. -1 — 1). pap. 5.99 *(978-1-5235-0207-3(X)*, 100207) Workman Publishing Co., Inc.

—Indestructibles: Home Sweet Home: Chew Proof · Rip Proof · Nontoxic · 100% Washable (Book for Babies, Newborn Books, Safe to Chew) 2018. (Indestructibles Ser.). (ENG.). 12p. (J). (gr. -1 — 1). pap. 5.99 *(978-1-5235-0208-0(8)*, 100208) Workman Publishing Co., Inc.

London, S. Keith & Osleeb, Rebecca. Defined Mind Vocabulary Accelerator: Music-Driven Vocabulary & Comprehension Tools for School / Test / SAT Prep, 1. 2004. 416p. (YA). pap. 25.00 *(978-0-9763767-0-5(9))* Defined Mind, Inc.

Lonely Planet Kids. Lonely Planet Kids First Words - English 1 1st Ed. Iwohn, Sebastien & Mansfield, Andy, illus. 2017. (Lonely Planet Kids Ser.). (ENG.). 208p. (J). (gr. 1-3). pap. 12.99 *(978-1-78701-279-0(4)*, 5716) Lonely Planet Global Ltd. IRL. Dist: Hachette Bk. Group.

Lonsdale, Mary, illus. First Words Sticker Book. 2003. 12p. (J). bds. *(978-1-85854-658-2(3))* Autumn Publishing, Ltd.

Look, Listen, & Speak-at the Mall. 2005. 80p. (gr. k-3). cd-rom 29.99 *(978-1-55799-951-1(1)*, EMC 2745) Evan-Moor Educational Pubs.

Look, Listen, & Speak-at the Supermarket. 2005. 80p. (gr. k-3). cd-rom 29.99 *(978-1-55799-950-4(3)*, EMC 2744) Evan-Moor Educational Pubs.

Look, Listen, & Speak-from Farm to You. 2005. 80p. (gr. k-3). cd-rom 29.99 *(978-1-55799-949-8(X)*, EMC 2743) Evan-Moor Educational Pubs.

Look, Listen, & Speak-Keeping Healthy. 2005. 80p. (gr. k-3). cd-rom 29.99 *(978-1-55799-948-1(1)*, EMC 2742) Evan-Moor Educational Pubs.

Look, Listen, & Speak-Transportation. 2005. 80p. (gr. k-3). cd-rom 29.99 *(978-1-55799-952-8(X)*, EMC 2746) Evan-Moor Educational Pubs.

Lubben, Amy & Williams, Rozanne Lanczak. Build-a-Skill Instant Books Word Families-Long Vowels. Shiotsu, Vicky & Faulkner, Stacey, eds. Campbell, Jenny & Tom, Darcy, illus. 2007. (J). 4.99 *(978-1-59198-409-2(2))* Creative Teaching Pr., Inc.

—Build-a-Skill Instant Books Word Families-Short Vowels. Shiotsu, Vicky & Faulkner, Stacey, eds. Campbell, Jenny & Tom, Darcy, illus. 2007. (J). 4.99 *(978-1-59198-408-5(4))* Creative Teaching Pr., Inc.

Lucero, Jaime. Bilingual Bingo. 2008. (SPA.). 80p. (gr. k-3). pap. 12.99 *(978-0-439-70067-2(1)*, Teaching Resources) Scholastic, Inc.

Lukoff, Kyle. A Storytelling of Ravens, 1 vol. Nelson, Natalie, illus. 2018. (ENG.). 32p. (J). (gr. k-4). 18.95 *(978-1-55498-912-6(4))* Groundwood Bks. CAN. Dist: Publishers Group West (PGW).

Lundquist, Joegil K. & Lundquist, Jeanne L. English from the Roots up, Volume II: Help for Reading, Writing, Spelling & S. A. T. Scores. 2011. (English from the Roots Up Ser.). (ENG., Illus.). 107p. (J). (gr. -1-3). 44.95 *(978-1-885942-30-2(3))* Cune Pr., LLC.

—English from the Roots up Volume II: Help for Reading, Writing, Spelling, & S. A. T. Scores, vol. 2, II. 2003. (Illus.). 125p. 29.95 net. *(978-1-885942-31-9(1))* Cune Pr., LLC.

Lunge-Larsen, Lise. Gifts from the Gods: Ancient Words & Wisdom from Greek & Roman Mythology. Hinds, Gareth, illus. 2011. (ENG.). 96p. (J). (gr. 5-7). 18.99 *(978-0-547-15229-5(9)*, 1051948, Clarion Bks.) HarperCollins Pubs.

Mac, Cola. Rhyming on Time. Bey, Charles, illus. 2011. 20p. pap. 24.95 *(978-1-4560-6940-7(3))* America Star Bks.

MagneTalk Match-Up Adventure Kit (with Barrier) Gb181. 2006. (J). 59.99 *(978-1-58650-616-2(1))* Super Duper Pubns.

MagneTalk Match-Up Adventure Kit (without Barrier) Gb182. 2006. (J). 59.99 *(978-1-58650-653-7(6))* Super Duper Pubns.

Mairi, Mackinnon. Phonics Workbook 1. 2012. (Very First Reading Workbooks Ser.). 36p. (J). pap. 7.99 *(978-0-7945-3115-7(6)*, Usborne) EDC Publishing.

—Phonics Workbook 2. 2012. (Very First Reading Workbooks Ser.). 36p. (J). pap. 7.99 *(978-0-7945-3116-4(4)*, Usborne) EDC Publishing.

Make Believe Ideas. First Words Sticker Activity Book. Machell, Dawn, illus. 2015. (ENG.). 56p. (J). (gr. -1-7). pap. 6.99 *(978-1-78393-830-8(7))* Make Believe Ideas GBR. Dist: Scholastic, Inc.

Maldonado, Premier, creator. House-Casa: English-Español. 2004. (SPA., Illus.). 20p. (J). bds. 6.00 *(978-0-9727886-1-8(1))* Osmosis, LLC.

Marrow, Lesley Mandel & Vacca, Richard T. Sadlier Phonics: Level C Grade 3. 2001st ed. 2004. (Sadlier Phonics Reading Program). (Illus.). 336p. (gr. 3-18). pap., tchr. ed. 64.00 net. *(978-0-8215-7013-5(7))* Sadlier, William H., Inc.

Marsh, Carole. Work Words: Job/Business/Career Words & Terms You Need to Know! 2012. (Carole Marsh's Careers Curriculum Ser.). (ENG., Illus.). 58p. (J). pap. 19.99 *(978-0-635-10556-1(X))* Gallopade International.

Martin, Dayna. Actions. 2018. (Illus.). 31p. (J). *(978-1-4896-9637-3(7)*, AV2 by Weigl) Weigl Pubs., Inc.

—Opposites. 2018. (Illus.). 31p. (J). *(978-1-4896-9633-5(4)*, AV2 by Weigl) Weigl Pubs., Inc.

—Sports. 2018. (Illus.). 31p. (J). *(978-1-4896-9661-8(X)*, AV2 by Weigl) Weigl Pubs., Inc.

—The Toddler's Handbook: Bilingual (English / Spanish) (Ingles / Espanol) Numbers, Colors, Shapes, Sizes, ABC Animals, Opposites, & Sounds, with over 100 Words That Every Kid Should Know (Engage Early Readers: Children's Learning Books) Roumanis, A. r., ed. I.t. ed. 2015. (SPA & ENG., Illus.). 48p. (J). pap. *(978-1-77226-225-4(0))* AD Classic.

Martin, John David. A Time to Plant: Workbook. 2005. (Rod & Staff's Readers Ser.). 145p. (gr. 5-18). 4.80 *(978-0-7399-0402-2(7)*, 11521) Rod & Staff Pubs., Inc.

Maskell, Hazell. Very First Words. 2009. (First Words Board Bks). 18p. (J). bds. 6.99 *(978-0-7945-2052-6(9)*, Usborne) EDC Publishing.

Mastering Sight Words (Gr. 1-2) 2003. (J). *(978-1-58232-091-5(8))* ECS Learning Systems, Inc.

McCarty, Diane Bischoff. Copywork for Children: For Grades 1-3. 2004. (Illus.). 63p. (J). *(978-0-9712124-1-1(4))* Angel Heart Children's Pr.

McKay, Sindy. Can You Find? (We Both Read - Level Pk-K) An ABC Book. 2015. (We Both Read - Level Pk -K Ser.). (ENG., Illus.). 41p. (J). 9.95 *(978-1-60115-279-4(5))* Treasure Bay, Inc.

—We Read Phonics-Magic Tricks. Johnson, Meredith, illus. 2011. (We Read Phonics Ser.). 32p. (J). (gr. 1-3). 9.95 *(978-1-60115-337-1(6))*; pap. 4.99 *(978-1-60115-338-8(4))* Treasure Bay, Inc.

—We Read Phonics-Matt & Sid. Reinhart, Larry, illus. 2010. 32p. (J). 9.95 *(978-1-60115-315-9(5))*; pap. 4.99 *(978-1-60115-316-6(3))* Treasure Bay, Inc.

—We Read Phonics-Pat, Cat, & Rat. Johnson, Meredith, illus. 2010. 32p. (J). 9.95 *(978-1-60115-311-1(2))*; pap. 4.99 *(978-1-60115-312-8(0))* Treasure Bay, Inc.

McNamara, Connie. My First IU Words Go Hoosiers. 2012. (ENG.). 16p. 10.99 *(978-0-06-219609-5(X)*, Dey Street Bks.) HarperCollins Pubs.

—My First Ohio State Words Go Buckeyes. 2012. (ENG.). 16p. 10.99 *(978-0-06-219605-7(7))* HarperCollins Pubs.

—My First University of Florida Words Go Gators. 2012. (ENG.). 16p. 10.99 *(978-0-06-219611-8(1))* HarperCollins Pubs.

—My First Wisconsin Words Go Badgers. 2012. (ENG.). 16p. 10.99 *(978-0-06-219606-4(5))* HarperCollins Pubs.

Meachen Rau, Dana. ¡a Volar! (Flying). 1 vol. 2008. (En Movimiento (on the Move) Ser.). (SPA., Illus.). 32p. (gr. k-1). lib. bdg. 25.50 *(978-0-7614-2425-3(3)*, 3ffa301d-8a07-42c4-985d-0334ceffc052) Cavendish Square Publishing LLC.

—At the Beach, 1 vol. 2008. (Fun Time Ser.). (ENG., Illus.). 24p. (gr. k-1). lib. bdg. 25.50 *(978-0-7614-2609-7(4)*, 81df4d12-166c-4e8d-857e-526ee8d52a8f) Cavendish Square Publishing LLC.

—Baker, 1 vol. 2008. (Jobs in Town Ser.). (ENG., Illus.). 24p. (gr. k-1). lib. bdg. 25.50 *(978-0-7614-2623-3(X)*, c6257c3d-6ea0-434f-bdfa-9c1ede4eaf68) Cavendish Square Publishing LLC.

—Climbing, 1 vol. 2007. (On the Move Ser.). (ENG., Illus.). 24p. (gr. k-1). lib. bdg. 25.50 *(978-0-7614-2318-8(4)*, a94a0757-5102-43c1-aa5b-f381cb8c39f6) Cavendish Square Publishing LLC.

—En la Playa (at the Beach), 1 vol. 2009. (Tiempo de la Diversión (Fun Time) Ser.). (SPA., Illus.). 24p. (gr. k-1). lib. bdg. 25.50 *(978-0-7614-2748-3(1)*, d4c12fb7-eb50-4738-a48d-55aac6da10e1) Cavendish Square Publishing LLC.

—Flying, 1 vol. 2007. (On the Move Ser.). (ENG., Illus.). 24p. (gr. k-1). lib. bdg. 25.50 *(978-0-7614-2319-5(2)*, aaa0cfda-52e3-4bba-97fc-79772464d4fb, Cavendish Square) Cavendish Square Publishing LLC.

—Un Panadero (Baker), 1 vol. 2009. (Trabajos en Pueblos y Ciudades (Jobs in Town) Ser.). (SPA., Illus.). 24p. (gr. k-1). lib. bdg. 25.50 *(978-0-7614-2781-0(3)*, 8f35c52e-75fc-4977-b2ed-b6d3b409abbb) Cavendish Square Publishing LLC.

—Rolling, 1 vol. 2007. (On the Move Ser.). (ENG., Illus.). 24p. (gr. k-1). lib. bdg. 25.50 *(978-0-7614-2314-0(1)*, 6fb0f09c-33a2-4974-85f7-dd404d1d5b9f, Cavendish Square) Cavendish Square Publishing LLC.

Mein Erstes Woerterbuch: Auf dem Bauernhof. (Duden Ser.). (GER.). 48p. (J). *(978-3-411-71071-3(3))* Bibliographisches Institut & F. A. Brockhaus AG DEU. Dist: International Bk. Import Service, Inc.

Mes 100 Premiers Mots. 2003. (First 100 Words Ser.).Tr. of My First 100 Words. (FRE.). 32p. 5.58 *(978-1-4054-1139-4(2))* Parragon, Inc.

Michael, Joan. The Five Senses/Opposites & Position Words, 4 bks., Set. Incl. Let's Play a Five Senses Guessing Game. Miller, Amanda. 18.00 *(978-0-531-14871-6(8))*; Let's Talk about Opposites, Morning to Night. Falk, Laine. 18.00 *(978-0-531-14872-3(6))*; (Illus.). 24p. (J). (gr. -1-3). 2007. (Let's Find Out Early Learning Bks.). 2007. 72.00 o.p. *(978-0-531-17574-3(X)*, Children's Pr.) Scholastic Library Publishing.

Miles Kelly Staff. Mix-Ups. 2003. (Illus.). 14p. 9.95 *(978-1-902947-83-9(5))* Miles Kelly Publishing, Ltd. GBR. Dist: Independent Pubs. Group.

Milet Publishing. My First Bilingual Book-Jobs (English-Spanish), 1 vol. 2012. (My First Bilingual Book Ser.). (ENG & SPA., Illus.). 24p. (J). (gr. k — 1). bds. 7.99 *(978-1-84059-712-7(7))* Milet Publishing.

Milet Publishing Staff. Jobs, 1 vol. 2012. (My First Bilingual Book Ser.). (ENG & FRE., Illus.). 24p. (J). (gr. k — 1). bds. 7.99 *(978-1-84059-704-2(6))*; bds. 7.99 *(978-1-84059-706-6(2))*; bds. 7.99 *(978-1-84059-711-0(9))* Milet Publishing.

—Jobs - Berufe, 1 vol. 2012. (My First Bilingual Book Ser.). (ENG & GER., Illus.). 24p. (J). (gr. k — 1). bds. 7.99 *(978-1-84059-705-9(4))* Milet Publishing.

—Jobs - My First Bilingual Book, 1 vol. 2012. (My First Bilingual Book Ser.). (ENG., Illus.). 24p. (J). (gr. k — 1). bds. 7.99 *(978-1-84059-701-1(1))* Milet Publishing.

—Jobs Empregos, 1 vol. 2012. (My First Bilingual Book Ser.). (ENG., Illus.). 24p. (J). (gr. k — 1). bds. 7.99 *(978-1-84059-709-7(7))* Milet Publishing.

—Music, 1 vol. 2012. (My First Bilingual Book Ser.). (ENG & POR., Illus.). 24p. (J). (gr. k — 1). bds. 8.99 *(978-1-84059-724-0(0))*; bds. 7.99 *(978-1-84059-716-5(X))*; bds. 8.99 *(978-1-84059-718-9(6))* Milet Publishing.

—Music - English-Spanish, 1 vol. 2012. (My First Bilingual Book Ser.). (ENG & SPA., Illus.). 24p. (J). (gr. k — 1). bds. 8.99 *(978-1-84059-728-8(3))* Milet Publishing.

—Music - My First Bilingual Book, 1 vol. 2012. (My First Bilingual Book Ser.). (ENG., Illus.). 24p. (J). (gr. k — 1). bds. 7.99 *(978-1-84059-725-7(9))*; bds. 7.99 *(978-1-84059-722-6(4))* Milet Publishing.

—La Musique, 1 vol. 2012. (My First Bilingual Book Ser.).Tr. of Music. (ENG & FRE., Illus.). 24p. (J). (gr. k — 1). bds. 7.99 *(978-1-84059-720-2(8))* Milet Publishing.

—My Bilingual Book - Sight, 1 vol. 2014. (My Bilingual Book Ser.). (ENG., Illus.). 24p. (J). (gr. -1-k). 9.95 *(978-1-84059-801-8(8))* Milet Publishing.

—My Bilingual Book - Smell, 1 vol. 2014. (My Bilingual Book Ser.). (ENG & CHI., Illus.). 24p. (J). (gr. -1-k). 9.95 *(978-1-84059-806-3(9))* Milet Publishing.

—My Bilingual Book-Hearing, 1 vol. 2014. (My Bilingual Book Ser.). (ENG., Illus.). 24p. (J). (gr. -1-k). 9.95 *(978-1-84059-779-0(8))*; 9.95 *(978-1-84059-785-1(2))*; 9.95 *(978-1-84059-774-5(7))* Milet Publishing.

—My Bilingual Book-Hearing (English-Arabic), 1 vol. 2014. (My Bilingual Book Ser.). (ENG & ARA., Illus.). 24p. (J). (gr. -1-k). 9.95 *(978-1-84059-772-1(0))* Milet Publishing.

—My Bilingual Book-Hearing (English-Bengali), 1 vol. 2014. (My Bilingual Book Ser.). (ENG & BEN., Illus.). 24p. (J). (gr. -1-k). 9.95 *(978-1-84059-773-8(9))* Milet Publishing.

—My Bilingual Book-Hearing (English-Farsi), 1 vol. 2014. (My Bilingual Book Ser.). (ENG., Illus.). 24p. (J). (gr. -1-k). 9.95 *(978-1-84059-775-2(5))* Milet Publishing.

—My Bilingual Book-Hearing (English-French), 1 vol. 2014. (My Bilingual Book Ser.). (ENG & FRE., Illus.). 24p. (J). (gr. -1-k). 9.95 *(978-1-84059-776-9(3))* Milet Publishing.

—My Bilingual Book-Hearing (English-German), 1 vol. 2014. (My Bilingual Book Ser.). (ENG & GER., Illus.). 24p. (J). (gr. -1-k). 9.95 *(978-1-84059-777-6(1))* Milet Publishing.

—My Bilingual Book-Hearing (English-Italian), 1 vol. 2014. (My Bilingual Book Ser.). (ENG & ITA., Illus.). 24p. (J). (gr. -1-k). 9.95 *(978-1-84059-778-3(X))* Milet Publishing.

—My Bilingual Book-Hearing (English-Polish), 1 vol. 2014. (My Bilingual Book Ser.). (ENG & POR., Illus.). 24p. (J). (gr. -1-k). 9.95 *(978-1-84059-780-6(1))* Milet Publishing.

—My Bilingual Book-Hearing (English-Portuguese), 1 vol. 2014. (My Bilingual Book Ser.). (ENG & POR., Illus.). 24p. (J). (gr. -1-k). 9.95 *(978-1-84059-781-3(X))* Milet Publishing.

—My Bilingual Book-Hearing (English-Russian), 1 vol. 2014. (My Bilingual Book Ser.). (ENG & RUS., Illus.). 24p. (J). (gr. -1-k). 9.95 *(978-1-84059-782-0(8))* Milet Publishing.

—My Bilingual Book-Hearing (English-Somali), 1 vol. 2014. (My Bilingual Book Ser.). (ENG., Illus.). 24p. (J). (gr. -1-k). 9.95 *(978-1-84059-783-7(6))* Milet Publishing.

—My Bilingual Book-Hearing (English-Urdu), 1 vol. 2014. (My Bilingual Book Ser.). (ENG., Illus.). 24p. (J). (gr. -1-k). 9.95 *(978-1-84059-786-8(0))* Milet Publishing.

—My Bilingual Book-Hearing (English-Vietnamese), 1 vol. 2014. (My Bilingual Book Ser.). (ENG., Illus.). 24p. (J). (gr. -1-k). 9.95 *(978-1-84059-787-5(9))* Milet Publishing.

—My Bilingual Book-Sight, 1 vol. 2014. (My Bilingual Book Ser.). (ENG., Illus.). 24p. (J). (gr. -1-k). 9.95 *(978-1-84059-795-0(X))* Milet Publishing.

—My Bilingual Book-Sight (English-Bengali), 1 vol. 2014. (My Bilingual Book Ser.). (ENG & BEN., Illus.). 24p. (J). (gr. -1-k). 9.95 *(978-1-84059-789-9(5))* Milet Publishing.

—My Bilingual Book-Sight (English-Chinese), 1 vol. 2014. (My Bilingual Book Ser.). (ENG & CHI., Illus.). 24p. (J). (gr. -1-k). 9.95 *(978-1-84059-790-5(9))* Milet Publishing.

—My Bilingual Book-Sight (English-Farsi), 1 vol. 2014. (My Bilingual Book Ser.). (ENG., Illus.). 24p. (J). (gr. -1-k). 9.95 *(978-1-84059-791-2(7))* Milet Publishing.

—My Bilingual Book-Sight (English-French), 1 vol. 2014. (My Bilingual Book Ser.). (ENG & FRE., Illus.). 24p. (J). (gr. -1-k). 9.95 *(978-1-84059-792-9(5))* Milet Publishing.

—My Bilingual Book-Sight (English-German), 1 vol. 2014. (My Bilingual Book Ser.). (ENG & GER., Illus.). 24p. (J). (gr. -1-k). 9.95 *(978-1-84059-793-6(3))* Milet Publishing.

—My Bilingual Book-Sight (English-Italian), 1 vol. 2014. (My Bilingual Book Ser.). (ENG & ITA., Illus.). 24p. (J). (gr. -1-k). 9.95 *(978-1-84059-794-3(1))* Milet Publishing.

—My Bilingual Book-Sight (English-Polish), 1 vol. 2014. (My Bilingual Book Ser.). (ENG & POR., Illus.). 24p. (J). (gr. -1-k). 9.95 *(978-1-84059-796-7(8))* Milet Publishing.

—My Bilingual Book-Sight (English-Portuguese), 1 vol. 2014. (My Bilingual Book Ser.). (ENG & POR., Illus.). 24p. (J). (gr. -1-k). 9.95 *(978-1-84059-797-4(6))* Milet Publishing.

—My Bilingual Book-Sight (English-Russian), 1 vol. 2014. (My Bilingual Book Ser.). (ENG & RUS., Illus.). 24p. (J). (gr. -1-k). 9.95 *(978-1-84059-798-1(4))* Milet Publishing.

—My Bilingual Book-Sight (English-Somali), 1 vol. 2014. (My Bilingual Book Ser.). (ENG., Illus.). 24p. (J). (gr. -1-k). 9.95 *(978-1-84059-799-8(2))* Milet Publishing.

—My Bilingual Book-Sight (English-Spanish), 1 vol. 2014. (My Bilingual Book Ser.). (ENG & SPA., Illus.). 24p. (J). (gr. -1-k). 9.95 *(978-1-84059-800-1(X))* Milet Publishing.

—My Bilingual Book-Sight (English-Urdu), 1 vol. 2014. (My Bilingual Book Ser.). (ENG., Illus.). 24p. (J). (gr. -1-k). 9.95 *(978-1-84059-802-5(6))* Milet Publishing.

—My Bilingual Book-Sight (English-Vietnamese), 1 vol. 2014. (My Bilingual Book Ser.). (ENG., Illus.). 24p. (J). (gr. -1-k). 9.95 *(978-1-84059-803-2(4))* Milet Publishing.

—My Bilingual Book-Smell, 1 vol. 2014. (My Bilingual Book Ser.). (ENG., Illus.). 24p. (J). (gr. -1-k). 9.95 *(978-1-84059-811-7(5))* Milet Publishing.

—My Bilingual Book-Smell (English-Arabic), 1 vol. 2014. (My Bilingual Book Ser.). (ENG & ARA., Illus.). 24p. (J). (gr. -1-k). 9.95 *(978-1-84059-804-9(2))* Milet Publishing.

—My Bilingual Book-Smell (English-Bengali), 1 vol. 2014. (My Bilingual Book Ser.). (ENG & BEN., Illus.). 24p. (J). (gr. -1-k). 9.95 *(978-1-84059-805-6(0))* Milet Publishing.

—My Bilingual Book-Smell (English-Farsi), 1 vol. 2014. (My Bilingual Book Ser.). (ENG., Illus.). 24p. (J). (gr. -1-k). 9.95 *(978-1-84059-807-0(7))* Milet Publishing.

—My Bilingual Book-Smell (English-Italian), 1 vol. 2014. (My Bilingual Book Ser.). (ENG & ITA., Illus.). 24p. (J). (gr. -1-k). 9.95 *(978-1-84059-810-0(7))* Milet Publishing.

—My Bilingual Book-Smell (English-Polish), 1 vol. 2014. (My Bilingual Book Ser.). (ENG & POR., Illus.). 24p. (J). (gr. -1-k). 9.95 *(978-1-84059-812-4(3))* Milet Publishing.

—My Bilingual Book-Smell (English-Russian), 1 vol. 2014. (My Bilingual Book Ser.). (ENG & RUS., Illus.). 24p. (J). (gr. -1-k). 9.95 *(978-1-84059-814-8(X))* Milet Publishing.

—My Bilingual Book-Smell (English-Somali), 1 vol. 2014. (My Bilingual Book Ser.). (ENG., Illus.). 24p. (J). (gr. -1-k). 9.95 *(978-1-84059-815-5(8))* Milet Publishing.

—My Bilingual Book-Smell (English-Turkish), 1 vol. 2014. (My Bilingual Book Ser.). (ENG., Illus.). 24p. (J). (gr. -1-k). 9.95 *(978-1-84059-817-9(4))* Milet Publishing.

—My Bilingual Book-Smell (English-Urdu), 1 vol. 2014. (My Bilingual Book Ser.). (ENG., Illus.). 24p. (J). (gr. -1-k). 9.95 *(978-1-84059-818-6(2))* Milet Publishing.

—My Bilingual Book-Smell (English-Vietnamese), 1 vol. 2014. (My Bilingual Book Ser.). (ENG., Illus.). 24p. (J). (gr. -1-k). 9.95 *(978-1-84059-819-3(0))* Milet Publishing.

—My Bilingual Book-Taste (English-Arabic), 1 vol. 2014. (My Bilingual Book Ser.). (ENG & ARA., Illus.). 24p. (J). (gr. -1-k). 9.95 *(978-1-84059-820-9(4))* Milet Publishing.

—My Bilingual Book-Taste (English-Bengali), 1 vol. 2014. (My Bilingual Book Ser.). (ENG & BEN., Illus.). 24p. (J). (gr. -1-k). 9.95 *(978-1-84059-821-6(2))* Milet Publishing.

—My Bilingual Book-Taste (English-Farsi), 1 vol. 2014. (My Bilingual Book Ser.). (ENG., Illus.). 24p. (J). (gr. -1-k). 9.95 *(978-1-84059-823-0(9))* Milet Publishing.

—My Bilingual Book-Taste (English-Italian), 1 vol. 2014. (My Bilingual Book Ser.). (ENG & ITA., Illus.). 24p. (J). (gr. -1-k). 9.95 *(978-1-84059-826-1(3))* Milet Publishing.

—My Bilingual Book-Taste (English-Korean), 1 vol. 2014. (My Bilingual Book Ser.). (ENG., Illus.). 24p. (J). (gr. -1-k). 9.95 *(978-1-84059-827-8(1))* Milet Publishing.

—My Bilingual Book-Taste (English-Polish), 1 vol. 2014. (My Bilingual Book Ser.). (ENG & POR., Illus.). 24p. (J). (gr. -1-k). 9.95 *(978-1-84059-828-5(X))* Milet Publishing.

—My Bilingual Book-Taste (English-Portuguese), 1 vol. 2014. (My Bilingual Book Ser.). (ENG & POR., Illus.). 24p. (J). (gr. -1-k). 9.95 *(978-1-84059-829-2(8))* Milet Publishing.

—My Bilingual Book-Taste (English-Russian), 1 vol. 2014. (My Bilingual Book Ser.). (ENG & RUS., Illus.). 24p. (J). (gr. -1-k). 9.95 *(978-1-84059-830-8(1))* Milet Publishing.

—My Bilingual Book-Taste (English-Somali), 1 vol. 2014. (My Bilingual Book Ser.). (ENG., Illus.). 24p. (J). (gr. -1-k). 9.95 *(978-1-84059-831-5(X))* Milet Publishing.

—My Bilingual Book-Taste (English-Turkish), 1 vol. 2014. (My Bilingual Book Ser.). (ENG., Illus.). 24p. (J). (gr. -1-k). 9.95 *(978-1-84059-833-9(6))* Milet Publishing.

—My Bilingual Book-Taste (English-Urdu), 1 vol. 2014. (My Bilingual Book Ser.). (ENG., Illus.). 24p. (J). (gr. -1-k). 9.95 *(978-1-84059-834-6(4))* Milet Publishing.

—My Bilingual Book-Taste (English-Vietnamese), 1 vol. 2014. (My Bilingual Book Ser.). (ENG., Illus.). 24p. (J). (gr. -1-k). 9.95 *(978-1-84059-835-3(2))* Milet Publishing.

—My Bilingual Book-Touch, 1 vol. 2014. (My Bilingual Book Ser.). (ENG., Illus.). 24p. (J). (gr. -1-k). 9.95 *(978-1-84059-843-8(3))* Milet Publishing.

—My Bilingual Book-Touch (English-Arabic), 1 vol. 2014. (My Bilingual Book Ser.). (ENG & ARA., Illus.). 24p. (J). (gr. -1-k). 9.95 *(978-1-84059-836-0(0))* Milet Publishing.

—My Bilingual Book-Touch (English-Bengali), 1 vol. 2014. (My Bilingual Book Ser.). (ENG & BEN., Illus.). 24p. (J). (gr. -1-k). 9.95 *(978-1-84059-837-7(9))* Milet Publishing.

—My Bilingual Book-Touch (English-Chinese), 1 vol. 2014. (My Bilingual Book Ser.). (ENG & CHI., Illus.). 24p. (J). (gr. -1-k). 9.95 *(978-1-84059-838-4(7))* Milet Publishing.

—My Bilingual Book-Touch (English-Farsi), 1 vol. 2014. (My Bilingual Book Ser.). (ENG., Illus.). 24p. (J). (gr. -1-k). 9.95 *(978-1-84059-839-1(5))* Milet Publishing.

—My Bilingual Book-Touch (English-German), 1 vol. 2014. (My Bilingual Book Ser.). (ENG & GER., Illus.). 24p. (J). (gr. -1-k). 9.95 *(978-1-84059-841-4(7))* Milet Publishing.

—My Bilingual Book-Touch (English-Italian), 1 vol. 2014. (My Bilingual Book Ser.). (ENG & ITA., Illus.). 24p. (J). (gr. -1-k). 9.95 *(978-1-84059-842-1(5))* Milet Publishing.

—My Bilingual Book-Touch (English-Portuguese), 1 vol. 2014. (My Bilingual Book Ser.). (ENG & POR., Illus.). 24p. (J). (gr. -1-k). 9.95 *(978-1-84059-845-2(X))* Milet Publishing.

—My Bilingual Book-Touch (English-Russian), 1 vol. 2014. (My Bilingual Book Ser.). (ENG & RUS., Illus.). 24p. (J). (gr. -1-k). 9.95 *(978-1-84059-846-9(8))* Milet Publishing.

—My Bilingual Book-Touch (English-Somali), 1 vol. 2014. (My Bilingual Book Ser.). (ENG., Illus.). 24p. (J). (gr. -1-k). 9.95 *(978-1-84059-847-6(6))* Milet Publishing.

—My Bilingual Book-Touch (English-Turkish), 1 vol. 2014. (My Bilingual Book Ser.). (ENG., Illus.). 24p. (J). (gr. -1-k). 9.95 *(978-1-84059-849-0(2))* Milet Publishing.

—My Bilingual Book-Touch (English-Urdu), 1 vol. 2014. (My Bilingual Book Ser.). (ENG., Illus.). 24p. (J). (gr. -1-k). 9.95 *(978-1-84059-850-6(6))* Milet Publishing.

—My Bilingual Book-Touch (English-Vietnamese), 1 vol. 2014. (My Bilingual Book Ser.). (ENG., Illus.). 24p. (J). (gr. -1-k). 9.95 *(978-1-84059-851-3(4))* Milet Publishing.

—My First Bilingual Book - Jobs, 1 vol. 2012. (My First Bilingual Book Ser.). (ENG & POR., Illus.). 24p. (J). (gr. k — 1). bds. 7.99 *(978-1-84059-708-0(9))* Milet Publishing.

—My First Bilingual Book - Opposites, 1 vol. 2012. (My First Bilingual Book Ser.). (ENG., Illus.). 24p. (J). (gr. k — 1). bds. 8.99 *(978-1-84059-746-2(1))*; bds. 7.99 *(978-1-84059-732-5(1))* Milet Publishing.

—My First Bilingual Book-Jobs, 1 vol. 2012. (My First Bilingual Book Ser.). (ENG., Illus.). 24p. (J). (gr. k — 1). bds. 7.99 *(978-1-84059-703-5(8))*; bds. 7.99 *(978-1-84059-700-4(3))* Milet Publishing.

T
U
V

—My First Bilingual Book-Jobs (English-Chinese), 1 vol. 2012. (My First Bilingual Book Ser.). (ENG., Illus.). 24p. (J). (gr. k — 1). bds. 7.99 *(978-1-84059-702-8(X))* Milet Publishing.

—My First Bilingual Book-Jobs (English-Korean), 1 vol. 2012. (My First Bilingual Book Ser.). (ENG., Illus.). 24p. (J). (gr. k — 1). bds. 7.99 *(978-1-84059-707-3(0))* Milet Publishing.

—My First Bilingual Book-Jobs (English-Russian), 1 vol. 2012. (My First Bilingual Book Ser.). (ENG., Illus.). 24p. (J). (gr. k — 1). bds. 7.99 *(978-1-84059-710-3(0))* Milet Publishing.

—My First Bilingual Book-Jobs (English-Turkish), 1 vol. 2012. (My First Bilingual Book Ser.). (ENG., Illus.). 24p. (J). (gr. k — 1). bds. 7.99 *(978-1-84059-713-4(5))* Milet Publishing.

—My First Bilingual Book-Jobs (English-Urdu), 1 vol. 2012. (My First Bilingual Book Ser.). (ENG., Illus.). 24p. (J). (gr. k — 1). bds. 7.99 *(978-1-84059-714-1(3))* Milet Publishing.

—My First Bilingual Book-Jobs (English-Vietnamese), 1 vol. 2012. (My First Bilingual Book Ser.). (ENG., Illus.). 24p. (J). (gr. k — 1). bds. 7.99 *(978-1-84059-715-8(1))* Milet Publishing.

—My First Bilingual Book-Music, 1 vol. 2012. (My First Bilingual Book Ser.). (ENG., Illus.). 24p. (J). (gr. k — 1). bds. 7.99 *(978-1-84059-717-2(8))* Milet Publishing.

—My First Bilingual Book-Music (English-Farsi), 1 vol. 2012. (My First Bilingual Book Ser.). (ENG., Illus.). 24p. (J). (gr. k — 1). bds. 7.99 *(978-1-84059-719-6(4))* Milet Publishing.

—My First Bilingual Book-Music (English-German), 1 vol. 2012. (My First Bilingual Book Ser.). (ENG & GER., Illus.). 24p. (J). (gr. k — 1). bds. 7.99 *(978-1-84059-721-9(6))* Milet Publishing.

—My First Bilingual Book-Music (English-Korean), 1 vol. 2012. (My First Bilingual Book Ser.). (ENG., Illus.). 24p. (J). (gr. k — 1). bds. 7.99 *(978-1-84059-723-3(2))* Milet Publishing.

—My First Bilingual Book-Music (English-Russian), 1 vol. 2012. (My First Bilingual Book Ser.). (ENG., Illus.). 24p. (J). (gr. k — 1). bds. 7.99 *(978-1-84059-726-4(7))* Milet Publishing.

—My First Bilingual Book-Music (English-Somali), 1 vol. 2012. (My First Bilingual Book Ser.). (ENG., Illus.). 24p. (J). (gr. k — 1). bds. 8.99 *(978-1-84059-727-1(5))* Milet Publishing.

—My First Bilingual Book-Music (English-Turkish), 1 vol. 2012. (My First Bilingual Book Ser.). (ENG., Illus.). 24p. (J). (gr. k — 1). bds. 7.99 *(978-1-84059-729-5(1))* Milet Publishing.

—My First Bilingual Book-Music (English-Urdu), 1 vol. 2012. (My First Bilingual Book Ser.). (ENG., Illus.). 24p. (J). (gr. k — 1). bds. 7.99 *(978-1-84059-730-1(5))* Milet Publishing.

—My First Bilingual Book-Music (English-Vietnamese), 1 vol. 2012. (My First Bilingual Book Ser.). (ENG., Illus.). 24p. (J). (gr. k — 1). bds. 7.99 *(978-1-84059-731-8(3))* Milet Publishing.

—My First Bilingual Book-Opposites, 1 vol. 2012. (My First Bilingual Book Ser.). (ENG., Illus.). 24p. (J). (gr. k — 1). bds. 8.99 *(978-1-84059-734-9(8))*; bds. 8.99 *(978-1-84059-737-0(2))*; bds. 7.99 *(978-1-84059-740-0(2))* Milet Publishing.

—My First Bilingual Book-Opposites (English-Bengali), 1 vol. 2012. (My First Bilingual Book Ser.). (ENG., Illus.). 24p. (J). (gr. k — 1). bds. 7.99 *(978-1-84059-733-2(X))* Milet Publishing.

—My First Bilingual Book-Opposites (English-Korean), 1 vol. 2012. (My First Bilingual Book Ser.). (ENG., Illus.). 24p. (J). (gr. k — 1). bds. 8.99 *(978-1-84059-739-4(9))* Milet Publishing.

—My First Bilingual Book-Opposites (English-Polish), 1 vol. 2012. (My First Bilingual Book Ser.). (ENG & POR., Illus.). 24p. (J). (gr. k — 1). bds. 7.99 *(978-1-84059-741-7(0))* Milet Publishing.

—My First Bilingual Book-Opposites (English-Russian), 1 vol. 2012. (My First Bilingual Book Ser.). (ENG., Illus.). 24p. (J). (gr. k — 1). bds. 7.99 *(978-1-84059-742-4(9))* Milet Publishing.

—My First Bilingual Book-Opposites (English-Vietnamese), 1 vol. 2012. (My First Bilingual Book Ser.). (ENG., Illus.). 24p. (J). (gr. k — 1). bds. 8.99 *(978-1-84059-747-9(X))* Milet Publishing.

—My First Bilingual Book-Sports, 1 vol. 2012. (My First Bilingual Book Ser.). (ENG., Illus.). 24p. (J). (gr. k — 1). bds. 7.99 *(978-1-84059-761-5(5))* Milet Publishing.

—My First Bilingual Book-Sports (English-Bengali), 1 vol. 2012. (My First Bilingual Book Ser.). (ENG., Illus.). 24p. (J). (gr. k — 1). bds. 7.99 *(978-1-84059-749-3(6))* Milet Publishing.

—My First Bilingual Book-Sports (English-Farsi), 1 vol. 2012. (My First Bilingual Book Ser.). (ENG., Illus.). 24p. (J). (gr. k — 1). bds. 7.99 *(978-1-84059-751-6(8))* Milet Publishing.

—My First Bilingual Book-Sports (English-German), 1 vol. 2012. (My First Bilingual Book Ser.). (ENG & GER., Illus.). 24p. (J). (gr. k — 1). bds. 7.99 *(978-1-84059-753-0(4))* Milet Publishing.

—My First Bilingual Book-Sports (English-Korean), 1 vol. 2012. (My First Bilingual Book Ser.). (ENG., Illus.). 24p. (J). (gr. k — 1). bds. 7.99 *(978-1-84059-755-4(0))* Milet Publishing.

—My First Bilingual Book-Sports (English-Polish), 1 vol. 2012. (My First Bilingual Book Ser.). (ENG & POR., Illus.). 24p. (J). (gr. k — 1). bds. 7.99 *(978-1-84059-756-1(9))* Milet Publishing.

—My First Bilingual Book-Sports (English-Russian), 1 vol. 2012. (My First Bilingual Book Ser.). (ENG., Illus.). 24p. (J). (gr. k — 1). bds. 7.99 *(978-1-84059-758-5(5))* Milet Publishing.

—My First Bilingual Book-Sports (English-Spanish), 1 vol. 2012. (My First Bilingual Book Ser.). (ENG & SPA., Illus.). 24p. (J). (gr. k — 1). bds. 7.99 *(978-1-84059-760-8(7))* Milet Publishing.

—My First Bilingual Book-Sports (English-Urdu), 1 vol. 2012. (My First Bilingual Book Ser.). (ENG., Illus.). 24p. (J). (gr. k — 1). bds. 7.99 *(978-1-84059-762-2(3))* Milet Publishing.

—My First Bilingual Book-Sports (English-Vietnamese), 1 vol. 2012. (My First Bilingual Book Ser.). (ENG., Illus.). 24p. (J). (gr. k — 1). bds. 7.99 *(978-1-84059-763-9(1))* Milet Publishing.

—Opposites, 1 vol. 2012. (My First Bilingual Book Ser.). (ENG., Illus.). 24p. (J). (gr. k — 1). bds. 8.99 *(978-1-84059-735-6(6))*; bds. 7.99 *(978-1-84059-743-1(7))*; bds. 8.99 *(978-1-84059-736-3(4))* Milet Publishing.

—Opposites - My First Bilingual Book, 1 vol. 2012. (My First Bilingual Book Ser.). (ENG., Illus.). 24p. (J). (gr. k — 1). bds. 8.99 *(978-1-84059-745-5(3))*; bds. 8.99 *(978-1-84059-738-7(0))* Milet Publishing.

—Sight - English-Arabic, 1 vol. 2014. (My Bilingual Book Ser.). (ENG & ARA., Illus.). 24p. (J). (gr. -1-k). 9.95 *(978-1-84059-788-2(7))* Milet Publishing.

—Smell / Das Riechen, 1 vol. 2014. (My Bilingual Book Ser.). (ENG & GER., Illus.). 24p. (J). (gr. -1-k). 9.95 *(978-1-84059-809-4(3))* Milet Publishing.

—Smell (English-French), 1 vol. 2014. (My Bilingual Book Ser.). (ENG & FRE., Illus.). 24p. (J). (gr. -1-k). 9.95 *(978-1-84059-808-7(5))* Milet Publishing.

—Smell O olfato, 1 vol. 2014. (My Bilingual Book Ser.). (ENG & POR., Illus.). 24p. (J). (gr. -1-k). 9.95 *(978-1-84059-813-1(1))* Milet Publishing.

—Sports, 1 vol. 2012. (My First Bilingual Book Ser.). (ENG., Illus.). 24p. (J). (gr. k — 1). bds. 7.99 *(978-1-84059-757-8(7))*; bds. 7.99 *(978-1-84059-750-9(X))*; bds. 7.99 *(978-1-84059-748-6(8))* Milet Publishing.

—Sports - My First Bilingual Book, 1 vol. 2012. (My First Bilingual Book Ser.). (ENG & FRE., Illus.). 24p. (J). (gr. k — 1). bds. 7.99 *(978-1-84059-752-3(6))*; bds. 7.99 *(978-1-84059-759-2(3))* Milet Publishing.

—Sports (English-Italian), 1 vol. 2012. (My First Bilingual Book Ser.). (ENG & ITA., Illus.). 24p. (J). (gr. k — 1). bds. 7.99 *(978-1-84059-754-7(2))* Milet Publishing.

—Taste - My Bilingual Book, 1 vol. 2014. (My Bilingual Book Ser.). (ENG & FRE., Illus.). 24p. (J). (gr. -1-k). 9.95 *(978-1-84059-824-7(7))* Milet Publishing.

—Taste / Das Schmecken, 1 vol. 2014. (My Bilingual Book Ser.). (ENG & GER., Illus.). 24p. (J). (gr. -1-k). 9.95 *(978-1-84059-825-4(5))* Milet Publishing.

—Touch - My Bilingual Book, 1 vol. 2014. (My Bilingual Book Ser.). (ENG & FRE., Illus.). 24p. (J). (gr. -1-k). 9.95 *(978-1-84059-840-7(9))* Milet Publishing.

Miller, Jonathan, illus. When I Grow Up. 2011. 16p. (J). *(978-1-58865-637-7(3))* Kidsbooks, LLC.

Miller, Susan A. My First 1000 Words. 2005. (My First Ser.). (Illus.). 96p. (J). 6.98 *(978-1-4127-1182-1(7)*, 1246993) Phoenix International Publications, Inc.

Minden, Cecilia. Seeing Black. 2018. (Learning My Colors Ser.). (ENG., Illus.). 16p. (J). (gr. -1-2). pap. 11.36 *(978-1-5341-2392-2(X)*, 210565, Cherry Blossom Press) Cherry Lake Publishing.

—Seeing Pink. 2018. (Learning My Colors Ser.). (ENG., Illus.). 16p. (J). (gr. -1-2). pap. 11.36 *(978-1-5341-2391-5(1)*, 210562, Cherry Blossom Press) Cherry Lake Publishing.

—Seeing Red. 2018. (Learning My Colors Ser.). (ENG., Illus.). 16p. (J). (gr. -1-2). pap. 11.36 *(978-1-5341-2390-8(3)*, 210559, Cherry Blossom Press) Cherry Lake Publishing.

—Seeing Tan. 2018. (Learning My Colors Ser.). (ENG., Illus.). 16p. (J). (gr. -1-2). pap. 11.36 *(978-1-5341-2393-9(8)*, 210568, Cherry Blossom Press) Cherry Lake Publishing.

—Up & Down. 2016. (21st Century Basic Skills Library: Animal Opposites Ser.). (ENG., Illus.). 24p. (J). (gr. k-3). 26.35 *(978-1-63470-468-1(1)*, 207603) Cherry Lake Publishing.

Mini My First Book of Words. 2004. (Early Learning Ser.). 18p. (J). bds. 2.99 *(978-1-85854-831-9(4))* Brimax Books Ltd. GBR. Dist: Byeway Bks.

Minsky, Michael. Greenwood Word Lists: One-Syllable Words. 2003. 168p. spiral bd. *(978-1-57035-770-1(6)*, 206WORD1) Cambium Education, Inc.

Mis Primeras 100 Palabras.Tr. of My First 100 Words in Spanish. (FRE & SPA.). 32p. (J). *(978-0-7525-8380-8(8))* Parragon, Inc.

Mitton, Tony. Amazing Machines: First Words. Parker, Ant, illus. 2018. (Amazing Machines Ser.). (ENG.). 22p. (J). bds. 9.99 *(978-0-7534-7439-6(5)*, 900192345, Kingfisher) Roaring Brook Pr.

Modéré, Armelle. My First English/Norwegian Dictionary of Sentences. 2008. (NOR & ENG., Illus.). 128p. (J). *(978-1-57534-048-7(8))* Skandisk, Inc.

Modéré, Armelle & Hokenson, Linda. My First English/Swedish Dictionary of Sentences. 2008. (SWE & ENG.). 128p. *(978-1-57534-049-4(6))* Skandisk, Inc.

Modeste, Caroline, illus. My First 1000 Words. 2016. (ENG.). 64p. (J). (gr. -1 — 1). 19.95 *(978-1-77085-797-1(4)*, e00e78fa-daa7-4871-8421-96bc61d330cc) Firefly Bks., Ltd.

Moncure, Jane Belk. My First Book. Thornburgh, Rebecca, illus. 2018. (Jane Belk Moncure's Sound Box Bks.). (ENG.). 32p. (J). (gr. -1-2). 35.64 *(978-1-5038-2302-0(4)*, 212157) Child's World, Inc, The.

Moore, Sonya. Kitchen Talk. 2011. 16p. 9.99 *(978-1-4567-5067-1(4))* AuthorHouse.

Morales, Yuyi. Nino Wrestles the World. 2015. (J). lib. bdg. 18.40 *(978-0-606-37276-3(8))* Turtleback.

The Moves Make the Man: Teaching Unit. 2003. 73p. (YA). ring bd. *(978-1-58049-433-5(1)*, TU4331) Prestwick Hse., Inc.

My Community. 2005. (Look, Listen, & Speak Ser.). 80p. (gr. k-3). cd-rom 29.99 *(978-1-55799-928-3(7)*, EMC 2741) Evan-Moor Educational Pubs.

My Community. 2004. cd-rom 89.99 *(978-0-9819585-1-4(6))* Social Skill Builder, Inc.

My Family & Me. 2005. (Look, Listen, & Speak Ser.). 80p. (gr. k-3). cd-rom 29.99 *(978-1-55799-924-5(4)*, EMC 2737) Evan-Moor Educational Pubs.

My First 100 Words. 2003. 32p. (J). 11.95 *(978-0-7525-7767-8(0))* Parragon, Inc.

My First 100 Words in Spanish/English. 2003. 32p. (J). 11.95 *(978-0-7525-7769-2(7))* Parragon, Inc.

My First Sight Words (Gr. K-1) 2003. (J). *(978-1-58232-090-8(X))* ECS Learning Systems, Inc.

My First Word Book about Things That Go. 2017. (My First Word Bks.). (ENG.). (J). bds. 9.99 *(978-0-7945-3932-0(7)*, Usborne) EDC Publishing.

My First Word Book Large Bd. 2004. 12p. (J). bds. 7.99 *(978-1-85854-467-0(X))* Brimax Books Ltd. GBR. Dist: Byeway Bks.

My First Words: English & Spanish Book 1. 2006. (SPA.). (J). bds. *(978-0-9785744-1-3(9))* LTL Media LLC.

My First Words: English & Spanish Book 2. 2006. (SPA.). (J). bds. *(978-0-9785744-2-0(7))* LTL Media LLC.

My Little Box of First Words. Date not set. (Illus.). (J). bds. 6.98 *(978-1-4054-0811-0(1))* Parragon, Inc.

My Nest, 6 vols. 8p. (gr. k-1). 21.50 *(978-0-322-02063-4(8))* Wright Group/McGraw-Hill.

Myers, Connie Ellis. Words to Say out Loud: A Safety Book for Children. 2007. (Illus.). 84p. (J). spiral bd. 19.99 *(978-0-9799127-0-2(9))* Say Out Loud, LLC.

Narváez, Concha López & Salmeron, Carmelo. Tomas Es Distinto a los Demas.Tr. of Tomas Is Different from the Others. (SPA.). 64p. (J). (gr. 2-4). *(978-84-216-3432-5(1))* Bruño, Editorial ESP. Dist: Lectorum Pubns., Inc.

National Geographic Kids. National Geographic Kids Look & Learn: Match! 2011. (ENG., Illus.). 24p. (J). (gr. -1-k). bds. 7.99 *(978-1-4263-0871-0(X)*, National Geographic Kids) Disney Publishing Worldwide.

—National Geographic Readers: Let's Play. 2017. (Readers Ser.). (Illus.). 96p. (J). (gr. -1-k). pap. 7.99 *(978-1-4263-2791-9(9)*, National Geographic Kids) Disney Publishing Worldwide.

National Geographic Learning. Vocabulary Builders Kit. 2004. (Avenues Ser.). (ENG.). (C). (gr. -1-2). 945.95 *(978-0-7362-2396-6(7))* CENGAGE Learning.

Nelson, J. Ron & Marchand-Martella, Nancy. The Multiple Meaning Vocabulary Program: Level I. 2005. (Illus.). 248p. (gr. 4-6). pap., stu. ed., wbk. ed. 10.95 *(978-1-59318-405-6(0)*, 267STU1) Cambium Education, Inc.

—The Multiple Meaning Vocabulary Program: Level II. 2005. (Illus.). 328p. (gr. 4-6). pap., stu. ed., wbk. ed. 10.95 *(978-1-59318-406-3(9))* Cambium Education, Inc.

—The Multiple Meaning Vocabulary Program Instructor's Manual: Level I & Level II. 2005. 64p. *(978-1-59318-422-3(0)*, 267TE) Cambium Education, Inc.

Neuman, Susan B. National Geographic Readers: Hop Bunny: Explore the Forest. 2014. (Readers Ser.). (ENG., Illus.). 24p. (J). (gr. -1-k). lib. bdg. 14.90 *(978-1-4263-1740-8(9)*, National Geographic Children's Bks.) Disney Publishing Worldwide.

Newmark Learning, compiled by. Complete Fluency Instruction & Practice Set Grades 1-3 with Audio CDs. 2009. (Fluency Instruction Practice Ser.). (gr. 1-3). 107.91 net. *(978-1-60719-099-8(0))* Newmark Learning LLC.

—Sight Word Readers 12 copy set with Rack Set A. 2009. (Sight Word Readers Set A Ser.). (J). 1095.12 net. *(978-1-60719-159-9(8))* Newmark Learning LLC.

Nickelodeon Staff, ed. Words - Dora the Explorer. 2010. (Write, Slide & Learn Ser.). 14p. (J). (gr. -1-1). 9.99 *(978-1-74184-519-8(X)*, Ideals Pubns.) Worthy Publishing.

Nunn, Daniel. In Front of or Behind: Where's Eddie?, 1 vol. 2012. (Hide & Seek Ser.). (ENG.). 24p. (J). (gr. -1-k). pap. 9.95 *(978-1-4109-4720-8(3)*, 119214, Raintree) Capstone.

—Inside or Outside: Where's Eddie?, 1 vol. 2012. (Hide & Seek Ser.). (ENG.). 24p. (J). (gr. -1-k). pap. 9.95 *(978-1-4109-4719-2(X)*, 119213, Raintree) Capstone.

—Left or Right: Where's Eddie?, 1 vol. 2012. (Hide & Seek Ser.). (ENG.). 24p. (J). (gr. -1-k). pap. 9.95 *(978-1-4109-4718-5(1)*, 119212, Raintree) Capstone.

Nussbaum, Ben. First Words Playtime. 2004. (ENG.). 36p. (J). 12.99 *(978-1-59069-410-7(4)*, 1A109) Studio Mouse LLC.

Orero, Maria Jesus. Nico y Sus Trajes. 2006. (Nico Collection). (SPA & ESP., Illus.). 12p. (gr. -1-2). per., bds. 6.99 *(978-84-272-6152-5(7))* Molino, Editorial ESP. Dist: Santillana USA Publishing Co., Inc.

Organic Baby Sleep. 2008. (Illus.). (J). (gr. -1-3). bds. *(978-0-312-50270-6(2))* Priddy Bks.

Orme, Helen. 800 Words. 2011. (I Love Reading Book & CD-ROM Packs Ser.). (ENG., Illus.). 96p. (J). (gr. k-2). pap. 16.95 *(978-1-84898-180-5(5)*, TickTock Books) Octopus Publishing Group GBR. Dist: Independent Pubs. Group.

Orshoski, Paul. We Read Phonics-Ant in Her Pants. Ebbeler, Jeffrey, illus. 2010. (ENG.). 32p. (J). pap. 4.99 *(978-1-60115-328-9(7))* Treasure Bay, Inc.

—We Read Phonics-Bugs on the Bus. Noiset, Michele, illus. 2010. 32p. (J). 9.95 *(978-1-60115-325-8(2))*; pap. 4.99 *(978-1-60115-326-5(0))* Treasure Bay, Inc.

—We Read Phonics-Sports Dream. Ebbeler, Jeffrey, illus. 2011. (We Read Phonics: Level 5-6 Ser.). 32p. (J). (ENG.). (gr. k-3). 17.44 *(978-1-60115-335-7(X))*; (gr. 1-3). pap. 4.99 *(978-1-60115-336-4(8))* Treasure Bay, Inc.

—We Read Phonics-Talent Night. Kulka, Joe, illus. 2011. (We Read Phonics Ser.). 32p. (J). (gr. 1-3). 9.95 *(978-1-60115-339-5(2))*; pap. 4.99 *(978-1-60115-340-1(6))* Treasure Bay, Inc.

O'Sullivan, Jill Korey. The Heinle Picture Dictionary for Children: British English. 2007. (ENG., Illus.). 160p. (C). (gr. 3-7). pap. 23.95 *(978-1-4240-0849-0(2))* Cengage Heinle.

O'Toole, Janet & Anness Publishing Staff. First Words: Lift the Flaps to Find Out about Words! Adams, Ben, illus. 2013. 16p. (J). (gr. -1-12). bds. 6.99 *(978-1-84322-795-3(9)*, Armadillo) Anness Publishing GBR. Dist: National Bk. Network.

Ottaiano, Mela. 240 Vocabulary Words Kids Need to Know: Grade 2, 1 vol. 2012. (ENG.). 80p. (gr. 2-2). pap., pap., pap. 12.99 *(978-0-545-46051-4(4)*, Teaching Resources) Scholastic, Inc.

Owen, Ruth. My Busy Day. 2017. (First Words & Pictures Ser.). (ENG., Illus.). 32p. (J). (gr. -1-2). lib. bdg. 29.32 *(978-1-911341-83-3(9)*, 32b3a571-e1e9-4a74-a80c-b3f296bfd487) Ruby Tuesday Books Limited GBR. Dist: Lerner Publishing Group.

—100 Words. 2011. (I Love Reading Book & CD-ROM Packs Ser.). (ENG., Illus.). 96p. (J). (gr. k-2). pap. 16.95 *(978-1-84898-178-2(3)*, TickTock Books) Octopus Publishing Group GBR. Dist: Independent Pubs. Group.

Panec, D. J. Riddle Rhymes (We Both Read - Level Pk-K) 2016. (We Both Read Level Pk-K Ser.). (ENG., Illus.). 42p. (J). 9.95 *(978-1-60115-277-0(9))* Treasure Bay, Inc.

Paragon Publishing Staff, ed. Words. 2003. (J). per. *(978-1-884907-41-8(5))* Paradise Pr., Inc.

Parragon Staff, ed. Words. Date not set. (Illus.). (J). bds. 5.98 *(978-0-7525-8559-8(2))* Parragon, Inc.

Patterson, Susan & Patterson, James. Big Words for Little Geniuses. Pan, Hsinping, illus. 2017. (Big Words for Little Geniuses Ser.: 1). (ENG.). 32p. (J). (gr. -1-1). 18.99 *(978-0-316-50293-1(6)*, Jimmy Patterson) Little Brown & Co.

Phillips, Dee. First Words. 2009. (Christmas Lift the Flap Ser.). (ENG.). 10p. (J). (gr. -1-k). bds. 5.95 *(978-1-84696-968-3(9)*, TickTock Books) Octopus Publishing Group GBR. Dist: Independent Pubs. Group.

Phillips, Jessica, illus. Zoom Along. 2018. (Zoom Along Ser.). (ENG.). 16p. (J). (gr. -1 — 1). bds. 15.99 *(978-1-77138-797-2(1))* Kids Can Pr., Ltd. CAN. Dist: Hachette Bk. Group.

Phillips, Mark. Pinocchio Intermediate Vocabulary Builder. 2004. (ENG.). 326p. pap. 16.95 *(978-0-9727439-2-1(8)*, 9780972743921) Cornell, A.J. Pubns.

Phonemic Awareness, Level 1. 2003. (Illus.). (J). spiral bd. *(978-1-58605-822-7(3)*, LeapFrog Schl. Hse.) LeapFrog Enterprises, Inc.

PI Kids. Disney Baby: Head to Toe! Head, Shoulders, Knees & Toes Sound Book. 2017. (ENG., Illus.). 20p. (J). bds. 18.99 *(978-1-5037-2567-6(7)*, 2607, PI Kids) Phoenix International Publications, Inc.

—Disney Pixar Incredibles 2: Look & Find. 2018. (ENG., Illus.). 24p. (J). 10.99 *(978-1-5037-3044-1(1)*, 2731, PI Kids) Phoenix International Publications, Inc.

Picthall, Chez. Flip Flaps Zoo. 2015. (Illus.). 18p. (J). bds. 9.99 *(978-1-907604-53-9(7))* Award Pubns. Ltd. GBR. Dist: Parkwest Pubns., Inc.

Picthall, Chez, creator. Flip Flaps Shapes. 2014. (ENG., Illus.). 32p. 10.00 *(978-1-906572-80-8(1))* Award Pubns. Ltd. GBR. Dist: Parkwest Pubns., Inc.

Picthall, Chez & Gunzl, Christiane. Words. 2014. (ENG., Illus.). 20p. pap. 8.95 *(978-1-907604-33-1(2))* Award Pubns. Ltd. GBR. Dist: Parkwest Pubns., Inc.

Picture/Word Cards. (gr. -1-12). 75.18 *(978-0-7362-0345-6(1))* CENGAGE Learning.

Pihl, Marshall R. Korean Word Book. 2004. (KOR., Illus.). 112p. pap. 14.95 *(978-1-57306-197-1(2))* Bess Pr., Inc.

Polansky, Marisa. Today I'm a Dancer. Lee, Maxine, illus. 2018. (Today I'm A... Ser.). (ENG.). 14p. (J). bds. 8.99 *(978-0-374-30440-9(8)*, 9780374304409, Farrar, Straus & Giroux (BYR)) Farrar, Straus & Giroux.

Powell, Marie. Dan Can! Cartwright, Amy, illus. 2016. (Word Families Ser.). (ENG.). 16p. (J). (gr. k-2). lib. bdg. 17.95 *(978-1-60753-924-7(1)*, 15537) Amicus.

—Go to Bed, Ted! Cartwright, Amy, illus. 2016. (Word Families Ser.). (ENG.). 16p. (J). (gr. k-2). lib. bdg. 17.95 *(978-1-60753-927-8(6)*, 15540) Amicus.

—The Map Trap. Cartwright, Amy, illus. 2016. (Word Families Ser.). (ENG.). 16p. (J). (gr. k-2). lib. bdg. 17.95 *(978-1-60753-928-5(4)*, 15541) Amicus.

—Nab the Crab. 2013. (Word Families Ser.). (ENG.). 16p. (J). (gr. k-2). lib. bdg. 25.65 *(978-1-60753-513-3(0)*, 16231) Amicus.

—Out for Trout. 2013. (Word Families Ser.). (ENG.). 16p. (J). (gr. k-2). lib. bdg. 25.65 *(978-1-60753-514-0(9)*, 16232) Amicus.

—Stop, Pop! Cartwright, Amy, illus. 2016. (Word Families Ser.). (ENG.). 16p. (J). (gr. k-2). lib. bdg. 17.95 *(978-1-60753-925-4(X)*, 15538) Amicus.

—When, Jen? Cartwright, Amy, illus. 2016. (Word Families Ser.). (ENG.). 16p. (J). (gr. k-2). lib. bdg. 17.95 *(978-1-60753-926-1(8)*, 15539) Amicus.

POWer Words Gr. 7-8. 2005. (YA). per. *(978-1-57022-521-5(4))* ECS Learning Systems, Inc.

POWer Words Gr. 9-12. 2005. (YA). per. *(978-1-57022-549-9(4))* ECS Learning Systems, Inc.

Practice Pals Bilingual Practice Book: First Words. 2006. (ENG & FRE., Illus.). 16p. (J). (gr. -1-1). spiral bd. *(978-1-930355-55-2(6))* Bright of America.

Prefixes, Suffixes, & Root Words (Gr. 2-3) 2003. (J). *(978-1-58232-123-3(X))* ECS Learning Systems, Inc.

Priddy, Roger. Alphaprints First Words. 2018. (Alphaprints Ser.). (ENG., Illus.). 14p. (J). bds. 9.99 *(978-0-312-52812-6(4)*, 900195209) St. Martin's Pr.

—Big Board First 100 Words. rev. ed. 2005. (First 100 Ser.). (ENG., Illus.). 14p. (J). (gr. -1 — 1). bds. 8.95 *(978-0-312-49541-1(2)*, 900034533) St. Martin's Pr.

—Bright Baby First Words. rev. ed. 2004. (Bright Baby Ser.). (ENG., Illus.). 26p. (J). (gr. -1 — 1). bds. 5.99 *(978-0-312-49388-2(6)*, 900028208) St. Martin's Pr.

—Bright Baby Touch & Feel: Bilingual Words / Palabras: English-Spanish Bilingual. 2008. (Bright Baby Touch & Feel Ser.). (SPA., Illus.). 10p. (J). (gr. -1 — 1). bds. 5.99 *(978-0-312-50216-4(8)*, 900051283) St. Martin's Pr.

—Bright Baby Touch & Feel Words. 2008. (Bright Baby Touch & Feel Ser.). (ENG.). 10p. (J). (gr. -1 — 1). bds. 4.99 *(978-0-312-50424-3(1)*, 900054924) St. Martin's Pr.

—First 100 Christmas Words. 2018. (First 100 Ser.). (ENG., Illus.). 24p. (J). bds. 6.99 *(978-0-312-52768-6(3)*, 900191839) St. Martin's Pr.

—First 100 Padded: First Farm Words. 2017. (First 100 Ser.). (ENG., Illus.). 24p. (J). bds. 5.99 *(978-0-312-52283-4(5)*, 900175466) St. Martin's Pr.

—First 100 Words: A Padded Board Book. 2011. (First 100 Ser.). (ENG., Illus.). 24p. (J). (— 1). bds. 5.99 *(978-0-312-51078-7(0)*, 900075564) St. Martin's Pr.

—First 100 Words Lift-The-Flap: Over 35 Fun Flaps to Lift & Learn. 2013. (First 100 Ser.). (ENG., Illus.). 14p. (J). (gr. -1 — 1). bds. 9.99 *(978-0-312-51689-5(4)*, 900126750) St. Martin's Pr.

—Hello Baby: Animals: A High-Contrast Board Book. 2013. (Hello Baby Ser.). (ENG., Illus.). 16p. (J). (gr. -1 — 1). bds. 5.99 *(978-0-312-51597-3(9)*, 900118659) St. Martin's Pr.

—Hello Baby: Faces: A High-Contrast Board Book. 2013. (Hello Baby Ser.). (ENG., Illus.). 16p. (J). (gr. -1 — 1). bds. 5.99 *(978-0-312-51600-0(2)*, 900118678) St. Martin's Pr.

—Hello Baby: Words: A High-Contrast Board Book. 2013. (Hello Baby Ser.). (ENG., Illus.). 16p. (J). (gr. -1 — 1). bds. 5.99 *(978-0-312-51598-0(7)*, 900118661) St. Martin's Pr.

—My Fun School Bus Lift-The-flap. 2018. (My Fun Flap Bks.). (ENG., Illus.). 10p. (J). bds. 10.99 *(978-0-312-52649-8(0)*, 900185562) St. Martin's Pr.

—Simple First Words Let's Talk. 2011. (Simple First Words Ser.). (ENG.). 12p. (J). (gr. -1 — 1). bds. 14.95 *(978-0-312-51421-1(2)*, 900081754) St. Martin's Pr.

—Wipe Clean: First Words. 2012. (Wipe Clean Ser.). (ENG., Illus.). 26p. (J). (gr. -1-1). bds. 8.95 *(978-0-312-51393-1(3)*, 900082333) St. Martin's Pr.

Publications International Ltd. Staff. My First Look & Find Early Learning. 2013. 18p. (gr. -1-1). bds. 7.98 *(978-1-4508-1897-1(8)*, 1450818978) Phoenix International Publications, Inc.

Publications International Ltd. Staff, ed. Baby's Words. 2010. (Illus.). 18p. (J). bds. 7.98 *(978-1-60553-964-5(3))* Publications International, Ltd.

—First Words (Listen & Learn Sound Book) 2011. 19p. (J). bds. 11.98 *(978-1-4508-1441-6(7))* Phoenix International Publications, Inc.

—My First Book Block - First Words. 2011. 12p. (J). bds. 3.75 net. *(978-1-4508-1666-3(5)*, 1450816665) Publications International, Ltd.

Publishing, Berlitz. Berlitz English Flash Cards. 2nd ed. 2018. (Berlitz Flashcards Ser.). 50p. (J). 9.99 *(978-1-78004-482-8(8)*, 3330, Berlitz Languages, Inc.) Berlitz Publishing.

¿Puedo Salir? 2003. (Coleccion Parvulitos). 63.50 *(978-0-8136-8103-0(0))* Modern Curriculum Pr.

Pulse- Fun with Vocabulary & Spelling. 2006. cd-rom 4.99 *(978-1-60245-041-7(2))* GDL Multimedia, LLC.

Purcell, Susan. Words, 1 vol. 2018. (My Book Of Ser.). (ENG.). 24p. (gr. k-1). 26.27 *(978-1-5081-9655-6(9)*, 809c7c4b-3bab-4f2a-ad2f-176f664fe929, Windmill Bks.) Rosen Publishing Group, Inc., The.

Rabbit's Book of Words. 2004. 12p. (J). bds. 2.99 *(978-1-85997-431-5(7))* Byeway Bks.

Rasinski, Timothy. Starting with Prefixes & Suffixes, 1 vol. rev. ed. 2013. (Getting to the Roots of Content-Area Vocabulary Ser.). (ENG., Illus.). 216p. (gr. 2-4). pap. 34.99 *(978-1-4258-1103-7(5))* Shell Educational Publishing.

—Understanding Word Nuances, Level 4. rev. ed. 2014. (Vocabulary Ladders Ser.). (ENG., Illus.). 144p. (gr. 4-4). pap. 19.99 *(978-1-4258-1303-1(8))* Shell Educational Publishing.

—Understanding Word Nuances, Level 5. rev. ed. 2014. (Vocabulary Ladders Ser.). (ENG., Illus.). 144p. (gr. 5-5). pap. 19.99 *(978-1-4258-1304-8(6))* Shell Educational Publishing.

—Understanding Word Nuances, Level 6. rev. ed. 2014. (Vocabulary Ladders Ser.). (ENG., Illus.). 144p. (gr. 6-6). pap. 19.99 *(978-1-4258-1305-5(4))* Shell Educational Publishing.

Rasinski, Timothy V. Daily Word Ladders: Grades 1-2 Grades 1-2. 2008. (ENG.). 176p. (gr. 1-2). pap. 19.99 *(978-0-545-07476-6(2)*, Teaching Resources) Scholastic, Inc.

—Daily Word Ladders: Grades 2-3. 2005. (Daily Word Ladders Ser.). (ENG., Illus.). 112p. (gr. 2-3). pap. 15.99 *(978-0-439-51383-8(9)*, Teaching Resources) Scholastic, Inc.

—Daily Word Ladders: Grades 4-6. 2005. (Daily Word Ladders Ser.). (ENG., Illus.). 112p. (gr. 4-6). pap. 15.99 *(978-0-439-77345-4(8)*, Teaching Resources) Scholastic, Inc.

Reaching into Space: Word Study: Suffixes, Level B. 2003. ("Plaid" Phonics & Stories Libraries). (gr. 2-3). 38.50 *(978-0-8136-9153-4(2))* Modern Curriculum Pr.

Reading Rods Prefixes & Suffixes: Instruction & Activity Book. 2003. (J). pap. 12.95 *(978-1-56911-107-9(3))* Learning Resources, Inc.

Reading Rods Prefixes & Suffixes Activity Cards. 2003. (J). pap. 12.95 *(978-1-56911-108-6(1))* Learning Resources, Inc.

Reading Rods Sentence Building Activity Cards, Set 2. 2003. (J). 19.95 *(978-1-56911-116-1(2))* Learning Resources, Inc.

Reading Rods Simple Sentences Activity Cards. 2003. (J). pap. 12.95 *(978-1-56911-111-6(1))* Learning Resources, Inc.

Reading Rods Simple Sentences Activity Cards, Set 2. 2003. (J). pap. 19.95 *(978-1-56911-112-3(X))* Learning Resources, Inc.

Reading Rods Simple Sentences Instruction & Activity Book. 2003. (J). pap. 12.95 *(978-1-56911-110-9(3))* Learning Resources, Inc.

Reading Rods Word Building Activity Book. 2003. (J). pap. 4.95 *(978-1-56911-119-2(7))* Learning Resources, Inc.

Reading Rods Word Building Activity Cards, Set 2. 2003. (J). 19.95 *(978-1-56911-115-4(4))* Learning Resources, Inc.

Reasoner, Charles. Colors in the Garden. Pitt, Sarah, illus. 2009. (3D Board Bks.). 12p. (J). (gr. -1-k). bds. 9.99 *(978-1-934650-40-0(4))* Just For Kids Pr., LLC.

Redmond, Diane. Peter & the Wolf Workbook. Bendall-Brunello, John, illus. 2012. (Collins Big Cat Ser.). (ENG.). 16p. (J). pap., wbk. ed. 5.99 *(978-0-00-747426-4(1))* HarperCollins Pubs. Ltd. GBR. Dist: Independent Pubs. Group.

Reeve, Christine E. Functional Vocabulary for Children Ben Likes All Kinds of Sports. 2005. (J). spiral bd. 14.95 *(978-0-7606-0627-8(7))* LinguiSystems, Inc.

—Functional Vocabulary for Children Dontel Learns about Transportation. 2005. (J). spiral bd. 14.95 *(978-0-7606-0625-4(0))* LinguiSystems, Inc.

—Functional Vocabulary for Children Jasmine Sets the Table. 2005. (J). spiral bd. 14.95 *(978-0-7606-0623-0(4))* LinguiSystems, Inc.

—Functional Vocabulary for Children Kira Likes to Go to Schools. 2005. (J). spiral bd. 14.95 *(978-0-7606-0628-5(5))* LinguiSystems, Inc.

—Functional Vocabulary for Children Michelle Goes for a Walk. 2005. (J). spiral bd. 14.95 *(978-0-7606-0624-7(2))* LinguiSystems, Inc.

—Functional Vocabulary for Children Ramon Plays on the Playground. 2005. (J). spiral bd. 14.95 *(978-0-7606-0626-1(9))* LinguiSystems, Inc.

—Functional Vocabulary for Children Sarah Goes to Bed. 2005. (J). spiral bd. 14.95 *(978-0-7606-0620-9(X))* LinguiSystems, Inc.

—Functional Vocabulary for Children Tyler Gets Cleaned Up. 2005. (J). spiral bd. 14.95 *(978-0-7606-0621-6(8))* LinguiSystems, Inc.

—Functional Vocabulary for Children Zoey Uses the Bathroom. 2005. (J). spiral bd. 14.95 *(978-0-7606-0622-3(6))* LinguiSystems, Inc.

Reid, Struan & Stowell, Louie. My First Pirate Book. Allen, Peter, illus. 2012. (My First Book Ser.). 16p. (J). ring bd. 6.99 *(978-0-7945-3226-4(4)*, Usborne) EDC Publishing.

Reiss, John J. Shapes. Reiss, John J., illus. 2016. (ENG., Illus.). 34p. (J). (gr. -1 — 1). bds. 8.99 *(978-1-4814-7645-4(9)*, Little Simon) Little Simon.

Reynolds, Edith. Working with Words. 2003. 132p. (YA). pap. 16.95 *(978-1-59330-093-7(X))* Aventine Pr.

Rhyming & Word Families Big Book. 2004. (J). pap. 39.95 *(978-1-56911-175-8(8))* Learning Resources, Inc.

Rhyming Words (Gr. 1-2) 2003. (J). *(978-1-58232-112-7(4))*; *(978-1-58232-117-2(5))* ECS Learning Systems, Inc.

Rhyming Words in Context (Gr. K-2) 2003. (J). *(978-1-58232-098-4(5))* ECS Learning Systems, Inc.

Rickards, Lynne. The Big City Yellow Band. Roberts, Ley Honor, illus. 2017. (Cambridge Reading Adventures Ser.). (ENG.). 16p. pap. 6.15 *(978-1-108-41079-3(0))* Cambridge Univ. Pr.

Rinker, Sherri Duskey. Cement Mixer's ABC: Goodnight, Goodnight, Construction Site. Lichtenheld, Tom & Long, Ethan, illus. 2018. (Goodnight, Goodnight, Construc Ser.). (ENG.). 20p. (J). (gr. -1 — 1). bds. 6.99 *(978-1-4521-5318-6(3))* Chronicle Bks. LLC.

RiverStream Readers - Pre-1. 2013. (RiverStream Readers Ser.: PK). 124p. (gr. -1-2). 11.49 *(978-1-62588-900-3(3))* Black Rabbit Bks.

Robles, D. & Minquini, Lourdes. Los 100 Mejores Acertijos Matematicos (The One Hundred Best Word Problems) (SPA., Illus.). 151p. (J). (gr. k-6). pap. 7.95 *(978-968-416-820-6(9)*, FN8209) Fernandez USA Publishing.

Rock 'n Learn. Animals Point & Name with 44 Rhymes. 2016. (ENG., Illus.). 32p. (J). bds. 8.99 *(978-1-941722-20-6(2))* Rock 'N Learn, Inc.

Rodriguez, Patty & Stein, Ariana. Guadalupe: First Words/Primeras Palabras, 1 vol. Reyes, Citlali, illus. 2018. 22p. (J). bds. 9.99 *(978-0-9861099-0-4(8))* Little Libros, LLC.

—La Llorona: Counting down / Contando Hacia Atras: Counting down - Contando Hacia Atras, 1 vol. Reyes, Citlali, illus. 2018. (ENG.). 22p. (J). bds. 9.99 *(978-0-9861099-2-8(4))* Little Libros, LLC.

Rofé, April, illus. The SENSEational Alphabet: See-Read, Touch-Feel, Scratch & Smell, Hear-Learn, Have Fun! 2006. (J). *(978-0-9779189-1-1(2))* Waldenhouse Pubs., Inc.

Roffey, C. My Red Busy Book. 2003. (Illus.). 12p. (J). 6.99 *(978-0-333-65970-0(8))* Macmillan Pubs., Ltd. GBR. Dist: Trafalgar Square Publishing.

Roffey, M. First Words Indoors. 2003. (Illus.). 12p. (J). 3.99 *(978-1-85292-227-6(3)*, Campbell Bks.) Pan Macmillan GBR. Dist: Trafalgar Square Publishing.

Rogala, Jennifer. Ways to Say the Words You've Heard. 2006. 28p. (J). per. 11.95 *(978-1-58939-864-1(5))* Virtualbookworm.com Publishing, Inc.

—When My Nose Runs, Where Does It Go? Nicholas, Jacob, illus. 2006. 36p. per. 11.95 *(978-1-58939-866-5(1))* Virtualbookworm.com Publishing, Inc.

Rolbin, Cyrus. Kana-OK! A New Approach to Learning the ABC's of Japanese: Hiragana & Katakana. 2004. (ENG., Illus.). 128p. pap. 9.95 *(978-4-7700-2988-1(8))* Kodansha International JPN. Dist: Kodansha America, Inc.

Rollason, Jane. Killer Bees Level 2 Elementary/Lower-intermediate American English. 2010. (Cambridge Experience Readers Ser.). (ENG., Illus.). 64p. pap. 14.75 *(978-0-521-14896-2(0))* Cambridge Univ. Pr.

Rookie Ready to Learn - First Science: Me & My World, 5 vols., Set. Incl. Germs. Oetting, Judy. Herr, Tad, illus. lib. bdg. 18.69 *(978-0-531-26500-0(5))*; Please, Wind? Greene, Carol. Sharp, Gene, illus. lib. bdg. 23.00 *(978-0-531-26502-4(1))*; Water Everywhere! Taylor-Butler, Christine. Manning, Maurie, illus. lib. bdg. 23.00 *(978-0-531-26504-8(8))*; 40p. (J). (gr. -1-k). (Rookie Ready to Learn Ser.). 2011. Set lib. bdg. 115.00 *(978-0-531-23850-9(4)*, Children's Pr.) Scholastic Library Publishing.

Rookie Ready to Learn - I Can!, 5 vols., Set. Incl. Best Mud Pie. Quinn, Lin. Rooney, Ronnie, illus. 40p. lib. bdg. 23.00 *(978-0-531-26425-6(4)*, Children's Pr.); I Can Do It All. Pearson, Mary E. Shelley, Jeff, illus. 32p. lib. bdg. 23.00 *(978-0-531-26429-4(7)*, Children's Pr.); I'll Do It Later. Ribke, Simone T. White, Lee, illus. 40p. lib. bdg. 23.00 *(978-0-531-26528-4(5)*, Children's Pr.); Splat! Pérez-Mercado, Mary Margaret. Torrey, Rich, illus. 40p. lib. bdg. 23.00 *(978-0-531-26373-0(8)*, Children's Pr.); Willie's Word World. Curry, Don L. Stromoski, Rick, illus. 40p. lib. bdg. 18.69 *(978-0-531-26374-7(6))*; (J). (gr. -1-1). 2011. (Rookie Ready to Learn Ser.). 2011. Set lib. bdg. 115.00 *(978-0-531-25150-8(0)*, Children's Pr.) Scholastic Library Publishing.

Rookie Ready to Learn - My Family & Friends, 5 vols., Set. Incl. Eat Your Peas, Louise! Snow, Pegeen. Venezia, Mike, illus. lib. bdg. 23.00 *(978-0-531-26527-7(7))*; I Do Not Want To. Schulz, Kathy. Rescek, Sanja, illus. lib. bdg. 23.00 *(978-0-531-26525-3(0))*; Just Like Always. Perry, Anne M. Lyon, Tammie, illus. lib. bdg. 23.00 *(978-0-531-26370-9(3))*; So Many Me's. Neasi, Barbara J. Ochoa, Ana, illus. lib. bdg. 23.00 *(978-0-531-26372-3(X))*; 40p. (J). (gr. -1-k). (Rookie Ready to Learn Ser.). 2011. Set lib. bdg. 115.00 *(978-0-531-24450-0(4)*, Children's Pr.) Scholastic Library Publishing.

Rookie Ready to Learn - Numbers & Shapes, 5 vols., Set. Incl. Number One Puppy. Wilson, Zachary. Pertile, Paula, illus. lib. bdg. 23.00 *(978-0-531-26448-5(3))*; Too Many Balloons. Matthias, Catherine. Sharp, Gene, illus. lib. bdg. 23.00 *(978-0-531-26449-2(1))*; 40p. (J). (gr. -1-k). (Rookie Ready to Learn Ser.). 2011. Set lib. bdg. 115.00 *(978-0-531-24300-8(1)*, Children's Pr.) Scholastic Library Publishing.

Rookie Ready to Learn - Out & About: In My Community, 5 vols., Set. Incl. Always Be Safe. Schulz, Kathy. 40p. lib. bdg. 25.00 *(978-0-531-27175-9(7))*; Joshua James Likes Trucks. Petrie, Catherine. Snyder, Joel, illus. 32p. lib. bdg. 18.69 *(978-0-531-27177-3(3))*; (J). (gr. -1-k). 2011. (Rookie Ready to Learn Ser.). 2011. Set lib. bdg. 115.00 *(978-0-531-25905-4(6)*, Children's Pr.) Scholastic Library Publishing.

Rooney, Anne. Working with Words. 2004. (QEB Learn Computing Ser.). (Illus.). 32p. (YA). (gr. 4-7). lib. bdg. 18.95 *(978-1-59566-036-1(0))* QEB Publishing Inc.

Rosa-Mendoza, Gladys. Jobs Around My Neighborhood/Oficios en Mi Vecindario. Iosa, Ann, illus. 2007. (English Spanish Foundations Ser.). 20p. (gr. -1-k). pap. 19.95 *(978-1-931398-81-7(X))* Me+Mi Publishing.

—Let's Go to the Zoo!/Vamos Al Zoologico! Elkerton, Andy, illus. 2007. (English Spanish Foundations Ser.). (ENG & SPA.). 20p. (J). (gr. -1-k). bds. 6.95 *(978-1-931398-20-6(8))* Me+Mi Publishing.

—Lupe Lupita, Where Are You?/Lupe Lupita Donde Estas? Ochoa, Ana, illus. 2007. (English Spanish Foundations Ser.). 20p. (gr. -1-k). pap. 19.95 *(978-1-931398-82-4(8))* Me+Mi Publishing.

—My House/Mi Casa. Borlasca, Hector, illus. (English Spanish Foundations Ser.). (gr. -1-1). 2007. per. 19.95 *(978-1-931398-84-8(4))* 2006. (ENG & SPA.). 20p. (J). bds. 6.95 *(978-1-931398-18-3(6))* Me+Mi Publishing.

—My School/Mi Escuela. Murphy, Terri, illus. 2007. (English Spanish Foundations Ser.). (ENG & SPA.). (J). (gr. -1-k). bds. 6.95 *(978-1-931398-23-7(2))* Me+Mi Publishing.

—My Senses/Mis Sentidos. Merer, Laura, illus. 2007. (English Spanish Foundations Ser.). (ENG & SPA.). 20p. (J). (gr. -1-k). bds. 6.95 *(978-1-931398-21-3(6))* Me+Mi Publishing.

—My Week/Mi Semana. Wesley, Milliana, ed. Grosshauser, Peter, illus. 2007. (English Spanish Foundations Ser.). (gr. -1-k). bds. 6.95 *(978-1-931398-25-1(9))* Me+Mi Publishing.

—Opposites. Cifuentes, Carolina, ed. McGeehan, Dan, illus. 2004. (English-Spanish Foundations Ser.: Vol. 5).Tr. of Opuestos. (ENG & SPA.). 20p. (J). (gr. -1-4). bds. 6.95 *(978-0-9679748-6-6(0))* Me+Mi Publishing.

—Who Lives in the Sea?/Qui'n Vive en el Mar? O'Neil, Sharron, illus. 2007. (English Spanish Foundations Ser.). (ENG & SPA.). 20p. (J). (gr. -1-k). bds. 6.95 *(978-1-931398-24-4(0))* Me+Mi Publishing.

Rozler, Lora. Lucky Me, 1 vol. Dolby, Jan, illus. 2017. (ENG.). 32p. (J). (gr. -1-3). 18.95 *(978-1-55455-410-2(1)*, 85a5f0f7-a2a7-4f52-b3a0-85a39c952feb) Fitzhenry & Whiteside, Ltd. CAN. Dist: Firefly Bks., Ltd.

Salzmann, Mary Elizabeth. Am I Happy? 2005. (Illus.). 23p. (J). pap. 48.42 *(978-1-59679-351-4(1))* ABDO Publishing Co.

—Come Home with Me! 2004. (Sight Words Ser.). (ENG., Illus.). 24p. (J). (gr. k-3). lib. bdg. 24.21 *(978-1-59197-465-9(8))* ABDO Publishing Co.

—Here Is a Zoo. 2005. (Illus.). 23p. (J). pap. 48.42 *(978-1-59679-379-8(1))* ABDO Publishing Co.

—I Am a Kitten. 2005. (Illus.). 23p. (J). pap. 48.42 *(978-1-59679-381-1(3))* ABDO Publishing Co.

—I See a Costume. 2005. (Illus.). 23p. (J). pap. 48.42 *(978-1-59679-385-9(6))* ABDO Publishing Co.

—It's Not Good, It's Great! 2003. (Sight Words Ser.). (ENG., Illus.). 24p. (J). (gr. k-3). lib. bdg. 24.21 *(978-1-59197-479-6(8)*, SandCastle) ABDO Publishing Co.

—Look at the Playground! 2005. (Illus.). 23p. (J). pap. 48.42 *(978-1-59679-399-6(6))* ABDO Publishing Co.

—Out for the Summer! 2004. (Sight Words Ser.). (ENG., Illus.). 24p. (J). (gr. k-3). lib. bdg. 24.21 *(978-1-59197-472-7(0)*, SandCastle) ABDO Publishing Co.

—The Parade Is Here! 2005. (Illus.). 23p. (J). pap. 48.42 *(978-1-59679-407-8(0))* ABDO Publishing Co.

—See the Farm! 2005. (Illus.). 23p. (J). pap. 48.42 *(978-1-59679-415-3(1))* ABDO Publishing Co.

—Snow & More Snow! 2004. (Sight Words Ser.). (ENG., Illus.). 24p. (J). (gr. k-3). lib. bdg. 24.21 *(978-1-59197-470-3(4)*, SandCastle) ABDO Publishing Co.

—They Are the Best! 2004. (Sight Words Ser.). (ENG., Illus.). 24p. (J). (gr. k-3). lib. bdg. 24.21 *(978-1-59197-474-1(7)*, SandCastle) ABDO Publishing Co.

—We Are at the Park. 2005. (Illus.). 23p. (J). pap. 48.42 *(978-1-59679-425-2(9))* ABDO Publishing Co.

—We Are Playing! 2005. (Illus.). 23p. (J). pap. 48.42 *(978-1-59679-427-6(5))* ABDO Publishing Co.

—We Look at Food. 2005. (Illus.). 23p. (J). pap. 48.42 *(978-1-59679-437-5(2))* ABDO Publishing Co.

—We See the Beach! 2005. (Illus.). 23p. (J). pap. 48.42 *(978-1-59679-441-2(0))* ABDO Publishing Co.

—Who Is This at the Beach? 2004. (Sight Words Ser.). (ENG., Illus.). 24p. (J). (gr. k-3). lib. bdg. 24.21 *(978-1-59197-480-2(1)*, SandCastle) ABDO Publishing Co.

Sanseri, Wanda. Play by the Sea. 2003. (J). 5.00 *(978-1-880045-26-8(5))* Back Home Industries.

Sather, Edgar, et al. People at Work: Listening/Communicative Skills/Vocabulary Building:Text/3 CDs. 2005. (gr. 9-12). pap., stu. ed. 28.00 incl. audio compact disk *(978-0-86647-210-4(X))* Pro Lingua Assocs., Inc.

—People at Work: Listening/Communicative Skills/Vocabulary Building:Text/3 CDs/Supplement. 2005. (gr. 9-12). pap., tchr. ed. 39.00 incl. audio compact disk *(978-0-86647-211-1(8))* Pro Lingua Assocs., Inc.

Saviola, Ava. Dinosaur's First Words, 1 vol. 2012. (Dinosaur School Ser.). (ENG., Illus.). 24p. (J). (gr. k-k). pap. 9.15 *(978-1-4339-7156-3(9)*, a62c71f0-ee52-4d2a-9398-90d12724a5ee); lib. bdg. 25.27 *(978-1-4339-7155-6(0)*, c8559f85-5f14-48ac-adce-8edb3a805be8) Stevens, Gareth Publishing LLLP.

Scheunemann, Pam. Big Bug, Little Bug. 2005. (Illus.). 23p. (J). 48.42 *(978-1-59679-357-6(0))* ABDO Publishing Co.

—Come & See My Game! 2005. (Illus.). 23p. (J). pap. 48.42 *(978-1-59679-363-7(5))* ABDO Publishing Co.

—Come for a Party! 2005. (Illus.). 23p. (J). pap. 48.42 *(978-1-59679-365-1(1))* ABDO Publishing Co.

—The Cow Said Meow! 2005. (Illus.). 23p. (J). pap. 48.42 *(978-1-59679-369-9(4))* ABDO Publishing Co.

—Is This a Flower? 2005. (Illus.). 23p. (J). pap. 48.42 *(978-1-59679-391-0(0))* ABDO Publishing Co.

—Look at Me! 2005. (Illus.). 23p. (J). pap. 48.42 *(978-1-59679-397-2(X))* ABDO Publishing Co.

—Meg & I. 2005. (Illus.). 23p. (J). 48.42 *(978-1-59679-401-6(1))* ABDO Publishing Co.

—The Puppy Is for Me! 2005. (Illus.). 23p. (J). pap. 48.42 *(978-1-59679-409-2(7))* ABDO Publishing Co.

—Rainy Day. 2005. (Illus.). 23p. (J). pap. 48.42 *(978-1-59679-411-5(9))* ABDO Publishing Co.

—This Is Not My Dog! 2005. (Illus.). 23p. (J). pap. 48.42 *(978-1-59679-419-1(4))* ABDO Publishing Co.

—We Like Music! 2005. (Illus.). 23p. (J). pap. 48.42 *(978-1-59679-433-7(X))* ABDO Publishing Co.

—We Like to Play! 2005. (Illus.). 23p. (J). pap. 48.42 *(978-1-59679-435-1(6))* ABDO Publishing Co.

Schmitt, Conrad. ¡Así Se Dice! 2009. (Glencoe Spanish Ser.). (SPA.). 160p. (gr. 6-12). pap., wbk. ed. 23.20 *(978-0-07-892935-9(0)*, 0078929350) McGraw-Hill Education.

—Asi Se Dice 2009, Level 1A. 2009. (Glencoe Spanish Ser.). (SPA.). 160p. (gr. 6-12). pap., wbk. ed. 23.20 *(978-0-07-892934-2(2)*, 0078929342) McGraw-Hill Education.

Scholastic. All about Me/ Todo Sobre Mí (Words Are Fun/Diverpalabras) (Bilingual) (Bilingual Edition) 2017. (Words Are Fun / Diverpalabras Ser.). (SPA.). 12p. (J). (gr. -1 — 1). bds. 8.95 *(978-0-531-23071-8(6)*, Children's Pr.) Scholastic Library Publishing.

Scholastic, Inc. Staff. First 100 Words. 2015. (Scholastic Early Learners Ser.). (ENG.). 14p. (J). (gr. -1 — 1). 9.99 *(978-0-545-90315-8(7)*, Cartwheel Bks.) Scholastic, Inc.

Scholastic Library Publishing. Rookie Ready to Learn Español. 2011. (Rookie Ready to Learn Español Ser.). (J). 276.00 *(978-0-531-28509-1(X)*, Children's Pr.) Scholastic Library Publishing.

School Zone. Wonder Words Flash Action Software. 2007. 128p. pap. 15.99 *(978-1-58947-112-2(1))* School Zone Publishing Co.

School Zone Publishing. Vocabulary Puzzles. 2003. (ENG.). cd-rom 19.99 *(978-1-58947-931-9(9))* School Zone Publishing Co.

School Zone Publishing Co. Make-A-Word Bingo Game. 2006. (ENG.). (J). 5.99 *(978-1-58947-496-3(1))* School Zone Publishing Co.

School Zone Publishing Company Staff. Big Activity Ages 8-Up: Word Searches, Crosswords, Puzzles, & Codes. 2004. (ENG.). 320p. (J). pap. 9.99 *(978-1-58947-422-2(8))* School Zone Publishing Co.

—Sight Word Fun! 1. deluxe ed. 2019. (ENG.). 64p. (J). (gr. 1-2). pap., wbk. ed. 4.49 *(978-1-58947-338-6(8)*, da167b2a-808e-460f-9c92-898142f5ef6d) School Zone Publishing Co.

—Sight Words: 55 Flash Cards, 56 vols. rev. ed. 2019. (ENG.). (J). (gr. k-2). 3.49 *(978-0-938256-87-8(4)*, 67317120-56f2-452d-a969-2351e2c50bb3) School Zone Publishing Co.

—Vocabulary Puzzles 2. (Illus.). (J). 19.99 incl. audio compact disk *(978-0-88743-968-1(3))* School Zone Publishing Co.

—Word Families, 56 vols. rev. ed. 2019. (ENG., Illus.). 56p. (J). (gr. -1-2). 3.49 *(978-0-938256-82-3(3)*, 7bf7f80e-fcb5-4752-a642-6c13fd5d395d) School Zone Publishing Co.

School Zone Staff. Bilingual Basic Sight Words, 56 vols. 2019. (SPA.). 54p. (J). 3.49 *(978-1-58947-982-1(3)*, 4ffe766e-2c98-4f5b-a53a-46e063870a6a) School Zone Publishing Co.

—Picture Words, 56 vols. 2019. (ENG.). 56p. (J). (gr. -1-k). 3.49 *(978-1-58947-480-2(5)*, 012ee4da-7847-4608-970c-9a62a477982d) School Zone Publishing Co.

School Zone Staff, ed. My First 100 Magnetic Words. 2006. (ENG.). 14p. (J). (gr. k-2). bds. 15.99 *(978-1-58947-318-8(3))* School Zone Publishing Co.

Schuh, Mari. Deer. 2019. (Spot Backyard Animals Ser.). (ENG.). 16p. (J). (gr. -1-2). lib. bdg. *(978-1-68151-544-1(X)*, 14504) Amicus.

—Geese. 2019. (Spot Backyard Animals Ser.). (ENG.). 16p. (J). (gr. -1-2). lib. bdg. *(978-1-68151-546-5(6)*, 14505) Amicus.

—Hawks. 2019. (Spot Backyard Animals Ser.). (ENG.). 16p. (J). (gr. -1-2). lib. bdg. *(978-1-68151-543-4(1)*, 14506) Amicus.

—Snakes. 2019. (Spot Backyard Animals Ser.). (ENG.). 16p. (J). (gr. -1-2). lib. bdg. *(978-1-68151-549-6(0)*, 14510) Amicus.

Schumacher, Bev. Critters. 2007.Tr. of Criaturas de la Naturaleza. 20p. (J). lib. bdg. 9.95 *(978-0-9768706-6-1(5))* Learning Props.

—Dress Up. 2007.Tr. of Vestirse. 20p. (J). lib. bdg. 9.95 *(978-0-9768706-4-7(9))* Learning Props.

—Patterns. 2007.Tr. of Los Disenos. 20p. (J). lib. bdg. 9.95 *(978-0-9768706-3-0(0))* Learning Props.

—Where Will You Find Me? 2007.Tr. of Donde Me Encontraras? 20p. (J). lib. bdg. 9.95 *(978-0-9768706-5-4(7))* Learning Props.

—Where Will You Find Me? / Donde Me Encontraras. 2008. (SPA.). 20p. (J). lib. bdg. 9.95 *(978-1-935292-07-4(2))* Learning Props.

Schwartz, Amy. Things That Make Me Happy. 2017. (100 Things Ser.). (ENG., Illus.). 24p. (J). (gr. -1 — 1). bds. 7.95 *(978-1-4197-2367-4(7)*, 1045010, Abrams Appleseed) Abrams, Inc.

Scott, Kimberley, illus. Wipe-Clean First Words. 2014. (ENG.). (J). (gr. k-2). pap. 7.99 *(978-0-7945-3331-1(0)*, Usborne) EDC Publishing.

Scrambled Word Building. 2003. (J). (gr. 1). pap., act. bk. ed. 12.95 *(978-1-56911-128-4(6))*; (gr. 2). pap., act. bk. ed. 12.95 *(978-1-56911-129-1(4))*; (gr. 3). pap., act. bk. ed. 12.95 *(978-1-56911-130-7(8))* Learning Resources, Inc.

Seal, Julia, illus. Farmyard Words. 2016. (ENG.). 12p. (J). (gr. -1 — 1). bds. 6.99 *(978-1-4998-0260-3(9))* Little Bee Books Inc.

Seelig, Renate, illus. Mein Kleiner Brockhaus: Erste Woerter. 28p. (J). (gr. -1-18). *(978-3-7653-2561-8(9))* Brockhaus, F. A., GmbH DEU. Dist: International Bk. Import Service, Inc.

Sentence Building Activity Cards (OCR) 2004. (J). 14.95 *(978-1-56911-195-6(2))* Learning Resources, Inc.

Shabanu. (J). pap., stu. ed. *(978-0-13-620295-0(0))* Prentice Hall (Schl. Div.).

Shannon, Rosemarie, et al, adapted by. Vocabulary Puzzles. 2003. (Kids Can Learn with Franklin Ser.). (ENG., Illus.). 32p. (J). (gr. 1-3). 3.95 *(978-1-55337-596-8(3))* Kids Can Pr., Ltd. CAN. Dist: Hachette Bk. Group.

Shaskan, Trisha Speed. If You Were a Compound Word, 1 vol. Gray, Sara, illus. 2008. (Word Fun Ser.). (ENG.). 24p. (J). (gr. 2-4). pap. 7.95 *(978-1-4048-4776-7(6)*, 95143, Picture Window Bks.) Capstone.

Shaw, Marie-Jose. Jumbo Vocabulary Development Yearbook: Grade 3. (Jumbo Vocabulary Ser.). 96p. (J). (gr. 3). 15.95 *(978-0-8209-0052-0(4)*, B JVDY 3) ESP, Inc.

Sheikh-Miller, Jonathan. Latin Words Sticker Book. Cartwright, Stephen, illus. 2006. (Latin Words Sticker Book Ser.). 16p. (J). (gr. 1). pap. 8.99 *(978-0-7945-1145-6(7)*, Usborne) EDC Publishing.

Shiotsu, Vicky. Build-a-Skill Instant Books Beginning & Ending Consonant Sounds. Faulkner, Stacey, ed. Campbell, Jenny & Tom, Darcy, illus. 2007. (J). 4.99 *(978-1-59198-416-0(5))* Creative Teaching Pr., Inc.

Short, Deborah J., et al. Avenues B: Photofile Picture Cards. 2003. (Avenues Ser.). (ENG.). (gr. 1-18). pap. 116.95 *(978-0-7362-1841-2(6))* CENGAGE Learning.

TUV

—Avenues C: Photofile Picture Cards. 2003. (Avenues Ser.). (ENG.). (gr. 2-18). pap. 110.95 *(978-0-7362-1890-0(4))* CENGAGE Learning.
—Avenues d: Photo File Picture Cards. 2003. (Avenues Ser.). (ENG.). (gr. 3-18). pap. 148.95 *(978-0-7362-1683-8(9))* CENGAGE Learning.
—Avenues e: Photofile Picture Cards. 2003. (Avenues Ser.). (ENG.). (gr. 4-18). pap. 148.95 *(978-0-7362-1719-4(3))* CENGAGE Learning.
—Avenues F: Photofile Picture Cards. 2003. (Avenues Ser.). (ENG.). (gr. 5-18). pap. 148.95 *(978-0-7362-1755-2(X))* CENGAGE Learning.
Shostak, Jerome. Vocabulary Workshop, Student Text, Level A. 2002nd ed. 2005. (Vocabulary Workshop Ser.). 192p. (YA). (gr. 6-18). stu. ed. 6.90 *(978-0-8215-7606-9(2))* Sadlier, William H. Inc.
—Vocabulary Workshop, Student Text, Level B. 2002nd ed. 2005. (Vocabulary Workshop Ser.). 192p. (YA). (gr. 7-18). stu. ed. 6.90 *(978-0-8215-7607-6(0))* Sadlier, William H. Inc.
—Vocabulary Workshop, Student Text, Level C. 2002nd ed. 2005. (Vocabulary Workshop Ser.). 182p. (YA). (gr. 8-18). stu. ed. 6.90 *(978-0-8215-7608-3(9))* Sadlier, William H. Inc.
Sickman, Kari. Rhyming & Sight Words. 2003. (Full-Color Literacy Activities Ser.). (ENG., Illus.). 176p. (gr. -1-1). pap. 24.99 *(978-0-7439-3236-3(6))* Teacher Created Resources, Inc.
Siede Preis Photography (Firm) Staff & Brian Warling Photography (Firm) Staff, contrib. by. First Words. 2003. (Lift-A-Flap Ser.). (Illus.). 12p. (J). bds. 12.98 *(978-0-7853-8624-7(6)*, 7188400) Publications International, Ltd.
Sight Word Fun. (Basic Skills Ser.). 48p. (gr. -1-2). 5.99 *(978-0-513-02335-2(6)*, TSD23356) Denison, T. S. & Co., Inc.
Sight Word Rhymes (Gr. K-2) 2003. (J). *(978-1-58232-093-9(4))* ECS Learning Systems, Inc.
Sight Word Stories (Gr. K-2) 2003. (J). *(978-1-58232-092-2(6))* ECS Learning Systems, Inc.
Sight Words (Gr. 1-2) 2003. (J). *(978-1-58232-039-7(X))* ECS Learning Systems, Inc.
Sight Words (Gr. K-1) 2003. (J). *(978-1-58232-031-1(4))* ECS Learning Systems, Inc.
Sight Words in Context (Gr. K-2) 2003. (J). *(978-1-58232-097-7(7))* ECS Learning Systems, Inc.
Sight Words Word Search (Gr. K-2) 2003. (J). *(978-1-58232-094-6(2))* ECS Learning Systems, Inc.
Sight Words/ESL Intro Kit. 2004. (ENG.). (J). 44.99 *(978-0-943343-75-4(5))* Learning Wrap-Ups, Inc.
Singhal, Sheetal. Opposites. Sona & Jacob, illus. 2007.Tr. of Vipareet Shabdh. (ENG, HIN, GUJ & PAN.). 32p. (J). pap. 8.00 *(978-0-9773645-9-6(3))* MeeraMasi, Inc.
SIPPS Beginning Hand-held Sight Word Cards. 2004. *(978-1-57621-457-2(5))* Center for the Collaborative Classroom.
SIPPS Beginning Sight Word Wall Cards. 2004. *(978-1-57621-456-5(7))* Center for the Collaborative Classroom.
SIPPS Beginning Sound Wall Cards. 2004. *(978-1-57621-454-1(0))* Center for the Collaborative Classroom.
Skidmore, Sharon, et al. Balanced Literacy Grade 5. 2008. per. 34.00 *(978-1-879097-34-6(6))* Kagan Publishing.
Small, Cathleen. Spelling & Vocabulary. 2019. (J). pap. *(978-1-5026-5359-8(1))* Cavendish Square Publishing LLC.
Snyders, Natalie, et al. Vocabulary Quick Take along Mini-Book: Ta230. 2011. (Illus.). 66p. (J). spiral bd. 12.95 net. *(978-1-58650-996-5(9))* Super Duper Pubns.
Solotareff, Gregoire. Nieve. 2003. (SPA.). 86p. 21.99 *(978-84-8470-039-5(9))* Corimbo, Editorial S.L. ESP. Dist: Lectorum Pubns., Inc.
Speechmark. Sequences: 6 & 8-Step for Children. 2013. (Colorcards Ser.). (ENG.). 99999p. (C). 41.95 *(978-0-86388-558-7(6)*, Y330133) Routledge.
Spelling & Vocabulary, Set. 2004. (gr. 2). 38.95 *(978-0-7403-0219-0(1)*, Horizons) Alpha Omega Pubns., Inc.
Spigarelli, Jane. Oxford Picture Dictionary Third Edition: Low-Beginning Workbook. 3rd ed. 2017. (ENG.). 272p. pap., wbk. ed. 24.20 *(978-0-19-451124-7(3))* Oxford Univ. Pr., Inc.
Stanek, Robert, pseud. Student's Classroom Handbook for the Kingdoms & the Elves of the Reaches. 2003. (ENG.). 128p. pap. 15.00 *(978-1-57545-033-9(X)*, Ruin Mist Pubns.) RP Media.
Star Bright Books. My First Words at Home: Burmese/English, 1 vol. 2012. (ENG., Illus.). 20p. (J). 6.95 *(978-1-59572-372-7(2))* Star Bright Bks., Inc.
—My First Words at Home: English, 1 vol. 2011. (ENG.). 20p. (J). (gr. -1). bds. 6.95 *(978-1-59572-281-2(5))* Star Bright Bks., Inc.
—My First Words at Home: Spanish/English, 1 vol. 2011. (ENG.). 32p. (J). bds. 6.95 *(978-1-59572-282-9(3))* Star Bright Bks., Inc.
Steck-Vaughn Staff. Vocabulary Connections, Level D. 2004. (Steck-Vaughn Vocabulary Connections Ser.). (ENG., Illus.). 144p. (gr. 4-4). pap., stu. ed. 21.90 *(978-0-7398-9171-1(5))* Houghton Mifflin Harcourt Publishing Co.
—Vocabulary Skills. 2003. (Vocabulary Skills Ser.). (ENG.). 96p. (gr. 2-2). pap., wbk. ed. 11.99 *(978-0-7398-6901-7(9))* Houghton Mifflin Harcourt Publishing Co.
—Vocabulary Skills, Grade 3. 2003. (Vocabulary Skills Ser.). (ENG.). 96p. (gr. 3-3). pap., wbk. ed. 11.99 *(978-0-7398-6902-4(7))* Houghton Mifflin Harcourt Publishing Co.
—Vocabulary Skills, Grade 4. 2003. (Vocabulary Skills Ser.). (ENG.). 96p. (gr. 4-4). pap. 11.99 *(978-0-7398-6903-1(5))* Houghton Mifflin Harcourt Publishing Co.
—Vocabulary Skills, Grade 5. 2003. (Vocabulary Skills Ser.). (ENG.). 96p. (gr. 5-5). pap. 11.99 *(978-0-7398-6904-8(3))* Houghton Mifflin Harcourt Publishing Co.
—Vocabulary Skills, Grade 6. 2003. (Vocabulary Skills Ser.). (ENG.). 96p. (gr. 6-6). pap. 11.99 *(978-0-7398-6905-5(1))* Houghton Mifflin Harcourt Publishing Co.
—Vocabulary Ventures. 2004. (gr. 1-2). pap. 14.99 *(978-0-7398-8561-1(8))*; (gr. 3-4). pap. 14.99 *(978-0-7398-8562-8(6))* Steck-Vaughn.
Steck-Vaughn Staff & Coulter, Barbara. Vocabulary Connections, Level C. 2004. (Steck-Vaughn Vocabulary Connections Ser.). (ENG., Illus.). 144p. (gr. 3-3). pap. 21.90 *(978-0-7398-9170-4(7))* Houghton Mifflin Harcourt Publishing Co.
Stella, Gaia. Welcome to My House: A Collection of First Words. 2017. (ENG., Illus.). 48p. (J). (gr. -1-k). 17.99 *(978-1-4521-5792-4(8))* Chronicle Bks. LLC.
Sterling Children's Staff. My First Football Book. 2015. (First Sports Ser.). (ENG., Illus.). 22p. (J). (— 1). bds. 7.95 *(978-1-4549-1488-4(2))* Sterling Publishing Co., Inc.
Sterling Children's, Sterling. My First Basketball Book. 2015. (First Sports Ser.). (Illus.). 22p. (J). (— 1). bds. 6.95 *(978-1-4549-1487-7(4))* Sterling Publishing Co., Inc.
Studio Mouse Staff. First Concepts, Pack. rev. ed. 2003. (ENG., Illus.). 60p. (J). (gr. -1-k). 12.99 *(978-1-59069-363-6(9)*, 1A502) Studio Mouse LLC.
Suen, Anastasia. Kittens. 2019. (Spot Baby Farm Animals Ser.). (ENG.). 16p. (J). (gr. -1-2). lib. bdg. *(978-1-68151-533-5(4)*, 14494) Amicus.
—Lambs. 2019. (Spot Baby Farm Animals Ser.). (ENG.). 16p. (J). (gr. -1-2). lib. bdg. *(978-1-68151-534-2(2)*, 14495) Amicus.
Sunshine TM Word Books Set: 1 Each of 4 Big Books. (gr. k-1). 125.50 *(978-0-7802-6930-9(6))*; Vol. 2. 125.50 *(978-0-7802-6984-2(5))* Wright Group/McGraw-Hill.
Sunshine TM Word Books Set: 1 Each of 4 Student Books. (Sunshine Ser.). (gr. k-1). 19.50 *(978-0-7802-3848-0(6))*; Vol. 2. 22.95 *(978-0-7802-6821-0(0))* Wright Group/McGraw-Hill.
Sunshine TM Word Books Set: 6 Each of 4 Student Books. (Sunshinetm Word Ser.). (gr. k-1). 116.95 *(978-0-7802-6820-3(2))*; Vol. 2. 150.95 *(978-0-7802-6822-7(9))* Wright Group/McGraw-Hill.
Swirnow, Linda. What's New at the Zoo? A PhotoPhOnics (c)Reader. 2009. 32p. pap. 12.99 *(978-1-4490-2218-1(9))* AuthorHouse.
Tam on Sam: Consonants m, s, t; Short Vowel a; -am, -at word families: Level A, 6 vols. (Wright Skills Ser.). 12p. (gr. k-3). 17.95 *(978-0-322-01445-9(X))* Wright Group/McGraw-Hill.
Tat Is Sad: Consonant d: Level A, 6 vols. (Wright Skills Ser.). 12p. (gr. k-3). 17.95 *(978-0-322-03105-0(2))* Wright Group/McGraw-Hill.
Teckentrup, Britta, illus. Grande y Pequeno. 2013. 14p. (J). (gr. -1-k). bds. 6.99 *(978-1-78285-034-2(1))* Barefoot Bks., Inc.
The Learning Company, The Learning. Curious George Adventures in Learning, Grade 1: Story-Based Learning. 2015. (Learning with Curious George Ser.). (ENG., Illus.). 320p. (J). (gr. -1-3). pap. 12.99 *(978-0-544-37323-5(5)*, 1590935, Clarion Bks.) HarperCollins Pubs.
—Curious George Adventures in Learning, Kindergarten: Story-Based Learning. 2015. (Learning with Curious George Ser.). (ENG., Illus.). 320p. (J). (gr. k — 1). pap. 12.99 *(978-0-544-37263-4(8)*, 1590934, Clarion Bks.) HarperCollins Pubs.
—Curious George Adventures in Learning, Pre-K: Story-Based Learning. 2015. (Learning with Curious George Ser.). (ENG., Illus.). 320p. (J). (gr. -1 — 1). pap. 12.99 *(978-0-544-37273-3(5)*, 1590933, Clarion Bks.) HarperCollins Pubs.
Thorne, Pat. My First Word Book. (Illus.). (J). (gr. -1-18). pap. 16.95 *(978-0-590-74011-1(3))* Scholastic, Inc.
El Tiempo. (Coleccion Planeta Vivo).Tr. of Weather. (SPA.). (J). (gr. 5-8). 12.00 *(978-84-342-1945-8(X))* Parramon Ediciones S.A. ESP. Dist: Distribuidora Norma, Inc.
Tiger Tales. 100 First Words. 2018. (My First Ser.). (ENG., Illus.). 24p. (J). (gr. -1-k). mass mkt. 4.99 *(978-1-68010-418-9(7))* Tiger Tales.
Tiger Tales Staff, creator. 100 First Animals. 2013. (My Big Book of Lift & Learn Ser.). (ENG., Illus.). 12p. (gr. -1). bds. 9.99 *(978-1-58925-608-5(5))* Tiger Tales.
—100 First Words. 2013. (My Big Book of Lift & Learn Ser.). (ENG., Illus.). 12p. (gr. -1). bds. 9.99 *(978-1-58925-607-1(7))* Tiger Tales.
Tilton, Patricia. Reproducible Little Books for Sight Words. 2004. (ENG.). 176p. (gr. k-2). pap. 18.99 *(978-0-7439-3225-7(0))* Teacher Created Resources, Inc.
Top That Publishing Staff, ed. Bobby Badgers Box of Books. 2005. (Illus.). 16p. bds. *(978-1-84510-542-6(7))* Top That! Publishing PLC.
—First Words. 2004. (Magnetic Play & Learn Ser.). (ENG., Illus.). 8p. (J). *(978-1-84510-049-0(2))* Top That! Publishing PLC.
Trattles, Patricia. Flying Butter. Swift, Gary, illus. 2005. (Rookie Reader: Compound Words Ser.). (ENG.). 24p. (J). (gr. k-2). 17.44 *(978-0-516-25150-9(3)*, Children's Pr.) Scholastic Library Publishing.
Tucker, Sian. My Book of First Words. Tucker, Sian, illus. 2003. (My Book of. . . Ser.). (Illus.). 48p. (YA). *(978-1-85602-439-6(3)*, Pavilion Children's Books) Pavilion Bks.
Tullet, Hervé. Press Here: Board Book Edition. 2019. (Herve Tullet Ser.). (ENG., Illus.). 46p. (J). (gr. -1-k). bds. 8.99 *(978-1-4521-7859-2(3))* Chronicle Bks. LLC.
Turhan, Sedat. Milet Flashwords English. Hagin, Sally, illus. 2005. (Milet Flashwords Ser.). (ENG.). 60p. (J). (gr. 4-7). 8.95 *(978-1-84059-455-3(1))* Milet Publishing.
Tuxworth, Nicola. Farm Animals. 2013. (ENG., Illus.). 12p. (J). (gr. -1-12). bds. 6.99 *(978-0-7548-2202-8(8))* Anness Publishing GBR. Dist: National Bk. Network.
—Messy. (J). (gr. -1-k). 2016. (Illus.). 20p. bds. 6.99 *(978-1-86147-690-6(6)*, Armadillo) 2013. (ENG.). 12p. bds. 6.99 *(978-0-7548-2209-7(5))* Anness Publishing GBR. Dist: National Bk. Network.
—Mix & Match. 2016. (Learn-a-Word Book Ser.). (Illus.). 20p. (J). (gr. -1-2). bds. 6.99 *(978-1-84322-862-2(9)*, Armadillo) Anness Publishing GBR. Dist: National Bk. Network.
—Nature. 2015. (Illus.). 20p. (J). (gr. -1-12). bds. 6.99 *(978-1-86147-411-7(3)*, Armadillo) Anness Publishing GBR. Dist: National Bk. Network.
—Things That Go. 2016. (Illus.). 20p. (J). (gr. -1-12). bds. 6.99 *(978-1-84322-752-6(5)*, Armadillo) Anness Publishing GBR. Dist: National Bk. Network.
Two Little Hands Productions, creator. Good Night, Alex & Leah. 2010. (ENG., Illus.). (J). *(978-1-933543-73-4(6))* Two Little Hands Productions LLC.
—What Do You See Outside? 2010. (ENG., Illus.). (J). *(978-1-933543-74-1(4))* Two Little Hands Productions LLC.
Tyler, Jenny. Baby's Very First Getting Dressed. 2009. (Baby's Very First Bks). 10p. (J). (gr. -1). bds. 6.99 *(978-0-7945-2609-2(8)*, Usborne) EDC Publishing.
—Baby's Very First Mealtime Book. 2009. (Baby's Very First Board Bks). 10p. (J). (gr. -1). bds. 6.99 *(978-0-7945-2607-8(1)*, Usborne) EDC Publishing.
Ultman, Suzy, illus. A to Z Menagerie: (ABC Baby Book, Sensory Alphabet Board Book for Babies & Toddlers, Interactive Book for Babies) 2019. (ENG.). 28p. (J). (gr. -1 — 1). 24.99 *(978-1-4521-7711-3(2))* Chronicle Bks. LLC.
Uncle Bill Is Feeling Ili, 6 vols. 8p. (gr. k-1). 21.50 *(978-0-322-02078-8(6))* Wright Group/McGraw-Hill.
Under the Clock, 6 vols. 8p. (gr. k-1). 21.50 *(978-0-322-02064-1(6))* Wright Group/McGraw-Hill.
University Games Staff. I Have. 2007. 32p. (J). *(978-1-57528-888-8(5))* Univ. Games.
Using the Right Words (Gr. 3+) 2003. (J). *(978-1-58232-053-3(5))* ECS Learning Systems, Inc.
Valentino, Catherine. Blue Ribbon Spelling & Vocabulary, Level 1. (J). pap. 7.95 *(978-0-86651-196-4(2))* Seymour, Dale Pubns.
Vaughn, Jim. Jumbo Vocabulary Development Yearbook: Grade 7. (Jumbo Vocabulary Ser.). 96p. (J). (gr. 7-9). 15.95 *(978-0-8209-0056-8(7)*, B JVDY J) ESP, Inc.
Vinopol, Corinne. Spell Well: CD-ROM American Sign Language Spelling Game. 2003. (YA). cd-rom 19.95 *(978-0-9752933-0-0(3))* Institute for Disabilities Research & Training, Inc.
VIP Tours, 10 vols. 2014. (VIP Tours Ser.). (ENG.). 48p. (J). (gr. 4-4). 165.35 *(978-1-62713-144-5(2)*, d446bcd3-e54c-4256-8ccd-e27945888dea, Cavendish Square) Cavendish Square Publishing LLC.
VocabuLáminas: VocabuLáminas Kit. (J). (gr. -1-2). 407.79 *(978-0-7362-2605-9(2))* CENGAGE Learning.
Vocabulary Centers. 2006. (J). 24.99 *(978-1-59673-152-3(4)*, EMC 3352); 24.99 *(978-1-59673-150-9(8)*, EMC 3350) Evan-Moor Educational Pubs.
Vocabulary Flip Chart. 2004. (Scott Foresman Reading Ser.). (gr. 1-18). suppl. ed. 109.15 *(978-0-673-62166-5(9))*; (gr. 2-18). suppl. ed. 109.15 *(978-0-673-62167-2(7))* Addison-Wesley Educational Pubs., Inc.
Vocabulary from Classical Roots. 2004. (Vocabulary from Classical Roots Ser.). (gr. 10-18). pap. 9.95 *(978-0-8388-2258-6(4))*; (gr. 11-18). pap. 9.95 *(978-0-8388-2260-9(6))*; (gr. 7-18). pap. 9.35 *(978-0-8388-2252-4(5))*; (gr. 8-18). pap. 9.35 *(978-0-8388-2254-8(1))*; (gr. 9-18). pap. 9.35 *(978-0-8388-2256-2(8))* Educators Publishing Service, Inc.
Vocabulary in Action: Level A; Testing Program (BLMs) 2004. (gr. 4-18). *(978-0-8294-1333-5(2))* Loyola Pr.
Vocabulary Vocabulary, Level A, Grades 10-11. 2005. (Vocabulary Workshop Ser.). 182p. (YA). (gr. 6-18). tchr. ed. 13.80 *(978-0-8215-7616-8(X))* Sadlier, William H. Inc.
Vocabulary Workshop: Test Generator CD-ROM, Level A, (Mac) 2005. (YA). (gr. 6-18). cd-rom 114.00 *(978-0-8215-0196-2(8))* Sadlier, William H. Inc.
Vocabulary Workshop: Test Generator CD-ROM, Level B, (Mac) 2005. (YA). (gr. 7-18). cd-rom 114.00 *(978-0-8215-0197-9(6))* Sadlier, William H. Inc.
Vocabulary Workshop: Test Generator CD-ROM, Level C, (Mac) 2005. (YA). (gr. 8-18). cd-rom 114.00 *(978-0-8215-0198-6(4))* Sadlier, William H. Inc.
Vocabulary Workshop, Level B. annot. ed. 2005. (Vocabulary Workshop Ser.). 182p. (YA). (gr. 7-18). tchr. ed. 13.80 *(978-0-8215-7617-5(8))* Sadlier, William H. Inc.
Vocabulary Workshop, Level C. annot. ed. 2005. (Vocabulary Workshop Ser.). 182p. (YA). (gr. 8-18). tchr. ed. 13.80 *(978-0-8215-7618-2(6))* Sadlier, William H. Inc.
Vocabulary Workshop Test Generator, Level A, PC Version: 2002. 2005. (Vocabulary Workshop Ser.). (YA). (gr. 6-18). cd-rom 114.00 *(978-0-8215-0186-3(0))* Sadlier, William H. Inc.
Vocabulary Workshop Test Generator, Level B, PC Version: 2002. 2005. (Vocabulary Workshop Ser.). (YA). (gr. 7-18). cd-rom 114.00 *(978-0-8215-0187-0(9))* Sadlier, William H. Inc.
Vocabulary Workshop Test Generator, Level C, PC Version: 2002. 2005. (Vocabulary Workshop Ser.). (YA). (gr. 8-18). cd-rom 114.00 *(978-0-8215-0188-7(7))* Sadlier, William H. Inc.
Los Volcanes. (Coleccion Planeta Vivo).Tr. of Volcanos. (SPA.). (YA). (gr. 5-8). 10.36 *(978-84-342-1943-4(3))* Parramon Ediciones S.A. ESP. Dist: Lectorum Pubns., Inc.
Wade, Angela. New York City. 2006. (Illus.). 8p. (J). pap. *(978-0-439-74035-7(5))* Scholastic, Inc.
Wall Words Word Search (Gr. 1-2) 2003. (J). *(978-1-58232-095-3(0))* ECS Learning Systems, Inc.
Watson, Richar, illus. My Book of Letters: For Ages 3+ 2016. (ENG.). 24p. (J). pap. *(978-1-78209-799-0(6))* Miles Kelly Publishing, Ltd.
Watt, Fiona. Baby's Very First Word Book. 2012. (Baby's Very First Word Book Ser.). 10p. (J). ring bd. 7.99 *(978-0-7945-2979-6(8)*, Usborne) EDC Publishing.
Weldon Owen Inc Staff & Weldon Owen Inc Staff, contrib. by. My First Emoji Feelings. 2016. (Illus.). (J). *(978-1-4351-6433-8(4))* Barnes & Noble, Inc.
Wernham, Sara & Lloyd, Sue. Dictionary. Wade, Sarah, illus. 2003. (Jolly Grammar Ser.: DICTIONARY). (ENG.). 300p. (J). pap. 15.50 *(978-1-84414-001-5(6)*, JL016, Jolly Learning) Jolly Learning, Ltd. GBR. Dist: American International Distribution Corp.
What a Spelling Test!, 6 Packs. (gr. -1-2). 27.00 *(978-0-7635-9483-1(0))* Rigby Education.
Wheeler, Kimberly. Emma's Extravagant Expedition. 2012. (ENG.). pap. *(978-1-4675-4236-4(9))* Independent Pub.
Where Do I Live? (Peek A Boo Pockets Ser.). 12p. (J). bds. *(978-2-7643-0108-1(1))* Phidal Publishing, Inc./Editions Phidal, Inc.
Wilbur, Richard. The Pig in the Spigot. Siebold, J. Otto, illus. 2004. (J). reprint ed. pap. 7.00 *(978-0-15-525066-6(3)*, Voyager Books/Libros Viajeros) Harcourt Children's Bks. CAN. Dist: Allen, Thomas & Son, Ltd.
William H. Sadlier Staff. Vocabulary Vocabulary Test Booklets, Level C, Form A. 2005. (Vocabulary Workshop Ser.). 64p. (gr. 8-9). 42.00 net. *(978-0-8215-7628-1(3))* Sadlier, William H. Inc.
—Vocabulary Vocabulary Test Booklets, Level D, Form A. 2002nd ed. 2005. (Vocabulary Workshop Ser.). 64p. (gr. 9-10). 42.00 net. *(978-0-8215-7629-8(1))* Sadlier, William H. Inc.
—Vocabulary Workshop: Test Booklet Form A; Level Purple. 2005. (Vocabulary Workshop 2005 Ser.). (gr. 2-3). 36.00 net. *(978-0-8215-0382-9(0))* Sadlier, William H. Inc.
—Vocabulary Workshop: Test Booklet Form B; Level Purple. 2005. (Vocabulary Workshop 2005 Ser.). (gr. 2-3). 36.00 net. *(978-0-8215-0392-8(8))* Sadlier, William H. Inc.
—Vocabulary Workshop: (with Answer Key to Tests, Forms A & B); Level Purple. annot. ed. 2005. (Vocabulary Workshop 2005 Ser.). (gr. 2-3). 15.00 net. *(978-0-8215-0372-0(3))* Sadlier, William H. Inc.
—Vocabulary Workshop Test Booklets. 2005. (Vocabulary Workshop Ser.). 64p. (gr. 12-18). 42.00 net. *(978-0-8215-7643-4(7))*;Level B, Form B. (gr. 7-8). 42.00 net. *(978-0-8215-7637-3(2))* Sadlier, William H. Inc.
—Vocabulary Workshop, Test Booklets, Cycle 1, Level Blue. 2006. (Vocabulary Workshop Ser.). (gr. 5-6). 42.00 net. *(978-0-8215-0438-3(X))* Sadlier, William H. Inc.
—Vocabulary Workshop, Test Booklets, Cycle 2, Level Blue. 2006. (Vocabulary Workshop Ser.). (gr. 5-6). 42.00 net. *(978-0-8215-0439-0(8))* Sadlier, William H. Inc.
—Vocabulary Workshop Test Booklets, Level A, Form A: 2002. 2005. (Vocabulary Workshop Ser.). 64p. (gr. 6-7). 42.00 net. *(978-0-8215-7626-7(7))* Sadlier, William H. Inc.
—Vocabulary Workshop Test Booklets, Level A, Form B: 2002. 2005. (Vocabulary Workshop Ser.). 64p. (gr. 6-7). 42.00 net. *(978-0-8215-7636-6(4))* Sadlier, William H. Inc.
—Vocabulary Workshop Test Booklets, Level B, Form A. 2005. (Vocabulary Workshop Ser.). 64p. (gr. 7-8). 42.00 net. *(978-0-8215-7627-4(5))* Sadlier, William H. Inc.
—Vocabulary Workshop Test Booklets, Level C, Form B. 2005. (Vocabulary Workshop Ser.). 64p. (gr. 8-9). 42.00 net. *(978-0-8215-7638-0(0))* Sadlier, William H. Inc.
—Vocabulary Workshop Test Booklets, Level E, Form A: 2002. 2005. (Vocabulary Workshop Ser.). 64p. (gr. 10-11). 42.00 net. *(978-0-8215-7630-4(5))* Sadlier, William H. Inc.
—Vocabulary Workshop Test Booklets, Level E, Form B. 2005. (Vocabulary Workshop Ser.). 64p. (gr. 10-11). 42.00 net. *(978-0-8215-7640-3(2))* Sadlier, William H. Inc.
—Vocabulary Workshop Test Booklets, Level F, Form A. 2005. (Vocabulary Workshop Ser.). 64p. (gr. 11-12). 42.00 net. *(978-0-8215-7631-1(3))* Sadlier, William H. Inc.
—Vocabulary Workshop Test Booklets, Level F, Form B. 2005. (Vocabulary Workshop Ser.). 64p. (gr. 11-12). 42.00 net. *(978-0-8215-7641-0(0))* Sadlier, William H. Inc.
—Vocabulary Workshop Test Booklets, Level G, Form A. 2005. (Vocabulary Workshop Ser.). 64p. (gr. 12-18). 42.00 net. *(978-0-8215-7632-8(1))* Sadlier, William H. Inc.
—Vocabulary Workshop Test Booklets, Level G, Form B. 2005. (Vocabulary Workshop Ser.). 64p. (gr. 11-12). 42.00 net. *(978-0-8215-7642-7(9))* Sadlier, William H. Inc.
—Vocabulary Workshop Test Booklets, Level H, Form A. 2005. (Vocabulary Workshop Ser.). 64p. (gr. 12-18). 42.00 net. *(978-0-8215-7633-5(X))* Sadlier, William H. Inc.
—Vocabulary Workshop, Test Booklets Level Orange Cycle 1. 2006. (Vocabulary Workshop Ser.). (gr. 4-18). 42.00 net. *(978-0-8215-0436-9(3))* Sadlier, William H. Inc.
—Vocabulary Workshop, Test Booklets Level Orange, Cycle 2. 2005. (Vocabulary Workshop Ser.). (gr. 4-18). 42.00 net. *(978-0-8215-0437-6(1))* Sadlier, William H. Inc.
—Vocabulary Workshop, TEST PREP Blackline Masters, Level A. 2005. (Vocabulary Workshop Ser.). (gr. 6-7). 29.00 net. *(978-0-8215-7676-2(3))* Sadlier, William H. Inc.
—Vocabulary Workshop TEST PREP Blackline Masters, Level B. 2005. (Vocabulary Workshop Ser.). 64p. (gr. 7-8). 29.00 net. *(978-0-8215-7677-9(1))* Sadlier, William H. Inc.
—Vocabulary Workshop TEST PREP Blackline Masters, Level C. 2005. (Vocabulary Workshop Ser.). 64p. (gr. 8-9). 29.00 net. *(978-0-8215-7678-6(X))* Sadlier, William H. Inc.
—Vocabulary Workshop TEST PREP Blackline Masters, Level D. 2005. (Vocabulary Workshop Ser.). 64p. (gr. 9-10). 29.00 net. *(978-0-8215-7679-3(8))* Sadlier, William H. Inc.
—Vocabulary Workshop TEST PREP Blackline Masters, Level E. 2005. (Vocabulary Workshop Ser.). 64p. (gr. 10-11). 29.00 net. *(978-0-8215-7680-9(1))* Sadlier, William H. Inc.
—Vocabulary Workshop TEST PREP Blackline Masters, Level F. 2005. (Vocabulary Workshop Ser.). 64p. (gr. 10-11). 29.00 net. *(978-0-8215-7681-6(X))* Sadlier, William H. Inc.
—Vocabulary Workshop TEST PREP Blackline Masters, Level G. 2005. (Vocabulary Workshop Ser.). 64p. (gr. 11-12). 29.00 net. *(978-0-8215-7682-3(8))* Sadlier, William H. Inc.
—Vocabulary Workswhop Test Booklets, Level D, Form B. 2005. (Vocabulary Workshop Ser.). 64p. (gr. 9-10). 42.00 net. *(978-0-8215-7639-7(9))* Sadlier, William H. Inc.
Williams, Garth. Baby's First Book. Williams, Garth, illus. 2007. (Little Golden Book Ser.). (Illus.). 24p. (J). (gr. -1-2). 5.99 *(978-0-375-83916-0(X)*, Golden Bks.) Random Hse. Children's Bks.
Williams, Rozanne Lanczak. Build-a-Skill Instant Books Sight Words, Part 1. Faulkner, Stacey, ed. Campbell, Jenny & Tom, Darcy, illus. 2007. (J). 4.99 *(978-1-59198-414-6(9))* Creative Teaching Pr., Inc.
—Build-a-Skill Instant Books Sight Words, Part 2. Faulkner, Stacey, ed. Campbell, Jenny & Tom, Darcy, illus. 2007. (J). 4.99 *(978-1-59198-415-3(7))* Creative Teaching Pr., Inc.
Wilson, P. R. Readle the Reading Beetle: The Journey to Love Read Land. 2007. 26p. pap. 8.95 *(978-0-7414-4318-2(X))* Infinity Publishing.
Wise, Sue. How Do I Say That? / ¿Cómo Se Dice?, 1 vol. 2005. (Reference Ser.). (ENG & SPA., Illus.). 32p. (gr. 2-4). pap. 11.50 *(978-0-8368-6583-7(9)*, 14d262c5-a77c-4846-8610-5f4700215d4d); lib. bdg. 28.67 *(978-0-8368-6259-1(7)*, d7f78b4d-090d-42e7-ae3b-d39e993c0815) Stevens, Gareth Publishing LLLP. (Gareth Stevens Learning Library).
Wong, Benedict Norbert. Lo & Behold: Words That Walk & Run. 2004. (Illus.). 40p. (J). (gr. 1-12). 16.95 *(978-0-9728192-2-0(3))* Taiji Arts Publishing.
Word Building Activity Cards (OCR) 2004. (J). 14.95 *(978-1-56911-194-9(4))* Learning Resources, Inc.
Word Endings in Context (Gr. K-2) 2003. (J). *(978-1-58232-099-1(3))* ECS Learning Systems, Inc.
Word Families Ad Libs. 2004. (J). pap. 10.95 *(978-1-56911-160-4(X))* Learning Resources, Inc.

Word Wall Words. 2004. (gr. k-18). suppl. ed. 39.70 (978-0-673-62182-5(0)); (gr. 1-18). suppl. ed. 220.50 (978-0-673-62183-2(9)); (gr. 2-18). suppl. ed. 220.50 (978-0-673-62184-9(7)); (gr. 3-18). suppl. ed. 220.50 (978-0-673-62185-6(5)) Addison-Wesley Educational Pubs., Inc.

Wordly Wise: Book 1. 2004. (Wordly Wise Ser.). pap., stu. ed. 8.70 (978-0-8388-0431-5(4)) Educators Publishing Service, Inc.

Wordly Wise: Book 2. 2004. (Wordly Wise Ser.). pap., stu. ed. 8.70 (978-0-8388-0432-2(2)) Educators Publishing Service, Inc.

Wordly Wise: Book 3. 2004. (Wordly Wise Ser.). pap., stu. ed. 8.70 (978-0-8388-0433-9(0)) Educators Publishing Service, Inc.

Wordly Wise: Book 4. 2004. (Wordly Wise Ser.). pap., stu. ed. 8.70 (978-0-8388-0434-6(9)) Educators Publishing Service, Inc.

Wordly Wise: Book 5. 2004. (Wordly Wise Ser.). pap., stu. ed. 8.70 (978-0-8388-0435-3(7)) Educators Publishing Service, Inc.

Wordly Wise: Book 6. 2004. (Wordly Wise Ser.). pap., stu. ed. 9.65 (978-0-8388-0436-0(5)) Educators Publishing Service, Inc.

Wordly Wise: Book 7. 2004. (Wordly Wise Ser.). pap., stu. ed. 9.65 (978-0-8388-0437-7(3)) Educators Publishing Service, Inc.

Wordly Wise: Book 8. 2004. (Wordly Wise Ser.). pap., stu. ed. 9.65 (978-0-8388-0438-4(1)) Educators Publishing Service, Inc.

Wordly Wise: Book 9. 2004. (Wordly Wise Ser.). pap., stu. ed. 9.65 (978-0-8388-0439-1(X)) Educators Publishing Service, Inc.

Wordly Wise: Book A. 2004. (Wordly Wise Ser.). pap., stu. ed. 6.70 (978-0-8388-0428-5(4)) Educators Publishing Service, Inc.

Wordly Wise: Book B. 2004. (Wordly Wise Ser.). pap., stu. ed. 6.70 (978-0-8388-0429-2(2)) Educators Publishing Service, Inc.

Wordly Wise: Book C. 2004. (Wordly Wise Ser.). pap., stu. ed. 6.70 (978-0-8388-0430-8(6)) Educators Publishing Service, Inc.

Wordly Wise 3000: Book 8. 2004. (Wordly Wise 3000 Ser.). pap., stu. ed. 10.62 net. (978-0-8388-2438-2(2)) Educators Publishing Service, Inc.

Wordly Wise 3000: Book 9. 2004. (Wordly Wise 3000 Ser.). pap., stu. ed. 9.65 (978-0-8388-2439-9(0)) Educators Publishing Service, Inc.

Wordly Wise 3000: Book A. 2004. (Wordly Wise 3000 Ser.). pap., stu. ed. 6.70 (978-0-8388-2425-2(0)) Educators Publishing Service, Inc.

Wordly Wise 3000: Book B. 2004. (Wordly Wise 3000 Ser.). pap., stu. ed. 6.70 (978-0-8388-2426-9(9)) Educators Publishing Service, Inc.

Wordly Wise 3000: Book C. 2004. (Wordly Wise 3000 Ser.). pap., stu. ed. 6.70 (978-0-8388-2427-6(7)) Educators Publishing Service, Inc.

Words are Fun. 2004. (Play & Learn Pads Ser.). 48p. (J). 3.99 (978-1-85997-722-4(7)) Byeway Bks.

Words for 3-5 Years. Date not set. (Play & Learn Ser.). (Illus.). 192p. (J). 3.98 (978-0-7525-6914-7(7)) Parragon, Inc.

Words for 5-7 Years. Date not set. (Play & Learn Ser.). (Illus.). 192p. (J). 3.98 (978-0-7525-6915-4(5)) Parragon, Inc.

Wordsearch. 2004. (Play & Learn Pads Ser.). 48p. (J). 3.99 (978-1-85997-716-3(2)) Byeway Bks.

Wordsearch Fun. 2004. (Play & Learn Pads Ser.). 48p. (J). 3.99 (978-1-85997-723-1(5)) Byeway Bks.

World Book, Inc. Staff, contrib. by. Letters to Words: A Supplement to Childcraft — The How & Why Library. 2012. (Illus.). 208p. (J). (978-0-7166-0627-7(5)) Univ. of Chicago Pr.

Wortgeschichte. (Duden-Schuelerduden Ser.). (GER.). 491p. (YA). 27.95 (978-3-411-02212-0(4), B2212E) Bibliographisches Institut & F. A. Brockhaus AG DEU. Dist: Continental Bk. Co., Inc.

Wotton, Joy. My First Word Book: Pictures & Words to Start Toddlers Reading & to Help Pre-Schoolers Develop Vocabulary Skills. Tulip, Jenny, illus. 2012. 200p. (J). (gr. -1-12). 9.99 (978-1-84322-617-8(0), Armadillo) Anness Publishing GBR. Dist: National Bk. Network.

Write on, Wipe off Writing. 2007. (Early Days: Copy & Learn Ser.). (Illus.). 40p. (978-1-84666-390-1(3)) Top That! Publishing PLC.

Wyldeck, Kathi. Grammar & Vocabulary Games for Children. 2007. 83p. pap. 12.95 (978-1-84799-930-6(1)); 81p. pap. 12.95 (978-1-84753-579-5(8)) Lulu Pr., Inc.

Yes I Can Staff. Words Are Everywhere. (J). 29.70 (978-0-8136-4402-8(X)) Modern Curriculum Pr.

Yoon, Salina, creator. Bug Buddies: A Sparkling Little Colors Book. 2005. (ENG., Illus.). 12p. (J). bds. 5.95 (978-1-58117-166-2(8), Intervisual/Piggy Toes) Bendon, Inc.

Yoyo Books, creator. Numbers. 2011. (Baby's First Library). (ENG., Illus.). 40p. (gr. -1-k). bds. (978-94-6033-702-4(3)) YoYo Bks.

Yoyo Books Staff. Words: Mini Baby's First Library. 2005. 42p. bds. (978-90-5843-803-4(1)) YoYo Bks.

Zakiyyah & Zakiyyah. Chatterworld My Numbers in Spanish/My Numbers in French: MIS Numeros en Espanol/Mes Mombres en Francais. 2006. (Illus.). 40p. (J). (gr. -1-3). 14.99 (978-0-9777085-0-5(0)) Little Linguists Press.

Ziefert, Harriet. Lower-Case Letters. Kido, Yukiko, illus. 2007. (I'm Going to Read(r) Ser.). (ENG.). 64p. (J). (gr. -1-1). pap. 5.95 (978-1-4027-5055-7(2)) Sterling Publishing Co., Inc.

—Sight Words. Roitman, Tanya, illus. 2007. (I'm Going to Read(r) Ser.). (ENG.). 64p. (J). (gr. -1-1). pap. 5.95 (978-1-4027-5058-8(7)) Sterling Publishing Co., Inc.

Zoo-Zológico Bilingual Board Book. 2008. (ENG & SPA., Illus.). (J). pap. 5.99 (978-0-9727886-8-7(9)) Osmosis, LLC.

VOCABULARY—FICTION

Alinas, Marv. A Crab in the Cab. Petelinsek, Kathleen, illus. 2018. (Rhyming Word Families Ser.). (ENG.). 24p. (J). (gr. -1-2). lib. bdg. 32.79 (978-1-5038-2348-8(2), 212183) Child's World, Inc, The.

—Kit's Banana Split. Petelinsek, Kathleen, illus. 2018. (Rhyming Word Families Ser.). (ENG.). 24p. (J). (gr. -1-2). lib. bdg. 32.79 (978-1-5038-2354-9(7), 212187) Child's World, Inc, The.

—The Rag Bag. Petelinsek, Kathleen, illus. 2018. (Rhyming Word Families Ser.). (ENG.). 24p. (J). (gr. -1-2). lib. bdg. 32.79 (978-1-5038-2349-5(0), 212194) Child's World, Inc, The.

Austin, Ruth. Happy Grumpy Loved: a Little Book of Feelings: Board Book. 2018. (ENG., Illus.). (J). (gr. -1). bds. 16.95 (978-1-946873-07-1(1)) Compendium, Inc., Publishing & Communications.

—Hide Seek Stinky Sweet: a Little Book of Opposites: Board Book. 2018. (ENG., Illus.). (gr. -1-k). bds. 12.95 (978-1-946873-08-8(X)) Compendium, Inc., Publishing & Communications.

Barnette, Brandon. Word Fanatics. 2012. 32p. pap. 14.50 (978-1-4669-2942-5(1)) Trafford Publishing.

Battle-Lavert, Gwendolyn. The Barber's Cutting Edge, 1 vol. Holbert, Raymond, illus. 2022. (ENG.). 32p. (J). (gr. -1-3). pap. 10.95 (978-0-89239-196-7(0), leelowcbp) Lee & Low Bks., Inc.

Benoit-Renard, Anne. Navani from Delhi. Rigaudie, Mylène, illus. 2014. (AV2 Fiction Readalong Ser.: Vol. 133). (ENG.). 32p. (J). (gr. -1-3). lib. bdg. 34.28 (978-1-4896-2271-6(3), AV2 by Weigl) Weigl Pubs., Inc.

Beobi & the Magic Coloring Book ABC First Words. 2005. (J). cd-rom 15.99 (978-0-9743847-8-8(X)) Cohn, Tricia.

Bizcochitos de Cumpleanos Story Pack. 2003. (Coleccion Parvulitos). (SPA., Illus.). 67.50 (978-0-8136-8531-1(1)) Modern Curriculum Pr.

Bober, Suzanne & Merberg, Julie. Mama, Baby, & Other First Words. 2010. (ENG.). 22p. (J). bds. 6.99 (978-1-935703-03-7(X)) Downtown Bookworks.

Boehm, Richard G., et al. Take-Home Review Books. 2003. (Harcourt Brace Social Studies). (gr. 1-18). 6.20 (978-0-15-310293-6(4)); (gr. 2-18). 6.20 (978-0-15-310294-3(2)) Harcourt Schl. Pubs.

Bolger, Kevin. Fun with Ed & Fred. Hodson, Ben, illus. 2016. (ENG.). 40p. (J). (gr. -1-3). 7.99 (978-0-06-228600-0(5), HarperCollins) HarperCollins Pubs.

Bonnet, Rosalinde, illus. Alphabet Picture Book. 2011. (Alphabet Picture Book Ser.). 26p. (J). ring bd. 11.99 (978-0-7945-2954-3(2), Usborne) EDC Publishing.

Brunetti, Ivan. Wordplay: TOON Level 1. 2017. (Illus.). 40p. (J). (gr. -1-3). 12.99 (978-1-943145-17-1(2), Toon Books) Astra Publishing Hse.

Capucilli, Alyssa Satin. Tulip & Rex Write a Story. 2015. (ENG., Illus.). 32p. (J). (gr. -1-3). 17.99 (978-0-06-209416-2(5), Tegen, Katherine Bks) HarperCollins Pubs.

Cardwell, Michelle. Seeing the World Through Different Eyes. 2009. 32p. pap. 12.99 (978-1-4389-9776-6(0)) AuthorHouse.

Carol Henson Keesee. The Angry Thunderstorm. Rachel Henson, illus. 2009. 40p. pap. 20.00 (978-1-4389-4334-3(2)) AuthorHouse.

Carter, David A. B Is for Box — the Happy Little Yellow Box: A Pop-Up Book. Carter, David A., illus. 2014. (ENG., Illus.). 18p. (J). (gr. -1). 14.99 (978-1-4814-0295-8(1), Little Simon) Little Simon.

Claire, Elizabeth. The New Boy Is Lost! An ESL Picture Novel 2004. Orig. Title: Where Is Taro? (Illus.). 70p. stu. ed. 12.00 (978-0-937630-12-9(8)) Eardley Pubns.

Clayton, Darcy M. Making Mouth Sounds All Day Long. Freeswick, Jill, illus. 2013. 36p. pap. 9.95 (978-1-889131-90-0(3), Castlebridge Bks.) Big Tent Bks.

Cooper, Susan. The Word Pirates. Kellogg, Steven, illus. 2019. 40p. (J). (gr. -1-3). 18.99 (978-0-8234-4359-8(0), Neal Porter Bks) Holiday Hse., Inc.

Cousins, Lucy. Maisy's Animals Los Animales de Maisy: A Maisy Dual Language Book. Cousins, Lucy, illus. 2009. (Maisy Ser.). (Illus.). 16p. (J). (gr. -1-2). bds. 6.99 (978-0-7636-4517-5(6)) Candlewick Pr.

—Maisy's Clothes la Ropa de Maisy: A Maisy Dual Language Book. Cousins, Lucy, illus. 2009. (Maisy Ser.). (Illus.). 16p. (J). (gr. -1-2). bds. 6.99 (978-0-7636-4518-2(4)) Candlewick Pr.

—Maisy's Food Los Alimentos de Maisy: A Maisy Dual Language Book. Cousins, Lucy, illus. 2009. (Maisy Ser.). (SPA., Illus.). 16p. (J). (gr. -1-2). bds. 5.99 (978-0-7636-4519-9(2)) Candlewick Pr.

Cowley, Joy. Space Aliens in Our School. Ming, Choo Hill, illus. 2004. (ENG.). 8p. (J). (gr. 1-1). pap. 4.67 (978-1-56270-755-2(8), Dominie Elementary) Savvas Learning Co.

Cox, Phil Roxbee. Fat Cat on a Mat. Tyler, Jenny, ed. Cartwright, Stephen, illus. rev. ed. 2006. (Phonics Readers Ser.). 16p. (J). (gr. -1-3). pap. 6.99 (978-0-7945-1502-7(9), Usborne) EDC Publishing.

Curry, Peter. Millie Goes Shopping. 2004. (First Words with Millie Ser.). (Illus.). 12p. (J). bds. 3.99 (978-1-85854-505-9(6)) Brimax Books Ltd. GBR. Dist: Byeway Bks.

D'Amico, Christine. Higgledy-Piggledy: Mabel's World. Bell-Myers, Darcy, illus. 2005. (ENG.). 32p. (J). 16.95 (978-0-9716631-1-4(4)) Attitude Pr. Inc.

D'Andrea, Deborah, creator. Words. 2006. (Picture Me Ser.). (Illus.). (J). (978-1-57151-768-5(5)) Playhouse Publishing.

Danylyshyn, Greg. A Crash of Rhinos: And Other Wild Animal Groups. Lomp, Stephan, illus. 2016. (ENG.). 40p. (J). (gr. -1-3). 17.99 (978-1-4814-3150-7(1), Little Simon) Little Simon.

Disculpe Usted, Senor. 2003. (SPA., Illus.). stu. ed. 35.50 (978-0-8136-8033-0(6)) Modern Curriculum Pr.

DK. My First Words. 2015. (My First Ser.). (ENG., Illus.). 36p. (J). (gr. -1 — 1). bds. 5.99 (978-1-4654-2899-8(2), DK Children) Dorling Kindersley Publishing, Inc.

A Donde Vamos? 2003. (Coleccion Parvulitos). (SPA., Illus.). (J). stu. ed. 35.50 (978-0-8136-8027-9(1)) Modern Curriculum Pr.

A Donde Vamos? Big Book. 2003. (Coleccion Parvulitos). (SPA., Illus.). 35.50 (978-0-8136-8029-3(8)) Modern Curriculum Pr.

A Donde Vamos? Story Pack. 2003. (Coleccion Parvulitos). (SPA., Illus.). 67.50 (978-0-8136-8524-3(9)) Modern Curriculum Pr.

Duncklee, John. Manchado & His Friends Manchado Y Sus Amigos. 2009. 52p. pap. 9.95 (978-1-4401-2496-9(5)) iUniverse, Inc.

Emigh, Karen. Bookworm: Discovering Idioms, Sayings & Expressions. Dana, Steve, illus. 2013. (ENG.). 32p. (J). pap. 11.95 (978-1-935274-88-9(0), P230827) Future Horizons, Inc.

Fallon, Jimmy & Lopez, Jennifer. Con Pollo: A Bilingual Playtime Adventure. Campos, Andrea, illus. 2022. (ENG.). 48p. (J). 18.99 (978-1-250-83041-8(9), 900252853) Feiwel & Friends.

farahay, m. l. The BUTTERFLY, the BEE & the SPIDER. 2009. (ENG.). 32p. pap. 6.94 (978-0-557-14043-5(9)) Lulu Pr., Inc.

—The BUTTERFLY, the BEE & the SPIDER, Sc3. 2009. (ENG.). 32p. pap. 14.94 (978-0-557-15287-2(9)) Lulu Pr., Inc.

Ford, Adam B. Jam-Bo, Litta-Girl, & the Bullies. Huddleston, Courtney, illus. 2013. 44p. pap. 12.95 (978-0-9794104-9-9(5)) H Bar Pr.

Forde, Patricia. The List. (List Ser.). (ENG.). 368p. (J). (gr. 5-8). 2018. pap. 9.99 (978-1-4926-6085-9(X)) 2017. 16.99 (978-1-4926-4796-6(9), 9781492647966) Sourcebooks, Inc.

Frasier, Debra. Miss Alaineus: A Vocabulary Disaster. Frasier, Debra, illus. 2007. (ENG., Illus.). 40p. (J). (gr. -1-3). pap. 7.99 (978-0-15-206053-4(7), 1198181, Clarion Bks.) HarperCollins Pubs.

Galassi, Isabel. I Want, 1 vol. 2009. 12p. pap. 24.95 (978-1-61546-535-4(9)) America Star Bks.

Garcia Orihuela, Luis & DIVINCENZO, Sofia & Yoselem. The Army of Words. GARCIA ORIHUELA, Luis, illus. 2012. 24p. pap. 19.99 (978-1-61196-934-4(4)) Pintos, Yoselem G.

Gottesfeld, Jeff. Party of Four. 2018. (Red Rhino Ser.). (ENG.). 76p. (J). (gr. 4-7). pap. 9.95 (978-1-62250-982-9(X)) Saddleback Educational Publishing, Inc.

Graham, Mark. Hello, I Am Fiona from Scotland. Sofilas, Mark, illus. 2014. (AV2 Fiction Readalong Ser.: Vol. 128). (ENG.). 32p. (J). (gr. -1-3). lib. bdg. 34.28 (978-1-4896-2253-2(5), AV2 by Weigl) Weigl Pubs., Inc.

Graham, Oakley. When I Dream of 123. 2014. (Illus.). (J). (978-1-4351-5468-1(1)) Barnes & Noble, Inc.

—When I Dream Of 123. Orkrania, Alexia & Fisher, Henry, illus. 2018. (Padded Board Bks.). (ENG.). 26p. (J). (gr. -1-1). bds. 9.99 (978-1-78700-257-9(8)) Top That! Publishing PLC GBR. Dist: Independent Pubs. Group.

Griffith, Christina. Why Jubilee & Ashanti go to the Doctor? 2011. 28p. pap. 13.54 (978-1-4269-7069-6(2)) Trafford Publishing.

Groeneweg, Nicole. One Word Pearl. Mitchell, Hazel, illus. 2013. 32p. (J). (gr. k-3). 17.95 (978-1-934133-53-8(1)) Charlesbridge Publishing, Inc.

Grosset and Dunlap Staff, contrib. by. The World of Dick & Jane Anderson. 2003. (Illus.). (J). 9.97 (978-0-448-43479-7(2), Grosset & Dunlap) Penguin Publishing Group.

Guy, Ginger Foglesong. Bravo! 2010. (ENG., Illus.). 32p. (J). (gr. -1-k). 17.99 (978-0-06-173180-8(3), Greenwillow Bks.) HarperCollins Pubs.

Hallowell, George & Holub, Joan. Wagons Ho! Avril, Lynne, illus. 2014. (AV2 Fiction Readalong Ser.: Vol. 153). (ENG.). 32p. (J). (gr. -1-3). lib. bdg. 34.28 (978-1-4896-2389-8(2), AV2 by Weigl) Weigl Pubs., Inc.

—Wagons Ho! Then & Now on the Oregon Trail. Avril, Lynne, illus. 2019. (ENG.). 32p. (J). (gr. -1-3). pap. 7.99 (978-0-8075-8613-6(7), 807586137) Whitman, Albert & Co.

Howard-Parham, Pam. Caillou Gets in Shape. Gillen, Lisa P., illus. l.t. ed. 2006. (HRL Board Book Ser.). (J). (gr. k-18). pap. 10.95 (978-1-57332-331-4(4), HighReach Learning, Incorporated) Carson-Dellosa Publishing, LLC.

Huisingh, Rosemary. At the Library. 2012. (Illus.). (J). (978-0-7606-1346-7(X)) LinguiSystems, Inc.

—Vocabulary Stories for Toddlers: Getting Ready for Bed. 2012. (Illus.). 10p. (978-0-7606-1345-0(1)) LinguiSystems, Inc.

—Vocabulary Stories for Toddlers: My Body's Just Right for Me. 2012. (Illus.). 10p. (978-0-7606-1347-4(8)) LinguiSystems, Inc.

—Vocabulary Stories for Toddlers: Seasons. 2012. (Illus.). (978-0-7606-1348-1(6)) LinguiSystems, Inc.

Husar, Jaco & Husar, Stephane. Hello, I Am Lily from New York City. Rigaudie, Mylène, illus. 2014. (AV2 Fiction Readalong Ser.: Vol. 129). (ENG.). 32p. (J). (gr. -1-3). lib. bdg. 34.28 (978-1-4896-2259-4(4), AV2 by Weigl) Weigl Pubs., Inc.

Husar, Stephane. Hello, I Am Charlie from London. Robert, Yannick, illus. 2014. (AV2 Fiction Readalong Ser.: Vol. 127). (ENG.). 32p. (J). (gr. -1-3). lib. bdg. 34.28 (978-1-4896-2256-3(X), AV2 by Weigl) Weigl Pubs., Inc.

—Hello, I Am Max from Sydney. Sofilas, Mark, illus. 2014. (AV2 Fiction Readalong Ser.: Vol. 130). (ENG.). 32p. (J). (gr. -1-3). lib. bdg. 34.28 (978-1-4896-2250-1(0), AV2 by Weigl) Weigl Pubs., Inc.

—Paolo from Rome. Le Grand, Claire, illus. 2014. (AV2 Fiction Readalong Ser.: Vol. 134). (ENG.). 32p. (J). (gr. -1-3). lib. bdg. 34.28 (978-1-4896-2274-7(8), AV2 by Weigl) Weigl Pubs., Inc.

James, Tamara. The World Is Your Oyster. Sancartier, Emma, illus. 2010. 50p. (J). (gr. -1-3). 16.95 (978-1-897476-22-2(1)) Simply Read Bks. CAN. Dist: Ingram Publisher Services.

Jansson, Tove. Moomin's Little Book of Words. 2011. (Moomins Ser.). (ENG., Illus.). 16p. (J). (gr. -1 — 1). bds. 9.99 (978-0-374-35048-2(5), 900070718, Farrar, Straus & Giroux (BYR)) Farrar, Straus & Giroux.

Jarrell, Pamela R. Time for Bed. Coillen, Lisa P., illus. l.t. ed. 2005. (HRL Board Book Ser.). (J). (gr. -1-k). pap. 10.95 (978-1-57332-325-3(X), HighReach Learning, Incorporated) Carson-Dellosa Publishing, LLC.

Johnston, Tony. The Magic of Letters. Minor, Wendell, illus. 2019. 32p. (J). (gr. -1-3). 18.99 (978-0-8234-4159-4(8), Neal Porter Bks) Holiday Hse., Inc.

Kelley, Maria Felicia. Buz Words: Discovering Words in Pairs. Kelley, Maria Felicia, illus. 2007. (Illus.). 32p. (J). (gr. -1-3). 14.95 (978-0-9650918-1-7(3)) April Arts Press & Productions.

Kennedy, Kevin. Ten Dollar Words for Kids. Fife, Jay, illus. 2013. 26p. pap. 11.95 (978-1-61244-244-0(7)) Halo Publishing International.

Kopley, Richard. The Remarkable David Wordsworth. Fazio, Michael, illus. 2013. 30p. (J). pap. (978-1-936172-67-2(4)) Eifrig Publishing.

Lederer, Susan. I Can Do That. Loehr, Jenny, illus. 2008. 28p. (J). per. 19.95 (978-0-9789347-0-5(9)) Children's Publishing.

Lederer, Suzy. I Can Say That. Loehr, Jenny, illus. l.t. ed. 2006. 32p. (J). (gr. -1-3). 19.95 incl. audio compact disk (978-0-9725803-7-3(9)) Children's Publishing.

Levy, Debbie. Yiddish Saves the Day. Borlasca, Hector, illus. 2019. (ENG.). 32p. (J). 17.95 (978-1-68115-544-9(3), 563e41f9-3396-4de3-bb96-a74b11225faf, Apples & Honey Pr.) Behrman Hse., Inc.

Lobato, Arcadio, illus. Volando por las Palabras. 2004.Tr. of Flying through Words. (SPA.). 48p. (J). 10.50 (978-84-263-5018-3(6)) Vives, Luis Editorial (Edelvives) ESP. Dist: Lectorum Pubns., Inc.

Long, Ethan. Up, Tall & High. Long, Ethan, illus. 2012. (Illus.). 44p. (J). (gr. -1-2). 18.99 (978-0-399-25611-0(3), G.P. Putnam's Sons Books for Young Readers) Penguin Young Readers Group.

Malepart, Celine, illus. When Pigs Fly: A Piggy Pop-up Book! 2008. (ENG.). 12p. 16.95 (978-1-58117-671-1(6), Intervisual/Piggy Toes) Bendon, Inc.

Melvin, Alice. The World of Alice Melvin: Me & You: A Book of Opposites. 2018. (ENG., Illus.). 20p. (J). (gr. -1 — 1). 9.99 (978-1-84976-585-5(5), 1325110) Tate Publishing, Ltd. GBR. Dist: Abrams, Inc.

—The World of Alice Melvin: My Day: A Book of Actions. 2018. (ENG., Illus.). 20p. (J). 9.99 (978-1-84976-586-2(3), 1325210) Tate Publishing, Ltd. GBR. Dist: Abrams, Inc.

Metzger, Steve. The Mixed-Up Alphabet. Ho, Jannie, illus. 2007. (J). (978-0-545-00098-7(X)) Scholastic, Inc.

A Mi Abuelita Le Gusta Correr. 2003. (Coleccion Parvulitos). (SPA., Illus.). stu. ed. 35.50 (978-0-8136-8141-2(3)) Modern Curriculum Pr.

A Mi Abuelita Le Gusta Correr Big Book. 2003. (Coleccion Parvulitos). (SPA., Illus.). 35.50 (978-0-8136-8535-9(4)) Modern Curriculum Pr.

Miller, Jonathan, illus. Winter, Spring, Summer, Fall. 2010. 16p. (J). (978-1-58865-578-3(4)) Kidsbooks, LLC.

Monalisa, DeGross. Donavan's Word Jar. 2014. (Trophy Chapter Bks). (ENG.). 80p. (J). (gr. 2-5). 9.24 (978-1-63245-337-2(1)) Lectorum Pubns., Inc.

Muench-Williams, Heather. Adam's Grouchy Day. Meier, Kerry L., illus. l.t. ed. 2005. (HRL Little Book Ser.). (J). (gr. -1-k). pap. 10.95 (978-1-57332-321-5(7)); pap. 10.95 (978-1-57332-320-8(9)) Carson-Dellosa Publishing, LLC. (HighReach Learning, Incorporated).

Mullican, Judy. Caillou & the Storyteller. Storch, Ellen N., illus. l.t. ed. 2006. (HRL Board Book Ser.). (J). (gr. k-18). pap. 10.95 (978-1-57332-330-7(6), HighReach Learning, Incorporated) Carson-Dellosa Publishing, LLC.

Nelson, Mary Beth & Linn, Laurent, illus. Elmo's Big Word Book: El Libro Grande de Palabras de Elmo. Barrett, John E., photos by. 2006. (Elmo's Big Word Book/el Libro Grande de Palabras de Elmo Ser.). (ENG.). 12p. (J). (gr. -1 — 1). bds. 8.95 (978-0-87358-906-2(8)) Cooper Square Publishing Llc.

Noyce, Pendred. Lost in Lexicon: An Adventure in Words & Numbers. Charles, Joan, illus. 2011. (ENG.). 368p. (J). (gr. 3). pap. 12.95 (978-0-9830219-2-6(9)) Mighty Media Pr.

O'Connor, Jane. Every Day Is Earth Day. 2010. (Fancy Nancy - I Can Read! Ser.). (J). lib. bdg. 13.55 (978-0-606-12294-8(X)) Turtleback.

—Fancy Nancy: Aspiring Artist. 2011. (Fancy Nancy Ser.). (ENG., Illus.). 32p. (J). (gr. -1-2). 12.99 (978-0-06-191526-0(2), HarperCollins) HarperCollins Pubs.

—Fancy Nancy: My Family History. 2010. (I Can Read Level 1 Ser.). (ENG., Illus.). 32p. (J). (gr. -1-3). pap. 5.99 (978-0-06-188271-5(2), HarperCollins) HarperCollins Pubs.

—Fancy Nancy: Nancy Clancy Seeks a Fortune. Glasser, Robin Preiss, illus. 2016. (Nancy Clancy Ser.: 7). (ENG.). 144p. (J). (gr. 1-5). 9.99 (978-0-06-226969-0(0), HarperCollins) HarperCollins Pubs.

—Fancy Nancy: Nancy Clancy, Soccer Mania. Glasser, Robin Preiss, illus. 2016. (Nancy Clancy Ser.: 6). (ENG.). 144p. (J). (gr. 1-5). pap. 4.99 (978-0-06-226966-9(6), HarperCollins) HarperCollins Pubs.

—Fancy Nancy: Nancy Clancy, Super Sleuth. 2013. (Nancy Clancy Ser.: 1). (J). lib. bdg. 14.75 (978-0-606-31795-5(3)) Turtleback.

—Fancy Nancy: Splendid Speller. Glasser, Robin Preiss, illus. 2011. (I Can Read Level 1 Ser.). (ENG.). 32p. (J). (gr. -1-3). 17.99 (978-0-06-200176-4(0), HarperCollins) HarperCollins Pubs.

—Fancy Nancy: Splendiferous Christmas. Glasser, Robin Preiss, illus. 2018. (Fancy Nancy Ser.). (ENG.). 32p. (J). (gr. -1-3). 9.99 (978-0-06-284726-3(0), HarperCollins) HarperCollins Pubs.

—Fancy Nancy: The Dazzling Book Report. 2009. (I Can Read Level 1 Ser.). (ENG., Illus.). 32p. (J). (gr. -1-3). pap. 4.99 (978-0-06-170368-3(0), HarperCollins) HarperCollins Pubs.

—Fancy Nancy: The Dazzling Book Report. Glasser, Robin Preiss & Enik, Ted, illus. 2009. (Fancy Nancy Ser.). 32p. lib. bdg. 14.00 (978-1-60686-531-6(5)) Perfection Learning Corp.

—Fancy Nancy: The Show Must Go On. 2009. (I Can Read Level 1 Ser.). (ENG., Illus.). 32p. (J). (gr. -1-3). pap. 5.99 (978-0-06-170372-0(9), HarperCollins) HarperCollins Pubs.

—Fancy Nancy & the Boy from Paris. Glasser, Robin Preiss, illus. 2008. (I Can Read Level 1 Ser.). (ENG.). 32p. (J). (gr. -1-3). 16.99 (978-0-06-123610-5(1)); pap. 4.99 (978-0-06-123609-9(8)) HarperCollins Pubs. (HarperCollins).

—Fancy Nancy & the Delectable Cupcakes. Glasser, Robin Preiss, illus. 2010. (I Can Read Level 1 Ser.). (ENG.). 32p. (J). (gr. -1-3). 17.99 (978-0-06-188269-2(0)); pap. 4.99 (978-0-06-188268-5(2)) HarperCollins Pubs. (HarperCollins).

—Fancy Nancy & the Fabulous Fashion Boutique. Glasser, Robin Preiss, illus. 2010. (Fancy Nancy Ser.). (ENG.). 32p. (J). (gr. -1-3). 17.99 (978-0-06-123592-4(X)); lib. bdg. 18.89 (978-0-06-123593-1(8)) HarperCollins Pubs. (HarperCollins).

—Fancy Nancy & the Late, Late, LATE Night. Glasser, Robin Preiss, illus. 2010. (Fancy Nancy Ser.). (ENG.). 24p. (J). (gr. -1-3). pap. 4.99 (978-0-06-170377-5(X), HarperFestival) HarperCollins Pubs.

—Fancy Nancy & the Late, Late, Late Night. 2010. (Fancy Nancy Picture Bks.). (J). lib. bdg. 13.55 (978-0-606-12312-9(1)) Turtleback.

—Fancy Nancy & the Mean Girl. Glasser, Robin Preiss, illus. 2011. (I Can Read Level 1 Ser.). (ENG.). 32p. (J). (gr. -1-3). 16.99 *(978-0-06-200178-8(7))*; pap. 4.99 *(978-0-06-200177-1(9))* HarperCollins Pubs. (HarperCollins).

—Fancy Nancy & the Mermaid Ballet. Glasser, Robin Preiss, illus. 2012. (Fancy Nancy Ser.). (ENG.). 32p. (J). (gr. -1-2). 18.99 *(978-0-06-170381-2(8)*, HarperCollins) HarperCollins Pubs.

—Fancy Nancy & the Sensational Babysitter. Glasser, Robin Preiss et al, illus. 2010. (Fancy Nancy Ser.). (ENG.). 24p. (J). (gr. -1-3). pap. 4.99 *(978-0-06-170378-2(8)*, HarperFestival) HarperCollins Pubs.

—Fancy Nancy & the Sensational Babysitter. 2010. (Fancy Nancy Picture Bks.). (J). lib. bdg. 13.55 *(978-0-606-14840-5(X))* Turtleback.

—Fancy Nancy & the Too-Loose Tooth. Glasser, Robin Preiss, illus. 2012. (I Can Read Level 1 Ser.). (ENG.). 32p. (J). (gr. -1-3). 17.99 *(978-0-06-208301-2(5))*; pap. 4.99 *(978-0-06-208302-9(3))* HarperCollins Pubs. (HarperCollins).

—Fancy Nancy & the Too-Loose Tooth. 2012. (Fancy Nancy - I Can Read! Ser.). (J). lib. bdg. 13.55 *(978-0-606-23551-8(5))* Turtleback.

—Fancy Nancy Big Book. Glasser, Robin Preiss, illus. 2009. (Fancy Nancy Ser.). (ENG.). 32p. (J). (gr. -1-3). pap. 24.99 *(978-0-06-171944-8(7)*, HarperFestival) HarperCollins Pubs.

—Fancy Nancy Collector's Quintet. 2009. (I Can Read Level 1 Ser.). (ENG., Illus.). (J). (gr. k-3). 19.99 *(978-0-06-171905-9(6)*, HarperCollins) HarperCollins Pubs.

—Fancy Nancy: Every Day Is Earth Day: A Springtime Book for Kids. Glasser, Robin Preiss et al, illus. 2010. (I Can Read Level 1 Ser.). (ENG.). 32p. (J). (gr. -1-3). 16.99 *(978-0-06-187327-0(6))*; pap. 5.99 *(978-0-06-187326-3(8))* HarperCollins Pubs. (HarperCollins).

—Fancy Nancy Explorer Extraordinaire. Glasser, Robin Preiss, illus. 2009. (Fancy Nancy Ser.). (ENG.). 32p. (J). (gr. -1-2). 12.99 *(978-0-06-168486-9(4)*, HarperCollins) HarperCollins Pubs.

—Fancy Nancy: Jojo & the Twins. Glasser, Robin Preiss, illus. 2018. (My First I Can Read Ser.). (ENG.). 32p. (J). (gr. -1-3). 16.99 *(978-0-06-237805-7(8))*; pap. 4.99 *(978-0-06-237804-0(X))* HarperCollins Pubs. (HarperCollins).

—Fancy Nancy: Nancy Clancy, Secret Admirer. Glasser, Robin Preiss, illus. 2013. (Nancy Clancy Ser.: 2). (ENG.). (J). (gr. 1-5). 144p. pap. 5.99 *(978-0-06-208420-0(8))*; 128p. 9.99 *(978-0-06-208295-4(7))* HarperCollins Pubs. (HarperCollins).

—Fancy Nancy: Nancy Clancy, Soccer Mania. Glasser, Robin Preiss, illus. 2015. (Nancy Clancy Ser.: 6). (ENG.). 128p. (J). (gr. 1-5). 9.99 *(978-0-06-226967-6(4)*, HarperCollins) HarperCollins Pubs.

—Fancy Nancy: Nancy Clancy, Super Sleuth. Glasser, Robin Preiss, illus. (Nancy Clancy Ser.: 1). (ENG.). (J). (gr. 1-5). 2013. 144p. pap. 5.99 *(978-0-06-208419-4(4))* 2012. 128p. 9.99 *(978-0-06-208293-0(0))* HarperCollins Pubs. (HarperCollins).

—Fancy Nancy: Nancy Clancy's Tres Charming Chapter Book Box Set: Books 1-3, 3 vols., Set. Glasser, Robin Preiss, illus. 2013. (Nancy Clancy Ser.). (ENG.). 384p. (J). (gr. 1-5). 24.99 *(978-0-06-227793-0(6)*, HarperCollins) HarperCollins Pubs.

—Fancy Nancy Ooh la la! It's Beauty Day. 2010. (Fancy Nancy Ser.). (ENG., Illus.). 40p. (J). (gr. -1-2). 12.99 *(978-0-06-191525-3(4)*, HarperCollins) HarperCollins Pubs.

—Fancy Nancy: Pajama Day. Glasser, Robin Preiss et al, illus. 2009. (I Can Read Level 1 Ser.). (ENG.). 32p. (J). (gr. -1-3). 16.99 *(978-0-06-170371-3(0)*, HarperCollins) HarperCollins Pubs.

—Fancy Nancy Pajama Day. 2009. (I Can Read Level 1 Ser.). (ENG., Illus.). 32p. (J). (gr. -1-3). pap. 4.99 *(978-0-06-170370-6(2)*, HarperCollins) HarperCollins Pubs.

—Fancy Nancy: Poison Ivy Expert. Glasser, Robin Preiss, illus. 2008. (I Can Read Level 1 Ser.). (ENG.). 32p. (J). (gr. -1-3). 16.99 *(978-0-06-123614-3(4))*; pap. 4.99 *(978-0-06-123613-6(6))* HarperCollins Pubs. (HarperCollins).

—Fancy Nancy: Spectacular Spectacles. Glasser, Robin Preiss, illus. 2010. (I Can Read Level 1 Ser.). (ENG.). 32p. (J). (gr. -1-3). pap. 4.99 *(978-0-06-188264-7(X)*, HarperCollins) HarperCollins Pubs.

—Fancy Nancy: Splendid Speller. Glasser, Robin Preiss, illus. 2011. (I Can Read Level 1 Ser.). (ENG.). 32p. (J). (gr. -1-3). pap. 4.99 *(978-0-06-200175-7(2)*, HarperCollins) HarperCollins Pubs.

—Fancy Nancy: Splendiferous Christmas: A Christmas Holiday Book for Kids. Glasser, Robin Preiss, illus. (Fancy Nancy Ser.). (ENG.). 32p. (J). (gr. -1-2). 2011. 18.99 *(978-0-06-123590-0(3))* 2009. lib. bdg. 18.89 *(978-0-06-123591-7(1))* HarperCollins Pubs. (HarperCollins).

—Fancy Nancy: Tea for Two. Glasser, Robin Preiss, illus. 2012. (Fancy Nancy Ser.). (ENG.). 24p. (J). (gr. -1-3). pap. 4.99 *(978-0-06-123597-9(0)*, HarperFestival) HarperCollins Pubs.

—Fancy Nancy: Tea Parties. Glasser, Robin Preiss, illus. 2009. (Fancy Nancy Ser.). (ENG.). 40p. (J). (gr. -1-2). 13.99 *(978-0-06-180174-7(7)*, HarperCollins) HarperCollins Pubs.

—Fancy Nancy: the 100th Day of School. Glasser, Robin Preiss, illus. 2009. (I Can Read Level 1 Ser.). (ENG.). 32p. (J). (gr. -1-3). 16.99 *(978-0-06-170375-1(3))*; pap. 4.99 *(978-0-06-170374-4(5))* HarperCollins Pubs. (HarperCollins).

—Fancy Nancy: the Dazzling Book Report. Glasser, Robin Preiss, illus. 2009. (I Can Read Level 1 Ser.). (ENG.). 32p. (J). (gr. -1-3). 16.99 *(978-0-06-170369-0(9)*, HarperCollins) HarperCollins Pubs.

—Fancy Nancy: the Show Must Go On. Glasser, Robin Preiss, illus. 2009. (I Can Read Level 1 Ser.). (ENG.). 32p. (J). (gr. -1-3). 16.99 *(978-0-06-170373-7(7)*, HarperCollins) HarperCollins Pubs.

—Fancy Nancy's Favorite Fancy Words: From Accessories to Zany. Glasser, Robin Preiss, illus. 2008. (Fancy Nancy Ser.). (ENG.). 32p. (J). (gr. -1-2). 12.99 *(978-0-06-154923-6(1)*, HarperCollins) HarperCollins Pubs.

—My Family History. 2010. (Fancy Nancy - I Can Read! Ser.). (J). lib. bdg. 13.55 *(978-0-606-14988-4(0))* Turtleback.

—Nancy Clancy, Secret Admirer. 2013. (Nancy Clancy Ser.: 2). (J). lib. bdg. 14.75 *(978-0-606-35045-7(4))* Turtleback.

—Nancy Clancy, Soccer Mania. Glasser, Robin Preiss, illus. 2016. (Nancy Clancy Ser.: 6). (ENG.). 144p. (J). (gr. 1-5). 14.75 *(978-0-606-39270-9(X))* Turtleback.

—Nancy Clancy, Star of Stage & Screen. 2016. (Nancy Clancy Ser.: 5). (J). lib. bdg. 14.75 *(978-0-606-38153-6(8))* Turtleback.

—Poison Ivy Expert. Glasser, Robin Preiss & Enik, Ted, illus. 2008. (Fancy Nancy - I Can Read! Ser.). 32p. (J). lib. bdg. 13.55 *(978-1-4364-5050-8(0))* Turtleback.

—Tea for Two. Glasser, Robin Preiss, illus. 2012. (Fancy Nancy Picture Bks.). (J). lib. bdg. 13.55 *(978-0-606-23577-8(9))* Turtleback.

O'Connor, Jane & Glasser, Robin Preiss. Fancy Nancy: My Family History. 2010. (I Can Read Level 1 Ser.). (ENG., Illus.). 32p. (J). (gr. -1-3). 16.99 *(978-0-06-188270-8(4)*, HarperCollins) HarperCollins Pubs.

—Fancy Nancy: Stellar Stargazer. 2011. (Fancy Nancy Ser.). (ENG., Illus.). 32p. (J). (gr. -1-2). 13.99 *(978-0-06-191523-9(8)*, HarperCollins) HarperCollins Pubs.

Paiva, Stela Maris Rezende. A Poesia Da Primeira Vez. Cardon, Laurent, illus. 2014. (POR.). 30p. (J). *(978-85-250-5613-9(8))* Globo, Editora SA.

Park, Linda Sue. Yaks Yak: Animal Word Pairs. Reinhardt, Jennifer Black, illus. 2016. (ENG.). 40p. (J). (gr. -1-3). 16.99 *(978-0-544-39101-7(2)*, 1593193, Clarion Bks.) HarperCollins Pubs.

Pecci, Mary. Pecci Reading Series: Primer. 2008. (Pecci Reading Ser.). pap. 9.95 *(978-0-943220-16-1(5))* Pecci Educational Pubs.

Priddy, Roger. First 100 Stickers: Words: Over 500 Stickers. 2015. (First 100 Ser.). (ENG.). 48p. (J). (gr. -1-1). pap. 9.99 *(978-0-312-51899-8(4)*, 900149124) St. Martin's Pr.

Pulver, Robin. Happy Endings: A Story about Suffixes. Reed, Lynn Rowe, illus. 2012. (ENG.). 32p. (J). (gr. -1-3). pap. 8.99 *(978-0-8234-2434-4(0))* Holiday Hse., Inc.

Quienes Son Tus Amigos? 2003. (Coleccion Parvulitos). (SPA., Illus.). stu. ed. 35.50 *(978-0-8136-8525-0(7))* Modern Curriculum Pr.

Reynolds, Peter. The Word Collector. 2018. (KOR.). (J). *(978-89-546-5172-1(0))* Munhak Dongne Publishing Corp.

Reynolds, Peter H. The Word Collector. Reynolds, Peter H., illus. 2018. (ENG., Illus.). 40p. (J). (gr. -1-3). 17.99 *(978-0-545-86502-9(6)*, Orchard Bks.) Scholastic, Inc.

Ricci, Christine. Dora in the Deep Sea. Roper, Robert, illus. 2003. (Dora the Explorer Ser.: Vol. 3). (ENG.). 24p. (J). pap. 3.99 *(978-0-689-85845-1(0)*, Simon Spotlight/Nickelodeon) Simon Spotlight/Nickelodeon.

Rosenthal, Marc. Big Bot, Small Bot: A Book of Robot Opposites. 2015. (ENG., Illus.). 24p. (J). (-k). 17.95 *(978-1-57687-750-0(7)*, powerHouse Bks.) powerHse. Bks.

Rowe, Chelsea H. Ebenezer Has a Word for Everything, 1 vol. DORMER, Frank, illus. 2018. 32p. (J). (gr. -1-3). 17.95 *(978-1-56145-848-6(1))* Peachtree Publishing Co. Inc.

Rubinger, Ami. I Dream of an Elephant. 2010. (ENG., Illus.). 28p. (J). (gr. -1-k). 13.95 *(978-0-7892-1058-6(4)*, 791058, Abbeville Kids) Abbeville Pr., Inc.

Sabatier-Morel, Francoise & Pellegrini, Isabelle. Marie from Paris. Camcam, Princesse, illus. 2014. (AV2 Fiction Readalong Ser.: Vol. 131). (ENG.). 32p. (J). (gr. -1-3). lib. bdg. 34.28 *(978-1-4896-2262-4(4)*, AV2 by Weigl) Weigl Pubs., Inc.

Saroyan, William & Tinkelman, Murray. Me. 2016. (ENG., Illus.). 64p. (gr. 1-3). pap. 9.99 *(978-0-486-81066-9(6)*, 810666) Dover Pubns., Inc.

Sasso, Sandy Eisenberg. When God Gave Us Words. Zoells, Darcy Day, illus. 2018. (ENG.). 32p. (J). (gr. -1-3). 16.00 *(978-1-947888-01-2(3)*, Flyaway Bks.) Westminster John Knox Pr.

Scarry, Richard. Richard Scarry's Best Little Word Book Ever! 2018. (Illus.). 26p. (J). (-k). bds. 7.99 *(978-1-5247-1855-8(6)*, Golden Bks.) Random Hse. Children's Bks.

—Richard Scarry's Best Little Word Book Ever! Scarry, Richard, illus. 2016. (Pictureback(R) Ser.). (Illus.). 24p. (J). (-k). pap. 4.99 *(978-0-385-39271-6(0)*, Random Hse. Bks. for Young Readers) Random Hse. Children's Bks.

Schmidt, Kristina Edelkamp. Miss Flavia & the Cookie Cottage. Cologne, Starla, illus. 2009. 28p. pap. 7.99 *(978-1-935125-61-7(3))* Robertson Publishing.

Schotter, Roni. The Boy Who Loved Words. Potter, Giselle, illus. 2006. (ENG.). 40p. (J). (gr. -1-3). 18.99 *(978-0-375-83601-5(2)*, Schwartz & Wade Bks.) Random Hse. Children's Bks.

Seuss, Dr. Hay un Molillo en Mi Bolsillo! Canetti, Yanitzia, tr. from ENG. 2007.Tr. of There's a Wocket in my Pocket! (SPA., Illus.). 26p. (J). (gr. k-3). 8.99 *(978-1-933032-25-2(1))* Lectorum Pubns., Inc.

Shannon, David. Oops! a Diaper David Book. Shannon, David, illus. 2005. (ENG., Illus.). 12p. (J). (gr. -1-k). bds. 6.99 *(978-0-439-68882-6(5)*, Blue Sky Pr., The) Scholastic, Inc.

Si Yo Tuviera un Cordel... 2003. (Coleccion Parvulitos). (SPA., Illus.). stu. ed. 35.50 *(978-0-8136-8530-4(3))* Modern Curriculum Pr.

Sierra, Judy. The Great Dictionary Caper. Comstock, Eric, illus. 2018. (ENG.). 40p. (J). (gr. -1-3). 17.99 *(978-1-4814-8004-8(9)*, Simon & Schuster/Paula Wiseman Bks.) Simon & Schuster/Paula Wiseman Bks.

Snicket, Lemony, pseud. 13 Words. Kalman, Maira, illus. (ENG.). 40p. (J). (gr. -1-3). 2014. pap. 7.99 *(978-0-06-166467-0(7))* 2010. 16.99 *(978-0-06-166465-6(0))* HarperCollins Pubs. (HarperCollins).

Stauffacher, Sue & Love, Comfort. Wireman. 2007. (Illus.). 159p. (J). pap. *(978-0-9709811-4-1(7))* Grand Valley State Univ.

Steinberg, Laya. Thesaurus Rex. Harter, Debbie, illus. (ENG.). 24p. (J). 2005. (gr. -1-2). pap. 9.99 *(978-1-84148-180-7(7))* 2003. 15.99 *(978-1-84148-042-8(8))* Barefoot Bks., Inc.

Stihler, Chérie B. & Stihler, Chérie B. Wiggle-Waggle Woof: Counting Sled Dogs in Alaska. Bania, Michael, illus. 2009. (Paws IV Ser.). (ENG.). 32p. (J). (gr. -1-2). pap. 10.99 *(978-1-57061-559-7(4)*, Little Bigfoot) Sasquatch Bks.

Storch, Ellen N. Here We Go! Storch, Ellen N., illus. l.t. ed. 2005. (HRL Board Book Ser.). (Illus.). (J). (gr. -1-k). pap. 10.95 *(978-1-57332-322-2(5)*, HighReach Learning, Incorporated) Carson-Dellosa Publishing, LLC.

Tiger Tales. My Busy Day. 2014. (My First Ser.). (ENG., Illus.). 12p. (J). (gr. -1-k). bds. 8.99 *(978-1-58925-590-6(9))* Tiger Tales.

Tiger Tales Staff, creator. Things That Go. 2014. (My First Jumbo Tab Bks.). (ENG., Illus.). 12p. (J). (gr. -1). bds. 8.99 *(978-1-58925-589-0(5))* Tiger Tales.

Tiger Tales Staff, ed. Easter Surprise: My First Lift & Learn. 2014. (ENG.). 10p. (J). bds. 7.99 *(978-1-58925-580-7(1))* Tiger Tales.

Van Fleet, Matthew. Heads. Van Fleet, Matthew, illus. 2010. (ENG., Illus.). 18p. (J). (gr. -1-1). 24.99 *(978-1-4424-0379-6(9)*, Simon & Schuster/Paula Wiseman Bks.) Simon & Schuster/Paula Wiseman Bks.

Van Slyke, Rebecca. Lexie the Word Wrangler. Hartland, Jessie, illus. 2017. 40p. (J). (gr. k-3). 18.99 *(978-0-399-16957-1(1)*, Nancy Paulsen Books) Penguin Young Readers Group.

Vonthron, Satanta C. Caillou's Community. Storch, Ellen N., illus. l.t. ed. 2006. (HRL Board Book Ser.). (J). (gr. k-18). pap. 10.95 *(978-1-57332-332-1(2)*, HighReach Learning, Incorporated) Carson-Dellosa Publishing, LLC.

Weston, Carol. Ava & Pip. 2015. (Ava & Pip Ser.: 1). (ENG.). 224p. (J). (gr. 5-7). pap. 10.99 *(978-1-4926-0183-8(7))* Sourcebooks, Inc.

Williams, Garth. Baby's First Book. Williams, Garth, illus. 2011. (Golden Baby Ser.). (Illus.). 24p. (J). (— 1). 6.99 *(978-0-375-85905-2(5)*, Golden Bks.) Random Hse. Children's Bks.

Wimmer, Sonja. The Word Collector. Brokenbrow, Jon, tr. Wimmer, Sonja, illus. 2012. (ENG., Illus.). 32p. (J). (gr. k-3). 18.95 *(978-84-15241-34-8(8))* Cuento de Luz SL ESP. Dist: Publishers Group West (PGW).

Yamada, Miho. Miyako from Tokyo. Camcam, Princesse, illus. 2014. (AV2 Fiction Readalong Ser.: Vol. 132). (ENG.). 32p. (J). (gr. -1-3). lib. bdg. 34.28 *(978-1-4896-2268-6(3)*, AV2 by Weigl) Weigl Pubs., Inc.

Yoyo. Learning Words. 2005. 40p. bds. *(978-90-5843-887-4(2))* YoYo Bks.

VOCAL CULTURE

see Voice

VOCATION, CHOICE OF

see Vocational Guidance

VOCATIONAL GUIDANCE

see also Blind—Education; Counseling; Deaf—Education; Educational Counseling; Job Hunting; Occupations; Professions

also subdivision Vocational Guidance under names of occupations, fields of endeavor, military services, and types of industries

Ames, Michelle. Librarians in Our Community, 1 vol. 2009. (On the Job Ser.). (ENG., Illus.). 24p. (J). (gr. 1-1). pap. 9.25 *(978-1-4358-2458-4(X)*, a836bbff-bc4b-42be-8e6c-5d12281bf9cf); lib. bdg. 26.27 *(978-1-4042-8072-4(3)*, 969eedb1-cc4f-4497-867b-19654afc4c30) Rosen Publishing Group, Inc., The. (PowerKids Pr.).

Anonymous. Book of Old-Time Trades & Tools. 2005. (ENG., Illus.). 320p. (gr. 3-7). per. 15.95 *(978-0-486-44342-3(6)*, 443426) Dover Pubns., Inc.

Antill, Sara. 10 Ways I Can Help My Community, 1 vol. 2012. (I Can Make a Difference Ser.). (ENG., Illus.). 24p. (J). (gr. 2-3). pap. 9.25 *(978-1-4488-6363-1(5)*, a06fb6f8-f55a-474b-b499-fe8ab15e6296); lib. bdg. 26.27 *(978-1-4488-6202-3(7)*, e3028fb1-b729-409f-9274-57aeff84d52f) Rosen Publishing Group, Inc., The. (PowerKids Pr.).

Apel, Melanie. Cool Careers Without College for Film & Television Buffs, 1 vol. 2nd ed. 2007. (Cool Careers Without College (2002-2006) Ser.). (ENG., Illus.). 144p. (YA). (gr. 7-7). lib. bdg. 41.13 *(978-1-4042-1429-3(1)*, 4e780e00-46b4-4ac3-a97b-870aa31075ec) Rosen Publishing Group, Inc., The.

—Cool Careers Without College for Film & TV Buffs. 2009. (Cool Careers Without College Ser.). 144p. (gr. 6-6). 66.50 *(978-1-61511-956-1(6))* Rosen Publishing Group, Inc., The.

Arment Jd, Laura B. Sixteen Things You Should Know about Work Now: A Guide for Young People. 2008. 48p. pap. 11.95 *(978-1-60145-569-7(0))* Booklocker.com, Inc.

Asher, Dana. Epidemiologists: Life Tracking Deadly Diseases, 1 vol. 2003. (Extreme Careers Ser.). (ENG., Illus.). 64p. (YA). (gr. 5-5). 37.13 *(978-0-8239-3633-5(3)*, c5e41a90-a61a-4b77-83c3-6467f633a8d2) Rosen Publishing Group, Inc., The.

Berman, Ron. Future Stars of America. 2006. (Future Stars Ser.). (Illus.). 90p. (gr. 3-8). pap. 9.95 *(978-0-9741997-4-0(5))* Scobre Pr. Corp.

Bickerstaff, Linda. Careers in Nutrition. 2009. (Careers in the New Economy Ser.). 144p. (gr. 7-7). 63.90 *(978-1-61511-818-2(7))* Rosen Publishing Group, Inc., The.

Books, Checkmark, creator. Research & Information Management: Follow the Fast Track to Career Success. 2nd rev. ed. 2007. (Mastering Career Skills Ser.). (ENG., Illus.). 128p. per. 12.95 *(978-0-8160-7118-0(7)*, P165515, Checkmark Bks.) Infobase Holdings, Inc.

Brezina, Corona. Careers as a Medical Examiner. 2009. (Careers in Forensics Ser.). 64p. (gr. 5-5). 58.50 *(978-1-61511-799-4(7)*, Rosen Reference) Rosen Publishing Group, Inc., The.

—Careers in Nanotechnology. 2009. (Cutting-Edge Careers Ser.). 64p. (gr. 7-7). 55.90 *(978-1-61512-100-7(5))* Rosen Publishing Group, Inc., The.

—Great Decision-Making Skills. (Work Readiness Ser.). 64p. (gr. 6-6). 2009. 58.50 *(978-1-60854-823-1(6))* 2008. (ENG., Illus.). (J). lib. bdg. 37.13 *(978-1-4042-1422-4(4)*, 579ab0d1-05c4-4216-ae41-34758eea89ec) Rosen Publishing Group, Inc., The.

—Jobs in Sustainable Energy, 1 vol. 2010. (Green Careers Ser.). (ENG., Illus.). 80p. (YA). (gr. 6-6). lib. bdg. 38.47 *(978-1-4358-3569-6(7)*, 848f836d-2c52-4bf5-b300-bbad9698cb46) Rosen Publishing Group, Inc., The.

Brindell Fradin, Dennis & Bloom Fradin, Judith. Earning, 1 vol. 2011. (Money Smart Ser.). (ENG.). 64p. (gr. 5-5). 35.50 *(978-1-60870-123-0(9)*, 385f22ff-c656-4f73-8283-a00f5f6e94f0) Cavendish Square Publishing LLC.

Brown, Marty. Webmaster. 2009. (Coolcareers. com Ser.). 48p. (gr. 5-8). 53.00 *(978-1-61511-985-1(X)*, Rosen Reference) Rosen Publishing Group, Inc., The.

Brown, Ruby. I Want to Be ... a Lion Tamer. Coburn, Alisa, illus. 2016. (ENG.). 22p. (J). bds. 8.99 *(978-1-61067-405-8(7))* Kane Miller.

Buell, Tonya. Cool Careers Without College for Web Surfers. 2007. (Cool Careers Without College Ser.). (Illus.). 144p. (J). (gr. 4-7). lib. bdg. 33.25 *(978-1-4042-0871-1(2))* Rosen Publishing Group, Inc., The.

Burnett, Betty. Cool Careers Without College for Math & Science Wizards. 2009. (Cool Careers Without College Ser.). 144p. (gr. 6-6). 66.50 *(978-1-61511-959-2(0))* Rosen Publishing Group, Inc., The.

Burns, Monique. Cool Careers Without College for People Who Love to Make Things Grow. 2009. (Cool Careers Without College Ser.). 144p. (gr. 6-6). 66.50 *(978-1-61511-975-2(2))* Rosen Publishing Group, Inc., The.

Byers, Ann. Jobs As Green Builders & Planners, 1 vol. 2010. (Green Careers Ser.). (ENG., Illus.). 80p. (YA). (gr. 6-6). lib. bdg. 38.47 *(978-1-4358-3566-5(2)*, 9d6c9578-1e22-413a-973a-16332280b1de) Rosen Publishing Group, Inc., The.

Byrd-Hill, Ida. Me & My Big Career, Hill, Karen, ed. Hill, Kevin, illus. 2010. (ENG.). 24p. (J). 14.95 *(978-0-9829610-0-1(6))* Upheaval Media, Inc.

Calling All Innovators: A Career for You (Spring 2016 Set Of 4) 2016. (Calling All Innovators: a Career for You Ser.). (J). lib. bdg. 120.00 *(978-0-531-21679-8(9)*, Children's Pr.) Scholastic Library Publishing.

Caraccilo, Dominic. E-Tailing: Careers Selling over the Web. 2009. (Library of E-Commerce & Internet Careers Ser.). 64p. (gr. 5-5). 58.50 *(978-1-60853-587-3(8))* Rosen Publishing Group, Inc., The.

Careers in the New Economy, 5 bk. set. 2005. (YA). (gr. 7-12). lib. bdg. 118.35 *(978-1-4042-0374-7(5))* Rosen Publishing Group, Inc., The.

Careers Set: Promising Careers, 8 vols. Incl. Careers in Alternative Medicine. Steinfeld, Alan. 192p. (YA). 2000. lib. bdg. 18.95 *(978-0-8239-2963-4(9)*, CAALME); Careers in Starting & Building Franchises. Frisch, Carlienne A. 192p. (YA). 1999. lib. bdg. 38.10 *(978-0-8239-2781-4(4)*, CAFRAN); Careers in the Fashion Industry. Giacobello, John. 122p. (J). 1999. lib. bdg. 18.95 *(978-0-8239-2890-3(X)*, CAFASH); Exploring Careers in Social Work. Simpson, Carolyn & Simpson, Dwain. 192p. (YA). 1999. lib. bdg. 31.95 *(978-0-8239-2879-8(9)*, CASOWO); (gr. 7-12). (Illus.). Set lib. bdg. 135.60 o.p. *(978-0-8239-9085-6(0))* Rosen Publishing Group, Inc., The.

Careers That Count. 2015. (Careers That Count Ser.). (ENG.). 32p. (J). (gr. 4-4). pap., pap., pap. 360.00 *(978-1-4994-1274-1(6)*, PowerKids Pr.) Rosen Publishing Group, Inc., The.

Cassedy, Patrice, tr. Finance. 2003. (Careers for the Twenty-First-Century Ser.). (ENG., Illus.). 112p. (J). 30.85 *(978-1-59018-520-9(X)*, Lucent Bks.) Cengage Gale.

Cefrey, Holly. Career Building Through Machinima: Using Video Games to Make Movies. 2009. (Digital Career Building Ser.). 64p. (gr. 6-6). 58.50 *(978-1-61512-168-7(4))* Rosen Publishing Group, Inc., The.

—Career Building Through Music, Video, & Software Mashups. 2009. (Digital Career Building Ser.). 64p. (gr. 6-6). 58.50 *(978-1-61512-169-4(2))* Rosen Publishing Group, Inc., The.

Christen, Carol & Blomquist, Jean M. What Color Is Your Parachute? for Teens. 2015. lib. bdg. 28.15 *(978-0-606-36433-1(1))* Turtleback.

Cool Careers: Adventure Careers, 8 vols., Set. Incl. Deep-Sea Fishing. Thomas, William David. lib. bdg. 28.67 *(978-0-8368-8881-2(2)*, 4a752227-67e7-4ef8-b9d3-8e0de4cf1289); Forest Firefighter. Thomas, William David. lib. bdg. 28.67 *(978-0-8368-8882-9(0)*, ecb97f57-c33b-4c32-9af5-f2c1b5ab0b78); Oil Rig Roughneck. Horn, Geoffrey M. lib. bdg. 28.67 *(978-0-8368-8883-6(9)*, cd9679ef-c36c-4e8b-a054-583fbba6e3df); Test Pilot. Horn, Geoffrey M. lib. bdg. 28.67 *(978-0-8368-8884-3(7)*, 2c3b9296-7cc2-41f2-848d-cdf3eaa3c846); Wildlife Photographer. Thomas, William David. lib. bdg. 28.67 *(978-0-8368-8885-0(5)*, 3e0a9aa4-db8f-4082-a587-e37c2419f096); (Illus.). (gr. 3-3). (Cool Careers: Adventure Careers Ser.). (ENG.). 32p. 2008. Set lib. bdg. 114.68 *(978-0-8368-8879-9(0)*, c69a710c-d12b-49c6-9104-931dea19f0dc) Stevens, Gareth Publishing LLLP.

Cool Careers: Cutting Edge Careers, 8 vols. 2008. (Cool Careers: Cutting Edge Ser.). (ENG.). 32p. (J). (gr. 3-3). lib. bdg. 114.68 *(978-1-4339-1998-5(2)*, 1534c2f5-0596-45f9-84c8-5d3d64d5edd6) Stevens, Gareth Publishing LLLP.

Cool Careers Without College, 8 bks., Set. Incl. Cool Careers Without College for People Who Love Everything Digital. Romano, Amy. lib. bdg. 41.13 *(978-1-4042-0748-6(1)*, 7f7dde33-9840-4d43-b336-316283e08ce9); Cool Careers Without College for People Who Love Houses. Beco, Alice. lib. bdg. 41.13 *(978-1-4042-0753-0(8)*, 4a3dc699-6a4a-4810-b8c5-21f06dc9ab67); Cool Careers Without College for People Who Love Manga, Comics, & Animation. Glass, Sherri & Wentzel, Jim. lib. bdg. 41.13 *(978-1-4042-0754-7(6)*, 880a3827-74e6-4da3-bd1e-e6c4da3b578e); Cool Careers Without College for People Who Love to Organize, Manage, & Plan. Greenberger, Robert. lib. bdg. 41.13 *(978-1-4042-0752-3(X)*, c24a8234-097f-470f-a137-549e907753df); Cool Careers Without College for People Who Love to Write. Roza, Greg. lib. bdg. 41.13 *(978-1-4042-0750-9(3)*, 757b472b-2759-410f-ba6e-81b3aeabf3a1); Cool Careers Without College for People Who Love Video Games. Croce, Nicholas. lib. bdg. 41.13 *(978-1-4042-0747-9(3)*, 894b1c7c-996b-4aa3-92c4-cf2b0580df6c); People Who Love to Buy Things. Santos, Edson. lib. bdg. 41.13 *(978-1-4042-0751-6(1)*, a6c84d0e-a368-479c-8c59-bc9bc5b54bcc); (Illus.). 144p. (YA). (gr. 7-7). 2006. 2006. 276.15 o.p. *(978-1-4042-1015-8(6))* Rosen Publishing Group, Inc., The.

Cool Careers Without College: Set 2, 16 vols. 2016. (Cool Careers Without College Ser.). (ENG.). 00104p. (J). (gr. 7-7). 328.96 *(978-1-5081-7360-1(5)*, 88f49afe-f726-47f0-bf34-a8cec5a4aa00, Rosen Young Adult) Rosen Publishing Group, Inc., The.

Cool Careers Without College: Set 3, 12 vols. 2017. (Cool Careers Without College Ser.). (ENG.). 112p. (gr. 7-7). 246.72 *(978-1-4994-6632-4(3),* b6dcb547-73fc-487c-89ab-61523ee5bd8b, Rosen Young Adult) Rosen Publishing Group, Inc., The.

Coolcareers.com, 6 vols. Incl. Hardware Engineer. Donelly, Karen. lib. bdg. 34.47 *(978-0-8239-3118-7(8),* 06030faf-7f38-4c89-af52-b8e647969a17); Webmaster. Brown, Marty. lib. bdg. 33.47 *(978-0-8239-3111-8(0),* 44468cb1-8a7a-4d79-b6af-c17cb159a735, Rosen Reference); 48p. (YA). (gr. 5-8). 1999. (Coolcareers. com Ser.). (ENG., Illus.). 2003. Set lib. bdg. 103.41 *(978-0-8239-9089-4(3),* 14132b81-ce54-4192-9462-b9ac898fb4e4, Rosen Reference) Rosen Publishing Group, Inc., The.

Coon, Nora. Teen Dream Jobs: How to Find the Job You Really Want Now! 2004. (Illus.). 132p. (YA). (gr. 8-12). per. 9.95 *(978-1-58270-093-9(1))* Beyond Words Publishing, Inc.

Cowen, Carla Romaine. E-Commerce: Careers in Multimedia. 2009. (Library of E-Commerce & Internet Careers Ser.). 64p. (gr. 5-5). 58.50 *(978-1-60853-586-6(X))* Rosen Publishing Group, Inc., The.

Craig, Tom. Internet: Technology, People, Process. 2003. (Media Wise Ser.). 64p. (J). lib. bdg. 28.50 *(978-1-58340-257-3(8))* Black Rabbit Bks.

Creative Careers, 12 vols. 2014. (Creative Careers Ser.). 48p. (J). (gr. 4-5). (ENG.). 201.60 *(978-1-4824-1184-3(9),* ff10c465-d6c2-4ce3-bf51-b255d4d9f160); pap. 84.30 *(978-1-4824-1557-5(7))* Stevens, Gareth Publishing LLLP.

Croce, Nicholas. Detectives: Life Investigating Crime. 2009. (Extreme Careers Ser.). 64p. (gr. 5-5). 58.50 *(978-1-61512-390-2(3),* Rosen Reference) Rosen Publishing Group, Inc., The.

Currie-McGhee, Leanne. Getting a Job. 2019. (Teen Life Skills Ser.). (ENG.). 64p. (J). (gr. 6-12). 41.27 *(978-1-68282-743-7(7))* ReferencePoint Pr., Inc.

Cutting-Edge Careers, 10 vols., Set. Incl. Careers in Artificial Intelligence. Greenberger, Robert. (Illus.). (YA). lib. bdg. 37.13 *(978-1-4042-0953-4(0),* c56562ac-f5dc-45c4-a4bd-52bbc1799d47); Careers in Biotechnology. Hall, Linley Erin. (Illus.). (J). lib. bdg. 37.13 *(978-1-4042-0954-1(9),* 4bf5176f-3b1a-4501-82cf-f65841dfd47c); Careers in Computer Gaming. Robinson, Matthew. (YA). lib. bdg. 37.13 *(978-1-4042-0958-9(1),* fa229cc2-5768-4824-9173-508787c7de44); Careers in Nanotechnology. Brezina, Corona. (Illus.). (J). lib. bdg. 37.13 *(978-1-4042-0955-8(7),* 0474880f-9ed4-498e-b39d-a6e3cb58ced6); Careers in Robotics. Kupperberg, Paul. (Illus.). lib. bdg. 37.13 *(978-1-4042-0956-5(5),* 0674229a-7605-4d1d-96ca-03ec582578cc); 64p. (gr. 7-7). 2007. (Cutting-Edge Careers Ser.). (ENG.). 2006. Set lib. bdg. 185.65 *(978-1-4042-0934-3(4),* 38dfb8dc-0b87-430f-8720-874eecc44eb8) Rosen Publishing Group, Inc., The.

Cutting-Edge STEM Careers, 8 vols. 2014. (Cutting-Edge STEM Careers Ser.). (ENG.). 128p. (YA). (gr. 9-9). 155.20 *(978-1-4777-7680-3(X),* d6f9191b-5f18-4660-8a66-8d6cf1074520) Rosen Publishing Group, Inc., The.

Dalton, Sarah, et al, eds. Encyclopedia of Careers & Vocational Guidance, 5 vols., Set. 15th rev. ed. 2010. 4128p. (C). (gr. 9). 249.95 *(978-0-8160-8313-8(4),* Ferguson Publishing Company) Infobase Holdings, Inc.

Digital Career Building, 12 vols., Set. 2008. (YA). (gr. 7-12). lib. bdg. 351.00 *(978-1-4042-1497-2(6))* Rosen Publishing Group, Inc., The.

Digital Career Building: Set 1, 8 vols. 2007. (Digital Career Building Ser.). (ENG.). (YA). (gr. 6-6). lib. bdg. 148.52 *(978-1-4042-1116-2(0),* 6179810d-2d60-41b4-8b1c-8c3556ba3c39) Rosen Publishing Group, Inc., The.

Digital Career Building: Set 2, 10 vols. 2007. (Digital Career Building Ser.). (ENG.). (YA). (gr. 6-6). lib. bdg. 185.65 *(978-1-4042-1478-1(X),* bcd58160-0f2f-449d-bda0-81a84ca60ca3) Rosen Publishing Group, Inc., The.

Dunn, Mary R. I Want to Be a Chef, 1 vol. 2008. (Dream Jobs Ser.). (ENG., Illus.). 24p. (YA). (gr. 2-3). lib. bdg. 26.27 *(978-1-4042-4471-9(9),* 24cafc67-d185-40bd-8f10-81bdeb18eafd) Rosen Publishing Group, Inc., The.

—Quiero Ser Chef, 1 vol. 2009. (Trabajos de Ensueño (Dream Jobs) Ser.).Tr. of I Want to Be a Chef. (SPA., Illus.). 24p. (J). (gr. 2-3). lib. bdg. 26.27 *(978-1-4042-8156-1(8),* 80cbb62b-7cd8-48d8-a397-70b684d051c8) Rosen Publishing Group, Inc., The.

—Quiero Ser Diseñador de Modas, 1 vol. 2009. (Trabajos de Ensueño (Dream Jobs) Ser.).Tr. of I Want to Be a Fashion Designer. (SPA., Illus.). 24p. (J). (gr. 2-3). lib. bdg. 26.27 *(978-1-4042-8154-7(1),* 0fe2bc84-5d75-4610-9b9b-06beaed5252c) Rosen Publishing Group, Inc., The.

EDITORS AT JIST. Young Person's Occupational Outlook Handbook. 7th rev. ed. 2010. (ENG.). 336p. 25.95 *(978-1-59357-743-8(5))* Kendall Hunt Publishing Co.

Ellis, Amy, des. Looking at Myself I. 2nd ed. 2003. (J). pap. *(978-1-887481-27-4(3),* LAM1KIT) CFKR Career Materials, Inc.

—Looking at Myself I Answer Folder. 2nd ed. 2003. (J). pap. *(978-1-887481-28-1(1))* CFKR Career Materials, Inc.

Ellis, Amy, rev. Major-Minor Finder: College to Career Planner. 2nd ed. 2003. (YA). *(978-1-887481-38-0(9))* CFKR Career Materials, Inc.

Environment. 2011. (ENG., Illus.). 128p. (gr. 4-9). 24.95 *(978-0-8160-8050-2(X),* P189796, Ferguson Publishing Company) Infobase Holdings, Inc.

Facts on File, Inc. Staff. Construction. 2010. (New Discovering Careers for Your Future Ser.). (Illus.). 128p. (gr. 4-9). 24.95 *(978-0-8160-8045-8(3),* Ferguson Publishing Company) Infobase Holdings, Inc.

Federal Forces: Careers As Federal Agents. 2015. (Federal Forces: Careers As Federal Agents Ser.). (ENG.). 32p. (J). (gr. 4-5). pap., pap., pap. 360.00 *(978-1-4994-1291-8(6),* PowerKids Pr.) Rosen Publishing Group, Inc., The.

Federal Forces: Careers As Federal Agents Set, 12 vols. 2015. (Federal Forces: Careers As Federal Agents Ser.). (ENG.). 32p. (J). (gr. 4-5). lib. bdg. 167.58 *(978-1-4994-0772-3(6),* eb0df0a9-f388-45ce-8222-a041ddf75735, PowerKids Pr.) Rosen Publishing Group, Inc., The.

Ferguson. History. 2006. (Discovering Careers for Your Future Ser.). (ENG., Illus.). 96p. (gr. 4-9). 21.95 *(978-0-89434-391-9(2),* P063147, Ferguson Publishing Company) Infobase Holdings, Inc.

Ferguson, creator. Automotives. 2009. (Ferguson's Careers in Focus Ser.). (ENG.). 188p. (gr. 6-12). 32.95 *(978-0-8160-7300-9(7),* P179101, Ferguson Publishing Company) Infobase Holdings, Inc.

—Business Managers. 2nd rev. ed. 2009. (Ferguson's Careers in Focus Ser.). (ENG.). 204p. (gr. 6-12). 32.95 *(978-0-8160-7296-5(5),* P179098, Ferguson Publishing Company) Infobase Holdings, Inc.

—Earth Science. 2nd rev. ed. 2008. (Ferguson's Careers in Focus Ser.). (ENG., Illus.). 188p. (gr. 6-12). 32.95 *(978-0-8160-7272-9(8),* P179079, Ferguson Publishing Company) Infobase Holdings, Inc.

—Library & Information Science. 2008. (Discovering Careers for Your Future Ser.). (ENG.). 91p. (gr. 4-9). 21.95 *(978-0-8160-7282-8(5),* P179086, Ferguson Publishing Company) Infobase Holdings, Inc.

—Math. 2nd rev. ed. 2008. (Discovering Careers for Your Future Ser.). (ENG.). 91p. (gr. 4-9). 21.95 *(978-0-8160-7278-1(7),* P179083, Ferguson Publishing Company) Infobase Holdings, Inc.

—Nonprofit Organizations. 2008. (Ferguson's Careers in Focus Ser.). (ENG.). 188p. (gr. 6-12). 32.95 *(978-0-8160-7289-7(2),* P179093, Ferguson Publishing Company) Infobase Holdings, Inc.

—Sports. 4th rev. ed. 2008. (Ferguson's Careers in Focus Ser.). (ENG.). 204p. (gr. 6-12). 32.95 *(978-0-8160-7287-3(6),* P179091, Ferguson Publishing Company) Infobase Holdings, Inc.

Ferguson Publishing. Encyclopedia of Careers & Vocational Guidance, 6. 17th ed. 2018. (ENG., Illus.). 6344p. (gr. 9). 299.95 *(978-0-8160-8514-9(5),* P560536) Ferguson Publishing.

Ferguson Publishing Staff. Career Discovery Encyclopedia. 7th rev. ed. 2009. 1728p. (gr. 4-9). 235.00 *(978-0-8160-7931-5(5),* Ferguson Publishing Company) Infobase Holdings, Inc.

Franks, Katie. Dream Jobs: Set 1, 8 vols. Incl. I Want to Be a Baseball Player. (J). lib. bdg. 26.27 *(978-1-4042-3622-6(8),* 164646bb-2da3-4e4f-92d5-798a0f66589f); I Want to Be a Basketball Player. (J). lib. bdg. 26.27 *(978-1-4042-3621-9(X),* a4f8b420-cda0-45fa-a2e2-5e45d03a75d6); I Want to Be a Movie Star. (YA). lib. bdg. 26.27 *(978-1-4042-3619-6(8),* 173dd864-0ee6-4483-b772-e364699a0208); I Want to Be a Race Car Driver. (J). lib. bdg. 26.27 *(978-1-4042-3623-3(6),* 87391c97-8ca6-46cb-9cd5-ea5e17a97521); (Illus.). 24p. (gr. 2-3). (Dream Jobs Ser.). (ENG.). 2006. Set lib. bdg. 105.08 *(978-1-4042-3598-4(1),* 75a959c7-dddc-45f9-bf28-32d74732aa6c) Rosen Publishing Group, Inc., The.

—Quiero Ser Beisbolista, 1 vol. 2009. (Trabajos de Ensueño (Dream Jobs) Ser.). (SPA.). 24p. (gr. 2-3). pap. 8.25 *(978-1-4358-3431-6(3),* 1ca5b70b-ed9f-4967-b8df-e8aacd86cfdf, PowerKids Pr.); (Illus.). 26.27 *(978-1-4042-8159-2(2),* 7cb20c69-64c7-4af3-a722-7b241a63009) Rosen Publishing Group, Inc., The.

Freedman, Jeri. Career Building Through Skinning & Modding. 2009. (Digital Career Building Ser.). 64p. (gr. 6-6). 58.50 *(978-1-61512-171-7(4))* Rosen Publishing Group, Inc., The.

—Careers in Child Care, 1 vol. 2014. (Essential Careers Ser.). (ENG.). 80p. (J). (gr. 6-6). 37.47 *(978-1-4777-7884-5(5),* fd38af77-7074-4324-936d-85dd11df456f, Rosen Young Adult) Rosen Publishing Group, Inc., The.

—Careers in Emergency Medical Response Teams' Search & Rescue Units. 2009. (Careers in Search & Rescue Operations Ser.). 64p. (gr. 5-8). 58.50 *(978-1-61511-805-2(5),* Rosen Reference) Rosen Publishing Group, Inc., The.

Fremont, Elenor. Odd Jobs: The Wackiest Jobs You've Never Heard Of. 2012. (ENG., Illus.). 80p. (J). (gr. 2-5). pap. 33.99 *(978-0-689-82934-5(5),* Simon & Schuster/Paula Wiseman Bks.) Simon & Schuster/Paula Wiseman Bks.

Furgang, Kathy. 20 Great Career-Building Activities Using Twitter, 1 vol. 2016. (Social Media Career Building Ser.). (ENG., Illus.). 64p. (J). (gr. 7-7). 36.13 *(978-1-5081-7268-0(4),* 0a46d648-5d86-451a-9cef-dde791debaca) Rosen Publishing Group, Inc., The.

Gabler, Laura R., ed. Career Exploration on the Internet: A Student's Guide to More Than 500 Web Sites. 2nd ed. 2006. (ENG., Illus.). 404p. 24.95 *(978-0-89434-305-6(X),* P101953, Ferguson Publishing Company) Infobase Holdings, Inc.

Gard, Carolyn. Cool Careers Without College for People Who Love to Sell Things. 2009. (Cool Careers Without College Ser.). 144p. (gr. 6-6). 66.50 *(978-1-61511-979-0(5))* Rosen Publishing Group, Inc., The.

Gareth Guides to an Extraordinary Life: Set 2, 12 vols. 2018. (Gareth Guides to an Extraordinary Life Ser.). (ENG.). 32p. (gr. 4-5). lib. bdg. 177.60 *(978-1-5382-2184-6(5),* e86ca806-0f87-4516-9b9c-e2d07fb4726d) Stevens, Gareth Publishing LLLP.

Gerry, Lisa M. 100 Things to Be When You Grow Up. 2017. (Illus.). 256p. (J). (gr. 3-7). pap. 9.99 *(978-1-4263-2711-7(0),* National Geographic Kids) Disney Publishing Worldwide.

Given-Wilson, Rachel & Watson, Stephanie. Your Future As a Police Officer, 1 vol. 2019. (High-Demand Careers Ser.). (ENG., Illus.). 80p. (J). (gr. 7-7). 37.47 *(978-1-5081-8792-9(4),* 052105ef-761b-434e-9219-6599ee8da09c) Rosen Publishing Group, Inc., The.

Goetchius, Alex. Career Building Through Social Networking, 4 vols. 2007. (Digital Career Building Ser.). (ENG.). 64p. (gr. 6-6). 74.26 *(978-1-61512-172-4(2),* 9fb82df7-77c6-45b3-b9de-7dd8bdab73e1) Rosen Publishing Group, Inc., The.

Goranson, Christopher. Careers as a Webmaster: Maintaining the Site. 2009. (Library of E-Commerce & Internet Careers Ser.). 64p. (gr. 5-5). 58.50 *(978-1-60853-579-8(7))* Rosen Publishing Group, Inc., The.

Gosling, Maureen, et al. You Can Be a Woman Movie Maker. I.t. ed. 2003. (Illus.). 80p. (J). 19.95 incl. DVD *(978-1-880599-64-8(3));* pap. 14.95 incl. DVD *(978-1-880599-63-1(5))* Cascade Pass, Inc.

Graham, Amy. Be Smart about Your Career: College, Income, & Careers, 1 vol. 2014. (Be Smart about Money & Financial Literacy Ser.). (ENG.). 48p. (gr. 8-9). lib. bdg. 25.27 *(978-0-7660-4286-5(3),* 4b9775f2-81ec-4397-b575-116672888b45) Enslow Publishing, LLC.

Great Careers in the Sports Industry: Set 2, 12 vols. 2014. (Great Careers in the Sports Industry Ser.). (ENG.). 160p. (YA). (gr. 7-7). 264.78 *(978-1-4777-7522-6(6),* ff8daf26-bee7-431d-aa0e-5c4750baa08a) Rosen Publishing Group, Inc., The.

Great Careers in the Sports Industry: Sets 1-2. 2014. (Great Careers in the Sports Industry Ser.). 160p. (YA). (gr. 7-12). 409.50 *(978-1-4777-8098-5(X))* Rosen Publishing Group, Inc., The.

Greenberger, Robert. Careers in Artificial Intelligence. (Cutting-Edge Careers Ser.). 64p. (gr. 7-7). 2009. 55.90 *(978-1-61512-098-7(X))* 2007. (ENG., Illus.). (YA). lib. bdg. 37.13 *(978-1-4042-0953-4(0),* c56562ac-f5dc-45c4-a4bd-52bbc1799d47) Rosen Publishing Group, Inc., The.

Gregory, Josh. Hydrologist. 2013. (21st Century Skills Library: Cool STEM Careers Ser.). (ENG., Illus.). 32p. (gr. 4-8). (J). pap. 14.21 *(978-1-62431-025-6(7),* 202457); 32.07 *(978-1-62431-001-0(X),* 202455) Cherry Lake Publishing.

Gustaitis, Joseph Alan. Arctic Trucker, 1 vol. 2011. (Dirty & Dangerous Jobs Ser.). (ENG., Illus.). 32p. (gr. 3-3). 31.21 *(978-1-60870-169-8(7),* 7ef75d26-21d1-484b-a635-d1be48f1168c) Cavendish Square Publishing LLC.

Haddock, Patricia. Careers in Banking & Finance. 2009. (Career Resource Library). 192p. (gr. 7-12). 63.90 *(978-1-60853-398-5(0))* Rosen Publishing Group, Inc., The.

Haegele, Katie. Cool Careers Without College for Nature Lovers. 2009. (Cool Careers Without College Ser.). 144p. (gr. 6-6). 66.50 *(978-1-61511-961-5(2));* 2nd ed. (ENG., Illus.). (J). (gr. 7-7). 41.13 *(978-1-4358-5245-7(1),* fd88bd8b-26f5-4390-86d5-d7c6a80dbf20) Rosen Publishing Group, Inc., The.

Hagler, Gina. Money-Making Opportunities for Teens Who Are Artistic, 1 vol. 2013. (Make Money Now! Ser.). (ENG., Illus.). 80p. (YA). (gr. 7-7). lib. bdg. 38.41 *(978-1-4488-9387-4(9),* c4f51914-1559-4110-b282-9142951b13c5) Rosen Publishing Group, Inc., The.

Hall, Linley Erin. Careers in Biotechnology. 2009. (Cutting-Edge Careers Ser.). 64p. (gr. 7-7). 55.90 *(978-1-61512-099-4(8))* Rosen Publishing Group, Inc., The.

Hand, Carol. Getting Paid to Produce Videos, 1 vol. 2016. (Turning Your Tech Hobbies into a Career Ser.). (ENG., Illus.). 80p. (J). (gr. 7-7). 37.47 *(978-1-5081-7292-5(7),* b40702c0-9655-4b46-b648-65d67ecf36a2) Rosen Publishing Group, Inc., The.

Harmon, Daniel E. Careers in Explosives & Arson Investigation. 2009. (Careers in Forensics Ser.). 64p. (gr. 5-5). 58.50 *(978-1-61511-803-8(9),* Rosen Reference) Rosen Publishing Group, Inc., The.

—Jobs in Environmental Cleanup & Emergency Hazmat Response, 1 vol. 2010. (Green Careers Ser.). (ENG., Illus.). 80p. (YA). (gr. 6-6). lib. bdg. 38.47 *(978-1-4358-3570-2(0),* 4e9364fd-9fe0-47fe-8634-46249a9de995) Rosen Publishing Group, Inc., The.

Hayhurst, Chris. Cool Careers Without College for Animal Lovers. 2009. (Cool Careers Without College Ser.). 144p. (gr. 6-6). 66.50 *(978-1-61511-955-4(8))* Rosen Publishing Group, Inc., The.

Heiman, Diane & Suneby, Liz. See What You Can Be: Explore Careers That Could Be for You! Wood, Tracey, illus. 2009. (ENG.). 108p. (gr. 4-7). spiral bd. 9.95 *(978-1-59369-277-3(3))* American Girl Publishing, Inc.

Heling, Kathryn. Clothesline Clues to Jobs People Do. 2014. 17.95 *(978-1-63419-654-3(6))* Perfection Learning Corp.

Heling, Kathryn & Hembrook, Deborah. Clothesline Clues to Jobs People Do. Davies, Andy Robert, illus. 2012. (ENG.). 40p. (J). (gr. -1-2). 15.99 *(978-1-58089-251-3(5))* Charlesbridge Publishing, Inc.

Henneberg, Susan. Money-Making Opportunities for Teens Who Like Working with Kids, 1 vol. 2013. (Make Money Now! Ser.). (ENG., Illus.). 80p. (YA). (gr. 7-7). lib. bdg. 38.41 *(978-1-4488-9385-0(2),* c76f2e72-638b-4924-91fd-5ee4d977b4e9) Rosen Publishing Group, Inc., The.

Hinton, Kerry. Cool Careers Without College for People Who Love Food. 2009. (Cool Careers Without College Ser.). 144p. (gr. 6-6). 66.50 *(978-1-61511-966-0(3));* 2nd ed. (ENG., Illus.). (J). (gr. 7-7). lib. bdg. 41.13 *(978-1-4358-5246-4(X),* 1ed74a3b-b2a8-43db-a4ac-17d13cfedda1) Rosen Publishing Group, Inc., The.

Hovanec, Erin. Careers as a Content Provider for the Web. 2009. (Library of E-Commerce & Internet Careers Ser.). 64p. (gr. 5-5). 58.50 *(978-1-60853-578-1(9))* Rosen Publishing Group, Inc., The.

Howard, Ayanna. On the Job with an Engineer. 2003. (Adventures in Science Ser.). (J). lib. bdg. *(978-1-58417-059-4(X))* Lake Street Pubs.

Howell, Sara. Chemists at Work, 1 vol. 2017. (Scientists at Work Ser.). (ENG., Illus.). 32p. (J). (gr. 2-3). pap. 13.90 *(978-1-68048-753-4(1),* b206361e-53b0-4c7b-b91a-bdbefac396d8, Britannica Educational Publishing) Rosen Publishing Group, Inc., The.

Hunt, Christopher. Victory after High School: Survive or Thrive — -You Choose! 2005. 144p. (YA). per. 16.95 *(978-0-9765973-4-6(9))* Adjust Communications.

JIST Works. Young Person's Occupational Outlook Handbook, Fifth Edition. 5th ed. 2004. (Illus.). 336p. pap. 19.95 *(978-1-59357-125-2(9),* J1259, JIST Works) JIST Publishing.

Jobs to Do. 2017. (J). *(978-0-7166-7949-3(3))* World Bk., Inc.

Jones, Molly. Top 10 Tips for Planning for a Career, 1 vol. 2012. (Tips for Success Ser.). (ENG., Illus.). 64p. (J). (gr. 6-6). 37.13 *(978-1-4488-6863-6(7),* a6f4d3f9-3d08-4a8c-a2a6-de2c5c2e61a5) Rosen Publishing Group, Inc., The.

Jones, Sarah. Film. 2003. (Media Wise Ser.). (Illus.). 64p. (J). lib. bdg. 28.50 *(978-1-58340-256-6(X))* Black Rabbit Bks.

Kallen, Stuart A. Careers If You Like the Outdoors. 2017. (ENG.). 80p. (YA). (gr. 5-12). 39.93 *(978-1-68282-140-4(4))* ReferencePoint Pr., Inc.

Kamberg, Mary-Lane. Getting a Job in the IT Industry, 1 vol. 2016. (Job Basics: Getting the Job You Need Ser.). (ENG., Illus.). 80p. (J). (gr. 8-8). 38.41 *(978-1-4777-8556-0(6),* 7a4b3c14-e710-450a-bfa8-243907ff473c) Rosen Publishing Group, Inc., The.

Koster, Lorraine. Students Beware: Life Does Not Begin At 21. 2008. 108p. 22.95 *(978-0-595-50442-8(6));* pap. 12.95 *(978-0-595-47703-6(8))* iUniverse, Inc.

Kupperberg, Paul. Careers in Robotics. 2009. (Cutting-Edge Careers Ser.). 64p. (gr. 7-7). 55.90 *(978-1-61512-101-4(3))* Rosen Publishing Group, Inc., The.

La Bella, Laura. What Degree Do I Need to Pursue a Career in Bookkeeping & Accounting?, 1 vol. 2014. (Right Degree for Me Ser.). (ENG.). 80p. (YA). (gr. 7-7). 37.80 *(978-1-4777-7861-6(6),* 2f81d636-3ccd-412e-9df3-a79d105d69ac, Rosen Young Adult) Rosen Publishing Group, Inc., The.

Learning a Trade, Preparing for a Career, 16 vols. 2014. (Learning a Trade, Preparing for a Career Ser.). (ENG.). 80p. (YA). (gr. 6-6). 299.76 *(978-1-4777-7738-1(5),* 2872ea91-f9f3-48dc-8448-6ef0f342349b) Rosen Publishing Group, Inc., The.

Levin, Judith N. Careers Creating Search Engines. 2009. (Cutting-Edge Careers Ser.). 64p. (gr. 7-7). 55.90 *(978-1-61512-097-0(1))* Rosen Publishing Group, Inc., The.

Levy, Janey. Careers in Criminal Profiling. 2009. (Careers in Forensics Ser.). 64p. (gr. 5-5). 58.50 *(978-1-61511-801-4(2),* Rosen Reference) Rosen Publishing Group, Inc., The.

Liebman, Dan. Quiero Ser Vaquero. 2003. (Quiero Ser.). (SPA., Illus.). 24p. (J). (gr. -1-2). pap. 5.99 *(978-1-55297-747-7(1),* 0199f65f-bfd6-4b5b-b530-883b8b2a5a06) Firefly Bks., Ltd.

Liebman, Dan & Liebman, Dan. Quiero Ser Guardian de Zoologico. 2003. (Quiero Ser.).Tr. of I Want to Be a Zookeeper. (SPA., Illus.). 24p. (J). (gr. -1-2). pap. 5.99 *(978-1-55297-730-9(7),* 5484bd85-1d9d-4f9f-b47a-e715b86f5738) Firefly Bks., Ltd.

Linn, Dennis, et al. What Is My Song? Miranda, Francisco, illus. 2005. (ENG.). 32p. (J). 16.95 *(978-0-8091-6722-7(0),* 6722-0) Paulist Pr.

Loh-Hagan, Virginia. Mortician. 2015. (Illus.). 32p. (J). pap. *(978-1-63470-052-8(X))* Cherry Lake Publishing.

Lüsted, Marcia Amidon. The Vo-Tech Track to Success in Human Services, 1 vol. 2014. (Learning a Trade, Preparing for a Career Ser.). (ENG.). 80p. (J). (gr. 6-6). 37.47 *(978-1-4777-7732-9(6),* 49146809-b410-478b-ad32-0b37ff7f9a2c) Rosen Publishing Group, Inc., The.

Mapua, Jeff. A Career in Customer Service & Tech Support, 1 vol. 2014. (Essential Careers Ser.). (ENG.). 80p. (J). (gr. 6-6). 37.47 *(978-1-4777-7886-9(1),* c3eb4179-7698-44bf-b2b9-cde294d3a78e, Rosen Young Adult) Rosen Publishing Group, Inc., The.

Mara, Wil. Robotics Engineer. 2015. (21st Century Skills Library: Cool STEAM Careers Ser.). (ENG., Illus.). 32p. (J). (gr. 4-7). pap. 14.21 *(978-1-63362-045-2(X),* 205937) Cherry Lake Publishing.

Marcovitz, Hal. Teens & Career Choices. Developed in Association with the Gallup Organization Staff, ed. 2013. (Gallup Youth Survey: Major Issues & Trends Ser.: 14). 112p. (J). (gr. 7-18). 24.95 *(978-1-4222-2950-7(5))* Mason Crest.

Marlowe, Christie. Presenting Yourself: Business Manners, Personality, & Etiquette. 2013. (Earning $50,000 - $100,000 with a High School Diploma or Less Ser.: 14). 64p. (J). (gr. 7-18). 22.95 *(978-1-4222-2898-2(3))* Mason Crest.

Marlowe, Christie & Morkes, Andrew. Presenting Yourself: How to Make a Great Impression. 2019. (Careers with Earning Potential Ser.). (Illus.). 80p. (J). (gr. 12). lib. bdg. 34.60 *(978-1-4222-4328-2(1))* Mason Crest.

Marsh, Carole. Heroes & Helpers Careers Book. 2003. (Heroes & Helper Ser.). 48p. (J). (gr. 2-8). pap. 9.95 *(978-0-635-01095-7(X))* Gallopade International.

Maybury, Richard J. Uncle Eric Talks about Personal, Career, & Financial Security. Williams, Jane A. & Daniels, Kathryn, eds. 2nd ed. 2004. ("Uncle Eric" Bk.: 1). (ENG., Illus.). 187p. pap. 14.95 *(978-0-942617-38-2(X))* Bluestocking Pr.

McAlpine, Margaret. Working with Children, 1 vol. 2005. (My Future Career Ser.). (ENG., Illus.). 64p. (gr. 4-6). lib. bdg. 29.67 *(978-0-8368-4241-8(3),* e9721b2f-8cea-47ec-be17-0891d59599d2, Gareth Stevens Learning Library) Stevens, Gareth Publishing LLLP.

Mcginty, Alice B. Software Designer. (Coolcareers. com Ser.). 48p. (gr. 5-8). 2009. 53.00 *(978-1-61511-984-4(1),* Rosen Reference) 2003. (ENG.). (YA). lib. bdg. 34.47 *(978-0-8239-4086-8(1),* 79b388f3-bb23-47b5-85eb-0d4b888f8dd9) Rosen Publishing Group, Inc., The.

Messina, Noreen E. Teenwork: Four Teens Tell All: A Guide for Finding Jobs. 2005. (Illus.). 126p. (gr. 6-12). per. 12.75 *(978-1-59070-598-8(X))* Goodheart-Willcox Pub.

Meyer, Jared. Working in a War Zone: Military Contractors. 2009. (Extreme Careers Ser.). 64p. (gr. 5-5). 58.50 *(978-1-61512-422-0(5),* Rosen Reference) Rosen Publishing Group, Inc., The.

Meyer, Susan. Careers As a Bookkeeper & Auditor, 1 vol. 2013. (Essential Careers Ser.). (ENG.). 80p. (YA). (gr. 6-6). 37.47 *(978-1-4777-1792-9(7),* f6157356-db72-4402-91fa-41dff1ca8ff9) Rosen Publishing Group, Inc., The.

Mezzanotte, Jim. Police, 1 vol. 2011. (Working Animals Ser.). (ENG.). 64p. (gr. 5-5). 31.21 *(978-1-60870-166-7(2),* a8196bcc-b54c-489c-b5e2-3d9dfe94873c) Cavendish Square Publishing LLC.

Moore, Elizabeth. Keeping Us Safe, 1 vol. 2011. (Wonder Readers Emergent Level Ser.). (ENG.). 8p. (gr. -1-1). (J). pap. 6.25 *(978-1-4296-7845-2(3),* 118158); pap. 35.94 *(978-1-4296-8232-9(9),* Capstone Pr.) Capstone.

Morgan, Genevieve. Undecided, 2nd Edition: Navigating Life & Learning after High School. 2nd rev. ed. 2020. (ENG., Illus.).

T U V

288p. (J). (gr. 9-12). 37.32 *(978-1-5415-9778-5(8),* 097e9832-5f6f-4890-96ca-690603c41cba, Zest Bks.) Lerner Publishing Group.

Morkes, Andrew. Professional Hackers. 2019. (Cool Careers in Science Ser.). (Illus.). 96p. (J). (gr. 12). lib. bdg. 34.60 *(978-1-4222-4300-8(1))* Mason Crest.

Morkes, Andrew & McKenna, Amy. Nontraditional Careers for Women & Men: More Than 30 Great Jobs for Women & Men with Apprenticeships Through Phds. 2011. (ENG., Illus.). vii, 280p. (J). pap. 19.95 *(978-0-9745251-9-8(7))* College & Career Pr., LLC.

Mozer, Mindy. Careers As a Commissioned Sales Representative, 1 vol. 2013. (Essential Careers Ser.). (ENG.). 80p. (YA). (gr. 6-6). 37.47 *(978-1-4777-1794-3(3),* 591954f5-9c30-4825-9ff3-64dfb57ba62a) Rosen Publishing Group, Inc., The.

Murdico, Suzanne J. Bomb Squad Experts: Life Defusing Explosive Devices. (Extreme Careers Ser.). 64p. (gr. 5-5). 2009. 58.50 *(978-1-61512-386-5(5),* Rosen Reference) 2004. (ENG., Illus.). (YA). lib. bdg. 37.13 *(978-0-8239-3968-8(5),* 297c9e52-9fbb-4eb2-8135-c4ba5f565b2b) Rosen Publishing Group, Inc., The.

Nagle, Jeanne M. Careers in Television. 2009. (Career Resource Library). 192p. (gr. 7-12). 63.90 *(978-1-60853-404-3(9))* Rosen Publishing Group, Inc., The.

Neale, Vivienne. Keep Your Options Open. (ENG., Illus.). x, 134p. (J). pap. 8.99 *(978-0-340-66088-1(0))* Hodder & Stoughton GBR. Dist: Trafalgar Square Publishing.

New Cool Careers Without College: Set 1, 12 vols. 2013. (Cool Careers Without College Ser.). (ENG.). 144p. (YA). (gr. 7-7). 246.72 *(978-1-4777-1831-5(1),* fa0e0bf1-88ec-44aa-9737-e47bd73591ad) Rosen Publishing Group, Inc., The.

Orr, Tamra B. Money-Making Opportunities for Teens Who Like Working Outside, 1 vol. 2013. (Make Money Now! Ser.). (ENG., Illus.). 80p. (YA). (gr. 7-7). lib. bdg. 38.41 *(978-1-4488-9383-6(6),* b870f6ad-bdc8-44e9-9b23-0389cffe871e) Rosen Publishing Group, Inc., The.

Owen, Ruth. Building Green Places: Careers in Planning, Designing, & Building. 2009. (Green-Collar Careers Ser.). (ENG., Illus.). 64p. (J). (gr. 5-8). pap. *(978-0-7787-4863-2(4));* lib. bdg. *(978-0-7787-4852-6(9))* Crabtree Publishing Co.

Parks, Peggy J. Veterinarian. 2004. (EXPLORING CAREERS Ser.). (ENG.). (J). 27.50 *(978-0-7377-2068-6(9),* Greenhaven Pr., Inc.) Cengage Gale.

—Writer. 2003. (Illus.). 48p. (J). 26.20 *(978-0-7377-2069-3(7),* Greenhaven Pr., Inc.) Cengage Gale.

Pasternak, Ceel. Cool Careers for Girls in Travel & Hospitality. 2003. (ENG., Illus.). 144p. (YA). (gr. 8-17). pap. 13.95 *(978-1-57023-192-6(3))* Impact Pubns.

Payment, Simone. Cool Careers Without College for People Who Love to Travel. 2009. (Cool Careers Without College Ser.). 144p. (gr. 6-6). 66.50 *(978-1-61511-980-6(9))* Rosen Publishing Group, Inc., The.

Penn, Maya S. You Got This! Unleash Your Awesomeness, Find Your Path, & Change Your World. 2016. (ENG., Illus.). 224p. 17.99 *(978-1-5011-2371-9(8),* North Star Way) Simon & Schuster.

Penna, Christine. Careers in Network Engineering. 2009. (Library of E-Commerce & Internet Careers Ser.). 64p. (gr. 5-5). 58.50 *(978-1-60853-581-1(9))* Rosen Publishing Group, Inc., The.

Perritano, John. The Most Disgusting Jobs on the Planet, 1 vol. 2012. (Disgusting Stuff Ser.). (ENG., Illus.). 48p. (J). (gr. 5-9). lib. bdg. 32.65 *(978-1-4296-7532-1(2),* 117106) Capstone.

Personal Services. 2nd rev. ed. 2007. (Ferguson's Careers in Focus Ser.). (ENG., Illus.). 192p. (gr. 6-12). 32.95 *(978-0-8160-6592-9(6),* P127106. Ferguson Publishing Company) Infobase Holdings, Inc.

Petley, Julian. Newspapers & Magazines. 2003. (Media Wise Ser.). (Illus.). 64p. (J). lib. bdg. 28.50 *(978-1-58340-258-0(6))* Black Rabbit Bks.

Publishing, Ferguson. Professional Sports Organizations. 2012. (Career Launcher Ser.). (ENG.). 130p. (gr. 9). 34.95 *(978-0-8160-7964-3(1),* P179133, Ferguson Publishing Company) Infobase Holdings, Inc.

Publishing, Ferguson, creator. Mathematics & Physics. 2003. (Ferguson's Careers in Focus Ser.). (ENG., Illus.). 192p. (gr. 6-12). 29.95 *(978-0-89434-413-8(7),* P053165, Ferguson Publishing Company) Infobase Holdings, Inc.

—Therapists. 2003. (Ferguson's Careers in Focus Ser.). (ENG.). 192p. (gr. 6-12). 29.95 *(978-0-89434-412-1(9),* P053164, Ferguson Publishing Company) Infobase Holdings, Inc.

Publishing, Ferguson, et al. Preparing for a Career in Sports. 2006. (What Can I Do Now? Ser.). (ENG., Illus.). 172p. (gr. 6-12). 22.95 *(978-0-89434-254-7(1),* P053083, Ferguson Publishing Company) Infobase Holdings, Inc.

—Preparing for a Career in the Environment. 2006. (What Can I Do Now? Ser.). (ENG., Illus.). 200p. (gr. 6-12). 22.95 *(978-0-89434-249-3(5),* P053078, Ferguson Publishing Company) Infobase Holdings, Inc.

Radomski, Kassandra Kathleen. So You Want to Be a U. S. Representative. 2019. (Being in Government Ser.). (ENG., Illus.). 32p. (J). (gr. 3-6). pap. 7.95 *(978-1-5435-7528-6(5),* 141058); lib. bdg. 27.99 *(978-1-5435-7196-7(4),* 140441) Capstone.

—So You Want to Be a U. S. Senator. 2019. (Being in Government Ser.). (ENG., Illus.). 32p. (J). (gr. 3-6). pap. 7.95 *(978-1-5435-7529-3(3),* 141060); lib. bdg. 27.99 *(978-1-5435-7195-0(6),* 140440) Capstone.

Rarus, Pat. Careers in E-Commerce. 2019. (E-Careers Ser.). (ENG.). 80p. (J). (gr. 6-12). 41.27 *(978-1-68282-611-9(2))* ReferencePoint Pr., Inc.

Rauf, Don. Working As a Hairstylist in Your Community, 1 vol. 2015. (Careers in Your Community Ser.). (ENG., Illus.). 80p. (J). (gr. 7-8). 37.47 *(978-1-4994-6121-3(6),* 96409e67-eec7-49c8-b783-077c39f1bc02, Rosen Young Adult) Rosen Publishing Group, Inc., The.

Reeves, Diane Lindsey. Business. 2017. (Bright Futures Press: World of Work Ser.). (ENG., Illus.). 32p. (J). (gr. 4-7). lib. bdg. 32.07 *(978-1-5341-0171-5(3),* 210154) Cherry Lake Publishing.

—Career Ideas for Kids Who Like Adventure & Travel. 2nd rev. ed. 2007. (Career Ideas for Kids Ser.). (ENG., Illus.). 208p. (gr. 4-9). 32.95 *(978-0-8160-6547-9(0),* P127238, Checkmark Bks.) Infobase Holdings, Inc.

—Finance. 2017. (Bright Futures Press: World of Work Ser.). (ENG., Illus.). 32p. (J). (gr. 4-7). lib. bdg. 32.07 *(978-1-5341-0173-9(X),* 210162) Cherry Lake Publishing.

—Find Your Future in Science. 2016. (Bright Futures Press: Find Your Future in STEAM Ser.). (ENG., Illus.). 32p. (J). (gr. 4-6). 32.07 *(978-1-63471-898-1(4),* 208913) Cherry Lake Publishing.

—Goofy Jobs. 2009. (Way Out Work Ser.). (ENG., Illus.). 48p. (gr. 3-5). 29.95 *(978-1-60413-130-7(6),* P173466, Ferguson Publishing Company) Infobase Holdings, Inc.

—Government. 2017. (Bright Futures Press: World of Work Ser.). (ENG., Illus.). 32p. (J). (gr. 4-7). lib. bdg. 32.07 *(978-1-5341-0174-6(8),* 210166) Cherry Lake Publishing.

—Gross Jobs. 2009. (Way Out Work Ser.). (ENG., Illus.). 48p. (gr. 3-5). 29.95 *(978-1-60413-131-4(4),* P173470, Ferguson Publishing Company) Infobase Holdings, Inc.

—Gutsy Jobs. 2009. (Way Out Work Ser.). (ENG., Illus.). 48p. (gr. 3-5). 29.95 *(978-1-60413-133-8(0),* P173469, Ferguson Publishing Company) Infobase Holdings, Inc.

—Hospitality & Tourism. 2017. (Bright Futures Press: World of Work Ser.). (ENG., Illus.). 32p. (J). (gr. 4-7). lib. bdg. 32.07 *(978-1-5341-0175-3(6),* 210170) Cherry Lake Publishing.

—Human Service. 2017. (Bright Futures Press: World of Work Ser.). (ENG., Illus.). 32p. (J). (gr. 4-7). lib. bdg. 32.07 *(978-1-5341-0176-0(4),* 210174) Cherry Lake Publishing.

—Marketing, Sales & Service. 2017. (Bright Futures Press: World of Work Ser.). (ENG., Illus.). 32p. (J). (gr. 4-7). lib. bdg. 32.07 *(978-1-5341-0177-7(2),* 210178) Cherry Lake Publishing.

Reeves, Diane Lindsey & White, Kelly. Choose a Career Adventure at the White House. 2016. (Bright Futures Press: Choose a Career Adventure Ser.). (ENG., Illus.). 32p. (J). (gr. 4-6). 32.07 *(978-1-63471-916-2(6),* 208985) Cherry Lake Publishing.

Reina, Mary. Earn Money. 2015. (Money & You Ser.). (ENG., Illus.). 24p. (J). (gr. -1-2). pap. 5.95 *(978-1-4914-2299-1(8),* 127761) Capstone.

Riley, Rowan. Great Careers with a High School Diploma: Hospitality, Human Services, & Tourism. 2008. (Great Careers with a High School Diploma Ser.). 93p. (C). (gr. 9). 32.95 *(978-0-8160-7048-0(2),* Ferguson Publishing Company) Infobase Holdings, Inc.

Rissman, Rebecca. You're Hired! Business Basics Every Babysitter Needs to Know, 1 vol. 2014. (Babysitter's Backpack Ser.). (ENG., Illus.). 32p. (J). (gr. 3-9). 28.65 *(978-1-4914-0766-0(2),* 125998) Capstone.

Rocha, Toni L. Careers in Magazine Publishing. 2009. (Career Resource Library). 192p. (gr. 7-12). 63.90 *(978-1-60853-399-2(9))* Rosen Publishing Group, Inc., The.

Roff, Jason T. Careers in E-Commerce: Software Development. 2009. (Library of E-Commerce & Internet Careers Ser.). 64p. (gr. 5-5). 58.50 *(978-1-60853-580-4(0))* Rosen Publishing Group, Inc., The.

Rose, Simon. Animal Caretaker. 2014. (J). *(978-1-4896-2982-1(3))* Weigl Pubs., Inc.

Rowe, Brooke. What's Your Dream Job? 2015. (Best Quiz Ever Ser.). (ENG., Illus.). 32p. (J). (gr. 4-8). 32.07 *(978-1-63470-035-1(X),* 206812) Cherry Lake Publishing.

Roza, Greg. Great Networking Skills. (Work Readiness Ser.). 64p. 2009. (gr. 6-6). 58.50 *(978-1-60854-826-2(0))* 2008. (Illus.). (YA). (gr. 8-12). lib. bdg. 35.45 *(978-1-4042-1420-0(8))* Rosen Publishing Group, Inc., The.

Ryan, Jerry & Ryan, Roberta. Preparing for Career Success ExamView(r) Test Generator. 3rd ed. (YA). cd-rom 99.95 *(978-1-59357-211-2(5),* J2115) JIST Publishing.

—Preparing for Career Success Student Activity Book. 3rd ed. 208p. (YA). pap. 8.95 *(978-1-59357-209-9(3),* J2093) JIST Publishing.

Ryan, Peter K. Powering up a Career in Robotics, 1 vol. 2015. (Preparing for Tomorrow's Careers Ser.). (ENG., Illus.). 80p. (J). (gr. 7-8). 37.47 *(978-1-4994-6085-8(6),* 19b0185e-c2ec-4238-af25-8410ba96d6f5, Rosen Young Adult) Rosen Publishing Group, Inc., The.

Sanna, Ellyn. Politician. 2004. (Careers with Character Ser.). (Illus.). 96p. (YA). (gr. 7-18). lib. bdg. 22.95 *(978-1-59084-320-8(7))* Mason Crest.

Santos, Edson. Cool Careers Without College for People who Love to Buy Things. 2009. (Cool Careers Without College Ser.). 144p. (gr. 6-6). 66.50 *(978-1-61511-971-4(X))* Rosen Publishing Group, Inc., The.

Sawyer, Sarah. Career Building Through Podcasting. 2009. (Digital Career Building Ser.). 64p. (gr. 6-6). 58.50 *(978-1-61512-170-0(6))* Rosen Publishing Group, Inc., The.

—Careers in DNA Analysis. 2009. (Careers in Forensics Ser.). 64p. (gr. 5-5). 58.50 *(978-1-61511-802-1(0),* Rosen Reference) Rosen Publishing Group, Inc., The.

Schwartz, Tina P. Writing & Publishing: The Ultimate Teen Guide. 2009. (It Happened to Me Ser.: 27). (ENG., Illus.). 282p. (gr. 9-18). instr.'s gde. ed. 62.00 *(978-0-8108-5647-9(6))* Scarecrow Pr., Inc.

Seuss. Maybe You Should Fly a Jet! Maybe You Should Be a Vet! Kennedy, Kelly, illus. 2020. (Beginner Books(R) Ser.). (ENG.). 48p. (J). (gr. -1-2). 9.99 *(978-1-9848-9406-9(4));* lib. bdg. 12.99 *(978-1-9848-9407-6(2))* Random Hse. Children's Bks. (Random Hse. Bks. for Young Readers).

Sheen, Barbara. Careers in Healthcare. 2014. (Exploring Careers). (ENG., Illus.). 80p. (J). lib. bdg. *(978-1-60152-648-9(2))* ReferencePoint Pr., Inc.

Snyder, Gail. Teen Guide to Starting a Business. 2016. (ENG.). 64p. (J). (gr. 5-12). lib. bdg. *(978-1-68282-088-9(2))* ReferencePoint Pr., Inc.

Sommers, Michael. Wildlife Photographers: Life Through a Lens. 2009. (Extreme Careers Ser.). 64p. (gr. 5-5). 58.50 *(978-1-61512-421-3(7),* Rosen Reference) Rosen Publishing Group, Inc., The.

Spaulding, Jeffrey. Career Building Through Digital Sampling & Remixing. 2009. (Digital Career Building Ser.). 64p. (gr. 6-6). 58.50 *(978-1-61512-165-6(X))* Rosen Publishing Group, Inc., The.

Steinfeld, Alan. Careers in Alternative Medicine. 2009. (Career Resource Library). 192p. (gr. 7-12). 63.90 *(978-1-60853-396-1(4))* Rosen Publishing Group, Inc., The.

Swaine, Meg. Career Building Through Interactive Online Games. 2009. (Digital Career Building Ser.). 64p. (gr. 6-6). 58.50 *(978-1-61512-167-0(6))* Rosen Publishing Group, Inc., The.

Syrewicz, Connor. Energizing Energy Markets: Clean Coal, Shale, Oil, Wind, & Solar. 2013. (Earning $50,000 - $100,000 with a High School Diploma or Less Ser.: 14). 64p. (J). (gr. 7-18). 22.95 *(978-1-4222-2894-4(0))* Mason Crest.

—Personal Assistant. 2013. (Earning $50,000 - $100,000 with a High School Diploma or Less Ser.: 14). 64p. (J). (gr. 7-18). 22.95 *(978-1-4222-2897-5(5))* Mason Crest.

Taylor, Charlotte. Ways to Make Money Working Outside, 1 vol. 2019. (Cash in on Your Skills Ser.). (ENG.). 80p. (gr. 7-7). pap. 18.60 *(978-1-9785-1548-2(0),* 6c65ffdb-9e47-4ee8-820a-5c8c71c2a457) Enslow Publishing, LLC.

Thompson, Elissa & Roza, Greg. Learn How to Network at Work, 1 vol. 2019. (Building Job Skills Ser.). (ENG.). 64p. (gr. 6-6). pap. 13.95 *(978-1-7253-4715-1(6),* 45d7a00f-3929-4905-8477-ec56b4e32982) Rosen Publishing Group, Inc., The.

Timmons, Angie. Ways to Make Money with Art, 1 vol. 2019. (Cash in on Your Skills Ser.). (ENG.). 80p. (gr. 7-7). pap. 18.60 *(978-1-9785-1542-0(1),* 5f6d14f2-3452-4789-8695-7e5bddfba5fe) Enslow Publishing, LLC.

Trabajo en Grupo Series: Set, 12 vols. 2003. (Trabajo en Grupo (Working Together) Ser.). (SPA., Illus.). (J). (gr. 1-2). lib. bdg. 157.62 *(978-0-8239-6915-9(0),* aef7c2a9-c32b-4f6b-933f-7a1c2545004f, Editorial Buenas Letras) Rosen Publishing Group, Inc., The.

Turner, Cherie. Adventure Tour Guides: Life on Extreme Outdoor Adventures. 2009. (Extreme Careers Ser.). 64p. (gr. 5-5). 58.50 *(978-1-61512-383-4(0),* Rosen Reference) Rosen Publishing Group, Inc., The.

Uschan, Michael V. Careers If You Like Government & Politics. 2016. (ENG.). 80p. (J). (gr. 5-12). lib. bdg. *(978-1-68282-000-1(9))* ReferencePoint Pr., Inc.

Ventura, Marne. Marine Biologist. 2019. (Jobs with Animals Ser.). (ENG., Illus.). 32p. (J). (gr. 4-6). pap. 7.95 *(978-1-5435-6046-6(6),* 140091); lib. bdg. 28.65 *(978-1-5435-5784-8(8),* 139740) Capstone.

Webber, Diane. Shot & Framed: Photographers at the Crime Scene. 2007. (24/7: Science Behind the Scenes Ser.). (ENG., Illus.). 64p. (YA). (gr. 9-12). 29.00 *(978-0-531-12063-7(5),* Watts, Franklin) Scholastic Library Publishing.

When I Grow Up. 2014. (When I Grow Up Ser.). 24p. (J). (gr. k-2). pap. 48.90 *(978-1-4824-1593-3(3))* Stevens, Gareth Publishing LLLP.

Wilcox, Christine. Careers in Environmental Conservation. 2017. (ENG.). 80p. (YA). (gr. 5-12). *(978-1-68282-203-6(6))* ReferencePoint Pr., Inc.

Willett, Edward. Careers in Outer Space: New Business Opportunities. 2009. (Career Resource Library). 192p. (gr. 7-12). 63.90 *(978-1-60853-401-2(4))* Rosen Publishing Group, Inc., The.

Williams, Anna Graf, et al. The Family Guide to the American Workplace. Williams, Anna Graf, ed. 2003. (Illus.). 272p. per. 31.00 *(978-0-9705790-4-1(7),* 866/332-5905) Learnovation, LLC.

Winning at Work Readiness, 10 vols. 2014. (Winning at Work Readiness Ser.). (ENG.). 64p. (YA). (gr. 6-6). 180.65 *(978-1-4777-7794-7(6),* 5f692016-e60d-4807-bd53-e978519f879f) Rosen Publishing Group, Inc., The.

Wood, Alix. Explosives Expert, 1 vol., 1. 2014. (World's Coolest Jobs Ser.). (ENG.). 32p. (J). (gr. 4-4). lib. bdg. 28.93 *(978-1-4777-6011-6(3),* d29aba82-d73a-47a8-95a0-1ff4bb54384c); pap. 11.00 *(978-1-4777-6012-3(1),* 2c2d58b1-30f9-42da-a685-eb93359ca587) Rosen Publishing Group, Inc., The. (PowerKids Pr.).

Wright, Dixie Lee. Job Smarts: 12 Steps to Job Success. 2nd ed. 2003. 80p. pap., wbk. ed. 13.95 *(978-1-59357-028-6(7),* JIST Works) JIST Publishing.

—Job Smarts Instructor's Manual: 12 Steps to Job Success for Students with Special Needs. 2nd ed. 2003. 96p. pap., tchr. ed. 29.95 *(978-1-59357-029-3(5),* JIST Works) JIST Publishing.

Yomtov, Nel. Transportation Planner. 2013. (21st Century Skills Library: Cool STEM Careers Ser.). (ENG., Illus.). 32p. (J). (gr. 4-8). 32.07 *(978-1-62431-008-9(7),* 202483); pap. 14.21 *(978-1-62431-032-4(X),* 202485) Cherry Lake Publishing.

—Urban Planner. 2015. (21st Century Skills Library: Cool STEAM Careers Ser.). (ENG., Illus.). 32p. (J). (gr. 4-7). 32.07 *(978-1-63362-009-4(3),* 205948) Cherry Lake Publishing.

VOCATIONS

see Professions

VOICE

see also Phonetics; Public Speaking; Singing; Speech

Comprehending & Verbalizing Visual Clues. 2003. 100p. (J). spiral bd. 28.00 *(978-1-886143-54-8(4))* Great Ideas for Teaching, Inc.

Feierabend, John M. The Book of Pitch Exploration: Can Your Voice Do This? 2004. (First Steps in Music Ser.). (ENG.). 33p. (J). pap. 11.95 *(978-1-57999-242-2(0));* (Illus.). (gr. -1-2). pap. 12.95 *(978-1-57999-265-1(X),* G-5276) G I A Pubns., Inc.

Verdick, Elizabeth. Voices Are Not for Yelling. Heinlen, Marieka, illus. 2015. (Best Behavior(r) Board Book Ser.). (ENG.). (J). 26p. (— 1). bds. 9.99 *(978-1-57542-500-9(9));* 40p. (gr. -1-2). pap. 11.99 *(978-1-57542-501-6(7))* Free Spirit Publishing Inc.

—Voices Are Not for Yelling / la Voz No Es para Gritar. Heinlen, Marieka, illus. 2017. (Best Behavior(r) Board Book Ser.). (ENG.). (J). (gr. -1 — 1). 26p. bds. 9.99 *(978-1-63198-194-4(3),* 81944); 40p. pap. 11.99 *(978-1-63198-191-3(9),* 81913) Free Spirit Publishing Inc.

VOLCANOES

Adams, Simon. My Best Book of Volcanoes. 2020. (Best Book Of Ser.). (ENG.). 32p. (J). pap. 7.99 *(978-0-7534-7539-3(1),* 900211379, Kingfisher) Roaring Brook Pr.

Alkire, Jessie. Super Simple Volcano Projects: Science Activities for Future Volcanologists. 2017. (Super Simple Earth Investigations Ser.). (ENG., Illus.). 32p. (J). (gr. k-4). lib. bdg. 34.21 *(978-1-5321-1240-9(8),* 27627, Super SandCastle) ABDO Publishing Co.

Anderson, Michael. Investigating Plate Tectonics, Earthquakes & Volcanoes, 1 vol. 2011. (Introduction to Earth Science Ser.). (ENG., Illus.). 88p. (J). (gr. 8-8). lib. bdg. 35.29 *(978-1-61530-504-9(1),* 772c2243-b29e-4dec-b31b-41c4c0e6f6be) Rosen Publishing Group, Inc., The.

Arlon, Penelope. Volcanoes & Other Forces of Nature. 2017. (LEGO Nonfiction Ser.). (ENG.). 64p. (J). (gr. 1-3). pap. 8.99 *(978-1-338-14913-5(X))* Scholastic, Inc.

Armentrout, David. Volcanoes. 2009. (ENG.). 32p. pap. 3.99 *(978-0-8249-1411-0(2),* Ideals Pubns.) Worthy Publishing.

Armour, Cy. Volcanoes!, 1 vol. 2nd rev. ed. 2011. (TIME for KIDS(r): Informational Text Ser.). (ENG.). 24p. (gr. 2-3). pap. 9.99 *(978-1-4333-3615-7(4))* Teacher Created Materials, Inc.

Aronin, Miriam. Saving Animals from Volcanoes. 2011. (Rescuing Animals from Disasters Ser.). 32p. (YA). (gr. 2-5). lib. bdg. 28.50 *(978-1-61772-291-2(X))* Bearport Publishing Co., Inc.

Ashworth, William B., Jr. Vulcan's Forge anda Fingal's Cave: Volcanoes, Basalt, & the Discovery of Geological Time. 2004. (Illus.). per. 20.00 *(978-0-9763590-0-5(6))* Linda Hall Library.

Bankier, William. The Mount St. Helens Volcano. Miller, Zachary N., ed. Taylor, Marjorie, illus. rev. ed. 2003. (Take Ten Ser.). 45p. (J). (gr. 4-12). pap. 4.95 *(978-1-58659-023-9(5))* Artesian Pr.

Barlow, Dave. Tome of Knowledge; Volcanoes. 2005. (ENG., Illus.). 20p. (YA). per. 4.95 *(978-0-9725230-9-7(X))* Wandering Sage Pubns., LLC.

Barr, Linda. Volcano! When a Mountain Explodes, 6 vols. 2003. (High Five Reading - Red Ser.). (ENG.). 48p. (gr. 3-4). pap. 54.00 *(978-0-7368-2836-9(2));* (Illus.). per. 9.00 *(978-0-7368-2826-0(5))* Capstone.

Bauer, Marion Dane. Volcano! Ready-To-Read Level 1. Wallace, John, illus. 2008. (Natural Disasters Ser.). (ENG.). 32p. (J). (gr. -1-1). pap. 4.99 *(978-1-4169-2549-1(X),* Aladdin) Simon & Schuster Children's Publishing.

Baynard, Kate Holland & Baynard, Holland Callaway. Holland Goes to Pompeii: A brief look at the buried city & its famous volcano named Vesuvius. 2010. 16p. 12.50 *(978-1-4490-4697-2(5))* AuthorHouse.

Benchmark Education Company. Volcanoes (Teacher Guide) Nature's Awesome Power. 2004. *(978-1-4108-2586-5(8))* Benchmark Education Co.

Benoit, Peter. The Krakatau Eruption. 2011. (J). pap. *(978-0-531-29027-9(1))* Children's Pr., Ltd.

—The Krakatau Eruption. 2011. (True Bks.). 48p. (J). (gr. 3-5). 29.00 *(978-0-531-20628-7(9));* (ENG., Illus.). pap. 6.95 *(978-0-531-28997-6(4))* Scholastic Library Publishing. (Children's Pr.).

Berg, Shannon. Hawaii Volcano Of 2018. 2019. (21st Century Disasters Ser.). (ENG., Illus.). 32p. (J). (gr. 2-3). pap. 9.95 *(978-1-64185-808-3(7),* 1641858087); lib. bdg. 31.35 *(978-1-64185-739-0(0),* 1641857390) North Star Editions. (Focus Readers).

Bodden, Valerie. Volcanoes. 2006. (Our World Ser.). (Illus.). 24p. (J). (gr. -1-3). lib. bdg. 16.95 *(978-1-58341-466-8(5),* Creative Education) Creative Co., The.

Branley, Franklyn M. Volcanoes. (J). Date not set. lib. bdg. 16.89 *(978-0-06-028012-3(3))* 2008. (ENG., Illus.). 40p. pap. 5.99 *(978-0-06-445189-5(5),* HarperCollins) HarperCollins Pubs.

Bredeson, Carmen. Fiery Volcano: The Eruption of Mount St. Helens, 1 vol. 2013. (Disasters: People in Peril Ser.). (ENG., Illus.). 48p. (gr. 5-7). 27.93 *(978-0-7660-4015-1(1),* d9e9dcfc-f9ef-4de1-93a5-e125f14434a8) Enslow Publishing, LLC.

Brooks, Susie. Earthquakes & Volcanoes, 1 vol. 2016. (Where on Earth? Ser.). (ENG.). 32p. (gr. 4-5). 27.93 *(978-1-4994-2256-6(3),* 29d6a1f5-1eeb-4c93-ae23-135e6a9e81ba, PowerKids Pr.) Rosen Publishing Group, Inc., The.

Brown, Laaren. Volcanoes: Run for Your Life! 2013. (Illus.). 32p. (J). *(978-0-545-62413-8(4))* Scholastic, Inc.

Bulletpoints Volcanoes & Earthquakes. 2005. (Illus.). (J). per. 4.99 *(978-1-933581-06-4(9))* Byeway Bks.

Chad, Jon. Science Comics: Volcanoes: Fire & Life. 2016. (Science Comics Ser.). (ENG., Illus.). 128p. (J). pap. 12.99 *(978-1-62672-360-3(5),* 900154792, First Second Bks.) Roaring Brook Pr.

Challen, Paul. Volcano Alert! 3rd rev. ed. 2011. (ENG., Illus.). 32p. (J). *(978-0-7787-1595-5(7));* (Disaster Alert! Ser.: No. 19). pap. *(978-0-7787-1628-0(7))* Crabtree Publishing Co.

Cimarusti, Nick. Exploring Volcanic Activity (Grade 4) rev. ed. 2018. (Smithsonian: Informational Text Ser.). (ENG., Illus.). 32p. (J). (gr. 3-5). pap. 11.99 *(978-1-4938-6703-5(2))* Teacher Created Materials, Inc.

Claybourne, Anna. Investigating Volcanoes. 2010. (Extreme! Ser.). (ENG.). 32p. (gr. 3-4). pap. 47.70 *(978-1-4296-5132-5(6),* Capstone Pr.) Capstone.

Close, Edward. Volcanoes: Fire from Below: Rocks & Minerals, 1 vol., 1. 2014. (Discovery Education: Earth & Space Science Ser.). (ENG.). 32p. (gr. 4-5). 28.93 *(978-1-4777-6186-1(1),* 3270ba6d-6f59-4262-ba70-a5f9203288d4, PowerKids Pr.) Rosen Publishing Group, Inc., The.

Cole, Joanna. Volcanoes & Earthquakes. 2014. (Magic School Bus Presents Ser.). lib. bdg. 17.20 *(978-0-606-36333-4(5))* Turtleback.

Cook, Mauliola. Discover Hawaii's Volcanoes: Birth by Fire. Orr, Katherine, illus. rev. ed. 2010. (ENG.). 44p. pap. *(978-1-59700-849-5(4))* Island Heritage Publishing.

Cook, Mauliola & Orr, Katherine. Discover His Birth by Fire Volcanoes. 2010. 44p. 9.95 *(978-1-59700-830-3(3))* Island Heritage Publishing.

Cooper, John. Volcanoes. 2016. (Wise Up Ser.). 32p. (gr. 2-6). 31.35 *(978-1-62588-342-1(0),* Smart Apple Media) Black Rabbit Bks.

Coss, Lauren. Volcanoes. 2013. (Earth in Action Ser.). (ENG., Illus.). 48p. (J). (gr. 4-8). pap. 18.50 *(978-1-62403-007-9(6),* 8682) ABDO Publishing Co.

The Crying Mountain: 6 Small Books. (Greetings Ser.: Vol. 1). 32p. (gr. 3-5). 31.00 *(978-0-7635-1841-7(7))* Rigby Education.

The Crying Mountain: Big Book. (Greetings Ser.: Vol. 1). 32p. (gr. 3-5). 31.00 (978-0-7635-3222-2(3)) Rigby Education.
Cunningham, Kevin. Volcanologist. 2015. (21st Century Skills Library: Cool STEAM Careers Ser.). (ENG., Illus.). 32p. (J). (gr. 4-7). 32.07 (978-1-63362-568-6(0), 206456) Cherry Lake Publishing.
Dayton, Connor. Volcanic Rocks. (Rocks & Minerals Ser.). 24p. (gr. 2-3). 2009. 42.50 (978-1-60852-503-4(1), PowerKids Pr.) 2007. (ENG., Illus.). (YA). lib. bdg. 26.27 (978-1-4042-3688-2(0), b601e067-75a8-47e3-bb40-10171ded1102) Rosen Publishing Group, Inc., The.
DK. DKfindout! Volcanoes. 2016. (DK Findout! Ser.). (ENG., Illus.). 64p. (J). (gr. 1-4). pap. 10.99 (978-1-4654-5425-6(X), DK Children) Dorling Kindersley Publishing, Inc.
—Ultimate Sticker Book: Volcano: More Than 250 Reusable Stickers. 2017. (Ultimate Sticker Book Ser.). (ENG.). 32p. (J). (gr. 1-4). pap. 6.99 (978-1-4654-5693-9(7), DK Children) Dorling Kindersley Publishing, Inc.
Dobeck, Maryann. Volcanoes Nature's Awesome Power: Set Of 6. 2010. (Navigators Ser.). (J). pap. 50.00 net. (978-1-4108-2571-1(X)) Benchmark Education Co.
—Volcanoes: Nature's Awesome Power & Volcanes: 6 English, 6 Spanish Adaptations: el poder asombroso de la Naturaleza. 2011. (ENG & SPA.). (J). 101.00 net. (978-1-4108-5737-8(9)) Benchmark Education Co.
Dodd, Emily. Volcanoes: Band 15/Emerald (Collins Big Cat), Bd. 15. 2015. (Collins Big Cat Ser.). (ENG., Illus.). 48p. (J). (gr. 3-4). pap. 11.99 (978-0-00-812786-2(7)) HarperCollins Pubs. Ltd. GBR. Dist: Independent Pubs. Group.
Duffield, Wendell A. What's So Hot about Volcanoes? Black, Bronze, illus. 2011. 96p. (J). pap. 16.00 (978-0-87842-574-7(8)) Mountain Pr. Publishing Co., Inc.
Dwyer, Helen. Volcanoes!, 1 vol. Chabluk, Stefan, illus. 2011. (Eyewitness Disaster Ser.). (ENG.). 32p. (gr. 3-3). 31.21 (978-1-60870-006-6(2), 2d4a809d-1387-46c6-91f0-c27b46932ec5) Cavendish Square Publishing LLC.
Dyan, Penelope. It's Hot, Hot, Hot! a Kid's Guide to Hawaiian Volcanoes National Park. Weigand, John D., illus. 2013. 34p. pap. 11.95 (978-1-61477-118-0(9)) Bellissima Publishing, LLC.
Earth's Crust. 2007. (Illus.). 48p. (J). (gr. 2-5). pap. 8.95 (978-0-8225-6585-7(4)) Lerner Publishing Group.
Encyclopaedia Britannica, Inc. Staff, compiled by. Britannica Illustrated Science Library: Volcanoes, 16 vols. 2008. (Illus.). (J). 29.95 (978-1-59339-400-4(4)) Encyclopaedia Britannica, Inc.
Farndon, John. Extreme Volcanoes. 2017. (When Nature Attacks Ser.). (ENG., Illus.). 32p. (J). (gr. 3-6). 27.99 (978-1-5124-3220-6(2), 184d1b3e-2de1-46be-a0fa-6110c01b4062, Hungry Tomato (r)) Lerner Publishing Group.
Farndon, John & Riley, Peter D. Volcanoes & Earthquakes & Other Facts about Planet Earth: Bulletpoints. 2003. (Bulletpoints Ser.). (Illus.). 40p. (J). pap. 6.95 (978-1-84236-238-9(0)) Miles Kelly Publishing, Ltd. GBR. Dist: Independent Pubs. Group.
Furgang, Kathy. Kilauea: Hawaii's Most Active Volcano. 2009. (Volcanoes of the World Ser.). 24p. (gr. 3-3). 42.50 (978-1-60854-729-6(9), PowerKids Pr.) Rosen Publishing Group, Inc., The.
—Krakatoa: History's Loudest Volcano. 2009. (Volcanoes of the World Ser.). 24p. (gr. 3-3). 42.50 (978-1-60854-730-2(2), PowerKids Pr.) Rosen Publishing Group, Inc., The.
—Mount Pelee: The Biggest Volcano Eruption of the 20th Century. 2009. (Volcanoes of the World Ser.). 24p. (gr. 3-3). 42.50 (978-1-60854-731-9(0), PowerKids Pr.) Rosen Publishing Group, Inc., The.
—Mount Vesuvius: Europe's Mighty Volcano of Smoke & Ash. 2009. (Volcanoes of the World Ser.). 24p. (gr. 3-3). 42.50 (978-1-60854-733-3(7), PowerKids Pr.) Rosen Publishing Group, Inc., The.
—National Geographic Kids Everything Volcanoes & Earthquakes: Earthshaking Photos, Facts, & Fun! 2013. (National Geographic Kids Everything Ser.). 64p. (J). (gr. 3-7). (ENG.). lib. bdg. 21.90 (978-1-4263-1365-3(9)); (Illus.). pap. 12.95 (978-1-4263-1364-6(0)) Disney Publishing Worldwide. (National Geographic Kids).
—Tambora: A Killer Volcamo from Indonesia. 2009. (Volcanoes of the World Ser.). 24p. (gr. 3-3). 42.50 (978-1-60854-734-0(5), PowerKids Pr.) Rosen Publishing Group, Inc., The.
—Volcanoes, 1 vol. 2019. (Investigate Earth Science Ser.). (ENG.). 24p. (gr. 2-2). pap. 10.95 (978-1-9785-0874-3(3), 3af99bb6-a5a3-4ebe-bf84-e214a00bbd22) Enslow Publishing, LLC.
Galat, Joan Marie. National Geographic Readers - Erupt! 100 Fun Facts about Volcanoes (L3) 100 Fun Facts about Volcanoes. 2017. (Readers Ser.). (Illus.). 48p. (J). (gr. 2-4). pap. 5.99 (978-1-4263-2910-4(5), National Geographic Kids) Disney Publishing Worldwide.
—National Geographic Readers: Erupt! 100 Fun Facts about Volcanoes (L3) 2017. (Readers Ser.). (ENG., Illus.). 48p. (J). (gr. 3-7). lib. bdg. 14.90 (978-1-4263-2911-1(3), National Geographic Kids) Disney Publishing Worldwide.
Gallant, Roy A. Plates: Restless Earth, 1 vol. 2003. (EarthWorks Ser.). (ENG., Illus.). 80p. (gr. 6-6). 36.93 (978-0-7614-1370-7(7), 6d2d872f-75ef-477b-a88a-4c22a1dd4203) Cavendish Square Publishing LLC.
Ganeri, Anita. Esos Violentos Volcanes. (Coleccion Esa Horrible Geografia).Tr. of Violent Volcanoes. (SPA., Illus.). 128p. (YA). (gr. 5-8). 9.95 (978-84-272-2151-2(7), ML1621) Molino, Editorial ESP. Dist: Lectorum Pubns., Inc.
—Volcanes y terremotos/Earthquakes & Volcanoes. 2011. 16p. pap. (978-607-404-319-8(1), Silver Dolphin en Español) Advanced Marketing, S. de R. L. de C. V.
—Volcanoes in Action, 1 vol. 2008. (Natural Disasters in Action Ser.). (ENG., Illus.). 48p. (gr. 5-5). pap. 11.75 (978-1-4358-5134-4(X), b9880d24-460b-47fa-ad51-4c5640d05a8d, Rosen Reference) Rosen Publishing Group, Inc., The.
Garbe, Suzanne. The Worst Volcanic Eruptions of All Time. 2012. (Epic Disasters Ser.). (ENG.). 32p. (gr. 3-4). pap. 47.70 (978-1-4296-8510-8(7)); (J). pap. 8.29 (978-1-4296-8016-5(4), 118348) Capstone. (Capstone Pr.).
Gazlay, Suzy. Be a Volcanologist, 1 vol. 2008. (Scienceworks! Ser.). (ENG.). 32p. (gr. 3-5). pap. 11.50 (978-0-8368-8937-6(1), 6a05fd29-036f-49ec-ac10-977da0cecef3, Gareth Stevens Learning Library) Stevens, Gareth Publishing LLLP.
Gedacht, Daniel C. Land & Resources in Ancient Rome. 2009. (Primary Sources of Ancient Civilizations Ser.). 24p. (gr. 3-3). 42.50 (978-1-60851-559-2(1), PowerKids Pr.) Rosen Publishing Group, Inc., The.
George, Michael. Volcanoes: The Fiery Mountains. 2003. (LifeViews Ser.). (Illus.). 32p. (J). lib. bdg. (978-1-58341-255-8(7), Creative Education) Creative Co., The.
Gilbert, Sara. Volcanoes. 2018. (Earth Rocks! Ser.). (ENG.). 24p. (J). (gr. 1-3). pap. 10.99 (978-1-62832-512-6(7), 19672, Creative Paperbacks); (Illus.). (978-1-60818-896-3(5), 19674, Creative Education) Creative Co., The.
—Les Volcans. 2018. (Vive la Terre! Ser.). (FRE., Illus.). 24p. (J). (978-1-77092-404-8(3), 19693) Creative Co., The.
Gilkerson, Patricia. My Adventure Inside a Volcano. 2006. 44p. (J). 8.99 (978-1-59092-443-3(6)) Blue Forge Pr.
Gill, Maria. Volcanic Eruptions. 2009. (ENG., Illus.). 24p. pap. 4.99 (978-1-59198-699-7(0)) Creative Teaching Pr., Inc.
Gilles, Renae & Rylands, Warren. Volcanoes. 2019. (Illus.). 24p. (J). (978-1-4896-8023-5(3), AV2 by Weigl) Weigl Pubs., Inc.
Giulieri, Anne. Volcano Bubbles. Kreinberg, Sylvia, illus. 2012. (Engage Literacy Blue Ser.). (ENG.). 16p. (J). (gr. k-2). pap. 36.94 (978-1-4296-8979-3(X), 18386, Capstone Pr.) Capstone.
—Volcano Bubbles, 1 vol. 2012. (Engage Literacy Blue Ser.). (ENG., Illus.). 16p. (J). (gr. k-2). pap. 6.99 (978-1-4296-8978-6(1), 119994, Capstone Pr.) Capstone.
Gonzales, Doreen. Volcanoes, 1 vol. 2012. (Killer Disasters Ser.). (ENG., Illus.). 24p. (J). (gr. 2-3). 26.27 (978-1-4488-7441-5(6), bf85cc16-e52d-43ea-985f-7772b6f3d8ad); pap. 9.25 (978-1-4488-7514-6(5), 5e1d49f6-fc0e-4f60-97c4-e0f0058c4010) Rosen Publishing Group, Inc., The. (PowerKids Pr.).
Gray-Wilburn, Renée. Volcanoes! Sotirovski, Aleksandar, illus. 2012. (First Graphics: Wild Earth Ser.). (ENG.). 24p. (gr. 1-2). pap. 35.70 (978-1-4296-8373-9(2)) Capstone.
Gray-Wilburn, Renée & Beehive Illustrations Staff. Volcanoes!, 1 vol. Sotirovski, Aleksandar, illus. 2012. (First Graphics: Wild Earth Ser.). (ENG.). 24p. (J). (gr. k-3). pap. 6.29 (978-1-4296-7953-4(0), 118285) Capstone.
Green, Emily K. Volcanoes. 2006. (Learning about the Earth Ser.). (ENG., Illus.). 24p. (J). (gr. k-3). lib. bdg. 26.95 (978-1-60014-041-9(6)) Bellwether Media.
—Volcanoes. 2011. (Blastoff! Readers: Learning about the Earth: Level 3 Ser.). (Illus.). 24p. (J). pap. 5.95 (978-0-531-20845-8(1), Children's Pr.) Scholastic Library Publishing.
Green, Jen. Understanding Volcanoes & Earthquakes, 1 vol. 2007. (Our Earth Ser.). (ENG., Illus.). 24p. (YA). (gr. 2-3). lib. bdg. 26.27 (978-1-4042-4276-0(7), 89ceaae2-18a5-4109-945c-d90f28802a08) Rosen Publishing Group, Inc., The.
—Volcanoes Around the World, 1 vol. (Geography Now! Ser.). (ENG.). 32p. (gr. 5-5). 2009. (J). pap. 11.00 (978-1-4358-2959-6(X), 4854469e-f7f9-4ed8-8aab-f1d15f0e9997, PowerKids Pr.) 2008. (YA). lib. bdg. 30.27 (978-1-4358-2873-5(9), 7bb8377b-7847-47e5-892c-78fd7d532ee6) Rosen Publishing Group, Inc., The.
Griffey, Harriet. Earthquakes & Other Natural Disasters. 2010. (DK Readers Level 4 Ser.). (ENG.). 48p. (J). (gr. 2-4). 16.19 (978-0-7566-5933-2(7)) Dorling Kindersley Publishing, Inc.
Group/McGraw-Hill, Wright. Forces of Nature: Level K, 6 vols., Vol. 2. (First Explorers Ser.). 24p. (gr. 1-2). 34.95 (978-0-7699-1458-9(6)) Shortland Pubns. (U. S. A.) Inc.
—Volcanoes: The Hottest Spots on Earth, 6 vols. (Book2WebTM Ser.). (gr. 4-8). 36.50 (978-0-322-04425-8(1)) Wright Group/McGraw-Hill.
Gullo, Arthur. Volcanoes. 2015. (J). lib. bdg. (978-1-62713-513-9(8)) 2014. (ENG.). 48p. (gr. 4-4). 33.07 (978-1-5026-0221-3(0), 96ac7b67-9a94-48c6-9197-def4c2aa1278) Cavendish Square Publishing LLC.
Hamalainen, Karina. Hawai'I Volcanoes (a True Book: National Parks) (Library Edition) 2018. (True Book (Relaunch) Ser.). (ENG., Illus.). 48p. (J). (gr. 3-5). lib. bdg. 31.00 (978-0-531-12933-3(0), Children's Pr.) Scholastic Library Publishing.
—Hawai'I Volcanoes National Park (Rookie National Parks) (Library Edition) 2018. (Rookie National Parks Ser.). (ENG., Illus.). 32p. (J). (gr. 1-2). lib. bdg. 25.00 (978-0-531-13320-0(6), Children's Pr.) Scholastic Library Publishing.
Hansen, Grace. Hawai'i Volcanoes National Park. 2018. (National Parks (Abdo Kids Jumbo) Ser.). (ENG., Illus.). 24p. (J). (gr. -1-2). lib. bdg. 32.79 (978-1-5321-8208-2(2), 29875, Abdo Kids) ABDO Publishing Co.
Harbo, Christopher L. The Explosive World of Volcanoes with Max Axiom, Super Scientist, 1 vol. Smith, Tod, illus. 2008. (Graphic Science Ser.). (ENG.). 32p. (J). (gr. 3-9). pap. 8.10 (978-1-4296-1770-3(5), 94817, Capstone Pr.) Capstone.
—The Explosive World of Volcanoes with Max Axiom Super Scientist: 4D an Augmented Reading Science Experience. Smith, Tod, illus. 2018. (Graphic Science 4D Ser.). (ENG.). 32p. (J). (gr. 3-9). pap. 7.95 (978-1-5435-2958-6(5), 138558); lib. bdg. 36.65 (978-1-5435-2947-0(X), 138536) Capstone. (Capstone Pr.).
—El Mundo Explosivo de Los Volcanes con Max Axiom, Supercientífico. Strictly Spanish, LLC., tr. Smith, Tod, illus. 2012. (Ciencia Gráfica Ser.). (SPA.). 32p. (J). (gr. 3-9). lib. bdg. 31.32 (978-1-4296-9237-3(5), 120244) Capstone.
Harris, Nicholas & Dennis, Peter. Volcano. 2006. (Illus.). 31p. (J). (978-0-7607-7530-1(3)) backpackbook.
Harris, Nicolas. Volcanoes Through Time, 1 vol. 2009. (Fast Forward Ser.). (ENG.). 32p. (YA). (gr. 4-4). lib. bdg. 28.93 (978-1-4358-2800-1(3), 379f6c00-8d18-4dbf-9342-8597147e2ae1) Rosen Publishing Group, Inc., The.
Harris, Terrell. Volcanoes Change the Land. 2013. (InfoMax Readers Ser.). (ENG.). 24p. (J). (gr. 2-3). pap. 49.50 (978-1-4777-2400-2(1)); (Illus.). pap. 8.25 (978-1-4777-2399-9(4), 9a5b6a5e-9c3b-44e4-8a93-3960044630b3) Rosen Publishing Group, Inc., The. (Rosen Classroom).
Hoffman, Steven M. Volcanoes & Earthquakes: Making & Moving Rock, 1 vol. 2011. (Rock It! Ser.). (ENG., Illus.). 24p. (J). (gr. 3-4). pap. 9.25 (978-1-4488-2704-6(3), 4f18e31f-8ad1-4c31-92b3-206812d80871); lib. bdg. 26.27 (978-1-4488-2559-2(8), f7b62daa-8a19-45dc-8ee7-851a593c75b0) Rosen Publishing Group, Inc., The. (PowerKids Pr.).
Holt, Rinehart and Winston Staff. Holt Science & Technology Chapter 9: Earth Science: Volcanoes. 5th ed. 2004. (Illus.). pap. 12.86 (978-0-03-030306-7(0)) Holt McDougal.
How a Volcano Is Formed: Level M, 6 vols. (Wonder Worldtm Ser.). 16p. 34.95 (978-0-7802-2913-6(4)) Wright Group/McGraw-Hill.
Howell, Izzi. Volcano Geo Facts. 2018. (Geo Facts Ser.). (Illus.). 32p. (J). (gr. 5-5). (978-0-7787-4395-8(0)) Crabtree Publishing Co.
Jackson, Tom. The Magic School Bus Presents: Volcanoes & Earthquakes: a Nonfiction Companion to the Original Magic School Bus Series. Bracken, Carolyn, illus. 2014. (Magic School Bus Presents Ser.). (ENG.). 32p. (J). (gr. 1-3). pap. 7.99 (978-0-545-68584-9(2), Scholastic Paperbacks) Scholastic, Inc.
Jennings, Terry J. Violent Volcanoes. 2009. (Amazing Planet Earth Ser.). 32p. (gr. 4-7). 31.35 (978-1-59920-374-4(X)) Black Rabbit Bks.
Kalman, Bobbie. Los Volcanes de la Tierra. 2009. (SPA.). 32p. (J). (978-0-7787-8244-5(1)); pap. (978-0-7787-8261-2(1)) Crabtree Publishing Co.
—Les Volcans. 2009. (FRE., Illus.). 32p. (J). pap. 9.95 (978-2-89579-250-5(X)) Bayard Canada Livres CAN. Dist: Crabtree Publishing Co.
Kalman, Bobbie & Aloian, Molly. Volcanoes on Earth. 2008. (Looking at Earth Ser.). (ENG., Illus.). 32p. (J). (gr. 3-7). pap. (978-0-7787-3215-0(0)); lib. bdg. (978-0-7787-3205-1(3)) Crabtree Publishing Co.
Katirgis, Jane & Ingber Drohan, Michele. Volatile Volcanoes, 1 vol. 2015. (Earth's Natural Disasters Ser.). (ENG.). 32p. (gr. 3-4). pap. 11.52 (978-0-7660-6801-8(3), cde05f65-abf8-4e4a-b9f8-aa92d024ad11) Enslow Publishing, LLC.
Keedle, Jayne. Volcanoes, 1 vol. 2008. (Ultimate 10: Natural Disasters Ser.). (ENG.). 48p. (YA). (gr. 3-3). lib. bdg. 33.67 (978-0-8368-9155-3(4), e7a5c288-8e4c-4f47-b0bd-47d871c49800) Stevens, Gareth Publishing LLLP.
Kerrod, Robin. Exploring Science: Volcanoes & Earthquakes - an Amazing Fact File & Hands-On Project Book. 2014. (ENG., Illus.). 64p. (J). (gr. 3-7). 12.99 (978-1-86147-306-6(0), Armadillo) Anness Publishing GBR. Dist: National Bk. Network.
Klepeis, Alicia Z. The Science of Volcanic Eruptions, 1 vol. 2019. (Science of Natural Disasters Ser.). (ENG.). 32p. (gr. 3-3). pap. 11.58 (978-1-5026-4658-3(7), 71c4c18b-850f-405a-93e2-cabff73f8da2) Cavendish Square Publishing LLC.
Koontz, Robin. The Science of a Tsunami. 2015. (21st Century Skills Library: Disaster Science Ser.). (ENG., Illus.). 32p. (J). (gr. 4-8). 32.07 (978-1-63362-483-2(8), 206840) Cherry Lake Publishing.
Kranz, Rachel. Mount St. Helens. 2011. (Early Connections Ser.). (J). (978-1-61672-643-0(1)) Benchmark Education Co.
Landau, Elaine. Volcanoes. 2009. (True Book(tm), a — Earth Science Ser.). (ENG., Illus.). 48p. (J). (gr. 2-5). 31.00 (978-0-531-16886-8(7)) Scholastic Library Publishing.
Latta, Sara L. Lava Scientist: Careers on the Edge of Volcanoes, 1 vol. 2009. (Wild Science Careers Ser.). (ENG., Illus.). 128p. (gr. 5-6). lib. bdg. 35.93 (978-0-7660-3049-7(0), e2064bd1-dec1-44e1-a9e8-cb688c03902a) Enslow Publishing, LLC.
—Volcanologists: Examining Active Volcanoes, 1 vol. 2015. (Extreme Science Careers Ser.). (ENG., Illus.). 128p. (gr. 7-7). lib. bdg. 38.93 (978-0-7660-6972-5(9), 5d207fe3-34bc-4d50-a404-862bb2e5be43) Enslow Publishing, LLC.
Law, Felicia & Bailey, Gerry. Escape from the Volcano. Noyes, Leighton, illus. 2015. (Science to the Rescue Ser.). (ENG.). 32p. (J). (gr. 4-4). (978-0-7787-1675-4(9)) Crabtree Publishing Co.
Lawrence, Ellen. How Do Volcanoes Make Rock? A Look at Igneous Rock. 2015. (Illus.). 24p. (J). lib. bdg. 26.99 (978-1-62724-298-1(8)) Bearport Publishing Co., Inc.
Leavitt, Amie Jane. Anatomy of a Volcanic Eruption. 2011. (Disasters Ser.). (ENG.). 48p. (J). (gr. 3-4). pap. 66.70 (978-1-4296-7358-7(3), 16844); (gr. 5-9). pap. 10.95 (978-1-4296-7357-0(5), 116889) Capstone.
Leigh, Autumn. Warning: Volcano! the Story of Mt. St. Helens. 2009. (Reading Room Collection 2 Ser.). 24p. (gr. 3-4). 42.50 (978-1-60852-000-8(5), PowerKids Pr.) Rosen Publishing Group, Inc., The.
Leitten, Emily. Lava, 1 vol. 2009. (Real Life Readers Ser.). (ENG.). 32p. (gr. 4-6). pap. 10.00 (978-1-4358-0231-5(4), 385231b6-8fa4-458e-a91e-ed3902241b9d, Rosen Classroom) Rosen Publishing Group, Inc., The.
Levine, Shar & Johnstone, Leslie. Volcanoes! 2007. (Illus.). 46p. (J). (978-1-60311-062-4(3)) Mud Puddle, Inc.
Levy, Janey. World's Worst Volcanic Eruptions. (Deadly Disasters Ser.). 24p. (gr. 2-3). 2009. 42.50 (978-1-61512-153-3(6), PowerKids Pr.) 2008. (ENG.). pap. 9.40 (978-1-4042-4536-5(7), f884b021-a87b-4149-92c0-ef3b5b4040e8, Rosen Classroom) 2008. (ENG., Illus.). (J). lib. bdg. 26.27 (978-1-4042-4512-9(X), 20c5ee96-da0c-4dda-82d3-8dd2a0dee5de) Rosen Publishing Group, Inc., The.
Levy, Matthys & Salvadori, Mario. Earthquakes, Volcanoes, & Tsunamis: Projects & Principles for Beginning Geologists. 2009. (ENG., Illus.). 160p. (J). (gr. 4). pap. 14.95 (978-1-55652-801-9(9)) Chicago Review Pr., Inc.
Lindop, Laurie. Probing Volcanoes. 2003. (Science on the Edge Ser.). (Illus.). 80p. (gr. 5-18). lib. bdg. 26.90 (978-0-7613-2700-4(2), Twenty-First Century Bks.) Lerner Publishing Group.
Loria, Laura. Volcanic Processes. 2017. (Let's Find Out! Our Dynamic Earth Ser.). (Illus.). 32p. (J). (gr. 6-10). 77.40 (978-1-5383-0030-5(3)) Rosen Publishing Group, Inc., The.
Lucarelli, Ariana. Volcanoes: Shaping Earth, 1 vol. 2013. (Rosen Readers Ser.). (ENG.). 24p. (J). (gr. 2-2). pap. 8.25 (978-1-4777-2412-5(5), e581916e-43c4-43da-8690-3f877ceb5428); pap. 49.50 (978-1-4777-2414-9(1)) Rosen Publishing Group, Inc., The. (Rosen Classroom).
Lunis, Natalie. Volcanoes. 2011. (Early Connections Ser.). (J). (978-1-61672-653-9(9)) Benchmark Education Co.
Malizia, Diana. A Visual Guide to Volcanoes & Earthquakes, 1 vol. 2017. (Visual Exploration of Science Ser.). (ENG., Illus.). 104p. (J). (gr. 8-8). 38.80 (978-1-5081-7708-1(2), 9dba5db8-5697-4cdd-bde9-d996834d11d7); pap. 18.65 (978-1-5081-7881-1(X), 0dd11e33-dad1-4f5c-ae6b-95cbdc77d2d6) Rosen Publishing Group, Inc., The. (Rosen Young Adult).
Manatt, Kathleen. Volcanologist. 2007. (21st Century Skills Library: Cool Science Careers Ser.). (ENG.). 32p. (gr. 4-8). pap. 14.21 (978-1-60279-085-8(X), 200646); (Illus.). lib. bdg. 32.07 (978-1-60279-050-6(7), 200018) Cherry Lake Publishing.
Mara, Wil. Why Do Volcanoes Erupt?, 1 vol. 2010. (Tell Me Why, Tell Me How Ser.). (ENG.). 32p. (gr. 3-3). 32.64 (978-0-7614-3989-9(7), 98188da6-bd9e-42b7-9d2c-b6a3f1b18060) Cavendish Square Publishing LLC.
Martin, Claudia. My Little Book of Volcanoes & Earthquakes. 2014. (Illus.). 64p. (J). (978-1-4351-5531-2(9)) Barnes & Noble, Inc.
Masters, Nancy Robinson. Volcanic Eruptions. 2012. (21st Century Skills Library: Real World Math Ser.). (ENG., Illus.). 32p. (gr. 4-8). (J). pap. 14.21 (978-1-61080-414-1(7), 201346); lib. bdg. 32.07 (978-1-61080-328-1(0), 201314) Cherry Lake Publishing.
Mattern, Joanne. Mauna Loa: El volcan en actividad más grande del mundo (Mauna Loa: World's Largest Active Volcano) 2009. (Maravillas naturales (Natures Greatest Hits) Ser.). (SPA.). 24p. (gr. 2-2). 42.50 (978-1-61514-364-1(5), Editorial Buenas Letras) Rosen Publishing Group, Inc., The.
—Mauna Loa: World's Largest Active Volcano. 2009. (Nature's Greatest Hits Ser.). 24p. (gr. 2-2). 42.50 (978-1-61514-841-7(8), PowerKids Pr.) Rosen Publishing Group, Inc., The.
Matthas, Seth. How Do Volcanoes Explode? Showing Events & Processes, 1 vol. 2017. (Computer Kids: Powered by Computational Thinking Ser.). (ENG.). 24p. (J). (gr. 3-4). 25.27 (978-1-5383-2402-8(4), da12dc40-fd72-4f48-9b45-e2ab9b449044, PowerKids Pr.); pap. (978-1-5081-3790-0(0), cf1ccef6-386e-4ebe-941a-3d8c3127c76e, Rosen Classroom) Rosen Publishing Group, Inc., The.
Maurer, Tracy Nelson. The World's Worst Volcanic Eruptions. 2019. (World's Worst Natural Disasters Ser.). (ENG., Illus.). 32p. (J). (gr. 3-9). lib. bdg. 27.32 (978-1-5435-5480-9(6), 139348, Capstone Pr.) Capstone.
Mayer, Cassie. Volcanoes. rev. ed. 2016. (Landforms Ser.). (ENG.). 24p. (J). (gr. -1-1). pap. 6.29 (978-1-4846-3589-6(2), 133659, Heinemann) Capstone.
Meachen Rau, Dana. Los Volcanes / Volcanoes, 1 vol. 2009. (Maravillas de la Naturaleza / Wonders of Nature Ser.). (ENG & SPA., Illus.). 32p. (gr. 1-2). lib. bdg. 25.50 (978-0-7614-2832-9(1), f7ce0e86-5ecc-4d5b-a928-fa2836797d7b) Cavendish Square Publishing LLC.
—Los Volcanes (Volcanoes), 1 vol. 2009. (Maravillas de la Naturaleza (Wonders of Nature) Ser.). (SPA., Illus.). 32p. (gr. 1-2). lib. bdg. 25.50 (978-0-7614-2808-4(9), 018a2962-b534-455a-bcb2-e6d476e5c878) Cavendish Square Publishing LLC.
—Volcanoes, 1 vol. 2008. (Wonders of Nature Ser.). (ENG.). 32p. (gr. 1-2). pap. 9.23 (978-0-7614-3330-9(9), 511aeea4-d358-4b1b-94b7-f99c20e71394); (Illus.). lib. bdg. 25.50 (978-0-7614-2670-7(1), 45f467bf-3a2a-4b95-a645-91379a2becc9) Cavendish Square Publishing LLC.
Meister, Cari. Volcanoes. 2015. (Illus.). 24p. (J). lib. bdg. (978-1-62031-227-8(1)) Jump! Inc.
Melin, Jen. Examining Volcanic Eruptions. 2015. (ENG., Illus.). 48p. (J). lib. bdg. 24.95 net. (978-1-934545-68-3(6)) Oliver Pr., Inc.
Millett, Peter. The Mountain of Fire 1 Pathfinders. Bacchin, Giorgio, illus. 2017. (Cambridge Reading Adventures Ser.). (ENG.). 24p. pap. 8.60 (978-1-108-40074-9(4)) Cambridge Univ. Pr.
Moore, David. National Geographic Science 1-2 (Earth Science: Land & Water): Explore on Your Own: the Island That Formed in One Day. 2009. (Illus.). 12p. (C). pap. 8.95 (978-0-7362-5522-6(2)) National Geographic School Publishing, Inc.
Morlock, Jeremy. Lava & Magma: How the Hawaiian Islands Formed, 1 vol. 2019. (Earth's History Through Rocks Ser.). (ENG.). 32p. (gr. 4-5). 27.93 (978-1-7253-0150-4(4), 7b7bfe53-2340-4e74-9f1f-c7adf9adbd14, PowerKids Pr.) Rosen Publishing Group, Inc., The.
Mountains of Fire. 2017. (Illus.). 40p. (J). (978-0-7166-3367-9(1)) World Bk., Inc.
Nargi, Lela. Absolute Expert: Volcanoes. 2018. (Absolute Expert Ser.). (Illus.). 112p. (J). (gr. 3-7). 14.99 (978-1-4263-3142-8(8)); (ENG., lib. bdg. 24.90 (978-1-4263-3143-5(6)) Disney Publishing Worldwide. (National Geographic Kids).
National Geographic Learning. Language, Literacy & Vocabulary - Reading Expeditions (Earth Science): Volcanoes. 2007. (ENG., Illus.). 36p. (J). pap. 20.95 (978-0-7922-5434-8(1)) CENGAGE Learning.
—Reading Expeditions (Science: Earth Science): Volcanoes & Earthquakes. 2007. (ENG., Illus.). 32p. (J). pap. 18.95 (978-0-7922-8874-9(2)) CENGAGE Learning.
—Reading Expeditions (Science: on Assignment): Surviving Volcanoes & Glaciers. 2007. (ENG., Illus.). 32p. (J). pap. 18.95 (978-0-7922-8448-2(8)) CENGAGE Learning.
Nault, Jennifer. Volcanoes. 2016. (Illus.). 24p. (J). (978-1-5105-1154-5(7)) SmartBook Media, Inc.
—Volcanoes. 2004. (Science Matters Ser.). (Illus.). 24p. (J). lib. bdg. 24.45 (978-1-59036-211-2(X)) Weigl Pubs., Inc.

Nestor, John. Volcanoes. 2009. (21st Century Skills Library: Real World Math Ser.). (ENG.). 32p. (gr. 4-8). lib. bdg. 32.07 *(978-1-60279-491-7(X)*, 200320) Cherry Lake Publishing.

Nuttall, Gina. Volcanoes & Earthquakes. 2004. (QEB Start Writing Ser.). (Illus.). 24p. (J). lib. bdg. 15.95 *(978-1-59566-018-3(6))* QEB Publishing Inc.

Ogden, Charlie. Surviving the Yellowstone Supervolcano, 1 vol. 2017. (Surviving the Impossible Ser.). (ENG.). 32p. (J). (gr. 4-5). pap. 11.50 *(978-1-5382-1455-8(5)*, 276510a3-dc80-4a05-9a0a-86ee47d954b7); lib. bdg. 28.27 *(978-1-5382-1426-8(1)*, c9deeb4b-5194-49e9-8841-ca52ee35aeff) Stevens, Gareth Publishing LLLP.

Olson, Elsie. Exploring Volcanoes: Volcanologists at Work! 2017. (Earth Detectives Ser.). (ENG.). 24p. (J). (gr. k-4). lib. bdg. 32.79 *(978-1-5321-1233-1(5)*, 27620, Super SandCastle) ABDO Publishing Co.

O'Meara, Donna. Into the Volcano: A Volcano Researcher at Work. 2007. (ENG., Illus.). 56p. (J). (gr. 3-7). 9.99 *(978-1-55337-693-4(5))* Kids Can Pr., Ltd. CAN. Dist: Hachette Bk. Group.

O'Neal, Claire. A Project Guide to Volcanoes. 2010. (Earth Science Projects for Kids Ser.). (Illus.). 48p. (J). (gr. 4-7). lib. bdg. 29.95 *(978-1-58415-868-4(9))* Mitchell Lane Pubs.

Oxlade, Chris. Volcanoes. 2010. (Unpredictable Nature Ser.). (Illus.). 48p. (J). (gr. 3-18). lib. bdg. 19.95 *(978-1-4222-2007-8(9))* Mason Crest.

Paiva, Johannah Gilman, ed. The Awesome Book of Volcanoes: Awesome. Thompson, Ian et al, illus. 2013. (World of Wonder: the Awesome Book Of Ser.). (ENG.). 32p. (J). (gr. 3-7). 7.99 *(978-1-77093-778-9(1))* Flowerpot Pr.

Person, Stephen. Devastated by a Volcano! 2010. (Disaster Survivors Ser.). (Illus.). 32p. (YA). (gr. 4-7). lib. bdg. 28.50 *(978-1-936087-50-1(2))* Bearport Publishing Co., Inc.

Peterson, Judy Monroe. Braving Volcanoes: Volcanologists. (Extreme Scientists Ser.). 24p. (gr. 2-3). 2009. 42.50 *(978-1-61512-449-7(7)*, PowerKids Pr.) 2008. (ENG., Illus.). (YA). lib. bdg. 26.27 *(978-1-4042-4525-9(1)*, 41cd929b-7e67-4a96-8247-c1000c7f6c93) Rosen Publishing Group, Inc., The.

Peyrols, Sylvaine, et al. Volcanoes. Stanley-Baker, Penelope, tr. Peyrols, Sylvaine et al, illus. 2013. (My First Discoveries Ser.). (ENG.). 32p. (J). (-k). 19.99 *(978-1-85103-420-8(X))* Moonlight Publishing, Ltd. GBR. Dist: Independent Pubs. Group.

Pierce, Nick. Volcanoes. 2013. (Worldwise Nature Ser.). (ENG., Illus.). 24p. (J). pap. *(978-1-911242-83-3(0))* Book Hse.

Pierce, Terry. Volcanoes A to Z Coloring Book. Villalobos, Ethel M., illus. 2003. 24p. pap. 4.95 *(978-1-57306-123-0(9))* Bess Pr., Inc.

Pirk, Wendy. Volcanoes, 1 vol. 2017. (Super Explorers Ser.). (ENG., Illus.). 64p. (J). pap. 6.99 *(978-1-926700-70-0(8)*, 630843e0-98ff-4fa8-8732-236f554d9172) Blue Bike Bks. CAN. Dist: Lone Pine Publishing USA.

Prager, Ellen J. National Geographic Kids: Volcano! 2016. (Jump into Science Ser.). (Illus.). 32p. (J). (gr. -1-k). pap. 7.99 *(978-1-4263-2366-9(2)*, National Geographic Kids) Disney Publishing Worldwide.

PRESS, Celebration. Blast Zone: The Eruption & Recovery of Mount St. Helens. 2003. (ENG.). (J). (gr. 6-8). pap. 37.95 *(978-0-7652-3245-8(6)*, Celebration Pr.) Savvas Learning Co.

Prokos, Anna. Don't Blow Your Top! A Look Inside Volcanoes. Selivanova, Elena, illus. 2017. (Imagine That! Ser.). (ENG.). 32p. (J). (gr. 2-4). E-Book 39.99 *(978-1-63440-160-9(3))* Red Chair Pr.

QEB Start Reading & Writing National Book Stores Edition: Volcanoes & Earthquakes. 2006. (J). per. *(978-1-59566-265-1(0))* QEB Publishing Inc.

Rathburn, Betsy. Volcanoes. 2019. (Natural Disasters Ser.). (ENG., Illus.). 24p. (J). (gr. k-3). pap. 7.99 *(978-1-61891-750-8(1)*, 12319, Blastoff! Readers) Bellwether Media.

René, Ellen. Investigating Volcanic Eruptions. (Science Detectives Ser.). 24p. (gr. 2-3). 2009. 42.50 *(978-1-60853-014-4(0)*, PowerKids Pr.) 2008. (ENG., Illus.). (J). lib. bdg. 26.27 *(978-1-4042-4481-8(6)*, 5fc7eed7-a8d6-4d18-8cbd-db25bab7dceb) Rosen Publishing Group, Inc., The.

Rice, William B. Los Volcanes. rev. ed. 2010. (Science: Informational Text Ser.). (SPA., Illus.). 32p. (gr. 3-5). pap. 11.99 *(978-1-4333-2154-2(8))* Teacher Created Materials, Inc.

Riley, Gail Blasser. Volcano! The 1980 Mount St. Helens Eruption. 2006. (X-Treme Disasters That Changed America Ser.). (Illus.). 32p. (J). (gr. 2-5). lib. bdg. 25.27 *(978-1-59716-072-8(5))* Bearport Publishing Co., Inc.

Riley, Joelle. Volcanoes. 2008. pap. 40.95 *(978-0-8225-9446-8(3))* Lerner Publishing Group.

Rose, Simon. Amazing Volcanoes Around the World. 2019. (Passport to Nature Ser.). (ENG., Illus.). 32p. (J). (gr. 4-6). lib. bdg. 28.65 *(978-1-5435-5779-4(1)*, 139735) Capstone.

Rowe, Brooke. Building a Volcano. Bane, Jeff, illus. 2016. (My Early Library: My Science Fun Ser.). (ENG.). 24p. (J). (gr. k-1). 30.64 *(978-1-63471-025-1(8)*, 208180) Cherry Lake Publishing.

Royston, Angela. The Science of Volcanoes, 1 vol. 2013. (Nature's Wrath: the Science Behind Natural Disasters Ser.). (ENG., Illus.). 48p. (gr. 5-5). 34.60 *(978-1-4339-8671-0(X)*, 1d0c98c2-15ed-4b5d-921f-f3ebb483d956); pap. 15.05 *(978-1-4339-8672-7(8)*, cd0e275a-2e53-48a9-b6a6-b2e1bdfb7b43) Stevens, Gareth Publishing LLLP. (Gareth Stevens Learning Library).

Rubin, Ken. Volcanoes & Earthquakes. 2007. (Insiders Ser.). (ENG., Illus.). 64p. (J). (gr. 3-7). 21.99 *(978-1-4169-3862-0(1)*, Simon & Schuster Bks. For Young Readers) Simon & Schuster Bks. For Young Readers.

Rusch, Elizabeth. Eruption! Volcanoes & the Science of Saving Lives. Uhlman, Tom, illus. 2017. (Scientists in the Field Ser.). (ENG.). 80p. (J). (gr. 5-7). pap. 10.99 *(978-0-544-93245-6(5)*, 1657947, Clarion Bks.) HarperCollins Pubs.

—Volcano Rising. Swan, Susan, illus. 2013. (ENG.). 32p. (J). (gr. 1-4). pap. 7.95 *(978-1-58089-409-8(7))* Charlesbridge Publishing, Inc.

—Will It Blow? Become a Volcano Detective at Mount St. Helens. Lewis, K. E., illus. 2017. 48p. (J). (gr. 1-4). pap. 14.99 *(978-1-63217-110-8(4)*, Little Bigfoot) Sasquatch Bks.

Schreiber, Anne. National Geographic Readers: Volcanoes! 2008. (Readers Ser.). (Illus.). 32p. (J). (gr. 1-3). pap. 4.99 *(978-1-4263-0285-5(1)*, National Geographic Kids); (ENG., lib. bdg. 15.99 *(978-1-4263-0287-9(8)*, National Geographic Children's Bks.) Disney Publishing Worldwide.

—Volcanoes (1 Hardcover/1 CD) 2017. (National Geographic Kids Ser.). (ENG.). (J). 29.95 *(978-1-4301-2669-0(8))* Live Oak Media.

—Volcanoes (1 Paperback/1 CD) 2017. (National Geographic Kids Ser.). (ENG.). (J). pap. 19.95 *(978-1-4301-2668-3(X))* Live Oak Media.

—Volcanoes (4 Paperbacks/1 CD), 4 vols. 2017. (National Geographic Kids Ser.). (ENG.). (J). pap. 31.95 *(978-1-4301-2670-6(1))* Live Oak Media.

The Science of a Volcanic Eruption. 2014. (21st Century Skills Library: Disaster Science Ser.). (ENG., Illus.). 32p. (J). (gr. 4-8). 32.07 *(978-1-63137-628-3(4)*, 205295) Cherry Lake Publishing.

Sengupta, Monalisa. Volcanoes & Earthquakes. (Wild Nature Ser.). 48p. (gr. 4-5). 2009. 53.00 *(978-1-60854-795-1(7)*, PowerKids Pr.) 2007. (ENG., Illus.). (YA). lib. bdg. 32.93 *(978-1-4042-3901-2(4)*, c4334696-d48f-40f0-87a9-4faa1e35aca0) Rosen Publishing Group, Inc., The.

Senior, Kathryn. Volcanoes. 2005. (What on Earth? Ser.). (ENG., Illus.). 32p. (J). (gr. 2-4). lib. bdg. 25.50 *(978-0-516-25324-4(7)*, Children's Pr.) Scholastic Library Publishing.

Shone, Rob. Volcanoes. (Graphic Natural Disasters Ser.). (ENG.). 48p. (gr. 5-5). 2009. (YA). 58.50 *(978-1-61513-008-5(X)*, Rosen Reference) 2007. (Illus.). pap. 14.05 *(978-1-4042-1975-5(7)*, d3612d48-0e36-4f7d-9be7-205e18386f56) Rosen Publishing Group, Inc., The.

—Volcanoes, 1 vol. Riley, Terry, illus. 2007. (Graphic Natural Disasters Ser.). (ENG.). 48p. (J). (gr. 5-5). lib. bdg. 37.13 *(978-1-4042-1988-5(9)*, 574bee2a-b4ca-4b2f-afca-bd7195505561) Rosen Publishing Group, Inc., The.

Sillet, Helen. The Awesome Power of Volcanoes & Earthquakes. 2005. (YA). pap. 12.95 *(978-1-4105-0421-0(2))*; cd-rom *(978-1-4105-0423-4(9))* Building Wings LLC.

—Understanding Volcanoes & Earthquakes. 2005. (YA). pap. 12.95 *(978-1-4105-0417-3(4))*; cd-rom *(978-1-4105-0419-7(0))* Building Wings LLC.

Silverstein, Alvin & Silverstein, Virginia. Volcanoes: The Science Behind Fiery Eruptions, 1 vol. 2009. (Science Behind Natural Disasters Ser.). (ENG., Illus.). 48p. (gr. 5-7). lib. bdg. 27.93 *(978-0-7660-2972-9(7)*, c23c5e2f-6bcb-48ec-bd57-d1c099effcbf) Enslow Publishing, LLC.

Simon, Seymour. Volcanoes. 2006. (ENG., Illus.). 32p. (J). (gr. k-4). pap. 9.99 *(978-0-06-087717-0(0)*, HarperCollins) HarperCollins Pubs.

—Volcanoes. 2006. (Illus.). 31p. (gr. k-4). 17.00 *(978-0-7569-6744-4(9))* Perfection Learning Corp.

Sisk, Maeve T. Mount Terror, 1 vol. 2014. (Scariest Places on Earth Ser.). (ENG.). 24p. (J). (gr. 2-3). 24.27 *(978-1-4824-1156-0(3)*, 9e6ae397-7da0-4a8d-a13c-c2a091aa8954) Stevens, Gareth Publishing LLLP.

Smith, Paula. Earthquakes, Eruptions, & Other Events That Change Earth. 2015. (Earth's Processes Close-Up Ser.). (ENG., Illus.). 24p. (J). (gr. 2-3). *(978-0-7787-1725-6(9))* Crabtree Publishing Co.

Souza, D. M. Volcanoes Inside & Out. Cormack, Allan & Drew-Brook, Deborah, illus. 2006. (On My Own Science Ser.). (ENG.). 48p. (J). (gr. 2-4). per. 7.99 *(978-1-57505-853-5(7)*, 874a7979-0aa4-420f-b264-7518f1db648e, First Avenue Editions) Lerner Publishing Group.

Souza, Dorothy M. Volcanoes Inside & Out. Cormack, Allan & Cormack, Deborah Drew Brook, illus. 2005. (On My Own Science Ser.). 48p. (J). (gr. 3-7). lib. bdg. 25.26 *(978-1-57505-761-3(1))* Lerner Publishing Group.

Spilsbury, Louise & Spilsbury, Richard. Volcano Melts Village, 1 vol. 2017. (Earth under Attack! Ser.). (ENG.). 48p. (J). (gr. 5-5). pap. 15.05 *(978-1-5382-1319-3(2)*, 653e8443-343e-407f-8420-15b2e38d1598) Stevens, Gareth Publishing LLLP.

—Volcano Melts Village, 1 vol. 2017. (Earth under Attack! Ser.). (ENG.). 48p. (J). (gr. 5-5). lib. bdg. 33.60 *(978-1-5382-1321-6(4)*, 071c4749-be7f-481d-bc30-7d493b3a0268) Stevens, Gareth Publishing LLLP.

Spilsbury, Richard & Spilsbury, Louise. Escape the Volcano. 2015. (Science Adventures Ser.). (ENG., Illus.). 32p. (J). (gr. 3-7). 31.35 *(978-1-62588-146-5(0))* Black Rabbit Bks.

Stamper, Judith Bauer. Volcanoes. 2010. (Illus.). 32p. (J). pap. *(978-0-545-28543-8(7))* Scholastic, Inc.

Stamper, Judith Bauer & Stamper, Judith. Voyage to the Volcano. 2003. (Magic School Bus Chapter Bks.: 15). (gr. 3-6). lib. bdg. 14.75 *(978-0-613-63363-5(6))* Turtleback.

Steele, Philip & Morris, Neil. Inside Volcanoes, 1 vol. 2006. (Inside Nature's Disasters Ser.). (ENG., Illus.). 36p. (gr. 4-6). lib. bdg. 28.67 *(978-0-8368-7250-7(9)*, d007bef0-561d-4404-9ef5-613371ab4c5b, Gareth Stevens Learning Library) Stevens, Gareth Publishing LLLP.

Steele, Philip, et al. Extreme Planet. 2014. (Illus.). 128p. (J). *(978-1-4351-5523-7(8))* Barnes & Noble, Inc.

Stewart, Melissa. Earthquakes & Volcanoes. 2008. (For Your Information Ser.). (Illus.). 80p. (J). (gr. 3-7). pap. 7.99 *(978-0-06-089950-9(6))* HarperCollins Pubs.

Stienecker, David. Blast Zone: The Eruption & Recovery of Mount St. Helens. 2003. (ENG., Illus.). 32p. (J). (gr. 6-8). pap. 7.97 net. *(978-0-7652-3265-6(0)*, Celebration Pr.) Savvas Learning Co.

Storey, Melinda. Volcanoes: A Comprehensive Hands-on Science Unit. Mitchell, Judy & Lindeen, Mary, eds. Armbrust, Janet, illus. 2007. (Nature's Fury Ser.). 32p. (J). pap. 6.95 *(978-1-57310-530-9(9))* Teaching & Learning Co.

Sutherland, Lin. Terremotos y Volcanes. Lopez-Izquierdo, Nieves, tr. 2003. (Exploradores de National Geographic Ser.). (SPA., Illus.). 64p. (gr. 4-7). *(978-970-651-716-6(2)*, 1610) Editorial Oceano De Mexico, S.A. DE C.V.

Tagliaferro, Linda. How Does a Volcano Become an Island? rev. ed. 2016. (How Does It Happen Ser.). (ENG.). 32p. (J). (gr. 3-5). pap. 8.29 *(978-1-4109-8530-9(X)*, 134115, Raintree) Capstone.

Tanumihardja, Pat. Amazing Islands Around the World. 2019. (Passport to Nature Ser.). (ENG., Illus.). 32p. (J). (gr. 4-6). lib. bdg. 28.65 *(978-1-5435-5777-0(5)*, 139733) Capstone.

Thoron, Joe. Volcanoes, 1 vol. 2007. (Kaleidoscope: Earth Science Ser.). (ENG., Illus.). 48p. (gr. 4-4). lib. bdg. 32.64 *(978-0-7614-2105-4(X)*, a9afe808-91dd-44d9-a334-77ac9f454931) Cavendish Square Publishing LLC.

Ticktock Media, Ltd. Staff. Violent Planet. 2008. (ENG.). 128p. (J). (gr. 4-7). pap. 12.95 *(978-1-84696-813-6(5)*, TickTock Books) Octopus Publishing Group GBR. Dist: Independent Pubs. Group.

Time For Kids, Editors. Time for Kids: Volcanoes! 2006. (Time for Kids Ser.). (ENG., Illus.). 32p. (J). (gr. 1-3). pap. 3.99 *(978-0-06-078223-8(4))* HarperCollins Pubs.

Time for Kids Magazine Staff, ed. Volcanoes! 2006. (Time for Kids Science Scoops Ser.). (Illus.). 32p. (gr. 1-3). 14.00 *(978-0-7569-6984-4(0))* Perfection Learning Corp.

Truett, Trudi Strain. Detecting Volcanic Eruptions. 2017. (Detecting Disasters Ser.). (ENG., Illus.). 32p. (J). (gr. 3-5). lib. bdg. 31.35 *(978-1-63517-006-1(0)*, 1635170060, Focus Readers) North Star Editions.

Trueno de la Tierra: 6 Small Books. (Saludos Ser.: Vol. 2). (SPA.). (gr. 3-5). 31.00 *(978-0-7635-2068-7(3))* Rigby Education.

Tuffen, Hugh & Waldron, Melanie. Volcanologist: The Coolest Jobs on the Planet, 1 vol. HL Studios, illus. 2014. (Coolest Jobs on the Planet Ser.). (ENG.). 48p. (J). (gr. 5-8). 35.32 *(978-1-4109-6643-8(7)*, 126143); pap. 8.99 *(978-1-4109-6649-0(6)*, 126148) Capstone. (Raintree).

Turnbull, Stephanie. Volcanoes. Tudor, Andy, illus. 2006. (Usborne Beginners Ser.). 32p. (J). (gr. 1). lib. bdg. 12.99 *(978-1-58086-949-2(1))*; 4.99 *(978-0-7945-1401-3(4))* EDC Publishing. (Usborne).

—Volcanoes. Tudor, Andy, illus. 2005. 32p. (J). pap. *(978-0-439-84610-3(2))* Scholastic, Inc.

Usborne Books Staff, creator. Volcanoes Kid Kit. 2006. (Kid Kits Ser.). (Illus.). (J). (gr. 1). 15.99 *(978-1-58086-981-2(5))* EDC Publishing.

Los Volcanes, 6 vols., Vol. 2. (Explorers. Exploradores Nonfiction Sets Ser.).Tr. of Volcanos. (SPA.). 32p. (gr. 3-6). 44.95 *(978-0-7699-0645-4(1))* Shortland Pubns. (U. S. A.) Inc.

Volcanoes. 3rd ed. 2018. (J). *(978-0-7166-9942-2(7))* World Bk., Inc.

Volcanoes: Level O, 6 vols., Vol. 2. (Explorers Ser.). 32p. (gr. 3-6). 44.95 *(978-0-7699-0609-6(5))* Shortland Pubns. (U. S. A.) Inc.

Walker, Sally M. Volcanoes. 2008. pap. 52.95 *(978-0-8225-9347-8(5))* 2007. (ENG., Illus.). 48p. (gr. 2-5). lib. bdg. 26.60 *(978-0-8225-6733-2(4)*, Lerner Pubns.) Lerner Publishing Group.

Watt, Fiona. Earthquakes & Volcanoes. Stockley, Corinne & Brooks, Felicity, eds. Gower, Jeremy & Shields, Chris, illus. rev. ed. 2007. (Geography Ser.). 32p. (YA). (gr. 8-12). pap. 7.99 *(978-0-7945-1531-7(2)*, Usborne) EDC Publishing.

Webster, Christine. Mauna Loa: The Largest Volcano in the United States. 2004. (Natural Wonders of the U. S. A. Ser.). (Illus.). 32p. (J). (gr. 3-6). per. 9.95 *(978-1-59036-162-7(8))* Weigl Pubs., Inc.

Whiting, Jim. The Volcanic Eruption on Santorini, 1650 BCE. 2007. (Natural Disasters Ser.). (Illus.). 32p. (J). (gr. 1-4). lib. bdg. 25.70 *(978-1-58415-568-3(X))* Mitchell Lane Pubs.

Winchester, Simon. The Day the World Exploded: The Earthshaking Catastrophe at Krakatoa. Chin, Jason, illus. 2008. 96p. (J). (gr. 5-9). lib. bdg. 23.89 *(978-0-06-123983-0(6))* HarperCollins Pubs.

Wiseman, Blaine. Volcanoes. 2014. (J). *(978-1-4896-3276-0(X))* Weigl Pubs., Inc.

Wonders of Creation: Volcanoes & Their. 2004. reprint ed. pap. 15.95 *(978-1-4191-9484-9(4))* Kessinger Publishing, LLC.

Wonders of Creation: Volcanoes & Their Phenomena. 2004. reprint ed. pap. 1.99 *(978-1-4192-9484-6(9))* Kessinger Publishing, LLC.

Woods, Michael & Woods, Mary B. Volcanoes. 2006. (Disasters up Close Ser.). (ENG., Illus.). 64p. (gr. 4-8). lib. bdg. 27.93 *(978-0-8225-4715-0(5)*, Lerner Pubns.) Lerner Publishing Group.

Woolf, Alex. The Science of Natural Disasters: the Devastating Truth about Volcanoes, Earthquakes, & Tsunamis (the Science of the Earth) (Library Edition) Rowland, Andy, illus. 2018. (Science Of... Ser.). (ENG.). 32p. (J). (gr. 3-7). lib. bdg. 29.00 *(978-0-531-22766-4(9)*, Watts, Franklin) Scholastic Library Publishing.

World Book, Inc. Staff, contrib. by. Volcanoes. (Illus.). 47p. (J). 2007. *(978-0-7166-9815-9(3))* 2nd ed. 2009. *(978-0-7166-9831-9(5))* World Bk., Inc.

Yomtov, Nel. When Volcanoes Erupt! O'Neill, Sean, illus. 2012. (Adventures in Science Ser.). (ENG.). 32p. (gr. 3-4). pap. 47.70 *(978-1-4296-8468-2(2)*, Capstone Pr.) Capstone.

Yomtov, Nelson. When Volcanoes Erupt!, 1 vol. O'Neill, Sean, illus. 2012. (Adventures in Science Ser.). (ENG.). 32p. (J). (gr. 3-9). pap. 8.10 *(978-1-4296-7990-9(5)*, 118322) Capstone.

Zeiger, Jennifer. Measuring Volcanic Activity. 2015. (Explorer Library: Science Explorer Ser.). (ENG., Illus.). 32p. (J). (gr. 4-8). lib. bdg. 32.07 *(978-1-63362-389-7(0)*, 206976) Cherry Lake Publishing.

—Measuring Volcanic Activity. 2018. (J). *(978-1-5105-3722-4(8))* SmartBook Media, Inc.

VOLCANOES—FICTION

Amillway, Alex. The Magma Conspiracy: Armed, Dangerous & Covered in Fur! 2013. (ENG., Illus.). 224p. (J). pap. 5.99 *(978-1-61067-159-0(7))* Kane Miller.

Avalon, Dawn. Bubbles. A Wet Dragon. 2006. 59p. pap. 8.21 *(978-1-4116-1177-1(2))* Lulu Pr., Inc.

Awdry, W. Thomas & the Volcano. 2015. (Thomas & Friends Step into Reading Ser.). lib. bdg. 14.75 *(978-0-606-36404-1(8))* Turtleback.

Bordiglioni, Stefano. Volcano!, 1 vol. Bertolucci, Federico, illus. 2009. (Dinodino's Dinosaur Adventures Ser.). (ENG.). 56p. (J). (gr. 1-2). 32.60 *(978-1-60754-712-9(0)*, 530591fb-ba8f-457a-8164-2dcd316cec2b); pap. 13.85 *(978-1-60754-717-4(1)*, 43a607e3-f610-4f50-9cdc-64fa024f5aad) Rosen Publishing Group, Inc., The. (Windmill Bks.).

Brasch, Nicolas. Escape from Pacaya, 1 vol. rev. ed. 2013. (Literary Text Ser.). (ENG., Illus.). 24p. (J). (gr. 1-3). pap. 8.99 *(978-1-4333-5529-5(9))* Teacher Created Materials, Inc.

—Hot Springs & Brown Bears, 1 vol. rev. ed. 2013. (Literary Text Ser.). (ENG., Illus.). 32p. (gr. 2-4). pap. 11.99 *(978-1-4333-5637-7(6))* Teacher Created Materials, Inc.

Brunson, Emma. Survivor Spirit Book: Megan's Ark. 2010. 204p. pap. 13.50 *(978-1-60911-834-1(0)*, Eloquent Bks.) Strategic Book Publishing & Rights Agency (SBPRA).

Catasús Jennings, Terry. Gopher to the Rescue! a Volcano Recovery Story, 1 vol. O'Keefe, Laurie, illus. 2012. (ENG.). 32p. (J). (gr. -1-4). 17.95 *(978-1-60718-131-6(2))*; pap. 9.95 *(978-1-60718-141-5(X))* Arbordale Publishing.

Cook, Sherry & Johnson, Terri. Vinnie Volcano, 26. Kuhn, Jesse, illus. I.t. ed. 2006. (Quirkles — Exploring Phonics through Science Ser.: 22). 32p. (J). 7.99 *(978-1-933815-21-3(3)*, Quirkles, The) Creative 3, LLC.

Coss, Lauren. Volcanoes. 2013. (Earth in Action Ser.). (ENG., Illus.). 48p. (J). (gr. 4-8). pap. 18.50 *(978-1-62403-007-9(6)*, 8682) ABDO Publishing Co.

COX, Margaret. The Emerald-fire. 2010. 166p. pap. 11.50 *(978-1-4461-3379-8(6))* Lulu Pr., Inc.

Crawford, Brian. The Evil Wind. 2017. (Survive Ser.). (ENG.). 192p. (YA). (gr. 5-12). lib. bdg. 31.42 *(978-1-68076-732-2(1)*, 25398, Epic Escape) EPIC Pr.

Crofoot, Betty & Arledge, Roo. The Great Celebration Ceremony - My Genie & Me Series Book 2. 2012. 84p. pap. 8.95 *(978-1-60862-430-0(7))* E-BookTime LLC.

Derubertis, Barbara. Victor Vicuna's Volcano Vacation. Alley, R. W., illus. 2011. (Animal Antics A to Z Set III Ser.). pap. 45.32 *(978-0-7613-8431-1(6))* Astra Publishing Hse.

deRubertis, Barbara. Victor Vicuna's Volcano Vacation. Alley, R. W., illus. 2011. (Animal Antics A to Z Ser.). 32p. (J). (gr. -1-3). pap. 7.95 *(978-1-57565-347-1(8)*, e2e7f138-2df7-44ad-b7e3-c5fb2ef2c3ed, Kane Press) Astra Publishing Hse.

deRubertis, Barbara & DeRubertis, Barbara. Victor Vicuna's Volcano Vacation. Alley, R. W., illus. 2012. (Animal Antics A to Z Ser.). 32p. (J). (gr. 2 — 1). cd-rom 7.95 *(978-1-57565-415-7(6))* Astra Publishing Hse.

Earhart, Kristin, et al. The Magic School Bus Inside a Volcano. Bracken, Carolyn, illus. 2012. 32p. (J). *(978-0-545-35685-5(7))* Scholastic, Inc.

George, Jean Craighead. Dear Katie, the Volcano Is a Girl. 32p. (J). pap. *(978-0-7868-1178-6(1))* Hyperion Bks. for Children.

Geraghty, Paul. Dinosaur in Danger. 2005. (Illus.). 40p. (J). pap. *(978-0-09-943865-6(8)*, Red Fox) Random House Children's Books.

Giulieri, Anne. The Volcano Sand Hill. Boyer, Susy, illus. 2012. (Engage Literacy Blue Ser.). (ENG.). 16p. (J). (gr. k-2). pap. 36.94 *(978-1-4296-8977-9(3)*, 18385); pap. 6.99 *(978-1-4296-8976-2(5)*, 119993) Capstone. (Capstone Pr.).

Godkin, Celia. When the Giant Stirred: Legend of a Volcanic Island, 1 vol. Godkin, Celia, illus. 2005. (ENG., Illus.). 40p. (J). (gr. k-2). pap. 14.95 *(978-1-55041-965-8(X)*, f0511b34-690e-4645-9ba7-f91ab12d04ce) Fitzhenry & Whiteside, Ltd. CAN. Dist: Firefly Bks., Ltd.

Greenway, Beth. Una Verdadera Princesa de Hawái. Yee, Tammy, illus. 2017. (SPA.). 32p. (J). (gr. 2-3). pap. 11.95 *(978-1-62855-950-7(0)*, 0e9b39f5-7b57-457e-903b-b4620d5a04b2) Arbordale Publishing.

Hayler, Kate. Volcano Alert! Team Mission: A Pop-up Book. Giraffe, Red & Doughty, Clare, illus. 2006. 10p. (J). (gr. k-4). reprint ed. 19.00 *(978-1-4223-5075-1(4))* DIANE Publishing Co.

Hoena, Blake. Can You Survive a Supervolcano Eruption? An Interactive Doomsday Adventure. Vanzo, Filippo, illus. 2016. (You Choose: Doomsday Ser.). (ENG.). 112p. (J). (gr. 3-7). lib. bdg. 32.65 *(978-1-4914-8108-0(0)*, 130599, Capstone Pr.) Capstone.

Kennedy, Marlane. Volcano Blast (Disaster Strikes #4) Madrid, Erwin, illus. 2015. (Disaster Strikes Ser.: 4). (ENG.). 128p. (J). (gr. 2-5). pap. 4.99 *(978-0-545-53047-7(4)*, Scholastic Paperbacks) Scholastic, Inc.

Lawrence, Margaret. Earthshakers, Top Blowers & High Rollers. 2012. 170p. pap. 36.95 *(978-1-937600-74-7(2))* Salem Author Services.

Lewis, Paul Owen. Frog Girl. 2004. (Illus.). 38p. (J). tchr. ed., tchr.'s planning gde. ed. 2.95 *(978-1-58246-009-3(4)*, Tricycle Pr.) Ten Speed Pr.

—Frog Girl. (ENG., Illus.). 32p. (J). (gr. -1-5). 18.95 *(978-1-55110-658-8(2))* Whitecap Bks., Ltd. CAN. Dist: Graphic Arts Ctr. Publishing Co.

Locke, Elsie. A Canoe in the Mist. 2005. (ENG.). 224p. *(978-1-86950-568-4(9))* HarperCollins Pubs. Australia.

Maddox, Jake. Volcano! A Survive! Story. Tiffany, Sean, illus. 2009. (Jake Maddox Sports Stories Ser.). (ENG.). 72p. (J). (gr. 3-6). 25.99 *(978-1-4342-1208-5(4)*, 95405, Stone Arch Bks.) Capstone.

Manushkin, Fran. Katie Blows Her Top. Lyon, Tammie, illus. 2018. (Katie Woo Ser.). (ENG.). 32p. (J). (gr. k-2). lib. bdg. 22.65 *(978-1-5158-2265-3(6)*, 136884, Picture Window Bks.) Capstone.

Marsh, Carole. The Curse of the Ancient Acropolis: Athens, Greece. 2008. (Carole Marsh Mysteries Ser.). 133p. (J). (gr. 3-5). per. 7.99 *(978-0-635-06470-7(7)*, Marsh, Carole Bks.) Gallopade International.

—The Voracious Volcano Mystery. 2008. (Masters of Disasters Ser.). (Illus.). 118p. (J). (gr. 3-5). 14.95 *(978-0-635-06466-0(9))*; per. 5.99 *(978-0-635-06463-9(4))* Gallopade International.

Messner, Kate. Journey Through Ash & Smoke (Ranger in Time #5) McMorris, Kelley, illus. 2017. (Ranger in Time Ser.: 5). (ENG.). 160p. (J). (gr. 2-5). pap. 5.99 *(978-0-545-90978-5(3)*, Scholastic Pr.) Scholastic, Inc.

Mullin, Mike. Ashen Winter. 2013. (Ashfall Ser.). (ENG.). 580p. (YA). (gr. 6). pap. 13.99 *(978-1-933718-98-9(6))* Tanglewood Pr.

—Ashfall. (Ashfall Ser.). (ENG.). 476p. (gr. 8). 2012. (YA). pap. 13.99 *(978-1-933718-74-3(9))* 2011. (J). 17.95 *(978-1-933718-55-2(2))* Tanglewood Pr.
leff, C. M. The Glue Volcano. 2008. 14p. pap. 24.95 *(978-1-60441-312-0(3))* America Star Bks.
)plinger, Jon & Cooke, Elizabeth. The Wicked Small People of Whiskey Bridge. 2011. 156p. (gr. 4-6). 22.95 *(978-1-4620-4948-6(6))*; pap. 12.95 *(978-1-4620-4947-9(8))* iUniverse, Inc.
)sborne, Mary Pope. Vacation under the Volcano. unabr. ed. 2004. (Magic Tree House Ser.: No. 13). 74p. (J). (gr. k-3). pap. 17.00 incl. audio *(978-0-8072-0782-6(9))*, LFTR 241 SP, Listening Library) Random Hse. Audio Publishing Group.
Pugin-Rodas, M. C. The Eight Ball Club: Ocean of Fire. 2007. (ENG., Illus.). 144p. pap. 15.95 *(978-0-9793761-2-2(2))* ESOL Publishing.
Slivensky, Katie. The Seismic Seven. 2018. (ENG., Illus.). 352p. (J). (gr. 3-7). 16.99 *(978-0-06-246318-0(7))*, HarperCollins) HarperCollins Pubs.
Snelling, Lauraine. What about Cimmaron? 2008. (J). 8.99 *(978-1-59166-872-5(7))* BJU Pr.
Stamper, Judith. Voyage to the Volcano. Speirs, John, illus. 2010. (Magic School Bus Science Chapter Bks.). (KOR.). 101p. (J). *(978-89-491-5322-3(X))* Biryongso Publishing Co.
—Voyage to the Volcano. Speirs, John, illus. 2003. (Magic School Bus Science Chapter Bks.). 87p. (gr. 3-6). 15.00 *(978-0-7569-1581-0(3))* Perfection Learning Corp.
Stevens, A. P. The Volcano: The Adventures of Antboy & Mr Cricket. Finn, N. K., ed. Deskcube, illus. 2008. (ENG.). 29p. pap. 9.95 *(978-0-9798886-0-1(3))* Mugsy and Sugar Pressed.
Tarshis, Lauren. I Survived the Destruction of Pompeii, AD 79. Dawson, Scott, illus. 2014. 95p. (J). *(978-0-545-77568-7(X))*, Scholastic Pr.) Scholastic, Inc.
—I Survived the Destruction of Pompeii, AD 79 (I Survived #10) 2014. (I Survived Ser.: 10). (ENG., Illus.). 112p. (J). (gr. 2-5). pap. 5.99 *(978-0-545-45939-6(7))* Scholastic, Inc.
—I Survived the Eruption of Mount St. Helens, 1980 (I Survived #14) 2016. (I Survived Ser.: 14). (ENG., Illus.). 112p. (J). (gr. 2-5). pap. 5.99 *(978-0-545-65852-2(7))*, Scholastic Paperbacks) Scholastic, Inc.
Teitelbaum, Michael, adapted by. Volcano to the Rescue! 2016. (Illus.). (J). *(978-1-5182-3165-0(9))*, Sizzle Pr.) Little Bee Books Inc.
Turner, Daniel. Cinnamon the Adventurous Guinea Pig Goes to Devil's Island. Skinner, Gayle, illus. 2013. (ENG.). 48p. (J). pap. 10.95 *(978-1-4787-1753-9(X))* Outskirts Pr., Inc.
Vern, Jules. A Journey to the Interior of the Earth. 2006. 196p. per. 13.95 *(978-1-59818-461-7(X))* Aegypan.
—Journey to the Interior of the Earth. 2006. 196p. 26.95 *(978-1-59818-557-7(8))* Aegypan.
—Voyage au Centre de la Terre.Tr. of Voyage to the Center of the Earth. (FRE.). (J). pap. 14.95 *(978-2-07-051437-3(4))* Gallimard, Editions FRA. Dist: Distribooks, Inc.
Viva, Frank. A Trip to the Top of the Volcano with Mouse: TOON Level 1. 2019. (Trips with Mouse Ser.). (Illus.). 36p. (J). (gr. -1-k). 12.99 *(978-1-943145-36-2(9))*, TOON Books) Astra Publishing Hse.
Westerman, Robert. Alohalani Kalikimaka Auntie: Sheet Music & Lyrics. Westerman, Robert, . 2006. (Illus.). 12p. (J). 6.95 *(978-0-9761992-1-2(1))* Gold Boy Music & Pubn.
Wilson, Wendy. The First Book of Red. 2005. 99p. pap. 19.95 *(978-1-4137-5570-1(4))* America Star Bks.
Withers, Pam. Mountainboard Maniacs, 1 vol. 2008. (Take It to the Xtreme Ser.: 10). (ENG.). 224p. (YA). (gr. 7-10). pap. 8.95 *(978-1-55285-915-5(0))*, 4fbe12e4-14b9-4b2f-9af7-46356e50c102) Whitecap Bks., Ltd. CAN. Dist: Firefly Bks., Ltd.

VOLGA RIVER AND VALLEY

Mattern, Joanne. The Volga River. 2012. (Illus.). 47p. (J). lib. bdg. 29.95 *(978-1-61228-312-8(8))* Mitchell Lane Pubs.

VOLLEYBALL

Abramovitz, Melissa. Volleyball, 1 vol. 2013. (Science Behind Sports Ser.). (ENG., Illus.). 128p. (gr. 7-7). lib. bdg. 41.03 *(978-1-4205-1157-4(2))*, ef719fc6-8958-4c89-8dfb-70b332329cc7, Lucent Pr.) Greenhaven Publishing LLC.
Ackerman, Jon. Make Me the Best Volleyball Player. 2016. (Make Me the Best Athlete Ser.). (ENG., Illus.). 48p. (J). (gr. 4-6). lib. bdg. 34.21 *(978-1-68078-492-3(7))*, 23793, SportsZone) ABDO Publishing Co.
Barth, Katrin & Heuchert, Richard. Learning Volleyball. 2006. (Illus.). 152p. (J). (gr. 4-7). pap. 14.95 *(978-1-84126-197-3(1))* Meyer & Meyer Sport, Ltd. GBR. Dist: Cardinal Pubs. Group.
Barth, Katrin & Linkerhand, Antje. Training Volleyball. 2007. (Illus.). 152p. (J). (gr. 4-7). pap. 14.95 *(978-1-84126-211-6(0))* Meyer & Meyer Sport, Ltd. GBR. Dist: Cardinal Pubs. Group.
Buckey, A. W. Women in Volleyball. 2020. (She's Got Game Ser.). (ENG., Illus.). 32p. (J). (gr. 3-5). pap. 9.95 *(978-1-64493-145-5(1))*, 1644931451); lib. bdg. 31.35 *(978-1-64493-066-3(8))*, 1644930668) North Star Editions. (Focus Readers).
Crossingham, John & Kalman, Bobbie. Spike It Volleyball. 2008. (Sports Starters Ser.). (ENG., Illus.). 32p. (J). (gr. 3-7). pap. *(978-0-7787-3175-7(8))*; lib. bdg. *(978-0-7787-3143-6(X))* Crabtree Publishing Co.
Dann, Sarah. Le Volleyball. 2011. (FRE., Illus.). 32p. (J). pap. 9.95 *(978-2-89579-413-4(8))* Bayard Canada CAN. Dist: Crabtree Publishing Co.
Derr, Aaron. Volleyball: An Introduction to Being a Good Sport. Angle, Scott, illus. 2017. (Start Smart (tm) — Sports Ser.). (ENG.). 32p. (J). (gr. k-3). lib. bdg. 26.65 *(978-1-63440-134-0(4))*, ba00301c-2a4a-4347-8c72-7ede82092e20); E-Book 39.99 *(978-1-63440-146-3(8))* Red Chair Pr.
Doeden, Matt. Volleyball. 2015. (Summer Olympic Sports Ser.). (ENG., Illus.). 32p. (J). (gr. 2-4). 19.95 *(978-1-60753-811-0(3))* Amicus Learning.
Dolphin, Colleen. Volleyball by the Numbers, 1 vol. 2010. (Team Sports by the Numbers Ser.). (ENG.). 24p. (J). (gr. k-3). lib. bdg. 29.93 *(978-1-60453-772-7(8))*, 14686, SandCastle) ABDO Publishing Co.
Douglas, Peter. Volleyball: Approaching the Net. 2017. (Preparing for Game Day Ser.: Vol. 10). (ENG.). 80p. (J). (gr. 7-12). 24.95 *(978-1-4222-3921-6(7))* Mason Crest.
Evdokimoff, Natasha. Volleyball. (For the Love of Sports Ser.). (Illus.). (J). (gr. 3-6). 2019. (ENG.). 24p. pap. 12.95 *(978-1-7911-0569-3(6))* 2019. (ENG., 24p. lib. bdg. 28.55 *(978-1-7911-0029-2(5))* 2010. 32p. pap. 11.95 *(978-1-60596-908-4(7))* 2010. 32p. lib. bdg. 25.70 *(978-1-60596-907-7(9))* Weigl Pubs., Inc.
Forest, Anne. Girls Play Volleyball, 1 vol. 2016. (Girls Join the Team Ser.). (ENG.). 24p. (J). (gr. 3-3). pap. 9.25 *(978-1-4994-2111-8(7))*, 4299e850-dc0e-4125-a16c-d6eeb3924f8b, PowerKids Pr.) Rosen Publishing Group, Inc., The.
Getting the Edge: Conditioning, Injuries, & Legal & Illicit Drugs, 14 vols., Set. Incl. Baseball & Softball. Sanna, Gabriel. lib. bdg. 24.95 *(978-1-4222-1730-6(2))*; Basketball. Vanderhoof, Gabrielle. lib. bdg. 24.95 *(978-1-4222-1731-3(0))*; Cheerleading. Vanderhoof, Gabrielle. lib. bdg. 24.95 *(978-1-4222-1732-0(9))*; Extreme Sports. Li, Wenfang. lib. bdg. 24.95 *(978-1-4222-1729-0(9))*; Football. McIntosh, J. S. lib. bdg. 24.95 *(978-1-4222-1733-7(7))*; Gymnastics. McIntosh, J. S. lib. bdg. 24.95 *(978-1-4222-1734-4(5))*; Hockey. Vanderhoof, Gabrielle. lib. bdg. 24.95 *(978-1-4222-1735-1(3))*; Lacrosse. Vanderhoof, Gabrielle. lib. bdg. 24.95 *(978-1-4222-1737-5(X))*; Martial Arts. McIntosh, J. S. lib. bdg. 24.95 *(978-1-4222-1738-2(8))*; Soccer. McIntosh, J. S. lib. bdg. 24.95 *(978-1-4222-1739-9(6))*; Track & Field. Vanderhoof, Gabrielle. lib. bdg. 24.95 *(978-1-4222-1740-5(X))*; Volleyball. Vanderhoof, Gabrielle. lib. bdg. 24.95 *(978-1-4222-1741-2(8))*; Wrestling. McIntosh, J. S. lib. bdg. 24.95 *(978-1-4222-1743-6(4))*; (YA). 2010. (Illus.). 96p. 2011. Set lib. bdg. 349.30 *(978-1-4222-1728-3(0))*, 1317895) Mason Crest.
Grozdanovic, Sava, et al. Volleyball for Boys & Girls. 2004. (Illus.). 168p. pap. 17.95 *(978-1-84126-126-3(2))* Meyer & Meyer Sport, Ltd. GBR. Dist: Cardinal Pubs. Group.
Jensen, Julie. Play-by-Play Volleyball. King, Andy, photos by. 2005. (Play-by-Play Ser.). (Illus.). 80p. (gr. 4-8). pap.; lib. bdg. 23.93 *(978-0-8225-9882-4(5))* Lerner Publishing Group.
Kortemeier, Todd. 12 Reasons to Love Volleyball. 2018. (Sports Report). (ENG.). 32p. (J). (gr. 3-6). 32.80 *(978-1-63235-432-7(2))*, 13795, 12-Story Library) Bookstaves, LLC.
—12 Reasons to Love Volleyball. 2018. (ENG.). 32p. (gr. 3-6). pap. 9.95 *(978-1-62143-553-2(9))* Pr. Room Editions LLC.
LeBoutillier, Nate. Volleyball. 2012. (Summer Olympic Legends Ser.). (ENG., Illus.). 48p. (J). (gr. 5-8). 35.65 *(978-1-60818-213-8(4))*, 22293, Creative Education) Creative Co., The.
McClellan, Ray. Volleyball. 2010. (My First Sports Ser.). (ENG., Illus.). 24p. (J). (gr. 2-5). lib. bdg. 26.95 *(978-1-60014-464-6(0))*, Blastoff! Readers) Bellwether Media.
McIntyre, Abigael & Giddens, Sandra. An Insider's Guide to Volleyball. 2014. (Sports Tips, Techniques, & Strategies Ser.). (Illus.). 48p. (J). (gr. 5-8). pap. 70.50 *(978-1-4777-8598-0(1))*, Rosen Reference) Rosen Publishing Group, Inc., The.
Miller, Kat & Manley, Claudia B. Volleyball: Girls Rocking It, 1 vol., 1. 2015. (Title IX Rocks! Ser.). (ENG., Illus.). 64p. (J). (gr. 6-6). 36.13 *(978-1-5081-7045-7(2))*, 86ed7e31-de2f-44ac-bf59-9071f936d0ddc, Rosen Young Adult) Rosen Publishing Group, Inc., The.
Monnig, Alex. Total Volleyball. 2016. (Total Sports Ser.). (ENG., Illus.). 64p. (J). (gr. 3-6). lib. bdg. 35.64 *(978-1-68078-508-1(7))*, 23839, SportsZone) ABDO Publishing Co.
Omoth, Tyler. First Source to Volleyball: Rules, Equipment, & Key Playing Tips. 2017. (First Sports Source Ser.). (ENG., Illus.). 24p. (J). (gr. 1-3). lib. bdg. 27.99 *(978-1-5157-8783-9(4))*, 136333, Capstone Pr.) Capstone.
Osborne, M. K. El Vóleibol. 2020. (Deportes Olímpicos de Verano Ser.). (SPA.). 32p. (J). (gr. 2-5). lib. bdg. *(978-1-68151-900-5(3))*, 10704) Amicus.
—Volleyball. 2nd ed. 2020. (Summer Olympic Sports Ser.). (ENG., Illus.). 32p. (J). (gr. 2-4). pap. 11.99 *(978-1-68152-554-9(2))*, 10753) Amicus.
Saxena, Shalini. Volleyball & Its Greatest Players, 1 vol. 2014. (Inside Sports Ser.). (ENG.). 80p. (YA). (gr. 6-6). 35.29 *(978-1-62275-594-3(4))*, a5955bbc-f3d1-4725-aaed-5461c5da89ab, Britannica Educational Publishing) Rosen Publishing Group, Inc., The.
Schuh, Mari. Volleyball. 2019. (Spot Sports Ser.). (ENG.). 16p. (J). (gr. -1-2). lib. bdg. *(978-1-68151-655-4(1))*, 10787) Amicus.
Schwartz, Heather E. Top Volleyball Tips. 2017. (Top Sports Tips Ser.). (ENG., Illus.). 32p. (J). (gr. 3-9). lib. bdg. 28.65 *(978-1-5157-4720-8(4))*, 134355, Capstone Pr.) Capstone.
Slupskiy, Leon. Volleyball with the Family: Fife Steps to Success. Synepolsky, I. & Belomlinsky, M., illus. 2003. 105/35p. (YA). pap. *(978-0-9728301-3-3(8))* Publishing Hse. Gelany.
Vanderhoof, Gabrielle. Volleyball. 2010. (Getting the Edge Ser.). 96p. (YA). lib. bdg. 24.95 *(978-1-4222-1741-2(8))* Mason Crest.
Watson, Stephanie. The Science Behind Soccer, Volleyball, Cycling, & Other Popular Sports. 2016. (Science of the Summer Olympics Ser.). (ENG., Illus.). 32p. (J). (gr. 3-9). lib. bdg. 28.65 *(978-1-4914-8160-8(9))*, 130639, Capstone Pr.) Capstone.

VOLUNTARISM

Ancona, George. Can We Help? Kids Volunteering to Help Their Communities. Ancona, George, illus. (ENG., Illus.). 48p. (J). (gr. k-3). 2019. 7.99 *(978-1-5362-0297-7(5))* 2015. 17.99 *(978-0-7636-7367-3(6))* Candlewick Pr.
Bartowski, Sara. Gavin Volunteers!, 1 vol. 2012. (InfoMax Readers Ser.). (ENG., Illus.). 24p. (J). (gr. 1-1). pap. 8.25 *(978-1-4488-9064-4(0))*, ccc08a8d-9c0b-45dc-b146-0df3b87a823e, Rosen Classroom) Rosen Publishing Group, Inc., The.
Born This Way Foundation Reporters & Gaga, Lady. Channel Kindness: Stories of Kindness & Community. 2020. (ENG.). 304p. (YA). 24.99 *(978-1-250-24558-8(3))*, 900212605) Feiwel & Friends.
Borus, Audrey. Volunteering: A How-To Guide, 1 vol. 2011. (Life: a How-To Guide Ser.). (ENG., Illus.). 128p. (gr. 6-7). pap. 13.88 *(978-1-59845-310-2(6))*, 35537eeb-72a2-47fa-8435-a0d963a3cea0); lib. bdg. 35.93 *(978-0-7660-3440-2(2))*, 5452a950-ee37-47eb-94bf-14ac14765e9e) Enslow Publishing, LLC.
Cane, Ella. Communities in My World, 1 vol. 2013. (My World Ser.). (ENG.). 24p. (J). (gr. -1-2). pap. 6.95 *(978-1-4765-3462-6(4))*, 123561) Capstone.
Clinton, Chelsea. It's Your World: Get Informed, Get Inspired & Get Going! (ENG., Illus.). (J). (gr. 5). 2017. 432p. pap. 9.99 *(978-0-399-54532-0(8))*, Puffin Books) 2015. 416p. 18.99 *(978-0-399-17612-8(8))*, Philomel Bks.) Penguin Young Readers Group.
—Start Now! You Can Make a Difference. 144p. (J). (gr. 2-5). 2020. 8.99 *(978-0-525-51438-1(4))*, Puffin Books) 2018. (Illus.). 16.99 *(978-0-525-51436-7(8))*, Philomel Bks.) Penguin Young Readers Group.
Cohn, Jessica. Hand to Heart: Improving Communities, 1 vol. 2nd rev. ed. (TIME for KIDS(r): Informational Text Ser.). (ENG., 48p. (gr. 4-5). 2013. Illus.). (J). lib. bdg. 29.96 *(978-1-4807-1118-1(7))* 2012. pap. 11.99 *(978-1-4333-4866-2(7))* Teacher Created Materials, Inc.
—Hand to Paw - Protecting Animals, 1 vol. 2nd rev. ed. 2012. (TIME for KIDS(r): Informational Text Ser.). (ENG.). 48p. (gr. 4-5). pap. 13.99 *(978-1-4333-4867-9(5))* Teacher Created Materials, Inc.
Connolly, Michael & Goolbis, Brie. Young Enough to Change the World: Stories of Kids & Teens Who Turned Their Dreams into Action, 750 vols. 2015. (ENG., Illus.). 144p. pap. 21.95 *(978-1-935826-38-5(7))* Kalindi Pr.
Duhig, Holly. Activism & Volunteering. 2018. (Our Values - Level 3 Ser.). 32p. (J). (gr. 5-6). *(978-0-7787-5436-7(7))* Crabtree Publishing Co.
Fischer, James. The Power to Do Good: Money & Charity. 2010. (Junior Library of Money). 64p. (YA). (gr. 7-18). pap. 9.95 *(978-1-4222-1888-4(0))*; lib. bdg. 22.95 *(978-1-4222-1769-6(8))* Mason Crest.
Gerdes, Louise I., ed. National Service, 1 vol. 2011. (Opposing Viewpoints Ser.). (ENG.). 248p. (gr. 10-12). pap. 34.80 *(978-0-7377-5234-2(3))*, 8ca1008b-ae90-4f33-9b9d-82039a815fbb); lib. bdg. 50.43 *(978-0-7377-5233-5(5))*, 6bb6047c-3918-4004-94c2-8cea7433c4e0) Greenhaven Publishing LLC. (Greenhaven Publishing).
Gregory, Helen. Team Work. 2011. (Wonder Readers Early Level Ser.). (ENG.). 16p. (gr. -1-1). pap. 35.94 *(978-1-4296-8166-7(7))*, Capstone Pr.) Capstone.
—Teamwork. 2011. (Wonder Readers Early Level Ser.). (ENG.). 16p. (J). (gr. -1-1). pap. 6.25 *(978-1-4296-7898-8(4))*, 118230, Capstone Pr.) Capstone.
Hoose, Philip M. It's Our World, Too. 2014. 23.95 *(978-1-63419-712-0(7))* Perfection Learning Corp.
How to Help: A Guide to Giving Back, 8 vols., Set. Incl. Celebrities Giving Back: A Guide to Giving Back. Reusser, Kayleen. lib. bdg. 29.95 *(978-1-58415-922-3(7))*; Volunteering in School: A Guide to Giving Back. O'Neal, Claire. lib. bdg. 29.95 *(978-1-58415-920-9(0))*; Ways to Help after a Natural Disaster: A Guide to Giving Back. Saul, Laya. lib. bdg. 29.95 *(978-1-58415-917-9(0))*; Ways to Help Children with Disabilities: A Guide to Giving Back. Gibson, Karen Bush. lib. bdg. 29.95 *(978-1-58415-916-2(2))*; Ways to Help Chronically Ill Children: A Guide to Giving Back. Gagne, Tammy. lib. bdg. 29.95 *(978-1-58415-919-3(7))*; Ways to Help Disadvantaged Youth: A Guide to Giving Back. Saul, Laya. lib. bdg. 29.95 *(978-1-58415-918-6(9))*; Ways to Help in Your Community: A Guide to Giving Back. O'Neal, Claire. lib. bdg. 29.95 *(978-1-58415-921-6(9))*; Ways to Help the Elderly: A Guide to Giving Back. Orr, Tamra. lib. bdg. 29.95 *(978-1-58415-915-5(4))*; (Illus.). 48p. (J). (gr. 4-8). 2010. 2010. Set lib. bdg. 239.60 *(978-1-58415-923-0(5))* Mitchell Lane Pubs.
Junior Library of Money, 14 vols., Set. Incl. All about Money: The History, Culture, & Meaning of Modern Finance. Simons, Rae. lib. bdg. 22.95 *(978-1-4222-1760-3(4))*; Banking Basics. Fischer, James. lib. bdg. 22.95 *(978-1-4222-1761-0(2))*; Cost of Living. Thompson, Helen. lib. bdg. 22.95 *(978-1-4222-1762-7(0))*; Earning Money: Jobs. Fischer, James. lib. bdg. 22.95 *(978-1-4222-1763-4(9))*; Entrepreneurship. Simons, Rae. lib. bdg. 22.95 *(978-1-4222-1764-1(7))*; Guide to Teaching Young Adults about Money. Simons, Rae. lib. bdg. 22.95 *(978-1-4222-1765-8(5))*; Investing Money. Thompson, Helen. lib. bdg. 22.95 *(978-1-4222-1766-5(3))*; Money & Relationships. Simons, Rae. lib. bdg. 22.95 *(978-1-4222-1767-2(1))*; Planning for Your Education. Fischer, James. lib. bdg. 22.95 *(978-1-4222-1768-9(X))*; Power to Do Good: Money & Charity. Fischer, James. lib. bdg. 22.95 *(978-1-4222-1769-6(8))*; Spending Money. Simons, Rae. lib. bdg. 22.95 *(978-1-4222-1770-2(1))*; Sustainable Lifestyles in a Changing Economy. Simons, Rae. lib. bdg. 22.95 *(978-1-4222-1771-9(X))*; Understanding Credit. Thompson, Helen. lib. bdg. 22.95 *(978-1-4222-1772-6(8))*; Understanding the Stock Market. Thompson, Helen. lib. bdg. 22.95 *(978-1-4222-1773-3(6))*; (YA). (gr. 7-18). 2010. (Illus.). 64p. 2011. Set lib. bdg. 321.30 *(978-1-4222-1759-7(0))* Mason Crest.
Kalman, Bobbie. Helpers in My Community. 2010. (My World Ser.). (ENG., Illus.). 24p. (J). (gr. k-2). *(978-0-7787-9444-8(X))*; (gr. 1-1). pap. *(978-0-7787-9488-2(1))* Crabtree Publishing Co.
Keppeler, Jill. Be an Activist! 2018. (Be the Change! Shaping Your Community Ser.). 32p. (gr. 3-4). 63.00 *(978-1-5382-2014-6(8))*; (ENG.). 28.27 *(978-1-5382-2011-5(3))*, 6889ca4c-159e-4870-973e-c6dee4dc560e); (ENG.). pap. 11.50 *(978-1-5382-2013-9(X))*, 977fb29c-8209-411a-a30f-72f27877c1fe) Stevens, Gareth Publishing LLLP.
Kreisman, Rachelle. Being a Good Citizen: A Kids' Guide to Community Involvement. Haggerty, Tim, illus. 2015. (Start Smart (tm) — Community Ser.). (ENG.). 32p. (J). (gr. 1-3). E-Book 39.99 *(978-1-937529-50-5(9))* Red Chair Pr.
Laidlaw, Rob. Cat Champions: Caring for Our Feline Friends. (ENG., Illus.). 64p. (J). (gr. 3-7). 2015. pap. 11.95 *(978-1-927485-54-5(1))* 2014. 15.95 *(978-1-927485-31-6(2))* Pajama Pr. CAN. Dist: Publishers Group West (PGW).
Lewis, Barbara A. The Kid's Guide to Service Projects: Over 500 Service Ideas for Young People Who Want to Make a Difference. 2nd rev. ed. 2009. (ENG., Illus.). 160p. (J). (gr. 3-18). pap. 14.99 *(978-1-57542-338-8(3))*, 23388) Free Spirit Publishing Inc.
Lindeen, Mary. Lend a Hand, 1 vol. 2011. (Wonder Readers Fluent Level Ser.). (ENG.). 16p. (gr. -1-2). (J). pap. 6.25 *(978-1-4296-7948-0(4))*, 118280); pap. 35.94 *(978-1-4296-8119-3(5))* Capstone. (Capstone Pr.).
Lopez, Anderson Elizabeth. Fantastic Kids: Helping Others (Level 3) 2017. (TIME for KIDS(r): Informational Text Ser.). (ENG., Illus.). 32p. (J). (gr. 3-4). pap. 12.99 *(978-1-4258-4972-6(5))* Teacher Created Materials, Inc.
Marcovitz, Hal. Teens & Voluntarism. 2008. (Gallup Youth Survey, Major Issues & Trends Ser.). (Illus.). 112p. (YA). (gr. 8-12). lib. bdg. 22.95 *(978-1-59084-877-7(2))* Mason Crest.
—Teens & Volunteerism. Developed in Association with the Gallup Organization Staff, ed. 2013. (Gallup Youth Survey: Major Issues & Trends Ser.: 14). 112p. (J). (gr. 7-18). 24.95 *(978-1-4222-2960-6(2))* Mason Crest.
Marsico, Katie. Rotary Clubs. 2016. (Community Connections: How Do They Help? Ser.). (ENG., Illus.). 24p. (J). (gr. 2-5). 29.21 *(978-1-63471-053-4(3))*, 208292) Cherry Lake Publishing.
Mills, Nathan & Pickman, Richard. Let's Volunteer!, 1 vol. 2012. (Rosen Readers Ser.). (ENG., Illus.). 24p. (J). (gr. 1-2). pap. 8.25 *(978-1-4488-8851-1(4))*, 95704de1-2dea-4c5f-aa8d-4d6f2b869ef7, Rosen Classroom) Rosen Publishing Group, Inc., The.
Mulder, Michelle. Home Sweet Neighborhood: Transforming Cities One Block at a Time, 1 vol. 2019. (Orca Footprints Ser.: 15). (ENG., Illus.). 48p. (J). (gr. 4-7). 19.95 *(978-1-4598-1691-6(9))* Orca Bk. Pubs. USA.
Muschal, Frank. Beyond Government. 2007. (21st Century Skills Library: Citizens & Their Governments Ser.). (ENG., Illus.). 32p. (gr. 4-8). lib. bdg. 32.07 *(978-1-60279-060-5(4))*, 200002) Cherry Lake Publishing.
Nelson, Maria. I Can Volunteer, 1 vol. 2013. (Kids of Character Ser.). (Illus.). 24p. (J). (gr. 1-2). (ENG.). pap. 9.15 *(978-1-4339-9038-0(5))*, c9377b38-dd43-4516-a6b1-e56206799a3c); (ENG., lib. bdg. 25.27 *(978-1-4339-9037-3(7))*, 2cc31920-756a-4ae9-8519-dfae3266583a); pap. 48.90 *(978-1-4339-9039-7(3))* Stevens, Gareth Publishing LLLP.
O'Neal, Claire. Volunteering in School: A Guide to Giving Back. 2010. (How to Help Ser.). (Illus.). 48p. (J). (gr. 4-8). lib. bdg. 29.95 *(978-1-58415-920-9(0))* Mitchell Lane Pubs.
Parker, Victoria. Helping the Environment, 1 vol. 2012. (I Can Make a Difference Ser.). (ENG., Illus.). 32p. (gr. 1-3). pap. 8.29 *(978-1-4329-5951-7(4))*, 117714, Heinemann) Capstone.
Pickman, Richard. Let's Volunteer!, 1 vol. 2012. (I'm an American Citizen Ser.). (ENG., Illus.). 24p. (J). (gr. 1-2). 26.27 *(978-1-4488-8589-3(2))*, 4cf68a2a-54bf-4876-bf52-1158745212bb, PowerKids Pr.) Rosen Publishing Group, Inc., The.
Rodgers, Kelly. Doing Your Part: Serving Your Community, 1 vol. rev. ed. 2014. (Social Studies: Informational Text Ser.). (ENG., Illus.). 32p. (J). (gr. 2-4). pap. 11.99 *(978-1-4333-7367-1(X))* Teacher Created Materials, Inc.
Rondeau, Amanda. Do Something in Your City, 1 vol. 2004. (Do Something about It! Ser.). 24p. (J). (gr. k-3). lib. bdg. 24.21 *(978-1-59197-571-7(9))*, SandCastle) ABDO Publishing Co.
—Do Something in Your Community. 2004. (Do Something about It! Ser.). (ENG., Illus.). 24p. (J). (gr. k-3). lib. bdg. 24.21 *(978-1-59197-572-4(7))*, SandCastle) ABDO Publishing Co.
—Do Something in Your Country, 1 vol. 2004. (Do Something about It! Ser.). (Illus.). 24p. (J). (gr. k-3). lib. bdg. 24.21 *(978-1-59197-573-1(5))*, SandCastle) ABDO Publishing Co.
—Do Something in Your State, 1 vol. 2004. (Do Something about It! Ser.). (Illus.). 24p. (J). (gr. k-3). lib. bdg. 24.21 *(978-1-59197-575-5(1))*, SandCastle) ABDO Publishing Co.
—Do Something in Your World, 1 vol. 2004. (Do Something about It! Ser.). (Illus.). 24p. (J). (gr. k-3). lib. bdg. 24.21 *(978-1-59197-576-2(X))*, SandCastle) ABDO Publishing Co.
Rondeau, Amanda & ABDO Publishing Company Staff. Do Something about It! (Set of 5 Titles) 2004. (Do Something about It! Ser.: 5). (Illus.). 24p. (J). (gr. k-3). 121.05 *(978-1-59197-570-0(0))*, SandCastle) ABDO Publishing Co.
Rondeau, Amanda & Scheunemann, Pam. Volunteering. 2003. (United We Stand Ser.). (Illus.). 24p. (J). (gr. k-3). lib. bdg. 24.21 *(978-1-57765-882-5(5))*, SandCastle) ABDO Publishing Co.
Ryan, Bernard, Jr. & Ryan, Bernard. Community Service for Teens: Caring for Animals. 2006. (ENG., Illus.). 96p. (gr. 6-12). 19.95 *(978-0-89434-227-1(4))*, P053067, Ferguson Publishing Company) Infobase Holdings, Inc.
—Community Service for Teens: Expanding Education & Literacy. 2006. (ENG., Illus.). 96p. (gr. 6-12). 19.95 *(978-0-89434-231-8(2))*, P053071, Ferguson Publishing Company) Infobase Holdings, Inc.
Saul, Laya. Ways to Help after a Natural Disaster: A Guide to Giving Back. 2010. (How to Help Ser.). (Illus.). 48p. (J). (gr. 4-8). lib. bdg. 29.95 *(978-1-58415-917-9(0))* Mitchell Lane Pubs.
Shava, Ryder. Akihiro Volunteers, 1 vol., 1. 2015. (Rosen REAL Readers: Social Studies Nonfiction / Fiction: Myself, My Community, My World Ser.). (ENG.). 12p. (J). (gr. k-1). pap. 6.33 *(978-1-5081-1764-3(0))*, 7f39a708-f978-4a1a-a86f-6ed0f0b1332a, Rosen Classroom) Rosen Publishing Group, Inc., The.
Smith, Paula. Be the Change in the World. 2014. (Be the Change! Ser.). (ENG., Illus.). 24p. (J). (gr. 2-3). *(978-0-7787-0622-9(2))*; pap. *(978-0-7787-0634-2(6))* Crabtree Publishing Co.
—Be the Change in Your School. 2014. (Be the Change! Ser.). (ENG., Illus.). 24p. (J). (gr. 2-3). *(978-0-7787-0626-7(5))*; pap. *(978-0-7787-0638-0(9))* Crabtree Publishing Co.
Sundem, Garth. Real Kids, Real Stories, Real Change: Courageous Actions Around the World. 2010. (ENG.). 176p. (J). (gr. 4-8). pap. 14.99 *(978-1-57542-350-0(2))*, 23500) Free Spirit Publishing Inc.
—Real Kids, Real Stories, Real Change: Courageous Actions Around the World. 2010. 20.00 *(978-1-60686-625-2(7))* Perfection Learning Corp.
Taylor, Charlotte. Volunteers: Making Our Country Better, 6 vols. 2020. (Being a U. S. Citizen Ser.). (ENG.). 24p. (J). (gr. 1-2). 56.10 *(978-1-9785-1759-2(9))* Enslow Publishing, LLC.

TUV

Volunteering: Do What You Like to Do. 2004. (YA). *(978-1-929888-38-2(4))* National Crime Prevention Council.

Weeldreyer, Laura. Everything You Need to Know about Volunteering. 2009. (Need to Know Library). 64p. (gr. 5-5). 58.50 *(978-1-60854-097-6(9))* Rosen Publishing Group, Inc., The.

VOLUNTARISM—FICTION

Anderson, Laurie Halse. Helping Hands. 2013. (Vet Volunteers Ser.: 15). (ENG.). 144p. (J). (gr. 3-7). pap. 7.99 *(978-0-14-241677-8(0)*, Puffin Books) Penguin Young Readers Group.

—Treading Water. 2014. (Vet Volunteers Ser.: 16). (ENG.). 192p. (J). (gr. 3-7). pap. 7.99 *(978-0-14-241678-5(9)*, Puffin Books) Penguin Young Readers Group.

Davis, Jacky. Ladybug Girl & the Rescue Dogs. Soman, David, illus. 2018. (Ladybug Girl Ser.). 40p. (J). (-k). 18.99 *(978-0-399-18640-0(9)*, Dial Bks) Penguin Young Readers Group.

Delle Donne, Elena. Full-Court Press. (Hoops Ser.: 2). (ENG.). (J). (gr. 3-7). 2019. 176p. pap. 7.99 *(978-1-5344-1235-4(2))* 2018. (Illus.). 160p. 17.99 *(978-1-5344-1234-7(4))* Simon & Schuster Bks. For Young Readers. (Simon & Schuster Bks. For Young Readers).

Grimes, Nikki. Almost Zero: A Dyamonde Daniel Book. Christie, R. Gregory, illus. 2010. (Dyamonde Daniel Book Ser.: 3). (ENG.). 128p. (J). (gr. 2-4). 12.99 *(978-0-399-25177-1(4)*, G.P. Putnam's Sons Books for Young Readers) Penguin Young Readers Group.

Grogan, Joy. Into the Fold. 2003. 156p. per. 15.00 *(978-0-9740321-6-0(6))* Open Bk. Publishing.

Gurtler, Janet. The Truth about Us: They Never Meant to Fall in Love. 2015. (ENG.). 320p. (YA). (gr. 8-12). pap. 9.99 *(978-1-4022-7800-6(4)*, 9781402278006) Sourcebooks, Inc.

Harp, Susan. Evie Goes Clean & Green. Siau, Jon, illus. 2013. 24p. (J). lib. bdg. 14.95 *(978-1-938730-09-2(7))* M.T. Publishing Co., Inc.

—Retrieving with Evie. Siau, John, illus. 2007. (ENG.). 24p. (J). lib. bdg. 12.95 *(978-1-932439-67-0(6))* M.T. Publishing Co., Inc.

Huser, Glen. Skinnybones & the Wrinkle Queen. 2013. 232p. pap. *(978-1-4596-6507-1(4))* ReadHowYouWant.com, Ltd.

Krulik, Nancy. Revenge of the Killer Worms. 2015. (George Brown, Class Clown Ser.: 16). lib. bdg. 14.75 *(978-0-606-37545-0(7))* Turtleback.

Lord, Cynthia. Jelly Bean. 2014. (Shelter Pet Squad Ser.: 1). lib. bdg. 16.00 *(978-0-606-36063-0(8))* Turtleback.

Lyon, George Ella. You & Me & Home Sweet Home. Anderson, Stephanie, illus. 2009. (ENG.). 48p. (J). (gr. -1-3). 19.99 *(978-0-689-87589-2(4)*, Atheneum/Richard Jackson Bks.) Simon & Schuster Children's Publishing.

Mikkelsen, Jon. The Empty Room. Lueth, Nathan, illus. 2008. (We Are Heroes Ser.). (ENG.). 40p. (J). (gr. 5-9). lib. bdg. 24.65 *(978-1-4342-0791-3(9)*, 95197, Stone Arch Bks.) Capstone.

—Kids Against Hunger. Lueth, Nathan, illus. 2008. (We Are Heroes Ser.). (ENG.). 40p. (J). (gr. 5-9). lib. bdg. 24.65 *(978-1-4342-0790-6(0)*, 95195, Stone Arch Bks.) Capstone.

Morgan, Melissa J. Freaky Tuesday #17, 17 vols. 2007. (Camp Confidential Ser.: 17). 160p. (J). (gr. 3-7). pap. 4.99 *(978-0-448-44651-6(0)*, Grosset & Dunlap) Penguin Young Readers Group.

Papp, Lisa. Madeline Finn & the Shelter Dog. 2019. (ENG., Illus.). 32p. (J). (gr. -1-3). 17.95 *(978-1-68263-075-4(7))* Peachtree Publishing Co. Inc.

Prentiss, Timothy. Miss Keen Needs Help. 2006. (Early Explorers Ser.). (J). pap. *(978-1-4108-6113-9(9))* Benchmark Education Co.

Randall, Angel. Snow Angels. 2011. (Illus.). 32p. (J). 17.99 *(978-1-60641-046-2(6)*, Shadow Mountain) Shadow Mountain Publishing.

Reinhardt, Dana. How to Build a House. 2009. (ENG.). 240p. (YA). (gr. 9-11). pap. 8.99 *(978-0-375-84454-6(6)*, Ember) Random Hse. Children's Bks.

Schraff, Anne. A Walk in the Park, 1 vol. 2013. (Urban Underground Ser.). (ENG.). 196p. (YA). (gr. 9-12). pap. 11.95 *(978-1-62250-043-7(1))* Saddleback Educational Publishing, Inc.

Schraff, Anne E. A Walk in the Park. 2013. (Urban Underground — Harriet Tubman High School Ser.). (YA). lib. bdg. 20.80 *(978-0-606-31585-2(3))* Turtleback.

Sotomayor, Sonia. Just Help! How to Build a Better World. Dominguez, Angela, illus. 2022. 32p. (J). (gr. -1-3). 17.99 *(978-0-593-20626-3(6)*, Philomel Bks.) Penguin Young Readers Group.

Stewart, Arlene. Weaving a Wish. 2017. (Friendship Bracelet Ser.: 2). (ENG.). 320p. (J). (gr. 4-7). pap. 6.99 *(978-1-4926-3771-4(8))* Sourcebooks, Inc.

Tamaki, Jillian. Our Little Kitchen. (ENG., Illus.). (J). (gr. -1 — 1). 2022. 36p. bds. 9.99 *(978-1-4197-4656-7(1)*, 1289810) 2020. 48p. 17.99 *(978-1-4197-4655-0(3)*, 1289801) Abrams, Inc. (Abrams Bks. for Young Readers).

Van Sycke, A. & Schwartz, Josh. The OC: 'twas the Night Before Chrismukkah. 2005. 206p. (YA). *(978-1-4156-3915-3(9))* Scholastic, Inc.

Walton, Phillip. Auto-B-Good - Citizen Miles: A Lesson in Citizenship. Rising Star Studios, illus. 2010. 48p. (J). pap. 7.95 *(978-1-936086-52-8(2))*; lib. bdg. 14.95 *(978-1-936086-46-7(8))* Rising Star Studios, LLC.

VON BRAUN, WERNHER, 1912-1977

Peak, Doris-Jean. Wernher Von Braun: Alabama's Rocket Scientist. 2009. (Alabama Roots Biography Ser.). (Illus.). 112p. (J). *(978-1-59421-044-0(6))* Seacoast Publishing, Inc.

Thomas, Rachael L. Wernher Von Braun: Revolutionary Rocket Engineer. 2018. (Space Crusaders Ser.). (ENG., Illus.). 32p. (J). (gr. 3-6). lib. bdg. 32.79 *(978-1-5321-1706-0(X)*, 30700, Checkerboard Library) ABDO Publishing Co.

VOTING

see Elections; Suffrage

VOYAGERS

see Explorers; Travelers

VOYAGES AND TRAVELS

ABDO Publishing Company Staff. Explore the Countries Set 2, 8 vols. 2014. (Explore the Countries Ser.: 8). (ENG.). 40p. (J). (gr. 2-5). lib. bdg. 285.12 *(978-1-62403-340-7(7)*, 1356, Big Buddy Bks.) ABDO Publishing Co.

Bowen, Richard. Captain James Cook: British Explorer. 2013. (People of Importance Ser.: 21). (Illus.). 32p. (J). (gr. 4-18). 19.95 *(978-1-4222-2843-2(6))* Mason Crest.

Chait, Baruch. The Lost Treasure of Tikkun Hamiddos Island. Pollack, Gadi, illus. (Good Middos Ser.: Vol. 2). 62p. 25.99 *(978-1-58330-478-5(9))* Feldheim Pubs.

Childress, Diana. Marco Polo's Journey to China. 2007. (Pivotal Moments in History Ser.). (ENG.). 160p. (gr. 9-12). lib. bdg. 38.60 *(978-0-8225-5903-0(X))* Lerner Publishing Group.

Claybourne, Anna. The Story of Exploration. McNee, Ian, illus. 2010. (Science Stories Ser.). 103p. (YA). (gr. 3-18). pap. 10.99 *(978-0-7945-2400-5(1)*, Usborne) EDC Publishing.

Cohen, Roger. Danger in the Desert: True Adventures of a Dinosaur Hunter. 2008. (Sterling Point Bks.). (ENG., Illus.). 189p. (J). (gr. 5-8). 21.19 *(978-1-4027-5706-8(9))* Sterling Publishing Co., Inc.

Collins UK. Collins Fascinating Facts - Explorers. 2016. (Collins Fascinating Facts Ser.). (ENG., Illus.). 72p. (J). (gr. 1-3). pap. 10.99 *(978-0-00-816926-8(8))* HarperCollins Pubs. Ltd. GBR. Dist: Independent Pubs. Group.

Cooke, Tim. Explore with Marco Polo. 2014. (Travel with the Great Explorers Ser.). (ENG., Illus.). 32p. (J). (gr. 4-5). *(978-0-7787-1428-6(4))* Crabtree Publishing Co.

—Maps & Exploration, 1 vol. 2010. (Understanding Maps of Our World Ser.). (ENG.). 48p. (gr. 6-8). (YA). lib. bdg. 33.67 *(978-1-4339-3512-1(0)*, 9538bc5b-4a7e-4b35-9a78-6c98d259ffa7); (Illus.). pap. 15.05 *(978-1-4339-3513-8(9)*, 2107db3e-d716-48e2-87b2-b052c0b8a0b7, Gareth Stevens Secondary Library) Stevens, Gareth Publishing LLLP.

Enchantment of the World, Second Series, 93 bks., Set. Incl. Belgium. Burgan, Michael. (J). 2000. 37.00 *(978-0-516-21006-3(8)*, Children's Pr.); Cambodia. Kras, Sara Louise. (YA). 2005. 39.00 *(978-0-516-23679-7(2))*; Chile. McNair, Sylvia. (J). 2000. 37.00 *(978-0-516-21007-0(6)*, Children's Pr.); Croatia. Hintz, Martin. (YA). 2004. 37.00 *(978-0-516-24253-8(9)*, Children's Pr.); Czech Republic. Milivcjevic, JoAnn. (YA). 2004. 37.00 *(978-0-516-24255-2(5)*, Children's Pr.); Enchantment of the World: Guatemala. Morrison, Marion. (YA). 2005. 39.00 *(978-0-516-23674-2(1))*; Enchantment of the World: Guyana. Morrison, Marion. (YA). 2003. 39.00 *(978-0-516-22377-3(1))*; Enchantment of the World: Hungary. Stalcup, Ann. (YA). 2005. 39.00 *(978-0-516-23683-4(0))*; Enchantment of the World: Luxembourg. Heinrichs, Ann. (YA). 2005. 39.00 *(978-0-516-23681-0(4))*; Enchantment of the World: Nicaragua. Morrison, Marion. (YA). 2002. 37.00 *(978-0-516-20963-0(9)*, Children's Pr.); Enchantment of the World: Tibet. Kummer, Patricia K. (YA). 2003. 39.00 *(978-0-516-22693-4(2))*; Enchantment of the World: United Arab Emirates. Augustin, Byron. (YA). 2002. 36.00 *(978-0-516-20473-4(4)*, Children's Pr.); Enchantment of the World: Vietnam. Willis, Terri. (YA). 2002. 39.00 *(978-0-516-22150-2(7))*; Ethiopia. Heinrichs, Ann & Heinrichs, Anne. (YA). 2005. 39.00 *(978-0-516-23680-3(6))*; Greenland. Blashfield, Jean F. (YA). 2005. 39.00 *(978-0-516-23678-0(4))*; Iceland. Somervill, Barbara A. (J). 2003. 37.00 *(978-0-516-22694-1(0)*, Children's Pr.); India. Swan, Erin Pembrey. (J). 2002. 37.00 *(978-0-516-21121-3(8)*, Children's Pr.); Indonesia. Orr, Tamra & Greenblatt, Miriam. (YA). 2005. 39.00 *(978-0-516-23684-1(9))*; Ireland. Blashfield, Jean F. & Blashfield, Jean. (YA). 2002. 39.00 *(978-0-516-21127-5(7))*; Lebanon. Willis, Terri. (YA). 2005. 39.00 *(978-0-516-23685-8(7))*; Monaco. Hintz, Martin. (YA). 2004. 39.00 *(978-0-516-24251-4(2))*; Panama. Augustin, Byron. (YA). 2005. 39.00 *(978-0-516-23676-6(8))*; Paraguay. Augustin, Byron. (YA). 2005. 39.00 *(978-0-516-23675-9(X))*; Portugal. Blauer, Ettagale. (YA). 2002. 37.00 *(978-0-516-21109-1(9)*, Children's Pr.); Scotland. Stein, R. Conrad. (YA). 2001. 39.00 *(978-0-516-21112-1(9))*; Singapore. Kummer, Patricia K. (YA). 2003. 39.00 *(978-0-516-22531-9(6))*; Syria. Kummer, Patricia K. (YA). 2005. 39.00 *(978-0-516-23677-3(6))*; Venezuela. Willis, Terri. (YA). 2003. 37.00 *(978-0-516-24214-9(8)*, Children's Pr.); Wales. Heinrichs, Ann. (J). 2003. 37.00 *(978-0-516-22288-2(0)*, Children's Pr.); (gr. 5-9). (Enchantment of the World Ser.). (Illus.). 144p. 2004. Set lib. bdg. 3348.00 o.p. *(978-0-516-20870-1(5)*, Children's Pr.) Scholastic Library Publishing.

Extreme Explorations! [Capstone Sole Source]. 2010. (Extreme Explorations! Ser.). 32p. lib. bdg. 155.94 *(978-1-4296-5856-0(8)*, Capstone Pr.) Capstone.

Feinstein, Stephen. Marco Polo: Amazing Adventures in China, 1 vol. 2009. (Great Explorers of the World Ser.). (ENG.). 112p. (gr. 6-7). pap. 13.88 *(978-0-7660-5430-1(6)*, 4d94171e-7792-48db-9a33-fa0fb79bcacf); (Illus.). lib. bdg. 35.93 *(978-1-59845-103-0(0)*, d387f151-8d23-47c6-a78f-fcb3f955c476) Enslow Publishing, LLC.

Flowers, Pam. Big-Enough Anna: The Little Sled Dog Who Braved the Arctic. Farnsworth, Bill, illus. 2003. (ENG.). 32p. (J). (gr. 1-3). pap. 12.99 *(978-0-88240-580-3(2)*, Alaska Northwest Bks.) West Margin Pr.

—Ellie's Long Walk: The True Story of Two Friends on the Appalachian Trail. Farnsworth, Bill, illus. 2012. (ENG.). 32p. (J). (gr. k-3). pap. 11.99 *(978-0-88240-885-9(2)*, West Winds Pr.) West Margin Pr.

Great Journeys (Group 3), 6 vols., Set. 2003. (Great Journeys Ser.). (ENG.). (gr. 6-6). 119.37 *(978-0-7614-1320-2(0)*, a42c0b90-7e6c-4927-93ab-7c43fcbac783, Cavendish Square) Cavendish Square Publishing LLC.

Hopping, Lorraine Jean. Crossing the Atlantic: One Family's Story. 2004. (ENG., Illus.). 16p. (J). (gr. 2-2). pap. 11.00 net. *(978-0-7652-5186-2(8))* Celebration Pr.

Journey to the New World: Individual Title Six-Packs. (Action Packs Ser.). 104p. (gr. 3-5). 44.00 *(978-0-7635-3301-4(7))* Rigby Education.

K. Williams, Megan. Maddy's Amazing African Birthday, 1 vol. Vallecchi, Alessandro & Vallecchi Williams, Maddalena, photos by. 2009. (ENG., Illus.). 32p. (J). (gr. 1-4). pap. 12.95 *(978-1-897187-47-0(5))* Second Story Pr. CAN. Dist: Orca Bk. Pubs. USA.

Khanduri, Kamini. The Great World Search. Hancock, David, illus. 2007. (Great Searches (EDC Hardcover) Ser.). 48p. (J). (gr. 3). lib. bdg. 16.99 *(978-1-58086-966-9(1)*, Usborne) EDC Publishing.

Koestler-Grack, Rachel A. Ferdinand Magellan. 2009. (Great Explorers Ser.). (ENG., Illus.). 112p. (gr. 6-12). 30.00 *(978-1-60413-422-3(4)*, P173421, Facts On File) Infobase Holdings, Inc.

Malam, John. Extreme Exploration. 2009. (Difficult & Dangerous Ser.). (ENG., Illus.). 32p. (J). (gr. 4-7). pap. *(978-1-897563-24-3(8))* Saunders Bk. Co.

McCarthy, Meghan. All That Trash: The Story of the 1987 Garbage Barge & Our Problem with Stuff. McCarthy, Meghan, illus. 2018. (ENG., Illus.). 48p. (J). (gr. -1-3). 19.99 *(978-1-4814-7752-9(8)*, Simon & Schuster/Paula Wiseman Bks.) Simon & Schuster/Paula Wiseman Bks.

McHaffie, Natalie. C-Growl: The Daring Little Airplane. McHaffie, Natalie, illus. 2004. (Illus.). 32p. 14.95 *(978-1-55125-015-1(2))* Vanwell Publishing, Ltd. CAN. Dist: Casemate Pubs. & Bk. Distributors, LLC.

Michels, Dia L. Visiting China. Bowles, Michael J. N., photos by. 2005. (Look What I See! Where Can I Be? Ser.: 5). (Illus.). 32p. (J). (gr. -1-3). 9.95 *(978-1-930775-15-2(6))* Platypus Media, L.L.C.

Mooney, Carla. Explorers of the New World: Discover the Golden Age of Exploration with 22 Projects. Casteel, Tom, illus. 2011. (Build It Yourself Ser.). (ENG.). 128p. (J). (gr. 3-7). 21.95 *(978-1-936313-44-0(8)*, 5c0fd946-518b-47b5-a211-07d30e207297); pap. 15.95 *(978-1-936313-43-3(X)*, c882736c-46ca-41f9-a8cf-0a57bee876e6) Nomad Pr.

Morley, Jacqueline. You Wouldn't Want to Explore with Marco Polo! A Really Long Trip You'd Rather Not Take. Antram, David, illus. 2009. (You Wouldn't Want to Ser.). (ENG.). 32p. (J). (gr. 3-12). 29.00 *(978-0-531-21327-8(7))* Scholastic Library Publishing.

National Geographic Learning. Reading Expeditions (Social Studies: World Explorers): Travels to Distant Lands 1000-1400. 2007. (Nonfiction Reading & Writing Workshops Ser.). (ENG., Illus.). 32p. (J). pap. 18.95 *(978-0-7922-4542-1(3))* CENGAGE Learning.

Nye, Naomi Shihab. I'll Ask You Three Times, Are You OK? Tales of Driving & Being Driven. 2007. (ENG.). 256p. (YA). (gr. 8-12). 17.99 *(978-0-06-085392-1(1)*, Greenwillow Bks.) HarperCollins Pubs.

—I'll Ask You Three Times, Are You Ok? Tales of Driving & Being Driven. 2007. 242p. (YA). (gr. 7-12). lib. bdg. 16.89 *(978-0-06-085393-8(X)*, Greenwillow Bks.) HarperCollins Pubs.

O'Donnell, Kerri. A Trip Around the World: Using Expanded Notation to Represent Numbers, 1 vol. (Math for the REAL World Ser.). 24p. (gr. 3-4). 2010. (ENG.). pap. 8.25 *(978-0-8239-8871-6(6)*, 9adcf479-ce83-461d-a589-6a335b077192) 2009. 45.00 *(978-1-60851-377-2(7))* 2003. (ENG.). (J). lib. bdg. 26.27 *(978-0-8239-8966-9(6)*, 697842ae-6984-43ae-a102-21fefafe427b) Rosen Publishing Group, Inc., The. (PowerKids Pr.).

Orme, David. Great Journeys. 2008. (Trailblazers Ser.). (ENG., Illus.). 36p. pap. *(978-1-84167-653-1(5))* Ransom Publishing Ltd.

Otfinoski, Steven. Marco Polo: To China & Back, 1 vol. 2003. (Great Explorations Ser.). (ENG., Illus.). 80p. (gr. 6-6). 36.93 *(978-0-7614-1480-3(0)*, bc412359-15d9-4a18-998c-a1ba06a718b2) Cavendish Square Publishing LLC.

—The Voyages of Christopher Columbus: Text Pairs. 2008. (Bridges/Navigators Ser.). (J). (gr. 5). 89.00 *(978-1-4108-8425-1(2))* Benchmark Education Co.

Powling, Chris. The Cave at the End of the World 4 Voyagers. Pinelli, Amerigo, illus. 2017. (Cambridge Reading Adventures Ser.). (ENG.). 32p. pap. 8.30 *(978-1-108-43979-4(9))* Cambridge Univ. Pr.

Reynolds, E. E. Unknown Ways: More Tales of Explorers, Pioneers & Travellers. Tresilian, S., illus. 2011. (ENG.). 126p. pap. 19.99 *(978-1-107-60027-0(8))* Cambridge Univ. Pr.

Rice, Dona Herweck. A Dónde Ir. 2nd rev. ed. 2011. (TIME for KIDS(r): Informational Text Ser.). (SPA.). 12p. (gr. k-1). 7.99 *(978-1-4333-4412-1(2))* Teacher Created Materials, Inc.

Richardson, Gillian. 10 Routes That Crossed the World. Rosen, Kim, illus. 2017. (ENG.). 164p. (J). (gr. 3-7). pap. 12.95 *(978-1-55451-875-3(X))* Annick Pr., Ltd. CAN. Dist: Publishers Group West (PGW).

Ripley's Believe It Or Not! Staff. Prepare to Be Shocked: Epic Endeavors. 2012. (Ripley's Disbelief & Shock Ser.). 36p. (J). (gr. 3-4). 19.95 *(978-1-4222-2568-4(2))* Mason Crest.

Russo, David Anson. Around the World: The Great Treasure Hunt. Russo, David Anson, illus. 2011. (ENG., Illus.). 28p. (J). (gr. 2-5). pap. 14.99 *(978-1-4424-4343-3(X)*, Simon & Schuster Bks. For Young Readers) Simon & Schuster Bks. For Young Readers.

Stefoff, Rebecca. Exploration, 1 vol. 2006. (World Historical Atlases Ser.). (ENG.). 48p. (gr. 5-5). 34.07 *(978-0-7614-1640-1(4)*, 9a6050d1-a28a-4480-8b86-bbd7278da14b) Cavendish Square Publishing LLC.

Stewart, David. You Wouldn't Want to Sail on the Titanic! 2013. (You Wouldn't Want To Ser.). lib. bdg. 20.80 *(978-0-606-31630-9(2))* Turtleback.

Stuckey, Rachel. Explore with Ibn Battuta. 2017. (Travel with the Great Explorers Ser.). (Illus.). 32p. (J). (gr. 4-5). *(978-0-7787-3908-1(2))*; pap. *(978-0-7787-3924-1(4))* Crabtree Publishing Co.

Synge, M. B. The Discovery of New Worlds, Book II of the Story of the World. 2007. 224p. 21.99 *(978-1-60206-621-2(3))*; per. 14.99 *(978-1-60206-620-5(5))* Cosimo, Inc.

Trzasko, Cheryl. Around the World in a Cement Boat: A Young Girl's True Adventure. 2013. 202p. (gr. 4-6). pap. 17.95 *(978-1-4759-7558-1(9))* iUniverse, Inc.

Turner, Tracey & Lenman, Jamie. Hard As Nails Travelers & Explorers. 2015. (Hard As Nails in History Ser.). (ENG., Illus.). 64p. (J). (gr. 4-5). *(978-0-7787-1521-4(3))* Crabtree Publishing Co.

Verhille, Alexandre & Tavernier, Sarah. Legendary Routes of the World. 2015. (ENG., Illus.). 18p. (J). (gr. k-4). 29.99 *(978-3-89955-759-6(X))* Die Gestalten Verlag DEU. Dist: Ingram Publisher Services.

Willems, Mo. You Can Never Find a Rickshaw When It Monsoons: The World on One Cartoon a Day. Willems, Mo, illus. 2006. (ENG., Illus.). 408p. (gr. 8-17). pap. 12.99 *(978-0-7868-3747-2(0))* Hyperion Pr.

Wittmann, Kelly. The Race to Sail Around the World. 2017. (Great Race: Fight to the Finish Ser.). 48p. (gr. 4-5). pap. 84.30 *(978-1-5382-0807-6(5))* Stevens, Gareth Publishing LLLP.

Zannos, Susan. The Life & Times of Marco Polo. 2004. (Biography from Ancient Civilizations Ser.). (Illus.). 48p. (J). (gr. 4-8). lib. bdg. 29.95 *(978-1-58415-264-4(8))* Mitchell Lane Pubs.

VOYAGES AND TRAVELS—FICTION

Abbott, Tony. The Copernicus Archives #1: Wade & the Scorpion's Claw. 2014. (Copernicus Archives Ser.: 1). (ENG.). 224p. (J). (gr. 3-7). pap. 3.99 *(978-0-06-231472-7(6)*, Tegen, Katherine Bks) HarperCollins Pubs.

—The Copernicus Archives #2: Becca & the Prisoner's Cross. 2015. (Copernicus Archives Ser.: 2). (ENG., Illus.). 208p. (J). (gr. 3-7). pap. 3.99 *(978-0-06-231474-1(2)*, Tegen, Katherine Bks) HarperCollins Pubs.

—The Copernicus Legacy: the Forbidden Stone. Perkins, Bill, illus. 2014. (Copernicus Legacy Ser.: 1). (ENG.). 432p. (J). (gr. 3-7). 16.99 *(978-0-06-219447-3(X)*, Tegen, Katherine Bks) HarperCollins Pubs.

—The Copernicus Legacy: the Golden Vendetta. 2015. (Copernicus Legacy Ser.: 3). (ENG., Illus.). 528p. (J). (gr. 3-7). 16.99 *(978-0-06-219449-7(6)*, Tegen, Katherine Bks) HarperCollins Pubs.

—The Forbidden Stone. 2014. (Illus.). 423p. (J). *(978-0-06-232811-3(5))* HarperCollins Pubs.

—The Golden Vendetta. 2016. (Copernicus Legacy Ser.: 3). (J). lib. bdg. 17.20 *(978-0-606-38764-4(1))* Turtleback.

—The Serpent's Curse. 2014. (Illus.). 496p. pap. 9.99 *(978-0-06-235159-3(1))* HarperCollins Pubs.

Aiken, Joan. Bridle the Wind. 2007. (ENG., Illus.). 352p. (J). (gr. 5-7). pap. 21.95 *(978-0-15-206058-9(8)*, 1198195, Clarion Bks.) HarperCollins Pubs.

Altman, Joel. Gapper's Grand Tour: A Voyage Through Great American Ball Park. Williams, Tim, illus. 2013. (ENG.). (J). (gr. -1-3). 14.95 *(978-1-62086-213-1(1))* Amplify Publishing Group.

Anaya, Rudolfo A. How Chile Came to New Mexico. Nasario, Garcia, tr. from ENG. Nicolas, Otero, illus. 2014. (SPA & ENG.). 48p. (J). (gr. -1-3). 24.95 *(978-1-936744-20-6(1)*, Rio Grande Bks.) LPD Pr.

Andrews, Jane. Each & All: The Seven Little Sisters Prove Their Sisterhood (Yesterday's Classics) 2009. 120p. pap. 8.95 *(978-1-59915-308-7(4))* Yesterday's Classics.

Andrews, Julie. Little Bo: The Story of Bonnie Boadicea, No. 2. 2011. (Illus.). (J). lib. bdg. 18.89 *(978-0-06-008912-2(1))* HarperCollins Pubs.

Applegate, Katherine. Endling #1: the Last. (Endling Ser.: 1). (ENG.). (J). (gr. 3-7). 2019. 416p. pap. 9.99 *(978-0-06-233554-8(5))* 2018. (Illus.). 400p. 17.99 *(978-0-06-233552-4(9))* HarperCollins Pubs. (HarperCollins).

Arena, Jen. Lady Liberty's Holiday. Hunt, Matt, illus. 2016. (ENG.). 40p. (J). (gr. k-3). 17.99 *(978-0-553-52067-5(9)*, Knopf Bks. for Young Readers) Random Hse. Children's Bks.

Arends, Donald L. Grandpa Grouper, the Fish with Glasses. 2006. (J). *(978-0-9768880-0-0(9))* Mission Manuscripts, Inc.

Arenstam, Peter. Nicholas: a New Hampshire Tale. Holman, Karen Busch, illus. 2009. (Nicholas Northeastern Ser.: 3). 144p. (J). (gr. k-7). 14.95 *(978-1-58726-521-1(4)*, Mitten Pr.) Ann Arbor Editions LLC.

—Nicholas: a Vermont Tale. Holman, Karen Busch, illus. 2010. (Nicholas Northeastern Ser.: 4). 144p. (J). (gr. k-7). 14.95 *(978-1-58726-522-8(2)*, Mitten Pr.) Ann Arbor Editions LLC.

Armstrong, Alan W. Looking for Marco Polo. Jessell, Tim, illus. 2011. (ENG.). 304p. (J). (gr. 4-6). lib. bdg. 21.19 *(978-0-375-93321-9(2)*, Yearling) Random Hse. Children's Bks.

Arnold, David. Kids of Appetite. 2017. (ENG.). 368p. (YA). (gr. 9). pap. 10.99 *(978-0-14-751366-3(9)*, Speak) Penguin Young Readers Group.

—Kids of Appetite. 2017. lib. bdg. 22.10 *(978-0-606-40491-4(0))* Turtleback.

Avi. Crispin: the End of Time. 2011. (ENG.). 240p. (J). (gr. 5). pap. 7.99 *(978-0-06-174083-1(7)*, Balzer & Bray) HarperCollins Pubs.

—The End of the Beginning: Being the Adventures of a Small Snail (and an Even Smaller Ant) Tusa, Tricia, illus. 2008. (ENG.). 144p. (J). (gr. 3-7). pap. 7.99 *(978-0-15-205532-5(0)*, 1196636, Clarion Bks.) HarperCollins Pubs.

Baccellia, Kim. Goddesses Can Wait. 2015. 196p. (YA). *(978-1-61271-297-0(5))* Zumaya Pubns. LLC.

Bakshi, Kelly. Myth-Busting Columbus. 2012. 24p. 18.95 *(978-1-61633-316-4(2))*; pap. 10.95 *(978-1-61633-317-1(0))* Guardian Angel Publishing, Inc.

Ballantyne, R. M. The Crew of the Water Wagtail. 2011. 146p. pap. 12.95 *(978-1-60664-550-5(1))* Rodgers, Alan Bks.

—Red Rooney: Or, the Last of the Crew. 2007. (R. M. Ballantyne Collection). (Illus.). 408p. 22.00 *(978-1-934554-08-1(1))* Vision Forum, Inc., The.

Barmettler, Timothy. The Contagious Yawn: A Journey Around the World. Hoover, William, illus. 2017. 41p. (J). pap. *(978-1-63293-189-4(3))* Sunstone Pr.

Barnhouse, Rebecca. The Book of the Maidservant. 2011. (ENG., Illus.). 240p. (J). (gr. 3-7). pap. 7.99 *(978-0-375-85857-4(1)*, Yearling) Random Hse. Children's Bks.

Barnum, P. T. Dick Broadhead: A Story of Perilous Adve. 2006. pap. 30.95 *(978-1-4286-1959-3(3))* Kessinger Publishing, LLC.

Barry, Rick. Kiriath's Quest. 2008. (J). 8.99 *(978-1-59166-905-0(7))* BJU Pr.

Baskin, Nora Raleigh. All We Know of Love. 2008. (ENG., Illus.). 208p. (YA). (gr. 9-12). 16.99 *(978-0-7636-3623-4(1))* Candlewick Pr.

Bateman, Rachel. Someone Else's Summer. 2018. (ENG.). 336p. (YA). (gr. 8-17). pap. 17.99 *(978-0-7624-6505-7(0)*, Running Pr. Kids) Running Pr.

Bauer, Sepp. The Christmas Rose. Wenz-Vietor, Else, illus. 2008. 48p. (J). (gr. -1-3). 12.95 *(978-1-58089-232-2(9))* Charlesbridge Publishing, Inc.

Bell, Loman. Old Glory. Bell, Loman, illus. 2012. (Illus.). 40p. pap. *(978-0-9866065-8-8(8))* Wood Islands Prints.

—Old Glory Faces the Hurricane. Bell, Loman, illus. 2013. (Illus.). 46p. pap. *(978-0-9918033-2-3(9))* Wood Islands Prints.

Bencastro, Mario. A Promise to Keep. Giersbach-Rascon, Susan, tr. from SPA. 2005. 134p. (J). (gr. 3-7). pap. 9.95 *(978-1-55885-457-4(6),* Piñata Books) Arte Publico Pr.

Berk, Sheryl & Berk, Carrie. Royal Icing: The Cupcake Club. 2014. (Cupcake Club Ser.: 6). 144p. (J). (gr. 3-7). pap. 12.99 *(978-1-4022-8333-8(4))* Sourcebooks, Inc.

Bethune, Helen. In a Whirl, 1 vol. rev. ed. 2013. (Literary Text Ser.). (ENG., Illus.). 28p. (gr. 2-3). pap. 9.99 *(978-1-4333-5561-5(2))* Teacher Created Materials, Inc.

—Sarah's Journal, 1 vol. rev. ed. 2013. (Literary Text Ser.). (ENG., Illus.). 28p. (gr. 2-3). pap. 9.99 *(978-1-4333-5568-4(X))* Teacher Created Materials, Inc.

Biddulph, Rob. Blown Away. Biddulph, Rob, illus. 2015. (ENG., Illus.). 40p. (J). (gr. -1-3). 17.99 *(978-0-06-236724-2(2),* HarperCollins) HarperCollins Pubs.

Billups, Ruth A. No Place for a Horse. 2008. 48p. pap. 16.95 *(978-1-60703-118-5(3))* America Star Bks.

Bingham, Jane, retold by. Around the World in Eighty Days. 2004. (Young Reading Gift Books Ser.). 64p. (J). (gr. 2-18). 8.95 *(978-0-7945-0826-5(X),* Usborne) EDC Publishing.

Bird, Helen. The Balloon Launch. Dimitri, Simona, illus. 2005. 32p. (J). lib. bdg. 9.00 *(978-1-4242-0887-6(4))* Fitzgerald Bks.

—Big Yellow Balloon, 1 vol. Dimitri, Simona, illus. 2009. (Get Set Readers Ser.). (ENG.). 32p. (J). (gr. 1-1). lib. bdg. 27.27 *(978-1-60754-268-1(4),* 324f9e19-b33f-4b51-a575-51bb0c56403e, Windmill Bks.) Rosen Publishing Group, Inc., The.

Biro, Val. Gumdrop's Magic Journey. (ENG., Illus.). 30p. (J). *(978-0-340-71455-3(7))* Hodder & Stoughton.

—Magic Journey. (ENG., Illus.). 30p. (J). pap. *(978-0-340-71441-6(7))* Hodder & Stoughton.

Blackstone, Stella. Bear Takes a Trip. Harter, Debbie, illus. 2012. (Bear Ser.). (ENG.). 24p. (J). (gr. -1-1). bds. 8.99 *(978-1-84686-757-6(6))* Barefoot Bks., Inc.

—My Granny Went to Market. Corr, Christopher, illus. 2006. (ENG.). 24p. (J). (gr. -1-2). pap. 9.99 *(978-1-905236-62-6(X))* Barefoot Bks., Inc.

—My Granny Went to Market: A Round-the-World Counting Rhyme. Corr, Christopher, illus. 2005. (ENG.). 24p. (J). 16.99 *(978-1-84148-792-2(9))* Barefoot Bks., Inc.

Blackstone, Stella & Harter, Debbie. Bear Takes a Trip. 2012. (Illus.). 24p. (J). (gr. -1-1). pap. 6.99 *(978-1-84686-756-9(8))* Barefoot Bks., Inc.

Blackstone, Stella & Parker, Elizabeth. L'Ours Fait un Voyage. Harter, Debbie, illus. 2013.Tr. of Bear Takes a Trip. (FRE & ENG.). 24p. (J). (gr. k-1). pap. 6.99 *(978-1-84686-946-4(3))* Barefoot Bks., Inc.

Blade, Adam. Vedra & Krimon the Twin Dragons. 2012. (Beast Quest Special Edition Ser.: 2). (Illus.). 187p. lib. bdg. 16.00 *(978-0-606-26187-6(7))* Turtleback.

Blume, Lesley M. M. The Wondrous Journals of Dr. Wendell Wellington Wiggins. Foote, David, illus. 2013. (ENG.). 256p. (J). (gr. 3-7). pap. 8.99 *(978-0-375-87218-1(3),* Knopf Bks. for Young Readers) Random Hse. Children's Bks.

Bohner, Charles H. Bold Journey: West with Lewis & Clark. 2004. (ENG.). 192p. (J). (gr. 5-7). pap. 7.99 *(978-0-618-43718-4(5),* 495901, Clarion Bks.) HarperCollins Pubs.

Bondoux, Anne-Laure. The Princetta. 2008. (ENG.). 448p. (YA). (gr. 6-12). pap. 10.99 *(978-1-59990-098-8(X),* 9781599900988, Bloomsbury USA Childrens) Bloomsbury Publishing USA.

Borgenicht, David & Lurie, Alexander. Deadly Seas: You Decide How to Survive! 2015. (WorstCase Scenario Ultimate Adventure Ser.). (ENG., Illus.). 204p. (gr. 3-8). 47.10 *(978-1-59920-981-4(0))* Black Rabbit Bks.

Brahmachari, Sita. Jasmine Skies. 2014. (ENG.). 336p. (J). (gr. 3-7). 16.99 *(978-0-8075-3782-4(9),* 807537829) Whitman, Albert & Co.

Brent, Isabelle. The Christmas Horse & the Three Wise Men. 2016. (Illus.). 28p. (J). (gr. k-3). 17.95 *(978-1-937786-61-8(7),* Wisdom Tales) World Wisdom, Inc.

Brooks, Susie. Choose Your Own Journey. Cottingham, Tracy, illus. 2017. (J). 11.99 *(978-1-61067-537-6(1))* Kane Miller.

Brown, Jeff. Flat Stanley's Worldwide Adventures #6: the African Safari Discovery. Pamintuan, Macky, illus. 2010. (Flat Stanley's Worldwide Adventures Ser.: 6). (ENG.). 112p. (J). (gr. 2-5). pap. 6.99 *(978-0-06-143000-8(5))*;No. 6. 15.99 *(978-0-06-143001-5(3))* HarperCollins Pubs. (HarperCollins).

Brown, Joneé M. The Corner of Rainbow. 2nd ed. 2017. (ENG.). 132p. (J). pap. 15.99 *(978-1-56229-318-5(4),* Christian Living Books, Inc.) Pneuma Life Publishing, Inc.

Buck, Alicia. Out of the Ashes. 2015. 281p. (YA). pap. 17.99 *(978-1-4621-1727-7(9))* Cedar Fort, Inc./CFI Distribution.

Bulla, Clyde Robert. A Lion to Guard Us. Chessare, Michele, illus. 2018. (ENG.). 128p. (J). (gr. 3-7). pap. 9.99 *(978-0-06-440333-7(5),* HarperCollins) HarperCollins Pubs.

Burnford, Sheila. The Incredible Journey. (J). (gr. 6-8). 18.95 *(978-0-88411-099-6(0))* Amereon Ltd.

Carle, Eric. Amigos. Carle, Eric, illus. 2016. (SPA., Illus.). 22p. (J). (— 1). bds. 7.99 *(978-0-399-54506-1(9))* Penguin Young Readers Group.

—Friends. Carle, Eric, illus. (ENG., Illus.). (J). (gr. -1-k). 2015. 24p. bds. 8.99 *(978-0-399-17206-9(8))* 2013. 32p. 18.99 *(978-0-399-16533-7(9))* Penguin Young Readers Group.

Carlson, Melody. Notes from a Spinning Planet — Papua New Guinea. 2007. (Notes from a Spinning Planet Ser.: 2). 240p. (YA). (gr. 7-12). per. 14.99 *(978-1-4000-7145-6(3),* WaterBrook Pr.) Crown Publishing Group, The.

Carmody, Isobelle. The Farseekers. 2003. (Obernewtyn Chronicles: Bk. 2). (Illus.). 316p. (J). 13.65 *(978-0-7569-4608-1(5))* Perfection Learning Corp.

Carrillo, P. S. Desert Passage. 2008. (ENG.). 192p. (YA). (gr. 6-18). pap. 10.95 *(978-1-55885-517-5(3),* Piñata Books) Arte Publico Pr.

Carter, Caela. My Best Friend, Maybe. 2014. (ENG.). 352p. (YA). (gr. 9). 17.99 *(978-1-59990-970-7(7),* 900095590, Bloomsbury USA Childrens) Bloomsbury Publishing USA.

Cerberus Jones, Cerberus. The Warriors of Brin-Hask: The Gateway. 2017. (ENG.). 160p. (J). pap. 5.99 *(978-1-61067-499-7(5))* Kane Miller.

Charles, Norma. The Girl in the Backseat. 2008. (ENG., Illus.). 184p. (YA). (gr. 7-18). per. *(978-1-55380-056-9(7))* Ronsdale Pr.

Cheng, Andrea. Shanghai Messenger, 1 vol. Young, Ed, illus. 2005. (ENG.). 40p. (J). (gr. 3-7). pap. 10.95 *(978-1-62014-230-1(9),* leelowbooks); 17.95 *(978-1-58430-238-4(0))* Lee & Low Bks., Inc.

Cheng, Jack. See You in the Cosmos. (ENG.). 320p. (J). (gr. 5). 2018. 8.99 *(978-0-399-18638-7(7),* Puffin Books) 2017. 17.99 *(978-0-399-18637-0(9),* Dial Bks) Penguin Young Readers Group.

Clough, Lisa. Nothing but Blue. 2013. (ENG.). 224p. (YA). (gr. 9-7). 16.99 *(978-0-618-95961-7(0),* 1021899, Clarion Bks.) HarperCollins Pubs.

Cohagan, Carolyn. The Lost Children. 2011. (ENG.). 320p. (J). (gr. 3-7). pap. 8.99 *(978-1-4169-8617-1(0),* Aladdin) Simon & Schuster Children's Publishing.

Cole, Dina. Meet Eddie the Equator. 2011. 28p. pap. 12.99 *(978-1-4634-6023-5(6))* AuthorHouse.

Colfer, Chris. Stranger Than Fanfiction. 2018. (ENG.). 320p. (YA). (gr. 9-17). pap. 10.99 *(978-0-316-38343-1(0))* Little, Brown Bks. for Young Readers.

Collingwood, Harry. The Cruise of The 'Esmeralda' 2009. 220p. pap. 15.95 *(978-1-60664-391-4(6))* Rodgers, Alan Bks.

—The Log of a Privateersman. 2008. 216p. 26.95 *(978-1-60664-899-5(3))*; pap. 15.95 *(978-1-60664-018-0(6))* Aegypan.

Cooney, Barbara. Miss Rumphius. Cooney, Barbara, illus. 2004. (Illus.). 28p. (J). (gr. k-2). reprint ed. pap. 6.00 *(978-0-7567-7107-2(2))* DIANE Publishing Co.

Cooper, Elisha. Train. Cooper, Elisha, illus. 2013. (ENG., Illus.). 40p. (J). (gr. -1-3). 18.99 *(978-0-545-38495-7(8),* Orchard Bks.) Scholastic, Inc.

Corder, Zizou. Lionboy. 2004. (ENG., Illus.). 304p. (J). (gr. 3-7). reprint ed. pap. 8.99 *(978-0-14-240226-9(5),* Puffin Books) Penguin Young Readers Group.

—Lionboy: the Truth, 3. 2006. (ENG., Illus.). 240p. (J). (gr. 3-7). 7.99 *(978-0-14-240705-9(4),* Puffin Books) Penguin Young Readers Group.

Cowley, Joy. Song of the River. Andrews, Kimberly, illus. 2019. (ENG.). 32p. (J). (gr. k-2). 17.99 *(978-1-77657-253-3(X),* 79bc1618-5da9-4d6e-bc66-c53f1dc2c0a2) Gecko Pr. NZL. Dist: Lerner Publishing Group.

Crawford, Neil. The Journeyers. 2006. (ENG.). 248p. (J). per. *(978-0-9778205-4-2(8))* Helm Publishing.

Creech, Sharon. Ruby Holler. 2012. (ENG.). 288p. (J). (gr. 3-7). pap. 7.99 *(978-0-06-056015-7(0),* HarperCollins) HarperCollins Pubs.

—Ruby Holler. 2004. (Joanna Cotler Bks.). 310p. (gr. 3-7). 17.00 *(978-0-7569-1940-5(1))* Perfection Learning Corp.

—Ruby Holler. 2012. (J). (gr. 3-6). 17.20 *(978-0-613-86272-1(4))* Turtleback.

Crockett, S. D. After the Snow. 2013. (After the Snow Ser.: 1). (ENG.). 320p. (YA). (gr. 7-12). pap. 13.99 *(978-1-250-01676-8(2),* 900087090) Square Fish.

Cronin, B. B. The Lost Cousins. 2019. (Illus.). 40p. (J). (gr. -1-2). 19.99 *(978-0-451-47908-2(4),* Viking Books for Young Readers) Penguin Young Readers Group.

Crowe, Ellie & Fry, Juliet. HOKU the Stargazer: The Exciting Pirate Adventure! Petosa-Sigel, Kristi, illus. 2009. (ENG.). 28p. (J). *(978-1-59700-601-9(7))* Island Heritage Publishing.

Crowley, James. Monsterland. 2018. lib. bdg. 19.65 *(978-0-606-41311-4(1))* Turtleback.

Crum, Sally. Race to Moonrise Rev. Carlson, Eric S., illus. 2nd ed. 2006. 98p. (J). 12.95 *(978-1-932738-31-5(2))* Western Reflections Publishing Co.

Cruz, Maria Colleen. Border Crossing. 2003. 128p. (J). pap. 9.95 *(978-1-55885-405-5(3),* Piñata Books) Arte Publico Pr.

—Border Crossing. 2006. 122p. (gr. 8-12). 19.95 *(978-0-7569-6587-7(X))* Perfection Learning Corp.

Culbertson, Kim. Instructions for a Broken Heart. 2011. (ENG.). 304p. (YA). (gr. 7-12). pap. 14.99 *(978-1-4022-4302-8(2))* Sourcebooks, Inc.

Cummings, Priscilla. Beetle Boddiker, 1 vol. 2009. (ENG., Illus.). 30p. (J). (gr. -1-3). 13.95 *(978-0-87033-602-7(9),* 3592, Cornell Maritime Pr./Tidewater Pubs.) Schiffer Publishing, Ltd.

—The Journey Back. 2013. 272p. (J). (gr. 5). pap. 8.99 *(978-0-14-242290-8(8),* Puffin Books) Penguin Young Readers Group.

Czekaj, Jef. Austin, Lost in America: A Geography Adventure. Czekaj, Jef, illus. 2015. (ENG., Illus.). 40p. (J). (gr. -1-3). 17.99 *(978-0-06-228017-6(1),* Balzer & Bray) HarperCollins Pubs.

Daly, Catherine. The Ghost of Christmas Past. 2012. 162p. (J). *(978-0-545-48422-0(7))* Scholastic, Inc.

Dao, Julie C. Kingdom of the Blazing Phoenix. 2019. (Rise of the Empress Ser.: 2). 384p. (YA). (gr. 9). pap. 10.99 *(978-1-5247-3834-1(4),* Penguin Books) Penguin Young Readers Group.

de Bonneval, Gwen. William & the Lost Spirit. Bonhomme, Matthieu, illus. 2013. (ENG.). 160p. (YA). (gr. 8-12). lib. bdg. 30.65 *(978-0-7613-8567-7(3),* 38866c96-abfc-4e7f-9449-c6a5f12f8f1a, Graphic Universe™) Lerner Publishing Group.

DiCamillo, Kate. Where Are You Going, Baby Lincoln? Tales from Deckawoo Drive, Volume Three. Van Dusen, Chris, illus. 2017. (Tales from Deckawoo Drive Ser.: 3). (ENG.). 112p. (J). (gr. 1-4). pap. 6.99 *(978-0-7636-9758-7(3))* Candlewick Pr.

Disney Press Staff, ed. Mickey's New Friend. 2011. (Illus.). 32p. (J). *(978-1-4231-4585-1(2))* Disney Pr.

Doktorski, Jennifer Salvato. How My Summer Went up in Flames. 2013. (ENG.). 320p. (YA). (gr. 9). 17.99 *(978-1-4424-5940-3(9))*; pap. 10.99 *(978-1-4424-5939-7(5))* Simon Pulse. (Simon Pulse).

Dragt, Tonke. The Letter for the King (winter Edition) 2018. (ENG., Illus.). 512p. (J). (gr. 3-7). pap. 15.95 *(978-1-78269-081-8(6),* Pushkin Children's Bks.) Steerforth Pr.

Draper, Rochelle. The Stone Wall Dragon. Draper, Rochelle, illus. 2007. (ENG., Illus.). 32p. (J). (gr. 1-17). 15.95 *(978-0-89272-690-5(3))* Down East Bks.

Duff, Hilary. Elixir. 2011. (Playaway Young Adult Ser.). (YA). 59.99 *(978-1-4417-7416-3(5))* Findaway World, LLC.

—Elixir. 2011. (Elixir Ser.). (ENG.). 336p. (YA). (gr. 9). pap. 12.99 *(978-1-4424-0854-8(5),* Simon & Schuster Bks. For Young Readers) Simon & Schuster Bks. For Young Readers.

Duggan, Matt. The Royal Woods. 2018. (ENG., Illus.). 158p. (J). (gr. 4-7). pap. *(978-0-9917115-7-4(2))* Duggan, Matt.

—The Royal Woods. 2010. (ENG., Illus.). 244p. (J). (gr. 4-7). pap. *(978-1-55470-060-8(4))* Me to We.

Easton, Kelly. Aftershock. 2007. (ENG.). 176p. (YA). (gr. 7-12). pap. 6.99 *(978-1-4169-0053-5(5),* McElderry, Margaret K. Bks.) McElderry, Margaret K. Bks.

Eboch, M. M. An Artful Escape. 2015. (Rourke's World Adventure Chapter Bks.). (ENG.). 96p. (gr. 3-5). 29.93 *(978-1-63430-395-8(4),* 9781634303958) Rourke Educational Media.

Egan, Tim. Dodsworth in London. Egan, Tim, illus. 2010. (Dodsworth Book Ser.). (ENG., Illus.). 48p. (J). (gr. 1-4). pap. 4.99 *(978-0-547-41440-9(4),* 1429469, Clarion Bks.) HarperCollins Pubs.

—Dodsworth in New York. 2009. (Dodsworth Book Ser.). (ENG., Illus.). 48p. (J). (gr. 1-4). pap. 4.99 *(978-0-547-24831-8(8),* 1100746, Clarion Bks.) HarperCollins Pubs.

—Dodsworth in New York. Egan, Tim, illus. 2007. (Dodsworth Ser.). (ENG., Illus.). 48p. (J). (gr. 1-3). 17.44 *(978-0-618-77708-2(3))* Houghton Mifflin Harcourt Publishing Co.

—Dodsworth in Paris. Egan, Tim, illus. 2011. (Dodsworth Ser.). (ENG., Illus.). 48p. (J). (gr. 1-3). 16.19 *(978-0-618-98062-8(8))* Houghton Mifflin Harcourt Publishing Co.

—Dodsworth in Paris (Reader) Egan, Tim, illus. 2010. (Dodsworth Book Ser.). (ENG., Illus.). 48p. (J). (gr. 1-4). pap. 4.99 *(978-0-547-33192-8(4),* 1417441, Clarion Bks.) HarperCollins Pubs.

—Dodsworth in Tokyo. Egan, Tim, illus. 2014. (Dodsworth Book Ser.). (ENG., Illus.). 48p. (J). (gr. 1-4). pap. 4.99 *(978-0-544-33915-6(0),* 1584486, Clarion Bks.) HarperCollins Pubs.

Elish, Dan. The School for the Insanely Gifted. 2011. (ENG.). 304p. (J). (gr. 3-7). 15.99 *(978-0-06-113873-7(8),* Balzer & Bray) HarperCollins Pubs.

Elissa, Barbara. The Remarkable Journey of Josh's Kippah. Zaman, Farida, illus. 2010. (ENG.). (J). (gr. -1-2). 24p. lib. bdg. 7.95 *(978-0-8225-9911-1(2),* 8e962b4b-1989-4e3d-819d-f40ffae64988); 32p. pap. 7.95 *(978-0-8225-9933-3(3))* Lerner Publishing Group. (Kar-Ben Publishing).

Erdrich, Louise. Chickadee. Erdrich, Louise, illus. (Birchbark House Ser.: 4). (ENG., Illus.). (J). (gr. 3-7). 2013. 224p. pap. 7.99 *(978-0-06-057792-6(4))* 2012. 208p. 16.99 *(978-0-06-057790-2(8))* HarperCollins Pubs. (HarperCollins).

—The Porcupine Year. Erdrich, Louise, illus. 2010. (Birchbark House Ser.: 3). (ENG., Illus.). 224p. (J). (gr. 3-7). pap. 9.99 *(978-0-06-441030-4(7),* HarperCollins) HarperCollins Pubs.

Evans, Douglas. Mvp* Magellan Voyage Project. Shelley, John, illus. 2008. (ENG.). 232p. (J). (gr. 4-7). pap. 10.95 *(978-1-59078-625-3(4),* Front Street) Astra Publishing Hse.

Evert, Lori. The Christmas Wish. Breiehagen, Per, illus. (Wish Book Ser.). (J). 2022. 32p. (— 1). bds. 10.99 *(978-0-593-56421-9(9))* 2013. 48p. (gr. -1-2). 18.99 *(978-0-449-81681-3(8))* 2013. (ENG.). 48p. (gr. -1-2). E-Book *(978-0-449-81942-5(6))* Random Hse. Children's Bks. (Random Hse. Bks. for Young Readers).

Fabrick, Harriet. Furello Journeys: Furello Questions. Date not set. (Illus.). 200p. (J). (gr. 7-9). wbk. ed. 12.95 *(978-0-9646698-9-5(7))* Wild Flower USA.

Faircloth, Sean. The Enchanted Globe. 2016. (ENG., Illus.). 224p. (J). (gr. 4-7). pap. 12.95 *(978-1-63431-101-4(9))* Pitchstone LLC.

Farrow, G. e. & Farrow, G. E. The Wallypug in London. 2011. 106p. 23.95 *(978-1-4638-9696-6(4))* Rodgers, Alan Bks.

Fayers, Claire. The Voyage to Magical North. 2016. (Accidental Pirates Ser.: 1). (ENG.). 320p. (J). 27.99 *(978-1-62779-420-6(4),* 900150098, Holt, Henry & Co. Bks. For Young Readers) Holt, Henry & Co.

Fejeran, Tony. Moana. Sastrawinata-Lemay, Griselda, illus. 2016. (J). *(978-1-5182-2105-7(X),* Golden Bks.) Random Hse. Children's Bks.

Findlay, Lisa. Gulliver in Lilliput. Caparo, Antonio Javier, illus. 2010. (Step into Reading Ser.). 48p. (J). (gr. k-3). pap. 4.99 *(978-0-375-86585-5(3),* Random Hse. Bks. for Young Readers) Random Hse. Children's Bks.

Findlay, Lisa & Swift, Jonathan. Gulliver in Lilliput. Caparó, Antonio Javier, illus. 2010. (Step into Reading: Step 3 Ser.). (ENG.). 48p. (J). (gr. k-2). lib. bdg. 16.19 *(978-0-375-96585-2(8))* Random Hse. Bks. for Young Readers.

Fleischman, Paul. Whirligig. 2010. (ENG.). 144p. (YA). (gr. 7-12). pap. 7.99 *(978-0-312-62911-3(7),* 900066875) Square Fish.

Fletcher, Susan. Journey of the Pale Bear. 2018. (ENG., Illus.). 304p. (J). (gr. 3-7). 18.99 *(978-1-5344-2077-9(0),* McElderry, Margaret K. Bks.) McElderry, Margaret K. Bks.

Flowers, J. J. Juan Pablo & the Butterflies. 2017. (ENG., Illus.). 224p. (YA). (gr. 9-12). 17.99 *(978-1-5072-0214-2(8),* Simon Pulse) Simon Pulse.

Ford, Sally. Bungee down Under. Dudley, Peter, illus. 2004. 40p. (J). 14.95 *(978-1-931807-26-5(4))* Randall, Peter E. Pub.

Forman, Gayle. Just One Day. 2013. (ENG.). 416p. (YA). (gr. 9). pap. 10.99 *(978-0-14-242295-3(9),* Speak) Penguin Young Readers Group.

—Just One Day. 2013. lib. bdg. 22.10 *(978-0-606-34405-0(5))* Turtleback.

—Just One Year. 2014. (ENG.). 352p. (YA). (gr. 9). pap. 10.99 *(978-0-14-242296-0(7),* Speak) Penguin Young Readers Group.

—Just One Year. 2014. lib. bdg. 22.10 *(978-0-606-36190-3(1))* Turtleback.

Fox, Robin C. & Fox, Carol White. The Traveling Adventures of the Robin & the Fox Around the World We Go! A Cruise Through the Mediterranean. 2013. 44p. pap. 20.45 *(978-1-4908-1763-7(8),* WestBow Pr.) Author Solutions, LLC.

Francoise. Fanchette & Jeannot: A Little Story with Pictures. 2011. 26p. 35.95 *(978-1-258-07322-0(6))* Literary Licensing, LLC.

Fraser, Chelsea Curtis. Around the World in Ten Days. l.t. ed. 2007. (ENG.). 208p. pap. 22.99 *(978-1-4346-3413-9(2))* Creative Media Partners, LLC.

Friedman, Laurie. Mallory on Board. Pollak, Barbara, illus. 2008. (Mallory Ser.: 7). (ENG.). 176p. (J). (gr. 2-5). per. 7.99 *(978-0-8225-9023-1(9),* b305bbdb-77de-4588-baa6-6905f8e2c64e, Darby Creek) Lerner Publishing Group.

Friesen, Jonathan. Both of Me, 1 vol. 2016. (ENG.). 256p. (YA). pap. 9.99 *(978-0-310-73187-0(9))* Blink.

Fromental, Jean-Luc. Oops! Jolivet, Joëlle, illus. 2010. (ENG.). 42p. (J). (gr. -1-3). 17.95 *(978-0-8109-8749-4(X),* 681701) Abrams, Inc.

Frossard, Claire, illus. Emma's Journey. Frossard, Etienne, photos by. 2010. (ENG.). 56p. (J). (gr. -1-3). 17.95 *(978-1-59270-099-8(3))* Enchanted Lion Bks., LLC.

Fruchter, Jason, illus. Space Race. 2017. (J). *(978-1-5182-2283-2(8),* Golden Bks.) Random Hse. Children's Bks.

Gaiman, Neil. Instructions. Vess, Charles, illus. (ENG.). 40p. (J). (gr. -1-3). 2015. 9.99 *(978-0-06-196032-1(2))* 2010. 16.99 *(978-0-06-196030-7(6))* 2010. lib. bdg. 15.89 *(978-0-06-196031-4(4))* HarperCollins Pubs. (HarperCollins).

Garfield, Henry. The Lost Voyage of John Cabot. 2007. (ENG., Illus.). 320p. (YA). (gr. 7). pap. 16.95 *(978-1-4169-5460-6(0),* Simon Pulse) Simon Pulse.

Garis, Howard Roger. Uncle Wiggily's Travels. Date not set. 192p. (J). 20.95 *(978-0-8488-2278-1(1))* Amereon Ltd.

Garland, Hamlin. Main-Travelled Roads. 2017. (ENG., Illus.). (J). 25.95 *(978-1-374-83930-4(2))* Capital Communications, Inc.

Gilligan, Alison. Search for the Black Rhino. Semionov, Vladimir, illus. 2011. (ENG.). 144p. (J). (gr. 4-8). pap. 7.99 *(978-1-937133-01-6(X))* Chooseco LLC.

Gownley, Jimmy. Her Permanent Record. Gownley, Jimmy, illus. 2012. (Amelia Rules! Ser.). (ENG., Illus.). 160p. (J). (gr. 2-7). 24.99 *(978-1-4169-8615-7(4))*; pap. 12.99 *(978-1-4169-8614-0(6))* Simon & Schuster Children's Publishing. (Atheneum Bks. for Young Readers).

—Her Permanent Record. 2012. (Amelia Rules! Ser.: 8). lib. bdg. 23.30 *(978-0-606-26885-1(5))* Turtleback.

Grahame, Kenneth. The Wind in the Willows. Ingpen, Robert R., illus. 2012. (Union Square Kids Illustrated Classics Ser.). (ENG.). 224p. (J). (gr. 2-8). 24.99 *(978-1-4027-8283-1(7))* Sterling Publishing Co., Inc.

Granson, Steven. Zando. 2009. 124p. pap. 10.95 *(978-1-4401-5658-8(1))* iUniverse, Inc.

Gravett, Emily. Meerkat Mail. Gravett, Emily, illus. 2007. (ENG., Illus.). 32p. (J). (gr. -1-3). 19.99 *(978-1-4169-3473-8(1),* Simon & Schuster Bks. For Young Readers) Simon & Schuster Bks. For Young Readers.

Gray, Michael Loyd. King Biscuit. 2013. (J). pap. *(978-1-938237-04-1(8))* Tempest Bk. Shop.

Greenawalt, Kelly. Princess Truly in My Magical, Sparkling Curls. Rauscher, Amariah, illus. 2018. (Princess Truly Ser.). (ENG.). 40p. (J). (gr. -1-k). 18.99 *(978-1-338-16719-1(7),* Orchard Bks.) Scholastic, Inc.

Greenwood, Diana. Insight, 1 vol. 2012. (ENG.). 224p. (YA). pap. 7.99 *(978-0-310-72315-8(9))* Zondervan.

Griggs, Terry. Nieve. Griggs-Burr, Alexander, illus. 2010. 264p. (J). (gr. 4-10). pap. 14.95 *(978-1-897231-87-6(3))* Biblioasis CAN. Dist: Consortium Bk. Sales & Distribution.

Gugger, Rebecca. Ida & the Whale. Röthlisberger, Simon, illus. 2019. (ENG.). 32p. (J). (gr. -1-2). 17.95 *(978-0-7358-4341-7(4))* North-South Bks., Inc.

Gutman, Dan. Flashback Four #2: the Titanic Mission. (Flashback Four Ser.: 2). (ENG.). (J). (gr. 3-7). 2018. 256p. pap. 7.99 *(978-0-06-223636-4(9))* 2017. (Illus.). 240p. 16.99 *(978-0-06-223635-7(0))* HarperCollins Pubs. (HarperCollins).

—You Only Die Twice. 2013. (Genius Files Ser.: 3). (J). lib. bdg. 17.20 *(978-0-606-35043-3(8))* Turtleback.

Haddix, Margaret Peterson. Torn. (Missing Ser.: 4). (ENG.). (J). (gr. 3-7). 2012. 368p. pap. 8.99 *(978-1-4169-8981-3(1))* 2011. 352p. 19.99 *(978-1-4169-8980-6(3))* Simon & Schuster Bks. For Young Readers. (Simon & Schuster Bks. For Young Readers).

—Torn. l.t. ed. 2011. (Missing Ser.: Bk. 4). (ENG.). 566p. 23.99 *(978-1-4104-4078-5(8))* Thorndike Pr.

—Torn. 2012. (Missing Ser.: 4). lib. bdg. 18.40 *(978-0-606-26333-7(0))* Turtleback.

Hagen, George. Gabriel Finley & the Lord of Air & Darkness. 2017. 288p. (J). (gr. 4-7). 16.99 *(978-0-399-55347-9(9),* Schwartz & Wade Bks.) Random Hse. Children's Bks.

Hale, Edward Everett. Last of the Peterkins with Others of the. 2006. pap. *(978-1-4068-1087-5(8))* Echo Library.

Hale, Lucretia Peabody. The Last of the Peterkins: With Others of Their Kin. 2017. (ENG., Illus.). (J). pap. 12.95 *(978-1-374-83451-4(3))* Capital Communications, Inc.

Hall, Lucy. From England to Jamestowne: A Journey to Find My Father. 2007. (J). *(978-0-9763706-5-9(4))* Tendril Pr., LLC.

Hampton, Francesca. Children's Voyage the Long Journey Home. 2010. 222p. pap. 13.96 *(978-0-557-23497-4(2))* Lulu Pr., Inc.

Handford, Martin. Where's Waldo? 2007. (Where's Waldo? Ser.). (Illus.). 24p. (gr. 4-7). lib. bdg. 18.40 *(978-1-4178-2424-3(7))* Turtleback.

—Where's Waldo? Deluxe Edition. Handford, Martin, illus. 25th anniv. deluxe ed. 2012. (Where's Waldo? Ser.). (ENG., Illus.). 32p. (J). (gr. k-4). 17.99 *(978-0-7636-4525-0(7))* Candlewick Pr.

—Where's Waldo? Destination: Everywhere! 12 Classic Scenes As You've Never Seen Them Before! Handford, Martin, illus. 2017. (Where's Waldo? Ser.). (ENG., Illus.). 32p. (J). (gr. k-4). 19.99 *(978-0-7636-9726-6(5))* Candlewick Pr.

—Where's Waldo? the Fantastic Journey: Deluxe Edition. Handford, Martin, illus. deluxe ed. 2013. (Where's Waldo? Ser.). (ENG., Illus.). 32p. (J). (gr. k-4). 17.99 *(978-0-7636-4528-1(1))* Candlewick Pr.

—Where's Waldo? the Great Picture Hunt. Handford, Martin, illus. 2006. (Where's Waldo? Ser.). (ENG., Illus.). 24p. (J). (gr. k-4). 17.99 *(978-0-7636-3043-0(8))* Candlewick Pr.

TUV

—Where's Waldo? the Wonder Book: Deluxe Edition. Handford, Martin, illus. 2014. (Where's Waldo? Ser.). (ENG., Illus.). 32p. (J). (gr. k-4). 17.99 *(978-0-7636-4530-4(3))* Candlewick Pr.

Hannibal, James R. The Clockwork Dragon. 2019. (Section 13 Ser.: 3). (ENG., Illus.). 432p. (J). (gr. 3-7). 17.99 *(978-1-4814-6715-5(8),* Simon & Schuster Bks. For Young Readers) Simon & Schuster Bks. For Young Readers.

Hatton, Libby. Pete Puffin's Wild Ride Cruising Alaska's Currents. Hatton, Libby, illus. 2008. (Illus.). (J). pap. 16.95 *(978-0-930931-92-6(0))* Alaska Geographic Assn.

Hecht, Tracey & Fieber, Sarah. The Thrilling Voyage. Bulpin, Chloe, illus. 2019. (Nocturnals Ser.: 4). (J). (gr. 1-7). 15.99 *(978-1-944020-21-7(7),* Fabled Films Pr. LLC) Fabled Films LLC.

Helget, Nicole. Wonder at the Edge of the World. 2015. (ENG., Illus.). 384p. (J). (gr. 3-7). 17.00 *(978-0-316-24510-4(0))* Little, Brown Bks. for Young Readers.

Heltzel, Anne. Charlie, Presumed Dead. 2016. (ENG.). 272p. (YA). (gr. 9). pap. 8.99 *(978-0-544-66869-0(3),* 1625496, Clarion Bks.) HarperCollins Pubs.

Hennessy, B. G. The Once upon a Time Map Book: Take a Tour of Six Enchanted Lands. Joyce, Peter, illus. 2010. (ENG.). 16p. (J). (gr. 1-4). pap. 9.99 *(978-0-7636-2682-2(1))* Candlewick Pr.

Hesse, Karen. Stowaway. unabr. ed. 2004. 328p. (J). (gr. 5-9). pap. 48.00 incl. audio *(978-0-8072-8760-6(1),* LYA 259 SP, Listening Library) Random Hse. Audio Publishing Group.

Hidden. 2014. (ENG., Illus.). 384p. (YA). (gr. 7). 17.99 *(978-1-4424-8300-2(8),* Simon & Schuster/Paula Wiseman Bks.) Simon & Schuster/Paula Wiseman Bks.

Himmelman, John. Albert Hopper, Science Hero. Himmelman, John, illus. 2020. (Albert Hopper, Science Hero Ser.: 1). (ENG., Illus.). 144p. (J). 13.99 *(978-1-250-23016-4(0),* 900209343, Holt, Henry & Co. Bks. For Young Readers) Holt, Henry & Co.

Hobbs, Will. Crossing the Wire. (ENG.). 224p. (J). (gr. 5-8). 2007. pap. 7.99 *(978-0-06-074140-2(6))* 2006. (Illus.). 16.99 *(978-0-06-074138-9(4))* HarperCollins Pubs. (HarperCollins).

—Crossing the Wire. 2007. (Illus.). 216p. (gr. 5-9). 17.00 *(978-0-7569-8053-5(4))* Perfection Learning Corp.

Hobbs, William. Jason's Gold. unabr. ed. 2004. 240p. (J). (gr. 5-9). pap. 38.00 incl. audio *(978-0-8072-8229-8(4),* Listening Library) Random Hse. Audio Publishing Group.

Hollier, Jo. Roary O'Rourke, Quest for the Secret of Bramble Castle. 2004. (J). pap. 9.95 *(978-1-59374-081-8(6))* Whiskey Creek Pr., LLC.

Holmes, Mary Tavener & Harris, John. A Giraffe Goes to Paris. 0 vols. Cannell, Jon, illus. 2012. (ENG.). 32p. (J). (gr. 1-4). 17.99 *(978-0-7614-5595-0(7),* 9780761455950, Two Lions) Amazon Publishing.

Hosford, Kate. How the Queen Found the Perfect Cup of Tea. Swiatkowska, Gabi, illus. 2017. (ENG.). 40p. (J). (gr. k-3). 18.99 *(978-1-4677-3904-7(9),* 7c02bedb-b44a-40c9-aa37-01918276516a); E-Book 29.32 *(978-1-5124-3272-5(5),* 9781512432725); E-Book 9.99 *(978-1-5124-3273-2(3),* 9781512432732); E-Book 29.32 *(978-1-4677-9563-0(1))* Lerner Publishing Group. (Carolrhoda Bks.).

Hughes, Devon. Unnaturals #2: Escape from Lion's Head. (Unnaturals Ser.: 2). (ENG.). 384p. (J). (gr. 3-7). 2018. pap. 6.99 *(978-0-06-225758-1(7))* 2017. 16.99 *(978-0-06-225757-4(9))* HarperCollins Pubs. (Tegen, Katherine Bks).

Hull, Maureen. Rainy Days with Bear. l.t. ed. 2012. 51p. (J). pap. *(978-1-4596-3453-4(5))* ReadHowYouWant.com, Ltd.

Hunter, Derek. Brainwash Escape Victims, Vol. 2. 2006. (ENG., Illus.). 144p. (YA). pap. 12.95 *(978-1-59362-051-6(9),* 87d8783e-e029-478f-affe-985db42c2370) Slave Labor Bks.

Hunter, Erin. Seekers: Return to the Wild #3: River of Lost Bears No. 3. 2013. (Seekers: Return to the Wild Ser.: 3). (ENG., Illus.). 320p. (J). (gr. 3-7). 16.99 *(978-0-06-199640-5(8),* HarperCollins) HarperCollins Pubs.

—Seekers: Return to the Wild #5: the Burning Horizon. 2015. (Seekers: Return to the Wild Ser.: 5). (ENG., Illus.). 304p. (J). (gr. 3-7). 16.99 *(978-0-06-199646-7(7),* HarperCollins) HarperCollins Pubs.

—Warriors Super Edition: Moth Flight's Vision. Barry, James L. & Richardson, Owen, illus. (Warriors Super Edition Ser.: 8). (ENG.). (J). (gr. 3-7). 2016. 544p. pap. 10.99 *(978-0-06-229149-3(1))* 2015. 528p. 18.99 *(978-0-06-229147-9(5))* HarperCollins Pubs. (HarperCollins).

—Warriors: the New Prophecy #3: Dawn. Stevenson, Dave, illus. 2015. (Warriors: the New Prophecy Ser.: 3). (ENG.). 400p. (J). (gr. 3-7). pap. 9.99 *(978-0-06-236704-4(8),* HarperCollins) HarperCollins Pubs.

Huser, Glen. Skinnybones & the Wrinkle Queen. 2013. 232p. pap. *(978-1-4596-6507-1(4))* ReadHowYouWant.com, Ltd.

Hyde, Catherine Ryan. Becoming Chloe. 2008. 224p. (YA). (gr. 9). pap. 8.99 *(978-0-375-83260-4(2),* Knopf Bks. for Young Readers) Random Hse. Children's Bks.

Jackson, Ciandress. Chloe the Jumbo Jet: Fantastic Friends Around the World. 2013. 24p. pap. 9.99 *(978-1-61286-195-1(4))* Avid Readers Publishing Group.

James, Helen Foster. With Love, Grandma. Brown, Petra, illus. 2018. (ENG.). 32p. (J). (gr. k-2). 15.99 *(978-1-58536-942-3(X),* 204330) Sleeping Bear Pr.

James, Laura. Fabio the World's Greatest Flamingo Detective: Mystery on the Ostrich Express. Fox, Emily, illus. 2020. (ENG.). 128p. (J). 16.99 *(978-1-5476-0459-3(X),* 900223954); pap. 6.99 *(978-1-5476-0458-6(1),* 900223951) Bloomsbury Publishing USA. (Bloomsbury Children's Bks.).

Jarman, Julia. The Magic Backpack. Gon, Adriano, illus. 2003. (Flying Foxes Ser.). (ENG.). 48p. (J). lib. bdg. *(978-0-7787-1487-3(X))* Crabtree Publishing Co.

—Stowaway!: Band 14/Ruby (Collins Big Cat) Oldroyd, Mark, illus. 2007. (Collins Big Cat Ser.). (ENG.). 48p. (J). (gr. 3-4). pap. 11.99 *(978-0-00-723088-4(5))* HarperCollins Pubs. Ltd. GBR. Dist: Independent Pubs. Group.

Jeffers, Oliver. Lost & Found. Jeffers, Oliver, illus. 2005. (ENG., Illus.). 32p. (J). (gr. -1-2). 18.99 *(978-0-399-24503-9(0),* Philomel Bks.) Penguin Young Readers Group.

Jensen Shaffer, Jody. A Chip off the Old Block. Miyares, Daniel, illus. 2018. 32p. (J). (gr. k-3). 17.99 *(978-0-399-17388-2(9),* Nancy Paulsen Books) Penguin Young Readers Group.

Johnson, Maureen. The Last Little Blue Envelope. (13 Little Blue Envelopes Ser.: 2). (ENG.). 288p. (YA). (gr. 8). 2016. Illus.). pap. 10.99 *(978-0-06-243912-3(X))* 2012. pap. 9.99 *(978-0-06-197681-0(4))* HarperCollins Pubs. (HarperTeen).

—13 Little Blue Envelopes. (13 Little Blue Envelopes Ser.: 1). (ENG., Illus.). (YA). (gr. 8-18). 2005. 336p. 17.99 *(978-0-06-054141-5(5))* 2010. 368p. reprint ed. pap. 9.99 *(978-0-06-054143-9(1))* HarperCollins Pubs. (HarperTeen).

—13 Little Blue Envelopes. 2007. 317p. 20.00 *(978-0-7569-7830-3(0))* Perfection Learning Corp.

Johnston, Tony. The Harmonica. Mazellan, Ron, illus. 2008. (ENG.). 32p. (J). (gr. 2-5). pap. 7.95 *(978-1-57091-489-8(3))* Charlesbridge Publishing, Inc.

Johnston, Tony & de Rhoads, Maria Elena Fontanot. Beast Rider. 2019. (ENG., Illus.). 176p. (J). (gr. 7-17). 18.99 *(978-1-4197-3363-5(X),* 1251301, Amulet Bks.) Abrams, Inc.

Jolivert, Immaculine. The Lamb Who Counted Clouds. Gillen, Rosemarie, illus. 2013. 24p. pap. 13.75 *(978-1-937260-91-0(7))* Sleepytown Pr.

Jones, Diana Wynne & Jones, Ursula. The Islands of Chaldea. 2015. (ENG.). 368p. (J). (gr. 3-7). pap. 10.99 *(978-0-06-229508-8(X),* Greenwillow Bks.) HarperCollins Pubs.

Jones, Frewin. Faerie Path #5: the Enchanted Quest. 2010. (Faerie Path Ser.: 5). (ENG.). 368p. (YA). (gr. 8-18). 16.99 *(978-0-06-087158-1(X),* HarperTeen) HarperCollins Pubs.

Judge, Chris. The Lonely Beast. Judge, Chris, illus. 2011. (ENG., Illus.). 32p. (J). (gr. -1-3). 16.95 *(978-0-7613-8097-9(3),* cf2839e0-7a8a-4af6-aa66-b9f0cacf9654) Lerner Publishing Group.

Karanja, Jedidah. My Language, My Experience. 2018. (ENG.). 58p. 41.39 *(978-1-9845-0255-1(7));* (Illus.). pap. 27.59 *(978-1-9845-0254-4(9))* Xlibris Corp.

Kargbo, Ms Mariatu. Three Themne Titi Girls. 2013. 24p. (J). pap. 24.95 *(978-1-63004-790-0(2))* America Star Bks.

Kaufmann, Kelli. Ned Redd, World Traveler: A Search-And-Find Adventure. Boyd, Aaron, illus. 2005. (J). *(978-1-58987-135-9(9))* Kindermusik International.

Keeling, Annie E. Andrew Golding A Tale of the Great Plague. 2004. reprint ed. pap. 15.95 *(978-1-4191-0694-1(5));* pap. 1.99 *(978-1-4192-0694-8(X))* Kessinger Publishing, LLC.

Kehret, Peg. Runaway Twin. 2011. (ENG.). 208p. (J). (gr. 5-18). 8.99 *(978-0-14-241849-9(8),* Puffin Books) Penguin Young Readers Group.

Kelby, Tom. Nathaniel's Journey: The King's Armory. Yaeger, Mark, illus. 2003. (J). per. *(978-1-930914-04-9(0))* Hands to the Plow, Inc.

Khanduri, Kamini. Usborne the Great World Search. Hancock, David, illus. rev. ed. 2005. (Great Searches (EDC Paperback) Ser.). 48p. (J). (gr. -1). pap. 8.99 *(978-0-7945-1030-5(2),* Usborne) EDC Publishing.

Kipling, Rudyard. The White Seal. Jones, Chuck, illus. 2006. (ENG.). 32p. (J). (gr. -1-3). 8.95 *(978-0-8249-6598-3(1),* Ideals Pubns.) Worthy Publishing.

Kirkpatrick, Katherine. Escape Across the Wide Sea. 2004. (ENG., Illus.). 224p. (J). (gr. 4-6). tchr. ed. 17.95 *(978-0-8234-1854-1(5))* Holiday Hse., Inc.

Korman, Gordon. Unsinkable (Titanic, Book 1), Bk. 1. 2011. (Titanic Ser.: 1). (ENG.). 176p. (J). (gr. 4-7). pap. 6.99 *(978-0-545-12331-0(3),* Scholastic Paperbacks) Scholastic, Inc.

Kotzwinkle, William, et al. Walter the Farting Dog Goes on a Cruise. Colman, Audrey, illus. 2008. (ENG.). 32p. (J). (gr. k-3). pap. 8.99 *(978-0-14-241142-1(6),* Puffin Books) Penguin Young Readers Group.

Kress, Adrienne. The Explorers: the Reckless Rescue. 2019. (Explorers Ser.: 2). (ENG.). 400p. (J). (gr. 3-7). 7.99 *(978-1-101-94012-9(3),* Yearling) Random Hse. Children's Bks.

LaFaye, A. Walking Home to Rosie Lee, 1 vol. Shepherd, Keith D., illus. 2019. (ENG.). 32p. (J). (gr. 1-6). pap. 11.95 *(978-1-941026-57-1(5),* 23353382, Cinco Puntos Press) Lee & Low Bks., Inc.

Lai, Remy. Fly on the Wall. Lai, Remy, illus. 2020. (ENG., Illus.). 336p. (J). 22.99 *(978-1-250-31411-6(9),* 900199489, Holt, Henry & Co. Bks. For Young Readers) Holt, Henry & Co.

—Fly on the Wall. Lai, Remy, illus. 2021. (ENG., Illus.). 336p. (J). pap. 12.99 *(978-1-250-31412-3(7),* 900199490) Square Fish.

Langen, Annette. Letters from Felix: A Little Rabbit on a World Tour. Droop, Constanza, illus. 2003. 47p. (J). 14.99 *(978-1-59384-034-1(9))* Parklane Publishing.

Langrish, Katherine. Troll Blood. 2008. (ENG., Illus.). 352p. (J). (gr. 5-8). 16.99 *(978-0-06-111674-2(2),* HarperCollins) HarperCollins Pubs.

—Troll Blood. Stevens, Tim & Wyatt, David, illus. 2008. 352p. (YA). (gr. 5-8). lib. bdg. 17.89 *(978-0-06-111675-9(0),* Eos) HarperCollins Pubs.

Larson, Hope. Knife's Edge. 2018. (Four Points Ser.: 2). (J). lib. bdg. 24.50 *(978-0-606-41086-1(4))* Turtleback.

Lasky, Kathryn. The River of Wind. 2007. (Guardians of Ga'Hoole Ser.: 13). lib. bdg. 17.20 *(978-1-4177-8261-1(7))* Turtleback.

Law, Ingrid. Savvy. 2011. 9.68 *(978-0-7848-3575-3(6),* Everbind) Marco Bk. Co.

—Savvy. 2010. (Illus.). 368p. (J). (gr. 4-7). 9.99 *(978-0-14-241433-0(6),* Puffin Books) Penguin Young Readers Group.

—Savvy. l.t. ed. 2011. (ENG.). 500p. 23.99 *(978-1-4104-3530-9(X))* Thorndike Pr.

—Savvy. 2010. lib. bdg. 18.40 *(978-0-606-14394-3(7))* Turtleback.

Leth, Kate. Adventure Time: Vol. 4. 2014. lib. bdg. 24.50 *(978-0-606-36119-4(7))* Turtleback.

Lisle, Holly. Ruby Key, Bk. 1. 2008. 384p. (J). *(978-0-545-00013-0(0),* Orchard Bks.) Scholastic, Inc.

Lo, Malinda. Huntress. 2012. (ENG.). 416p. (YA). (gr. 9-17). pap. 11.99 *(978-0-316-03999-4(3))* Little, Brown Bks. for Young Readers.

London, Jack. The Mutiny of the 'ElsinoreApos. 2006. 264p. per. 15.95 *(978-1-59818-834-9(8))* Aegypan.

Lynch, Brian. Minions: The Junior Novel. 2015. (Illus.). 130p. (J). *(978-0-316-30625-6(8))* Little Brown & Co.

—Minions: The Junior Novel. 2015. (J). lib. bdg. 17.20 *(978-0-606-37222-0(9))* Turtleback.

Ma, Jyoti & Devi, Chandra. Sparkling Together: Starbright & His Earthling Friends. 2004. (ENG., Illus.). 96p. (J). pap. 19.95 *(978-0-932040-54-1(3),* ddc1ee5d-f71a-4c3b-8b79-8b3ee127a8bb) Integral Yoga Pubns.

Malnor, Carol & Fuller, Sandy. The Blues Go Birding at Wild America's Shores, 1 vol. Schroeder, Louise, illus. 2010. (ENG.). 36p. (J). (gr. k-4). pap. 8.99 *(978-1-58469-132-7(8),* Dawn Pubns.) Sourcebooks, Inc.

—The Blues Go Extreme Birding, 1 vol. Schroeder, Louise, illus. 2011. (ENG.). 36p. (J). (gr. k-4). 16.95 *(978-1-58469-133-4(6),* Dawn Pubns.) Sourcebooks, Inc.

Malnor, Carol & Fuller, Sandy F. The BLUES Go Extreme Birding, 1 vol. Schroeder, Louise, illus. 2011. (ENG.). 36p. (J). (gr. k-4). pap. 8.95 *(978-1-58469-134-1(4))* Take Heart Pubns.

Malnor, Carol L. & Fuller, Sandy F. The BLUES Go Birding at Wild America's Shores, 1 vol. Schroeder, Louise, illus. 2010. (ENG.). 36p. (J). 16.95 *(978-1-58469-131-0(X))* Take Heart Pubns.

Mama Doo. Trevor's Adventure in Button Land, 1 vol. 2008. (ENG.). 47p. pap. 24.95 *(978-1-60672-349-4(9))* America Star Bks.

Marillier, Juliet. Raven Flight: A Shadowfell Novel. 2014. (Shadowfell Ser.). (ENG.). 416p. (YA). (gr. 7). pap. 9.99 *(978-0-375-87197-9(7),* Ember) Random Hse. Children's Bks.

—Shadowfell. 2013. (Shadowfell Ser.). (ENG., Illus.). 416p. (YA). (gr. 7). pap. 14.99 *(978-0-375-87196-2(9),* Ember) Random Hse. Children's Bks.

Martin, Rafe. Birdwing. 2007. (ENG.). 384p. (J). (gr. 7-12). pap. 7.99 *(978-0-439-21168-0(9),* Levine, Arthur A. Bks.) Scholastic, Inc.

Martinez, David & Benchmark Education Co., LLC. My Whale of a Tale. 2014. (Text Connections Ser.). (J). (gr. 3). *(978-1-4509-9651-8(5))* Benchmark Education Co.

Martinez, Rafael. El Deseo de Aurelio. Martinez, Enrique, illus. 2006. (la Orilla del Viento Ser.). (SPA.). 48p. (J). (gr. 8-10). pap. *(978-968-16-7988-0(1))* Fondo de Cultura Economica.

Mason-Black, Jennifer. Devil & the Bluebird. 2016. (ENG.). 336p. (J). (gr. 8-17). 17.95 *(978-1-4197-2000-0(7),* 1135901, Amulet Bks.) Abrams, Inc.

Mateboer, Hans. Peter the Cruise Ship. 2007. (Illus.). 32p. (J). 16.95 *(978-0-9759487-1-2(7))* Mateboer, Johannes Aart.

Mattick, Lindsay & Greenhut, Josh. Winnie's Great War. Blackall, Sophie, illus. (ENG.). 256p. (J). (gr. 3-7). 2019. pap. 7.99 *(978-0-316-44709-6(9))* 2018. 16.99 *(978-0-316-44712-6(9))* Little, Brown Bks. for Young Readers.

McCartney, Paul. Hey Grandude! Durst, Kathryn, illus. 2019. (ENG.). 32p. (J). (gr. -1-1). 17.99 *(978-0-525-64867-3(4),* Random Hse. Bks. for Young Readers) Random Hse. Children's Bks.

McCooke, Valerie J. Grandfather's Chest. 2012. 40p. pap. 32.70 *(978-1-4771-0543-6(3))* Xlibris Corp.

McDonnell, Kathleen. The Shining World, 1 vol. 2003. (Notherland Journeys Ser.: 2). (ENG.). 236p. (J). (gr. 7-9). pap. 6.95 *(978-1-896764-79-5(7))* Second Story Pr. CAN. Dist: Orca Bk. Pubs. USA.

Mead, Richelle. The Emerald Sea. 2018. (Glittering Court Ser.: 3). (ENG.). 496p. (YA). (gr. 7). 19.99 *(978-1-59514-845-2(0),* Razorbill) Penguin Young Readers Group.

Melton, Marcia. Joe Henry's Journey. 2014. (Illus.). 169p. (J). pap. 12.00 *(978-1-937849-20-7(1))* Raven Publishing Inc. of Montana.

Meyer, Carolyn. The True Adventures of Charley Darwin. 2011. (ENG., Illus.). 336p. (YA). (gr. 7-12). 24.94 *(978-0-15-206194-4(0))* Harcourt Children's Bks.

—The True Adventures of Charley Darwin. 2011. (ENG., Illus.). 336p. (YA). (gr. 7). pap. 9.99 *(978-0-547-41564-2(8),* 1429780, Clarion Bks.) HarperCollins Pubs.

Meyer, Kim Shapiro. The Journey of the Coconut. Shapiro, Pepper, illus. 2012. 36p. pap. 24.95 *(978-1-4626-8641-4(9))* America Star Bks.

Meyer, L. A. Mississippi Jack: Being an Account of the Further Waterborne Adventures of Jacky Faber, Midshipman, Fine Lady, & Lily of the West. (Bloody Jack Adventures Ser.: 5). (ENG., Illus.). 624p. (YA). (gr. 7-12). 2007. 17.00 *(978-0-15-206003-9(0),* 1198027) 2nd ed. 2010. pap. 8.99 *(978-0-15-206632-1(2),* 1099015) HarperCollins Pubs. (Clarion Bks.).

Michael, Morpurgo. El reino de kensuke. 2006. (SPA., Illus.). 155p. (J). (gr. 5-8). 16.99 *(978-84-7901-420-9(2))* RBA Libros, S.A. ESP. Dist: Santillana USA Publishing Co., Inc.

Miller, Pat Zietlow. Wherever You Go. Wheeler, Eliza, illus. 2019. (ENG.). 26p. (J). (gr. -1 — 1). bds. 7.99 *(978-0-316-48794-8(5))* Little, Brown Bks. for Young Readers.

Mills, G. Riley. Son of the Sea. 2012. 22.95 *(978-0-7414-7515-2(4));* pap. 11.95 *(978-0-7414-7514-5(6))* Infinity Publishing.

Minshall, Caleigh. Blue: Voyage to the Sky. 2005. 54p. (J). pap. 19.95 net. *(978-1-59975-284-6(0))* Independent Pub.

Mitchell, Laine. We're Going on a Santa Hunt. Shea, Louis, illus. 2017. (J). *(978-1-338-25514-0(2))* Scholastic, Inc.

Moran, Paul & Forizs, Gergely. Where's the Llama? An Around-The-World Adventure. 2019. (ENG.). 48p. (J). pap. 9.99 *(978-1-4494-9729-3(2))* Andrews McMeel Publishing.

Morgan, Anna. Daughters of the Ark, 1 vol. 2005. (ENG., Illus.). 200p. (J). (gr. 5-12). pap. 9.95 *(978-1-896764-92-4(4))* Second Story Pr. CAN. Dist: Orca Bk. Pubs. USA.

Morgen, A. M. The Inventors at No. 8. (ENG., Illus.). (J). (gr. 3-7). 2019. 368p. pap. 7.99 *(978-0-316-47151-0(8))* 2018. 352p. 16.99 *(978-0-316-47149-7(6))* Little, Brown Bks. for Young Readers.

Moriarty, Jaclyn. The Extremely Inconvenient Adventures of Bronte Mettlestone. 2018. (ENG., Illus.). 384p. (J). (gr. 3-7). 17.99 *(978-1-338-25584-3(3),* Levine, Arthur A. Bks.) Scholastic, Inc.

Morpurgo, Michael. Kensuke's Kingdom. 2004. (ENG.). 176p. (J). (gr. 4-7). mass mkt. 7.99 *(978-0-439-59181-2(3),* Scholastic Paperbacks) Scholastic, Inc.

—Twist of Gold. 2004. (ENG.). 304p. (J). pap. 8.99 *(978-0-7497-4687-2(4))* Farshore GBR. Dist: Trafalgar Square Publishing.

Moss, Marissa. Amelia's Family Ties. Moss, Marissa, illus. 2013. (Amelia Ser.). (ENG., Illus.). (J). 5.99 *(978-1-4169-1293-4(2),* Simon & Schuster/Paula Wiseman Bks.) Simon & Schuster/Paula Wiseman Bks.

Mull, Brandon. Keys to the Demon Prison. 2010. (Fablehaven Ser.: 5). (ENG., Illus.). 600p. (J). (gr. 3). 21.99 *(978-1-60641-238-1(8),* 5033746, Shadow Mountain) Shadow Mountain Publishing.

Murdock, Catherine Gilbert. The Book of Boy: A Newbery Honor Award Winner. 2018. (ENG., Illus.). 288p. (J). (gr. 3-7). 16.99 *(978-0-06-268620-6(8),* Greenwillow Bks.) HarperCollins Pubs.

Murphy, Patricia & Hoena, Blake A. A Visit To... rev. ed. 2018. (Visit To... Ser.). (ENG.). 24p. (J). (gr. -1-2). 175.92 *(978-1-5435-0901-4(0),* 27775, Capstone Pr.) Capstone.

Naylor, Phyllis Reynolds. Emily's Fortune. 1. 2011. (Emily Ser.: 1). 160p. (J). (gr. 3-7). 6.99 *(978-0-375-84492-8(9),* Yearling) Random Hse. Children's Bks.

Nielson, Kelli S. Stone Mage Wars, Book 1: Journey to the Fringe. 2011. (YA). 17.99 *(978-1-60908-833-0(6))* Deseret Bk. Co.

Novel Units. The Incredible Journey Novel Units Student Packet. 2019. (ENG.). (YA). pap. 13.99 *(978-1-56137-469-4(5),* Novel Units, Inc.) Classroom Library Co.

—Journey Novel Units Teacher Guide. 2019. (ENG.). (YA). pap. 12.99 *(978-1-56137-485-4(7),* Novel Units, Inc.) Classroom Library Co.

O'Byrne, Nicola. What's Next Door? O'Byrne, Nicola, illus. 2018. (ENG., Illus.). 32p. (J). (gr. -1-2). 15.99 *(978-0-7636-9634-4(X))* Candlewick Pr.

Odgers, Sally. Journey to the Center of the Earth, 1 vol. rev. ed. 2013. (Literary Text Ser.). (ENG., Illus.). 24p. (J). (gr. 2-3). pap. 8.99 *(978-1-4333-5527-1(2))* Teacher Created Materials, Inc.

Oliver, Lauren. Liesl & Po. Acedera, Kei, illus. 2012. (ENG.). 336p. (J). (gr. 3-7). pap. 7.99 *(978-0-06-201452-8(8),* HarperCollins) HarperCollins Pubs.

—Liesl & Po. 2012. (J). lib. bdg. 17.20 *(978-0-606-26853-0(7))* Turtleback.

Oneill, Elizabeth. Alfred Visits Maryland. 2008. 24p. (J). pap. 12.00 *(978-0-9799121-7-7(2))* Funny Bone Bks.

—Alfred Visits Oregon. 2008. 24p. pap. 12.00 *(978-0-9799121-8-4(0))* Funny Bone Bks.

—Alfred Visits Vermont. 2008. 24p. pap. 12.00 *(978-0-9799121-9-1(9))* Funny Bone Bks.

Optic, Oliver, pseud. Outward Bound. 2007. 180p. (gr. 4-7). per. *(978-1-4068-4343-9(1))* Echo Library.

—Outward Bound: Or Young America Afloat. l.t. ed. 2007. (ENG.). 274p. pap. 23.99 *(978-1-4264-9153-5(0))* Creative Media Partners, LLC.

—Sunny Shores; or, Young America in Italy & Austria a Story of Travel & Adventure by William T Adams. 2006. 428p. per. 26.99 *(978-1-4255-4627-4(7))* Michigan Publishing.

Orme, David. Deadly Virus, Set. 2008. (Starchasers Ser.). (ENG., Illus.). 48p. pap. *(978-1-84167-767-5(1))* Ransom Publishing Ltd.

—Galactic Shopping Mall, Set. 2008. (Starchasers Ser.). (ENG., Illus.). 48p. pap. *(978-1-84167-764-4(7))* Ransom Publishing Ltd.

—Jungle Planet, Set. 2008. (Starchasers Ser.). (ENG., Illus.). 48p. pap. *(978-1-84167-768-2(X))* Ransom Publishing Ltd.

—Lost Explorers, Set. 2008. (Starchasers Ser.). (ENG., Illus.). 48p. pap. *(978-1-84167-763-7(9))* Ransom Publishing Ltd.

—Planet of the Vampires, Set. 2008. (Starchasers Ser.). (ENG., Illus.). 48p. pap. *(978-1-84167-765-1(5))* Ransom Publishing Ltd.

Osborne, Mary Pope. Eve of the Emperor Penguin. Murdocca, Sal, illus. 2009. (Magic Tree House (R) Merlin Mission Ser.: 12). (ENG.). 144p. (J). (gr. 2-5). 6.99 *(978-0-375-83734-0(5),* Random Hse. Bks. for Young Readers) Random Hse. Children's Bks.

Oso Se Va de Viaje. 2014. (ENG & SPA., Illus.). (J). *(978-1-78285-088-5(0))* Barefoot Bks., Inc.

Oulton, Harry. Heather's Piglets. 2017. (Pig Called Heather Ser.: 3). (ENG., Illus.). 240p. (J). (gr. 4-7). pap. 8.99 *(978-1-84812-479-0(1))* Bonnier Publishing GBR. Dist: Independent Pubs. Group.

—The Return of a Pig Called Heather. 2017. (Pig Called Heather Ser.: 2). (ENG., Illus.). 192p. (J). (gr. 4-7). pap. 8.99 *(978-1-84812-473-8(2))* Bonnier Publishing GBR. Dist: Independent Pubs. Group.

Parker, Emma. Sam the Traveling Snail. 2010. (Illus.). pap. *(978-1-877561-19-1(3))* First Edition Ltd.

Parker, Richard. Voyage to Tasmani. Seward, Prudence, illus. 2011. 128p. 40.95 *(978-1-258-08572-8(0))* Literary Licensing, LLC.

Patterson, James. The Nerdiest, Wimpiest, Dorkiest I Funny Ever. 2018. (I Funny Ser.: 6). (ENG., Illus.). 336p. (J). (gr. 3-7). 13.99 *(978-0-316-34961-1(5),* Jimmy Patterson) Little Brown & Co.

Paulsen, Gary. Tucket's Travels: Francis Tucket's Adventures in the West, 1847-1849 (Books 1-5) 2003. (Francis Tucket Bks.: Bks. 1-5). (ENG.). 560p. (J). (gr. 3-7). pap. 9.99 *(978-0-440-41967-9(0),* Yearling) Random Hse. Children's Bks.

Paver, Michelle. Chronicles of Ancient Darkness #1: Wolf Brother. Taylor, Geoff, illus. 2006. (Chronicles of Ancient Darkness Ser.: 1). (ENG.). 320p. (J). (gr. 5-9). reprint ed. per. 9.99 *(978-0-06-072827-4(2),* Tegen, Katherine Bks) HarperCollins Pubs.

—Chronicles of Ancient Darkness #2: Spirit Walker, 2. Taylor, Geoff, illus. 2007. (Chronicles of Ancient Darkness Ser.: 2). (ENG.). 384p. (J). (gr. 5-8). pap. 7.99 *(978-0-06-072830-4(2),* Tegen, Katherine Bks) HarperCollins Pubs.

—Gods & Warriors. 2013. (Gods & Warriors Ser.: 1). (ENG.). 336p. (J). (gr. 5). pap. 8.99 *(978-0-14-242284-7(3),* Puffin Books) Penguin Young Readers Group.

—HERMANO LOBO: CRÓNICAS DE LA PREHISTORIA I. 2005. (SPA., Illus.). 222p. 17.25 *(978-84-7888-933-4(7))* Emece Editores ESP. Dist: Ediciones Universal.

—Wolf Brother, 6 vols. 2005. (Chronicles of Ancient Darkness Ser.: 1). (J). 89.75 *(978-1-4193-3811-3(0));* 91.75 *(978-1-4193-3809-0(9));* 76.75 *(978-1-4193-2628-8(7));* 73.75 *(978-1-4193-2630-1(9))* Recorded Bks., Inc.

Pene du Bois, William. The Twenty-One Balloons (Puffin Modern Classics) 2005. (Puffin Modern Classics Ser.).

(Illus.). 192p. (J). (gr. 3-7). pap. 7.99 (978-0-14-240330-3(X), Puffin Books) Penguin Young Readers Group.

Phelan, Matt. Around the World. Phelan, Matt, illus. 2011. (ENG., Illus.). 240p. (J). (gr. 4-7). 24.99 (978-0-7636-3619-7(3)) Candlewick Pr.

Place, Francois. The Last Giants. Place, Francois, illus. 2018. (ENG.). 80p. (J). (gr. -1-3). pap. 14.95 (978-1-56792-621-7(5)) Godine, David R. Pub.

Pon, Cindy. Silver Phoenix. 2011. (Silver Phoenix Ser.: 1). (ENG.). 368p. (YA). (gr. 9). pap. 8.99 (978-0-06-173024-5(6), Greenwillow Bks.) HarperCollins Pubs.

Priceman, Marjorie. How to Make a Cherry Pie & See the U. S. A. 2013. lib. bdg. 18.40 (978-0-606-32190-7(X)) Turtleback.

Prineas, Sarah. The Magic Thief: Found. Caparo, Antonio Javier, illus. 2011. (Magic Thief Ser.: 3). (ENG.). 384p. (J). (gr. 5). pap. 7.99 (978-0-06-137595-8(0), HarperCollins) HarperCollins Pubs.

Rae, Kristin. Wish You Were Italian: An If Only Novel. 2014. (If Only... Ser.). (ENG.). 352p. (YA). (gr. 7). pap. 9.99 (978-1-61963-286-8(1), 900131800, Bloomsbury USA Childrens) Bloomsbury Publishing USA.

Rapp, Adam. Punkzilla. 2009. (ENG., Illus.). 256p. (YA). (gr. 9). 16.99 (978-0-7636-3031-7(4)) Candlewick Pr.

Razzell, Mary. Runaway at Sea. unabr. ed. 2005. (ENG., Illus.). 150p. (YA). (gr. 7-9). (978-1-55017-327-7(8), 908e7792-56f8-417c-9398-8f228ed75aef) Harbour Publishing Co., Ltd.

Rees, Celia. Witch Child. unabr. ed. 2004. (Young Adult Cassette Librariestm Ser.). 304p. (J). (gr. 5-9). pap. 40.00 incl. audio (978-0-8072-1198-4(2), S YA 343 SP, Listening Library) Random Hse. Audio Publishing Group.

Rewa. Molly May on the High Seas. (Illus.). 9.95 (978-0-9726375-1-0(6)) Little Red Cat Publishing.

Riel, Jørn, et al. The Snowstorm. Cann, Helen, illus. 2012. 128p. (J). (gr. 4-6). pap. 9.99 (978-1-84686-797-2(5)) Barefoot Bks., Inc.

Riggs, Ransom. A Map of Days. 2018. (Miss Peregrine's Peculiar Children Ser.: 4). (ENG.). 496p. (YA). (gr. 7). 22.99 (978-0-7352-3214-3(8), Dutton Books for Young Readers) Penguin Young Readers Group.

Riggs, Sandy. Joe Boat. 2006. (Reader's Clubhouse Level 2 Reader Ser.). (Illus.). 24p. (J). (gr. k-1). pap. 3.99 (978-0-7641-3296-4(2)) Sourcebooks, Inc.

Riordan, Rick. Kane Chronicles, the, Book One: Red Pyramid: the Graphic Novel, the-Kane Chronicles, the, Book One, Bk. 1. 2012. (Kane Chronicles Ser.: 1). (ENG., Illus.). 192p. (J). (gr. 5-9). pap. 12.99 (978-1-4231-5069-5(4), Disney-Hyperion) Disney Publishing Worldwide.

—Kane Chronicles, the, Book One: Red Pyramid, the-Kane Chronicles, the, Book One. 2010. (Kane Chronicles Ser.: 1). (ENG., Illus.). 528p. (J). (gr. 5-9). 19.99 (978-1-4231-1338-6(1), Disney-Hyperion) Disney Publishing Worldwide.

—Kane Chronicles, the, Book One: Red Pyramid, the-The Kane Chronicles, Book One. 2018. (Kane Chronicles Ser.: 1). (ENG., Illus.). 576p. (J). (gr. 5-9). pap. 9.99 (978-1-368-01358-1(9), Disney-Hyperion) Disney Publishing Worldwide.

—Kane Chronicles, the, Book Three: Serpent's Shadow: the Graphic Novel, the-Kane Chronicles, the, Book Three. 2017. (Kane Chronicles Ser.). (ENG., Illus.). 160p. (J). (gr. 5-9). 21.99 (978-1-4847-8132-6(5)); pap. 14.99 (978-1-4847-8234-7(8)) Disney Publishing Worldwide. (Disney-Hyperion).

—Kane Chronicles, the, Book Three: Serpent's Shadow, the-Kane Chronicles, the, Book Three, Bk. 3. 2012. (Kane Chronicles Ser.: 3). (ENG.). 416p. (J). (gr. 5-9). 19.99 (978-1-4231-4057-3(5), Disney-Hyperion) Disney Publishing Worldwide.

—Kane Chronicles, the, Book Two: Throne of Fire, the-Kane Chronicles, the, Book Two. (Kane Chronicles Ser.: 2). (ENG., (J). (gr. 5-9). 2018. Illus.). 528p. pap. 9.99 (978-1-368-01359-8(7))Bk. 2. 2011. 464p. 18.99 (978-1-4231-4056-6(7)) Disney Publishing Worldwide. (Disney-Hyperion).

—The Red Pyramid. l.t. ed. 2018. (Kane Chronicles Ser.: 1). (ENG.). (J). pap. 15.99 (978-1-4328-5029-6(6)) Cengage Gale.

—The Red Pyramid. 2009. (Kane Chronicles: Bk. 1). 11.04 (978-0-7848-3733-7(3), Everbind) Marco Bk. Co.

—The Red Pyramid. 2012. 20.00 (978-1-61383-660-6(0)) Perfection Learning Corp.

—The Red Pyramid. 2010. pap. (978-0-545-40016-9(3)) Scholastic, Inc.

—The Red Pyramid. l.t. ed. 2010. (Kane Chronicles: Bk. 1). (ENG.). 671p. 23.95 (978-1-4104-2536-2(3)) Thorndike Pr.

—The Red Pyramid. (Kane Chronicles Ser.: 1). (J). 2018. lib. bdg. 20.85 (978-0-606-41205-6(0)) 2012. lib. bdg. 24.50 (978-0-606-37510-8(4)) 2011. lib. bdg. 20.85 (978-0-606-39216-7(5)) Turtleback.

—The Serpent's Shadow. 2012. 416p. (978-0-14-133568-1(8), Puffin) Penguin Bks., Ltd.

—The Serpent's Shadow. l.t. ed. 2012. (Kane Chronicles: Bk. 3). (ENG.). 521p. (gr. 5-12). 23.99 (978-1-4104-4789-0(8)) Thorndike Pr.

—The Serpent's Shadow. 2018. (Kane Chronicles Ser.: 3). (J). lib. bdg. 20.85 (978-0-606-41206-3(9)) Turtleback.

—The Throne of Fire. l.t. ed. 2011. (Kane Chronicles Ser.: 2). (ENG.). 591p. lib. bdg. 23.99 (978-1-4328-4405-9(9)) Cengage Gale.

—The Throne of Fire. 2011. (Kane Chronicles: Bk. 2). 452p. (J). pap. (978-1-4231-5059-6(7)) Disney Pr.

—The Throne of Fire. 2nd ed. 2012. (ENG.). 464p. (YA). (gr. 5-9). pap. 9.99 (978-1-4231-6703-7(1)) Hyperion Bks. for Children.

—The Throne of Fire. 2011. (Kane Chronicles: Bk. 2). (ENG., Illus.). 451p. 28.25 (978-0-85757-231-8(8)); 2nd ed. 554p. pap. (978-0-14-133566-7(1)) Penguin Publishing Group. (Puffin).

—The Throne of Fire. l.t. ed. 2011. (Kane Chronicles: Bk. 2). (ENG.). 589p. 23.99 (978-1-4104-3607-8(1)) Thorndike Pr.

—The Throne of Fire. (Kane Chronicles Graphic Novels Ser.: 2). 2015. lib. bdg. 24.50 (978-0-606-37509-2(0)) 2018. (J). lib. bdg. 20.85 (978-0-606-41204-9(2)) 2012. (J). lib. bdg. 20.85 (978-0-606-39217-4(3)) Turtleback.

Riordan, Rick & Collar, Orpheus. Serpent's Shadow. 2017. (Kane Chronicles Graphic Novels Ser.: 3). (J). lib. bdg. 24.50 (978-0-606-40604-8(2)) Turtleback.

Robert, Bulla Clyde & Clyde, Bulla. A Lion to Guard Us. 2014. (Trophy Bk Ser.). (ENG.). 128p. (J). (gr. 3-7). 10.24 (978-1-63245-324-2(X)) Lectorum Pubns., Inc.

Roberts, Willo Davis. Surviving Summer Vacation: How I Visited Yellowstone Park with the Terrible Rupes. 2015. (ENG., Illus.). 208p. (J). (gr. 3-7). pap. 6.99 (978-1-4814-3718-9(6), Aladdin) Simon & Schuster Children's Publishing.

Robinson, Christian. Another. Robinson, Christian, illus. 2019. (ENG., Illus.). 56p. (J). (gr. -1-3). 17.99 (978-1-5344-2167-7(X), Atheneum Bks. for Young Readers) Simon & Schuster Children's Publishing.

Roy, Philip. Seas of South Africa. 2013. (ENG.). 250p. pap. 11.95 (978-1-55380-247-1(0)) Ronsdale Pr. CAN. Dist: SPD-Small Pr. Distribution.

—Submarine Outlaw. 2008. (ENG., Illus.). 254p. pap. 10.95 (978-1-55380-058-3(3)) Ronsdale Pr. CAN. Dist: SPD-Small Pr. Distribution.

Rubalcaba, Jill. The Wadjet Eye. 2006. (ENG.). 160p. (J). (gr. 5-7). pap. 7.99 (978-0-618-68927-9(3), 100486, Clarion Bks.) HarperCollins Pubs.

Rushdie, Salman. Luka & the Fire of Life. 2009. 14.75 (978-0-7848-3731-3(7), Everbind) Marco Bk. Co.

—Luka & the Fire of Life. 2011. (ENG.). 224p. (J). mass mkt. 7.99 (978-0-8129-8196-4(0)) Random Hse., Inc.

—Luka & the Fire of Life: A Novel. 2011. (ENG.). 240p. (J). (gr. 7). pap. 17.00 (978-0-679-78347-3(4), Random Hse. Trade Paperbacks) Random House Publishing Group.

Said. The Seven Voyages of Sinbad the Sailor. Kheiriyeh, Rashin, illus. 2015. (ENG.). 64p. (J). (gr. k-2). 19.95 (978-0-7358-4240-3(X)) North-South Bks., Inc.

Sanderson, Ruth. The Snow Princess. 2017. (Ruth Sanderson Collection). (ENG., Illus.). 32p. (J). (gr. -1-3). pap. 8.95 (978-1-56656-098-6(5), Crocodile Bks.) Interlink Publishing Group, Inc.

Sante, Andrew R. The Silver Heart Chronicles: The Voyage. 2012. 50p. 24.99 (978-1-4771-4700-9(4)); pap. 15.99 (978-1-4771-4699-6(7)) Xlibris Corp.

Savit, Gavriel. The Way Back. 2020. (ENG.). 368p. (YA). (gr. 7). 18.99 (978-1-9848-9462-5(5), Knopf Bks. for Young Readers) Random Hse. Children's Bks.

Say, Allen. Grandfather's Journey. 2008. (ENG.). 32p. (J). (gr. -1-3). pap. 7.99 (978-0-547-14178-7(5), Sandpiper) Houghton Mifflin Harcourt Trade & Reference Pubs.

—Grandfather's Journey. 2011. (J). (gr. k-5). 29.95 (978-0-545-10696-2(6)); 18.95 (978-0-545-12708-0(4)) Weston Woods Studios, Inc.

—Grandfather's Journey: A Caldecott Award Winner. Say, Allen, illus. 2008. (ENG., Illus.). 32p. (J). (gr. -1-3). 7.99 (978-0-547-07680-5(0), 1042044, Clarion Bks.) HarperCollins Pubs.

—Grandfather's Journey 20th Anniversary: A Caldecott Award Winner. Say, Allen, illus. 20th anniv. ed. 2013. (ENG., Illus.). 32p. (J). (gr. -1-3). 18.99 (978-0-544-05050-1(9), 1532595, Clarion Bks.) HarperCollins Pubs.

Schaaf, Ron. Tiger's Quest: Rounding Cape Horn. 2007. (J). (978-0-9787555-0-8(2)) Hickory Tales Publishing.

Schomer-Wendel, Gretchen & Schomer, Adam Anthony. All Around Town, 1 vol. Renthrope, Damon, illus. 2009. (Becka & the Big Bubble Ser.). (ENG.). 32p. (J). (gr. 1-2). lib. bdg. 27.27 (978-1-60754-104-2(1), d0c1c60d-ea83-44d6-b3b9-914d5d09e595, Windmill Bks.) Rosen Publishing Group, Inc., The.

—Becka Goes to India, 1 vol. Renthrope, Damon, illus. 2009. (Becka & the Big Bubble Ser.). (ENG.). 32p. (J). (gr. 1-2). lib. bdg. 27.27 (978-1-60754-110-3(6), a51681e0-5005-4e43-93bb-cb63d3dee051, Windmill Bks.) Rosen Publishing Group, Inc., The.

—Becka Goes to San Francisco, 1 vol. Renthrope, Damon, illus. 2009. (Becka & the Big Bubble Ser.). (ENG.). 32p. (J). (gr. 1-2). 27.27 (978-1-60754-107-3(6), 170513f4-02aa-46b8-9669-835833a908e1); pap. 11.55 (978-1-60754-108-0(4), 786c09a2-f35f-4e17-a27d-fb3874f3785c) Rosen Publishing Group, Inc., The. (Windmill Bks.).

—Becka Goes to the North Pole, 1 vol. Renthrope, Damon, illus. 2009. (Becka & the Big Bubble Ser.). (ENG.). 32p. (J). (gr. 1-2). lib. bdg. 27.27 (978-1-60754-116-5(5), dc207ff7-b36b-4fc4-8048-4f53104e6923, Windmill Bks.) Rosen Publishing Group, Inc., The.

Service, Pamela F. The Wizards of Wyrd World. Gorman, Mike, illus. 2015. (Way-Too-Real Aliens Ser.: 3). (ENG.). 112p. (J). (gr. 4-6). E-Book 53.32 (978-1-4677-5962-5(7), 9781467759625, Lerner Digital) Lerner Publishing Group.

Shan, Darren, pseud. The Thin Executioner. 2011. (ENG.). 512p. (YA). (gr. 10-17). pap. 23.99 (978-0-316-07864-1(6)) Little, Brown Bks. for Young Readers.

Sharp, Margery. The Rescuers. Williams, Garth, illus. 2016. (ENG.). 160p. (J). (gr. 4-7). pap. 11.99 (978-1-68137-007-1(7), NYRB Kids) New York Review of Bks., Inc., The.

Shearer, Alex. Sky Run. 2014. (Cloud Hunters Ser.). (ENG.). 288p. (J). (gr. 2-7). 14.95 (978-1-62873-593-2(7), Sky Pony Pr.) Skyhorse Publishing Co., Inc.

Shepherd, David & Plummer, William K. We Were There at the Driving of the Golden Spike. 2013. (ENG., Illus.). 192p. (J). (gr. 3-8). pap. 7.99 (978-0-486-49259-9(1), 492591) Dover Pubns., Inc.

Sherrard, Valerie. Driftwood, 1 vol. 2013. (ENG.). 200p. (J). (gr. 4-6). pap. 9.95 (978-1-55455-305-1(9), 10d7acab-2e6a-47c1-beb3-19e3d2a87524) Trifolium Bks., Inc. CAN. Dist: Firefly Bks., Ltd.

Shondalae. The Great Giver of Life, No. 8. 2008. 49p. pap. 16.95 (978-1-60672-071-4(6)) America Star Bks.

Sidney, Margaret. Five Little Peppers Abroad. (J). 24.95 (978-0-8488-1475-5(4)) Amereon Ltd.

Skerwarski, N. D. Freddy Freckles: Friends, Flags, Facts & Fun. Wooten, Neal, illus. 2007. 52p. (J). pap. 16.99 (978-0-9800675-3-8(7)) Mirror Publishing.

Skinner, Daphne. All Aboard! Smath, Jerry, illus. 2007. (Math Matters Ser.). 32p. (J). (gr. 1-3). pap. 5.99 (978-1-57565-239-9(0), e3538b34-f443-4ff3-8b7e-a181e945e25c, Kane Press) Astra Publishing Hse.

Skye, Obert. Leven Thumps & the Wrath of Ezra. 2008. (Leven Thumps Ser.: Bk. 4). (Illus.). 388p. (J). 19.95 (978-1-59038-963-8(8), Shadow Mountain) Shadow Mountain Publishing.

—The Ruins of Alder. Sowards, Ben, illus. 2010. (Leven Thumps Ser.: 5). (ENG.). 416p. (J). (gr. 4-9). pap. 10.99 (978-1-4169-9093-2(3), Aladdin) Simon & Schuster Children's Publishing.

—The Wrath of Ezra. Sowards, Ben, illus. 2009. (Leven Thumps Ser.: 4). (ENG.). 464p. (J). (gr. 4-9). pap. 10.99 (978-1-4169-9092-5(5), Aladdin) Simon & Schuster Children's Publishing.

Slanina, Anne Maro. Annie Mouse's Route 66 Adventure: A Photo Journal, vols. 6, vol. 5. Collins, Kelsey, illus. 2011. (ENG.). 48p. (J). pap. 14.99 (978-0-9793379-6-3(8)) Annie Mouse Bks.

SLAY, Jenette. ABBY, the Easter Chicken. 2008. 29p. 13.96 (978-1-4357-1062-7(2)) Lulu Pr., Inc.

Smith, Maggie. Counting Our Way to Maine. 2008. (ENG., Illus.). 32p. (J). (gr. -1-3). 15.95 (978-0-89272-775-9(6)) Down East Bks.

Snell, Gordon. The King of Quizzical Island. McKee, David, illus. 2009. (ENG.). 40p. (J). (gr. -1-3). 16.99 (978-0-7636-3857-3(9)) Candlewick Pr.

Sonberg, Caryn. Six Dogs & a Police Officer. Dorenkamp, Michelle, illus. 2006. 31p. pap. 8.40 (978-1-55501-776-7(2)) Ballard & Tighe Pubs.

Soto, Gary. Pacific Crossing. 2003. (ENG., Illus.). 144p. (J). (gr. 3-7). pap. 7.99 (978-0-15-204696-5(8), 261567, Clarion Bks.) HarperCollins Pubs.

star, celina. Paw Prints on the Road. 2008. (ENG.). 79p. pap. 9.96 (978-0-557-02420-9(X)) Lulu Pr., Inc.

Stead, Philip C. Sebastian & the Balloon. Stead, Philip C., illus. 2014. (ENG., Illus.). 40p. (J). (gr. -1-2). 19.99 (978-1-59643-930-6(0), 900122420) Roaring Brook Pr.

Stevenson, Robert Louis. Treasure Island. (Young Collector's Illustrated Classics Ser.). (Illus.). 192p. (J). (gr. 3-7). 9.95 (978-1-56156-456-9(7)) Kidsbooks, LLC.

—Treasure Island: With Story of the Treasure of Normon Island. Date not set. (J). (gr. 5-6). reprint ed. lib. bdg. 22.95 (978-0-89190-236-2(8), American Reprint Co.) Amereon Ltd.

Stilton, Gerónimo & Stilton, Thea. Thea Stilton & the Ghost of the Shipwreck. 2010. (Thea Stilton Ser.: 3). lib. bdg. 19.65 (978-0-606-06843-7(0)) Turtleback.

Stockton, Frank Richard. Round-about Rambles in Lands of Fact & Fancy. 2006. pap. (978-1-4068-3083-5(6)) Echo Library.

Stoffels, Karlijn. Heartsinger. 2009. (YA). pap. (978-0-545-06968-7(8), Levine, Arthur A. Bks.) Scholastic, Inc.

Stone, Nic. Clean Getaway. (ENG., Illus.). 240p. (J). (gr. 3-7). 2021. 7.99 (978-1-9848-9300-0(9), Yearling) 2020. 16.99 (978-1-9848-9297-3(5), Crown Books For Young Readers) Random Hse. Children's Bks.

Summers, Susan. The Greatest Gift: The Story of the Other Wise Man. Morris, Jackie, illus. 2011. 30p. (J). 16.99 (978-1-84686-578-7(6)) Barefoot Bks., Inc.

Sussman, Joni Kibort. Grover Goes to Israel. Leigh, Tom, illus. 2019. (ENG.). 12p. (J). (gr. -1 — 1). bds. 5.99 (978-1-5415-2920-5(0), f0313eea-2851-49fb-8a60-b6fb74d402f5, Kar-Ben Publishing) Lerner Publishing Group.

Swift, Jonathan. Classic Starts(r): Gulliver's Travels: Retold from the Jonathan Swift Original. Akib, Jamel, illus. 2006. (Classic Starts(r) Ser.). 160p. (J). (gr. 2-4). 6.95 (978-1-4027-2662-0(7)) Sterling Publishing Co., Inc.

—Viajes de Gulliver. 2003. (Advanced Reading Ser.). (SPA.). 344p. (J). 11.95 (978-84-670-0095-5(3)) Espasa Calpe, S.A. ESP. Dist: Planeta Publishing Corp.

Tabilio, Marco. Marco Polo: Dangers & Visions. Tabilio, Marco, illus. 2017. (ENG., Illus.). 208p. (YA). (gr. 9-12). pap. 11.99 (978-1-5124-3069-1(2), 275e57e8-881a-4e55-8d5f-f96fde9d19bf, Graphic Universe™) Lerner Publishing Group.

Tait, A. L., pseud. Beyond the Edge of the Map. 2022. (Mapmaker Chronicles Ser.). (ENG.). 272p. (J). (gr. 3-7). 13.99 (978-0-7344-1774-9(8), Lothian Children's Bks.) Hachette Australia AUS. Dist: Hachette Bk. Group.

—Breath of the Dragon. 2017. (Mapmaker Chronicles Ser.). (ENG., Illus.). 239p. (J). (978-1-61067-702-8(1)) Kane Miller.

—Breath of the Dragon: Mapmaker Chronicles. 2018. (ENG., Illus.). 240p. (J). pap. 5.99 (978-1-61067-624-3(6)) Kane Miller.

—Race to the End of the World. 2018. (ENG., Illus.). 240p. (J). pap. 5.99 (978-1-61067-622-9(X)) Kane Miller.

Taylor, G. P. The Shadowmancer Returns: The Curse of Salamander Street. 2008. (ENG.). 256p. (gr. 7-12). pap. 17.99 (978-1-59979-084-8(X), 084X, Realms) Charisma Media.

Taylor, Mark. Henry the Castaway. Booth, Graham, illus. 2010. 48p. (J). (gr. -1-3). 18.95 (978-1-930900-47-9(3)) Purple Hse. Pr.

Thorpe, Kiki. Finding Tinker Bell #1: Beyond Never Land (Disney: the Never Girls) Christy, Jana, illus. 2018. (Never Girls Ser.: 1). (ENG.). 128p. (J). (gr. 1-4). 6.99 (978-0-7364-3599-4(9), RH/Disney) Random Hse. Children's Bks.

Tompert, Ann. Little Fox Goes to the End of the World, 0 vols. Bryant, Laura J., illus. 2012. (ENG.). 32p. (J). (gr. -1-3). 16.99 (978-0-7614-5703-9(8), 9780761457039, Two Lions) Amazon Publishing.

Tonatiuh, Duncan. Pancho Rabbit & the Coyote: A Migrant's Tale. 2013. (ENG., Illus.). 32p. (J). (gr. 1-4). 18.99 (978-1-4197-0583-0(0), 692601, Abrams Bks. for Young Readers) Abrams, Inc.

Travis, Lucille. The Far Journey. 2009. 160p. (J). (gr. 4-7). 8.99 (978-1-60682-023-0(0)) BJU Pr.

Troupe, Thomas Kingsley. The Dark Lens. 2015. (Tartan House Ser.). (ENG.). 96p. (J). (gr. 3-6). (978-1-63235-054-1(8), 11681, 12-Story Library) Bookstaves, LLC.

—The Squadron. 2015. (Tartan House Ser.). (ENG.). 96p. (J). (gr. 3-6). (978-1-63235-057-2(2), 11684, 12-Story Library) Bookstaves, LLC.

Twain, Mark, pseud. The Adventures of Huckleberry Finn: With a Discussion of Friendship. Lauter, Richard, tr. Lauter, Richard, illus. 2003. (Values in Action Illustrated Classics Ser.). (J). (978-1-59203-042-2(4)) Learning Challenge, Inc.

—Classic Starts(r): the Adventures of Huckleberry Finn: Retold from the Mark Twain Original. Andreasen, Dan, illus. 2006. (Classic Starts(r) Ser.). 160p. (J). (gr. 2-4). 7.99 (978-1-4027-2499-2(3)) Sterling Publishing Co., Inc.

Uss, Christina. The Adventures of a Girl Called Bicycle. 2018. (Illus.). 320p. (J). (gr. 3-7). 16.99 (978-0-8234-4007-8(9), Margaret Ferguson Books) Holiday Hse., Inc.

Vern, Jules. Around the World in 80 Days. 2019. (ENG.). 86p. (J). (gr. 3-7). pap. 15.95 (978-0-88145-820-6(1)) Broadway Play Publishing Inc.

—Around the World in 80 Days. 2017. (ENG., Illus.). (J). (gr. -1-1). 24.95 (978-1-374-83142-1(5)); pap. 14.95 (978-1-374-83141-4(7)) Capital Communications, Inc.

—Around the World in 80 Days. 2019. (ENG., Illus.). 438p. (J). (gr. 3-7). pap. 30.99 (978-1-7233-4606-4(3)) CreateSpace Independent Publishing Platform.

—Around the World in 80 Days. 2004. (Young Reading Series Two Ser.). 64p. (J). (gr. 2-18). pap. 5.95 (978-0-7945-0741-1(7), Usborne) EDC Publishing.

—Around the World in 80 Days. 2019. (ENG.). 156p. (J). (gr. 3-7). pap. (978-1-989201-86-2(5)) East India Publishing Co.

—Around the World in 80 Days. (ENG.). (J). 2020. 238p. (gr. 2-4). pap. 6.99 (978-1-940177-79-3(0)) 2019. 438p. (gr. 3-7). pap. 29.99 (978-1-6925-6751-4(9)) 2019. 438p. (gr. 3-7). pap. 25.99 (978-1-6918-7736-2(0)) Independently Published.

—Around the World in 80 Days. 2018. (VIE.). (J). (gr. 3-7). pap. (978-604-77-4585-2(7)) Thegioi Publishing Hse.

—Around the World in 80 Days. 2018. (ENG., Illus.). 152p. (J). 19.99 (978-1-5154-3363-7(3)) Wilder Pubns., Corp.

—Dick Sand. Munro, George, tr. 2008. 296p. 29.95 (978-1-60664-752-3(0)) Rodgers, Alan Bks.

—Dick Sands: The Boy Captain. ELLEN E. FREWER, tr. 2007. (ENG.). 298p. pap. 21.99 (978-1-4264-3403-7(0)) Creative Media Partners, LLC.

—Dick Sands: The Boy Captain. Frewer, Ellen E., tr. l.t. ed. 2007. (ENG.). 328p. pap. 24.99 (978-1-4264-3453-2(7)) Creative Media Partners, LLC.

—The English at the North Pole. 2009. 160p. 24.95 (978-1-60664-684-7(2)); pap. 13.95 (978-1-60664-313-6(4)) Rodgers, Alan Bks.

—The Field of Ice: Part II of the Adventures of Captain Hatteras. 2007. (ENG.). 154p. pap. 19.99 (978-1-4264-3591-1(6)) Creative Media Partners, LLC.

—Le Tour du Monde en 80 Jours.Tr. of Around the World in 80 Days. (FRE.). (J). pap. 19.95 (978-2-07-051436-6(6)) Gallimard, Editions FRA. Dist: Distribooks, Inc.

—La Vuelta Al Mundo en 80 Dias. 2012. 132p. pap. 9.99 (978-1-60796-466-7(X)) Meirovich, Igal.

Viva, Frank. A Trip to the Top of the Volcano with Mouse: TOON Level 1. 2019. (Trips with Mouse Ser.). (Illus.). 36p. (J). (gr. -1-k). 12.99 (978-1-943145-36-2(9), TOON Books) Astra Publishing Hse.

Voigt, Cynthia. The Tale of Birle. 2015. (Tales of the Kingdom Ser.: 2). (ENG., Illus.). 416p. (YA). (gr. 7). 19.99 (978-1-4424-8356-9(3), Atheneum Bks. for Young Readers) Simon & Schuster Children's Publishing.

Wahl, Jan. Cobweb Castle. 2014. (ENG., Illus.). 32p. (J). 14.95 (978-0-7649-6801-3(7)) Pomegranate Communications, Inc.

—The Long Tail Journey. Gapaillard, Laurent, illus. 2015. (ENG.). 48p. (J). (gr. 2-5). 18.99 (978-1-56846-230-1(1), 20827, Creative Editions) Creative Co., The.

Walfish, Miriam. The Jewel & the Journey. 2007. 208p. (J). 16.95 (978-1-932443-81-3(9)) Judaica Pr., Inc., The.

Wallace, Brandon. The Journey Home. (Wilder Boys Ser.). (ENG., Illus.). 208p. (J). 2017. (gr. 4-8). pap. 8.99 (978-1-4814-3266-5(4)) 2016. (gr. 3-7). 17.99 (978-1-4814-3267-2(2)) Simon & Schuster Children's Publishing. (Aladdin).

—Wilder Boys. 2017. (Wilder Boys Ser.). (ENG.). 256p. (J). (gr. 4-8). pap. 8.99 (978-1-4814-3263-4(X), Simon & Schuster/Paula Wiseman Bks.) Simon & Schuster/Paula Wiseman Bks.

Watson, Jude. Underworld. 2005. (Star Wars Ser.: No. 3). 137p. (J). lib. bdg. 20.00 (978-1-4242-0776-3(2)) Fitzgerald Bks.

Weaver, Anne H. The Voyage of the Beetle: A Journey Around the World with Charles Darwin & the Search for the Solution to the Mystery of Mysteries, As Narrated by Rosie, an Articulate Beetle. Lawrence, George, tr. Lawrence, George, illus. 2004. (Roman Mysteries Ser.). 80p. (J). (gr. 5-8). lib. bdg. 26.90 (978-0-7613-2923-7(4), Millbrook Pr.) Lerner Publishing Group.

Webb, Steve. City Kitty Cat. Le Huche, Magali, illus. 2015. (ENG.). 32p. (J). (gr. -1-3). 17.99 (978-1-4814-4331-9(3), Simon & Schuster Bks. For Young Readers) Simon & Schuster Bks. For Young Readers.

Weber, John. Orphan. 2010. 266p. (YA). (gr. 7-18). 16.95 (978-1-934813-38-6(9)) Westside Bks.

Welch, Jenna Evans. Love & Luck. (ENG.). (YA). (gr. 7). 2019. 336p. pap. 11.99 (978-1-5344-0101-3(6)) 2018. (Illus.). 320p. 18.99 (978-1-5344-0100-6(8)) Simon Pulse. (Simon Pulse).

Wendel, Gretchen Schomer & Schomer, Adam Anthomy. Becka & the Big Bubble: Becka Goes to San Diego. Renthrope, Damon, illus. 2008. 32p. (J). (gr. -1-3). 11.99 (978-1-933754-51-2(6)) Waterside Pr.

Wendel, Gretchen Schomer & Schomer, Adam Anthony. Becka Goes to Chicago. Renthrope, Damon, illus. 2008. (ENG.). 36p. (J). (gr. -1-3). 11.99 (978-1-933754-52-9(4)) Waterside Publishing.

Weston Woods Staff, creator. Grandfather's Journey. 2011. 38.75 (978-0-545-12710-3(6)) Weston Woods Studios, Inc.

Whelan, Gloria. Parade of Shadows. 2007. 304p. (J). (gr. 5-18). lib. bdg. 16.89 (978-0-06-089029-2(0)) HarperCollins Pubs.

—Yuki & the One Thousand Carriers. Nascimbene, Yan, illus. 2008. (Tales of the World Ser.). (ENG.). 40p. (J). (gr. 1-4). 17.95 (978-1-58536-352-0(9), 202139) Sleeping Bear Pr.

Where's Waldo: the Complete Set. 2006. (J). 82.94 (978-0-7636-3510-7(3)) Candlewick Pr.

White, E. B. Stuart Little. Date not set. 141p. 18.95 (978-0-8488-2602-4(7)) Amereon Ltd.

—Stuart Little. 2008. (J). 34.99 (978-0-7393-7101-5(0)) Findaway World, LLC.

—Stuart Little. Williams, Garth, illus. 60th anniv. ed. 2005. (ENG.). 144p. (J). (gr. 3-7). 18.99 *(978-0-06-026395-9(4)*, HarperCollins) HarperCollins Pubs.
—Stuart Little. 131p. (J). pap. 5.95 *(978-0-8072-8333-2(9))*; 2004. (gr. 3-7). pap. 29.00 incl. audio *(978-0-8072-8332-5(0)*, YA165SP) Random Hse. Audio Publishing Group. (Listening Library).
—Stuart Little 75th Anniversary Edition. Williams, Garth, illus. 60th anniv. ed. 2020. (ENG.). 144p. (J). (gr. 3-7). pap. 9.99 *(978-0-06-440056-5(5)*, HarperCollins) HarperCollins Pubs.
—Stuart Little: Full Color Edition. Williams, Garth & Wells, Rosemary, illus. 60th anniv. ed. 2005. (ENG.). 144p. (J). (gr. 3-7). pap. 9.99 *(978-0-06-441092-2(7)*, HarperCollins) HarperCollins Pubs.
White, E. B. & White, E. Stuart Little. 2005. (J). (gr. 3-6). lib. bdg. 17.20 *(978-0-8085-3806-6(3))* Turtleback.
Whitney, A. D. T. Sights & Insights: Patience Strong's Story of over the Way. Vol. 1. 2006. 356p. per. 26.99 *(978-1-4255-3625-1(5))* Michigan Publishing.
—Sights & Insights: Patience Strong's Story of over the Way. Vol. 2. 2006. 344p. per. 23.99 *(978-1-4255-3480-6(5))* Michigan Publishing.
Wiggins, Bethany. Cured: A Stung Novel. 2015. (ENG.). 320p. (YA). (gr. 7). pap. 10.99 *(978-0-8027-3787-8(0)*, 900139083, Bloomsbury USA Childrens) Bloomsbury Publishing USA.
Wildavsky, Rachel. The Secret of Rover. Caparo, Antonio, illus. 2015. (ENG.). 360p. (J). (gr. 4-8). pap. 7.95 *(978-1-4197-1968-4(8)*, 681103, Amulet Bks.) Abrams, Inc.
Wildsmith, Brian. Daisy, 1 vol. Wildsmith, Brian, illus. 2018. (ENG., Illus.). 48p. (J). *(978-1-59572-803-6(1))* Star Bright Bks., Inc.
Wishinsky, Frieda. No Frogs for Dinner, 1 vol. Hendry, Linda, illus. 2012. (ENG.). 32p. (J). (gr. k-1). pap. 6.95 *(978-1-55455-189-7(7)*, 227e000a-9bdf-497e-98a8-e88fa5d29738) Trifolium Bks., Inc. CAN. Dist: Firefly Bks., Ltd.
Wurge, B. B. The Last Notebook of Leonardo. 2010. (LeapKids Ser.). (ENG., Illus.). 154p. (J). (gr. 1-7). pap. 9.95 *(978-1-935248-14-9(6))* Leapfrog Pr.
Yonge, Charlotte M. Little Lucy's Wonderful Globe. 2008. 152p. 36.95 *(978-0-548-97272-4(9))* Kessinger Publishing, LLC.
Yonge, Charlotte Mary. Little Lucy's Wonderful Globe. 2016. (ENG., Illus.). (J). 22.95 *(978-1-358-12109-8(5))* Creative Media Partners, LLC.
—Little Lucys Wonderful Globe. 2017. (ENG., Illus.). 78p. (J). *(978-3-7326-1919-1(2))*; pap. *(978-3-7326-1918-4(4))* Klassik Literatur. ein Imprint der Salzwasser Verlag GmbH.
Yoon, Salina. Penguin's Big Adventure. 2015. (Penguin Ser.). (ENG., Illus.). 40p. (J). (gr. -1-1). 14.99 *(978-0-8027-3828-8(1)*, 900141990, Bloomsbury USA Childrens) Bloomsbury Publishing USA.
Young, Judy Dockrey & Young, Richard Dockrey. 1492, New World Tales. 2013. (ENG., Illus.). 267p. (J). (gr. 3-5). pap. 16.95 *(978-1-939160-73-7(1))* August Hse. Pubs., Inc.
Young, Rebecca. Teacup. Ottley, Matt, illus. 2016. (ENG.). 40p. (J). (gr. -1-3). 17.99 *(978-0-7352-2777-4(2)*, Dial Bks) Penguin Young Readers Group.
Zahler, Diane. Sleeping Beauty's Daughters. 2013. 216p. (J). lib. bdg. *(978-0-06-200497-0(2))* Harper & Row Ltd.
—A True Princess. (ENG.). (J). (gr. 3-7). 2012. 208p. pap. 6.99 *(978-0-06-182503-3(4))* 2011. 192p. 15.99 *(978-0-06-182501-9(8))* HarperCollins Pubs. (HarperCollins).
Zarcinas, Scott. The Golden Chalice: A Pilgrim's Chronicle. 2013. 200p. pap. *(978-0-9875975-9-5(0))* DoctorZed Publishing.

VOYAGES AROUND THE WORLD

see also Adventure and Adventurers; Aeronautics—Flights; Discoveries in Geography; Explorers; Northwest Passage; Overland Journeys to the Pacific; Scientific Expeditions; Seafaring Life; Shipwrecks; Travel; Travelers; Yachts and Yachting
also names of countries, continents, etc. with the subdivision Description and Travel (e.g. United States—Description and Travel); also names of regions (e.g. Antarctic Regions)

Bailey, Katharine. Ferdinand Magellan: Circumnavigating the World, 1 vol. 2005. (In the Footsteps of Explorers Ser.). (ENG., Illus.). 32p. (J). (gr. 4-7). pap. *(978-0-7787-2452-0(2))* Crabtree Publishing Co.
Benduhn, Tea. Life on the Edge, 6 vols., Set. Incl. Living in Deserts. lib. bdg. 24.67 *(978-0-8368-8341-1(1)*, e330f4b0-61b5-4c24-a5ab-823f1e161b22); Living in Mountains. lib. bdg. 24.67 *(978-0-8368-8342-8(X)*, 692c984e-65f8-4989-a97e-75d9e4490122); Living in Polar Regions. lib. bdg. 24.67 *(978-0-8368-8343-5(8)*, c9a8930b-dec2-4db8-ac00-f9c294df0f52); Living in Tropical Rain Forests. lib. bdg. 24.67 *(978-0-8368-8344-2(6)*, 3f407531-1650-49a6-adef-8e3f8c2ce084); (Illus.). (gr. 2-4). (Life on the Edge Ser.). (ENG.). 24p. 2007. Set lib. bdg. 74.01 *(978-0-8368-8340-4(3)*, 89ade30e-f4f5-4ac5-be9b-6b9227c06803, Weekly Reader Leveled Readers) Stevens, Gareth Publishing LLLP.
Bergreen, Laurence. Magellan: over the Edge of the World: Over the Edge of the World. 2017. (ENG., Illus.). 224p. (J). (gr. 5-9). 21.99 *(978-1-62672-120-3(3)*, 900138153) Roaring Brook Pr.
Bishop, Gavin. Cook's Cook: The Cook Who Cooked for Captain Cook. Bishop, Gavin, illus. 2018. (ENG., Illus.). 40p. (J). (gr. 2-5). 17.99 *(978-1-77657-204-5(1)*, e2449563-7c30-4acd-8902-61ffc86a7867) Gecko Pr. NZL. Dist: Lerner Publishing Group.
Burnett, Betty. Ferdinand Magellan: The First Voyage Around the World. 2009. (Library of Explorers & Exploration Ser.). 112p. (gr. 5-8). 66.50 *(978-1-60853-602-3(5)*, Rosen Reference) Rosen Publishing Group, Inc., The.
Castaldo, Nancy. The Race Around the World (Totally True Adventures) How Nellie Bly Chased an Impossible Dream... Lowe, Wesley, illus. 2015. (Totally True Adventures Ser.). (ENG.). 112p. (J). (gr. 2-5). 4.99 *(978-0-553-52278-5(7)*, Random Hse. Bks. for Young Readers) Random Hse. Children's Bks.
Connelly, Jack. Ferdinand Magellan: Circumnavigating the Globe, 1 vol. 2014. (Incredible Explorers Ser.). (ENG., Illus.). 64p. (YA). (gr. 7-7). 35.93 *(978-1-5026-0132-2(X)*, cdab139a-95e5-4d90-a4a0-38ef2cf6ab67) Cavendish Square Publishing LLC.
Dalrymple, Lisa. Explore with James Cook. 2015. (Travel with the Great Explorers Ser.). (ENG., Illus.). 32p. (J). (gr. 4-5). *(978-0-7787-1701-0(1))* Crabtree Publishing Co.
Fandel, Jennifer. Ferdinand Magellan. 2003. (Explorers of the Unknown Ser.). (J). *(978-1-58417-036-5(0))*; pap. *(978-1-58417-099-0(9))* Lake Street Pubs.
Gould, Jane H. Ferdinand Magellan, 1 vol. 2013. (Jr. Graphic Famous Explorers Ser.). (ENG., Illus.). 24p. (J). (gr. 2-3). pap. 11.60 *(978-1-4777-0123-2(0)*, e3cb2c07-ada3-43c9-aede-62dac39b22fe); lib. bdg. 28.93 *(978-1-4777-0069-3(2)*, 3784f612-3280-40e5-9727-85860ff7d0c1) Rosen Publishing Group, Inc., The. (PowerKids Pr.).
Hoogenboom, Lynn. Ferdinand Magellan. 2009. (Primary Source Library of Famous Explorers Ser.). 24p. (gr. 4-4). 42.50 *(978-1-60854-120-1(7)*, PowerKids Pr.) Rosen Publishing Group, Inc., The.
—Ferdinand Magellan: A Primary Source Biography, 1 vol. 2005. (Primary Source Library of Famous Explorers Ser.). (ENG., Illus.). 24p. (YA). (gr. 4-4). lib. bdg. 26.27 *(978-1-4042-3039-2(4)*, 6cec0d74-c482-4963-a018-6bd8b889fdc8) Rosen Publishing Group, Inc., The.
Justice, William E. Kodoku. Rivera, Hanae, illus. 2012. (ENG.). 32p. (J). 16.95 *(978-1-59714-173-4(9))* Heyday.
Kramer, S. A. & Who HQ. Who Was Ferdinand Magellan? 2004. (Who Was? Ser.). (Illus.). 112p. (J). (gr. 3-7). pap. 6.99 *(978-0-448-43105-5(X)*, Penguin Workshop) Penguin Young Readers Group.
Kramer, Sydelle. Who Was Ferdinand Magellan? Wolf, Elizabeth, illus. 2004. (Who Was... ? Ser.). 105p. (J). (gr. 3-7). 12.65 *(978-0-7569-4615-9(8))* Perfection Learning Corp.
Lace, William W. Captain James Cook. 2009. (Great Explorers Ser.). (ENG., Illus.). 112p. (gr. 6-12). 30.00 *(978-1-60413-416-2(X)*, P173422, Facts On File) Infobase Holdings, Inc.
—Sir Francis Drake. 2009. (Great Explorers Ser.). (ENG., Illus.). 112p. (gr. 6-12). 30.00 *(978-1-60413-417-9(8)*, P173414, Facts On File) Infobase Holdings, Inc.
Landau, Elaine. Ferdinand Magellan. 2005. (History Maker Bios Ser.). (Illus.). 48p. (J). (gr. 3-7). lib. bdg. 26.60 *(978-0-8225-2942-2(4)*, Lerner Pubns.) Lerner Publishing Group.
Lonely, Planet. Around the World in 50 Ways Cande, Camel, or Cable Car... You Choose!, 1 vol. 2018. (ENG., Illus.). 164p. (J). pap. ***(978-1-78657-755-9(0))*** Lonely Planet Global Ltd.
Macdonald, Fiona. The Story of Magellan. Mark Bergin, illus. 2017. (Explorers Ser.). 32p. (gr. 3-6). 31.35 *(978-1-910706-90-9(6))* Book Hse. GBR. Dist: Black Rabbit Bks.
Malam, John. Extreme Exploration. 2009. (Difficult & Dangerous Ser.). (ENG., Illus.). 32p. (J). (gr. 4-7). pap. *(978-1-897563-24-3(8))* Saunders Bk. Co.
Marsh, Carole. Ferdinand Magellan, World Voyager. 2004. 12p. (gr. k-4). 2.95 *(978-0-635-02373-5(3))* Gallopade International.
Meyer, Susan. Ferdinand Magellan, 1 vol. 2016. (Spotlight on Explorers & Colonization Ser.). (ENG., Illus.). 48p. (J). (gr. 6-6). pap. 12.75 *(978-1-4777-8800-4(X)*, 6615c7db-b16f-4a3f-9c78-51e8a7c1dae2) Rosen Publishing Group, Inc., The.
Morlock, Rachael. Magellan Sails Around the World, 1 vol. 2018. (Real-Life Scientific Adventures Ser.). (ENG.). 32p. (gr. 4-5). 29.27 *(978-1-5081-6854-6(7)*, e078633b-3d16-45f3-9e72-0d445088ecc0, PowerKids Pr.) Rosen Publishing Group, Inc., The.
Morriss, Roger. Captain Cook & His Exploration of the Pacific. 2010. (History of Exploration Ser.). 48p. 32.80 *(978-1-84898-303-8(4))* Black Rabbit Bks.
Powell, Marie. Explore with Ferdinand Magellan. 2014. (Travel with the Great Explorers Ser.). (ENG., Illus.). 32p. (J). (gr. 4-5). *(978-0-7787-1425-5(X))* Crabtree Publishing Co.
Rice, Dona Herweck. Lugares del Mundo. 2nd rev. ed. 2012. (TIME for KIDS(r): Informational Text Ser.).Tr. of Places Around the World. (SPA.). 20p. (gr. 1-2). 8.99 *(978-1-4333-4433-6(5))* Teacher Created Materials, Inc.
—Places Around the World. 1 vol. 2nd rev. ed. 2011. (TIME for KIDS(r): Informational Text Ser.). (ENG., Illus.). 20p. (gr. 1-2). 8.99 *(978-1-4333-3600-3(6))* Teacher Created Materials, Inc.
Royston, Angela & Hawksley, Gerald. My Big Book of the World. Hawksley, Gerald, illus. 2017. (Illus.). 40p. (J). (gr. k-6). 12.99 *(978-1-84322-893-6(9)*, Armadillo) Anness Publishing GBR. Dist: National Bk. Network.
Sisk, Siobhan. Would You Dare Sail Around the World?, 1 vol. 2016. (Would You Dare? Ser.). (ENG.). 32p. (J). (gr. 1-2). lib. bdg. 28.27 *(978-1-4824-5828-2(4)*, 5d0d713e-d7d2-4224-bf4c-930c27b46dd8) Stevens, Gareth Publishing LLLP.
Smith, Dan. Lonely Planet Kids Around the World in 50 Ways 1. Castle, Frances, illus. 2018. (Lonely Planet Kids Ser.). (ENG.). 164p. (J). (gr. 4-7). pap. 15.99 *(978-1-78657-756-6(9)*, 5553) Lonely Planet Global Ltd. IRL. Dist: Hachette Bk. Group.
Thermes, Jennifer. Charles Darwin's Around-The-World Adventure. 2016. (ENG., Illus.). 48p. (J). (gr. k-2). 19.99 *(978-1-4197-2120-5(8)*, 1117901, Abrams Bks. for Young Readers) Abrams, Inc.
Thomas, Isabel. Little Guides to Great Lives: Ferdinand Magellan. Adillon, Dalia, illus. 2019. (Little Guides to Great Lives Ser.). (ENG.). 64p. (J). (gr. 2-6). 11.99 *(978-1-78627-401-4(9)*, King, Laurence Publishing) Orion Publishing Group, Ltd. GBR. Dist: Hachette Bk. Group.
Waldman, Stuart. Magellan's World. Manchess, Gregory, illus. 2007. (Great Explorers Ser.). (ENG.). 48p. (J). (gr. 4-8). 22.95 *(978-1-931414-19-7(X)*, 53d8c30d-8502-40e6-85b4-31411556e104) Mikaya Pr.
Yomtov, Nel. Ferdinand Magellan Sails Around the World. 2015. (Extraordinary Explorers Ser.). (ENG., Illus.). 24p. (J). (gr. 3-8). lib. bdg. 29.95 *(978-1-62617-292-0(7)*, Black Sheep) Bellwether Media.

VOYAGES, IMAGINARY

McNulty, Faith. If You Decide to Go to the Moon. Kellogg, Steven, illus. 2005. (ENG.). 48p. (J). (gr. -1-k). 18.99 *(978-0-590-48359-9(5)*, Scholastic Pr.) Scholastic, Inc.

VOYAGES, IMAGINARY—FICTION

Benton, Jim. The Frandidate, No. 7. Benton, Jim, illus. 2008. (Franny K. Stein, Mad Scientist Ser.: 7). (ENG., Illus.). 128p. (J). (gr. 2-5). 17.99 *(978-1-4169-0233-1(3)*, Simon & Schuster Bks. For Young Readers) Simon & Schuster Bks. For Young Readers.
Clark, Eleanor Linton, et al. Dodo's Dream Boat or the Voyage of the Seven Seas. 2008. (Illus.). 45p. (J). *(978-0-9816873-2-2(6))* West Barnstable Pr.
Swift, Jonathan. Gulliver's Travels. Date not set. (J). (gr. 5-6). reprint ed. lib. bdg. 26.95 *(978-0-89190-845-6(5)*, American Reprint Co.) Amereon Ltd.
—Gulliver's Travels. 2004. (Young Reading Ser.). (Illus.). 64p. (J). (gr. 2-18). pap. 5.95 *(978-0-7945-0329-1(2)*, Usborne) EDC Publishing.
—Gulliver's Travels. (Young Collector's Illustrated Classics Ser.). (Illus.). 192p. (J). (gr. 3-7). 9.95 *(978-1-56156-457-6(5))* Kidsbooks, LLC.
Van den Ende, Peter. The Wanderer. 2020. (ENG., Illus.). 96p. (J). (gr. 3-9). 21.99 *(978-1-64614-017-6(6))* Levine Querido.

VOYAGES TO THE MOON

see Space Flight to the Moon

VULTURES

Abbott, Henry. Buzzards, 1 vol., 1. 2015. (Raptors! Ser.). (ENG., Illus.). 24p. (J). (gr. 3-4). pap. 9.25 *(978-1-5081-4236-2(X)*, be1a79dc-ff1e-4ff9-b089-86efc22775e5, PowerKids Pr.) Rosen Publishing Group, Inc., The.
Barrett, Tracy. Vultures, 1 vol. 2012. (Animals, Animals Ser.). (ENG., Illus.). 48p. (gr. 5-5). 32.64 *(978-0-7614-4880-8(2)*, 0a8de912-5c8e-45c6-bb87-c2ca55013b5a) Cavendish Square Publishing LLC.
Chung, Liz. Vultures, 1 vol., 1. 2015. (Raptors! Ser.). (ENG., Illus.). 24p. (J). (gr. 3-4). pap. 9.25 *(978-1-5081-4254-6(8)*, 6043f946-7d08-4fb8-b4e0-962d64f5b264, PowerKids Pr.) Rosen Publishing Group, Inc., The.
Coleman, Miriam. Vultures Eat Rotting Corpses!, 1 vol., 1. 2013. (Disgusting Animal Dinners Ser.). (ENG.). 24p. (J). (gr. 2-3). 26.27 *(978-1-4777-2886-4(4)*, fd2c4255-c0d6-4add-b2d4-d9867c17e074, PowerKids Pr.) Rosen Publishing Group, Inc., The.
Dunn, Mary R. Turkey Vultures. 2015. (Birds of Prey Ser.). (ENG., Illus.). 24p. (J). (gr. -1-2). pap. 6.95 *(978-1-4914-2312-7(9)*, 127770, Capstone Pr.) Capstone.
Early Macken, JoAnn. Vultures, 1 vol. (Animals That Live in the Desert (First Edition) Ser.). (ENG., 24p. (gr. 1-1). 2006. Illus.). lib. bdg. 25.27 *(978-0-8368-4831-1(4)*, ebda7d12-b630-44a1-a699-ef247365b5cf) 2nd rev. ed. 2009. (J). pap. 9.15 *(978-1-4339-2453-8(6)*, 252b5665-7b80-49d2-bca8-08ac4a24db50) 2nd rev. ed. 2009. (J). lib. bdg. 25.27 *(978-1-4339-2392-0(0)*, c469570e-18cf-4e4e-8bed-68f78ad7f3d4) Stevens, Gareth Publishing LLLP. (Weekly Reader Leveled Readers).
—Vultures / Buitres, 1 vol. (Animals That Live in the Desert / Animales Del Desierto (First Edition) Ser.). 24p. (gr. 1-1). 2005. (ENG & SPA., Illus.). pap. 9.15 *(978-0-8368-4852-6(7)*, 57f91509-deeb-455b-bc50-cf882c4f8668, Weekly Reader Leveled Readers) 2nd rev. ed. 2009. (SPA & ENG.). (J). pap. 9.15 *(978-1-4339-2461-3(7)*, 55b2acd7-6271-4717-a4bd-227803871f2a, Weekly Reader Leveled Readers) 2nd rev. ed. 2009. (SPA & ENG.). (J). lib. bdg. 25.27 *(978-1-4339-2424-8(2)*, db5f7654-cef2-4e51-8bc5-322534223973) Stevens, Gareth Publishing LLLP.
Gish, Melissa. Vultures. 2012. (Living Wild Ser.). (ENG., Illus.). 48p. (J). (gr. 4-7). 23.95 *(978-1-60818-171-1(5)*, 21897, Creative Education) Creative Co., The.
Kissock, Heather. Vulture. 2015. (Illus.). 24p. (J). *(978-1-4896-4125-0(4))* Weigl Pubs., Inc.
Lanser, Amanda. California Condor. 2016. (Back from near Extinction Ser.). (ENG., Illus.). 48p. (J). (gr. 4-8). lib. bdg. 35.64 *(978-1-68078-465-7(X)*, 23867) ABDO Publishing Co.
Lundgren, Julie. Vultures. 2009. (Illus.). 24p. (J). pap. 7.95 *(978-1-60694-774-6(5))* Rourke Educational Media.
Lynch, Wayne. Vultures. Neidigh, Sherry, illus. Lynch, Wayne, photos by. 2005. (Our Wild World Ser.). (ENG.). 48p. (J). (gr. 2-5). pap. 7.95 *(978-1-55971-918-6(4))* Cooper Square Publishing Llc.
Lynch, Wayne, contrib. by. Vultures. 2005. (Our Wild World Ser.). (ENG., Illus.). 48p. (J). (gr. 2-5). 10.95 *(978-1-55971-917-9(6))* Cooper Square Publishing Llc.
Magellan, Marta. Those Voracious Vultures. Weaver, Steve et al, illus. 2008. (Those Amazing Animals Ser.). (ENG.). 55p. (J). (gr. -1-12). 14.95 *(978-1-56164-424-7(2))* Pineapple Pr., Inc.
Markle, Sandra. Los Buitres. 2007. (Animales carroñeros (Animal Scavengers) Ser.). (SPA., Illus.). (J). (gr. -1-3). 39p. lib. bdg. 25.26 *(978-0-8225-7731-7(3))*; 40p. per. 7.95 *(978-0-8225-7735-5(6))* Lerner Publishing Group. (Ediciones Lerner).
—Los Buitres; Vultures. 2008. pap. 46.95 *(978-0-8225-9355-3(6))* Lerner Publishing Group.
—Vultures. (Animal Scavengers Ser.). (Illus.). (gr. 3-7). 2006. 39p. (J). pap. 7.95 *(978-0-8225-3471-6(1)*, First Avenue Editions) 2005. (ENG., 40p. lib. bdg. 25.26 *(978-0-8225-3195-1(X)*, Lerner Pubns.) Lerner Publishing Group.
O'Donnell, Kerri. Vultures. (Ugly Animals Ser.). 24p. (gr. 2-3). 2009. 42.50 *(978-1-60854-605-3(5)*, PowerKids Pr.) 2006. (ENG., Illus.). (J). lib. bdg. 26.27 *(978-1-4042-3526-7(4)*, 55484f1e-4bc8-4a69-9001-0111f0abb77f) Rosen Publishing Group, Inc., The.
Riggs, Kate. Vultures. 2015. (Amazing Animals Ser.). (ENG., Illus.). 24p. (J). (gr. 1-4). *(978-1-60818-492-7(7)*, 21148, Creative Education) Creative Co., The.
Shaffer, Lindsay. Bearded Vultures. 2019. (Animals of the Mountains Ser.). (ENG., Illus.). 24p. (J). (gr. k-3). lib. bdg. 26.95 *(978-1-64487-012-9(6)*, Blastoff! Readers) Bellwether Media.
Sommer, Nathan. Vultures. 2018. (Birds of Prey Ser.). (ENG., Illus.). 24p. (J). (gr. 3-7). lib. bdg. 26.95 *(978-1-62617-882-3(8)*, Epic Bks.) Bellwether Media.
Waxman, Laura Hamilton. California Condors: Wide-Winged Soaring Birds. 2016. (Comparing Animal Traits Ser.). (ENG., Illus.). 32p. (J). (gr. 2-4). pap. 8.99 *(978-1-4677-9639-2(5)*, ed50e2e2-c24c-4baf-9948-42aead2e6ec4) Lerner Publishing Group.
Wechsler, Doug. Vultures. 2009. (Really Wild Life of Animals Ser.). 24p. (gr. 3-4). 42.50 *(978-1-60854-212-3(2)*, PowerKids Pr.) Rosen Publishing Group, Inc., The.

VULTURES—FICTION

Del Riego, Erica. The Heart of Life. 2010. 36p. pap. 17.75 *(978-1-4389-7572-6(4))* AuthorHouse.
Hanson, Jonathan. Victor el Zopilote Renuente! Duffek, Kim Kanoa, illus. 2012. 36p. (J). pap. 16.95 *(978-1-886679-46-7(0))* Arizona Sonora Desert Museum Pr.
—Victor, the Reluctant Vulture. Duufek, Kim Kanoa, illus. 2012. 36p. (J). pap. 16.95 *(978-1-886679-45-0(2))* Arizona Sonora Desert Museum Pr.
Johnson, Calvin. Buzzy the Vegetarian Vulture. Ciresi-Abremski, M. Kathleen, illus. 2012. 28p. pap. 12.95 *(978-1-61493-109-6(7))* Peppertree Pr., The.
McAuliffe, Nichola. Attila, Loolagax & the Eagle. Collins, Ross, tr. Collins, Ross, illus. 2003. 128p. (J). pap. 10.99 *(978-0-7475-6499-7(X))* Bloomsbury Publishing Plc GBR. Dist: Independent Pubs. Group.
McDermott, Gerald. Jabutí the Tortoise: A Trickster Tale from the Amazon. McDermott, Gerald, illus. 2005. (ENG., Illus.). 32p. (J). (gr. -1-3). pap. 8.99 *(978-0-15-205374-1(3)*, 1196181, Clarion Bks.) HarperCollins Pubs.
Perry, Dakota. Vulture Itus, 1 vol. 2009. 20p. pap. 24.95 *(978-1-60836-087-1(3))* America Star Bks.
Pilkey, Dav. Ricky Ricotta's Mighty Robot vs. the Video Vultures from Venus (Ricky Ricotta's Mighty Robot #3) Santat, Dan, illus. 2014. (Ricky Ricotta's Mighty Robot Ser.: 3). (ENG.). 128p. (J). (gr. -1-3). pap. 5.99 *(978-0-545-63011-5(8))* Scholastic, Inc.
Quantz, Daniel, et al. Duel to the Death with the Vulture. 2006. (Spider-Man Ser.: No. 1). (ENG., Illus.). 24p. (J). (gr. 2-6). 31.36 *(978-1-59961-012-2(4)*, 13607, Marvel Age) Spotlight.
Willard, Hugh. The Goodwill Vultures Club: No Time for Play. Holjes, Kerry, ed. Eason, D. M, illus. 2013. 140p. pap. 9.99 *(978-1-935711-30-8(X))* Peak City Publishing, LLC.
—The Goodwill Vultures Club: The Gift of the Vulture. Dozier, Dolly, ed. Eason, D. M, illus. 2013. 128p. pap. 9.99 *(978-1-935711-34-6(2))* Peak City Publishing, LLC.

W

WAGNER, RICHARD, 1813-1883

Getzinger, Donna & Felsenfeld, Daniel. Richard Wagner & German Opera. 2004. (Classical Composers Ser.). (Illus.). 144p. (YA). (gr. 6-12). 26.95 *(978-1-931798-24-2(9))* Reynolds, Morgan Inc.
Whiting, Jim. The Life & Times of Richard Wagner. 2004. (Masters of Music Ser.). (Illus.). 48p. (gr. 4-8). lib. bdg. 20.95 *(978-1-58415-278-1(8))* Mitchell Lane Pubs.

WALD, LILLIAN, 1867-1940

Kaplan, Paul. Lillian Wald: America's Great Social & Healthcare Reformer, 1 vol. 2018. (ENG., Illus.). 112p. (gr. 6-7). 14.95 *(978-1-4556-2349-5(0)*, Pelican Publishing) Arcadia Publishing.

WALES

Carradice, Phil. A Child's Dylan Thomas. 2014. (ENG., Illus.). 32p. (gr. 4-6). pap. 13.99 *(978-1-84851-749-3(1))* Gomer Pr. GBR. Dist: Independent Pubs. Group, Casemate Pubs. & Bk. Distributors, LLC.
Evans, Robin. Pecyn Lluniau a Llyfr Athrawon. 2005. (WEL., Illus.). 8p. pap. *(978-1-85644-873-4(8))* CAA.
Heinrichs, Ann. Wales. 2003. (Enchantment of the World Ser.). (ENG., Illus.). 144p. (J). (gr. 5-9). 37.00 *(978-0-516-22288-2(0)*, Children's Pr.) Scholastic Library Publishing.
Hestler, Anna & Spilling, Jo-Ann. Wales, 1 vol. 2nd rev. ed. 2011. (Cultures of the World (Second Edition)(r) Ser.). (ENG., Illus.). 144p. (gr. 5-5). lib. bdg. 49.79 *(978-1-60870-457-6(2)*, 9f8a7cf1-54e8-49a8-984b-d0ef8a452f37) Cavendish Square Publishing LLC.
Hestler, Anna, et al. Wales, 1 vol. 3rd ed. 2020. (Cultures of the World (Third Edition)(r) Ser.). (ENG.). 144p. (gr. 5-5). 48.79 *(978-1-5026-5583-7(7)*, 1e3335dd-c3f5-4c92-a4a0-ca9429f3cad9) Cavendish Square Publishing LLC.
Meirion, Dafydd, et al. Anturio Ar Ynys Môn: Sawl Taith Stori I TI AC I'r Teulu. 2005. (WEL., Illus.). 84p. pap. *(978-0-86381-863-9(3))* Gwasg Carreg Gwalch.
Sonneborn, Liz. Wales (Enchantment of the World) (Library Edition) 2018. (Enchantment of the World. Second Ser.). (ENG., Illus.). 144p. (J). (gr. 5-9). lib. bdg. 40.00 *(978-0-531-23592-8(0)*, Children's Pr.) Scholastic Library Publishing.
Stevens, Catrin, et al. Yr Oesoedd Canol Cythryblus. 2005. (WEL., Illus.). 144p. pap. 4.99 *(978-1-84323-423-4(8))* Gomer Pr. GBR. Dist: Gomer Pr.
Sullivan, Laura. Black Bart Roberts, 1 vol. 2014. (True-Life Pirates Ser.). (ENG.). 48p. (gr. 4-4). lib. bdg. 33.07 *(978-1-5026-0207-7(5)*, 01a2fd0b-19f9-48b7-836a-deaeffa57ba2) Cavendish Square Publishing LLC.
Thomas, Dylan. A Child's Christmas in Wales. Raskin, Ellen, illus. 2003. (New Directions Paperbook Ser.: Vol. 972). (ENG.). 32p. reprint ed. pap. 8.00 *(978-0-8112-1560-2(1))* New Directions Publishing Corp.

WALES—FICTION

Anrias, Donnan. Targ - the King of Eagles. 2005. 138p. (YA). per. 23.00 *(978-1-4116-1923-4(4))* Lulu Pr., Inc.
Armour, Michael C. Orca Song. Lee, Katie, illus. (ENG.). 32p. (J). (gr. -1-2). pap. 6.95 *(978-1-59249-479-8(X)*, S4004) Soundprints.
Billingsley, Franny. Chime. 2011. (Playaway Young Adult Ser.). (YA). 59.99 *(978-1-61707-143-0(9))* Findaway World, LLC.
—Chime. 2012. (ENG.). 320p. (YA). (gr. 7-12). 26.19 *(978-0-8037-3552-1(9)*, Dial) Penguin Publishing Group.

-ond, Nancy. A String in the Harp. 2006. (ENG.). 384p. (J). (gr. 5-9). pap. 8.99 *(978-1-4169-2771-6(9),* Aladdin) Simon & Schuster Children's Publishing.
-oyce, Frank Cottrell. Framed. 2006. 306p. (J). (gr. 3-7). lib. bdg. 17.89 *(978-0-06-073403-9(5))* HarperCollins Pubs.
-rodien-Jones, Chris. The Dreamkeepers. 2009. (ENG.). 148p. (YA). (gr. 7). pap. 8.99 *(978-1-4424-0221-8(0),* Simon & Schuster Bks. For Young Readers) Simon & Schuster Bks. For Young Readers.
—The Glass Puzzle. 2013. (Illus.). 319p. (J). *(978-0-385-74298-6(3),* Delacorte Pr) Random House Publishing Group.
Carpenter, Suzanne. Barti & Bel Whizz Around Wales. 2003. (ENG., Illus.). 32p. pap. 12.95 *(978-1-84323-238-4(3))* Beekman Bks., Inc.
Coats, J. Anderson. The Wicked & the Just. 2013. (ENG.). 352p. (YA). (gr. 7). pap. 9.99 *(978-0-544-02221-8(1),* 1528479, Clarion Bks.) HarperCollins Pubs.
Cooper, Susan. The Dark Is Rising. 2007. (YA). 1.25 *(978-1-4193-7923-9(2))* Recorded Bks., Inc.
Cottrell Boyce, Frank. Framed. 2008. (ENG., Illus.). 320p. (J). (gr. 3). per. 8.99 *(978-0-06-073404-6(3),* HarperCollins) HarperCollins Pubs.
Davie, Jan. Arthur's Amulet. 2004. 86p. pap. *(978-1-84401-228-2(X))* Athena Pr.
Davies, Christie. Dewi the Dragon. 2006. (ENG.). 96p. (J). pap. 9.95 *(978-0-86243-770-1(9))* Y Lolfa GBR. Dist: Dufour Editions, Inc.
Davies, Elgan Philip & Ceredigion, Cymdeithas Lyfrau. Olion Hen Elyn. 2005. (WEL.). 200.0p. pap. *(978-1-84512-004-7(3))* Cymdeithas Lyfrau Ceredigion.
Davies, Linda. Longbow Girl. 2016. (ENG.). 336p. (YA). (gr. 7). 17.99 *(978-0-545-85345-3(1),* Chicken Hse., The) Scholastic, Inc.
Davies, Nicola. King of the Sky. Carlin, Laura, illus. 2017. (ENG.). 48p. (J). (gr. -1-3). 18.99 *(978-0-7636-9568-2(8))* Candlewick Pr.
Eames, Marion. Baner Beca. 2005. (WEL.). 80p. pap. *(978-0-86243-729-9(6))* Y Lolfa.
Eynon, Bob & Wen, Dref. Crwydro'r Môr Mawr. 2005. (WEL.). 80p. pap. *(978-1-85596-656-7(5))* Dref Wen.
Grainger, A. J. The Sisterhood. 2019. (ENG., Illus.). 304p. (YA). (gr. 7). 18.99 *(978-1-4814-2906-1(X),* Simon & Schuster Bks. For Young Readers) Simon & Schuster Bks. For Young Readers.
Holliday, Susan. Riding the Storm. l.t. ed. 2007. 164p. per. *(978-1-905665-22-8(9))* Pollinger In Print.
Huws, Emily & Gomer, Gwasg. CAE Berllan. 2005. (WEL.). 28.0p. 5.99 *(978-1-85902-998-5(1))* Gomer Pr. GBR. Dist: Gomer Pr.
Jenkins, Mike. Child of Dust. 2005. (ENG.). 192p. pap. 15.95 *(978-1-84323-491-3(2))* Beekman Bks., Inc.
Jones, Frewin. Warrior Princess. 2009. (YA). 346p. lib. bdg. 17.89 *(978-0-06-087144-4(X));* (ENG.). 352p. (gr. 7-18). 16.99 *(978-0-06-087143-7(1))* HarperCollins Pubs. (Eos).
—Warrior Princess #2: Destiny's Path. 2010. (Warrior Princess Ser.: 2). (ENG.). 352p. (YA). (gr. 8). pap. 8.99 *(978-0-06-087148-2(2),* HarperTeen) HarperCollins Pubs.
—Warrior Princess #3: the Emerald Flame. 2010. (Warrior Princess Ser.: 3). (ENG.). 352p. (YA). (gr. 8-18). 16.99 *(978-0-06-087149-9(0),* HarperTeen) HarperCollins Pubs.
Jones, Jac. In Chatter Wood. Jones, Jac, illus. 2004. (ENG., Illus.). 40p. pap. 13.95 *(978-1-84323-290-2(1))* Beekman Bks., Inc.
Jones, Margaret. Nat. 2004. (ENG., Illus.). 112p. pap. 13.95 *(978-1-84323-327-5(4))* Beekman Bks., Inc.
Jones, T. Llew. Storïau Cwm-Pen-Llo. 2005. (WEL., Illus.). 100p. pap. *(978-0-86381-750-2(5))* Gwasg Carreg Gwalch.
LaFevers, R. L. The Wyverns' Treasure. 2012. (Nathaniel Fludd, Beastologist Ser.: 3). lib. bdg. 16.00 *(978-0-606-24516-6(2))* Turtleback.
Lewis, Caryl & Lolfa, Y. Iawn Boi? 2005. (WEL.). 80p. pap. *(978-0-86243-699-5(0))* Y Lolfa.
Milway, Alex. Operation Robot Storm: The Mythical 9th Division. 2013. (ENG., Illus.). 224p. (J). pap. 5.99 *(978-1-61067-074-6(4))* Kane Miller.
Morgan, Gwyn & Owen, Dai. Babi Ben. 2005. (WEL., Illus.). 64p. pap. *(978-1-85596-611-6(5))* Dref Wen.
Morris, Jackie. The Seal Children. rev. ed. 2019. (ENG., Illus.). 32p. (J). (gr. k-3). 18.99 *(978-1-910959-47-3(2))* Otter-Barry Bks. GBR. Dist: Independent Pubs. Group.
Oldfield, Matt. Bale: From the Playground to the Pitch. 2018. (Ultimate Football Heroes Ser.). (ENG., Illus.). 176p. (J). (gr. 2-7). pap. 11.99 *(978-1-78606-801-9(X))* Blake, John Publishing, Ltd. GBR. Dist: Independent Pubs. Group.
Orca Song. (Illus.). 32p. (J). (gr. -1-2). 6.95 incl. reel tape *(978-1-59249-488-0(9),* SC4004) Soundprints.
Orme, David & Baines, Menna. Llanast Llyr. 2005. (WEL., Illus.). 32p. *(978-1-901358-16-2(X))* CAMFA.
Orme, Helen. Wet! 2008. (Siti's Sisters Ser.). (ENG., Illus.). 36p. pap. *(978-1-84167-688-3(8))* Ransom Publishing Ltd.
Rea, Emma. Top Dog. 2014. (ENG.). 122p. (J). pap. 8.95 *(978-1-84851-824-7(2))* Gomer Pr. GBR. Dist: Casemate Pubs. & Bk. Distributors, LLC.
Riggs, Ransom. Miss Peregrine's Home for Peculiar Children. (Miss Peregrine's Peculiar Children Ser.: 1). (Illus.). (YA). (gr. 9). 2013. 384p. pap. 14.99 *(978-1-59474-603-1(6))* 2011. 352p. 18.99 *(978-1-59474-476-1(9))* Quirk Bks.
—Miss Peregrine's Home for Peculiar Children. l.t. ed. 2012. (ENG.). 484p. (J). (gr. 8-12). 23.99 *(978-1-4104-5023-4(6))* Thorndike Pr.
—Miss Peregrine's Home for Peculiar Children. 2013. (Miss Peregrine's Peculiar Children Ser.: 1). (SWE.). lib. bdg. 22.10 *(978-0-606-32081-8(4))* Turtleback.
—Miss Peregrine's Home for Peculiar Children (Movie Tie-In Edition) 2016. (Miss Peregrine's Peculiar Children Ser.: 1). (Illus.). 392p. (YA). (gr. 9). pap. 11.99 *(978-1-59474-902-5(7))* Quirk Bks.
—Miss Peregrine's Peculiar Children Boxed Set, 3 vols. 2015. (Miss Peregrine's Peculiar Children Ser.). (Illus.). 1216p. (YA). (gr. 9). 44.97 *(978-1-59474-890-5(X))* Quirk Bks.
Riggs, Ransom, et al. Miss Peregrine's Home for Peculiar Children. 2011. pap. *(978-1-59474-574-4(9))* Quirk Bks.
Roberts, Esyllt Nest & Owen, Carys Eurwen. Dinas Emrys. 2005. (WEL., Illus.). 36p. pap. *(978-0-86381-439-6(5))* Gwasg Carreg Gwalch.
—Rhita Gawr. 2005. (WEL., Illus.). 36p. pap. *(978-0-86381-624-6(X))* Gwasg Carreg Gwalch.
Sanderson, Whitney. Horse Diaries #15: Lily. Sanderson, Ruth, illus. 2018. (Horse Diaries: 15). 160p. (J). (gr. 3-7). pap. 7.99 *(978-1-5247-6654-2(2),* Random Hse. Bks. for Young Readers) Random Hse. Children's Bks.
Skuse, C. J. Rockoholic. 2012. (YA). *(978-0-545-44251-0(6))* Scholastic, Inc.
Stone, Reuben. Guardians of the Cambrian Lode: An Ancient People - A Timeless Quest. 2005. 254p. (YA). (gr. 8-12). per. 7.99 *(978-0-9550034-0-0(7))* Bethania Bks. GBR. Dist: Send The Light Distribution LLC.
Sullivan, Jenny. A Guardian What? 2006. (ENG.). 84p. (J). pap. 7.50 *(978-1-84323-646-7(X))* Gomer Pr. GBR. Dist: Casemate Pubs. & Bk. Distributors, LLC.
—The Magic Apostrophe. 2003. (ENG.). 216p. pap. 19.95 *(978-1-85902-116-3(6))* Beekman Bks., Inc.
Togden, Ra Chel. The Legendary Rabbit of Death - Volume One [Paperback]. 2013. 108p. pap. *(978-1-898185-27-7(1))* Aro Bks. worldwide.
Twigg, Aeres. The Green Hawk. 2003. (ENG., Illus.). 88p. (J). pap. 12.95 *(978-1-85902-787-5(3))* Beekman Bks., Inc.

WALKER, MARY EDWARDS, 1832-1919

Gaines, Alison. Mary Edwards Walker: The Only Female Medal of Honor Recipient, 1 vol. 2017. (Fearless Female Soldiers, Explorers, & Aviators Ser.). (ENG.). 128p. (YA). (gr. 9-9). 47.36 *(978-1-5026-2745-2(0),* 4f3af724-2a96-4315-a3da-8590d2a2d372) Cavendish Square Publishing LLC.
Negley, Keith. Mary Wears What She Wants. Negley, Keith, illus. 2019. (ENG., Illus.). 48p. (J). (gr. -1-3). 18.99 *(978-0-06-284679-2(5),* Balzer & Bray) HarperCollins Pubs.

WALKING

see also Hiking

Barraclough, Sue. Move & Run. 2012. (Healthy Habits Ser.). (ENG., Illus.). 24p. (gr. 1-3). lib. bdg. 24.25 *(978-1-59771-308-5(2))* Sea-To-Sea Pubns.
Benjamin, Tina. Let's Walk in the Woods, 1 vol. 2015. (Let's Go Outdoors! Ser.). (ENG.). 24p. (J). (gr. k-k). lib. bdg. 24.27 *(978-1-4824-2635-9(8),* 57baae28-3833-466a-81e1-506c135b02a0); (Illus.). pap. 9.15 *(978-1-4824-2633-5(1),* 9ab691c2-921b-422b-a365-ab6e35e72503) Stevens, Gareth Publishing LLLP.
Bruce, Dan Wingfoot. The Thru-Hiker's Handbook 2004: #1 Guide for Long-Distance Hikes on the Appalachian Trail. 2004. (Illus.). 184p. per. 15.95 *(978-0-9707916-5-8(8))* Ctr. for Appalachian Trail Studies.
Caminando: Individual Title Six-Packs. (Literatura 2000 Ser.). (SPA.). (gr. 2-3). 33.00 *(978-0-7635-1085-5(8))* Rigby Education.
Dahl, Michael. Locomotion! March, Hop, Skip, Gallop, Run. Hughes, Beth, illus. 2018. (Creative Movement Ser.). (ENG.). 24p. (J). (gr. -1-2). lib. bdg. 33.99 *(978-1-68410-243-3(X),* 138433) Cantata Learning.
Loh-Hagan, Virginia. Vanishing Hitchhiker. 2018. (Urban Legends: Don't Read Alone! Ser.). (ENG., Illus.). 32p. (J). (gr. 4-8). pap. 14.21 *(978-1-5341-0863-9(7),* 210816); lib. bdg. 32.07 *(978-1-5341-0764-9(9),* 210815) Cherry Lake Publishing. (45th Parallel Press).
Meter, Pete O. & Meter, Pete. Walk the Walk: The Kid's Book of Pedometer Challenges. 2008. (ENG., Illus.). 56p. (J). (gr. 4). spiral bd. 12.95 *(978-1-60433-048-9(1),* Applesauce Pr.) Cider Mill Pr. Bk. Pubs., LLC.
Oregon Center for Applied Science, creator. Walk Smart: Children's Pedestrian Safety Program. 2005. (J). cd-rom 19.95 *(978-1-933898-10-0(0))* Oregon Ctr. for Applied Science, Inc.
Schuette, Sarah L. Pedestrian Safety. 2019. (Staying Safe! Ser.). (ENG., Illus.). 24p. (J). (gr. -1-2). 24.65 *(978-1-9771-0872-2(5),* 140483, Pebble) Capstone.
Sesame Street Staff, creator. Sesame Street: Elmo & Me! Boxed Set. 2011. 40p. (J). bds. 12.99 *(978-1-60745-166-2(2))* Flying Frog Pubs.
Thoreau, Henry D. Walking. Clifton Johnson, illus. 2010. 100p. pap. 3.49 *(978-1-60386-305-6(2),* Watchmaker Publishing) Wexford College Pr.
Votry, Kim & Waller, Curt. Out for a Walk. 2003. (Baby's First Signs Bks.). (ENG., Illus.). 16p. (J). pap. 6.95 *(978-1-56368-146-2(3))* Gallaudet Univ. Pr.
Walking in the City. (J). 26.20 *(978-0-8136-8422-2(6));* 26.20 *(978-0-8136-8423-9(4));* (gr. -1-3). 59.50 *(978-0-8136-7966-2(4))* Modern Curriculum Pr.

WALL STREET (NEW YORK, N.Y.)—FICTION

Standish, Burt L. Frank Merriwell in Wall Street. Rudman, Jack, ed. 2003. (Frank Merriwell Ser.). pap. 9.95 *(978-0-8373-9159-5(8))* Merriwell, Frank Inc.

WALLACE, ALFRED RUSSEL, 1823-1913

Colson, Mary. Charles Darwin & Alfred Russel Wallace. 2014. (Dynamic Duos of Science Ser.). 48p. (YA). (gr. 5-8). pap. 84.30 *(978-1-4824-1280-2(2))* Stevens, Gareth Publishing LLLP.

WALLACE, GEORGE C. (GEORGE CORLEY), 1919-1998

Yeager, Alice. George C. Wallace: Alabama Political Power. 2003. (Alabama Roots Biography Ser.). (Illus.). 104p. (J). pap. *(978-1-59421-003-7(9))* Seacoast Publishing, Inc.

WALLACE, LEW, 1827-1905

Boomhower, Ray E. The Sword & the Pen: A Life of Lew Wallace. 2005. (Illus.). x, 164p. (J). 15.95 *(978-0-87195-185-4(1))* Indiana Historical Society.

WALLACE AND GROMIT (FICTITIOUS CHARACTERS)—FICTION

Abnett, Dan. Wallace & Gromit: a Pier Too Far. Hansen, Jimmy, illus. 2005. (Wallace & Gromit Ser.). (ENG.). 48p. 12.95 *(978-1-84023-953-9(0),* Titan Bks.) Titan Bks. Ltd. GBR. Dist: Penguin Random Hse. LLC.
Rimmer, Ian. Wallace & Gromit: the Bootiful Game. Williamson, Brian, illus. 2005. (Wallace & Gromit Ser.). (ENG.). 48p. pap. 8.95 *(978-1-84023-948-5(4),* Titan Bks.) Titan Bks. Ltd. GBR. Dist: Penguin Random Hse. LLC.

WALLENBERG, RAOUL, 1912-1947

Idzikowski, Lisa. Raoul Wallenberg: Rescuer of Hungarian Jews During the Holocaust. 2017. (Spotlight on Civic Courage: Heroes of Conscience Ser.). (Illus.). 48p. (J). (gr. 10-15). 70.50 *(978-1-5383-8118-2(4));* (ENG., (gr. 6-6). pap. 12.75 *(978-1-5383-8117-5(6),* ea8d7ac5-a3fc-4a6d-9d1d-32106a23dec7) Rosen Publishing Group, Inc., The.
Simon, Emma & Streissguth, Thomas. Raoul Wallenberg, 1 vol., 1. 2015. (Holocaust Ser.). (ENG., Illus.). 112p. (J). (gr. 7-7). 38.80 *(978-1-4994-6242-5(5),* 80ac7adc-988d-44a6-975f-71ad0b70e651, Rosen Young Adult) Rosen Publishing Group, Inc., The.

WALRUSES

Barrett, Tracy. Walruses, 1 vol. 2012. (Animals, Animals Ser.). (ENG., Illus.). 48p. (gr. 5-5). 32.64 *(978-0-7614-4881-5(0),* c789a6ff-e194-4d59-b354-c4d41f0a2ff7) Cavendish Square Publishing LLC.
Berger, Melvin & Berger, Gilda. Sea Horses. 2003. (Scholastic Reader Ser.). (Illus.). (J). pap. *(978-0-439-47392-7(6))* Scholastic, Inc.
Bodden, Valerie. Walruses. 2016. (Amazing Animals Ser.). (ENG.). 24p. (J). (gr. 1-3). pap. 9.99 *(978-1-62832-221-7(7),* 20445, Creative Paperbacks); (Illus.). 28.50 *(978-1-60818-615-0(6),* 20447, Creative Education) Creative Co., The.
Drumlin, Sam. Walruses, 1 vol. 2013. (PowerKids Readers: Sea Friends Ser.). (ENG., Illus.). 24p. (J). (gr. k-k). pap. 9.25 *(978-1-4488-9742-1(4),* 03dfb78f-f455-41ec-a2c5-0565770b5f43); lib. bdg. 26.27 *(978-1-4488-9642-4(8),* a7d07335-fe8f-4200-b53f-5c6b84c04579) Rosen Publishing Group, Inc., The. (PowerKids Pr.).
—Walruses: Las Morsas, 1 vol. Alamán, Eduardo, tr. 2013. (PowerKids Readers: Los Amigos Del Mar / Sea Friends Ser.). (SPA & ENG., Illus.). 24p. (J). (gr. k-k). lib. bdg. 26.27 *(978-1-4488-9977-7(X),* aaf34480-eba5-4a19-a7cf-aecb899ce62a, PowerKids Pr.) Rosen Publishing Group, Inc., The.
Gish, Ashley. Walruses. 2019. (X-Books: Marine Mammals Ser.). (ENG.). 32p. (J). (gr. 3-5). pap. 9.99 *(978-1-62832-756-4(1),* 19225, Creative Paperbacks) Creative Co., The.
Gish, Melissa. Living Wild: Walruses. 2014. (Living Wild Ser.). (ENG., Illus.). 48p. (J). (gr. 4-7). pap. 12.00 *(978-0-89812-844-4(7),* 21647, Creative Paperbacks) Creative Co., The.
—Walruses. 2013. (Living Wild Ser.). (ENG., Illus.). 48p. (J). (gr. 4-7). 35.65 *(978-1-60818-291-6(6),* 21646, Creative Education) Creative Co., The.
Group/McGraw-Hill, Wright. I am the Walrus: Level N, 6 vols. (Autumn Leaves Ser.). 128p. (gr. 3-6). 36.95 *(978-0-322-06734-9(0))* Wright Group/McGraw-Hill.
Hansen, Grace. Walrus Migration. 2017. (Animal Migration Ser.). (ENG., Illus.). 24p. (J). (gr. -1-2). lib. bdg. 32.79 *(978-1-5321-0032-1(9),* 25144, Abdo Kids) ABDO Publishing Co.
Hirschmann, Kris. The Walrus. 2003. (Illus.). 48p. (J). 23.70 *(978-0-7377-1557-6(X),* Greenhaven Pr., Inc.) Cengage Gale.
Hodgkins, Fran. Do Seals Ever ...? Leggitt, Marjorie, illus. 2017. 32p. (J). (gr. -1-3). 16.95 *(978-1-60893-467-6(5))* Down East Bks.
Jackson, Tom. Walrus. 2008. (Nature's Children Ser.). (Illus.). 52p. (J). *(978-0-7172-6246-5(4))* Grolier, Ltd.
King, Zelda. Walruses. (Illus.). 24p. (J). 2012. 49.50 *(978-1-4488-5142-3(4),* PowerKids Pr.) 2011. (ENG., (gr. 2-3). pap. 9.25 *(978-1-4488-5141-6(6),* 6f7ddcc0-7284-4908-b4cc-04bd95b64d97, PowerKids Pr.) 2011. (ENG., (gr. 2-3). lib. bdg. 26.27 *(978-1-4488-5005-1(3),* 77987145-73ad-4f74-9d82-14381dc00b8f) Rosen Publishing Group, Inc., The.
Laughlin, Kara L. Walruses. 2017. (In the Deep Blue Sea Ser.). (ENG.). 24p. (J). (gr. k-3). lib. bdg. 32.79 *(978-1-5038-1694-7(X),* 211528) Child's World, Inc, The.
Macheske, Felicia. Big & Blubbery: Walrus. 2016. (Guess What Ser.). (ENG., Illus.). 24p. (J). (gr. k-2). 30.64 *(978-1-63470-719-0(2),* 207587) Cherry Lake Publishing.
Markovics, Joyce. My Skin Is Gray & Wrinkly (Walrus) 2014. (Zoo Clues Ser.). 24p. (J). (gr. -1-3). lib. bdg. 26.99 *(978-1-62724-109-0(4))* Bearport Publishing Co., Inc.
Markovics, Joyce L. Mi Piel Es Gris y Arrugada. 2015. (Pistas de Animales Ser.). (SPA.). 24p. (J). (gr. -1-3). lib. bdg. 26.99 *(978-1-62724-585-2(5))* Bearport Publishing Co., Inc.
Meister, Cari. Walruses. 2012. (ENG., Illus.). 24p. (J). lib. bdg. 25.65 *(978-1-62031-013-7(9))* Jump! Inc.
Miller, Sara Swan. Walruses of the Arctic. 2009. (Brrr! Polar Animals Ser.). 24p. (gr. 2-3). 42.50 *(978-1-61511-757-4(1),* PowerKids Pr.) Rosen Publishing Group, Inc., The.
Murray, Julie. Walruses. 2019. (Animal Kingdom Ser.). (ENG., Illus.). 32p. (J). (gr. 2-5). lib. bdg. 34.21 *(978-1-5321-1658-2(6),* 32427, Big Buddy Bks.) ABDO Publishing Co.
Nugent, Samantha. Walrus. 2015. (Illus.). 34p. (J). *(978-1-4896-4129-8(7))* Weigl Pubs., Inc.
Owen, Ruth. Walruses, 1 vol. 2013. (Polar Animals: Life in the Freezer Ser.). (ENG., Illus.). 32p. (J). (gr. 2-3). pap. 11.00 *(978-1-4777-0227-7(X),* 93deaed4-f173-4d31-ad3f-1ef6859a6c26); lib. bdg. 29.93 *(978-1-4777-0220-8(2),* c44302a5-fd14-4aee-ae9e-dea02bf0d56e) Rosen Publishing Group, Inc., The. (Windmill Bks.).
Paniaq, Herve. Animals Illustrated: Walrus, 1 vol. Shannon, Ben, illus. 2017. (Animals Illustrated Ser.: 4). (ENG.). 32p. (J). (gr. 1-3). 12.95 *(978-1-77227-142-3(X))* Inhabit Media Inc. CAN. Dist: Consortium Bk. Sales & Distribution.
Person, Stephen. Walrus: Tusk, Tusk. 2011. (Built for Cold Ser.). 32p. (YA). (gr. 1-4). lib. bdg. 28.50 *(978-1-61772-133-5(6));* (J). (gr. 4-5). lib. bdg., E-Book 49.22 *(978-1-61772-223-3(5))* Bearport Publishing Co., Inc.
Proudfit, Benjamin. Walruses, 1 vol. 2019. (Ocean Animals Ser.). (ENG.). 24p. (gr. k-k). pap. 9.15 *(978-1-5382-4473-9(X),* b2e5efbc-f904-4efc-a9f3-e635f89a183c) Stevens, Gareth Publishing LLLP.
Read, Tracy C. Exploring the World of Seals & Walruses. 2011. (Exploring the World Of Ser.). (ENG., Illus.). 24p. (J). (gr. 3-7). 16.95 *(978-1-55407-784-7(2),* 869a160e-bf4a-4da2-8356-79ceabdca1d0); pap. 6.95 *(978-1-55407-797-7(4),* 7cd2e8c5-ab0a-45f4-b309-a26ab05b26a6) Firefly Bks., Ltd.
Schuetz, Kari. Walruses. 2016. (Ocean Life up Close Ser.). (ENG., Illus.). 24p. (J). (gr. k-3). 26.95 *(978-1-62617-424-5(5),* Blastoff! Readers) Bellwether Media.
Sexton, Colleen. Walruses. 2007. (Oceans Alive Ser.). (ENG., Illus.). 24p. (J). (gr. k-3). lib. bdg. 26.95 *(978-1-60014-110-2(2))* Bellwether Media.
Soundprints Staff, ed. Oceanic Collection III: Beluga Whale, Harp Seal, Walrus & Lobster Books, 4 micro bks. (Smithsonian Oceanic Collection). (Illus.). 128p. (J). (gr. -1-2). 18.95 *(978-1-56899-633-2(0))* Soundprints.
Weber, Valerie J. Walruses, 1 vol. 2008. (Animals That Live in the Ocean Ser.). (ENG., Illus.). 24p. (J). (gr. 1-1). lib. bdg. 25.27 *(978-0-8368-9566-7(5),* 9116a86c-886d-4dc7-9fd9-ecfd261739f9, Weekly Reader Leveled Readers) Stevens, Gareth Publishing LLLP.
—Walruses / Morsas, 1 vol. 2008. (Animals That Live in the Ocean / Animales Que Viven en el Océano Ser.). 24p. (gr. 1-1). (ENG & SPA.). (J). lib. bdg. 25.27 *(978-0-8368-9568-1(1),* 1de07039-9504-4536-8a12-576eab82686f); (SPA & ENG.). pap. 9.15 *(978-0-8368-9578-0(9),* 2e86ca2c-e4d9-410f-a816-e5401612ff82) Stevens, Gareth Publishing LLLP. (Weekly Reader Leveled Readers).

WALRUSES—FICTION

Bradford, Arthur. Benny's Brigade. Hanawalt, Lisa, illus. 2012. (ENG.). 48p. (J). 19.95 *(978-1-936365-61-6(8),* d90f3ed6-666e-4056-88ba-efe956ba2f74) McSweeney's Publishing.
Cook, Sherry & Johnson, Terri. Watery William, 26. Kuhn, Jesse, illus. l.t. ed. 2006. (Quirkles — Exploring Phonics through Science Ser.: 23). 32p. (J). 7.99 *(978-1-933815-22-0(1),* Quirkles, The) Creative 3, LLC.
Derrick, Patricia. Mr. Walrus & the Old School Bus. Martinez, J-P Loppo, illus. 2007. 32p. 18.95 incl. audio compact disk *(978-1-933818-13-9(1))* Animalations.
Savage, Stephen. Where's Walrus? Savage, Stephen, illus. 2011. (ENG., Illus.). 32p. (J). (gr. -1 — 1). 17.99 *(978-0-439-70049-8(3),* Scholastic Pr.) Scholastic, Inc.
Simpson, D. C. Closer to the Void: Ozy & Millie 2006-2007. 2008. 127p. pap. 12.45 *(978-1-4357-0504-3(1))* Lulu Pr., Inc.
Underwood, Deborah. Walrus in the Bathtub. Hunt, Matt, illus. 2018. 40p. (J). (gr. -1-3). 17.99 *(978-0-8037-4101-0(4),* Dial Bks) Penguin Young Readers Group.
Walker, Anna. Lottie & Walter. Walker, Anna, illus. 2019. (ENG., Illus.). 40p. (J). (gr. -1-3). 17.99 *(978-1-328-47038-6(5),* 1714020, Clarion Bks.) HarperCollins Pubs.
Walker, Rhonda. Willie Out West. 2013. 24p. pap. 12.95 *(978-1-4497-9848-2(9),* WestBow Pr.) Author Solutions, LLC.
Wampol, Pam & Woodard, Heather. Oscar's Dreamzz: The Story of Santa's First Elf. 2013. 40p. pap. *(978-1-4602-0414-6(X))* FriesenPress.
Young, Carol. Little Walrus Warning. Stuart, Walter, illus. (Smithsonian Oceanic Collection). (J). 2009. 24.95 incl. audio compact disk *(978-1-59249-667-9(9))* 2005. (ENG.). 32p. (gr. -1-2). 8.95 *(978-1-59249-070-7(0),* SC4009) 2005. (ENG.). 32p. (gr. -1-3). 6.95 *(978-1-56899-937-1(2),* S4009) Soundprints.

WANAMAKER, JOHN, 1838-1922

Burt, Olive Woolley. John Wanamaker: Boy Merchant. Lees, Harry H., illus. 2011. 192p. 42.95 *(978-1-258-08290-1(X))* Literary Licensing, LLC.

WAR

see also Aeronautics, Military; Armies; Battles; Disarmament; International Law; Military Art and Science; Military Weapons; Naval Art and Science; Peace; Soldiers; Submarine Warfare

also names of wars, battles, etc., e.g. United States—History—Civil War; Gettysburg, Battle of, 1863

Agnew, Kate, ed. War & Peace: A Collection of Classic Poetry & Prose. 2011. (ENG.). 176p. (J). (gr. 7). 9.95 *(978-1-84046-570-9(0),* Wizard Books) Icon Bks., Ltd. GBR. Dist: Publishers Group West (PGW).
Anderson, Judith. War & Conflict. 2010. (Media Power Ser.). 48p. (J). 35.65 *(978-1-60753-116-6(2))* Amicus Learning.
Anderson, Judith & Flinthart, Dirk. War & Conflict. 2011. (Inside Crime Ser.). 48p. (YA). (gr. 5-9). lib. bdg. 34.25 *(978-1-59920-399-7(5))* Black Rabbit Bks.
Barker, Geoff. War. 2010. (Voices Ser.). (YA). (gr. 5-9). 34.25 *(978-1-59920-278-5(6))* Black Rabbit Bks.
Barnham, Kay. The Fact or Fiction Behind Battles & Wars, 1 vol. 2015. (Fact or Phony? Ser.). (ENG.). 96p. (J). (gr. 5-6). lib. bdg. 34.93 *(978-1-4824-4268-7(X),* 1304b0b1-00b6-4ce4-94be-15152c58d1b3) Stevens, Gareth Publishing LLLP.
Biographies of War, 20 vols. 2015. (Biographies of War Ser.). (ENG.). 112p. (YA). (gr. 7-8). 354.70 *(978-1-68048-198-3(3),* a9d2faa0-400b-4dc0-96e0-2a14ffbc9f9f, Britannica Educational Publishing) Rosen Publishing Group, Inc., The.
Brownell, Richard. The War in Afghanistan, 1 vol. 2011. (Hot Topics Ser.). (ENG., Illus.). 112p. (gr. 7-7). lib. bdg. 41.03 *(978-1-4205-0554-2(8),* 812653c3-2471-47bc-bb13-6dd2ba969de5, Lucent Pr.) Greenhaven Publishing LLC.
Broyles, Janell. Chemical Biological Incident Response Force, 1 vol. 2008. (Inside Special Operations Ser.). (ENG., Illus.). 64p. (J). (gr. 6-6). lib. bdg. 37.13 *(978-1-4042-1751-5(7),* fc902811-3dad-40c9-9f30-8c61f23fd82c) Rosen Publishing Group, Inc., The.
Connolly, Sean. War. 2003. (In Time of Need Ser.). (Illus.). 32p. (YA). (gr. 5-9). lib. bdg. 27.10 *(978-1-58340-391-4(4))* Black Rabbit Bks.
Curley, Robert, ed. The Science of War: Strategies, Tactics, & Logistics, 4 vols. 2011. (Britannica Guide to War Ser.). (ENG.). 192p. (YA). (gr. 10-10). 77.64 *(978-1-61530-794-4(X),* 79a21116-9393-438b-9b25-775e9325de71) Rosen Publishing Group, Inc., The.
—War on Land, 4 vols. 2011. (Britannica Guide to War Ser.). (ENG.). 192p. (YA). (gr. 10-10). 77.64 *(978-1-61530-799-9(0),* ebfde4b3-c36f-4d8e-b040-c302c735ffea) Rosen Publishing Group, Inc., The.

W X Y Z

DiConsiglio, John. Reporting Live. 2011. (Illus.). 112p. (J). *(978-0-531-22552-3(6))* Scholastic, Inc.

Doyle, Bill H. Behind Enemy Lines: Under Fire in the Middle East. 2011. 136p. (J). pap. *(978-0-545-33463-1(2))* Scholastic, Inc.

Early American Wars, 8 vols., Set. Incl. American Revolutionary War. Marston, Daniel & O'Neill, Robert John. lib. bdg. 38.47 *(978-1-4488-1331-5(X),* 97fdd7f5-b6c0-4a56-9c61-1c0f72d38d88); Texas War of Independence. Huffines, Alan C. & O'Neill, Robert. lib. bdg. 38.47 *(978-1-4488-1332-2(8),* 36cb7ba9-dc13-4896-8a71-3cada86c271c); War of 1812: The Fight for American Trade Rights. Benn, Carl & O'Neill, Robert. lib. bdg. 38.47 *(978-1-4488-1333-9(6),* d72506c9-ca2b-4440-b2de-85ad9710d12d); (YA). (gr. 10-10). 2011. (Early American Wars Ser.). (ENG., Illus.). 96p. 2010. Set lib. bdg. 153.88 *(978-1-4488-1387-2(5),* 2707729f-2e44-4276-a727-6c417d4c68f7) Rosen Publishing Group, Inc., The.

Engdahl, Sylvia, ed. War, 1 vol. 2010. (Issues on Trial Ser.). (ENG.). 224p. (gr. 10-12). 49.93 *(978-0-7377-4949-6(0),* a69aa804-e6c6-4e7d-85e0-5dd2f63002fd, Greenhaven Publishing) Greenhaven Publishing LLC.

Gagne, Tammy. Ghosts of War. 2018. (Ghosts & Hauntings Ser.). (ENG., Illus.). 32p. (J). (gr. 4-6). lib. bdg. 28.65 *(978-1-5435-4147-2(X),* 139101, Capstone Pr.) Capstone.

Gray, Leon. Dirty Bombs & Shell Shock: Biology Goes to War. 2017. (STEM on the Battlefield Ser.). (ENG., Illus.). 48p. (J). (gr. 4-6). 31.99 *(978-1-5124-3928-1(2),* e3d92160-3b28-4128-b1e2-61be5de64d96, Lerner Pubns.) Lerner Publishing Group.

Green, John. Horses in Battle. 2011. (Dover World History Coloring Bks.). (ENG., Illus.). 32p. (gr. 3-8). pap. 3.99 *(978-0-486-47608-7(1),* 476081) Dover Pubns., Inc.

Haugen, David M., ed. War, 1 vol. 2014. (Opposing Viewpoints Ser.). (ENG.). 264p. (gr. 10-12). pap. 34.80 *(978-0-7377-6972-2(6),* 7ef71523-0e28-4b17-825e-2a6201adf309); lib. bdg. 50.43 *(978-0-7377-6971-5(8),* b25d024a-eaf4-4f36-83e2-6747f946c3ef) Greenhaven Publishing LLC. (Greenhaven Publishing).

Haulley, Fletcher. Critical Perspectives on 9/11, 1 vol. 2004. (Critical Anthologies of Nonfiction Writing Ser.). (ENG.). 176p. (J). (gr. 8-8). lib. bdg. 42.47 *(978-1-4042-0060-9(6),* 3b3fe485-b729-4454-b7a5-4c5a477535d8) Rosen Publishing Group, Inc., The.

History's Greatest Rivals, 12 vols. 2014. (History's Greatest Rivals Ser.). (ENG.). 48p. (J). (gr. 6-8). lib. bdg. 201.60 *(978-1-4824-2229-0(8),* 3eba2b66-1d1c-49a2-8d94-dd602dfe9de3) Stevens, Gareth Publishing LLLP.

Hoffman, Mary. Lines in the Sand: New Writing on War & Peace. Lassiter, Rhiannon, ed. 2003. (ENG., Illus.). 288p. (J). (gr. 2-18). pap. 8.95 *(978-0-9729529-1-0(8))* Disinformation Co. Ltd., The.

Homer, illus. Classic Starts(r): the Iliad. 2014. (Classic Starts(r) Ser.). 160p. (J). (gr. 2-4). 7.99 *(978-1-4549-0612-4(X))* Sterling Publishing Co., Inc.

Hunt, Jilly. The Fight Against War & Terrorism. 2017. (Beyond the Headlines! Ser.). (ENG., Illus.). 48p. (J). (gr. 4-8). lib. bdg. 35.99 *(978-1-4846-4142-2(6),* 136196, Heinemann) Capstone.

The Interwar Years, 12 vols. 2017. (Interwar Years Ser.). (ENG.). 128p. (gr. 9-9). lib. bdg. 284.16 *(978-1-5026-2880-0(5),* 37411a28-ae2e-4647-8810-e02e3d17550d, Cavendish Square) Cavendish Square Publishing LLC.

Keating, Susan. Native American Rivalries. Johnson, Troy, ed. 2013. (Native American Life Ser.: 15). 64p. (J). (gr. 5-18). 19.95 *(978-1-4222-2975-0(0))* Mason Crest.

Kenney, Karen Latchana. The Spoils of War. 2007. (Shockwave: History & Politics Ser.). (ENG., Illus.). 36p. (J). (gr. 4-6). 25.00 *(978-0-531-17757-0(2),* Children's Pr.) Scholastic Library Publishing.

Kiland, Taylor Baldwin. Strategic Inventions of the War on Terror, 1 vol. 2016. (Tech in the Trenches Ser.). (ENG.). 112p. (YA). (gr. 9-9). lib. bdg. 44.50 *(978-1-5026-2349-2(8),* 19b0b883-3688-49a3-adc3-fdac8e231f64) Cavendish Square Publishing LLC.

Lawrence, Blythe. War & Terrorism in the Twenty-First Century. 2019. (Defining Events of the Twenty-First Century Ser.). (ENG.). 80p. (J). (gr. 6-12). 41.27 *(978-1-68282-609-6(0))* ReferencePoint Pr., Inc.

Lloyd Kyi, Tanya. Extreme Battlefields: When War Meets the Forces of Nature. Shannon, Drew, illus. 2016. (ENG.). 136p. (J). (gr. 4-8). pap. 14.95 *(978-1-55451-793-0(1))* Annick Pr., Ltd. CAN. Dist: Publishers Group West (PGW).

Lobel, Anita. No Pretty Pictures: A Child of War. 2008. (J). (gr. 5-8). lib. bdg. 18.40 *(978-0-613-28590-2(5))* Turtleback.

Loh-Hagan, Virginia. Amazons vs. Gladiators. 2019. (Battle Royale: Lethal Warriors Ser.). (ENG., Illus.). 32p. (J). (gr. 4-8). pap. 14.21 *(978-1-5341-5049-2(8),* 213503); lib. bdg. 32.07 *(978-1-5341-4763-8(2),* 213502) Cherry Lake Publishing. (45th Parallel Press).

Mapua, Jeff. Weaponizing Poop, 1 vol. 2017. (Power of Poop Ser.). (ENG.). 32p. (gr. 3-4). pap. 11.52 *(978-0-7660-9093-4(0),* e438156d-0d04-4bea-90f1-32437ae65716) Enslow Publishing, LLC.

Marsh, Carole. War What Kids Should Know. 2003. 32p. (gr. 2-8). pap. 7.95 *(978-0-635-01715-4(6))* Gallopade International.

Nelson, Sheila & Zoldak, Joyce. In Defense of Our Country: Survivors of Military Conflict. 2009. (J). pap. 24.95 *(978-1-4222-1465-7(6))* Mason Crest.

Nelson, Sheila, et al. In Defense of Our Country: Survivors of Military Conflict. 2010. (Survivors Ser.). 128p. (YA). (gr. 7-12). 24.95 *(978-1-4222-0452-8(9))* Mason Crest.

Parker, Steve. A Brief Illustrated History of Warfare. 2017. (ENG., Illus.). 32p. (J). pap. *(978-1-4747-2708-2(5))* Capstone.

Phillips, Larissa. Cochise: Jefe Apache, 1 vol. de la Vega, Eida, tr. 2003. (Grandes Personajes en la Historia de Los Estados Unidos (Famous People in American History) Ser.). (SPA., Illus.). 32p. (gr. 3-4). pap. 10.00 *(978-0-8239-4223-7(6),* 78727065-ac30-44c5-8197-d0ca1e0721c8); (J). lib. bdg. 29.13 *(978-0-8239-4129-2(9),* 792cb486-94fb-48f0-bcc7-1ac55441242a, Editorial Buenas Letras) Rosen Publishing Group, Inc., The.

Pramas, Chris. Orc Warfare, 1 vol. 2017. (Creature Warfare Ser.). (ENG.). 72p. (YA). (gr. 8-8). 38.80 *(978-1-5081-7624-4(8),* 97ef44d7-da30-4b4b-96ee-2220642abb8e, Rosen Young Adult) Rosen Publishing Group, Inc., The.

Rivera, Sheila. Rebuilding Iraq. 2004. (War in Iraq Ser.). (Illus.). 48p. (gr. 4-8). lib. bdg. 27.07 *(978-1-59197-498-7(4),* Abdo & Daughters) ABDO Publishing Co.

Road to War: Causes of Conflict, 5 vols., Set. Incl. Causes of the American Revolution. Strum, Richard M. 64p. (J). lib. bdg. 22.95 *(978-1-59556-001-8(7));* Causes of the Civil War. Epperson, James F. 64p. (J). lib. bdg. 22.95 *(978-1-59556-002-5(5));* Causes of the Iraq War. Gallagher, Jim. 72p. (J). lib. bdg. 22.95 *(978-1-59556-009-4(2));* Causes of World War I. Ziff, John. 72p. (J). lib. bdg. 22.95 *(978-1-59556-003-2(3));* Causes of World War II. Corrigan, Jim. 64p. lib. bdg. 22.95 *(978-1-59556-004-9(1));* (gr. 4-18). 2005. (Road to War Ser.). (Illus.). 64p. 2005. Set lib. bdg. 114.75 *(978-1-59556-000-1(9))* OTTN Publishing.

Rosenberg, Aaron. The Yom Kippur War, 1 vol. 2003. (War & Conflict in the Middle East Ser.). (ENG., Illus.). 64p. (gr. 5-5). lib. bdg. 37.13 *(978-0-8239-4553-5(7),* 7d1cacad-9868-41a6-8420-0e787722507c) Rosen Publishing Group, Inc., The.

Spilsbury, Louise. Global Conflict. Kai, Hanane, illus. 2018. (ENG.). 32p. (J). (gr. 1-2). 9.99 *(978-1-4380-5021-8(6))* Sourcebooks, Inc.

Spilsbury, Richard. Geronimo, 1 vol. Faure, Florence, illus. 2013. (Hero Journals). (ENG.). 48p. (J). (gr. 4-6). pap. 9.95 *(978-1-4109-5367-4(X),* 123251, Raintree) Capstone.

Summers, Elizabeth. Tools of War. 2015. (Tools of War Ser.). (ENG.). 32p. (J). (gr. 1-2). 117.28 *(978-1-4914-6657-5(X),* 22901, Capstone Pr.) Capstone.

Turner, Tracy. Conquerors. 2015. (Head-To-Head Ser.). (ENG., Illus.). 24p. (gr. 3-8). 28.50 *(978-1-62588-152-6(5))* Black Rabbit Bks.

Urrutia, Maria Cristina & Orozco, Rebeca. Cinco de Mayo. 2nd ed. 2008. (ENG., Illus.). 32p. (J). (gr. 4). pap. 7.95 *(978-0-88899-877-4(5))* Groundwood Bks. CAN. Dist: Publishers Group West (PGW).

Verrept, Paul. El Pequeno Soldado. Bourgeois, Elodie, tr. Verrept, Paul, illus. 2004. (SPA., Illus.). 26p. (J). (gr. -1-3). 17.99 *(978-84-261-3306-9(1))* Juventud, Editorial ESP. Dist: Lectorum Pubns., Inc.

Voices of War, 16 vols. 2014. (Voices of War Ser.). (ENG.). 48p. (J). (gr. 4-4). 264.56 *(978-1-62713-126-1(4),* 0398d67f-10de-4a73-bf13-4da4116c64be, Cavendish Square) Cavendish Square Publishing LLC.

Walker, Niki. Why Do We Fight? Conflict, War, & Peace. 2019. (ENG., Illus.). 80p. (J). pap. 14.95 *(978-1-77147-354-5(1))* Owlkids Bks. Inc. CAN. Dist: Publishers Group West (PGW).

Walter, Virginia A. War & Peace: A Guide to Literature & New Media, Grades 4-8, 1 vol. 2006. (Children's & Young Adult Literature Reference Ser.). (ENG.). 288p. pap. 50.00 *(978-1-59158-271-7(7),* 900322242, Libraries Unlimited) ABC-CLIO, LLC.

Watkins, Christine, ed. Biological Warfare, 1 vol. 2010. (Opposing Viewpoints Ser.). (ENG., Illus.). 232p. (J). (gr. 10-12). 50.43 *(978-0-7377-4757-7(9),* f3c07527-24f4-487e-9ad1-106fe4ee0118); pap. 34.80 *(978-0-7377-4758-4(7),* 7dfd5d81-6f20-44d5-ad61-67870f9074c8) Greenhaven Publishing LLC. (Greenhaven Publishing).

Wheeler, Sherrie Leigh. Defending Americ: A Children's Guide to Understanding the Circumstances & Sacrifices of War. 2012. 32p. pap. 24.95 *(978-1-4626-9758-8(5))* America Star Bks.

Why War Happened, 12 vols. 2016. (Why War Happened Ser.). 48p. (ENG.). (gr. 6-8). lib. bdg. 201.60 *(978-1-4824-5119-1(0),* 11ff654d-c601-4edf-ac2b-fea673038f6e); (gr. 8-6). pap. 84.30 *(978-1-4824-5329-4(0))* Stevens, Gareth Publishing LLLP.

Willett, Edward. The Iran-Iraq War, 1 vol. 2003. (War & Conflict in the Middle East Ser.). (ENG., Illus.). 64p. (gr. 5-5). lib. bdg. 37.13 *(978-0-8239-4547-4(2),* 8d76c917-17dd-40dd-a160-3c30293d73f0) Rosen Publishing Group, Inc., The.

World Book, Inc. Staff, contrib. by. Wooden Spears to Military Drones: A Timeline of Warfare. 2016. (Illus.). 40p. (J). *(978-0-7166-3544-4(5))* World Bk.-Childcraft International.

Yomtov, Nel. War on Terror Technology. 2017. (War Technology Ser.). (ENG., Illus.). 48p. (J). (gr. 4-8). lib. bdg. 35.64 *(978-1-5321-1191-4(6),* 25958) ABDO Publishing Co.

Young-Brown, Fiona. Declaring War, 1 vol. 2018. (How Government Works). (ENG.). 64p. (J). (gr. 5-5). pap. 16.28 *(978-1-5026-4050-5(3),* 1b3c6910-eaf0-4944-bf40-9c5c153c81cd) Cavendish Square Publishing LLC.

Zullo, Allan. The Secret Agent & Other Spy Kids. 2006. 147p. (J). pap. *(978-0-439-84835-0(0))* Scholastic, Inc.

24/7 Goes to War: On the Battlefield, 4 vols., Set. Incl. Gettysburg: The Bloodiest Battle of the Civil War. Johnson, Jennifer. lib. bdg. 22.44 *(978-0-531-25528-5(X));* Pearl Harbor: The U. S. Enters World War II. Dougherty, Steve. lib. bdg. 22.44 *(978-0-531-25525-4(5));* 64p. (J). (gr. 5-8). 2009. Set lib. bdg. 116.00 *(978-0-531-20550-1(9),* Watts, Franklin) Scholastic Library Publishing.

WAR—FICTION

Alcorn, Anita C. Caught in the Crossfire: A Boy's View of the Battle of Mill Springs, KY. 2006. 48p. pap. 8.95 *(978-0-7414-3581-1(0))* Infinity Publishing.

Altsheler, Joseph A. The Forest Runners: A Story of the Great War Trail in Early Kentucky. 2006. (Young Trailers Ser.: Vol. 2). (J). reprint ed. pap. *(978-1-4065-0810-9(1))* Dodo Pr.

Appleton, Victor. Tom Swift & his War Tank. 2005. 27.95 *(978-1-4218-1505-3(2),* 1st World Library - Literary Society) 1st World Publishing, Inc.

Armstrong, Jennifer. Shattered: Stories of Children & War. 2003. (ENG.). 176p. (YA). (gr. 7). mass mkt. 6.99 *(978-0-440-23765-5(3),* Laurel Leaf) Random Hse. Children's Bks.

Atwater-Rhodes, Amelia. The Shapeshifters: The Kiesha'ra of the Den of Shadows. 2010. (Kiesha'ra Ser.). (ENG.). 976p. (YA). (gr. 7). pap. 14.99 *(978-0-385-73950-4(8),* Delacorte Pr.) Random Hse. Children's Bks.

Avery, Pat McGrath. Tommy's War: A Parent Goes to War, 1. Ray, Eric, illus. 2003. 36p. (J). per. 5.95 *(978-0-9663276-8-7(3))* Red Engine Pr.

Bacigalupi, Paolo. The Drowned Cities. 2013. (ENG.). 464p. (J). (gr. 10-17). pap. 12.99 *(978-0-316-05622-9(7))* 2012. 448p. (YA). 17.99 *(978-0-316-20037-0(9))* Little, Brown Bks. for Young Readers.

—The Drowned Cities. 2012. 352p. *(978-1-59606-506-2(0))* Subterranean Pr.

—The Drowned Cities. 2013. (J). lib. bdg. 22.10 *(978-0-606-31749-8(X))* Turtleback.

Backer, Charles. Fireclaw. 2010. 288p. pap. 15.49 *(978-1-4520-1229-2(6))* AuthorHouse.

Barchers, Suzanne. The Brave Servant: A Tale from China. Han, Yu-Mei, illus. 2013. (Tales of Honor Ser.). (ENG.). 32p. (J). (gr. 1-3). pap. 8.99 *(978-1-937529-57-4(6),* 5347fe48-e5c0-4a2c-8c2c-1f8f58064513); E-Book 39.99 *(978-1-936163-89-2(6))* Red Chair Pr.

Bates, Gordon. The Khaki Boys over the Top: Doing & Daring for Uncle Sam. 2017. (ENG., Illus.). (J). 23.95 *(978-1-374-94649-1(4));* pap. 13.95 *(978-1-374-94648-4(6))* Capital Communications, Inc.

Bauer, Deidre. Silver Mountain. 2008. 38p. pap. 8.00 *(978-0-8059-7672-4(8))* Dorrance Publishing Co., Inc.

Beacham, Travis. Pacific Rim: Tales from Year Zero. 2013. (ENG., Illus.). 128p. (gr. 8-17). 24.99 *(978-0-7851-5394-8(2))* Legendary Comics.

Beckwith, Kathy & Lyon, Lea. Playing War, 1 vol. 2005. (ENG., Illus.). 32p. (J). (gr. 2-6). 16.95 *(978-0-88448-267-3(7),* 884267) Tilbury Hse. Pubs.

Beddor, Frank. ArchEnemy: The Looking Glass Wars, Book Three, 3 vols. 2010. (Looking Glass Wars Ser.: 3). (ENG.). 384p. (YA). (gr. 7-18). 10.99 *(978-0-14-241689-1(4),* Speak) Penguin Young Readers Group.

—Seeing Redd: The Looking Glass Wars, Book Two. 2008. (Looking Glass Wars Ser.: 2). (ENG.). 400p. (YA). (gr. 7-18). 11.99 *(978-0-14-241209-1(0),* Speak) Penguin Young Readers Group.

Belanger, Jeff. Ghosts of War: Restless Spirits of Soldiers, Spies, & Saboteurs, 1 vol. 2009. (Haunted: Ghosts & the Paranormal Ser.). (ENG.). 240p. (YA). (gr. 8-8). lib. bdg. 42.47 *(978-1-4358-5177-1(3),* 80b8eed3-9a0c-4bf2-a065-ebd27d18ff2e) Rosen Publishing Group, Inc., The.

Bell, Hilari. The Goblin War. 2011. (ENG.). 304p. (J). (gr. 8). 17.99 *(978-0-06-165105-2(2),* HarperTeen) HarperCollins Pubs.

Benary-Isbert, Margot. Rowan Farm. 2008. (J). (gr. 5-12). 25.00 *(978-0-8446-6475-0(8))* Smith, Peter Pub., Inc.

Berry, Julie. All the Truth That's in Me. 2014. lib. bdg. 20.85 *(978-0-606-36191-0(X))* Turtleback.

Birmajer, Marcelo. Una Vida Más: Noticias Extranas IV. 2004. (SPA.). 111p. (J). pap. 9.95 *(978-958-04-7081-6(2))* Norma S.A. COL. Dist: Lectorum Pubns., Inc.

Black, Judith. Home Front. (YA). 12.00 *(978-0-9701073-7-4(4))* Black, Judith Storyteller.

Bollen, Christine. Flying with the Geese, 1 vol. Matyuschenko, Tanya, illus. 2010. 34p. 24.95 *(978-1-4489-4401-9(5))* PublishAmerica, Inc.

Bowen, Carl. Shadow Squadron: Elite Infantry. Tortosa, Wilson, illus. 2013. (Shadow Squadron Ser.). (ENG.). 224p. (J). pap., pap., pap. 8.95 *(978-1-62370-032-4(9),* 124212, Capstone Young Readers) Capstone.

Bowler, Bill. Troy. 2nd ed. 2013. (ENG., Illus.). 40p. pap. 11.00 *(978-0-19-424970-6(0))* Oxford Univ. Pr., Inc.

Bowman, Patrick. Arrow Through the Axes. 2014. (ENG.). 200p. pap. 11.95 *(978-1-55380-323-2(X))* Ronsdale Pr. CAN. Dist: SPD-Small Pr. Distribution.

—Cursed by the Sea God. 2013. (ENG., Illus.). 200p. pap. 11.95 *(978-1-55380-186-3(5))* Ronsdale Pr. CAN. Dist: SPD-Small Pr. Distribution.

Brennan, Herbie. The Faeman Quest, 5. 2012. (Faerie Wars Chronicles Ser.). (ENG.). 368p. (YA). (gr. 7-12). 26.19 *(978-1-59990-476-4(4),* 900065985) Bloomsbury Publishing USA.

Brereton, F. S. With Joffre at Verdun: A Story of the Western Front. Webb, Arch, illus. 2012. 240p. *(978-1-78139-196-9(3))* Benediction Classics.

Brudlos, Christopher. Alpha Shade Chapter One. Brudlos, Joseph, illus. 2005. (YA). per. 24.95 net. *(978-0-9768705-0-0(9))* Alpha Shade, Inc.

Buckley, Michael. The Council of Mirrors. (Sisters Grimm Ser.: 9). 2018. lib. bdg. 19.65 *(978-0-606-41062-5(7))* 2013. (J). lib. bdg. 18.40 *(978-0-606-31650-7(7))* Turtleback.

—The Council of Mirrors (the Sisters Grimm #9) 10th Anniversary Edition. 10th ed. 2018. (Sisters Grimm Ser.). (ENG., Illus.). 304p. (J). (gr. 3-7). pap. 9.99 *(978-1-4197-2009-3(0),* 696406, Amulet Bks.) Abrams, Inc.

—The Everafter War. 2018. (Sisters Grimm Ser.: 7). (J). lib. bdg. 19.65 *(978-0-606-41064-9(3))* Turtleback.

Bullock, Robert. Sam Marsh & the Battle of the Cloudships: The Sam Marsh Stories - Part 2. 2012. 224p. pap. 13.97 *(978-1-61897-348-1(7),* Strategic Bk. Publishing) Strategic Book Publishing & Rights Agency (SBPRA).

Bunting, Eve. Gleam & Glow. Sylvada, Peter, illus. 2005. (ENG.). 32p. (J). (gr. -1-3). reprint ed. pap. 7.99 *(978-0-15-205380-2(8),* 1196199, Clarion Bks.) HarperCollins Pubs.

Caballero, Erica. Mount Mole. 2006. pap. 10.00 *(978-1-4257-2301-9(2))* Xlibris Corp.

Calabrese, Diane Marie. My Dad's off to War. Swope, Brenda, illus. 2011. 28p. pap. 24.95 *(978-1-4560-0942-7(7))* America Star Bks.

Camus, William. Azules Contra Grises. (Barco de Vapor). (SPA.). 200p. (YA). (gr. 5-8). 7.95 *(978-84-348-1455-4(2))* SM Ediciones ESP. Dist: AIMS International Bks., Inc.

Cantwell, Michael. The Rising of the Fifth Sun. 2012. 120p. (gr. 4-6). 20.95 *(978-1-4620-7203-3(8));* pap. 10.95 *(978-1-4620-7201-9(1))* iUniverse, Inc.

Castner, K. D. Daughters of Ruin. 2017. (ENG.). 320p. (YA). (gr. 9). pap. 11.99 *(978-1-4814-3666-3(X),* McElderry, Margaret K. Bks.) McElderry, Margaret K. Bks.

Chacko, Miss Hannah. The Lie. 2009. 372p. pap. 25.50 *(978-0-557-06829-6(0))* Lulu Pr., Inc.

Chapman, Kelly. A Warrior Prince for God. 2010. (ENG., Illus.). 32p. (J). (gr. -1-3). 14.99 *(978-0-7369-2895-3(2),* 6928953) Harvest Hse. Pubs.

—A Warrior Prince for God Curriculum Leader's Guide. Ebbeler, Jeff, illus. 2009. pap. 12.99 *(978-0-7369-2899-1(5))* Harvest Hse. Pubs.

Chee, Traci. The Storyteller. 2019. (Reader Ser.: 3). 544p. (YA). (gr. 7). pap. 10.99 *(978-0-14-751807-1(5),* Penguin Books) Penguin Young Readers Group.

Chickasaw Adventures: War with the Creeks. 2005. (J). *(978-1-4265-0001-5(7))* Layne Morgan Media, Inc.

Chima, Cinda Williams. Shadowcaster. (YA). 2018. (Shattered Realms Ser.: 2). (ENG.). 576p. (gr. 8). pap. 10.99 *(978-0-06-238098-2(2),* HarperTeen) 2017. (Shattered Realms Ser.: 2). (ENG., Illus.). 560p. (gr. 8). 18.99 *(978-0-06-238097-5(4),* HarperTeen) 2017. (Illus.). 560p. *(978-0-06-266291-0(0))* 2017. (Illus.). 551p. *(978-0-06-269044-9(2))* HarperCollins Pubs.

—Stormcaster. (Shattered Realms Ser.: 3). (ENG.). (YA). (gr. 8). 2019. 560p. pap. 10.99 *(978-0-06-238101-9(6))* 2018. 544p. 18.99 *(978-0-06-238100-2(8))* HarperCollins Pubs. (HarperTeen).

Coakley, Lena. Witchlanders. 2012. (ENG., Illus.). 416p. (YA). (gr. 7). pap. 11.99 *(978-1-4424-2005-2(7),* Atheneum Bks. for Young Readers) Simon & Schuster Children's Publishing.

—Witchlanders. 2011. (ENG., Illus.). 416p. (YA). (gr. 7-12). 16.99 *(978-1-4424-2004-5(9))* Simon & Schuster, Inc.

Cole, Barbara H. Anna & Natalie, 1 vol. Himler, Ronald, illus. 2007. (ENG.). 32p. (J). 16.95 *(978-1-59572-105-1(3))* Star Bright Bks., Inc.

Colfer, Chris. The Land of Stories: a Grimm Warning. 2014. (Land of Stories Ser.: 3). (ENG.). (J). (gr. 3-7). 480p. 19.99 *(978-0-316-40681-9(3));* 768p. 50.99 *(978-0-316-40964-3(2))* Little, Brown Bks. for Young Readers.

Collingwood, Harry. Across the Spanish Main. 2011. 204p. 26.95 *(978-1-4638-9643-0(3))* Rodgers, Alan Bks.

Collins, Suzanne. Gregor & the Code of Claw (the Underland Chronicles #5) 2013. (Underland Chronicles Ser.: 5). (ENG., Illus.). 416p. (J). (gr. 4-7). pap. 7.99 *(978-0-439-79144-1(8),* Scholastic Paperbacks) Scholastic, Inc.

—Gregor & the Marks of Secret. 2007. (Underland Chronicles Ser.: 4). 343p. (gr. 4-7). lib. bdg. 18.40 *(978-1-4177-8358-8(3))* Turtleback.

—Gregor & the Marks of Secret (the Underland Chronicles #4) 2013. (Underland Chronicles Ser.: 4). (ENG., Illus.). 352p. (J). (gr. 4-7). 7.99 *(978-0-439-79146-5(4),* Scholastic Paperbacks) Scholastic, Inc.

Cook, Kajsa. Discoveries in the Shriver Family Attic: How a Woman & Her Children Dealt with the Battle of Gettysburg. 2009. (Illus.). 122p. (J). (gr. 4-8). pap. 8.95 *(978-1-57249-398-8(4),* White Mane Kids) White Mane Publishing Co., Inc.

Cooney, Caroline B. Goddess of Yesterday. 2009. (ENG.). 272p. (YA). (gr. 7). pap. 8.99 *(978-0-385-73865-1(X),* Ember) Random Hse. Children's Bks.

Cooper, Michelle. The FitzOsbornes at War. 2013. (Montmaray Journals: 3). (ENG.). 560p. (YA). (gr. 7). pap. 12.99 *(978-0-307-93058-3(0),* Ember) Random Hse. Children's Bks.

Costa, T. L. Playing Tyler. 2013. (ENG.). 304p. (J). (gr. 9). pap. 9.99 *(978-1-908844-61-3(2),* Strange Chemistry) Watkins Media Limited GBR. Dist: Penguin Random Hse. LLC.

Cox, Greg. Riese: Kingdom Falling. 2013. (ENG., Illus.). 288p. (YA). (gr. 7). pap. 9.99 *(978-1-4424-2970-3(4),* Simon & Schuster Bks. For Young Readers) Simon & Schuster Bks. For Young Readers.

Cullen, James J. A Micro-Classic Trilogy: The Hero of Troy, the Trojan Horse & Ulysses & the Cyclops. 2004. (ENG.). 52p. pap. 15.99 *(978-1-4134-1790-6(6))* Xlibris Corp.

D'Adamo, Francesco. My Brother Johnny. 2008. (ENG.). 200p. pap. 16.95 *(978-0-9551566-3-2(7))* Aurora Metro Pubns. Ltd. GBR. Dist: Publishers Group West (PGW).

Dafoe, Daniel & Perry, John Jasiel. Atalantis Major. 2011. 54p. 15.95 *(978-1-4638-9670-6(0))* Rodgers, Alan Bks.

Davidson, Halsey. Navy Boys Behind the Big Guns: Or, Sinking the German U-Boats. 2017. (ENG., Illus.). (J). pap. 13.95 *(978-1-374-82701-1(0))* Capital Communications, Inc.

—Navy Boys Behind the Big Guns or Sinking the German U-Boats. 2007. 108p. per. *(978-1-4068-1847-5(X))* Echo Library.

Deforges, Regine. La Bicyclette Bleue, Level C. (FRE.). (YA). (gr. 7-12). 9.95 *(978-0-88436-990-5(0),* 40304) EMC/Paradigm Publishing.

DiMarco, Carol & Bowman, Sharon. The Tale of Two Kingdoms. 2009. (ENG.). 88p. (J). pap. 10.99 *(978-1-59092-170-8(4))* Blue Forge Pr.

Dixon, Chuck. Airboy Archives Volume 1, Vol. 1. Truman, Timothy et al, illus. 2014. (Airboy Ser.: 1). 308p. pap. 29.99 *(978-1-61377-900-2(3),* 9781613779002) Idea & Design Works, LLC.

Dorling Kindersley Publishing Staff. The Invincible Iron Man: The Rise of Iron Man. 2010. (DK Readers Level 4 Ser.). (ENG., Illus.). 48p. (J). (gr. 2-4). 16.19 *(978-0-7566-5784-0(9))* Dorling Kindersley Publishing, Inc.

Driscoll, James R. The Brighton Boys with the Flying Corps. 2005. 152p. pap. 11.95 *(978-1-59540-820-4(7),* 1st World Library - Literary Society) 1st World Publishing, Inc.

Dumas. The Count of Monte Cristo. 2011. (ENG., Illus.). (J). 33.99 *(978-1-61382-823-6(3))* Simon & Brown.

Dumas, Alexander. The Count of Monte Cristo. 2017. (ENG., Illus.). (YA). pap. 21.95 *(978-1-376-31008-5(2))* Creative Media Partners, LLC.

Dumas, Alexandre. The Count of Monte Cristo. (ENG.). (YA). 2019. 806p. (gr. 8-12). 35.95 *(978-1-01-115034-2(4),* Wentworth Pr.) 2019. 806p. (gr. 8-12). pap. 26.95 *(978-1-01-115033-5(6),* Wentworth Pr.) 2018. 584p. (gr. 8-12). 51.95 *(978-0-353-59549-1(7))* 2018. 802p. (gr. 8-12). 59.95 *(978-0-353-51395-2(4))* 2018. 584p. (gr. 8-12). pap. 36.95 *(978-0-353-59548-4(9))* 2018. 802p. (gr. 8-12). pap. 44.95 *(978-0-353-51394-5(6))* 2018. (Illus.). 802p. 35.95 *(978-0-343-47947-3(8))* 2018. (Illus.). 584p. 30.95 *(978-0-343-56311-0(8))* 2018. (Illus.). 802p. pap. 26.95 *(978-0-343-47946-6(X))* 2018. (Illus.). 584p. pap. 21.95 *(978-0-343-56310-3(X))* 2018. (Illus.). 702p. (gr. 8-12). pap. 23.95 *(978-1-377-26137-9(9))* Creative Media Partners, LLC.

—The Count of Monte Cristo. 2010. (ENG., illus.). 486p. (YA). (gr. 8-12). pap. 18.95 *(978-1-936136-94-0(5))* Pacific Publishing Studio.
—The Count of Monte-Cristo. 2017. (ENG.). (YA). (gr. 8-12). 352p. pap. *(978-3-337-37798-4(X))*; 298p. pap. *(978-3-337-37799-1(8))*; 300p. pap. *(978-3-337-37800-4(5))*; 352p. pap. *(978-3-337-37801-1(3))*; 352p. pap. *(978-3-337-37802-8(1))* Creation Pubs.
—The Count of Monte-Cristo. 2018. (ENG.). 686p. (YA). (gr. 8-12). 54.95 *(978-0-353-42870-6(1))*; (gr. 8-12). pap. 39.95 *(978-0-353-42869-0(8))*; (Illus.). 32.95 *(978-0-343-37964-3(3))* Creative Media Partners, LLC.
Dumas, Alexandre. The Man in the Iron Mask. 2008. (Bring the Classics to Life Ser.). (ENG., Illus.). 72p. (gr. 5-12). pap., act. bk. ed. 10.95 *(978-1-55576-359-6(6)*, EDCTR-509B) EDCON Publishing Group.
Ellis, Deborah. Parvana's Journey, 1 vol. 2015. (Breadwinner Ser.: 2). (ENG., Illus.). 200p. (J). (gr. 5-9). pap. 10.99 *(978-1-55498-770-2(9))* Groundwood Bks. CAN. Dist: Publishers Group West (PGW).
Entwistle, Charles. The Promise. 2004. 114p. (YA). per. 9.95 *(978-0-9709104-2-4(8))* Hickory Tales Publishing.
Esseltine, Christopher R. Caleb's Quest. 2008. (J). pap. 13.99 *(978-1-59955-104-3(7))* Cedar Fort, Inc./CFI Distribution.
Falkner, Brian. The Assault (Recon Team Angel #1) 2013. (Recon Team Angel Ser.: 1). (ENG.). 304p. (YA). (gr. 7). pap. 9.99 *(978-0-375-87190-0(X)*, Ember) Random Hse. Children's Bks.
Fan, Nancy Y. Sword Quest. Rioux, Jo-Anne, illus. 2008. (Swordbird Ser.). 176p. (J). (gr. 3-7). 15.99 *(978-0-06-124335-6(3))* HarperCollins Pubs.
Fan, Nancy Yi. Sword Quest. Rioux, Jo-Anne, illus. 2008. (Swordbird Ser.). 288p. (J). (gr. 3-7). lib. bdg. 16.89 *(978-0-06-124336-3(1))* HarperCollins Pubs.
—Swordbird. 2008. (J). 54.99 *(978-1-60514-800-7(8))* Findaway World, LLC.
—Swordbird. Zug, Mark, illus. 2008. (Swordbird Ser.: 1). (ENG.). 256p. (J). (gr. 3-7). pap. 6.99 *(978-0-06-113101-1(6)*, HarperCollins) HarperCollins Pubs.
Fine, Sarah. The Cursed Queen. 2017. (Impostor Queen Ser.: 2). (ENG., Illus.). 432p. (YA). (gr. 7). 19.99 *(978-1-4814-4193-3(0)*, McElderry, Margaret K. Bks.) McElderry, Margaret K. Bks.
—Of Dreams & Rust. 2016. (ENG.). 304p. (YA). (gr. 9). pap. 11.99 *(978-1-4424-8362-0(8)*, McElderry, Margaret K. Bks.) McElderry, Margaret K. Bks.
Flanagan, John. The Battle for Skandia. 2009. (Ranger's Apprentice Ser.: 4). lib. bdg. 19.65 *(978-0-606-02208-8(2))* Turtleback.
—The Battle for Skandia: Book Four. (Ranger's Apprentice Ser.: 4). (ENG.). (J). (gr. 5-18). 2008. 304p. 18.99 *(978-0-399-24457-5(3)*, Philomel Bks.)Bk. 4. 2009. 336p. 9.99 *(978-0-14-241340-1(2)*, Viking Books for Young Readers) Penguin Young Readers Group.
—The Battle of Hackham Heath. 2017. (Ranger's Apprentice: the Early Years Ser.: 2). (ENG.). 368p. (J). (gr. 5). 8.99 *(978-0-14-242733-0(0)*, Puffin Books) Penguin Young Readers Group.
—The Burning Bridge. 2007. (Ranger's Apprentice Ser.: 2). 262p. lib. bdg. 19.65 *(978-1-4177-9330-3(9))* Turtleback.
—The Burning Bridge: Book Two, Bk. 2. 2007. (Ranger's Apprentice Ser.: 2). (ENG., Illus.). 304p. (J). (gr. 5-18). 9.99 *(978-0-14-240842-1(5)*, Puffin Books) Penguin Young Readers Group.
—Erak's Ransom: Book Seven, Bk. 7. 2011. (Ranger's Apprentice Ser.: 7). (ENG.). 416p. (J). (gr. 5-18). 9.99 *(978-0-14-241525-2(1)*, Puffin Books) Penguin Young Readers Group.
—The Kings of Clonmel: Book Eight, Bk. 8. 2011. (Ranger's Apprentice Ser.: 8). (ENG., Illus.). 400p. (J). (gr. 5-18). 9.99 *(978-0-14-241857-4(9)*, Puffin Books) Penguin Young Readers Group.
—The Lost Stories. 2013. (Ranger's Apprentice Ser.: 11). lib. bdg. 19.65 *(978-0-606-31700-9(7))* Turtleback.
—The Lost Stories: Book Eleven. 2013. (Ranger's Apprentice Ser.: 11). (ENG.). 464p. (J). (gr. 5). pap. 8.99 *(978-0-14-242195-6(2)*, Puffin Books) Penguin Young Readers Group.
—The Siege of Macindaw: Book Six, Bk. 6. (Ranger's Apprentice Ser.: 6). (ENG.). (J). (gr. 5-18). 2010. 336p. 9.99 *(978-0-14-241524-5(3)*, Puffin Books) 2009. 304p. 18.99 *(978-0-399-25033-0(6)*, Viking Books for Young Readers) Penguin Young Readers Group.
Fontes, Justine & Fontes, Ron. The Trojan Horse: The Fall of Troy [a Greek Myth]. Purcell, Gordon, illus. 2015. (Graphic Myths & Legends Ser.). (ENG.). 48p. (J). (gr. 4-8). E-Book 53.32 *(978-1-4677-5985-4(6)*, 9781467759854, Lerner Digital) Lerner Publishing Group.
Foreman, Michael. El Jardin del Nino: Una Historia de Esperanza. Diego, Rapi & Flores, Martha, illus. 2009. (SPA.). 30p. (J). (gr. 1-3). 14.99 *(978-1-933032-56-6(1))* Lectorum Pubns., Inc.
Freedman, Claire. Dinosaurs Love Underpants. Cort, Ben, illus. 2009. (Underpants Bks.). (ENG.). 32p. (J). (gr. -1-2). 18.99 *(978-1-4169-8938-7(2)*, Aladdin) Simon & Schuster Children's Publishing.
Frost, Helen. Crossing Stones. 2009. (ENG., Illus.). 192p. (YA). (gr. 7-18). 19.99 *(978-0-374-31653-2(8)*, 900050356, Farrar, Straus & Giroux (BYR)) Farrar, Straus & Giroux.
Fulton-Vengco, Aletha. Felicidad & Her Pen Pal Kamar. 2009. 33p. 13.90 *(978-0-578-02728-9(3))* Vengco, Aletha Fulton.
Fussell, Sandy. Samurai Kids #2: Owl Ninja. James, Rhian Nest, illus. 2011. (Samurai Kids Ser.: 2). (ENG.). 272p. (J). (gr. 4-7). 15.99 *(978-0-7636-5003-2(X))* Candlewick Pr.
Gentry, Nancy. Little Blue, Little Gray. Keaggy, Sarah, illus. 2012. 56p. pap. 10.00 *(978-0-9846244-9-2(X))* O'More Publishing.
Geras, Adèle. Troy. 2004. 368p. (J). (gr. 8-18). pap. 48.00 incl. audio *(978-0-8072-2288-1(7)*, Listening Library) Random Hse. Audio Publishing Group.
Gerstein, Mordicai. The Old Country. rev. ed. 2005. (ENG.). 130p. (J). (gr. 4-6). 18.69 *(978-1-59643-047-1(8))* Roaring Brook Pr.
Glessner, Gordon. Water Wars, Secrets Revealed. 2012. 24p. 12.00 *(978-0-9859603-0-8(2))* Laughing Rhino Bks.
Goldsmith, Connie. Dogs at War: Military Canine Heroes. 2017. (ENG., Illus.). 104p. (YA). (gr. 6-12). E-Book 9.99 *(978-1-5124-3905-2(3)*, 9781512439052); E-Book 54.65 *(978-1-5124-3906-9(1)*, 9781512439069); E-Book 54.65 *(978-1-5124-2852-0(3))* Lerner Publishing Group. (Twenty-First Century Bks.).
Gonzalez Jensen, Margarita. Botas Negras. Sanchez, Enrique O., illus. (SPA.). (J). (gr. 2-4). 3.96 net. *(978-0-590-26842-4(2))* Scholastic, Inc.
Goodman, Alison. The Last Dragoneye. 2012. (Eon Ser.: 2). lib. bdg. 23.30 *(978-0-606-23648-5(1))* Turtleback.
Grant, Michael. Front Lines. 2016. (Front Lines Ser.: 1). (ENG.). 576p. (YA). (gr. 9). 18.99 *(978-0-06-234215-7(0)*, Tegen, Katherine Bks) HarperCollins Pubs.
Green, Roger Lancelyn. The Tale of Troy. 2012. (Puffin Classics Ser.). (ENG., Illus.). 240p. (J). (gr. 5). pap. 7.99 *(978-0-14-134196-5(3)*, Puffin Books) Penguin Young Readers Group.
Griffin, Paul. The Orange Houses. 2011. (ENG.). 160p. (YA). (gr. 9-12). 22.44 *(978-0-8037-3346-6(1)*, Dial) Penguin Publishing Group.
Guest, Jacqueline. Belle of Batoche, 1 vol. 2004. (Orca Young Readers Ser.). (ENG., Illus.). 144p. (J). (gr. 4-7). pap. 9.95 *(978-1-55143-297-7(8)*, 1551432978) Orca Bk. Pubs. USA.
Haar, Jaap Ter & Mearns, Martha. Boris. Poortvliet, Rien, illus. 2009. (J). pap. *(978-0-921100-72-0(8))* Inheritance Pubns.
Haddix, Margaret Peterson. The Always War. (ENG.). (YA). (gr. 7). 2012. 224p. pap. 8.99 *(978-1-4169-9527-2(7))* 2011. 208p. 16.99 *(978-1-4169-9526-5(9))* Simon & Schuster Bks. For Young Readers. (Simon & Schuster Bks. For Young Readers).
Haibara, Yak & Haibara, Yak. Sengoku Basara: Samurai Legends Volume 2: Samurai Legends Volume 2, 2 vols. 2013. (ENG., Illus.). 424p. (YA). pap. 19.99 *(978-1-926778-59-4(6)*, d748e1c6-88c3-40b7-ab2f-84ecedb6a598) URON Entertainment Corp. CAN. Dist: Diamond Comic Distributors, Inc.
Hamley, Dennis. Very Far from Here. 2007. 208p. per. *(978-1-904529-33-0(X)*, Back to Front) Solidus.
Hand, Elizabeth. A New Threat. 2004. (Star Wars Ser.: Vol. 5). 139p. (J). lib. bdg. 20.00 *(978-1-4242-0781-7(9))* Fitzgerald Bks.
Hardy, Janice. The Healing Wars: Book II: Blue Fire. (Healing Wars Ser.: II). (ENG.). (J). (gr. 5). 2011. 400p. pap. 7.99 *(978-0-06-174744-1(0))*Bk. 2. 2010. 384p. 16.99 *(978-0-06-174741-0(6))* HarperCollins Pubs. (Balzer & Bray).
—The Shifter. 2009. (Healing Wars Ser.). 384p. (J). (gr. 5-18). lib. bdg. 17.89 *(978-0-06-176177-5(X))* HarperCollins Pubs.
Harrell, Deborah A. Pintos Hope. 2003. 124p. (YA). pap. 10.95 *(978-0-595-26514-5(6)*, Writers Club Pr.) iUniverse, Inc.
Harris, Christine. The Silver Path. (Illus.). (J). (ENG & VIE.). 26p. *(978-1-85430-327-1(9)*, 93381); (CHI & ENG., 32p. *(978-1-85430-323-3(6)*, 93425) Little Tiger Pr. Group.
Hartman, Rachel. Shadow Scale: A Companion to Seraphina. 2018. (Seraphina Ser.: 2). (ENG.). 624p. (YA). (gr. 7). pap. 12.99 *(978-0-375-86624-1(8)*, Ember) Random Hse. Children's Bks.
Hayes, Clair W. The Boy Allies at Verdun or Saving France from the Enemy. 2007. 124p. (gr. -1-7). per. *(978-1-4068-1712-6(0))* Echo Library.
—The Boy Allies in the Balkan Campaign or the Struggle to Save a Nation. 2007. 128p. per. *(978-1-4068-1714-0(7))* Echo Library.
Haze, Armand. Beautiful Blossom. 2012. 322p. 29.95 *(978-1-4626-7056-7(3))* America Star Bks.
Heibel, Dorothy. Message for a Spy. 2004. (Illus.). 94p. (J). pap. *(978-1-932663-07-5(X))* History Compass, LLC.
Henty, A. G. With Frederick the Great. 2007. 324p. 98.99 *(978-1-4280-7565-8(8))*; per. 92.99 *(978-1-4280-7566-5(6))* IndyPublish.com.
Henty, George. By Sheer Pluck: A Tale of the Ashanti War. 2007. (ENG.). 246p. pap. 20.99 *(978-1-4264-3065-7(5))* Creative Media Partners, LLC.
—For Name & Fame: Or Through Afghan Passes. 2007. (ENG.). 240p. per. 20.99 *(978-1-4346-4487-9(1))* Creative Media Partners, LLC.
—True to the Old Flag: A Tale of the American War of Independence. 2004. reprint ed. pap. 1.99 *(978-1-4192-9123-4(8))*; pap. 27.95 *(978-1-4191-9123-7(3))* Kessinger Publishing, LLC.
—With Buller in Natal: Or a Born Leader. l.t. ed. 2007. (ENG.). 324p. pap. 24.99 *(978-1-4264-9739-1(3))* Creative Media Partners, LLC.
Hidalgo, Pablo. The Phantom Menace. 2012. (Star Wars Ser.). (ENG.). 64p. (J). (gr. -1-3). pap. 9.99 *(978-0-545-38986-0(0))* Scholastic, Inc.
Hinwood, Christine. The Returning. 2013. (ENG.). 320p. (YA). (gr. 9-12). 24.94 *(978-0-8037-3528-6(6)*, Dial) Penguin Publishing Group.
Holmes, Oliver Wendell, Sr. Grandmother's Story of Bunker Hill Battle. 2009. 45p. pap. 14.80 *(978-0-557-05927-0(5))* Lulu Pr., Inc.
Holmes, Sara. Operation Yes. 2009. 234p. (J). pap. *(978-0-545-20418-7(6))* Scholastic, Inc.
Homer. The Iliad. Tsilis, Thanos, illus. 2013. (Greek Classics Ser.). (ENG.). 64p. pap. 7.95 *(978-1-906230-53-1(6))* Real Reads Ltd. GBR. Dist: Casemate Pubs. & Bk. Distributors, LLC.
Hubble, Miles & Bryant, Justin. Bob & the Fowl War: Book One in the Poultry Series. 2008. 140p. pap. 11.95 *(978-1-4401-0857-0(9))* iUniverse, Inc.
Hunter, Erin. Warriors: Omen of the Stars #2: Fading Echoes. 2010. (Warriors: Omen of the Stars Ser.: 2). (ENG., Illus.). 352p. (J). (gr. 3-7). 16.99 *(978-0-06-155512-1(6)*, HarperCollins) HarperCollins Pubs.
Hunter, John P. Red Thunder: Secrets, Spies, & Scoundrels at Yorktown. 2006. 234p. (J). (gr. 6-8). 7.95 *(978-0-87935-231-8(0))* Colonial Williamsburg Foundation.
Ikeda, Daisaku. The Cherry Tree. McCaughrean, Geraldine, tr. from JPN. Wildsmith, Brian, illus. 2013. 6.95 *(978-1-935523-57-4(0))* World Tribune Pr.
Jacques, Brian. The Long Patrol: A Tale from Redwall. Curless, Allan, illus. 2004. (Redwall Ser.: 10). (ENG.). 368p. (J). (gr. 5-5). 9.99 *(978-0-14-240245-0(1)*, Firebird) Penguin Young Readers Group.
Jinks, Catherine. Babylonne. 2008. (ENG., Illus.). 400p. (YA). (gr. 7). 18.99 *(978-0-7636-3650-0(9))* Candlewick Pr.
Jones, Frewin. Warrior Princess. 2009. (YA). 346p. lib. bdg. 17.89 *(978-0-06-087144-4(X))*; (ENG.). 352p. (gr. 7-18). 16.99 *(978-0-06-087143-7(1))* HarperCollins Pubs. (Eos).
—Warrior Princess #2: Destiny's Path. 2010. (Warrior Princess Ser.: 2). (ENG.). 352p. (YA). (gr. 8). pap. 8.99 *(978-0-06-087148-2(2)*, HarperTeen) HarperCollins Pubs.
—Warrior Princess #3: the Emerald Flame. 2010. (Warrior Princess Ser.: 3). (ENG.). 352p. (YA). (gr. 8-18). 16.99 *(978-0-06-087149-9(0)*, HarperTeen) HarperCollins Pubs.
Khanduri, K. Tales of the trojan War. 2005. (Illus.). 144p. (J). pap. 4.95 *(978-0-7945-0323-9(3)*, Usborne) EDC Publishing.
Kincaid, S. J. Insignia. (Insignia Ser.: 1). (ENG.). (YA). (gr. 8). 2013. 480p. pap. 10.99 *(978-0-06-209300-4(2))* 2012. 464p. 17.99 *(978-0-06-209299-1(5))* HarperCollins Pubs. (Tegen, Katherine Bks).
—Vortex. 2013. (Insignia Ser.: 2). (ENG.). 400p. (YA). (gr. 8). 17.99 *(978-0-06-209302-8(9)*, Tegen, Katherine Bks) HarperCollins Pubs.
Krokos, Dan. The Black Stars. 2015. (Planet Thieves Ser.: 2). (ENG., Illus.). 304p. (J). (gr. 3-8). pap. 17.99 *(978-0-7653-7668-8(7)*, 900134306, Starscape) Doherty, Tom Assocs., LLC.
—The Planet Thieves. 2014. (Planet Thieves Ser.: 1). (ENG., Illus.). 256p. (J). (gr. 3-7). pap. 16.99 *(978-0-7653-7538-4(9)*, 900131710, Starscape) Doherty, Tom Assocs., LLC.
LaFleur, Suzanne. Beautiful Blue World. 2017. (ENG., Illus.). 240p. (J). (gr. 3-7). pap. 8.99 *(978-0-307-98032-8(4)*, Yearling) Random Hse. Children's Bks.
Lalonde, Carolyn. Hide Tommy Turkey. Lalonde, Johnathan, illus. 2005. 20p. (J). 9.60 *(978-1-4120-4893-4(1))* Trafford Publishing.
Lawlor, Laurie. Wind on the River. 2004. 156p. (J). lib. bdg. 16.92 *(978-1-4242-0771-8(1))* Fitzgerald Bks.
Leicht, Martin & Neal, Isla. Mothership. 2012. (Ever-Expanding Universe Ser.: 1). (ENG., Illus.). 320p. (YA). (gr. 9). 16.99 *(978-1-4424-2960-4(7)*, Simon & Schuster Bks. For Young Readers) Simon & Schuster Bks. For Young Readers.
—A Stranger Thing. 2013. (Ever-Expanding Universe Ser.: 2). (ENG., Illus.). 288p. (YA). (gr. 9). 17.99 *(978-1-4424-2963-5(1)*, Simon & Schuster Bks. For Young Readers) Simon & Schuster Bks. For Young Readers.
Lesler, Rebecca. The Truth of the Magic Stone, 1 vol. 2009. 107p. pap. 19.95 *(978-1-60836-422-0(4))* America Star Bks.
Lindsay, Fitzroy A. My Daddy Came Home Long after the War. 2012. 28p. pap. 19.99 *(978-1-4685-6010-7(7))* AuthorHouse.
Littell, William Adams. Guillaume. 2008. 74p. pap. 10.00 *(978-0-8059-7757-8(0))* Dorrance Publishing Co., Inc.
Lobel, Anita. Potatoes, Potatoes. 2004. 40p. (J). 15.99 *(978-0-06-023927-5(1))*; lib. bdg. 16.89 *(978-0-06-023928-2(X))* HarperCollins Pubs.
Lon Rogers. The Between Season. 2009. 280p. pap. 17.95 *(978-1-4401-8368-3(6))* iUniverse, Inc.
Lu, Marie. Legend. aut. ltd. collector's ed. 2013. (Legend Trilogy: Bk. 1). (Illus.). 306p. (YA). mass mkt. 100.00 net. *(978-1-934267-38-7(4))* Gauntlet, Inc.
—Legend. 2011. (Legend Trilogy: Bk. 1). (ENG.). (YA). (gr. 8-12). 54.99 *(978-1-61657-044-6(X)*, Penguin AudioBooks) Penguin Publishing Group.
—Legend. (Legend Ser.: 1). (ENG.). (YA). (gr. 7). 2013. 352p. pap. 12.99 *(978-0-14-242207-6(X)*, Speak) 2011. 320p. 19.99 *(978-0-399-25675-2(X)*, G.P. Putnam's Sons Books for Young Readers) Penguin Young Readers Group.
—Legend. l.t. ed. 2012. (Legend Trilogy: Bk. 1). (ENG.). 394p. (J). (gr. 7-12). 23.99 *(978-1-4104-4606-0(9))* Thorndike Pr.
—Legend. (Legend Graphic Novels Ser.: 1). 2015. lib. bdg. 26.95 *(978-0-606-38424-7(3))* 2013. lib. bdg. 20.85 *(978-0-606-31701-6(5))* Turtleback.
—Legend: the Graphic Novel. 2015. (Legend Ser.: 1). (ENG., Illus.). 160p. (YA). (gr. 7). pap. 15.99 *(978-0-399-17189-5(4)*, G.P. Putnam's Sons Books for Young Readers) Penguin Young Readers Group.
—Prodigy. l.t. ed. 2013. (Legend Trilogy: Bk. 2). (ENG.). 486p. 23.99 *(978-1-4104-5512-3(2))* Thorndike Pr.
—Prodigy. 2014. (Legend Ser.: 2). lib. bdg. 20.85 *(978-0-606-35716-6(5))* Turtleback.
—Prodigy: A Legend Novel. (Legend Ser.: 2). (ENG.). (YA). (gr. 7). 2014. Illus.). 416p. pap. 12.99 *(978-0-14-242755-2(1)*, Speak) 2013. 384p. 19.99 *(978-0-399-25676-9(8)*, G.P. Putnam's Sons Books for Young Readers) Penguin Young Readers Group.
—Prodigy: the Graphic Novel. 2016. (Legend Ser.: 2). (ENG., Illus.). 160p. (YA). (gr. 7). pap. 14.99 *(978-0-399-17190-1(8)*, G.P. Putnam's Sons Books for Young Readers) Penguin Young Readers Group.
Lundquist, Jenny. The Princess in the Opal Mask. 2013. (ENG.). 352p. (YA). (gr. 8-17). pap. 18.99 *(978-0-7624-5109-8(2)*, Running Pr. Kids) Running Pr.
Lynch, Chris. Free-Fire Zone. 2012. 183p. (J). *(978-0-545-49427-4(3)*, Scholastic Pr.) Scholastic, Inc.
—Free-Fire Zone. 2013. (Vietnam Ser.: 3). lib. bdg. 18.40 *(978-0-606-31963-8(8))* Turtleback.
—I Pledge Allegiance. 2011. 183p. (YA). *(978-0-545-38415-5(X))* Scholastic, Inc.
—I Pledge Allegiance. 2013. (Vietnam Ser.: 1). lib. bdg. 17.20 *(978-0-606-31961-4(1))* Turtleback.
—The Right Fight. 2014. 189p. (YA). *(978-0-545-63728-2(7)*, Scholastic Pr.) Scholastic, Inc.
—Sharpshooter. 2012. (J). *(978-0-545-43650-2(8)*, Scholastic Pr.);2. (Vietnam Ser.: 2). (ENG.). 192p. (gr. 6-8). 22.44 *(978-0-545-27026-7(X))* Scholastic, Inc.
—Sharpshooter. 2013. (Vietnam Ser.: 2). lib. bdg. 18.40 *(978-0-606-31962-1(X))* Turtleback.
Maddox, Joseph & Maddox, Diana. See You in Hell. 2004. 215p. (YA). pap. 14.95 *(978-0-7414-1872-2(X))* Infinity Publishing.
Mann, J. Albert. Scar: A Revolutionary War Tale. 2016. (ENG.). 144p. (J). (gr. 4-7). 17.99 *(978-1-62979-465-5(1)*, Calkins Creek) Highlights Pr., c/o Highlights for Children, Inc.
Manning, Matthew K. Go Slow. Lima, Dijo & Furuzono, Carlos, illus. 2016. (EOD Soldiers Ser.). (ENG.). 40p. (J). (gr. 4-8). lib. bdg. 26.65 *(978-1-4965-3109-4(4)*, 132175, Stone Arch Bks.) Capstone.
—The List. Lima, Rico et al, illus. 2016. (EOD Soldiers Ser.). (ENG.). 40p. (J). (gr. 4-8). lib. bdg. 26.65 *(978-1-4965-3110-0(8)*, 132176, Stone Arch Bks.) Capstone.
—The Mist. Lima, Rico & Bello, Thiago Dal, illus. 2016. (EOD Soldiers Ser.). (ENG.). 40p. (J). (gr. 4-8). lib. bdg. 26.65 *(978-1-4965-3108-7(6)*, 132174, Stone Arch Bks.) Capstone.
—Two Sides. Lima, Dijo & Furuzono, Carlos, illus. 2016. (EOD Soldiers Ser.). (ENG.). 40p. (J). (gr. 4-8). lib. bdg. 26.65 *(978-1-4965-3107-0(8)*, 132173, Stone Arch Bks.) Capstone.
—U. S. Special Forces: Ghosts of the Night. Enecio, Jeremy, illus. 2016. (U. S. Special Ops Ser.). (ENG.). 96p. (J). (gr. 3-4). E-Book 31.99 *(978-1-4965-3477-4(8)*, 69904); lib. bdg. 26.65 *(978-1-4965-3475-0(1)*, 132571) Capstone. (Stone Arch Bks.).
Marsden, John. Tomorrow, When the War Began (Tomorrow #1) 2006. (Tomorrow Ser.: 1). (ENG.). 304p. (J). (gr. 7-7). 12.99 *(978-0-439-82910-6(0)*, Scholastic Paperbacks) Scholastic, Inc.
Mason, Prue. Camel Rider. 2007. (ENG.). 208p. (J). (gr. 5-8). 15.95 *(978-1-58089-314-5(7))* Charlesbridge Publishing, Inc.
—Camel Rider. 2011. 9.49 *(978-0-7848-3618-7(3)*, Everbind) Marco Bk. Co.
Matson, Erik. Robobattlepets - Home Invasion. 2012. 144p. pap. 7.99 *(978-0-9841187-6-2(4))* Asteroid Publishing.
Matthews, Dave & Smith, Clete. If We Were Giants. Caparo, Antonio, illus. 2021. 48p. (J). (gr. 3-7). pap. 7.99 *(978-1-368-01869-2(6)*, Disney-Hyperion) Disney Publishing Worldwide.
Matthews, L. S. Fish. 2006. 183p. (gr. 5-9). 16.50 *(978-0-7569-6626-3(4))* Perfection Learning Corp.
Maxwell, Ruth H. Eighteen Roses Red: A Young Girl's Heroic Mission in the Revolutionary War. 2006. (American Revolution Adventures Ser.). 126p. (J). (gr. 3-7). per. 8.95 *(978-1-57249-380-3(1)*, White Mane Kids) White Mane Publishing Co., Inc.
McCormick, Patricia. Purple Heart. 2009. (ENG.). 208p. (YA). (gr. 8-18). 16.99 *(978-0-06-173090-0(4)*, Balzer & Bray) HarperCollins Pubs.
McCutcheon, John. Flowers for Sarajevo, 1 vol. Caldwell, Kristy, illus. 2017. 32p. (J). (gr. 2-5). 19.95 *(978-1-56145-943-8(7))* Peachtree Publishing Co. Inc.
McElroy, Lisa Tucker. Love, Lizzie: Letters to a Military Mom. Paterson, Diane, illus. 2009. (ENG.). 32p. (J). (gr. -1-3). pap. 7.99 *(978-0-8075-4778-6(6)*, 807547786) Whitman, Albert & Co.
McKee, David. Six Men. 2011. (ENG., Illus.). 44p. (J). (gr. -1-3). 16.95 *(978-0-7358-4050-8(4))* North-South Bks., Inc.
McMullan, Kate. Hit the Road, Helen! 2013. (Myth-O-Mania Ser.: Bk. 9). (ENG.). 240p. (J). (gr. 4-8). lib. bdg. 26.65 *(978-1-4342-4990-6(5)*, 122230, Stone Arch Bks.) Capstone.
Mead, Alice. Year of No Rain. 2005. (Illus.). 129p. (gr. 4-7). 15.50 *(978-0-7569-5158-0(5))* Perfection Learning Corp.
Menchen, Antonio Martinez. Fosco. (SPA.). 104p. (YA). (gr. 5-8). *(978-84-204-4101-6(5)*, AF1750) Ediciones Alfaguara ESP. Dist: Lectorum Pubns., Inc.
Merrill, Jean. The Pushcart War. 2006. (J). 1.25 *(978-1-4193-8348-9(5))* Recorded Bks., Inc.
Messner, Kate. D-Day: Battle on the Beach (Ranger in Time #7) McMorris, Kelley, illus. 2018. (Ranger in Time Ser.: 7). (ENG.). 160p. (J). (gr. 2-5). pap. 6.99 *(978-1-338-13390-5(X)*, Scholastic Pr.) Scholastic, Inc.
Mikaelsen, Ben. Tree Girl. 2004. 240p. (J). lib. bdg. 17.89 *(978-0-06-009005-0(7)*, Rayo) HarperCollins Pubs.
Monsters of Men (with Bonus Short Story) Chaos Walking: Book Three. 2014. (Chaos Walking Ser.: 3). (ENG., Illus.). 656p. (YA). (gr. 9). pap. 14.00 *(978-0-7636-7619-3(5))* Candlewick Pr.
Moskowitz, Hannah. A History of Glitter & Blood. 2015. (ENG., Illus.). 280p. (YA). (gr. 9-17). 18.99 *(978-1-4521-2942-6(8))* Chronicle Bks. LLC.
Moverley, Richard. The Reluctant Rajput. Dean, David, illus. 2005. (Yellow Go Bananas Ser.). (ENG.). 48p. (J). (gr. 3-4). lib. bdg. *(978-0-7787-2723-1(8))* Crabtree Publishing Co.
Mull, Brandon. Champion of the Titan Games, vol. 4. 2020. (Dragonwatch Ser.: 4). (ENG., Illus.). 544p. (J). (gr. 5). 19.99 *(978-1-62972-788-2(1)*, 5240661) Deseret Bk. Co.
—Champion of the Titan Games: A Fablehaven Adventure. 2021. (Dragonwatch Ser.: 4). (ENG., Illus.). 544p. (J). (gr. 3-8). pap. 9.99 *(978-1-4814-8508-1(3)*, Aladdin) Simon & Schuster Children's Publishing.
Muller, Seth. The Day of Storms, 3 vols. Dubay, Tayloe, ed. Whitethorne, Bahe, Jr., illus. 2010. (Keepers of the WindClaw Chronicles: Bk. 3). 224p. (J). pap. 12.95 *(978-1-893354-10-4(5))* Salina Bookshelf Inc.
—The Mockingbird's Manual. Tayloe, McConnell Dubay, ed. Whitethorne, Bahe, Jr., illus. 2009. (Keepers of the WindClaw Chronicles: Bk. 1). (ENG.). 128p. (J). (gr. 4-7). pap. 12.95 *(978-1-893354-04-3(0))* Salina Bookshelf Inc.
Myers, Walter Dean. Fallen Angels. 2008. (ENG.). 336p. (J). (gr. 7). pap. 10.99 *(978-0-545-05576-5(8)*, Scholastic Paperbacks) Scholastic, Inc.
—Invasion. (ENG.). 224p. (YA). 2015. (gr. 7). pap. 12.99 *(978-0-545-38429-2(X))* 2013. E-Book *(978-0-545-57659-8(8))* Scholastic, Inc. (Scholastic Pr.).
—Patrol: An American Soldier in Vietnam. Grifalconi, Ann, illus. 2005. (ENG.). 40p. (J). (gr. 3-7). pap. 7.99 *(978-0-06-073159-5(1)*, HarperCollins) HarperCollins Pubs.
—Sunrise over Fallujah. 2011. 9.04 *(978-0-7848-3413-8(X)*, Everbind) Marco Bk. Co.
—Sunrise over Fallujah. 2009. (ENG.). 320p. (J). (gr. 7-12). 10.99 *(978-0-439-91625-7(9)*, Scholastic Pr.) Scholastic, Inc.
—Sunrise over Fallujah. l.t. ed. 2008. 468p. (YA). 23.95 *(978-1-4104-1019-1(6))* Thorndike Pr.
Nilsson, Troy, 2nd. Hiroshima Stones: The Shadow Stones of Hiroshima. Nilsson, Troy, 2nd, illus. 2003. (Illus.). 248p. (YA). pap. 9.95 *(978-0-9724771-0-9(1)*, Nilsson, Troy) Nilsson Media.
North, Julian. Fate of Order: Age of Order Saga Book 3. 2017. (ENG.). 278p. (YA). pap. *(978-0-9992658-1-9(4))* Plebeian Media.
Novel Units. A Separate Peace Novel Units Student Packet. 2019. (ENG.). (J). pap. 13.99 *(978-1-56137-400-7(8)*, Novel Units, Inc.) Classroom Library Co.
—A Separate Peace Novel Units Teacher Guide. 2019. (ENG.). (YA). (gr. 9-12). pap. 12.99 *(978-1-56137-399-4(0)*, BK8553, Novel Units, Inc.) Classroom Library Co.

W X Y Z

Oakes, Colleen. War of the Cards. (Queen of Hearts Ser.: 3). (ENG.). (YA). (gr. 8). 2018. 368p. pap. 9.99 *(978-0-06-240980-5(8))* 2017. 352p. 17.99 *(978-0-06-240979-9(4))* HarperCollins Pubs. (HarperTeen).
O'Hearn, Kate. War of the Realms. (Valkyrie Ser.: 3). (ENG.). 384p. (J). (gr. 4-8). 2019. pap. 8.99 *(978-1-4814-4744-7(0))* 2018. (Illus.). 18.99 *(978-1-4814-4743-0(2))* Simon & Schuster Children's Publishing. (Aladdin).
Onyebuchi, Tochi. War Girls. 2019. (ENG.). 464p. (YA). (gr. 7). 18.99 *(978-0-451-48167-2(4)*, Razorbill) Penguin Young Readers Group.
Optic, Oliver, pseud. Fighting for the Right. 2007. 136p. per. *(978-1-4068-3635-6(4))* Echo Library.
—Stand by the Union. 2007. 140p. (gr. 4-7). per. *(978-1-4068-4345-3(8))* Echo Library.
—A Victorious Union: The Blue & the Gray-Afloat Book 6. 2017. (ENG., Illus.). (J). 24.95 *(978-1-374-97059-5(X))*; pap. 14.95 *(978-1-374-97058-8(1))* Capital Communications, Inc.
—Within the Enemy's Lines. 2007. 132p. (gr. 4-7). per. *(978-1-4068-4348-4(2))* Echo Library.
Orzechowski, Shawneen. Sarah's Secret: Civil War Deserter at Fredericksburg. 2011. 104p. (J). pap. 8.95 *(978-1-57249-400-8(X)*, White Mane Kids) White Mane Publishing Co., Inc.
Osborne, Mary Pope. World at War 1944. Murdocca, Sal, illus. 2017. (Magic Tree House Super Edition Ser.: 1). 208p. (J). (gr. 2-5). 6.99 *(978-0-553-50885-7(7)*, Random Hse. Bks. for Young Readers) Random Hse. Children's Bks.
Pacat, C. S. Kings Rising. 2016. (Captive Prince Trilogy Ser.: 3). (ENG., Illus.). 356p. pap. 17.00 *(978-0-425-27399-9(7)*, Berkley) Penguin Publishing Group.
Palmer, W. G. Awaiting Whisperland: The Calling of Galahad Green. 2007. 340p. 29.95 *(978-0-595-68248-5(0))*; per. 19.95 *(978-0-595-43560-9(2))* iUniverse, Inc.
Parker, Robert. Edenville Owls. 2008. 194p. (gr. 4-6). 18.00 *(978-0-7569-8920-0(5))* Perfection Learning Corp.
Parry, Rosanne. Heart of a Shepherd. 2010. 176p. (J). (gr. 3-7). pap. 7.99 *(978-0-375-84803-2(7)*, Yearling) Random Hse. Children's Bks.
Patton, Jack. The Butterfly Rebellion. 2016. (Battle Bugs Ser.: 9). (ENG., Illus.). 128p. (J). (gr. 2-5). pap. 4.99 *(978-0-545-94515-8(1)*, Scholastic Paperbacks) Scholastic, Inc.
Peet, Mal. Life: an Exploded Diagram. 2018. (ENG.). 400p. (YA). (gr. 9). pap. 10.99 *(978-1-5362-0362-2(9))* Candlewick Pr.
Penning, L. & Nelson, Marietjie. The Hero of Spionkop. 2006. (Illus.). 166p. (YA). pap. *(978-1-894666-92-3(5))* Inheritance Pubns.
—The Lion of Modderspruit. 2004. (Illus.). 142p. (YA). pap. *(978-1-894666-91-6(7))* Inheritance Pubns.
Peyton, Km. Far from Home. 2014. (ENG., Illus.). 183p. (J). (gr. 4-7). pap. 5.99 *(978-0-7945-3292-5(6)*, Usborne) EDC Publishing.
Phillips, Dee. Blast, 1 vol. unabr. ed. 2010. (Right Now! Ser.). (ENG.). 45p. (YA). (gr. 9-12). pap. 10.75 *(978-1-61651-245-3(8))* Saddleback Educational Publishing, Inc.
Pochenko. Conspiracy Prophecy II: WWIII & Rumors of WWIV in Revelation. 2003. 230p. (YA). pap. 14.95 *(978-0-595-26419-3(0)*, Writer's Showcase Pr.) iUniverse, Inc.
Porter, Sarah. The Twice Lost. 2014. (Lost Voices Trilogy Ser.: 3). (ENG.). 480p. (YA). (gr. 7). pap. 9.99 *(978-0-547-48255-2(8)*, 1439698, Clarion Bks.) HarperCollins Pubs.
Pratchett, Terry. Only You Can Save Mankind. 224p. (J). (gr. 3-7). 2006. (Johnny Maxwell Trilogy Ser.: 1). (ENG.). per. 7.99 *(978-0-06-054187-3(3)*, Clarion Bks.) 2005. 15.99 *(978-0-06-054185-9(7))* HarperCollins Pubs.
—Only You Can Save Mankind. 2006. (Johnny Maxwell Trilogy). 207p. (J). (gr. 3-7). 13.65 *(978-0-7569-6933-2(6))* Perfection Learning Corp.
Raether, Erin F. When Auntie Angie Left for Iraq & Remi Came to Stay. 2008. 15p. pap. 24.95 *(978-1-4241-8735-5(4))* America Star Bks.
Ransom, Marty. Our Father, Our Soldier, Our Hero. 2011. 36p. pap. 24.95 *(978-1-4626-1377-9(2))* America Star Bks.
Reedy, Trent. Burning Nation. 2015. 417p. (YA). *(978-0-545-75282-4(5))* Scholastic, Inc.
Reiter, David P. Las Armas de Fuego. Rosales-Martinez, Guadalupe, tr. from ENG. Murphy, Patrick J., illus. 2010. Tr. of Real Guns. (SPA.). 32p. (YA). *(978-1-921479-44-1(2))* Interactive Pubns. Pty, Ltd.
Richards, Elizabeth. Phoenix: A Black City Novel. 2nd ed. 2014. (Black City Novel Ser.: 2). 368p. (YA). (gr. 9). pap. 9.99 *(978-0-14-751137-9(2)*, Speak) Penguin Young Readers Group.
Robertson, William P. & Rimer, David. The Battling Bucktails at Fredericksburg. 2005. (WM Kids Ser.: Vol. 16). (Illus.). 154p. (J). (gr. 4-7). per. 7.95 *(978-1-57249-345-2(3)*, White Mane Kids) White Mane Publishing Co., Inc.
Rogers, Lon. The Between Season. 2009. 280p. 27.95 *(978-1-4401-8370-6(8))* iUniverse, Inc.
Roop, Peter & Roop, Connie. An Eye for an Eye. 2004. 168p. (J). lib. bdg. 16.92 *(978-1-4242-0772-5(X))* Fitzgerald Bks.
Rosoff, Meg. How I Live Now. (ENG.). (YA). (gr. 7). 2013. 208p. pap. 9.99 *(978-0-449-81960-9(4)*, Ember) 2006. 224p. reprint ed. pap. 9.99 *(978-0-553-37605-0(5)*, Lamb, Wendy Bks.) Random Hse. Children's Bks.
Roy, Jennifer & Fadhil, Ali. Playing Atari with Saddam Hussein: Based on a True Story. (ENG.). 176p. (J). (gr. 5-7). 2019. pap. 9.99 *(978-0-358-10882-5(9)*, 1748840) 2018. (Illus.). 16.99 *(978-0-544-78507-6(X)*, 1638613) HarperCollins Pubs. (Clarion Bks.).
Sanderson, Brandon. Calamity. 2016. (Reckoners Ser.: 3). (ENG.). 432p. (YA). (gr. 7-10). 19.99 *(978-0-385-74360-0(2)*, Delacorte Pr.) Random House Publishing Group.
—Firefight. (Reckoners Ser.: 2). (ENG.). (YA). (gr. 7). 2020. 496p. 10.99 *(978-0-593-30713-7(5)*, Delacorte Pr.) 2016. 464p. pap. 11.99 *(978-0-385-74359-4(9)*, Ember) 2015. 432p. 19.99 *(978-0-385-74358-7(0)*, Delacorte Pr.) Random Hse. Children's Bks.
—Firefight. 2016. (Reckoners Ser.: 2). lib. bdg. 22.10 *(978-0-606-38447-6(2))* Turtleback.
—The Reckoners Series Hardcover Boxed Set: Steelheart; Firefight; Calamity, 3 vols. 2016. (Reckoners Ser.). (ENG.). (YA). (gr. 7). 59.97 *(978-0-399-55168-0(9)*, Delacorte Pr.) Random Hse. Children's Bks.
—Steelheart. 2013. 386p. (YA). *(978-0-385-38371-4(1)*, Delacorte Pr) Random House Publishing Group.
—Steelheart. (Reckoners Ser.: 1). (ENG.). (YA). (gr. 7). 2020. 496p. 9.99 *(978-0-593-30712-0(7)*, Delacorte Pr.) 2014. 432p. pap. 11.99 *(978-0-385-74357-0(2)*, Ember) 2013. 400p. 19.99 *(978-0-385-74356-3(4)*, Delacorte Pr.) Random Hse. Children's Bks.
—Steelheart. 2014. (Reckoners Ser.: 1). lib. bdg. 20.85 *(978-0-606-36027-2(1))* Turtleback.
—STEELHEART (TRILOGÍA DE LOS RECKONERS 1) (SPA.). 416p. pap. 27.95 *(978-84-666-5296-4(5))* Ediciones B ESP. Dist: Spanish Pubs., LLC.
—Steelheart(Spanish Edition), Vol. 2. 2021. (Trilogía de Los Reckoners / the Reckoners Ser.: 1). (SPA.). 416p. pap. 14.95 *(978-84-9070-095-2(3))* Ediciones B Mexico MEX. Dist: Penguin Random Hse. LLC.
Savage, J. Scott. Gears of Revolution. 2016. (Mysteries of Cove Ser.: 2). (ENG., Illus.). 352p. (J). (gr. 3-6). 17.99 *(978-1-62972-223-8(5)*, 5155663, Shadow Mountain) Shadow Mountain Publishing.
Scheffler, Stephanie. Elise the Patriot: A Revolutionary War Story. 2008. 108p. 20.95 *(978-0-595-51324-6(7))*; pap. 10.95 *(978-0-595-52582-9(2))* iUniverse, Inc.
Shadow, Jak. The F. E. A. R. Agency. 2006. (F. E. A. R. Adventures S. Ser.). (ENG., Illus.). 80p. (J). 4.00 *(978-1-84046-726-0(6)*, Wizard Books) Icon Bks., Ltd. GBR. Dist: Publishers Group Canada.
Shakespeare, William. Henry V: The Graphic Novel, 1 vol. 2010. (Classic Graphic Novel Collection). (ENG.). 144p. (gr. 7-10). 41.03 *(978-1-4205-0371-5(5)*, 665ec24a-d53b-4f54-8d96-0eb5fcde0627, Lucent Pr.) Greenhaven Publishing LLC.
Sherman, M. Zachary. Blood Brotherhood, 1 vol. Casas, Fritz, illus. 2011. (Bloodlines Ser.). (ENG.). 88p. (J). (gr. 4-8). pap. 6.95 *(978-1-4342-3098-0(8)*, 114738, Stone Arch Bks.) Capstone.
—Fighting Phantoms, 1 vol. Casas, Fritz, illus. 2011. (Bloodlines Ser.). (ENG.). 88p. (J). (gr. 4-8). lib. bdg. 27.32 *(978-1-4342-2560-3(7)*, 113619, Stone Arch Bks.) Capstone.
—Heart of the Enemy, 1 vol. Cage, Josef, illus. 2012. (Bloodlines Ser.). (ENG.). 88p. (J). (gr. 4-8). lib. bdg. 27.32 *(978-1-4342-3767-5(2)*, 117028, Stone Arch Bks.) Capstone.
Singer, Sarah Jane. Two Bullets for Sergeant Franks. 2003. (Illus.). 112p. (YA). pap. 7.99 *(978-0-9721216-9-9(2)*, 0972121692) Computer Classics (R).
Smith, Andrew. Rabbit & Robot. 2018. (ENG., Illus.). 448p. (YA). (gr. 9). 18.99 *(978-1-5344-2220-9(X)*, Simon & Schuster Bks. For Young Readers) Simon & Schuster Bks. For Young Readers.
Smith, Mary P. Wells. The Young Puritans in King Philip's War. Bridgman, L. J., illus. 2011. 396p. 54.95 *(978-1-258-05550-9(3))* Literary Licensing, LLC.
Smith, Melinda. Soldiers for Battle. 2008. 192p. 24.50 *(978-1-60693-398-5(1)*, Eloquent Bks.) Strategic Book Publishing & Rights Agency (SBPRA).
Smucker, Barbara. Nubes Negras. (SPA.). (YA). (gr. 5-8). pap. *(978-84-279-3148-0(4)*, NG3493) Noguer y Caralt Editores, S. A. ESP. Dist: Lectorum Pubns., Inc.
Snyder, Maria V. Dawn Study. 2017. (Chronicles of Ixia Ser.: 9). (ENG.). 480p. pap. 19.99 *(978-0-7783-1985-6(7)*, Mira Bks.) Harlequin Enterprises ULC CAN. Dist: HarperCollins Pubs.
Somper, Justin. Immortal War. 2013. (Vampirates Ser.: 6). (J). lib. bdg. 22.10 *(978-0-606-26696-3(8))* Turtleback.
—Vampirates: Immortal War. 2013. (Vampirates Ser.: 6). (ENG.). 512p. (J). (gr. 3-7). pap. 23.99 *(978-0-316-03325-1(1))* Little, Brown Bks. for Young Readers.
Spillebeen, Geert. Kipling's Choice. 2007. (ENG.). 160p. (YA). (gr. 7-9). pap. 12.95 *(978-0-618-80035-3(2)*, 496440, Clarion Bks.) HarperCollins Pubs.
—Kipling's Choice. Edelstein, Terese, tr. 2007. 147p. (YA). (gr. 7-9). 15.65 *(978-0-7569-8061-0(5))* Perfection Learning Corp.
Spradlin, Michael P. Into the Killing Seas. 2015. (J). (ENG.). 224p. (gr. 3-7). 16.99 *(978-0-545-72602-3(6)*, Scholastic Pr.); 185p. *(978-0-545-83764-4(2))* Scholastic, Inc.
Star Wars Staff & Valois, Rob. Sticker Storyteller. 2008. (Star Wars). (ENG.). 48p. (J). (gr. 1-3). pap. 12.99 *(978-0-448-45058-2(5))* Penguin Publishing Group.
Steele, William O. The Perilous Road: A Newbery Honor Award Winner. 2004. (ENG., Illus.). 176p. (J). (gr. 3-7). 17.00 *(978-0-15-205203-4(8)*, 1195690); pap. 9.99 *(978-0-15-205204-1(6)*, 1195693) HarperCollins Pubs. (Clarion Bks.).
Steinlage, Ben. Bird Boy. 2011. 290p. pap. 17.95 *(978-1-4327-6667-2(8))* Outskirts Pr., Inc.
Stevenson, Robert Louis. The Black Arrow. l.t. ed. 2005. 448p. pap. *(978-1-84637-164-6(3))* Echo Library.
Stewart, E. J. The Lyre Birds. 2008. 214p. pap. 16.95 *(978-0-615-18762-4(5))* Leaf & Vine Bks.
Strang, Herbert. With Marlborough to Malplaquet. 2006. pap. *(978-1-4068-3126-9(3))* Echo Library.
Strasser, Todd. Price of Duty. 2018. (ENG., Illus.). 192p. (YA). (gr. 9). 17.99 *(978-1-4814-9709-1(X)*, Simon & Schuster Bks. For Young Readers) Simon & Schuster Bks. For Young Readers.
—Price of Duty. 2019. (ENG.). 192p. (YA). (gr. 9). pap. 11.99 *(978-1-4814-9710-7(3))* Simon & Schuster, Inc.
Trout, Robert J. Drumbeat: The Story of a Civil War Drummer Boy. 2007. 190p. (J). (gr. 4-9). pap. 12.95 *(978-1-57249-390-2(9)*, White Mane Kids) White Mane Publishing Co., Inc.
Valente, Catherynne M. The Glass Town Game. Green, Rebecca, illus. (ENG.). (J). (gr. 5). 2018. 560p. pap. 9.99 *(978-1-4814-7697-3(1))* 2017. 544p. 17.99 *(978-1-4814-7696-6(3))* McElderry, Margaret K. Bks. (McElderry, Margaret K. Bks.).
—Glass Town Game. 2017. (ENG.). (J). (gr. 5). pap. 12.99 *(978-1-5344-1771-7(0))* Simon & Schuster.
Vaugelade, Anais. The War. Rouffiac, Marie-Christine & Streissguth, Thomas, trs. from FRE. Vaugelade, Anais, illus. 2005. (Picture Bks.). (Illus.). 32p. (J). (gr. k-2). 15.25 *(978-1-57505-562-6(7))* Lerner Publishing Group.
Walker, Alice. Why War Is Never a Good Idea. Vitale, Stefano, illus. 2007. 32p. (J). (gr. -1-3). lib. bdg. 17.89 *(978-0-06-075386-3(2))* HarperCollins Pubs.
Wells, Dan. Ruins. 2014. (Partials Sequence Ser.: 3). (ENG.). 464p. (YA). (gr. 9). 17.99 *(978-0-06-207110-1(6)*, Balzer & Bray) HarperCollins Pubs.
Westerfeld, Scott. Behemoth. Thompson, Keith, illus. (Leviathan Trilogy Ser.). (ENG.). (YA). (gr. 7). 2011. 512p. pap. 14.99 *(978-1-4169-7176-4(9))* 2010. 496p. 18.99 *(978-1-4169-7175-7(0))* Simon Pulse. (Simon Pulse).
—Behemoth. l.t. ed. 2010. (Leviathan Trilogy: Bk. 2). (ENG., Illus.). 540p. 23.99 *(978-1-4104-3066-3(9))* Thorndike Pr.
—Behemoth. 2011. (Leviathan Ser.: 2). lib. bdg. 24.50 *(978-0-606-22407-9(6))* Turtleback.
—Goliath, 8 vols. 2011. (YA). 122.75 *(978-1-4618-0617-2(8))*; 122.75 *(978-1-4618-0614-1(3))*; 305.75 *(978-1-4618-0618-9(6))*; 1.25 *(978-1-4640-3062-8(6))*; 124.75 *(978-1-4618-0613-4(5))* Recorded Bks., Inc.
—Goliath. Thompson, Keith, illus. (Leviathan Trilogy Ser.). (ENG.). (YA). (gr. 7). 2012. 576p. pap. 14.99 *(978-1-4169-7178-8(5))* 2011. 560p. 24.99 *(978-1-4169-7177-1(7))* Simon Pulse. (Simon Pulse).
—Goliath. 2012. (Leviathan Ser.: 3). lib. bdg. 24.50 *(978-0-606-26355-9(1))* Turtleback.
—Leviathan. Thompson, Keith, illus. (Leviathan Trilogy Ser.). (ENG.). (YA). (gr. 7-18). 2010. 464p. pap. 14.99 *(978-1-4169-7174-0(2))* 2009. 448p. 24.99 *(978-1-4169-7173-3(4))* Simon Pulse. (Simon Pulse).
—Leviathan. l.t. ed. 2010. (Leviathan Trilogy: Bk. 1). (ENG.). 525p. 23.95 *(978-1-4104-2572-0(X))* Thorndike Pr.
Wiechman, Kathy Cannon. Like a River: A Civil War Novel. 2015. (ENG.). 336p. (J). (gr. 4-7). 18.99 *(978-1-62979-209-5(8)*, Calkins Creek) Highlights Pr., c/o Highlights for Children, Inc.
Williams, John Joseph. Vak's War. 2013. 102p. (J). pap. *(978-1-78299-323-0(1))* FeedARead.com.
Williams, Mary. Brothers in Hope: The Story of the Lost Boys of Sudan, 1 vol. Christie, R. Gregory, illus. 2013. (ENG.). 40p. (J). (gr. 2-5). 20.95 *(978-1-58430-232-2(1)*, leelowbooks) Lee & Low Bks., Inc.
Wilson, John. Germania. 2008. (ENG., Illus.). 280p. (YA). (gr. 7-18). *(978-1-55470-112-4(0))* Me to We.
Wolf-Morgenländer, Karl. Ragtag. 2009. (ENG.). 240p. (J). (gr. 5-7). 16.00 *(978-0-547-07424-5(7)*, 1041670, Clarion Bks.) HarperCollins Pubs.
Wolfe, Robert Hewitt. The Final Drop: Billy Smith & the Goblins, Book 3. 2020. (Billy Smith & the Goblins Ser.: 3). (ENG., Illus.). 336p. (J). pap. 16.99 *(978-1-68162-618-5(7))*; (YA). 31.99 *(978-1-68162-619-2(5))* Turner Publishing Co.
Wolverton, Barry. Neversink. Nielson, Sam, illus. 2012. xiii, 287p. (J). *(978-0-06-202792-4(1))* Longman Publishing.
Wright, Pauline. Why Did My Dad Go to War? 2008. 48p. pap. 19.49 *(978-1-4343-4677-3(3))* AuthorHouse.
Yancey, Rick. The Infinite Sea. 2015. (5th Wave Ser.: 2). lib. bdg. 22.10 *(978-0-606-38204-5(6))* Turtleback.
—The Infinite Sea: The Second Book of the 5th Wave. 2015. (5th Wave Ser.: 2). (ENG.). 352p. (YA). (gr. 9-12). pap. 12.99 *(978-1-101-99698-0(6)*, Penguin Books) Penguin Young Readers Group.
—The Last Star. 2017. (5th Wave Ser.: 3). lib. bdg. 22.10 *(978-0-606-40098-5(2))* Turtleback.
—The Last Star: The Final Book of the 5th Wave. 2016. (5th Wave Ser.: 3). (ENG.). 352p. (YA). (gr. 9). 18.99 *(978-0-399-16243-5(7)*, G.P. Putnam's Sons Books for Young Readers) Penguin Young Readers Group.
—The 5th Wave. 2015. (5th Wave Ser.: Vol. 1). (ENG.). (YA). (gr. 9). lib. bdg. 21.60 *(978-1-62765-623-8(5))* Perfection Learning Corp.
—The 5th Wave. l.t. ed. 2016. (5th Wave Ser.: 1). 630p. pap. 12.99 *(978-1-59413-981-9(4)*, Large Print Pr.) Thorndike Pr.
—The 5th Wave. 2015. (5th Wave Ser.: 1). lib. bdg. 22.10 *(978-0-606-36640-3(7))*; lib. bdg. 22.10 *(978-0-606-37680-8(1))* Turtleback.
—The 5th Wave: The First Book of the 5th Wave Series. 2015. (5th Wave Ser.: 1). (ENG.). 512p. (YA). (gr. 9). pap. 12.99 *(978-0-14-242583-1(4)*, Penguin Books) Penguin Young Readers Group.
—The 5th Wave Collection, 3 vols. 2017. (5th Wave Ser.). (ENG.). (YA). (gr. 9). pap., pap., pap. 35.97 *(978-0-425-29032-3(8)*, Speak) Penguin Young Readers Group.
Yardi, Robin. The Midnight War of Mateo Martinez. 2018. (ENG.). 184p. (J). (gr. 3-6). pap. 9.99 *(978-1-5415-1483-6(1)*, db266dd5-e965-4980-9ce2-73d5fa151b04, Carolrhoda Bks.) Lerner Publishing Group.
Young, Adrienne. Sky in the Deep. (Sky & Sea Ser.: 1). (ENG.). (YA). 2019. 368p. pap. 11.99 *(978-1-250-16846-7(5)*, 900187700) 2018. 352p. 18.99 *(978-1-250-16845-0(7)*, 900187699) St. Martin's Pr. (Wednesday Bks.).
—Sky in the Deep. l.t. ed. 2020. (Sky & Sea Ser.: 1). (ENG.). lib. bdg. 22.99 *(978-1-4328-7818-4(2))* Thorndike Pr.
Zerfing, Robert A. The Silencer: A U. N. Conspiracy Novel. 2nd ed. 2003. 326p. (YA). per. 14.95 *(978-0-9747881-0-4(4))* Clawfoot Publishing.

WAR CORRESPONDENTS

see Reporters and Reporting

WAR CRIME TRIALS

Kacer, Kathy. To Look a Nazi in the Eye: A Teen's Account of a War Criminal Trial, 1 vol. 2017. (ENG., Illus.). 240p. (YA). (gr. 9-13). pap. 13.95 *(978-1-77260-040-7(7))* Second Story Pr. CAN. Dist: Orca Bk. Pubs. USA.
Sachs, Ruth. Adolf Eichmann: Engineer of Death. 2009. (Holocaust Biographies Ser.). 112p. (gr. 7-12). 63.90 *(978-1-61513-380-2(1))* Rosen Publishing Group, Inc., The.

WAR OF 1812

see United States—History—War of 1812

WAR OF 1914

see World War, 1914-1918

WAR OF 1939-1945

see World War, 1939-1945

WAR OF SECESSION, U.S., 1861-1865

see United States—History—Civil War, 1861-1865

WAR OF THE AMERICAN REVOLUTION

see United States—History—Revolution, 1775-1783

WAR POETRY

Dieterman, Nicole. A Child's View of War: A Collection of Poems by Nicole Dieterman. 2003. mass mkt. 12.95 *(978-0-9742472-0-5(0))* Pleiness Publishing.
Greenfield, Eloise. When the Horses Ride By: Children in the Times of War, 1 vol. Gilchrist, Jan Spivey, illus. 2006. (ENG.) 40p. (J). (gr. 2-6). pap. 14.95 *(978-1-60060-454-6(4)*, leelowbooks); (gr. 4-7). 17.95 *(978-1-58430-249-0(6))* Lee & Low Bks., Inc.
Wade, Stephen. The War Poets: The Secrets of Poems from the Great War. 2003. (Studymates Ser.). (ENG., Illus.). 128p. pap. 27.50 *(978-1-84285-030-5(X))* GLMP Ltd. GBR. Dist: Chicago Distribution Ctr.

WAR SHIPS

see Warships

WARFARE, SUBMARINE

see Submarine Warfare

WARLOCKS

see Witches; Wizards

WARREN, EARL, 1891-1974

Branscomb, Leslie Wolf. Earl Warren. 2011. (Supreme Court Justices Ser.). (Illus.). 112p. 28.95 *(978-1-59935-158-2(7))* Reynolds, Morgan Inc.

WARS

see Military History; Naval History; War

WARSAW (POLAND)

Beyer, Mark. Emmanuel Ringelblum: Historian of the Warsaw Ghetto. 2009. (Holocaust Biographies Ser.). 112p. (gr. 7-12). 63.90 *(978-1-61513-384-0(4))* Rosen Publishing Group, Inc., The.
Brophy Down, Susan. Irena Sendler: Bringing Life to Children of the Holocaust. 2012. (ENG.). 112p. (J). pap. *(978-0-7787-2556-5(1))*; (Illus.). *(978-0-7787-2553-4(7))* Crabtree Publishing Co.
Callahan, Kerry P. Mordechai Anielewicz: Hero of the Warsaw Ghetto Uprising. 2009. (Holocaust Biographies Ser.). 112p. (gr. 7-12). 63.90 *(978-1-61513-389-5(5))* Rosen Publishing Group, Inc., The.
Freedman, Jeri. The Warsaw Ghetto & Uprising, 1 vol. 2014. (Documentary History of the Holocaust Ser.). (ENG.). 80p. (YA). (gr. 7-7). 37.47 *(978-1-4777-7605-6(2)*, 0d8ae687-16a1-4b29-bdca-8131f389d9f6) Rosen Publishing Group, Inc., The.
Greenspan, Judy. Irena Sendler: Get to Know the World War II Rescuer. 2019. (People You Should Know Ser.). (ENG., Illus.). 32p. (J). (gr. 3-6). pap. 7.95 *(978-1-5435-7465-4(3)*, 140905); lib. bdg. 29.99 *(978-1-5435-7183-7(2)*, 140434) Capstone.
Jacobs Altman, Linda. The Warsaw Ghetto Uprising: Striking a Blow Against the Nazis, 1 vol. 2012. (Holocaust Through Primary Sources Ser.). (ENG., Illus.). 128p. (gr. 6-7). pap. 13.88 *(978-1-59845-347-8(5)*, 4cf23899-8f03-417e-a3d3-9527718511a7); lib. bdg. 35.93 *(978-0-7660-3320-7(1)*, 410c3b67-7f83-48a7-b9cb-5af796e0193f) Enslow Publishing, LLC.
Spielman, Gloria. Janusz Korczak's Children. Archambault, Matthew, illus. 2007. (Kar-Ben for Older Readers Ser.). (ENG.). 40p. (J). (gr. 3-7). lib. bdg. 17.95 *(978-1-58013-255-8(3)*, Kar-Ben Publishing) Lerner Publishing Group.
Vaughan, Marcia. Irena's Jars of Secrets, 1 vol. Mazellan, Ron, illus. 2011. (ENG.). 40p. (J). 18.95 *(978-1-60060-439-3(0))* Lee & Low Bks., Inc.

WARSAW (POLAND)—FICTION

Dalager, Stig. David's Story. 2010. (ENG., Illus.). 280p. (J). (gr. 10). pap. 16.99 *(978-1-906582-04-3(1))* Aurora Metro Pubns. Ltd. GBR. Dist: Publishers Group West (PGW).
Orlev, Uri. Run, Boy, Run. 10th ed. 2007. (ENG.). 192p. (YA). (gr. 5-18). 7.99 *(978-0-618-95706-4(5)*, 1021443, Clarion Bks.) HarperCollins Pubs.
Spinelli, Jerry. Milkweed. 2010. (ENG.). 240p. (YA). (gr. 7). pap. 10.99 *(978-0-375-86147-5(5)*, Ember) Random Hse. Children's Bks.

WARSHIPS

see also Aircraft Carriers; Submarines (Ships)
also names of countries with the subhead Navy (e.g. United States—Navy)

Adams, Simon. Warships. 2009. (War Machines Ser.). (YA). (gr. 5-9). 28.50 *(978-1-59920-225-9(5))* Black Rabbit Bks.
Alpert, Barbara. Military Ships. 2012. (Military Machines Ser.). (ENG.). 24p. (gr. k-1). pap. 41.70 *(978-1-4296-8316-6(3)*, Capstone Pr.) Capstone.
Alvarez, Carlos. Arleigh Burke Destroyers. 2010. (Military Machines Ser.). (ENG., Illus.). 24p. (J). (gr. 3-7). lib. bdg. 26.95 *(978-1-60014-331-1(8))* Bellwether Media.
—Ticonderoga Cruisers. 2010. (Military Machines Ser.). (ENG., Illus.). 24p. (J). (gr. 3-7). lib. bdg. 26.95 *(978-1-60014-321-2(0))* Bellwether Media.
Barton, Chris. Dazzle Ships: World War I & the Art of Confusion. Ngai, Victo, illus. 2017. (ENG.). 36p. (J). (gr. 2-5). lib. bdg. 19.99 *(978-1-5124-1014-3(4)*, f606e87d-56aa-4cff-b87c-c59ad06e0b83, Millbrook Pr.) Lerner Publishing Group.
Bodden, Valerie. Battleships. 2012. (J). 25.65 *(978-1-60818-124-7(3)*, Creative Education) Creative Co., The.
Boutland, Craig. Attack Vehicles at Sea: Ships, Submarines, & Patrol Boats. 2019. (Military Machines in the War on Terrorism Ser.). (ENG., Illus.). 32p. (J). (gr. 3-9). lib. bdg. 28.65 *(978-1-5435-7381-7(9)*, 140670) Capstone.
Brook, Henry. Warships IR. 2012. (Discovery Adventures Ser.). 80p. (J). pap. 8.99 *(978-0-7945-3289-5(6)*, Usborne) EDC Publishing.
Cohn, Jessica. Military Machines, 1 vol. 2013. (Machines in Motion Ser.). 48p. (J). (gr. 3-3). (ENG.). pap. 15.05 *(978-1-4339-9605-4(7)*, be9e9466-a0fb-4133-90ce-0e6fa7147cdd); pap. 84.30 *(978-1-4339-9606-1(5))*; (ENG., Illus.). lib. bdg. 34.61 *(978-1-4339-9604-7(9)*, 5d11d558-1934-40ca-a0e1-e03398e71ffc) Stevens, Gareth Publishing LLLP.

Polson, Rob Scott. Warships, 1 vol. 2013. (Ultimate Machines Ser.). (ENG., Illus.). 24p. (J). (gr. 5-5). pap. 9.25 *(978-1-4777-0113-3(3),* 302adbb7-370a-4a59-8c8e-185630247e2c); lib. bdg. 26.27 *(978-1-4777-0064-8(1),* aa254728-7983-4f7a-b760-8be997dd08c2) Rosen Publishing Group, Inc., The. (PowerKids Pr.).

Cooke, Tim. Warships. 2012. (Ultimate Military Machines Ser.). (Illus.). 32p. (gr. 4-7). lib. bdg. 31.35 *(978-1-59920-824-4(5))* Black Rabbit Bks.

Curley, Robert, ed. War at Sea & in the Air, 4 vols. 2011. (Britannica Guide to War Ser.). (ENG.). 200p. (YA). (gr. 10-10). 77.64 *(978-1-61530-798-2(2),* c4de5df6-cdd9-40c1-bdbc-76b007752164) Rosen Publishing Group, Inc., The.

Dartford, Mark. Warships. 2003. (Military Hardware in Action Ser.). (ENG., Illus.). 48p. (gr. 5-9). lib. bdg. 25.26 *(978-0-8225-4703-7(1))* Lerner Publishing Group.

Dell, Pamela & Delmar, Pete. The Science of Military Vehicles, 1 vol. 2012. (Science of War Ser.). (ENG., Illus.). 48p. (J). (gr. 6-9). pap. 9.10 *(978-0-7565-4525-3(0),* 1337566, Compass Point Bks.) Capstone.

Delmar, Pete. Vehicles of the Civil War, 1 vol. 2013. (War Vehicles Ser.). (ENG.). 32p. (J). (gr. 3-9). 28.65 *(978-1-4296-9912-9(4),* 120625, Capstone Pr.) Capstone.

Doman, Mary Kate. Big Military Machines, 1 vol. 2011. (All about Big Machines Ser.). (ENG., Illus.). 24p. (gr. -1-1). pap. 10.35 *(978-1-59845-243-3(6),* 13847093-d60d-4a47-bd72-f54ea6741012, Enslow Publishing) Enslow Publishing, LLC.

Dougherty, Martin J. Modern Warships up Close, 1 vol., 1. Pearson, Colin, illus. 2015. (Military Technology: Top Secret Clearance Ser.). (ENG.). 224p. (YA). (gr. 7-8). 46.80 *(978-1-5081-7084-6(3),* 0756c2e6-a9ad-461f-9d16-aa0462c7dfce, Rosen Young Adult) Rosen Publishing Group, Inc., The.

—Sea Warfare, 1 vol. 2010. (Modern Warfare Ser.). (ENG., Illus.). 32p. (J). (gr. 3-5). lib. bdg. 28.67 *(978-1-4339-2734-8(9),* 45af19c0-ebb4-47bd-acbf-dcc391772edf) Stevens, Gareth Publishing LLLP.

Fighting Ships. 2003. (Illus.). 32p. (YA). pap. *(978-1-904516-33-0(5),* Pavilion Children's Books) Pavilion Bks.

Finn, Denny Von. Arleigh Burke Destroyers. 2014. (Military Vehicles Ser.). (ENG., Illus.). 24p. (J). (gr. 3-7). lib. bdg. 26.95 *(978-1-62617-080-3(0),* Epic Bks.) Bellwether Media.

Garstecki, Julia. Embarcaciones Militares. 2017. (Tecnología Militar Ser.). (SPA., Illus.). 32p. (J). (gr. 4-6). lib. bdg. *(978-1-68072-583-4(1),* 10591, Bolt) Black Rabbit Bks.

—Military Ships. 2017. (Military Tech Ser.). (ENG., Illus.). 32p. (J). (gr. 4-6). lib. bdg. *(978-1-68072-166-9(6),* 10516, Bolt) Black Rabbit Bks.

Green, Phillip. Littoral Combat Ships. 2011. (Military Machines Ser.). (ENG., Illus.). 24p. (J). (gr. 3-7). lib. bdg. 26.95 *(978-1-60014-580-3(9),* Torque Bks.) Bellwether Media.

Hale, Nathan. Nathan Hale's Hazardous Tales: Big Bad Ironclad! 2012. (Nathan Hale's Hazardous Tales Ser.). (ENG., Illus.). 128p. (J). (gr. 3-7). 14.99 *(978-1-4197-0395-9(1),* 1000001, Amulet Bks.) Abrams, Inc.

Jackson, Kay. Navy Ships in Action. 2009. (Amazing Military Vehicles Ser.). 24p. (gr. 3-3). 42.50 *(978-1-61511-321-7(5),* PowerKids Pr.); (ENG.). (YA). lib. bdg. 26.27 *(978-1-4358-2750-9(3),* 523d6f08-b4d1-43dc-99e5-2bb597717ec3); (ENG., Illus.). (J). pap. 9.25 *(978-1-4358-3160-5(8),* 5d5e7e6c-4d00-4310-94b9-fa0d804c174b, PowerKids Pr.) Rosen Publishing Group, Inc., The.

Jackson, Robert. Warships: Inside & Out, 1 vol. 2011. (Weapons of War Ser.). (ENG.). 160p. (YA). (gr. 7-7). lib. bdg. 47.80 *(978-1-4488-5981-8(6),* c11a3e72-39e6-4e1c-8360-f45fbdc25aeb) Rosen Publishing Group, Inc., The.

Ku Rhee, Helena. The Turtle Ship, 1 vol. Kong-Savage, Colleen, illus. 2018. (ENG.). 32p. (J). (gr. k-2). 19.95 *(978-1-885008-90-9(2),* leelowshens, Shen's Bks.) Lee & Low Bks., Inc.

Marsico, Katie. A a True Book - Engineering Wonders (NEW SUBSET): Warships. 2016. (True Book(tm) — Engineering Wonders Ser.). (ENG., Illus.). 48p. (J). pap. 6.95 *(978-0-531-22274-4(8),* Children's Pr.) Scholastic Library Publishing.

Mavrikis, Peter. Battleships, 1 vol., 1. 2015. (What's Inside? Ser.). (ENG.). 48p. (J). (gr. 3-4). pap. 12.75 *(978-1-5081-4603-2(9),* 379da148-d3e3-4201-8f17-e490b7ec05a0, PowerKids Pr.) Rosen Publishing Group, Inc., The.

—Battleships & Aircraft Carriers. 2014. (Illus.). 48p. (J). *(978-1-4351-5367-7(7))* Barnes & Noble, Inc.

—Classic Warships. 2014. (Illus.). 48p. (J). *(978-1-4351-5368-4(5))* Barnes & Noble, Inc.

—Classic Warships, 1 vol., 1. 2015. (What's Inside? Ser.). (ENG.). 48p. (J). (gr. 3-4). pap. 12.75 *(978-1-5081-4607-0(1),* e27a33e8-4aa1-4e26-b62d-bda371e8f20a, PowerKids Pr.) Rosen Publishing Group, Inc., The.

Meister, Cari. Totally Amazing Facts about Military Sea & Air Vehicles. 2017. (Mind Benders Ser.). (ENG., Illus.). 112p. (J). (gr. 3-6). lib. bdg. 23.99 *(978-1-5157-4526-6(0),* 134242, Capstone Pr.) Capstone.

Mighty Military Machines, 12 vols. 2014. (Mighty Military Machines Ser.). (ENG.). 32p. (J). (gr. 1-1). lib. bdg. 161.58 *(978-1-4824-1649-7(2),* 3b196470-0e28-407f-9aa8-79f6d010a63e) Stevens, Gareth Publishing LLLP.

Miles, John C. Fighting Forces of World War II at Sea. 2019. (Fighting Forces of World War II Ser.). (ENG., Illus.). 32p. (J). (gr. 3-9). lib. bdg. 28.65 *(978-1-5435-7481-4(5),* 141002) Capstone.

Mueller, Richard. Naval Warfare of the Future. (Library of Future Weaponry Ser.). 64p. (gr. 6-6). 2009. 58.50 *(978-1-60853-640-5(8))* 2006. (ENG., Illus.). (J). lib. bdg. 37.13 *(978-1-4042-0526-0(8),* 79362953-5812-48a5-999a-e68a85d71840) Rosen Publishing Group, Inc., The.

Parker, Steve. Military Machines. 2010. (How It Works Ser.). 40p. (J). (gr. 3-18). lib. bdg. 19.95 *(978-1-4222-1797-9(3))* Mason Crest.

Riggs, Kate. Battleships. 2016. (Seedlings Ser.). (ENG., Illus.). 24p. (J). (gr. k-2). pap. 8.99 *(978-1-62832-245-3(4),* 20519, Creative Paperbacks); (gr. -1-k). 28.50 *(978-1-60818-660-0(1),* 20521, Creative Education) Creative Co., The.

Ross, David. The World's Most Powerful Battleships, 1 vol. 2016. (World's Most Powerful Machines Ser.). (ENG., Illus.). 224p. (J). (gr. 9-9). 46.80 *(978-1-4994-6598-3(X),* 3655d8a3-d6fc-4ac8-aa1c-521122d2fa33) Rosen Publishing Group, Inc., The.

Scheff, Matt. Destroyers: A 4D Book. 2018. (Mighty Military Machines Ser.). (ENG., Illus.). 24p. (J). (gr. -1-2). lib. bdg. 24.65 *(978-1-9771-0110-5(0),* 138301, Pebble) Capstone.

Stark, William N. Mighty Military Ships. 2016. (Military Machines on Duty Ser.). (ENG., Illus.). 24p. (J). (gr. 1-3). lib. bdg. 27.99 *(978-1-4914-8846-1(8),* 131473, Capstone Pr.) Capstone.

Stone, Lynn M. Battleships. 2005. (Fighting Forces Ser.). (Illus.). 32p. (J). (gr. 4-8). lib. bdg. 19.95 *(978-1-59515-461-3(2),* 1244403) Rourke Educational Media.

West, David. Modern Warships & Submarines, 1 vol. Pang, Alex, illus. 2011. (Machines Close-Up Ser.). (ENG.). 32p. (gr. 4-4). 31.21 *(978-1-60870-110-0(7),* 4bec0be5-c9bd-4986-8690-2b3f3a283437) Cavendish Square Publishing LLC.

—Warships. West, David, illus. 2019. (War Machines Ser.). (ENG., Illus.). 32p. (J). (gr. 5-6). pap. *(978-0-7787-6685-8(3),* 7ceed681-b56c-4161-b08c-b4c7052b13ee); lib. bdg. *(978-0-7787-6678-0(0),* ad024fd2-1862-41fb-aa20-de2e16f1906a) Crabtree Publishing Co.

Zuehlke, Jeffrey. Warships. 2005. (Pull Ahead Books — Mighty Movers Ser.). (ENG., Illus.). 32p. (J). (gr. k-3). per. 7.99 *(978-0-8225-2906-4(8),* 229b3389-84ef-4536-905f-faefd21acd3c, First Avenue Editions) Lerner Publishing Group.

101 Great Warships, 1 vol. 2010. (101 Greatest Weapons of All Times Ser.). (ENG., Illus.). 112p. (YA). (gr. 10-10). lib. bdg. 39.80 *(978-1-4358-3596-2(4),* 2547f3cf-7a4d-4c99-ae64-1fa789705d29) Rosen Publishing Group, Inc., The.

WARSHIPS—FICTION

Appleton, Victor. Tom Swift & His Aerial Warship or the. 2006. pap. *(978-1-4065-0894-9(2))* Dodo Pr.

—Tom Swift & His Aerial Warship or the Naval Terror of the Seas. 2005. reprint ed. pap. 24.95 *(978-0-7661-9446-5(9))* Kessinger Publishing, LLC.

—The Tom Swift Omnibus #6: Tom Swift & His Giant Cannon, Tom Swift & His Photo Telephone, Tom Swift & His Aerial Warship. 2007. 296p. per. 12.99 *(978-1-60459-108-0(0))* Wilder Pubns., Corp.

WASHINGTON, BOOKER T., 1856-1915

Asim, Jabari. Fifty Cents & a Dream: Young Booker T. Washington. 2012. (ENG., Illus.). 48p. (J). (gr. -1-3). 18.99 *(978-0-316-08657-8(6))* Little, Brown Bks. for Young Readers.

Braun, Eric. Booker T. Washington: Great American Educator, 1 vol. Martin, Cynthia, illus. 2006. (Graphic Biographies Ser.). (ENG.). 32p. (J). (gr. 3-9). per. 8.10 *(978-0-7368-6190-8(4),* 87896, Capstone Pr.) Capstone.

Brimner, Larry Dane. Booker T. Washington: Getting into the Schoolhouse, 1 vol. 2009. (American Heroes Ser.). (ENG.). 48p. (gr. 3-3). lib. bdg. 32.64 *(978-0-7614-3063-6(6),* 03eab1a3-95bb-48ec-8714-ed0c9c2df0d3) Cavendish Square Publishing LLC.

Buckley, James. Who Was Booker T. Washington? 2019. (Who HQ Ser.). (ENG.). 108p. (J). (gr. 2-3). 16.36 *(978-1-64310-858-2(1))* Penworthy Co., LLC, The.

—Who Was Booker T. Washington? 2018. (Who Was...? Ser.). lib. bdg. 16.00 *(978-0-606-40896-7(7))* Turtleback.

Buckley, James & Who HQ. Who Was Booker T. Washington? Murray, Jake, illus. 2018. (Who Was? Ser.). 112p. (J). (gr. 3-7). 5.99 *(978-0-448-48851-6(5),* Penguin Workshop) Penguin Young Readers Group.

Haldy, Emma E. Booker T. Washington. Bane, Jeff, illus. 2016. (My Early Library: My Itty-Bitty Bio Ser.). (ENG.). 24p. (J). (gr. k-1). 30.64 *(978-1-63471-018-3(5),* 208152) Cherry Lake Publishing.

Hurt, Avery Elizabeth. Booker T. Washington: Civil Rights Leader & Education Advocate, 1 vol. 2019. (African American Trailblazers Ser.). (ENG.). 128p. (gr. 9-9). pap. 22.16 *(978-1-5026-4557-9(2),* 40dea83a-65cc-4a3c-87e7-9270ea1546b1) Cavendish Square Publishing LLC.

Levy, Janey. Booker T. Washington, 1 vol. 2020. (Heroes of Black History Ser.). (ENG.). 32p. (gr. 3-4). pap. 11.50 *(978-1-5382-5806-4(4),* 0ce043d7-55d6-4c42-a43a-0b95eb487076) Stevens, Gareth Publishing LLLP.

Mckissack, Patricia & Mckissack, Fredrick. Booker T. Washington: African-American Leader, 1 vol. 2013. (Famous African Americans Ser.). (ENG.). 24p. (gr. 1-2). pap. 10.35 *(978-1-4644-0194-7(2),* 1d182b7d-f75f-4ef5-9aa4-31409abd86db); (Illus.). lib. bdg. 25.27 *(978-0-7660-4100-4(X),* 9bdb3866-8eb0-4af7-8822-47fe7ad84434) Enslow Publishing, LLC. (Enslow Elementary).

Slade, Suzanne. With Books & Bricks: How Booker T. Washington Built a School. Tadgell, Nicole, illus. 2014. (ENG.). 32p. (J). (gr. -1-3). 17.99 *(978-0-8075-0897-8(7),* 807508977) Whitman, Albert & Co.

Whiting, Jim. Booker T. Washington. 2010. (Transcending Race in America Ser.). (Illus.). 64p. (YA). (gr. 4-8). lib. bdg. 22.95 *(978-1-4222-1608-8(X))* Mason Crest.

Wukovits, John F. Booker T. Washington & Education, 1 vol. 2008. (Lucent Library of Black History Ser.). (ENG., Illus.). 112p. (gr. 7-7). 41.03 *(978-1-4205-0052-3(X),* aaded95a-09c2-43f7-83c5-a6e173afeb7c, Lucent Pr.) Greenhaven Publishing LLC.

WASHINGTON, GEORGE, 1732-1799

Abbey, Jed. The Life of George Washington, 1 vol. 2012. (InfoMax Readers Ser.). (ENG., Illus.). 24p. (J). (gr. 1-1). pap. 8.25 *(978-1-4488-8986-0(3),* 7d07b071-19ae-41e8-9060-ff114c5e7394, Rosen Classroom) Rosen Publishing Group, Inc., The.

Abnett, Dan. George Washington & the American Revolution. (Jr. Graphic Biographies Ser.). (ENG.). 24p. (gr. 2-3). 2009. (J). 47.90 *(978-1-61513-813-5(7),* PowerKids Pr.) 2006. (Illus.). (J). lib. bdg. 28.93 *(978-1-4042-3395-9(4),* f5ebb962-806c-4e30-beef-2ed75efa306a) 2006. (Illus.). pap. 10.60 *(978-1-4042-2148-2(4),* 27420dd3-e201-4cdf-8332-ff4d4b4b3df1, PowerKids Pr.) Rosen Publishing Group, Inc., The.

—George Washington y la Guerra de Independencia, 1 vol. 2009. (Historietas Juveniles: Biografías (Jr. Graphic Biographies) Ser.). (SPA., Illus.). 24p. (gr. 2-3). pap. 10.60 *(978-1-4358-3322-7(8),* a38fe106-c9b7-4c5c-9508-fd86a6c2150a); (YA). 28.93 *(978-1-4358-8564-6(3),* 97102909-4df6-44a2-b6ce-f4870ffe0e02) Rosen Publishing Group, Inc., The.

Abraham, Philip. How to Draw the Life & Times of George Washington. (Kid's Guide to Drawing the Presidents of the United States of America Ser.). 32p. (gr. 4-4). 2009. 50.50 *(978-1-61511-140-4(9),* PowerKids Pr.) 2005. (ENG., Illus.). (YA). 30.27 *(978-1-4042-2978-5(7),* 01f6367d-53e7-4aef-af91-e848c1d203e7) Rosen Publishing Group, Inc., The.

Abraham, Philip & Turner, Cherie. How to Draw the Life & Times of George Washington, 1 vol. 2004. (Extreme Careers Ser.). (ENG.). 64p. (YA). (gr. 5-5). lib. bdg. 37.13 *(978-1-4042-0364-8(8),* 2d865cf3-8843-4031-8a7f-f27328c5456a, PowerKids Pr.) Rosen Publishing Group, Inc., The.

Adler, David A. A Parade for George Washington. O'Brien, John, illus. 2020. 32p. (J). (gr. -1-3). 17.99 *(978-0-8234-4252-2(7))* Holiday Hse., Inc.

—A Picture Book of George Washington. Wallner, John & Wallner, Alexandra, illus. 2018. (Picture Book Biography Ser.). 32p. (J). (gr. -1-3). pap. 7.99 *(978-0-8234-4059-7(1))* Holiday Hse., Inc.

Albee, Sarah. George Washington: The First President. Ko, Chin, illus. 2017. (I Can Read Level 2 Ser.). 32p. (J). (ENG.). (gr. -1-3). pap. 4.99 *(978-0-06-243266-7(4),* HarperCollins); *(978-1-5182-5283-9(4))* HarperCollins Pubs.

—George Washington: the First President. Ko, Chin, illus. 2017. (I Can Read Level 2 Ser.). (ENG.). 32p. (J). (gr. -1-3). 16.99 *(978-0-06-243267-4(2),* HarperCollins) HarperCollins Pubs.

Allen, Thomas B. George Washington, Spymaster: How the Americans Outspied the British & Won the Revolutionary War. 2007. (Illus.). 192p. (J). (gr. 5-9). per. 7.95 *(978-1-4263-0041-7(7),* National Geographic Kids) Disney Publishing Worldwide.

—Remember Valley Forge: Patriots, Tories, & Redcoats Tell Their Stories. 2015. (Illus.). 64p. (J). (gr. 5-9). pap. 7.99 *(978-1-4263-2250-1(X),* National Geographic Kids) Disney Publishing Worldwide.

Armentrout, David & Armentrout, Patricia. George Washington. 2004. (Discover the Life of an American Legend Ser.). (Illus.). 24p. (J). (gr. 2-5). 20.64 *(978-1-58952-662-4(7))* Rourke Educational Media.

Baldwin, James. Four Great Americans. 2006. pap. *(978-1-4065-0509-2(9))* Dodo Pr.

—Four Great Americans: Washington Franklin Webster Lincoln: a Book for Young Americans. 2017. (ENG., Illus.). (J). (gr. 3-7). 23.95 *(978-1-374-89694-9(2));* pap. 13.95 *(978-1-374-89693-2(4))* Capital Communications, Inc.

—Four Great Americans: Washington, Franklin, Webster, Lincoln. a Book for Young Americans. 2017. (ENG., Illus.). (J). (gr. 3-7). pap. *(978-0-649-58735-3(9))* Trieste Publishing Pty Ltd.

Benchmark Education Company. George Washington & the American Revolution (Teacher Guide) 2005. *(978-1-4108-4681-5(4))* Benchmark Education Co.

Biskup, Agnieszka. George Washington: The Rise of America's First President, 1 vol. Mallea, Cristian & Mallea, Cristian, illus. 2012. (American Graphic Ser.). (ENG.). 32p. (J). (gr. 3-9). lib. bdg. 31.32 *(978-1-4296-8621-1(9),* 118642) Capstone.

Botones para el General Washington (Buttons for General Washington) 2006. (J). pap. 6.95 *(978-0-8225-6617-5(6),* Ediciones Lerner) Lerner Publishing Group.

Boyd, Bentley. George Washington Leads the Way. 2011. (Mount Vernon Comix Ser.). (Illus.). 24p. (J). (gr. 3-9). pap. 6.95 *(978-1-933122-44-1(7))* Chester Comix, LLC.

Brannon, Barbara. Discover George Washington. 2005. (J). pap. *(978-1-4108-5158-1(3))* Benchmark Education Co.

Britton, Tamara L. George Washington, 1 vol. (United States Presidents *2017 Ser.). (ENG., Illus.). 40p. (J). 2016. (gr. 2-5). lib. bdg. 35.64 *(978-1-68078-122-9(7),* 21861, Big Buddy Bks.) 2009. (gr. 3-6). 34.21 *(978-1-60453-479-5(6),* 15121, Checkerboard Library) ABDO Publishing Co.

Carr, Aaron. Washington Monument. 2013. (J). *(978-1-62127-205-2(2));* pap. *(978-1-62127-209-0(5))* Weigl Pubs., Inc.

Castrovilla, Selene. Revolutionary Friends: General George Washington & the Marquis de Lafayette. Kozjan, Drazen, illus. 2013. (ENG.). 40p. (J). (gr. 2-5). 16.99 *(978-1-59078-880-6(X),* Calkins Creek) Highlights Pr., c/o Highlights for Children, Inc.

Chandra, Deborah & Comora, Madeleine. George Washington's Teeth. Cole, Brock, illus. 2007. (ENG.). 40p. (J). (gr. -1-3). pap. 8.99 *(978-0-312-37604-8(9),* 900048324) Square Fish.

Cheney, Lynne. When Washington Crossed the Delaware: A Wintertime Story for Young Patriots. Fiore, Peter M., illus. 2012. (ENG.). 40p. (J). (gr. k-4). 7.99 *(978-1-4424-4423-2(1),* Simon & Schuster/Paula Wiseman Bks.) Simon & Schuster/Paula Wiseman Bks.

—When Washington Crossed the Delaware: When Washington Crossed the Delaware. 2004. (ENG., Illus.). 32p. (J). (gr. k-4). 19.99 *(978-0-689-87043-9(4),* Simon & Schuster/Paula Wiseman Bks.) Simon & Schuster/Paula Wiseman Bks.

Collard, Sneed B., III. American Heroes, 6 vols., Group 3. Incl. Cesar Chavez. 32.64 *(978-0-7614-4055-0(0),* abfe4b16-e58b-4817-8708-b7bdbc77951d); George Washington. 32.64 *(978-0-7614-4060-4(7),* 2757fb59-5b7f-48ba-b248-ebe59643b8d1); Jacob Lawrence. 32.64 *(978-0-7614-4058-1(5),* 19d54f3f-2d13-43c3-a7af-77244e0ba9a9); Lady Bird Johnson. 32.64 *(978-0-7614-4056-7(9),* 1b484198-89c3-48ec-b434-f596e2cfb712); Phillis Wheatley. (Illus.). 32.64 *(978-0-7614-4057-4(7),* b5aabf94-bd02-4815-9f30-a3d8be34143b); Sitting Bull. 32.64 *(978-0-7614-4059-8(3),* d331b804-8748-40a1-a55d-cc9e79408f93); 48p. (gr. 3-3). 2010. (American Heroes 3 Ser.). 2009. Set lib. bdg. 179.57 o.p. *(978-0-7614-4054-3(2),* Cavendish Square) Cavendish Square Publishing LLC.

—George Washington, 1 vol. 2010. (American Heroes Ser.). (ENG.). 48p. (gr. 3-3). 32.64 *(978-0-7614-4060-4(7),* 2757fb59-5b7f-48ba-b248-ebe59643b8d1) Cavendish Square Publishing LLC.

Collier, James Lincoln. The George Washington You Never Knew. Copeland, Greg, illus. 2004. (You Never Knew Ser.). (ENG.). 80p. (J). (gr. 4-6). pap. 6.95 *(978-0-516-25833-1(8),* Children's Pr.) Scholastic Library Publishing.

Corporate Contributor Staff & Aloian, Molly. George Washington: Hero of the American Revolution. 2012. (ENG.). 48p. (J). *(978-0-7787-0799-8(7))* Crabtree Publishing Co.

Crabtree Staff & Aloian, Molly. George Washington: Hero of the American Revolution. 2012. (ENG., Illus.). 48p. (J). pap. *(978-0-7787-0810-0(1))* Crabtree Publishing Co.

Dayton, Connor. Presidents' Day, 1 vol. 2012. (American Holidays Ser.). (ENG., Illus.). 24p. (J). (gr. 1-1). pap. 9.25 *(978-1-4488-6242-9(6),* 2561629b-cfaa-442a-80cd-8c3650d2d59c); lib. bdg. 26.27 *(978-1-4488-6142-2(X),* 82401d5e-c56c-405b-9b30-4fdbd5f9a52d) Rosen Publishing Group, Inc., The. (PowerKids Pr.).

Dean, Arlan. Crossing the Delaware: George Washington & the Battle of Trenton. 2009. (Great Moments in American History Ser.). 32p. (gr. 3-3). 47.90 *(978-1-61513-140-2(X))* Rosen Publishing Group, Inc., The.

Dean, Sheri. Presidents' Day, 1 vol. (Our Country's Holidays (First Edition) Ser.). (ENG., Illus.). 24p. (gr. k-2). 2006. pap. 9.15 *(978-0-8368-6515-8(4),* a373ec74-336e-49ac-9c56-6c78673d92b5, Weekly Reader Leveled Readers) 2005. lib. bdg. 24.67 *(978-0-8368-6508-0(1),* d6994cbb-bbd2-4f33-9fb2-913147a5eba5) Stevens, Gareth Publishing LLLP.

Dipiazza, Francesca. When Did George Washington Fight His First Military Battle? And Other Questions about the French & Indian War. 2011. (Six Questions of American History Ser.). (ENG.). 48p. (gr. 4-6). pap. 56.72 *(978-0-7613-7643-9(7))* Lerner Publishing Group.

Dodson Wade, Mary. Presidents' Day, 1 vol. 2016. (Story of Our Holidays Ser.). (ENG., Illus.). 32p. (gr. 3-3). pap. 11.52 *(978-0-7660-8345-5(4),* 062ea253-ce24-487f-a0a8-1def4836fc84) Enslow Publishing, LLC.

Dolan, Edward F. George Washington, 1 vol. 2008. (Presidents & Their Times Ser.). (ENG., Illus.). 96p. (gr. 6-6). lib. bdg. 36.93 *(978-0-7614-2427-7(X),* cd0e6306-5e7f-48f3-821e-9706b4b1c5a7) Cavendish Square Publishing LLC.

Duling, Kaitlyn. George Washington, 1 vol. 2017. (Great Military Leaders Ser.). (ENG.). 128p. (YA). (gr. 9-9). 47.36 *(978-1-5026-2784-1(1),* bff19b63-d71d-426b-a194-d1610cdd3180) Cavendish Square Publishing LLC.

Dunbar, Erica Armstrong & Van Cleve, Kathleen. Never Caught, the Story of Ona Judge: George & Martha Washington's Courageous Slave Who Dared to Run Away; Young Readers Edition. 2019. (ENG., Illus.). 272p. (J). (gr. 4-8). 19.99 *(978-1-5344-1617-8(X),* Aladdin) Simon & Schuster Children's Publishing.

Dyan, Penelope. This Is the House George Built! a Kid's Guide to Mount Vernon. Weigand, John D., photos by. 2009. (Illus.). 44p. pap. 11.95 *(978-1-935118-83-1(8))* Bellissima Publishing, LLC.

Edison, Erin. George Washington, 1 vol. 2012. (Presidential Biographies Ser.). (ENG., Illus.). 24p. (J). (gr. -1-2). lib. bdg. 27.32 *(978-1-4296-8737-9(1),* 119530, Capstone Pr.) Capstone.

—The Washington Monument: A 4D Book. 2018. (National Landmarks Ser.). (ENG., Illus.). 24p. (J). (gr. 1-3). lib. bdg. 27.99 *(978-1-5435-3133-6(4),* 138738, Capstone Pr.) Capstone.

Edwards, Roberta. Who Was George Washington? 2009. (Who Was...? Ser.). lib. bdg. 16.00 *(978-0-606-04042-6(0))* Turtleback.

Edwards, Roberta & Who HQ. Who Was George Washington? Kelley, True, illus. 2009. (Who Was? Ser.). 112p. (J). (gr. 3-7). pap. 5.99 *(978-0-448-44892-3(0),* Penguin Workshop) Penguin Young Readers Group.

Egan, Tracie. George Washington, 1 vol. 2003. (Primary Sources of Famous People in American History Ser.). (ENG., Illus.). 32p. (gr. 3-4). lib. bdg. 29.13 *(978-0-8239-4111-7(6),* 83c1d84a-028e-43d2-8a6d-b92a42ae615e, Rosen Reference) Rosen Publishing Group, Inc., The.

—George Washington: Padre de la Patria, 1 vol. 2003. (Grandes Personajes en la Historia de Los Estados Unidos (Famous People in American History) Ser.). (SPA.). 32p. (gr. 3-4). pap. 10.00 *(978-0-8239-4229-9(5),* b074e87f-15d9-4a7a-bf4f-9c638418e7b2, Rosen Classroom); (Illus.). lib. bdg. 29.13 *(978-0-8239-4135-3(3),* f48d0b7b-f6de-4849-8a09-87ae1b9d2aa7, Editorial Buenas Letras) Rosen Publishing Group, Inc., The.

—George Washington: Padre de la patria (George Washington: Father of the American Nation) 2009. (Grandes personajes en la historia de los Estados Unidos (Famous People in American History) Ser.). (SPA.). 32p. (gr. 2-3). 47.90 *(978-1-61512-800-6(X),* Editorial Buenas Letras) Rosen Publishing Group, Inc., The.

—George Washington: The Father of the American Nation. (Primary Sources of Famous People in American History Ser.). 32p. 2009. (gr. 2-3). 47.90 *(978-1-60851-683-4(0))* 2003. (ENG., Illus.). (gr. 3-4). pap. 10.00 *(978-0-8239-4183-4(3),*

WXYZ

82e308a1-7f2a-4c95-9bd6-ac18995af2e5) Rosen Publishing Group, Inc., The.

Finegan, Jeffrey E., Sr. Colonel Washington & Me: George Washington, His Slave William Lee & Their Incredible Journey Together. Nikolopoulos, Stephanie, ed. 2012. (ENG., Illus.). 32p. (J). 16.95 (978-0-9852819-0-8(1)) Seigle Bks.

Freedman, Russell. Washington at Valley Forge. 2020. (Illus.). 112p. (J). (gr. 5). pap. 14.99 (978-0-8234-4508-0(9)) Holiday Hse., Inc.

Gaff, Jackie. George Washington: The Life of an American Patriot, 1 vol. 2005. (Graphic Nonfiction Biographies Ser.). (ENG., Illus.). 48p. (YA). (gr. 4-6). lib. bdg. 37.13 (978-1-4042-0236-8(6), 6309c903-837f-4795-a83c-03b9fb9476ef) Rosen Publishing Group, Inc., The.

Gedacht, Daniel C. George Washington: Leader of a New Nation. (Library of American Lives & Times Ser.). 112p. (gr. 5-5). 2009. 69.20 (978-1-60853-484-5(7)) 2003. (ENG., Illus.). (J). lib. bdg. 38.27 (978-0-8239-6622-6(4), cc7bd966-2ad0-441a-b726-1adbbf4f7df3) Rosen Publishing Group, Inc., The.

Gilpin, Caroline Crosson. National Geographic Readers: George Washington. 2014. (Readers Bios Ser.). (Illus.). 32p. (J). (gr. 1-3). pap. 4.99 (978-1-4263-1468-1(X), National Geographic Kids) Disney Publishing Worldwide.

Goddu, Krystyna Poray. George Washington's Presidency. 2016. (Presidential Powerhouses Ser.). (ENG., Illus.). 104p. (YA). (gr. 6-12). 35.99 (978-1-4677-7924-1(5), 5ef17340-8503-4d31-9be2-86617a0a3921); E-Book 54.65 (978-1-4677-8598-3(9)) Lerner Publishing Group. (Lerner Pubns.).

Gosman, Gillian. George Washington, 1 vol. 2011. (Life Stories Ser.). (Illus.). 24p. (J). (gr. 3-3). (ENG.). pap. 9.25 (978-1-4488-2751-0(5), 6b3ec24a-8848-4d8d-b62d-34dc2df64d9c, PowerKids Pr.); (ENG., lib. bdg. 26.27 (978-1-4488-2581-3(4), 44b4d329-a6e9-4b5e-88ff-2844593ba48b, PowerKids Pr.); (SPA & ENG., lib. bdg. 26.27 (978-1-4488-3215-6(2), 58af38af-7a01-4498-8784-0f44b808ec4b) Rosen Publishing Group, Inc., The.

Gregory, Josh. George Washington: The 1st President. 2015. (First Look at America's Presidents Ser.). (ENG.). 24p. (J). (gr. -1-3). lib. bdg. 26.99 (978-1-62724-552-4(9)) Bearport Publishing Co., Inc.

Group/McGraw-Hill, Wright. George Washington: A Quiet Leader, 6 vols. (Book2WebTM Ser.). (gr. 4-8). 36.50 (978-0-322-04461-6(8)) Wright Group/McGraw-Hill.

Haldy, Emma E. George Washington. Bane, Jeff, illus. 2017. (My Early Library: My Itty-Bitty Bio Ser.). (ENG.). 24p. (J). (gr. k-1). lib. bdg. 30.64 (978-1-63472-152-3(7), 209180) Cherry Lake Publishing.

—George Washington SP. Bane, Jeff, illus. 2018. (My Early Library: Mi Mini Biografía (My Itty-Bitty Bio) Ser.). (SPA.). 24p. (J). (gr. k-1). lib. bdg. 30.64 (978-1-5341-2996-2(0), 212032) Cherry Lake Publishing.

Hamilton, Lynn. Presidents' Day. 2015. (Illus.). 24p. (J). (978-1-5105-0116-4(9)) SmartBook Media, Inc.

—Presidents' Day. (American Celebrations Ser.). (Illus.). 24p. (J). 2010. (gr. 3-5). pap. 11.95 (978-1-60596-931-2(1)) 2010. (gr. 3-5). lib. bdg. 18.99 (978-1-60596-773-8(4)) 2004. (gr. 1-3). lib. bdg. 24.45 (978-1-59036-108-5(3)) 2004. (gr. 1-3). per. 8.95 (978-1-59036-169-6(5)) Weigl Pubs., Inc.

Hansen, Grace. George Washington, 1 vol. 2014. (United States President Biographies (Abdo Kids Jumbo) Ser.). (ENG.). 24p. (J). (gr. -1-2). lib. bdg. 32.79 (978-1-62970-089-2(4), 1720, Abdo Kids) ABDO Publishing Co.

Harness, Cheryl. George Washington. 2006. (Illus.). 48p. (J). (gr. 3-7). per. 8.99 (978-0-7922-5490-4(2), National Geographic Kids) Disney Publishing Worldwide.

Harris, Duchess & Wyskowski, Lindsay. Oney Ona Judge: Escape from Slavery & the President's House. 2018. (Freedom's Promise Ser.). (ENG., Illus.). 48p. (J). (gr. 4-8). lib. bdg. 35.64 (978-1-5321-1773-2(6), 30834) ABDO Publishing Co.

Herweck, Dona. George Washington, 1 vol. 2nd rev. ed. (TIME for KIDS(r): Informational Text Ser.). (ENG., 28p. (gr. 2-3). 2013. Illus.). (J). lib. bdg. 23.96 (978-1-4807-1061-0(X)) 2011. pap. 10.99 (978-1-4333-3640-9(5)) Teacher Created Materials, Inc.

Hollar, Sherman, contrib. by. George Washington, 1 vol. 2012. (Pivotal Presidents: Profiles in Leadership Ser.). (ENG., Illus.). 80p. (gr. 8-8). (J). lib. bdg. 36.47 (978-1-61530-939-9(X), 5406dae3-454b-476c-bd1c-9cfe62bfa85b); (YA). 72.94 (978-1-61530-956-6(X), 6d4e4612-5ccc-4364-9d13-da5d6b06182c) Rosen Publishing Group, Inc., The.

Hooks, Gwendolyn. Ona Judge Outwits the Washingtons: An Enslaved Woman Fights for Freedom. Agoussoye, Simone, illus. 2019. (ENG.). 40p. (J). (gr. 3-6). 18.95 (978-1-5435-1280-9(1), 137745, Capstone Editions) Capstone.

Houran, Lori Haskins. My Little Golden Book about George Washington. Garofoli, Viviana, illus. 2016. (Little Golden Book Ser.). 24p. (J). (gr. -1-3). 5.99 (978-1-101-93969-7(9), Golden Bks.) Random Hse. Children's Bks.

Joseph, Natalie. Visit the Washington Monument, 1 vol. 2012. (Landmarks of Liberty Ser.). (ENG., Illus.). 24p. (J). (gr. 2-3). pap. 9.15 (978-1-4339-6406-0(6), 130dd795-86ce-4a1d-93f6-77823ceb51ee, Gareth Stevens Learning Library); lib. bdg. 25.27 (978-1-4339-6404-6(X), 3fab3373-810b-45bb-a181-a617975fb9ac) Stevens, Gareth Publishing LLLP.

Jurmain, Suzanne Tripp. George Did It. Day, Larry, illus. 2007. (gr. -1-3). 17.00 (978-0-7569-8161-7(1)) Perfection Learning Corp.

Kaiser, Lori. George Washington. Kaiser, Lori, illus. 2012. (Illus.). 26p. pap. (978-0-9836651-7-5(6)) Roxby Media Ltd.

Katirgis, Jane & Egan, Tracie. Meet George Washington: America's First President, 1 vol. 2019. (Introducing Famous Americans Ser.). (ENG.). 32p. (gr. 3-4). pap. 11.53 (978-1-9785-1122-4(1), 4e427baa-29bf-4aa7-9083-aa9e57796dac) Enslow Publishing, LLC.

Katz, Vladimir. A Timeline of the Life of George Washington. (Timelines of American History Ser.). 32p. (gr. 4-4). 2009. 47.90 (978-1-60854-388-5(9)) 2004. (ENG., Illus.). lib. bdg. 29.13 (978-0-8239-4538-2(3), 2fa8f672-9994-452f-b005-cfc1b954837f) Rosen Publishing Group, Inc., The. (Rosen Reference).

Kawa, Katie. 20 Fun Facts about George Washington. 2017. (Fun Fact File: Founding Fathers Ser.). 32p. (gr. 2-3). pap. 63.00 (978-1-5382-0272-2(7)) Stevens, Gareth Publishing LLLP.

Keating, Frank. George: George Washington, Our Founding Father. Wimmer, Mike, illus. 2012. (Mount Rushmore Presidential Ser.). (ENG.). 32p. (J). (gr. 1-4). 17.99 (978-1-4169-5482-8(1), Simon & Schuster/Paula Wiseman Bks.) Simon & Schuster/Paula Wiseman Bks.

Kirkman, Marissa. The Life & Times of George Washington & the American Revolution. 2016. (Life & Times Ser.). (ENG., Illus.). 24p. (J). (gr. 1-3). lib. bdg. 27.99 (978-1-5157-2476-6(X), 132848, Capstone Pr.) Capstone.

Kissock, Heather. Washington Monument. 2017. (Illus.). 24p. (J). (978-1-5105-0608-4(X)) SmartBook Media, Inc.

Kraus, Stephanie. George Washington & His Right-Hand Man (Alexander Hamilton) rev. ed. 2017. (Social Studies: Informational Text Ser.). (ENG., Illus.). 32p. (J). (gr. 4-8). pap. 11.99 (978-1-4258-6356-2(6)) Teacher Created Materials, Inc.

Kravitz, Danny. The Untold Story of Washington's Surprise Attack: The Daring Crossing of the Delaware River. 2015. (What You Didn't Know about the American Revolution Ser.). (ENG.). 64p. (J). (gr. 5-9). 35.32 (978-0-7565-4973-2(6), 127219, Compass Point Bks.) Capstone.

Krensky, Stephen. George Washington's First Victory: Ready-To-Read Level 2. Hearn, Diane Dawson, illus. 2005. (Ready-To-Read Childhood of Famous Americans Ser.). (ENG.). 32p. (J). (gr. k-2). pap. 4.99 (978-0-689-85942-7(2), Simon Spotlight) Simon Spotlight.

Landau, Elaine. General Washington Crosses the Delaware: Would You Join the American Revolution?, 1 vol. 2014. (What Would You Do? Ser.). (ENG.). 48p. (gr. 3-4). 27.93 (978-0-7660-6315-0(1), c1b912c5-4351-47ec-a62e-2ca9aed546a5); pap. 11.53 (978-0-7660-6316-7(X), a3e7fa61-2614-4da4-b415-b0c379dc668d, Enslow Elementary) Enslow Publishing, LLC.

—George Washington Crosses the Delaware: Would You Risk the Revolution?, 1 vol. 2009. (What Would You Do? Ser.). (ENG., Illus.). 48p. (gr. 3-3). pap. 11.53 (978-1-59845-195-5(2), 98c4ac0a-48e3-4485-a5d1-eb75e1358676); lib. bdg. 27.93 (978-0-7660-2904-0(2), 842b7348-ded7-40fe-9d38-b4aee15fa2cd) Enslow Publishing, LLC. (Enslow Elementary).

—The Washington Monument. 2004. (Cornerstones of Freedom Ser.). (ENG.). 48p. (YA). (gr. 4-7). 26.00 (978-0-516-24238-5(5)) Scholastic Library Publishing.

Leighton, Marian. George Washington. Salvador, Martin, illus. 2005. (Heroes of America Ser.). 239p. (gr. 3-8). lib. bdg. 27.07 (978-1-59679-262-3(0), Abdo & Daughters) ABDO Publishing Co.

Levin, Jack E. & Levin, Mark R. George Washington: the Crossing. 2013. (ENG., Illus.). 64p. 18.00 (978-1-4767-3193-3(4), Threshold Editions) Threshold Editions.

Levy, Janey. Before George Washington Was President, 1 vol. 2018. (Before They Were President Ser.). (ENG.). 24p. (gr. 2-3). lib. bdg. 24.27 (978-1-5382-2912-5(9), 2e7aa5d5-9059-4ab8-9cc2-c0e16b0731d5) Stevens, Gareth Publishing LLLP.

—Slavery at Mount Vernon, 1 vol. 2016. (Hidden History Ser.). (ENG., Illus.). 32p. (J). (gr. 4-5). pap. 11.50 (978-1-4824-5802-2(0), 7c4da709-75cc-4d55-99aa-2cc697c29e15) Stevens, Gareth Publishing LLLP.

Lusted, Marcia Amidon. Revolution & the New Nation: 1750-Early 1800s. 2007. (Presidents of the United States Ser.). (Illus.). 48p. (J). (gr. 4-7). lib. bdg. 29.05 (978-1-59036-739-1(1)); per. 10.95 (978-1-59036-740-7(5)) Weigl Pubs., Inc.

Malaspina, Ann. Phillis Sings Out Freedom: The Story of George Washington & Phillis Wheatley. Keeter, Susan, illus. 2012. (J). 34.28 (978-1-61913-149-1(8)) Weigl Pubs., Inc.

Maloof, Torrey. George Washington & the Men Who Shaped America. rev. ed. 2016. (Social Studies: Informational Text Ser.). (ENG., Illus.). 32p. (gr. 4-8). pap. 11.99 (978-1-4938-3081-7(3)) Teacher Created Materials, Inc.

Manolis, Kay & Todd, Anne. George Washington: A Life of Self-Discipline. 2007. (People of Character Ser.). (ENG., Illus.). 24p. (J). (gr. 2-5). lib. bdg. 26.95 (978-1-60014-094-5(7)) Bellwether Media.

Marcovitz, Hal. Liberty Bell: Let Freedom Ring. 2015. (Illus.). 48p. (J). (978-1-4222-3117-3(8)) Mason Crest.

—The Washington Monument. 2004. (American Symbols & Their Meanings Ser.). (Illus.). 48p. (J). (gr. 4-18). lib. bdg. 19.95 (978-1-59084-028-3(3)) Mason Crest.

—Washington Monument: Memorial to a Founding Father. Moreno, Barry, ed. 2014. (Patriotic Symbols of America Ser.: 20). 48p. (J). (gr. 4-18). lib. bdg. 20.95 (978-1-4222-3137-1(2)) Mason Crest.

Margaret, Amy. Presidents' Day. 2009. (Library of Holidays Ser.). 24p. (gr. 2-3). 42.50 (978-1-60853-716-7(1), PowerKids Pr.) Rosen Publishing Group, Inc., The.

Massie, Elizabeth. George Washington. 2016. (Spring Forward Ser.). (J). (gr. 1). (978-1-4900-9409-0(1)) Benchmark Education Co.

McClafferty, Carla Killough. Buried Lives: The Enslaved People of George Washington's Mount Vernon. 2018. (ENG., Illus.). 168p. (J). (gr. 5-7). 24.99 (978-0-8234-3697-2(7)) Holiday Hse., Inc.

Mcpherson, Stephanie Sammartino. Martha Washington: Legendary First Lady of the United States, 1 vol. 2014. (Legendary American Biographies Ser.). (ENG.). 96p. (gr. 6-6). 29.60 (978-0-7660-6475-1(1), afd97b4a-9287-4fc5-a030-e63ea9ca3b05) Enslow Publishing, LLC.

Mead, David. Little George Washington Learns about Responsibility: Responsibility. Sharp, Chris, illus. 2004. (American Virtues for Kids Ser.). (J). bds. 6.95 (978-0-9746440-1-1(3), Ideals Pubns.) Worthy Publishing.

Meloche, Renee Taft. Heroes of History for Young Readers - George Washington: America's Patriot. Pollard, Brian, illus. 2006. (Heroes of History Ser.). (ENG.). 32p. (J). 8.99 (978-1-932096-28-6(0)) Emerald Bks.

—Heroes of History for Young Readers - George Washington Carver: America's Scientist. Pollard, Bryan, illus. 2006. (Heroes for Young Readers Ser.). (ENG.). 32p. (J). (gr. 1-4). 8.99 (978-1-932096-17-0(5)) Emerald Bks.

Meltzer, Brad. I Am George Washington. Eliopoulos, Christopher, illus. 2016. (Ordinary People Change the World Ser.). 40p. (J). (gr. k-4). 15.99 (978-0-525-42848-0(8), Dial Bks) Penguin Young Readers Group.

Meltzer, Brad. Soy George Washington. Eliopoulos, Christopher, illus. 2023.Tr. of I Am George Washington. (SPA.). 40p. (J). (gr. k-3). pap. 14.99 **(978-1-5433-8605-9(9))** Vista Higher Learning, Inc.

Micklos, John & Micklos, John, Jr. From Thirteen Colonies to One Nation, 1 vol. 2008. (Revolutionary War Library). (ENG., Illus.). 48p. (J). (gr. 3-3). lib. bdg. 27.93 (978-0-7660-3015-2(6), c96af7cf-f967-42c2-80d4-67636f4de9d3, Enslow Elementary) Enslow Publishing, LLC.

—The Making of the United States from Thirteen Colonies: Through Primary Sources, 1 vol. 2013. (American Revolution Through Primary Sources Ser.). (ENG.). 48p. (gr. 4-6). pap. 11.53 (978-1-4644-0191-6(8), 34f4b0d8-053b-4331-ab55-77e8baf3d2c8); (Illus.). (J). 27.93 (978-0-7660-4133-2(6), 451c891d-fc74-4e1d-a855-d24b94dd42cd) Enslow Publishing, LLC.

—Washington's Crossing the Delaware & the Winter at Valley Forge: Through Primary Sources, 1 vol. 2013. (American Revolution Through Primary Sources Ser.). (ENG., Illus.). 48p. (J). (gr. 4-6). 27.93 (978-0-7660-4132-5(8), 22bf5158-e47c-42c7-9d03-25ec224712b2); pap. 11.53 (978-1-4644-0190-9(X), c759c386-064d-4048-9796-e54bc92199cf) Enslow Publishing, LLC.

Mikoley, Kate. George Washington Wasn't the First President: Exposing Myths about US Presidents. 2019. (Exposed! More Myths about American History Ser.). (ENG.). 32p. (gr. 2-3). 63.00 (978-1-5382-3751-9(2)) Stevens, Gareth Publishing LLLP.

Miller, Brandon Marie. George Washington for Kids: His Life & Times with 21 Activities. 2007. (For Kids Ser.: 22). (ENG., Illus.). 144p. (J). (gr. 4-7). pap. 18.99 (978-1-55652-655-8(5)) Chicago Review Pr., Inc.

Miller, Chuck. George Washington. 2003. (America's Founders Ser.). (J). pap. (978-1-58417-080-8(8)); lib. bdg. (978-1-58417-017-4(4)) Lake Street Pubs.

Mills, Nathan & Hill, Laura. George Washington Leads the Country, 1 vol. 2012. (Rosen Readers Ser.). (ENG., Illus.). 24p. (J). (gr. 1-1). pap. 8.25 (978-1-4488-8767-5(4), e11372f9-2c65-4e3b-8b69-fd6cb772fb91, Rosen Classroom) Rosen Publishing Group, Inc., The.

Mooney, Carla. George Washington: 25 Great Projects You Can Build Yourself. Carbaugh, Samuel, illus. 2010. (Build It Yourself Ser.). (ENG.). 128p. (J). (gr. 3-7). 21.95 (978-1-934670-64-4(2), 14bb8ad7-0628-4a6b-8e67-672face52822) Nomad Pr.

Murphy, Frank. George Washington & the General's Dog. Walz, Richard, illus. 2015. 48p. pap. 5.00 (978-1-61003-605-4(0)) Center for the Collaborative Classroom.

—George Washington & the General's Dog. 2003. (J). 1.25 (978-1-4025-4103-2(1)) Recorded Bks., Inc.

Murphy, Jim. The Crossing: How George Washington Saved the American Revolution. 2016. (ENG.). 96p. (J). (gr. 4-7). pap. 14.99 (978-0-439-69187-1(7)) Scholastic, Inc.

Murray, Robb. The Washington Monument: Myths, Legends, & Facts, 1 vol. 2014. (Monumental History Ser.). (ENG.). 32p. (J). (gr. 3-6). 27.99 (978-1-4914-0206-1(7), 125789, Capstone Pr.) Capstone.

Nagle, Jeanne. How George Washington Fought the Revolutionary War, 1 vol. 2017. (Presidents at War Ser.). (ENG.). 128p. (gr. 8-8). lib. bdg. 38.93 (978-0-7660-8523-7(6), 525f9128-4e87-4008-8471-cda23af7b720) Enslow Publishing, LLC.

Nelson, Maria. The Life of George Washington, 1 vol. 2012. (Famous Lives Ser.). (ENG.). 24p. (J). (gr. 1-2). pap. 9.15 (978-1-4339-6351-3(5), 04b50bd1-3b14-4e89-9569-56cc24340b3d) Stevens, Gareth Publishing LLLP.

—The Life of George Washington / la Vida de George Washington, 1 vol. 2012. (Famous Lives / Vidas Extraordinarias Ser.). (ENG & SPA., Illus.). 24p. (J). (gr. 1-2). 25.27 (978-1-4339-6655-2(7), f4783f2b-ef40-42a4-bf3c-4941cf9ca8de) Stevens, Gareth Publishing LLLP.

Nelson, Robin. George Washington: A Life of Leadership. 2006. (Pull Ahead Bks.). (Illus.). 32p. (J). (gr. 3-7). lib. bdg. 22.60 (978-0-8225-3474-7(6), Lerner Pubns.) Lerner Publishing Group.

—George Washington: Una Vida de Liderazgo. 2006. (Libros para Avanzar Ser.). (ENG & SPA., Illus.). 32p. (J). (gr. 3-7). lib. bdg. 22.60 (978-0-8225-6235-1(9), Ediciones Lerner) Lerner Publishing Group.

—George Washington: Una vida de liderazgo (A Life of Leadership) 2006. (Libros para Avanzar-Biografías (Pull Ahead Books-Biographies Ser.). (Illus.). 32p. (J). (gr. -1-3). per. 6.95 (978-0-8225-6555-0(2), Ediciones Lerner) Lerner Publishing Group.

Norwich, Grace. I Am George Washington (I Am #5) 2012. (I Am Ser.: 5). (ENG.). 128p. (J). (gr. 3-5). pap. 5.99 (978-0-545-48435-0(9)) Scholastic, Inc.

Olesen, Andrew. George Washington: The First President of the United States, 1 vol. 2015. (Spotlight on American History Ser.). (ENG., Illus.). 24p. (J). (gr. 4-6). pap. 11.00 (978-1-4994-1751-7(9), 4fbc47f3-6d10-49d7-bbac-8141eaab4641, PowerKids Pr.) Rosen Publishing Group, Inc., The.

Palazzo-Craig, Janet. The Making of the American Flag: Betsy Ross & George Washington. 2009. (Great Moments in American History Ser.). 32p. (gr. 3-3). 47.90 (978-1-61513-155-6(8)) Rosen Publishing Group, Inc., The.

Parker, Christi E. George Washington, 1 vol. rev. ed. 2004. (Social Studies: Informational Text Ser.). (ENG.). 24p. (gr. 4-8). pap. 10.99 (978-0-7439-8749-3(7)) Teacher Created Materials, Inc.

Pelleschi, Andrea. George Washington, 1 vol. 2012. (Jr. Graphic Founding Fathers Ser.). (ENG., Illus.). 24p. (J). (gr. 2-3). pap. 11.60 (978-1-4488-7991-5(4), af978e28-1877-4c21-8638-55bad2dc85c0); lib. bdg. 28.93 (978-1-4488-7897-0(7), bc4d46dd-3b20-4d80-b64a-a9f9f821ad5d) Rosen Publishing Group, Inc., The. (PowerKids Pr.).

Rand, Casey. George Washington, 1 vol. Oxford Designers and Illustrators, illus. 2012. (American Biographies Ser.). (ENG.). 48p. (J). (gr. 4-6). lib. bdg. 35.32 (978-1-4329-6452-8(6), 119051, Heinemann) Capstone.

Ransom, Candice. George Washington. 2018. (Founding Fathers Ser.). (ENG., Illus.). 24p. (J). (gr. 1-1). pap. 8.95 (978-1-63517-817-3(7), 1635178177) North Star Editions.

—George Washington. 2018. (Founding Fathers Ser.). (ENG., Illus.). 24p. (J). (gr. k-3). lib. bdg. 31.36 (978-1-5321-6022-6(4), 28676, Pop! Cody Koala) Pop!

—George Washington & the Story of the U. S. Constitution. Reeves, Jeni, illus. 2011. (History Speaks: Picture Books Plus Reader's Theater Ser.). 48p. pap. 56.72 (978-0-7613-7632-3(1)); (ENG.). (gr. 2-4). 27.93 (978-0-7613-5877-0(3), Millbrook Pr.); (ENG.). (gr. 2-4). pap. 9.95 (978-0-7613-7116-8(8)) Lerner Publishing Group.

Rauf, Don. Washington's Farewell Address, 1 vol. 2016. (Let's Find Out! Primary Sources Ser.). (ENG., Illus.). 32p. (J). (gr. 2-3). lib. bdg. 26.06 (978-1-5081-0407-0(7), 8aea0638-2193-4c99-bb41-0151eb8a6b8a) Rosen Publishing Group, Inc., The.

Regan, Michael. George Washington & the American Presidency. 2017. (Foundations of Our Nation Ser.). (ENG., Illus.). 32p. (J). (gr. 3-5). pap. 9.95 (978-1-63517-313-0(2), 1635173132); lib. bdg. 31.35 (978-1-63517-248-5(9), 1635172489) North Star Editions. (Focus Readers).

RJF Publishing Staff & Schaffer, Julia. The Washington Monument. 2009. (Symbols of American Freedom Ser.). 48p. (gr. 4-6). 30.00 (978-1-60413-517-6(4), Chelsea Clubhse.) Infobase Holdings, Inc.

Rockwell, Anne. Big George: How a Shy Boy Became President Washington. Phelan, Matt, illus. 2015. (ENG.). 48p. (J). (gr. 1-4). pap. 8.99 (978-0-544-58246-0(2), 1613675, Clarion Bks.) HarperCollins Pubs.

Roop, Peter & Roop, Connie. Botones Para el General Washington. Hanson, Peter E., illus. 2006. (Yo Solo - Historia (on My Own - History) Ser.).Tr. of Buttons for General Washington. (SPA.). 48p. (gr. 2-4). lib. bdg. 25.26 (978-0-8225-6261-0(8)) Lerner Publishing Group.

—Buttons for General Washington, 4 bks., Set. unabr. ed. 2007. (Readalongs for Beginning Readers Ser.). (J). (gr. 2-3). pap. 37.95 incl. audio (978-1-59519-931-7(4)) Live Oak Media.

—Buttons for General Washington, 4 bks., Set. Hanson, Peter E., illus. unabr. ed. 2007. (Readalongs for Beginning Readers Ser.). (J). (gr. 2-3). pap. 39.95 incl. audio compact disk (978-1-59519-935-5(7)) Live Oak Media.

Saddleback Educational Publishing Staff, ed. George Washington, 1 vol. unabr. ed. 2007. (Graphic Biographies Ser.). (ENG., Illus.). 25p. (YA). (gr. 4-12). pap. 9.75 (978-1-59905-223-6(7)) Saddleback Educational Publishing, Inc.

Schanzer, Rosalyn. George vs. George. 2007. (ENG.). 64p. (J). (gr. 4-7). 17.75 (978-1-5311-7657-0(7)) Perfection Learning Corp.

—George vs. George: The American Revolution As Seen from Both Sides. 2007. (Illus.). 64p. (J). (gr. 3-7). per. 6.95 (978-1-4263-0042-4(5), National Geographic Kids) Disney Publishing Worldwide.

—George vs. George: The Revolutionary War As Seen by Both Sides. 2004. (Illus.). 64p. (J). (gr. 3-7). 16.95 (978-0-7922-7349-3(4), National Geographic Children's Bks.) Disney Publishing Worldwide.

Schubert, Barbara. George Washington. 2009. pap. 13.25 (978-1-60559-060-8(6)) Hameray Publishing Group, Inc.

Snyder, Gail. George Washington. 2004. (Childhoods of the Presidents Ser.). (Illus.). 48p. (J). (gr. 4-18). lib. bdg. 17.95 (978-1-59084-270-6(7)) Mason Crest.

Spender, Nick. George Washington & the Winter at Valley Forge, 1 vol. 2011. (Graphic Heroes of the American Revolution Ser.). (ENG.). 24p. (J). (gr. 3-3). pap. 9.15 (978-1-4339-6014-7(1), 212546e8-51ff-4148-864f-6777e830450c, Gareth Stevens Learning Library); (Illus.). lib. bdg. 26.60 (978-1-4339-6174-8(1), a7d37558-8404-4d5a-9b25-9d6db992cc36) Stevens, Gareth Publishing LLLP.

Stevens, C. M. The Wonderful Story of Washington & Th. 2004. reprint ed. pap. 24.95 (978-1-4179-2621-3(X)) Kessinger Publishing, LLC.

Strand, Jennifer. George Washington. 2016. (Legendary Leaders Ser.). (ENG.). 24p. (J). (gr. -1-2). 49.94 (978-1-68079-405-2(1), 23026, Abdo Zoom-Launch) ABDO Publishing Co.

Strum, Richard. Henry Knox: Washington's Artilleryman. 2006. (Forgotten Heroes of the American Revolution Ser.). (Illus.). 88p. (J). (gr. 5-11). lib. bdg. 23.95 (978-1-59556-013-1(0)) OTTN Publishing.

Strum, Richard M. Henry Knox: Washington's Artilleryman. 2006. (J). pap. (978-1-59556-018-6(1)) OTTN Publishing.

Thomas, Peggy. Farmer George Plants a Nation. Johnson, Layne, illus. (ENG.). 40p. (J). (gr. 2-5). 2013. pap. 9.99 (978-1-62091-029-0(2)) 2008. 17.95 (978-1-59078-460-0(X)) Highlights Pr., c/o Highlights for Children, Inc. (Calkins Creek).

Wachter, Joanne. George Washington & the American Revolution. 2005. (J). pap. (978-1-4108-4633-4(4)) Benchmark Education Co.

West, David. George Washington: The Life of an American Patriot. 2009. (Graphic Nonfiction Biographies Ser.). (Illus.). 48p. (YA). (gr. 4-5). 58.50 (978-1-61513-017-7(9), Rosen Reference) Rosen Publishing Group, Inc., The.

Weston Woods Staff, creator. George Washington's Mother. 2011. 38.75 *(978-0-439-72669-6(7))*; 18.95 *(978-0-439-72667-2(0))* Weston Woods Studios, Inc.

White, Becky. Betsy Ross. Lloyd, Megan, illus. 2019. (I Like to Read Ser.). 32p. (J). (gr. -1-3). pap. 7.99 *(978-0-8234-4523-3(2))* Holiday Hse., Inc.

Williamson, Mary. The Life of George Washington. 2004. (ENG.). 128p. per. 6.95 *(978-1-930367-91-3(0)*, CLP29870) Christian Liberty Pr.

WASHINGTON, GEORGE, 1732-1799—FICTION

Burgess, Linda, text. Mount Vernon's Magnificent Menagerie: And the Very Mysterious Guest. 2012. (ENG., Illus.). 48p. (J). 15.95 *(978-0-931917-31-8(X))* Mount Vernon Ladies' Assn. of the Union.

Carson, Jana. We Both Read-The Boy Who Carried the Flag. Westerman, Johanna, illus. 2010. (We Both Read Ser.). 44p. (J). (gr. 2-5). 9.95 *(978-1-60115-247-3(7))*; pap. 5.99 *(978-1-60115-248-0(5))* Treasure Bay, Inc.

Cherry, Jason. Sassafras in the Window, 1 vol. 2009. 44p. pap. 24.95 *(978-1-61582-209-6(7))* America Star Bks.

Deutsch, Stacia & Cohon, Rhody. Washington's War. Francis, Guy, illus. 2015. (Blast to the Past Ser.: 7). (ENG.). 128p. (J). (gr. 2-5). pap. 6.99 *(978-1-4424-9540-1(5)*, Simon & Schuster/Paula Wiseman Bks.) Simon & Schuster/Paula Wiseman Bks.

Grandpa Dennis, as told by. George Washington's Smallest Army: The Miracle Before Trenton. 2009. 216p. (J). pap. 17.49 *(978-1-4389-3147-0(6))* AuthorHouse.

Heald, Robin. Liberty Saves the Day! Elkerton, Andy, illus. 2017. (J). *(978-0-87935-290-5(6))* Colonial Williamsburg Foundation.

Hedstrom-Page, Deborah. From Colonies to Country with George Washington. Martinez, Sergio, illus. 2007. (My American Journey Ser.). 82p. (J). (gr. 3-9). 9.99 *(978-0-8054-3265-7(5))* B&H Publishing Group.

Hemphill, Kris. Ambush in the Wilderness. 2003. (Adventures in America Ser.). (Illus.). 90p. (gr. 4). 14.95 *(978-1-893110-34-2(6))* Silver Moon Pr.

Henry, Marguerite. Cinnabar, the One o'Clock Fox. Dennis, Wesley, illus. (ENG.). 144p. (J). (gr. 3-7). 2015. 19.99 *(978-1-4814-0401-3(6))* 2014. pap. 7.99 *(978-1-4814-0400-6(8))* Simon & Schuster Children's Publishing. (Aladdin).

Hutton, John. Flowers for Mr. President. 2012. (Illus.). (J). *(978-0-9789608-3-4(1))* Salem Academy & College.

Kalb, Deborah. George Washington & the Magic Hat: George Washington & the Magic Hat, 1 vol. Lunsford, Robert, illus. 2016. (President & Me Ser.: 1). (ENG.). 144p. (gr. 3-6). pap. 12.99 *(978-0-7643-5110-5(9)*, 7365) Schiffer Publishing, Ltd.

—John Adams & the Magic Bobblehead: John Adams & the Magic Bobblehead, 1 vol. Lunsford, Robert, illus. 2018. (President & Me Ser.: 2). (ENG.). 144p. (gr. 3-6). pap. 12.99 *(978-0-7643-5556-1(2)*, 9948) Schiffer Publishing, Ltd.

Kennedy Center, The. Chasing George Washington. Hoyt, Ard, illus. 2011. (ENG.). 80p. (J). (gr. 2-5). pap. 5.99 *(978-1-4169-4861-2(9)*, Simon & Schuster Bks. For Young Readers) Simon & Schuster Bks. For Young Readers.

Kennedy Center, The, et al. Chasing George Washington. Hoyt, Ard, illus. 2009. (ENG.). 80p. (J). (gr. 2-5). 12.99 *(978-1-4169-4858-2(9)*, Simon & Schuster Bks. For Young Readers) Simon & Schuster Bks. For Young Readers.

Klimo, Kate. Dog Diaries #6: Sweetie. Jessell, Tim, illus. 2015. (Dog Diaries: 6). 160p. (J). (gr. 2-5). pap. 7.99 *(978-0-385-39240-2(0)*, Random Hse. Bks. for Young Readers) Random Hse. Children's Bks.

Limbaugh, Rush & Adams Limbaugh, Kathryn. Rush Revere & the Presidency. 2016. (Rush Revere Ser.: 5). (ENG., Illus.). 272p. (gr. 4-7). 21.00 *(978-1-5011-5689-2(6)*, Threshold Editions) Threshold Editions.

McNamara, Margaret. George Washington's Birthday: A Mostly True Tale. Blitt, Barry, illus. 2012. (ENG.). 40p. (J). (gr. -1-3). 17.99 *(978-0-375-84499-7(6)*, Schwartz & Wade Bks.) Random Hse. Children's Bks.

Orgill, Roxane. Siege: How General Washington Kicked the British Out of Boston & Launched a Revolution. 2018. (ENG., Illus.). 240p. (J). (gr. 5). 17.99 *(978-0-7636-8851-6(7))* Candlewick Pr.

Osborne, Mary Pope. Revolutionary War on Wednesday. unabr. ed. 2004. (Magic Tree House Ser.: No. 22). 69p. (J). (gr. k-3). pap. 17.00 incl. audio *(978-0-8072-0931-8(7)*, S FTR 254 SP, Listening Library) Random Hse. Audio Publishing Group.

Perry, Fred. Time Lincoln, Vol. 1. 2011. (ENG.). 122p. (YA). pap., pap. 19.95 *(978-0-9831823-7-5(X)*, cd022291-ebe4-480a-87a0-41bd78130b2d) Antarctic Pr., Inc.

Potter, David. The Left Behinds: the IPhone That Saved George Washington. 2016. (Left Behinds Ser.: 1). (ENG.). 368p. (J). (gr. 3-7). 8.99 *(978-0-385-39059-0(9)*, Yearling) Random Hse. Children's Bks.

Rinaldi, Ann. The Family Greene. 2011. (ENG.). 256p. (YA). (gr. 7). pap. 14.95 *(978-0-547-57723-4(0)*, 1458519, Clarion Bks.) HarperCollins Pubs.

—Taking Liberty: The Story of Oney Judge, George Washington's Runaway Slave. 2004. (ENG., Illus.). 272p. (YA). (gr. 7). mass mkt. 8.99 *(978-0-689-85188-9(X)*, Simon Pulse) Simon Pulse.

Roop, Peter & Roop, Connie. The Top-Secret Adventure of John Darragh, Revolutionary War Spy. 2010. pap. 51.02 *(978-0-7613-6923-3(6))* Lerner Publishing Group.

—The Top-Secret Adventure of John Darragh, Revolutionary War Spy. Trover, Zachary, illus. 2010. (History's Kid Heroes Ser.). (ENG.). 32p. (gr. 3-5). lib. bdg. 26.60 *(978-0-7613-6174-9(X))* Lerner Publishing Group.

Scieszka, Jon. Oh Say, I Can't See #15, No. 15. McCauley, Adam, illus. 2007. (Time Warp Trio Ser.: 15). 80p. (J). (gr. 2-4). 5.99 *(978-0-14-240808-7(5)*, Puffin Books) Penguin Young Readers Group.

Stratemeyer, Edward. With Washington in the West or A Soldier Boy's Battles in the Wilderness. Shute, A. B., illus. 2004. reprint ed. pap. 30.95 *(978-1-4179-2977-1(4))* Kessinger Publishing, LLC.

Turner, Diane D. My Name Is Oney Judge. Massey, Cal, illus. 2010. (J). pap. *(978-0-88378-321-4(5))* Third World Press.

WASHINGTON, MARTHA, 1731-1802

Dunbar, Erica Armstrong & Van Cleve, Kathleen. Never Caught, the Story of Ona Judge: George & Martha Washington's Courageous Slave Who Dared to Run Away; Young Readers Edition. 2019. (ENG.). 272p. (J). (gr. 4-8). 19.99 *(978-1-5344-1617-8(X)*, Aladdin) Simon & Schuster Children's Publishing.

Hooks, Gwendolyn. Ona Judge Outwits the Washingtons: An Enslaved Woman Fights for Freedom. Agoussoye, Simone, illus. 2019. (ENG.). 40p. (J). (gr. 3-6). 18.95 *(978-1-5435-1280-9(1)*, 137745, Capstone Editions) Capstone.

Larkin, Tanya. What Was Cooking in Martha Washington's Presidential Mansion? 2009. (Cooking Throughout American History Ser.). 24p. (gr. 3-3). 42.50 *(978-1-61511-953-0(1)*, PowerKids Pr.) Rosen Publishing Group, Inc., The.

Lee, Sally. Martha Washington, 1 vol. 2010. (First Ladies Ser.). (ENG.). 24p. (J). (gr. -1-2). pap. 7.29 *(978-1-4296-5605-4(0)*, 114107); (gr. -1-2). lib. bdg. 27.32 *(978-1-4296-5011-3(7)*, 112960); (gr. k-1). pap. 43.74 *(978-1-4296-5606-1(9)*, 15475) Capstone. (Capstone Pr.).

Manera, Alexandria. Martha Washington. 2003. (Women of the Revolution Ser.). (J). pap. *(978-1-58417-087-7(5))*; lib. bdg. *(978-1-58417-024-2(7))* Lake Street Pubs.

Mcpherson, Stephanie Sammartino. Martha Washington: Legendary First Lady of the United States, 1 vol. 2014. (Legendary American Biographies Ser.). (ENG.). 96p. (gr. 6-6). 29.60 *(978-0-7660-6475-1(1)*, afd97b4a-9287-4fc5-a030-e63ea9ca3b05) Enslow Publishing, LLC.

Ransom, Candice. Martha Washington. Ritz, Karen, illus. 2003. (On My Own Biographies Ser.). 48p. (J). 25.26 *(978-0-87614-918-8(2)*, Carolrhoda Bks.); (ENG.). (gr. 2-4). per. 8.99 *(978-0-87614-107-6(6)*, 4c0f38f4-4630-4dd2-a209-c0d6e8fec56b, First Avenue Editions) Lerner Publishing Group.

Strand, Jennifer. Martha Washington. 2017. (First Ladies (Launch!) Ser.). (ENG., Illus.). 24p. (J). (gr. -1-2). lib. bdg. 31.36 *(978-1-5321-2020-6(6)*, 25290, Abdo Zoom-Launch) ABDO Publishing Co.

WASHINGTON (D.C.)

Benchmark Education Company. The United States Government (Teacher Guide) 2005. *(978-1-4108-4640-2(7))* Benchmark Education Co.

Braithwaite, Jill. The White House. 2003. (Pull Ahead Books — American Symbols Ser.). (ENG., Illus.). 32p. (J). (gr. k-3). pap. 7.99 *(978-0-8225-3758-8(3)*, 00f7b1ad-6a5c-44b4-b2d9-5635ee7ac294, First Avenue Editions) Lerner Publishing Group.

Brown, Vanessa. District of Columbia. 2009. (Bilingual Library of the United States of America Ser.). (ENG & SPA.). 32p. (gr. 2-2). 47.90 *(978-1-60853-351-0(4)*, Editorial Buenas Letras) Rosen Publishing Group, Inc., The.

Carr, Aaron. Lincoln Memorial. 2013. (J). *(978-1-62127-202-1(8))*; pap. *(978-1-62127-206-9(0))* Weigl Pubs., Inc.

—Washington Monument. 2013. (J). *(978-1-62127-205-2(2))*; pap. *(978-1-62127-209-0(5))* Weigl Pubs., Inc.

Curlee, Lynn. Capital. Curlee, Lynn, illus. 2003. (ENG., Illus.). 48p. (J). (gr. 3-7). 19.99 *(978-0-689-84947-3(8)*, Atheneum Bks. for Young Readers) Simon & Schuster Children's Publishing.

Dougherty, Rachel. A Raccoon at the White House: Ready-To-Read Level 2. Sanson, Rachel, illus. 2018. (Tails from History Ser.). (ENG.). 32p. (J). (gr. k-2). 17.99 *(978-1-5344-0542-4(9))*; pap. 4.99 *(978-1-5344-0541-7(0))* Simon Spotlight. (Simon Spotlight).

Douglas, Lloyd G. The White House. 2003. (Welcome Bks.). (ENG., Illus.). 24p. (J). (gr. -1-2). pap. 4.95 *(978-0-516-27878-0(9)*, Children's Pr.) Scholastic Library Publishing.

Drouot, Lucile Danis, illus. Washington, D. C. Monsters: A Search & Find Book. 2017. (ENG.). 22p. (J). (gr. -1). bds. 9.99 *(978-2-924734-06-3(1))* City Monsters Bks. CAN. Dist: Publishers Group West (PGW).

Eldridge, Alison & Eldridge, Stephen. The White House: An American Symbol, 1 vol. 2012. (All about American Symbols Ser.). (ENG.). 24p. (gr. -1-1). 25.27 *(978-0-7660-4062-5(3)*, 79e314ad-ddb0-4055-8358-566f1484a2f2, Enslow Publishing) Enslow Publishing, LLC.

Elish, Dan. Washington, D. C., 1 vol. 2nd rev. ed. 2007. (Celebrate the States (Second Edition) Ser.). (ENG., Illus.). 144p. (gr. 6-6). lib. bdg. 39.79 *(978-0-7614-2352-2(4)*, 263a3d6a-e664-4694-a069-92bce1a8f41b) Cavendish Square Publishing LLC.

Falk, Laine. What's in Washington, D. C. ? (Scholastic News Nonfiction Readers: American Symbols) 2009. (Scholastic News Nonfiction Readers Ser.). (ENG.). 24p. (J). (gr. 1-2). pap. 6.95 *(978-0-531-22429-8(5)*, Children's Pr.) Scholastic Library Publishing.

Farris, Christine King. March On! The Day My Brother Martin Changed the World. Ladd, London, illus. 2011. (J). (gr. 2-7). 29.95 *(978-0-545-10689-4(3))* Weston Woods Studios, Inc.

Figueroa, Acton. Washington, D. C., 1 vol. 2003. (World Almanac(r) Library of the States Ser.). (ENG., Illus.). 48p. (gr. 4-6). pap. 15.05 *(978-0-8368-5333-9(4)*, 0a9f666a-2a96-41f2-9ca2-a85a1388ff7c); lib. bdg. 33.67 *(978-0-8368-5162-5(5)*, 8ba3dab1-7607-42ce-9157-94ac251141f0) Stevens, Gareth Publishing LLLP. (Gareth Stevens Learning Library).

Gamble, Adam. Good Night Washington DC. Veno, Joe, illus. 2006. (Good Night Our World Ser.). (ENG.). 20p. (J). (gr. k — 1). bds. 9.95 *(978-0-9777979-1-2(0))* Good Night Bks.

Gelletly, LeeAnne. The Mid-Atlantic States: Delaware, Maryland, & Washington, D. C. 2015. (Let's Explore the States Ser.). (Illus.). 64p. (J). (gr. 5). 23.95 *(978-1-4222-3327-6(8))* Mason Crest.

Group/McGraw-Hill, Wright. Washington D. C. Heartbeat of a Nation, 6 vols. (Book2WebTM Ser.). (gr. 4-8). 36.50 *(978-0-322-04457-9(X))* Wright Group/McGraw-Hill.

HARCOURT. A Kid's Guide to Washington, D. C: Revised & Updated Edition. Brown, Richard, illus. rev. ed. 2008. (ENG.). 160p. (J). (gr. 1-4). pap. 15.99 *(978-0-15-206125-8(8)*, 1198393, Clarion Bks.) HarperCollins Pubs.

Hargrove, Julia. Tomb of the Unknowns. 2003. (Historic Monuments Ser.). (Illus.). 48p. (J). pap. 6.95 *(978-1-57310-405-0(1))* Teaching & Learning Co.

Heinrichs, Ann. Washington, DC. Kania, Matt, illus. 2017. (U. S. A. Travel Guides). (ENG.). 40p. (J). (gr. 2-5). lib. bdg. 38.50 *(978-1-5038-1991-7(4)*, 211625) Child's World, Inc, The.

Hicks, Terry Allan. Washington, D. C., 1 vol. Santoro, Christopher, illus. 2007. (It's My State! (First Edition)(r) Ser.). (ENG.). 80p. (gr. 4-4). lib. bdg. 34.07 *(978-0-7614-1929-7(2)*, 5d74eef8-f9a1-4fba-b36d-90a794674429) Cavendish Square Publishing LLC.

—Washington, D. C., 1 vol. 2nd rev. ed. 2014. (It's My State! (Second Edition)(r) Ser.). (ENG.). 80p. (gr. 4-4). lib. bdg. 35.93 *(978-1-62712-242-9(7)*, 7e6f978d-9506-4e96-b6a1-dfa1c90f644f) Cavendish Square Publishing LLC.

Hicks, Terry Allan & Jones Waring, Kerry. Washington, D. C. The Nation's Capital, 1 vol. 3rd rev. ed. 2016. (It's My State! (Third Edition)(r) Ser.). (ENG., Illus.). 80p. (J). (gr. 4-4). 35.93 *(978-1-62713-253-4(8)*, 28fe18e9-ae85-46e7-9f41-0d3b428427ef) Cavendish Square Publishing LLC.

Hill, Isabel. Urban Animals of Washington, D. C. 2013. (ENG., Illus.). 40p. (J). 17.99 *(978-1-59572-658-2(6))* Star Bright Bks., Inc.

Horn, Geoffrey M. Washington, D. C., 1 vol. 2005. (Portraits of the States Ser.). (ENG., Illus.). 32p. (gr. 3-5). pap. 11.50 *(978-0-8368-4695-9(8)*, f25390fb-774b-44ae-8dc7-9552c4251de5); lib. bdg. 28.67 *(978-0-8368-4676-8(1)*, b14ee624-8a4f-41a8-bc16-3866a12e3a8f) Stevens, Gareth Publishing LLLP. (Gareth Stevens Learning Library).

Johnson, Etta. The United States Government. 2005. (J). pap. *(978-1-4108-4592-4(3))* Benchmark Education Co.

Johnston, Joyce. Washington D. C. 2nd exp. rev. ed. 2003. (Hello U. S. A. Ser.). (Illus.). 84p. (J). (gr. 3-6). 25.26 *(978-0-8225-4091-5(6)*, Lerner Pubns.) Lerner Publishing Group.

—Washington, D.C. 2012. (J). lib. bdg. 25.26 *(978-0-7613-4492-6(6)*, Lerner Pubns.) Lerner Publishing Group.

Kent, Deborah. America the Beautiful: Washington D. C. (Revised Edition) rev. ed. 2011. (America the Beautiful, Third Ser.). (ENG.). 144p. (J). pap. 12.95 *(978-0-531-22915-6(7)*, Children's Pr.) Scholastic Library Publishing.

Kopp, Megan. Washington, DC. 2017. (Illus.). 24p. (J). *(978-1-4896-7299-5(0)*, AV2 by Weigl) Weigl Pubs., Inc.

Linde, Barbara M. Building Washington, D. C. Measuring the Area of Rectangular Spaces, 1 vol. 2010. (Math for the REAL World Ser.). (ENG., Illus.). 32p. (gr. 4-5). pap. 10.00 *(978-0-8239-8867-9(8)*, 3daef751-1840-4cc8-945c-e5f310d4da72, PowerKids Pr.) Rosen Publishing Group, Inc., The.

—Building Washington, DC: Measuring the Area of Rectangular Shapes, 1 vol. 2003. (PowerMath: Proficiency Ser.). (ENG., Illus.). 32p. (YA). (gr. 4-5). lib. bdg. 28.93 *(978-0-8239-8980-5(1)*, 57cac86a-0ca7-45ac-869c-d2a8177f66f3) Rosen Publishing Group, Inc., The.

Lusted, Marcia Amidon. The District of Columbia: The Nation's Capital, 1 vol. 2010. (Our Amazing States Ser.). (ENG.). 24p. (J). (gr. 3-3). pap. 9.25 *(978-1-4488-0772-7(7)*, a608de80-02b1-4ac9-b50f-df86855654e5); lib. bdg. 26.27 *(978-1-4488-0667-6(4)*, 00d88e66-aeaf-4e32-9097-0fd3746cc8b7) Rosen Publishing Group, Inc., The. (PowerKids Pr.).

Marcovitz, Hal. The Lincoln Memorial. 2004. (American Symbols & Their Meanings Ser.). (Illus.). 48p. (J). (gr. 4-18). lib. bdg. 19.95 *(978-1-59084-029-0(1))* Mason Crest.

—The Washington Monument. 2004. (American Symbols & Their Meanings Ser.). (Illus.). 48p. (J). (gr. 4-18). lib. bdg. 19.95 *(978-1-59084-028-3(3))* Mason Crest.

—The White House. 2004. (American Symbols & Their Meanings Ser.). (Illus.). 48p. (J). (gr. 4-18). lib. bdg. 19.95 *(978-1-59084-024-5(0))* Mason Crest.

Mattern, Joanne. Washington, D. C., 1 vol. 2007. (Cities Set 2 Ser.). (Illus.). 32p. (gr. -1-3). 27.07 *(978-1-59679-725-3(8)*, Checkerboard Library) ABDO Publishing Co.

Melmed, Laura Krauss. Capital! Washington D. C. from a to Z. Lessac, Frane, illus. 2006. (ENG.). 48p. (J). (gr. 1-6). 7.99 *(978-0-06-113614-6(X)*, HarperCollins) HarperCollins Pubs.

Orr, Tamra. The National Zoo. 2017. (Smithsonian Field Trips Ser.). (ENG., Illus.). 32p. (J). (gr. 2-5). pap. 7.95 *(978-1-5157-7990-2(4)*, 136053, Capstone Pr.) Capstone.

Rappoport, Bernice. The Community of Washington, D. C. Set Of 6. 2010. (Navigators Ser.). (J). pap. 44.00 net. *(978-1-4108-5094-2(3))* Benchmark Education Co.

—The Community of Washington, D. C. Text Pairs. 2008. (Bridges/Navigators Ser.). (J). (gr. 3). 81.00 *(978-1-4108-8356-8(6))* Benchmark Education Co.

Ribke, Simone T. Washington, D. C. Hamilton, Harriet, tr. 2006. (Rookie Espanol: Geografia: Estados (Geography: States) Ser.). (SPA., Illus.). 31p. (J). (gr. k-2). per. 5.95 *(978-0-516-25049-6(3)*, Children's Pr.) Scholastic Library Publishing.

—Washington, D. C. 2005. (Rookie Español Geografía Ser.). (SPA., Illus.). 32p. (J). (gr. k-2). lib. bdg. 19.50 *(978-0-516-25248-3(8)*, Children's Pr.) Scholastic Library Publishing.

Rice, Dona & Wilder, Nellie. Solving Problems as the Zoo. rev. ed. 2019. (Smithsonian: Informational Text Ser.). (ENG., Illus.). 24p. (J). (gr. 1-2). pap. 8.99 *(978-1-4938-6657-1(5))* Teacher Created Materials, Inc.

Robertson, Charles J. American Louvre: A History of the Renwick Gallery Building. 2015. (ENG., Illus.). 108p. pap. 24.95 *(978-1-907804-81-6(1))* Giles, D. Ltd. GBR. Dist: Consortium Bk. Sales & Distribution.

Segal, Robin. ABC in Washington, DC. 2007. (All 'Bout Cities Ser.). (ENG.). 32p. (J). (gr. k — 1). 12.95 *(978-0-9719697-7-3(9))* Murray Hill Bks., LLC.

Silate, Jennifer. The United States Capitol, 1 vol. 2005. (Primary Sources of American Symbols Ser.). (ENG., Illus.). 24p. (J). (gr. 3-3). lib. bdg. 26.27 *(978-1-4042-2694-4(X)*, 5bb4d991-6590-4bff-88bb-72dc94d90bf4) Rosen Publishing Group, Inc., The.

—The White House, 1 vol. 2005. (Primary Sources of American Symbols Ser.). (ENG., Illus.). 24p. (J). (gr. 3-3). lib. bdg. 26.27 *(978-1-4042-2695-1(8)*, 5e07579f-ac16-4a0d-acb7-e7a6cbae7d70) Rosen Publishing Group, Inc., The.

Swain, Gwenyth. Riding to Washington. Geister, David, illus. 2007. (Tales of Young Americans Ser.). (ENG.). 40p. (J). (gr. 1-4). 17.95 *(978-1-58536-324-7(3)*, 202128) Sleeping Bear Pr.

Weintraub, A. How to Draw District of Columbia's Sights & Symbols. 2009. (Kid's Guide to Drawing America Ser.). 32p. (gr. k-k). 50.50 *(978-1-61511-053-7(4)*, PowerKids Pr.) Rosen Publishing Group, Inc., The.

Zschock, Martha Day. Journey Around Washington D. C. from a to Z. 2004. (Journey Around... Ser.: Bk. 5). (ENG., Illus.). 32p. (J). (gr. 1-6). 17.95 *(978-1-889833-62-0(2)*, Commonwealth Editions) Applewood Bks.

WASHINGTON (D.C.)—CAPITOL

see United States Capitol (Washington, D.C.)

WASHINGTON (D.C.)—FICTION

Alexander, Kwame. Rebound. (Crossover Ser.). (ENG.). (J). (gr. 5-7). 2021. 432p. pap. 10.99 *(978-0-358-49483-6(4)*, 1806547) 2018. (Illus.). 416p. 16.99 *(978-0-544-86813-7(7)*, 1648717) HarperCollins Pubs. (Clarion Bks.).

—Rebound. 2021. (Crossover Ser.). (ENG.). 432p. (gr. 4-7). 26.19 *(978-1-5364-6794-9(4))* Houghton Mifflin Harcourt Publishing Co.

—Rebound. 2021. (Crossover Ser.). (ENG.). 432p. lib. bdg. 20.80 *(978-1-6636-3127-5(1))* Perfection Learning Corp.

Ali, Khayyam Esab. The Wormhole Kids Visit President Kennedy. 2004. (ENG., Illus.). 56p. (J). per. 7.95 *(978-1-59526-231-8(8))* Aeon Publishing Inc.

Amato, Mary. Invisible Lines. Caparó, Antonio Javier, illus. 2011. (ENG.). 336p. (gr. 4-6). lib. bdg. 22.44 *(978-1-60684-043-6(6))* Farshore GBR. Dist: Children's Plus, Inc.

Angleberger, Tom. Emperor Pickletine Rides the Bus. 2014. (Origami Yoda Files Ser.: 6). (J). lib. bdg. 25.70 *(978-0-606-36168-2(5))* Turtleback.

—Emperor Pickletine Rides the Bus (Origami Yoda #6) 2016. (Origami Yoda Ser.). (ENG., Illus.). 240p. (J). (gr. 3-7). pap. 7.95 *(978-1-4197-2201-1(8)*, 1074103, Amulet Bks.) Abrams, Inc.

Barnes, Jennifer Lynn. The Fixer. 2016. (ENG.). 400p. (YA). pap. 11.99 *(978-1-61963-598-2(4)*, 900141877, Bloomsbury USA Childrens) Bloomsbury Publishing USA.

Barnes, Peter W. Woodrow, the White House Mouse. Barnes, Cheryl Shaw, illus. 2012. (ENG.). 40p. (J). (gr. k-3). 17.99 *(978-1-59698-788-3(X)*, Little Patriot Pr.) Regnery Publishing.

Barry, Dave. The Worst Class Trip Ever. 2015. (Class Trip Ser.). (ENG.). 224p. (J). (gr. 3-7). 13.99 *(978-1-4847-0849-1(0))* Disney Pr.

—The Worst Class Trip Ever. 2020. (Penworthy Picks YA Fiction Ser.). (ENG.). 214p. (J). (gr. 6-8). 17.49 *(978-1-64697-236-4(8))* Penworthy Co., LLC, The.

Barry, Dave & Barry, Dave. The Worst Class Trip Ever. 2019. (Class Trip Ser.). (ENG.). 224p. (J). (gr. 3-7). pap. 9.99 *(978-1-368-04059-4(4))* Little, Brown Bks. for Young Readers.

Battle, Cleaton D. A Saturday Surprise. Cooper, Emmanuel, illus. 2006. 68p. (J). pap. 11.95 *(978-1-59663-504-3(5)*, Castle Keep Pr.) Rock, James A. & Co. Pubs.

Beck-Jacobson, Darlene. Wheels of Change. 2014. (ENG., Illus.). 197p. (J). (gr. 2-5). 15.95 *(978-1-939547-13-2(X)*, fea434e9-1ddd-40eb-b4bd-f71744c8d3e9) Creston Bks.

Benchmark Education Co., LLC. A Trip to Washington, D. C. A Capital Idea Teacher's Guide. 2013. (Reader's Theater Word Plays Ser.). *(978-1-4509-9037-0(1))* Benchmark Education Co.

Blackwood, Gary. Second Sight. 2007. (ENG.). 288p. (J). (gr. 5-18). 8.99 *(978-0-14-240747-9(X)*, Puffin Books) Penguin Young Readers Group.

Blackwood, Gary L. Second Sight. 2007. (Illus.). 279p. (J). (gr. 5-9). 14.65 *(978-0-7569-8132-7(8))* Perfection Learning Corp.

Bolden, Tonya. Inventing Victoria. (ENG.). (YA). 2020. 288p. pap. 10.99 *(978-1-5476-0317-6(8)*, 900211265) 2019. (Illus.). 272p. 17.99 *(978-1-68119-807-1(X)*, 900187338) Bloomsbury Publishing USA. (Bloomsbury Young Adult).

—Saving Savannah. 2020. (ENG., Illus.). 272p. (YA). 17.99 *(978-1-68119-804-0(5)*, 900187335, Bloomsbury Young Adult) Bloomsbury Publishing USA.

Bond, Thomas A. Mill Creek Kids. 2009. 132p. pap. 14.99 *(978-1-60791-634-5(7))* Salem Author Services.

Bowen, Carl. Back Burn. Lee, Marc, illus. 2016. (Firestormers Ser.). (ENG.). 112p. (J). (gr. 4-8). lib. bdg. 27.32 *(978-1-4965-3305-0(4)*, 132446, Stone Arch Bks.) Capstone.

Bradford, Chris. Bodyguard: Recruit (Book 1), Bk. 1. 2017. (Bodyguard Ser.: 1). (ENG.). 272p. (J). (gr. 5). pap. 8.99 *(978-1-5247-3697-2(X)*, Philomel Bks.) Penguin Young Readers Group.

Bradley, F. T. Double Vision: Code Name 711. 2015. (Double Vision Ser.: 2). (ENG.). 272p. (J). (gr. 3-7). pap. 6.99 *(978-0-06-210441-0(1)*, HarperCollins) HarperCollins Pubs.

Brezenoff, Steve. Field Trip Mysteries: the Ghost Who Haunted the Capitol. Canga, Chris, illus. 2010. (Field Trip Mysteries Ser.). 88p. (J). (gr. 3-6). 25.32 *(978-1-4342-2140-7(7)*, 102870); pap. 5.95 *(978-1-4342-2772-0(3)*, 114039) Capstone. (Stone Arch Bks.).

Brown, Jeff. Flat Stanley's Worldwide Adventures #9: the US Capital Commotion. Pamintuan, Macky, illus. 2011. (Flat Stanley's Worldwide Adventures Ser.: 9). (ENG.). 112p. (J). (gr. 2-5). 15.99 *(978-0-06-157436-8(8))*; pap. 6.99 *(978-0-06-143019-0(6))* HarperCollins Pubs. (HarperCollins).

Cabot, Meg. All-American Girl. 2008. (All-American Girl Ser.: 1). (ENG.). 416p. (YA). (gr. 8). pap. 10.99 *(978-0-06-147989-2(6)*, HarperTeen) HarperCollins Pubs.

—All-American Girl. 2008. (All-American Girl Ser.: Vol. 1). 398p. (YA). (gr. 7-12). 19.65 *(978-1-4178-2386-4(0))* Turtleback.

—Ready or Not. (All-American Girl Ser.: 2). 2008. (ENG.). 336p. (YA). (gr. 8). pap. 10.99 *(978-0-06-147996-0(9)*, HarperTeen) 2005. (ENG.). 256p. (J). (gr. 7-18). 16.99 *(978-0-06-072450-4(1))* 2nd ed. 2005. 256p. (J). (gr. 7-18). lib. bdg. 16.89 *(978-0-06-072451-1(X))* HarperCollins Pubs.

Caletti, Deb. The Queen of Everything. 2008. (ENG.). 352p. (YA). (gr. 7-12). pap. 11.99 *(978-1-4169-5781-2(2)*, Simon Pulse) Simon Pulse.

W X Y Z

Catasús Jennings, Terry. Gopher to the Rescue! a Volcano Recovery Story, 1 vol. O'Keefe, Laurie, illus. 2012. (ENG.). 32p. (J). (gr. -1-4). 17.95 *(978-1-60718-131-6(2))*; pap. 9.95 *(978-1-60718-141-5(X))* Arbordale Publishing.

Cobot, Meg. All-American Girl. 2004. 416p. (J). (gr. 7-18). pap. 44.00 incl. audio *(978-0-8072-2281-2(X)*, Listening Library) Random Hse. Audio Publishing Group.

Cohn, Rachel. You Know Where to Find Me. 2009. (ENG.). 224p. (YA). (gr. 7). pap. 8.99 *(978-0-689-87860-2(5)*, Simon & Schuster Bks. For Young Readers) Simon & Schuster Bks. For Young Readers.

—You Know Where to Find Me. 2008. (ENG.). 204p. (YA). (gr. 7-12). 22.44 *(978-0-689-87859-6(1))* Simon & Schuster, Inc.

Davis, Rachel. My Life at Mapleleaf Cabin. 2nd ed. 2004. (YA). per. 10.00 *(978-0-9741176-8-3(4))* Wu Li Turtle Corp.

De Los Heros, Luis & Wilson, Elizabeth. Chifa Chi's Little Adventure in Washington Dc. 2010. (ENG.). 40p. pap. 21.99 *(978-0-557-23085-3(3))* Lulu Pr., Inc.

Dee, Barbara. Everything I Know about You. 2018. (ENG., Illus.). 320p. (J). (gr. 4-8). 18.99 *(978-1-5344-0507-3(0)*, Aladdin) Simon & Schuster Children's Publishing.

Deflitch, Jennifer L. Delia the Dragonfly's Grand Adventures: Delia Goes to Washington D. C. 2012. 28p. (-18). pap. 24.95 *(978-1-62709-290-6(0))* America Star Bks.

DeVillers, Julia. Cleared for Takeoff. Pooler, Paige, illus. 2012. (Liberty Porter, First Daughter Ser.: 3). (ENG.). 224p. (J). (gr. 3-7). pap. 7.99 *(978-1-4169-9131-1(X)*, Simon & Schuster/Paula Wiseman Bks.) Simon & Schuster/Paula Wiseman Bks.

—Liberty Porter, First Daughter, 1. Pooler, Paige, illus. 2009. (Liberty Porter, First Daughter Ser.: 1). (ENG.). 176p. (J). (gr. 3-7). 15.99 *(978-1-4169-9126-7(3)*, Aladdin) Simon & Schuster Children's Publishing.

—Liberty Porter, First Daughter. Pooler, Paige, illus. 2010. (Liberty Porter, First Daughter Ser.: 1). (ENG.). 192p. (J). (gr. 3-7). pap. 7.99 *(978-1-4169-9127-4(1)*, Simon & Schuster/Paula Wiseman Bks.) Simon & Schuster/Paula Wiseman Bks.

—New Girl in Town. Pooler, Paige, illus. 2011. (Liberty Porter, First Daughter Ser.: 2). (ENG.). 224p. (J). (gr. 3-7). pap. 7.99 *(978-1-4169-9129-8(8)*, Simon & Schuster/Paula Wiseman Bks.) Simon & Schuster/Paula Wiseman Bks.

Earnhart, Hugh. A Day in D. C. with the Forest Friends. Ertel, Susan, illus. 2016. (ENG.). (J). 16.95 *(978-1-939710-53-6(7))* Orange Frazer Pr.

Ehrenberg, Pamela. Ethan, Suspended. 2009. (ENG.). 272p. (J). (gr. 6-9). pap. 8.50 *(978-0-8028-5317-2(X))* 2007. 266p. (YA). (gr. 7-18). 16.00 *(978-0-8028-5324-0(2)*, Eerdmans Bks For Young Readers) Eerdmans, William B. Publishing Co.

Emerson, Alice B. Betty Gordon in Washington. 2004. reprint ed. pap. 20.95 *(978-1-4191-0977-5(4))*; pap. 1.99 *(978-1-4192-0977-2(9))* Kessinger Publishing, LLC.

Emmer, E. R. Me, Minerva & the Flying Flora. Huerta, Catherine, illus. 2nd rev. ed. 2003. (Going to Ser.). Orig. Title: Me, Minera & the Flying Car. (ENG.). 133p. (J). (gr. 4-8). pap. 6.95 *(978-1-893577-10-7(4))* Four Corners Publishing Co., Inc.

Evans, Shane W. We March. Evans, Shane W., illus. 2012. (ENG., Illus.). 32p. (J). (gr. -1-3). 18.99 *(978-1-59643-539-1(9)*, 900061341) Roaring Brook Pr.

Everett, Forrest. Dear Santa, Love, Washington: An Evergreen State Christmas Celebration - with Real Letters! Quang Phuc, Pham, illus. 2018. (ENG.). 32p. (J). (gr. 1-4). 16.99 *(978-1-64170-039-9(4)*, 550039) Familius LLC.

Fisher, Anne. Look What Brains Can Do! 2005. reprint ed. pap. 20.95 *(978-1-4179-9453-3(3))* Kessinger Publishing, LLC.

Florence, Leigh Anne. Mr. Dogwood Goes to Washington. Asher, James, illus. 2008. (Woody the Kentucky Wiener Ser.). 56p. (J). (gr. 2-8). pap. 12.95 *(978-0-9741417-5-6(5))* HotDiggetyDog Pr.

Flores-Scott, Patrick. Jumped In. 2014. (ENG., Illus.). 304p. (YA). (gr. 7). pap. 15.99 *(978-1-250-05398-5(6)*, 900137223) Square Fish.

Frederick, Heather Vogel. The Black Paw, 1. 2013. (Spy Mice Ser.: 1). (ENG., Illus.). 224p. (J). (gr. 3-6). pap. 7.99 *(978-1-4424-6701-9(0))* Simon & Schuster, Inc.

Friedman, Laurie. Red, White & True Blue Mallory. Kalis, Jennifer, illus. (Mallory Ser.: 11). (ENG.). 184p. (J). (gr. 2-5). 2010. pap. 7.99 *(978-0-7613-3945-5(9)*, 126fea1d-13ec-4070-9e5e-70227e5a6a73) 2009. 15.95 *(978-0-8225-8882-5(X)*, 25f4d989-183f-4ef3-89d8-84c63c627d23) Lerner Publishing Group. (Darby Creek).

Furtney, Charles S. Tryconnel: An Antebellum Adventure along the C & O Canal. 2004. (Illus.). iii, 156p. (J). pap. *(978-0-9711835-3-7(8))* Local History Co., The.

Gibbs, Stuart. Spy School Secret Service. 2018. (Spy School Ser.). (ENG.). 368p. (J). (gr. 3-7). pap. 8.99 *(978-1-4814-7783-3(8)*, Simon & Schuster Bks. For Young Readers) Simon & Schuster Bks. For Young Readers.

Goguen, Martha. Sissy Goes to Washington. Fowler, Faith, illus. 2013. 36p. pap. *(978-1-897435-59-5(2))* Agio Publishing Hse.

Goldsberry, Booty. Scaredy-Cat, I'm Not. 2007. (ENG., Illus.). 40p. (gr. 4-7). pap. 9.95 *(978-0-9792875-0-3(2))* Goldsberry, Booty.

Gottesfeld, Jeff. Choices. 2014. (Campus Confessions Ser.: 3). (YA). lib. bdg. 20.80 *(978-0-606-34000-7(9))* Turtleback.

—Frenemies. 2014. (Campus Confessions Ser.: 2). (YA). lib. bdg. 20.80 *(978-0-606-33999-5(X))* Turtleback.

Gray, Mila. Run Away with Me. (ENG.). 368p. (YA). (gr. 11). 2018. pap. 12.99 *(978-1-4814-9097-9(4))* 2017. (Illus.). 17.99 *(978-1-4814-9096-2(6))* Simon Pulse. (Simon Pulse).

Green, S. E. Killer Instinct. 2014. (ENG., Illus.). 272p. (YA). (gr. 9). 17.99 *(978-1-4814-0285-9(4)*, Simon Pulse) Simon Pulse.

—Killer Within. 2015. (ENG.). 304p. (YA). (gr. 9). 17.99 *(978-1-4814-0288-0(9)*, Simon Pulse) Simon Pulse.

Harmon, Michael. Under the Bridge. 2013. (ENG.). 272p. (YA). (gr. 9). pap. 8.99 *(978-0-375-85930-4(6)*, Ember) Random Hse. Children's Bks.

Hicks, Deron R. The Van Gogh Deception. 2018. (Lost Art Mysteries Ser.). (ENG.). 320p. (J). (gr. 5-7). pap. 9.99 *(978-1-328-63517-4(1)*, 1735316, Clarion Bks.) HarperCollins Pubs.

Hope, Laura Lee. The Bobbsey Twins in Washington. 2005. 27.95 *(978-1-4218-0974-8(5)*, 1st World Library - Literary Society) 1st World Publishing, Inc.

—The Bobbsey Twins in Washington. 2007. 256p. 29.95 *(978-1-4344-8591-5(9))*; per. 17.95 *(978-1-4344-8590-8(0))* Wildside Pr., LLC.

Jacobs, Lily. The Littlest Bunny in Washington: An Easter Adventure. Dunn, Robert, illus. 2015. (Littlest Bunny Ser.). (ENG.). 32p. (J). (gr. -1-3). 9.99 *(978-1-4926-1231-5(6)*, Hometown World) Sourcebooks, Inc.

—The Littlest Bunny in Washington, DC: An Easter Adventure. Dunn, Robert, illus. 2015. (Littlest Bunny Ser.). (ENG.). 32p. (J). (gr. -1-3). 9.99 *(978-1-4926-1234-6(0)*, Hometown World) Sourcebooks, Inc.

James, Eric. Santa's Sleigh Is on Its Way to Washington: A Christmas Adventure. Dunn, Robert, illus. 2015. (Santa's Sleigh Is on Its Way Ser.). (ENG.). 32p. (J). (gr. k-2). 12.99 *(978-1-4926-2760-9(7)*, Hometown World) Sourcebooks, Inc.

—Santa's Sleigh Is on Its Way to Washington, D. C. A Christmas Adventure. Dunn, Robert, illus. 2016. (Santa's Sleigh Is on Its Way Ser.). (ENG.). 32p. (J). (gr. k-2). 12.99 *(978-1-4926-4363-0(7)*, 9781492643630, Hometown World) Sourcebooks, Inc.

—The Spooky Express Washington. Piwowarski, Marcin, illus. 2017. (Spooky Express Ser.). (ENG.). 32p. (J). (gr. k-6). 9.99 *(978-1-4926-5409-4(4)*, Hometown World) Sourcebooks, Inc.

—The Spooky Express Washington, D. C. Piwowarski, Marcin, illus. 2017. (Spooky Express Ser.). (ENG.). 32p. (J). (gr. k-6). 9.99 *(978-1-4926-5410-0(8)*, Hometown World) Sourcebooks, Inc.

—Tiny the Washington, D.C. 2018. (Tiny the Easter Bunny Ser.). (ENG.). 40p. (J). (gr. k-3). 9.99 *(978-1-4926-5976-1(2)*, Hometown World) Sourcebooks, Inc.

Keffer, Ann. The Seventh Chair. 2007. 76p. (J). per. 8.95 *(978-0-595-45917-9(X))* iUniverse, Inc.

Kehret, Peg & the Cat, Pete. The Stranger Next Door. 2008. (Pete the Cat Ser.: 1). (ENG.). 176p. (J). (gr. 3-7). 5.99 *(978-0-14-241248-0(1)*, Puffin Books) Penguin Young Readers Group.

Kelly, Katy. Lucy Rose: Here's the Thing about Me. Rex, Adam, illus. 2006. (Lucy Rose Ser.: 1). 160p. (J). (gr. 3-7). reprint ed. per. 7.99 *(978-0-440-42026-2(1)*, Yearling) Random Hse. Children's Bks.

—Lucy Rose: Working Myself to Pieces & Bits. Ferguson, Peter, illus. 2008. (Lucy Rose Ser.: 4). (ENG.). 208p. (J). (gr. 3-7). 6.99 *(978-0-440-42166-3(1)*, Yearling) Random Hse. Children's Bks.

—Melonhead. Johnson, Gillian, illus. (Melonhead Ser.: 1). (J). 2010. 240p. (gr. 3-7). 8.99 *(978-0-440-42187-0(X)*, Yearling)1. 2009. (ENG.). 224p. (gr. 4-6). lib. bdg. 22.44 *(978-0-385-90426-1(6)*, Delacorte Pr.) Random Hse. Children's Bks.

—Melonhead & the Big Stink. 2011. (Melonhead Ser.: 2). 224p. (J). (gr. 3-7). 7.99 *(978-0-375-84527-7(5)*, Yearling) Random Hse. Children's Bks.

—Melonhead & the Undercover Operation. Johnson, Gillian, illus. 2012. (Melonhead Ser.: 3). 256p. (J). (gr. 3-7). 7.99 *(978-0-375-84528-4(3)*, Yearling) Random Hse. Children's Bks.

Krishnaswami, Uma. The Problem with Being Slightly Heroic. Halpin, Abigail, illus. (ENG.). 288p. (J). (gr. 3-7). 2014. pap. 7.99 *(978-1-4424-2329-9(3)*, Atheneum Bks. for Young Readers) 2013. 16.99 *(978-1-4424-2328-2(5))* Simon & Schuster Children's Publishing.

Krulik, Nancy. Go Fetch! 2014. (Magic Bone Ser.: 5). (Illus.). 111p. (J). lib. bdg. 14.75 *(978-0-606-35701-2(7))* Turtleback.

—Go Fetch! #5. Braun, Sebastien, illus. 2014. (Magic Bone Ser.: 5). 128p. (J). (gr. 1-3). 6.99 *(978-0-448-48094-7(8)*, Grosset & Dunlap) Penguin Young Readers Group.

Labrecque, Candida. A Riverside Walk with Grandma. Labrecque, Candida & Labrecque, Candida, illus. l.t. ed. 2006. (Illus.). 23p. (J). per. 11.95 *(978-1-59879-137-2(0))* Lifevest Publishing, Inc.

Lee, Margaret A. Grandpa, What Are Lasers? 2012. 32p. pap. 19.99 *(978-1-4685-6343-6(2))* AuthorHouse.

Leray, Merrill. The House of Lady Chase. 2009. 70p. pap. 15.99 *(978-1-4415-4381-3(3))* Xlibris Corp.

Lewis, J. Patrick & Zappitello, Beth. First Dog's White House Christmas. Bowers, Tim, illus. 2010. (ENG.). 32p. (J). (gr. 1-4). 15.95 *(978-1-58536-503-6(3)*, 202197) Sleeping Bear Pr.

Marchi, C. You Can Grow Old with Me: A True Story. 2011. 24p. (gr. -1). pap. 12.95 *(978-1-4520-3716-5(7))* AuthorHouse.

Marciano, John Bemelmans. Madeline at the White House. (Madeline Ser.). (Illus.). (J). (gr. -1-2). 2020. 34p. bds. 9.99 *(978-0-593-11800-9(6)*, Viking Books for Young Readers) 2016. 48p. pap. 9.99 *(978-1-101-99780-2(X)*, Puffin Books) 2011. 48p. 19.99 *(978-0-670-01228-2(9)*, Viking Books for Young Readers) Penguin Young Readers Group.

—Madeline at the White House. 2016. (Madeline Ser.). lib. bdg. 19.65 *(978-0-606-38845-0(1))* Turtleback.

Marsh, Carole. The White House Christmas Mystery. 2009. (Real Kids, Real Places Ser.). 146p. (J). 18.99 *(978-0-635-06996-2(2)*, Marsh, Carole Mysteries) Gallopade International.

McCarthy, Peggy & Rivers, Julia. Not for the Meek. 2013. (ENG.). 130p. (J). pap. 10.95 *(978-1-4327-9157-5(5))* Outskirts Pr., Inc.

Mcgill, Leslie. Fighter. 2014. (Cap Central Ser.: 1). (YA). lib. bdg. 20.80 *(978-0-606-35737-1(8))* Turtleback.

—Hacker. 2014. (Cap Central Ser.: 3). (YA). lib. bdg. 20.80 *(978-0-606-35739-5(4))* Turtleback.

—Running Scared. 2014. (Cap Central Ser.: 2). (YA). lib. bdg. 20.80 *(978-0-606-35738-8(6))* Turtleback.

McLean, Hope. Catch Us If You Can, 1. 2013. (Jewel Society Ser.: 1). (ENG.). 144p. (J). (gr. 4-6). 18.69 *(978-0-545-60762-9(0))* Scholastic, Inc.

McPherson, Missie & O'Neill, Elizabeth. Alfred Visits Washington, D. C. 2005. (ENG., Illus.). 24p. (J). (gr. -1-3). pap. 12.00 *(978-0-9771836-1-6(0))* Funny Bone Bks.

Meddaugh, Susan. White House Dog. 2011. (Martha Speaks: Chapter Bks.). (ENG., Illus.). 96p. (J). (gr. 1-4). 18.69 *(978-0-547-39359-9(8))*; pap. 5.99 *(978-0-547-21076-6(0))* Houghton Mifflin Harcourt Publishing Co.

Messner, Kate. Capture the Flag, 1. 2013. (ENG.). 240p. (J). (gr. 3-7). pap. 8.99 *(978-0-545-41974-1(3)*, Scholastic Paperbacks) Scholastic, Inc.

Monroe, Ella. Truth or Dare: A Capital Girls Novel. 2013. (Capital Girls Ser.: 3). (ENG.). 304p. (YA). (gr. 8). pap. 20.99 *(978-0-312-62304-3(6)*, 900076855, St. Martin's Griffin) St. Martin's Pr.

Myers, Anna. Assassin. 2007. (ENG.). 224p. (YA). (gr. 7). per. 10.99 *(978-0-8027-9643-1(5)*, 900044867, Bloomsbury USA Childrens) Bloomsbury Publishing USA.

—Assassin. 2011. (ENG.). 192p. (YA). (gr. 4-6). 22.44 *(978-0-8027-8989-1(7)*, 9780802789891) 2005. (J). *(978-978-080-278-3(9))* Walker & Co.

Nez, John Abbott. The Twelve Days of Christmas in Washington. 2017. (Twelve Days of Christmas in America Ser.). (ENG., Illus.). 22p. (J). (-k). bds. 7.95 *(978-1-4549-2795-2(X))* Sterling Publishing Co., Inc.

Osborne, Mary Pope. Abe Lincoln at Last! 2013. (Magic Tree House Merlin Missions Ser.: 19). lib. bdg. 16.00 *(978-0-606-35563-6(4))* Turtleback.

Patterson, James. Ali Cross. (Ali Cross Ser.: 1). (ENG.). (J). (gr. 5-9). 2020. 336p. pap. 8.99 *(978-0-316-70568-4(3))* 2019. 320p. 16.99 *(978-0-316-53041-5(7))* Little Brown & Co. (Jimmy Patterson).

—Public School Superhero. 2015. (ENG., Illus.). 304p. (J). (gr. 3-7). 13.99 *(978-0-316-32214-0(8)*, Jimmy Patterson) Little Brown & Co.

Patterson, James & Tebbetts, Chris. Public School Superhero. Thomas, Cory, illus. 2016. (ENG.). 304p. (J). (gr. 3-7). pap. 8.99 *(978-0-316-26598-0(5)*, Jimmy Patterson) Little Brown & Co.

Patterson, James, et al. Public School Superhero. 2015. *(978-0-316-34231-5(9))* Little, Brown Bks. for Young Readers.

Pence, Charlotte. Marlon Bundo's Day in the Life of the Vice President. Pence, Karen, illus. 2018. (ENG.). 40p. (J). (gr. -1-3). 18.99 *(978-1-62157-776-8(7)*, Regnery Kids) Regnery Publishing.

Ponti, James. Framed! 2016. (Framed! Ser.: 1). (ENG., Illus.). 304p. (J). (gr. 3-7). 19.99 *(978-1-4814-3630-4(9)*, Aladdin) Simon & Schuster Children's Publishing.

Powell, Gail. The Adventures of Harold J. Kat. 2008. 40p. pap. 16.99 *(978-1-4259-6334-7(X))* AuthorHouse.

Ransom, Candice. The Twelve Days of Christmas in Washington, D. C. Hollander, Sarah, illus. 2018. (Twelve Days of Christmas in America Ser.). (ENG.). 22p. (J). (-k). bds. 7.95 *(978-1-4549-2966-6(9))* Sterling Publishing Co., Inc.

Roy, Ron. Capital Mysteries #10: the Election-Day Disaster. Bush, Timothy, illus. 2008. (Capital Mysteries Ser.: 10). (ENG.). 96p. (J). (gr. 1-4). 5.99 *(978-0-375-84805-6(3)*, Random Hse. Bks. for Young Readers) Random Hse. Children's Bks.

—Capital Mysteries #14: Turkey Trouble on the National Mall. Bush, Timothy, illus. 2012. (Capital Mysteries Ser.: 14). 96p. (J). (gr. 1-4). 6.99 *(978-0-307-93220-4(6)*, Random Hse. Bks. for Young Readers) Random Hse. Children's Bks.

—Capital Mysteries #3: the Skeleton in the Smithsonian. Bush, Timothy, illus. 2003. (Capital Mysteries Ser.: 3). (ENG.). 96p. (J). (gr. 1-4). 5.99 *(978-0-307-26517-3(X)*, Random Hse. Bks. for Young Readers) Random Hse. Children's Bks.

—Capital Mysteries #4: a Spy in the White House. Bush, Timothy, illus. 2004. (Capital Mysteries Ser.: 4). 96p. (J). (gr. 1-4). 6.99 *(978-0-375-82557-6(6)*, Random Hse. Bks. for Young Readers) Random Hse. Children's Bks.

—Capital Mysteries #5: Who Broke Lincoln's Thumb? Bush, Timothy, illus. 2005. (Capital Mysteries Ser.: 5). 96p. (J). (gr. 1-4). per. 5.99 *(978-0-375-82558-3(4)*, Random Hse. Bks. for Young Readers) Random Hse. Children's Bks.

—Capital Mysteries #7: Trouble at the Treasury. Bush, Timothy, illus. 2006. (Capital Mysteries Ser.: 7). 96p. (J). (gr. 1-4). per. 6.99 *(978-0-375-83969-6(0)*, Random Hse. Bks. for Young Readers) Random Hse. Children's Bks.

—Capital Mysteries #8: Mystery at the Washington Monument. Bush, Timothy, illus. 2007. (Capital Mysteries Ser.: 8). (ENG.). 96p. (J). (gr. 1-4). per. 5.99 *(978-0-375-83970-2(4)*, Random Hse. Bks. for Young Readers) Random Hse. Children's Bks.

—The Election-Day Disaster. Bush, Timothy, illus. 2008. (Capital Mysteries Ser.: No. 10). 87p. (gr. 1-4). 15.00 *(978-0-7569-8802-9(0))* Perfection Learning Corp.

—Mystery at the Washington Monument. Bush, Timothy, illus. 2007. (Capital Mysteries Ser.: No. 8). 87p. (gr. 1-4). 15.00 *(978-0-7569-7845-7(9))* Perfection Learning Corp.

—Mystery at the Washington Monument, 8. Bush, Timothy, illus. 2007. (Capital Mysteries Ser.: No. 8). (ENG.). 87p. (J). (gr. 3-6). lib. bdg. 17.44 *(978-0-375-93970-9(9))* Random House Publishing Group.

—A Spy in the White House, 4. Bush, Timothy, tr. Bush, Timothy, illus. 2004. (Capital Mysteries Ser.: No. 4). (ENG.). 86p. (J). (gr. 2-4). lib. bdg. 17.44 *(978-0-375-92557-3(0))* Random House Publishing Group.

—A Thief at the National Zoo. Bush, Timothy, illus. 2008. (Capital Mysteries Ser.: No. 9). 87p. (gr. k-3). 15.00 *(978-0-7569-8329-1(0))* Perfection Learning Corp.

—A to Z Mysteries Super Edition 3: White House White-Out. Gurney, John Steven, illus. 2008. (to Z Mysteries Ser.: 3). 144p. (J). (gr. 1-4). 6.99 *(978-0-375-84721-9(9)*, Random Hse. Bks. for Young Readers) Random Hse. Children's Bks.

—White House White-Out. Gurney, John, illus. 2008. (A to Z Mysteries Ser.: No. 3). 124p. (gr. 1-4). 15.00 *(978-0-7569-8799-2(7))* Perfection Learning Corp.

—Who Broke Lincoln's Thumb?, 5. Bush, Timothy, illus. 2005. (Capital Mysteries Ser.: No. 5). (ENG.). 86p. (J). (gr. 2-4). lib. bdg. 17.44 *(978-0-375-92558-0(9))* Random House Publishing Group.

Rutledge, Eddie. Amani's World: Amani Goes to Washington D. C. Anderson, Susan, illus. 2009. 16p. pap. 8.75 *(978-1-4490-2095-8(X))* AuthorHouse.

Salazar, L. J. Chin & the Magic Stones: Book One - Becoming Guardians. 2009. 108p. 20.95 *(978-0-595-63627-3(6))*; pap. 10.95 *(978-0-595-53157-8(1))* iUniverse, Inc.

Sauls, Lynn B. Gabriel Goes to Washington: Through Big Brown Eyes; the Adventures of Gabriel the Poodle. Sauls, Lynn B., illus. 2013. (Illus.). 26p. pap. 9.99 *(978-0-9893216-1-7(4))* Sauls, Lynn.

Scheffler, Stephanie. Elizabeth & the War of 1812. 2010. 292p. (YA). 28.95 *(978-1-4502-3539-6(5))*; (ENG.). pap. 18.95 *(978-1-4502-3540-2(9))* iUniverse, Inc.

Skewes, John & Fox, Andrew. Larry Gets Lost in Washington, DC. Skewes, John, illus. 2014. (Larry Gets Lost Ser.). (ENG., Illus.). 32p. (J). (gr. -1-2). 17.99 *(978-1-57061-899-4(2)*, Little Bigfoot) Sasquatch Bks.

Smallman, Steve. Santa Is Coming to Washington. Dunn, Robert, illus. (ENG.). (J). 2012. 32p. (-3). 9.99 *(978-1-4022-7524-1(2)*, Sourcebooks Jabberwocky) 2nd ed. 2019. 40p. (gr. -1-3). 12.99 *(978-1-7282-0111-5(X)*, Hometown World) Sourcebooks, Inc.

Smith, Lindsay. Skandal. 2016. (Sekret Ser.: 2). (ENG.). 352p. (YA). pap. 20.99 *(978-1-250-07369-3(3)*, 900150800) Square Fish.

Smith, Roland. Beneath. 2015. (ENG., Illus.). 272p. (J). (gr. 4-7). 16.99 *(978-0-545-56486-1(7)*, Scholastic Pr.) Scholastic, Inc.

Smith, Yeardley. I, Lorelei. 2009. 352p. (J). (gr. 3-7). lib. bdg. 17.89 *(978-0-06-149345-4(7)*, Geringer, Laura Book) HarperCollins Pubs.

Stewart, Emma. The Adventures of Fillmore the Gerbil. 2008. 24p. pap. 13.50 *(978-1-60693-033-5(8)*, Eloquent Bks.) Strategic Book Publishing & Rights Agency (SBPRA).

Stinson, Kathy. The Man with the Violin. Petricic, Dusan, illus. 2016. 32p. (J). (gr. k-3). pap. 9.95 *(978-1-55451-564-6(5))* Annick Pr., Ltd. CAN. Dist: Publishers Group West (PGW).

Stone, Peter. The Perfect Candidate. 2018. (ENG., Illus.). 384p. (YA). (gr. 7). 18.99 *(978-1-5344-2217-9(X)*, Simon & Schuster Bks. For Young Readers) Simon & Schuster Bks. For Young Readers.

—The Perfect Candidate. 2019. (ENG.). 384p. (YA). (gr. 7). pap. 12.99 *(978-1-5344-2218-6(8))* Simon & Schuster, Inc.

Stossel, Sage. On the Loose in Washington, D. C. 2013. (Find the Animals Ser.). (ENG., Illus.). 28p. (J). (gr. -1-3). 14.95 *(978-1-938700-14-9(7)*, Commonwealth Editions) Applewood Bks.

Sully, Katherine. Night-Night Washington. Poole, Helen, illus. 2017. (Night-Night Ser.). (ENG.). 20p. (J). (gr. -1-1). bds. 9.99 *(978-1-4926-4766-9(7)*, 9781492647669, Hometown World) Sourcebooks, Inc.

—Night-Night Washington, D. C. Poole, Helen, illus. 2017. (Night-Night Ser.). (ENG.). 20p. (J). (gr. -1-1). bds. 9.99 *(978-1-4926-4773-7(X)*, 9781492647737, Hometown World) Sourcebooks, Inc.

Sutton, Margaret. Discovery at Dragon's Mouth #31, No. 31. 2008. (Judy Bolton Ser.). (ENG., Illus.). 196p. (gr. 4-7). pap. 14.95 *(978-1-4290-9051-3(0))* Applewood Bks.

—Whispered Watchword #32, No. 32. 2008. (Judy Bolton Ser.). (ENG., Illus.). 196p. (gr. 4-7). pap. 14.95 *(978-1-4290-9052-0(9))* Applewood Bks.

Swain, Gwenyth & Whelan, Gloria. Voices for Freedom. Geister, David et al, illus. 2013. (American Adventures Ser.). (ENG.). 72p. (J). (gr. 3-6). 6.99 *(978-1-58536-886-0(5)*, 202900) Sleeping Bear Pr.

Thomson, Melissa. Keena Ford & the Field Trip Mix-Up. 2010. (Keena Ford Ser.: 2). 112p. (J). (gr. 1-3). 6.99 *(978-0-14-241572-6(3)*, Puffin Books) Penguin Young Readers Group.

Trueit, Trudi. Explorer Academy: the Nebula Secret (Book 1) (Explorer Academy Ser.: 1). (Illus.). (J). (gr. 3-7). 2019. 216p. pap. 9.99 *(978-1-4263-3810-6(4))* 2018. 208p. 16.99 *(978-1-4263-3159-6(2))* 2018. (ENG., 208p. lib. bdg. 26.90 *(978-1-4263-3160-2(6))* Disney Publishing Worldwide. (Under the Stars).

Trueman, Terry. No Right Turn. 2009. (ENG.). 176p. (YA). (gr. 9). pap. 8.99 *(978-0-06-057493-2(3)*, HarperTeen) HarperCollins Pubs.

Turnage, Cyndy. A Trip to Washington, D. C. A Capital Idea. Fagan, Martin, illus. 2013. (Reader's Theater Word Plays Ser.). (J). (gr. 1-2). *(978-1-4509-8941-1(1))* Benchmark Education Co.

Warner, Penny. The Hunt for the Missing Spy. 2016. (Code Busters Club Ser.: 5). (ENG.). 168p. (J). (gr. 3-6). E-Book 26.65 *(978-1-5124-0305-3(9)*, Darby Creek) Lerner Publishing Group.

Wildavsky, Rachel. The Secret of Rover. Caparo, Antonio, illus. 2015. (ENG.). 360p. (J). (gr. 4-8). pap. 7.95 *(978-1-4197-1968-4(8)*, 681103, Amulet Bks.) Abrams, Inc.

Wiles, Deborah. Countdown. (Sixties Trilogy Ser.). (ENG.). 400p. (J). (gr. 4-7). 2010. 21.99 *(978-0-545-10605-4(2)*, Scholastic Pr.)1. 2013. pap. 9.99 *(978-0-545-10606-1(0)*, Scholastic Paperbacks) Scholastic, Inc.

Yasso, C. D. The Adventures of Penn & Penelope in Washington, Dc. 2012. (ENG.). 32p. 15.75 *(978-1-105-64108-4(2))* Lulu Pr., Inc.

WASHINGTON (D.C.)—HISTORY

Aretha, David. The Story of the Civil Rights March on Washington for Jobs & Freedom in Photographs, 1 vol. 2014. (Story of the Civil Rights Movement in Photographs Ser.). (ENG.). 48p. (gr. 5-6). lib. bdg. 27.93 *(978-0-7660-4238-4(3)*, a31e10d2-c298-4e27-939e-f160f74c3113) Enslow Publishing, LLC.

Benduhn, Tea, et al. Washington, 1 vol. 3rd rev. ed. 2014. (It's My State! (Third Edition)(r) Ser.). (ENG.). 80p. (gr. 4-4). 35.93 *(978-1-5026-0007-3(2)*, cc719396-2156-4123-8250-5b66ccc57b2e) Cavendish Square Publishing LLC.

Bolden, Tonya. Capital Days: Michael Shiner's Journal & the Growth of Our Nation's Capital. 2015. (ENG., Illus.). 96p. (J). (gr. 5-9). 21.95 *(978-1-4197-0733-9(7)*, 1056601, Abrams Bks. for Young Readers) Abrams, Inc.

Butterfield, Moira. Lonely Planet Kids City Trails - Washington DC 1. Bruff, Alex & Taylor, Matt, illus. 2017. (Lonely Planet Kids Ser.). (ENG.). 104p. (J). (gr. 4-7). pap. 12.99 *(978-1-78657-962-1(6)*, 5658) Lonely Planet Global Ltd. IRL. Dist: Hachette Bk. Group.

Carole Marsh. Washington Dc Coloring & Activity Book. 2004. (City Bks.). 24p. (gr. k-5). pap. 3.95 *(978-0-635-02232-5(X))* Gallopade International.

—Washington Indians. 2004. (Washington Experienc Ser.). lib. bdg. 29.95 *(978-0-635-02339-1(3))*; 36p. (gr. 3-8). pap. 7.95 *(978-0-635-02338-4(5))* Gallopade International.

Chang, Kirsten. The Lincoln Memorial. 2019. (Symbols of American Freedom Ser.). (ENG., Illus.). 24p. (J). (gr. k-3).

pap. 7.99 *(978-1-61891-493-4(6)*, 12143, Blastoff! Readers) Bellwether Media.
—The Washington Monument. 2019. (Symbols of American Freedom Ser.). (ENG., Illus.). 24p. (J). (gr. k-3). pap. 7.99 *(978-1-61891-495-8(2)*, 12145, Blastoff! Readers) Bellwether Media.
Conley, Kate. Engineering the Space Needle. 2017. (Building by Design Set 2 Ser.). (ENG., Illus.). 48p. (J). (gr. 4-8). lib. bdg. 35.64 *(978-1-5321-1377-2(3)*, 27675) ABDO Publishing Co.
Cunningham, Alvin Robert. Washington Is Burning! The War of 1812. 2003. (Reading Essentials in Social Studies). (Illus.). 48p. (J). 9.00 *(978-0-7891-5896-3(5))* Perfection Learning Corp.
Currie, Karen. District of Columbia: The Nation's Capital. 2012. (J). 27.13 *(978-1-61913-337-2(7))*; pap. 27.13 *(978-1-61913-338-9(5))* Weigl Pubs., Inc.
Dyan, Penelope. Abraham Lincoln Was Here! a Kid's Guide to Washington D C. Weigand, John D., photos by. 2009. (Illus.). 44p. pap. 11.95 *(978-1-935118-82-4(X))* Bellissima Publishing, LLC.
Edison, Erin. The Lincoln Memorial: A 4D Book. 2018. (National Landmarks Ser.). (ENG., Illus.). 24p. (J). (gr. 1-3). lib. bdg. 27.99 *(978-1-5435-3130-5(X)*, 138735, Capstone Pr.) Capstone.
—The Vietnam Veterans Memorial: A 4D Book. 2018. (National Landmarks Ser.). (ENG., Illus.). 24p. (J). (gr. 1-3). lib. bdg. 27.99 *(978-1-5435-3132-9(6)*, 138737, Capstone Pr.) Capstone.
—The Washington Monument: A 4D Book. 2018. (National Landmarks Ser.). (ENG., Illus.). 24p. (J). (gr. 1-3). lib. bdg. 27.99 *(978-1-5435-3133-6(4)*, 138738, Capstone Pr.) Capstone.
Epstein, Brad M. Washington D. C. 101: My First City-Board-book. I.t. ed. 2009. (ENG., Illus.). 24p. (J). 9.95 *(978-1-60730-004-5(4)*, 101 Bk.) Michaelson Entertainment.
Esbaum, Jill. Cherry Blossoms Say Spring. 2012. (Illus.). (J). (gr. -1-k). pap. 5.95 *(978-1-4263-0984-7(8)*, National Geographic Kids) Disney Publishing Worldwide.
Fejto, Raphael & Fejto, Raphael. The Fork. 2016. (Little Inventions Ser.). (ENG., Illus.). 32p. (J). (gr. 3-5). 9.95 *(978-1-77085-745-2(1)*, 0f7ef054-f0a3-46ac-8bd2-5c3bcebf58f5) Firefly Bks., Ltd.
Figley, Marty Rhodes. Washington Is Burning. Orback, Craig, illus. (On My Own History Ser.). 48p. (J). (gr. 2-4). 2007. (ENG.). per. 8.99 *(978-0-8225-6050-0(X)*, 220511bf-9018-498f-8ff3-a73d591dfbeb, First Avenue Editions) 2006. lib. bdg. 25.26 *(978-1-57505-875-7(8))* Lerner Publishing Group.
Fox, Frances Margaret. Washington D C , the Nation's Capital: Romance, Adventure, Achievement. Vincent, Andrew M. & Higgie, Will K., illus. 2012. 394p. 53.95 *(978-1-258-23323-5(1))* Literary Licensing, LLC.
Furman, Elina. Washington, D. C. 2009. (From Sea to Shining Sea, Second Ser.). (ENG.). 80p. (J). pap. 7.95 *(978-0-531-21145-8(2)*, Children's Pr.) Scholastic Library Publishing.
Gaspar, Joe. The White House / la Casa Blanca, 1 vol. Alamn, Eduardo, ed. 2013. (PowerKids Readers: Símbolos de América / American Symbols Ser.). (ENG & SPA.). 24p. (J). (gr. k-k). 26.27 *(978-1-4777-1206-1(2)*, e0883af7-8068-4cae-8704-cccfacd383c4, PowerKids Pr.) Rosen Publishing Group, Inc., The.
Hamilton, John. Washington, DC, 1 vol. 2016. (United States of America Ser.). (ENG., Illus.). 48p. (J). (gr. 5-9). 34.21 *(978-1-68078-351-3(3)*, 21687, Abdo & Daughters) ABDO Publishing Co.
Hirsch, Rebecca E. What's Great about Washington, DC? 2015. (Our Great States Ser.). (ENG., Illus.). 32p. (J). (gr. 2-5). lib. bdg. 26.65 *(978-1-4677-3859-0(X)*, 35e909c5-fead-4a27-9068-301c9c996ca5, Lerner Pubns.) Lerner Publishing Group.
Hoena, B. A. Washington, D.C: The U.S. Capital. 2014. (Illus.). 32p. (J). *(978-0-531-29158-0(8))* Bellwether Media.
Hoena, Blake. Washington, D. C. 2013. (Exploring the States Ser.). (ENG., Illus.). 32p. (J). (gr. 3-7). lib. bdg. 27.95 *(978-1-62617-048-3(7)*, Blastoff! Readers) Bellwether Media.
Hopkinson, Deborah. Sweet Land of Liberty, 1 vol. Jenkins, Leonard, illus. 2019. 32p. (J). (gr. 1-4). pap. 7.95 *(978-1-68263-124-9(9))* Peachtree Publishing Co. Inc.
Ingram, Scott. The 1963 Civil Rights March, 1 vol. 2004. (Landmark Events in American History Ser.). (ENG., Illus.). 48p. (gr. 5-8). lib. bdg. 33.67 *(978-0-8368-5392-6(X)*, c81073e3-f41f-4b6e-9e6d-c9becae83512, Gareth Stevens Secondary Library) Stevens, Gareth Publishing LLLP.
Jakobsen, Kathy. My Washington, DC. 2016. (ENG., Illus.). 40p. (J). (gr. -1-3). 18.99 *(978-0-316-12612-0(8))* Little, Brown Bks. for Young Readers.
Jerome, Kate B. Lucky to Live in Washington. 2017. (Arcadia Kids Ser.). (ENG., Illus.). 32p. (J). 16.99 *(978-0-7385-2774-1(2))* Arcadia Publishing.
—The Wise Animal Handbook Washington. 2017. (Arcadia Kids Ser.). (ENG., Illus.). 32p. (J). 16.99 *(978-0-7385-2848-9(X))* Arcadia Publishing.
Johnson, Robin. March on Washington. 2013. (ENG.). 48p. (J). *(978-0-7787-1101-8(3))*; pap. *(978-0-7787-1121-6(8))* Crabtree Publishing Co.
Kellaher, Karen. Washington, D. C. (a True Book: My United States) (Library Edition) 2018. (True Book (Relaunch) Ser.). (ENG., Illus.). 48p. (J). (gr. 3-5). lib. bdg. 31.00 *(978-0-531-23172-2(0)*, Children's Pr.) Scholastic Library Publishing.
Kent, Deborah. America the Beautiful: Washington, D. C. (Revised Edition) 2014. (America the Beautiful, Third Ser. (Revised Edition) Ser.). (ENG., Illus.). 144p. (J). lib. bdg. 40.00 *(978-0-531-28298-4(8))* Scholastic Library Publishing.
Kissock, Heather. Lincoln Memorial. 2017. (Illus.). 24p. (J). *(978-1-5105-0602-2(0))* SmartBook Media, Inc.
—Washington Monument. 2017. (Illus.). 24p. (J). *(978-1-5105-0608-4(X))* SmartBook Media, Inc.
—White House. 2017. (Illus.). 24p. (J). *(978-1-5105-0611-4(X))* SmartBook Media, Inc.
Klemm, Rebecca & Rebecca Klemm Charitable Foundation. NumbersAlive! Books for Young Travelers. 2012. (ENG.). pap. 13.95 *(978-0-9853667-0-4(2))* NumbersAlive! Pr.
Korrell, Emily B. Awesome Adventures at the Smithsonian: The Official Kids Guide to the Smithsonian Institution. 2013. (Illus.). 128p. (gr. 2-5). pap. 14.95 *(978-1-58834-349-9(9)*, Smithsonian Bks.) Smithsonian Institution Scholarly Pr.
Krull, Kathleen. What Was the March on Washington? 2013. (What Was... Ser.). lib. bdg. 16.00 *(978-0-606-29974-9(2))* Turtleback.
Krull, Kathleen & Who HQ. What Was the March on Washington? Tomkinson, Tim, illus. 2013. (What Was? Ser.). 112p. (J). (gr. 3-7). pap. 5.99 *(978-0-448-46287-5(7)*, Penguin Workshop) Penguin Young Readers Group.
Linde, Barbara M. Building Washington, D. C. Measuring the Area of Rectangular Shapes. 2009. (PowerMath: Proficiency Ser.). 32p. (gr. 4-5). 47.90 *(978-1-60851-390-1(4)*, PowerKids Pr.) Rosen Publishing Group, Inc., The.
—The Lincoln Memorial, 1 vol. 2018. (Symbols of America Ser.). (ENG.). 24p. (gr. 1-2). 24.27 *(978-1-5382-2899-9(8)*, ec4147a1-3f4f-4d4e-a904-02d3f9a65154) Stevens, Gareth Publishing LLLP.
—The Washington Monument, 1 vol. 2018. (Symbols of America Ser.). (ENG.). 24p. (gr. 1-2). 24.27 *(978-1-5382-2900-2(5)*, b34cd5fd-492c-47e8-be87-894a5e7b5914) Stevens, Gareth Publishing LLLP.
—The White House, 1 vol. 2018. (Symbols of America Ser.). (ENG.). 24p. (gr. 1-2). lib. bdg. 24.27 *(978-1-5382-2901-9(3)*, 96153e96-1365-4456-a742-d208641df833) Stevens, Gareth Publishing LLLP.
Lunis, Natalie & Taylor, Troy. A Haunted Capital. 2015. (Illus.). 32p. (J). lib. bdg. 28.50 *(978-1-62724-243-1(0))* Bearport Publishing Co., Inc.
Maloof, Torrey. You Are There! March on Washington, August 28, 1963. 2nd rev. ed. 2017. (TIME(r): Informational Text Ser.). (ENG., Illus.). 32p. (gr. 6-8). pap. 13.99 *(978-1-4938-3929-2(2))* Teacher Created Materials, Inc.
Marcovitz, Hal. Lincoln Memorial: Shrine to an American Hero. Moreno, Barry, ed. 2014. (Patriotic Symbols of America Ser.: 20). (Illus.). 48p. (J). (gr. 4-18). 20.95 *(978-1-4222-3127-2(5))* Mason Crest.
Marsh, Carole. Exploring Washington Through Project-Based Learning: Geography, History, Government, Economics & More. 2016. (Washington Experience Ser.). (ENG.). (J). pap. 9.99 *(978-0-635-12371-8(1))* Gallopade International.
—I'm Reading about Washington. 2014. (Washington Experience Ser.). (ENG., Illus.). (J). pap., pap. 8.99 *(978-0-635-11322-1(8))* Gallopade International.
Mattern, Joanne. Washington, D. C. (Rookie Read-About American Symbols) (Library Edition) 2014. (Rookie Read-About American Symbols Ser.). (ENG., Illus.). 32p. (J). (gr. 1-2). lib. bdg. 25.00 *(978-0-531-21569-2(5)*, Children's Pr.) Scholastic Library Publishing.
Nelson, Kristin L. The Lincoln Memorial. 2010. (Lightning Bolt Bks.). (Illus.). 32p. (J). (gr. k-2). lib. bdg. 25.26 *(978-0-7613-6018-6(2)*, Lerner Pubns.) Lerner Publishing Group.
—The Washington Monument. (Lightning Bolt Bks.). (Illus.). 32p. (J). (gr. k-2). 2010. lib. bdg. 25.26 *(978-0-7613-6019-3(0)*, Lerner Pubns.) 2003. (ENG., pap. 7.99 *(978-0-8225-3759-5(1)*, 4a0d1f3a-9731-4c87-b938-ac6605d7826f, First Avenue Editions) Lerner Publishing Group.
O'Connor, Jane. If the Walls Could Talk: Family Life at the White House. Hovland, Gary, illus. 2004. (ENG.). 48p. (J). (gr. 1-4). 19.99 *(978-0-689-86863-4(4)*, Simon & Schuster/Paula Wiseman Bks.) Simon & Schuster/Paula Wiseman Bks.
O'Neal, Claire. Washington, D. C. 2009. (Class Trip Ser.). (Illus.). 48p. (J). (gr. 2-5). lib. bdg. 29.95 *(978-1-58415-809-7(3))* Mitchell Lane Pubs.
Owens, Tom. Washington, D.C. 2003. (Reading Essentials in Social Studies). (Illus.). 48p. (J). pap. 9.00 *(978-0-7891-5839-0(6))* Perfection Learning Corp.
Panchyk, Richard. Washington, DC, History for Kids: The Making of a Capital City, with 21 Activities. 2016. (For Kids Ser.: 58). (ENG., Illus.). 144p. (J). (gr. 4). pap. 16.99 *(978-1-61373-006-5(3))* Chicago Review Pr., Inc.
Publications International Ltd. Staff. Yesterday & Today Seattle. 2008. 192p. 19.95 *(978-1-4127-1577-5(6))* Publications International, Ltd.
Rajczak, Michael. Haunted! the White House. 2013. (History's Most Haunted Ser.). 32p. (J). (gr. 3-6). pap. 63.00 *(978-1-4339-9270-4(1))* Stevens, Gareth Publishing LLLP.
Rodgers, Kelly. Our Nation's Capital: Washington, DC, 1 vol. rev. ed. 2014. (Social Studies: Informational Text Ser.). (ENG., Illus.). 32p. (gr. 2-4). pap. 11.99 *(978-1-4333-7362-6(9))* Teacher Created Materials, Inc.
Ruffin, Frances E. The Lincoln Memorial, 1 vol. 2005. (Places in American History Ser.). (ENG., Illus.). 24p. (gr. 2-4). pap. 9.15 *(978-0-8368-6418-2(2)*, 6077f5f0-4f2d-49bc-ae23-0d36382a36a4); lib. bdg. 24.67 *(978-0-8368-6411-3(5)*, 61b9d970-2d0f-42ee-948b-8a392a052d9d) Stevens, Gareth Publishing LLLP. (Weekly Reader Leveled Readers).
Sasek, Miroslav. This Is Washington, D. C. A Children's Classic. 2011. (This Is ... Ser.). (ENG., Illus.). 64p. (J). (gr. 2-12). 17.95 *(978-0-7893-2232-6(3))* Universe Publishing.
Schuh, Mari. The White House. 2018. (Symbols of American Freedom Ser.). (ENG.). 24p. (J). (gr. k-3). lib. bdg. 26.95 *(978-1-62617-890-8(9)*, Blastoff! Readers) Bellwether Media.
Silate, Jennifer. The White House. 2009. (Primary Sources of American Symbols Ser.). 24p. (gr. 3-3). 42.50 *(978-1-60851-512-7(5)*, PowerKids Pr.) Rosen Publishing Group, Inc., The.
Silverman, Steve. The Story of the Washington Wizards. 2010. (NBA — A History of Hoops Ser.). 48p. (YA). (gr. 5-18). 23.95 *(978-1-58341-965-6(9)*, Creative Education) Creative Co., The.
Skewes, John. Larry Loves Washington, DC! A Larry Gets Lost Book. 2016. (Larry Gets Lost Ser.). (Illus.). 20p. (J). (— 1). bds. 10.99 *(978-1-63217-048-4(5)*, Little Bigfoot) Sasquatch Bks.
Smith, Jr, Charles R. Brick by Brick. 2012. (ENG., Illus.). 32p. (J). (gr. -1-3). 17.99 *(978-0-06-192082-0(7)*, Amistad) HarperCollins Pubs.
Smith, Charles R., Jr. Brick by Brick. Cooper, Floyd, illus. 2015. (ENG.). 32p. (J). (gr. -1-3). pap. 8.99 *(978-0-06-192084-4(3)*, Amistad) HarperCollins Pubs.
Sonneborn, Liz. District of Columbia: Past & Present, 1 vol. 2010. (United States: Past & Present Ser.). (ENG.). 48p. (YA). (gr. 5-5). pap. 12.75 *(978-1-4358-9528-7(2)*, 9825c07d-fd4e-4060-8ffe-805e49860d54); lib. bdg. 34.47 *(978-1-4358-9501-0(0)*, b9052fd3-75d0-4364-bbe0-53b6d7123e28) Rosen Publishing Group, Inc., The. (Rosen Reference).
Stine, Megan & Who HQ. Where Is the White House? Groff, David, illus. 2015. (Where Is? Ser.). 112p. (J). (gr. 3-7). 5.99 *(978-0-448-48355-9(6)*, Penguin Workshop) Penguin Young Readers Group.
Sutcliffe, Jane. The White House Is Burning: August 24 1814. Farquharson, Alexander, illus. 2014. 128p. (J). (gr. 4-7). 19.95 *(978-1-58089-656-6(1))* Charlesbridge Publishing, Inc.
Thomas, William. District of Columbia. 2011. (Guide to American States Ser.). (Illus.). 48p. (YA). (gr. 3-6). 29.99 *(978-1-61690-821-8(1))* Weigl Pubs., Inc.
—District of Columbia: The Nation's Capital. 2016. (J). *(978-1-4896-4839-6(9))* Weigl Pubs., Inc.

WASHINGTON (D.C.)—WHITE HOUSE

see White House (Washington, D.C.)

WASHINGTON (STATE)

Applegate, Katherine. Ivan: the Remarkable True Story of the Shopping Mall Gorilla. Karas, G. Brian, illus. 2014. (ENG.). 40p. (J). (gr. -1-3). 18.99 *(978-0-544-25230-1(6)*, 1566586, Clarion Bks.) HarperCollins Pubs.
Boekhoff, P. M. Washington, 1 vol. 2005. (Portraits of the States Ser.). (ENG., Illus.). 32p. (gr. 3-5). pap. 11.50 *(978-0-8368-4656-0(7)*, 61ae08f0-6307-4e97-8328-ea6df2d7d51c); lib. bdg. 28.67 *(978-0-8368-4637-9(0)*, f677eb73-e66a-4d9f-ac9c-3f81c874c26c) Stevens, Gareth Publishing LLLP. (Gareth Stevens Learning Library).
Bragg, Lynn. A River Lost. 2009. (Act Ser.). (ENG., Illus.). 32p. (Orig.). (gr. 2-8). pap. 11.95 *(978-0-88839-383-8(0))* Hancock Hse. Pubs.
Bredeson, Carmen. Fiery Volcano: The Eruption of Mount St. Helens, 1 vol. 2013. (Disasters: People in Peril Ser.). (ENG., Illus.). 48p. (gr. 5-7). 27.93 *(978-0-7660-4015-1(1)*, d9e9dcfc-f9ef-4de1-93a5-e125f14434a8) Enslow Publishing, LLC.
Harmon, Daniel E. Washington: Past & Present. 2009. (Illus.). 48p. (J). 70.50 *(978-1-4358-5589-2(2))*; (ENG., (gr. 5-5). pap. 12.75 *(978-1-4358-5588-5(4)*, 521f6da9-3381-467f-b364-bb5d5174df54); (ENG., (gr. 5-5). lib. bdg. 34.47 *(978-1-4358-5295-2(8)*, 3d6dcbcf-4254-4dae-b602-0b056952ba95) Rosen Publishing Group, Inc., The. (Rosen Reference).
Heinrichs, Ann. Washington. Kania, Matt, illus. 2017. (U. S. A. Travel Guides). (ENG.). 40p. (J). (gr. 2-5). lib. bdg. 38.50 *(978-1-5038-1987-0(6)*, 211624) Child's World, Inc, The.
Hood, Karen Jean Matsko. Washington State: Activity & Coloring Book. I.t. ed. 2014. (Educational Activity & Coloring Book Ser.). (J). 19.95 *(978-1-930948-56-3(5))* Whispering Pine Pr. International, Inc.
Kranz, Rachel. Mount St. Helens. 2011. (Early Connections Ser.). (J). *(978-1-61672-643-0(1))* Benchmark Education Co.
Labella, Susan. Washington. 2006. (Rookie Read-About Geography Ser.). (ENG., Illus.). 32p. (J). (gr. 1-2). lib. bdg. 20.50 *(978-0-516-24993-3(2)*, Children's Pr.) Scholastic Library Publishing.
Marsh, Carole. Washington Current Events Projects: 30 Cool, Activities, Crafts, Experiments & More for Kids to Do to Learn about Your State! 2003. (Washington Experience Ser.). 32p. (gr. k-8). pap. 5.95 *(978-0-635-02066-6(1)*, Marsh, Carole Bks.) Gallopade International.
—Washington Geography Projects: 30 Cool, Activities, Crafts, Experiments & More for Kids to Do to Learn about Your State! 2003. (Washington Experience Ser.). 32p. (gr. k-5). pap. 5.95 *(978-0-635-01865-6(9)*, Marsh, Carole Bks.) Gallopade International.
—Washington Government Projects: 30 Cool, Activities, Crafts, Experiments & More for Kids to Do to Learn about Your State! 2003. (Washington Experience Ser.). 32p. (gr. k-5). pap. 5.95 *(978-0-635-01966-0(3)*, Marsh, Carole Bks.) Gallopade International.
—Washington People Projects: 30 Cool, Activities, Crafts, Experiments & More for Kids to Do to Learn about Your State! 2003. (Washington Experience Ser.). 32p. (gr. k-5). pap. 5.95 *(978-0-635-02016-1(5)*, Marsh, Carole Bks.) Gallopade International.
—Washington Symbols & Facts Projects: 30 Cool, Activities, Crafts, Experiments & More for Kids to Do to Learn about Your State! 2003. (Washington Experience Ser.). 32p. (gr. k-5). pap. 5.95 *(978-0-635-01916-5(7)*, Marsh, Carole Bks.) Gallopade International.
McConaghy, Lorraine & Bentley, Judy. Free Boy: A True Story of Slave & Master. 2013. (V Ethel Willis White Bks.). (ENG., Illus.). 112p. (J). pap. 18.95 *(978-0-295-99271-6(9))* Univ. of Washington Pr.
McDaniel, Melissa. Washington (a True Book: My United States) (Library Edition) 2018. (True Book (Relaunch) Ser.). (ENG., Illus.). 48p. (J). (gr. 3-5). lib. bdg. 31.00 *(978-0-531-23584-3(X)*, Children's Pr.) Scholastic Library Publishing.
McHugh, Erin. State Shapes: Washington. Schrier, Alfred, illus. 2008. (ENG.). 48p. (J). (gr. -1-17). 9.95 *(978-1-57912-775-6(4)*, 81775, Black Dog & Leventhal Pubs. Inc.) Hachette Bks.
Moench, Megan Hansen. Know Your State Activity Book Washington, 1 vol. 2015. (ENG., Illus.). 272p. (J). pap. 14.99 *(978-1-4236-4059-2(4))* Gibbs Smith, Publisher.
Murray, Julie. Washington, 1 vol. 2006. (Buddy Book Ser.). (ENG., Illus.). 32p. (gr. 2-4). 27.07 *(978-1-59197-706-3(1)*, Buddy Bks.) ABDO Publishing Co.
Otfinoski, Steven. Washington, 1 vol. Santoro, Christopher, illus. 2003. (It's My State! (First Edition)(r) Ser.). (ENG.). 80p. (gr. 4-4). 34.07 *(978-0-7614-1522-0(X)*, 738616e9-3341-419b-b542-e3d6571e3c28) Cavendish Square Publishing LLC.
Powell, E. Sandy. Washington. (J). 2012. lib. bdg. 25.26 *(978-0-7613-4562-6(0)*, Lerner Pubns.) 2nd exp. rev. ed. 2003. (Illus.). 84p. (gr. 3-6). pap. 6.95 *(978-0-8225-4155-4(6))* Lerner Publishing Group.
Smith, Roland. E Is for Evergreen: A Washington State Alphabet. Ayriss, Linda Holt, illus. 2004. (Discover America State by State Ser.). (ENG.). 40p. (J). (gr. 1-3). 17.95 *(978-1-58536-143-4(7)*, 202003) Sleeping Bear Pr.
Stefoff, Rebecca. Washington, 1 vol. (Celebrate the States (First Edition) Ser.). (ENG., 144p. (gr. 6-6). 2004. Illus.). lib. bdg. 39.79 *(978-0-7614-0422-4(8)*, 9dd74abb-13bc-4b0a-90de-e4afbe1b5554) 2nd rev. ed. 2008. lib. bdg. 39.79 *(978-0-7614-2561-8(6)*, 05d27159-fa4c-4f86-a326-1ecfbaec0c3d) Cavendish Square Publishing LLC.
Way, Jennifer. Washington. 2009. (Bilingual Library of the United States of America Ser.). (ENG & SPA.). 32p. (gr. 2-2). 47.90 *(978-1-60853-391-6(3)*, Editorial Buenas Letras) Rosen Publishing Group, Inc., The.
Weintraub, A. How to Draw Washington's Sights & Symbols. 2009. (Kid's Guide to Drawing America Ser.). 32p. (gr. k-k). 50.50 *(978-1-61511-103-9(4)*, PowerKids Pr.) Rosen Publishing Group, Inc., The.

WASHINGTON (STATE)—FICTION

Alexie, Sherman. The Absolutely True Diary of a Part-Time Indian. 2011. 10.36 *(978-0-7848-3391-9(5))* 2009. 14.44 *(978-0-7848-3800-6(3))* Marco Bk. Co. (Everbind).
—The Absolutely True Diary of a Part-Time Indian. Forney, Ellen, illus. 2008. 230p. 25.00 *(978-1-60686-072-4(0))* Perfection Learning Corp.
—The Absolutely True Diary of a Part-Time Indian. 2008. (YA). 1.25 *(978-1-4281-8291-2(8))*; 78.49 *(978-1-4361-0259-9(6))*; 57.75 *(978-1-4281-8294-3(2))*; 68.75 *(978-1-4281-8300-1(0))*; 70.75 *(978-1-4281-8298-1(5))*; 55.75 *(978-1-4281-8296-7(9))*; 212.75 *(978-1-4281-8295-0(0))* Recorded Bks., Inc.
—The Absolutely True Diary of a Part-Time Indian. I.t. ed. 2008. (Thorndike Literacy Bridge Ser.). (ENG., Illus.). 301p. (YA). (gr. 7-12). 23.95 *(978-1-4104-0499-2(4))* Thorndike Pr.
—The Absolutely True Diary of a Part-Time Indian. 2009. (YA). lib. bdg. 28.15 *(978-0-606-07296-0(9))* Turtleback.
—The Absolutely True Diary of a Part-Time Indian (National Book Award Winner) (ENG., Illus.). (YA). (gr. 7-17). 2009. 288p. pap. 16.99 *(978-0-316-01369-7(2))* 2007. 320p. 21.99 *(978-0-316-01368-0(4))* Little, Brown Bks. for Young Readers.
Banerjee, Anjali. Seaglass Summer. 2011. (ENG.). 176p. (J). (gr. 4-6). lib. bdg. 22.44 *(978-0-385-90555-8(6)*, Lamb, Wendy Bks.); (Illus.). (gr. 3-7). pap. 7.99 *(978-0-375-84399-0(X)*, Yearling) Random Hse. Children's Bks.
Barr, Ellisa. Outage, 0 vols. 2015. (Powerless Nation Ser.: 1). (ENG.). 218p. (YA). (gr. 7-12). pap. 9.99 *(978-1-4778-2994-3(6)*, 9781477829943, Skyscape) Amazon Publishing.
Bond, Katherine Grace. The Summer of No Regrets. 2012. (ENG.). 304p. (YA). (gr. 7-12). pap. 18.99 *(978-1-4022-6504-4(2))* Sourcebooks, Inc.
Brainerd, Debbi. The Tree That Came Home: An IslandWood Story Inspired by the True Story of a 92-Foot Beam That Returned to Bainbridge Island, Washington. Zecca, Katherine, illus. 2008. 63p. (J). pap. *(978-0-9821633-0-6(4))* IslandWood.
Brothers, Marilee. Moon Rise. 2009. (YA). pap. 14.95 *(978-0-9821756-9-9(8)*, Bell Bridge Bks.) BelleBks., Inc.
—Moon Spun. 2010. 246p. pap. 14.95 *(978-1-935661-95-5(7)*, Bell Bridge Bks.) BelleBks., Inc.
—Moonstone. 2008. 236p. (YA). pap. 14.95 *(978-0-9802453-4-9(6)*, Bell Bridge Bks.) BelleBks., Inc.
—Shadow Moon. 2011. 230p. (YA). pap. *(978-1-61194-058-9(3))* BelleBks., Inc.
Caletti, Deb. The Fortunes of Indigo Skye. (ENG.). (YA). (gr. 7). 2009. 320p. pap. 9.99 *(978-1-4169-1008-4(5))* 2008. 304p. 15.99 *(978-1-4169-1007-7(7))* Simon Pulse. (Simon Pulse).
—Love Is All You Need: Wild Roses; the Nature of Jade. 2013. (ENG.). 608p. (YA). (gr. 7-7). pap. 11.99 *(978-1-4424-6636-4(7)*, Simon Pulse) Simon Pulse.
—Stay. (ENG.). (YA). (gr. 7). 2012. 336p. pap. 9.99 *(978-1-4424-0374-1(8))* 2011. 320p. 16.99 *(978-1-4424-0373-4(X))* Simon Pulse. (Simon Pulse).
—Wild Roses. 2008. (ENG.). 320p. (YA). (gr. 7-12). pap. 8.99 *(978-1-4169-5782-9(0)*, Simon Pulse) Simon Pulse.
Calhoun, Dia. After the River the Sun. Slater, Kate, illus. 2013. (ENG.). 368p. (J). (gr. 4-7). 16.99 *(978-1-4424-3985-6(8))* Simon & Schuster Children's Publishing.
—Eva of the Farm. Slater, Kate, illus. (ENG.). (J). (gr. 4-7). 2013. 272p. pap. 6.99 *(978-1-4424-1701-4(3))* 2012. 256p. 16.99 *(978-1-4424-1700-7(5))* Simon & Schuster Children's Publishing. (Atheneum Bks. for Young Readers).
Chen, Justina. Lovely, Dark, & Deep. 2018. (ENG.). 352p. (YA). (gr. 7-7). 18.99 *(978-1-338-13406-3(X)*, Levine, Arthur A. Bks.) Scholastic, Inc.
Coats, J. Anderson. The Many Reflections of Miss Jane Deming. 2017. (ENG., Illus.). 288p. (J). (gr. 5-7). 16.99 *(978-1-4814-6496-3(5)*, Atheneum Bks. for Young Readers) Simon & Schuster Children's Publishing.
Cook, Eileen. Unraveling Isobel. 2012. (ENG.). 320p. (YA). (gr. 9). pap. 9.99 *(978-1-4424-1328-3(X)*, Simon Pulse) Simon Pulse.
Dashner, James. The Journal of Curious Letters. Beus, Bryan, illus. 2008. (13th Reality Ser.: Bk. 1). 434p. (J). (gr. 4-7). 17.95 *(978-1-59038-831-0(3)*, Shadow Mountain) Shadow Mountain Publishing.
—The Journal of Curious Letters. Beus, Bryan, illus. 2009. (13th Reality Ser.: 1). (ENG.). 528p. (J). (gr. 3-7). pap. 9.99 *(978-1-4169-9152-6(2)*, Aladdin) Simon & Schuster Children's Publishing.
Davis, Heather. The Clearing. 2010. (ENG., Illus.). 224p. (YA). (gr. 9). pap. 13.99 *(978-0-547-26367-0(8)*, 1406284, Clarion Bks.) HarperCollins Pubs.
Derting, Kimberly. The Body Finder. 2011. (Body Finder Ser.: 1). (ENG.). 352p. (YA). (gr. 9). pap. 10.99 *(978-0-06-177983-1(0)*, HarperCollins) HarperCollins Pubs.
—Desires of the Dead. 2012. (Body Finder Ser.: 2). (ENG.). 384p. (YA). (gr. 9). pap. 8.99 *(978-0-06-177986-2(5)*, HarperCollins) HarperCollins Pubs.
Deuker, Carl. Gym Candy. 2008. (ENG., Illus.). 320p. (YA). (gr. 7). pap. 11.99 *(978-0-547-07631-7(2)*, 1042009, Clarion Bks.) HarperCollins Pubs.
—Gym Candy. 2008. 313p. 19.00 *(978-1-60686-376-3(2))* Perfection Learning Corp.
Emerson, Alice. Betty Gordon in Washington. 2005. pap. 14.95 *(978-1-59605-610-7(X)*, Cosimo Classics) Cosimo, Inc.

W X Y Z

Forman, Gayle. I Was Here. l.t. ed. 2015. 420p. 24.99 *(978-1-4104-8255-6(3))* Cengage Gale.

—I Was Here. 2016. (ENG.). 304p. (YA). (gr. 9). pap. 10.99 *(978-0-14-751403-5(7),* Speak) Penguin Young Readers Group.

—I Was Here. 2016. lib. bdg. 22.10 *(978-0-606-38404-9(9))* Turtleback.

Francis, JennaKay. The Ferry Boat. Woodward II, Ed, illus. 2013. 12p. pap. 8.95 *(978-1-61633-426-0(6))* Guardian Angel Publishing, Inc.

Frazier, Sundee T. Brendan Buckley's Universe & Everything in It. 2008. (ENG.). 208p. (J). (gr. 3-7). 7.99 *(978-0-440-42206-8(X),* Yearling) Random Hse. Children's Bks.

Frazier, Sundee Tucker. Brendan Buckley's Universe & Everything in It, 1. 2008. (Brendan Buckley Ser.). (ENG.). 208p. (J). (gr. 4-6). lib. bdg. 21.19 *(978-0-385-90445-2(2),* Delacorte Pr.) Random Hse. Children's Bks.

Gamble, Adam & Jasper, Mark. Good Night Washington State. Kelly, Cooper, illus. 2012. (Good Night Our World Ser.). (ENG.). 20p. (J). (gr. -1-k). bds. 9.95 *(978-1-60219-072-6(0))* Good Night Bks.

Goode, Suzi. The Lost Wizard Series Bk 1. 2007. pap. 11.95 *(978-1-59374-817-3(5))* Whiskey Creek Pr., LLC.

Grace, Amanda. But I Love Him. 2011. (ENG.). 264p. (YA). (gr. 9-12). pap. 9.95 *(978-0-7387-2594-9(3),* 0738725943, Flux) North Star Editions.

Gurtler, Janet. If I Tell. 2011. (ENG.). 256p. (YA). (gr. 7-12). pap. 12.99 *(978-1-4022-6103-9(9))* Sourcebooks, Inc.

Hayes, Ned. The Eagle Tree: A Novel. 2016. (ENG.). 270p. pap. 14.95 *(978-1-5039-3664-5(3),* 9781503936645, Little A) Amazon Publishing.

Hill, Janet Muirhead. Kendall's Storm. Leonhard, Herb, illus. 2011. (J). pap. 12.00 *(978-0-9820893-0-9(9))* Raven Publishing Inc. of Montana.

Holm, Jennifer L. Boston Jane: an Adventure. 2010. (Boston Jane Ser.: 1). (ENG.). 272p. (J). (gr. 3-7). 8.99 *(978-0-375-86204-5(8),* Yearling) Random Hse. Children's Bks.

—Boston Jane: the Claim. 2010. (Boston Jane Ser.: 3). (ENG.). 224p. (J). (gr. 3-7). pap. 8.99 *(978-0-375-86206-9(4),* Yearling) Random Hse. Children's Bks.

—Boston Jane: Wilderness Days. 2010. (Boston Jane Ser.: 2). (ENG.). 256p. (J). (gr. 3-7). pap. 8.99 *(978-0-375-86205-2(6),* Yearling) Random Hse. Children's Bks.

—The Claim. 2010. (Boston Jane Ser.: No. 3). (ENG.). 224p. (J). (gr. 4-6). lib. bdg. 22.44 *(978-0-375-96206-6(9))* Random House Publishing Group.

—Our Only May Amelia. 2019. (ENG., Illus.). 272p. (J). (gr. 3-7). pap. 9.99 *(978-0-06-288177-9(9),* HarperCollins) HarperCollins Pubs.

—Our Only May Amelia. unabr. ed. 2004. 253p. (J). (gr. 5-9). pap. 36.00 incl. audio *(978-0-8072-8366-0(5),* YA191SP, Listening Library) Random Hse. Audio Publishing Group.

—The Trouble with May Amelia. Gustavson, Adam, illus. (ENG.). 224p. (J). (gr. 3-7). 2012. pap. 5.99 *(978-1-4169-1374-0(2))*2. 2011. 17.99 *(978-1-4169-1373-3(4))* Simon & Schuster Children's Publishing. (Atheneum Bks. for Young Readers).

—Wilderness Days. 2004. (Boston Jane Ser.: No. 2). 256p. (J). (gr. 5-18). pap. 5.99 *(978-0-06-440881-3(7),* Harper Trophy) HarperCollins Pubs.

—Wilderness Days. 2010. (Boston Jane Ser.: No. 2). (ENG.). 256p. (J). (gr. 4-6). lib. bdg. 22.44 *(978-0-375-96205-9(0))* Random House Publishing Group.

—Wilderness Days. unabr. ed. 2004. (Boston Jane Ser.: No. 2). 288p. (J). (gr. 5-9). pap. 38.00 incl. audio *(978-0-8072-0787-1(X),* S YA 307 SP, Listening Library) Random Hse. Audio Publishing Group.

Holsather, Kent. Henry of York: The Secret of Juan de Vega. Holsather, Bill, illus. 2003. 176p. (YA). (gr. 5-18). 22.95 *(978-0-9729101-0-1(7));* 2nd ed. per. 12.95 *(978-0-9729101-1-8(5))* Lonejack Mountain Pr.

Hood, Karen Jean Matsko. Washington State: Activity & Coloring Book. 2014. (J). spiral bd. 19.95 *(978-1-59649-434-3(4))* Whispering Pine Pr. International, Inc.

James, Eric. Tiny the Washington Easter Bunny. 2018. (Tiny the Easter Bunny Ser.). (ENG.). 40p. (J). (gr. k-3). 9.99 *(978-1-4926-5975-4(4),* Hometown World) Sourcebooks, Inc.

Johnson, Joy. Harry the Woodpecker's Search for a Home. Johnson, Craig, illus. 2013. 28p. (J). pap. 9.95 *(978-0-9785191-7-9(5))* Orange Spot Publishing.

Johnston, Wayne M. North Fork. 2016. (ENG.). 210p. (YA). (gr. 7-12). pap. 14.95 *(978-1-936364-20-6(4))* Black Heron Pr.

Katcher, Brian. The Improbable Theory of Ana & Zak. 2016. (ENG.). 352p. (YA). (gr. 8). pap. 9.99 *(978-0-06-227278-2(0),* Tegen, Katherine Bks) HarperCollins Pubs.

Kehret, Peg. The Ghost's Grave. 2007. 224p. pap. 5.99 *(978-0-14-280819-1(9),* Puffin) Penguin Publishing Group.

—The Ghost's Grave. 2007. (ENG.). 224p. (J). (gr. 5-18). 7.99 *(978-0-14-240819-3(0),* Puffin Books) Penguin Young Readers Group.

Kocsis, Konrád Hayward. The Adventures of the Krusaders & the Legend of Wilde Island. 2012. 238p. pap. 16.97 *(978-1-61897-106-7(9),* Strategic Bk. Publishing) Strategic Book Publishing & Rights Agency (SBPRA).

Larson, Kirby. Dash (Dogs of World War II) 2016. (Dogs of World War II Ser.). (ENG.). 256p. (J). (gr. 3-7). pap. 8.99 *(978-0-545-41636-8(1),* Scholastic Paperbacks) Scholastic, Inc.

Llewellyn, Tom. The Bottle Imp of Bright House. Grimly, Gris, illus. 2018. (ENG.). 224p. (J). (gr. 3-7). 17.99 *(978-0-8234-3969-0(0))* Holiday Hse., Inc.

—The Shadow of Seth: A Seth Anomundy Murder Mystery. 2015. (Seth Anomundy Murder Mysteries Ser.: 1). (ENG.). 192p. (YA). pap. 18.99 *(978-1-929345-18-2(6),* Poisoned Pen Press) Sourcebooks, Inc.

Madson, Trish. W Is for Washington: An Evergreen State ABC Primer. Miles, David W., illus. 2016. (ENG.). 20p. (J). (gr. -1 — 1). bds. 12.95 *(978-1-944822-02-6(X),* 552202) Familius LLC.

Mathews, Temple. The Sword of Armaggeddon. 2010. ix, 291p. *(978-1-935618-17-1(2))* BenBella Bks.

McKenzie, Paige. The Haunting of Sunshine Girl. 2016. (Haunting of Sunshine Girl Ser.: Vol. 1). (ENG.). 320p. (YA). (gr. 7-17). lib. bdg. 21.80 *(978-1-5311-8307-3(7))* Perfection Learning Corp.

—The Haunting of Sunshine Girl: Book One. 2016. (Haunting of Sunshine Girl Ser.: 1). (ENG.). 320p. (YA). (gr. 7-17). pap. 10.99 *(978-1-60286-302-6(4))* Hachette Bk. Group.

—The Haunting of Sunshine Girl: Book One. 2015. (Haunting of Sunshine Girl Ser.: 1). (ENG.). 304p. (YA). (gr. 7-17). 16.00 *(978-1-60286-272-2(9))* Hachette Bks.

Mentyka, Sharon. Chasing at the Surface: A Novel. 2016. (ENG., Illus.). 228p. (J). (gr. 3-7). pap. 12.99 *(978-1-943328-60-4(9),* West Winds Pr.) West Margin Pr.

Merrick, Rebecca. Rain Harbor. 2011. 276p. 47.95 *(978-1-258-07693-1(4))* Literary Licensing, LLC.

Meyer, Stephenie. Amanecer / Breaking Dawn. 2008. (Saga Crepusculo / the Twilight Saga Ser.: 4).Tr. of Breaking Dawn. (SPA.). 832p. (YA). (gr. 9-12). pap. 23.95 *(978-607-11-0033-7(X),* Alfaguara) Penguin Random House Grupo Editorial ESP. Dist: Penguin Random Hse. LLC.

—Breaking Dawn. 2008. (Twilight Saga Ser.: 4). (ENG.). 768p. (YA). (gr. 7-17). 24.99 *(978-0-316-06792-8(X))* Little, Brown Bks. for Young Readers.

—Breaking Dawn. 2010. (Twilight Saga Ser.: 4). (YA). lib. bdg. 29.40 *(978-0-606-23108-4(0))* Turtleback.

—Eclipse. 2007. (Twilight Saga Ser.: 3). (ENG.). 640p. (YA). (gr. 7-17). 22.99 *(978-0-316-16020-9(2))* Little, Brown Bks. for Young Readers.

—Eclipse. 2008. 576p. *(978-1-904233-91-6(0),* Atom Books) Little, Brown Book Group Ltd.

—Eclipse. 2011. (Twilight Saga: Bk. 3). 13.08 *(978-0-7848-3531-9(4),* Everbind) Marco Bk. Co.

—Eclipse. 2010. (Twilight Saga: Bk. 3). 629p. (YA). (gr. 9-12). 22.10 *(978-1-60686-303-9(7))* Perfection Learning Corp.

—Eclipse. 2007. (Twilight Saga Spanish Ser.: 3). (SPA.). 637p. (gr. 7-12). lib. bdg. 28.15 *(978-1-4177-9862-9(9))* Turtleback.

—New Moon. 2008. (Twilight Saga: Bk. 2). 563p. (gr. 9-12). 21.00 *(978-1-60686-336-7(3))* Perfection Learning Corp.

—New Moon. 2006. (Twilight Saga Ser.: 2). (ENG.). 608p. (J). (gr. 7-17). 24.99 *(978-0-316-16019-3(9))* Little, Brown Bks. for Young Readers.

—New Moon. 2011. (Twilight Saga: Bk. 2). 11.72 *(978-0-7848-3535-7(7),* Everbind) Marco Bk. Co.

—The Short Second Life of Bree Tanner: An Eclipse Novella. 2010. (Twilight Saga Ser.). (ENG.). 192p. (YA). (gr. 7-17). 17.99 *(978-0-316-12558-1(X))* Little, Brown Bks. for Young Readers.

—Twilight. 2008. (Twilight Saga: Bk. 1). (CHI.). 375p. (YA). pap. *(978-7-5448-0333-5(3))* Jieli Publishing Hse.

—Twilight. 2005. (Twilight Saga Ser.: 1). (ENG.). 544p. (YA). (gr. 7-17). 24.99 *(978-0-316-16017-9(2))* Little, Brown Bks. for Young Readers.

—Twilight. 2008. 480p. pap. *(978-1-905654-34-5(0),* Atom Books) Little, Brown Book Group Ltd.

—Twilight. 2009. (Twilight Saga: Bk. 1). 11.72 *(978-0-7848-1934-0(3),* Everbind) Marco Bk. Co.

—Twilight. (Twilight Saga: Bk. 1). 2010. 498p. (YA). (gr. 9-12). 20.10 *(978-1-60686-352-7(5))* 2006. 21.00 *(978-0-7569-6825-0(9))* Perfection Learning Corp.

—Twilight. (Twilight Ser.: 1). (YA). 2007. 1.25 *(978-1-4193-9974-9(8))* 2006. 87.75 *(978-1-4193-9975-6(6))* Recorded Bks., Inc.

—Twilight. 2006. (Twilight Saga Ser.: 1). (Illus.). 498p. (YA). (gr. 9-12). lib. bdg. 28.15 *(978-1-4177-5591-2(1))* Turtleback.

—The Twilight Saga Collection Set, 4 vols. 2008. (ENG.). 2560p. (YA). (gr. 7-17). 92.00 *(978-0-316-03184-4(4))* Little, Brown Bks. for Young Readers.

Ness, Patrick. The Rest of Us Just Live Here. (YA). 2016. (ENG.). 336p. (gr. 9). pap. 12.99 *(978-0-06-240317-9(6),* Quill Tree Bks.) 2015. (ENG.). 336p. (gr. 9-12). 17.99 *(978-0-06-240316-2(8),* Quill Tree Bks.) 2015. 352p. *(978-1-4063-3116-5(3))* HarperCollins Pubs.

O'Neill, Elizabeth. Alfred Visits Washington State. 2009. 24p. (J). pap. 12.00 *(978-0-9822288-4-5(8))* Funny Bone Bks.

Palka, Yvonne. Dragon Fire Ocean Mist. 2009. pap. 12.95 *(978-0-9817668-0-5(3))* Heartrock Pr.

Patterson, James. Ali Cross: the Secret Detective. 2022. (Ali Cross Ser.: 3). (ENG.). 272p. (J). (gr. 5-9). 16.99 *(978-0-316-40991-9(X),* Jimmy Patterson) Little Brown & Co.

Reed, Amy. Crazy. (ENG., (YA). (gr. 9). 2013. Illus.). 416p. pap. 9.99 *(978-1-4424-1348-1(4))* 2012. 384p. 16.99 *(978-1-4424-1347-4(6))* Simon Pulse. (Simon Pulse).

Robinson, Gary. Tribal Journey. 2013. (PathFinders Ser.). (ENG.). 96p. (YA). (gr. 8-12). pap. 9.95 *(978-1-939053-01-5(3),* 7th Generation) BPC.

Rushford, Patricia H. Secrets of Ghost Island. 2007. (J). *(978-88-02-46255-4(0))* Moody Pubs.

Sampson, Jeff. Vesper. 2011. (Deviants Ser.: 1). (ENG.). 304p. (YA). (gr. 8-18). 16.99 *(978-0-06-199276-6(3),* Balzer & Bray) HarperCollins Pubs.

Sargent, Dave & Sargent, Pat. Whiskers: (Roan) Pride & Peace, 30 vols., Vol. 59. Lenoir, Jane, illus. 2003. (Saddle up Ser.: Vol. 59). 42p. (J). pap. 10.95 *(978-1-56763-806-6(6))* Ozark Publishing.

Scott, Mindi. Live Through This. 2012. (ENG.). 304p. (YA). (gr. 9). pap. 9.99 *(978-1-4424-4060-9(0));* 17.99 *(978-1-4424-4059-3(7))* Simon Pulse. (Simon Pulse).

The Secret of Bunratty Castle: Individual Title Six-Packs. (Action Packs Ser.). 104p. (gr. 3-5). 44.00 *(978-0-7635-3302-1(5))* Rigby Education.

Shepard, Sara. The Good Girls. 2015. (Perfectionists Ser.: 2). (ENG.). 368p. (YA). (gr. 9). 17.99 *(978-0-06-207452-2(0),* HarperTeen); 341p. (J). *(978-0-06-239115-5(1))* HarperCollins Pubs.

—The Perfectionists. 2014. (Perfectionists Ser.: 1). (ENG.). 336p. (YA). (gr. 9). 17.99 *(978-0-06-207469-0(5),* HarperTeen) HarperCollins Pubs.

—The Perfectionists TV Tie-In Edition. 2019. (ENG.). 352p. (YA). (gr. 9). pap. 10.99 *(978-0-06-296756-5(8),* HarperTeen) HarperCollins Pubs.

Smiley, Jess Smart, abr. 12 Little Elves Visit Washington, Volume 2. 2016. (12 Little Elves Ser.: 2). (ENG., Illus.). 32p. (J). (gr. k-3). 16.95 *(978-1-942934-71-4(8),* 553471) Familius LLC.

Snelling, Lauraine. What about Cimmaron? 2008. (J). 8.99 *(978-1-59166-872-5(7))* BJU Pr.

Sullivan, Jacqueline Levering. Annie's War. 2007. (Illus.). 183p. (J). (gr. 3-7). 15.00 *(978-0-8028-5325-7(0),* Eerdmans Bks For Young Readers) Eerdmans, William B. Publishing Co.

Tarshis, Lauren. I Survived the Eruption of Mount St. Helens, 1980 (I Survived #14) 2016. (I Survived Ser.: 14). (ENG., Illus.). 112p. (J). (gr. 2-5). pap. 5.99 *(978-0-545-65852-2(7),* Scholastic Paperbacks) Scholastic, Inc.

Vaughan, Richard & Crews, Marcia. Three Bears of the Pacific Northwest. Trammell, Jeremiah, illus. 2016. (Pacific Northwest Fairy Tales Ser.). 20p. (J). (— 1). bds. 10.99 *(978-1-63217-076-7(0),* Little Bigfoot) Sasquatch Bks.

Vaughan, Richard Lee & Vaughn, Marcia. Three Bears of the Pacific Northwest. Trammell, Jeremiah, illus. 2011. (Pacific Northwest Fairy Tales Ser.). (ENG.). 32p. (J). (gr. -1-2). 17.99 *(978-1-57061-684-6(1),* Little Bigfoot) Sasquatch Bks.

Wenberg, Michael. Stringz. 2010. 216p. (YA). (gr. 6-10). 16.95 *(978-1-934813-33-1(8))* Westside Bks.

Wilsdon, Christina. On the Trail of Bigfoot in Washington. McCreary, Jane, illus. 2006. 26p. (J). 7.99 *(978-1-59939-012-3(4))* Cornerstone Pr.

Wolf, Jennifer Shaw. Dead Girls Don't Lie. (ENG.). 2014. 368p. (YA). (gr. 9). pap. 12.99 *(978-0-8027-3753-3(6),* 900135679) 2013. 304p. E-Book 7.99 *(978-0-8027-3450-1(2))* Bloomsbury Publishing USA. (Bloomsbury USA Childrens).

WASHINGTON (STATE)—HISTORY

Bauer, Marion Dane. Celebrating Washington State: 50 States to Celebrate. Canga, C. B., illus. 2014. (ENG.). 40p. (J). (gr. 1-4). pap. 4.99 *(978-0-544-28948-2(X),* 1572173, Clarion Bks.) HarperCollins Pubs.

Conkling, Winifred. Passenger on the Pearl: The True Story of Emily Edmonson's Flight from Slavery. 2016. (ENG., Illus.). 176p. (YA). (gr. 7-10). pap. 10.95 *(978-1-61620-550-8(4),* 73550) Algonquin Young Readers.

Downey, Tika. Washington: The Evergreen State, 1 vol. 2009. (Our Amazing States Ser.). (ENG., Illus.). 24p. (J). (gr. 3-3). pap. 9.25 *(978-1-4358-3346-3(5),* 8710054d-0610-48a2-be50-343fd02a5fef); lib. bdg. 26.27 *(978-1-4042-8113-4(4),* 302d4048-b823-46c7-9c5d-cbbf140ff48d) Rosen Publishing Group, Inc., The. (PowerKids Pr.).

Freedman, Deborah K. & Tacoma Historical Society. Rising up from Tacoma's Twenty-One Disasters & Defeats: Based on Topics Chosen by the 2012-2013 Students of Seabury Middle School. 2015. (Illus.). 48p. (J). pap. 6.99 *(978-0-9846234-4-0(2))* Tacoma Historical Society.

Gish, Melissa. Washington. 2009. (This Land Called America Ser.). 32p. (YA). (gr. 3-6). 19.95 *(978-1-58341-800-0(8))* Creative Co., The.

Hamilton, John. Washington, 1 vol. 2016. (United States of America Ser.). (ENG., Illus.). 48p. (J). (gr. 5-9). 34.21 *(978-1-68078-350-6(5),* 21685, Abdo & Daughters) ABDO Publishing Co.

Johnson, Anna Maria, et al. Washington: The Evergreen State, 1 vol. 2019. (It's My State! (Fourth Edition)(r) Ser.). (ENG.). 80p. (gr. 4-4). pap. 18.64 *(978-1-5026-4456-5(8),* 1244882c-ce73-4c5f-a945-a300f37abf7f) Cavendish Square Publishing LLC.

Kleinmartin, Hex, et al. Washington. 2015. (J). lib. bdg. *(978-1-62712-757-8(7))* Cavendish Square Publishing LLC.

Leigh, Autumn. Warning: Volcano! the Story of Mt. St. Helens. 2009. (Reading Room Collection 2 Ser.). 24p. (gr. 3-4). 42.50 *(978-1-60852-000-8(5),* PowerKids Pr.) Rosen Publishing Group, Inc., The.

Marsh, Carole. Washington History Projects: 30 Cool, Activities, Crafts, Experiments & More for Kids to Do to Learn about Your State! 2003. (Washington Experience Ser.). 32p. (gr. k-5). pap. 5.95 *(978-0-635-01816-8(0),* Marsh, Carole Bks.) Gallopade International.

Otfinoski, Steven & Benduhn, Tea. Washington, 1 vol. 2nd rev. ed. 2011. (It's My State! (Second Edition)(r) Ser.). (ENG.). 80p. (gr. 4-4). lib. bdg. 34.07 *(978-1-60870-061-5(5),* 2f85ab4b-6161-404e-97e2-b9ed868a1385) Cavendish Square Publishing LLC.

Pratt, Laura. Washington: The Evergreen State. 2012. (J). *(978-1-61913-415-7(2));* pap. *(978-1-61913-416-4(0))* Weigl Pubs., Inc.

Stein, R. Conrad. America the Beautiful: Washington (Revised Edition) 2014. (America the Beautiful, Third Ser. (Revised Edition) Ser.). (ENG., Illus.). 144p. (J). lib. bdg. 40.00 *(978-0-531-28297-7(X))* Scholastic Library Publishing.

Strudwick, Leslie. Washington. 2011. (Guide to American States Ser.). (Illus.). 48p. (YA). (gr. 3-6). 29.99 *(978-1-61690-820-1(3))* Weigl Pubs., Inc.

—Washington: The Evergreen State. 2016. (Illus.). 48p. (J). *(978-1-5105-2099-8(6))* SmartBook Media, Inc.

—Washington: The Evergreen State. 2016. (J). *(978-1-4896-4959-1(X))* Weigl Pubs., Inc.

The Washington Journey: New 7th Grade Textbook, 1 vol. l.t. ed. 2009. 281p. (gr. 7-9). 47.95 *(978-1-4236-0622-2(1))* Gibbs Smith, Publisher.

The Washington Journey Program Kit: All program components for the Washington Journey, 1 vol. 2009. 129.95 *(978-1-4236-0735-9(X))* Gibbs Smith, Publisher.

Washington, Our Home: New 4th Grade Textbook, 1 vol. l.t. ed. 2009. 218p. (gr. 4-4). 47.95 *(978-1-4236-0614-7(0))* Gibbs Smith, Publisher.

Washington, Our Home Program Kit: All program components for Washington, Our Home, 1 vol. 2009. (gr. 4-4). 169.95 *(978-1-4236-0734-2(1))* Gibbs Smith, Publisher.

Way, Jennifer. Washington, 1 vol. Brusca, Maria Cristina, tr. 2005. (Bilingual Library of the United States of America Ser.: Set 2). (ENG & SPA., Illus.). 32p. (J). (gr. 2-2). lib. bdg. 28.93 *(978-1-4042-3113-9(7),* 515e277c-3485-4406-b552-667917e7201a) Rosen Publishing Group, Inc., The.

The Wonderful Washington Events Guide, 2006. 2005. (YA). per. 21.95 *(978-1-881005-49-0(6))* Gail's Guides.

Ziff, John. Northwest: Idaho, Oregon, Washington, Vol. 19. 2015. (Let's Explore the States Ser.). (Illus.). 64p. (J). (gr. 5). 23.95 *(978-1-4222-3331-3(6))* Mason Crest.

WASHINGTON MONUMENT (WASHINGTON, D.C.)

Aboff, Marcie; Peattie. The Washington Monument. Peattie, Cindy, ed. 2016. (Spring Forward Ser.). (ENG.). (J). (gr. 1). 7.02 net. *(978-1-4900-6025-5(1))* Benchmark Education Co.

Ashley, Susan. The Washington Monument, 1 vol. 2004. (Places in American History Ser.). (ENG., Illus.). 24p. (gr. 2-4). pap. 9.15 *(978-0-8368-4151-0(4),* 547d763f-7d2b-4752-aecd-39c122e10340); lib. bdg. 24.67 *(978-0-8368-4144-2(1),* 186daaba-3f29-4939-9870-8d97bbb8d4dc) Stevens, Gareth Publishing LLLP. (Weekly Reader Leveled Readers).

Carr, Aaron. Washington Monument. 2013. (J). *(978-1-62127-205-2(2));* pap. *(978-1-62127-209-0(5))* Weigl Pubs., Inc.

Chang, Kirsten. The Washington Monument. 2019. (Symbols of American Freedom Ser.). (ENG., Illus.). 24p. (J). (gr. k-3). pap. 7.99 *(978-1-61891-495-8(2),* 12145, Blastoff! Readers) Bellwether Media.

Dittmer, Lori. Washington Monument. 2019. (Landmarks of America Ser.). (ENG.). 24p. (J). (gr. 1-4). pap. 8.99 *(978-1-62832-692-5(1),* 18986, Creative Paperbacks) Creative Co., The.

Edison, Erin. The Washington Monument: A 4D Book. 2018. (National Landmarks Ser.). (ENG., Illus.). 24p. (J). (gr. 1-3). lib. bdg. 27.99 *(978-1-5435-3133-6(4),* 138738, Capstone Pr.) Capstone.

Joseph, Natalie. Visit the Washington Monument, 1 vol. 2012. (Landmarks of Liberty Ser.). (ENG., Illus.). 24p. (J). (gr. 2-3). pap. 9.15 *(978-1-4339-6406-0(6),* 130dd795-86ce-4a1d-93f6-77828ceb51ee, Gareth Stevens Learning Library); lib. bdg. 25.27 *(978-1-4339-6404-6(X),* 3fab3373-810b-45bb-a181-a617975fb9ac) Stevens, Gareth Publishing LLLP.

Kissock, Heather. Washington Monument. 2017. (Illus.). 24p. (J). *(978-1-5105-0608-4(X))* SmartBook Media, Inc.

Landau, Elaine. The Washington Monument. 2004. (Cornerstones of Freedom Ser.). (ENG.). 48p. (YA). (gr. 4-7). 26.00 *(978-0-516-24238-5(5))* Scholastic Library Publishing.

Linde, Barbara M. The Washington Monument, 1 vol. 2018. (Symbols of America Ser.). (ENG.). 24p. (gr. 1-2). 24.27 *(978-1-5382-2900-2(5),* b34cd5fd-492c-47e8-be87-894a5e7b5914) Stevens, Gareth Publishing LLLP.

Marcovitz, Hal. The Washington Monument. 2004. (American Symbols & Their Meanings Ser.). (Illus.). 48p. (J). (gr. 4-18). lib. bdg. 19.95 *(978-1-59084-028-3(3))* Mason Crest.

—Washington Monument: Memorial to a Founding Father. Moreno, Barry, ed. 2014. (Patriotic Symbols of America Ser.: 20). 48p. (J). (gr. 4-18). lib. bdg. 20.95 *(978-1-4222-3137-1(2))* Mason Crest.

Murray, Robb. The Washington Monument: Myths, Legends, & Facts, 1 vol. 2014. (Monumental History Ser.). (ENG.). 32p. (J). (gr. 3-6). 27.99 *(978-1-4914-0206-1(7),* 125789, Capstone Pr.) Capstone.

Nelson, Kristin L. The Washington Monument. (Lightning Bolt Bks.). (gr. k-2). 2010. (Illus.). 32p. (J). lib. bdg. 25.26 *(978-0-7613-6019-3(0),* Lerner Pubns.) 2010. pap. 45.32 *(978-0-7613-6994-3(5))* 2003. (ENG., Illus.). 32p. (J). pap. 7.99 *(978-0-8225-3759-5(1),* 4a0d1f3a-9731-4c87-b938-ac6605d7826f, First Avenue Editions) Lerner Publishing Group.

RJF Publishing Staff & Schaffer, Julia. The Washington Monument. 2009. (Symbols of American Freedom Ser.). 48p. (gr. 4-6). 30.00 *(978-1-60413-517-6(4),* Chelsea Clubhse.) Infobase Holdings, Inc.

WASHINGTON NATIONALS (BASEBALL TEAM)

Bodden, Valerie. Bryce Harper: Big Time. 2013. (Big Time Ser.). (ENG.). 24p. (J). (gr. 1-4). 23.09 *(978-1-60818-474-3(9),* 21702) Creative Co., The.

Epstein, Brad. Washington Nationals 101. 2008. (My First Team Board Bks.). (ENG., Illus.). 22p. (J). (gr. -1). bds. *(978-1-932530-86-5(X),* 101 Bk.) Michaelson Entertainment.

Goessling, Ben. Washington Nationals, 1 vol. 2015. (Inside MLB Ser.). (ENG.). 48p. (J). (gr. 3-6). lib. bdg. 34.21 *(978-1-62403-489-3(6),* 17141, SportsZone) ABDO Publishing Co.

Goodman, Michael E. The Story of the Washington Nationals. 2011. (Baseball: the Great American Game Ser.). (Illus.). 48p. (J). (gr. 5-8). lib. bdg. 34.25 *(978-1-60818-060-8(3),* Creative Education) Creative Co., The.

Hawkes, Brian. The Story of the Washington Nationals. 2007. (Baseball, the Great American Game Ser.). (Illus.). 48p. (YA). (gr. 4-7). lib. bdg. 32.80 *(978-1-58341-553-5(X))* Creative Co., The.

Raum, Elizabeth. Pro Sports Biographies: Bryce Harper. 2017. (Pro Sports Biographies Ser.). (ENG., Illus.). 24p. (J). (gr. 1-3). pap. 10.99 *(978-1-68152-166-4(0),* 14794) Amicus.

—Pro Sports Biographies: Cam Newton. 2017. (Pro Sports Biographies Ser.). (ENG.). 24p. (J). (gr. 1-3). pap. 10.99 *(978-1-68152-168-8(7),* 14795) Amicus.

Stewart, Mark. The Washington Nationals. 2012. (Team Spirit Ser.). 48p. (J). (gr. 3-6). lib. bdg. 29.27 *(978-1-59953-501-2(7))* Norwood Hse. Pr.

WASHINGTON REDSKINS (FOOTBALL TEAM)

Epstein, Brad M. Washington Redskins 101. 2010. (ENG., Illus.). 24p. (J). bds. *(978-1-60730-131-8(8),* 101 Bk.) Michaelson Entertainment.

Frisch, Aaron. Washington Redskins. 2011. (Super Bowl Champions Ser.). (J). (gr. 1-3). 24.25 *(978-1-60818-030-1(1))* Creative Co., The.

—Washington Redskins. 2014. (Super Bowl Champions Ser.). (ENG., Illus.). 24p. (J). (gr. 1-4). 18.95 *(978-1-60818-389-0(0),* 21591, Creative Editions) Creative Co., The.

Gilbert, Sara. The Story of the Washington Redskins. 2013. (Illus.). 48p. (J). 35.65 *(978-1-60818-323-4(8),* Creative Education) Creative Co., The.

Goodman, Michael E. The History of the Washington Redskins. 2004. (NFL Today Ser.). (Illus.). 32p. (YA). (gr. 5-9). 18.95 *(978-1-58341-317-3(0))* Creative Co., The.

—The Story of the Washington Redskins. 2009. (NFL Today Ser.). 48p. (YA). (gr. 5-9). 22.95 *(978-1-58341-774-4(5))* Creative Co., The.

Mack, Larry. The Washington Redskins Story. 2016. (NFL Teams Ser.). (ENG., Illus.). 32p. (J). (gr. 3-7). lib. bdg. 26.95 *(978-1-62617-386-6(9),* Torque Bks.) Bellwether Media.

Smolka, Bo. Washington Redskins, 1 vol. 2016. (NFL up Close Ser.). (ENG., Illus.). 32p. (J). (gr. 3-9). lib. bdg. 32.79 *(978-1-68078-237-0(1),* 22075, SportsZone) ABDO Publishing Co.

Storm, Marysa. Highlights of the Washington Redskins. 2019. (Team Stats — Football Edition Ser.). (ENG., Illus.). 32p. (J). (gr. 4-6). lib. bdg. *(978-1-68072-890-3(3),* 12836, Bolt) Black Rabbit Bks.

Temple, Ramey. Washington Redskins. (Illus.). 32p. (J). 2015. pap. *(978-1-4896-0907-6(5))* 2014. (ENG., (gr. 4-7). lib. bdg. 28.55 *(978-1-4896-0906-9(7)*, AV2 by Weigl) Weigl Pubs., Inc.

Whiting, Jim. The Story of the Washington Redskins. 2019. (NFL Today Ser.). (ENG.). 48p. (J). (gr. 3-6). *(978-1-64026-161-7(3)*, 19099, Creative Education) Creative Co., The.

—Washington Redskins. rev. ed. 2019. (NFL Today Ser.). (ENG.). 48p. (J). (gr. 4-7). pap. 12.00 *(978-1-62832-724-3(3)*, 22680, Creative Paperbacks) Creative Co., The.

Zappa, Marcia. Washington Redskins, 1 vol. 2015. (NFL's Greatest Teams Ser.). (ENG.). 32p. (J). (gr. 2-5). 34.21 *(978-1-62403-592-0(2)*, 17211, Big Buddy Bks.) ABDO Publishing Co.

WASPS

Berne, Emma Carlson. Yellow Jackets. 2014. (Scavengers: Eating Nature's Trash Ser.). (Illus.). 24p. (J). (gr. k-5). pap. 49.50 *(978-1-4777-6594-4(8)*, PowerKids Pr.) Rosen Publishing Group, Inc., The.

Black, Nessa. Wasps. 2019. (Spot Creepy Crawlies Ser.). (ENG.). 16p. (J). (gr. -1-2). lib. bdg. *(978-1-68151-541-0(5)*, 14502) Amicus.

Byerly, Robbie. Wasps (1-3Y) Byerly, Robbie, illus. 2016. (1-3Y Bugs Ser.). (ENG., Illus.). 20p. (J). pap. 8.00 *(978-1-61406-690-3(6))* American Reading Co.

Chang, Kirsten. Bee or Wasp? 2019. (Spotting Differences Ser.). (ENG., Illus.). 24p. (J). (gr. k-3). lib. bdg. 26.95 *(978-1-64487-031-0(2)*, Blastoff! Readers) Bellwether Media.

Dibble, Traci. Bees & Wasps. 2014. (1G Bugs Ser.). (ENG., Illus.). 24p. (J). pap. 8.00 *(978-1-63437-095-0(3))* American Reading Co.

George, Lynn. Wasps: Nest Builders, 1 vol. 2010. (Animal Architects Ser.). (ENG.). 24p. (J). (gr. 2-3). pap. 9.25 *(978-1-4488-1347-6(6)*, 683f1c15-c101-4ba1-af83-3a407dad4145); lib. bdg. 26.27 *(978-1-4488-0693-5(3)*, 6ba2ea4e-13cf-4675-93e8-38e4b52b79d0) Rosen Publishing Group, Inc., The. (PowerKids Pr.).

Gish, Ashley. Wasps. 2018. (X-Books: Insects Ser.). (ENG.). 32p. (J). (gr. 3-5). pap. 9.99 *(978-1-62832-621-5(2)*, 20010, Creative Paperbacks); *(978-1-60818-994-6(5)*, 20002, Creative Education) Creative Co., The.

Green, Jen. Wasps. 2009. (Illus.). 52p. (J). *(978-0-7172-8077-3(2))* Grolier, Ltd.

Harris, Monica. Paper Wasp. 2003. (Bug Bks.). (Illus.). 32p. (J). lib. bdg. 22.79 *(978-1-4034-0767-2(3))* Heinemann-Raintree.

Maclaine, James. Bees & Wasps. 2013. (Beginner's Nature Ser.). 32p. (J). ring bd. 4.99 *(978-0-7945-3360-1(4)*, Usborne) EDC Publishing.

McAneney, Caitie. Jewel Wasps Take Over!, 1 vol. 2017. (Insects: Six-Legged Nightmares Ser.). (ENG.). 24p. (J). (gr. 2-3). pap. 9.15 *(978-1-5382-1267-7(6)*, 7ee8616b-17a9-4b74-bbec-7d3fee6104ba) Stevens, Gareth Publishing LLLP.

McKinney, Devon. Watch Out for Wasps!, 1 vol., 1. 2015. (Wild Backyard Animals Ser.). (ENG., Illus.). 24p. (J). (gr. 3-4). pap. 9.25 *(978-1-5081-4270-6(X)*, af27ba0e-55fa-4ffd-a9fc-d6e3f25269ad, PowerKids Pr.) Rosen Publishing Group, Inc., The.

Morgan, Sally. Bees & Wasps. 2006. (Animal Lives (QEB Publishing) Ser.). (Illus.). 32p. (J). (gr. 4-7). lib. bdg. 19.95 *(978-1-59566-202-6(2))* QEB Publishing Inc.

Morgan, Sally & Teacher Created Resources Staff. Bees & Wasps. 2007. (Animal Lives (QEB Publishing) Ser.). (ENG., Illus.). 32p. (gr. 2-9). pap. 7.99 *(978-1-4206-8112-3(5))* Teacher Created Resources, Inc.

Orr, Tamra. Wasp or Bee. 2019. (21st Century Junior Library: Which Is Which? Ser.). (ENG., Illus.). 24p. (J). (gr. 2-5). pap. 12.79 *(978-1-5341-5023-2(4)*, 213399); lib. bdg. 30.64 *(978-1-5341-4737-9(3)*, 213398) Cherry Lake Publishing.

Pallotta, Jerry. Hornet vs. Wasp (Who Would Win?) Bolster, Rob, illus. 2020. (Who Would Win? Ser.: 10). (ENG.). 32p. (J). (gr. 1-4). pap. 4.99 *(978-0-545-45190-1(6))* Scholastic, Inc.

Patterson, Jack K. Wasps, 1 vol. 2018. (Creepy Crawlers Ser.). (ENG.). 24p. (gr. 1-1). lib. bdg. 25.93 *(978-1-5026-4271-4(9)*, e0bc1b39-23e6-4dfc-8d9c-26ee7cc1e7b7) Cavendish Square Publishing LLC.

Perish, Patrick. Wasps. 2017. (Insects up Close Ser.). (ENG., Illus.). 24p. (J). (gr. k-3). lib. bdg. 26.95 *(978-1-62617-668-3(X)*, Blastoff! Readers) Bellwether Media.

Rockwood, Leigh. Tell Me the Difference Between a Bee & a Wasp, 1 vol. 2013. (How Are They Different? Ser.). (ENG., Illus.). 24p. (J). (gr. 2-3). pap. 9.25 *(978-1-4488-9736-0(X)*, ac810d45-9124-4701-a6f9-0d088afc626d); lib. bdg. 26.27 *(978-1-4488-9639-4(8)*, 9aa23ca3-9039-4f7a-b97b-c1635592b633) Rosen Publishing Group, Inc., The. (PowerKids Pr.).

Rustad, Martha E. H. Wasps. 2007. (World of Insects Ser.). (ENG., Illus.). 24p. (J). (gr. k-3). lib. bdg. 26.95 *(978-1-60014-076-1(9))* Bellwether Media.

Scarborough, Kate, et al. A Wasp Builds a Nest: See Inside a Paper Wasp's Nest & Watch It Grow. 2016. (ENG., Illus.). 24p. (J). (gr. 1-3). 12.95 *(978-1-77085-695-0(1)*, 61931f51-be0f-4a51-9d83-59d68bc61a86) Firefly Bks., Ltd.

Schuh, Mari. Wasps. 2014. (Illus.). 24p. (J). lib. bdg. 25.65 *(978-1-62031-088-5(0)*, Bullfrog Bks.) Jump! Inc.

Taylor, Trace. Wasps. 2009. (2G Bugs Ser.). (ENG.). 12p. (J). (gr. k-2). pap. 9.60 *(978-1-59301-853-5(3))* American Reading Co.

Terp, Gail. Is It a Bee or a Wasp? 2019. (Can You Tell the Difference? Ser.). (ENG.). 24p. (J). (gr. 2-4). pap. 8.99 *(978-1-64466-052-2(0)*, 12901); (Illus.). (gr. 4-6). lib. bdg. *(978-1-68072-897-2(0)*, 12900) Black Rabbit Bks. (Hi Jinx).

WASTE (ECONOMICS)

Berry, Joy. Help Me Be Good about Being Wasteful. 2009. (Help Me Be Good Ser.). 32p. pap. 7.95 *(978-1-60577-105-2(8))* Berry, Joy Enterprises.

Berry, Joy Wilt. A Book about Being Wasteful. 2005. (Illus.). (J). *(978-0-7172-8587-7(1))* Scholastic, Inc.

Chancellor, Deborah. Food Waste. 2010. (Reduce, Reuse, Recycle! Ser.). 32p. (J). (gr. 1-5). E-Book 50.50 *(978-1-4488-0363-7(2))*; (ENG.). (gr. 2-3). pap. 11.60 *(978-1-61532-240-4(X)*, 5eaf02ec-7488-4fce-ba21-6b48fa0fc1fc, PowerKids Pr.); (ENG., Illus.). (gr. 3-8). lib. bdg. 30.27 *(978-1-61532-233-6(7)*, e3a159aa-1f5c-4de8-97dc-5e05b8ae18a4) Rosen Publishing Group, Inc., The.

WASTE DISPOSAL

see Refuse and Refuse Disposal; Sewage Disposal; Waste Products

WASTE PRODUCTS

see also Refuse and Refuse Disposal

Bellamy, Rufus. Waste & Pollution. 2010. (Sustaining Our Environment Ser.). 48p. (J). 35.65 *(978-1-60753-139-5(9))* Amicus Learning.

Berg, Shannon. E-Waste in Guiyu, China. 2019. (21st Century Disasters Ser.). (ENG., Illus.). 32p. (J). (gr. 2-3). pap. 9.95 *(978-1-64185-807-6(9)*, 1641858079); lib. bdg. 31.35 *(978-1-64185-738-3(2)*, 1641857382) North Star Editions. (Focus Readers).

Bone, Emily & Pratt, Leonie. Recycling Things to Make & Do. 2010. (Activity Book Ser.). 32p. (J). pap. 6.99 *(978-0-7945-2675-7(6)*, Usborne) EDC Publishing.

Holt, Rinehart and Winston Staff. Environmental Science Chptr. 19: Waste. 4th ed. Date not set. pap. 11.20 *(978-0-03-068081-6(6))* Holt McDougal.

Junk: A Journey Through the Dark Matter of the Genome. (Jump Ser.). (Illus.). 36p. (J). (gr. 2-6). pap. *(978-1-882210-37-4(9))* Action Publishing, Inc.

Knighton, Kate. Why Shouldn't I Eat Junk Food? Larkum, Adam, illus. 2008. (Usborne Ser.). 48p. (J). (gr. 4-7). pap. 6.99 *(978-0-7945-1953-7(9)*, Usborne) EDC Publishing.

Llimós, Anna. Earth-Friendly Christmas Crafts in 5 Easy Steps, 1 vol. 2013. (Earth-Friendly Crafts in 5 Easy Steps Ser.). (ENG., Illus.). 32p. (gr. 3-3). lib. bdg. 26.61 *(978-0-7660-4188-2(3)*, a9038f4b-0ad4-4f5a-a927-16064efe25e4) Enslow Publishing, LLC.

—Earth-Friendly Crafts from Recycled Stuff in 5 Easy Steps, 1 vol. 2013. (Earth-Friendly Crafts in 5 Easy Steps Ser.). (ENG., Illus.). 32p. (J). (gr. 3-3). lib. bdg. 26.61 *(978-0-7660-4190-5(5)*, 28cd6699-08cf-4b63-8868-5a334a8446db) Enslow Publishing, LLC.

Shea, John M. Where Does the Recycling Go?, 1 vol. 2012. (Everyday Mysteries Ser.). (ENG., Illus.). 24p. (J). (gr. 2-2). 25.27 *(978-1-4339-6333-9(7)*, e300e315-c160-46d4-9967-9fbdeb65869f); pap. 9.15 *(978-1-4339-6335-3(3)*, 75b80f61-341c-46cb-b78b-3556f4fcef4e) Stevens, Gareth Publishing LLLP.

Walker, Kate. Paper, 1 vol. Vanzet, Gaston, illus. 2011. (Recycling Ser.). (ENG.). 32p. (J). (gr. 1-1). 31.21 *(978-1-60870-132-2(8)*, a3565ec0-8196-4c27-9514-eee8dbf2b6ed) Cavendish Square Publishing LLC.

Watson, Stephanie. Making Good Choices about Recycling & Reuse. 2009. (J). 77.70 *(978-1-4358-5607-3(4))*, Rosen Reference); (ENG.). 64p. (YA). (gr. 6-6). pap. 13.95 *(978-1-4358-5606-6(6)*, b7aebf9a-55e7-45e5-81db-cb9ec8392e72, Rosen Reference); (ENG., Illus.). 64p. (YA). (gr. 6-6). lib. bdg. 37.13 *(978-1-4358-5312-6(1)*, daa45e5f-85c2-4435-854b-f137897b0622) Rosen Publishing Group, Inc., The.

WATCHES

see Clocks and Watches

WATER

see also Floods; Fog; Glaciers; Hydraulic Engineering; Ice; Lakes; Ocean; Rain and Rainfall; Rivers; Snow

Aleo, Karen. Living Things Need Water. 2019. (What Living Things Need Ser.). (ENG., Illus.). 24p. (J). (gr. -1-2). pap. 6.95 *(978-1-9771-1038-1(X)*, 141114); lib. bdg. 24.65 *(978-1-9771-0887-6(3)*, 140495) Capstone. (Pebble).

Amson-Bradshaw, Georgia. Water Cycle Geo Facts. 2018. (Geo Facts Ser.). (Illus.). 32p. (J). (gr. 5-5). *(978-0-7787-4394-1(2))* Crabtree Publishing Co.

Anderson, Nancy. Water & Life, 1 vol. 2016. (Rosen REAL Readers: STEM & STEAM Collection). (ENG.). 8p. (gr. k-1). pap. 5.46 *(978-1-5081-2380-4(2)*, 6b72ba77-33cc-455a-acf8-c5df5d3973cf, Rosen Classroom) Rosen Publishing Group, Inc., The.

Asch, Frank. Water. 2014. 17.00 *(978-1-63419-750-2(X))* Perfection Learning Corp.

Ayer, Paula & Banyard, Antonia. Water Wow! A Visual Exploration. 2016. (Visual Exploration Ser.). (ENG., Illus.). 64p. (J). (gr. 3-7). pap. 12.95 *(978-1-55451-821-0(0))* Annick Pr., Ltd. CAN. Dist: Publishers Group West (PGW).

Bailey, Gerry. Water, 1 vol. 2009. (Simply Science Ser.). (ENG., Illus.). 32p. (YA). (gr. 3-5). lib. bdg. 28.67 *(978-1-4339-0037-2(8)*, bd8d8f6d-887b-45d8-96cb-6f274e57d44a) Stevens, Gareth Publishing LLLP.

Ball, Nate. Let's Investigate with Nate #1: The Water Cycle. Hargis, Wes, illus. 2017. (Let's Investigate with Nate Ser.: 1). (ENG.). 40p. (J). (gr. -1-3). pap. 7.99 *(978-0-06-235739-7(5)*, HarperCollins) HarperCollins Pubs.

Barker, Geoff. Water. 2010. (World at Risk Ser.). (YA). (gr. 5-9). 34.25 *(978-1-59920-379-9(0))* Black Rabbit Bks.

Barnham, Kay & Frost, Maddie. The Great Big Water Cycle Adventure. 2018. (ENG., Illus.). 32p. (J). (gr. k-3). 10.99 *(978-1-4380-5044-7(5))* Sourcebooks, Inc.

Bates, Matthew. The Ways We Use Water, 1 vol. 2012. (InfoMax Readers Ser.). (ENG., Illus.). 24p. (J). (gr. 1-1). pap. 8.25 *(978-1-4488-9013-2(6)*, 2f32597b-697b-411c-a780-0a840bf8d20c, Rosen Classroom) Rosen Publishing Group, Inc., The.

Beasley, Ava. What's the Water Cycle? Working in a Loop, 1 vol. 2017. (Computer Kids: Powered by Computational Thinking Ser.). (ENG.). 24p. (J). (gr. 3-4). 25.27 *(978-1-5383-2445-5(8)*, bb80cd9b-55ca-41a3-9f07-aa29b3638ead, PowerKids Pr.); pap. *(978-1-5383-5313-4(X)*, e968a9a7-05fd-4a98-9b93-8d7bf8e60fe5, Rosen Classroom) Rosen Publishing Group, Inc., The.

Benchmark Education Company. Water on Earth (Teacher Guide) 2005. *(978-1-4108-4637-2(7))* Benchmark Education Co.

Benchmark Education Company, LLC Staff, compiled by. Water. 2006. spiral bd. 375.00 *(978-1-4108-6792-6(7))* Benchmark Education Co.

—Water & Weather. 2006. spiral bd. 330.00 *(978-1-4108-7018-6(9))* 2006. (J). 206.00 *(978-1-4108-7056-8(1))* 2005. (J). spiral bd. 265.00 *(978-1-4108-5759-0(X))* Benchmark Education Co.

—Water & Weather: Theme Set. 2006. (J). 215.00 *(978-1-4108-7132-9(0))* Benchmark Education Co.

Bethea, Nikole Brooks. The Water Cycle. 3rd rev. ed. 2012. (ENG., Illus.). 118p. (gr. 6-12). 35.00 *(978-1-60413-943-3(9)*, P189955, Facts On File) Infobase Holdings, Inc.

Blokland, Suzanne & Hammer, Randy. God's Blue Earth: Teaching Kids to Celebrate the Sacred Gift of Water. 2013. (Illus.). viii, 134p. (J). *(978-0-8298-1941-0(X))* Pilgrim Pr., The/United Church Pr.

Bodden, Valerie. Water Rides. 2012. (Illus.). 24p. (J). 25.65 *(978-1-60818-115-5(4)*, Creative Education) Creative Co., The.

Boelts, Maribeth. A World of Water. Grudzina, Rebecca; Boelts, ed. 2016. (Spring Forward Ser.). (ENG.). (J). (gr. 2). 7.20 net. *(978-1-4900-6028-6(6))* Benchmark Education Co.

Bond, Janice & Fiebelkorn, Claire. Water on Earth, 1 vol. 2012. (InfoMax Readers Ser.). (ENG., Illus.). 24p. (J). (gr. 1-1). pap. 8.25 *(978-1-4488-9034-7(9)*, 6bd646c2-9498-4977-9389-72d3e5ac4172, Rosen Classroom) Rosen Publishing Group, Inc., The.

Brannon, Barbara. Discover Water. 2005. (J). pap. *(978-1-4108-5125-3(7))* Benchmark Education Co.

Burstein, John. Outstanding Oils & Wonderful Water. 2009. (Slim Goodbody's Nutrition Edition Ser.). (ENG., Illus.). 24p. (J). (gr. k-3). pap. *(978-0-7787-5061-1(2))*; lib. bdg. *(978-0-7787-5046-8(9))* Crabtree Publishing Co.

Burton, Margie, et al. Water. 2011. (Early Connections Ser.). (J). *(978-1-61672-313-2(0))* Benchmark Education Co.

—Water Goes up! Water Comes Down! 2011. (Early Connections Ser.). (J). *(978-1-61672-510-5(9))* Benchmark Education Co.

—We Use Water. 2011. (Early Connections Ser.). (J). *(978-1-61672-274-6(6))* Benchmark Education Co.

Canavan, Roger. You Wouldn't Want to Live Without Clean Water! Antram, David, illus. 2014. (You Wouldn't Want to Live Without... Ser.). (ENG.). 32p. (J). lib. bdg. 29.00 *(978-0-531-21219-6(X)*, Watts, Franklin) Scholastic Library Publishing.

Capstone Classroom & Stead, Tony. What If You Didn't Have Running Water? 2017. (What's the Point? Reading & Writing Expository Text Ser.). (ENG., Illus.). 32p. (J). (gr. 5-5). pap. 7.95 *(978-1-4966-0735-5(X)*, 132370, Capstone Classroom) Capstone.

Cardenas, Ernesto A. Bodies of Water. 2009. pap. 4.95 *(978-1-60698-062-0(9))* Milo Educational Bks. & Resources.

—Water Cycle. 2009. pap. 4.95 *(978-1-60698-096-5(3))* Milo Educational Bks. & Resources.

Carlson-Berne, Emma. From River to Raindrop: The Water Cycle. 2017. (Start to Finish, Second Ser.). (ENG., Illus.). 24p. (J). (gr. k-3). 23.99 *(978-1-5124-3442-2(6)*, 4901946c-a454-473c-b27e-1314009e947f, Lerner Pubns.); pap. 7.99 *(978-1-5124-5623-3(3)*, 8428878e-bfdd-49d3-9017-abee0a4a0a88) Lerner Publishing Group.

Centore, Michael. Water. 2017. (Illus.). 64p. (J). *(978-1-4222-3746-5(X))* Mason Crest.

Cobb, Vicki. Squirts & Spurts: Science Fun with Water. Haefele, Steve, illus. 2007. (Science Fun with Vicki Cobb Ser.). 48p. (J). (gr. 4-7). per. 7.95 *(978-0-8225-7024-0(6)*, First Avenue Editions) Lerner Publishing Group.

Cole, Joanna. At the Waterworks. 2004. (Magic School Bus Original Ser.). (gr. k-3). lib. bdg. 17.20 *(978-0-8335-1744-9(9))* Turtleback.

Cornell, Kari. Water. 2016. (Illus.). 24p. (J). *(978-0-87659-700-2(2))* Gryphon Hse., Inc.

Croce, Nicholas, ed. Oceanography & Hydrology, 4 vols. 2016. (Study of Science Ser.). (ENG.). 128p. (gr. 8-8). 75.64 *(978-1-68048-234-8(3)*, 96d12eab-a568-4566-9eb3-2548ddcc99d2); 1. (Illus.). (J). 37.82 *(978-1-68048-235-5(1)*, 25fc15e1-5523-4168-b9fe-063e7abbf388) Rosen Publishing Group, Inc., The. (Britannica Educational Publishing).

Danielson, Ethan. Our Water Experiment, 1 vol. 2012. (InfoMax Readers Ser.). (ENG., Illus.). 24p. (J). (gr. 1-1). pap. 8.25 *(978-1-4488-9031-6(4)*, 2110a722-362c-4906-a940-553afcc975d3, Rosen Classroom) Rosen Publishing Group, Inc., The.

Dawson, Emily C. How Animals Find Water. 2010. (Amicus Readers. Our Animal World (Level 1) Ser.). (ENG.). 24p. (J). (gr. k-2). lib. bdg. 25.65 *(978-1-60753-011-4(2)*, 17166) Amicus.

Dayton, Connor. Water. 2014. (Four Elements Ser.). (Illus.). 32p. (J). (gr. k-3). pap. 60.00 *(978-1-4777-9265-0(1))* Windmill Bks.

Del Moral, Susana. Agua Por Todas Partes. Zaidi, Nadeem, illus. 2006. (SPA.). 8p. (J). (gr. -1). *(978-970-718-452-7(3)*, Silver Dolphin en Español) Advanced Marketing, S. de R. L. de C. V.

Delaunois, Angèle. Water's Children: Celebrating the Resource That Unites Us All. Woods, Erin, tr. from FRE. Frischeteau, Gérard, illus. 2017. (ENG.). 32p. (J). (gr. k-3). 16.95 *(978-1-77278-015-4(4))* Pajama Pr. CAN. Dist: Publishers Group West (PGW).

Delta Education. Sci Res Bk Foss Grade 3 Next Gen Ea. 2014. (Illus.). 274p. (J). lib. bdg. *(978-1-62571-375-9(4))* Delta Education, LLC.

Dickmann, Nancy. The Water Cycle, 1 vol. 2015. (Earth Figured Out Ser.). (ENG., Illus.). 32p. (gr. 4-4). pap. 11.58 *(978-1-5026-0858-1(8)*, 174efc33-505f-4891-b11b-aa5bd8ee0773) Cavendish Square Publishing LLC.

Disney Publishing Staff. The Wonders of Water, 15 vols. 2003. (It's Fun to Learn Ser.). (Illus.). 32p. (J). (gr. -1-3). 3.99 *(978-1-57973-137-3(6))* Advance Pubs. LLC.

Donovan, Emily. Exploring Earth's Water Cycle, 1 vol. 2018. (Spotlight on Weather & Natural Disasters Ser.). (ENG.). 24p. (gr. 4-6). 27.93 *(978-1-5081-6896-6(2)*, 890bfd7b-4401-45d5-b307-6e741a1079fb, PowerKids Pr.) Rosen Publishing Group, Inc., The.

Duke, Shirley. The Earth & the Role of Water. 2012. (Let's Explore Science Ser.). (ENG.). 48p. (gr. 4-6). pap. 10.95 *(978-1-61810-259-1(1)*, 9781618102591) Rourke Educational Media.

Duke, Shirley Smith. The Water Cycle. 2016. (J). *(978-1-4896-5298-0(1))* Weigl Pubs., Inc.

Dutton, Michael. The Water Cycle Coloring Book. 2012. (Dover Nature Coloring Book Ser.). (ENG.). 32p. (J). (gr. 2-5). pap. 3.99 *(978-0-486-47988-0(9)*, 479889) Dover Pubns., Inc.

Edom, H. Science Activities, Vol. 1. 2010. (Science Activities Ser.). 72p. (J). 13.99 *(978-0-7945-2752-5(3)*, Usborne) EDC Publishing.

Enz, Tammy Laura Lynn. Liquid Planet: Exploring Water on Earth with Science Projects. 2016. (ENG., Illus.). 32p. (J). lib. bdg. *(978-1-4747-0325-3(9))* Capstone.

Everything Changes Interactive Packages: Water Changes. (Pebble Soup Explorations Ser.). (gr. -1-18). 52.00 *(978-0-7578-5239-8(4))* Rigby Education.

Farndon, John. Buoyancy, 1 vol. 2003. (Science Experiments Ser.). (ENG.). 32p. (gr. 4-4). 32.64 *(978-0-7614-1467-4(3)*, 693b0f08-f824-44fd-9a45-128cd947eeca) Cavendish Square Publishing LLC.

Faucets & Water Sets: 1 Each of 3 Big Books. (Sunshinetm Science Ser.). (gr. 1-2). 111.50 *(978-0-7802-2814-6(6))* Wright Group/McGraw-Hill.

Firely, G. M. The Raindrop. Holmes, Joshua D., illus. 2004. 21p. pap. 24.95 *(978-1-4137-3388-4(3))* PublishAmerica, Inc.

Flood, Nancy Bo. Water Runs Through This Book. 2015. (ENG., Illus.). 64p. (J). (gr. 3-7). pap. 19.95 *(978-1-936218-13-4(5))* Fulcrum Publishing.

Flynn, Claire E. Water World: Earth's Water Cycle. (Science Scope Ser.). 2009. 32p. (gr. 5-5). 47.90 *(978-1-60853-058-8(2)*, PowerKids Pr.) 2009. (J). pap. 60.00 *(978-1-4358-0194-3(6)*, PowerKids Pr.) 2009. (ENG.). 32p. (J). (gr. 5-5). lib. bdg. 28.93 *(978-1-4358-2999-2(9)*, 1ad4824c-ff8c-4bea-9176-65edee03df95, PowerKids Pr.) 2008. (ENG.). 32p. (gr. 5-6). pap. 10.00 *(978-1-4358-0193-6(8)*, 64e4e526-88ed-4849-8710-880ac90d2464, Rosen Classroom) Rosen Publishing Group, Inc., The.

Flynn, James. Water. 2003. (Matter & Materials Ser.). (J). pap. *(978-1-58417-167-6(7))*; lib. bdg. *(978-1-58417-161-4(8))* Lake Street Pubs.

Franklin, Yvonne. Las Charcas. rev. ed. 2010. (Science: Informational Text Ser.).Tr. of Ponds. (SPA., Illus.). 32p. (gr. 2-4). pap. 11.99 *(978-1-4333-2144-3(0))* Teacher Created Materials, Inc.

Fredericks, Carrie & Manheim, James M., eds. Water, 1 vol. 2006. (Fueling the Future Ser.). (ENG., Illus.). 120p. (gr. 10-12). lib. bdg. 46.23 *(978-0-7377-3593-2(7)*, d3408400-e909-4905-a248-7e2d7ce23342, Greenhaven Publishing) Greenhaven Publishing LLC.

Fridell, Ron. Protecting Earth's Water Supply. 2015. (Saving Our Living Earth Ser.). (ENG., Illus.). 72p. (J). (gr. 4-7). E-Book 46.65 *(978-1-5124-1051-8(9)*, Lerner Pubns.) Lerner Publishing Group.

Furgang, Kathy. Water All Around. 2011. (Early Connections Ser.). (J). *(978-1-61672-606-5(7))* Benchmark Education Co.

—Water All Around: Set Of 6. 2011. (Early Connections Ser.). (J). pap. 37.00 net. *(978-1-4108-1071-7(2))* Benchmark Education Co.

Galla, Nicole. Water & Ice, 1 vol. 2008. (Real Life Readers Ser.). (ENG.). 8p. (gr. k-1). pap. 5.15 *(978-1-4042-7979-7(2)*, acc3e291-c5a2-423b-b0fa-832b12a1b854, Rosen Classroom) Rosen Publishing Group, Inc., The.

Gallant, Roy A. Water: Our Precious Resource, 1 vol. 2003. (EarthWorks Ser.). (ENG., Illus.). 80p. (gr. 6-6). 36.93 *(978-0-7614-1365-3(0)*, f859ed09-07af-4af8-87e8-4d94c3af3a84) Cavendish Square Publishing LLC.

Gallardo, Mary, illus. & as told by. The Tiny Little Raindrop. Gallardo, Mary, as told by. 2007. 32p. (J). 15.99 *(978-0-9779763-0-0(0))* Blue Cat Bks.

Garbe, Suzanne. The Science Behind Wonders of the Water: Exploding Lakes, Ice Circles, & Brinicles. 2016. (Science Behind Natural Phenomena Ser.). (ENG., Illus.). 32p. (J). (gr. 3-9). lib. bdg. 28.65 *(978-1-5157-0776-9(8)*, 132116, Capstone Pr.) Capstone.

Gardner, Robert. Earth's Cycles: Great Science Projects about the Water Cycle, Photosynthesis, & More, 1 vol. 2011. (Team Green Science Projects Ser.). (ENG., Illus.). 112p. (gr. 5-6). lib. bdg. 35.93 *(978-0-7660-3644-4(8)*, edf667ee-761c-46b7-8690-18782b6b9449) Enslow Publishing, LLC.

—Science Fair Projects about Water & Soil, 1 vol. 2016. (Hands-On Science Ser.). (ENG.). 48p. (gr. 4-4). pap. 12.70 *(978-0-7660-8211-3(3)*, a401950b-3da0-424a-a345-84a667eafd0f) Enslow Publishing, LLC.

—Water: Green Science Projects for a Sustainable Planet, 1 vol. 2011. (Team Green Science Projects Ser.). (ENG., Illus.). 128p. (gr. 5-6). lib. bdg. 35.93 *(978-0-7660-3645-1(6)*, 649f9824-3db9-48ab-a0c9-fbe53efa7f04) Enslow Publishing, LLC.

Goodstein, Madeline. Water Science Fair Projects, Using the Scientific Method, 1 vol. 2010. (Chemistry Science Projects Using the Scientific Method Ser.). (ENG., Illus.). 160p. (gr. 5-6). 38.60 *(978-0-7660-3411-2(9)*, b7265f9f-93d9-4164-aef1-d23f5ec2f4be) Enslow Publishing, LLC.

Gordon, Sharon. Mojado, Seco / Wet, Dry, 1 vol. 2008. (Exactamente lo Opuesto / Just the Opposite Ser.). (ENG & SPA., Illus.). 24p. (gr. k-1). lib. bdg. 25.50 *(978-0-7614-2450-5(4)*, 7dce8a20-236b-4a2f-8c91-c1712ceda405) Cavendish Square Publishing LLC.

—Mojado, Seco (Wet, Dry), 1 vol. 2008. (Exactamente lo Opuesto (Just the Opposite) Ser.). (SPA., Illus.). 24p. (gr. k-1). lib. bdg. 25.50 *(978-0-7614-2370-6(2)*, 627444d3-31b6-4961-936c-7f75ceaae11d) Cavendish Square Publishing LLC.

—Wet, Dry, 1 vol. (Just the Opposite Ser.). (ENG.). 24p. (gr. k-1). 2008. pap. 9.23 *(978-0-7614-3285-2(X)*, f621d150-b5a8-4e40-bb36-2b8da27f7231) 2003. (Illus.). lib. bdg. 25.50 *(978-0-7614-1572-5(6)*,

WXYZ

c9d48325-609d-4791-a2bb-34f6f7950bce, Cavendish Square) Cavendish Square Publishing LLC.

Green, Jen. How the Water Cycle Works, 1 vol. 2007. (Our Earth Ser.). (ENG., Illus.). 24p. (J). (gr. 2-3). lib. bdg. 26.27 *(978-1-4042-4273-9(2),* 06829138-f16e-428e-93ea-9d995b598a9f) Rosen Publishing Group, Inc., The.

—Water. 2010. (Reduce, Reuse, Recycle! Ser.). 32p. (J). (gr. 1-5). E-Book 50.50 *(978-1-4488-0368-2(3));* (ENG.). (gr. 2-3). pap. 11.60 *(978-1-61532-246-6(9),* 67428810-de31-4197-b81c-07c13b65647d, PowerKids Pr.); (ENG., Illus.). (gr. 2-3). lib. bdg. 30.27 *(978-1-61532-235-0(3),* f717bea8-0cff-4bd0-877e-a264202146c6) Rosen Publishing Group, Inc., The.

Greene, Carol. I Love Our Water, 1 vol. 2012. (I Love Our Earth Ser.). (ENG., Illus.). 24p. (gr. 3-3). 25.27 *(978-0-7660-4042-7(9),* ac54492f-cef8-4c24-804c-2735fe77a98a); pap. 10.35 *(978-1-4644-0138-1(1),* c8017531-f892-4a1d-a0a4-f8dbf938b075) Enslow Publishing, LLC.

Gregoire, Maryellen. What Is Water?, 1 vol. 2011. (Wonder Readers Emergent Level Ser.). (ENG.). 8p. (gr. -1-1). (J). pap. 6.25 *(978-1-4296-7849-0(6),* 118162); pap. 35.94 *(978-1-4296-8238-1(8),* Capstone Pr.) Capstone.

Gregory, Josh. Hydrologist. 2013. (21st Century Skills Library: Cool STEM Careers Ser.). (ENG., Illus.). 32p. (gr. 4-8). (J). pap. 14.21 *(978-1-62431-025-6(7),* 202457); 32.07 *(978-1-62431-001-0(X),* 202455) Cherry Lake Publishing.

Hammersmith, Craig. The Water Cycle. 2011. (Earth & Space Science Ser.). (ENG.). 24p. (J). (gr. k-1). pap. 44.74 *(978-1-4296-7146-0(7),* 16715, Capstone Pr.) Capstone.

Harman, Rebecca. The Water Cycle: Evaporation, Condensation & Erosion. rev. ed. 2016. (Earth's Processes Ser.). (ENG.). 32p. (J). (gr. 3-6). pap. 8.29 *(978-1-4846-3820-0(4),* 134717, Heinemann) Capstone.

Hayes, Amy. Earth's Hydrosphere, 1 vol. 2018. (Understanding Earth's Systems Ser.). (ENG.). 32p. (gr. 5-5). 27.93 *(978-1-5383-2987-0(5),* 848837f8-df91-4e8a-92de-e6b89edc0634); pap. 11.00 *(978-1-5383-2989-4(1),* bd1517ef-514e-41e3-a0f8-e147d0a38ab6) Rosen Publishing Group, Inc., The. (PowerKids Pr.).

Heitkamp, Kristina Lyn. The Water Cycle. 2017. (Let's Find Out! Our Dynamic Earth Ser.). 32p. (J). (gr. 6-10). 77.40 *(978-1-5383-0031-2(1))* Rosen Publishing Group, Inc., The.

Hewitt, Sally. Water, 1 vol. 2007. (Good for Me Ser.). (ENG., Illus.). 24p. (J). (gr. 1-2). lib. bdg. 26.27 *(978-1-4042-4291-3(0),* 035ab89b-a467-444b-b2d4-7724f2cb67a0, PowerKids Pr.) Rosen Publishing Group, Inc., The.

Higgins, Nadia. Bodies of Water. Infante, Sara, illus. 2017. (Water All Around Us Ser.). (ENG.). 24p. (J). (gr. 1-3). 33.99 *(978-1-68410-011-8(9),* 31529) Cantata Learning.

—Hop on the Water Cycle. Infante, Sara, illus. 2017. (Water All Around Us Ser.). (ENG.). 24p. (J). (gr. 1-3). 33.99 *(978-1-68410-035-4(6),* 31530) Cantata Learning.

Hill, E. C. Earth: the Water Planet: Text Pairs. 2008. (Bridges/Navigators Ser.). (J). (gr. 5). 94.00 *(978-1-4108-8414-5(7))* Benchmark Education Co.

Hodge, Judith. Riches from Earth & Las riquezas de la Tierra: 6 English, 6 Spanish Adaptations. 2011. (ENG & SPA.). (J). 97.00 net. *(978-1-4108-5716-3(6))* Benchmark Education Co.

Hudd, Emily. How Long Is the Water Cycle? 2019. (How Long Does It Take? Ser.). (ENG., Illus.). 32p. (J). (gr. 3-6). pap. 7.95 *(978-1-5435-7543-9(9),* 141075); lib. bdg. 27.99 *(978-1-5435-7294-0(4),* 140611) Capstone.

Hume, Desmond. Earth's Water, 1 vol. 2012. (Exploring Earth & Space Ser.). (ENG., Illus.). 24p. (J). (gr. 1-2). 26.27 *(978-1-4488-8568-8(X),* 15e08b03-ca50-43da-b546-119a1ec2a6cd, PowerKids Pr.) Rosen Publishing Group, Inc., The.

Hunt, Santana. The Water Cycle, 1 vol. 2019. (Look at Nature's Cycles Ser.). (ENG.). 32p. (gr. 2-2). pap. 11.50 *(978-1-5382-4122-6(6),* 46b88a4f-fd79-498a-81dc-1b40d428c5b8) Stevens, Gareth Publishing LLLP.

Hutson-Thompson, Holliday & Staggs, Kelley. Water Wonderful: An Activity Book for Grade K-3. 2010. (J). 21.00 *(978-1-58321-810-5(6))* American Water Works Assn.

Ipcizade, Catherine. The Water Cycle: A 4D Book. 2018. (Cycles of Nature Ser.). (ENG., Illus.). 24p. (J). (gr. -1-2). lib. bdg. 29.32 *(978-1-9771-0039-9(2),* 138181, Capstone Pr.) Capstone.

Issues, Evidence & You - Water Mega Module Complete Materials Package. 2003. (Illus.). tchr. ed., ring bd. *(978-1-887725-42-2(3));* (YA). tchr. ed., stu. ed., per. *(978-1-887725-60-6(1))* Lab-Aids, Inc.

James, Emily. The Simple Science of Water. 2017. (Simply Science Ser.). (ENG., Illus.). 32p. (J). (gr. -1-2). lib. bdg. 27.99 *(978-1-5157-7080-0(X),* 135504, Capstone Pr.) Capstone.

Johnson, Heather Domjan. The Itsy Bitsy Water Cycle. 2007. (J). lib. bdg. 19.95 *(978-1-933732-21-3(0))* Big Ransom Studio.

—Itsy Bitsy Water Cycle Audiobook. 2007. (J). lib. bdg. 24.95 *(978-1-933732-22-0(9))* Big Ransom Studio.

Jones, Tammy. In the Water. 2009. (Sight Word Readers Set A Ser.). (J). 3.49 net. *(978-1-60719-142-1(3))* Newmark Learning LLC.

Just Add Water: Individual Title Six-Packs. (Discovery World Ser.). 12p. (gr. k-1). 28.00 *(978-0-7635-8451-1(7))* Rigby Education.

Kalman, Bobbie. Hogares de los Seres Vivos. 2008.Tr. of Living Things Need Water. (SPA.). 24p. (J). pap. *(978-0-7787-8687-0(0))* Crabtree Publishing Co.

—Rapping about Bodies of Water. 2012. (ENG., Illus.). 24p. (J). *(978-0-7787-2795-8(5));* pap. *(978-0-7787-2802-3(1))* Crabtree Publishing Co.

—Water Changes. 2011. (ENG.). 16p. (J). *(978-0-7787-9559-9(4));* pap. *(978-0-7787-9584-1(5))* Crabtree Publishing Co.

Kalman, Bobbie & Sjonger, Rebecca. El Ciclo del Agua. 2006. (Libro de Bobbie Kalman Ser.). (SPA., Illus.). 32p. (J). (gr. 3-7). pap. *(978-0-7787-8388-6(X));* lib. bdg. *(978-0-7787-8374-9(X))* Crabtree Publishing Co.

—Le Cycle de L'eau. Briere, Marie-Josee, tr. from ENG. rev. ed. 2007. (Petit Monde Vivant Ser.). (FRE., Illus.). 32p. (J). (gr. 1-7). pap. 10.95 *(978-2-89579-127-0(9))* Bayard Canada Livres CAN. Dist: Crabtree Publishing Co.

—The Water Cycle, 1 vol. 2006. (Nature's Changes Ser.). (ENG., Illus.). 32p. (J). (gr. 3-7). pap. *(978-0-7787-2310-3(0))* Crabtree Publishing Co.

—Water Cycle. 2008. (ENG.). 32p. (J). *(978-0-7787-7719-9(7)); (978-0-7787-7720-5(0))* Crabtree Publishing Co.

Kalz, Jill. Water. 2003. 24p. (J). lib. bdg. 21.35 *(978-1-58340-302-0(7))* Black Rabbit Bks.

Kids: Healthy Water Healthy People. 2005. (SPA.). (J). 1.00 *(978-1-888631-40-1(6))* Project WET Foundation.

Kids: The Water Story. 2004. (J). 1.00 *(978-1-888631-31-9(7))* Project WET Foundation.

Kids: Water, Every Drop Counts. 2004. (J). 1.00 *(978-1-888631-35-7(X))* Project WET Foundation.

KociendaGenevieve. WATER: VITAL FOR LIFE LOW INTERMEDIATE BOOK WITH ONLINE ACCESS, 1 vol. 2014. (ENG., Illus.). 24p. (J). pap., E-Book, E-Book 9.50 *(978-1-107-62251-7(4))* Cambridge Univ. Pr.

Koemer, Sandy, et al. Water Adventures Around the World, 10 vols. 2008. (ENG.). 30p. (J). (gr. 3-5). pap. 25.00 *(978-1-58321-558-6(1))* American Water Works Assn.

Koontz, Robin. Water Goes Round: The Water Cycle, 1 vol. Davidson, Chris, illus. 2010. (First Graphics: Nature Cycles Ser.). (ENG.). 24p. (J). (gr. 1-3). pap. 6.29 *(978-1-4296-6231-4(X),* 115386) Capstone.

—Water Goes Round: The Water Cycle. Davidson, Chris, illus. 2010. (First Graphics: Nature Cycles Ser.). (ENG.). 24p. (J). (gr. 1-2). pap. 38.74 *(978-1-4296-6400-4(2),* 16147) Capstone.

Koontz, Robin Michal. Water Goes Round: The Water Cycle, 1 vol. Davidson, Chris, illus. 2010. (First Graphics: Nature Cycles Ser.). (ENG.). 24p. (J). (gr. 1-3). lib. bdg. 24.65 *(978-1-4296-5364-0(7),* 113792) Capstone.

Krajnik, Elizabeth. Making Dams & Reservoirs, 1 vol. 2018. (Impacting Earth: How People Change the Land Ser.). (ENG.). 24p. (gr. 2-2). pap. 9.25 *(978-1-5383-4192-6(1),* b5134104-39eb-490d-b137-0a0b74b0efc1, PowerKids Pr.) Rosen Publishing Group, Inc., The.

Lauw, Darlene & Puay, Lim Cheng. Water. 2003. (Science Alive! Ser.). (ENG., Illus.). 32p. (J). (gr. 3-6). lib. bdg. 22.44 *(978-0-7787-0567-3(6))* Crabtree Publishing Co. CAN. Dist: Children's Plus, Inc.

Lawrence, Ellen. Covered in Water. 2016. (Drip, Drip, Drop: Earth's Water Ser.: 6). (ENG., Illus.). 24p. (J). (gr. -1-3). 26.99 *(978-1-943553-26-6(2))* Bearport Publishing Co., Inc.

—Say Hello to H2O. 2016. (Drip, Drip, Drop: Earth's Water Ser.). (ENG., Illus.). 24p. (J). (gr. -1-3). 26.99 *(978-1-943553-21-1(1))* Bearport Publishing Co., Inc.

—The Water Beneath Your Feet. 2016. (Drip, Drip, Drop: Earth's Water Ser.). (ENG., Illus.). 24p. (J). (gr. -1-3). 26.99 *(978-1-943553-24-2(6))* Bearport Publishing Co., Inc.

—Wet, Blue, & Good for You. 2016. (Drip, Drip, Drop: Earth's Water Ser.). (ENG., Illus.). 24p. (J). (gr. -1-3). 26.99 *(978-1-943553-25-9(4))* Bearport Publishing Co., Inc.

—What Is the Water Cycle? (Weather Wise Ser.). 24p. (J). (gr. -1-3). 2018. (ENG.). 7.99 *(978-1-64280-092-0(9))* 2012. lib. bdg. 26.99 *(978-1-61772-402-2(5))* Bearport Publishing Co., Inc.

—What's So Fresh about Fresh Water? 2016. (Drip, Drip, Drop: Earth's Water Ser.). (ENG., Illus.). 24p. (J). (gr. -1-3). 26.99 *(978-1-943553-23-5(8))* Bearport Publishing Co., Inc.

Lawson, Barbara Spilman. Water, Water Everywhere. 2016. (Spring Forward Ser.). (J). (gr. 2). *(978-1-4900-9446-5(6))* Benchmark Education Co.

Lerner, K. Lee, et al. UXL Encyclopedia of Water Science, 3 vols. 2004. (Illus.). xlviii, 510p. (J). *(978-0-7876-7673-5(X)); (978-0-7876-7674-2(8)); (978-0-7876-7675-9(6))* Cengage Gale. (UXL).

Levete, Sarah. A Tale of One Well in Malawi. 2010. (Big Picture: Climate Ser.). (ENG.). 24p. (gr. 1-2). pap. 41.70 *(978-1-4296-5973-4(4),* Capstone Pr.) Capstone.

Levine, Shar. Bathtub Science. 2003. (Illus.). 80p. pap. 10.95 *(978-0-8069-7243-5(2))* Sterling Publishing Co., Inc.

Lilly, Melinda. Water & Ice. (Read & Do Science Ser.). (Illus.). (J). 20.64 *(978-1-58952-639-6(2))* Rourke Educational Media.

Linde, Barbara M. The Water Cycle, 1 vol. 2016. (Where's the Water? Ser.). (ENG.). 24p. (J). (gr. 2-3). pap. 9.15 *(978-1-4824-4688-3(X),* 26f26572-0668-4304-9bc0-4abbfa504b8a) Stevens, Gareth Publishing LLLP.

—Water on Earth. 2005. (J). pap. *(978-1-4108-4589-4(3))* Benchmark Education Co.

Lindeen, Mary. Water. 2017. (BeginningtoRead Ser.). (ENG.). 32p. (J). (-2). 22.60 *(978-1-59953-875-4(X));* pap. 13.26 *(978-1-68404-094-0(9))* Norwood Hse. Pr.

Llewellyn, Claire. Water Pink a Band. 2016. (Cambridge Reading Adventures Ser.). (ENG., Illus.). 16p. pap. 7.95 *(978-1-107-57584-4(2))* Cambridge Univ. Pr.

Lundberg, Constance. Why We Need Water, 1 vol. 2008. (Real Life Readers Ser.). (ENG.). 12p. (gr. 1-2). pap. 5.90 *(978-1-4042-7915-5(6),* 0d0232a7-3142-4f90-90c8-f07835e9de23, Rosen Classroom) Rosen Publishing Group, Inc., The.

Madgwick, Wendy. Water Play: 18 Easy-to-Follow Experiments for Learning Fun - Find Out About Rain, Ice & How Water Works! 2014. (Illus.). 270p. (J). (gr. -1-12). 8.99 *(978-1-86147-351-6(6),* Armadillo) Anness Publishing GBR. Dist: National Bk. Network.

Maloof, Torrey. Water Cycle, 1 vol. rev. ed. 2014. (Science: Informational Text Ser.). (ENG.). 32p. (gr. 2-3). pap. 10.99 *(978-1-4807-4612-1(6))* Teacher Created Materials, Inc.

Markovics, Pearl. In the Pond. 2019. (Farm Charm Ser.). (ENG.). 16p. (J). (gr. -1-1). 6.99 *(978-1-64280-375-4(8))* Bearport Publishing Co., Inc.

Martin, Emmett. What Is Wet?, 1 vol. 2019. (Let's Learn Textures! Ser.). (ENG.). 24p. (gr. k-k). pap. 9.15 *(978-1-5382-4449-4(7),* 3a394020-31ee-4211-b648-265a2e4bffa0) Stevens, Gareth Publishing LLLP.

Martineau, Susan. Bubbles in the Bathroom, 1 vol. Noyes, Leighton, illus. 2011. (Everyday Science Experiments Ser.). (ENG.). 24p. (J). (gr. 3-4). pap. 11.60 *(978-1-61533-409-4(2),* 395c269d-ee23-444c-a024-a7deb7dacbf5); lib. bdg. 29.93 *(978-1-61533-371-4(1),* 6a9d661a-982b-45ba-89af-e04e396513a0) Rosen Publishing Group, Inc., The. (Windmill Bks.).

Masters, Nancy Robinson. How Did That Get to My House? Water. 2009. (Community Connections: How Did That Get to My House? Ser.). (ENG.). 24p. (gr. 2-5). lib. bdg. 29.21 *(978-1-60279-475-7(8),* 200252) Cherry Lake Publishing.

Maurer, Daniel D. Do You Really Want to Skate on Thin Ice? A Book about States of Matter. Alberini, Teresa, illus. 2016. (Adventures in Science Ser.). (ENG.). 24p. (J). (gr. 1-4). lib. bdg. 20.95 *(978-1-60753-958-2(6),* 15631) Amicus.

McAllan, Kate. Water Is Precious, 1 vol. 2012. (Discovery Education: the Environment Ser.). (ENG., Illus.). 32p. (J). (gr. 4-5). pap. 11.00 *(978-1-4488-7981-6(7),* 8ee3ee2d-ea43-461f-8235-603ea9a8ad1d); lib. bdg. 28.93 *(978-1-4488-7893-2(4),* c2771473-9672-4afc-b68d-3551d08b816d) Rosen Publishing Group, Inc., The. (PowerKids Pr.).

McClure, Jason & Willis, John. Water. 2016. (Illus.). 24p. (J). *(978-1-5105-1058-6(3))* Lightbox, The.

McGill, Jordan. Water Science Fair Projects. 2011. (J). *(978-1-61690-332-9(5));* (gr. 3-5). pap. 12.95 *(978-1-61690-656-6(1),* AV2 by Weigl); (Illus.). 24p. (gr. 3-6). 27.13 *(978-1-61690-652-8(9))* Weigl Pubs., Inc.

McKenzie, Precious. Water World. 2011. (Green Earth Science Discovery Library). (ENG., Illus.). 24p. (gr. k-2). pap. 9.95 *(978-1-61741-971-3(0),* 9781617419713) Rourke Educational Media.

McKinney, Barbara Shaw. Water Words Rhymed & Defined. Stich, Carlolyn R., illus. 2007. 30p. (J). (gr. 4-7). 19.95 *(978-0-9712692-8-6(9))* EDCO Publishing, Inc.

Meachen Rau, Dana. El Agua / Water, 1 vol. 2010. (Los Ciclos de la Naturaleza / Nature's Cycles Ser.). (ENG & SPA.). 32p. (gr. 1-2). lib. bdg. 25.50 *(978-0-7614-4792-4(X),* 51be9ac4-dc68-41a3-bf43-a11b143825a2) Cavendish Square Publishing LLC.

—Water, 1 vol. 2010. (Nature's Cycles Ser.). (ENG.). 32p. (gr. 1-2). 25.50 *(978-0-7614-4099-4(2),* 43c76e68-1bd4-4b50-91db-32856615d919) Cavendish Square Publishing LLC.

—Waterfalls, 1 vol. 2008. (Wonders of Nature Ser.). (ENG.). 32p. (gr. 1-2). pap. 9.23 *(978-0-7614-3331-6(7),* 26af678c-edbf-437a-b390-267255df2ca6) Cavendish Square Publishing LLC.

Meredith, Susan Markowitz. Hooray for Water! 2016. (Spring Forward Ser.). (J). (gr. 2). *(978-1-4900-2250-5(3))* Benchmark Education Co.

Mezzanotte, Jim. Cómo Cambia el Agua (How Water Changes), 1 vol. 2006. (Estados de la Materia (States of Matter) Ser.). (SPA., Illus.). 24p. (gr. 2-4). pap. 9.15 *(978-0-8368-7407-5(2),* 71d9691d-bd51-40b8-8324-4c48dc0ca88d); lib. bdg. 24.67 *(978-0-8368-7402-0(1),* 7141fdfc-9c04-4921-a293-56f64fb0fc43) Stevens, Gareth Publishing LLLP. (Weekly Reader Leveled Readers).

—How Water Changes, 1 vol. (States of Matter Ser.). (ENG., 24p. (gr. 2-4). 2007. Illus.). lib. bdg. 24.67 *(978-0-8368-6798-5(X),* 24160952-1a1f-470a-9a41-9db129c6b3ee) 2006. pap. 9.15 *(978-0-8368-6803-6(X),* b4b60f7e-b668-499a-bedb-9157fd8d9cf0) Stevens, Gareth Publishing LLLP. (Weekly Reader Leveled Readers).

Michele, Tracey. Earth's Land & Water. 2011. (Learn-Abouts Ser.). (Illus.). 16p. (J). pap. 7.95 *(978-1-59920-593-9(9))* Black Rabbit Bks.

Mills, Nathan & Hume, Desmond. Earth's Water. 2012. (Rosen Readers Ser.). (ENG., Illus.). 24p. (J). (gr. 1-2). pap. 49.50 *(978-1-4488-8819-1(0));* pap. 8.25 *(978-1-4488-8818-4(2),* e27b16cf-f8a0-4147-9b24-98e3204f4715) Rosen Publishing Group, Inc., The. (Rosen Classroom).

Mills, Nathan & McCann, Margaret. How We Use Water, 1 vol. 2012. (Rosen Readers Ser.). (ENG., Illus.). 24p. (J). (gr. 1-1). pap. 8.25 *(978-1-4488-8794-1(1),* 3117a6ad-d5ab-43e3-b540-7d9821c92c30, Rosen Classroom) Rosen Publishing Group, Inc., The.

Modules: Earth Science; Earth's Waters TE. 2005. (gr. 6-12). *(978-0-618-33418-6(1),* 2-01008) Holt McDougal.

Moore, Rob. Why Does Water Evaporate?, 1 vol. 2010. (Solving Science Mysteries Ser.). (ENG., Illus.). 24p. (gr. 4-5). (J). pap. 9.25 *(978-1-61531-915-2(8),* 37bce3e2-1a32-434a-8d3a-ac813df3bde7, PowerKids Pr.); (YA). lib. bdg. 26.27 *(978-1-61531-892-6(5),* a61ea7af-15fc-4977-80d6-6c83a0a62c8d) Rosen Publishing Group, Inc., The.

—Why Does Water Evaporate? All about Heat & Temperature. 2010. (Illus.). 24p. (J). 49.50 *(978-1-61531-916-9(6),* 1307166, PowerKids Pr.) Rosen Publishing Group, Inc., The.

Morgan, Sally. Earth's Water Cycle. 2011. (Earth Cycles Ser.). 32p. (YA). (gr. 3-6). lib. bdg. 28.50 *(978-1-59920-523-6(8))* Black Rabbit Bks.

—The Water Cycle, 1 vol. 2008. (Nature's Cycles Ser.). (ENG.). 32p. (J). (gr. 5-5). lib. bdg. 30.27 *(978-1-4358-2868-1(2),* d51ffee7-f315-458b-92cc-dc0173f746e2, PowerKids Pr.) Rosen Publishing Group, Inc., The.

Nadeau, Isaac. Learing about the Water Cycle with Graphic Organizers, 1 vol. 2004. (Graphic Organizers in Science Ser.). (ENG., Illus.). 24p. (J). (gr. 4-5). lib. bdg. 26.27 *(978-1-4042-2808-5(X),* 057bcad9-cc89-4c56-bba7-bfc7317670d1, PowerKids Pr.) Rosen Publishing Group, Inc., The.

—Learning about the Water Cycle with Graphic Organizers, 1 vol. 2005. (Graphic Organizers in Science & Social Studies). (ENG., Illus.). 24p. (gr. 4-5). pap. 8.25 *(978-1-4042-5046-8(8),* e0a67dfd-2032-4eb0-8482-51f314d6ea60, PowerKids Pr.) Rosen Publishing Group, Inc., The.

—Water in Glaciers. 2009. (Water Cycle Ser.). 24p. (gr. 4-4). 42.50 *(978-1-60854-268-0(8),* PowerKids Pr.) Rosen Publishing Group, Inc., The.

—Water in Plants & Animals. 2009. (Water Cycle Ser.). 24p. (gr. 4-4). 42.50 *(978-1-60854-270-3(X),* PowerKids Pr.) Rosen Publishing Group, Inc., The.

—Water in the Atmosphere. 2009. (Water Cycle Ser.). 24p. (gr 4-4). 42.50 *(978-1-60854-272-7(6),* PowerKids Pr.) Rosen Publishing Group, Inc., The.

—Water under Ground. 2009. (Water Cycle Ser.). 24p. (gr. 4-4). 42.50 *(978-1-60854-273-4(4),* PowerKids Pr.) Rosen Publishing Group, Inc., The.

Nagy, Frances. Science with Water. 2007. (Usborne Science Activities Ser.). (Illus.). 24p. (J). (gr. 1). lib. bdg. 13.99 *(978-1-58086-976-8(9));* pap. 5.99 *(978-0-7945-1484-6(7))* EDC Publishing. (Usborne).

Nelson, Penelope S. The Water Cycle. 2018. (Weather Watch Ser.). (ENG., Illus.). 24p. (J). (gr. 1-1). pap. 8.95 *(978-1-63517-843-2(6),* 1635178436) North Star Editions.

—The Water Cycle. 2018. (Weather Watch Ser.). (ENG., Illus.). 24p. (J). (gr. k-3). lib. bdg. 31.36 *(978-1-5321-6055-4(0),* 28742, Pop! Cody Koala) Pop!

Nelson, Robin. El Ciclo Del Agua. 2003. (Mi Primer Paso al Mundo Real Ser.). (SPA., Illus.). 24p. (J). (gr. k-2). lib. bdg. 18.60 *(978-0-8225-4866-9(6))* Lerner Publishing Group.

—¿Dónde Hay Agua? Castañer, Mercedes P. & Fitzpatrick, Julia, trs. 2003. (Mi Primer Paso Al Mundo Real - el Agua (First Step Nonfiction - Water) Ser.). (SPA., Illus.). 24p. (gr. k-2). lib. bdg. 23.93 *(978-0-8225-4868-3(2))* Lerner Publishing Group.

—Earth's Water Cycle. 2010. (First Step Nonfiction — Discovering Nature's Cycles Ser.). (gr. k-2). (ENG., Illus.). 24p. (J). pap. 6.99 *(978-0-7613-5680-6(0),* f701d169-8c76-49fd-90a9-ca383d03acd0); pap. 33.92 *(978-0-7613-6913-4(9));* (ENG.). 24p. lib. bdg. 23.93 *(978-0-7613-4581-7(7))* Lerner Publishing Group.

—Flotar y Hundirse. Translations.com Staff, tr. from ENG. 2007. (Mi Primer Paso Al Mundo Real - Fuerzas y Movimiento (First Step Nonfiction - Forces & Motion) Ser.). (SPA., Illus.). 24p. (gr. k-2). lib. bdg. 23.93 *(978-0-8225-7808-6(5),* Ediciones Lerner) Lerner Publishing Group.

—Freezing & Melting. 2003. (First Step Nonfiction — Water Ser.). (Illus.). 24p. (J). (gr. k-2). (ENG.). pap. 6.99 *(978-0-8225-4591-0(8),* 45fa9ba6-a3d8-49c4-bf5e-0360baaa3084); lib. bdg. 18.60 *(978-0-8225-4590-3(X))* Lerner Publishing Group.

—Que Es el Agua? Castañer, Mercedes & Fitzpatrick, Julia, trs. 2003. (Mi Primer Paso Al Mundo Real - el Agua (First Step Nonfiction - Water) Ser.). (SPA., Illus.). 24p. (gr. k-2). lib. bdg. 23.93 *(978-0-8225-4869-0(0))* Lerner Publishing Group.

—Se Congela y Se Derrite. Castañer, Mercedes & Fitzpatrick, Julia, trs. 2003. (Mi Primer Paso Al Mundo Real - el Agua (First Step Nonfiction - Water) Ser.). (SPA., Illus.). 24p. (gr. k-2). lib. bdg. 23.93 *(978-0-8225-4865-2(8))* Lerner Publishing Group.

—Water. 2005. (First Step Nonfiction — What Earth Is Made Of Ser.). (ENG., Illus.). 24p. (J). (gr. k-2). pap. 6.99 *(978-0-8225-5377-9(5),* 13568681-e624-4971-a5f0-164f54f5eec1) Lerner Publishing Group.

—Water: By Robin Nelson. 2005. (First Step Nonfiction Ser.). (Illus.). 23p. (J). (gr. 3-7). lib. bdg. 18.60 *(978-0-8225-2600-1(X),* Lerner Pubns.) Lerner Publishing Group.

—What Is Water? 2003. (First Step Nonfiction Ser.). (Illus.). 24p. (J). (gr. k-2). lib. bdg. 18.60 *(978-0-8225-4588-0(8))* Lerner Publishing Group.

—Where Is Water? (Illus.). 24p. 2009. 5.95 *(978-0-8225-4593-4(4))* 2003. (J). lib. bdg. 18.60 *(978-0-8225-4592-7(6))* Lerner Publishing Group.

Nunn, Daniel. Water, 1 vol. 2012. (Why Living Things Need Ser.). (ENG.). 24p. (gr. -1-1). pap. 6.29 *(978-1-4329-5923-4(9),* 117625, Heinemann) Capstone.

Olien, Rebecca. Water Sources. 2016. (Water in Our World Ser.). (ENG., Illus.). 24p. (J). (gr. 1-3). lib. bdg. 27.99 *(978-1-4914-8277-3(X),* 130762, Capstone Pr.) Capstone.

Ostopowich, Melanie. Oceans, Lakes, & Rivers. 2016. *(978-1-4896-5794-7(0))* Weigl Pubs., Inc.

Our World of Water, 12 vols. 2017. (Our World of Water Ser.). (ENG.). (J). (gr. 1-1). lib. bdg. 155.58 *(978-1-5026-3225-8(X),* 401f6888-a7e7-4c0c-9587-190660082f7a) Cavendish Square Publishing LLC.

Owen, Ruth. Energy from Oceans & Moving Water: Hydroelectric, Wave, & Tidal Power, 1 vol. 2013. (Power: Yesterday, Today, Tomorrow Ser.). (ENG., Illus.). 32p. (J). (gr. 4-5). 28.93 *(978-1-4777-0269-7(5),* 082b8e2a-3050-4b12-8c95-a38b68862ffa); pap. 12.75 *(978-1-4777-0277-2(6),* 3cfb63f7-dc77-4b0c-b218-a7d78982331c) Rosen Publishing Group, Inc., The. (PowerKids Pr.).

Oxlade, Chris. Experiments with Air & Water, 1 vol. 2014. (Excellent Science Experiments Ser.). (ENG., Illus.). 32p. (J). (gr. 4-5). lib. bdg. 29.27 *(978-1-4777-5793-2(7),* aee3547d-3207-48a5-8617-388e6640f6b1, PowerKids Pr.) Rosen Publishing Group, Inc., The.

—Water, 1 vol. 2012. (How Does My Home Work? Ser.). (ENG.). 24p. (J). (gr. k-1). lib. bdg. 25.99 *(978-1-4329-6567-9(0),* 119219, Heinemann) Capstone.

Parker, Steve. Tabletop Scientist — the Science of Water: Projects & Experiments with Water Science & Power. 2013. (Dover Science for Kids Ser.). (ENG., Illus.). 32p. (J). (gr. 5). pap. 6.99 *(978-0-486-49262-9(1),* 492621) Dover Pubns., Inc.

—Water Power, 1 vol. 2004. (Science Files: Energy Ser.). (ENG., Illus.). 32p. (gr. 3-5). lib. bdg. 28.67 *(978-0-8368-4033-9(X),* f2ac92e5-2984-47a2-b48d-c0b408dbc486, Gareth Stevens Learning Library) Stevens, Gareth Publishing LLLP.

Paul, Miranda. Water Is Water: A Book about the Water Cycle. Chin, Jason, illus. 2015. (ENG.). 40p. (J). (gr. 1-5). 19.99 *(978-1-59643-984-9(X),* 900128158) Roaring Brook Pr.

Pendergast, George. The Water Cycle at Work, 1 vol. 2015. (Cycles in Nature Ser.). (ENG.). 24p. (J). (gr. 1-2). lib. bdg. 24.27 *(978-1-4824-1670-1(0),* 1b152afb-de0d-4f27-80bc-9ce0ce50fcb6) Stevens, Gareth Publishing LLLP.

Perritano, John. Freshwater Resources, Vol. 12. 2015. (North American Natural Resources Ser.). (Illus.). 64p. (J). (gr. 7). lib. bdg. 23.95 *(978-1-4222-3381-8(2))* Mason Crest.

etersen, Christine. A Project Guide to Earth's Waters. 2010. (Earth Science Projects for Kids Ser.). (Illus.). 48p. (J). (gr. 4-7). lib. bdg. 29.95 *(978-1-58415-871-4(9))* Mitchell Lane Pubs.
Pond Ecosystem. 2012. (Nature Trail Ser.). (ENG., Illus.). 32p. (J). (gr. k-5). 23.95 *(978-1-4488-6627-4(8)*, PowerKids Pr.) Rosen Publishing Group, Inc., The.
ortis, Antoinette. Hey, Water! 2019. (ENG., Illus.). 48p. (J). (gr. -1-3). 18.99 *(978-0-8234-4155-6(5)*, Neal Porter Bks) Holiday Hse., Inc.
roudfit, Benjamin. Why Do Ice Cubes Float?, 1 vol. 2015. (Everyday Mysteries Ser.). (ENG.). 24p. (J). (gr. 1-2). pap. 9.15 *(978-1-4824-3852-9(6)*, 60c10cf3-6efa-49a7-83ab-ad456b0ba00b) Stevens, Gareth Publishing LLLP.
ursiow, Frances. The Water Cycle. 2015. (Illus.). 24p. (J). *(978-1-5105-0056-3(1))* SmartBook Media, Inc.
—The Water Cycle. (Illus.). 24p. 2016. (J). *(978-1-4896-5800-5(9))* 2010. (J). (gr. 3-5). pap. 11.95 *(978-1-61690-009-0(1))* 2010. (YA). (gr. 3-6). lib. bdg. 25.70 *(978-1-61690-003-8(2))* 2005. (J). (gr. 3-7). lib. bdg. 24.45 *(978-1-59036-306-5(X)*, 1251285) Weigl Pubs., Inc.
Ranola-Collier, Jean. Living Water. 2013. 24p. pap. *(978-1-4602-0682-9(7))* FriesenPress.
Rees, Peter. Why Do Raindrops Fall? Level 3 Factbook. 2010. (Cambridge Young Readers Ser.). (ENG., Illus.). 16p. pap. 6.00 *(978-0-521-13714-0(4))* Cambridge Univ. Pr.
René, Ellen. Investigating Why It Rains. (Science Detectives Ser.). 24p. (gr. 2-3). 2009. 42.50 *(978-1-60853-016-8(7)*, PowerKids Pr.) 2008. (ENG., Illus.). (J). lib. bdg. 26.27 *(978-1-4042-4483-2(2)*, 0a9b1aef-d552-431d-afcc-ce00381d844d) Rosen Publishing Group, Inc., The.
Rice, Dona & Wilder, Nellie. Making Water Safe. rev. ed. 2019. (Smithsonian: Informational Text Ser.). (ENG., Illus.). 24p. (J). (gr. 1-2). pap. 8.99 *(978-1-4938-6656-4(7))* Teacher Created Materials, Inc.
Rice, Dona Herweck. Agua. 2nd rev. ed. 2011. (TIME for KIDS(r): Informational Text Ser.). (SPA.). 12p. (gr. k-1). 7.99 *(978-1-4333-4415-2(7))* Teacher Created Materials, Inc.
—Water, 1 vol. 2nd rev. ed. (TIME for KIDS(r): Informational Text Ser.). (ENG., 12p. (gr. k-1). 2013. Illus.). (J). lib. bdg. 15.96 *(978-1-4807-1015-3(6))* 2011. 7.99 *(978-1-4333-3576-1(X))* Teacher Created Materials, Inc.
—Water Bodies, 1 vol. rev. ed. 2014. (Science: Informational Text Ser.). (ENG.). 32p. (gr. 2-3). pap. 10.99 *(978-1-4807-4609-1(6))* Teacher Created Materials, Inc.
Rice, Willam B. Water Scientists, 1 vol. rev. ed. 2007. (Science: Informational Text Ser.). (ENG.). 32p. (gr. 4-6). pap. 12.99 *(978-0-7439-0556-5(3))* Teacher Created Materials, Inc.
Rice, William B. Struggle for Survival: Water. 2016. (Time for Kids Nonfiction Readers Ser.). (ENG.). (J). (gr. 5-8). lib. bdg. 20.85 *(978-0-606-39539-7(3))* Turtleback.
Richards, Jon. Water & Boats. (Science Factory Ser.). 32p. (gr. 4-5). 2009. 50.50 *(978-1-60853-023-6(X)*, PowerKids Pr.) 2007. (ENG., Illus.). (YA). lib. bdg. 30.27 *(978-1-4042-3909-8(X)*, 47a4bd89-250d-4d0c-ab8f-f2f64340a610) Rosen Publishing Group, Inc., The.
Rieger, Linda. Water Party. Bianchi, John, illus. 2008. 20p. (J). *(978-0-9779427-3-2(2))* Pathways into Science.
Rivera, Andrea. Water. 2016. (Our Renewable Earth Ser.). (ENG., Illus.). 24p. (J). (gr. -1-2). lib. bdg. 31.36 *(978-1-68079-942-2(8)*, 24188, Abdo Zoom-Launch) ABDO Publishing Co.
Rookie Read-About Geography: Bodies of Water, 7 bks., Set. Incl. Lake Tahoe. Zollman, Pam. lib. bdg. 20.50 *(978-0-516-25036-6(1))*; Missouri River. Taylor-Butler, Christine. lib. bdg. 20.50 *(978-0-516-25037-3(X))*; (Illus.). 32p. (J). (gr. 1-2). 2006. 2006. 136.50 o.p. *(978-0-516-25414-2(6)*, Children's Pr.) Scholastic Library Publishing.
Rose, Simon. Estuaries. 2014. (Illus.). 32p. (J). *(978-1-62127-485-8(3))* Weigl Pubs., Inc.
Rossiter, Brienna. Wet & Dry. 2019. (Opposites Ser.). (ENG., Illus.). 16p. (J). (gr. k-1). 25.64 *(978-1-64185-352-1(2)*, 1641853522, Focus Readers) North Star Editions.
Roth, Jennifer A. Just Add Water: Science Projects You Can Sink, Squirt, Splash, Sail. 2007. (Experiment with Science Ser.). (ENG., Illus.). 32p. (J). (gr. 3-6). 27.00 *(978-0-531-18545-2(1)*, Children's Pr.) Scholastic Library Publishing.
Royston, Angela. Experiments with Water. 2016. (One-Stop Science Ser.). 32p. (gr. 2-5). 31.35 *(978-1-62588-142-7(8)*, Smart Apple Media) Black Rabbit Bks.
—Water: Let's Look at a Puddle, 1 vol. 2005. (J). (ENG.). 24p. pap. *(978-1-4109-1832-1(7))*; lib. bdg. *(978-1-4109-1823-9(8))* Steck-Vaughn.
Salas, Laura Purdie. Water Can Be ... Dabija, Violeta, illus. 2014. (Can Be ... Bks.). (ENG.). 32p. (J). (gr. k-2). 17.99 *(978-1-4677-0591-2(8)*, 440e5b1f-cc6f-4978-bfff-995a8f2467b9, Millbrook Pr.) Lerner Publishing Group.
Sayre, April Pulley. Raindrops Roll. Sayre, April Pulley, photos by. 2015. (Weather Walks Ser.). (ENG., Illus.). 40p. (J). (gr. -1-3). 18.99 *(978-1-4814-2064-8(X)*, Beach Lane Bks.) Beach Lane Bks.
Schmauss, Judy Kentor. Shockwave: Wicked & Wonderful Water. 2007. (Shockwave: Economics & Geography Ser.). (ENG., Illus.). 36p. (J). (gr. 3-5). 25.00 *(978-0-531-17751-8(3)*, Children's Pr.) Scholastic Library Publishing.
Schnell, Lisa. Water All Around. 2018. (I Wonder Ser.). (ENG., Illus.). 16p. (gr. -1-2). lib. bdg. 28.50 *(978-1-64156-187-7(4)*, 9781641561877) Rourke Educational Media.
Schomp, Virginia. 24 Hours in a Pond, 1 vol. 2013. (Day in an Ecosystem Ser.). (ENG.). 48p. (gr. 4-4). 34.07 *(978-1-60870-894-9(2)*, ffb6226d-7e9e-4575-b4eb-556a10443f4a) Cavendish Square Publishing LLC.
Selwyn, Josephine. When Does Water Turn into Ice? 2012. (Level F Ser.). (ENG., Illus.). 16p. (J). (gr. k-2). pap. 7.95 *(978-1-927136-59-1(8)*, 19436) RiverStream Publishing.
Shookuhi, Aminjon. Where Does the Water Come From? Khodjibaev, Karim & Khodjibaeva, Moukhabbat, trs. Seabaugh, Jan, illus. 2009. 88p. (J). pap. 15.95 *(978-0-9740551-2-1(3))* Smith, Viveca Publishing.
Sian Revision Water Cycle. 2004. (J). *(978-1-59242-081-0(8))* Delta Education, LLC.
Silverman, Buffy. Saving Water: The Water Cycle. rev. ed. 2016. (Do It Yourself Ser.). (ENG.). 48p. (J). (gr. 3-6). pap. 8.99 *(978-1-4846-3695-4(3)*, 134107, Heinemann) Capstone.
Simon, Charnan. Water. 2009. (Explorer Library: Science Explorer Ser.). (ENG., Illus.). 32p. (gr. 4-8). lib. bdg. 32.07 *(978-1-60279-529-7(0)*, 200298) Cherry Lake Publishing.
Simon, Charnan & Kazunas, Ariel. Junior Scientists: Experiment with Water. 2010. (Explorer Junior Library: Science Explorer Junior Ser.). (ENG., Illus.). 32p. (gr. 3-6). lib. bdg. 32.07 *(978-1-60279-838-0(9)*, 200542) Cherry Lake Publishing.
Simon, Seymour. Water. 2017. (ENG., Illus.). 40p. (J). (gr. 1-5). 17.99 *(978-0-06-247055-3(8))*; pap. 7.99 *(978-0-06-247054-6(X))* HarperCollins Pubs. (HarperCollins).
Slade, Suzanne. Water on the Move. (Cycles in Nature Ser.). (gr. 3-3). 2009. 24p. 42.50 *(978-1-61512-117-5(X))* 2007. 28p. pap. 21.25 *(978-1-4358-3829-1(7))* 2007. (ENG., Illus.). 24p. (J). lib. bdg. 25.27 *(978-1-4042-3492-5(6)*, 935dd452-5176-44a4-83a8-af773edd2b1b) Rosen Publishing Group, Inc., The. (PowerKids Pr.).
Smith, Michael. It Starts with a Raindrop: Comienza con una Gota de Lluvia. Goley, Jonathon & Alvarenga, Angela, illus. 2016. (ENG & SPA.). 33p. (J). *(978-0-9973947-1-9(4))* East West Discovery Pr.
Smuskiewicz, Alfred J. Properties of Water, 1 vol. 2007. (Gareth Stevens Vital Science Library: Earth Science Ser.). (ENG., Illus.). 48p. (gr. 5-8). pap. 15.05 *(978-0-8368-7875-2(2)*, e6e9e858-7b83-4555-92da-ddba07d17cb6); lib. bdg. 29.67 *(978-0-8368-7764-9(0)*, 60e7d4b8-deff-4d35-943f-3f650299232d) Stevens, Gareth Publishing LLLP. (Gareth Stevens Secondary Library).
Sohn, Emily & Townsend, Laura. Water. 2019. (IScience Ser.). (ENG., Illus.). 32p. (J). (gr. 3-4). 23.94 *(978-1-68450-954-6(8))* Norwood Hse. Pr.
Spilsbury, Louise. What Are Rivers, Lakes, & Oceans?, 1 vol., 1. 2013. (Let's Find Out! Earth Science Ser.). (ENG.). 32p. (gr. 2-3). 27.04 *(978-1-62275-281-2(3)*, a6c9cc56-3a58-4842-9d8e-5982216028d9) Rosen Publishing Group, Inc., The.
—What Is the Water Cycle?, 1 vol., 1. 2013. (Let's Find Out! Earth Science Ser.). (ENG.). 32p. (gr. 2-3). 27.04 *(978-1-62275-261-4(9)*, 185f7d7b-776d-41c7-aaf4-5f9adb0c2d6c) Rosen Publishing Group, Inc., The.
Spilsbury, Richard & Spilsbury, Louise. The Water Cycle, 1 vol. 2018. (Flowchart Smart Ser.). (ENG.). 48p. (gr. 4-5). pap. 15.05 *(978-1-5382-3479-2(3)*, 906a80f5-1f55-4579-ab37-c7b723b0c411) Stevens, Gareth Publishing LLLP.
Stearns, Carolyn. Where Did All the Water Go?, 1 vol. 2009. (ENG., Illus.). 30p. (J). (gr. 4-7). 12.95 *(978-0-87033-506-8(5)*, 3750, Cornell Maritime Pr./Tidewater Pubs.) Schiffer Publishing, Ltd.
Stewart, Melissa. National Geographic Readers: Water. 2014. (Readers Ser.). (Illus.). 48p. (J). (gr. 1-3). pap. 4.99 *(978-1-4263-1474-2(4)*, National Geographic Kids) Disney Publishing Worldwide.
Strauss, Rochelle. One Well: The Story of Water on Earth. Woods, Rosemary, illus. 2007. (CitizenKid Ser.). (ENG.). 32p. (J). (gr. 3-7). 19.99 *(978-1-55337-954-6(3))* Kids Can Pr., Ltd. CAN. Dist: Hachette Bk. Group.
Sullivan, Martha. Pitter & Patter, 1 vol. Morrison, Cathy, illus. 2015. 32p. (J). (gr. k-4). pap. 8.95 *(978-1-58469-509-7(9)*, Dawn Pubns.) Sourcebooks, Inc.
Sundance/Newbridge LLC Staff. Amazing Water. 2007. (Early Science Ser.). (gr. k-3). 18.95 *(978-1-4007-6296-5(0))*; pap. 6.10 *(978-1-4007-6292-7(8))* Sundance/Newbridge Educational Publishing.
Taylor-Butler, Christine. Hydrology: The Study of Water. 2012. (True Book: Earth Science Ser.). (ENG., Illus.). 48p. (J). (gr. 3-5). lib. bdg. 21.19 *(978-0-531-24677-1(9)*, Children's Pr.) Scholastic Library Publishing.
—Hydrology (a True Book: Earth Science) 2012. (True Book (Relaunch) Ser.). (ENG., Illus.). 48p. (J). (gr. 3-5). pap. 6.95 *(978-0-531-28271-7(6)*, Children's Pr.) Scholastic Library Publishing.
—Water Everywhere! Manning, Maurie, illus. 2011. (Rookie Ready to Learn - First Science Ser.). 40p. (J). (gr. -1-k). lib. bdg. 23.00 *(978-0-531-26504-8(8)*, Children's Pr.) Scholastic Library Publishing.
Taylor, Kim. Water. (Illus.). 32p. (YA). (gr. 3-18). lib. bdg. 27.10 *(978-1-931983-79-2(8))* Chrysalis Education.
Valat, Pierre-Marie. Water. Valat, Pierre-Marie, illus. 2012. (ENG., Illus.). 36p. (J). (gr. -1-k). spiral bd. 19.99 *(978-1-85103-403-1(X))* Moonlight Publishing, Ltd. GBR. Dist: Independent Pubs. Group.
Vogt, Gregory. The Hydrosphere: Agent of Change. 2007. (Earth's Spheres Ser.). (ENG., Illus.). 80p. (gr. 6-8). lib. bdg. 29.27 *(978-0-7613-2839-1(4))* Lerner Publishing Group.
Waldman, Neil. The Snowflake: A Water Cycle Story. Waldman, Neil, illus. 2003. (Illus.). 32p. lib. bdg. 23.90 *(978-0-7613-1762-3(7)*, Millbrook Pr.) Lerner Publishing Group.
Walker, Kate. Water, 1 vol. Hopgood, Andrew, illus. 2012. (Investigating Earth Ser.). (ENG.). 32p. (gr. 2-2). 31.21 *(978-1-60870-562-7(5)*, 26875fb1-3940-4bd4-9b0f-b0022104af9b) Cavendish Square Publishing LLC.
Walton, Ruth. Let's Drink Some Water. 2013. (Let's Find Out Ser.). (ENG., Illus.). 32p. (gr. k-5). 28.50 *(978-1-59771-384-9(8))* Sea-To-Sea Pubns.
Warhol, Tom. Water, 1 vol. 2007. (Earth's Biomes Ser.). (ENG., Illus.). 80p. (gr. 6-6). lib. bdg. 36.93 *(978-0-7614-2192-4(0)*, aa77649f-877b-40a3-9b6a-4129375b4904) Cavendish Square Publishing LLC.
Water. (Jump Ser.). (Illus.). 32p. (J). (gr. 2-7). pap. 4.95 *(978-1-882210-29-9(8))* Action Publishing, Inc.
Water, Vol. 5. 2005. (Our Seasons & Weather Ser.). (YA). (gr. k-3). 178.20 *(978-0-7368-4202-0(0)*, Pebble) Capstone.
Water. 2004. (Illus.). lib. bdg. 7.95 *(978-0-8225-4753-2(8))* Lerner Publishing Group.
Water All Around. 2005. (Water All Around Ser.). (ENG., Illus.). 24p. (gr. 1-2). lib. bdg. 49.30 *(978-0-7368-3811-5(2)*, Capstone Pr.) Capstone.
Webster, Christine. Glaciers. 2015. (Illus.). 24p. (J). *(978-1-5105-0050-1(2))* SmartBook Media, Inc.
—Glaciers. 2016. (Illus.). 24p. (J). *(978-1-4896-5791-6(6))* Weigl Pubs., Inc.
Der Weg des Wassers.Tr. of Characteristics of Water. (GER., Illus.). (YA). 31.95 *(978-3-411-09131-7(2))* Bibliographisches Institut & F. A. Brockhaus AG DEU. Dist: Continental Bk. Co., Inc.
Wells, Robert E. Did a Dinosaur Drink This Water? 2012. (J). *(978-1-61913-113-2(7))* Weigl Pubs., Inc.
—Did a Dinosaur Drink This Water? Wells, Robert E., illus. 2006. (Wells of Knowledge Science Ser.). (ENG., Illus.). 32p. (J). (gr. -1-3). 8.99 *(978-0-8075-8840-6(7)*, 807588407) Whitman, Albert & Co.
—Why Do Elephants Need the Sun? Wells, Robert E., illus. 2012. (Wells of Knowledge Science Ser.). (ENG., Illus.). 32p. (J). (gr. -1-3). pap. 8.99 *(978-0-8075-9082-9(7)*, 807590827) Whitman, Albert & Co.
Where's the Water?, 12 vols. 2016. (Where's the Water? Ser.). 24p. (ENG.). (gr. 2-3). lib. bdg. 145.62 *(978-1-4824-4604-3(9)*, 0af26894-7f1f-4c5d-a509-e74419c7eac5); (gr. 3-2). pap. 48.90 *(978-1-4824-5304-1(5))* Stevens, Gareth Publishing LLLP.
Whittaker, Helen & Lewis, Helen. Water: Information & Projects to Reduce Your Environmental Footprint, 1 vol. Porcellato, Nives, illus. 2012. (Living Green Ser.). (ENG.). 32p. (gr. 4-4). 31.21 *(978-1-60870-576-4(5)*, 2c97bbc9-66ca-42f5-968e-d2883ae31cad) Cavendish Square Publishing LLC.
Who Likes Water? KinderWords Individual Title Six-Packs. (Kinderstarters Ser.). 8p. (gr. -1-1). 21.00 *(978-0-7635-8713-0(3))* Rigby Education.
Wilder, Nellie. On Water, 1 vol. rev. ed. 2014. (Science: Informational Text Ser.). (ENG., Illus.). 24p. (J). (gr. -1-1). pap. 9.99 *(978-1-4807-4533-9(2))* Teacher Created Materials, Inc.
—Staying Afloat. rev. ed. 2019. (Smithsonian: Informational Text Ser.). (ENG., Illus.). 20p. (J). (gr. k-1). 7.99 *(978-1-4938-6636-6(2))* Teacher Created Materials, Inc.
Wood, Ira. Water, Ice, & Steam. (Rosen Real Readers Big Bookstm Ser.). (ENG., Illus.). 12p. (gr. 1-2). 2006. 33.50 *(978-1-4042-6215-7(6))* 2005. pap. 5.90 *(978-0-8239-6353-9(5)*, 19241861-0961-442d-9575-cb4dddcd1adc) Rosen Publishing Group, Inc., The.
World Book, Inc. Staff, contrib. by. Fabled Waters. 2017. (Illus.). 40p. (J). *(978-0-7166-3369-3(8))* World Bk., Inc.
Yanez, Anthony & Guillory, Mike. A Wild Ride on the Water Cycle. 2014. (ENG., Illus.). 28p. (J). (gr. -1-4). 19.95 *(978-1-939055-80-4(6)*, da5a384d-bd8a-40c4-b1f5-17a756f79d3c) Night Heron Media.
Yasuda, Anita. Explore Water! 25 Great Projects, Activities, Experiments. Stone, Bryan, illus. 2011. (Explore Your World Ser.). (ENG.). 96p. (J). (gr. k-4). pap. 12.95 *(978-1-936313-42-6(1)*, baedaabf-fa86-4ca2-858d-88d225cdef2a) Nomad Pr.
Yates, Irene. Water. 2004. (Activities for 3-5 Year Olds Ser.). (Illus.). 32p. pap. 11.00 *(978-1-897675-25-0(9))* Brilliant Pubns. GBR. Dist: Parkwest Pubns., Inc.
Ylvisake, Anne. Land & Water: World Rivers. (Fact Finders Ser.). (Illus.). (J). (gr. 3-4). lib. bdg. 90.40 *(978-0-7368-2559-7(2))* Capstone.
York, M. J. A Pond in Spring. 2017. (Welcoming the Seasons Ser.). (ENG.). 24p. (J). (gr. -1-2). lib. bdg. 32.79 *(978-1-5038-1656-5(7)*, 211502) Child's World, Inc, The.

WATER—CONSERVATION

see Water Conservation

WATER—POLLUTION

see also Refuse and Refuse Disposal; Sewage Disposal also Petroleum Pollution of Water and similar headings

Benchmark Education Company. Ocean Pollution (Teacher Guide) 2005. *(978-1-4108-4678-5(4))* Benchmark Education Co.
Brannon, Barbara. Discover Ocean Pollution. 2005. (J). pap. *(978-1-4108-5140-6(0))* Benchmark Education Co.
Bullard, Lisa. Watch over Our Water. Xin, Xiao, illus. 2011. (Planet Protectors Ser.). pap. 39.62 *(978-0-7613-8657-5(2)*, Millbrook Pr.) Lerner Publishing Group.
—Watch over Our Water. Zheng, Xin, illus. 2011. (Cloverleaf Books (tm) — Planet Protectors Ser.). (ENG.). 24p. (J). (gr. k-2). pap. 8.99 *(978-0-7613-8517-2(7)*, d8a73cbe-a1c6-4fcc-b79a-0ad7cd86e2c5, Millbrook Pr.) Lerner Publishing Group.
Castellano, Peter. Water Conservation, 1 vol. 2016. (Where's the Water? Ser.). (ENG., Illus.). 24p. (J). (gr. 2-3). pap. 9.15 *(978-1-4824-4692-0(8)*, c03dedbd-df21-49ef-8d04-e0eb438dcebe) Stevens, Gareth Publishing LLLP.
Cooper, Candy J. & Aronson, Marc. Poisoned Water: How the Citizens of Flint, Michigan, Fought for Their Lives & Warned the Nation. 2020. (ENG., Illus.). 256p. (J). 18.99 *(978-1-5476-0232-2(5)*, 900204200, Bloomsbury Children's Bks.) Bloomsbury Publishing USA.
Farrell, Courtney. Save the Planet: Keeping Water Clean. 2010. (Explorer Library: Language Arts Explorer Ser.). (ENG.). 32p. (gr. 4-8). pap. 14.21 *(978-1-60279-668-3(8)*, 200915) Cherry Lake Publishing.
—Save the Planet: Keeping Water Clean. 2010. (Explorer Library: Language Arts Explorer Ser.). (ENG., Illus.). 32p. (gr. 4-8). lib. bdg. 32.07 *(978-1-60279-659-1(9)*, 200352) Cherry Lake Publishing.
Faust, Daniel R. Desastres Ecológicos: los Derrames de Petróleo y el MedioAmbiente, 1 vol. 2009. (Historietas Juveniles: Peligros Del Medioambiente (Jr. Graphic Environmental Dangers) Ser.). (SPA., Illus.). 24p. (gr. 4-4). pap. 10.60 *(978-1-4358-8469-4(8)*, 45598d3b-0bc0-4b0d-be3b-50c9905819ef, PowerKids Pr.) Rosen Publishing Group, Inc., The.
—Desastres Ecológicos: Los Derrames de Petróleo y el Medio Ambiente = Sinister Sludge: Oil Spills & the Environment, 1 vol. 2009. (Historietas Juveniles: Peligros Del Medioambiente (Jr. Graphic Environmental Dangers) Ser.). (SPA., Illus.). 24p. (YA). (gr. 4-4). lib. bdg. 28.93 *(978-1-4358-8468-7(X)*, bbf3bb69-9c5a-4ed8-8ad3-cadb2e6e85ed) Rosen Publishing Group, Inc., The.
Feinstein, Stephen. Conserving & Protecting Water: What You Can Do, 1 vol. 2010. (Green Issues in Focus Ser.). (ENG., Illus.). 128p. (gr. 6-7). lib. bdg. 35.93 *(978-0-7660-3346-7(5)*, 8daff8ad-4883-40a9-9dfe-2d6906e23a9b) Enslow Publishing, LLC.
—Drying Up: Running Out of Water, 1 vol. 2015. (End of Life As We Know It Ser.). (ENG., Illus.). 144p. (gr. 7-8). lib. bdg. 38.93 *(978-0-7660-7286-2(X)*, a8a4288f-6356-4ecb-bb25-6012d6a5b9b9) Enslow Publishing, LLC.
Fridell, Ron. Protecting Earth's Water Supply. 2009. pap. 58.95 *(978-0-7613-4694-4(5))* 2008. 72p. (YA). (gr. 4-7). lib. bdg. 30.60 *(978-0-8225-7557-3(4))* Lerner Publishing Group.
Goldish, Meish. Poisoned Water: Minamata, Japan. 2017. (Eco-Disasters Ser.). (ENG., Illus.). 32p. (J). (gr. 2-7). 19.95 *(978-1-68402-224-3(X))* Bearport Publishing Co., Inc.
Greene, Carol. I Love Our Water, 1 vol. 2012. (I Love Our Earth Ser.). (ENG., Illus.). 24p. (gr. 3-3). 25.27 *(978-0-7660-4042-7(9)*, ac54492f-cef8-4c24-804c-2735fe77a98a); pap. 10.35 *(978-1-4644-0138-1(1)*, c8017531-f892-4a1d-a0a4-f8dbf938b075) Enslow Publishing, LLC.
Harper, Joel. All the Way to the Ocean. Spusta, Marq, illus. 2006. (J). 14.95 *(978-0-9714254-1-5(8))* Freedom Three Publishing.
Haynes, Danielle. Chemical Catastrophes. 2017. (Unnatural Disasters Ser.). 32p. (J). (gr. 4-5). pap. 63.00 *(978-1-5382-0417-7(7))* Stevens, Gareth Publishing LLLP.
Head, Honor. Poisoned Rivers & Lakes, 1 vol. 2018. (Totally Toxic Ser.). (ENG.). 48p. (gr. 4-5). pap. 15.05 *(978-1-5382-3500-3(5)*, ab036dd4-0190-431c-a938-f8e84f087c3f) Stevens, Gareth Publishing LLLP.
Heos, Bridget. Polluted Water & Your Vital Organs, 1 vol. 2012. (Incredibly Disgusting Environments Ser.). (ENG., Illus.). 48p. (YA). (gr. 5-8). pap. 12.75 *(978-1-4488-8424-7(1)*, e69bd04d-bd42-4a1c-acd0-a4e010d9d172); lib. bdg. 34.47 *(978-1-4488-8412-4(8)*, a94ba9c4-2157-49f3-8db6-caec2e9af78f) Rosen Publishing Group, Inc., The.
Hustad, Douglas. How Can We Reduce Manufacturing Pollution? 2016. (Searchlight Books (tm) — What Can We Do about Pollution? Ser.). (ENG., Illus.). 40p. (J). (gr. 3-5). 30.65 *(978-1-4677-9518-0(6)*, adce80d6-7d6f-4168-8fa2-f709ff6fc26b, Lerner Pubns.) Lerner Publishing Group.
Kallen, Stuart A. Running Dry: The Global Water Crisis. 2015. (ENG., Illus.). 64p. (YA). (gr. 6-12). lib. bdg. 33.32 *(978-1-4677-2646-7(X)*, 70ee290d-49fb-44e6-bc09-1ec7d4122681); E-Book 50.65 *(978-1-4677-6308-0(X))* Lerner Publishing Group. (Twenty-First Century Bks.).
La Bella, Laura. Not Enough to Drink: Pollution, Drought, & Tainted Water Supplies. 2009. (Extreme Environmental Threats Ser.). 64p. (gr. 6-6). 58.50 *(978-1-61512-432-9(2))*; (ENG.). (YA). lib. bdg. 37.13 *(978-1-4358-5020-0(3)*, cf0dacbb-bb36-4473-8051-c316c07cd725); (ENG., Illus.). (J). pap. 13.95 *(978-1-4358-5376-8(8)*, 3351956c-73e1-4fab-83f5-891c2435bd86) Rosen Publishing Group, Inc., The.
Labrecque, Ellen. Clean Water. 2017. (21st Century Skills Library: Global Citizens: Environmentalism Ser.). (ENG., Illus.). 32p. (J). (gr. 4-7). lib. bdg. 32.07 *(978-1-63472-870-6(X)*, 209906) Cherry Lake Publishing.
Lawrence, Ellen. Poisoned Rivers & Lakes. 2014. (Science Slam: Green World, Clean World Ser.). 24p. (J). (gr. -1-3). lib. bdg. 26.99 *(978-1-62724-105-2(1))* Bearport Publishing Co., Inc.
Mason, Paul. How Big Is Your Water Footprint?, 1 vol. 2010. (Environmental Footprints Ser.). (ENG.). 32p. (gr. 4-4). 31.21 *(978-0-7614-4417-6(3)*, e2f94c3a-54ad-427b-9c22-753812749646) Cavendish Square Publishing LLC.
Minden, Cecilia. Kids Can Keep Water Clean. 2010. (21st Century Basic Skills Library: Kids Can Ser.). (ENG., Illus.). 24p. (gr. k-3). lib. bdg. 26.35 *(978-1-60279-872-4(9)*, 200610) Cherry Lake Publishing.
Newman, Patricia. Plastic, Ahoy! Investigating the Great Pacific Garbage Patch. Crawley, Annie, illus. 2014. (ENG.). 48p. (J). (gr. 3-6). lib. bdg. 30.65 *(978-1-4677-1283-5(3)*, 79120d0d-5b42-47f6-80e4-e7af8c1d8d00, Millbrook Pr.) Lerner Publishing Group.
Ostopowich, Melanie. Water Pollution. 2015. (Illus.). 24p. (J). *(978-1-5105-0058-7(8))* SmartBook Media, Inc.
—Water Pollution. 2016. 24p. (J). *(978-1-4896-5803-6(3))* 2010. (Illus.). 24p. (J). (gr. 3-5). pap. 11.95 *(978-1-61690-010-6(5))* 2010. (Illus.). 32p. (YA). (gr. 3-6). lib. bdg. 25.70 *(978-1-61690-004-5(0))* 2005. (Illus.). 24p. (J). (gr. 3-7). lib. bdg. 24.45 *(978-1-59036-307-2(8))* Weigl Pubs., Inc.
Parsons, Michelle Hyde. Ocean Pollution. 2005. (J). pap. *(978-1-4108-4630-3(X))* Benchmark Education Co.
Price, Sean. Water Pollution, 1 vol. 2009. (Saving Our World Ser.). (ENG.). 32p. (gr. 4-4). lib. bdg. 31.21 *(978-0-7614-3221-0(3)*, 6787cd87-6e9c-459f-b741-dae6aba4dc56) Cavendish Square Publishing LLC.
Spilsbury, Louise. Threats to Our Water Supply. 2009. (J). 70.50 *(978-1-4358-5481-9(0))*; (ENG.). 48p. (YA). (gr. 5-5). pap. 12.75 *(978-1-4358-5480-2(2)*, c40b1ed0-a7d0-4b4c-9bd5-543d9b6c912c); (ENG., Illus.). 48p. (J). (gr. 5-5). lib. bdg. 34.47 *(978-1-4358-5352-2(0)*, f45f6412-95ab-4ff3-9d8d-e29a74ec15a3) Rosen Publishing Group, Inc., The.
Tyler, Madeline. Surviving in a World Without Water, 1 vol. 2018. (Surviving the Impossible Ser.). (ENG.). 32p. (gr. 4-5). pap. 11.50 *(978-1-5382-3522-5(6)*, 2acc52d8-fb9c-4a1f-8eaa-dc78bf6cb414) Stevens, Gareth Publishing LLLP.

WATER—POLLUTION—FICTION

Allen, Nancy. Trouble in Troublesome Creek. Crawford, K., illus. 2011. (ENG.). 32p. (gr. -1-3). pap. 11.95 *(978-1-933176-36-9(9))* Red Rock Pr., Inc.

Allen, Nancy Kelly. Trouble in Troublesome Creek: A Troublesome Creek Kids Story. Crawford, K. Michael, illus. 2010. (ENG.). 32p. (J). (gr. -1-3). 16.95 *(978-1-933176-32-1(6))* Red Rock Pr., Inc.

Anthony, Fortuna. Tim Tim the River Crayfish. 2011. 40p. (gr. -1). pap. 19.99 *(978-1-4269-6068-0(9))* Trafford Publishing.

Atwell, Debby. River. 2004. (ENG., Illus.). 32p. (J). (gr. -1-3). reprint ed. pap. 6.95 *(978-0-618-43952-2(8)*, 490912, Clarion Bks.) HarperCollins Pubs.

Bardhan-Quallen, Sudipta. Purrmaids #6: Quest for Clean Water. Wu, Vivien, illus. 2019. (Purrmaids Ser.: 6). (ENG.). 96p. (J). (gr. 1-4). pap. 6.99 *(978-0-525-64637-2(X)*, Random Hse. Bks. for Young Readers) Random Hse. Children's Bks.

Covey, Richard D. & Pappas, Diane H. Let's Keep Our Oceans, Rivers, & Lakes Clean. 2009. (Planet Earth Patrol Ser.). (Illus.). (J). *(978-0-545-06105-6(9))* Scholastic, Inc.

Dombek, Jeff. How the Oysters Saved the Bay, 1 vol. 2013. (ENG., Illus.). 32p. (J). (gr. -1-3). 16.99 *(978-0-7643-4283-7(5)*, 4791) Schiffer Publishing, Ltd.

Gordon, Pauline C. The Adventures of the Droplet Twins. 2013. 136p. *(978-1-4602-1343-8(2))*; pap. *(978-1-4602-1344-5(0))* FriesenPress.

Gratz, Alan. Something Rotten, 1. 2007. (Horatio Wilkes Mystery Ser.). (ENG.). 208p. (J). (gr. 7-12). 21.19 *(978-0-8037-3216-2(3))* Penguin Young Readers Group.

Kline, Trish & Donev, Mary. Coming Home: KA Reader 8. 2007. (Illus.). 32p. (J). per. 20.00 *(978-1-934307-01-4(7))* Ghost Hunter Productions.

Lee, WonKyeong. Green River. Yang, HyeWon, illus. 2014. (MySELF Bookshelf Ser.). (ENG.). 32p. (J). (gr. k-2). lib. bdg. 25.27 *(978-1-59953-660-6(9))* Norwood Hse. Pr.

Lindstrom, Carole. We Are Water Protectors. Goade, Michaela, illus. 2020. (ENG.). 40p. (J). 17.99 *(978-1-250-20355-7(4)*, 900200518) Roaring Brook Pr.

McCurdie, Trevor. A Dolphin's Wish: How You Can Help Make a Difference & Save Our Oceans. Battistel, Cinzia, illus. 2020. (ENG.). 32p. (J). (gr. -1-3). 17.99 *(978-1-7282-0522-9(0))* Sourcebooks, Inc.

Meadows, Daisy. Milly the River Fairy. 2014. (Rainbow Magic — the Earth Fairies Ser.). lib. bdg. 14.75 *(978-0-606-35835-4(8))* Turtleback.

Patterson, James & Grabenstein, Chris. Max Einstein: Rebels with a Cause. Johnson, Beverly, illus. 2019. (Max Einstein Ser.: 2). (ENG.). 320p. (J). (gr. 3-9). 14.99 *(978-0-316-48816-7(X)*, Jimmy Patterson) Little Brown & Co.

Petty, Kate Reed. The Leak. Bell, Andrea & Bell, Andrea, illus. 2021. (ENG.). 240p. (J). 23.99 *(978-1-250-21795-0(4)*, 900207080); pap. 14.99 *(978-1-250-21796-7(2)*, 900207081) Roaring Brook Pr. (First Second Bks.).

Roddy, Lee. The Ghost Dog of Stoney Ridge. 2008. (D. J. Dillon Adventure Ser.: No. 4). (J). 7.99 *(978-0-88062-268-4(7))* Mott Media.

Shaw, Daniel, illus. Journey to Pansophigus. 2005. (J). per. 9.95 *(978-0-9772168-0-2(2))* Water Lily Pr., Inc.

Taylor-Butler, Christine. Water Everywhere! Manning, Maurie J., illus. 2005. (Rookie Reader Skill Set Ser.). (ENG.). 24p. (J). (gr. 1-2). per. 4.95 *(978-0-516-25285-8(2)*, Children's Pr.) Scholastic Library Publishing.

WATER—PURIFICATION

Evert, Franklin. Water & Other Forces for Good. 2017. (Text Connections Guided Close Reading Ser.). (J). (gr. 2). *(978-1-4900-1833-1(6))* Benchmark Education Co.

Flynn, Riley. Water Isn't Wasted! How Does Water Become Safe to Drink? 2018. (Story of Sanitation Ser.). (ENG., Illus.). 32p. (J). (gr. 3-6). pap. 7.95 *(978-1-5435-3116-9(4)*, 138724); lib. bdg. 27.99 *(978-1-5435-3112-1(1)*, 138709) Capstone. (Capstone Pr.).

Head, Honor. Poisoned Rivers & Lakes, 1 vol. 2018. (Totally Toxic Ser.). (ENG.). 48p. (gr. 4-5). pap. 15.05 *(978-1-5382-3500-3(5)*, ab036dd4-0190-431c-a938-f8e84f087c3f) Stevens, Gareth Publishing LLLP.

Heos, Bridget. Polluted Water & Your Vital Organs, 1 vol. 2012. (Incredibly Disgusting Environments Ser.). (ENG., Illus.). 48p. (YA). (gr. 5-8). pap. 12.75 *(978-1-4488-8424-7(1)*, e69bd04d-bd42-4a1c-acd0-a4e010d9d172); lib. bdg. 34.47 *(978-1-4488-8412-4(8)*, a94ba9c4-2157-49f3-8db6-caec2e9af78f) Rosen Publishing Group, Inc., The.

Hicks, Dwayne. Finding Water in the Wild, 1 vol., 1. 2015. (Wilderness Survival Skills Ser.). (ENG., Illus.). 24p. (J). (gr. 3-4). pap. 9.25 *(978-1-5081-4311-6(0)*, fb837d9a-2d75-461f-8b4e-36e02ef1b92f, PowerKids Pr.) Rosen Publishing Group, Inc., The.

Kallen, Stuart A. Real-World STEM: Global Access to Clean Water. 2017. (ENG.). 80p. (YA). (gr. 5-12). *(978-1-68282-243-2(5))* ReferencePoint Pr., Inc.

—Science & Sustainable Water. 2017. (ENG.). 80p. (YA). (gr. 5-12). *(978-1-68282-257-9(5))* ReferencePoint Pr., Inc.

Lawrence, Ellen. Poisoned Rivers & Lakes. 2014. (Science Slam: Green World, Clean World Ser.). 24p. (J). (gr. -1-3). lib. bdg. 26.99 *(978-1-62724-105-2(1))* Bearport Publishing Co., Inc.

Olien, Rebecca. Cleaning Water. 2016. (Water in Our World Ser.). (ENG., Illus.). 24p. (J). (gr. 1-3). lib. bdg. 27.99 *(978-1-4914-8278-0(8)*, 130763, Capstone Pr.) Capstone.

Water for the World, 6 Packs. (gr. k-1). 23.00 *(978-0-7635-8852-6(0))* Rigby Education.

Yomtov, Nel. Water/Wastewater Engineer. 2015. (21st Century Skills Library: Cool STEAM Careers Ser.). (ENG., Illus.). 32p. (J). (gr. 4-7). pap. 14.21 *(978-1-63362-049-0(2)*, 205953) Cherry Lake Publishing.

WATER ANIMALS

see Freshwater Animals; Marine Animals

WATER BIRDS

Murphy, Julie. Sea Birds, 1 vol. 2010. (Weird, Wild, & Wonderful Ser.). (ENG.). 24p. (J). (gr. 2-3). lib. bdg. 24.67 *(978-1-4339-3579-4(1)*, f380d282-ce0a-4cb8-a848-8a29997509ba, Gareth Stevens Learning Library) Stevens, Gareth Publishing LLLP.

WATERCOLOR PAINTING

Bolte, Mari. Watercolors, 1 vol. Ice, Dawn, illus. 2013. (Paint It Ser.). (ENG.). 32p. (J). (gr. 3-9). 28.65 *(978-1-4765-3108-3(0)*, 123090, Capstone Pr.) Capstone.

Dutta-Yean, Tutu & Maire, Lucy Bedoya. Twelve Treasures of the East: Legends & Folk Tales from Asia. Dutta-Yean, Tutu, ed. Konatich, James, illus. 2005. (J). per. *(978-0-9768436-0-3(9)*, 20) Maire, Lucy Bedoya.

Editors of Klutz. Watercolor Crush, 1 vol. 2016. (ENG.). 54p. (J). (gr. 3-7). 18.99 *(978-1-338-03756-2(0))* Klutz.

Giddy Up Staff. Go Diego Go Water Wow! Book. 2009. 4p. (J). 6.99 *(978-1-59524-215-0(5))* Giddy Up, LLC.

Top That Publishing Staff, ed. Sketching with Watercolor Pencils. 2005. (Illus.). 48p. *(978-1-84510-300-2(9))* Top That! Publishing PLC.

—Watercolor Painting. 2004. (Art Tricks Ser.). (Illus.). 48p. *(978-1-84510-318-7(1))* Top That! Publishing PLC.

Wood, Alix. Watercolors, 1 vol. 2018. (Make a Masterpiece Ser.). (ENG.). 32p. (J). (gr. 3-4). pap. 11.50 *(978-1-5382-3572-0(2)*, 5ff10823-1fad-4df5-a584-eda8bd586b9b); lib. bdg. 28.27 *(978-1-5382-3574-4(9)*, 15b8b564-5121-4dce-98bf-e0ab72198bee) Stevens, Gareth Publishing LLLP.

WATER CONSERVATION

see also Water-Supply

Bailey, Gerry. Water, 1 vol. 2009. (Simply Science Ser.). (ENG., Illus.). 32p. (YA). (gr. 3-5). lib. bdg. 28.67 *(978-1-4339-0037-2(8)*, bd8d8f6d-887b-45d8-96cb-6f274e57d44a) Stevens, Gareth Publishing LLLP.

Barker, Geoff. Water. 2010. (World at Risk Ser.). (YA). (gr. 5-9). 34.25 *(978-1-59920-379-9(0))* Black Rabbit Bks.

Barnham, Kay. Save Water. 2007. (Rise & Shine Ser.). (ENG., Illus.). 32p. (J). (gr. 3-7). pap. *(978-0-7787-3671-4(7))* Crabtree Publishing Co.

Bodden, Valerie. Water for Life. 2010. (Earth Issues Ser.). 48p. (YA). (gr. 5-18). 23.95 *(978-1-58341-986-1(1)*, Creative Education) Creative Co., The.

Boothroyd, Jennifer. Be Water-Wise, Super Grover! 2020. (Go Green with Sesame Street (r) Ser.). (ENG., Illus.). 32p. (J). (gr. -1-2). 27.99 *(978-1-5415-7259-1(9)*, e0b191c0-9488-45e4-b222-f496e432a2f8, Lerner Pubns.) Lerner Publishing Group.

Bullard, Lisa. Go Green by Caring for Water. Zheng, Xin, illus. 2018. (Go Green (Early Bird Stories (tm)) Ser.). (ENG.). 24p. (J). (gr. k-2). pap. 9.99 *(978-1-5415-2711-9(9)*, 750cd29e-8d86-47e9-a9d3-3e471adcf07d); lib. bdg. 29.32 *(978-1-5415-2017-2(3)*, 06e26007-951a-4ac0-b93e-30d6c34687de, Lerner Pubns.) Lerner Publishing Group.

Castellano, Peter. Water Conservation, 1 vol. 2016. (Where's the Water? Ser.). (ENG., Illus.). 24p. (J). (gr. 2-3). pap. 9.15 *(978-1-4824-4692-0(8)*, c03dedbd-df21-49ef-8d04-e0eb438dcebe) Stevens, Gareth Publishing LLLP.

Conrad, Steve, intro. Enough Water? A Guide to What We Have & How We Use It. 2016. (ENG., Illus.). 72p. (J). (gr. 4-7). pap. 9.95 *(978-1-77085-818-3(0)*, 0b69b466-21ed-46b4-9719-14fc5a7036aa) Firefly Bks., Ltd.

David, Sarah B. Reducing Your Carbon Footprint at Home. 2009. (Your Carbon Footprint Ser.). 48p. (gr. 5-5). 53.00 *(978-1-60854-910-8(0)*, Rosen Reference) Rosen Publishing Group, Inc., The.

Feinstein, Stephen. Conserving & Protecting Water: What You Can Do, 1 vol. 2010. (Green Issues in Focus Ser.). (ENG., Illus.). 128p. (gr. 6-7). lib. bdg. 35.93 *(978-0-7660-3346-7(5)*, 8daff8ad-4883-40a9-9dfe-2d6906e23a9b) Enslow Publishing, LLC.

—Drying Up: Running Out of Water, 1 vol. 2015. (End of Life As We Know It Ser.). (ENG., Illus.). 144p. (gr. 7-8). lib. bdg. 38.93 *(978-0-7660-7286-2(X)*, a8a4288f-6356-4ecb-bb25-6012d6a5b9b9) Enslow Publishing, LLC.

Fridell, Ron. Protecting Earth's Water Supply. 2009. pap. 58.95 *(978-0-7613-4694-4(5))* 2008. 72p. (YA). (gr. 4-7). lib. bdg. 30.60 *(978-0-8225-7557-3(4))* Lerner Publishing Group.

Green, Jen. Saving Water, 1 vol. 2011. (Sherlock Bones Looks at the Environment Ser.). (ENG., Illus.). 32p. (YA). (gr. 5-5). lib. bdg. 29.93 *(978-1-61533-347-9(9)*, 3da7bb94-cbaf-414d-8da8-c83d2d3e92e3, Windmill Bks.) Rosen Publishing Group, Inc., The.

—Saving Water, 1 vol. 2004. (Improving Our Environment Ser.). (ENG., Illus.). 32p. (gr. 3-5). lib. bdg. 28.67 *(978-0-8368-4431-3(9)*, 5ebe1d15-295c-400b-b504-aae639d30530, Gareth Stevens Learning Library) Stevens, Gareth Publishing LLLP.

—Why Should I Save Water? Gordon, Mike, illus. 2005. (Why Should I? Bks.). (ENG.). 32p. (J). (gr. -1-2). pap. 7.99 *(978-0-7641-3157-8(5))* Sourcebooks, Inc.

Hawes, Alison. Water Wise! 2010. (ENG.). 32p. (J). *(978-0-7787-9904-7(2))*; pap. *(978-0-7787-9925-2(5))* Crabtree Publishing Co.

Heos, Bridget. Follow That Paper! A Paper Recycling Journey. Westgate, Alex, illus. 2016. (Keeping Cities Clean Ser.). (ENG.). 24p. (J). (gr. 1-4). lib. bdg. 20.95 *(978-1-60753-962-9(4)*, 15654) Amicus.

Hock, Peggy A. Our Earth: Saving Water. 2009. (Scholastic News Nonfiction Readers: Conservation Ser.). (ENG.). 24p. (J). (gr. k-3). 21.19 *(978-0-531-13836-6(4)*, Children's Pr.) Scholastic Library Publishing.

Hurt, Avery Elizabeth. Engineering Solutions for Drought, 1 vol. 2019. (Preparing for Disaster Ser.). (ENG.). 48p. (gr. 5-5). pap. 12.75 *(978-1-7253-4772-4(5)*, 4200e1fa-6697-4c3e-ab26-2b3a4a128bb5) Rosen Publishing Group, Inc., The.

Hutmacher, Kimberly. The Wonderful Water Cycle. 2012. (My Science Library). (ENG.). 24p. (gr. 4-5). pap. 8.95 *(978-1-61810-237-9(0)*, 9781618102379) Rourke Educational Media.

Kallen, Stuart A. Running Dry: The Global Water Crisis. 2015. (ENG., Illus.). 64p. (YA). (gr. 6-12). lib. bdg. 33.32 *(978-1-4677-2646-7(X)*, 70ee290d-49fb-44e6-bc09-1ec7d4122681); E-Book 50.65 *(978-1-4677-6308-0(X))* Lerner Publishing Group. (Twenty-First Century Bks.).

Knight, M. J. Why Should I Turn off the Tap? 2009. (One Small Step Ser.). (YA). (gr. 2-5). 28.50 *(978-1-59920-264-8(6))* Black Rabbit Bks.

Labrecque, Ellen. Clean Water. 2017. (21st Century Skills Library: Global Citizens: Environmentalism Ser.). (ENG., Illus.). 32p. (J). (gr. 4-7). lib. bdg. 32.07 *(978-1-63472-870-6(X)*, 209906) Cherry Lake Publishing.

Llewellyn, Claire. Stop Water Waste. 2005. (Illus.). 32p. (YA). (gr. 1-18). lib. bdg. 27.10 *(978-1-932333-24-4(X))* Chrysalis Education.

Mason, Jenny. 10 Cosas Que Puedes Hacer para Ahorrar Aqua (Rookie Star: Make a Difference) 2017. (Rookie Star Ser.). (SPA., Illus.). 32p. (J). (gr. 2-3). pap. 5.95 *(978-1-338-18779-3(1)*, Children's Pr.) Scholastic Library Publishing.

—10 Cosas Que Puedes Hacer para Ahorrar Aqua (Rookie Star: Make a Difference) (Library Edition) 2017. (Rookie Star Ser.). (SPA., Illus.). 32p. (J). (gr. 2-3). lib. bdg. 25.00 *(978-0-531-22858-6(4)*, Children's Pr.) Scholastic Library Publishing.

—10 Things You Can Do to Save Water (Rookie Star: Make a Difference) (Library Edition) 2016. (Rookie Star Ser.). (ENG., Illus.). 32p. (J). (gr. 2-3). lib. bdg. 25.00 *(978-0-531-22651-3(4)*, Children's Pr.) Scholastic Library Publishing.

Minden, Cecilia. Kids Can Use Less. 2010. (21st Century Basic Skills Library: Kids Can Ser.). (ENG., Illus.). 24p. (gr. k-3). lib. bdg. 26.35 *(978-1-60279-869-4(9)*, 200604) Cherry Lake Publishing.

National Geographic Learning. Reading Expeditions (Science: Earth Science): Wonders of Water. 2006. (Nonfiction Reading & Writing Workshops Ser.). (ENG., Illus.). 32p. (J). pap. 18.95 *(978-0-7922-4572-8(5))* CENGAGE Learning.

Olien, Rebecca. Saving Water. 2016. (Water in Our World Ser.). (ENG., Illus.). 24p. (J). (gr. 1-3). lib. bdg. 27.99 *(978-1-4914-8279-7(6)*, 130764, Capstone Pr.) Capstone.

Peterson, Megan Cooley. How Water Gets from Treatment Plants to Toilet Bowls. 2016. (Here to There Ser.). (ENG., Illus.). 24p. (J). (gr. -1-2). lib. bdg. 27.32 *(978-1-4914-8435-7(7)*, 130867, Capstone Pr.) Capstone.

Reynolds, Alison. Let's Save Water. Hopgood, Andrew, illus. 2009. (Save Our Planet! Ser.). 12p. (J). (gr. -1-3). bds. 11.40 *(978-1-60754-413-5(X))* Windmill Bks.

Rieger, Linda. Start the Clean Up. Bianchi, John, illus. 2008. 20p. (J). *(978-0-9779427-5-6(9))* Pathways into Science.

Robertson, Joanne. The Water Walker, 1 vol. 2017. (ENG & OJI., Illus.). 36p. (J). (gr. 1-3). 18.95 *(978-1-77260-038-4(5))* Second Story Pr. CAN. Dist: Orca Bk. Pubs. USA.

Rosenberg, Pam. Watershed Conservation. 2008. (21st Century Skills Library: Global Perspectives Ser.). (ENG., Illus.). 32p. (gr. 4-8). lib. bdg. 32.07 *(978-1-60279-131-2(7)*, 200111) Cherry Lake Publishing.

Roza, Greg. Reducing Your Carbon Footprint on Vacation. 2009. (Your Carbon Footprint Ser.). 48p. (gr. 5-5). 53.00 *(978-1-60854-913-9(5)*, Rosen Reference) Rosen Publishing Group, Inc., The.

Sawyer, Ava. Humans & the Hydrosphere: Protecting Earth's Water Sources. 2017. (Humans & Our Planet Ser.). (ENG., Illus.). 32p. (J). (gr. 3-6). lib. bdg. 27.99 *(978-1-5157-7198-2(9)*, 135555, Capstone Pr.) Capstone.

Sherman, Jill. Fresh Water, 1 vol. 2017. (Let's Learn about Natural Resources Ser.). (ENG.). 24p. (gr. 1-2). 24.27 *(978-0-7660-9235-8(6)*, 037b692b-adfb-40d8-b278-8fcfa2ad1a56) Enslow Publishing, LLC.

Steele, Philip. Saving Water & Energy. 2009. (Now We Know About... Ser.). (ENG., Illus.). 24p. (J). (gr. k-3). pap. *(978-0-7787-4740-6(9))*; lib. bdg. *(978-0-7787-4723-9(9))* Crabtree Publishing Co.

Tyler, Madeline. Surviving in a World Without Water, 1 vol. 2018. (Surviving the Impossible Ser.). (ENG.). 32p. (gr. 4-5). pap. 11.50 *(978-1-5382-3522-5(6)*, 2acc52d8-fb9c-4a1f-8eaa-dc78bf6cb414) Stevens, Gareth Publishing LLLP.

Walters, Abby. Saving Water. Fiorentino, Chiara, illus. 2017. (I Help My Friends Ser.). (ENG.). 24p. (gr. -1-2). 28.50 *(978-1-68342-744-5(0)*, 9781683427445) Rourke Educational Media.

Your Carbon Footprint, 12 vols., Set. Incl. On the Move: Green Transportation. Furgang, Kathy & Furgang, Adam. lib. bdg. 34.47 *(978-1-4042-1773-7(8)*, 4350af81-a9f6-4345-845b-09e5923144c1); Reducing Your Carbon Footprint at Home. Ganchy, Sally. lib. bdg. 34.47 *(978-1-4042-1772-0(X)*, c1b55bf1-02c4-4bbb-9886-2f441ed88906); Reducing Your Carbon Footprint at School. Nagle, Jeanne. lib. bdg. 34.47 *(978-1-4042-1774-4(6)*, 65472741-3c09-4ade-b61d-f957ab7e97b8); Reducing Your Carbon Footprint in the Kitchen. Hall, Linley Erin. lib. bdg. 34.47 *(978-1-4042-1776-8(2)*, 72d24f36-8fb5-4098-8c0b-4b96b4418379); Reducing Your Carbon Footprint on Vacation. Roza, Greg. lib. bdg. 34.47 *(978-1-4042-1777-5(0)*, 0fcc1d0b-b782-478d-b5fb-792b5c4b6600); Smart Shopping: Shopping Green. Nagle, Jeanne. lib. bdg. 34.47 *(978-1-4042-1775-1(4)*, c91fdd48-1034-40bb-a5a8-cff6b9d007a2); (Illus.). 48p. (YA). (gr. 5-5). 2008. (Your Carbon Footprint Ser.). (ENG.). 2008. Set lib. bdg. 206.82 *(978-1-4042-1880-2(7)*, 82d1547c-d4b7-4afc-b404-e6497dd88511) Rosen Publishing Group, Inc., The.

WATER FOWL

see Water Birds

WATER PLANTS

see Marine Plants

WATER POLLUTION

see Water—Pollution

WATER POLO

Egan, Tracie. Water Polo: Rules, Tips, Strategy, & Safety. 2009. (Sports from Coast to Coast Ser.). 48p. (gr. 6-6). 53.00 *(978-1-60853-132-5(5)*, Rosen Reference) Rosen Publishing Group, Inc., The.

WATER POWER

Alkire, Jessie. Water Energy: Putting Water to Work. 2018. (Earth's Energy Innovations Ser.). (ENG., Illus.). 24p. (J). (gr. k-4). lib. bdg. 32.79 *(978-1-5321-1575-2(X)*, 29004, Super SandCastle) ABDO Publishing Co.

Bailey, Diane. Hydropower. 2014. (Harnessing Energy Ser.). (ENG.). 48p. (J). (gr. 5-8). *(978-1-60818-410-1(2)*, 21352, Creative Education) Creative Co., The.

Bard, Jonathan. Hydroelectricity: Harnessing the Power of Water, 1 vol. 2017. (Powered up! a STEM Approach to Energy Sources Ser.). (ENG.). 24p. (J). (gr. 3-3). 25.27 *(978-1-5081-6427-2(4)*, 8e24cb72-ffb1-41c7-9b85-0276e95929e7, PowerKids Pr.) Rosen Publishing Group, Inc., The.

Benduhn, Tea. Energía Del Agua (Water Power), 1 vol. 2008. (Energía para el Presente (Energy for Today) Ser.). (SPA.). 24p. (gr. 3-3). (J). lib. bdg. 24.67 *(978-0-8368-9270-3(4)*, 70d44206-a175-4a35-8833-67c084f638d1); pap. 9.15 *(978-0-8368-9369-4(7)*, 6a68c971-c1c7-4552-8d4d-4390e40bade4) Stevens, Gareth Publishing LLLP. (Weekly Reader Leveled Readers).

—Water Power, 1 vol. 2008. (Energy for Today Ser.). (ENG.). 24p. (gr. 3-3). (J). lib. bdg. 24.67 *(978-0-8368-9264-2(X)*, 31418883-593d-4e1b-8b3f-326adad1666d); pap. 9.15 *(978-0-8368-9363-2(8)*, c87b4b7d-252b-4b89-b63d-ca9abd556395) Stevens, Gareth Publishing LLLP. (Weekly Reader Leveled Readers).

Borgert-Spaniol, Megan. Water Energy Projects: Easy Energy Activities for Future Engineers! 2018. (Earth's Energy Experiments Ser.). (ENG., Illus.). 32p. (J). (gr. k-4). lib. bdg. 34.21 *(978-1-5321-1566-0(0)*, 28986, Super SandCastle) ABDO Publishing Co.

Brearley, Laurie. Water Power: Energy from Rivers, Waves, & Tides (a True Book: Alternative Energy) 2018. (True Book (Relaunch) Ser.). (ENG., Illus.). 48p. (J). (gr. 3-5). pap. 7.95 *(978-0-531-23944-5(6)*, Children's Pr.) Scholastic Library Publishing.

—Water Power: Energy from Rivers, Waves, & Tides (a True Book: Alternative Energy) (Library Edition) 2018. (True Book (Relaunch) Ser.). (ENG., Illus.). 48p. (J). (gr. 3-5). lib. bdg. 31.00 *(978-0-531-23687-1(0)*, Children's Pr.) Scholastic Library Publishing.

Currie, Stephen. Hydropower. 2010. (Compact Research Ser.). 96p. (YA). (gr. 7-12). 41.27 *(978-1-60152-122-4(7))* ReferencePoint Pr., Inc.

currie, stephen. What Is the Future of Hydropower? 2012. (Illus.). 80p. (J). lib. bdg. *(978-1-60152-276-4(2)*, 1346139) ReferencePoint Pr., Inc.

Dickmann, Nancy. Energy from Water: Hydroelectric, Tidal, & Wave Power. 2016. (Next Generation Energy Ser.). (ENG., Illus.). 32p. (J). (gr. 5-8). *(978-0-7787-2380-6(1))* Crabtree Publishing Co.

Doeden, Matt. Finding Out about Hydropower. 2014. (Searchlight Books (tm) — What Are Energy Sources? Ser.). (ENG., Illus.). 40p. (J). (gr. 3-5). pap. 9.99 *(978-1-4677-4555-0(3)*, ce95f064-58ac-44f4-87f8-43138dc057d1) Lerner Publishing Group.

Goodman, Polly. Understanding Water Power, 1 vol. 2010. (World of Energy Ser.). (ENG.). 48p. (J). (gr. 5-6). lib. bdg. 34.60 *(978-1-4339-4130-6(9)*, 6e9da3df-ae1e-4410-a3e0-9c8dc5161556, Gareth Stevens Learning Library) Stevens, Gareth Publishing LLLP.

Grady, Colin. Hydropower, 1 vol. 2016. (Saving the Planet Through Green Energy Ser.). (ENG., Illus.). 24p. (gr. 3-3). pap. 10.35 *(978-0-7660-8284-7(9)*, 7d2aeac8-82d3-4230-8e07-415ec3f89ceb) Enslow Publishing, LLC.

Graham, Ian. From Falling Water to Electric Car: An Energy Journey Through the World of Electricity. 2015. (Energy Journeys Ser.). (ENG., Illus.). 48p. (J). (gr. 3-6). 35.99 *(978-1-4846-0884-5(4)*, 127968, Heinemann) Capstone.

Hansen, Amy. Hydropower: Making a Splash!, 1 vol. 2010. (Powering Our World Ser.). (ENG.). 24p. (J). (gr. 3-3). pap. 9.25 *(978-1-4358-9746-5(3)*, 5888c0e1-c27c-4331-bd89-0f833077529c, PowerKids Pr.) Rosen Publishing Group, Inc., The.

Hansen, Amy S. Hydropower: Making a Splash! 2010. (Powering Our World Ser.). 24p. (J). (gr. 2-5). E-Book 42.50 *(978-1-4488-0203-6(2))*; (ENG., Illus.). (gr. 3-3). lib. bdg. 26.27 *(978-1-4358-9329-0(8)*, 6b47b901-a097-4f3a-bb49-29f543e5d185, PowerKids Pr.) Rosen Publishing Group, Inc., The.

Harris, William. Water Makes Hydropower. 2003. (From Resource to Energy Source Ser.). (J). *(978-1-58417-286-4(X))*; pap. *(978-1-58417-287-1(8))* Lake Street Pubs.

Jennings, Terry Catasús. Hydroelectric Energy. 2016. (Alternative Energy Ser.). (ENG., Illus.). 48p. (J). (gr. 4-8). lib. bdg. 35.64 *(978-1-68078-455-8(2)*, 23847) ABDO Publishing Co.

Mahaney, Ian. Water Power. 2007. 28p. pap. 21.25 *(978-1-4358-3826-0(2)*, PowerKids Pr.) Rosen Publishing Group, Inc., The.

Mahaney, Ian F. Water Power, 1 vol. 2006. (Journeys Ser.). (ENG., Illus.). 24p. (gr. 3-3). pap. 7.05 *(978-1-4042-2190-1(5)*, a1f4ba28-158c-4ff7-842d-424a169bd58a, PowerKids Pr.) Rosen Publishing Group, Inc., The.

Marquardt, Meg. Hydrogen Fuel Cells. 2016. (Alternative Energy Ser.). (ENG., Illus.). 48p. (J). (gr. 4-8). lib. bdg. 35.64 *(978-1-68078-456-5(0)*, 23849) ABDO Publishing Co.

Morris, Neil. Water Power. 2007. (Energy Sources Ser.). (Illus.). 32p. (YA). (gr. 4-7). lib. bdg. 28.50 *(978-1-58340-909-1(2))* Black Rabbit Bks.

—Water Power: Now & in the Future. 2010. (J). 34.25 *(978-1-59920-343-0(X))* Black Rabbit Bks.

Newman, Patricia. Water Power. 2013. (Explorer Library: Language Arts Explorer Ser.). (ENG.). 32p. (gr. 4-8). pap. 14.21 *(978-1-61080-924-5(6)*, 202577); (Illus.). 32.07 *(978-1-61080-899-6(1)*, 202575); (Illus.). E-Book 49.21 *(978-1-61080-974-0(2)*, 202578) Cherry Lake Publishing.

Olson, Elsie. Water Energy. 2018. (Earth's Energy Resources Ser.). (ENG., Illus.). 24p. (J). (gr. -1-3). lib. bdg. 29.93 *(978-1-5321-1557-8(1)*, 28968, SandCastle) ABDO Publishing Co.

Orr, Tamra B. Hydroelectric Energy. 2007. (21st Century Skills Library: Power Up! Ser.). (ENG., Illus.). 32p. (gr. 4-8). lib. bdg. 32.07 *(978-1-60279-049-0(3)*, 200054) Cherry Lake Publishing.

aris, Stephanie. Pop! Air & Water Pressure, 1 vol. 2nd rev. ed. 2013. (TIME for KIDS(r): Informational Text Ser.). (ENG., Illus.). 64p. (J). (gr. 4-8). pap. 14.99 *(978-1-4333-4939-3(6))* Teacher Created Materials, Inc.

hillips, Cynthia & Priwer, Shana. Dams & Waterways. 2014. (ENG., Illus.). 112p. (C). (gr. 6-18). lib. bdg. 180.00 *(978-0-7656-8122-5(6),* Y181910) Routledge.

ipe, Jim. Water Power. 2011. (J). 28.50 *(978-1-59604-216-2(8))* Black Rabbit Bks.

ne Power of Water: Individual Title Six-Packs. (gr. k-1). 23.00 *(978-0-7635-8848-9(2))* Rigby Education.

ichards, Julie. Water Energy, 1 vol. 2010. (Energy Choices Ser.). (ENG.). 32p. (gr. 3-3). 31.21 *(978-0-7614-4429-9(7),* c529b3b9-4fd1-4917-93d2-edd996e81973) Cavendish Square Publishing LLC.

lodger, Marguerite. Hydroelectric Power: Power from Moving Water, 1 vol. 2010. (ENG., Illus.). 32p. (J). pap. *(978-0-7787-2934-1(6));* lib. bdg. *(978-0-7787-2920-4(6))* Crabtree Publishing Co.

SchreyerKarmel. Water Power: The Greatest Force on Earth, 1 vol. 2014. (ENG., Illus.). 28p. (J). pap., E-Book, E-Book 9.50 *(978-1-107-68897-1(3))* Cambridge Univ. Pr.

Solway, Andrew. Water Power, 1 vol. 2007. (Energy for the Future & Global Warming Ser.). (ENG.). 32p. (gr. 3-3). pap. 12.70 *(978-0-8368-8413-5(2),* 74d2d4bf-a78d-4487-8435-0b76b4d2404b); lib. bdg. 29.67 *(978-0-8368-8404-3(3),* 4156a92b-09ad-4bf3-ba3a-5502850c3e20) Stevens, Gareth Publishing LLLP.

Spilsbury, Louise. Dams & Hydropower, 1 vol. 2011. (Development or Destruction? Ser.). (ENG., Illus.). 48p. (J). (gr. 5-5). 34.47 *(978-1-4488-6990-9(0),* a6e483f2-0b56-4963-9122-092e35faf17a); pap. 12.75 *(978-1-4488-6994-7(3),* bc78f95b-a5d7-43ad-a3d5-65e05a0afc1f) Rosen Publishing Group, Inc., The. (Rosen Reference).

Spilsbury, Louise & Spilsbury, Richard. Under the Ocean, 1 vol. 2016. (Science on Patrol Ser.). (ENG.). 48p. (J). (gr. 4-5). pap. 15.05 *(978-1-4824-5988-3(4),* 05e823a2-c9c9-4c11-b818-3b1ea2cd2c06) Stevens, Gareth Publishing LLLP.

Spilsbury, Richard & Spilsbury, Louise. The Pros & Cons of Water Power, 1 vol. 2007. (Energy Debate Ser.). (ENG., Illus.). 48p. (YA). (gr. 6-6). lib. bdg. 34.47 *(978-1-4042-3743-8(7),* 940418f1-c08e-42f7-b877-970bb721e4e9) Rosen Publishing Group, Inc., The.

—Water, Waves, & Tidal Power, 1 vol. 2011. (Let's Discuss Energy Resources Ser.). (ENG., Illus.). 32p. (YA). (gr. 4-5). lib. bdg. 30.27 *(978-1-4488-5263-5(3),* 0e3c9a06-1302-4e56-99e3-fc7afef4ac06) Rosen Publishing Group, Inc., The.

Webster, Christine. Water Power. 2015. (Illus.). 24p. (J). *(978-1-5105-0060-0(X))* SmartBook Media, Inc.

—Water Power. 24p. 2016. (J). *(978-1-4896-5806-7(8))* 2010. (Illus.). (J). (gr. 3-5). pap. 11.95 *(978-1-61690-011-3(3))* 2010. (Illus.). (YA). (gr. 3-6). lib. bdg. 25.70 *(978-1-61690-005-2(9))* 2005. (Illus.). (J). (gr. 3-7). lib. bdg. 24.45 *(978-1-59036-308-9(6))* Weigl Pubs., Inc.

Whiting, Jim. The Science of Lighting a City: Electricity in Action. 2010. (Action Science Ser.). (ENG.). 32p. (gr. 3-4). pap. 47.70 *(978-1-4296-5077-9(X),* Capstone Pr.) Capstone.

WATER PURIFICATION

see Water—Purification

WATER RESOURCES DEVELOPMENT

see also Irrigation; Water Power; Water-Supply

Bodden, Valerie. Water for Life. 2010. (Earth Issues Ser.). 48p. (YA). (gr. 5-18). 23.95 *(978-1-58341-986-1(1),* Creative Education) Creative Co., The.

Harris, William. Water Makes Hydropower. 2003. (From Resource to Energy Source Ser.). (J). *(978-1-58417-286-4(X));* pap. *(978-1-58417-287-1(8))* Lake Street Pubs.

Sawvel, Patty Jo, ed. Water Resource Management, 1 vol. 2008. (Introducing Issues with Opposing Viewpoints Ser.). (ENG., Illus.). 160p. (gr. 7-10). 43.63 *(978-0-7377-3979-4(7),* 4bd541df-75aa-4321-8c09-13b34b36daeb, Greenhaven Publishing) Greenhaven Publishing LLC.

WATER SPORTS

see Aquatic Sports

WATER-SUPPLY

see also Dams; Irrigation; Water—Pollution; Water—Purification; Water Conservation

Aldridge, Rebecca. The Hoover Dam. 2009. (Building America: Then & Now Ser.). (ENG., Illus.). 120p. (gr. 5-8). 35.00 *(978-1-60413-069-0(5),* P161625, Facts On File) Infobase Holdings, Inc.

Allyn, Daisy. Where Does the Bathwater Go?, 1 vol. 2012. (Everyday Mysteries Ser.). (ENG.). 24p. (J). (gr. 2-2). pap. 9.15 *(978-1-4339-6323-0(X),* 2d06de41-03f9-4f92-bea1-b8e370ea0bc1); lib. bdg. 25.27 *(978-1-4339-6321-6(3),* a5239926-1bfa-4203-ab44-9deebd1dcc69) Stevens, Gareth Publishing LLLP.

AWWA Staff, compiled by. The Store of Drinking Water - Teacher's Guide. 2011. (ENG.). 70p. (YA). pap. 18.00 *(978-1-58321-820-4(3))* American Water Works Assn.

—Story of Drinking Water (the) 5th ed. 2011. 24p. (J). 22.00 *(978-1-58321-812-9(2))* American Water Works Assn.

Barnham, Kay. Save Water. 2007. (Rise & Shine Ser.). (ENG., Illus.). 32p. (J). (gr. 3-7). pap. *(978-0-7787-3671-4(7))* Crabtree Publishing Co.

Berlatsky, Noah, ed. Water, 1 vol. 2011. (Global Viewpoints Ser.). (ENG., Illus.). 224p. (gr. 10-12). pap. 32.70 *(978-0-7377-5667-8(5),* 6be11062-3d4c-49e0-b1c7-084e82871b22, Greenhaven Publishing) Greenhaven Publishing LLC.

Bodden, Valerie. Water for Life. 2010. (Earth Issues Ser.). 48p. (YA). (gr. 5-18). 23.95 *(978-1-58341-986-1(1),* Creative Education) Creative Co., The.

Bowden, Rob. Food & Water. 2010. (Development Without Damage Ser.). (YA). (gr. 5-9). 34.25 *(978-1-59920-248-8(4))* Black Rabbit Bks.

Bright, Michael. From Raindrop to Tap. 2016. (Source to Resource Ser.). (ENG., Illus.). 32p. (J). (gr. 3-6). *(978-0-7787-2708-8(4))* Crabtree Publishing Co.

Bringing Water to People: 6 Small Books. (Greetings Ser.: Vol. 3). 32p. (gr. 3-5). 31.00 *(978-0-7635-1821-9(2))* Rigby Education.

Bringing Water to People: Big Book. (Greetings Ser.: Vol. 3). 32p. (gr. 3-5). 31.00 *(978-0-7635-3269-7(X))* Rigby Education.

Castellano, Peter. Water Conservation, 1 vol. 2016. (Where's the Water? Ser.). (ENG., Illus.). 24p. (J). (gr. 2-3). pap. 9.15 *(978-1-4824-4692-0(8),* c03dedbd-df21-49ef-8d04-e0eb438dcebe) Stevens, Gareth Publishing LLLP.

Cherry, Lynne. A River Ran Wild. 2005. 17.00 *(978-0-7569-5231-0(X))* Perfection Learning Corp.

cohen, judith L. & friend, robyn. Future Engineering: The Clean Water Challenge. katz, david A., illus. 2015. 44p. (J). pap. 7.00 *(978-1-935999-08-9(7))* Cascade Pass, Inc.

Cohen, Judith L. & Friend, Robyn. Los Angeles' Water Future. Katz, David A., illus. 2015. 40p. (J). pap. 7.00 *(978-1-935999-11-9(7))* Cascade Pass, Inc.

Cole, Joanna. The Magic School Bus at the Waterworks. Degen, Bruce, illus. 2004. (Magic School Bus Ser.). (ENG.). 40p. (J). (gr. -1-3). pap. 8.99 *(978-0-590-40360-3(5),* Scholastic Pr.) Scholastic, Inc.

Cooper, Candy J. & Aronson, Marc. Poisoned Water: How the Citizens of Flint, Michigan, Fought for Their Lives & Warned the Nation. 2020. (ENG., Illus.). 256p. (J). 18.99 *(978-1-5476-0232-2(5),* 900204200, Bloomsbury Children's Bks.) Bloomsbury Publishing USA.

Dittmer, Lori. Hoover Dam. 2019. (Landmarks of America Ser.). (ENG.). 24p. (J). (gr. 1-4). *(978-1-64026-126-6(5),* 18973, Creative Education); pap. 8.99 *(978-1-62832-689-5(1),* 18974, Creative Paperbacks) Creative Co., The.

Feinstein, Stephen. Conserving & Protecting Water: What You Can Do, 1 vol. 2010. (Green Issues in Focus Ser.). (ENG., Illus.). 128p. (gr. 6-7). lib. bdg. 35.93 *(978-0-7660-3346-7(5),* 8daff8ad-4883-40a9-9dfe-2d6906e23a9b) Enslow Publishing, LLC.

—Drying Up: Running Out of Water, 1 vol. 2015. (End of Life As We Know It Ser.). (ENG., Illus.). 144p. (gr. 7-8). lib. bdg. 38.93 *(978-0-7660-7286-2(X),* a8a4288f-6356-4ecb-bb25-6012d6a5b9b9) Enslow Publishing, LLC.

Flynn, Riley. Water Isn't Wasted! How Does Water Become Safe to Drink? 2018. (Story of Sanitation Ser.). (ENG., Illus.). 32p. (J). (gr. 3-6). pap. 7.95 *(978-1-5435-3116-9(4),* 138724); lib. bdg. 27.99 *(978-1-5435-3112-1(1),* 138709) Capstone. (Capstone Pr.).

Furgang, Kathy. Zoom in on Water & Sewage Systems, 1 vol. 2017. (Zoom in on Engineering Ser.). (ENG.). 24p. (gr. 2-2). pap. 10.95 *(978-0-7660-8840-5(5),* f596da04-3edd-4812-8c38-ea3864bfb9c6); lib. bdg. 25.60 *(978-0-7660-8714-9(X),* 691d8a52-7224-45eb-bc11-18dde139506a) Enslow Publishing, LLC.

Geiger, Beth. Clean Water. 2009. (Sally Ride Science Ser.). (ENG., Illus.). 40p. (J). (gr. 2-6). pap. 9.99 *(978-1-59643-577-3(1),* 900063913) Roaring Brook Pr.

Goldish, Meish. The Hoover Dam. 2016. (American Places: from Vision to Reality Ser.). (ENG., Illus.). 32p. (J). (gr. 2-7). 28.50 *(978-1-944102-45-6(0))* Bearport Publishing Co., Inc.

Green, Jen. Saving Water, 1 vol. 2004. (Improving Our Environment Ser.). (ENG., Illus.). 32p. (gr. 3-5). lib. bdg. 28.67 *(978-0-8368-4431-3(9),* 5ebe1d15-295c-400b-b504-aae639d30530, Gareth Stevens Learning Library) Stevens, Gareth Publishing LLLP.

Hamilton, Robert M. Should We Pay for Water?, 1 vol. 2017. (Points of View Ser.). (ENG.). 24p. (gr. 3-3). pap. 9.25 *(978-1-5345-2348-7(0),* a083f7af-1ff6-43cb-a1ad-fcb6d024034e); lib. bdg. 26.23 *(978-1-5345-2330-2(8),* f9ea4edd-0dfb-4789-8f61-6e42aa32d704) Greenhaven Publishing LLC.

Hawes, Alison. Water Wise! 2010. (ENG.). 32p. (J). *(978-0-7787-9904-7(2));* pap. *(978-0-7787-9925-2(5))* Crabtree Publishing Co.

Hellebuyck, Adam & Medvinsky, Mike. Moving Water in Minecraft. 2019. (21st Century Skills Innovation Library: Minecraft & STEAM Ser.). (ENG., Illus.). 32p. (J). (gr. 4-8). pap. 14.21 *(978-1-5341-3970-1(2),* 212709) Cherry Lake Publishing.

—Moving Water in Minecraft: Engineering. 2019. (21st Century Skills Innovation Library: Minecraft & STEAM Ser.). (ENG., Illus.). 32p. (J). (gr. 4-8). lib. bdg. 32.07 *(978-1-5341-4314-2(9),* 212708) Cherry Lake Publishing.

Heos, Bridget. Follow That Paper! A Paper Recycling Journey. Westgate, Alex, illus. 2016. (Keeping Cities Clean Ser.). (ENG.). 24p. (J). (gr. 1-4). lib. bdg. 20.95 *(978-1-60753-962-9(4),* 15654) Amicus.

Hewitt, Sally. Using Water. 2008. (Green Team Ser.). (ENG., Illus.). 32p. (J). (gr. 3-4). pap. *(978-0-7787-4104-6(4));* lib. bdg. *(978-0-7787-4097-1(8))* Crabtree Publishing Co.

Hock, Peggy. Our Earth: Saving Water (Scholastic News Nonfiction Readers: Conservation) 2008. (Scholastic News Nonfiction Readers Ser.). (ENG., Illus.). 24p. (J). (gr. 1-2). pap. 6.95 *(978-0-531-20436-8(7),* Children's Pr.) Scholastic Library Publishing.

Hock, Peggy A. Our Earth: Saving Water. 2009. (Scholastic News Nonfiction Readers: Conservation Ser.). (ENG.). 24p. (J). (gr. k-3). 21.19 *(978-0-531-13836-6(4),* Children's Pr.) Scholastic Library Publishing.

Hofer, Charles. How Do Irrigation Systems Work?, 1 vol. 2016. (STEM Waterworks Ser.). (ENG., Illus.). 32p. (J). (gr. 5-5). pap. 12.75 *(978-1-4994-2007-4(2),* c68aa25c-7843-40f0-8deb-14a4d24b4aaf, PowerKids Pr.) Rosen Publishing Group, Inc., The.

How Faucets Work. (Sunshinetm Science Ser.). 24p. (gr. 1-2). 37.50 *(978-0-7802-2778-1(6))* Wright Group/McGraw-Hill.

How Faucets Work: 6 Each of 1 Student Book, 6 vols. (Sunshinetm Science Ser.). 24p. (gr. 1-2). 41.95 *(978-0-7802-2688-3(7))* Wright Group/McGraw-Hill.

Hunter, Rebecca. Water Supply. 2012. (Eco Alert! Ser.). (ENG., Illus.). 32p. (gr. 4-6). lib. bdg. 28.50 *(978-1-59771-300-9(7))* Sea-To-Sea Pubns.

Hutmacher, Kimberly. The Wonderful Water Cycle. 2012. (My Science Library). (ENG.). 24p. (gr. 4-5). pap. 8.95 *(978-1-61810-237-9(0),* 9781618102379) Rourke Educational Media.

Kallen, Stuart A. Real-World STEM: Global Access to Clean Water. 2017. (ENG.). 80p. (YA). (gr. 5-12). *(978-1-68282-243-2(5))* ReferencePoint Pr., Inc.

—Running Dry: The Global Water Crisis. 2015. (ENG., Illus.). 64p. (YA). (gr. 6-12). lib. bdg. 33.32 *(978-1-4677-2646-7(X),* 70ee290d-49fb-44e6-bc09-1ec7d4122681); E-Book 50.65 *(978-1-4677-6308-0(X))* Lerner Publishing Group. (Twenty-First Century Bks.).

—Science & Sustainable Water. 2017. (ENG.). 80p. (YA). (gr. 5-12). *(978-1-68282-257-9(5))* ReferencePoint Pr., Inc.

Kegley, David E. Where Does Rain Come From? 2009. (Reading Room Collection 2 Ser.). 24p. (gr. 3-4). 42.50 *(978-1-60852-003-9(X),* PowerKids Pr.) Rosen Publishing Group, Inc., The.

Kerley, Barbara. A Cool Drink of Water. 2006. (Barbara Kerley Photo Inspirations Ser.). (Illus.). 32p. (J). (gr. -1-k). pap. 7.95 *(978-0-7922-5489-8(9),* National Geographic Kids) Disney Publishing Worldwide.

La Bella, Laura. Not Enough to Drink: Pollution, Drought, & Tainted Water Supplies. 2009. (Extreme Environmental Threats Ser.). 64p. (gr. 6-6). 58.50 *(978-1-61512-432-9(2));* (ENG.). (YA). lib. bdg. 37.13 *(978-1-4358-5020-0(3),* cf0dacbb-bb36-4473-8051-c316c07cd725); (ENG., Illus.). (J). pap. 13.95 *(978-1-4358-5376-8(8),* 3351956c-73e1-4fab-83f5-891c2435bd86) Rosen Publishing Group, Inc., The.

Labrecque, Ellen. Clean Water. 2017. (21st Century Skills Library: Global Citizens: Environmentalism Ser.). (ENG., Illus.). 32p. (J). (gr. 4-7). lib. bdg. 32.07 *(978-1-63472-870-6(X),* 209906) Cherry Lake Publishing.

Laidlaw, Jill. Water. 2010. (Sustaining Our Environment Ser.). (Illus.). 48p. 35.65 *(978-1-60753-140-1(2))* Amicus Learning.

Linde, Barbara M. The Water Cycle, 1 vol. 2016. (Where's the Water? Ser.). (ENG.). 24p. (J). (gr. 2-3). pap. 9.15 *(978-1-4824-4688-3(X),* 26f26572-0668-4304-9bc0-4abbfa504b8a) Stevens, Gareth Publishing LLLP.

—What Is Wastewater?, 1 vol. 2016. (Where's the Water? Ser.). (ENG.). 24p. (gr. 2-3). pap. 9.15 *(978-1-4824-4696-8(0),* 3ed49099-6e84-4d4c-b108-c0a5e54cdedc) Stevens, Gareth Publishing LLLP.

Mason, Jenny. 10 Cosas Que Puedes Hacer para Ahorrar Aqua (Rookie Star: Make a Difference) 2017. (Rookie Star Ser.). (SPA., Illus.). 32p. (J). (gr. 2-3). pap. 5.95 *(978-1-338-18779-3(1),* Children's Pr.) Scholastic Library Publishing.

—10 Cosas Que Puedes Hacer para Ahorrar Aqua (Rookie Star: Make a Difference) (Library Edition) 2017. (Rookie Star Ser.). (SPA., Illus.). 32p. (J). (gr. 2-3). lib. bdg. 25.00 *(978-0-531-22858-6(4),* Children's Pr.) Scholastic Library Publishing.

—10 Things You Can Do to Save Water (Rookie Star: Make a Difference) (Library Edition) 2016. (Rookie Star Ser.). (ENG., Illus.). 32p. (J). (gr. 2-3). lib. bdg. 25.00 *(978-0-531-22651-3(4),* Children's Pr.) Scholastic Library Publishing.

Masters, Nancy Robinson. How Did That Get to My House? Water. 2009. (Community Connections: How Did That Get to My House? Ser.). (ENG.). 24p. (gr. 2-5). lib. bdg. 29.21 *(978-1-60279-475-7(8),* 200252) Cherry Lake Publishing.

Nardo, Don. Roman Roads & Aqueducts. 2014. (History's Great Structures). (ENG., Illus.). 80p. (J). lib. bdg. *(978-1-60152-634-2(2))* ReferencePoint Pr., Inc.

National Geographic Learning. Reading Expeditions (Science: Earth Science): Wonders of Water. 2006. (Nonfiction Reading & Writing Workshops Ser.). (ENG., Illus.). 32p. (J). pap. 18.95 *(978-0-7922-4572-8(5))* CENGAGE Learning.

Nelson, Robin. Usamos el Agua. 2003. (Primeros Pasos Ser.). (SPA., Illus.). 23p. (J). pap. 6.95 *(978-0-8225-4825-6(9),* Ediciones Lerner) Lerner Publishing Group.

—We Use Water. 2003. (First Step Nonfiction - Water Ser.). (ENG., Illus.). 24p. (J). (gr. k-2). lib. bdg. 23.93 *(978-0-8225-4594-1(2))* Lerner Publishing Group.

Newton, David E. The Global Water Crisis: A Reference Handbook, 1 vol. 2016. (Contemporary World Issues Ser.). (ENG., Illus.). 376p. (C). 66.00 *(978-1-4408-3980-1(8),* 794742) ABC-CLIO, LLC.

Nichols, Susan, ed. The Politics of Water Scarcity, 1 vol. 2017. (Opposing Viewpoints Ser.). (ENG.). 192p. (gr. 10-12). pap. 34.80 *(978-1-5345-0052-5(9),* 7855dd5c-017c-4b05-94d8-27cd5c61baa1); lib. bdg. 50.43 *(978-1-5345-0054-9(5),* 6b56ae33-5540-421f-9471-ed4431b46bf2) Greenhaven Publishing LLC.

Olien, Rebecca. Cleaning Water. 2016. (Water in Our World Ser.). (ENG., Illus.). 24p. (J). (gr. 1-3). lib. bdg. 27.99 *(978-1-4914-8278-0(8),* 130763, Capstone Pr.) Capstone.

—Water Sources. 2016. (Water in Our World Ser.). (ENG., Illus.). 24p. (J). (gr. 1-3). lib. bdg. 27.99 *(978-1-4914-8277-3(X),* 130762, Capstone Pr.) Capstone.

Parker, Russ. Water Supplies in Crisis, 1 vol. 2009. (Planet in Crisis Ser.). (ENG.). 32p. (gr. 5-5). (YA). lib. bdg. 30.47 *(978-1-4358-5250-1(8),* 02531a76-01c5-47ba-81c6-81ebed62c22f); (Illus.). (J). pap. 11.00 *(978-1-4358-0680-1(8),* 8c7785d7-d91b-4b68-be4a-098fe6061202) Rosen Publishing Group, Inc., The. (Rosen Reference).

Perritano, John. Freshwater Resources, Vol. 12. 2015. (North American Natural Resources Ser.). (Illus.). 64p. (J). (gr. 7). lib. bdg. 23.95 *(978-1-4222-3381-8(2))* Mason Crest.

Peterson, Megan Cooley. How Water Gets from Treatment Plants to Toilet Bowls. 2016. (Here to There Ser.). (ENG., Illus.). 24p. (J). (gr. -1-2). lib. bdg. 27.32 *(978-1-4914-8435-7(7),* 130867, Capstone Pr.) Capstone.

Rice, Dona & Wilder, Nellie. Making Water Safe. rev. ed. 2019. (Smithsonian: Informational Text Ser.). (ENG., Illus.). 24p. (J). (gr. 1-2). pap. 8.99 *(978-1-4938-6656-4(7))* Teacher Created Materials, Inc.

Rieger, Linda. Water in Our House. Bianchi, John, illus. 2008. 20p. (J). *(978-0-9779427-6-3(7))* Pathways into Science.

Rosenberg, Pam. Watershed Conservation. 2008. (21st Century Skills Library: Global Perspectives Ser.). (ENG., Illus.). 32p. (gr. 4-8). lib. bdg. 32.07 *(978-1-60279-131-2(7),* 200111) Cherry Lake Publishing.

Roza, Greg. How Do Aqueducts Work?, 1 vol. 2016. (STEM Waterworks Ser.). (ENG., Illus.). 32p. (J). (gr. 5-5). pap. 12.75 *(978-1-4994-1991-7(0),* 95c8bfa7-9d5f-45a0-b47b-31322e98acd7, PowerKids Pr.) Rosen Publishing Group, Inc., The.

Santos, Rita. Our Water Supply, 1 vol. 2019. (Exploring Infrastructure Ser.). (ENG.). 48p. (gr. 3-4). 29.60 *(978-1-9785-0336-6(9),* 0859bff7-3f96-447e-b0c2-003b78e5f4d8) Enslow Publishing, LLC.

Sawyer, Ava. Humans & the Hydrosphere: Protecting Earth's Water Sources. 2017. (Humans & Our Planet Ser.). (ENG., Illus.). 32p. (J). (gr. 3-6). lib. bdg. 27.99 *(978-1-5157-7198-2(9),* 135555, Capstone Pr.) Capstone.

Sévigny, Eric, illus. Caillou: Every Drop Counts! 2011. (Ecology Club Ser.). (ENG.). 24p. (J). (gr. -1-1). pap. 5.99 *(978-2-89450-772-8(0))* Caillouet, Gerry.

Shaw, Daniel. Southwest Aquatic Habitats: On the Trail of Fish in a Desert. 2013. (Barbara Guth Worlds of Wonder Science Series for Young Readers Ser.). (ENG., Illus.). 112p. (J). 34.95 *(978-0-8263-5309-2(6),* P225266) Univ. of New Mexico Pr.

Shea, Therese. How Do Reservoirs Work?, 1 vol. 2016. (STEM Waterworks Ser.). (ENG., Illus.). 32p. (J). (gr. 5-5). pap. 12.75 *(978-1-4994-2011-1(0),* cbe301ee-9803-4edc-a3b1-7b209a52e5ee, PowerKids Pr.) Rosen Publishing Group, Inc., The.

Spilsbury, Louise. Threats to Our Water Supply. 2009. (J). 70.50 *(978-1-4358-5481-9(0));* (ENG.). 48p. (YA). (gr. 5-5). pap. 12.75 *(978-1-4358-5480-2(2),* c40b1ed0-a7d0-4b4c-9bd5-543d9b6c912c); (ENG., Illus.). 48p. (J). (gr. 5-5). lib. bdg. 34.47 *(978-1-4358-5352-2(0),* f45f6412-95ab-4ff3-9d8d-e29a74ec15a3) Rosen Publishing Group, Inc., The.

Stone, Andrew & Bryan, Jessica. Well... What's All That Drilling About? Pender, Rachel, illus. 2007. 40p. (J). 7.95 *(978-0-9641186-3-8(7))* American Ground Water Trust.

Tyler, Madeline. Surviving in a World Without Water, 1 vol. 2018. (Surviving the Impossible Ser.). (ENG.). 32p. (gr. 4-5). pap. 11.50 *(978-1-5382-3522-5(6),* 2acc52d8-fb9c-4a1f-8eaa-dc78bf6cb414) Stevens, Gareth Publishing LLLP.

Walton, Ruth. Let's Drink Some Water. 2013. (Let's Find Out Ser.). (ENG., Illus.). 32p. (gr. k-5). 28.50 *(978-1-59771-384-9(8))* Sea-To-Sea Pubns.

Watching Every Drop, 6 Packs. (gr. k-1). 23.00 *(978-0-7635-8851-9(2))* Rigby Education.

Welton, Jude. Water Supplies. 2005. (Action for the Environment Ser.). (Illus.). 32p. (J). (gr. 4-7). lib. bdg. 27.10 *(978-1-58340-601-4(8),* 1247299) Black Rabbit Bks.

Why Do We Need Water? 2014. (Natural Resources Close-Up Ser.). (ENG., Illus.). 24p. (J). (gr. 1-1). *(978-0-7787-0494-2(7))* Crabtree Publishing Co.

Workman, James G. Water. 2009. (Diminishing Resources Ser.). 111p. (J). lib. bdg. 28.95 *(978-1-59935-115-5(3))* Reynolds, Morgan Inc.

World Book, Inc. Staff, contrib. by. Food, Water, & Climate Change. 2015. (Illus.). 48p. (J). *(978-0-7166-2712-8(4))* World Bk., Inc.

WATER-SUPPLY ENGINEERING

Edwards, Erika. Levees & Seawalls, 1 vol. 2016. (Technology Takes on Nature Ser.). (ENG.). 32p. (J). (gr. 3-4). pap. 11.50 *(978-1-4824-5775-9(X),* 05c2c31f-08c7-4827-968a-67dc6deb82b5) Stevens, Gareth Publishing LLLP.

Koehntopp, James. Hydraulics for Kids. 2019. (J). 27.99 *(978-0-578-61820-3(6))* Koehntopp, James.

WATER WORKS

see Waterworks

WATERGATE AFFAIR, 1972-1974

Archer, Jules. Watergate: A Story of Richard Nixon & the Shocking 1972 Scandal. rev. ed. 2015. (Jules Archer History for Young Readers Ser.). (ENG., Illus.). 344p. (J). (gr. 6-6). 16.99 *(978-1-63220-606-0(4),* Sky Pony Pr.) Skyhorse Publishing Co., Inc.

Elish, Dan. The Watergate Scandal. 2004. (Cornerstones of Freedom Ser.). (ENG., Illus.). 48p. (J). 26.00 *(978-0-516-24239-2(3),* Children's Pr.) Scholastic Library Publishing.

Fremon, David K. The Watergate Scandal in United States History, 1 vol. 2014. (In United States History Ser.). (ENG., Illus.). 96p. (gr. 5-6). (J). pap. 13.88 *(978-0-7660-6108-8(6),* 620b45c8-e671-4b5c-b7d8-6d22b4045811); 31.61 *(978-0-7660-6107-1(8),* 7733f69b-38ff-41c5-8ffe-24a281bb7dcc) Enslow Publishing, LLC.

Honders, Christine. Watergate & the Resignation of President Nixon, 1 vol. 2018. (American History Ser.). (ENG.). 104p. (gr. 7-7). 41.03 *(978-1-5345-6427-5(6),* 09e66a89-585c-4750-b227-8241dc49ea84, Lucent Pr.) Greenhaven Publishing LLC.

Meter, Larry A. Van. United States V. Nixon. 2007. (Great Supreme Court Decisions Ser.). (ENG., Illus.). 112p. (gr. 5-9). lib. bdg. 32.95 *(978-0-7910-9381-8(6),* P124639, Facts On File) Infobase Holdings, Inc.

Noble, William. Presidential Power on Trial: From Watergate to All the President's Men, 1 vol. 2009. (Famous Court Cases That Became Movies Ser.). (ENG., Illus.). 128p. (gr. 6-7). lib. bdg. 35.93 *(978-0-7660-3058-9(X),* ccd06e6e-8d4e-4e9b-bf78-58d3af9a0a5a) Enslow Publishing, LLC.

Thiel, Kristin. Watergate & Investigative Journalism, 1 vol. 2018. (Fourth Estate: Journalism in North America Ser.). (ENG.). 112p. (gr. 8-8). lib. bdg. 44.50 *(978-1-5026-3487-0(2),* 3df255b5-d062-46f5-b0de-6952b8fcf69f) Cavendish Square Publishing LLC.

Tracy, Kathleen. The Watergate Scandal. 2006. (Monumental Milestones Ser.). (Illus.). 48p. (YA). (gr. 4-7). lib. bdg. 29.95 *(978-1-58415-470-9(5))* Mitchell Lane Pubs.

Uschan, Michael V. Watergate, 1 vol. 2009. (American History Ser.). (ENG., Illus.). 104p. (gr. 7-7). 41.03 *(978-1-4205-0135-3(6),* 25c4e805-a3e4-4787-8933-293ffb81b51e, Lucent Pr.) Greenhaven Publishing LLC.

WXYZ

WATERLOO, BATTLE OF, WATERLOO, BELGIUM, 1815

Roberts, Russell. Battle of Waterloo. 2011. (Technologies & Strategies in Battle Ser.). (Illus.). 48p. (J). (gr. 4-7). lib. bdg. 29.95 *(978-1-61228-076-9(5))* Mitchell Lane Pubs.

WATERMELONS

National Geographic Learning. Windows on Literacy Step up (Science: Plants Around Us): Watermelons. 2007. (ENG., Illus.). 8p. pap. 9.95 *(978-0-7922-8455-0(0))* National Geographic School Publishing, Inc.

WATERSHIP DOWN (IMAGINARY PLACE)—FICTION

Adams, Richard. Watership Down: A Novel. 2005. (ENG., Illus.). 496p. pap. 19.99 *(978-0-7432-7770-9(8),* Scribner) Scribner.

WATERWAYS

see also Canals; Rivers

Hinman, Bonnie. Infrastructure of America's Inland Waterways. 2018. lib. bdg. 29.95 *(978-1-68020-144-4(1))* Mitchell Lane Pubs.

Honders, Christine. How Do Canals Work?, 1 vol. 2016. (STEM Waterworks Ser.). (ENG.). 32p. (J). (gr. 5-5). pap. 12.75 *(978-1-4994-1995-5(3),* e63422c8-4045-4ce1-b55f-e2d33abc89c7, PowerKids Pr.) Rosen Publishing Group, Inc., The.

Janin, Hunt & Carlson, Ursula. Historic Nevada Waters: Four Rivers, Three Lakes, Past & Present, 1 vol. 2019. (ENG., Illus.). 216p. pap. 55.00 *(978-1-4766-7261-8(X),* f5be9a78-5b76-4226-ab29-5fd869b7827f) McFarland & Co., Inc. Pubs.

Laplante, Walter. Waterways of the Great Lakes. 2014. (Exploring the Great Lakes Ser.). (Illus.). 32p. (J). (gr. 3-6). pap. 63.00 *(978-1-4824-1195-9(4))* Stevens, Gareth Publishing LLLP.

McAneney, Caitie. 20 Fun Facts about Famous Canals & Seaways, 1 vol. 2019. (Fun Fact File: Engineering Marvels Ser.). (ENG.). 32p. (gr. 2-3). pap. 11.50 *(978-1-5382-4654-2(6),* 9f8c4691-f0c1-46b3-84ea-a41d1865e01e0) Stevens, Gareth Publishing LLLP.

Mitten, Ellen. Aguas Navegables (Waterways) 2009. (Pequeño mundo Geografía (Little World Geography) Ser.). (ENG & SPA., Illus.). 24p. (J). (gr. k-2). lib. bdg. 22.79 *(978-1-60694-587-2(4))* Rourke Educational Media.

Phillips, Cynthia & Priwer, Shana. Dams & Waterways. 2014. (ENG., Illus.). 112p. (C). (gr. 6-18). lib. bdg. 180.00 *(978-0-7656-8122-5(6),* Y181910) Routledge.

Radley, Gail. Waterways. Sherlock, Jean & Matheny, Jean, illus. 2005. (Vanishing from Ser.). 32p. (gr. 6-12). lib. bdg. 22.60 *(978-1-57505-408-7(6))* Lerner Publishing Group.

Rand McNally. Map It! Jr Waterways Boardbook. 2018. (Map It! Jr Ser.). (ENG., Illus.). 20p. (J). bds. *(978-0-528-02034-6(X))* Rand McNally Canada.

WATERWORKS

see also Water-Supply

Cole, Joanna. At the Waterworks. 2004. (Magic School Bus Original Ser.). (gr. k-3). lib. bdg. 17.20 *(978-0-8335-1744-9(9))* Turtleback.

Murphy, Kevin. Water for Hartford: The Story of the Hartford Water Works & the Metropolitan District Commission. 2004. (Illus.). xxi, 318p. 29.95 *(978-0-9749352-0-1(4))* Shining Tramp Pr.

STEM Waterworks, 12 vols. 2016. (STEM Waterworks Ser.). 32p. (gr. 5-5). (ENG.). 167.58 *(978-1-4994-1979-5(1),* a856d036-4349-4485-99bc-3b2bdd9c7437); pap. 70.50 *(978-1-4994-2459-1(0))* Rosen Publishing Group, Inc., The. (PowerKids Pr.).

WATIE, STAND, 1806-1871—FICTION

Novel Units. Rifles for Watie Novel Units Teacher Guide. 2019. (ENG.). (YA). pap. 12.99 *(978-1-56137-598-1(5),* Novel Units, Inc.) Classroom Library Co.

WATT, JAMES, 1736-1819

Whiting, Jim. James Watt & the Steam Engine. 2005. (Uncharted, Unexplored, & Unexplained Ser.). (Illus.). 48p. (J). (gr. 4-8). lib. bdg. 29.95 *(978-1-58415-371-9(7))* Mitchell Lane Pubs.

WAVES

see also Light; Ocean Waves; Radiation

Cain, Marie Mowery. Under the Waves. 2013. (Big Books, Blue Ser.). (ENG & SPA., Illus.). 16p. pap. 33.00 *(978-1-59246-005-2(4))* Big Books, by George!

Dickmann, Nancy. Harnessing Wave & Tidal Energy, 1 vol. 2016. (Future of Power Ser.). (ENG.). 32p. (J). (gr. 4-5). pap. 11.00 *(978-1-4994-3213-8(5),* c12dcabf-35bb-471d-a583-2ffae4844273, PowerKids Pr.) Rosen Publishing Group, Inc., The.

Diehn, Andi. Waves. Li, Hui, illus. 2018. (Picture Book Science Ser.). (ENG.). 32p. (J). (gr. k-3). 19.95 *(978-1-61930-633-2(6),* 649e5428-b49d-40f7-a275-11bb05ef344d) Nomad Pr.

Gardner, Robert. Light, Sound, & Waves Science Fair Projects, Using the Scientific Method, 1 vol. 2010. (Physics Science Projects Using the Scientific Method Ser.). (ENG., Illus.). 160p. (gr. 5-6). 38.60 *(978-0-7660-3416-7(X),* a9e26572-5a3f-47d1-bd08-f3116b6e00ac) Enslow Publishing, LLC.

Gerdes, Louise I., ed. Wave & Tidal Power, 1 vol. 2010. (At Issue Ser.). (ENG.). 120p. (gr. 10-12). 41.03 *(978-0-7377-4900-7(8),* 24e3fa32-8c53-41f5-8754-40044c0ff2a4, Greenhaven Publishing) Greenhaven Publishing LLC.

Holt, Rinehart and Winston Staff. Holt Science & Technology Chapter 20: Physical Science: The Energy of Waves. 5th ed. 2004. (Illus.). pap. 13.13 *(978-0-03-030431-6(8))* Harcourt Trade Pubs.

Hudak, Heather. Waves & Information Transfer, 1 vol. 2017. (Catch a Wave Ser.). (ENG., Illus.). 32p. (J). (gr. 4-4). pap. *(978-0-7787-2970-9(2))* Crabtree Publishing Co.

Hudak, Heather C. What Are Waves? 2017. (Catch a Wave Ser.). (Illus.). 32p. (J). (gr. 4-4). *(978-0-7787-2964-8(8))* Crabtree Publishing Co.

Hurt, Avery Elizabeth. How Do Waves Move?, 1 vol. 2018. (How Does It Move? Forces & Motion Ser.). (ENG.). 32p. (gr. 3-3). 30.21 *(978-1-5026-3771-0(5),* 74c01042-a3bd-41d1-8837-2764d13a5a74) Cavendish Square Publishing LLC.

Ivancic, Linda. What Is a Wave?, 1 vol. 2015. (Unseen Science Ser.). (ENG., Illus.). 32p. (gr. 3-3). pap. 11.58 *(978-1-5026-0917-5(7),* c9d64beb-62b9-406b-88e9-c8366f32ee77) Cavendish Square Publishing LLC.

Mansfield, Cheryl. Focus on Waves. 2017. (Hands-On STEM Ser.). (ENG., Illus.). 32p. (J). (gr. 2-3). pap. 9.95 *(978-1-63517-352-9(3),* 1635173523); lib. bdg. 31.35 *(978-1-63517-287-4(X),* 163517287X) North Star Editions. (Focus Readers).

Mara, Wil. How Do Waves Form?, 1 vol. 2011. (Tell Me Why, Tell Me How Ser.). (ENG.). 32p. (gr. 3-3). 32.64 *(978-0-7614-4829-7(2),* 1a822fc2-a20c-4d91-849a-d8746b360741) Cavendish Square Publishing LLC.

McPartland, Randall. Understanding Waves & Wave Motion. 2015. (J). lib. bdg. *(978-1-62713-431-6(X))* Cavendish Square Publishing LLC.

Solway, Andrew. Exploring Sound, Light, & Radiation, 1 vol. 2007. (Exploring Physical Science Ser.). (ENG., Illus.). 48p. (YA). (gr. 6-6). lib. bdg. 34.47 *(978-1-4042-3746-9(1),* 00bfa945-8d0e-4dbe-832a-882598e802ba) Rosen Publishing Group, Inc., The.

Thompson, Lisa. Wild Waves. 2003. (Real Deal Ser.). (Illus.). 32p. (J). pap. *(978-0-7608-6690-0(2))* Sundance/Newbridge Educational Publishing.

Wright, Holly. Wave. 2004. (J). *(978-0-9743690-7-5(1))* Britt Allcroft Productions.

WAXES

Meister, Cari. From Wax to Crayons. Pinilla, Albert, illus. 2019. (Who Made My Stuff? Ser.). (ENG.). 24p. (J). (gr. 1-4). lib. bdg. *(978-1-68151-698-1(5),* 10850) Amicus.

Snyder, Inez. Wax to Crayons. 2003. (Welcome Bks.). (ENG., Illus.). 24p. (J). (gr. -1-2). 19.00 *(978-0-516-24267-5(9),* Children's Pr.) Scholastic Library Publishing.

WAYNE, ANTHONY, 1745-1796—FICTION

Rinaldi, Ann. The Family Greene. 2011. (ENG.). 256p. (YA). (gr. 7). pap. 14.95 *(978-0-547-57723-4(0),* 1458519, Clarion Bks.) HarperCollins Pubs.

—A Ride into Morning: The Story of Tempe Wick. 2003. (Great Episodes Ser.). (ENG.). 368p. (YA). (gr. 5-7). pap. 21.95 *(978-0-15-204683-5(6),* Clarion Bks.) HarperCollins Pubs.

WEAPONS

see also Firearms; Military Weapons

Benoit, Peter. Cornerstones of Freedom, Third Series: the Nuclear Age. 2012. (Cornerstones of Freedom, Third Ser.). (ENG., Illus.). 64p. (J). pap. 8.95 *(978-0-531-28162-8(0),* Children's Pr.) Scholastic Library Publishing.

Bergin, Mark. Warfare in the 16th to 19th Centuries. 2015. (Warriors Ser.). (Illus.). 48p. (gr. 4-7). 37.10 *(978-1-62588-357-5(9))* Black Rabbit Bks.

Brezina, Corona. Weapons of Mass Destruction: Proliferation & Control. 2009. (Library of Weapons of Mass Destruction Ser.). 64p. (gr. 5-5). 58.50 *(978-1-60853-959-8(8))* Rosen Publishing Group, Inc., The.

Chapman, Caroline. Battles & Weapons: Exploring History Through Art. 2007. (Picture That Ser.). (ENG., Illus.). 64p. (J). (gr. 3-5). 19.95 *(978-1-58728-588-2(6))* Cooper Square Publishing Llc.

Clarke, Catriona. Armor. McKenna, Terry, illus. 2007. (Usborne Beginners Ser.). 32p. (J). (gr. -1-3). 4.99 *(978-0-7945-1578-2(9),* Usborne) EDC Publishing.

Clint, Marc. Aztec Warriors. 2011. (History's Greatest Warriors Ser.). (ENG., Illus.). 24p. (J). (gr. 3-7). lib. bdg. 26.95 *(978-1-60014-626-8(0),* Torque Bks.) Bellwether Media.

Cunningham, Anne C., ed. Revisiting Nuclear Power, 1 vol. 2017. (Global Viewpoints Ser.). (ENG.). 256p. (gr. 10-12). pap. 32.70 *(978-1-5345-0127-0(4),* 4b981fe4-ece3-470f-9735-7f0384df1301); lib. bdg. 47.83 *(978-1-5345-0129-4(0),* 9c57ee34-27d3-4a55-b553-162d1c67c94b) Greenhaven Publishing LLC.

Curley, Robert, ed. Weapons of Mass Destruction, 1 vol. 2011. (Britannica Guide to War Ser.). (ENG.). 168p. (YA). (gr. 10-10). lib. bdg. 38.82 *(978-1-61530-687-9(0),* 706d8077-14b4-4bbe-82fa-691d6d50d87e) Rosen Publishing Group, Inc., The.

—Weapons Of Mass Destruction, 4 vols. 2011. (Britannica Guide to War Ser.). (ENG.). 168p. (YA). (gr. 10-10). 77.64 *(978-1-61530-800-2(8),* 4b19c8d5-194b-484c-a30b-ee08c45de842) Rosen Publishing Group, Inc., The.

Egan, Tracie. Weapons of Mass Destruction & North Korea, 1 vol. 2004. (Library of Weapons of Mass Destruction Ser.). (ENG., Illus.). 64p. (J). (gr. 5-5). lib. bdg. 37.13 *(978-1-4042-0296-2(X),* 92b49345-de0d-4fe7-9fdc-4f194164ad58) Rosen Publishing Group, Inc., The.

Fact Atlas: Arms & Armor. 2009. (FACT ATLAS Ser.). 72p. (J). 14.95 *(978-0-8437-1901-7(X))* Hammond World Atlas Corp.

Fowler, Will. The Story of Ancient Weapons, 1 vol. 2010. (Journey Through History Ser.). (ENG.). 64p. (YA). (gr. 5-6). lib. bdg. 37.13 *(978-1-4488-0623-2(2),* 6c53eee1-ccaa-46c3-aa3a-f2d958a54521, Rosen Reference) Rosen Publishing Group, Inc., The.

—The Story of Modern Weapons & Warfare, 1 vol. 2011. (Journey Through History Ser.). (ENG.). 64p. (J). (gr. 5-6). lib. bdg. 37.13 *(978-1-4488-4793-8(1),* f339e89b-6e8a-4873-a241-f7feca6f668d) Rosen Publishing Group, Inc., The.

Gifford, Clive. The Arms Trade. 2004. (World Issues Ser.). (J). lib. bdg. 28.50 *(978-1-59389-154-1(7))* Chrysalis Education.

Gurstelle, William. The Art of the Catapult: Build Greek Ballistae, Roman Onagers, English Trebuchets, & More Ancient Artillery. 2nd ed. 2018. (ENG., Illus.). 192p. (J). (gr. 5). pap. 16.99 *(978-0-912777-33-7(8))* Chicago Review Pr., Inc.

Hudak, Heather C. Nuclear Weapons & the Arms Race. 2018. (Uncovering the Past: Analyzing Primary Sources Ser.). (Illus.). 48p. (J). (gr. 5-6). *(978-0-7787-4801-4(4))* Crabtree Publishing Co.

Ives, Rob. Break the Siege: Make Your Own Catapults. Paul de Quay, John, illus. 2016. (Tabletop Wars Ser.). (ENG.). 32p. (J). (gr. 3-6). 27.99 *(978-1-5124-0638-2(4),* a8306ca7-addc-424a-b9ff-4d743266fa27, Hungry Tomato (r)) Lerner Publishing Group.

—Ready, Aim, Launch! Make Your Own Small Launchers. Paul de Quay, John, illus. 2016. (Tabletop Wars Ser.). (ENG.). 32p. (J). (gr. 3-6). lib. bdg. 27.99 *(978-1-5124-0636-8(8),* 96405206-b643-4dfc-86e2-461253d95971, Hungry Tomato (r)) Lerner Publishing Group.

—Surprise the Enemy: Make Your Own Traps & Triggers. Paul de Quay, John, illus. 2016. (Tabletop Wars Ser.). (ENG.). 32p. (J). (gr. 3-6). lib. bdg. 27.99 *(978-1-5124-0637-5(6),* f63cb0ca-af47-48c7-9b12-95a800ff3094, Hungry Tomato (r)) Lerner Publishing Group.

Jackson, Robert. The 101 Greatest Weapons of All Times, 4 vols., Set. Incl. 101 Great Bombers. lib. bdg. 39.80 *(978-1-4358-3594-8(8),* 498f2041-80ea-4067-b71e-6d3a98383b23); 101 Great Tanks. lib. bdg. 39.80 *(978-1-4358-3595-5(6),* baffb633-ab21-4909-9b67-6e2899b82c94); 101 Great Warships. lib. bdg. 39.80 *(978-1-4358-3596-2(4),* 2547f3cf-7a4d-4c99-ae64-1fa789705d29); (YA). (gr. 10-10). 2010. (Illus.). 112p. 2010. Set lib. bdg. 152.40 *(978-1-4358-3604-4(9))* Rosen Publishing Group, Inc., The.

Loveless, Antony. Bomb & Mine Disposal Officers, 1 vol. 2009. (World's Most Dangerous Jobs Ser.). (ENG., Illus.). 32p. (J). (gr. 3-6). pap. *(978-0-7787-5109-0(0))*; lib. bdg. *(978-0-7787-5095-6(7))* Crabtree Publishing Co.

Lusted, Marcia Amidon. Ninja Science: Camouflage, Weapons, & Stealthy Attacks. 2016. (Warrior Science Ser.). (ENG., Illus.). 32p. (J). (gr. 3-9). lib. bdg. 28.65 *(978-1-4914-8115-8(3),* 130606, Capstone Pr.) Capstone.

McClintock Miller, Shannon & Hoena, Blake. A Low-Tech Mission. Brown, Alan, illus. 2018. (Adventures in Makerspace Ser.). (ENG.). 32p. (J). (gr. 3-5). 30.65 *(978-1-4965-7744-3(2),* 138430); pap. 7.95 *(978-1-4965-7748-1(5),* 139047) Capstone. (Stone Arch Bks.).

Owen, Ruth. Ready, Aim, Fire!, 1 vol., 1. 2014. (DIY for Boys Ser.). (ENG.). 32p. (J). (gr. 4-4). 30.17 *(978-1-4777-6286-8(8),* 40f84193-aa13-43a6-add9-84e0b4cea448, PowerKids Pr.) Rosen Publishing Group, Inc., The.

Parker, Helen. Weird Weapons Intermediate Book with Online Access, 1 vol. 2014. (ENG., Illus.). 28p. (J). pap., E-Book, E-Book 9.50 *(978-1-107-65200-2(6))* Cambridge Univ. Pr.

Ripley, Tim. Torpedoes, Missiles, & Cannons: Physics Goes to War. 2017. (STEM on the Battlefield Ser.). (ENG., Illus.). 48p. (J). (gr. 4-6). 31.99 *(978-1-5124-3926-7(6),* 4886172c-1774-4b59-99e0-1607c2641e75, Lerner Pubns.) Lerner Publishing Group.

Rivera, Sheila. Weapons of Mass Destruction. 2003. (World in Conflict-the Middle East Ser.). 32p. (gr. 4-8). 27.07 *(978-1-59197-421-5(6),* Abdo & Daughters) ABDO Publishing Co.

Staeger, Rob. Native American Tools & Weapons. Johnson, Troy, ed. 2013. (Native American Life Ser.: 15). 64p. (J). (gr. 5-18). 19.95 *(978-1-4222-2977-4(7))* Mason Crest.

The Library of Weapons of Mass Destruction: Set 1, 8 vols. 2004. (Library of Weapons of Mass Destruction Ser.). (ENG.). (J). (gr. 5-5). 148.52 *(978-1-4042-0382-2(6),* 91a281d3-3fff-4e76-aa68-6514f2f4fcbb) Rosen Publishing Group, Inc., The.

The Library of Weapons of Mass Destruction: Set 2, 10 vols. 2004. (Library of Weapons of Mass Destruction Ser.). (ENG.). (YA). (gr. 5-5). 185.65 *(978-1-4042-0383-9(4),* 38481970-c4b7-4192-b55b-eb2d3db3ab11) Rosen Publishing Group, Inc., The.

The Library of Weapons of Mass Destruction: Sets 1 & 2, 18 vols. 2004. (Library of Weapons of Mass Destruction Ser.). (ENG.). (YA). (gr. 5-5). lib. bdg. 334.17 *(978-1-4042-0384-6(2),* bc6eeffb-e12b-4e98-846c-4c9f454faa39) Rosen Publishing Group, Inc., The.

Turner, Tracy. Weapons of War. 2015. (Head-To-Head Ser.). (ENG., Illus.). 24p. (gr. 3-8). 28.50 *(978-1-62588-151-9(7))* Black Rabbit Bks.

Weapons & Warfare. 2003. (Illus.). 32p. (YA). pap. *(978-1-904516-31-6(9),* Pavilion Children's Books) Pavilion Bks.

Wood, Alix. Biological Weapons, 1 vol., 1. 2015. (Today's High-Tech Weapons Ser.). (ENG.). 32p. (J). (gr. 4-5). pap. 11.00 *(978-1-5081-4671-1(3),* 049bc24a-37ff-49be-b981-05cac6aa5058, PowerKids Pr.) Rosen Publishing Group, Inc., The.

—Chemical Weapons, 1 vol., 1. 2015. (Today's High-Tech Weapons Ser.). (ENG.). 32p. (J). (gr. 4-5). pap. 11.00 *(978-1-5081-4679-7(9),* eebbe6d6-3163-46f5-9c5d-65a98a9f61b7, PowerKids Pr.) Rosen Publishing Group, Inc., The.

—Nuclear Weapons, 1 vol., 1. 2015. (Today's High-Tech Weapons Ser.). (ENG.). 32p. (J). (gr. 4-5). pap. 11.00 *(978-1-5081-4687-2(X),* d5d2b181-315a-4ca7-b7c6-46ea252b3dae, PowerKids Pr.) Rosen Publishing Group, Inc., The.

Woods, Mary B. & Woods, Michael. Ancient Warfare: From Clubs to Catapults. 2005. (Ancient Technology Ser.). (Illus.). 96p. (gr. 6-12). 25.26 *(978-0-8225-2999-6(8))* Lerner Publishing Group.

Wright, Susan. Weapons of Mass Destruction: Illicit Trade & Trafficking. 2009. (Library of Weapons of Mass Destruction Ser.). 64p. (gr. 5-5). 58.50 *(978-1-60853-960-4(1))* Rosen Publishing Group, Inc., The.

WEASELS

Beer, Amy-Jane. Weasels. 2008. (Nature's Children Ser.). (Illus.). 52p. (J). *(978-0-7172-6263-2(4))* Grolier, Ltd.

Borgert-Spaniol, Megan. Weasels. 2012. (Backyard Wildlife Ser.). (ENG., Illus.). 24p. (J). (gr. k-3). lib. bdg. 26.95 *(978-1-60014-725-8(9),* Blastoff! Readers) Bellwether Media.

McLellan, Joe. Nikik & Wapus Save the People, 1 vol. Traverse, Jackie, illus. 2015. (ENG.). 32p. (J). mass mkt. 10.95 *(978-1-894717-70-0(8),* baddc49e-5bc9-4569-a55f-6ed5d2b298d0) Pemmican Pubns., Inc. CAN. Dist: Firefly Bks., Ltd.

Meister, Cari. Do You Really Want to Meet a Weasel? Fabbri, Daniele, illus. 2018. (Do You Really Want to Meet ... ? Ser.). (ENG.). 24p. (J). (gr. 1-4). pap. 8.99 *(978-1-68152-313-2(2),* 15040); lib. bdg. *(978-1-68151-393-5(5),* 15034) Amicus.

WEASELS—FICTION

Chartrand, Lili. The Smelly Story of Hazel the Weasel, 1 vol. Eid, Jean-Paul, illus. 2009. (Rainy Day Readers Ser.). (ENG.). 32p. (J). (gr. 1-2). 27.27 *(978-1-60754-379-4(6),* 1a0dac32-12f0-49c2-800c-cfed51f6cb4b); pap. 11.55 *(978-1-60754-380-0(X),* 088407fe-92c8-48f5-8fe7-7550f159d1ea) Rosen Publishing Group, Inc., The. (Windmill Bks.).

Florence, Debbi Michiko. Dorothy & Toto the Disappearing Picnic. Roe, Monika, illus. 2016. (Dorothy & Toto Ser.). (ENG.). 40p. (J). (gr. k-2). lib. bdg. 21.32 *(978-1-4795-8704-9(4),* 130953) Capstone.

Green, K. S. A Winter's Tail: Book Three of the Weasel Chronicles. 2005. (ENG.). 64p. pap. 22.99 *(978-1-59926-758-6(6))* Xlibris Corp.

Jackson, Bobby L. Boon the Raccoon & Easel the Weasel. Rodriguez, Christina, illus. 2004. 32p. (J). pap. 11.95 *(978-1-884242-03-8(0),* BREW2NED); 19.95 *(978-1-884242-02-1(2),* BREW2NED) Multicultural Pubns.

Marcellino, Fred, illus. The Wainscott Weasel. 2014. (ENG.). 208p. (J). (gr. 2-7). 16.99 *(978-1-4814-1010-6(5),* Atheneum Bks. for Young Readers) Simon & Schuster Children's Publishing.

Neumann, Jeanne L. Wendell the Weasel. 2008. 16p. per. 24.95 *(978-1-4241-9922-8(0))* America Star Bks.

Pittman, Samuel, II. Alligator Jazz, 1 vol. Bailey, Sheila, illus. 2018. (ENG.). 32p. (J). (gr. -1-3). 16.99 *(978-1-4556-2422-5(5),* Pelican Publishing) Arcadia Publishing.

Price, Dann. Wesley the Weasel Can't Stop His Sneezel. 2013. 24p. pap. 10.95 *(978-1-4626-9427-3(6))* America Star Bks.

Sabo, J. Train Wrecker. 2011. 28p. pap. 24.95 *(978-1-4626-4379-0(5))* America Star Bks.

Sargent, Dave & Sargent, Pat. Bandit: I Help Others, 56 vols., Vol. 14. Huff, Jeane, illus. 2003. (Animal Pride Ser.: 14). 42p. (J). lib. bdg. 20.95 *(978-1-56763-785-4(X))* Ozark Publishing.

WEATHER

see also Climate; Meteorology; Rain and Rainfall; Snow; Storms; Weather Control; Winds

ABDO Publishing Company Staff & Doudna, Kelly. Weather, 1 vol. 2003. (Weather Ser.: 6). (ENG.). 24p. (J). (gr. k-3). lib. bdg. 145.26 *(978-1-57765-532-9(X),* SandCastle) ABDO Publishing Co.

AIMS Education Foundation. Weather Sense: Moisture. 2008. 272p. (J). pap. 21.95 *(978-1-932093-00-1(1))* AIMS Education Foundation.

Alkire, Jessie. Super Simple Weather Projects: Science Activities for Future Meteorologists. 2017. (Super Simple Earth Investigations Ser.). (ENG., Illus.). 32p. (J). (gr. k-4). lib. bdg. 34.21 *(978-1-5321-1241-6(6),* 27628, Super SandCastle) ABDO Publishing Co.

Allaby, Michael. The World's Weather. 2012. (ENG., Illus.). 48p. (J). 15.00 *(978-1-899762-81-1(7))* Award Pubns. Ltd. GBR. Dist: Parkwest Pubns., Inc.

Andersen, Jill. Keeping Track of the Weather, 1 vol. 2016. (Rosen REAL Readers: STEM & STEAM Collection). (ENG.). 12p. (gr. k-1). pap. 6.33 *(978-1-5081-2422-1(1),* ec3a340c-f4a1-4c04-9e63-83b6dfdcc110, Rosen Classroom) Rosen Publishing Group, Inc., The.

Anderson, Michael. Investigating Earth's Weather, 1 vol. 2011. (Introduction to Earth Science Ser.). (ENG.). 88p. (J). (gr. 8-8). lib. bdg. 35.29 *(978-1-61530-499-8(1),* 14e9f14f-a357-40c5-803b-edeee98e4589) Rosen Publishing Group, Inc., The.

—Investigating the Global Climate, 1 vol. 2011. (Introduction to Earth Science Ser.). (ENG., Illus.). 88p. (J). (gr. 8-8). lib. bdg. 35.29 *(978-1-61530-496-7(7),* 3178b8a2-74b9-451e-a893-2865d7d93a9f) Rosen Publishing Group, Inc., The.

Appleby, Alex. It's Hailing!, 1 vol. 2013. (What's the Weather? Ser.). 24p. (J). (gr. k-k). (ENG.). pap. 9.15 *(978-1-4339-9393-0(7),* 367fa6b4-a465-4c52-890d-77b0dc943363); pap. 48.90 *(978-1-4339-9394-7(5))*; (ENG., Illus.). lib. bdg. 25.27 *(978-1-4339-9392-3(9),* 99e457a6-1548-4ba4-b795-a819fea36e4b) Stevens, Gareth Publishing LLLP.

—It's Hailing! / ¡Está Granizando!, 1 vol. 2013. (What's the Weather? / ¿Qué Tiempo Hace? Ser.). (SPA & ENG., Illus.). 24p. (J). (gr. k-k). 25.27 *(978-1-4339-9462-3(3),* cf4c67db-e3f5-4c61-b4ee-3d9575efe83e) Stevens, Gareth Publishing LLLP.

—It's Rainy!, 1 vol. 2013. (What's the Weather? Ser.). (Illus.). 24p. (J). (gr. k-k). (ENG.). pap. 9.15 *(978-1-4339-9397-8(X),* 426cff56-be4b-4831-92af-abef6d481e97); (ENG., lib. bdg. 25.27 *(978-1-4339-9396-1(1),* fc75c5bd-7018-48f7-a368-88b8494e8663); pap. 48.90 *(978-1-4339-9398-5(8))* Stevens, Gareth Publishing LLLP.

—It's Rainy! / ¡Está Lloviendo!, 1 vol. 2013. (What's the Weather? / ¿Qué Tiempo Hace? Ser.). (SPA & ENG., Illus.). 24p. (J). (gr. k-k). 25.27 *(978-1-4339-9460-9(7),* 7dae9155-2b86-45b5-8f7e-08e0a94ec6ff) Stevens, Gareth Publishing LLLP.

—It's Snowing!, 1 vol. 2013. (What's the Weather? Ser.). 24p. (J). (gr. k-k). (ENG.). 25.27 *(978-1-4339-9400-5(3),* a6105c64-914b-4df2-8023-527dbb5b97ea); (ENG.). pap. 9.15 *(978-1-4339-9401-2(1),* 9dee1de7-57db-4d52-ad1f-83321d0ea882); pap. 48.90 *(978-1-4339-9402-9(X))* Stevens, Gareth Publishing LLLP.

—It's Snowing! / ¡Está Nevando!, 1 vol. 2013. (What's the Weather? / ¿Qué Tiempo Hace? Ser.). (SPA & ENG., Illus.). 24p. (J). (gr. k-k). 25.27 *(978-1-4339-9458-6(5),* 0c42ee97-da26-4587-9e9b-e13f5c79f888) Stevens, Gareth Publishing LLLP.

—It's Stormy!, 1 vol. 2013. (What's the Weather? Ser.). (Illus.). 24p. (J). (gr. k-k). (ENG.). pap. 9.15 *(978-1-4339-9405-0(4),* dac5a8a5-20d7-4865-af7e-bac5a4525e1e); (ENG., lib. bdg. 25.27 *(978-1-4339-9404-3(6),* af3958a4-fa27-4cb9-bb36-d2c567bf69ba); pap. 48.90 *(978-1-4339-9406-7(2))* Stevens, Gareth Publishing LLLP.

—It's Stormy! / ¡Es una Tormenta!, 1 vol. 2013. (What's the Weather? / ¿Qué Tiempo Hace? Ser.). (ENG & SPA., Illus.). 24p. (J). (gr. k-k). lib. bdg. 25.27 *(978-1-4339-9456-2(9),* 881e49f6-4583-44dd-911a-54ab9d049a5b) Stevens, Gareth Publishing LLLP.

—It's Sunny!, 1 vol. 2013. (What's the Weather? Ser.). 24p. (J). (gr. k-k). (ENG.). pap. 9.15 *(978-1-4339-9409-8(7),* f49b7ca5-5325-4950-8c3c-e713362a2050); pap. 48.90 *(978-1-4339-9410-4(0))*; (ENG., Illus.). lib. bdg. 25.27 *(978-1-4339-9408-1(9),* 31813962-5f96-414b-92f3-7e80d26cfd59) Stevens, Gareth Publishing LLLP.
—It's Sunny! / ¡Está Soleado!, 1 vol. 2013. (What's the Weather? / ¿Qué Tiempo Hace? Ser.). (SPA & ENG., Illus.). 24p. (J). (gr. k-k). 25.27 *(978-1-4339-9454-8(2),* 8520c099-825c-40d9-9a9e-704fd347d662) Stevens, Gareth Publishing LLLP.
—It's Windy!, 1 vol. 2013. (What's the Weather? Ser.). (Illus.). 24p. (J). (gr. k-k). (ENG.). 25.27 *(978-1-4339-9412-8(7),* eeeee899-d36c-4d58-b45c-19a149ce3f97); (ENG., pap. 9.15 *(978-1-4339-9413-5(5),* a4a54a5f-35d9-49f3-b961-d321d021d3bf); pap. 48.90 *(978-1-4339-9414-2(3))* Stevens, Gareth Publishing LLLP.
—It's Windy! / ¡Está Ventoso!, 1 vol. 2013. (What's the Weather? / ¿Qué Tiempo Hace? Ser.). (SPA & ENG., Illus.). 24p. (J). (gr. k-k). 25.27 *(978-1-4339-9452-4(6),* ae6c9bf0-db7a-4c8c-945a-3b8e69bee130) Stevens, Gareth Publishing LLLP.
Amer, Elizabeth. Weather Detectives. 2004. (Illus.). (J). (gr. 4-6). 40.00 *(978-1-57336-404-1(5),* I2065) Interaction Pubs., Inc.
Arnold, Tedd. Fly Guy Presents: Weather. 2016. (Illus.). (J). *(978-1-338-04666-3(7))* Scholastic, Inc.
—Fly Guy Presents: Weather (Scholastic Reader, Level 2) Arnold, Tedd, illus. 2016. (Scholastic Reader, Level 2 Ser.). (ENG.). 32p. (J). (gr. k-2). 5.99 *(978-0-545-85187-9(4))* Scholastic, Inc.
—Weather. 2016. (Fly Guy Presents Ser.). (ENG.). 32p. (J). (gr. k-2). 13.55 *(978-0-606-39161-0(4))* Turtleback.
Artell, Mike. Weather Whys. 2nd ed. 2005. (Illus.). 96p. (J). pap. 14.95 *(978-1-59647-001-9(1))* Good Year Bks.
Aspen-Baxter, Linda & Kissock, Heather. Los Arcoiris, with Code. 2012. (Mirando Al Cielo Ser.). (SPA., Illus.). 24p. (J). (gr. k-2). lib. bdg. 27.13 *(978-1-61913-216-0(8),* AV2 by Weigl) Weigl Pubs., Inc.
Aucoin, Lee. Weather. rev. ed. 2009. (Early Literacy Ser.). (ENG., Illus.). 16p. (gr. -1-1). 19.99 *(978-1-4333-1457-5(6))*; 6.99 *(978-1-4333-1456-8(8))* Teacher Created Materials, Inc.
Austen, Elizabeth. Playing with Wind. rev. ed. 2019. (Smithsonian: Informational Text Ser.). (ENG., Illus.). 20p. (J). (gr. k-1). 7.99 *(978-1-4938-6643-4(5))* Teacher Created Materials, Inc.
Baker, Theo. Warning, Wild Weather Ahead. 2017. *(978-0-515-15895-3(X),* Grosset & Dunlap) Penguin Young Readers Group.
Banqueri, Eduardo. Weather, 1 vol. 2007. (Field Guides). (ENG., Illus.). 64p. (gr. 3-3). 26.93 *(978-1-59270-059-2(4),* f6c3ef4a-ce94-4d28-88bf-0bb027fa2dcd) Cavendish Square Publishing LLC.
Barwick. Sail Main5 Weather Alert Nf. 2003. (Rigby Sails Ser.). (ENG.). 32p. (gr. 5-5). pap. 9.50 *(978-0-7578-8020-9(7))* Rigby Education.
Basher, Simon & Green, Dan. Basher Basics: Weather: Whipping up a Storm! Basher, Simon, illus. 2012. (Basher Basics Ser.). (ENG., Illus.). 64p. (J). (gr. 3-7). pap. 8.99 *(978-0-7534-6826-5(3),* 900081920, Kingfisher) Roaring Brook Pr.
Bassett, John. Experiments with Weather & Climate, 1 vol. 2010. (Cool Science Ser.). (ENG.). 32p. (J). (gr. 4-5). lib. bdg. 30.67 *(978-1-4339-3447-6(7),* b6404fb4-d5ec-441d-b851-0b1096427786); (Illus.). pap. 11.50 *(978-1-4339-3448-3(5),* b7038e34-d0de-4e53-a498-51ea5e8d667a) Stevens, Gareth Publishing LLLP. (Gareth Stevens Learning Library).
Bauer, Marion Dane. Rainbow: Ready-To-Read Level 1. Wallace, John, illus. 2016. (Weather Ready-To-Reads Ser.). (ENG.). 32p. (J). (gr. -1-1). pap. 4.99 *(978-1-4814-6336-2(5),* Simon Spotlight) Simon Spotlight.
Bearport Publishing. Weather Watch. 2018. (ENG.). 16p. (J). (gr. -1-1). 47.70 *(978-1-64280-133-0(X))* Bearport Publishing Co., Inc.
Beckett, Sydney. My Favorite Season, 1 vol. 2012. (InfoMax Readers Ser.). (ENG., Illus.). 16p. (J). (gr. k-k). pap. 7.00 *(978-1-4488-8914-3(6),* b56957f0-0829-4f26-9600-1ab2d449d39d, Rosen Classroom) Rosen Publishing Group, Inc., The.
Bell, Samantha. Weather. Bane, Jeff, illus. 2018. (Mi Mini Biografía (My Itty-Bitty Bio): My Early Library). (ENG.). 24p. (J). (gr. k-1). pap. 12.79 *(978-1-5341-0822-6(X),* 210652); lib. bdg. 30.64 *(978-1-5341-0723-6(1),* 210651) Cherry Lake Publishing.
Benchmark Education Company. Weather & Climate (Teacher Guide) 2005. *(978-1-4108-4635-8(0))* Benchmark Education Co.
—Weathering & Erosion (Teacher Guide) 2005. *(978-1-4108-4648-8(2))* Benchmark Education Co.
Benchmark Education Company, LLC Staff, compiled by. Science Theme: Weather. 2005. spiral bd. 115.00 *(978-1-4108-5316-5(0))* Benchmark Education Co.
—Water & Weather. 2006. spiral bd. 330.00 *(978-1-4108-7018-6(9))* 2006. (J). 206.00 *(978-1-4108-7056-8(1))* 2005. (J). spiral bd. 265.00 *(978-1-4108-5759-0(X))* Benchmark Education Co.
—Water & Weather: Theme Set. 2006. (J). 215.00 *(978-1-4108-7132-9(0))* Benchmark Education Co.
—Weather & Seasons. 2006. (J). 265.00 *(978-1-4108-7031-5(6))* Benchmark Education Co.
Berger, Melvin & Berger, Gilda. Hurricanes Have Eyes but Can't See: And Other Amazing Facts about Wild Weather. 2003. (Illus.). 48p. (J). *(978-0-439-54980-6(9))* Scholastic, Inc.
Bernay, Emma & Berne, Emma Carlson. The Seasons of the Year. Palin, Tim, illus. 2019. (Patterns of Time Ser.). (ENG.). 24p. (J). (gr. -1-2). 33.99 *(978-1-68410-410-9(6),* 141220) Cantata Learning.
Berry, Joy. Good Answers to Tough Questions Disasters. Bartholomew, illus. 2010. (Good Answers to Tough Questions Ser.). (ENG.). 48p. (J). (gr. k-7). pap. 7.99 *(978-1-60577-510-4(X))* Berry, Joy Enterprises.
Best, Arthur. Temperature, 1 vol. 2018. (Properties of Matter Ser.). (ENG.). 24p. (J). (gr. 1-1). 25.93 *(978-1-5026-4274-5(3),* bd4d92e9-26cb-41a3-bf4c-1ace5832b66f) Cavendish Square Publishing LLC.
Big Picture. 2010. (Big Picture Ser.). (ENG.). 24p. (gr. 1-2). pap. 333.60 *(978-1-4296-5829-4(0),* Capstone Pr.) Capstone.
Birch, Robin. How Weather Works, 1 vol. 2010. (Weather & Climate Ser.). (ENG.). 32p. (gr. 3-3). 31.21 *(978-0-7614-4466-4(1),* 05521072-c53e-403d-b7c5-69cd9253ac4d) Cavendish Square Publishing LLC.
—Living with Weather, 1 vol. 2010. (Weather & Climate Ser.). (ENG.). 32p. (gr. 3-3). 31.21 *(978-0-7614-4465-7(3),* a53b4211-ec73-4527-a8f1-08835f3b5011) Cavendish Square Publishing LLC.
Biskup, Agnieszka. Understanding Global Warming with Max Axiom Super Scientist: 4D an Augmented Reading Science Experience. Martin, Cynthia & Martin, Cynthia, illus. 2018. (Graphic Science 4D Ser.). (ENG.). 32p. (J). (gr. 3-9). pap. 7.95 *(978-1-5435-2964-7(X),* 138564); lib. bdg. 36.65 *(978-1-5435-2953-1(4),* 138542) Capstone. (Capstone Pr.).
Bix, Jasper. Winter Weather, 1 vol. 2015. (Winter Fun Ser.). (ENG., Illus.). 24p. (J). (gr. k-k). pap. 9.15 *(978-1-4824-3767-6(8),* f11ed2d1-2bb4-4645-a70a-9f03864ca145) Stevens, Gareth Publishing LLLP.
Boerger, Kristin & Boyett, Suzi. Let's Read about Rain, 1 vol. 2007. (Let's Read about Weather Ser.). (ENG., Illus.). 12p. (gr. k-1). lib. bdg. 17.67 *(978-0-8368-7805-9(1),* 9f7e82b3-9971-480c-80b9-eccc43628edf, Weekly Reader Leveled Readers) Stevens, Gareth Publishing LLLP.
—Llueve (Let's Read about Rain), 1 vol. 2007. (¿Qué Tiempo Hace? (Let's Read about Weather) Ser.). (SPA., Illus.). 12p. (J). (gr. k-1). pap. 5.10 *(978-0-8368-8118-9(4),* 080a1481-b458-45a4-9709-aa38bcfcc80f, Weekly Reader Leveled Readers); lib. bdg. 17.67 *(978-0-8368-8113-4(3),* 51543699-d46e-4d13-9358-cd5d202f65dc) Stevens, Gareth Publishing LLLP.
Boothroyd, Jennifer. How Does Weather Change? 2014. (First Step Nonfiction — Let's Watch the Weather Ser.). (ENG., Illus.). 24p. (J). (gr. k-2). pap. 6.99 *(978-1-4677-4495-9(6),* 031c43b3-1478-4691-ae39-a17c1ca26b47) Lerner Publishing Group.
—Save Energy, Bert & Ernie! 2020. (Go Green with Sesame Street (r) Ser.). (ENG., Illus.). 32p. (J). (gr. -1-2). 27.99 *(978-1-5415-7257-7(2),* bab28574-527a-4ce6-aa72-b08f4610abaf, Lerner Pubns.) Lerner Publishing Group.
—What Is Climate? 2014. (First Step Nonfiction — Let's Watch the Weather Ser.). (ENG., Illus.). 24p. (J). (gr. k-2). lib. bdg. 23.99 *(978-1-4677-3918-4(9),* 6434e1eb-1024-4e2c-94c3-7c5360548920, Lerner Pubns.) Lerner Publishing Group.
—What Is Today's Weather? 2014. (First Step Nonfiction — Let's Watch the Weather Ser.). (ENG., Illus.). 24p. (J). (gr. k-2). pap. 6.99 *(978-1-4677-4500-0(6),* 1ef483d3-0a2a-4e3b-96e1-f387e3950e74); lib. bdg. 23.99 *(978-1-4677-3916-0(2),* 61026b9e-bfff-4bfe-8ceb-6f28ef7ac492, Lerner Pubns.) Lerner Publishing Group.
Boyett, Suzi. Let's Read about Snow, 1 vol. 2007. (Let's Read about Weather Ser.). (ENG., Illus.). 12p. (gr. k-1). lib. bdg. 17.67 *(978-0-8368-7806-6(X),* 8446ee61-df99-4f0f-a2a9-841c13b20e53, Weekly Reader Leveled Readers) Stevens, Gareth Publishing LLLP.
—Nieva (Let's Read about Snow), 1 vol. 2007. (¿Qué Tiempo Hace? (Let's Read about Weather) Ser.). (SPA., Illus.). 12p. (J). (gr. k-1). pap. 5.10 *(978-0-8368-8119-6(2),* b81ea23f-fc30-4ff7-84a3-dc67ecd09832, Weekly Reader Leveled Readers); lib. bdg. 17.67 *(978-0-8368-8114-1(1),* 32ac75d2-62b5-48f3-9e48-7838537e05f3) Stevens, Gareth Publishing LLLP.
Brannon, Barbara. Discover Weather. 2005. (J). pap. *(978-1-4108-5123-9(0))* Benchmark Education Co.
Brannon, Cecelia H. A Look at Erosion & Weathering, 1 vol. 2015. (Rock Cycle Ser.). (ENG., Illus.). 32p. (gr. 3-4). 26.93 *(978-0-7660-7280-0(0),* 2dd815c7-534d-4d09-8b99-844b95b668a9) Enslow Publishing, LLC.
Branson, Sam. Let's Measure the Weather, 1 vol. 2012. (InfoMax Readers Ser.). (ENG., Illus.). 24p. (J). (gr. 1-1). pap. 8.25 *(978-1-4488-9019-4(5),* f489e9d2-876c-4746-9278-0dfe9e0e73d3, Rosen Classroom) Rosen Publishing Group, Inc., The.
Bredeson, Carmen. Weird but True Weather, 1 vol. 2012. (Weird but True Science Ser.). (ENG., Illus.). 24p. (gr. k-2). pap. 10.35 *(978-1-59845-372-0(6),* cecda73b-16f5-4141-8b7d-dc6f9996d22d, Enslow Elementary); lib. bdg. 25.27 *(978-0-7660-3862-2(9),* c30685f5-ef88-4a4b-a5d7-0768a530d02b) Enslow Publishing, LLC.
Bright, Michael. Weather Explained, 1 vol. 2014. (Guide for Curious Minds Ser.). (ENG.). 152p. (YA). (gr. 8-8). 42.41 *(978-1-4777-8129-6(3),* 7d9dd675-bcf1-49cf-9076-a50a1ce99ecc, Rosen Young Adult) Rosen Publishing Group, Inc., The.
Brinker, Spencer. A Rainy Day. 2018. (Weather Watch Ser.). (ENG., Illus.). 16p. (J). (gr. -1-1). 6.99 *(978-1-64280-135-4(6))* Bearport Publishing Co., Inc.
—A Snowy Day. 2018. (Weather Watch Ser.). (ENG., Illus.). 16p. (J). (gr. -1-1). 6.99 *(978-1-64280-136-1(4))* Bearport Publishing Co., Inc.
—A Stormy Day. 2018. (Weather Watch Ser.). (ENG., Illus.). 16p. (J). (gr. -1-1). 6.99 *(978-1-64280-137-8(2))*; 16.96 *(978-1-64280-000-5(7))* Bearport Publishing Co., Inc.
—A Sunny Day. 2018. (Weather Watch Ser.). (ENG.). 16p. (J). (gr. -1-1). 6.99 *(978-1-64280-134-7(8))*; (Illus.). 16.96 *(978-1-64280-001-2(5))* Bearport Publishing Co., Inc.
—A Windy Day. 2018. (Weather Watch Ser.). (ENG., Illus.). 16p. (J). (gr. -1-1). 6.99 *(978-1-64280-138-5(0))* Bearport Publishing Co., Inc.
Brooke, Samantha. Rock Man vs. Weather Man. 2018. (Scholastic Readers Ser.). (ENG.). 31p. (J). (gr. -1-k). 13.89 *(978-1-64310-248-1(6))* Penworthy Co., LLC, The.
—Rock Man vs. Weather Man (the Magic School Bus Rides Again: Scholastic Reader, Level 2) Artful Doodlers Ltd., illus. 2018. (Scholastic Reader, Level 2 Ser.). (ENG.). 32p. (J). (gr. k-2). pap. 5.99 *(978-1-338-25378-8(6))* Scholastic, Inc.
Bullard, Lisa. Blizzards. 2009. pap. 40.95 *(978-0-7613-4767-5(4))* Lerner Publishing Group.
Bundey, Nikki. Drought & People. 2005. (Science of Weather Ser.). (Illus.). 32p. (gr. 4-6). lib. bdg. 21.27 *(978-1-57505-498-8(1))* Lerner Publishing Group.
—Drought & the Earth. 2005. (Science of Weather Ser.). (Illus.). 32p. (gr. 4-6). lib. bdg. 21.27 *(978-1-57505-473-5(6))* Lerner Publishing Group.
—Storms & People. 2005. (Science of Weather Ser.). (Illus.). 32p. (gr. 4-6). lib. bdg. 21.27 *(978-1-57505-499-5(X))* Lerner Publishing Group.
Burton, Margie, et al. Changing Weather. 2011. (Early Connections Ser.). (J). *(978-1-61672-517-4(6))* Benchmark Education Co.
—Changing Weather & Cambios en el Clima: 6 English, 6 Spanish Adaptations. 2011. (J). spiral bd. 75.00 net. *(978-1-4108-5623-4(2))* Benchmark Education Co.
—Weather. 2011. (Early Connections Ser.). (J). *(978-1-61672-275-3(4))* Benchmark Education Co.
Cain, Marie Mowery. It's a Matter of Weather. 2013. (Big Books, Red Ser.). (ENG & SPA., Illus.). 16p. pap. 33.00 *(978-1-59246-213-1(8))* Big Books, by George!
Cali, Jennifer. Rookie Preschool: Rookie Learn about Nauture: What's the Weather? Miller, Edward, illus. 2009. (Rookie Preschool Ser.). (ENG.). 24p. (J). (gr. -1). lib. bdg. 23.00 *(978-0-531-24410-4(5))* Scholastic Library Publishing.
—What's the Weather? Miller, Edward, illus. 2009. (Rookie Preschool-NEW Ser.). (ENG.). 24p. (J). pap. 6.95 *(978-0-531-24585-9(3))* Scholastic Library Publishing.
Callery, Sean. The Magic School Bus Presents: Wild Weather: a Nonfiction Companion to the Original Magic School Bus Series. Bracken, Carolyn, illus. 2014. (Magic School Bus Presents Ser.). (ENG.). 32p. (J). (gr. -1-3). pap. 7.99 *(978-0-545-68367-8(X))* Scholastic, Inc.
Canavan, Roger. You Wouldn't Want to Live Without Extreme Weather! 2015. (You Wouldn't Want to Live Without Ser.). lib. bdg. 20.80 *(978-0-606-36711-0(X))* Turtleback.
—You Wouldn't Want to Live Without Extreme Weather! (You Wouldn't Want to Live Without...) Bergin, Mark, illus. 2015. (You Wouldn't Want to Live Without... Ser.). (ENG.). 32p. (J). (gr. 3). pap. 9.95 *(978-0-531-21408-4(7),* Watts, Franklin) Scholastic Library Publishing.
Capstone Classroom & Stead, Tony. What If the Rainbow Included Different Colors? 2017. (What's the Point? Reading & Writing Expository Text Ser.). (ENG., Illus.). 16p. (J). (gr. k-k). pap. 6.95 *(978-1-4966-0758-4(9),* 132393, Capstone Classroom) Capstone.
Cardenas, Ernesto & Saavedra, Patricia. El estado del Tiempo. l.t. ed. 2006. (SPA., Illus.). 16p. pap. 4.95 *(978-1-933668-22-2(9))* Milo Educational Bks. & Resources.
Cardenas, Ernesto A. Weather. 2009. pap. 4.95 *(978-1-60698-098-9(X))* Milo Educational Bks. & Resources.
—What Is the Weather Like Today? 2009. 23.95 *(978-1-60698-053-8(X))*; pap. 4.95 *(978-1-60698-051-4(3))* Milo Educational Bks. & Resources.
Carson, Mary Kay. Weather Projects for Young Scientists: Experiments & Science Fair Ideas. 2007. (ENG., Illus.). 144p. (J). (gr. 4-7). pap. 16.95 *(978-1-55652-629-9(6))* Chicago Review Pr., Inc.
—What Makes a Tornado Twist? And Other Questions about Weather. Mackay, Louis, illus. 2014. (Good Question! Ser.). (ENG.). 32p. (J). (gr. 1). pap. 6.95 *(978-1-4549-0683-4(9))* Sterling Publishing Co., Inc.
Casado, Dami & Casado, Alicia. El Otoño. 2005. (Brujita Mo y las Cuatro Estaciones Ser.). (SPA & ESP., Illus.). 14p. (J). per., bds. 7.99 *(978-84-272-6236-2(1))* Molino, Editorial ESP. Dist: Santillana USA Publishing Co., Inc.
Chancellor, Deborah & Goldsmith, Mike. The Weather. 2009. (ENG., Illus.). 24p. (J). (gr. k-4). lib. bdg. *(978-0-7787-4724-6(7))* Crabtree Publishing Co.
Chancellor, Debroah. The Weather. 2009. (Now We Know About... Ser.). (ENG., Illus.). 24p. (J). (gr. k-3). pap. *(978-0-7787-4741-3(7))* Crabtree Publishing Co.
Charlesworth, Liza. Science Vocabulary Reader Set: Wild Weather. 2007. (Science Vocabulary Readers Ser.). (ENG., Illus.). (gr. 1-2). 74.99 *(978-0-545-01598-1(7))* Scholastic, Inc.
Child's Play. Ocean Deep. Hatfield, Richard, illus. 2011. (Information Bks.). 14p. (J). (gr. -1-3). spiral bd. *(978-0-85953-929-6(6))* Child's Play International Ltd.
Cipriano, Jeri. El tiempo a Prueba. 2011. (SPA.). 32p. (J). pap. 49.00 net. *(978-1-4108-2340-3(7),* A23407) Benchmark Education Co.
Clarke, Catriona. Weather. Slane, Andrea & Chen, Kuo Kang, illus. 2006. (Beginners Science: Level 2 Ser.). 32p. (J). (gr. 1-3). 4.99 *(978-0-7945-1253-8(4),* Usborne) EDC Publishing.
—Weather: Level 7. Chen, Kuo Kang, illus. 2006. (Usborne Beginners Ser.). 32p. (J). (gr. 4-7). lib. bdg. 12.99 *(978-1-58086-892-1(4),* Usborne) EDC Publishing.
Claybourne, Anna. Extreme Earth. 2014. (100 Facts You Should Know Ser.). 48p. (J). (gr. 4-6). pap. 84.95 *(978-1-4824-1262-8(4))* Stevens, Gareth Publishing LLLP.
Close, Edward. All about the Weather, 1 vol., 1. 2014. (Discovery Education: Earth & Space Science Ser.). (ENG.). 32p. (gr. 4-5). 28.93 *(978-1-4777-6190-8(X),* 9dd15a12-b9ed-4982-a376-0eafbab672ab, PowerKids Pr.) Rosen Publishing Group, Inc., The.
Coan, Sharon. Changing Weather. 2nd rev. ed. 2015. (TIME for KIDS(r): Informational Text Ser.). (ENG., Illus.). 12p. (gr. -1-k). 7.99 *(978-1-4938-2054-2(0))* Teacher Created Materials, Inc.
—El Clima Cambiante. 2nd rev. ed. 2016. (TIME for KIDS(r): Informational Text Ser.). (SPA., Illus.). 12p. (gr. -1-k). 7.99 *(978-1-4938-2963-7(7))* Teacher Created Materials, Inc.
Cole, Joanna. Wild Weather. 2014. (Magic School Bus Presents Ser.). lib. bdg. 17.20 *(978-0-606-35817-0(X))* Turtleback.
Conangla, Maria Mercè & Soler, Jaume. Feelings Forecasters: A Creative Approach to Managing Emotions, 1 vol. 2018. (ENG.). 64p. (gr. 3-6). 16.99 *(978-0-7643-5624-7(0),* 9923) Schiffer Publishing, Ltd.
Cook, Mindy. The Animals' Guide to Weather Around the World & Other Natural Wonders. Regier, Melanie B., illus. 2015. (J). pap. *(978-0-692-03128-5(6))* Baron Ridge Productions.
Cortland, D J. A Week of Weather: Learning to Collect & Record Data on a Pictograph, 1 vol. (Math for the REAL World Ser.). (ENG., Illus.). 8p. (gr. k-1). 2010. pap. 5.15 *(978-0-8239-8887-7(2),* 81e8c645-b482-4be4-9341-3b280759a48e) 2004. 29.95 *(978-0-8239-7630-0(0))* Rosen Publishing Group, Inc., The.
Cousins, Lucy. Maisy's Wonderful Weather Book: A Maisy First Science Book. 2011. (Maisy Ser.). (ENG., Illus.). 16p. (J). (gr. -1-2). 16.99 *(978-0-7636-5096-4(X))* Candlewick Pr.
Cox Cannons, Helen. Rain, 1 vol. 2014. (Weather Wise Ser.). (ENG., Illus.). 24p. (J). (gr. -1-1). pap. 5.99 *(978-1-4846-0555-4(1),* 126646, Heinemann) Capstone.
—Snow, 1 vol. 2014. (Weather Wise Ser.). (ENG., Illus.). 24p. (J). (gr. -1-1). pap. 5.99 *(978-1-4846-0556-1(X),* 126647, Heinemann) Capstone.
—Sunshine, 1 vol. 2014. (Weather Wise Ser.). (ENG., Illus.). 24p. (J). (gr. -1-1). pap. 5.99 *(978-1-4846-0557-8(8),* 126648, Heinemann) Capstone.
—Thunder & Lightning, 1 vol. 2014. (Weather Wise Ser.). (ENG., Illus.). 24p. (J). (gr. -1-1). 25.32 *(978-1-4846-0548-6(9),* 126643, Heinemann) Capstone.
—Wind, 1 vol. 2014. (Weather Wise Ser.). (ENG., Illus.). 24p. (J). (gr. -1-1). pap. 5.99 *(978-1-4846-0559-2(4),* 126650, Heinemann) Capstone.
Crane, Cody. Heating & Cooling (Rookie Read-About Science: Physical Science) (Library Edition) 2019. (Rookie Read-About Science Ser.). (ENG., Illus.). 32p. (J). (gr. 1-2). lib. bdg. 25.00 *(978-0-531-13407-8(5),* Children's Pr.) Scholastic Library Publishing.
Crook, Jennifer. Mrs. Crook's Kindergarten Sings about the Weather: Musical Colors Series. 2003. (Musical Colors Rhyming Story Coloring Book Ser.). (ENG., Illus.). 21p. (J). spiral bd. 14.95 *(978-1-931844-05-5(4),* PP1017) Piano Pr.
D'Aubuisson, Elisabeth. Snowy Days, 1 vol. 2006. (What's the Weather? Ser.). (ENG., Illus.). 24p. (J). (gr. 2-3). lib. bdg. 26.27 *(978-1-4042-3684-4(8),* 83c99a91-7552-4051-ad32-e2c62d68eb2d, PowerKids Pr.) Rosen Publishing Group, Inc., The.
d'Aubuisson, Elisabeth. Snowy Days. 2009. (What's the Weather? Ser.). 24p. (gr. 2-3). 42.50 *(978-1-60854-776-0(0),* PowerKids Pr.) Rosen Publishing Group, Inc., The.
D'Aubuisson, Elisabeth. Sunny Days, 1 vol. 2006. (What's the Weather? Ser.). (ENG., Illus.). 24p. (J). (gr. 2-3). lib. bdg. 26.27 *(978-1-4042-3685-1(6),* e95182c4-4aed-4ee2-9e8c-9458a2300595, PowerKids Pr.) Rosen Publishing Group, Inc., The.
d'Aubuisson, Elisabeth. Sunny Days. 2009. (What's the Weather? Ser.). 24p. (gr. 2-3). 42.50 *(978-1-60854-777-7(9),* PowerKids Pr.) Rosen Publishing Group, Inc., The.
D'Aubuisson, Elisabeth. What's the Weather?, 8 vols., Set. Incl. Rainy Days. lib. bdg. 26.27 *(978-1-4042-3682-0(1),* c8e12711-da4b-4ca1-90d4-9b3bc4ab2dfe); Snowy Days. lib. bdg. 26.27 *(978-1-4042-3684-4(8),* 83c99a91-7552-4051-ad32-e2c62d68eb2d); Sunny Days. lib. bdg. 26.27 *(978-1-4042-3685-1(6),* e95182c4-4aed-4ee2-9e8c-9458a2300595); Windy Days. lib. bdg. 26.27 *(978-1-4042-3683-7(X),* a567d377-a966-4617-855a-6138ea37ad85); (Illus.). 24p. (J). (gr. 2-3). (What's the Weather? Ser.). (ENG.). 2006. Set lib. bdg. 105.08 *(978-1-4042-3609-7(0),* 7736b602-1218-4dd8-b4a2-04418227e139, PowerKids Pr.) Rosen Publishing Group, Inc., The.
—Windy Days, 1 vol. 2006. (What's the Weather? Ser.). (ENG., Illus.). 24p. (J). (gr. 2-3). lib. bdg. 26.27 *(978-1-4042-3683-7(X),* a567d377-a966-4617-855a-6138ea37ad85, PowerKids Pr.) Rosen Publishing Group, Inc., The.
d'Aubuisson, Elisabeth. Windy Days. 2009. (What's the Weather? Ser.). 24p. (gr. 2-3). 42.50 *(978-1-60854-778-4(7),* PowerKids Pr.) Rosen Publishing Group, Inc., The.
David, Alex. Drowning: Rising Oceans & Frequent Floods, 1 vol. 2019. (Taking Action on Climate Change Ser.). (ENG.). 64p. (gr. 6-6). pap. 16.28 *(978-1-5026-5228-7(5),* 54d26c0e-b0f5-43b6-9f2e-6af6f57d2e9b) Cavendish Square Publishing LLC.
—Dying Off: Endangered Plants & Animals, 1 vol. 2019. (Taking Action on Climate Change Ser.). (ENG.). 64p. (J). (gr. 6-6). pap. 16.28 *(978-1-5026-5231-7(5),* c4398af3-9733-40db-8ab6-30e00844d2a7) Cavendish Square Publishing LLC.
Davis, Brangien. Air & Weather, 1 vol. 2007. (Gareth Stevens Vital Science Library: Earth Science Ser.). (ENG., Illus.). 48p. (gr. 5-8). pap. 15.05 *(978-0-8368-7871-4(X),* f510d0ba-fa74-4150-9287-cd896edd3ddf); lib. bdg. 29.67 *(978-0-8368-7760-1(8),* 469e2ca1-ceb4-4cd0-a21a-a860fa967d66) Stevens, Gareth Publishing LLLP. (Gareth Stevens Secondary Library).
Daynes, Katie. See Inside Weather & Climate IR. 2015. (See Inside Board Bks.). (ENG.). 16p. (J). (gr. k-5). 14.99 *(978-0-7945-2161-5(4),* Usborne) EDC Publishing.
de Seve, Karen. National Geographic Little Kids First Big Book of Weather. 2017. (Illus.). 128p. (J). (gr. -1-k). 14.99 *(978-1-4263-2719-3(6),* National Geographic Kids) Disney Publishing Worldwide.
Dewitt, Lynda. What Will the Weather Be? Croll, Carolyn, illus. 2015. (Let's-Read-And-Find-Out Science 2 Ser.). (ENG.). 32p. (J). (gr. -1-3). pap. 7.99 *(978-0-06-238198-9(9),* HarperCollins) HarperCollins Pubs.
DK. Eyewonder: Weather: Open Your Eyes to a World of Discovery. 2016. (Eye Wonder Ser.). (ENG., Illus.). 56p. (J). (gr. k-4). 10.99 *(978-1-4654-4472-1(6),* DK Children) Dorling Kindersley Publishing, Inc.
—Weather & the Seasons. 2019. (Projects to Make & Do Ser.). (ENG., Illus.). 32p. (J). (-k). 8.99 *(978-1-4654-6649-5(5),* DK Children) Dorling Kindersley Publishing, Inc.
Donnelly, Karen. Droughts of the Past & the Future. 2009. (Earth's Changing Weather & Climate Ser.). 24p. (gr. 4-4). 42.50 *(978-1-61512-244-8(3),* PowerKids Pr.) Rosen Publishing Group, Inc., The.
Dorion, Christiane. How the Weather Works: A Hands-On Guide to Our Changing Climate. Young, Beverley, illus. 2011. (Explore the Earth Ser.). (ENG.). 20p. (J). (gr. 2-5). 19.99 *(978-0-7636-5262-3(8),* Templar) Candlewick Pr.
Doubleday Entertainment USA - Sun: Weather Watch. 2006. (J). per. 7.95 *(978-1-59566-229-3(4))* QEB Publishing Inc.
Duling, Kaitlyn. It's Raining Fish & Other Cool Weather Facts. 2019. (Mind-Blowing Science Facts Ser.). (ENG., Illus.). 32p.

W
X
Y
Z

(J). (gr. 4-6). lib. bdg. 28.65 *(978-1-5435-5770-1(8)*, 139726) Capstone.

Eckart, Edana. Welcome Books: Watching the Weather. 2004. (Wel-Watching Nature Ser.). (ENG., Illus.). 24p. (J). (gr. -1-2). pap. 4.95 *(978-0-516-25940-6(7)*, Children's Pr.) Scholastic Library Publishing.

Edison, Erin. Weather Basics. 2011. (Weather Basics Ser.). (ENG.). 24p. (J). (gr. -1-2). pap., pap., pap. 43.74 *(978-1-4296-7089-0(4)*, 16682, Capstone Pr.) Capstone.

—Weather Basics Classroom Collection. 2011. (Weather Basics Ser.). (ENG.). 24p. (J). (gr. k-1). pap., pap. 268.44 *(978-1-4296-7090-6(8)*, 16683, Capstone Pr.) Capstone.

Editors of Kingfisher. Wild Weather. 2016. (It's All About... Ser.). (ENG., Illus.). 32p. (J). pap. 5.99 *(978-0-7534-7269-9(4)*, 900156437, Kingfisher) Roaring Brook Pr.

Encyclopaedia Britannica, Inc. Staff. Britannica Illustrated Science Library Series (18 Title Series), 18 vols. 2010. 599.00 *(978-1-61535-423-8(9))* Encyclopaedia Britannica, Inc.

Estigarribia, Diana. Learning about Weather with Graphic Organizers. (Graphic Organizers in Science Ser.). 24p. 2009. (gr. 3-4). 42.50 *(978-1-61513-053-5(5))* 2005. (ENG., Illus.). (gr. 4-5). pap. 8.25 *(978-1-4042-5036-9(0)*, 9d36b3d0-5184-4038-9424-7aaa47e03fcb) 2004. (ENG., Illus.). (J). (gr. 4-5). lib. bdg. 26.27 *(978-1-4042-2803-0(9)*, 31ea50a6-83d3-48a9-8118-0caf3ff01497) Rosen Publishing Group, Inc., The. (PowerKids Pr.).

Evans, David & Williams, Claudette. Seasons & Weather. (Let's Explore Science Ser.). (Illus.). (J). 12.95 *(978-0-590-74592-5(1))* Scholastic, Inc.

Eye on the Sky. 2015. (Eye on the Sky Ser.). (ENG.). 32p. (J). (gr. 3-4). pap., pap., pap. 378.00 *(978-1-4824-3460-6(1))*; lib. bdg. 169.62 *(978-1-4824-2551-2(3)*, 978cb9ab-1b15-45b4-8663-0c6d508f1bfc) Stevens, Gareth Publishing LLLP.

Felix, Rebecca. How's the Weather in Fall? 2013. (21st Century Basic Skills Library: Let's Look at Fall Ser.). (ENG.). 24p. (gr. k-3). (J). pap. 12.79 *(978-1-61080-927-6(0)*, 202589); (Illus.). 26.35 *(978-1-61080-902-3(5)*, 202587); (Illus.). E-Book 43.50 *(978-1-61080-977-1(7)*, 202590) Cherry Lake Publishing.

—How's the Weather in Summer? 2014. (21st Century Basic Skills Library: Let's Look at Summer Ser.). (ENG., Illus.). 24p. (J). (gr. k-3). 26.35 *(978-1-63137-596-5(2)*, 205167) Cherry Lake Publishing.

—How's the Weather in Winter? 2014. (21st Century Basic Skills Library: Let's Look at Winter Ser.). (ENG., Illus.). 24p. (J). (gr. k-3). 26.35 *(978-1-63137-605-4(5)*, 205203) Cherry Lake Publishing.

Ferris, Diane J. Weather Watcher. 2009. (Illus.). 20p. pap. 13.00 *(978-1-4490-1218-2(3))* AuthorHouse.

Forces Of Nature. 2009. (Illus.). 47p. (J). *(978-0-7166-9822-7(6))* World Bk., Inc.

Foxxe, Ellen. The Rising Seas: Shorelines under Threat, 1 vol. 2006. (Extreme Environmental Threats Ser.). (ENG., Illus.). 64p. (YA). (gr. 6-6). lib. bdg. 37.13 *(978-1-4042-0742-4(2)*, 9ee61077-f555-4f36-9d80-a817106910de) Rosen Publishing Group, Inc., The.

Franchino, Vicky. Droughts. 2012. (21st Century Skills Library: Real World Math Ser.). (ENG., Illus.). 32p. (gr. 4-8). (J). pap. 14.21 *(978-1-61080-407-3(4)*, 201339); lib. bdg. 32.07 *(978-1-61080-322-9(1)*, 201300) Cherry Lake Publishing.

Fretland VanVoorst, Jenny. El Clima en la Primavera. 2015.Tr. of Weather in Spring. (SPA., Illus.). 24p. (J). lib. bdg. *(978-1-62031-252-0(2)*, Bullfrog Bks.) Jump! Inc.

—Weather in Spring. 2015. (Illus.). 24p. (J). lib. bdg. *(978-1-62031-238-4(7)*, Bullfrog Bks.) Jump! Inc.

Furgang, Kathy. National Geographic Kids Everything Weather: Facts, Photos, & Fun That Will Blow You Away. 2012. (National Geographic Kids Everything Ser.). (Illus.). 64p. (J). (gr. 3-7). pap. 12.95 *(978-1-4263-1058-4(7)*, National Geographic Kids); (ENG., lib. bdg. 25.90 *(978-1-4263-1063-8(3)*, National Geographic Children's Bks.) Disney Publishing Worldwide.

—What Will the Weather Be? Set Of 6. 2010. (Early Connections Ser.). (J). pap. 37.00 net. *(978-1-4108-1073-1(9))* Benchmark Education Co.

Furgang, Kathy, rev. Zoom in on Weather Maps, 1 vol. 2017. (Zoom in on Maps Ser.). (ENG.). 24p. (gr. 2-2). 25.60 *(978-0-7660-9224-2(0)*, 85b035de-646e-47b5-9229-581a69128d55) Enslow Publishing, LLC.

Gaertner, Meg. Spring Weather. 2020. (Spring Is Here Ser.). (ENG., Illus.). 16p. (J). (gr. k-1). pap. 7.95 *(978-1-64493-104-2(4)*, 1644931044); lib. bdg. 25.64 *(978-1-64493-025-0(0)*, 1644930250) North Star Editions. (Focus Readers).

Gaffney, Timothy R. Storm Scientist: Careers Chasing Severe Weather, 1 vol. 2010. (Wild Science Careers Ser.). (ENG., Illus.). 112p. (gr. 5-6). lib. bdg. 35.93 *(978-0-7660-3050-3(4)*, 583909e9-419d-4dba-a2d3-dad1bde33be4) Enslow Publishing, LLC.

Galiano, Dean. Clouds, Rain & Snow. 2003. (Weather Watchers' Library). (Illus.). 48p. (YA). (gr. 5-8). lib. bdg. 23.95 *(978-0-8239-3092-0(0)*, WECLRA, Rosen Reference) Rosen Publishing Group, Inc., The.

—Thunderstorms & Lightning. (Weather Watcher's Library). 48p. (gr. 5-8). 2009. 53.00 *(978-1-60854-275-8(0))* 2003. (Illus.). (YA). lib. bdg. 23.95 *(978-0-8239-3093-7(9)*, WETHLI) Rosen Publishing Group, Inc., The. (Rosen Reference).

Garbe, Suzanne. Threatening Skies: History's Most Dangerous Weather, 1 vol. 2013. (Dangerous History Ser.). (ENG.). 32p. (J). (gr. 3-9). 28.65 *(978-1-4765-0128-4(9)*, 122205, Capstone Pr.) Capstone.

Gardner, Robert. Easy Genius Science Projects with Weather: Great Experiments & Ideas, 1 vol. 2008. (Easy Genius Science Projects Ser.). (ENG., Illus.). 128p. (J). (gr. 5-6). lib. bdg. 35.93 *(978-0-7660-2924-8(7)*, fe626b97-ebcc-4bb8-9384-cd0e1f203d33) Enslow Publishing, LLC.

—Experiments with Weather, 1 vol. 2017. (Science Whiz Experiments Ser.). (ENG.). 128p. (gr. 5-5). lib. bdg. 38.93 *(978-0-7660-8686-9(0)*, d33e1278-5207-4921-9e9e-616c74c84401) Enslow Publishing, LLC.

—Science Fair Projects about Weather, 1 vol. 2016. (Hands-On Science Ser.). (ENG.). 48p. (gr. 4-4). pap. 12.70 *(978-0-7660-8204-5(0)*, a8eb04cd-1b8e-43f0-9782-9b369eaa9cab) Enslow Publishing, LLC.

—Weather Science Fair Projects, Using the Scientific Method, 1 vol. 2010. (Earth Science Projects Using the Scientific Method Ser.). (ENG., Illus.). 160p. (gr. 5-6). 38.60 *(978-0-7660-3424-2(0)*, 34a7cbfa-d54e-4758-ac49-3f4518437a9a) Enslow Publishing, LLC.

Gardner, Robert & Tocci, Salvatore. Ace Your Weather Science Project: Great Science Fair Ideas, 1 vol. 2009. (Ace Your Physics Science Project Ser.). (ENG., Illus.). 104p. (gr. 5-6). lib. bdg. 35.93 *(978-0-7660-3223-1(X)*, abb9e9fa-ea2b-4d59-8dc1-544cfff132b9) Enslow Publishing, LLC.

Geatches, Hazel, ed. Sunny & Rainy. 2012. (ENG., Illus.). 40p. pap. 11.00 *(978-0-19-464680-2(7))* Oxford Univ. Pr., Inc.

Gerry, Lisa M. Explore My World: Weather. 2018. (Explore My World Ser.). (Illus.). 32p. (J). (gr. -1-k). pap. 4.99 *(978-1-4263-3155-8(X))*; (ENG., lib. bdg. 14.90 *(978-1-4263-3156-5(8))* Disney Publishing Worldwide. (National Geographic Kids).

Ghigna, Charles. Raindrops Fall All Around. Watson, Laura, illus. 2015. (Springtime Weather Wonders Ser.). (ENG.). 24p. (J). (gr. -1-2). lib. bdg. 22.65 *(978-1-4795-6030-1(8)*, 127289, Picture Window Bks.) Capstone.

Gibbons, Gail. Weather Words & What They Mean (New Edition) 2019. (Illus.). 32p. (J). (gr. -1-3). 18.99 *(978-0-8234-4171-6(7))*; pap. 8.99 *(978-0-8234-4190-7(3))* Holiday Hse., Inc.

Gleisner, Jenna Lee. How's the Weather in Spring? 2014. (21st Century Basic Skills Library: Let's Look at Spring Ser.). (ENG., Illus.). 24p. (J). (gr. k-3). pap. 12.79 *(978-1-62431-681-4(6)*, 203129) Cherry Lake Publishing.

Gleisner, Jenna Lee & Willis, John. Weather. 2018. (Illus.). 24p. (J). *(978-1-4896-9584-0(2)*, AV2 by Weigl) Weigl Pubs., Inc.

Goldstein, Natalie. Drought & Heat Waves: A Practical Survival Guide. 2009. (Library of Emergency Preparedness Ser.). 64p. (gr. 6-6). 29.25 *(978-1-60853-592-7(4)*, Rosen Reference) Rosen Publishing Group, Inc., The.

Goodenow, Ellen A. My Weather Journal. 2003. (Shutterbug Bks.). (Illus.). 16p. pap. 4.10 *(978-0-7398-7654-1(6))* Steck-Vaughn.

Gosman, Gillian. What Do You Know about Earth's Atmosphere?, 1 vol. 2013. (20 Questions: Earth Science Ser.). 24p. (J). (ENG.). (gr. 2-3). pap. 9.25 *(978-1-4488-9856-5(0)*, 1f65b808-2a20-4f78-b141-c59ea5038f4c); (ENG.). (gr. 2-3). lib. bdg. 26.27 *(978-1-4488-9699-8(1)*, 0540c873-a86d-4d23-835c-cae6cd899c6d); (gr. 3-6). pap. 49.50 *(978-1-4488-9857-2(9))* Rosen Publishing Group, Inc., The. (PowerKids Pr.).

—What Do You Know about Weather & Climate?, 1 vol. 2013. (20 Questions: Earth Science Ser.). (ENG., Illus.). 24p. (J). (gr. 2-3). pap. 9.25 *(978-1-4488-9860-2(9)*, c81583e3-9aac-448f-b16b-9cc88a69dad6, PowerKids Pr.) Rosen Publishing Group, Inc., The.

Grayson, Augustus. What Is the Weather Today?, 1 vol. 2012. (InfoMax Readers Ser.). (ENG., Illus.). 16p. (J). (gr. k-k). pap. 7.00 *(978-1-4488-8968-6(5)*, 93bf9ae5-677e-4658-b57b-7df8de71b385, Rosen Classroom) Rosen Publishing Group, Inc., The.

Greathead, Helen. Perilous Places, 1 vol. 2016. (What Would You Choose? Ser.). (ENG.). 32p. (J). (gr. 4-5). pap. 11.50 *(978-1-4824-6116-9(1)*, 45540eb6-0c66-4cc3-b3e6-02cca8ea9ad4) Stevens, Gareth Publishing LLLP.

Greek, Joe. Weather & Climate. 2017. (Let's Find Out! Our Dynamic Earth Ser.). (Illus.). 32p. (J). (gr. 6-10). 77.40 *(978-1-5383-0032-9(X))* Rosen Publishing Group, Inc., The.

—What Is the Atmosphere & How Does It Circulate?, 1 vol. 2014. (Let's Find Out! Weather Ser.). (ENG.). 32p. (J). (gr. 2-3). 26.06 *(978-1-62275-783-1(1)*, 7fa3f9b5-50d2-4f49-9b03-199a582ec3ae, Britannica Educational Publishing) Rosen Publishing Group, Inc., The.

Green, Jen. Weather & Seasons, 1 vol. 2007. (Our Earth Ser.). (ENG., Illus.). 24p. (J). (gr. 2-3). lib. bdg. 26.27 *(978-1-4042-4272-2(4)*, 292c8d5e-5eb9-4a04-ad80-3f6d4410b662) Rosen Publishing Group, Inc., The.

Group/McGraw-Hill, Wright. Forces of Nature: Level K, 6 vols., Vol. 2. (First Explorers Ser.). 24p. (gr. 1-2). 34.95 *(978-0-7699-1458-9(6))* Shortland Pubns. (U. S. A.) Inc.

—Winter Weather: Collection 2. (Storyteller Interactive Writing Cards Ser.). (J). (gr. 3-6). *(978-0-322-09341-6(4))* Wright Group/McGraw-Hill.

Haddon, Jean. It's a Beautiful Day! Enright, Vicky, illus. 2005. (Silly Millies Ser.). 32p. (J). per. 5.95 *(978-0-7613-2397-6(X)*, First Avenue Editions) Lerner Publishing Group.

—It's a Beautiful Day! Enright, Vicky, tr. Enright, Vicky, illus. 2005. (Silly Millies Level 2 Ser.). (ENG.). 32p. (J). (gr. 1-3). lib. bdg. 21.27 *(978-0-7613-2834-6(3)*, Millbrook Pr.) Lerner Publishing Group.

Hall, Julie. Weather: Grades 2 & 3. (Illus.). (J). pap., wbk. ed. 4.99 *(978-0-88743-962-9(4))* School Zone Publishing Co.

Hand, Carol. Science Lab: Weather Patterns. 2011. (Explorer Library: Language Arts Explorer Ser.). (ENG.). 32p. (gr. 4-8). pap. 14.21 *(978-1-61080-299-4(3)*, 201221) Cherry Lake Publishing.

—Science Lab: Weather Patterns. 2011. (Explorer Library: Language Arts Explorer Ser.). (ENG., Illus.). 32p. (gr. 4-8). lib. bdg. 32.07 *(978-1-61080-210-9(1)*, 201196) Cherry Lake Publishing.

—Weather Myths, Busted! 2017. (Science Myths, Busted! Ser.). (ENG., Illus.). 32p. (J). (gr. 3-6). pap. 9.95 *(978-1-63235-357-3(1)*, 11820); lib. bdg. 32.80 *(978-1-63235-307-8(5)*, 11812) Bookstaves, LLC. (12-Story Library).

Hansen, Grace. El Clima (Weather), 6 vols. 2015. (Clima (Weather) Ser.: Vol. 6). (SPA.). 24p. (J). (gr. -1-2). lib. bdg. 196.74 *(978-1-68080-349-5(2)*, 18652, Abdo Kids) ABDO Publishing Co.

—Wind, 1 vol. 2015. (Weather Ser.). (ENG., Illus.). 24p. (J). (gr. -1-2). 32.79 *(978-1-62970-936-9(0)*, 18330, Abdo Kids) ABDO Publishing Co.

Harper, Kathryn. Dressing for the Weather Green Band. Sims, Sean, illus. 2016. (Cambridge Reading Adventures Ser.). (ENG.). 16p. pap. 7.95 *(978-1-316-50324-9(0))* Cambridge Univ. Pr.

Harris, Caroline. Discover Science: Weather. 2017. (Discover Science Ser.). (ENG.). 56p. (J). pap. 7.99 *(978-0-7534-7336-8(4)*, 9780753473368, Kingfisher) Roaring Brook Pr.

Heckt, Jackie. What the Clouds Are Telling You, 1 vol. 2013. (Rosen Readers Ser.). (ENG.). 24p. (J). (gr. 2-2). pap. 8.25 *(978-1-4777-2309-8(9)*, c2a312ec-6f83-421f-9974-c2055b971483); pap. 49.50 *(978-1-4777-2310-4(2))* Rosen Publishing Group, Inc., The. (Rosen Classroom).

Herriges, Ann. Clouds. 2006. (Weather Ser.). (ENG., Illus.). 24p. (J). (gr. k-3). lib. bdg. 26.95 *(978-1-60014-024-2(6))* Bellwether Media.

—Lightning. 2006. (Weather Ser.). (ENG., Illus.). 24p. (J). (gr. k-3). lib. bdg. 26.95 *(978-1-60014-025-9(4))* Bellwether Media.

—Lightning. 2011. (Blastoff! Readers Ser.). 24p. (J). pap. 5.95 *(978-0-531-27621-1(X)*, Children's Pr.) Scholastic Library Publishing.

—Rain. 2006. (Weather Ser.). (ENG., Illus.). 24p. (J). (gr. k-3). lib. bdg. 26.95 *(978-1-60014-027-3(0))* Bellwether Media.

—Rain. 2011. (Blastoff! Readers Ser.). 24p. (J). pap. 5.95 *(978-0-531-27622-8(8)*, Children's Pr.) Scholastic Library Publishing.

—Snow. 2006. (Weather Ser.). (ENG., Illus.). 24p. (J). (gr. k-3). lib. bdg. 26.95 *(978-1-60014-029-7(7))* Bellwether Media.

—Snow. 2011. (Blastoff! Readers Ser.). 24p. (J). pap. 5.95 *(978-0-531-27623-5(6)*, Children's Pr.) Scholastic Library Publishing.

—Sunshine. 2006. (Weather Ser.). (ENG., Illus.). 24p. (J). (gr. k-3). lib. bdg. 26.95 *(978-1-60014-028-0(9))* Bellwether Media.

—Wind. 2006. (Weather Ser.). (ENG., Illus.). 24p. (J). (gr. k-3). lib. bdg. 26.95 *(978-1-60014-026-6(2))* Bellwether Media.

—Wind. 2011. (Blastoff! Readers Ser.). 24p. (J). pap. 5.95 *(978-0-531-27624-2(4)*, Children's Pr.) Scholastic Library Publishing.

Hewitt, Sally. Weather. 2010. (Starting Geography Ser.). 32p. (J). (gr. 2-5). 28.50 *(978-1-60753-130-2(5))* Amicus Learning.

Hirsch, Rebecca E. Using Climate Maps. 2016. (Searchlight Books (tm) — What Do You Know about Maps? Ser.). (ENG., Illus.). 40p. (J). (gr. 3-5). 30.65 *(978-1-5124-0950-5(2)*, 3911df2a-67ab-44f8-bb0d-ae78ee67b509, Lerner Pubns.) Lerner Publishing Group.

Hirschmann, Kris & Herndon, Ryan, compiled by. Guinness World Records, up Close. 2007. (Illus.). 47p. *(978-0-439-89828-7(5))* Scholastic, Inc.

Hot & Cold Weather, 6 vols. (Sunshinetm Science Ser.). 24p. (gr. 1-2). 37.50 *(978-0-7802-1380-7(7))* Wright Group/McGraw-Hill.

Houghton Gosman, Gillian. What Do You Know about Weather & Climate?, 1 vol. 2013. (20 Questions: Earth Science Ser.). (ENG.). 24p. (J). (gr. 2-3). 26.27 *(978-1-4488-9701-8(7)*, 8b63e8ea-389c-4e43-89d7-c5b76ce3a83a, PowerKids Pr.) Rosen Publishing Group, Inc., The.

Howell, Izzi. Climate Change Eco Facts. 2019. (Eco Facts Ser.). (ENG.). 32p. (J). (gr. 5-5). pap. *(978-0-7787-6357-4(9)*, e8769ca0-a843-470e-aa23-9e539fea9b08) Crabtree Publishing Co.

Howell, Laura. Introduction to Weather & Climate Change. 2004. (Geography Ser.). (ENG., Illus.). 96p. (J). pap. 14.95 *(978-0-7945-0629-2(1))* EDC Publishing.

—Introduction to Weather & Climate Change. Furnival, Keith, illus. 2004. (Geography Ser.). 96p. (J). (gr. 5). lib. bdg. 22.95 *(978-1-58086-613-2(1)*, Usborne) EDC Publishing.

Jackson, Randy. Get Ready for Hazardous Weather: Learning Through Puzzles, Games & Exercises. 2004. 40p. (YA). 3.50 *(978-0-9742794-2-8(0))* HazardousWeather Preparedness Institute.

James, Trisha. I Know the Weather, 1 vol. 2017. (What I Know Ser.). (ENG.). 24p. (J). (gr. k-k). pap. 9.15 *(978-1-4824-6313-2(X)*, 8c351dc9-1320-4690-87b0-2ac0c881a5f7) Stevens, Gareth Publishing LLLP.

Jaycox, Jaclyn. Totally Amazing Facts about Weather. 2018. (Mind Benders Ser.). (ENG.). 112p. (J). (gr. 3-6). lib. bdg. 23.99 *(978-1-5157-7764-9(2)*, 135968, Capstone Pr.) Capstone.

Jennings, Terry. Extreme Weather. 2009. (Amazing Planet Earth Ser.). (ENG.). 32p. (J). (gr. 3-6). 31.35 *(978-1-59920-369-0(3)*, 19256, Smart Apple Media) Black Rabbit Bks.

Jennings, Terry J. The Weather: Rain. 2004. (J). lib. bdg. 27.10 *(978-1-59389-143-5(1))* Chrysalis Education.

—The Weather: Wind. 2004. (J). lib. bdg. 27.10 *(978-1-59389-146-6(6))* Chrysalis Education.

Johnson, Robin. What Is Weather? 2012. (ENG.). 24p. (J). *(978-0-7787-0756-1(3))*; (Illus.). pap. *(978-0-7787-0763-9(6))* Crabtree Publishing Co.

Jones, Tammy. I Like the Spring! 2009. (Sight Word Readers Set A Ser.). (J). 3.49 net. *(978-1-60719-138-4(5))* Newmark Learning LLC.

—Look at the Weather. 2009. (Sight Word Readers Set A Ser.). (J). *(978-1-60719-140-7(7))* Newmark Learning LLC.

Kallio, Jamie. 12 Things to Know about Wild Weather. 2015. (Today's News Ser.). (ENG., Illus.). 32p. (J). (gr. 3-6). 32.80 *(978-1-63235-035-0(1)*, 11613, 12-Story Library) Bookstaves, LLC.

Kalman, Maira & Handler, Daniel. Weather, Weather. Meister, Sarah Hermanson, ed. 2016. (ENG., Illus.). 64p. (gr. -1-2). 17.95 *(978-1-63345-014-1(7)*, 1645401) Museum of Modern Art.

Kampff, Joseph. What Are Weather Instruments?, 1 vol. 2014. (Let's Find Out! Weather Ser.). (ENG.). 32p. (J). (gr. 2-3). 26.06 *(978-1-62275-791-6(2)*, 4f1d1ad2-b0b6-41cf-963e-34946339f375, Britannica Educational Publishing) Rosen Publishing Group, Inc., The.

Kelley, K. C. Weather. 2018. (Spot Awesome Nature Ser.). (ENG.). 16p. (J). (gr. -1-2). pap. 7.99 *(978-1-68152-244-9(6)*, 14827) Amicus.

Kerrod, Robin. Find Out about Weather: With 15 Projects & More Than 260 Pictures. 2013. (Illus.). 64p. (J). (gr. -1-12). 9.99 *(978-1-84322-871-4(8))* Anness Publishing GBR. Dist: National Bk. Network.

Kesselring, Susan. With Weather. 2018. (J). pap. *(978-1-4896-9980-0(5)*, AV2 by Weigl) Weigl Pubs., Inc.

Kirmes, William. The Year the Snow Didn't Melt. 2011. 32p. (gr -1). pap. 12.95 *(978-1-4567-5460-0(2))* AuthorHouse.

Kjelle, Marylou Morano. A Project Guide to Wind, Weather, & the Atmosphere. 2010. (Earth Science Projects for Kids Ser.). (Illus.). 48p. (J). (gr. 4-7). lib. bdg. 29.95 *(978-1-58415-869-1(7))* Mitchell Lane Pubs.

Klepeis, Alicia Z. The Sun & the Weather. 2019. (Power of the Sun Ser.). (ENG.). 32p. (gr. 3-3). 63.48 *(978-1-5026-4671-2(4))* Cavendish Square Publishing LLC.

Kosara, Tori. Wild Weather Around the World. 2010. (Illus.). 46p. (J). pap. *(978-0-545-32147-1(6))* Scholastic, Inc.

Krajnik, Elizabeth. How Earth's Landscape Affects the Weather, 1 vol. 2018. (Spotlight on Weather & Natural Disasters Ser.). (ENG.). 24p. (gr. 4-6). 27.93 *(978-1-5081-6901-7(2)*, 8a0a703e-0f3c-4a21-917d-173fb50e10f8, PowerKids Pr.) Rosen Publishing Group, Inc., The.

Kudlinski, Kathleen V. Boy, Were We Wrong about the Weather! Serra, Sebastià, illus. 2015. 32p. (J). (gr. -1-3). 18.99 *(978-0-8037-3793-8(9)*, Dial Bks) Penguin Young Readers Group.

Ladd, Karol. The Glad Scientist Learn about the Weather. 2004. (Glad Scientist Ser.). pap., act. bk. ed. 6.99 *(978-0-8054-0830-0(4))* B&H Publishing Group.

LaFontaine, Bruce. All about the Weather. 2004. (Dover Science for Kids Coloring Bks.). (ENG., Illus.). 48p. (J). (gr. 3-8). pap. 4.99 *(978-0-486-43036-2(7)*, 430367) Dover Pubns., Inc.

Langston-George, Rebecca. A Primary Source History of the Dust Bowl. 2015. (Primary Source History Ser.). (ENG., Illus.). 32p. (J). (gr. 3-6). lib. bdg. 27.99 *(978-1-4914-1840-6(0)*, 127278, Capstone Pr.) Capstone.

Larrick, Nancy. Rain, Hail, Sleet & Snow. Yap, Weda, illus. 2011. 68p. 36.95 *(978-1-258-08878-1(9))* Literary Licensing, LLC.

Law, Felicia & Way, Steve. Weather, 1 vol. 2008. (Simply Science Ser.). (ENG., Illus.). 32p. (YA). (gr. 3-5). lib. bdg. 28.67 *(978-0-8368-9233-8(X)*, 99818c37-1384-48cc-8aef-70b4b49bd88b) Stevens, Gareth Publishing LLLP.

Lawrence, Ellen. Weather. 2016. (FUN-Damental Experiments Ser.). (ENG., Illus.). 24p. (J). (gr. -1-3). 26.99 *(978-1-943553-18-1(1))* Bearport Publishing Co., Inc.

—What Is Weather? (Weather Wise Ser.). 24p. (J). (gr. -1-3). 2018. (ENG.). 7.99 *(978-1-64280-093-7(7))* 2012. lib. bdg. 26.99 *(978-1-61772-405-3(X))* Bearport Publishing Co., Inc.

Lee, Sally. Cold Weather: A 4D Book. 2018. (All Kinds of Weather Ser.). (ENG., Illus.). 24p. (J). (gr. -1-2). lib. bdg. 24.65 *(978-1-9771-0188-4(7)*, 138715, Pebble) Capstone.

—Snowy Weather: A 4D Book. 2018. (All Kinds of Weather Ser.). (ENG., Illus.). 24p. (J). (gr. -1-2). lib. bdg. 24.65 *(978-1-9771-0186-0(0)*, 138712, Pebble) Capstone.

—Sunny Weather: A 4D Book. 2018. (All Kinds of Weather Ser.). (ENG., Illus.). 24p. (J). (gr. -1-2). lib. bdg. 24.65 *(978-1-9771-0185-3(2)*, 138710, Pebble) Capstone.

—Windy Weather: A 4D Book. 2018. (All Kinds of Weather Ser.). (ENG., Illus.). 24p. (J). (gr. -1-2). lib. bdg. 24.65 *(978-1-9771-0187-7(9)*, 138713, Pebble) Capstone.

LernerClassroom Editors. First Step Nonfiction-Kinds of Weather Teaching Guide. 2009. pap. 7.95 *(978-0-8225-5397-7(X))* Lerner Publishing Group.

—First Step Nonfiction-Weather Teaching Guide. 2009. pap. 7.95 *(978-0-8225-5539-1(5))* Lerner Publishing Group.

Let's Find Out! Weather, 12 vols. 2014. (Let's Find Out! Weather Ser.). (ENG.). 32p. (J). (gr. 2-3). lib. bdg. 156.36 *(978-1-62275-799-2(8)*, 2155d5d8-0cee-4ab2-9a82-e5b0cbbe77c0, Britannica Educational Publishing) Rosen Publishing Group, Inc., The.

Let's Read about Weather, 4 vols. 2007. (Let's Read about Weather Ser.). (ENG.). 12p. (gr. k-1). lib. bdg. 35.34 *(978-0-8368-7804-2(3)*, 0dab96fc-c7fb-4f72-a940-ac7405fed28d, Weekly Reader Leveled Readers) Stevens, Gareth Publishing LLLP.

Levete, Sarah. Catastrophic Weather. 2010. (Protecting Our Planet Ser.). (ENG., Illus.). 32p. (J). (gr. 3-6). *(978-0-7787-5210-3(0))*; pap. *(978-0-7787-5227-1(5))* Crabtree Publishing Co.

Levey, Richard H. Dust Bowl! The 1930s Black Blizzards. 2005. (X-Treme Disasters That Changed America Ser.). 32p. (J). lib. bdg. 28.50 *(978-1-59716-007-0(5))* Bearport Publishing Co., Inc.

Levy, Janey. Dangerous Climates, 1 vol. 2019. (Mother Nature Is Trying to Kill Me! Ser.). (ENG.). 24p. (gr. 2-3). pap. 9.15 *(978-1-5382-3958-2(2)*, bcff7503-fd61-4ff9-a8d0-55972db76291) Stevens, Gareth Publishing LLLP.

Life Nature's Fury. 2008. (Time Inc. Home Entertainment Library-Bound Titles Ser.). (ENG.). 144p. (gr. 5-12). lib. bdg. 39.93 *(978-0-7613-4051-5(3)*, Twenty-First Century Bks.) Lerner Publishing Group.

Lilly, Melinda. Hot & Cold. 2005. (Read & Do Science Ser.). (ENG.). 24p. (gr. 1-4). pap. 8.95 *(978-1-62717-259-2(9)*, 9781627172592) Rourke Educational Media.

Linde, Barbara M. Weather & Climate. 2005. (J). pap. *(978-1-4108-4587-0(7))* Benchmark Education Co.

Lindeen, Mary. Reduce, Reuse, & Recycle, Oscar! 2020. (Go Green with Sesame Street (r) Ser.). (ENG., Illus.). 32p. (J). (gr. -1-2). 27.99 *(978-1-5415-7262-1(9)*, 8d67ccbb-0588-4603-842d-1cf059143f85, Lerner Pubns.) Lerner Publishing Group.

—Weather near You. 2017. (Beginning-To-Read Ser.). (ENG.). 32p. (J). (gr. k-2). pap. 13.26 *(978-1-68404-092-6(2))*; (Illus.). 22.60 *(978-1-59953-873-0(3))* Norwood Hse. Pr.

Litchfield, Jo. Weather. Maynard, Marc, illus. 2008. (Usborne Look & Say Ser.). 12p. (J). (gr. -1-3). bds. 7.99 *(978-0-7945-1989-6(X)*, Usborne) EDC Publishing.

Llewellyn, Claire. The Weather Today Red Band. Jonatronix, illus. 2016. (Cambridge Reading Adventures Ser.). (ENG.). 16p. pap. 7.95 *(978-1-107-57676-6(8))* Cambridge Univ. Pr.

Lonsdale, Mary, illus. Whatever the Weather: When the Snow Comes. 2004. (Whatever the Weather Ser.). 10p. (J). bds.

4.99 (978-1-85854-103-7(4)) Brimax Books Ltd. GBR. Dist: Byeway Bks.

-Whatever the Weather: When the Sun Shines. 2004. (Whatever the Weather Ser.). 10p. (J). bds. 4.99 (978-1-85854-105-1(0)) Brimax Books Ltd. GBR. Dist: Byeway Bks.

-Whatever the Weather: When the Wind Blows. 2004. (Whatever the Weather Ser.). 10p. (J). bds. 4.99 (978-1-85854-102-0(6)) Brimax Books Ltd. GBR. Dist: Byeway Bks.

owel, Margaret. Weather Tools: A Content Area Reader-science. 2005. (Sadlier Phonics Reading Program). (Illus.). 12p. (gr. k-2). 25.20 (978-0-8215-7814-8(6)) Sadlier, William H. Inc.

ynn, Saundra. Am I Like the Weather? 2009. 52p. pap. 20.49 (978-1-4490-4510-4(3)) AuthorHouse.

lachajewski, Sarah. Storms, Floods, & Erosion, 1 vol. 2018. (Spotlight on Weather & Natural Disasters Ser.). (ENG., Illus.). 24p. (J). (gr. 4-6). 27.93 (978-1-5081-6911-6(X), 5247fc9a-d754-4bc2-9106-f7db16a5660f, PowerKids Pr.) Rosen Publishing Group, Inc., The.

—Weather & Climate Around the World, 1 vol. 2018. (Spotlight on Weather & Natural Disasters Ser.). (ENG.). 24p. (gr. 4-6). 27.93 (978-1-5081-6920-8(9), 393c23a4-ab85-4e6e-9a6e-62901d41aef0, PowerKids Pr.) Rosen Publishing Group, Inc., The.

Mack, Lorrie & Dorling Kindersley Publishing Staff. Weather. 2004. (DK Eye Wonder Ser.). (ENG.). 48p. (J). (gr. 3-6). lib. bdg. 22.44 (978-0-7566-0324-3(2)) Dorling Kindersley Publishing, Inc.

Madgwick, Wendy. Up in the Air: 17 Easy-to-Follow Experiments for Learning Fun - Find Out about Flight & How Weather Works! 2014. (Illus.). 270p. (J). (gr. -1-12). 8.99 (978-1-86147-350-9(8), Armadillo) Anness Publishing GBR. Dist: National Bk. Network.

Mahaney, Ian F. Weather Maps. (Map It! Ser.). 24p. (gr. 3-4). 2009. 42.50 (978-1-61514-359-7(9), PowerKids Pr.) 2006. (ENG., Illus.). (YA). lib. bdg. 26.27 (978-1-4042-3057-6(2), 468eadb2-92e9-41b7-99b4-127fbde017e4) Rosen Publishing Group, Inc., The.

Make It Work Geography, 4 vol. set. 2003. (gr. 4-8). 59.00 (978-0-7166-5124-6(6)) World Bk., Inc.

Making a Weather Chart: KinderFacts Individual Title Six-Packs. (Kinderstarters Ser.). 8p. (gr. -1-1). 21.00 (978-0-7635-8753-6(2)) Rigby Education.

Malavolti, Angela. You Are a Twisting Tornado. Stiffler, Michael, illus. 2011. 28p. (J). 16.99 (978-0-9834092-0-5(X)) Jungle Wagon Pr.

Malizia, Diana. A Visual Guide to Weather & Climate, 1 vol. 2017. (Visual Exploration of Science Ser.). (ENG.). 104p. (YA). (gr. 8-8). 38.80 (978-1-5081-7706-7(6), e8be2f97-4b7c-4694-9e82-f7737a5eff3f); pap. 18.65 (978-1-5081-7882-8(8), 3bd3a88f-ce21-47b6-8d7e-0ef9b2ec3bf4) Rosen Publishing Group, Inc., The. (Rosen Young Adult).

Malloy, Devin. WeatherTalk: Conversation Cards for the Entire Family. 2008. (Tabletalk Conversation Cards Ser.). (Illus.). (J). (gr. 4-7). 6.00 (978-1-57281-632-9(5)) U.S. Games Systems, Inc.

Maloof, Torrey. Extreme Weather, 1 vol. 2015. (Science: Informational Text Ser.). (ENG., Illus.). 32p. (J). (gr. 3-4). pap. 11.99 (978-1-4807-4647-3(9)) Teacher Created Materials, Inc.

—Weathering & Erosion, 1 vol. rev. ed. 2014. (Science: Informational Text Ser.). (ENG.). 32p. (gr. 2-3). pap. 10.99 (978-1-4807-4611-4(8)) Teacher Created Materials, Inc.

Manolis, Kay. Blizzards. 2008. (Extreme Weather Ser.). (ENG., Illus.). 24p. (J). (gr. 2-5). lib. bdg. 26.95 (978-1-60014-183-6(8)) Bellwether Media.

Marsico, Katie. Scholastic News Nonfiction Readers: Wild Weather Days. 2006. (Scholastic News Nonfiction Readers Ser.). (ENG., Illus.). 24p. (J). (gr. 1-2). lib. bdg. 22.00 (978-0-531-16771-7(2)) Scholastic Library Publishing.

Martin, Emmett. Exploring the Weather, 1 vol. 2018. (So into Science! Ser.). (ENG.). 24p. (gr. k-k). 24.27 (978-1-5382-2889-0(0), 46bc1b8b-5015-47e8-9076-9063e1135ba5) Stevens, Gareth Publishing LLLP.

Mattern, Joanne. What Are Weather & Climate?, 1 vol. 2014. (Let's Find Out! Weather Ser.). (ENG.). 32p. (J). (gr. 2-3). 26.06 (978-1-62275-779-4(3), cb6e0160-cc8e-4374-8411-2169bf2dc9b5, Britannica Educational Publishing) Rosen Publishing Group, Inc., The.

Maynard, Christopher & Martin, Terry. Why Does Lightning Strike? Questions Children Ask about Weather. (Why Bks.). (Illus.). 24p. (J). pap. 10.99 (978-0-590-24945-4(2)) Scholastic, Inc.

McAneney, Caitie. Graphing the Weather, 1 vol. 2013. (Rosen Readers Ser.). (ENG.). 24p. (J). (gr. 3-3). pap. 8.25 (978-1-4777-2441-5(9), 3535d5ff-f2c5-4f4d-8baa-e4df9702d4a7, Rosen Classroom) Rosen Publishing Group, Inc., The.

—Precipitation, 1 vol. 2016. (Where's the Water? Ser.). (ENG., Illus.). 24p. (J). (gr. 2-3). pap. 9.15 (978-1-4824-4684-5(7), 66e210d4-eb3d-4435-aef4-00076d9214c8); lib. bdg. 24.27 (978-1-4824-4686-9(3), cd38b477-9d2c-4857-aea9-a25f63db3ed2) Stevens, Gareth Publishing LLLP.

—20 Fun Facts about Weather, 1 vol. 2017. (Fun Fact File: Earth Science Ser.). (ENG.). 32p. (J). (gr. 2-3). pap. 11.50 (978-1-5382-1193-9(9), afc8a026-daed-4203-be71-c2de997be78f) Stevens, Gareth Publishing LLLP.

McAneney, Caitlin. Graphing the Weather. 2013. (Rosen Readers Ser.). (ENG.). 24p. (J). (gr. 3-4). pap. 49.50 (978-1-4777-2443-9(5), Rosen Classroom) Rosen Publishing Group, Inc., The.

McAuliffe, Bill. Forecasting. 2017. (X-Books: Weather Ser.). (ENG., Illus.). 32p. (J). (gr. 3-6). pap. 9.99 (978-1-62832-427-3(9), 20406, Creative Paperbacks) Creative Co., The.

McDonald, Jill. Hello, World! Weather. 2016. (Hello, World! Ser.). (Illus.). 26p. (J). (— 1). bds. 8.99 (978-0-553-52101-6(2), Doubleday Bks. for Young Readers) Random Hse. Children's Bks.

McDonnell, Rory. Matemáticas con el Tiempo / Math with Weather, 1 vol. de la Vega, Eida, tr. 2016. (¡Matemáticas en Todas Partes! / Math Is Everywhere! Ser.). (ENG & SPA.). 24p. (gr. k-k). lib. bdg. 24.27 (978-1-4824-5212-9(X), 8f9cd20b-92eb-4f25-937d-14a8e1f8e051) Stevens, Gareth Publishing LLLP.

McHale, Scarlett. Brady Makes a Weather Graph, 1 vol. 2013. (InfoMax Readers Ser.). (ENG., Illus.). 24p. (J). (gr. 3-3). pap. 8.25 (978-1-4777-2460-6(5), 26d846c0-5d3a-4250-91d4-658dcbe8357a, Rosen Classroom) Rosen Publishing Group, Inc., The.

McMahon, Michael. Why Does Thunder Clap?, 1 vol. 2010. (Solving Science Mysteries Ser.). (ENG., Illus.). 24p. (gr. 4-5). (J). pap. 9.25 (978-1-4488-0407-8(8), 80cf9159-c55a-49dc-983e-35c0654e51b3, PowerKids Pr.); (YA). 26.27 (978-1-4488-0406-1(X), 51889875-75fb-491b-9f44-d5a9a3a9caff) Rosen Publishing Group, Inc., The.

Meachen Rau, Dana. Air, 1 vol. 2009. (Earth Matters Ser.). (ENG.). 32p. (gr. 1-2). pap. 9.23 (978-0-7614-3568-6(9), a5644f2f-f85a-49aa-a04c-5df4e8acdcb5); lib. bdg. 25.50 (978-0-7614-3042-1(3), 023fb073-70cd-415c-8471-980deef96c0a) Cavendish Square Publishing LLC.

—El Aire / Air, 1 vol. 2010. (Nuestro Planeta Es Importante / Earth Matters Ser.). (ENG & SPA.). 32p. (gr. 1-2). lib. bdg. 25.50 (978-0-7614-3488-7(7), d838b490-a186-4917-b660-ffe12fd51b8a) Cavendish Square Publishing LLC.

—El Aire (Air), 1 vol. 2010. (Nuestro Planeta Es Importante (Earth Matters) Ser.). (SPA.). 32p. (gr. 1-2). lib. bdg. 25.50 (978-0-7614-3464-1(X), 4c62faa2-77ae-42a5-be89-cc5226e992b5) Cavendish Square Publishing LLC.

Mehling, Randi. Weather, & How It Works. 2007. (Scientific American Ser.). (ENG., Illus.). 72p. (gr. 5-9). lib. bdg. 30.00 (978-0-7910-9053-4(1), P114520, Facts On File) Infobase Holdings, Inc.

Meister, Cari. Droughts. 2015. (Illus.). 24p. (J). lib. bdg. (978-1-62031-224-7(7)) Jump! Inc.

Meses y Estaciones. (Coleccion Picaros Peluchines). (SPA.). (J). 5.50 (978-950-11-0401-1(X), SGM401) Sigmar ARG. Dist: Continental Bk. Co., Inc.

Michaels, Pat. W Is for Wind: A Weather Alphabet. Rose, Melanie, illus. rev. ed. (Science Alphabet Ser.). (ENG.). 40p. (J). (gr. 1-4). 2006. pap. 7.95 (978-1-58536-330-8(8), 202293) 2005. 16.95 (978-1-58536-237-0(9), 202061) Sleeping Bear Pr.

Michele, Tracey. Measure the Weather. 2011. (Learn-Abouts Ser.). (Illus.). 16p. (J). pap. 7.95 (978-1-59920-641-7(2)) Black Rabbit Bks.

Milbourne, Anna. The Snowy Day. Temporin, Elena, illus. 2005. 24p. (J). (gr. -1-3). 9.99 (978-0-7945-1147-0(3), Usborne) EDC Publishing.

Mills, Nathan & Frampton, Callie. Tools Tell the Weather, 1 vol. 2012. (Rosen Readers Ser.). (ENG., Illus.). 24p. (J). (gr. 1-1). pap. 8.25 (978-1-4488-8800-9(X), 475f84a4-211d-4937-9a2a-cc5f53ea5114, Rosen Classroom) Rosen Publishing Group, Inc., The.

Mills, Nathan & Waters, Grace. The Changing Weather, 1 vol. 2012. (Rosen Readers Ser.). (ENG., Illus.). 16p. (J). (gr. k-k). pap. 7.00 (978-1-4488-8749-1(6), 1c4643ef-4b38-49b5-9626-dfec64dd1d26, Rosen Classroom) Rosen Publishing Group, Inc., The.

Mogil, H. Michael & Levine, Barbara G. Extreme Weather. 2011. (Insiders Ser.). (ENG., Illus.). 64p. (J). (gr. 3-7). 19.99 (978-1-4424-3274-1(8), Simon & Schuster Bks. For Young Readers) Simon & Schuster Bks. For Young Readers.

Montgomery, Sharon, text. Your Invisible Bodies: A Reference Book for Children & Adults about Human Energy Fields. 2011. (Illus.). (978-0-9811089-2-6(X)) Words By Montgomery.

Mooney, Carla. Becoming Invisible: From Camouflage to Cloaks. 2010. (Great Idea Ser.). 48p. (J). (gr. 4-6). lib. bdg. 26.60 (978-1-59953-378-0(2)) Norwood Hse. Pr.

—Climate & Weather. 2012. (Let's Explore Science Ser.). (ENG.). 48p. (gr. 4-6). pap. 10.95 (978-1-61810-258-4(3), 9781618102584) Rourke Educational Media.

Moore, Phillip. What Is Weather? 2012. (Level B Ser.). (ENG., Illus.). 16p. (J). (gr. k-2). pap. 7.95 (978-1-927136-16-4(4), 19424) RiverStream Publishing.

Morris, Neil. Weather. 2003. (Knowledge Masters Ser.). (Illus.). 32p. (YA). pap. incl. cd-rom (978-1-903954-52-2(5), Pavilion Children's Books) Pavilion Bks.

Murray, Julie. Blizzards. 2017. (Wild Weather Ser.). (ENG., Illus.). 24p. (J). (gr. k-4). lib. bdg. 31.36 (978-1-5321-2085-5(0), 26768, Abdo Zoom-Dash) ABDO Publishing Co.

National Geographic Kids. National Geographic Kids Look & Learn: Look Outside! 2017. (Look & Learn Ser.). (Illus.). 24p. (J). (gr. -1-k). bds. 6.99 (978-1-4263-2702-5(1), National Geographic Kids) Disney Publishing Worldwide.

National Geographic Learning. Reading Expeditions (Science: Earth Science): Extreme Weather. 2007. (ENG., Illus.). 32p. (J). pap. 18.95 (978-0-7922-4575-9(X)) CENGAGE Learning.

—Reading Expeditions (Science: Earth Science): Introduction to Weather. 2007. (Nonfiction Reading & Writing Workshops Ser.). (ENG., Illus.). 32p. (J). pap. 18.95 (978-0-7922-4800-2(7)) CENGAGE Learning.

—Reading Expeditions (Science: Earth Science): Weather & Climate. 2006. (Nonfiction Reading & Writing Workshops Ser.). (ENG., Illus.). 32p. (J). pap. 18.95 (978-0-7922-8876-3(9)) CENGAGE Learning.

Newson, Lesley & Wadsworth, Pamela. Rhagor Am Greigiau, Pridd a Thywydd. 2005. (WEL., Illus.). 24p. pap. (978-1-85596-238-5(1)) Dref Wen.

Nunn, Daniel. True or False? Weather. 2013. (True or False? Ser.). (ENG.). 24p. (J). (gr. -1-1). lib. bdg. 25.32 (978-1-4109-5070-3(0), 121300, Raintree) Capstone.

Oard, Michael. The New Weather Book. 2015. (Illus.). 96p. (J). (gr. 9-12). 18.99 (978-0-89051-861-8(0), Master Books) New Leaf Publishing Group.

OLIVER, Clare. Weather. 2014. (100 Facts You Should Know Ser.). 48p. (J). (gr. 4-6). pap. 84.95 (978-1-4824-1273-4(X)) Stevens, Gareth Publishing LLLP.

Ord, Michael. The Weather Book. 2006. (Wonders of Creation Ser.). 72p. pap. 3.99 (978-1-893345-59-1(9)) Answers In Genesis.

Orero, Maria Jesus. Nico y Las Estaciones. 2006. (Nico Collection). (SPA & ESP., Illus.). 12p. (gr. -1-2). per., bds. 6.99 (978-84-272-6154-9(3)) Molino, Editorial ESP. Dist: Santillana USA Publishing Co., Inc.

Orme, Helen. Weather. 2010. (Science Everywhere! Ser.). 24p. 24.25 (978-1-84898-293-2(3)) Black Rabbit Bks.

Orr, Tamra B. It Snows. 2015. (Tell Me Why Library). (ENG., Illus.). 24p. (gr. 2-5). 29.21 (978-1-63188-998-1(2), 205904) Cherry Lake Publishing.

—Weather. 2009. (Explorer Library: Science Explorer Ser.). (ENG., Illus.). 32p. (gr. 4-8). lib. bdg. 32.07 (978-1-60279-528-0(2), 200294) Cherry Lake Publishing.

Osborne, Mary Pope. Twisters & Other Terrible Storms: A Nonfiction Companion to Magic Tree House #23: Twister on Tuesday. Osborne, Will & Murdocca, Sal, illus. 2003. (Magic Tree House (R) Fact Tracker Ser.: 8). 128p. (J). (gr. 2-5). 6.99 (978-0-375-81358-0(6), Random Hse. Bks. for Young Readers) Random Hse. Children's Bks.

Owen, Ruth. Science & Craft Projects with Weather, 1 vol. 2013. (Get Crafty Outdoors Ser.). (ENG., Illus.). 32p. (J). (gr. 2-3). 30.27 (978-1-4777-0244-4(X), e641b76d-7079-4d7f-be39-794b3ed78831); pap. 12.75 (978-1-4777-0251-2(2), 9a0898fe-fbdf-42c2-be9a-3d6c6a53639c) Rosen Publishing Group, Inc., The. (PowerKids Pr.).

Oxlade, Chris. Why Why Why Do Tornadoes Spin. 2008. 32p. pap. (978-1-84810-004-6(3)) Miles Kelly Publishing, Ltd.

—Why Why Why... Do Tornadoes Spin? 2010. (Why Why Why Ser.). 32p. (J). (gr. 1-3). lib. bdg. 18.95 (978-1-4222-1586-9(5)) Mason Crest.

—Wild Weather: Band 11/Lime. 2015. (Collins Big Cat Ser.). (ENG.). 32p. (J). (gr. 2-2). pap. 10.99 (978-0-00-759128-2(4)) HarperCollins Pubs. Ltd. GBR. Dist: Independent Pubs. Group.

Palmer, Kristin. Wild Weather Trivia. 2013. (Ultimate Trivia Challenge Ser.). 32p. (J). (gr. 2-5). pap. 63.00 (978-1-4339-8306-1(0)); (ENG., Illus.). pap. 11.50 (978-1-4339-8305-4(2), b4b685c9-7bbb-42c1-be76-3726c9e1a534); (ENG., Illus.). lib. bdg. 27.92 (978-1-4339-8304-7(4), e3b194af-62a6-4e12-ba46-69b661cd7d5b) Stevens, Gareth Publishing LLLP.

Paris, Stephanie. Pop! Air & Water Pressure, 1 vol. 2nd rev. ed. 2013. (TIME for KIDS(r): Informational Text Ser.). (ENG., Illus.). 64p. (J). (gr. 4-8). lib. bdg. 31.96 (978-1-4333-7438-8(2)) Teacher Created Materials, Inc.

Parker, Janice. Weather. 2016. (Illus.). 48p. (J). (978-1-5105-2243-5(3)) SmartBook Media, Inc.

—Weather. 2008. (Science Q & A Ser.). (Illus.). 48p. (YA). (gr. 5-8). pap. 10.95 (978-1-59036-953-1(X)); lib. bdg. 29.05 (978-1-59036-952-4(1)) Weigl Pubs., Inc.

—Weather Q & A. 2013. (J). (978-1-62127-417-9(9)); pap. (978-1-62127-423-0(3)) Weigl Pubs., Inc.

Pebble Books: Our Seasons & Weather. 2005. (YA). (gr. k-3). 712.80 (978-0-7368-4219-8(5), Pebble) Capstone.

Pendergast, George. A Year of Seasons, 1 vol. 2015. (Cycles in Nature Ser.). (ENG., Illus.). 24p. (J). (gr. 1-2). lib. bdg. 24.27 (978-1-4824-1654-1(9), bb89c215-9098-495f-8027-3358f8510d0f) Stevens, Gareth Publishing LLLP.

Peppas, Lynn. How Do Clouds Form?, 1 vol. 2012. (Clouds Close-Up Ser.). (ENG., Illus.). 24p. (J). (gr. 2-2). pap. (978-0-7787-4480-1(9)) Crabtree Publishing Co.

—What Are Cirrus Clouds? 2012. (ENG.). 24p. (J). (978-0-7787-4473-3(6)); (Illus.). (gr. 2-2). pap. (978-0-7787-4478-8(7)) Crabtree Publishing Co.

—What Are Cumulus Clouds?, 1 vol. 2012. (Clouds Close-Up Ser.). (ENG., Illus.). 24p. (J). (gr. 2-2). pap. (978-0-7787-4479-5(5)) Crabtree Publishing Co.

—What Are Stratus Clouds? 2012. (ENG.). 24p. (J). (978-0-7787-4476-4(0)); (Illus.). (gr. 2-2). pap. (978-0-7787-4481-8(7)) Crabtree Publishing Co.

Perritano, John. The Ultimate Book of Dangerous Weather. 2019. (Ultimate Danger Ser.). (Illus.). 80p. (J). (gr. 12). lib. bdg. 34.60 (978-1-4222-4230-8(7)) Mason Crest.

—Wild Weather. 2018. (Red Rhino Nonfiction Ser.). lib. bdg. 20.80 (978-0-606-41254-4(9)) Turtleback.

Peters, Katie. Look at the Rain. 2019. (Let's Look at Weather (Pull Ahead Readers — Nonfiction) Ser.). (ENG., Illus.). 16p. (J). (gr. -1-1). pap. 8.99 (978-1-5415-7323-9(4), 44224a3b-1d8f-4ff9-aca2-b3152aace4fb); lib. bdg. 27.99 (978-1-5415-5835-9(9), 4ecdff1b-df8d-4cfd-8ad2-c35aad74414a) Lerner Publishing Group. (Lerner Pubns.).

—So Many Clouds. 2019. (Let's Look at Weather (Pull Ahead Readers — Nonfiction) Ser.). (ENG., Illus.). 16p. (J). (gr. -1-1). pap. 8.99 (978-1-5415-7322-2(6), 4d8b8862-503a-4379-9567-9dc5ac82e74d); lib. bdg. 27.99 (978-1-5415-5836-6(7), 586a0519-c360-4c9a-b7b1-bb17760de623) Lerner Publishing Group. (Lerner Pubns.).

—The Sun Shines Everywhere. 2019. (Let's Look at Weather (Pull Ahead Readers — Nonfiction) Ser.). (ENG., Illus.). 16p. (J). (gr. -1-1). pap. 8.99 (978-1-5415-7325-3(0), d85b8b82-d262-4284-abf2-2c8b033f8b43); lib. bdg. 27.99 (978-1-5415-5837-3(5), ac652e28-538a-4c55-b992-3989c72d4990) Lerner Publishing Group. (Lerner Pubns.).

—When the Wind Blows. 2019. (Let's Look at Weather (Pull Ahead Readers — Nonfiction) Ser.). (ENG., Illus.). 16p. (J). (gr. -1-1). pap. 8.99 (978-1-5415-7326-0(9), 346e51a9-4d43-4ba8-aa05-e8f9619c48cc); lib. bdg. 27.99 (978-1-5415-5833-5(2), 98aa2769-5367-4fd3-a5e2-8ee7fa9645a4) Lerner Publishing Group. (Lerner Pubns.).

Peterson, Christy. Earth Day & the Environmental Movement: Standing up for Earth. 2020. (ENG., Illus.). 120p. (YA). (gr. 6-12). 37.32 (978-1-5415-5281-4(4), bf83b4b0-89e7-4e20-8075-d6db93d1fb55, Twenty-First Century Bks.) Lerner Publishing Group.

Poole, Hilary W. The Ultimate Book of Dangerous Places. 2019. (Illus.). 80p. (J). (978-1-4222-4224-7(2)) Mason Crest.

Powell, Jillian. Projects with Weather & Seasons, 1 vol. 2014. (Make & Learn Ser.). (ENG., Illus.). 32p. (J). (gr. 4-4). lib. bdg. 29.27 (978-1-4777-7181-5(6), 2f54b9ed-114d-48e3-a826-76e46cead893, PowerKids Pr.) Rosen Publishing Group, Inc., The.

Pugliano-Martin, Carol. Summer to Fall. 2006. (Early Explorers Ser.). (J). pap. (978-1-4108-6102-3(3)) Benchmark Education Co.

Purdie, Kate. Sunshine & Drought, 1 vol. 2010. (Weatherwise Ser.). (ENG.). 32p. (gr. 4-4). (J). pap. 11.60 (978-1-61532-278-7(7), c3a6e697-fb3b-48d5-b174-35946350cac0, PowerKids Pr.); (Illus.). (YA). lib. bdg. 30.27 (978-1-61532-266-4(3), 785fa62e-ff1f-4efc-9d6b-9d894d8ef4e7) Rosen Publishing Group, Inc., The.

¿Qué Tiempo Hace?, 8 vols. 2007. (¿Qué Tiempo Hace? (Let's Read about Weather) Ser.). (SPA.). 12p. (gr. k-1). lib. bdg. 70.68 (978-0-8368-8110-3(9), a63b955c-6f6d-4394-8d19-c3bbba139f1b) Stevens, Gareth Publishing LLLP.

Quin, Caroline & Pearce, Sue. Weather. 2004. (Activities for 3-5 Year Olds Ser.). (Illus.). 32p. pap. 11.00 (978-1-897675-39-7(9)) Brilliant Pubns. GBR. Dist: Parkwest Pubns., Inc.

Rabe, Tish. Oh Say Can You Say What's the Weather Today? All about Weather. Ruiz, Aristides, illus. 2004. (Cat in the Hat's Learning Library). (ENG.). 48p. (J). (gr. -1-3). 9.99 (978-0-375-82276-6(3), Random Hse. Bks. for Young Readers) Random Hse. Children's Bks.

Raby, Charlotte. Collins Big Cat Phonics for Letters & Sounds - Pit Pat: Band 01A/Pink A, Bd. 1A. 2018. (Collins Big Cat Phonics Ser.). (ENG., Illus.). 16p. (J). (gr. -1-k). pap. 6.99 (978-0-00-825130-7(4)) HarperCollins Pubs. Ltd. GBR. Dist: Independent Pubs. Group.

Rain or Shine: Level O, 6 vols. (Explorers Ser.). 32p. (gr. 3-6). 44.95 (978-0-7699-0596-9(X)) Shortland Pubns. (U. S. A.) Inc.

Randolph, Joanne. What Are the Elements of Weather?, 1 vol. 2014. (Let's Find Out! Weather Ser.). (ENG., Illus.). 32p. (J). (gr. 2-3). 26.06 (978-1-62275-775-6(0), 125f6a15-526e-4e5f-8cc3-85f9d9509607, Britannica Educational Publishing) Rosen Publishing Group, Inc., The.

Randolph, Joanne, ed. Air Pressure Driving the Weather!, 1 vol. 2017. (Weather Report). (ENG.). 32p. (gr. 3-3). pap. 11.52 (978-0-7660-9005-7(1), 074abaa8-d097-4da8-9688-d1101b89b3a0) Enslow Publishing, LLC.

—Extreme Weather Ahead!, 1 vol. 2017. (Weather Report). (ENG.). 32p. (gr. 3-3). pap. 11.52 (978-0-7660-9009-5(4), c7fae254-da58-4a45-b270-5282ed63b1a4) Enslow Publishing, LLC.

—Northern Lights Sighting!, 1 vol. 2017. (Weather Report). (ENG.). 32p. (gr. 3-3). pap. 11.52 (978-0-7660-9021-7(3), 5645c0d3-8637-4709-9f75-f9cf894a4557) Enslow Publishing, LLC.

Rattini, Kristin Baird. National Geographic Readers - Weather. 2013. (Readers Ser.). (Illus.). 32p. (J). (gr. -1-k). pap. 5.99 (978-1-4263-1348-6(9), National Geographic Kids) Disney Publishing Worldwide.

—National Geographic Readers: Weather. 2013. (Readers Ser.). (ENG., Illus.). 32p. (J). (gr. -1-k). lib. bdg. 14.90 (978-1-4263-1349-3(7), National Geographic Kids) Disney Publishing Worldwide.

Rees, Peter. Why Do Raindrops Fall? Level 3 Factbook. 2010. (Cambridge Young Readers Ser.). (ENG., Illus.). 16p. pap. 6.00 (978-0-521-13714-0(4)) Cambridge Univ. Pr.

Regan, Lisa. A Cool Kid's Field Guide to Weather. Hutchinson, Tim, illus. 2009. (Cool Kid's Field Guide Ser.). 26p. (J). (gr. 1-3). spiral bd. 6.99 (978-0-8416-7147-8(8)) Hammond World Atlas Corp.

Rice, Dona. ¿Qué Tipo de Tiempo? rev. ed. 2010. (Early Literacy Ser.). (SPA., Illus.). 16p. (gr. k-1). (J). 6.99 (978-1-4333-1498-8(3)); 19.99 (978-1-4333-1499-5(1)) Teacher Created Materials, Inc.

—What Kind of Weather?, 1 vol. 2009. (Early Literacy Ser.). (ENG., Illus.). 16p. (gr. k-1). 6.99 (978-1-4333-1458-2(4)) Teacher Created Materials, Inc.

Rice, Dona Herweck. El Tiempo. 2nd rev. ed. 2011. (TIME for KIDS(r): Informational Text Ser.). (SPA.). 12p. (gr. k-1). 7.99 (978-1-4333-4414-5(9)) Teacher Created Materials, Inc.

—Weather, 1 vol. 2nd rev. ed. (TIME for KIDS(r): Informational Text Ser.). (ENG., 12p. (gr. k-1). 2013. Illus.). (J). lib. bdg. 15.96 (978-1-4807-1014-6(8)) 2011. 7.99 (978-1-4333-3575-4(1)) Teacher Created Materials, Inc.

Riechmann, Annie & Smith, Dawn Suzette. Whatever the Weather: Science Experiments & Art Activities That Explore the Wonders of Weather. 2016. (Illus.). 216p. pap. 19.95 (978-1-61180-231-3(8), Roost Books) Shambhala Pubns., Inc.

RIGBY. Look Out the Window: First Grade Big Books. 2003. (Rigby on Our Way to English Ser.). (ENG.). 16p. (gr. 1-1). pap. 50.70 (978-0-7578-1501-0(4)) Rigby Education.

—What Is the Weather Outside? First Grade Big Books. 2003. (Rigby on Our Way to English Ser.). (ENG.). 16p. (gr. 1-1). pap. 50.70 (978-0-7578-1507-2(3)) Rigby Education.

Rigby Education Staff. Hot & Cold. (Sails Literacy Ser.). (Illus.). 16p. (gr. 1-2). 27.00 (978-0-7635-9920-1(4), 699204C99) Rigby Education.

Robertson, Charmaine. Severe Weather, 1 vol. 2016. (Rosen REAL Readers: STEM & STEAM Collection). (ENG.). 12p. (gr. k-1). pap. 6.33 (978-1-5081-2425-2(6), f793ca67-8f7a-43e5-975f-0c4eace24957, Rosen Classroom) Rosen Publishing Group, Inc., The.

Rogers, Paul. What Will the Weather Be Like Today? Kazuko, illus. 2011. (Houghton Mifflin Reading Ser.). 38p. (J). pap. 61.35 (978-0-618-03420-8(X)) Houghton Mifflin Harcourt Trade & Reference Pubs.

Roker, Al. Al Roker's Extreme Weather: Tornadoes, Typhoons, & Other Weather Phenomena. 2017. (ENG., Illus.). 48p. (J). (gr. 3-7). 16.99 (978-0-06-248499-4(0), HarperCollins) HarperCollins Pubs.

Rookie Ready to Learn - Seasons & Weather, 5 vols., Set. Incl. Animal Babies. Hamsa, Bobbie. Dunnington, Tom, illus. 40p. lib. bdg. 23.00 (978-0-531-25640-4(5)); Going to the Beach. Kittinger, Jo S. Warren, Shari, illus. 32p. lib. bdg. 23.00 (978-0-531-25641-1(3)); Pumpkin Fever. Simon, Charnan. Bryan-Hunt, Jan, illus. 40p. lib. bdg. 23.00 (978-0-531-25643-5(X)); Snow Joe. Greene, Carol. Sharp, Paul, illus. 40p. lib. bdg. 23.00 (978-0-531-25644-2(8)); (J). (gr. -1-k). (Rookie Ready to Learn Ser.). 2011. Set lib. bdg. 115.00 (978-0-531-26724-0(5), Children's Pr.) Scholastic Library Publishing.

Rosa-Mendoza, Gladys. The Weather. Cifuentes, Carolina, ed. Hullinger, C. D., illus. 2004. (English-Spanish Foundations Ser.: Vol. 6). Orig. Title: El Tiempo. (ENG & SPA.). 20p. (J). (gr. -1-4). bds. 6.95 (978-0-9679748-5-9(2)) Me+Mi Publishing.

—The Weather, 1 vol. Hullinger, C. D., illus. 2010. (My World Ser.). Orig. Title: El Tiempo. (ENG.). 24p. (J). (gr. k-1). pap. 9.15 (978-1-61533-043-0(7), 9ee53439-d8f9-4de1-86dc-0f429826775c); lib. bdg. 27.27 (978-1-60754-955-0(7), dcfb05c6-3db8-4541-b372-eb91bed0f506) Rosen Publishing Group, Inc., The. (Windmill Bks.).

Rose, Emma. Warning! Set: Extreme Weather, 6 vols. 2004. (Phonics Readers Books 37-72 Ser.). (ENG.). 8p. (gr. k-1). pap. 35.70 (978-0-7368-4074-3(5)) Capstone.

Ross, Kathy. Crafts for Kids Who Are Learning about Weather. Barger, Jan, illus. 2006. (Crafts for Kids Who Are Learning about Ser.). 47p. (J). (gr. 3-6). lib. bdg. 25.26 (978-0-7613-2796-7(7)) Lerner Publishing Group.

Rowell, Rebecca. Weather & Climate Through Infographics. Dean, Venitia, illus. 2013. (Super Science Infographics Ser.). (ENG.). 32p. (J). (gr. 3-5). lib. bdg. 26.65 (978-1-4677-1292-7(2), 643f07a8-6cce-4132-89eb-9d7cd5d35c42, Lerner Pubns.) Lerner Publishing Group.

Rustad, Martha E. H. Diversión en el Clima de Otoño (Fall Weather Fun) Enright, Amanda, illus. 2019. (Diversión en Otoño (Fall Fun) (Early Bird Stories (tm) en Español) Ser.). (SPA.). 24p. (J). (gr. k-2). 29.32 (978-1-5415-4084-2(0), ee58ccd5-fdd2-49cd-bc7a-6832ac236e29, Ediciones Lerner) Lerner Publishing Group.

—Fall Weather Fun. Enright, Amanda, illus. 2018. (Fall Fun (Early Bird Stories (tm)) Ser.). (ENG.). 24p. (J). (gr. k-2). pap. 9.99 (978-1-5415-2722-5(4), 09a3c235-0999-4d43-a779-5f0770bec0f6); lib. bdg. 29.32 (978-1-5415-2005-9(X), f42426aa-be25-452e-bb6a-21f841f1de5c, Lerner Pubns.) Lerner Publishing Group.

—Rainbows. 2017. (Amazing Sights of the Sky Ser.). (ENG., Illus.). 24p. (J). (gr. -1-2). pap. 6.95 (978-1-5157-6756-5(6), 135293, Capstone Pr.) Capstone.

—Today Is a Hot Day. 2017. (What Is the Weather Today? Ser.). (ENG., Illus.). 24p. (J). (gr. -1-2). lib. bdg. 24.65 (978-1-5157-4923-3(1), 134539, Pebble) Capstone.

—Today Is a Rainy Day. 2017. (What Is the Weather Today? Ser.). (ENG., Illus.). 24p. (J). (gr. -1-2). lib. bdg. 24.65 (978-1-5157-4921-9(5), 134537, Pebble) Capstone.

—Today Is a Snowy Day. 2017. (What Is the Weather Today? Ser.). (ENG., Illus.). 24p. (J). (gr. -1-2). lib. bdg. 24.65 (978-1-5157-4919-6(3), 134535, Pebble) Capstone.

—Today Is a Sunny Day. 2017. (What Is the Weather Today? Ser.). (ENG., Illus.). 24p. (J). (gr. -1-2). lib. bdg. 24.65 (978-1-5157-4920-2(7), 134536, Pebble) Capstone.

—Today Is a Windy Day. 2017. (What Is the Weather Today? Ser.). (ENG., Illus.). 24p. (J). (gr. k-2). pap. 6.29 (978-1-4966-0945-8(X), 134532, Pebble) Capstone.

—Weather in Spring, 1 vol. 2012. (All about Spring Ser.). (ENG.). 24p. (J). (gr. -1-2). pap. 7.29 (978-1-4296-9364-6(9), 120387); (gr. k-1). pap. 43.74 (978-1-4296-9365-3(7), 18577) Capstone. (Capstone Pr.).

—What Is the Weather Today? 2017. (What Is the Weather Today? Ser.). (ENG., Illus.). 24p. (J). (gr. k-2). pap., pap., pap. 45.84 (978-1-4966-0955-7(7), 26007, Pebble) Capstone.

—When Will It Rain? Noticing Weather Patterns. Conger, Holli, illus. 2015. (Cloverleaf Books (tm) — Nature's Patterns Ser.). (ENG.). 24p. (J). (gr. k-2). 25.32 (978-1-4677-8557-0(1), 79b34a2b-c15d-4a2d-a7c5-b41e3ea68f59, Millbrook Pr.) Lerner Publishing Group.

Salas, Laura Purdie. Colors of Weather. 2011. (Colors All Around Ser.). (ENG.). 32p. (gr. 1-2). pap. 47.70 (978-1-4296-6158-4(5), Capstone Pr.) Capstone.

Santos, Rita, ed. Geoengineering: Counteracting Climate Change, 1 vol. 2018. (Global Viewpoints Ser.). (ENG.). 176p. (gr. 10-12). 47.83 (978-1-5345-0346-5(3), 9a0dca9e-bd78-4ff1-98bd-6af222801c74) Greenhaven Publishing LLC.

Scholastic Clubs US Weather Watch Pack (exc. Snow) Weather Watch. 2006. (J). pap. 31.80 (978-1-59566-320-7(7)) QEB Publishing Inc.

Schuetz, Kristin. Humidity. 2015. (Understanding Weather Ser.). (ENG., Illus.). 24p. (J). (gr. k-3). lib. bdg. 26.95 (978-1-62617-252-4(8), Blastoff! Readers) Bellwether Media.

Schuh, Mari. I Feel Fall Weather. 2016. (First Step Nonfiction — Observing Fall Ser.). (ENG., Illus.). 24p. (J). (gr. k-2). 23.99 (978-1-5124-0797-6(6), 8fb0eb1f-79e9-4770-a953-bd2d0a2c359d, Lerner Pubns.) Lerner Publishing Group.

—Weather in Fall. 2013. (ENG., Illus.). 24p. (J). lib. bdg. 25.65 (978-1-62031-061-8(9)) Jump! Inc.

The Science of Weather. 2004. (Illus.). lib. bdg. 7.95 (978-0-8225-4341-1(9)) Lerner Publishing Group.

Sengupta, Monalisa. Wild Weather. (Wild Nature Ser.). 48p. (gr. 4-5). 2009. 53.00 (978-1-60854-796-8(5), PowerKids Pr.) 2007. (ENG., Illus.). (YA). lib. bdg. 32.93 (978-1-4042-3902-9(2), 7ced16c0-db87-452f-a550-cdc4f4e0410b) Rosen Publishing Group, Inc., The.

Sesame Workshop Staff. Toddler Time Explore Seasons with Cookie Monster. 2011. (J). (gr. k-1). pap. 3.99 (978-1-59922-883-9(1)) Twin Sisters IP, LLC.

Shea, Therese M. Freaky Weather Stories, 1 vol. 2015. (Freaky True Science Ser.). (ENG.). 32p. (J). (gr. 4-5). pap. 11.50 (978-1-4824-2968-8(3), b3c64bfa-3c3a-417a-9da9-882b0b3dd071) Stevens, Gareth Publishing LLLP.

Shoals, James. Extreme Weather. 2019. (Illus.). 48p. (J). (978-1-4222-4355-8(9)) Mason Crest.

Shofner, Melissa Raé. Weather & Natural Disasters, 1 vol. 2016. (Spotlight on Earth Science Ser.). (ENG.). 24p. (J). (gr. 4-6). pap. 11.00 (978-1-4994-2547-5(3), 26838812-6f83-43bd-b67e-37beffbea773, PowerKids Pr.) Rosen Publishing Group, Inc., The.

Shulman, Mark. Wicked Weather. 2007. (Illus.). 48p. (J). per. 6.99 (978-0-696-23689-1(3)) Meredith Bks.

Sian Revision Weather Wise. 2004. (J). (978-1-59242-085-8(0)) Delta Education, LLC.

Silverstein, Alvin, et al. Weather & Climate. 2007. (Science Concepts, Second Ser.). (Illus.). 96p. (J). (gr. 6-8). lib. bdg. 31.93 (978-0-8225-6796-7(2), Twenty-First Century Bks.) Lerner Publishing Group.

Simon, Seymour. Weather. 2006. (ENG., Illus.). 40p. (J). (gr. k-4). pap. 8.99 (978-0-06-088439-0(8), HarperCollins) HarperCollins Pubs.

Singer, Marilyn. On the Same Day in March. 2014. 17.00 (978-1-63419-675-8(9)) Perfection Learning Corp.

Slade, Suzanne. How Do Tornadoes Form? And Other Questions Kids Have about Weather, 1 vol. Pillo, Cary, illus. 2010. (Kids' Questions Ser.). (ENG.). 24p. (J). (gr. k-2). pap. 7.49 (978-1-4048-6731-4(7), 115556, Picture Window Bks.) Capstone.

Smith, Alastair & Clarke, Phillip. Weather: With Internet Links. 2006. (Usborne Spotter's Guides). (Illus.). 64p. (J). (gr. 2). lib. bdg. 13.99 (978-1-58086-915-7(7), Usborne) EDC Publishing.

Smith, Ben. Who Listens to the Weather Forecast? 2012. (Level D Ser.). (ENG., Illus.). 16p. (J). (gr. k-2). pap. 7.95 (978-1-927136-36-2(9), 19452) RiverStream Publishing.

Snedeker, Joseph. The Everything KIDS' Weather Book: From Tornadoes to Snowstorms, Puzzles, Games, & Facts That Make Weather for Kids Fun! 2012. (Everything(r) Kids Ser.). (ENG., Illus.). 144p. pap. 9.99 (978-1-4405-5036-2(0), Everything) Adams Media Corp.

Sohn, Emily. Air & Weather. 2019. (IScience Ser.). (ENG., Illus.). 24p. (J). (gr. k-2). pap. 13.26 (978-1-68404-356-9(5)) Norwood Hse. Pr.

—Experiments in Earth Science & Weather with Toys & Everyday Stuff. 2015. (Fun Science Ser.). (ENG., Illus.). 24p. (J). (gr. 1-3). lib. bdg. 27.99 (978-1-4914-5035-2(5), 128759, Capstone Pr.) Capstone.

Spalding, Maddie. Weather in Summer. 2018. (Welcoming the Seasons Ser.). (ENG.). 24p. (J). (gr. -1-2). lib. bdg. 32.79 (978-1-5038-2383-9(0), 212226) Child's World, Inc, The.

Spalding, Maddie & Willis, John. Weather. 2018. (Illus.). 24p. (J). pap. (978-1-4896-9686-1(5), AV2 by Weigl) Weigl Pubs., Inc.

Spilsbury, Louise. Threats to Our Water Supply. 2009. (J). 70.50 (978-1-4358-5481-9(0)); (ENG.). 48p. (YA). (gr. 5-5). pap. 12.75 (978-1-4358-5480-2(2), c40b1ed0-a7d0-4b4c-9bd5-543d9b6c912c); (ENG., Illus.). 48p. (J). (gr. 5-5). lib. bdg. 34.47 (978-1-4358-5352-2(0), f45f6412-95ab-4ff3-9d8d-e29a74ec15a3) Rosen Publishing Group, Inc., The.

—What Is Weather?, 1 vol., 1. 2013. (Let's Find Out! Earth Science Ser.). (ENG.). 32p. (gr. 2-3). 27.04 (978-1-62275-276-8(7), 9b45661a-9f43-48d4-86c0-42b40e909488) Rosen Publishing Group, Inc., The.

Spilsbury, Richard. Ask an Expert: Climate Change. 2010. (Crabtree Connections Ser.). (ENG.). 24p. (J). (gr. 3-6). (978-0-7787-9938-2(7)); pap. (978-0-7787-9960-3(3)) Crabtree Publishing Co.

Spilsbury, Richard & Spilsbury, Louise. Weather & Seasons, 1 vol. 2018. (Flowchart Smart Ser.). (ENG.). 48p. (gr. 4-5). pap. 15.05 (978-1-5382-3482-2(3), 47e5a693-74a0-4796-a037-bcdc2e31bef0) Stevens, Gareth Publishing LLLP.

Squire, Ann O. Extreme Weather (a True Book: Extreme Science) (Library Edition) 2014. (True Book (Relaunch) Ser.). (ENG.). 48p. (J). (gr. 3-5). lib. bdg. 31.00 (978-0-531-20743-7(9), Children's Pr.) Scholastic Library Publishing.

Staff, Gareth Editorial Staff. Weather & Climate, 1 vol. 2004. (Discovery Channel School Science: Our Planet Earth Ser.). (ENG., Illus.). 32p. (gr. 5-7). lib. bdg. 28.67 (978-0-8368-3386-7(4), dc80d651-0b67-4d66-8be7-b34068a9c905, Gareth Stevens Learning Library) Stevens, Gareth Publishing LLLP.

Steck-Vaughn Staff. Stormy Weather. 2003. pap. 4.10 (978-0-7398-7637-4(6)) Steck-Vaughn.

Stein, Paul. Droughts of the Future. 2009. (Library of Future Weather & Climate Ser.). 64p. (gr. 5-5). 58.50 (978-1-60853-644-3(0)) Rosen Publishing Group, Inc., The.

Steps To Literacy Staff, compiled by. Weather Series: Capv210. 2005. (ENG., Illus.). (J). pap. (978-1-60015-015-9(2)) Steps To Literacy, LLC.

—What Kind of Day Is It? Collection: Capv204. 2005. (ENG., Illus.). (J). pap. (978-1-60015-014-2(4)) Steps To Literacy, LLC.

Stille, Darlene R. Weather, 1 vol. 2012. (Science Behind Ser.). (ENG.). 32p. (J). (gr. 2-4). pap. 8.29 (978-1-4109-4498-6(0), 117691, Raintree) Capstone.

Storad, Conrad J. Studying Weather & Climates. 2011. (My Science Library). (ENG., Illus.). 24p. (gr. 2-3). pap. 9.95 (978-1-61741-951-5(6), 9781617419515) Rourke Educational Media.

—What's the Weather Like Today? 2011. (My Science Library). (ENG., Illus.). 24p. (gr. 1-2). pap. 9.95 (978-1-61741-939-3(7), 9781617419393) Rourke Educational Media.

Stradling, Jan. Erosion & Weathering: Level K, 6 vols., Vol. 2. (First Explorers Ser.). 24p. (gr. 1-2). 34.95 (978-0-7699-1457-2(8)) Shortland Pubns. (U. S. A.) Inc.

Strain Trueit, Trudi. Stormy Days, 1 vol. 2010. (Weather Watch Ser.). (ENG.). 24p. (gr. k-1). 25.50 (978-0-7614-4016-1(X), 6024ae98-d454-46fb-90a1-06a60b28470a) Cavendish Square Publishing LLC.

—Windy Days, 1 vol. 2010. (Weather Watch Ser.). (ENG.). 24p. (gr. k-1). 25.50 (978-0-7614-4020-8(8), 6b467ae4-419d-4039-a563-ac25908586d2) Cavendish Square Publishing LLC.

Sundance/Newbridge LLC Staff. Our Sun, Our Weather. 2007. (Early Science Ser.). (gr. k-3). 18.95 (978-1-4007-6531-7(5)); pap. 6.10 (978-1-4007-6527-0(7)) Sundance/Newbridge Educational Publishing.

—Who Cares about the Weather? 2007. (Early Science Ser.). (gr. k-3). 18.95 (978-1-4007-6413-6(0)); pap. 6.10 (978-1-4007-6409-9(2)) Sundance/Newbridge Educational Publishing.

Teckentrup, Britta. Look at the Weather. Tanaka, Shelley, tr. from GER. 2018. Orig. Title: Alle Wetter. (ENG., Illus.). 152p. (J). (gr. 1-6). 21.95 (978-1-77147-286-9(3)) Owlkids Bks. Inc. CAN. Dist: Publishers Group West (PGW).

This or That? Weather, 6 vols. 2015. (This or That? Weather Ser.: 6). (ENG.). 24p. (J). (gr. k-4). lib. bdg. 196.74 (978-1-62403-952-2(9), 19560, Super SandCastle) ABDO Publishing Co.

Tiempo extremo (Wild Weather), 8 vols. 2009. (Tiempo Extremo (Wild Weather) Ser.). (SPA.). 24p. (J). (gr. 1-1). lib. bdg. 98.68 (978-1-4339-2359-3(9), 93a8f119-be67-4ffd-88c8-366348ff1d16, Weekly Reader Leveled Readers) Stevens, Gareth Publishing LLLP.

Time for Kids Editors. TIME for Kids Weather Kit. 2013. (ENG.). 48p. (J). (gr. 3-17). 21.95 (978-1-61893-011-8(7)) Time Inc. Bks.

Time for Kids Magazine Staff, ed. Storms! 2006. (Time for Kids Science Scoops Ser.). (Illus.). 32p. (gr. 1-3). 14.00 (978-0-7569-6674-4(4)) Perfection Learning Corp.

Top That Publishing Staff, ed. Weather Watch. 2004. (Fun Kits Ser.). (Illus.). 48p. (J). (978-1-84510-131-2(6)) Top That! Publishing PLC.

Townsend, John. Is Our Weather Getting Worse? 2010. (Crabtree Connections Ser.). (ENG.). 24p. (J). (gr. 3-6). (978-0-7787-9957-3(3)); pap. (978-0-7787-9979-5(4)) Crabtree Publishing Co.

Trumbauer, Lisa. Weathering & Erosion. 2005. (J). pap. (978-1-4108-4600-6(8)) Benchmark Education Co.

Vail, Grace. More Freaky Weather Stories, 1 vol. 2019. (Freaky True Science Ser.). (ENG.). 32p. (gr. 4-5). pap. 11.50 (978-1-5382-4074-8(2), 5b669164-55c7-492b-92c6-e77ac1d84f03) Stevens, Gareth Publishing LLLP.

Vilardi, Debbie. What Makes a Rainbow? 2019. (Science Questions Ser.). (ENG., Illus.). 24p. (J). (gr. 1-1). pap. 8.95 (978-1-64185-586-0(X), 164185586X) North Star Editions.

—What Makes a Rainbow? 2018. (Science Questions Ser.). (ENG., Illus.). 24p. (J). (gr. k-3). lib. bdg. 31.36 (978-1-5321-6215-2(4), 30213, Pop! Cody Koala) Pop!

Wadsworth, Pamela. Creigiau, Pridd a Thywydd. 2005. (WEL., Illus.). 24p. pap. (978-1-85596-237-8(3)) Dref Wen.

Wadsworth, Pamela & Tate, Sylvia. Golwg Gyntaf Ar Greigiau, Pridd a Thywydd. 2005. (WEL., Illus.). 24p. pap. (978-1-85596-253-8(5)) Dref Wen.

Waldron, Melanie. Mapping the Land & Weather, 1 vol. 2013. (Let's Get Mapping! Ser.). (ENG., Illus.). 32p. (J). (gr. 2-4). pap. 8.29 (978-1-4109-4909-7(5), 120891, Raintree) Capstone.

Walker, Kate. Weather, 1 vol. 2012. (Investigating Earth Ser.). (ENG.). 32p. (gr. 2-2). 31.21 (978-1-60870-563-4(3), 97378983-e1f3-442c-9e51-51aeb7e1192c) Cavendish Square Publishing LLC.

Walker, Nan. Weather. 2010. (Illus.). 24p. (J). (978-0-545-27360-2(9)) Scholastic, Inc.

Wallace, Jessica. Weather: KinderConcepts Individual Title Six-Packs. Ross, Christine, illus. (Kinderstarters Ser.). 8p. (gr. -1-1). 21.00 (978-0-7635-8725-3(7)) Rigby Education.

Weather. (Jump Ser.). (Illus.). 32p. (J). (gr. 2-7). pap. (978-1-882210-25-1(5)) Action Publishing, Inc.

Weather. 2005. (Our Seasons & Weather Ser.). (YA). (gr. k-3). 118.80 (978-0-7368-4198-6(9), Pebble) Capstone.

Weather, 6 bks., Set. Incl. Scholastic News Nonfiction Readers: Wild Weather Days. Marsico, Katie. lib. bdg. 22.00 (978-0-531-16771-7(2)); Sunny Weather Days. Rosenberg, Pam. lib. bdg. 22.00 (978-0-531-16770-0(4)); 24p. (J). (gr. 1-2). (Scholastic News Nonfiction Readers Ser.). (Illus.). 2006. 114.00 o.p. (978-0-531-12473-4(8), Children's Pr.) Scholastic Library Publishing.

Weather: Individual Title Six-Packs. (Chiquilibros Ser.). (gr. k-1). 23.00 (978-0-7635-0416-8(5)) Rigby Education.

Weather & Seasons Classroom Library. (gr. k-2). lib. bdg. 128.95 (978-0-7368-1828-5(6), Red Brick Learning) Capstone.

Weather & Seasons Complete Program. (gr. k-2). 642.95 (978-0-7368-1829-2(4), Red Brick Learning) Capstone.

Weather Around You, 8 vols. 2004. (Weather Around You Ser.). (ENG.). 24p. (gr. 2-4). lib. bdg. 98.68 (978-0-8368-4298-2(7), a8dc19a4-77d5-4271-9c3e-8056399bc68f, Weekly Reader Leveled Readers) Stevens, Gareth Publishing LLLP.

Weather Facts. 2004. (Pocket Guides). 160p. (J). pap. 6.95 (978-0-328-09817-0(5), Scott Foresman) Addison Wesley Schl.

Weather Instructional Guide. 2009. (Grade 8: Science Exit Project Kits Ser.). spiral bd. (978-1-4042-4024-7(1), Rosen Classroom) Rosen Publishing Group, Inc., The.

The Weather Report. 2017. (Weather Report). 32p. (gr. 3-3). pap. 63.12 (978-0-7660-9036-1(1)); (ENG.). lib. bdg. 161.58 (978-0-7660-9035-4(3), c561aa13-341e-43df-9a3a-f0a8b4126f7e) Enslow Publishing, LLC.

Weather Sets: 1 Each of 3 Big Books. (Sunshinetm Science Ser.). (gr. 1-2). (978-0-7802-1451-4(X)) Wright Group/McGraw-Hill.

Weather Sets: 1 Each of 3 Student Books. (Sunshinetm Science Ser.). (gr. 1-2). 20.95 (978-0-7802-1753-9(5)) Wright Group/McGraw-Hill.

Weather Update [Kaplan]. 2010. (Weather Update Ser.). pap. 41.70 (978-1-4296-5972-7(6), Capstone Pr.) Capstone.

Weather Watching: Level P, 6 vols., Vol. 3. (Explorers Ser.). 32p. (gr. 3-6). 44.95 (978-0-7699-0618-8(4)) Shortland Pubns. (U. S. A.) Inc.

West, David & Parker, Steve. Natural Disasters, 1 vol. 2011. (ENG., Illus.). 32p. (J). pap. (978-0-7787-7581-2(X)); pap. (978-0-7787-7579-9(8)); lib. bdg. (978-0-7787-7576-8(3)) Crabtree Publishing Co.

Wetterer, Margaret K. & Wetterer, Charles M. Caminando Bajo la Nieve; the Snow Walker. 2008. pap. 40.95 (978-0-8225-9699-8(7)) Lerner Publishing Group.

What a Week!, 6 packs. (gr. -1-2). 23.00 (978-0-7635-9010-9(X)) Rigby Education.

What Do You Know about Weather & Climate? 2013. (20 Questions: Earth Science Ser.). 24p. (J). (gr. 3-6). pap. 49.50 (978-1-4488-9861-9(7), PowerKids Pr.) Rosen Publishing Group, Inc., The.

What Kind of Day Is It?, Vol. 2. 2005. (Our Seasons & Weather Ser.). (YA). (gr. k-3). 178.20 (978-0-7368-4199-3(7), Pebble) Capstone.

What's the Weather?, 12 vols. 2013. (What's the Weather? Ser.). 24p. (J). (gr. k-k). (ENG.). 151.62 (978-1-4339-9669-6(3), a0e15481-a6d4-464c-83da-72332602c43f); pap. 293.40 (978-1-4339-9840-9(8)); pap. 48.90 (978-1-4339-9839-3(4)) Stevens, Gareth Publishing LLLP.

What's the Weather? / Qu Tiempo Hace?, 12 vols. 2013. (What's the Weather? / ¿Qué Tiempo Hace? Ser.). (SPA & ENG.). 24p. (J). (gr. k-k). 151.62 (978-1-4339-9670-2(7), f165c08b-e743-4128-9c91-af3b2c72492b) Stevens, Gareth Publishing LLLP.

What's the Weather Like?, 10 vols. 2016. (What's the Weather Like? Ser.). 24p. (gr. 1-1). (ENG.). 126.35 (978-1-4994-2429-4(9), 3721797a-4eb7-4499-b526-8abad1c4c5a0); pap. 41.25 (978-1-4994-2493-5(0)) Rosen Publishing Group, Inc., The. (PowerKids Pr.).

Wild Weather, 12 vols. 2009. (Wild Weather Ser.). (ENG.). 24p. (J). (gr. 1-1). lib. bdg. 148.02 (978-1-4339-2352-4(1), 5a9fa7d4-ddf2-484a-8a8d-bd548d22614b, Weekly Reader Leveled Readers) Stevens, Gareth Publishing LLLP.

Wilder, Nellie. Changing Weather, 1 vol. rev. ed. 2014. (Science: Informational Text Ser.). (ENG., Illus.). 24p. (J). (gr. -1-1). pap. 9.99 (978-1-4807-4531-5(6)) Teacher Created Materials, Inc.

—What Is the Weather?, 1 vol. rev. ed. 2014. (Science: Informational Text Ser.). (ENG., Illus.). 24p. (J). (gr. k-1). pap. 9.99 (978-1-4807-4530-8(8)) Teacher Created Materials, Inc.

Williams, Judith. ¿Cómo el Sol Afecta el Clima? / How Does the Sun Make Weather?, 1 vol. 2010. (Me Gusta el Clima / I Like Weather! Ser.). (SPA & ENG.). 24p. (gr. k-2). 26.60 (978-0-7660-3237-8(X), a5804d2a-7141-4c80-82e1-0756de08fa84, Enslow Elementary) Enslow Publishing, LLC.

—Does the Sun Make Weather?, 1 vol. 2014. (How Does Weather Happen? Ser.). (ENG.). 24p. (gr. k-1). pap. 10.35 (978-0-7660-6396-9(8), f3048efa-0c10-4365-bbde-f8bf6f6cc97c); lib. bdg. 24.27 (978-0-7660-6395-2(X), 2c9f6f04-a162-494a-8215-f5d95f2ecef6) Enslow Publishing, LLC. (Enslow Elementary).

Williams, Zella. Experiments on the Weather. (Do-It-Yourself Science Ser.). 24p. (gr. 2-3). 2009. 47.90 (978-1-61512-188-5(9), PowerKids Pr.) 2007. (ENG., Illus.). (J). lib. bdg. 28.93 (978-1-4042-3663-9(5), c9b75c6c-a02f-404c-a62f-8a8dd51b24cd) Rosen Publishing Group, Inc., The.

Woods, Michael. Droughts. 2009. pap. 8.95 (978-0-8225-6864-3(0)) Lerner Publishing Group.

Workman, James G. Water. 2009. (Diminishing Resources Ser.). 111p. (J). lib. bdg. 28.95 (978-1-59935-115-5(3)) Reynolds, Morgan Inc.

World Book, Inc. Staff, contrib. by. Droughts. 2nd ed. 2009. (Illus.). 47p. (J). (978-0-7166-9819-7(6)) World Bk., Inc.

—Forces of Nature. 2007. (J). (978-0-7166-9806-7(4)) World Bk., Inc.

—Learning about Weather. 2011. (J). (978-0-7166-0235-4(0)) World Bk., Inc.

—Weather. (J). 2019. (978-0-7166-3770-7(7)) 2007. (978-0-7166-7732-1(6)) World Bk., Inc.

—Weather & Climate Change. (Illus.). 47p. (J). 2019. (978-0-7166-2767-8(1)) 2015. (978-0-7166-2707-4(8)) World Bk., Inc.

Wynne, Patricia J. & Silver, Donald M. My First Book about Weather. 2016. (Dover Science for Kids Coloring Bks.). (ENG.). 48p. (J). (gr. 3-6). pap. 5.99 (978-0-486-79872-1(0), 798720) Dover Pubns., Inc.

York, M. J. & Willis, John. Weather. 2018. (Illus.). 24p. (J). pap. (978-1-4896-9674-8(1), AV2 by Weigl) Weigl Pubs., Inc.

York, Penelope, et al. Natural World. 2017. (Illus.). (J). (978-1-4654-7288-5(6)) Dorling Kindersley Publishing, Inc.

Zuchora-Walske, Christine. The Dust Bowl: A History Perspectives Book. 2013. (Perspectives Library). (ENG., Illus.). 32p. (J). (gr. 4-8). 32.07 (978-1-62431-417-9(1), 202788); pap. 14.21 (978-1-62431-493-3(7), 202790) Cherry Lake Publishing.

—Weather Robots. 2014. (Lightning Bolt Books (r) — Robots Everywhere! Ser.). (ENG., Illus.). 32p. (J). (gr. 1-3). pap. 9.99 (978-1-4677-4511-6(1), 433d8598-01ff-4b84-aa23-72ae68fbc476) Lerner Publishing Group.

100 Facts You Should Know: Set 3, 12 vols. 2015. (100 Facts You Should Know Ser.). (ENG.). 48p. (J). (gr. 4-5). lib. bdg. 201.60 (978-1-4824-2564-2(5), aeb433a2-ed76-43e5-861f-e862e450f456) Stevens, Gareth Publishing LLLP.

WEATHER—FICTION

Adamson, Ged. Ava & the Rainbow (Who Stayed) 2018. (ENG., Illus.). 40p. (J). (gr. -1-3). 18.99 (978-0-06-267080-9(8), HarperCollins) HarperCollins Pubs.

Agell, Charlotte. Mud, Sand, & Snow, 1 vol. 2019. (ENG., Illus.). 24p. (J). bds. 10.95 (978-1-944762-63-6(9), d78dec78-9cf2-4564-827f-b22713342f84) Islandport Pr., Inc.

Aki. The Weather Girls. Aki, illus. 2018. (ENG., Illus.). 32p. (J). 17.99 (978-1-62779-620-0(7), 900156981, Holt, Henry & Co. Bks. For Young Readers) Holt, Henry & Co.

Bailey, Dawn Wentz. Joey & the Mighty Oak. 2008. 20p. pap. 24.95 (978-1-60813-377-2(X)) PublishAmerica, Inc.

Barclay, Jane. How Cold Was It? 2004. (Illus.). (J). (gr. k-3). spiral bd. (978-0-616-01538-4(0)) Canadian National Institute for the Blind/Institut National Canadien pour les Aveugles.

—How Cold Was It? Donato, Janice, illus. 2004. (J). (gr. k-3). spiral bd. (978-0-616-11862-7(7)) Canadian National Institute for the Blind/Institut National Canadien pour les Aveugles.

Barrett, Judi. Pickles to Pittsburgh: Cloudy with a Chance of Meatballs 2/ Book & CD. Barrett, Ron, illus. 2012. (ENG.). 32p. (J). (gr. -1-3). pap. 9.99 (978-1-4424-4459-1(2), Little Simon) Little Simon.

Barrett, Judith. Cloudy with a Chance of Meatballs. Barrett, Ron, illus. 2011. (Classic Board Bks.). (ENG.). 34p. (J). (gr. -1-k). bds. 8.99 (978-1-4424-3023-5(0), Little Simon) Little Simon.

—Cloudy with a Chance of Meatballs. Barrett, Ron, illus. 2009. 9.00 (978-1-55744-455-4(2), Everbind) Marco Bk. Co.

Cloudy with a Chance of Meatballs: Book & CD. Barrett, Ron, illus. 2012. (ENG.). 32p. (J). (gr. -1-3). pap. 10.99 *(978-1-4424-4337-2(5),* Little Simon) Little Simon.

Cloudy with a Chance of Meatballs 3: Planet of the Pies. Mones, Isidre, illus. 2013. (ENG.). 32p. (J). (gr. -1-3). 18.99 *(978-1-4424-9027-7(6),* Atheneum Bks. for Young Readers) Simon & Schuster Children's Publishing.

-Pickles to Pittsburgh: Cloudy with a Chance of Meatballs 2. Barrett, Ron, illus. 2013. (Classic Board Bks.). (ENG.). 34p. (J). (gr. -1-k). bds. 7.99 *(978-1-4424-6493-3(3),* Little Simon) Little Simon.

-Pickles to Pittsburgh: The Sequel to Cloudy with a Chance of Meatballs. Barrett, Ron, illus. 2004. 26p. (gr. -1-3). 17.00 *(978-0-7569-4215-1(2))* Perfection Learning Corp.

atson, Susann. Scaredy: A Cloud Afraid of Thunder. 2010. 16p. pap. 9.95 *(978-1-61633-053-8(8))* Guardian Angel Publishing, Inc.

ecker, Brooke. The Adventures of Sammy Snowflake, Vol. 1. Gentry, Kyle, illus. 2007. (ENG.). 64p. (gr. 4-7). 19.95 *(978-0-9795260-0-8(0))* Courtyard Publishing, LLC.

Beech, Sandy. Weather's Here, Wish You Were Great, 2. Holder, Jimmy, illus. 2005. (Castaways Ser.). (ENG.). 185p. (J). (gr. 3-6). 17.44 *(978-0-689-87597-7(5))* Simon & Schuster, Inc.

Bishop, Celeste. Hace Sol / It's Sunny, 1 vol. 2016. (¿Qué Tiempo Hace? / What's the Weather Like? Ser.). (ENG & SPA., Illus.). 24p. (J). (gr. 1-1). lib. bdg. 25.27 *(978-1-4994-2330-3(6),* 5aa8873c-8fa0-4d64-8a76-23d926fa4242, PowerKids Pr.) Rosen Publishing Group, Inc., The.

—Hace Sol (It's Sunny), 1 vol. 2016. (¿Qué Tiempo Hace? (What's the Weather Like?) Ser.). (SPA., Illus.). 24p. (J). (gr. 1-1). lib. bdg. 25.27 *(978-1-4994-2326-6(8),* 4d67c389-7b95-43fb-af6c-5473cc0e649e, PowerKids Pr.) Rosen Publishing Group, Inc., The.

—Hace Viento / It's Windy, 1 vol. 2016. (¿Qué Tiempo Hace? / What's the Weather Like? Ser.). (ENG & SPA., Illus.). 24p. (J). (gr. 1-1). lib. bdg. 25.27 *(978-1-4994-2337-2(3),* fdc1cc58-0e3a-4bad-9cc0-3ec3a212c05a, PowerKids Pr.) Rosen Publishing Group, Inc., The.

—Hace Viento (It's Windy), 1 vol. 2016. (¿Qué Tiempo Hace? (What's the Weather Like?) Ser.). (SPA., Illus.). 24p. (J). (gr. 1-1). lib. bdg. 25.27 *(978-1-4994-2333-4(0),* df02b9cb-ce6f-45a4-8f20-2220830d0ea7, PowerKids Pr.) Rosen Publishing Group, Inc., The.

—It's Sunny, 1 vol. 2016. (What's the Weather Like? Ser.). (ENG.). 24p. (gr. 1-1). pap. 9.25 *(978-1-4994-2359-4(4),* 52804292-377c-4bd7-9298-91acdc0f5ed0, PowerKids Pr.) Rosen Publishing Group, Inc., The.

Blackstone, Stella. Bear in Sunshine - Oso Bajo el Sol. Harter, Debbie, illus. 2009. (Bear Ser.). (ENG.). 24p. (J). (gr. -1-1). pap. 8.99 *(978-1-84686-389-9(9))* Barefoot Bks., Inc.

Blcom, Jan, et al. You Track it Weather Lab. Free Jenna Staff, ed. 2012. (ENG.). 12p. 14.99 *(978-1-60380-087-7(5))* becker&mayer! books.

Blotnick, Elihu. The Fog Line. Robinson, Barbara J., illus. 2009. (Mr. Blot Ser.: No. 3). (ENG.). 56p. (YA). (gr. 6-18). pap. 9.00 *(978-0-915090-12-9(0),* California Street) Firefall Editions.

Bolton, Nicola Joanne. The WeatherGens. 2010. (ENG.). 89p. pap. 10.50 *(978-1-4452-7936-7(3))* Lulu Pr., Inc.

Bonnell, Kris. Clouds Tell the Weather. 2007. (J). pap. 5.95 *(978-1-933727-47-9(0))* Reading Reading Bks., LLC.

Brooke, Samantha. Rock Man vs. Weather Man. 2018. (Illus.). 31p. (J). *(978-1-5444-0658-9(4))* Scholastic, Inc.

Cameron, Anne. The Storm Tower Thief. Jamieson, Victoria, illus. 2014. (Lightning Catcher Ser.: 2). (ENG.). 432p. (J). (gr. 3-7). 16.99 *(978-0-06-211279-8(1),* Greenwillow Bks.) HarperCollins Pubs.

Celano, June. Dripsy the Cloud. 2008. 28p. per. 24.95 *(978-1-4241-9958-7(1))* America Star Bks.

Cottrell, Kim. Jimmy Has the Bugaloo Zoo Flu. 2009. 32p. pap. 12.99 *(978-1-4389-5209-3(0))* AuthorHouse.

Cousins, Lucy. Maisy's Wonderful Weather Book. Cousins, Lucy, illus. 2006. (Maisy Ser.). (ENG., Illus.). 14p. (J). (gr. -1). 11.99 *(978-0-7636-2987-8(1))* Candlewick Pr.

Crews, Donald. Cloudy Day Sunny Day. Crews, Donald, illus. 2003. (Green Light Readers Level 1 Ser.). (ENG., Illus.). 24p. (J). (gr. -1-3). pap. 4.99 *(978-0-15-204850-1(2),* 1194645, Clarion Bks.) HarperCollins Pubs.

—Cloudy Day Sunny Day. 2003. (Green Light Readers Level 1 Ser.). (gr. -1-2). 13.50 *(978-0-613-62277-6(4))* Turtleback.

Darlison, Aleesah. Ellabeth's Light. Brailsford, Jill, illus. 2017. (Unicorn Riders Ser.). (ENG.). 112p. (J). (gr. 3-5). pap. 5.95 *(978-1-4795-6559-7(8),* 128549, Picture Window Bks.) Capstone.

Dean, Janice. Freddy the Frogcaster. 2013. (Freddy the Frogcaster Ser.). (ENG., Illus.). 40p. (J). (gr. -1-3). 16.99 *(978-1-62157-084-4(3),* Regnery Kids) Regnery Publishing.

—Freddy the Frogcaster & the Big Blizzard. 2014. (Freddy the Frogcaster Ser.). (ENG., Illus.). 40p. (J). (gr. k-3). 16.99 *(978-1-62157-254-1(4),* Regnery Kids) Regnery Publishing.

Depken, Kristen L. Save the Rainbow! (Shimmer & Shine) Aikins, Dave, illus. 2018. (Step into Reading Ser.). (ENG.). 24p. (J). (gr. -1-1). pap. 5.99 *(978-0-525-57751-5(3));* lib. bdg. 12.99 *(978-0-525-57752-2(1))* Random Hse. Children's Bks. (Random Hse. Bks. for Young Readers).

Doherty, Ellen. Mondo & Gordo Weather the Storm: Set Of 6. 2010. (Early Connections Ser.). (J). pap. 39.00 net. *(978-1-4108-1556-9(0))* Benchmark Education Co.

Dreyer, Dylan. Misty the Cloud: a Very Stormy Day. Butcher, Rosie, illus. 2021. 40p. (J). (gr. -1-2). (ENG.). lib. bdg. 21.99 *(978-0-593-18040-2(2));* 19.99 *(978-0-593-18038-9(0))* Random Hse. Children's Bks. (Random Hse. Bks. for Young Readers).

Durant, Alan & Lucas, Kath. Bird Flies South. 2005. (Illus.). 32p. (J). lib. bdg. 9.00 *(978-1-4242-0888-3(2))* Fitzgerald Bks.

Durst, Sarah Beth. Spark. 2019. (ENG.). 320p. (J). (gr. 5-7). 17.99 *(978-1-328-97342-9(5),* 1708139, Clarion Bks.) HarperCollins Pubs.

Ellis, Melody A. An Unexpected Hero. 2009. 48p. pap. 16.95 *(978-1-60749-834-6(0))* America Star Bks.

Etherly, L. D. Winter Arrives This Summer. 2012. 34p. pap. 12.95 *(978-0-9833877-1-8(0))* Inkspil Publishing.

Evans, Catrin & Evans, Guto. Peiriant y Tywydd. 2005. (WEL., Illus.). 36p. *(978-0-86243-412-0(2))* Y Lolfa.

Falcon, David. Weather or Not? LaGrange, Tiffany, illus. 2009. 28p. pap. 12.95 *(978-1-936051-24-3(9))* Peppertree Pr., The.

Fox, Alex. Windsock Wesley & His Wild & Wonderful Weather MacHine, Living in Cloud. Bazzoni, Lainie M. A., illus. 2010. 48p. pap. 16.50 *(978-1-60911-873-0(1),* Eloquent Bks.) Strategic Book Publishing & Rights Agency (SBPRA).

Furgang, Kathy. Unlucky Stanley & Stanley no tiene Suerte: 6 English, 6 Spanish Adaptations. 2011. (ENG & SPA.). (J). 75.00 net. *(978-1-4108-5633-3(X))* Benchmark Education Co.

Galloway, Emily Ledford. Nimby the Cloud. 2008. 32p. pap. 24.95 *(978-1-60441-779-1(X))* America Star Bks.

Garcia, Kami & Stohl, Margaret. Beautiful Chaos. 2012. (Beautiful Creatures Ser.: 3). (ENG.). 528p. (YA). (gr. 7-17). pap. 16.99 *(978-0-316-12351-8(X))* Little, Brown Bks. for Young Readers.

George, Kallie. A True Home. Graegin, Stephanie, illus. 2017. (Heartwood Hotel Ser.: 1). (ENG.). 176p. (J). (gr. 2-5). 14.99 *(978-1-4847-3161-1(1))* Disney Pr.

George, Olivia. The Weather. Fletcher, Rusty, illus. 2005. (My First Reader Ser.). (ENG.). 32p. (J). (gr. k-1). lib. bdg. 18.50 *(978-0-516-24880-6(4),* Children's Pr.) Scholastic Library Publishing.

Gliori, Debi. Little Bear & the Wish Fish. (ENG., Illus.). 32p. (J). (gr. -1-2). pap. *(978-0-7112-0986-2(3))* ReiseArt Buchhandlung GmbH.

Gratz, Alan. Two Degrees. 2022. (ENG.). 384p. (J). (gr. 3-7). 17.99 *(978-1-338-73567-3(5),* Scholastic Pr.) Scholastic, Inc.

Graves, Kassie. Brave Little Sailboat. Graves, Kassie, illus. 2003. (Illus.). 20p. (J). 14.95 *(978-0-9728019-0-4(1))* Bright Eyes Pr.

Gray, P. J. The Lab Book 3, 1 vol. 2014. (Trippin' Ser.). (ENG.). 64p. (YA). (gr. 9-12). pap. 10.75 *(978-1-62250-933-1(1))* Saddleback Educational Publishing, Inc.

Guru Animation Studio Ltd., illus. True & the Rainbow Kingdom: the Great Rainbow Race. 2019. (True & the Rainbow Kingdom Ser.). 24p. (J). (gr. -1-1). 3.99 *(978-2-89802-033-9(8),* CrackBoom! Bks.) Chouette Publishing CAN. Dist: Publishers Group West (PGW).

Hammond, Rebecca. Winds Cove. 2004. 248p. (YA). pap. 6.99 *(978-1-932307-00-9(1),* Ambassador International) Emerald Hse. Group, Inc.

Harper, Jamie. Miss Mingo Weathers the Storm. Harper, Jamie, illus. (Miss Mingo Ser.). (ENG., Illus.). 40p. (J). (gr. -1-3). 2017. 6.99 *(978-0-7636-9514-9(9))* 2012. 15.99 *(978-0-7636-4931-9(7))* Candlewick Pr.

Hill, Julia. Cyril the Serious Cirrus Cloud. (ENG., Illus.). (J). 2018. 26p. 19.95 *(978-1-949231-43-4(7))* 2017. pap. 9.95 *(978-1-947825-18-5(6))* Yorkshire Publishing Group.

Hines, Ken, illus. Searching for an Oasis: Featuring Barrel Bob & Cousin Fishhook. 2019. 44p. (J). pap. *(978-1-63293-248-8(2))* Sunstone Pr.

Horácek, Petr. A Surprise for Tiny Mouse. Horácek, Petr, illus. 2015. (ENG., Illus.). 16p. (J). (— 1). bds. 8.99 *(978-0-7636-7967-5(4))* Candlewick Pr.

Hoshino, Felicia. Sora & the Cloud. 2012. (ENG., Illus.). 40p. (J). (gr. -1-3). 15.95 *(978-1-59702-027-5(3))* Immedium.

Howell. Wesley-Hampton Academy - The Weatherman. 2008. 179p. 28.29 *(978-0-615-15346-9(1))* Howell, Steven.

Hughes, Shirley. Alfie Weather. Hughes, Shirley, illus. 2007. (Alfie Ser.). (Illus.). 48p. (J). (gr. -1-k). pap. 15.99 *(978-0-09-940425-5(7),* Red Fox) Random House Children's Books GBR. Dist: Independent Pubs. Group.

Jackson, Richard. This Beautiful Day. Lee, Suzy., illus. 2017. (ENG.). 40p. (J). (gr. -1-3). 15.99 *(978-1-4814-4139-1(6),* Atheneum/Caitlyn Dlouhy Books) Simon & Schuster Children's Publishing.

Jansson, Tove & Jansson, Lars. Moomin & the Comet. 2013. (Moomin Stories Ser.). (J). lib. bdg. 20.80 *(978-0-606-31881-5(X))* Turtleback.

Johnston, Tony. Winter Is Coming. LaMarche, Jim, illus. 2014. (ENG.). 40p. (J). (gr. -1-3). 19.99 *(978-1-4424-7251-8(0),* Simon & Schuster Bks. For Young Readers) Simon & Schuster Bks. For Young Readers.

Kapai, Tommy. Cuzzies Find the Rainbow's End. Henry, Mike, illus. 2006. (ENG.). 32p. (gr. -1-3). pap. 9.00 *(978-0-9582517-0-9(3),* 2990) Huia Pubs. NZL. Dist: Univ. of Hawaii Pr.

Kaplan, Madeline. Planet Earth Gets Well. 2008. (ENG.). 24p. pap. 9.99 *(978-1-4196-8986-4(X))* CreateSpace Independent Publishing Platform.

Knowles, Kent. Lucius & the Storm. Knowles, Kent, illus. 2007. (Illus.). 32p. (J). (gr. -1-3). 15.95 *(978-1-60108-005-9(0))* Red Cygnet Pr.

Korba, Joanne. Wild Weather. 2005. (J). pap. *(978-1-4108-4218-3(5))* Benchmark Education Co.

Krensky, Stephen. Just in Case. Hobai, Ioana, illus. 2017. (J). *(978-0-7680-8422-1(9))* SAE Intl.

Leblanc, Louise. Leo's Skiing Surprise. Prud'homme, Jules, illus. 2007. (Formac First Novels Ser.). (ENG.). 64p. (J). (gr. 2-5). 14.95 *(978-0-88780-738-1(0),* 738); 4.95 *(978-0-88780-736-7(4),* 736) Formac Publishing Co., Ltd. CAN. Dist: Formac Lorimer Bks. Ltd.

Lin, Grace. Ling & Ting: Together in All Weather. 2016. (ENG.). 48p. (J). (gr. 1-4). pap. 4.99 *(978-0-316-33548-5(7))* Little, Brown Bks. for Young Readers.

Look Out the Window: Individual Title Six-Packs. (Story Steps Ser.). (gr. k-2). 29.00 *(978-0-7635-9587-6(X))* Rigby Education.

MacKay, Elly. Red Sky at Night. 2018. (Illus.). 40p. (J). (gr. -1-2). 17.99 *(978-1-101-91783-1(0),* Tundra Bks.) Tundra Bks. CAN. Dist: Penguin Random Hse. LLC.

Maddox, Jake. Blizzard! A Survive! Story, 1 vol. Tiffany, Sean, illus. 2009. (Jake Maddox Sports Stories Ser.). (ENG.). 72p. (J). (gr. 3-6). 25.99 *(978-1-4342-1206-1(8),* 95403, Stone Arch Bks.) Capstone.

Mae, Darcie. Sammy & Robert Go Home for the Holidays. 2011. 44p. pap. 24.95 *(978-1-4560-5702-2(2))* America Star Bks.

Malavolti, Angela. You Are a Twisting Tornado. Stiffler, Michael, illus. 2011. 28p. (J). 16.99 *(978-0-9834092-0-5(X))* Jungle Wagon Pr.

Marshall, Rita. Wake up, Weather. Felix, Monique, illus. 2016. (ENG.). 14p. (J). (gr. -1-k). bds. 8.99 *(978-1-56846-286-8(7),* 20562, Creative Editions) Creative Co., The.

May, Eleanor. Let's Go, Snow! Pillo, Cary, illus. 2017. (Math Matters Ser.). 32p. (J). (gr. k-4). pap. 5.99 *(978-1-57565-807-0(0),* c10b9d6d-d8c6-494f-882f-04311f6945c8, Kane Press) Astra Publishing Hse.

McKee, David. Elmer's Weather. 2018. (Elmer Ser.). (ENG., Illus.). 10p. (J). (— 1). bds. 9.99 *(978-1-78344-606-3(4))* Andersen Pr. GBR. Dist: Independent Pubs. Group.

McNeely, Marian Hurd & L., Jean. The Jumping-Off Place. 2008. (ENG., Illus.). 320p. (J). pap. 15.95 *(978-0-9798940-4-6(2),* P240879, South Dakota State Historical Society Pr.) South Dakota Historical Society Pr.

Meadows, Daisy. Hayley the Rain Fairy. 2007. (Rainbow Magic — the Weather Fairies Ser.: 7). (Orig.). lib. bdg. 14.75 *(978-1-4177-7082-3(1))* Turtleback.

Milz, Cynthia A. Waiting for the Last Leaf to Fall. 2008. 20p. per. 24.95 *(978-1-4241-8965-6(9))* America Star Bks.

Montes, Hugo & Montes, Michelle. Young Eagles Armor Academy: Caught in the Storm, V02. 2010. 76p. (J). pap. 5.99 *(978-1-60683-022-2(8))* Harrison House Pubs.

Morrison, Toni & Morrison, Slade. Little Cloud & Lady Wind. Qualls, Sean, illus. 2010. (ENG.). 32p. (J). pap. 7.99 *(978-1-4169-8524-2(7),* Simon & Schuster Bks. For Young Readers) Simon & Schuster Bks. For Young Readers.

—Little Cloud & Lady Wind. Qualls, Sean, illus. 2010. (ENG.). 32p. (J). (gr. -1-3). 19.99 *(978-1-4169-8523-5(9),* Simon & Schuster/Paula Wiseman Bks.) Simon & Schuster/Paula Wiseman Bks.

Mullaly Hunt, Lynda. Shouting at the Rain. 2019. 288p. (J). (gr. 5). 17.99 *(978-0-399-17515-2(6),* Nancy Paulsen Books) Penguin Young Readers Group.

Naraynan, Manjula. The Grey Grey Cloud. 2010. (Illus.). 32p. pap. 14.49 *(978-1-4490-8507-0(5))* AuthorHouse.

The North Pole Is Sinking! 2005. (J). 9.99 *(978-0-9773674-0-5(1))* Blue State Pr.

Parker, Emma. What Will the Weather Be Today? 2010. (Illus.). pap. *(978-1-877547-90-4(5))* First Edition Ltd.

Parry, Jo. Rainbow Fairies. 2009. (Wow! Bks.). (Illus.). (J). bds. 12.99 *(978-1-934650-25-7(0))* Just For Kids Pr., LLC.

Passey, Marion. Sneezles & Wheezles. Harston, Jerry, illus. 2006. 32p. (J). (gr. -1-3). 15.99 *(978-1-55517-912-0(6))* Cedar Fort, Inc./CFI Distribution.

Pearson, Henrik Barkley de. The Secret of the Rainbow. 2011. 92p. pap. 51.99 *(978-1-4568-1291-1(2))* Xlibris Corp.

Phinney, Patty McCoy. Makayla's Rainbow. 2011. 94p. pap. 19.95 *(978-1-4560-7529-3(2))* America Star Bks.

Randolph, Joanne. Stormy: a Storm Cloud's Story, 1 vol. 2009. (Nature Stories Ser.). (ENG., Illus.). 24p. (J). (gr. 1-2). lib. bdg. 27.27 *(978-1-60754-092-2(4),* 142ee8c3-dd4d-4709-9be4-7c3b114fc8b3, Windmill Bks.) Rosen Publishing Group, Inc., The.

Ras. Oh No, the Leaves Are Moving! 2011. 24p. pap. 15.99 *(978-1-4568-5030-2(X))* Xlibris Corp.

Rice, Dona. What Kind of Weather? 2009. (Early Literacy Ser.). (ENG., Illus.). 16p. (gr. k-1). 19.99 *(978-1-4333-1459-9(2))* Teacher Created Materials, Inc.

Rice, Karen. The Forbidden Sneeze. 2011. 28p. pap. 24.95 *(978-1-4626-3488-0(5))* America Star Bks.

Ross, Fiona. Chilly Milly Moo. 2011. (ENG., Illus.). 32p. (J). (gr. -1-2). 15.99 *(978-0-7636-5693-5(3))* Candlewick Pr.

Ross, Tony. El Tiempo. 2006. (Little Princess Ser.).Tr. of Weather. (SPA.). (J). (gr. -1-k). bds. 7.95 *(978-968-19-1487-5(2),* AT33281) Lectorum Pubns., Inc.

Ruckman, Ivy. Night of the Twisters. 2003. (ENG.). 160p. (J). (gr. 3-6). reprint ed. pap. 9.99 *(978-0-06-440176-0(6),* HarperCollins) HarperCollins Pubs.

Rudolph, Miriam. A Frozen Dream. 2009. 28p. pap. 12.00 *(978-1-60693-962-8(9),* Eloquent Bks.) Strategic Book Publishing & Rights Agency (SBPRA).

Ruffenach, Jessie, ed. Baby Learns about Weather. Thomas, Peter, tr. from ENG. Blacksheep, Beverly, illus. 2005. (NAV & ENG.). 16p. (J). (gr. 4-7). 7.95 *(978-1-893354-62-3(8))* Salina Bookshelf Inc.

Rylant, Cynthia. Gooseberry Park & the Master Plan. Howard, Arthur, illus. 2015. (Gooseberry Park Ser.). (ENG.). 128p. (J). (gr. 3-7). 16.99 *(978-1-4814-0449-5(0),* Beach Lane Bks.) Beach Lane Bks.

Schirmer, Jodi L. It Is a Good Day: Clay. 2009. 23p. (J). pap. 11.95 *(978-1-4327-4018-4(0))* Outskirts Pr., Inc.

Schmidt, Karen Lee. Carl's Nose. 2006. (ENG., Illus.). 40p. (J). (gr. -1-3). 16.00 *(978-0-15-205049-8(3),* 1195252, Clarion Bks.) HarperCollins Pubs.

Smith, Gloria. Annie Elf & Bo Bo Robin. 2012. 24p. 24.95 *(978-1-62709-650-8(7))* America Star Bks.

Smith, Jennifer E. The Storm Makers. Helquist, Brett, illus. 2013. (ENG.). 384p. (J). (gr. 3-7). pap. 19.99 *(978-0-316-17959-1(0))* Little, Brown Bks. for Young Readers.

Stout, Shawn K. Fiona Finkelstein, Big-Time Ballerina!! Martini, Angela, illus. 2010. (ENG.). 192p. (J). pap. 4.99 *(978-1-4169-7109-2(2),* Simon & Schuster/Paula Wiseman Bks.) Simon & Schuster/Paula Wiseman Bks.

Thiebaux, Tamara. When Heaven Smiled on Our World, 1 vol. 2020. (ENG.). 32p. (J). (gr. 2-5). pap. 14.95 *(978-1-55041-286-4(8),* afc2e0d3-0386-4bd5-bf3f-ad95d879ac29) Fitzhenry & Whiteside, Ltd. CAN. Dist: Firefly Bks., Ltd.

Thompson, Chad. The Itsy Bitsy Spider. 2009. (Early Literacy Ser.). (ENG., Illus.). 16p. (gr. k-1). 19.99 *(978-1-4333-1455-1(X))* Teacher Created Materials, Inc.

Thompson, Kate. Switchers. 220p. (J). (gr. 4-7). pap. 5.99 *(978-0-8072-1553-1(8));* 2004. (Switchers Ser.: Vol. 1). (gr. 5-9). pap. 38.00 incl. audio *(978-0-8072-8138-3(7),* YA115SP) Random Hse. Audio Publishing Group. (Listening Library).

Vischer, Frans. A Very Fuddles Christmas. Vischer, Frans, illus. 2013. (ENG., Illus.). 32p. (J). (gr. -1-2). 18.99 *(978-1-4169-9156-4(5),* Aladdin) Simon & Schuster Children's Publishing.

Voake, Steve. Daisy Dawson on the Farm. Meserve, Jessica, illus. 2013. (Daisy Dawson Ser.). (ENG.). 96p. (J). (gr. 1-4). pap. 7.99 *(978-0-7636-6340-7(9))* Candlewick Pr.

Voght, Victor A. Fun with Huff & Puff, 1 vol. 2009. 15p. pap. 24.95 *(978-1-60749-853-7(7))* America Star Bks.

Warren, Jordan L. Jo's Rainy Sad Day. 2011. 28p. pap. 15.99 *(978-1-4568-4161-4(0))* Xlibris Corp.

White, Carolyn. Snowff & the Rowdy-Cloudy Bunch. 2006. (Snowff the Snowflake Kid Adventure Ser.). (J). 24.95 *(978-1-893563-05-6(7))* AARO Publishing.

—Snowff Visits Razorteeth Village. 2006. (Illus.). 72p. (J). 24.95 *(978-1-893563-10-0(3))* AARO Publishing.

—Snowff's MIST.erious Journey (Snowff the Snowflake Kid Adventure, 1) 2006. (J). 24.95 *(978-1-893563-00-1(6))* AARO Publishing.

White, Kathryn. Snowshoe the Hare. Rivers, Ruth, illus. 2005. (Red Go Bananas Ser.). (ENG.). 48p. (J). (gr. 2-3). lib. bdg. *(978-0-7787-2677-7(0),* 1253648) Crabtree Publishing Co.

Wilks, Mike. The Weather Works. Wilks, Mike, illus. 2016. (ENG., Illus.). 32p. (J). 17.95 *(978-0-7649-7538-7(2))* Pomegranate Communications, Inc.

Yaccarino, Dan. Where the Four Winds Blow. Yaccarino, Dan, illus. 2003. (Illus.). 104p. (J). 17.89 *(978-0-06-623627-8(4),* Cotler, Joanna Books) HarperCollins Pubs.

Zee, Ginger. Chasing Helicity: First She Has to Face the Storm. 2018. *(978-1-368-02030-5(5))* Disney Publishing Worldwide.

Zuchora-Walske, Christine. Weather Robots. 2014. (Lightning Bolt Books (r) — Robots Everywhere! Ser.). (ENG., Illus.). 32p. (J). (gr. 1-3). lib. bdg. 29.32 *(978-1-4677-4057-9(8),* 62878b01-b114-4a48-bc17-cf0f99a490e3, Lerner Pubns.) Lerner Publishing Group.

WEATHER CONTROL

Brimner, Larry Dane. The Rain Wizard: The Amazing, Mysterious, True Life of Charles Mallory Hatfield. 2015. (ENG., Illus.). 80p. (J). (gr. 4-7). 16.95 *(978-1-59078-990-2(3),* Calkins Creek) Highlights Pr., c/o Highlights for Children, Inc.

Scirri, Kaitlin. The Science of Controlling Electricity & Weather, 1 vol. 2018. (Science of Superpowers Ser.). (ENG.). 48p. (J). (gr. 4-4). 33.07 *(978-1-5026-3796-3(0),* b66bd2b4-672a-4355-b63a-80fef333e8a5) Cavendish Square Publishing LLC.

WEATHER FORECASTING

And Now for the Weather! Individual Title Six-Packs. (Bookweb Ser.). 32p. (gr. 5-18). 34.00 *(978-0-7635-3799-9(3))* Rigby Education.

Arnold, Tedd. Fly Guy Presents: Weather. 2016. (Illus.). (J). *(978-1-338-04666-3(7))* Scholastic, Inc.

Birch, Robin. Watching Weather, 1 vol. 2010. (Weather & Climate Ser.). (ENG.). 32p. (gr. 3-3). 31.21 *(978-0-7614-4470-1(X),* 79d39cce-3ae8-4307-a029-3bf68fbf4f77) Cavendish Square Publishing LLC.

Boothroyd, Jennifer. What Is a Forecast? 2014. (First Step Nonfiction — Let's Watch the Weather Ser.). (ENG., Illus.). 24p. (J). (gr. k-2). pap. 6.99 *(978-1-4677-4497-3(2),* 59d1d9eb-e0e4-483b-a680-5df76fd86c33); lib. bdg. 23.99 *(978-1-4677-3920-7(0),* d8d3676a-fede-497a-8b18-8e97e18f8062, Lerner Pubns.) Lerner Publishing Group.

Breen, Mark. The Kids' Book of Weather Forecasting. 2008. (ENG., Illus.). 144p. (J). (gr. 2-7). pap. 14.99 *(978-0-8249-6823-6(9),* Ideals Pubns.) Worthy Publishing.

Coleman, Miriam. Using the Weather to Learn about Earth, 1 vol. 2015. (Earth Science Detectives Ser.). (ENG., Illus.). 24p. (J). (gr. 3-3). lib. bdg. 25.27 *(978-1-4777-5958-5(1),* b441000b-03aa-478b-b128-7ac88440ef3e, PowerKids Pr.) Rosen Publishing Group, Inc., The.

Davies, Monika. Tracking the Weather, 1 vol. 2015. (Science: Informational Text Ser.). (ENG., Illus.). 32p. (gr. 3-4). pap. 11.99 *(978-1-4807-4648-0(7))* Teacher Created Materials, Inc.

Davis, Graeme. Floods. 2012. (21st Century Skills Library: Real World Math Ser.). (ENG., Illus.). 32p. (gr. 4-8). lib. bdg. 32.07 *(978-1-61080-324-3(8),* 201304) Cherry Lake Publishing.

Dixon, Dale. Let's Track the Storm: What Will Happen?, 1 vol. 2017. (Computer Science for the Real World Ser.). (ENG.). 8p. (gr. k-1). pap. *(978-1-5383-5059-1(9),* d43a4294-35fa-4de8-b720-4ef1823e5392, Rosen Classroom) Rosen Publishing Group, Inc., The.

Felix, Rebecca. How's the Weather in Fall? 2013. (21st Century Basic Skills Library: Let's Look at Fall Ser.). (ENG.). 24p. (gr. k-3). (J). pap. 12.79 *(978-1-61080-927-6(0),* 202589); (Illus.). 26.35 *(978-1-61080-902-3(5),* 202587); (Illus.). E-Book 43.50 *(978-1-61080-977-1(7),* 202590) Cherry Lake Publishing.

Fleisher, Paul. Doppler Radar, Satellites, & Computer Models: The Science of Weather Forecasting. 2010. (Weatherwise Ser.). (Illus.). 48p. (YA). (gr. 4-7). lib. bdg. 29.27 *(978-0-8225-7535-1(3))* Lerner Publishing Group.

Franchino, Vicky. Droughts. 2012. (21st Century Skills Library: Real World Math Ser.). (ENG., Illus.). 32p. (gr. 4-8). lib. bdg. 32.07 *(978-1-61080-322-9(1),* 201300) Cherry Lake Publishing.

Friestad, Kathleen M., et al. The Kids' Book of Weather Forecasting. Kline, Michael, illus. 2008. 160p. (J). 16.99 *(978-0-8249-6822-9(0),* Ideals Pubns.) Worthy Publishing.

Furgang, Adam. Adapting to Intense Storms, 1 vol. 2012. (Science to the Rescue: Adapting to Climate Change Ser.). (ENG.). 64p. (YA). (gr. 5-5). lib. bdg. 37.13 *(978-1-4488-6848-3(3),* c045314e-926b-4937-bc06-968d50fa9119, Rosen Reference) Rosen Publishing Group, Inc., The.

Hayes, Amy & Lyman, Geraldine. Meteorology & Forecasting the Weather, 1 vol. 2018. (Spotlight on Weather & Natural Disasters Ser.). (ENG.). 24p. (gr. 4-6). 27.93 *(978-1-5081-6906-2(3),* 3736b68f-52cd-4442-a0d2-0fab19f34695, PowerKids Pr.) Rosen Publishing Group, Inc., The.

Hoena, Blake A. If It's Really Cold... & Other Weather Predictions. 2012. (If Bks.). (ENG.). 32p. (J). (gr. 1-2). pap. 48.60 *(978-1-4296-9248-9(0),* 18503, Capstone Pr.) Capstone.

Jackson, Randy, et al. Tropical Weather Tracking Book. 2004. (YA). 7.95 *(978-0-9742794-1-1(2))* HazardousWeather Preparedness Institute.

Kudlinski, Kathleen V. Boy, Were We Wrong about the Weather! Serra, Sebastià, illus. 2015. 32p. (J). (gr. -1-3). 18.99 *(978-0-8037-3793-8(9),* Dial Bks) Penguin Young Readers Group.

Lawrence, Ellen. What Is Weather? (Weather Wise Ser.). 24p. (J). (gr. -1-3). 2018. (ENG.). 7.99 *(978-1-64280-093-7(7))*

2012. lib. bdg. 26.99 *(978-1-61772-405-3(X))* Bearport Publishing Co., Inc.

Levine, Shar & Johnstone, Leslie. Wonderful Weather. Harpster, Steve, illus. 2005. (First Science Experiments Ser.). (ENG.). 48p. (J). (gr. 2-4). 17.44 *(978-0-8069-7249-7(1))* Sterling Publishing Co., Inc.

Maurer, Daniel D. Do You Really Want to Drive in a Blizzard? A Book about Predicting Weather. Alberini, Teresa, illus. 2016. (Adventures in Science Ser.). (ENG.). 24p. (J). (gr. 1-4). lib. bdg. 20.95 *(978-1-60753-959-9(4),* 15630) Amicus.

McAuliffe, Bill. Forecasting. (X-Books: Weather Ser.). (ENG., (J). 2017. Illus.). 32p. (gr. 3-6). pap. 9.99 *(978-1-62832-427-3(9),* 20406, Creative Paperbacks) 2017. (Illus.). 32p. (gr. 3-6). *(978-1-60818-824-6(8),* 20405, Creative Education) 2010. 48p. (gr. 5-8). lib. bdg. 23.95 *(978-1-58341-927-4(6),* 22283) Creative Co., The.

National Geographic Learning. Reading Expeditions (Science: Earth Science): Extreme Weather. 2007. (ENG., Illus.). 32p. (J). pap. 18.95 *(978-0-7922-4575-9(X))* CENGAGE Learning.

Nelson, Penelope S. Forecasting Weather. 2018. (Weather Watch Ser.). (ENG., Illus.). 24p. (J). (gr. 1-1). pap. 8.95 *(978-1-63517-841-8(X),* 163517841X) North Star Editions.

—Forecasting Weather. 2018. (Weather Watch Ser.). (ENG., Illus.). 24p. (J). (gr. k-3). lib. bdg. 31.36 *(978-1-5321-6053-0(4),* 28738, Pop! Cody Koala) Pop!

Orr, Tamra B. Forecasting a Flood. 2014. (Explorer Library: Science Explorer Ser.). (ENG., Illus.). 32p. (J). (gr. 4-8). 32.07 *(978-1-62431-778-1(2),* 203308) Cherry Lake Publishing.

Randolph, Joanne, ed. Tornado Alert!, 1 vol. 2017. (Weather Report). (ENG.). 32p. (gr. 3-3). pap. 11.52 *(978-0-7660-9025-5(6),* 5d7dd9f4-d240-43f3-a372-9effc285941a) Enslow Publishing, LLC.

Schuetz, Kristin. Forecasts. 2015. (Understanding Weather Ser.). (ENG., Illus.). 24p. (J). (gr. k-3). lib. bdg. 26.95 *(978-1-62617-251-7(X),* Blastoff! Readers) Bellwether Media.

Schwartz, Heather E. Tracking a Storm. rev. ed. 2018. (Smithsonian: Informational Text Ser.). (ENG., Illus.). 32p. (J). (gr. 3-5). pap. 11.99 *(978-1-4938-6704-2(0))* Teacher Created Materials, Inc.

Sears, Kathleen. Weather 101: From Doppler Radar & Long-Range Forecasts to the Polar Vortex & Climate Change, Everything You Need to Know about the Study of Weather. 2017. (Adams 101 Ser.). (ENG., Illus.). 256p. 15.99 *(978-1-5072-0463-4(9))* Adams Media Corp.

Sharkawy, Azza. Predict It! 2014. (Science Sleuths Ser.). (ENG., Illus.). 24p. (J). (gr. 2-2). *(978-0-7787-0773-8(3))* Crabtree Publishing Co.

Shea, Therese M. Freaky Weather Stories, 1 vol. 2015. (Freaky True Science Ser.). (ENG.). 32p. (J). (gr. 4-5). pap. 11.50 *(978-1-4824-2968-8(3),* b3c64bfa-3c3a-417a-9da9-882b0b3dd071) Stevens, Gareth Publishing LLLP.

Sievert, Terri. Forecasting Weather. 2011. (Earth & Space Science Ser.). (ENG.). 24p. (J). (gr. k-1). pap. 44.74 *(978-1-4296-7144-6(0),* 16713, Capstone Pr.) Capstone.

Sohn, Emily. Weather & the Water Cycle. 2019. (iScience Ser.). (ENG., Illus.). 48p. (J). (gr. 5-6). pap. 13.26 *(978-1-68404-409-2(X))* Norwood Hse. Pr.

Somervill, Barbara A. Hurricanes. 2012. (21st Century Skills Library: Real World Math Ser.). (ENG., Illus.). 32p. (gr. 4-8). lib. bdg. 32.07 *(978-1-61080-325-0(6),* 201302) Cherry Lake Publishing.

Steinberg, Lynnae D. What Is Weather Forecasting?, 1 vol. 2014. (Let's Find Out! Weather Ser.). (ENG.). 32p. (J). (gr. 2-3). 26.06 *(978-1-62275-795-4(5),* 8eb990f5-5cfb-4a53-bdfd-f052da5ec02d, Britannica Educational Publishing) Rosen Publishing Group, Inc., The.

Sundance/Newbridge LLC Staff. Predicting the Weather. 2004. (Reading PowerWorks Ser.). (gr. 1-3). 37.50 *(978-0-7608-9245-9(8));* pap. 6.10 *(978-0-7608-9246-6(6))* Sundance/Newbridge Educational Publishing.

Waunsch, John. My Very, Very First Weather Book. 2013. 56p. 23.99 *(978-1-62697-903-1(0));* pap. 12.99 *(978-1-62697-764-8(X))* Salem Author Services.

Wills, Susan & Wills, Steven R. Meteorology: Predicting the Weather. 2003. (Innovators Ser.: Vol. 12). (Illus.). 144p. (gr. 5-18). lib. bdg. 21.95 *(978-1-881508-61-8(7))* Oliver Pr., Inc.

WEATHER SATELLITES

see Meteorological Satellites

WEAVING

see also Basket Making; Beadwork; Textile Industry
also names of woven articles, e.g. Carpets

Howell, Vickie. Finger Knitting Fun: 28 Cute, Clever, & Creative Projects for Kids. 2015. (ENG., Illus.). 96p. (J). (gr. 2-8). pap. 22.99 *(978-1-63159-070-2(7),* 215621, Quarry Bks.) Quarto Publishing Group USA.

Rodee, Marian. Weaving of the Southwest, 1 vol. 2nd rev. ed. 2003. (ENG., Illus.). 248p. (gr. 10-13). pap. 29.95 *(978-0-7643-1854-2(3),* 2181) Schiffer Publishing, Ltd.

Switzer, Chris. Projects for Alpaca & Llama. 2004. 16.00 *(978-0-9642663-2-2(6))* Switzer Land Enterprises.

Weston Woods Staff, creator. Charlie Needs a Cloak. 2004. 38.75 *(978-1-55592-383-9(6));* 13.95 *(978-1-55592-382-2(8))* Weston Woods Studios, Inc.

WEB SITES

Anniss, Matt. What Is a Website & How Do I Use It?, 1 vol. 2013. (Practical Technology Ser.). (ENG.). 48p. (J). (gr. 5-5). 29.44 *(978-1-62275-072-6(1),* f0d91f3f-0cc9-4221-843d-421538fc0d36); pap. 15.05 *(978-1-62275-073-3(X),* 8598ddc2-065b-4666-ba67-4077bf70fa5f) Rosen Publishing Group, Inc., The.

Anniss, Matthew. Create Your Own Web Site or Blog. 2016. (Media Genius Ser.). (ENG., Illus.). 48p. (J). (gr. 5-8). lib. bdg. 35.99 *(978-1-4109-8111-0(8),* 131005, Raintree) Capstone.

Atkins, Marcie Flinchum. Build a Website (Rookie Get Ready to Code) (Library Edition) 2019. (Rookie Get Ready to Code Ser.). (ENG., Illus.). 32p. (J). (gr. 1-2). lib. bdg. 25.00 *(978-0-531-13226-5(9),* Children's Pr.) Scholastic Library Publishing.

Bailer, Darice. Will & Wendy Build a Website with Digital Tools. O'Neill, Sean, illus. 2014. (Writing Builders Ser.). (ENG.). 32p. (J). (gr. 2-4). pap. 11.94 *(978-1-60357-558-4(8));* lib. bdg. 25.27 *(978-1-59953-584-5(X))* Norwood Hse. Pr.

Bingham, Jane, et al. The Usborne Internet-Linked Encyclopedia of World History: Prehistoric, Ancient, Medieval, Last 500 Years. 2004. (World History Ser.). (ENG., Illus.). 1p. (J). (gr. 3-18). 39.95 *(978-0-7460-4168-0(3))* EDC Publishing.

Brown, Tracy. Facebook Safety & Privacy. 2013. (21st Century Safety & Privacy Ser.). 64p. (J). (gr. 5-8). pap. 77.70 *(978-1-4488-9581-6(2));* (ENG., Illus.). (gr. 6-6). 37.12 *(978-1-4488-9569-4(3),* 039c65c6-d600-440b-977f-0379fa761bc5); (ENG., Illus.). (gr. 6-6). pap. 13.95 *(978-1-4488-9580-9(4),* 19a209d0-0877-4cb9-89ba-86b146c1d093) Rosen Publishing Group, Inc., The.

Collier Hillstrom, Laurie. Online Social Networks, 1 vol. 2010. (Technology 360 Ser.). (ENG., Illus.). 128p. (gr. 7-10). lib. bdg. 41.53 *(978-1-4205-0167-4(4),* 4b34a57f-5d9e-4bfe-8e0c-657d2181fe1e, Lucent Pr.) Greenhaven Publishing LLC.

Doherty, Gillian. Birds. 2004. (Discovery Program Ser.). (SPA., Illus.). 64p. (J). (gr. 2-18). lib. bdg. 16.95 *(978-1-58086-334-6(5))* EDC Publishing.

Ekman, Joseph Anthony. Kids Ultimate Online Homework Resource Guide 2004. 2003. spiral bd. 14.95 *(978-0-9745406-0-3(9))* Duke Publishing & Software Corp.

Fontichiaro, Kristin. Blog It! 2012. (Explorer Library: Information Explorer Ser.). (ENG.). 32p. (gr. 4-8). pap. 14.21 *(978-1-61080-656-5(5),* 202266); (Illus.). 32.07 *(978-1-61080-482-0(1),* 202092) Cherry Lake Publishing.

—Starting Your Own Blog. Petelinsek, Kathleen, illus. 2013. (Explorer Junior Library: Information Explorer Junior Ser.). (ENG.). 24p. (J). (gr. 1-4). 32.07 *(978-1-62431-133-8(4),* 202852) Cherry Lake Publishing.

Fontichiaro, Kristin & Truesdell, Ann. Learning & Sharing with a Wiki. Petelinsek, Kathleen, illus. 2013. (Explorer Junior Library: Information Explorer Junior Ser.). (ENG.). 24p. (J). (gr. 1-4). pap. 12.79 *(978-1-62431-264-9(0),* 202850) Cherry Lake Publishing.

Fromm, Megan. Gathering & Sharing Digital Information, 1 vol. 2014. (Media Literacy Ser.). (ENG.). 48p. (YA). (gr. 6-6). 33.47 *(978-1-4777-8062-6(9),* 92199e94-8489-499b-8204-35689ea99924, Rosen Reference) Rosen Publishing Group, Inc., The.

Gilbert, Sara. The Story of Facebook. (Built for Success Ser.). (ENG.). 48p. (J). (gr. 5-9). 2013. pap. 12.00 *(978-0-89812-761-4(0),* 21877, Creative Paperbacks) 2012. (Illus.). 23.95 *(978-1-60818-176-6(6),* 21873, Creative Education) Creative Co., The.

—The Story of Google. 2008. (Built for Success Ser.). (ENG.). 48p. (J). (gr. 5-8). pap. 12.00 *(978-0-89812-755-3(6),* 22118, Creative Paperbacks) Creative Co., The.

—The Story of Twitter. 2014. (Built for Success Ser.). (ENG.). 48p. (J). (gr. 5-8). *(978-1-60818-398-2(X),* 21293, Creative Education) Creative Co., The.

Goldsworthy, Steve. Mark Zuckerberg. 2012. (J). *(978-1-61913-872-8(7));* pap. *(978-1-61913-873-5(5))* Weigl Pubs., Inc.

Gray, Leon. What Is a Blog & How Do I Use It?, 1 vol. 2013. (Practical Technology Ser.). (ENG.). 48p. (J). (gr. 5-5). 29.44 *(978-1-62275-066-5(7),* d1bd9361-1cd2-40b5-992a-ecbdaa57d8ec); pap. 15.05 *(978-1-62275-067-2(5),* 393a160a-c332-40b2-8ac6-7860d22c580f) Rosen Publishing Group, Inc., The.

—What Is a Social Network & How Do I Use It?, 1 vol. 2013. (Practical Technology Ser.). (ENG.). 48p. (J). (gr. 5-5). 29.44 *(978-1-62275-075-7(6),* 31071949-f1fd-43a2-8d61-37745ec08e06); pap. 15.05 *(978-1-62275-076-4(4),* de071c83-e30f-41a1-bd75-ecaac63b23b4) Rosen Publishing Group, Inc., The.

—What Is a Wiki & How Do I Use It?, 1 vol. 2013. (Practical Technology Ser.). (ENG.). 48p. (J). (gr. 5-5). 29.44 *(978-1-62275-069-6(1),* 41e53043-b05c-471c-a89e-e7882d45ee53); pap. 15.05 *(978-1-62275-070-2(5),* 2d09830f-0456-4e47-a8c0-5cf6cbc8037a) Rosen Publishing Group, Inc., The.

Green, Julie. Shooting Video to Make Learning Fun. 2010. (Explorer Library: Information Explorer Ser.). (ENG., Illus.). 32p. (gr. 4-8). lib. bdg. 32.07 *(978-1-60279-955-4(5),* 200635) Cherry Lake Publishing.

Hasday, Judy L. Facebook & Mark Zuckerberg. 2012. (Business Leaders Ser.). (Illus.). 112p. (YA). (gr. 7-12). 28.95 *(978-1-59935-176-6(5))* Reynolds, Morgan Inc.

Hawthorne, Kate & Sheppard, Daniela. The Young Person's Guide to the Internet: The Essential Website Reference Book for Young People, Parents & Teachers. 2nd ed. 2005. (ENG., Illus.). 224p. (C). (gr. 3-7). per. 43.95 *(978-0-415-34505-7(7),* RU42390) Routledge.

Henneberg, Susan. Twitter Safety & Privacy: A Guide to Microblogging. 2013. (21st Century Safety & Privacy Ser.). 64p. (J). (gr. 5-8). pap. 77.70 *(978-1-4488-9589-2(8));* (ENG.). (gr. 6-6). 37.12 *(978-1-4488-9572-4(3),* 54f42b65-0b6b-43ae-b6f0-59cb028d3bd4); (ENG.). (gr. 6-6). pap. 13.95 *(978-1-4488-9588-5(X),* 1076435a-33ff-4123-9681-c1fb214a28a1) Rosen Publishing Group, Inc., The.

Hudak, Heather C. Digital Data Security. 2019. (Get Informed — Stay Informed Ser.). (Illus.). 48p. (J). (gr. 5-6). *(978-0-7787-5331-5(X))* Crabtree Publishing Co.

Kling, Andrew A. Web 2. 0, 1 vol. 2011. (Technology 360 Ser.). (ENG., Illus.). 128p. (gr. 7-10). lib. bdg. 41.53 *(978-1-4205-0171-1(2),* ea9c1bb5-5a6d-42fa-9726-173387a004eb, Lucent Pr.) Greenhaven Publishing LLC.

Kurzius, Alexa. Building a Website (a True Book: Get Ready to Code) (Library Edition) 2019. (True Book (Relaunch) Ser.). (ENG., Illus.). 48p. (J). (gr. 3-5). lib. bdg. 31.00 *(978-0-531-12732-2(X),* Children's Pr.) Scholastic Library Publishing.

Lent, Colleen Van. More Web Design with HTML5. 2015. (21st Century Skills Innovation Library: Makers As Innovators Ser.). (ENG., Illus.). 32p. (J). (gr. 4-8). lib. bdg. 32.07 *(978-1-63188-868-7(4),* 206052) Cherry Lake Publishing.

—Web Design with HTML5. 2014. (21st Century Skills Innovation Library: Makers As Innovators Ser.). (ENG., Illus.). 32p. (J). (gr. 4-8). 32.07 *(978-1-63137-773-0(6),* 205335) Cherry Lake Publishing.

Lent, Colleen Van & Lent, Christopher van. Making a Web Page. 2018. (21st Century Skills Innovation Library: Makers As Innovators Junior Ser.). (ENG.). 24p. (J). (gr. 2-5). pap. 12.79 *(978-1-5341-0879-0(3),* 210880); (Illus.). lib. bdg. 30.64 *(978-1-5341-0780-9(0),* 210879) Cherry Lake Publishing.

Mark Zuckerberg & Facebook. 2011. (Graphic Nonfiction Biographies Ser.). (ENG.). 48p. (YA). (gr. 5-8). *(978-1-4488-5547-6(0),* Rosen Reference) Rosen Publishing Group, Inc., The.

Martin, Chris. Build Your Own Web Site, 1 vol. 2013. (Quick Expert's Guide Ser.). 64p. (J). (gr. 5-5). (ENG.). 37.12 *(978-1-4777-2823-9(6),* ca74eba1-f015-4b2a-b524-aa8c910e28f8); (ENG.). pap. 13.95 *(978-1-4777-2825-3(2),* 47d2db16-62cc-4767-abd5-a72161e4931e); pap. 77.70 *(978-1-4777-2826-0(0))* Rosen Publishing Group, Inc., The. (Rosen Reference).

Noll, Elizabeth. Coding in the Internet. 2018. (Coding Is Everywhere Ser.). (ENG., Illus.). 24p. (J). (gr. k-3). pap. 7.99 *(978-1-61891-478-1(2),* 12131, Blastoff! Readers) Bellwether Media.

Pascaretti, Vicki & Wilkie, Sara. Team up Online. 2010. (Explorer Library: Information Explorer Ser.). (ENG., Illus.). 32p. (gr. 4-8). lib. bdg. 32.07 *(978-1-60279-644-7(0),* 200347) Cherry Lake Publishing.

Poolos, Jamie. Designing, Building, & Maintaining Web Sites, 1 vol. 2010. (Digital & Information Literacy Ser.). (ENG.). 48p. (YA). (gr. 6-6). pap. 12.75 *(978-1-4488-0594-5(5),* ca90975d-06f8-4d51-b21a-7526dc132c8c); lib. bdg. 33.47 *(978-1-4358-9424-2(3),* 3f196503-6ce1-4349-8e89-a868e982dd37) Rosen Publishing Group, Inc., The. (Rosen Reference).

Raatma, Lucia. Blogs. 2010. (21st Century Skills Innovation Library: Innovation in Entertainment Ser.). (ENG., Illus.). 32p. (gr. 4-8). lib. bdg. 32.07 *(978-1-60279-635-5(1),* 200339) Cherry Lake Publishing.

Sack, Rebekah. So You Want to Start a Blog: A Step-By-Step Guide to Starting a Fun & Profitable Blog. 2017. (ENG.). 180p. (YA). (gr. 8-12). lib. bdg. 34.95 *(978-1-62023-230-9(8),* bdda44f9-2f74-48fd-b4f2-44f05298a0c9) Atlantic Publishing Group, Inc.

Sack, Rebekah & Atlantic Publishing Group. So You Want to Start a Blog: A Step-By-Step Guide to Starting a Fun & Profitable Blog. 2017. (ENG., Illus.). 180p. (YA). pap. 19.95 *(978-1-62023-217-0(0),* 8a9aa940-2132-4d5b-88d8-e8527614bb16) Atlantic Publishing Group, Inc.

Schwartz, Heather E. Safe Social Networking, 6 vols. 2013. (Tech Safety Smarts Ser.). (ENG.). 32p. (J). (gr. 3-4). pap. 48.60 *(978-1-62065-803-1(8),* 19384, Capstone Pr.) Capstone.

Scott, Celicia. Twitter: How Jack Dorsey Changed the Way We Communicate. 2014. (Wizards of Technology Ser.: 10). 64p. (J). (gr. 7-18). 23.95 *(978-1-4222-3187-6(9))* Mason Crest.

Truesdell, Ann. Learning & Sharing with a Wiki. Petelinsek, Kathleen, illus. 2013. (Explorer Junior Library: Information Explorer Junior Ser.). (ENG.). 24p. (J). (gr. 1-4). 32.07 *(978-1-62431-132-1(6),* 202848) Cherry Lake Publishing.

—Wonderful Wikis. 2012. (Explorer Library: Information Explorer Ser.). (ENG.). 32p. (gr. 4-8). pap. 14.21 *(978-1-61080-654-1(9),* 202264); (Illus.). 32.07 *(978-1-61080-480-6(5),* 202090) Cherry Lake Publishing.

Truesdell, Ann & Fontichiaro, Kristin. Starting Your Own Blog. Petelinsek, Kathleen, illus. 2013. (Explorer Junior Library: Information Explorer Junior Ser.). (ENG.). 24p. (J). (gr. 1-4). pap. 12.79 *(978-1-62431-265-6(9),* 202854) Cherry Lake Publishing.

Waters, Rosa. Pinterest(r): How Ben Silbermann & Evan Sharp Changed the Way We Share What We Love. 2014. (Wizards of Technology Ser.: 10). 64p. (J). (gr. 7-18). 23.95 *(978-1-4222-3185-2(2))* Mason Crest.

Wolny, Philip. Foursquare & Other Location-Based Services: Checking in, Staying Safe, & Being Savvy, 1 vol. 2011. (Digital & Information Literacy Ser.). (ENG.). 48p. (YA). (gr. 6-6). pap. 12.75 *(978-1-4488-5615-2(9),* c80c836f-767d-4461-aa13-53a01b6a4750); lib. bdg. 33.47 *(978-1-4488-5554-4(3),* 59857962-7386-4c8a-87cc-4b3b0ed63608) Rosen Publishing Group, Inc., The. (Rosen Reference).

—Google & You: Maximizing Your Google Experience, 1 vol. 2011. (Digital & Information Literacy Ser.). (ENG.). 48p. (YA). (gr. 6-6). pap. 12.75 *(978-1-4488-5613-8(2),* 8c485daa-dc01-4e7f-a381-f44e6b264dca); lib. bdg. 33.47 *(978-1-4488-5553-7(5),* 415cf6f2-9bd0-40c6-bf0b-50bb75cdd634) Rosen Publishing Group, Inc., The. (Rosen Reference).

Woog, Adam. Mark Zuckerberg: Facebook Creator, 1 vol. 2009. (Innovators Ser.). (ENG., Illus.). 48p. (gr. 4-8). 34.58 *(978-0-7377-4566-5(5),* fa57e9a5-7e01-4325-bf58-0f3f491babcb, KidHaven Publishing) Greenhaven Publishing LLC.

WEB SITES—DESIGN

Aho, Kirsti & Underwood, Dale, contrib. by. Town Website Project Using Macromedia Dreamweaver MX 2004: Communicating Information & Ideas on the Web. 2003. (YA). ring bd. 10.00 *(978-0-9742273-3-7(1))* Macromedia, Inc.

Amihud, Zohar. Look Mom! I Built My Own Web Site. 2nd ed. 2006. (Illus.). 204p. (YA). (gr. 7). per. 18.95 *(978-0-9760111-1-8(5))* BookChamp LLC.

Brown, Marty. Webmaster. 2009. (Coolcareers. com Ser.). 48p. (gr. 5-8). 53.00 *(978-1-61511-985-1(X),* Rosen Reference) Rosen Publishing Group, Inc., The.

Bussell, Linda. Exploring SOLID FIGURES on the Web, 1 vol. 2008. (Math in Our World - Level 3 Ser.). (ENG.). 24p. (gr. 3-3). (J). lib. bdg. 24.67 *(978-0-8368-9287-1(9),* 5a49f005-e334-4429-ba7a-24e6b2e17a0d); pap. 9.15 *(978-0-8368-9386-1(7),* 04218b48-57a4-43c8-831a-1fb85bec42b5) Stevens, Gareth Publishing LLLP. (Weekly Reader Leveled Readers).

Career Building Through Using Search Engine Optimization Techniques. 2013. (Digital Career Building Ser.). 64p. (YA). (gr. 7-12). pap. 77.70 *(978-1-4777-1746-2(3))* Rosen Publishing Group, Inc., The.

Endsley, Kezia. Website Design, 1 vol. 2014. (High-Tech Jobs Ser.). (ENG., Illus.). 96p. (YA). (gr. 8-8). 44.50 *(978-1-5026-0111-7(7),* f69c6deb-2957-4540-823c-c759f0630476) Cavendish Square Publishing LLC.

Fischer, James. Computer Math. 2013. (Math 24/7 Ser.: 10). 48p. (J). (gr. 5-18). 19.95 *(978-1-4222-2904-0(1))* Mason Crest.

Freedman, Jeri. Career Building Through Skinning & Modding. 2009. (Digital Career Building Ser.). 64p. (gr. 6-6). 58.50 *(978-1-61512-171-7(4))* Rosen Publishing Group, Inc., The.

Furgang, Adam. Coding Activities for Building Websites with HTML, 1 vol. 2021. (Code Creator Ser.). (ENG.). 64p. (gr. 7-7). pap. 13.95 *(978-1-7253-4113-5(1),* 9a363563-239c-4f9f-917d-101574e25ada) Rosen Publishing Group, Inc., The.

Hatter, Clyde, et al. Create with Code: Build Your Own Website. Lucken, Gary, illus. 2017. 93p. (J). *(978-1-338-14634-9(3))* Scholastic, Inc.

Kallen, Stuart A. Careers in Social Media. 2019. (E-Careers Ser.). (ENG.). 80p. (J). (gr. 6-12). 41.27 *(978-1-68282-617-1(1))* ReferencePoint Pr., Inc.

Leigh, Anna. Design & Build Your Own Website. 2018. (Digital Makers (Alternator Books (r)) Ser.). (ENG., Illus.). 32p. (J). (gr. 3-6). 29.32 *(978-1-5124-8342-0(7),* 0e05c602-626a-4a2e-bc34-30ec54492faf, Lerner Pubns.) Lerner Publishing Group.

Poolos, J. Designing, Building, & Maintaining Websites, 1 vol. 2nd ed. 2017. (Digital & Information Literacy Ser.). (ENG.). 48p. (J). (gr. 6-6). pap. 12.75 *(978-1-4994-3899-4(0),* 9edd023d-3044-4f7e-bb21-b539f6425e68, Rosen Reference) Rosen Publishing Group, Inc., The.

Press, Ferguson. Internet. 2nd rev. ed. 2012. (Career Launcher Ser.). (ENG.). 160p. (gr. 9). 34.95 *(978-0-8160-7951-3(X),* P179120, Ferguson Publishing Company) Infobase Holdings, Inc.

Selfridge, Benjamin. A Kid's Guide to Creating Web Pages for Home & School. 2008. 128p. pap. 17.95 *(978-1-59363-334-9(3))* Prufrock Pr.

Selfridge, Benjamin & Selfridge, Peter. A Kid's Guide to Creating Web Pages for Home & School. 2004. (Illus.). 128p. (J). (gr. 5-10). pap. 19.95 *(978-1-56976-180-9(9),* Zephyr Pr.) Chicago Review Pr., Inc.

Suen, Anastasia. Career Building Through Using Search Engine Optimization Techniques, 1 vol. 2013. (Digital Career Building Ser.). (ENG.). 64p. (YA). (gr. 6-6). 37.13 *(978-1-4777-1726-4(9),* 798f9948-20e9-48cd-a6d8-dc1ea7118e3d); pap. 13.95 *(978-1-4777-1744-8(7),* c38dcdd6-1949-4b2d-85c3-f5d79f4fe2bb) Rosen Publishing Group, Inc., The.

Underwood, Dale & Aho, Kirsti. Town Website Project for Macromedia Dreamweaver MX 2004: Communicating Information & Ideas on the Web, 2 bks. Dharkar, Anuja & McCain, Malinda, eds. Morgan, Mark & Gallenson, Ann, illus. 2003. 39p. spiral bd. 10.00 *(978-0-9742273-8-2(2),* Macromedia Education) Macromedia, Inc.

Vanden-Heuvel, John C., Sr. & Ostrovsky, Andrey. ABCs of the Web. Holmes, Tom, illus. 2016. (ENG.). 28p. (J). (gr. -1-3). bds. 8.99 *(978-1-4998-0312-9(5))* Little Bee Books Inc.

Young Rewired State. Get Coding!: Learn HTML, CSS & JavaScript & Build a Website, App & Game. 2017. (ENG., Illus.). 208p. (J). (gr. 4-7). pap. 12.99 *(978-0-7636-9276-6(X))* Candlewick Pr.

WEBSTER, DANIEL, 1782-1852

Baldwin, James. Four Great Americans. 2006. pap. *(978-1-4065-0509-2(9))* Dodo Pr.

—Four Great Americans: Washington Franklin Webster Lincoln: a Book for Young Americans. 2017. (ENG., Illus.). (J). (gr. 3-7). 23.95 *(978-1-374-89694-9(2));* pap. 13.95 *(978-1-374-89693-2(4))* Capital Communications, Inc.

—Four Great Americans: Washington, Franklin, Webster, Lincoln. a Book for Young Americans. 2017. (ENG., Illus.). (J). (gr. 3-7). pap. *(978-0-649-58735-3(9))* Trieste Publishing Pty Ltd.

WEBSTER, NOAH, 1758-1843

Anderson, Beth. An Inconvenient Alphabet: Ben Franklin & Noah Webster's Spelling Revolution. Baddeley, Elizabeth, illus. 2018. (ENG.). 48p. (J). (gr. -1-3). 17.99 *(978-1-5344-0555-4(0),* Simon & Schuster/Paula Wiseman Bks.) Simon & Schuster/Paula Wiseman Bks.

Ferris, Jeri Chase. Noah Webster & His Words. Kirsch, Vincent X., illus. 2015. (ENG.). 32p. (J). (gr. 1-4). 7.99 *(978-0-544-58242-2(X),* 1613671, Clarion Bks.) HarperCollins Pubs.

Maurer, Tracy Nelson. Noah Webster's Fighting Words. Catusanu, Mircea, illus. 2017. (ENG.). 40p. (J). (gr. 2-5). E-Book 30.65 *(978-1-5124-2839-1(6),* Millbrook Pr.) Lerner Publishing Group.

Melis, Luisanna Fodde. Noah Webster & the First American Dictionary. 2009. (Library of American Lives & Times Ser.). 112p. (gr. 5-5). 69.20 *(978-1-60853-495-1(2))* Rosen Publishing Group, Inc., The.

Proudfit, Isabel. Noah Webster, Father of the Dictionary. 2008. (Illus.). 224p. (J). pap. 15.95 *(978-0-9801563-0-0(0))* Bradford Pr., Inc.

Reef, Catherine. Noah Webster: Man of Many Words. 2015. (ENG., Illus.). 224p. (J). (gr. 5-7). 18.99 *(978-0-544-12983-2(0),* 1544739, Clarion Bks.) HarperCollins Pubs.

Shea, Pegi Deitz. Noah Webster: Weaver of Words. Vachula, Monica, illus. 2009. (ENG.). 40p. (J). (gr. 2-5). 18.99 *(978-1-59078-441-9(3),* Calkins Creek) Highlights Pr., c/o Highlights for Children, Inc.

WEDDINGS

see Etiquette; Marriage; Marriage Customs and Rites

WEIGHT CONTROL

see also Diet; Exercise

Allman, Toney. Food in Schools. rev. ed. 2014. (Matters of Opinion Ser.). (ENG.). 64p. (J). (gr. 4-6). pap. 14.60 *(978-1-60357-584-3(7))* Norwood Hse. Pr.

—Obesity. 2008. (21st Century Skills Library: Health at Risk Ser.). (ENG., Illus.). 32p. (gr. 4-8). lib. bdg. 32.07 *(978-1-60279-285-2(2),* 200134) Cherry Lake Publishing.

Bartell, Susan S. Dr. Susan's Girls-Only Weight Loss Guide: The Easy, Fun Way to Look & Feel Good! 2006. (ENG., Illus.). 272p. (J). (gr. 7-12). per. 14.95 *(978-0-9721502-0-0(X))* Parent Positive Pr.

Brauchner, Elizabeth. Weight Management. McDonnell, Mary Ann & Forman, Sara, eds. 2013. (Young Adult's Guide to the Science of Health Ser.: 15). 128p. (J). (gr. 7-18). 24.95 *(978-1-4222-2818-0(5))* Mason Crest.

Boudreau, Helene. Real Mermaids Don't Need High Heels. 2013. (ENG.). 240p. (J). (gr. 4-8). pap. 10.99 *(978-1-4022-6458-0(5))* Sourcebooks, Inc.

Chandler, Matt. Understanding Obesity. 2019. (21st Century Skills Library: Upfront Health Ser.). (ENG.). 32p. (J). (gr. 4-8). pap. 14.21 *(978-1-5341-5085-0(4)*, 213647); (Illus.). lib. bdg. 32.07 *(978-1-5341-4799-7(3)*, 213646) Cherry Lake Publishing.

Currie-McGhee, Leanne K. Childhood Obesity, 1 vol. 2012. (Nutrition & Health Ser.). (ENG., Illus.). 104p. (gr. 7-10). lib. bdg. 37.33 *(978-1-4205-0723-2(0)*, 60f4b4f8-cf07-4b89-99d6-ae006c234235, Lucent Pr.) Greenhaven Publishing LLC.

Dweck, Joey. Losing for Good. 2005. (YA). per. 19.95 *(978-0-9754448-6-3(7))* Weight Loss Buddy, Inc.

Edwards, Hazel & Alexander, Goldie. Talking about Your Weight, 1 vol. 2010. (Healthy Living Ser.). (ENG., Illus.). 32p. (YA). (gr. 3-4). lib. bdg. 28.67 *(978-1-4339-3655-5(0)*, a8867b6a-ae51-4e96-8b40-b52e3aba4cc8) Stevens, Gareth Publishing LLLP.

Engdahl, Sylvia, ed. Obesity, 1 vol. 2014. (Opposing Viewpoints Ser.). (ENG.). 232p. (gr. 10-12). lib. bdg. 50.43 *(978-0-7377-7278-4(6)*, 769d31d4-a0da-43b6-a1fc-9577c47fb098, Greenhaven Publishing) Greenhaven Publishing LLC.

Esherick, Joan. Emotions & Eating. Garcia, Victor, ed. 2014. (Understanding Obesity Ser.: 10). 104p. (J). (gr. 7-18). lib. bdg. 24.95 *(978-1-4222-3059-6(7))* Mason Crest.

—Looking & Feeling Good in Your Body. Garcia, Victor, ed. 2014. (Understanding Obesity Ser.: 10). (Illus.). 104p. (J). (gr. 7-18). lib. bdg. 24.95 *(978-1-4222-3063-3(5))* Mason Crest.

Faulkner, Nicholas & Williams, Kara. Conquering Diet Drug Abuse, 1 vol., 1. 2015. (Conquering Eating Disorders Ser.). (ENG.). 64p. (J). (gr. 6-6). 36.13 *(978-1-4994-6197-8(6)*, 116ea6b4-0205-4457-86b1-c357c9c8afba, Rosen Young Adult) Rosen Publishing Group, Inc., The.

Favor, Lesli J. & Massie, Elizabeth. Weighing In: Nutrition & Weight Management, 1 vol. 2010. (Food & You Ser.). (ENG.). 32p. (gr. 5-5). 31.21 *(978-0-7614-4367-4(3)*, 8bcc9d94-97c1-4fc7-8954-1f45ff54c7a6) Cavendish Square Publishing LLC.

Ford, Jean. Health Issues Caused by Obesity. Garcia, Victor, ed. 2014. (Understanding Obesity Ser.: 10). 104p. (J). (gr. 7-18). lib. bdg. 24.95 *(978-1-4222-3062-6(7))* Mason Crest.

Ford, Jean & Libal, Autumn. No Quick Fix: Fad Diets & Weight-Loss Miracles. Garcia, Victor, ed. 2014. (Understanding Obesity Ser.: 10). (Illus.). 104p. (YA). (gr. 7-18). lib. bdg. 24.95 *(978-1-4222-3065-7(1))* Mason Crest.

Friedman, Lauri S., ed. Obesity, 1 vol. 2010. (Introducing Issues with Opposing Viewpoints Ser.). (ENG.). 144p. (gr. 7-10). 43.63 *(978-0-7377-5083-6(9)*, 3c2f02b8-b8bf-4627-8f42-853d39a4a6cc, Greenhaven Publishing) Greenhaven Publishing LLC.

Gay, Kathlyn. Am I Fat? The Obesity Issue for Teens, 1 vol. 2006. (Issues in Focus Today Ser.). (ENG., Illus.). 112p. (gr. 6-7). lib. bdg. 35.93 *(978-0-7660-2527-1(6)*, d821e5cd-fc0d-406e-b08d-686fa5594eb2) Enslow Publishing, LLC.

—Are You Fat? The Obesity Issue for Teens, 1 vol. 2014. (Got Issues? Ser.). (ENG., Illus.). 112p. (gr. 6-7). lib. bdg. 38.93 *(978-0-7660-4322-0(3)*, da651fb9-b91a-4747-89b1-2e7ad5a905e9) Enslow Publishing, LLC.

—Do You Know What to Eat?, 1 vol. 2015. (Got Issues? Ser.). (ENG., Illus.). 128p. (gr. 7-7). 38.93 *(978-0-7660-6987-9(7)*, cf7df775-dba4-4875-9619-8c16ea63285f) Enslow Publishing, LLC.

Gillard, Arthur, ed. Dieting, 1 vol. 2014. (Issues That Concern You Ser.). (ENG., Illus.). 112p. (gr. 7-10). lib. bdg. 43.63 *(978-0-7377-6938-8(6)*, ab68bd51-fd41-426e-98f9-63312c9ed534, Greenhaven Publishing) Greenhaven Publishing LLC.

Greene, Meg. Obesity. 2008. (Gallup Major Trends & Events Ser.). (Illus.). 112p. (YA). (gr. 7-18). lib. bdg. 22.95 *(978-1-59084-967-5(1))* Mason Crest.

Griffith, M. Christopher & Griffith, Jeana R. The Tale of Two Athletes: The Story of Jumper & the Thumper a True Story on Understanding & Combating Childhood Obesity. 2012. 60p. pap. 24.99 *(978-1-4685-4014-7(9))* AuthorHouse.

Haerens, Margaret, ed. Obesity, 1 vol. 2011. (Global Viewpoints Ser.). (ENG., Illus.). 232p. (gr. 10-12). 47.83 *(978-0-7377-5660-9(8)*, 26b03a41-abcb-4fb9-a9cc-8d5229cfadea); pap. 32.70 *(978-0-7377-5661-6(6)*, f555206d-2c3a-4c5d-bd58-d709e47c8352) Greenhaven Publishing LLC. (Greenhaven Publishing).

Harmon, Daniel E. Obesity. (Coping in a Changing World Ser.). 112p. (gr. 7-7). 2009. 63.90 *(978-1-61512-021-5(1))* 2007. (ENG.). (YA). lib. bdg. 39.80 *(978-1-4042-0949-7(2)*, be64f74d-f2e3-4dde-b01b-6087cdfad575) Rosen Publishing Group, Inc., The.

Hicks, Terry Allan. Obesity, 1 vol. 2009. (Health Alert Ser.). (ENG.). 64p. (gr. 4-4). lib. bdg. 35.50 *(978-0-7614-2911-1(5)*, 4e68d304-05a3-44ae-92ff-e77723006809) Cavendish Square Publishing LLC.

Hidalgo-Robert, Alberto. Fat No More: A Teenager's Victory over Obesity. 2012. (J). pap. 16.95 *(978-1-55885-745-2(1)*, Piñata Books) Arte Publico Pr.

Hunt, Jamie. Tired of Being Teased: Obesity & Others. 2010. (Kids & Obesity Ser.). 48p. (YA). lib. bdg. 19.95 *(978-1-4222-1711-5(6))* Mason Crest.

Hunter, William. Nature & Nurture: The Causes of Obesity. 2015. (Illus.). 104p. (YA). *(978-1-4222-3056-5(2))* Mason Crest.

—Nature & Nurture: The Causes of Obesity. Garcia, Victor, ed. 2014. (Understanding Obesity Ser.: 10). 104p. (J). (gr. 7-18). lib. bdg. 24.95 *(978-1-4222-3064-0(3))* Mason Crest.

—Surgery & Medicine for Weight Loss. Garcia, Victor, ed. 2014. (Understanding Obesity Ser.: 10). 104p. (J). (gr. 7-18). lib. bdg. 24.95 *(978-1-4222-3066-4(X))* Mason Crest.

Juettner, Bonnie. Childhood Obesity. 2009. (In Controversy Ser.). (YA). (gr. 7-12). 43.93 *(978-1-60152-083-8(2))* ReferencePoint Pr., Inc.

Kallen, Stuart. Obesity. 2016. (Matters of Opinion Ser.). (ENG., Illus.). 64p. (J). (gr. 4-6). pap. 14.60 *(978-1-60357-859-2(5))* Norwood Hse. Pr.

Kallen, Stuart A. Obesity. 2016. (Matters of Opinion Ser.). (ENG., Illus.). 64p. (J). (gr. 4-6). lib. bdg. 27.93 *(978-1-59953-756-6(7))* Norwood Hse. Pr.

Kern, Merilee A. Making Healthy Choices: A Story to Inspire Fit, Weight-Wise Kids (Boys' Edition) 2007. (J). pap. 11.95 *(978-1-58736-742-7(4))* Wheatmark, Inc.

—Making Healthy Choices: A Story to Inspire Fit, Weight-Wise Kids (Girls' Edition) 2007. (J). pap. 11.95 *(978-1-58736-743-4(2))* Wheatmark, Inc.

Kids & Obesity, 10 vols., Set. Incl. Does Television Make You Fat? Lifestyle & Obesity. Simons, Rae. (Illus.). pap. 7.95 *(978-1-4222-1900-3(3))*; Too Many Sunday Dinners: Family & Diet. Simons, Rae. pap. 7.95 *(978-1-4222-1901-0(1))*; Truth about Diets: What's Right for You? Hunt, Jamie. pap. 7.95 *(978-1-4222-1898-3(8))*; Weighted Down: When Being Overweight makes You Sick. Thompson, Helen. (Illus.). pap. 7.95 *(978-1-4222-1896-9(1))*; 48p. (YA). 2009. 2011. Set pap. 79.50 *(978-1-4222-1893-8(7))*; Set lib. bdg. 199.50 *(978-1-4222-1705-4(1))* Mason Crest.

Langwith, Jacqueline, ed. Childhood Obesity, 1 vol. 2012. (Perspectives on Diseases & Disorders Ser.). (ENG., Illus.). 152p. (gr. 10-12). lib. bdg. 45.93 *(978-0-7377-6350-8(7)*, 29bb355a-c624-40b1-b6e9-f3a3ba77fef6, Greenhaven Publishing) Greenhaven Publishing LLC.

LeMay, DiDi. Freddy's French Fries Fiasco. 2012. (ENG.). (J). pap. *(978-1-4675-2963-1(X))* Independent Pub.

Libal, Autumn. Discrimination & Prejudice. Garcia, Victor, ed. 2014. (Understanding Obesity Ser.: 10). 104p. (J). (gr. 7-18). lib. bdg. 24.95 *(978-1-4222-3058-9(9))* Mason Crest.

—Fast Food & the Obesity Epidemic. Garcia, Victor, ed. 2014. (Understanding Obesity Ser.: 10). 104p. (J). (gr. 7-18). lib. bdg. 24.95 *(978-1-4222-3061-9(9))* Mason Crest.

—Fats, Sugars, & Empty Calories: The Fast Food Habit. 2007. (Obesity Ser.). (Illus.). 104p. (YA). (gr. 4-7). lib. bdg. 23.95 *(978-1-59084-943-9(4))* Mason Crest.

Lite, Lori. Children's Wellness Curriculum: Lessons, Stories & Techniques Designed to Decrease Bullying, Anxiety, Anger & Obesity While Promoting Self-Esteem & Healthy Food Choices. 2007. (J). (gr. k-5). 89.95 incl. audio compact disk *(978-0-9787781-2-5(X)*, 5) Stress Free Kids.

Lluch, Alex A. Lose 10 Pounds in Two Weeks. 2011. 360p. pap. 16.95 *(978-1-936061-17-4(1))* WS Publishing.

—Lose up to 10 Pounds in 2 Weeks Pocket Guide. 2011. 220p. pap., pupil's gde. ed. 11.95 *(978-1-936061-40-2(6))* WS Publishing.

Lombardo, Michelle. Balancing the Energy Equation: One Step at a Time! Herron, Mark, illus. 2003. (J). lib. bdg. 17.95 *(978-1-931212-51-9(1))* OrganWise Guys Inc., The.

—Pepto's Place: Where Every Portion Size Is OrganWise! Herron, Mark, illus. 2003. 32p. (J). lib. bdg. 17.95 *(978-1-931212-50-2(3))* OrganWise Guys Inc., The.

Mattern, Joanne. Obesity: Causes & Consequences. 2005. (Behind the News Ser.). (Illus.). 112p. (J). (gr. 5-18). lib. bdg. 24.95 *(978-1-881508-67-0(6))* Oliver Pr., Inc.

McMahon, Christina & Marcovitz, Hal. The Dangers of Diet Drugs, 1 vol. 2016. (Drug Education Library). (ENG.). 104p. (YA). (gr. 7-7). 39.08 *(978-1-5345-6005-5(X)*, efa39f03-96c9-4f3d-bba1-d8bf4a4ef5f5, Lucent Pr.) Greenhaven Publishing LLC.

Murphy, Wendy B. Weight & Health. 2008. (Twenty-First Century Medical Library). (ENG., Illus.). 112p. (gr. 6-12). lib. bdg. 33.26 *(978-0-8225-6784-4(9))* Lerner Publishing Group.

Nakaya, Andrea C. Thinking Critically: Obesity. 2017. (ENG., Illus.). 80p. (J). (gr. 5-12). *(978-1-68282-267-8(2))* ReferencePoint Pr., Inc.

Newman Jimerson, Maxine. Childhood Obesity, 1 vol. 2008. (Diseases & Disorders Ser.). (ENG., Illus.). 112p. (J). (gr. 7-7). lib. bdg. 41.53 *(978-1-59018-997-9(3)*, f5e53500-226b-420f-b217-cb57dad981b4, Lucent Pr.) Greenhaven Publishing LLC.

Obesity: Modern-Day Epidemic, 10 vols., Set. Incl. Diet & Your Emotions: The Comfort Food Falsehood. Esherick, Joan. (J). 2004. lib. bdg. 23.95 *(978-1-59084-950-7(7))*; Fats, Sugars, & Empty Calories: The Fast Food Habit. Libal, Autumn. (YA). 2007. lib. bdg. 23.95 *(978-1-59084-943-9(4))*; Medications & Surgeries for Weight Loss: When Dieting Isn't Enough. Hunter, William. (YA). 2007. lib. bdg. 23.95 *(978-1-59084-947-7(7))*; (gr. 4-7). (Illus.). 104p. 2005. Set lib. bdg. 239.50 *(978-1-59084-941-5(8))* Mason Crest.

Owens, Peter. Teens Health & Obesity. 2008. (Gallup Youth Survey, Major Issues & Trends Ser.). (Illus.). 112p. (YA). (gr. -1-7). lib. bdg. 22.95 *(978-1-59084-872-2(1))* Mason Crest.

—Teens, Health & Obesity. Developed in Association with the Gallup Organization Staff, ed. 2013. (Gallup Youth Survey: Major Issues & Trends Ser.: 14). (Illus.). 112p. (J). (gr. 7-18). 24.95 *(978-1-4222-2961-3(0))* Mason Crest.

Parsons, William B., Jr. Tough Talk about Fat! How to Reach & Maintain Your Ideal Weight. 2003. 134p. per. 12.95 *(978-0-9662568-9-5(1))* Lilac Pr.

Robbins, Lynette. How to Deal with Obesity, 1 vol. 2009. (Kids' Health Ser.). (ENG.). 24p. (gr. 2-3). (J). pap. 9.25 *(978-1-4358-3423-1(2)*, 26f83424-edb2-4d87-935d-669a29344b35, PowerKids Pr.); (Illus.). (YA). lib. bdg. 26.27 *(978-1-4042-8143-1(6)*, 6f482a59-33a3-44af-b4a3-5e38bc49f99c) Rosen Publishing Group, Inc., The.

Roberts, Jeremy. Drugs & Dieting. 2009. (Drug Abuse Prevention Library). 64p. (gr. 5-5). 58.50 *(978-1-60853-428-9(6))* Rosen Publishing Group, Inc., The.

Sanna, Ellyn. Big Portions, Big Problems. Garcia, Victor, ed. 2014. (Understanding Obesity Ser.: 10). (Illus.). 104p. (J). (gr. 7-18). lib. bdg. 24.95 *(978-1-4222-3057-2(0))* Mason Crest.

Sartori, Rosanne Sheritz. A New Start: One Child's Struggle with Obesity. 2004. (Illus.). 88p. (J). per. 19.95 *(978-1-931636-33-9(8))* National Ctr. For Youth Issues.

Scherer, Lauri S., ed. Obesity, 1 vol. 2013. (Issues That Concern You Ser.). (ENG., Illus.). 120p. (gr. 7-10). lib. bdg. 43.63 *(978-0-7377-6298-3(5)*, 2bd42a5b-0812-4480-97d0-f4a709b3037f, Greenhaven Publishing) Greenhaven Publishing LLC.

Simons, Rae. Does Television Make You Fat? Lifestyle & Obesity. (Kids & Obesity Ser.). (Illus.). 48p. (YA). 2010. lib. bdg. 19.95 *(978-1-4222-1712-2(4))* 2009. pap. 7.95 *(978-1-4222-1900-3(3))* Mason Crest.

—I Eat When I'm Sad: Food & Feelings. 2010. (Kids & Obesity Ser.). 48p. (YA). lib. bdg. 19.95 *(978-1-4222-1714-6(0))* Mason Crest.

—Too Many Sunday Dinners: Family & Diet. (Kids & Obesity Ser.). 48p. (YA). 2010. lib. bdg. 19.95 *(978-1-4222-1713-9(2))* 2009. pap. 7.95 *(978-1-4222-1901-0(1))* Mason Crest.

Snyder, Gail. Kids & Obesity. 2018. (Diseases & Disorders of Youth Ser.). (ENG.). 80p. (YA). (gr. 6-12). 39.93 *(978-1-68282-403-0(9))* ReferencePoint Pr., Inc.

Stewart, Gail. Fat in America. 2007. (Ripped from the Headlines Ser.). 64p. (J). (gr. 7-12). 23.95 *(978-1-60217-002-5(9))* Erickson Pr.

Tecco, Betsy Dru. Food for Fuel: The Connection Between Food & Physical Activity. (Library of Nutrition Ser.). 48p. 2009. (gr. 5-8). 53.00 *(978-1-60853-766-2(8)*, Rosen Reference) 2007. (ENG., Illus.). (gr. 5-8). per. 12.75 *(978-1-4042-1635-8(9)*, 030297f5-d816-480a-aa89-080d24465e77) 2004. (Illus.). (J). lib. bdg. 26.50 *(978-1-4042-0303-7(6))* Rosen Publishing Group, Inc., The.

Thompson, Helen. Weighted Down: When Being Overweight makes You Sick. (Kids & Obesity Ser.). (Illus.). 48p. (YA). 2010. lib. bdg. 19.95 *(978-1-4222-1708-5(6))* 2009. pap. 7.95 *(978-1-4222-1896-9(1))* Mason Crest.

Williams, Kara. Diet Drugs, 1 vol. 2007. (Danger Zone: Dieting & Eating Disorders Ser.). (ENG., Illus.). 64p. (YA). (gr. 5-6). lib. bdg. 37.13 *(978-1-4042-1994-6(3)*, 491527cc-5c75-4d55-9285-96cd954254a4) Rosen Publishing Group, Inc., The.

Zahensky, Barbara. Diet Fads. 2009. (Danger Zone: Dieting & Eating Disorders Ser.). 64p. (gr. 5-6). 55.90 *(978-1-61512-124-3(2))* Rosen Publishing Group, Inc., The.

Zahensky, Barbara A. Diet Fads, 1 vol. 2007. (Danger Zone: Dieting & Eating Disorders Ser.). (ENG., Illus.). 64p. (YA). (gr. 5-6). lib. bdg. 37.13 *(978-1-4042-1999-1(4)*, 320c05d7-afce-4006-a5e1-995188bacd97) Rosen Publishing Group, Inc., The.

WEIGHT CONTROL—FICTION

Aliano, Kimberly Potenzone. Chubby ... Is Everywhere! 2009. (ENG.). 38p. pap. 16.99 *(978-1-4490-0505-4(5))* AuthorHouse.

Babich, Elaine. You Never Called Me Princess. 2012. 210p. pap. 14.00 *(978-1-105-70209-9(X))* Lulu.com GBR. Dist: Lulu Pr., Inc.

Barson, Kelly. 45 Pounds (More or Less) 2014. 272p. (YA). (gr. 7). pap. 9.99 *(978-0-14-242265-6(7)*, Speak) Penguin Young Readers Group.

Bently, Peter. The Yoga Ogre. Rickerty, Simon, illus. 2012. (ENG.). 32p. (J). 15.99 *(978-1-84738-902-2(3))* Simon & Schuster, Ltd. GBR. Dist: Simon & Schuster, Inc.

Brown, Gladys. The Adventures of King Flapjack. 2005. 36p. pap. 13.95 *(978-1-4116-2694-2(X))* Lulu Pr., Inc.

Bunting, Eve. My Dog Jack Is Fat, 0 vols. Rex, Michael, illus. 2012. (ENG.). 32p. (J). (gr. 1-3). 16.99 *(978-0-7614-5809-8(3)*, 9780761458098, Two Lions) Amazon Publishing.

Caple, Kathy. Starring Hillary. Caple, Kathy, illus. 2003. (Picture Bks.). (Illus.). 28p. (J). (gr. -1-3). 15.95 *(978-1-57505-261-8(X)*, Carolrhoda Bks.) Lerner Publishing Group.

Capper, Ann. Big Thighs, Tight Jeans (Should Jan Go O. 2005. pap. 11.95 *(978-0-7414-2676-5(5))* Infinity Publishing.

Carlson-Berne, Emma. Under Pressure. 2013. (Counterattack Ser.). (ENG.). 104p. (YA). (gr. 6-12). pap. 7.95 *(978-1-4677-0718-3(X)*, a24134f3-ade8-4ba8-a4d0-709bb61425e1); lib. bdg. 27.99 *(978-1-4677-0303-1(6)*, b0cbbeaf-429b-4c39-a3d0-609184a04d33) Lerner Publishing Group. (Darby Creek).

Carter, Catherine. Anna's Choice. Pittman, Gail, illus. 2005. 24p. (J). (gr. 3-7). 12.95 *(978-1-893062-79-5(1))* Quail Ridge Pr., Inc.

Cohn, Rachel. You Know Where to Find Me. 2009. (ENG.). 224p. (YA). (gr. 7). pap. 8.99 *(978-0-689-87860-2(5)*, Simon & Schuster Bks. For Young Readers) Simon & Schuster Bks. For Young Readers.

—You Know Where to Find Me. 2008. (ENG.). 204p. (YA). (gr. 7-12). 22.44 *(978-0-689-87859-6(1))* Simon & Schuster, Inc.

Colbert, June. The King of Large. 2005. 160p. pap. *(978-0-7344-0615-6(0)*, Lothian Children's Bks.) Hachette Australia.

DeClements, Barthe. Nothing's Fair in Fifth Grade. 2008. (ENG.). 144p. (J). (gr. 3-7). 7.99 *(978-0-14-241349-4(6)*, Puffin Books) Penguin Young Readers Group.

deVos, Kelly. Fat Girl on a Plane. 2018. (ENG.). 384p. (YA). 18.99 *(978-0-373-21253-8(4)*, Harlequin Teen) Harlequin Enterprises ULC CAN. Dist: HarperCollins Pubs.

Gonzales Bertrand, Diane. Sofia & the Purple Dress / Sofia y el Vestido Morado. Baeza Ventura, Gabriela, tr. Fields, Lisa, illus. 2012. (SPA & ENG.). (J). 17.95 *(978-1-55885-701-8(X)*, Piñata Books) Arte Publico Pr.

Griffith, Jeana R. The Tale of Two Athletes: the Story of Jumper & the Thumper: Workbook: Steps to Tackle Childhood Obesity. 2012. 68p. pap. 13.95 *(978-1-4772-4086-1(1))* AuthorHouse.

Hardy, Zoey. Everything Changes. 2005. 316p. per. 9.95 *(978-0-9765423-0-8(7))* Eudon Publishing.

Helen, Grace. Santa's Way. 2012. 32p. pap. 24.95 *(978-1-4626-7356-8(2))* America Star Bks.

Jackson, A. Isaiah J. Jiffy: You, You, You. Bully! 2005. 50p. pap. 16.95 *(978-1-4137-8524-1(7))* PublishAmerica, Inc.

Kramer, Paul. Maggie Goes on a Diet. 2011. (ENG.). 44p. (J). (gr. 1-7). 15.95 *(978-0-9819745-5-2(4))* Aloha Wellness Pubs.

Lane, Melaina. Chubs. . Another Day at School. 2011. 20p. 9.14 *(978-1-4251-7330-2(6))* Trafford Publishing.

Lang, Diane & Buchanan, Michael. The Fat Boy Chronicles. 2010. (Fat Boy Chronicles Ser.). (ENG.). 224p. (J). (gr. 7-11). pap. 9.95 *(978-1-58536-543-2(2)*, 202220) Sleeping Bear Pr.

Liberto, Lorenzo. Matt the Rat Fights Back / Ratón Mateo se Defiende. Gomez, Rocio, tr. from ENG. Torres, Irving, illus. 2005. (Matt the Rat Ser. / La Serie de Ratón Mateo). (ENG & SPA.). 32p. (J). lib. bdg. 20.00 *(978-0-9743668-4-5(6))* Harvest Sun Pr., LLC.

Lipsyte, Robert. One Fat Summer. rev. ed. 2004. (ENG.). 240p. (YA). (gr. 8-18). pap. 8.99 *(978-0-06-447073-5(3)*, HarperTeen) HarperCollins Pubs.

Lowry, Brigid. Things You Either Hate or Love: A Novel. 2007. (ENG.). 192p. (YA). (gr. 8-12). pap. 18.99 *(978-0-312-36308-6(7)*, 900040880, St. Martin's Griffin) St. Martin's Pr.

Mackler, Carolyn. The Earth, My Butt, & Other Big Round Things. 2018. (ENG.). 288p. (YA). pap. 11.99 *(978-1-68119-798-2(7)*, 900187324, Bloomsbury USA Childrens) Bloomsbury Publishing USA.

—The Universe Is Expanding & So Am I. 2019. (ENG.). 304p. (YA). pap. 10.99 *(978-1-68119-982-5(3)*, 900194721, Bloomsbury Young Adult) Bloomsbury Publishing USA.

Marino, Peter. Dough Boy. (ENG.). 176p. (gr. 7-12). 2007. (YA). pap. 6.95 *(978-0-8234-2096-4(5))* 2005. (J). 17.95 *(978-0-8234-1873-2(1))* Holiday Hse., Inc.

Mauzy, Barbara E. Don't Be a Schwoe: Fitness: Fitness, 1 vol. 2013. (ENG., Illus.). 64p. (J). (gr. -1-3). 16.99 *(978-0-7643-4295-0(9)*, 4777) Schiffer Publishing, Ltd.

May, Eleanor. The Great Shape-up. 2008. pap. 34.95 *(978-1-58013-763-8(6))* Astra Publishing Hse.

Menon, Sandhya. There's Something about Sweetie. (ENG.). (YA). (gr. 7). 2020. 400p. pap. 12.99 *(978-1-5344-1679-6(X))* 2019. (Illus.). 384p. 18.99 *(978-1-5344-1678-9(1))* Simon Pulse. (Simon Pulse).

Morgan McKinney Was Portly, Not Skinny: A Christmas Story. 2nd ed. 2003. (Illus.). 50p. (J). per. 59.95 *(978-0-9654843-3-6(5)*, 1) MacGregor, Doug.

Murphy, Julie. Dear Sweet Pea. 2019. (ENG.). 288p. (J). (gr. 3-7). 16.99 *(978-0-06-247307-3(7))*; E-Book *(978-0-06-247309-7(3)*, 9780062473097) HarperCollins Pubs. (Balzer & Bray).

—Dumplin' (Dumplin' Ser.: 1). (ENG.). (YA). (gr. 8). 2017. 400p. pap. 10.99 *(978-0-06-232719-2(4))* 2015. 384p. 17.99 *(978-0-06-232718-5(6))* HarperCollins Pubs. (Balzer & Bray).

—Dumplin'. 2017. (YA). lib. bdg. 20.85 *(978-0-606-39647-9(0))* Turtleback.

—Dumplin' Movie Tie-In Edition. movie tie-in ed. 2018. (Dumplin' Ser.: 1). (ENG.). 400p. (YA). (gr. 8). pap. 9.99 *(978-0-06-293467-3(8)*, Balzer & Bray) HarperCollins Pubs.

Olsen, Judith K. I Can Hardly Wait. 2006. 100p. (J). pap. 7.95 *(978-1-59800-999-6(0))* Outskirts Pr., Inc.

Paley, Sasha. Huge. 2008. (ENG.). 272p. (YA). (gr. 7-12). pap. 8.99 *(978-1-4169-5795-9(2)*, Simon & Schuster Bks. For Young Readers) Simon & Schuster Bks. For Young Readers.

Patneaude, David. Colder Than Ice. 2003. (ENG.). 168p. (J). (gr. 4-6). 18.69 *(978-0-8075-8135-3(6))* Whitman, Albert & Co.

Perl, Lila. Me & Fat Glenda. 2014. (Fat Glenda Ser.). (ENG.). 200p. (gr. 3). pap. 12.95 *(978-1-939601-03-2(7))* Ig Publishing, Inc.

Rivera, Lassen. Soy Gordito. Alvarez, Mrinali, illus. 2006. (SPA.). 28p. 8.95 *(978-0-8477-1565-7(5))* Univ. of Puerto Rico Pr.

Sachs, Marilyn. The Fat Girl. 2nd ed. 2007. (ENG.). 240p. (YA). (gr. 9-12). per. 8.95 *(978-0-7387-1000-6(8)*, 0738710008, Flux) North Star Editions.

Sackier, Shelley. Dear OPL. 2015. (ENG.). 240p. (J). (gr. 5-8). pap. 12.99 *(978-1-4926-0859-2(9)*, 9781492608592) Sourcebooks, Inc.

Schechter, Lynn R. My Big Fat Secret: How Jenna Takes Control of Her Emotions & Eating. Chin, Jason, illus. 2009. 64p. (J). (gr. 3-7). 14.95 *(978-1-4338-0540-0(5))*; pap. 9.95 *(978-1-4338-0541-7(3))* American Psychological Assn. (Magination Pr.).

Schraff, Anne. Going for Gold. 2008. 124p. lib. bdg. 13.95 *(978-0-7569-8403-8(3))* Perfection Learning Corp.

Seymour's Weight Loss Challenge! 2004. (J). *(978-0-9777159-2-3(2))* Health New England.

Supplee, Suzanne. Artichoke's Heart. 2009. 288p. (YA). (gr. 7-18). 8.99 *(978-0-14-241427-9(1)*, Speak) Penguin Young Readers Group.

Walton, K. M. Empty. 2013. (ENG., Illus.). 272p. (YA). (gr. 9). pap. 12.99 *(978-1-4424-5358-6(3)*, Simon Pulse) Simon Pulse.

Whytock, Cherry. My Cup Runneth Over: The Life of Angelica Cookson Potts. Whytock, Cherry, illus. 2012. (ENG., Illus.). 192p. (YA). (gr. 7). pap. 9.99 *(978-1-4424-6055-3(5)*, Simon Pulse) Simon Pulse.

—My Scrumptious Scottish Dumplings: The Life of Angelica Cookson Potts. Whytock, Cherry, illus. 2006. (ENG., Illus.). 192p. (YA). mass mkt. 5.99 *(978-0-689-86552-7(X)*, Simon Pulse) Simon Pulse.

Willis, Jeanne. Flabby Cat & Slobby Dog. Ross, Tony, illus. 2009. (Andersen Press Picture Bks). (ENG.). 32p. (J). (gr. -1-3). 16.95 *(978-0-7613-5151-1(5)*, Carolrhoda Bks.) Lerner Publishing Group.

WEIGHTS AND MEASURES

Here are entered works on a system of standard units of measure. Works on the science of measurement or of weights and measures are entered under Metrology. Works on a quantity taken as a standard of measurement are entered under Units of Measurement. Works on the force exerted by the gravitational field on a body are entered under Weight (Physics).

see also Measurement; Metric System; Metrology

Aboff, Marcie. If You Were an Inch or a Centimeter, 1 vol. Dillard, Sarah, illus. 2009. (Math Fun Ser.). (ENG.). 24p. (J). (gr. 2-4). pap. 7.95 *(978-1-4048-5199-3(2)*, 95507, Picture Window Bks.) Capstone.

Adamson, Heather & Adamson, Thomas K. How Do You Measure Weight? 2010. (Measure It! Ser.). (ENG.). 32p. (J). (gr. 1-2). pap. 48.60 *(978-1-4296-6460-8(6)*, 16215, Capstone Pr.) Capstone.

Adamson, Thomas K. & Adamson, Heather. ¿Cómo Mides los Líquidos? 2011. (Mídelo/Measure It Ser.).Tr. of How Do You Measure Liquids? (MUL.). 32p. (J). (gr. -1-2). 27.99 *(978-1-4296-6890-3(3)*, 116505, Capstone Pr.) Capstone.

WXYZ

—How Do You Measure Weight?, 1 vol. 2010. (Measure It! Ser.). (ENG.). 32p. (J). (gr. -1-2). pap. 8.10 *(978-1-4296-6333-5(2),* 115534) Capstone.

Adler, David A. The Metric System. Miller, Edward, illus. 2020. 32p. (J). (gr. 2-5). 18.99 *(978-0-8234-4096-2(6))* Holiday Hse., Inc.

—Perimeter, Area, & Volume: A Monster Book of Dimensions. Miller, Edward, illus. 2013. (ENG.). 32p. (J). (gr. 2-5). pap. 8.99 *(978-0-8234-2763-5(3))* Holiday Hse., Inc.

Alvarez, Jordan. Heavy or Light? Describe & Compare Measurable Attributes. 2013. (Rosen Math Readers Ser.). (ENG.). 16p. (J). (gr. k-1). pap. 42.00 *(978-1-4777-1651-9(3));* (illus.). pap. 7.00 *(978-1-4777-1650-2(5),* 51aa4c1a-7cb6-4bb7-965c-182024d628cc) Rosen Publishing Group, Inc., The. (Rosen Classroom).

Amstutz, Lisa J. Scales & Balances. 2019. (Science Tools Ser.). (ENG., Illus.). 24p. (J). (gr. k-2). pap. 6.95 *(978-1-9771-0061-0(9),* 138212); lib. bdg. 27.32 *(978-1-9771-0057-3(0),* 138208) Capstone. (Pebble).

Anderson, Jill. Measuring with Sebastian Pig & Friends on a Road Trip, 1 vol. 2009. (Math Fun with Sebastian Pig & Friends! Ser.). (ENG., Illus.). 32p. (gr. k-2). lib. bdg. 26.60 *(978-0-7660-3362-7(7),* faff3f3a-d90f-4294-b1aa-8e80bde5b720) Enslow Publishing, LLC.

Baer, T. H. Measuring Weight, 1 vol. 2015. (Measure It! Ser.). (ENG.). 24p. (J). (gr. 1-2). pap. 9.15 *(978-1-4824-3876-5(3),* acfb24b9-928c-4dbc-80e4-38ae65e3632c); lib. bdg. 24.27 *(978-1-4824-3878-9(X),* 07d5e4c8-c3b5-4788-bda6-cdf3baf0b67a) Stevens, Gareth Publishing LLLP.

Baron, Jessica. What's in the Garden? Learning to Compare Two Sets of Objects, 1 vol. 2010. (Math for the REAL World Ser.). (ENG., Illus.). 8p. (gr. k-1). pap. 5.15 *(978-0-8239-8860-0(0),* b191e9d6-405e-412d-b552-eee25bfe1bde) Rosen Publishing Group, Inc., The.

Benjamin, Lindsay. Measurement Action! 2005. (Yellow Umbrella Fluent Level Ser.). (ENG., Illus.). 16p. (gr. k-1). pap. 35.70 *(978-0-7368-5322-4(7),* Capstone Pr.) Capstone.

Burton, Margie, et al. Looking Down. 2011. (Early Connections Ser.). (J). *(978-1-61672-260-9(6))* Benchmark Education Co.

—What Can You Measure with A Lollipop? 2011. (Early Connections Ser.). (J). *(978-1-61672-545-7(1))* Benchmark Education Co.

Bussiere, Desirée. What in the World Is a Ton? & Other Weight & Volume Measurements, 1 vol. 2013. (Let's Measure Ser.). (ENG.). 24p. (J). (gr. -1-3). lib. bdg. 29.93 *(978-1-61783-599-5(4),* 11115, SandCastle) ABDO Publishing Co.

Cardenas, Ernesto & Saavedra, Patricia. Medición. l.t. ed. 2006.Tr. of Measurement. (SPA., Illus.). 16p. pap. 4.95 *(978-1-933668-14-7(8))* Milo Educational Bks. & Resources.

Chapman, Joan. Heavy & Light: Learning to Compare Weights of Objects, 1 vol. 2010. (Math for the REAL World Ser.). (ENG., Illus.). 8p. (gr. k-1). pap. 5.15 *(978-0-8239-8844-0(9),* d813d4e2-b543-4c4e-97a3-f529b5258d53) Rosen Publishing Group, Inc., The.

Chrismer, Melanie. Math Tools. 2006. (Rookie Read-About Math Ser.). (ENG., Illus.). 32p. (J). (gr. 1-2). lib. bdg. 20.50 *(978-0-516-24961-2(4),* Children's Pr.) Scholastic Library Publishing.

Cleary, Brian P. On the Scale, a Weighty Tale. Gable, Brian, illus. (Math Is CATegorical (r) Ser.). (ENG.). 32p. (gr. k-3). 2010. (J). pap. 7.99 *(978-1-58013-845-1(4),* b48d6f41-79fa-4546-8bd9-fb9a013c034b, Millbrook Pr.) 2008. 16.95 *(978-0-8225-7851-2(4))* Lerner Publishing Group.

—On the Scale, A Weighty Tale. 2010. pap. 39.62 *(978-0-7613-6997-4(X))* Lerner Publishing Group.

Cobb, Vicki. I Fall Down. Gorton, Julia, illus. 2004. (ENG.). 40p. (J). (gr. -1-3). 18.99 *(978-0-688-17842-0(1),* HarperCollins) HarperCollins Pubs.

Dearborne, Hilary. Heavy & Light: Describe & Compare Measurable Attributes. 2013. (InfoMax Math Readers Ser.). (ENG.). 16p. (J). (gr. k-1). pap. 42.00 *(978-1-4777-1941-1(5));* (illus.). pap. 7.00 *(978-1-4777-1940-4(7),* f683a02e-3dd0-45ab-b8d2-cac2fdec30fe) Rosen Publishing Group, Inc., The. (Rosen Classroom).

Doudna, Kelly. It's My Pleasure to Measure the Treasure!, 1 vol. 2007. (Science Made Simple Ser.). (Illus.). 24p. (J). (gr. k-3). lib. bdg. 24.21 *(978-1-59928-602-0(5),* SandCastle) ABDO Publishing Co.

—It's Time to Dance, We Can Use a Balance!, 1 vol. 2007. (Science Made Simple Ser.). (Illus.). 24p. (J). (gr. k-3). lib. bdg. 24.21 *(978-1-59928-608-2(4),* SandCastle) ABDO Publishing Co.

—Let's Be Kids & Measure Liquids!, 1 vol. 2007. (Science Made Simple Ser.). (Illus.). 24p. (J). (gr. k-3). lib. bdg. 24.21 *(978-1-59928-610-5(6),* SandCastle) ABDO Publishing Co.

Dowdy, Penny. Measurement. 2008. (My Path to Math Ser.). (ENG., Illus.). 24p. (J). (gr. k-3). pap. *(978-0-7787-4359-0(4))* Crabtree Publishing Co.

Elliott, Cathy. How Much Does It Weigh? 2008. (Discovering & Exploring Science Ser.). (Illus.). 16p. (J). (gr. -1-3). lib. bdg. 12.95 *(978-0-7569-8416-8(5))* Perfection Learning Corp.

First, Rachel. Weigh It! Fun with Weight, 1 vol. 2015. (Math Beginnings Ser.). (ENG., Illus.). 24p. (J). (gr. -1-3). 29.93 *(978-1-62403-936-2(7),* 19299, SandCastle) ABDO Publishing Co.

Fosnot, Catherine Twomey. Measuring for the Art Show: Addition on the Open Number Line. 2008. (ENG.). 80p. (gr. 1-2). pap. 31.25 *(978-0-325-01010-6(2),* E01010, Firsthand) Heinemann.

Furgang, Kathy. Measuring Length: Set Of 6. 2011. (Early Connections Ser.). (J). pap. 37.00 net. *(978-1-4108-1088-5(7))* Benchmark Education Co.

Gardner, Robert. How Big Is Big? Science Projects with Volume, 1 vol. 2014. (Hot Science Experiments Ser.). (ENG.). 48p. (gr. 3-4). 26.93 *(978-0-7660-6620-5(7),* 59e2ffbd-3dfa-44d1-a217-89a1d798828c) Enslow Publishing, LLC.

—How Heavy Is Heavy? Science Projects with Weight, 1 vol. 2014. (Hot Science Experiments Ser.). (ENG.). 48p. (gr. 3-4). 26.93 *(978-0-7660-6600-7(2),* 6a136b12-c3ea-40af-8e30-a924c9a4b6ba) Enslow Publishing, LLC.

—How High Is High? Science Projects with Height & Depth, 1 vol. 2014. (Hot Science Experiments Ser.). (ENG.). 48p. (gr. 3-4). 26.93 *(978-0-7660-6595-6(2),* 3cad5a94-5695-4045-846d-a3bd3ab5b215) Enslow Publishing, LLC.

Hirschmann, Kris. Is a Paw a Foot? All about Measurement. 2006. (Artist Collection: the Dog Ser.). (ENG., Illus.). 32p. (J). (gr. -1-3). pap. 3.99 *(978-0-439-92213-5(5))* Scholastic, Inc.

Holland, Gini. Light & Heavy, 1 vol. 2007. (I Know Opposites Ser.). (ENG.). 16p. (gr. k-2). pap. 6.30 *(978-0-8368-8300-8(4),* ea0db15f-bf99-4a4b-a119-794ec756dc91); lib. bdg. 21.67 *(978-0-8368-8295-7(4),* dc8e6bda-1299-4499-af24-7e18bbd09502) Stevens, Gareth Publishing LLLP. (Weekly Reader Leveled Readers).

—Light & Heavy / Ligero y Pesado, 1 vol. 2007. (I Know Opposites / Conceptos Contrarios Ser.). (SPA & ENG.). 16p. (gr. k-2). lib. bdg. 21.67 *(978-0-8368-8305-3(5),* eacf24b2-3f0e-4bbb-a1dc-8b5bf5e2685f, Weekly Reader Leveled Readers) Stevens, Gareth Publishing LLLP.

Ithaca, Sciencenter, NY. How Small Is Nano? 2009. 24p. 11.20 *(978-0-578-00197-5(7))* Sciencenter.

Jeffries, Joyce. Heavy & Light, 1 vol. 2013. (Dinosaur School Ser.). (ENG., Illus.). 24p. (gr. k-k). 25.27 *(978-1-4339-8087-9(8),* 1f9d2c59-08ed-48da-9978-ee55e27c4205); pap. 9.15 *(978-1-4339-8088-6(6),* 1d755ca5-8145-47eb-8203-b7aff10753d9) Stevens, Gareth Publishing LLLP.

Keman, Elizabeth. How Long Is It? Learning to Measure with Nonstandard Units, 1 vol. 2010. (Math for the REAL World Ser.). (ENG., Illus.). 8p. (gr. k-1). pap. 5.15 *(978-0-8239-8843-3(0),* 1dbf9ccf-271c-45ec-bd57-21c05ac62a0d) Rosen Publishing Group, Inc., The.

Loughran, Donna. A Day at Mini-Golf: What's the Length? 2013. (iMath Ser.). (Illus.). 24p. (J). (gr. k-2). lib. bdg. 21.27 *(978-1-59953-556-2(4))* Norwood Hse. Pr.

Loughran, Donna & Brunner-Jass, Renata. Field of Play: Measuring Distance, Rate, & Time. 2013. (iMath Ser.). (Illus.). 48p. (J). (gr. 5-6). lib. bdg. 23.94 *(978-1-59953-571-5(8))* Norwood Hse. Pr.

Mattern, Joanne. Let's Visit Canada: The Metric System, 1 vol. (Math for the REAL World Ser.). (ENG., Illus.). 24p. (gr. 3-4). 2010. pap. 8.25 *(978-0-8239-8872-3(4),* f9be11d4-924a-4fdb-997d-c99cee4f5851) 2003. (J). lib. bdg. 26.27 *(978-0-8239-8967-6(4),* 9bf4cca3-fae9-4499-902c-688170c1dfd3) Rosen Publishing Group, Inc., The. (PowerKids Pr.).

McGraw Hill. Key to Measurement, Book 1: English Units of Length, Bk. 1. 2012. (Key To... workbooks Ser.: Bk. 1). (ENG.). 48p. (gr. 6-8). spiral bd. 6.32 *(978-1-55953-021-7(9),* 1559530219) McGraw-Hill Education.

—Key to Measurement, Book 2: Measuring Length & Perimeter Using English Units, 2. 2012. (Key To... workbooks Ser.: Bk. 2). (ENG.). 48p. (gr. 6-8). spiral bd. 6.32 *(978-1-55953-022-4(7),* 1559530227) McGraw-Hill Education.

—Key to Metric Measurement, Book 2: Measuring Length & Perimeter Using Metric Units, Bk. 2. 2012. (Key To... workbooks Ser.: Bk. 2). (ENG., Illus.). 48p. (gr. 6-8). spiral bd., wbk. ed. 6.32 *(978-1-55953-326-3(9),* 1559533269) McGraw-Hill Education.

Metz, Lorijo. Using Scales & Balances, 1 vol. 2013. (Science Tools Ser.). (ENG., Illus.). 24p. (J). (gr. 2-3). 26.27 *(978-1-4488-9686-8(X),* 54300f7c-04b8-46f2-9f19-293f21528331); pap. 9.25 *(978-1-4488-9830-5(7),* 86d17a2d-4e01-4791-8191-642fa9f111d7) Rosen Publishing Group, Inc., The. (PowerKids Pr.).

Minden, Cecilia. What Does It Weigh? 2010. (21st Century Basic Skills Library: Measurements Ser.). (ENG., Illus.). 24p. (gr. k-3). lib. bdg. 26.35 *(978-1-60279-849-6(4),* 200564) Cherry Lake Publishing.

Murphy, Stuart J. Mighty Maddie. Lum, Bernice, illus. 2004. (MathStart Ser.). 40p. (J). 15.99 *(978-0-06-053159-1(2));* (ENG.). (gr. -1-3). pap. 6.99 *(978-0-06-053161-4(4),* HarperCollins) HarperCollins Pubs.

Nsrc. Science & Technology for Children Books: Measuring Time. 2004. (Illus.). 64p. (J). *(978-1-933008-09-7(1))* Smithsonian Science Education Ctr. (SSEC).

O'Hara, Nicholas. Sort It by Weight, 1 vol. 2015. (Sort It Out! Ser.). (ENG., Illus.). 24p. (J). (gr. k-1). pap. 9.15 *(978-1-4824-2585-7(8),* b92528c8-faf8-4207-8246-974f5a11f0eb) Stevens, Gareth Publishing LLLP.

Pallotta, Jerry. Hershey's Weights & Measures. Bolster, Rob, illus. 2003. (Hershey's Ser.). (ENG.). 32p. (J). 16.99 *(978-0-439-38876-4(7),* Cartwheel Bks.) Scholastic, Inc.

—Weights & Measures. Bolster, Rob, illus. 2008. 32p. (J). pap. *(978-0-545-06448-4(1))* Scholastic, Inc.

Pluckrose, Henry. Capacity (Math Counts: Updated Editions) (Library Edition) 2018. (Math Counts, New & Updated Ser.). (ENG., Illus.). 32p. (J). (gr. k-3). lib. bdg. 25.00 *(978-0-531-17506-4(5),* Children's Pr.) Scholastic Library Publishing.

—Weight (Math Counts: Updated Editions) (Library Edition) 2018. (Math Counts, New & Updated Ser.). (ENG., Illus.). 32p. (J). (gr. k-3). lib. bdg. 25.00 *(978-0-531-17515-6(4),* Children's Pr.) Scholastic Library Publishing.

Rauen, Amy. Vamos a Encontrar lo Más Corto y lo Más Largo (Finding Shortest & Longest), 1 vol. 2008. (Matemáticas para Empezar (Getting Started with Math) Ser.). (SPA.). 16p. (gr. k-1). pap. 6.30 *(978-0-8368-8997-0(5),* 39b1fe38-e780-47d3-bb74-446b0fa25f41); (Illus.). lib. bdg. 21.67 *(978-0-8368-8992-5(4),* 8576efdd-56dd-41f9-b23c-60a1bfa2b984) Stevens, Gareth Publishing LLLP. (Weekly Reader Leveled Readers).

Reinke, Beth Bence. Measuring Weight. Petelinsek, Kathleen, illus. 2014. (Explorer Junior Library: Math Explorer Junior Ser.). (ENG.). 24p. (J). (gr. 1-4). 32.07 *(978-1-62431-652-4(2),* 203120) Cherry Lake Publishing.

Rivera, Sheila. Balance. 2006. (First Step Nonfiction — Simple Tools Ser.). (ENG., Illus.). 8p. (J). (gr. k-2). pap. 5.99 *(978-0-8225-5716-6(9),* 9718c004-5140-4b85-a280-43c980b0e8da) Lerner Publishing Group.

—Scale. 2007. (First Step Nonfiction — Simple Tools Ser.). (ENG., Illus.). 8p. (J). (gr. k-2). pap. 5.99 *(978-0-8225-6854-4(3),* a39ebd51-154c-4d94-81cc-0d6452af7fa5) Lerner Publishing Group.

Rozines Roy, Jennifer & Roy, Gregory. Measuring at Home, 1 vol. 2008. (Math All Around Ser.). (ENG.). 32p. (gr. 2-2). pap. 9.23 *(978-0-7614-3384-2(8),* 637568df-c407-48e7-b5eb-88a842cb6dd2) Cavendish Square Publishing LLC.

Rustad, Martha E. H. Measuring Weight. 2019. (Measuring Masters Ser.). (ENG., Illus.). 24p. (J). (gr. -1-2). lib. bdg. 27.32 *(978-1-9771-0370-3(7),* 139344, Capstone Pr.) Capstone.

Salzmann, Mary Elizabeth. What in the World Is an Ounce? CD & Book. 2010. (Let's Measure CD+Book Ser.). 24p. (gr. k-3). audio compact disk 42.70 *(978-1-61613-318-4(X),* SandCastle) ABDO Publishing Co.

Sargent, Brian. How Heavy Is It? 2005. (Rookie Read-About Math Ser.). (ENG., Illus.). 32p. (J). (gr. 1-2). lib. bdg. 20.50 *(978-0-516-25267-4(4),* Children's Pr.) Scholastic Library Publishing.

Schrier, Allyson Valentine. Is It Heavier Than an Elephant? 2008. (Discovering & Exploring Science Ser.). (Illus.). 16p. (J). (gr. -1-3). lib. bdg. 12.95 *(978-0-7569-8438-0(6))* Perfection Learning Corp.

Schwartz, David M. Millions to Measure. Kellogg, Steven, illus. (ENG.). 40p. (J). (gr. k-7). 2003. 17.99 *(978-0-688-12916-3(1))* 2006. reprint ed. pap. 7.99 *(978-0-06-084806-4(5))* HarperCollins Pubs. (HarperCollins).

Science & Technology for Children Books, Measuring Time Set. 8 vols. 2004. (Illus.). 64p. (J). *(978-1-933008-21-9(0))* Smithsonian Science Education Ctr. (SSEC).

Sullivan, Erin Ash. Measuring Matter: Text Pairs. 2008. (Bridges/Navigators Ser.). (J). (gr. 3). 94.00 *(978-1-4108-8367-4(1))* Benchmark Education Co.

Sullivan, Navin. Weight, 1 vol. 2007. (Measure Up! Ser.). (ENG., Illus.). 48p. (gr. 4-4). lib. bdg. 34.07 *(978-0-7614-2324-9(9),* 2a69846f-af63-49fe-a21d-3b102aed822d) Cavendish Square Publishing LLC.

Sweeney, Joan. Me & the Measure of Things. Kath, Katie, illus. 2019. 32p. (J). (gr. -1-2). 12.99 *(978-1-9848-2959-7(9),* Knopf Bks. for Young Readers) Random Hse. Children's Bks.

Trumbauer, Lisa. Animal Giants. 2005. (Yellow Umbrella Fluent Level Ser.). (ENG., Illus.). 16p. (gr. k-1). pap. 35.70 *(978-0-7368-5328-6(6),* Capstone Pr.) Capstone.

Vogel, Julia. Weight. 2018. (Illus.). 24p. (J). *(978-1-4896-5886-9(6),* AV2 by Weigl) Weigl Pubs., Inc.

Weakland, Mark. How Heavy? Wacky Ways to Compare Weight, 1 vol. Bolton, Bill, illus. 2013. (Wacky Comparisons Ser.). (ENG.). 24p. (J). (gr. -1-2). pap. 8.95 *(978-1-4795-1912-5(X),* 123619, Picture Window Bks.) Capstone.

Woodford, Chris. Weight, 1 vol. 2012. (Measure up Math Ser.). (ENG., Illus.). 32p. (J). (gr. 4-4). pap. 11.50 *(978-1-4339-7462-5(2),* 58f52030-2ee6-4c35-9da2-7f44b7a7e798); lib. bdg. 29.27 *(978-1-4339-7461-8(4),* d69b232e-1c9f-4b97-831f-82a259050eed) Stevens, Gareth Publishing LLLP.

WELDING

Rathburn, Betsy. Welders. 2020. (Community Helpers Ser.). (ENG., Illus.). 24p. (J). (gr. k-3). pap. 7.99 *(978-1-61891-790-4(0),* 12575, Blastoff! Readers) Bellwether Media.

WELFARE STATE

see Economic Policy

WELFARE WORK

see Social Service

WELLS, H. G. (HERBERT GEORGE), 1866-1946

Boerst, William J. Time Machine: The Story of H. G. Wells. 2004. (World Writers Ser.). (Illus.). 112p. (YA). (gr. 6-12). 23.95 *(978-1-883846-40-4(4),* First Biographies) Reynolds, Morgan Inc.

H. G. Wells: First Citizen of the Future. 2014. (ENG.). 192p. (J). (gr. 3-7). pap. 13.95 *(978-1-59077-356-7(X))* Evans, M. & Co., Inc.

WELLS, IDA B., 1862-1931

see Wells-Barnett, Ida B., 1862-1931

WELLS-BARNETT, IDA B., 1862-1931

Bailey, Diane. Ida B. Wells: Discovering History's Heroes. 2019. (Jeter Publishing Ser.). (ENG.). 160p. (J). (gr. 2-5). pap. 6.99 *(978-1-5344-2484-5(9),* Aladdin) Simon & Schuster Children's Publishing.

—Ida B. Wells: Discovering History's Heroes. 2019. (Jeter Publishing Ser.). (ENG.). 160p. (J). (gr. 2-5). E-Book *(978-1-5344-2486-9(5));* (Illus.). 18.99 *(978-1-5344-2485-2(7))* Simon & Schuster/Paula Wiseman Bks. (Simon & Schuster/Paula Wiseman Bks.).

Dray, Philip. Yours for Justice, Ida B. Wells: The Daring Life of a Crusading Journalist, 1 vol. Alcorn, Stephen, illus. 2008. 48p. (J). (gr. 5-9). 18.95 *(978-1-56145-417-4(6))* Peachtree Publishing Co. Inc.

Hinman, Bonnie. Eternal Vigilance: The Story of Ida B. Wells-Barnett. 2011. (Civil Rights Leaders Ser.). 128p. (gr. 6-10). lib. bdg. 28.95 *(978-1-59935-111-7(0))* Reynolds, Morgan Inc.

Jones, Naomi E. Ida B. Wells-Barnett: Suffragette & Social Activist, 1 vol. 2019. (African American Trailblazers Ser.). (ENG.). 128p. (gr. 9-9). pap. 22.16 *(978-1-5026-4560-9(2),* cb519ffa-ab7a-438d-b1e0-9a25e98d89c7) Cavendish Square Publishing LLC.

Mckissack, Patricia & Mckissack, Fredrick. Ida B. Wells-Barnett: Fighter for Justice, 1 vol. 2013. (Famous African Americans Ser.). (ENG.). 24p. (gr. k-2). pap. 10.35 *(978-1-4644-0198-5(5),* eb7e9a8e-6b17-4790-bf93-adb0f9aff98b, Enslow Elementary); (Illus.). 25.27 *(978-0-7660-4108-0(5),* f37a0a7c-6b05-4e1f-9f84-ee2615e0615f) Enslow Publishing, LLC.

Morretta, Alison. Ida B. Wells-Barnett & the Crusade Against Lynching, 1 vol. 2016. (Primary Sources of the Civil Rights Movement Ser.). (ENG., Illus.). 64p. (gr. 6-6). 35.93 *(978-1-5026-1874-0(5),* 44127a2f-3bba-4d97-985b-e0917805406e) Cavendish Square Publishing LLC.

Myers, Walter Dean. Ida B. Wells: Let the Truth Be Told. Christensen, Bonnie, illus. 2008. (ENG.). 40p. (J). (gr. -1-3). 17.99 *(978-0-06-027705-5(X),* Amistad) HarperCollins Pubs.

Welch, Catherine A. Ida B. Wells-Barnett: Powerhouse with a Pen. 2005. (Trailblazers Biographies Ser.). (Illus.). 112p. (gr. 5-9). 27.93 *(978-1-57505-352-3(7))* Lerner Publishing Group.

WELLS

see also Petroleum; Water-Supply

Shoveller, Herb. Ryan & Jimmy: And the Well in Africa That Brought Them Together. 2008. (CitizenKid Ser.). (ENG., Illus.). 56p. (J). (gr. 3-7). pap. 10.99 *(978-1-55453-271-1(X))* Kids Can Pr., Ltd. CAN. Dist: Hachette Bk. Group.

Stone, Andrew & Bryan, Jessica. Well... What's All That Drilling About? Pender, Rachel, illus. 2007. 40p. (J). 7.95 *(978-0-9641186-3-8(7))* American Ground Water Trust.

WELLS—FICTION

Ar ôl y Parti. 2005. (WEL., Illus.). 14p. pap. *(978-1-85644-994-6(7))* CAA.

Gogarty, Brian. Shamrock Sean & the Wishing Well. Burchartz, Roxanne, illus. 2007. (ENG.). 12p. (J). pap. 7.95 *(978-0-86278-967-1(2))* O'Brien Pr., Ltd., The. IRL. Dist: Dufour Editions, Inc.

Hemenway, Stephen J. The Stinkells in Stankwell. Piela, Shaun, illus. 2007. (ENG.). 50p. per. 15.99 *(978-1-4257-7290-1(0))* Xlibris Corp.

Kimberly, Anne. Dark Well of Decision. 2007. 136p. per. 7.99 *(978-0-9800356-5-0(1))* Highland Pr. Publishing.

Lin, Joyce, tr. The frog in the Well. Caprio, Pattie, illus. 2008. (ENG & CHI.). 36p. (J). 14.95 *(978-0-9801305-1-5(4))* CE Bilingual Bks. LLC.

Peeler, Gail. Jackson's Magic Wishing Well. 2008. 25p. 35.50 *(978-1-4357-2950-6(1))* Lulu Pr., Inc.

WELLS, FARGO & COMPANY

Moody, Ralph. Wells Fargo. 2005. (ENG., Illus.). 186p. (J). pap. 13.95 *(978-0-8032-8303-9(2),* MOOWEX, Bison Bks.) Univ. of Nebraska Pr.

WELSH LANGUAGE

Campbell, Rod. Jyngl: Sefyll-I-Fyny. 2005.Tr. of Pop-Up Jungle. (WEL., Illus.). 14p. *(978-1-85596-166-1(0))* Dref Wen.

Davies, Helen Emanuel & Cooper, Anne Lloyd. Torri Gair. 2005. (WEL., Illus.). 16p. pap. *(978-1-85644-545-0(3))* CAA.

Emlyn, Non ap. Hamddena. 2005. (WEL., Illus.). 20p. pap. *(978-1-86085-603-7(9))* ICA Video.

—Hamddena - Llyfr 1 Lefel 3/4. 2005. (WEL., Illus.). 20p. pap. *(978-1-86085-600-6(4))* ICA Video.

—Hamddena - Llyfr 3 Lefel 5/6. 2005. (WEL., Illus.). 20p. pap. *(978-1-86085-602-0(0))* ICA Video.

Gliori, Debi. Mr. Arth Yn Gwarchod. 2005.Tr. of Mr Bear Babysits. (WEL., Illus.). 32p. pap. *(978-1-85596-139-5(3))* Dref Wen.

Gruffydd, Stella. Haws Dweud: Gweithgareddau Llefaredd, Darllen Ac Ysgrifennu I Blant Cyfnod Allweddol 2. 2005. (WEL., Illus.). 152p. pap. *(978-1-85644-601-3(8))* CAA.

Hughes, Mair Wynn. Y Dewis. 2005. (WEL., Illus.). 16p. pap. *(978-1-85644-747-8(2))* CAA.

Jones, Marlis. Wyn Melangell. 2005. (WEL., Illus.). 16p. pap. *(978-1-85644-744-7(8))* CAA.

Jones, Marlis & Jên, Ruth. Cuddio'r Colur. 2005. (WEL., Illus.). 16p. pap. *(978-1-85644-547-4(X))* CAA.

Lasarus, Gwen. Hud Hen Hanes. 2005. (WEL., Illus.). 16p. pap. *(978-1-85644-745-4(6))* CAA.

Lewis, D. Geraint. A Shorter Welsh Dictionary. 2005. (ENG.). 344p. pap. 13.99 *(978-1-84323-099-1(2))* Gomer Pr. GBR. Dist: Independent Pubs. Group, Casemate Pubs. & Bk. Distributors, LLC.

Lewis, Sian & Thomas, Rhianedd. Cris Croes. 2005. (WEL., Illus.). 16p. pap. *(978-1-85644-544-3(5))* CAA.

Maelor, Gwawr, et al. Tân Yn y Jyngl. 2005. (WEL., Illus.). 16p. pap. *(978-1-85644-842-0(8))* CAA.

Richards, Aled. Stori Dda. 2005. (WEL., Illus.). 16p. pap. *(978-1-85644-746-1(4))* CAA.

Richards, Aled & Pritchard, Richard Huw. Am y Copa. 2005. (WEL., Illus.). 16p. pap. *(978-1-85644-549-8(6))* CAA.

Roberts, Eirlys. Dweud ein Dweud. 2005. (WEL., Illus.). 72p. pap. *(978-1-85644-906-9(8))* CAA.

Roberts, Heulwen. Anifeiliaid Anwes. 2005. (WEL., Illus.). 16p. pap. *(978-1-85644-778-2(2))* CAA.

University of Wales, Aberystwyth, Centre for Educational Studies Staff, contrib. by. Arch Noa: Casgliad o Sbardunau Ac Ymarferion Ar Thema Creaduriaid. 2005. (WEL., Illus.). 72p. pap. *(978-1-85644-959-5(9))* CAA.

WENCESLAS, DUKE OF BOHEMIA, APPROXIMATELY 907-929

Manson, Christopher, illus. Good King Wenceslas. 2004. 25p. (J). (gr. k-4). reprint ed. 15.00 *(978-0-7567-8226-9(0))* DIANE Publishing Co.

WEREWOLVES

Baker, Linda R. American Werewolves, 1 vol. 2019. (Creatures of the Paranormal Ser.). (ENG.). 48p. (J). (gr. 5-5). pap. 12.70 *(978-1-9785-1362-4(3),* aa8ca474-51fb-43bd-b21b-b08b8f84aa9a) Enslow Publishing, LLC.

Beaumont, Steve. Drawing Werewolves & Other Gothic Ghouls, 1 vol. 2011. (Drawing Legendary Monsters Ser.). (ENG., Illus.). 32p. (J). (gr. 4-4). 30.27 *(978-1-4488-3254-5(3),* b198716e-8499-413e-b6ea-3faf8c5b3776, PowerKids Pr.) Rosen Publishing Group, Inc., The.

Bennett, Adelaide. Ancient Werewolves & Vampires: The Roots of the Teeth. 2010. (Making of a Monster Ser.). (Illus.). 64p. (YA). (gr. 7-18). pap. 9.95 *(978-1-4222-1955-3(0));* lib. bdg. 22.95 *(978-1-4222-1802-0(3))* Mason Crest.

—Global Legends & Lore: Vampires & Werewolves Around the World. 2010. (Making of a Monster Ser.). 64p. (YA). (gr. 7-18). pap. 9.95 *(978-1-4222-1963-8(1))* Mason Crest.

Castellano, Peter. Werewolves, 1 vol. 2015. (Monsters! Ser.). (ENG., Illus.). 32p. (J). (gr. 1-2). pap. 11.50 *(978-1-4824-4098-0(9),* 9cc22ccb-7666-4ccd-ab2c-b5284f1650c8) Stevens, Gareth Publishing LLLP.

heatham, Mark. Werewolves!, 1 vol. 2012. (Jr. Graphic Monster Stories Ser.). (ENG.). 24p. (J). (gr. 2-3). pap. 11.60 *(978-1-4488-6399-0(6),* e38ca169-0ef1-4608-a20e-62764773e5c0); lib. bdg. 28.93 *(978-1-4488-6220-7(5),* 36ed8516-73cf-4d8f-8ac3-411a2e18a679) Rosen Publishing Group, Inc., The. (PowerKids Pr.).
avis, Graeme. Hunting Werewolves, 1 vol. 2016. (Monster Hunting Ser.). (ENG., Illus.). 88p. (YA). (gr. 8-8). 38.80 *(978-1-4994-6534-1(3),* 870804f9-bb35-4e55-a4ac-98b9463e38b2, Rosen Young Adult) Rosen Publishing Group, Inc., The.
schbach, Christina. Werewolves. 2018. (Mythical Creatures Ser.). (ENG., Illus.). 32p. (J). (gr. 2-3). pap. 9.95 *(978-1-64185-008-7(6),* 1641850086); lib. bdg. 31.35 *(978-1-63517-906-4(8),* 1635179068) North Star Editions. (Focus Readers).
—Werewolves. 2018. 32p. (J). *(978-1-4896-9863-6(9),* AV2 by Weigl) Weigl Pubs., Inc.
tingoff, Kim. Howling at the Moon: Vampires & Werewolves in the New World. 2010. (Making of a Monster Ser.). (Illus.). 64p. (YA). (gr. 7-18). pap. 9.95 *(978-1-4222-1958-4(5));* lib. bdg. 22.95 *(978-1-4222-1805-1(8))* Mason Crest.
—The Science of the Beast: The Facts Behind the Fangs. 2010. (Making of a Monster Ser.). (Illus.). 64p. (YA). (gr. 7-18). pap. 9.95 *(978-1-4222-1961-4(5));* lib. bdg. 22.95 *(978-1-4222-1808-2(2))* Mason Crest.
Ferrell, David L. Shape-Shifters!, 1 vol., 1. 2013. (Jr. Graphic Monster Stories Ser.). (ENG.). 24p. (J). (gr. 2-3). 28.93 *(978-1-4777-6219-6(1),* 19577d9b-5e19-427b-be73-aa34b979f4c4, PowerKids Pr.) Rosen Publishing Group, Inc., The.
Frisch, Aaron. Werewolves. 2013. (Illus.). 24p. (J). 25.65 *(978-1-60818-249-7(5),* Creative Education) Creative Co., The.
Gaertner, Meg. Shapeshifters. 2019. (Monster Histories Ser.). (ENG., Illus.). 32p. (J). (gr. 4-6). pap. 7.95 *(978-1-5435-7502-6(1),* 141032); lib. bdg. 30.65 *(978-1-5435-7125-7(5),* 140407) Capstone.
Harmon, Daniel E. Werewolves, 1 vol. 2015. (Greatest Movie Monsters Ser.). (ENG., Illus.). 48p. (J). (gr. 5-6). 33.47 *(978-1-4994-3521-4(5),* 01e8d145-644e-43d8-bfe5-88a8e26b68eb, Rosen Central) Rosen Publishing Group, Inc., The.
hirschmann, kris. The Werewolf. 2011. 80p. (YA). lib. bdg. 43.93 *(978-1-60152-238-2(X))* ReferencePoint Pr., Inc.
Jeffrey, Gary. Werewolves, 1 vol. 2011. (Graphic Mythical Creatures Ser.). (ENG., Illus.). 24p. (J). (gr. 3-3). 26.60 *(978-1-4339-6049-9(4),* ce53366f-ea7a-4c52-b221-902775431582); pap. 9.15 *(978-1-4339-6051-2(6),* fe117a65-dd9e-4b13-9d8d-77598d9dccfd, Gareth Stevens Learning Library) Stevens, Gareth Publishing LLLP.
Kallen, Stuart A. Werewolves. 2010. (Mysterious & Unknown Ser.). 104p. (YA). (gr. 7-12). lib. bdg. 43.93 *(978-1-60152-097-5(2))* ReferencePoint Pr., Inc.
Kespert, Deborah. 3-D Chillers: Vampires, Zombies, & Werewolves. 2012. (3-D Chillers Ser.). (ENG.). 48p. (J). (gr. 3-7). pap. 7.99 *(978-0-545-38779-8(5),* Scholastic Paperbacks) Scholastic, Inc.
Krensky, Stephen. Werewolves. 2006. (Monster Chronicles Ser.). (ENG., Illus.). 48p. (gr. 4-7). lib. bdg. 26.60 *(978-0-8225-5922-1(6))* Lerner Publishing Group.
Lestrade, Ursula & Hachette Children's Group. The Werewolf Hunter's Guide. 2012. (Monster Tracker Ser.). (ENG.). 32p. (gr. 4-6). lib. bdg. 28.50 *(978-1-59771-318-4(X))* Sea-To-Sea Pubns.
Loh-Hagan, Virginia. Werewolves. 2016. (Magic, Myth, & Mystery Ser.). (ENG., Illus.). 32p. (J). (gr. 4-8). 32.07 *(978-1-63471-110-4(6),* 208551, 45th Parallel Press) Cherry Lake Publishing.
Martin, Nicholas. Fighting the Fangs: A Guide to Vampires & Werewolves. 2010. (Making of a Monster Ser.). (Illus.). 64p. (YA). (gr. 7-18). pap. 9.95 *(978-1-4222-1957-7(7));* lib. bdg. 22.95 *(978-1-4222-1804-4(X))* Mason Crest.
O'Hearn, Michael. Vampires vs. Werewolves: Battle of the Bloodthirsty Beasts. Kendree, McLean, illus. 2011. (Monster Wars Ser.). (ENG.). 32p. (gr. 3-4). pap. 47.70 *(978-1-4296-7266-5(8),* Capstone Pr.) Capstone.
Owen, Ruth. Werewolves & Other Shape-Shifters. 2013. (Not near Normal: the Paranormal Ser.). 32p. (J). (gr. 3-8). lib. bdg. 28.50 *(978-1-61772-695-8(8))* Bearport Publishing Co., Inc.
Peabody, Erin. Werewolves. Rivas, Victor, illus. 2017. (Behind the Legend Ser.). (ENG.). 128p. (J). (gr. 2-5). pap. 9.99 *(978-1-4998-0458-4(X))* Little Bee Books Inc.
Pearson, Marie. Werewolves. 2019. (Monster Histories Ser.). (ENG., Illus.). 32p. (J). (gr. 4-6). pap. 7.95 *(978-1-5435-7504-0(8),* 141034); lib. bdg. 30.65 *(978-1-5435-7127-1(1),* 140410) Capstone.
Peter Pauper Press Staff, et al. Vampires, Werewolves, Zombies: From the papers of Herr Doktor Max Sturm & Baron Ludwig Von Drang. Waldman, Bruce, illus. 2010. 168p. 9.95 *(978-1-59359-647-7(2))* Peter Pauper Pr. Inc.
Roby, Cynthia A. Werewolves, 1 vol. 2015. (Creatures of Fantasy Ser.). (ENG., Illus.). 64p. (gr. 6-6). 35.93 *(978-1-5026-0510-8(4),* 9af62a0d-ae77-4239-ab3b-c3d0b1957b21) Cavendish Square Publishing LLC.
Sanna, Emily. Pop Monsters: The Modern-Day Craze for Vampires & Werewolves. 2010. (Making of a Monster Ser.). 64p. (YA). (gr. 7-18). pap. 9.95 *(978-1-4222-1959-1(3))* Mason Crest.
Shea, Therese M. Werewolves Do Word Problems!, 1 vol. 2018. (Monsters Do Math! Ser.). (ENG.). 24p. (gr. 2-3). 24.27 *(978-1-5382-2936-1(6),* 6e9aae4f-4e11-4669-b314-4481536296df) Stevens, Gareth Publishing LLLP.
Spencer, Liv. Love Bites: The Unofficial Saga of Twilight. 2010. (ENG., Illus.). 203p. (YA). (gr. 7). pap. 14.95 *(978-1-55022-930-1(3),* 5794965c-1c31-4a08-9c84-7624b5b00c5d) ECW Pr. CAN. Dist: Baker & Taylor Publisher Services (BTPS).
Stefoff, Rebecca. Vampires, Zombies, & Shape-Shifters, 1 vol. 2008. (Secrets of the Unexplained Ser.). (ENG., Illus.). 96p. (gr. 6-6). lib. bdg. 36.93 *(978-0-7614-2635-6(3),* 8bdd50c7-d277-4665-b7a9-aadf279eaf73) Cavendish Square Publishing LLC.
Stewart, Sheila. The Psychology of Our Dark Side: Humans' Love Affair with Vampires & Werewolves. 2010. (Making of a Monster Ser.). (Illus.). 64p. (YA). (gr. 7-18). pap. 9.95 *(978-1-4222-1960-7(7));* lib. bdg. 22.95 *(978-1-4222-1807-5(4))* Mason Crest.
Ticktock Media, Ltd. Staff. Undead: Zombies, Vampires, Werewolves. 2008. (ENG.). 96p. (J). (gr. 4-7). pap. 9.95 *(978-1-84696-797-9(X),* TickTock Books) Octopus Publishing Group GBR. Dist: Independent Pubs. Group.
Tieck, Sarah. Werewolves, 1 vol. 2015. (Creepy Creatures Ser.). (ENG., Illus.). 32p. (J). (gr. 2-5). 34.21 *(978-1-62403-768-9(2),* 17838, Big Buddy Bks.) ABDO Publishing Co.
Townsend, John. Werewolf Attack. 2008. (ENG., Illus.). 32p. (J). (gr. 5-9). pap. *(978-0-7787-3795-7(0));* lib. bdg. *(978-0-7787-3773-5(X))* Crabtree Publishing Co.
Uhl, Xina M. Werewolves. 2017. (Strange but True Ser.). (ENG.). (J). (gr. 4-7). pap. 9.95 *(978-1-68072-482-0(7));* 32p. pap. 9.99 *(978-1-64466-219-9(1),* 11491); (Illus.). 32p. lib. bdg. *(978-1-68072-185-0(2),* 10553) Black Rabbit Bks. (Bolt).
Weakland, Mark Andrew & Collins, Terry Lee. Truth Behind Werewolves. 2016. (ENG., Illus.). 24p. (J). pap. *(978-1-4062-8896-4(9))* Capstone.
West, David & Ganeri, Anita. Werewolves & Other Shape-Shifters, 1 vol. West, David & Ganeri, Anita, illus. 2010. (Dark Side Ser.). (ENG., Illus.). 32p. (J). (gr. 4-5). pap. 11.50 *(978-1-4488-1572-2(X),* 192e2ee5-d4a3-4ebc-b727-d6ac6a9d549a); lib. bdg. 30.27 *(978-1-61531-900-8(X),* 045bc1b9-d613-47bd-8fba-a6bf35724e13) Rosen Publishing Group, Inc., The. (PowerKids Pr.).

WEREWOLVES—FICTION

Adams, Leon. Jewel of Light. 2008. 182p. pap. 14.00 *(978-1-4357-1538-7(1))* Lulu Pr., Inc.
Arcayena-Nguyen, Rachelle. Who Me? a Werewolf: Chronicles of Timothy North. 2011. 138p. pap. 24.95 *(978-1-4560-4234-9(3))* America Star Bks.
Armstrong, Kelley. The Reckoning. 2011. (Darkest Powers Ser.: 3). (ENG.). 416p. (YA). (gr. 8). pap. 10.99 *(978-0-06-145056-3(1),* HarperCollins) HarperCollins Pubs.
Banks, Steven. Middle School Bites. Fearing, Mark, illus. 2020. (Middle School Bites Ser.: 1). 304p. (J). (gr. 3-7). 13.99 *(978-0-8234-4543-1(7))* Holiday Hse., Inc.
Barnes, Jennifer Lynn. Taken by Storm. 2013. (Raised by Wolves Ser.: Bk. 3). (ENG.). 320p. (YA). (gr. 7-12). pap. 9.99 *(978-1-60684-497-7(0),* 32809e95-8dfc-4a1a-8465-a1efc501e2eb, Carolrhoda Lab™) Lerner Publishing Group.
Beastly Boys Staff, et al. Battle of the Zombies. 2012. (Awfully Beastly Business Ser.: 5). (ENG., Illus.). 208p. (J). (gr. 4-7). pap. 8.99 *(978-0-85707-522-2(5))* Simon & Schuster, Ltd. GBR. Dist: Simon & Schuster, Inc.
Bell, C. D. Weregirl. Greene, Dot, illus. 2016. (ENG.). 400p. (YA). (gr. 8-12). 17.99 *(978-1-937133-55-9(9))* Chooseco LLC.
Bently, Peter. Casketball Capers, 1. Harrison, Chris, illus. 2011. (Vampire School Ser.: 1). (ENG.). 96p. (J). (gr. 1-4). 17.44 *(978-0-8075-8462-0(2))* Whitman, Albert & Co.
Bernstein, Nina. Magic by the Book, 4 vols. unabr. ed. 2005. (J). 65.75 *(978-1-4193-3607-2(X),* 42048) Recorded Bks., Inc.
Bird, Benjamin. Scare Ball. Fabicka, Patrycja, illus. 2019. (Boo Bks.). (ENG.). 32p. (J). (gr. k-2). lib. bdg. 22.65 *(978-1-5158-4487-7(0),* 140583, Picture Window Bks.) Capstone.
Blakley-Cartwright, Sarah & Johnson, David Leslie. Red Riding Hood. 2011. (ENG.). 352p. (J). (gr. 10-17). pap. 18.99 *(978-0-316-17604-0(4),* Poppy) Little, Brown Bks. for Young Readers.
Blevins, Wiley. Rapunzel & the Werewolf. Cox, Steve, illus. 2017. (Scary Tales Retold Ser.). (ENG.). 24p. (J). (gr. k-3). lib. bdg. 27.99 *(978-1-63440-167-8(0),* 708c337e-1f1e-459a-a99c-51a30e017a25) Red Chair Pr.
Carriger, Gail. Waistcoats & Weaponry. 2015. (Finishing School Ser.: 3). (ENG.). 320p. (YA). (gr. 7-17). pap. 18.99 *(978-0-316-19025-1(X))* Little, Brown Bks. for Young Readers.
Carver, Peter, ed. The Horrors: Terrifying Tales Book 2, 1 vol. 2006. (Terrifying Tales Ser.: 2). (ENG.). 184p. (YA). (gr. 8-12). per. 9.95 *(978-0-88995-338-3(4),* f8ceb222-f86d-48a4-884d-afca410ab5da) Trifolium Bks., Inc. CAN. Dist: Firefly Bks., Ltd.
Casanova, Mary. Curse of a Winter Moon. 2014. (ENG.). 144p. pap. 9.95 *(978-0-8166-9207-1(6))* Univ. of Minnesota Pr.
Collins, Tim. Notes from a Hairy-Not-Scary Werewolf. Pinder, Andrew, illus. 2013. (ENG.). 288p. (J). (gr. 5-9). 12.99 *(978-1-4424-8207-4(9),* Aladdin) Simon & Schuster Children's Publishing.
—Prince of Dorkness: More Notes from a Totally Lame Vampire. Pinder, Andrew, illus. 2011. (ENG.). 336p. (J). (gr. 5-9). 12.99 *(978-1-4424-3388-5(4),* Aladdin) Simon & Schuster Children's Publishing.
Cremer, Andrea. Bloodrose. 2012. (Nightshade Ser.: 3). lib. bdg. 22.10 *(978-0-606-26635-2(6))* Turtleback.
—Snakeroot. 2014. (Nightshade Ser.: 4). (ENG.). 352p. (YA). (gr. 9). pap. 10.99 *(978-0-14-750860-7(6),* Speak) Penguin Young Readers Group.
Dahl, Michael. Werewolf Skin. Sinkovec, Igor, illus. 2015. (Igor's Lab of Fear Ser.). (ENG.). 40p. (J). (gr. 4-8). lib. bdg. 23.99 *(978-1-4965-0458-6(5),* 128483, Stone Arch Bks.) Capstone.
Dent, Sue. Never Ceese: Can Two Who Were Wronged Make It Right? 2006. 336p. (YA). lib. bdg. 17.99 *(978-1-59958-017-3(9))* Journey Stone Creations, LLC.
Donbavand, Tommy. Attack of the Trolls. 2012. (Scream Street Ser.: 8). lib. bdg. 16.00 *(978-0-606-31471-8(7))* Turtleback.
—Scream Street: Attack of the Trolls. 2012. (Scream Street Ser.: 8). (ENG., Illus.). 128p. (J). (gr. 3-7). pap. 5.99 *(978-0-7636-5760-4(3))* Candlewick Pr.
—Scream Street: Fang of the Vampire. Cartoon Saloon, Ltd., illus. 2009. (Scream Street Ser.: 1). (ENG.). 160p. (J). (gr. 3-7). pap. 7.99 *(978-0-7636-4608-0(3))* Candlewick Pr.
—Scream Street: Flesh of the Zombie, Bk. 4. Cartoon Saloon, Ltd., illus. 2010. (Scream Street Ser.: 4). (ENG.). 128p. (J). (gr. 3-7). pap. 5.99 *(978-0-7636-4637-0(7))* Candlewick Pr.
—Scream Street: Heart of the Mummy, Bk. 3. Cartoon Saloon, Ltd., illus. 2010. (Scream Street Ser.: 3). (ENG.). 128p. (J). (gr. 3-7). pap. 5.99 *(978-0-7636-4636-3(9))* Candlewick Pr.
—Scream Street: Invasion of the Normals. 2012. (Scream Street Ser.: 7). (ENG., Illus.). 128p. (J). (gr. 3-7). pap. 5.99 *(978-0-7636-5759-8(X))* Candlewick Pr.
—Terror of the Nightwatchman. 2014. (Scream Street Ser.: 9). lib. bdg. 16.00 *(978-0-606-35872-9(2))* Turtleback.
—Wolf. 2012. (Stoke Books Titles Ser.). 64p. (J). (gr. 5-8). pap. 45.32 *(978-0-7613-9225-5(4));* pap. 7.95 *(978-1-78112-034-7(X));* lib. bdg. 22.60 *(978-1-78112-033-0(1))* Stoke Bks.
Doyle, Bill. The Zombie at the Finish Line, 4. Lee, Jared, illus. 2013. (Scream Team Ser.). (ENG.). 96p. (J). (gr. 2-4). 17.44 *(978-0-545-47978-3(9))* Scholastic, Inc.
Dunne, Colin. Werewolf. 128p. (J). pap. 7.95 *(978-0-233-99580-9(3))* Andre Deutsch GBR. Dist: Trans-Atlantic Pubns., Inc.
Epstein, Adam Jay & Jacobson, Andrew. Secrets of the Crown. 2012. (Familiars Ser.: 2). (ENG.). 400p. (J). (gr. 3-7). pap. 7.99 *(978-0-06-196113-7(2),* HarperCollins) HarperCollins Pubs.
Evans, Sandra. This Is Not a Werewolf Story. 2016. (ENG., Illus.). 352p. (J). (gr. 4-7). 18.99 *(978-1-4814-4480-4(8),* Atheneum Bks. for Young Readers) Simon & Schuster Children's Publishing.
Feasey, Steve. Blood Wolf: Wereling Book #3, 3. 2011. (Wereling Ser.: 3). (ENG.). 304p. (YA). (gr. 8-12). pap. 18.99 *(978-0-312-65352-1(2),* 900069508) Feiwel & Friends.
—Dark Moon: A Wereling Novel. 2011. (Wereling Ser.: 2). (ENG.). 336p. (YA). (gr. 7-18). pap. 19.99 *(978-0-312-64643-1(7),* 900068714) Feiwel & Friends.
Fisher, Rusty. Littlest Werewolf's Story, 1 vol. 2014. (Story Time for Little Monsters Ser.). (ENG.). 24p. (J). (gr. -1-4). lib. bdg. 31.36 *(978-1-62402-021-6(6),* 628, Looking Glass Library) Magic Wagon.
Fontes, Justine & Fontes, Ron. Casebook: Werewolves, 1 vol. 2009. (Top Secret Graphica Mysteries Ser.). (ENG., Illus.). 48p. (YA). (gr. 4-4). 33.93 *(978-1-60754-609-2(4),* 96c3fbfe-b878-4f9d-a3b6-ab8e6871b315); pap. 12.75 *(978-1-60754-611-5(6),* 795e26db-5522-44f5-8e38-b2700805851f) Rosen Publishing Group, Inc., The. (Windmill Bks.).
French, Jackie. My Uncle Wal the Werewolf. King, Stephen Michael, illus. 2018. (Wacky Families Ser.: 05). (ENG.). 128p. 5.99 *(978-0-207-20013-7(0),* HarperCollins) HarperCollins Pubs.
Garfield, Henry. Tartabull's Throw. 2015. (ENG., Illus.). 272p. (YA). (gr. 7). pap. 12.99 *(978-1-4814-7510-5(X),* Atheneum Bks. for Young Readers) Simon & Schuster Children's Publishing.
Gibbons, Alan. Night Hunger. 2013. (ENG.). 64p. (YA). (gr. 6-12). pap. 6.95 *(978-1-78112-179-5(6));* lib. bdg. 22.60 *(978-1-78112-178-8(8))* Lerner Publishing Group.
Grant, Tess. Flying in the Dark. 2013. 186p. pap. 10.99 *(978-1-62237-167-9(4))* Turquoise Morning Pr.
Grau, Sheila. Dr. Critchlore's School for Minions: Book One. Sutphin, Joe, illus. 2016. (Dr. Critchlore's School for Minions Ser.). (ENG.). 304p. (J). (gr. 3-7). pap. 7.95 *(978-1-4197-2029-1(5),* 1091603, Amulet Bks.) Abrams, Inc.
Graves, Judith. Second Skin. 2011. 280p. (J). pap. 16.99 *(978-1-61603-006-3(2))* Leap Bks.
—Under My Skin. Cox, Val, illus. 2010. 328p. (YA). (gr. 8-18). pap. 16.99 *(978-1-61603-000-1(3))* Leap Bks.
Gray, Claudia. Fateful. 2012. (ENG.). 352p. (YA). (gr. 9). pap. 9.99 *(978-0-06-200621-9(5),* HarperTeen) HarperCollins Pubs.
Haesche, Richard, Sr. The Werewolf Syndrome. 3rd ed. 2007. (ENG.). 218p. (YA). pap. 9.95 *(978-0-9798536-0-9(5))* Kreative X-Pressions Pubns.
Haig, Matt. To Be a Cat. Curtis, Stacy, illus. (ENG.). 304p. (J). (gr. 3-7). 2014. pap. 8.99 *(978-1-4424-5406-4(7))* 2013. 16.99 *(978-1-4424-5405-7(9))* Simon & Schuster Children's Publishing.
Hall, Tim. Shadow of the Wolf. 2016. (ENG.). 480p. (YA). (gr. 9). pap. 9.99 *(978-1-338-03250-5(X))* Scholastic, Inc.
Hawthorne, Rachel. Dark Guardian #4: Shadow of the Moon. 2010. (Dark Guardian Ser.: 4). (ENG.). 256p. (YA). (gr. 9-18). pap. 8.99 *(978-0-06-196290-5(2),* HarperTeen) HarperCollins Pubs.
Herman, Gail. Scooby-Doo in up, up, & Away!, 1 vol. 2015. (Scooby-Doo! Ser.). (ENG., Illus.). 32p. (J). (gr. k-4). lib. bdg. 31.36 *(978-1-61479-412-7(X),* 19451, Picture Bk.) Spotlight.
Holder, Nancy & Viguie, Debbie. Unleashed. 2012. (Wolf Spring Chronicles Ser.: 1). (ENG.). 400p. (YA). (gr. 7). pap. 9.99 *(978-0-385-74099-9(9),* Ember) Random Hse. Children's Bks.
Hopkins, Ellen, ed. A New Dawn: Your Favorite Authors on Stephenie Meyer's Twilight Series: Completely Unauthorized. 2009. (Illus.). 200p. (J). (gr. 9-12). pap. 12.95 *(978-1-933771-93-9(3),* SmartPop) BenBella Bks.
Hueller, P. W. Wolf High. 2015. (Tartan House Ser.). (ENG.). 96p. (J). (gr. 3-6). *(978-1-63235-055-8(6),* 11682, 12-Story Library) Bookstaves, LLC.
Ireland, Justina. Tiffany Donovan vs. the Poison Werewolves. Champion, Tyler, illus. 2018. (Devils' Pass Ser.). (ENG.). 128p. (J). (gr. 4-8). lib. bdg. 25.99 *(978-1-4965-6525-9(8),* 138528, Stone Arch Bks.) Capstone.
Jobling, Curtis. Nest of Serpents. 2015. (Wereworld Ser.: 4). (ENG.). 512p. (J). (gr. 5). 9.99 *(978-0-14-242193-2(6),* Puffin Books) Penguin Young Readers Group.
—Rage of Lions. 2013. (Wereworld Ser.: 2). lib. bdg. 19.65 *(978-0-606-30041-4(4))* Turtleback.
—Rise of the Wolf. 2012. (Wereworld Ser.: 1). (ENG.). 432p. (J). (gr. 5-18). pap. 9.99 *(978-0-14-242108-6(1),* Puffin Books) Penguin Young Readers Group.
—Rise of the Wolf. 2012. (Wereworld Ser.: 1). lib. bdg. 19.65 *(978-0-606-26084-8(6))* Turtleback.
—Shadow of the Hawk. 2013. (Wereworld Ser.: 3). (ENG.). 496p. (J). (gr. 5). pap. 9.99 *(978-0-14-242192-5(8),* Puffin Books) Penguin Young Readers Group.
—Shadow of the Hawk. 2013. (Wereworld Ser.: 3). lib. bdg. 19.65 *(978-0-606-30044-5(9))* Turtleback.
—Storm of Sharks. 2015. (Wereworld Ser.: 5). (ENG.). 480p. (J). (gr. 5). 9.99 *(978-0-14-242577-0(X),* Puffin Books) Penguin Young Readers Group.
Johnson, Christine. Nocturne. 2011. (ENG.). 368p. (YA). (gr. 7). 16.99 *(978-1-4424-0776-3(X),* Simon Pulse) Simon Pulse.
—Nocturne: A Claire de Lune Novel. 2012. (ENG.). 384p. (YA). (gr. 7). pap. 9.99 *(978-1-4424-0777-0(8),* Simon Pulse) Simon Pulse.
Keswick, Kitty. Freaksville. Cox, Val, illus. 2010. 328p. (YA). (gr. 8-12). pap. 16.99 *(978-1-61603-001-8(1))* Leap Bks.
Klause, Annette Curtis. Blood & Chocolate. 2007. (ENG.). 288p. (YA). (gr. 7). pap. 9.99 *(978-0-385-73421-9(2),* Ember) Random Hse. Children's Bks.
Kovalkova-McKenna, Svetlana & McKenna, Konstantin. Oberon. 2009. 44p. pap. 7.26 *(978-0-557-06114-3(8))* Lulu Pr., Inc.
Kruger, Kat. The Night Has Claws. 2013. 280p. pap. *(978-0-9917937-5-4(7))* Fierce Ink Pr. Co-Op, Ltd.
Long, Chad M. The Lycan Journal. 2007. (Illus.). 141p. (YA). per. 12.95 *(978-0-615-15295-0(3))* Long Stories LLC.
Long, Chad Michael, illus. The Lycan Journal. Long, Chad Michael, . 2nd ed. 2007. 141p. (YA). per. 12.95 *(978-0-615-18961-1(X))* Long Stories LLC.
Longmeyer, C. M. My Life As a Third Grade Werewolf. Blanding, Dexter, illus. 2014. (ENG.). (J). (gr. 2-3). pap. 7.99 *(978-0-635-11144-9(6))* Gallopade International.
Luper, Eric. The Haunted Howl. Weber, Lisa K., illus. 2016. (Key Hunters Ser.: 3). (ENG.). 128p. (J). (gr. 2-5). pap. 4.99 *(978-0-545-82211-4(4),* Scholastic Paperbacks) Scholastic, Inc.
Lyons, Jayne. 100% Wolf. Rivas, Victor, illus. (ENG.). 256p. (J). (gr. 2-7). 2010. pap. 8.99 *(978-1-4424-0252-2(0))* 2009. 16.99 *(978-1-4169-7474-1(1))* Simon & Schuster Children's Publishing. (Atheneum Bks. for Young Readers).
Manoa, J. By the Blood... #6. 2017. (Werewolf Council Ser.). (ENG.). 208p. (YA). (gr. 5-12). lib. bdg. 32.84 *(978-1-68076-503-8(5),* 25416, Epic Escape) EPIC Pr.
—The Hidden Blade #2. 2017. (Werewolf Council Ser.). (ENG.). 208p. (YA). (gr. 5-12). lib. bdg. 32.84 *(978-1-68076-499-4(3),* 25408, Epic Escape) EPIC Pr.
—Never Alone #1. 2017. (Werewolf Council Ser.). (ENG.). 208p. (YA). (gr. 5-12). 51.42 *(978-1-68076-554-0(X),* 26509, Epic Escape) EPIC Pr.
—Nobilitate Nobis #3. 2017. (Werewolf Council Ser.). (ENG.). 208p. (YA). (gr. 5-12). lib. bdg. 32.84 *(978-1-68076-500-7(0),* 25410, Epic Escape) EPIC Pr.
—Pointed Hand #5. 2017. (Werewolf Council Ser.). (ENG.). 208p. (YA). (gr. 5-12). lib. bdg. 32.84 *(978-1-68076-502-1(7),* 25414, Epic Escape) EPIC Pr.
—Wolfland #4. 2017. (Werewolf Council Ser.). (ENG.). 208p. (YA). (gr. 5-12). lib. bdg. 32.84 *(978-1-68076-501-4(9),* 25412, Epic Escape) EPIC Pr.
Mary-Todd, Jonathan. Lock-In. 2011. (Night Fall (tm) Ser.). (ENG.). 112p. (YA). (gr. 6-12). lib. bdg. 27.99 *(978-0-7613-7743-6(3),* 428ca348-d51c-42f6-9130-f956c338417f, Darby Creek) Lerner Publishing Group.
MaryAnn, Aunt. Spooky Journey down Riverside Drive the Night of the Full Moon. 2010. (ENG.). 40p. pap. 15.95 *(978-0-557-31081-4(4))* Lulu Pr., Inc.
Meyer, Stephenie. Amanecer / Breaking Dawn. 2008. (Saga Crepusculo / the Twilight Saga Ser.: 4). Tr. of Breaking Dawn. (SPA.). 832p. (YA). (gr. 9-12). pap. 23.95 *(978-607-11-0033-7(X),* Alfaguara) Penguin Random House Grupo Editorial ESP. Dist: Penguin Random Hse. LLC.
—Breaking Dawn. 2008. (Twilight Saga Ser.: 4). (ENG.). 768p. (YA). (gr. 7-17). 24.99 *(978-0-316-06792-8(X))* Little, Brown Bks. for Young Readers.
—Breaking Dawn. 2010. (Twilight Saga Ser.: 4). (YA). lib. bdg. 29.40 *(978-0-606-23108-4(0))* Turtleback.
—Eclipse. 2007. (Twilight Saga Ser.: 3). (ENG.). 640p. (YA). (gr. 7-17). 22.99 *(978-0-316-16020-9(2))* Little, Brown Bks. for Young Readers.
—Eclipse. 2008. 576p. *(978-1-904233-91-6(0),* Atom Books) Little, Brown Book Group Ltd.
—Eclipse. 2011. (Twilight Saga: Bk. 3). 13.08 *(978-0-7848-3531-9(4),* Everbind) Marco Bk. Co.
—Eclipse. 2010. (Twilight Saga: Bk. 3). 629p. (YA). (gr. 9-12). 22.10 *(978-1-60686-303-9(7))* Perfection Learning Corp.
—Eclipse. 2007. (Twilight Saga Spanish Ser.: 3). (SPA.). 637p. (gr. 7-12). lib. bdg. 28.15 *(978-1-4177-9862-9(9))* Turtleback.
—New Moon. 2008. (Twilight Saga: Bk. 2). 563p. (gr. 9-12). 21.00 *(978-1-60686-336-7(3))* Perfection Learning Corp.
—New Moon. 2006. (Twilight Saga Ser.: 2). (ENG.). 608p. (J). (gr. 7-17). 24.99 *(978-0-316-16019-3(9))* Little, Brown Bks. for Young Readers.
—New Moon. 2011. (Twilight Saga: Bk. 2). 11.72 *(978-0-7848-3535-7(7),* Everbind) Marco Bk. Co.
—The Short Second Life of Bree Tanner: An Eclipse Novella. 2010. (Twilight Saga Ser.). (ENG.). 192p. (YA). (gr. 7-17). 17.99 *(978-0-316-12558-1(X))* Little, Brown Bks. for Young Readers.
—The Twilight Saga Collection Set, 4 vols. 2008. (ENG.). 2560p. (YA). (gr. 7-17). 92.00 *(978-0-316-03184-4(4))* Little, Brown Bks. for Young Readers.
Millar, Martin. Lonely Werewolf Girl. 2008. (ENG.). 560p. per. 16.95 *(978-0-9796636-6-6(0),* Soft Skull Pr.) Counterpoint Pr.
Mounteer, J. B. Camp (Were) Wolf. 2007. (ENG.). 24p. per. 16.99 *(978-1-4259-9185-2(8))* AuthorHouse.
North, Laura. Cinderella: The Terrible Truth. Dreidemy, Joëlle, illus. 2014. (Race Ahead with Reading Ser.). (ENG.). 32p. (J). (gr. 2-2). *(978-0-7787-1326-5(1))* Crabtree Publishing Co.
O'Callaghan, G. The Eternals. 2007. 376p. per. *(978-1-84693-055-3(3))* Best Global Publishing Ltd.
O'Shea, M.J. Cold Moon [Library Edition]. 2nd ed. 2014. 180p. pap. 14.99 *(978-1-62798-460-7(7),* Harmony Ink Pr.) Dreamspinner Pr.
Park, Devin & Lee, Claudia. Howl Michigan. 2011. 138p. pap. 24.95 *(978-1-4560-8895-8(5))* America Star Bks.
Peacock, Kathleen. Hemlock. 2013. (Shifters Novel Ser.: 1). (ENG.). 432p. (YA). (gr. 9). pap. 9.99 *(978-0-06-204866-0(X),* Tegen, Katherine Bks) HarperCollins Pubs.

W X Y Z

—Thornhill. 2015. (Shifters Novel Ser.: 2). (ENG.). 368p. (YA). (gr. 9). pap. 9.99 *(978-0-06-204869-1(4))*, Tegen, Katherine Bks) HarperCollins Pubs.

Pearce, Jackson. Sisters Red. 2011. (Fairy Tale Retelling Ser.). (ENG.). 352p. (YA). (gr. 10-17). pap. 18.99 *(978-0-316-06867-3(5))* Little, Brown Bks. for Young Readers.

—Sweetly. 2012. (Fairy Tale Retelling Ser.). (ENG.). 336p. (YA). (gr. 10-17). pap. 17.99 *(978-0-316-06866-6(7))* Little, Brown Bks. for Young Readers.

Perez, Marlene. Dead Is a State of Mind. 2009. (Dead Is Ser.: 2). (ENG., Illus.). 192p. (YA). (gr. 7-18). pap. 7.99 *(978-0-15-206210-1(6)*, 1063350, Clarion Bks.) HarperCollins Pubs.

Price, Jennifer L. Half Moon: Phases of the Moon: Book 2, 1 vol. 2009. 252p. pap. 27.95 *(978-1-4489-2193-5(7))* PublishAmerica, Inc.

Reisz, Kristopher. Unleashed. 2010. (ENG.). 352p. (YA). (gr. 9). pap. 9.99 *(978-1-4424-0637-7(2)*, Simon Pulse) Simon Pulse.

Reynolds, J. H. Monsterstreet #1: the Boy Who Cried Werewolf. 2019. (ENG.). 176p. (J). (gr. 3-7). 16.99 *(978-0-06-286935-7(3))*; pap. 5.99 *(978-0-06-286934-0(5))* HarperCollins Pubs. (Tegen, Katherine Bks).

Richemont, Enid. The Night of the Were-Boy. 2015. (Race Further with Reading Ser.). (ENG., Illus.). 48p. (J). (gr. 3-3). *(978-0-7787-2087-4(X))* Crabtree Publishing Co.

Riviello, Linda. Werewolves, Vampires & Ghosts... Oh My! 2009. (J). pap. 12.95 *(978-1-61623-088-3(6))* Independent Pub.

Robertson, Andrea. Bloodrose: A Nightshade Novel. 2012. (Nightshade Ser.: 3). (ENG.). 432p. (YA). (gr. 9). pap. 12.99 *(978-0-14-242370-7(X)*, Speak) Penguin Young Readers Group.

—Nightshade: Book 1. 2011. (Nightshade Ser.: 1). (ENG.). 496p. (YA). (gr. 9-18). pap. 12.99 *(978-0-14-241980-9(X)*, Speak) Penguin Young Readers Group.

Rowleym'Lin. Knights of Right, BK 3: The Warrior's Guard. 2010. 80p. (J). pap. 6.99 *(978-1-60641-240-4(X)*, Shadow Mountain) Shadow Mountain Publishing.

Sampson, Jeff. Vesper. 2011. (Deviants Ser.: 1). (ENG.). 304p. (YA). (gr. 8-18). 16.99 *(978-0-06-199276-6(3)*, Balzer & Bray) HarperCollins Pubs.

Sander, Sonia. Werewolf Watch. 2012. (Scooby Doo Reader Ser.). lib. bdg. 13.55 *(978-0-606-23961-5(8))* Turtleback.

Schreiber, Ellen. Full Moon Kisses. 2013. (Full Moon Ser.: 3). (ENG.). 224p. (YA). (gr. 8). pap. 9.99 *(978-0-06-198654-3(2)*, Tegen, Katherine Bks) HarperCollins Pubs.

—Magic of the Moonlight, 2. 2012. (Full Moon Ser.: 2). (ENG.). 256p. (YA). (gr. 8-12). pap. 9.99 *(978-0-06-198656-7(9)*, Tegen, Katherine Bks) HarperCollins Pubs.

—Once in a Full Moon. 2011. (Full Moon Ser.: 1). (ENG.). 320p. (YA). (gr. 8). pap. 9.99 *(978-0-06-198652-9(6)*, Tegen, Katherine Bks) HarperCollins Pubs.

Shan, Darren, pseud. Blood Beast. 2008. (Demonata Ser.: 5). (ENG.). 224p. (J). (gr. 10-17). pap. 12.99 *(978-0-316-00378-0(6))* Little, Brown Bks. for Young Readers.

—Dark Calling. 2010. (Demonata Ser.: 9). (ENG.). 224p. (J). (gr. 10-17). pap. 13.99 *(978-0-316-04872-9(0))* Little, Brown Bks. for Young Readers.

—Death's Shadow. 2009. (Demonata Ser.: 7). (ENG.). 240p. (J). (gr. 10-17). pap. 14.99 *(978-0-316-00382-7(4))* Little, Brown Bks. for Young Readers.

—Demon Apocalypse. 2009. (Demonata Ser.: 6). (ENG.). 208p. (J). (gr. 10-17). pap. 12.99 *(978-0-316-00380-3(8))* Little, Brown Bks. for Young Readers.

—Wolf Island. 2010. (Demonata Ser.: 8). (ENG.). 216p. (J). (gr. 10-17). pap. 13.99 *(978-0-316-04881-1(X))* Little, Brown Bks. for Young Readers.

Shusterman, Neal. Red Rider's Hood. 2006. (Dark Fusion Ser.: 3). (ENG.). 192p. (YA). (gr. 7-18). 7.99 *(978-0-14-240678-6(3)*, Speak) Penguin Young Readers Group.

Sirod, G. p. & Sirod, G. P. Scabs. 2010. 190p. pap. *(978-1-84923-457-3(4))* YouWriteOn.

Smith, Cynthia Leitich. Blessed. 2011. (Tantalize Ser.: 3). (ENG., Illus.). 480p. (YA). (gr. 9-18). 17.99 *(978-0-7636-4326-3(2))* Candlewick Pr.

—Diabolical. 2012. (Tantalize Ser.: 4). (ENG., Illus.). 368p. (YA). (gr. 9-12). 17.99 *(978-0-7636-5118-3(4))* Candlewick Pr.

—Tantalize. 2008. (Tantalize Ser.: 1). (ENG., Illus.). 336p. (YA). (gr. 9). pap. 9.99 *(978-0-7636-4059-0(X))* Candlewick Pr.

Specter, Baron. To Werewolf or Not to Werewolf, 1 vol. Kneupper, Setch, illus. 2012. (Graveyard Diaries). (ENG.). 128p. (J). (gr. 2-5). 38.50 *(978-1-61641-901-1(6)*, 9180, Calico Chapter Bks.) ABDO Publishing Co.

Speer, Cindy Lynn. Unbalanced. 2010. 241p. pap. *(978-1-934841-90-7(0))* Zumaya Pubns. LLC.

St. Crow, Lili. Betrayals, 10 vols. 2010. (Strange Angels Ser.: 2). (YA). 95.75 *(978-1-4407-7156-9(1))* Recorded Bks., Inc.

—Betrayals. 2009. (Strange Angels Ser.: 2). lib. bdg. 20.85 *(978-0-606-09020-9(7))* Turtleback.

—Betrayals: A Strange Angels Novel, 2. 2009. (Strange Angels Ser.: 2). (ENG., Illus.). 304p. (YA). (gr. 7-18). pap. 26.19 *(978-1-59514-252-8(5)*, Razorbill) Penguin Young Readers Group.

—Defiance, 4. 2011. (Strange Angels Ser.: 4). (ENG.). 304p. (YA). (gr. 7-18). 26.19 *(978-1-59514-392-1(0)*, Razorbill) Penguin Young Readers Group.

—Jealousy, 10 vols. 2010. (Strange Angels Ser.: 3). (J). 86.75 *(978-1-4498-2774-8(8))*; 209.75 *(978-1-4498-2772-4(1))*; 1.25 *(978-1-4498-2777-9(2))*; 83.75 *(978-1-4498-2776-2(4))*; 68.75 *(978-1-4498-2773-1(X))* Recorded Bks., Inc.

—Jealousy. 2010. (Strange Angels Ser.: 3). lib. bdg. 20.85 *(978-0-606-14566-4(4))* Turtleback.

—Jealousy: A Strange Angels Novel. 2010. (Strange Angels Ser.: 3). (ENG.). 320p. (YA). (gr. 7-18). 9.99 *(978-1-59514-290-0(8)*, Razorbill) Penguin Young Readers Group.

—Strange Angels, 9 vols. 2009. (Strange Angels Ser.: 1). (J). 181.75 *(978-1-4407-6194-2(9))*; 117.75 *(978-1-4407-6197-3(3))*; 114.75 *(978-1-4407-6199-7(X))*; 87.75 *(978-1-4407-6193-5(0))*; 84.75 *(978-1-4407-6195-9(7))* Recorded Bks., Inc.

—Strange Angels. 2009. (Strange Angels Ser.: 1). lib. bdg. 20.85 *(978-0-606-08957-9(8))* Turtleback.

Stine, R. L. The Werewolf of Fever Swamp. 2009. (Goosebumps Ser.: 11). lib. bdg. 17.20 *(978-0-606-00241-7(3))* Turtleback.

Strange, Jason. Full Moon Horror, 1 vol. Parks, Phil & Dal Lago, Alberto, illus. 2011. (Jason Strange Ser.). (ENG.). 72p. (J). (gr. 3-6). pap. 6.25 *(978-1-4342-3434-6(7)*, 116455, Stone Arch Bks.) Capstone.

Thompson, Paul B. The Battle for the Brightstone: Book III of the Brightstone Saga, 1 vol. 2014. (Brightstone Saga Ser.). (ENG.). 176p. (J). (gr. 5-6). 39.93 *(978-0-7660-3984-1(6)*, e9149e38-6bf6-4e58-a2bb-da562639cd41) Enslow Publishing, LLC.

—The Fortune-Teller: Book II of the Brightstone Saga, 1 vol. 2013. (Brightstone Saga Ser.). (ENG.). 160p. (J). (gr. 5-6). 39.93 *(978-0-7660-3983-4(8)*, 33708694-74f5-4c14-b5c4-80a8adbdb9e3); pap. 13.88 *(978-1-4644-0265-4(5)*, 495c2983-5c39-40c9-9230-c735fb19d132) Enslow Publishing, LLC.

Troupe, Thomas Kingsley. The Misplaced Mummy, 1 vol. Gilpin, Stephen, illus. 2014. (Furry & Flo Ser.). (ENG.). 128p. (J). (gr. 2-3). 25.32 *(978-1-4342-6396-4(7)*, 123874, Stone Arch Bks.) Capstone.

—The Skeletons in City Park, 1 vol. Gilpin, Stephen, illus. 2014. (Furry & Flo Ser.). (ENG.). 128p. (J). (gr. 2-3). 25.32 *(978-1-4342-6397-1(5)*, 123875, Stone Arch Bks.) Capstone.

—The Solemn Golem. Gilpin, Stephen, illus. 2015. (Furry & Flo Ser.). (ENG.). 128p. (J). (gr. 2-3). lib. bdg. 25.32 *(978-1-4342-9646-7(6)*, 126933, Stone Arch Bks.) Capstone.

—The Voiceless Vampire. Gilpin, Stephen, illus. 2015. (Furry & Flo Ser.). (ENG.). 128p. (J). (gr. 2-3). lib. bdg. 25.32 *(978-1-4342-9645-0(8)*, 126932, Stone Arch Bks.) Capstone.

VanDerveuten, Robin M. Keepers of the Fairy Moon. 2013. 200p. *(978-1-4602-1429-9(3))*; pap. *(978-1-4602-1430-5(7))* FriesenPress.

Warner, Gertrude Chandler, creator. The Legend of the Howling Werewolf. 2018. (Boxcar Children Mysteries Ser.: 148). (ENG., Illus.). 128p. (J). (gr. 2-5). 12.99 *(978-0-8075-0740-7(7)*, 807507407); pap. 6.99 *(978-0-8075-0741-4(5)*, 807507415) Random Hse. Children's Bks. (Random Hse. Bks. for Young Readers).

Young, Jessica. Howl at the Moon: a Branches Book (Haggis & Tank Unleashed #3) Burks, James, illus. 2017. (Haggis & Tank Unleashed Ser.: 3). (ENG.). 80p. (J). (gr. k-2). pap. 5.99 *(978-1-338-04525-3(3))* Scholastic, Inc.

Zornow, Jeff. Werewolf, 1 vol. Zornow, Jeff, illus. 2007. (Graphic Horror Ser.). (ENG., Illus.). 32p. (J). (gr. 3-6). 32.79 *(978-1-60270-062-8(1)*, 9078, Graphic Planet - Fiction) Magic Wagon.

WESLEY, JOHN, 1703-1791

Benge, Janet & Benge, Geoff. Christian Heroes - Then & Now - John Wesley: The World, His Parish. 2007. (Christian Heroes Ser.). (ENG.). 190p. (YA). (gr. 3-7). pap. 11.99 *(978-1-57658-382-1(1))* YWAM Publishing.

WEST, BENJAMIN, 1738-1820

Brenner, Barbara. The Boy Who Loved to Draw: Benjamin West. Dunrea, Olivier, illus. 2003. (ENG.). 48p. (J). (gr. -1-3). pap. 6.99 *(978-0-618-31089-0(4)*, 482065, Clarion Bks.) HarperCollins Pubs.

WEST, JERRY, 1938-

Ramen, Fred. Jerry West. 2009. (Basketball Hall of Famers Ser.). 112p. (gr. 5-8). 63.90 *(978-1-61511-532-7(3)*, Rosen Reference) Rosen Publishing Group, Inc., The.

WEST (U.S.)

see also Northwest, Pacific; Pacific States

Allison, Pamela S. Emerald's Journal: A summer with Hatchlings. Cepeda, Joseph C., photos by. 2007. (Illus.). 24p. (J). lib. bdg. 16.95 *(978-0-9793474-1-2(6))* Sand Sage Pr.

Andrews, Barbara. Discover the West Region. 2006. (J). pap. *(978-1-4108-6437-6(5))* Benchmark Education Co.

—The West Region. 2006. (J). pap. *(978-1-4108-6434-5(0))* Benchmark Education Co.

Barkan, Joanne. A Western Activity Book & Libro de actividades del Oeste: 6 English, 6 Spanish Adaptations. 2011. (ENG & SPA.). (J). 101.00 net. *(978-1-4108-5734-7(4))* Benchmark Education Co.

Bodden, Valerie. Through the American West. 2011. (Great Expeditions Ser.). (ENG., Illus.). 48p. (J). (gr. 5-8). 35.65 *(978-1-60818-065-3(4)*, 22151, Creative Education) Creative Co., The.

Carlson, Lisa, illus. Calamity Jane. 2007. (On My Own Folklore Ser.). 48p. (J). (gr. -1-3). per. 6.95 *(978-0-8225-6480-5(7)*, First Avenue Editions) Lerner Publishing Group.

Criscione, Rachel Damon. The Mustang. 2009. (Library of Horses Ser.). 24p. (gr. 3-3). 42.50 *(978-1-60853-722-8(6)*, PowerKids Pr.) Rosen Publishing Group, Inc., The.

Demund, Tom. From Slave to Superstar of the Wild West: The Awesome Story of Jim Beckwourth. 2007. (Illus.). 154p. (J). 18.95 *(978-0-9786904-0-3(0))* Legends of the West Publishing Co.

Drinkard, Lawson. Riding on a Range: Western Activities for Kids. Lee, Fran, illus. 2003. (ENG.). 64p. (YA). pap. 9.99 *(978-1-58685-036-4(9))* Gibbs Smith, Publisher.

Exploring the West Classroom Library. (gr. 2-5). lib. bdg. 49.95 *(978-0-7368-4514-4(3)*, Red Brick Learning) Capstone.

Gilbert, Sara. Calamity Jane. 2005. (Legends of the West (Creative Education) Ser.). (Illus.). 48p. (J). (gr. 5-9). lib. bdg. 21.95 *(978-1-58341-337-1(5)*, Creative Education) Creative Co., The.

Glasscock, Sarah. The Western States: Set Of 6. 2011. (Navigators Ser.). (J). pap. 48.00 net. *(978-1-4108-6254-9(2))* Benchmark Education Co.

—The Western States: Text Pairs. 2008. (Bridges/Navigators Ser.). (J). (gr. 4). 89.00 *(978-1-4108-8398-8(1))* Benchmark Education Co.

Gondosch, Linda. Where Did Sacagawea Join the Corps of Discovery? And Other Questions about the Lewis & Clark Expedition. 2011. (Six Questions of American History Ser.). (ENG.). 48p. (gr. 4-6). pap. 56.72 *(978-0-7613-7644-6(5))*; (Illus.). (J). pap. 11.99 *(978-0-7613-7131-1(1)*, 061f662a-a998-4abe-ac16-604cd15f7710) Lerner Publishing Group.

Granfield, Linda. Cowboy: An Album. (J). 9.99 *(978-1-55054-230-1(3)*, Da Capo Pr. Inc.) Hachette Bks.

Johmann, Carol A. The Lewis & Clark Expedition: Join the Corps of Discovery to Explore Uncharted Territory. 2008. (ENG., Illus.). 112p. (J). (gr. 4-6). pap. 14.25 *(978-1-885593-73-3(2)*, Ideals Pubns.) Worthy Publishing.

Knowlton, Laurie Lazzaro. Cowgirl Alphabet, 1 vol. Knowlton, Charlotte & Coates, Kathy, illus. 2011. (ABC Ser.). (ENG.). 32p. (J). (gr. k-3). 16.99 *(978-1-58980-669-6(7)*, Pelican Publishing) Arcadia Publishing.

Krohn, Katherine E. Women of the Wild West. 2003. (Biography Ser.). (Illus.). 112p. (YA). (gr. 6-18). pap. 7.95 *(978-0-8225-9690-5(3)*, Carolrhoda Bks.) Lerner Publishing Group.

Latham, Frank. Jed Smith: Trail Blazer of the West. McHugh, Michael J., ed. Murch, Frank, illus. 2003. 121p. pap. 6.95 *(978-1-930367-86-9(4))* Christian Liberty Pr.

Levy, Janey. Lewis & Clark in Their Own Words, 1 vol., Vol. 1. 2014. (Eyewitness to History Ser.). (ENG.). 32p. (J). (gr. 4-5). 29.27 *(978-1-4339-9929-1(3)*, f6377acd-b9ac-4838-8b85-72be01888a2b); pap. 11.50 *(978-1-4339-9930-7(7)*, a1e4799d-12bc-438c-9624-9fddec8edc01) Stevens, Gareth Publishing LLLP.

Manheimer, Ann S. James Beckwourth: Legendary Mountain Man. 2005. (Trailblazer Biographies Ser.). (ENG., Illus.). 112p. (J). (gr. 5-9). lib. bdg. 31.93 *(978-1-57505-892-4(8)*, Twenty-First Century Bks.) Lerner Publishing Group.

Marsh, Carole. John C. Fremont. 2004. 12p. (gr. k-4). 2.95 *(978-0-635-02380-3(6))* Gallopade International.

Miller, Reagan & Walker, Robert. What's in the West? Crabtree Publishing Staff, ed. 2011. (ENG.). 32p. (J). (gr. 3-6). pap. *(978-0-7787-1833-8(6))* Crabtree Publishing Co.

—What's in the West? 2011. (ENG.). 32p. (J). lib. bdg. *(978-0-7787-1827-7(1))* Crabtree Publishing Co.

Miller, Robert H. Reflections of a Black Cowboy: Buffalo Soldiers. 2004. (J). pap. 9.95 *(978-0-940975-69-9(6)*, Sankofa Bks.) Just Us Bks., Inc.

—Reflections of a Black Cowboy: Cowboys. 2004. (J). pap. 9.95 *(978-0-940975-70-5(X)*, Sankofa Bks.) Just Us Bks., Inc.

Moran, Margaret. Cowhands & Cattle Trails & Los vaqueros y el arreo de Ganado: 6 English, 6 Spanish Adaptations. 2011. (ENG & SPA.). (J). 97.00 net. *(978-1-4108-5700-2(X))* Benchmark Education Co.

Mulhall, Jill K. Lewis & Clark. rev. ed. 2017. (Social Studies: Informational Text Ser.). (ENG., Illus.). 32p. (gr. 4-8). pap. 11.99 *(978-1-4938-3886-8(5))* Teacher Created Materials, Inc.

National Geographic Learning. Language, Literacy & Vocabulary - Reading Expeditions (U. S. Regions): Explore the West. 2007. (Avenues Ser.). (ENG., Illus.). 36p. (J). pap. 20.95 *(978-0-7922-5461-4(9))* CENGAGE Learning.

—Reading Expeditions (Social Studies: Readings about America): the West Today. 2007. (ENG., Illus.). 32p. (J). pap. 18.95 *(978-0-7922-4536-0(9))* CENGAGE Learning.

—Reading Expeditions (Social Studies: Travels Across America): the West. 2007. (Avenues Ser.). (ENG., Illus.). 32p. (J). pap. 18.95 *(978-0-7922-8682-0(0))* CENGAGE Learning.

Penn, Sarah. Nat Love: Vaquero Afroamericano, 1 vol. 2003. (Grandes Personajes en la Historia de Los Estados Unidos (Famous People in American History) Ser.). (SPA., Illus.). 32p. (J). (gr. 3-4). pap. 10.00 *(978-0-8239-4234-3(1)*, 97b78651-a0c4-4862-8de1-6901458d5d5f, Rosen Classroom) Rosen Publishing Group, Inc., The.

Ross, Michael Elsohn. Exploring the Earth with John Wesley Powell. Smith, Wendy, illus. 2005. (Naturalist's Apprentice Biographies Ser.). 48p. (gr. 3-6). lib. bdg. 19.93 *(978-1-57505-254-0(7))* Lerner Publishing Group.

Sanford, William R. & Green, Carl R. Buffalo Bill Cody: Courageous Wild West Showman, 1 vol. 2013. (Courageous Heroes of the American West Ser.). (ENG., Illus.). 48p. (J). (gr. 5-7). pap. 11.53 *(978-1-4644-0090-2(3)*, ca598850-b688-4425-8bbf-58bbc7301998) Enslow Publishing, LLC.

—Calamity Jane: Courageous Wild West Woman, 1 vol. 2013. (Courageous Heroes of the American West Ser.). (ENG., Illus.). 48p. (J). (gr. 5-7). pap. 11.53 *(978-1-4644-0093-3(8)*, 3294d813-6625-4898-b0e3-ec98e86bcdec) Enslow Publishing, LLC.

Santillo, LuAnn. Wild West, 6 vols. Santillo, LuAnn, ed. 2003. (Half-Pint Kids Readers Ser.). (Illus.). 42p. (J). (gr. -1-1). pap. 6.95 *(978-1-59256-077-6(6))* Half-Pint Kids, Inc.

Savage, Candace. Born to Be a Cowgirl: A Spirited Ride Through the Old West. 2004. (Illus.). *(978-1-55054-838-9(7)*, Da Capo Pr. Inc.) Hachette Bks.

Savage, Jeff. Fearless Scouts: True Tales of the Wild West, 1 vol. 2012. (True Tales of the Wild West Ser.). (ENG., Illus.). 48p. (gr. 5-7). lib. bdg. 25.27 *(978-0-7660-4024-3(0)*, 2b158bfd-477d-4d23-ae67-76b93dbaa2c3) Enslow Publishing, LLC.

—Pioneering Women: True Tales of the Wild West, 1 vol. 2012. (True Tales of the Wild West Ser.). (ENG., Illus.). 48p. (gr. 5-7). lib. bdg. 25.27 *(978-0-7660-4022-9(4)*, ca454646-a36b-4509-8760-686725fe879c) Enslow Publishing, LLC.

Sechrist, Darren. Taming the West. 2008. (ENG., Illus.). 32p. (J). pap. *(978-0-7787-4215-9(6))* Crabtree Publishing Co.

Smith-Llera, Danielle. People & Places of the West. 2016. (United States by Region Ser.). (ENG., Illus.). 32p. (J). (gr. 3-6). lib. bdg. 27.99 *(978-1-5157-2441-4(7)*, 132822, Capstone Pr.) Capstone.

Stefoff, Rebecca. Opening of the West, 1 vol. 2003. (American Voices From Ser.). (ENG., Illus.). 160p. (gr. 6-6). 41.21 *(978-0-7614-1201-4(8)*, 80e9629c-104d-4ab6-89f2-29c5a462eded) Cavendish Square Publishing LLC.

Stuckey, Rachel. Go West with Famous Trailblazers. 2016. (ENG.). 32p. (J). *(978-0-7787-2324-0(0))* Crabtree Publishing Co.

Vann, Donna. Wild West Adventures. 2006. (Adventure Ser.). (ENG., Illus.). 96p. (J). per. 8.99 *(978-1-84550-065-8(2)*, 022fcbc9-e8f2-45c7-a720-4619344ecbc4) Christian Focus Pubns. GBR. Dist: Baker & Taylor Publisher Services (BTPS).

Visca, Curt. How to Draw Cartoon Symbols of the Wild West. 2009. (Kid's Guide to Drawing Ser.). 24p. (gr. 3-3). 47.90 *(978-1-61511-021-6(6)*, PowerKids Pr.) Rosen Publishing Group, Inc., The.

Williams, Colleen Madonna Flood. My Adventure in the Wild West. 2007. 44p. (J). 8.99 *(978-1-59092-439-6(8))* Blue Forge Pr.

WEST (U.S.)—FICTION

Abnett, Dan. Dragon Frontier. 2015. (Dragon Frontier Ser.). (ENG., Illus.). 336p. (J). (gr. 4). pap. 12.99 *(978-0-14-134296-2(X))* Penguin Bks., Ltd. GBR. Dist: Independent Pubs. Group.

Abnett, Dan & Lanning, Andy. Dragon Frontier: Burning Moon. 2nd ed. 2015. (Dragon Frontier Ser.: 2). (ENG.). 352p. (J). (gr. 4). pap. 12.99 *(978-0-14-134298-6(6))* Penguin Bks., Ltd. GBR. Dist: Independent Pubs. Group.

Alger, Horatio. Frank & Fearless or the Fortunes of Jasper Kent. 2007. 228p. 20.99 *(978-1-4280-7465-1(1))*; per. 14.99 *(978-1-4280-7470-5(8))* IndyPublish.com.

Anderson, Connie Kingrey. Haunted Cattle Drive. 2013. (Creepers Mysteries Ser.: Bk. 1). (ENG.). 112p. (J). pap. 7.99 *(978-1-935793-00-7(4))* Movies for the Ear, LLC.

Anderson, Suzette. Cybertreks: Wildest West. 2004. 196p. pap. 13.95 *(978-0-595-30840-8(6))* iUniverse, Inc.

Arrigan, Mary. Pa Jinglebob - The Fastest Knitter in the West. Paul, Korky, illus. 2005. (Red Bananas Ser.). (ENG.). 48p. (J). lib. bdg. *(978-0-7787-1072-1(6))* Crabtree Publishing Co.

—Pa Jinglebob & the Grabble Gang. 2006. (Red Bananas Ser.). (ENG., Illus.). 48p. (J). (gr. -1-3). lib. bdg. *(978-0-7787-1074-5(2))* Crabtree Publishing Co.

Arrigan, Mary & Paul, Korky. PA Jinglebob: The Fastest Knitter in the West. 2005. (Red Bananas Ser.). (ENG., Illus.). 48p. (J). (gr. 1-3). *(978-0-7787-1088-2(2))* Crabtree Publishing Co.

ber, Gail. Time of the Cats. 2013. 132p. pap. 11.99 *(978-1-4582-1232-0(7)*, Abbott Pr.) Author Solutions, LLC.

Berenstain, Jan & Berenstain, Stan. The Berenstain Bears Out West. Berenstain, Jan, illus. 2006. (I Can Read Level 1 Ser.). (ENG., Illus.). 32p. (J). (gr. k-3). pap. 4.99 *(978-0-06-058354-5(1)*, HarperCollins) HarperCollins Pubs.

Bietz, Barbara. The Sundown Kid: A Southwestern Shabbat. 2017. (ENG., Illus.). 32p. (J). (gr. k-2). pap. 8.95 *(978-1-939160-94-2(4))* August Hse. Pubs., Inc.

Blakeslee, Ann R. A Different Kind of Hero, 1 vol. 2005. (ENG.). 32p. (YA). pap. 5.95 *(978-0-7614-5147-1(1))* Marshall Cavendish Corp.

Blanchet, Deborah A. The Hat. 2009. 122p. 29.99 *(978-1-4415-4624-1(3))*; pap. 19.99 *(978-1-4415-4623-4(5))* Xlibris Corp.

Bloomfield, Susanne George & Reed, Eric Melvin, eds. Adventures in the West: Stories for Young Readers. 2007. (ENG., Illus.). 302p. (J). (gr. 3-7). pap. 19.95 *(978-0-8032-5974-4(3)*, BLOADX, Bison Bks.) Univ. of Nebraska Pr.

Bly, Stephen A. The Lost Wagon Train. 2005. (Retta Barre's Oregon Trail Ser.: Vol. 1). 110p. pap. 5.99 *(978-1-58134-391-5(4)*, Crossway Bibles) Crossway.

Bostick, B. k. Huber Hill & the Dead Man's Treasure. 2011. (J). *(978-1-59955-911-7(0)*, Bonneville Bks.) Cedar Fort, Inc./CFI Distribution.

Bowman, Erin. Retribution Rails. (ENG.). (YA). (gr. 9). 2019. 400p. pap. 9.99 *(978-1-328-60367-8(9)*, 1732075) 2017. (Illus.). 384p. 17.99 *(978-0-544-91888-7(6)*, 1655796) HarperCollins Pubs. (Clarion Bks.).

Bruchac, Joseph. Sacajawea. 2008. (ENG., Illus.). 208p. (YA). (gr. 7). pap. 7.99 *(978-0-15-206455-6(9)*, 1199286, Clarion Bks.) HarperCollins Pubs.

Buffalo Storm. 2014. (ENG., Illus.). 32p. (J). (gr. -1-3). pap. 7.99 *(978-0-544-33921-7(5)*, 1584492, Clarion Bks.) HarperCollins Pubs.

Burgess, Thornton W. Old Mother West Wind's "When" Stories. (J). 21.95 *(978-0-8488-0387-2(6))* Amereon Ltd.

Byars, Betsy. The Golly Sisters Go West. Truesdell, Sue, illus. 2003. (I Can Read Level 3 Ser.). (ENG.). 64p. (J). (gr. k-3). pap. 4.99 *(978-0-06-444132-2(6)*, HarperCollins) HarperCollins Pubs.

Byars, Betsy & Byars, B. The Golly Sisters Go West. 2003. (I Can Read! Level 3 Ser.). (J). (gr. k-3). lib. bdg. 13.55 *(978-0-8335-4709-5(7))* Turtleback.

Campbell, Roy. Song of the Jackalope. Bosworth, David, illus. 2nd ed. 2006. 140p. (YA). pap. 12.95 *(978-1-933538-04-4(X))* Bridgeway Bks.

Cannon, A. E. Charlotte's Rose. 2011. (ENG., Illus.). 256p. (gr. 4). pap. 9.95 *(978-1-60781-141-1(3)*, P196472) Univ. of Utah Pr.

Carson, William G. B. & Carson, William C., texts. Peter Becomes a Trail Man: The Story of a Boy's Journey on the Santa Fe Trail: A Novel. 2018. (Illus.). 191p. (J). pap. *(978-1-63293-226-6(1))* Sunstone Pr.

Cole, Gwen. Ride On. 2018. (ENG.). 280p. (YA). (gr. 6-12). 16.99 *(978-1-5107-2993-3(3)*, Sky Pony Pr.) Skyhorse Publishing Co., Inc.

Collins, Tim. The Long-Lost Secret Diary of the World's Worst Dinosaur Hunter. 2018. (Long-Lost Secret Diary Ser.). (ENG., Illus.). 216p. (J). (gr. 4-5). pap. 9.99 *(978-1-63163-196-2(9)*, 1631631969); lib. bdg. 28.50 *(978-1-63163-195-5(0)*, 1631631950) North Star Editions. (Jolly Fish Pr.).

Coren, Alan. Arthur the Kid. 2004. (Illus.). 64p. *(978-0-903895-76-7(5)*, Robson Bks. Ltd.) Pavilion Bks.

—Buffalo Arthur. 2004. (Illus.). 64p. *(978-0-903895-75-0(7)*, Robson Bks. Ltd.) Pavilion Bks.

—Railroad Arthur. 2004. (Illus.). 64p. *(978-0-903895-92-7(7)*, Robson Bks. Ltd.) Pavilion Bks.

Cushman, Karen. Rodzina. 2020.Tr. of Rodzina. (ENG.). 240p. (J). (gr. 3-7). pap. 7.99 *(978-0-358-09751-8(7)*, 1747610, Clarion Bks.) HarperCollins Pubs.

Dale, Elizabeth. Cara the Cowgirl. Lombardo, Serena, illus. 2021. (Early Bird Readers — Gold (Early Bird Stories (tm)) Ser.). (ENG.). 32p. (J). (gr. k-3). 30.65 *(978-1-5415-9007-6(4)*, 2c85c67a-e715-4717-9395-1ee97d95bee3, Lerner Pubns.) Lerner Publishing Group.

Davies, Robert, adapted by. Lit a Shuck for Texas: Adapted Louis l'Amour Short Stories Series. 2003. (Adapted Louis

L'Amour Short Stories Ser.). (Illus.). 56p. (YA). (978-1-57035-983-5(0), 233LIT) Cambium Education, Inc.
-Merrano of the Dry Country: Adapted Louis l'Amour Short Story Series. 2003. (Adapted Louis L'Amour Short Stories Ser.). (Illus.). 60p. (J). (978-1-57035-985-9(7), 233MERRANO) Cambium Education, Inc.
-A Trail to the West: Adapted Louis l'Amour Short Stories Series. 2003. (Adapted Louis L'Amour Short Stories Ser.). (Illus.). 56p. (J). (978-1-57035-984-2(9), 233TRAIL) Cambium Education, Inc.
undy, Melanie Richardson. Westward Ho with Ollie Ox! Date not set. (Illus.). 56p. (J). (gr. k-5). per. 12.95 (978-0-9674491-4-2(6)) M D C T Publishing.
rickson, John. The Case of the Black-Hooded Hangmans. Holmes, Gerald L., illus. 2011. (Hank the Cowdog Ser.). (ENG.). 113p. (J). (gr. 3-6). pap. 5.99 (978-1-59188-124-7(2)) Maverick Bks., Inc.
—The Case of the Burrowing Robot. Holmes, Gerald L., illus. 2011. (Hank the Cowdog Ser.). (ENG.). 125p. (J). (gr. 3-6). pap. 5.99 (978-1-59188-142-1(0)) Maverick Bks., Inc.
—The Case of the Car-Barkaholic Dog. Holmes, Gerald L., illus. 2011. (Hank the Cowdog Ser.). (ENG.). 115p. (J). (gr. 3-6). pap. 5.99 (978-1-59188-117-9(X)) Maverick Bks., Inc.
—The Case of the Deadly Ha-Ha Game. Holmes, Gerald L., illus. 2011. (Hank the Cowdog Ser.). (ENG.). 128p. (J). (gr. 3-6). pap. 5.99 (978-1-59188-137-7(4)) Maverick Bks., Inc.
—The Case of the Double Bumblebee Sting. Holmes, Gerald L., illus. 2011. (Hank the Cowdog Ser.: No. 22). (ENG.). 114p. (J). (gr. 3-6). pap. 5.99 (978-1-59188-122-3(6)) Maverick Bks., Inc.
—The Case of the Falling Sky. Holmes, Gerald L., illus. 2011. (Hank the Cowdog Ser.: No. 45). (ENG.). 129p. (J). (gr. 3-6). pap. 5.99 (978-1-59188-145-2(5)) Maverick Bks., Inc.
—The Case of the Fiddle-Playing Fox. Holmes, Gerald L., illus. 2011. (Hank the Cowdog Ser.: No. 12). (ENG.). 118p. (J). (gr. 3-6). pap. 5.99 (978-1-59188-112-4(9)) Maverick Bks., Inc.
—The Case of the Halloween Ghost. Holmes, Gerald L., illus. 2011. (Hank the Cowdog Ser.). (ENG.). 123p. (J). (gr. 3-6). pap. 5.99 (978-1-59188-109-4(9)) Maverick Bks., Inc.
—The Case of the Haystack Kitties. Holmes, Gerald L., illus. 2011. (Hank the Cowdog Ser.). (ENG.). 123p. (J). (gr. 3-6). pap. 5.99 (978-1-59188-130-8(7)) Maverick Bks., Inc.
—The Case of the Hooking Bull. Holmes, Gerald L., illus. 2011. (Hank the Cowdog Ser.). (ENG.). 119p. (J). (gr. 3-6). pap. 5.99 (978-1-59188-118-6(8)) Maverick Bks., Inc.
—The Case of the Kidnapped Collie. Holmes, Gerald L., illus. 2011. (Hank the Cowdog Ser.). (ENG.). 113p. (J). (gr. 3-6). pap. 5.99 (978-1-59188-126-1(9)) Maverick Bks., Inc.
—The Case of the Midnight Rustler. Holmes, Gerald L., illus. 2011. (Hank the Cowdog Ser.: No. 19). (ENG.). 113p. (J). (gr. 3-6). pap. 5.99 (978-1-59188-119-3(6)) Maverick Bks., Inc.
—The Case of the Missing Bird Dog. Holmes, Gerald L., illus. 2011. (Hank the Cowdog Ser.: No. 40). (ENG.). 126p. (J). (gr. 3-6). pap. 5.99 (978-1-59188-140-7(4)) Maverick Bks., Inc.
—The Case of the Missing Cat. Holmes, Gerald L., illus. 2011. (Hank the Cowdog Ser.: No. 15). (ENG.). 114p. (J). (gr. 3-6). pap. 5.99 (978-1-59188-115-5(3)) Maverick Bks., Inc.
—The Case of the Monkey Burglar. Holmes, Gerald L., illus. 2011. (Hank the Cowdog Ser.: No. 48). (ENG.). 129p. (J). (gr. 3-6). pap. 5.99 (978-1-59188-148-3(X)) Maverick Bks., Inc.
—The Case of the Most Ancient Bone. Holmes, Gerald L., illus. 2011. (Hank the Cowdog Ser.). (ENG.). 239p. (J). (gr. 3-6). pap. 5.99 (978-1-59188-150-6(1)) Maverick Bks., Inc.
—The Case of the Night-Stalking Bone Monster. Holmes, Gerald L., illus. 2011. (Hank the Cowdog Ser.). (ENG.). 115p. (J). (gr. 3-6). pap. 5.99 (978-1-59188-127-8(7)) Maverick Bks., Inc.
—The Case of the One-Eyed Killer Stud Horse. Holmes, Gerald L., illus. 2011. (Hank the Cowdog Ser.: No. 8). (ENG.). 120p. (J). (gr. 3-6). pap. 5.99 (978-1-59188-108-7(0)) Maverick Bks., Inc.
—The Case of the Raging Rottweiler. Holmes, Gerald L., illus. 2011. (Hank the Cowdog Ser.). (ENG.). 131p. (J). (gr. 3-6). pap. 5.99 (978-1-59188-136-0(6)) Maverick Bks., Inc.
—The Case of the Saddle House Robbery. Holmes, Gerald L., illus. 2011. (Hank the Cowdog Ser.: No. 35). (ENG.). 125p. (J). (gr. 3-6). pap. 5.99 (978-1-59188-135-3(8)) Maverick Bks., Inc.
—The Case of the Shipwrecked Tree. Holmes, Gerald L., illus. 2011. (Hank the Cowdog Ser.: No. 41). (ENG.). 119p. (J). (gr. 3-6). pap. 5.99 (978-1-59188-141-4(2)) Maverick Bks., Inc.
—The Case of the Tender Cheeping Chickies. Holmes, Gerald L., illus. 2011. (Hank the Cowdog Ser.). (ENG.). 129p. (J). (gr. 3-6). pap. 5.99 (978-1-59188-147-6(1)) Maverick Bks., Inc.
—The Case of the Tricky Trap. Holmes, Gerald L., illus. 2011. (Hank the Cowdog Ser.). (ENG.). 126p. (J). (gr. 3-6). pap. 5.99 (978-1-59188-146-9(3)) Maverick Bks., Inc.
—The Case of the Twisted Kitty. Holmes, Gerald L., illus. 2004. (Hank the Cowdog Ser.: No. 43). 131p. (J). lib. bdg. 17.00 (978-1-4242-1600-0(1)) Fitzgerald Bks.
—The Case of the Twisted Kitty. Holmes, Gerald L., illus. 2011. (Hank the Cowdog Ser.). (ENG.). 131p. (J). (gr. 3-6). pap. 5.99 (978-1-59188-143-8(9)) Maverick Bks., Inc.
—The Case of the Vampire Cat. Holmes, Gerald L., illus. 2011. (Hank the Cowdog Ser.). (ENG.). 115p. (J). (gr. 3-6). pap. 5.99 (978-1-59188-121-6(8)) Maverick Bks., Inc.
—The Case of the Vampire Vacuum Sweeper. Holmes, Gerald L., illus. 2011. (Hank the Cowdog Ser.). (ENG.). 119p. (J). (gr. 3-6). pap. 5.99 (978-1-59188-129-2(3)) Maverick Bks., Inc.
—The Case of the Vanishing Fishhook. Holmes, Gerald L., illus. 2011. (Hank the Cowdog Ser.: No. 31). (ENG.). 124p. (J). (gr. 3-6). pap. 5.99 (978-1-59188-131-5(5)) Maverick Bks., Inc.
—The Curse of the Incredible Priceless Corncob. Holmes, Gerald L., illus. 2011. (Hank the Cowdog Ser.: No. 7). (ENG.). 127p. (J). (gr. 3-6). pap. 5.99 (978-1-59188-107-0(2)) Maverick Bks., Inc.
—The Dungeon of Doom. Holmes, Gerald L., illus. 2004. (Hank the Cowdog Ser.: No. 44). 122p. (J). lib. bdg. 17.00 (978-1-4242-1601-7(X)) Fitzgerald Bks.
—The Dungeon of Doom. Holmes, Gerald L., illus. 2011. (Hank the Cowdog Ser.). (ENG.). 122p. (J). (gr. 3-6). pap. 5.99 (978-1-59188-144-5(7)) Maverick Bks., Inc.
—Every Dog Has His Day. Holmes, Gerald L., illus. 2011. (Hank the Cowdog Ser.). (ENG.). 118p. (J). (gr. 3-6). pap. 5.99 (978-1-59188-110-0(2)) Maverick Bks., Inc.
—Faded Love. Holmes, Gerald L., illus. 2011. (Hank the Cowdog Ser.: No. 5). (ENG.). 125p. (J). (gr. 3-6). pap. 5.99 (978-1-59188-105-6(6)) Maverick Bks., Inc.
—The Fling. Holmes, Gerald L., illus. 2011. (Hank the Cowdog Ser.). (ENG.). 126p. (J). (gr. 3-6). pap. 5.99 (978-1-59188-138-4(2)) Maverick Bks., Inc.
—The Garbage Monster from Outer Space. Holmes, Gerald L., illus. 2011. (Hank the Cowdog Ser.). (ENG.). 126p. (J). (gr. 3-6). pap. 5.99 (978-1-59188-132-2(3)) Maverick Bks., Inc.
—It's a Dog's Life. Holmes, Gerald L., illus. (Hank the Cowdog Ser.: No. 3). (J). 100p. (gr. 2-5). 9.95 (978-0-916941-04-8(3)); 2011. (ENG.). 127p. (gr. 3-6). pap. 5.99 (978-1-59188-103-2(X)) Maverick Bks., Inc.
—Let Sleeping Dogs Lie. Holmes, Gerald L., illus. 2011. (Hank the Cowdog Ser.: No. 6). (ENG.). 129p. (J). (gr. 3-6). pap. 5.99 (978-1-59188-106-3(4)) Maverick Bks., Inc.
—Lost in the Blinded Blizzard. Holmes, Gerald L., illus. 2011. (Hank the Cowdog Ser.). (ENG.). 115p. (J). (gr. 3-6). pap. 5.99 (978-1-59188-116-2(1)) Maverick Bks., Inc.
—Lost in the Dark Unchanted Forest. Holmes, Gerald L., illus. 2011. (Hank the Cowdog Ser.). (ENG.). 124p. (J). (gr. 3-6). pap. 5.99 (978-1-59188-111-7(0)) Maverick Bks., Inc.
—Moonlight Madness. Holmes, Gerald L., illus. 2011. (Hank the Cowdog Ser.: No. 23). (ENG.). 114p. (J). (gr. 3-6). pap. 5.99 (978-1-59188-123-0(4)) Maverick Bks., Inc.
—The Mopwater Files. Holmes, Gerald L., illus. 2011. (Hank the Cowdog Ser.). (ENG.). 111p. (J). (gr. 3-6). pap. 5.99 (978-1-59188-128-5(5)) Maverick Bks., Inc.
—Murder in the Middle Pasture. Holmes, Gerald L., illus. 2011. (Hank the Cowdog Ser.). (ENG.). 120p. (J). (gr. 3-6). pap. 5.99 (978-1-59188-104-9(8)) Maverick Bks., Inc.
—The Original Adventures of Hank the Cowdog. Holmes, Gerald L., illus. (ENG.). 127p. (J). (gr. 3-6). 2012. (Hank the Cowdog Ser.: Vol. 1). 15.99 (978-1-59188-201-5(X)) 2011. (Hank the Cowdog Ser.: No. 1). pap. 5.99 (978-1-59188-101-8(3)) Maverick Bks., Inc.
—The Phantom in the Mirror. Holmes, Gerald L., illus. 2011. (Hank the Cowdog Ser.: No. 20). (ENG.). 114p. (J). (gr. 3-6). pap. 5.99 (978-1-59188-120-9(X)) Maverick Bks., Inc.
—The Quest for the Great White Quail. Holmes, Gerald L., illus. 2011. (Hank the Cowdog Ser.). (ENG.). 123p. (J). (gr. 3-6). pap. 5.99 (978-1-59188-152-0(8)) Maverick Bks., Inc.
—The Return of the Charlie Monsters. Holmes, Gerald L., illus. 2014. 128p. (J). pap. (978-1-59188-163-6(3)) Maverick Bks., Inc.
—The Secret Laundry Monster Files. Holmes, Gerald L., illus. 2011. (Hank the Cowdog Ser.). (ENG.). 128p. (J). (gr. 3-6). pap. 5.99 (978-1-59188-139-1(0)) Maverick Bks., Inc.
—Slim's Good-Bye. Holmes, Gerald L., illus. 2011. (Hank the Cowdog Ser.). (ENG.). 132p. (J). (gr. 3-6). pap. 5.99 (978-1-59188-134-6(X)) Maverick Bks., Inc.
—The Wounded Buzzard on Christmas Eve. Holmes, Gerald L., illus. 2011. (Hank the Cowdog Ser.: No. 13). (ENG.). 112p. (J). (gr. 3-6). pap. 5.99 (978-1-59188-113-1(7)) Maverick Bks., Inc.
Fitzgerald, John D. Brave Buffalo Fighter. 2003. (Young Adult Bookshelf Ser.). (ENG.). 192p. pap. 11.95 (978-1-883937-59-1(0)) Ignatius Pr.
Fleischman, Sid. Jim Ugly. Smith, Jos. A., illus. 2003. (ENG.). 144p. (J). (gr. 3-7). pap. 6.99 (978-0-06-052121-9(X), Greenwillow Bks.) HarperCollins Pubs.
Frank, John. Toughest Cowboy: Toughest Cowboy. 2004. (ENG., Illus.). 48p. (J). (gr. 1-3). 19.99 (978-0-689-83461-5(6), Simon & Schuster Bks. For Young Readers) Simon & Schuster Bks. For Young Readers.
Garland, Sherry. The Buffalo Soldier, 1 vol. Himler, Ronald, illus. 2006. (ENG.). 32p. (J). (gr. k-3). 16.99 (978-1-58980-391-6(4), Pelican Publishing) Arcadia Publishing.
Goscinny, René. The Daltons Always on the Run. Morris, illus. 2012. (Lucky Luke Ser.: 34). 48p. (J). (gr. 3-12). pap. 11.95 (978-1-84918-119-8(5)) CineBook GBR. Dist: National Bk. Network.
—The Wagon Train. Morris, Jean, illus. 2008. (Lucky Luke Ser.: 9). 48p. pap. 11.95 (978-1-905460-40-3(6)) CineBook GBR. Dist: National Bk. Network.
Goscinny, René & Morris Publishing Company Staff. The Grand Duke. 2011. (Lucky Luke Ser.: 29). (Illus.). 48p. (J). (gr. -1-12). pap. 11.95 (978-1-84918-083-2(0)) CineBook GBR. Dist: National Bk. Network.
—The Singing Wire. 2012. (Lucky Luke Ser.: 35). (Illus.). 48p. (J). (gr. 3-9). pap. 11.95 (978-1-84918-123-5(3)) CineBook GBR. Dist: National Bk. Network.
Grace & the Guiltless. 2014. (Wanted Ser.). (ENG.). 272p. (YA). 16.95 (978-1-63079-001-1(X), 126762, Switch Pr.) Capstone.
Guzman, Lila & Guzman, Rick. Lorenzo's Revolutionary Quest. 2003. 176p. (J). pap. 9.95 (978-1-55885-392-8(8), Piñata Books) Arte Publico Pr.
Hahn, Mary Downing. The Gentleman Outlaw & Me — Eli. 2007. (ENG.). 224p. (YA). (gr. 7-7). pap. 6.99 (978-0-618-83000-8(6), 100560, Clarion Bks.) HarperCollins Pubs.
Heaton, Layce D. The Many Tracks of Lap'n Tap, 1. Heaton, Layce D., illus. 2006. (Illus.). 32p. (J). lib. bdg. 18.95 (978-0-9761128-3-9(3)) KB Bks. & More.
Hemphill, Helen. The Adventurous Deeds of Deadwood Jones. 2011. (ENG.). 232p. (J). (gr. 5-9). pap. 7.95 (978-1-59078-896-7(6), Front Street) Astra Publishing Hse.
Henry, Marguerite. San Domingo: The Medicine Hat Stallion. Lougheed, Robert, illus. 2016. (ENG.). 288p. (J). (gr. 3-7). 19.99 (978-1-4814-6211-2(3), Aladdin) Simon & Schuster Children's Publishing.
Henty, George. Captain Bayley's Heir: A Tale of the California Gold Fields. 2011. 314p. pap. 19.95 (978-1-61179-115-0(4)) Fireship Pr.
—A Tale of the Western Plains. Pearse, Alfred, illus. 2006. (Dover Children's Classics Ser.). (ENG.). 352p. (YA). (gr. 3-8). per. 16.95 (978-0-486-45261-6(1), 452611) Dover Pubns., Inc.
Hergé. Land of Black Gold. Orig. Title: Tintin au Pays de l'Or Noir. (Illus.). 62p. (J). 19.95 (978-0-8288-5048-3(8)) French & European Pubns., Inc.
—Tintin au Pays de l'Or Noir.Tr. of Land of Black Gold. (FRE.). (J). (gr. 7-9). 24.95 (978-0-8288-5091-9(7)) French & European Pubns., Inc.
—Tintin en el Pais del Oro Negro.Tr. of Land of Black Gold. (SPA., Illus.). 62p. (J). 24.95 (978-0-8288-4995-1(1)) French & European Pubns., Inc.
Hermes, Patricia. Horse Diaries #3: Koda. Sanderson, Ruth, illus. 2009. (Horse Diaries: 3). 160p. (J). (gr. 3-7). pap. 7.99 (978-0-375-85199-5(2), Random Hse. Bks. for Young Readers) Random Hse. Children's Bks.
Hirsch, Andy. Varmints. 2016. (J). lib. bdg. 29.40 (978-0-606-39563-2(6)) Turtleback.
Hope, Laura Lee. The Bobbsey Twins in the Great West. 2005. 27.95 (978-1-4218-0365-4(8), 1st World Library - Literary Society) 1st World Publishing, Inc.
Ives, David. Scrib. 2005. 208p. (J). (gr. 5-18). lib. bdg. 17.89 (978-0-06-059842-6(5)) HarperCollins Pubs.
James, Will. Home Ranch. rev. ed. (Tumbleweed Ser.). (Illus.). 302p. (J). (gr. 4). pap. (978-0-87842-406-1(7), 802) Mountain Pr. Publishing Co., Inc.
—Look-See with Uncle Bill. rev. ed. (Illus.). 190p. (J). (gr. 4). pap. (978-0-87842-458-0(X), 814) Mountain Pr. Publishing Co., Inc.
—Smokey Vol. 1: The Cowhorse. rev. ed. (Tumbleweed Ser.). (Illus.). 260p. (J). (gr. 4-7). 36.00 (978-0-87842-414-6(8), 805) Mountain Pr. Publishing Co., Inc.
—Smoky Cowhorse, the Cowhorse. 2011. 9.00 (978-0-7848-3460-2(1), Everbind) Marco Bk. Co.
—Smoky the Cowhorse. 2008. (ENG., Illus.). 336p. (J). (gr. 3-7). pap. 8.99 (978-1-4169-4941-1(0), Aladdin) Simon & Schuster Children's Publishing.
Johnson, Erin. Her Cold Revenge. 2015. (Wanted Ser.). (ENG.). 272p. (YA). (gr. 9-9). 16.95 (978-1-63079-007-3(9), 127377, Switch Pr.) Capstone.
Karr, Kathleen. The Great Turkey Walk. 2004. 199p. (gr. 4-7). 18.00 (978-0-7569-4124-6(5)) Perfection Learning Corp.
Kimmel, Eric A. The Great Texas Hamster Drive, 0 vols. Whatley, Bruce, illus. 2012. (ENG.). 40p. (J). (gr. -1-3). 16.99 (978-0-7614-5357-4(1), 9780761453574, Two Lions) Amazon Publishing.
LaFaye, A. Follow Me down to Nicodemus Town: Based on the History of the African American Pioneer Settlement. Tadgell, Nicole, illus. 2019. (ENG.). 32p. (J). (gr. -1-3). 16.99 (978-0-8075-2535-7(9), 807525359) Whitman, Albert & Co.
Lee, Stacey. Under a Painted Sky. 2016. lib. bdg. 22.10 (978-0-606-38391-2(3)) Turtleback.
McCall, Edith. Stories of American Steamboats. Borja, Robert, illus. 2011. 126p. 40.95 (978-1-258-10111-4(4)) Literary Licensing, LLC.
McKernan, Victoria. The Devil's Paintbox, 1. 2010. (Devil's Paintbox Ser.). (ENG.). 368p. (J). (gr. 9-12). lib. bdg. 22.44 (978-0-375-93750-7(1)) Random House Publishing Group.
—The Devil's Paintbox. (ENG.). (YA). (gr. 9). 2013. 384p. pap. 9.99 (978-0-449-81655-4(9), Ember) 2010. 368p. mass mkt. 8.99 (978-0-440-23962-8(1), Laurel Leaf) Random Hse. Children's Bks.
McKissack, Patricia. Away West. James, Gordon C., illus. 2006. (Scraps of Time Ser.). (ENG.). 144p. (J). (gr. 3-7). 7.99 (978-0-14-240688-5(0), Puffin Books) Penguin Young Readers Group.
McLelland, Brad & Sylvester, Louis. The Fang of Bonfire Crossing: Legends of the Lost Causes. 2020. (Legends of the Lost Causes Ser.: 2). (ENG.). 400p. (J). pap. 20.99 (978-1-250-23360-8(7), 900174394) Square Fish.
Messner, Kate. Rescue on the Oregon Trail (Ranger in Time #1) McMorris, Kelley, illus. 2015. (Ranger in Time Ser.: 1). (ENG.). 144p. (J). (gr. 2-5). pap. 5.99 (978-0-545-63914-9(X), Scholastic Pr.) Scholastic, Inc.
Miller, Christopher & Miller, Allan. The Legend of Gid the Kid & the Black Bean Bandits, 2 bks., Bk.1. Miller, Christopher & Miller, Allan, illus. 2007. (Heroes of Promise Ser.: Bk. 1). (ENG., Illus.). 32p. (J). (gr. 1-5). 12.99 (978-1-59317-202-2(8)) Warner Pr., Inc.
Morrow, Sherry. Woman of the Mountains. 268p. (YA). pap. 22.00 (978-1-58982-611-3(6)) American Bk. Publishing Group.
Mortensen, Lori. Cowpoke Clyde Rides the Range. Austin, Michael Allen, illus. 2016. (ENG.). 32p. (J). (gr. -1-3). 16.99 (978-0-544-37030-2(9), 1596763, Clarion Bks.) HarperCollins Pubs.
Moss, Marissa. Amelia's Are-We-There-Yet Longest Ever Car Trip. Moss, Marissa, illus. (Amelia Ser.). (ENG., Illus.). 40p. (J). (gr. 2-5). 2012. pap. 8.99 (978-1-4169-1287-3(8)) 2006. 14.99 (978-1-4169-0906-4(0)) Simon & Schuster/Paula Wiseman Bks. (Simon & Schuster/Paula Wiseman Bks.).
Myers, Walter Dean. The Righteous Revenge of Artemis Bonner. 2003. (J). (gr. 5-18). 23.00 (978-0-8446-7250-2(5)) Smith, Peter Pub., Inc.
Nayeri, Daniel. Straw House, Wood House, Brick House, Blow: Four Novellas by Daniel Nayeri. 2011. (ENG., Illus.). 432p. (YA). (gr. 9). 19.99 (978-0-7636-5526-6(0)) Candlewick Pr.
Naylor, Phyllis Reynolds. Emily's Fortune, 1. 2011. (Emily Ser.: 1). 160p. (J). (gr. 3-7). 6.99 (978-0-375-84492-8(9), Yearling) Random Hse. Children's Bks.
Nell Nugget & the Cow Caper. 2008. (Illus.). 32p. (J). pap. 14.95 (978-0-9792820-2-7(0)) Toe The Line.
Nislick, June Levitt. Zayda Was a Cowboy. 2005. (ENG.). 88p. pap. 11.95 (978-0-8276-0817-7(9)) Jewish Pubn. Society.
Nixon, Hershell H. The Long Way West. 2003. (ENG., Illus.). 175p. 16.95 (978-0-89672-508-9(1), P171827) Texas Tech Univ. Pr.
Nolen, Jerdine. Thunder Rose. Nelson, Kadir, illus. 2007. (ENG.). 32p. (J). (gr. k-3). pap. 8.99 (978-0-15-206006-0(5), 1198036, Clarion Bks.) HarperCollins Pubs.
—Thunder Rose. Nelson, Kadir, illus. 2007. (gr. k-3). 17.00 (978-0-7569-8199-0(9)) Perfection Learning Corp.
Novara, Joe. Road Wrangler: Cowboys on Wheels. Lawson, Robert & Spatrisano, Kimberly, illus. 2007. 112p. (J). pap. 8.95 (978-1-58980-507-1(0), Pelican Publishing) Arcadia Publishing.
O'Hearn, Michael. The el Dorado Map. 2015. (Middle-Grade Novels Ser.). (ENG.). 320p. (J). (gr. 4-6). lib. bdg. 26.65 (978-1-4965-0158-5(6), 127931, Stone Arch Bks.) Capstone.
Oliveira, Luis. The Children of Hope 3. 2008. (ENG.). 56p. pap. 15.49 (978-0-578-00420-4(8)) Desktop Prepress Services.
Osborne, Mary Pope. Ghost Town at Sundown. unabr. ed. 2004. (Magic Tree House Ser.: No. 10). 73p. (J). (gr. k-3). pap. 17.00 incl. audio (978-0-8072-0535-8(4), Listening Library) Random Hse. Audio Publishing Group.
Paulsen, Gary. Tucket's Travels: Francis Tucket's Adventures in the West, 1847-1849 (Books 1-5) 2003. (Francis Tucket Bks.: Bks. 1-5). (ENG.). 560p. (J). (gr. 3-7). pap. 9.99 (978-0-440-41967-9(0), Yearling) Random Hse. Children's Bks.
Payne, Stephen. Teenage Stories of the West. 2011. 252p. 46.95 (978-1-258-09964-0(0)) Literary Licensing, LLC.
Pierce, Mary E. Permilia: A Western Children's Book. Dobler, Shirley Jean, illus. 2013. 62p. (J). 25.00 (978-1-936617-15-9(3)) Lemon Pr. LLC.
Pierpoint, Eric. The Last Ride of Caleb O'Toole. 2013. (ENG., Illus.). 304p. (J). (gr. 4-7). pap. 11.99 (978-1-4022-8171-6(4), 9781402281716) Sourcebooks, Inc.
Reeve, Kirk. Sun Father, Corn Mother: A Novel. 2015. 168p. (YA). pap. (978-1-63293-091-0(9)) Sunstone Pr.
Reid, Mayne. The Boy Hunters or Adventures in Search of a White Buffalo. 2005. reprint ed. pap. 30.95 (978-1-4179-0412-9(7)) Kessinger Publishing, LLC.
Roberts, Nancy. Ghosts of the Wild West: Including Five Never-Before-published Stories. 2nd fac. ed. 2008. (ENG., Illus.). 120p. (gr. 3-7). 24.99 (978-1-57003-731-3(0), P146720) Univ. of South Carolina Pr.
Rose, Caroline Starr. Ride on, Will Cody! A Legend of the Pony Express. Lillington, Joe, illus. 2017. (ENG.). 32p. (J). (gr. -1-3). 16.99 (978-0-8075-7068-5(0), 807570680) Whitman, Albert & Co.
Rowe, Gordon J. Showdown at Pecos. 2004. (Illus.). 32p. (gr. -1-3). 11.95 (978-1-57197-192-0(0)) Pentland Pr., Inc.
Rylant, Cynthia. Henry & Mudge & the Tumbling Trip: Ready-To-Read Level 2. Bracken, Carolyn, illus. (Henry & Mudge Ser.: 27). (ENG.). 40p. (J). (gr. k-2). 2006. pap. 4.99 (978-0-689-83452-3(7)) 2005. 17.99 (978-0-689-81180-7(2)) Simon Spotlight. (Simon Spotlight).
Sargent, Dave & Sargent, Pat. Ginger: (Lilac Roan) Be Likeable, 30 vols., Vol. 27. Lenoir, Jane, illus. 2003. (Saddle up Ser.: Vol. 27). 42p. (J). pap. 10.95 (978-1-56763-812-7(0)); lib. bdg. 23.60 (978-1-56763-811-0(2)) Ozark Publishing.
Schaefer, Jack. Stubby Pringle's Christmas. Bjorklund, Lorence, illus. 2017. (ENG.). 48p. pap. 16.95 (978-0-8263-5865-3(9), P544562) Univ. of New Mexico Pr.
Schnetzler, Pattie L. Fast 'n Snappy. Manning, Jane K., tr. Manning, Jane K., illus. 2004. (Carolrhoda Picture Books Ser.). 32p. (J). (gr. k-3). 16.95 (978-1-57505-539-8(2)) Lerner Publishing Group.
—Widdermaker. Sealock, Rick, illus. 2005. 32p. (gr. k-2). 15.95 (978-0-87614-647-7(7)) Lerner Publishing Group.
Scieszka, Jon. The Good, the Bad, & the Goofy. Smith, Lane, illus. 2005. (Time Warp Trio Ser.: No. 3). 70p. (gr. 4-7). 15.00 (978-0-7569-5876-3(8)) Perfection Learning Corp.
—The Good, the Bad, & the Goofy #3. Smith, Lane, illus. 2004. (Time Warp Trio Ser.: 3). 80p. (J). (gr. 2-4). pap. 5.99 (978-0-14-240046-3(7), Puffin Books) Penguin Young Readers Group.
Selfors, Suzanne. Spirit Riding Free: Lucky & the Mustangs of Miradero. 2017. (ENG.). 272p. (J). (gr. 3-7). 14.99 (978-0-316-50623-6(0)) Little, Brown Bks. for Young Readers.
Shire, Poppy. Magic Pony Carousel #3: Star the Western Pony. Berg, Ron, illus. 2007. (Magic Pony Carousel Ser.: 3). (ENG.). 96p. (J). (gr. 2-5). pap. 3.99 (978-0-06-083785-3(3), HarperCollins) HarperCollins Pubs.
Simon, Leslie. Wish You Were Here: An Essential Guide to Your Favorite Music Scenes — From Punk to Indie & Everything in Between. 2009. (ENG., Illus.). 256p. pap. 17.99 (978-0-06-157371-2(X), Dey Street Bks.) HarperCollins Pubs.
Smith, Andrew. Ghost Medicine. 2010. (ENG.). 384p. (YA). (gr. 8-13). pap. 19.99 (978-0-312-62912-0(5), 900066876) Square Fish.
Smith, Roland. The Captain's Dog: My Journey with the Lewis & Clark Tribe. 2008. (Great Episodes Ser.). (ENG., Illus.). 304p. (J). (gr. 5-7). pap. 8.99 (978-0-15-202696-7(7), 1193556, Clarion Bks.) HarperCollins Pubs.
Sneve, Virginia Driving Hawk. The Chichi Hoohoo Bogeyman. 2nd ed. 2008. (ENG., Illus.). 64p. (J). (gr. -1). pap. 9.95 (978-0-8032-1745-4(5), SNEC2X, Bison Bks.) Univ. of Nebraska Pr.
Sperry, Armstrong. Wagons Westward: The Old Trail to Santa Fe. Sperry, Armstrong, illus. 2005. (Illus.). 200p. (YA). (gr. 6-11). reprint ed. pap. 15.00 (978-0-7567-9693-8(8)) DIANE Publishing Co.
Steig, Jeanne. Tales from Gizzard's Grill. Turner, Sandy, illus. 2004. 80p. (J). 17.89 (978-0-06-000960-1(8), Cotler, Joanna Books) HarperCollins Pubs.
Stein, David Ezra. Cowboy Ned & Andy. Stein, David Ezra, illus. (ENG., Illus.). 32p. (J). (gr. -1-1). 2011. 6.99 (978-1-4424-3619-0(0)) 2006. 16.99 (978-1-4169-0041-2(1)) Simon & Schuster/Paula Wiseman Bks. (Simon & Schuster/Paula Wiseman Bks.).
Toni Eubanks. Journey Home. 2010. 52p. pap. 8.95 (978-1-4401-8246-4(9)) iUniverse, Inc.
Uribe Urbieta, Kirmen & Lete, Nere. Garmendia & the Black Rider. 2015. (Illus.). 93p. (J). pap. (978-1-935709-64-0(X)) Ctr. for Basque Studies.
Van Dyne, Edith. Aunt Jane's Nieces Out West. 2004. reprint ed. pap. 21.95 (978-1-4191-0826-6(3)) Kessinger Publishing, LLC.
Vande Velde, Vivian. Ghost of a Hanged Man, 1 vol. 2003. (ENG.). 32p. (J). (gr. 5). pap. 5.95 (978-0-7614-5154-9(4)) Marshall Cavendish Corp.
Velasco, M. G. Cardslinger. 2019. (ENG., Illus.). 360p. (J). (gr. 4-8). 17.99 (978-1-5415-5464-1(7), daf09fa5-43d7-45d4-8097-588f77b22e4f, Carolrhoda Bks.) Lerner Publishing Group.
Vens, William D. Alias Pecos Bill. 2003. per. 13.95 (978-1-891929-92-2(5)) Four Seasons Pubs.
Vo, Nancy. The Outlaw, 1 vol. 2018. (Crow Stories Trilogy Ser.: 1). (ENG., Illus.). 42p. (J). (gr. k-3). 17.95 (978-1-77306-016-3(3)) Groundwood Bks. CAN. Dist: Publishers Group West (PGW).

Webber, Gail. Time of the Cats. 2013. 132p. 28.95 *(978-1-4582-1233-7(5),* Abbott Pr.) Author Solutions, LLC.

White, Ramy Allison. Sunny Boy in the Far West. Hastings, Howard L., illus. 2011. 216p. 44.95 *(978-1-258-09942-8(X))* Literary Licensing, LLC.

Wilson, Diane Lee. Black Storm Comin' 2006. (ENG.). 240p. (J). (gr. 5-9). pap. 8.99 *(978-0-689-87138-2(4),* McElderry, Margaret K. Bks.) McElderry, Margaret K. Bks.

Winfield, Arthur M. The Rover Boys Out West. 2007. 228p. 26.95 *(978-1-4218-4140-3(1));* per. 11.95 *(978-1-4218-4238-7(6))* 1st World Publishing, Inc. (1st World Library - Literary Society).

Wolf, Allan. New Found Land: Lewis & Clark's Voyage of Discovery. 2007. (ENG., Illus.). 512p. (YA). (gr. 7-9). per. 19.99 *(978-0-7636-3288-5(0))* Candlewick Pr.

Wrede, Patricia C. Across the Great Barrier. 2011. (Frontier Magic Ser.: 2). (ENG.). 352p. (J). (gr. 7-7). 16.99 *(978-0-545-03343-5(8),* Scholastic Pr.) Scholastic, Inc.

Yep, Laurence. The Traitor. 2004. (Golden Mountain Chronicles). 310p. (J). (gr. 5). 14.65 *(978-0-7569-3457-6(5))* Perfection Learning Corp.

Young, Judy & Scillian, Devin. Westward Journeys. Farnsworth, Bill et al, illus. 2013. (American Adventures Ser.). (ENG.). 96p. (J). (gr. 3-6). pap. 6.99 *(978-1-58536-860-0(1),* 202367) Sleeping Bear Pr.

WEST (U.S.)—HISTORY

Alagna, Magdalena. Wyatt Earp: Lawman of the American West, 1 vol. 2003. (Famous People in American History / Grandes Personajes en la Historia de Los Estados Unidos Ser.). (ENG & SPA., Illus.). 32p. (gr. 2-3). lib. bdg. 29.13 *(978-0-8239-4171-1(X),* 091fb1b1-cbbc-4827-8f0a-484aaffea1a9, Editorial Buenas Letras) Rosen Publishing Group, Inc., The.

Anderson, Dale. The Civil War in the West (1861-July 1863), 1 vol. 2004. (World Almanac(r) Library of the Civil War Ser.). (ENG., Illus.). 48p. (gr. 5-8). pap. 15.05 *(978-0-8368-5592-0(2),* f1a73c48-7757-40ac-bab0-b107533729d6); lib. bdg. 33.67 *(978-0-8368-5583-8(3),* a497de3e-669b-4027-92d0-df03b0280971) Stevens, Gareth Publishing LLLP. (Gareth Stevens Secondary Library).

Arnéz, Lynda. My Wagon Train Adventure, 1 vol. 2015. (My Place in History Ser.). (ENG., Illus.). 24p. (J). (gr. 2-3). pap. 9.15 *(978-1-4824-4002-7(4),* 123566d3-91e8-4ad7-bc2b-ead566925690) Stevens, Gareth Publishing LLLP.

Aronin, Miriam. How Many People Traveled the Oregon Trail? And Other Questions about the Trail West. 2012. (Six Questions of American History Ser.). (ENG.). 48p. (gr. 4-6). pap. 56.72 *(978-0-7613-9237-8(8));* (Illus.). (J). pap. 11.99 *(978-0-7613-8566-0(5),* cb80b72c-4ecb-42fa-980f-9c951f655ece); (Illus.). (J). lib. bdg. 30.65 *(978-0-7613-5332-4(1),* feb9aceb-5243-49a1-b0d3-f994e3938250, Lerner Pubns.) Lerner Publishing Group.

Baker, Brynn. Buffalo Soldiers: Heroes of the American West. 2015. (Military Heroes Ser.). (ENG., Illus.). 32p. (J). (gr. 3-6). lib. bdg. 27.99 *(978-1-4914-4838-0(5),* 128723, Capstone Pr.) Capstone.

Baptiste, Tracey. If You Were a Kid in the Wild West (If You Were a Kid) (Library Edition) Raish, Jason, illus. 2018. (If You Were a Kid Ser.). (ENG.). 32p. (J). (gr. 2-4). lib. bdg. 26.00 *(978-0-531-23215-6(8),* Children's Pr.) Scholastic Library Publishing.

Barkan, Joanne. Settling the West 1862-1890: Set Of 6. 2011. (Navigators Ser.). (J). pap. 50.00 net. *(978-1-4108-2566-7(3))* Benchmark Education Co.

—A Western Activity Book: Set Of 6. 2011. (Navigators Ser.). (J). pap. 50.00 net. *(978-1-4108-2579-7(5))* Benchmark Education Co.

Barnett, Tracy. The Buffalo Soldiers. 2004. (History of the Old West Ser.). (Illus.). 64p. (YA). (gr. 5-18). lib. bdg. 19.95 *(978-1-59084-072-6(0))* Mason Crest.

Benchmark Education Co., LLC. Gold & the Settling of the West. 2014. (PRIME Ser.). (J). (gr. 6-8). pap. *(978-1-4509-9493-4(8))* Benchmark Education Co.

—Westward Expansion. 2014. (PRIME Ser.). (J). (gr. 6-8). pap. *(978-1-4509-9492-7(X))* Benchmark Education Co.

Benchmark Education Company. Settling the West (Teacher Guide) 1862 To 1890. 2004. *(978-1-4108-2581-0(7))* Benchmark Education Co.

Berman, Ruth. American Bison. rev. ed. 2008. (Nature Watch Ser.). (ENG., Illus.). 48p. (gr. 4-8). 27.93 *(978-0-8225-7513-9(2),* Lerner Pubns.) Lerner Publishing Group.

Bliss, John. Pioneers to the West, 1 vol. 2011. (Children's True Stories: Migration Ser.). (ENG.). 32p. (J). (gr. 3-5). pap. 8.29 *(978-1-4109-4082-7(9),* 114620, Raintree) Capstone.

Bloom Fradin, Judith & Brindell Fradin, Dennis. The Lewis & Clark Expedition, 1 vol. 2008. (Turning Points in U. S. History Ser.). (ENG., Illus.). 48p. (gr. 4-4). lib. bdg. 34.07 *(978-0-7614-2044-6(4),* 7f2d646f-467e-4a5c-ab42-787f757e9373) Cavendish Square Publishing LLC.

Bornemann Spies, Karen. Buffalo Bill Cody: Legend of the Wild West, 1 vol. 2014. (Legendary American Biographies Ser.). (ENG.). 96p. (gr. 6-6). 29.60 *(978-0-7660-6450-8(6),* aa6858bf-b38b-4ffd-8af0-5e9f93e88d65); pap. 13.88 *(978-0-7660-6451-5(4),* b6001603-e87d-49d8-9217-04aaf37d967a) Enslow Publishing, LLC.

Bougie, Matt. Life As a Pony Express Rider in the Wild West, 1 vol. 2017. (Life As... Ser.). (ENG.). 32p. (gr. 3-3). pap. 11.58 *(978-1-5026-3047-6(8),* 28e222f3-7275-4195-8fcd-3769a491db99) Cavendish Square Publishing LLC.

Braidich, Victoria. Making History: A Covered Wagon, 1 vol. 2005. (Content-Area Literacy Collections). (ENG.). 24p. (gr. 3-4). pap. 8.85 *(978-1-4042-5589-0(3),* 42736b4c-1aa8-4a79-a315-ec5a5e77ef3f) Rosen Publishing Group, Inc., The.

Britton, Arthur K. Life in the Wild West, 1 vol. 2013. (What You Didn't Know about History Ser.). (ENG., Illus.). 24p. (J). (gr. 2-3). pap. 9.15 *(978-1-4339-8440-2(7),* 29edb12a-9cea-4e2a-b29d-69352bac9683); lib. bdg. 25.27 *(978-1-4339-8439-6(3),* c9297c62-12f8-4121-a600-f4d2435ce6ff) Stevens, Gareth Publishing LLLP.

Brook, Henry. Wild West. 2008. (True Stories Ser.). 160p. (YA). pap. 4.99 *(978-0-7945-2197-4(5),* Usborne) EDC Publishing.

Brown, Dee. Saga of the Sioux: An Adaptation from Dee Brown's Bury My Heart at Wounded Knee. 2014. (ENG., Illus.). 224p. (J). (gr. 5-9). pap. 14.99 *(978-1-250-05067-0(7),* 900134138) Square Fish.

Bryant, Jill. Wagon Train. 2003. (Real Life Stories Ser.). (Illus.). 24p. (J). lib. bdg. 24.45 *(978-1-59036-082-8(6))* Weigl Pubs., Inc.

—Women in the West. 2003. (Real Life Stories Ser.). (Illus.). 24p. (J). lib. bdg. 24.45 *(978-1-59036-083-5(4))* Weigl Pubs., Inc.

Buffalo Bill Cody. 2010. (ENG., Illus.). 136p. (gr. 6-12). 35.00 *(978-1-60413-528-2(X),* P179304, Facts On File) Infobase Holdings, Inc.

Burger, James P. Mountain Men of the West. 2009. (Library of the Westward Expansion Ser.). 24p. (gr. 3-4). 42.50 *(978-1-60853-937-6(7),* PowerKids Pr.) Rosen Publishing Group, Inc., The.

Burlingame, Jeff. Jesse James: I Will Never Surrender, 1 vol. 2008. (Americans: the Spirit of a Nation Ser.). (ENG., Illus.). 128p. (gr. 5-6). lib. bdg. 35.93 *(978-0-7660-3353-5(8),* d2c6626d-19eb-49c0-9525-bdde4d7388ea) Enslow Publishing, LLC.

Byers, Ann. Life As a Homesteader in the American West, 1 vol. 2016. (Life As... Ser.). (ENG., Illus.). 32p. (gr. 3-3). 30.21 *(978-1-5026-1787-3(0),* 84c36979-4d22-41c5-8662-4711540ae137) Cavendish Square Publishing LLC.

Callery, Sean. The Dark History of America's Old West, 1 vol. 2011. (Dark Histories Ser.). (ENG.). 64p. (gr. 5-5). 35.50 *(978-1-60870-086-8(0),* ab883aea-2530-45bd-8ce6-bfe1e124ab05) Cavendish Square Publishing LLC.

Calvert, Patricia. Kit Carson: He Led the Way, 1 vol. 2007. (Great Explorations Ser.). (ENG., Illus.). 80p. (gr. 6-6). lib. bdg. 36.93 *(978-0-7614-2223-5(4),* 963e1330-9bef-4967-b147-72bb2846fbe9) Cavendish Square Publishing LLC.

Christopher, Nick. The Dream of Manifest Destiny: Immigrants & the Westward Expansion, 1 vol., 1. 2015. (Spotlight on Immigration & Migration Ser.). (ENG., Illus.). 24p. (J). (gr. 4-5). pap. 11.00 *(978-1-5081-4071-9(5),* c3c88689-d9f8-432c-a97c-a01dd9104c81, PowerKids Pr.) Rosen Publishing Group, Inc., The.

Clinton, Greg. The Louisiana Purchase, 1 vol. 2015. (Expanding America Ser.). (ENG., Illus.). 96p. (YA). (gr. 8-8). lib. bdg. 44.50 *(978-1-5026-0962-5(2),* f35c0639-c860-46a9-9a7f-2ff61ac97757) Cavendish Square Publishing LLC.

Collins, Kathleen. Jesse James: Bank Robber of the American West. (Primary Sources of Famous People in American History Ser.). 32p. (gr. 2-3). 2009. 47.90 *(978-1-60851-690-2(3))* 2003. (ENG & SPA., Illus.). lib. bdg. 29.13 *(978-0-8239-4160-5(4),* 1e40f58b-78c2-4e1f-911d-e6cd70abd37f, Editorial Buenas Letras) Rosen Publishing Group, Inc., The.

—Jesse James: Bank Robber of the American West / Legendario bandido del oeste Americano. 2009. (Famous People in American History/Grandes personajes en la historia de los Estados Unidos Ser.). (ENG & SPA.). 32p. (gr. 2-3). 47.90 *(978-1-61512-547-0(7),* Editorial Buenas Letras) Rosen Publishing Group, Inc., The.

—Jesse James: Legendario Bandido del Oeste Americano, 1 vol. 2003. (Grandes Personajes en la Historia de Los Estados Unidos (Famous People in American History) Ser.). (SPA.). 32p. (gr. 3-4). pap. 10.00 *(978-0-8239-4230-5(9),* 6e7f9fb2-76bb-47aa-a222-9838d6e7e24b, Rosen Classroom) Rosen Publishing Group, Inc., The.

—Jesse James: Legendario bandido del oeste americano (Jesse James: Bank Robber of the American West) 2009. (Grandes personajes en la historia de los Estados Unidos (Famous People in American History) Ser.). (SPA.). 32p. (gr. 2-3). 47.90 *(978-1-61512-801-3(8),* Editorial Buenas Letras) Rosen Publishing Group, Inc., The.

Collins, Terry. Into the West: Causes & Effects of U. S. Westward Expansion, 1 vol. 2013. (Cause & Effect Ser.). (ENG.). 32p. (J). (gr. 3-6). 27.99 *(978-1-4765-0237-3(4),* 122291); pap. 8.95 *(978-1-4765-3403-9(9),* 123534) Capstone.

Conant, Susan Sens. Lewis & Clark's Journey of Discovery: A Guide for Young Explorers. Lynn, Rick, illus. 2004. 48p. (J). pap. *(978-0-9725584-1-9(1))* Little Blue Pr.

Cooke, Tim. Butch Cassidy & the Sundance Kid: Notorious Outlaws of the West, 1 vol. 2015. (Wanted! Famous Outlaws Ser.). (ENG., Illus.). 48p. (J). (gr. 6-8). pap. 15.05 *(978-1-4824-4255-7(8),* e3198923-d01b-44f3-b297-abfabac1b545) Stevens, Gareth Publishing LLLP.

—Jesse James: A Notorious Bank Robber of the Wild West, 1 vol. 2015. (Wanted! Famous Outlaws Ser.). (ENG., Illus.). 48p. (J). (gr. 6-8). pap. 15.05 *(978-1-4824-4259-5(0),* 5c82e94b-70dd-4a3b-9df6-f4ad8812d3cb) Stevens, Gareth Publishing LLLP.

Copeland, Peter F., et al. Big Book of the Old West to Color. 2008. (Dover American History Coloring Bks.). (ENG., Illus.). 144p. (gr. 3-8). 9.95 *(978-0-486-46679-8(5),* 466795) Dover Pubns., Inc.

Corrigan, Jim. Civil War in the West. 2004. (History of the Old West Ser.). (Illus.). 64p. (YA). (gr. 5-18). lib. bdg. 19.95 *(978-1-59084-067-2(4))* Mason Crest.

Craats, Rennay. Ranching. 2003. (Real Life Stories Ser.). (Illus.). 24p. (J). lib. bdg. 24.45 *(978-1-59036-081-1(8))* Weigl Pubs., Inc.

Curtis, Suzanne. John Wesley Powell: American Hero. 2013. (ENG & SPA., Illus.). 78p. (J). pap. 8.95 *(978-0-86541-178-4(6))* Filter Pr., LLC.

Davis, Hasan. The Journey of York: The Unsung Hero of the Lewis & Clark Expedition. Harris, Alleanna, illus. (ENG.). 40p. (J). (gr. 3-4). 2021. pap. 7.95 *(978-1-5435-1286-1(0),* 137749) 2019. lib. bdg. 17.95 *(978-1-5435-1282-3(8),* 137748) Capstone. (Capstone Editions).

Dean, Arlan. The Mormon Pioneer Trail: From Nauvoo, Illinois to the Great Salt Lake, Utah. 2009. (Famous American Trails Ser.). 24p. (gr. 3-3). 42.50 *(978-1-61512-488-6(8),* PowerKids Pr.) Rosen Publishing Group, Inc., The.

—The Oregon Trail: From Independence, Missouri to Oregon City, Oregon. 2009. (Famous American Trails Ser.). 24p. (gr. 3-3). 42.50 *(978-1-61512-490-9(X),* PowerKids Pr.) Rosen Publishing Group, Inc., The.

—The Overland Trail: From Atchison, Kansas to Ft. Bridger, Wyoming. 2009. (Famous American Trails Ser.). 24p. (gr. 3-3). 42.50 *(978-1-61512-491-6(8),* PowerKids Pr.) Rosen Publishing Group, Inc., The.

Ditchfield, Christin. The Lewis & Clark Expedition. 2006. (True Bks.). (ENG., Illus.). 48p. (J). (gr. 3-7). pap. 6.95 *(978-0-516-25222-3(4),* Children's Pr.) Scholastic Library Publishing.

Domnauer, Teresa. The Lewis & Clark Expedition (Cornerstones of Freedom: Third Series) 2012. (Cornerstones of Freedom. Third Ser.). (ENG., Illus.). 64p. (J). (gr. 4-6). pap. 8.95 *(978-0-531-28159-8(0),* Children's Pr.) Scholastic Library Publishing.

—Life in the West (a True Book: Westward Expansion) 2010. (True Book (Relaunch) Ser.). (ENG., Illus.). 48p. (J). (gr. 3-5). pap. 6.95 *(978-0-531-21246-2(7),* Children's Pr.) Scholastic Library Publishing.

—True Books: Life in the West. 2010. (True Book Ser.). (ENG.). 48p. (J). (gr. 2-5). 29.00 *(978-0-531-20583-9(5))* Scholastic Library Publishing.

—True Books: Westward Expansion. 2010. (True Book Ser.). (ENG., Illus.). 48p. (J). (gr. 2-5). 29.00 *(978-0-531-20586-0(X))* Scholastic Library Publishing.

Doudna, Kelly. Cowboys! Rough & Rowdy Riders. 2017. (History's Hotshots Ser.). (ENG., Illus.). 32p. (J). (gr. 3-6). lib. bdg. 32.79 *(978-1-5321-1271-3(8),* 27595, Checkerboard Library) ABDO Publishing Co.

Edwards, Judith. The Journey of Lewis & Clark in United States History, 1 vol. 2014. (In United States History Ser.). (ENG., Illus.). 96p. (gr. 5-6). 31.61 *(978-0-7660-6058-6(6),* 892fda6b-0126-4fa2-ae2f-26993dcaf615) Enslow Publishing, LLC.

Ellis, Edward S. The Life of Kit Carson: Hunter, Trapper, Guide, Indian Agent & Colonel U. S. A. 2007. 176p. per. *(978-1-4065-2477-2(8))* Dodo Pr.

Engle, Stephen Douglas. The Civil War: The Siege of Vicksburg & Other Western Battles, 1861-July 1863, 1 vol. O'Neill, Robert, ed. 2010. (Civil War: Essential Histories Ser.). (ENG.). 96p. (YA). (gr. 10-10). lib. bdg. 38.47 *(978-1-4488-0390-3(X),* d25be999-12c6-4c0b-a8e7-928196cdb50d) Rosen Publishing Group, Inc., The.

Engsberg Cunningham, Meghan. Jesse James: Outlaw, 1 vol. Lapegue, Matias, illus. 2016. (American Legends & Folktales Ser.). (ENG.). 32p. (gr. 3-3). 30.21 *(978-1-5026-2197-9(5),* e7040c0a-5b11-44f5-88ee-79d91f517313) Cavendish Square Publishing LLC.

Evan-Moor Educational Publishers. Moving West Grade 4-6+ 2003. (History Pockets Ser.). (ENG., Illus.). 96p. (J). (gr. 4-6). pap., tchr. ed., suppl. ed. 17.99 *(978-1-55799-902-3(3),* EMC 3704) Evan-Moor Educational Pubs.

Expansionism. 2010. (Extraordinary Jobs Ser.). (ENG., Illus.). 128p. (gr. 6-12). 45.00 *(978-1-60413-221-2(3),* P179248, Facts On File) Infobase Holdings, Inc.

Faber, Harold. John Charles Frémont: Pathfinder to the West, 1 vol. 2003. (Great Explorations Ser.). (ENG., Illus.). 80p. (gr. 6-6). 36.93 *(978-0-7614-1481-0(9),* 3e4bbf2f-84e0-4ea8-a1d0-512b8d5cf8c6) Cavendish Square Publishing LLC.

Favor, Lesli J. A Historical Atlas of America's Manifest Destiny. (United States: Historical Atlases of the Growth of a New Nation Ser.). 64p. (gr. 5-5). 2009. 61.20 *(978-1-60854-250-5(5))* 2004. (ENG., Illus.). (J). lib. bdg. 37.13 *(978-1-4042-0201-6(3),* 7e0d0682-29df-4e8b-ad8c-c06cddc7ee7f) Rosen Publishing Group, Inc., The.

Foran, Jill. Homesteading. 2003. (Real Life Stories Ser.). (Illus.). 24p. (J). lib. bdg. 24.45 *(978-1-59036-079-8(6))* Weigl Pubs., Inc.

Fox, Suzanne G. Meriwether Lewis & William Clark: The Corp of Discovery & the Exploration of the American Frontier. 2009. (Library of American Lives & Times Ser.). 112p. (gr. 5-5). 69.20 *(978-1-60853-493-7(6))* Rosen Publishing Group, Inc., The.

Frazier, Neta. Path to the Pacific: The Story of Sacagawea. 2017. (Great Leaders & Events Ser.). (ENG.). (J). (gr. 4-8). lib. bdg. 35.99 *(978-1-942875-44-4(4))* Quarto Publishing Group USA.

Fredericks, Anthony D. P Is for Prairie Dog: A Prairie Alphabet. Bowles, Doug, illus. 2011. (Science Alphabet Ser.). (ENG.). 32p. (J). (gr. 1-4). 16.95 *(978-1-58536-508-1(4),* 202201) Sleeping Bear Pr.

Frisch, Aaron. Jesse James. 2005. (Legends of the West (Creative Education) Ser.). (Illus.). 48p. (J). (gr. 5-9). lib. bdg. 21.95 *(978-1-58341-338-8(3),* Creative Education) Creative Co., The.

Ganeri, Anita. On Expedition with Lewis & Clark. 2010. (ENG.). 32p. (J). (gr. 3-5). *(978-0-7787-9896-5(8));* (Crabtree Connections Ser.: No. 2). pap. *(978-0-7787-9917-7(4))* Crabtree Publishing Co.

George, Enzo. The Expanding Frontier. 2015. (J). lib. bdg. *(978-1-62713-489-7(1))* 2014. (ENG.). 48p. (gr. 4-4). lib. bdg. 33.07 *(978-1-5026-0248-0(2),* fba6921a-3a7b-4c53-9a95-475306e8cf70) Cavendish Square Publishing LLC.

George, Lynn. What Do You Know about Westward Expansion? 2009. (20 Questions: History Ser.). 24p. (gr. 2-3). 42.50 *(978-1-60854-960-3(7),* PowerKids Pr.) Rosen Publishing Group, Inc., The.

George-Warren, Holly. The Cowgirl Way: Hats off to America's Women of the West. 2015. (ENG., Illus.). 128p. (J). (gr. 5-7). pap. 9.99 *(978-0-544-45595-5(9),* 1599320, Clarion Bks.) HarperCollins Pubs.

Gibby, Shauna. Exploring the Pioneer Trail: A Flashlight Discovery Book. Nelson, Casey, illus. 2019. (J). 16.99 *(978-1-62972-575-8(7))* Deseret Bk. Co.

Gingrich, Callista. From Sea to Shining Sea. Arciero, Susan, illus. 2014. (Ellis the Elephant Ser.: 4). (ENG.). 40p. (J). (gr. -1-3). 14.99 *(978-1-62157-253-4(6),* Regnery Kids) Regnery Publishing.

Graubart, Norman D. Bison in American History, 1 vol. 2014. (How Animals Shaped History Ser.). (ENG., Illus.). 24p. (J). (gr. 2-3). 25.27 *(978-1-4777-6757-3(6),* a8ce9800-c84b-4499-9f79-17483d981494, PowerKids Pr.) Rosen Publishing Group, Inc., The.

Green, John. Horses of the Old West. 2007. (Dover Animal Coloring Bks.). (ENG., Illus.). 32p. (gr. 3-8). 3.99 *(978-0-486-45675-1(7),* 456757) Dover Pubns., Inc.

Harris, Irene. The Homestead ACT & Westward Expansion: Settling the Western Frontier, 1 vol. 2016. (Spotlight on American History Ser.). (ENG., Illus.). 24p. (gr. 4-6). 27.93 *(978-1-5081-4943-9(7),* 571ee341-dae6-43a8-8ad2-8a526a36b53f, PowerKids Pr.) Rosen Publishing Group, Inc., The.

Harrison, Peter. The Amazing History of the Wild West: Find Out about the Brave Pioneers Who Tamed the American Frontier, Shown in 300 Exciting Pictures. 2016. (ENG., Illus.). 64p. (J). (gr. -1-12). 12.99 *(978-1-86147-766-8(X),* Armadillo) Anness Publishing GBR. Dist: National Bk. Network.

Harrison, Peter & Hunt, Norman Bancroft. The Amazing World of the Wild West: Discover the Trailblazing History of Cowboys, Outlaws & Native Americans. 2010. (Illus.). 64p. (J). (gr. 4-7). pap. 12.99 *(978-1-84476-609-3(8),* Hermes House) Anness Publishing GBR. Dist: National Bk. Network.

Harvey, Dan. Rocky Mountain: Colorado, Utah, Wyoming, Vol. 19. 2015. (Let's Explore the States Ser.). (Illus.). 64p. (J). (gr. 5). 23.95 *(978-1-4222-3332-0(4))* Mason Crest.

Hatt, Christine. The American West. 2004. (Questioning History Ser.). (J). lib. bdg. 28.50 *(978-1-58340-443-0(0))* Black Rabbit Bks.

Hill, William E. The California Trail: Yesterday & Today. 2017. (Illus.). xviii, 343p. *(978-0-87004-604-9(7))* Caxton Pr.

Hinman, Bonnie. Famous Lawmen, 1 vol. 2016. (Wild West Ser.). (ENG., Illus.). 48p. (J). (gr. 4-8). lib. bdg. 35.64 *(978-1-68078-255-4(X),* 22111) ABDO Publishing Co.

Hooker, Forrestine Cooper. Child of the Fighting Tenth: On the Frontier with the Buffalo Soldiers. Wilson, Steve, ed. 2011. (ENG., Illus.). 296p. pap. 21.95 *(978-0-8061-4080-3(1),* P643251) Univ. of Oklahoma Pr.

James, Will. The Will James Cowboy Book, Vol. 1. rev. ed. (Illus.). 128p. (J). (gr. 4). *(978-0-87842-469-6(5),* 816) Mountain Pr. Publishing Co., Inc.

Jeffrey, Gary. The Oregon Trail, 1 vol. Poluzzi, Allesandro, illus. 2012. (Graphic History of the American West Ser.). (ENG.). 24p. (J). (gr. 3-3). pap. 9.15 *(978-1-4339-6745-0(6),* 6cef5d54-63c3-4008-83af-ed9d14b18589, Gareth Stevens Learning Library); lib. bdg. 26.60 *(978-1-4339-6743-6(X),* 0ad4de6b-3511-4850-a21f-171ad1720118) Stevens, Gareth Publishing LLLP.

—The Pony Express, 1 vol. Riley, Terry, illus. 2012. (Graphic History of the American West Ser.). (ENG.). 24p. (J). (gr. 3-3). pap. 9.15 *(978-1-4339-6749-8(9),* 48a12229-d95d-4464-944d-8821c5729f53, Gareth Stevens Learning Library); lib. bdg. 26.60 *(978-1-4339-6747-4(2),* fbe13987-bdb7-456a-ab4a-454d8ec20547) Stevens, Gareth Publishing LLLP.

Kalman, Bobbie. A Visual Dictionary of the Old West. 2007. (Visual Dictionaries Ser.). (ENG., Illus.). 32p. (J). (gr. 3-7). pap. *(978-0-7787-3523-6(0));* lib. bdg. *(978-0-7787-3503-8(6))* Crabtree Publishing Co.

Keller, Susanna. The True Story of Lewis & Clark, 1 vol. 2013. (What Really Happened? Ser.). (ENG., Illus.). 24p. (J). (gr. 2-3). pap. 9.25 *(978-1-4488-9846-6(3),* e0a93e44-5e16-4d0a-8805-6b38d2ae6877); lib. bdg. 26.27 *(978-1-4488-9694-3(0),* 45b0e550-b940-425e-969e-33f6fe3bf16f) Rosen Publishing Group, Inc., The. (PowerKids Pr.).

Kimmel, Elizabeth Cody. As Far as the Eye Can Reach: Lewis & Clark's Westward Quest. 2005. (Illus.). 119p. (YA). (gr. 4-8). reprint ed. 5.00 *(978-0-7567-9660-0(1))* DIANE Publishing Co.

King, David C. Westward Expansion. 2012. (American Heritage, American Voices Ser.). (ENG.). 146p. (J). (gr. 5-9). pap. 22.95 *(978-1-118-43608-0(3),* Wiley) Wiley, John & Sons, Inc.

Klar, Jeremy. The Louisiana Purchase & Westward Expansion, 1 vol., 1. 2015. (Early American History Ser.). (ENG., Illus.). 80p. (J). (gr. 8-8). lib. bdg. 35.47 *(978-1-68048-271-3(8),* 8edb574c-c4f3-43ba-b586-ea3500ead70c, Britannica Educational Publishing) Rosen Publishing Group, Inc., The.

Klepeis, Alicia Z. Lewis & Clark & Exploring the Louisiana Purchase, 1 vol. 2017. (Primary Sources of Westward Expansion Ser.). (ENG., Illus.). 64p. (gr. 6-6). 35.93 *(978-1-5026-2639-4(X),* 4c1afc12-b4ad-4ebd-a36d-64694b2924f9) Cavendish Square Publishing LLC.

Künstler, Mort, illus. The Wild West: 1804-1890. 2016. (ENG.). 48p. (J). (gr. 2-6). 13.95 *(978-0-7892-1260-3(9),* 791260, Abbeville Kids) Abbeville Pr., Inc.

LaClair, Teresa. Americans Move West (1846-1860) 2013. (Illus.). 48p. (J). pap. *(978-1-4222-2417-5(1))* Mason Crest.

—Americans Move West (1846-1860) Rakove, Jack N., ed. 2012. (How America Became America Ser.). (Illus.). 48p. (J). (gr. 3-4). 19.95 *(978-1-4222-2403-8(1))* Mason Crest.

—Americans Move West, 1846-1860. 2019. *(978-1-5105-3600-5(0))* SmartBook Media, Inc.

Langley, Andrew. 100 Things You Should Know about the Wild West. 2004. (Mosaic of Magical Information Ser.). (Illus.). 48p. (YA). (gr. 3-18). lib. bdg. 19.95 *(978-1-59084-458-8(0))* Mason Crest.

Langley, Andrew & Kelly, Miles. The Wild West. Kelly, Richard, ed. 2017. (Illus.). 48p. (J). pap. 9.95 *(978-1-84810-240-8(2))* Miles Kelly Publishing, Ltd. GBR. Dist: Parkwest Pubns., Inc.

Lassieur, Allison. Westward Expansion: An Interactive History Adventure. rev. ed. 2016. (You Choose: History Ser.). (ENG., Illus.). 112p. (J). (gr. 3-7). pap. 6.95 *(978-1-5157-4259-3(8),* 134014, Capstone Pr.) Capstone.

Lawrence, Blythe. The Lewis & Clark Expedition. 2018. (Expansion of Our Nation Ser.). (ENG., Illus.). 32p. (J). (gr. 3-5). pap. 9.95 *(978-1-63517-983-5(1),* 1635179831); lib. bdg. 31.35 *(978-1-63517-882-1(7),* 1635178827) North Star Editions. (Focus Readers).

—The Lewis & Clark Expedition. 2018. (Illus.). 32p. (J). *(978-1-4896-9870-4(1),* AV2 by Weigl) Weigl Pubs., Inc.

Levy, Janey. Life on a Wagon Train. 2003. (Rosen Real Readers Big Bookstm Ser.). (ENG.). 16p. (gr. 2-3). 37.95 *(978-1-4042-6224-9(5))* Rosen Publishing Group, Inc., The.

ghtfoot, D. J. Trail Fever: The Life of a Texas Cowboy. Bobbish, John, illus. exp. ed. 2003. 88p. (J). (gr. 3-18). pap. 12.95 *(978-0-9728768-0-3(4))* Seven Rivers Publishing.
nette, Rachel. Meriwether Lewis & William Clark, 1 vol. 2013. (Pioneer Spirit: the Westward Expansion Ser.). 24p. (J). (ENG.). (gr. 2-3). 26.27 *(978-1-4777-0783-8(2),* c3379d73-e58a-46ba-a505-004b5518497d); (gr. 3-6). pap. 49.50 *(978-1-4777-0900-9(2));* (ENG., Illus.). (gr. 2-3). pap. 9.25 *(978-1-4777-0899-6(5),* a7e102b5-f175-4b5e-9fee-d0fde36daf27) Rosen Publishing Group, Inc., The. (PowerKids Pr.).
arsh, Carole. Lewis & Clark Go on a Hike. 2003. 32p. (J). (gr. 3-8). pap. 5.95 *(978-0-635-02122-9(6))* Gallopade International.
attern, Joanne. The Gateway Arch: Celebrating Western Expansion. 2017. (Core Content Social Studies — Let's Celebrate America Ser.). (ENG., Illus.). 32p. (J). (gr. 2-5). pap. 8.99 *(978-1-63440-238-5(3),* a460910d-62ac-482a-b5c1-70a8fc8929b4); lib. bdg. 26.65 *(978-1-63440-228-6(6),* 87a0f930-7e15-4ac0-9985-faabb8adeab8) Red Chair Pr.
Maynard, Charles W. Fort Laramie. 2009. (Famous Forts Throughout American History Ser.). 24p. (gr. 3-4). 42.50 *(978-1-61512-516-6(7),* PowerKids Pr.) Rosen Publishing Group, Inc., The.
—Jedediah Smith: Mountain Man of the American West. 2009. (Famous Explorers of the American West Ser.). 24p. (gr. 3-4). 42.50 *(978-1-61512-501-2(9),* PowerKids Pr.) Rosen Publishing Group, Inc., The.
—Jim Bridger: Frontiersman & Mountain Guide. 2009. (Famous Explorers of the American West Ser.). 24p. (gr. 3-4). 42.50 *(978-1-61512-502-9(7),* PowerKids Pr.) Rosen Publishing Group, Inc., The.
—Zebulon Pike: Soldier-Explorer of the American Southwest. 2009. (Famous Explorers of the American West Ser.). 24p. (gr. 3-4). 42.50 *(978-1-61512-506-7(X),* PowerKids Pr.) Rosen Publishing Group, Inc., The.
McIntosh, Kenneth. Saloons, Shootouts, & Spurs: The Wild West in The 1800's. 2009. (Daily Life in America in the 1800s Ser.). 64p. (YA). (gr. 7-18). pap. 9.95 *(978-1-4222-1862-4(7));* lib. bdg. 22.95 *(978-1-4222-1789-4(2))* Mason Crest.
McNeese, Tim. The Oregon Trail. 2009. (ENG., Illus.). 152p. (gr. 6-12). 35.00 *(978-1-60413-027-0(X),* P161434, Facts On File) Infobase Holdings, Inc.
Micklos, John, Jr. Bold Riders: The Story of the Pony Express. 2015. (Adventures on the American Frontier Ser.). (ENG., Illus.). 32p. (J). (gr. 3-6). pap. 7.95 *(978-1-4914-4910-3(1),* 128745, Capstone Pr.) Capstone.
Miller, Brandon Marie. Women of the Frontier: 16 Tales of Trailblazing Homesteaders, Entrepreneurs, & Rabble-Rousers. 2013. (Women of Action Ser.: 3). (ENG., Illus.). 256p. (J). (gr. 7). 19.95 *(978-1-883052-97-3(1))* Chicago Review Pr., Inc.
Monceaux, Morgan & Katcher, Ruth. My Heroes, My People: African Americans & Native Americans in Thewest. Monceaux, Morgan, illus. 2004. (Illus.). 63p. (J). (gr. k-4). reprint ed. 18.00 *(978-0-7567-7868-2(9))* DIANE Publishing Co.
Morley, Jacqueline. The Story of Lewis & Clark. David Antram, illus. 2017. (Explorers Ser.). 32p. (gr. 3-6). 31.35 *(978-1-910706-89-3(2))* Book Hse. GBR. Dist: Black Rabbit Bks.
—You Wouldn't Want to... Be an American Pioneer! Antram, David, illus. rev. ed. 2012. (ENG.). 32p. (J). lib. bdg. 29.00 *(978-0-531-27500-9(0))* Scholastic Library Publishing.
—You Wouldn't Want to Explore with Lewis & Clark! An Epic Journey You'd Rather Not Make. Bergin, Mark, illus. 2013. (You Wouldn't Want to... Ser.). (ENG.). 32p. (J). 29.00 *(978-0-531-25942-9(0),* Watts, Franklin) Scholastic Library Publishing.
—You Wouldn't Want to Explore with Lewis & Clark! An Epic Journey You'd Rather Not Make. 2013. (You Wouldn't Want To Ser.). lib. bdg. 20.80 *(978-0-606-31633-0(7))* Turtleback.
Morlock, Rachael. Lewis & Clark Explore the Louisiana Territory, 1 vol. 2018. (Real-Life Scientific Adventures Ser.). (ENG.). 32p. (gr. 4-5). 29.27 *(978-1-5081-6850-8(4),* 7235896b-7bfb-4480-91b5-538c4973a4fc, PowerKids Pr.) Rosen Publishing Group, Inc., The.
Morretta, Alison. Homesteading & Settling the Frontier, 1 vol. 2017. (Primary Sources of Westward Expansion Ser.). (ENG., Illus.). 64p. (gr. 6-6). 35.93 *(978-1-5026-2641-7(1),* 22112011-f2e5-4bce-b0ee-f7e1b45b5bc3) Cavendish Square Publishing LLC.
Mulhall, Jill K. Expanding the Nation, 1 vol. rev. ed. 2005. (Social Studies: Informational Text Ser.). (ENG.). 24p. (gr. 4-8). pap. 10.99 *(978-0-7439-8905-3(8))* Teacher Created Materials, Inc.
National Geographic Learning. Reading Expeditions (Social Studies: Travels Across America's Past): the West: Its History & People. 2007. (Nonfiction Reading & Writing Workshops Ser.). (ENG., Illus.). 32p. (J). pap. 18.95 *(978-0-7922-8617-2(0))* CENGAGE Learning.
—Reading Expeditions (Social Studies: Voices from America's Past): Cowboys & Cattle Drives. 2007. (ENG., Illus.). 40p. (J). pap. 21.95 *(978-0-7922-4550-6(4))* CENGAGE Learning.
The New South & the Old West: 1866-1890. 2010. (ENG., Illus.). 136p. (gr. 5-8). 35.00 *(978-1-60413-354-7(6),* P178885, Facts On File) Infobase Holdings, Inc.
Nolan, Frederick. Trailblazing the Way West. 2015. (Wild West Ser.). (Illus.). 64p. (J). (gr. 9-12). 39.95 *(978-1-78404-081-9(9))* Arcturus Publishing GBR. Dist: Black Rabbit Bks.
Nolan, Frederick W. Gunslingers & Cowboys. 2015. (Wild West Ser.). (Illus.). 64p. (J). (gr. 9-12). 39.95 *(978-1-78404-078-9(9))* Arcturus Publishing GBR. Dist: Black Rabbit Bks.
—Outlaws & Rebels. 2015. (Wild West Ser.). (Illus.). 64p. (J). (gr. 9-12). 39.95 *(978-1-78404-080-2(0))* Arcturus Publishing GBR. Dist: Black Rabbit Bks.
O'Brien, Cynthia. Go West with Miners, Prospectors, & Loggers. 2016. (ENG.). 32p. (J). *(978-0-7787-2328-8(3))* Crabtree Publishing Co.
O'Hara, Megan. Plains Communities Past & Present, 1 vol. 2014. (Who Lived Here? Ser.). (ENG., Illus.). 24p. (J). (gr. 1-3). lib. bdg. 27.99 *(978-1-4765-4061-0(6),* 124137) Capstone.
Olson, Steven. The Oregon Trail: A Primary Source History of the Route to the American West. 2009. (Primary Sources in American History Ser.). 64p. (gr. 5-8). 58.50 *(978-1-60851-501-1(X))* Rosen Publishing Group, Inc., The.
Olson, Tod. How to Get Rich on a Texas Cattle Drive: In Which I Tell the Honest Truth about Rampaging Rustlers, Stampeding Steers & Other Fateful Hazards on the Wild Chisolm Trail. 2010. (How to Get Rich Ser.). (Illus.). 48p. (J). (gr. 3-7). 18.95 *(978-1-4263-0524-5(9),* National Geographic Kids) Disney Publishing Worldwide.
O'Neill, Robert John & Glatthaar, Joseph T. The Civil War: Sherman's Capture of Atlanta & Other Western Battles, 1863-1865, 1 vol. 2010. (Civil War: Essential Histories Ser.). (ENG.). 96p. (YA). (gr. 10-10). lib. bdg. 38.47 *(978-1-4488-0389-7(6),* e8238cfa-f9a6-4398-b6df-9d64c756955d) Rosen Publishing Group, Inc., The.
Orr, Tamra. The Lewis & Clark Expedition: A Primary Source History of the Journey of the Corps of Discovery. 2009. (Primary Sources in American History Ser.). 64p. (gr. 5-8). 58.50 *(978-1-60851-498-4(6))* Rosen Publishing Group, Inc., The.
Osborne, Mary Pope & Boyce, Natalie Pope. Wild West. 2018. (Magic Tree House Fact Trackers Ser.: 38). lib. bdg. 17.20 *(978-0-606-40924-7(6))* Turtleback.
—Wild West: A Nonfiction Companion to Magic Tree House #10: Ghost Town at Sundown. Mones, Isidre, illus. 2018. (Magic Tree House (R) Fact Tracker Ser.: 38). 128p. (J). (gr. 2-5). 6.99 *(978-1-101-93645-0(2),* Random Hse. Bks. for Young Readers) Random Hse. Children's Bks.
Osmundson, Linda. How the West Was Drawn: Women's Art, 1 vol. 2014. (How the West Was Drawn Ser.). (ENG., Illus.). 32p. (J). (gr. k-7). 16.99 *(978-1-4556-1878-1(0),* Pelican Publishing) Arcadia Publishing.
Otfinoski, Steven. A Primary Source History of Westward Expansion. 2015. (Primary Source History Ser.). (ENG., Illus.). 32p. (J). (gr. 3-6). lib. bdg. 27.99 *(978-1-4914-1841-3(9),* 127277, Capstone Pr.) Capstone.
Paprocki, Greg, illus. V Is for Vittles: A Wild West Alphabet, 1 vol. 2016. (BabyLit Ser.). (ENG.). 32p. (J). (— 1). bds. 12.99 *(978-1-4236-4251-0(1))* Gibbs Smith, Publisher.
Pascal, Janet B. What Was the Wild West? 2017. (What Was... Ser.). lib. bdg. 16.00 *(978-0-606-39775-9(2))* Turtleback.
Pascal, Janet B. & Who HQ. What Was the Wild West? Marchesi, Stephen, illus. 2017. (What Was? Ser.). (ENG.). 112p. (J). (gr. 3-7). 5.99 *(978-0-399-54424-8(0),* Penguin Workshop) Penguin Young Readers Group.
Patent, Dorothy Hinshaw. The Lewis & Clark Trail: Then & Now. Muñoz, William, photos by. 2006. (Illus.). 60p. (J). (gr. 4-8). reprint ed. 20.00 *(978-1-4223-5732-3(5))* DIANE Publishing Co.
Patrick, Bethanne Kelly. Forts of the West. 2004. (History of the Old West Ser.). (Illus.). 64p. (YA). (gr. 5-18). lib. bdg. 19.95 *(978-1-59084-071-9(2))* Mason Crest.
Penn, Sarah. Nat Love: African American Cowboy, 1 vol. 2003. (Primary Sources of Famous People in American History Ser.). (ENG., Illus.). 32p. (J). (gr. 3-4). pap. 10.00 *(978-0-8239-4188-9(4),* 6be498a9-1f80-45ca-847a-fd10fdb2527e); lib. bdg. 29.13 *(978-0-8239-4116-2(7),* d002c57f-e32f-47ee-a27c-8b7d13c4c2af, Rosen Reference) Rosen Publishing Group, Inc., The.
Perritano, John. True Books: the Lewis & Clark Expedition. 2010. (True Book Ser.). (ENG., Illus.). 48p. (J). (gr. 2-5). 29.00 *(978-0-531-20582-2(7))* Scholastic Library Publishing.
Phillips, Larissa. Wild Bill Hickok: Legend of the American Wild West, 1 vol. 2003. (Famous People in American History / Grandes Personajes en la Historia de Los Estados Unidos Ser.). (ENG & SPA., Illus.). 32p. (gr. 2-3). lib. bdg. 29.13 *(978-0-8239-4170-4(1),* 1320d7dc-508d-4207-bcad-b7e733e160e1, Editorial Buenas Letras) Rosen Publishing Group, Inc., The.
—Wild Bill Hickok: Legend of the American Wild West / Leyenda del oeste Americano. 2009. (Famous People in American History/Grandes personajes en la historia de los Estados Unidos Ser.). (ENG & SPA.). 32p. (gr. 2-3). 47.90 *(978-1-61512-557-9(4),* Editorial Buenas Letras) Rosen Publishing Group, Inc., The.
—Wild Bill Hickok: Legend of the Wild West. 2009. (Primary Sources of Famous People in American History Ser.). 32p. (gr. 2-3). 47.90 *(978-1-60851-740-4(3))* Rosen Publishing Group, Inc., The.
—Wild Bill Hickok: Leyenda del oeste americano (Wild Bill Hickok: Legend of the American Wild West) 2009. (Grandes personajes en la historia de los Estados Unidos (Famous People in American History) Ser.). (SPA.). 32p. (gr. 2-3). 47.90 *(978-1-61512-810-5(7),* Editorial Buenas Letras) Rosen Publishing Group, Inc., The.
Porterfield, Jason. The Homestead Act of 1862, 1 vol. 2004. (Primary Sources in American History Ser.). (ENG., Illus.). 64p. (J). (gr. 5-8). lib. bdg. 37.13 *(978-1-4042-0178-1(5),* dfe77c85-c064-4a78-9d4c-7d8d1afb26e0) Rosen Publishing Group, Inc., The.
—The Homestead Act Of 1862: A Primary Source History of the Settlement of the American Heartland in the Late 19th Century. 2009. (Primary Sources in American History Ser.). 64p. (gr. 5-8). 58.50 *(978-1-60851-496-0(X))* Rosen Publishing Group, Inc., The.
Primary Sources of Westward Expansion, 12 vols. 2017. (Primary Sources of Westward Expansion Ser.). (ENG.). 64p. (gr. 6-6). lib. bdg. 215.58 *(978-1-5026-2646-2(2),* bf5577d4-f518-4906-9728-c9abc40b0b4f, Cavendish Square) Cavendish Square Publishing LLC.
Quasha, Jennifer. Covered Wagons: Hands-on Projects about America's Westward Expansion. 2009. (Great Social Studies Projects Ser.). 24p. (gr. 3-3). 42.50 *(978-1-61513-208-9(2),* PowerKids Pr.) Rosen Publishing Group, Inc., The.
Raabe, Emily. Buffalo Soldiers & the Western Frontier. 2009. (Westward Ho! Ser.). 24p. (gr. 2-3). 42.50 *(978-1-60854-759-3(0),* PowerKids Pr.) Rosen Publishing Group, Inc., The.
—Pioneers: Life as a Homesteader. 2009. (Westward Ho! Ser.). 24p. (gr. 2-3). 42.50 *(978-1-60854-761-6(2),* PowerKids Pr.) Rosen Publishing Group, Inc., The.
—Thomas Jefferson & the Louisiana Purchase. 2009. (Westward Ho! Ser.). 24p. (gr. 2-3). 42.50 *(978-1-60854-763-0(9),* PowerKids Pr.) Rosen Publishing Group, Inc., The.
Rae, Thelma. Pioneer Families. 2009. (Reading Room Collection 1 Ser.). 16p. (gr. 2-3). 37.50 *(978-1-60851-948-4(1),* PowerKids Pr.) Rosen Publishing Group, Inc., The.
Rajczak Nelson, Kristen. Life on a Wagon Train, 1 vol. 2013. (What You Didn't Know about History Ser.). (ENG., Illus.). 24p. (J). (gr. 2-3). pap. 9.15 *(978-1-4339-8445-7(8),* 9b458fc3-3d4c-4a1d-a23f-1647e3661dab); lib. bdg. 25.27 *(978-1-4339-8444-0(X),* cd79e9b1-b73f-4f37-9a43-5ef18bc1fd78) Stevens, Gareth Publishing LLLP.
—20 Fun Facts about Pioneer Women, 1 vol. 2015. (Fun Fact File: Women in History Ser.). (ENG., Illus.). 32p. (J). (gr. 2-3). 27.93 *(978-1-4824-2806-3(7),* a193b127-d4d8-4801-84a3-e4a62a08cf9b) Stevens, Gareth Publishing LLLP.
Randolph, Ryan. A Bank Robber's End: The Death of Jesse James. 2009. (Great Moments in American History Ser.). 32p. (gr. 3-3). 47.90 *(978-1-61513-138-9(8))* Rosen Publishing Group, Inc., The.
Randolph, Ryan P. Black Cowboys. 2009. (Library of the Westward Expansion Ser.). 24p. (gr. 3-4). 42.50 *(978-1-60853-933-8(4),* PowerKids Pr.) Rosen Publishing Group, Inc., The.
—Wild West Lawmen & Outlaws. 2009. (Library of the Westward Expansion Ser.). 24p. (gr. 3-4). 42.50 *(978-1-60853-944-4(X),* PowerKids Pr.) Rosen Publishing Group, Inc., The.
Ratliff, Thomas. You Wouldn't Want to Be a Pony Express Rider! A Dusty, Thankless Job You'd Rather Not Do. Bergin, Mark, illus. 2012. (ENG.). 32p. (J). lib. bdg. 29.00 *(978-0-531-20872-4(9))* Scholastic Library Publishing.
Rau, Dana Meachen. A True Book: the West. 2012. (True Book: U. S. Regions Ser.). (ENG., Illus.). 48p. (J). (gr. 3-5). 21.19 *(978-0-531-24855-3(0),* Children's Pr.) Scholastic Library Publishing.
Rea, Amy C. The Trail of Tears, 1 vol. 2016. (Wild West Ser.). (ENG., Illus.). 48p. (J). (gr. 4-8). lib. bdg. 35.64 *(978-1-68078-260-8(6),* 22121) ABDO Publishing Co.
Rice, Dona Herweck. Bad Guys & Gals of the Wild West, 1 vol. 2nd rev. ed. 2013. (TIME for KIDS(r): Informational Text Ser.). (ENG., Illus.). 64p. (J). (gr. 5-8). pap. 14.99 *(978-1-4333-4903-4(5));* lib. bdg. 31.96 *(978-1-4333-7426-5(9))* Teacher Created Materials, Inc.
Rice, Katelyn. The Great Leap Westward. rev. ed. 2017. (Social Studies: Informational Text Ser.). (ENG., Illus.). 32p. (gr. 4-8). pap. 11.99 *(978-1-4938-3791-5(5))* Teacher Created Materials, Inc.
—Settling & Unsettling the West (America in The 1800s) rev. ed. 2017. (Social Studies: Informational Text Ser.). (ENG., Illus.). 32p. (gr. 4-8). pap. 11.99 *(978-1-4938-3797-7(4))* Teacher Created Materials, Inc.
Riddle, John. The Pony Express. 2004. (History of the Old West Ser.). (Illus.). 64p. (YA). (gr. 5-18). lib. bdg. 19.95 *(978-1-59084-061-0(5))* Mason Crest.
Robinson, Kate. Lewis & Clark: Exploring the American West, 1 vol. 2009. (Great Explorers of the World Ser.). (ENG., Illus.). 112p. (gr. 6-7). 35.93 *(978-1-59845-124-5(3),* 5a91466e-b841-429e-a58d-e2b90c9c3a72) Enslow Publishing, LLC.
Roza, Greg. Westward Expansion, 1 vol. 2011. (Story of America Ser.). (ENG., Illus.). 32p. (J). (gr. 4-5). pap. 11.50 *(978-1-4339-4781-0(1),* a461c41e-ac53-4d94-b48f-966439839c9a); lib. bdg. 29.27 *(978-1-4339-4780-3(3),* 22526696-52e7-4d1f-8437-511ab40fc7a0) Stevens, Gareth Publishing LLLP. (Gareth Stevens Learning Library).
Russo, Kristin J. Viewpoints on the Oregon Trail & Westward Expansion. 2018. (Perspectives Library: Viewpoints & Perspectives Ser.). (ENG., Illus.). 48p. (J). (gr. 5-8). lib. bdg. 39.21 *(978-1-5341-2967-2(7),* 211912) Cherry Lake Publishing.
Sandler, Martin W. Iron Rails, Iron Men, & the Race to Link the Nation: the Story of the Transcontinental Railroad. 2015. (ENG., Illus.). 224p. (J). (gr. 5). 24.99 *(978-0-7636-6527-2(4))* Candlewick Pr.
Sanford, Carl R. & Sanford, William R. Outlaws & Lawmen of the Wild West, 10 bks., Set. (Illus.). (YA). (gr. 4-10). lib. bdg. 169.50 *(978-0-89490-391-5(8))* Enslow Publishing, LLC.
Sanford, William R. & Green, Carl R. Kit Carson: Courageous Mountain Man, 1 vol. 2013. (Courageous Heroes of the American West Ser.). (ENG., Illus.). 48p. (J). (gr. 5-7). pap. 11.53 *(978-1-4644-0094-0(6),* c76bd838-258d-431a-a120-4cfb04bb164f) Enslow Publishing, LLC.
—Zebulon Pike: Courageous Rocky Mountain Explorer, 1 vol. 2013. (Courageous Heroes of the American West Ser.). (ENG., Illus.). 48p. (J). (gr. 5-7). lib. bdg. 25.27 *(978-0-7660-4012-0(7),* 05a2fcff-67b5-48be-a735-82bd326fcd47) Enslow Publishing, LLC.
Savage, Jeff. American Cowboys: True Tales of the Wild West, 1 vol. 2012. (True Tales of the Wild West Ser.). (ENG., Illus.). 48p. (gr. 5-7). pap. 11.53 *(978-1-4644-0027-8(X),* a4e300e6-66b9-40d4-ae60-a1b500d3ed7f) Enslow Publishing, LLC.
—Daring Pony Express Riders: True Tales of the Wild West, 1 vol. 2012. (True Tales of the Wild West Ser.). (ENG., Illus.). 48p. (gr. 5-7). pap. 11.53 *(978-1-4644-0031-5(8),* ca5e0880-db02-4c69-884a-4fd104eb36de); lib. bdg. 25.27 *(978-0-7660-4023-6(2),* e694efd9-a05f-4e1f-bda0-8f114b3b5b2f) Enslow Publishing, LLC.
—Fearless Scouts: True Tales of the Wild West, 1 vol. 2012. (True Tales of the Wild West Ser.). (ENG., Illus.). 48p. (gr. 5-7). pap. 11.53 *(978-1-4644-0032-2(6),* 1e23d9c1-b183-4644-b14d-d34ef5487bc1) Enslow Publishing, LLC.
—Quick-Draw Gunfighters: True Tales of the Wild West, 1 vol. 2012. (True Tales of the Wild West Ser.). (ENG., Illus.). 48p. (gr. 5-7). pap. 11.53 *(978-1-4644-0029-2(6),* aac891de-4be3-4d12-acc9-87ad5075d450); lib. bdg. 25.27 *(978-0-7660-4021-2(6),* c1f8bdce-fe0e-487c-ae9f-9adf9572c8d4) Enslow Publishing, LLC.
Schwartz, Heather E. Outlaws, Gunslingers, & Thieves. 2015. (ShockZone (tm) — Villains Ser.). (ENG., Illus.). 32p. (J). (gr. 5-8). E-Book 46.65 *(978-1-4677-6004-1(8),* 9781467760041, Lerner Digital) Lerner Publishing Group.
Sebree, Chet'la. Historical Sources on Westward Expansion, 1 vol. 2019. (America's Story Ser.). (ENG.). 144p. (gr. 8-8). pap. 22.16 *(978-1-5026-5216-4(1),* 70f5ac93-c3cf-4e5f-8cf3-72a6b322efe2); lib. bdg. 47.36 *(978-1-5026-5217-1(X),* 39dc7542-fb48-46d6-acaf-f591e1e15aa5) Cavendish Square Publishing LLC.
Sechrist, Darren. Taming the West. 2008. (ENG., Illus.). 32p. (J). lib. bdg. *(978-0-7787-4188-6(5))* Crabtree Publishing Co.
—Westward, Ho!, 1 vol. 2008. (ENG., Illus.). 32p. (J). pap. *(978-0-7787-4217-3(2))* Crabtree Publishing Co.
Shea, Therese M. The Louisiana Purchase & the Lewis & Clark Expedition. 2017. (Westward Expansion: America's Push to the Pacific Ser.). (Illus.). 48p. (J). (gr. 10-14). 84.30 *(978-1-5383-0013-8(3));* (ENG., (gr. 6-7). pap. 15.05 *(978-1-68048-790-9(6),* e3a8ec93-25d6-4e7e-82ab-fe30c88fb8d1) Rosen Publishing Group, Inc., The. (Britannica Educational Publishing).
Sheinkin, Steve. Which Way to the Wild West? Everything Your Schoolbooks Didn't Tell You about Westward Expansion. 2015. (J). lib. bdg. 20.85 *(978-0-606-37589-4(9))* Turtleback.
Sioux, Tracee. Immigrants & the Westward Expansion. (Primary Sources of Immigration & Migration in America Ser.). 24p. (gr. 3-4). 2009. 42.50 *(978-1-60851-776-3(4))* 2003. (ENG., Illus.). (J). lib. bdg. 26.27 *(978-0-8239-6824-4(3),* 6225d3c4-75d1-4473-b59b-6a1feb937d7b) Rosen Publishing Group, Inc., The. (PowerKids Pr.).
Smalley, Carol Parenzan. Lewis & Clark. 2008. (What's So Great About... ? Ser.). (Illus.). 32p. (YA). (gr. 2-4). lib. bdg. 25.70 *(978-1-58415-725-0(9))* Mitchell Lane Pubs.
Smith, Jeff. William Clark: Explorer & Diplomat. 2016. (ENG., Illus.). 48p. (J). pap. 27.00 *(978-1-61248-178-4(7))* Truman State Univ. Pr.
Somervill, Barbara A. It's Cool to Learn about the United States: West. 2011. (Explorer Library: Social Studies Explorer Ser.). (ENG., Illus.). 48p. (gr. 4-8). lib. bdg. 34.93 *(978-1-61080-182-9(2),* 201158) Cherry Lake Publishing.
Souza, D. M. John Wesley Powell. 2004. (Watts Library). (ENG., Illus.). 64p. (J). (gr. 5-7). pap. 8.95 *(978-0-531-16653-6(8),* Watts, Franklin) Scholastic Library Publishing.
—Watts Library: John C. Frémont. 2004. (Watts Library). (ENG., Illus.). 80p. (J). (gr. 5-7). pap. 8.95 *(978-0-531-16652-9(X),* Watts, Franklin) Scholastic Library Publishing.
St. George, Judith & Who HQ. What Was the Lewis & Clark Expedition? Foley, Tim, illus. 2014. (What Was? Ser.). 112p. (J). (gr. 3-7). pap. 5.99 *(978-0-448-47901-9(X),* Penguin Workshop) Penguin Young Readers Group.
Staeger, Rob. The Boom Towns. 2004. (History of the Old West Ser.). (Illus.). 64p. (YA). (gr. 5-18). lib. bdg. 19.95 *(978-1-59084-068-9(2))* Mason Crest.
Steele, Christy. Famous Wagon Trails, 1 vol. 2004. (America's Westward Expansion Ser.). (ENG., Illus.). 48p. (gr. 5-8). pap. 15.05 *(978-0-8368-5795-5(X),* 960f15d9-0f17-470d-96a8-1bb79b286c9a); lib. bdg. 33.67 *(978-0-8368-5788-7(7),* cdb80fe3-5c8f-4fd5-b8ec-0282bee0fc85) Stevens, Gareth Publishing LLLP. (Gareth Stevens Secondary Library).
—Pioneer Life in the American West, 1 vol. 2004. (America's Westward Expansion Ser.). (ENG., Illus.). 48p. (gr. 5-8). pap. 15.05 *(978-0-8368-5797-9(6),* 1e313d11-4bc8-4653-8fba-dbedc6dc962e); lib. bdg. 33.67 *(978-0-8368-5790-0(9),* fe0283bd-a406-4492-b189-30c5021396a2) Stevens, Gareth Publishing LLLP. (Gareth Stevens Secondary Library).
Stefoff, Rebecca. Texas & the Far West, 1 vol. 2003. (North American Historical Atlases Ser.). (ENG., Illus.). 48p. (gr. 5-5). 32.64 *(978-0-7614-1345-5(6),* 0ac39afa-f94c-43f2-bb35-12911614d67a) Cavendish Square Publishing LLC.
—The Wild West, 1 vol. 2007. (American Voices From Ser.). (ENG., Illus.). 160p. (gr. 6-6). lib. bdg. 41.21 *(978-0-7614-2170-2(X),* d98d8496-a771-43e2-9b03-98c032965b89) Cavendish Square Publishing LLC.
Stoltman, Joan. 20 Fun Facts about Westward Expansion, 1 vol. 2018. (Fun Fact File: U. S. History! Ser.). (ENG.). 32p. (gr. 2-3). pap. 11.50 *(978-1-5382-1919-5(0),* 5a247029-dcc4-48e0-b42c-9d50f95dca60); lib. bdg. 27.93 *(978-1-5382-1921-8(2),* 6fc1b9f0-d70b-4b5a-91f9-771df24f3eb9) Stevens, Gareth Publishing LLLP.
Strand, Jennifer. Lewis & Clark. 2016. (Pioneering Explorers Ser.). (ENG.). 24p. (J). (gr. -1-2). 49.94 *(978-1-68079-411-3(6),* 23032, Abdo Zoom-Launch) ABDO Publishing Co.
Streissguth, Tom. Perspectives on Westward Expansion. 2018. (Perspectives on US History Ser.). (ENG., Illus.). 32p. (J). (gr. 3-6). 32.80 *(978-1-63235-404-4(7),* 13726, 12-Story Library) Bookstaves, LLC.
Sullivan, Laura. Life As an Explorer with Lewis & Clark, 1 vol. 2015. (Life As... Ser.). (ENG., Illus.). 32p. (gr. 3-3). pap. 11.58 *(978-1-5026-1078-2(7),* a7c1a42e-2fae-40ab-84e6-53fd8a16109c) Cavendish Square Publishing LLC.
Torr, James D., ed. Westward Expansion. 2003. (Interpreting American History Through Primary Documents Ser.x). (Illus.). 208p. (J). 32.45 *(978-0-7377-1134-9(5),* Greenhaven Pr., Inc.) Cengage Gale.
The True History of the Wild West. 2015. (True History of the Wild West Ser.). (ENG.). 32p. (J). (gr. 5-5). pap., pap., pap. 360.00 *(978-1-4994-1325-0(4),* PowerKids Pr.) Rosen Publishing Group, Inc., The.
Uhl, Xina M. The Railroad, the Telegraph, & Other Technologies. 2017. (Westward Expansion: America's Push to the Pacific Ser.). (Illus.). 48p. (J). (gr. 10-14). 84.30

WXYZ

(978-1-5383-0016-9(8), Britannica Educational Publishing) Rosen Publishing Group, Inc., The.
—Settlers, Traders, & Trails. 2017. (Westward Expansion: America's Push to the Pacific Ser.). 48p. (J). (gr. 10-14). 84.30 *(978-1-5383-0017-6(6)*, Britannica Educational Publishing) Rosen Publishing Group, Inc., The.
Uhl, Xina M. & Moriarty, J. T. A Primary Source Investigation of Manifest Destiny, 1 vol. 2018. (Uncovering American History Ser.). (ENG.). 64p. (gr. 6-6). pap. 13.95 *(978-1-5081-8402-7(X)*, 8169a5e4-5279-4dda-94a0-7bc352d2a016, Rosen Reference) Rosen Publishing Group, Inc., The.
Waldman, Stuart. The Last River: John Wesley Powell & the Colorado River Exploring Expedition. Manchess, Gregory, illus. 2015. (ENG.). 48p. (J). (gr. 4-8). pap. 12.95 *(978-1-931414-58-6(0)*, 801deecd-d05d-466d-9a20-9b35acbd1225) Mikaya Pr.
Walsh, Steve. Zebulon Montgomery Pike: Explorer & Military Officer. 2011. (ENG & SPA., Illus.). 54p. (J). pap. 8.95 *(978-0-86541-123-4(9))* Filter Pr., LLC.
West, David. Lots of Things You Want to Know about Cowboys. 2015. (Lots of Things You Want to Know About Ser.). (ENG., Illus.). 24p. (J). 28.50 *(978-1-62588-089-5(8)*, 19300, Smart Apple Media) Black Rabbit Bks.
White, Katherine. The 2000-2002 Forest Fires in the Western United States. (Tragic Fires Throughout History Ser.). 48p. (gr. 5-8). 2009. 53.00 *(978-1-60854-580-3(6))* 2003. (ENG., Illus.). (J). lib. bdg. 34.47 *(978-0-8239-4488-0(3)*, e3127e3f-a037-4890-9295-e1a6c27ebc2f) Rosen Publishing Group, Inc., The. (Rosen Reference).
Wild Bill Hickok. 2010. (ENG., Illus.). 112p. (gr. 6-12). 35.00 *(978-1-60413-593-0(X)*, P179307, Facts On File) Infobase Holdings, Inc.
The Wild West, 7 vols. 2016. (Wild West Ser.). (ENG.). 48p. (J). (gr. 4-8). lib. bdg. 285.12 *(978-1-68078-254-7(1)*, 22109) ABDO Publishing Co.
Williams, Jean K. The Perils of the Santa Fe Trail. 2017. (Landmarks in U. S. History Ser.). (ENG., Illus.). 32p. (J). (gr. 3-6). lib. bdg. 27.99 *(978-1-5157-7117-3(2)*, 135518, Capstone Pr.) Capstone.
Wiseman, Blaine. The West. 2016. (Illus.). 48p. (J). *(978-1-5105-1144-6(X))* SmartBook Media, Inc.
Yasuda, Anita. Explore the Wild West! With 25 Great Projects. Stone, Bryan, illus. 2012. (Explore Your World Ser.). (ENG.). 96p. (J). (gr. k-4). pap. 12.95 *(978-1-936749-71-3(8)*, e991a54b-7869-4fe9-8fdf-88ad79cb1b2a) Nomad Pr.
—Exploring the West. 2017. (Exploring America's Regions Ser.). (ENG., Illus.). 48p. (J). (gr. 4-8). lib. bdg. 35.64 *(978-1-5321-1385-7(4)*, 27683) ABDO Publishing Co.

WEST INDIES

Duhgam, P. Island Hopping with Anancy. 24p. *(978-976-8184-11-5(6))* LMH Publishing, Ltd.
Hernandez, Romel. The Caribbean Islands: Facts & Figures. (Caribbean Today Ser.). 64p. (YA). 2010. (Illus.). (gr. 9-12). 21.95 *(978-1-4222-0622-5(X))* 2006. (gr. 7-18). pap. 9.95 *(978-1-4222-0689-8(0))* Mason Crest.
Kozleski, Lisa. The Leeward Islands. 2010. (Caribbean Today Ser.). (Illus.). 64p. (YA). (gr. 7-18). 21.95 *(978-1-4222-0627-0(0))* Mason Crest.
Kras, Sara Louise. Antigua & Barbuda, 1 vol. 2nd ed. 2008. (Cultures of the World (First Edition)(r) Ser.). (ENG., Illus.). 144p. (J). (gr. 5-5). lib. bdg. 49.79 *(978-0-7614-2570-0(5)*, 33f66be0-aa05-4ab6-a89c-2e569dbd3751) Cavendish Square Publishing LLC.
Orr, Tamra. The Windward Islands. (Caribbean Today Ser.). 64p. (YA). 2010. (Illus.). (gr. 9-12). 21.95 *(978-1-4222-0630-0(0))* 2006. (gr. 7-18). pap. 9.95 *(978-1-4222-0697-3(1))* Mason Crest.
Spenceley, Angela. Virgin Islands Coloring Book. 2006. (Illus.). 24p. (J). 2.00 net. *(978-0-9778913-9-9(9))* Coconut Pr., LLC.

WEST INDIES—FICTION

Francis, Claudia Elizabeth Ruth. Island Issues. 2003. 196p. per. 15.00 net. *(978-1-931934-18-3(5))* Back Yard Pub.
Hann, Harry Henry & Johnson, Nancy. Down in the Tropics. Langille, Elaine, illus. 2013. 48p. pap. 14.99 *(978-0-9891323-0-5(7))* Goin' Native, Inc.
Rolt-Wheeler, Francis. Plotting in Pirate Seas. 2017. (ENG., Illus.). (J). 23.95 *(978-1-374-91224-3(7))* Capital Communications, Inc.
—Plotting in Pirate Seas. 2018. (ENG., Illus.). 142p. (J). 14.99 *(978-1-5154-2242-6(9))* Wilder Pubns., Corp.
Sari. Jeanne-Marie Goes to Market: A Story of the West Indies. 2011. 26p. 35.95 *(978-1-258-10346-0(X))* Literary Licensing, LLC.
Spencer, Hannah. With All Best Wishes, Mrs Butterbean. 2008. 28p. pap. 13.50 *(978-1-60693-138-7(5)*, Eloquent Bks.) Strategic Book Publishing & Rights Agency (SBPRA).

WEST INDIES—HISTORY

Kozleski, Lisa. Leeward Islands, Vol. 11. Henderson, James D., ed. 2015. (Discovering the Caribbean: History, Politics, & Culture Ser.). (Illus.). 64p. (J). (gr. 7). lib. bdg. 22.95 *(978-1-4222-3314-6(6))* Mason Crest.
Longman Publishing Staff & Norman, Alma. The People Who Came, Bk. 1. 2nd ed. Date not set. (ENG., Illus.). 96p. pap. 9.95 *(978-0-582-76648-8(6))* Addison-Wesley Longman, Ltd. GBR. Dist: Trans-Atlantic Pubns., Inc.
Orr, Tamra. Windward Islands, Vol. 11. Henderson, James D., ed. 2015. (Discovering the Caribbean: History, Politics, & Culture Ser.). (Illus.). 64p. (J). (gr. 7). lib. bdg. 22.95 *(978-1-4222-3318-4(9))* Mason Crest.

WEST POINT (MILITARY ACADEMY)

see United States Military Academy

WEST VIRGINIA

Brown, Jonatha A. West Virginia, 1 vol. 2006. (Portraits of the States Ser.). (ENG.). 32p. (gr. 3-5). pap. 11.50 *(978-0-8368-4728-4(8)*, 78121169-cb36-4612-8c1e-4c267d7a10d2); (Illus.). lib. bdg. 28.67 *(978-0-8368-4711-6(3)*, 09b285d0-193f-4583-92d4-412008e4885a) Stevens, Gareth Publishing LLLP. (Gareth Stevens Learning Library).
Cribben, Patrick & Heinemann Library Staff. Uniquely West Virginia, 1 vol. 2004. (State Studies). (ENG., Illus.). 48p. pap. 8.99 *(978-1-4034-4734-0(9)*, Heinemann) Capstone.
Di Piazza, Domenica. West Virginia. 2012. (J). lib. bdg. 25.26 *(978-0-7613-4517-6(5)*, Lerner Pubns.) Lerner Publishing Group.
Fein, E. How to Draw West Virginia's Sights & Symbols. 2009. (Kid's Guide to Drawing America Ser.). 32p. (gr. k-k). 50.50 *(978-1-61511-104-6(2)*, PowerKids Pr.) Rosen Publishing Group, Inc., The.
Fontes, Justine & Fontes, Ron. West Virginia, 1 vol. 2003. (World Almanac(r) Library of the States Ser.). (ENG., Illus.). 48p. (gr. 4-6). pap. 15.05 *(978-0-8368-5334-6(2)*, c04acb29-a7d6-46a0-ad6a-285a5f9137ba); lib. bdg. 33.67 *(978-0-8368-5163-2(3)*, 72842fee-6c9c-4867-88b7-d8424cc51d22) Stevens, Gareth Publishing LLLP. (Gareth Stevens Learning Library).
Heinrichs, Ann. West Virginia. Kania, Matt, illus. 2017. (U. S. A. Travel Guides). (ENG.). 40p. (J). (gr. 2-5). lib. bdg. 38.50 *(978-1-5038-1988-7(4)*, 211626) Child's World, Inc, The.
Hoffman, Nancy & Hart, Joyce. West Virginia, 1 vol. 2nd rev. ed. 2008. (Celebrate the States (Second Edition) Ser.). (ENG.). 144p. (gr. 6-6). lib. bdg. 39.79 *(978-0-7614-2562-5(4)*, efe44c3f-7b8a-43b3-b895-df0252139f7c) Cavendish Square Publishing LLC.
Koontz, Robin Michal. West Virginia: The Mountain State, 1 vol. 2010. (Our Amazing States Ser.). (ENG., Illus.). 24p. (J). (gr. 3-3). pap. 9.25 *(978-1-4488-0736-9(0)*, c33920a1-aec9-4cba-9144-06bda272a686); lib. bdg. 26.27 *(978-1-4488-0652-2(6)*, f7f56cab-d4dd-4981-aedc-c1c825c1633e) Rosen Publishing Group, Inc., The. (PowerKids Pr.).
Labella, Susan. West Virginia. 2006. (Rookie Read-About Geography Ser.). (ENG., Illus.). 32p. (J). (gr. 1-2). lib. bdg. 20.50 *(978-0-516-24994-0(0)*, Children's Pr.) Scholastic Library Publishing.
Marsh, Carole. West Virginia Current Events Projects: 30 Cool, Activities, Crafts, Experiments & More for Kids to Do to Learn about Your State! 2003. (West Virginia Experience Ser.). 32p. (gr. k-8). pap. 5.95 *(978-0-635-02067-3(X)*, Marsh, Carole Bks.) Gallopade International.
—West Virginia Government Projects: 30 Cool, Activities, Crafts, Experiments & More for Kids to Do to Learn about Your State! 2003. (West Virginia Experience Ser.). 32p. (gr. k-5). pap. 5.95 *(978-0-635-01967-7(1)*, Marsh, Carole Bks.) Gallopade International.
—West Virginia People Projects: 30 Cool, Activities, Crafts, Experiments & More for Kids to Do to Learn about Your State! 2003. (West Virginia Experience Ser.). 32p. (gr. k-5). pap. 5.95 *(978-0-635-02017-8(3)*, Marsh, Carole Bks.) Gallopade International.
—West Virginia Symbols & Facts Projects: 30 Cool, Activities, Crafts, Experiments & More for Kids to Do to Learn about Your State! 2003. (West Virginia Experience Ser.). 32p. (gr. k-5). pap. 5.95 *(978-0-635-01917-2(5)*, Marsh, Carole Bks.) Gallopade International.
Murray, Julie. West Virginia, 1 vol. 2006. (Buddy Book Ser.). (ENG., Illus.). 32p. (gr. 2-4). 27.07 *(978-1-59197-707-0(X)*, Buddy Bks.) ABDO Publishing Co.
Parker, Bridget. West Virginia. 2016. (States Ser.). (ENG., Illus.). 32p. (J). (gr. 3-6). lib. bdg. 27.99 *(978-1-5157-0437-9(8)*, 132048, Capstone Pr.) Capstone.
Petreycik, Rick. West Virginia, 1 vol. Santoro, Christopher, illus. 2007. (It's My State! (First Edition)(r) Ser.). (ENG.). 80p. (gr. 4-4). lib. bdg. 34.07 *(978-0-7614-2216-7(1)*, 84f0e253-1165-49fe-bffc-b880d4c8e823) Cavendish Square Publishing LLC.
Riehle, Mary Ann McCabe. M Is for Mountain State: A West Virginia Alphabet. Bryant, Laura J., illus. 2004. (Discover America State by State Ser.). (ENG.). 40p. (J). (gr. 1-3). 18.99 *(978-1-58536-151-9(8)*, 202011) Sleeping Bear Pr.
Schwabacher, Martin. West Virginia (a True Book: My United States) (Library Edition) 2018. (True Book (Relaunch) Ser.). (ENG., Illus.). 48p. (J). (gr. 3-5). 31.00 *(978-0-531-23585-0(8)*, Children's Pr.) Scholastic Library Publishing.
Somervill, Barbara A. From Sea to Shining Sea: West Virgina. 2008. (ENG.). 80p. (J). pap. 7.95 *(978-0-531-20818-2(4)*, Children's Pr.) Scholastic Library Publishing.
—West Virginia. 2003. (From Sea to Shining Sea Ser.: 2). (ENG., Illus.). 80p. (J). 30.50 *(978-0-516-22389-6(5)*, Children's Pr.) Scholastic Library Publishing.
Way, Jennifer. West Virginia. 2009. (Bilingual Library of the United States of America Ser.). (ENG & SPA.). 32p. (gr. 2-2). 47.90 *(978-1-60853-392-3(1)*, Editorial Buenas Letras) Rosen Publishing Group, Inc., The.

WEST VIRGINIA—FICTION

Atwell, A. Erika Laura. 2008. 157p. pap. 24.95 *(978-1-60703-006-5(3))* PublishAmerica, Inc.
Bauer, Joan. Close to Famous. 2012. (ENG.). 272p. (J). (gr. 5-8). 8.99 *(978-0-14-242017-1(4)*, Puffin Books) Penguin Young Readers Group.
Cummings, John Michael. The Night I Freed John Brown. 2016. (ENG.). 256p. pap. 16.99 *(978-1-940425-96-2(4)*, P501745, Vandalia Pr.) West Virginia Univ. Pr.
—Ugly to Start With. 2011. (ENG.). 176p. pap. 16.99 *(978-1-935978-08-4(X)*, P502175, Vandalia Pr.) West Virginia Univ. Pr.
Dunham, Wendy. Hope Girl. 2016. (ENG.). 144p. (J). (gr. 2-6). pap. 8.99 *(978-0-7369-6495-1(9)*, 6964951) Harvest Hse. Pubs.
—My Name Is River. 2015. (ENG.). 144p. (J). (gr. 2-6). pap. 8.99 *(978-0-7369-6461-6(4)*, 6964616) Harvest Hse. Pubs.
Ehrenberg, Pamela. Tillmon County Fire. 2009. 192p. (YA). (gr. 9-18). pap. 9.00 *(978-0-8028-5345-5(5)*, Eerdmans Bks For Young Readers) Eerdmans, William B. Publishing Co.
Faine, Edward Allan. More Little Ned Stories. 2003. 112p. (J). pap. 6.95 *(978-0-9716911-2-4(6))* IM Pr.
Hahn, Mary Downing. Witch Catcher. 2011. (ENG.). 240p. (J). (gr. 5-7). pap. 7.99 *(978-0-547-57714-2(1)*, 1458462, Clarion Bks.) HarperCollins Pubs.
Hedrick, Helen Groves. Tails, Trails & Pies: An Appalachian Cattle Drive. Spiker, Sue Ann Maxwell, illus. 2008. 32p. 15.95 *(978-0-929915-87-6(9))* Headline Bks., Inc.
Heidecker, Rosemary. Emmie. 2011. 144p. pap. 17.99 *(978-1-4567-3708-5(2))* AuthorHouse.
Jacobs, Lily. The Littlest Bunny in West Virginia: An Easter Adventure. Dunn, Robert, illus. 2015. (Littlest Bunny Ser.). (ENG.). 32p. (J). (gr. -1-3). 9.99 *(978-1-4926-1237-7(5)*, Hometown World) Sourcebooks, Inc.
James, Eric. Santa's Sleigh Is on Its Way to West Virginia: A Christmas Adventure. Dunn, Robert, illus. 2016. (Santa's Sleigh Is on Its Way Ser.). (ENG.). 32p. (J). (gr. k-2). 12.99 *(978-1-4926-4364-7(5)*, 9781492643647, Hometown World) Sourcebooks, Inc.
—The Spooky Express West Virginia. Piwowarski, Marcin, illus. 2017. (Spooky Express Ser.). (ENG.). 32p. (J). (gr. k-6). 9.99 *(978-1-4926-5411-7(6)*, Hometown World) Sourcebooks, Inc.
Kennedy, Marlane. The Dog Days of Charlotte Hayes. 2009. (ENG., Illus.). 240p. (J). (gr. 3-7). 16.99 *(978-0-06-145241-3(6)*, Greenwillow Bks.) HarperCollins Pubs.
Kincaid, Tracy. The Adventures of Casey the Lost Suitcase. 2007. (Illus.). 32p. (J). (gr. -1-3). 16.95 *(978-0-929915-67-8(4))* Headline Bks., Inc.
Laskas, Gretchen Moran. The Miner's Daughter. 2007. (ENG.). 256p. (YA). (gr. 7-12). 19.99 *(978-1-4169-1262-0(2)*, Simon & Schuster Bks. For Young Readers) Simon & Schuster Bks. For Young Readers.
Martin, T. Michael. The End Games. 2014. (ENG.). 400p. (YA). (gr. 9). pap. 9.99 *(978-0-06-220181-2(6)*, Balzer & Bray) HarperCollins Pubs.
Mills, Lauren A. Minna's Patchwork Coat. 2015. (ENG., Illus.). 288p. (J). (gr. 3-7). 17.00 *(978-0-316-40621-5(X))* Little, Brown Bks. for Young Readers.
Oneill, Elizabeth. Alfred Visits West Virginia. 2009. 24p. (J). pap. 12.00 *(978-0-9822288-2-1(1))* Funny Bone Bks.
Rand, Johnathan. American Chillers #23 Wicked Velociraptors of West Virginia. 2008. 208p. (J). pap. 5.99 *(978-1-893699-94-6(3))* AudioCraft Publishing, Inc.
Reynolds Naylor, Phyllis. The Girls Take Over. 2004. (Boys Against Girls Ser.: No. 8). 146p. (J). (gr. 4-7). 13.65 *(978-0-7569-2804-9(4))* Perfection Learning Corp.
—Shiloh. 144p. (J). (Shiloh Ser.: No. 1). (gr. 4-7). pap. 4.99 *(978-0-8072-8330-1(4))*;No. 1. 2004. (gr. 3-7). pap. 29.00 incl. audio *(978-0-8072-8329-5(0)*, YA164SP) Random Hse. Audio Publishing Group. (Listening Library).
—Shiloh Season. unabr. ed. 2004. (Shiloh Ser.: No. 2). 120p. (J). (gr. 3-7). pap. 29.00 incl. audio *(978-0-8072-8707-1(5)*, YA242SP, Listening Library) Random Hse. Audio Publishing Group.
Rylant, Cynthia. Missing May. unabr. ed. 2004. 89p. (J). (gr. 5-9). pap. 29.00 incl. audio *(978-0-8072-8701-9(6)*, YA240SP, Listening Library) Random Hse. Audio Publishing Group.
—Missing May (Scholastic Gold), 1 vol. 2004. (ENG.). 128p. (J). (gr. 4-7). pap. 6.99 *(978-0-439-61383-5(3)*, Scholastic Paperbacks) Scholastic, Inc.
Shank, Marilyn Sue. Child of the Mountains. 2013. 272p. (J). (gr. 4-7). 7.99 *(978-0-375-87331-7(7)*, Yearling) Random Hse. Children's Bks.
Sully, Katherine. Night-Night West Virginia. Poole, Helen, illus. 2017. (Night-Night Ser.). (ENG.). 20p. (J). (gr. -1-1). bds. 9.99 *(978-1-4926-5475-9(2)*, Hometown World) Sourcebooks, Inc.
Wach, Martin. The Great West Virginia Snow Adventure: Teddy Bear Guardians of the Rain Forest. 2006. (Illus.). 32p. (J). 16.95 *(978-0-929915-42-5(9))* Headline Bks., Inc.
Watts, Jeri. A Piece of Home. Yum, Hyewon, illus. 2016. (ENG.). 32p. (J). (gr. k-3). 17.99 *(978-0-7636-6971-3(7))* Candlewick Pr.
Wyatt, Melissa. Funny How Things Change. 2009. (ENG.). 208p. (YA). (gr. 9-13). 27.99 *(978-0-374-30233-7(2)*, 900048651, Farrar, Straus & Giroux (BYR)) Farrar, Straus & Giroux.
Yolen, Jane. Snow in Summer. 2013. (ENG.). 272p. (J). (gr. 5). pap. 7.99 *(978-0-14-242197-0(9)*, Puffin Books) Penguin Young Readers Group.

WEST VIRGINIA—HISTORY

Byers, Ann. West Virginia: Past & Present, 1 vol. 2010. (United States: Past & Present Ser.). (ENG.). 48p. (YA). (gr. 5-5). pap. 12.75 *(978-1-4358-9526-3(6)*, 619b6edf-79be-4bb0-a21f-8d0a922bfc71); lib. bdg. 34.47 *(978-1-4358-9499-0(5)*, 0814291c-3615-4719-8752-7d4de6a0de76) Rosen Publishing Group, Inc., The. (Rosen Reference).
Carole Marsh. West Virginia Indians. 2004. (West Virginia Experi Ser.). 36p. (gr. 3-8). pap. 7.95 *(978-0-635-02340-7(7))* Gallopade International.
Davidson, Tish. Atlantic: North Carolina, Virginia, West Virginia, Vol. 19. 2015. (Let's Explore the States Ser.). (Illus.). 64p. (J). (gr. 5). 23.95 *(978-1-4222-3320-7(0))* Mason Crest.
Fluharty, Linda Cunningham. Civil War - West Virginia: Union Lives Lost. 2004. (Illus.). 175p. lib. bdg. 35.00 *(978-0-9759097-1-3(1))* Fluharty, Linda Cunningham.
Hallock, Marilyn R. Central Glass Company: The First Thirty Years, 1863-1893, 1 vol. 2003. (ENG., Illus.). 176p. 39.95 *(978-0-7643-1762-0(8)*, 1821) Schiffer Publishing, Ltd.
Hamilton, John. West Virginia, 1 vol. 2016. (United States of America Ser.). (ENG., Illus.). 48p. (J). (gr. 5-9). 34.21 *(978-1-68078-352-0(1)*, 21689, Abdo & Daughters) ABDO Publishing Co.
Hanel, Rachael. West Virginia. 2009. (This Land Called America Ser.). (Illus.). 32p. (YA). (gr. 3-6). 19.95 *(978-1-58341-801-7(6))* Creative Co., The.
Heinrichs, Ann. America the Beautiful: West Virginia (Revised Edition) 2014. (America the Beautiful, Third Ser. (Revised Edition) Ser.). (ENG.). 144p. (J). lib. bdg. 40.00 *(978-0-531-28299-1(6))* Scholastic Library Publishing.
Lawton, Val. West Virginia. 2011. (Guide to American States Ser.). (Illus.). 48p. (YA). (gr. 3-6). 29.99 *(978-1-61690-822-5(0))*; (J). *(978-1-61690-497-5(6))* Weigl Pubs., Inc.
—West Virginia: The Mountain State. 2016. (J). *(978-1-4896-4962-1(X))* Weigl Pubs., Inc.
Marsh, Carole. Exploring West Virginia Through Project-Based Learning: Geography, History, Government, Economics & More. 2016. (West Virginia Experience Ser.). (ENG.). (J). pap. 9.99 *(978-0-635-12372-5(X))* Gallopade International.
—West Virginia History Projects: 30 Cool, Activities, Crafts, Experiments & More for Kids to Do to Learn about Your State! 2003. (West Virginia Experience Ser.). 32p. (gr. k-5). pap. 5.95 *(978-0-635-01817-5(9)*, Marsh, Carole Bks.) Gallopade International.
—West Virginia Native Americans: A Kid's Look at Our State's Chiefs, Tribes, Reservations, Powwows, Lore & More from the Past & the Present. 2004. (West Virginia Experi Ser.). (Illus.). 36p. (J). (gr. 3-8). 29.95 *(978-0-635-02341-4(5))* Gallopade International.
Owings, Lisa. West Virginia. 2013. (Exploring the States Ser.). (ENG., Illus.). 32p. (J). (gr. 3-7). lib. bdg. 27.95 *(978-1-62617-049-0(5)*, Blastoff! Readers) Bellwether Medi
Petreycik, Rick. West Virginia, 1 vol. 2nd rev. ed. 2014. (It's My State! (Second Edition)(r) Ser.). (ENG.). 80p. (gr. 4-4). pap. 18.64 *(978-1-62712-486-7(1)*, df39f6ea-9123-4a90-ac3e-71ec39a9bbb7); (Illus.). lib. bdg. 35.93 *(978-1-62712-224-5(9)*, e3b1aa55-8e9d-47b2-85f0-a25514642fdb) Cavendish Square Publishing LLC.
Petreycik, Rick & Boehme, Gerry. West Virginia: The Mountain State, 1 vol. 3rd rev. ed. 2016. (It's My State! (Third Edition)(r) Ser.). (ENG.). 80p. (gr. 4-4). 35.93 *(978-1-62713-256-5(2)*, 6c44798e-6a8c-427f-a438-4489d351ff0f) Cavendish Square Publishing LLC.
Phillips, Margaret Coull. West Virginia. 2003. (Seeds of a Nation Ser.). (Illus.). 48p. (J). (gr. 3-5). 23.70 *(978-0-7377-1567-5(7)*, Kidhaven) Cengage Gale.
Pratt, Laura. West Virginia: The Mountain State. 2012. (J). *(978-1-61913-417-1(9))*; pap. *(978-1-61913-418-8(7))* Weigl Pubs., Inc.
Roxburgh, Ellis. The Raid on Harpers Ferry. 2017. (Rebellions, Revolts, & Uprisings Ser.). 48p. (gr. 5-5). pap. 84.30 *(978-1-5382-0754-3(0))* Stevens, Gareth Publishing LLLP.
Schraff, Anne. John Brown: We Came to Free the Slaves, 1 vol. 2008. (Americans: the Spirit of a Nation Ser.). (ENG., Illus.). 128p. (gr. 5-6). lib. bdg. 35.93 *(978-0-7660-3355-9(4)*, 4d2d0bf1-4734-41ec-b384-c08076340bc5) Enslow Publishing, LLC.
Smucker, Anna. History of West Virginia. 2004. (Illus.). per. 7.95 *(978-1-891852-39-8(6))* Quarrier Pr.
Way, Jennifer. West Virginia/Virginia Occidental, 1 vol. Brusca, Maria Cristina, tr. 2005. (Bilingual Library of the United States of America Ser.: Set 2). (ENG & SPA., Illus.). 32p. (J). (gr. 2-2). lib. bdg. 28.93 *(978-1-4042-3114-6(5)*, cf5abb94-a69b-4e31-9ced-2ea7a6b7526a) Rosen Publishing Group, Inc., The.
Yomtov, Nel. John Brown: Defending the Innocent or Plotting Terror?, 1 vol. 2013. (Perspectives on History Ser.). (ENG., Illus.). 32p. (J). (gr. 3-6). 27.99 *(978-1-4765-0244-1(7)*, 122298) Capstone.
Zaunders, Bo. The Great Bridge-Building Contest. Munro, Roxie, illus. 2006. 30p. (J). (gr. 4-8). reprint ed. 17.00 *(978-1-4223-5239-7(0))* DIANE Publishing Co.

WESTINGHOUSE, GEORGE, 1846-1914

Winchell, Mike. The Electric War: Edison, Tesla, Westinghouse, & the Race to Light the World. 2019. (ENG., Illus.). 272p. (YA). 19.99 *(978-1-250-12016-8(0)*, 900172928, Holt, Henry & Co. Bks. For Young Readers) Holt, Henry & Co.

WETLAND ECOLOGY

Ake, Anne. Everglades: An Ecosystem Facing Choices & Challenges. 2017. 122p. (J). (gr. -1-12). pap. 19.95 *(978-1-68334-032-4(9))* Pineapple Pr., Inc.
Aloian, Molly & Kalman, Bobbie. Un Hábitat de Pantano. 2007. (Introduction a Los Habitats Ser.). (SPA., Illus.). 32p. (J). (gr. 3-7). lib. bdg. *(978-0-7787-8328-2(6))*; (gr. k-3). pap. *(978-0-7787-8352-7(9))* Crabtree Publishing Co.
—A Wetland Habitat. 2006. (Introducing Habitats Ser.). (ENG., Illus.). 32p. (J). (gr. -1-3). pap. *(978-0-7787-2983-9(4))* Crabtree Publishing Co.
Barghoorn, Linda. Map & Track Wetlands. 2019. (Map & Track Biomes & Animals Ser.). (Illus.). 32p. (J). (gr. 4-5). *(978-0-7787-6186-0(X))*; pap. *(978-0-7787-5383-4(2))* Crabtree Publishing Co.
Bennett, Doraine. Coastal Plain. 2009. (J). *(978-1-935077-51-0(1))*; pap. *(978-1-935077-52-7(X))* State Standards Publishing, LLC.
Benoit, Peter. A True Book: Wetlands. 2011. (True Bk Ser.). (ENG.). 48p. (J). pap. 6.95 *(978-0-531-28100-0(0)*, Children's Pr.) Scholastic Library Publishing.
—Wetlands. 2011. (True Bks.). 48p. (J). (gr. 3-5). 29.00 *(978-0-531-20551-8(7)*, Children's Pr.) Scholastic Library Publishing.
Bow, James. Wetlands Inside Out. 2014. (Ecosystems Inside Out Ser.). (ENG., Illus.). 32p. (J). (gr. 4-5). *(978-0-7787-0641-0(9))* Crabtree Publishing Co.
Dunphy, Madeleine. Here Is the Wetland. McLoughlin, Wayne, illus. 2007. (Web of Life Ser.: 6). (ENG.). 32p. (J). (gr. -1-3). pap. 9.95 *(978-0-9773795-8-3(2))* Web of Life Children's Bks.
Early Macken, JoAnn. Wetlands / Terrenos Pantanosos, 1 vol. 2005. (Water Habitats / Hábitats Acuáticos Ser.). (SPA & ENG., Illus.). 24p. (gr. k-2). pap. 9.15 *(978-0-8368-6039-9(X)*, 180850d3-e649-4c69-a15f-609acb17a47b, Weekly Reader Leveled Readers) Stevens, Gareth Publishing LLLP.
Franchino, Vicky. Florida Wetlands. 2016. (Community Connections: Getting to Know Our Planet Ser.). (ENG., Illus.). 24p. (J). (gr. 2-5). 29.21 *(978-1-63470-516-5(5)*, 207795) Cherry Lake Publishing.
Frisch, Aaron. Wetlands. 2008. (Our World Ser.). (Illus.). 24p. (J). (gr. -1-3). lib. bdg. 24.25 *(978-1-58341-575-7(0)*, Creative Education) Creative Co., The.
Hale, Wendy A. & Lantz, Peggy. The Wetlands of Florida. 2014. (Florida Water Story Ser.). (Illus.). 36p. (J). (gr. -1-12). pap. 11.95 *(978-1-56164-705-7(5))* Pineapple Pr., Inc.
Heos, Bridget. Do You Really Want to Visit a Wetland? Fabbri, Daniele, illus. 2014. (Do You Really Want to Visit Earth's Biomes? Ser.). (ENG.). 24p. (J). (gr. 1-4). lib. bdg. 27.10 *(978-1-60753-454-9(1)*, 15889) Amicus.
Johnson, Robin. Everglades Research Journal. 2017. (Ecosystems Research Journal Ser.). (Illus.). 32p. (J). (gr. 4-5). *(978-0-7787-3469-7(2))*; (ENG., pap. *(978-0-7787-3494-9(3))* Crabtree Publishing Co.
Kalman, Bobbie & Bishop, Amanda. Les Terres Humides. 2004. (Petit Monde Vivant Ser.). (FRE., Illus.). 32p. (J). pap. 9.95 *(978-2-89579-014-3(0))* Bayard Canada Livres CAN. Dist: Crabtree Publishing Co.
Kalman, Bobbie & Burns, Kylie. Wetland Food Chains, 1 vol. 2006. (Food Chains Ser.). (ENG., Illus.). 32p. (J). (gr. -1-3). pap. *(978-0-7787-1999-1(5))* Crabtree Publishing Co.
Kurtz, Kevin. A Day in a Forested Wetland, 1 vol. Neidigh, Sherry, illus. 2018. (ENG.). 32p. (J). (gr. k-3). 17.95

(978-1-62855-912-5(8), 9781628559125) Arbordale Publishing.
arsen, Laurel. One Night in the Everglades. Turley, Joyce Mihran, illus. 2012. (Long Term Ecological Research Ser.). (ENG.). 32p. (J). (gr. 3-7). 15.95 (978-0-9817700-4-8(5)) Taylor Trade Publishing.
eeson, Cole. Wetland/Swamp. 2003. (Wild America Habitats Ser.). (Illus.). 24p. (J). 21.20 (978-1-56711-810-0(0), Blackbirch Pr., Inc.) Cengage Gale.
arais, Vivian. Life in a Swamp: A Wetlands Habitat, 1 vol. 2008. (Real Life Readers Ser.). (ENG.). 24p. (gr. 3-3). pap. 8.25 (978-1-4358-0141-7(5), bf64001c-344b-4fcc-8dc3-f99daa53a6a7, Rosen Classroom) Rosen Publishing Group, Inc., The.
lebane, Jeanie. At the Marsh in the Meadow. Guerlais, Gérald, illus. 2016. (ENG.). 32p. (J). (gr. 1-3). 17.99 (978-1-58536-958-4(6), 204028) Sleeping Bear Pr.
erdew, Laura. Bringing Back Our Wetlands. 2017. (Conservation Success Stories Ser.). (ENG., Illus.). 112p. (J). (gr. 6-12). lib. bdg. 41.36 (978-1-5321-1318-5(8), 27526, Essential Library) ABDO Publishing Co.
Pettiford, Rebecca. Wetland Food Chains. 2016. (Who Eats What?). (Illus.). 24p. (J). (gr. 2-5). lib. bdg. (978-1-62031-305-3(7), Pogo) Jump! Inc.
Pyers, Greg. Biodiversity of Wetlands, 1 vol. 2012. (Biodiversity Ser.). (ENG.). 32p. (gr. 4-4). 31.21 (978-1-60870-533-7(1), a3bf7518-647c-4931-b8ad-5e0299fa30c7) Cavendish Square Publishing LLC.
Rivera, Sheila. Wetland. 2005. (Illus.). 24p. (J). pap. 5.95 (978-0-8225-5370-0(8)) Lerner Publishing Group.
Sidabras, Kimberly. Wetlands, Vol. 5. 2018. (World's Biomes Ser.). (Illus.). 80p. (J). (gr. 7). 33.27 (978-1-4222-4040-3(1)) Mason Crest.
Stewart, Melissa. Life in a Wetland. Maka, Stephen, photos by. 2003. (Ecosystems in Action Ser.). (ENG., Illus.). 72p. (gr. 5-9). lib. bdg. 26.60 (978-0-8225-4687-0(6)) Lerner Publishing Group.
Stone, Lynn M. Wetlands. 2003. (Rourke Discovery Library). (Illus.). 24p. (J). 20.64 (978-1-58952-688-4(0)) Rourke Educational Media.
Sundance/Newbridge LLC Staff. Wetlands. 2007. (Early Science Ser.). (gr. k-3). 18.95 (978-1-4007-6450-1(5)); pap. 6.10 (978-1-4007-6446-4(7)) Sundance/Newbridge Educational Publishing.
Taylor, Trace & Zorzi, Gina. This Is a Wetland. 2011. (Power 100 - Ecosystems Ser.). 28p. (J). (gr. k-2). pap. 7.95 (978-1-61541-450-5(9)) American Reading Co.
Wallace, Marianne D. America's Wetlands: Guide to Plants & Animals. 2004. (America's Ecosystems Ser.). (ENG., Illus.). 48p. (J). (gr. 3-6). pap. 11.95 (978-1-55591-484-4(5)) Fulcrum Publishing.
Watson, Galadriel Findlay. Wetlands. (J). 2011. (gr. 5-8). pap. 13.95 (978-1-61690-649-8(9), AV2 by Weigl) 2011. (Illus.). 32p. (gr. 2-5). 28.55 (978-1-61690-643-6(X)) 2005. (Illus.). 32p. (gr. 4-6). lib. bdg. 26.00 (978-1-59036-349-2(3)) Weigl Pubs., Inc.
World Book, Inc. Staff, contrib. by. Forests & Wetlands. 2008. (J). (978-0-7166-1401-2(4)) World Bk., Inc.

WETLANDS

see also Marshes

Arnold, Quinn M. Wetlands. (Seedlings Ser.). (ENG., Illus.). 24p. (J). 2017. (gr. k-2). pap. 10.99 (978-1-62832-351-1(5), 20752, Creative Paperbacks) 2016. (gr. -1-k). (978-1-60818-798-0(5), 20754, Creative Education) Creative Co., The.
Barghoorn, Linda. Map & Track Wetlands. 2019. (Map & Track Biomes & Animals Ser.). (Illus.). 32p. (J). (gr. 4-5). (978-0-7787-6186-0(X)); pap. (978-0-7787-5383-4(2)) Crabtree Publishing Co.
Benoit, Peter. A True Book: Wetlands. 2011. (True Bk Ser.). (ENG.). 48p. (J). pap. 6.95 (978-0-531-28100-0(0), Children's Pr.) Scholastic Library Publishing.
—Wetlands. 2011. (True Bks.). 48p. (J). (gr. 3-5). 29.00 (978-0-531-20551-8(7), Children's Pr.) Scholastic Library Publishing.
Best, Arthur. Bayous, 1 vol. 2017. (Our World of Water Ser.). (ENG.). 24p. (gr. 1-1). pap. 9.22 (978-1-5026-3086-5(9), 18cf39f4-7a83-4222-a58f-c227bb8d75a7) Cavendish Square Publishing LLC.
—Wetlands, 1 vol. 2017. (Our World of Water Ser.). (ENG.). 24p. (gr. 1-1). pap. 9.22 (978-1-5026-3106-0(7), 9ed6441b-e9c3-4579-b7a4-ec46b5e40604) Cavendish Square Publishing LLC.
Bethea, Nikole Brooks. Wetland Ecosystems, 1 vol. 2015. (Ecosystems of the World Ser.). (ENG., Illus.). 48p. (J). (gr. 4-8). 35.64 (978-1-62403-858-7(1), 18086) ABDO Publishing Co.
Campbell, Andrew. Protecting Wetlands, 1 vol. 2005. (Protecting Habitats Ser.). (ENG., Illus.). 32p. (gr. 4-6). lib. bdg. 28.67 (978-0-8368-4996-7(5), d737d04f-4913-4047-a7fc-e61c83b6c74d, Gareth Stevens Learning Library) Stevens, Gareth Publishing LLLP.
Chambers, Catherine. Threatened Wetlands. 2010. (Protecting Our Planet Ser.). (ENG., Illus.). 32p. (J). (gr. 3-6). (978-0-7787-5214-1(3)); pap. (978-0-7787-5231-8(3)) Crabtree Publishing Co.
Clarke, Penny. Scary Creatures of the Wetlands. 2008. (Scary Creatures Ser.). (ENG.). 32p. (J). 27.00 (978-0-531-21749-8(3), Watts, Franklin) Scholastic Library Publishing.
Early Macken, JoAnn. Wetlands, 1 vol. 2005. (Water Habitats Ser.). (ENG., Illus.). 24p. (J). (gr. k-2). pap. 9.15 (978-0-8368-4894-6(2), 8f576269-239f-452d-950c-e0282dbc7545); lib. bdg. 24.67 (978-0-8368-4887-8(X), d00ee805-3af4-47f6-81b7-f5b3ccbb91f9) Stevens, Gareth Publishing LLLP. (Weekly Reader Leveled Readers).
—Wetlands / Terrenos Pantanosos, 1 vol. 2005. (Water Habitats / Hábitats Acuáticos Ser.). (SPA & ENG., Illus.). 24p. (gr. k-2). pap. 9.15 (978-0-8368-6039-9(X), 180850d3-e649-4c69-a15f-609acb17a47b); lib. bdg. 24.67 (978-0-8368-6032-0(2), 82530860-c79-4cc0-bfa9-93dd88840735) Stevens, Gareth Publishing LLLP. (Weekly Reader Leveled Readers).
Endres, Hollie. Wetlands. 2007. (Learning about the Earth Ser.). (ENG., Illus.). 24p. (J). (gr. k-3). lib. bdg. 26.95 (978-1-60014-116-4(1)) Bellwether Media.
Endres, Hollie J. Wetlands. 2011. (Blastoff! Readers: Learning about the Earth: Level 3 Ser.). (Illus.). 24p. (J). pap. 5.95 (978-0-531-26039-5(9), Children's Pr.) Scholastic Library Publishing.
Franklin, Yvonne. Los Pantanos. rev. ed. 2010. (Science: Informational Text Ser.). (SPA., Illus.). 32p. (gr. 2-4). pap. 11.99 (978-1-4333-2140-5(8)) Teacher Created Materials, Inc.
Gardeski, Christina Mia. All about Wetlands. 2018. (Habitats Ser.). (ENG., Illus.). 24p. (J). (gr. -1-2). lib. bdg. 22.65 (978-1-5157-9759-3(7), 136869, Pebble) Capstone.
Gordon, Sharon. Animales de Los Humedales (Wetland Animals), 1 vol. 2010. (Animales Salvajes (Wild Animals) Ser.). (SPA.). 24p. (gr. k-1). lib. bdg. 25.50 (978-0-7614-3433-7(X), 35976bc4-5b6c-4707-a678-aedbf585098c) Cavendish Square Publishing LLC.
—Wetland Animals, 1 vol. 2009. (Wild Animals Ser.). (ENG.). 24p. (gr. k-1). pap. 9.23 (978-0-7614-3512-9(3), fbdb9cb1-43a1-49b8-bf39-130f7321fbfd) Cavendish Square Publishing LLC.
Grack, Rachel. Alligators. 2019. (Animals of the Wetlands Ser.). (ENG., Illus.). 24p. (J). (gr. k-3). lib. bdg. 26.95 (978-1-62617-985-1(9), Blastoff! Readers) Bellwether Media.
—Herons. 2019. (Animals of the Wetlands Ser.). (ENG., Illus.). 24p. (J). (gr. k-3). lib. bdg. 26.95 (978-1-62617-988-2(3), Blastoff! Readers) Bellwether Media.
Hale, Wendy A. & Lantz, Peggy. The Wetlands of Florida. 2014. (Florida Water Story Ser.). (Illus.). 36p. (J). (gr. -1-12). pap. 11.95 (978-1-56164-705-7(5)) Pineapple Pr., Inc.
Head, Honor. Poisoned Wetlands, 1 vol. 2018. (Totally Toxic Ser.). (ENG.). 48p. (gr. 4-5). pap. 15.05 (978-1-5382-3497-6(1), ef1b4358-f6f7-4965-9c34-7d4a5c530517) Stevens, Gareth Publishing LLLP.
Heos, Bridget. Do You Really Want to Visit a Wetland? Fabbri, Daniele, illus. 2014. (Do You Really Want to Visit Earth's Biomes? Ser.). (ENG.). 24p. (J). (gr. 1-4). lib. bdg. 27.10 (978-1-60753-454-9(1), 15889) Amicus.
Johnson, Rebecca L. A Journey into a Wetland. Saroff, Phyllis V., illus. 2004. (Biomes of North America Ser.). (J). pap. 8.95 (978-0-8225-2047-4(8)); 48p. (gr. 3-6). lib. bdg. 23.93 (978-1-57505-593-0(7)) Lerner Publishing Group.
Kalman, Bobbie. What Are Wetlands? 2003. (Science of Living Things Ser.). (ENG., Illus.). 32p. (J). (gr. 3-6). lib. bdg. 24.94 (978-0-86505-993-1(4)) Crabtree Publishing Co. CAN. Dist: Children's Plus, Inc.
Kalman, Bobbie & Burns, Kylie. Cadenas Alimentarias de los Pantanos. 2007. (Cadenas Alimentarias Ser.). (SPA., Illus.). 32p. (J). (gr. 3-7). lib. bdg. (978-0-7787-8532-3(7)) Crabtree Publishing Co.
Kanfush, Philip M. Emma's Wetlands Adventure: The Story of the Monastery Run Imporvement Project Wetlands at Saint Vincent. 2006. (J). pap. 12.95 (978-0-9708216-9-0(7)) St. Vincent Archabbey Pubns.
Kavanagh, James & Waterford Press Staff. My First Wetlands Nature. Leung, Raymond, illus. 2011. (Nature Activity Book Ser.). (ENG.). 32p. (J). (gr. 2-4). act. bk. ed. 6.95 (978-1-58355-591-0(9)) Western National Parks Assn.
Kinsner, Kathy. The Everglades. 2011. (Early Connections Ser.). (J). (978-1-61672-675-1(X)) Benchmark Education Co.
Kurtz, Kevin & Neidigh, Sherry. Un Día en el Bosque Del Humedal. Neidigh, Sherry, illus. 2018.Tr. of Day in a Forested Wetland. (SPA., Illus.). 32p. (J). (gr. 2-3). pap. 11.95 (978-1-62855-914-9(4), b8c24ca2-38fd-4bc7-8af1-66d0d31aa7c3) Arbordale Publishing.
Leeson, Cole. Wetland/Swamp. 2003. (Wild America Habitats Ser.). (Illus.). 24p. (J). 21.20 (978-1-56711-810-0(0), Blackbirch Pr., Inc.) Cengage Gale.
Levy, Janey. Discovering Wetlands, 1 vol. 2007. (World Habitats Ser.). (ENG., Illus.). 32p. (J). (gr. 4-5). lib. bdg. 28.93 (978-1-4042-3784-1(4), de6b399b-3ff7-4331-9346-f231d0bc10af, PowerKids Pr.) Rosen Publishing Group, Inc., The.
Looye, Juliette, text. I Live near a Wetland. 2004. (Illus.). 16p. (J). pap. (978-0-7367-1940-7(7)) Zaner-Bloser, Inc.
Mack, Dave. What Lives in a Marsh? 2013. (InfoMax Readers Ser.). (ENG.). 24p. (J). (gr. 3-4). pap. 49.50 (978-1-4777-2580-1(6)); (Illus.). pap. 8.25 (978-1-4777-2579-5(2), fdbe6572-6c0d-4c75-a263-0bf99cb24307) Rosen Publishing Group, Inc., The. (Rosen Classroom).
Mebane, Jeanie. At the Marsh in the Meadow. Guerlais, Gérald, illus. 2016. (ENG.). 32p. (J). (gr. 1-3). 17.99 (978-1-58536-958-4(6), 204028) Sleeping Bear Pr.
Nichols, Catherine. Wetlands, 1 vol. 2003. (We Can Read about Nature! Ser.). (ENG., Illus.). 32p. (gr. 1-2). 25.50 (978-0-7614-1434-6(7), b92705fa-2b00-42ef-aca9-cea1bababa03) Cavendish Square Publishing LLC.
Perdew, Laura. Bringing Back Our Wetlands. 2017. (Conservation Success Stories Ser.). (ENG., Illus.). 112p. (J). (gr. 6-12). lib. bdg. 41.36 (978-1-5321-1318-5(8), 27526, Essential Library) ABDO Publishing Co.
Project WET Foundation, prod. Kids: Celebrate Wetlands Activity Guide. 2003. (ENG.). (J). 1.00 (978-1-888631-25-8(2)) Project WET Foundation.
Rice, William & Franklin, Yvonne. Wetlands, 1 vol. rev. ed. 2009. (Science: Informational Text Ser.). (ENG.). 32p. (J). (gr. 2-4). pap. 11.99 (978-1-4333-0316-6(7)) Teacher Created Materials, Inc.
Rivera, Sheila. Wetland. 2005. (First Step Nonfiction Ser.). (Illus.). 23p. (J). (gr. 3-7). lib. bdg. 18.60 (978-0-8225-2598-1(4), Lerner Pubns.) Lerner Publishing Group.
Scrace, Carolyn. Life in the Wetlands. 2005. (What on Earth? Ser.). (ENG., Illus.). 32p. (J). (gr. 2-4). 25.50 (978-0-516-25318-3(2), Children's Pr.) Scholastic Library Publishing.
Sherk, Beth Larson. The Three Sisters. 2012. (Illus.). 35p. (J). 14.95 (978-1-62086-091-5(0)) Amplify Publishing Group.
Sill, Cathryn. About Habitats: Wetlands, 1 vol. Sill, John, illus. 2013. (About Habitats Ser.: 2). 48p. (J). (gr. -1-2). pap. 8.99 (978-1-56145-689-5(6)) Peachtree Publishing Co. Inc.
Spilsbury, Richard & Spilsbury, Louise. At Home in the Wetlands, 1 vol., 1. 2015. (Home in the Biome Ser.). (ENG.). 32p. (J). (gr. 3-4). pap. 11.00 (978-1-5081-4569-1(5), 65d52ad3-b1c6-40b0-b06a-74d91e99e8c1, PowerKids Pr.) Rosen Publishing Group, Inc., The.
Stone, Lynn M. Wetlands. 2003. (Rourke Discovery Library). (Illus.). 24p. (J). 20.64 (978-1-58952-688-4(0)) Rourke Educational Media.
Taylor, Barbara. Inland Water Habitats, 1 vol. 2006. (Exploring Habitats Ser.). (ENG., Illus.). 36p. (gr. 4-6). lib. bdg. 28.67 (978-0-8368-7254-5(1), d5eee19e-6b4a-47df-8bbd-8d823741e325, Gareth Stevens Learning Library) Stevens, Gareth Publishing LLLP.
Wallace, Marianne D. America's Wetlands: Guide to Plants & Animals. 2004. (America's Ecosystems Ser.). (ENG., Illus.). 48p. (J). (gr. 3-6). pap. 11.95 (978-1-55591-484-4(5)) Fulcrum Publishing.
World Book, Inc. Staff, contrib. by. Forests & Wetlands. 2008. (J). (978-0-7166-1401-2(4)) World Bk., Inc.

WETLANDS—FICTION

Szymanski, Lois. Wild Colt, 1 vol. 2012. (ENG., Illus.). 40p. (J). 16.99 (978-0-7643-3975-2(3), 4445) Schiffer Publishing, Ltd.
Ter Haar, Carol. Chris T. Saves the Wetlands. 2008. (J). 20.00 (978-0-9768310-2-0(3)) BIC Alliance.

WHALES

Adamson, Heather. Orcas. 2017. (Ocean Life up Close Ser.). (ENG., Illus.). 24p. (J). (gr. k-3). lib. bdg. 26.95 (978-1-62617-643-0(4), Blastoff! Readers) Bellwether Media.
Adamson, Thomas K. Great White Shark vs. Killer Whale. 2020. (Animal Battles Ser.). (ENG.). 24p. (J). (gr. 3-7). lib. bdg. 26.95 (978-1-64487-157-7(2), Torque Bks.) Bellwether Media.
Allyn, Daisy. Killer Whales Are Not Whales!, 1 vol. 2014. (Confusing Creature Names Ser.). (ENG.). 24p. (J). (gr. 1-2). 24.27 (978-1-4824-0961-1(5), 15bca321-9070-41da-92ac-1ba3ca0ce53b) Stevens, Gareth Publishing LLLP.
Animal Watch: Whales. (J). (gr. 1-3). 75.00 (978-0-669-15103-9(3)); pap. 10.75 (978-0-669-15879-3(8)) Houghton Mifflin Harcourt School Pubs.
Antill, Sara. A Whale's Life. (Illus.). 24p. (J). 2012. 49.50 (978-1-4488-5105-8(X), PowerKids Pr.) 2011. (ENG., (gr. 2-3). pap. 9.25 (978-1-4488-5104-1(1), 17d7d596-9a46-4629-ba43-67475e3064fd, PowerKids Pr.) 2011. (ENG., (gr. 2-3). lib. bdg. 26.27 (978-1-4488-4978-9(0), 596c32ec-53c1-40ae-a6f6-15ca9dffc3c9) Rosen Publishing Group, Inc., The.
Atlantic, Leonard. 200-Year-Old Bowhead Whales!, 1 vol. 2016. (World's Longest-Living Animals Ser.). (ENG., Illus.). 24p. (J). (gr. 1-2). pap. 9.15 (978-1-4824-5631-8(1), c4e86d25-4dd1-4d24-ae74-5972d36e5f9e) Stevens, Gareth Publishing LLLP.
Avery, Logan. Amazing Animals: Narwhals: Addition (Grade 1) 2018. (Mathematics in the Real World Ser.). (ENG., Illus.). 24p. (J). (gr. 1-2). pap. 9.99 (978-1-4258-5680-9(2)) Teacher Created Materials, Inc.
—Narvales. rev. ed. 2019. (Mathematics in the Real World Ser.). (SPA., Illus.). 24p. (J). (gr. 1-2). pap. 9.99 (978-1-4258-2842-4(6)) Teacher Created Materials, Inc.
Baskes Litwin, Laura. Was Moby Dick Real?, 1 vol. 2017. (I Want to Know Ser.). (ENG.). 32p. (gr. 3-3). 26.93 (978-0-7660-9197-9(X), 400c14a4-e209-46fc-ad0d-a1654504d67f) Enslow Publishing, LLC.
Batten, Mary. Baby Orca. Rallis, Chris, illus. 2016. 32p. (J). (-k). bds. 5.99 (978-0-448-48839-4(6), Grosset & Dunlap) Penguin Young Readers Group.
Battistoni, I. What a Whale! Learning the WH Sound. 2009. (PowerPhonics Ser.). 24p. (gr. 1-1). 39.90 (978-1-60851-478-6(1), PowerKids Pr.) Rosen Publishing Group, Inc., The.
Beaton, Kathryn. Discover Beluga Whales. 2015. (21st Century Basic Skills Library: Splash! Ser.). (ENG., Illus.). 24p. (J). (gr. 2-4). 26.35 (978-1-63362-596-9(6), 206568) Cherry Lake Publishing.
Becker, John E. Gray Whales. 2004. (Returning Wildlife Ser.). (ENG., Illus.). 48p. (J). (gr. 4-7). 27.50 (978-0-7377-2293-2(2), Greenhaven Pr., Inc.) Cengage Gale.
Berger, Melvin & Berger, Gilda. Whales. 2013. (Illus.). 16p. (J). pap. (978-0-545-35168-3(5)) Scholastic, Inc.
Berne, Emma Carlson. Whale Sharks: Bulletproof! 2013. (Animal Superpowers Ser.). (Illus.). 24p. (J). (gr. k-5). pap. 49.50 (978-1-4777-0840-8(5), PowerKids Pr.) Rosen Publishing Group, Inc., The.
Best, B. J. Humpback Whales, 1 vol. 2016. (Migrating Animals Ser.). (ENG., Illus.). 24p. (J). (gr. 1-1). pap. 9.81 (978-1-5026-2110-8(X), d0eab785-284e-4776-8f46-57ff0a34439c); lib. bdg. 27.36 (978-1-5026-2112-2(6), 2fb69ea2-818b-4d93-845a-c194456fe86e) Cavendish Square Publishing LLC.
Bjorklund, Ruth. Blue Whales. 2013. (ENG.). 48p. (J). 28.00 (978-0-531-23355-9(3)) Scholastic Library Publishing.
Blake, Carly. Why Why Why... Do Dolphins Squeak? 2010. (Why Why Why Ser.). 32p. (J). (gr. 1-3). lib. bdg. 18.95 (978-1-4222-1581-4(4)) Mason Crest.
Block, Cheryl. True Blue Friend. Takeshita, Gene, illus. 2006. 32p. (J). 21.95 (978-0-9761625-2-0(0)) Block Publishing.
Books Are Fun 8 Title Animal Lives Set: Whales. 2006. (J). (978-1-59566-308-5(8)) QEB Publishing Inc.
Bowley, Catherine. Giants of the Ocean Gold Band. 2016. (Cambridge Reading Adventures Ser.). (ENG., Illus.). 24p. pap. 8.80 (978-1-107-55165-7(X)) Cambridge Univ. Pr.
Brannon, Cecelia H. Baby Whales at the Zoo, 1 vol. 2016. (All about Baby Zoo Animals Ser.). (ENG.). 24p. (gr. k-1). 24.27 (978-0-7660-7563-4(X), 697d132b-f6a3-4b73-95d9-a25e2f958fc9) Enslow Publishing, LLC.
Burleigh, Robert. Trapped! (1 Hardcover/1 CD) A Whale's Rescue. Minor, Wendell, illus. 2017. (ENG.). (J). (gr. -1-1). 29.95 (978-1-4301-2684-3(1)) Live Oak Media.
—Trapped! a Whale's Rescue. Minor, Wendell, illus. 2018. 32p. (J). (gr. -1-1). pap. 8.99 (978-1-58089-559-0(X)) Charlesbridge Publishing, Inc.
Burling, Alexis. Humpback Whale Migration. 2018. (Natural Phenomena Ser.). (ENG., Illus.). 32p. (J). (gr. 3-5). pap. 9.95 (978-1-64185-010-0(8), 1641850108); lib. bdg. 31.35 (978-1-63517-908-8(4), 1635179084) North Star Editions. (Focus Readers).
Butterfield, Moira. The Life Cycle of the Orca: Band 16/Sapphire. 2017. (Collins Big Cat Ser.). (ENG., Illus.). 56p. (J). pap. 8.99 (978-0-00-820890-5(5)) HarperCollins Pubs. Ltd. GBR. Dist: Independent Pubs. Group.
Camm, Martin, illus. Meyers Buch der Wale und Delfine. (GER.). 48p. (978-3-411-07451-8(5)) Bibliographisches Institut & F. A. Brockhaus AG DEU. Dist: i. b. d., Ltd.
Cantor, Rachel Anne. Beluga Whale. 2016. (Weird but Cute Ser.). (ENG., Illus.). 24p. (J). (gr. -1-3). 26.99 (978-1-62724-851-8(X)) Bearport Publishing Co., Inc.
Capone, Lisa. Inland: The True Story of a North Atlantic Humpback Whale. 2011. (ENG., Illus.). 50p. (J). pap. 14.95 (978-0-945980-92-6(2)) North Country Pr.
Carlson Berne, Emma. Whale Sharks: Bulletproof!, 1 vol. 2013. (Animal Superpowers Ser.). (ENG., Illus.). 24p. (J). (gr. 2-3). 26.27 (978-1-4777-0749-4(2), 34895ed8-b653-454e-8038-06915541b890); pap. 9.25 (978-1-4777-0839-2(1), 450ab626-e528-4094-847e-fac9476b4c27) Rosen Publishing Group, Inc., The. (PowerKids Pr.).
Carmichael, L. E. Humpback Whales: A Journey to Warm Waters. 2016. (Illus.). 32p. (J). (978-1-4896-4519-7(5)) Weigl Pubs., Inc.
Carr, Aaron. Humpback Whale. 2014. (Illus.). 24p. (J). (978-1-62127-284-7(2)) Weigl Pubs., Inc.
—Narwhal. 2014. (J). (978-1-4896-2637-0(9)) Weigl Pubs., Inc.
Catt, Thessaly. Migrating with the Humpback Whale, 1 vol. 2011. (Animal Journeys Ser.). (ENG., Illus.). 24p. (J). (gr. 2-3). pap. 9.25 (978-1-4488-2670-4(5), 6a8797e5-08f0-4643-a2b3-9340cd957458, PowerKids Pr.); lib. bdg. 26.27 (978-1-4488-2543-1(1), f928972a-b648-4b57-9775-71a5041a33fd) Rosen Publishing Group, Inc., The.
Claybourne, Anna. Orcas, 1 vol. 2013. (Animal Abilities Ser.). (ENG.). 32p. (J). (gr. 2-4). pap. 8.95 (978-1-4109-5246-2(0), 122582, Raintree) Capstone.
Cleave, Andrew. Whales & Dolphins. 2019. (Creatures of the Ocean Ser.). (Illus.). 80p. (J). (gr. 12). lib. bdg. 34.60 (978-1-4222-4311-4(7)) Mason Crest.
Cohen Christopherson, Sara. Top 50 Reasons to Care about Whales & Dolphins: Animals in Peril, 1 vol. 2010. (Top 50 Reasons to Care about Endangered Animals Ser.). (ENG., Illus.). 104p. (gr. 5-6). 35.93 (978-0-7660-3453-2(4), c9ad608d-43a5-4824-aa3e-08eb0562c260) Enslow Publishing, LLC.
Coleman, Clara. Whales Work Together, 1 vol. 2017. (Animal Teamwork Ser.). (ENG.). 24p. (J). (gr. 3-3). 25.27 (978-1-5081-5544-7(5), b044088f-0777-4766-88ce-0fe0785b3e86, PowerKids Pr.) Rosen Publishing Group, Inc., The.
Cooper, Jason. Great Whale. 2003. (Life Cycles II Ser.). (Illus.). 24p. (J). 25.64 (978-1-58952-709-6(7)) Rourke Educational Media.
Coughlan, Billy. Not Without My Whale. Karabatzia, Villie, illus. 2019. (Early Bird Readers — Green (Early Bird Stories (tm)) Ser.). (ENG.). 32p. (J). (gr. k-3). 30.65 (978-1-5415-4204-4(5), 8f981220-0b58-4e5f-9c0b-823a7ebf46de); pap. 9.99 (978-1-5415-7409-0(5), 31c2d9b7-aeb3-47e4-8c7a-058f9da6326c) Lerner Publishing Group. (Lerner Pubns.).
Davidson, Susanna. Whales & Dolphins: Internet-Linked. 2009. (Discovery Nature Ser.). 48p. (YA). (gr. 3-18). 8.99 (978-0-7945-2376-3(5), Usborne) EDC Publishing.
Davidson, Susannah. Whales & Dolphins. 2004. (Discovery Program Ser.). (Illus.). 48p. (J). lib. bdg. 16.95 (978-1-58086-478-7(3)) EDC Publishing.
Davidson, Susannah, et al. Whales & Dolphins. Woodcock, John, illus. 2003. (Usborne Discovery Ser.). 48p. (J). pap. (978-0-439-57780-9(2)); pap. (978-0-439-56060-3(8)) Scholastic, Inc.
Davies, Nicola. Big Blue Whale. Maland, Nick, illus. 2015. 32p. pap. 7.00 (978-1-61003-542-2(9)) Center for the Collaborative Classroom.
—Big Blue Whale with Audio: Read, Listen & Wonder. Maland, Nick, illus. 2008. (Read, Listen, & Wonder Ser.). (ENG.). 32p. (J). (gr. -1-3). pap. 8.99 (978-0-7636-3822-1(6)) Candlewick Pr.
Desmond, Jenni, creator. The Blue Whale. 2015. (Illus.). 48p. (J). (gr. -1-4). 17.95 (978-1-59270-165-0(5)) Enchanted Lion Bks., LLC.
Drumlin, Sam. Orcas, 1 vol. 2013. (PowerKids Readers: Sea Friends Ser.). (ENG., Illus.). 24p. (J). (gr. k-k). pap. 9.25 (978-1-4488-9748-3(3), 9c9fa7ca-7731-44b6-a4d4-7b95ad34b819); lib. bdg. 26.27 (978-1-4488-9645-5(2), 179d669a-7e12-43f4-a755-2fd3e3edc307) Rosen Publishing Group, Inc., The. (PowerKids Pr.).
—Orcas: Las Orcas, 1 vol. Alamán, Eduardo, tr. 2013. (PowerKids Readers: Los Amigos Del Mar / Sea Friends Ser.). (SPA & ENG., Illus.). 24p. (J). (gr. k-k). lib. bdg. 26.27 (978-1-4488-9975-3(3), f6da1596-456e-4060-95cc-765850f8a552, PowerKids Pr.) Rosen Publishing Group, Inc., The.
Dunn, Joeming & Denham, Brian. Shamu: The 1st Killer Whale in Captivity, 1 vol. 2011. (Famous Firsts: Animals Making History Ser.). (ENG., Illus.). 32p. (J). (gr. 3-8). 32.79 (978-1-61641-642-3(4), 1332269, Graphic Planet - Fiction) Magic Wagon.
Einstein, Erin. Whales & Dolphins of Canada, 1 vol. 2014. (KidsWorld Ser.). (ENG., Illus.). 64p. (J). pap. 6.99 (978-0-9938401-5-9(9), 435f211e-3a5b-498a-b0a8-24a13369b3cd) KidsWorld Bks. CAN. Dist: Lone Pine Publishing USA.
Fact Atlas: Dolphins & Whales. 2009. (FACT ATLAS Ser.). 72p. (J). 14.95 (978-0-8437-1865-2(X)) Hammond World Atlas Corp.
Furgang, Kathy. Beluga Whales, 1 vol. 2019. (Life at the Poles Ser.). (ENG.). 24p. (gr. 2-2). pap. 10.35 (978-1-9785-1205-4(8), 4c44ee71-a3d5-42dc-a9dc-e3f63b341b14) Enslow Publishing, LLC.
Geistdoerfer, Patrick. Las Ballenas y Otros Mamíferos Marinos / Whales & Other Sea Mammals. Boucher, Joelle, illus.

2018. (Altea Benjamin Ser.). (SPA.). 32p. (J). (gr. 3-7). pap. 10.99 *(978-1-947783-60-7(2),* Altea) Penguin Random House Grupo Editorial ESP. Dist: Penguin Random Hse. LLC.

Gilkerson, Patricia. My Adventure with Whales. 2009. (ENG.). 44p. (J). 8.99 *(978-1-59092-475-4(4))* Blue Forge Pr.

Gill, Shelley. If I Were a Whale. Brooks, Erik, illus. 2017. (If I Were Ser.). 22p. (J). (— 1). bds. 10.99 *(978-1-63217-104-7(X),* Little Bigfoot) Sasquatch Bks.

Gish, Ashley. Blue Whales. 2019. (X-Books: Marine Mammals Ser.). (ENG.). 32p. (J). (gr. 3-5). pap. 9.99 *(978-1-62832-751-9(0),* 19205, Creative Paperbacks) Creative Co., The.

Gish, Melissa. Killer Whales. (X-Books: Predators Ser.). (ENG.). (J). 2017. Illus.). 32p. (gr. 3-6). *(978-1-60818-818-5(3),* 20387, Creative Education) 2010. 48p. (gr. 5-8). 23.95 *(978-1-58341-971-7(3),* 22184, Creative Education) 2010. 48p. (gr. 5-8). pap. 12.00 *(978-0-89812-554-2(5),* 22209, Creative Paperbacks) Creative Co., The.

—Living Wild: Whales. 2012. (Living Wild Ser.). (ENG., Illus.). 48p. (J). (gr. 4-7). pap. 12.00 *(978-0-89812-676-1(2),* 22214, Creative Paperbacks) Creative Co., The.

—Whales. 2011. (Living Wild Ser.). (ENG., Illus.). 48p. (J). (gr. 5-8). 35.65 *(978-1-60818-084-4(0),* 22199, Creative Education) Creative Co., The.

—X-Books: Killer Whales. 2017. (X-Bks.). (ENG., Illus.). 32p. (J). (gr. 3-7). pap. 9.99 *(978-1-62832-421-1(X),* 20388, Creative Paperbacks) Creative Co., The.

Green, Jen. Whales. 2008. (Nature's Children Ser.). (Illus.). 52p. *(978-0-7172-6264-9(2))* Grolier, Ltd.

Greenberg, Daniel A. Whales, 1 vol. 2003. (Animal Ways Ser.). (ENG., Illus.). 112p. (gr. 6-6). 38.36 *(978-0-7614-1389-9(8),* 31f31c5d-64eb-4977-a6a0-dec65fe4f52c) Cavendish Square Publishing LLC.

Greenberg, Daniel A. & Hess, Nina. Whales, 1 vol. 2010. (Animals Ser.). (ENG.). 24p. (gr. 3-3). 26.93 *(978-0-7614-4346-9(0),* 3b845a97-a2e3-4682-bb4b-71cc4453fb81) Cavendish Square Publishing LLC.

Gunderson, Megan M. Beluga Whales, 1 vol. 2010. (Whales Ser.). (ENG.). 24p. (J). (gr. 3-6). 31.36 *(978-1-61613-446-4(1),* 15267, Checkerboard Library) ABDO Publishing Co.

—Blue Whales, 1 vol. 2010. (Whales Ser.). (ENG., Illus.). 24p. (J). (gr. 3-6). 31.36 *(978-1-61613-447-1(X),* 1315320, Checkerboard Library) ABDO Publishing Co.

—Gray Whales, 1 vol. 2010. (Whales Ser.). (ENG., Illus.). 24p. (J). (gr. 3-6). 31.36 *(978-1-61613-448-8(8),* 1315321, Checkerboard Library) ABDO Publishing Co.

—Humpback Whales, 1 vol. 2010. (Whales Ser.). (ENG.). 24p. (J). (gr. 3-6). 31.36 *(978-1-61613-449-5(6),* 15273, Checkerboard Library) ABDO Publishing Co.

—Killer Whales, 1 vol. 2010. (Whales Ser.). (ENG.). 24p. (J). (gr. 3-6). 31.36 *(978-1-61613-450-1(X),* 15275, Checkerboard Library) ABDO Publishing Co.

—Sperm Whales, 1 vol. 2010. (Whales Ser.). (ENG.). 24p. (J). (gr. 3-6). 31.36 *(978-1-61613-451-8(8),* 15277, Checkerboard Library) ABDO Publishing Co.

Gustafson, Sarah. Whales, Dolphins, & More Marine Mammals. 2005. (Illus.). 48p. (J). pap. *(978-0-439-71189-0(4))* Scholastic, Inc.

Halfmann, Janet. Narwhal: The Unicorn of the Sea. Petruccio, Steven James, illus. 2008. (ENG.). 32p. (J). (gr. -1-2). 19.95 *(978-1-59249-872-7(8))* Soundprints.

—Narwhal: Unicorn of the Sea. Petruccio, Steven James, illus. 2008. (ENG.). 32p. (J). (gr. -1-2). pap. 9.95 *(978-1-59249-871-0(X))* Soundprints.

Haney, Johannah. Whales, 1 vol. 2009. (Endangered! Ser.). (ENG.). 48p. (gr. 3-3). lib. bdg. 32.64 *(978-0-7614-2990-6(5),* 0b87e2a0-ccb1-4e77-95af-6aac0e997680) Cavendish Square Publishing LLC.

Hansen, Grace. Ballenas (Whales), 1 vol. 2016. (Vida en el Océano (Ocean Life) Ser.). (SPA., Illus.). 24p. (J). (gr. -1-2). lib. bdg. 32.79 *(978-1-68080-750-9(1),* 22662, Abdo Kids) ABDO Publishing Co.

—Blue Whales, 1 vol. 2016. (Super Species Ser.). (ENG., Illus.). 24p. (J). (gr. -1-2). lib. bdg. 32.79 *(978-1-68080-542-0(8),* 21364, Abdo Kids) ABDO Publishing Co.

—Humpback Whale Migration. 2017. (Animal Migration Ser.). (ENG., Illus.). 24p. (J). (gr. -1-2). lib. bdg. 32.79 *(978-1-5321-0028-4(0),* 25136, Abdo Kids) ABDO Publishing Co.

—Whales, 1 vol. 2015. (Ocean Life Ser.). (ENG.). 24p. (J). (gr. -1-2). lib. bdg. 32.79 *(978-1-62970-713-6(9),* 17225, Abdo Kids) ABDO Publishing Co.

—Whales. 2017. (Ocean Life Ser.). (ENG.). 24p. (J). (gr. -1-2). pap. 7.95 *(978-1-4966-1257-1(4),* 135005, Capstone Classroom) Capstone.

Hardyman, Robyn. Whales. 2008. (World of Animals Ser.). (ENG.). 32p. (J). (gr. 2-4). 31.35 *(978-1-933834-34-4(X),* 16827) Brown Bear Bks.

Harris, Caroline. Discover Science: Whales & Dolphins. 2012. (Discover Science Ser.). (ENG., Illus.). 56p. (J). (gr. 1-3). pap. 22.44 *(978-0-7534-6716-9(X),* 9780753467169) Kingfisher Publications, plc GBR. Dist: Children's Plus, Inc.

Herriges, Ann. Whales. 2006. (Oceans Alive Ser.). (ENG., Illus.). 24p. (J). (gr. k-3). lib. bdg. 26.95 *(978-1-60014-023-5(8))* Bellwether Media.

Hirsch, Rebecca E. Humpback Whales: Musical Migrating Mammals. 2015. (Comparing Animal Traits Ser.). (ENG., Illus.). 32p. (gr. 2-4). 39.99 *(978-1-4677-8925-7(9),* Lerner Digital); (J). lib. bdg. 26.65 *(978-1-4677-5579-5(6),* 93a38a0e-168b-4fc6-aace-d2e3f7a14801, Lerner Pubns.) Lerner Publishing Group.

Hodson, Sally. Granny's Clan: A Tale of Wild Orcas. Jones, Ann, illus. 2012. 32p. (J). (gr. k-4). pap. 8.99 *(978-1-58469-172-3(7),* Dawn Pubns.) Sourcebooks, Inc.

—Granny's Clan: A Tale of Wild Orcas. Jones, Ann, illus. 2012. (ENG.). 32p. (J). (gr. 1-4). 24.94 *(978-1-58469-171-6(9))* Take Heart Pubns.

Hoyt, Erich. Whale Rescue: Changing the Future for Endangered Wildlife. 2005. (Firefly Animal Rescue Ser.). (ENG., Illus.). 64p. (J). (gr. 5-8). 19.95 *(978-1-55297-601-2(7),* 94c7ea98-0753-45fd-bc61-5899a1757dd0); pap. 9.95 *(978-1-55297-600-5(9),* bf5cb8f6-3a29-4fb0-b8bf-28c7119d92d5) Firefly Bks., Ltd.

Idzikowski, Lisa. How Whales Grow Up, 1 vol. 2018. (Animals Growing Up Ser.). (ENG.). 24p. (gr. 1-2). 24.27 *(978-0-7660-9663-9(7),* a617ff87-07f8-4f72-bfd6-0e5f28f191b9) Enslow Publishing, LLC.

Imbriaco, Alison. The Sperm Whale: Help Save This Endangered Species!, 1 vol. 2008. (Saving Endangered Species Ser.). (ENG., Illus.). 128p. (gr. 6-7). lib. bdg. 37.27 *(978-1-59845-071-2(9),* 62ab9d09-76ce-4951-a6db-5df2276922d9, MyReportLinks.com Bks.) Enslow Publishing, LLC.

Jaycox, Jaclyn. Killer Whales Are Awesome. 2019. (Polar Animals Ser.). (ENG., Illus.). 32p. (J). (gr. -1-2). 27.99 *(978-1-9771-0816-6(4),* 140444, Pebble) Capstone.

—Narwhals Are Awesome. 2019. (Polar Animals Ser.). (ENG., Illus.). 32p. (J). (gr. -1-2). pap. 7.95 *(978-1-9771-0997-2(7),* 140940, Pebble) Capstone.

Johnson, Elizabeth R. Beluga Whales. 2016. (Sea Life Ser.). (ENG., Illus.). 24p. (J). (gr. -1-2). lib. bdg. 27.32 *(978-1-5157-2081-2(0),* 132683, Capstone Pr.) Capstone.

—Orcas. 2017. (J). *(978-1-5157-2083-6(7))* Capstone.

Jones, Michael P. Whales — The Gentle Giants: Calendar 1988. (Illus.). (J). 10.00 *(978-0-89904-211-4(2));* 25.00 *(978-0-89904-213-8(9))* Crumb Elbow Publishing.

Jones, Tracy. Whales & Dolphins. 2011. (Illus.). 16p. (J). *(978-0-545-24793-1(4))* Scholastic, Inc.

Kalman, Bobbie. Wonderful Whales. 2005. (Living Ocean Ser.). (ENG., Illus.). 32p. (J). (gr. 3-4). lib. bdg. *(978-0-7787-1302-9(4))* Crabtree Publishing Co.

Kalman, Bobbie & Thal, Karuna. Les Rorquals. 2005. (Petit Monde Vivant Ser.). (FRE., Illus.). 32p. (J). pap. 9.95 *(978-2-89579-049-5(3))* Bayard Canada Livres CAN. Dist: Crabtree Publishing Co.

Kant, Tanya. The Migration of a Whale. Bergin, Mark, illus. 2008. (Amaze Ser.). (ENG.). 32p. (J). (gr. k-3). 27.00 *(978-0-531-24049-6(5));* pap. 8.95 *(978-0-531-23803-5(2))* Scholastic Library Publishing. (Children's Pr.).

Karpik, Joanasie. Animals Illustrated: Bowhead Whale, 1 vol. Uehara, Sho, illus. 2018. (Animals Illustrated Ser.: 5). (ENG.). 28p. (J). (gr. 1-3). 12.95 *(978-1-77227-162-1(4))* Inhabit Media Inc. CAN. Dist: Consortium Bk. Sales & Distribution.

Kennedy, Paul E. Fun with Whales Stencils. 2008. (Dover Stencils Ser.). (ENG., Illus.). (J). (gr. -1-5). pap. 1.50 *(978-0-486-46687-3(6))* Dover Pubns., Inc.

Kennington, Tammy. Beluga Whales. 2014. (21st Century Skills Library: Exploring Our Oceans Ser.). (ENG., Illus.). 32p. (J). (gr. 3-6). 32.07 *(978-1-62431-603-6(4),* 203196) Cherry Lake Publishing.

Kerrod, Robin. Exploring Nature: Whales & Dolphins. 2014. (ENG., Illus.). 64p. (J). (gr. 3-7). 12.99 *(978-1-84322-912-4(9),* Armadillo) Anness Publishing GBR. Dist: National Bk. Network.

—Whales & Dolphins. 2008. (Nature Watch Ser.). (Illus.). 64p. (J). (gr. 4-7). 14.99 *(978-0-7548-1875-5(6))* Anness Publishing GBR. Dist: National Bk. Network.

Killer Whales, 6 bks. 2005. (Animal Predators Ser.). (Illus.). 40p. (J). (gr. 3-6). pap. 46.95 *(978-0-8225-5492-9(5))* Lerner Publishing Group.

Kinder, Cando. Birth of Whale Read-Along. (J). 7.95 incl. audio *(978-0-8136-0649-1(7))* Modern Curriculum Pr.

King, Zelda. Orcas. (Illus.). 24p. (J). 2012. 49.50 *(978-1-4488-5146-1(7),* PowerKids Pr.) 2011. (ENG., (gr. 2-3). pap. 9.25 *(978-1-4488-5145-4(9),* b71f157c-e4f7-4925-a027-85c51ff040ad, PowerKids Pr.) 2011. (ENG., (gr. 2-3). lib. bdg. 26.27 *(978-1-4488-5335-9(4),* 38e81d71-5af2-46e5-97a5-9f6a37d8f723) Rosen Publishing Group, Inc., The.

Kissock, Heather. Orcas. 2017. (Illus.). 24p. (J). *(978-1-5105-0593-3(8))* SmartBook Media, Inc.

Klepeis, Alicia Z. Orcas on the Hunt. 2017. (Searchlight Books (tm) — Predators Ser.). (ENG., Illus.). 32p. (J). (gr. 3-5). lib. bdg. 30.65 *(978-1-5124-3398-2(5),* 14e49824-8d59-4cfc-a9dd-84dbda627270, Lerner Pubns.) Lerner Publishing Group.

Kluth, Paula & Schwarz, Patrick. Pedro's Whale, 1 vol. 2010. (Illus.). 32p. (J). 18.95 *(978-1-59857-160-8(5))* Brookes Publishing.

Krajnik, Elizabeth. Orcas, 1 vol. 2019. (Killers of the Animal Kingdom Ser.). (ENG.). 24p. (gr. 3-3). pap. 9.25 *(978-1-7253-0617-2(4),* eb286b77-9173-402d-b50d-a6322c062105, PowerKids Pr.) Rosen Publishing Group, Inc., The.

Kratt, Chris & Kratt, Martin. Wild Sea Creatures: Sharks, Whales & Dolphins! (Wild Kratts) 2014. (Step into Reading Ser.). (Illus.). 32p. (J). (gr. -1-1). 5.99 *(978-0-553-49901-8(7),* Random Hse. Bks. for Young Readers) Random Hse. Children's Bks.

Lajiness, Katie. Humpback Whales: Super Singers. 2018. (Awesome Animal Powers Ser.). (ENG., Illus.). 32p. (J). (gr. 2-5). lib. bdg. 34.21 *(978-1-5321-1500-4(8),* 28854, Big Buddy Bks.) ABDO Publishing Co.

Landau, Elaine. Beluga Whales: Animals of the Snow & Ice, 1 vol. 2010. (Animals of the Snow & Ice Ser.). (ENG., Illus.). 32p. (gr. 3-3). lib. bdg. 26.60 *(978-0-7660-3459-4(3),* 64ee8369-2619-4439-a1e4-f0aca04c55c3) Enslow Publishing, LLC.

Laughlin, Kara L. Whales. 2017. (In the Deep Blue Sea Ser.). (ENG.). 24p. (J). (gr. k-3). lib. bdg. 32.79 *(978-1-5038-1695-4(8),* 211529) Child's World, Inc, The.

Leaf, Christina. Humpback Whales. 2016. (Ocean Life up Close Ser.). (ENG., Illus.). 24p. (J). (gr. k-3). 26.95 *(978-1-62617-417-7(2));* pap. 7.99 *(978-1-61891-265-7(8),* 12055) Bellwether Media. (Blastoff! Readers).

—Narwhal. 2014. (Extremely Weird Animals Ser.). (ENG., Illus.). 24p. (J). (gr. 3-8). lib. bdg. 27.95 *(978-1-62617-075-9(4),* Pilot Bks.) Bellwether Media.

Lee, Justin. How to Draw Whales. 2009. (Kid's Guide to Drawing Ser.). 24p. (gr. 3-3). 47.90 *(978-1-61511-042-1(9),* PowerKids Pr.) Rosen Publishing Group, Inc., The.

Leon, Vicki. A Pod of Killer Whales: The Mysterious Life of the Intelligent Orca. Foott, Jeff, photos by. 2nd ed. 2006. (Jean-Michel Cousteau Presents Ser.). (ENG., Illus.). 48p. (J). (gr. 4-9). pap. 9.95 *(978-0-9766134-7-3(6))* London Town Pr.

Lindeen, Carol K. & Lugtu, Carol J. Whales [Scholastic]. 2010. (Under the Sea Ser.). 24p. pap. 0.50 *(978-1-4296-5065-6(6),* Capstone Pr.) Capstone.

Lindsey, Marta. Little Gray's Great Migration, 1 vol. Gabriel, Andrea, illus. 2015. (ENG.). 32p. (J). (gr. k-3). 17.95 *(978-1-62855-452-6(5))* Arbordale Publishing.

Little & Large Sticker Activity Whales & Dolphins. 2008. 24p. pap. *(978-1-84810-064-0(7))* Miles Kelly Publishing, Ltd.

Lourie, Peter. Whaling Season: A Year in the Life of an Arctic Whale Scientist. 2015. (Scientists in the Field Ser.). (ENG., Illus.). 80p. (J). (gr. 5-7). pap. 9.99 *(978-0-544-58241-5(1),* 1613670, Clarion Bks.) HarperCollins Pubs.

Lunde, Darrin. Hello, Baby Beluga. Wynne, Patricia J., illus. (ENG.). (J). 2016. 14p. (— 1). bds. 7.99 *(978-1-58089-525-5(5))* 2011. 32p. (gr. -1-2). pap. 6.95 *(978-1-57091-740-0(X))* Charlesbridge Publishing, Inc.

Lunis, Natalie. Humpback Whale: The Singer. 2011. (Animal Loudmouths: Noisy Animals Ser.). 24p. (YA). (gr. k-3). lib. bdg. 26.99 *(978-1-61772-280-6(4))* Bearport Publishing Co., Inc.

—Killer Whale: The World's Largest Dolphin. 2010. (More SuperSized! Ser.). (Illus.). 24p. (J). (gr. k-3). lib. bdg. 26.99 *(978-1-936087-27-3(8))* Bearport Publishing Co., Inc.

MacIntire, Francis. Jumbo Blue Whales, 1 vol. 2017. (Great Big Animals Ser.). (ENG.). 24p. (J). (gr. k-k). pap. 9.15 *(978-1-5382-0907-3(1),* 3d83fdc0-cc4c-4b08-baf4-bc42b958e811) Stevens, Gareth Publishing LLLP.

MacMillan, Dianne M. Humpback Whales. 2003. (Nature Watch Ser.). (ENG., Illus.). 48p. (J). (gr. 4-8). 27.93 *(978-1-57505-347-9(0))* Lerner Publishing Group.

Malam, John. Killer Whales. 2008. (Scary Creatures Ser.). (ENG., Illus.). 32p. (J). (gr. 2-7). 27.00 *(978-0-531-20447-4(2))* Scholastic Library Publishing.

—Scary Creatures: Killer Whale. 2008. (Scary Creatures Ser.). (ENG., Illus.). 32p. (J). (gr. 2-7). pap. 8.95 *(978-0-531-21006-2(5),* Watts, Franklin) Scholastic Library Publishing.

Mann, Dionna L. Orcas (Nature's Children) (Library Edition) 2019. (Nature's Children, Fourth Ser.). (ENG., Illus.). 48p. (J). (gr. 3-5). lib. bdg. 30.00 *(978-0-531-12718-6(4),* Children's Pr.) Scholastic Library Publishing.

Markle, Sandra. Killer Whales. 2005. (Animal Predators Ser.). (Illus.). 40p. (J). (gr. 4-6). pap. 7.95 *(978-1-57505-743-9(3))* Lerner Publishing Group.

—Ranger Rick: I Wish I Was an Orca. 2017. (I Can Read Level 1 Ser.). (ENG., Illus.). 32p. (J). (gr. -1-3). 16.99 *(978-0-06-243208-7(7),* HarperCollins) HarperCollins Pubs.

—Ranger Rick: I Wish I Was an Orca. 2017. (I Can Read Level 1 Ser.). (ENG., Illus.). 32p. (J). (gr. -1-3). pap. 4.99 *(978-0-06-243207-0(9),* HarperCollins) HarperCollins Pubs.

Marsh, Laura. National Geographic Readers: Great Migrations Whales. 2010. (Readers Ser.). (Illus.). 48p. (J). (gr. 3-7). (ENG.). 14.90 *(978-1-4263-0746-1(2));* pap. 4.99 *(978-1-4263-0745-4(4))* Disney Publishing Worldwide. (National Geographic Kids).

Marsico, Katie. Narwhal, 1 vol. 2011. (Day in the Life: Polar Animals Ser.). (ENG.). 24p. (J). (gr. k-2). pap. 6.79 *(978-1-4329-5339-3(7),* 116049, Heinemann) Capstone.

McAneney, Caitie. Blue Whale: The Largest Marine Mammal, 1 vol. 2019. (Animal Record Breakers Ser.). (ENG.). 24p. (gr. 2-3). pap. 9.25 *(978-1-7253-0862-6(2),* 7b92fe7c-4e27-4265-aab1-c7deb9aca76d, PowerKids Pr.) Rosen Publishing Group, Inc., The.

McDowell, Pamela. Manta Rays. 2014. (J). *(978-1-4896-1074-4(X))* Weigl Pubs., Inc.

McNeill, Michele Babineau. Whales. 2008. (Illus.). 32p. (J). *(978-0-545-08465-9(2))* Scholastic, Inc.

Meachen Rau, Dana. Adivina Quien Caza / Guess Who Hunts, 1 vol. 2010. (Adivina Quién / Guess Who? Ser.). (ENG & SPA.). 32p. (gr. k-2). 25.50 *(978-0-7614-3486-3(0),* 132d9597-ef03-484e-9c0b-32337d0bb8de) Cavendish Square Publishing LLC.

—Adivina Quien Caza (Guess Who Hunts), 1 vol. 2010. (Adivina Quién (Guess Who?) Ser.). (SPA.). 32p. (gr. k-2). lib. bdg. 25.50 *(978-0-7614-3461-0(5),* fbd402d3-57fe-4d46-a29e-44b9baa6c315) Cavendish Square Publishing LLC.

—La Ballena en el Océano (the Whale in the Water), 1 vol. 2008. (Naturaleza (Nature) Ser.). (SPA., Illus.). 24p. (gr. k-1). lib. bdg. 25.50 *(978-0-7614-2412-3(1),* 30e98702-8486-46eb-90bd-fb5a8a0df021) Cavendish Square Publishing LLC.

—Guess Who Hunts, 1 vol. 2009. (Guess Who? Ser.). (ENG.). 32p. (gr. k-1). pap. 9.23 *(978-0-7614-3562-4(X),* f8ef0d53-4f3d-4093-8282-acc8cf6f5028); lib. bdg. 25.50 *(978-0-7614-2907-4(7),* 19f9df62-bd09-4218-b641-fe6bf1782640) Cavendish Square Publishing LLC.

—The Whale in the Water, 1 vol. 2007. (Nature Ser.). (ENG., Illus.). 24p. (gr. k-1). lib. bdg. 25.50 *(978-0-7614-2307-2(9),* dfc0c4d8-4bd6-4289-bbd2-4592fb5ffdb1, Cavendish Square) Cavendish Square Publishing LLC.

Meister, Cari. Do You Really Want to Meet an Orca? Fabbri, Daniele, illus. 2016. (Do You Really Want to Meet ... ? Ser.). (ENG.). 24p. (J). (gr. 1-4). pap. 8.99 *(978-1-68152-118-3(0),* 15599); lib. bdg. 20.95 *(978-1-60753-947-6(0),* 15593) Amicus.

—Whales. 2012. (Illus.). 24p. (J). lib. bdg. 25.65 *(978-1-62031-009-0(0))* Jump! Inc.

Miettunen, Anita. Big Blue Forever: The Story of Canada's Largest Blue Whale Skeleton, 1 vol. 2017. (ENG., Illus.). 64p. (J). (gr. 4-8). 24.95 *(978-0-88995-542-4(5),* 3600583b-4458-4a48-9715-0394a623fff9) Trifolium Bks., Inc. CAN. Dist: Firefly Bks., Ltd.

Miller, Sara Swan. Whales of the Arctic. 2009. (Brrr! Polar Animals Ser.). 24p. (gr. 2-3). 42.50 *(978-1-61511-760-4(1),* PowerKids Pr.); (ENG.). (J). lib. bdg. 26.27 *(978-1-4358-2743-1(0),* 87e7ee32-261d-4342-8f1e-f2362e4f228d); (ENG., Illus.). (J). pap. 9.25 *(978-1-4358-3147-6(0),* 8e24246d-b65c-4ce3-887d-8e7d66275c95, PowerKids Pr.) Rosen Publishing Group, Inc., The.

Miller-Schroeder, Patricia. Blue Whales. 2013. (Illus.). 48p. (J). *(978-1-61913-423-2(3))* Weigl Pubs., Inc.

—Blue Whales, with Code. 2012. (Animals on the Brink Ser.). (ENG., Illus.). 48p. (J). (gr. 5-9). pap. 14.95 *(978-1-61913-424-9(1),* AV2 by Weigl) Weigl Pubs., Inc.

Morgan, Sally. Whales. 2015. (Animal Lives Ser.). (ENG., Illus.). 24p. (J). (gr. 3-5). 23.99 *(978-1-939581-86-0(9),* 86dba210-67d7-40f7-8abc-f2dce9d90174) QEB Publishing Inc.

Morgan, Sally & Teacher Created Resources Staff. Whales. 2006. (Animal Lives Ser.). (ENG., Illus.). 32p. (gr. -1-3). pap. 7.99 *(978-1-4206-8157-4(5))* Teacher Created Resources, Inc.

Murray, Julie. Beluga Whales. 2019. (Animal Kingdom Ser.). (ENG.). 32p. (J). (gr. 2-5). lib. bdg. 34.21 *(978-1-5321-1616-2(0),* 32343, Big Buddy Bks.) ABDO Publishing Co.

—Blue Whales. 2019. (Animal Kingdom Ser.). (ENG., Illus.). 32p. (J). (gr. 2-5). lib. bdg. 34.21 *(978-1-5321-1619-3(5),* 32349, Big Buddy Bks.) ABDO Publishing Co.

—Humpback Whales. 2019. (Animal Kingdom Ser.). (ENG.). 32p. (J). (gr. 2-5). lib. bdg. 34.21 *(978-1-5321-1638-4(1),* 32387, Big Buddy Bks.) ABDO Publishing Co.

—Orca Whale Pod. 2018. (Animal Groups (Abdo Kids Junior) Ser.). (ENG., Illus.). 24p. (J). (gr. -1-2). lib. bdg. 31.36 *(978-1-5321-0783-2(8),* 28127, Abdo Kids) ABDO Publishing Co.

Nagelhout, Ryan. Whales, 1 vol. 2013. (Underwater World Ser.). (ENG., Illus.). 24p. (J). (gr. k-k). pap. 9.15 *(978-1-4339-8583-6(7),* 30e5d687-ed95-42bb-9b9a-f0904a477332); lib. bdg. 25.27 *(978-1-4339-8582-9(9),* bb20c4c6-2bcb-47d8-861c-986c594107de) Stevens, Gareth Publishing LLLP.

—Whales / Ballenas, 1 vol. 2013. (Underwater World / el Mundo Submarino Ser.). (SPA & ENG., Illus.). 24p. (J). (gr. k-k). lib. bdg. 25.27 *(978-1-4339-8788-5(0),* 7523670d-fd27-43f3-9c71-3d8ca2c7a908) Stevens, Gareth Publishing LLLP.

Nicklin, Linda & Nicklin, Flip. Face to Face with Whales. 2010. (Face to Face with Animals Ser.). (Illus.). 32p. (J). (gr. 3-7). pap. 6.95 *(978-1-4263-0697-6(0),* National Geographic Kids) Disney Publishing Worldwide.

Nuzzolo, Deborah & Parham, Donna. Whales K-3, 1. 2003. (Illus.). 28p. (J). (gr. k-3). tchr.'s training gde. ed. 5.99 *(978-1-893698-33-8(5),* T15) SeaWorld, Inc.

O'Connell, Jennifer. The Eye of the Whale: A Rescue Story, 1 vol. 2013. (Tilbury House Nature Book Ser.: 0). (ENG., Illus.). 32p. (J). (gr. 1-7). 17.95 *(978-0-88448-335-9(5),* 884335) Tilbury Hse. Pubs.

O'Keefe, Emily. Humpback Whale. 2016. (Back from near Extinction Ser.). (ENG., Illus.). 48p. (J). (gr. 4-8). lib. bdg. 35.64 *(978-1-68078-469-5(2),* 23875) ABDO Publishing Co.

Oldfield, Dawn Bluemel. Killer Whale: Water Bullet! 2010. (Blink of an Eye: Superfast Animals Ser.). 24p. (J). (gr. k-3). lib. bdg. 26.99 *(978-1-936087-92-1(8))* Bearport Publishing Co., Inc.

O'Loughlin, Chloe & Borrowman, Mary. The Rescue of Nanoose, 1 vol. Wang, Jacqueline, illus. 2004. (ENG.). 32p. (J). pap. *(978-1-894898-20-1(6))* TouchWood Editions.

Osborne, Mary Pope & Boyce, Natalie Pope. Narwhals & Other Whales: A Nonfiction Companion to Magic Tree House #33: Narwhal on a Sunny Night. Mones, Isidre, illus. 2020. (Magic Tree House (R) Fact Tracker Ser.: 42). 128p. (J). (gr. 2-5). lib. bdg. 12.99 *(978-1-9848-9321-5(1),* Random Hse. Bks. for Young Readers) Random Hse. Children's Bks.

Owen, Ruth. Beluga Whales, 1 vol. 2013. (Polar Animals: Life in the Freezer Ser.). (ENG., Illus.). 32p. (gr. 2-3). 29.93 *(978-1-4777-0221-5(0),* 2f3f6636-b012-4e6a-ad46-17b201443c2c); pap. 11.00 *(978-1-4777-0229-1(6),* e4b45467-0c60-4011-98af-4f6a53d2320b) Rosen Publishing Group, Inc., The. (Windmill Bks.).

—Blue Whales, 1 vol., 1. 2013. (Dr. Bob's Amazing World of Animals Ser.). (ENG.). 32p. (J). (gr. 2-3). 31.27 *(978-1-4777-9028-1(4),* 9090a58d-4e16-4c69-855d-b716153752f1, Windmill Bks.) Rosen Publishing Group, Inc., The.

—Orca Calves. 2012. (Water Babies Ser.). 24p. (J). (gr. -1-3). lib. bdg. 25.65 *(978-1-61772-600-2(1))* Bearport Publishing Co., Inc.

Paige, Joy. The Blue Whale: World's Largest Mammal. 2009. (Record-Breaking Animals Ser.). 24p. (gr. 1-1). 42.50 *(978-1-60852-437-2(X),* PowerKids Pr.) Rosen Publishing Group, Inc., The.

Pallotta, Jerry. Whale vs. Giant Squid (Who Would Win?) Bolster, Rob, illus. 2016. (Who Would Win? Ser.). (ENG.). 32p. (J). (gr. 1-3). pap. 3.99 *(978-0-545-30173-2(4))* Scholastic, Inc.

—Who Would Win? Killer Whale vs. Great White Shark. Bolster, Rob, illus. 2015. (Who Would Win? Ser.). (ENG.). 32p. (J). (gr. 2-5). pap. 3.99 *(978-0-545-16075-9(8))* Scholastic, Inc.

Parker, Steve. Wales & Dolphins. 2010. (Remarkable Man & Beast Ser.). (Illus.). 48p. (J). (gr. 3-18). lib. bdg. 19.95 *(978-1-4222-1978-2(X))* Mason Crest.

—Whales & Dolphins, 1 vol. 2015. (100 Facts You Should Know Ser.). (ENG., Illus.). 48p. (J). (gr. 4-5). pap. 15.05 *(978-1-4824-3211-4(0),* 8339ce0d-049b-4e05-a568-94c9ca5a0f3a) Stevens, Gareth Publishing LLLP.

Parker, Steve & Dewan, Ted. Inside the Whale & Other Animals. (Illus.). (J). 18.95 *(978-0-590-73869-9(0))* Scholastic, Inc.

Payment, Simone. Saving the Endangered Blue Whale, 1 vol., 1. 2015. (Conservation of Endangered Species Ser.). (ENG., Illus.). 32p. (J). (gr. 2-3). pap. 13.90 *(978-1-5081-0052-2(7),* c3e96b0b-d0d7-47b8-a843-249e00d41efc, Britannica Educational Publishing) Rosen Publishing Group, Inc., The.

Ploch, Melissa. Amazing Animals: Wild Whales: Addition & Subtraction (Grade 3) 2017. (Mathematics in the Real World Ser.). (ENG., Illus.). 32p. (J). (gr. 3-4). pap. 11.99 *(978-1-4807-5795-0(0))* Teacher Created Materials, Inc.

Portman, Michael. Whales in Danger, 1 vol. 2011. (Animals at Risk Ser.). (ENG., Illus.). 24p. (J). (gr. 2-3). 25.27 *(978-1-4339-5814-4(7),* 50d7b480-d9b7-48fd-9e1f-84442dedea57); pap. 9.15 *(978-1-4339-5816-8(3),*

054b2f30-44d6-4c5f-ad63-77df65d12390) Stevens, Gareth Publishing LLLP. (Gareth Stevens Learning Library).
ringle, Laurence. Whales! Strange & Wonderful. Henderson, Meryl Learnihan, illus. 2012. (Strange & Wonderful Ser.). (ENG.). 32p. (J). (gr. 2-5). pap. 9.95 *(978-1-59078-917-9(2),* Astra Young Readers) Astra Publishing Hse.
aatma, Lucia. A Pod of Whales. 2019. (Animal Groups Ser.). (ENG., Illus.). 24p. (J). (gr. -1-2). pap. 6.95 *(978-1-9771-1048-0(7),* 141124); lib. bdg. 27.32 *(978-1-9771-0952-1(7),* 140550) Capstone. (Pebble).
aff, Courtney Granet. Giant of the Sea: The Story of a Sperm Whale. Gould, Shawn, illus. 2005. (Smithsonian Oceanic Collection). (ENG.). 32p. (J). (gr. -1-2). 15.95 *(978-1-931465-71-7(1),* B4023) Soundprints.
ake, Jody Sullivan. Beluga Whales up Close [Scholastic]. 2011. (Whales & Dolphins up Close Ser.). 24p. pap. 0.50 *(978-1-4296-6322-9(7),* Capstone Pr.) Capstone.
—Blue Whales up Close [Scholastic]. 2011. (Whales & Dolphins up Close Ser.). 24p. pap. 0.50 *(978-1-4296-6324-3(3),* Capstone Pr.) Capstone.
—Killer Whales up Close [Scholastic]. 2011. (Whales & Dolphins up Close Ser.). 24p. pap. 0.50 *(978-1-4296-6323-6(5),* Capstone Pr.) Capstone.
Rao, Lisa. Whales. 2008. (Smart Animals! Ser.). (Illus.). 32p. (J). (gr. 2-5). lib. bdg. 28.50 *(978-1-59716-579-2(4))* Bearport Publishing Co., Inc.
Read, Nicholas. A Whale's World, 1 vol. McAllister, Ian, photos by. 2018. (My Great Bear Rainforest Ser.: 4). (ENG., Illus.). 32p. (J). (gr. 1-3). 19.95 *(978-1-4598-1273-4(5))* Orca Bk. Pubs. USA.
Read, Tracy C. & Read, Tracy C. Exploring the World of Whales. 2017. (Exploring the World Of Ser.). (ENG., Illus.). 24p. (J). (gr. 3-7). 16.95 *(978-1-77085-948-7(9),* 3b0964da-2d7e-4177-89d5-814fba3384d8); pap. 6.95 *(978-1-77085-949-4(7),* 23eca179-7676-4147-b91b-463748bddba2) Firefly Bks., Ltd.
Reher, Matt. Blue Whale Babies. 2015. (2G Marine Life Ser.). (ENG., Illus.). 24p. (J). pap. 8.00 *(978-1-63437-084-4(8))* American Reading Co.
—Orcas Have to Eat. 2016. (1G Predator Animals Ser.). (ENG., Illus.). 36p. (J). pap. 9.60 *(978-1-63437-102-5(X))* American Reading Co.
Reiter, Chris & Katirgis, Jane. Endangered Blue Whales, 1 vol. 2015. (Wildlife at Risk Ser.). (ENG.). 48p. (J). (gr. 6-6). pap. 12.70 *(978-0-7660-6888-9(9),* 680bc321-599b-4555-b7ba-c85c7cd98bff); (Illus.). 29.60 *(978-0-7660-6890-2(0),* 00e9f3f6-f985-47b8-a750-d0238fe2fd40) Enslow Publishing, LLC.
Riehecky, Janet. Killer Whales: On the Hunt. rev. ed. 2016. (Killer Animals Ser.). (ENG.). 32p. (J). (gr. 3-9). pap. 7.95 *(978-1-5157-6240-9(8),* 135062) Capstone.
Riggs, Kate. Amazing Animals: Whales. 2014. (Amazing Animals Ser.). (ENG., Illus.). 24p. (J). (gr. 1-4). lib. bdg. 7.50 *(978-1-60818-351-7(3),* 21482) Creative Co., The.
—Amazing Animals: Killer Whales. 2012. (Amazing Animals Ser.). (ENG., Illus.). 24p. (J). (gr. 1-3). pap. 9.99 *(978-0-89812-694-5(0),* 23049, Creative Paperbacks) Creative Co., The.
—Amazing Animals: Whales. 2014. (Amazing Animals Ser.). (ENG.). 24p. (J). (gr. 1-3). pap. 9.99 *(978-0-89812-930-4(3),* 21483, Creative Paperbacks) Creative Co., The.
—Killer Whales. (Seedlings Ser.). (ENG., Illus.). 24p. (J). 2017. (gr. -1-k). *(978-1-60818-869-7(8),* 20342) 2012. (gr. 1-4). 25.65 *(978-1-60818-109-4(X),* 23048) Creative Co., The. (Creative Education).
—Seedlings: Killer Whales. 2017. (Seedlings Ser.). (ENG., Illus.). 24p. (J). (gr. -1-1). pap. 9.99 *(978-1-62832-484-6(8),* 20343, Creative Paperbacks) Creative Co., The.
—Seedlings: Whales. 2015. (Seedlings Ser.). (ENG.). 24p. (J). (gr. -1-1). pap. 10.99 *(978-1-62832-117-3(2),* 21262, Creative Paperbacks) Creative Co., The.
—Whales. 2015. (Seedlings Ser.). (ENG.). 24p. (J). (gr. -1-k). *(978-1-60818-517-7(6),* 21261, Creative Education) Creative Co., The.
Ripley's Believe It Or Not!, compiled by. Ripley Twists: Whales & Dolphins. 2014. (Twist Ser.: 11). (ENG., Illus.). 48p. (J). 12.95 *(978-1-60991-114-0(8))* Ripley Entertainment, Inc.
Rose, Simon. Belugas. 2010. (Illus.). 24p. *(978-1-55388-674-7(7));* pap. *(978-1-55388-675-4(5))* Weigl Educational Pubs. Ltd.
Rosenthal, Sue. Whales. McGinty, Mick, illus. 2003. (Magic School Bus Fact Finder Ser.). (ENG.). 96p. (J). pap. 4.99 *(978-0-439-38174-1(6))* Scholastic, Inc.
Roumanis, Alexis. Blue Marlin. 2014. (J). *(978-1-4896-1086-7(3))* Weigl Pubs., Inc.
Rountree, Monica, tr. Ballenas. 2003. (Zoobooks Ser.). Orig. Title: Whales. (SPA., Illus.). 24p. (J). (gr. 1-7). lib. bdg. 15.95 *(978-1-888153-84-2(9))* National Wildlife Federation.
Royston, Angela. Blue Whales. (Amazing Animals Ser.). (Illus.). 24p. (J). 2009. (gr. 2-4). pap. 8.95 *(978-1-60596-149-1(3))* 2009. (gr. 2-4). lib. bdg. 24.45 *(978-1-60596-148-4(5))* 2003. lib. bdg. 21.35 *(978-1-58340-226-9(8))* Weigl Pubs., Inc.
Ruffin, Fran. Whales / Ballenas. 2009. (My World of Animals / Yo y los animales Ser.). (ENG & SPA.). 24p. (gr. 1-1). 37.50 *(978-1-61514-719-9(5),* Editorial Buenas Letras) Rosen Publishing Group, Inc., The.
Ruffin, Frances E. Whales: Ballenas, 1 vol. Beullens, Nathalie, tr. 2003. (My World of Animals / Yo y Los Animales Ser.). (ENG & SPA., Illus.). 24p. (J). (gr. 1-1). lib. bdg. 22.27 *(978-1-4042-7520-1(7),* bdf7cffd-a5f3-48f2-9bf0-32d2539a782f, PowerKids Pr.) Rosen Publishing Group, Inc., The.
Sayre, April Pulley. Here Come the Humpbacks! Hogan, Jamie, illus. 2013. 40p. (J). (gr. -1-3). (ENG.). pap. 7.95 *(978-1-58089-406-7(2));* lib. bdg 17.95 *(978-1-58089-405-0(4))* Charlesbridge Publishing, Inc.
Scherm, Deedra. The Whale & Jonah: A Story of Obedience & Forgiveness. Dreyer, Laura, illus. 2007. (ENG.). 20p. 7.99 *(978-1-934789-00-1(3))* Lemon Vision Productions.
Schuetz, Kari. Humpback Whale Migration. 2018. (Animals on the Move Ser.). (ENG., Illus.). 24p. (J). (gr. k-3). lib. bdg. 26.95 *(978-1-62617-816-8(X),* Blastoff! Readers) Bellwether Media.
Schuh, Mari. It's a Narwhal! 2018. (Bumba Books (r) — Polar Animals Ser.). (ENG., Illus.). 24p. (J). (gr. -1-1). pap. 8.99 *(978-1-5415-2694-5(5),* 876f51ae-5f03-4204-8b62-d844b86caea3); lib. bdg. 26.65 *(978-1-5124-8282-9(X),* 236cfa20-dc4d-47e4-9609-1de10ab706d2, Lerner Pubns.) Lerner Publishing Group.
—It's an Orca! 2018. (Bumba Books (r) — Polar Animals Ser.). (ENG., Illus.). 24p. (J). (gr. -1-1). pap. 8.99 *(978-1-5415-2698-3(8),* 9a034ec5-40b1-46e6-9f47-ca0ccd397817) Lerner Publishing Group.
—Orcas. 2017. (Black & White Animals Ser.). (ENG., Illus.). 24p. (J). (gr. -1-2). lib. bdg. 22.65 *(978-1-5157-3373-7(4),* 133369, Capstone Pr.) Capstone.
—Whales. 2019. (Spot Ocean Animals Ser.). (ENG.). 16p. (J). (gr. -1-2). lib. bdg. *(978-1-68151-635-6(7),* 10767) Amicus.
Sea 3D Whales& Dolphins. 2008. (Illus.). 24p. (J). spiral bd. 19.95 *(978-0-9759629-1-6(4))* ETN, Inc.
Simon, Charnan & Kazunas, Ariel. Killer Whales. 2012. (ENG., Illus.). 48p. (J). lib. bdg. 28.00 *(978-0-531-26834-6(9))* Scholastic Library Publishing.
Simon, Seymour. Penguins. 2007. (Illus.). 32p. (J). (gr. k-4). lib. bdg. 17.89 *(978-0-06-028396-4(3))* HarperCollins Pubs.
Spence, Kelly. Bringing Back the Humpback Whale. 2018. (Animals Back from the Brink Ser.). (Illus.). 32p. (J). (gr. 4-4). *(978-0-7787-4905-9(3))* Crabtree Publishing Co.
Spilsbury, Louise. Save the Humpback Whale, 1 vol., 1. 2013. (Animal SOS! Ser.). (ENG.). 32p. (J). (gr. 2-3). pap. 11.00 *(978-1-4777-6034-5(2),* af34f87a-efdf-4d13-a095-4a041e5cde53, Windmill Bks.) Rosen Publishing Group, Inc., The.
Spilsbury, Richard & Spilsbury, Louise. Dolphin & Whale Pods, 1 vol. 2013. (Animal Armies Ser.). (ENG., Illus.). 32p. (J). (gr. 2-3). pap. 11.00 *(978-1-4777-0332-8(2),* e6c8189f-0bfe-459b-a898-9d38d24899bd); lib. bdg. 28.93 *(978-1-4777-0305-2(5),* 4e49d25a-e183-4752-8fde-23b46539b795) Rosen Publishing Group, Inc., The. (PowerKids Pr.).
Statts, Leo. Beluga Whales. 2016. (Polar Animals Ser.). (ENG.). 24p. (J). (gr. -1-2). 49.94 *(978-1-68079-354-3(3),* 22975, Abdo Zoom-Launch) ABDO Publishing Co.
—Killer Whales. 2016. (Ocean Animals Ser.). (ENG., Illus.). 24p. (J). (gr. -1-2). lib. bdg. 31.36 *(978-1-68079-912-5(6),* 24128, Abdo Zoom-Launch) ABDO Publishing Co.
Stefoff, Rebecca. Whale Sharks. 2015. (Illus.). 48p. (J). pap. *(978-1-62712-955-8(3))* Musa Publishing.
Suen, Anastasia. Orcas. 2020. (Spot Arctic Animals Ser.). (ENG.). 16p. (J). (gr. -1-1). pap. 7.99 *(978-1-68152-524-2(0),* 10723) Amicus.
Szymanski, Jennifer. National Geographic Readers: Whales (PreReader) 2020. (Readers Ser.). (Illus.). 24p. (J). (gr. -1-k). pap. 4.99 *(978-1-4263-3713-0(2));* (ENG., lib. bdg. 14.90 *(978-1-4263-3714-7(0))* Disney Publishing Worldwide. (National Geographic Kids).
The Tale of a White Whale: Digraph wh: Level B, 6 vols. (Wright Skills Ser.). 16p. (gr. k-3). 17.95 *(978-0-322-01474-9(3))* Wright Group/McGraw-Hill.
Taylor, Trace. Whales. 2012. (Marine Life Ser.). (ENG.). 12p. (J). (gr. k-2). pap. 8.00 *(978-1-59301-762-0(6))* American Reading Co.
Taylor, Trace & Sánchez, Lucía M. Ballenas: Whales. 2015. (2G Animales Marinos Ser.). (SPA.). 12p. (J). (gr. k-2). pap. 8.00 *(978-1-61541-280-8(8))* American Reading Co.
Taylor, Trace & Sanchez, Lucia M. Ballenas (Whales) 2011. (poder de 100 - Animales marinos Ser.). 12p. pap. 39.62 *(978-1-61541-281-5(6))* American Reading Co.
Terp, Gail. Killer Whales. 2016. (Wild Animal Kingdom Ser.). (ENG.). 32p. (J). (gr. 4-6). pap. 9.99 *(978-1-64466-170-3(5),* 10397); (Illus.). 31.35 *(978-1-68072-052-5(X),* 10396) Black Rabbit Bks. (Bolt).
—Killer Whales. 2018. (Wild Animal Kingdom Ser.). (ENG., Illus.). 32p. (gr. 2-7). pap. 9.95 *(978-1-68072-309-0(X))* RiverStream Publishing.
Thomas, Isabel. Shark vs. Killer Whale. 2017. (Animal Rivals Ser.). (ENG., Illus.). 24p. (J). (gr. k-2). lib. bdg. 25.99 *(978-1-4846-4071-5(3),* 135682, Heinemann) Capstone.
Thomson, Sarah L. Amazing Whales! (I Can Read Level 2 Ser.). (ENG., Illus.). 32p. (J). (gr. k-3). 2006. pap. 4.99 *(978-0-06-054467-6(8),* HarperCollins) 2005. 15.99 *(978-0-06-054465-2(1))* HarperCollins Pubs.
—Amazing Whales! Wildlife Conservation Society, photos by. 2006. (I Can Read Bks.). (Illus.). (gr. -1-3). 14.00 *(978-0-7569-6665-2(5))* Perfection Learning Corp.
Tracqui, Valérie. The Whale. 2004. (Animal Close-Ups Ser.). (Illus.). 28p. (J). pap. 6.95 *(978-1-57091-625-0(X))* Charlesbridge Publishing, Inc.
Trapped! a Whale's Rescue. 2015. (ENG., Illus.). 32p. (J). (gr. -1-1). lib. bdg. 17.95 *(978-1-58089-558-3(1))* Charlesbridge Publishing, Inc.
Tunby, Benjamin. The Whale's Journey. 2018. (Lightning Bolt Books (r) — Amazing Migrators Ser.). (ENG., Illus.). 24p. (J). (gr. 1-3). pap. 9.99 *(978-1-5415-1184-2(0),* e8ab70ba-7587-494c-9fef-cf3d01fd4d49); lib. bdg. 29.32 *(978-1-5124-8635-3(3),* 8d194249-9510-4d54-8d69-359c2aa32404, Lerner Pubns.) Lerner Publishing Group.
Turnbull, Stephanie. Whale. 2013. (Big Beasts Ser.). (Illus.). 24p. (J). (gr. k-3). 28.50 *(978-1-59920-838-1(5))* Black Rabbit Bks.
Valice, Kim Perez. The Orca Scientists. 2018. (Scientists in the Field Ser.). (ENG., Illus.). 80p. (J). (gr. 5-7). 18.99 *(978-0-544-89826-4(5),* 1653794, Clarion Bks.) HarperCollins Pubs.
Vastola, P. Huge Animals: Learning the Long U Sound. 2009. (PowerPhonics Ser.). 24p. (gr. 1-1). 39.90 *(978-1-60851-445-8(5),* PowerKids Pr.) Rosen Publishing Group, Inc., The.
Weber, Valerie J. Whales / Ballenas, 1 vol. 2008. (Animals That Live in the Ocean / Animales Que Viven en el Océano Ser.). (ENG & SPA.). 24p. (J). (gr. 1-1). lib. bdg. 25.27 *(978-0-8368-9569-8(X),* abd00aaa-37d5-4f85-a775-f8a7ad79666f, Weekly Reader Leveled Readers) Stevens, Gareth Publishing LLLP.
—Whales / Ballenas, 1 vol. 2008. (Animals That Live in the Ocean / Animales Que Viven en el Océano Ser.). (SPA & ENG.). 24p. (gr. 1-1). pap. 9.15 *(978-0-8368-9579-7(7),* 5ed4b476-547a-4ca0-9e72-3bc29d66f8f7, Weekly Reader Leveled Readers) Stevens, Gareth Publishing LLLP.
Weber, Valerie J. & Weber, Valerie J. Whales, 1 vol. 2008. (Animals That Live in the Ocean Ser.). (ENG., Illus.). 24p. (J). (gr. 1-1). lib. bdg. 25.27 *(978-0-8368-9567-4(3),* 62d23f93-cad3-44d7-a5ce-e810e6a55ff7, Weekly Reader Leveled Readers) Stevens, Gareth Publishing LLLP.
Weingarten, E. T. Hunting with Killer Whales, 1 vol., Vol. 1. 2014. (Animal Attack! Ser.). (ENG.). 32p. (J). (gr. 2-3). 25.27 *(978-1-4824-0496-8(6),* bbe543bd-5593-4b36-9d25-933aaa018928) Stevens, Gareth Publishing LLLP.
West, David. Whales & Other Mammals, 1 vol. 2017. (Inside Animals Ser.). (ENG.). 24p. (J). (gr. 3-3). 26.27 *(978-1-5081-9392-0(4),* cf834669-04b1-4c76-b99c-16c8f1fb8301, Windmill Bks.) Rosen Publishing Group, Inc., The.
West, David, contrib. by. Whales & Other Mammals, 1 vol. 2017. (Inside Animals Ser.). (ENG.). 24p. (J). (gr. 3-3). pap. 9.25 *(978-1-5081-9431-6(9),* 3a530a54-c08e-42dc-9967-b8e8d8aa04bf, Windmill Bks.) Rosen Publishing Group, Inc., The.
Westerskov, Kim, photos by. Whales. 2004. (Illus.). 32p. (J). *(978-0-7685-2109-2(2))* Dominie Pr., Inc.
Wexo, John Bonnett. Whales. rev. ed. 2003. (Illus.). 24p. (J). (gr. 1-7). 10.95 *(978-1-888153-97-2(0),* Zoo Bks.) National Wildlife Federation.
The Whale: Review & Practice Book for Level B, 6 vols. (Wright Skills Ser.). 16p. (gr. k-3). 26.50 *(978-0-322-03100-5(1))* Wright Group/McGraw-Hill.
The Whale Watchers, 6, Pack. (gr. 1-2). 22.00 *(978-0-7635-9181-6(5))* Rigby Education.
Whales: Level N, 6 vols. (Wonder Worldtm Ser.). 48p. 34.95 *(978-0-7802-2915-0(0))* Wright Group/McGraw-Hill.
Whales & Dolphins. (Eyes on Nature Ser.). 32p. (J). (gr. 1). pap. *(978-1-882210-56-5(5))* Action Publishing, Inc.
Whales & Dolphins. (Eyes on Nature Ser.). (Illus.). 32p. (J). (gr. 1-18). 7.95 *(978-1-56156-423-1(0))* Kidsbooks, LLC.
Whales & Dolphins, 1 vol. 2014. (Animal Q & A Ser.). (ENG., Illus.). 24p. (J). (gr. 2-2). lib. bdg. 26.27 *(978-1-4777-9202-5(3),* cb7e0175-d908-494b-a11e-1e93ef4dba73, Windmill Bks.) Rosen Publishing Group, Inc., The.
Whales & Dolphins Pack [Scholastic]. 2011. (Whales & Dolphins up Close Ser.). 24p. pap. 2.00 *(978-1-4296-6325-0(1),* Capstone Pr.) Capstone.
Whales in American History. 2014. (How Animals Shaped History Ser.). (Illus.). 24p. (J). (gr. k-5). pap. 49.50 *(978-1-4777-6630-9(8),* PowerKids Pr.) Rosen Publishing Group, Inc., The.
Wildlife Education, Ltd Staff, contrib. by. Whales. 2006. (Critters Up Close Ser.). (Illus.). (J). bds. 5.95 *(978-1-932396-17-1(9))* National Wildlife Federation.
Williams, Alwena & Drake, Gwasg Addysgol. Morfilod. 2005. (WEL., Illus.). 20p. *(978-0-86174-101-4(3))* Drake Educational Assocs. Ltd.
Williams, Heather DiLorenzo & Rylands, Warren. Humpback Whales. 2019. (Illus.). 24p. (J). *(978-1-4896-8159-1(0),* AV2 by Weigl) Weigl Pubs., Inc.
Willis, John. Orca. 2015. (Illus.). 24p. (J). *(978-1-4896-4109-0(2))* Weigl Pubs., Inc.
World Book, Inc. Staff, contrib. by. Blue Whales & Other Baleen Whales. 2005. (World Book's Animals of the World Ser.). (Illus.). 64p. (J). *(978-0-7166-1264-3(X))* World Bk., Inc.
A World of Whales, 6 vols. (Book2WebTM Ser.). (gr. 4-8). 36.50 *(978-0-322-02969-9(4))* Wright Group/McGraw-Hill.
Worth, Bonnie. A Whale of a Tale! All about Porpoises, Dolphins, & Whales. Ruiz, Aristides, illus. 2006. (Cat in the Hat's Learning Library). (ENG.). 48p. (J). (gr. -1-3). 9.99 *(978-0-375-82279-7(8),* Random Hse. Bks. for Young Readers) Random Hse. Children's Bks.
Young, Karen Romano. Whale Quest: Working Together to Save Endangered Species. 2017. (ENG., Illus.). 128p. (YA). (gr. 6-12). 37.32 *(978-1-4677-9246-2(2),* d01d29c7-a672-4e54-9f3c-b314b5746a33, Twenty-First Century Bks.) Lerner Publishing Group.
Zayarny, Jack. Humpback Whales. 2014. (J). pap. *(978-1-4896-1079-9(0))* Weigl Pubs., Inc.

WHALES—FICTION

Abler, Amanda. The Spirit of Springer: The Real-Life Rescue of an Orphaned Orca. Hastings, Levi, illus. 2020. 48p. (J). (gr. 2-5). 18.99 *(978-1-63217-212-9(7),* Little Bigfoot) Sasquatch Bks.
Adams, Jennifer. Moby Dick Playset: A BabyLit(TM) Ocean Primer Board Book & Playset, 1 vol. Oliver, Alison, illus. 2015. (ENG.). 22p. (J). 19.99 *(978-1-4236-3871-1(9))* Gibbs Smith, Publisher.
Al-Ghani, K. I. Baby Blue Has the Blues, 1 vol. 2011. (ENG., Illus.). 32p. (J). (gr. -1-3). 16.99 *(978-0-7643-3732-1(7),* 4089, Schiffer Publishing Ltd) Schiffer Publishing, Ltd.
Aldrich, Sandra D. Lenny Lobster Saves the Day. 2012. 38p. 19.95 *(978-1-4626-9817-2(4))* America Star Bks.
—Trouble in the Park. 2012. 28p. 19.95 *(978-1-4626-8818-0(7))* America Star Bks.
Alexander, Kwame. Surf's Up. Miyares, Daniel, illus. (ENG.). (J). (— 1). 2018. 24p. bds. 7.95 *(978-0-7358-4313-4(9))* 2016. 32p. 18.95 *(978-0-7358-4220-5(5))* North-South Bks., Inc.
Anderson, M. T. Whales on Stilts! Cyrus, Kurt, illus. 2010. (Pals in Peril Tale Ser.). (ENG.). (J). (gr. 5-9). 224p. pap. 8.99 *(978-1-4424-0701-5(8));* 1. 208p. 17.99 *(978-1-4424-0695-7(X))* Beach Lane Bks. (Beach Lane Bks.).
Anderson, Matthew. Whales on Stilts! Cyrus, Kurt, illus. 2006. (M. T. Anderson's Thrilling Tales Ser.). 188p. (gr. 5-9). 15.95 *(978-0-7569-7213-4(2))* Perfection Learning Corp.
Anthony, Mike. The Adventures of Henry the Patchwork Whale, 1 vol. 2010. 20p. 24.95 *(978-1-60813-076-4(2))* PublishAmerica, Inc.
Apte, Sunita. Ride the Whale: A Surfer Tall Tale. Reed, Kyle, illus. 2006. 16p. (J). pap. *(978-0-439-74638-0(8))* Scholastic, Inc.
Armstrong, Kim. Petunia in Manhattan. 2009. 50p. pap. 12.99 *(978-1-935436-97-3(X))* Rodaian Pr.
Barnett, Mac. Billy Twitters & His Blue Whale Problem. Rex, Adam, illus. 2009. (ENG.). 48p. (J). (gr. -1-3). 18.99 *(978-0-7868-4958-1(4))* Little, Brown Bks. for Young Readers.
Because of Walter, 6 Packs. (Action Packs Ser.). 104p. (gr. 3-5). 44.00 *(978-0-7635-8402-3(9))* Rigby Education.
Bernay, Emma & Berne, Emma Carlson. Orca in Open Water. Madrid, Erwin, illus. 2019. (Seaside Sanctuary Ser.). (ENG.). 112p. (J). (gr. 3-7). lib. bdg. 25.99 *(978-1-4965-7862-4(7),* 139401, Stone Arch Bks.) Capstone.
Blume, Rebecca. Baby Whales. Blume, Rebecca, illus. 2007. (Illus.). 8p. (J). 5.00 *(978-0-9785427-2-6(X))* Liberty Artists Management.
Bonnell, Kris. The Little Boat. 2006. (J). pap. 5.95 *(978-1-933727-34-9(9))* Reading Reading Bks., LLC.
Booth, Christina. Welcome Home, Whales. 2021. (ENG., Illus.). 32p. (J). 17.95 *(978-1-7331212-8-6(5))* Blue Dot Pubns. LLC.
Botelho, R. J. G. A. R. T. H. Book IV: A Whale of a Tale. 2007. 104p. per. 19.95 *(978-1-4241-8799-7(0))* America Star Bks.
Brown, Joy. Spy Hopping. 2008. 48p. pap. 24.95 *(978-1-60474-525-2(8))* America Star Bks.
Burks, James. Bird & Squirrel on Ice. 2014. (Illus.). 125p. (J). *(978-0-605-86251-7(6),* Graphix) Scholastic, Inc.
Carbone, Courtney. Break the Ice!/Everest Saves the Day! (PAW Patrol) MJ Illustrations, illus. 2017. (Step into Reading Ser.). (ENG.). 48p. (J). (gr. -1-1). pap. 5.99 *(978-1-5247-6400-5(0),* Random Hse. Bks. for Young Readers) Random Hse. Children's Bks.
Carnavas, Peter. Blue Whale Blues. Carnavas, Peter, illus. 2016. (ENG., Illus.). 32p. (J). 11.99 *(978-1-61067-458-4(8))* Kane Miller.
Chronicle Books. Baby Orca: Finger Puppet Book (Puppet Book for Babies, Baby Play Book, Interactive Baby Book) Huang, Yu-Hsuan, illus. 2019. (Baby Animal Finger Puppets Ser.: 16). (ENG.). 12p. (J). (gr. -1 — 1). 7.99 *(978-1-4521-7079-4(7))* Chronicle Bks. LLC.
Collier, Kevin Scott. Journeys of Hope, Pearl of Wisdom. Collier, Kevin Scott, illus. 2006. (Illus.). 28p. (J). E-Book 9.95 incl. cd-rom *(978-1-933090-31-3(6))* Guardian Angel Publishing, Inc.
Curran, Steven Earl. Whales used to Fly in the Sky. 2005. 9.00 *(978-0-8059-8086-8(5))* Dorrance Publishing Co., Inc.
Dadey, Debby & Dadey, Debbie. Whale of a Tale, Bk. 3. Avakyan, Tatevik, illus. 2015. (Mermaid Tales Ser.). (ENG.). 120p. (J). (gr. 1-4). 31.36 *(978-1-61479-324-3(7),* 17146, Chapter Bks.) Spotlight.
Dalmatian Press Staff. A Little Whale Tale. 2008. (ENG.). 8p. bds. 4.95 *(978-1-58117-713-8(5),* Intervisual/Piggy Toes) Bendon, Inc.
Dalmatian Press Staff, adapted by. Moby Dick. (J). 9.95 *(978-1-56156-308-1(0))* Kidsbooks, LLC.
David, Jamie. Johann Sebastian Humpbach. David, Jamie, illus. 2009. (Illus.). 167p. pap. 14.95 *(978-0-615-31840-0(1))* Chai Yo Maui Pr.
Davidge, James. Driftwood Saves the Whales. 2009. (ENG., Illus.). 200p. (YA). 10.95 *(978-1-897411-01-8(4))* Bayeux Arts, Inc. CAN. Dist: Chicago Distribution Ctr.
Davies, Benji. The Storm Whale. Davies, Benji, illus. 2014. (ENG., Illus.). 32p. (J). (gr. -1-3). 18.99 *(978-0-8050-9967-6(0),* 900128170, Holt, Henry & Co. Bks. For Young Readers) Holt, Henry & Co.
Davies, Nicola. Whale Boy. 2014. 272p. (J). (gr. 2-4). pap. 10.99 *(978-0-440-87015-9(1))* Transworld Publishers Ltd. GBR. Dist: Independent Pubs. Group.
Davis, Buddy. Whale of a Story: Adventures on the High Seas. 2003. 40p. (J). 14.99 *(978-0-89051-390-3(2),* Master Books) New Leaf Publishing Group.
Davis, Maggie Steincrohn. A Garden of Whales. O'Connell, Jennifer Barrett, illus. 25th ed. 2008. (ENG.). 32p. (J). (gr. -1-2). reprint ed. pap. 7.95 *(978-0-944475-35-5(3),* 61f17095-d550-40e5-9c43-6c12190a31e6) Firefly Bks., Ltd.
Donaldson, Julia. The Snail & the Whale. 2004. (ENG., Illus.). 32p. (J). (gr. -1-2). 18.99 *(978-0-8037-2922-3(7),* Dial Bks) Penguin Young Readers Group.
—The Snail & the Whale. Scheffler, Axel, illus. 2006. (ENG.). 32p. (J). (gr. -1-2). reprint ed. pap. 8.99 *(978-0-14-240580-2(9),* Puffin Books) Penguin Young Readers Group.
Douglas, Babette. Kiss a Me: A Little Whale Watching. Rockwell, Barry, illus. 2006. (Kiss a Me Teacher Creature Stories Ser.). (J). (gr. 3-7). 9.99 *(978-1-890343-08-8(0))* Kiss A Me Productions, Inc.
—Kiss a Me Goes to School. Rockwell, Barry, illus. 2006. (Kiss a Me Teacher Creature Stories Ser.). (J). (gr. -1-3). 9.99 *(978-1-890343-09-5(9))* Kiss A Me Productions, Inc.
—Kiss a Me to the Rescue. Rockwell, Barry, illus. 2006. (Kiss a Me Teacher Creature Stories Ser.). (J). (gr. -1-3). 9.99 *(978-1-890343-11-8(0))* Kiss A Me Productions, Inc.
Dove, Emily. Wendell the Narwhale. 2016. (ENG., Illus.). 36p. (J). 16.95 *(978-1-927018-66-8(8))* Simply Read Bks. CAN. Dist: Ingram Publisher Services.
Dunn, Richard & Sprick, Jessica. Whales: Read Well Level K Unit 18 Storybook. Koontz, Robin Michal, illus. 2003. (Read Well Level K Ser.). 20p. (J). *(978-1-57035-689-6(0),* 55589) Cambium Education, Inc.
Edwardson, Debby Dahl. Whale Snow. Patterson, Annie, illus. 2004. (ENG.). 32p. (J). (gr. -1-3). pap. 7.95 *(978-1-57091-394-5(3))* Charlesbridge Publishing, Inc.
Eisner, Will & Melville, Herman. Moby Dick. 2003. (ENG., Illus.). 32p. (J). pap. 7.95 *(978-1-56163-294-7(5))* NBM Publishing Co.
Elliott, Jenny. Save Me. 2015. (ENG.). 336p. (YA). (gr. 7-12). pap. 10.99 *(978-1-250-06147-8(4),* 900141885) Feiwel & Friends.
Evans, Sally. Sea Treasure. Richardson, Linda, illus. 2004. (J). 16.95 *(978-1-59094-073-0(3),* 1590940733, Jawbreakers for Kids) Jawbone Publishing Corp.
Ferry, Beth & Mundorff, Lisa. A Small Blue Whale. 2017. (ENG., Illus.). 32p. (J). (-k). 17.99 *(978-1-5247-1337-9(6));* lib. bdg. 20.99 *(978-1-5247-1338-6(4))* Random Hse. Children's Bks. (Knopf Bks. for Young Readers).
Fogliano, Julie. If You Want to See a Whale. 2013. (ENG., Illus.). 32p. (J). (gr. -1-2). 18.99 *(978-1-59643-731-9(6),* 900076361) Roaring Brook Pr.
Gabriele, Ben. The Tale of a Whale Named Snow. 2018. (ENG., Illus.). 48p. (J). (gr. k-6). pap. 10.99 *(978-1-948801-53-9(1))* Bookwhip.

W X Y Z

—The Tale of a Whale Named Snow. 2014. (ENG.). 18.00 *(978-0-938271-07-9(5))*; pap. 15.00 *(978-0-938271-06-2(7))*; pap. 15.00 *(978-0-938271-08-6(3))*; (J). 18.00 *(978-0-938271-05-5(9))* Press North America.

—The Tale of a Whale Named Snow. 2013. 50p. pap. 31.99 *(978-1-4836-9269-2(8))* Xlibris Corp.

Garner, Alan. The Owl Service. 2006. (Odyssey Classics Ser.). (ENG., Illus.). 240p. (J). (gr. 7-12). pap. 14.95 *(978-0-15-205618-6(1))* Houghton Mifflin Harcourt Publishing Co.

George, Joshua. Tiny Whale. Pinillos, Puy, illus. 2018. (Picture Bks.). (ENG.). 32p. (J). (gr. -1-k). 16.99 *(978-1-78700-457-3(0))* Willow Tree Bks. GBR. Dist: Independent Pubs. Group.

Gerstein, Mordicai. The Boy & the Whale. Gerstein, Mordicai, illus. 2017. (ENG., Illus.). 40p. (J). 18.99 *(978-1-62672-505-8(5)*, 900159303) Roaring Brook Pr.

Ghent, Rena. The Adventures of Billy the Whale. 2009. 28p. pap. 13.99 *(978-1-4490-3456-6(X))* AuthorHouse.

Gibbes, Lesley. Fluke. Dawson, Michelle, illus. 2019. 32p. pap. 6.99 *(978-1-921504-96-9(X)*, Working Title Pr.) HarperCollins Pubs. Australia AUS. Dist: HarperCollins Pubs.

Gill, Shelley. Big Blue. Barrow, Ann, illus. 2005. 32p. (J). (gr. k-3). 7.95 *(978-1-57091-667-0(5))* Charlesbridge Publishing, Inc.

Gleasner, Diana C. Popoki, the Hawaiian Cat: An Amazing Adventure with the Whale. Winton, Andrea Evans, illus. 2004. (J). *(978-0-9651185-7-6(6))* Gleasner, Bill & Diana Inc.

Gray, Rick & Gray, Coral. Evangel Meets Orsen Whale. Headley, Aaron, illus. 2007. (ENG.). 32p. (J). (gr. -1-3). 14.95 *(978-0-9790210-1-5(4))* Evening Star Enterprise, Inc.

Green, Yuko. Naia & Kohola. 2010. 20p. pap. 6.95 *(978-1-59700-803-7(6))* Island Heritage Publishing.

Greenburg, J. C. Andrew Lost #6: in the Whale. Reed, Mike, illus. 2003. (Andrew Lost Ser.: 6). (ENG.). 96p. (J). (gr. 1-4). 4.99 *(978-0-375-82524-8(X)*, Random Hse. Bks. for Young Readers) Random Hse. Children's Bks.

Gugger, Rebecca. Ida & the Whale. Röthlisberger, Simon, illus. 2019. (ENG.). 32p. (J). (gr. -1-2). 17.95 *(978-0-7358-4341-7(4))* North-South Bks., Inc.

Heinz, Brian. Mocha Dick: the Legend & Fury. Enos, Randall, illus. 2014. (ENG.). 32p. (J). (gr. 1-3). 18.99 *(978-1-56846-242-4(5)*, 21314, Creative Editions) Creative Co., The.

Hensley, Annemarie. Freeman Out of Water. 2011. 32p. pap. 14.99 *(978-1-4520-5864-1(4))* AuthorHouse.

Hernandez, Ruben. Elisa Escuchaba el Canto de Las Ballenas. Corichi, Yadhira, illus. rev. ed. 2003. (Castillo de la Lectura Blanca Ser.). (SPA & ENG.). 48p. (J). (gr. 1-3). pap. 6.95 *(978-970-20-0141-6(2))* Castillo, Ediciones, S. A. de C. V. MEX. Dist: Macmillan.

Hicks, Bob. Narvick the Whark (or a Shwale) 2003. (Illus.). cd-rom 9.95 *(978-0-9729703-0-3(4))* Kidderature Publishing.

Highley, Rainey Marie. The Long Lost Tale of the Dragon & the Whale. 2013. 28p. pap. 16.95 *(978-1-4808-0151-6(8))* Archway Publishing.

Hill, Ros. Shamoo, a Whale of a Cow. 2013. (ENG., Illus.). 34p. pap. 12.95 *(978-1-59687-941-6(6)*, Milk & Cookies) ibooks, Inc.

—Shamooo: A Whale of a Cow. Hill, Ros, illus. 2005. (Illus.). 32p. (J). 15.95 *(978-0-689-04634-6(0)*, Milk & Cookies) ibooks, Inc.

Holden, Pam. Baby Whale's Mistake, 1 vol. Aziz, Lamia, illus. 2009. (Red Rocket Readers Ser.). (ENG.). 16p. (gr. 2-2). pap. *(978-1-877363-87-0(1))* Flying Start Bks.

—Watch Out for Whales, 1 vol. Aziz, Lamia, illus. 2009. (Red Rocket Readers Ser.). (ENG.). 23p. (gr. 2-2). pap. *(978-1-877363-63-4(4)*, Red Rocket Readers) Flying Start Bks.

—Whale Rescue, 1 vol. Aziz, Lamia, illus. 2009. (Red Rocket Readers Ser.). (ENG.). 23p. (gr. 2-2). pap. *(978-1-877363-79-5(0))* Flying Start Bks.

Horacek, Petr. Puffin Peter. Horacek, Petr, illus. 2013. (ENG., Illus.). 40p. (J). (gr. -1-2). 17.99 *(978-0-7636-6572-2(X))* Candlewick Pr.

How the Whale Got His Throat. 2017. (Picture Bks.). (ENG.). (J). 9.99 *(978-0-7945-3869-9(X)*, Usborne) EDC Publishing.

Howell, Troy. Whale in a Fishbowl. Jones, Richard, illus. 2018. 40p. (J). (gr. -1-3). 17.99 *(978-1-5247-1518-2(2)*, Schwartz & Wade Bks.) Random Hse. Children's Bks.

Ilyas, Adnan. The Tale of Five Whales. 2010. 12p. 8.50 *(978-1-4389-5888-0(9))* AuthorHouse.

Irwin, Bindi & Kunz, Chris. A Whale of a Time, 5. 2011. (Bindi's Wildlife Adventures Ser.: 5). (ENG.). 112p. (J). (gr. 3-6). pap. 8.99 *(978-1-4022-5928-9(X)*, Sourcebooks Jabberwocky) Sourcebooks, Inc.

Iwasa, Megumi. Dear Professor Whale. Takabatake, Jun, illus. 2018. (ENG.). 104p. (J). (gr. k-3). 16.99 *(978-1-77657-206-9(8)*, 99e443a3-c963-40f9-861a-c55409bd2ce8) Gecko Pr. NZL. Dist: Lerner Publishing Group.

Jacobson, Bonny B. Whale Fables. 2011. 68p. pap. 31.99 *(978-1-4535-9956-3(8))* Xlibris Corp.

James, Simon. Querido Salvatierra. de la Vega, Eida, tr. from ENG. 2003.Tr. of Dear Mr. Blueberry. (SPA.). (J). (gr. k-2). pap. 8.99 *(978-1-930332-45-4(9))* Lectorum Pubns., Inc.

Johnson, Grace. The Little Fish Who Was Afraid to Swim. 2008. 36p. pap. 15.49 *(978-1-4389-2262-1(0))* AuthorHouse.

Johnston, Johanna. Whale's Way. Weisgard, Leonard, illus. 2015. 48p. 20.00 *(978-1-85124-428-7(X))* Bodleian Library GBR. Dist: Chicago Distribution Ctr.

Joy, Linda. Little Wave & the Mystery of the Lost Whale. 2011. 28p. pap. 15.99 *(978-1-4628-9711-7(8))* Xlibris Corp.

Judith Anne Moody. Golden Eye & the Killer Cat. 2009. 248p. pap. 19.49 *(978-1-4251-7684-6(4))* Trafford Publishing.

Keefer, Mikal. Everywhere I Go, God Is with Me. Perez, Nomar, illus. 2017. (Best of Li'l Buddies Ser.). (ENG.). 16p. (J). bds. 6.99 *(978-1-4707-4857-9(6))* Group Publishing, Inc.

Kelly, Lynne. Song for a Whale. 2020. (Penworthy Picks YA Fiction Ser.). (ENG.). 298p. (J). (gr. 6-8). 19.96 *(978-1-64697-227-2(9))* Penworthy Co., LLC, The.

—Song for a Whale. 2019. (ENG.). (J). (gr. 3-7). 304p. 8.99 *(978-1-5247-7026-6(4)*, Yearling); (Illus.). 320p. 17.99 *(978-1-5247-7023-5(X)*, Delacorte Bks. for Young Readers) Random Hse. Children's Bks.

Kita, Suzanne. Three Whales: Who Won the Heart of the World. Sundram, Steve, illus. 2010. (ENG.). 40p. (J). (gr. 3). *(978-1-59700-761-0(7))* Island Heritage Publishing.

Lanan, Jessica. The Fisherman & the Whale. Lanan, Jessica, illus. 2019. (ENG., Illus.). 48p. (J). (gr. -1-3). 17.99 *(978-1-5344-1574-4(2)*, Simon & Schuster Bks. For Young Readers) Simon & Schuster Bks. For Young Readers.

Lindsey, Marta. Little Gray's Great Migration, 1 vol. Gabriel, Andrea, illus. 2015. (SPA.). 32p. (J). (gr. 2-3). pap. 11.95 *(978-1-62855-468-7(1)*, 17f460f3-c10e-4f01-b492-2c0d238dd1ca) Arbordale Publishing.

Lingemann, Linda. Beluga Passage. Weiman, Jon, illus. 2011. (Smithsonian Oceanic Collection Ser.). (ENG.). 32p. (J). (gr. -1-3). 19.95 *(978-1-60727-645-6(3))* Soundprints.

Lum, Leimomi o. Kamahae Kuamoo Mookini. The Legend of Kuamo'o Mo'okini & Hamumu the Great Whale. Kam, Kathleen, illus. 2004. 24p. (J). 12.95 *(978-1-58178-036-9(2))* Bishop Museum Pr.

Magoon, Scott. Breathe. Magoon, Scott, illus. 2014. (ENG., Illus.). 40p. (J). (gr. -1-3). 18.99 *(978-1-4424-1258-3(5)*, Simon & Schuster/Paula Wiseman Bks.) Simon & Schuster/Paula Wiseman Bks.

Malone, Cheryl Lawton. Dario & the Whale. Masseva, Bistra, illus. 2016. (ENG.). 32p. (J). (gr. -1-3). 16.99 *(978-0-8075-1463-4(2)*, 807514632) Whitman, Albert & Co.

Manning, Sara. Wally the Whale: A Tale about a Whale with Seizures. 2011. 40p. pap. 18.46 *(978-1-4634-4160-9(6))* AuthorHouse.

Marino, Gianna. Following Papa's Song. 2014. (Illus.). 40p. (J). (gr. -1-k). 18.99 *(978-0-670-01315-9(3)*, Viking Books for Young Readers) Penguin Young Readers Group.

McDonald, Jill, illus. Ghoulish Gang. 2008. (ENG.). 12p. (J). 9.95 *(978-1-58117-782-4(6)*, Intervisual/Piggy Toes) Bendon, Inc.

McKee, David. Elmer & the Whales. McKee, David, illus. 2014. (Elmer Ser.). (ENG., Illus.). 32p. (J). (gr. -1-3). 16.95 *(978-1-4677-3453-0(5)*, 38181d9e-acb0-45e5-8042-73782a258a4d) Lerner Publishing Group.

McNulty, Faith & Shiffman, Lena. Le Chant des Baleines. (Hello Reader! Ser.). (FRE., Illus.). 40p. (J). pap. 5.99 *(978-0-590-16027-8(3))* Scholastic, Inc.

Meadows, Daisy. Whitney the Whale Fairy. 2011. (Illus.). 64p. (J). *(978-0-545-28876-7(2))* Scholastic, Inc.

Meister, Cari. The Stranded Orca, 1 vol. Harpster, Steve, illus. 2012. (Ocean Tales Ser.). (ENG.). 32p. (J). (gr. 2-3). lib. bdg. 22.65 *(978-1-4342-4026-2(6)*, 118411, Stone Arch Bks.) Capstone.

Melville, Herman. Cities of the Fantastic: Brusel. Eisner, Will, illus. 2003. (Cities of the Fantastic Ser.). (ENG.). 120p. 19.95 *(978-1-56163-291-6(0))* NBM Publishing Co.

—Classic Starts(r): Moby-Dick. Freeberg, Eric, illus. 2010. (Classic Starts(r) Ser.). 160p. (J). (gr. 2-4). 7.99 *(978-1-4027-6644-2(0))* Sterling Publishing Co., Inc.

—Moby Dick. Eisner, Will, illus. 2003. (ENG.). 32p. (J). (gr. 4-7). 15.95 *(978-1-56163-293-0(7))* NBM Publishing Co.

—Moby Dick. 2008. (Bring the Classics to Life Ser.). (Illus.). 72p. (gr. 5-12). pap., act. bk. ed. 10.95 *(978-1-55576-326-8(X)*, EDCTR-508B) EDCON Publishing Group.

—Moby Dick. 2007. (SPA.). (YA). *(978-987-1129-68-3(8))* Grupo Visor E.A.S.A.

—Moby Dick. 2003. (Historias de Siempre Ser.). (SPA., Illus.). 92p. (J). (gr. 5-8). pap. 9.95 *(978-84-204-5732-1(9))* Santillana USA Publishing Co., Inc.

—Moby Dick: With a Discussion of Determination. 2003. (Values in Action Illustrated Classics Ser.). (Illus.). 190p. (J). *(978-1-59203-033-0(5))* Learning Challenge, Inc.

—Moby Dick, Grades 5-12. adapted ed. pap., tchr. ed. 4.95 *(978-0-8359-0123-9(8))* Globe Fearon Educational Publishing.

—Moby Dick, or the Whale. 2005. (J). Pt. 1. cd-rom *(978-1-4105-0265-0(1))*Pt. 2. pap. 9.95 *(978-1-4105-0267-4(8))* Vol. 1. pap. 9.95 *(978-1-4105-0263-6(5))* Vol. 2. cd-rom *(978-1-4105-0269-8(4))* Building Wings LLC.

Melville, Herman. & Huth, Michael. Moby Dick. 2004. (Veröffentlichung der Maximilian-Gesellschaft für die Jahre 2004/2005 Ser.). (GER., Illus.). 92p. (J). *(978-3-921743-52-2(4))* Maximilian-Gesellschaft e. V.

Melville, Herman., et al. Moby Dick. (Classics Illustrated Ser.). (Illus.). 52p. (YA). pap. 4.95 *(978-1-57209-003-3(0))* Classics International Entertainment, Inc.

Mentyka, Sharon. Chasing at the Surface: A Novel. 2016. (ENG., Illus.). 228p. (J). (gr. 3-7). pap. 12.99 *(978-1-943328-60-4(9)*, West Winds Pr.) West Margin Pr.

Mikaelsen, Ben. Stranded. rev. ed. 2010. (ENG.). 288p. (J). (gr. 3-7). pap. 7.99 *(978-1-4231-3362-9(5))* Hyperion Bks. for Children.

Moniz, Michael. The Boy & the Whale. 2013. (ENG., Illus.). 36p. (J). (gr. -1-3). 16.95 *(978-1-927018-14-9(5))* Simply Read Bks. CAN. Dist: Ingram Publisher Services.

Morris, Dudley. Mike the Monk. 2011. 58p. 36.95 *(978-1-258-02967-8(7))* Literary Licensing, LLC.

Murrow, Vita. The Whale. Murrow, Ethan, illus. 2016. (ENG.). 32p. (J). (gr. -1-3). 17.99 *(978-0-7636-7965-1(8)*, Templar) Candlewick Pr.

Ness, Patrick. And the Ocean Was Our Sky. Cai, Rovina, illus. 2018. (ENG.). 160p. (YA). (gr. 8). 19.99 *(978-0-06-286072-9(0)*, Quill Tree Bks.) HarperCollins Pubs.

—And the Ocean Was Our Sky. 2018. (Illus.). 160p. (YA). pap. *(978-0-06-287744-4(5)*, HarperTeen) HarperCollins Pubs.

Nikolet, C. T. From Bullies to Friends. Howe, Cindy T., illus. 2008. 25p. pap. 24.95 *(978-1-60610-121-6(8))* America Star Bks.

O'Brien, Kevin J. My Macaroni Whales. 2012. 28p. pap. 15.99 *(978-1-4691-4988-2(5))* Xlibris Corp.

Oppel, Kenneth. Peg & the Whale. 2004. (Illus.). (J). (gr. k-3). spiral bd. *(978-0-616-07245-5(7))* Canadian National Institute for the Blind/Institut National Canadien pour les Aveugles.

Park, Sunny. Bboonk, the Minke Whale. 2012. 20p. pap. 17.99 *(978-1-4685-6363-4(7))* AuthorHouse.

Parks, M. Elizabeth. The Sea Cow. 2013. (Illus.). 44p. pap. 16.95 *(978-0-9824565-2-1(2))* Sibyl Merritt.

Paul, Ruth. Little Hector & the Big Blue Whale. 2018. (Little Hector Ser.: 1). (Illus.). 24p. (J). (gr. -1-k). 15.99 *(978-0-14-377152-4(3))* Penguin Group New Zealand, Ltd. NZL. Dist: Independent Pubs. Group.

Pearl, Barbara. Whale of a Tale. 2005. (Illus.). 32p. (J). 14.95 *(978-0-9647924-7-0(8))* Crane Bks.

Peratrovich, Roy, Jr. Little Whale: A Story of the Last Tlingit War Canoe. Peratrovich, Roy, Jr., illus. 2016. (ENG., Illus.). 64p. pap. 18.95 *(978-1-60223-295-2(4))* Univ. of Alaska Pr.

Peterson, Brenda. Wild Orca: The Oldest, Wisest Whale in the World. Minor, Wendell, illus. 2018. (ENG.). 40p. (J). 18.99 *(978-1-250-11069-5(6)*, 900169711, Holt, Henry & Co. Bks. For Young Readers) Holt, Henry & Co.

Pfister, Marcus. The Rainbow Fish Colors. 2013. (Rainbow Fish Ser.). (ENG., Illus.). 12p. (J). (gr. -1-k). bds. 7.95 *(978-0-7358-4147-5(0))* North-South Bks., Inc.

Plumberg, William. The Legend of Peggy Postue: The Girl with the Upturned Nose. 2011. 28p. pap. 15.99 *(978-1-4568-9635-5(0))* Xlibris Corp.

Posner-Sanchez, Andrea. As Big As a Whale (Disney Junior: Doc Mcstuffins) RH Disney, illus. 2014. (Little Golden Book Ser.). (ENG.). 24p. (J). (-k). 5.99 *(978-0-7364-3087-6(3)*, Golden/Disney) Random Hse. Children's Bks.

Presley, Daniel & Polders, Claire. A Whale in Paris. McGuire, Erin, illus. (ENG.). (J). (gr. 5). 2019. pap. 7.99 *(978-1-5344-1916-2(0))* 2018. 17.99 *(978-1-5344-1915-5(2))* Simon & Schuster Children's Publishing. (Atheneum Bks. for Young Readers).

Rae, Lisa. A Distinguished Old Bentley Drove down to the Sea, 1 vol. Pickersgill, Peter, illus. 2007. (ENG.). 28p. (J). (gr. -1-2). pap. *(978-1-897174-05-0(5))* Breakwater Bks., Ltd.

Raschka, Chris, illus. Whaley Whale. 2014. (Thingy Things Ser.). (ENG.). 24p. (J). (gr. -1-k). 6.95 *(978-1-4197-1058-2(3)*, 1073201, Abrams Appleseed) Abrams, Inc.

Ratcliff, Charline. The Princess, the Toad & the Whale. 2012. (ENG.). 36p. (J). (-18). pap. 12.95 *(978-1-4787-1672-3(X))* Outskirts Pr., Inc.

Rebal, Tara. Sarah Sue Smith: A Crooked Wharf Adventure. 2010. 52p. pap. 22.49 *(978-1-4520-7165-7(9))* AuthorHouse.

Reed, J. Mac & Briggs-Greenberg, Ruthie. Sea of Echoes. 2015. (ENG., Illus.). 32p. (J). (gr. 3-7). 15.95 *(978-1-63076-107-3(9))* Taylor Trade Publishing.

Riner, Sherry. Wally the Whale Learns How to Be a Winner. Morris, Lillie, illus. 2004. 43p. pap. 24.95 *(978-1-4137-3129-3(5))* PublishAmerica, Inc.

Rivers, Karen. A Possibility of Whales. 2019. (ENG.). 288p. (gr. 3-7). pap. 8.95 *(978-1-61620-926-1(7)*, 73926) Algonquin Young Readers.

Rml. An Interesting Crew. 2012. 16p. (-18). pap. 15.99 *(978-1-4772-8699-9(3))* AuthorHouse.

Rylant, Cynthia. The Whale. McDaniels, Preston, illus. 2004. (Lighthouse Family Ser.: 2). (ENG.). 64p. (J). (gr. 1-5). pap. 5.99 *(978-0-689-84883-4(8)*, Simon & Schuster Bks. For Young Readers) Simon & Schuster Bks. For Young Readers.

Scholes, Katherine. El Niño y la Ballena. Violi, Daniela, illus. 2019. (SPA.). 78p. (J). (gr. 2-4). pap. 11.99 *(978-958-04-6020-6(5)*, Norma) Norma S.A. COL. Dist: Lectorum Pubns., Inc.

Scotton, Rob. Splat the Cat: A Whale of a Tale. 2013. (I Can Read Level 1 Ser.). (ENG., Illus.). 32p. (J). (gr. -1-3). pap. 4.99 *(978-0-06-209022-5(4)*, HarperCollins) HarperCollins Pubs.

—Splat the Cat: a Whale of a Tale. Scotton, Rob, illus. 2013. (I Can Read Level 1 Ser.). (ENG., Illus.). 32p. (J). (gr. -1-3). 16.99 *(978-0-06-209024-9(0)*, HarperCollins) HarperCollins Pubs.

—A Whale of a Tale. 2013. (Splat the Cat: I Can Read Ser.). (J). lib. bdg. 13.55 *(978-0-606-31814-3(3))* Turtleback.

Skurzynski, Gloria. Mysteries in Our National Parks: Out of the Deep: A Mystery in Acadia National Park. 2008. (Mysteries in Our National Park Ser.). (Illus.). 160p. (J). (gr. 3-7). pap. 4.99 *(978-1-4263-0251-0(7)*, National Geographic Kids) Disney Publishing Worldwide.

Smith, John D. H. The Whale Whisperers, 1 vol. Smith, Anne, illus. 2009. 17p. pap. 24.95 *(978-1-60749-211-5(3))* America Star Bks.

Smith, Laverne Byrd. Pokey the Playful Whale: (who wanted to live on Land) 2010. (Illus.). 36p. pap. 25.50 *(978-1-4490-7620-7(3))* AuthorHouse.

Snowden, Gary. Hank & Kale Visit the Aquarium. Smith, William E., illus. 2012. 24p. pap. 8.99 *(978-1-938768-05-7(1))* Gypsy Pubns.

Sommer, Bill & Tilghman, Natalie Haney. A 52-Hertz Whale. 2015. (ENG.). 200p. (YA). (gr. 8-12). E-Book 27.99 *(978-1-4677-8811-3(2)*, Carolrhoda Lab™) Lerner Publishing Group.

Speight, Peter. Wally the Whale. 2013. 28p. pap. *(978-1-78222-170-8(0))* Paragon Publishing, Rothersthorpe.

Spinelli, Eileen. Jonah's Whale. Giuliano Ferri, illus. 2012. (ENG.). 32p. (J). 16.00 *(978-0-8028-5382-0(X)*, Eerdmans Bks For Young Readers) Eerdmans, William B. Publishing Co.

Starfall Education. Jake's Tale. Starfall Education, ed. 2004. (ENG., Illus.). 8p. (J). pap. *(978-1-59577-006-6(2))* Starfall Education.

Steig, William. Amos & Boris. 2011. 8.30 *(978-0-7848-3427-5(X)*, Everbind) Marco Bk. Co.

—Amos & Boris. Steig, William, illus. 2009. (ENG., Illus.). 32p. (J). (gr. k-3). pap. 8.99 *(978-0-312-53566-7(X)*, 900054745) Square Fish.

—Amos & Boris. 2009. (J). (gr. -1-2). lib. bdg. 18.40 *(978-0-8085-2709-1(6))* Turtleback.

Sweeney, Joyce. Waiting for June, 0 vols. 2012. (ENG.). 158p. (YA). (gr. 7-12). pap. 7.99 *(978-0-7614-5329-1(6)*, 9780761453291, Skyscape) Amazon Publishing.

Tate, Suzanne. Katie K. Whale: A Whale of a Tale. Melvin, James, illus. 2004. (Suzanne Tate's Nature Ser.: No. 17). 32p. (J). per. 10.95 *(978-1-878405-47-0(0))* Nags Head Art, Inc.

Tempest, Annabel, illus. Moby Dick: a BabyLit(TM) Storybook: A BabyLit(TM) Storybook, 1 vol. 2017. (BabyLit Ser.). 28p. (gr. -1-k). 12.99 *(978-1-4236-4784-3(X))* Gibbs Smith, Publisher.

Thomas, Doris. Through the Eyes of the Orcas. 2010. 146p. pap. 14.90 *(978-3-8391-6582-9(2))* Bks. on Demand.

Tobin, Deborah. Tangled in the Bay, 1 vol. Domm, Jeffrey, illus. 2003. (ENG.). 32p. (J). (gr. 4-7). pap. 10.95 *(978-1-55109-441-0(X)*, d8ebfd3e-031b-4110-875b-a86121d8ac85) Nimbus Publishing, Ltd. CAN. Dist: Baker & Taylor Publisher Services (BTPS).

Trechsel, Kelli. A Whale Set Sail. Renfroe, Leisa, illus. 2011. 28p. (J). pap. 14.95 *(978-1-936085-42-2(9))* Decent Hill.

Turk, Evan. Heartbeat. Turk, Evan, illus. 2018. (ENG., Illus.). 56p. (J). (gr. -1-3). 19.99 *(978-1-4814-3520-8(5)*, Atheneum Bks. for Young Readers) Simon & Schuster Children's Publishing.

Van Dusen, Chris. Down to the Sea with Mr. Magee: (Kids Book Series, Early Reader Books, Best Selling Kids Books) 2006. (Mr. Magee Ser.). (ENG., Illus.). 36p. (J). (gr. -1-7). pap. 8.99 *(978-0-8118-5225-8(3))* Chronicle Bks. LLC.

Van Scoyoc, Pam. I Could Catch a Whale/ Yo Podria Pescar una Ballena. Santillan-Cruz, Sylvia R., tr. Lewis, R. J., illus. l.t. ed. 2005. (ENG & SPA.). 32p. (J). (gr. k-2). lib. bdg. 16.98 *(978-0-9663629-5-4(0))* By Grace Enterprises.

Velmans, Hester. Isabel of the Whales. 2006. (ENG.). 192p. (J). (gr. 3-7). per. 6.99 *(978-0-440-42025-5(3)*, Yearling) Random Hse. Children's Bks.

Verne, Jules. Dick Sand. Munro, George, tr. 2008. 296p. 29.95 *(978-1-60664-752-3(0))* Rodgers, Alan Bks.

—Dick Sands: The Boy Captain. ELLEN E. FREWER, tr. 2007. (ENG.). 298p. pap. 21.99 *(978-1-4264-3403-7(0))* Creative Media Partners, LLC.

—Dick Sands: The Boy Captain. Frewer, Ellen E., tr. l.t. ed. 2007. (ENG.). 328p. pap. 24.99 *(978-1-4264-3453-2(7))* Creative Media Partners, LLC.

—The English at the North Pole. 2009. 160p. 24.95 *(978-1-60664-684-7(2))*; pap. 13.95 *(978-1-60664-313-6(4))* Rodgers, Alan Bks.

Volke, Gordon. The Little Lost Whale. Bowler, Colin, illus. 2004. 24p. pap. 7.00 *(978-1-84161-118-1(2))* Ravette Publishing, Ltd. GBR. Dist: Parkwest Pubns., Inc.

Waters, Summer. River Rescue (Silver Dolphins, Book 10), Book 10. 2010. (Silver Dolphins Ser.: 10). (ENG.). 176p. (J). (gr. 2-4). pap. 7.99 *(978-0-00-736750-4(3)*, HarperCollins Children's Bks.) HarperCollins Pubs. Ltd. GBR. Dist: HarperCollins Pubs.

Weaver, Jo. Little Whale, 1 vol. 2018. (ENG., Illus.). 32p. (J). (gr. -1-2). 17.95 *(978-1-68263-049-5(8))* Peachtree Publishing Co. Inc.

Westaway, Kylie. A Whale in the Bathtub. Jellett, Tom, illus. 2016. (ENG.). 40p. (J). (gr. -1-3). 16.99 *(978-0-544-53535-0(9)*, 1608120, Clarion Bks.) HarperCollins Pubs.

Whale Mail. 2003. (J). spiral bd. 9.95 *(978-0-89610-126-5(6))* Island Heritage Publishing.

Wiederhold, Kathryn. Ravenwhale. 2011. 40p. pap. 24.95 *(978-1-4626-2027-2(2))* America Star Bks.

Willems, Mo. A Big Guy Took My Ball!-An Elephant & Piggie Book. 2013. (Elephant & Piggie Book Ser.: 19). (ENG., Illus.). 64p. (J). (gr. 1-3). 10.99 *(978-1-4231-7491-2(7)*, Hyperion Books for Children) Disney Publishing Worldwide.

Wilson, Bob. Stanley Bagshaw & the Twenty Two Ton Whale. 2006. (Stanley Bagshaw Ser.). (Illus.). 32p. (J). (gr. k-2). pap. 6.95 *(978-1-903015-50-6(2))* Barn Owl Bks, London GBR. Dist: Independent Pubs. Group.

Yolen, Jane. The Stranded Whale. Cataldo, Melanie, illus. 2015. (ENG.). 32p. (J). (gr. k-4). 15.99 *(978-0-7636-6953-9(9))* Candlewick Pr.

Young, Ed. Mighty Moby. 2017. (ENG., Illus.). 40p. (J). (gr. -1-3). 18.99 *(978-0-316-29936-7(7))* Little, Brown Bks. for Young Readers.

Zalme, Ron, illus. A Humpback Whale Tale. 2006. (Go, Diego, Go! Ser.: Vol. 2). (ENG.). 24p. (J). (gr. -1-2). pap. 3.99 *(978-1-4169-1511-9(7)*, Simon Spotlight/Nickelodeon) Simon Spotlight/Nickelodeon.

Zurchin, Cynthia, et al. The Whale Done School: Transforming a School's Culture by Catching Students Doing Things Right. 2012. 124p. pap. 14.95 *(978-1-4685-9536-9(9))* AuthorHouse.

WHALING

Cook, Peter & Salariya, David. Sail on a 19th-Century Whaling Ship! Grisly Tasks You'd Rather Not Do. Antram, David, illus. 2004. (You Wouldn't Want to Ser.). (ENG.). (J). 29.00 *(978-0-531-12356-0(1))* Scholastic Library Publishing.

Currie, Stephen. Thar She Blows: American Whaling in the Nineteenth Century. 2005. (People's History Ser.). (Illus.). 96p. (gr. 6-18). lib. bdg. 26.60 *(978-0-8225-0646-1(7))* Lerner Publishing Group.

Faiella, Graham. Moby Dick & the Whaling Industry of the 19th Century. 2009. (Looking at Literature Through Primary Sources Ser.). 64p. (gr. 5-8). 58.50 *(978-1-61514-305-4(X))* Rosen Publishing Group, Inc., The.

Herold, Vickey. A Whaling Community: Nantucket. 2006. (J). pap. *(978-1-4108-6426-0(X))* Benchmark Education Co.

Philbrick, Nathaniel. In the Heart of the Sea (Young Readers Edition) The True Story of the Whaleship Essex. 2015. (Illus.). 208p. (J). (gr. 3-7). 8.99 *(978-1-101-99776-5(1)*, Puffin Books) Penguin Young Readers Group.

Prohibited! Individual Title Six-Packs. (Bookweb Ser.). 32p. (gr. 6-18). 34.00 *(978-0-7578-0908-8(1))* Rigby Education.

Sandler, Martin W. The Impossible Rescue: The True Story of an Amazing Arctic Adventure. 2014. (ENG.). 176p. (J). (gr. 5). pap. 16.99 *(978-0-7636-7093-1(6))* Candlewick Pr.

Whales in American History. 2014. (How Animals Shaped History Ser.). (Illus.). 24p. (J). (gr. k-5). pap. 49.50 *(978-1-4777-6630-9(8)*, PowerKids Pr.) Rosen Publishing Group, Inc., The.

WHALING—FICTION

Brook, Henry. Moby Dick. 2010. (Usborne Classics Retold Ser.). 144p. (J). 6.99 *(978-0-7945-2761-7(2)*, Usborne) EDC Publishing.

Chalker Browne, Susan. The Land of a Thousand Whales, 1 vol. Keating, Nancy, illus. 2007. (ENG.). 32p. (J). (gr. 3-7). pap. *(978-1-897174-08-1(X))* Breakwater Bks., Ltd.

Dalmatian Press Staff, adapted by. Moby Dick. (J). 9.95 *(978-1-56156-308-1(0))* Kidsbooks, LLC.

Edwardson, Debby Dahl. Whale Snow. Patterson, Annie, illus. 2004. (ENG.). 32p. (J). (gr. -1-3). pap. 7.95 *(978-1-57091-394-5(3))* Charlesbridge Publishing, Inc.

sner, Will & Melville, Herman. Moby Dick. 2003. (ENG., Illus.). 32p. (J). pap. 7.95 (978-1-56163-294-7(5)) NBM Publishing Co.

ederick, Heather Vogel. The Voyage of Patience Goodspeed. 2004. (Aladdin Historical Fiction Ser.). 219p. (J). (gr. 3-7). 13.65 (978-0-7569-2943-5(1)) Perfection Learning Corp.

-The Voyage of Patience Goodspeed. 2004. (ENG., Illus.). 224p. (J). (gr. 3-7). pap. 8.99 (978-0-689-84869-8(2), Simon & Schuster Bks. For Young Readers) Simon & Schuster Bks. For Young Readers.

yde, Heidi Smith. Emanuel & the Whale Oil Lamp. Akib, Jamel, illus. 2012. (Hanukkah Ser.). (ENG.). 32p. (J). (gr. -1-1). lib. bdg. 17.95 (978-0-7613-6625-6(3), Kar-Ben Publishing) Lerner Publishing Group.

olivet, Joëlle, illus. Moby-Dick: A Pop-Up Book from the Novel by Herman Melville (Pop up Books for Adults & Kids, Classic Books for Kids, Interactive Books for Adults & Children) 2019. (ENG.). 16p. 40.00 (978-1-4521-7384-9(2)) Chronicle Bks. LLC.

Kassirer, Sue. Thar She Blows! Whaling in The 1860s. Fridell, Pat, illus. 2007. 32p. (J). 15.00 (978-1-4223-6721-6(5)) DIANE Publishing Co.

Melville, Herman. Cities of the Fantastic: Brusel. Eisner, Will, illus. 2003. (Cities of the Fantastic Ser.). (ENG.). 120p. 19.95 (978-1-56163-291-6(0)) NBM Publishing Co.

—Classic Starts(r): Moby-Dick. Freeberg, Eric, illus. 2010. (Classic Starts(r) Ser.). 160p. (J). (gr. 2-4). 7.99 (978-1-4027-6644-2(0)) Sterling Publishing Co., Inc.

—Moby Dick. Eisner, Will, illus. 2003. (ENG.). 32p. (J). (gr. 4-7). 15.95 (978-1-56163-293-0(7)) NBM Publishing Co.

—Moby Dick. 2008. (Bring the Classics to Life Ser.). (Illus.). 72p. (gr. 5-12). pap., act. bk. ed. 10.95 (978-1-55576-326-8(X), EDCTR-508B) EDCON Publishing Group.

—Moby Dick. 2019. (ENG.). 320p. (J). (gr. 3-7). (978-1-989631-64-5(9)) OMNI Publishing.

—Moby Dick. Elphinstone, Katy, illus. 2014. (Travel & Adventure Ser.). (ENG.). 64p. pap. 7.95 (978-1-906230-72-2(2)) Real Reads Ltd. GBR. Dist: Casemate Pubs. & Bk. Distributors, LLC.

—Moby Dick. 2003. (Historias de Siempre Ser.). (SPA., Illus.). 92p. (J). (gr. 5-8). pap. 9.95 (978-84-204-5732-1(9)) Santillana USA Publishing Co., Inc.

—Moby Dick: Or, the Whale. 2019. (ENG.). 316p. (YA). (gr. 7-12). pap. 12.18 (978-1-6995-4001-5(2)) Independently Published.

—Moby Dick: Or, the Whale. 2010. 528p. pap. 12.95 (978-1-59594-840-3(6), Wingspan Pr.) WingSpan Publishing.

—Moby Dick: With a Discussion of Determination. 2003. (Values in Action Illustrated Classics Ser.). (Illus.). 190p. (J). (978-1-59203-033-0(5)) Learning Challenge, Inc.

—Moby Dick, Grades 5-12. adapted ed. pap., tchr. ed. 4.95 (978-0-8359-0123-9(8)) Globe Fearon Educational Publishing.

—Moby Dick, or the Whale. 2005. (J). Pt. 1. cd-rom (978-1-4105-0265-0(1))Pt. 2. pap. 9.95 (978-1-4105-0267-4(8)) Vol. 1. pap. 9.95 (978-1-4105-0263-6(5)) Vol. 2. cd-rom (978-1-4105-0269-8(4)) Building Wings LLC.

Melville, Herman., creator. Moby Dick. 2020. (ENG.). 582p. (J). (gr. 3-7). pap. (978-0-371-37815-1(X)) HardPr.

Melville, Herman. & Huth, Michael. Moby Dick. 2004. (Veröffentlichung der Maximilian-Gesellschaft für die Jahre 2004/2005 Ser.). (GER., Illus.). 92p. (J). (978-3-921743-52-2(4)) Maximilian-Gesellschaft e. V.

Melville, Herman., et al. Moby Dick. (Classics Illustrated Ser.). (Illus.). 52p. (YA). pap. 4.95 (978-1-57209-003-3(0)) Classics International Entertainment, Inc.

Prins, Piet. Stefan Derksen's Polar Adventure. 2004. (Illus.). 237p. (J). pap. (978-1-894666-67-1(4)) Inheritance Pubns.

Rivera, Raquel. Tuk & the Whale, 1 vol. Gerber, Mary Jane, illus. 2008. (ENG.). 96p. (J). (gr. 3-5). pap. 9.95 (978-0-88899-891-0(0)) Groundwood Bks. CAN. Dist: Publishers Group West (PGW).

Stevenson, Robert Louis. Moby Dick. 2014. (Graphic Classics Ser.). (Illus.). 48p. (gr. 3-6). 37.10 (978-1-908973-88-7(9)) Book Hse. GBR. Dist: Black Rabbit Bks.

Tempest, Annabel, illus. Moby Dick: a BabyLit(TM) Storybook: A BabyLit(TM) Storybook, 1 vol. 2017. (BabyLit Ser.). 28p. (gr. -1-k). 12.99 (978-1-4236-4784-3(X)) Gibbs Smith, Publisher.

Thompson, Gare. A Whaling Community: Set of 6: New Bedford, Mass. 2011. (Navigators Ser.). (J). pap. 44.00 net. (978-1-4108-6248-8(8)) Benchmark Education Co.

WHEAT

Brannon, Cecelia H. Wheat, 1 vol. 2017. (All about Food Crops Ser.). (ENG.). 24p. (gr. k-1). lib. bdg. 24.27 (978-0-7660-8585-5(6), b4cf4289-50c4-4047-a98c-7cb84a5b4fe5) Enslow Publishing, LLC.

Etingoff, Kim. Dairy Products. 2013. (Illus.). 48p. (J). (978-1-4222-2741-1(3)) Mason Crest.

Hayes, Amy. Turning Wheat into Bread, 1 vol. 2015. (Step-By-Step Transformations Ser.). (ENG., Illus.). 24p. (gr. 1-1). pap. 9.23 (978-1-5026-0445-3(0), 3207a7be-7dae-4b30-b794-56dd3bad7702) Cavendish Square Publishing LLC.

Heos, Bridget. From Wheat to Bread. 2018. (Who Made My Lunch? Ser.). (ENG., Illus.). 24p. (J). (gr. k-3). pap. 10.99 (978-1-68152-143-5(1), 14773) Amicus.

—From Wheat to Bread. Coleman, Stephanie Fizer, illus. 2017. (Who Made My Lunch? Ser.). (ENG.). 24p. (J). (gr. 1-4). 20.95 (978-1-68151-118-4(5), 14654) Amicus.

Lackey, Jennifer. The Biography of Wheat. 2007. (How Did That Get Here? Ser.). (ENG., Illus.). 32p. (J). (gr. 3-7). lib. bdg. (978-0-7787-2495-7(6)); (gr. 2-9). pap. (978-0-7787-2531-2(6)) Crabtree Publishing Co.

Levenson, George. Bread Comes to Life: A Garden of Wheat & a Loaf to Eat. Thaler, Shmuel, photos by. 2008. (Illus.). 32p. (J). (gr. -1-2). pap. 7.99 (978-1-58246-273-8(9), Tricycle Pr.) Random Hse. Children's Bks.

Nelson, Maria. I'm Allergic to Wheat, 1 vol. 2014. (I'm Allergic Ser.). (ENG.). 24p. (J). (gr. 1-2). 24.27 (978-1-4824-0989-5(5), aa1c6795-8f3b-4ef8-b964-436abf552fb7) Stevens, Gareth Publishing LLLP.

Owen, Ruth. Bread! Life on a Wheat Farm, 1 vol. 2012. (Food from Farmers Ser.). (ENG.). 32p. (J). (gr. 1-2). pap. 12.75 (978-1-61533-544-2(7), 2b5b6c5f-71d0-49bb-8c8e-2b1b5e70220d); lib. bdg. 29.93 (978-1-61533-532-9(3), a64e569c-8322-4320-9d7e-6511088356da) Rosen Publishing Group, Inc., The. (Windmill Bks.).

Ridley, Sarah. Seeds to Bread. 2018. (Where Food Comes From Ser.). (Illus.). 24p. (J). (gr. 3-3). (978-0-7787-5128-1(7)) Crabtree Publishing Co.

Singer, Jane E. Wheat. 2013. (Feeding the World Ser.: 8). (Illus.). 48p. (J). (gr. 4-18). 19.95 (978-1-4222-2749-7(9)) Mason Crest.

Taus-Bolstad, Stacy. From Wheat to Bread. 2012. (Start to Finish, Second Ser.: No. 2). (ENG., Illus.). 24p. (J). (gr. k-3). pap. 7.99 (978-1-58013-970-0(1), 03fd3b43-ac84-4e27-af84-8f2030217f11) Lerner Publishing Group.

Welvaert, Scott R. Follow That Crop: From the Farmer's Field to Our Grocery Store. 2003. (From Here to There Ser.). (J). (978-1-58417-194-2(4)); pap. (978-1-58417-195-9(2)) Lake Street Pubs.

WHEATLEY, PHILLIS, 1753-1784

Clinton, Catherine. Phillis's Big Test. Qualls, Sean, illus. 2008. (ENG.). 32p. (J). (gr. -1-3). 16.00 (978-0-618-73739-0(1), 596218, Clarion Bks.) HarperCollins Pubs.

Collard, Sneed B., III. American Heroes, 6 vols., Group 3. Incl. Cesar Chavez. 32.64 (978-0-7614-4055-0(0), abfe4b16-e58b-4817-8708-b7bdbc77951d); George Washington. 32.64 (978-0-7614-4060-4(7), 2757fb59-5b7f-48ba-b248-ebe59643b8d1); Jacob Lawrence. 32.64 (978-0-7614-4058-1(5), 19d54f3f-2d13-43c3-a7af-77244e0ba9a9); Lady Bird Johnson. 32.64 (978-0-7614-4056-7(9), 1b484198-89c3-48ec-b434-f596e2cfb712); Phillis Wheatley. (Illus.). 32.64 (978-0-7614-4057-4(7), b5aabf94-bd02-4815-9f30-a3d8be34143b); Sitting Bull. 32.64 (978-0-7614-4059-8(3), d331b804-8748-40a1-a55d-cc9e79408f93); 48p. (gr. 3-3). 2010. (American Heroes 3 Ser.). 2009. Set lib. bdg. 179.57 o.p. (978-0-7614-4054-3(2), Cavendish Square) Cavendish Square Publishing LLC.

—Phillis Wheatley, 1 vol. 2010. (American Heroes Ser.). (ENG., Illus.). 48p. (gr. 3-3). 32.64 (978-0-7614-4057-4(7), b5aabf94-bd02-4815-9f30-a3d8be34143b) Cavendish Square Publishing LLC.

Corporate Contibutor Staff & Aloian, Molly. Phillis Wheatley: Poet of the Revolutionary Era. 2012. (ENG.). 48p. (J). (978-0-7787-0803-2(9)); pap. (978-0-7787-0814-8(4)) Crabtree Publishing Co.

Doak, Robin S. Phillis Wheatley: The Inspiring Life Story of the American Poet. 2016. (Inspiring Stories Ser.). (ENG., Illus.). 112p. (J). (gr. 5-7). lib. bdg. 38.65 (978-0-7565-5166-7(8), 128794, Compass Point Bks.) Capstone.

Jarnow, Jesse. Phillis Wheatley, 1 vol. 2003. (Primary Sources of Famous People in American History Ser.). (ENG., Illus.). 32p. (J). (gr. 3-4). lib. bdg. 29.13 (978-0-8239-4119-3(1), e4040339-04fc-4aa7-8995-5cc37f904356, Rosen Reference) Rosen Publishing Group, Inc., The.

—Phillis Wheatley: African American Poet / Poeta Afroamericana. 2009. (Famous People in American History/Grandes personajes en la historia de los Estados Unidos Ser.). (ENG & SPA.). 32p. (gr. 2-3). 47.90 (978-1-61512-554-8(X), Editorial Buenas Letras) Rosen Publishing Group, Inc., The.

—Phillis Wheatley: Poeta afroamericana (Phillis Wheatley: African American Poet) 2009. (Grandes personajes en la historia de los Estados Unidos (Famous People in American History) Ser.). (SPA.). 32p. (gr. 2-3). 47.90 (978-1-61512-807-5(7), Editorial Buenas Letras) Rosen Publishing Group, Inc., The.

Jarnow, Jesse & Moriarty, J. T. Phillis Wheatley, 1 vol. 2003. (Primary Sources of Famous People in American History Ser.). (ENG., Illus.). 32p. (J). (gr. 3-4). pap. 10.00 (978-0-8239-4191-9(4), 6948aa9e-1aea-4182-8015-183b51df0027) Rosen Publishing Group, Inc., The.

Katirgis, Jane & Moriarty, J. T. Meet Phillis Wheatley: Poet & Former Slave, 1 vol. 2019. (Introducing Famous Americans Ser.). (ENG.). 32p. (J). (gr. 3-4). pap. 11.53 (978-1-9785-1126-2(4), e57e4207-e764-4677-a83d-24c49043b4d7) Enslow Publishing, LLC.

Kent, Jacqueline C. Phillis Wheatley. 2003. (Women of the Revolution Ser.). (J). pap. (978-1-58417-089-1(1)); lib. bdg. (978-1-58417-026-6(3)) Lake Street Pubs.

Lasky, Kathryn. A Voice of Her Own: A Story of Phillis Wheatley, Slave Poet. 2012. lib. bdg. 14.75 (978-0-606-26940-7(1)) Turtleback.

—A Voice of Her Own: Candlewick Biographies: The Story of Phillis Wheatley, Slave Poet. Lee, Paul, illus. 2012. (Candlewick Biographies Ser.). (ENG.). 48p. (J). (gr. 3-7). 14.99 (978-0-7636-6427-5(8)); pap. 6.99 (978-0-7636-6091-8(4)) Candlewick Pr.

Malaspina, Ann. Phillis Sings Out Freedom: The Story of George Washington & Phillis Wheatley. Keeter, Susan, illus. 2012. (J). 34.28 (978-1-61913-149-1(8)) Weigl Pubs., Inc.

Marsh, Carole. Phillis Wheatley. 2003. 12p. (gr. k-4). 2.95 (978-0-635-02371-1(7)) Gallopade International.

McLeese, Don. Phillis Wheatley. 2004. (Heroes of the American Revolution Ser.). (Illus.). 32p. (J). (gr. -1 — 1). pap. 5.95 (978-1-59515-320-3(9)) Rourke Educational Media.

McLendon, Jacquelyn. Phillis Wheatley: A Revolutionary Poet. 2009. (Library of American Lives & Times Ser.). 112p. (gr. 5-5). 69.20 (978-1-60853-499-9(5)) Rosen Publishing Group, Inc., The.

Mclendon, Jacquelyn & Roza, Greg. Katie's Candy, 1 vol. 2006. (Neighborhood Readers Ser.). (ENG.). 8p. (gr. k-1). pap. 5.90 (978-1-4042-5750-4(0), 620702a6-809e-46da-8310-163f80c1e17a) Rosen Publishing Group, Inc., The.

Moriarty, J. T. Phillis Wheatley: African American Poet. 2009. (Primary Sources of Famous People in American History Ser.). 32p. (gr. 2-3). 47.90 (978-1-60851-717-6(9)) Rosen Publishing Group, Inc., The.

—Phillis Wheatley: African American Poet = Poeta Afroamericana, 1 vol. 2003. (Famous People in American History / Grandes Personajes en la Historia de Los Estados Unidos Ser.). (ENG & SPA., Illus.). 32p. (J). (gr. 3-4). lib. bdg. 29.13 (978-0-8239-4167-4(1), d6c50ca0-35d0-44e5-b6e3-2c186c5b8a60, Editorial Buenas Letras) Rosen Publishing Group, Inc., The.

Pickford, Susan B. Expectations: The Life of Phillis Wheatley. 18p. (J). (gr. 5-9). pap., wbk. ed. 10.00 (978-1-878668-67-7(6)) History Compass, LLC.

Roza, Greg. Guide My Pen: The Poems of Phillis Wheatley. (Great Moments in American History Ser.). 32p. (gr. 3-3). 2009. 47.90 (978-1-61513-133-4(7)) 2003. (ENG., Illus.). (J). lib. bdg. 29.13 (978-0-8239-4381-4(X), 893e7e99-5c63-4123-9adb-02e4e0b7c4c9, Rosen Reference) Rosen Publishing Group, Inc., The.

Smith, Emily. Phillis Wheatley (America's Early Years) rev. ed. 2016. (Social Studies: Informational Text Ser.). (ENG., Illus.). 32p. (gr. 4-8). pap. 11.99 (978-1-4938-3882-0(2)) Teacher Created Materials, Inc.

Smith, Emily R. & Conklin, Wendy. Phillis Wheatley. 2020. (Social Studies: Informational Text Ser.). (SPA., Illus.). 32p. (J). (gr. 3-5). pap. 11.99 (978-0-7439-1362-1(0)) Teacher Created Materials, Inc.

Watson-Doost, Valeria. Phillis Wheatley. 2008. (ENG.). 35p. pap. 21.50 (978-0-557-03153-5(2)) Lulu Pr., Inc.

WHEELS

Allyn, Daisy. Wheels & Axles, 1 vol. 2013. (Simple Machine Science Ser.). (ENG., Illus.). 24p. (gr. 1-2). 25.27 (978-1-4339-8156-2(4), 1177abb3-b1c7-4422-bf6d-71d2dbbd698b); pap. 9.15 (978-1-4339-8157-9(2), 2248143c-4b8f-476c-8765-c0e4432d2c94) Stevens, Gareth Publishing LLLP.

Bailey, Gerry. Rolling Along: Wheels & Axles. Spoor, Mike, illus. 2014. (Robotx Get Help from Simple Machines Ser.). (ENG.). 32p. (J). (gr. 2-3). (978-0-7787-0418-8(1)); pap. (978-0-7787-0424-9(6)) Crabtree Publishing Co.

Banting, Erinn. All about Wheels & Axles. 2017. (Illus.). 24p. (J). (978-1-5105-0963-4(1)) SmartBook Media, Inc.

—Wheels & Axles. 2013. (J). (978-1-62127-429-2(2)); pap. (978-1-62127-435-3(7)) Weigl Pubs., Inc.

Bodden, Valerie. Ferris Wheels. 2012. (Illus.). 24p. (J). 25.65 (978-1-60818-113-1(8), Creative Education) Creative Co., The.

—Wheels & Axles. 2011. (Simple Machine Ser.). 24p. (J). (gr. 1-3). 24.25 (978-1-60818-013-4(1)) Creative Co., The.

Cardenas, Ernesto A. Wheels & Motors. 2009. 19.95 (978-1-60698-023-1(8)); pap. 3.95 (978-1-60698-021-7(1)) Milo Educational Bks. & Resources.

Challen, Paul. Get to Know Wheels & Axles. 2009. (Get to Know Simple Machines Ser.). (ENG., Illus.). 32p. (J). (gr. 2-3). pap. (978-0-7787-4488-7(4)); lib. bdg. (978-0-7787-4471-9(X)) Crabtree Publishing Co.

Close, Edward. Wheels, Wings, & Motors, 1 vol., 1. 2014. (Discovery Education: How It Works). (ENG.). 32p. (gr. 4-5). 28.93 (978-1-4777-6313-1(9), 803af42f-58c3-43fd-81fa-5099de611187, PowerKids Pr.) Rosen Publishing Group, Inc., The.

Cobb, Annie & Jones, Davy. Ruedas! Jones, Davy, illus. 2003. (Road to Reading Ser.). (Illus.). (J). lib. bdg. 11.99 (978-0-375-91500-0(1), Golden Bks.) Random Hse. Children's Bks.

De Medeiros, Michael & Banting, Erinn. Wheels & Axles. 2009. (Science Matters Ser.). (Illus.). 24p. (J). (gr. 3-5). pap. 8.95 (978-1-60596-034-0(9)) Weigl Pubs., Inc.

Dickmann, Nancy. Wheels & Axles. 2018. (Simple Machines Ser.). (ENG., Illus.). 24p. (J). (gr. 2-4). (978-1-78121-403-9(4), 16691) Brown Bear Bks.

Erinn, Banting. Wheels & Axles. 2009. (Science Matters Ser.). (Illus.). 24p. (J). (gr. 3-5). lib. bdg. 24.45 (978-1-60596-033-3(0)) Weigl Pubs., Inc.

Feldman, Roseann & Walker, Sally M. Put Wheels & Axles to the Test. 2011. (Searchlight Books How Do Simple Machines Work Ser.). (ENG., Illus.). (gr. 3-5). pap. 51.01 (978-0-7613-8402-1(2)) Lerner Publishing Group.

Feldmann, Roseann & Walker, Sally M. Put Wheels & Axles to the Test. 2011. (Searchlight Books (tm) — How Do Simple Machines Work? Ser.). (ENG., Illus.). 40p. (J). (gr. 3-5). pap. 9.99 (978-0-7613-7870-9(7), 5d110c1c-8347-4b9c-adb8-bcdf4e36772c) Lerner Publishing Group.

Gardner, Robert. Simple Machine Experiments Using Seesaws, Wheels, Pulleys, & More: One Hour or Less Science Experiments, 1 vol. 2012. (Last-Minute Science Projects Ser.). (ENG.). 48p. (gr. 5-6). 27.93 (978-0-7660-3957-5(9), c71e592f-1768-45fd-8ff8-e7bb096193fc) Enslow Publishing, LLC.

Geatches, Hazel, ed. Wheels. 2012. (ENG., Illus.). 32p. pap. 11.00 (978-0-19-464631-4(9)) Oxford Univ. Pr., Inc.

Gosman, Gillian. Wheels & Axles in Action, 1 vol. 2010. (Simple Machines at Work Ser.). (ENG.). 24p. (J). (gr. 2-3). pap. 9.25 (978-1-4488-1301-8(8), b7224d3a-4b64-49d1-babf-d3202dff721b); lib. bdg. 26.27 (978-1-4488-0684-3(4), 4173fcba-c319-4334-89c4-01122490dcab) Rosen Publishing Group, Inc., The. (PowerKids Pr.).

How Things Work Interactive Packages: Wheels on the Bus. (Pebble Soup Explorations Ser.). (gr. -1-18). 52.00 (978-0-7578-5244-2(0)) Rigby Education.

LaMachia, Dawn. Wheels & Axles at Work, 1 vol. 2015. (Zoom in on Simple Machines Ser.). (ENG.). 24p. (gr. 2-2). 25.60 (978-0-7660-6748-6(3), 078e701e-b15e-4c0f-bc7d-363a0888df7f); pap. 10.95 (978-0-7660-6746-2(7), 5cee8c48-c518-4c40-aae1-f3523b988988) Enslow Publishing, LLC.

Manolis, Kay. Wheels & Axles. 2009. (Simple Machines Ser.). (ENG., Illus.). 24p. (J). (gr. 2-5). lib. bdg. 26.95 (978-1-60014-347-2(4), Blastoff! Readers) Bellwether Media.

Mattern, Joanne. Wheels & Axles. 2019. (Simple Machines Fun! Ser.). (ENG., Illus.). 24p. (J). (gr. k-3). lib. bdg. 26.95 (978-1-62617-996-7(4), Blastoff! Readers) Bellwether Media.

Mezzanotte, Jim. Cómo Funcionan Las Ruedas y Los Ejes (How Wheels & Axles Work), 1 vol. 2006. (Cómo Funcionan Las Máquinas Simples (How Simple Machines Work) Ser.). (SPA., Illus.). 24p. (gr. 2-4). pap. 9.15 (978-0-8368-7451-8(X), 298f3066-2824-456c-81ae-b84d8a98ce55); lib. bdg. 24.67 (978-0-8368-7446-4(3), 635d35a0-7760-4abe-8808-7eb0c7e5572f) Stevens, Gareth Publishing LLLP. (Weekly Reader Leveled Readers).

—How Wheels & Axles Work, 1 vol. 2006. (How Simple Machines Work Ser.). (ENG., Illus.). 24p. (gr. 2-4). pap. 9.15 (978-0-8368-7355-9(6), 939fd8d5-32cf-4dca-861d-9d77bf0359c5); lib. bdg. 24.67 (978-0-8368-7350-4(5), 957f009d-3bd7-4bc3-ac0b-af2fa48e3930) Stevens, Gareth Publishing LLLP. (Weekly Reader Leveled Readers).

Miller, Tim & Sjonger, Rebecca. Wheels & Axles in My Makerspace. 2017. (Simple Machines in My Makerspace Ser.). (ENG., Illus.). 32p. (J). (gr. 3-4). (978-0-7787-3375-1(0)) Crabtree Publishing Co.

Oxlade, Chris. Simple Experiments with Wheels & Axles, 1 vol. 2013. (Science Experiments with Simple Machines Ser.). (ENG.). 32p. (J). (gr. 2-3). 31.17 (978-1-61533-754-5(7), f20d8034-caf6-4904-b63c-c3548d2e2bb0); pap. 12.75 (978-1-61533-825-2(X), 9561e978-f36e-4a8b-92e4-dbfa4b2bd1d6) Rosen Publishing Group, Inc., The. (Windmill Bks.).

—Simple Experiments with Wheels & Axles. 2013. (Science Experiments with Simple Machines Ser.). 32p. (J). (gr. k-3). pap. 70.50 (978-1-61533-826-9(8)) Windmill Bks.

—Wheels. 2009. (Simple Machines (Smart Apple Media Paperback) Ser.). (Illus.). 32p. (J). pap. 7.95 (978-1-59920-204-4(2)) Black Rabbit Bks.

Prince, April Jones. What Do Wheels Do All Day? Laroche, Giles, illus. 2006. (ENG.). 32p. (J). (gr. -1-3). 17.99 (978-0-618-56307-4(5), 593931, Clarion Bks.) HarperCollins Pubs.

—What Do Wheels Do All Day?/¿Qué Hacen Las Ruedas Todo el día? Board Book: Bilingual English-Spanish. Laroche, Giles, illus. 2013.Tr. of What Do Wheels Do All Day? (ENG.). 32p. (J). (— 1). bds. 5.99 (978-0-547-99625-7(X), 1525533, Clarion Bks.) HarperCollins Pubs.

Randolph, Joanne. Wheels & Axles in My World, 1 vol. 2006. (Journeys Ser.). (ENG.). 24p. (gr. k-2). pap. 7.05 (978-1-4042-8427-2(3), 27fa068d-8e9a-4d09-80a0-b6ac1c5228d2, Rosen Classroom) Rosen Publishing Group, Inc., The.

—Wheels & Axles in My World: Ejes y Ruedas en Mi Mundo, 1 vol. 2005. (My World of Science / la Ciencia en Mi Mundo Ser.). (ENG & SPA.). 24p. (J). (gr. 2-2). 22.27 (978-1-4042-3325-6(3), 7a96327d-1324-482a-8470-843977f3d90d) Rosen Publishing Group, Inc., The.

Rockwell, Anne. Big Wheels. 2006. (ENG., Illus.). 11p. (J). (gr. -1-1). bds. 8.99 (978-0-8027-8903-7(X), 900039441, Bloomsbury USA Childrens) Bloomsbury Publishing USA.

Rosa y el Escarabajo: Individual Title Six-Packs. (Literatura 2000 Ser.). (SPA.). (gr. 2-3). 33.00 (978-0-7635-1250-7(8)) Rigby Education.

Round & Round, 6 Packs. (gr. k-1). 23.00 (978-0-7635-9057-4(6)) Rigby Education.

Rustad, Martha E. H. Wheels & Axles. 2018. (Simple Machines Ser.). (ENG., Illus.). 24p. (J). (gr. -1-2). lib. bdg. 22.65 (978-1-5435-0076-9(5), 137027, Capstone Pr.) Capstone.

Schuh, Mari. Hauling a Pumpkin: Wheels & Axles vs. Lever. 2015. (First Step Nonfiction — Simple Machines to the Rescue Ser.). (ENG., Illus.). 24p. (J). (gr. k-2). pap. 6.99 (978-1-4677-8304-0(8), e7f4a3c6-fb07-4757-abc5-aeecbf1664db) Lerner Publishing Group.

—Holding a Door Open: Wedge vs. Wheels & Axles. 2015. (First Step Nonfiction — Simple Machines to the Rescue Ser.). (ENG., Illus.). 24p. (J). (gr. k-2). E-Book 35.99 (978-1-4677-8303-3(X), Lerner Pubns.) Lerner Publishing Group.

Scott, Natalie. Wheels Make it Work, 1 vol. 2008. (Real Life Readers Ser.). (ENG.). 12p. (gr. 1-2). pap. 5.90 (978-1-4042-7923-0(7), b062b2b5-2769-4edf-994b-f7402e279c74, Rosen Classroom) Rosen Publishing Group, Inc., The.

ShackletonCaroline. THE WHEEL LOW INTERMEDIATE BOOK WITH ONLINE ACCESS, 1 vol. 2014. (ENG., Illus.). 28p. (J). pap., E-Book, E-Book 9.50 (978-1-107-66739-6(9)) Cambridge Univ. Pr.

Sian Revision Wheels at Work. 2004. (Science in A Nutshell Ser.). (J). (978-1-59242-087-2(7)) Delta Education, LLC.

Smith, Sian. Wheels & Axles, 1 vol. 2012. (How Toys Work Ser.). (ENG.). 24p. (gr. -1-1). pap. 6.29 (978-1-4329-6591-4(3), 119235, Heinemann) Capstone.

Taylor, Trace. Wheels. Taylor, Trace, illus. 2009. (1-3Y Getting Around Ser.). (ENG., Illus.). 16p. (J). pap. 8.00 (978-1-61406-201-1(3)) American Reading Co.

Tieck, Sarah. Wheels & Axles, 1 vol. 2006. (Simple Machines Ser.). (ENG., Illus.). 24p. (gr. -1-3). 25.65 (978-1-59679-819-9(X), Buddy Bks.) ABDO Publishing Co.

Walker, Sally M. & Feldmann, Roseann. Wheels & Axles. 2005. (Early Bird Physics Ser.). (Illus.). 48p. (gr. 3-6). lib. bdg. 25.26 (978-0-8225-2219-5(5)) Lerner Publishing Group.

Weakland, Mark. Fred Flintstone's Adventures with Wheels & Axles: Bedrock & Roll! Brown, Alan, illus. 2016. (Flintstones Explain Simple Machines Ser.). (ENG.). 24p. (J). (gr. k-2). lib. bdg. 27.99 (978-1-4914-8474-6(8), 130923) Capstone.

—Gears Go, Wheels Roll. 2010. (Science Starts Ser.). (ENG.). 32p. (J). (gr. 1-2). pap. 48.60 (978-1-4296-6144-7(5), 16036, Capstone Pr.) Capstone.

Wells, Robert E. How Do You Lift a Lion? 2012. (J). 34.28 (978-1-61913-159-0(5)) Weigl Pubs., Inc.

Wheels: Individual Title Six-Packs. (Literatura 2000 Ser.). (gr. k-1). 28.00 (978-0-7635-0077-1(1)); 16p. 27.00 (978-0-7635-4446-1(9)) Rigby Education.

Woods, Michael & Woods, Mary B. Ancient Machine Technology: From Wheels to Forges. 2011. (Technology in Ancient Cultures Ser.). (ENG.). 96p. (gr. 6-12). lib. bdg. 31.93 (978-0-7613-6523-5(0)) Lerner Publishing Group.

WHISKEY REBELLION, PA., 1794

Schiel, Katy. The Whiskey Rebellion: An Early Challenge to America's New Government. (Life in the New American Nation Ser.). 32p. (gr. 4-4). 2009. 47.90

(978-1-61514-289-7(4)) 2003. (ENG., Illus.). pap. 10.00 *(978-0-8239-4262-6(7)*, ccdb6263-16e0-4fcf-891d-08b22fac56f1) 2003. (ENG., Illus.). lib. bdg. 29.13 *(978-0-8239-4044-8(6)*, 45767c13-023c-49f0-98c7-a918ad520b87, Rosen Reference) Rosen Publishing Group, Inc., The.

WHITE HOUSE (WASHINGTON, D.C.)

Arnold, Tedd. Fly Guy Presents: the White House (Scholastic Reader, Level 2) Arnold, Tedd, illus. 2016. (Scholastic Reader, Level 2 Ser.). (ENG., Illus.). 32p. (J). (gr. k-2). pap. 4.99 *(978-0-545-91737-7(9))* Scholastic, Inc.

Ashley, Susan. The White House, 1 vol. 2004. (Places in American History Ser.). (ENG., Illus.). 24p. (gr. 2-4). pap. 9.15 *(978-0-8368-4152-7(2)*, 4ea8d8d2-7318-48aa-ad29-d3c09860beea); lib. bdg. 24.67 *(978-0-8368-4145-9(X)*, 97d0acb8-2dc2-49e9-92b3-e0d3d1e66f35) Stevens, Gareth Publishing LLLP. (Weekly Reader Leveled Readers).

Becker, Cynthia Simmelink. Lights On! Ike Hoover Electrifies the White House. Hummel, Benjamin, illus. 2017. (ENG.). 40p. (J). 19.95 *(978-0-86541-244-6(8))* Filter Pr., LLC.

Blake, Kevin. The White House. 2016. (American Places: from Vision to Reality Ser.). (ENG., Illus.). 32p. (J). (gr. 2-7). 28.50 *(978-1-944102-42-5(6))* Bearport Publishing Co., Inc.

Braithwaite, Jill. The White House. 2010. (Lightning Bolt Books (r) — Famous Places Ser.). (ENG., Illus.). 32p. (J). (gr. 1-3). pap. 9.99 *(978-0-7613-6054-4(9)*, 6ac5bb17-5d51-4699-838c-b3f17528f5ff); pap. 45.32 *(978-0-7613-6995-0(3))* Lerner Publishing Group.

Carr, Aaron. The White House. 2016. (American Icons Ser.). (ENG., Illus.). (J). (gr. k-2). lib. bdg. 27.13 *(978-1-4896-0532-0(0)*, AV2 by Weigl) Weigl Pubs., Inc.

Cesky, Brittany. The White House. 2018. (US Symbols Ser.). (ENG., Illus.). 24p. (J). (gr. 1-1). pap. 8.95 *(978-1-63517-838-8(X)*, 163517838X) North Star Editions.

—The White House. 2018. (US Symbols Ser.). (ENG., Illus.). 24p. (J). (gr. k-3). lib. bdg. 31.36 *(978-1-5321-6050-9(X)*, 28732, Pop! Cody Koala) Pop!

Clay, Kathryn. The White House: Introducing Primary Sources. 2017. (Introducing Primary Sources Ser.). (ENG., Illus.). 32p. (J). (gr. -1-2). pap. 6.95 *(978-1-5157-6361-1(7)*, 135118); lib. bdg. 28.65 *(978-1-5157-6356-7(0)*. 135115) Capstone. (Capstone Pr.).

Connors, Kathleen. What's It Like to Live in the White House?, 1 vol. 2014. (White House Insiders Ser.). (ENG.). 24p. (J). (gr. 2-3). 24.27 *(978-1-4824-1110-2(5)*, 0e5887f2-5ddf-45cd-8ed2-be6de588169d) Stevens, Gareth Publishing LLLP.

—What's It Like to Work in the White House?, 1 vol. 2014. (White House Insiders Ser.). (ENG.). 24p. (J). (gr. 2-3). 24.27 *(978-1-4824-1115-7(6)*, 0dd36628-cd81-446f-890d-894eb628f8c8) Stevens, Gareth Publishing LLLP.

Davidson, Janice. Inside the White House. 2013. (InfoMax Readers Ser.). (ENG.). 24p. (J). (gr. 2-3). pap. 49.50 *(978-1-4777-2270-1(X))*; (Illus.). pap. 8.25 *(978-1-4777-2269-5(6)*, b632b5af-347a-439b-a074-0de1bcf38096) Rosen Publishing Group, Inc., The. (Rosen Classroom).

Davis, Gibbs. First Kids. Comport, Sally Wern, illus. 2009. (Step into Reading: Step 4 Ser.). (ENG.). 48p. (J). (gr. 1-3). lib. bdg. 16.19 *(978-0-375-92218-3(0))* Random House Publishing Group.

—First Kids. Comport, Sally Wern, illus. 2004. (Step into Reading Ser.). (ENG.). 48p. (J). (gr. 2-4). pap. 4.99 *(978-0-375-82218-6(6)*, Random Hse. Bks. for Young Readers) Random Hse. Children's Bks.

Douglas, Lloyd G. The White House. 2003. (Welcome Bks.). (ENG., Illus.). 24p. (J). (gr. -1-2). pap. 4.95 *(978-0-516-27878-0(9)*, Children's Pr.) Scholastic Library Publishing.

Eldridge, Alison & Eldridge, Stephen. The White House: An American Symbol, 1 vol. 2012. (All about American Symbols Ser.). (ENG.). 24p. (gr. -1-1). 25.27 *(978-0-7660-4062-5(3)*, 79e314ad-ddb0-4055-8358-566f1484a2f2); (Illus.). pap. 10.35 *(978-1-4644-0050-6(4)*, d4022209-cb74-403a-9b14-a017d8525bb8) Enslow Publishing, LLC. (Enslow Publishing).

Flynn, Sarah Wassner. 1,000 Facts about the White House. 2017. (1,000 Facts About Ser.). (Illus.). 96p. (J). (gr. 3-7). 14.99 *(978-1-4263-2873-2(7)*, National Geographic Kids) Disney Publishing Worldwide.

Freeman, Martha. The Case of the Diamond Dog Collar, 2. 2nd ed. 2012. (First Kids Mysteries Ser.: 2). (ENG.). 144p. (J). (gr. 2-4). 21.19 *(978-0-8234-2337-8(9))* Holiday Hse., Inc.

Fuentes, Marco. A Visit to the White House. 2016. (Spring Forward Ser.). (J). (gr. k). *(978-1-4900-3711-0(X))* Benchmark Education Co.

Gagne, Tammy. Ghosts of the White House. 2018. (Ghosts & Hauntings Ser.). (ENG., Illus.). 32p. (J). (gr. 4-6). lib. bdg. 28.65 *(978-1-5435-4150-2(X)*, 139104, Capstone Pr.) Capstone.

Gaspar, Joe. The White House, 1 vol. 2013. (PowerKids Readers: American Symbols Ser.). (Illus.). 24p. (J). (gr. k-k). (ENG.). pap. 9.25 *(978-1-4777-0817-0(0)*, 716e9627-c9dd-437c-8456-1d67438e9cb2); (ENG., lib. bdg. 26.27 *(978-1-4777-0738-8(7)*, b2b77777-5333-4eb9-b6b9-aef20d85fb19); pap. 49.50 *(978-1-4777-0818-7(9))* Rosen Publishing Group, Inc., The. (PowerKids Pr.).

—The White House / la Casa Blanca, 1 vol. Alamn, Eduardo, ed. 2013. (PowerKids Readers: Símbolos de América / American Symbols Ser.). (ENG & SPA.). 24p. (J). (gr. k-k). 26.27 *(978-1-4777-1206-1(2)*, e0883af7-8068-4cae-8704-cccfacd383c4, PowerKids Pr.) Rosen Publishing Group, Inc., The.

Gilbert, H. K. Reporting for Duty: A Day at the White House. 2009. 50p. pap. 9.95 *(978-1-4401-5686-1(7))* iUniverse, Inc.

Healy, Nick. The White House. 2003. (J). pap. *(978-1-58417-120-1(0))*; lib. bdg. *(978-1-58417-056-3(5))* Lake Street Pubs.

Herrington, Lisa M. The White House (Rookie Read-About American Symbols) (Library Edition) 2014. (Rookie Read-About American Symbols Ser.). (ENG., Illus.). 32p. (J). (gr. 1-2). lib. bdg. 25.00 *(978-0-531-21567-8(9)*, Children's Pr.) Scholastic Library Publishing.

Hess, Debra. The White House, 1 vol. (Symbols of America Ser.). (ENG.). 40p. (gr. 3-3). 2008. pap. 9.23 *(978-0-7614-3394-1(5)*, 78d1cc54-bf2e-4dee-85fe-37161aa93683) 2005. (Illus.). lib. bdg. 32.64 *(978-0-7614-1712-5(5)*, 6264dc64-d378-4419-8d34-025935ad25b6, Cavendish Square) Cavendish Square Publishing LLC.

Hicks, Terry Allan. Symbols of America Group 2, 12 vols., Set. Incl. Bald Eagle. lib. bdg. 32.64 *(978-0-7614-2133-7(5)*, 4cc77ac4-353f-4135-8229-fee1fad1bf3b); Capitol. lib. bdg. 32.64 *(978-0-7614-2132-0(7)*, 983498dc-4064-4d9b-a5fd-9541490d6e2c); Declaration of Independence. lib. bdg. 32.64 *(978-0-7614-2135-1(1)*, b672c79b-ebcf-460a-bf6f-c79934c3be91); Ellis Island. lib. bdg. 32.64 *(978-0-7614-2134-4(3)*, eadd5cdd-45bd-4dab-99b1-a60a5a76c2ba); Pledge of Allegiance. lib. bdg. 32.64 *(978-0-7614-2136-8(X)*, 4f80c1f0-d3ea-4dd5-b747-5d88842745e5); Uncle Sam. lib. bdg. 32.64 *(978-0-7614-2137-5(8)*, e6f9da10-1cd5-4edb-8cd5-0e9e233d21ec); (Illus.). 40p. (gr. 3-3). (Symbols of America Ser.). (ENG.). 2007. Set lib. bdg. 195.84 *(978-0-7614-2130-6(0)*, b2a0354a-8705-48f9-b041-df7983c1050e, Cavendish Square) Cavendish Square Publishing LLC.

House, Katherine L. The White House for Kids: A History of a Home, Office, & National Symbol, with 21 Activities. 2014. (For Kids Ser.: 46). (ENG., Illus.). 144p. (J). (gr. 4). pap. 16.95 *(978-1-61374-461-1(7))* Chicago Review Pr., Inc.

Kennedy, Marge. Pets at the White House. 2009. (Scholastic News Nonfiction Readers Ser.). (Illus.). 24p. (J). (gr. 1-2). 22.00 *(978-0-531-21096-3(0))* Scholastic Library Publishing.

—Scholastic News Nonfiction Readers: Let's Visit the White House, 6 vols., Set. Incl. Having Fun at the White House. Kennedy, Marge M. (Illus.). (gr. 1-2). 22.00 *(978-0-531-21095-6(2))*; Pets at the White House. (Illus.). (gr. 1-2). 22.00 *(978-0-531-21096-3(0))*; See Inside the White House. (Illus.). (gr. 1-2). 22.00 *(978-0-531-21097-0(9))*; Story of the White House. Kennedy, Marge M. (Illus.). (gr. 1-2). 22.00 *(978-0-531-21094-9(4))*; Time to Eat at the White House. (gr. k-3). 21.19 *(978-0-531-21098-7(7)*, Children's Pr.); Who Works at the White House? (Illus.). (gr. 1-2). 22.00 *(978-0-531-21099-4(5))*; 24p. (J). 2009. Set lib. bdg. 132.00 *(978-0-531-27902-1(2)*, Children's Pr.) Scholastic Library Publishing.

—See Inside the White House. 2009. (Scholastic News Nonfiction Readers Ser.). (Illus.). 24p. (J). (gr. 1-2). 22.00 *(978-0-531-21097-0(9))* Scholastic Library Publishing.

—Time to Eat at the White House. 2009. (Scholastic News Nonfiction Readers: Let's Visit the White House Ser.). (ENG.). 24p. (J). (gr. k-3). 21.19 *(978-0-531-21098-7(7)*, Children's Pr.); (gr. 1-3). pap. 6.95 *(978-0-531-22436-6(8))* Scholastic Library Publishing.

—Who Works at the White House? 2009. (Scholastic News Nonfiction Readers Ser.). (Illus.). 24p. (J). (gr. 1-2). 22.00 *(978-0-531-21099-4(5))* Scholastic Library Publishing.

Kennedy, Marge M. & Kennedy, Marge. Having Fun at the White House. 2009. (Scholastic News Nonfiction Readers Ser.). (Illus.). 24p. (J). (gr. 1-2). 22.00 *(978-0-531-21095-6(2))* Scholastic Library Publishing.

—The Story of the White House. 2009. (Scholastic News Nonfiction Readers Ser.). (Illus.). 24p. (J). (gr. 1-2). 22.00 *(978-0-531-21094-9(4))* Scholastic Library Publishing.

Kissock, Heather. White House. 2017. (Illus.). 24p. (J). *(978-1-5105-0611-4(X))* SmartBook Media, Inc.

Linde, Barbara M. The White House, 1 vol. 2018. (Symbols of America Ser.). (ENG.). 24p. (gr. 1-2). lib. bdg. 24.27 *(978-1-5382-2901-9(3)*, 96153e96-1365-4456-a742-d208641df833) Stevens, Gareth Publishing LLLP.

Marcovitz, Hal. The White House. 2004. (American Symbols & Their Meanings Ser.). (Illus.). 48p. (J). (gr. 4-18). lib. bdg. 19.95 *(978-1-59084-024-5(0))* Mason Crest.

—The White House: The Home of the U. S. President. Moreno, Barry, ed. 2014. (Patriotic Symbols of America Ser.: 20). 48p. (J). (gr. 4-18). lib. bdg. 20.95 *(978-1-4222-3134-0(8))* Mason Crest.

Markovics, Joyce. White & Majestic: What Am I? 2018. (American Place Puzzlers Ser.). (ENG.). 24p. (J). (gr. -1-3). E-Book 41.36 *(978-1-68402-543-5(5))* Bearport Publishing Co., Inc.

Markovics, Joyce L. White & Majestic: What Am I? 2018. (American Place Puzzlers Ser.). (ENG.). 24p. (J). (gr. -1-3). lib. bdg. 26.99 *(978-1-68402-485-8(4))* Bearport Publishing Co., Inc.

Marsh, Carole. The Obama Family - Life in the White House: President Barack Obama, First Lady Michelle Obama, First Children Malia & Sasha. 2008. (Here & Now Ser.). 32p. (J). (gr. 2-9). pap. 8.99 *(978-0-635-07051-7(0))* Gallopade International.

Modifica, Lisa. A Timeline of the White House. (Timelines of American History Ser.). 32p. (gr. 4-4). 2009. 47.90 *(978-1-60854-393-9(5))* 2004. (ENG., Illus.). lib. bdg. 29.13 *(978-0-8239-4543-6(X)*, d525a8ac-c718-47fa-8248-0b89d5f2071f) Rosen Publishing Group, Inc., The. (Rosen Reference).

Morrison, Jennifer. The White House. 2009. (Structural Wonders Ser.). (Illus.). 32p. (J). (gr. 4-6). lib. bdg. 9.95 *(978-1-60596-664-9(9))*; lib. bdg. 26.00 *(978-1-60596-663-2(0))* Weigl Pubs., Inc.

Morrison, Jessica. The White House. 2019. (Structural Wonders of the World Ser.). (ENG., Illus.). 24p. (J). (gr. 4-7). pap. 12.95 *(978-1-4896-9948-0(1))*; lib. bdg. 28.55 *(978-1-4896-9947-3(3))* Weigl Pubs., Inc.

Morrison, Jessica & Kissock, Heather. The White House. 2012. (J). 27.13 *(978-1-61913-253-5(2))*; pap. 12.95 *(978-1-61913-259-7(1))* Weigl Pubs., Inc.

Murray, Julie. The Statue of Liberty. 2016. (US Landmarks Ser.). (ENG., Illus.). 24p. (J). (gr. -1-2). lib. bdg. 31.36 *(978-1-68080-914-5(8)*, 23303, Abdo Kids) ABDO Publishing Co.

—The White House. 2016. (US Landmarks Ser.). (ENG., Illus.). 24p. (J). (gr. -1-2). lib. bdg. 31.36 *(978-1-68080-916-9(4)*, 23307, Abdo Kids) ABDO Publishing Co.

Nagelhout, Ryan. 20 Fun Facts about the White House, 1 vol. 2013. (Fun Fact File: U. S. History! Ser.). (ENG.). 32p. (J). (gr. 2-3). pap. 11.50 *(978-1-4339-9204-9(3)*, 1bf1c4bf-cd86-47c6-b2ab-6fa6c844db87) Stevens, Gareth Publishing LLLP.

N.C.B.L.A. Our White House: Looking in, Looking Out. 2010. (ENG., Illus.). 256p. (J). (gr. 5). pap. 16.99 *(978-0-7636-4609-7(1))* Candlewick Pr.

Newport, Chelsea. Visiting the White House, 1 vol. 2013. (Rosen Readers Ser.). (ENG.). 24p. (J). (gr. 2-2). pap. 8.25 *(978-1-4777-2246-6(7)*, 05d69d93-8398-48f4-a587-ee9cbf123739); pap. 49.50 *(978-1-4777-2247-3(5))* Rosen Publishing Group, Inc., The. (Rosen Classroom).

O'Connor, Jane. If the Walls Could Talk: Family Life at the White House. Hovland, Gary, illus. 2004. (ENG.). 48p. (J). (gr. 1-4). 19.99 *(978-0-689-86863-4(4)*, Simon & Schuster/Paula Wiseman Bks.) Simon & Schuster/Paula Wiseman Bks.

Osborne, Mary Pope. Abe Lincoln at Last! Murdocca, Sal, illus. 2013. (Magic Tree House (R) Merlin Mission Ser.: 19). 144p. (J). (gr. 2-5). 6.99 *(978-0-375-86797-2(X)*, Random Hse. Bks. for Young Readers) Random Hse. Children's Bks.

Owings, Lisa. Ghosts in the White House. 2016. (Ghost Stories Ser.). (ENG., Illus.). 24p. (J). (gr. 3-7). 26.95 *(978-1-62617-432-0(6)*, Epic Bks.) Bellwether Media.

Petruccio, Steven James. The History of the White House Coloring Book. 2010. (Dover American History Coloring Bks.). (ENG.). 32p. (gr. 3-5). pap. 3.99 *(978-0-486-47556-1(5)*, 475565) Dover Pubns., Inc.

Proudfit, Benjamin. Building the White House, 1 vol. 2014. (What You Didn't Know about History Ser.). (ENG., Illus.). 24p. (J). (gr. 2-3). pap. 9.15 *(978-1-4824-1930-6(0)*, f84a1f35-deea-4db3-b4f1-7e0f34387bc8) Stevens, Gareth Publishing LLLP.

Rajczak, Michael. Haunted! the White House. 2013. (History's Most Haunted Ser.). 32p. (J). (gr. 3-6). pap. 63.00 *(978-1-4339-9270-4(1))*; (ENG., Illus.). pap. 11.50 *(978-1-4339-9269-8(8)*, ff2c13ad-7756-402c-8ab7-fd60677fda72); (ENG., Illus.). lib. bdg. 29.27 *(978-1-4339-9268-1(X)*, e7723c10-e0c2-4641-9840-656ecedda926) Stevens, Gareth Publishing LLLP.

Reeves, Diane Lindsey & White, Kelly. Choose a Career Adventure at the White House. 2016. (Bright Futures Press: Choose a Career Adventure Ser.). (ENG., Illus.). 32p. (J). (gr. 4-6). 32.07 *(978-1-63471-916-2(6)*, 208985) Cherry Lake Publishing.

Sabuda, Robert. The White House: a Pop-Up of Our Nation's Home. Sabuda, Robert, illus. 2015. (ENG., Illus.). 12p. (J). (gr. -1-3). bds. 29.99 *(978-0-545-54089-6(5)*, Orchard Bks.) Scholastic, Inc.

Schuh, Mari. The White House. 2018. (Symbols of American Freedom Ser.). (ENG., Illus.). 24p. (J). (gr. k-3). pap. 7.99 *(978-1-61891-476-7(6)*, 12129, Blastoff! Readers) Bellwether Media.

Silate, Jennifer. The White House. (Primary Sources of American Symbols Ser.). 24p. (gr. 3-3). 2009. 42.50 *(978-1-60851-512-7(5)*, PowerKids Pr.) 2005. (ENG., Illus.). (J). lib. bdg. 26.27 *(978-1-4042-2695-1(8)*, 5e07579f-ac16-4a0d-acb7-e7a6cbae7d70) Rosen Publishing Group, Inc., The.

Smith, Jr, Charles R. Brick by Brick. 2012. (ENG., Illus.). 32p. (J). (gr. -1-3). 17.99 *(978-0-06-192082-0(7)*, Amistad) HarperCollins Pubs.

Smith, A. g. & Smith, A. G. The White House Cut & Assemble. 2010. (Dover Children's Activity Bks.). (ENG., Illus.). 20p. (J). (gr. 3-6). pap. 9.99 *(978-0-486-47681-0(2)*, 476812) Dover Pubns., Inc.

Smith, Charles R., Jr. Brick by Brick. 2015. (J). lib. bdg. 17.20 *(978-0-606-37371-5(3))* Turtleback.

Stevens, Stewart, Sr. The White House Chandeliers: My Experiences While Working for Seven U. S. Presidents. 2016. (ENG., Illus.). xi, 127p. (gr. 6-17). pap. 25.00 *(978-0-9974925-0-7(3))* Lightning Fast Bk. Publishing.

Stine, Megan. Where Is the White House? 2015. (Where Is... ? Ser.). lib. bdg. 16.00 *(978-0-606-36591-8(5))* Turtleback.

Stine, Megan & Who HQ. Where Is the White House? Groff, David, illus. 2015. (Where Is? Ser.). 112p. (J). (gr. 3-7). 5.99 *(978-0-448-48355-9(6)*, Penguin Workshop) Penguin Young Readers Group.

Sutcliffe, Jane. The White House Is Burning: August 24 1814. Farquharson, Alexander, illus. 2014. 128p. (J). (gr. 4-7). 19.95 *(978-1-58089-656-6(1))* Charlesbridge Publishing, Inc.

White House Insiders, 12 vols. 2014. (White House Insiders Ser.). 24p. (J). (gr. 2-3). (ENG.). 145.62 *(978-1-4824-1089-1(3)*, b1ee5fec-e3f4-4e88-9397-a1a9a2efdf91); pap. 41.70 *(978-1-4824-1595-7(X))* Stevens, Gareth Publishing LLLP.

20 Fun Facts about the White House. 2013. (Fun Fact File: US History! Ser.). 32p. (J). (gr. 3-6). pap. 63.00 *(978-1-4339-9205-6(1))* Stevens, Gareth Publishing LLLP.

WHITMAN, MARCUS, 1802-1847—FICTION

Frazier, Neta. The Stout-Hearted Seven: Orphaned on the Oregon Trail. 2017. (Great Leaders & Events Ser.). (ENG.). (J). (gr. 4-8). lib. bdg. 35.99 *(978-1-942875-43-7(6))* Quarto Publishing Group USA.

WHITMAN, NARCISSA (PRENTISS), 1808-1847

Harness, Cheryl. The Tragic Tale of Narcissa Whitman & a Faithful History of the Oregon Trail (Direct Mail Edition) 2006. (Cheryl Harness Histories Ser.). (Illus.). 144p. (J). (gr. 5-9). 16.95 *(978-0-7922-5920-6(3)*, National Geographic Kids) Disney Publishing Worldwide.

WHITMAN, WALT, 1819-1892

Beene, Alex. Reading & Interpreting the Works of Walt Whitman, 1 vol. 2017. (Lit Crit Guides). (ENG.). 160p. (gr. 8-8). lib. bdg. 41.60 *(978-0-7660-8495-7(7)*, f54ac705-4d96-473b-9d95-d3b13dfc7162) Enslow Publishing, LLC.

Burleigh, Robert. O Captain, My Captain: Walt Whitman, Abraham Lincoln, & the Civil War. Hundley, Sterling, illus. 2019. (ENG.). 64p. (J). (gr. 5-17). 19.99 *(978-1-4197-3358-1(3)*, 1120101, Abrams Bks. for Young Readers) Abrams, Inc.

Kerley, Barbara. Walt Whitman: Words for America, 1 vol. Selznick, Brian, illus. 2004. (ENG.). 56p. (gr. 2-5). 19.99 *(978-0-439-35791-3(8)*, Scholastic Pr.) Scholastic, Inc.

Loewen, Nancy. Walt Whitman. 2014. (Voices in Poetry Ser.). (ENG., Illus.). 48p. (J). (gr. 5-8). pap. 12.00 *(978-1-62832-057-2(5)*, 21459, Creative Paperbacks) Creative Co., The.

—Walt Whitman. Day, Rob, illus. 2014. (Voices in Poetry Ser.) (ENG.). 48p. (J). (gr. 5-8). 35.65 *(978-1-60818-329-6(7)*, 21458, Creative Education) Creative Co., The.

Riggs, Thomas, ed. Democracy in the Poetry of Walt Whitman 1 vol. 2012. (Social Issues in Literature Ser.). (ENG., Illus.). 208p. (gr. 10-12). pap. 33.00 *(978-0-7377-6378-2(7)*, 6114475f-97be-4af3-a3d8-c2d667f1f68c); lib. bdg. 48.03 *(978-0-7377-6377-5(9)*, 85d35420-c323-4feb-93bb-bc58110970c2) Greenhaven Publishing LLC. (Greenhaven Publishing).

WHITNEY, ELI, 1765-1825

Bethea, Nikole Brooks. The Invention of the Cotton Gin. 2017. (Engineering That Made America Ser.). (ENG.). 32p. (J). (gr. 3-6). lib. bdg. 35.64 *(978-1-5038-1642-8(7)*, 211158) Child's World, Inc, The.

Cefrey, Holly. The Inventions of Eli Whitney: The Cotton Gin. 2009. (19th Century American Inventors Ser.). 24p. (gr. 2-3). 42.50 *(978-1-60854-951-1(8)*, PowerKids Pr.) Rosen Publishing Group, Inc., The.

Garcia, Tracy J. Eli Whitney, 1 vol. 2013. (Jr. Graphic American Inventors Ser.). (ENG., Illus.). 24p. (J). (gr. 2-3). pap. 11.60 *(978-1-4777-0135-5(4)*, e51cf43c-c88e-44fc-a0fa-5bdbd5c6cdaa); lib. bdg. 28.93 *(978-1-4777-0075-4(7)*, b6538853-61ed-4ace-97a8-8ab78d25319a) Rosen Publishing Group, Inc., The. (PowerKids Pr.).

Gibson, Karen Bush. Eli Whitney. 2006. (Profiles in American History Ser.). (Illus.). 48p. (J). (gr. 3-7). lib. bdg. 29.95 *(978-1-58415-434-1(9))* Mitchell Lane Pubs.

Gunderson, Jessica Sarah & Barnett, Charles, III. Eli Whitney & the Cotton Gin, 1 vol. Acerno, Gerry, illus. 2007. (Inventions & Discovery Ser.). (ENG.). 32p. (J). (gr. 3-9). per. 8.10 *(978-0-7368-7895-1(5)*, 93892, Capstone Pr.) Capstone.

Huff, Regan A. Eli Whitney: The Cotton Gin & American Manufacturing. 2009. (Library of American Lives & Times Ser.). 112p. (gr. 5-5). 69.20 *(978-1-60853-478-4(2))* Rosen Publishing Group, Inc., The.

Mitchell, Barbara. Maker of Machines: A Story about Eli Whitney. Jones, Jan Naimo, tr. Jones, Jan Naimo, illus. 2004. (Creative Minds Biographies Ser.). (ENG.). 64p. (gr. 4-8). 22.60 *(978-1-57505-603-6(8)*, Carolrhoda Bks.) Lerner Publishing Group.

Welch, Catherine A. Eli Whitney: History Maker Bios Set. 2008. pap. 52.95 *(978-0-8225-9388-1(2))* Lerner Publishing Group.

WHITTIER, JOHN GREENLEAF, 1807-1892

Cody, Sherwin. Four American Poets. 2009. 198p. pap. 14.14 *(978-0-217-47860-1(3))* General Bks. LLC.

WHITTLING

see Wood-Carving

WIESEL, ELIE, 1928-2016

Dakers, Diane. Elie Wiesel: Holocaust Survivor & Messenger for Humanity. 2012. (ENG., Illus.). 112p. (J). *(978-0-7787-2552-7(9))*; pap. *(978-0-7787-2555-8(3))* Crabtree Publishing Co.

Houghton, Sarah. Elie Wiesel: A Holocaust Survivor Cries Out for Peace. 2003. (High Five Reading - Green Ser.). (ENG., Illus.). 48p. (J). (gr. 3-4). per. 9.00 *(978-0-7368-2833-8(8))* Capstone.

—Elie Wiesel Set: A Holocaust Survivor Cries Out for Peace, 6. 2003. (High Five Reading - Green Ser.). (ENG.). 48p. (gr. 3-4). pap. 54.00 *(978-0-7368-2843-7(5))* Capstone.

Koestler-Grack, Rachel. Elie Wiesel: Witness for Humanity, 1 vol. 2009. (Life Portraits Ser.). (ENG., Illus.). 112p. (J). (gr. 6-8). lib. bdg. 38.67 *(978-1-4339-0054-9(8)*, 74f0f7fc-d07c-4729-897a-72060673239c) Stevens, Gareth Publishing LLLP.

Night. 2009. (ENG.). 136p. (gr. 9-18). 30.00 *(978-1-60413-198-7(5)*, P161630, Facts On File) Infobase Holdings, Inc.

Silverman, Jean. Elie Wiesel, 1 vol., 1. 2015. (Holocaust Ser.). (ENG., Illus.). 112p. (J). (gr. 7-7). 38.80 *(978-1-4994-6250-0(6)*, 3c7de5a5-2a46-4002-8d93-2430a51d6ef9, Rosen Young Adult) Rosen Publishing Group, Inc., The.

WIGMAKERS

Sullivan, Laura. The Colonial Wigmaker, 1 vol. 2015. (Colonial People Ser.). (ENG.). 48p. (gr. 4-4). 34.07 *(978-1-5026-0480-4(9)*, 353e7018-3711-49c1-95c9-e4d18934ccb3) Cavendish Square Publishing LLC.

WILBERFORCE, WILLIAM, 1759-1833

Belmonte, Kevin. Travel with William Wilberforce: The Friend of Humanity. 2006. (Travel With... Ser.). (Illus.). 128p. per. 15.00 *(978-1-84625-027-9(7))* DayOne Pubns. GBR. Dist: Send The Light Distribution LLC.

Benge, Janet & Benge, Geoff. Heroes of History - William Wilberforce: Take up the Fight. 2015. (ENG.). 218p. (YA). pap. 11.99 *(978-1-62486-057-7(5))* Emerald Bks.

Edwards, Andrew & Thornton, Fleur. Wilberforce: 24 Ready to Use Lesson Plans: an Activity Book. 2007. (Illus.). 32p. (J). (gr. 3-7). pap. 4.99 *(978-0-89221-672-7(7))* New Leaf Publishing Group.

WILD ANIMALS

see Animals

WILD BOAR

Avett, Harper. Wild Boars, 1 vol. 2016. (Creatures of the Forest Habitat Ser.). (ENG.). 24p. (J). (gr. 3-3). pap. 9.25 *(978-1-4994-2718-9(2)*, 10649b23-50ef-46ca-a261-d61973169071, PowerKids Pr.) Rosen Publishing Group, Inc., The.

Somervill, Barbara A. Wild Boar. 2009. (21st Century Skills Library: Animal Invaders Ser.). (ENG., Illus.). 32p. (gr. 4-8). lib. bdg. 32.07 *(978-1-60279-329-3(8)*, 200225) Cherry Lake Publishing.

Thatcher, Henry. Wild Boars & Teacup Pigs, 1 vol., 1. 2014. (Big Animals, Small Animals Ser.). (ENG.). 32p. (J). (gr. 2-3). 28.93 *(978-1-4777-6097-0(0)*, 7a0dd1bf-b5d4-4132-bd56-9ad2af6a712b, PowerKids Pr.) Rosen Publishing Group, Inc., The.

ILD BOAR—FICTION

lgus, Walter C. Emma & the Wild Boar. Howarth, Craig, illus. 2006. (ENG.). 46p. per. 17.99 (978-1-4257-1088-0(3)) Xlibris Corp.

ILD FLOWERS

edeson, Carmen & Cousins, Lindsey. Can You Find These Flowers?, 1 vol. 2012. (All about Nature Ser.). (ENG.). 24p. (gr. -1-1). 25.27 (978-0-7660-3976-6(5), fd0dd33c-9d2e-4fc8-a899-bd84615a2e89, Enslow Publishing) Enslow Publishing, LLC.

ooke, Arthur O. Flowers of the Farm. 2007. (ENG., Illus.). 80p. per. (978-1-4065-1515-2(9)) Dodo Pr.

orey, Pamela. Wild Flowers of the United States & Canada. 2004. (World Book's Science & Nature Guides Ser.). (Illus.). 80p. (J). (978-0-7166-4220-6(4)) World Bk., Inc.

Gallagher, Belinda. British Garden Life Handbook. Kelly, Richard, ed. 2017. (ENG., Illus.). 224p. (J). pap. 14.99 (978-1-78209-128-8(9)) Miles Kelly Publishing, Ltd. GBR. Dist: Parkwest Pubns., Inc.

Green, Jen. Wild Flowers, 1 vol., 1. 2015. (Adventures in Nature Ser.). (ENG.). 32p. (J). (gr. 3-4). pap. 11.00 (978-1-5081-4594-3(6), 98bedb46-b6ea-41a8-9f59-81aa41bfb756, PowerKids Pr.) Rosen Publishing Group, Inc., The.

Green, John. Wildflowers GemGlow Stained Glass Coloring Book. 2009. (Dover Flower Coloring Bks.). (ENG., Illus.). 32p. (J). (gr. 1-5). pap. 7.99 (978-0-486-47148-8(9), 471489) Dover Pubns., Inc.

Kavanagh, James & Waterford Press Staff. Hawaii Trees & Wildflowers: A Folding Pocket Guide to Familiar Species. Leung, Raymond, illus. 2017. (Wildlife & Nature Identification Ser.). (ENG.). 12p. 7.95 (978-1-58355-509-5(9)) Waterford Pr., Inc.

Kukolax, Andy. Ultralight Wildflower Guide to the Central Montana Rocky Mountains: Wildflower Montana. 2003. (Illus.). 64p. pap. 19.95 (978-0-9729940-0-2(9)) Diamond Springs Pr.

Romero, Libby. Wildflowers. 2018. (Illus.). 160p. (J). (gr. 3-7). pap. 12.99 (978-1-4263-2995-1(4), National Geographic Kids) Disney Publishing Worldwide.

Ruggiero, M. Wild Flowers of North America. rev. ed. 2004. (Spotter's Guides). (ENG.). 64p. (J). pap. 5.95 (978-0-7945-0256-0(3)) EDC Publishing.

Voake, Charlotte. A Little Guide to Wild Flowers. 2007. (Illus.). 80p. (J). (gr. -1-2). pap. 16.99 (978-1-903919-11-8(8)) Transworld Publishers Ltd. GBR. Dist: Independent Pubs. Group.

Wildflowers. (Color & Learn Ser.). 36p. (J). (gr. 1-5). pap. (978-1-882210-02-2(6)) Action Publishing, Inc.

WILD FOWL

see Water Birds

WILD LIFE CONSERVATION

see Wildlife Conservation

WILDEBEESTS

see Gnus

WILDER, LAURA INGALLS, 1867-1957

Anderson, William. Laura Ingalls Wilder: A Biography. 2007. (Little House Nonfiction Ser.). (ENG., Illus.). 256p. (J). (gr. 3-7). pap. 9.99 (978-0-06-088552-6(1), HarperCollins) HarperCollins Pubs.

—Laura's Album: A Remembrance Scrapbook of Laura Ingalls Wilder. 2017. (Little House Nonfiction Ser.). (ENG., Illus.). 80p. (J). (gr. 3-7). 21.99 (978-0-06-245934-3(1), HarperCollins) HarperCollins Pubs.

Benge, Janet & Benge, Geoff. Heroes of History - Laura Ingalls Wilder: A Storybook Life. 2005. (Heroes of History Ser.). (ENG., Illus.). 192p. (YA). (gr. 4-7). pap. 11.99 (978-1-932096-32-3(9)) Emerald Bks.

Brezina, Corona. Laura Ingalls Wilder: Children's Author. 2017. (Britannica Beginner Bios Ser.). 32p. (J). (gr. 6-10). 77.40 (978-1-5383-0024-4(9), Britannica Educational Publishing) Rosen Publishing Group, Inc., The.

Collins, Carolyn Strom. The World of Little House. 2015. (Little House Nonfiction Ser.). (ENG., Illus.). 160p. (J). (gr. 3). 29.99 (978-0-06-243049-6(1), HarperCollins) HarperCollins Pubs.

Demuth, Patricia Brennan. Who Was Laura Ingalls Wilder? 2013. (Who Was... ? Ser.). lib. bdg. 16.00 (978-0-606-32134-1(9)) Turtleback.

Demuth, Patricia Brennan & Who HQ. Who Was Laura Ingalls Wilder? Foley, Tim, illus. 2013. (Who Was? Ser.). 112p. (J). (gr. 3-7). 6.99 (978-0-448-46706-1(2), Penguin Workshop) Penguin Young Readers Group.

Hill, Pamela Smith. Laura Ingalls Wilder: A Writer's Life. 2007. (South Dakota Biography Ser.). (ENG., Illus.). 244p. per. 12.95 (978-0-9777955-6-7(X), P233276, South Dakota State Historical Society Pr.) South Dakota Historical Society Pr.

Ingalls, Laura. Aquellos Años Dorado. 2003. (SPA., Illus.). 222p. (gr. 5-8). pap. 12.99 (978-84-279-3255-5(3)) Noguer y Caralt Editores, S. A. ESP. Dist: Lectorum Pubns., Inc.

Leaf, Christina. Laura Ingalls Wilder. 2015. (Children's Storytellers Ser.). (ENG., Illus.). 24p. (J). (gr. 2-5). lib. bdg. 26.95 (978-1-62617-269-2(2), Blastoff! Readers) Bellwether Media.

Mara, Wil. Laura Ingalls Wilder. 2003. (Rookie Biographies Ser.). (ENG., Illus.). 32p. (J). (gr. 1-2). 20.50 (978-0-516-22855-6(2), Children's Pr.) Scholastic Library Publishing.

Rajczak Nelson, Kristen. Laura Ingalls Wilder in Her Own Words, 1 vol. 2015. (Eyewitness to History Ser.). (ENG., Illus.). 32p. (J). (gr. 4-5). pap. 11.50 (978-1-4824-4070-6(9), 3dea84d2-3841-49e7-b25e-7baac428a4a5) Stevens, Gareth Publishing LLLP.

Rice, Dona Herweck. Laura Ingalls Wilder: Pioneer Woman (America in The 1800s) rev. ed. 2017. (Social Studies: Informational Text Ser.). (ENG., Illus.). 32p. (gr. 4-8). pap. 11.99 (978-1-4938-3798-4(2)) Teacher Created Materials, Inc.

Scraper, Katherine. Laura Ingalls Wilder. 2011. (Early Connections Ser.). (J). (978-1-61672-555-6(9)) Benchmark Education Co.

—Laura Ingalls Wilder & Laura Ingalls Wilder (Spanish) 6 English, 6 Spanish Adaptations. 2011. (ENG & SPA.). (J). 75.00 net. (978-1-4108-5620-3(8)) Benchmark Education Co.

Walker, Barbara M. The Little House Cookbook: New Full-Color Edition: Frontier Foods from Laura Ingalls Wilder's Classic Stories. Williams, Garth, illus. 2018. (Little House Nonfiction Ser.). (ENG.). 304p. (J). (gr. 3-7). 26.99 (978-0-06-247079-9(5), HarperCollins) HarperCollins Pubs.

Wilder, Laura Ingalls. A Little House Traveler: Writings from Laura Ingalls Wilder's Journeys Across America. 2011. (Little House Nonfiction Ser.). (ENG., Illus.). 368p. (J). (gr. 5). pap. 7.99 (978-0-06-072492-4(7), HarperCollins) HarperCollins Pubs.

WILDERNESS SURVIVAL

Abdo, Kenny. How to Survive the Wild. 2018. (How to Survive Ser.). (ENG., Illus.). 24p. (J). (gr. 2-8). lib. bdg. 31.36 (978-1-5321-2328-3(0), 28423, Abdo Zoom-Fly) ABDO Publishing Co.

Arburthnott, Gill. Wonderful Wilderness: Band 15/Emerald. 2017. (Collins Big Cat Ser.). (ENG.). 48p. (J). pap. 8.99 (978-0-00-820885-1(9)) HarperCollins Pubs. Ltd. GBR. Dist: Independent Pubs. Group.

Awa, Solomon. How to Build an Iglu & a Qamutiik: Inuit Tools & Techniques, 1 vol. Breithaupt, Andrew, illus. 2013. (ENG & IKU.). 32p. (J). (gr. 4-8). 12.95 (978-1-927095-31-7(X)) Inhabit Media Inc. CAN. Dist: Consortium Bk. Sales & Distribution.

Bailey, Diane. Survival Skills, Vol. 10. 2016. (Great Outdoors! Ser.). (Illus.). 48p. (J). (gr. 5). 20.95 (978-1-4222-3574-4(2)) Mason Crest.

Bath, Louella. Making Fire in the Wild, 1 vol., 1. 2015. (Wilderness Survival Skills Ser.). (ENG., Illus.). 24p. (J). (gr. 3-4). pap. 9.25 (978-1-5081-4320-8(X), d6ee8652-7255-4157-a20d-3cb19c2f33c0, PowerKids Pr.) Rosen Publishing Group, Inc., The.

Bell, Samantha. Deserted Islands. 2018. (J). (978-1-4896-9777-6(2), AV2 by Weigl) Weigl Pubs., Inc.

—How to Survive in the Wilderness. 2015. (Survival Guides). (ENG.). 24p. (J). (gr. 2-5). 32.79 (978-1-60973-160-1(3), 208796) Child's World, Inc, The.

—How to Survive on a Deserted Island. 2015. (Survival Guides). (ENG.). 24p. (J). (gr. 2-5). 32.79 (978-1-60973-162-5(X), 208797) Child's World, Inc, The.

—The Wilderness. 2018. (Illus.). 24p. (J). (978-1-4896-9797-4(7), AV2 by Weigl) Weigl Pubs., Inc.

Bowman, Chris. Survive in the Mountains. 2016. (Survival Zone Ser.). (ENG., Illus.). 24p. (J). (gr. 3-7). 26.95 (978-1-62617-446-7(6), Torque Bks.) Bellwether Media.

—Survive in the Woods. 2016. (Survival Zone Ser.). (ENG., Illus.). 24p. (J). (gr. 3-7). 26.95 (978-1-62617-447-4(4), Torque Bks.) Bellwether Media.

Braun, Eric. Fighting to Survive in the Wilderness: Terrifying True Stories. 2019. (Fighting to Survive Ser.). (ENG., Illus.). 64p. (J). (gr. 4-9). pap. 8.95 (978-0-7565-6234-2(1), 140934); lib. bdg. 35.32 (978-0-7565-6187-1(6), 140667) Capstone. (Compass Point Bks.).

Brown, Alex. Mountain Adventures. 2009. (Difficult & Dangerous Ser.). (J). 28.50 (978-1-59920-157-3(7)) Black Rabbit Bks.

—Mountain Adventures. 2009. (Difficult & Dangerous Ser.). (ENG., Illus.). 32p. (J). pap. (978-1-897563-25-0(6)) Saunders Bk. Co.

Brown Bear Books. Survivors: Into the Wilderness. 2012. (Mission Impossible Ser.). (ENG.). 32p. (J). (gr. 4-6). lib. bdg. 31.35 (978-1-936333-27-1(9), 16755) Brown Bear Bks.

Brush, Jim & Scarborough, Kate. Extreme Survival. 2012. (Fast Facts Ser.). (ENG., Illus.). 32p. (gr. 4-6). pap. 28.50 (978-1-59771-325-2(2)) Sea-To-Sea Pubns.

Champion, Neil. Finding Your Way. 2010. (Survive Alive Ser.). (ENG.). 32p. (J). (gr. 3-7). lib. bdg. 28.50 (978-1-60753-038-1(4), 17221) Amicus.

—Finding Your Way. 2012. (ENG., Illus.). 32p. (gr. 3-7). pap. 8.95 (978-1-926722-56-6(6)) Saunders Bk. Co. CAN. Dist: RiverStream Publishing.

—Making Shelter. 2010. (Survive Alive Ser.). (ENG.). 32p. (J). (gr. 3-7). lib. bdg. 28.50 (978-1-60753-041-1(4), 17225) Amicus.

—Making Shelter. 2012. (ENG., Illus.). 32p. (gr. 3-7). pap. 8.95 (978-1-926722-59-7(0)) Saunders Bk. Co. CAN. Dist: RiverStream Publishing.

—Tools & Crafts. 2010. (Survive Alive Ser.). (ENG.). 32p. (J). (gr. 3-7). lib. bdg. 28.50 (978-1-60753-042-8(2), 17226) Amicus.

—Tools & Crafts. 2012. (ENG., Illus.). 32p. (gr. 3-7). pap. 8.95 (978-1-926722-60-3(4)) Saunders Bk. Co. CAN. Dist: RiverStream Publishing.

Champion, Neil & Ganeri, Anita. Finding Food & Water. 2011. (How the World Makes Music Ser.). 32p. (gr. 4-7). lib. bdg. 31.35 (978-1-59920-478-9(9)) Black Rabbit Bks.

—Tools & Crafts. 2011. (How the World Makes Music Ser.). 32p. (gr. 4-7). lib. bdg. 31.35 (978-1-59920-481-9(9)) Black Rabbit Bks.

Decker, William. Getting Rescued in the Wild, 1 vol., 1. 2015. (Wilderness Survival Skills Ser.). (ENG., Illus.). 24p. (J). (gr. 3-4). pap. 9.25 (978-1-5081-4315-4(3), 3c49584a-ed0f-4af3-9262-7143fac68c5a, PowerKids Pr.) Rosen Publishing Group, Inc., The.

Doeden, Matt. Can You Survive the Wilderness? An Interactive Survival Adventure. 2012. (You Choose: Survival Ser.). (ENG.). 112p. (gr. 3-4). pap. 41.70 (978-1-4296-8480-4(1)); (J). pap. 6.95 (978-1-4296-7996-1(4), 118328); (Illus.). (J). lib. bdg. 32.65 (978-1-4296-7542-0(X), 117119) Capstone. (Capstone Pr.).

Ganeri, Anita. Brass Instruments. 2011. (How the World Makes Music Ser.). (ENG.). 32p. (J). (gr. 4-7). lib. bdg. 31.35 (978-1-59920-477-2(0), 19295, Smart Apple Media) Black Rabbit Bks.

Goldish, Meish. Lost in the Woods. 2015. (Illus.). 32p. (J). lib. bdg. 28.50 (978-1-62724-293-6(7)) Bearport Publishing Co., Inc.

Green, Jen. Extreme Survival. 2010. (Unpredictable Nature Ser.). (Illus.). 48p. (J). (gr. 3-18). lib. bdg. 19.95 (978-1-4222-1999-7(2)) Mason Crest.

Grylls, Bear. Extreme Planet: Exploring the Most Extreme Stuff on Earth. 2017. (Illus.). 123p. (J). (978-1-61067-754-7(4)) Kane Miller.

Grylls, Bear, ed. Bear Grylls Survival Camp. 2019. (Illus.). 121p. (J). 12.99 (978-1-61067-755-4(2)) Kane Miller.

Gulati, Annette. Amazing Human Feats of Survival. 2018. (Superhuman Feats Ser.). (ENG., Illus.). 32p. (J). (gr. 4-6). lib. bdg. 28.65 (978-1-5435-4122-9(4), 139076, Capstone Pr.) Capstone.

Hanel, Rachael. Can You Survive Antarctica? An Interactive Survival Adventure, 1 vol. 2011. (You Choose: Survival Ser.). (ENG., 112p. (J). (gr. 3-7). Illus.). lib. bdg. 32.65 (978-1-4296-6589-6(0), 115710); pap. 41.70 (978-1-4296-7346-4(X), 16839); pap. 6.95 (978-1-4296-7345-7(1), 116884) Capstone. (Capstone Pr.).

Hicks, Dwayne. Finding Water in the Wild, 1 vol., 1. 2015. (Wilderness Survival Skills Ser.). (ENG., Illus.). 24p. (J). (gr. 3-4). pap. 9.25 (978-1-5081-4311-6(0), fb837d9a-2d75-461f-8b4e-36e02ef1b92f, PowerKids Pr.) Rosen Publishing Group, Inc., The.

Jankowski, Susan. True Wilderness Rescue Stories, 1 vol. 2011. (True Rescue Stories Ser.). (ENG.). 48p. (gr. 5-7). lib. bdg. 25.27 (978-0-7660-3666-6(9), 7e9d8a43-e1d4-4d66-9292-252a9206954b) Enslow Publishing, LLC.

King, Vickie. Search Dogs & You, a Wilderness Safety Guide from American Search Dogs. 2009. 32p. pap. 13.00 (978-1-60860-105-9(6), Strategic Bk. Publishing) Strategic Book Publishing & Rights Agency (SBPRA).

Lassieur, Allison. Can You Survive Being Lost at Sea? An Interactive Survival Adventure. 2013. (You Choose: Survival Ser.). (ENG.). 112p. (J). (gr. 3-4). pap. 41.70 (978-1-62065-712-6(0), 19306, Capstone Pr.) Capstone.

Lewis, Brenda Ralph. Wilderness Rescue with the U. S. Search & Rescue Task Force. 2004. (Rescue & Prevention Ser.). (Illus.). 96p. (YA). (gr. 7-18). lib. bdg. 22.95 (978-1-59084-404-5(1)) Mason Crest.

Loh-Hagan, Virginia. Ada Blackjack: Castaway. 2018. (True Survival Ser.). (ENG., Illus.). 32p. (J). (gr. 4-8). pap. 14.21 (978-1-5341-0873-8(4), 210856); lib. bdg. 32.07 (978-1-5341-0774-8(6), 210855) Cherry Lake Publishing. (45th Parallel Press).

—Deserted Island Hacks. 2019. (Could You Survive? Ser.). (ENG., Illus.). 32p. (J). (gr. 4-8). pap. 14.21 (978-1-5341-5066-9(8), 213571); lib. bdg. 32.07 (978-1-5341-4780-5(2), 213570) Cherry Lake Publishing. (45th Parallel Press).

Mack, Dave. Making Shelter in the Wild, 1 vol., 1. 2015. (Wilderness Survival Skills Ser.). (ENG., Illus.). 24p. (J). (gr. 3-4). pap. 9.25 (978-1-5081-4323-9(4), 24b10d35-e6af-4c85-a0ec-85be868c3bd0, PowerKids Pr.) Rosen Publishing Group, Inc., The.

Mathias, Adeline. How a Young Brave Survived. Hamilton, Penny, ed. 2009. (ENG., Illus.). 30p. (J). pap. 5.95 (978-1-934594-04-9(0)) Salish Kootenia College Pr.

McNab, Chris. Survival in the Wilderness. Carney, John, ed. 2014. (Extreme Survival in the Military Ser.: 12). 64p. (J). (gr. 7-18). lib. bdg. 23.95 (978-1-4222-3087-9(2)) Mason Crest.

Nickens, T. Edward. Field & Stream's Guide to Outdoor Survival, 1 vol. of, The Editors of Field and Stream, ed. 2014. (Field & Stream's Guide to the Outdoors Ser.). (ENG., Illus.). 96p. (J). (gr. 6-8). 37.60 (978-1-4824-2304-4(9), aa112e67-b232-467b-94e1-32bb8d2d3b94) Stevens, Gareth Publishing LLLP.

O'DellKathryn. SURVIVAL GUIDE: LOST IN THE MOUNTAINS LOW INTERMEDIATE BOOK WITH ONLINE ACCESS, 1 vol. 2014. (ENG., Illus.). 28p. (J). pap., E-Book, E-Book 9.50 (978-1-107-64328-4(7)) Cambridge Univ. Pr.

Owen, Ruth. Desert Survival Guide. 2010. (ENG., Illus.). 32p. (J). pap. (978-0-7787-7554-6(2)); lib. bdg. (978-0-7787-7532-4(1)) Crabtree Publishing Co.

—Roughing It, 1 vol., 1. 2014. (DIY for Boys Ser.). (ENG.). 32p. (J). (gr. 4-4). 30.17 (978-1-4777-6278-3(7), 3e848547-55ca-4bee-9efb-893d3489ce4d, PowerKids Pr.) Rosen Publishing Group, Inc., The.

Paulsen, Gary. Gone to the Woods: Surviving a Lost Childhood. 2021. (ENG.). 368p. (J). 18.99 (978-0-374-31415-6(2), 900225840, Farrar, Straus & Giroux (BYR)) Farrar, Straus & Giroux.

Puri, Devi. Making Tools in the Wild, 1 vol., 1. 2015. (Wilderness Survival Skills Ser.). (ENG., Illus.). 24p. (J). (gr. 3-4). pap. 9.25 (978-1-5081-4327-7(7), 02893825-db41-49fe-a002-f056d4748ba1, PowerKids Pr.) Rosen Publishing Group, Inc., The.

Rice, William B. Survival! Desert, 1 vol. 2nd rev. ed. 2012. (TIME for KIDS(r): Informational Text Ser.). (ENG., Illus.). 48p. (gr. 4-5). pap. 13.99 (978-1-4333-4818-1(7)) Teacher Created Materials, Inc.

—Survival! Jungle, 1 vol. 2nd rev. ed. 2012. (TIME for KIDS(r): Informational Text Ser.). (ENG., Illus.). 48p. (gr. 4-5). pap. 13.99 (978-1-4333-4820-4(9)) Teacher Created Materials, Inc.

—Survival! Ocean, 1 vol. 2nd rev. ed. 2012. (TIME for KIDS(r): Informational Text Ser.). (ENG., Illus.). 48p. (gr. 4-5). pap. 13.99 (978-1-4333-4819-8(5)) Teacher Created Materials, Inc.

Shone, Rob. Defying Death in the Mountains, 1 vol. Spender, Nik, illus. 2010. (Graphic Survival Stories Ser.). (ENG.). 48p. (YA). (gr. 5-5). 37.13 (978-1-4358-3532-0(8), 07fd218d-4cd0-4b93-9f8e-bc58bdcb39b9); pap. 15.05 (978-1-61532-866-6(1), 0ff7e3c8-0165-4567-b4ab-294b843bb172) Rosen Publishing Group, Inc., The. (Rosen Reference).

—Defying Death in the Wilderness. Field, James, illus. 2010. (Graphic Survival Stories Ser.). 48p. (YA). 58.50 (978-1-4488-0068-1(4)); (ENG.). (gr. 5-5). 37.13 (978-1-4358-3531-3(X), 209e8784-d74b-4cc4-8c23-6eb2c697a9d2); (ENG.). (gr. 5-5). pap. 15.05 (978-1-61532-865-9(3), 4a7ff7a6-0c26-49c3-9713-854e0a80fb0d) Rosen Publishing Group, Inc., The. (Rosen Reference).

Smith, L. Survival Skills. 2008. (Survival Skills Ser.). 48p. (J). pap. 5.99 (978-0-7945-2218-6(1), Usborne) EDC Publishing.

Spilsbury, Louise. How to Survive in the Arctic & Antarctica, 1 vol. 2012. (Tough Guides). (ENG., Illus.). 32p. (J). (gr. 4-5). pap. 11.00 (978-1-4488-7931-1(0), 0129535c-14f4-473c-96bc-b28f0785be89); lib. bdg. 28.93 (978-1-4488-7866-6(7), 28868d93-7882-4c13-a732-09956e89d72a) Rosen Publishing Group, Inc., The. (PowerKids Pr.).

—How to Survive in the Ocean, 1 vol. 2012. (Tough Guides). (ENG., Illus.). 32p. (J). (gr. 4-5). pap. 11.00 (978-1-4488-7933-5(7), e1ffd3c7-233b-4f90-a287-bf63f10838a1); lib. bdg. 28.93 (978-1-4488-7868-0(3), 9aacc0bc-de93-46a0-be92-d9ef5d73a68e) Rosen Publishing Group, Inc., The. (PowerKids Pr.).

—How to Survive on a Mountain, 1 vol. 2012. (Tough Guides). (ENG., Illus.). 32p. (J). (gr. 4-5). pap. 11.00 (978-1-4488-7936-6(1), 47227724-b281-4cca-8dc2-29baac1bb2f4); lib. bdg. 28.93 (978-1-4488-7871-0(3), a92196a4-9d79-44e2-83fd-cb506f4f1fba) Rosen Publishing Group, Inc., The. (PowerKids Pr.).

Turnbull, Stephanie. Cold! 2015. (Survival Challenge Ser.). (ENG., Illus.). 24p. (J). (gr. 2-5). 28.50 (978-1-62588-213-4(0), 17422) Black Rabbit Bks.

—Cold! 2015. (ENG., Illus.). 24p. (J). pap. 8.95 (978-1-77092-238-9(5)) RiverStream Publishing.

—Emergency! 2015. (Survival Challenge Ser.). (ENG., Illus.). 24p. (J). (gr. 2-5). 28.50 (978-1-62588-214-1(9), 17423) Black Rabbit Bks.

—Emergency! 2015. (ENG., Illus.). 24p. (J). pap. 8.95 (978-1-77092-239-6(3)) RiverStream Publishing.

—Hungry! 2015. (Survival Challenge Ser.). (ENG.). 24p. (J). (gr. 2-5). 28.50 (978-1-62588-215-8(7), 17424) Black Rabbit Bks.

—Hungry! 2015. (ENG., Illus.). 24p. (J). pap. 8.95 (978-1-77092-240-2(7)) RiverStream Publishing.

—Lost! 2015. (Survival Challenge Ser.). (ENG.). 24p. (J). (gr. 2-5). 28.50 (978-1-62588-216-5(5), 17425) Black Rabbit Bks.

—Lost! 2015. (ENG., Illus.). 24p. (J). pap. 8.95 (978-1-77092-241-9(5)) RiverStream Publishing.

—Stranded! 2015. (Survival Challenge Ser.). (ENG.). 24p. (J). (gr. 2-5). 28.50 (978-1-62588-217-2(3), 17426) Black Rabbit Bks.

—Stranded! 2015. (ENG., Illus.). 24p. (J). pap. 8.95 (978-1-77092-242-6(3)) RiverStream Publishing.

—Thirsty! 2015. (Survival Challenge Ser.). (ENG.). 24p. (J). (gr. 2-5). 28.50 (978-1-62588-218-9(1), 17427) Black Rabbit Bks.

—Thirsty! 2015. (ENG., Illus.). 24p. (J). pap. 8.95 (978-1-77092-243-3(1)) RiverStream Publishing.

Wadsworth, Ginger. Survival in the Snow. Orback, Craig, illus. 2011. 48p. (J). pap. 6.95 (978-0-7613-3941-0(8), First Avenue Editions) Lerner Publishing Group.

Wilson, Patrick. Survival Equipment. Carney, John, ed. 2014. (Extreme Survival in the Military Ser.: 12). 64p. (J). (gr. 7-18). lib. bdg. 23.95 (978-1-4222-3085-5(6)) Mason Crest.

—Surviving by Trapping, Fishing, & Eating Plants. Carney, John, ed. 2014. (Extreme Survival in the Military Ser.: 12). (Illus.). 64p. (J). (gr. 7-18). lib. bdg. 23.95 (978-1-4222-3088-6(0)) Mason Crest.

Zoldak, Joyce. Danger in the Deep: Survivors of Shark Attacks. 2009. (J). pap. 25.95 (978-1-4222-1475-6(3)) Mason Crest.

WILDERNESS SURVIVAL—FICTION

Armstrong, Kelley. The Calling. 2013. (Darkness Rising Ser.: 2). (ENG.). 352p. (YA). (gr. 8). pap. 10.99 (978-0-06-179706-4(5), HarperCollins) HarperCollins Pubs.

—The Calling: Number 2 in Series. 2012. (Darkness Rising Ser.: Bk. 2). (ENG.). 336p. pap. (978-1-907410-47-5(3)) Atom Pr.

Bates, Sonya Spreen. Marsh Island, 1 vol. Charko, Kasia, illus. 2009. (Orca Echoes Ser.). (ENG.). 64p. (J). (gr. 1-3). pap. 6.95 (978-1-55469-117-3(6)) Orca Bk. Pubs. USA.

Carter, Ally. Not If I Save You First. (ENG.). 304p. (gr. 7). 2019. (J). pap. 10.99 (978-1-338-13415-5(9)) 2018. (YA). 18.99 (978-1-338-13414-8(0)) Scholastic, Inc. (Scholastic Pr.).

Cook, Trish. Outward Blonde. 2016. (ENG.). 279p. (YA). pap. 9.99 (978-1-945293-04-7(7)) Adaptive Studios.

Daher, Anita. On the Trail of the Bushman, 1 vol. 2009. (Orca Young Readers Ser.). (ENG.). 128p. (J). (gr. 4-7). pap. 7.95 (978-1-55469-013-8(7)) Orca Bk. Pubs. USA.

Eustache, Harold. Shuswap Journey. 2004. (Shuswap Journey Ser.). (ENG.). 176p. pap. 15.95 (978-1-894778-15-2(4)) Theytus Bks., Ltd. CAN. Dist: Univ. of Toronto Pr.

Gaetz, Dayle Campbell. Spoiled Rotten. 2006. (Orca Currents Ser.). 103p. (gr. 5-9). 19.95 (978-0-7569-6875-5(5)) Perfection Learning Corp.

George, Jean Craighead. My Side of the Mountain. l.t. ed. 2003. (LRS Large Print Cornerstone Ser.). 205p. (J). lib. bdg. 32.95 (978-1-58118-114-2(0)) LRS.

—My Side of the Mountain (Puffin Modern Classics) 2004. (Puffin Modern Classics Ser.). (ENG., Illus.). 192p. (J). (gr. 3-7). 8.99 (978-0-14-240111-8(0), Puffin Books) Penguin Young Readers Group.

Gilliland, Hap. Alone in the Wilderness. 2003. (Illus.). 160p. (YA). (gr. 6-10). pap. 14.95 (978-0-87961-257-3(6)) Naturegraph Pubs., Inc.

Goerzen, Christy. Explore, 1 vol. 2009. (Orca Currents Ser.). (ENG.). 128p. (J). (gr. 4-7). pap. 9.95 (978-1-55469-119-7(2)) Orca Bk. Pubs. USA.

Goodspeed, Betsy. The Reluctant Mountaineer. 2004. 230p. (YA). per. (978-1-59196-617-3(5)) Instant Pub.

Graham, D. A. The Island. 2019. (Reality Show Ser.). (ENG.). 112p. (YA). (gr. 6-12). 26.65 (978-1-5415-4028-6(X), e3805319-9caa-4001-aac1-c88c098367dc, Darby Creek) Lerner Publishing Group.

Gutman, Dan. Getting Air. (ENG.). 240p. (J). (gr. 3-7). 2008. pap. 7.99 (978-0-689-87681-3(5)) 2007. 16.99 (978-0-689-87680-6(7)) Simon & Schuster Bks. For Young Readers. (Simon & Schuster Bks. For Young Readers).

Hobbs, Will. Wild Man Island. 2003. (ENG.). 192p. (J). (gr. 5-18). pap. 6.99 (978-0-380-73310-1(2), HarperCollins) HarperCollins Pubs.

Holmes, Kathryn. The Distance Between Lost & Found. 2016. (ENG.). 320p. (YA). (gr. 8). pap. 9.99 (978-0-06-231727-8(X), HarperTeen) HarperCollins Pubs.

Hughey, Sue C. Herby's Secret Formula. Hughey, Sue C., illus. 2013. (Illus.). 232p. pap. 11.95 (978-0-9840358-1-6(8)) Associated Arts Pub.

Hunter, Erin. The Apprentice's Quest. 2017. (Warriors — a Vision of Shadows Ser.: 1). (J). lib. bdg. 18.40 (978-0-606-39643-1(8)) Turtleback.

—Warriors: a Vision of Shadows #1: the Apprentice's Quest. (Warriors: a Vision of Shadows Ser.: 1). (ENG., Illus.). (J). (gr. 3-7). 2017. 352p. pap. 9.99 (978-0-06-238639-7(5)) 2016. 336p. 16.99 (978-0-06-238637-3(9)) 2016. 336p. lib. bdg.

W X Y Z

17.89 *(978-0-06-238638-0(7))* HarperCollins Pubs. (HarperCollins).
Key, Watt. Alabama Moon. (Alabama Moon Ser.: 1). (ENG.). (J). (gr. 5-9). 2008. 304p. pap. 8.99 *(978-0-312-38428-9(9),* 900053363) 2010. 320p. pap. 8.99 *(978-0-312-64480-2(9),* 900068607) Square Fish.
London, Jonathan. Grizzly Peak. London, Sean, illus. 2017. (Aaron's Wilderness Ser.). (ENG.). 174p. (YA). 24.99 *(978-1-943328-85-7(4),* West Winds Pr.) West Margin Pr.
Maddox, Jake. Volcano! A Survive! Story. Tiffany, Sean, illus. 2009. (Jake Maddox Sports Stories Ser.). (ENG.). 72p. (J). (gr. 3-6). 25.99 *(978-1-4342-1208-5(4),* 95405, Stone Arch Bks.) Capstone.
McCabe, James Dabney, Jr. Planting the Wilderness or, the Pioneer Boys: a Story of Frontier Life. 2007. pap. 27.95 *(978-1-4304-8187-4(0))* Kessinger Publishing, LLC.
Mills, Charles. Storm on Shadow Mountain. 2003. 127p. (J). 7.99 *(978-0-8163-1993-0(6))* Pacific Pr. Publishing Assn.
Monninger, Joseph. Stay Alive #1: Crash. 2014. (Stay Alive Ser.: 1). (ENG.). 208p. (J). (gr. 3-7). pap. 5.99 *(978-0-545-56348-2(8),* Scholastic Paperbacks) Scholastic, Inc.
Osborne, Mary Pope. Adaline Falling Star. unabr. ed. 2004. (Middle Grade Cassette Librariestm Ser.). 176p. (J). (gr. 3-7). pap. 29.00 incl. audio *(978-0-8072-1195-3(8),* S YA 319 SP, Listening Library) Random Hse. Audio Publishing Group.
Patterson, James & Tebbetts, Chris. Middle School: Save Rafe! Park, Laura, illus. 2014. (Middle School Ser.: 6). (ENG.). 288p. (J). (gr. 3-7). 13.99 *(978-0-316-32212-6(1),* Jimmy Patterson) Little Brown & Co.
Paulsen, Gary. Brian's Return. unabr. ed. 2004. (Middle Grade Cassette Librariestm Ser.). 115p. (J). (gr. 5-9). pap. 29.00 incl. audio *(978-0-8072-0658-4(X),* S YA 292 SP, Listening Library) Random Hse. Audio Publishing Group.
—Hatchet. 2006. (ENG., Illus.). 192p. (J). (gr. 5-9). pap. 8.99 *(978-1-4169-3647-3(5),* Simon & Schuster Bks. For Young Readers) Simon & Schuster Bks. For Young Readers.
—Hatchet. 2006. (ENG., Illus.). 208p. (YA). (gr. 7-9). mass mkt. 8.99 *(978-1-4169-3646-6(7),* Simon Pulse) Simon Pulse.
—Hatchet: 20th Anniversary Edition. Willis, Drew, illus. 20th anniv. ed. 2007. (ENG.). 192p. (J). (gr. 5-9). 19.99 *(978-1-4169-2508-8(2),* Simon & Schuster Bks. For Young Readers) Simon & Schuster Bks. For Young Readers.
—Northwind. 2022. (ENG.). 256p. (J). 18.99 *(978-0-374-31420-0(9),* 900225846, Farrar, Straus & Giroux (BYR)) Farrar, Straus & Giroux.
—Northwind. 2024. (ENG.). 256p. (gr. 6-8). 24.94 ***(978-1-5364-8333-8(8))*** Square Fish.
Paulsen, Gary. The River. unabr. ed. 2004. (Middle Grade Cassette Librariestm Ser.). 132p. (J). (gr. 5-9). pap. 29.00 incl. audio *(978-0-8072-8704-0(0),* S YA 241 SP, Listening Library) Random Hse. Audio Publishing Group.
Petersen, P. J. Wild River. 2013. 128p. (J). (gr. 4-7). 7.99 *(978-0-375-84624-3(7),* Yearling) Random Hse. Children's Bks.
Rock, Jonathan. Out of Bounds Bk. 1, Bk. 1. 2013. (Survival Squad Ser.: 1). (Illus.). 272p. (J). (gr. 4-7). pap. 10.99 *(978-1-86230-965-4(5),* Red Fox) Random House Children's Books GBR. Dist: Independent Pubs. Group.
—Search & Rescue: 'For Anyone Thinking of Becoming a Scout, Go for It, Come & Join the Big Adventure' 2013. (Survival Squad Ser.: 2). (Illus.). 256p. (J). (gr. 4-7). pap. 15.99 *(978-1-86230-966-1(3),* Red Fox) Random House Children's Books GBR. Dist: Independent Pubs. Group.
Roddy, Lee. Escape down the Raging Rapids. 2008. (D. J. Dillon Adventure Ser.: No. 10). (Illus.). 117p. (J). 7.99 *(978-0-88062-274-5(1))* Mott Media.
—The Legend of the White Raccoon. 2008. (D. J. Dillon Adventure Ser.: No. 6). (Illus.). 105p. (J). 7.99 *(978-0-88062-270-7(9))* Mott Media.
—Mad Dog of Lobo Mountain. 2008. (D. J. Dillon Adventure Ser.: No. 5). (J). 7.99 *(978-0-88062-269-1(5))* Mott Media.
Rorby, Ginny. Lost in the River of Grass. 2012. (ENG.). 264p. (YA). (gr. 7-12). pap. 9.99 *(978-0-7613-8498-4(7),* 12ae2bd5-22e5-4761-8bde-ed56322fd477, Carolrhoda Lab™) Lerner Publishing Group.
Schwarz, S. L. Treasure at Lure Lake. 2016. (Illus.). 185p. (J). *(978-1-4621-2600-2(6))* Cedar Fort, Inc./CFI Distribution.
Shotz, Jennifer Li. Scout: Storm Dog. 2019. (Scout Ser.: 3). (ENG.). 192p. (J). (gr. 3-7). pap. 7.99 *(978-0-06-280264-4(X),* HarperCollins) HarperCollins Pubs.
Spradlin, Michael P. Denali Storm: A 4D Book. Karkavelas, Spiros, illus. 2018. (Pararescue Corps Ser.). (ENG.). 128p. (J). (gr. 4-8). lib. bdg. 27.32 *(978-1-4965-5203-7(2),* 136213, Stone Arch Bks.) Capstone.
Troupe, Thomas Kingsley. Lost - A Wild Tale of Survival. Fagan, Kirbi, illus. 2016. (Survive! Ser.). (ENG.). 56p. (J). (gr. 4-8). lib. bdg. 25.32 *(978-1-4965-2557-4(4),* 130516, Stone Arch Bks.) Capstone.
Turnbull, Ann & Giblin, James Cross. Maroo of the Winter Caves: A Winter & Holiday Book for Kids. 20th anniv. ed. 2004. (ENG., Illus.). 144p. (J). (gr. 3-7). pap. 7.99 *(978-0-618-44299-7(5),* 100368, Clarion Bks.) HarperCollins Pubs.
VanRiper, Gary & VanRiper, Justin. Escape from Black Bear Mountain. 2008. (Adirondack Kids Ser.: Vol. 8). 70p. (J). (gr. 2-7). pap. 9.95 *(978-0-9707044-8-1(8))* Adirondack Kids Pr.
Weaver, Will. Memory Boy. 2012. Orig. Title: The Boy on Platform One. (ENG.). 240p. (YA). (gr. 8-12). pap. 8.99 *(978-0-06-201814-4(0),* HarperTeen) HarperCollins Pubs.
Wedekind, Annie. Samirah's Ride: the Story of an Arabian Filly. 2010. (Breyer Horse Collection: 3). (ENG.). 128p. (J). (gr. 4-7). pap. 15.99 *(978-0-312-62268-8(6),* 900066204) Feiwel & Friends.
Withers, Pam. Camp Wild. 1 vol. 2006. (Orca Currents Ser.). (ENG.). 112p. (J). (gr. 4-7). 14.95 *(978-1-55143-557-2(8))* Orca Bk. Pubs. USA.
—Camp Wild. 2006. (Orca Currents Ser.). 104p. (gr. 5-9). lib. bdg. 19.95 *(978-0-7569-6878-6(X))* Perfection Learning Corp.
Woods, Shirley & Wood, Muriel. Tooga: Story of a Polar Bear, 1 vol. 2004. (ENG., Illus.). 32p. (J). (gr. 3-4). pap. 7.95 *(978-1-55041-900-9(5),* e6c34d50-a508-4bd7-a89a-c4051840ab4d) Clockwise Pr. CAN. Dist: Firefly Bks., Ltd.

WILDLIFE CONSERVATION

see also Birds—Protection; Endangered Species; Forests and Forestry; Game Protection; National Parks and Reserves

Allgor, Marie. Endangered Animals of Africa, 1 vol. 2011. (Save Earth's Animals! Ser.). (ENG.). 24p. (J). (gr. 2-3). pap. 9.25 *(978-1-4488-2640-7(3),* aeb00fab-c5fa-4f7d-b521-7506b1bc8b7d); (Illus.). lib. bdg. 26.27 *(978-1-4488-2528-8(8),* 3b285c3a-8064-427b-8be7-5f8a56a4dbfa) Rosen Publishing Group, Inc., The. (PowerKids Pr.).
—Endangered Animals of Antarctica & the Arctic, 1 vol. 2011. (Save Earth's Animals! Ser.). (ENG., Illus.). 24p. (J). (gr. 2-3). pap. 9.25 *(978-1-4488-2652-0(7),* b8c4e7ba-ef01-4d97-90ff-1348aa6c8284); lib. bdg. 26.27 *(978-1-4488-2534-9(2),* 3f0a08e6-91a1-4a34-b6dc-328679992ce2) Rosen Publishing Group, Inc., The. (PowerKids Pr.).
—Endangered Animals of Asia, 1 vol. 2011. (Save Earth's Animals! Ser.). (ENG.). 24p. (J). (gr. 2-3). pap. 9.25 *(978-1-4488-2642-1(X),* efb73c90-bf96-4669-8b5e-b99f474fe798); (Illus.). lib. bdg. 26.27 *(978-1-4488-2529-5(6),* aab825e3-21cc-4b26-8619-498cbcf3dc86) Rosen Publishing Group, Inc., The. (PowerKids Pr.).
—Endangered Animals of Australia, 1 vol. 2011. (Save Earth's Animals! Ser.). (ENG.). 24p. (J). (gr. 2-3). pap. 9.25 *(978-1-4488-2644-5(6),* a271f6c1-4ceb-44dc-8372-9672608ec893); (Illus.). lib. bdg. 26.27 *(978-1-4488-2530-1(X),* c53f121a-20cf-428a-b998-1879db2a9066) Rosen Publishing Group, Inc., The. (PowerKids Pr.).
—Endangered Animals of Europe, 1 vol. 2011. (Save Earth's Animals! Ser.). (ENG., Illus.). 24p. (J). (gr. 2-3). 26.27 *(978-1-4488-2531-8(8),* 1e3a2ec3-c80f-432c-826a-86108050fd6d); pap. 9.25 *(978-1-4488-2646-9(2),* 402a7b0f-1f35-425b-8b73-fe14898b897f) Rosen Publishing Group, Inc., The. (PowerKids Pr.).
—Endangered Animals of North America, 1 vol. 2011. (Save Earth's Animals! Ser.). (ENG., Illus.). 24p. (J). (gr. 2-3). 26.27 *(978-1-4488-2532-5(6),* 17080219-fb7e-41bb-872b-1a3a96820527); pap. 9.25 *(978-1-4488-2648-3(9),* b923a14f-9fc4-4cb5-97dd-6a807ac18db8) Rosen Publishing Group, Inc., The. (PowerKids Pr.).
—Endangered Animals of South America, 1 vol. 2011. (Save Earth's Animals! Ser.). (ENG.). 24p. (J). (gr. 2-3). pap. 9.25 *(978-1-4488-2650-6(0),* 9e6571d4-cc55-45ee-ba11-bc136aff2e4a); (Illus.). lib. bdg. 26.27 *(978-1-4488-2533-2(4),* 764661f1-994b-4c98-b09d-41cbb93b6bd7) Rosen Publishing Group, Inc., The. (PowerKids Pr.).
—Endangered Desert Animals, 1 vol. 2012. (Save Earth's Animals! Ser.). (ENG., Illus.). 24p. (J). (gr. 2-3). 26.27 *(978-1-4488-7423-1(8),* 12e5cf85-15af-4a02-a877-c6124c5ecdac); pap. 9.25 *(978-1-4488-7496-5(3),* cb3d40f5-679e-4c19-97af-e570273dc52d) Rosen Publishing Group, Inc., The. (PowerKids Pr.).
—Endangered Forest Animals, 1 vol. 2012. (Save Earth's Animals! Ser.). (ENG., Illus.). 24p. (J). (gr. 2-3). pap. 9.25 *(978-1-4488-7497-2(1),* 41e088e3-9df3-457b-83c2-7333f3251060); lib. bdg. 26.27 *(978-1-4488-7424-8(6),* 4f7ab03b-db1f-4f25-b403-763df8377716) Rosen Publishing Group, Inc., The. (PowerKids Pr.).
—Endangered Grassland Animals, 1 vol. 2012. (Save Earth's Animals! Ser.). (ENG., Illus.). 24p. (J). (gr. 2-3). pap. 9.25 *(978-1-4488-7498-9(X),* 7f63ac50-718f-477c-8220-e30354fc9322); lib. bdg. 26.27 *(978-1-4488-7425-5(4),* e7985484-0614-4563-9f1f-27e8335f1ff1) Rosen Publishing Group, Inc., The. (PowerKids Pr.).
—Endangered Rain Forest Animals, 1 vol. 2012. (Save Earth's Animals! Ser.). (ENG., Illus.). 24p. (J). (gr. 2-3). pap. 9.25 *(978-1-4488-7495-8(5),* 7afae836-4dbc-4901-859e-5a085a48a1cb); lib. bdg. 26.27 *(978-1-4488-7422-4(X),* 8e980b0e-bcd3-41c9-8700-132c89a44f91) Rosen Publishing Group, Inc., The. (PowerKids Pr.).
—Endangered Tundra Animals, 1 vol. 2012. (Save Earth's Animals! Ser.). (ENG., Illus.). 24p. (J). (gr. 2-3). pap. 9.25 *(978-1-4488-7494-1(7),* 2bf75c81-2a1b-40d2-9752-1df0a540f6e0); lib. bdg. 26.27 *(978-1-4488-7421-7(1),* ddae7440-71ec-44fd-8b02-0b69d2b99bfb) Rosen Publishing Group, Inc., The. (PowerKids Pr.).
Bailey, Diane. Battling Wildlife Poachers: The Fight to Save Elephants, Rhinos, Lions, Tigers, & More. 2017. (Illus.). 64p. (J). *(978-1-4222-3874-5(1))* Mason Crest.
—Saving Marine Mammals: Whales, Dolphins, Seals, & More. 2017. (Illus.). 64p. (J). *(978-1-4222-3878-3(4))* Mason Crest.
Barr, Catherine. Red Alert! Endangered Animals Around the World. Wilson, Anne, illus. 2018. (ENG.). 48p. (J). (gr. k-3). 17.99 *(978-1-58089-839-3(4))* Charlesbridge Publishing, Inc.
Bath, Louella. Saving Endangered Animals, 1 vol. 2016. (Global Guardians Ser.). (ENG.). 24p. (J). (gr. 3-3). 25.27 *(978-1-4994-2936-7(3),* 7d10fcc0-0c21-491b-8f72-d9ad4d961830); pap. 9.25 *(978-1-4994-2753-0(0),* c2ab248b-d330-4703-998c-2c5f803bfb26) Rosen Publishing Group, Inc., The. (PowerKids Pr.).
Becker, John E. Frenemies for Life: Cheetahs & Anatolian Shepherd Dogs. 2010. 56p. (YA). (gr. 5-8). pap. 8.95 *(978-0-9841554-1-5(4));* lib. bdg. 18.95 *(978-0-9841554-0-8(6))* Columbus Zoo & Aquarium, The.
Bell, Samantha S. 12 Amphibians Back from the Brink. 2015. (Back from the Brink Ser.). (ENG., Illus.). 32p. (J). (gr. 3-6). 32.80 *(978-1-63235-000-8(9),* 11527, 12-Story Library) Bookstaves, LLC.
—12 Amphibians Back from the Brink. 2015. (ENG., Illus.). 32p. (J). pap. 9.95 *(978-1-63235-060-2(2))* RiverStream Publishing.
—12 Insects Back from the Brink. 2015. (Back from the Brink Ser.). (ENG., Illus.). 32p. (J). (gr. 3-6). 32.80 *(978-1-63235-002-2(5),* 11529, 12-Story Library) Bookstaves, LLC.
—12 Reptiles Back from the Brink. 2015. (Back from the Brink Ser.). (ENG., Illus.). 32p. (J). (gr. 3-6). 32.80 *(978-1-63235-005-3(X),* 11532, 12-Story Library) Bookstaves, LLC.
Blewett, Ashlee Brown. National Geographic Kids Chapters: Hoot, Hoot, Hooray! And More True Stories of Amazing Animal Rescues. 2015. (NGK Chapters Ser.). (Illus.). 112p. (J). (gr. 3-7). pap. 5.99 *(978-1-4263-2054-5(X),* National Geographic Kids) Disney Publishing Worldwide.
Bow, James. Saving Endangered Plants & Animals. 2008. (Science Solves It Ser.). (ENG., Illus.). 32p. (J). (gr. 3-7). pap. *(978-0-7787-4177-0(X),* 1286291) Crabtree Publishing Co.
Brown, Vinson. The Californian Wildlife Region. 3rd rev. ed. 2003. (Illus.). 302p. (J). pap. 14.95 *(978-0-87961-201-6(0))* Naturegraph Pubs., Inc.
Bruchac, Joseph. Buffalo Song, 1 vol. Farnsworth, Bill, illus. (J). 2014. (ENG.). 40p. (gr. 1-6). 18.95 *(978-1-58430-280-3(1),* leelowbooks) 2008. Lee & Low Bks., Inc.
Burroughs, Caleb. Animal Rescue Adventure. 2006. (Illus.). (J). pap. 24.98 *(978-1-4127-6491-9(2))* Publications International, Ltd.
Burton, L. Devere. Fish & Wildlife: Principles of Zoology & Ecology. 3rd rev. ed. 2009. (ENG.). 416p. (C). 221.95 *(978-1-4354-1963-6(4))* Delmar Cengage Learning.
Capek, Michael. Jane Goodall: Primatologist & Conservationist. 2017. (Women in Science Ser.). (ENG., Illus.). 112p. (J). (gr. 6-12). lib. bdg. 41.36 *(978-1-5321-1043-6(X),* 25662, Essential Library) ABDO Publishing Co.
Capstone Press. Animals on the Edge. 2010. (Animals on the Edge Ser.). (ENG.). 32p. lib. bdg. 103.96 *(978-1-4296-5923-9(8),* Capstone Pr.) Capstone.
Carson, Mary Kay. Emi & the Rhino Scientist. 2010. (Scientists in the Field Ser.). (ENG., Illus.). 64p. (J). (gr. 5-7). pap. 9.99 *(978-0-547-40850-7(1),* 1428813, Clarion Bks.) HarperCollins Pubs.
—Park Scientists: Gila Monsters, Geysers, & Grizzly Bears in America's Own Backyard. 2017. (Scientists in the Field Ser.). (ENG., Illus.). 80p. (J). (gr. 5-7). pap. 9.99 *(978-1-328-74090-8(0),* 1677131, Clarion Bks.) HarperCollins Pubs.
Castaldo, Nancy F. Back from the Brink: Saving Animals from Extinction. 2018. (ENG., Illus.). 176p. (J). (gr. 5-7). 17.99 *(978-0-544-95343-7(6),* 1660625, Clarion Bks.) HarperCollins Pubs.
Centore, Michael. Saving Ocean Animals: Sharks, Turtles, Coral, & Fish. 2017. (Illus.). 64p. (J). *(978-1-4222-3879-0(2))* Mason Crest.
Chancellor, Deborah. Save the Animals. Ewen, Diane, illus. 2020. 32p. (J). *(978-0-7787-7285-9(3))* Crabtree Publishing Co.
Christian, Peggy. Chocolate, a Glacier Grizzly. Cottone-Kolthoff, Carol, illus. (Humane Society of the United States Animal Tales Ser.). 32p. (J). (gr. 1-5). 34.95 incl. audio *(978-1-882728-64-0(5));* pap. 19.95 incl. audio *(978-1-882728-69-5(6));* pap. 9.95 incl. audio *(978-1-882728-67-1(X))* Benefactory, Inc., The.
Clendening, John. Wildlife Preserves, 1 vol. 2014. (Animal Rescue Ser.). (ENG., Illus.). 32p. (J). (gr. 4-4). 27.93 *(978-1-4777-7015-3(1),* 7af7663c-4a64-4cff-8277-d4b8c5cd66fa, PowerKids Pr.) Rosen Publishing Group, Inc., The.
Clinton, Chelsea. Don't Let Them Disappear: 12 Endangered Species Across the Globe. Marino, Gianna, illus. 2019. 40p. (J). (gr. -1-3). 17.99 *(978-0-525-51432-9(5),* Philomel Bks.) Penguin Young Readers Group.
Coey, Julia. Animal Hospital: Rescuing Urban Wildlife. 2015. (ENG., Illus.). 64p. (J). (gr. 4-7). 19.95 *(978-1-77085-572-4(6),* fbd56c36-066a-41d4-9764-049b69cfa1b2) Firefly Bks., Ltd.
Cohn, Jessica. Hand to Paw - Protecting Animals, 1 vol. 2nd rev. ed. 2012. (TIME for KIDS(r): Informational Text Ser.). (ENG.). 48p. (gr. 4-5). pap. 13.99 *(978-1-4333-4867-9(5))* Teacher Created Materials, Inc.
Cram101 Textbook Reviews Staff & L. DeVere Burton. Studyguide for Fish & Wildlife: Principles of Zoology & Ecology by L. Devere Burton, Isbn 9781435419636. 3rd ed. 2014. (ENG.). 216p. (C). pap. 30.95 *(978-1-4784-1055-3(8))* Cram101 Inc.
Crum, Anna-Maria. Animal Behaviorists & Conductistas de Animales: 6 English, 6 Spanish Adaptations. 2011. (ENG & SPA.). (J). 89.00 net. *(978-1-4108-5679-1(8))* Benchmark Education Co.
Crump, Marty. Amphibians & Reptiles: An Introduction to Their Natural History & Conservation, 1 vol. 2011. (ENG., Illus.). 272p. (J). 29.95 *(978-1-935778-20-2(X))* McDonald & Woodward Publishing Co., The.
deMarin, Layne. Save the Animals. 2011. (Wonder Readers Fluent Level Ser.). (ENG.). 16p. (gr. -1-2). pap. 35.94 *(978-1-4296-8144-5(6),* Capstone Pr.) Capstone.
Discover Series: Science, Nature, Wildlife, 11 bks. (Illus.). (J). (gr. 3-6). lib. bdg. 175.45 *(978-1-56674-935-0(2))* Forest Hse. Publishing Co., Inc.
Doak, Robin S. Jane Goodall: Chimpanzee Protector, 1 vol. 2014. (Women in Conservation Ser.). (ENG., Illus.). 48p. (J). (gr. 3-6). pap. 8.99 *(978-1-4846-0474-8(1),* 126604, Heinemann) Capstone.
Dunne, Abbie. Endangered & Threatened Animals. 2016. (Life Science Ser.). (ENG., Illus.). 24p. (J). (gr. -1-2). lib. bdg. 27.32 *(978-1-5157-0945-9(0),* 132259, Capstone Pr.) Capstone.
Einhorn, Kama. Welcome, Wombat. 2018. (True Tales of Rescue Ser.). (ENG., Illus.). 160p. (J). (gr. 3-7). 14.99 *(978-1-328-76702-8(7),* 1680370, Clarion Bks.) HarperCollins Pubs.
Emminizer, Theresa. What If Mountain Lions Disappeared?, 1 vol. 2019. (Life Without Animals Ser.). (ENG.). 24p. (gr. 1-2). 24.27 *(978-1-5382-3816-5(0),* 546f18cd-bbca-4dc3-a062-ecc8f4a4e389) Stevens, Gareth Publishing LLLP.
Faust, Daniel R. Desastres Ecológicos: los Derrames de Petróleo y el MedioAmbiente, 1 vol. 2009. (Historietas Juveniles: Peligros Del Medioambiente (Jr. Graphic Environmental Dangers) Ser.). (SPA., Illus.). 24p. (gr. 4-4). pap. 10.60 *(978-1-4358-8469-4(8),* 45598d3b-0bc0-4b0d-be3b-50c9905819ef, PowerKids Pr.) Rosen Publishing Group, Inc., The.
—Desastres Ecológicos: Los Derrames de Petróleo y el Medio Ambiente = Sinister Sludge: Oil Spills & the Environment, 1 vol. 2009. (Historietas Juveniles: Peligros Del Medioambiente (Jr. Graphic Environmental Dangers) Ser.). (SPA., Illus.). 24p. (YA). (gr. 4-4). lib. bdg. 28.93 *(978-1-4358-8468-7(X),* bbf3bb69-9c5a-4ed8-8ad3-cadb2e6e85ed) Rosen Publishing Group, Inc., The.
Frankenhuyzen, Robbyn Smith van. Saving Samantha: A True Story. Frankenhuyzen, Gijsbert van, illus. 2004. (Hazel Ridge Farm Stories Ser.). (ENG.). 48p. (J). (gr. 1-4). 17.95 *(978-1-58536-220-2(4),* 202050) Sleeping Bear Pr.
Furstinger, Nancy. 12 Mammals Back from the Brink. 2015. (Back from the Brink Ser.). (ENG., Illus.). 32p. (J). (gr. 3-6). 32.80 *(978-1-63235-003-9(3),* 11530, 12-Story Library) Bookstaves, LLC.
—12 Marine Animals Back from the Brink. 2015. (Back from the Brink Ser.). (ENG., Illus.). 32p. (J). (gr. 3-6). 32.80 *(978-1-63235-004-6(1),* 11531, 12-Story Library) Bookstaves, LLC.
Gagne, Tammy. Day by Day with Bindi Sue Irwin. 2012. 32p. (J). (gr. -1-2). lib. bdg. 25.70 *(978-1-61228-326-5(8))* Mitchell Lane Pubs.
Ganeri, Anita. Endangered Animals, 1 vol. 2017. (Last Chance to Save Ser.). (ENG.). 32p. (J). (gr. 4-5). 27.93 *(978-1-5383-2283-3(8),* 8c2865fd-ec76-499a-8550-af8bcb194636); pap. 11.00 *(978-1-5383-2382-3(6),* 1ed75d0a-e5f3-440d-b9cf-12cdba0357d7) Rosen Publishing Group, Inc., The. (PowerKids Pr.).
Gazlay, Suzy. Managing Green Spaces: Careers in Wilderness & Wildlife Management. 2009. (Green-Collar Careers Ser.). (ENG., Illus.). 64p. (J). (gr. 5-8). pap. *(978-0-7787-4866-3(9));* lib. bdg. *(978-0-7787-4855-7(3))* Crabtree Publishing Co.
Gibson, Brylee. Wildlife Detectives. 2007. (Connectors Ser.). (gr. 2-5). pap. *(978-1-877453-18-2(8))* Global Education Systems Ltd.
Global Issues: Habitat Preservation (below-Level) 2012. (Global Issues Ser.). (Illus.). 32p. (J). pap. 13.95 *(978-0-7362-9778-3(2))* National Geographic School Publishing, Inc.
Goldish, Meish. Wildlife Rehabilitators to the Rescue. 2013. (Work of Heroes: First Responders in Action Ser.). 32p. (J). (gr. 1-6). lib. bdg. 28.50 *(978-1-61772-748-1(2))* Bearport Publishing Co., Inc.
Golkar, Golriz. Bindi Irwin. 2018. (Influential People Ser.). (ENG., Illus.). 32p. (J). (gr. 4-6). lib. bdg. 28.65 *(978-1-5435-4132-8(1),* 139086, Capstone Pr.) Capstone.
Greene, Carol. I Love Our Animals, 1 vol. 2012. (I Love Our Earth Ser.). (ENG., Illus.). 24p. (gr. 3-3). 25.27 *(978-0-7660-4038-0(0),* 47bd78a3-c119-45d4-9f17-60567cd3a99c); pap. 10.35 *(978-1-4644-0139-8(X),* 6613b2f8-102b-4fcb-9d73-d9b239e3f93e) Enslow Publishing, LLC. (Enslow Elementary).
Hamilton, Garry. Rhino Rescue: Changing the Future for Endangered Wildlife. 2006. (Firefly Animal Rescue Ser.). (ENG., Illus.). 64p. (J). (gr. 5-12). 19.95 *(978-1-55297-912-9(1),* 3efa896e-2844-4e37-b806-73507d921231); pap. 9.95 *(978-1-55297-910-5(5),* 85419e7f-8341-4487-be71-880fe5e24002) Firefly Bks., Ltd.
Hansen, Grace. Jane Goodall: Activista y Experta en Chimpancés (Spanish Version) 2016. (Biografías: Personas Que Han Hecho Historia (History Maker Biographies) Ser.). (SPA., Illus.). 24p. (J). (gr. -1-2). lib. bdg. 32.79 *(978-1-68080-739-4(0),* 22640, Abdo Kids) ABDO Publishing Co.
Hemstock, Annie Wendt. Hunting Laws & Safety, 1 vol. 2014. (Open Season Ser.). (ENG.). 32p. (J). (gr. 4-5). lib. bdg. 28.93 *(978-1-4777-6725-2(8),* 52036a8f-afa6-4a08-8e73-89f0010d6a19, PowerKids Pr.) Rosen Publishing Group, Inc., The.
Hibbert, Clare. Elephant Orphans, 1 vol. 2014. (Save the Animals Ser.). (ENG.). 32p. (J). (gr. 4-5). pap. 11.00 *(978-1-4777-5896-0(8),* c93578ac-294b-4ef0-b0ce-6e85ede5217d, PowerKids Pr.) Rosen Publishing Group, Inc., The.
—Save the Animals, 1 vol. 2015. (Save the Animals Ser.). (ENG.). 32p. (J). 60.00 *(978-1-4994-0316-9(X),* PowerKids Pr.) Rosen Publishing Group, Inc., The.
Hickman, Pamela. Birds of Prey Rescue: Changing the Future for Endangered Wildlife. 2006. (Firefly Animal Rescue Ser.). (ENG., Illus.). 64p. (J). (gr. 5-12). 19.95 *(978-1-55407-145-6(3),* 8148d705-8787-40f1-93fe-c1da39837536); pap. 9.95 *(978-1-55407-144-9(5),* 4150dbbe-59ac-4303-86a9-a5913a596d1e) Firefly Bks., Ltd.
Hogan, Zeb. National Geographic Kids Chapters: Monster Fish! True Stories of Adventures with Animals. 2017. (NGK Chapters Ser.). (Illus.). 112p. (J). (gr. 3-7). pap. 6.99 *(978-1-4263-2703-2(X),* National Geographic Kids) Disney Publishing Worldwide.
Hopkins, Andy & Potter, Joc. Oxford Bookworms Factfiles: Animals in Danger: Level 1: 400-Word Vocabulary. 3rd ed. 2008. (ENG., Illus.). 64p. pap. 11.00 *(978-0-19-423379-8(0))* Oxford Univ. Pr., Inc.
Houston, Dick. Bulu: African Wonder Dog. 2011. 336p. (J). (gr. 3-7). 7.99 *(978-0-375-84724-0(3),* Yearling) Random Hse. Children's Bks.
Houts, Michelle. Silent Swoop: An Owl, an Egg, & a Warm Shirt Pocket. Hoeffner, Deb, illus. 2019. 32p. (J). (gr. -1-3). 16.95 *(978-1-58469-646-9(X),* Dawn Pubns.) Sourcebooks, Inc.
Hunter, Rebecca. Saving Wildlife. 2012. (Eco Alert! Ser.). (ENG., Illus.). 32p. (J). (gr. 4-6). lib. bdg. 28.50 *(978-1-59771-298-9(1))* Sea-To-Sea Pubns.
Jackson, Donna M. The Wildlife Detectives: How Forensic Scientists Fight Crimes Against Nature. Shattil, Wendy & Rozinski, Bob, photos by. 2005. (Scientists in the Field Ser.). (Illus.). 47p. (gr. 3-7). 20.00 *(978-0-7569-5191-7(7))* Perfection Learning Corp.

zynka, Kitson. National Geographic Kids Mission: Panda Rescue: All about Pandas & How to Save Them. 2016. (NG Kids Mission: Animal Rescue Ser.). (Illus.). 112p. (J). (gr. 5-9). pap. 12.99 *(978-1-4263-2088-0(4)*, National Geographic Kids) Disney Publishing Worldwide.
enkins, Martin. Can We Save the Tiger? White, Vicky, illus. 2014. (ENG.). 56p. (J). (gr. k-3). 9.99 *(978-0-7636-7378-9(1))* Candlewick Pr.
alman, Bobbie. Big Challenges That Animals Face. 2016. (Big Science Ideas Ser.). (ENG., Illus.). 32p. (J). (gr. 3-6). lib. bdg. *(978-0-7787-2781-1(5))* Crabtree Publishing Co.
avanagh, James & Waterford Press Staff. Grasslands Wildlife: A Folding Pocket Guide to Familiar Species Found in Prairie Grasslands. Leung, Raymond, illus. 2010. (Wildlife & Nature Identification Ser.). (ENG.). 12p. 7.95 *(978-1-58355-510-1(2))* Waterford Pr., Inc.
Keats Curtis, Jennifer. Animal Helpers: Raptor Centers, 1 vol. 2015. (Animal Helpers Ser.). (ENG., Illus.). 32p. (J). (gr. 2-5). 17.95 *(978-1-62855-447-2(9))* Arbordale Publishing.
Kenyon, Linda. Rainforest Bird Rescue: Changing the Future for Endangered Wildlife. 2006. (Firefly Animal Rescue Ser.). (ENG., Illus.). 64p. (J). (gr. 5-12). 19.95 *(978-1-55407-153-1(4)*, 5f5391f3-e92a-4443-9f37-ebc59bad0fb4); pap. 9.95 *(978-1-55407-152-4(6)*, 8aebe428-2efd-46f5-bbb7-1a18ed239dc3) Firefly Bks., Ltd.
Kimberly. Ocean Friends "Sing-A-Long" 2009. (ENG.). 28p. pap. 13.99 *(978-1-4415-3386-9(9))* Xlibris Corp.
Kinsner, Kathy. Doomed to Disappear? Endangered Species & Condenadas a desaparecer? Especies en peligro de Extinción: 6 English, 6 Spanish Adaptations. 2011. (ENG & SPA.). (J). 97.00 net. *(978-1-4108-5698-2(4))* Benchmark Education Co.
Kirk, Daniel. Rhino in the House: The Story of Saving Samia. 2017. (ENG., Illus.). 40p. (J). (gr. -1-3). 17.95 *(978-1-4197-2316-2(2)*, 1157201) Abrams, Inc.
Kortemeier, Todd. Saving Endangered Species. 2017. (Science Frontiers Ser.). (ENG., Illus.). 32p. (J). (gr. 3-6). pap. 9.95 *(978-1-63235-396-2(2)*, 11881, 12-Story Library) Bookstaves, LLC.
—Saving Endangered Species. 2017. (Illus.). 32p. (J). *(978-1-62143-520-4(2))* Pr. Room Editions LLC.
Labrecque, Ellen. Wildlife Conservation. 2017. (21st Century Skills Library: Global Citizens: Environmentalism Ser.). (ENG., Illus.). 32p. (J). (gr. 4-7). lib. bdg. 32.07 *(978-1-63472-866-9(1)*, 209890) Cherry Lake Publishing.
Lasky, Kathryn. Interrupted Journey: Saving Endangered Sea Turtles. Knight, Christopher G., photos by. 2006. (ENG., Illus.). 48p. (J). (gr. 1-4). 7.99 *(978-0-7636-2883-3(2))* Candlewick Pr.
Leaman, Louisa & The Born Free Foundation, The Born. Elephant Rescue: True-Life Stories. 2017. (Born Free... Bks.). (ENG., Illus.). 96p. (J). (gr. 2-6). pap. 6.99 *(978-1-4380-0987-2(9))* Sourcebooks, Inc.
Levete, Sarah. Habitats & Wildlife in Danger. 2010. (Protecting Our Planet Ser.). (ENG., Illus.). 32p. (J). (gr. 3-6). *(978-0-7787-5213-4(5))*; pap. *(978-0-7787-5230-1(5))* Crabtree Publishing Co.
Lourie, Peter. The Manatee Scientists: Saving Vulnerable Species. 2016. (Scientists in the Field Ser.). (ENG., Illus.). 80p. (J). (gr. 5-7). pap. 10.99 *(978-0-544-22529-9(5)*, 1563372, Clarion Bks.) HarperCollins Pubs.
Love, Ann & Drake, Jane. Rewilding: Giving Nature a Second Chance. 2017. (ENG., Illus.). 88p. (J). (gr. 4-7). 19.95 *(978-1-55451-962-0(4))*; pap. 12.95 *(978-1-55451-961-3(6))* Annick Pr., Ltd. CAN. Dist: Publishers Group West (PGW).
MacCarald, Clara. How Do Wildlife Crossings Save Animals? 2018. (How'd They Do That? Ser.). (ENG., Illus.). 32p. (J). (gr. 4-6). lib. bdg. 28.65 *(978-1-5435-4138-0(0)*, 139092, Capstone Pr.) Capstone.
MacDonald, Lisa. Raising Clouded Leopards (Grade 3) rev. ed. 2018. (Smithsonian: Informational Text Ser.). (ENG., Illus.). 32p. (J). (gr. 3-4). pap. 11.99 *(978-1-4938-6676-2(1))* Teacher Created Materials, Inc.
Machajewski, Sarah. The Return of the Mountain Gorilla. 2017. (Bouncing Back from Extinction Ser.). 32p. (J). (gr. 9-10). 60.00 *(978-1-5081-5603-1(4)*, PowerKids Pr.) Rosen Publishing Group, Inc., The.
Malnor, Carol & Malnor, Bruce. Earth Heroes: Champions of Wild Animals, 1 vol. Hovemann, Anisa Claire, illus. 2011. (ENG.). 144p. (J). (gr. 5-8). pap. 12.95 *(978-1-58469-123-5(9)*, Dawn Pubns.) Sourcebooks, Inc.
Markle, Sandra. The Great Leopard Rescue: Saving the Amur Leopards. 2016. (Sandra Markle's Science Discoveries Ser.). (ENG., Illus.). 48p. (J). (gr. 4-6). 33.32 *(978-1-4677-9247-9(0)*, 3561c0d3-eabe-4129-b277-24d7098ea0a8); E-Book 47.99 *(978-1-4677-9755-9(3))* Lerner Publishing Group. (Millbrook Pr.).
Marsico, Katie. World Wildlife Fund. 2016. (Community Connections: How Do They Help? Ser.). (ENG., Illus.). 24p. (J). (gr. 2-5). 29.21 *(978-1-63471-055-8(X)*, 208300) Cherry Lake Publishing.
Meissner, David. Habitat Rescue & Rescate del Hábitat: 6 English, 6 Spanish Adaptations. 2011. (ENG & SPA.). (J). 89.00 net. *(978-1-4108-5676-0(3))* Benchmark Education Co.
Montgomery, Sy. The Great White Shark Scientist. 2016. (Scientists in the Field Ser.). (ENG., Illus.). 80p. (J). (gr. 5-7). 18.99 *(978-0-544-35298-8(X)*, 1586364, Clarion Bks.) HarperCollins Pubs.
Nagelhout, Ryan. Saving the Chesapeake Bay, 1 vol. 2013. (Exploring the Chesapeake Bay Ser.). (ENG., Illus.). 32p. (J). (gr. 3-4). pap. 11.50 *(978-1-4339-9785-3(1)*, 8d856c30-b5c6-4731-a3b6-785bfd7a2aea); lib. bdg. 29.27 *(978-1-4339-9784-6(3)*, 49d2e09a-fd80-4a58-8dd1-de1f29a70604) Stevens, Gareth Publishing LLLP.
Nagle, Jeanne. Endangered Wildlife: Habitats in Peril. 2009. (Extreme Environmental Threats Ser.). 64p. (gr. 6-6). 58.50 *(978-1-61512-429-9(2))* Rosen Publishing Group, Inc., The.
Nagle, Jeanne M. Endangered Wildlife: Habitats in Peril, 1 vol. 2009. (Extreme Environmental Threats Ser.). (ENG.). 64p. (gr. 6-6). (YA). lib. bdg. 37.13 *(978-1-4358-5019-4(X)*, 859770df-7abd-4dfc-a43a-b69f6d6eff40); (Illus.). (J). pap. 13.95 *(978-1-4358-5375-1(X)*, b4a30223-5cac-4572-98bb-2c63265f0d24) Rosen Publishing Group, Inc., The.
Newland, Sonya. Desert Animals. 2011. (Saving Wildlife Ser.). 32p. (YA). (gr. 3-6). lib. bdg. 28.50 *(978-1-59920-655-4(2))* Black Rabbit Bks.
—Ocean Animals. 2011. (Saving Wildlife Ser.). 32p. (YA). (gr. 3-6). lib. bdg. 28.50 *(978-1-59920-658-5(7))* Black Rabbit Bks.
—Polar Animals. 2011. (Saving Wildlife Ser.). 32p. (gr. 4-7). lib. bdg. 31.35 *(978-1-59920-659-2(5))* Black Rabbit Bks.
—Rain Forest Animals. 2011. (Saving Wildlife Ser.). 32p. (gr. 4-7). lib. bdg. 31.35 *(978-1-59920-660-8(9))* Black Rabbit Bks.
Newman, Patricia. Zoo Scientists to the Rescue. Crawley, Annie, photos by. 2017. (ENG., Illus.). 64p. (J). (gr. 4-8). lib. bdg. 33.32 *(978-1-5124-1571-1(5)*, 85e5e5e1-e4d4-40b1-a39a-cfa8a6664d14, Millbrook Pr.) Lerner Publishing Group.
O'Connell, Jennifer. The Eye of the Whale: A Rescue Story, 1 vol. 2013. (Tilbury House Nature Book Ser.: 0). (ENG., Illus.). 32p. (J). (gr. 1-7). 17.95 *(978-0-88448-335-9(5)*, 884335) Tilbury Hse. Pubs.
O'Connor, Karen. Animals on the Verge of Extinction. 2013. (Animal 911: Environmental Threats Ser.). 48p. (J). (gr. 3-5). pap. 84.30 *(978-1-4339-9716-7(9))*; (ENG.). (gr. 4-4). pap. 15.05 *(978-1-4339-9715-0(0)*, a94847c6-8f57-458a-bce5-360f8a712b7b); (ENG., Illus.). (gr. 4-4). lib. bdg. 34.61 *(978-1-4339-9714-3(2)*, a4fb8d05-f0db-4fca-be47-0d40ebe21d8d) Stevens, Gareth Publishing LLLP.
O'Neal, Claire. Threat to the Bengal Tiger. 2008. (On the Verge of Extinction Ser.). (Illus.). 32p. (J). (gr. 1-5). lib. bdg. 25.70 *(978-1-58415-688-8(0))* Mitchell Lane Pubs.
Orr, Tamra B. Battling Extinction. 2014. (Explorer Library: Science Explorer Ser.). (ENG., Illus.). 32p. (J). (gr. 4-8). 32.07 *(978-1-62431-780-4(4)*, 203316) Cherry Lake Publishing.
Parker, Russ. Wildlife Crisis, 1 vol. 2009. (Planet in Crisis Ser.). (ENG.). 32p. (gr. 5-5). (YA). lib. bdg. 30.47 *(978-1-4358-5255-6(9)*, eb5625be-2252-4fb9-b50b-9ff4df3f1495); (Illus.). (J). pap. 11.00 *(978-1-4358-0685-6(9)*, a4f3c5d9-bb0f-4f3f-898c-594351c6a297) Rosen Publishing Group, Inc., The. (Rosen Reference).
Parks, Peggy J. Science & Sustainable Wildlife Habitats. 2017. (Science & Sustainability Ser.). (ENG.). 80p. (YA). (gr. 5-12). *(978-1-68282-259-3(1))* ReferencePoint Pr., Inc.
Patent, Dorothy Hinshaw. Call of the Osprey. Muñoz, William, illus. (Scientists in the Field Ser.). (ENG.). 80p. (J). (gr. 5-7). 2020. pap. 10.99 *(978-0-358-10547-3(1)*, 1748671) 2015. 18.99 *(978-0-544-23268-6(2)*, 1564093) HarperCollins Pubs. (Clarion Bks.).
—Saving the Tasmanian Devil: How Science Is Helping the World's Largest Marsupial Carnivore Survive. 2019. (Scientists in the Field Ser.). (ENG., Illus.). 80p. (J). (gr. 5-7). 18.99 *(978-0-544-99148-4(6)*, 1666537, Clarion Bks.) HarperCollins Pubs.
Patterson, Virginia Sharpe. Dickey Downy: The Autobiography of a Bird. 2007. 106p. pap. 10.99 *(978-1-4346-2478-9(1))*; 116p. pap. 11.99 *(978-1-4346-2479-6(X))* Creative Media Partners, LLC.
Posewitz, James. Rifle in Hand: How Wild America Was Saved. 2004. (Illus.). 128p. per. 9.95 *(978-1-931832-41-0(2)*, 8667872363) Riverbend Publishing.
Rich, Mari. Rescuing Primates: Gorillas, Chimps, & Monkeys. 2017. (Illus.). 64p. (J). *(978-1-4222-3877-6(6))* Mason Crest.
Robinson, Jill & Bekoff, Marc. Jasper's Story: Saving Moon Bears. Frankenhuyzen, Gijsbert van, illus. 2013. (ENG.). 40p. (J). (gr. 1-4). 17.99 *(978-1-58536-798-6(2)*, 202359) Sleeping Bear Pr.
Rose, Deborah Lee & Kelly, Susan. Jimmy the Joey: The True Story of an Amazing Koala Rescue. 2013. (Baby Animal Tales Ser.). (Illus.). 32p. (J). (gr. -1-k). 16.95 *(978-1-4263-1371-4(3)*, National Geographic Kids) Disney Publishing Worldwide.
Royston, Angela. Mountain Food Chains, 1 vol. 2014. (Food Chains & Webs Ser.). (ENG., Illus.). 32p. (J). (gr. 1-3). 29.99 *(978-1-4846-0519-6(5)*, 126629, Heinemann) Capstone.
Salmansohn, Pete. Saving Birds: Heroes Around the World, 1 vol. 2005. (ENG., Illus.). 40p. (gr. 3-6). 16.95 *(978-0-88448-237-6(5))* Tilbury Hse. Pubs.
Save the Animals, 12 vols. 2014. (Save the Animals Ser.). (ENG.). 32p. (J). (gr. 4-5). lib. bdg. 167.58 *(978-1-4777-5726-0(0)*, 8486018f-980b-4275-99fd-e469b70d39a6, PowerKids Pr.) Rosen Publishing Group, Inc., The.
Saving the Chesapeake Bay. 2013. (Exploring the Chesapeake Bay Ser.). 32p. (J). (gr. 3-6). pap. 63.00 *(978-1-4339-9786-0(X))* Stevens, Gareth Publishing LLLP.
Shepherd, Jodie. Jane Goodall. 2015. (Rookie Biographies(tm) Ser.). (ENG.). 32p. (J). lib. bdg. 25.00 *(978-0-531-21413-8(3)*, Children's Pr.) Scholastic Library Publishing.
Shields, Amy. National Geographic Readers: Saving Animal Babies. 2013. (Readers Ser.). (Illus.). 32p. (J). (gr. 1-3). pap. 4.99 *(978-1-4263-1040-9(4)*, National Geographic Kids); (ENG., lib. bdg. 13.90 *(978-1-4263-1041-6(2)*, National Geographic Children's Bks.) Disney Publishing Worldwide.
Simpson, Phillip. How Can We Save the Cheetah? A Problem & Solution Text, 1 vol. 2014. (Text Structures Ser.). (ENG.). 32p. (J). (gr. 1-3). pap. 7.99 *(978-1-4846-0415-1(6)*, 126583, Heinemann) Capstone.
Slade, Suzanne. What Can We Do about Endangered Animals? 2009. (J). 49.50 *(978-1-4358-2478-2(4)*, PowerKids Pr.); (ENG.). 24p. (J). (gr. 2-3). pap. 9.25 *(978-1-4358-2477-5(6)*, 64446bc6-963c-4fe8-88a9-8d8dd655ea96, PowerKids Pr.); (ENG., Illus.). 24p. (YA). (gr. 2-3). lib. bdg. 26.27 *(978-1-4042-8080-9(4)*, 91676f0f-9ce1-4120-9cbc-20b428f4aa14) Rosen Publishing Group, Inc., The.
Snyder, Trish. Alligator & Crocodile Rescue: Changing the Future for Endangered Wildlife. 2006. (Firefly Animal Rescue Ser.). (ENG., Illus.). 64p. (J). (gr. 5-12). 19.95 *(978-1-55297-920-4(2)*, 51f16bee-b6b2-4af2-ae47-436b70848f89); pap. 9.95 *(978-1-55297-919-8(9)*, dbe618eb-6205-4b0e-8cc9-4e4f35502c4b) Firefly Bks., Ltd.
Stamper, Judith Bauer. Eco Dogs. 2016. (Dog Heroes Ser.). (ENG.). 32p. (J). (gr. 2-7). pap. 7.99 *(978-1-944998-63-9(2))* Bearport Publishing Co., Inc.
Stetson, Emily. Create a Wildlife Habitat for Urban & Suburban Small Spaces. 2004. (ENG., Illus.). 128p. (J). pap. 12.95 *(978-0-8249-8665-0(2)*, Ideals Pubns.) Worthy Publishing.
Strain Truit, Trudi. Wildlife Conservationist, 1 vol. 2014. (Careers with Animals Ser.). (ENG., Illus.). 64p. (gr. 5-5). pap. 16.28 *(978-1-62712-468-3(3)*, e0daea08-e212-4696-bd51-65ff180daf32); lib. bdg. 36.93 *(978-1-62712-467-6(5)*, c042c9cb-0c62-4b60-8e68-e373b52220b4) Cavendish Square Publishing LLC.
Swanson, Diane. Why Seals Blow Their Noses: Canadian Wildlife in Fact & Fiction, 1 vol. Penhale, Douglas, illus. (ENG.). 80p. (J). pap. 12.95 *(978-1-55110-038-8(X))* Whitecap Bks., Ltd. CAN. Dist: Graphic Arts Ctr. Publishing Co.
Thimmesh, Catherine. Camp Panda: Helping Cubs Return to the Wild. 2018. (ENG., Illus.). 64p. (J). (gr. 5-7). 17.99 *(978-0-544-81891-0(1)*, 1642679, Clarion Bks.) HarperCollins Pubs.
Thomas, Keltie. Bear Rescue: Changing the Future for Endangered Wildlife. 2006. (Firefly Animal Rescue Ser.). (ENG., Illus.). 64p. (J). (gr. 5-12). 19.95 *(978-1-55297-922-8(9)*, 82c525b7-5c27-4514-931f-1230ffc081e7); pap. 9.95 *(978-1-55297-921-1(0)*, bb7b50ec-cae9-4673-82e2-9be98fd4bee9) Firefly Bks., Ltd.
Torres, John. Threat to the Giant Panda. 2008. (On the Verge of Extinction Ser.). (Illus.). 32p. (J). (gr. 2-5). lib. bdg. 25.70 *(978-1-58415-689-5(9))* Mitchell Lane Pubs.
Tupper, Susan. Fran & Frederick Hamerstrom: Wildlife Conservation Pioneers. 2016. (Badger Biographies Ser.). (ENG., Illus.). 136p. (J). (gr. 4-6). pap. 12.95 *(978-0-87020-732-7(6))* Wisconsin Historical Society.
Waeschle, Amy. Daring Wildfire Rescues. 2018. (Rescued! Ser.). (ENG., Illus.). 32p. (J). (gr. 3-9). pap. 7.95 *(978-1-5435-0116-2(8)*, 137069, Capstone Pr.) Capstone.
Watkins, Sue. Getting Involved! A Guide to Hunting & Conservation for Kids. 2011. (Illus.). 128p. pap. 12.95 *(978-1-57157-377-3(1))* Safari Pr., Inc.
Weitzman, Elizabeth. 10 Cosas Que Puedes Hacer para Proteger a Los Animales (Rookie Star: Make a Difference) 2017. (Rookie Star Ser.). (SPA., Illus.). 32p. (J). (gr. 2-3). pap. 5.95 *(978-1-338-18778-6(3)*, Children's Pr.) Scholastic Library Publishing.
—10 Cosas Que Puedes Hacer para Proteger a Los Animales (Rookie Star: Make a Difference) (Library Edition) 2017. (Rookie Star Ser.). (SPA., Illus.). 32p. (J). (gr. 2-3). lib. bdg. 25.00 *(978-0-531-22857-9(6)*, Children's Pr.) Scholastic Library Publishing.
—10 Things You Can Do to Protect Animals. 2016. (Rookie Star — Make a Difference Ser.). (ENG., Illus.). 32p. (J). lib. bdg. 25.00 *(978-0-531-22652-0(2)*, Children's Pr.) Scholastic Library Publishing.
Wells, Robert E. Can We Share the World with Tigers? Wells, Robert E., illus. 2012. (Wells of Knowledge Science Ser.). (ENG., Illus.). 32p. (J). (gr. -1-3). 16.99 *(978-0-8075-1055-1(6)*, 807510556) Whitman, Albert & Co.
Wildlife at Risk. 2015. (Wildlife at Risk Ser.). (ENG.). 48p. (J). (gr. 6-6). pap., pap., pap. 421.20 *(978-0-7660-6689-2(4))*; lib. bdg. 177.60 *(978-0-7660-6688-5(6)*, 75691550-c8ea-4b22-9f45-123655305bbf) Enslow Publishing, LLC.
Woolf, Alex. Jane Goodall (Women in Science) (Library Edition) Lundie, Isobel, illus. 2019. (Women in Science Ser.). (ENG.). 32p. (J). (gr. 2-3). lib. bdg. 29.00 *(978-0-531-23535-5(1)*, Watts, Franklin) Scholastic Library Publishing.
World Book, Inc. Staff, contrib. by. Code Red: Animals in Peril: A Supplement to Childcraft-The How & Why Library. 2011. (Illus.). 206p. (J). *(978-0-7166-0626-0(7))* World Bk., Inc.
—Endangered Animals of Europe. 2014. (J). *(978-0-7166-5624-1(8))* World Bk., Inc.

WILDLIFE CONSERVATION—FICTION

Aguirre, Jorge. Trees for the Okapis: Little Green Nickelodeon. Mawhinney, Art, illus. 2010. (Go Diego Go! Ser.). (ENG.). 24p. (J). (gr. -1-1). 17.44 *(978-1-4169-9090-1(9))* Simon & Schuster, Inc.
Applegate, Katherine. Willodeen. 2023. (SPA.). 220p. (J). (gr. 2-4). pap. 13.95 ***(978-607-557-486-8(7))*** Editorial Oceano de Mexico MEX. Dist: Independent Pubs. Group.
—Willodeen. Santoso, Charles, illus. 2021. (ENG.). 272p. (J). 16.99 *(978-1-250-14740-0(9)*, 900181551) Feiwel & Friends.
Arnold, Marsha Diane. Galapagos Girl: A Bi-Lingual Celebration of the Gal�pagos Islands, 1 vol. Dominguez, Angela, illus. 2018. (ENG.). 40p. (J). (gr. -1-3). 19.95 *(978-0-89239-413-5(7)*, leelowcbp, Children's Book Press) Lee & Low Bks., Inc.
Ball Sr., Frank J. Bryanna Global Warrior: Attack of the Alaska Aerial Wolf Hunters, 1 vol. Pelton, Bonnie L., illus. 2009. 23p. pap. 24.95 *(978-1-61582-587-5(8))* America Star Bks.
Barr, Brady & Keats Curtis, Jennifer. Hasta la Vista, Cocodrilo: el Diario de Alexa. Detwiler, Susan, illus. 2016. (SPA.). 32p. (J). (gr. 2-3). pap. 11.95 *(978-1-62855-836-4(9)*, 3f8213bc-7d57-4d95-ab47-784cd803357f) Arbordale Publishing.
Bernay, Emma & Berne, Emma Carlson. A Dolphin Named Star. Madrid, Erwin, illus. 2019. (Seaside Sanctuary Ser.). (ENG.). 112p. (J). (gr. 3-7). lib. bdg. 25.99 *(978-1-4965-7859-4(7)*, 139398, Stone Arch Bks.) Capstone.
Blake, Quentin. Loveykins. 2003. (ENG., Illus.). 32p. (J). (gr. -1-3). 15.95 *(978-1-56145-282-8(3))* Peachtree Publishing Co. Inc.
Brooks, John. Balloons, Sea Creatures, & Me. 2006. 34p. (J). 14.58 *(978-0-9661789-3-7(9))* Lulu Pr., Inc.
Cochard, David, illus. The Legend of Honey Hollow. 2008. 46p. (J). 16.99 *(978-0-979444-0-6(6))* Joey Publishing.
Cohn, Diana. Crane Boy, 1 vol. Youme, illus. 2015. (ENG.). 40p. (J). (gr. 2-5). 17.95 *(978-1-941026-16-8(8)*, 23353382, Cinco Puntos Press) Lee & Low Bks., Inc.
Collins, Yvonne & Rideout, Sandy. The Black Sheep. 2007. 348p. (J). *(978-1-4287-4665-7(X))* Hyperion Pr.
Cousteau, Fabien & Fraioli, James O. Great White Shark Adventure. St.Pierre, Joe, illus. 2019. (Fabien Cousteau Expeditions Ser.). (ENG.). 112p. (J). (gr. 3-7). 12.99 *(978-1-5344-2087-8(8)*, McElderry, Margaret K. Bks.) McElderry, Margaret K. Bks.
Cry of the Falcon. 2006. 208p. (J). pap. 9.95 *(978-0-9788541-0-2(1))* m.d. hughes.
Dillard, Mary Gregory. Jeepers Creepers! The Squirrels Are Coming. 2007. 85p. pap. 19.95 *(978-1-4241-9951-8(4))* America Star Bks.
Doerr, Bonnie J. Kenzie's Key. Aberle, Xylena Apotheloz, illus. 2003. 211p. (J). 16.95 *(978-0-9619155-6-8(0))* Laurel & Herbert, Inc.
Draper, Sharon M. The Backyard Animal Show. Watson, Jesse Joshua, illus. 2012. (Clubhouse Mysteries Ser.: 5). (ENG.). 128p. (J). (gr. 3-7). pap. 6.99 *(978-1-4424-5022-6(3)*, Aladdin) Simon & Schuster Children's Publishing.
—The Backyard Animal Show. Watson, Jesse Joshua, illus. 2012. (Clubhouse Mysteries Ser.: 5). (ENG.). 128p. (J). (gr. 3-7). 17.99 *(978-1-4424-5023-3(1)*, Simon & Schuster/Paula Wiseman Bks.) Simon & Schuster/Paula Wiseman Bks.
Dunlap, Jim. Sam Snake Says. Holland, Kathy, illus. 2008. 35p. pap. 24.95 *(978-1-60672-709-6(5))* America Star Bks.
Ferguson, Pamela. Sunshine Picklelime. Slade, Christian, illus. 2011. (ENG.). 240p. (J). (gr. 4-6). 21.19 *(978-0-375-86175-8(0))* Random House Publishing Group.
Frankenhuyzen, Robbyn Smith van. Kelly of Hazel Ridge. Frankenhuyzen, Gijsbert van, illus. 3rd rev. ed. 2006. (Hazel Ridge Farm Stories Ser.). (ENG.). 48p. (J). (gr. 1-4). 17.95 *(978-1-58536-268-4(9)*, 202082) Sleeping Bear Pr.
George, Jean Craighead. Frightful's Mountain. 2014. (ENG.). 272p. (J). (gr. 4-8). 11.24 *(978-1-63245-351-8(7))* Lectorum Pubns., Inc.
Graham, Bob. How to Heal a Broken Wing. Graham, Bob, illus. 2017. (ENG., Illus.). 40p. (J). (gr. -1-2). 8.99 *(978-0-7636-9841-6(5))* Candlewick Pr.
Harlow, Patty Fayerweather. Rock with Rodney and, Party with Perky to Preserve Wildlife. 2006. (Illus.). 96p. (J). per. 16.95 *(978-1-60002-002-5(X)*, 3583) Mountain Valley Publishing, LLC.
Harris, Godfrey. Credit the Crocodile: A Tale of Survival in the African Wild. 2017. (ENG., Illus.). 260p. (YA). *(978-0-935047-89-9(1))* Americas Group, The.
Haylock, Heather. Granny Mcflitter, the Champion Knitter. Chisholm, Lael, illus. 2018. (Granny Mcflitter Ser.). 32p. (J). (gr. k-2). 16.99 *(978-0-14-377054-1(3))* Penguin Group New Zealand, Ltd. NZL. Dist: Independent Pubs. Group.
Henry, Marguerite. Mustang: Wild Spirit of the West. Lougheed, Robert, illus. 2016. (ENG.). 240p. (J). (gr. 3-7). 19.99 *(978-1-4814-5222-9(3)*, Simon & Schuster/Paula Wiseman Bks.) Simon & Schuster/Paula Wiseman Bks.
Hiaasen, Carl. Scat. 2011. 10.54 *(978-0-7848-3574-6(8)*, Everbind) Marco Bk. Co.
—Scat. 2010. 19.00 *(978-1-60686-585-9(4))* Perfection Learning Corp.
—Scat. (ENG.). 400p. (J). (gr. 5). 2012. 8.99 *(978-0-440-42104-7(7)*, Yearling) 2010. pap. 9.99 *(978-0-375-83487-5(7)*, Ember) Random Hse. Children's Bks.
—Scat. 2012. lib. bdg. 18.40 *(978-0-606-26532-4(5))* Turtleback.
Irwin, Bindi & Kunz, Chris. Croc Capers: Bindi Wildlife Adventures. 2012. (Bindi's Wildlife Adventures Ser.: 7). (ENG.). 112p. (J). (gr. 3-6). pap. 5.99 *(978-1-4022-7373-5(8)*, Sourcebooks Jabberwocky) Sourcebooks, Inc.
Jules, Jacqueline. The Generous Fish. Tyrrell, Frances, illus. 2020. 40p. (J). (gr. k-3). 16.95 *(978-1-937786-79-3(X)*, Wisdom Tales) World Wisdom, Inc.
Keats Curtis, Jennifer. Baby Bear's Adoption, 1 vol. V. Jones, Veronica, illus. 2018. (ENG & SPA.). 32p. (J). (gr. k-3). 17.95 *(978-1-60718-726-4(4)*, 9781607187264) Arbordale Publishing.
—Baby Owl's Rescue, 1 vol. Jacques, Laura, illus. 2009. (ENG.). 32p. (J). (gr. -1-3). 16.95 *(978-1-934359-95-2(5)*, 9781934359952) Arbordale Publishing.
Knight, Richard John & Walker, Richard. Winter Shadow. Johnson, Richard, illus. 2009. 80p. (J). (gr. 3-9). 16.99 *(978-1-84686-116-1(0))* Barefoot Bks., Inc.
Lamperd, Laurel. Battle for Boodicuttup Creek. 2008. 64p. pap. *(978-1-84923-238-8(5))* YouWriteOn.
Lewis, J. M. The Adventures of Gabby & Coyote Girl. 2007. 64p. per. 7.95 *(978-1-4327-1511-3(9))* Outskirts Pr., Inc.
Loebel-Fried, Caren. Manu, the Boy Who Loved Birds. 2020. (ENG., Illus.). 48p. (J). 16.99 *(978-0-8248-8272-3(5)*, 13537, Latitude 20) Univ. of Hawaii Pr.
—ʻo Manu, Ke Keiki Aloha Manu. Tolentino, Blaine Namahana, tr. from ENG. 2020. (HAW., Illus.). 48p. (J). 16.99 *(978-0-8248-8343-0(8)*, 13794, Latitude 20) Univ. of Hawaii Pr.
Lumry, Amanda & Hurwitz, Laura. Riddle of the Reef. 2009. (Illus.). 32p. (J). *(978-0-545-06848-2(7)*, Scholastic Pr.) Scholastic, Inc.
—Tigers in Terai. McIntyre, Sarah, illus. 2nd rev. ed. 2007. (Adventures of Riley (Unnumbered) Ser.). 36p. (J). (gr. -1-3). 15.95 *(978-1-60040-003-2(5))* Centro Bks., LLC.
—Tigers in Terai. McIntyre, Sarah, illus. 2nd ed. 2007. 36p. *(978-0-9748411-6-8(1))* Eaglemont Pr.
Lyle-Soffe, Shari. Trouble Finds Rooter & Snuffle. Collier, Kevin Scott, illus. 2008. 20p. pap. 9.95 *(978-1-933090-72-6(3))* Guardian Angel Publishing, Inc.
Messer, Celeste M. Forever & Always. Hoeffner, Deb, illus. 2004. 82-92p. 4.95 *(978-0-9710145-0-3(7))* AshleyAlan Enterprises.
Meunier, Sylvain. Raffi's Animal Rescue. Cummins, Sarah, tr. Eudes-Pascal, Elisabeth, illus. 2007. (ENG.). 64p. (J). (gr. 2-5). *(978-0-88780-742-8(9))* Formac Publishing Co., Ltd.
Mikaelsen, Ben. Stranded. rev. ed. 2010. (ENG.). 288p. (J). (gr. 3-7). pap. 7.99 *(978-1-4231-3362-9(5))* Hyperion Bks. for Children.
Novel Units. The Weirdo Novel Units Student Packet. 2019. (ENG.). (J). pap., stu. ed. 13.99 *(978-1-56137-815-9(1)*, Novel Units, Inc.) Classroom Library Co.
Poke-A-Dot: Wheels on the Bus. 2017. (ENG.). (J). 15.99 *(978-1-60169-420-1(2))* Innovative Kids.
Prager, Ellen. The Shark Rider. Caparo, Antonio Javier, illus. 2015. (Tristan Hunt & the Sea Guardians Ser.: 2). (ENG.).

WXYZ

326p. (J). (gr. 3-7). pap. 9.95 *(978-1-938063-51-0(1))*, Mighty Media Junior Readers) Mighty Media Pr.

—Stingray City. Caparo, Antonio Javier, illus. 2016. (Tristan Hunt & the Sea Guardians Ser.: 3). (ENG.). 292p. (J). (gr. 2-7). pap. 9.95 *(978-1-938063-70-1(8)*, Mighty Media Junior Readers) Mighty Media Pr.

Ralph, Donna J. Critter Chronicles: Stories of Critters in a Colorado Wildlife Rehabilitator's Life. 2007. 200p. per. 16.95 *(978-0-595-47858-3(1))* iUniverse, Inc.

Smith, Lauren. Ashley Enright & the Mystery at Miller's Pond. 2006. (ENG.). 60p. per. 16.95 *(978-1-4241-5268-1(2))* America Star Bks.

St. John, Lauren. Dolphin Song. 2008. (Legend of the Animal Healer Ser.). (ENG.). 246p. (J). (gr. 4-6). 21.19 *(978-0-8037-3214-8(7))* Penguin Young Readers Group.

—The Elephant's Tale. 2011. (Legend of the Animal Healer Ser.). (ENG.). (J). 208p. (gr. 4-6). 21.19 *(978-0-8037-3291-9(0))*; 240p. (gr. 3-7). 6.99 *(978-0-14-241879-6(X)*, Puffin Books) Penguin Young Readers Group.

—The White Giraffe. 2008. (ENG., Illus.). 208p. (J). (gr. 2-5). 8.99 *(978-0-14-241152-0(3)*, Puffin Books) Penguin Young Readers Group.

Stauffacher, Sue. Hide & Seek, 3. Lamont, Priscilla, illus. 2012. (Animal Rescue Team Ser.). (ENG.). 160p. (J). (gr. 2-5). lib. bdg. 18.69 *(978-0-375-95849-6(5)*, Knopf Bks. for Young Readers) Random Hse. Children's Bks.

Taylor, Theodore. The Weirdo. 2006. (Illus.). 292p. (gr. 7-12). 18.00 *(978-0-7569-6752-9(X))* Perfection Learning Corp.

Townsend, Wendy. Blue Iguana. 2014. 188p. 18.95 *(978-1-60898-157-1(6))* namelos llc.

Watson, J. A. Hatchling Hero: A Sea Turtle Defender's Journal. Olbey, Arpad, illus. 2018. (Science Squad Ser.). (ENG.). 192p. (J). (gr. 3-4). 28.50 *(978-1-63163-160-3(8)*, 1631631608); pap. 9.99 *(978-1-63163-161-0(6)*, 1631631616) North Star Editions. (Jolly Fish Pr.).

Wight, Tamra. Mystery of the Eagle's Nest, 1 vol. DiRocco, Carl, illus. 2016. (Cooper & Packrat Ser.: 2). (ENG.). 175p. (J). pap. 14.95 *(978-1-939017-08-6(4)*, c7142407-34bd-4d1b-bcf3-928882aa5d83) Islandport Pr., Inc.

Wildsmith, Brian. Hunter & His Dog, 1 vol. 2008. (ENG., Illus.). 32p. (J). 16.95 *(978-1-59572-123-5(1))* Star Bright Bks., Inc.

Wyss, Tyan. African Dream. Immelman, Sarita, illus. 2006. 48p. (J). pap. 15.95 *(978-1-58939-915-0(3))* Virtualbookworm.com Publishing, Inc.

WILLIAM I, KING OF ENGLAND, 1027 OR 1028-1087

Abbott, Jacob. History of William the Conqueror. 2003. 291p. 89.00 *(978-0-7950-4508-0(5))* New Library Press LLC.

Hamilton, Janice. The Norman Conquest of England. 2007. (Pivotal Moments in History Ser.). (ENG., Illus.). 160p. (J). (gr. 9-12). lib. bdg. 38.60 *(978-0-8225-5902-3(1))* Lerner Publishing Group.

Harkins, Susan Sales & Harkins, William H. The Life & Times of William the Conqueror. 2008. (Biography from Ancient Civilizations Ser.). (Illus.). 48p. (J). (gr. 4-8). lib. bdg. 29.95 *(978-1-58415-700-7(3))* Mitchell Lane Pubs.

Hilliam, Paul. William the Conqueror: First Norman King of England. (Leaders of the Middle Ages Ser.). 112p. (gr. 5-8). 2009. 66.50 *(978-1-61513-903-3(6)*, Rosen Reference) 2004. (ENG., Illus.). (J). lib. bdg. 39.80 *(978-1-4042-0166-8(1)*, e4013b6a-5a33-4369-8293-4f8962f75b49) Rosen Publishing Group, Inc., The.

Ross, Stewart. Will's Dream. Shields, Susan, illus. (ENG.). 28p. pap. 9.99 *(978-0-7502-2965-4(9))* Hodder & Stoughton GBR. Dist: Trafalgar Square Publishing.

WILLIAMS, HANK, 1923-1953

Bailey, Tom. Hank Williams Sr: Country Music Legend. 2008. (Illus.). 104p. (J). *(978-1-59421-043-3(8))* Seacoast Publishing, Inc.

WILLIAMS, ROGER, 1604?-1683

Marsh, Carole. Roger Williams. 2003. 12p. (gr. k-4). 2.95 *(978-0-635-02361-2(X))* Gallopade International.

The Puritans, Algonkians & Roger Williams (NCHS) (J). (gr. 5-8). spiral bd., tchr.'s planning gde. ed. 13.50 *(978-0-382-44447-0(7))* Cobblestone Publishing Co.

The Puritans, Algonkians & Roger Williams (NCHS) Grades 5-8. (J). tchr. ed. 18.00 *(978-0-382-44537-8(6))* Cobblestone Publishing Co.

WILLIAMS, SERENA, 1981-

Anniss, Matt. Venus & Serena Williams in the Community, 1 vol., 1. 2013. (Making a Difference: Athletes Who Are Changing the World Ser.). (ENG.). 48p. (J). (gr. 5-5). 29.44 *(978-1-62275-170-9(1)*, 4be2f4ca-7b11-4468-8ea7-cefe4c598471) Rosen Publishing Group, Inc., The.

Apps, Roy. EDGE: Sporting Heroes: Serena Williams. 2018. (EDGE: Sporting Heroes Ser.). (ENG.). 48p. (J). (gr. 2-4). 12.99 *(978-1-4451-5338-4(6)*, Franklin Watts) Hachette Children's Group GBR. Dist: Hachette Bk. Group.

Bailey, Diane. Venus & Serena Williams: Tennis Champions, 1 vol. 2010. (Sports Families Ser.). 48p. (gr. 5-5). (ENG.). (J). pap. 12.75 *(978-1-4358-8520-2(1)*, d6c0759c-676f-4178-b999-6834ea6d1c26, Rosen Reference); (YA). lib. bdg., E-Book 53.00 *(978-1-4488-0124-4(9))*; (ENG., Illus.). (YA). lib. bdg. 34.47 *(978-1-4358-3552-8(2)*, 241aae56-ad15-4a0f-97ba-c0b7fd676cf3) Rosen Publishing Group, Inc., The.

Boehme, Gerry. Serena Williams: Setting New Standards, 1 vol. 2017. (At the Top of Their Game Ser.). (ENG.). 128p. (YA). (gr. 9-9). 44.50 *(978-1-5026-2762-9(0)*, 78dcc698-6dda-4e4e-b2be-ab32c963e2d9) Cavendish Square Publishing LLC.

Bradley, Michael. Serena Williams, 1 vol. 2006. (All-Stars Ser.). (ENG., Illus.). 48p. (gr. 4-4). 34.07 *(978-0-7614-1760-6(5)*, eaaed1f9-01fa-49a4-88ab-92b4e111e18f) Cavendish Square Publishing LLC.

Brown, Jonatha A. Venus & Serena Williams, 1 vol. 2004. (People We Should Know Ser.). (ENG., Illus.). 24p. (gr. 2-4). pap. 9.15 *(978-0-8368-4477-1(7)*, 8255fb18-05b5-4f15-b369-e441cf7f355e); lib. bdg. 24.67 *(978-0-8368-4470-2(X)*, 91512202-a7bb-4e33-a448-ac0fa1d73d33) Stevens, Gareth Publishing LLLP. (Weekly Reader Leveled Readers).

—Venus y Serena Williams, 1 vol. 2004. (Gente Que Hay Que Conocer (People We Should Know) Ser.).Tr. of Venus & Serena Williams. (SPA.). 24p. (gr. 2-4). lib. bdg. 24.67 *(978-0-8368-4586-0(2)*, e46f018e-bcdf-4a86-8be0-35f7d475c1c5, Weekly Reader Leveled Readers) Stevens, Gareth Publishing LLLP.

Bryant, Howard. Sisters & Champions: the True Story of Venus & Serena Williams. Cooper, Floyd, illus. 2018. 32p. (J). (gr. -1-3). 17.99 *(978-0-399-16906-9(7)*, Philomel Bks.) Penguin Young Readers Group.

Buckley, James, Jr. & Who HQ. Who Are Venus & Serena Williams? Thomson, Andrew, illus. 2017. (Who Was? Ser.). 112p. (J). (gr. 3-7). 6.99 *(978-0-515-15803-8(8)*, Penguin Workshop) Penguin Young Readers Group.

Christopher, Matt. Serena Williams: Legends in Sports. 2017. (ENG., Illus.). 144p. (J). (gr. 3-7). pap. 7.99 *(978-0-316-47180-0(1))* Little, Brown Bks. for Young Readers.

Cline-Ransome, Lesa. Game Changers: The Story of Venus & Serena Williams. Ransome, James E., illus. 2018. (ENG.). 48p. (J). (gr. -1-3). 17.99 *(978-1-4814-7684-3(X)*, Simon & Schuster/Paula Wiseman Bks.) Simon & Schuster/Paula Wiseman Bks.

Donaldson, Madeline. Venus & Serena Williams. (Amazing Athletes Ser.). 32p. 2007. (Illus.). (J). (gr. -1-3). per. 6.95 *(978-0-8225-8857-3(9)*, First Avenue Editions) 2005. (Illus.). (gr. 3-4). lib. bdg. 22.60 *(978-0-8225-3316-0(2))* 2nd rev. ed. 2011. (J). pap. 45.32 *(978-0-7613-7654-5(2))* Lerner Publishing Group.

—Venus & Serena Williams. rev. ed. 2007. (Amazing Athletes Ser.). (ENG., Illus.). 32p. (gr. 2-5). lib. bdg. 25.26 *(978-0-8225-7595-5(7))* Lerner Publishing Group.

Dorrie, Roxanne. Venus & Serena Williams: The Smashing Sisters, 6 vols. 2003. (High Five Reading - Red Ser.). (ENG.). 48p. (gr. 3-4). pap. 54.00 *(978-0-7368-2837-6(0))*; (Illus.). per. 9.00 *(978-0-7368-2827-7(3))* Capstone.

Engsberg Cunningham, Meghan. Serena Williams: International Tennis Superstar, 1 vol. 2016. (Leading Women Ser.). (ENG.). 112p. (YA). (gr. 7-7). 41.64 *(978-1-5026-2014-9(6)*, dcc24e1d-7677-4af8-8d0e-efec16cc05bd) Cavendish Square Publishing LLC.

Fuller, Barbara. Great Britain, 1 vol. 2nd ed. 2005. (Cultures of the World (First Edition)(r) Ser.). (ENG., Illus.). 144p. (gr. 5-5). 49.79 *(978-0-7614-1845-0(8)*, 802b64c1-df2d-4fc2-8fbf-b2dc4c280095) Cavendish Square Publishing LLC.

Goddu, Krystyna Poray. Serena Williams. 2019. (Player Profiles Ser.). (ENG., Illus.). 32p. (J). (gr. 4-6). lib. bdg. *(978-1-68072-877-4(6)*, 12788, Bolt) Black Rabbit Bks.

Gray, Karlin. Serena: the Littlest Sister. Ahanonu, Monica, illus. 2019. (ENG.). 40p. (J). 18.99 *(978-1-62414-694-7(5)*, 900197962) Page Street Publishing Co.

Hoena, Blake. Serena Williams: Athletes Who Made a Difference. LeDoyen, Sam, illus. 2020. (Athletes Who Made a Difference Ser.). (ENG.). 32p. (J). (gr. 3-6). 27.99 *(978-1-5415-7818-0(X)*, 004897ce-e80b-449f-bed7-0f55f0c5eaa1); pap. 8.99 *(978-1-7284-0296-3(4)*, e27a1a4d-c61a-46c5-b659-5555d51aab7f) Lerner Publishing Group. (Graphic Universe™).

Marcovitz, Hal. Venus & Serena Williams. 2012. (Role Model Athletes Ser.). 64p. (J). (gr. 7). 22.95 *(978-1-4222-2714-5(6))* Mason Crest.

Moening, Kate. Serena Williams: Tennis Star. 2019. (Women Leading the Way Ser.). (ENG., Illus.). 24p. (J). (gr. k-3). pap. 7.99 *(978-1-61891-725-6(0)*, 12306); lib. bdg. 26.95 *(978-1-64487-102-7(5))* Bellwether Media. (Blastoff! Readers).

Monnig, Alex. Serena Williams: Tennis Legend. 2017. (Playmakers Set 6 Ser.). (ENG., Illus.). 32p. (J). (gr. 2-6). lib. bdg. 32.79 *(978-1-5321-1152-5(5)*, 25880, SportsZone) ABDO Publishing Co.

—Serena Williams vs. Billie Jean King. 2017. (Versus Ser.). (ENG., Illus.). 32p. (J). (gr. 3-6). lib. bdg. 32.79 *(978-1-5321-1357-4(9)*, 27655, SportsZone) ABDO Publishing Co.

Morgan, Terri. Venus & Serena Williams: Grand Slam Sisters. (Sports Achievers Biographies Ser.). (Illus.). 2005. 80p. (gr. 7-12). lib. bdg. 22.60 *(978-0-8225-3684-0(6))* 2003. 64p. (J). (gr. 4-9). pap. 5.95 *(978-0-8225-9866-4(3)*, Carolrhoda Bks.) Lerner Publishing Group.

Morganelli, Adrianna. Serena Williams. 2018. (Superstars! Ser.). (ENG.). 32p. (J). (gr. 4-4). *(978-0-7787-4842-7(1))*; pap. *(978-0-7787-4871-7(5))* Crabtree Publishing Co.

Nagelhout, Ryan. Serena Williams, 1 vol. 2016. (Sports MVPs Ser.). (ENG., Illus.). 24p. (J). (gr. 1-2). 24.27 *(978-1-4824-4642-5(1)*, 3df0797d-66d6-4999-a80c-7c344c256a31) Stevens, Gareth Publishing LLLP.

Pina, Andrew & Uschan, Michael V. Serena Williams: Tennis Ace, 1 vol. 2016. (People in the News Ser.). (ENG.). 104p. (YA). (gr. 7-7). lib. bdg. 41.03 *(978-1-5345-6027-7(0)*, cf1324ab-ac03-4396-81b9-5344f7bfee7a, Lucent Pr.) Greenhaven Publishing LLC.

Porter, Esther. Serena Williams. 2016. (Women in Sports Ser.). (ENG., Illus.). 24p. (J). (gr. -1-2). pap. 6.95 *(978-1-4914-8569-9(8)*, 131188, Capstone Pr.) Capstone.

Rajczak Nelson, Kristen. Serena Williams: Tennis Star, 1 vol. 2016. (Junior Biographies Ser.). (ENG., Illus.). 24p. (gr. 3-4). pap. 10.35 *(978-0-7660-8181-9(8)*, 4f19a894-4607-4463-a256-637865324581) Enslow Publishing, LLC.

Raum, Elizabeth. Pro Sports Biographies: Serena Williams. 2017. (Pro Sports Biographies Ser.). (ENG., Illus.). 24p. (J). (gr. -1-3). pap. 10.99 *(978-1-68152-170-1(9)*, 14801) Amicus.

—Serena Williams. 2017. (Pro Sports Biographies Ser.). (ENG., Illus.). 24p. (J). (gr. 1-4). 20.95 *(978-1-68151-139-9(8)*, 14682) Amicus.

Roza, Greg. Venus & Serena Williams: The Sisters of Tennis, 1 vol. 2005. (Content-Area Literacy Collections). (ENG.). 24p. (gr. 3-4). pap. 8.85 *(978-1-4042-5537-1(0)*, 44f3d653-ae53-4481-a480-842bc236f82f) Rosen Publishing Group, Inc., The.

Shepherd, Jodie. Serena Williams: A Champion on & off the Court. 2016. (Rookie Biographies(tm) Ser.). (ENG., Illus.). 32p. (J). lib. bdg. 25.00 *(978-0-531-21684-2(5)*, Children's Pr.) Scholastic Library Publishing.

Swanson, June. Venus & Serena Williams. Burke, Susan S., illus. 2003. (You Must Be Joking! Riddle Bks.). 32p. (J). (gr. 2-5). pap. 5.95 *(978-0-8225-9842-8(6))* Lerner Publishing Group.

Todd, Anne M. Venus & Serena Williams. 2009. (Women of Achievement Ser.). (ENG., Illus.). 144p. (gr. 6-12). 35.00 *(978-1-60413-461-2(5)*, P167315, Facts On File) Infobase Holdings, Inc.

Uschan, Michael V. Serena Williams, 1 vol. 2011. (People in the News Ser.). (ENG.). 104p. (gr. 7-7). lib. bdg. 41.03 *(978-1-4205-0488-0(6)*, 7784970d-96df-4bb7-8427-1f6f8f564684, Lucent Pr.) Greenhaven Publishing LLC.

Venus & Serena Williams. 2015. (Quotes from the Greatest Athletes Ser.). (ENG., Illus.). 24p. (J). lib. bdg. 12.95 *(978-1-4896-3385-9(5))*; lib. bdg. 28.55 *(978-1-4896-3384-2(7))* Weigl Pubs., Inc. (AV2 by Weigl).

Watson, Galadriel Findlay. Venus & Serena Williams. 2005. (Great African American Women for Kids Ser.). (Illus.). 24p. (J). (gr. 2-3). lib. bdg. 24.45 *(978-1-59036-332-4(9))*; (gr. 3-7). per. 8.95 *(978-1-59036-338-6(8))* Weigl Pubs., Inc.

Wetzel, Dan. Epic Athletes: Serena Williams. Leong, Sloane, illus. 2019. (Epic Athletes Ser.: 3). (ENG.). 176p. (J). 16.99 *(978-1-250-29578-1(5)*, 900195301, Holt, Henry & Co. Bks. For Young Readers) Holt, Henry & Co.

—Epic Athletes: Serena Williams. Leong, Sloane, illus. 2020. (Epic Athletes Ser.: 3). (ENG.). 192p. (J). pap. 7.99 *(978-1-250-25072-8(2)*, 900198023) Square Fish.

Wiener, Gary. Serena vs. Venus vs. Sharapova vs. Navratilova, 1 vol. 2019. (Who's the GOAT? Using Math to Crown the Champion Ser.). (ENG.). 64p. (gr. 5-5). pap. 13.95 *(978-1-7253-4852-3(7)*, c8f75790-1401-4543-b648-5f866c2f00d9) Rosen Publishing Group, Inc., The.

Williams, Serena & Williams, Venus. Venus & Serena: Serving from the Hip: 10 Rules for Living, Loving, & Winning. 2005. (ENG., Illus.). 144p. (YA). (gr. 7). pap. 14.00 *(978-0-618-57653-1(3)*, 498418, Clarion Bks.) HarperCollins Pubs.

Winter, Jeanette. Sisters: Venus & Serena Williams. Winter, Jeanette, illus. 2019. (ENG., Illus.). 48p. (J). (gr. -1-3). 17.99 *(978-1-5344-3121-8(7)*, Beach Lane Bks.) Beach Lane Bks.

WILLIAMS, TENNESSEE, 1914-1983

Hermann, Spring. Reading & Interpreting the Works of Tennessee Williams, 1 vol. 2016. (Lit Crit Guides). (ENG.). 176p. (gr. 6-6). lib. bdg. 41.60 *(978-0-7660-8346-2(2)*, 99b4258e-b7ee-43f5-9622-845660327cc0) Enslow Publishing, LLC.

Novel Units. A Streetcar Named Desire Novel Units Student Packet. 2019. (ENG.). (YA). pap. 13.99 *(978-1-58130-951-5(1)*, Novel Units, Inc.) Classroom Library Co.

Tracy, Kathleen. Tennessee Williams. 2007. (Poets & Playwrights Ser.). (Illus.). 112p. (J). (gr. 3-7). lib. bdg. 37.10 *(978-1-58415-427-3(6))* Mitchell Lane Pubs.

WILLIAMS, TED, 1918-2002

McCormack, Shaun. Ted Williams. (Baseball Hall of Famers Ser.). 112p. (gr. 5-8). 2009. 63.90 *(978-1-61511-517-4(X))* 2003. (ENG., Illus.). (J). lib. bdg. 39.80 *(978-0-8239-3783-7(6)*, 708d1b8b-c734-4136-ae80-efc96ac06acd) Rosen Publishing Group, Inc., The. (Rosen Reference).

Tavares, Matt. There Goes Ted Williams: Candlewick Biographies: The Greatest Hitter Who Ever Lived. Tavares, Matt, illus. 2015. (Candlewick Biographies Ser.). (ENG., Illus.). 48p. (J). (gr. 1-4). 14.99 *(978-0-7636-7655-1(1))* Candlewick Pr.

WILLIAMS, VENUS, 1980-

Anniss, Matt. Venus & Serena Williams in the Community, 1 vol., 1. 2013. (Making a Difference: Athletes Who Are Changing the World Ser.). (ENG.). 48p. (J). (gr. 5-5). 29.44 *(978-1-62275-170-9(1)*, 4be2f4ca-7b11-4468-8ea7-cefe4c598471) Rosen Publishing Group, Inc., The.

Bailey, Diane. Venus & Serena Williams: Tennis Champions, 1 vol. 2010. (Sports Families Ser.). 48p. (gr. 5-5). (ENG.). (J). pap. 12.75 *(978-1-4358-8520-2(1)*, d6c0759c-676f-4178-b999-6834ea6d1c26, Rosen Reference); (YA). lib. bdg., E-Book 53.00 *(978-1-4488-0124-4(9))*; (ENG., Illus.). (YA). lib. bdg. 34.47 *(978-1-4358-3552-8(2)*, 241aae56-ad15-4a0f-97ba-c0b7fd676cf3) Rosen Publishing Group, Inc., The.

Bradley, Michael. Venus Williams, 1 vol. 2005. (All-Stars Ser.). (ENG., Illus.). 48p. (gr. 4-4). lib. bdg. 34.07 *(978-0-7614-1630-2(7)*, aae35196-fb4a-4f79-9337-bc954d02fea4) Cavendish Square Publishing LLC.

Brown, Jonatha A. Venus & Serena Williams, 1 vol. 2004. (People We Should Know Ser.). (ENG., Illus.). 24p. (gr. 2-4). pap. 9.15 *(978-0-8368-4477-1(7)*, 8255fb18-05b5-4f15-b369-e441cf7f355e); lib. bdg. 24.67 *(978-0-8368-4470-2(X)*, 91512202-a7bb-4e33-a448-ac0fa1d73d33) Stevens, Gareth Publishing LLLP. (Weekly Reader Leveled Readers).

—Venus y Serena Williams, 1 vol. 2004. (Gente Que Hay Que Conocer (People We Should Know) Ser.).Tr. of Venus & Serena Williams. (SPA.). 24p. (gr. 2-4). lib. bdg. 24.67 *(978-0-8368-4586-0(2)*, e46f018e-bcdf-4a86-8be0-35f7d475c1c5, Weekly Reader Leveled Readers) Stevens, Gareth Publishing LLLP.

Bryant, Howard. Sisters & Champions: the True Story of Venus & Serena Williams. Cooper, Floyd, illus. 2018. 32p. (J). (gr. -1-3). 17.99 *(978-0-399-16906-9(7)*, Philomel Bks.) Penguin Young Readers Group.

Buckley, James, Jr. & Who HQ. Who Are Venus & Serena Williams? Thomson, Andrew, illus. 2017. (Who Was? Ser.). 112p. (J). (gr. 3-7). 6.99 *(978-0-515-15803-8(8)*, Penguin Workshop) Penguin Young Readers Group.

Cline-Ransome, Lesa. Game Changers: The Story of Venus & Serena Williams. Ransome, James E., illus. 2018. (ENG.). 48p. (J). (gr. -1-3). 17.99 *(978-1-4814-7684-3(X)*, Simon & Schuster/Paula Wiseman Bks.) Simon & Schuster/Paula Wiseman Bks.

Donaldson, Madeline. Venus & Serena Williams. (Amazing Athletes Ser.). 32p. 2007. (Illus.). (J). (gr. -1-3). per. 6.95 *(978-0-8225-8857-3(9)*, First Avenue Editions) 2005. (Illus.). (gr. 3-4). lib. bdg. 22.60 *(978-0-8225-3316-0(2))* 2nd rev. ed. 2011. (J). pap. 45.32 *(978-0-7613-7654-5(2))* Lerner Publishing Group.

—Venus & Serena Williams. rev. ed. 2007. (Amazing Athletes Ser.). (ENG., Illus.). 32p. (gr. 2-5). lib. bdg. 25.26 *(978-0-8225-7595-5(7))* Lerner Publishing Group.

Dorrie, Roxanne. Venus & Serena Williams: The Smashing Sisters, 6 vols. 2003. (High Five Reading - Red Ser.). (ENG.). 48p. (gr. 3-4). pap. 54.00 *(978-0-7368-2837-6(0))*; (Illus.). per. 9.00 *(978-0-7368-2827-7(3))* Capstone.

Feldman, Heather. Venus Williams: Campeona de Tenis (Tennis Champion) 2009. (Superestrellas del Deporte (Superstars of Sports) Ser.). (SPA.). 24p. (gr. 1-2). 42.50 *(978-1-60853-229-2(1)*, Editorial Buenas Letras) Rosen Publishing Group, Inc., The.

—Venus Williams: Tennis Champion. 2009. (Sports Superstars Ser.). 24p. (gr. 1-1). 42.50 *(978-1-60853-183-7(X)*, PowerKids Pr.) Rosen Publishing Group, Inc., The.

—Venus Williams: Tennis Champion / Campeona de Tenis. 2009. (Superstars of Sports/Superestrellas del deporte Ser.). (ENG & SPA.). 24p. (gr. 1-2). 42.50 *(978-1-60853-241-4(0)*, Editorial Buenas Letras) Rosen Publishing Group, Inc., The.

Franzen, Lenore. Venus Williams. 2003. (Ovations Ser.). (Illus.). 32p. (J). *(978-1-58341-249-7(2)*, Creative Education) Creative Co., The.

Marcovitz, Hal. Venus & Serena Williams. 2012. (Role Model Athletes Ser.). 64p. (J). (gr. 7). 22.95 *(978-1-4222-2714-5(6))* Mason Crest.

Morgan, Terri. Venus & Serena Williams: Grand Slam Sisters. (Sports Achievers Biographies Ser.). (Illus.). 2005. 80p. (gr. 7-12). lib. bdg. 22.60 *(978-0-8225-3684-0(6))* 2003. 64p. (J). (gr. 4-9). pap. 5.95 *(978-0-8225-9866-4(3)*, Carolrhoda Bks.) Lerner Publishing Group.

Roza, Greg. Venus & Serena Williams: The Sisters of Tennis, 1 vol. 2005. (Content-Area Literacy Collections). (ENG.). 24p. (gr. 3-4). pap. 8.85 *(978-1-4042-5537-1(0)*, 44f3d653-ae53-4481-a480-842bc236f82f) Rosen Publishing Group, Inc., The.

Sandler, Michael. Tennis: Victory for Venus Williams. 2006. (Upsets & Comebacks Ser.). (Illus.). 32p. (J). (gr. 3-6). lib. bdg. 28.50 *(978-1-59716-170-1(5))* Bearport Publishing Co., Inc.

Swanson, June. Venus & Serena Williams. Burke, Susan S., illus. 2003. (You Must Be Joking! Riddle Bks.). 32p. (J). (gr. 2-5). pap. 5.95 *(978-0-8225-9842-8(6))* Lerner Publishing Group.

Todd, Anne M. Venus & Serena Williams. 2009. (Women of Achievement Ser.). (ENG., Illus.). 144p. (gr. 6-12). 35.00 *(978-1-60413-461-2(5)*, P167315, Facts On File) Infobase Holdings, Inc.

Venus & Serena Williams. 2015. (Quotes from the Greatest Athletes Ser.). (ENG., Illus.). 24p. (J). lib. bdg. 12.95 *(978-1-4896-3385-9(5))*; lib. bdg. 28.55 *(978-1-4896-3384-2(7))* Weigl Pubs., Inc. (AV2 by Weigl).

Watson, Galadriel Findlay. Venus & Serena Williams. 2005. (Great African American Women for Kids Ser.). (Illus.). 24p. (J). (gr. 2-3). lib. bdg. 24.45 *(978-1-59036-332-4(9))*; (gr. 3-7). per. 8.95 *(978-1-59036-338-6(8))* Weigl Pubs., Inc.

Wiener, Gary. Serena vs. Venus vs. Sharapova vs. Navratilova, 1 vol. 2019. (Who's the GOAT? Using Math to Crown the Champion Ser.). (ENG.). 64p. (gr. 5-5). pap. 13.95 *(978-1-7253-4852-3(7)*, c8f75790-1401-4543-b648-5f866c2f00d9) Rosen Publishing Group, Inc., The.

Williams, Serena & Williams, Venus. Venus & Serena: Serving from the Hip: 10 Rules for Living, Loving, & Winning. 2005. (ENG., Illus.). 144p. (YA). (gr. 7). pap. 14.00 *(978-0-618-57653-1(3)*, 498418, Clarion Bks.) HarperCollins Pubs.

Wilson, Mike. The Williams Sisters: Venus & Serena. 2005. (ENG., Illus.). 32p. pap. 8.50 *(978-0-340-84876-0(6))* Cambridge Univ. Pr.

Winter, Jeanette. Sisters: Venus & Serena Williams. Winter, Jeanette, illus. 2019. (ENG., Illus.). 48p. (J). (gr. -1-3). 17.99 *(978-1-5344-3121-8(7)*, Beach Lane Bks.) Beach Lane Bks.

WILLIAMSBURG (VA.)

Chorao, Kay. D Is for Drums: A Colonial Williamsburg ABC. 2004. (ENG., Illus.). 32p. (J). (gr. -1-1). 16.95 *(978-0-8109-4927-0(X))* Abrams, Inc.

McNeese, Tim. Williamsburg. 2007. (ENG., Illus.). 112p. (gr. 5-9). lib. bdg. 30.00 *(978-0-7910-9333-7(6)*, P124643, Facts On File) Infobase Holdings, Inc.

Rudolph, Ellen K. Willi Gets a History Lesson: In Virginia's Historic Triangle. Rudolph, Ellen K., photos by. 2007. (ENG., Illus.). 80p. pap. 24.00 *(978-0-9791348-0-7(3))* EKR Pubns.

WILLIAMSBURG (VA.)—FICTION

Elliott, L. M. Give Me Liberty. 2008. (ENG., Illus.). 384p. (J). (gr. 4-8). pap. 7.99 *(978-0-06-074423-6(5)*, Tegen, Katherine Bks) HarperCollins Pubs.

Nixon, Joan Lowery. Ann's Story, 1747. 2004. (J). *(978-0-87935-198-4(5))* Colonial Williamsburg Foundation.

—Caesar's Story, 1759. 2004. (J). *(978-0-87935-199-1(3))* Colonial Williamsburg Foundation.

—John's Story, 1775. 2004. (J). *(978-0-87935-228-8(0))* Colonial Williamsburg Foundation.

—Maria's Story, 1773. 2004. (J). *(978-0-87935-227-1(2))* Colonial Williamsburg Foundation.

—Nancy's Story, 1765. 2004. (J). *(978-0-87935-225-7(6))* Colonial Williamsburg Foundation.

—Will's Story, 1771. 2004. (J). *(978-0-87935-226-4(4))* Colonial Williamsburg Foundation.

Tripp, Valerie. Felicity Story Collection. Andreasen, Dan, illus. 2008. (ENG.). 404p. (J). 29.95 *(978-1-59369-452-4(0))* American Girl Publishing, Inc.

Trumbore, Cindy. Three Cheers for Liberty! Elkerton, Andy, illus. 2016. 126p. (J). pap. *(978-0-87935-287-5(6))* Colonial Williamsburg Foundation.

WILLIAMSBURG (VA.)—HISTORY

Bauley, Thomas K. Williamsburg A-Z: An Alphabetical Journey, 1 vol. 2010. (ENG., Illus.). 32p. 19.99 *(978-0-7643-3671-3(1)*, 3981) Schiffer Publishing, Ltd.

Chorao, Kay. D Is for Drums: A Colonial Williamsburg A. B. C. 2004. (J). 16.95 *(978-0-87935-197-7(7))* Colonial Williamsburg Foundation.
—D Is for Drums: A Colonial Williamsburg ABC. 2004. (ENG., Illus.). 32p. (J). (gr. -1-1). 16.95 *(978-0-8109-4927-0(X))* Abrams, Inc.
—D Is for Drums: A Colonial Williamsburg ABC. Chorao, Kay, illus. 2006. (Illus.). 30p. (J). (gr. k-4). reprint ed. 17.00 *(978-1-4223-5240-3(4))* DIANE Publishing Co.
Colonial Williamsburg Foundation & Kostyal, K. M. 1776: A New Look at Revolutionary Williamsburg. 2009. (Illus.). 48p. (J). (gr. 3-7). 17.95 *(978-1-4263-0517-7(6))*, National Geographic Kids) Disney Publishing Worldwide.
Markovics, Joyce. Historic & Lively: What Am I? 2018. (American Place Puzzlers Ser.). (ENG.). 24p. (J). (gr. -1-3). lib. bdg. 26.99 *(978-1-68402-482-7(X))* Bearport Publishing Co., Inc.
Mattern, Joanne. Historic Williamsburg: A Revolutionary City. 2017. (Core Content Social Studies — Let's Celebrate America Ser.). (ENG., Illus.). 32p. (J). (gr. 2-5). pap. 8.99 *(978-1-63440-229-3(4),* 99e20e4a-31a1-4a48-a7b9-14f319e76fb9) Red Chair Pr.
Varela, Barry. The Young Patriots' Guide to Colonial Williamsburg's Historic Area. 2010. (J). pap. *(978-0-87935-245-5(0))* Colonial Williamsburg Foundation.

WILLOW—FICTION

Hegamin, Tonya Cherie. Willow. 2014. (ENG.). 384p. (YA). (gr. 9). 16.99 *(978-0-7636-5769-7(7))* Candlewick Pr.
Martin, Ann M. Keeping Secrets, 7. 2009. (Main Street Ser.: 7). (ENG.). 208p. (J). (gr. 4-6). 21.19 *(978-0-439-86885-3(8))* Scholastic, Inc.
The Willow Pattern: Individual Title Six-Packs. (Action Packs Ser.). 104p. (gr. 3-5). 44.00 *(978-0-7635-2996-3(6))* Rigby Education.

WILLS—FICTION

Diggle, David Mark. Sammy: Leaves His Mark. Diggle, Daniel James, illus. 2011. 24p. (J). pap. *(978-0-9871657-3-2(9))* Diggle de Doo Productions Pty, Ltd.
Keene, Carolyn. The Bungalow Mystery #3, No. 3. 2014. (Nancy Drew Ser.: 3). 192p. (J). (gr. 3-7). 7.99 *(978-0-448-47971-2(0),* Grosset & Dunlap) Penguin Young Readers Group.
—The Hidden Staircase #2, No. 2. 2014. (Nancy Drew Ser.: 2). 192p. (J). (gr. 3-7). 9.99 *(978-0-448-47970-5(2),* Grosset & Dunlap) Penguin Young Readers Group.
—The Mystery at Lilac Inn #4. 2014. (Nancy Drew Ser.: 4). 192p. (J). (gr. 3-7). 10.99 *(978-0-448-47972-9(9),* Grosset & Dunlap) Penguin Young Readers Group.
—The Secret of the Old Clock #1, Bk. 1. 2014. (Nancy Drew Ser.: 1). 192p. (J). (gr. 3-7). 9.99 *(978-0-448-47969-9(9),* Grosset & Dunlap) Penguin Young Readers Group.

WILSON, SAMUEL, 1766-1854

Friesen, Helen Lepp. Uncle Sam with Code. 2012. (AV2 American Icons Ser.). (ENG., Illus.). 24p. (J). (gr. -1-3). pap. 12.95 *(978-1-61913-304-4(0),* AV2 by Weigl) Weigl Pubs., Inc.
Hicks, Terry Allan. Uncle Sam, 1 vol. (Symbols of America Ser.). (ENG., Illus.). 40p. (gr. 3-3). 2008. pap. 9.23 *(978-0-7614-3379-8(1),* 36ed5508-6ab2-4d17-b3bd-5437c8515901, Cavendish Square) 2007. lib. bdg. 32.64 *(978-0-7614-2137-5(8),* e6f9da10-1cd5-4edb-8cd5-0e9e233d21ec) Cavendish Square Publishing LLC.
Marcovitz, Hal. Uncle Sam: International Symbol of America. Moreno, Barry, ed. 2014. (Patriotic Symbols of America Ser.: 20). 48p. (J). (gr. 4-18). lib. bdg. 20.95 *(978-1-4222-3135-7(6))* Mason Crest.
Monroe, Tyler. Uncle Sam, 1 vol. 2013. (U. S. Symbols Ser.). (ENG.). 24p. (J). (gr. -1-2). 27.32 *(978-1-4765-3086-4(6),* 123063); pap. 7.95 *(978-1-4765-3535-7(3),* 123581) Capstone.

WILSON, WOODROW, 1856-1924

Aronin, Miriam. Woodrow Wilson. 2016. (First Look at America's Presidents Ser.). (ENG., Illus.). 24p. (J). (gr. -1-3). 26.99 *(978-1-943553-30-3(0))* Bearport Publishing Co., Inc.
Ashby, Ruth. Woodrow & Edith Wilson, 1 vol. 2004. (Presidents & First Ladies Ser.). (ENG., Illus.). 48p. (gr. 5-8). lib. bdg. 33.67 *(978-0-8368-5759-7(3),* 08a66539-4499-45c2-9cb6-cafc5a450a33, World Almanac Library) Stevens, Gareth Publishing LLLP.
Crompton, Samuel Willard. How Woodrow Wilson Fought World War I, 1 vol. 2017. (Presidents at War Ser.). (ENG.). 128p. (gr. 8-8). lib. bdg. 38.93 *(978-0-7660-8529-9(5),* 64acc819-1e5c-4ab3-bc93-b627f6f32da0) Enslow Publishing, LLC.
Dommermuth-Costa, Carol. Woodrow Wilson. 2003. (Presidential Leaders Ser.). (Illus.). 112p. (J). 29.27 *(978-0-8225-0094-0(9),* Lerner Pubns.) Lerner Publishing Group.
Gaines, Ann. Woodrow Wilson. 2003. (Great American Presidents Ser.). (ENG., Illus.). 100p. (gr. 5-8). 30.00 *(978-0-7910-7597-5(4),* P113900, Facts On File) Infobase Holdings, Inc.
Harmon, Daniel E. Woodrow Wilson. 2004. (Childhoods of the Presidents Ser.). (Illus.). 48p. (J). (gr. 4-18). lib. bdg. 17.95 *(978-1-59084-277-5(4))* Mason Crest.
Huddle, Lorena. Woodrow Wilson, 1 vol. 2017. (Pivotal Presidents: Profiles in Leadership Ser.). (ENG., Illus.). 80p. (J). (gr. 8-8). lib. bdg. 36.47 *(978-1-68048-635-3(7),* e35b543f-74c9-482f-8d07-267b266ea228, Britannica Educational Publishing) Rosen Publishing Group, Inc., The.
Lukes, Bonnie L. Woodrow Wilson & the Progressive Era. 2006. (World Leaders Ser.). (Illus.). 192p. (J). (gr. 6-10). lib. bdg. 26.95 *(978-1-931798-79-2(6))* Reynolds, Morgan Inc.
Marsico, Katie. Woodrow Wilson, 1 vol. 2011. (Presidents & Their Times Ser.). (ENG.). 96p. (gr. 6-6). 36.93 *(978-0-7614-4815-0(2),* 03eb9ec5-0cf2-4556-9379-b3d42426852e) Cavendish Square Publishing LLC.
Mis, M. S. How to Draw the Life & Times of Woodrow Wilson. 2009. (Kid's Guide to Drawing the Presidents of the United States of America Ser.). 32p. (gr. 4-4). 50.50 *(978-1-61511-168-8(9),* PowerKids Pr.) Rosen Publishing Group, Inc., The.
Mis, Melody S. How to Draw the Life & Times of Woodrow Wilson, 1 vol. 2005. (Kid's Guide to Drawing the Presidents of the United States of America Ser.). (ENG., Illus.). 32p. (YA). (gr. 4-4). 30.27 *(978-1-4042-3004-0(1),* 242bf2d5-bd7f-402d-87e1-47edfe543e9b) Rosen Publishing Group, Inc., The.
Rumsch, BreAnn. Woodrow Wilson, 1 vol. 2016. (United States Presidents *2017 Ser.). (ENG., Illus.). 40p. (J). (gr. 2-5). lib. bdg. 35.64 *(978-1-68078-123-6(5),* 21863, Big Buddy Bks.) ABDO Publishing Co.
Schwartz, Eric. A World Contender. 2006. (How America Became America Ser.). (Illus.). 96p. (YA). lib. bdg. 22.95 *(978-1-59084-911-8(6))* Mason Crest.
Venezia, Mike. Woodrow Wilson: Twenty-Eighth President. Venezia, Mike, illus. 2007. (Getting to Know the U. S. Presidents Ser.). (Illus.). 32p. (J). (gr. 3-7). pap. 7.95 *(978-0-516-25462-3(6),* Children's Pr.) Scholastic Library Publishing.
Waxman, Laura Hamilton. Woodrow Wilson. 2006. (History Maker Biographies Ser.). (ENG., Illus.). 48p. (gr. 3-6). lib. bdg. 27.93 *(978-0-8225-6053-1(4),* Lerner Pubns.) Lerner Publishing Group.
Zamosky, Lisa. Woodrow Wilson, 1 vol. rev. ed. 2007. (Social Studies: Informational Text Ser.). (ENG.). 32p. (gr. 4-8). pap. 11.99 *(978-0-7439-0665-4(9))* Teacher Created Materials, Inc.

WIND

see Winds

WIND INSTRUMENTS

see also Bands (Music)

Fraser, Dot & Fraser, Noel. Abracadabra Brass - Abracadabra Tutors: Abracadabra Brass - Bass Clef: the Way to Learn Through Songs & Tunes. Sebba, Jane, ed. Shulman, Dee & Tinkler, Dennis, illus. 2005. (Abracadabra Ser.). (ENG.). 64p. (J). pap. 13.95 *(978-0-7136-7184-1(X))* HarperCollins Pubs. Ltd. GBR. Dist: Independent Pubs. Group.
Ganeri, Anita. Brass Instruments. 2011. (ENG., Illus.). 32p. (J). pap. 10.95 *(978-1-77092-029-3(3))* Saunders Bk. Co. CAN. Dist: RiverStream Publishing.
—Wind Instruments. 2011. (ENG., Illus.). 32p. (J). pap. 10.95 *(978-1-77092-034-7(X))* Saunders Bk. Co. CAN. Dist: RiverStream Publishing.
Hussey, Christopher. Abracadabra Brass - Abracadabra Christmas: Trumpet Showstoppers, 1 vol. 2015. (Abracadabra Ser.). (ENG.). 32p. (J). pap. 22.95 incl. audio compact disk *(978-1-4729-2052-2(X))* HarperCollins Pubs. Ltd. GBR. Dist: Independent Pubs. Group.
—Abracadabra Woodwind - Abracadabra Christmas: Clarinet Showstoppers, 1 vol. 2015. (Abracadabra Ser.). (ENG.). 32p. (J). (gr. k-4). pap. 22.95 incl. audio compact disk *(978-1-4729-2053-9(8))* HarperCollins Pubs. Ltd. GBR. Dist: Independent Pubs. Group.
Kenney, Karen Latchana. Buzzing Breath. Heinsz, Joshua, illus. 2019. (Physics of Music Ser.). (ENG.). 24p. (J). (gr. k-2). lib. bdg. 33.99 *(978-1-68410-342-3(8),* 140262) Cantata Learning.
Landau, Elaine. Is the Clarinet for You? 2010. (Ready to Make Music Ser.). (ENG.). 40p. (gr. 4-6). lib. bdg. 27.93 *(978-0-7613-5421-5(2),* Lerner Pubns.) Lerner Publishing Group.
Nunn, Daniel. Brass, 1 vol. 2011. (Instruments & Music Ser.). (ENG.). 24p. (J). (gr. -1-1). pap. 6.29 *(978-1-4329-5065-1(7),* 115118, Heinemann) Capstone.
Pollock, Malcolm & Hussey, Christopher. Abracadabra Woodwind - Abracadabra Flute Technique (Pupil's Book with CD), 1 vol. 2015. (Abracadabra Ser.). (ENG.). 48p. (J). (gr. 1-3). pap. 15.95 incl. audio compact disk *(978-1-4081-9344-0(2))* HarperCollins Pubs. Ltd. GBR. Dist: Independent Pubs. Group.
Sharth, Sharon. Saxophones. 2019. (Musical Instruments Ser.). (ENG.). 24p. (J). (gr. 3-6). lib. bdg. 32.79 *(978-1-5038-3192-6(2),* 213321) Child's World, Inc, The.
Steynor, Ali & Jolly, Hattie. Get Set! Flute Pieces Book 1 with CD, 1 vol. 2015. (Get Set! Ser.). (ENG.). 48p. (J). (gr. k-4). pap. 15.95 incl. audio compact disk *(978-1-4729-0909-1(7))* HarperCollins Pubs. Ltd. GBR. Dist: Independent Pubs. Group.
—Get Set! Flute Tutor Book 1 with CD, 1 vol. 2015. (Get Set! Ser.). (ENG., Illus.). 48p. (J). pap. 15.95 incl. audio compact disk *(978-1-4729-0906-4(9))* HarperCollins Pubs. Ltd. GBR. Dist: Independent Pubs. Group.
Storey, Rita. The Recorder & Other Wind Instruments. 2010. (J). 28.50 *(978-1-59920-213-6(1))* Black Rabbit Bks.
Temple, Bob. Trombones. 2019. (Musical Instruments Ser.). (ENG.). 24p. (J). (gr. 3-6). lib. bdg. 32.79 *(978-1-5038-3185-8(X),* 213322) Child's World, Inc, The.
—Tubas. 2019. (Musical Instruments Ser.). (ENG.). 24p. (J). (gr. 3-6). lib. bdg. 32.79 *(978-1-5038-3194-0(9),* 213324) Child's World, Inc, The.

WIND POWER

Alkire, Jessie. Wind Energy: Putting the Air to Work. 2018. (Earth's Energy Innovations Ser.). (ENG., Illus.). 24p. (J). (gr. k-4). lib. bdg. 32.79 *(978-1-5321-1576-9(8),* 29006, Super SandCastle) ABDO Publishing Co.
—Wind Energy Projects: Easy Energy Activities for Future Engineers! 2018. (Earth's Energy Experiments Ser.). (ENG., Illus.). 32p. (J). (gr. k-4). lib. bdg. 34.21 *(978-1-5321-1567-7(9),* 28988, Super SandCastle) ABDO Publishing Co.
Allen, Kathy. Wind Power. 2013. (Explorer Library: Language Arts Explorer Ser.). (ENG.). 32p. (gr. 4-8). (J). pap. 14.21 *(978-1-61080-925-2(4),* 202581); (Illus.). 32.07 *(978-1-61080-900-9(9),* 202579); (Illus.). E-Book 49.21 *(978-1-61080-975-7(0),* 202582) Cherry Lake Publishing.
Armentrout, David & Armentrout, Patricia. Energía Del Viento. 2012. (Let's Explore Science Ser.). (SPA.). 48p. (gr. 4-8). pap. 10.95 *(978-1-61810-474-8(8),* 9781618104748) Rourke Educational Media.
Bailey, Diane. Wind Power. 2014. (Harnessing Energy Ser.). (ENG.). 48p. (J). (gr. 5-8). pap. 12.00 *(978-0-89812-999-1(0),* 21365, Creative Paperbacks); lib. bdg. 35.65 *(978-1-60818-413-2(7),* 21364, Creative Education) Creative Co., The.
Benduhn, Tea. Energía Del Viento (Wind Power), 1 vol. 2008. (Energía para el Presente (Energy for Today) Ser.). (SPA.). 24p. (gr. 3-3). (J). lib. bdg. 24.67 *(978-0-8368-9271-0(2),* ad1981df-5e0b-4325-993e-accf14cf9c0e); pap. 9.15 *(978-0-8368-9370-0(0),* 0591f092-3690-49d4-a213-36265b53e37f) Stevens, Gareth Publishing LLLP. (Weekly Reader Leveled Readers).
—Wind Power, 1 vol. 2008. (Energy for Today Ser.). (ENG.). 24p. (gr. 3-3). pap. 9.15 *(978-0-8368-9364-9(6),* 50cfe103-a721-4711-9f15-d135553da3b1, Weekly Reader Leveled Readers) Stevens, Gareth Publishing LLLP.
Dickmann, Nancy. Harnessing Wind Energy, 1 vol. 2016. (Future of Power Ser.). (ENG., Illus.). 32p. (J). (gr. 4-5). pap. 11.00 *(978-1-4994-3215-2(1),* 8b269d6d-69b1-4c51-9790-512021b6335d, PowerKids Pr.) Rosen Publishing Group, Inc., The.
Dobson, Clive. Wind Power: 20 Projects to Make with Paper. 2010. (ENG., Illus.). 96p. (J). (gr. 5-12). 24.95 *(978-1-55407-659-8(5),* 2927e174-eac4-483a-9f98-0a756ba461d2); pap. 12.95 *(978-1-55407-749-6(4),* a28fb5b0-3f6f-49cf-818a-7e45578ec9f3) Firefly Bks., Ltd.
Dodd, Emily. Wind Power: Band 13/Topaz. 2017. (Collins Big Cat Ser.). (ENG., Illus.). 32p. (J). pap. 9.99 *(978-0-00-820880-6(8))* HarperCollins Pubs. Ltd. GBR. Dist: Independent Pubs. Group.
Drummond, Allan. Energy Island: How One Community Harnessed the Wind & Changed Their World. Drummond, Allan, illus. 2011. (Green Power Ser.). (ENG., Illus.). 40p. (J). (gr. 1-5). 19.99 *(978-0-374-32184-0(1),* 900065067, Farrar, Straus & Giroux (BYR)) Farrar, Straus & Giroux.
—Energy Island: How One Community Harnessed the Wind & Changed Their World. Drummond, Allan, illus. 2015. (Green Power Ser.). (ENG., Illus.). 40p. (J). (gr. 1-5). 9.99 *(978-1-250-05676-4(4),* 900139047) Square Fish.
Felix, Rebecca. Wind Energy. 2018. (Earth's Energy Resources Ser.). (ENG., Illus.). 24p. (J). (gr. -1-3). lib. bdg. 29.93 *(978-1-5321-1558-5(X),* 28970, SandCastle) ABDO Publishing Co.
Fitzgerald, Stephanie. Wind Power. 2010. (ENG.). 48p. (gr. 3-6). 30.00 *(978-1-60413-780-4(0),* P197783, Facts On File) Infobase Holdings, Inc.
Francis, Amy, ed. Wind Farms, 1 vol. 2015. (At Issue Ser.). (ENG.). 96p. (gr. 10-12). pap. 28.80 *(978-0-7377-7204-3(2),* 19ce6f36-2b1a-441c-ab98-2914c8c5308f, Greenhaven Publishing) Greenhaven Publishing LLC.
Gaertner, Meg. Make a Wind-Powered Car. 2018. (Make Your Own Ser.). (ENG., Illus.). 32p. (J). (gr. 2-4). 26.60 *(978-1-59953-922-5(5))* Norwood Hse. Pr.
Goodman, Polly. Understanding Wind Power, 1 vol. 2010. (World of Energy Ser.). (ENG.). 48p. (J). (gr. 5-6). lib. bdg. 34.60 *(978-1-4339-4133-7(3),* e4309d75-b52a-48e7-8e2d-d5dd14f924ed, Gareth Stevens Learning Library) Stevens, Gareth Publishing LLLP.
Grady, Colin. Wind Energy, 1 vol. 2016. (Saving the Planet Through Green Energy Ser.). (ENG.). 24p. (gr. 3-3). pap. 10.35 *(978-0-7660-8296-0(2),* 5ce62c39-a64f-4ac0-954f-1abb8003b926) Enslow Publishing, LLC.
Hansen, Amy. Wind Energy: Blown Away!, 1 vol. 2010. (Powering Our World Ser.). (ENG.). 24p. (J). (gr. 3-3). pap. 9.25 *(978-1-4358-9742-7(0),* fa5316fd-7c8e-4a9f-869d-6da0d643daa1, PowerKids Pr.) Rosen Publishing Group, Inc., The.
Hansen, Amy S. Wind Energy: Blown Away! 2010. (Powering Our World Ser.). 24p. (J). (gr. 2-5). E-Book 42.50 *(978-1-4488-0199-2(0));* (ENG., Illus.). (gr. 3-3). lib. bdg. 26.27 *(978-1-4358-9327-6(1),* 2e940f3e-811b-4294-a035-1664fcefc166, PowerKids Pr.) Rosen Publishing Group, Inc., The.
Hirsch, Rebecca E. Birds vs. Blades? Offshore Wind Power & the Race to Protect Seabirds. 2016. (ENG., Illus.). 48p. (J). (gr. 4-6). 33.32 *(978-1-4677-9520-3(8),* c97ebf24-0680-45a6-a995-4218462a64bb); E-Book 50.65 *(978-1-5124-1111-9(6))* Lerner Publishing Group. (Millbrook Pr.).
Iwinski, Melissa. Shockwave: Science: the Wind at Work. 2007. (Shockwave: Technology & Manufacturing Ser.). (ENG., Illus.). 36p. (J). (gr. 3-5). 25.00 *(978-0-531-17586-6(3),* Children's Pr.) Scholastic Library Publishing.
Kopp, Megan. Energy from Wind: Wind Farming. 2015. (Next Generation Energy Ser.). (ENG., Illus.). 32p. (J). (gr. 5-5). *(978-0-7787-1983-0(9))* Crabtree Publishing Co.
Lachner, Elizabeth. Wind Power, 1 vol. 2018. (Exploring Energy Technology Ser.). (ENG.). 48p. (gr. 6-6). pap. 15.05 *(978-1-5081-0624-1(X),* a9ac8a95-4e41-4551-aeab-a8dc53fa3aa6, Britannica Educational Publishing) Rosen Publishing Group, Inc., The.
Land-Sailing Venus Rover: Meet NASA Inventor Geoffrey Landis & His Team's. 2017. (J). *(978-0-7166-6160-3(8))* World Bk., Inc.
Mara, Wil. Wind Turbine Service Technician. 2013. (21st Century Skills Library: Cool STEM Careers Ser.). (ENG.). 32p. (gr. 4-8). (J). pap. 14.21 *(978-1-62431-027-0(3),* 202465); (Illus.). 32.07 *(978-1-62431-003-4(6),* 202463) Cherry Lake Publishing.
McCann, Shawn, illus. Catch the Wind. 2008. 38p. (J). pap. *(978-1-59298-244-8(1))* Beaver's Pond Pr., Inc.
Morlock, Theresa. Wind Farms: Harnessing the Power of Wind, 1 vol. 2017. (Powered up! a STEM Approach to Energy Sources Ser.). (ENG.). 24p. (J). (gr. 3-3). 25.27 *(978-1-5081-6424-1(X),* 59c5f444-ab32-4c03-b377-63d3d636a72a, PowerKids Pr.) Rosen Publishing Group, Inc., The.
Morris, Neil. Wind Power. 2010. (J). 34.25 *(978-1-59920-344-7(8))* 2007. (Illus.). 32p. (YA). (gr. 4-7). lib. bdg. 28.50 *(978-1-58340-910-7(6))* Black Rabbit Bks.
Muschal, Frank. Energy from Wind, Sun, & Tides. 2007. (21st Century Skills Library: Power Up! Ser.). (ENG.). 32p. (gr. 4-8). pap. 14.21 *(978-1-60279-096-4(5),* 200657); (Illus.). lib. bdg. 32.07 *(978-1-60279-046-9(9),* 200052) Cherry Lake Publishing.
Nazzaro, Robin M. Wind Power: Impacts on Wildlife & Government Responsibilities for Regulating Development & Protecting Wildlife. 2006. (Illus.). 59p. (C). pap. 20.00 *(978-1-4223-0354-2(3))* DIANE Publishing Co.
O'Neal, Claire. How to Use Wind Power to Light & Heat Your Home. 2009. (Tell Your Parents Ser.). (Illus.). 48p. (J). (gr. 4-7). lib. bdg. 29.95 *(978-1-58415-762-5(3))* Mitchell Lane Pubs.
Owen, Ruth. Energy from the Wind: Generating Power with Wind Turbines, 1 vol. 2013. (Power: Yesterday, Today, Tomorrow Ser.). (ENG., Illus.). 32p. (J). (gr. 4-5). 28.93 *(978-1-4777-0271-0(7),* 584288de-df3b-4a4f-bec4-c3375b2802be); pap. 12.75 *(978-1-4777-0281-9(4),* 2a685c37-323d-471b-977c-36900e239b92) Rosen Publishing Group, Inc., The. (PowerKids Pr.).
Parks, Peggy J. Wind Power. 2009. (Compact Research Ser.). 96p. (YA). (gr. 7-12). 43.93 *(978-1-60152-080-7(8))* ReferencePoint Pr., Inc.
Pipe, Jim. Wind Power. 2010. (J). 28.50 *(978-1-59604-212-4(5))* Black Rabbit Bks.
Pluckrose, Henry. Air. 2007. (Let's Explore: Elements Ser.). (Illus.). 32p. (J). (gr. 4-7). lib. bdg. 27.10 *(978-1-59771-033-6(4))* Sea-To-Sea Pubns.
Richards, Julie. Wind Energy, 1 vol. 2010. (Energy Choices Ser.). (ENG.). 32p. (gr. 3-3). 31.21 *(978-0-7614-4430-5(0),* 31a68318-6339-462f-bbf4-f70d9d1011ee) Cavendish Square Publishing LLC.
Rivera, Andrea. Wind Power. 2016. (Our Renewable Earth Ser.). (ENG., Illus.). 24p. (J). (gr. -1-2). lib. bdg. 31.36 *(978-1-68079-943-9(6),* 24190, Abdo Zoom-Launch) ABDO Publishing Co.
Saunders, Nigel. Wind Power, 1 vol. 2007. (Energy for the Future & Global Warming Ser.). (ENG., Illus.). 32p. (J). (gr. 3-3). pap. 12.70 *(978-0-8368-8414-2(0),* ac251819-63cd-4bd9-9f04-4e24c39a77c1); lib. bdg. 29.67 *(978-0-8368-8405-0(1),* 69993bcb-a7e9-496f-ba5e-60d2344ee22b) Stevens, Gareth Publishing LLLP.
Spalding, Maddie. The Science of Wind Energy. 2018. (ENG.). 80p. (YA). (gr. 5-12). *(978-1-68282-309-5(1))* ReferencePoint Pr., Inc.
Spilsbury, Richard & Spilsbury, Louise. The Pros & Cons of Wind Power, 1 vol. 2007. (Energy Debate Ser.). (ENG., Illus.). 48p. (YA). (gr. 6-6). lib. bdg. 34.47 *(978-1-4042-3745-2(3),* d6ab95d9-2ed2-4580-b96c-180165ea6794) Rosen Publishing Group, Inc., The.
—Wind Power, 1 vol. 2011. (Let's Discuss Energy Resources Ser.). (ENG., Illus.). 32p. (J). (gr. 4-5). lib. bdg. 30.27 *(978-1-4488-5264-2(1),* 3202a94b-a29f-4ee8-91ec-4172fb0f5f75) Rosen Publishing Group, Inc., The.
Walker, Niki. Generating Wind Power, 1 vol. 2006. (Energy Revolution Ser.). (ENG., Illus.). 32p. (J). (gr. 3-7). pap. *(978-0-7787-2927-3(3))* Crabtree Publishing Co.
Ziem, Matt. Wind Power: Sailboats, Windmills, & Wind Turbines (a True Book: Alternative Energy) 2018. (True Book (Relaunch) Ser.). (ENG., Illus.). 48p. (J). (gr. 3-5). pap. 7.95 *(978-0-531-23945-2(4),* Children's Pr.) Scholastic Library Publishing.

WINDMILLS

Cartlidge, Cherese. Home Windmills. 2009. (Great Idea Ser.). (ENG., Illus.). 48p. (J). (gr. 4-6). lib. bdg. 26.60 *(978-1-59953-192-2(5))* Norwood Hse. Pr.
Doeden, Matt. Finding Out about Wind Energy. 2014. (Searchlight Books (tm) — What Are Energy Sources? Ser.). (ENG., Illus.). 40p. (J). (gr. 3-5). pap. 9.99 *(978-1-4677-4558-1(8),* 49dcd6db-b31c-4dc5-b0b4-bbd59237d414) Lerner Publishing Group.
Friedman, Mark. What Does It Do? Windmill. 2011. (Community Connections: What Does It Do? Ser.). (ENG., Illus.). 24p. (gr. 2-5). lib. bdg. 29.21 *(978-1-61080-118-8(0),* 201126) Cherry Lake Publishing.
Kamkwamba, William. The Boy Who Harnessed the Wind: Creating Currents of Electricity & Hope. 2009. 14.44 *(978-0-7848-3872-3(0),* Everbind) Marco Bk. Co.
Kamkwamba, William & Mealer, Bryan. The Boy Who Harnessed the Wind: Picture Book Edition. Zunon, Elizabeth, illus. 2012. 32p. (J). (gr. 1-3). 18.99 *(978-0-8037-3511-8(1),* Dial Bks) Penguin Young Readers Group.
—The Boy Who Harnessed the Wind: Young Readers Edition. Hymas, Anna, illus. 304p. (J). (gr. 5). 2016. (ENG.). 9.99 *(978-0-14-751042-6(2),* Puffin Books) 2015. 18.99 *(978-0-8037-4080-8(8),* Dial Bks) Penguin Young Readers Group.
McCook, William. Windmills of the World. Harris, Coy F., ed. 2003. (Illus.). 109p. (YA). reprint ed. pap. 24.95 *(978-0-9679480-1-0(0))* American Wind Power Ctr.
Woelfle, Gretchen. The Wind at Work: An Activity Guide to Windmills. 2nd ed. 2013. (ENG., Illus.). 160p. (J). (gr. 4). pap. 16.95 *(978-1-61374-100-9(6))* Chicago Review Pr., Inc.

WINDOWS, STAINED GLASS

see Glass Painting and Staining

WINDS

see also Hurricanes; Storms; Tornadoes

Alpert, Barbara. How to Make a Wind Speed Meter: A 4D Book. 2019. (Hands-On Science Fun Ser.). (ENG., Illus.). 24p. (J). (gr. -1-2). lib. bdg. 29.32 *(978-1-9771-0227-0(1),* 139240, Capstone Pr.) Capstone.
Appleby, Alex. It's Windy!, 1 vol. 2013. (What's the Weather? Ser.). (Illus.). 24p. (J). (gr. k-k). (ENG.). 25.27 *(978-1-4339-9412-8(7),* eeeee899-d36c-4d58-b45c-19a149ce3f97); (ENG., pap. 9.15 *(978-1-4339-9413-5(5),* a4a54a5f-35d9-49f3-b961-d321d021d3bf); pap. 48.90 *(978-1-4339-9414-2(3))* Stevens, Gareth Publishing LLLP.
—It's Windy! / ¡Está Ventoso!, 1 vol. 2013. (What's the Weather? / ¿Qué Tiempo Hace? Ser.). (SPA & ENG., Illus.). 24p. (J). (gr. k-k). 25.27 *(978-1-4339-9452-4(6),* ae6c9bf0-db7a-4c8c-945a-3b8e69bee130) Stevens, Gareth Publishing LLLP.
Austen, Elizabeth. Playing with Wind. rev. ed. 2019. (Smithsonian: Informational Text Ser.). (ENG., Illus.). 20p. (J). (gr. k-1). 7.99 *(978-1-4938-6643-4(5))* Teacher Created Materials, Inc.
Bauer, Marion Dane. Wind. Wallace, John, illus. 2005. (Ready-to-Read Ser.). 32p. (gr. -1-1). 14.00 *(978-0-7569-5622-6(6))* Perfection Learning Corp.
—Wind: Ready-To-Read Level 1. Wallace, John, illus. 2003. (Weather Ready-To-Reads Ser.). (ENG.). 32p. (J). (gr. -1-1).

WXYZ

pap. 4.99 *(978-0-689-85443-9(9)*, Simon Spotlight) Simon Spotlight.

Benchmark Education Co., LLC. The Wind Big Book. 2014. (Shared Reading Foundations Ser.). (J). (gr. -1). *(978-1-4509-9441-5(5))* Benchmark Education Co.

Berkes, Marianne. Daisylocks, 1 vol. Morrison, Cathy, illus. 2014. (ENG.). 32p. (J). (gr. -1-3). pap. 9.95 *(978-1-62855-215-7(8))* Arbordale Publishing.

—Daisylocks: Spanish, 1 vol. Morrison, Cathy, illus. 2014. (SPA.). 32p. (J). (gr. k-1). pap. 11.95 *(978-1-62855-224-9(7)*, 3976660f-096a-4e71-a5c9-796e1e7dccbb) Arbordale Publishing.

Blaisdell, Molly. Can You See the Wind? 2008. (Discovering & Exploring Science Ser.). (Illus.). 16p. (J). (gr. -1-3). lib. bdg. 12.95 *(978-0-7569-8412-0(2))* Perfection Learning Corp.

Boerger, Kristin. Hace Viento (Let's Read about Wind), 1 vol. 2007. (¿Qué Tiempo Hace? (Let's Read about Weather) Ser.). (SPA., Illus.). 12p. (J). (gr. k-1). pap. 5.10 *(978-0-8368-8117-2(6)*, f9bd83f8-b828-4a34-a92c-b0e00be90c03, Weekly Reader Leveled Readers); lib. bdg. 17.67 *(978-0-8368-8112-7(5)*, 3c376bb3-af1b-40cf-b2fb-02a769b8d188) Stevens, Gareth Publishing LLLP.

—Let's Read about Wind, 1 vol. 2007. (Let's Read about Weather Ser.). (ENG., Illus.). 12p. (gr. k-1). pap. 5.10 *(978-0-8368-7813-4(2)*, 6858a819-8a66-46ef-9510-10635b051ffd); lib. bdg. 17.67 *(978-0-8368-7808-0(6)*, 211573cc-101b-495f-aaa3-5e937c18c6d9) Stevens, Gareth Publishing LLLP. (Weekly Reader Leveled Readers).

Borngraber, Elizabeth & Bard, Mariel. Air Masses & Fronts, 1 vol. 2018. (Spotlight on Weather & Natural Disasters Ser.). (ENG.). 24p. (gr. 4-6). 27.93 *(978-1-5081-6866-9(0)*, 1e90ddb0-f083-420f-ae36-8a9072cf9203, PowerKids Pr.) Rosen Publishing Group, Inc., The.

Brinker, Spencer. A Windy Day. 2018. (Weather Watch Ser.). (ENG., Illus.). 16p. (J). (gr. -1-1). 6.99 *(978-1-64280-138-5(0))* Bearport Publishing Co., Inc.

Brooke, Samantha. Blowing in the Wind. 2018. (Illus.). 32p. (J). *(978-1-5444-0657-2(6))* Scholastic, Inc.

Bundey, Nikki. Wind & People. 2005. (Science of Weather Ser.). (Illus.). 32p. (gr. 4-6). lib. bdg. 21.27 *(978-1-57505-495-7(7))* Lerner Publishing Group.

Cain, Marie Mowery. Air Power. 2013. (Big Books, Red Ser.). (ENG & SPA., Illus.). 16p. pap. 33.00 *(978-1-59246-210-0(3))* Big Books, by George!

Canizares, Susan & Chessen, Betsey. Wind: El Viento. 2005. (Illus.). (J). *(978-0-439-66391-5(1))* Scholastic, Inc.

Cardenas, Ernesto A. Wind. 2009. 19.95 *(978-1-60698-026-2(2))*; pap. 3.95 *(978-1-60698-024-8(6))* Milo Educational Bks. & Resources.

Clark, Stacy. When the Wind Blows. Sneed, Brad, illus. 2015. (ENG.). 32p. (J). (gr. -1-3). 16.95 *(978-0-8234-3069-7(3))* Holiday Hse., Inc.

Cobb, Vicki. I Face the Wind. Gorton, Julia, illus. 2003. (ENG.). 40p. (J). (gr. -1-3). 17.99 *(978-0-688-17840-6(5)*, HarperCollins) HarperCollins Pubs.

Cole, Joanna & Capeci, Anne. The Magic School Bus Rides the Wind (Scholastic Reader, Level 2) Bracken, Carolyn, illus. 2007. (Scholastic Reader, Level 2 Ser.). (ENG.). 32p. (J). (gr. -1-3). pap. 4.99 *(978-0-439-80108-9(7)*, Cartwheel Bks.) Scholastic, Inc.

Cox Cannons, Helen. Wind, 1 vol. 2014. (Weather Wise Ser.). (ENG., Illus.). 24p. (J). (gr. -1-1). pap. 5.99 *(978-1-4846-0559-2(4)*, 126650, Heinemann) Capstone.

D'Aubuisson, Elisabeth. Windy Days, 1 vol. 2006. (What's the Weather? Ser.). (ENG., Illus.). 24p. (J). (gr. 2-3). lib. bdg. 26.27 *(978-1-4042-3683-7(X)*, a567d377-a966-4617-855a-6138ea37ad85, PowerKids Pr.) Rosen Publishing Group, Inc., The.

d'Aubuisson, Elisabeth. Windy Days. 2009. (What's the Weather? Ser.). 24p. (gr. 2-3). 42.50 *(978-1-60854-778-4(7)*, PowerKids Pr.) Rosen Publishing Group, Inc., The.

Dinmont, Kerry. Abby Flies a Kite: A Book about Wind. 2017. (My Day Readers Ser.). (ENG.). 24p. (J). (gr. -1-2). lib. bdg. 32.79 *(978-1-5038-2014-2(9)*, 211861) Child's World, Inc, The.

Eckart, Edana. Watching the Wind. 2004. (Welcome Bks.). (ENG., Illus.). 24p. (J). (gr. -1-2). pap. 4.95 *(978-0-516-25941-3(5)*, Children's Pr.) Scholastic Library Publishing.

Edison, Erin. Wind, 1 vol. 2011. (Weather Basics Ser.). (ENG.). 24p. (J). (gr. -1-2). pap. 7.29 *(978-1-4296-7082-1(7)*, 116758); (gr. k-1). pap. 43.74 *(978-1-4296-7088-3(6)*, 16681, Capstone Pr.) Capstone.

Eggleton, Jill. The Wonder of the Wind. 2007. (Connectors Ser.). (gr. 2-5). pap. *(978-1-877453-19-9(6))* Global Education Systems Ltd.

Farris Naff, Clay, ed. Wind, 1 vol. 2006. (Fueling the Future Ser.). (ENG., Illus.). 128p. (gr. 10-12). lib. bdg. 46.23 *(978-0-7377-3580-2(5)*, cd8f1f47-3702-454d-8953-2a07b1fb49e0, Greenhaven Publishing) Greenhaven Publishing LLC.

Ganeri, Anita. Wind, 1 vol. 2004. (Weather Around You Ser.). (ENG., Illus.). 24p. (gr. 2-4). lib. bdg. 24.67 *(978-0-8368-4302-6(9)*, 575427cb-0147-4b09-8e4c-518ae549b33b, Weekly Reader Leveled Readers) Stevens, Gareth Publishing LLLP.

Hansen, Grace. El Viento. 2016. (Clima Ser.). (SPA.). 24p. (J). (gr. -1-2). pap. 7.95 *(978-1-4966-0697-6(3)*, 131741, Capstone Classroom) Capstone.

—Wind, 1 vol. 2015. (Weather Ser.). (ENG., Illus.). 24p. (J). (gr. -1-2). 32.79 *(978-1-62970-936-9(0)*, 18330, Abdo Kids) ABDO Publishing Co.

Hardyman, Robyn. Wind & Storms, 1 vol. 2010. (Weatherwise Ser.). (ENG.). 32p. (gr. 4-4). (J). pap. 11.60 *(978-1-61532-282-4(5)*, 451a6f1b-4ce1-4d0e-8b3c-b843c3234799, PowerKids Pr.); (Illus.). (YA). lib. bdg. 30.27 *(978-1-61532-267-1(1)*, a27bc644-0045-4ae3-83f3-85c6303f9421) Rosen Publishing Group, Inc., The.

Herriges, Ann. Wind. 2006. (Weather Ser.). (ENG., Illus.). 24p. (J). (gr. k-3). lib. bdg. 26.95 *(978-1-60014-026-6(2))* Bellwether Media.

—Wind. 2011. (Blastoff! Readers Ser.). 24p. (J). pap. 5.95 *(978-0-531-27624-2(4)*, Children's Pr.) Scholastic Library Publishing.

Ikids Staff. Why Does the Wind Blow? Science Made Simple! Pérez, Sara Rojo, illus. 2009. (ENG.). 20p. (J). (gr. -1-1). 9.99 *(978-1-58476-934-7(3))* Innovative Kids.

Ivancic, Linda. What Is Wind?, 1 vol. 2015. (Unseen Science Ser.). (ENG., Illus.). 32p. (gr. 3-3). pap. 11.58 *(978-1-5026-0923-6(1)*, 2b96b2af-0a70-478a-a62a-1f01a2f35481) Cavendish Square Publishing LLC.

Jennings, Terry J. The Weather: Wind. 2004. (J). lib. bdg. 27.10 *(978-1-59389-146-6(6))* Chrysalis Education.

Johnson, Robin. What Is Wind?, 1 vol. 2012. (ENG., Illus.). 24p. (J). pap. *(978-0-7787-0764-6(4))* Crabtree Publishing Co.

Kjelle, Marylou Morano. A Project Guide to Wind, Weather, & the Atmosphere. 2010. (Earth Science Projects for Kids Ser.). (Illus.). 48p. (J). (gr. 4-7). lib. bdg. 29.95 *(978-1-58415-869-1(7))* Mitchell Lane Pubs.

Lee, Sally. Windy Weather: A 4D Book. 2018. (All Kinds of Weather Ser.). (ENG., Illus.). 24p. (J). (gr. -1-2). lib. bdg. 24.65 *(978-1-9771-0187-7(9)*, 138713, Pebble) Capstone.

Lonsdale, Mary, illus. Whatever the Weather: When the Wind Blows. 2004. (Whatever the Weather Ser.). 10p. (J). bds. 4.99 *(978-1-85854-102-0(6))* Brimax Books Ltd. GBR. Dist: Byeway Bks.

Lowery, Lawrence F. How Does the Wind Blow? 2013. (I Wonder Why Ser.). (ENG., Illus.). 36p. (J). (gr. k-3). pap. 29.99 *(978-1-938946-13-4(8))* National Science Teachers Assn.

Murphy, Patricia J. How Does the Wind Blow?, 1 vol. (Tell Me Why, Tell Me How Ser.). (ENG.). 32p. (gr. 3-3). 2008. pap. 9.23 *(978-0-7614-3363-7(5)*, 9b5a0a23-581a-4f75-92d8-f9b64ea06257) 2007. (Illus.). lib. bdg. 32.64 *(978-0-7614-2107-8(6)*, 62d25e93-c50f-4c2f-80f6-3497fba705a7) Cavendish Square Publishing LLC.

Nelson, Robin. Un Día Con Viento. Translations.com Staff, tr. from ENG. 2006. (Mi Primer Paso Al Mundo Real - el Estado Del Tiempo (First Step Nonfiction - Weather) Ser.).Tr. of Windy Day. (SPA., Illus.). 24p. (gr. k-2). lib. bdg. 23.93 *(978-0-8225-6214-6(6)*, Ediciones Lerner) Lerner Publishing Group.

—Un Día con Viento (A Windy Day) 2006. (Mi Primer Paso al Mundo Real Ser.). (Illus.). 23p. (J). (gr. -1-3). per. 5.95 *(978-0-8225-6549-9(8)*, Ediciones Lerner) Lerner Publishing Group.

—Windy. (First Step Nonfiction — Kinds of Weather Ser.). (ENG., Illus.). 8p. (J). (gr. k-2). 2005. pap. 5.99 *(978-0-8225-5364-9(3)*, 3d203d9c-47ad-449a-a648-b5739097f3ef) 2015. E-Book 23.99 *(978-1-5124-1040-2(3))* Lerner Publishing Group.

O'Mara, Mary. Monsoon! an Extreme Weather Season. (Science Kaleidoscope Ser.). 32p. (gr. 4-4). 2009. 47.90 *(978-1-60853-038-0(8)*, PowerKids Pr.) 2008. (ENG.). pap. 10.00 *(978-1-4358-0159-2(8)*, 4c6a010c-8c26-4ff9-8c02-7601601825f8, Rosen Classroom) Rosen Publishing Group, Inc., The.

Orr, Tamra B. The Wind Blows. 2015. (Tell Me Why Library). (ENG., Illus.). 24p. (J). (gr. 2-5). 29.21 *(978-1-63362-618-8(0)*, 206656) Cherry Lake Publishing.

Peters, Katie. When the Wind Blows. 2019. (Let's Look at Weather (Pull Ahead Readers — Nonfiction) Ser.). (ENG., Illus.). 16p. (J). (gr. -1-1). pap. 8.99 *(978-1-5415-7326-0(9)*, 346e51a9-4d43-4ba8-aa05-e8f9619c48cc); lib. bdg. 27.99 *(978-1-5415-5833-5(2)*, 98aa2769-5367-4fd3-a5e2-8ee7fa9645a4) Lerner Publishing Group. (Lerner Pubns.).

Randolph, Joanne, ed. Jet Stream Steering the Winds!, 1 vol. 2017. (Weather Report). (ENG.). 32p. (gr. 3-3). pap. 11.52 *(978-0-7660-9017-0(5)*, d21f363a-b4f7-4271-b99e-92bdce070772) Enslow Publishing, LLC.

Rossiter, Brienna. Wind. 2019. (Weather Ser.). (ENG., Illus.). 16p. (J). (gr. k-1). pap. 7.95 *(978-1-64185-863-2(X)*, 164185863X); lib. bdg. 25.64 *(978-1-64185-794-9(3)*, 1641857943) North Star Editions. (Focus Readers).

Rustad, Martha E. H. Today Is a Windy Day. 2017. (What Is the Weather Today? Ser.). (ENG., Illus.). 24p. (J). (gr. k-2). pap. 6.29 *(978-1-4966-0945-8(X)*, 134532, Pebble) Capstone.

Sánchez, Lucía M. Viento. Taylor, Trace, illus. 2010. (1B Nuestro Mundo Natural Ser.). (SPA.). 40p. (J). pap. 9.60 *(978-1-61406-207-3(2))* American Reading Co.

Sherman, Josepha. Gusts & Gales: A Book about Wind, 1 vol. Wesley, Omarr, illus. 2003. (Amazing Science: Weather Ser.). (ENG.). 24p. (J). (gr. -1-3). per. 8.95 *(978-1-4048-0338-1(6)*, 92650, Picture Window Bks.) Capstone.

Sherman, Josepha & Picture Window Books Staff. Sopla y Silba: Un Libro Sobre el Viento, 1 vol. Robledo, Sol, tr. Wesley, Omarr, illus. 2007. (Ciencia Asombrosa: el Tiempo Ser.). (SPA.). 24p. (J). (gr. -1-3). 27.32 *(978-1-4048-3217-6(3)*, 93788, Picture Window Bks.) Capstone.

Strain Trueit, Trudi. Windy Days, 1 vol. 2010. (Weather Watch Ser.). (ENG.). 24p. (gr. k-1). 25.50 *(978-0-7614-4020-8(8)*, 6b467ae4-419d-4039-a563-ac25908586d2) Cavendish Square Publishing LLC.

Whelan, Piper & Willis, John. Wind. 2017. (Illus.). 24p. *(978-1-5105-1048-7(6))* SmartBook Media, Inc.

Williams, Judith. How Come It's Windy?, 1 vol. 2014. (How Does Weather Happen? Ser.). (ENG.). 24p. (gr. k-1). pap. 10.35 *(978-0-7660-6391-4(7)*, 1fbfc47b-eeae-457c-9dc5-a4559aceeb39); lib. bdg. 24.27 *(978-0-7660-6390-7(9)*, ce0e2ebb-2c49-4ed8-9298-2cff6b593960) Enslow Publishing, LLC. (Enslow Elementary).

—¿Por Qué Hace Viento? / Why Is It Windy?, 1 vol. 2010. (Me Gusta el Clima / I Like Weather! Ser.). (SPA & ENG.). 24p. (gr. k-2). 26.60 *(978-0-7660-3240-8(X)*, e9686edb-29dd-4685-b7ee-96f3ee3ba292, Enslow Elementary) Enslow Publishing, LLC.

The Wind: Level D, 6 vols. (Wonder Worldtm Ser.). 16p. 24.95 *(978-0-7802-1057-8(3))* Wright Group/McGraw-Hill.

Wind & Storms: 6 Each of 1 Student Book, 6 vols. (Sunshinetm Science Ser.). 24p. (gr. 1-2). 41.95 *(978-0-7802-1376-0(9))* Wright Group/McGraw-Hill.

Wind & Storms: Big Book. (Sunshinetm Science Ser.). 24p. (gr. 1-2). 37.50 *(978-0-7802-1377-7(7))* Wright Group/McGraw-Hill.

WINDS—FICTION

Aesop, Aesop. The Wind & the Sun. 2012. (J). 29.99 *(978-1-61913-108-8(0))* Weigl Pubs., Inc.

Andrade, Marcia. Gust's Maze. 2010. 142p. pap. 11.50 *(978-1-60911-101-4(X)*, Eloquent Bks.) Strategic Book Publishing & Rights Agency (SBPRA).

Asch, Frank & Asch, Devin. Like a Windy Day. Asch, Frank & Asch, Devin, illus. 2008. (ENG., Illus.). 32p. (J). (gr. -1-3). pap. 7.99 *(978-0-15-206403-7(6)*, 1199168, Clarion Bks.) HarperCollins Pubs.

Birdsall, Jeanne. Flora's Very Windy Day. Phelan, Matt, illus. 2013. (ENG.). 32p. (J). (gr. -1-3). pap. 7.99 *(978-0-547-99485-7(0)*, 1525240, Clarion Bks.) HarperCollins Pubs.

Bishop, Celeste. It's Windy, 1 vol. 2016. (What's the Weather Like? Ser.). (ENG.). 24p. (gr. 1-1). pap. 9.25 *(978-1-4994-2363-1(2)*, 884d3570-3d48-40dc-946d-8eef2bc92f26, PowerKids Pr.) Rosen Publishing Group, Inc., The.

Busy Little Breezie. 2006. (J). per. 7.95 *(978-0-9742714-2-2(X))* I C Creative, Inc.

Cepeda, Joe. Up. (I Like to Read Ser.). (ENG.). 32p. (J). (gr. -1-3). 2017. 4.99 *(978-0-8234-3887-7(2))* 2016. (Illus.). 7.99 *(978-0-8234-3689-7(6))* Holiday Hse., Inc.

Collins, Terry. The Wind Blows. 2010. (ENG.). 33p. pap. 15.95 *(978-0-557-48340-2(9))* Lulu Pr., Inc.

Cowley, Joy. Big Bear & Little Bear: Wind. Lam, Amy, illus. 2013. (ENG.). 8p. pap. *(978-1-927186-20-6(X)*, Joy Cowley Club) Flying Start Bks.

—Smarty No Pants. 2009. pap. 8.25 *(978-1-60559-239-8(0))* Hameray Publishing Group, Inc.

Del Negro, Janice M. Willa & the Wind, 1 vol. Solomon, Heather M., illus. 2005. (ENG.). 32p. (J). (gr. k-3). 16.95 *(978-0-7614-5232-4(X))* Marshall Cavendish Corp.

Derby, Sally. Whoosh Went the Wind!, 0 vols. Nguyen, Vincent, illus. 2013. (ENG.). 32p. (J). (gr. -1-3). pap. 9.99 *(978-1-4778-1677-6(1)*, 9781477816776, Two Lions) Amazon Publishing.

di Chiara, Francesca, illus. The Sun & the Wind. 2007. (First Reading Level 1 Ser.). 32p. (J). (gr. -1-3). 8.99 *(978-0-7945-1811-0(7)*, Usborne) EDC Publishing.

Disney Publishing Staff. Blow, Wind, Blow, 15 vols. 2003. (It's Fun to Learn Ser.). (Illus.). 32p. (J). (gr. -1-3). 3.99 *(978-1-57973-134-2(1))* Advance Pubs. LLC.

Dixon, Pamela. A Windy Day Walk. Horner, Maree, illus. 2016. (ENG.). 32p. (J). (gr. 1-4). *(978-0-473-34486-3(6))* Lizzy Web Bks.

Dwyer, Mindy. It's Only the Wind. 2017. (ENG., Illus.). 32p. (J). (gr. k-3). 16.99 *(978-1-5132-6074-7(X)*, West Winds Pr.) West Margin Pr.

—Just Close Your Eyes. 2005. (J). *(978-0-88240-592-6(6))*; pap. *(978-0-88240-593-3(4))* West Margin Pr. (Alaska Northwest Bks.).

Ehlert, Lois. Leaf Man. 2005. (ENG., Illus.). 40p. (J). (gr. -1-3). 19.99 *(978-0-15-205304-8(2)*, 1195981, Clarion Bks.) HarperCollins Pubs.

—Leaf Man Big Book. Ehlert, Lois, illus. 2014. (ENG., Illus.). 40p. (J). (gr. -1-3). pap. 26.99 *(978-0-544-33916-3(9)*, 1584487, Clarion Bks.) HarperCollins Pubs.

Erin, Bethany. The Wind & the Blows. 2010. 24p. pap. 11.99 *(978-1-4490-7569-9(X))* AuthorHouse.

Evyindson, Peter. The Wish Wind, 1 vol. Wolsak, Wendy, illus. 2015. (ENG.). 32p. (J). pap. 7.95 *(978-0-921827-03-0(2)*, 133ad96f-e78d-4ad8-b708-27c5d35b1767) Pemmican Pubns., Inc. CAN. Dist: Firefly Bks., Ltd.

Felix, Monique, illus. The Wind. 2012. (Mouse Book Ser.). (ENG.). 32p. (J). (gr. -1-k). 12.99 *(978-1-56846-227-1(1)*, 22055, Creative Editions) Creative Co., The.

Gates, Margo. A Windy Day. Jennings, Sarah, illus. 2019. (Let's Look at Weather (Pull Ahead Readers — Fiction) Ser.). (ENG.). 16p. (J). (gr. -1-1). 27.99 *(978-1-5415-5843-4(X)*, dd9f6631-c415-4b45-9893-ce5743d87b45, Lerner Pubns.) Lerner Publishing Group.

Ghosh, Ronojoy. Ollie & the Wind. 2017. (Illus.). 32p. (J). (gr. k-2). 14.99 *(978-0-14-378506-4(0))* Random Hse. Australia AUS. Dist: Independent Pubs. Group.

Gibbins, Desiree. The Book Keeper's Oracle. 2008. 212p. pap. 14.49 *(978-1-4389-0791-8(5))* AuthorHouse.

Glencoe Staff. Catch the Wind. (J). (gr. 6). wbk. ed. *(978-0-02-132670-9(3))* Macmillan Publishing Co., Inc.

Grahame, Kenneth. The Wind in the Willows. 2012. (ENG., Illus.). 280p. *(978-1-904919-51-3(0)*, Collector's Library, The) Pan Macmillan.

Greene, Carol. Please, Wind? Sharp, Gene, illus. 2011. (Rookie Ready to Learn - First Science Ser.). 40p. (J). (gr. -1-k). lib. bdg. 23.00 *(978-0-531-26502-4(1)*, Children's Pr.) Scholastic Library Publishing.

Hancock, Susan G. The Wind & Little Cloud. Simmons, Robert, illus. 2006. (J). (ENG.). 40p. spiral bd. 17.95 *(978-0-9741743-3-4(5))*; 48p. (gr. -1-3). per. 10.95 *(978-0-9741743-0-3(0))* Perlycross Pubs.

Herbauts, Anne, creator. What Color Is the Wind? 2016. (Illus.). 48p. (J). (gr. k). pap. 21.95 *(978-1-59270-221-3(X))* Enchanted Lion Bks., LLC.

Hunter, Rhonda. Chinook & Winter, 1 vol. Lamontagne, Jayce, illus. 2017. (ENG.). 40p. (J). (gr. 2-4). pap. 10.95 *(978-1-926506-01-2(4)*, 33c8a013-2ae3-492b-874e-3f5d42bd7279) Pemmican Pubns., Inc. CAN. Dist: Firefly Bks., Ltd.

Joseph, O'Day E. I Like Wind! Foster, Ron, illus. 2007. 28p. (J). (gr. -1-3). *(978-1-929039-42-5(5))* Ambassador Bks., Inc.

Leibenkop, T. The Sovereign of the Northern Winds. 2009. 30p. pap. 13.50 *(978-1-60693-847-8(9)*, Eloquent Bks.) Strategic Book Publishing & Rights Agency (SBPRA).

Levine, Gail Carson. Ever. 2011. (ENG.). 272p. (J). (gr. 3-7). pap. 7.99 *(978-0-06-122964-0(4)*, HarperCollins) HarperCollins Pubs.

Marshall, Linda Elovitz. Good Night, Wind: A Yiddish Folktale. Doliveux, Maelle, illus. 2019. 32p. (J). (gr. -1-3). 18.99 *(978-0-8234-3788-7(4))* Holiday Hse., Inc.

Mattern, Carrie. Papa, Why Does the Wind Blow? 2009. 24p. pap. 15.95 *(978-1-4490-0809-3(7))* AuthorHouse.

Mencio, Anna. The Day the Wind Changed. 2012. 24p. pap. 28.03 *(978-1-4691-8232-2(7))* Xlibris Corp.

Messenger, Shannon. Let the Sky Fall. 2013. (Sky Fall Ser.: 1). (ENG., Illus.). 432p. (YA). (gr. 7). pap. 12.99 *(978-1-4424-5042-4(8)*, Simon Pulse) Simon Pulse.

—Let the Storm Break. 2014. (Sky Fall Ser.: 2). (ENG., Illus.). 400p. (YA). (gr. 7). 17.99 *(978-1-4424-5044-8(4)*, Simon Pulse) Simon Pulse.

—Let the Wind Rise. (Sky Fall Ser.: 3). (ENG., Illus.). (YA). (gr. 7). 2017. 432p. pap. 12.99 *(978-1-4814-4655-6(X))* 2016. 416p. 19.99 *(978-1-4814-4654-9(1))* Simon Pulse. (Simon Pulse).

Michaels, Fern, et al. Silver Bells. l.t. ed. 2008. (YA). 34.95 *(978-1-59722-823-7(0))* Thorndike Pr.

Milbourne, Anna. The Windy Day. Temporin, Elena, illus. 2007 (Picture Bks). 24p. (J). (gr. -1-3). 9.99 *(978-0-7945-1616-1(5)*, Usborne) EDC Publishing.

Montgomery, L. M. Ana la de Alamos Ventosos. Fantín de Bellocq, Constanza, tr. (Ana la de Tejas Verdes Ser.: 4).Tr. of Anne of Windy Poplars. (SPA.). 288p. (J). (gr. 5-8). *(978-84-7888-636-4(2)*, SAL3944) Emece Editores ESP. Dist: Lectorum Pubns., Inc.

Morrison, Toni & Morrison, Slade. Little Cloud & Lady Wind. Qualls, Sean, illus. 2010. (ENG.). 32p. (J). pap. 7.99 *(978-1-4169-8524-2(7)*, Simon & Schuster Bks. For Young Readers) Simon & Schuster Bks. For Young Readers.

—Little Cloud & Lady Wind. Qualls, Sean, illus. 2010. (ENG.). 32p. (J). (gr. -1-3). 19.99 *(978-1-4169-8523-5(9)*, Simon & Schuster/Paula Wiseman Bks.) Simon & Schuster/Paula Wiseman Bks.

Nana, Old. Just Right. 2013. 24p. pap. 11.50 *(978-1-62857-212-4(4)*, Strategic Bk. Publishing) Strategic Book Publishing & Rights Agency (SBPRA).

Nash, Margaret. Hetty's New Hat. Impey, Martin, illus. 2005. (Reading Corner Ser.). 24p. (J). (gr. k-3). lib. bdg. 22.80 *(978-1-59771-007-7(5))* Sea-To-Sea Pubns.

Noble, Trinka Hakes. The Legend of Michigan. Frankenhuyzen, Gijsbert van, illus. 2006. (Myths, Legends, Fairy & Folktales Ser.). (ENG.). 48p. (J). (gr. 2-5). 17.95 *(978-1-58536-278-3(6)*, 202089) Sleeping Bear Pr.

peddi, radhika. Kickkide. 2010. 44p. pap. 19.70 *(978-0-557-16435-6(4))* Lulu Pr., Inc.

Ras. Oh No, the Leaves Are Moving! 2011. 24p. pap. 15.99 *(978-1-4568-5030-2(X))* Xlibris Corp.

Reyes, Yazmin. Fairies vs. Wizards: The Last Battle, 1 vol. 2009. 48p. pap. 16.95 *(978-1-4489-9527-1(2))* America Star Bks.

Rhema, Dan. Bluegrass Breeze. Leonard, Michael, illus. 2004. (J). per. 19.95 *(978-0-9729835-1-8(1))* Mesquite Tress Pr., LLC.

Rice, T. F. The Wind Being. 2007. (ENG.). 28p. 15.95 *(978-0-615-17173-9(7))* Hidden Valley Farm Pub.

Rink, Cynthia A. Where Does the Wind Blow? Rink, Cynthia A., illus. 2004. (Sharing Nature with Children Book Ser.). (Illus.). 32p. (J). (gr. k-5). 16.95 *(978-1-58469-041-2(0))* Take Heart Pubns.

Rink, Cynthia A., illus. Where Does the Wind Blow? 2004. (Sharing Nature with Children Book Ser.). 32p. (J). pap. 7.95 *(978-1-58469-040-5(2))* Take Heart Pubns.

Ritz, Lee F. The Sun & the Wind. Hale, Randy, illus. 2013. 62p. 23.99 *(978-1-940840-00-0(7))* Ritz, Lee Pubns.

Roller, Pat Kellogg. Pink Hat's Adventure with Kites. Salazar, Riana, illus. Roller, John, photos by. 2009. 36p. pap. 10.95 *(978-1-59858-957-3(1))* Dog Ear Publishing, LLC.

Scanlon, Liz Garton. Kate, Who Tamed the Wind. White, Lee, illus. 2018. 40p. (J). (gr. -1-3). 18.99 *(978-1-101-93479-1(4)*, Schwartz & Wade Bks.) Random Hse. Children's Bks.

Spalding, Andrea. Sarah May & the New Red Dress. 2004. (Illus.). (J). (gr. k-3). spiral bd. *(978-0-616-01782-1(0))* Canadian National Institute for the Blind/Institut National Canadien pour les Aveugles.

Spurr, Elizabeth. In the Wind, 1 vol. Oliphant, Manelle, illus. 2016. (In the Weather Ser.). 22p. (J). (gr. -1 — 1). bds. 6.99 *(978-1-56145-854-7(6))* Peachtree Publishing Co. Inc.

Swenson, Jamie A. A Fall Ball for All. Fedele, Chiara, illus. 2018. (ENG.). 32p. (J). (gr. k-2). 19.99 *(978-1-5124-9803-5(3)*, 58a720c8-25c5-494b-baa5-616ae97cfa71, Millbrook Pr.) Lerner Publishing Group.

The Library Fairy. The Magical Tree & Musical Wind. Faust, Laurie A., illus. 2008. 32p. pap. 16.95 *(978-1-59858-604-6(1))* Dog Ear Publishing, LLC.

Thompson, Carol. Wind. Thompson, Carol, illus. 2014. (Whatever the Weather Ser.). (Illus.). 12p. (J). (gr. k-k). spiral bd. *(978-1-84643-682-6(6))* Child's Play International Ltd.

Thompson, Lauren. Mouse's First Fall. Erdogan, Buket, illus. 2010. (Classic Board Bks.). (ENG.). 34p. (J). (gr. -1 — 1). bds. 8.99 *(978-1-4169-9477-0(7)*, Little Simon) Little Simon.

—Mouse's First Fall. 2006. (ENG., Illus.). 32p. (J). (gr. -1-1). 18.99 *(978-0-689-85837-6(X)*, Simon & Schuster Bks. For Young Readers) Simon & Schuster Bks. For Young Readers.

—Mouse's First Spring. Erdogan, Buket, illus. 2012. (Classic Board Bks.). (ENG.). 34p. (J). (gr. -1-3). bds. 8.99 *(978-1-4424-3431-8(7)*, Little Simon) Little Simon.

—Mouse's First Spring. Erdogan, Buket, illus. 2005. (ENG.). 32p. (J). (gr. -1-3). 19.99 *(978-0-689-85838-3(8)*, Simon & Schuster Bks. For Young Readers) Simon & Schuster Bks. For Young Readers.

Westall, Robert. Voces en el Viento. (SPA.). 9.95 *(978-958-04-4700-9(4))* Norma S.A. COL. Dist: Distribuidora Norma, Inc.

White, Loricia. Little Tail's Rhyming Roots. 2012. 74p. pap. 19.95 *(978-1-4626-6885-4(2))* America Star Bks.

Willems, Ashley. The Boy & the Wind. 2013. 52p. pap. 20.99 *(978-1-4525-8369-3(2)*, Balboa Pr.) Author Solutions, LLC.

Wolff, Ferida. It Is the Wind. Ransome, James E., illus. Date not set. (ENG.). 32p. (J). (gr. -1-1). pap. 5.99 *(978-0-06-443530-7(X))* HarperCollins Pubs.

Wright, Maureen. Sneeze, Big Bear, Sneeze!, 0 vols. Hillenbrand, Will, illus. 2012. (ENG.). 32p. (J). (gr. -1-2). 16.99 *(978-0-7614-5959-0(6)*, 9780761459590, Two Lions) Amazon Publishing.

Yildirim, Rabia. Wind, Rain & Snow. 2013. (ENG., Illus.). 53p. (J). (gr. k-1). pap. 9.95 *(978-1-59784-284-6(2)*, Tughra Bks.) Blue Dome, Inc.

lotow, Charlotte. When the Wind Stops. 2004. (Illus.). (J). (gr. 2-4). spiral bd. *(978-0-616-01823-1(1))*; spiral bd. *(978-0-616-01822-4(3))* Canadian National Institute for the Blind/Institut National Canadien pour les Aveugles.

INE AND WINE MAKING

umenthal, Karen. Bootleg: Murder, Moonshine, & the Lawless Years of Prohibition. 2013. (ENG., Illus.). 176p. (YA). (gr. 7-12). pap. 14.99 *(978-1-250-03427-4(2),* 900120600) Square Fish.

ohnston, Jack. The Vineyard Book. Manion, Moira, illus. 2005. 48p. (J). 25.00 *(978-0-9629880-0-4(6))* ACME Pr.

WINFREY, OPRAH, 1954-

lter, Judy. Oprah Winfrey. 2007. (21st Century Skills Library: Life Skills Biographies Ser.). (ENG., Illus.). 48p. (gr. 4-8). lib. bdg. 34.93 *(978-1-60279-069-8(8),* 200045) Cherry Lake Publishing.

lashfield, Jean F. Oprah Winfrey, 1 vol. 2004. (Trailblazers of the Modern World Ser.). (ENG., Illus.). 48p. (gr. 5-8). pap. 15.05 *(978-0-8368-5247-9(8),* a22221d7-89d8-49af-83a7-22a6b0cab35d, Gareth Stevens Secondary Library) Stevens, Gareth Publishing LLLP.

Brown, Jonatha A. Oprah Winfrey, 1 vol. 2004. (Gente Que Hay Que Conocer (People We Should Know) Ser.). (Illus.). 24p. (gr. 2-4). (SPA.). pap. 9.15 *(978-0-8368-4361-3(4),* 599563fd-105d-49cc-a311-743e8790647b); (ENG., pap. 9.15 *(978-0-8368-4319-4(3),* fbcee122-e549-46da-95ea-bb42649dd f91); (ENG., lib. bdg. 24.67 *(978-0-8368-4312-5(6),* 43b47061-bca8-4d08-a25f-dbffe54c2a5c); (SPA., lib. bdg. 24.67 *(978-0-8368-4354-5(1),* 9f142926-aec3-4ed2-bbdb-a5384aa293d2) Stevens, Gareth Publishing LLLP. (Weekly Reader Leveled Readers).

Dakers, Diane. Oprah Winfrey: Media Legend & Inspiration to Millions. 2015. (Crabtree Groundbreaker Biographies Ser.). (ENG., Illus.). 112p. (J). (gr. 6-6). *(978-0-7787-2559-6(6))* Crabtree Publishing Co.

Feinstein, Stephen. Oprah Winfrey, 1 vol. 2008. (African-American Heroes Ser.). (ENG., Illus.). 24p. (gr. k-2). lib. bdg. 25.27 *(978-0-7660-2764-0(3),* cee298c1-8449-466d-8e96-d4140c4f3b38, Enslow Elementary) Enslow Publishing, LLC.

Hudak, Heather C. Oprah Winfrey. (Remarkable People Ser.). (Illus.). 24p. (J). 2009. (gr. 4-6). pap. 8.95 *(978-1-60596-631-1(2))* 2009. (gr. 4-6). lib. bdg. 24.45 *(978-1-60596-630-4(4))* 2005. (gr. 2-3). lib. bdg. 24.45 *(978-1-59036-335-5(3))* 2005. (gr. 3-7). per. 8.95 *(978-1-59036-341-6(8))* Weigl Pubs., Inc.

Jeffrey, Gary. Oprah Winfrey: The Life of a Media Superstar. (Graphic Nonfiction Biographies Ser.). (ENG.). 48p. (gr. 4-5). 2009. (YA). 58.50 *(978-1-61513-024-5(1),* Rosen Reference) 2006. (Illus.). pap. 14.05 *(978-1-4042-0925-1(5),* dfe24bc1-ccb8-4441-998e-642f45a7299f) Rosen Publishing Group, Inc., The.

Jones Donatelli, Jen. Oprah Winfrey: Celebrity with Heart, 1 vol. 2010. (Celebrities with Heart Ser.). (ENG., Illus.). 128p. (gr. 6-7). 35.93 *(978-0-7660-3406-8(2),* 45681157-7380-4747-8990-fef0284426ea); pap. 13.88 *(978-1-59845-206-8(1),* 69b2101f-ce1b-4592-83f6-0aeacdea60ab) Enslow Publishing, LLC.

Kramer, Barbara & Who HQ. Who Is Oprah Winfrey? Putra, Dede, illus. 2019. (Who Was? Ser.). 112p. (J). (gr. 3-7). 5.99 *(978-1-5247-8750-9(7),* Penguin Workshop) Penguin Young Readers Group.

Krohn, Katherine E. Oprah Winfrey. (Just the Facts Biographies Ser.). (Illus.). 112p. 2004. (ENG.). (gr. 5-12). lib. bdg. 27.93 *(978-0-8225-2472-4(4))* 2003. (J). (gr. 6-18). pap. 7.95 *(978-0-8225-5000-6(8))* Lerner Publishing Group.

Lee, T. S. The Oprah Winfrey Story: The First Oprah Winfrey Comic Biography. 2010. 190p. (J). pap. 14.95 *(978-0-9819542-6-4(X))* DASANBOOKS.

Lies, Anne. Oprah Winfrey: Media Mogul, 1 vol. 2011. (Essential Lives Set 6 Ser.). (ENG., Illus.). 112p. (J). (gr. 6-12). lib. bdg. 41.36 *(978-1-61714-786-9(9),* 6737, Essential Library) ABDO Publishing Co.

Oliver, Alison. Be Bold, Baby: Oprah. Oliver, Alison, illus. 2018. (Be Bold, Baby Ser.). (ENG., Illus.). 20p. (J). (— 1). bds. 9.99 *(978-1-328-51990-0(2),* 1720771, Clarion Bks.) HarperCollins Pubs.

Oprah Winfrey. 2004. (Illus.). 112p. pap. 9.95 *(978-0-8225-5320-5(1))* Lerner Publishing Group.

Orr, Tamra B. Oprah Winfrey. 2019. (ENG., Illus.). 32p. (J). 26.50 *(978-1-62469-428-8(4))* Purple Toad Publishing, Inc.

Paprocki, Sherry Beck. Oprah Winfrey. 2008. (ENG.). 112p. (gr. 6-12). pap. 11.95 *(978-1-60413-326-4(0),* P158537, Checkmark Bks.) Infobase Holdings, Inc.

Strand, Jennifer. Oprah Winfrey. 2016. (Great Women Ser.). (ENG.). 24p. (J). (gr. -1-2). 49.94 *(978-1-68079-392-5(6),* 23013, Abdo Zoom-Launch) ABDO Publishing Co.

Westen, Robin. Oprah Winfrey: A Biography of a Billionaire Talk Show Host, 1 vol. 2013. (African-American Icons Ser.). (ENG.). 104p. (gr. 6-7). pap. 13.88 *(978-1-59845-394-2(7),* 99e8a3c3-1b4f-4e69-b81f-cc51601d4701); lib. bdg. 30.61 *(978-0-7660-3991-9(9),* 4e1bceb1-a92b-4385-bb79-25a31e0cc23c) Enslow Publishing, LLC.

Woog, Adam. Oprah Winfrey, 1 vol. 2009. (People in the News Ser.). (ENG., Illus.). 104p. (gr. 7-7). lib. bdg. 41.03 *(978-1-4205-0128-5(3),* 9460f4da-ea85-438e-aff2-ba1b136ec734, Lucent Pr.) Greenhaven Publishing LLC.

WINNIE-THE-POOH (FICTITIOUS CHARACTER)—FICTION

Bendon Publishing International Staff. Pooh Workbook Bindup #1040. 2004. pap. 9.99 *(978-1-59394-323-3(7))* Bendon, Inc.

Benedictus, David. Return to the Hundred Acre Wood. Burgess, Mark, illus. 2009. (Winnie-The-Pooh Ser.). (ENG.). 216p. (J). (gr. 3-7). 21.99 *(978-0-525-42160-3(2),* Dutton Books for Young Readers) Penguin Young Readers Group.

Bergner, Bobby. Why kitty Is afraid of Poo: A cautionary Tale. Bergner, Bobby, illus. 2008. (Illus.). 20p. 12.99 *(978-0-615-21301-9(4))* Bergner, Bobby.

Canfield, Nancy Lee. A Rose for My Mother: A Memoir. Grey, Andrew, illus. 2010. (ENG.). 300p. pap. 21.95 *(978-1-4502-3123-7(3))* iUniverse, Inc.

Classic Sticker Stories: Winnie-the-Pooh. (Illus.). 80p. (J). pap. 14.95 *(978-0-525-46782-3(3))* Penguin Publishing Group.

de Alba, Arlette, tr. Musica en Casa: Libro de Cuentos. 2005. (Disney Winnie the Pooh (SilverDolphin) Ser.). (SPA., Illus.). 38p. (J). (gr. -1-7). incl. audio compact disk *(978-970-718-290-5(3),* Silver Dolphin en Español) Advanced Marketing, S. de R. L. de C. V.

—Winnie Pooh Tesoros para Llevar. 2006. (Disney Winnie the Pooh (SilverDolphin) Ser.). (Illus.). 24p. (J). (gr. -1-k). bds. *(978-970-718-358-2(6),* Silver Dolphin en Español) Advanced Marketing, S. de R. L. de C. V.

Disney Books. Disney Baby: Peekaboo Winnie the Pooh. 2016. (ENG., Illus.). 10p. (J). (gr. -1 — 1). bds. 8.99 *(978-1-4847-7824-1(3),* Disney Press Books) Disney Publishing Worldwide.

—Winnie the Pooh: a Gift for Pooh. 2012. (ENG.). 24p. (J). (gr. -1-k). pap. 5.99 *(978-1-4231-3592-0(X),* Disney Press Books) Disney Publishing Worldwide.

—Winnie the Pooh: Pooh's Honey Trouble. 2012. (ENG.). 16p. (J). (gr. -1-k). bds. 6.99 *(978-1-4231-3579-1(2),* Disney Press Books) Disney Publishing Worldwide.

—Winnie the Pooh: Pooh's Secret Garden. 2012. (ENG., Illus.). 24p. (J). (gr. -1-k). pap. 4.99 *(978-1-4231-4845-6(2),* Disney Press Books) Disney Publishing Worldwide.

—Winnie the Pooh: Sweet Dreams, Roo. 2012. (ENG., Illus.). 24p. (J). (gr. -1-k). bds. 6.99 *(978-1-4231-4843-2(6),* Disney Press Books) Disney Publishing Worldwide.

—5-Minute Winnie the Pooh Stories. 2017. (5-Minute Stories Ser.). (ENG., Illus.). 192p. (J). (gr. 1-3). 12.99 *(978-1-368-01399-4(6),* Disney Press Books) Disney Publishing Worldwide.

Disney Staff. Winnie the Pooh. (FRE.). 96p. (J). (gr. k-5). pap. 9.95 *(978-0-7859-8848-9(3))* French & European Pubns., Inc.

DK. Ultimate Sticker Book: Winnie the Pooh. (Ultimate Sticker Book Ser.). (ENG.). 16p. (J). (gr. k-4). 2011. pap. 6.99 *(978-0-7566-7212-6(0))* 2004. pap. 6.99 *(978-0-7894-9996-7(7))* Dorling Kindersley Publishing, Inc. (DK Children).

Ferguson, Don. Winnie the Pooh's A to ZZZZ. Wakeman, Bill & Langley, Bill, illus. 2009. 32p. (gr. -1-2). pap. 4.99 *(978-0-7868-4094-6(3))* Disney Pr.

Gaines, Isabel & Milne, Alan Alexander. Pooh's Leaf Pile. Rigol, Francesc, illus. 2012. (J). *(978-1-4351-4190-2(3))* Disney Pr.

Galvin, Laura. Pooh & Friends Colors & Shapes. 2008. (ENG.). 24p. (J). (gr. -1). 4.99 *(978-1-59069-736-8(7))* Studio Mouse LLC.

Galvin, Laura Gates. Best Book of Pooh, Ever: Reading to Grow. rev. ed. 2005. (Reading to Grow Ser.). (ENG., Illus.). 40p. (J). (gr. -1-3). 12.99 *(978-1-59069-450-3(3),* 1A701) Studio Mouse LLC.

—Counting Fun Winnie the Pooh. 2009. (Leanring Anywhere Pooh & Friends Ser.). (ENG.). 24p. (J). (gr. -1). 7.99 *(978-1-59069-859-4(2))* Studio Mouse LLC.

—Winnie the Pooh Bedtime ABCs. 2008. (ENG.). 20p. (J). (gr. -1-3). 9.99 *(978-1-59069-656-9(5))* Studio Mouse LLC.

Galvin, Laura Gates & Studio Mouse Staff. Write-with-Me Alphabet. Giblin, Brian E., ed. 2011. (Write-with-Me Ser.). (ENG., Illus.). 28p. (J). 15.99 *(978-1-59069-921-8(1))* Studio Mouse LLC.

Here Comes Winter! 2003. (J). per. *(978-1-57657-967-1(0))* Paradise Pr., Inc.

Hinkler Studios Staff., ed. Winnie the Pooh: ABC & First Words. 2011. 12p. 9.99 *(978-1-74183-872-5(X))* Hinkler Bks. Pty, Ltd. AUS. Dist: Ideals Pubns.

Izquierdo, Ana, tr. Caritas Felices: Winnie-the-Pooh. 2007. (Disney Winnie the Pooh (SilverDolphin) Ser.). (SPA., Illus.). 10p. (J). (gr. -1). bds. *(978-970-718-393-3(4),* Silver Dolphin en Español) Advanced Marketing, S. de R. L. de C. V.

LeapFrog Staff. Lots & Lots of Honeypots. 2003. (Illus.). (J). spiral bd. 14.99 *(978-1-59319-002-6(6))* LeapFrog Enterprises, Inc.

Little Red Riding Pooh: A Fairy Tale Friend a Board Book & Plush Figure. 2004. (Pooh's Fairy Tale Theater Ser.). 12p. (J). 6.99 *(978-0-7364-2239-0(0),* RH/Disney) Random Hse. Children's Bks.

Mattick, Lindsay. Finding Winnie: The True Story of the World's Most Famous Bear (Caldecott Medal Winner) Blackall, Sophie, illus. 2015. (ENG.). 56p. (J). (gr. -1-3). 18.99 *(978-0-316-32490-8(6))* Little, Brown Bks. for Young Readers.

Mattick, Lindsay & Greenhut, Josh. Winnie's Great War. Blackall, Sophie, illus. (ENG.). 256p. (J). (gr. 3-7). 2019. pap. 7.99 *(978-0-316-44709-6(9))* 2018. 16.99 *(978-0-316-44712-6(9))* Little, Brown Bks. for Young Readers.

Milne, A. A. Positively Pooh: Timeless Wisdom from Pooh. 2008. (Winnie-The-Pooh Ser.). (ENG., Illus.). 120p. (J). (gr. 3-7). 23.00 *(978-0-525-47931-4(7),* Dutton Books for Young Readers) Penguin Young Readers Group.

—Winnie the Pooh: Deluxe Edition. Shepard, Ernest H., illus. 80th anniv. deluxe ed. 2009. (Winnie-The-Pooh Ser.). (ENG.). 176p. (J). (gr. 3-7). 19.99 *(978-0-525-47768-6(3),* Dutton Books for Young Readers) Penguin Young Readers Group.

—Winnie the Pooh: Eeyore Has a Birthday. Shepard, E. H., illus. 2016. (ENG.). 48p. (J). 9.99 *(978-1-4052-8294-9(0))* Farshore GBR. Dist: HarperCollins Pubs.

—Winnie the Pooh: Piglet Meets Heffalump. Shepard, E. H., illus. 2016. (ENG.). 48p. (J). 9.99 *(978-1-4052-8134-8(0))* Farshore GBR. Dist: HarperCollins Pubs.

—Winnie the Pooh: Pooh Goes Visiting. Shepard, E. H., illus. 2016. (ENG.). 48p. (J). 9.99 *(978-1-4052-8133-1(2))* Farshore GBR. Dist: HarperCollins Pubs.

—Winnie the Pooh & the Wrong Bees. Shepard, E. H., illus. 2016. (ENG.). 48p. (J). 9.99 *(978-1-4052-8132-4(4))* Farshore GBR. Dist: HarperCollins Pubs.

—Winnie-The-Pooh: Piglet Does a Very Grand Thing. Shepard, E. H., illus. 2017. (ENG.). 48p. (J). 9.99 ***(978-1-4052-8613-8(X))*** Farshore GBR. Dist: HarperCollins Pubs.

—Winnie-The-Pooh (Puffin Modern Classics) Shepard, Ernest H., illus. 2005. (Winnie-The-Pooh Ser.). (ENG.). 176p. (J). (gr. 3-7). 7.99 *(978-0-14-240467-6(5),* Puffin Books) Penguin Young Readers Group.

—Winnie the Pooh's 1,2,3. Shepard, Ernest H., illus. 2009. (Winnie-The-Pooh Ser.). 18p. (J). (gr. -1 — 1). bds. 7.99 *(978-0-525-42084-2(3),* Dutton Books for Young Readers) Penguin Young Readers Group.

—Winnie the Pooh's Colors. Shepard, Ernest H., illus. 2009. (Winnie-The-Pooh Ser.). (ENG.). 20p. (J). (gr. -1 — 1). bds. 7.99 *(978-0-525-42083-5(5),* Dutton Books for Young Readers) Penguin Young Readers Group.

—The World of Pooh: The Complete Winnie-The-Pooh & the House at Pooh Corner. Shepard, Ernest H., illus. 2010. (Winnie-The-Pooh Ser.). (ENG.). 384p. (J). (gr. 3-7). 26.99 *(978-0-525-44447-3(5),* Dutton Books for Young Readers) Penguin Young Readers Group.

Milne, Alan Alexander. In Which a House Is Built at Pooh Corner for Eeyore. Shepard, Ernest H., illus. unabr. ed. (Classic Pooh Treasury Ser.). (J). incl. audio *(978-1-57375-527-6(3),* 71394) Audioscope.

—In Which Christopher Robin Gives Pooh a Party. Shepard, Ernest H., illus. unabr. ed. (Winnie-the-Pooh Ser.). (J). incl. audio *(978-1-57375-046-2(8),* 70554) Audioscope.

—In Which Pooh Goes Visiting & Gets into a Tight Place & in Which Pooh & Piglet Go Hunting & Nearly Catch a Woozle. Shepard, Ernest H., illus. unabr. ed. (Winnie-the-Pooh Ser.). (J). incl. audio *(978-1-57375-001-1(8),* 70014) Audioscope.

—In Which Tigger Is Unbounced. Shepard, Ernest H., illus. unabr. ed. (Classic Pooh Treasury Ser.). (J). incl. audio *(978-1-57375-528-3(1),* 71404) Audioscope.

—In Which We Are Introduced to Winnie the Pooh & Some Bees, & the Stories Begin. Shepard, Ernest H., illus. unabr. ed. (Winnie-the-Pooh Ser.). (J). incl. audio *(978-1-57375-000-4(X),* 70004) Audioscope.

—Pu Baut ein Haus.Tr. of Pooh Builds a House. (GER.). (J). pap. 12.95 *(978-3-423-07395-0(0))* Deutscher Taschenbuch Verlag GmbH & Co KG DEU. Dist: Distribooks, Inc.

—A Smackerel of Pooh: Ten Favorite Stories & Poems. Shepard, Ernest H., illus. 2006. 79p. (J). (gr. k-4). 16.00 *(978-1-4223-5283-0(8))* DIANE Publishing Co.

—Winnie Puh. Meddemmen, John, tr. Shepard, Ernest H., illus.Tr. of Winnie the Pooh. (ITA.). 164p. pap. 29.95 *(978-88-7782-278-9(3))* Salani ITA. Dist: Distribooks, Inc.

—Winnie the Pooh & When We Were Young. Shepard, Ernest H., illus. 32p. (J). Boxed set. pap. incl. audio compact disk *(978-1-57375-583-2(4),* 71512)Set. pap. incl. audio *(978-1-57375-652-5(0),* 71514) Audioscope.

Mouse Works Staff. Winnie the Pooh's Touch & Feel Book. 2nd ed. 2005. 10p. (J). 6.99 *(978-0-7364-1021-2(X))* Hyperion Pr.

Parragon Staff. Celebrate the Year with Winnie the Pooh. 2010. (Disney Diecut Classics). (Illus.). 72p. (J). (gr. -1-1). *(978-1-4075-8902-2(4))* Parragon, Inc.

—My Book of Winnie the Pooh. 2010. (Disney Diecut Classics). (Illus.). 72p. (J). (gr. -1-1). *(978-1-4075-8904-6(0))* Parragon, Inc.

—Once upon a Time with Winnie the Pooh. 2010. (Disney Diecut Classics). 72p. (J). (gr. -1-1). *(978-1-4075-8905-3(9))* Parragon, Inc.

Pooh & Friends Numbers & Counting. 2007. (ENG., Illus.). 26p. (J). (gr. -1-1). 16.99 *(978-1-59069-502-9(X),* 1A1000) Studio Mouse LLC.

Publications International Ltd. Staff. My 1St Libraries Winnie the Pooh. 2011. 10p. (J). bds. 13.98 *(978-1-4508-0870-5(0))* Phoenix International Publications, Inc.

Publications International Ltd. Staff, creator. Pooh Surprise Sing-along. 2007. (Surprise Mirror Book Ser.). (Illus.). (gr. -1-k). 15.98 *(978-1-4127-7418-5(7))* Publications International, Ltd.

Publications International Ltd. Staff, ed. My First Look & Find Winnie The Pooh. 2011. 18p. (J). bds. 9.98 *(978-1-4508-0734-0(8))* Phoenix International Publications, Inc.

—My Friends Tigger & Pooh. 2008. (J). bds. 5.98 *(978-1-4127-8483-2(2))* Publications International, Ltd.

—Play a Sound 10 Stories Winnie the Pooh. 2009. 24p. (J). 17.98 *(978-1-4127-5370-8(8),* PIL Kids) Publications International, Ltd.

—Pooh's Heffalump Movie. 2004. (Illus.). 24p. (J). 15.98 *(978-1-4127-3555-1(6),* 7259300) Publications International, Ltd.

—A Ring-A-Ling Day! 2009. 12p. (J). bds. 11.98 *(978-1-4127-9614-9(8),* PIL Kids) Publications International, Ltd.

—Winnie the Pooh. 2007. (J). 15.98 *(978-1-4127-8351-4(8))* Publications International, Ltd.

—Winnie the Pooh: I Love You Winnie the Pooh. 2011. 12p. (J). bds. 10.98 *(978-1-4508-0767-8(4))* Phoenix International Publications, Inc.

—Winnie the Pooh: Super Look & Find Activity Pad. 2011. 64p. (J). 10.98 *(978-1-4508-1866-7(8))* Publications International, Ltd.

—Winnie the Pooh: Super Look & Find Activity Pad with Stickers. 2011. 64p. (J). 10.98 *(978-1-4508-0869-9(7))* Publications International, Ltd.

—Winnie the Pooh Drum Sound. 2011. 14p. (J). bds. 20.98 *(978-1-4508-0911-5(1))* Phoenix International Publications, Inc.

—Winnie the Pooh (Find-A-Friend Book) 2011. 14p. (J). bds. 17.98 *(978-1-4508-0694-7(5))* Phoenix International Publications, Inc.

—Winnie the Pooh Large Look & Find Activity Pad. 2011. 64p. (J). *(978-1-4508-0868-2(9))* Publications International, Ltd.

—Winnie The Pooh Large Play A Sound. 2011. 24p. (J). 12.98 *(978-1-4508-0570-4(1))* Publications International, Ltd.

—9 Button Record Story Pooh Friends & Fun. 2011. 18p. 19.98 *(978-1-4508-1994-7(X))* Publications International, Ltd.

Rudnick, Elizabeth & Disney Books. Christopher Robin: the Novelization. 2018. (ENG., Illus.). 288p. (J). (gr. 3-7). pap. 8.99 *(978-1-368-02590-4(0),* Disney Press Books) Disney Publishing Worldwide.

Studio Mouse, ed. Disney Time to Learn with Pooh: Flat Learn & Carry 4 Board Books & CD. rev. ed. 2007. (ENG.). 12.99 *(978-1-59069-626-2(3))* Studio Mouse LLC.

Studio Mouse Staff. Pooh & Eeyore. 2008. (ENG., Illus.). 36p. (J). (gr. -1). 7.99 *(978-1-59069-418-3(X))* Studio Mouse LLC.

—Pooh & Eeyore, Pooh & Tigger. rev. ed. 2004. (Friends Collection). (ENG., Illus.). 36p. (J). (gr. -1-3). 15.99 *(978-1-59069-390-2(6),* 1A302) Studio Mouse LLC.

—Pooh & Friends ABCs & 123s: First Concepts. rev. ed. 2007. (ENG., Illus.). 24p. (J). (gr. -1-3). 4.99 *(978-1-59069-606-4(9))* Studio Mouse LLC.

—Pooh & Piglet. 2008. (ENG., Illus.). 36p. (J). (gr. -1). 7.99 *(978-1-59069-419-0(8))* Studio Mouse LLC.

—Pooh & Roo. 2008. (ENG., Illus.). 36p. (J). (gr. -1). 7.99 *(978-1-59069-420-6(1))* Studio Mouse LLC.

—Pooh & Tigger. 2008. (ENG., Illus.). 36p. (J). (gr. -1). 7.99 *(978-1-59069-417-6(1))* Studio Mouse LLC.

—Winnie Pooh y sus amigos Ejercicios: Puffy Book with CD. rev. ed. 2007. (ESP & ENG.). 36p. (J). 14.99 *(978-1-59069-528-9(3))* Studio Mouse LLC.

ToyBox Innovations, creator. Disney's Winnie the Pooh: Winnie the Pooh Springtime with Roo/Pooh's Heffalump Movie/Piglet's Big Movie. unabr. ed. 2005. (Disney's Read along Collection Ser.). (ENG.). (J). pap. *(978-0-7634-1147-3(7))* Walt Disney Records.

Willis, Jeanne, et al. The Best Bear in All the World. Burgess, Mark, illus. 2016. (Winnie-The-Pooh Ser.). (ENG.). 128p. (J). (gr. 3-7). 21.99 *(978-0-399-18747-6(2),* Dutton Books for Young Readers) Penguin Young Readers Group.

Winnie the Pooh. The Close-up Day. 2010. 16p. 5.99 *(978-1-4231-3096-3(0))* Disney Pr.

—Goodbye, Honeypot! 2010. 12p. 6.99 *(978-1-4231-3098-7(7))* Disney Pr.

Winnie, The pooh. Pooh Invents a New Game: Pooh Invents a New Game. 2017. (ENG., Illus.). 48p. (J). 9.99 ***(978-1-4052-8612-1(1))*** Farshore GBR. Dist: HarperCollins Pubs.

Winnie the Pooh. Spring Cleaning. 2010. 32p. pap. 4.99 *(978-1-4231-3072-7(3))* Disney Pr.

—Winnie the Pooh Nature's True Colors. 2009. 10.95 *(978-1-4231-3097-0(9))* Disney Pr.

Winnie the Pooh. (Sing-Along Ser.). (J). 11.99 incl. audio *(978-1-55723-933-4(9))* Walt Disney Records.

Winnie the Pooh: Party in the Wood. 2011. 32p. pap. 4.99 *(978-1-4231-5386-3(3))* Disney Pr.

Winnie the Pooh & a Day for Eeyore (Read-Along Ser.). (J). 7.99 incl. audio *(978-1-55723-176-5(1))* Walt Disney Records.

Zolotow, Charlotte. Growing up Stories for 5-6 Year Olds. 114p. (J). (gr. -1-17). 19.99 *(978-0-7868-0519-8(6))* Disney Pr.

WINNING AND LOSING—FICTION

Arena, Felice. Little Athletics! Jellett, Tom, illus. 2018. (Sporty Kids Ser.). 80p. (J). (gr. 1-3). 8.99 *(978-0-14-378318-3(1))* Random Hse. Australia AUS. Dist: Independent Pubs. Group.

Bowen, Fred. Playoff Dreams, 1 vol. rev. ed. 2009. (Fred Bowen Sports Story Ser.: 3). (Illus.). 112p. (J). (gr. 2-6). pap. 6.95 *(978-1-56145-507-2(5))* Peachtree Publishing Co. Inc.

Catalanotto, Peter. Emily's Art. Catalanotto, Peter, illus. 2006. (ENG., Illus.). 32p. (J). (gr. k-3). 8.99 *(978-1-4169-2688-7(7),* Atheneum Bks. for Young Readers) Simon & Schuster Children's Publishing.

Chaconas, Dori. Good Sports. McCue, Lisa, illus. 2010. (Cork & Fuzz Ser.: 3). 32p. (J). (gr. 1-3). mass mkt. 4.99 *(978-0-14-241713-3(0),* Penguin Young Readers) Penguin Young Readers Group.

Christopher, Matt. Body Check. 2003. (ENG.). 144p. (J). (gr. 3-7). pap. 10.99 *(978-0-316-13405-7(8))* Little, Brown Bks. for Young Readers.

—Body Check. 2004. (Matt Christopher Sports Ser.). 138p. (gr. 3-7). 15.00 *(978-0-7569-2984-8(9))* Perfection Learning Corp.

Cooper, Ann Goode. Zebordee Goes to the Races. Jessee, Diana, illus. 2005. 32p. (J). (gr. -1-3). *(978-1-933251-01-1(8))* Parkway Pubs., Inc.

Gilman, Grace. Dixie Wins the Race. Rogers, Jacqueline, illus. 2012. (I Can Read Level 1 Ser.). (ENG.). 32p. (J). (gr. -1-3). pap. 4.99 *(978-0-06-208614-3(6),* HarperCollins) HarperCollins Pubs.

Krensky, Stephen. I Can Do It Myself! Gillingham, Sara, illus. 2012. (Empowerment Ser.). (ENG.). 12p. (J). (gr. -1 — 1). bds. 7.99 *(978-1-4197-0400-0(1),* 1033001, Abrams Appleseed) Abrams, Inc.

Lupica, Mike. Shoot-Out. 2018. (ENG.). 208p. (J). (gr. 3-7). pap. 8.99 *(978-0-451-47934-1(3),* Puffin Books) Penguin Young Readers Group.

Magee, Helen. What's French for Help, George? l.t. ed. 2007. pap. *(978-1-905665-68-6(7))* Pollinger In Print.

Martin, R. T. Pod Racer. 2017. (Level Up Ser.). (ENG.). 112p. (YA). (gr. 6-12). pap. 7.99 *(978-1-5124-5358-4(7),* ca2a9320-8539-4cd2-b818-bbab252d30a7); lib. bdg. 26.65 *(978-1-5124-3988-5(6),* c051e999-497c-4d60-b57b-c3aac1520b93) Lerner Publishing Group. (Darby Creek).

Marwood, Lorraine. Jamie Wins Again. Hocking, Geoff, illus. 2004. iv, 36p. (J). pap. *(978-0-7608-6743-3(7))* Sundance/Newbridge Educational Publishing.

Mazeroski, Kelly. Maz, You're Up! Lauso, Judith, illus. 2010. 24p. (J). pap. 12.95 *(978-0-936340-18-0(5))* Historical Society of Western Pennsylvania.

Miles, Brenda S. & Sweet, Susan D. Chicken or Egg: Who Comes First? Melon + Mandarina, Melon +, illus. 2017. (ENG.). 32p. (J). *(978-1-4338-2719-8(0))* American Psychological Assn.

Paley, Dan. Luigi & the Barefoot Races, 1 vol. Boyd, Aaron, illus. 2015. (ENG.). 32p. (J). (gr. -1-2). 16.95 *(978-0-88448-397-7(5),* 884397) Tilbury Hse. Pubs.

Park, Barbara. Junie B. Jones #27: Dumb Bunny. Brunkus, Denise, illus. 2009. (Junie B. Jones Ser.: 27). (ENG.). 128p. (J). (gr. 1-4). 5.99 *(978-0-375-83810-1(4),* Random Hse. Bks. for Young Readers) Random Hse. Children's Bks.

Purciello, Gerard. The Year They Won: A Tale of the Boston Red Sox. 2005. 112p. (J). (gr. 5-9). per. *(978-0-9746481-5-6(9))* Brown Barn Bks.

Rayner, Robert. Miss Little's Losers, 1 vol. 2003. (Lorimer Sports Stories Ser.). (ENG.). 128p. (J). (gr. 4-8). 16.95 *(978-1-55028-811-7(3),* 811) James Lorimer & Co. Ltd., Pubs. CAN. Dist: Formac Lorimer Bks. Ltd.

Shea, Bob. Cheetah Can't Lose. 2013. (ENG., Illus.). 40p. (J). (gr. -1-3). 17.99 *(978-0-06-173083-2(1),* Balzer & Bray) HarperCollins Pubs.

Simon, Charnan. Me Gusta Ganar! Translations.com Staff, tr. from ENG. Handelman, Dorothy, photos by. 2007. (Lecturas para niños de Verdad - Nivel 1 (Real Kids Readers - Level 1) Ser.).Tr. of I Like to Win! (SPA., Illus.). 32p. (J). (gr. k-2). per.

WXYZ

5.95 *(978-0-8225-7801-7(8)*, Ediciones Lerner) Lerner Publishing Group.
—Me Gusta Ganar; I Like to Win. 2008. pap. 34.95 *(978-0-8225-9499-4(4))* Lerner Publishing Group.
Steers, Billy. Tractor Mac You're a Winner. 2015. (Tractor Mac Ser.). (ENG., Illus.). 32p. (J). (gr. -1-k). 8.99 *(978-0-374-30104-0(2)*, 900138382, Farrar, Straus & Giroux (BYR)) Farrar, Straus & Giroux.
—You're a Winner. 2016. (Tractor Mac Ser.). (ENG.). 24p. (J). (gr. -1-k). 14.75 *(978-0-606-39283-9(1))* Turtleback.
Suen, Anastasia. A Prize Inside: A Robot & Rico Story, 1 vol. Laughead, Michael, illus. 2009. (Robot & Rico Ser.). (ENG.). 32p. (J). (gr. 1-2). pap. 6.25 *(978-1-4342-1749-3(3)*, 102221, Stone Arch Bks.) Capstone.
Wong, Janet S. Alex & the Wednesday Chess Club. Schuett, Stacey, illus. 2004. (ENG.). 40p. (J). (gr. -1-3). 19.99 *(978-0-689-85890-1(6)*, McElderry, Margaret K. Bks.) McElderry, Margaret K. Bks.

WINTER

Abeel, Samantha. My Thirteenth Winter: a Memoir, 1 vol. 2005. (ENG., Illus.). 208p. (gr. 4-7). pap. 7.99 *(978-0-439-33905-6(7)*, Scholastic Paperbacks) Scholastic, Inc.
Aloian, Molly. How Do We Know It Is Winter? 2013. (ENG., Illus.). 24p. (J). *(978-0-7787-0962-6(0))*; (gr. 2-2). pap. *(978-0-7787-0966-4(3))* Crabtree Publishing Co.
Anderson, Maxine. Explore Winter! 25 Great Ways to Learn about Winter. Frederick-Frost, Alexis, illus. 2007. (Explore Your World Ser.). (ENG.). 96p. (J). (gr. k-4). pap. 12.95 *(978-0-9785037-5-8(9)*, 6b43068d-c9ea-4565-b6bc-8147144d3e3b) Nomad Pr.
Anderson, Sheila. Are You Ready for Winter? 2010. (Lightning Bolt Books (r) — Our Four Seasons Ser.). (ENG., Illus.). 32p. (J). (gr. 1-3). pap. 9.99 *(978-0-7613-5669-1(X)*, 2d4e8a07-2436-4364-8fc4-7921cb6ad942) Lerner Publishing Group.
Appleby, Alex. ¿Qué Sucede en Invierno? / What Happens in Winter?, 1 vol., Vol. 1. 2013. (Cuatro Estaciones Estupendas / Four Super Seasons Ser.). (SPA & ENG.). 24p. (J). (gr. k-k). 25.27 *(978-1-4824-0132-5(0)*, d8b53b9b-a8b9-4f7b-b6c0-b503bb196a6e) Stevens, Gareth Publishing LLLP.
Barklem, Jill. Cuento de Invierno.Tr. of Winter Story. (SPA.). 32p. (J). 8.95 *(978-84-233-2617-4(9))* Ediciones Destino ESP. Dist: Planeta Publishing Corp.
Barnham, Kay. Winter, 1 vol. 2010. (Seasons Ser.). (ENG.). 24p. (J). (gr. 1-1). lib. bdg. 26.27 *(978-1-61532-568-9(9)*, c3c880e6-e09e-401c-b375-340333616ef22, PowerKids Pr.) Rosen Publishing Group, Inc., The.
Berger, Melvin & Berger, Gilda. Cold Weather. 2010. (Illus.). 16p. (J). *(978-0-545-16084-1(7))* Scholastic, Inc.
Bix, Jasper. Winter Holidays, 1 vol. 2015. (Winter Fun Ser.). (ENG., Illus.). 24p. (J). (gr. k-k). pap. 9.15 *(978-1-4824-3763-8(5)*, 7c397d6e-c071-4b2e-905b-3cd59ae30dbc) Stevens, Gareth Publishing LLLP.
—Winter Weather, 1 vol. 2015. (Winter Fun Ser.). (ENG., Illus.). 24p. (J). (gr. k-k). pap. 9.15 *(978-1-4824-3767-6(8)*, f11ed2d1-2bb4-4645-a70a-9f03864ca145) Stevens, Gareth Publishing LLLP.
Brode, Robyn. December, 1 vol. 2nd rev. ed. 2009. (Months of the Year (Second Edition) Ser.). (ENG.). 24p. (J). (gr. 1-1). pap. 9.15 *(978-1-4339-2105-6(7)*, 83a76c1f-6a45-4a74-824b-536bbc8c9cab); lib. bdg. 24.67 *(978-1-4339-1928-2(1)*, 69e9a58f-73cb-4324-8e45-3c0953dbe872) Stevens, Gareth Publishing LLLP. (Weekly Reader Leveled Readers).
—December / Diciembre, 1 vol. 2009. (Months of the Year / Meses Del Ano Ser.). (ENG & SPA.). 24p. (J). (gr. 1-1). pap. 9.15 *(978-1-4339-2117-9(0)*, 3b06ac47-d44d-4347-8e3c-7c1fdf22247b); lib. bdg. 24.67 *(978-1-4339-1940-4(0)*, 7da791ed-2b48-408e-818d-ce6b301fbd5b) Stevens, Gareth Publishing LLLP. (Weekly Reader Leveled Readers).
—February, 1 vol. 2nd rev. ed. 2009. (Months of the Year (Second Edition) Ser.). (ENG.). 24p. (J). (gr. 1-1). pap. 9.15 *(978-1-4339-2095-0(6)*, fad4d013-a112-437f-b2d8-4d82ebc6c7a7); lib. bdg. 24.67 *(978-1-4339-1918-3(4)*, e35fc70b-2438-453f-ac90-08fbbeac70d6) Stevens, Gareth Publishing LLLP. (Weekly Reader Leveled Readers).
—February / Febrero, 1 vol. 2009. (Months of the Year / Meses Del Ano Ser.). (ENG & SPA.). 24p. (J). (gr. 1-1). pap. 9.15 *(978-1-4339-2107-0(3)*, bb90e354-93e6-41f4-8331-1a1781090645); lib. bdg. 24.67 *(978-1-4339-1930-5(3)*, 80e531d7-2cdb-4419-9e61-5ab6ac4d7abd) Stevens, Gareth Publishing LLLP. (Weekly Reader Leveled Readers).
—January, 1 vol. 2nd rev. ed. 2009. (Months of the Year (Second Edition) Ser.). (ENG.). 24p. (J). (gr. 1-1). pap. 9.15 *(978-1-4339-2094-3(8)*, 597faa33-9fd9-4084-ae57-542e675298e6); lib. bdg. 24.67 *(978-1-4339-1917-6(6)*, c125702c-12f7-4be4-98fc-9bb9b92af5a3) Stevens, Gareth Publishing LLLP. (Weekly Reader Leveled Readers).
—January / Enero, 1 vol. 2009. (Months of the Year / Meses Del Ano Ser.). (ENG & SPA.). 24p. (J). (gr. 1-1). pap. 9.15 *(978-1-4339-2106-3(5)*, ab729847-401e-41a7-a7ac-37a33e21a3ae); lib. bdg. 24.67 *(978-1-4339-1929-9(X)*, 622b9688-bbf2-476c-9d4f-96d6af31c399) Stevens, Gareth Publishing LLLP. (Weekly Reader Leveled Readers).
Bryant, Margaret A., et al. Learning about Winter with Children's Literature. 2006. (ENG., Illus.). 160p. (J). (gr. k-3). pap. 14.95 *(978-1-56976-205-9(8)*, Zephyr Pr.) Chicago Review Pr., Inc.
Butterworth Moira. Winter. James, Helen, illus. 2005. (Seasons (Smart Apple Media) Ser.). 32p. (YA). (gr. 2-4). lib. bdg. 27.10 *(978-1-58340-617-5(4))* Black Rabbit Bks.
Carlson-Voiles, Polly. Someone Walks By. 2008. 32p. (J). (gr. 1-2). 18.95 *(978-0-9801045-5-4(6))* Raven Productions, Inc.
—Someone Walks By: The Wonders of Winter Wildlife. 2008. 32p. (J). (gr. 1-2). pap. 9.95 *(978-0-9801045-6-1(4))* Raven Productions, Inc.
Carr, Aaron. Winter. 2013. pap. 17.95 *(978-1-62127-495-7(0))* Weigl Pubs., Inc.
Casado, Dami & Casado, Alicia. El Invierno. 2005. (Brujita Mo y las Cuatro Estaciones Ser.). (ESP., Illus.). 14p. (J). per., bds. 7.99 *(978-84-272-6237-9(X))* Molino, Editorial ESP. Dist: Santillana USA Publishing Co., Inc.
Charron, Ashley. Hello Green Mountains: It's a Winter Wonderland. 2013. 26p. 21.95 *(978-1-4787-2416-2(1))* Outskirts Pr., Inc.
Clay, Kathryn & Rustad, Martha E. H. Celebrate Winter. 2015. (Celebrate Winter Ser.). (ENG.). 24p. (J). (gr. k-1). 90.60 *(978-1-4914-6918-7(8)*, 22971, Pebble) Capstone.
Coleman, Karlyn. Where Are All the Minnesotans? Hartman, Carrie, illus. 2017. (ENG.). 32p. (J). 16.95 *(978-1-68134-040-1(2))* Minnesota Historical Society Pr.
Collinson, Clare. Winter. 2010. (Thinking about the Seasons Ser.). 32p. 28.50 *(978-1-59771-262-0(0))* Sea-To-Sea Pubns.
DeGezelle, Terri. Exploring Winter. 2012. (Exploring the Seasons Ser.). (ENG.). 24p. (gr. k-1). pap. 41.70 *(978-1-4296-8353-1(8)*, Capstone Pr.) Capstone.
Early Macken, JoAnn. Winter, 1 vol. 2005. (Seasons of the Year Ser.). (ENG., Illus.). 16p. (gr. k-1). pap. 6.30 *(978-0-8368-6361-1(5)*, 60cf79e6-2c1b-4bbd-8c66-4df9495d0acb); lib. bdg. 21.67 *(978-0-8368-6356-7(9)*, b5ddda00-eb4d-4f43-a133-82feae22dd33) Stevens, Gareth Publishing LLLP. (Weekly Reader Leveled Readers).
—Winter / Invierno, 1 vol. 2005. (Seasons of the Year / Las Estaciones Del Año Ser.). 16p. (gr. k-1). (SPA & ENG.). pap. 6.30 *(978-0-8368-6540-0(5)*, 6173dcff-ec6e-49a2-9829-c4f2d3167ec6); (ENG & SPA., Illus.). lib. bdg. 21.67 *(978-0-8368-6535-6(9)*, 23dd7801-c25e-49a3-85c1-80300c9c7b61) Stevens, Gareth Publishing LLLP. (Weekly Reader Leveled Readers).
Enslow, Brian. Winter Colors, 1 vol. 2011. (All about Colors of the Seasons Ser.). (ENG., Illus.). 24p. (gr. -1-1). pap. 10.35 *(978-1-59845-268-6(1)*, 968f2c41-0740-4028-adab-357a1443ef59, Enslow Publishing) Enslow Publishing, LLC.
Esbaum, Jill. Winter Wonderland. 2010. (Illus.). 16p. (J). (gr. -1-k). pap. 5.95 *(978-1-4263-0714-0(4)*, National Geographic Kids) Disney Publishing Worldwide.
Felix, Rebecca. How's the Weather in Winter? 2014. (21st Century Basic Skills Library: Let's Look at Winter Ser.). (ENG., Illus.). 24p. (J). (gr. k-3). 26.35 *(978-1-63137-605-4(5)*, 205203) Cherry Lake Publishing.
—We Celebrate Hanukkah in Winter. 2014. (21st Century Basic Skills Library: Let's Look at Winter Ser.). (ENG., Illus.). 24p. (J). (gr. k-3). 26.35 *(978-1-63137-610-8(1)*, 205223) Cherry Lake Publishing.
—We See Snowflakes in Winter. 2014. (21st Century Basic Skills Library: Let's Look at Winter Ser.). (ENG., Illus.). 24p. (J). (gr. k-3). 26.35 *(978-1-63137-612-2(8)*, 205231) Cherry Lake Publishing.
—What Do People Do in Winter? 2014. (21st Century Basic Skills Library: Let's Look at Winter Ser.). (ENG., Illus.). 24p. (J). (gr. k-3). 26.35 *(978-1-63137-606-1(3)*, 205207) Cherry Lake Publishing.
—What Happens to Plants in Winter? 2014. (21st Century Basic Skills Library: Let's Look at Winter Ser.). (ENG., Illus.). 24p. (J). (gr. k-3). 26.35 *(978-1-63137-608-5(X)*, 205215) Cherry Lake Publishing.
Flatt, Lizann. Sizing up Winter. Barron, Ashley, illus. 2018. (Math in Nature Ser.: 3). (ENG.). 32p. (J). (gr. k-3). pap. 8.95 *(978-1-77147-339-2(8))* Owlkids Bks. Inc. CAN. Dist: Publishers Group West (PGW).
Fowler, Allan. How Do You Know It's Winter? 2013. (Rookie Read-about Science Ser.). (gr. k-3). 15.95 *(978-0-613-37393-7(6))* Turtleback.
Gagliardi, Sue. Get Outside in Winter. 2019. (Get Outside Ser.). (ENG., Illus.). 32p. (J). (gr. 2-3). pap. 9.95 *(978-1-64185-392-7(1)*, 1641853921); lib. bdg. 31.35 *(978-1-64185-334-7(4)*, 1641853344) North Star Editions. (Focus Readers).
Gardner, Kate. Snow Falls. Scott, Brandon James, illus. 2020. (ENG.). 32p. (J). (gr. -1-2). 17.99 *(978-1-101-91921-7(3)*, Tundra Bks.) Tundra Bks. CAN. Dist: Penguin Random Hse. LLC.
George, Jean Craighead. Winter Moon. 2003. (J). (gr. 3-7). 20.75 *(978-0-8446-7244-1(0))* Smith, Peter Pub., Inc.
Ghigna, Charles. Making 10. Saburi, Misa, illus. 2017. (Winter Math Ser.). (ENG.). 24p. (J). (gr. -1-3). 33.99 *(978-1-68410-037-8(2)*, 31594) Cantata Learning.
Glaser, Rebecca. Winter. 2012. (ENG., Illus.). 24p. (J). lib. bdg. 25.65 *(978-1-62031-017-5(1))* Jump! Inc.
Gleisner, Jenna Lee. Animals in Winter. 2018. (Welcoming the Seasons Ser.). (ENG.). 24p. (J). (gr. -1-2). lib. bdg. 32.79 *(978-1-5038-2386-0(5)*, 212229) Child's World, Inc, The.
—A Fun Winter Day. 2018. (Welcoming the Seasons Ser.). (ENG.). 24p. (J). (gr. -1-2). lib. bdg. 32.79 *(978-1-5038-2384-6(9)*, 212227) Child's World, Inc, The.
—A Lake in Winter. 2018. (Welcoming the Seasons Ser.). (ENG.). 24p. (J). (gr. -1-2). lib. bdg. 32.79 *(978-1-5038-2385-3(7)*, 212228) Child's World, Inc, The.
—Plants in Winter. 2018. (Welcoming the Seasons Ser.). (ENG.). 24p. (J). (gr. -1-2). lib. bdg. 32.79 *(978-1-5038-2388-4(1)*, 212231) Child's World, Inc, The.
—Sports in Winter. 2018. (Welcoming the Seasons Ser.). (ENG.). 24p. (J). (gr. -1-2). lib. bdg. 32.79 *(978-1-5038-2389-1(X)*, 212232) Child's World, Inc, The.
—Weather in Winter. 2018. (Welcoming the Seasons Ser.). (ENG.). 24p. (J). (gr. -1-2). lib. bdg. 32.79 *(978-1-5038-2390-7(3)*, 212233) Child's World, Inc, The.
—Winter Solstice. 2018. (Welcoming the Seasons Ser.). (ENG.). 24p. (J). (gr. -1-2). lib. bdg. 32.79 *(978-1-5038-2391-4(1)*, 212234) Child's World, Inc, The.
Graham Lotz, Anne & Lotz Wright, Rachel-Ruth. Preparing to Meet Jesus: A 21-Day Challenge to Move from Salvation to Transformation. 2023. (ENG.). 208p. E-Book *(978-0-525-65228-1(0)*, NAL) Crown Publishing Group, The.
Group/McGraw-Hill, Wright. Winter Weather: Collection 2. (Storyteller Interactive Writing Cards Ser.). (J). (gr. k-3). *(978-0-322-09341-6(4))* Wright Group/McGraw-Hill.
Herriges, Ann. Winter. 2006. (Seasons Ser.). (ENG., Illus.). 24p. (J). (gr. k-3). lib. bdg. 26.95 *(978-1-60014-030-3(0))* Bellwether Media.
—Winter. 2011. (Blastoff! Readers: Seasons: Level 3 Ser.). (Illus.). 24p. (J). pap. 5.95 *(978-0-531-26249-8(9)*, Children's Pr.) Scholastic Library Publishing.
Herrington, Lisa M. How Do You Know It's Winter? 2013. (ENG.). 32p. (J). 23.00 *(978-0-531-29949-4(X))* Scholastic Library Publishing.
Jackson, Ellen. The Winter Solstice. Ellis, Jan Davey, illus. 2003. (ENG.). 32p. (J). (gr. 3-6). pap. 9.99 *(978-0-7613-0297-1(2)*, 776e86ea-aefb-49db-b3c0-f879e788c1a5, First Avenue Editions) Lerner Publishing Group.
Jeffries, Joyce. Dinosaurs in the Winter, 1 vol. 2014. (Dinosaur School Ser.). (ENG.). 24p. (J). (gr. k-k). 25.27 *(978-1-4824-0717-4(5)*, a4bf570a-2127-442b-8817-6a25597fdc5a) Stevens, Gareth Publishing LLLP.
Jones, Jennifer Berry. Who Lives in the Snow? Powell, Consie, illus. 2012. (ENG.). 32p. (J). (gr. -1-3). pap. 8.95 *(978-1-57098-444-0(1))* Rinehart, Roberts Pubs.
Kalz, Jill. Winter. 2005. (My First Look at Seasons Ser.). (Illus.). 24p. (J). (gr. k-3). lib. bdg. 15.95 *(978-1-58341-365-4(0)*, Creative Education) Creative Co., The.
Kramer, Nash. Why Do You Change in Winter? 2012. (Level F Ser.). (ENG., Illus.). 16p. (J). (gr. k-2). pap. 7.95 *(978-1-927136-57-7(1)*, 19462) RiverStream Publishing.
Lapenta, Marilyn. Winter Punches to Nut Crunches. 2013. (Yummy Tummy Recipes: Seasons Ser.). 24p. (J). (gr. 1-6). lib. bdg. 26.99 *(978-1-61772-743-6(1))* Bearport Publishing Co., Inc.
Latta, Sara L. Why Is It Winter?, 1 vol. 2012. (Why Do We Have Seasons? Ser.). (ENG., Illus.). 24p. (J). (gr. k-2). 25.27 *(978-0-7660-3988-9(9)*, db8e83fd-6c54-419a-a375-58ee8ee4bc33); pap. 10.35 *(978-1-59845-391-1(2)*, 6815eee9-38c1-4c79-8926-22e29bbefa47, Enslow Elementary) Enslow Publishing, LLC.
Lee, Sally. Cold Weather: A 4D Book. 2018. (All Kinds of Weather Ser.). (ENG., Illus.). 24p. (J). (gr. -1-2). lib. bdg. 24.65 *(978-1-9771-0188-4(7)*, 138715, Pebble) Capstone.
Lim, Annalees. 10-Minute Seasonal Crafts for Winter, 1 vol. 2014. (10-Minute Seasonal Crafts Ser.). (ENG., Illus.). 24p. (J). (gr. 2-3). lib. bdg. 28.93 *(978-1-4777-9218-6(X)*, d544e267-c87d-4760-a9b5-fb59d83dca62, Windmill Bks.) Rosen Publishing Group, Inc., The.
Lindeen, Mary. Winter! 2015. (BeginningtoRead Ser.). (ENG., Illus.). 32p. (J). (gr. k-2). lib. bdg. 22.60 *(978-1-59953-682-8(X))* Norwood Hse. Pr.
—Winter. 2015. (Beginning-To-Read Ser.). (ENG., Illus.). 32p. (J). (gr. k-2). pap. 13.26 *(978-1-60357-742-7(4))* Norwood Hse. Pr.
Loughrey, Anita. Owl's Winter Rescue. Howarth, Daniel, illus. 2016. (J). *(978-1-4351-6415-4(6))* Barnes & Noble, Inc.
Lowrie, Paul. Hooray for Minnesota Winters. 2008. 19.95 *(978-0-9755801-9-6(1))* Questmarc Publishing.
MacDonald, Margaret. What Do People Do in Winter? 2011. (Learn-Abouts: Level 10 Ser.). (Illus.). 16p. (J). pap. 7.95 *(978-1-59920-601-1(3))* Black Rabbit Bks.
Macken, JoAnn Early. What We Do in Winter. 2018. (Seasons Can Be Fun (LOOK! Books (tm)) Ser.). (ENG., Illus.). 24p. (J). (gr. -1-3). pap. 8.99 *(978-1-63440-361-0(4)*, 5b18b416-5ac2-4bb7-81f4-b379314e5a42); lib. bdg. 25.32 *(978-1-63440-309-2(6)*, 646349ec-233f-4ccd-9981-925096d58d2e) Red Chair Pr.
McGee, Randel. Fun & Festive Winter Crafts: Snow Globes, Groundhog Puppets, & Fairy Masks, 1 vol. 2014. (Fun & Festive Crafts for the Seasons Ser.). (ENG., Illus.). 48p. (gr. 3-3). lib. bdg. 26.93 *(978-0-7660-4317-6(7)*, f8555d59-0ec6-4eeb-bd59-49a998919660, Enslow Elementary) Enslow Publishing, LLC.
Meister, Cari. Winter Is Wonderful, 1 vol. Lingenfelter, Jim, illus. 2010. (First Graphics: Seasons Ser.). (ENG.). 24p. (J). (gr. 1-3). lib. bdg. 24.65 *(978-1-4296-4732-8(9)*, 103276) Capstone.
Minden, Cecilia. What Can I See in the Winter? 2018. (Seasons Ser.). (ENG.). 16p. (J). (gr. -1-2). pap. 11.36 *(978-1-5341-2876-7(X)*, 211549, Cherry Blossom Press) Cherry Lake Publishing.
Moon, Walt K. ¡el Invierno Es Divertido! (Winter Is Fun!) 2017. (Bumba Books (r) en Español — Diviértete con Las Estaciones (Season Fun) Ser.). (SPA., Illus.). 24p. (J). (gr. -1-1). 26.65 *(978-1-5124-2863-6(9)*, 6a1560b8-2617-43f2-98a3-48e81151b8e6, Ediciones Lerner) Lerner Publishing Group.
—Winter Is Fun! 2016. (Bumba Books (r) — Season Fun Ser.). (ENG., Illus.). 24p. (J). (gr. -1-1). lib. bdg. 26.65 *(978-1-5124-1410-3(7)*, 6e390b2c-438e-4339-8fee-428acd489554, Lerner Pubns.) Lerner Publishing Group.
Moskal, G. I Like Winter: Learning the ER Sound. 2009. (PowerPhonics Ser.). 24p. (gr. 1-1). 39.90 *(978-1-60851-451-9(X)*, PowerKids Pr.) Rosen Publishing Group, Inc., The.
Murray, Julie. El Invierno. 2016. (Las Estaciones Ser.). (SPA.). 24p. (J). (gr. -1-2). pap. 7.95 *(978-1-4966-0713-3(9)*, 131746, Capstone Classroom) Capstone.
—Winter, 1 vol. 2015. (Seasons Ser.). (ENG., Illus.). 24p. (J). (gr. -1-2). 31.36 *(978-1-62970-922-2(0)*, 18302, Abdo Kids) ABDO Publishing Co.
Orr, Tamra B. Polar Vortex & Climate Change. 2017. (Perspectives Library: Modern Perspectives Ser.). (ENG., Illus.). 32p. (J). (gr. 4-7). lib. bdg. 32.07 *(978-1-63472-862-1(9)*, 209874) Cherry Lake Publishing.
Owen, Ruth. How Do You Know It's Winter? (Signs of the Seasons Ser.). 24p. (J). 2016. (ENG., Illus.). (gr. k-3). pap. 7.99 *(978-1-944998-51-6(9))* 2012. (gr. -1-3). lib. bdg. 26.99 *(978-1-61772-397-1(5))* Bearport Publishing Co., Inc.
Peters, Katie. Winter Fun. 2019. (Seasons All Around Me (Pull Ahead Readers — Nonfiction) Ser.). (ENG., Illus.). 16p. (J). (gr. -1-1). pap. 8.99 *(978-1-5415-7347-5(1)*, eeaed2e3-0b79-4877-9525-e3ae86394391); lib. bdg. 27.99 *(978-1-5415-5869-4(3)*, 177f8cda-46f2-4478-9683-55e02492ae7c) Lerner Publishing Group. (Lerner Pubns.).
Pettiford, Rebecca. Winter. 2018. (Seasons of the Year Ser.). (ENG., Illus.). 24p. (J). (gr. k-3). pap. 7.99 *(978-1-61891-304-3(2)*, 12100, Blastoff! Readers) Bellwether Media.
Pfeffer, Wendy. The Shortest Day: Celebrating the Winter Solstice. Reisch, Jesse, illus. 2014. 40p. (J). (gr. 1-4). 8.99 *(978-0-14-751284-0(0)*, Puffin Books) Penguin Young Readers Group.
Posner, Renee & Quinton, Sasha. Suzy Season Loves Winte D'Argo, Laura, illus. 2003. (Be Mine Bears Ser.). (J). bds. 4.99 *(978-1-58209-353-6(9))* Bks. Are Fun, Ltd.
Preparing for Winter, Vol. 3. 2005. (Our Seasons & Weather Ser.). (YA). (gr. k-3). 118.80 *(978-0-7368-4200-6(4)*, Pebble) Capstone.
Priddy, Roger. Bright Baby Touch & Feel Winter. 2011. (Bright Baby Touch & Feel Ser.). (ENG., Illus.). 10p. (J). (gr. -1 — 1) bds. 5.99 *(978-0-312-50976-7(6)*, 900078359) St. Martin's Pr.
Rau, Dana Meachen. Creating Winter Crafts. Petelinsek, Kathleen, illus. 2013. (How-To Library). (ENG.). 32p. (J). (gr. 3-6). 32.07 *(978-1-62431-150-5(4)*, 202920); pap. 14.21 *(978-1-62431-282-3(9)*, 202922) Cherry Lake Publishing.
Roca, Nuria. El Invierno. 2004. (Estaciones / Seasons Ser.).Tr. of Winter. (SPA., Illus.). 36p. (J). (gr. k-3). 21.19 *(978-0-7641-2732-8(2)*, B.E.S. Publishing) Peterson's.
Rotner, Shelley. Hello Winter! 2019. 32p. (J). (gr. -1-3). pap. 7.99 *(978-0-8234-4434-2(1))* Holiday Hse., Inc.
Rustad, Martha E. H. All about Animals in Winter. 2015. (Celebrate Winter Ser.). (ENG., Illus.). 24p. (J). (gr. -1-2). lib. bdg. 22.65 *(978-1-4914-6005-4(9)*, 128932, Pebble) Capstone.
—Animals in Fall: Preparing for Winter. Enright, Amanda, illus. 2011. (Fall's Here! Ser.). pap. 39.62 *(978-0-7613-8643-8(2))*; (ENG.). 24p. (J). pap. 8.99 *(978-0-7613-8506-6(1)*, e3374981-72a3-48e0-84b7-91cda7b64625) Lerner Publishing Group. (Millbrook Pr.).
Sabuda, Robert, illus. Winter's Tale: Winter's Tale. 2005. (ENG.). 12p. (J). (gr. -1-3). 39.99 *(978-0-689-85363-0(7)*, Little Simon) Little Simon.
Sams, Carl R., II & Stoick, Jean. Happy Bird Day! Sams, Carl R., II & Stoick, Jean, photos by. 2012. (ENG., Illus.). 14p. (J). bds. 7.95 *(978-0-9827625-2-3(6))* Sams, II, Carl R. Photography, Inc.
Sayre, April Pulley. Best in Snow. 2016. (Weather Walks Ser.). (ENG., Illus.). 40p. (J). (gr. -1-3). 18.99 *(978-1-4814-5916-7(3)*, Beach Lane Bks.) Beach Lane Bks.
Scholastic. Touch & Feel Winter: Scholastic Early Learners (Touch & Feel) 2017. (Scholastic Early Learners Ser.). (ENG.). 14p. (J). (gr. -1 — 1). bds. 6.99 *(978-1-338-16145-8(8)*, Cartwheel Bks.) Scholastic, Inc.
Schuette, Sarah L. Let's Look at Winter: A 4D Book. rev. ed. 2018. (Investigate the Seasons Ser.). (ENG., Illus.). 24p. (J). (gr. -1-2). lib. bdg. 29.32 *(978-1-5435-0845-1(6)*, 137608, Capstone Pr.) Capstone.
Schuh, Mari. L'hiver. 2019. (Spot les Saisons Ser.). (FRE.). 16p. (J). (gr. -1-2). *(978-1-77092-442-0(6)*, 14537) Amicus.
—El Invierno. 2019. (Estaciones Ser.). (SPA.). 16p. (J). (gr. -1-2). lib. bdg. *(978-1-68151-629-5(2)*, 14530) Amicus.
—Winter. 2019. (Spot Seasons Ser.). (ENG.). 16p. (J). (gr. -1-2). lib. bdg. *(978-1-68151-553-3(9)*, 14514) Amicus.
Shepherd, Jodie. Colores Del Invierno Crayola (r) (Crayola (r) Winter Colors) 2018. (Estaciones Crayola (r) (Crayola (r) Seasons) Ser.). (SPA., Illus.). 24p. (J). (gr. -1-3). 29.32 *(978-1-5415-0956-6(0)*, a6e43e28-0ae8-44dc-a978-7d4cdbc89819, Ediciones Lerner) Lerner Publishing Group.
Smith, Sian. What Can You See in Winter?, 1 vol. 2014. (Seasons Ser.). (ENG.). 24p. (J). (gr. -1-1). pap. 5.99 *(978-1-4846-0356-7(7)*, 126442, Heinemann) Capstone.
Stewart, Mark. Blizzards & Winter Storms, 1 vol. 2008. (Ultimate 10: Natural Disasters Ser.). (ENG.). 48p. (YA). (gr. 3-3). lib. bdg. 33.67 *(978-0-8368-9150-8(3)*, 9550c152-1cbb-4db1-a2f5-7dd71c58b1b2) Stevens, Gareth Publishing LLLP.
Storey, Rita. Art for Winter, 1 vol. 2017. (Outdoor Art Room Ser.). (ENG., Illus.). 32p. (J). (gr. 3-3). 30.27 *(978-1-5081-9420-0(3)*, c3e94546-1edd-4c9f-adcf-52f749c6b00f); pap. 12.75 *(978-1-5081-9469-9(6)*, 23ba28d5-87eb-4584-beb9-1a125b7f5688) Rosen Publishing Group, Inc., The. (Windmill Bks.).
Turnbull, Stephanie. Winter. 2013. (Seasons Ser.). (Illus.). 24p. (gr. 1-4). 25.65 *(978-1-59920-850-3(4))* Black Rabbit Bks.
Wearing, Judy. Winter: WOW Study of Day & Seasons. 2010. (J). *(978-1-60596-765-3(3))*; pap. *(978-1-60596-769-1(6))* Weigl Pubs., Inc.
Wearing, Judy & Diemer, Lauren. Winter. 2010. (Illus.). 24p. (J). pap. 9.95 *(978-1-61690-049-6(0))*; (gr. 2-4). lib. bdg. 25.70 *(978-1-61690-045-8(8))* Weigl Pubs., Inc.
Winter Sunshine: Level P, 6 vols. (Wonder Worldtm Ser.). 48p. 39.95 *(978-0-7802-7080-0(0))* Wright Group/McGraw-Hill.
Winter Survival: Individual Title Six-Packs. (Action Packs Ser.). 104p. (gr. 3-5). 44.00 *(978-0-7635-8400-9(2))* Rigby Education.
World Book, Inc. Staff, contrib. by. Winter Celebrations. 2003. (World Book's Celebrations & Rituals Around the World Ser.). (Illus.). 46p. (J). *(978-0-7166-5013-3(4))* World Bk., Inc.

WINTER—FICTION

Abbott, Jacob. Jonas on a Farm in Winter (Illustrated E. 2006. pap. *(978-1-4065-0358-6(4))* Dodo Pr.
Albrecht, Sally K., et al. Snow Way Out! a Vacation in Winter's Wonderland: A Mini-Musical for Unison & 2-Part Voices (Teacher's Handbook) 2009. (ENG.). 68p. pap. 34.99 *(978-0-7390-5835-0(5))* Alfred Publishing Co., Inc.
Alcott, Louisa. Jack & Jill. 2005. 29.95 *(978-1-4218-1069-0(7))*; 320p. pap. 14.95 *(978-1-4218-1169-7(3))* 1st World Publishing, Inc. (1st World Library - Literary Society).
—Jack & Jill. Date not set. 352p. (YA). 25.95 *(978-0-8488-2671-0(X))* Amereon Ltd.
—Jack & Jill. 2005. pap. *(978-1-4065-0100-1(X))* Dodo Pr.
—Jack & Jill. 2013. (Works of Louisa May Alcott). 425p. reprint ed. lthr. 79.00 *(978-0-7812-1638-8(9))* Reprint Services Corp.
—Jack & Jill: A Village Story. 2012. (Applewood Bks.). (ENG., Illus.). 364p. (gr. 3-9). pap. 17.95 *(978-1-4290-9310-1(2))* Applewood Bks.
Allison, Samuel Buel. An American Robinson Crusoe. 2006. pap. *(978-1-4065-0803-1(9))* Dodo Pr.
Anbinder, Adrienne. Clarence Blooms in Winter. Pickman, Marian, illus. 2009. 40p. pap. 16.99 *(978-1-4389-7028-8(5))* AuthorHouse.

na, Holly. The Ice Castle. Santos, Genevieve, illus. 2017. (Daisy Dreamer Ser.: 5). (ENG.). 128p. (J). (gr. k-4). 17.99 *(978-1-4814-9893-7(2))*; pap. 6.99 *(978-1-4814-9892-0(4))* Little Simon. (Little Simon).
kinson, Elizabeth. Lisa's Totally Unforgettable Winter. 2006. (ENG.). 56p. per. 16.95 *(978-1-4241-6249-9(1))* America Star Bks.
vaz, Huda. Freeze-Land: A New Beginning. 2013. 110p. pap. 11.99 *(978-1-4808-0267-4(0))* Archway Publishing.
ak, Robyn. Lucky Little Bison. 2012. 12p. pap. 15.99 *(978-1-4685-4734-4(8))* AuthorHouse.
aker, Keith. No Two Alike. Baker, Keith, illus. 2011. (ENG., Illus.). 40p. (J). (gr. -1-2). 19.99 *(978-1-4424-1742-7(0))*, Beach Lane Bks.) Beach Lane Bks.
auer, Marion Dane. Winter Dance: A Winter & Holiday Book for Kids. Jones, Richard, illus. 2017. (ENG.). 40p. (J). (gr. -1-3). 16.99 *(978-0-544-31334-7(8))*, 1581571, Clarion Bks.) HarperCollins Pubs.
Berenstain, Jan & Berenstain, Mike. The Berenstain Bears' Winter Wonderland: A Winter & Holiday Book for Kids. Berenstain, Jan & Berenstain, Mike, illus. 2011. (Berenstain Bears Ser.). (ENG., Illus.). 16p. (J). (gr. -1-1). pap. 6.99 *(978-0-06-057427-7(5))*, HarperFestival) HarperCollins Pubs.
Berger, Carin. Finding Spring: A Springtime Book for Kids. Berger, Carin, illus. 2015. (ENG., Illus.). 40p. (J). (gr. -1-3). 17.99 *(978-0-06-225019-3(1))*, Greenwillow Bks.) HarperCollins Pubs.
Berner, Rotraut Susanne. All Around Bustletown: Winter. 2019. (All Around Bustletown Ser.). (ENG., Illus.). 14p. (J). (-k). bds. 14.95 *(978-3-7913-7415-4(X))* Prestel Verlag GmbH & Co KG. DEU. Dist: Penguin Random Hse. LLC.
Biggs, Brian. Henry Goes Skating. Abbott, Simon, illus. 2012. (My First I Can Read Ser.). (J). lib. bdg. 13.55 *(978-0-606-26852-3(9))* Turtleback.
Birney, Betty G. Winter According to Humphrey. 2013. (Humphrey Ser.: 9). (ENG.). 176p. (J). (gr. 3-7). pap. 7.99 *(978-0-14-242759-0(4))*, Puffin Books) Penguin Young Readers Group.
—Winter According to Humphrey. 2013. (According to Humphrey Ser.: 9). lib. bdg. 16.00 *(978-0-606-32138-9(1))* Turtleback.
Bogart, Mike. Ice Warriors, 1 vol. 2010. 72p. pap. 19.95 *(978-1-4489-3885-8(6))* America Star Bks.
Bratun, Katy. Gingerbread Mouse: A Christmas Holiday Book for Kids. Bratun, Katy, illus. 2007. (ENG., Illus.). 32p. (J). (gr. -1-3). per. 7.99 *(978-0-06-009082-1(0))*, HarperCollins) HarperCollins Pubs.
Brett, Jan. Jan Brett's Christmas Treasury. Brett, Jan, illus. 2018. (Illus.). 256p. (J). (gr. -1-3). 42.00 *(978-0-525-51718-4(9))*, G.P. Putnam's Sons Books for Young Readers) Penguin Young Readers Group.
—The Snowy Nap. Brett, Jan, illus. 2018. (Illus.). 32p. (J). (gr. -1-3). 18.99 *(978-0-399-17073-7(1))*, G.P. Putnam's Sons Books for Young Readers) Penguin Young Readers Group.
Brett, Jan & Moore, Clement Clarke. The Night Before Christmas. Brett, Jan, illus. 2011. (Illus.). 32p. (J). (gr. -1-k). 20.00 *(978-0-399-25670-7(9))*, G.P. Putnam's Sons Books for Young Readers) Penguin Young Readers Group.
Brooks, Amy. Princess Polly's Gay Winter. 2018. (ENG., Illus.). 106p. (YA). (gr. 7-12). pap. *(978-93-5297-533-4(2))* Alpha Editions.
—Princess Polly's Gay Winter. 2004. reprint ed. pap. 1.99 *(978-1-4192-4299-1(7))*; pap. 15.95 *(978-1-4191-4299-4(2))* Kessinger Publishing, LLC.
Butcher, Kristin. Winter Road. 2018. (Orca Currents Ser.). lib. bdg. 20.80 *(978-0-606-41267-4(0))* Turtleback.
Cammuso, Frank. Frozen Fiasco. 2015. (Misadventures of Salem Hyde Ser.: 5). (J). lib. bdg. 17.15 *(978-0-606-37433-0(7))* Turtleback.
Campbell, Mari & Jennings, Randy. Maggiemoosetracks: Christmas Star. 2013. 106p. pap. 21.00 *(978-0-9895205-4-6(4))* MaggieMooseTracks.
Caple, Kathy. Hillary to the Rescue. Caple, Kathy, illus. 2003. (Picture Bks.). (Illus.). 32p. (J). (gr. -1-3). 15.95 *(978-1-57505-420-9(5))*, Carolrhoda Bks.) Lerner Publishing Group.
Carr, Annie Roe. Nan Sherwood's Winter Holidays. 2018. (ENG., Illus.). 176p. (YA). (gr. 7-12). pap. *(978-93-5297-487-0(5))* Alpha Editions.
—Nan Sherwood's Winter Holidays. 2007. 124p. per. *(978-1-4068-4397-2(0))* Echo Library.
—Nan Sherwoods Winter Holidays or Rescuin. 2007. pap. *(978-1-4065-1296-0(6))* Dodo Pr.
Carriger, Candace. Inside My Garden. Allen, Cassandra, illus. 2011. 46p. (J). pap. 11.95 *(978-0-9816047-5-6(7))* Sadie Bks.
Carter, David A. Snow Bugs: A Wintery Pop-Up Book. Carter, David A., illus. 2009. (David Carter's Bugs Ser.). (ENG., Illus.). 20p. (J). (gr. -1-3). 14.99 *(978-1-4169-5054-7(0))*, Little Simon) Little Simon.
Chandler, Jean. The Poky Little Puppy's Wonderful Winter Day. DiCicco, Sue, illus. 2017. (Little Golden Book Ser.). (J). (-k). 24p. 5.99 *(978-0-399-55292-2(8))*; *(978-1-5379-5880-4(1))* Random Hse. Children's Bks. (Golden Bks.).
Child's Play. Winter. Busby, Ailie, illus. 2015. (Seasons Ser.: 4). 12p. (J). (gr. 1-1). spiral bd. *(978-1-84643-745-8(8))* Child's Play International Ltd.
Chou, Joey, illus. Olaf's Frozen Adventure. 2017. (J). *(978-1-5379-5893-4(3))*, Golden Bks.) Random Hse. Children's Bks.
Christensen, Gerda & Evans, Carol. Troll Peter & His Family Prepare for Winter & Other Stories: Troll Peter's Adventures Book 4. 2011. 40p. pap. *(978-1-4269-7312-3(8))* Trafford Publishing (UK) Ltd.
Christiansen, Candace. The Mitten Tree. Greenstein, Elaine, illus. 2008. (ENG.). 32p. pap. 7.95 *(978-1-55591-698-5(8))* Fulcrum Publishing.
Chronicle Books & ImageBooks. Little Turkey: Finger Puppet Book: (Finger Puppet Book for Toddlers & Babies, Baby Books for First Year, Animal Finger Puppets) 2010. (Little Finger Puppet Board Bks.). (ENG., Illus.). 12p. (J). (gr. -1 — 1). 7.99 *(978-0-8118-7513-4(X))* Chronicle Bks. LLC.
Clark, Kent & Snider, Brandon T. Peter Powers & the Sinister Snowman Showdown! Bardin, Dave, illus. 2017. (Peter Powers Ser.: 5). (ENG.). 128p. (J). (gr. 1-5). pap. 5.99 *(978-0-316-54628-7(3))* Little, Brown Bks. for Young Readers.
Cobb, Amy. Birdhouse Builder. Neonakis, Alexandria, illus. 2017. (Libby Wimbley Ser.). (ENG.). 32p. (J). (gr. -1-3). lib. bdg. 32.79 *(978-1-5321-3023-6(6))*, 25524, Calico Chapter Bks) Magic Wagon.
Conforto, Lisa. The Very Compromising Adventures of Thumby Blackstone, 1 vol. 2010. 34p. 24.95 *(978-1-4512-0270-0(9))* PublishAmerica, Inc.
Cooper, Mimi. Me Versus Snow. 2006. 17p. 9.99 *(978-1-4116-8257-3(2))* Lulu Pr., Inc.
Corum, Stephanie J. Goats with Coats. 2008. 32p. pap. 12.99 *(978-1-4343-9302-9(X))* AuthorHouse.
Crandall, Janet. Winter on the Farm. 2006. (J). per. 9.95 *(978-1-59872-612-1(9))* Instant Pub.
Crane, Christine E. It's Winter the First Day of Spring on Summer Street. 2009. 20p. pap. 14.00 *(978-1-4490-1099-7(7))* AuthorHouse.
Crockett, S. D. After the Snow. 2013. (After the Snow Ser.: 1). (ENG.). 320p. (YA). (gr. 7-12). pap. 13.99 *(978-1-250-01676-8(2))*, 900087090) Square Fish.
Curious George Windy Delivery. 2014. (Curious George Ser.). (ENG., Illus.). 24p. (J). (gr. -1-3). pap. 4.99 *(978-0-544-32076-5(X))*, 1582515, Clarion Bks.) HarperCollins Pubs.
Currie, Robin. Tuktuk: un Cuento Sobre la Tundra. Saroff, Phyllis, illus. 2016. (SPA.). 32p. (J). (gr. k-1). pap. 11.95 *(978-1-62855-881-4(4))*, 2725d00e-b868-4d78-a464-ad4a5ecafa4c) Arbordale Publishing.
Czajak, Paul. Monster Needs a Christmas Tree. Grieb, Wendy, illus. 2014. (Monster & Me Ser.). (ENG.). 32p. (J). (-k). 16.95 *(978-1-938063-46-6(5))*, Mighty Media Kids) Mighty Media Pr.
Debowski, Sharon. The Snowman, the Owl, & the Groundhog. 2007. (J). lib. bdg. 15.95 *(978-1-60227-468-6(1))*; (Illus.). 32p. (gr. -1-4). 14.95 *(978-1-60227-470-9(3))* Above the Clouds Publishing.
DePrisco, Dorothea. Mini Snowbears Winter Day. 2006. (ENG.). 10p. (J). 4.95 *(978-1-58117-506-6(X))*, Intervisual/Piggy Toes) Bendon, Inc.
Disney Books. Olaf's Frozen Adventure: Olaf's Journey: A Light-Up Board Book. 2017. (Light-Up Board Book Ser.). (ENG., Illus.). 10p. (J). (gr. -1-k). bds. 12.99 *(978-1-368-00674-3(4))*, Disney Press Books) Disney Publishing Worldwide.
Disney Editors. Anna's Act of Love. 2013. (Frozen 8X8 Ser.). (Illus.). (J). lib. bdg. 14.75 *(978-0-606-32204-1(3))* Turtleback.
Doyle, Brian. Spud in Winter, 1 vol. 2nd. ed. 2006. (ENG.). 176p. (J). (gr. 4-7). pap. 5.95 *(978-0-88899-755-5(8))* Groundwood Bks. CAN. Dist: Publishers Group West (PGW).
Doyle, Eugenie. Sleep Tight Farm: A Farm Prepares for Winter. Stadtlander, Becca, illus. 2016. (ENG.). 36p. (J). (gr. -1-k). 16.99 *(978-1-4521-2901-3(0))* Chronicle Bks. LLC.
Duncan Gurley, Ann. Esbe's Halo. 2009. 108p. (J). pap. 15.95 *(978-1-4327-3453-4(9))* Outskirts Pr., Inc.
Dunham, Wendy. Winter Snow Fun: God Gives Us Friends When We're Ready for Adventure. 2018. (Tales of Buttercup Grove Ser.). (ENG., Illus.). 64p. (J). (gr. -1-2). 12.99 *(978-0-7369-7207-9(2))*, 6972079) Harvest Hse. Pubs.
Dunn, Hunter S. A Winter's Dream. Ellis, Joey, illus. 2004. 65p. (J). 19.95 *(978-0-9761732-0-5(4))* Dunn, Hunter.
Dunshee, Gloria Fjare. Will & the Magic Snowman. 2010. 32p. pap. 11.95 *(978-0-9828231-1-8(8))* WillGo Pr.
Ford, J. Neil. The Doodle Bug Story. 2010. (ENG.). 32p. (YA). pap. 17.49 *(978-1-4535-3510-3(1))* Xlibris Corp.
Fordham, Walter. Ilian. Krizmanic, Tatjana, illus. 2012. 42p. pap. *(978-0-9813889-5-3(7))* Publish Yourself.
Frampton, Caytie. Bernard's Winter Nap. 2004. 21p. pap. 24.95 *(978-1-4137-3083-8(3))* PublishAmerica, Inc.
Fraser, Christine Marion. Rhanna. (ENG., Illus.). 320p. (J). (gr. k-6). pap. 11.95 *(978-0-340-76565-4(8))* Hodder & Stoughton GBR. Dist: Trafalgar Square Publishing.
Freedman, Claire. Little Bear's Special Friend. Kolanovic, Dubravka, illus. 2007. (J). *(978-0-545-06757-7(X))* Scholastic, Inc.
Freedman, Claire & Cabban, Vanessa. Gooseberry Goose. 2003. (Illus.). 32p. (J). (gr. -1-2). tchr. ed. 15.95 *(978-1-58925-030-7(3))* Tiger Tales.
Friedman, Becky. Daniel's Winter Adventure. Fruchter, Jason, illus. 2016. (Daniel Tiger's Neighborhood 8X8 Ser.). (ENG.). 24p. (J). (gr. -1-2). 13.55 *(978-0-606-39247-1(5))* Turtleback.
Galbraith, Kathryn O. Winter Babies. Pons, Adela, illus. 2018. (Babies in the Park Ser.). 20p. (J). (gr. -1 — 1). bds. 6.99 *(978-1-68263-067-9(6))* Peachtree Publishing Co. Inc.
Gavin, Ciara. Bear Is Not Tired. 2016. (Illus.). 32p. (J). (gr. -1-2). 16.99 *(978-0-385-75476-7(0))*, Knopf Bks. for Young Readers) Random Hse. Children's Bks.
George, Kallie. The Greatest Gift. Graegin, Stephanie, illus. 2017. (Heartwood Hotel Ser.: 2). (ENG.). 176p. (J). (gr. 2-5). 14.99 *(978-1-4847-3234-2(0))* Hyperion Bks. for Children.
—The Greatest Gift. 2017. (Heartwood Hotel Ser.: 2). (J). lib. bdg. 16.00 *(978-0-606-39967-8(4))* Turtleback.
Ghigna, Charles. I See Winter, 1 vol. Jatkowska, Agnieszka, illus. 2011. (I See Ser.). (ENG.). 24p. (J). (gr. -1 — 1). pap. 6.10 *(978-1-4048-6850-2(X))*, 116431, Picture Window Bks.) Capstone.
—Snow Wonder. Woolf, Julia, illus. 2008. (Step into Reading Ser.: Vol. 2). 24p. (J). (gr. -1-1). 4.99 *(978-0-375-85586-3(6))*, Random Hse. Bks. for Young Readers) Random Hse. Children's Bks.
Gladstone, James. My Winter City, 1 vol. Clement, Gary, illus. 2019. (ENG.). 32p. (J). (gr. k-2). 19.95 *(978-1-77306-010-1(4))* Groundwood Bks. CAN. Dist: Publishers Group West (PGW).
Grandma Sue. Bubba the Bear. 2010. 12p. pap. 8.49 *(978-1-4490-1813-9(0))* AuthorHouse.
Green, K. S. A Winter's Tail: Book Three of the Weasel Chronicles. 2005. (ENG.). 64p. pap. 22.99 *(978-1-59926-758-6(6))* Xlibris Corp.
Green, Poppy. Winter's No Time to Sleep! Bell, Jennifer A., illus. 2015. (Adventures of Sophie Mouse Ser.: 6). (ENG.). 128p. (J). (gr. k-4). pap. 6.99 *(978-1-4814-4199-5(X))*, Little Simon) Little Simon.
—Winter's No Time to Sleep! Bell, Jennifer A., illus. 2017. (Adventures of Sophie Mouse Ser.). (ENG.). 128p. (J). (gr. k-4). lib. bdg. 31.36 *(978-1-5321-4115-7(7))*, 26988, Chapter Bks.) Spotlight.
Hadcroft, Will. Anne Droyd & the Ghosts of Winter Hill. 2013. 210p. pap. *(978-0-9560537-2-5(6))* Nordic.
Hader, Berta and Elmer. The Big Snow & Other Stories: A Treasury of Caldecott Award Winning Tales. 2015. (ENG., Illus.). 160p. (J). (gr. 1-4). pap. 14.99 *(978-0-486-78163-1(1))*, 781631) Dover Pubns., Inc.
Hamilton, Pamela Greenhalgh. Snow Day. 2011. 34p. (J). pap. 18.95 *(978-1-4327-5743-4(1))* Outskirts Pr., Inc.
Hannan, Peter. The Greatest Snowman in the World! Hannan, Peter, illus. 2010. (ENG., Illus.). 32p. (J). (gr. -1-3). 16.99 *(978-0-06-128480-9(7))*, HarperCollins) HarperCollins Pubs.
Hartley Bellows, Carol. Icabog Bear. 2009. 24p. pap. 15.50 *(978-1-4389-3856-1(X))* AuthorHouse.
Hawley, Mabel C. Four Little Blossoms & Their Winter Fun. 2007. 96p. per. *(978-1-4068-1705-8(8))* Echo Library.
Hayes, Karel. The Winter Visitors. 2007. (ENG., Illus.). 32p. (J). (gr. -1-3). 17.95 *(978-0-89272-750-6(0))* Down East Bks.
Heinz, Brian J. A Coming of Winter in the Adirondacks. Healy, Maggie, illus. 2011. (ENG.). 32p. (J). 19.95 *(978-1-59531-038-5(X))* North Country Bks., Inc.
Henkes, Kevin. Winter Is Here. Dronzek, Laura, illus. 2018. (ENG.). 40p. (J). (gr. -1-3). 17.99 *(978-0-06-274718-1(5))*; lib. bdg. 18.89 *(978-0-06-274719-8(3))* HarperCollins Pubs. (Greenwillow Bks.).
Here Comes Winter! 2003. (J). per. *(978-1-57657-967-1(0))* Paradise Pr., Inc.
Herring, Bruce D. The Wizard of Wonderland, 1 vol. 2010. 192p. pap. 24.95 *(978-1-4489-5844-3(X))* America Star Bks.
Hest, Amy. You Can Do It, Sam. Jeram, Anita, illus. 2007. (Sam Bks.). (ENG.). 32p. (J). (gr. -1-k). pap. 6.99 *(978-0-7636-3688-3(6))* Candlewick Pr.
Hillert, Margaret. Feliz Navidad, Querido Dragón. Pullan, Jack, illus. 2017. (BeginningtoRead Ser.).Tr. of Merry Christmas, Dear Dragon. (ENG & SPA.). 32p. (J). (-2). 22.60 *(978-1-59953-838-9(5))* Norwood Hse. Pr.
—It's Winter, Dear Dragon. Schimmell, David, illus. 2009. (BeginningtoRead Ser.). 32p. (J). (gr. k-2). lib. bdg. 22.60 *(978-1-59953-314-8(6))* Norwood Hse. Pr.
—Merry Christmas, Dear Dragon. 2016. (BeginningtoRead Ser.). (ENG., Illus.). 32p. (J). (-2). lib. bdg. 22.60 *(978-1-59953-775-7(3))* Norwood Hse. Pr.
Homberg, Ruth. Tiana's Winter Treats (Disney Princess) Disney Storybook Art Team, Disney Storybook, illus. 2018. (Step into Reading Ser.). (ENG.). 24p. (J). (gr. -1-1). pap. 5.99 *(978-0-7364-3870-4(X))*, RH/Disney) Random Hse. Children's Bks.
Hudson, Katy. A Loud Winter's Nap. Hudson, Katy, illus. 2017. (ENG., Illus.). 32p. (J). (gr. -1-1). 15.95 *(978-1-62370-869-6(9))*, 135087, Capstone Young Readers) Capstone.
Huizenga, Nathaniel. Justice in Winter: Justice the Dog Series. 2009. 28p. pap. 13.99 *(978-1-4389-7361-6(6))* AuthorHouse.
Hunter, Erin. Warriors: the Broken Code #1: Lost Stars. (Warriors: the Broken Code Ser.: 1). (ENG.). (J). (gr. 3-7). 2020. 320p. pap. 7.99 *(978-0-06-282353-3(1))* 2019. (Illus.). 304p. 18.99 *(978-0-06-282351-9(5))* 2019. (Illus.). 304p. lib. bdg. 18.89 *(978-0-06-282352-6(3))* HarperCollins Pubs. (HarperCollins).
Hunter, Rhonda. Chinook & Winter, 1 vol. Lamontagne, Jayce, illus. 2017. (ENG.). 40p. (J). (gr. 2-4). pap. 10.95 *(978-1-926506-01-2(4))*, 33c8a013-2ae3-492b-874e-3f5d42bd7279) Pemmican Pubns., Inc. CAN. Dist: Firefly Bks., Ltd.
Hurley, Wes. How the Winter Frog Came to Was: Or, How to Get a Nice Surprise on Thanksgiving! Lee, Susan, illus. 2007. 36p. per. 24.95 *(978-1-4241-8395-1(2))* America Star Bks.
Jakobs, D. Holly, Jolly Harmony. 2013. (Passport to Reading Level 2 Ser.). (J). lib. bdg. 14.75 *(978-0-606-32276-8(0))* Turtleback.
Jakobs, D. & Williams, Merriwether. Holly, Jolly Harmony. 2017. (My Little Pony Leveled Readers Ser.). (ENG.). 32p. (J). (gr. -1-3). lib. bdg. 31.36 *(978-1-5321-4092-1(4))*, 26965) Spotlight.
Jansson, Tove. Moomin Winter. 2018. (Moomin Ser.). (ENG., Illus.). 60p. (J). pap. 9.95 *(978-1-77046-310-3(0))*, 900190487) Drawn & Quarterly Pubns. CAN. Dist: Macmillan.
—Moominland Midwinter. Warburton, Thomas, tr. Jansson, Tove, illus. 2010. (Moomins Ser.: 5). (ENG., Illus.). 160p. (J). (gr. 4-7). pap. 9.99 *(978-0-312-62541-2(3))*, 900066518) Square Fish.
—Moomin's Winter Follies. 2012. (Moomin Ser.). (ENG., Illus.). 48p. (J). (gr. 4-7). pap. 9.95 *(978-1-77046-098-0(5))*, 900087417) Drawn & Quarterly Pubns. CAN. Dist: Macmillan.
—Moominvalley in November. Hart, Kingsley, tr. Jansson, Tove, illus. 2010. (Moomins Ser.: 8). (ENG., Illus.). 208p. (J). (gr. 4-7). pap. 8.99 *(978-0-312-62544-3(8))*, 900066522) Square Fish.
Jeffries, Joyce. It's Winter, 1 vol. 2016. (Four Seasons Ser.). (ENG., Illus.). 24p. (gr. 1-1). pap. 9.25 *(978-1-5081-5191-3(1))*, 364db628-3177-4083-bec6-3aa2c311e6da, PowerKids Pr.) Rosen Publishing Group, Inc., The.
Jenkins, Emily. Lemonade in Winter: A Book about Two Kids Counting Money. Karas, G. Brian, illus. 2012. 40p. (J). (gr. -1-2). 18.99 *(978-0-375-85883-3(0))*, Schwartz & Wade Bks.) Random Hse. Children's Bks.
Jocelyn, Marthe. Ready for Winter. 2008. (Ready for Ser.). (Illus.). 16p. (J). (gr. -1-k). 7.99 *(978-0-88776-848-4(2))*, Tundra Bks.) Tundra Bks. CAN. Dist: Penguin Random Hse. LLC.
Johnson, Andi. Hailey Snowstorm. 2004. (Illus.). 16p. 9.00 *(978-1-84161-113-6(1))* Ravette Publishing, Ltd. GBR. Dist: Parkwest Pubns., Inc.
Johnson, Christine. Deep in Alaska. Johnson, Gary R., illus. 2013. (ENG.). 42p. pap. 13.95 *(978-1-60223-215-0(6))* Univ. of Alaska Pr.
Johnson, Crockett. Time for Spring. Johnson, Crockett, illus. 2016. (ENG., Illus.). 40p. (J). (gr. -1-3). 14.99 *(978-0-06-243033-5(5))*, HarperCollins) HarperCollins Pubs.
Jordan, Apple. Winter Wishes (Disney Princess) Marrucchi, Elisa, illus. 2006. (Step into Reading Ser.). (ENG.). 32p. (J). (gr. k-3). per. 5.99 *(978-0-7364-2409-7(1))*, RH/Disney) Random Hse. Children's Bks.
Joyce, William. Jack Frost. Joyce, William, illus. 2015. (Guardians of Childhood Ser.). (ENG., Illus.). 48p. (J). (gr. -1-3). 19.99 *(978-1-4424-3043-3(5))*, Atheneum Bks. for Young Readers) Simon & Schuster Children's Publishing.
Judge, Chris. The Snow Beast. Judge, Chris, illus. 2015. (ENG., Illus.). 32p. (J). (gr. -1-3). 17.99 *(978-1-4677-9313-1(2))*, a711d3a5-9c18-4a5e-a4f5-dd8ef98bb756) Lerner Publishing Group.
Katz, Karen. Baby Loves Winter! A Karen Katz Lift-The-Flap Book. Katz, Karen, illus. 2013. (ENG., Illus.). 14p. (J). (gr. -1 — 1). bds. 6.99 *(978-1-4424-5213-8(7))*, Little Simon) Little Simon.
Kelley, Marty, illus. Winter Woes. 2003. 32p. (J). 12.95 *(978-1-55933-306-1(5))* Zino Pr. Children's Bks.
Kemp, Michelle. Flutter by Butterfly. 2012. 28p. pap. 24.95 *(978-1-4626-6181-7(5))* America Star Bks.
Keyes, Diane. Spirit of the Snowpeople. Stevens, Helen, illus. 2008. (ENG.). 32p. (J). (gr. -1-3). 15.95 *(978-0-89272-710-0(1))* Down East Bks.
Kirby, Matthew J. Icefall. 2013. (ENG.). 336p. (J). (gr. 3-7). pap. 10.99 *(978-0-545-27425-8(7))*, Scholastic Paperbacks) Scholastic, Inc.
Knudsen, Michelle. Winter Is for Snowflakes. Denise & Fernando, illus. 2003. (Please Read to Me Ser.). (ENG.). 24p. (J). (gr. -1-1). 16.19 *(978-0-375-82215-5(1))* Random House Publishing Group.
Kohara, Kazuno. Here Comes Jack Frost. Kohara, Kazuno, illus. 2011. (ENG., Illus.). 32p. (J). (gr. -1-1). pap. 9.99 *(978-0-312-60446-2(7))*, 900076478) Square Fish.
Kratt, Chris & Kratt, Martin. Wild Winter Creatures! (Wild Kratts) Random House, illus. 2017. (Step into Reading Ser.). 32p. (J). (gr. -1-1). 4.99 *(978-1-101-93906-2(0))*, Random Hse. Bks. for Young Readers) Random Hse. Children's Bks.
Krensky, Stephen. Chaucer's First Winter. Cole, Henry, illus. (ENG.). 32p. (J). (gr. -1-1). 2010. 9.99 *(978-1-4424-1658-1(0))* 2009. 17.99 *(978-1-4169-9026-0(7))* Simon & Schuster Bks. For Young Readers. (Simon & Schuster Bks. For Young Readers).
Kroll, Linda. Winter, Awake!, 1 vol. Lieberherr, Ruth, illus. rev. ed. 2003. 32p. (J). pap. 11.95 *(978-0-88010-528-6(3))* SteinerBooks, Inc.
Lagonegro, Melissa. A Tale of Two Sisters (Disney Frozen) RH Disney, illus. 2013. (Step into Reading Ser.). (ENG.). 32p. (J). (gr. -1-1). 5.99 *(978-0-7364-3120-0(9))*, RH/Disney) Random Hse. Children's Bks.
Lamba, Marie. A Day So Gray. Marley, Alea, illus. 2019. (ENG.). 32p. (J). (gr. -1-3). 17.99 *(978-1-328-69599-4(9))*, 1671314, Clarion Bks.) HarperCollins Pubs.
Landis, Mary M. Winter Days with the Treelo Triplets. 2012. (Illus.). 218p. (J). *(978-0-7399-2447-1(8))* Rod & Staff Pubs., Inc.
Laughing Elephant Staff, ed. The Truth about Snow People. 2005. (Classic Children's Bks.). (ENG., Illus.). 32p. (J). (gr. -1-3). 17.95 *(978-1-59583-052-4(9))*, 9781595830524) Laughing Elephant.
Lester, James D. Corn Flower in Blowing Snow on the Great Plains: Third in a Fiction Series Based on the Four Seasons. 2019. (ENG., Illus.). 118p. (J). (gr. 8-12). pap. 16.95 *(978-1-63293-273-0(3))* Sunstone Pr.
Levine, Rhoda. Arthur. Aison, Everett, illus. 2015. 48p. (J). (gr. -1-2). 15.95 *(978-1-59017-935-2(8))*, NYR Children's Collection) New York Review of Bks., Inc., The.
London, Jonathan. Little Fox in the Snow. Miyares, Daniel, illus. 2018. (ENG.). 40p. (J). (gr. -1-3). 16.99 *(978-0-7636-8814-1(2))* Candlewick Pr.
Luciani, Brigitte. Peace & Quiet: Book 4, No. 4. Tharlet, Eve, illus. 2012. (Mr. Badger & Mrs. Fox Ser.: 4). (ENG.). 32p. (J). (gr. k-3). pap. 7.99 *(978-0-8225-9163-4(4))*, c88a3e3a-49bd-4fd8-af9b-b8ad48fd6eb9, Graphic Universe™) Lerner Publishing Group.
MacLean, Kerry Lee, creator. Pigs Ski over Colorado: The Top Ten Reasons Winter is the Piggies Favorite Season. 2005. (J). per. 15.95 *(978-0-9652998-7-9(2))* On the Spot! Bks.
Maclear, Kyo. The Wish Tree. Turnham, Chris, illus. 2016. (ENG.). 40p. (J). (gr. -1 — 1). 16.99 *(978-1-4521-5065-9(6))* Chronicle Bks. LLC.
Mapel, Tiffany. Bears Don't Ski. Harder, Miki, illus. 2018. (J). *(978-0-692-96831-4(8))* Rock Wren Pr.
Marie, Barbara. Snowy & Felix Find Christmas. 2009. 24p. pap. 11.49 *(978-1-4389-7392-0(6))* AuthorHouse.
Marino Walters, Jennifer. Wonderful Winter. Nez, John, illus. 2016. (Seasons Ser.). (ENG.). 24p. (J). (gr. -1 — 1). lib. bdg. 25.32 *(978-1-63440-046-6(1))*, 8ddc45ac-25da-4bdf-ab3f-80c90e8aad36, Rocking Chair Kids) Red Chair Pr.
Marshall, Natalie. Millie-Mae: In Winter. 2014. (Illus.). (J). *(978-1-4351-5613-5(7))* Barnes & Noble, Inc.
Mason, Jane B. & Stephens, Sarah Hines. Snowfall Surprise. 2009. (Candy Apple Ser.: 21). (ENG.). 144p. (J). (gr. 3-7). 5.99 *(978-0-545-10067-0(4))*, Scholastic Paperbacks) Scholastic, Inc.
Matthews, Caitlin & Barefoot Books. Fireside Stories: Tales for a Winter's Eve. Cann, Helen, illus. 2015. 96p. (J). (gr. 2-6). 19.99 *(978-1-78285-251-3(4))* Barefoot Bks., Inc.
Matthews, Caitlin, et al. Fireside Stories: Tales for a Winter's Eve. 2007. (ENG., Illus.). 96p. (J). (gr. -1-5). 19.99 *(978-1-84686-065-2(2))* Barefoot Bks., Inc.
McAllister, Angela. Brave Bitsy & the Bear. Beeke, Tiphanie, illus. 2006. (ENG.). 32p. (J). (gr. -1-3). 16.00 *(978-0-618-63994-6(2))*, 100459, Clarion Bks.) HarperCollins Pubs.
—Winter's Child. Baker-Smith, Grahame, illus. 2015. (ENG.). 40p. (J). (gr. -1-2). 16.99 *(978-0-7636-7964-4(X))*, Templar) Candlewick Pr.
McCollum, Kimberly. Gloves in a Hat. 2011. 16p. (gr. -1). pap. 8.32 *(978-1-4567-3430-5(X))* AuthorHouse.
McCracken, Harold. Pirate of the North. Tonk, Ernest, illus. 2011. 224p. 44.95 *(978-1-258-09631-1(5))* Literary Licensing, LLC.
McDonald, Megan. Ant & Honey Bee: a Pair of Friends in Winter. Karas, G. Brian, illus. (Candlewick Sparks Ser.). (ENG.). 64p. (J). (gr. k-4). 2014. pap. 4.99 *(978-0-7636-6862-4(1))* 2013. 14.99 *(978-0-7636-5712-3(3))* Candlewick Pr.

W X Y Z

McGregor, John. Daisy & Her Autumn & Winter Adventures. 2012. (Illus.). 77p. pap. 13.50 *(978-1-78035-482-8(7),* Fastprint Publishing) Upfront Publishing Ltd. GBR. Dist: Printondemand-worldwide.com.
Meadows, Daisy. Magic Animal Friends: Mia Floppyear's Snowy Adventure: Special 3. 2022. (Magic Animal Friends Ser.). (ENG., Illus.). 176p. (J). (gr. k-2). pap. 8.99 *(978-1-4083-3887-2(4),* Orchard Bks.) Hachette Children's Group GBR. Dist: Hachette Bk. Group.
Menear, Linda. The Little Groundhog Discovers the True Meaning of Christmas. 2011. 24p. pap. 24.95 *(978-1-4626-3288-6(2))* America Star Bks.
Meschenmoser, Sebastian. Waiting for Winter. 2015. (ENG., Illus.). 58p. (J). (gr. k-3). 10.99 *(978-1-61067-435-5(9))* Kane Miller.
Messner, Kate. Over & under the Snow. Neal, Christopher Silas, illus. 2014. (Over & Under Ser.). (ENG.). 44p. (J). (gr. -1-3). 8.99 *(978-1-4521-3646-2(7))* Chronicle Bks. LLC.
Miller, Pat Zietlow. Wide-Awake Bear. Kim, Jean, illus. 2018. (ENG.). 40p. (J). (gr. -1-3). 17.99 *(978-0-06-235603-1(8),* HarperCollins) HarperCollins Pubs.
Milligan, Bryce. Comanche Captive. 2005. (Illus.). 168p. (YA). (gr. 7). per. *(978-1-57168-849-1(8))* Eakin Pr.
Miska & the Long, Cold Winter. 2004. (Literacy Think-Togethers Ser.). 16-24p. (gr. 2-3). pap. 31.50 *(978-0-322-06357-0(4))* Wright Group/McGraw-Hill.
Mitton, Tony. Snowy Bear. Brown, Alison, illus. (ENG.). (J). 2016. 26p. bds. 7.99 *(978-1-68119-084-6(2),* 900158411) 2015. 32p. (gr. -1-1). 16.99 *(978-1-61963-905-8(X),* 900151395) Bloomsbury Publishing USA. (Bloomsbury USA Childrens).
Muench-Williams, Heather. A Cold Winter Day. Crowell, Knox, illus. l.t. ed. 2006. (HRL Board Book Ser.). (J). (gr. -1-k). pap. 10.95 *(978-1-57332-326-0(8),* HighReach Learning, Incorporated) Carson-Dellosa Publishing, LLC.
Muller, Marie. 'Twas the Night Before Winter. 2009. 24p. pap. 12.99 *(978-1-4389-6984-8(8))* AuthorHouse.
Nelson, Steve & Rollins, Jack. Frosty the Snowman. Williams, Sam, illus. 2013. (ENG.). 16p. (J). (gr. -1-k). bds. 9.99 *(978-0-545-45005-8(5),* Cartwheel Bks.) Scholastic, Inc.
Neubecker, Robert. Winter Is for Snow. 2020. (ENG., Illus.). 30p. (J). (gr. -1 — 1). bds. 7.99 *(978-1-368-04543-8(X))* Hyperion Bks. for Children.
Nicholas, Nicki. Peter & Lil on a Winter's Day. 2011. 24p. pap. *(978-1-4269-7316-1(0))* Trafford Publishing (UK) Ltd.
Nolan, Allia Zobel. God's Winter Wonderland. Mitchell, Melanie, illus. 2006. 10p. (J). bds. 8.99 *(978-0-8254-5526-1(X))* Kregel Pubns.
Nona Theresa Perez - Bayanin. Nadia Mei's First Winter in the Forest & Meeting with First Friends. 2012. 28p. pap. 21.99 *(978-1-4771-0596-2(4))* Xlibris Corp.
Nuzum, K. A. The Leanin' Dog. (ENG.). 256p. (J). (gr. 3-7). 2010. pap. 7.99 *(978-0-06-113936-9(X))* 2008. 15.99 *(978-0-06-113934-5(3))* HarperCollins Pubs. (HarperCollins).
Oceanak, Karla. Hotdogger. Spanjer, Kendra, illus. 2013. (Aldo Zelnick Comic Novel Ser.: 8). (ENG.). 160p. (J). (gr. 3-7). 12.95 *(978-1-934649-37-4(6))* Bailiwick Pr.
Off to School: Individual Title Six-Packs. (Story Steps Ser.). (gr. k-2). 29.00 *(978-0-7635-9577-7(2))* Rigby Education.
Ohanesian, Diane. Snuggle down Deep. Bornoff, Emily, illus. 2018. (ENG.). 32p. (J). (gr. -1-3). 16.99 *(978-1-4998-0651-9(5))* Little Bee Books Inc.
On a Cold, Cold Day: 6 Small Books. (gr. k-3). 24.00 *(978-0-7635-6231-1(9))* Rigby Education.
Orsi, Tea. Tinker Bell & the Secret of the Wings. 2014. (Disney Fairies Graphic Novels Ser.: 15). (J). lib. bdg. 18.40 *(978-0-606-35533-9(2))* Turtleback.
Osborne, M. D. The Rescue of Mr. Goldsmith. l.t. ed. 2005. (Illus.). 40p. (J). 12.95 *(978-0-9762852-1-2(5))* Wooden Shoe Pr.
Pak, Kenard. Goodbye Autumn, Hello Winter. Pak, Kenard, illus. 2017. (ENG., Illus.). 32p. (J). 18.99 *(978-1-62779-416-9(6),* 900149958, Holt, Henry & Co. Bks. For Young Readers) Holt, Henry & Co.
Palmer, Deokie Savie. My Little Baby Sister & I, on a Cold Winter Day. 2007. 38p. 17.95 *(978-1-4303-2061-6(3))* Lulu Pr., Inc.
Partridge, Helen L. Blinky: The Bear Who Wouldn't Hibernate. 2008. 32p. per. 24.95 *(978-1-4241-9261-8(7))* America Star Bks.
Paulsen, Gary. Brian's Winter. 2012. (Hatchet Adventure Ser.: 3). (ENG.). 176p. (YA). (gr. 5). pap. 10.99 *(978-0-307-92958-7(2),* Ember) Random Hse. Children's Bks.
—Brian's Winter. 2012. lib. bdg. 20.85 *(978-0-606-23879-3(4))* Turtleback.
Pendziwol, Jean E. Once upon a Northern Night, 1 vol. Arsenault, Isabelle, illus. 2013. (ENG.). 36p. (J). (gr. k-2). 17.95 *(978-1-55498-138-0(7))* Groundwood Bks. CAN. Dist: Publishers Group West (PGW).
Perkins, Lynne Rae. Wintercake: A Winter & Holiday Book for Kids. Perkins, Lynne Rae, illus. 2019. (ENG., Illus.). 48p. (J). (gr. 1-5). 17.99 *(978-0-06-289487-8(0),* Greenwillow Bks.) HarperCollins Pubs.
Petty, Dev. I Don't Want to Go to Sleep. Boldt, Mike, illus. 2018. 32p. (J). (gr. -1-2). 18.99 *(978-1-5247-6896-6(0),* Doubleday Bks. for Young Readers) Random Hse. Children's Bks.
Pratchett, Terry. Wintersmith. (YA). 2015. (Tiffany Aching Ser.: 3). (ENG.). 416p. (gr. 8). pap. 10.99 *(978-0-06-243528-6(0),* Clarion Bks.) 2007. (Tiffany Aching Ser.: 3). (ENG.). 464p. (gr. 8-12). per. 9.99 *(978-0-06-089033-9(9),* Clarion Bks.) 2006. (Discworld Novels Ser.). 323p. (gr. 7-12). 16.99 *(978-0-06-089031-5(2),* HarperTeen) 2006. (Discworld Novels Ser.). 323p. (gr. 7-12). lib. bdg. 17.89 *(978-0-06-089032-2(0),* HarperTeen) HarperCollins Pubs.
—Wintersmith. 2007. 450p. (gr. 7). 19.00 *(978-0-7569-8091-7(7))* Perfection Learning Corp.
Princess Rosa's Winter: Level M, 6 vols. 128p. (gr. 2-3). 49.95 *(978-0-7699-0986-8(8))* Shortland Pubns. (U. S. A.) Inc.
Rabe, Tish. Big Snowman, Little Snowman (Disney Frozen) RH Disney, illus. 2013. (Step into Reading Ser.). (ENG.). 32p. (J). (gr. -1-1). 5.99 *(978-0-7364-3119-4(5),* RH/Disney) Random Hse. Children's Bks.
Rey, H. A. Curious George a Winter's Nap: A Winter & Holiday Book for Kids. 2010. (Curious George TV Ser.). (ENG., Illus.). 24p. (J). (gr. -1-3). pap. 4.99 *(978-0-547-23590-5(9),* 1083308, Clarion Bks.) HarperCollins Pubs.
Rey, H. A. & Rey, Margret. Three Tales for a Winter's Night. 2012. (Curious George TV Tie-In 8x8 Ser.). lib. bdg. 18.40 *(978-0-606-26603-1(8))* Turtleback.
RH Disney. Anna's Act of Love/Elsa's Icy Magic (Disney Frozen), 2 bks. in 1. RH Disney, illus. 2013. (Pictureback(R) Ser.). (ENG., Illus.). 24p. (J). (gr. -1-2). 4.99 *(978-0-7364-3061-6(X),* RH/Disney) Random Hse. Children's Bks.
Rose, Andrea. A Home for Abby. 2011. 24p. pap. 12.79 *(978-1-4634-2121-2(4))* AuthorHouse.
Rose, Deborah Lee. The Twelve Days of Winter: A School Counting Book. Armstrong-Ellis, Carey F., illus. 2019. (ENG.). 32p. (J). (gr. -1-3). pap. 5.99 *(978-1-4197-3845-6(3),* 574803, Abrams Bks. for Young Readers) Abrams, Inc.
Rosen, Robert. Our Snowy Day. Curzon, Brett, illus. 2017. (Seasons Around Me Ser.). (ENG.). 24p. (gr. -1-2). pap. 9.95 *(978-1-68342-797-1(1),* 9781683427971) Rourke Educational Media.
Rudolph, Miriam. A Frozen Dream. 2009. 28p. pap. 12.00 *(978-1-60693-962-8(9),* Eloquent Bks.) Strategic Book Publishing & Rights Agency (SBPRA).
Russell-Gilmer, Phyllis A. Where Do Crickets Go When Winter Comes? Jones, Chamira, illus. 2009. 32p. (J). 16.95 *(978-1-934363-10-2(3))* Zoe Life Christian Communications.
Rylant, Cynthia. Annie & Snowball & the Wintry Freeze: Ready-To-Read Level 2. Stevenson, Suçie & Stevenson, Suçie, illus. (Annie & Snowball Ser.: 8). (ENG.). 40p. (J). (gr. k-2). 2011. pap. 4.99 *(978-1-4169-7206-8(4))* 2010. 17.99 *(978-1-4169-7205-1(6))* Simon Spotlight. (Simon Spotlight).
—Little Penguins. Robinson, Christian, illus. 2016. 40p. (J). (gr. -1-2). 18.99 *(978-0-553-50770-6(2),* Schwartz & Wade Bks.) Random Hse. Children's Bks.
—Mr. Putter & Tabby Hit the Slope. Howard, Arthur, illus. (Mr. Putter & Tabby Ser.). (ENG.). 40p. (J). (gr. 1-4). 2017. pap. 5.99 *(978-1-328-74060-1(3),* 1677037) 2016. 14.99 *(978-0-15-206427-3(3),* 1199224) HarperCollins Pubs. (Clarion Bks.).
—Poppleton in Winter. Teague, Mark, illus. 2008. 48p. (gr. -1-3). 14.00 *(978-0-7569-8910-1(8))* Perfection Learning Corp.
—Poppleton in Winter (Scholastic Reader, Level 3) Teague, Mark, illus. 2008. (Scholastic Reader, Level 3 Ser.). (ENG.). 48p. (J). (gr. -1-3). pap. 3.99 *(978-0-545-06823-9(1),* Cartwheel Bks.) Scholastic, Inc.
Sabuda, Robert, illus. Winter in White: Winter in White. 2007. (ENG.). 18p. (J). (gr. -1-3). 17.99 *(978-0-689-85365-4(3),* Little Simon) Little Simon.
Salmieri, Daniel. Bear & Wolf. 2018. (Illus.). 48p. (J). (gr. -1-3). 17.95 *(978-1-59270-238-1(4))* Enchanted Lion Bks., LLC.
Sams, Carl R. First Snow in the Woods. Stoick, Jean, photos by. 2007. (ENG., Illus.). 49p. (J). (gr. -1-3). 19.95 *(978-0-9770108-6-8(4))* Sams, II, Carl R. Photography, Inc.
Sams II, Carl R. A Magical Winter. 2016. (ENG., Illus.). (J). 19.95 *(978-0-9827625-8-5(5))* Sams, II, Carl R. Photography, Inc.
Sander, Sonia, adapted by. Dragon's Snowy Day. 2005. (Scholastic Reader Ser.). (Illus.). 32p. (J). pap. *(978-0-439-80163-8(X))* Scholastic, Inc.
Sapp, Karen. Rookie Preschool: Rookie Learn about Nauture: Who Is Sleeping? 2009. (Rookie Preschool-NEW Ser.). (ENG.). 24p. (J). pap. 6.95 *(978-0-531-24586-6(1));* (gr. -1). lib. bdg. 23.00 *(978-0-531-24411-1(3))* Scholastic Library Publishing. (Children's Pr.).
Sargent, Dave. Sammy's First Winter #10, 10 vols. 2007. (Little Stinker Ser.: 10). (J). lib. bdg. 23.60 *(978-1-59381-300-0(7))* Ozark Publishing.
—Sammy's First Winter #10 (PB), 10 vols. 2007. (Little Stinker Ser.: 10). (J). pap. 10.95 *(978-1-59381-301-7(5))* Ozark Publishing.
Scotton, Rob. Splat the Cat & the Snowy Day Surprise. 2014. (Splat the Cat Ser.). (ENG., Illus.). 16p. (J). (gr. -1-3). pap. 7.99 *(978-0-06-197864-7(7),* HarperFestival) HarperCollins Pubs.
Shaw, Gina. Waiting for Snow. Barton, Patrice, illus. 2010. 48p. (J). pap. *(978-0-545-24385-8(8))* Scholastic, Inc.
Sherman, Marcia A. The Splendid, Blended Family. 2007. 24p. 13.95 *(978-0-615-17159-3(1))* Pumpkin Seeds Pr.
Silvestro, Annie. Mice Skating. White, Teagan, illus. 2017. (Mice Skating Ser.: 1). 32p. (J). (gr. -1). 17.99 *(978-1-4549-1632-1(X))* Sterling Publishing Co., Inc.
Smith, John D. H. The Whale Whisperers, 1 vol. Smith, Anne, illus. 2009. 17p. pap. 24.95 *(978-1-60749-211-5(3))* America Star Bks.
Smith, Richard B. & Bernard, Felix. Walking in a Winter Wonderland. Hopgood, Tim, illus. 2016. (ENG.). 32p. (J). 18.99 *(978-1-62779-304-9(6),* 900146038, Holt, Henry & Co. Bks. For Young Readers) Holt, Henry & Co.
Snow Rabbit, Spring Rabbit: a Book of Changing Seasons. (ENG.). (J). (gr. -1 — 1). 2013. 24p. bds. 7.99 *(978-0-307-97790-8(0))* 2011. 32p. 16.99 *(978-0-375-86786-6(4))* Random Hse. Children's Bks. (Knopf Bks. for Young Readers).
Sommer, Cindy. Saving Kate's Flowers, 1 vol. Allen Klein, Laurie, illus. 2016. (ENG.). 32p. (J). (gr. k-3). 17.95 *(978-1-62855-870-8(9))* Arbordale Publishing.
Spinelli, Eileen. Now It Is Winter. DePalma, Mary Newell, illus. 2004. 32p. (J). 16.00 *(978-0-8028-5244-1(0))* Eerdmans, William B. Publishing Co.
Spurr, Elizabeth. In the Snow, 1 vol. Oliphant, Manelle, illus. 2017. (In the Weather Ser.). 22p. (J). (gr. -1 — 1). bds. 6.99 *(978-1-56145-855-4(4))* Peachtree Publishing Co. Inc.
Stones, Yvonne. Olivia's Magical Moment. 2010. 36p. pap. 16.99 *(978-1-4490-8045-7(6))* AuthorHouse.
Strange, Jason. Zombie Winter, 1 vol. Parks, Phil, illus. 2011. (Jason Strange Ser.). (ENG.). 72p. (J). (gr. 3-6). pap. 6.25 *(978-1-4342-3095-9(3),* 114735, Stone Arch Bks.) Capstone.
—Zombie Winter, 1 vol. Soleiman, Serg & Parks, Phil, illus. 2011. (Jason Strange Ser.). (ENG.). 72p. (J). (gr. 3-6). lib. bdg. 25.32 *(978-1-4342-2964-9(5),* 114197, Stone Arch Bks.) Capstone.
Stringer, Lauren. Winter Is the Warmest Season: A Winter & Holiday Book for Kids. Stringer, Lauren, illus. 2006. (ENG., Illus.). 40p. (J). (gr. -1-3). 18.99 *(978-0-15-204967-6(3),* 1194999, Clarion Bks.) HarperCollins Pubs.
Swenson, Jamie. Woof & Quack in Winter (Reader) A Winter & Holiday Book for Kids. Sias, Ryan, illus. 2017. (Green Light Readers Level 1 Ser.). (ENG.). 32p. (J). (gr. -1-3). pap. 4.99 *(978-0-544-95902-6(7),* 1661277, Clarion Bks.) HarperCollins Pubs.
Teckentrup, Britta. Sleep Tight Little Bear. 2014. (ENG., Illus.). 40p. (J). (gr. -1-2). 17.95 *(978-0-7358-4180-2(2))* North-South Bks., Inc.
Thomas Nelson Publishing Staff. Cozy, Snowy Cuddles Touch & Feel, 1 vol. 2018. (ENG., Illus.). 10p. (J). bds. 8.99 *(978-1-4002-0978-1(1),* Tommy Nelson) Nelson, Thomas Inc.
Thomas, Patricia. Red Sled. Demarest, Chris L., illus. 2013. (ENG.). 32p. (J). (gr. -1-k). pap. 6.95 *(978-1-62091-592-9(8),* Astra Young Readers) Astra Publishing Hse.
Thompson, Lauren. Mouse Loves Snow. 2018. (Ready-To-Read Ser.). (ENG.). 32p. (J). (gr. -1-1). 13.89 *(978-1-64310-618-2(X))* Penworthy Co., LLC, The.
—Mouse Loves Snow: Ready-To-Read Pre-Level 1. Erdogan, Buket, illus. 2017. (Mouse Ser.). (ENG.). 32p. (J). (gr. -1-k). 17.99 *(978-1-5344-0182-2(2));* pap. 4.99 *(978-1-5344-0181-5(4))* Simon Spotlight. (Simon Spotlight).
—Mouse's First Snow. Erdogan, Buket, illus. 2011. (Classic Board Bks.). (ENG.). 34p. (J). (gr. -1 — 1). bds. 7.99 *(978-1-4424-2651-1(9),* Little Simon) Little Simon.
Trimble, Irene. Winter Fun for Everyone! (Disney Princess) RH Disney, illus. 2015. (Pictureback(R) Ser.). (ENG.). 16p. (J). (gr. -1-2). 5.99 *(978-0-7364-3416-4(X),* RH/Disney) Random Hse. Children's Bks.
Urbanovic, Jackie. Duck at the Door: An Easter & Springtime Book for Kids. Urbanovic, Jackie, illus. 2011. (Max the Duck Ser.: 1). (ENG., Illus.). 32p. (J). (gr. -1-2). pap. 8.99 *(978-0-06-121440-0(X),* HarperCollins) HarperCollins Pubs.
Van Stockum, Hilda. A Day on Skates: The Story of a Dutch Picnic. Van Stockum, Hilda, illus. 2007. (Illus.). 40p. (J). (gr. 1). 19.95 *(978-1-932350-18-0(7))* Bethlehem Bks.
Vance, Colleen. The Flip Flop Family. Kinra, Richa, illus. 2013. (ENG.). (J). (gr. -1-3). 14.95 *(978-1-62086-275-9(1))* Amplify Publishing Group.
Vaughan, Garth. Tommy's New Block Skates PB, 1 vol. Smith, David Preston, illus. 2007. (ENG.). 36p. (J). (gr. 1-3). pap. 12.95 *(978-1-55109-620-9(X),* 1d8ca434-d869-49ba-aaa1-01edef613a79) Nimbus Publishing, Ltd. CAN. Dist: Baker & Taylor Publisher Services (BTPS).
Vogel, Vin. The Thing about Yetis. 2015. (Illus.). 32p. (J). (gr. -1-k). 16.99 *(978-0-8037-4170-6(7),* Dial Bks) Penguin Young Readers Group.
Waits, Kristine. Sweet Sam Shares. 2008. (ENG.). 36p. pap. 14.98 *(978-0-557-01679-2(7))* Lulu Pr., Inc.
Wilder, Laura Ingalls. The Long Winter: A Newbery Honor Award Winner. Williams, Garth, illus. 2008. (Little House Ser.: 6). (ENG.). 352p. (J). (gr. 3-7). pap. 9.99 *(978-0-06-440006-0(9),* HarperCollins) HarperCollins Pubs.
Willard, Nancy. A Starlit Snowfall. Pinkney, Jerry, illus. 2011. (ENG.). 32p. (J). (gr. -1-3). 6.99 *(978-0-316-18366-6(0))* Little, Brown Bks. for Young Readers.
Williamson, Greg. How Do I Cure This Cold? Popko, Wendy, illus. 2005. (J). 7.99 *(978-0-9666076-4-2(3))* Peerless Publishing, L.L.C.
Wilson, CeCe. Snow: Snow Much Fun!, 1 vol. 2015. (Rosen REAL Readers: STEM & STEAM Collection). (ENG.). 8p. (gr. k-1). pap. 5.46 *(978-1-4994-9551-5(X),* bad94dab-5784-49d5-9552-b7bd9f1609dc, Rosen Classroom) Rosen Publishing Group, Inc., The.
Wingart, Ramona A. Where Is Brother Beaver?, 1 vol. 2010. 30p. 24.95 *(978-1-4489-4773-7(1))* PublishAmerica, Inc.
Winter Beauty. 2005. (J). 8.00 *(978-0-9769843-0-6(X))* Simmons, Kristina.
Wolff, Ashley. Baby Bear Counts One. Wolff, Ashley, illus. 2013. (Baby Bear Ser.). (ENG., Illus.). 40p. (J). (gr. -1-1). 19.99 *(978-1-4424-4158-3(5),* Beach Lane Bks.) Beach Lane Bks.
Woods, Emily. Thingamafig B Quaxindehouse: Best Friends. 2011. 24p. pap. 12.99 *(978-1-4634-4853-0(8))* AuthorHouse.
Worcester, Daryl D. Traves Travislot's Going South for the Winter. 2011. 46p. pap. 16.95 *(978-1-4626-1091-4(9))* America Star Bks.
Wright, Maureen. Sleep, Big Bear, Sleep!, 0 vols. Hillenbrand, Will, illus. 2012. (ENG.). 32p. (J). (gr. -1-2). 16.99 *(978-0-7614-5560-8(4),* 9780761455608, Two Lions) Amazon Publishing.
Yeoman, John. The Bear's Winter House. Blake, Quentin, illus. 2010. (ENG.). 32p. (J). (gr. k-k). pap. 12.99 *(978-1-84270-916-0(X))* Andersen Pr. GBR. Dist: Independent Pubs. Group.
Yeomans, Ellen. Some Snow Is... Offermann, Andrea, illus. 2019. 32p. (J). (gr. -1-3). 17.99 *(978-0-399-54754-6(1),* G.P. Putnam's Sons Books for Young Readers) Penguin Young Readers Group.
Yolen, Jane & Stemple, Heidi E. Y. Sleep, Black Bear, Sleep. Dyer, Brooke, illus. 2007. 32p. (J). (gr. -1-1). (ENG.). 15.99 *(978-0-06-081560-8(4),* HarperCollins); lib. bdg. 16.89 *(978-0-06-081561-5(2))* HarperCollins Pubs.

WINTER—POETRY

Hines, Anna Grossnickle. Winter Lights: A Season in Poems & Quilts. Hines, Anna Grossnickle, illus. 2005. (Illus.). 32p. (J). lib. bdg. 17.89 *(978-0-06-000818-5(0))* HarperCollins Pubs.
Prelutsky, Jack. It's Snowing! It's Snowing! Abolafia, Yossi, illus. 2007. (I Can Read Bks.). 48p. (gr. -1-3). 14.00 *(978-0-7569-8057-3(7))* Perfection Learning Corp.
Whipple, Laura. A Snowflake Fell: Poems about Winter. Hori, Hatsuki, illus. 2003. 40p. (J). 16.99 *(978-1-84148-033-6(9))* Barefoot Bks., Inc.

WINTER SPORTS

see also Hockey; Skating; Skis and Skiing

Abdo, Kenny. Snocross. 2017. (Action Sports (Fly!) Ser.). (ENG., Illus.). 24p. (J). (gr. 2-8). lib. bdg. 31.36 *(978-1-5321-2095-4(8),* 26778, Abdo Zoom-Fly) ABDO Publishing Co.
Adams, C. On My Sled: Learning the SL Sound. 2009. (PowerPhonics Ser.). 24p. (gr. 1-1). 39.90 *(978-1-60851-465-6(X),* PowerKids Pr.) Rosen Publishing Group, Inc., The.
Bix, Jasper. Let's Go Sledding!, 1 vol. 2015. (Winter Fun Ser.). (ENG., Illus.). 24p. (J). (gr. k-k). pap. 9.15 *(978-1-4824-3759-1(7),* e48972ac-4769-4352-bdb9-31d3ae094663) Stevens, Gareth Publishing LLLP.
Butler, Erin K. Extreme Snow & Ice Sports. 2017. (Sports to the Extreme Ser.). (ENG., Illus.). 32p. (J). (gr. 3-9). lib. bdg. 28.65 *(978-1-5157-7859-2(2),* 135994, Capstone Pr.) Capstone.
Gagliardi, Sue. Get Outside in Winter. 2019. (Get Outside Ser.). (ENG., Illus.). 32p. (J). (gr. 2-3). pap. 9.95 *(978-1-64185-392-7(1),* 1641853921); lib. bdg. 31.35 *(978-1-64185-334-7(4),* 1641853344) North Star Editions. (Focus Readers).
Hedlund, Stephanie F. Snowboarding. 2003. (X-Treme Sports Ser.). 32p. (J). (gr. k-6). 27.07 *(978-1-57765-929-7(5),* Checkerboard Library) ABDO Publishing Co.
Johnson, Robin. Bobsleigh, Luge, & Skeleton. 2009. (Winter Olympic Sports Ser.). (ENG., Illus.). 32p. (J). (gr. 3-6). lib. bdg. *(978-0-7787-4024-7(2));* (gr. 4-6). pap. *(978-0-7787-4043-8(9))* Crabtree Publishing Co.
—Ice Hockey & Curling. 2009. (Winter Olympic Sports Ser.). (ENG., Illus.). 32p. (J). (gr. 3-6). lib. bdg. *(978-0-7787-4023-0(4))* Crabtree Publishing Co.
Labrecque, Ellen. Nordic Skiing. 2018. (21st Century Skills Library: Global Citizens: Olympic Sports Ser.). (ENG.). 32p. (J). (gr. 4-7). pap. 14.21 *(978-1-5341-0850-9(5),* 210764); (Illus.). lib. bdg. 32.07 *(978-1-5341-0751-9(7),* 210763) Cherry Lake Publishing.
Luke, Andrew. Snow Sports. 2017. 48p. (J). *(978-1-4222-3708-3(7))* Mason Crest.
Marsh, Carole. I'm Reading about the Iditarod. 2016. (I'm Reading About Ser.). (ENG., Illus.). (J). pap. 7.99 *(978-0-635-12204-9(9))* Gallopade International.
McClellan, Ray. Snocross. 2008. (Action Sports Ser.). (ENG., Illus.). 24p. (J). (gr. 3-7). lib. bdg. 26.95 *(978-1-60014-143-0(9))* Bellwether Media.
McKinney, John & Bailey, Diane. Snow Sports, Vol. 10. 2016. (Great Outdoors! Ser.). (Illus.). 48p. (J). (gr. 5). 20.95 *(978-1-4222-3573-7(4))* Mason Crest.
McNeil, Niki, et al. HOCPP 1143 Winter Sports. 2007. spiral bd. 14.00 *(978-1-60308-143-6(7))* In the Hands of a Child.
Rajczak, Kristen. Racing the Iditarod. 2014. (Illus.). 32p. (J). *(978-1-4824-3292-3(7),* 1368191) Stevens, Gareth Publishing LLLP.
Rigby Education Staff. Gliders & Sliders. (Sails Literacy Ser.). (Illus.). 16p. (gr. 1-2). 27.00 *(978-0-7635-9922-5(0),* 699220C99) Rigby Education.
Sticker Winter Sports. 2017. (Sticker Dressing Ser.). (ENG.). (J). pap. 9.99 *(978-0-7945-3937-5(8),* Usborne) EDC Publishing.
Tomljanovic, Tatiana. Skiing. 2020. (J). *(978-1-7911-1840-2(2),* AV2 by Weigl) Weigl Pubs., Inc.
Waxman, Laura Hamilton. Bobsled & Luge. 2017. (Winter Olympic Sports Ser.). (ENG.). 32p. (J). (gr. 2-5). 20.95 *(978-1-68151-150-4(9),* 14691) Amicus.
—Figure Skating. 2017. (Winter Olympic Sports Ser.). (ENG.). 32p. (J). (gr. 2-5). 20.95 *(978-1-68151-148-1(7),* 14692) Amicus.
—Ice Hockey & Curling. 2017. (Winter Olympic Sports Ser.). (ENG., Illus.). 32p. (J). (gr. 2-5). 20.95 *(978-1-68151-149-8(5),* 14693) Amicus.
—Winter Olympic Sports: Bobsled & Luge. 2017. (Winter Olympic Sports Ser.). (ENG.). 32p. (J). (gr. 2-5). pap. 9.99 *(978-1-68152-181-7(4),* 14810) Amicus.
—Winter Olympic Sports: Ice Hockey & Curling. 2017. (Winter Olympic Sports Ser.). (ENG., Illus.). 32p. (J). (gr. 2-5). pap. 9.99 *(978-1-68152-180-0(6),* 14812) Amicus.
Whitelaw, Ian. DK Readers L4: Snow Dogs! Racers of the North. 2008. (DK Readers Level 4 Ser.). (ENG.). 48p. (J). (gr. 3-7). 4.99 *(978-0-7566-4081-1(4),* DK Children) Dorling Kindersley Publishing, Inc.
—Snow Dogs! Racers of the North. 2008. (DK Readers Level 4 Ser.). (ENG.). 48p. (J). (gr. 2-4). 16.19 *(978-0-7566-4082-8(2))* Dorling Kindersley Publishing, Inc.

WINTER SPORTS—FICTION

Blake, Robert J. Akiak: A Tale from the Iditarod. Blake, Robert J., illus. 2004. (Illus.). 40p. (J). (gr. k-3). reprint ed. pap. 7.99 *(978-0-14-240185-9(4),* Puffin Books) Penguin Young Readers Group.
Bowes, Lisa. Lucy Tries Luge, 1 vol. Hearne, James, illus. 2015. (Lucy Tries Sports Ser.: 1). (ENG.). 32p. (J). (gr. 1-3). pap. 12.95 *(978-1-4598-1019-8(8))* Orca Bk. Pubs. USA.
Brown, Jeff. Flat Stanley's Worldwide Adventures #4: the Intrepid Canadian Expedition. Pamintuan, Macky, illus. 2009. (Flat Stanley's Worldwide Adventures Ser.: 4). (ENG.). 112p. (J). (gr. 2-5). 15.99 *(978-0-06-142997-2(X),* HarperCollins) HarperCollins Pubs.
—Flat Stanley's Worldwide Adventures #4: the Intrepid Canadian Expedition Vol. 4. Pamintuan, Macky, illus. 2009. (Flat Stanley's Worldwide Adventures Ser.: 4). (ENG.). 112p. (J). (gr. 2-5). pap. 4.99 *(978-0-06-142996-5(1),* HarperCollins) HarperCollins Pubs.
Bunting, Eve. Snowboarding on Monster Mountain. Ritz, Karen, illus. 2003. (ENG.). 64p. (J). 15.95 *(978-0-8126-2704-6(0))* Cricket Bks.
Christopher, Matt. Snowboard Champ. 2004. (ENG.). 160p. (J). (gr. 3-7). pap. 10.99 *(978-0-316-79643-9(3))* Little, Brown Bks. for Young Readers.
Fames, Catherine. Snowblind. 2004. 108p. (J). *(978-1-59166-329-4(6))* BJU Pr.
Ferguson, Donald. The Chums of Scranton High at Ice Hockey. 2007. 124p. per. *(978-1-4065-2361-4(5))* Dodo Pr.
—Chums of Scranton High at Ice Hockey. 2006. 25.95 *(978-1-4218-2936-4(3));* pap. 10.95 *(978-1-4218-3036-0(1))* 1st World Publishing, Inc.
Gürth, Per-Henrik & Gürth, Per-Henrik. Snowy Sports: Ready, Set, Play! Gürth, Per-Henrik & Gürth, Per-Henrik, illus. 2009. (ENG., Illus.). 24p. (J). (gr. -1-2). 14.95 *(978-1-55337-367-4(7))* Kids Can Pr., Ltd. CAN. Dist: Hachette Bk. Group.
Kiefer, Kit. Jake the Grizz & the World's Fastest Snowboard. 2010. (ENG.). (J). pap. *(978-0-9774802-9-6(1))* Cornerstone Pr.
Klein, Abby. Ready, Set, Snow! (Ready, Freddy! #16), Vol. 16. McKinley, John, illus. 2009. (Ready, Freddy! Ser.: 16). (ENG.). 96p. (J). (gr. -1-3). pap. 5.99 *(978-0-439-89596-5(0))* Scholastic, Inc.
Krensky, Stephen. The Three Little Pigs' Sledding Adventure. Shortley, Michele, illus. 2011. 28p. (J). pap. *(978-0-7680-3486-8(8))* SAE Intl.

ster, Helen. Tacky & the Winter Games: A Winter & Holiday Book for Kids. Munsinger, Lynn, illus. 2007. (Tacky the Penguin Ser.). (ENG.). 32p. (J). (gr. -1-3). 7.99 *(978-0-618-95674-6(3),* 1021437, Clarion Bks.) HarperCollins Pubs.

addox, Jake. Half-Pipe Prize, 1 vol. Mourning, Tuesday, illus. 2009. (Jake Maddox Girl Sports Stories Ser.). (ENG.). 72p. (J). (gr. 3-6). 25.32 *(978-1-4342-1607-6(1),* 95781, Stone Arch Bks.) Capstone.

itchey, Kate. Goofy's Sledding Contest. 2013. (Mickey & Friends World of Reading Ser.). (J). lib. bdg. 13.55 *(978-0-606-32293-5(0))* Turtleback.

haw, Gina. Waiting for Snow. Barton, Patrice, illus. 2010. 48p. (J). pap. *(978-0-545-24385-8(8))* Scholastic, Inc.

tilton, Thea. Thea Stilton Mouseford Academy #10: A Dream on Ice. 2016. (Illus.). 128p. (J). *(978-0-545-91797-1(2))* Scholastic, Inc.

WIRE

wanson, Jennifer. The Shocking Truth about Electricity. Lum, Bernice, illus. 2012. (LOL Physical Science Ser.). (ENG.). 32p. (J). (gr. 3-4). pap. 49.60 *(978-1-4296-9301-1(0),* 18532, Capstone Pr.) Capstone.

WISCONSIN

Apps, Jerry. Tents, Tigers & the Ringling Brothers. 2006. (Badger Biographies Ser.). (ENG., Illus.). 128p. (J). (gr. 3-7). per. 12.95 *(978-0-87020-374-9(6))* Wisconsin Historical Society.

Blashfield, Jean F. America the Beautiful, Third Series: Wisconsin (Revised Edition) 2014. (America the Beautiful Ser.: 3). (ENG.). 144p. (J). lib. bdg. 40.00 *(978-0-531-24874-4(7))* Scholastic Library Publishing.

Bratvold, Gretchen. Wisconsin. 2012. (J). lib. bdg. 25.26 *(978-0-7613-4518-3(3),* Lerner Pubns.) Lerner Publishing Group.

Cohen, Sheila & Terman Cohen, Sheila. Mai Ya's Long Journey. 2005. (Badger Biographies Ser.). (ENG., Illus.). 96p. (J). (gr. 3-7). per. 12.95 *(978-0-87020-365-7(7))* Wisconsin Historical Society.

Dornfeld, Margaret. Wisconsin, 1 vol. Santoro, Christopher, illus. 2003. (It's My State! (First Edition)(r) Ser.). (ENG.). 80p. (gr. 4-4). 34.07 *(978-0-7614-1524-4(6),* f9d66cfe-d513-4613-9fb0-d664ead6b666) Cavendish Square Publishing LLC.

Flatt, Lizann. Life in a Farming Community, 1 vol. 2009. (Learn about Rural Life Ser.). (ENG., Illus.). 32p. (J). (gr. 3-4). pap. *(978-0-7787-5084-0(1))* Crabtree Publishing Co.

Franchino, Vicky. Wisconsin (a True Book: My United States) (Library Edition) 2018. (True Book (Relaunch) Ser.). (ENG., Illus.). 48p. (J). (gr. 3-5). 31.00 *(978-0-531-23173-9(9),* Children's Pr.) Scholastic Library Publishing.

Gamble, Adam & Jasper, Mark. Count to Sleep Wisconsin. Veno, Joe, illus. 2014. (Count to Sleep Ser.). (ENG.). 20p. (J). (— 1). bds. 9.95 *(978-1-60219-328-4(2))* Good Night Bks.

Hantula, Richard & Dornfeld, Margaret. Wisconsin, 1 vol. 3rd rev. ed. 2014. (It's My State! (Third Edition)(r) Ser.). (ENG.). 80p. (gr. 4-4). lib. bdg. 35.93 *(978-1-62712-760-8(7),* 7601e24f-64cb-4103-ae34-d403faf558a8) Cavendish Square Publishing LLC.

Jacobson, Bob. Ole Evinrude & His Outboard Motor. 2009. (Badger Biographies Ser.). (ENG., Illus.). 78p. (J). (gr. 3-7). pap. 12.95 *(978-0-87020-420-3(3))* Wisconsin Historical Society.

Lantier, Pat. Wisconsin, 1 vol. 2005. (Portraits of the States Ser.). (ENG., Illus.). 32p. (gr. 3-5). pap. 11.50 *(978-0-8368-4657-7(5),* a60083c9-8e6b-48f0-96bf-49e6e0bd1f47); lib. bdg. 28.67 *(978-0-8368-4638-6(9),* ce6d5971-c2a2-48e4-b215-20940949c38d) Stevens, Gareth Publishing LLLP. (Gareth Stevens Learning Library).

Malone, Bobbie & Rosebrough, Amy. Water Panthers, Bears, & Thunderbirds: Exploring Wisconsin's Effigy Mounds. 2003. (ENG., Illus.). 48p. (J). (gr. 4-7). pap. 12.95 *(978-0-87020-357-2(6))* Wisconsin Historical Society.

Malone, Bobbie, et al. Wisconsin: Our State, Our Story. 2016. (Illus.). x, 252p. (J). *(978-0-87020-796-9(2))* Wisconsin Historical Society.

Marsh, Carole. My First Book about Wisconsin. 2004. (Wisconsin Experience! Ser.). (Illus.). 32p. (J). (gr. k-4). pap. 7.95 *(978-0-7933-9539-2(9))* Gallopade International.

—Wisconsin Current Events Projects: 30 Cool, Activities, Crafts, Experiments & More for Kids to Do to Learn about Your State! 2003. (Wisconsin Experience Ser.). 32p. (gr. k-8). pap. 5.95 *(978-0-635-02068-0(8),* Marsh, Carole Bks.) Gallopade International.

—The Wisconsin Experience Pocket Guide. 2004. (Wisconsin Experience! Ser.). (Illus.). 96p. (J). (gr. 3-8). pap. 6.95 *(978-0-7933-9538-5(0))* Gallopade International.

—Wisconsin Geography Projects: 30 Cool, Activities, Crafts, Experiments & More for Kids to Do to Learn about Your State! 2003. (Wisconsin Experience Ser.). 32p. (gr. k-5). pap. 5.95 *(978-0-635-01867-0(5),* Marsh, Carole Bks.) Gallopade International.

—Wisconsin Government Projects: 30 Cool, Activities, Crafts, Experiments & More for Kids to Do to Learn about Your State! 2003. (Wisconsin Experience Ser.). 32p. (gr. k-5). pap. 5.95 *(978-0-635-01968-4(X),* Marsh, Carole Bks.) Gallopade International.

—Wisconsin Jeopardy! Answers & Questions about Our State! 2004. (Wisconsin Experience! Ser.). (Illus.). 32p. (J). (gr. 3-8). pap. 7.95 *(978-0-7933-9540-8(2))* Gallopade International.

—Wisconsin "Jography" A Fun Run Thru Our State! 2004. (Wisconsin Experience! Ser.). (Illus.). 32p. (J). (gr. 3-8). pap. 7.95 *(978-0-7933-9541-5(0))* Gallopade International.

—Wisconsin People Projects: 30 Cool, Activities, Crafts, Experiments & More for Kids to Do to Learn about Your State! 2003. (Wisconsin Experience Ser.). 32p. (gr. k-5). pap. 5.95 *(978-0-635-02018-5(1),* Marsh, Carole Bks.) Gallopade International.

—Wisconsin Symbols & Facts Projects: 30 Cool, Activities, Crafts, Experiments & More for Kids to Do to Learn about Your State! 2003. (Wisconsin Experience Ser.). 32p. (gr. k-5). pap. 5.95 *(978-0-635-01918-9(3),* Marsh, Carole Bks.) Gallopade International.

—Wisconsin's Big Activity Book. 2004. (Wisconsin Experience! Ser.). (Illus.). 96p. (J). (gr. 2-6). pap. 9.95 *(978-0-7933-9542-2(9))* Gallopade International.

—The Wonderful Wisconsin Coloring Book. 2004. (Wisconsin Experience! Ser.). (Illus.). 32p. (J). (gr. k-2). pap. 3.95 *(978-0-7933-9543-9(7))* Gallopade International.

Micklos, John, Jr., et al. Wisconsin: The Badger State, 1 vol. 2018. (It's My State! (Fourth Edition)(r) Ser.). (ENG.). 80p. (J). (gr. 4-4). pap. 18.64 *(978-1-5026-4446-6(0),* a2402df7-633f-4847-a312-abb55dcfa5d1) Cavendish Square Publishing LLC.

Micklos, John, et al. Wisconsin: The Badger State, 1 vol. 2018. (It's My State! (Fourth Edition)(r) Ser.). (ENG.). 80p. (J). (gr. 4-4). 35.93 *(978-1-5026-2628-8(4),* a99f6bda-50b8-42ef-bd7c-80d90f875530) Cavendish Square Publishing LLC.

Murray, Julie. Wisconsin, 1 vol. 2006. (Buddy Book Ser.). (ENG., Illus.). 32p. (gr. 2-4). 27.07 *(978-1-59197-708-7(8),* Buddy Bks.) ABDO Publishing Co.

Obregón, José María. Wisconsin. 2009. (Bilingual Library of the United States of America Ser.). (SPA.). 32p. (gr. 2-2). 47.90 *(978-1-60853-393-0(X),* Editorial Buenas Letras) Rosen Publishing Group, Inc., The.

Parker, Bridget. Wisconsin. 2016. (States Ser.). (ENG., Illus.). 32p. (J). (gr. 3-6). lib. bdg. 27.99 *(978-1-5157-0438-6(6),* 132049, Capstone Pr.) Capstone.

Peters, S. True. How to Draw Wisconsin's Sights & Symbols. 2009. (Kid's Guide to Drawing America Ser.). 32p. (gr. k-k). 50.50 *(978-1-61511-105-3(0),* PowerKids Pr.) Rosen Publishing Group, Inc., The.

Rechner, Amy. Wisconsin. 2013. (Exploring the States Ser.). (ENG., Illus.). 32p. (J). (gr. 3-7). lib. bdg. 27.95 *(978-1-62617-050-6(9),* Blastoff! Readers) Bellwether Media.

Trumbauer, Lisa. Rookie Read-About Geography: Wisconsin. 2003. (Rookie Read-About Geography Ser.). (ENG., Illus.). 32p. (J). 20.50 *(978-0-516-22745-0(9),* Children's Pr.) Scholastic Library Publishing.

Wargin, Kathy-jo. B Is for Badger: A Wisconsin Alphabet. Graef, Renée, illus. 2004. (Discover America State by State Ser.). (ENG.). 40p. (J). (gr. 1-3). 18.99 *(978-1-58536-135-9(6),* 201997) Sleeping Bear Pr.

Wittekind, Erika. What's Great about Wisconsin? 2014. (Our Great States Ser.). (ENG., Illus.). 32p. (J). (gr. 2-5). lib. bdg. 26.65 *(978-1-4677-3390-8(3),* f3a6b7fb-be01-4421-8cc2-d9b29f7800da, Lerner Pubns.) Lerner Publishing Group.

Zeinert, Karen & Hart, Joyce. Wisconsin, 1 vol. 2nd rev. ed. 2007. (Celebrate the States (Second Edition) Ser.). (ENG., Illus.). 144p. (gr. 6-6). lib. bdg. 39.79 *(978-0-7614-2157-3(2),* 017a0ad0-b23c-42a0-980e-f8c756700f3d) Cavendish Square Publishing LLC.

WISCONSIN—FICTION

Addy, Sharon. In Grandpa's Woods. Akins, Tamlyn, illus. 2004. (J). *(978-1-931599-42-9(4),* Trails Bks.) Bower Hse.

Alger, Horatio. Strive & Succeed. 2007. 172p. 24.95 *(978-1-4344-8359-1(2));* per. 14.95 *(978-1-4344-8358-4(4))* Wildside Pr., LLC.

Anderson, Jodi Lynn. The Vanishing Season. (ENG.). (YA). (gr. 9). 2019. 288p. pap. 9.99 *(978-0-06-288337-7(2))* 2014. 272p. 17.99 *(978-0-06-200327-0(5))* HarperCollins Pubs. (HarperCollins).

Aryal, Aimee. Go, Pack, Go! De Angel, Miguel, illus. 2007. 24p. (J). (gr. -1-3). 14.95 *(978-1-932888-94-2(2))* Amplify Publishing Group.

Atkinson, Elizabeth. I, Emma Freke. 2012. (ENG.). 240p. (J). (gr. 4-7). 10.99 *(978-0-7613-8500-4(2),* 4c09ccbf-9456-48aa-8415-47bb3cfd891b, Carolrhoda Bks.) Lerner Publishing Group.

Baker, Amanda, illus. The Cheesehead Night Before Christmas. 2007. 40p. (J). per. 19.95 *(978-0-9797781-0-0(7))* Dreams 2 Wings LLC.

Berenato, Dave. Medlocks: The Peractio Blackout. 2011. 284p. (gr. 10-12). 27.95 *(978-1-4620-5219-6(3));* pap. 17.95 *(978-1-4620-5217-2(7))* iUniverse, Inc.

Bick, Ilsa J. Draw the Dark. (ENG.). 344p. (YA). (gr. 9-12). 2011. pap. 9.95 *(978-0-7613-8131-0(7),* 308f22d6-6abe-45af-b28c-b962f2cb5485) 2010. 16.95 *(978-0-7613-5686-8(X))* Lerner Publishing Group. (Carolrhoda Lab™).

—The Sin-Eater's Confession. 2014. (ENG., Illus.). 296p. (YA). (gr. 9-12). pap. 9.95 *(978-1-4677-3705-0(4),* d1d2a2d6-a315-4ec1-843c-4b7c1da54080, Carolrhoda Lab™) Lerner Publishing Group.

Birdsall, Bridget. Double Exposure. 2014. (ENG.). 304p. (J). (gr. 6-6). 16.95 *(978-1-62914-606-5(4),* Sky Pony Pr.) Skyhorse Publishing Co., Inc.

Bjornson, Nancy. Sleds, Skins & Snow. 2007. (J). *(978-1-930596-83-2(9))* Amherst Pr.

Brink, Carol Ryrie. Caddie Woodlawn. 2006. (ENG., Illus.). 288p. (J). (gr. 3-7). pap. 7.99 *(978-1-4169-4028-9(6),* Aladdin) Simon & Schuster Children's Publishing.

Brookins, Cara. Doris Free. Barrow, Ann, illus. 2006. 127p. (J). pap. *(978-1-59336-333-8(8))* Mondo Publishing.

Busteed, Kerri J. Will's Bow Hunting Adventure. Byers, Leon, illus. 2012. 108p. pap. 30.00 *(978-1-61897-207-1(3),* Strategic Bk. Publishing) Strategic Book Publishing & Rights Agency (SBPRA).

Cameron, Ann. The Secret Life of Amanda K. Woods. 2014. (ENG.). 208p. (J). (gr. 5-9). pap. 14.99 *(978-1-250-04419-8(7),* 900128307) Square Fish.

Carlson, Sarah. Everything's Not Fine. 2020. 304p. (YA). (ENG.). 31.99 *(978-1-68442-411-5(9));* pap. 17.99 *(978-1-68442-410-8(0))* Turner Publishing Co.

Carter, Alden R. Walkaway. 2008. (ENG.). 192p. (YA). (gr. 7-18). 16.95 *(978-0-8234-2106-0(6))* Holiday Hse., Inc.

Charbonneau, Joelle. Need. 2017. (ENG.). 352p. (YA). (gr. 7). pap. 9.99 *(978-0-544-93883-0(6),* 1658459, Clarion Bks.) HarperCollins Pubs.

Clarissa - Evaluation Guide: Evaluation Guide. 2006. (J). *(978-1-55942-402-8(8))* Witcher Productions.

Cumbie, Patricia. Where People Like Us Live. 2008. 224p. (YA). (gr. 7-18). lib. bdg. 17.89 *(978-0-06-137598-9(5),* Geringer, Laura Book) HarperCollins Pubs.

Daly, Maureen. Seventeenth Summer. 2010. (ENG.). 384p. (YA). (gr. 7). pap. 10.99 *(978-1-4169-9463-3(7),* Simon Pulse) Simon Pulse.

DeKeyser, Stacy. The Rhino in Right Field. 2018. (Washington Park Stories Ser.). (ENG., Illus.). 272p. (J). (gr. 3-7). 18.99 *(978-1-5344-0626-1(3),* McElderry, Margaret K. Bks.) McElderry, Margaret K. Bks.

Enright, Elizabeth. Thimble Summer. 2006. 21.75 *(978-0-8446-7281-6(5))* Smith, Peter Pub., Inc.

—Thimble Summer. Enright, Elizabeth, illus. 2008. (ENG., Illus.). 144p. (J). (gr. 3-7). pap. 8.99 *(978-0-312-38002-1(X),* 900050525) Square Fish.

Erdrich, Louise. The Porcupine Year. Erdrich, Louise, illus. 2010. (Birchbark House Ser.: 3). (ENG., Illus.). 224p. (J). (gr. 3-7). pap. 9.99 *(978-0-06-441030-4(7),* HarperCollins) HarperCollins Pubs.

Farrey, Brian. With or Without You. 2011. (ENG., Illus.). 368p. (YA). (gr. 11-18). pap. 8.99 *(978-1-4424-0699-5(2),* Simon Pulse) Simon Pulse.

Fleming, Vicki & Dipietro, Kara. North Woods Numbers. 2010. 28p. pap. 13.99 *(978-1-4490-8420-2(6))* AuthorHouse.

Freeman, Meryl. The Voyages of Galley Cat. 2008. 36p. pap. 24.95 *(978-1-60474-632-7(7))* America Star Bks.

Gliori, Debi. No Matter What Padded Board Book. Gliori, Debi, illus. 2017. (ENG., Illus.). 24p. (J). (— 1). bds. 8.99 *(978-0-544-91584-8(4),* 1655572, Clarion Bks.) HarperCollins Pubs.

Groethe, Kd. The Virtual Adventures of Megan & Timmy. 2012. 230p. (gr. 4-6). 27.99 *(978-1-4685-5050-4(0));* pap. 16.95 *(978-1-4685-5049-8(7))* AuthorHouse.

Hannigan, Katherine. Ida B: ... & Her Plans to Maximize Fun, Avoid Disaster, & (Possibly) Save the World. 2004. (ENG.). 256p. (J). (gr. 4-18). 17.99 *(978-0-06-073024-6(2),* Greenwillow Bks.) HarperCollins Pubs.

—Ida B: ... And Her Plans to Maximize Fun, Avoid Disaster, & (Possibly) Save the World. 2004. 256p. (gr. 4-18). lib. bdg. 16.89 *(978-0-06-073025-3(0))* HarperCollins Pubs.

—Ida B: ... & Her Plans to Maximize Fun, Avoid Disaster, & (Possibly) Save the World. 2011. (ENG.). 272p. (J). (gr. 5-9). reprint ed. pap. 7.99 *(978-0-06-073026-0(9),* Greenwillow Bks.) HarperCollins Pubs.

Hawke, Jay Jordan. Onwaachige the Dreamer. 2016. (ENG., Illus.). (YA). 24.99 *(978-1-63533-058-8(0),* Harmony Ink Pr.) Dreamspinner Pr.

Henkes, Kevin. Bird Lake Moon. (ENG.). 192p. (J). (gr. 3-7). 2010. pap. 6.99 *(978-0-06-147079-0(1))* 2008. 17.99 *(978-0-06-147076-9(7))* HarperCollins Pubs. (Greenwillow Bks.).

—The Year of Billy Miller. Henkes, Kevin, illus. 2015. (ENG., Illus.). (J). (gr. 3-7). lib. bdg. 17.60 *(978-1-62765-762-4(2))* Perfection Learning Corp.

—The Year of Billy Miller. 2015. (J). lib. bdg. 18.40 *(978-0-606-36977-0(5))* Turtleback.

—The Year of Billy Miller: A Newbery Honor Award Winner. Henkes, Kevin, illus. 2013. (ENG., Illus.). 240p. (J). (gr. 3-7). 17.99 *(978-0-06-226812-9(0));* lib. bdg. 17.89 *(978-0-06-226813-6(9))* HarperCollins Pubs. (Greenwillow Bks.).

Hijuelos, Oscar. Dark Dude. 2009. (ENG., Illus.). 464p. (YA). (gr. 8-18). pap. 14.99 *(978-1-4169-4945-9(3),* Atheneum Bks. for Young Readers) Simon & Schuster Children's Publishing.

Hysen, Sylvia. A Very Dairy Christmas. 2005. 290p. 24.95 *(978-0-9763365-6-3(1))* 1st Impression Publishing.

Jacobs, Lily. The Littlest Bunny in Wisconsin: An Easter Adventure. Dunn, Robert, illus. 2015. (Littlest Bunny Ser.). (ENG.). 32p. (J). (gr. -1-3). 9.99 *(978-1-4926-1240-7(5),* Hometown World) Sourcebooks, Inc.

James, Eric. Santa's Sleigh Is on Its Way to Wisconsin: A Christmas Adventure. Dunn, Robert, illus. 2015. (Santa's Sleigh Is on Its Way Ser.). (ENG.). 32p. (J). (gr. k-2). 12.99 *(978-1-4926-2755-5(0),* Hometown World) Sourcebooks, Inc.

—The Spooky Express Wisconsin. Piwowarski, Marcin, illus. 2017. (Spooky Express Ser.). (ENG.). 32p. (J). (gr. k-6). 9.99 *(978-1-4926-5412-4(4),* Hometown World) Sourcebooks, Inc.

—Tiny the Wisconsin Easter Bunny. 2018. (Tiny the Easter Bunny Ser.). (ENG.). 40p. (J). (gr. k-3). 9.99 *(978-1-4926-5978-5(9),* Hometown World) Sourcebooks, Inc.

James, Steven. Blur, 0 vols. 2014. (Blur Trilogy Ser.: 1). (ENG.). 368p. (YA). (gr. 7-12). pap. 9.99 *(978-1-4778-4727-5(8),* 9781477847275, Skyscape) Amazon Publishing.

Johnson, Lois Walfrid. The Creeping Shadows. 2009. (Orig.). (J). 8.99 *(978-0-88062-277-6(6))* Mott Media.

—Disaster on Windy Hill. 2009. (J). 8.99 *(978-0-88062-284-4(9))* Mott Media.

—Grandpa's Stolen Treasure. 2009. (Orig.). (J). 8.99 *(978-0-88062-281-3(4))* Mott Media.

—The Runaway Clown. 2009. (Orig.). (J). 8.99 *(978-0-88062-282-0(2))* Mott Media.

—Trouble at Wild River. 2009. (J). 8.99 *(978-0-88062-279-0(2))* Mott Media.

Kopetz, Mark. Red Herrings at Rock Island: A Door County Mystery. 2005. 15.00 *(978-0-940473-42-3(9))* Caxton, Wm Ltd.

LaBree Stute, Lela. The Sunnyset Pugs. 2010. 34p. pap. 19.99 *(978-0-557-41751-3(1))* Lulu Pr., Inc.

Liebig, Nelda Johnson. Carrie & the Boarding House. 2005. 127p. (J). (gr. 3-7). 10.95 *(978-1-883953-35-5(9))* Great Lakes Literary, LLC.

Maddox, Jake. Snowboard Struggle. 2016. (Jake Maddox JV Ser.). (ENG., Illus.). 96p. (J). (gr. 4-6). lib. bdg. 26.65 *(978-1-4965-3980-9(X),* 133203, Stone Arch Bks.) Capstone.

Maxwell, William. The Heavenly Tenants. Karasz, Ilonka, illus. 2017. (ENG.). 64p. pap. 16.95 *(978-0-486-81529-9(3))* Dover Pubns., Inc.

Meaney, Flynn. The Boy Recession. 2012. (ENG.). 256p. (YA). (gr. 10-17). 32.99 *(978-0-316-10213-1(X),* Poppy) Little, Brown Bks. for Young Readers.

Merkel, Ruth Vitrano. Ann: 1833-1897. 2006. (Hannah's Girls Ser.). (Illus.). 112p. (J). (gr. 4-7). per. 9.99 *(978-0-8280-1951-4(7))* Review & Herald Publishing Assn.

—Grace: 1890-1973, 6. 2006. (Hannah's Girls Ser.). (Illus.). 128p. (J). (gr. 4-7). per. 9.99 *(978-0-8280-1953-8(3))* Review & Herald Publishing Assn.

—Marilla 1851-1916, 6 bks. 2006. (Hannah's Girls Ser.). (Illus.). 144p. (J). (gr. 4-7). per. 9.99 *(978-0-8280-1952-1(5))* Review & Herald Publishing Assn.

—Ruthie: Born 1931. 2007. (Hannah's Girls Ser.). (Illus.). 144p. (J). (gr. 4-7). per. 9.99 *(978-0-8280-1954-5(1))* Review & Herald Publishing Assn.

Miller-Lachmann, Lyn. Gringolandia. 2009. (ENG.). 288p. (gr. 7-17). 18.95 *(978-1-931896-49-8(6))* Curbstone Pr.

Murdock, Catherine Gilbert. Front & Center. 2011. (ENG.). 288p. (YA). (gr. 7). pap. 9.99 *(978-0-547-40305-2(4),* 1428144, Clarion Bks.) HarperCollins Pubs.

Nation, Kay. Jamie Learns to Love. 2006. pap. 10.00 *(978-1-4257-0534-3(0))* Xlibris Corp.

Nelson, Bruce. Captain Black Licorice. 2004. (Illus.). 60p. (J). per. 7.95 *(978-1-59466-026-9(3))* Port Town Publishing.

Olin, Sean. Killing Britney. 2005. (ENG.). 240p. (YA). (gr. 9-12). pap. 9.99 *(978-0-689-87778-0(1),* Simon Pulse) Simon Pulse.

Oliver, Andrew. Haunted Hill. 2006. (Sam & Stephanie Mystery Ser.). 268p. (J). (gr. 5-9). per. 12.95 *(978-0-9661009-7-6(2))* Adams-Pomeroy Pr.

—If Photos Could Talk. 2005. (Sam & Stephanie Mystery Ser.). 264p. (J). per. 12.95 *(978-0-9661009-6-9(4))* Adams-Pomeroy Pr.

—Scrambled. 2007. 288p. (J). per. 12.95 *(978-0-9661009-8-3(0))* Adams-Pomeroy Pr.

Óscar, Hijuelos. Dark Dude. 2010. (SPA.). 430p. (YA). (gr. 9-18). 19.99 *(978-84-441-4316-3(2))* Everest Editora ESP. Dist: Lectorum Pubns., Inc.

Paulsen, Gary. The Island. 2006. (Point Ser.). 202p. (gr. 7-12). 16.00 *(978-0-7569-6382-8(6))* Perfection Learning Corp.

Pellowski, Anne & Sharpe, Roseanne. First Farm in the Valley: Anna's Story. 2008. (ENG., Illus.). 183p. (J). (gr. 3-9). pap. 12.95 *(978-1-932350-24-1(1))* Ignatius Pr.

Pferdehirt, Julia. Wisconsin Forest Tales. 2004. (Illus.). vii, 152p. (J). *(978-1-931599-47-4(5),* Trails Bks.) Bower Hse.

Qualey, Marsha. Thin Ice. 2007. 214p. (YA). *(978-0-9793444-0-4(9))* Quercus Pr.

Riordan, Robert. Medicine for Wildcat: A Story of the Friendship between a Menominee Indian & Frontier Priest Samuel Mazzuchelli. 2006. (Illus.). 132p. (YA). per. 14.95 *(978-0-9774934-0-1(7))* Sinsinawa Dominicans, Inc.

Rousselow, Jeff. Bury the Dead. 2009. 244p. pap. 15.26 *(978-0-557-07129-6(1))* Lulu Pr., Inc.

Sales, Leila. Once Was a Time. 2016. (ENG., Illus.). 272p. (J). (gr. 5-17). 16.99 *(978-1-4521-4009-4(X))* Chronicle Bks. LLC.

—Once Was a Time: (Middle Grade Fiction Books, Friendship Stories for Young Adults, Middle Grade Novels in Verse) 2017. (ENG.). 340p. (J). (gr. 5-9). pap. 7.99 *(978-1-4521-6139-6(9))* Chronicle Bks. LLC.

Schaefer, Laura. The Secret Ingredient. Rim, Sujean, illus. (ENG.). 240p. (J). (gr. 4-8). 2012. pap. 6.99 *(978-1-4424-1960-5(1))* 2011. 15.99 *(978-1-4424-1959-9(8))* Simon & Schuster/Paula Wiseman Bks. (Simon & Schuster/Paula Wiseman Bks.).

—The Teashop Girls. Rim, Sujean, illus. 2009. (ENG.). 272p. (J). (gr. 4-9). pap. 8.99 *(978-1-4169-6794-1(X),* Simon & Schuster/Paula Wiseman Bks.) Simon & Schuster/Paula Wiseman Bks.

Smallman, Steve. Santa Is Coming to Wisconsin. Dunn, Robert, illus. (ENG.). (J). 2012. 32p. (-3). 9.99 *(978-1-4022-7533-3(1),* Sourcebooks Jabberwocky) 2nd ed. 2019. 40p. (gr. -1-3). 12.99 *(978-1-7282-0114-6(4),* Hometown World) Sourcebooks, Inc.

Smith, Jennifer E. The Storm Makers. Helquist, Brett, illus. 2013. (ENG.). 384p. (J). (gr. 3-7). pap. 19.99 *(978-0-316-17959-1(0))* Little, Brown Bks. for Young Readers.

Sully, Katherine. Night-Night Wisconsin. Poole, Helen, illus. 2016. (Night-Night Ser.). (ENG.). 20p. (J). (gr. -1-1). bds. 9.99 *(978-1-4926-4217-6(7),* 9781492642176, Hometown World) Sourcebooks, Inc.

Timberlake, Amy. One Came Home. 2014. (Illus.). 272p. (J). (gr. 5-7). 8.99 *(978-0-375-87345-4(7),* Yearling) Random Hse. Children's Bks.

Tougas, Shelley. Finders Keepers. 2016. (ENG.). 304p. (J). (gr. 3-7). 18.40 *(978-0-606-39290-7(4))* Turtleback.

Wargin, Kathy-jo. The Legend of Old Abe. Caple, Laurie, illus. 2006. (Myths, Legends, Fairy & Folktales Ser.). (ENG.). 40p. (J). (gr. 2-5). 17.95 *(978-1-58536-232-5(8),* 202057) Sleeping Bear Pr.

Warner, Gertrude Chandler, creator. The Mystery of the Runaway Ghost. 2004. (Boxcar Children Mysteries Ser.: 98). (ENG., Illus.). 144p. (J). (gr. 2-5). pap. 5.99 *(978-0-8075-5551-4(7),* 807555517, Random Hse. Bks. for Young Readers) Random Hse. Children's Bks.

Wilder, Laura Ingalls. Little House in the Big Woods. Williams, Garth, illus. 2008. (Little House Ser.: 1). (ENG.). 256p. (J). (gr. 3-7). pap. 9.99 *(978-0-06-440001-5(8),* HarperCollins) HarperCollins Pubs.

—Little House in the Big Woods. 2007. (Little House Ser.). 224p. (J). (gr. 3-7). pap. 6.99 *(978-0-06-088537-3(8),* Harper Trophy) HarperCollins Pubs.

Wilkes, Maria D. Little House in Brookfield. abr. ed. 2007. (Little House Ser.). (ENG.). 144p. (J). (gr. 3-7). pap. 6.99 *(978-0-06-114821-7(0),* HarperCollins) HarperCollins Pubs.

—Little Town at the Crossroads. 2007. (Little House Ser.). 159p. (J). (gr. 3-7). per. 5.99 *(978-0-06-114822-4(9),* Harper Trophy) HarperCollins Pubs.

WISCONSIN—HISTORY

Ball, Jacqueline A. Wildfire! The 1871 Peshtigo Firestorm. 2005. (X-Treme Disasters That Changed America Ser.). 32p. (J). lib. bdg. 28.50 *(978-1-59716-011-7(3))* Bearport Publishing Co., Inc.

Bollow, Ludmilla. Lulu's Christmas Story: A True Story of Faith & Hope During the Great Depression. 2014. (ENG.). 256p. (gr. 7). 22.95 *(978-0-9911938-5-1(7))* Titletown Publishing, LLC.

Carole Marsh. Wisconsin Indians. 2004. (Wisconsin Experience Ser.). 36p. (gr. 3-8). 29.95 *(978-0-635-02343-8(1));* pap. 7.95 *(978-0-635-02342-1(3))* Gallopade International.

Davis, Susan Burdick. Old Forts & Real Folks. 2006. pap. 31.95 *(978-1-4286-5582-9(4))* Kessinger Publishing, LLC.

Dornfeld, Margaret & Hantula, Richard. Wisconsin, 1 vol. 2nd rev. ed. 2011. (It's My State! (Second Edition)(r) Ser.).

W X Y Z

(ENG.). 80p. (gr. 4-4). lib. bdg. 34.07 (978-1-60870-062-2(3), 38ebdd80-c72f-4b9a-b477-30e86af04a96) Cavendish Square Publishing LLC.

Galiano, Dean. Wisconsin, 1 vol. Brusca, Maria Cristina, tr. 2005. (Bilingual Library of the United States of America Ser.: Set 2). (ENG & SPA., Illus.). 32p. (J). (gr. 2-2). lib. bdg. 28.93 (978-1-4042-3115-3(3), ff271199-479d-4b17-b384-ab6741a02d6a) Rosen Publishing Group, Inc., The.

Gamble, Adam & Jasper, Mark. Good Night Wisconsin. Kelly, Cooper, illus. 2012. (Good Night Our World Ser.). (ENG.). 20p. (J). (gr. k — 1). bds. 9.95 (978-1-60219-064-1(X)) Good Night Bks.

Hamilton, John. Wisconsin, 1 vol. 2016. (United States of America Ser.). (ENG., Illus.). 48p. (J). (gr. 5-9). 34.21 (978-1-68078-353-7(X), 21691, Abdo & Daughters) ABDO Publishing Co.

Henry, Marcia. Madeline Island ABC Coloring Book. Parsons, Sally, illus. 2008. (ENG.). 32p. (J). (gr. k-6). pap. 6.95 (978-0-9817723-0-1(7)) Univ. of Wisconsin Pr.

Heos, Bridget. Wisconsin: Past & Present. 2009. (J). 70.50 (978-1-4358-5585-4(X)); (ENG.). 48p. (gr. 5-5). pap. 12.75 (978-1-4358-5584-7(1), 9a5e3740-34f4-4c47-95fa-b6c70082b380); (ENG., Illus.). 48p. (gr. 5-5). lib. bdg. 34.47 (978-1-4358-5293-8(1), 9c9b3842-841e-4d81-a20f-3bca0094368a) Rosen Publishing Group, Inc., The. (Rosen Reference).

Holtz, Monica Stauber. Behind the Zoo: Find Out What the Animals Eat & Do at Irvine Park Zoo, Chippewa Falls, Wisconsin. Opatz, Shane, illus. Opatz, Shane, photos by. 2011. (J). (978-0-9837617-1-6(X)) Holtz Creative Enterprises.

Jerome, Kate B. Lucky to Live in Wisconsin. 2017. (Arcadia Kids Ser.). (ENG., Illus.). 32p. (J). 16.99 (978-0-7385-2787-1(4)) Arcadia Publishing.

—The Wise Animal Handbook Wisconsin. 2017. (Arcadia Kids Ser.). (ENG., Illus.). 32p. (J). 16.99 (978-0-7385-2849-6(8)) Arcadia Publishing.

Knickelbine, Scott. The Great Peshtigo Fire: Stories & Science from America's Deadliest Fire. 2012. (ENG., Illus.). 88p. (J). pap. 15.95 (978-0-87020-499-9(8)) Wisconsin Historical Society.

Loew, Patty, et al. Native People of Wisconsin, Rev. TG & Student Materials. 2016. (New Badger History Ser.). (ENG.). (J). (gr. 4-6). cd-rom 49.95 (978-0-87020-749-5(0)) Wisconsin Historical Society.

Lorbiecki, Marybeth. Things Natural, Wild, & Free: The Life of Aldo Leopold. 2011. (ENG., Illus.). 112p. (J). (gr. 4-7). pap. 12.95 (978-1-55591-474-5(8)) Fulcrum Publishing.

Lusted, Marcia Amidon. Wisconsin: The Badger State, 1 vol. 2009. (Our Amazing States Ser.). (ENG., Illus.). 24p. (J). (gr. 3-3). pap. 9.25 (978-1-4358-3366-1(X), 37277aa6-4d72-4c26-b78d-2e25be64866a); lib. bdg. 26.27 (978-1-4042-8120-2(7), acd9f651-0753-4f30-9adc-f91563b4c8eb) Rosen Publishing Group, Inc., The. (PowerKids Pr.).

Madeline Island Abc Book. 2008. (ENG., Illus.). 52p. (gr. -1-4). pap. 18.95 (978-1-4243-3753-8(4), P153692) Univ. of Wisconsin Pr.

Malone, Bobbie. Wisconsin: Our State, Our Story. 2008. (J). pap. (978-0-87020-396-1(7)) Wisconsin Historical Society.

Malone, Bobbie & Oberle, Kori. Wisconsin: Our State, Our Story. 2008. (Illus.). x, 246p. (J). (978-0-87020-512-5(9)) Wisconsin Historical Society.

Manger, Barbara & Smith, Janine. Mary Nohl: A Lifetime in Art. 2013. (Badger Biographies Ser.). (ENG., Illus.). 128p. (J). pap. 12.95 (978-0-87020-577-4(3)) Wisconsin Historical Society.

Marsh, Carole. Exploring Wisconsin Through Project-Based Learning: Geography, History, Government, Economics & More. 2016. (Wisconsin Experience Ser.). (ENG.). (J). pap. 9.99 (978-0-635-12373-2(8)) Gallopade International.

—Wisconsin History Projects: 30 Cool, Activities, Crafts, Experiments & More for Kids to Do to Learn about Your State! 2003. (Wisconsin Experience Ser.). 32p. (gr. k-5). pap. 5.95 (978-0-635-01818-2(7), Marsh, Carole Bks.) Gallopade International.

O'Neill, Elizabeth. Alfred Visits Wisconsin. 2009. 24p. (J). pap. 12.00 (978-0-9841507-0-0(6)) Funny Bone Bks.

Parker, Janice. Wisconsin. 2011. (Guide to American States Ser.). (Illus.). 48p. (YA). (gr. 3-6). 29.99 (978-1-61690-823-2(8)); (978-1-61690-498-2(4)) Weigl Pubs., Inc.

—Wisconsin: The Badger State. 2016. (Illus.). 48p. (J). (978-1-5105-2101-8(1)) SmartBook Media, Inc.

—Wisconsin: The Badger State. 2016. (J). (978-1-4896-4965-2(4)) Weigl Pubs., Inc.

Peterson, Sheryl. Wisconsin. 2009. (This Land Called America Ser.). (Illus.). 32p. (YA). (gr. 3-6). 19.95 (978-1-58341-802-4(4)) Creative Co., The.

Pferdehirt, Julia. Freedom Train North: Stories of the Underground Railroad in Wisconsin. Butler, Jerry, illus. Date not set. (J). (gr. 3-8). pap. 10.00 (978-0-9664925-0-7(1)) Living History Pr.

Pratt, Laura. Wisconsin: The Badger State. 2012. (J). (978-1-61913-419-5(5)); pap. (978-1-61913-420-1(9)) Weigl Pubs., Inc.

Uschan, Michael V. Wisconsin. 2003. (Seeds of a Nation Ser.). (Illus.). 48p. (J). (gr. 3-5). 23.70 (978-0-7377-1481-4(6), Kidhaven) Cengage Gale.

Wargin, Kathy-jo. Little Wisconsin. Monroe, Michael Glenn, illus. 2012. (Little State Ser.). (ENG.). 20p. (J). (gr. -1-1). bds. 9.95 (978-1-58536-209-7(3), 202275) Sleeping Bear Pr.

Wittekind, Erika. What's Great about Wisconsin? 2014. (Our Great States Ser.). (ENG., Illus.). 32p. (J). (gr. 2-5). pap. 7.95 (978-1-4677-4540-6(5), a8472a32-9d2d-47b0-81d7-337e5d652b99) Lerner Publishing Group.

Ziff, John. Western Great Lakes: Illinois, Minnesota, Wisconsin, Vol. 19. 2015. (Let's Explore the States Ser.). (Illus.). 64p. (J). (gr. 5). 23.95 (978-1-4222-3338-2(3)) Mason Crest.

WISHBONE (FICTITIOUS CHARACTER)—FICTION

Williamson, Barbara. Wishbone. 2007. (Illus.). 24p. (J). per. 12.95 (978-1-60002-197-8(2), 4216) Mountain Valley Publishing, LLC.

Worley, Roger. The Wishbone Journal. 2003. 173p. pap. 24.95 (978-1-4137-0101-2(9)) America Star Bks.

WIT AND HUMOR

see also Comedy; Humorists; Nonsense Verses; Satire also American Wit and Humor; English Wit and Humor

Aalgaard, Wendy. Venezuela in Pictures. 2nd ed. 2004. (Visual Geography Series, Second Ser.). (ENG., Illus.). 80p. (gr. 5-12). lib. bdg. 31.93 (978-0-8225-1172-4(X)) Lerner Publishing Group.

Andreu Iglesias, Cesar & Hernández, Juan A. A Mal Tiempo, Buena Cara: El Humor en el Periodismo Puertorriqueno. l.t. ed. 2003. (SPA., Illus.). 48p. pap. (978-0-9743102-0-6(4)) Casa de Periodistas Editorial.

ARISE Foundation Staff. Life Skills Curriculum: ARISE Life Isn't Fair (Instructor's Manual) 2011. 78p. (J). pap. 29.95 (978-1-58614-296-4(8)) Arise Foundation.

Austen, Catherine. 26 Tips for Surviving Grade 6, 1 vol. 2011. (ENG., Illus.). 168p. (J). (gr. 5-7). 16.95 (978-1-55277-925-5(4), 925) James Lorimer & Co. Ltd., Pubs. CAN. Dist: Formac Lorimer Bks. Ltd.

Baines, Nigel, illus. The Little Book of Christmas Jokes. 2016. (ENG.). 128p. (J). (gr. k-2). pap. 6.95 (978-1-78344-487-8(8)) Andersen Pr. GBR. Dist: Independent Pubs. Group.

Balestier, Courtney. Would You Rather... ? Super Secrets! Over 300 Fiercely Fascinating Questions to Ask Your Friends. Heimberg, Justin & Gomberg, David, eds. 2011. (Would You Rather... ? Ser.). (ENG.). 192p. (gr. 4-9). pap. 9.95 (978-1-934734-69-8(1)) Seven Footer Pr.

Barfield, Mike. The Ultimate Spell-Caster: Over 60 Million Marvelously Silly Spells. 2018. (ENG., Illus.). 100p. (J). (gr. 1-7). 14.99 (978-1-78627-310-9(1), King, Laurence Publishing) Orion Publishing Group, Ltd. GBR. Dist: Hachette Bk. Group.

—The Ultimate Wisecrack Generator: Over 60 Million Hilarious Zingers & Stingers. 2017. (ENG.). 100p. (J). (gr. 1-4). 14.99 (978-1-78627-030-6(7), King, Laurence Publishing) Orion Publishing Group, Ltd. GBR. Dist: Hachette Bk. Group.

Barlow, Steve & Skidmore, Steve. The Lost Diary of Shakespeare's Ghostwriter. 2011. (ENG., Illus.). 128p. pap. 7.99 (978-0-00-694588-8(0), HarperCollins Children's Bks.) HarperCollins Pubs. Ltd. GBR. Dist: HarperCollins Pubs.

Barnham, Kay & Connolly, Sean. The Animal Antics Joke Book, 1 vol. 2011. (Laugh Out Loud Ser.). (ENG., Illus.). 32p. (J). (gr. 2-3). pap. 12.75 (978-1-61533-400-1(9), 3f066ba9-59e5-4994-9654-ae27b6af498f); lib. bdg. 31.27 (978-1-61533-362-2(2), df1760ad-1a2e-4b6f-83e0-301540f5809e) Rosen Publishing Group, Inc., The. (Windmill Bks.).

—The Funny Food Joke Book, 1 vol. 2011. (Laugh Out Loud Ser.). (ENG., Illus.). 32p. (J). (gr. 2-3). pap. 12.75 (978-1-61533-403-2(3), a22370b6-7b2e-414f-a0c8-29113f3eb174, Windmill Bks.) Rosen Publishing Group, Inc., The.

—The Monster Fun Joke Book, 1 vol. 2011. (Laugh Out Loud Ser.). (ENG., Illus.). 32p. (J). (gr. 2-3). pap. 12.75 (978-1-61533-398-1(3), fe4175c7-b7a9-426f-878a-c0f5c7f93969); lib. bdg. 31.27 (978-1-61533-360-8(6), b00319c7-afe0-4283-8d27-0bd80c32c935) Rosen Publishing Group, Inc., The. (Windmill Bks.).

—The Outer Space Joke Book, 1 vol. 2011. (Laugh Out Loud Ser.). (ENG., Illus.). 32p. (J). (gr. 2-3). pap. 12.75 (978-1-61533-402-5(5), b79a49da-623f-4f20-958c-4896bcbf9363); lib. bdg. 31.27 (978-1-61533-364-6(9), 3acc742e-a0f6-4c6b-b9c7-c08d77541edf) Rosen Publishing Group, Inc., The. (Windmill Bks.).

—The School's Cool Joke Book, 1 vol. 2011. (Laugh Out Loud Ser.). (ENG., Illus.). 32p. (J). (gr. 2-3). pap. 12.75 (978-1-61533-401-8(7), b95376d3-5406-4ba7-bcb3-48c0fd97f665); lib. bdg. 31.27 (978-1-61533-363-9(0), 47c4bf90-8d8d-47de-98cc-4997e5b9c337) Rosen Publishing Group, Inc., The. (Windmill Bks.).

—The Silly Safari Joke Book, 1 vol. 2011. (Laugh Out Loud Ser.). (ENG., Illus.). 32p. (J). (gr. 2-3). pap. 12.75 (978-1-61533-399-8(1), 8bf2e128-caf7-4326-abe5-eecff101f793, Windmill Bks.) Rosen Publishing Group, Inc., The.

Barrett, Judi. Animals Should Definitely Not Wear Clothing. Barrett, Ron, illus. 2012. (Classic Board Bks.). (ENG.). 36p. (J). (gr. -1 — 1). bds. 8.99 (978-1-4424-3334-2(5), Little Simon) Little Simon.

—Lots More Animals Should Definitely Not Wear Clothing. Barrett, Ron, illus. 2018. (ENG.). 40p. (J). (gr. -1-3). 17.99 (978-1-4814-8866-2(X), Atheneum/Caitlyn Dlouhy Books) Simon & Schuster Children's Publishing.

Bathroom Readers' Institute. The Funniest Joke Book Ever! 2016. (ENG., Illus.). 128p. (J). (gr. 3-7). pap. 4.99 (978-1-62686-584-6(1), Portable Pr.) Printers Row Publishing Group.

—The Grossest Joke Book Ever! 2016. (ENG., Illus.). 128p. (J). (gr. 3-7). pap. 4.99 (978-1-62686-585-3(X), Portable Pr.) Printers Row Publishing Group.

Behnke, Alison. South Korea in Pictures. 2nd ed. 2005. (Visual Geography Ser.). (Illus.). 80p. (YA). (gr. 7-12). 27.93 (978-0-8225-1174-8(6)) Lerner Publishing Group.

Bender, Mike & Chernack, Doug. Everything Is Awkward. 2016. (ENG., Illus.). 40p. (J). (gr. k-4). 14.99 (978-0-399-54984-7(6), Crown Books For Young Readers) Random Hse. Children's Bks.

Beth, Georgia. World's Best (and Worst) Knock-Knock Jokes. 2018. (Laugh Your Socks Off! Ser.). (ENG., Illus.). 24p. (J). (gr. 1-4). pap. 6.99 (978-1-5415-1172-9(7), bf7a1d6d-e412-4172-b9fe-c7086bee1cc8); 26.65 (978-1-5124-8348-2(6), e20735cd-797d-4012-a54d-c6a175bc9796, Lerner Pubns.) Lerner Publishing Group.

—World's Best (and Worst) Riddles. 2018. (Laugh Your Socks Off! Ser.). (ENG., Illus.). 24p. (J). (gr. 1-4). pap. 6.99 (978-1-5415-1174-3(3), 2fc96074-f036-4170-a5ae-360aa7ce7b72) Lerner Publishing Group.

Bird, Benjamin. A Baby's Guide to Surviving Dad. Americo, Tiago, illus. 2016. (Baby Survival Guides). (ENG.). 24p. (J). (gr. -1-1). 6.95 (978-1-62370-610-4(6), 130713, Capstone Young Readers) Capstone.

—A Baby's Guide to Surviving Mom. Americo, Tiago, illus. 2016. (Baby Survival Guides). (ENG.). 24p. (J). (gr. -1-1). 6.95 (978-1-62370-611-1(4), 130714, Capstone Young Readers) Capstone.

Bird, Nicky. Knock-Knock Jokes: Bird Brains, 1 vol. 2016. (Knock-Knock Jokes Ser.: 1). (ENG., Illus.). 64p. (J). pap. 6.99 (978-1-926677-96-5(X), a68670be-417c-4e37-a065-28f59709e9b7) Folklore Publishing CAN. Dist: Lone Pine Publishing USA.

—Knock-Knock Jokes: Bug Brains, 1 vol. 2016. (Knock-Knock Jokes Ser.: 2). (ENG., Illus.). 64p. (J). pap. 6.99 (978-1-926677-97-2(8), adb1defc-f00b-4d6a-a118-e07f6a50d6ac) Folklore Publishing CAN. Dist: Lone Pine Publishing USA.

—Knock-Knock Jokes: Monkey Madness, 1 vol. 2016. (Knock-Knock Jokes Ser.: 3). (ENG., Illus.). 64p. (J). pap. 6.99 (978-1-926677-98-9(6), 59fe252c-2d94-446f-9639-0d620b8a2388) Folklore Publishing CAN. Dist: Lone Pine Publishing USA.

Birtles. Dumb Jokes For Smart Kids. (Illus.). 96p. (J). pap. 5.95 (978-1-85479-649-3(6)) O'Mara, Michael Bks., Ltd. GBR. Dist: Trans-Atlantic Pubns., Inc.

Blank, Eva, et al. Jokelopedia: The Biggest, Best, Silliest, Dumbest Joke Book Ever! Wright, Mike, illus. 3rd ed. 2016. (ENG.). 288p. (J). (gr. 2-7). pap. 10.99 (978-0-7611-8997-8(1), 18997) Workman Publishing Co., Inc.

Boone, Brian. Hysterical Jokes for Minecrafters: Blocks, Boxes, Blasts, & Blow-Outs. 2017. (Jokes for Minecrafters Ser.). (ENG., Illus.). 176p. (J). (gr. k). pap. 7.99 (978-1-5107-1882-1(6), Sky Pony Pr.) Skyhorse Publishing Co., Inc.

—The Jokiest Joking Trivia Book Ever Written ... No Joke! 1,001 Surprising Facts to Amaze Your Friends. Brack, Amanda, illus. 2018. (Jokiest Joking Joke Bks.). (ENG.). 272p. (J). pap. 12.99 (978-1-250-19976-8(X), 900195020) St. Martin's Pr.

—Sidesplitting Jokes for Minecrafters: Ghastly Golems & Ghoulish Ghasts. 2017. (Illus.). 176p. (J). (gr. k). pap. 7.99 (978-1-5107-1883-8(4), Sky Pony Pr.) Skyhorse Publishing Co., Inc.

—Uproarious Riddles for Minecrafters: Mobs, Ghasts, Biomes, & More. Brack, Amanda, illus. 2018. (Jokes for Minecrafters Ser.). (ENG.). 184p. (J). (gr. 1-6). pap. 7.99 (978-1-5107-2717-5(5), Sky Pony Pr.) Skyhorse Publishing Co., Inc.

Borgenicht, David. Monkeyfarts! Wacky Jokes Every Kid Should Know. 2012. (Illus.). 96p. (J). (gr. 1-4). 8.99 (978-1-59474-605-5(2)) Quirk Bks.

Boyer, Crispin. That's Gross! Icky Facts That Will Test Your Gross-Out Factor. 2012. (Illus.). 176p. (J). (gr. 3-7). pap. 12.95 (978-1-4263-1066-9(8)); (ENG., lib. bdg. 21.95 (978-1-4263-1127-7(3)) Disney Publishing Worldwide. (National Geographic Kids).

Bozzo, Linda. Corny Thanksgiving Jokes to Tickle Your Funny Bone, 1 vol. 2013. (Funnier Bone Jokes Ser.). (ENG.). 48p. (gr. 3-3). pap. 11.53 (978-1-4644-0178-7(0), 09759e79-9fcb-45be-97c0-581d92bedb47, Enslow Elementary); lib. bdg. 25.27 (978-0-7660-4120-2(4), 9f7dc287-12e7-425a-9eb8-e40bec15d261) Enslow Publishing, LLC.

—Food Jokes to Tickle Your Funny Bone, 1 vol. 2011. (Funny Bone Jokes Ser.). (ENG., Illus.). 48p. (gr. 3-3). pap. 11.53 (978-0-7660-5986-3(3), 8be353d8-ae98-4f32-9567-8a8bc2d391e9); lib. bdg. 25.27 (978-0-7660-3541-6(7), a25e8942-7e6b-4086-8c29-287aacfb15cc) Enslow Publishing, LLC. (Enslow Elementary).

—Funny Valentine's Day Jokes to Tickle Your Funny Bone, 1 vol. 2013. (Funnier Bone Jokes Ser.). (ENG., Illus.). 48p. (gr. 3-3). 25.27 (978-0-7660-4119-6(0), 3ae1143f-9de9-4d6f-90f5-5ab10ea77ab6); pap. 11.53 (978-1-4644-0177-0(2), 1977fa87-4eb4-4cb5-979a-59013147afae, Enslow Elementary) Enslow Publishing, LLC.

—Gross Body Jokes to Tickle Your Funny Bone, 1 vol. 2011. (Funny Bone Jokes Ser.). (ENG., Illus.). 48p. (gr. 3-3). pap. 11.53 (978-0-7660-5987-0(1), 3248e264-46d4-42eb-899d-78a2294a6fa3); lib. bdg. 25.27 (978-0-7660-3540-9(9), a3f3b464-03b6-40a8-a7ff-3143ff098e81) Enslow Publishing, LLC. (Enslow Elementary).

—Kooky Halloween Jokes to Tickle Your Funny Bone, 1 vol. 2013. (Funnier Bone Jokes Ser.). (ENG.). 48p. (gr. 3-3). 25.27 (978-0-7660-4118-9(2), 618b2a6c-0823-44e8-a6f8-e939465f7b70); pap. 11.53 (978-1-4644-0176-3(4), e9d2a2d8-fb21-403c-b932-a22d8e377800, Enslow Elementary) Enslow Publishing, LLC.

Braun, Eric. How to Outsmart a Martian. 2019. (How to Outsmart ... Ser.). (ENG.). 24p. (J). (gr. 2-4). pap. 8.99 (978-1-64466-059-1(8), 12953); (Illus.). (gr. 4-6). lib. bdg. (978-1-68072-922-1(5), 12952) Black Rabbit Bks. (Hi Jinx).

—How to Outsmart a Ninja. 2019. (How to Outsmart ... Ser.). (ENG.). 24p. (J). (gr. 2-4). pap. 8.99 (978-1-64466-061-4(X), 12961); (Illus.). (gr. 4-6). lib. bdg. (978-1-68072-923-8(3), 12960) Black Rabbit Bks. (Hi Jinx).

—How to Outsmart a Vampire. 2019. (How to Outsmart ... Ser.). (ENG., Illus.). 24p. (J). (gr. 2-4). pap. 8.99 (978-1-64466-062-1(8), 12965); (gr. 4-6). lib. bdg. (978-1-68072-924-5(1), 12964) Black Rabbit Bks. (Hi Jinx).

—How to Outsmart a Werewolf. 2019. (How to Outsmart ... Ser.). (ENG., Illus.). 24p. (J). (gr. 2-4). pap. 8.99 (978-1-64466-063-8(6), 12969); (gr. 4-6). lib. bdg. (978-1-68072-925-2(X), 12968) Black Rabbit Bks. (Hi Jinx).

—How to Outsmart an Evil Villain. 2019. (How to Outsmart ... Ser.). (ENG., Illus.). 24p. (J). (gr. 2-4). pap. 8.99 (978-1-64466-060-7(1), 12957); (gr. 4-6). lib. bdg. (978-1-68072-926-9(8), 12956) Black Rabbit Bks. (Hi Jinx).

Brewer, Paul. You Must Be Joking! Lots of Cool Jokes, Plus 17 1/2 Tips for Remembering, Telling, & Making up Your Own Jokes. 2003. (ENG., Illus.). 128p. (J). 17.95 (978-0-8126-2661-2(3)) Cricket Bks.

Brewer, Paul, illus. You Must Be Joking, Two! Even Cooler Jokes, Plus 11 1/2 Tips for Laughing Yourself into Your Own Stand-Up Comedy Routine. 2007. (ENG.). 128p. (J). (gr. k-5). 17.95 (978-0-8126-2752-7(0)) Cricket Bks.

Brinkley, Laquita. Aww Hell Naw Let Me Explain! The Top 100 Frequently Used Excuses Americans Say to Try to Escape Ticket or Tow. 2009. (ENG.). 60p. 24.99 (978-1-4500-0082-6(7)); pap. 15.99 (978-1-4500-0081-9(9), Xlibris Corp.

Browning. Mega Joke Book For Kids. (Illus.). 162p. (J). pap. 9.95 (978-1-85479-249-5(0)) O'Mara, Michael Bks., Ltd. GBR. Dist: Trans-Atlantic Pubns., Inc.

The Bunty Annual 2005. 2004. (Illus.). 128p. (J). 9.95 (978-0-85116-849-4(3)) Thomson, D.C. & Co., Ltd. GBR. Dist: APG Sales & Distribution Services.

Burns, Diane L. Horsing Around: Jokes to Make Ewe Smile. Gable, Brian, illus. 2005. (Make Me Laugh! Ser.). 32p. (J). (gr. k-3). lib. bdg. 19.93 (978-1-57505-662-3(3)) Lerner Publishing Group.

Burns, Diane L. & Scholten, Dan. Horsing Around: Jokes to Make Ewe Smile. Gable, Brian, illus. 2004. (Make Me Laugh! Ser.). 32p. (J). (gr. -1-3). per. 4.95 (978-1-57505-737-8(9)) Lerner Publishing Group.

Burns, Diane L., et al. Backyard Beasties: Jokes to Snake You Smile. Gable, Brian, illus. 2004. (Make Me Laugh! Ser.). 32p. (J). (gr. k-3). lib. bdg. 19.93 (978-1-57505-646-3(1)) Lerner Publishing Group.

—Jordan in Pictures. Gable, Brian, illus. 2nd ed. 2005. (Visual Geography Series, Second Ser.). (ENG.). 80p. (gr. 5-12). 31.93 (978-0-8225-1173-1(8)) Lerner Publishing Group.

Burton, Jeffrey. Laugh Out Loud I Ruff Jokes. 2017. (Laugh Out Loud Ser.). (ENG., Illus.). 208p. (J). (gr. k-2). pap. 6.99 (978-1-5344-0029-0(X), Little Simon) Little Simon.

Burton, Jeffrey & Naundorff, Brittany. Laugh Out Loud. 2017. (Illus.). (978-1-5379-7454-5(8), Little Simon) Little Simon.

Capstone Press. Joke Books. 2010. (Joke Bks.). (ENG.). 32p. lib. bdg. 123.90 (978-1-4296-5942-0(4), Pebble) Capstone.

Carlson-Berne, Emma. World's Best (and Worst) Animal Jokes. 2018. (Laugh Your Socks Off! Ser.). (ENG., Illus.). 24p. (J). (gr. 1-4). pap. 6.99 (978-1-5415-1171-2(9), 6a1394bf-e82f-44a4-9813-ef2888735c8b); 26.65 (978-1-5124-8351-2(6), fa5d7dff-8024-4668-9546-534e26a71cee, Lerner Pubns.) Lerner Publishing Group.

—World's Best (and Worst) Spooky Jokes. 2018. (Laugh Your Socks Off! Ser.). (ENG., Illus.). 24p. (J). (gr. 1-4). pap. 6.99 (978-1-5415-1178-1(6), e6088a55-3440-46ed-a275-cf23928ace6b); 26.65 (978-1-5124-8352-9(4), c1f5d5fa-3b20-4d50-bbce-afcc64f96dab, Lerner Pubns.) Lerner Publishing Group.

—World's Best (and Worst) Sports Jokes. 2018. (Laugh Your Socks Off! Ser.). (ENG., Illus.). 24p. (J). (gr. 1-4). pap. 6.99 (978-1-5415-1179-8(4), 23ee1258-de3d-4a55-9d20-82d8b7184721); 26.65 (978-1-5124-8353-6(2), bbaba351-7770-4a04-bce9-adb87fdaddce, Lerner Pubns.) Lerner Publishing Group.

Caswell, Deanna. Making Secret Codes & Messages. 2018. (Spy Kid Ser.). (ENG., Illus.). 24p. (J). (gr. 4-6). lib. bdg. 28.50 (978-1-68072-588-9(2), 12474, Hi Jinx) Black Rabbit Bks.

Charney, Steve. Hocus-Jokus: 50 Funny Magic Tricks Complete with Jokes. 2003. (Illus.). ix, 132p. (J). (978-0-88166-376-1(X)) Meadowbrook Pr.

Chirp Magazine, The Editors of. Joking Around with Chirp. Kain, Bob, illus. 2013. (ENG.). 96p. (J). (gr. -1-3). pap. 11.95 (978-1-926973-65-4(8)) Owlkids Bks. Inc. CAN. Dist: Publishers Group West (PGW).

Chmielewski, Gary. The Animal Zone. Caputo, Jim, illus. rev. ed. 2007. (Funny Zone Ser.). (ENG.). 24p. (J). (gr. 2-4). pap. 11.94 (978-1-60357-677-2(0)) Norwood Hse. Pr.

—Animal Zone. Caputo, Jim, illus. rev. ed. 2007. (Funny Zone Ser.). (ENG.). 24p. (J). (gr. 2-4). lib. bdg. 22.60 (978-1-59953-139-7(9)) Norwood Hse. Pr.

—The Classroom Zone. Caputo, Jim, illus. rev. ed. 2007. (Funny Zone Ser.). (ENG.). 24p. (J). (gr. 2-4). pap. 11.94 (978-1-60357-680-2(0)) Norwood Hse. Pr.

—The Computer Zone. Caputo, Jim, illus. rev. ed. 2009. (Funny Zone Ser.). (ENG.). 24p. (J). (gr. 2-4). pap. 11.94 (978-1-60357-684-0(3)) Norwood Hse. Pr.

—The Computer Zone: Jokes, Riddles, Tongue Twisters & Daffynitions. Caputo, Jim, illus. rev. ed. 2009. (Funny Zone Ser.). (ENG.). 24p. (J). (gr. 2-4). lib. bdg. 22.60 (978-1-59953-300-1(6)) Norwood Hse. Pr.

—The Fright Zone. Caputo, Jim, illus. rev. ed. 2009. (Funny Zone Ser.). (ENG.). 24p. (J). (gr. 2-4). pap. 11.94 (978-1-60357-685-7(1)) Norwood Hse. Pr.

—The Fright Zone: Jokes, Riddles, Tongue Twisters & Daffynitions. Caputo, Jim, illus. rev. ed. 2009. (Funny Zone Ser.). (ENG.). 24p. (J). (gr. 2-4). lib. bdg. 22.60 (978-1-59953-298-1(0)) Norwood Hse. Pr.

—The Ghost Zone. Caputo, Jim, illus. rev. ed. 2009. (Funny Zone Ser.). (ENG.). 24p. (J). (gr. 2-4). pap. 11.94 (978-1-60357-686-4(X)) Norwood Hse. Pr.

—The Ghost Zone: Jokes, Riddles, Tongue Twisters & Daffynitions. Caputo, Jim, illus. rev. ed. 2009. (Funny Zone Ser.). (ENG.). 24p. (J). (gr. 2-4). lib. bdg. 22.60 (978-1-59953-297-4(2)) Norwood Hse. Pr.

—The History Zone. Caputo, Jim, illus. rev. ed. 2007. (Funny Zone Ser.). (ENG.). 24p. (J). (gr. 2-4). pap. 11.94 (978-1-60357-678-9(9)) Norwood Hse. Pr.

—History Zone. Caputo, Jim, illus. rev. ed. 2007. (Funny Zone Ser.). (ENG.). 24p. (J). (gr. 2-4). lib. bdg. 22.60 (978-1-59953-141-0(0)) Norwood Hse. Pr.

—Let's Eat in the Funny Zone. Caputo, Jim, illus. rev. ed. 2007. (Funny Zone Ser.). (ENG.). 24p. (J). (gr. 2-4). pap. 11.94 (978-1-60357-681-9(9)) Norwood Hse. Pr.

—Let's Eat in the Funny Zone: Jokes, Riddles, Tongue Twisters & Daffynitions. Caputo, Jim, illus. rev. ed. 2007. (Funny Zone Ser.). (ENG.). 24p. (J). (gr. 2-4). lib. bdg. 22.60 (978-1-59953-181-6(X)) Norwood Hse. Pr.

—Let's Go in the Funny Zone. Caputo, Jim, illus. rev. ed. 2007. (Funny Zone Ser.). (ENG.). 24p. (J). (gr. 2-4). pap. 11.94 (978-1-60357-682-6(7)) Norwood Hse. Pr.

—Let's Go in the Funny Zone: Jokes, Riddles, Tongue Twisters & Daffynitions. Caputo, Jim, illus. rev. ed. 2007. (Funny Zone Ser.). (ENG.). 24p. (J). (gr. 2-4). lib. bdg. 22.60 (978-1-59953-182-3(8)) Norwood Hse. Pr.

The Medical Zone. Caputo, Jim, illus. rev. ed. 2009. (Funny Zone Ser.). (ENG.). 24p. (J). (gr. 2-4). pap. 11.94 *(978-1-60357-687-1(8))* Norwood Hse. Pr.
-The Medical Zone: Jokes, Riddles, Tongue Twisters & Daffynitions. Caputo, Jim, illus. rev. ed. 2009. (Funny Zone Ser.). (ENG.). 24p. (J). (gr. 2-4). lib. bdg. 22.60 *(978-1-59953-299-8(9))* Norwood Hse. Pr.
-The Science Zone. Caputo, Jim, illus. rev. ed. 2007. (Funny Zone Ser.). (ENG.). 24p. (J). (gr. 2-4). pap. 11.94 *(978-1-60357-683-3(5))* Norwood Hse. Pr.
-The Science Zone: Jokes, Riddles, Tongue Twisters & Daffynitions. Caputo, Jim, illus. rev. ed. 2007. (Funny Zone Ser.). (ENG.). 24p. (J). (gr. 2-4). lib. bdg. 22.60 *(978-1-59953-183-0(6))* Norwood Hse. Pr.
-The Sports Zone. Caputo, Jim, illus. rev. ed. 2007. (Funny Zone Ser.). (ENG.). 24p. (J). (gr. 2-4). pap. 11.94 *(978-1-60357-679-6(7))*; lib. bdg. 22.60 *(978-1-59953-144-1(5))* Norwood Hse. Pr.
Christopher, Clara. Animal Jokes, Riddles, & Games. 2016. (ENG., Illus.). 32p. (J). *(978-0-7787-2387-5(9))* Crabtree Publishing Co.
Cleary, Brian P. Chips & Cheese & Nana's Knees: What Is Alliteration? Goneau, Martin, illus. 2017. (Words Are CATegorical (r) Ser.). (ENG.). 32p. (J). (gr. 2-5). 7.99 *(978-1-5124-3421-7(3),* 59e432c1-1075-4832-9637-2172a8180406, Millbrook Pr.) Lerner Publishing Group.
Cliff Road Books Staff & Sweetwater Press Staff, contrib. by. Jokes & Riddles for Kids of All Ages, 3 vols. 2004. (Illus.). *(978-1-58173-312-9(7))*; *(978-1-60261-115-3(7))*; *(978-1-58173-313-6(5))* Cliff Road Bks.
Cole, William. Monster Knock Knocks. 2012. (ENG.). 112p. (Orig.). (J). (gr. 3-6). pap. 6.99 *(978-1-4424-7438-3(6),* Simon Pulse) Simon Pulse.
Cole, William Edward. Cole's Funny Picture Book No. 2011. 976p. pap. *(978-1-84902-480-8(4))* Benediction Classics.
Compiled by Barbour Staff, Compiled by. 999 Super Silly, Awesomely Hilarious, Funny Bone-Tickling Jokes for Kids. 2018. (ENG.). 224p. (J). pap. 4.99 *(978-1-68322-561-4(9),* Barbour Bks.) Barbour Publishing, Inc.
Connolly, Sean. The Fun on the Farm Joke Book, 1 vol. 2013. (Laugh Out Loud Ser.). (ENG., Illus.). 32p. (J). (gr. 2-3). pap. 12.75 *(978-1-61533-654-8(0),* 4411dc72-2bec-4eb9-8931-38a229b9c898, Windmill Bks.) Rosen Publishing Group, Inc., The.
—The Hysterical History Joke Book, 1 vol. 2013. (Laugh Out Loud Ser.). (ENG., Illus.). 32p. (gr. 2-3). pap. 12.75 *(978-1-61533-656-2(7),* 45eff5c7-4c06-4436-b867-26445dc93062, Windmill Bks.) Rosen Publishing Group, Inc., The.
—The Jolly Jungle Joke Book, 1 vol. 2013. (Laugh Out Loud Ser.). (ENG., Illus.). 32p. (J). (gr. 2-3). pap. 12.75 *(978-1-61533-658-6(3),* 7cc40f00-7f5d-4ef0-9ac6-028f4667ba38, Windmill Bks.) Rosen Publishing Group, Inc., The.
—Laugh Out Loud! The Silly Spells Joke Book, 1 vol. 2013. (Laugh Out Loud Ser.). (ENG., Illus.). 32p. (J). (gr. 2-3). pap. 12.75 *(978-1-61533-662-3(1),* ac89c5ed-2713-4ee6-9512-aad8f408078d, Windmill Bks.) Rosen Publishing Group, Inc., The.
—The Out to Sea Joke Book, 1 vol. 2013. (Laugh Out Loud Ser.). (ENG., Illus.). 32p. (J). (gr. 2-3). pap. 12.75 *(978-1-61533-660-9(5),* 11ae99e9-4648-469c-a748-e90815f33218, Windmill Bks.) Rosen Publishing Group, Inc., The.
Connolly, Sean & Harris, Joseph. The Crazy Computers Joke Book, 1 vol. 2013. (Laugh Out Loud Ser.). (ENG., Illus.). 32p. (J). (gr. 2-3). pap. 12.75 *(978-1-61533-652-4(4),* 282d9131-5620-459a-9f34-8eb2a9695790); lib. bdg. 31.27 *(978-1-61533-643-2(5),* 187c0a6e-bbc5-4a9c-ac86-69450b8786b2) Rosen Publishing Group, Inc., The. (Windmill Bks.).
Corchin, Dj. The Marching Band Nerds Handbook. Dougherty, Dan, illus. 2012. 136p. 22.95 *(978-0-9834876-7-8(7))*; pap. 12.95 *(978-0-9819645-7-7(5))* phazelFOZ Co., LLC., The.
Crosbie, Duncan & Potter, Tony, compiled by. Irish Jokes. 2003. (ENG., Illus.). 60p. 11.95 *(978-0-7171-3532-5(2))* M.H. Gill & Co. U. C. IRL. Dist: Dufour Editions, Inc.
Crotts, Barbara. Gemini Cricket: John Glenn - First Person to Orbit the Earth. Khory, Emil, illus. 2011. 56p. pap. 10.03 *(978-1-4269-6213-4(4))* Trafford Publishing.
Crowe, Sharon. Daniel & the Big Belly Button. 2009. 23p. (J). pap. 17.95 *(978-1-4327-1549-6(6))* Outskirts Pr., Inc.
Dahl, Michael. Knock Your Socks Off: A Book of Knock-Knock Jokes, 1 vol. Haugen, Ryan & Jensen, Brian, illus. 2010. (Michael Dahl Presents Super Funny Joke Bks.). (ENG.). 80p. (J). (gr. 1-3). 25.32 *(978-1-4048-5774-2(5),* 102654, Picture Window Bks.) Capstone.
—Laff-O-Tronic Monster Jokes! Collins, Daryll et al, illus. 2013. (Laff-O-Tronic Joke Books! Ser.). (ENG.). 96p. (J). (gr. k-3). pap. 29.70 *(978-1-4342-6239-4(1),* 20045, Stone Arch Bks.) Capstone.
—Laff-O-Tronic School Jokes! Holgate, Douglas & Collins, Daryll, illus. 2013. (Laff-O-Tronic Joke Books! Ser.). (ENG.). 96p. (J). (gr. k-3). pap. 29.70 *(978-1-4342-6240-0(5),* 20044, Stone Arch Bks.) Capstone.
—Laff-O-Tronic School Jokes!, 1 vol. Collins, Daryll et al, illus. 2013. (Laff-O-Tronic Joke Books! Ser.). (ENG.). 96p. (J). (gr. 1-3). 25.32 *(978-1-4342-6022-2(4),* 123163, Stone Arch Bks.) Capstone.
—Laugh-Out-Loud Jokes to Tell Your Friends. 2018. (Jokes, Tricks, & Other Funny Stuff Ser.). (ENG., Illus.). 32p. (J). (gr. 3-9). lib. bdg. 27.32 *(978-1-5435-0342-5(X),* 137193, Capstone Pr.) Capstone.
—Puzzling Riddles to Stump Your Friends. 2018. (Jokes, Tricks, & Other Funny Stuff Ser.). (ENG., Illus.). 32p. (J). (gr. 3-9). lib. bdg. 27.32 *(978-1-5435-0339-5(X),* 137191, Capstone Pr.) Capstone.
—School Jokes! 2013. (Laff-O-Tronic Joke Books! Ser.). (ENG., Illus.). 96p. (J). (gr. 1-3). pap. 4.95 *(978-1-4342-6192-2(1),* 123486, Stone Arch Bks.) Capstone.
—Scooby-Doo Animal Jokes. Jeralds, Scott, illus. 2015. (Scooby-Doo Joke Bks.). (ENG.). 64p. (J). (gr. 2-6). lib. bdg. 22.65 *(978-1-4342-9683-2(0),* 126991, Stone Arch Bks.) Capstone.
—Scooby-Doo on the Go Jokes. Jeralds, Scott, illus. 2015. (Scooby-Doo Joke Bks.). (ENG.). 64p. (J). (gr. 2-6). lib. bdg. 22.65 *(978-1-4342-9684-9(9),* 126992, Stone Arch Bks.) Capstone.
—Scooby-Doo's Laugh-Out-Loud Jokes! Jeralds, Scott, illus. 2015. (Scooby-Doo Joke Bks.). (ENG.). 224p. (J). (gr. 2-6). pap., pap., pap. 9.95 *(978-1-62370-182-6(1),* 126993, Capstone Young Readers) Capstone.
Dahl, Michael & Lemke, Donald. DC Super Heroes Animal Jokes. 2018. (DC Super Heroes Joke Bks.). (ENG., Illus.). 64p. (J). (gr. 2-6). lib. bdg. 23.32 *(978-1-4965-5762-9(X),* 136754, Stone Arch Bks.) Capstone.
—DC Super Heroes Joke Books. 2018. (DC Super Heroes Joke Bks.). (ENG.). 64p. (J). (gr. 2-6). 101.28 *(978-1-4965-5777-3(8),* 27414, Stone Arch Bks.) Capstone.
—DC Super Heroes Knock-Knock Jokes. 2018. (DC Super Heroes Joke Bks.). (ENG., Illus.). 64p. (J). (gr. 2-6). lib. bdg. 23.32 *(978-1-4965-5764-3(6),* 136756, Stone Arch Bks.) Capstone.
—DC Super Heroes Monster Jokes. 2018. (DC Super Heroes Joke Bks.). (ENG., Illus.). 64p. (J). (gr. 2-6). lib. bdg. 23.32 *(978-1-4965-5763-6(8),* 136755, Stone Arch Bks.) Capstone.
—DC Super Heroes School Jokes. 2018. (DC Super Heroes Joke Bks.). (ENG., Illus.). 64p. (J). (gr. 2-6). lib. bdg. 23.32 *(978-1-4965-5761-2(1),* 136753, Stone Arch Bks.) Capstone.
—DC Super Heroes World's Greatest Jokes: Featuring Batman, Superman, Wonder Woman, & More! 2018. (DC Super Heroes Ser.). (ENG., Illus.). 224p. (J). (gr. 2-6). pap., pap., pap. 9.95 *(978-1-68436-002-4(1),* 136780, Stone Arch Bks.) Capstone.
Dahl, Michael & Sullivan, Alesha. Jokes, Tricks, & Other Funny Stuff. 2018. (Jokes, Tricks, & Other Funny Stuff Ser.). (ENG.). 32p. (J). (gr. 3-9). 117.28 *(978-1-5435-0360-9(8),* 27632, Capstone Pr.) Capstone.
Dahl, Michael & Ziegler, Mark. Laughs for a Living: Jokes about Doctors, Teachers, Firefighters, & Other People Who Work, 1 vol. Haugen, Ryan & Jensen, Brian, illus. 2010. (Michael Dahl Presents Super Funny Joke Bks.). (ENG.). 80p. (J). (gr. 1-3). 25.32 *(978-1-4048-5771-1(0),* 102651, Picture Window Bks.) Capstone.
Dahl, Michael, et al. The Everything Kids' Giant Book of Jokes, Riddles, & Brain Teasers. 2010. (Everything(r) Kids Ser.). (ENG., Illus.). 304p. pap. 10.99 *(978-1-4405-0633-8(7),* Everything) Adams Media Corp.
Davis, James (Jim) W. Out-takes of 55 Years of Camping 2004. (Illus.). 168p. (YA). per. 5.95 *(978-0-9760960-0-9(5))* Davis, James (Jim).
Degen, Bruce. Snow Joke. 2014. 24p. pap. *(978-0-8234-3223-3(8))* Holiday Hse., Inc.
deGroat, Diane. April Fool! Watch Out at School! deGroat, Diane, illus. 2009. (Gilbert Ser.). (Illus.). 32p. (J). (gr. -1-3). lib. bdg. 18.89 *(978-0-06-143043-5(9))* HarperCollins Pubs.
DeTellis, Luc. Who's There: 101 Knock Knock Jokes for Kids. 2003. pap. 5.95 *(978-0-9722774-1-9(2))* Muscatello Publishing.
—Who's There Again? 101 More Knock Knock Jokes for Kids. 2004. 108p. (J). per. 6.99 *(978-0-9722774-3-3(9))* Muscatello Publishing.
Dewin, Howard & Barba, M. J. Scooby-Doo! A to Z Ultimate Joke Book. 2011. (Illus.). 63p. (J). pap. *(978-0-545-37944-1(X))* Scholastic, Inc.
Dinneen, John. The Practical Joker's Handbook. (ENG., Illus.). 80p. (J). pap. 4.95 *(978-0-330-34634-4(2),* Pan) Pan Macmillan GBR. Dist: Trafalgar Square Publishing.
—The Practical Joker's Handbook 2. Maddison, Lucy, illus. (ENG.). 80p. (J). pap. 4.95 *(978-0-330-35524-7(4),* Pan) Pan Macmillan GBR. Dist: Trafalgar Square Publishing.
Dipiazza, Francesca. Turkey in Pictures. 2nd ed. 2004. (Visual Geography Series, Second Ser.). (ENG., Illus.). 80p. (gr. 5-12). 31.93 *(978-0-8225-1169-4(X))* Lerner Publishing Group.
Doering, Jennie Spray. Beach Riddles. Pica, Steve, illus. 2006. (Silly Millies Level 3 Ser.). (ENG.). 32p. (gr. 1-3). lib. bdg. 21.27 *(978-0-7613-2885-8(8),* Millbrook Pr.) Lerner Publishing Group.
Dreams that Lye Within. 2005. (YA). *(978-1-59872-101-0(1))* Instant Pub.
Dunn, S. K., compiled by. Just Joking! 1001 Jokes to Crack You Up. 2007. (Illus.). 208p. (J). *(978-0-545-03271-1(7))* Scholastic, Inc.
Editors of Kingfisher. Sidesplitters Christmas Crackups. 2010. (Sidesplitters Ser.). (ENG., Illus.). 144p. (J). (gr. 1-4). pap. 16.19 *(978-0-7534-3045-3(2),* 9780753430453) Kingfisher Publications, plc GBR. Dist: Children's Plus, Inc.
Editors of Portable Press. The Spookiest Tricks & Treats Joke Book Ever! 2019. (ENG., Illus.). 256p. (J). (gr. 3-7). pap. 8.99 *(978-1-68412-941-6(9),* Portable Pr.) Printers Row Publishing Group.
—The Wackiest Joke Book Ever! 2017. (ENG., Illus.). 128p. (J). (gr. 3-7). pap. 4.99 *(978-1-62686-380-4(6),* Portable Pr.) Printers Row Publishing Group.
—The Wackiest Joke Book That'll Knock-Knock You Over! 2018. (ENG., Illus.). 256p. (J). (gr. 3-7). pap. 8.99 *(978-1-68412-278-3(3),* Portable Pr.) Printers Row Publishing Group.
Editors of Portable Press, ed. The Funniest & Grossest Joke Book Ever! 2017. (ENG., Illus.). 256p. (J). (gr. 3-7). pap. 8.99 *(978-1-68412-128-1(0),* Portable Pr.) Printers Row Publishing Group.
Einstein, Nicholle. Animal Knock-Knock Jokes, 1 vol. 2014. (KidsWorld Ser.). (ENG., Illus.). 64p. (J). pap. 6.99 *(978-0-9938401-7-3(5),* 79ce649f-6280-4fb4-ae8b-56b0dc1685a1) KidsWorld Bks. CAN. Dist: Lone Pine Publishing USA.
—Animal Riddles, 1 vol. 2016. (KidsWorld Ser.). (ENG., Illus.). 64p. (J). pap. 6.99 *(978-0-9940069-6-7(5),* 8edf66ca-bc2a-4c9c-93a5-0de4972dbb54) KidsWorld Bks. CAN. Dist: Lone Pine Publishing USA.
—Dinosaur Jokes, 1 vol. 2016. (KidsWorld Ser.). (ENG., Illus.). 64p. (J). pap. 6.99 *(978-0-9940069-7-4(7),* adcbf8a8-e01c-4dd1-893f-a492729c4dab) KidsWorld Bks. CAN. Dist: Lone Pine Publishing USA.
Elling, Brian & Who HQ. Knock! Knock! Who Was There? Thomson, Andrew, illus. 2018. (Who Was? Ser.). 128p. (J). (gr. 3-7). 6.99 *(978-0-515-15932-5(8),* Penguin Workshop) Penguin Young Readers Group.
Elliott, Rob. The Complete Laugh-Out-Loud Jokes for Kids: A 4-In-1 Collection. 2016. (ENG.). 256p. 12.99 *(978-0-8007-2829-8(7))* Revell.
—Laugh-Out-Loud a+ Jokes for Kids. 2018. (Laugh-Out-Loud Jokes for Kids Ser.). (ENG., Illus.). 128p. (J). (gr. 1-5). pap. 6.99 *(978-0-06-274872-0(6),* HarperCollins) HarperCollins Pubs.
—Laugh-Out-Loud Adventure Jokes for Kids. 2019. (Laugh-Out-Loud Jokes for Kids Ser.). (ENG., Illus.). 144p. (J). (gr. 1-5). pap. 4.99 *(978-0-06-274870-6(X),* HarperCollins) HarperCollins Pubs.
—Laugh-Out-Loud Animal Jokes for Kids. 2014. (ENG.). 128p. (J). pap. 5.99 *(978-0-8007-2375-0(9))* Revell.
—Laugh-Out-Loud Awesome Jokes for Kids. Gearbox, illus. 2017. (Laugh-Out-Loud Jokes for Kids Ser.). (ENG.). 128p. (J). (gr. 1-5). pap. 4.99 *(978-0-06-249795-6(2),* HarperCollins) HarperCollins Pubs.
—Laugh-Out-Loud Christmas Jokes for Kids: A Christmas Holiday Book for Kids. Gearbox, illus. 2016. (Laugh-Out-Loud Jokes for Kids Ser.). (ENG.). 144p. (J). (gr. 1-5). pap. 8.99 *(978-0-06-249791-8(X),* HarperCollins) HarperCollins Pubs.
—Laugh-Out-Loud Holiday Jokes for Kids: 2-In-1 Collection of Spooky Jokes & Christmas Jokes: a Christmas Holiday Book for Kids. Gearbox, illus. 2016. (Laugh-Out-Loud Jokes for Kids Ser.). (ENG.). 272p. (J). (gr. 1-5). 10.99 *(978-0-06-256976-9(7),* HarperCollins) HarperCollins Pubs.
—Laugh-Out-Loud Road Trip Jokes for Kids. Gearbox, illus. 2017. (Laugh-Out-Loud Jokes for Kids Ser.). (ENG.). 128p. (J). (gr. 1-5). pap. 6.99 *(978-0-06-249793-2(6),* HarperCollins) HarperCollins Pubs.
—Laugh-Out-Loud Spooky Jokes for Kids. 2016. (Laugh-Out-Loud Jokes for Kids Ser.). (ENG., Illus.). 128p. (J). (gr. 1-5). pap. 6.99 *(978-0-06-249788-8(X),* HarperCollins) HarperCollins Pubs.
—Laugh-Out-Loud Spooky Jokes for Kids () 2016. (Laugh-Out-Loud Jokes for Kids Ser.). 128p. (J). (gr. 1-5). pap. 4.99 *(978-0-06-266105-0(1))* HarperCollins Pubs.
—Laugh-Out-Loud Springtime Jokes for Kids. 2019. (Laugh-Out-Loud Jokes for Kids Ser.). (ENG., Illus.). 128p. (J). (gr. 1-5). pap. 6.99 *(978-0-06-287220-3(6),* HarperCollins) HarperCollins Pubs.
—Laugh-Out-Loud Ultimate Jokes for Kids: 2-In-1 Collection of Awesome Jokes & Road Trip Jokes. Gearbox, illus. 2017. (Laugh-Out-Loud Jokes for Kids Ser.). (ENG.). 256p. (J). (gr. 1-5). 10.99 *(978-0-06-256977-6(5),* HarperCollins) HarperCollins Pubs.
—More Laugh-Out-Loud Jokes for Kids. 2014. (ENG.). 128p. (J). pap. 4.99 *(978-0-8007-8821-6(4))* Revell.
Enright, Amanda. My First Joke Book. 2018. (ENG.). 96p. (J). pap. 9.99 *(978-1-78828-520-9(4),* 1fd35e6e-05fa-41d5-afa3-5901002ed1ad) Arcturus Publishing GBR. Dist: Baker & Taylor Publisher Services (BTPS).
Eshleman, William & Kimball, Paige. Prank & Pray You Get Away! over 60 Fun Jokes to Play on Your Sibling. 2012. 154p. pap. 13.95 *(978-0-9849322-0-7(8))* Find Your Way Publishing, Inc.
Farshore. The Ultimate Unicorn Joke Book. 2018. (ENG., Illus.). 96p. (J). (gr. k-2). pap. 7.99 *(978-1-4052-9433-1(7),* Red Shed) Farshore GBR. Dist: HarperCollins Pubs.
Figglehorn, Fred & Fisher, J. J. Fred-Tastically Funny Jokes. 2012. (Illus.). 64p. (J). pap. *(978-0-545-35603-9(2))* Scholastic, Inc.
Fitch, Sheree. There Were Monkeys in My Kitchen. braille ed. 2004. (Illus.). (J). (gr. k-3). spiral bd. *(978-0-616-01639-8(5))* Canadian National Institute for the Blind/Institut National Canadien pour les Aveugles.
Fleischman, Sid. Jim Ugly. Smith, Jos. A., illus. 2003. (ENG.). 144p. (J). (gr. 3-7). pap. 6.99 *(978-0-06-052121-9(X),* Greenwillow Bks.) HarperCollins Pubs.
Friedman, Sharon. Grin & Bear It: Zoo Jokes to Make You Roar. Gable, Brian, illus. 2005. (Make Me Laugh! Ser.). 32p. (J). (gr. k-3). lib. bdg. 19.93 *(978-1-57505-660-9(7))* Lerner Publishing Group.
Gallo, Tina. Lettuce In! And Other Knock-Knock Jokes. Chollat, Emilie, illus. 2011. (Little Simon Sillies Ser.). (ENG.). 20p. (J). (gr. -1-1). 5.99 *(978-1-4424-1404-4(9),* Little Simon) Little Simon.
Garstecki, Julia. Goofy, Nutty Jokes about Parents & Teachers. 2018. (Just for Laughs Ser.). (ENG., Illus.). 24p. (J). (gr. 4-6). lib. bdg. *(978-1-68072-327-4(8),* 12092, Hi Jinx) Black Rabbit Bks.
—Make Your Own Drinkable Blood. 24p. (J). 2019. (Illus.). pap. *(978-1-68072-757-9(5))* 2018. (ENG.). (gr. 4-6). pap. 8.99 *(978-1-64466-310-3(4),* 12535, Hi Jinx) Black Rabbit Bks.
—Make Your Own Fake Poo. 24p. (J). 2019. (Illus.). pap. *(978-1-68072-761-6(3))* 2018. (ENG.). (gr. 4-6). pap. 8.99 *(978-1-64466-314-1(7),* 12551, Hi Jinx) Black Rabbit Bks.
—Make Your Own Fake Skin. 24p. (J). 2019. (Illus.). pap. *(978-1-68072-758-6(3))* 2018. (ENG.). (gr. 1-3). pap. 8.99 *(978-1-64466-311-0(2),* 12539, Hi Jinx) Black Rabbit Bks.
—Make Your Own Fake Snot. 24p. (J). 2019. (Illus.). pap. *(978-1-68072-759-3(1))* 2018. (ENG.). (gr. 4-6). pap. 8.99 *(978-1-64466-312-7(0),* 12543, Hi Jinx) Black Rabbit Bks.
—Make Your Own Fake Vomit. (J). 2019. pap. *(978-1-68072-762-3(1))* 2018. (ENG.). 24p. (gr. 4-6). pap. 8.99 *(978-1-64466-315-8(5),* 12555, Hi Jinx) 2018. (ENG.). 24p. (gr. 4-6). lib. bdg. 28.50 *(978-1-68072-631-2(5),* 12554, Hi Jinx) Black Rabbit Bks.
—Make Your Own Farting Goo. 24p. (J). 2019. (Illus.). pap. *(978-1-68072-760-9(5))* 2018. (ENG.). (gr. 1-3). pap. 8.99 *(978-1-64466-313-4(9),* 12547, Hi Jinx) Black Rabbit Bks.
—Silly, Smelly Animal Jokes. 2018. (Just for Laughs Ser.). (ENG., Illus.). 24p. (J). (gr. 4-6). lib. bdg. *(978-1-68072-330-4(8),* 12101, Hi Jinx) Black Rabbit Bks.
—Terribly Tricky Tongue Twisters. 2018. (Just for Laughs Ser.). (ENG., Illus.). 24p. (J). (gr. 4-6). lib. bdg. *(978-1-68072-331-1(6),* 12104, Hi Jinx) Black Rabbit Bks.
Gatacre, Sophie. Please Don't Call Me Mad! 2005. Orig. Title: Don't Call Me Mad. (YA). pap. 9.99 *(978-0-9746697-1-7(7))* Three Cents Publishing.
Gibeau, Claire Janvier. Homonyms. 2009. 40p. pap. 16.99 *(978-1-4490-3367-5(9))* AuthorHouse.
Gifford, Clive. 1001 Really Ridiculously Silly Jokes. 2018. (ENG., Illus.). 256p. (J). (gr. 1-7). 9.99 *(978-1-4449-4445-7(2))* Hachette Children's Group GBR. Dist: Hachette Bk. Group.
Gogol, Nikolai. The Nose. 2011. (ENG.). 42p. (gr. 4-7). pap. 7.95 *(978-1-60664-520-8(X))* Rodgers, Alan Bks.
Gonzales, Doreen. Silly Cat Jokes to Tickle Your Funny Bone, 1 vol. 2014. (Funniest Bone Animal Jokes Ser.). (ENG.). 48p. (gr. 3-3). 18.61 *(978-0-7660-5991-7(X),* 27d95da5-0516-4960-82a0-afaa12b9d08d); (Illus.). pap. 11.53 *(978-0-7660-5992-4(8),* 9f229f62-990f-4000-9e56-bc70a2004c6b, Enslow Elementary) Enslow Publishing, LLC.
Goode, Ben. The Fine Art of Worrying: The Official Guide Book for Worry Warts. 2003. (YA). per. 9.95 *(978-1-885027-21-4(4))* Apricot Pr.
Greening, Rosie. It's Fun to Be a Furmaid. Lynch, Stuart, illus. 2018. (ENG.). 12p. (J). (gr. -1 — 1). bds. 10.99 *(978-1-78692-965-5(1))* Make Believe Ideas GBR. Dist: Scholastic, Inc.
Griffiths, Andy. The Treehouse Joke Book. Denton, Terry, illus. 2020. (Treehouse Bks.). (ENG.). 304p. (J). pap. 10.99 *(978-1-250-25950-9(9),* 900221044) Feiwel & Friends.
—What Body Part Is That? A Wacky Guide to the Funniest, Weirdest, & Most Disgustingest Parts of Your Body. Denton, Terry, illus. 2013. (ENG.). 208p. (J). (gr. 3-7). pap. 12.99 *(978-1-250-03406-9(X),* 900120576) Square Fish.
Grossman, Bill. Cowboy Ed. Wint, Florence, illus. 2004. 28p. (J). (gr. -1-3). reprint ed. *(978-0-7567-7851-4(4))* DIANE Publishing Co.
Guess, Alison. No Bones about It, Skeleton Jokes. White, David, illus. 2008. 88p. pap. 9.95 *(978-0-9817572-4-7(3))* Peppertree Pr., The.
Gumm, Merry L. Help! I'm in Middle School... How Will I Survive? 2005. (Illus.). 80p. (J). per. 9.95 *(978-0-9761724-5-1(3),* B-HMS) NSR Pubns.
Gutman, Dan. My Weird School: Jokes, Games, & Puzzles. Paillot, Jim, illus. 2018. (My Weird School Ser.). (ENG.). 192p. (J). (gr. 1-5). pap. 5.99 *(978-0-06-279687-5(9),* HarperCollins) HarperCollins Pubs.
Hall, Katy, pseud & Eisenberg, Lisa. Dino Riddles. Rubel, Nicole, illus. 2003. (Easy-to-Read Ser.). 40p. (J). (gr. -1-3). 11.65 *(978-0-7569-2823-0(0))* Perfection Learning Corp.
Hawley, Shane. ABC Death. Erkkinen, Joel, illus. 2018. (Button Poetry Ser.). (ENG.). 72p. (J). 16.00 *(978-1-943735-46-4(8))* Button Poetry.
Healy, Shay. Beastly Jokes. 2005. (ENG., Illus.). 96p. (J). pap. 10.00 *(978-0-86278-923-7(0))* O'Brien Pr., Ltd., The IRL. Dist: Dufour Editions, Inc.
—More Beastly Jokes. 2005. (ENG., Illus.). 96p. (J). pap. 10.00 *(978-0-86278-924-4(9))* O'Brien Pr., Ltd., The IRL. Dist: Dufour Editions, Inc.
Heimberg, Justin & Gomberg, David. Radically Repulsive: Over 400 Crazy Questions! 2010. (Would You Rather... ? Ser.). (ENG., Illus.). 216p. (J). (gr. 2-18). pap. 9.95 *(978-1-934734-42-1(X))* Seven Footer Pr.
—Would You Rather... ? Terrifically Twisted: Over 300 Crazy Questions! 2012. (Would You Rather... ? Ser.). (ENG., Illus.). 224p. pap. 9.95 *(978-1-934734-25-4(X))* Seven Footer Pr.
—Would You Rather... ? Wonderfully Weird: Over 400 Crazy Questions! 2013. (Would You Rather... ? Ser.). (ENG.). 224p. (gr. 2-7). pap. 9.95 *(978-1-934734-92-6(6))* Seven Footer Pr.
Heimberg, Justin & Gomberg, David, eds. Would You Rather... ? LOL: Over 300 Intensely Intriguing Questions to Ask Your Friends. 2011. (Would You Rather... ? Ser.). (ENG.). 192p. (gr. 7-18). pap. 9.95 *(978-1-934734-26-1(8))* Seven Footer Pr.
Highlights, creator. Best Kids' Jokes Ever! Volume 1, Vol. 1. 2018. (Highlights Joke Bks.). (ENG., Illus.). 128p. (J). (gr. 1-4). pap. 5.99 *(978-1-68437-244-7(5),* Highlights) Highlights Pr., c/o Highlights for Children, Inc.
—Best Kids' Jokes Ever! Volume 2, Vol. 2. 2018. (Highlights Joke Bks.). (ENG., Illus.). 128p. (J). (gr. 1-4). pap. 5.99 *(978-1-68437-243-0(7),* Highlights) Highlights Pr., c/o Highlights for Children, Inc.
—Best Kids' Knock-Knock Jokes Ever! Volume 1, Vol. 1. 2018. (Highlights Joke Bks.). (ENG., Illus.). 128p. (J). (gr. 1-4). pap. 5.99 *(978-1-68437-245-4(3),* Highlights) Highlights Pr., c/o Highlights for Children, Inc.
—Best Kids' Knock-Knock Jokes Ever! Volume 2, Vol. 2. 2018. (Highlights Joke Bks.). (Illus.). 128p. (J). (gr. 1-4). pap. 5.99 *(978-1-68437-246-1(1),* Highlights) Highlights Pr., c/o Highlights for Children, Inc.
—Knock Knock! The BIGGEST, Best Joke Book EVER. 2017. (Highlights Laugh Attack! Joke Bks.). (ENG., Illus.). 352p. (J). (gr. 1-4). pap. 9.99 *(978-1-62979-889-9(4),* Highlights) Highlights Pr., c/o Highlights for Children, Inc.
—Laugh Attack! The BIGGEST, Best Joke Book EVER. 2016. (Highlights Laugh Attack! Joke Bks.). (ENG., Illus.). 352p. (J). (gr. 1-4). pap. 9.99 *(978-1-62979-553-9(4),* 1402602, Highlights) Highlights Pr., c/o Highlights for Children, Inc.
Hoena, Blake. Sport Illustrated Kids Baseball Jokes! Collins, Daryll, illus. 2017. (Sports Illustrated Kids All-Star Jokes! Ser.). (ENG.). 64p. (J). (gr. 2-6). lib. bdg. 22.65 *(978-1-4965-5092-7(7),* 136060, Stone Arch Bks.) Capstone.
—Sports Illustrated Kids All-Star Jokes! 2017. (Sports Illustrated Kids All-Star Jokes!). (ENG., Illus.). 64p. (J). (gr. 2-6). 98.60 *(978-1-4965-5106-1(0),* 26970, Stone Arch Bks.) Capstone.
Hogan, Christa C. Laugh Out Loud Knock Knock Jokes. 2018. (Just for Laughs Ser.). (ENG.). 24p. (J). (gr. 4-6). lib. bdg. *(978-1-68072-328-1(6),* 12095, Hi Jinx) Black Rabbit Bks.
—Scary, Spooky Jokes about Monsters. 2018. (Just for Laughs Ser.). (ENG., Illus.). 24p. (J). (gr. 4-6). lib. bdg. *(978-1-68072-329-8(4),* 12098, Hi Jinx) Black Rabbit Bks.
Hollow, Michele C. Animal Jokes to Tickle Your Funny Bone, 1 vol. 2011. (Funny Bone Jokes Ser.). (ENG., Illus.). 48p. (gr. 3-3). pap. 11.53 *(978-0-7660-5985-6(5),* 6ac136ee-50b0-4626-9752-11d6ca140dcf); lib. bdg. 25.27 *(978-0-7660-3544-7(1),* 4de0b97d-0602-4ee3-9798-c46016309308) Enslow Publishing, LLC. (Enslow Elementary).
Hollow, Michele C., et al. Hilarious Jokes for Minecrafters: Mobs, Zombies, Skeletons, & More. 2016. (Jokes for Minecrafters Ser.). (ENG., Illus.). 176p. (J). (gr. k). pap. 7.99

W X Y Z

(978-1-5107-0632-3(1), Sky Pony Pr.) Skyhorse Publishing Co., Inc.

—Jokes for Minecrafters: Booby Traps, Bombs, Boo-Boos, & More. 2016. (Jokes for Minecrafters Ser.). (ENG., Illus.). 176p. (J). (gr. k). pap. 7.99 *(978-1-5107-0633-0(X)*, Sky Pony Pr.) Skyhorse Publishing Co., Inc.

Howell, Laura. Hundreds of Silly Jokes. 2008. (Activity Cards Ser.). (Illus.). 50p. (J). 9.99 *(978-0-7945-2384-8(6)*, Usborne) EDC Publishing.

Howell, Laura, ed. Animal Jokes. Rolland, Leonard Le, illus. 2004. (Jokes Ser.). 96p. (J). pap. 6.95 *(978-0-7945-0655-1(0)*, Usborne) EDC Publishing.

—Jokes. 2009. (Kid Kits Ser.). 50p. (J). 15.99 *(978-1-60130-161-1(8)*, Usborne) EDC Publishing.

—The Usborne Book of Really Awful Jokes: About School & Other Stuff. Le Rolland, Leonard, illus. 2005. (Usborne Ser.). 288p. (J). (gr. -1-7). per. 10.95 *(978-0-7945-0578-3(3)*, Usborne) EDC Publishing.

—The Usborne Book of Silly Jokes. Le Rolland, Leonard, illus. 2003. (Jokes Ser.). 96p. (J). (gr. 4-7). pap. 6.95 *(978-0-7945-0395-6(0)*, Usborne) EDC Publishing.

Isler, Linda Germano. It's Elementary, Funny Things Kids Say in School. Santitoro, Theresa & Tumminello, Giovanna, illus. 2010. 32p. pap. 9.95 *(978-1-936343-00-3(2))* Peppertree Pr., The.

Jobo Jobo, Jobo. Jokes from the Back Seat: Humor for Kids! 2019. (Illus.). 128p. (J). (gr. 2-6). pap. 4.99 *(978-1-947597-14-3(0))* Walnut Street Bks.

Jumbo Shrimp, the Ultimate Oxymoron Book. 2003. per. 19.95 *(978-0-9745049-0-2(4))* Fein, Bruce.

Just Joking, 12 vols. 2016. (Just Joking Ser.). 48p. (ENG.). (gr. 2-3). 197.58 *(978-1-4994-8094-8(6)*, 61c16fca-e6ca-488f-8d7b-f5503aed9bed); (gr. 3-2). pap. 70.50 *(978-1-5081-9277-0(4))* Rosen Publishing Group, Inc., The. (Windmill Bks.).

Just Kidding! 2014. (Just Kidding! Ser.). 24p. (J). (gr. 2-3). pap. 48.90 *(978-1-4824-1545-2(3))* Stevens, Gareth Publishing LLLP.

Kay, Edward. Stinky Science: Why the Smelliest Smells Smell So Smelly. Shiell, Mike, illus. 2019. (ENG.). 44p. (J). (gr. 3-7). 17.99 *(978-1-77138-382-0(8))* Kids Can Pr., Ltd. CAN. Dist: Hachette Bk. Group.

Keating, Eliza. Folk of Feodora's Lane: There is a Lane... ... . 2010. 68p. pap. 11.95 *(978-1-4327-5659-8(1))* Outskirts Pr., Inc.

Keller, Charles. Super Knock-Knocks. Harpster, Steve, illus. 2003. (Giggle Fit Ser.). (ENG.). 48p. (J). (gr. k-3). 16.19 *(978-1-4027-0863-3(7))* Sterling Publishing Co., Inc.

Keller, Charles & Rosenbloom, Joseph. The Gigantic Book of Giggles. 2004. (Illus.). 255p. (J). pap. 4.98 *(978-1-4027-1535-8(8)*, Sterling/Main St.) Sterling Publishing Co., Inc.

Kids, National Geographic. Just Joking Sidesplitters. 2019. (Just Joking Ser.). 208p. (J). (gr. 3-7). (ENG.). lib. bdg. 17.90 *(978-1-4263-3311-8(0))*; (Illus.). pap. 7.99 *(978-1-4263-3310-1(2))* Disney Publishing Worldwide. (National Geographic Kids).

—Just Joking Sports. 2018. (Just Joking Ser.). (Illus.). 208p. (J). (gr. 3-7). pap. 7.99 *(978-1-4263-2979-1(2)*, National Geographic Kids) Disney Publishing Worldwide.

King, Joe. The Funniest Animal Joke Book Ever. Baines, Nigel, illus. 2015. (ENG.). 96p. (J). pap. 9.99 *(978-1-78344-233-1(6))* Andersen Pr. GBR. Dist: Independent Pubs. Group.

Kirby, Robert. Kirby Soup for the Soul. Bagley, Pat, illus. 2003. 127p. per. 9.95 *(978-0-9744860-2-4(7))* White Horse Bks.

Klutz Editors. Scratch Off Carabiners: Punch Lines; Truth or Dare; Your Future. 2005. (ENG.). 40p. (J). (gr. 1-18). 3.95 *(978-1-57054-878-9(1))* Klutz.

Kowitt, Holly. Off-The-Hook Big Book of Really Dumb School Jokes. 2007. (Illus.). (J). *(978-0-439-93335-3(8))* Scholastic, Inc.

—Too Funny! 234 Laugh-Out-Loud Jokes. 2008. (Illus.). 63p. (J). pap. *(978-0-439-67172-9(8))* Scholastic, Inc.

Krieger, Emily. Real or Fake? Far-Out Fibs, Fishy Facts, & Phony Photos to Test for the Truth. 2016. (Illus.). 208p. (J). (gr. 3-7). pap. 7.99 *(978-1-4263-2405-5(7)*, National Geographic Kids) Disney Publishing Worldwide.

—Real or Fake? 3. 2018. (Illus.). 208p. (J). (gr. 3-7). (ENG.). lib. bdg. 17.90 *(978-1-4263-3005-6(7))*; Vol. 3. pap. 7.99 *(978-1-4263-3004-9(9))* Disney Publishing Worldwide. (National Geographic Kids).

Krull, Kathleen & Brewer, Paul. Lincoln Tells a Joke: How Laughter Saved the President (and the Country) Innerst, Stacy, illus. 2010. (ENG.). 40p. (J). (gr. 1-4). 17.99 *(978-0-15-206639-0(X)*, 1199695, Clarion Bks.) HarperCollins Pubs.

Laffin, Ima. Knock Knock Jokes. 2016. (Big Buddy Jokes Ser.). (ENG., Illus.). 32p. (J). (gr. 2-5). lib. bdg. 34.21 *(978-1-68078-512-8(5)*, 23573, Big Buddy Bks.) ABDO Publishing Co.

—Monster Jokes. 2016. (Big Buddy Jokes Ser.). (ENG., Illus.). 32p. (J). (gr. 2-5). lib. bdg. 34.21 *(978-1-68078-513-5(3)*, 23575, Big Buddy Bks.) ABDO Publishing Co.

LaRoche, Amelia. Amusing Animal Jokes to Tickle Your Funny Bone, 1 vol. 2014. (Funniest Bone Animal Jokes Ser.). (ENG.). 48p. (gr. 3-3). 18.61 *(978-0-7660-5968-9(5)*, a41500cb-a5ba-4252-bd72-4b9af2eea608); (Illus.). pap. 11.53 *(978-0-7660-5969-6(3)*, d16e37c0-ee7a-4916-bf2b-e58ef12941c4, Enslow Elementary) Enslow Publishing, LLC.

—April Fool's Day Jokes to Tickle Your Funny Bone, 1 vol. 2013. (Funnier Bone Jokes Ser.). (ENG.). 48p. (gr. 3-3). pap. 11.53 *(978-1-4644-0180-0(2)*, c39fd82c-171a-4fdf-af66-e9cc6e5a05b6, Enslow Elementary); lib. bdg. 25.27 *(978-0-7660-4122-6(0)*, 2ed40a51-cc28-40e0-bbd8-42f503dc7e83) Enslow Publishing, LLC.

—Fowl Chicken Jokes to Tickle Your Funny Bone, 1 vol. 2014. (Funniest Bone Animal Jokes Ser.). (ENG., Illus.). 48p. (gr. 3-3). 18.61 *(978-0-7660-5963-4(4)*, 3fdfe874-9dae-4905-a3a3-e47318286092, Enslow Elementary) Enslow Publishing, LLC.

—Ho-Ho-Ho Christmas Jokes to Tickle Your Funny Bone, 1 vol. 2013. (Funnier Bone Jokes Ser.). (ENG.). 48p. (gr. 3-3). 25.27 *(978-0-7660-4123-3(9)*, 7ee30063-5dbe-4c3f-9f75-8f92b56e518c); pap. 11.53 *(978-1-4644-0181-7(0)*, a2bc9345-0bae-4e87-b6be-728b5c57645b, Enslow Elementary) Enslow Publishing, LLC.

Laughter. 2004. per. 9.95 *(978-0-9760484-0-4(X))* Dennison, Donna.

Laughter is the Best Medicine: Individual Title Six-Packs. (Action Packs Ser.). 120p. (gr. 3-5). 44.00 *(978-0-7635-8433-7(9))* Rigby Education.

Le Rolland, L. & Smith, Alastair. Classroom Jokes. 2004. (What's Happening Ser.). (ENG.). 96p. (J). pap. 6.95 *(978-0-7945-0391-8(8))* EDC Publishing.

Lee, Cyl. Really Silly Jokes. 2016. (Big Buddy Jokes Ser.). (ENG., Illus.). 32p. (J). (gr. 2-5). lib. bdg. 34.21 *(978-1-68078-514-2(1)*, 23577, Big Buddy Bks.) ABDO Publishing Co.

—Ridiculous Riddles. 2016. (Big Buddy Jokes Ser.). (ENG., Illus.). 32p. (J). (gr. 2-5). lib. bdg. 34.21 *(978-1-68078-515-9(X)*, 23579, Big Buddy Bks.) ABDO Publishing Co.

Leet, Karen M. Gross Pranks, 1 vol. 2013. (Gross Guides). (ENG., Illus.). 32p. (J). (gr. 3-9). 28.65 *(978-1-4296-9922-8(1)*, 120633, Capstone Pr.) Capstone.

Lewis, J. Patrick. National Geographic Kids Just Joking: Animal Riddles. 2015. (Illus.). 208p. (J). (gr. 3-7). pap. 7.99 *(978-1-4263-1869-6(3)*, National Geographic Kids) Disney Publishing Worldwide.

Lewis, J. Patrick & Yolen, Jane. Last Laughs: Animal Epitaphs. Timmins, Jeffrey Stewart, illus. 2012. (ENG.). 32p. (J). (gr. 2-5). 16.95 *(978-1-58089-260-5(4))* Charlesbridge Publishing, Inc.

Lindley, Sally. Stellar Space Jokes, 1 vol. 2016. (Just Joking Ser.). (ENG., Illus.). 48p. (J). (gr. 2-3). lib. bdg. 32.93 *(978-1-5081-9258-9(8)*, 01e10806-754b-44cd-b1a7-dbacf1497c57, Windmill Bks.) Rosen Publishing Group, Inc., The.

Lisboa, David M. The World Best Jokes. 2004. 160p. 12.00 *(978-0-9752740-0-2(7))* Lisboa, David.

Little Bee Books. The Gross Book of Jokes. 2015. (ENG., Illus.). 144p. (J). (gr. 2-5). pap. 7.99 *(978-1-4998-0162-0(9))* Little Bee Books Inc.

Loh-Hagan, Virginia. Epic Fails. 2017. (Stranger Than Fiction Ser.). (ENG., Illus.). 32p. (J). (gr. 4-8). lib. bdg. 32.07 *(978-1-63472-893-5(9)*, 209998, 45th Parallel Press) Cherry Lake Publishing.

Lowenstein Niven, Felicia. Brainless Birthday Jokes to Tickle Your Funny Bone, 1 vol. 2013. (Funnier Bone Jokes Ser.). (ENG.). 48p. (gr. 3-3). pap. 11.53 *(978-1-4644-0179-4(9)*, 4be80e9a-20d2-4fda-a195-8ce56151829c, Enslow Elementary); lib. bdg. 25.27 *(978-0-7660-4121-9(2)*, afe6568d-6813-4d05-a109-86821d729afd) Enslow Publishing, LLC.

—Ha-Ha Holiday Jokes to Tickle Your Funny Bone, 1 vol. 2011. (Funny Bone Jokes Ser.). (ENG., Illus.). 48p. (gr. 3-3). pap. 11.53 *(978-0-7660-5988-7(X)*, 8ed1ac86-eb04-496e-97cc-38c8e1d49a06); lib. bdg. 25.27 *(978-0-7660-3542-3(5)*, 3a5d3fc2-6537-477c-897a-7d7720158629) Enslow Publishing, LLC. (Enslow Elementary).

—Hilarious Huge Animal Jokes to Tickle Your Funny Bone, 1 vol. 2014. (Funniest Bone Animal Jokes Ser.). (ENG., Illus.). 48p. (gr. 3-3). 18.61 *(978-0-7660-5948-1(0)*, 4c42a900-955f-4243-b68f-95fc04664a3f, Enslow Elementary) Enslow Publishing, LLC.

—Hysterical Dog Jokes to Tickle Your Funny Bone, 1 vol. 2014. (Funniest Bone Animal Jokes Ser.). (ENG., Illus.). 48p. (gr. 3-3). 18.61 *(978-0-7660-5958-0(8)*, d346db23-9418-417d-9101-e2f41bc90af1); pap. 11.53 *(978-0-7660-5959-7(6)*, f02b4de2-9e75-4e2b-a982-ad6ea8db86ba, Enslow Elementary) Enslow Publishing, LLC.

—Weird Science Jokes to Tickle Your Funny Bone, 1 vol. 2011. (Funny Bone Jokes Ser.). (ENG., Illus.). 48p. (gr. 3-3). pap. 11.53 *(978-0-7660-5990-0(1)*, df548541-ead5-445d-92b3-521c3ec77c77); lib. bdg. 25.27 *(978-0-7660-3543-0(3)*, aa730b1d-cf4e-4d49-9fb6-0c476eb5842c) Enslow Publishing, LLC. (Enslow Elementary).

MacLennan, David. Christmas Jokes for Kids, 1 vol. 2013. (ENG., Illus.). 240p. (J). pap. 14.95 *(978-1-926677-91-0(9)*, fa57fd94-d6b5-4365-9ca6-545baa84b460) Folklore Publishing CAN. Dist: Lone Pine Publishing USA.

—Jokes for Canadian Kids, 1 vol. 2011. (ENG.). 168p. (J). pap. 14.95 *(978-1-926677-45-3(5)*, 9d18a265-a5ca-4ded-bd0b-5b68c2d02765) Folklore Publishing CAN. Dist: Lone Pine Publishing USA.

Mad Libs. Diary of a Wimpy Kid Mad Libs: World's Greatest Word Game. 2015. (Mad Libs Ser.). (ENG.). 48p. (J). (gr. 3-7). pap. 5.99 *(978-0-8431-8353-5(5)*, Mad Libs) Penguin Young Readers Group.

—Mad Libs Mania: World's Greatest Word Game. 2015. (Mad Libs Ser.). 240p. (J). (gr. 3-7). bds. 8.99 *(978-0-8431-8289-7(X)*, Mad Libs) Penguin Young Readers Group.

—Meow Libs: World's Greatest Word Game. 2015. (Mad Libs Ser.). 48p. (J). (gr. 3-7). bds. 5.99 *(978-0-8431-8292-7(X)*, Mad Libs) Penguin Young Readers Group.

Make Believe Ideas Editors. Big Joke Mash-Up! 2017. (ENG., Illus.). 128p. (J). pap. 12.99 *(978-1-68412-025-3(X)*, Silver Dolphin Bks.) Readerlink Distribution Services, LLC.

Manushkin, Fran. Katie Woo's Crazy Critter Jokes. 2017. (Katie Woo's Joke Bks.). (ENG., Illus.). 32p. (J). (gr. k-2). pap. 5.95 *(978-1-5158-0975-3(7)*, 134783); lib. bdg. 21.32 *(978-1-5158-0971-5(4)*, 134779) Capstone. (Picture Window Bks.).

—Katie Woo's Funny Friends & Family Jokes. 2017. (Katie Woo's Joke Bks.). (ENG., Illus.). 32p. (J). (gr. k-2). lib. bdg. 21.32 *(978-1-5158-0973-9(0)*, 134781, Picture Window Bks.) Capstone.

—Katie Woo's Hilarious Holiday Jokes. 2017. (Katie Woo's Joke Bks.). (ENG., Illus.). 32p. (J). (gr. k-2). lib. bdg. 21.32 *(978-1-5158-0972-2(2)*, 134780, Picture Window Bks.) Capstone.

—Katie Woo Joke Books. 2017. (Katie Woo's Joke Bks.). (ENG.). 32p. (J). (gr. k-2). pap., pap., pap. 23.80 *(978-1-5158-0992-0(7)*, 26126, Picture Window Bks.) Capstone.

—Katie Woo's Silly School Jokes. 2017. (Katie Woo's Joke Bks.). (ENG., Illus.). 32p. (J). (gr. k-2). pap. 5.95 *(978-1-5158-0978-4(1)*, 134786, Picture Window Bks.) Capstone.

Marchesani, Laura. Teachers Rule! Mad Libs: World's Greatest Word Game. 2015. (Mad Libs Ser.). 48p. (J). (gr. 3-7). bds. 5.99 *(978-0-8431-8334-4(9)*, Mad Libs) Penguin Young Readers Group.

Mayer, Kristin. Alvin & the Chipmunks: Joke Book. 2012. 48p. *(978-0-545-48121-2(X))* Scholastic, Inc.

Mitchell, Susan K. Humorous Small Critter Jokes to Tickle Your Funny Bone, 1 vol. 2014. (Funniest Bone Animal Jokes Ser.). (ENG., Illus.). 48p. (gr. 3-3). 18.61 *(978-0-7660-6032-6(2)*, bdd9b487-3e92-4943-a58d-7ad1edf73231, Enslow Elementary) Enslow Publishing, LLC.

Montgomery, Monte. Kid Confidential: An Insider's Guide to Grown-Ups. Storms, Patricia, illus. 2012. (ENG.). 160p. (J). (gr. 3-6). 24.94 *(978-0-8027-8643-2(X)*, 9780802786432) Walker & Co.

Moore, Hugh. School Jokes. 2016. (Big Buddy Jokes Ser.). (ENG., Illus.). 32p. (J). (gr. 2-5). lib. bdg. 34.21 *(978-1-68078-516-6(8)*, 23581, Big Buddy Bks.) ABDO Publishing Co.

—Sports Jokes. 2016. (Big Buddy Jokes Ser.). (ENG., Illus.). 32p. (J). (gr. 2-5). lib. bdg. 34.21 *(978-1-68078-517-3(6)*, 23583, Big Buddy Bks.) ABDO Publishing Co.

Musgrave, Ruth A. National Geographic Kids Just Joking 3: 300 Hilarious Jokes about Everything, Including Tongue Twisters, Riddles, & More! 2013. (Just Joking Ser.: 3). (Illus.). 208p. (J). (gr. 3-7). pap. 8.99 *(978-1-4263-1098-0(6)*, National Geographic Kids) Disney Publishing Worldwide.

Mutchnick, Brenda & Casden, Ron. A Noteworthy Tale. Penney, Ian, illus. 2004. 30p. (J). (gr. k-4). reprint ed. 19.00 *(978-0-7567-7654-1(6))* DIANE Publishing Co.

Myers, Bill. My Life As Alien Monster Bait, 1 vol. 2019. (Incredible Worlds of Wally Mcdoogle Ser.: 2). (ENG.). 144p. (J). pap. 8.99 *(978-0-7852-3114-1(5)*, Tommy Nelson) Nelson, Thomas Inc.

Myers, Robert. 365 Knock-Knock Jokes. Toohey, Eileen N., illus. 2006. 128p. (J). (gr. 1-4). per. 5.95 *(978-1-4027-4108-1(1))* Sterling Publishing Co., Inc.

Namm, Diane. Laugh Out Loud Jokes. Becker, Wayne, illus. 2004. (Laugh-A-Long Readers Ser.). (J). *(978-0-7607-5281-4(8))* Barnes & Noble, Inc.

—Slithery Squirmy Jokes. Becker, Wayne, illus. 2004. (Laugh-A-Long Readers Ser.). (J). *(978-0-7607-5282-1(6))* Barnes & Noble, Inc.

National Geographic Kids. Just Joking: Jumbo: 1,000 Giant Jokes & 1,000 Funny Photos Add up to Big Laughs. 2017. (Just Joking Ser.). (ENG., Illus.). 288p. (J). (gr. 3-7). lib. bdg. 24.90 *(978-1-4263-2880-0(X)*, National Geographic Kids) Disney Publishing Worldwide.

—Just Joking Jumbo: 1,000 Giant Jokes & 1,000 Funny Photos Add up to Big Laughs. 2017. (Just Joking Ser.). (Illus.). 288p. (J). (gr. 3-7). pap. 14.99 *(978-1-4263-2879-4(6)*, National Geographic Kids) Disney Publishing Worldwide.

—Just Joking LOL. 2017. (Just Joking Ser.). (Illus.). 208p. (J). (gr. 3-7). pap. 7.99 *(978-1-4263-2845-9(1)*, National Geographic Kids) Disney Publishing Worldwide.

—Just Joking Sports. 2018. (Just Joking Ser.). (ENG., Illus.). 208p. (J). (gr. 3-7). lib. bdg. 17.90 *(978-1-4263-2980-7(6)*, National Geographic Kids) Disney Publishing Worldwide.

—National Geographic Kids Just Joking: 300 Hilarious Jokes, Tricky Tongue Twisters, & Ridiculous Riddles. 2012. 208p. (J). (gr. 3-7). (ENG.). lib. bdg. 14.90 *(978-1-4263-0944-1(9)*, National Geographic Children's Bks.); (Illus.). pap. 7.95 *(978-1-4263-0930-4(9)*, National Geographic Kids) Disney Publishing Worldwide.

—National Geographic Kids Just Joking: Collector's Set\ 2013. (Just Joking Ser.). (Illus.). 624p. (J). (gr. 3-7). 23.95 *(978-1-4263-1614-2(3)*, National Geographic Kids) Disney Publishing Worldwide.

—National Geographic Kids Just Joking 2: 300 Hilarious Jokes about Everything, Including Tongue Twisters, Riddles, & More. 2012. (Just Joking Ser.: 2). (Illus.). 208p. (J). (gr. 3-7). pap. 8.99 *(978-1-4263-1016-4(1)*, National Geographic Kids) Disney Publishing Worldwide.

—National Geographic Kids Just Joking 5: 300 Hilarious Jokes about Everything, Including Tongue Twisters, Riddles, & More! 2014. (Just Joking Ser.: 5). (Illus.). 208p. (J). (gr. 3-7). pap. 7.99 *(978-1-4263-1504-6(X)*, National Geographic Kids) Disney Publishing Worldwide.

—National Geographic Kids Just Joking 6: 300 Hilarious Jokes, about Everything, Including Tongue Twisters, Riddles, & More! 2014. (Just Joking Ser.: 6). (Illus.). 208p. (J). (gr. 3-7). pap. 8.99 *(978-1-4263-1735-4(2)*, National Geographic Kids) Disney Publishing Worldwide.

—National Geographic Kids Just Joking Cats. 2016. (Just Joking Ser.). (Illus.). 208p. (J). (gr. 3-7). pap. 7.99 *(978-1-4263-2327-0(1)*, National Geographic Kids) Disney Publishing Worldwide.

—National Geographic Kids Just Joking Gross. 2017. (Illus.). 208p. (J). (gr. 3-7). pap. 7.99 *(978-1-4263-2717-9(X)*, National Geographic Kids) Disney Publishing Worldwide.

Nelson, Maria. Jokes & More about Bees, 1 vol. 2014. (Just Kidding! Ser.). (ENG., Illus.). 24p. (J). (gr. 2-3). 24.27 *(978-1-4824-0538-5(5)*, f4fc694a-79a9-428c-a198-91bd5c1fd79f) Stevens, Gareth Publishing LLLP.

—Jokes & More about Dogs, 1 vol. 2014. (Just Kidding! Ser.). (ENG., Illus.). 24p. (J). (gr. 2-3). pap. 9.15 *(978-1-4824-0542-2(3)*, 3d123ea5-b995-4b35-9bb2-8871da22fd4c) Stevens, Gareth Publishing LLLP.

—Jokes & More about Fish, 1 vol. 2014. (Just Kidding! Ser.). (ENG., Illus.). 24p. (J). (gr. 2-3). pap. 9.15 *(978-1-4824-0546-0(6)*, a3ed83d4-2194-420c-900f-fc381bb1d145) Stevens, Gareth Publishing LLLP.

—Jokes & More about Horses, 1 vol. 2014. (Just Kidding! Ser.). (ENG., Illus.). 24p. (J). (gr. 2-3). 24.27 *(978-1-4824-0548-4(2)*, 4bfdeaad-60f2-4349-917a-5bf21e2cce9e) Stevens, Gareth Publishing LLLP.

—Jokes & More about Monkeys & Apes, 1 vol. 2014. (Just Kidding! Ser.). (ENG., Illus.). 24p. (J). (gr. 2-3). 24.27 *(978-1-4824-0550-7(4)*, 7a8f9c65-11de-4e79-9f65-872f24850b77) Stevens, Gareth Publishing LLLP.

—Jokes & More about Snakes, 1 vol. 2014. (Just Kidding! Ser.). (ENG., Illus.). 24p. (J). (gr. 2-3). 24.27 *(978-1-4824-0554-5(7)*, cf6b3783-2716-46ac-ab0b-bf9cb2096268) Stevens, Gareth Publishing LLLP.

Nelson, Thomas. Joke-Tionary Jokes, 1 vol. 2019. (Knock-Knock Rocks Ser.). (ENG.). 128p. (J). pap. 4.99 *(978-1-4002-1437-2(8)*, Tommy Nelson) Nelson, Thomas Inc.

—Lol-Apalooza Jokes: More Than 444 Jokes for Kids, 1 vol. 2019. (Knock-Knock Rocks Ser.). (ENG., Illus.). 128p. (J). pap. 4.99 *(978-1-4002-1438-9(6)*, Tommy Nelson) Nelson, Thomas Inc.

—Super-Funny ROFL Jokes: More Than 444 Jokes for Kids, 1 vol. 2019. (Knock-Knock Rocks Ser.). (ENG.). 128p. (J). pap 4.99 *(978-1-4002-1434-1(3)*, Tommy Nelson) Nelson, Thomas Inc.

Nuevas Adivinanzas. 2003. (SPA.). (J). pap. *(978-956-13-1304-0(9)*, AB8001) Bello, Andres CHL. Dist: Lectorum Pubns., Inc.

O'Doherty, David. Danger Is Still Everywhere: Beware of the Dog! Judge, Chris, illus. 2018. (Danger Is Everywhere Ser.: 2). (ENG.). 256p. (J). (gr. 3-7). pap. 14.99 *(978-0-316-50185-9(9))* Little, Brown Bks. for Young Readers.

Oscar's New Home. 12p. (J). bds. *(978-2-7643-0050-3(6))* Phidal Publishing, Inc./Editions Phidal, Inc.

Pallotta, Jerry. A Giraffe Did One. Mai-Wyss, Tatjana, illus. 2012. (ENG.). 32p. (J). (gr. 1-4). 15.95 *(978-1-58536-641-5(2)*, 202328) Sleeping Bear Pr.

Parr, todd. The Underwear Book. 2012. (ENG., Illus.). 32p. (J). (gr. -1-1). pap. 8.99 *(978-0-316-18831-9(X))* Little, Brown Bks. for Young Readers.

Pastis, Stephan. Suit Your Selfie: A Pearls Before Swine Collection. 2017. (Pearls Before Swine Kids Ser.: 5). (ENG.). (J). 176p. pap. 9.99 *(978-1-4494-8375-3(5))*; (Illus.). (gr. 3-6). 35.99 *(978-1-4494-9403-2(X))* Andrews McMeel Publishing.

Pattison, Rosie Gowsell. National Geographic Kids Just Joking 4: 300 Hilarious Jokes about Everything, Including Tongue Twisters, Riddles, & More!, Vol. 4. 2013. (Just Joking Ser.: 4). (Illus.). 208p. (J). (gr. 3-7). pap. 7.95 *(978-1-4263-1378-3(0)*, National Geographic Kids) Disney Publishing Worldwide.

Paxton, Rain. Children's Joke Book. 2012. 12p. pap. 12.68 *(978-1-4669-2312-6(1))* Trafford Publishing.

Peirce, Lincoln. Big Nate Boredom Buster. Peirce, Lincoln, illus. 2014. (Big Nate Activity Book Ser.: 1). (ENG., Illus.). 224p. (J). (gr. 3-7). pap. 7.99 *(978-0-06-233800-6(5)*, HarperCollins) HarperCollins Pubs.

Pellowski, Michael J. Joke & Riddle Bonanza. 2012. (Illus.). 96p. (J). (gr. 3-6). pap. 17.44 *(978-1-4027-8837-6(1))* Sterling Publishing Co., Inc.

—Joke & Riddle Gold Mine. 2017. (Illus.). 96p. (J). (gr. k-7). pap. 6.95 *(978-1-4549-2228-5(1))* Sterling Publishing Co., Inc.

—Joke & Riddle Jackpot. Reed, Chris, illus. 2010. (Jokes & Riddles Ser.). (ENG.). 96p. (J). (gr. k-3). 17.44 *(978-1-4027-7849-0(X))* Sterling Publishing Co., Inc.

—Lunchroom Laughs Joke Book. Davis, Tim, illus. 2005. (ENG.). 128p. (gr. 2-6). per. 3.99 *(978-1-58196-032-7(8)*, Darby Creek) Lerner Publishing Group.

—Mega-Funny Jokes & Riddles. 2019. (Joke Bks.). (ENG., Illus.). 96p. (J). (gr. 2-4). 16.69 *(978-1-64310-786-8(0))* Penworthy Co., LLC, The.

—Out of This World Jokes & Riddles. 2019. (Joke Bks.). (ENG.). 96p. (J). (gr. 2-4). 16.69 *(978-1-64310-787-5(9))* Penworthy Co., LLC, The.

—Wild & Wacky Pet Jokes & Riddles. 2019. (Joke Bks.). (ENG., Illus.). 96p. (J). (gr. 2-4). 16.69 *(978-1-64310-788-2(7))* Penworthy Co., LLC, The.

Peterson, Megan Cooley. Pranks to Play Around Town. 2018. (Humorous Hi Jinx Ser.). (ENG., Illus.). 24p. (J). (gr. 4-6). lib. bdg. *(978-1-68072-333-5(2)*, 12110, Hi Jinx) Black Rabbit Bks.

—Pranks to Play at School. 2018. (Humorous Hi Jinx Ser.). (ENG., Illus.). 24p. (J). (gr. 4-6). lib. bdg. *(978-1-68072-334-2(0)*, 12113, Hi Jinx) Black Rabbit Bks.

—Pranks to Play on Holidays. 2018. (Humorous Hi Jinx Ser.). (ENG., Illus.). 24p. (J). (gr. 4-6). lib. bdg. *(978-1-68072-335-9(9)*, 12116, Hi Jinx) Black Rabbit Bks.

—Pranks to Play on Your Brothers & Sisters. 2018. (Humorous Hi Jinx Ser.). (ENG., Illus.). 24p. (J). (gr. 4-6). lib. bdg. *(978-1-68072-336-6(7)*, 12119, Hi Jinx) Black Rabbit Bks.

—Pranks to Play on Your Parents. 2018. (Humorous Hi Jinx Ser.). (ENG.). 24p. (J). (gr. 4-6). lib. bdg. *(978-1-68072-337-3(5)*, 12122, Hi Jinx) Black Rabbit Bks.

—Pranks to Play Outside. 2018. (Humorous Hi Jinx Ser.). (ENG., Illus.). 24p. (J). (gr. 4-6). lib. bdg. *(978-1-68072-338-0(3)*, 12125, Hi Jinx) Black Rabbit Bks.

Peterson, Scott K. Let the Fun Begin: Nifty Knock-Knocks, Playful Puns, & More. Gable, Brian, illus. 2005. (Make Me Laugh! Ser.). 32p. (J). (gr. k-3). lib. bdg. 19.93 *(978-1-57505-661-6(5))* Lerner Publishing Group.

Phillips, Bob. All-Time Awesome Collection of Good Clean Jokes for Kids. 2006. (Illus.). 366p. (J). (gr. 3-12). per. 10.99 *(978-0-7369-1777-3(2))* Harvest Hse. Pubs.

—Awesome Knock-Knock Jokes for Kids. 2006. (ENG.). 112p. (J). (gr. 2-6). per. 4.99 *(978-0-7369-1714-8(4)*, 6917144) Harvest Hse. Pubs.

—The Best Ever Knock-Knock Jokes for Kids. 2010. (ENG.). 112p. (J). (gr. 2-6). pap. 4.99 *(978-0-7369-2772-7(7)*, 6927727) Harvest Hse. Pubs.

—Slam Dunk Jokes for Kids. 2004. 160p. (J). pap. 4.99 *(978-0-7369-1346-1(7))* Harvest Hse. Pubs.

—Super Duper Knock-Knock Jokes for Kids. 2014. (ENG.). 112p. (J). (gr. 2-6). pap. 4.99 *(978-0-7369-5863-9(0)*, 6958639) Harvest Hse. Pubs.

Phillips, Bob & Russo, Steve. Fabulous & Funny Clean Jokes for Kids. 2nd ed. 2004. 176p. (YA). reprint ed. pap. 4.99 *(978-0-7369-1365-2(3))* Harvest Hse. Pubs.

Phunny, U. R. Animal Jokes. 2016. (Big Buddy Jokes Ser.). (ENG., Illus.). 32p. (J). (gr. 2-5). lib. bdg. 34.21

(978-1-68078-510-4(9), 23569, Big Buddy Bks.) ABDO Publishing Co.
—Dinosaur Jokes. 2016. (Big Buddy Jokes Ser.). (ENG., Illus.). 32p. (J). (gr. 2-5). lib. bdg. 34.21 (978-1-68078-511-1(7), 23571, Big Buddy Bks.) ABDO Publishing Co.
erce, Terry. Greatest Goofiest Jokes. Jones, Buck, illus. 2010. (Jokes & Riddles Ser.). (ENG.). 96p. (J). (gr. k-3). 17.44 (978-1-4027-7847-6(3)) Sterling Publishing Co., Inc.
irk, Wendy. Laugh Out Loud Cats: Fun Facts & Jokes, 1 vol. 2018. (IThink Ser.: 4). (ENG., Illus.). 64p. (J). pap. 6.99 (978-1-897206-17-1(8), 79973a2d-aa12-4dce-8373-03cc284e2cc1) Folklore Publishing CAN. Dist: Lone Pine Publishing USA.
—Laugh Out Loud Dogs: Fun Facts & Jokes, 1 vol. 2018. (IThink Ser.: 5). (ENG., Illus.). 64p. (J). pap. 6.99 (978-1-897206-15-7(1), c8dfeb62-1508-417a-855e-f9d062e02eb9) Folklore Publishing CAN. Dist: Lone Pine Publishing USA.
—Laugh Out Loud Farm Animals: Fun Facts & Jokes, 1 vol. 2018. (IThink Ser.: 6). (ENG., Illus.). 64p. (J). pap. 6.99 (978-1-897206-19-5(4), fa87e031-6009-477b-9c55-3be3f7809488) Folklore Publishing CAN. Dist: Lone Pine Publishing USA.
Practical Pranks. 2004. (Formula Fun Ser.). (Illus.). 48p. (J). (978-1-84229-579-3(9)) Top That! Publishing PLC.
Publishing, Arcturus. Knock Knock! Who's There? 500 Hilarious Jokes for Kids. 2017. (ENG.). 256p. (J). (gr. 2-7). pap. 9.99 (978-1-78428-478-7(5), ab052288-af11-4d6d-9a54-b96b4a7b6165) Arcturus Publishing GBR. Dist: Baker & Taylor Publisher Services (BTPS).
Quackenbush, Robert. Henry's Awful Mistake. Quackenbush, Robert, illus. rev. deluxe ed. 2005. (Illus.). 40p. (J). (gr. k-2). reprint ed. 12.95 (978-0-9712757-0-6(X)) Quackenbush, Robert Studios.
—Henry's Awful Mistake. Quackenbush, Robert, illus. 2019. (Henry Duck Ser.). (ENG., Illus.). 48p. (J). (gr. -1-3). 18.99 (978-1-5344-1540-9(8), Aladdin) Simon & Schuster Children's Publishing.
Ransford, Sandy. Jokes & Pranks, 3 vols. 2003. (Wicked Wallets Ser.). (ENG., Illus.). 24p. (YA). (978-1-84347-040-3(3), Pavilion Children's Books) Pavilion Bks.
—2001 A Joke Odyssey: The Millennium Joke Book. 2003. (ENG., Illus.). 288p. (J). pap. 8.99 (978-0-330-34988-8(0), Pan) Pan Macmillan GBR. Dist: Trafalgar Square Publishing.
Rayner, Shoo. The Christmas Stocking Joke Book. 2017. (ENG., Illus.). (J). (gr. 2-6). pap. (978-1-908944-32-0(3)) Rayner, Shoo.
—The Monster Joke Book: Band 12/Copper (Collins Big Cat) Rayner, Shoo, illus. 2007. (Collins Big Cat Ser.). (ENG., Illus.). 32p. (J). (gr. 2-4). pap. 10.99 (978-0-00-723075-4(3)) HarperCollins Pubs. Ltd. GBR. Dist: Independent Pubs. Group.
Read, Howard & Chantler, Chris. Little Howard's Big Book. 2011. (ENG., Illus.). 128p. (J). 15.99 (978-0-00-739125-7(0)) HarperCollins Pubs. Ltd. GBR. Dist: Independent Pubs. Group.
Regan, Lisa. Underwater Riddles, 1 vol. 2014. (Riddle Me This! Ser.). (ENG.). 32p. (J). (gr. 2-3). lib. bdg. 30.27 (978-1-4777-9177-6(9), 71eaa4bf-7dd3-4e66-babf-de831586fb17, Windmill Bks.) Rosen Publishing Group, Inc., The.
Reid, Alastair. Ounce, Dice, Trice. Shahn, Ben, illus. 2009. 64p. (J). (gr. k-4). 15.95 (978-1-59017-320-6(1), NYR Children's Collection) New York Review of Bks., Inc., The.
Rhatigan, Joe. Wacky Things about the Human Body: Weird & Amazing Facts about Our Bodies! Perrett, Lisa, illus. 2019. (Wacky Things Ser.). (ENG.). 32p. (J). (gr. 3-5). lib. bdg. 27.99 (978-1-942875-72-7(X), ddf77205-f86f-45c3-b2ed-470e122cfe80, Walter Foster Jr) Quarto Publishing Group USA.
Rice, Dona Herweck. Communicate! Tongue Twisters (Level 2) 2017. (TIME for KIDS(r): Informational Text Ser.). (ENG., Illus.). 28p. (gr. 2-3). pap. 10.99 (978-1-4258-4965-8(2)) Teacher Created Materials, Inc.
Richards, Kitty. Phineas & Ferb Laughapalooza Joke Book. 2011. (ENG., Illus.). (J). (-3). pap. (978-1-4075-8486-7(3)) Parragon Bk. Service Ltd.
Rissinger, Matt & Yates, Philip. Nuttiest Knock-Knocks Ever. Long, Ethan, illus. 2008. (Jokes & Riddles Ser.). (ENG.). 96p. (J). (gr. k-3). 17.44 (978-1-4027-4256-9(8)) Sterling Publishing Co., Inc.
Ristas. Chistes para Ninos, Vol. II.Tr. of Jokes for Children. (SPA.). (J). 6.98 (978-970-643-265-0(5)) Selector, S.A. de C.V. MEX. Dist: Spanish Pubs., LLC.
Robinson, Barbara. The Best School Year Ever. 2005. (Best Ever Ser.). (ENG.). 176p. (J). (gr. 3-18). pap. 7.99 (978-0-06-440492-1(7), HarperCollins) HarperCollins Pubs.
Roche, May. The Jokiest Joking Bathroom Joke Book Ever Written ... No Joke! 1,001 Hilarious Potty Jokes to Make You Laugh While You Go. Brack, Amanda, illus. 2018. (Jokiest Joking Joke Bks.). (ENG.). 240p. (J). pap. 19.99 (978-1-250-19003-1(7), 900192349) St. Martin's Pr.
Rocks, Tim, illus. Bathroom Jokes: For Kids of All Ages. 2006. 288p. pap. (978-1-58173-601-4(0)) Sweetwater Pr.
—Gross-Out Jokes: For Kids of All Ages. 2006. 288p. pap. (978-1-58173-602-1(9)) Sweetwater Pr.
—Knock-Knock Jokes: For Kids of All Ages. 2006. 288p. pap. (978-1-58173-600-7(2)) Sweetwater Pr.
Rodger, Anne-Marie. Sports Jokes, Riddles, & Games. 2016. (ENG., Illus.). 32p. (J). (978-0-7787-2390-5(9)) Crabtree Publishing Co.
Rodger, Ellen. Monster & Creepy-Crawly Jokes, Riddles, & Games. 2016. (ENG., Illus.). 32p. (J). (978-0-7787-2389-9(5)) Crabtree Publishing Co.
Rodger, Marguerite. Around the World in Jokes, Riddles, & Games. 2016. (ENG., Illus.). 32p. (J). (978-0-7787-2388-2(7)) Crabtree Publishing Co.
Rogers, J. Ellen. Hairy Legs & Wagon Wheels. 2011. 28p. pap. 15.99 (978-1-4628-7819-2(9)) Xlibris Corp.
Romain, Trevor. Bullying Is a Pain in the Brain. Mark, Steve, illus. rev. ed. 2016. (Laugh & Learn(r) Ser.). (ENG.). 112p. (J). (gr. 2-7). pap. 10.99 (978-1-63198-065-7(3)) Free Spirit Publishing Inc.
Roop, Peter & Roop, Connie. Holiday Howlers: Jokes for Punny Parties. Gable, Brian, illus. 2004. (Make Me Laugh! Ser.). 32p. (J). (gr. k-3). lib. bdg. 19.93 (978-1-57505-645-6(3)) Lerner Publishing Group.
Rothman, Joel & Stein, Frank N. Shut up & Straighten the Bolt in Your Neck: For Monster Kids Ages 7-11. 2007. (Illus.). 80p. (J). (gr. 2-6). pap. 6.95 (978-1-930596-71-9(5)) Amherst Pr.
Rusick, Jessica. World's Best (and Worst) Creepy Critter Jokes. 2020. (Laugh Your Socks Off! Ser.). (ENG., Illus.). 24p. (J). (gr. 1-4). pap. 6.99 (978-1-5415-8906-3(8), 5b7acc3a-aadc-4a15-850e-9c863baf3d0c); lib. bdg. 26.65 (978-1-5415-7695-7(0), caf2026a-6e85-4da1-a9ed-4ff84a77a9d9) Lerner Publishing Group. (Lerner Pubns.).
—World's Best (and Worst) Gross Jokes. 2020. (Laugh Your Socks Off! Ser.). (ENG., Illus.). 24p. (J). (gr. 1-4). pap. 6.99 (978-1-5415-8907-0(6), b0e80dc4-67d7-40fe-8978-59992a5ce6f4); lib. bdg. 26.65 (978-1-5415-7697-1(7), 08bf0269-5133-454d-8bf5-4654fa6e84bb) Lerner Publishing Group. (Lerner Pubns.).
—World's Best (and Worst) Monster Jokes. 2020. (Laugh Your Socks Off! Ser.). (ENG., Illus.). 24p. (J). (gr. 1-4). pap. 6.99 (978-1-5415-8908-7(4), 4f81f277-eb4b-4b40-8ade-78ec80cb5925); lib. bdg. 26.65 (978-1-5415-7698-8(5), 4437a81a-9571-461c-bdeb-e2a0327c8648) Lerner Publishing Group. (Lerner Pubns.).
—World's Best (and Worst) School Jokes. 2020. (Laugh Your Socks Off! Ser.). (ENG., Illus.). 24p. (J). (gr. 1-4). pap. 6.99 (978-1-5415-8909-4(2), 55c757c7-6620-4cf8-9663-b5454cd86f60); lib. bdg. 26.65 (978-1-5415-7696-4(9), 1ee5f050-9638-49b7-917c-e5e30300c6ce) Lerner Publishing Group. (Lerner Pubns.).
Santini, Nicky. Christes y Sorpresas prar Ninos.Tr. of Jokes & Surprises for Kids. (SPA.). (J). 6.98 (978-968-403-937-7(9)) Selector, S.A. de C.V. MEX. Dist: Spanish Pubs., LLC.
Scanlon, Allison. Great Grilled Cheese! My Sandwich Is on Fire! 2010. 36p. (J). 15.49 (978-1-4490-5634-6(2)) AuthorHouse.
Scheunemann, Pam. Ape Cape, 1 vol. 2004. (Rhyming Riddles Ser.). (Illus.). 24p. (J). (gr. k-3). lib. bdg. 24.21 (978-1-59197-457-4(7), SandCastle) ABDO Publishing Co.
—Chipper Flipper, 1 vol. 2004. (Rhyming Riddles Ser.). (ENG., Illus.). 24p. (J). (gr. k-3). lib. bdg. 24.21 (978-1-59197-458-1(5), SandCastle) ABDO Publishing Co.
—Cooler Ruler, 1 vol. 2004. (Rhyming Riddles Ser.). (Illus.). 24p. (J). (gr. k-3). lib. bdg. 24.21 (978-1-59197-459-8(3), SandCastle) ABDO Publishing Co.
—Loud Crowd, 1 vol. 2004. (Rhyming Riddles Ser.). (Illus.). 24p. (J). (gr. k-3). lib. bdg. 24.21 (978-1-59197-461-1(5), SandCastle) ABDO Publishing Co.
—Overdue Kangaroo, 1 vol. 2004. (Rhyming Riddles Ser.). (ENG., Illus.). 24p. (J). (gr. k-3). lib. bdg. 24.21 (978-1-59197-462-8(3), SandCastle) ABDO Publishing Co.
Scholastic. Get the Giggles (Scholastic Reader, Level 1) A First Joke Book. Davies, Bronwen, illus. 2014. (Scholastic Reader, Level 1 Ser.). (ENG.). 32p. (J). (gr. -1-2). pap. 3.99 (978-0-545-54087-2(9)) Scholastic, Inc.
Schultz, Sam. Don't Kid Yourself: Relatively Great (Family) Jokes. Gable, Brian, illus. 2004. (Make Me Laugh! Ser.). 32p. (J). (gr. k-3). lib. bdg. 19.93 (978-1-57505-641-8(0)) Lerner Publishing Group.
—Ivan to Make You Laugh: Jokes about Novel, Nifty, & Notorious Names. Gable, Brian, illus. 2005. (Make Me Laugh! Ser.). 32p. (J). (gr. k-3). lib. bdg. 19.93 (978-1-57505-659-3(3)) Lerner Publishing Group.
—Monster Mayhem: Jokes to Scare You Silly. Gable, Brian, illus. 2004. (Make Me Laugh! Ser.). 32p. (J). (gr. k-3). lib. bdg. 19.93 (978-1-57505-642-5(9)) Lerner Publishing Group.
—Schoolyard Snickers: Classy Jokes That Make the Grade. Gable, Brian, illus. 2004. (Make Me Laugh! Ser.). (ENG.). 32p. (J). (gr. k-3). lib. bdg. 17.44 (978-1-57505-643-2(7), Lerner Pubns.) Lerner Publishing Group.
Schwartz, Joel. Noses are Red. 2006. pap. (978-0-9785885-0-2(9)) Schwartz, Joel.
Scott, Jerry & Borgman, Jim. Extra Cheesy Zits: A Zits Treasury. 2016. (Zits Ser.: 33). (ENG., Illus.). 208p. pap. 18.99 (978-1-4494-7982-4(0)) Andrews McMeel Publishing.
Seaburn, Paul. Jestercises & Gamestorms. 2004. (J). pap. 5.50 (978-1-931334-39-6(0)) Pieces of Learning.
Searight Dibert, Tracy. Detective Pancake. 2010. 24p. pap. 12.99 (978-1-4490-2264-8(2)) AuthorHouse.
Sendak, Maurice. Pierre: A Cautionary Tale in Five Chapters & a Prologue. Sendak, Maurice, illus. 2018. (ENG., Illus.). 48p. (J). (gr. -1-3). pap. 7.95 (978-0-06-285442-1(9), HarperCollins) HarperCollins Pubs.
Shores, Erika L. More Funny Knock-Knock Jokes, 1 vol. 2012. (Joke Bks.). (ENG.). 24p. (J). (gr. -1-2). lib. bdg. 24.65 (978-1-4296-7564-2(0), 117161, Pebble) Capstone.
Silverthorne, Sandy. Crack Yourself up Jokes for Kids. 2018. (ENG., Illus.). 144p. (J). mass mkt. 4.99 (978-0-8007-2969-1(2)) Revell.
—More Crack Yourself up Jokes for Kids. 2019. (ENG., Illus.). 144p. (J). mass mkt. 5.99 (978-0-8007-2970-7(6)) Revell.
Simon, Francesca. Horrid Henry's Joke Book. Ross, Tony, illus. 2010. (Horrid Henry Ser.: 0). (ENG.). 112p. (J). (gr. 2-5). pap. 8.99 (978-1-4022-4425-4(8), 9781402244254, Sourcebooks Jabberwocky) Sourcebooks, Inc.
Singleton, Glen. Crazy Book of Gross Jokes. 2004. (Illus.). 192p. pap. (978-1-74121-544-1(7)) Hinkler Bks. Pty, Ltd.
—1001 Even More Cool Jokes. (Illus.). 208p. pap. (978-1-86515-868-6(2)) Hinkler Bks. Pty, Ltd.
Sky Pony Editors. Belly Laugh Jokes for Kids: 350 Hilarious Jokes. Straker, Bethany, illus. 2015. (ENG.). 144p. (J). (gr. k). 9.99 (978-1-63450-156-9(X), Sky Pony Pr.) Skyhorse Publishing Co., Inc.
—Belly Laugh Knock-Knock Jokes for Kids: 350 Hilarious Knock-Knock Jokes. Straker, Bethany, illus. 2015. 144p. (J). (gr. k). 9.99 (978-1-63220-437-0(1), Sky Pony Pr.) Skyhorse Publishing Co., Inc.
—Belly Laugh Riddles & Puns for Kids: 350 Hilarious Riddles & Puns. Straker, Bethany, illus. 2016. (ENG.). 144p. (J). (gr. k). 9.99 (978-1-5107-1198-3(8), Sky Pony Pr.) Skyhorse Publishing Co., Inc.
Sky Pony Press. Belly Laugh Fart Jokes for Kids: 350 Hilarious Fart Jokes. Paterson, Alex, illus. 2018. (ENG.). 128p. (J). (gr. k-7). 9.99 (978-1-5107-3361-9(2), Sky Pony Pr.) Skyhorse Publishing Co., Inc.
Snider, Brandon T. How to Be Annoying: A Joke Book. 2013. (Annoying Orange Ser.). (ENG., Illus.). 112p. (J). (gr. 1-5). pap. 7.99 (978-0-06-223615-9(6)) HarperCollins Pubs.
—This or That? 2017. (Illus.). 208p. (J). (gr. 3-5). pap. 8.95 (978-1-4549-2102-8(1)) Sterling Publishing Co., Inc.
Stewart, Melissa. Creepy, Crawly Jokes about Spiders & Other Bugs: Laugh & Learn about Science, 1 vol. 2012. (Super Silly Science Jokes Ser.). (ENG., Illus.). 48p. (gr. 3-3). pap. 11.53 (978-1-4644-0167-1(5), 4bc0b2c7-14fd-47bb-abc6-fc190a4e298b, Enslow Elementary) Enslow Publishing, LLC.
—Dino-Mite Jokes about Prehistoric Life: Laugh & Learn about Science, 1 vol. 2012. (Super Silly Science Jokes Ser.). (ENG., Illus.). 48p. (gr. 3-3). pap. 11.53 (978-1-4644-0164-0(0), fcb38932-c04e-4cc8-a6d0-e39df21d9349, Enslow Elementary); E-Book 27.93 (978-1-4645-1071-7(7), 9dfabe43-9af7-41c0-a3dc-f3e3c04f4273) Enslow Publishing, LLC.
—Mountains of Jokes about Rocks, Minerals, & Soil: Laugh & Learn about Science, 1 vol. 2012. (Super Silly Science Jokes Ser.). (ENG., Illus.). 48p. (gr. 3-3). 27.93 (978-0-7660-3969-8(2), 1cc8ef19-0107-46c2-b155-5031ae51e3d6); pap. 11.53 (978-1-4644-0165-7(9), ce1e7d3c-4d14-492d-9092-27c0308a6bdc) Enslow Publishing, LLC. (Enslow Elementary).
—Out of This World Jokes about the Solar System: Laugh & Learn about Science, 1 vol. 2012. (Super Silly Science Jokes Ser.). (ENG., Illus.). 48p. (gr. 3-3). 27.93 (978-0-7660-3970-4(6), 99233040-4496-45ad-bb73-36080281dc68); pap. 11.53 (978-1-4644-0166-4(7), 38758e1d-7cfd-48fa-a58d-84cb396ad05d) Enslow Publishing, LLC. (Enslow Elementary).
—Shockingly Silly Jokes about Electricity & Magnetism: Laugh & Learn about Science, 1 vol. 2012. (Super Silly Science Jokes Ser.). (ENG., Illus.). 48p. (gr. 3-3). 27.93 (978-0-7660-3967-4(6), d5b832bf-1f6c-4c9c-89cc-5ee874c0abe6, Enslow Elementary); pap. 11.53 (978-1-4644-0163-3(2), 5e6385bd-46c0-410f-87bf-b7a42d69523b, Enslow Elementary); E-Book 27.93 (978-1-4645-1070-0(9), 320b8a20-5108-4e26-b724-7facebf205d4) Enslow Publishing, LLC.
—Wacky Weather & Silly Season Jokes: Laugh & Learn about Science, 1 vol. 2012. (Super Silly Science Jokes Ser.). (ENG., Illus.). 48p. (gr. 3-3). 27.93 (978-0-7660-3971-1(4), 8142fad7-bee4-4e97-9244-d8557e33bd4a); pap. 11.53 (978-1-4644-0168-8(3), a121e01c-5704-4a53-880f-de452be6ecb8) Enslow Publishing, LLC. (Enslow Elementary).
Strecker, Michael. Jokes for Crescent City Kids, 1 vol. Smith, Vernon, illus. 2018. (ENG.). 64p. (gr. k-2). pap. 8.95 (978-1-4556-2427-0(6), Pelican Publishing) Arcadia Publishing.
Streissguth, Tom. Costa Rica in Pictures. 2nd ed. 2005. (Visual Geography Ser.). (Illus.). 80p. (YA). (gr. 7-12). 27.93 (978-0-8225-1168-7(1)) Lerner Publishing Group.
Sullivan, Alesha. Funny Tricks & Practical Jokes to Play on Your Friends. 2018. (Jokes, Tricks, & Other Funny Stuff Ser.). (ENG., Illus.). 32p. (J). (gr. 3-9). lib. bdg. 27.32 (978-1-5435-0340-1(3), 137192, Capstone Pr.) Capstone.
Swanson, June. Punny Places: Jokes That Go the Extra Mile. Gable, Brian, illus. 2004. (Make Me Laugh! Ser.). 32p. (J). (gr. k-3). lib. bdg. 19.93 (978-1-57505-647-0(X)) Lerner Publishing Group.
Swerling, Lisa & Lazar, Ralph. The World's Best Jokes for Kids Volume 1: Every Single One Illustrated. 2019. (ENG., Illus.). 128p. (J). pap. 6.99 (978-1-4494-9798-9(5)) Andrews McMeel Publishing.
—The World's Best Jokes for Kids Volume 2: Every Single One Illustrated. 2019. (ENG., Illus.). 128p. (J). pap. 6.99 (978-1-4494-9799-6(3)) Andrews McMeel Publishing.
Swift, Jonathan. Gulliver's Travels. 2008. (Bring the Classics to Life Ser.). (Illus.). 72p. (gr. 4-12). pap., act. bk. ed. 10.95 (978-1-55576-065-6(1), EDCTR-404B) EDCON Publishing Group.
Tait, Chris. Ridiculous Knock-Knocks. Zahnd, Mark, illus. 2010. (Jokes & Riddles Ser.). (ENG.). 96p. (J). (gr. k-3). 17.44 (978-1-4027-7852-0(X)) Sterling Publishing Co., Inc.
—Ridiculous Tongue Twisters. Jones, Buck, illus. 2010. (Jokes & Riddles Ser.). (ENG.). 96p. (J). (gr. k-3). 17.44 (978-1-4027-7854-4(6)) Sterling Publishing Co., Inc.
Temko, Florence. Funny Money. Davis, Tim, illus. 2005. 48p. (J). (gr. -1-3). per. 4.99 (978-1-58196-037-2(9), Darby Creek) Lerner Publishing Group.
Thaler, Mike. In the Big Inning Bible Riddles from the Back Pew. Lee, Jared, illus. 2010. (Tales from the Back Pew Ser.). (ENG.). 32p. (J). (gr. k-2). 17.44 (978-0-310-71597-9(0)) Zonderkidz.
—Oinkers Away. 2014. (ENG.). 96p. (J). (gr. 3-7). pap. 13.99 (978-1-4814-2542-1(0), Simon Pulse) Simon Pulse.
—School Riddles from the Black Lagoon. Lee, Jared, illus. 2007. (J). pap. (978-0-545-01758-9(0)) Scholastic, Inc.
The Child of Achievement(tm) Awards, compiled by. The Giggle-A-Day Joke Book. 2011. (ENG., Illus.). 112p. pap. 7.99 (978-0-00-711591-4(1), HarperCollins Children's Bks.) HarperCollins Pubs. Ltd. GBR. Dist: HarperCollins Pubs.
Thomas, Marian. Comedy Writer. (Illus.). 48p. (J). (gr. 3-6). pap. (978-1-875739-84-4(X)) Wizard Bks.
Thornley, Stew. Sports Jokes to Tickle Your Funny Bone, 1 vol. 2011. (Funny Bone Jokes Ser.). (ENG., Illus.). 48p. (gr. 3-3). pap. 11.53 (978-0-7660-5989-4(8), 5cd763bd-c0cd-4e17-9dd1-c1fe53a1cb5b); lib. bdg. 25.27 (978-0-7660-3545-4(X), 1cef6c60-9ffd-4c15-9fe9-b2da18455c9f) Enslow Publishing, LLC. (Enslow Elementary).
Tize W. Clark. Street Jokes: 1st Edition. 2012. (ENG.). 150p. (YA). per. 14.95 (978-0-9766770-2-4(4)) BAU Publishing Group.
Top That Publishing Staff, ed. Practical Jokes. 2004. (I-Quest Ser.). (Illus.). 48p. (J). per. (978-1-84510-194-7(4)) Top That! Publishing PLC.
Troupe, Thomas Kingsley. Surviving a Bigfoot Attack. 2018. (Survival Guides You Didn't Know You Needed Ser.). (ENG., Illus.). 24p. (J). (gr. 4-6). lib. bdg. (978-1-68072-341-0(3), 12134, Hi Jinx) Black Rabbit Bks.
—Surviving a Zombie Attack. 2018. (Survival Guides You Didn't Know You Needed Ser.). (ENG., Illus.). 24p. (J). (gr. 4-6). lib. bdg. (978-1-68072-344-1(8), 12143, Hi Jinx) Black Rabbit Bks.
—Surviving an Alien Attack. 2018. (Survival Guides You Didn't Know You Needed Ser.). (ENG., Illus.). 24p. (J). (gr. 4-6). lib. bdg. (978-1-68072-339-7(1), 12128, Hi Jinx) Black Rabbit Bks.
—Surviving in the Jungle. 2018. (Survival Guides You Didn't Know You Needed Ser.). (ENG., Illus.). 24p. (J). (gr. 4-6). lib. bdg. (978-1-68072-340-3(5), 12131, Hi Jinx) Black Rabbit Bks.
Vernon, Steve. Maritime Monsters, 1 vol. Solway, Jeff, illus. 2nd ed. 2019. (ENG.). 48p. (J). pap. 11.95 (978-1-77108-814-5(1), 818dc097-1af7-4fa2-8e0d-94838d134121) Nimbus Publishing, Ltd. CAN. Dist: Baker & Taylor Publisher Services (BTPS).
Vilsaint, Fequiere. Jokes, Riddles & Proverbs: In Haitian Creole. Date not set. 28p. (J). (gr. 3-6). wbk. ed. 2.50 (978-1-881839-54-5(0)) Educa Vision Inc.
Wagner, Kathi. The Jokiest Joking Joke Book Ever Written... No Joke! 2015. (Jokiest Joking Joke Bks.). (ENG., Illus.). 368p. (J). pap. 9.99 (978-1-250-08615-0(9), 900157445) St. Martin's Pr.
Walton, Rick. The Sky's the Limit: Naturally Funny Jokes. Gable, Brian, illus. 2005. (Make Me Laugh! Ser.). 32p. (J). (gr. k-3). lib. bdg. 19.93 (978-1-57505-663-0(1)) Lerner Publishing Group.
Walton, Rick & Walton, Ann. Can You Match This? Jokes about Unlikely Pairs. Hanson, Joan, illus. (Make Me Laugh! Joke Bks.). 36p. (J). reprint ed. pap. 2.95 (978-0-8225-9565-6(6), Lerner Pubns.) Lerner Publishing Group.
—Foul Play: Sports Jokes That Won't Strike Out. Gable, Brian, illus. 2005. (Make Me Laugh! Ser.). 32p. (J). (gr. k-3). lib. bdg. 19.93 (978-1-57505-666-1(6)) Lerner Publishing Group.
—Kiss a Frog! Jokes about Fairy Tales, Knights, & Dragons. Hanson, Joan, illus. 40p. (J). (gr. 1-4). reprint ed. pap. 2.95 (978-0-8225-9566-3(4), Lerner Pubns.) Lerner Publishing Group.
—Magical Mischief: Jokes That Shock & Amaze. Gable, Brian, illus. 2005. (Make Me Laugh! Ser.). 32p. (J). (gr. k-3). lib. bdg. 19.93 (978-1-57505-664-7(X)) Lerner Publishing Group.
Walton, Rick, et al. Real Classy: Silly School Jokes. Gable, Brian, illus. 2005. (Make Me Laugh! Ser.). 32p. (J). (gr. k-3). lib. bdg. 19.93 (978-1-57505-665-4(8)) Lerner Publishing Group.
Wee Society. Wee Hee Hee: A Collection of Pretty Funny Jokes & Pictures. 2018. (Wee Society Ser.). (Illus.). 64p. (J). (gr. k-4). 22.00 (978-1-5247-5996-4(1), Clarkson Potter) Potter/Ten Speed/Harmony/Rodale.
Weitzman, Et Al. & Weitzman, Ilana. Jokelopedia: The Biggest, Best, Silliest, Dumbest Joke Book Ever! 2016. lib. bdg. 20.80 (978-0-606-39012-5(X)) Turtleback.
West, Mira. If Beaumont Could Speak. 2009. 28p. pap. 9.99 (978-1-60693-447-0(3), Eloquent Bks.) Strategic Book Publishing & Rights Agency (SBPRA).
West, Tracey. 365 Silly Jokes for Kids. West, Simon, ed. Stroud, Joanne, illus. 2013. 100p. pap. (978-1-910094-05-1(6)) Magic Oxygen.
Whelon, Chuck. Funny Families, 1 vol. 2018. (Joking Around Ser.). (ENG.). 32p. (J). (gr. 2-3). 28.93 (978-1-5081-9559-7(5), c948443c-702d-481b-bc87-717f782564d2, Windmill Bks.) Rosen Publishing Group, Inc., The.
—Hysterical History, 1 vol. 2018. (Joking Around Ser.). (ENG.). 32p. (J). (gr. 2-3). 28.93 (978-1-5081-9563-4(3), bd84ce67-2ee8-40ef-b4ab-49aa8ff7cafd, Windmill Bks.) Rosen Publishing Group, Inc., The.
—Merry Magic, 1 vol. 2018. (Joking Around Ser.). (ENG.). 32p. (J). (gr. 2-3). 28.93 (978-1-5081-9567-2(6), 13ac97c2-5922-4010-8891-7036a6966396, Windmill Bks.) Rosen Publishing Group, Inc., The.
—Nutty Nature, 1 vol. 2018. (Joking Around Ser.). (ENG.). 32p. (J). (gr. 2-3). 28.93 (978-1-5081-9571-9(4), b6a96487-ff24-4d47-ab9a-48c057e13fb1, Windmill Bks.) Rosen Publishing Group, Inc., The.
—Witty Wandering, 1 vol. 2018. (Joking Around Ser.). (ENG.). 32p. (J). (gr. 2-3). 28.93 (978-1-5081-9575-7(7), 16f71a38-4299-4f9a-9a79-89516479a127, Windmill Bks.) Rosen Publishing Group, Inc., The.
Wilcox, Jean K. & Cameron, E. Jane. AbuLLard's ABC's of Branding: 26 Concepts That Capture the Essence of Good Brand Management Kopervas, Gary & Hanes, Don, illus. unabr. ed. 2003. 64p. 19.95 (978-0-9745612-0-2(7), CPN-BMS-001) CattLeLogos Brand Management Systems.
Wing, Natasha. Lettuce Laugh: 600 Corny Jokes about Food. 2018. (Illus.). 96p. (J). (gr. k-7). pap. 6.95 (978-1-4549-3125-6(6)) Sterling Publishing Co., Inc.
Winn, Whee. Lots of Animal Jokes for Kids, 1 vol. 2020. (ENG., Illus.). 128p. (J). pap. 4.99 (978-0-310-76952-1(3)) Zonderkidz.
—Lots of Christmas Jokes for Kids, 1 vol. 2018. (ENG., Illus.). 128p. (J). pap. 4.99 (978-0-310-76710-7(5)) Zonderkidz.
—Lots of Knock-Knock Jokes for Kids, 1 vol. 2016. (ENG., Illus.). 128p. (J). pap. 4.99 (978-0-310-75062-8(8)) Zonderkidz.
Winter, Judy A. Joke Books, 8 vols., Set. Incl. Jokes about Bugs. (ENG.). 24p. (J). (gr. -1-2). 2010. lib. bdg. 24.65 (978-1-4296-4997-1(6), 112943, Pebble); (Joke Bks.). (ENG.). 24p. 2010. 135.90 o.p. (978-1-4296-5272-8(1), 170505, Pebble) Capstone.
—Jokes about Bugs, 1 vol. 2010. (Joke Bks.). (ENG.). 24p. (J). (gr. -1-2). lib. bdg. 24.65 (978-1-4296-4997-1(6), 112943, Pebble) Capstone.
Winterbottom, Julie. Pranklopedia: The Funniest, Grossest, Craziest, Not-Mean Pranks on the Planet! 2016. lib. bdg. 20.80 (978-0-606-39013-2(8)) Turtleback.

Wodehouse, Pelham Grenville. Mike at Wrykyn. 2013. 189p. reprint ed. lthr. 69.00 *(978-0-7426-3265-3(2))* Classic Bks.

Wullie, Oor. Oor Wullie's Big Bucket of Laughs Joke Book. 2015. (ENG., Illus.). 192p. (J). (gr. 4-7). pap. 9.95 *(978-1-910230-00-8(6))* Black and White Publishing Ltd. GBR. Dist: Independent Pubs. Group.

Wynne-Jones, Tim. Mischief City. (J). 16.95 *(978-0-88899-049-5(9),* Libros Tigrillo) Groundwood Bks. CAN. Dist: Publishers Group West (PGW).

Yoe, Craig. Lol: A Load of Laughs & Jokes for Kids. Yoe, Craig, illus. 2017. (ENG., Illus.). 288p. (J). (gr. k-4). pap. 5.99 *(978-1-4814-7818-2(4),* Little Simon) Little Simon.

Yolen, Jane & Lewis, J. Patrick. Last Laughs: Prehistoric Epitaphs. Timmins, Jeffrey Stewart, illus. 2017. 32p. (J). (gr. 2-5). 16.99 *(978-1-58089-706-8(1))* Charlesbridge Publishing, Inc.

Z, Elena Dianna. 102 Awesome School Jokes. 2008. 48p. pap. 13.95 *(978-1-4327-1356-0(6))* Outskirts Pr., Inc.

Ziegler, Mark & Dahl, Michael. The Funny Farm: Jokes about Dogs, Cats, Ducks, Snakes, Bears, & Other Animals, 1 vol. Haberstroh, Anne et al, illus. 2010. (Michael Dahl Presents Super Funny Joke Bks.). (ENG.). 80p. (J). (gr. 1-3). 25.32 *(978-1-4048-5772-8(9),* 102652, Picture Window Bks.) Capstone.

Zuehlke, Jeffrey. Ethiopia in Pictures. 2nd ed. 2004. (Visual Geography Series, Second Ser.). (ENG., Illus.). 80p. (gr. 5-12). 31.93 *(978-0-8225-1170-0(3))* Lerner Publishing Group.

Zullo, Allan. Worlds Dumbest Crooks 2: True Tales of Goofs, Giggles & Gaffes. 2009. 127p. (J). pap. *(978-0-545-11664-0(3))* Scholastic, Inc.

WIT AND HUMOR, PICTORIAL

Archie Superstars. Archie's Even Funnier Kids' Joke Book. 2013. (Archie's Joke Bks.: 2). (Illus.). 192p. (J). (gr. 4-7). 6.99 *(978-1-936975-67-9(X))* Archie Comic Pubns., Inc.

Esos Prodigiosos Actores. 2003. (Coleccion Esa Gran Cultura).Tr. of Dreadful Drama. (SPA., Illus.). (YA). pap. 7.96 *(978-84-272-2138-3(X))* Molino, Editorial ESP. Dist: Lectorum Pubns., Inc.

Frazee, Marla. Why Did the Chicken Cross the Road? 2006. (Illus.). 32p. (J). lib. bdg. 16.99 *(978-0-8037-3203-2(1),* Dial) Penguin Publishing Group.

Pastis, Stephan. The Croc Ate My Homework: A Pearls Before Swine Collection. 2014. (Pearls Before Swine Kids Ser.: 2). (ENG., Illus.). 224p. (J). pap. 9.99 *(978-1-4494-3636-0(6))* Andrews McMeel Publishing.

Peirce, Lincoln. Epic Big Nate. 2016. (Big Nate Ser.). (ENG., Illus.). 472p. 50.00 *(978-1-4494-7195-8(1))* Andrews McMeel Publishing.

Smith, Elwood, illus. How to Draw with Your Funny Bone. 2015. 40p. (J). (gr. 1-4). 17.99 *(978-1-56846-243-1(3),* 21096, Creative Editions) Creative Co., The.

Thaler, Richard H. Catzilla: Cat Riddles, Cat Jokes, & Cartoons. 2014. (ENG., Illus.). 128p. (J). (gr. 3-7). pap. 13.99 *(978-1-4814-2543-8(9),* Simon Pulse) Simon Pulse.

Thebo, Patricia J. Uncle Looker & the Hurricane. 2003. (Illus.). 50p. (J). (gr. k-9). 16.50 *(978-0-9725706-0-2(8))* Seaforth Publishing.

120 Ways to Annoy Your Mother (and Influence People) 2014. (Illus.). 224p. (J). (gr. 6-9). pap. 19.95 *(978-0-500-29146-7(2),* 529146) Thames & Hudson.

WITCHCRAFT

see also Charms; Occultism

Aronson, Marc. Witch-Hunt: Mysteries of the Salem Witch Trials. 2005. (Illus.). 272p. (YA). (gr. 7-12). 16.65 *(978-0-7569-5659-2(5))* Perfection Learning Corp.

Bloom Fradin, Judith & Brindell Fradin, Dennis. The Salem Witch Trials, 1 vol. 2009. (Turning Points in U. S. History Ser.). (ENG.). 48p. (gr. 4-4). lib. bdg. 34.07 *(978-0-7614-3013-1(X),* b2c5e336-94b8-47b6-be36-ca80b68e06c0) Cavendish Square Publishing LLC.

Ceanadach, Siusaidh. Let's Talk about Pagan Festivals. 2012. (ENG., Illus.). 59p. (J). (gr. -1-12). pap. 9.95 *(978-1-78099-463-5(X),* Moon Bks.) Hunt, John Publishing Ltd. GBR. Dist: National Bk. Network.

Crewe, Sabrina & Uschan, Michael V. The Salem Witch Trials, 1 vol. 2004. (Events That Shaped America Ser.). (ENG., Illus.). 32p. (J). (gr. 3-5). lib. bdg. 28.67 *(978-0-8368-3406-2(2),* e3ca2228-b8b1-46d3-a6b0-e7331d447fb7, Gareth Stevens Learning Library) Stevens, Gareth Publishing LLLP.

Della, Jamie. The Book of Spells: The Magick of Witchcraft [a Spell Book for Witches]. rev. ed. 2019. (Illus.). 224p. (gr. 7). 15.99 *(978-1-9848-5702-6(9),* Ten Speed Pr.) Potter/Ten Speed/Harmony/Rodale.

Doeden, Matt. The Salem Witch Trials: An Interactive History Adventure, 1 vol. 2010. (You Choose: History Ser.). (ENG.). 112p. (J). (gr. 3-7). pap. 6.95 *(978-1-4296-6272-7(7),* 115418, Capstone Pr.) Capstone.

Dowswell, Paul. The Amazing History of Wizards & Witches: Discover a World of Magic & Mystery, with over 340 Exciting Pictures. 2016. (Illus.). 64p. (J). (gr. -1-12). 12.99 *(978-1-86147-731-6(7))* Anness Publishing, Inc.

Dowswell, Paul & Greenwood, Susan. The Amazing World of Witches: Discover the Spellbinding History of Witches, Wizardry , Magic & Mystery. 2010. (Illus.). 64p. (J). (gr. 4-7). pap. 12.99 *(978-1-84476-669-7(1))* Anness Publishing GBR. Dist: National Bk. Network.

Dunn, Joeming W. The Salem Witch Trials, 1 vol. Martin, Cynthia, illus. 2008. (Graphic History Ser.). (ENG.). 32p. (J). (gr. 3-8). 32.79 *(978-1-60270-186-1(5),* 9064, Graphic Planet - Fiction) Magic Wagon.

Ellis, Stacy. A Wiccan ABC Book for Babies. 2005. (Illus.). (J). pap. 13.00 *(978-0-9773731-2-3(6))* MaestroMedia Pr.

Fremon, David K. The Salem Witchcraft Trials in United States History, 1 vol. 2014. (In United States History Ser.). (ENG.). 96p. (gr. 5-5). 31.61 *(978-0-7660-6340-2(2),* 84da000c-3b46-4045-a734-89409036475a) Enslow Publishing, LLC.

Giordano, Geraldine. Everything You Need to Know about Wicca: Ancient Beliefs for a Modern World. 2009. (Need to Know Library). 64p. (gr. 5-5). 58.50 *(978-1-60854-098-3(7))* Rosen Publishing Group, Inc., The.

Graves, Lisa. History's Witches. Graves, Lisa, illus. 2013. (Women in History Ser.). (ENG., Illus.). 28p. (J). (gr. 5-12). pap. 19.99 *(978-1-62395-516-8(5))* Xist Publishing.

Guiley, Rosemary ellen. Witches & Wiccans: Mysteries, Legends & Unexplained Phenomena. 2009. (ENG.). 120p. (gr. 6-12). pap. 10.95 *(978-0-7910-9896-7(6),* P160499, Checkmark Bks.) Infobase Holdings, Inc.

Hill, Raine. Growing up Pagan: A Workbook for Wiccan Families, 1 vol. 2009. (ENG., Illus.). 64p. pap., wbk. ed. 19.99 *(978-0-7643-3143-5(4),* 3354, Red Feather) Schiffer Publishing, Ltd.

Holub, Joan. What Were the Salem Witch Trials? 2015. (What Was... Ser.). lib. bdg. 16.00 *(978-0-606-36761-5(6))* Turtleback.

Holub, Joan & Who HQ. What Were the Salem Witch Trials? Putra, Dede, illus. 2015. (What Was? Ser.). 112p. (J). (gr. 3-7). 7.99 *(978-0-448-47905-7(2),* Penguin Workshop) Penguin Young Readers Group.

Horne, Fiona. Witchin': A Handbook for Teen Witches. 2003. (Illus.). 224p. pap. *(978-0-00-713695-7(1),* HarperThorsons) HarperCollins Pubs. Ltd.

Kent, Deborah. Dark Days in Salem: The Witchcraft Trials. 2019. (J). pap. *(978-1-9785-1521-5(9))* Enslow Publishing, LLC.

—Witchcraft Trials: Fear, Betrayal, & Death in Salem, 1 vol. 2008. (America's Living History Ser.). (ENG., Illus.). 128p. (gr. 5-6). lib. bdg. 35.93 *(978-0-7660-2906-4(9),* f48e6595-9950-45a0-840a-3eb1e5d882b5) Enslow Publishing, LLC.

Landau, Elaine. The Salem Witchcraft Trials: Would You Join the Madness?, 1 vol. 2014. (What Would You Do? Ser.). (ENG., Illus.). 48p. (gr. 3-3). lib. bdg. 27.93 *(978-0-7660-4224-7(3),* 44869b5a-9de4-4083-b291-075d1611321f, Enslow Elementary) Enslow Publishing, LLC.

Light, Kate. Questions & Answers about the Salem Witch Trials, 1 vol. 2018. (Eye on Historical Sources Ser.). (ENG.). 32p. (gr. 4-4). 27.93 *(978-1-5383-4123-0(9),* 3f08d66a-28ec-44e9-a1b1-a3a68d59a8c8, PowerKids Pr.) Rosen Publishing Group, Inc., The.

Loh-Hagan, Virginia. Witches. 2016. (Magic, Myth, & Mystery Ser.). (ENG., Illus.). 32p. (J). (gr. 4-8). 32.07 *(978-1-63471-112-8(2),* 208559, 45th Parallel Press) Cherry Lake Publishing.

MacBain, Jenny. The Salem Witch Trials: A Primary Source History of the Witchcraft Trials in Salem, Massachusetts. 2009. (Primary Sources in American History Ser.). 64p. (gr. 5-8). 58.50 *(978-1-60851-503-5(6))* Rosen Publishing Group, Inc., The.

Manoy, Laureen. Where to Park Your Broomstick: A Teen's Guide to Witchcraft. 2004. (Illus.). 311p. (YA). (gr. 7-11). reprint ed. pap. 13.00 *(978-0-7567-7048-8(3))* DIANE Publishing Co.

Martin, Michael J. The Salem Witch Trials, 1 vol. Bascle, Brian, illus. 2005. (Graphic History Ser.). (ENG.). 32p. (J). (gr. 3-9). per. 8.10 *(978-0-7368-5246-3(8),* 86992, Capstone Pr.) Capstone.

Mills, J. Elizabeth. Witches in America, 1 vol. 2011. (America's Supernatural Secrets Ser.). (ENG.). 48p. (YA). (gr. 5-5). pap. 12.75 *(978-1-4488-5580-3(2),* 10fff987-c177-40a0-bb70-04b8f3431928); lib. bdg. 34.47 *(978-1-4488-5531-5(4),* 5f308f51-6417-4621-a2fa-0aee7d9a8999) Rosen Publishing Group, Inc., The.

Nardo, Don & Dellaccio, Tanya. The Salem Witch Trials: A Crisis in Puritan New England, 1 vol. 2016. (American History Ser.). (ENG.). 104p. (YA). (gr. 7-7). lib. bdg. 41.03 *(978-1-5345-6039-0(4),* a54bb4c3-1439-472d-bb47-a5595491e3a6, Lucent Pr.) Greenhaven Publishing LLC.

Olivares, Katie Lydon. ABC Book of Shadows. l.t. ed. 2005. (Illus.). 30p. (J). bds. 9.99 *(978-0-9768573-0-3(8))* Itty Bitty Witch Works.

Parks, Peggy J. Witches. 2007. (Mysterious & Unknown Ser.). (Illus.). 96p. (YA). (gr. 7-12). lib. bdg. 43.93 *(978-1-60152-031-9(X))* ReferencePoint Pr., Inc.

Pipe, Jim. Be a Salem Witch! Bizarre Accusations You'd Rather Not Face. 2009. (You Wouldn't Want to Ser.). (ENG., Illus.). 32p. (J). (gr. 3-18). 29.00 *(978-0-531-20821-2(4),* Watts, Franklin) Scholastic Library Publishing.

—You Wouldn't Want to Be a Salem Witch! 2009. (You Wouldn't Want To Ser.). lib. bdg. 20.80 *(978-0-606-04265-9(2))* Turtleback.

Pizer, Carol. Witchcraft. 2015. (Red Rhino Nonfiction Ser.). (J). lib. bdg. 20.80 *(978-0-606-37205-3(9))* Turtleback.

Rieth, Velvet. My First Little Workbook of Wicca: A Child's Guide to Wicca Through Interactive Play. 2007. (J). per. 16.95 *(978-0-9794533-0-4(5),* Full Circle Pr.) WillowTree Pr., L.L.C.

Roby, Cynthia A. Witches, 1 vol. 2015. (Creatures of Fantasy Ser.). (ENG., Illus.). 64p. (gr. 6-6). 35.93 *(978-1-5026-0930-4(4),* daafdb8f-3317-4d63-95d2-4d93797f6455) Cavendish Square Publishing LLC.

Roleff, Tamara L., ed. Black Magic & Witches. 2003. (Illus.). 127p. (J). pap. 18.70 *(978-0-7377-1319-0(4),* Greenhaven Pr., Inc.) Cengage Gale.

Smith, Andrea P. The Salem Witch Trials. (Illus.). 24p. 2012. 63.60 *(978-1-4488-5215-4(3))* 2011. (ENG., (gr. 2-3). pap. 11.60 *(978-1-4488-5214-7(5),* 361277c1-75d9-4d13-aef9-4cbffbd3e9c5) 2011. (ENG., (gr. 2-3). lib. bdg. 28.93 *(978-1-4488-5188-1(2),* f2f49013-fd8c-4d4a-b602-c5f1b365aff3) Rosen Publishing Group, Inc., The. (PowerKids Pr.).

Solotareff, Gregoire. Dictionary of Witches. 2017. (ENG., Illus.). 192p. (J). (gr. 7-12). pap. 14.95 *(978-1-77085-995-1(0),* 87fc7ca2-7763-40f9-ae49-9ed044c23fdd) Firefly Bks., Ltd.

Stefoff, Rebecca. Witches & Witchcraft, 1 vol. 2008. (Secrets of the Unexplained Ser.). (ENG., Illus.). 96p. (gr. 6-6). lib. bdg. 36.93 *(978-0-7614-2637-0(X),* 3906f7e4-dd22-4eff-bb42-71c5ffc4fc53) Cavendish Square Publishing LLC.

Stern, Steven L. Witchcraft in Salem. (HorrorScapes Ser.). 32p. (gr. 4-9). 2018. (ENG.). (J). 7.99 *(978-1-64280-077-7(5))* 2010. (Illus.). (YA). lib. bdg. 28.50 *(978-1-936088-00-3(2))* Bearport Publishing Co., Inc.

Teen Spirit Wicca. 2014. (ENG., Illus.). 221p. (J). (gr. -1-12). pap. 22.95 *(978-1-78279-059-4(4),* Soul Rocks Bks.) Hunt, John Publishing Ltd. GBR. Dist: National Bk. Network.

von Zumbusch, Amelie. The True Story of the Salem Witch Hunts. 2009. (What Really Happened? Ser.). 24p. (gr. 2-3). 42.50 *(978-1-60854-770-8(1),* PowerKids Pr.) Rosen Publishing Group, Inc., The.

Wallis, Jeffrey. Trials in Salem. 2005. (Houghton Mifflin Social Studies Leveled Readers). (Illus.). 16p. (J). pap. *(978-0-618-56037-0(8))* Houghton Mifflin Harcourt Publishing Co.

Wood, Alix. Witch Trials, 1 vol. Wood, Alix, illus. 2013. (Why'd They Do That? Strange Customs of the Past Ser.). (Illus.). 32p. (J). (gr. 4-5). (ENG.). 29.27 *(978-1-4339-9592-7(1),* 425dc6ef-0497-4c4a-939c-fa4ad98139bf); (ENG., pap. 11.50 *(978-1-4339-9593-4(X),* 72cb3174-752a-4735-a5d4-013f54e12a80); pap. 63.00 *(978-1-4339-9594-1(8))* Stevens, Gareth Publishing LLLP.

WITCHCRAFT—FICTION

Anonymous. Jay's Journal. Sparks, Beatrice, ed. (Anonymous Diaries). (ENG.). 240p. (YA). 2012. (gr. 9). 17.99 *(978-1-4424-8094-0(7))* 2010. (gr. 7). pap. 11.99 *(978-1-4424-1993-3(8))* Simon Pulse. (Simon Pulse).

Armstrong, Kelley. The Gathering. (Darkness Rising Ser.: 1). (ENG.). (YA). (gr. 8). 2012. 384p. pap. 9.99 *(978-0-06-179703-3(0))* 2011. 368p. 17.99 *(978-0-06-179702-6(2))* HarperCollins Pubs. (HarperCollins).

—The Gathering, 7 vols. (Darkness Rising Ser.: Bk. 1). (YA). 100.75 *(978-1-4498-6186-5(5));* 1.25 *(978-1-4498-6189-6(X));* 2013. 102.75 *(978-1-4498-6184-1(9))* Recorded Bks., Inc.

Balian, Lorna. Humbug Witch, 1 vol. (ENG., Illus.). 32p. (J). 2004. pap. 4.95 *(978-1-59572-009-2(X))* 2003. 13.99 *(978-1-932065-32-9(6),* 1-718-784-9112) Star Bright Bks., Inc.

Bolger, Kevin. Zombiekins 2. Blecha, Aaron, illus. 2011. (J). 10.99 *(978-1-59514-432-4(3),* Razorbill) Penguin Publishing Group.

Brian, Kate, pseud. The Book of Spells: A Private Prequel. 2011. (Private Ser.). (ENG.). 320p. (YA). (gr. 9). pap. 9.99 *(978-1-4424-1237-8(2),* Simon & Schuster Bks. For Young Readers) Simon & Schuster Bks. For Young Readers.

Burg, Shana. Laugh with the Moon. 2013. (Illus.). 256p. (J). (gr. 5-6). pap. 7.99 *(978-0-440-42210-5(8),* Yearling) Random Hse. Children's Bks.

Burge, Constance M. Seasons of the Witch, Vol. 1. Simon and Schuster Children's Staff, ed. 2003. (Charmed Ser.). (ENG.). 192p. (YA). pap. *(978-0-689-86545-9(7))* Gallery Pr., The.

Burgis, Stephanie. Renegade Magic, 2. 2012. (Kat, Incorrigible Ser.: 2). (ENG., Illus.). 336p. (J). (gr. 5-9). 16.99 *(978-1-4169-9449-7(1),* Atheneum Bks. for Young Readers) Simon & Schuster Children's Publishing.

Cabot, Meg. Jinx. 2007. (gr. 7-12). 262p. (YA). lib. bdg. 17.89 *(978-0-06-083765-5(9));* (ENG.). 272p. (J). 16.99 *(978-0-06-083764-8(0))* HarperCollins Pubs. (HarperTeen).

Cajoleas, Jimmy. The Good Demon. (ENG.). 2019. 336p. (YA). (gr. 8-17). pap. 10.99 *(978-1-4197-3899-9(2),* 1195803) 2018. (Illus.). 320p. (gr. 9-17). 18.99 *(978-1-4197-3127-3(0),* 1195801) Abrams, Inc. (Amulet Bks.).

Clement-Moore, Rosemary. Texas Gothic. 2012. (ENG.). 416p. (YA). (gr. 9). pap. 10.99 *(978-0-385-73694-7(0),* Ember) Random Hse. Children's Bks.

Dahl, Roald. Las Brujas. Date not set.Tr. of Witches. (SPA.). 208p. 15.95 *(978-84-204-3655-5(0))* Ediciones Alfaguara ESP. Dist: Santillana USA Publishing Co., Inc.

—Las Brujas. Blake, Quentin, illus. 2003.Tr. of Witches. (SPA.). 200p. (YA). (gr. 5-8). pap. 12.95 *(978-958-24-0100-9(1))* Santillana USA Publishing Co., Inc.

DeKeyser, Stacy. The Brixen Witch. Nickle, John, illus. (ENG.). 208p. (J). (gr. 3-7). 2013. pap. 6.99 *(978-1-4424-3329-8(9))* 2012. 15.99 *(978-1-4424-3328-1(0))* McElderry, Margaret K. Bks. (McElderry, Margaret K. Bks.).

DeLuca, Laura. Destiny. 2011. (ENG.). 276p. (YA). pap. 12.95 *(978-0-9826747-2-7(4))* Free Focus Publishing.

Duble, Kathleen Benner. The Sacrifice. 2007. (ENG.). 224p. (J). (gr. 5-9). pap. 8.99 *(978-0-689-87651-6(3),* McElderry, Margaret K. Bks.) McElderry, Margaret K. Bks.

Duce, Gillian. Magic & Mayhem. 2006. (ENG.). 212p. per. *(978-1-894936-64-4(7))* Saga Bks.

Duncan, Lois. Summer of Fear. 2011. (ENG.). 256p. (YA). (gr. 7-17). pap. 14.99 *(978-0-316-09907-3(4))* Little, Brown Bks. for Young Readers.

Elliott, Jenny. Save Me. 2015. (ENG.). 336p. (YA). (gr. 7-12). pap. 10.99 *(978-1-250-06147-8(4),* 900141885) Feiwel & Friends.

Flora, James. Grandpa's Witched up Christmas. 2018. (Feral Kids Ser.). (ENG., Illus.). 32p. (J). 17.95 *(978-1-62731-068-0(1))* Feral Hse.

Gailey, Sarah. When We Were Magic. 2020. (ENG.). 352p. (YA). (gr. 9). 18.99 *(978-1-5344-3287-1(6),* Simon Pulse) Simon Pulse.

Gallagher, Diana G. & Burge, Constance M. Trickery Treat. 2008. (Charmed Ser.). (ENG.). 208p. (YA). (gr. 8-12). mass mkt. 6.99 *(978-1-4169-3670-1(X))* Pocket Books.

Gibbs, Gretchen. The Book of Maggie Bradstreet. 2012. (Bradstreet Chronicles). (ENG.). 183p. (YA). pap. 9.99 *(978-0-9852948-0-9(9))* Glenmere Pr.

Greenburg, Dan. It's Itchcraft! Davis, Jack E., illus. 2004. (Zack Files Ser.). 118p. lib. bdg. 15.00 *(978-0-7569-2238-2(0))* Perfection Learning Corp.

—Zack Files 30: It's Itchcraft! SuperSpecial, 30 vols. Davis, Jack E., illus. 2003. (Zack Files Ser.: 30). (ENG.). 128p. (J). (gr. 2-5). pap. 4.99 *(978-0-448-42888-8(1),* Grosset & Dunlap) Penguin Young Readers Group.

Hanna, Nicholas. Coven of Rats. 2007. (ENG.). 223p. pap. 15.95 *(978-0-615-14369-9(5))* Hanna, Nicholas.

Hansen, Lynne. A Time for Witches. 2007. (YA). *(978-1-4114-9671-2(X),* Spark Publishing Group) Sterling Publishing Co., Inc.

Hearn, Julie. The Minister's Daughter. 2006. (ENG.). 272p. (YA). (gr. 7-12). pap. 7.99 *(978-0-689-87691-2(2),* Atheneum Bks. for Young Readers) Simon & Schuster Children's Publishing.

Hemphill, Stephanie. Wicked Girls: A Novel of the Salem Witch Trials. (YA). 2013. (ENG.). 432p. (gr. 8). pap. 10.99 *(978-0-06-185330-2(5),* Balzer & Bray) 2010. 336p. (gr. 7-18). lib. bdg. 17.89 *(978-0-06-185329-6(1))* HarperCollins Pubs.

Hightman, J. P. Spirit. 2008. 224p. (gr. 7-18). (ENG.). (J). 16.9 *(978-0-06-085063-0(9));* (YA). lib. bdg. 17.89 *(978-0-06-085064-7(7))* HarperCollins Pubs. (HarperTeen).

Hoffmann, Alice. Nightbird. 2016. (ENG., Illus.). 208p. (J). (gr. 5). pap. 7.99 *(978-0-385-38961-7(2),* Yearling) Random Hse Children's Bks.

—Nightbird. 2016. lib. bdg. 18.40 *(978-0-606-38451-3(0))* Turtleback.

Hulme-Cross, Benjamin. The Stone Witch. Evergreen, Nelson illus. 2015. (Dark Hunter Ser.). (ENG.). 64p. (J). (gr. 4-8). pap. 4.99 *(978-1-4677-8089-6(8),* ba40e2dd-741d-4adb-87c8-e2b4d6162eea, Darby Creek) Lerner Publishing Group.

Hunter, Mollie. The Thirteenth Member. 2008. (J). (gr. 6-9). 24.75 *(978-0-8446-6362-3(X))* Smith, Peter Pub., Inc.

Jones, Diana Wynne. The Chronicles of Chrestomanci Vol. 1: Charmed Life; The Lives of Christopher Chant, Vol. 1. 2007. (Chrestomanci Ser.). (YA). (gr. 5-8). lib. bdg. 19.65 *(978-0-613-31070-3(5))* Turtleback.

—The Chronicles of Chrestomanci, Volume I, Vol. 1. 2007. (Chronicles of Chrestomanci Ser.: Nos. 1-2). (ENG.). 608p. (YA). (gr. 8-12). pap. 10.99 *(978-0-06-447268-5(X),* Greenwillow Bks.) HarperCollins Pubs.

—The Chronicles of Chrestomanci, Volume II, Vol. 2. 2007. (Chronicles of Chrestomanci Ser.: Nos. 3-4). (ENG.). 560p. (YA). (gr. 8-12). pap. 8.99 *(978-0-06-447269-2(8),* Greenwillow Bks.) HarperCollins Pubs.

—The Chronicles of Chrestomanci, Volume III, Vol. 3. 2008. (Chronicles of Chrestomanci Ser.: 3). (ENG.). 688p. (YA). (gr. 8-18). pap. 8.99 *(978-0-06-114832-3(6),* Greenwillow Bks.) HarperCollins Pubs.

—Conrad's Fate. 2006. (ENG., Illus.). 352p. *(978-0-00-719087-4(5))* HarperCollins Children's Bks.

—Conrad's Fate. (J). 2006. (Chronicles of Chrestomanci Ser.: 3). (ENG.). 400p. (gr. 3-7). per. 6.99 *(978-0-06-074745-9(5),* Greenwillow Bks.) 2005. (Chrestomanci Ser.: No. 5). 384p. (gr. k-17). lib. bdg. 17.89 *(978-0-06-074744-2(7))* 2005. (Chrestomanci Ser.: No. 5). 384p. (gr. 5-18). 16.99 *(978-0-06-074743-5(9))* HarperCollins Pubs.

—Conrad's Fate: Read-Along/Homework Pack, 6 vols. 2005. (Chrestomanci Ser.: No. 5). (J). (gr. 5-8). 86.75 *(978-1-4193-3551-8(0),* 42039) Recorded Bks., Inc.

—The Pinhoe Egg. (J). 2007. (Chronicles of Chrestomanci Ser.: 6). (ENG.). 480p. (gr. 3-7). per. 7.99 *(978-0-06-113126-4(1),* Greenwillow Bks.) 2006. (Chrestomanci Ser.: No. 6). 528p. lib. bdg. 18.89 *(978-0-06-113125-7(3))* HarperCollins Pubs.

Karmaniolos, Ellie. Groomilda, the Witch. 2016. (ENG., Illus.). 24p. (J). pap. 24.19 *(978-1-5245-1857-8(3))* Xlibris Corp.

Konigsburg, E. L. Jennifer, Hecate, Macbeth, William McKinley, & Me, Elizabeth. (J). (gr. 3-6). 177p. pap. 4.99 *(978-0-8072-1524-1(4));* 117p. pap. 4.99 *(978-0-8072-1417-6(5))* Random Hse. Audio Publishing Group. (Listening Library).

—Jennifer, Hecate, Macbeth, William Mckinley, & Me, Elizabeth. 2007. (ENG., Illus.). 128p. (J). (gr. 3-7). pap. 8.99 *(978-1-4169-3396-0(4),* Atheneum Bks. for Young Readers) Simon & Schuster Children's Publishing.

Kreie, Chris. The Rookie Trap. 2019. (League of the Paranormal Ser.). (ENG.). 120p. (YA). (gr. 6-12). pap. 7.99 *(978-1-5415-7297-3(1),* d5045536-ee69-4a9a-a677-0a898fd75bc7); lib. bdg. 26.65 *(978-1-5415-5684-3(4),* 4ee2a27a-b9b1-42e0-808c-32cb611d5060) Lerner Publishing Group. (Darby Creek).

Lachtman, Ofelia Dumas. The Trouble with Tessa. 2005. 122p. (J). (gr. 3-7). per. 9.95 *(978-1-55885-448-2(7),* Piñata Books) Arte Publico Pr.

Latimer, E. Witches of Ash & Ruin. 2020. (ENG.). 384p. (YA). (gr. 9-17). 18.99 *(978-1-368-05225-2(8))* Disney Publishing Worldwide.

MacHale, D. J. Black Moon Rising (the Library Book 2) (Library: 2). 304p. (J). (gr. 3-7). 2018. pap. 7.99 *(978-1-101-93260-5(0),* Yearling) 2017. 16.99 *(978-1-101-93257-5(0),* Random Hse. Bks. for Young Readers) Random Hse. Children's Bks.

Martin, Ann M. Karen's Witch: a Graphic Novel (Baby-Sitters Little Sister #1) (Adapted Edition), Vol. 1. Farina, Katy, illus. adapted ed. 2019. (Baby-Sitters Little Sister Graphix Ser.: 1). (ENG.). 144p. (J). (gr. 2-5). pap. 10.99 *(978-1-338-31519-6(6),* Graphix) Scholastic, Inc.

Martinez, Roland L. The Evil Leaf. 2009. 232p. 24.99 *(978-1-4490-0916-8(6));* pap. 14.90 *(978-1-4490-0917-5(4))* AuthorHouse.

Monahan, Hillary. The Hollow Girl. 2017. ix, 261p. (YA). *(978-1-5247-0188-8(2),* Delacorte Pr.) Random Hse. Children's Bks.

Moore, Daniel. Abdallah Jones & the DisappearingDust. 2006. (ENG.). 168p. pap. 17.00 *(978-0-615-13570-0(6))* Ecstatic Exchange, The.

Myracle, Lauren. Rhymes with Witches. (ENG.). (YA). (gr. 8-17). 2006. 272p. pap. 7.95 *(978-0-8109-9215-3(9))* 2005. 224p. 16.95 *(978-0-8109-5859-3(7),* Amulet Bks.) Abrams, Inc.

Naylor, Phyllis Reynolds. Witch Weed. 2004. (ENG., Illus.). 192p. (J). (gr. 3-7). pap. 9.99 *(978-0-689-85381-4(5),* Simon & Schuster/Paula Wiseman Bks.) Simon & Schuster/Paula Wiseman Bks.

Novel Units. The Witch of Blackbird Pond Novel Units Student Packet. 2019. (ENG.). (J). pap. 13.99 *(978-1-56137-534-9(9),* Novel Units, Inc.) Classroom Library Co.

Ocelot, Michel. Kirikou et la Sorciere. pap. 14.95 *(978-2-01-321877-1(X))* Hachette Groupe Livre FRA. Dist: Distribooks, Inc.

Papineau, Lucie. Baby Witch, Yuck! 2004. (Illus.). (J). (gr. -1-18). spiral bd. *(978-0-616-03052-3(5));* spiral bd. *(978-0-616-04560-2(3))* Canadian National Institute for the Blind/Institut National Canadien pour les Aveugles.

Parra, B. A. Tyler Trio Adventure Salem Witch Hunt. 2007. (ENG.). 124p. pap. *(978-0-615-14720-8(8))* Parra, Beverly.

Preussler, Otfried. Krabat & the Sorcerer's Mill. Bell, Anthea, tr. 2014. (ENG.). 264p. (J). (gr. 3-7). 17.95 *(978-1-59017-778-5(9),* NYR Children's Collection) New York Review of Bks., Inc., The.

eynolds Naylor, Phyllis. The Witch Returns. 2005. (Witch Ser.: No. 6). 186p. (J). (gr. 1-7). 12.65 *(978-0-7569-5504-5(1))* Perfection Learning Corp.
naldi, Ann. A Break with Charity: A Story about the Salem Witch Trials. 2003. (Great Episodes Ser.). (ENG.). 320p. (YA). (gr. 7-8). pap. 8.99 *(978-0-15-204682-8(8),* 1194109, Clarion Bks.) HarperCollins Pubs.
owling, J. K. Harry Potter à l'École des Sorciers. Menard, Jean-François, tr. from ENG. 2007. (Harry Potter Ser.: Year 1).Tr. of Harry Potter & the Sorcerer's Stone. 311p. (J). per. 14.95 *(978-2-07-061236-9(8))* Gallimard, Editions FRA. Dist: Distribooks, Inc.
cholastic. Hidden Creatures. Warner Bros Staff, illus. 2018. (ENG.). 64p. (J). (gr. 1-1). pap. 12.99 *(978-1-338-28094-4(5))* Scholastic, Inc.
harpe, Tess, et al. Toil & Trouble: 15 Tales of Women & Witchcraft. 2018. (ENG.). 416p. (YA). 18.99 *(978-1-335-01627-0(9),* Harlequin Teen) Harlequin Enterprises ULC CAN. Dist: HarperCollins Pubs.
mith, L. J. The Secret Circle: The Initiation & the Captive Part I TV Tie-In Edition. movie tie-in ed. 2011. (Secret Circle Ser.). (ENG.). 416p. (YA). (gr. 8). pap. 9.99 *(978-0-06-211900-1(1),* HarperTeen) HarperCollins Pubs.
—The Secret Circle: the Captive Part II & the Power. 2012. (Secret Circle Ser.: Vols. 1-2). (ENG.). 416p. (YA). (gr. 8). pap. 10.99 *(978-0-06-167135-7(5),* HarperTeen) HarperCollins Pubs.
—Spellbinder. 2016. (Night World Ser.: 3). (ENG., Illus.). 256p. (YA). (gr. 9). 13.99 *(978-1-4814-8681-1(0),* Simon Pulse) Simon Pulse.
Smith, Sasha Peyton. The Witch Haven. 2022. (ENG., Illus.). 464p. (YA). (gr. 9). pap. 13.99 *(978-1-5344-5439-2(X),* Simon & Schuster Bks. For Young Readers) Simon & Schuster Bks. For Young Readers.
Snyder, Zilpha Keatley. The Witches of Worm. 2009. 9.00 *(978-0-7848-3612-5(4),* Everbind) Marco Bk. Co.
—The Witches of Worm. Raible, Alton, illus. 2009. (ENG.). (J). (gr. 3-7). 192p. 19.99 *(978-1-4169-9531-9(5));* 208p. pap. 8.99 *(978-1-4169-9053-6(4))* Simon & Schuster Children's Publishing. (Atheneum Bks. for Young Readers).
—The Witches of Worm. 2006. 22.75 *(978-0-8446-7290-8(4))* Smith, Peter Pub., Inc.
Speare, Elizabeth George. The Witch of Blackbird Pond. 2011. (ENG.). 272p. (J). (gr. 5-7). pap. 8.99 *(978-0-547-55029-9(4),* 1450238, Clarion Bks.) HarperCollins Pubs.
—The Witch of Blackbird Pond. Random House Publishing Group.
—The Witch of Blackbird Pond. 2004. 223p. (J). (gr. 4-7). pap., tchr.'s planning gde. ed. 38.00 incl. audio *(978-0-8072-0862-5(0),* Listening Library) Random Hse. Audio Publishing Group.
Spence, Craig. Josh & the Magic Vial. 2006. (ENG.). 396p. (J). per. 17.95 *(978-1-897235-10-2(0))* Thistledown Pr., Ltd. CAN. Dist: Univ. of Toronto Pr.
Stolarz, Laurie Faria. Red Is for Remembrance. 2005. (Stolarz Ser.: 4). (ENG.). 336p. (YA). (gr. 9-12). pap. 11.99 *(978-0-7387-0760-0(0),* 0738707600, Flux) North Star Editions.
—Red Is for Remembrance. l.t. ed. 2008. (Blue Is for Nightmares Ser.: Bk. 4). 385p. (YA). (gr. 7). 22.95 *(978-1-4104-0339-1(4))* Thorndike Pr.
—Silver Is for Secrets. 2005. (Stolarz Ser.: 3). (ENG.). 288p. (YA). (gr. 9-12). pap. 11.99 *(978-0-7387-0631-3(0),* 0738706310, Flux) North Star Editions.
—White Is for Magic. 2004. (Stolarz Ser.: 2). (ENG.). 312p. (YA). (gr. 9-12). pap. 11.99 *(978-0-7387-0443-2(1),* 0738704431, Flux) North Star Editions.
Stone, Kelsey. The Predahil Chronicles. 2005. (YA). per. 6.49 *(978-1-59196-995-2(6))* Instant Pub.
Thompson, Paul B. The Devil's Door: A Salem Witchcraft Story, 1 vol. 2011. (Historical Fiction Adventures Ser.). (ENG., Illus.). 160p. (J). (gr. 3-5). 31.93 *(978-0-7660-3387-0(2),* b032300a-5660-4f10-8e33-a57d5745824e); pap. 13.88 *(978-1-59845-214-3(2),* b6288c2c-d77e-4e8d-8d6c-4dae679dbf24) Enslow Publishing, LLC.
Vande Velde, Vivian. Dragon's Bait. 2003. (ENG., Illus.). 208p. (YA). (gr. 7-12). pap. 13.95 *(978-0-15-216663-2(7),* 1201591, Clarion Bks.) HarperCollins Pubs.
—Magic Can Be Murder. 2009. (ENG.). 208p. (YA). (gr. 7). pap. 12.99 *(978-0-547-25872-0(0),* 1402326, Clarion Bks.) HarperCollins Pubs.
Vega, Danielle. The Merciless. 2014. (Merciless Ser.: 1). (ENG.). 288p. (YA). (gr. 9). 17.99 *(978-1-59514-722-6(5),* Razorbill) Penguin Young Readers Group.
Verano, M. Book of Shadows. (Diary of a Haunting Ser.). (ENG.). (YA). (gr. 9). 2018. 304p. pap. 12.99 *(978-1-4814-9203-4(9))* 2017. (Illus.). 288p. 17.99 *(978-1-4814-9202-7(0))* Simon Pulse. (Simon Pulse).
Walton, Rick. Pig Pigger Piggest. Holder, Jimmy, illus. 2003. (ENG.). 32p. (J). (gr. 1). reprint ed. pap. 6.99 *(978-1-58685-318-1(X))* Gibbs Smith, Publisher.
White, Paul. Jungle Doctor Spots a Leopard. rev. ed. 2008. (Flamingo Fiction 9-13s Ser.). (ENG., Illus.). 176p. (J). (gr. 5-7). per. 8.99 *(978-1-84550-301-7(5),* 19e1be96-5b42-4620-a898-bc67dd924342) Christian Focus Pubns. GBR. Dist: Baker & Taylor Publisher Services (BTPS).
Wigington, Patti. Summer's Ashes. 2007. (ENG.). 208p. (gr. 8-12). per. 15.00 *(978-0-9766805-9-8(9))* Keene Publishing.
Williams, Kate M. The Babysitters Coven. (Babysitters Coven Ser.: 1). (ENG.). 368p. (YA). (gr. 7). 2020. pap. 10.99 *(978-0-525-70740-0(9),* Ember) 2019. 18.99 *(978-0-525-70737-0(9),* Delacorte Pr.) Random Hse. Children's Bks.
Wrede, Patricia. Snow White & Rose Red. 2009. (ENG.). 288p. (YA). (gr. 7-18). 8.99 *(978-0-14-241121-6(3),* Firebird) Penguin Young Readers Group.

WITCHES

Alexander, Audrey. Witches & Wicca. 2015. (J). *(978-1-61900-072-8(5))* Eldorado Ink.
Beaumont, Steve. How to Draw Witches & Wizards. (Drawing Fantasy Art Ser.). 32p. (J). (gr. 4-5). 2009. 50.50 *(978-1-61512-195-3(1),* PowerKids Pr.) 2007. (ENG., Illus.). (J). lib. bdg. 30.27 *(978-1-4042-3857-2(3),* 8973b3b3-47ed-4314-8583-1b6ec68c04b8) Rosen Publishing Group, Inc., The.
—How to Draw Wizards, Warriors, Orcs & Elves. 2007. (Illus.). 143p. pap. 7.99 *(978-0-7858-2345-2(X),* Chartwell) Book Sales, Inc.
Braun, Eric. The Truth about Witches, 1 vol. Squier, Robert, illus. 2010. (Fairy-Tale Superstars Ser.). (ENG.). 32p. (J). (gr. 1-3). lib. bdg. 27.99 *(978-1-4048-6160-2(2),* 112946, Picture Window Bks.) Capstone.
Brinker, Spencer. The Witch's Things: A Counting to 20 Rhyme. 2015. (Illus.). 32p. (J). lib. bdg. 28.50 *(978-1-62724-333-9(X))* Bearport Publishing Co., Inc.
Broutin, Christian & Delafosse, Claude. Let's Look at Fairies, Witches, Giants & Dragons. 2012. (ENG., Illus.). 38p. (J). (gr. k-3). spiral bd. 11.99 *(978-1-85103-358-4(0))* Moonlight Publishing, Ltd. GBR. Dist: Independent Pubs. Group.
Burton, Bonnie. J. K. Rowling's Wizarding World: Movie Magic Volume Three: Amazing Artifacts. 2017. (J. K. Rowling's Wizarding World Ser.). (ENG., Illus.). 96p. (J). (gr. 5). 29.99 *(978-0-7636-9584-2(X))* Candlewick Pr.
Castellano, Peter. Witches, 1 vol. 2015. (Monsters! Ser.). (ENG.). 32p. (J). (gr. 1-2). pap. 11.50 *(978-1-4824-4102-4(0),* fa2fd925-baf4-438f-8cce-b31b026d6abe) Stevens, Gareth Publishing LLLP.
Cheatham, Mark. Witches!, 1 vol. 2012. (Jr. Graphic Monster Stories Ser.). (ENG.). 24p. (J). (gr. 2-3). pap. 11.60 *(978-1-4488-6407-2(0),* 712d0ef3-48f6-4b19-8bdd-06fa249ffaf4); lib. bdg. 28.93 *(978-1-4488-6224-5(8),* 83db396e-833d-4344-9428-c992d8cd2d4f) Rosen Publishing Group, Inc., The. (PowerKids Pr.).
Frisch, Aaron. Witches. 2013. (Illus.). 24p. (J). 25.65 *(978-1-60818-250-3(9),* Creative Education) Creative Co., The.
Graves, Lisa. History's Witches. Graves, Lisa, illus. 2013. (Women in History Ser.). (ENG., Illus.). 28p. (J). (gr. 5-12). pap. 19.99 *(978-1-62395-516-8(5))* Xist Publishing.
Guiley, Rosemary ellen. Witches & Wiccans: Mysteries, Legends & Unexplained Phenomena. 2009. (ENG.). 120p. (gr. 6-12). pap. 10.95 *(978-0-7910-9896-7(6),* P160499, Checkmark Bks.) Infobase Holdings, Inc.
Hill, Raine. Growing up Pagan: A Workbook for Wiccan Families, 1 vol. 2009. (ENG., Illus.). 64p. pap., wbk. ed. 19.99 *(978-0-7643-3143-5(4),* 3354, Red Feather) Schiffer Publishing, Ltd.
Kerns, Ann. Wizards & Witches. 2009. (Fantasy Chronicles Ser.). (ENG., Illus.). 48p. (gr. 4-7). lib. bdg. 27.93 *(978-0-8225-9983-8(X))* Lerner Publishing Group.
Leblanc, Catherine. How to Outwit Witches. Garrigue, Roland, illus. 2013. (ENG.). 32p. (J). (gr. -1). 14.99 *(978-1-60887-193-3(2))* Insight Editions.
Loh-Hagan, Virginia. Witches. 2016. (Magic, Myth, & Mystery Ser.). (ENG., Illus.). 32p. (J). (gr. 4-8). 32.07 *(978-1-63471-112-8(2),* 208559, 45th Parallel Press) Cherry Lake Publishing.
Lynette, Rachel. Witches, 1 vol. 2007. (Mysterious Encounters Ser.). (ENG., Illus.). 48p. (gr. 4-8). lib. bdg. 29.13 *(978-0-7377-3643-4(7),* 80e1603d-0394-4c56-b58d-8d51e2c0f91a, KidHaven Publishing) Greenhaven Publishing LLC.
Marsico, Katie. Magic Monsters: From Witches to Goblins. 2017. (Monster Mania Ser.). (ENG., Illus.). 32p. (J). (gr. 2-5). 26.65 *(978-1-5124-2595-6(8),* 6ee6e0ef-68ff-4a76-ab82-2ae5adf99180); E-Book 39.99 *(978-1-5124-2815-5(9));* E-Book 39.99 *(978-1-5124-3822-2(7),* 9781512438222); E-Book 4.99 *(978-1-5124-3821-5(9),* 9781512438215) Lerner Publishing Group. (Lerner Pubns.).
Narayan, Natasha. Witches, Wizards & Warlocks of London. 2004. (Of London Ser.). (ENG., Illus.). 96p. (J). pap. 8.99 *(978-1-904153-12-2(7))* Watling St., Ltd. GBR. Dist: Independent Pubs. Group.
Netzley, Patricia D. Do Witches Exist? 2015. (ENG., Illus.). 80p. (J). lib. bdg. *(978-1-60152-862-9(0))* ReferencePoint Pr., Inc.
Nye, Kimara. The Four Little Pigs. Bruchnalski, Marcin, illus. 2019. (Early Bird Readers — Purple (Early Bird Stories (tm)) Ser.). (ENG.). 32p. (J). (gr. k-3). 30.65 *(978-1-5415-4227-3(4),* 60cefd4f-6003-46ef-a1b5-4f0a01fafd6e); pap. 9.99 *(978-1-5415-7422-9(2),* 22486836-c7a2-484e-b99a-2e87d84aedc9) Lerner Publishing Group. (Lerner Pubns.).
O'Hearn, Michael. Ghosts vs. Witches: Tussle of the Tricksters. Moffet, Patricia, illus. 2011. (Monster Wars Ser.). (ENG.). 32p. (gr. 3-4). pap. 47.70 *(978-1-4296-7262-7(5),* Capstone Pr.) Capstone.
Parks, Peggy J. Witches. 2007. (Mysterious & Unknown Ser.). (Illus.). 96p. (YA). (gr. 7-12). lib. bdg. 43.93 *(978-1-60152-031-9(X))* ReferencePoint Pr., Inc.
Rawson, Christopher. Stories of Witches. Cartwright, Stephen, illus. 2004. (Young Reading Ser.: Vol. 1). 48p. (J). (gr. 2-18). lib. bdg. 13.95 *(978-1-58086-630-9(1),* Usborne) EDC Publishing.
Roby, Cynthia A. Witches, 1 vol. 2015. (Creatures of Fantasy Ser.). (ENG., Illus.). 64p. (gr. 6-6). 35.93 *(978-1-5026-0930-4(4),* daafdb8f-3317-4d63-95d2-4d93797f6455) Cavendish Square Publishing LLC.
Solotareff, Gregoire. Dictionary of Witches. 2017. (ENG., Illus.). 192p. (J). (gr. 7-12). pap. 14.95 *(978-1-77085-995-1(0),* 87fc7ca2-7763-40f9-ae49-9ed044c23fdd) Firefly Bks., Ltd.
Stefoff, Rebecca. Witches & Witchcraft, 1 vol. 2008. (Secrets of the Unexplained Ser.). (ENG., Illus.). 96p. (gr. 6-6). lib. bdg. 36.93 *(978-0-7614-2637-0(X),* 3906f7e4-dd22-4eff-bb42-71c5ffo4fc53) Cavendish Square Publishing LLC.
Stempie, Heidi E. Y. Witch Haunts. 2016. (Scary Places Ser.). (ENG., Illus.). 32p. (J). (gr. 4-8). 28.50 *(978-1-944102-39-5(6))* Bearport Publishing Co., Inc.
Susaeta, Equipo. LAS BRUJAS. (SPA.). (J). 3.48 *(978-84-305-9406-1(X))* Susaeta Ediciones, S.A. ESP. Dist: AIMS International Bks., Inc.
Tieck, Sarah. Witches, 1 vol. 2015. (Creepy Creatures Ser.). (ENG.). 32p. (J). (gr. 2-5). 34.21 *(978-1-62403-769-6(0),* 17840, Big Buddy Bks.) ABDO Publishing Co.
Timmons-Hanselka, Angela. American Witches, 1 vol. 2019. (Creatures of the Paranormal Ser.). (ENG.). 48p. (J). (gr. 5-5). pap. 12.70 *(978-1-9785-1365-5(8),* 3b9b5422-fbad-41d8-926e-0c14b63d94e3) Enslow Publishing, LLC.
Turner, Patrenia. My Little Golden Book About Queen Patrenialla: A Fairy-Tail About the Queen of England Patrenia Turner. Turner, Troyius, ed. 2017. (Little Golden Book Ser.). (Illus.). pap. 4.99 *(978-0-578-19815-6(0))* The Sleeping Bear Pr.
—Queen Patrenialla: A Fairy-Tail About the Queen of England Patrenia Turner. Turner, Troyius, ed. 2017. (Illus.). pap. *(978-0-578-19814-9(2))* The Sleeping Bear Pr.
Turner, Queen of England Patrenia. Queen Patrenialla - A Canadian Story Poem. Turner, Keeng of England Troyius, ed. 2015. (Illus.). pap. *(978-0-578-18000-7(6))* Royalty Patrenia Turner Publications.
West, David & Ganeri, Anita. Witches & Warlocks, 1 vol. West, David & Ganeri, Anita, illus. 2010. (Dark Side Ser.). (ENG., Illus.). 32p. (J). (gr. 4-5). lib. bdg. 30.27 *(978-1-61531-901-5(8),* ef537589-8edf-4413-9a47-f3f1c077b5ea, PowerKids Pr.) Rosen Publishing Group, Inc., The.

WITCHES—FICTION

Adams, Adrienne. A Woggle of Witches. Adams, Adrienne, illus. 2017. (ENG., Illus.). 32p. (J). (gr. -1-3). 13.99 *(978-1-5344-1246-0(8),* Aladdin) Simon & Schuster Children's Publishing.
Adams, Alane. The Blue Witch: The Witches of Orkney, Book One. 2018. (Witches of Orkney Ser.: 1). (ENG., Illus.). 216p. (J). (gr. 2-6). pap. 12.95 *(978-1-943006-77-9(6))* SparkPr. (a Bks.parks Imprint).
—The Raven God: The Legends of Orkney Series. 2017. (Legends of Orkney Ser.: 3). (ENG., Illus.). 344p. (J). (gr. 4-7). pap. 16.95 *(978-1-943006-36-6(9))* SparkPr. (a Bks.parks Imprint).
Adams, Denise H. Itchy the Witch. Adams, Denise H., illus. 2007. (Illus.). 32p. (J). (gr. -1-3). 13.99 *(978-1-59879-385-7(3))* Lifevest Publishing, Inc.
Aikins, Dave, illus. Dora Saves the Snow Princess. 2008. (Dora the Explorer Ser.: 27). (ENG.). 24p. (J). (gr. -1-2). pap. 3.99 *(978-1-4169-5866-6(5),* Simon Spotlight/Nickelodeon) Simon Spotlight/Nickelodeon.
Alcántara, Ricardo. Huy, Que Miedo! 13th ed. 2003. (SPA., Illus.). 44p. *(978-84-236-2559-8(1),* ED6263) Edebé ESP. Dist: Lectorum Pubns., Inc.
Alexander, R. C. Unfamiliar Magic. 2011. 368p. (J). (gr. 3-7). pap. 8.99 *(978-0-375-85855-0(5),* Yearling) Random Hse. Children's Bks.
Alexander, Susanne L. Adventures of the Pixies of Penny Brook Village: Reeza's Revenge. 2007. 174p. (J). pap. 12.95 *(978-0-7414-4292-5(2))* Infinity Publishing.
Almeida, Jose-Gabriel. Lodiville: Adventure Land. 2008. 52p. pap. 16.95 *(978-1-60563-989-5(3))* America Star Bks.
Alton, Steve. The Firehills. 2005. (ENG.). 192p. (YA). (gr. 5-12). 15.95 *(978-1-57505-798-9(0),* Carolrhoda Bks.) Lerner Publishing Group.
—The Malifex. 2003. (Middle Readers Ser.). (Illus.). 182p. (J). (gr. 3-7). 14.95 *(978-0-8225-0959-2(8))* Lerner Publishing Group.
Anderson, Al. Adventures with Bingo Borden. Agora Publications Staff, tr. Kurzyca, Krystyna Emilia, illus. 2010. 77p. (J). pap. 9.50 *(978-1-887250-46-7(8))* Agora Pubns., Inc.
Anderson, Clay. Mary Margaret Hammersmith & the Lady of the Roundtable, 1 vol. 2009. 134p. pap. 24.95 *(978-1-4489-1892-8(8))* America Star Bks.
Andrews, Natalie. Clara's Witch. 2004. (ENG.). 272p. (YA). pap. 22.50 *(978-1-920731-62-5(8))* Fremantle Pr. AUS. Dist: Independent Pubs. Group.
Anthony, Horowitz. Raven's Gate. 2005. (SWE.). 288p. pap. *(978-1-84428-619-5(3))* Walker Bks., Ltd.
Archie Superstars. The Complete Sabrina the Teenage Witch: 1962-1971. 2017. (Sabrina's Spellbook Ser.: 1). (Illus.). 512p. (J). (gr. 4-7). pap. 9.99 *(978-1-936975-94-5(7))* Archie Comic Pubns., Inc.
Arden, Alys. The Romeo Catchers. 2017. (Casquette Girls Ser.: 2). (ENG., Illus.). 604p. (YA). (gr. 7-12). pap. 12.95 *(978-1-5039-4000-0(4),* 9781503940000, Skyscape) Amazon Publishing.
Argyle, Amber. Winter Queen. 2013. 256p. 21.99 *(978-0-9857394-4-7(4))* Starling Publishing.
Ashby, Mandy Anne. Mindy's Adventure with the Pussycat Witches: Playing in the Rain. 2011. (Illus.). 28p. pap. 20.66 *(978-1-4567-8788-2(8))* AuthorHouse.
Ashby, Norman. Magic Fireplace. 2003. (Illus.). 50p. pap. *(978-1-84401-066-0(4))* Athena Pr.
Asquith, Ros. Trixie Gets the Witch Factor. 2007. (Trixie Ser.). (ENG., Illus.). 176p. (J). (gr. 3-6). pap. 13.95 *(978-0-00-725910-6(7))* HarperCollins Pubs. Ltd. GBR. Dist: Independent Pubs. Group.
Attia, Stephan. Other Christmas Stories. 2009. 42p. pap. 19.68 *(978-0-557-11189-3(7))* Lulu Pr., Inc.
Atwater-Rhodes, Amelia. Persistence of Memory. 2010. (Den of Shadows Ser.: 5). (ENG.). 224p. (YA). (gr. 7). pap. 8.99 *(978-0-440-24004-4(2),* Delacorte Pr.) Random Hse. Children's Bks.
Baker, E. D. Dragon's Breath: Read-Along/Homework Pack, 6 vols. unabr. ed. 2005. (Frog Princess Ser.: 2). (SPA.). (J). (gr. 5-8). 78.75 *(978-1-4193-3563-1(4),* 42041) Recorded Bks., Inc.
Barnhill, Kelly. The Girl Who Drank the Moon (Winner of the 2017 Newbery Medal) (ENG.). 400p. (J). (gr. 5-9). 2019. pap. 9.95 *(978-1-61620-746-5(9),* 73746) 2016. 18.99 *(978-1-61620-567-6(9),* 73567) Algonquin Young Readers.
—The Girl Who Drank the Moon (Winner of the 2017 Newbery Medal) - Gift Edition. 2019. (ENG., Illus.). 416p. (gr. 5-9). 19.95 *(978-1-61620-997-1(6),* 73997) Algonquin Young Readers.
—La Niña Que Bebió la Luna. Onoda, Yuta, illus. 2018.Tr. of Girl Who Drank the Moon. (SPA.). 424p. pap. 17.95 *(978-1-64101-210-2(2),* Loqueleo) Santillana USA Publishing Co., Inc.
—The Witch's Boy. 2014. (ENG.). 400p. (J). (gr. 4-7). 37.99 *(978-1-61620-351-1(X),* 73351) Algonquin Young Readers.
Barraclough, Lindsey. The Mark of Cain. 2016. (ENG.). 496p. (YA). (gr. 9). 17.99 *(978-0-7636-7864-7(3))* Candlewick Pr.
Batham, Matthew. Lightsleep. 2006. 167p. pap. *(978-1-904623-39-7(5))* WritersPrintShop.
Baum, L. Frank. 8 Books In: L. Frank Baum's Oz Series, volume 2 of 2. Little Wizard Stories of Oz, Tik-Tok of Oz, the Scarecrow of Oz, Rinkitink in Oz, the Lost P. 2008. 812p. pap. *(978-1-905921-09-6(8))* Shoes & Ships & Sealing Wax Ltd.
Baxter, Nicola. Witches, Wizards & Magicians. Morton, Ken, illus. 2012. 80p. (J). (gr. k-4). pap. 9.99 *(978-1-84322-807-3(6))* Anness Publishing GBR. Dist: National Bk. Network.
Begler, Pete. The Fearless Travelers' Guide to Wicked Places. 2017. (ENG., Illus.). 384p. (J). (gr. 4-8). 14.95 *(978-1-62370-799-6(4),* 133339, Capstone Young Readers) Capstone.
Bell, Hilari. The Goblin Gate. (ENG.). (YA). (gr. 8). 2011. 400p. pap. 8.99 *(978-0-06-165104-5(4))* 2010. 384p. 16.99 *(978-0-06-165102-1(8))* HarperCollins Pubs. (HarperTeen).
—The Goblin Wood. 2004. (Illus.). 371p. (J). (gr. 5-9). 14.65 *(978-0-7569-3253-4(X))* Perfection Learning Corp.
Beltz, Temre. The Tragical Tale of Birdie Bloom. (ENG., Illus.). (J). (gr. 3-7). 2020. 384p. pap. 7.99 *(978-0-06-283584-0(X))* 2019. 368p. 16.99 *(978-0-06-283583-3(1))* HarperCollins Pubs. (HarperCollins).
Bennett, Anna Elizabeth. Little Witch: 60th Anniversary Edition. Stone, Helen, illus. 60th anniv. ed. 2013. 128p. (J). (gr. k-3). pap. 12.95 *(978-1-61608-964-1(4),* 608964, Sky Pony Pr.) Skyhorse Publishing Co., Inc.
BeSwitched. 2004. (YA). mass mkt. 7.99 *(978-0-9759784-0-5(3))* Breezy Reads.
Biederman, Ashley. The Witches Keys. 2012. 250p. 28.99 *(978-1-105-52163-8(X))* Lulu Pr., Inc.
Bishop, Debbie. MYST of the Lost Shadow Boys. 2008. (ENG.). 228p. (J). (gr. 4-9). pap. 6.99 *(978-1-932431-79-7(9))* Left Field Angel Gate.
Blacker, Terence & Ross, Tony. En la Carcel. 2003. (Serafina the Little Witch Ser.). (SPA., Illus.). 72p. (J). 7.95 *(978-84-8453-011-4(6))* Ediciones del Bronce ESP. Dist: Planeta Publishing Corp.
—Estrella de la Tele. 2003. (Serafina the Little Witch Ser.). (SPA.). 80p. (J). 7.95 *(978-84-8453-066-4(3))* Ediciones del Bronce ESP. Dist: Planeta Publishing Corp.
—Fuera de Control. 2003. (Serafina the Little Witch Ser.). (SPA., Illus.). 72p. (J). 7.95 *(978-84-8453-049-7(3))* Ediciones del Bronce ESP. Dist: Planeta Publishing Corp.
—Una Intrusa en el Hospital. 2003. (Serafina the Little Witch Ser.). (SPA., Illus.). 72p. (J). 7.95 *(978-84-8453-010-7(8))* Ediciones del Bronce ESP. Dist: Planeta Publishing Corp.
—Un Mundo de Problemas. 2003. (Serafina the Little Witch Ser.). (SPA.). 80p. (J). 7.95 *(978-84-8453-009-1(4))* Ediciones del Bronce ESP. Dist: Planeta Publishing Corp.
Blevins, Wiley. Hansel & Gretel & the Haunted Hut. Cox, Steve, illus. 2016. (Scary Tales Retold Ser.). (ENG.). 24p. (J). (gr. k-3). pap. 6.99 *(978-1-63440-097-8(6),* 3901e723-1a08-42ee-a75c-16f968d8bfca); lib. bdg. 27.99 *(978-1-63440-096-1(8),* 5cfd02df-7edf-431d-873a-53668e90ccdf) Red Chair Pr.
Bredin, Henrietta & McEwen, Priscilla. The Prince & the Goosegirl: A Story with Activities Based on the Opera by Humperdinck. 2006. (Illus.). 30p. (J). (gr. k-4). reprint ed. pap. 17.00 *(978-1-4223-5538-1(1))* DIANE Publishing Co.
Brezenoff, Steve. Witch Mayor, 1 vol. Percival, Tom, illus. 2012. (Ravens Pass Ser.). (ENG.). 96p. (J). (gr. 3-6). lib. bdg. 25.32 *(978-1-4342-3791-0(5),* 117090, Stone Arch Bks.) Capstone.
Brignull, Irena. The Hawkweed Prophecy. 2017. (Hawkweed Ser.: 1). (ENG.). 384p. (YA). (gr. 7-17). pap. 10.99 *(978-1-60286-313-2(X))* Hachette Bk. Group.
Briley, Randy. Mr Underneath. 2013. 134p. pap. 12.99 *(978-0-9896269-0-3(3))* Raven Mad Studios.
Brinkerhoff, Phillip. To the Magical Pond. 2004. 116p. (YA). pap. 11.95 *(978-0-7414-1982-8(3))* Infinity Publishing.
Brinson, Julie L. Princess Olivia & the Leap Frog, 1 vol. Brinson, Connor J., illus. 2009. 22p. pap. 24.95 *(978-1-60813-802-9(X))* America Star Bks.
Broadribb, Donald. Marcia. 2009. 423p. 39.47 *(978-1-4092-6754-6(7))* Lulu Pr., Inc.
Brokamp, Elizabeth. Back to School, Picky Little Witch!, 1 vol. Welling, Peter, illus. 2014. (Picky Little Witch Ser.). (ENG.). 32p. (J). (gr. k-3). 16.99 *(978-1-4556-1887-3(X),* Pelican Publishing) Arcadia Publishing.
Brothers, Marilee. Moon Rise. 2009. (YA). pap. 14.95 *(978-0-9821756-9-9(8),* Bell Bridge Bks.) BelleBks., Inc.
—Moon Spun. 2010. 246p. pap. 14.95 *(978-1-935661-95-5(7),* Bell Bridge Bks.) BelleBks., Inc.
—Moonstone. 2008. 236p. (YA). pap. 14.95 *(978-0-9802453-4-9(6),* Bell Bridge Bks.) BelleBks., Inc.
—Shadow Moon. 2011. 230p. (YA). pap. *(978-1-61194-058-9(3))* BelleBks., Inc.
Brown, Anne. The Dumari Chronicles: Year One: Year One. 2007. 376p. (YA). per. 20.95 *(978-0-595-45725-0(8))* iUniverse, Inc.
Brown, Lisa. Vampire Boy's Good Night. Brown, Lisa, illus. 2010. (ENG., Illus.). 32p. (J). (gr. -1-2). 16.99 *(978-0-06-114011-2(2),* HarperCollins) HarperCollins Pubs.
Brunn Emanuele, Susan. Brooms Are Out! 2009. 24p. pap. 12.99 *(978-1-4490-2227-3(8))* AuthorHouse.
Bryant, Ann. The Lost Broomstick. 2011. (Tadpoles Ser.: No. 37). (ENG., Illus.). 24p. (J). (gr. k-3). pap. *(978-0-7787-0594-9(3))* Crabtree Publishing Co.
Buckmaster, Heath L. Box of Hair: A Fairy Tale, 3 bks., Bk. 1. (Illus.). (YA). 2007. 102p. pap. 12.99 *(978-0-9771802-5-7(5))* 2008. 108p. lib. bdg. 25.00 *(978-0-9771802-4-0(7))* Transaltar Publishing.
—Box of Hair: A Fairy Tale. 2008. 104p. pap. 12.50 *(978-1-4357-2690-1(1))* Lulu Pr., Inc.
Burge, Constance M. Seasons of the Witch, Vol. 1. Simon and Schuster Children's Staff, ed. 2003. (Charmed Ser.). (ENG.). 192p. (YA). pap. *(978-0-689-86545-9(7))* Gallery Pr., The.
Burge, Constance M., creator. The Warren Witches. 2005. (Charmed Ser.). (ENG.). 320p. (YA). pap. *(978-0-689-87876-3(1))* Gallery Pr., The.
Burns, A. M. Witches. 2016. (ENG., Illus.). (J). 24.99 *(978-1-63477-996-8(7),* Harmony Ink Pr.) Dreamspinner Pr.
Busch, Jean. Aiden & the Frog Prince, 1 vol. 2009. 48p. pap. 16.95 *(978-1-60836-892-1(0))* America Star Bks.
Butler, Erin. Blood Hex. 2013. 260p. pap. *(978-1-77130-351-4(4))* Evernight Publishing.

W
X
Y
Z

Cajoleas, Jimmy. Goldeline. (ENG.). (J). (gr. 5). 2019. 272p. pap. 6.99 *(978-0-06-249876-2(2))* 2017. 256p. 16.99 *(978-0-06-249875-5(4))* HarperCollins Pubs. (HarperCollins).

Cammuso, Frank. Cookie Catastrophe. 2014. (Misadventures of Salem Hyde Ser.: 3). (J). lib. bdg. 17.15 *(978-0-606-36149-1(9))* Turtleback.

—The Misadventures of Salem Hyde: Book Two: Big Birthday Bash. 2014. (Misadventures of Salem Hyde Ser.). (ENG., Illus.). 96p. (J). (gr. 1-4). 14.95 *(978-1-4197-1025-4(7),* 1044801, Amulet Bks.) Abrams, Inc.

—The Misadventures of Salem Hyde: Spelling Trouble. 2013. (Misadventures of Salem Hyde Ser.: 1). (J). lib. bdg. 17.15 *(978-0-606-33440-2(8))* Turtleback.

Campana, Augustine. The Last Fairy. 2008. 204p. (gr. -1 — 1). 24.95 *(978-0-595-50892-1(8))*; pap. 14.95 *(978-0-595-52086-2(3))* iUniverse, Inc.

Canfield, Andrea. Sassy the Seahag. Hallinan, Susan, illus. 2003. Orig. Title: Sassy the Seahag. (J). per. *(978-0-9721327-3-2(2))* One Foot in the Grave Media.

Cardwell, Helen. Amber Janusson: Protector of the Magic Lands. 2003. 136p. pap. 11.95 *(978-0-595-29436-7(7))* iUniverse, Inc.

Carretero, Mónica. Witches Handbook. Brokenbrow, Jon, tr. Carretero, Mónica, illus. 2012. (ENG., Illus.). 32p. (J). (gr. k-3). 14.95 *(978-84-15241-06-5(2))* Cuento de Luz SL ESP. Dist: Publishers Group West (PGW).

Carter, Amy. The Not So Wicked, Wicked Witch! 2009. 24p. pap. 15.95 *(978-1-4327-3781-8(3))* Outskirts Pr., Inc.

Catalano, Nikki. Mitsu: The Dark Witch & the Dream Wilderness. 2010. 88p. pap. 25.13 *(978-1-4251-7411-8(6))* Trafford Publishing.

Chance, Kim. Keeper. 2018. (Keeper Duology Ser.). (ENG.). 408p. (YA). (gr. 9-12). pap. 14.99 *(978-1-63583-012-5(5),* 1635830125, Flux) North Star Editions.

—Keeper. 2018. lib. bdg. 26.95 *(978-0-606-41244-5(1))* Turtleback.

Chapman, Lara. Accidentally Evil. 2015. (Mix Ser.). (ENG., Illus.). 240p. (J). (gr. 4-8). pap. 7.99 *(978-1-4814-0110-4(6),* Aladdin) Simon & Schuster Children's Publishing.

—The XYZs of Being Wicked. 2014. (Mix Ser.). (ENG., Illus.). 272p. (J). (gr. 4-8). pap. 6.99 *(978-1-4814-0107-4(6),* Aladdin) Simon & Schuster Children's Publishing.

—The XYZs of Being Wicked. 2014. (Mix Ser.). (ENG., Illus.). 272p. (J). (gr. 4-8). 17.99 *(978-1-4814-0108-1(4),* Simon & Schuster/Paula Wiseman Bks.) Simon & Schuster/Paula Wiseman Bks.

Chew, Ruth. A Matter-Of-Fact Magic Book: No Such Thing As a Witch. 2013. (Matter-Of-Fact Magic Book Ser.). (Illus.). 128p. (J). (gr. 2-5). 5.99 *(978-0-449-81562-5(5),* Random Hse. Bks. for Young Readers) Random Hse. Children's Bks.

—A Matter-Of-Fact Magic Book: the Wednesday Witch. 2015. (Matter-Of-Fact Magic Book Ser.). (Illus.). 144p. (J). (gr. 2-5). pap. 5.99 *(978-0-449-81556-4(0),* Random Hse. Bks. for Young Readers) Random Hse. Children's Bks.

—A Matter-Of-Fact Magic Book: Witch's Broom. 2015. (Matter-Of-Fact Magic Book Ser.). (Illus.). 144p. (J). (gr. 2-5). pap. 5.99 *(978-0-449-81578-6(1),* Random Hse. Bks. for Young Readers) Random Hse. Children's Bks.

Christian, Cheryl. Witches, 1 vol. Williams, Wish, illus. 2011. (ENG.). 32p. (J). pap. 5.95 *(978-1-59572-283-6(1))* Star Bright Bks., Inc.

Chupeco, Rin. The Bone Witch. 2018. (Bone Witch Ser.: 1). 448p. (YA). (gr. 6-12). pap. 12.99 *(978-1-4926-5278-6(4))* Sourcebooks, Inc.

—The Heart Forger: Bone Witch #2. (Bone Witch Ser.: 2). (YA). (gr. 8-12). 2019. 544p. pap. 10.99 *(978-1-4926-6808-4(7))* 2018. (ENG., Illus.). 528p. 17.99 *(978-1-4926-3585-7(5))* Sourcebooks, Inc.

—The Shadowglass: Bone Witch #3. (Bone Witch Ser.: 3). 480p. (YA). (gr. 8-12). 2020. pap. 12.99 *(978-1-4926-9332-1(4))* 2019. (ENG., Illus.). 17.99 *(978-1-4926-6060-6(4))* Sourcebooks, Inc.

Cinebook. Halloween. Jeffrey, Erica, tr. 2007. (Melusine Ser.: 2). (Illus.). 48p. (J). (gr. 4-7). pap. 11.95 *(978-1-905460-34-2(1))* CineBook GBR. Dist: National Bk. Network.

Clark, Isabelle. The Enchanted Forest of Hope. 2009. 44p. pap. 18.50 *(978-1-4389-7781-2(6))* AuthorHouse.

Clarke, Jane. Creaky Castle. Fox, Christyan, illus. 2013. *(978-1-4351-4951-9(3))* Barnes & Noble, Inc.

Coakley, Lena. Witchlanders. 2012. (ENG., Illus.). 416p. (YA). (gr. 7). pap. 11.99 *(978-1-4424-2005-2(7),* Atheneum Bks. for Young Readers) Simon & Schuster Children's Publishing.

—Witchlanders. 2011. (ENG., Illus.). 416p. (YA). (gr. 7-12). 16.99 *(978-1-4424-2004-5(9))* Simon & Schuster, Inc.

Cochran, Molly. Legacy, 1. 2011. (Legacy Ser.). (ENG.). 432p. (YA). (gr. 9-12). 17.99 *(978-1-4424-1739-7(0))* Simon & Schuster, Inc.

—Poison. 2012. (Legacy Ser.). (ENG.). 368p. (YA). (gr. 9). 17.99 *(978-1-4424-5050-9(9),* Simon & Schuster/Paula Wiseman Bks.) Simon & Schuster/Paula Wiseman Bks.

Cochrane, Ian. Shian & the Corryvreckan. 2013. (Illus.). 96p. pap. *(978-1-909465-09-1(7))* Cloister Hse. Pr., The.

Coe, Mary. The Prince of Betherland. 2007. 100p. pap. 9.95 *(978-1-4303-2521-5(6))* Lulu Pr., Inc.

Coe, Mary E. The Prince of Betherland. 2008. 117p. 24.95 *(978-0-557-03112-2(5))* Lulu Pr., Inc.

Cohen, Caron Lee. Broom, Zoom! Ruzzier, Sergio, illus. 2010. (ENG.). 32p. (J). (gr. -1-3). 17.99 *(978-1-4169-9113-7(1),* Simon & Schuster Bks. For Young Readers) Simon & Schuster Bks. For Young Readers.

Colfer, Chris. A Tale of Sorcery... 2021. (ENG., (J). (gr. 3-7). (Tale of Magic... Ser.: 3). Illus.). 496p. 18.99 *(978-0-316-05599-4(9))*; 576p. 20.99 *(978-0-316-30096-4(9))* Little, Brown Bks. for Young Readers.

—A Tale of Witchcraft... Dorman, Brandon, illus. 2020. 432p. (J). *(978-0-316-59120-1(3))* Little Brown & Co.

—A Tale of Witchcraft... (Tale of Magic... Ser.: 2). (ENG.). (J). (gr. 3-7). 2021. 464p. pap. 9.99 *(978-0-316-52354-7(2))* 2020. (Illus.). 448p. 18.99 *(978-0-316-52356-1(9))* 2020. 528p. pap. 26.99 *(978-0-316-54175-6(3))* Little, Brown Bks. for Young Readers.

Coll, Ivar Da. Medias Dulces. (SPA.). (J). (gr. 3-5). 7.95 *(978-958-04-3398-9(4),* NR7686) Norma S.A. COL. Dist: Lectorum Pubns., Inc., Distribuidora Norma, Inc.

Columbus, Chris & Vizzini, Ned. House of Secrets: Battle of the Beasts. Call, Greg, illus. 2014. (House of Secrets Ser.: 2). (ENG.). 480p. (J). (gr. 3-7). 17.99 *(978-0-06-219249-3(3),* Balzer & Bray) HarperCollins Pubs.

Condenzio, John. Cocoa the Witch Cat. 2013. 20p. pap. 24.95 *(978-1-62709-264-7(1))* America Star Bks.

Connolly, Tina. Seriously Wicked. 2016. (YA). lib. bdg. 20.85 *(978-0-606-38783-5(8))* Turtleback.

Coombes, Patrick. The Witch's Assistant. 2013. 34p. pap. *(978-1-909593-74-9(5))* Legend Pr.

Cooper, Bernice Soroka. The Little Elf-Frog. 2012. 24p. pap. 17.99 *(978-1-4772-9525-0(9))* AuthorHouse.

Corderoy, Tracey. The Great Granny Cake Contest! Hubble Bubble. Berger, Joe, illus. 2017. (Hubble Bubble Ser.). (ENG.). 128p. (J). (gr. 1-4). pap. 6.99 *(978-0-7636-8849-3(5))* Candlewick Pr.

—The Wacky Winter Wonderland! Hubble Bubble. Berger, Joe, illus. 2017. (Hubble Bubble Ser.). (ENG.). 128p. (J). (gr. 1-4). 14.99 *(978-0-7636-9624-5(2))* Candlewick Pr.

Córdova, Zoraida. Bruja Born. 2019. (Brooklyn Brujas Ser.: 2). (ENG.). 352p. (YA). (gr. 8-12). pap. 10.99 *(978-1-7282-0986-9(2))* Sourcebooks, Inc.

—Labyrinth Lost. 2017. (Brooklyn Brujas Ser.: 1). (ENG.). 352p. (YA). (gr. 8-12). pap. 10.99 *(978-1-4926-2316-8(4))* Sourcebooks, Inc.

Coughlin, Jennie Rose. The Purple Scarf. Howes, Bryan Arthur, illus. 2008. 20p. per. 24.95 *(978-1-60441-733-3(1))* America Star Bks.

Coven, Wanda. Heidi Heckelbeck 3 Books In 1! Heidi Heckelbeck Has a Secret; Heidi Heckelbeck Casts a Spell; Heidi Heckelbeck & the Cookie Contest. Burris, Priscilla, illus. 2014. (Heidi Heckelbeck Ser.). (ENG.). 384p. (J). (gr. k-4). pap. 8.99 *(978-1-4814-2771-5(7),* Little Simon) Little Simon.

—Heidi Heckelbeck & the Big Mix-Up. Burris, Priscilla, illus. 2016. (Heidi Heckelbeck Ser.: 18). (ENG.). 128p. (J). (gr. k-4). pap. 5.99 *(978-1-4814-7169-5(4),* Little Simon) Little Simon.

—Heidi Heckelbeck & the Christmas Surprise. Burris, Priscilla, illus. 2013. (Heidi Heckelbeck Ser.: 9). (ENG.). 128p. (J). (gr. k-2). 17.99 *(978-1-4424-8125-1(0))*; pap. 6.99 *(978-1-4424-8124-4(2))* Little Simon. (Little Simon).

—Heidi Heckelbeck & the Christmas Surprise. 2013. (Heidi Heckelbeck Ser.: 9). lib. bdg. 14.75 *(978-0-606-32325-3(2))* Turtleback.

—Heidi Heckelbeck & the Cookie Contest. Burris, Priscilla, illus. 2012. (Heidi Heckelbeck Ser.: 3). (ENG.). 128p. (J). (gr. k-4). 17.99 *(978-1-4424-4166-8(6))*; pap. 6.99 *(978-1-4424-4165-1(8))* Little Simon. (Little Simon).

—Heidi Heckelbeck & the Cookie Contest. 2012. (Heidi Heckelbeck Ser.: 3). lib. bdg. 16.00 *(978-0-606-26328-3(4))* Turtleback.

—Heidi Heckelbeck & the Magic Puppy. Burris, Priscilla, illus. 2017. (Heidi Heckelbeck Ser.: 20). (ENG.). 128p. (J). (gr. k-4). pap. 5.99 *(978-1-4814-9521-9(6),* Little Simon) Little Simon.

—Heidi Heckelbeck & the Never-Ending Day. Burris, Priscilla, illus. 2017. (Heidi Heckelbeck Ser.: 21). (ENG.). 128p. (J). (gr. k-4). 17.99 *(978-1-4814-9525-7(9))*; pap. 6.99 *(978-1-4814-9524-0(0))* Little Simon. (Little Simon).

—Heidi Heckelbeck & the Secret Admirer. Burris, Priscilla, illus. 2012. (Heidi Heckelbeck Ser.: 6). (ENG.). 128p. (J). (gr. k-4). 17.99 *(978-1-4424-4175-0(5))*; pap. 6.99 *(978-1-4424-4174-3(7))* Little Simon. (Little Simon).

—Heidi Heckelbeck & the Secret Admirer. 2012. (Heidi Heckelbeck Ser.: 6). lib. bdg. 16.00 *(978-0-606-26905-6(3))* Turtleback.

—Heidi Heckelbeck & the Snoopy Spy. Burris, Priscilla, illus. 2018. (Heidi Heckelbeck Ser.: 23). (ENG.). 128p. (J). (gr. k-4). 17.99 *(978-1-5344-1111-1(9))*; pap. 6.99 *(978-1-5344-1110-4(0))* Little Simon. (Little Simon).

—Heidi Heckelbeck & the Tie-Dyed Bunny. 2014. (Heidi Heckelbeck Ser.: 10). lib. bdg. 16.00 *(978-0-606-35429-5(8))* Turtleback.

—Heidi Heckelbeck & the Wacky Tacky Spirit Week. Burris, Priscilla, illus. 2019. (Heidi Heckelbeck Ser.: 27). (ENG.). 128p. (J). (gr. k-4). 16.99 *(978-1-5344-4636-6(2),* Little Simon) Little Simon.

—Heidi Heckelbeck Casts a Spell. Burris, Priscilla, illus. 2012. (Heidi Heckelbeck Ser.: 2). (ENG.). 128p. (J). (gr. k-4). 17.99 *(978-1-4424-4088-3(0))*; pap. 6.99 *(978-1-4424-3567-4(4))* Little Simon. (Little Simon).

—Heidi Heckelbeck Casts a Spell. 2012. (Heidi Heckelbeck Ser.: 2). lib. bdg. 16.00 *(978-0-606-26327-6(6))* Turtleback.

—The Heidi Heckelbeck Collection (Boxed Set) A Bewitching Four-Book Boxed Set: Heidi Hecklebeck Has a Secret; Heidi Hecklebeck Casts a Spell; Heidi Hecklebeck & the Cookie Contest; Heidi Hecklebeck in Disguise. Burris, Priscilla, illus. 2013. (Heidi Heckelbeck Ser.). (ENG.). 512p. (J). (gr. k-4). pap. 23.99 *(978-1-4424-8976-9(6),* Little Simon) Little Simon.

—Heidi Heckelbeck Gets Glasses. Burris, Priscilla, illus. 2012. (Heidi Heckelbeck Ser.: 5). (ENG.). 128p. (J). (gr. k-4). 17.99 *(978-1-4424-4172-9(0))*; pap. 6.99 *(978-1-4424-4171-2(2))* Little Simon. (Little Simon).

—Heidi Heckelbeck Gets Glasses. 2012. (Heidi Heckelbeck Ser.: 5). lib. bdg. 16.00 *(978-0-606-26888-2(X))* Turtleback.

—Heidi Heckelbeck Goes to Camp! Burris, Priscilla, illus. 2013. (Heidi Heckelbeck Ser.: 8). (ENG.). 128p. (J). (gr. k-4). 17.99 *(978-1-4424-6481-0(X))*; pap. 6.99 *(978-1-4424-6480-3(1))* Little Simon. (Little Simon).

—Heidi Heckelbeck Goes to Camp! 2013. (Heidi Heckelbeck Ser.: 8). lib. bdg. 16.00 *(978-0-606-32031-3(8))* Turtleback.

—Heidi Heckelbeck Has a New Best Friend. Burris, Priscilla, illus. 2018. (Heidi Heckelbeck Ser.: 22). (ENG.). 128p. (J). (gr. k-4). 17.99 *(978-1-5344-1108-1(9))*; pap. 6.99 *(978-1-5344-1107-4(0))* Little Simon. (Little Simon).

—Heidi Heckelbeck Has a Secret. Burris, Priscilla, illus. 2012. (Heidi Heckelbeck Ser.: 1). (ENG.). 128p. (J). (gr. k-4). 17.99 *(978-1-4424-4087-6(2))*; pap. 6.99 *(978-1-4424-3565-0(8))* Little Simon. (Little Simon).

—Heidi Heckelbeck Has a Secret. 2012. (Heidi Heckelbeck Ser.: 1). lib. bdg. 16.00 *(978-0-606-26326-9(8))* Turtleback.

—Heidi Heckelbeck in Disguise. Burris, Priscilla, illus. 2012. (Heidi Heckelbeck Ser.: 4). (ENG.). 128p. (J). (gr. k-2). 17.99 *(978-1-4424-4169-9(0))*; pap. 6.99 *(978-1-4424-4168-2(2))* Little Simon. (Little Simon).

—Heidi Heckelbeck in Disguise. 2012. (Heidi Heckelbeck Ser.: 4). lib. bdg. 16.00 *(978-0-606-26329-0(2))* Turtleback.

—Heidi Heckelbeck Is a Flower Girl. Burris, Priscilla, illus. 2014. (Heidi Heckelbeck Ser.: 11). (ENG.). 128p. (J). (gr. k-4). pap. 6.99 *(978-1-4814-0498-3(9),* Little Simon) Little Simon.

—Heidi Heckelbeck Is Not a Thief! Burris, Priscilla, illus. 2015. (Heidi Heckelbeck Ser.: 13). (ENG.). 128p. (J). (gr. k-4). pap. 5.99 *(978-1-4814-2324-3(X),* Little Simon) Little Simon.

—Heidi Heckelbeck Is Ready to Dance! Burris, Priscilla, illus. 2013. (Heidi Heckelbeck Ser.: 7). (ENG.). 128p. (J). (gr. k-2). pap. 6.99 *(978-1-4424-5191-9(2))*; 17.99 *(978-1-4424-5192-6(0))* Little Simon. (Little Simon).

—Heidi Heckelbeck Is Ready to Dance! 2013. (Heidi Heckelbeck Ser.: 7). lib. bdg. 16.00 *(978-0-606-27033-5(7))* Turtleback.

—Heidi Heckelbeck Is So Totally Grounded! Burris, Priscilla, illus. 2018. (Heidi Heckelbeck Ser.: 24). (ENG.). 128p. (J). (gr. k-4). 16.99 *(978-1-5344-2645-0(0))*; pap. 5.99 *(978-1-5344-2644-3(2))* Little Simon. (Little Simon).

—Heidi Heckelbeck Is the Bestest Babysitter! Burris, Priscilla, illus. 2015. (Heidi Heckelbeck Ser.: 16). (ENG.). 128p. (J). (gr. k-4). pap. 6.99 *(978-1-4814-4630-3(4),* Little Simon) Little Simon.

—Heidi Heckelbeck Lends a Helping Hand. Burris, Priscilla, illus. 2019. (Heidi Heckelbeck Ser.: 26). (ENG.). 128p. (J). (gr. k-4). pap. 5.99 *(978-1-5344-4529-1(3),* Little Simon) Little Simon.

—Heidi Heckelbeck Makes a Wish. 2016. (Heidi Heckelbeck Ser.: 17). lib. bdg. 16.00 *(978-0-606-38962-4(8))* Turtleback.

—Heidi Heckelbeck Makes a Wish: Super Special! Burris, Priscilla, illus. 2016. (Heidi Heckelbeck Ser.: 17). (ENG.). 160p. (J). (gr. k-4). pap. 6.99 *(978-1-4814-6613-4(5),* Little Simon) Little Simon.

—Heidi Heckelbeck Might Be Afraid of the Dark. Burris, Priscilla, illus. 2015. (Heidi Heckelbeck Ser.: 15). (ENG.). 128p. (J). (gr. k-4). pap. 6.99 *(978-1-4814-4627-3(4),* Little Simon) Little Simon.

—Heidi Heckelbeck Says "Cheese!" Burris, Priscilla, illus. 2015. (Heidi Heckelbeck Ser.: 14). (ENG.). 128p. (J). (gr. k-4). pap. 6.99 *(978-1-4814-2327-4(4),* Little Simon) Little Simon.

—Heidi Heckelbeck Tries Out for the Team. Burris, Priscilla, illus. 2017. (Heidi Heckelbeck Ser.: 19). (ENG.). 128p. (J). (gr. k-4). pap. 6.99 *(978-1-4814-7172-5(4),* Little Simon) Little Simon.

Coven, Wanda. Worst Broommate Ever! Abramskaya, Anna, illus. 2023. (Middle School & Other Disasters Ser.: 1). (ENG.). 352p. (J). (gr. 3-7). 14.99 ***(978-1-6659-2528-0(0),*** Simon Spotlight) Simon Spotlight.

Crenshaw, Glenda. Friends of the Enchanted Forest: How they Save Christmas. 2011. 28p. pap. 15.47 *(978-1-4520-0512-6(5))* AuthorHouse.

Crommett, Lora. The Blue Witch Who Dared to Be Different. 2013. 64p. 14.99 *(978-1-62951-025-5(4))* Mockingbird Lane Pr.

Crump, Fred, Jr. Ebonita & the Seven Boyz. 2010. 32p. (J). 12.95 *(978-1-934056-71-4(5))* UMI (Urban Ministries, Inc.).

Cummins, Molly. The Jewel of Fez. 2006. 141p. pap. 24.95 *(978-1-4241-1044-5(0))* PublishAmerica, Inc.

Dahl, Roald. The Witches. Blake, Quentin, illus. 2007. (ENG.). 224p. (J). (gr. 3-7). 8.99 *(978-0-14-241011-0(X),* Puffin Books) Penguin Young Readers Group.

—The Witches. 2007. (SWE., Illus.). 206p. (gr. 4-7). 17.00 *(978-0-7569-8229-4(4))* Perfection Learning Corp.

Daily, Lorrie Ann. The Castlewood Twins, the Magic Begins. 2008. 196p. pap. 12.95 *(978-0-9820479-8-9(3))* Peppertree Pr., The.

Daines, Julie. Unraveled: A Tale of True Love. 2014. 192p. (J). pap. 14.99 *(978-1-62108-627-7(5))* Covenant Communications, Inc.

D'Angelo, Elaina R. The Magic Book of E, 1 vol. 2010. 48p. pap. 16.95 *(978-1-4489-3949-7(6))* America Star Bks.

Davies, Anna. Wrecked. 2013. (ENG., Illus.). 336p. (YA). (gr. 9). pap. 9.99 *(978-1-4424-3279-6(9),* Simon & Schuster Bks. For Young Readers) Simon & Schuster Bks. For Young Readers.

De Blumenthal, Verra X. K. Folk Tales from the Russian. 2008. 88p. pap. 8.95 *(978-1-60664-152-1(2))* Aegypan.

Deane, Nancy Lou. Meg's Secret. 2011. 148p. (gr. 4-6). pap. 14.69 *(978-1-4567-8884-1(1))* AuthorHouse.

deGroat, Diane. Trick or Treat, Smell My Feet. deGroat, Diane, illus. 2008. (Illus.). (J). (gr. -1-7). pap. 16.95 incl. audio *(978-1-4301-0425-4(2))* Live Oak Media.

del Rio, Tania. Sabrina the Teenage Witch: the Magic Within 1. 2013. (Sabrina Manga Ser.: 1). (Illus.). 256p. (J). (gr. 4-7). 10.99 *(978-1-936975-39-6(4))* Archie Comic Pubns., Inc.

—Sabrina the Teenage Witch: the Magic Within 3. 2013. (Sabrina Manga Ser.: 3). (Illus.). 256p. (J). (gr. 4-7). pap. 10.99 *(978-1-936975-60-0(2))* Archie Comic Pubns., Inc.

—Sabrina the Teenage Witch: the Magic Within 4. 2014. (Sabrina Manga Ser.: 4). (Illus.). 272p. (J). (gr. 4-7). pap. 10.99 *(978-1-936975-76-1(9))* Archie Comic Pubns., Inc.

Delaney, Joseph. The Last Apprentice: a Coven of Witches. Arrasmith, Patrick, illus. (Last Apprentice Short Fiction Ser.: 2). (ENG.). 240p. (YA). (gr. 8). 2011. pap. 10.99 *(978-0-06-196040-6(3))* 2010. 16.99 *(978-0-06-196038-3(1))* HarperCollins Pubs. (Greenwillow Bks.).

—The Last Apprentice: Attack of the Fiend (Book 4) Arrasmith, Patrick, illus. 2009. (Last Apprentice Ser.: 4). (ENG.). 576p. (YA). (gr. 8-18). pap. 9.99 *(978-0-06-089129-9(7),* Greenwillow Bks.) HarperCollins Pubs.

—The Last Apprentice: Curse of the Bane (Book 2) (Last Apprentice Ser.: 2). (ENG., Illus.). (YA). (gr. 8-9). 2007. 496p. pap. 9.99 *(978-0-06-076623-8(9))* 2006. 480p. 18.99 *(978-0-06-076621-4(2))* HarperCollins Pubs. (Greenwillow Bks.).

—The Last Apprentice: Grimalkin the Witch Assassin (Book 9), Bk. 9. Arrasmith, Patrick, illus. 2013. (Last Apprentice Ser.: 9). (ENG.). 416p. (YA). (gr. 8). pap. 10.99 *(978-0-06-208208-4(6),* Greenwillow Bks.) HarperCollins Pubs.

—The Last Apprentice: Night of the Soul Stealer (Book 3), Bk. 3. 2008. (Last Apprentice Ser.: 3). (ENG.). 528p. (YA). (gr. 8-18). pap. 9.99 *(978-0-06-076626-9(3),* Greenwillow Bks.) HarperCollins Pubs.

—The Last Apprentice: Rage of the Fallen (Book 8) Bk. 8. Arrasmith, Patrick, illus. 2012. (Last Apprentice Ser.: 8). (ENG.). 416p. (YA). (gr. 8). pap. 10.99 *(978-0-06-202758-0(1),* Greenwillow Bks.) HarperCollins Pubs.

—The Last Apprentice: Revenge of the Witch (Book 1), Bk. 1. Arrasmith, Patrick, illus. (Last Apprentice Ser.: 1). (ENG.). (YA). (gr. 8). 2005. 368p. 18.99 *(978-0-06-076618-4(2))* 2006. 384p. reprint ed. pap. 10.99 *(978-0-06-076620-7(4))* HarperCollins Pubs. (Greenwillow Bks.).

—The Last Apprentice: Rise of the Huntress (Book 7) Bk. 7, Bk. 7. Arrasmith, Patrick, illus. 2011. (Last Apprentice Ser.: 7). (ENG.). 464p. (YA). (gr. 8). pap. 10.99 *(978-0-06-171512-9(3),* Greenwillow Bks.) HarperCollins Pubs.

—The Last Apprentice: the Spook's Tale: And Other Horrors. (Last Apprentice Short Fiction Ser.: 1). (ENG.). 176p. (YA). (gr. 8-18). 2010. pap. 9.99 *(978-0-06-173031-3(9))* 2009. 16.99 *(978-0-06-173028-3(9))* HarperCollins Pubs. (Greenwillow Bks.).

—The Last Apprentice: Wrath of the Bloodeye (Book 5) (Last Apprentice Ser.: 5). (ENG., (YA). (gr. 8-18). 2009. Illus.). 544p. pap. 10.99 *(978-0-06-134461-9(3))*Bk. 5. 2008. 528p. 17.99 *(978-0-06-134459-6(1))* HarperCollins Pubs. (Greenwillow Bks.).

—A New Darkness. 2014. (ENG.). 352p. (YA). (gr. 8). 17.99 *(978-0-06-233453-4(0),* Greenwillow Bks.) HarperCollins Pubs.

Demolin, G. The Blaue Hexe. 2010. (Illus.). 44p. pap. 21.22 *(978-1-4520-5516-9(5))* AuthorHouse.

Dennard, Susan. Sightwitch: A Tale of the Witchlands. 2018. (Witchlands Ser.: 3). (ENG., Illus.). 240p. (YA). 16.99 *(978-1-250-18352-1(9),* 900190887, Tor Teen) Doherty, Tom Assocs., LLC.

—Truthwitch. 2016. (Witchlands Ser.: Vol. 1). (ENG.). (gr. 8-12). pap. 12.99 *(978-0-7653-9022-6(1),* Tor Teen) Doherty, Tom Assocs., LLC.

—Truthwitch. 2017. (Witchlands Ser.: 1). (YA). lib. bdg. 20.85 *(978-0-606-39586-1(5))* Turtleback.

—Truthwitch: The Witchlands. 2017. (Witchlands Ser.: 1). (ENG.). 432p. (YA). pap. 10.99 *(978-0-7653-7929-0(5),* 900141949, Tor Teen) Doherty, Tom Assocs., LLC.

—Windwitch. 2017. (Witchlands Ser.). (ENG., Illus.). 380p. (gr. 8-12). pap. 12.99 *(978-0-7653-9579-5(7),* Tor Teen) Doherty, Tom Assocs., LLC.

—Windwitch: The Witchlands. (Witchlands Ser.: 2). (ENG.). (YA). 2018. 400p. pap. 10.99 *(978-0-7653-7931-3(7),* 900141951) 2017. (Illus.). 384p. 18.99 *(978-0-7653-7930-6(9),* 900141950) Doherty, Tom Assocs., LLC. (Tor Teen).

dePaola, Tomie. Strega Nona & the Twins: Ready-To-Read Level 1. dePaola, Tomie, illus. 2017. (Strega Nona Book Ser.). (ENG., Illus.). 32p. (J). (gr. -1-1). pap. 4.99 *(978-1-4814-8137-3(1),* Simon Spotlight) Simon Spotlight.

—Strega Nona Does It Again. 2017. lib. bdg. 19.65 *(978-0-606-39784-1(1))* Turtleback.

—Strega Nona Takes a Vacation. dePaola, Tomie, illus. 2003. (Illus.). 32p. (J). (gr. -1-3). pap. 8.99 *(978-0-14-250076-7(3),* Puffin Books) Penguin Young Readers Group.

—Strega Nona Takes a Vacation. dePaola, Tomie, illus. 2003. (Illus.). (J). (gr. -1-3). 13.65 *(978-0-7569-1469-1(8))* Perfection Learning Corp.

—Strega Nona's Gift. dePaola, Tomie, illus. 2011. (Illus.). 32p. (J). (gr. -1-3). 17.99 *(978-0-399-25649-3(0),* Nancy Paulsen Books) Penguin Young Readers Group.

—Strega Nona's Harvest. dePaola, Tomie, illus. (Illus.). 32p. (J). (gr. -1-3). 2012. (ENG.). mass mkt. 8.99 *(978-0-14-242338-7(6),* Puffin Books) 2009. 17.99 *(978-0-399-25291-4(6),* G.P. Putnam's Sons Books for Young Readers) Penguin Young Readers Group.

—Strega Nona's Magic Lessons. dePaola, Tomie, illus. 2017. (Strega Nona Book Ser.). (ENG., Illus.). 32p. (J). (gr. -1-3). 17.99 *(978-1-4814-7759-8(5),* Simon & Schuster Bks. For Young Readers) Simon & Schuster Bks. For Young Readers.

—Strega Nona's Magic Ring. dePaola, Tomie, illus. (Strega Nona Book Ser.). (ENG., Illus.). 32p. (J). (gr. -1-3). 2019. 7.99 *(978-1-5344-3017-4(2))* 2018. 17.99 *(978-1-4814-7761-1(7))* Simon & Schuster Bks. For Young Readers. (Simon & Schuster Bks. For Young Readers).

dePaola, Tomie, illus. Strega Nona & the Twins. 2017. (J). *(978-1-5379-5057-0(6),* Simon Spotlight) Simon Spotlight.

Deutsch, Barry. Hereville: How Mirka Got Her Sword. 2012. (Hereville Ser.). (ENG., Illus.). 144p. (J). (gr. 3-7). pap. 12.99 *(978-1-4197-0619-6(5),* 667403) Abrams, Inc.

—Hereville: How Mirka Met a Meteorite. 2012. (Hereville Ser.). (ENG., Illus.). 128p. (J). (gr. 3-7). 17.95 *(978-1-4197-0398-0(6),* 1004001, Amulet Bks.) Abrams, Inc.

Devlin, Wende. Old Black Witch! Devlin, Harry, illus. 2012. (ENG.). 32p. (J). (gr. -1-3). 18.95 *(978-1-930900-62-2(7))* Purple Hse. Pr.

Dietrich, Sean, illus. Hansel & Gretel: The Graphic Novel, 1 vol. 2008. (Graphic Spin Ser.). (ENG.). 40p. (J). (gr. 3-6). pap. 5.95 *(978-1-4342-0863-7(X),* 95224, Stone Arch Bks.) Capstone.

Ditchfield, Lily K & Zielski, Juile A. The Witches That Saved the Dogs. 2009. 26p. pap. 12.95 *(978-1-60264-494-6(2))* Virtualbookworm.com Publishing, Inc.

DiTerlizzi, Tony. Kenny & the Book of Beasts. DiTerlizzi, Tony, illus. (Kenny & the Dragon Ser.). (ENG., Illus.). (J). (gr. 3-7). 2021. 240p. pap. 8.99 *(978-1-4424-8650-8(3))* 2020. 224p. 17.99 *(978-1-4169-8316-3(3))* Simon & Schuster Bks. For Young Readers. (Simon & Schuster Bks. For Young Readers).

Diver, Lucienne. Fangtabulous. 2017. (Vamped Ser.: Vol. 4). (ENG., Illus.). (YA). pap. 14.95 *(978-1-62268-121-1(5))* Bella Rosa Bks.

Dixon, Joyce Ann. The Witches' Cat, 1 vol. 2010. 48p. pap. 16.95 *(978-1-4489-7030-8(X))* America Star Bks.

Doeden, Matt. Hansel & Gretel: An Interactive Fairy Tale Adventure. Miramon, Sabrina, illus. 2017. (You Choose: Fractured Fairy Tales Ser.). (ENG.). 112p. (J). (gr. 3-7). lib. bdg. 32.65 *(978-1-5157-6944-6(5),* 135418, Capstone Pr.) Capstone.

Dokey, Cameron & Burge, Constance M. Truth & Consequences. 2003. (Charmed Ser.). (ENG., Illus.). 208p. (YA). mass mkt. 6.99 *(978-0-689-85791-1(8))* Pocket Books.

ɔn, Lari. The Witch's Guide to Magical Combat, 40 vols. 2017. (Spellchasers Ser.: 3). (Illus.). 272p. (J). 9.95 *(978-1-78250-307-1(2)*, Kelpies) Floris Bks. GBR. Dist: Consortium Bk. Sales & Distribution.

ɔnaldson, Julia. Room on the Broom. Scheffler, Axel, illus. 2003. (ENG.). 32p. (J). (gr. -1-2). pap. 7.99 *(978-0-14-250112-2(3)*, Puffin Books) Penguin Young Readers Group.

-Room on the Broom in Scots. Robertson, James, tr. Scheffler, Axel, illus. 2014. 32p. (J). (-k). pap. 10.99 *(978-1-84502-753-7(1))* Black and White Publishing Ltd. GBR. Dist: Independent Pubs. Group.

ɔonbavand, Tommy. Scream Street: Blood of the Witch. 2009. (Scream Street Ser.: 2). (ENG., Illus.). 128p. (J). (gr. 3-7). pap. 5.99 *(978-0-7636-4607-3(5))* Candlewick Pr.

ɔowell, Frances O'Roark. Falling In. 2012. (ENG., Illus.). 256p. (J). (gr. 3-7). pap. 8.99 *(978-1-4424-2205-6(X)*, Atheneum Bks. for Young Readers) Simon & Schuster Children's Publishing.

ɔoyen, Denise. The Pomegranate Witch. Moser, Barry, illus. 2013. (J). *(978-0-375-87057-6(1))*; lib. bdg. *(978-0-375-97057-3(6))* Random Hse., Inc.

—The Pomegranate Witch: (Halloween Children's Books, Early Elementary Story Books, Scary Stories for Kids) Wheeler, Eliza, illus. 2017. (ENG.). 40p. (J). (gr. k-3). 16.99 *(978-1-4521-4589-1(X))* Chronicle Bks. LLC.

ɔoyle, Marissa. Betraying Season. 2010. (ENG.). 336p. (YA). (gr. 9-13). pap. 19.99 *(978-0-312-62916-8(8)*, 900066880) Square Fish.

—Courtship & Curses. 2013. (ENG.). 368p. (YA). (gr. 9-13). pap. 19.99 *(978-1-250-02744-3(6)*, 900098317) Square Fish.

Dyer, Jill. The Plant of the Zorks. 2005. 11p. 6.65 *(978-1-4116-6641-2(0))* Lulu Pr., Inc.

EDCON Publishing Group Staff. Jack & the Beanstalk - The Stubborn Witch - Rapunzel - Betsy - The Magic Bus. l.t. ed. 2008. (Classic Children's Tales Ser.). 32p. (gr. k-4). pap. 8.95 *(978-1-55576-551-4(3))* EDCON Publishing Group.

Edwards, Marnie. Magical Mix-Ups: Pets & Parties. Hodgkinson, Leigh, illus. 2013. (Magical Mix-Ups Ser.: 3). (ENG.). 96p. (J). (gr. 2-5). pap. 6.99 *(978-0-7636-6371-1(9))* Candlewick Pr.

Egan, Kate, adapted by. World's Apart. 2005. (W. I. T. C. H. Ser.: Bk. 14). 134p. (J). lib. bdg. 16.92 *(978-1-4242-0788-6(6))* Fitzgerald Bks.

Ele, Delores. Horse Bones: The Adventures of Daisy & Maisy. 2012. 56p. pap. 15.99 *(978-1-4771-4113-7(8))* Xlibris Corp.

Elgert, C. J. The Elder Brothers & the Dragon's Portal. 2011. 236p. (gr. 4-6). 25.95 *(978-1-4620-1467-5(4))*; pap. 15.95 *(978-1-4620-1466-8(6))* iUniverse, Inc.

Elkerton, Andy. Viking Adventures: Bitra & the Witch. 2022. (Viking Adventures Ser.). (ENG., Illus.). 32p. (J). (gr. 1-3). pap. 9.99 *(978-1-4451-5841-9(8)*, Franklin Watts) Hachette Children's Group GBR. Dist: Hachette Bk. Group.

Elliot, Rachel. The Friendly Witch. Broadley, Leo, illus. 2015. (ENG.). 28p. (J). (gr. -1-3). 7.99 *(978-1-85733-725-9(5))* Lerner Publishing Group.

Elliott, Zetta. The Dragon Thief. Geneva B, Geneva, illus. 2019. (Dragons in a Bag Ser.: 2). 176p. (J). (gr. 3-7). 16.99 *(978-1-5247-7049-5(3)*, Random Hse. Bks. for Young Readers) Random Hse. Children's Bks.

Epstein, Alex. The Circle Cast: The Lost Years of Morgan le Fey, 1 vol. 2011. (ENG., Illus.). 240p. (YA). (gr. 8-12). pap. 12.95 *(978-1-896580-63-0(7))* Tradewind Bks. CAN. Dist: Orca Bk. Pubs. USA.

Ernshaw, Shea. The Wicked Deep. (ENG.). (YA). (gr. 9). 2019. 336p. pap. 12.99 *(978-1-4814-9735-0(9))* 2018. (Illus.). 320p. 19.99 *(978-1-4814-9734-3(0))* Simon Pulse. (Simon Pulse).

Evans, Catrin & Evans, Guto. Peiriant y Tywydd. 2005. (WEL., Illus.). 36p. *(978-0-86243-412-0(2))* Y Lolfa.

Evans, Robert J. Dorothy's Mystical Adventures in Oz. 2004. reprint ed. pap. 1.99 *(978-1-4192-1658-9(9))* Kessinger Publishing, LLC.

Falter, Laury. Residue. 2013. (Residue Ser.: bk.1). 306p. pap. 12.99 *(978-0-9855110-0-5(1))* William & William Publishing.

Fiedler, Lisa. A Dark Descent. Giacobino, Sebastian, illus. 2018. (Ages of Oz Ser.). (ENG.). 368p. (J). (gr. 3-7). 17.99 *(978-1-4814-6974-6(6)*, McElderry, Margaret K. Bks.) McElderry, Margaret K. Bks.

Fisher, Rusty. Littlest Witch's Story, 1 vol. 2014. (Story Time for Little Monsters Ser.). (ENG., Illus.). 24p. (J). (gr. -1-4). lib. bdg. 31.36 *(978-1-62402-022-3(4)*, 630, Looking Glass Library) Magic Wagon.

Flinn, Alex. Bewitching. (Kendra Chronicles Ser.: 2). (ENG.). (YA). (gr. 8). 2013. 368p. pap. 9.99 *(978-0-06-202416-9(7))* 2012. 352p. 17.99 *(978-0-06-202414-5(0))* HarperCollins Pubs. (HarperTeen).

—A Kiss in Time. 2010. (ENG.). 400p. (YA). (gr. 8-18). pap. 9.99 *(978-0-06-087421-6(X)*, HarperTeen) HarperCollins Pubs.

—Mirrored. 2015. (Kendra Chronicles Ser.: 3). (ENG.). 384p. (YA). (gr. 8). 17.99 *(978-0-06-213451-6(5)*, HarperTeen) HarperCollins Pubs.

Flood, Heather. Mousey Mousey & the Witches' Revenge. 2012. 220p. pap. *(978-1-909359-03-1(3))* My Voice Publishing.

Forsyth, Kate. Battle of the Heroes. 2016. (Illus.). 188p. (J). pap. 5.99 *(978-1-61067-418-8(9))* Kane Miller.

—The Drowned Kingdom. 2016. (Illus.). 185p. (J). pap. 5.99 *(978-1-61067-417-1(0))* Kane Miller.

Foxlee, Karen. A Most Magical Girl. 2017. (ENG.). 304p. (J). (gr. 3-7). 8.99 *(978-0-553-51288-5(9)*, Yearling) Random Hse. Children's Bks.

Freeman, David. The Whispery Witch. Beers, Robert Lee, illus. 2012. 24p. pap. 24.95 *(978-1-4137-9620-9(6))* PublishAmerica, Inc.

Freese, Thomas. Halloween Sleepwalker, 1 vol. 2013. (ENG., Illus.). 64p. (J). (gr. -1-3). 16.99 *(978-0-7643-4399-5(8)*, 4866) Schiffer Publishing, Ltd.

French, Vivian. The Bag of Bones: The Second Tale from the Five Kingdoms. Collins, Ross, illus. 2009. (Tales from the Five Kingdoms Ser.: 2). (ENG.). 256p. (J). (gr. 3-7). 14.99 *(978-0-7636-4255-6(X))* Candlewick Pr.

Friel, Maeve. Brewing up (Witch-In-Training, Book 4), Book 4. Reed, Nathan, illus. 2011. (Witch-In-Training Ser.: 4). (ENG.). 96p. pap. 5.99 *(978-0-00-713344-4(8)*, HarperCollins Children's Bks.) HarperCollins Pubs. Ltd. GBR. Dist: HarperCollins Pubs.

—Broomstick Battles (Witch-In-Training, Book 5), Book 5. Reed, Nathan, illus. 2011. (Witch-In-Training Ser.: 5). (ENG.). 96p. pap. 5.99 *(978-0-00-718524-5(3)*, HarperCollins Children's Bks.) HarperCollins Pubs. Ltd. GBR. Dist: HarperCollins Pubs.

—The Broomstick Collection: Books 1-4 (Witch-In-Training), Bks 1-4. Reed, Nathan, illus. 2006. (Witch-In-Training Ser.). (ENG.). 368p. (gr. 2-4). 11.99 *(978-0-00-724072-2(4)*, HarperCollins Children's Bks.) HarperCollins Pubs. Ltd. GBR. Dist: HarperCollins Pubs.

—Charming or What? (Witch-In-Training, Book 3), Book 3. Reed, Nathan, illus. 2011. (Witch-In-Training Ser.: 3). (ENG.). 96p. pap. 5.99 *(978-0-00-713343-7(X)*, HarperCollins Children's Bks.) HarperCollins Pubs. Ltd. GBR. Dist: HarperCollins Pubs.

—Flying Lessons (Witch-In-Training, Book 1), Book 1. Reed, Nathan, illus. 2011. (Witch-In-Training Ser.: 1). (ENG.). 96p. pap. 5.99 *(978-0-00-713341-3(3)*, HarperCollins Children's Bks.) HarperCollins Pubs. Ltd. GBR. Dist: HarperCollins Pubs.

—The Last Task (Witch-In-Training, Book 8), Book 8. Reed, Nathan, illus. 2011. (Witch-In-Training Ser.: 8). (ENG.). 96p. (gr. 4-7). pap. 5.99 *(978-0-00-718527-6(8)*, HarperCollins Children's Bks.) HarperCollins Pubs. Ltd. GBR. Dist: HarperCollins Pubs.

—Moonlight Mischief (Witch-In-Training, Book 7), Book 7. Reed, Nathan, illus. 2011. (Witch-In-Training Ser.: 7). (ENG.). 96p. per. 5.99 *(978-0-00-718526-9(X)*, HarperCollins Children's Bks.) HarperCollins Pubs. Ltd. GBR. Dist: HarperCollins Pubs.

—Spelling Trouble (Witch-In-Training, Book 2) Vol. 2, Book 2. Reed, Nathan, illus. 2011. (Witch-In-Training Ser.: 2). (ENG.). 96p. pap. 5.99 *(978-0-00-713342-0(1)*, HarperCollins Children's Bks.) HarperCollins Pubs. Ltd. GBR. Dist: HarperCollins Pubs.

—Witch Switch (Witch-In-Training, Book 6), Book 6. Reed, Nathan, illus. 2011. (Witch-In-Training Ser.: 6). (ENG.). 96p. pap. 5.99 *(978-0-00-718525-2(1)*, HarperCollins Children's Bks.) HarperCollins Pubs. Ltd. GBR. Dist: HarperCollins Pubs.

Gaichies, Sarah. Angela & the Prince. 2011. (FRE & ENG., Illus.). 96p. pap. 32.26 *(978-1-4567-8999-2(6))* AuthorHouse.

Gardner, Sally. Operation Bunny: Book One. Roberts, David, illus. 2014. (Wings & Co Ser.: 1). (ENG.). 208p. (J). (gr. 2-5). pap. 8.99 *(978-1-250-05053-3(7)*, 900134108) Square Fish.

Garza, Xavier & Villarroel, Carolina. Zulema & the Witch Owl/Zulema y la Bruja Lechuza. Garza, Xavier, illus. 2009. (SPA & ENG., Illus.). 32p. (J). (gr. -1-4). 16.95 *(978-1-55885-515-1(7)*, Piñata Books) Arte Publico Pr.

George, Ben W. Wanda the Witch's Broom: How an Old School Witch Learns New Tricks. 2011. 24p. pap. 12.99 *(978-1-4634-4380-1(3))* AuthorHouse.

George, Jessica Day. Princess of Glass. 2011. (Twelve Dancing Princesses Ser.). (ENG.). 272p. (YA). (gr. 7). pap. 10.99 *(978-1-59990-659-1(7)*, 900074740, Bloomsbury USA Childrens) Bloomsbury Publishing USA.

Geragotelis, Brittany. Life's a Witch. 2013. (Life's a Witch Ser.). (ENG., Illus.). 320p. (YA). (gr. 9). 16.99 *(978-1-4424-6655-5(3)*, Simon & Schuster Bks. For Young Readers) Simon & Schuster Bks. For Young Readers.

—What the Spell. (Life's a Witch Ser.). (ENG., Illus.). (YA). (gr. 9). 2014. 352p. pap. 9.99 *(978-1-4424-6707-1(X))* 2013. 336p. 16.99 *(978-1-4424-6815-3(7))* Simon & Schuster Bks. For Young Readers. (Simon & Schuster Bks. For Young Readers).

—The Witch Is Back. 2014. (Life's a Witch Ser.). (ENG., Illus.). 352p. (YA). (gr. 9). 17.99 *(978-1-4424-6688-3(X)*, Simon & Schuster Bks. For Young Readers) Simon & Schuster Bks. For Young Readers.

—The Witch Is Back. 2015. (Life's a Witch Ser.). (ENG., Illus.). 352p. (YA). (gr. 9). pap. 11.99 *(978-1-4424-6691-3(X))* Simon & Schuster Children's Publishing.

Gerber, Carole. 10 Busy Brooms. Fleming, Michael, illus. (J). 2018. 26p. (— 1). 7.99 *(978-1-5247-6899-7(5))* 2016. 32p. (gr. -1-2). 12.99 *(978-0-553-53341-5(X))* Random Hse. Children's Bks. (Doubleday Bks. for Young Readers).

Gibbs, Gretchen. The Book of Maggie Bradstreet. 2012. (Bradstreet Chronicles). (ENG.). 183p. (YA). pap. 9.99 *(978-0-9852948-0-9(9))* Glenmere Pr.

Gilbert, Julie. Into the Storm: A Mermaid's Journey. Fagan, Kirbi, illus. 2017. (Dark Waters Ser.). (ENG.). 160p. (J). (gr. 5-9). lib. bdg. 26.65 *(978-1-4965-4171-0(5)*, 133769, Stone Arch Bks.) Capstone.

Gill, David Macinnis. Uncanny. 2017. (ENG., Illus.). 544p. (YA). (gr. 9). 17.99 *(978-0-06-229016-8(9)*, Greenwillow Bks.) HarperCollins Pubs.

Gilson. Melusine Vol. 3: The Vampires' Ball. 2008. (Melusine Ser.: 3). (Illus.). 48p. (J). (gr. 4-7). pap. 11.95 *(978-1-905460-69-4(4))* CineBook GBR. Dist: National Bk. Network.

—Melusine - Hocus Pocus. Clarke & Clarke, illus. 2007. (Melusine Ser.: 1). 48p. (J). (gr. -1-12). per. 9.99 *(978-1-905460-20-5(1))* CineBook GBR. Dist: National Bk. Network.

Glasser, Frederick. Monsters Come Out Tonight! Miller, Edward, illus. 2019. (Festive Flaps Ser.). (ENG.). 18p. (J). (gr. -1-k). bds. 9.99 *(978-1-4197-3722-0(8)*, 1277110, Abrams Appleseed) Abrams, Inc.

Gliori, Debi. Witch Baby & Me. 2010. (Illus.). 256p. (J). (gr. 2-4). pap. 12.99 *(978-0-552-55676-7(9))* Transworld Publishers Ltd. GBR. Dist: Independent Pubs. Group.

—Witch Baby & Me on Stage. 2011. (Illus.). 336p. (J). (gr. 2-4). pap. 7.99 *(978-0-552-55679-8(3))* Transworld Publishers Ltd. GBR. Dist: Independent Pubs. Group.

Gogonya, Carol. The African Mermaid & Other Stories. 2011. 40p. pap. 32.70 *(978-1-4568-5416-4(X))* Xlibris Corp.

Goodman, John. Percy's Magical Adventures. 2005. (Illus.). 170p. pap. *(978-1-84401-556-6(4))* Athena Pr.

Gore, Jim. Witch Snatchit & Mr Grabbit. 2005. (Illus.). 80p. pap. *(978-1-84401-486-6(X))* Athena Pr.

Gormley, Greg. Fairy Tale Frankie & the Tricky Witch. Lenton, Steven, illus. 2016. (ENG.). 32p. (J). (gr. -1-1). 17.99 *(978-1-4814-6625-7(9)*, Aladdin) Simon & Schuster Children's Publishing.

Granata, Nancy. The Perfect Porch for Witch Watching. 2008. 52p. pap. 22.49 *(978-1-4389-0107-7(0))* AuthorHouse.

Grandoit, Jean. In the Quest for Inshalla: Simbies of the Caribbean at the World Under. 2010. 68p. pap. 25.49 *(978-1-4520-3900-8(3))* AuthorHouse.

Grant, Holly. The Witch's Glass. Portillo, Josie, illus. 2017. (League of Beastly Dreadfuls Ser.: Bk. 3). 305p. (J). pap. *(978-1-101-93369-5(0))* Random Hse., Inc.

Gratton, Tessa. Strange Grace. 2018. (ENG., Illus.). 400p. (YA). (gr. 7). 18.99 *(978-1-5344-0208-9(X)*, McElderry, Margaret K. Bks.) McElderry, Margaret K. Bks.

Gray, Claudia. Steadfast. 2015. (Spellcaster Ser.: 2). (ENG.). 368p. (YA). (gr. 8). pap. 9.99 *(978-0-06-196123-6(X)*, HarperTeen) HarperCollins Pubs.

Gray, Rev. Maxine A. Children's Lessons on Morality: Don't Use Your Friends. 2013. 24p. pap. 14.99 *(978-1-4669-8831-6(2))* Trafford Publishing.

Greban, Tanguy. Sarah So Small. Greban, Quentin, illus. 2004. (ENG.). 32p. (J). (gr. 4-7). 16.95 *(978-1-59687-179-3(2))* IBks., Inc.

—Sarah So Small. Greban, Quentin, illus. 2004. 32p. (J). 16.95 *(978-0-689-03594-4(2)*, Milk & Cookies) ibooks, Inc.

Green, Sally. Half Bad. 2015. (Half Bad Trilogy Ser.: 1). (ENG.). 464p. (YA). (gr. 7). pap. 11.99 *(978-0-14-751146-1(1)*, Speak) Penguin Young Readers Group.

Greenberg, Nicki. The Cursed First Term of Zelda Stitch. Bad Teacher. Worse Witch. 2017. (ENG., Illus.). 272p. (J). (gr. 2-6). pap. 13.99 *(978-1-76029-490-8(X))* Allen & Unwin AUS. Dist: Independent Pubs. Group.

—Zelda Stitch Term Two: Too Much Witch. 2019. (ENG.). 288p. (J). (gr. 2-6). pap. 12.99 *(978-1-76052-367-1(4)*, A&U Children's) Allen & Unwin AUS. Dist: Independent Pubs. Group.

Gregory, Caroline. Puppy Stew. Suorsa, Michael, illus. 2009. (ENG.). 28p. (J). pap. 8.99 *(978-0-9772025-9-1(3))* Sortis Publishing.

Griffin, Sarah Maria. Other Words for Smoke. 2019. (ENG.). 352p. (YA). (gr. 9). 17.99 *(978-0-06-240891-4(7)*, Greenwillow Bks.) HarperCollins Pubs.

Gripari, Pierre. Le Gentil Petit Diable: Et Autres Contes de la Rue Broca. Rosado, Puig, illus. 2007. (Folio Junior Ser.). 142p. (J). per. *(978-2-07-061255-0(4))* National Round Table on the Environment & the Economy (NRTEE)/Table ronde nationale sur l'environnement et l'economie (TRNEE).

Gritton, Steve. The Kandy Witch. 2007. (Illus.). (J). 18.95 *(978-0-9795361-0-6(3))* Bad Frog Art/SMG Bks.

Guerin, F. A. The Witch at NO46: Verbrola. 2011. (Illus.). 140p. pap. 14.69 *(978-1-4567-7118-8(3))* AuthorHouse.

Guerrera, Jeannette D. The Christmas Witch. 2012. 24p. pap. 17.99 *(978-1-4685-6226-2(6))* AuthorHouse.

Gummelt, Donna & Melchiorre, Dondino. Michelina the Magical Musical Good Witch of the Forest. Wall, Randy Hugh, ed. Varela, Juan D., tr. Varela, Juan D., illus. 2006. (SPA.). 34p. (J). 14.95 *(978-0-9764798-6-4(9))* Story Store Collection Publishing.

Gutenberg, S. R. Abby Longbotham & the Quilt. 2008. 28p. pap. 24.95 *(978-1-4241-9428-5(8))* America Star Bks.

Hahn, Mary Downing. Took: A Ghost Story. 2016. (ENG.). 272p. (J). (gr. 5-7). pap. 9.99 *(978-0-544-81310-6(3)*, 1641903, Clarion Bks.) HarperCollins Pubs.

—Witch Catcher. 2011. (ENG.). 240p. (J). (gr. 5-7). pap. 7.99 *(978-0-547-57714-2(1)*, 1458462, Clarion Bks.) HarperCollins Pubs.

Hardie, Samantha. Samantha's Oracle: A Fortune Teller for Teenage Witches. (Illus.). 80p. 12.95 *(978-1-55285-282-8(2))* Whitecap Bks., Ltd. CAN. Dist: Graphic Arts Ctr. Publishing Co.

Hardinge, Frances. Verdigris Deep. 2018. (ENG.). 304p. (gr. 8-17). pap. 10.99 *(978-1-4197-2878-5(4)*, 1172203, Amulet Bks.) Abrams, Inc.

Hargreaves, Roger. Little Miss Sunshine & the Wicked Witch. 2007. (Mr. Men & Little Miss Ser.). (ENG., Illus.). 32p. (J). (gr. -1-2). mass mkt. 4.99 *(978-0-8431-2490-3(3)*, Price Stern Sloan) Penguin Young Readers Group.

Harper, Benjamin. Bird Boy: A Grimm & Gross Retelling. Banks, Timothy, illus. 2018. (Michael Dahl Presents: Grimm & Gross Ser.). (ENG.). 64p. (J). (gr. 3-5). lib. bdg. 21.99 *(978-1-4965-7317-9(X)*, 138921, Stone Arch Bks.) Capstone.

—Hansel & Gretel & Zombies: A Graphic Novel. Cano, Fernando, illus. 2016. (Far Out Fairy Tales Ser.). (ENG.). 40p. (J). (gr. 3-6). lib. bdg. 25.32 *(978-1-4965-2509-3(4)*, 130481, Stone Arch Bks.) Capstone.

Harris, Christine. Four Tails: An Anthology of Four Tales for Children. 2011. (Illus.). 92p. (gr. -1). pap. 12.10 *(978-1-4520-7643-0(X))* AuthorHouse.

Hartley, James. Berlina's Quest. Legge, Barbara, ed. Kelsey, Amanda, illus. 2013. 146p. (J). pap. 17.99 *(978-1-61572-948-7(8))* Damnation Bks.

Hautzig, Deborah. Little Witch Learns to Read. Wickstrom, Sylvie, illus. 2003. (Step into Reading Ser.). 48p. (J). (gr. k-3). pap. 5.99 *(978-0-375-82179-0(1)*, Random Hse. Bks. for Young Readers) Random Hse. Children's Bks.

Havard, Amanda. The Survivors. 2011. (ENG.). (YA). 294p. 21.99 *(978-0-9833190-0-9(6))*; 300p. pap. 11.99 *(978-0-9833190-2-3(2))* Chafie Pr., LLC.

Hawkins, Rachel. Demonglass, 2. 2012. (Hex Hall Novel Ser.: 2). (ENG.). 384p. (J). (gr. 5-9). pap. 8.99 *(978-1-4231-2844-1(3))* Hyperion Bks. for Children.

Hayden, Jeanne. Last Minute Wilma & Her Toad Soup. 2009. 24p. pap. 14.95 *(978-1-4327-3857-0(7))* Outskirts Pr., Inc.

Haynes, Lori. The Wallenda Witches Flying School. 2005. (Illus.). 24p. (J). pap. 13.13 *(978-0-9746959-4-5(7)*, 2000) Falcon Publishing LTD.

Hayter, Rhonda. The Witchy Worries of Abbie Adams. 2011. (ENG.). 224p. (gr. 4-6). 21.19 *(978-0-8037-3468-5(9))* Penguin Young Readers Group.

Healy, Christopher. The Hero's Guide to Saving Your Kingdom. Harris, Todd, illus. 2013. (Hero's Guide Ser.: 1). (ENG.). 480p. (J). (gr. 3-7). pap. 7.99 *(978-0-06-211745-8(9)*, Waldon Pond Pr.) HarperCollins Pubs.

Heible, Beverly. A Christmas Party on River Row. 2012. 98p. 22.95 *(978-1-62709-018-6(5))* America Star Bks.

Heidi Heckelbeck Gets the Sniffles. 2014. (Heidi Heckelbeck Ser.: 12). (ENG., Illus.). 128p. (J). (gr. k-4). pap. 6.99 *(978-1-4814-1362-6(7)*, Little Simon) Little Simon.

Henderson, Jason. Alex Van Helsing: The Triumph of Death. 2012. (Alex Van Helsing Ser.: 3). (ENG.). 320p. (YA). (gr. 8). 17.99 *(978-0-06-195103-9(X)*, HarperTeen) HarperCollins Pubs.

Henning, Sarah. Sea Witch. (ENG.). 2019. 384p. (YA). (gr. 8). pap. 10.99 *(978-0-06-243880-5(8))* 2018. 368p. (YA). (gr. 8). 17.99 *(978-0-06-243877-5(8))* 2018. 368p. (J). *(978-0-00-830084-5(4))* HarperCollins Pubs. (Tegen, Katherine Bks).

—Sea Witch Rising. 2019. (ENG.). 416p. (YA). (gr. 8). 17.99 *(978-0-06-293147-4(4)*, Tegen, Katherine Bks) HarperCollins Pubs.

Henry, James. The Cabinet of Curiosities. 2010. 240p. pap. 21.50 *(978-0-9559851-0-2(2))* Blue Cat GBR. Dist: Lulu Pr., Inc.

Heppermann, Christine & Koertge, Ron. Maya's Story. Marcero, Deborah, illus. 2018. (Backyard Witch Ser.: 3). (ENG.). 192p. (J). (gr. 3-7). pap. 5.99 *(978-0-06-233845-7(5)*, Greenwillow Bks.) HarperCollins Pubs.

Hillert, Margaret. Witch Who Went for a Walk. 2016. (BeginningtoRead Ser.). (ENG., Illus.). 32p. (J). (gr. 1-2). 22.60 *(978-1-59953-810-5(5))* Norwood Hse. Pr.

—The Witch Who Went for a Walk. Mernie Gallagher-Cole, illus. 2016. (Beginning-To-Read Ser.). (ENG.). 32p. (J). (gr. k-2). pap. 13.26 *(978-1-60357-951-3(6))* Norwood Hse. Pr.

Hoena, Blake. The Horrible Hex. Bardin, Dave, illus. 2018. (Monster Heroes Ser.). (ENG.). 32p. (J). (gr. k-2). lib. bdg. 21.32 *(978-1-4965-6413-9(8)*, 138260, Stone Arch Bks.) Capstone.

—Witch's Brew. Bardin, Dave, illus. 2016. (Monster Heroes Ser.). (ENG.). 32p. (J). (gr. k-2). lib. bdg. 21.32 *(978-1-4965-3756-0(4)*, 133082, Stone Arch Bks.) Capstone.

Hoepfner, John P. The Tale of Magic Pixie Dust. 2011. 34p. pap. 16.95 *(978-1-4560-6811-0(3))* PublishAmerica, Inc.

Holder, Nancy & Viguie, Debbie. Wicked: Witch & Curse. 2009. *(978-1-4351-2000-6(0))* Barnes & Noble, Inc.

Holder, Nancy, et al. Resurrection. 2009. (Wicked Ser.). (ENG.). 416p. (YA). (gr. 9-18). pap. 9.99 *(978-1-4169-7227-3(7)*, Simon Pulse) Simon Pulse.

—Wicked: Witch & Curse. 2008. (Wicked Ser.). (ENG.). 672p. (YA). (gr. 9). pap. 14.99 *(978-1-4169-7119-1(X)*, Simon Pulse) Simon Pulse.

—Wicked 2: Legacy & Spellbound. 2008. (Wicked Ser.). (ENG.). 672p. (YA). (gr. 9). pap. 13.99 *(978-1-4169-7117-7(3)*, Simon Pulse) Simon Pulse.

Horwitz, Sarah Jean. The Dark Lord Clementine. 2019. (ENG.). 336p. (J). (gr. 4-8). 17.95 *(978-1-61620-894-3(5)*, 73894) Algonquin Young Readers.

Howard, Arthur. Hoodwinked. Howard, Arthur, illus. 2005. (ENG., Illus.). 32p. (J). (gr. -1-3). pap. 7.00 *(978-0-15-205386-4(7)*, 1196217, Clarion Bks.) HarperCollins Pubs.

Howell, Robert. Third Times the Charm. 2007. (ENG.). 224p. (gr. 4-7). per. 12.95 *(978-1-897235-20-1(8))* Thistledown Pr., Ltd. CAN. Dist: Univ. of Toronto Pr.

Human, Deborah. Pinky Promise. 2009. 40p. (J). pap. 11.99 *(978-0-9818374-0-6(9))* Writing Bench LLC., The.

Hume, Maureen. The Pizza Gang: Facing the Witch. 2009. 80p. pap. 9.95 *(978-1-60860-337-4(7)*, Eloquent Bks.) Strategic Book Publishing & Rights Agency (SBPRA).

Hurd, Pamela. Switch Witch: An Old Fashioned Witch Learns a New Trick. 2011. 20p. pap. 11.99 *(978-1-4634-4587-4(3))* AuthorHouse.

Hurley, Crystal. The Witch with an Itch. 2008. 24p. pap. 24.95 *(978-1-60703-339-4(9))* America Star Bks.

Hutchings, Paul. Halloween Tails. 2012. 24p. pap. 24.95 *(978-1-4626-7106-9(3))* America Star Bks.

Ibbotson, Eva. Not Just a Witch. Hawkes, Kevin, illus. 2004. (ENG.). 192p. (J). (gr. 3-7). pap. 5.99 *(978-0-14-240232-0(X)*, Puffin Books) Penguin Young Readers Group.

Isbell, Shaun. The Mouse & the Witch, 1 vol. 2009. 56p. pap. 16.95 *(978-1-61546-892-8(7))* PublishAmerica, Inc.

Ivy, Maggie, illus. Beware the Bell Witch. 2018. (Haunted States of America Ser.). (ENG.). 136p. (J). (gr. 3-4). pap. 7.99 *(978-1-63163-204-4(3)*, 1631632043, Jolly Fish Pr.) North Star Editions.

Jablonski, Carla. Shadow of the Sphinx. 2007. (Charmed Ser.). (ENG.). 192p. (YA). pap. 14.95 *(978-1-4169-6756-9(7)*, Gallery Bks.) Gallery Bks.

Jantha, A. W. Hocus Pocus & the AllNew Sequel. 2018. (ENG., Illus.). 528p. (YA). (gr. 9-12). 12.99 *(978-1-368-02003-9(8)*, Disney-Hyperion) Disney Publishing Worldwide.

Jaycox, Jaclyn. Witch's Stew. Gatti, Giada, illus. 2019. (Boo Bks.). (ENG.). 32p. (J). (gr. k-2). lib. bdg. 21.32 *(978-1-5158-4482-2(X)*, 140578, Picture Window Bks.) Capstone.

Jessup, VonDa. Wanda the Witch at the Happy Haunted House. 2008. (Illus.). 44p. pap. 18.50 *(978-1-60693-149-3(0)*, Eloquent Bks.) Strategic Book Publishing & Rights Agency (SBPRA).

Jones, Chris. Cameron Jack & the Key to the Universe. 2010. (Illus.). 136p. pap. 10.99 *(978-1-4490-6547-8(3))* AuthorHouse.

Jones, Diana Wynne. Earwig & the Witch. Zelinsky, Paul O., illus. 2012. (ENG.). 128p. (J). (gr. 3-7). 15.99 *(978-0-06-207511-6(X)*, Greenwillow Bks.) HarperCollins Pubs.

Jones, J. J. Flute Tudor & the Secret Order. 2012. 304p. 22.95 *(978-1-4575-1302-2(1))* Dog Ear Publishing, LLC.

Jordan, Annie Laurie. Bogwaddle Pond. La Grange, Myrtle, illus. 2004. 25p. pap. 24.95 *(978-1-4137-2013-6(7))* PublishAmerica, Inc.

Jordan, Jennifer. Silly Tilly Witch: And Other Stories. Guile, Gill, illus. 2004. (Early Learning Ser.). 18p. (J). bds. 2.99 *(978-1-85854-825-8(X))* Brimax Books Ltd. GBR. Dist: Byeway Bks.

Joyce, Rita. Wandawillie. 2005. (J). lib. bdg. 17.95 *(978-1-59094-095-2(4))* Jawbone Publishing Corp.

Kaaberbøl, Lene. Heartbreak Island. 2005. (W. I. T. C. H. Adventures Ser.: Bk. 3). (Illus.). 105p. (J). lib. bdg. 11.00 *(978-1-4242-0786-2(X))* Fitzgerald Bks.

Kaaberbol, Lene. Wildwitch 4 - Bloodling. 2017. (Wildwitch Ser.: 4). (ENG., Illus.). 200p. (J). (gr. 3-7). pap. 9.99

(978-1-78269-086-3(7), Pushkin Children's Bks.) Steerforth Pr.

Kadono, Eiko. Kiki's Delivery Service: The Classic That Inspired the Beloved Animated Film. Balistrieri, Emily, tr. from JPN. Onoda, Yuta, illus. 2020. (ENG.). 208p. (J). (gr. 5). 16.99 (978-1-9848-9666-7(0)); lib. bdg. 19.99 (978-1-9848-9668-1(7)) Random Hse. Children's Bks. (Delacorte Bks. for Young Readers).

Kakinouchi, Narumi. My Codename is Charmer, Vol. 3. 208p. pap. 12.95 (978-1-932575-08-8(1)) International Comics & Entertainment L.L.C.

Kane, Gillian. The Witch Who Liked to Wear Pink. Povey, Andrea, illus. 2013. 24p. pap. 11.50 (978-1-62516-315-8(0), Strategic Bk. Publishing) Strategic Book Publishing & Rights Agency (SBPRA).

Karsten, Dylan. The Witch & the Wand: Practicing the W Sound, 1 vol. 2016. (Rosen Phonics Readers Ser.). (ENG., Illus.). 12p. (J). (gr. -1-2). pap. (978-1-5081-3046-8(9), 7d6a8226-9103-4af2-93ef-bbf8c10a8225, Rosen Classroom) Rosen Publishing Group, Inc., The.

Kats, Jewel. Hansel & Gretel: A Fairy Tale with a Down Syndrome Twist. Lenart, Claudia, illus. 2014. 37p. (J). (978-1-61599-251-5(0)) Loving Healing Pr., Inc.

Kayser, Megan. Finishing What I Didn't Start. 2006. 108p. pap. 19.95 (978-1-4241-1271-5(0)) PublishAmerica, Inc.

Kidwell, Justina. The Enchanted Garden & the Curse of the Evil Witch: The Kent Boys' Adventures. 2009. 68p. pap. 19.95 (978-1-60749-163-7(X)) America Star Bks.

Kiernan, Celine. Begone the Raggedy Witches (the Wild Magic Trilogy, Book One) (Wild Magic Trilogy Ser.: 1). (ENG.). 288p. (J). (gr. 4-7). 2019. pap. 7.99 (978-1-5362-0874-0(4)) 2018. 15.99 (978-0-7636-9996-3(9)) Candlewick Pr.

Kimmel, Elizabeth Cody. ParaNormaN. 2012. (ENG.). (J). (gr. 4-7). 64.99 (978-1-61969-450-7(6)) Findaway World, LLC.

Kimmel, Eric A. Hank & Gertie: A Pioneer Hansel & Gretel Story. Penny, Mara, illus. 2018. (ENG.). 32p. (J). (gr. 1-3). 16.99 (978-1-5132-6122-5(3), West Winds Pr.) West Margin Pr.

Kladstrup, Kristin. Garden Princess. 2015. (ENG.). 272p. (J). (gr. 5). pap. 7.99 (978-0-7636-7668-1(3)) Candlewick Pr.

Kohara, Kazuno. Ghosts in the House! Kohara, Kazuno, illus. 2010. (ENG., Illus.). 32p. (J). (gr. -1-1). pap. 8.99 (978-0-312-60886-6(1), 900065181) Square Fish.

Kok, Gemma. Explore. 2008. 44p. pap. 18.50 (978-1-4092-2058-9(3)) Lulu Pr., Inc.

—Explore (Printed in black & White) 2008. 44p. pap. 8.00 (978-1-4092-2530-0(5)) Lulu Pr., Inc.

Konigsburg, E. L. Jennifer, Hecate, Macbeth, William McKinley, & Me, Elizabeth. 2011. 8.32 (978-0-7848-3469-5(5), Everbind) Marco Bk. Co.

Korba, Joanna. Sleepless Beauty. 2006. (J). pap. (978-1-4108-7171-8(1)) Benchmark Education Co.

Kovalkova-McKenna, Svetlana. Vasilisa & the Queen of Asps. 2009. 63p. pap. 8.02 (978-0-557-05710-8(8)) Lulu Pr., Inc.

Krulik, Nancy. Witch Switch: Super Special. John and Wendy, illus. 2006. (Katie Kazoo, Switcheroo Ser.: No. 4). (ENG.). 160p. (J). (gr. 2-4). pap. 4.99 (978-0-448-44330-0(9), Grosset & Dunlap) Penguin Young Readers Group.

Kulper, Kendall. Drift & Dagger. 2015. (ENG.). 368p. (YA). (gr. 7-17). 18.00 (978-0-316-40453-2(5)) Little, Brown Bks. for Young Readers.

—Salt & Storm. 2014. (ENG.). 416p. (YA). E-Book (978-0-316-40456-3(X)) Little Brown & Co.

Kurtagich, Dawn. Teeth in the Mist. 2019. (ENG., Illus.). 464p. (J). (gr. 9-17). 18.99 (978-0-316-47847-2(4)) Little, Brown Bks. for Young Readers.

Lagron, Camille. Tatian. 2012. 302p. pap. 12.99 (978-0-9856698-0-5(2)) Camas Pr.

Laky, Esther. Just Fairy Tales. 2010. 95p. pap. 11.80 (978-0-557-01926-7(5)) Lulu Pr., Inc.

Lanagan, Margo. The Brides of Rollrock Island. 2013. (ENG.). 320p. (YA). (gr. 9). pap. 9.99 (978-0-375-87336-2(8), Ember) Random Hse. Children's Bks.

Lane, Leonie. The Retford Witch Catchers. 2005. 144p. per. (978-1-84667-002-2(0)) Derwent Pr., The.

Larson, M. A. The Warrior Princess of Pennyroyal Academy. 2018. (Pennyroyal Ser.: 3). lib. bdg. 19.65 (978-0-606-41312-1(X)) Turtleback.

Laughlin, Florence. The Little Leftover Witch. 2013. (ENG.). 96p. (J). (gr. 3-7). 15.99 (978-1-4424-8677-5(5)); pap. 6.99 (978-1-4424-8672-0(4)) Simon & Schuster Bks. For Young Readers. (Simon & Schuster Bks. For Young Readers).

Launchbury, Jane. Witch & Wizard Stories. 2012. (ENG., Illus.). 64p. (J). 9.95 (978-1-84135-103-2(2)) Award Pubns. Ltd. GBR. Dist: Parkwest Pubns., Inc.

Laura Grey Wahl. The Magic Town of Stuart Easterly. 2009. 16p. pap. 15.00 (978-1-4389-4703-7(8)) AuthorHouse.

Lawlor, Ashley. Ashley & the First Day of School. 2012. 24p. pap. 24.95 (978-1-4626-6518-1(7)) America Star Bks.

LeGette, M. L. The Unicorn Girl. 2008. (ENG.). 416p. pap. 10.00 (978-1-4196-8696-2(8)) CreateSpace Independent Publishing Platform.

Legrand, Claire. Foxheart. Zollars, Jaime, illus. 2016. (ENG.). 480p. (J). (gr. 3-7). 16.99 (978-0-06-242773-1(3), Greenwillow Bks.) HarperCollins Pubs.

Lemire, Lillie. A Young Witch's Magical Adventure. 2006. (ENG.). 48p. per. 16.95 (978-1-4241-5413-5(8)) America Star Bks.

Lenagh, Cecilia. La Brujita Fregona. (Raton de Biblioteca Coleccion). (SPA., Illus.). 64p. (J). (gr. 3-5). 7.95 (978-84-88061-83-6(8)) Serres, Ediciones, S. L. ESP. Dist: Lectorum Pubns., Inc.

Lenhard, Elizabeth. Different Path. 2004. (W. I. T. C. H. Ser.: Bk. 13). 158p. (J). lib. bdg. 16.92 (978-1-4242-0791-6(6)) Fitzgerald Bks.

Lewis, C. S. The Lion, the Witch & the Wardrobe. 2008. (Chronicles of Narnia Ser.: 2). (J). 18.40 (978-0-613-94066-5(0)) Turtleback.

Loewen, Nancy. Trust Me, Hansel & Gretel Are Sweet! The Story of Hansel & Gretel As Told by the Witch. Bock, Janna Rose, illus. 2016. (Other Side of the Story Ser.). (ENG.). 24p. (J). (gr. -1-3). lib. bdg. 27.99 (978-1-4795-8623-3(4), 130445, Picture Window Bks.) Capstone.

Lou, Rachel. The Bridge. 2016. (ENG., Illus.). (YA). (gr. 8-12). 24.99 (978-1-63477-964-7(9), Harmony Ink Pr.) Dreamspinner Pr.

Lowe, Natasha. The Courage of Cat Campbell. 2015. (Poppy Pendle Ser.). (ENG., Illus.). 288p. (J). (gr. 3-7). 16.99 (978-1-4814-1870-6(X), Simon & Schuster/Paula Wiseman Bks.) Simon & Schuster/Paula Wiseman Bks.

—The Marvelous Magic of Miss Mabel. (Poppy Pendle Ser.). (ENG.). (J). (gr. 3-7). 2017. 304p. pap. 8.99 (978-1-4814-6534-2(1)) 2016. (Illus.). 288p. 16.99 (978-1-4814-6533-5(3)) Simon & Schuster/Paula Wiseman Bks. (Simon & Schuster/Paula Wiseman Bks.).

—The Power of Poppy Pendle. (Poppy Pendle Ser.). (ENG., 272p. (J). (gr. 3-7). 2013. Illus.). pap. 8.99 (978-1-4424-4926-8(8)) 2012. 16.99 (978-1-4424-4679-3(X)) Simon & Schuster/Paula Wiseman Bks. (Simon & Schuster/Paula Wiseman Bks.).

Luberto, Bradley. Clide & Druce: A Repulsive Tale of Trolls & Tax Money. 2006. (ENG.). 48p. per. 16.95 (978-1-4241-5012-0(4)) PublishAmerica, Inc.

Lück, Stefanie. Carla's Worlds. 2010. 222p. pap. 20.90 (978-3-8391-4857-0(X)) Bks. on Demand.

Lucke, Deb. Knee-Deep in Niceness. 2016. (Lunch Witch Ser.: 2). (ENG.). 180p. (J). (gr. 2-5). 26.95 (978-0-606-39301-0(3)) Turtleback.

Lyle, Patrice. The Case of the Invisible Witch. 2013. 194p. pap. 9.99 (978-1-61603-034-6(8)) Leap Bks.

MacCullough, Carolyn. Once a Witch. 2010. (ENG.). 320p. (YA). (gr. 7). pap. 17.99 (978-0-547-41730-1(6), 1430229, Clarion Bks.) HarperCollins Pubs.

—Once a Witch. 2009. (ENG.). 304p. (YA). (gr. 7-12). 24.94 (978-0-547-22399-5(4)) Houghton Mifflin Harcourt Publishing Co.

MacDonald, George. Stephen Archer & Other Tales. 2008. 212p. 26.95 (978-1-60664-985-5(X)) Aegypan.

Manning, Jane. Cat Nights. Manning, Jane, illus. 2008. (Illus.). 32p. (J). lib. bdg. 17.89 (978-0-06-113889-8(4), Greenwillow Bks.) HarperCollins Pubs.

Manning, Matthew K. The Salem Witch Showdown. Neely, Scott, illus. 2017. (You Choose Stories: Scooby-Doo Ser.). (ENG.). 112p. (J). (gr. 2-6). lib. bdg. 32.65 (978-1-4965-4334-9(3), 134223, Stone Arch Bks.) Capstone.

Marciano, John Bemelmans. The Secret Janara. Blackall, Sophie, illus. 2019. (Witches of Benevento Ser.: 6). 144p. (J). (gr. 3-7). 13.99 (978-0-425-29154-2(5), Viking Books for Young Readers) Penguin Young Readers Group.

Marlow, Layn. The Witch with a Twitch. Dreidemy, Joëlle, illus. (Tiger Tales Ser.). (J). (gr. -1-2). 2006. 28p. pap. 6.95 (978-1-58925-400-8(7)) 2005. 32p. 15.95 (978-1-58925-052-9(4)) Tiger Tales.

Marrone, Amanda. Only the Stars Know Her Name: Salem's Lost Story of Tituba's Daughter. 2019. (ENG.). 304p. (J). (gr. 4-9). 16.99 (978-1-4998-0890-2(9), Yellow Jacket) Bonnier Publishing USA.

Marsh, Katherine. The Door by the Staircase. Murphy, Kelly, illus. 2017. (ENG.). 288p. (J). (gr. 3-7). pap. 7.99 (978-1-4231-3785-6(X)) Hyperion Bks. for Children.

Martin, Gary. The Witch of Endor, 1 vol. Cariello, Sergio, illus. 2008. (Z Graphic Novels / Son of Samson Ser.). (ENG.). 160p. (J). pap. 6.99 (978-0-310-71283-1(1)) Zonderkidz.

Martin, W. Lyon. Aidan's First Full Moon Circle: A Magical Child Story. Martin, W. Lyon, illus. 2008. (Illus.). 32p. (J). (gr. -1-1). lib. bdg. 16.95 (978-0-9796834-4-2(0)) Shades of White.

Martinez, Roland L. The Evil Leaf. 2009. 232p. 24.99 (978-1-4490-0916-8(6)); pap. 14.90 (978-1-4490-0917-5(4)) AuthorHouse.

Masters, H. Pink Feathers,Murky Pools & a Witch: A Lellaland Adventure. Lie, Vivian, illus. 2003. 52p. pap. (978-1-84401-098-1(8)) Athena Pr.

Mayo, Jason. Do Witches Make Fishes? 2010. 36p. pap. 16.99 (978-1-4520-6944-9(1)) AuthorHouse.

Mc Shane, Mary. Karena the Fairy & the Bat Colony. 2011. 344p. (gr. 4-6). pap. 19.95 (978-1-4620-5295-0(9)) iUniverse, Inc.

McClymer, Kelly. Competition's a Witch. 2007. (ENG.). 256p. (YA). (gr. 7-18). pap. 8.99 (978-1-4169-1645-1(8), Simon Pulse) Simon Pulse.

—The Salem Witch Tryouts. 2006. (ENG.). 272p. (YA). (gr. 7-12). pap. 12.99 (978-1-4169-1644-4(X), Simon Pulse) Simon Pulse.

McGhee, Alison. The Sweetest Witch Around. Bliss, Harry, illus. 2014. (ENG.). 32p. (J). (gr. -1-3). 15.99 (978-1-4424-7833-6(0), Simon & Schuster/Paula Wiseman Bks.) Simon & Schuster/Paula Wiseman Bks.

Mcghee, Alison. A Very Brave Witch. Bliss, Harry, illus. 2007. (J). (gr. -1-3). 24.95 incl. audio (978-0-545-04268-0(2)) Scholastic, Inc.

—A Very Brave Witch. 2011. (J). (gr. -1-3). 29.95 (978-0-545-04267-3(4)) Weston Woods Studios, Inc.

McGhee, Alison. A Very Brave Witch. Bliss, Harry, illus. (ENG.). 32p. (J). (gr. -1-3). 2011. 7.99 (978-0-689-86731-6(X)) 2009. 9.99 (978-1-4169-8670-6(7)) 2006. 19.99 (978-0-689-86730-9(1)) Simon & Schuster/Paula Wiseman Bks. (Simon & Schuster/Paula Wiseman Bks.).

McGowan, Keith. The Witch's Guide to Cooking with Children: A Modern-Day Retelling of Hansel & Gretel, 1. Tanaka, Yoko, illus. 2011. (ENG.). 192p. (J). (gr. 4-6). pap. 12.99 (978-0-312-67486-1(4), 900072904) Square Fish.

Mckenzie, Riford. The Witches of Dredmoore Hollow, 0 vols. unabr. ed. 2013. (ENG.). 274p. (J). (gr. 5-7). pap. 9.99 (978-1-4778-1702-5(6), 9781477817025, Two Lions) Amazon Publishing.

McLean, Matthew. A Bewitching Summer, 1 vol. 2009. 100p. pap. 19.95 (978-1-60836-686-6(3)) America Star Bks.

McLemore, Anna-Marie. When the Moon Was Ours: A Novel. 2018. (ENG.). 288p. (YA). pap. 10.99 (978-1-250-16010-2(3), 900185827, Wednesday Bks.) St. Martin's Pr.

McMullan, Kate. Sir Lancelot, Where Are You? #6, 6. Basso, Bill, illus. 2003. (Dragon Slayers' Academy Ser.: 6). (ENG.). 112p. (J). (gr. 2-5). 5.99 (978-0-448-43278-6(1), Grosset & Dunlap) Penguin Young Readers Group.

Meadows, Daisy. Chloe Slipperslide's Secret. 2016. (Magic Animal Friends Ser.: 11). lib. bdg. 14.75 (978-0-606-38801-6(X)) Turtleback.

—Evie Scruffypup's Big Surprise (Magic Animal Friends #10), 1 vol. 2016. (Magic Animal Friends Ser.: 1). (ENG., Illus.). 112p. (J). (gr. 2-5). pap. 4.99 (978-0-545-94077-1(X), Scholastic Paperbacks) Scholastic, Inc.

—Evie Scruffypup's Surprise. 2016. (Magic Animal Friends Ser.: 10). lib. bdg. 14.75 (978-0-606-38800-9(1)) Turtleback.

—Grace Woollyhop's Musical Mystery. 2016. (Magic Animal Friends Ser.: 12). lib. bdg. 14.75 (978-0-606-38802-3(8)) Turtleback.

—Magic Animal Friends: Mia Floppyear's Snowy Adventure: Special 3. 2022. (Magic Animal Friends Ser.). (ENG., Illus.). 176p. (J). (gr. k-2). pap. 8.99 (978-1-4083-3887-2(4), Orchard Bks.) Hachette Children's Group GBR. Dist: Hachette Bk. Group.

Meddaugh, Susan. The Witches' Supermarket with Stickers. Meddaugh, Susan, illus. 2014. (Martha Speaks Ser.). (ENG., Illus.). 32p. (J). (gr. -1-3). pap. 6.99 (978-0-544-32358-2(0), 1582864, Clarion Bks.) HarperCollins Pubs.

Meriano, Anna. Love Sugar Magic: a Dash of Trouble. Ortega, Mirelle, illus. (Love Sugar Magic Ser.: 1). (ENG.). (J). (gr. 3-7). 2019. 336p. pap. 7.99 (978-0-06-249847-2(9)) 2018. 320p. 16.99 (978-0-06-249846-5(0)) HarperCollins Pubs. (Waldon Pond Pr.).

—Love Sugar Magic: a Sprinkle of Spirits. Ortega, Mirelle, illus. (Love Sugar Magic Ser.: 2). (ENG.). (J). (gr. 3-7). 2020. 336p. pap. 9.99 (978-0-06-249852-6(5)) 2019. 320p. 16.99 (978-0-06-249849-6(5)) HarperCollins Pubs. (Waldon Pond Pr.).

Meroto, Tina. The Tooth Gnashing Witch. 2007. (ENG., Illus.). 48p. (J). 18.95 (978-84-96788-82-4(2)) OQO, Editora ESP. Dist: Baker & Taylor Bks.

Miceli, Mary Anne. Boston North Shore's ... Salem's Golden Broomstick. 2013. 44p. pap. 20.00 (978-0-9888654-0-2(8)) Miceli, Mary Anne.

Milburn, Trish. White Witch. 2012. 188p. pap. 12.95 (978-1-61194-083-1(4), Bell Bridge Bks.) BelleBks., Inc.

Miyazaki, Hayao. Kiki's Delivery Service Film Comic, Vol. 3, Vol. 3. 2006. (Kiki's Delivery Service Film Comics Ser.: 3). (ENG., Illus.). 152p. pap. 9.99 (978-1-59116-784-6(1)) Viz Media.

—Kiki's Delivery Service Film Comic, Vol. 4. 2006. (Kiki's Delivery Service Film Comics Ser.: 4). Orig. Title: Majo No Takkyubin. (ENG., Illus.). 152p. pap. 9.99 (978-1-4215-0595-4(9)) Viz Media.

—Kiki's Delivery Service Picture Book. 2006. (Kiki's Delivery Service Picture Book Ser.). (ENG., Illus.). 112p. (J). pap. 19.99 (978-1-4215-0596-1(7)) Viz Media.

Mlynowski, Sarah. Frogs & French Kisses. 2007. (Magic in Manhattan Ser.: 2). (ENG.). 304p. (YA). (gr. 7). pap. 8.99 (978-0-385-73185-0(X), Delacorte Pr.) Random Hse. Children's Bks.

—Parties & Potions. 2010. (Magic in Manhattan Ser.: 4). (ENG., Illus.). 368p. (YA). (gr. 7). pap. 10.99 (978-0-385-73646-6(0), Ember) Random Hse. Children's Bks.

—Spells & Sleeping Bags. 2008. (Magic in Manhattan Ser.: 3). (ENG.). 320p. (YA). (gr. 7-12). pap. 8.99 (978-0-385-73388-5(7), Delacorte Pr.) Random Hse. Children's Bks.

Mogg, Kylan. Trip to the Mall. 2017. (ENG., Illus.). (J). pap. 9.95 (978-1-946977-89-2(6)) Yorkshire Publishing Group.

Moore, Victor L. The Pentacle of Northumbria. 2013. 432p. pap. (978-1-78222-073-2(9)) Paragon Publishing, Rothersthorpe.

Moriarty, Chris. The Inquisitor's Apprentice. Geyer, Mark Edward, illus. 2013. (ENG.). 352p. (J). (gr. 5-7). pap. 7.99 (978-0-547-85084-9(0), 1501042, Clarion Bks.) HarperCollins Pubs.

Morita, Kisetsu. I've Been Killing Slimes for 300 Years & Maxed Out My Level, Vol. 3. 2018. (I've Been Killing Slimes for 300 Years & Maxed Out My Level Ser.: 3). (ENG., Illus.). 208p. (J). (gr. 8-17). pap. 14.00 (978-1-9753-2931-0(7), 9781975329310, Yen Pr.) Yen Pr. LLC.

Morrison, Megan. Grounded: The Tale of Rapunzel. 2015. (Illus.). 374p. (J). (978-0-545-75468-2(2)) Scholastic, Inc.

Moss, Ronald. The Wizard Next Door. 2009. 198p. pap. 14.95 (978-1-60911-077-2(3), Eloquent Bks.) Strategic Book Publishing & Rights Agency (SBPRA).

Mould, Chris. Pip & the Wood Witch Curse: A Spindlewood Tale, Bk. 1. 2012. (Spindlewood Tales Ser.: Book 1). (ENG.). 176p. (J). (gr. 3-7). 12.99 (978-0-8075-6548-3(2), 807565482) Whitman, Albert & Co.

Muncaster, Harriet. Happy Halloween, Witch's Cat! 2015. (ENG., Illus.). 32p. (J). (gr. -1-3). 15.99 (978-0-06-222916-8(8), HarperCollins) HarperCollins Pubs.

—I Am a Witch's Cat. 2014. (ENG., Illus.). 32p. (J). (gr. -1-3). 15.99 (978-0-06-222914-4(1), HarperCollins) HarperCollins Pubs.

Murphy, Jill. A Bad Spell for the Worst Witch. Murphy, Jill, illus. 2014. (Worst Witch Ser.: 2). (ENG., Illus.). 128p. (J). (gr. 3-7). pap. 6.99 (978-0-7636-7252-2(1)) Candlewick Pr.

—The Worst Witch & the Wishing Star. Murphy, Jill, illus. 2015. (Worst Witch Ser.: 7). (ENG., Illus.). 208p. (J). (gr. 3-7). 14.99 (978-0-7636-7000-9(6)) Candlewick Pr.

—The Worst Witch Saves the Day. Murphy, Jill, illus. 2014. (Worst Witch Ser.: 5). (ENG., Illus.). 160p. (J). (gr. 3-7). pap. 6.99 (978-0-7636-7255-3(6)) Candlewick Pr.

—The Worst Witch to the Rescue. Murphy, Jill, illus. (Worst Witch Ser.: 6). (ENG., Illus.). 176p. (J). (gr. 3-7). 2015. pap. 6.99 (978-0-7636-7862-3(7)) 2014. 14.99 (978-0-7636-6999-7(7)) Candlewick Pr.

Murray, Diana. Grimelda & the Spooktacular Pet Show. Ross, Heather, illus. 2017. (ENG.). 40p. (J). (gr. -1-3). 16.99 (978-0-06-226449-7(4), Tegen, Katherine Bks) HarperCollins Pubs.

—Grimelda: the Very Messy Witch. Ross, Heather, illus. 2016. (ENG.). 32p. (J). (gr. -1-3). 16.99 (978-0-06-226448-0(6), Tegen, Katherine Bks) HarperCollins Pubs.

Naifeh, Ted. Courtney Crumrin Vol. 5: The Witch Next Door. 2014. (Courtney Crumrin Ser.: 5). (ENG., Illus.). 144p. (J). 24.99 (978-1-934964-96-5(4), 9781934964965, Lion Forge) Oni Pr., Inc.

Nardone, Frank. Something's Brewing in Salem. 2013. 164p. pap. 9.99 (978-0-9884024-1-6(6)) Dragon Tree Bks.

Neff, Henry H. The Fiend & the Forge: Book Three of the Tapestry. 2011. (Tapestry Ser.: 3). (ENG., Illus.). 560p. (J). (gr. 3-7). 9.99 (978-0-375-83899-6(6), Yearling) Random Hse. Children's Bks.

—The Maelstrom: Book Four of the Tapestry, Bk. 4. Neff, Henry H., illus. 2013. (Tapestry Ser.: 4). (Illus.). 480p. (J). (gr. 3-7). 8.99 (978-0-375-87148-1(9), Yearling) Random Hse. Children's Bks.

—The Second Siege: Book Two of the Tapestry. 2010. (Tapestry Ser.: 2). (ENG., Illus.). 512p. (J). (gr. 3-7). 9.99 (978-0-375-83897-2(X), Yearling) Random Hse. Children's Bks.

Nicol, James. The Apprentice Witch (Unabridged Edition), 7 vols. unabr. ed. 2017. (ENG.). 2p. (J). (gr. 3-7). audio compact disk 34.99 (978-1-338-15972-1(0), Chicken Hse., The) Scholastic, Inc.

Niemann, Christoph. The Pet Dragon: A Story about Adventure, Friendship, & Chinese Characters. Niemann, Christoph, illus. 2008. (ENG., Illus.). 40p. (J). (gr. -1-3). 18.99 (978-0-06-157776-5(6), Greenwillow Bks.) HarperCollins Pubs.

North, Laura. Hansel & Gretel & the Green Witch. Jevons, Chris, illus. 2015. (Tadpoles: Fairytale Twists Ser.). (ENG.). 32p. (J). (gr. 1-2). (978-0-7787-1928-1(6)) Crabtree Publishing Co.

North, Lynne. Gerties Gets It Right. 2008. 204p. pap. (978-1-84923-231-9(8)) YouWriteOn.

Nowicki, Colin J. Lamia High: Moon of Destiny, 1 vol. 2010. 186p. pap. 24.95 (978-1-4512-8561-1(2)) America Star Bks.

Oakes, Cory Putman. Witchtown. 2017. (ENG.). 320p. (YA). (gr. 7). 17.99 (978-0-544-76557-3(5), 1635515, Clarion Bks.) HarperCollins Pubs.

O'Connor, Jane. Lulu & the Witch Baby. Sinclair, Bella, illus. 2014. (I Can Read Level 2 Ser.). (ENG.). 48p. (J). (gr. -1-3). pap. 4.99 (978-0-06-230516-9(6), HarperCollins) HarperCollins Pubs.

—Lulu Goes to Witch School. 2013. (I Can Read Level 2 Ser.). (ENG., Illus.). 48p. (J). (gr. -1-3). 16.99 (978-0-06-223351-6(3), HarperCollins) HarperCollins Pubs.

—Lulu Goes to Witch School: A Halloween Book for Kids. Sinclair, Bella, illus. 2013. (I Can Read Level 2 Ser.). (ENG.). 48p. (J). (gr. -1-3). pap. 4.99 (978-0-06-223350-9(5), HarperCollins) HarperCollins Pubs.

Olin, Marilyn. Mom, Mac & Cheese, Please! Pantic, Dunja, illus. 2013. (ENG.). 28p. (J). (gr. -1-k). 16.95 (978-1-62087-995-5(6), 620995, Sky Pony Pr.) Skyhorse Publishing Co., Inc.

Oliver, Ilanit. Ten Flying Brooms. Poling, Kyle, illus. 2015. (ENG.). 24p. (J). (gr. k-2). 17.44 (978-1-4844-5738-2(2)); (gr. -1-k). 4.99 (978-0-545-81336-5(0), Cartwheel Bks.) Scholastic, Inc.

Ortega, Claribel A. The Golden Frog Games (Witchlings 2) 2023. (Witchlings Ser.). (ENG.). 384p. (J). (gr. 3-7). 17.99 (978-1-338-74579-5(4), Scholastic Pr.) Scholastic, Inc.

—Witchlings. (Witchlings Ser.). (ENG.). 352p. (J). (gr. 3-7). 2023. pap. 8.99 (978-1-338-74553-5(0)) 2022. 17.99 (978-1-338-74552-8(2), Scholastic Pr.) Scholastic, Inc.

Ostertag, Molly Knox. The Witch Boy: a Graphic Novel (the Witch Boy Trilogy #1) 2017. (Witch Boy Ser.). (ENG., Illus.). 224p. (J). (gr. 3-7). 27.99 (978-1-338-08952-3(8)); pap. 12.99 (978-1-338-08951-6(X)) Scholastic, Inc. (Graphix).

Owen, Joanne. Martha Mayhem & the Witch from the Ditch. Ross, Tony, illus. 2017. (Martha Mayhem Ser.). (ENG.). 192p. (J). (gr. 2-4). pap. 9.99 **(978-1-84812-536-0(4))** Piccadilly Pr., Ltd. GBR. Dist: Independent Pubs. Group.

Owen, Margaret. The Merciful Crow. 2019. (Merciful Crow Ser.: 1). (ENG., Illus.). 384p. (YA). 18.99 (978-1-250-19192-2(0), 900192893, Holt, Henry & Co. Bks. For Young Readers) Holt, Henry & Co.

—The Merciful Crow. 2020. (Merciful Crow Ser.: 1). (ENG.). 400p. (YA). pap. 10.99 (978-1-250-25094-0(3), 900192894) Square Fish.

Owen, Sarah. The Enchanted Tales. 2009. 39p. pap. 26.50 (978-1-4452-5948-2(6)) Lulu Pr., Inc.

Paige, Danielle. Dorothy Must Die. (Dorothy Must Die Ser.: 1). (ENG.). (YA). (gr. 9-12). 2014. 464p. 17.99 (978-0-06-228067-1(8)) 9th ed. 2015. 480p. pap. 12.99 (978-0-06-228068-8(6)) HarperCollins Pubs. (HarperCollins).

—Dorothy Must Die. 2015. (Dorothy Must Die Ser.: 1). (YA). lib. bdg. 20.85 (978-0-606-36510-9(9)) Turtleback.

—Dorothy Must Die 2-Book Box Set: Dorothy Must Die, the Wicked Will Rise. 2016. (Dorothy Must Die Ser.). (ENG.). 800p. (YA). (gr. 9). pap. 19.98 (978-0-06-256982-0(1), HarperCollins) HarperCollins Pubs.

—Dorothy Must Die Stories: No Place Like Oz, the Witch Must Burn, the Wizard Returns. 2015. (Dorothy Must Die Novella Ser.). (ENG., Illus.). 416p. (YA). (gr. 9). pap. 10.99 (978-0-06-228079-4(1), HarperCollins) HarperCollins Pubs.

—Dorothy Must Die Stories: No Place Like Oz, the Witch Must Burn, the Wizard Returns. 2015. (Dorothy Must Die Ser.). (YA). lib. bdg. 20.85 (978-0-606-37248-0(2)) Turtleback.

—Dorothy Must Die Stories Volume 2: Heart of Tin, the Straw King, Ruler of Beasts. 2016. (Dorothy Must Die Novella Ser.). (ENG.). 336p. (YA). (gr. 9). pap. 10.99 (978-0-06-240397-1(4), HarperCollins) HarperCollins Pubs.

—The Wicked Will Rise. (Dorothy Must Die Ser.: 2). (ENG.). (YA). (gr. 9). 2016. 320p. pap. 12.99 (978-0-06-228071-8(6)) 2015. 304p. 17.99 (978-0-06-228070-1(8)) HarperCollins Pubs. (HarperCollins).

—The Wicked Will Rise. 2016. (Dorothy Must Die Ser.: 2). (YA). lib. bdg. 20.85 (978-0-606-38170-3(8)) Turtleback.

—Yellow Brick War. 2016. (Dorothy Must Die Ser.: 3). (ENG.). 288p. (YA). (gr. 9-12). 18.99 (978-0-06-228073-2(2), HarperCollins) HarperCollins Pubs.

Palatini, Margie. Piggie Pie! Book & CD, 1 vol. Fine, Howard, illus. 2008. (ENG.). 32p. (J). (gr. -1-3). audio 10.99 (978-0-547-18178-3(7), 1055919, Clarion Bks.) HarperCollins Pubs.

Palmer, Jennie. The Wompananny Witches Make One Mean Pizza. 2017. (ENG., Illus.). 40p. (J). (gr. -1-2). 16.95 (978-1-4197-2642-2(0), 1189501, Abrams Bks. for Young Readers) Abrams, Inc.

Pardoe, David. Jasper Tippett's Amazing Journey to Page 42. 2006. (Illus.). 132p. pap. (978-1-84401-785-0(0)) Athena Pr.

Parker, Emma. The Wickedest Witch. 2010. (Illus.). pap. (978-1-877561-17-7(7)) First Edition Ltd.

Pascoe, Sara. Being a Witch, & Other Things I Didn't Ask For. Lindsey, Alexander, ed. 2nd ed. 2017. (Historicalnovelsociety. Org/Reviews/Ratchet-The-Rel Ser.). (ENG., Illus.). 369p. (YA). (gr. 7-12). pap. (978-0-9935747-3-3(4)) Trindles & Green, Ltd.

scual, P. V. The Beautiful Witch. 2004. (J). per. 28.95 *(978-1-58939-603-6(0))* Virtualbookworm.com Publishing, Inc.

atterson, James. The Fire. 2011. (Playaway Children Ser.). (ENG.). (YA). (gr. 8-12). 59.99 *(978-1-61113-385-1(8))* Hachette Audio.

The Gift. 2010. (Witch & Wizard Ser.: No. 2). (J). 59.99 *(978-1-60941-012-4(2))* Findaway World, LLC.

-The Gift. 2014. lthr. 79.00 *(978-1-62715-523-6(6))* Leatherbound Bestsellers.

-Witch & Wizard. 2014. lthr. 79.00 *(978-1-62715-529-8(5))* Leatherbound Bestsellers.

-Witch & Wizard. 2010. (Witch & Wizard Ser.: 1). (YA). lib. bdg. 20.85 *(978-0-606-15119-1(2))* Turtleback.

atterson, James & Charbonnet, Gabrielle. Witch & Wizard. (Witch & Wizard Ser.: 1). (ENG.). (J). (gr. 5-17). 2011. 368p. mass mkt. 8.99 *(978-0-446-56243-0(2))* 2010. 336p. pap. 11.99 *(978-0-316-03834-8(2))* 2009. 320p. 34.99 *(978-0-316-03624-5(2))* Little Brown & Co. (Jimmy Patterson).

—Witch & Wizard. 2011. (Witch & Wizard Ser.: 1). lib. bdg. 18.45 *(978-0-606-26452-5(3))* Turtleback.

Patterson, James & Dembowski, Jill. The Fire. 2011. (Witch & Wizard Ser.: 3). (ENG.). (YA). (gr. 5-17). 352p. 35.99 *(978-0-316-10190-5(7))*; 448p. 30.99 *(978-0-316-19620-8(7))* Little Brown & Co. (Jimmy Patterson).

—The Kiss. 2013. (YA). (Witch & Wizard Ser.: 4). (ENG.). 384p. (gr. 7-17). pap. 10.99 *(978-0-316-10176-9(1)*, Jimmy Patterson); (Witch & Wizard Ser.: 4). (ENG.). 368p. (gr. 7-17). 35.99 *(978-0-316-10191-2(5)*, Jimmy Patterson); 357p. *(978-0-316-22640-0(8))* Little Brown & Co.

—The Kiss. 2013. (Witch & Wizard Ser.: 4). (YA). lib. bdg. 20.85 *(978-0-606-32281-2(7))* Turtleback.

Patterson, James & Raymond, Emily. The Lost. (YA). 2015. (Witch & Wizard Ser.: 5). (ENG.). 384p. (gr. 7-17). pap. 10.99 *(978-0-316-20774-4(8)*, Jimmy Patterson) 2014. (Witch & Wizard Ser.: 5). (ENG.). 384p. (gr. 7-17). 36.99 *(978-0-316-20770-6(5)*, Jimmy Patterson) 2014. 355p. *(978-0-316-24266-0(7))* 2014. (Witch & Wizard Ser.: 5). (ENG.). 480p. (gr. 7-17). 39.99 *(978-0-316-24002-4(8)*, Jimmy Patterson) Little Brown & Co.

—The Lost. 2015. (Witch & Wizard Ser.: 5). (YA). lib. bdg. 20.85 *(978-0-606-37528-3(7))* Turtleback.

Patterson, James & Rust, Ned. The Gift. (Witch & Wizard Ser.: 2). (ENG.). (gr. 5-17). 2012. 352p. mass mkt. 7.99 *(978-0-446-56245-4(9))* 2011. 400p. pap. 10.99 *(978-0-316-03835-5(0))* 2010. 352p. 17.99 *(978-0-316-03625-2(0))* Little Brown & Co. (Jimmy Patterson).

—The Gift. 2012. (Witch & Wizard Ser.: 2). lib. bdg. 18.40 *(978-0-606-26451-8(5))* Turtleback.

Pau Pau. The Princess' Adventure. 2007. 52p. pap. 16.95 *(978-1-60441-069-3(8))* America Star Bks.

Paulk, William. The Creatures of Vision City: Pokie's Party, Book One. 2009. 48p. pap. 10.99 *(978-1-4389-5659-6(2))* AuthorHouse.

PC Treasures Staff, prod. Hansel & Gretel. 2007. (J). *(978-1-60072-030-7(7))* PC Treasures, Inc.

Peace, Bob. The Wicked Witch Pop Quiz. Rasheed, M., illus. 2013. 132p. pap. 12.95 *(978-0-9824741-4-3(8))* Sojourner Publishing, Inc.

Pearce, Jackson. Sweetly. 2012. (Fairy Tale Retelling Ser.). (ENG.). 336p. (YA). (gr. 10-17). pap. 17.99 *(978-0-316-06866-6(7))* Little, Brown Bks. for Young Readers.

Pearce, Margaret. A Belinda Robinson Novel Book 1: Belinda & the Witch's Cat. 2013. 82p. pap. *(978-1-922066-58-9(3))* Writers Exchange E-Publishing.

Pearson, Kimberly Ann. Mystling Glen Book I: The Tale of A Prince. 2009. 207p. pap. 14.95 *(978-1-4327-4169-3(1))* Outskirts Pr., Inc.

Perkins, T. J. Four Little Witches, 1 vol. Pinero, Eimi, illus. 2015. (ENG.). 40p. (J). 12.99 *(978-0-7643-4943-0(0)*, 6691, Red Feather) Schiffer Publishing, Ltd.

Perry, Adam. The Magicians of Elephant County. Perry, Adam, illus. 2018. (ENG., Illus.). 384p. (J). (gr. 3-7). 16.99 *(978-0-06-279535-9(X)*, HarperCollins) HarperCollins Pubs.

Perry, Pete. The Secret of Bedside Manor. 2009. (Illus.). 140p. pap. 36.49 *(978-1-4389-6668-7(7))* AuthorHouse.

Petrlik, Andrea, illus. Hansel & Gretel. (Flip-Up Fairy Tales Ser.). 24p. (J). 2007. (gr. -1-2). *(978-1-84643-090-9(9))* 2006. (gr. 1-2). *(978-1-904550-73-0(8))* Child's Play International Ltd.

Philpot, Graham, illus. Hansel & Gretel. 2007. (First Fairy Tales Ser.). 32p. (J). (gr. -1-3). lib. bdg. 28.50 *(978-1-59771-075-6(X))* Sea-To-Sea Pubns.

Pierce, Meredith Ann. The Pearl of the Soul of the World. 2008. (Darkangel Trilogy Ser.: Bk. 3). (ENG.). 256p. (YA). (gr. 7-17). per. 15.99 *(978-0-316-06724-9(5))* Little, Brown Bks. for Young Readers.

Pike, Christopher, pseud. Black Knight. 2014. (Witch World Ser.: 2). (ENG., Illus.). 464p. (YA). (gr. 9). 19.99 *(978-1-4424-6733-0(9))*; pap. 11.99 *(978-1-4424-6734-7(7))* Simon Pulse. (Simon Pulse).

—Red Queen. 2014. (Witch World Ser.: 1). (ENG., Illus.). 560p. (YA). (gr. 9). pap. 11.99 *(978-1-4424-3029-7(X)*, Simon Pulse) Simon Pulse.

—Witch World. 2012. (Witch World Ser.: 1). (ENG.). 528p. (YA). (gr. 9). 17.99 *(978-1-4424-3028-0(1)*, Simon Pulse) Simon Pulse.

—The Witch's Revenge. 2015. (Spooksville Ser.: 6). (ENG., Illus.). 128p. (J). (gr. 3-7). pap. 7.99 *(978-1-4814-1069-4(5)*, Aladdin) Simon & Schuster Children's Publishing.

Pinkwater, Daniel M. The Yggyssey: How Iggy Wondered What Happened to All the Ghosts, Found Out Where They Went, & Went There. Brown, Calef, illus. 2009. (ENG.). 256p. (J). (gr. 4-6). 18.69 *(978-0-618-59445-0(0))* Houghton Mifflin Harcourt Publishing Co.

Plourde, Paulette. Smitty Moose, Petey & Me - Episode One, the Witch. Golen, Jessica, illus. l.t. ed. 2005. 32p. (J). per. 9.95 *(978-1-59879-038-2(2))* Lifevest Publishing, Inc.

Poore, Michael. Two Girls, a Clock, & a Crooked House. 2019. (Illus.). 304p. (J). (gr. 3-7). 16.99 *(978-0-525-64416-3(4)*, Random Hse. Bks. for Young Readers) Random Hse. Children's Bks.

Popper, Garry. Worm's Eye View: A Witch's Tale. Forshaw, John, illus. 2004. 48p. 7.00 *(978-1-84161-025-2(9))* Ravette Publishing, Ltd. GBR. Dist: Parkwest Pubns., Inc.

Pounder, Sibéal & Pounder, Sibéal. Witch Wars. Anderson, Laura Ellen, illus. 2016. (Witch Wars Ser.). (ENG.). 272p. (J). 16.99 *(978-1-61963-925-6(4)*, 900152463, Bloomsbury USA Childrens) Bloomsbury Publishing USA.

Powell, J. Frederick. Puffy & the Witch's Revenge. 2004. (Illus.). 96p. pap. *(978-1-84401-329-6(4))* Athena Pr.

Powell, Laura. Witch Fire. 2013. (ENG.). 336p. (YA). (gr. 7). 17.99 *(978-1-61963-006-2(0)*, 900098189, Bloomsbury USA Childrens) Bloomsbury Publishing USA.

Pratchett, Terry. A Hat Full of Sky. 2015. (Tiffany Aching Ser.: 2). (ENG.). 400p. (YA). (gr. 8). pap. 10.99 *(978-0-06-243527-9(2)*, Clarion Bks.) HarperCollins Pubs.

—A Hat Full of Sky. 2005. 407p. (gr. 7). 19.00 *(978-0-7569-5126-9(7))* Perfection Learning Corp.

—A Hat Full of Sky. 2005. (Discworld Ser.: 32). 407p. (YA). 19.65 *(978-1-4177-2658-5(X))* Turtleback.

—I Shall Wear Midnight. (Tiffany Aching Ser.: 4). (ENG.). (YA). (gr. 8). 2015. 464p. pap. 12.99 *(978-0-06-243529-3(9))* 2011. 368p. pap. 11.99 *(978-0-06-143306-1(3))* HarperCollins Pubs. (Clarion Bks.).

—The Wee Free Men. (Tiffany Aching Ser.: 1). (ENG.). (YA). (gr. 8). 2015. 352p. pap. 15.99 *(978-0-06-243526-2(4))* 2006. 400p. reprint ed. pap. 10.99 *(978-0-06-001238-0(2))* HarperCollins Pubs. (Clarion Bks.).

—The Wee Free Men. 2004. 19.00 *(978-0-7569-3252-7(1))* Perfection Learning Corp.

—The Wee Free Men. 2006. (Discworld Ser.: 28). (YA). 19.65 *(978-1-4176-2764-6(6))* Turtleback.

—Wintersmith. (YA). 2015. (Tiffany Aching Ser.: 3). (ENG.). 416p. (gr. 8). pap. 10.99 *(978-0-06-243528-6(0)*, Clarion Bks.) 2007. (Tiffany Aching Ser.: 3). (ENG.). 464p. (gr. 8-12). per. 9.99 *(978-0-06-089033-9(9)*, Clarion Bks.) 2006. (Discworld Novels Ser.). 323p. (gr. 7-12). 16.99 *(978-0-06-089031-5(2)*, HarperTeen) 2006. (Discworld Novels Ser.). 323p. (gr. 7-12). lib. bdg. 17.89 *(978-0-06-089032-2(0)*, HarperTeen) HarperCollins Pubs.

—Wintersmith. 2007. 450p. (gr. 7). 19.00 *(978-0-7569-8091-7(7))* Perfection Learning Corp.

Preble, Joy. Dreaming Anastasia. 2009. (Dreaming Anastasia Ser.: 1). 320p. (YA). (gr. 7-12). pap. 13.99 *(978-1-4022-1817-0(6))* Sourcebooks, Inc.

—Haunted, 2. 2011. (Dreaming Anastasia Ser.: 2). 304p. (YA). (gr. 7-12). pap. 9.99 *(978-1-4022-4468-1(1))* Sourcebooks, Inc.

Preussler, Otfried. The Little Witch. Bell, Anthea, tr. Gebhardt-Gayler, Winnie, illus. 2015. (ENG.). 144p. (J). (gr. k-4). 16.95 *(978-1-59017-934-5(X)*, NYR Children's Collection) New York Review of Bks., Inc., The.

Price, Margaret Evans, illus. Hansel & Gretel: Shape Book. 2005. (Children's Die-Cut Shape Book Ser.). (ENG.). 16p. (J). (gr. -1-3). 9.95 *(978-1-59583-012-8(X)*, 9781595830128, Green Tiger Pr.) Laughing Elephant.

The Princess & the Magic Locket. (My Tooth Is Loose!). (Illus.). 32p. (J). *(978-1-4054-1022-9(1))* Parragon, Inc.

Randall, Thomas. The Waking: A Winter of Ghosts. 2011. (YA). pap. 9.99 *(978-1-59990-252-4(4)*, Bloomsbury USA Childrens) Bloomsbury Publishing USA.

Ravenwolf, Silver. Jóvenes y brujas. 2004. (SPA.). 352p. pap. *(978-84-7720-753-5(4))* Ediciones Obelisco.

Rawson, C. Stories of Witches. 2004. (Young Reading Ser.: Vol. 1). 48p. (J). (gr. 2-18). pap. 5.95 *(978-0-7945-0647-6(X))* EDC Publishing.

Rees, Celia. Witch Child. unabr. ed. 2004. (Young Adult Cassette Librariestm Ser.). 304p. (J). (gr. 5-9). pap. 40.00 incl. audio *(978-0-8072-1198-4(2)*, S YA 343 SP, Listening Library) Random Hse. Audio Publishing Group.

Reid, Isabelle. Serafina Moon. 2009. 48p. pap. *(978-1-84923-771-0(9))* YouWriteOn.

Reisfeld, Randi. Trouble with Trix (Winx Club), 2. Golden Books, illus. 2012. (Winx Club: Chapter Bks.). (ENG.). 128p. (J). (gr. 2-5). 17.44 *(978-0-307-97995-7(4))* Random House Publishing Group.

Riding, Will. Ebenezer's Tale. 2008. (Illus.). 188p. pap. 14.49 *(978-1-4343-9694-5(0))* AuthorHouse.

Riveros, Gabriela. El Encargo de Fernanda. Castillo, Jesus, illus. rev. ed. 2006. (Castillo de la Lectura Blanca Ser.). (SPA & ENG.). 64p. (J). (gr. k-2). pap. 6.95 *(978-970-20-0126-3(9))* Castillo, Ediciones, S. A. de C. V. MEX. Dist: Macmillan.

Roberts, Roxanne. Angel Wings, Faery Dust & Other Magical Things: A Story about Witches, Warlocks & Such. 2011. 24p. pap. 11.50 *(978-1-61204-072-1(1)*, Eloquent Bks.) Strategic Book Publishing & Rights Agency (SBPRA).

Rockley, Frank. Tinderbox Cottage. 2010. 136p. pap. 10.99 *(978-1-4490-3120-6(X))* AuthorHouse.

Rojo, Sara, illus. Baba Yaga: the Flying Witch. 2008. (Usborne First Reading: Level 4 Ser.). 48p. (J). 8.99 *(978-0-7945-2078-6(2)*, Usborne) EDC Publishing.

Rose, Alice. Maria Dracula: A Fantasy Novel for Children. 2007. (ENG., Illus.). 191p. pap. 13.50 *(978-0-615-15099-4(3))* DUENDE Bks.

Rowling, J. K. The Tales of Beedle the Bard. Rowling, J. K., illus. 2008. (ENG., Illus.). 128p. *(978-0-7475-9987-6(4))* Bloomsbury Publishing Plc.

—The Tales of Beedle the Bard. GrandPré, Mary, illus. collector's ed. 2008. 184p. *(978-0-9560109-0-2(3))* Children's High Level Group.

—The Tales of Beedle the Bard. 2017. (ENG.). 128p. (J). (gr. 3-3). 12.99 *(978-1-338-12568-9(0)*, Levine, Arthur A. Bks.) Scholastic, Inc.

—The Tales of Beedle the Bard. 2017. (ENG.). (J). (gr. 3). lib. bdg. 24.50 *(978-0-606-39695-0(0))* Turtleback.

Sage, Angie. TodHunter Moon, Book Three: StarChaser. Zug, Mark, illus. 2016. (World of Septimus Heap Ser.: 3). (ENG.). 496p. (J). (gr. 3-7). 17.99 *(978-0-06-227251-5(9)*, Tegen, Katherine Bks) HarperCollins Pubs.

Samwell, Cynthia A. Witches Anonymous. 2006. (Illus.). 84p. pap. *(978-1-84401-660-0(9))* Athena Pr.

Sandoval, John. The Witches of Ruidoso. 2013. (ENG.). 120p. (YA). pap. 12.95 *(978-1-55885-766-7(4)*, Piñata Books) Arte Publico Pr.

Santoro, Scott. Which Way to Witch School? Santoro, Scott, illus. (ENG., Illus.). 32p. (J). (gr. -1-2). 2012. pap. 5.99 *(978-0-06-078183-5(1))* 2010. 16.99 *(978-0-06-078181-1(5))* HarperCollins Pubs. (HarperCollins).

Scharf, J. L. Grace & the Ice Prince: The Diamond Heart Quest. 2006. (ENG.). 262p. (J). per. 16.95 *(978-1-897235-09-6(7))* Thistledown Pr., Ltd. CAN. Dist: Univ. of Toronto Pr.

Schliewen, Richard. Paulina's Teddy Bear Journey. Visaya, Artemio, illus. 2012. 104p. 24.95 *(978-1-62709-055-1(X))* America Star Bks.

Schlitz, Laura Amy. Splendors & Glooms. (ENG.). 400p. (J). 2017. (gr. 5-9). pap. 10.99 *(978-0-7636-9449-4(5))* 2012. (Illus.). (gr. 4-7). 17.99 *(978-0-7636-5380-4(2))* Candlewick Pr.

—Splendors & Glooms. 2014. (ENG.). (J). (gr. 4-7). lib. bdg. 18.60 *(978-1-62765-443-2(7))* Perfection Learning Corp.

—Splendors & Glooms. 2014. lib. bdg. 18.40 *(978-0-606-35170-6(1))* Turtleback.

Schoffstall, John. Half-Witch: A Novel. 2019. (ENG.). 336p. (YA). pap. 14.95 *(978-1-61873-167-8(X)*, Big Mouth Hse.) Small Beer Pr.

Schwab, V. E. The near Witch. 2020. 320p. pap. 16.99 *(978-1-78909-114-4(4))* 2019. 360p. 19.99 *(978-1-78909-112-0(8))* Titan Bks. Ltd. GBR. (Titan Bks.). Dist: Penguin Random Hse. LLC.

Seduction. 2014. (Legacy Ser.). (ENG., Illus.). 416p. (YA). (gr. 9). 17.99 *(978-1-4814-0023-7(1)*, Simon & Schuster/Paula Wiseman Bks.) Simon & Schuster/Paula Wiseman Bks.

Seever, Berni. A Supernatural Tale. 2007. 62p. pap. 20.00 *(978-1-4196-7788-5(8))* CreateSpace Independent Publishing Platform.

Serafin, Jordan. Bella: The Crooked Hat Witch. Rubino, Alisa A., illus. 2004. (J). *(978-0-932991-57-7(2))* Place In The Woods, The.

Serrano, Tomas. Salfon el Limpiador de Tejados. (SPA.). 48p. (J). (gr. 1-3). pap. *(978-84-264-3746-4(X))* Editorial Lumen ESP. Dist: Lectorum Pubns., Inc.

Shannon, George. A Very Witchy Spelling Bee. Fearing, Mark, illus. 2013. (ENG.). 32p. (J). (gr. -1-3). 16.99 *(978-0-15-206696-3(9)*, 1199789, Clarion Bks.) HarperCollins Pubs.

Shea, Therese M. Witches Add!, 1 vol. 2018. (Monsters Do Math! Ser.). (ENG.). 24p. (gr. 2-3). 24.27 *(978-1-5382-2937-8(4)*, 4cd94879-b423-4c27-99c4-d954350e116b) Stevens, Gareth Publishing LLLP.

Shepherd, Audrey. Morgana the Recession Witch. 2010. (ENG., Illus.). 48p. pap. *(978-1-84748-783-4(1))* Athena Pr.

Shepherd, Megan. Grim Lovelies. (Grim Lovelies Ser.). (ENG.). (YA). (gr. 9). 2019. 448p. pap. 9.99 *(978-0-358-10823-8(3)*, 1748887) 2018. 384p. 17.99 *(978-1-328-80918-6(8)*, 1688543) HarperCollins Pubs. (Clarion Bks.).

—Midnight Beauties. 2019. (Grim Lovelies Ser.). (ENG.). 448p. (YA). (gr. 9). 17.99 *(978-1-328-81190-5(5)*, 1688554, Clarion Bks.) HarperCollins Pubs.

Shields, Gillian. Eternal. 2012. (Immortal Ser.: 3). (ENG.). 384p. (YA). (gr. 8). pap. 9.99 *(978-0-06-200040-8(3)*, Tegen, Katherine Bks) HarperCollins Pubs.

—Immortal. 2010. (Immortal Ser.: 1). (ENG.). 384p. (YA). (gr. 8-12). pap. 8.99 *(978-0-06-137583-5(7)*, Tegen, Katherine Bks) HarperCollins Pubs.

Shults, Sylvia. Double Double Love & Trouble. 2013. 150p. pap. 12.99 *(978-0-9848931-3-3(X))* Dark Continents Publishing.

Shurtliff, Liesl. Red: the (Fairly) True Tale of Red Riding Hood. 2017. (ENG.). 272p. (J). (gr. 3-7). 8.99 *(978-0-385-75586-3(4)*, Yearling) Random Hse. Children's Bks.

Simmons, H. Two Tales from Our Corner Lot. 2004. 68p. pap. 19.95 *(978-1-4137-5251-9(9))* America Star Bks.

Simmons, Steven J. Alice & Greta: A Tale of Two Witches. Moore, Cyd, illus. 2019. 32p. (J). (gr. -1-2). 16.99 *(978-1-62354-110-1(7))* Charlesbridge Publishing, Inc.

Simpson, C. E. Eighth Grade Witch. Utomo, Gabhor, illus. 2014. (ENG.). 144p. (J). (gr. 4-8). mass mkt. 6.99 *(978-1-937133-45-0(1))* Chooseco LLC.

Skye, Evelyn. The Crown's Fate. (Crown's Game Ser.: 2). (ENG.). 432p. (YA). (gr. 8). 2018. pap. 10.99 *(978-0-06-242262-0(6))* 2017. 17.99 *(978-0-06-242261-3(8))* HarperCollins Pubs. (Balzer & Bray).

Skye Toggles. Bella the Witch & Her Worries. 2010. 36p. pap. 16.99 *(978-1-4490-6803-5(0))* AuthorHouse.

Slade, Anthea. Titch the Witch. 2018. (ENG., Illus.). 30p. (J). *(978-1-5289-2466-5(5))*; pap. *(978-1-5289-2467-2(3))* Austin Macauley Pubs. Ltd.

Sloat, Teri. Zip! Zoom! on a Broom. Bonnet, Rosalinde, illus. (ENG.). (J). (gr. -1 — 1). 2019. 24p. bds. 7.99 *(978-0-316-25672-8(2))* 2017. 40p. 16.99 *(978-0-316-25673-5(0))* Little, Brown Bks. for Young Readers.

Smith, Ann Pierce. Esmerelda Hedgepath's First Date. 2010. 16p. 12.50 *(978-1-4520-3493-5(1))* AuthorHouse.

Smith, Audrey. The Halloween Misfits. 2004. 23p. (J). pap. 9.95 incl. audio compact disk *(978-0-9722673-4-2(4))* Audrey Productions.

Smith, Cleveland W. Billabongo. 2008. 172p. pap. *(978-1-84923-100-8(1))* YouWriteOn.

Smith, L. J. The Secret Circle: Temptation, Vol. 6. 2013. (Secret Circle Ser.: 6). (ENG.). 288p. (YA). (gr. 8). 17.99 *(978-0-06-213047-1(1)*, HarperTeen) HarperCollins Pubs.

—The Secret Circle: the Divide, Vol. 4. 2013. (Secret Circle Ser.: 4). (ENG.). 320p. (YA). (gr. 8). pap. 10.99 *(978-0-06-213041-9(2)*, HarperTeen) HarperCollins Pubs.

—The Secret Circle: the Hunt. 2013. (Secret Circle Ser.: 5). (ENG.). 288p. (YA). (gr. 8). pap. 10.99 *(978-0-06-213043-3(9)*, HarperTeen) HarperCollins Pubs.

—The Secret Circle: the Initiation & the Captive Part I, Pt. 1. 2012. (Secret Circle Ser.: Vols. 1 - 2). (ENG.). 416p. (YA). (gr. 8). pap. 10.99 *(978-0-06-167085-5(5)*, HarperTeen) HarperCollins Pubs.

—The Secret Circle: the Temptation. 2014. (Secret Circle Ser.: 6). (ENG.). 304p. (YA). (gr. 8). pap. 9.99 *(978-0-06-213045-7(5)*, HarperTeen) HarperCollins Pubs.

Smith, L. J. & Kevin Williamson & Julie Plec, Kevin Williamson. The Vampire Diaries: Stefan's Diaries #6: the Compelled. 2012. (Vampire Diaries: Stefan's Diaries: 6). (ENG.). 256p. (YA). (gr. 9). pap. 11.99 *(978-0-06-211398-6(4)*, HarperTeen) HarperCollins Pubs.

Snowe, Olivia. Dandelion & the Witch, 1 vol. Lamoreaux, Michelle, illus. 2014. (Twicetold Tales Ser.). (ENG.). 128p. (J). (gr. 3-6). 25.32 *(978-1-4342-9147-9(2)*, 125595, Stone Arch Bks.) Capstone.

—The Girl & the Seven Thieves, 1 vol. Lamoreaux, Michelle, illus. 2013. (Twicetold Tales Ser.). (ENG.). 128p. (J). (gr. 3-6). 8.95 *(978-1-4342-6280-6(4)*, 123724); lib. bdg. 25.32 *(978-1-4342-6018-5(6)*, 123159) Capstone. (Stone Arch Bks.).

Sobat, Gail Sidonie. A Winter's Tale. 2004. (Ingamald Ser.: 2). (ENG.). 176p. pap. 16.95 *(978-1-894283-45-8(7))* Great Plains Pubns. CAN. Dist: Publishers Group Canada.

Sobel, Gerrie. Jacob & His Magical Flying Bears, a Halloween Story. Torres, Dottie, illus. 2009. 32p. pap. 12.95 *(978-1-936051-42-7(7))* Peppertree Pr., The.

Soper, Stuart A. The P. U'Trid & S. Pooky Pickles Company. 2013. 400p. (J). pap. 21.50 *(978-1-61204-724-9(6)*, Strategic Bk. Publishing) Strategic Book Publishing & Rights Agency (SBPRA).

Sorenson, Jack R. Eibhlin & Her Dragon, 1 vol. 2009. 131p. pap. 24.95 *(978-1-60749-634-2(8))* America Star Bks.

Spotswood, Jessica. Born Wicked. 2013. (Cahill Witch Chronicles Ser.: 1). (ENG.). 352p. (YA). (gr. 7). pap. 10.99 *(978-0-14-242187-1(1)*, Speak) Penguin Young Readers Group.

—Born Wicked. 2013. lib. bdg. 22.10 *(978-0-606-26729-8(8))* Turtleback.

Stadelmann, Amy Marie. Olive & Beatrix: The Super-Smelly Moldy Blob, Vol. 2. Stadelmann, Amy Marie, illus. 2016. (Olive & Beatrix Ser.: 2). (ENG., Illus.). 80p. (J). (gr. k-2). 15.99 *(978-0-545-81485-0(5))* Scholastic, Inc.

Stanley, Pauline. The Children & the Witches Magic. 2010. (Illus.). 48p. pap. 10.49 *(978-1-4490-9544-4(5))* AuthorHouse.

Steig, William. Wizzil. Blake, Quentin, illus. 2014. 32p. pap. 8.00 *(978-1-61003-221-6(7))* Center for the Collaborative Classroom.

—Wizzil. 2015. (J). lib. bdg. 18.40 *(978-0-606-36445-4(5))* Turtleback.

Steinkellner, Emma. The Okay Witch. Steinkellner, Emma, illus. 2019. (Okay Witch Ser.: 1). (ENG., Illus.). 272p. (J). (gr. 3-7). 20.99 *(978-1-5344-3146-1(2))*; pap. 12.99 *(978-1-5344-3145-4(4))* Simon & Schuster Children's Publishing. (Aladdin).

Stephens, Helen. Witchety Sticks & the Magic Buttons. Stephens, Helen, illus. 2010. (ENG., Illus.). 32p. (J). (gr. -1-k). pap. 8.99 *(978-1-4169-1107-4(3)*, Simon & Schuster Children's) Simon & Schuster, Ltd. GBR. Dist: Simon & Schuster, Inc.

Stewart, Mary. The Little Broomstick. pap. *(978-0-440-44897-6(2))* Random Hse. Children's Bks.

Stilton, Geronimo. The Search for Treasure (Geronimo Stilton & the Kingdom of Fantasy #6), Volume 6. 2014. (Geronimo Stilton & the Kingdom of Fantasy Ser.: 6). (ENG., Illus.). 320p. (J). (gr. 2-5). 16.99 *(978-0-545-65604-7(4)*, Scholastic Paperbacks) Scholastic, Inc.

Storm, Falcon. Natalie the Not-So-Nasty: Tales from upon A. Time Series. 2013. (ENG.). 82p. pap. 9.95 *(978-1-62253-072-4(1))* Evolved Publishing.

Strega Nona. 2005. (J). *(978-1-59564-834-1(8))* Steps To Literacy, LLC.

Stuart, Lisa Marie. The Little Cat, the Wonderful Witch, & the Clever Mouse. Potter, Lori, illus. 2008. 60p. pap. 21.95 *(978-1-59858-691-6(2))* Dog Ear Publishing, LLC.

Sundstrom, Dainel H. The Return of Oz. 2007. pap. 10.00 *(978-0-8059-8944-1(7))* Dorrance Publishing Co., Inc.

Symes, Ruth. Bella Donna: Too Many Spells. Lindsay, Marion, illus. 2016. (ENG.). 192p. (J). (gr. 1-5). pap. 7.99 *(978-1-63450-155-2(1)*, Sky Pony Pr.) Skyhorse Publishing Co., Inc.

Tagg, Christine. Who Will You Meet on Scary Street? Nine Pop-up Nightmares! Fuge, Charles, illus. 2004. 20p. (J). reprint ed. 15.00 *(978-0-7567-8003-6(9))* DIANE Publishing Co.

Tatcheva, Eva. Witch Zelda's Birthday Cake: A Wild & Wicked Pop-up, Pull-the-Tab Book. Tatcheva, Eva, illus. 2004. (Illus.). 12p. (J). (gr. k-3). reprint ed. 18.00 *(978-0-7567-7225-3(7))* DIANE Publishing Co.

Tate, N. F. The Witch of Hambone: Books 1 And 2. 2009. (Illus.). 120p. pap. 33.49 *(978-1-4490-0621-1(3))* AuthorHouse.

Tenney, Shawna J. C., illus. Brunhilda's Backwards Day. 2016. (ENG.). 32p. (J). (gr. -1-k). 16.99 *(978-1-63450-691-5(X)*, Sky Pony Pr.) Skyhorse Publishing Co., Inc.

Thame, Val. Witches in Secret. l.t. ed. 2007. 100p. per. *(978-1-905665-26-6(1))* Pollinger In Print.

Thomas, Valerie. Winnie's Big Bad Robot. Paul, Korky, illus. 2015. (ENG.). 32p. *(978-0-19-273874-5(7))* Oxford Univ. Pr.

Thompson, Colin. The Floods #2: School Plot. Scrambly, Crab, illus. 2008. (Floods Ser.). (J). (ENG.). 224p. 15.99 *(978-0-06-113861-4(4))*; 256p. lib. bdg. 16.89 *(978-0-06-113855-3(X))* HarperCollins Pubs.

—The Floods Family Files. Thompson, Colin, illus. 2012. (Floods Ser.: 1). (ENG., Illus.). 32p. (J). (gr. 4-7). pap. 12.99 *(978-1-86471-942-0(7))* Random Hse. Australia AUS. Dist: Independent Pubs. Group.

—Good Neighbors. Scrambly, Crab, illus. 2008. (Floods Ser.: No. 1). 214p. (J). (gr. 3-7). 15.99 *(978-0-06-113196-7(2))* HarperCollins Pubs.

Thompson, Jill. Magic Trixie. 2008. (ENG., Illus.). 96p. (J). (gr. 3-7). pap. 8.99 *(978-0-06-117045-4(3))* HarperCollins Pubs.

—Magic Trixie & the Dragon. 2009. (ENG., Illus.). 96p. (J). (gr. 3-7). pap. 7.99 *(978-0-06-117050-8(X))* HarperCollins Pubs.

Thompson, Richard. The Follower, 1 vol. Springett, Martin, illus. 2003. (ENG.). 32p. (J). (gr. 1-3). pap. 7.95 *(978-1-55041-880-4(7)*, f8727bf0-bf98-46d5-9fd8-544bd1cbf8bb) Fitzhenry & Whiteside, Ltd. CAN. Dist: Firefly Bks., Ltd.

Tiger Tales. Five Little Pumpkins. Mantle, Ben, illus. 2010. (ENG.). 24p. (J). (gr. -1-k). bds. 8.95 *(978-1-58925-856-3(8))* Tiger Tales.

Tomos, Angharad. Ceridwen. 2005. (WEL., Illus.). 48.0p. pap. 1.95 *(978-0-86243-066-5(6))* Y Lolfa GBR. Dist: Dufour Editions, Inc.

WXYZ

—Cosyn. 2005. (WEL., Illus.). 24p. pap. (978-0-86243-566-0(8)) Y Lolfa.

—Rala Rwdins (Cyfres Rwdlan) Tomos, Angharad, illus. 2005. (WEL., Illus.). 48p. pap. 1.95 (978-0-86243-065-8(8)) Y Lolfa GBR. Dist: Dufour Editions, Inc.

Tozier, Christopher. Olivia Brophie & the Pearl of Tagelus. 2013. (ENG.). 208p. (J). (gr. -1-12). pap. 12.95 (978-1-56164-519-0(2)) Pineapple Pr., Inc.

Trent, Tiffany. The Unnaturalists. (ENG., (YA). (gr. 7). 2013. Illus.). 336p. pap. 9.99 (978-1-4424-2207-0(6)) 2012. 320p. 16.99 (978-1-4424-2206-3(8)) Simon & Schuster Bks. For Young Readers. (Simon & Schuster Bks. For Young Readers).

Trotter, Bob. The Curious Tale of Marmalade Tuttle. 2008. 116p. pap. 12.95 (978-1-60693-014-4(1), Eloquent Bks.) Strategic Book Publishing & Rights Agency (SBPRA).

Troulis, Jennifer. Penelope & Priscilla & the City of the Banished. 2007. (J). per. 14.95 (978-0-9768602-1-1(X)) Twin Monkeys Pr.

Tyrrell, Melissa. Hansel & Gretel. McMullen, Nigel, illus. 2005. (Fairytale Friends Ser.). 12p. (J). bds. 5.95 (978-1-58117-152-5(8), Intervisual/Piggy Toes) Bendon, Inc.

Umansky, Kaye. Clover Twig & the Perilous Path. Wright, Johanna, illus. 2013. (ENG.). 272p. (J). (gr. 3-7). pap. 15.99 (978-1-250-02727-6(6), 900098299) Square Fish.

—Pongwiffy. Smedley, Chris, illus. 2007. (ENG.). 192p. (J). (gr. 3-7). pap. 10.95 (978-1-4169-6832-0(6), Simon & Schuster/Paula Wiseman Bks.) Simon & Schuster/Paula Wiseman Bks.

Valentino, Serena. Mother Knows Best-Villains, Book 5. 2018. (Villains Ser.: 5). (ENG.). 400p. (YA). (gr. 7-12). 17.99 (978-1-368-00902-7(6), Disney Press Books) Disney Publishing Worldwide.

—Poor Unfortunate Soul-Villains, Book 3. 2016. (Villains Ser.: 3). (ENG., Illus.). 224p. (YA). (gr. 7-12). 17.99 (978-1-4847-2405-7(4), Disney Press Books) Disney Publishing Worldwide.

Van, Muon Thi. Clever Little Witch. Yum, Hyewon, illus. 2019. (ENG.). 40p. (J). (gr. -1-1). 17.99 (978-1-4814-8171-7(1)); E-Book (978-1-4814-8172-4(X)) McElderry, Margaret K. Bks. (McElderry, Margaret K. Bks.).

Van Nostrand, Michele. The Little Witch. 2013. 24p. pap. 13.00 (978-1-4525-8329-7(3), Balboa Pr.) Author Solutions, LLC.

Vande Velde, Vivian. Three Good Deeds. 2007. (ENG., Illus.). 160p. (J). (gr. 4-6). 22.44 (978-0-15-205382-6(4)) Harcourt Children's Bks.

—Three Good Deeds. 2007. (ENG., Illus.). 160p. (J). (gr. 5-7). pap. 7.99 (978-0-15-205455-7(3), 1196414, Clarion Bks.) HarperCollins Pubs.

—Witch Dreams, 0 vols. 2013. (ENG.). 128p. (J). (gr. 5-9). pap. 7.99 (978-0-7614-5460-1(8), 9780761454601, Two Lions) Amazon Publishing.

Vandepeer, Helen. Gifts. 2008. 76p. pap. 35.80 (978-0-557-03191-7(5)) Lulu Pr., Inc.

Vant, Jeanie. The Witch's Cat. Vant, Tim, illus. 2010. 24p. pap. 11.50 (978-1-60976-051-9(4), Eloquent Bks.) Strategic Book Publishing & Rights Agency (SBPRA).

Viz Media. Fairy Dreams. 2013. (Winx Club Ser.: 5). lib. bdg. 17.20 (978-0-606-26987-2(8)) Turtleback.

Wadsworth, Peter. The Wicked Witch of the Woods. 2012. (Illus.). 28p. pap. 8.49 (978-1-78035-481-1(9), Fastprint Publishing) Upfront Publishing Ltd. GBR. Dist: Printondemand-worldwide.com.

Walker, Chris, creator. Collision Course Goad by Zombienose. 2005. (Illus.). 60p. (YA). 13.95 (978-0-9768670-0-5(1)) Icecat Bks.

Wallace Ii, James C. & Wallace, Amanda D. The Emerald Slippers of Oz. 2013. 156p. pap. 14.99 (978-0-578-12511-4(0)) Scientia Est Vox Pr.

Wallace, Jessica. The Present 6 Packs. KinderConcepts. Gardner, Marjory, illus. (Kinderstarters Ser.). 8p. (gr. -1-1). 21.00 (978-0-7635-8720-8(6)) Rigby Education.

Walser, David. Meg & the Romans. Pienkowski, Jan, illus. 2017. 32p. (J). (-k). pap. 11.99 (978-0-241-29875-6(X)) Penguin Bks., Ltd. GBR. Dist: Independent Pubs. Group.

Walstead, Alice. How to Catch a Witch. Joyce, Megan, illus. 2022. (How to Catch Ser.). 40p. (J). (gr. k-5). 10.99 (978-1-7282-1035-3(6)) Sourcebooks, Inc.

Washington, Linda & Pyykkonen, Carrie. Secrets of the Wee Free Men & Discworld: The Myths & Legends of Terry Pratchett's Multiverse. 2008. (ENG., Illus.). 288p. (YA). (gr. 8-13). pap. 22.99 (978-0-312-37243-9(4), 900044690, St. Martin's Griffin) St. Martin's Pr.

Watson, Sally. Witch of the Glens. 2004. (YA). pap. 12.95 (978-1-59511-001-5(1), 800-691-7779) Image Cascade Publishing.

Wax, Wendy. City Witch, Country Switch, 0 vols. Gibala-Broxholm, Scott, illus. 2013. (ENG.). 42p. (J). (gr. -1-3). pap. 9.99 (978-1-4778-1676-9(3), 9781477816769, Two Lions) Amazon Publishing.

Webb, Holly. Rose. 2013. (Rose Ser.: 1). (ENG.). 240p. (J). (gr. 3-6). pap. 12.99 (978-1-4022-8581-3(7), 9781402285813) Sourcebooks, Inc.

Wees, Alyssa. The Waking Forest. 2019. 304p. (YA). (gr. 7). 17.99 (978-0-525-58116-1(2), Delacorte Pr.) Random Hse. Children's Bks.

Weston Woods Staff, creator. Hansel & Gretel. 2011. 38.75 (978-0-439-80425-7(6)) Weston Woods Studios, Inc.

Wetherby, Mark. The Tales of Mossy Dell. 2009. (Illus.). 88p. pap. 10.49 (978-1-4389-7726-3(3)) AuthorHouse.

Whalen, Erin T. Charlie Gets Spooked, 3 vols. 2004. (Illus.). 32p. (J). (gr. k-3). 16.95 (978-1-929265-04-6(2)); pap. 8.95 (978-1-929265-05-3(0)) Lily & Co. Publishing.

White, J. A. The Thickety #3: Well of Witches. Offermann, Andrea, illus. 2017. (Thickety Ser.: 3). (ENG.). 528p. (J). (gr. 5). pap. 7.99 (978-0-06-225731-4(5), Tegen, Katherine Bks) HarperCollins Pubs.

—The Thickety #4: The Last Spell. Offermann, Andrea, illus. 2017. (Thickety Ser.: 4). (ENG.). 512p. (J). (gr. 5). 16.99 (978-0-06-238139-2(3), Tegen, Katherine Bks) HarperCollins Pubs.

Widow's Broom (25th Anniversary Edition) 25th ed. 2018. (ENG., Illus.). 32p. (J). (gr. -1-3). 18.99 (978-1-328-47019-5(9), 1714512, Clarion Bks.) HarperCollins Pubs.

Wilde, Terry Lee. The Vampire... in My Dreams. 2008. (ENG.). 244p. (YA). (gr. 7-12). pap. 13.00 (978-1-59998-837-5(2)) Samhain Publishing, LTD.

Williams, Guana Dunbar. The Wacky Winter Witch. William, Icebergg Dunbar, illus. 2003. (J). per. (978-0-9740673-1-5(8)) Graphix Network.

Williams, John Joseph. The Frightened Garden. 2013. 98p. (J). pap. (978-1-78299-167-0(0)) FeedARead.com.

Wilson, N. D. The Door Before (100 Cupboards Prequel) 2018. (100 Cupboards Ser.). 256p. (J). (gr. 3-7). 8.99 (978-0-449-81680-6(X), Yearling) Random Hse. Children's Bks.

Wilson, W. Shane. Little Monsters. 2009. 99p. pap. 11.96 (978-0-557-20687-2(1)) Lulu Pr., Inc.

Woollvin, Bethan. Hansel & Gretel. 2018. (ENG., Illus.). 32p. (J). (gr. k-4). 16.95 (978-1-68263-073-0(0)) Peachtree Publishing Co. Inc.

Wrede, Patricia C. Searching for Dragons. unabr. ed. 2004. (Enchanted Forest Chronicles: Bk. 2). 242p. (J). (gr. 5-18). pap. 38.00 incl. audio (978-0-8072-0670-6(9), Listening Library) Random Hse. Audio Publishing Group.

Yolen, Jane. Baba Yaga. Date not set. 32p. (J). (gr. -1-1). pap. 5.99 (978-0-06-443599-4(7)) HarperCollins Pubs.

—The Flying Witch. Vagin, Vladimir, illus. 2003. 40p. (J). (gr. -1-1). 15.99 (978-0-06-028536-4(2)) HarperCollins Pubs.

Yolen, Jane & Stemple, Heidi E. Y. The Salem Witch Trials: An Unsolved Mystery from History. Roth, Roger, Sr. & Roth, Roger, illus. 2004. (Unsolved Mystery from History Ser.). (ENG.). 32p. (J). (gr. 1-5). 18.99 (978-0-689-84620-5(7), Simon & Schuster Bks. For Young Readers) Simon & Schuster Bks. For Young Readers.

Zera, Beata. Little Puppy Swifty & Elle. 2008. 64p. pap. 21.99 (978-1-4257-6703-7(6)) Xlibris Corp.

Ziegler, Argentina Palacios, tr. Dora y la Princesa de la Nieve (Dora Saves the Snow Princess) Aikins, Dave, illus. 2008. (Dora la Exploradora Ser.). (SPA.). 24p. (J). (gr. -1-2). pap. 3.99 (978-1-4169-5870-3(3), Libros Para Ninos) Libros Para Ninos.

WIZARDS

Beahm, George. The Whimsic Alley Book of Spells: Mythical Incantations for Wizards of All Ages. Goldin, Stan, ed. 2007. (ENG., Illus.). 192p. (YA). pap. 14.95 (978-1-57174-535-4(1)) Hampton Roads Publishing Co., Inc.

Beaumont, Steve. How to Draw Witches & Wizards. (Drawing Fantasy Art Ser.). 32p. (gr. 4-5). 2009. 50.50 (978-1-61512-195-3(1), PowerKids Pr.) 2007. (ENG., Illus.). (J). lib. bdg. 30.27 (978-1-4042-3857-2(3), 8973b3b3-47ed-4314-8583-1b6ec68c04b8) Rosen Publishing Group, Inc., The.

—How to Draw Wizards, Warriors, Orcs & Elves. 2007. (Illus.). 143p. pap. 7.99 (978-0-7858-2345-2(X), Chartwell) Book Sales, Inc.

Clark, Jennifer. The Wizard's Workshop. 2018. (ENG.). (J). pap. 13.99 (978-1-4621-2167-0(5)) Cedar Fort, Inc./CFI Distribution.

Doherty, Gillian. 1001 Wizard Things to Spot. Gower, Teri, illus. 2008. (Usborne 1001 Things to Spot Ser.). 31p. (J). (gr. 4-7). 9.99 (978-0-7945-1860-8(5), Usborne) EDC Publishing.

Dooling, Sandra. Sorcerers, Spells, & Magic!, 1 vol., 1. 2013. (Jr. Graphic Monster Stories Ser.). (ENG.). 24p. (J). (gr. 2-3). 28.93 (978-1-4777-6211-0(6), 3647e898-4c6a-4fa0-952d-13c56c8fc89d, PowerKids Pr.) Rosen Publishing Group, Inc., The.

Kerns, Ann. Wizards & Witches. 2009. (Fantasy Chronicles Ser.). (ENG., Illus.). 48p. (gr. 4-7). lib. bdg. 27.93 (978-0-8225-9983-8(X)) Lerner Publishing Group.

Kilby, Janice Eaton, et al. The Book of Wizard Craft: In Which the Apprentice Finds Spells, Potions, Fantastic Tales & 50 Enchanting Things to Make. Burnett, Lindy, illus. 2019. (Books of Wizard Craft Ser.: 1). 144p. (J). (gr. 3-7). lthr. 19.95 (978-1-4549-3547-6(2)) Sterling Publishing Co., Inc.

Lee, Puck Hee. The Wizard Monk of Kamayut & Six Other True Stories. 2005. 48p. per. 10.00 (978-1-4134-8216-4(3)) Xlibris Corp.

Lehotsky, Chris. Wizards, 1 vol. 2016. (Creatures of Fantasy Ser.). (ENG., Illus.). 64p. (gr. 6-6). 35.93 (978-1-5026-1856-6(7), 5c6d8983-a063-4d35-bd92-ef72b0cd7df2) Cavendish Square Publishing LLC.

Mahoney, Emily. Learn Capitalization with Wizards, 1 vol. 2020. (Grammar Magic! Ser.). (ENG.). 24p. (gr. 2-3). pap. 9.15 (978-1-5382-4727-3(5), 747219ca-b071-411f-855b-eaf3afdd2ca1) Stevens, Gareth Publishing LLLP.

McIntee, David A. & McIntee, Lesley. Wizards, 1 vol. 2015. (Heroes & Legends Ser.). (ENG., Illus.). 88p. (J). (gr. 8-8). 38.80 (978-1-4994-6176-3(3), af5d3ef0-3f65-4293-a2b5-2dd769b24e36, Rosen Young Adult) Rosen Publishing Group, Inc., The.

Narayan, Natasha. Witches, Wizards & Warlocks of London. 2004. (Of London Ser.). (ENG., Illus.). 96p. (J). pap. 8.99 (978-1-904153-12-2(7)) Watling St., Ltd. GBR. Dist: Independent Pubs. Group.

Savage, Candace. Wizards: An Amazing Journey Through the Last Great Age of Magic. 2003. (ENG., Illus.). 80p. (J). (gr. 4-7). 17.95 (978-1-55054-943-0(X)) Greystone Books Ltd. CAN. Dist: Publishers Group West (PGW).

WIZARDS—FICTION

Abbott, Tony. The Chariot of Queen Zara (the Secrets of Droon #27) Merrell, David, illus. 2004. (Geronimo Stilton Ser.: 27). (ENG.). 128p. (J). (gr. 2-5). E-Book 7.99 (978-0-545-41840-9(2), Scholastic Paperbacks) Scholastic, Inc.

—Queen of Shadowthorn (the Secrets of Droon #31) 2018. (True Book (Relaunch) Ser.: 31). (ENG.). 128p. (J). (gr. 3-5). E-Book 31.00 (978-0-545-41844-7(5), Scholastic Paperbacks) Scholastic, Inc.

Alton, Steve. The Firehills. 2005. (ENG.). 192p. (YA). (gr. 5-12). 15.95 (978-1-57505-798-9(0), Carolrhoda Bks.) Lerner Publishing Group.

—The Malifex. 2003. (Middle Readers Ser.). (Illus.). 182p. (J). (gr. 3-7). 14.95 (978-0-8225-0959-2(8)) Lerner Publishing Group.

Ambrosio, Stefano. Mouse Magic. Pastrovicchio, Lorenzo, illus. 2010. (ENG.). 112p. (J). 24.99 (978-1-60886-550-5(9)); Vol. 1. pap. 9.99 (978-1-60886-541-3(X)) BOOM! Studios.

—Wizards of Mickey - Grand Tournament, Vol. 2. Pastrovicchio, Lorenzo & Magic Eye Studios, illus. 2010. (Wizards of Mickey Ser.). (ENG.). 128p. (J). (gr. 3-6). pap. 9.99 (978-1-60886-564-2(9)) BOOM! Studios.

Anderson, Scoular. Bubble Trouble (Wizzbang Wizard, Book 2). Book 2. Anderson, Scoular, illus. 2010. (Wizzbang Wizard Ser.: 2). (ENG., Illus.). 96p. (gr. 2-4). pap. 5.99 (978-0-00-719006-5(9), HarperCollins Children's Bks.) HarperCollins Pubs. Ltd. GBR. Dist: HarperCollins Pubs.

—Dragon Danger / Grasshopper Glue (Wizzbang Wizard) Anderson, Scoular, illus. 2011. (Wizzbang Wizard Ser.). (ENG., Illus.). 192p. (gr. 2-4). pap. 7.99 (978-0-00-719007-2(7), HarperCollins Children's Bks.) HarperCollins Pubs. Ltd. GBR. Dist: HarperCollins Pubs.

—Super Splosh (Wizzbang Wizard, Book 1), Book 1. Anderson, Scoular, illus. 2011. (Wizzbang Wizard Ser.: 1). (ENG., Illus.). 96p. (gr. 2-4). pap. 5.99 (978-0-00-719005-8(0), HarperCollins Children's Bks.) HarperCollins Pubs. Ltd. GBR. Dist: HarperCollins Pubs.

Anfuso, Dennis & Lindsay, Alan. Oz House. 2012. (ENG.). 321p. pap. 19.95 (978-1-57433-041-0(1)) Interset Pr.

Appleton, Victor. Tom Swift Omnibus #5: Tom Swift in Captivity, Tom Swift & His Wizard Camera, Tom Swift & His Great Searchlight. 2007. 312p. 24.95 (978-1-60459-106-4(4)); per. 12.99 (978-1-60459-105-7(6)) Wilder Pubns., Corp.

Baker, E. D. A Prince among Frogs. 2nd ed. 2015. (Tales of the Frog Princess Ser.). (ENG.). 240p. (YA). (gr. 3-6). pap. 9.99 (978-1-61963-624-8(7), 900142485, Bloomsbury USA Childrens) Bloomsbury Publishing USA.

Banerjee, Anjali. The Silver Spell. Fiegenshuh, Emily, illus. 2005. (Knights of the Silver Dragon Ser.: Bk. 8). 174p. (J). (978-1-4156-1645-1(0), Mirrorstone) Wizards of the Coast.

Barron, T. A. Doomraga's Revenge: Book 7, 7 vols., Bk. 7. 2011. (Merlin Saga Ser.: 7). (ENG.). 272p. (J). (gr. 5-18). 8.99 (978-0-14-241925-0(7), Puffin Books) Penguin Young Readers Group.

—The Dragon of Avalon: Book 6, Bk. 6. 2011. (Merlin Saga Ser.: 6). (ENG.). 336p. (J). (gr. 5-18). 8.99 (978-0-14-241924-3(9), Puffin Books) Penguin Young Readers Group.

—The Eternal Flame: Book 11, 11 vols. 2011. (Merlin Saga Ser.: 11). (ENG.). 416p. (J). (gr. 5-18). 9.99 (978-0-14-241929-8(X), Puffin Books) Penguin Young Readers Group.

—The Lost Years: Book 1, Bk. 1. 2011. (Merlin Saga Ser.: 1). (ENG.). 352p. (J). (gr. 5-18). 9.99 (978-0-14-241889-5(7), Puffin Books) Penguin Young Readers Group.

—The Lost Years of Merlin. unabr. ed. 2004. (Lost Years of Merlin Ser.: Bk. 1). 284p. (J). (gr. 5-9). pap. 46.00 incl. audio (978-0-8072-8766-8(0), YA261SP, Listening Library) Random Hse. Audio Publishing Group.

—The Raging Fires: Book 3, Bk. 3. 2011. (Merlin Saga Ser.: 3). (ENG.). 288p. (J). (gr. 5-18). 8.99 (978-0-14-241921-2(4), Puffin Books) Penguin Young Readers Group.

—The Seven Songs: Book 2, Bk. 2. 2011. (Merlin Saga Ser.: 2). (ENG.). 336p. (J). (gr. 5-18). 9.99 (978-0-14-241920-5(6), Puffin Books) Penguin Young Readers Group.

—Ultimate Magic: Book 8, 8 vols., Bk. 8. 2011. (Merlin Saga Ser.: 8). (ENG.). 256p. (J). (gr. 5-18). 8.99 (978-0-14-241926-7(5), Puffin Books) Penguin Young Readers Group.

—The Wizard's Wings: Book 5, Bk. 5. 2011. (Merlin Saga Ser.: 5). (ENG.). 384p. (J). (gr. 5-18). 8.99 (978-0-14-241923-6(0), Puffin Books) Penguin Young Readers Group.

Batham, Matthew. Lightsleep. 2006. 167p. pap. (978-1-904623-39-7(5)) WritersPrintShop.

Baum, L. Frank. Adventures in Oz: Dorothy & the Wizard in Oz, the Road to Oz, the Emerald City of Oz. 2007. 296p. 24.95 (978-1-60459-017-3(3)); per. 12.95 (978-1-60459-016-6(5)) Wilder Pubns., Corp.

—Adventures in Oz: The Patchwork Girl of Oz, Little Wizard Stories of Oz, Tik-Tok of Oz. 2007. 268p. 24.95 (978-1-60459-019-7(X)); per. 12.99 (978-1-60459-018-0(1)) Wilder Pubns., Corp.

—Complete Book of Oz: The Wonderful Wizard of Oz, the Marvelous Land of Oz, & Ozma of Oz, Vol. 1. 2009. 268p. (J). 24.95 (978-1-60459-711-0(9)) Wilder Pubns., Corp.

—Dorothy & the Wizard in Oz. 2019. (ENG.). (J). 142p. pap. 6.99 (978-0-368-73134-1(0)); 98p. pap. 10.71 (978-0-368-25974-6(9)) Blurb, Inc.

—Dorothy & the Wizard in Oz. (ENG.). (J). 2019. 244p. pap. 9.99 (978-1-7121-7489-0(4)) 2019. 244p. pap. 11.99 (978-1-7016-1879-4(6)) 2019. 332p. pap. 14.99 (978-1-6996-1197-5(1)) 2019. 334p. pap. 19.99 (978-1-6949-5664-4(4)) 2019. 276p. pap. 19.99 (978-1-6935-2914-6(9)) 2019. 334p. pap. 19.99 (978-1-6907-1041-7(1)) 2019. 482p. pap. 30.99 (978-1-6865-0513-3(2)) 2019. 244p. pap. 15.99 (978-1-0861-6605-7(1)) 2019. 296p. pap. 19.99 (978-1-0828-0289-8(1)) 2019. 334p. pap. 21.99 (978-1-0804-6450-0(6)) 2019. 488p. pap. 26.99 (978-1-0756-3610-3(8)) 2019. 260p. pap. 18.99 (978-1-0723-4222-9(7)) 2019. 336p. pap. 19.99 (978-1-0704-5458-0(3)) 2019. 402p. pap. 24.99 (978-1-0994-9744-5(2)) 2019. 246p. pap. 15.99 (978-1-0989-5773-5(3)) 2019. 190p. pap. 10.99 (978-1-0979-8618-7(7)) 2019. 402p. pap. 24.99 (978-1-0968-8175-9(6)) 2019. 334p. pap. 21.99 (978-1-0936-9118-4(2)) 2019. 246p. pap. 15.99 (978-1-0931-9183-7(X)) 2019. 282p. pap. 18.99 (978-1-0917-8010-1(2)) 2019. 282p. pap. 16.99 (978-1-7965-5884-5(2)) 2019. (Illus.). 184p. pap. 14.00 (978-1-7938-3201-6(3)) 2018. (Illus.). 470p. pap. 30.99 (978-1-7915-2681-8(0)) Independently Published.

—Dorothy & the Wizard in Oz, 1 vol. 2nd ed. 2016. (Wizard of Oz Collection). (ENG., Illus.). 172p. (J). (gr. 4-8). 7.99 (978-1-78226-308-1(X), 29ba1016-650a-4197-a7b9-28139a06af9f) Sweet Cherry Publishing GBR. Dist: Baker & Taylor Publisher Services (BTPS).

—Dorothy & the Wizard in Oz. 2017. (ENG., Illus.). (J). pap. (978-0-649-07630-7(3)) Trieste Publishing Pty Ltd.

—Dorothy & the Wizard of Oz. 2005. pap. (978-1-4065-0075-2(5)) Dodo Pr.

—Dorothy & the Wizard of Oz. 2004. (Twelve-Point Ser.). lib. bdg. 24.00 (978-1-58287-273-5(2)); lib. bdg. 25.00 (978-1-58287-769-3(6)) North Bks.

—Glinda of Oz. 2007. 108p. 22.95 (978-1-60312-591-8(4)) Aegypan.

—Large Hardback 1: L. Frank Baum's Original Oz Series. Wonderful Wizard of Oz, Marvelous Land of Oz, Ozma of Oz, Dorothy & the Wizard I. 2011. 1194p. (978-1-905921-22-5(5)) Shoes & Ships & Sealing Wax Ltd.

—Little Wizard Stories of Oz. Neill, John R., illus. 2011. (Dover Children's Classics Ser.). (ENG.). 160p. (J). (gr. 3-5). pap. 14.99 (978-0-486-47644-5(8)) Dover Pubns., Inc.

—La Mirinda Sorchisto de Oz. Broadribb, Donald, tr. Denslow, W. W., illus. 2012. 278p. pap. 24.00 (978-1-59569-245-0(2)) Mondial.

—The Treasury of Oz. 2007. 784p. 49.99 (978-1-60459-028-9(9)) Wilder Pubns., Corp.

—The Tresury of Oz: The Wonderful Wizard of Oz, the Marvelous Land of Oz, Ozma of Oz, Dorothy & the Wizard in Oz, the Road to Oz, the Emerald City Of. 2007. 548p. per. 19.49 (978-1-60459-029-6(7)) Wilder Pubns., Corp.

—The Wizard of Oz. Evangelista, Mauro, illus. 2007. (Usborne Young Reading: Series Two Ser.). 64p. (J). (gr. 3-7). 8.99 (978-0-7945-1457-0(X), Usborne) EDC Publishing.

—The Wizard of Oz. 2004. reprint ed. pap. 19.95 (978-1-4191-8832-9(1)) Kessinger Publishing, LLC.

—The Wizard of Oz. Denslow, W. W., illus. 2012. (Stepping Stone Book(TM) Ser.). 112p. (J). (gr. 1-4). 6.99 (978-0-375-86994-5(8), Random Hse. Bks. for Young Readers) Random Hse. Children's Bks.

—The Wizard of Oz: And Other Wonderful Books of Oz: the Emerald City of Oz & Glinda of Oz (Penguin Classics Deluxe Edition) Sumpter, Rachell, illus. deluxe ed. 2012. (Penguin Classics Deluxe Edition Ser.). 432p. (gr. 5). pap. 17.00 (978-0-14-310663-0(5), Penguin Classics) Penguin Publishing Group.

—The Wonderful Wizard of Oz. 2005. 180p. 26.95 (978-1-4218-0652-5(5), 1st World Library - Literary Society) 1st World Publishing, Inc.

—The Wonderful Wizard of Oz. 2007. (ENG.). 134p. pap. 19.99 (978-1-4264-4884-3(8)); 374p. pap. 18.99 (978-1-4264-4841-6(4)) Creative Media Partners, LLC.

—The Wonderful Wizard of Oz. Denslow, W. W. & Menten, Ted, illus. 2010. (Dover Read & Listen Ser.). (ENG.). 112p. (J). (gr. 1-5). pap. 14.99 (978-0-486-47725-1(8), 477258) Dover Pubns., Inc.

—The Wonderful Wizard of Oz: A Classic Story about Cooperation. 2003. (Illus.). 32p. per. 3.95 (978-0-9747133-5-9(X), Values to Live By Classic Stories) Thomas, Frederic Inc.

Baum, L. Frank & Neill, John R. III. Dorothy & the Wizard in Oz. 2018. (ENG., Illus.). 228p. (J). pap. 14.95 (978-1-378-96327-2(X)) Creative Media Partners, LLC.

Baxter, Nicola. Witches, Wizards & Magicians. Morton, Ken, illus. 2012. 80p. (J). (gr. k-4). pap. 9.99 (978-1-84322-807-3(6)) Anness Publishing GBR. Dist: National Bk. Network.

Benjamin, A. H. Shamwood. 2006. 140p. pap. 24.95 (978-1-4137-9193-8(X)) PublishAmerica, Inc.

Bennett, Jeffrey. El Mago Que Salvó el Mundo. Collier-Morales, Roberta, illus. 2011. (SPA.). 32p. (J). (gr. 2-4). 15.00 (978-0-9721819-5-2(4)) Big Kid Science.

—The Wizard Who Saved the World. Collier-Morales, Roberta, illus. 2011. (ENG.). 32p. (J). (gr. 2-4). 15.00 (978-0-9721819-4-5(6)) Big Kid Science.

Bergsma, Jody. Wizard. 2nd ed. 2008. (Illus.). 32p. (J). 15.95 (978-0-9740190-9-3(7)) Illumination Arts Publishing Co., Inc.

Birney, Betty G. The Princess & the Peabodys. 2007. (ENG.). 256p. (J). (gr. 5-9). 15.99 (978-0-06-084720-3(4)) HarperCollins Pubs.

Bishop, Desmond. The Wizard of Zee. 2012. 194p. pap. 14.95 (978-1-61897-447-1(5), Strategic Bk. Publishing) Strategic Book Publishing & Rights Agency (SBPRA).

Blackwood, Sage. Jinx's Fire. (Jinx Ser.: 3). (ENG.). 400p. (J). (gr. 3-7). 2016. pap. 9.99 (978-0-06-212997-0(X)) 2015. 16.99 (978-0-06-212996-3(1)) HarperCollins Pubs. (Tegen, Katherine Bks).

—Jinx's Magic. 2014. (Jinx Ser.: 2). (ENG.). 400p. (J). (gr. 3-7). 16.99 (978-0-06-212993-2(7), Tegen, Katherine Bks) HarperCollins Pubs.

Blade, Adam. Beast Quest: Master Your Destiny 2: the Dagger of Doom. 2014. (Beast Quest Ser.). (ENG., Illus.). 128p. (J). (gr. 2-4). 5.99 (978-1-4083-1406-7(1), Orchard Bks.) Hachette Children's Group GBR. Dist: Hachette Bk. Group.

—Beast Quest: Master Your Destiny 3: the Pirate's Curse. 2016. (Beast Quest Ser.). (ENG., Illus.). 144p. (J). (gr. 2-4). pap. 5.99 (978-1-4083-1840-9(7), Orchard Bks.) Hachette Children's Group GBR. Dist: Hachette Bk. Group.

—Vedra & Krimon the Twin Dragons. 2012. (Beast Quest Special Edition Ser.: 2). (Illus.). 187p. lib. bdg. 16.00 (978-0-606-26187-6(7)) Turtleback.

Blashfield, Jean F. Realm of the Enchanter. 2007. (Paths of Doom Ser.). (Illus.). 127p. (J). per. 4.99 (978-1-931567-73-2(5)) Margaret Weis Productions, Ltd.

Blunden, Alan. Tommy & the Garden Shed. 2008. 104p. pap. (978-1-84923-111-4(7)) YouWriteOn.

Brittain, Bill. The Wizards & the Monster. Date not set. 96p. (J). (gr. 2-5). pap. 4.25 (978-0-06-442003-7(5)) HarperCollins Pubs.

Brodhead, Kimberly. Gaden's Tower: Book One. 2007. 164p. per. 24.95 (978-1-60441-038-9(8)) America Star Bks.

Brown, Ruth E. The Goontoff Kingdom Chronicles: The Bogus King. 2011. 46p. pap. 16.95 (978-1-4560-8346-5(5)) America Star Bks.

Bucay, Jorge. The King & the Magician. Gusti, illus. 2014. (ENG.). 52p. (J). (gr. -1). 14.95 (978-0-7892-1204-7(8), 791204, Abbeville Kids) Abbeville Pr., Inc.

Card, Orson Scott. Stonefather. Kidd, Tom, illus. 2008. 112p. 35.00 (978-1-59606-194-1(4)) Subterranean Pr.

Carter, Grant Matthew. The Disaster Caster. Morling, Donovan, illus. 2012. 38p. pap. 16.00 (978-1-4349-8432-6(X), RoseDog Bks.) Dorrance Publishing Co., Inc.

Catipon, Atreyu. The Wizard's Magic Hat. 2012. 26p. 16.00 (978-1-61863-390-3(2)) Bookstand Publishing.

Chance, Kim. Keeper. 2018. (Keeper Duology Ser.). (ENG.). 408p. (YA). (gr. 9-12). pap. 14.99 (978-1-63583-012-5(5), 1635830125, Flux) North Star Editions.

—Keeper. 2018. lib. bdg. 26.95 (978-0-606-41244-5(1)) Turtleback.

ima, Cinda Williams. The Crimson Crown. 2013. (Seven Realms Novel Ser.: 4). (ENG.). 624p. (YA). (gr. 7-17). pap. 11.99 *(978-1-4231-5214-9(X))* Little, Brown Bks. for Young Readers.
-The Demon King. 2010. (Seven Realms Novel Ser.: 1). (ENG.). 528p. (YA). (gr. 7-17). pap. 12.99 *(978-1-4231-2136-7(8))* Little, Brown Bks. for Young Readers.
-The Dragon Heir. 2009. (Heir Chronicles Ser.: 3). (ENG., Illus.). 528p. (YA). (gr. 7-17). pap. 11.99 *(978-1-4231-1071-2(4))* Little, Brown Bks. for Young Readers.
-The Enchanter Heir. 2013. (Heir Chronicles Ser.: 4). (ENG.). 464p. (YA). (gr. 7-12). E-Book 45.00 *(978-1-4231-8789-9(X))* Little, Brown Bks. for Young Readers.
-The Exiled Queen. 2011. (Seven Realms Novel Ser.: 2). (ENG.). 608p. (YA). (gr. 7-17). pap. 11.99 *(978-1-4231-2137-4(6))* Little, Brown Bks. for Young Readers.
-The Gray Wolf Throne. 2012. (Seven Realms Novel Ser.: 3). (ENG.). 544p. (YA). (gr. 7-17). pap. 11.99 *(978-1-4231-2138-1(4))* Little, Brown Bks. for Young Readers.
—The Sorcerer Heir. 2016. (Heir Chronicles Ser.: 5). (ENG.). 560p. (YA). (gr. 7-12). pap. 11.99 *(978-1-4231-9475-0(6))* Little, Brown Bks. for Young Readers.
—The Warrior Heir. 2007. (Heir Chronicles Ser.: 1). (ENG.). 448p. (YA). (gr. 7-17). pap. 11.99 *(978-0-7868-3917-9(1))* Little, Brown Bks. for Young Readers.
—The Warrior Heir. 2006. (Heir Chronicles: No. 1). 1.00 *(978-1-4294-0323-8(3))* Recorded Bks., Inc.
—The Wizard Heir. 2008. (Heir Chronicles Ser.: 2). (ENG.). 480p. (YA). (gr. 7-17). pap. 12.99 *(978-1-4231-0488-9(9))* Little, Brown Bks. for Young Readers.
Clare, Cassandra & Chu, Wesley. The Red Scrolls of Magic. 2020. (Eldest Curses Ser.: 1). (ENG.). 384p. (YA). (gr. 9). pap. 14.99 *(978-1-4814-9509-7(7)*, McElderry, Margaret K. Bks.) McElderry, Margaret K. Bks.
—The Red Scrolls of Magic. 2019. (Eldest Curses Ser.: 1). (ENG., Illus.). 368p. (YA). (gr. 9). 24.99 *(978-1-4814-9508-0(9)*, SAGA Press) Simon & Schuster Bks. For Young Readers.
Clark, Platte F. Bad Unicorn. 2013. (Bad Unicorn Trilogy Ser.: 1). (ENG., Illus.). 432p. (J). (gr. 3-7). 18.99 *(978-1-4424-5012-7(6)*, Aladdin) Simon & Schuster Children's Publishing.
—Good Ogre. 2015. (Bad Unicorn Trilogy Ser.: 3). (ENG., Illus.). 384p. (J). (gr. 3-7). 17.99 *(978-1-4424-5018-9(5)*, Aladdin) Simon & Schuster Children's Publishing.
Cluess, Jessica. A Shadow Bright & Burning (Kingdom on Fire, Book One) 2017. (Kingdom on Fire Ser.: 1). (ENG.). 432p. (YA). (gr. 7). pap. 9.99 *(978-0-553-53593-8(5)*, Ember) Random Hse. Children's Bks.
Cole, Bob. Power Reading: Chapter Books/Wizard of OZ. Sirrell, Terri, illus. 2004. 94p. (J). (gr. 3-4). vinyl bd. 39.95 *(978-1-883186-64-7(1)*, PPCL1) National Reading Styles Institute, Inc.
—Power Reading: Comic Book/Wizard of OZ. Sirrell, Terri, illus. 2005. 60p. (J). (gr. 3-4). vinyl bd. 39.95 *(978-1-883186-80-7(3)*, PPCLC1) National Reading Styles Institute, Inc.
Colebourn, Craig. The Knights of Videnland: Passing the Torch. 2007. 428p. per. 23.95 *(978-0-595-46989-5(2))* iUniverse, Inc.
Connolly, MarcyKate. Monstrous. 2016. (J). lib. bdg. 18.40 *(978-0-606-38136-9(8))* Turtleback.
Cook, Jeremy. The Illusion Stick. 2008. 115p. pap. 19.95 *(978-1-60474-705-8(6))* America Star Bks.
Coonan, Candace N. The Darkest Hour: Tales from Fadreama: Book 1. 2012. 328p. (gr. 4-6). pap. 19.11 *(978-1-4669-3565-5(0))* Trafford Publishing.
Cooper, Susan. The Word Pirates. Kellogg, Steven, illus. 2019. 40p. (J). (gr. -1-3). 18.99 *(978-0-8234-4359-8(0)*, Neal Porter Bks) Holiday Hse., Inc.
Cormier, Shawn P. Nomadin. 2003. 296p. (YA). per. 12.95 *(978-0-9740151-0-1(5))* Pine View Pr.
Cox, R. The Lonely Wizard Named Wizzy: The Apprentice. 2009. 16p. pap. 8.49 *(978-1-4490-2236-5(7))* AuthorHouse.
Croggon, Alison. The Singing: Book Four of Pellinor. 2017. (Pellinor Ser.). (ENG.). 496p. (J). (gr. 7). pap. 9.99 *(978-0-7636-9446-3(0))* Candlewick Pr.
Cyrus, Kurt. Be a Good Dragon. Cyrus, Kurt, illus. 2018. (ENG., Illus.). 32p. (J). (gr. k-3). 16.99 *(978-1-58536-383-4(9)*, 204395) Sleeping Bear Pr.
Daily, Lorrie Ann. The Castlewood Twins, the Magic Begins. 2008. 196p. pap. 12.95 *(978-0-9820479-8-9(3))* Peppertree Pr., The.
Darlison, Aleesah. Ellabeth's Light. Brailsford, Jill, illus. 2017. (Unicorn Riders Ser.). (ENG.). 112p. (J). (gr. 3-5). pap. 5.95 *(978-1-4795-6559-7(8)*, 128549, Picture Window Bks.) Capstone.
Davis, Graeme. Re-Read Harry Potter & the Chamber of Secrets Today! an Unauthorized Guide. 2008. 112p. pap. 15.49 *(978-1-934840-72-6(6))* Nimble Bks. LLC.
Disney Press Staff. School's Out. 2010. 128p. pap. 4.99 *(978-1-4231-2677-5(7))* Disney Pr.
Dokey, Cameron. Golden: A Retelling Of "Rapunzel" 2007. (Once upon a Time Ser.). (ENG.). 192p. (YA). (gr. 7-9). mass mkt. 8.99 *(978-1-4169-3926-9(1)*, Simon Pulse) Simon Pulse.
Donaldson, Julia. Superworm. Scheffler, Axel, illus. 2014. (ENG.). 32p. (J). (gr. -1-3). 16.99 *(978-0-545-59176-8(7)*, Levine, Arthur A. Bks.) Scholastic, Inc.
Downer, Ann. The Dragon of Never-Was. Rayyan, Omar, illus. 2008. (ENG.). 320p. (J). (gr. 3-6). pap. 14.99 *(978-1-4169-5453-8(8)*, Atheneum Bks. for Young Readers) Simon & Schuster Children's Publishing.
—Hatching Magic. Rayyan, Omar, illus. 2004. 242p. 16.00 *(978-0-7569-3481-1(8))* Perfection Learning Corp.
Dozier, Kim. The Backwards Wizard. Dozier, Ashlyn McCauley & Dozier, Makenna Joy, illus. l.t. ed. 2005. (ENG.). 28p. (J). 10.00 *(978-0-9745839-4-5(4)*, Fun to Read Bks. with Royally Good Morals) MKADesigns.
Drischel, Candy L. Restless with the Dark Moon Rising. 2008. 105p. pap. 19.95 *(978-1-60610-421-7(7))* America Star Bks.
Duane, Diane. Games Wizards Play. 2017. (Young Wizards Ser.: 10). (ENG.). 640p. (YA). (gr. 7). pap. 8.99 *(978-0-544-81323-6(5)*, 1641929, Clarion Bks.) HarperCollins Pubs.
—High Wizardry. 7 vols. (Young Wizards Ser.: 3). (J). 2006. 90.75 *(978-1-4025-9917-0(X))* 2004. 93.75 *(978-1-4025-8355-1(9))* Recorded Bks., Inc.
—A Wizard Alone: The Sixth Book in the Young Wizards Series. (Young Wizards Ser.: 6). (ENG., (J). (gr. 5-7). 2005. Illus.). 348p. pap. 6.95 *(978-0-15-205509-7(6)*, 1196571) 2003. 352p. pap. 8.99 *(978-0-15-204911-9(8)*, 1194830) HarperCollins Pubs. (Clarion Bks.).
—Wizards at War Bk. 8: The Eighth Book in the Young Wizards Series. 2007. (Young Wizards Ser.: 8). (ENG., Illus.). 560p. (J). (gr. 7-9). pap. 8.99 *(978-0-15-205223-2(2)*, 1195741, Clarion Bks.) HarperCollins Pubs.
—The Wizard's Dilemma: The Fifth Book in the Young Wizards Series. 2005. (Young Wizards Ser.: 5). (ENG., Illus.). 432p. (J). (gr. 5-7). pap. 6.95 *(978-0-15-205491-5(X)*, 1196520, Clarion Bks.) HarperCollins Pubs.
Dunn, Edward Grieves. Crinkles Academy for Wizards. 2008. 424p. pap. *(978-1-906210-98-4(5))* Grosvenor Hse. Publishing Ltd.
Edwards, Garth. The Blue Wizard. Stasyuk, Max, illus. 2011. (Adventures of Titch & Mitch Ser.). (J). pap. *(978-0-9567449-9-9(0))* Inside Pocket Publishing, Ltd.
—The #05 Blue Wizard. Stasyuk, Max, illus. 2011. (Adventures of Titch & Mitch, the Ser.). (J). pap. *(978-0-7613-8425-0(1))* Inside Pocket Publishing, Ltd.
Elgert, C. J. The Elder Brothers & the Dragon's Portal. 2011. 236p. (gr. 4-6). 25.95 *(978-1-4620-1467-5(4))*; pap. 15.95 *(978-1-4620-1466-8(6))* iUniverse, Inc.
Eliotte, Lisa J. The Adventures of Derby Doodle. 2009. 640p. pap. 25.99 *(978-1-4389-3058-9(5))* AuthorHouse.
Ellis, Larry & Ellis, Denise Brown. Antigua: The Land of Fairies Wizards & Heroes. 2007. (ENG.). 300p. 28.49 *(978-1-4343-1400-0(6))*; per. 17.99 *(978-1-4259-9782-3(1))* AuthorHouse.
Ende, Michael. The Night of Wishes: Or the Satanarchaeolidealcohellish Notion Potion. Schwarzbauer, Heike & Takvorian, Rick, trs. Kehn, Regina, illus. 2017. 216p. (J). (gr. 3-7). 16.95 *(978-1-68137-188-7(X)*, NYR Children's Collection) New York Review of Bks., Inc., The.
Epstein, Adam Jay & Jacobson, Andrew. Circle of Heroes. (Familiars Ser.: 3). (ENG.). 336p. (J). (gr. 3-7). 2013. pap. 7.99 *(978-0-06-196116-8(7))* 2012. (Illus.). 16.99 *(978-0-06-196114-4(0))* HarperCollins Pubs. (HarperCollins).
—The Familiars. (Familiars Ser.: 1). (ENG.). (J). (gr. 3-7). 2011. 384p. pap. 9.99 *(978-0-06-196110-6(8))* 2010. (Illus.). 368p. 17.99 *(978-0-06-196108-3(6))* HarperCollins Pubs. (HarperCollins).
—Secrets of the Crown. (Familiars Ser.: 2). (ENG.). (J). (gr. 3-7). 2012. 400p. pap. 7.99 *(978-0-06-196113-7(2))* 2011. 384p. 16.99 *(978-0-06-196111-3(6))* HarperCollins Pubs. (HarperCollins).
Eubank, Patricia Reeder. The Princess & the Snarls. Eubank, Patricia Reeder, illus. 2006. (ENG., Illus.). 32p. (J). (gr. k-3). 16.95 *(978-0-8249-5536-6(6)*, Ideals Pubns.) Worthy Publishing.
Fagan, Deva. Rival Magic. 2021. (ENG.). 320p. (J). (gr. 3-7). pap. 7.99 *(978-1-5344-3906-1(4)*, Atheneum Bks. for Young Readers) Simon & Schuster Children's Publishing.
Feasey, Steve. Dark Moon: A Wereling Novel. 2011. (Wereling Ser.: 2). (ENG.). 336p. (YA). (gr. 7-18). pap. 19.99 *(978-0-312-64643-1(7)*, 900068714) Feiwel & Friends.
Fernandez, David R. Lady Godiva & the Legend of the Black Rose. 2008. (Illus.). 32p. (J). pap. 8.99 *(978-0-9817521-4-3(4))* Mirror Publishing.
Fischer, David. Heir to Oswyn. 2011. 66p. pap. 19.95 *(978-1-4626-2581-9(9))* America Star Bks.
Flannigan, Liz. Cara & the Wizard, 2 vols. Docampo, Valeria, illus. 2013. (Magic Stories Ser.). 48p. (J). (gr. 1-4). pap. 8.99 *(978-1-84686-780-4(0))* Barefoot Bks., Inc.
Fletcher, Pamela. Who Is Freddy Farlittle? 2011. 40p. pap. 16.99 *(978-1-4634-1086-5(7))* AuthorHouse.
Flood, Tony. Jody Richards & the Secret Potion. 2nd ed. 2012. 146p. pap. *(978-0-9569682-9-6(5))* My Voice Publishing.
Födi, Lee Edward. Kendra Kandlestar & the Crack in Kazah. Födi, Lee Edward, illus. 2011. (ENG., Illus.). 282p. (J). (gr. 4-7). 16.95 *(978-1-61254-018-4(X))* Brown Books Publishing Group.
Forman, M. L. Adventurers Wanted, Book 1: Slathbog's Gold. 2011. (Adventurers Wanted Ser.: 1). (ENG.). 416p. (J). (gr. 5). mass mkt. 9.99 *(978-1-60641-681-5(2)*, 5053131, Shadow Mountain) Shadow Mountain Publishing.
—Adventurers Wanted, Book 2: The Horn of Moran. 2011. 400p. 39.99 *(978-1-60641-255-8(8))* Deseret Bk. Co.
—Adventurers Wanted, Book 2: The Horn of Moran. 2012. (Adventurers Wanted Ser.: 2). (ENG.). 384p. (J). (gr. 5). pap. 9.99 *(978-1-60908-911-5(1)*, 5069125, Shadow Mountain) Shadow Mountain Publishing.
—Adventurers Wanted, Book 3: Albrek's Tomb. 2013. (Adventurers Wanted Ser.: 3). (ENG.). 504p. (J). (gr. 5). pap. 9.99 *(978-1-60907-339-8(8)*, 5097801, Shadow Mountain) Shadow Mountain Publishing.
—Adventurers Wanted, Book 4: Sands of Nezza. 2013. (Adventurers Wanted Ser.: 4). (ENG.). 400p. (J). (gr. 5). 19.99 *(978-1-60907-329-9(0)*, 5097486, Shadow Mountain) Shadow Mountain Publishing.
—Adventurers Wanted, Book 3: Albrek's Tomb. 2012. x, 494p. (YA). 19.99 *(978-1-60908-892-7(1))* Deseret Bk. Co.
Forman, Mark. The Horn of Moran. 2011. 400p. (YA). (gr. 3-18). 18.99 *(978-0-60641-226-8(4)*, Shadow Mountain) Shadow Mountain Publishing.
—Slathbog's Gold. 2009. (Adventurers Wanted Ser.: Bk. 1). 432p. (J). 17.95 *(978-1-60641-029-5(6)*, Shadow Mountain) Shadow Mountain Publishing.
Forward, Toby. Dragonborn. 2013. (Dragonborn Ser.: 1). (ENG.). 368p. (J). (gr. 3-6). pap. 9.99 *(978-1-59990-983-7(9)*, 900096406, Bloomsbury USA Childrens) Bloomsbury Publishing USA.
—Starborn: A Dragonborn Novel. 2017. (Dragonborn Ser.). (ENG.). 448p. (J). pap. 9.99 *(978-1-68119-277-2(2)*, 900165494, Bloomsbury USA Childrens) Bloomsbury Publishing USA.
Foxlee, Karen. A Most Magical Girl. 2017. (ENG.). 304p. (J). (gr. 3-7). 8.99 *(978-0-553-51288-5(9)*, Yearling) Random Hse. Children's Bks.
Fridolfs, Derek. Black Adam & the Eternity War. Levins, Tim, illus. 2018. (Justice League Ser.). (ENG.). 88p. (J). (gr. 2-6). lib. bdg. 27.32 *(978-1-4965-5981-4(9)*, 137330, Stone Arch Bks.) Capstone.
Frost, C. Amethyst. Mourning under the Bridge. 2012. 280p. pap. 9.99 *(978-0-9847236-2-1(5))* Frost, C. A.
Gallego García, Laura & Peden, Margaret Sayers. The Valley of the Wolves. 2006. 247p. (J). pap. *(978-0-439-58554-5(6)*, Levine, Arthur A. Bks.) Scholastic, Inc.
Garner, Alan. The Moon of Gomrath: A Tale of Alderley. 2006. (ENG., Illus.). 216p. (J). (gr. 4-8). pap. 13.95 *(978-0-15-205630-8(0))* Houghton Mifflin Harcourt Publishing Co.
—The Weirdstone of Brisingamen: A Tale of Alderley. 2006. (ENG., Illus.). 288p. (J). (gr. 4-8). pap. 16.95 *(978-0-15-205636-0(X))* Houghton Mifflin Harcourt Publishing Co.
George, Jessica Day. Fridays with the Wizards. 2016. (Tuesdays at the Castle Ser.: 4). (ENG.). 240p. (YA). 16.99 *(978-1-61963-429-9(5)*, 900135951, Bloomsbury USA Childrens) Bloomsbury Publishing USA.
Gogonya, Carol. The African Mermaid & Other Stories. 2011. 40p. pap. 32.70 *(978-1-4568-5416-4(X))* Xlibris Corp.
Goodyear-Brown, Paris. Gabby the Gecko. 2003. per. *(978-1-932203-54-7(0))* Sundog, Ltd.
Gordon, Sylvia. Further Adventures of the Potty Wizard & His Cat, Muddles. 2009. (Illus.). 60p. pap. 10.49 *(978-1-4389-6819-3(1))* AuthorHouse.
Grace, N. B. Rev It Up! 9th ed. 2010. (Wizards of Waverly Place Ser.: No. 9). 128p. (J). (gr. 3-7). pap. 4.99 *(978-1-4231-2676-8(9))* Disney Pr.
Graham, Deborah. The Magic Comes Back: A Max & Sam Adventure. 2012. 66p. (gr. 2-4). pap. 8.95 *(978-1-4759-4758-8(5))* iUniverse, Inc.
Grove, Malachai. The Return of Malachai. 2011. 24p. pap. 14.99 *(978-1-4567-6257-5(5))* AuthorHouse.
Haining, Peter. Magicians' Circle. 2012. 348p. (-18). pap. *(978-1-4596-4365-9(8))* ReadHowYouWant.com, Ltd.
Hamley, Dennis. Hawk's Vision. 2006. 116p. per. *(978-1-904529-20-0(8)*, Back to Front) Solidus.
Helm, Julie G. Merlin for Sherman. Cary, Debbi G., photos by. 2010. (Illus.). 84p. pap. 26.49 *(978-1-4520-5183-3(6))* AuthorHouse.
Henderson, Hugh. VanDland. 2012. 112p. pap. 10.95 *(978-1-61204-859-8(5)*, Strategic Bk. Publishing) Strategic Book Publishing & Rights Agency (SBPRA).
Hook, Carol A. Before There Were Stars: An Orange Dragon. 2009. 48p. pap. 8.95 *(978-1-4401-5475-1(9))* iUniverse, Inc.
Hounam, Donald. A Dangerous Magic. 2017. (ENG., Illus.). 352p. (YA). (gr. 5-12). 17.99 *(978-1-5124-3232-9(6)*, ce27e1d0-1960-495f-a52b-2d7bd78c0eca, Carolrhoda Lab™) Lerner Publishing Group.
James, Kari, adapted by. Barbie & the Magic of Pegasus: A Junior Novelization. 2005. (Illus.). 72p. pap. *(978-0-439-78542-6(1))* Scholastic, Inc.
Joe Thomson-Swift. The Magic Stone. 2011. 92p. pap. *(978-1-908105-83-7(6))* Grosvenor Hse. Publishing Ltd.
Jones, Diana Wynne. House of Many Ways. 2008. 404p. (J). 9.99 *(978-0-06-147798-0(2)*, Greenwillow Bks.) HarperCollins Pubs.
—House of Many Ways. 2009. (J). 1.25 *(978-1-4361-6123-7(1))*; 79.75 *(978-1-4361-6128-2(2))*; 100.75 *(978-1-4361-6132-9(0))*; 245.75 *(978-1-4361-6127-5(4))*; 102.75 *(978-1-4361-6130-5(4))* Recorded Bks., Inc.
—Howl's Moving Castle. 2008. (World of Howl Ser.: 1). (ENG.). 448p. (J). (gr. 3-7). pap. 11.99 *(978-0-06-147878-9(4)*, Greenwillow Bks.) HarperCollins Pubs.
—Howl's Moving Castle. 2009. 9.00 *(978-0-7848-2484-9(3)*, Everbind) Marco Bk. Co.
—Howl's Moving Castle, 8 vols. 2008. (YA). 101.75 *(978-1-4361-5953-1(9))*; 179.75 *(978-1-4361-5948-7(2))*; 104.75 *(978-1-4361-5951-7(2))*; 1.25 *(978-1-4361-5944-9(X))*; 75.75 *(978-1-4361-5949-4(0))*; 78.75 *(978-1-4361-5947-0(4))* Recorded Bks., Inc.
Jones, J. J. Flute Tudor & the Secret Order. 2012. 304p. 22.95 *(978-1-4575-1302-2(1))* Dog Ear Publishing, LLC.
Jones, Marcia & Dadey, Debbie. Wizards Do Roast Turkeys. Dreidemy, Joëlle, illus. 2007. 64p. (J). pap. *(978-0-545-00235-6(4))* Scholastic, Inc.
Joyce, William. E. Aster Bunnymund & the Warrior Eggs at the Earth's Core! Joyce, William, illus. (Guardians Ser.: 2). (ENG., Illus.). (J). (gr. 2-6). 2018. 288p. pap. 8.99 *(978-1-4424-3051-8(6))*Bk. 2. 2012. 272p. 18.99 *(978-1-4424-3050-1(8))* Simon & Schuster Children's Publishing. (Atheneum Bks. for Young Readers).
Joyce, William & Geringer, Laura. Nicholas St. North & the Battle of the Nightmare King. Joyce, William, illus. 2018. (Guardians Ser.: 1). (ENG., Illus.). 256p. (J). (gr. 2-6). pap. 8.99 *(978-1-4424-3049-5(4)*, Atheneum Bks. for Young Readers) Simon & Schuster Children's Publishing.
—Nicholas St. North & the Battle of the Nightmare King, Bk. 1. Joyce, William, illus. 2011. (Guardians Ser.: 1). (ENG., Illus.). 240p. (J). (gr. 2-6). 18.99 *(978-1-4424-3048-8(6)*, Atheneum Bks. for Young Readers) Simon & Schuster Children's Publishing.
K., J. Harry Potter e Il Prigioniero Di Azkaban. (Harry Potter Ser.: Year 3). (ITA.). pap. 32.95 *(978-88-7782-852-1(8))* Salani ITA. Dist: Distribooks, Inc.
Kent, Elizabeth. The Enchanted Adventures of the Caroline Kemps. 2007. 148p. pap. 24.95 *(978-1-4241-9915-0(8))* America Star Bks.
Kent, Jaden. Ella & Owen 1: the Cave of Aaaaah! Doom! Bodnaruk, Iryna, illus. 2017. (Ella & Owen Ser.: 1). (ENG.). 112p. (J). (gr. k-3). pap. 5.99 *(978-1-4998-0368-6(0))* Little Bee Books Inc.
Kilgore, Lee. Widga's Quest, 1 vol. 2009. 48p. pap. 16.95 *(978-1-4489-2517-9(7))* America Star Bks.
King, J. R. Arianna Kelt & the Renegades of Time: Deluxe Edition, Wizards of Skyhall Book 2. 2008. (ENG.). 252p. (YA). per. 15.95 *(978-1-57545-120-6(4))* RP Media.
—Arianna Kelt & the Renegades of Time: Signature Edition, Wizards of Skyhall Book 2. 2008. (ENG.). 256p. (J). 18.95 *(978-1-57545-165-7(4)*, Reagent Pr. Echo) RP Media.
—Arianna Kelt & the Wizards of Skyhall. (J). 2008. (ENG.). 200p. 18.95 *(978-1-57545-164-0(6)*, Reagent Pr. Echo) 2006. (Illus.). 200p. pap. 11.95 *(978-1-57545-115-2(8))* 2006. (Illus.). 148p. per. 18.95 *(978-1-57545-106-0(9)*, Reagent Pr. Echo) RP Media.
—Arianna Kelt & the Wizards of Skyhall: Deluxe Edition, Wizards of Skyhall Book 1. 2008. (ENG.). 200p. (YA). per. 14.95 *(978-1-57545-170-1(0))* RP Media.
Kinton, P. D. Wishing for Wizards & Chips for Te. 2010. 28p. pap. *(978-1-907211-26-3(8))* Grosvenor Hse. Publishing Ltd.
Klett, David E. Rachel & the Wizard of Lake Lure: The Lake Lure Chronicles - Book 2. 2006. (Illus.). (J). lib. bdg. 17.95 *(978-0-9779325-1-1(6))* Five Oaks Pr.
Koller, Jackie French. A Wizard Named Nell. 2003. (ENG., Illus.). 208p. (J). (gr. 3-7). pap. 11.95 *(978-0-689-85591-7(5)*, Aladdin) Simon & Schuster Children's Publishing.
—The Wizard's Apprentice. 2003. (ENG., Illus.). 192p. (J). (gr. 3-7). pap. 9.99 *(978-0-689-85592-4(3)*, Aladdin) Simon & Schuster Children's Publishing.
—The Wizard's Scepter. 2012. (ENG., Illus.). 176p. (J). (gr. 3-7). pap. 9.99 *(978-0-689-85593-1(1)*, Aladdin) Simon & Schuster Children's Publishing.
Korczak, Janusz. Kaytek the Wizard. Lloyd-Jones, Antonia, tr. 2012. (ENG.). 272p. (J). (gr. 4-7). 17.95 *(978-0-9838685-0-7(6))* Flashlight Pr.
Kositsky, Lynne. Minerva's Voyage. 2009. (ENG., Illus.). 240p. (YA). (gr. 6-18). pap. 10.99 *(978-1-55488-439-1(X))* Dundurn Pr. CAN. Dist: Publishers Group West (PGW).
Kumin, Maxine & Sexton, Anne. The Wizard's Tears. Katz, Keren, illus. 2019. 48p. (J). (gr. k-4). 18.95 *(978-1-60980-875-4(4)*, Triangle Square) Seven Stories Pr.
Lacle, Tony. A Man Called Avalon. 2006. 156p. per. 15.63 *(978-1-4120-5609-0(8))* Trafford Publishing.
Lamb, Enelle. Christopher Collin & the True Okemus - the Adventure Begins. 2009. (ENG.). 123p. pap. 13.00 *(978-0-557-05783-2(3))* Lulu Pr., Inc.
Landy, Derek. Dark Days (Skulduggery Pleasant, Book 4), Book 4. (ENG.). 416p. pap. *(978-0-00-732597-9(5))* HarperCollins Children's Bks.
—Death Bringer (Skulduggery Pleasant, Book 6) 2018. (Skulduggery Pleasant Ser.: 6). (ENG.). 608p. (J). 7.99 *(978-0-00-826638-7(7)*, HarperCollins Children's Bks.) HarperCollins Pubs. Ltd. GBR. Dist: HarperCollins Pubs.
—The Faceless Ones. (Skulduggery Pleasant Ser.: 3). (ENG.). 432p. (J). (gr. 5). 2010. pap. 7.99 *(978-0-06-124093-5(1))* 2009. 16.99 *(978-0-06-124091-1(5))* HarperCollins Pubs.
—Mortal Coil (Skulduggery Pleasant, Book 5) 2018. (Skulduggery Pleasant Ser.: 5). (ENG.). 576p. (J). 7.99 *(978-0-00-826636-3(0)*, HarperCollins Children's Bks.) HarperCollins Pubs. Ltd. GBR. Dist: HarperCollins Pubs.
—Playing with Fire. 2008. (Skulduggery Pleasant Ser.: 2). (ENG.). 400p. (J). (gr. 5-9). 16.99 *(978-0-06-124088-1(5))* HarperCollins Pubs.
—Scepter of the Ancients. Percival, Tom, illus. 2008. (Skulduggery Pleasant Ser.: 1). (ENG.). 416p. (J). (gr. 5). pap. 7.99 *(978-0-06-123117-9(7))* HarperCollins Pubs.
Launchbury, Jane. Witch & Wizard Stories. 2012. (ENG., Illus.). 64p. (J). 9.95 *(978-1-84135-103-2(2))* Award Pubns. Ltd. GBR. Dist: Parkwest Pubns., Inc.
Le Guin, Ursula. K. Tehanu. 2012. (Earthsea Cycle Ser.: 4). (ENG., Illus.). 320p. (YA). (gr. 7). pap. 11.99 *(978-1-4424-5996-0(4)*, Atheneum Bks. for Young Readers) Simon & Schuster Children's Publishing.
Le Guin, Ursula K. A Wizard of Earthsea. 2012. (Earthsea Cycle Ser.: Vol. 1). (ENG.). (YA). (gr. 7). lib. bdg. 19.60 *(978-1-68065-210-9(9))* Perfection Learning Corp.
—A Wizard of Earthsea. 2012. (Earthsea Ser.: 1). lib. bdg. 19.65 *(978-0-606-26624-6(0))* Turtleback.
Lee, Brian. Bouncey the Elf & Friends - Bedtime St. 2005. (ENG., Illus.). 53p. pap. *(978-0-7552-1023-7(9))* Authors OnLine, Ltd.
Lehane, Pearse. The Train That Never Came. 2008. 328p. pap. *(978-1-84923-249-4(0))* YouWriteOn.
Levine, Gail Carson. The Two Princesses of Bamarre. (J). 2012. (ENG.). 272p. (gr. 3-7). pap. 9.99 *(978-0-06-440966-7(X)*, HarperCollins) 2004. (Illus.). 304p. (gr. 7-18). reprint ed. pap. 6.99 *(978-0-06-057580-9(8))* HarperCollins Pubs.
Levinson, Marilyn. Rufus & Magic Run Amok, 1 vol. 2005. (ENG.). 32p. (YA). pap. 5.95 *(978-0-7614-5176-1(5))* Marshall Cavendish Corp.
Lobel, Arnold. The Arnold Lobel Treasury. 2014. (ENG., Illus.). 160p. (J). (gr. 1-4). pap. 14.99 *(978-0-486-78078-8(3)*, 780783) Dover Pubns., Inc.
Loiske, Jennifer, et al. Tales of an Old Wizard. 2013. (ENG.). 116p. pap. 10.58 *(978-1-291-30601-9(3))* Lulu Pr., Inc.
Luberto, Bradley. Clide & Druce: A Repulsive Tale of Trolls & Tax Money. 2006. (ENG.). 48p. per. 16.95 *(978-1-4241-5012-0(4))* PublishAmerica, Inc.
Lutz II, William. Seeking Mason. 2009. 212p. pap. 14.00 *(978-0-557-03737-7(9))* Lulu Pr., Inc.
Malaspina, Ann. The Mouse & the Wizard: A Hindu Folktale. Sylvaine, Jenny, illus. 2013. (Folktales from Around the World Ser.). (ENG.). 24p. (J). (gr. k-3). 32.79 *(978-1-62323-633-5(9)*, 206384) Child's World, Inc, The.
Malchow, Hal & Malchow, Alex. The Sword of Darrow. 2011. 372p. (J). (gr. 3-7). pap. 12.99 *(978-1-935618-47-8(4))* BenBella Bks.
Malloy, Chris. Wizard Academies - A Special Kind of Talent. 2007. (ENG.). 142p. pap. 19.95 *(978-0-615-18505-7(3))* Wizard Academies, LLC.
Martin, Dick. The Ozmapolitan of Oz. 2006. (J). 24.95 *(978-1-930764-11-8(1))* International Wizard of Oz Club, The.
McCarthy, Cory & Capetta, A. R. Once & Future. (ENG.). (YA). (gr. 9-17). 2020. 384p. pap. 10.99 *(978-0-316-44926-7(1))* 2019. 368p. 18.99 *(978-0-316-44927-4(X))* Little Brown & Co. (Jimmy Patterson).
McCullough, Karen. Wizard's Bridge. 2004. pap. 13.75 *(978-0-9759653-0-6(1)*, ImaJinn Bks.) BelleBks., Inc.
McDowell, Andrew. Beyond the Forest. 2007. 286p. pap. 16.95 *(978-0-7414-4238-3(8))* Infinity Publishing.
McGowan, Maureen. Cinderella: Ninja Warrior. 2010. 320p. pap. 8.95 *(978-1-60747-778-5(5)*, Pickwick Pr.) Phoenix Bks., Inc.
McGraw, Eloise Jarvis & McGraw, Lauren Lynn. The Forbidden Fountain of Oz. 2006. (J). 24.95 *(978-1-930764-12-5(X))* International Wizard of Oz Club, The.

W X Y Z

McKillip, Patricia A. The Forgotten Beasts of Eld. 2006. (ENG., Illus.). 352p. (YA). (gr. 7-12). pap. 16.95 *(978-0-15-205536-3(3))* Houghton Mifflin Harcourt Publishing Co.

Memling, Carl. The Sword in the Stone (Disney) RH Disney, illus. 2015. (Little Golden Book Ser.). (ENG.). 24p. (J). (-k). 5.99 *(978-0-7364-3374-7(0)*, Golden/Disney) Random Hse. Children's Bks.

Mertz, Alyssa. The Lucky Farm Boy, 1 vol. Crum, A. M., illus. 2009. 28p. pap. 24.95 *(978-1-60813-892-0(5))* PublishAmerica, Inc.

Metz, Diana. Brinn & the Dragons of Pallan Cliffs. 2003. 352p. (J). pap. *(978-0-9718431-2-7(0))* M.O.T.H.E.R. Publishing Co., Inc., The.

Mitchell, N. J. W. Saraly & the Dragons. 2003. 124p. pap. 10.95 *(978-0-595-30264-2(5))* iUniverse, Inc.

Moffitt, Sara. Merlin & the Frog Meet Chatty & Noble. 2011. 25p. (J). pap. 18.95 *(978-1-4327-5921-6(3))* Outskirts Pr., Inc.

Mongredien, Sue. Oliver Moon & the Broomstick Battle. 2011. (Oliver Moon, Junior Wizard Ser.). (ENG.). 94p. (J). (gr. 2-5). 17.44 *(978-0-7945-3038-9(9))* EDC Publishing.

—Oliver Moon & the Dragon Disaster. 2011. (Oliver Moon Ser.). 94p. (J). pap. 4.99 *(978-0-7945-3036-5(2)*, Usborne) EDC Publishing.

—Oliver Moon & the Monster Mystery. 2011. (Oliver Moon, Junior Wizard Ser.). (ENG.). 89p. (J). (gr. 2-5). 17.44 *(978-0-7945-3095-2(8))* EDC Publishing.

—Oliver Moon & the Nipperbat Nightmare. 2011. (Oliver Moon, Junior Wizard Ser.). (ENG.). 94p. (J). (gr. 2-5). 17.44 *(978-0-7945-3037-2(0))* EDC Publishing.

—Oliver Moon & the Spell Off. 2011. (Oliver Moon, Junior Wizard Ser.). (ENG.). 93p. (J). (gr. 2-5). 17.44 *(978-0-7945-3093-8(1))* EDC Publishing.

—Oliver Moon's Fangtastic Sleepover. 2011. (Oliver Moon, Junior Wizard Ser.). (ENG.). 92p. (J). (gr. 2-5). 17.44 *(978-0-7945-3094-5(X))* EDC Publishing.

Morpurgo, Michael. Toto: the Dog-Gone Amazing Story of the Wizard of Oz. Chichester Clark, Emma, illus. 2017. (ENG.). 284p. (J). 17.99 *(978-0-00-825256-4(4)*, HarperCollins Children's Bks.) HarperCollins Pubs. Ltd. GBR. Dist: HarperCollins Pubs.

Morris, J. S. The Jewel. 2007. (ENG.). 204p. pap. 22.95 *(978-1-4357-0140-3(2))* Lulu Pr., Inc.

Morrissey, Dean & Krensky, Stephen. The Wizard Mouse. Morrissey, Dean, illus. 2011. (ENG., Illus.). 32p. (J). (gr. k-4). 16.99 *(978-0-06-008066-2(3))* HarperCollins Pubs.

Moss, Ronald. The Wizard Next Door. 2009. 198p. pap. 14.95 *(978-1-60911-077-2(3)*, Eloquent Bks.) Strategic Book Publishing & Rights Agency (SBPRA).

Mulholland, Marie. A Study Guide for the Necklace of Terrersylvanous. 2007. 38p. (J). ring bd. 11.95 *(978-0-9797715-0-7(1))* Sonic Sword Productions.

Mull, Brandon. Beyonders the Complete Set (Boxed Set) A World Without Heroes; Seeds of Rebellion; Chasing the Prophecy, Set. 2013. (Beyonders Ser.). (ENG., Illus.). 1456p. (J). (gr. 3-7). 59.99 *(978-1-4424-8593-8(0)*, Aladdin) Simon & Schuster Children's Publishing.

—Chasing the Prophecy. (Beyonders Ser.: 3). (ENG.). (J). (gr. 3-7). 2014. 528p. pap. 9.99 *(978-1-4169-9797-9(0))* 2013. 512p. 21.99 *(978-1-4169-9796-2(2))* Simon & Schuster Children's Publishing. (Aladdin).

—Seeds of Rebellion. (Beyonders Ser.: 2). (ENG., Illus.). 512p. (J). (gr. 3-7). 2013. pap. 9.99 *(978-1-4169-9795-5(4))* 2012. 21.99 *(978-1-4169-9794-8(6))* Simon & Schuster Children's Publishing. (Aladdin).

—Seeds of Rebellion. 2012. (Beyonders Ser.: Bk. 2). (ENG., Illus.). 512p. (J). pap. 10.99 *(978-1-4424-4965-7(9)*, Simon & Schuster/Paula Wiseman Bks.) Simon & Schuster/Paula Wiseman Bks.

—Seeds of Rebellion. 2013. (Beyonders Ser.: 2). lib. bdg. 19.65 *(978-0-606-27030-4(2))* Turtleback.

—A World Without Heroes. (J). 2011. (Beyonders Ser.: 1). 1.25 *(978-1-4640-0920-4(1))* (Beyonders Ser.: 1). 92.75 *(978-1-4618-0338-6(1))* 2011. (Beyonders Ser.: 1). 124.75 *(978-1-4618-0353-9(5))* 2011. 122.75 *(978-1-4618-0363-8(2))* Recorded Bks., Inc.

—A World Without Heroes. (Beyonders Ser.: 1). (ENG.). (J). (gr. 3-7). 2012. 512p. pap. 9.99 *(978-1-4169-9793-1(8))* 2011. 464p. 21.99 *(978-1-4169-9792-4(X))* Simon & Schuster Children's Publishing. (Aladdin).

—A World Without Heroes. 2011. (Beyonders Ser.: Bk. 1). (ENG.). 464p. (J). pap. 10.99 *(978-1-4424-3530-8(5)*, Simon & Schuster/Paula Wiseman Bks.) Simon & Schuster/Paula Wiseman Bks.

—A World Without Heroes. 2012. (Beyonders Ser.: 1). lib. bdg. 19.65 *(978-0-606-23675-1(9))* Turtleback.

Negrin, Fabian, illus. Wizard Tales. 2003. 96p. 19.95 *(978-1-55285-558-4(9))* Whitecap Bks., Ltd. CAN. Dist: Graphic Arts Ctr. Publishing Co.

Nguyen, Thao. Consequences: A Chance for Hope. 2012. 60p. pap. 15.99 *(978-1-4691-8794-5(9))* Xlibris Corp.

Nix, Garth. Frogkisser! 2019. (ENG.). 384p. (YA). (gr. 7-7). pap. 12.99 *(978-1-338-05209-1(8))* Scholastic, Inc.

Novel Units. Harry Potter & the Prisoner of Azkaban Novel Units Student Packet. 2019. (Harry Potter Ser.: Year 3). (ENG.). (J). pap., stu. ed. 13.99 *(978-1-58130-657-6(1)*, Novel Units, Inc.) Classroom Library Co.

—Harry Potter & the Prisoner of Azkaban Novel Units Teacher Guide. 2019. (Harry Potter Ser.: Year 3). (ENG.). (J). pap., tchr. ed. 12.99 *(978-1-58130-656-9(3)*, Novel Units, Inc.) Classroom Library Co.

Ogilvy, Ian. Measle & the Dragodon. 2006. 344p. (J). (gr. 3-8). per. 6.99 *(978-0-06-058690-4(7)*, Harper Trophy) HarperCollins Pubs.

—Measle & the Wrathmonk. 2004. 224p. (J). (gr. 4-6). 15.99 *(978-0-06-058685-0(0))* HarperCollins Pubs.

Okugas, Juanaiga. The tales of Mew the Cat. 2011. 92p. pap. 35.30 *(978-1-4567-3480-0(6))* AuthorHouse.

Osborne, Mary Pope. El Invierno Del Hechicero Del Hielo. 2015. (Casa De árbol Ser.: 32). (SPA., Illus.). 144p. (J). (gr. 2-4). pap. 6.99 *(978-1-63245-535-2(8))* Lectorum Pubns., Inc.

Parsons, Colin. Wizards' Kingdom. 2005. (ENG., Illus.). 117p. pap. *(978-1-84401-522-1(X))* Athena Pr.

Patterson, James. The Fire. 2011. (Playaway Children Ser.). (ENG.). (YA). (gr. 8-12). 59.99 *(978-1-61113-385-1(8))* Hachette Audio.

—The Gift. 2010. (Witch & Wizard Ser.: No. 2). (J). 59.99 *(978-1-60941-012-4(2))* Findaway World, LLC.

—The Gift. 2014. lthr. 79.00 *(978-1-62715-523-6(6))* Leatherbound Bestsellers.

—Witch & Wizard. 2014. lthr. 79.00 *(978-1-62715-529-8(5))* Leatherbound Bestsellers.

—Witch & Wizard. 2010. (Witch & Wizard Ser.: 1). (YA). lib. bdg. 20.85 *(978-0-606-15119-1(2))* Turtleback.

Patterson, James & Charbonnet, Gabrielle. Witch & Wizard. (Witch & Wizard Ser.: 1). (ENG.). (J). (gr. 5-17). 2011. 368p. mass mkt. 8.99 *(978-0-446-56243-0(2))* 2010. 336p. pap. 11.99 *(978-0-316-03834-8(2))* 2009. 320p. 34.99 *(978-0-316-03624-5(2))* Little Brown & Co. (Jimmy Patterson).

—Witch & Wizard. 2011. (Witch & Wizard Ser.: 1). lib. bdg. 18.45 *(978-0-606-26452-5(3))* Turtleback.

Patterson, James & Dembowski, Jill. The Fire. 2011. (Witch & Wizard Ser.: 3). (ENG.). (YA). (gr. 5-17). 352p. 35.99 *(978-0-316-10190-5(7))*; 448p. 30.99 *(978-0-316-19620-8(7))* Little Brown & Co. (Jimmy Patterson).

—The Kiss. 2013. (Witch & Wizard Ser.: 4). (ENG.). (YA). (gr. 7-17). 384p. pap. 10.99 *(978-0-316-10176-9(1))*; 368p. 35.99 *(978-0-316-10191-2(5))* Little Brown & Co. (Jimmy Patterson).

—The Kiss. 2013. (Witch & Wizard Ser.: 4). (YA). lib. bdg. 20.85 *(978-0-606-32281-2(7))* Turtleback.

Patterson, James & Raymond, Emily. The Lost. (YA). 2015. (Witch & Wizard Ser.: 5). (ENG.). 384p. (gr. 7-17). pap. 10.99 *(978-0-316-20774-4(8)*, Jimmy Patterson) 2014. (Witch & Wizard Ser.: 5). (ENG.). 384p. (gr. 7-17). 36.99 *(978-0-316-20770-6(5)*, Jimmy Patterson) 2014. 355p. *(978-0-316-24266-0(7))* 2014. (Witch & Wizard Ser.: 5). (ENG.). 480p. (gr. 7-17). 39.99 *(978-0-316-24002-4(8)*, Jimmy Patterson) Little Brown & Co.

—The Lost. 2015. (Witch & Wizard Ser.: 5). (YA). lib. bdg. 20.85 *(978-0-606-37528-3(7))* Turtleback.

Patterson, James & Rust, Ned. The Gift. (Witch & Wizard Ser.: 2). (ENG.). (gr. 5-17). 2012. 352p. mass mkt. 7.99 *(978-0-446-56245-4(9))* 2011. 400p. pap. 10.99 *(978-0-316-03835-5(0))* 2010. 352p. 17.99 *(978-0-316-03625-2(0))* Little Brown & Co. (Jimmy Patterson).

—The Gift. 2012. (Witch & Wizard Ser.: 2). lib. bdg. 18.40 *(978-0-606-26451-8(5))* Turtleback.

Paul, Donita K. Two Renegade Realms, 1 vol. 2014. (Realm Walkers Ser.). (ENG.). 416p. (YA). pap. 13.99 *(978-0-310-73581-6(5))* Zondervan.

Pearse, Asha, illus. Wizard of Oz. 2017. (10 Minute Classics Ser.). (ENG.). 32p. (J). (gr. 1-4). 16.99 *(978-1-4867-1221-2(5)*, 341fccfd-893b-4e64-bc14-77b725bee85d) Flowerpot Pr.

—Wizard of Oz. 2017. (ENG.). 32p. (J). (gr. 1-5). *(978-1-4867-1269-4(X))* Flowerpot Children's Pr. Inc.

—Wizard of Oz. 2014. (ENG.). 16p. (J). (gr. -1-4). 7.99 *(978-1-4867-0009-7(8))* Flowerpot Children's Pr. Inc. CAN. Dist: Cardinal Pubs. Group.

Perry, Pete. The Secret of Bedside Manor. 2009. (Illus.). 140p. pap. 36.49 *(978-1-4389-6668-7(7))* AuthorHouse.

Pickering, Sean & Morrill, Scott. The Adventures of Danny & Spike: Underground. 2007. 92p. per. 9.95 *(978-0-595-44365-9(6))* iUniverse, Inc.

Pierce, Tamora. In the Hand of the Goddess. 2014. (Song of the Lioness Ser.: 2). (ENG., Illus.). 288p. (YA). (gr. 7). 21.99 *(978-1-4814-3960-2(X)*, Atheneum Bks. for Young Readers) Simon & Schuster Children's Publishing.

Plourde, Lynn. The Blizzard Wizard. Aardema, John, illus. 2010. (ENG.). 32p. (J). (gr. -1-3). 16.95 *(978-0-89272-789-6(6))* Down East Bks.

Price, Nick, illus. The Wonderful Wizard of Oz. 2009. (ENG.). 12p. (J). 8.95 *(978-1-58117-856-2(5)*, Intervisual/Piggy Toes) Bendon, Inc.

Princess Madeline & the Dragon. 2013. (Illus.). 118p. (YA). pap. 5.99 *(978-1-62375-070-1(9)*, Caliburn Bks.) MQuills Publishing.

Prineas, Sarah. Lost. 2009. (Magic Thief Ser.: 2). (J). 88.75 *(978-1-4407-3133-4(0))*; 130.75 *(978-1-4407-3129-7(2))*; 1.25 *(978-1-4407-3131-0(4))*; 132.75 *(978-1-4407-3127-3(6))*; 110.75 *(978-1-4407-3125-9(X))*; (SPA.). 265.75 *(978-1-4407-3124-2(1))*; 112.75 *(978-1-4407-3123-5(3))* Recorded Bks., Inc.

—The Magic Thief. Caparo, Antonio Javier, illus. (Magic Thief Ser.: 1). (ENG.). (J). (gr. 5-9). 2008. 432p. 16.99 *(978-0-06-137587-3(X))*1 2009. 448p. pap. 7.99 *(978-0-06-137590-3(X))* HarperCollins Pubs. (HarperCollins).

—The Magic Thief: Found. Caparo, Antonio Javier, illus. 2011. (Magic Thief Ser.: 3). (ENG.). 384p. (J). (gr. 5). pap. 7.99 *(978-0-06-137595-8(0)*, HarperCollins) HarperCollins Pubs.

—The Magic Thief: Home. Caparo, Antonio Javier, illus. 2015. (Magic Thief Ser.: 4). (ENG.). 416p. (J). (gr. 3-7). pap. 8.99 *(978-0-06-220956-6(6)*, HarperCollins) HarperCollins Pubs.

—The Magic Thief: Lost. Caparo, Antonio Javier, illus. (Magic Thief Ser.: 2). (ENG.). (J). (gr. 5-18). 2009. 400p. 17.99 *(978-0-06-137589-7(6))*2 2010. 416p. pap. 8.99 *(978-0-06-137592-7(6))* HarperCollins Pubs. (HarperCollins).

Pritchard, G. Rosemary Sage & the Man in Black. 2005. 78p. pap. 16.95 *(978-1-4137-9809-8(8))* PublishAmerica, Inc.

Rawson, C. Wizards. 2004. (Young Reading Ser.). (Illus.). 48p. (J). (gr. 2-18). pap. 5.95 *(978-0-7945-0328-4(4)*, Usborne) EDC Publishing.

Reardon, A. C. Gaiish: The adventure of Isabelle & Eva. 2011. 168p. pap. 14.69 *(978-1-4567-7818-7(8))* AuthorHouse.

Roberts, Roxanne. Angel Wings, Faery Dust & Other Magical Things: A Story about Witches, Warlocks & Such. 2011. 24p. pap. 11.50 *(978-1-61204-072-1(1)*, Eloquent Bks.) Strategic Book Publishing & Rights Agency (SBPRA).

Robinson, Robin, illus. L. Frank Baum's the Wonderful Wizard of Oz. 2013. (Penguin Young Readers, Level 4 Ser.). 48p. (J). (gr. 3-4). mass mkt. 5.99 *(978-0-448-45588-4(9)*, Penguin Young Readers) Penguin Young Readers Group.

Rodriguez, AJ. Theodore Da Baer. 2004. 113p. pap. 19.95 *(978-1-4137-5247-2(0))* America Star Bks.

—Theodore Da Baer Ii: A New Beginning. 2006. 207p. pap. 24.95 *(978-1-4241-1125-1(0))* America Star Bks.

Rogers, Tom, adapted by. The Secret Spell Book. 2017. (Illus.). 31p. (J). *(978-1-5182-3831-4(9))* Disney Publishing Worldwide.

Rose, Christine & Rose, Ethan. Rowan of the Wood. 2008. 240p. (YA). pap. 14.95 *(978-0-9817443-1-5(1))* Dalton Publishing GBR. Dist: Midpoint Trade Bks., Inc.

Round, Suzanne. The Dragonfire Crystal. 2011. 154p. pap. *(978-0-7552-1359-7(9))* Authors OnLine, Ltd.

Rowe, W. W. The Wizard's Wayward Wand. 2010. (ENG.). 99p. (J). (gr. 3-7). pap. 12.95 *(978-0-9843754-0-0(6))* Sanctuary Publishing, Inc.

Rowling, J. K. Fantastic Beasts & Where to Find Them. 2017. (ENG.). 128p. (J). (gr. 3). 12.99 *(978-1-338-13231-1(8)*, Levine, Arthur A. Bks.) Scholastic, Inc.

—Hare Pota Me Te Whatu Manapou [Harry Potter & the Philosopher's Stone]. Blake, Leon Heketu, tr. 2021. (Kotahi Rau Pukapuka Ser.: 1). 328p. pap. 24.99 *(978-1-86940-914-2(0))* Auckland Univ. Pr. NZL. Dist: Independent Pubs. Group.

—Harrius Potter et Philosophi Lapis: (Harry Potter & the Philosopher's Stone) 2003. (Harry Potter Ser.).Tr. of Harry Potter & the Philosopher's Stone. (LAT., Illus.). 256p. (YA). (gr. 7). 29.99 *(978-1-58234-825-4(1)*, 900020066, Bloomsbury USA Childrens) Bloomsbury Publishing USA.

—Harry Potter à l'École des Sorciers. Menard, Jean-François, tr. from ENG. 2007. (Harry Potter Ser.: Year 1).Tr. of Harry Potter & the Sorcerer's Stone. 311p. (J). per. 14.95 *(978-2-07-061236-9(8))* Gallimard, Editions FRA. Dist: Distribooks, Inc.

—Harry Potter & the Chamber of Secrets. 2009. 9.64 *(978-0-7848-1444-4(9)*, Everbind) Marco Bk. Co.

—Harry Potter & the Chamber of Secrets. unabr. ed. 2004. (Harry Potter Ser.: Year 2). 352p. (J). (gr. 3-18). pap. 46.00 incl. audio *(978-0-8072-8207-6(3)*, S YA 137 SP, Listening Library) Random Hse. Audio Publishing Group.

—Harry Potter & the Chamber of Secrets. (Harry Potter Ser.: 2). (J). 2006. 1.25 *(978-1-4193-8079-2(6))* 2003. 78.75 *(978-1-4025-6698-1(0))* Recorded Bks., Inc.

—Harry Potter & the Chamber of Secrets. (Harry Potter Ser.: Year 2). (RUS., Illus.). 28.95 *(978-5-8451-0947-7(7))* Rosmen-Izdat RUS. Dist: Distribooks, Inc.

—Harry Potter & the Chamber of Secrets, Bk. 2. Selznick, Brian & GrandPré, Mary, illus. 2018. (Harry Potter Ser.: 2). (ENG.). 368p. (J). (gr. 3). pap. 12.99 *(978-1-338-29915-1(8)*, Levine, Arthur A. Bks.) Scholastic, Inc.

—Harry Potter & the Chamber of Secrets, Bk. 2. Kay, Jim, illus. 2016. (Harry Potter Ser.: 2). (ENG.). 272p. (J). (gr. 3). 39.99 *(978-0-545-79132-8(4)*, Levine, Arthur A. Bks.) Scholastic, Inc.

—Harry Potter & the Chamber of Secrets. l.t. ed. 2003. (Harry Potter Ser.: Year 2). (ENG.). 466p. pap. 13.95 *(978-1-59413-001-4(9))* Thorndike Pr.

—Harry Potter & the Chamber of Secrets (Latin) Harrius Potter et Camera Secretorum. Needham, Peter, tr. 2016. (Harry Potter Ser.). (LAT.). 288p. 29.99 *(978-1-4088-6911-6(X)*, 900210040, Bloomsbury Children's Bks.) Bloomsbury Publishing USA.

—Harry Potter & the Deathly Hallows. (Illus.). 2008. 832p. pap. *(978-0-7475-9586-1(0))* 2007. (ENG., 608p. *(978-0-7475-9106-1(7))* Bloomsbury Publishing Plc.

—Harry Potter & the Deathly Hallows. Menard, Jean-François, tr. 2017. (FRE.). 896p. (J). (gr. 4-10). pap. *(978-2-07-058523-6(9))* Gallimard, Editions.

—Harry Potter & the Deathly Hallows. braille ed. 2007. (Harry Potter Ser.: Year 7). (J). (gr. 4-7). 34.99 *(978-0-939173-57-0(3))* National Braille Pr.

—Harry Potter & the Deathly Hallows. 2010. 25.00 *(978-1-60686-882-9(9))* Perfection Learning Corp.

—Harry Potter & the Deathly Hallows, 17 vols. 2007. (Harry Potter Ser.: 7). (YA). 129.79 *(978-1-4281-6654-7(8))*; 131.75 *(978-1-4281-6652-3(1))* Recorded Bks., Inc.

—Harry Potter & the Deathly Hallows, Bk. 7. Selznick, Brian & GrandPré, Mary, illus. 2018. (Harry Potter Ser.: 7). (ENG.). 784p. (J). (gr. 3). pap. 16.99 *(978-1-338-29920-5(4)*, Levine, Arthur A. Bks.) Scholastic, Inc.

—Harry Potter & the Deathly Hallows, 7 vols., Bk. 7. GrandPré, Mary, illus. 2007. (Harry Potter Ser.: 7). (ENG.). 784p. (J). (gr. 3-9). 37.99 *(978-0-545-01022-1(5)*, Levine, Arthur A. Bks.) Scholastic, Inc.

—Harry Potter & the Deathly Hallows. l.t. ed. 2009. (ENG.). 970p. pap. 14.95 *(978-1-59413-355-8(7)*, Large Print Pr.) 2007. (Harry Potter Ser.: Year 7). (Illus.). 969p. (J). (gr. 4-7). 34.95 *(978-0-7862-9665-1(8))* Thorndike Pr.

—Harry Potter & the Deathly Hallows. (Harry Potter (Kazu Kibuishi Illustrations) Ser.: 7). 2013. lib. bdg. 29.40 *(978-0-606-32351-2(1))* 2009. lib. bdg. 26.95 *(978-0-606-00420-6(3))* Turtleback.

—Harry Potter & the Deathly Hallows. Bar-hillel, Gili, tr. from ENG. 2007. (Harry Potter Ser.: Year 7). (HEB., Illus.). 568p. (J). (gr. 4-7). pap. *(978-965-482-635-8(6))* Yediot Aharonot Bks., Miscal.

—Harry Potter & the Goblet of Fire. 2009. 10.24 *(978-0-7848-1587-8(9)*, Everbind) Marco Bk. Co.

—Harry Potter & the Goblet of Fire. (Harry Potter Ser.: 4). (J). 2006. 1.25 *(978-1-4193-8531-5(3))* 2003. 101.75 *(978-1-4025-6702-5(2))* Recorded Bks., Inc.

—Harry Potter & the Goblet of Fire. Kay, Jim, illus. 2019. (Harry Potter Ser.: 4). (ENG.). 464p. (J). (gr. 3). 47.99 *(978-0-545-79142-7(1)*, Levine, Arthur A. Bks.) Scholastic, Inc.

—Harry Potter & the Goblet of Fire, Bk. 4. Selznick, Brian & GrandPré, Mary, illus. 2018. (Harry Potter Ser.: 4). (ENG.). 768p. (J). (gr. 3). pap. 14.99 *(978-1-338-29917-5(4)*, Levine, Arthur A. Bks.) Scholastic, Inc.

—Harry Potter & the Goblet of Fire. GrandPré, Mary, illus. l.t. ed. 2003. (Harry Potter Ser.: Vol. 4). (ENG.). 936p. pap. 11.66 *(978-1-59413-003-8(5))* Thorndike Pr.

—Harry Potter & the Half-Blood Prince. 2005. audio compact disk *(978-0-7475-8258-8(0))* Bloomsbury Publishing Plc.

—Harry Potter & the Half-Blood Prince, 9 vols. braille ed. 2005. (Harry Potter Ser.: Year 6). (J). (gr. 4-8). 29.99 *(978-0-939173-39-6(5)*, HALF) National Braille Pr.

—Harry Potter & the Half-Blood Prince. GrandPré, Mary, illus. 2006. (Harry Potter Ser.: Year 6). 652p. (gr. 4-8). 23.00 *(978-0-7569-6765-9(1))* Perfection Learning Corp.

—Harry Potter & the Half-Blood Prince. (Harry Potter Ser.: 6). (J). 2007. 1.25 *(978-1-4193-5430-4(2))* 2006. 110.75 *(978-1-4193-5436-6(1))* 2006. 193.75 *(978-1-4193-5432-8(9))* 2005. 113.75 *(978-1-4193-5434-2(5))* Recorded Bks., Inc.

—Harry Potter & the Half-Blood Prince, Bk. 6. Selznick, Brian & GrandPré, Mary, illus. 2018. (Harry Potter Ser.: 6). (ENG.). 688p. (J). (gr. 3). pap. 14.99 *(978-1-338-29919-9(0)*, Levine, Arthur A. Bks.) Scholastic, Inc.

—Harry Potter & the Half-Blood Prince, Bk. 6. GrandPré, Mary, illus. 2005. (Harry Potter Ser.: 6). (ENG.). 672p. (J). (gr. 3-8). 32.99 *(978-0-439-78454-2(9)*, Levine, Arthur A. Bks.) Scholastic, Inc.

—Harry Potter & the Half-Blood Prince. l.t. ed. (Illus.). (J). (gr. 4-7). 2007. (ENG.). 832p. per. 14.95 *(978-1-59413-221-6(6))* 2005. (Harry Potter Ser.: Year 6). 831p. 29.95 *(978-0-7862-7745-2(9))* Thorndike Pr. (Large Print Pr.).

—Harry Potter & the Half-Blood Prince. 2013. (Harry Potter (Kazu Kibuishi Illustrations) Ser.: 6). lib. bdg. 26.95 *(978-0-606-32350-5(3))* Turtleback.

—Harry Potter & the Half Blood Prince - Chinese Language. 2005. (Harry Potter Ser.: Year 6). (CHI.). 496p. (YA). (gr. 4-8). pap. 28.95 *(978-7-02-005323-0(8)*, HAP06) People's Literature Publishing Hse. CHN. Dist: Chinasprout, Inc.

—Harry Potter & the Order of the Phoenix. 768p. (J). (gr. 6-10). pap. *(978-0-7475-6107-1(9))* Bloomsbury Publishing Plc.

—Harry Potter & the Order of the Phoenix. 2008. *(978-977-14-2697-4(4))* Nahdat Misr Bkshop for Printing and Pubs.

—Harry Potter & the Order of the Phoenix, 13 vols. braille ed. 2003. (Harry Potter Ser.: Year 5). (YA). 29.99 *(978-0-939173-38-9(7))* National Braille Pr.

—Harry Potter & the Order of the Phoenix. 2003. (Harry Potter Ser.: Year 5). (CHI.). 575p. (YA). pap. 26.95 *(978-7-02-004327-9(5)*, HAP05) People's Literature Publishing Hse. CHN. Dist: Chinasprout, Inc.

—Harry Potter & the Order of the Phoenix. 2004. (Harry Potter Ser.). 870p. (gr. 4-6). 16.49 *(978-0-7569-4163-5(6))* Perfection Learning Corp.

—Harry Potter & the Order of the Phoenix. 2003. (ENG.). 768p. *(978-1-55192-570-7(2))* Raincoast Bk. Distribution.

—Harry Potter & the Order of the Phoenix. 2004. (JPN.). (J). (gr. 6-10). *(978-4-915512-51-3(7))* Sayzansha.

—Harry Potter & the Order of the Phoenix, Bk. 5. Selznick, Brian & GrandPré, Mary, illus. 2018. (Harry Potter Ser.: 5). (ENG.). 912p. (J). (gr. 3). pap. 14.99 *(978-1-338-29918-2(2)*, Levine, Arthur A. Bks.) Scholastic, Inc.

—Harry Potter & the Order of the Phoenix, Bk. 5. GrandPré, Mary, illus. 2003. (Harry Potter Ser.: 5). (ENG.). 896p. (gr. 3-7). 32.99 *(978-0-439-35806-4(X)*, Levine, Arthur A. Bks.) Scholastic, Inc.

—Harry Potter & the Order of the Phoenix. l.t. ed. 2003. (Harry Potter Ser.: Year 5). 1093p. 29.95 *(978-0-7862-5778-2(4)*, Large Print Pr.) Thorndike Pr.

—Harry Potter & the Order of the Phoenix. GrandPré, Mary, illus. l.t. ed. 2003. (Thorndike Young Adult Ser.). (ENG.). 1232p. (J). (gr. 4-7). per. 14.95 *(978-1-59413-112-7(0)*, Large Print Pr.) Thorndike Pr.

—Harry Potter & the Order of the Phoenix. 2004. (Harry Potter Ser.: 5). lib. bdg. 24.50 *(978-0-613-99916-8(9))* Turtleback.

—Harry Potter & the Philosopher's Stane: Harry Potter & the Philosopher's Stone in Scots. Fitt, Matthew, tr. 2015. (SCO.). 320p. (J). (gr. 4-6). pap. 14.95 *(978-1-78530-154-4(3))* Black and White Publishing Ltd. GBR. Dist: Independent Pubs. Group.

—Harry Potter & the Philosopher's Stone. 2014. (ENG., Illus.). 352p. *(978-1-4088-5589-8(5))* Bloomsbury Publishing Plc.

—Harry Potter & the Philosopher's Stone (Irish) 2015. (ENG.). 272p. (J). *(978-1-4088-6619-1(6)*, 283017, Bloomsbury Children's Bks.) Bloomsbury Publishing Plc.

—Harry Potter & the Philosopher's Stone (Latin) Harrius Potter et Philosophi Lapis (Latin) Needham, Peter, tr. 2015. (LAT.). 256p. (J). *(978-1-4088-6618-4(8)*, 283019, Bloomsbury Children's Bks.) Bloomsbury Publishing Plc.

—Harry Potter & the Prisoner of Azkaban. 2009. 9.64 *(978-0-7848-1542-7(9)*, Everbind) Marco Bk. Co.

—Harry Potter & the Prisoner of Azkaban. 2005. (Harry Potter Ser.: Year 3). (CHI.). 260p. (YA). pap. 16.95 *(978-7-02-003345-4(8)*, HAP03) People's Literature Publishing Hse. CHN. Dist: Chinasprout, Inc.

—Harry Potter & the Prisoner of Azkaban, 10 vols. 2003. (Harry Potter Ser.: 3). (J). 84.75 *(978-1-4025-6700-1(6))* Recorded Bks., Inc.

—Harry Potter & the Prisoner of Azkaban, Bk. 3. Selznick, Brian & GrandPré, Mary, illus. 2018. (Harry Potter Ser.: 3). (ENG.). 464p. (J). (gr. 3). pap. 12.99 *(978-1-338-29916-8(6)*, Levine, Arthur A. Bks.) Scholastic, Inc.

—Harry Potter & the Prisoner of Azkaban. l.t. ed. 2003. (Harry Potter Ser.: Year 3). (ENG.). 592p. pap. 13.95 *(978-1-59413-002-1(7)*, Large Print Pr.) Thorndike Pr.

—Harry Potter & the Prisoner of Azkaban. 2013. (Harry Potter (Kazu Kibuishi Illustrations) Ser.: 3). lib. bdg. 24.50 *(978-0-606-32347-5(3))* Turtleback.

—Harry Potter & the Sorcerer's Stone. 2014. (ENG.). lthr. 79.00 *(978-1-62715-772-8(7))* Leatherbound Bestsellers.

—Harry Potter & the Sorcerer's Stone. 2009. 8.44 *(978-0-7848-2438-2(X))*; 10.84 *(978-0-7848-1357-7(4))* Marco Bk. Co. (Everbind).

—Harry Potter & the Sorcerer's Stone. 2003. (Harry Potter Ser.: Year 1). (CHI.). 191p. (YA). pap. 14.95 *(978-7-02-003343-0(1)*, HAP01) People's Literature Publishing Hse. CHN. Dist: Chinasprout, Inc.

—Harry Potter & the Sorcerer's Stone. (Harry Potter Ser.: 1). (J). 2004. 1.25 *(978-1-4025-6757-5(X))* 2003. 80.75 *(978-1-4025-6696-7(4))* Recorded Bks., Inc.

—Harry Potter & the Sorcerer's Stone, Bk. 1. Selznick, Brian & GrandPré, Mary, illus. 2018. (Harry Potter Ser.: 1). (ENG.). 336p. (J). (gr. 3). pap. 12.99 *(978-1-338-29914-4(X)*, Levine, Arthur A. Bks.) Scholastic, Inc.

—Harry Potter & the Sorcerer's Stone, Bk. 1. Kay, Jim, illus. 2015. (Harry Potter Ser.: 1). (ENG.). 256p. (J). (gr. 3). 39.99 *(978-0-545-79035-2(2)*, Levine, Arthur A. Bks.) Scholastic, Inc.

—Harry Potter & the Sorcerer's Stone. 2013. (Harry Potter (Kazu Kibuishi Illustrations) Ser.: 1). lib. bdg. 24.50 *(978-0-606-32345-1(7))* Turtleback.

—Harry Potter e a Camara Secreta. (Harry Potter Ser.: Year 2).Tr. of Harry Potter & the Chamber of Secrets. (POR.). pap. 28.95 *(978-85-325-1166-9(X))* Rocco, Editora, Ltda BRA. Dist: Distribooks, Inc.
—Harry Potter e a Pedra Filosofal. (Harry Potter Ser.: Year 1).Tr. of Harry Potter & the Philosopher's Stone. (POR.). pap. 28.95 *(978-85-325-1101-0(5))* Rocco, Editora, Ltda BRA. Dist: Distribooks, Inc.
—Harry Potter e a Prisioneiro de Azkaban. (Harry Potter Ser.: Year 3).Tr. of Harry Potter & the Prisoner of Azkaban. (POR.). pap. 29.95 *(978-85-325-1206-2(2))* Rocco, Editora, Ltda BRA. Dist: Distribooks, Inc.
—Harry Potter e o Cálice de Fogo. (Harry Potter Ser.: Year 4).Tr. of Harry Potter & the Goblet of Fire. (POR.). pap. 38.95 *(978-85-325-1252-9(6))* Rocco, Editora, Ltda BRA. Dist: Distribooks, Inc.
—Harry Potter et la Coupe de Feu. (Harry Potter Ser.: Year 4).Tr. of Harry Potter & the Goblet of Fire. (FRE., Illus.). 766p. pap. 19.95 *(978-2-07-054351-9(X))* Gallimard, Editions FRA. Dist: Distribooks, Inc.
—Harry Potter Signature Hardback Boxed Set X 7, 7 vols., Set. 2011. (ENG.). 7p. *(978-1-4088-2594-5(5))* Bloomsbury Publishing Plc.
—Harry Potter y el Prisionero de Azkaban. 2015. (Harry Potter Spanish Ser.: 3).Tr. of Harry Potter & the Prisoner of Azkaban. (SPA.). (gr. 3-6). lib. bdg. 28.10 *(978-0-613-35958-0(5))* Turtleback.
—The Tales of Beedle the Bard. Rowling, J. K., illus. 2008. (ENG., Illus.). 128p. *(978-0-7475-9987-6(4))* Bloomsbury Publishing Plc.
—The Tales of Beedle the Bard. GrandPré, Mary, illus. collector's ed. 2008. 184p. *(978-0-9560109-0-2(3))* Children's High Level Group.
—The Tales of Beedle the Bard. 2017. (ENG.). 128p. (J). (gr. 3-3). 12.99 *(978-1-338-12568-9(0))*, Levine, Arthur A. Bks.) Scholastic, Inc.
—The Tales of Beedle the Bard. 2017. (ENG.). (J). (gr. 3). lib. bdg. 24.50 *(978-0-606-39695-0(0))* Turtleback.
Rowling, J. K. & Scamander, Newt. Fantastic Beasts & Where to Find Them. Gill, Olivia Lomenech, illus. 2017. (ENG.). 160p. (J). (gr. 3-3). 34.99 *(978-1-338-21679-0(1)*, Levine, Arthur A. Bks.) Scholastic, Inc.
Rowling, J.k. Harry Potter y el prisionero de Azkaban (Harry Potter 3) 2004. (Harry Potter Ser.: Year 3). (SPA., Illus.). 360p. (gr. 3-18). 17.95 *(978-84-7888-519-0(6)*, SAL1889) Emece Editores ESP. Dist: Lectorum Pubns., Inc.
—Harry Potter y la cámara secreta (Harry Potter 2) 2004. (Harry Potter Ser.: Year 2). (SPA., Illus.). 288p. (YA). (gr. 3-18). 15.95 *(978-84-7888-495-7(5)*, SAL4595) Emece Editores ESP. Dist: Lectorum Pubns., Inc.
—Harry Potter y la piedra filosofal (Harry Potter 1) 2004. (Harry Potter Ser.: Year 1). (SPA., Illus.). 256p. (YA). (gr. 7-18). 15.95 *(978-84-7888-445-2(9)*, SAL2819) Emece Editores ESP. Dist: Lectorum Pubns., Inc.
Rowntree, G. M. Wizards Spell Magic in the Legends of Mere Leander. 2010. 291p. pap. 32.50 *(978-1-4452-6812-5(4))* Lulu Pr., Inc.
—Wizards Spell Magic in the Legends of Mere Leander - US Trade Size. 2010. (ENG.). 291p. pap. 24.95 *(978-1-4452-9266-3(1))* Lulu Pr., Inc.
Ruth, Nick. The Dark Dreamweaver. Concannon, Sue, illus. 2007. (Remin Chronicles: 1). (ENG.). 256p. (J). (gr. 4-7). per. 11.95 *(978-0-9745603-5-9(9))* Imaginator Pr.
Ryan, Brittney. The Legend of Holly Claus. Long, Laurel, illus. 2004. (Julie Andrews Collection). 544p. (J). (gr. 4-18). 16.99 *(978-0-06-058511-2(0))*; lib. bdg. 17.89 *(978-0-06-058514-3(5))* HarperCollins Pubs. (Julie Andrews Collection).
Ryan, Carrie & Davis, John Parke. The Map to Everywhere. 2015. (Map to Everywhere Ser.: 1). (J). lib. bdg. 18.45 *(978-0-606-37521-4(X))* Turtleback.
Sage, Angie. Darke, 12 vols. (Septimus Heap Ser.: 6). (J). 131.75 *(978-1-4498-6218-3(7))*; 1.25 *(978-1-4498-6226-8(8))*; 297.75 *(978-1-4498-6217-6(9))*; 2013. 92.75 *(978-1-4498-6225-1(X))*; 2011. 131.75 *(978-1-4498-6222-0(5))*; 2011. 133.75 *(978-1-4498-6220-6(9))* Recorded Bks., Inc.
—Darke. Zug, Mark, illus. 2012. (Septimus Heap Ser.: 6). (J). lib. bdg. 18.40 *(978-0-606-26264-4(4))* Turtleback.
—Flyte. (Septimus Heap Ser.: 2). (J). 2009. 84.49 *(978-1-4361-5831-2(1))* 2008. 1.25 *(978-1-4193-9383-9(9))* 2006. 114.75 *(978-1-4193-9386-0(3))* 2006. 133.75 *(978-1-4193-9390-7(1))* 2006. 131.75 *(978-1-4193-9392-1(8))* 2006. 282.75 *(978-1-4193-9387-7(1))* 2006. 111.75 *(978-1-4193-9388-4(X))* Recorded Bks., Inc.
—Fyre. Zug, Mark, illus. 2013. 702p. (J). *(978-0-06-224697-4(6))* HarperCollins Pubs.
—Fyre. 2014. (Septimus Heap Ser.: 7). (J). lib. bdg. 18.40 *(978-0-606-35067-9(5))* Turtleback.
—Magyk. Zug, Mark, illus. 2007. (Septimus Heap Ser.: Bk. 1). 564p. (gr. 4-7). 18.00 *(978-0-7569-7760-3(6))* Perfection Learning Corp.
—Magyk. (Septimus Heap Ser.: 1). (J). 2008. 79.75 *(978-1-4361-0584-2(6))* 2007. 1.25 *(978-1-4193-2619-6(8))* 2006. 123.75 *(978-1-4193-3807-6(2))* 2005. 126.75 *(978-1-4193-3805-2(6))* 2005. 106.75 *(978-1-4193-2622-6(8))* 2005. 103.75 *(978-1-4193-2624-0(4))* Recorded Bks., Inc.
—Magyk. 2006. (Septimus Heap Ser.: 1). (J). lib. bdg. 18.40 *(978-1-4177-3321-7(7))* Turtleback.
—Physik, 11 vols. 2007. (Septimus Heap Ser.: 3). (J). 113.75 *(978-1-4281-4576-4(1))*; (SPA.). 131.75 *(978-1-4281-4582-5(6))*; 133.75 *(978-1-4281-4580-1(X))*; 1.25 *(978-1-4281-4573-3(7))*; 111.75 *(978-1-4281-4578-8(8))*; 277.75 *(978-1-4281-4577-1(X))* Recorded Bks., Inc.
—Physik. 2008. (Septimus Heap Ser.: 3). (J). lib. bdg. 18.40 *(978-1-4178-1565-4(5))* Turtleback.
—Queste. Zug, Mark, illus. 2009. (Septimus Heap Ser.: 4). 596p. (J). lib. bdg. 18.40 *(978-0-606-02607-9(X))* Turtleback.
—Septimus Heap, Set. Zug, Mark, illus. 2007. (Septimus Heap Ser.: Bks. 1-2). (J). (gr. 4). pap. 15.99 *(978-0-06-136195-1(X)*, Tegen, Katherine Bks) HarperCollins Pubs.
—Septimus Heap, Book Five: Syren. Zug, Mark, illus. (Septimus Heap Ser.: 5). (ENG.). (J). (gr. 4). 2011. 656p. pap. 8.99 *(978-0-06-088212-9(3))* 2009. 640p. lib. bdg. 18.89 *(978-0-06-088211-2(5))* 2009. 640p. 17.99 *(978-0-06-088210-5(7))* HarperCollins Pubs. (Tegen, Katherine Bks).
—Septimus Heap, Book Four: Queste. Zug, Mark, illus. (Septimus Heap Ser.: 4). (ENG.). (J). (gr. 4). 2009. 624p. pap. 10.99 *(978-0-06-088209-9(3))* 2008. 608p. 18.99 *(978-0-06-088207-5(7))* HarperCollins Pubs. (Tegen, Katherine Bks).
—Septimus Heap, Book One: Magyk. Zug, Mark, illus. (Septimus Heap Ser.: 1). (ENG.). (J). (gr. 4-18). 2005. 576p. 18.99 *(978-0-06-057731-5(2))* 2005. 576p. lib. bdg. 18.89 *(978-0-06-057732-2(0))* 2006. 608p. reprint ed. pap. 7.99 *(978-0-06-057733-9(9))* HarperCollins Pubs. (Tegen, Katherine Bks).
—Septimus Heap, Book Seven: Fyre. Zug, Mark, illus. 2013. (Septimus Heap Ser.: 7). (ENG.). 720p. (J). (gr. 3-7). 18.99 *(978-0-06-124245-8(4)*, Tegen, Katherine Bks) HarperCollins Pubs.
—Septimus Heap, Book Six: Darke. Zug, Mark, illus. 2012. (Septimus Heap Ser.: 6). (ENG.). 656p. (J). (gr. 4). pap. 7.99 *(978-0-06-124244-1(6)*, Tegen, Katherine Bks) HarperCollins Pubs.
—Septimus Heap, Book Three: Physik. Zug, Mark, illus. (Septimus Heap Ser.: 3). (ENG.). (J). (gr. 4-7). 2007. 560p. 18.99 *(978-0-06-057737-7(1))*Bk. 3. 2008. 576p. pap. 9.99 *(978-0-06-057739-1(8))* HarperCollins Pubs. (Tegen, Katherine Bks).
—Septimus Heap, Book Two: Flyte. Zug, Mark, illus. (Septimus Heap Ser.: 2). (ENG.). 544p. (J). (gr. 4-7). 2007. pap. 8.99 *(978-0-06-057736-0(3))* 2006. 17.99 *(978-0-06-057734-6(7))* HarperCollins Pubs. (Tegen, Katherine Bks).
—TodHunter Moon, Book One: PathFinder. Zug, Mark, illus. 2014. (World of Septimus Heap Ser.: 1). (ENG.). 480p. (J). (gr. 3-7). 17.99 *(978-0-06-227245-4(4)*, Tegen, Katherine Bks) HarperCollins Pubs.
—TodHunter Moon, Book Three: StarChaser. Zug, Mark, illus. 2016. (World of Septimus Heap Ser.: 3). (ENG.). 496p. (J). (gr. 3-7). 17.99 *(978-0-06-227251-5(9)*, Tegen, Katherine Bks) HarperCollins Pubs.
—TodHunter Moon, Book Two: SandRider. Zug, Mark, illus. 2015. (World of Septimus Heap Ser.: 2). (ENG.). 480p. (J). (gr. 3-7). 17.99 *(978-0-06-227248-5(9)*, Tegen, Katherine Bks) HarperCollins Pubs.
Santillo, LuAnn. Look at Me. Santillo, LuAnn, ed. 2003. (Half-Pint Kids Readers Ser.). (Illus.). 7p. (J). (gr. -1-1). pap. 1.00 *(978-1-59256-052-3(0))* Half-Pint Kids, Inc.
Santore, Charles. Wizard of Oz Coloring Book: The Classic Edition. 2017. (Classic Edition Ser.). (ENG., Illus.). 52p. (J). (gr. 1). pap. 10.99 *(978-1-60433-706-8(0)*, Applesauce Pr.) Cider Mill Pr. Bk. Pubs., LLC.
Sarrasin, Alex. The Guardians of Neoegypti: Book One. 2007. 300p. per. 18.95 *(978-0-595-45710-6(X))* iUniverse, Inc.
Seal, Caitlin. Twice Dead. 2019. 336p. (YA). (gr. 7). pap. 12.99 *(978-1-62354-105-7(0)*, Charlesbridge Teen) Charlesbridge Publishing, Inc.
—Twice Dead: The Necromancer's Song. 2018. (Necromancer's Song Ser.: 1). (Illus.). 336p. (YA). (gr. 7). 17.99 *(978-1-58089-807-2(6)*, Charlesbridge Teen) Charlesbridge Publishing, Inc.
Shakespeare, William. The Tempest: The Graphic Novel, 1 vol. 2011. (Classic Graphic Novel Collection). (ENG.). 144p. (gr. 7-10). lib. bdg. 41.03 *(978-1-4205-0632-7(3)*, 33031fef-3bcc-4f2b-b6b1-9b876d12a7ce, Lucent Pr.) Greenhaven Publishing LLC.
Shapiro D., Brian. Plaquetooth. 2008. 28p. pap. 13.99 *(978-1-4343-8913-8(8))* AuthorHouse.
Shaw, Stephanie. Schnitzel: A Cautionary Tale for Lazy Louts. Barry, Kevin M., illus. 2016. (ENG.). 32p. (J). (gr. k-3). 17.99 *(978-1-58536-957-7(8)*, 204104) Sleeping Bear Pr.
Sherman, Delia. The Evil Wizard Smallbone. 2018. (ENG.). 416p. (J). (gr. 3-7). pap. 8.99 *(978-1-5362-0365-3(3))* Candlewick Pr.
Shi, Charleston. The Quest of the Phoenix: Book 1, the Phoenix & the Yeti. 2009. 168p. pap. 14.95 *(978-1-60844-173-0(3))* Dog Ear Publishing, LLC.
—The Quest of the Phoenix: Book Two, Storm of the Kraken. 2010. 180p. pap. 14.95 *(978-1-60844-352-9(3))* Dog Ear Publishing, LLC.
Shue, Jenna. Animal Island. Herzog, Inge, illus. 2005. 27p. (J). (gr. -1-3). per. 14.95 *(978-1-4259-0039-7(9))* AuthorHouse.
Simon, Elizabeth. Tyler Adams & the Adventures of Bravura: the First Quest. 2009. (ENG.). 49p. pap. 19.95 *(978-0-557-06290-4(X))* Lulu Pr., Inc.
Simon, Morris. Wizards Keep. 2007. 124p. pap. 4.99 *(978-1-931567-67-1(0))* Margaret Weis Productions, Ltd.
Skye, Obert. Apprentice Needed. 2019. (Wizard for Hire Ser.: 2). (ENG., Illus.). 416p. (J). (gr. 5-9). 17.99 *(978-1-62972-529-1(3)*, 5211782, Shadow Mountain) Shadow Mountain Publishing.
—Wizard for Hire. 2018. (Wizard for Hire Ser.: 1). (ENG.). 416p. (J). (gr. 5-9). 17.99 *(978-1-62972-412-6(2)*, 5194480, Shadow Mountain) Shadow Mountain Publishing.
Smith, M. a. & Smith, M. A. A Boy & His Wizard. Freeland, Devon & Contreras-Freeland, Gina, illus. 2009. 32p. pap. 8.95 *(978-1-60076-152-2(6))* StoneGarden.net Publishing.
Smith, Sasha Peyton. The Witch Haven. 2022. (ENG., Illus.). 464p. (YA). (gr. 9). pap. 13.99 *(978-1-5344-5439-2(X)*, Simon & Schuster Bks. For Young Readers) Simon & Schuster Bks. For Young Readers.
Somtow, S. P. The Wizard's Apprentice. 2018. (ENG., Illus.). 144p. (YA). (gr. 7). pap. 13.00 *(978-1-940999-27-2(8))*; pap. 13.00 *(978-1-940999-28-9(6))* Diplodocus Pr.
Sonneborn, Scott. Prisoner of the Ring, 1 vol. Schoening, Dan, illus. 2011. (Green Lantern Ser.). (ENG.). 56p. (J). (gr. 3-6). pap. 4.95 *(978-1-4342-3410-0(X)*, 116423); lib. bdg. 26.65 *(978-1-4342-2624-2(7)*, 113669) Capstone. (Stone Arch Bks.).
St-Onge, Donna Na-Tasa Katherine. The Eye of Isis, 1 vol. 2009. 155p. pap. 24.95 *(978-1-60836-986-7(2))* America Star Bks.
St-Onge, Julie-Ann. Passage to Fairywell. 2008. 80p. pap. 19.95 *(978-1-60441-172-0(4))* America Star Bks.
Stanek, Robert, pseud. The Kingdoms & the Elves of the Reaches: Signature, Keeper Martin's Tales, Bk. 1. 2007. (Illus.). 240p. (YA). 35.00 *(978-1-57545-128-2(X))* RP Media.
—The Kingdoms & the Elves of the Reaches II: Keeper Martin's Tales, Book 2. 2008. (Keeper Martin's Tales (Playaway) Ser.). (J). 54.99 *(978-1-60514-649-2(8))* Findaway World, LLC.
—The Kingdoms & the Elves of the Reaches II: Signature, Keeper Martin's Tales, Bk. 2. 2007. (Illus.). 244p. (J). (gr. 4-7). 35.00 *(978-1-57545-129-9(8))* RP Media.
—The Kingdoms & the Elves of the Reaches III: Signature, Keeper Martin's Tales, Bk. 3. 2008. (Illus.). 244p. (J). (gr. 4-7). 35.00 *(978-1-57545-130-5(1))* RP Media.
Stanley, P. "Olivia". The Dreadful Noises of Landoshar. 2008. 44p. pap. 12.26 *(978-0-557-02381-3(5))* Lulu Pr., Inc.
Stansberry, Don. Inky & the Missing Gold. 2007. (Illus.). 128p. (YA). per. 15.95 *(978-0-929915-10-4(0)*, Publisher Page) Headline Bks., Inc.
Stilton, Geronimo. The Enchanted Charms (Geronimo Stilton & the Kingdom of Fantasy #7) 2015. (Geronimo Stilton & the Kingdom of Fantasy Ser.: 7). (ENG., Illus.). 320p. (J). (gr. 2-5). 16.99 *(978-0-545-74615-1(9)*, Scholastic Paperbacks) Scholastic, Inc.
—The Wizard's Wand (Geronimo Stilton & the Kingdom of Fantasy #9) 2016. (Geronimo Stilton & the Kingdom of Fantasy Ser.: 9). (ENG., Illus.). 320p. (J). (gr. 2-5). 16.99 *(978-1-338-03291-8(7)*, Scholastic Paperbacks) Scholastic, Inc.
Stilton, Thea. The Secret of the Crystal Fairies (Thea Stilton: Special Edition #7) A Geronimo Stilton Adventure. 2018. (Thea Stilton Ser.: 7). (ENG., Illus.). 320p. (J). (gr. 2-5). 14.99 *(978-1-338-26859-1(7)*, Scholastic Paperbacks) Scholastic, Inc.
Stine, R. L. The Wizard of Ooze (Goosebumps HorrorLand #17) 2010. (Goosebumps Horrorland Ser.: 17). (ENG., Illus.). 160p. (J). (gr. 3-7). pap. 6.99 *(978-0-545-16198-5(3)*, Scholastic Paperbacks) Scholastic, Inc.
Sutton, Laurie S. The Crystal Quest. Lozano, Omar, illus. 2019. (You Choose Stories: Wonder Woman Ser.). (ENG.). 112p. (J). (gr. 2-6). pap. 6.95 *(978-1-4965-8441-0(4)*, 140966); lib. bdg. 32.65 *(978-1-4965-8351-2(5)*, 140645) Capstone. (Stone Arch Bks.).
Sutton, S. A. A Hero for Quale. 2009. 72p. pap. 9.99 *(978-1-60860-189-9(7)*, Strategic Bk. Publishing) Strategic Book Publishing & Rights Agency (SBPRA).
Terry, Frederick H. Gingerbread for All Seasons. 2009. 32p. pap. 14.95 *(978-1-4490-4476-3(X))* AuthorHouse.
Terry Lowey's Children's Stories Staff. The Secret of the Wizard's Wand. 2007. (Illus.). 24p. (J). 18.95 *(978-0-9792695-0-9(4))* Terry Lowey's Children's Stories, LLC.
Thomas, Sherry. The Immortal Heights. 2015. (Elemental Trilogy Ser.: 3). (ENG.). 448p. (YA). (gr. 9). 17.99 *(978-0-06-220735-7(0)*, Balzer & Bray) HarperCollins Pubs.
Thompson, Colin. The Floods #2: School Plot. Scrambly, Crab, illus. 2008. (Floods Ser.). (J). (ENG.). 224p. 15.99 *(978-0-06-113861-4(4))*; 256p. lib. bdg. 16.89 *(978-0-06-113855-3(X))* HarperCollins Pubs.
—The Floods Family Files. Thompson, Colin, illus. 2012. (Floods Ser.: 1). (ENG., Illus.). 32p. (J). (gr. 4-7). pap. 12.99 *(978-1-86471-942-0(7))* Random Hse. Australia AUS. Dist: Independent Pubs. Group.
—Good Neighbors. Scrambly, Crab, illus. 2008. (Floods Ser.: No. 1). 214p. (J). (gr. 3-7). 15.99 *(978-0-06-113196-7(2))* HarperCollins Pubs.
Thompson, Paul B. The Battle for the Brightstone: Book III of the Brightstone Saga, 1 vol. 2014. (Brightstone Saga Ser.). (ENG.). 176p. (J). (gr. 5-6). 39.93 *(978-0-7660-3984-1(6)*, e9149e38-6bf6-4e58-a2bb-da562639cd41) Enslow Publishing, LLC.
Thompson, Ruth Plumly. The Enchanted Island of Oz. 2006. (J). 24.95 *(978-1-930764-10-1(3))* International Wizard of Oz Club, The.
—The Wonder Book. 2006. (J). 24.95 *(978-1-930764-15-6(4))* International Wizard of Oz Club, The.
—Yankee in Oz. 2006. (J). 24.95 *(978-1-930764-13-2(8))* International Wizard of Oz Club, The.
Titelman, Becky. The Wonky Witch & the Witching Well. 2009. 364p. pap. 19.99 *(978-1-4490-2673-8(7))* AuthorHouse.
Tulien, Sean. The Not-So-Evil Wizard. Cunyat, Pol, illus. 2016. (Thud & Blunder Ser.). (ENG.). 56p. (J). (gr. 1-3). lib. bdg. 23.99 *(978-1-4965-3221-3(X)*, 132416, Stone Arch Bks.) Capstone.
Vande Velde, Vivian. The Book of Mordred. 2007. (ENG.). 352p. (YA). (gr. 7-12). pap. 8.99 *(978-0-618-80916-5(3)*, 497456, Clarion Bks.) HarperCollins Pubs.
—Wizard at Work. 2004. (ENG., Illus.). 144p. (J). (gr. 5-7). pap. 10.95 *(978-0-15-205309-3(3)*, 1195997, Clarion Bks.) HarperCollins Pubs.
Wallace Ii, James C. & Wallace, Amanda D. The Emerald Slippers of Oz. 2013. 156p. pap. 14.99 *(978-0-578-12511-4(0))* Scientia Est Vox Pr.
Wasson, Christopher. Quest for Adlaremzee Molair Nopeeoh. 2003. 120p. pap. 19.95 *(978-1-4137-0117-3(5))* America Star Bks.
Waterfield, Susan. Spunkie's Magical Garden. 2012. 32p. pap. 14.95 *(978-1-257-77576-7(6))* Lulu Pr., Inc.
West, Tracey. Call of the Sound Dragon: a Branches Book (Dragon Masters #16) Loveridge, Matt, illus. 2020. (Dragon Masters Ser.: 16). (ENG.). 96p. (J). (gr. 1-3). pap. 5.99 *(978-1-338-54028-4(9))* Scholastic, Inc.
—Call of the Sound Dragon: a Branches Book (Dragon Masters #16) (Library Edition) Loveridge, Matt, illus. 2020. (Dragon Masters Ser.: 16). (ENG.). 96p. (J). (gr. 1-3). lib. bdg. 24.99 *(978-1-338-54029-1(7))* Scholastic, Inc.
—Chill of the Ice Dragon, 9. 2019. (Branches Early Ch Bks). (ENG.). 89p. (J). (gr. 2-3). 15.36 *(978-0-87617-974-1(X))* Penworthy Co., LLC, The.
—Chill of the Ice Dragon, 9. 2018. (Branches: Dragon Masters Ser.). (ENG.). 96p. (gr. 1-4). 18.69 *(978-1-5364-3194-0(X))* Scholastic, Inc.
—Chill of the Ice Dragon: a Branches Book (Dragon Masters #9), 1 vol. de Polonia, Nina, illus. 2018. (Dragon Masters Ser.: 9). (ENG.). 96p. (J). (gr. 1-3). pap. 5.99 *(978-1-338-16986-7(6))* Scholastic, Inc.
—Eye of the Earthquake Dragon, 13. 2019. (Branches Early Ch Bks). (ENG.). 90p. (J). (gr. 2-3). 15.36 *(978-1-64697-098-8(5))* Penworthy Co., LLC, The.
—Eye of the Earthquake Dragon, 13. 2019. (Branches: Dragon Masters Ser.). (ENG.). 96p. (gr. 1-4). 18.69 *(978-1-5364-5484-0(2))* Scholastic, Inc.
—Eye of the Earthquake Dragon: a Branches Book (Dragon Masters #13) Griffo, Daniel, illus. 2019. (Dragon Masters Ser.: 13). (ENG.). 96p. (J). (gr. 1-3). pap. 5.99 *(978-1-338-26371-8(4))* Scholastic, Inc.
—Flight of the Moon Dragon, 6. 2016. (Branches: Dragon Masters Ser.). (ENG.). 96p. (gr. 1-4). 17.44 *(978-1-4844-9296-3(X))* Scholastic, Inc.
—Flight of the Moon Dragon. Jones, Damien, illus. 2016. (Dragon Masters Ser.: bk.6). (ENG.). 96p. (J). (gr. 1-3). 14.75 *(978-0-606-39155-9(X))* Turtleback.
—Flight of the Moon Dragon: a Branches Book (Dragon Masters #6) Jones, Damien, illus. 2016. (Dragon Masters Ser.: 6). (ENG.). 96p. (J). (gr. 1-3). pap. 4.99 *(978-0-545-91392-8(6))* Scholastic, Inc.
—Fortress of the Stone Dragon: a Branches Book (Dragon Masters #17) Loveridge, Matt, illus. 2020. (Dragon Masters Ser.). (ENG.). 96p. (J). (gr. 1-3). pap. 5.99 *(978-1-338-54031-4(9))* Scholastic, Inc.
—Fortress of the Stone Dragon: a Branches Book (Dragon Masters #17) (Library Edition) Loveridge, Matt, illus. 2020. (Dragon Masters Ser.). (ENG.). 96p. (J). (gr. 1-3). 24.99 *(978-1-338-54032-1(7))* Scholastic, Inc.
—Future of the Time Dragon, 15. 2020. (Branches: Dragon Masters Ser.). (ENG.). 96p. (gr. 1-4). 18.69 *(978-1-5364-6188-6(1))* Scholastic, Inc.
—Future of the Time Dragon: a Branches Book (Dragon Masters #15) Griffo, Daniel, illus. 2020. (Dragon Masters Ser.: 15). (ENG.). 96p. (J). (gr. 1-3). pap. 5.99 *(978-1-338-54025-3(4))* Scholastic, Inc.
—Future of the Time Dragon: a Branches Book (Dragon Masters #15) (Library Edition) Griffo, Daniel, illus. 2020. (Dragon Masters Ser.: 15). (ENG.). 96p. (J). (gr. 1-3). 24.99 *(978-1-338-54026-0(2))* Scholastic, Inc.
—Land of the Spring Dragon: a Branches Book (Dragon Masters #14) Loveridge, Matt, illus. 2019. (Dragon Masters Ser.: 14). (ENG.). 96p. (J). (gr. 1-3). pap. 4.99 *(978-1-338-26374-9(9))* Scholastic, Inc.
—Land of the Spring Dragon: a Branches Book (Dragon Masters #14) (Library Edition) Loveridge, Matt, illus. 2019. (Dragon Masters Ser.: 14). (ENG.). 96p. (J). (gr. 1-3). 24.99 *(978-1-338-26375-6(7))* Scholastic, Inc.
—Power of the Fire Dragon: a Branches Book (Dragon Masters #4) Howells, Graham, illus. 2015. (Dragon Masters Ser.: 4). (ENG.). 96p. (J). (gr. 1-3). pap. 5.99 *(978-0-545-64631-4(6))* Scholastic, Inc.
—Rise of the Earth Dragon. 2014. (Dragon Masters Ser.: 1). lib. bdg. 14.75 *(978-0-606-36050-0(6))* Turtleback.
—Rise of the Earth Dragon: a Branches Book (Dragon Masters #1) Howells, Graham, illus. 2014. (Dragon Masters Ser.: 1). (ENG.). 96p. (J). (gr. 1-3). pap. 5.99 *(978-0-545-64623-9(5))* Scholastic, Inc.
—Rise of the Earth Dragon: a Branches Book (Dragon Masters #1) (Library Edition), Vol. 1. Howells, Graham, illus. 2014. (Dragon Masters Ser.: 1). (ENG.). 96p. (J). (gr. 1-3). 24.99 *(978-0-545-64624-6(3))* Scholastic, Inc.
—Roar of the Thunder Dragon, 8. 2019. (Branches Early Ch Bks). (ENG.). 88p. (J). (gr. 2-3). 15.36 *(978-0-87617-975-8(8))* Penworthy Co., LLC, The.
—Roar of the Thunder Dragon. 2017. (Dragon Masters — Branches Ser.: 8). lib. bdg. 14.75 *(978-0-606-40668-0(9))* Turtleback.
—Roar of the Thunder Dragon: a Branches Book (Dragon Masters #8) Jones, Damien, illus. 2017. (Dragon Masters Ser.: 8). (ENG.). 96p. (J). (gr. 1-3). pap. 5.99 *(978-1-338-04292-4(0))* Scholastic, Inc.
—Roar of the Thunder Dragon: a Branches Book (Dragon Masters #8) (Library Edition) Jones, Damien, illus. 2017. (Dragon Masters Ser.: 8). (ENG.). 96p. (J). (gr. 1-3). lib. bdg. 15.99 *(978-1-338-04293-1(9))* Scholastic, Inc.
—Saving the Sun Dragon. 2014. (Dragon Masters Ser.: 2). lib. bdg. 14.75 *(978-0-606-36051-7(4))* Turtleback.
—Saving the Sun Dragon: a Branches Book (Dragon Masters #2) Jones, Damien, illus. 2014. (Dragon Masters Ser.: 2). (ENG.). 96p. (J). (gr. 1-3). pap. 5.99 *(978-0-545-64625-3(1))* Scholastic, Inc.
—Saving the Sun Dragon: a Branches Book (Dragon Masters #2) (Library Edition) Jones, Damien, illus. 2014. (Dragon Masters Ser.: 2). (ENG.). 96p. (J). (gr. 1-3). 15.99 *(978-0-545-64626-0(X))* Scholastic, Inc.
—Search for the Lightning Dragon. 2017. (Dragon Masters Ser.: 7). lib. bdg. 14.75 *(978-0-606-39713-1(2))* Turtleback.
—Search for the Lightning Dragon: a Branches Book (Dragon Masters #7) Jones, Damien, illus. 2017. (Dragon Masters Ser.: 7). (ENG.). 96p. (J). (gr. 1-3). pap. 4.99 *(978-1-338-04288-7(2))* Scholastic, Inc.
—Search for the Lightning Dragon: a Branches Book (Dragon Masters #7) (Library Edition) Jones, Damien, illus. 2017. (Dragon Masters Ser.: 7). (ENG.). 96p. (J). (gr. 1-3). lib. bdg. 24.99 *(978-1-338-04289-4(0))* Scholastic, Inc.
—Secret of the Water Dragon. 2015. (Dragon Masters Ser.: 3). lib. bdg. 14.75 *(978-0-606-39886-2(4))* Turtleback.
—Secret of the Water Dragon: a Branches Book (Dragon Masters #3) Jones, Damien, illus. 2015. (Dragon Masters Ser.: 3). (ENG.). 96p. (J). (gr. 1-3). pap. 5.99 *(978-0-545-64628-4(6))* Scholastic, Inc.
—Shine of the Silver Dragon, 11. 2019. (Branches Early Ch Bks). (ENG.). 90p. (J). (gr. 2-3). 15.36 *(978-0-87617-976-5(6))* Penworthy Co., LLC, The.
—Shine of the Silver Dragon. Polonia, Nina de, illus. 2018. (Dragon Masters Ser.: 11). (ENG.). 96p. (J). (gr. 1-3). 15.99 *(978-1-338-26366-4(8))* Scholastic, Inc.
—Shine of the Silver Dragon: a Branches Book (Dragon Masters #11) de Polonia, Nina, illus. 2018. (Dragon Masters Ser.: 11). (ENG.). 96p. (J). (gr. 1-3). pap. 4.99 *(978-1-338-26365-7(X))* Scholastic, Inc.
—Treasure of the Gold Dragon, 12. 2019. (Branches Early Ch Bks). (ENG.). 90p. (J). (gr. 2-3). 15.36 *(978-0-87617-977-2(4))* Penworthy Co., LLC, The.
—Treasure of the Gold Dragon: a Branches Book (Dragon Masters #12) Foresti, Sara, illus. 2018. (Dragon Masters Ser.: 12). (ENG.). 96p. (J). (gr. 1-3). pap. 4.99 *(978-1-338-26368-8(4))* Scholastic, Inc.
—Treasure of the Gold Dragon: a Branches Book (Dragon Masters #12) (Library Edition) Foresti, Sara, illus. 2018.

(Dragon Masters Ser.: 12). (ENG.). 96p. (J). (gr. 1-3). lib. bdg. 15.99 *(978-1-338-26369-5(2))* Scholastic, Inc.

Wexler, Django. The Forbidden Library. 2015. (Forbidden Library: 1). (ENG., Illus.). 400p. (J). (gr. 5). 8.99 *(978-0-14-242681-4(4),* Puffin Books) Penguin Young Readers Group.

Whisp, Kennilworthy, pseud. Quidditch Through the Ages. 2017. (ENG.). 128p. (J). (gr. 3-3). 12.99 *(978-1-338-12574-0(5),* Levine, Arthur A. Bks.) Scholastic, Inc.

—Quidditch Through the Ages. 2017. (ENG.). (J). (gr. 3). lib. bdg. 24.50 *(978-0-606-39694-3(2))* Turtleback.

Willow, Tirissa & the Necklace of Nulidor. 2009. 338p. pap. 17.95 *(978-1-4327-4013-9(X))* Outskirts Pr., Inc.

Wilson, Karma. Baby Cakes. Williams, Sam, illus. 2006. (ENG.). 32p. (J). (gr. -1 — 1). bds. 8.99 *(978-1-4169-0289-8(9),* Little Simon) Little Simon.

Wilson, Wendy. The First Book of Red. 2005. 99p. pap. 19.95 *(978-1-4137-5570-1(4))* America Star Bks.

Wind, Chuck T. The Test of Love. 2011. 24p. pap. 24.95 *(978-1-4626-2398-3(0))* America Star Bks.

Wizard Academies I: The Heart of Darkness. 2006. 658p. pap. 24.96 *(978-1-4116-7787-6(0))* Lulu Pr., Inc.

Wizards of Waverly Place Insider's Guide. 2009. 128p. pap. 8.99 *(978-1-4231-2473-3(1))* Disney Pr.

Wrede, Patricia C. Talking to Dragons. unabr. ed. 2004. (Enchanted Forest Chronicles: Bk. 4). 255p. (J). (gr. 6-18). pap. 38.00 incl. audio *(978-0-8072-0983-7(X),* S YA 385 SP, Listening Library) Random Hse. Audio Publishing Group.

Yagmin, Daniel, Jr., illus. Norton B. Nice. 2009. (J). *(978-1-60108-018-9(2))* Red Cygnet Pr.

Yolen, Jane. Wizard's Hall. 144p. (J). (gr. 3-5). pap. 6.00 *(978-0-8072-1544-9(9),* Listening Library) Random Hse. Audio Publishing Group.

Zimmerman, Diana S. Kandide & the Secret of the Mists, Bk. 1. Gadd, Maxine, illus. 2008. (Calabiyau Chronicles Ser.). 290p. (J). (gr. 4-7). pap. 9.99 *(978-0-9794328-2-8(0))* Noesis Publishing.

WOLFE, THOMAS, 1900-1938

Boffa, Laura. Writing Home: The Story of Author Thomas Wolfe. 2016. (Illus.). 32p. (J). (gr. -1-12). 15.95 *(978-1-63076-133-2(8))* Taylor Trade Publishing.

Prince, Jennifer S. The Life & Times of Asheville's Thomas Wolfe. 2016. (True Tales for Young Readers Ser.). (ENG., Illus.). 116p. (YA). pap. 17.00 *(978-0-86526-484-7(8),* 01OSPS) Univ. of North Carolina Pr.

WOLVERINE

Borgert-Spaniol, Megan. Wolverines. (Illus.). 24p. (J). 2014. *(978-0-531-21818-1(X))* 2013. (ENG., lib. bdg. 26.95 *(978-1-60014-916-0(2),* Blastoff! Readers) Bellwether Media.

Carr, Aaron. Wolverine. 2014. (J). *(978-1-4896-2645-5(X))* Weigl Pubs., Inc.

Gish, Melissa. Living Wild: Wolverines. 2015. (Living Wild Ser.). (ENG., Illus.). 48p. (J). (gr. 5-8). pap. 12.00 *(978-1-62832-007-7(9),* 21390, Creative Paperbacks) Creative Co., The.

—Wolverines. 2014. (Living Wild Ser.). (ENG.). 48p. (J). (gr. 4-7). *(978-1-60818-421-7(8),* 21389, Creative Education) Creative Co., The.

Markle, Sandra. Los Glotones. 2007. (Animales carroñeros (Animal Scavengers) Ser.). (SPA., Illus.). (J). (gr. -1-3). 39p. lib. bdg. 25.26 *(978-0-8225-7732-4(1));* 40p. per. 7.95 *(978-0-8225-7736-2(4))* Lerner Publishing Group. (Ediciones Lerner).

—Los Glotones; Wolverines. 2008. pap. 46.95 *(978-0-8225-9453-6(6))* Lerner Publishing Group.

—Wolverines. 2005. (Animal Scavengers Ser.). (ENG., Illus.). 40p. (J). (gr. 3-6). lib. bdg. 25.26 *(978-0-8225-3198-2(4),* Lerner Pubns.) Lerner Publishing Group.

Markovics, Joyce L. Wolverine: Super Strong. 2011. (Built for Cold Ser.). 32p. (YA). (gr. 1-4). lib. bdg. 28.50 *(978-1-61772-131-1(X));* (J). (gr. 4-5). lib. bdg., E-Book 49.22 *(978-1-61772-224-0(3))* Bearport Publishing Co., Inc.

McIntyre, Sandra. Wolverines. 2010. (Illus.). 24p. *(978-1-55388-671-6(2));* pap. *(978-1-55388-672-3(0))* Weigl Educational Pubs. Ltd.

Pallotta, Jerry. Wolverine vs. Tasmanian Devil (Who Would Win?) Bolster, Rob, illus. 2020. (Who Would Win? Ser.). (ENG.). 32p. (J). (gr. 1-4). pap. 4.99 *(978-0-545-45189-5(2))* Scholastic, Inc.

Rathburn, Betsy. Wolverines. 2018. (North American Animals Ser.). (ENG., Illus.). 24p. (J). (gr. k-3). lib. bdg. 26.95 *(978-1-62617-731-4(7),* Blastoff! Readers) Bellwether Media.

Stewart, Melissa. National Geographic Readers: Wolverines (L3) 2018. (Readers Ser.). (Illus.). 48p. (J). (gr. 3-7). pap. 4.99 *(978-1-4263-3222-7(X));* (ENG., lib. bdg. 14.90 *(978-1-4263-3223-4(8))* Disney Publishing Worldwide. (National Geographic Kids).

Swanson, Diane. Welcome to the World of Wolverines, 1 vol. 2007. (Welcome to the World Ser.: 0). (ENG., Illus.). 32p. (J). (gr. -1-2). pap. 7.95 *(978-1-55285-840-0(5),* 7c4e8e9b-a77d-4db2-b695-57fd4248eec2) Whitecap Bks., Ltd. CAN. Dist: Firefly Bks., Ltd.

WOLVERINE—FICTION

Caballero, Erica. Mount Mole. 2006. pap. 10.00 *(978-1-4257-2301-9(2))* Xlibris Corp.

Jacques, Brian. Rakkety Tam. 2004. (Redwall Ser.). 1.00 *(978-1-4175-5517-8(3))* Recorded Bks., Inc.

—Rakkety Tam: A Tale from Redwall. 2006. (Redwall Ser.: 17). (ENG., Illus.). 384p. (J). (gr. 5-18). 9.99 *(978-0-14-240683-0(X),* Firebird) Penguin Young Readers Group.

McCracken, Harold. Pirate of the North. Tonk, Ernest, illus. 2011. 224p. 44.95 *(978-1-258-09631-1(5))* Literary Licensing, LLC.

McIntyre, Sandra. Les Carcajous: Les Animaux du Canada. Karvonen, Tanjah, tr. from ENG. 2011. (FRE.). 24p. (gr. 3-6). *(978-1-77071-417-5(0))* Weigl Educational Pubs. Ltd.

Skurzynski, Gloria. Mysteries in Our National Parks: Buried Alive! A Mystery in Denali National Park. 2008. (Mysteries in Our National Park Ser.). (Illus.). 160p. (J). (gr. 3-7). pap. 4.99 *(978-1-4263-0252-7(5),* National Geographic Kids) Disney Publishing Worldwide.

Skurzynski, Gloria & Ferguson, Alane. Buried Alive. 2003. (Mysteries in Our National Park Ser.: No. 12). (ENG.). 160p. (J). (gr. 3-7). 15.95 *(978-0-7922-6966-3(7),* National Geographic Children's Bks.) National Geographic Society.

WOLVES

Absolute Expert: Wolves. 2020. (ENG.). (J). *(978-1-4263-3852-6(X))* National Geographic Society.

Albertson, Al. Gray Wolves. 2020. (Animals of the Forest Ser.). (ENG., Illus.). 24p. (J). (gr. k-3). lib. bdg. 26.95 *(978-1-64487-126-3(2),* Blastoff! Readers) Bellwether Media.

Animal Watch: Wolves. (J). (gr. 1-3). 75.00 *(978-0-669-15881-6(X))* Houghton Mifflin Harcourt School Pubs.

Banner, Melanie Jane. Smoke: A Wolf's Story, 1 vol. 2003. (ENG., Illus.). 160p. (J). (gr. 4-7). pap. 9.95 *(978-1-55041-322-9(8),* d3611c0c-b979-49d4-b7cb-835d1a6fe9a2) Fitzhenry & Whiteside, Ltd. CAN. Dist: Firefly Bks., Ltd.

Barnes, J. Lou. The Secret Lives of Wolves, 1 vol. 2007. (Secret Lives of Animals Ser.). (ENG., Illus.). 32p. (gr. 3-5). lib. bdg. 28.67 *(978-0-8368-7660-4(1),* f4671ccd-b666-4771-999e-c0f7749ca3df, Gareth Stevens Learning Library) Stevens, Gareth Publishing LLLP.

Bergeron, Alain M., et al. Les Loups. 2008. (FRE., Illus.). 64p. (J). pap. 8.95 *(978-2-89435-375-2(8))* Quintin Pubs./Editions Michel Quintin CAN. Dist: Crabtree Publishing Co.

Bjorklund, Ruth. Wolves, 1 vol. 2009. (Endangered! Ser.). (ENG.). 48p. (gr. 3-3). lib. bdg. 32.64 *(978-0-7614-2993-7(X),* 54ef9bc6-07e7-4326-a10b-dc66f8fc0af7) Cavendish Square Publishing LLC.

Black, Robyn Hood. Wolves. Howard, Colin, illus. 2008. (ENG.). 24p. (J). (gr. 3-18). 19.95 *(978-1-58117-817-3(4),* Intervisual/Piggy Toes) Bendon, Inc.

Borgert-Spaniol, Megan. Jackals. 2013. (Animal Safari Ser.). (ENG., Illus.). 24p. (J). (gr. k-3). lib. bdg. 26.95 *(978-1-60014-910-8(3),* Blastoff! Readers) Bellwether Media.

Bozzo, Linda. How Wolves Grow Up. 2019. (Animals Growing Up Ser.). (ENG.). 24p. (gr. 1-2). 56.10 *(978-1-9785-0835-4(2))* Enslow Publishing, LLC.

Brandenburg, Jim. Face to Face with Wolves. 2018. (Face to Face with Animals Ser.). (Illus.). 32p. (J). (gr. 3-7). pap. 6.99 *(978-1-4263-3056-8(1),* National Geographic Kids) Disney Publishing Worldwide.

Brandenburg, Jim & Brandenburg, Judy. Face to Face with Wolves. 2010. (Face to Face (Paperback National Geographic) Ser.). (ENG.). (J). (gr. 2-5). lib. bdg. 17.55 *(978-1-62765-573-6(5))* Perfection Learning Corp.

Brannon, Cecelia H. Baby Wolves at the Zoo, 1 vol. 2015. (All about Baby Zoo Animals Ser.). (ENG., Illus.). 24p. (gr. k-1). pap. 10.35 *(978-0-7660-7162-9(6),* e441e719-5115-413d-82bd-b0dc1b7b62ed) Enslow Publishing, LLC.

Brown Bear Books. Wolves. 2012. (Animal Families Ser.). (ENG., Illus.). 32p. (J). (gr. 3-6). 31.35 *(978-1-78121-006-2(3),* 16429) Brown Bear Bks.

Butz, Christopher. Red Wolves. 2003. (Endangered Plants & Animals of North America Ser.). (J). pap. *(978-1-58417-213-0(4));* lib. bdg. *(978-1-58417-212-3(6))* Lake Street Pubs.

Carmichael, L. E. Fox Talk. Bronson, Jody, illus. 2013. 62p. *(978-0-9881638-5-0(3))* Ashby-BP Publishing.

Carter, James. The Story of the Wolf: Band 17/Diamond. 2017. (Collins Big Cat Ser.). (ENG., Illus.). 56p. (J). pap. 11.99 *(978-0-00-820896-7(4))* HarperCollins Pubs. Ltd. GBR. Dist: Independent Pubs. Group.

Chang, Kirsten. Wolf or Coyote? 2019. (Spotting Differences Ser.). (ENG., Illus.). 24p. (J). (gr. k-3). lib. bdg. 26.95 *(978-1-64487-037-2(1),* Blastoff! Readers) Bellwether Media.

Christopher, Nick. Arctic Wolves of the Tundra. 2017. (Animals of the Tundra Ser.). 24p. (gr. 1-2). 49.50 *(978-1-5345-2215-2(8),* KidHaven Publishing) Greenhaven Publishing LLC.

Clark, Willow. Wolves: Life in the Pack, 1 vol. 2011. (Animal Families Ser.). (ENG.). 24p. (J). (gr. 1-1). pap. 9.25 *(978-1-4488-2616-2(0),* 735ad011-4885-4465-b652-f7b94f7f4f90); (Illus.). lib. bdg. 26.27 *(978-1-4488-2515-8(6),* ad6b4f2d-8dc4-49c2-acfe-221cadcc56b4) Rosen Publishing Group, Inc., The. (PowerKids Pr.).

—Wolves: Lobos: Life in the Pack: Vida en la Manada, 1 vol. 2011. (Animal Families / Familias de Animales Ser.). (SPA & ENG., Illus.). 24p. (gr. 1-1). lib. bdg. 26.27 *(978-1-4488-3141-8(5),* e536be35-bd4e-4dd8-9ad8-15a590c75650, PowerKids Pr.) Rosen Publishing Group, Inc., The.

Clarke, Penny. Wolves. Hersey, Bob, illus. 2004. (Scary Creatures Ser.). (ENG.). 32p. (J). (gr. 2-4). pap. 6.95 *(978-0-531-16749-6(6),* Watts, Franklin) Scholastic Library Publishing.

Claybourne, Anna. A Pack of Wolves: And Other Canine Groups, 1 vol. 2012. (Animals in Groups Ser.). (ENG.). 48p. (J). (gr. 4-6). pap. 9.95 *(978-1-4329-6489-4(5),* 119076, Heinemann) Capstone.

Clever Coyote & other Wild Dogs: Level L, 6 vols. 128p. (gr. 2-3). 40.50 *(978-0-7699-1033-8(5))* Shortland Pubns. (U. S. A.) Inc.

Cohn, Scotti. One Wolf Howls, 1 vol. Detwiler, Susan, illus. 2009. (ENG.). 32p. (J). (gr. -1-3). 16.95 *(978-1-934359-92-1(0))* Arbordale Publishing.

Dahl, Michael. Wolves, 1 vol. 2012. (North American Animals Ser.). (ENG.). 24p. (J). (gr. -1-2). lib. bdg. 27.32 *(978-1-4296-7701-1(5),* 117298); (gr. k-1). pap. 41.70 *(978-1-4296-8361-6(9),* Capstone Pr.) Capstone.

DeLallo, Laura. Arctic Wolf: The High Arctic. 2011. (Built for Cold Ser.). 32p. (YA). (gr. 1-4). lib. bdg. 28.50 *(978-1-61772-132-8(8));* (J). (gr. 4-5). lib. bdg., E-Book 49.22 *(978-1-61772-219-6(7))* Bearport Publishing Co., Inc.

Dibble, Traci. Wolves. 2011. (Predator Animals Ser.). 16p. pap. 39.62 *(978-1-61541-364-5(2))* American Reading Co.

Dibble, Traci & Sanchez, Lucia M. Lobos: Wolves. 2011. (Animales depredadores (Predator Animals) Ser.). (SPA.). 16p. (J). pap. 6.95 *(978-1-61541-365-2(0))* American Reading Co.

Dibble, Traci & Washington, Joi. Wolves. Washington, Joi, illus. 2010. (1-3Y Animals Ser.). (ENG., Illus.). 16p. (J). (gr. k-2). pap. 9.60 *(978-1-61541-363-8(4))* American Reading Co.

Dutcher, Jamie. A Friend for Lakota: The Incredible True Story of a Wolf Who Braved Bullying. 2015. (Baby Animal Tales Ser.). (Illus.). 32p. (J). (gr. -1-k). 16.99 *(978-1-4263-2082-8(5),* National Geographic Kids) Disney Publishing Worldwide.

—Running with Wolves: Our Story of Life with the Sawtooth Pack. 2019. (Illus.). 160p. (J). (gr. 5-9). 16.99 *(978-1-4263-3358-3(7),* National Geographic Kids) Disney Publishing Worldwide.

Dutcher, Jim. National Geographic Kids Chapters: Living with Wolves! True Stories of Adventures with Animals. 2016. (NGK Chapters Ser.). (Illus.). 112p. (J). (gr. 3-7). pap. 5.99 *(978-1-4263-2563-2(0),* National Geographic Kids) Disney Publishing Worldwide.

—Running with Wolves: Our Story of Life with the Sawtooth Pack. 2019. (ENG., Illus.). 160p. (J). (gr. 5-9). lib. bdg. 26.90 *(978-1-4263-3359-0(5),* National Geographic Kids) Disney Publishing Worldwide.

Einstein, Sheila. Wolves, 1 vol. 2017. (KidsWorld Ser.). (ENG., Illus.). 64p. (J). pap. 6.99 *(978-1-988183-10-7(3),* 1c6c213a-9530-44ab-871d-da0174040675) KidsWorld Bks. CAN. Dist: Lone Pine Publishing USA.

Field, Nancy & Karasov, Corliss. Discovering Wolves. Hunkel, Cary, illus. 2011. (Discovering Nature Library). (ENG.). 40p. (J). (gr. 3-8). pap. 6.95 *(978-0-941042-39-0(1))* Dog-Eared Pubns.

Flaherty, William. Animals Illustrated: Arctic Wolf. Bigham, Sean, illus. 2018. (Animals Illustrated Ser.: 6). (ENG.). 24p. (J). (gr. 1-3). 12.95 *(978-1-77227-213-0(2))* Inhabit Media Inc. CAN. Dist: Consortium Bk. Sales & Distribution.

Fleischer, Jayson. These Are Wolves. Washington, Joi, illus. 2016. (2G Predator Animals Ser.). (ENG.). 28p. (J). (gr. k-2). pap. 8.00 *(978-1-61541-508-3(4))* American Reading Co.

Furstinger, Nancy. We Need Wolves. 2019. (Animal Files Ser.). (ENG., Illus.). 32p. (J). (gr. 3-5). pap. 9.95 *(978-1-64185-373-6(5),* 1641853735); lib. bdg. 31.35 *(978-1-64185-315-6(8),* 1641853158) North Star Editions. (Focus Readers).

Gagne, Tammy. Gray Wolf. 2016. (Back from near Extinction Ser.). (ENG., Illus.). 48p. (J). (gr. 4-8). lib. bdg. 35.64 *(978-1-68078-467-1(6),* 23871) ABDO Publishing Co.

Gangemi, Alphia. Hunting with Wolves, 1 vol. 2012. (Animal Attack! Ser.). (ENG., Illus.). 24p. (J). (gr. 2-3). 25.27 *(978-1-4339-7083-2(X),* 8f74a6fd-bd62-4a0c-9eaa-20970ede0e85); pap. 9.15 *(978-1-4339-7084-9(8),* e38edf15-ff23-4250-8a02-b3139c5d574c) Stevens, Gareth Publishing LLLP. (Gareth Stevens Learning Library).

Gardner, Jane P. Jackals. 2013. (Wild Canine Pups Ser.). 24p. (J). (gr. -1-3). lib. bdg. 25.65 *(978-1-61772-929-4(9))* Bearport Publishing Co., Inc.

George, Jean Craighead. Autumn Moon. 2003. (J). (gr. 3-7). 20.75 *(978-0-8446-7241-0(6))* Smith, Peter Pub., Inc.

—The Wolves Are Back. 2008. (J). (gr. 1-4). 28.95 incl. audio compact disk *(978-1-4301-0594-7(1))* Live Oak Media.

—The Wolves Are Back. Minor, Wendell, illus. 2008. (J). (gr. 1-4). 25.95 incl. audio *(978-1-4301-0591-6(7))* Live Oak Media.

—The Wolves Are Back. Minor, Wendell, illus. 2008. (ENG.). 32p. (J). (gr. -1-3). 17.99 *(978-0-525-47947-5(3),* Dutton Books for Young Readers) Penguin Young Readers Group.

Gilbert, Sara. Dire Wolves. 2017. (Ice Age Mega Beasts Ser.). (ENG., Illus.). 24p. (J). (gr. 1-4). pap. 8.99 *(978-1-62832-373-3(6),* 20069, Creative Paperbacks); *(978-1-60818-765-2(9),* 20071, Creative Education) Creative Co., The.

Gilkerson, Patricia. My Adventure with Wolves. 2009. (ENG.). 44p. (J). 8.99 *(978-1-59092-476-1(2))* Blue Forge Pr.

Giudice, Stephanie. Wolves Like to Eat. 2017. (1-3Y Mammals Ser.). (ENG., Illus.). 12p. (J). pap. 9.60 *(978-1-64053-089-8(4),* ARC Pr. Bks.) American Reading Co.

Godkin, Celia. The Wolves Return. Godkin, Celia, illus. 2017. (ENG., Illus.). 32p. (J). (gr. 1-3). 17.95 *(978-1-77278-011-6(1))* Pajama Pr. CAN. Dist: Publishers Group West (PGW).

Goecke, Michael P. Dire Wolf, 1 vol. 2003. (Prehistoric Animals Ser.). (ENG.). 24p. (gr. k-4). 25.65 *(978-1-57765-966-2(X),* Buddy Bks.) ABDO Publishing Co.

Goldish, Meish. Gray Wolves: Return to Yellowstone. 2016. (America's Animal Comebacks Ser.). (ENG., Illus.). 32p. (J). (gr. 2-7). pap. 7.99 *(978-1-944998-72-1(1))* Bearport Publishing Co., Inc.

—Red Wolves: And Then There Were (Almost) None. 2007. (America's Animal Comebacks Ser.). (Illus.). 32p. (YA). (gr. 2-5). lib. bdg. 25.27 *(978-1-59716-742-0(8))* Bearport Publishing Co., Inc.

Grack, Rachel. Wolves. 2018. (North American Animals Ser.). (ENG.). 24p. (J). (gr. 1-4). pap. 8.99 *(978-1-68152-339-2(6),* 15124); lib. bdg. *(978-1-68151-419-2(2),* 15116) Amicus.

Green, Emily. Wolves. 2011. (Backyard Wildlife Ser.). (ENG., Illus.). 24p. (J). (gr. k-3). lib. bdg. 26.95 *(978-1-60014-563-6(9),* Blastoff! Readers) Bellwether Media.

—Wolves. 2011. (Backyard Wildlife Ser.). 24p. (J). (gr. k-1). lib. bdg. 22.00 *(978-0-531-20489-4(8),* Children's Pr.) Scholastic Library Publishing.

Green, Jen. Exploring Nature: Examine the Wonderful World of Wolves, Jackals, Coyotes, Foxes & Other Wild Dogs, Shown in 190 Exciting Images: Wolves - Life in the Wild. 2015. (ENG., Illus.). 64p. (J). (gr. 3-7). 12.99 *(978-1-86147-395-0(8),* Armadillo) Anness Publishing GBR. Dist: National Bk. Network.

—Wolves. 2010. (Amazing Animal Hunters Ser.). 32p. (J). 28.50 *(978-1-60753-050-3(3))* Amicus Learning.

—Wolves. 2008. (Nature's Children Ser.). (Illus.). 52p. pap. *(978-0-7172-6266-3(9))* Grolier, Ltd.

—Wolves. 2012. (ENG., Illus.). 32p. (gr. 3-5). pap. 8.95 *(978-1-926722-54-2(X))* Saunders Bk. Co. CAN. Dist: RiverStream Publishing.

Green, Jen & Martineau, Susan. Wolves. 2011. (Positive Steps Ser.). (Illus.). 32p. (J). (gr. 2-5). lib. bdg. 31.35 *(978-1-59920-490-1(8))* Black Rabbit Bks.

Greenberg, Daniel A. Wolves, 1 vol. 2003. (Animals, Animals Ser.). (ENG., Illus.). 48p. (gr. 5-5). 32.64 *(978-0-7614-1447-6(9),* 961c5a25-85aa-4179-b5ee-9d3b6a71363b) Cavendish Square Publishing LLC.

Gregory, Josh. Red Wolves. 2014. (Nature's Children Ser.). (ENG.). 48p. (J). lib. bdg. 28.00 *(978-0-531-21227-1(0))* Scholastic Library Publishing.

Halfpenny, James C. Yellowstone Wolves in the Wild. 2003. (ENG., Illus.). 104p. per. 19.95 *(978-1-931832-26-7(9),* 8667872363) Riverbend Publishing.

Hamilton, S. L. Wolves. 2010. (Xtreme Predators Ser.). (ENG.). 32p. (J). (gr. 3-9). 32.79 *(978-1-60453-995-0(X),* 15734, Abdo & Daughters) ABDO Publishing Co.

Harrington, Fred H. The Ethiopian Wolf. 2009. (Library of Wolves & Wild Dogs Ser.). 24p. (gr. 3-3). 42.50 *(978-1-60853-972-7(5),* PowerKids Pr.) Rosen Publishing Group, Inc., The.

—The Red Wolf. 2009. (Library of Wolves & Wild Dogs Ser.). 24p. (gr. 3-3). 42.50 *(978-1-60853-974-1(1),* PowerKids Pr.) Rosen Publishing Group, Inc., The.

Havard, Christian. The Wolf: Night Howler. Jacana Agency, photos by. 2006. (Animal Close-Ups Ser.). (Illus.). 28p. (Orig.). (J). (gr. -1-3). pap. 6.95 *(978-1-57091-630-4(6))* Charlesbridge Publishing, Inc.

Heinz, Brian. The Wolves. Fuchs, Bernie, illus. 2005. 32p. (J). lib. bdg. 15.99 *(978-0-936335-11-7(4))* Ballyhoo BookWorks, Inc.

Hirsch, Rebecca E. Gray Wolves: Howling Pack Mammals. 2015. (Comparing Animal Traits Ser.). (ENG., Illus.). 32p. (gr. 2-4). 39.99 *(978-1-4677-8923-3(2),* Lerner Digital) Lerner Publishing Group.

Hudak, Heather C. Wolves. 2008. (Backyard Animals Ser.). (Illus.). 24p. (J). (gr. 4-7). lib. bdg. 24.45 *(978-1-60596-005-0(5))* Weigl Pubs., Inc.

Hudak, Heather C., ed. Wolves. 2008. (Backyard Animals Ser.). (Illus.). 24p. (J). (gr. 4-7). pap. 8.95 *(978-1-60596-011-1(X))* Weigl Pubs., Inc.

Jazynka, Kitson. National Geographic Kids Mission: Wolf Rescue: All about Wolves & How to Save Them. 2014. (Illus.). 128p. (J). (gr. 5-9). pap. 12.99 *(978-1-4263-1494-0(9),* National Geographic Kids) Disney Publishing Worldwide.

Johnson, Jinny. Gray Wolf. 2014. (North American Mammals Ser.). (ENG.). 24p. (J). (gr. 1-4). 28.50 *(978-1-62588-038-3(3),* 17372) Black Rabbit Bks.

—Gray Wolf. 2014. (North American Mammals Ser.). (ENG., Illus.). 24p. (J). (gr. -1-4). pap. 8.95 *(978-1-77092-173-3(7))* Saunders Bk. Co. CAN. Dist: RiverStream Publishing.

Kalman, Bobbie. Baby Wolves. 2010. (Fun to Learn about Baby Animals Ser.). (ENG.). 24p. (J). (gr. k-3). *(978-0-7787-4895-3(2));* pap. *(978-0-7787-4900-4(2))* Crabtree Publishing Co.

—Endangered Wolves, 1 vol. 2004. (Earth's Endangered Animals Ser.). (ENG., Illus.). 32p. (J). pap. *(978-0-7787-1900-7(6))* Crabtree Publishing Co.

—Wolf Family Adventures. 2016. (Animal Family Adventures Ser.). (ENG., Illus.). 32p. (J). (gr. 1-3). *(978-0-7787-2234-2(1))* Crabtree Publishing Co.

Keats Curtis, Jennifer. The Lucky Litter: Wolf Pups Rescued from Wildfire, 1 vol. Gomes, John, photos by. 2015. (Illus.). 32p. (J). (gr. 2-3). (SPA.). pap. 11.95 *(978-1-62855-720-6(6),* 5e9c3f2f-0e65-4218-b81c-fded60a85f87); (ENG., 17.95 *(978-1-62855-718-3(4))* Arbordale Publishing.

Kelley, K. C. Baby Tigers. 2018. (Spot Baby Animals Ser.). (ENG.). 16p. (J). (gr. -1-2). pap. 7.99 *(978-1-68152-257-9(8),* 14848) Amicus.

Kissock, Heather. Wolves. 2016. (Illus.). 24p. (J). *(978-1-4896-5402-1(X))* Weigl Pubs., Inc.

Koestler-Grack, Rachel A. Los Lobos. 2019. (SPA.). (J). lib. bdg. *(978-1-68151-625-7(X))* Amicus Learning.

Lawrence, Ellen. A Wolf's Life. 2012. (Science Slam: Animal Diaries-Life Cycles Ser.). 24p. (J). (gr. -1-3). lib. bdg. 26.99 *(978-1-61772-597-5(8))* Bearport Publishing Co., Inc.

Lawton, Carol L. Votive Reliefs. 2017. (Athenian Agora Ser.: XXXVIII). (ENG., Illus.). 248p. (C). 150.00 *(978-0-87661-238-5(9))* American Schl. of Classical Studies at Athens.

Leaf, Christina. Gray Wolves. 2015. (North American Animals Ser.). (ENG., Illus.). 24p. (J). (gr. k-3). lib. bdg. 26.95 *(978-1-62617-188-6(2),* Blastoff! Readers) Bellwether Media.

Leblanc, Catherine. How to Ward off Wolves. Garrigue, Roland, illus. 2013. (ENG.). 32p. (J). (gr. -1). 14.99 *(978-1-60887-194-0(0))* Insight Editions.

Linde, Barbara. Coyotes & Wolves Are Not Pets! 2013. (When Pets Attack! Ser.). 32p. (J). (gr. 3-6). pap. 63.00 *(978-1-4339-9295-7(7))* Stevens, Gareth Publishing LLLP.

Linde, Barbara M. Coyotes & Wolves Are Not Pets!, 1 vol. 2013. (When Pets Attack! Ser.). (ENG.). 32p. (J). (gr. 3-4). 29.27 *(978-1-4339-9293-3(0),* b8b9b399-2c3b-4ec7-b9ea-cdd11dca1c8c); pap. 11.50 *(978-1-4339-9294-0(9),* 67d42064-3b53-4f64-a6e7-b6109e6280e8) Stevens, Gareth Publishing LLLP.

Los Lobos (Wolves) 2006. (J). pap. 7.95 *(978-0-8225-6626-7(5),* Ediciones Lerner) Lerner Publishing Group.

Los Lobos: Individual Title Six-Packs. (Literatura 2000 Ser.). (SPA.). (gr. 2-3). 33.00 *(978-0-7635-1262-0(1))* Rigby Education.

MacLaine, James. Wolves. Francis, John & Scott, Kimberley, illus. 2013. (Usborne Beginners Ser.). (ENG.). 32p. (J). 4.99 *(978-0-7945-3402-8(3),* Usborne) EDC Publishing.

Markle, Sandra. Los Lobos. Translations.com Staff, tr. from ENG. 2006. (Animales Depredadores (Animal Predators) Ser.). (SPA., Illus.). 40p. (gr. 3-6). lib. bdg. 25.26 *(978-0-8225-6489-8(0),* Ediciones Lerner) Lerner Publishing Group.

—Los Lobos; Wolves. 2008. pap. 46.95 *(978-0-8225-7090-5(4))* Lerner Publishing Group.

—Wolves. (Animal Predators Ser.). (ENG., Illus.). 40p. (gr. 3-6). 2005. (J). pap. 8.99 *(978-1-57505-748-4(4),* 923970c7-af2d-4284-8b60-850796bc93db, First Avenue Editions) 2004. lib. bdg. 26.60 *(978-1-57505-732-3(8))* Lerner Publishing Group.

Marsh, Laura. National Geographic Readers: Wolves. 2012. (Readers Ser.). (Illus.). 32p. (J). (gr. 1-3). pap. 4.99 *(978-1-4263-0913-7(9));* (ENG., lib. bdg. 14.90 *(978-1-4263-0914-4(7))* Disney Publishing Worldwide. (National Geographic Kids).

Mattern, Joanne. Wolves & Coyotes. 2018. (Core Content Science — Animal Look-Alikes Ser.). (ENG., Illus.). 32p. (J). (gr. 2-4). lib. bdg. 23.99 *(978-1-63440-291-0(X),* dac646bc-81df-44f0-8ab5-42a77b4aaf34) Red Chair Pr.

cDonnell, Rory. Word Problems with Wolves, 1 vol. 2017. (Animal Math Ser.). (ENG.). 24p. (J). (gr. 1-2). pap. 9.15 (978-1-5382-0868-7(7), 528811d4-0b4b-40f3-9742-31d35fc5b8ab) Stevens, Gareth Publishing LLLP.

cDowell, Pamela. Lobos. 2013. (Animales en Mi Patio Ser.). (SPA., Illus.). 24p. (J). (gr. -1-3). lib. bdg. 27.13 (978-1-62127-599-2(X), AV2 by Weigl) Weigl Pubs., Inc.

-Wolves. 2012. (J). pap. 12.95 (978-1-61913-274-0(5)); 27.13 (978-1-61913-270-2(2)) Weigl Pubs., Inc.

lcLeese, Don. Gray Wolves. 2010. (Eye to Eye with Endangered Species Ser.). (ENG., Illus.). 24p. (gr. 3-6). pap. 8.95 (978-1-61590-511-9(1), 9781615905119) Rourke Educational Media.

leinking, Mary. Gray Wolves. 2013. (Wild Canine Pups Ser.). 24p. (J). (gr. -1-3). lib. bdg. 25.65 (978-1-61772-926-3(4)) Bearport Publishing Co., Inc.

leister, Cari. Do You Really Want to Meet a Wolf? Fabbri, Daniele, illus. 2016. (Do You Really Want to Meet ... ? Ser.). (ENG.). 24p. (J). (gr. 1-4). pap. 8.99 (978-1-68152-120-6(2), 15601); lib. bdg. 20.95 (978-1-60753-949-0(7), 15595) Amicus.

—Wolves. 2015. (J). lib. bdg. 25.65 (978-1-62031-170-7(4), Bullfrog Bks.) Jump! Inc.

Miller, Sara Swan. Wolves. (Paws & Claws Ser.). 24p. (gr. 2-3). 2009. 42.50 (978-1-60851-155-6(3)) 2008. (ENG., Illus.). (J). lib. bdg. 26.27 (978-1-4042-4161-9(2), 380a1daf-322d-4f17-9d07-bef6b46df6b9) Rosen Publishing Group, Inc., The. (PowerKids Pr.).

Moore Niver, Heather. Wolves after Dark, 1 vol. 2015. (Animals of the Night Ser.). (ENG.). 32p. (gr. 3-3). pap. 11.52 (978-0-7660-7416-3(1), 8409f738-d541-497a-9069-013295ab8892); (Illus.). 26.93 (978-0-7660-7418-7(8), de764e5c-88b1-47b9-8a9e-0119e8e87a0d) Enslow Publishing, LLC.

Murray, Julie. Wolf Pack. 2018. (Animal Groups (Abdo Kids Junior) Ser.). (ENG., Illus.). 24p. (J). (gr. -1-2). lib. bdg. 31.36 (978-1-5321-0784-9(6), 28129, Abdo Kids) ABDO Publishing Co.

O'Brien, Cynthia. Bringing Back the Gray Wolf. 2018. (Animals Back from the Brink Ser.). (Illus.). 32p. (J). (gr. 4-4). (978-0-7787-4903-5(7)) Crabtree Publishing Co.

Olson, Bethany. Baby Wolves. 2013. (Super Cute! Ser.). (ENG., Illus.). 24p. (J). (gr. k-3). lib. bdg. 26.95 (978-1-60014-934-4(0), Blastoff! Readers) Bellwether Media.

Owen, Ruth. Wolves, 1 vol. 2012. (Dr. Bob's Amazing World of Animals Ser.). (ENG., Illus.). 32p. (J). (gr. 2-3). pap. 12.75 (978-1-61533-558-9(7), 52ee62b6-945d-4e07-97da-1f98abae5913); lib. bdg. 31.27 (978-1-61533-549-7(8), 1b2fc8ee-ed82-42ac-a3b2-2c5b21c7dd42) Rosen Publishing Group, Inc., The. (Windmill Bks.).

Patent, Dorothy Hinshaw. When the Wolves Returned: Restoring Nature's Balance in Yellowstone. Hartman, Dan, illus. Hartman, Dan, photos by. 2008. (ENG.). 40p. (J). (gr. 1-4). 19.99 (978-0-8027-9686-8(9), 900045639, Bloomsbury USA Childrens) Bloomsbury Publishing USA.

Peterson, Brenda. Lobos: A Wolf Family Returns to the Wild. Musselman, Annie Marie, photos by. 2018. (Illus.). 32p. (J). (gr. k-4). 17.99 (978-1-63217-084-2(1), Little Bigfoot) Sasquatch Bks.

Pfeffer, Wendy & American Museum of Natural History Staff. Wolf Pup, Level 1. 2011. (Amer Museum of Nat History Easy Readers Ser.: 4). (ENG., Illus.). 32p. (J). (gr. -1-k). pap. 4.99 (978-1-4027-7785-1(X)) Sterling Publishing Co., Inc.

Read, Nicholas. The Sea Wolves: Living Wild in the Great Bear Rainforest, 1 vol. McAllister, Ian, photos by. 2010. (ENG., Illus.). 128p. (J). (gr. 4-7). pap. 19.95 (978-1-55469-206-4(7)) Orca Bk. Pubs. USA.

Read, Tracy C. Exploring the World of Wolves. 2010. (Exploring the World Of Ser.). (ENG., Illus.). 24p. (J). (gr. 4-7). 16.95 (978-1-55407-646-8(3), 6402f0fe-7c64-4d12-82b1-0380d0e481ba); pap. 6.95 (978-1-55407-655-0(2), 49f9f417-af98-429f-9e80-c804a870986a) Firefly Bks., Ltd.

Reher, Matt. Orcas: The Wolves of the Seas. 2016. (1B Animal Behaviors Ser.). (ENG., Illus.). 28p. (J). pap. 9.60 (978-1-63437-587-0(4)) American Reading Co.

—When the Wolves Came Back. 2017. (2B Wild Animals Ser.). (ENG., Illus.). 32p. (J). pap. 9.60 (978-1-63437-201-5(8)) American Reading Co.

—Wolf Babies Eat. 2011. (1G Predator Animals Ser.). (ENG., Illus.). 28p. (J). pap. 8.00 (978-1-63437-572-6(6)) American Reading Co.

—Wolves Eat. 2017. (1G Mammals Ser.). (ENG., Illus.). 24p. (J). pap. 8.00 (978-1-63437-013-4(9)) American Reading Co.

Riggs, Kate. Amazing Animals - Wolves. 2011. (Amazing Animals Ser.). (ENG.). 24p. (J). (gr. 1-4). 24.25 (978-1-58341-991-5(8), 23065) Creative Co., The.

—Seedlings: Wolves. 2014. (Seedlings Ser.). (ENG.). 24p. (J). (gr. -1-k). pap. 10.99 (978-0-89812-890-1(0), 21691, Creative Paperbacks) Creative Co., The.

—Wolves. 2013. (Seedlings Ser.). (ENG.). 24p. (J). (gr. -1-k). 25.65 (978-1-60818-345-6(9), 21690, Creative Education) Creative Co., The.

—Wolves. 2010. (ENG., Illus.). 24p. (J). pap. 8.95 (978-1-926853-71-0(7)) Saunders Bk. Co. CAN. Dist: Creative Co., The.

Royston, Angela. Wolf, 1 vol. 2013. (Top of the Food Chain Ser.). (ENG.). 32p. (J). (gr. 2-3). 29.92 (978-1-61533-738-5(5), c39bb11b-12dc-484b-b05c-1eac54a02651); pap. 11.00 (978-1-61533-793-4(8), d069294c-85da-4d51-b10d-05c15bee1476) Rosen Publishing Group, Inc., The. (PowerKids Pr.).

—Wolves. (Amazing Animals Ser.). (Illus.). 24p. (J). 2009. (gr. 2-4). pap. 8.95 (978-1-60596-157-6(4)) 2009. (gr. 2-4). lib. bdg. 24.45 (978-1-60596-156-9(6)) 2003. lib. bdg. 24.45 (978-1-58340-228-3(4)) Weigl Pubs., Inc.

Rue, Leonard Lee. Wolves, Vol. 12. 2018. (Animals in the Wild Ser.). (Illus.). 80p. (J). (gr. 7). 33.27 (978-1-4222-4175-2(0)) Mason Crest.

—Wolves - PB: A Portrait of the Animal World. 2013. (Portrait of the Animal World Ser.). (Illus.). 80p. pap. 9.95 (978-1-59764-326-9(2)) New Line Bks.

Rustad, Martha E. H. A Pack of Wolves. 2019. (Animal Groups Ser.). (ENG., Illus.). 24p. (J). (gr. -1-2). pap. 6.95 (978-1-9771-1046-6(0), 141122); lib. bdg. 29.32 (978-1-9771-0950-7(0), 140548) Capstone. (Pebble).

Saxena, Shalini. Saving the Endangered Gray Wolf, 1 vol., 1. 2015. (Conservation of Endangered Species Ser.). (ENG., Illus.). 32p. (J). (gr. 2-3). pap. 13.90 (978-1-5081-0055-3(1), d5231bb8-6897-423e-807f-63c54964867c, Britannica Educational Publishing) Rosen Publishing Group, Inc., The.

Scieszka, Jon. The True Story of the 3 Little Pigs. Smith, Lane, illus. 2011. (J). (gr. -1-3). 29.95 (978-0-545-09457-3(7)); 18.95 (978-0-545-09459-7(3)) Weston Woods Studios, Inc.

Searl, Duncan. Wolves. 2007. (Smart Animals! Ser.). (Illus.). 32p. (J). (gr. 2-5). lib. bdg. 28.50 (978-1-59716-370-5(8), 1265961) Bearport Publishing Co., Inc.

Seymour, Simon. Wolves. 2014. (ENG.). 32p. (J). (gr. k-4). 11.24 (978-1-63245-273-3(1)) Lectorum Pubns., Inc.

Shea, Abigail. Wolves in Danger, 1 vol. 2013. (Animals at Risk Ser.). (ENG.). 24p. (J). (gr. 2-3). pap. 9.15 (978-1-4339-9179-0(9), fad2c68e-c213-48a0-8e34-ce0a89a5738f); (Illus.). lib. bdg. 25.27 (978-1-4339-9178-3(0), 2d623ae2-7d20-4fbc-9b89-eab8f38446e9) Stevens, Gareth Publishing LLLP.

Silverman, Buffy. Can You Tell a Coyote from a Wolf? 2012. (Animal Look-Alikes Ser.). 32p. (gr. k-2). pap. 45.32 (978-0-7613-9253-8(X)) Lerner Publishing Group.

Simon, Charnan. Wolves. 2012. (Nature's Children Ser.). (ENG., Illus.). 48p. (J). pap. 6.95 (978-0-531-21084-0(7)); (gr. 3-5). lib. bdg. 28.00 (978-0-531-20909-7(1)) Scholastic Library Publishing. (Children's Pr.).

Simon, Seymour. Wolves. 2009. (ENG., Illus.). 32p. (J). (gr. k-4). pap. 7.99 (978-0-06-162657-9(0), HarperCollins) HarperCollins Pubs.

Sisk, Maeve T. Arctic Wolves, 1 vol. 2010. (Animals That Live in the Tundra Ser.). (ENG.). 24p. (J). (gr. 1-1). pap. 9.15 (978-1-4339-3894-8(4), abd8c40f-4f69-4fe7-9aa7-7609ce4107e5); lib. bdg. 25.27 (978-1-4339-3893-1(6), e87511cd-fde6-4719-b552-5b8b3e354c39) Stevens, Gareth Publishing LLLP.

Slade, Suzanne. What If There Were No Gray Wolves? A Book about the Temperate Forest Ecosystem, 1 vol. Schwartz, Carol, illus. 2010. (Food Chain Reactions Ser.). (ENG.). 24p. (J). (gr. 2-4). pap. 9.95 (978-1-4048-6395-8(8), 114146, Picture Window Bks.) Capstone.

Sommer, Nathan. Grizzly Bear vs. Wolf Pack. 2020. (Animal Battles Ser.). (ENG.). 24p. (J). (gr. 3-7). lib. bdg. 26.95 (978-1-64487-158-4(0), Torque Bks.) Bellwether Media.

Spilsbury, Richard & Spilsbury, Louise. Wolf Packs, 1 vol. 2013. (Animal Armies Ser.). (ENG., Illus.). 32p. (J). (gr. 2-3). pap. 11.00 (978-1-4777-0336-6(5), 1fd407df-66b6-4d92-b7b0-5853c01c539c); lib. bdg. 28.93 (978-1-4777-0307-6(1), 16ea7335-fdb0-4840-bdf8-19d9333b6997) Rosen Publishing Group, Inc., The. (PowerKids Pr.).

Staff, Gareth Editorial Staff. Wolves, 1 vol. 2004. (All about Wild Animals Ser.). (ENG., Illus.). 32p. (gr. 2-4). lib. bdg. 28.67 (978-0-8368-4124-4(7), 806715c5-07a9-486f-8193-e316620d5a5a, Gareth Stevens Learning Library) Stevens, Gareth Publishing LLLP.

Stone, Lynn M. Gray Wolves. 2004. (Early Bird Nature Bks.). (Illus.). 47p. (J). 25.26 (978-0-8225-3050-3(3), Lerner Pubns.) Lerner Publishing Group.

Strauss, Holden. Wolves, 1 vol. 2016. (Wild Canines Ser.). (ENG., Illus.). 24p. (J). (gr. 3-3). pap. 9.25 (978-1-4994-2023-4(4), c2324a16-c102-49b3-83fa-287e7a4cf75d, PowerKids Pr.) Rosen Publishing Group, Inc., The.

Tanner, S. The Wild Wolf: Learning the W Sound. 2009. (PowerPhonics Ser.). 24p. (gr. 1-1). 39.90 (978-1-60851-473-1(0), PowerKids Pr.) Rosen Publishing Group, Inc., The.

Terp, Gail. Gray Wolves. 2016. (Wild Animal Kingdom Ser.). (ENG.). 32p. (J). (gr. 4-6). pap. 9.99 (978-1-64466-169-7(1), 10393); (Illus.). 31.35 (978-1-68072-051-8(1), 10392) Black Rabbit Bks. (Bolt).

—Gray Wolves. 2018. (Wild Animal Kingdom Ser.). (ENG., Illus.). 32p. (gr. 2-7). pap. 9.95 (978-1-68072-308-3(1)) RiverStream Publishing.

Washington, Joi & Fleischer, Jayson. These Are Wolves. 2011. (ARC Press / Power 100 - Predator Animals Ser.). pap. 45.32 (978-1-61541-509-0(2)) American Reading Co.

Wexo, John Bonnett. Wolves. rev. ed. 2003. (Illus.). 24p. (J). (gr. 1-7). 10.95 (978-1-932396-01-0(2), Zoo Bks.) National Wildlife Federation.

Wildlife Education. Wolves. 2007. (Illus.). 10p. (J). pap. (978-1-932396-33-1(0), Critters Up Close) National Wildlife Federation.

Wilsdon, Christina. Wolves. 2006. (J). 7.99 (978-1-59939-031-4(0)) Cornerstone Pr.

—Wolves, 1 vol. 2010. (Amazing Animals Ser.). (ENG.). 48p. (J). (gr. 3-5). pap. 11.50 (978-1-4339-4032-3(9), a4deb562-0758-4f6d-a565-b9773f87deb0); lib. bdg. 30.67 (978-1-4339-4031-6(0), a8cfc0d5-4199-4f65-9d31-dab1c37ee992) Stevens, Gareth Publishing LLLP. (Gareth Stevens Learning Library).

Wimmer, Teresa. Wolves. 2009. (Living Wild Ser.). (ENG., Illus.). 48p. (J). (gr. 5-8). 22.95 (978-1-58341-744-7(3), 22200, Creative Education) Creative Co., The.

Wolf: Killer King of the Forest. 2013. (Top of the Food Chain Ser.). 32p. (J). (gr. k-5). pap. 60.00 (978-1-61533-794-1(6), PowerKids Pr.) Rosen Publishing Group, Inc., The.

Wolves: Easyreads - Level 1, 6 bks. 2005. (Animal Predators Ser.). (Illus.). 40p. (J). (gr. 3-6). pap. 46.95 (978-0-8225-5494-3(1)) Lerner Publishing Group.

Wolves: Easyreads - Level 1, 6 Packs. (Literatura 2000 Ser.). (gr. 2-3). 33.00 (978-0-7635-0271-3(5)) Rigby Education.

Wolves & Coyotes. (Eyes on Nature Ser.). 32p. (J). (gr. 1). pap. (978-1-882210-57-2(3)) Action Publishing, Inc.

Wolves & Coyotes. (Eyes on Nature Ser.). (Illus.). 32p. (J). (gr. 1-18). 7.95 (978-1-56156-424-8(9)) Kidsbooks, LLC.

Wolves in Danger. 2013. (Animals at Risk Ser.). 24p. (J). (gr. 2-5). pap. 48.90 (978-1-4339-9180-6(2)) Stevens, Gareth Publishing LLLP.

World Book, Inc. Staff, contrib. by. Harry the Wolf. 2017. (Illus.). 31p. (J). (978-0-7166-3522-2(4)) World Bk., Inc.

Zeiger, Jennifer. Coyotes. 2013. (ENG.). 48p. (J). 28.00 (978-0-531-23356-6(1)); pap. 6.95 (978-0-531-25154-6(3)) Scholastic Library Publishing.

WOLVES—FICTION

Adams, Elizabeth. The Boy Who Cried Wolf, 1 vol. 2012. (ENG., Illus.). 24p. (J). pap. (978-0-7787-7902-5(5)) Crabtree Publishing Co.

Aesop, Aesop. The Sheperd Boy & the Wolf. 2012. (J). 29.99 (978-1-61913-107-1(2)) Weigl Pubs., Inc.

—The Wolf in Sheep's Clothing: A Tale about Appearances. 2006. (J). (978-1-59939-086-4(8), Reader's Digest Young Families, Inc.) Studio Fun International.

Afanasyev, Alexander. The Tale of Tsarevich Ivan, the Firebird, & the Grey Wolf. 2017. (ENG., Illus.). 25p. (J). (978-1-910880-43-2(4)) Planet, The.

—The Tale of Tsarevich Ivan, the Firebird, & the Grey Wolf. Bilibin, Ivan, illus. 2013. 28p. pap. (978-1-909115-50-7(9)) Planet, The.

Alexander, Jed. Red. 2018. (ENG., Illus.). 32p. (J). (gr. -1-3). 15.95 (978-1-944903-11-4(9), 1313501, Cameron Kids) Cameron + Co.

Alily, Joseph. Untold- the Never Ending Tales: The Boy & the Wolf - Children's Story. 2006. 10.00 (978-0-8059-8133-9(0)) Dorrance Publishing Co., Inc.

Anderson, Derek. Ten Hungry Pigs: An Epic Lunch Adventure. Anderson, Derek, illus. 2016. (ENG., Illus.). 40p. (J). (gr. -1-k). 17.99 (978-0-545-16848-9(1)) Scholastic, Inc.

Anderson, Max Elliot. Legend of the White Wolf. 2005. (Illus.). 125p. (J). (gr. -1-7). pap. 10.95 (978-0-9752880-3-0(2)) Baker Trittin Pr.

Andrews, Julie & Hamilton, Emma Walton. Dragon. 2004. (Julie Andrews Collection). 192p. (J). (gr. 4-18). 16.99 (978-0-06-057119-1(5)); lib. bdg. 17.89 (978-0-06-057120-7(9)) HarperCollins Pubs. (Julie Andrews Collection).

Archer, Dosh. Big Bad Wolf. Archer, Dosh, illus. 2015. (Urgency Emergency! Ser.). (ENG., Illus.). 48p. (J). (gr. k-2). pap. 9.99 (978-0-8075-8351-7(0), 807583510) Whitman, Albert & Co.

Atwater-Rhodes, Amelia. Wolfcry. 2008. (Kiesha'ra Ser.: Bk. 4). (ENG.). 208p. (YA). (gr. 9-12). pap. 7.99 (978-0-440-23886-7(2), Delacorte Pr.) Random Hse. Children's Bks.

Austin, Jeanne J. Unlikely Friends. 2009. 24p. pap. 14.99 (978-1-4343-2348-4(X)) AuthorHouse.

Avi. The Good Dog. 2003. 243p. (gr. 3-7). 17.00 (978-0-7569-1389-2(6)) Perfection Learning Corp.

—Old Wolf. Floca, Brian, illus. 2015. (ENG.). 160p. (J). (gr. 3-7). 17.99 (978-1-4424-9921-8(4)) Simon & Schuster Children's Publishing.

Bad Boys. 2007. (J). (gr. k-3). 27.95 incl. audio (978-0-8045-6956-9(8)); 29.95 incl. audio compact disk (978-0-8045-4179-4(5)) Spoken Arts, Inc.

Baguley, Elizabeth. Just Like Brothers. Blanz, Aurélie, illus. 2018. (ENG.). 32p. (J). (gr. -1-2). 16.99 (978-1-78285-345-9(6)) Barefoot Bks., Inc.

Baker, Olaf. Dusty Star. 2011. (Illus.). 168p. pap. 12.99 (978-1-61203-233-7(8)) Bottom of the Hill Publishing.

Bargach, Naim. Wolfen: Beware, even, of little Wolves... 2008. 56p. per. 8.95 (978-1-4327-1802-2(9)) Outskirts Pr., Inc.

Barnett, Mac. The Wolf, the Duck, & the Mouse. Klassen, Jon, illus. 2017. (ENG.). 40p. (J). (gr. -1-3). 18.99 (978-0-7636-7754-1(X)) Candlewick Pr.

Bauer, Marion Dane. Runt. 2004. 138p. (gr. 4-7). 17.00 (978-0-7569-3203-9(3)) Perfection Learning Corp.

—Runt. 2004. (ENG.). 144p. (J). (gr. 3-7). reprint ed. 7.99 (978-0-440-41978-5(6), Yearling) Random Hse. Children's Bks.

Bedard, Michael. The Wolf of Gubbio. 2004. (Illus.). (J). (gr. k-3). spiral bd. (978-0-616-07213-4(9)) Canadian National Institute for the Blind/Institut National Canadien pour les Aveugles.

Belloni, Giulia. Anything Is Possible. Trevisan, Marco, illus. 2013. (ENG.). 32p. (J). (gr. -1-3). 16.95 (978-1-926973-91-3(7), Owlkids) Owlkids Bks. Inc. CAN. Dist: Publishers Group West (PGW).

Bentley, Sue. Cloud Capers #3, 3 vols., 3. Swan, Angela, illus. 2009. (Magic Puppy Ser.: 3). (ENG.). 128p. (J). (gr. 1-3). 6.99 (978-0-448-45046-9(1), Grosset & Dunlap) Penguin Young Readers Group.

—Magic Puppy #5 Party Dreams. 5th ed. 2008. (Illus.). 128p. (J). pap. (978-0-14-132379-4(5), Puffin) Penguin Bks., Ltd.

—Magic Puppy #6 a Forest Charm. 2008. (Illus.). 128p. (J). pap. (978-0-14-132380-0(9), Puffin) Penguin Bks., Ltd.

—A New Beginning #1, No. 1. Swan, Angela, illus. 2009. (Magic Puppy Ser.: 1). (ENG.). 128p. (J). (gr. 1-3). pap. 6.99 (978-0-448-45044-5(5), Grosset & Dunlap) Penguin Young Readers Group.

—Snowy Wishes. 2013. (Magic Puppy Ser.). lib. bdg. 16.00 (978-0-606-32124-2(1)) Turtleback.

Bently, Peter. The Great Sheep Shenanigans. Matsuoka, Mei, illus. 2012. (Andersen Press Picture Bks). (ENG.). 32p. (J). (gr. -1-3). 16.95 (978-0-7613-8990-3(3)) Lerner Publishing Group.

Bergren, Lisa Tawn. God Gave Us Thankful Hearts. Hohn, David, illus. 2016. (ENG.). 40p. (J). (gr. -1-2). 10.99 (978-1-60142-874-5(X), WaterBrook Pr.) Crown Publishing Group, The.

Bernard, Greg. Alpha Summer. 2005. (YA). per. 12.95 (978-0-926147-21-8(8)) Loonfeather Pr.

Bevis, Mary. Wolf Song. Powell, Consie, illus. 2007. 32p. (gr. 1-2). 18.95 (978-0-9794202-0-7(2)); pap. 12.95 (978-0-9794202-1-4(0)) Raven Productions, Inc.

Biddle, Charles, Jr. The Three Little Pigs. Malak, Annabel, illus. 2011. (ENG.). 16p. pap. 12.95 (978-2-89558-409-4(5), 9782895584094) Editions Alexandre Stanke CAN. Dist: Baker & Taylor Publisher Services (BTPS).

Black, Holly & Clare, Cassandra. The Copper Gauntlet (Magisterium #2), 1 vol. (Magisterium Ser.: 2). (ENG.). 272p. (J). (gr. 3-7). 2016. pap. 8.99 (978-0-545-52229-8(3)) 2015. 17.99 (978-0-545-52228-1(5), Scholastic Pr.) Scholastic, Inc.

Blackford, Andy. The Three Little Pigs & the New Neighbor. Zlatic, Tomislav, illus. 2014. (Tadpoles: Fairytale Twists Ser.). (ENG.). 32p. (J). (gr. 1-2). (978-0-7787-0447-8(5)); pap. (978-0-7787-0482-9(3)) Crabtree Publishing Co.

Blair, Eric. The Boy Who Cried Wolf, 1 vol. Silverman, Dianne, illus. 2011. (My First Classic Story Ser.). (ENG.). 24p. (J). (gr. k-3). pap. 7.10 (978-1-4048-7364-3(3), 118579, Picture Window Bks.) Capstone.

—El Lobo y Los Siete Cabritos: Versión Del Cuento de Los Hermanos Grimm. Abello, Patricia, tr. Petrusek, Brett, illus. 2006. (Read-It! Readers en Español: Cuentos de Hadas Ser.). (SPA.). 32p. (J). (gr. k-3). 22.65 (978-1-4048-1645-9(3), 86680, Picture Window Bks.) Capstone.

Blanco, César. Hoky the Caring Wolf. Brokenbrow, Jon, tr. Bk, Blanca, illus. 2013. (ENG.). 32p. (J). (gr. k-3). 15.95 (978-84-15241-92-8(5)) Cuento de Luz SL ESP. Dist: Publishers Group West (PGW).

Blevins, Wiley. Little Dead Riding Hood. Cox, Steve, illus. 2016. (Scary Tales Retold Ser.). (ENG.). 24p. (J). (gr. k-3). lib. bdg. 27.99 (978-1-63440-102-9(6), e26b8b13-9493-4352-be1a-df0096c02601) Red Chair Pr.

Bradford, Karleen. Ghost Wolf. Cormack, Allan & Drew-Brook, Deborah, illus. 2005. 59p. (J). lib. bdg. 20.00 (978-1-4242-1254-5(5)) Fitzgerald Bks.

—Ghost Wolf, 1 vol. Drew-Brook, Deborah & Cormack, Allan, illus. 2005. (Orca Echoes Ser.). (ENG.). 64p. (J). (gr. 1-3). per. 6.95 (978-1-55143-341-7(9)) Orca Bk. Pubs. USA.

Bradman, Tony. Mr. Wolf Bounces Back [Scholastic]. Warburton, Sarah, illus. 2009. (After Happily Ever After Ser.). (ENG.). 56p. (gr. 2-3). pap. 4.99 (978-1-4342-1676-2(4), Stone Arch Bks.) Capstone.

Brave M.A., Kathryn A. & Lavin, Paul J. A Fit ting Fairy Tale. 2006. 60p. pap. 16.95 (978-1-4241-2992-8(3)) PublishAmerica, Inc.

Brightwood, Laura, illus. Wolf under the Bed. Brightwood, Laura, . 2007. (J). DVD (978-1-934409-04-6(9)) 3-C Institute for Social Development.

Broach, Elise. The Wolf Keepers. Ratterree, Alice, illus. 2018. (ENG.). 368p. (J). pap. 15.99 (978-1-250-16501-5(6), 900186931) Square Fish.

Brown, Carron, ed. The Three Little Pigs & Little Red Riding Hood: Two Tales & Their Histories, 1 vol. 2009. (World of Fairy Tales Ser.). (ENG., Illus.). 32p. (J). (gr. 1-2). pap. 11.55 (978-1-60754-641-2(8), f11044f7-61ec-4d84-b6c3-6bebc70efb3a); lib. bdg. 27.27 (978-1-60754-640-5(X), dd97079b-c28b-4ca3-abf6-5e8b46ef1003) Rosen Publishing Group, Inc., The. (Windmill Bks.).

Brown, Ken. What's the Time, Grandma Wolf?, 1 vol. 2015. (ENG., Illus.). 32p. (J). (gr. -1-k). pap. 7.95 (978-1-56145-891-2(0)) Peachtree Publishing Co. Inc.

Brun-Cosme, Nadine. Big Wolf & Little Wolf: The Little Leaf That Wouldn't Fall. Tallec, Olivier, illus. 2009. 32p. (J). (gr. -1-2). 16.95 (978-1-59270-088-2(8)); 16.95 (978-1-59270-084-4(5)) Enchanted Lion Bks., LLC.

—Big Wolf & Little Wolf, Such a Beautiful Orange! Tallec, Olivier, illus. 2011. 32p. (J). (gr. -1-3). 16.95 (978-1-59270-106-3(X)) Enchanted Lion Bks., LLC.

Bryan, Ed, illus. Little Red Riding Hood: a Nosy Crow Fairy Tale. 2017. (ENG.). 32p. (J). (gr. -1-2). 9.99 (978-0-7636-9331-2(6)) Candlewick Pr.

Bryant, Ann. Tag. 2009. (ENG., Illus.). 24p. (J). pap. (978-0-7787-3900-5(7)); lib. bdg. (978-0-7787-3869-5(8)) Crabtree Publishing Co.

Burgess, Melvin. The Cry of the Wolf. 2012. (ENG.). 128p. (YA). (gr. 7). pap. 12.99 (978-1-84939-375-1(3)) Andersen Pr. GBR. Dist: Independent Pubs. Group.

Burgess, Thornton W. The Adventures of Danny Meadow Mouse. 2009. (gr. 4-7). 108p. 22.95 (978-1-60664-649-6(4)); 104p. pap. 9.95 (978-1-60664-274-0(X)) Rodgers, Alan Bks.

Butler, Dori. A Sheep in Wolf's Clothing. 2006. (J). pap. (978-1-4108-6185-6(6)) Benchmark Education Co.

Caballero, Erica. Mount Mole. 2006. pap. 10.00 (978-1-4257-2301-9(2)) Xlibris Corp.

The Call of the Wild Guide. 16.47 (978-0-13-425968-0(8)) Prentice Hall PTR.

Calmenson, Stephanie. Our Principal Is a Wolf! A QUIX Book. Blecha, Aaron, illus. 2018. (Our Principal Ser.). (ENG.). 64p. (J). (gr. k-3). 16.99 (978-1-4814-6669-1(0)); pap. 5.99 (978-1-4814-6668-4(2)) Simon & Schuster Children's Publishing. (Aladdin).

Campbell, Mari. Maggiemoosetracks: Making Friends. Katsumoto, Sayaka, tr. Jennings, Randy, illus. 2013. 108p. pap. 21.99 (978-0-9895205-6-0(0)) MaggieMooseTracks.

—Maggiemoosetracks: Wolf Pack. Jennings, Randy, illus. 2013. 106p. pap. 21.00 (978-0-9895205-5-3(2)) MaggieMooseTracks.

Campos, Jacqueline. The Adventures of Lil' Wolf, Twinkie, to. 2005. 63p. pap. 16.95 (978-1-4137-8494-7(1)) PublishAmerica, Inc.

Carlson-Voiles, Polly. Summer of the Wolves. 2013. (ENG.). 352p. (J). (gr. 5-7). pap. 7.99 (978-0-544-02276-8(9), 1528497, Clarion Bks.) HarperCollins Pubs.

Carter, Aimée. Simon Thorn & the Wolf's Den. 2017. (Simon Thorn Ser.: 1). (J). lib. bdg. 18.40 (978-0-606-39595-3(4)) Turtleback.

Carter, Anne Laurel. The Shepherd's Granddaughter, 1 vol. 2008. (ENG.). 224p. (YA). (gr. 8-9). pap. 9.95 (978-0-88899-903-0(8)) Groundwood Bks. CAN. Dist: Publishers Group West (PGW).

Casanova, Mary. Wolf Shadows. 2nd ed. 2009. (J). (978-0-9793444-1-1(7)) Quercus Press.

—Wolf Shadows. 2013. (Fesler-Lampert Minnesota Heritage Ser.). (ENG.). 136p. pap. 9.95 (978-0-8166-9031-2(6)) Univ. of Minnesota Pr.

Chandler, Kristen. Wolves, Boys & Other Things That Might Kill Me. 2011. (ENG.). 283p. (YA). (gr. 7-12). 24.94 (978-0-670-01142-1(8)) Penguin Young Readers Group.

Child, Lauren. Beware of the Storybook Wolves. 2012. (ENG., Illus.). 32p. (J). (gr. -1-k). pap. 9.99 (978-1-4083-1480-7(0), Orchard Bks.) Hachette Children's Group GBR. Dist: Hachette Bk. Group.

Clanton, Connie, illus. The Boy Who Cried Wolf: The Boy Who Cried Wolf. 2012. (SGN, ARA, BOS, CHI & ENG.). 32p. (J). pap. 19.95 incl. DVD (978-0-9818139-1-2(7)) ASL Tales.

Clark, Anthony. Little Wolf's Book of Badness. 2008. (Oberon Modern Plays Ser.). (ENG.). 96p. (J). pap. 14.95 (978-1-84002-823-2(8), 900241395) Oberon Bks., Ltd. GBR. Dist: Macmillan.

Cleveland, Marie. Prowlers in Peril: A Storybook Land Adventure, 1 vol. 2010. 52p. pap. 16.95 (978-1-4489-5204-5(2)) America Star Bks.

W X Y Z

Clish, Marian L. A Wolf's Tale. Anderson, Jan, illus. unabr. l.t. ed. (J). (gr. k-5). pap. 14.95 incl. audio compact disk *(978-1-928632-01-6(7))* Writers Marketplace:Consulting, Critiquing & Publishing.

Collins, Lynette. Margie & Wolf: Catch Us If You Can. 2017. (ENG.). 60p. 41.39 *(978-1-5434-0358-9(1))*; (Illus.). pap. 27.59 *(978-1-5434-0356-5(5))* Xlibris Corp.

—Margie & Wolf: How Zoe Became Forget Me Not. 2018. (ENG.). 76p. pap. 13.79 *(978-1-9845-0389-3(8))* Xlibris Corp.

—Margie & Wolf: New Friends. 2018. (ENG.). 68p. 44.84 *(978-1-5434-0856-0(7))*; (Illus.). pap. 31.04 *(978-1-5434-0855-3(9))* Xlibris Corp.

—Margie & Wolf: The Hidden Caves. 2019. (ENG.). 64p. 41.39 *(978-1-9845-0492-0(4))*; (Margie & Wolf Ser.: Bk. 6). pap. 27.59 *(978-1-9845-0491-3(6))* Xlibris Corp.

—Margie & Wolf: The Series. 2016. (ENG.). 260p. (gr. 1-1). 40.31 *(978-1-5245-1645-1(7))*; pap. 24.19 *(978-1-5245-1644-4(9))* Xlibris Corp.

—Margie & Wolf: The Storm. 2019. (ENG.). 154p. pap. 20.69 *(978-1-7960-0150-1(3))* Xlibris Corp.

—Margie & Wolf: The Surprise Party. 2018. (ENG.). 56p. 41.39 *(978-1-9845-0104-2(6))*; pap. 27.59 *(978-1-9845-0103-5(8))* Xlibris Corp.

—Margie & Wolf: Through Her Eyes. 2019. (ENG.). 120p. pap. 20.69 *(978-1-7960-0215-7(1))* Xlibris Corp.

—Margie & Wolf: When They Were Free. (ENG.). 2019. 96p. pap. 13.79 *(978-1-7960-0256-0(9))* 2017. (Illus.). pap. 32.25 *(978-1-5245-2168-4(X))* Xlibris Corp.

—Margie & Wolf: Zoe Has Come Home. 2019. (ENG.). 128p. pap. 20.69 *(978-1-7960-0129-7(5))* Xlibris Corp.

Connelly, Erin. Watch Out for Wolves! 2017. (Text Connections Guided Close Reading Ser.). (J). (gr. 1). *(978-1-4900-1820-1(4))* Benchmark Education Co.

Connolly, Brian A. Hawk. 2007. 156p. 20.95 *(978-1-60264-030-6(0))*; 160p. per. 13.95 *(978-1-60264-029-0(7))* Virtualbookworm.com Publishing, Inc.

—Wolf Journal: A Novel. 2005. 164p. 20.95 *(978-1-58939-795-8(9))*; 168p. per. 13.95 *(978-1-58939-794-1(0))* Virtualbookworm.com Publishing, Inc.

Conway, David. The Great Fairy Tale Disaster. Williamson, Melanie, illus. 2012. (ENG.). 32p. (J). (gr. -1-2). 17.99 *(978-1-58925-111-3(3))* Tiger Tales.

Cordell, Matthew. Wolf in the Snow. 2017. (ENG., Illus.). 48p. (J). 18.99 *(978-1-250-07636-6(6)*, 900152144) Feiwel & Friends.

—Wolf in the Snow. 2018. (CHI.). (gr. -1-1). *(978-986-189-861-2(1))* Grimm Cultural Ent., Co., Ltd.

Corentin, Philippe. Chaf! 2005. (SPA.). (J). 9.95 *(978-84-8470-131-6(X))* Corimbo, Editorial S.L. ESP. Dist: Iaconi, Mariuccia Bk. Imports.

—El Ogro, el Lobo, la Niña y el Pastel. 2004. (SPA.). 32p. (J). (gr. k-2). 19.99 *(978-84-8470-157-6(3))* Corimbo, Editorial S.L. ESP. Dist: Lectorum Pubns., Inc.

Costamagna, Beatrice, illus. Wolf Crunch! 2016. (Crunchy Board Bks.). (ENG.). 12p. (J). (gr. -1-1). bds. 7.99 *(978-1-4998-0200-9(5))* Little Bee Books Inc.

Crabtree, Zona Mae. White Dove. 2005. (Corn Cave Ser.: 3). (ENG., Illus.). (YA). per. 8.00 *(978-0-9726826-2-6(7))* Owl Hollow Publishing.

Crayton, Tina Lorice. The Lost Sheep. 2010. (ENG.). 24p. pap. 10.50 *(978-1-4490-7707-5(2))* AuthorHouse.

Crayton, Tina Lorice (Anderson). The Wolf in Sheep's Clothing: The Impostor. 2011. 20p. 10.50 *(978-1-4567-3011-6(8))* AuthorHouse.

Cresswell, Helen. Sophie & the Seawolf. (ENG., Illus.). 32p. (J). *(978-0-340-65608-2(5))* Hodder & Stoughton.

Cummins, Amanda Lynn. The Wolf: The Untold Story. 2005. (Illus.). 32p. (J). (gr. 5-6). 10.00 *(978-0-9670947-7-9(1))* Green Sheet Inc., The.

Dahl, Roald, et al. Collins Musicals - Roald Dahl's Little Red Riding Hood & the Wolf: a Howling Hilarious Musical, 1 vol. Baiton, Janice & Daley, Michelle, eds. Blake, Quentin & Eccles, Jane, illus. 2005. (and C Black Musicals Ser.). (ENG.). 56p. (J). (gr. 2-6). pap. 42.95 incl. cd-rom *(978-0-7136-6958-9(6))* HarperCollins Pubs. Ltd. GBR. Dist: Independent Pubs. Group.

Dance, Jennifer. Red Wolf. 2014. (ENG., Illus.). 256p. (YA). pap. 12.99 *(978-1-4597-0810-5(5)*, 9781459708105) Dundurn Pr. CAN. Dist: Ingram Publisher Services.

Dawson, Willow. The Wolf-Birds. 2015. (ENG., Illus.). 40p. (J). (gr. k-4). 17.95 *(978-1-77147-054-4(2)*, Owlkids) Owlkids Bks. Inc. CAN. Dist: Publishers Group West (PGW).

De Luca, Daniela. Harry the Wolf. 2008. (It's a Wildlife, Buddy! Ser.). (ENG., Illus.). 30p. (J). (gr. -1-1). 12.95 *(978-88-89272-60-2(0))* McRae Bks. Srl ITA. Dist: Independent Pubs. Group.

De Velasco, Miguel Martin Fernandez. Pabluras y Gris. (SPA.). 112p. (YA). (gr. 5-8). *(978-84-279-3178-7(6)*, NG3679) Noguer y Caralt Editores, S. A. ESP. Dist: Lectorum Pubns., Inc.

deRubertis, Barbara. Lana Llama's Little Lamb. Alley, R. W., illus. 2011. (Animal Antics A to Z Ser.). 32p. (J). pap. 45.32 *(978-0-7613-7658-3(5))*; (ENG.). lib. bdg. 22.60 *(978-1-57565-333-4(8))* Astra Publishing Hse.

deRubertis, Barbara & DeRubertis, Barbara. Lana Llama's Little Lamb. Alley, R. W., illus. 2012. (Animal Antics A to Z Ser.). 32p. (J). (gr. 2 — 1). cd-rom 7.95 *(978-1-57565-405-8(9))* Astra Publishing Hse.

Dewolfe, Jeannee'. The Adventures of Billy Chicken Toes & the Wolf: Add Your Own Art Children's Books. 2012. 56p. pap. 11.97 *(978-1-61204-921-2(4)*, Strategic Bk. Publishing) Strategic Book Publishing & Rights Agency (SBPRA).

Dodd, Emma. Wish. Dodd, Emma, illus. (Emma Dodd's Love You Bks.). (ENG., Illus.). (J). (— 1). 2017. 22p. bds. 9.99 *(978-0-7636-9643-6(9))* 2015. 24p. 14.99 *(978-0-7636-8009-1(5))* Candlewick Pr.

Don, Lari. The Hungry Wolf: A Story from North America. Williamson, Melanie, illus. 2013. (Animal Stories Ser.). 48p. (J). (gr. 1-4). pap. 8.99 *(978-1-84686-872-6(6))* Barefoot Bks., Inc.

Donovan, Kevin. Billy & His Friends Tame a Wild Wolf. 2003. (Illus.). 32p. 10.95 *(978-0-9641338-1-5(4))* Billy the Bear & His Friends, Inc.

Dorfman, Ariel. The Rabbits' Rebellion. Riddell, Chris, illus. 2020. (ENG.). 64p. (J). (gr. 2). 13.95 *(978-1-60980-937-9(8)*, Triangle Square) Seven Stories Pr.

Dudley, Maywill. The Story of Little Red Riding Hood. 2005. reprint ed. pap. 15.95 *(978-1-4191-5430-0(3))* Kessinger Publishing, LLC.

Dyckman, Ame. Wolfie the Bunny. OHora, Zachariah, illus. 2015. (ENG.). 40p. (J). (gr. -1-3). 18.99 *(978-0-316-22614-1(9))* Little, Brown Bks. for Young Readers.

Early, Alan. Arthur Quinn & the Fenris Wolf. 2012. (Father of Lies Chronicles Ser.: 2). (ENG.). 384p. (J). pap. 9.99 *(978-1-85635-998-6(0))* Mercier Pr., Ltd., The IRL. Dist: Casemate Pubs. & Bk. Distributors, LLC.

Eash, Sara. Adeline. 2011. 28p. pap. 15.99 *(978-1-4568-7099-7(8))* Xlibris Corp.

Edwards, Julie Andrews & Hamilton, Emma Walton. Dragon: Hound of Honor. 2005. (ENG.). 208p. (J). (gr. 4-18). pap. 7.99 *(978-0-06-057121-4(7)*, HarperCollins) HarperCollins Pubs.

Eichler, Ken. Swift Eagle's Vision Quest, 1 vol. 2009. 95p. pap. 19.95 *(978-1-60703-649-4(5))* America Star Bks.

Evans, Claire. The Three Little Superpigs. Evans, Claire, illus. 2018. (Three Little Superpigs Ser.). (ENG., Illus.). 40p. (J). (gr. -1-k). 16.99 *(978-1-338-24545-5(7)*, Scholastic Pr.) Scholastic, Inc.

—The Three Little Superpigs: Once upon a Time. Evans, Claire, illus. 2019. (Three Little Superpigs Ser.). (ENG., Illus.). 40p. (J). (gr. -1-k). 14.99 *(978-1-338-24548-6(1)*, Scholastic Pr.) Scholastic, Inc.

Evans, Sandra. This Is Not a Werewolf Story. 2016. (ENG., Illus.). 352p. (J). (gr. 4-7). 18.99 *(978-1-4814-4480-4(8)*, Atheneum Bks. for Young Readers) Simon & Schuster Children's Publishing.

Faria, N. K. The Little Smart Rabbit & the Greedy Wolf: Finding Carrots. 2009. (Illus.). 24p. pap. 11.49 *(978-1-4490-1004-1(0))* AuthorHouse.

Farrell, Liam. The Return of the Big Bad Wolf. Myler, Terry, illus. 2004. (ENG.). 64p. (J). pap. *(978-1-901737-48-6(9)*, Anvil Bks.) Mercier Pr., Ltd., The.

—The True Story of the Three Little Pigs & the Big Bad Wolf. 2nd rev. ed. 2012. (ENG.). 192p. (J). pap. 13.95 *(978-1-85635-955-9(7))* Mercier Pr., Ltd., The IRL. Dist: Dufour Editions, Inc.

Farrow, Stephanie, ed. Blue Wolf & Friends Storybook, 1 Vol., Units 1-4. l.t. ed. 2004. (Illus.). 93p. *(978-0-9758759-2-6(2))* Progressive Language, Inc.

Farshtey, Greg. Beware of the Wolves. 2013. (LEGO Legends of Chima Chapter Bks.: 2). lib. bdg. 14.75 *(978-0-606-32014-6(8))* Turtleback.

Fearnley, Jan. Mr Wolf's Pancakes. 2008. (ENG., Illus.). 32p. (J). (gr. -1-2). 12.95 *(978-1-4052-3872-4(0))* Farshore GBR. Dist: Independent Pubs. Group.

Flaxman, Andrew. Little Red Riding Hood: The Classic Grimm's Fairy Tale, 1 vol. Delisa, Patricia, illus. 2006. 32p. (J). (gr. -1-3). 14.95 *(978-0-88010-571-2(2)*, Bell Pond Bks.) SteinerBooks, Inc.

Fraser, W. A. The Gold Wolf. 2004. reprint ed. pap. 1.99 *(978-1-4192-6404-7(4))* Kessinger Publishing, LLC.

Freeman, Martha. Goldilocks, Go Home! Sevilla, Marta, illus. 2019. 96p. (J). (gr. 2-5). 16.99 *(978-0-8234-3857-0(0))* Holiday Hse., Inc.

Freitag, Fred. On Hills & Meadows by the River. 2013. 28p. pap. 24.95 *(978-1-63000-584-9(3))* America Star Bks.

Frontiera, Deborah K. Eric & the Enchanted Leaf / Eric y la Hoja Encantada: A Visit with Canis Lupis / una Visita con Canis Lupis. Santillan-Cruz, Silvia R., tr. Scott, Korey, illus. 2nd l.t. ed. 2005. (SPA & ENG.). 32p. (J). lib. bdg. 16.95 *(978-0-9663629-8-5(5))* By Grace Enterprises.

Gaiches, Sarah. Mirabelle the Lost Kitten. 2010. (Illus.). 76p. pap. 24.99 *(978-1-4490-5593-6(1))* AuthorHouse.

Gaiman, Neil. Los Lobos de la Pared. McKean, Dave, illus. 2006.Tr. of Wolves in the Wall. (SPA.). 64p. 22.95 *(978-1-59497-222-5(2))* Public Square Bks.

—The Wolves in the Walls. McKean, Dave, illus. 2003. (ENG.). 56p. (J). (gr. 3-7). 18.99 *(978-0-380-97827-4(X)*, HarperCollins) HarperCollins Pubs.

George, Jean Craighead. Julie. Minor, Wendell, illus. 2019. (Julie of the Wolves Ser.: 2). (ENG.). 256p. (J). (gr. 3-7). pap. 9.99 *(978-0-06-288431-2(X)*, HarperCollins) HarperCollins Pubs.

—Julie of the Wolves. l.t. ed. 2004. (Beeler Mystery Ser.). 32.95 *(978-1-58118-121-0(3))* LRS.

—Julie of the Wolves: A Newbery Award Winner. Schoenherr, John, illus. (Julie of the Wolves Ser.: 1). (ENG.). (J). (gr. 8-18). 2019. 224p. pap. 9.99 *(978-0-06-440058-9(1))* 2003. 208p. pap. 8.99 *(978-0-06-054095-1(8))* HarperCollins Pubs. (HarperCollins).

—Julie y los Lobos. 26th ed. 2003.Tr. of Julie & the Wolves. (SPA., Illus.). 184p. (J). (gr. 5-8). pap. 12.95 *(978-84-204-4887-9(7)*, AF0842) Santillana USA Publishing Co., Inc.

—Julie's Wolf Pack. 2019. (Julie of the Wolves Ser.: 3). (ENG.). 208p. (J). (gr. 3-7). pap. 7.99 *(978-0-06-288432-9(8)*, HarperCollins) HarperCollins Pubs.

Godkin, Celia. Wolf Island, 1 vol. 2006. (ENG., Illus.). 32p. (J). (gr. k-3). pap. 14.95 *(978-1-55455-008-1(4)*, bec3993c-da6a-4c5e-a699-38c5d4716861) Fitzhenry & Whiteside, Ltd. CAN. Dist: Firefly Bks., Ltd.

Goetze, Jutta. Howl. 2007. 96p. (YA). pap. *(978-1-4207-0740-3(X))* Sundance/Newbridge Educational Publishing.

Golden, Christopher & Lebbon, Tim. The Wild. Ruth, Greg, illus. 2011. (Secret Journeys of Jack London Ser.: 1). (ENG.). 368p. (YA). (gr. 5-18). 15.99 *(978-0-06-186317-2(3)*, HarperTeen) HarperCollins Pubs.

Gordon, Mike, illus. Little Red Riding Hood. 2007. (Picture Book Classics Ser.). 24p. (J). (gr. 1-4). 9.99 *(978-0-7945-1787-8(0)*, Usborne) EDC Publishing.

Grant, V. F. Stories from Grimley Forest. 2011. 48p. (gr. 1-2). pap. 19.50 *(978-1-4567-4709-1(6))* AuthorHouse.

Gravett, Emily. Wolf Won't Bite! Gravett, Emily, illus. 2012. (ENG., Illus.). 32p. (J). (gr. -1-1). 19.99 *(978-1-4424-2763-1(9)*, Simon & Schuster Bks. For Young Readers) Simon & Schuster Bks. For Young Readers.

—Wolves. Gravett, Emily, illus. 2006. (ENG., Illus.). 40p. (J). (gr. k-3). 19.99 *(978-1-4169-1491-4(9)*, Simon & Schuster Bks. For Young Readers) Simon & Schuster Bks. For Young Readers.

Grimm, Jacob & Grimm, Wilhelm K. Little Red Riding Hood: Caperucita Roja. Surges, James, tr. Estrada, Pau, illus. 2006. 22p. (J). (gr. k-4). reprint ed. 15.00 *(978-0-7567-9994-6(5))* DIANE Publishing Co.

Grimm, Wilhelm K. & Grimm, Jacob. Little Red Cap. Zwerger, Lisbeth, illus. 37p. (J). (gr. k-2). pap. 5.95 *(978-0-8072-1285-1(7)*, Listening Library) Random Hse. Audio Publishing Group.

Grotholt, Yannick. Wings for a Lion. 2015. (LEGO Legends of Chima Graphic Novels Ser.: 5). (J). lib. bdg. 18.40 *(978-0-606-37293-0(8))* Turtleback.

Gunderson, Jessica. No Lie, Pigs (and Their Houses) Can Fly! The Story of the Three Little Pigs As Told by the Wolf. Bernardini, Cristian, illus. 2016. (Other Side of the Story Ser.). (ENG.). 24p. (J). (gr. -1-3). lib. bdg. 27.99 *(978-1-4795-8621-9(8)*, 130443, Picture Window Bks.) Capstone.

Haesche, Richard, Sr. Ghost Wolf. 2007. (ENG.). 207p. (YA). 10.99 *(978-0-9798536-5-4(6))* Kreative X-Pressions Pubns.

Hahm, Ji-seul. Prokofiev's Peter & the Wolf. Lupton, David, illus. 2016. (Music Storybooks Ser.). (ENG.). 44p. (J). (gr. 3-5). 29.32 *(978-1-925247-39-8(2)*, f25f94ec-ce49-43d6-8868-fb807d406b1b, Big and SMALL) ChoiceMaker Pty. Ltd., The AUS. Dist: Lerner Publishing Group.

Harrison, Paul. Three Blind Mice Team up with the Three Little Pigs. Epelbaum, Mariano, illus. 2016. (Fairy Tale Mix-Ups Ser.). (ENG.). 24p. (J). (gr. k-2). lib. bdg. 23.99 *(978-1-4109-8301-5(3)*, 132996, Raintree) Capstone.

Harrison, Paula. The Star Wolf. Williams, Sophy, illus. 2018. (Secret Rescuers Ser.: 5). (ENG.). 112p. (J). (gr. 2-5). 16.99 *(978-1-4814-7617-1(3))*; pap. 5.99 *(978-1-4814-7616-4(5))* Simon & Schuster Children's Publishing. (Aladdin).

Harrison, Troon. Eye of the Wolf, 1 vol. (ENG.). 212p. (YA). (gr. 6-11). 2004. pap. 6.95 *(978-1-55005-073-8(7)*, 753d8ac9-629b-4b74-8736-45297fbb471e) 2003. (Illus.). 12.95 *(978-1-55005-072-1(9)*, 73690e76-b286-4e77-9bac-14d07944494d) Trifolium Bks., Inc. CAN. Dist: Firefly Bks., Ltd.

Hartman, Bob. The Wolf Who Cried Boy. Raglin, Tim, illus. 2004. (ENG.). 32p. (J). (gr. k-3). pap. 7.99 *(978-0-14-240159-0(5)*, Puffin Books) Penguin Young Readers Group.

—The Wolf Who Cried Boy. Raglin, Tim, illus. 2004. (Picture Puffins Ser.). (gr. k-3). 17.00 *(978-0-7569-2950-3(4))* Perfection Learning Corp.

—The Wolf Who Cried Boy. Rayla, Tim, illus. 2004. (J). (gr. 1-3). spiral bd. *(978-0-616-14574-6(8))* Canadian National Institute for the Blind/Institut National Canadien pour les Aveugles.

Hartnett, Sonya. Stripes of the Sidestep Wolf. 2005. (ENG.). 208p. (YA). (gr. 7-18). 16.99 *(978-0-7636-2644-0(9))* Candlewick Pr.

Heede, Sylvia Vanden. What Dog Knows. Tolman, Marije, illus. 2016. 128p. (J). pap. 19.99 *(978-1-77657-037-9(5))* Gecko Pr. NZL. Dist: Lerner Publishing Group.

Helakoski, Leslie. Big Chickens. Cole, Henry, illus. 2008. 32p. (J). (gr. -1-k). pap. 8.99 *(978-0-14-241057-8(8)*, Puffin Books) Penguin Young Readers Group.

Hennessy, B. G. The Boy Who Cried Wolf. Kulikov, Boris, illus. 2006. (ENG.). 40p. (J). (gr. -1-3). 19.99 *(978-0-689-87433-8(2)*, Simon & Schuster Bks. For Young Readers) Simon & Schuster Bks. For Young Readers.

—The Boy Who Cried Wolf. Kulikov, Boris, illus. 2011. (J). (gr. -1-2). 29.95 *(978-0-545-09452-8(6))* Weston Woods Studios, Inc.

Herget, Gundi & Garlid, Ann. Arnold the Brave. Renger, Nikolai, illus. 2018. (ENG.). 32p. (J). 16.99 *(978-1-4413-2650-8(2)*, 9de439e7-7f69-4835-bb80-46c50697dede) Peter Pauper Pr. Inc.

Hillert, Margaret. Little Red Riding Hood. (Illus.). (J). 6.00 *(978-0-87895-680-7(8))* Modern Curriculum Pr.

—Wolves: For the Earliest Reader. Starfall Education, ed. Sloan, Monty, photos by. 2006. (ENG., Illus.). 32p. (J). *(978-1-59577-037-0(2))*; pap. *(978-1-59577-038-7(0))* Starfall Education.

Holden, Pam. The Big Bad Wolf, 1 vol. Hawley, Kelvin, illus. 2009. (Red Rocket Readers Ser.). (ENG.). 20p. (gr. 2-2). pap. *(978-1-877363-56-6(1)*, Red Rocket Readers) Flying Start Bks.

—Don't Cry Wolf, 1 vol. Hatam, Samer, illus. 2015. (ENG.). 16p. (-1). pap. *(978-1-77654-130-0(8)*, Red Rocket Readers) Flying Start Bks.

Holdren, Mark W. Spirit Wolf. 2004. (Illus.). 158p. reprint ed. pap. 13.95 *(978-0-9760648-0-0(4))* Powell Hill Pr.

Holmes, Sara. The Wolf Hour. 2017. 310p. (J). pap. *(978-0-545-10798-3(9))*, Levine, Arthur A. Bks.) Scholastic, Inc.

Holmes, Sara Lewis. The Wolf Hour. 2017. (ENG.). 320p. (J). (gr. 3-7). 16.99 *(978-0-545-10797-6(0)*, Levine, Arthur A. Bks.) Scholastic, Inc.

Hoover, Helen. Great Wolf & the Good Woodsman. Bowen, Betsy, illus. 2005. (Fesler-Lampert Minnesota Heritage Ser.). (ENG.). 40p. (J). (gr. -1-7). 14.95 *(978-0-8166-4445-2(4))* Univ. of Minnesota Pr.

Hopkins, Suzette. Little Wolf's Christmas. Taylor, Jill, illus. 2004. (Little Wolf & Friends Ser.). 19p. (J). 12.95 *(978-1-932133-72-1(0))* Writers' Collective, The.

Howker, Janni. Walk with a Wolf with Audio: Read, Listen, & Wonder. Fox-Davies, Sarah, illus. 2008. (Read, Listen, & Wonder Ser.). (ENG.). 32p. (J). (gr. -1-3). pap. 8.99 *(978-0-7636-3875-7(7))* Candlewick Pr.

Hub, Ulrich & Ragg-Kirkby, Helena. Becoming the Wolf. Mühle, Jörg, illus. 2012. (ENG.). 64p. (J). 12.00 *(978-0-8028-5409-4(5)*, Eerdmans Bks For Young Readers) Eerdmans, William B. Publishing Co.

Hunter, Erin. Survivors: the Gathering Darkness #5: the Exile's Journey. Kubinyi, Laszlo & Green, Julia, illus. (Survivors: the Gathering Darkness Ser.: 5). (ENG.). 320p. (J). (gr. 3-7). 2019. pap. 9.99 *(978-0-06-234351-2(3))* 2018. 16.99 *(978-0-06-234349-9(1))* 2018. lib. bdg. 17.89 *(978-0-06-234350-5(5))* HarperCollins Pubs. (HarperCollins).

Irvin-Marston, Hope. My Little Book of Timber Wolves. Magdalena-Brown, Maria, illus. 2nd ed. 2004. (ENG.). 32p. (J). pap. 7.95 *(978-0-89317-052-3(6)*, WW-0526, Windward Publishing) Finney Co., Inc.

Jakubsen, Ryan. Portals III , Band of Rogues. 2011. 128p. pap. 10.00 *(978-0-9846320-0-8(X))* Alabaster Bk. Pub.

Jarman, Julia. Little Bad Riding Hood. Cope, Jane, illus. 2014. (Tadpoles: Fairytale Twists Ser.). (ENG.). 32p. (J). (gr. 1-2). *(978-0-7787-0442-3(4))*; pap. *(978-0-7787-0450-8(5))* Crabtree Publishing Co.

Johnson, Sandi. White Wolf at Dawn. Johnson, Britt, ed. Sturgen, Bobbi, illus. 2014. (ENG.). 30p. (J). (gr. k-5). pap. 12.99 *(978-1-929063-72-7(5)*, 171) Moons & Stars Publishing For Children.

Jones, Noah Z. Little Red Quacking Hood. 2014. (Princess Pink & the Land of Fake-Believe Ser.: 2). lib. bdg. 14.75 *(978-0-606-36048-7(4))* Turtleback.

—Little Red Quacking Hood: a Branches Book (Princess Pink & the Land of Fake-Believe #2) Jones, Noah Z., illus. 2014. (Princess Pink & the Land of Fake-Believe Ser.: 2). (ENG., Illus.). 80p. (J). (gr. k-2). pap. 6.99 *(978-0-545-63841-8(0))* Scholastic, Inc.

—The Three Little Pugs: a Branches Book (Princess Pink & the Land of Fake-Believe #3) Jones, Noah Z., illus. 2015. (Princess Pink & the Land of Fake-Believe Ser.: 3). (ENG., Illus.). 80p. (J). (gr. k-2). pap. 5.99 *(978-0-545-84857-2(1))* Scholastic, Inc.

Jungman, Ann. Lucy & the Big Bad Wolf. Littlewood, Karin, illus. 2005. 120p. (J). (gr. -1-6). pap. 4.95 *(978-1-903015-39-1(1))* Barn Owl Bks, London GBR. Dist: Independent Pubs. Group.

Kantner, Seth. Pup & Pokey. Hill, Beth, illus. 2014. (ENG.). 48p. pap. 15.95 *(978-1-60223-241-9(5))* Univ. of Alaska Pr.

Kasza, Keiko. The Dog Who Cried Wolf. Kasza, Keiko, illus. 2009. (Illus.). 32p. (J). (gr. -1-2). pap. 7.99 *(978-0-14-241305-0(4)*, Puffin Books) Penguin Young Readers Group.

Kaufman, Amie. Elementals: Ice Wolves. Szabo, Levente, illus. 2019. (Elementals Ser.: 1). (ENG.). 368p. (J). (gr. 3-7). pap. 7.99 *(978-0-06-245799-8(3)*, HarperCollins) HarperCollins Pubs.

Kellum, Rebecca L. The Conceited Little Girl. 2007. 24p. per. 24.95 *(978-1-4241-9810-8(0))* America Star Bks.

Keough, Rob. Wolf Summer. 2009. (Gem Lakes Ser.: 2). (ENG., Illus.). 192p. (YA). pap. 11.95 *(978-1-894283-87-8(2)*, Great Plains Teen Fiction) Great Plains Pubns. CAN. Dist: Independent Pubs. Group.

Kimmel, Eric A. Little Red Hot, 0 vols. Huliska-Beith, Laura, illus. 2013. (ENG.). 32p. (J). (gr. -1-3). 17.99 *(978-1-4778-1638-7(0)*, 9781477816387, Two Lions) Amazon Publishing.

—The Three Little Tamales, 0 vols. Docampo, Valeria, illus. 2012. (ENG.). 40p. (J). (gr. -1-3). 17.99 *(978-0-7614-5519-6(1)*, 9780761455196, Two Lions) Amazon Publishing.

Kimura & North, Lucy. One Stormy Night. Abe, Hiroshi, illus. 2005. 48p. (J). (gr. 1-3). 16.00 *(978-4-7700-2970-6(5))* Kodansha International JPN. Dist: Cheng & Tsui Co.

—One Sunny Day, 2 vols., Vol. 2. Abe, Hiroshi, illus. 2005. 48p. (J). 16.00 *(978-4-7700-2971-3(3))* Kodansha International JPN. Dist: Cheng & Tsui Co.

Kitamura, Satoshi. Por el Hilo se Saca el Ovillo. Kitamura, Satoshi, illus. 2003. (Picture Books Collection). (SPA., Illus.). 32p. (J). (gr. k-3). 14.95 *(978-84-372-2357-5(1))* Altea, Ediciones, S.A. - Grupo Santillana ESP. Dist: Santillana USA Publishing Co., Inc.

Knapman, Timothy. Time Now to Dream. Oxenbury, Helen, illus. 2017. (ENG.). 32p. (J). (gr. -1-2). 16.99 *(978-0-7636-9078-6(3))* Candlewick Pr.

Knight, Richard. Winter Shadow. Johnson, Richard, illus. 2011. 80p. (J). (gr. 1-5). pap. 9.99 *(978-1-84686-624-1(3))* Barefoot Bks., Inc.

Knight, Richard John & Walker, Richard. Winter Shadow. Johnson, Richard, illus. 2009. 80p. (J). (gr. 3-9). 16.99 *(978-1-84686-116-1(0))* Barefoot Bks., Inc.

Knopp, Sue, creator. Study Guide for Wolf Journal: A Novel. 2005. 60p. per. 7.95 *(978-1-58939-827-6(0))* Virtualbookworm.com Publishing, Inc.

Knox nee Ramsamugh, Lorna. Fire the Wolf & His Magical Kingdom, 1 vol. 2010. 24p. pap. 24.95 *(978-1-4489-6677-6(9))* PublishAmerica, Inc.

Koch, Claus. The Three Little Wolves & the Big Bad Boar. 2011. 68p. pap. 9.99 *(978-1-4520-5321-9(9))* AuthorHouse.

Koster, Gloria. Little Red Ruthie: A Hanukkah Tale. Eastland, Sue, illus. 2017. (ENG.). 32p. (J). (gr. -1-3). 17.99 *(978-0-8075-4646-8(1)*, 807546461) Whitman, Albert & Co.

Kramer, Alan. The Three Little Pigs Wise up & the Princess Prince & the Vegetables. 2011. (Navigators Ser.). (J). pap. *(978-1-61672-962-2(7))* Benchmark Education Co.

Krensky, Stephen. Big Bad Wolves at School. Sneed, Brad, illus. 2007. (ENG.). 32p. (J). (gr. -1-3). 18.99 *(978-0-689-83799-9(2)*, Simon & Schuster Bks. For Young Readers) Simon & Schuster Bks. For Young Readers.

—Big Bad Wolves at School. 2008. (J). (gr. k-3). 27.95 incl. audio *(978-0-8045-6966-8(5))* Spoken Arts, Inc.

—The Three Little Pigs' Sledding Adventure. Shortley, Michele, illus. 2011. 28p. (J). pap. *(978-0-7680-3486-8(8))* SAE Intl.

Kubler, Annie, illus. What's the Time, Mr Wolf? 2003. (Finger Puppet Bks.). 24p. (J). (gr. 1-1). *(978-0-85953-944-9(X))* Child's Play International Ltd.

Kvasnosky, Laura McGee. Little Wolf's First Howling. Kvasnosky, Laura McGee & McGee, Kate Harvey, illus. 2017. (ENG.). 32p. (J). (gr. -1-2). 17.99 *(978-0-7636-8971-1(8))* Candlewick Pr.

Ladybird. Little Red Riding Hood: Ladybird Readers Level 2, Vol. 2. 2016. (Ladybird Readers Ser.). (Illus.). 48p. (J). (gr. 2-4). pap. 9.99 *(978-0-241-25446-2(9))* Penguin Bks., Ltd. GBR. Dist: Independent Pubs. Group.

Ladybird, Ladybird. Ladybird Tales Peter & the Wolf. 2016. (Ladybird Tales Ser.). (Illus.). 48p. (J). (gr. k-2). 9.99 *(978-0-7232-9448-1(8))* Penguin Bks., Ltd. GBR. Dist: Independent Pubs. Group.

Langton, Jane. Saint Francis & the Wolf. Plume, Ilse, illus. 2019. (ENG.). 32p. (J). (gr. -1-3). 17.95 *(978-1-56792-320-9(8))* Godine, David R. Pub.

Lasky, Kathryn. Frost Wolf. 2011. (Wolves of the Beyond Ser.: 4). (ENG., Illus.). 288p. (J). (gr. 3-7). 17.99 *(978-0-545-09316-3(3)*, Scholastic Pr.) Scholastic, Inc.

Frost Wolf. 2012. (Wolves of the Beyond Ser.: 4). lib. bdg. 17.20 *(978-0-606-26739-7(5))* Turtleback.
—Lone Wolf (Wolves of the Beyond #1) 2011. (Wolves of the Beyond Ser.: 1). (ENG.). 240p. (J). (gr. 3-7). pap. 8.99 *(978-0-545-09311-8(2))* Scholastic, Inc.
—Shadow Wolf (Wolves of the Beyond #2) 2011. (Wolves of the Beyond Ser.: 2). (ENG.). 288p. (J). (gr. 3-7). pap. 8.99 *(978-0-545-09313-2(9)*, Scholastic Pr.) Scholastic, Inc.
—Spirit Wolf (Wolves of the Beyond #5) (Wolves of the Beyond Ser.: 5). (ENG.). 240p. (J). (gr. 3-7). 2013. illus.). pap. 7.99 *(978-0-545-27971-0(2))* 2012. 16.99 *(978-0-545-27961-1(5))* Scholastic, Inc. (Scholastic Pr.).
—Star Wolf. 2014. (Wolves of the Beyond Ser.: 6). (ENG.). 256p. (J). (gr. 3-7). pap. 7.99 *(978-0-545-27972-7(0)*, Scholastic Paperbacks) Scholastic, Inc.
—Watch Wolf. 2012. (Wolves of the Beyond Ser.: 3). (ENG.). 240p. (J). (gr. 3-7). pap. 7.99 *(978-0-545-09315-6(5))* Scholastic, Inc.
Latimer, Alex. Woolf. Latimer, Patrick, illus. 2017. (ENG.). 32p. (J). (gr. k-2). pap. 9.99 *(978-1-84365-340-0(0)*, Pavilion Children's Books) Pavilion Bks. GBR. Dist: HarperCollins Pubs.
Laurel Carter, Anne. The Shepherd's Granddaughter. 2013. 236p. pap. *(978-1-4596-6490-6(6))* ReadHowYouWant.com, Ltd.
Lauren, Child. Cuidado con los cuentos de lobos. 2004. (SPA., Illus.). 36p. (J). (gr. -1-3). 17.99 *(978-84-95040-80-0(8))* Serres, Ediciones, S. L. ESP. Dist: Lectorum Pubns., Inc.
Lee, George Douglas. The Wolf Who Cried Boy. Lee, Brenda Donaloio, ed. Lee, George Douglas, illus. 2012. (Illus.). 46p. pap. 15.95 *(978-0-9848486-2-1(2))* Electric Theatre Radio Hour.
Lee, Ji-yeong. Tchaikovsky's Swan Lake. Pacheco, Gabriel, illus. 2016. (Music Storybooks Ser.). (ENG.). 44p. (J). (gr. 3-5). pap. 9.99 *(978-1-925247-11-4(2)*, 9f5264d9-18d9-44d5-80a4-89189b93ca5a, Big and SMALL) ChoiceMaker Pty. Ltd., The AUS. Dist: Lerner Publishing Group.
Lefèvre, A. M. Hugan Fach Goch. 2005. (WEL., Illus.). 10p. *(978-0-86381-645-1(2))* Gwasg Carreg Gwalch.
Lester, Helen. The Sheep in Wolf's Clothing. Munsinger, Lynn, illus. 2014. (Laugh-Along Lessons Ser.). (ENG.). 32p. (J). (gr. -1-3). 8.99 *(978-0-544-23300-3(X)*, 1563484, Clarion Bks.) HarperCollins Pubs.
Levine, Gail Carson. Betsy Red Hoodie. Nash, Scott, illus. 2010. (ENG.). 40p. (J). (gr. -1-3). 17.99 *(978-0-06-146870-4(3)*, HarperCollins) HarperCollins Pubs.
—Betsy Who Cried Wolf. Nash, Scott, illus. 2005. (ENG.). 40p. (J). (gr. -1-3). reprint ed. pap. 7.99 *(978-0-06-443640-3(3)*, HarperCollins) HarperCollins Pubs.
Little Bear, Shena. How the lone wolf got her Name. 2008. 80p. pap. 9.95 *(978-0-578-00171-5(3))* Stone Castle Publishing.
Little Red Riding Hood: 6 Small Books. (gr. k-2). 23.00 *(978-0-7635-8510-5(6))* Rigby Education.
Little Red Riding Hood: Individual Title Six-Packs. (Story Steps Ser.). (gr. k-2). 32.00 *(978-0-7635-9841-9(0))* Rigby Education.
Liz, Pichon. Three Horrid Little Pigs. Liz, Pichon, illus. 2010. (ENG., Illus.). 32p. (J). pap. 7.95 *(978-1-58925-423-7(6))* Tiger Tales.
Loewen, Nancy. The Boy Who Cried Wolf, Narrated by the Sheepish but Truthful Wolf. Moreno, Juan M., illus. 2018. (Other Side of the Fable Ser.). (ENG.). 24p. (J). (gr. -1-3). lib. bdg. 27.99 *(978-1-5158-2869-3(7)*, 138407, Picture Window Bks.) Capstone.
London, Jack. The Call of the Wild, 1 vol. VanArsdale, Anthony, illus. 2010. (Calico Illustrated Classics Ser.). (ENG.). 112p. (J). (gr. 2-5). 38.50 *(978-1-60270-742-9(1)*, 3985, Calico Chapter Bks.) ABDO Publishing Co.
—The Call of the Wild. 2014. iv, 96p. (J). pap. *(978-1-4677-4602-1(9)*, First Avenue Editions) Lerner Publishing Group.
—The Call of the Wild. 2003. (Aladdin Classics Ser.). (ENG.). 160p. (J). (gr. 4-7). mass mkt. 6.99 *(978-0-689-85674-7(1)*, Aladdin) Simon & Schuster Children's Publishing.
—The Call of the Wild. Clift, Eva, tr. Clift, Eva, illus. 2003. (Values in Action Illustrated Classics Ser.). (J). *(978-1-59203-047-7(5))* Learning Challenge, Inc.
—Classic Starts(r): White Fang. Andreasen, Dan, illus. 2006. (Classic Starts(r) Ser.). 160p. (J). (gr. 2-4). 6.95 *(978-1-4027-2500-5(0))* Sterling Publishing Co., Inc.
—Colmillo Blanco. 2003. (Advanced Reading Ser.: Vol. 56).Tr. of White Fang. (SPA., Illus.). 268p. (J). (gr. 4-7). 11.95 *(978-84-239-9030-6(3))* Espasa Calpe, S.A. ESP. Dist: Planeta Publishing Corp.
—Colmillo Blanco. 2019.Tr. of White Fang. (SPA.). 266p. (J). pap. 10.95 *(978-1-7012-1834-5(8))* Independently Published.
—Colmillo Blanco.Tr. of White Fang. (SPA.). (J). 8.00 *(978-958-04-7143-1(6))* Norma S.A. COL. Dist: Distribuidora Norma, Inc.
—Colmillo Blanco. 2019.Tr. of White Fang. (SPA., Illus.). 80p. (J). (gr. 3-7). pap. *(978-970-643-743-3(6))* Selector, S.A. de C.V.
—Colmillo Blanco. 2006. (Clasicos Juveniles Ser.).Tr. of White Fang. (SPA., Illus.). 279p. pap. 13.95 *(978-84-263-5246-0(4))* Vives, Luis Editorial (Edelvives) ESP. Dist: Lectorum Pubns., Inc.
—White Fang. 2005. 28.95 *(978-1-4218-1472-8(2))*; 276p. pap. 13.95 *(978-1-4218-1572-5(9))* 1st World Publishing, Inc. (1st World Library - Literary Society).
—White Fang. 2005. (ENG.). 176p. (gr. 3-7). per. 14.95 *(978-1-59818-531-7(4))* Aegypan.
—White Fang. 2019. (ENG.). 206p. (J). (gr. 4-6). pap. *(978-93-5329-567-7(X))* Alpha Editions.
—White Fang. 2020. (ENG.). 166p. (J). (gr. 3-7). 19.95 *(978-1-64799-431-0(4))* Bibliotech Pr.
—White Fang. Beck, Ian, illus. 2019. (Alma Junior Classics Ser.). (ENG.). 288p. (J). pap. 10.00 *(978-1-84749-801-4(9)*, 900210529, Alma Classics) Bloomsbury Publishing USA.
—White Fang. 2019. (ENG.). (J). (gr. 4-6). 198p. pap. 7.99 *(978-0-368-43217-0(3))*; 96p. pap. 10.52 *(978-0-368-26333-0(9))*; 98p. pap. 10.71 *(978-0-368-26336-1(3))* Blurb, Inc.
—White Fang. (ENG.). (J). 2018. 336p. 44.95 *(978-0-344-17275-5(9))* 2018. 336p. pap. 27.95 *(978-0-344-17274-8(0))* 2018. (Illus.). 336p. 26.95 *(978-0-342-20703-9(2))* 2018. (Illus.). 336p. pap. 16.95 *(978-0-342-20702-2(4))* 2018. (Illus.). 344p. pap. 16.95 *(978-1-376-57966-6(9))* 2017. (Illus.). pap. 16.95 *(978-1-375-65127-1(7))* 2015. (Illus.). (gr. 5). 26.95 *(978-1-296-70309-7(6))* Creative Media Partners, LLC.
—White Fang. 2005. 120p. per. 5.95 *(978-1-4209-2246-2(7))* Digireads.com Publishing.
—White Fang. (ENG.). (J). 2019. 134p. (gr. 3-7). pap. 8.99 *(978-1-7086-8994-0(X))* 2019. 412p. (gr. 3-7). pap. 16.99 *(978-1-7030-6773-6(8))* 2019. 218p. (gr. 3-7). pap. 13.00 *(978-1-7012-8215-5(1))* 2019. 672p. (gr. 4-6). pap. 42.99 *(978-1-6973-2281-1(6))* 2019. 412p. (gr. 4-6). pap. 24.99 *(978-1-6929-6334-7(1))* 2019. 202p. (gr. 4-6). pap. 14.99 *(978-1-0890-3572-5(1))* 2019. 672p. (gr. 5-8). pap. 37.99 *(978-1-6951-7789-5(4))* 2019. 432p. (gr. 4-6). pap. 25.99 *(978-1-0869-8883-3(3))* 2019. 430p. (gr. 4-6). pap. 24.99 *(978-1-6867-3779-4(3))* 2019. 412p. (gr. 4-6). pap. 26.99 *(978-1-0799-6278-9(6))* 2019. 702p. (gr. 4-6). pap. 39.99 *(978-1-0781-6856-4(3))* 2019. 672p. (gr. 4-6). pap. 43.99 *(978-1-0824-1524-1(3))* 2019. 400p. (gr. 4-6). pap. 24.99 *(978-1-0710-7091-8(6))* 2019. 432p. (gr. 4-6). pap. 25.99 *(978-1-0711-1895-5(1))* 2019. 398p. (gr. 4-6). pap. 26.99 *(978-1-0728-1554-9(0))* 2019. 672p. (gr. 4-6). pap. 37.99 *(978-1-0994-4619-1(8))* 2019. 270p. (gr. 4-6). pap. 16.99 *(978-1-0954-8384-8(6))* 2019. 270p. (gr. 4-6). pap. 15.99 *(978-1-0962-7309-7(8))* 2019. 412p. (gr. 4-6). pap. 24.99 *(978-1-0921-7190-8(8))* 2019. 412p. (gr. 4-6). pap. 24.99 *(978-1-7965-9581-9(0))* 2018. (Illus.). 426p. pap. 28.99 *(978-1-7920-5016-9(X))* 2018. (Illus.). 426p. pap. 28.99 *(978-1-7920-0647-0(0))* 2018. 190p. pap. 7.99 *(978-1-7241-4812-4(5))* Independently Published.
—White Fang. 2019. (ENG.). 170p. (J). (gr. 3-7). pap. *(978-1-7947-1766-4(8))* Lulu Pr., Inc.
—White Fang. 2019. (ENG., Illus.). 160p. (J). (gr. 4-6). pap. 4.95 *(978-1-68422-385-5(7))* Martino Fine Bks.
—White Fang. 2019. (ENG.). 232p. (J). (gr. 4-6). pap. *(978-1-5287-1224-8(2))* Read Bks.
—White Fang. (ENG., Illus.). (J). 2018. 226p. 26.22 *(978-1-7317-0648-5(0))* 2018. 226p. pap. 14.16 *(978-1-7317-0649-2(9))* 2018. 226p. 13.50 *(978-1-7317-0243-2(4))* 2018. 226p. pap. 6.71 *(978-1-7317-0244-9(2))* 2018. 226p. 13.50 *(978-1-61382-453-5(X))* 2018. 226p. pap. 6.71 *(978-1-61382-468-9(8))* 2010. 15.99 *(978-1-61382-978-3(7))* Simon & Brown.
—White Fang. 2006. (Aladdin Classics Ser.). (ENG., Illus.). 368p. (J). (gr. 4-7). pap. 7.99 *(978-1-4169-1414-3(5)*, Aladdin) Simon & Schuster Children's Publishing.
—White Fang. 2018. (ENG., Illus.). 174p. (J). 19.99 *(978-1-5154-2882-4(6))* Wilder Pubns., Corp.
—White Fang, 1 vol. VanArsdale, Anthony, illus. 2011. (Calico Illustrated Classics Ser.: No. 3). (ENG.). 112p. (J). (gr. 2-5). 38.50 *(978-1-61641-112-1(0)*, 4031, Calico Chapter Bks.) ABDO Publishing Co.
—White Fang. 2004. reprint ed. pap. 1.99 *(978-1-4192-9386-3(9))*; pap. 22.95 *(978-1-4191-9386-6(4))* Kessinger Publishing, LLC.
—White Fang: With a Discussion of Resilience. Walker, Karen, illus. 2003. (Values in Action Illustrated Classics Ser.). 191p. (J). *(978-1-59203-038-5(6))* Learning Challenge, Inc.
London, Jack, creator. White Fang. 2016. (ENG., Illus.). (J). (gr. 1-4). pap. *(978-1-318-79441-6(2))* HardPr.
London, Jack. & Gruyer, Paul. Croc-Blanc. 2019.Tr. of White Fang. (FRE.). 170p. (J). pap. *(978-2-322-12786-3(8))* Books on Demand GmbH.
London, Jonathan. The Eyes of Gray Wolf. Van Zyle, Jon, illus. 2016. (ENG.). 32p. (J). (gr. k-3). pap. 12.99 *(978-1-943328-72-7(2)*, West Winds Pr.) West Margin Pr.
—The Seasons of Little Wolf. Van Zyle, Jon, illus. (ENG.). 32p. (J). (gr. k-3). 2016. pap. 11.99 *(978-1-941821-74-9(X))* 2014. 16.99 *(978-1-941821-06-0(5))* West Margin Pr. (West Winds Pr.).
Lupano, Wilfrid. The Wolf in Underpants. Cauuet, Paul & Itoïz, Mayana, illus. 2019. (Wolf in Underpants Ser.). (ENG.). 40p. (J). (gr. 2-5). 27.99 *(978-1-5415-2818-5(2)*, 0046f7d7-8e39-4319-a96e-ede58ecb8129, Graphic Universe™) Lerner Publishing Group.
Mackaman, Audrey. Cavall in Camelot #2: Quest for the Grail. 2019. (ENG., Illus.). 256p. (J). (gr. 3-7). 17.99 *(978-0-06-249453-5(8)*, HarperCollins) HarperCollins Pubs.
Mackinnon, Mairi. The Boy Who Cried Wolf. 2009. (First Reading Level 3 Ser.). 48p. (J). 6.99 *(978-0-7945-2472-2(9)*, Usborne) EDC Publishing.
Mann, Greyson. Wolves vs. Zombies: Secrets of an Overworld Survivor, #3. Sandford, Grace, illus. 2017. (Secrets of an Overworld Survivor Ser.). (ENG.). 112p. (J). (gr. 1-4). 13.99 *(978-1-5107-1331-4(X)*, Sky Pony Pr.) Skyhorse Publishing Co., Inc.
Martín Fernández de Velasco, Miguel. Pabluras. (SPA.). 120p. (YA). (gr. 5-8). *(978-84-279-3146-6(8)*, NG3678) Noguer y Caralt Editores, S. A. ESP. Dist: Lectorum Pubns., Inc.
Martin, Nicole. The Werewolf. 2006. 146p. pap. 14.99 *(978-1-4120-8802-2(X))* Trafford Publishing.
Mawhinney, Art, illus. Diego's Wolf Pup Rescue. 2006. (Go, Diego, Go! Ser.: 1). (ENG.). 24p. (J). (gr. -1-2). pap. 3.99 *(978-1-4169-1559-1(1)*, Simon Spotlight/Nickelodeon) Simon Spotlight/Nickelodeon.
Mazula, Derek. A Driften's Tale. 2009. 48p. pap. 24.99 *(978-1-4490-2782-7(2))* AuthorHouse.
McCleery, William. Wolf Story. Chappell, Warren, illus. 2012. 88p. (J). (gr. k-4). 16.95 *(978-1-59017-589-7(1)*, NYR Children's Collection) New York Review of Bks., Inc., The.
McDonald, Avril. The Wolf & the Baby Dragon, 1 vol. Minina, Tatiana, illus. 2016. (Feel Brave Ser.). (ENG.). 32p. (J). pap. 12.95 *(978-1-78583-021-1(X))* Crown Hse. Publishing LLC.
—The Wolf's Colourful Coat, 1 vol. Minina, Tatiana, illus. 2016. (Feel Brave Ser.). (ENG.). 32p. (J). pap. 12.95 *(978-1-78583-020-4(1))* Crown Hse. Publishing LLC.
McNaughton, Colin. Cyfres Meurig y Mochyn: M. W. S. G. Williams, Dylan, tr. 2005.Tr. of S. W. A. L. K. (WEL., Illus.). 32p. *(978-1-902416-62-5(7))* Cymdeithas Lyfrau Ceredigion.
—Gôl! Williams, Dylan, tr. McNaughton, Colin, illus. 2005.Tr. of Goal! (WEL., Illus.). 30p. *(978-0-948930-79-9(9))* Cymdeithas Lyfrau Ceredigion.
McNaughton, Colin, et al. Wps! 2005.Tr. of Oops! (WEL., Illus.). 28p. *(978-1-902416-29-8(5))* Cymdeithas Lyfrau Ceredigion.
Mcwilliams, Ronnie. The Leaf People: Philip & the Wolf. 2011. 16p. (gr. 1-2). pap. 9.36 *(978-1-4567-6583-5(3))* AuthorHouse.
Meddaugh, Susan. The Best Place. 2004. (ENG., Illus.). 32p. (J). (gr. -1-3). reprint ed. pap. 5.95 *(978-0-618-44882-1(9)*, 491413, Clarion Bks.) HarperCollins Pubs.
Mejuto Rial, Eva. RUN PUMPKIN, RUN. 2007. (ENG., Illus.). 36p. (J). 17.95 *(978-84-96788-88-6(1))* OQO, Editora ESP. Dist: Baker & Taylor Bks.
Menard, Michele R. Who Do I Think You Are? 2013. 26p. pap. 10.95 *(978-0-9887969-5-9(3))* Four Menards, The.
Milani, Mino. El Ultimo Lobo. (Barco de Vapor).Tr. of Last Wolf. (SPA.). 144p. (YA). (gr. 5-8). *(978-84-348-4520-6(2))* SM Ediciones.
Moore, Natalia. The Wolf Who Learned to Be Good. Moore, Natalia, illus. 2017. (ENG., Illus.). 32p. (J). (gr. -1-3). 16.99 *(978-0-8075-9204-5(8)*, 807592048) Whitman, Albert & Co.
Mortimer, Rachael. Red Riding Hood & the Sweet Little Wolf. Pichon, Liz, illus. 2013. (ENG.). 32p. 12.95 *(978-1-58925-117-5(2))* Tiger Tales.
Murphy, Jill. On the Way Home. 2nd rev. ed. 2007. (ENG., Illus.). 32p. (J). (gr. k-2). pap. 11.95 *(978-0-230-01584-5(0))* Pan Macmillan GBR. Dist: Independent Pubs. Group.
Murray, Donna. Mottsie, Wolf of Great Price. 2003. 80p. pap. 19.95 *(978-1-4137-0080-0(2))* America Star Bks.
Naumann-Villemin, Christine. When a Wolf Is Hungry. Di Giacomo, Kris, illus. 2017. (ENG.). 34p. (J). 16.00 *(978-0-8028-5482-7(6)*, Eerdmans Bks For Young Readers) Eerdmans, William B. Publishing Co.
Night, P. J. You Can't Come in Here!, 2. 2011. (You're Invited to a Creepover Ser.: 2). (ENG.). 160p. (J). (gr. 3-7). pap. 7.99 *(978-1-4424-2095-3(2)*, Simon Spotlight) Simon & Schuster Children's Publishing.
—You Can't Come in Here! 2018. (You're Invited to a Creepover Ser.: 2). (ENG.). 160p. (J). (gr. 3-7). 17.99 *(978-1-5344-1658-1(7)*, Simon Spotlight) Simon Spotlight.
—You Can't Come in Here!, 1 vol. 2013. (You're Invited to a Creepover Ser.). (ENG.). 160p. (J). (gr. 3-6). lib. bdg. 31.36 *(978-1-61479-066-2(3)*, 15854, Chapter Bks.) Spotlight.
Nobisso, Josephine. Francis Woke up Early. Hyde, Maureen, illus. 2011. (ENG.). 32p. (J). (gr. k-2). 17.95 *(978-0-940112-20-9(5))*; pap. 9.95 *(978-0-940112-22-3(1))* Gingerbread Hse.
Norris-Gooding, S. M. The Legend of Kerloup. 2011. 340p. (gr. -1). pap. 23.03 *(978-1-4343-5229-3(3))* AuthorHouse.
North, Laura. The Big Bad Wolf & the Robot Pig. 2014. (Race Ahead with Reading Ser.). (ENG., Illus.). 32p. (J). (gr. 2-2). *(978-0-7787-1291-6(5))* Crabtree Publishing Co.
Novel Units. Julie of the Wolves Novel Units Student Packet. 2019. (ENG.). (J). (gr. 4-7). pap. 13.99 *(978-1-56137-821-0(6)*, Novel Units, Inc.) Classroom Library Co.
—White Fang Novel Units Student Packet. 2019. (ENG.). (J). pap. 13.99 *(978-1-56137-527-1(6)*, Novel Units, Inc.) Classroom Library Co.
Numeroff, Laura Joffe. The Chicken Sisters. Collicott, Sharleen, illus. abr. ed. 2003. (J). (gr. -1-2). 28.95 incl. audio compact disk *(978-1-59112-533-4(2))* Live Oak Media.
Oliver, Alison. Moon. Oliver, Alison, illus. 2018. (ENG., Illus.). 40p. (J). (gr. -1-3). 17.99 *(978-1-328-78160-4(7)*, 1683178, Clarion Bks.) HarperCollins Pubs.
Once upon a Time Spanish Version-Little Red Riding Hood. 2005. (J). *(978-1-57022-562-8(1))* ECS Learning Systems, Inc.
Once upon a Time Spanish Version-the Boy Who Cried Wolf. 2005. (J). *(978-1-57022-557-4(5))* ECS Learning Systems, Inc.
Orihuela, Luz. Caperucita Roja: Little Red Riding Hood. Sarfatti, Esther, tr. Rovira, Francesc, illus. 2006. (Bilingual Tales Ser.). (ENG & SPA.). 24p. (J). (gr. -1-3). pap. 3.99 *(978-0-439-77375-1(X)*, Scholastic en Espanol) Scholastic, Inc.
Palatini, Margie. Bad Boys. Cole, Henry, illus. 40p. (J). (gr. -1-2). 2003. lib. bdg. 16.89 *(978-0-06-000103-2(8))* 2003. (ENG.). 15.99 *(978-0-06-000102-5(X)*, Tegen, Katherine Bks) 2006. (ENG.). reprint ed. 8.99 *(978-0-06-000104-9(6)*, Tegen, Katherine Bks) HarperCollins Pubs.
—Bad Boys Get Cookie! Cole, Henry, illus. 2006. 32p. (J). (gr. -1-3). 18.89 *(978-0-06-074437-3(5))*; (ENG.). 17.99 *(978-0-06-074436-6(7)*, Tegen, Katherine Bks) HarperCollins Pubs.
—Bad Boys Get Cookie! 2007. (J). (gr. k-3). 27.95 incl. audio compact disk *(978-0-8045-6957-6(6))*; 29.95 incl. audio compact disk *(978-0-8045-4180-0(9))* Spoken Arts, Inc.
—Bad Boys Get Henpecked! Cole, Henry, illus. 2009. (ENG.). 32p. (J). (gr. -1-2). 17.99 *(978-0-06-074433-5(2)*, Tegen, Katherine Bks) HarperCollins Pubs.
Parker, Emma. Little Red Riding Hood. 2010. (Illus.). pap. *(978-1-877561-01-6(0))* First Edition Ltd.
Parker, Vic, ed. The Wolf & His Shadow & Other Fables. 2014. (Aesop's Fables Ser.). 40p. (J). (gr. 2-5). pap. 84.95 *(978-1-4824-0793-8(0))* Stevens, Gareth Publishing LLLP.
—The Wolf in Sheep's Clothing & Other Fables. 2014. (Aesop's Fables Ser.). 40p. (J). (gr. 2-5). pap. 84.95 *(978-1-4824-1261-1(6))* Stevens, Gareth Publishing LLLP.
Parry, Rosanne. A Wolf Called Wander. 2021. (Voice of the Wilderness (Trade) Ser.). (ENG.). 272p. (gr. 3-6). 22.44 *(978-1-5364-6706-2(5))* HarperCollins Pubs.
—A Wolf Called Wander. Armiño, Mónica, illus. (Voice of the Wilderness Novel Ser.). (ENG.). 256p. (J). (gr. 3-7). 2021. pap. 7.99 *(978-0-06-289594-3(X))* 2019. 16.99 *(978-0-06-289593-6(1))* HarperCollins Pubs. (Greenwillow Bks.).
—A Wolf Called Wander. Armiño, Mónica, illus. 2019. (ENG.). 256p. lib. bdg. 18.80 *(978-1-6636-3081-0(X))* Perfection Learning Corp.
Paver, Michelle. Chronicles of Ancient Darkness #1: Wolf Brother. Taylor, Geoff, illus. 2006. (Chronicles of Ancient Darkness Ser.: 1). (ENG.). 320p. (J). (gr. 5-9). reprint ed. per. 9.99 *(978-0-06-072827-4(2)*, Tegen, Katherine Bks) HarperCollins Pubs.
—Chronicles of Ancient Darkness #2: Spirit Walker, 2. Taylor, Geoff, illus. 2007. (Chronicles of Ancient Darkness Ser.: 2). (ENG.). 384p. (J). (gr. 5-8). pap. 7.99 *(978-0-06-072830-4(2)*, Tegen, Katherine Bks) HarperCollins Pubs.
—Chronicles of Ancient Darkness #3: Soul Eater. Taylor, Geoff, illus. 2008. (Chronicles of Ancient Darkness Ser.: 3). (ENG.). 352p. (J). (gr. 5). pap. 7.99 *(978-0-06-072833-5(7)*, Tegen, Katherine Bks) HarperCollins Pubs.
—HERMANO LOBO: CRÓNICAS DE LA PREHISTORIA I. 2005. (SPA., Illus.). 222p. 17.25 *(978-84-7888-933-4(7))* Emece Editores ESP. Dist: Ediciones Universal.
—Wolf Brother, 6 vols. 2005. (Chronicles of Ancient Darkness Ser.: 1). (J). 89.75 *(978-1-4193-3811-3(0))*; 76.75 *(978-1-4193-2628-8(7))*; 91.75 *(978-1-4193-3809-0(9))*; 73.75 *(978-1-4193-2630-1(9))* Recorded Bks., Inc.
Pennart, Geoffroy de. EL LOBO SENTIMENTAL. 2004. (SPA.). 36p. (J). (gr. k-2). 20.99 *(978-84-8470-120-0(4))* Corimbo, Editorial S.L. ESP. Dist: Lectorum Pubns., Inc.
Percival, Tom. The Magic Looking Glass. 2017. (Little Legends Ser.: 4). (ENG.). 192p. (J). (gr. 2-5). pap. 8.99 *(978-1-4926-4259-6(2)*, Sourcebooks Jabberwocky) Sourcebooks, Inc.
Peter L. Ward. Freya & the Fenris-Wolf. 2010. 184p. 24.50 *(978-1-4269-2511-5(5))*; pap. 14.50 *(978-1-4269-2510-8(7))* Trafford Publishing.
Pichon, Liz. The Three Horrid Little Pigs. Pichon, Liz, illus. 2008. (Illus.). 32p. (J). (gr. -1-2). 15.95 *(978-1-58925-077-2(X))* Tiger Tales.
Pignat, Caroline. Timber Wolf, 1 vol. 2011. (ENG.). 214p. (J). (gr. 4-6). pap. 12.95 *(978-0-88995-459-5(3)*, 0ffb0656-7a0b-44d3-b9dd-070a83a437ae) Red Deer Pr. CAN. Dist: Firefly Bks., Ltd.
Pilney, Dovie. Charlie the Cocky Rooster: Another Adventure. 2008. 52p. pap. 20.95 *(978-1-4389-3517-1(X))* AuthorHouse.
Ponting, Susan. The Revenge of BB Wolf. 2011. 140p. (gr. -1). 28.98 *(978-1-4567-7528-5(6))*; (Illus.). pap. 17.23 *(978-1-4567-7011-2(X))* AuthorHouse.
Poole, Stephanie. Adopted by Wolves. 2009. 52p. pap. 15.99 *(978-1-4415-1032-7(X))* Xlibris Corp.
popular, Cancionero. Juguemos en el bosque. 2004. (SPA., Illus.). 28p. (J). (gr. k-18). pap. 6.50 *(978-980-257-282-3(9))* Ekare, Ediciones VEN. Dist: Iaconi, Mariuccia Bk. Imports.
Porter, Harry. Wolf. Stites, Theresa, illus. 2012. 28p. pap. 14.99 *(978-0-9838018-5-6(1))* 4RV Pub.
Publications International Ltd. Staff. Sweet Dreams Padded Treasury. 2013. 320p. (J). bds. *(978-1-4127-6333-2(9)*, 1412763339) Phoenix International Publications, Inc.
Raines, Kristy. Grizzer the Goofy Wolf. Raines, Morgan, illus. 2007. (ENG.). 80p. per. 11.95 *(978-1-59594-132-9(0)*, Wingspan Pr.) WingSpan Publishing.
Rameaka, T. Mystery of Wolf Den Cave. 2005. 74p. pap. 19.95 *(978-1-4137-5551-0(8))* America Star Bks.
Ramos, Mario. I Am So Clever. Ramos, Mario, illus. 2019. (ENG., Illus.). 48p. (J). (gr. k-2). 17.99 *(978-1-77657-248-9(3)*, 7adf32d6-48a7-4e35-994f-d3e6bca3b7ce) Gecko Pr. NZL. Dist: Lerner Publishing Group.
—I Am So Handsome. 2012. (ENG., Illus.). 32p. (gr. -1-4). 17.95 *(978-1-877579-19-6(X))* Gecko Pr. NZL. Dist: Lerner Publishing Group.
Ransom, Jeanie Franz. Big Red & the Little Bitty Wolf: A Story about Bullying. Zivoin, Jennifer, illus. 2016. 32p. (J). *(978-1-4338-2048-9(X)*, Magination Pr.) American Psychological Assn.
Redmond, Diane. Peter & the Wolf: Band 09/Gold (Collins Big Cat) Bendall-Brunello, John, illus. 2007. (Collins Big Cat Ser.). (ENG.). 24p. (J). (gr. 1-2). pap. 9.99 *(978-0-00-718674-7(6))* HarperCollins Pubs. Ltd. GBR. Dist: Independent Pubs. Group.
Reilly, Carmel & Miesen, Christina. The Call of the Wolf. 2008. (Rigby Focus Forward: Level H Ser.). (Illus.). 24p. (J). (gr. 4-7). pap. *(978-1-4190-3722-1(6)*, Rigby) Pearson Education Australia.
Richards, Pat. Bardolph Bedivere Wolf Returns. Richards, Charles, illus. 2007. 42p. (J). *(978-0-9790796-4-1(0))* PJR Assocs., Ltd.
Rigby Education Staff. Red Riding Hood: Jumbled Tumble. (gr. k-2). 26.00 *(978-0-7635-2416-6(6))* Rigby Education.
Robberecht, Thierry. The Wolf Who Fell Out of a Book, 1 vol. 2017. (ENG., Illus.). 24p. (J). 14.99 *(978-1-4236-4797-3(1))* Gibbs Smith, Publisher.
Robinson, Hilary. Goldilocks & the Wolf. Sanfilippo, Simona, illus. 2012. (ENG.). 32p. (J). *(978-0-7787-8023-6(6))*; pap. *(978-0-7787-8034-2(1))* Crabtree Publishing Co.
—Three Pigs & a Gingerbread Man. Sanfilippo, Simona, illus. 2012. (ENG.). 32p. (J). *(978-0-7787-8026-7(0))*; pap. *(978-0-7787-8037-3(6))* Crabtree Publishing Co.
Roddy, Lee. Tracked by the Wolf Pack. 2006. (Ladd Family Adventure Ser.: Vol. 15). (J). 7.99 *(978-0-88062-264-6(4))* Mott Media.
Romeu, Emma. Here Comes the Grey Wolf. Vigil, Luis Gerardo Sanchez & Broeck, Fabricio Vanden, illus. 2004. (Colección Animales de América / Animals of the Americas Ser.). (SPA.). 32p. (gr. 3-5). pap. 11.95 *(978-1-59437-843-0(6))* Santillana USA Publishing Co., Inc.
Roscoe, Alessandra Pontes. JK, o Lobo-Guará. Oliveira, Jô, illus. 2010. (POR.). 29p. (J). *(978-85-06-06063-6(X))* Companhia Melhoramentos de Sao Paulo Industrias de Papel.
Rosen, Michael J. In the Quiet, Noisy Woods. Won, Annie, illus. 2019. 40p. (J). (gr. -1-2). 17.99 *(978-1-5247-6665-8(8)*, Doubleday Bks. for Young Readers) Random Hse. Children's Bks.
Roy, Ron. A to Z Mysteries: the White Wolf. Gurney, John Steven, illus. 2004. (to Z Mysteries Ser.: 23). 96p. (J). (gr. 1-4). pap. 6.99 *(978-0-375-82480-7(4)*, Random Hse. Bks. for Young Readers) Random Hse. Children's Bks.
Rozanski, Bonnie. Borderline. 2007. (ENG.). 208p. (YA). (gr. 10). pap. 22.95 *(978-0-88984-293-9(0))* Porcupine's Quill, Inc. CAN. Dist: Univ. of Toronto Pr.
Rundell, Katherine. The Wolf Wilder. 2015. (ENG., Illus.). 240p. (J). (gr. 3-7). 19.99 *(978-1-4814-1942-0(0)*, Simon & Schuster Bks. For Young Readers) Simon & Schuster Bks. For Young Readers.
Salmieri, Daniel. Bear & Wolf. 2018. (Illus.). 48p. (J). (gr. -1-3). 17.95 *(978-1-59270-238-1(4))* Enchanted Lion Bks., LLC.
Sanders, Alex. Un Lobo! (SPA.). 36p. *(978-84-95150-34-9(4))* Corimbo, Editorial S.L.

W X Y Z

—Un Lobo! (SPA.). 36p. 16.95 *(978-84-95150-24-0(7))* Corimbo, Editorial S.L. ESP. Dist: Distribooks, Inc.
Sargent, Dave & Sargent, Pat. Bo Bo's Big Imagination, 10 vols., Vol. 13. Robinson, Laura, illus. 2004. (Learn to Read Ser.: 10).Tr. of Gran Imaginacion de Bo Bo. 18p. (J). pap. 10.95 *(978-1-56763-822-6(8))* Ozark Publishing.
Sargent, Pat L. Topper: Son of Barney, 8. Lenoir, Jane, illus. 2007. (Barney the Bear Killer Ser.: 7). 147p. (YA). lib. bdg. 25.25 *(978-1-56763-425-9(7))* Ozark Publishing.
—Topper, Son of Barney #7, 6 vols. 2007. (Barney the Bear Killer Ser.: 7). (YA). pap. 9.95 *(978-1-56763-426-6(5))*; lib. bdg. 26.25 *(978-1-59381-609-4(X))* Ozark Publishing.
Schwartz, Corey Rosen. Ninja Red Riding Hood. Santat, Dan, illus. 2014. 40p. (J). (gr. k-3). 18.99 *(978-0-399-16354-8(9))*, G.P. Putnam's Sons Books for Young Readers) Penguin Young Readers Group.
Scieszka, Jon. The True Story of the 3 Little Pigs / la Verdadera Historiade Los TresCerditos. 2009. 64p. (J). (gr. k-3). pap. 8.99 *(978-0-14-241447-7(6)*, Puffin Books) Penguin Young Readers Group.
Scott, Victoria. Hear the Wolves. 2017. (ENG.). 240p. (J). (gr. 3-7). 16.99 *(978-1-338-04358-7(7)*, Scholastic Pr.) Scholastic, Inc.
Scraper, Katherine. The Boy Who Cried Wolf: An Aesop's Fable. 2006. (J). pap. *(978-1-4108-6166-5(X))* Benchmark Education Co.
Scuderi. Lo Que el Lobo le Conto a la Luna. 2004.Tr. of What the Wolf Told the Moon. (SPA., Illus.). (J). 20.99 *(978-84-261-3275-8(8))* Juventud, Editorial ESP. Dist: Lectorum Pubns., Inc.
Seidler, Tor. Firstborn. Sheban, Chris, illus. 2015. (ENG.). 240p. (J). (gr. 4-9). 16.99 *(978-1-4814-1017-5(2)*, Atheneum Bks. for Young Readers) Simon & Schuster Children's Publishing.
Sesame Street Staff. Fairly Furry 2 bk Big Red Riding Hood 3 Little Grouches. 2007. 15.99 *(978-1-59069-625-5(5))* Studio Mouse LLC.
Shurtliff, Liesl. Red: the (Fairly) True Tale of Red Riding Hood. 2017. (ENG.). 272p. (J). (gr. 3-7). 8.99 *(978-0-385-75586-3(4)*, Yearling) Random Hse. Children's Bks.
Sierra, Judy. Tell the Truth, B. B. Wolf. Seibold, J. Otto, illus. 2010. 40p. (J). (gr. -1-2). 17.99 *(978-0-375-85620-4(X)*, Knopf Bks. for Young Readers) Random Hse. Children's Bks.
Simone, Yve. Little Valentine. 2013. 72p. pap. 28.99 *(978-1-4817-0496-0(6))* AuthorHouse.
Singh, Jay. Once upon a Time in a Forest Far Away. 2009. 394p. pap. 33.12 *(978-1-4251-9122-1(3))* Trafford Publishing.
Smallman, Steve. The Lamb Who Came for Dinner. Dreidemy, Joëlle, illus. 2007. 32p. (J). (gr. -1-2). 15.95 *(978-1-58925-067-3(2))* Tiger Tales.
Smith, Carrie. The Boy Who Cried Wolf: Classic Tales Edition. Kelley, Gerald, illus. 2011. (Classic Tales Ser.). (J). *(978-1-936258-59-8(5))* Benchmark Education Co.
Smith, Lynda Faye. The Revenge of the Big Bad Wolf. 2012. pap. 9.95 *(978-0-7414-6529-0(9))* Infinity Publishing.
Smith, Sherry. The Wolf & the Shield: An Adventure with Saint Patrick. McNally, Nicholas, illus. 2016. 118p. (J). pap. *(978-0-8198-8356-8(5))* Pauline Bks. & Media.
Smith, Stephanie & Smith, Stephanie A. Gray Wolf Pup's Adventure. Hynes, Robert, illus. 2nd ed. 2003. (ENG.). 32p. (J). (gr. 1-3). 12.95 *(978-1-931465-43-4(6)*, PS2077) Soundprints.
Snell, Roy J. Triple Spies. 2017. (ENG., Illus.). (J). (gr. -1-7). 22.95 *(978-1-374-95345-1(8))* Capital Communications, Inc.
—Triple Spies. 2008. 112p. (gr. -1-7). 22.95 *(978-1-60664-743-1(1))* Rodgers, Alan Bks.
Solotareff, Gregoire. Wolfy. Solotareff, Gregoire, illus. 2018. (ENG., Illus.). 36p. (J). (gr. k-3). 16.99 *(978-1-77657-156-7(8)*, ec1c4bfa-8b2a-4390-b247-9888ff858b66) Gecko Pr. NZL. Dist: Lerner Publishing Group.
Sommer, Carl. No One Will Ever Know. Budwine, Greg, illus. 2014. (J). pap. *(978-1-57537-962-3(7))* Advance Publishing, Inc.
—No One Will Ever Know. 2003. (Another Sommer-Time Story Ser.). (Illus.). 48p. (J). (gr. 1-4). 16.95 incl. audio *(978-1-57537-555-7(9))* Advance Publishing, Inc.
—No One Will Ever Know. Westbrook, Dick, illus. 2003. (Another Sommer-Time Story Ser.). (ENG.). 48p. (J). (gr. 1-4). 16.95 incl. audio compact disk *(978-1-57537-506-9(0))* Advance Publishing, Inc.
—No One Will Ever Know(Nadie Se Va a Enterar) Westbrook, Dick, illus. 2009. (Another Sommer-Time Story Bilingual Ser.). (SPA & ENG.). 48p. (J). lib. bdg. 16.95 *(978-1-57537-163-4(4))* Advance Publishing, Inc.
Soni, Parwinder Singh, illus. Little Red Riding Hood. 2010. (J). *(978-1-60617-132-5(1))* Teaching Strategies, LLC.
Sorgini, Linda. Little Red Riding Hood. Malak, Annabel, illus. 2011. (ENG.). 16p. cd-rom 12.95 *(978-2-89558-408-7(7)*, 9782895584087) Editions Alexandre Stanke CAN. Dist: Baker & Taylor Publisher Services (BTPS).
StacyPlays. Wild Rescuers: Guardians of the Taiga. 2018. (Wild Rescuers Ser.: 1). (ENG., Illus.). 224p. (J). (gr. 3-7). 17.99 *(978-0-06-279637-0(2)*, HarperCollins) HarperCollins Pubs.
—Wild Rescuers: Escape to the Mesa. 2019. (Wild Rescuers Ser.: 2). (ENG., Illus.). 224p. (J). (gr. 3-7). 17.99 *(978-0-06-279640-0(2)*, HarperCollins) HarperCollins Pubs.
—Wild Rescuers: Guardians of the Taiga. (Wild Rescuers Ser.: 1). (J). (gr. 3-7). 2075. 224p. 12.99 *(978-0-06-291274-9(7))* 2019. (ENG.). 240p. pap. 7.99 *(978-0-06-279638-7(0)*, HarperCollins) HarperCollins Pubs.
Stiefvater, Maggie. Forever. l.t. ed. 2011. (Shiver Trilogy: Bk. 3). (ENG.). 597p. 23.99 *(978-1-4104-3606-1(3))* Thorndike Pr.
—Forever. 2014. (Wolves of Mercy Falls Ser.: 3). lib. bdg. 20.85 *(978-0-606-36649-6(0))* Turtleback.
—Forever (Shiver, Book 3) 2014. (Shiver Ser.: 3). (ENG.). 416p. (YA). (gr. 9). pap. 10.99 *(978-0-545-68280-0(0))* Scholastic, Inc.
—Forever (Shiver, Book 3) (Unabridged Edition), 1 vol. unabr. ed. 2011. (Shiver Ser.: 3). (ENG.). 5p. (YA). (gr. 8). audio compact disk 79.99 *(978-0-545-31555-5(7))* Scholastic, Inc.
—Hunted (Spirit Animals, Book 2), Bk. 2. 2014. (Spirit Animals Ser.: 2). (ENG., Illus.). 192p. (J). (gr. 3-7). 13.99 *(978-0-545-52244-1(7)*, Scholastic Pr.) Scholastic, Inc.
—Linger. 2014. (Shiver Ser.). (ENG.). (YA). (gr. 9). lib. bdg. 20.60 *(978-1-68065-091-4(2))* Perfection Learning Corp.
—Linger. l.t. ed. 2011. (Shiver Trilogy: Bk. 2). (ENG.). 488p. pap. 23.99 *(978-1-4104-3447-0(8))* Thorndike Pr.
—Linger (Shiver, Book 2), 1 vol. 2014. (Shiver Ser.: 2). (ENG.). 384p. (YA). (gr. 9). pap. 10.99 *(978-0-545-68279-4(7))* Scholastic, Inc.
—Shiver. 2011. (Shiver Trilogy: Bk. 1). 9.64 *(978-0-7848-3572-2(1)*, Everbind) Marco Bk. Co.
—Shiver. (ENG.). (gr. 9). 2014. (Shiver Ser.). (YA). lib. bdg. 20.60 *(978-1-68065-090-7(4))* 2010. (Shiver Trilogy: Bk. 1). 392p. 20.00 *(978-1-60686-750-1(4))* Perfection Learning Corp.
—Shiver. l.t. ed. 2010. (Shiver Trilogy: Bk. 1). (ENG.). 506p. 23.95 *(978-1-4104-2667-3(X))* Thorndike Pr.
—Shiver. 2014. (Wolves of Mercy Falls Ser.: 1). lib. bdg. 20.85 *(978-0-606-36647-2(4))* Turtleback.
—Shiver (Shiver, Book 1), 1 vol. 2014. (Shiver Ser.: 1). (ENG.). 416p. (YA). (gr. 9). pap. 12.99 *(978-0-545-68278-7(9))* Scholastic, Inc.
—Sinner (Shiver) 2015. (Shiver Ser.). (ENG.). 368p. (YA). (gr. 9). pap. 12.99 *(978-0-545-65459-3(9))* Scholastic, Inc.
Stine, Faye. Wolf: A Story of the Wild. 2012. (ENG.). 64p. pap. 10.95 *(978-1-4787-2054-6(9))* Outskirts Pr., Inc.
Stockham, Jess, illus. The Boy Who Cried Wolf. 2011. (Flip-Up Fairy Tales Ser.). 24p. (J). *(978-1-84643-407-5(6))*; (gr. 2-2). *(978-1-84643-368-9(1))* Child's Play International Ltd.
—Little Red Riding Hood. 2005. (Flip-Up Fairy Tales Ser.). 24p. (J). pap. *(978-1-904550-22-8(3))* Child's Play International Ltd.
Storr, Catherine. The Complete Polly & the Wolf. Watts, Marjorie-Ann & Bennett, Jill, illus. 2016. (ENG.). 304p. (J). (gr. 3-7). 17.95 *(978-1-68137-001-9(8)*, NYR Children's Collection) New York Review of Bks., Inc., The.
Sweet, Melissa. Carmine: A Little More Red. 2008. (ENG., Illus.). 40p. (J). (gr. -1-3). pap. 6.95 *(978-0-618-99717-6(2)*, 1028081, Clarion Bks.) HarperCollins Pubs.
Talbott, Hudson. From Wolf to Woof: The Story of Dogs. Talbott, Hudson, illus. 2016. (Illus.). 40p. (J). (gr. k-3). 16.99 *(978-0-399-25404-8(8)*, Nancy Paulsen Books) Penguin Young Readers Group.
Taplin, Sam. Little Red Riding Hood. 2008. (First Fairytales Look & Say Ser.). 12p. (J). (gr. -1). bds. 9.99 *(978-0-7945-2199-8(1)*, Usborne) EDC Publishing.
Taylor, Christine. Red Riding Hood & the Toad. 2009. (Illus.). 44p. (gr. -1 — 1). 18.49 *(978-1-4389-3483-9(1))* AuthorHouse.
Taylor, Sean. Small Bad Wolf. Lewis, Jan, illus. 2004. (I Am Reading Ser.). 45p. (J). (gr. -1-3). 11.60 *(978-0-7569-5400-0(2))* Perfection Learning Corp.
Teague, Mark. The Three Little Pigs & the Somewhat Bad Wolf. Teague, Mark, illus. 2013. (ENG., Illus.). 48p. (J). (gr. -1-k). 18.99 *(978-0-439-91501-4(5)*, Orchard Bks.) Scholastic, Inc.
Tong, Reia D. The Lonely Gourmet: Juan the Vegetarian Wolf. 2010. 44p. pap. 16.99 *(978-1-4490-9466-9(X))* AuthorHouse.
Tremblay, Marc. Le Petit Frere du Chaperon Rouge. Fil et al, illus. 2004. (était une Fois Ser.). (FRE.). 24p. (J). (gr. -1). pap. *(978-2-89021-698-3(5))* Diffusion du livre Mirabel (DLM).
Trivizas, Eugene. The Three Little Wolves & the Big Bad Pig. 2004. (ENG., Illus.). 16p. (J). 24.95 *(978-1-4052-0669-3(1))* Farshore GBR. Dist: Trafalgar Square Publishing.
—The Three Little Wolves & the Big Bad Pig: A Pop-up Storybook. Oxenbury, Helen, illus. 2006. 16p. (J). (gr. k-4). reprint ed. 27.00 *(978-0-7567-9913-7(9))* DIANE Publishing Co.
—Los Tres Lobitos y el Cochino Feroz. Oxenbury, Helen, illus. 2003. (SPA.). 32p. (J). (gr. k-3). pap. 12.99 *(978-980-257-246-5(2)*, EK1366) Ekare, Ediciones VEN. Dist: Lectorum Pubns., Inc., Kane Miller.
Tsaliovich, Anatoly. Of Wolves & Lambs & Others. Burke, Daniel, illus. 2005. 73p. (YA). pap. 12.99 *(978-0-9773816-0-9(9))* ATInternational Pubs.
Tucker, Stephen. Little Red Riding Hood, 2 vols. Sharratt, Nick, illus. 2017. (Lift-The-Flap Fairy Tales Ser.). (ENG.). 24p. (J). (gr. -1-1). 10.99 *(978-1-5098-2815-9(X))* Pan Macmillan GBR. Dist: Independent Pubs. Group.
Tyler, William H. The Little Wolf Cubs' Christmas Gift. 2011. 48p. pap. *(978-1-4269-7443-4(4))* Trafford Publishing (UK) Ltd.
Van Slyke, Rebecca. Lana Lynn Howls at the Moon, 1 vol. Sandu, Anca, illus. 2019. 32p. (J). (gr. -1-3). 16.95 *(978-1-68263-050-1(1))* Peachtree Publishing Co. Inc.
Vanalstine, Carrie. Frizzy Izzy Yelp! 2012. 32p. pap. 11.95 *(978-1-4685-4609-5(0))* AuthorHouse.
Velez, Walter, illus. Little Red Riding Hood: A Tale about Staying Safe. 2006. (J). 6.99 *(978-1-59939-021-5(3))* Cornerstone Pr.
Vidal, Séverine. Mega Wolf. Barroux, Stephane, illus. 2015. (Mega Hero Bks.). (ENG.). 28p. (J). (gr. k-2). 12.95 *(978-1-77085-637-0(4)*, 84473abb-1b4f-4565-adad-e4da1d803377) Firefly Bks., Ltd.
Visconti, Guido. El Lobo con Correa (Wolf on a Leash), 1 vol. 2005. (Lobo con Correa (Wolf on a Leash) Ser.). (SPA., Illus.). 24p. (gr. k-2). lib. bdg. 26.67 *(978-0-8368-6262-1(7)*, cda37ef6-64fa-4cf0-8069-37bbf681f841, Gareth Stevens Learning Library) Stevens, Gareth Publishing LLLP.
Wallace, R. Mike. Saunter. 2009. 36p. pap. 10.75 *(978-1-60693-994-9(7)*, Strategic Bk. Publishing) Strategic Book Publishing & Rights Agency (SBPRA).
Weston, Robert Paul. Dust City. 2011. (ENG.). 299p. (YA). (gr. 7-12). 24.94 *(978-1-59514-296-2(7))* Penguin Young Readers Group.
Weston Woods Staff, creator. Red Riding Hood. 2011. 18.95 *(978-0-439-72882-9(7))*; 29.95 *(978-0-439-73518-6(1))*; 38.75 *(978-0-439-72883-6(5))* Weston Woods Studios, Inc.
—The True Story of the 3 Little Pigs. 2011. 38.75 *(978-0-545-09460-3(7))* Weston Woods Studios, Inc.
Whatley, Bruce. Wait! No Paint! 2005. (ENG., Illus.). 32p. (J). (gr. -1-3). pap. 7.99 *(978-0-06-443546-8(6)*, HarperCollins) HarperCollins Pubs.
Wheeler, Lisa. Invasion of the Pig Sisters: Ready-To-Read Level 3. Ansley, Frank, illus. 2006. (Fitch & Chip Ser.: 4). (ENG.). 48p. (J). (gr. 1-3). pap. 4.99 *(978-0-689-84958-9(3)*, Simon Spotlight) Simon Spotlight.
—Invasion of the Pig Sisters: Ready-To-Read Level 3. Ansley, Frank, illus. 2006. (Fitch & Chip Ser.: 4). (ENG.). 48p. (J). (gr. 1-3). 16.99 *(978-0-689-84953-4(2)*, Simon Spotlight) Simon Spotlight.
—New Pig in Town: Ready-To-Read Level 3. Ansley, Frank, illus. 2003. (Fitch & Chip Ser.: 1). (ENG.). 48p. (J). (gr. 1-3). 16.99 *(978-0-689-84950-3(8)*, Atheneum/Richard Jackson Bks.) Simon & Schuster Children's Publishing.
—Who's Afraid of Granny Wolf? Ready-To-Read Level 3. Ansley, Frank, illus. 2004. (Fitch & Chip Ser.: 3). (ENG.). 48p. (J). (gr. 1-3). 16.99 *(978-0-689-84952-7(4)*, Simon Spotlight) Simon Spotlight.
—Who's Afraid of Granny Wolf? Ready-To-Read Level 3. Ansley, Frank, illus. 2006. (Fitch & Chip Ser.: 3). (ENG.). 48p. (J). (gr. 1-3). pap. 4.99 *(978-0-689-84957-2(5)*, Simon Spotlight) Simon Spotlight.
White, Kathy. Little Green Riding Hood. 2006. (J). pap. *(978-1-4108-6182-5(1))* Benchmark Education Co.
White, Mark. The Wolf in Sheep's Clothing: A Retelling of Aesop's Fable, 1 vol. Rojo Pérez, Sara, illus. (My First Classic Story Ser.). (ENG.). 24p. (J). (gr. k-3). 2013. pap. 7.10 *(978-1-4795-1857-9(3)*, 123448) 2011. lib. bdg. 23.32 *(978-1-4048-6509-9(8)*, 114191) Capstone. (Picture Window Bks.).
Whybrow, Ian. Dear Little Wolf. Ross, Tony, illus. 2005. (Little Wolf Adventures Ser.). 64p. (gr. 3-6). pap., lib. bdg. 14.95 *(978-0-87614-902-7(6))* Lerner Publishing Group.
—Little Wolf, Forest Detective. Ross, Tony, illus. 2005. (Middle Grade Fiction Ser.). 112p. (J). (gr. 3-6). 14.95 *(978-1-57505-413-1(2))*; pap. 6.95 *(978-1-57505-829-0(4))* Lerner Publishing Group.
—Little Wolf, Pack Leader. Ross, Tony, illus. 2005. (Little Wolf Adventures Ser.). 126p. (gr. 3-6). 14.95 *(978-1-57505-400-1(0))* Lerner Publishing Group.
—Little Wolf, Terror of the Shivery Sea. Ross, Tony, illus. 2004. (Little Wolf Adventures Ser.). (ENG.). 144p. (J). (gr. 3-6). 14.95 *(978-1-57505-629-6(1))* Lerner Publishing Group.
—Little Wolf's Diary of Daring Deeds. Ross, Tony, illus. (Middle Grade Fiction Ser.). 132p. (gr. 3-6). 2005. 14.95 *(978-1-57505-411-7(6))* 2003. (J). pap. 6.95 *(978-0-87614-536-4(5)*, Carolrhoda Bks.) Lerner Publishing Group.
—Little Wolf's Handy Book of Poems. Ross, Tony, illus. 2005. (Little Wolf Adventures Ser.). 80p. (gr. 3-6). pap., lib. bdg. 14.95 *(978-0-87614-927-0(1))* Lerner Publishing Group.
—Little Wolf's Haunted Hall for Small Horrors. Ross, Tony, illus. (Middle Grade Fiction Ser.). (J). 2005. 132p. (gr. 3-6). 14.95 *(978-1-57505-412-4(4))* 2004. 125p. (gr. 4-7). per. 6.95 *(978-1-57505-794-1(8))* Lerner Publishing Group.
—Lobito Aprende a Ser Malo. Azaola, Miguel, tr. from ENG. Ross, Tony, illus. 2007. (Ediciones Lerner Single Titles Ser.). (SPA.). 136p. (J). (gr. 3-6). per. 6.95 *(978-0-8225-8644-9(4)*, Ediciones Lerner) Lerner Publishing Group.
—Malicia para Principiantes: Una Aventura de Lobito y Apestosito. Quintana, Joela, tr. Ross, Tony, illus. 2005. (Libros Ilustrados (Picture Bks.)). (SPA.). 32p. (J). (gr. k-2). 16.95 *(978-0-8225-3211-8(5)*, Ediciones Lerner) Lerner Publishing Group.
—What's the Time, Little Wolf? A Little Wolf & Smellybreff Adventure. Ross, Tony, illus. 2006. 32p. (J). (gr. -1-3). lib. bdg. 15.95 *(978-1-57505-939-6(8)*, Carolrhoda Bks.) Lerner Publishing Group.
Whybrow, Ian & Ross, Tony. Badness for Beginners: A Little Wolf & Smellybreff Adventure. 2005. (Illus.). 32p. (J). (gr. -1-3). 16.95 *(978-1-57505-861-0(8)*, Carolrhoda Bks.) Lerner Publishing Group.
Williams, M. J. Alora & the Howling Guff. 2010. 132p. pap. 10.68 *(978-1-4520-3207-8(6))* AuthorHouse.
Williamson, Melanie. El magnifico plan de Lobo/ Wolf's Magnificent Plan. Williamson, Melanie, illus. 2008. (SPA., Illus.). 29p. 20.95 *(978-84-263-6837-9(9))* Vives, Luis Editorial (Edelvives) ESP. Dist: Baker & Taylor Bks.
Willson, Sarah. What's with Dad? Marantz, Larissa & DiPaolo, Katharine, illus. 2006. (Ready-To-Read Level 3 Ser.). (ENG.). 32p. (J). (gr. 1-3). 16.19 *(978-1-4169-0669-8(X))* Simon & Schuster, Inc.
Wilson, Troy. Little Red Reading Hood & the Misread Wolf. Campana, Ilaria, illus. 2019. (ENG.). 32p. (J). (gr. -1-3). 17.99 *(978-0-7624-9266-4(X)*, Running Pr. Kids) Running Pr.
Wilson, W. Shane. War for Ice. 2010. 158p. pap. 13.99 *(978-0-557-23572-8(3))* Lulu Pr., Inc.
Winter, Milo, illus. The Three Little Pigs - Shape Book. 2008. (Children's Die-Cut Shape Book Ser.). (ENG.). 16p. (J). (gr. -1-3). per. 10.95 *(978-1-59583-265-8(3)*, 9781595832658, Green Tiger Pr.) Laughing Elephant.
Wood, Maryrose. The Incorrigible Children of Ashton Place: Book IV Bk. IV: The Interrupted Tale. Wheeler, Eliza, illus. 2013. (Incorrigible Children of Ashton Place Ser.: 4). (ENG.). 400p. (J). (gr. 3-7). 16.99 *(978-0-06-179122-2(9)*, Balzer & Bray) HarperCollins Pubs.
Woodington, Artie. Elroy, the Big Bad Wolf: The product of his Environment. 2011. 48p. pap. 16.95 *(978-1-4560-7229-2(3))* America Star Bks.
Woollvin, Bethan. Little Red, 1 vol. 2016. (ENG., Illus.). 32p. (J). (gr. k-4). 18.99 *(978-1-56145-917-9(8))* Peachtree Publishing Co. Inc.
Yanez-Arellano, Katherine. The Gunny Wolf Story. 2009. 28p. pap. 12.95 *(978-1-4269-1594-9(2))* Trafford Publishing.
Young, Ed. Lon Po Po: A Red-Riding Hood Story from China. unabr. ed. 2006. (J). (gr. k-4). 18.95 *(978-0-439-87366-6(5)*, WPCD690); (Illus.). 29.95 *(978-0-439-87367-3(3)*, WHCD690) Weston Woods Studios, Inc.
Young, Judy. The Wolves of Slough Creek. 2019. (Wild World of Buck Bray Ser.). (ENG., Illus.). 240p. (J). (gr. 3-6). pap. 9.99 *(978-1-5341-1021-2(6)*, 204662);Bk. 3. 16.99 *(978-1-5341-1020-5(8)*, 204651) Sleeping Bear Pr.
Zuill, Andrea. Wolf Camp. Zuill, Andrea, illus. 2018. (ENG., Illus.). 40p. (J). (gr. -1-3). pap. 8.99 *(978-1-9848-5165-9(9)*, Schwartz & Wade Bks.) Random Hse. Children's Bks.

WOMBATS

Einhorn, Kama. Welcome, Wombat. 2018. (True Tales of Rescue Ser.). (ENG., Illus.). 160p. (J). (gr. 3-7). 14.99 *(978-1-328-76702-8(7)*, 1680370, Clarion Bks.) HarperCollins Pubs.
Fishman, Jon M. Meet a Baby Wombat. 2017. (Lightning Bolt Books (r) — Baby Australian Animals Ser.). (ENG., Illus.). 24p. (J). (gr. 1-3). 29.32 *(978-1-5124-3387-6(X)*, af5df9c8-0156-4317-af80-073a384f7f88, Lerner Pubns.); pap. 9.99 *(978-1-5124-5592-2(X)*, 9f4c5cc7-d18c-41f1-a03a-a6eb8fde7dbc) Lerner Publishing Group.
Gates, Margo. Wombats. 2013. (Animal Safari Ser.). (ENG., Illus.). 24p. (J). (gr. k-3). lib. bdg. 26.95 *(978-1-60014-917-7(0)*, Blastoff! Readers) Bellwether Media
George, Lynn. Wombats: Burrow Builders, 1 vol. 2010. (Animal Architects Ser.). (ENG.). 24p. (J). (gr. 2-3). pap. 9.25 *(978-1-4488-1355-1(7)*, 8ad1832e-63ae-4622-9bce-c744eb7fb21a); lib. bdg. 26.27 *(978-1-4488-0697-3(6)*, be735e25-473b-469a-87d6-6a275889cb15) Rosen Publishing Group, Inc., The. (PowerKids Pr.).
Kras, Sara Louise. Wombats: A 4D Book. rev. ed. 2018. (Australian Animals Ser.). (ENG., Illus.). 24p. (J). (gr. -1-2). lib. bdg. 29.32 *(978-1-9771-0003-0(1)*, 138165, Capstone Pr.) Capstone.
Murray, Julie. Wombats. (Nocturnal Animals (Abdo Kids Junior) Ser.). (ENG., Illus.). (J). 2017. 24p. (gr. -1-2). lib. bdg. 31.36 *(978-1-5321-0409-1(X)*, 26535, Abdo Kids) 2011. 32p. (gr. 2-5). 34.21 *(978-1-61783-015-0(1)*, 2882, Big Buddy Bks.) ABDO Publishing Co.
—Wombats (Wombats) 2018. (Animales Nocturnos (Nocturnal Animals) Ser.). (SPA., Illus.). 24p. (J). (gr. -1-2). lib. bdg. 31.36 *(978-1-5321-8020-0(9)*, 28255, Abdo Kids) ABDO Publishing Co.
Phillips, Dee. Wombat's Burrow. 2014. (Science Slam: the Hole Truth Ser.). 24p. (J). (gr. -1-3). lib. bdg. 26.99 *(978-1-62724-091-8(8))* Bearport Publishing Co., Inc.

WOMBATS—FICTION

Chambers, Susannah. The Snow Wombat. Jackson, Mark, illus. 2016. (ENG.). 32p. (J). (gr. -1-1). 16.99 *(978-1-76011-381-0(6))* Allen & Unwin AUS. Dist: Independent Pubs. Group.
—The Snow Wombat. Jackson, Mark, illus. 2019. (ENG.). 32p. (J). (gr. -1-k). bds. 9.99 *(978-1-76063-293-9(7))* Allen & Unwin AUS. Dist: Independent Pubs. Group.
Churchill, Vicki & Fuge, Charles. Sometimes I Like to Curl up in a Ball. 2003. (ENG., Illus.). 22p. (J). (gr. -1-k). bds. 8.99 *(978-1-4027-0870-1(X))* Sterling Publishing Co., Inc.
French, Jackie. Diary of a Baby Wombat. Whatley, Bruce, illus. 2010. (ENG.). 32p. (J). (gr. -1-3). 16.99 *(978-0-547-43005-8(1)*, 1432352, Clarion Bks.) HarperCollins Pubs.
—Diary of a Wombat. Whatley, Bruce, illus. 2009. (ENG.). 32p. (J). (gr. -1-3). pap. 9.99 *(978-0-547-07669-0(X)*, 1042035, Clarion Bks.) HarperCollins Pubs.
French, Jackie & Whatley, Bruce. Diary of a Wombat Board Book. 2007. (ENG., Illus.). 16p. (J). bds. *(978-0-7322-8662-0(X))* HarperCollins Pubs. Australia.
—Grandma Wombat. 2021. (Illus.). 32p. pap. 7.99 *(978-0-7322-9960-6(8)*, HarperCollins) HarperCollins Pubs.
—Wombat Goes to School. 2020. (ENG.). 32p. pap. 7.99 *(978-0-7322-9903-3(9)*, HarperCollins) HarperCollins Pubs.
—Wombat Wins. 2021. (Illus.). 32p. pap. 7.99 *(978-0-7322-9958-3(6)*, HarperCollins) HarperCollins Pubs.
Lester, Helen. Batter up Wombat. Munsinger, Lynn, illus. 2006. (ENG.). 32p. (J). (gr. k-3). 24.80 *(978-1-4287-0160-1(5)*, Follettbound) Follett School Solutions.
McAllister, Angela. Dyna Lle'r Wyt Ti! Williams, Dylan & Jones, Gwen Angharad, trs. from ENG. 2005.Tr. of Found You, Little Wombat! (WEL., Illus.). 24p. *(978-1-902416-90-8(2))* Cymdeithas Lyfrau Ceredigion.
Treml, Renee. Once I Heard a Little Wombat. 2020. 24p. (J). (-k). bds. 11.99 *(978-1-76089-054-4(5)*, Picture Puffin) Penguin Random Hse. AUS. Dist: Independent Pubs. Group.
—One Very Tired Wombat. 2020. 24p. (J). (gr. -1-k). bds. 11.99 *(978-1-76089-052-0(9)*, Picture Puffin) Penguin Random Hse. AUS. Dist: Independent Pubs. Group.
—One Very Tired Wombat. Treml, Renee, illus. 2014. (ENG., Illus.). 32p. (J). (gr. -1-k). pap. 9.99 *(978-1-74275-579-3(8))* Random Hse. Australia AUS. Dist: Independent Pubs. Group.
—Wombat Big, Puggle Small. 2020. 24p. (J). (gr. -1-k). bds. 11.99 *(978-1-76089-055-1(3)*, Picture Puffin) Penguin Random Hse. AUS. Dist: Independent Pubs. Group.

WOMEN

see also Girls; Mothers

Andrews Henningfeld, Diane, ed. Should Women Be Allowed to Serve in Combat in the U. S. Armed Forces?, 1 vol. 2007. (At Issue Ser.). (ENG., Illus.). 120p. (gr. 10-12). pap. 28.80 *(978-0-7377-3939-8(8)*, 9da6ac82-283a-4d5b-a38f-2840fc18b8ee); lib. bdg. 41.03 *(978-0-7377-3938-1(X)*, 4ca8de6e-1a60-4ec2-8685-ceef046ae2bf) Greenhaven Publishing LLC. (Greenhaven Publishing).
—Women in Islam, 1 vol. 2010. (At Issue Ser.). (ENG.). 112p. (gr. 10-12). 41.03 *(978-0-7377-4904-5(0)*, 8ef301b2-aaaf-4d22-ae92-2f4628ff6168); pap. 28.80 *(978-0-7377-4905-2(9)*, b364b0f8-e2cd-4fa8-a59a-2bd7af1fa1bf) Greenhaven Publishing LLC. (Greenhaven Publishing).
Angelou, Maya. My Painted House, My Friendly Chicken, & Me. Courtney-Clarke, Margaret, illus. 2003. (ENG.). 48p. (J). (gr. -1-2). 8.99 *(978-0-375-82567-5(3)*, Crown Books For Young Readers) Random Hse. Children's Bks.
—My Painted House, My Friendly Chicken, & Me. 2003. (gr. k-3). lib. bdg. 18.40 *(978-0-613-71911-7(5))* Turtleback.
Bevis, Mary. Old Woman Winter. Powell, Consie, illus. 2010. 32p. (J). (gr. 1-2). pap. 9.95 *(978-0-9819307-6-3(X))* Raven Productions, Inc.
Burling, Alexis. Everything You Need to Know about Confronting Violence Against Women, 1 vol. 2018. (Need to Know Library). (ENG.). 64p. (gr. 6-6). 36.13 *(978-1-5081-7916-0(6)*, 22a2518b-f1e7-442b-9f7f-33e2c4fb90d8) Rosen Publishing Group, Inc., The.
Butterfield, Moira. Lady of the Manor. 2009. (Medieval Lives Ser.). 32.80 *(978-1-59920-169-6(0))* Black Rabbit Bks.
Chaterjee. With Our Own Minds: Women Organizing & Developing on Indian Plantation. 2010. (Gender, Culture, &

Global Politics Ser.: 10). (ENG.). (gr. 13). 85.00 (978-0-8153-3701-0(9)) Routledge.

ompiled by Barbour Staff, Compiled by. The Prayer Map for Women: A Creative Journal. 2018. (Faith Maps Ser.). (ENG.). 176p. spiral bd. 7.99 (978-1-68322-557-7(0), Barbour Bks.) Barbour Publishing, Inc.

rockett, Chelsea. Above All Else: 60 Devotions for Young Women, 1 vol. 2019. (ENG.). 208p. (YA). 15.99 (978-0-310-76726-8(1)) Zondervan.

urst Johnson, Claudia, ed. Women's Issues in Alice Walker's the Color Purple, 1 vol. 2011. (Social Issues in Literature Ser.). (ENG., Illus.). 168p. (gr. 10-12). lib. bdg. 48.03 (978-0-7377-5270-0(X), a7ab5455-2128-477c-95b5-c8a6ca6d2ca9); pap. 33.00 (978-0-7377-5271-7(8), a743f4bc-7f17-40d9-829a-0178fa4438f1) Greenhaven Publishing LLC. (Greenhaven Publishing).

sherick, Joan. Women in the World of Africa. 2006. (Women's Issues Ser.). (Illus.). 112p. (YA). lib. bdg. 22.95 (978-1-59084-857-9(8)) Mason Crest.

vans, Christine. Objectification of Women in the Media. 2019. (Women & Society Ser.). (ENG.). 80p. (J). (gr. 6-12). (978-1-68282-543-3(4)) ReferencePoint Pr., Inc.

risch, Aaron. Witches. 2013. (Illus.). 24p. (J). 25.65 (978-1-60818-250-3(9), Creative Education) Creative Co., The.

George, Elizabeth. Living Your Faith: A Journey Through James. 2018. (ENG.). 144p. (J). (gr. 2-7). pap. 10.99 (978-0-7369-6441-8(X), 6964418) Harvest Hse. Pubs.

Heing, Bridey. ISIS Brides, 1 vol. 2017. (Crimes of ISIS Ser.). (ENG.). 104p. (gr. 8-8). 38.93 (978-0-7660-9213-6(5), 45dd4a6e-487c-4514-b402-10bf802ec914) Enslow Publishing, LLC.

Jensen, Kelly. Here We Are: Feminism for the Real World. 2017. (ENG., Illus.). 240p. (YA). (gr. 9-12). pap. 17.95 (978-1-61620-586-7(5), 73586) Algonquin Young Readers.

Katz, Naomi. Beautiful-Being an Empowered Young Woman. 2016. (ENG., Illus.). 154p. (J). pap. 16.95 (978-1-59687-441-1(4), ipicturebooks) ibooks, Inc.

Korté, Steve & Who HQ. What Is the Story of Wonder Woman? Murray, Jake, illus. 2019. (What Is the Story Of? Ser.). (ENG.). 112p. (J). (gr. 3-7). 6.99 (978-1-5247-8827-8(9), Penguin Workshop) Penguin Young Readers Group.

Koya, Lena & Kamberg, Mary-Lane. Female Body Image & Self-Perception, 1 vol. 2017. (Women in the World Ser.). (ENG., Illus.). 112p. (J). (gr. 6-6). 38.80 (978-1-5081-7726-5(0), f3982b64-a3de-4ae1-bf79-0fc07d713210) Rosen Publishing Group, Inc., The.

Lawrence, Sandra. Anthology of Amazing Women: Trailblazers Who Dared to Be Different. Collins, Nathan, illus. 2018. (ENG.). 128p. (J). (gr. 3-7). 17.99 (978-1-4998-0690-8(6)) Little Bee Books Inc.

Lee Stone, Tanya. Who Says Women Can't Be Computer Programmers? The Story of Ada Lovelace. Priceman, Marjorie, illus. 2018. (ENG.). 40p. (J). 18.99 (978-1-62779-299-8(6), 900145930, Holt, Henry & Co. Bks. For Young Readers) Holt, Henry & Co.

Lewis, Anna M. Women of Steel & Stone: 22 Inspirational Architects, Engineers, & Landscape Designers. 2014. (Women of Action Ser.: 6). (ENG., Illus.). 272p. (YA). (gr. 7). 19.95 (978-1-61374-508-3(7)) Chicago Review Pr., Inc.

Libal, Autumn. Women in the Hispanic World. 2006. (Women's Issues, Global Trends Ser.). (Illus.). 112p. (YA). lib. bdg. 22.95 (978-1-59084-858-6(6)) Mason Crest.

Loh-Hagan, Virginia. Girl Bosses. 2019. (History's Yearbook Ser.). (ENG., Illus.). 32p. (J). (gr. 4-8). pap. 14.21 (978-1-5341-5078-2(1), 213619); lib. bdg. 32.07 (978-1-5341-4792-8(6), 213618) Cherry Lake Publishing. (45th Parallel Press).

—Katherine Johnson. Bane, Jeff, illus. 2018. (Mi Mini Biografía (My Itty-Bitty Bio): My Early Library). (ENG.). 24p. (J). (gr. k-1). pap. 12.79 (978-1-5341-0809-7(2), 210600); lib. bdg. 30.64 (978-1-5341-0710-6(X), 210599) Cherry Lake Publishing.

—Mary Jackson. Bane, Jeff, illus. 2018. (Mi Mini Biografía (My Itty-Bitty Bio): My Early Library). (ENG.). 24p. (J). (gr. k-1). pap. 12.79 (978-1-5341-0811-0(4), 210608); lib. bdg. 30.64 (978-1-5341-0712-0(6), 210607) Cherry Lake Publishing.

Lowery, Zoe & Bezdecheck, Bethany. Women in Relationships, 1 vol. 2017. (Women in the World Ser.). (ENG., Illus.). 112p. (J). (gr. 6-6). 38.80 (978-1-5081-7443-1(1), 2bce7e4e-dc1d-4251-8cda-4c1d34532f13, Rosen Young Adult) Rosen Publishing Group, Inc., The.

Lowery, Zoe & Mills, J. Elizabeth. Social Roles & Stereotypes, 1 vol. 2017. (Women in the World Ser.). (ENG., Illus.). 112p. (J). (gr. 6-6). 38.80 (978-1-5081-7441-7(5), 461dd125-e5a7-4467-9223-6b78b507b25a, Rosen Young Adult) Rosen Publishing Group, Inc., The.

Lüsted, Marcia Amidon. The Fight for Women's Rights, 1 vol. 2019. (Activism in Action: a History Ser.). (ENG.). 112p. (gr. 8-8). pap. 18.65 (978-1-5081-8552-9(2), 0d2973da-0004-447c-be57-a7e61a77cd52) Rosen Publishing Group, Inc., The.

Maring, Therese Kauchak. A Smart Girl's Guide: Sports & Fitness: How to Use Your Body & Mind to Play & Feel Your Best. Roe, Monika, illus. 2018. (American Girl(r) Wellbeing Ser.). (ENG.). 112p. (J). pap. 12.99 (978-1-68337-062-8(7)) American Girl Publishing, Inc.

Marquardt, Meg. Women in E-Sports. 2018. (ESports: Game On! Ser.). (ENG.). 48p. (J). (gr. 5-8). 29.27 (978-1-59953-966-9(7)) Norwood Hse. Pr.

Marriott, Emma. Violence Against Women. 2016. (Behind the News Ser.). (Illus.). 48p. (J). (gr. 6-9). (978-0-7787-2590-9(1)) Crabtree Publishing Co.

Martz, Sandra, ed. When I Am an Old Woman I Shall Wear Purple: Petite Version. 2nd gif. rev. ed. 2006. (Illus.). 64p. (C). pap. 47.70 (978-1-57601-093-8(7)) Nodin Pr.

Muise, Doris. Wild Woman Alphabet, 1 vol. 2017. (ENG., Illus.). 72p. (J). (gr. 1-3). 24.95 (978-1-926886-48-0(8)) Theytus Bks., Ltd. CAN. Dist: Orca Bk. Pubs. USA.

National Institute on Alcohol Abuse and Alcoholism (U S). Alcohol: a Women's Health Issue: A Women's Health Issue. 2017. (ENG.). 20p. (YA). (gr. 10-5). pap. 8.00 (978-0-16-093721-7(3), National Institute on Alcohol Abuse & Alcoholism) United States Government Printing Office.

Nyman, Debbie & Wortzman, Ricki. The 10 Most Notable Elected Female Leaders. 2008. 14.99 (978-1-55448-527-7(4)) Scholastic Library Publishing.

Parkinson, Siobhan. Rocking the System: Fearless & Amazing Irish Women Who Made History. Luke, Bren, illus. 2019. (ENG.). 180p. (J). (gr. 4-7). 15.99 (978-1-910411-96-4(5)) Little Island IRL. Dist: Consortium Bk. Sales & Distribution.

Parks, Catherine. Empowered: How God Shaped 11 Women's Lives (and Can Shape Yours Too) Brookshire, Breezy, illus. 2019. (ENG.). 208p. (J). (gr. 2-8). pap. 14.99 (978-1-5359-3455-8(7), 005809927, B&H Kids) B&H Publishing Group.

Phelps, Ethel Johnston, ed. Kamala: Feminist Folktales from Around the World. Boynton, Suki, illus. 2016. (Feminist Folktales Ser.: 2). (ENG.). 192p. (J). (gr. 2-7). 14.95 (978-1-55861-940-1(2)) Feminist Pr. at The City Univ. of New York.

—Sea Girl: Feminist Folktales from Around the World. Boynton, Suki, illus. 2017. (Feminist Folktales Ser.: 3). (ENG.). 168p. (J). (gr. 2-7). 14.95 (978-1-55861-418-5(4)) Feminist Pr. at The City Univ. of New York.

Pitman, Gayle E. & Beith, Laura Huliska. Feminism from a to Z. 2017. (ENG., Illus.). 288p. (J). pap. (978-1-4338-2721-1(2), Magination Pr.) American Psychological Assn.

Rajczak, Kristen. Women in Business, 1 vol. 2015. (Women Groundbreakers Ser.). (ENG.). 32p. (J). (gr. 4-5). pap. 11.00 (978-1-4994-1040-2(9), 43f5ebe3-2031-4d5e-8214-e776468fa611, PowerKids Pr.) Rosen Publishing Group, Inc., The.

Rajczak Nelson, Kristen. 20 Fun Facts about Women in Ancient Egypt, 1 vol. 2015. (Fun Fact File: Women in History Ser.). (ENG., Illus.). 32p. (J). (gr. 2-3). pap. 11.50 (978-1-4824-2812-4(1), f76f8868-c622-4d95-b7f1-2c0d268431d6) Stevens, Gareth Publishing LLLP.

Rauf, Don. Female Serial Killers, 1 vol. 2015. (Psychology of Serial Killers Ser.). (ENG.). 128p. (gr. 9-9). lib. bdg. 38.93 (978-0-7660-7288-6(6), 4d14cd2f-39ad-4f5f-bdf6-ae44dc30e4d4) Enslow Publishing, LLC.

Roberts, Kathryn, ed. Violence Against Women, 1 vol. 2018. (Global Viewpoints Ser.). (ENG.). 200p. (gr. 10-12). 47.83 (978-1-5345-0392-2(7), 93ff679c-fb75-4355-b7ab-65392a5e5d0b) Greenhaven Publishing LLC.

Robertson, David A. Betty: The Helen Betty Osborne Story, 1 vol. Henderson, Scott B., illus. 2015. (ENG.). 30p. (YA). (gr. 7-12). pap. (978-1-55379-544-5(X), 155379544X, HighWater Pr.) Portage & Main Pr.

Sideman, Jill, intro. Women in Science. 2005. (Women in Science Ser.). (Illus.). 112p. (gr. 6-12). 120.00 (978-0-7910-7250-9(9), Facts On File) Infobase Holdings, Inc.

Stewart, Sheila. Sometimes My Mom Drinks Too Much. (Kids Have Troubles Too Ser.). (Illus.). 48p. (YA). (gr. 5-18). 2010. lib. bdg. 19.95 (978-1-4222-1704-7(3)) 2009. pap. 7.95 (978-1-4222-1917-1(8)) Mason Crest.

Sugar Snap Studio & Ford, Jessie. ABC for Me: ABC What Can She Be? Girls Can Be Anything They Want to Be, from a to Z, Volume 5. 2018. (ABC for Me Ser.: 5). (ENG., Illus.). 36p. (J). (gr. -1-1). bds. 16.95 (978-1-63322-624-1(7), 304575, Walter Foster Jr) Quarto Publishing Group USA.

Tech Girls: Set 2, 14 vols. 2018. (Tech Girls Ser.). (ENG.). 80p. (gr. 7-7). lib. bdg. 262.29 (978-1-5081-8089-0(X), 0d9f7abd-9e0e-40c2-b675-94611be11a61) Rosen Publishing Group, Inc., The.

Thimmesh, Catherine. Girls Think of Everything: Stories of Ingenious Inventions by Women. Sweet, Melissa, illus. (ENG.). (J). (gr. 3-7). 2018. 112p. 17.99 (978-1-328-77253-4(5), 1681294) 2022. 128p. reprint ed. pap. 9.99 (978-0-618-19563-3(7), 410515) HarperCollins Pubs. (Clarion Bks.).

Wambach, Abby. Wolfpack (Young Readers Edition) 2020. (ENG., Illus.). 112p. (J). 16.99 (978-1-250-76686-1(9), 900232554) Roaring Brook Pr.

Waters, Sophie. Seeing the Gynecologist, 1 vol. 2007. (Girls' Health Ser.). (ENG., Illus.). 48p. (YA). (gr. 5-6). lib. bdg. 34.47 (978-1-4042-1948-9(X), b2f139bd-2ffa-4532-91fd-2952992e1c6e) Rosen Publishing Group, Inc., The.

Waycott, Flora, illus. She Believed She Could, So She Did: A Journal of Powerful Quotes from Powerful Women. 2018. 208p. (J). (gr. 3-7). pap. 12.95 (978-1-4549-2837-9(9)) Sterling Publishing Co., Inc.

Weatherford, Carole Boston. Dorothea Lange. 2018. (2019 Av2 Fiction Ser.). (ENG.). 32p. (J). lib. bdg. 34.28 (978-1-4896-8255-0(4), AV2 by Weigl) Weigl Pubs., Inc.

Wolfe, Helen. Terrific Women Teachers, 1 vol. 2011. (Women's Hall of Fame Ser.: 17). (ENG., Illus.). 118p. (J). (gr. 4-8). pap. 10.95 (978-1-897187-86-9(6)) Second Story Pr. CAN. Dist: Orca Bk. Pubs. USA.

WOMEN—BIOGRAPHY

Abbott, L. A. House by the Side of the Road: Stories of 20th Century Farm Life beside Illinois' Lincoln Highway. Abbott Gidel, Susan & Abbott Landow, Jan, eds. 2005. (Illus.). 120p. (YA). per. 14.95 (978-0-9766820-0-4(1)) Pines Publishing.

Abirached, Zeina. I Remember Beirut. Abirached, Zeina, illus. 2014. (ENG., Illus.). 96p. (YA). (gr. 8-12). pap. 11.99 (978-1-4677-4458-4(1), 69b3f232-512a-4c66-8514-4517324523a0, Graphic Universe™) Lerner Publishing Group.

Adams, Colleen. The Courage of Helen Keller. 2009. (Reading Room Collection 2 Ser.). 24p. (gr. 3-4). 42.50 (978-1-60851-992-7(9), PowerKids Pr.) Rosen Publishing Group, Inc., The.

—The True Story of Pocahontas, 1 vol. 2008. (What Really Happened? Ser.). (ENG., Illus.). 24p. (J). (gr. 2-3). lib. bdg. 26.27 (978-1-4042-4475-7(1), f0084636-13eb-497c-aee5-c454b0859aa2) Rosen Publishing Group, Inc., The.

Adiletta, Dawn. Elizabeth Cady Stanton: Women's Suffrage & the First Vote. (Library of American Lives & Times Ser.). 112p. (gr. 5-5). 2009. 69.20 (978-1-60853-479-1(0)) 2004. (ENG., Illus.). (J). lib. bdg. 38.27 (978-1-4042-2647-0(8), c7dcb355-12ad-4a2b-9bd6-5e815734870e) Rosen Publishing Group, Inc., The.

Alagna, Magdalena. Mae Jemison: The First African American Woman in Space. 2009. (Women Hall of Famers in Mathematics & Science Ser.). 112p. (gr. 5-8). 63.90 (978-1-60854-813-2(9), Rosen Reference) Rosen Publishing Group, Inc., The.

Aller, Susan Bivin. Anne Hutchinson. 2010. (History Maker Biographies Ser.). (ENG.). 48p. (gr. 3-6). lib. bdg. 27.93 (978-0-7613-5208-2(2), Lerner Pubns.) Lerner Publishing Group.

Allman, Toney. Women Scientists & Inventors. 2016. (ENG.). 80p. (YA). (gr. 5-12). (978-1-68282-032-2(7)) ReferencePoint Pr., Inc.

Anderson, Kirsten & Who HQ. Who Is Judy Blume? Hammond, Ted, illus. 2018. (Who Was? Ser.). 112p. (J). (gr. 3-7). 6.99 (978-0-448-48849-3(3), Penguin Workshop) Penguin Young Readers Group.

Ardagh, Philip. Marie Curie. 7th ed. 2003. (ENG., Illus.). 64p. (J). pap. 6.99 (978-0-330-37571-9(7), Pan) Pan Macmillan GBR. Dist: Trafalgar Square Publishing.

Atwood, Kathryn J. Courageous Women of the Vietnam War: Medics, Journalists, Survivors, & More. 2018. (Women of Action Ser.: 21). (ENG., Illus.). 240p. (YA). (gr. 7). 19.99 (978-1-61373-074-4(8)) Chicago Review Pr., Inc.

—Women Heroes of World War II: 32 Stories of Espionage, Sabotage, Resistance, & Rescue. 2nd ed. 2019. (Women of Action Ser.: 24). (Illus.). 352p. (YA). (gr. 7). 21.99 (978-1-64160-006-4(3)) Chicago Review Pr., Inc.

Aykroyd, Clarissa. Julia Alvarez: Novelist & Poet, 1 vol. 2007. (Twentieth Century's Most Influential Hispanics Ser.). (ENG., Illus.). 104p. (gr. 7-10). lib. bdg. 35.73 (978-1-4205-0022-6(8), 5f0a7dcf-db0a-44bd-ba38-8566bd198e0c, Lucent Pr.) Greenhaven Publishing LLC.

Bach, Nancy. Maria Montessori & Her Quiet Revolution: A Picture Book about Maria Montessori & Her School Method. Lätti, Leo, illus. 2013. 24p. pap. (978-1-938712-10-4(2)) Roxby Media Ltd.

Ball, Heather. Astonishing Women Artists, 1 vol. 2007. (Women's Hall of Fame Ser.: 10). (ENG., Illus.). 120p. (J). (gr. 4-8). pap. 10.95 (978-1-897187-23-4(8)) Second Story Pr. CAN. Dist: Orca Bk. Pubs. USA.

—Great Women Leaders, 1 vol. 2004. (Women's Hall of Fame Ser.: 4). (ENG., Illus.). 100p. (J). (gr. 4-8). pap. 10.95 (978-1-896764-81-8(9)) Second Story Pr. CAN. Dist: Orca Bk. Pubs. USA.

—Remarkable Women Writers, 1 vol. 2006. (Women's Hall of Fame Ser.: 8). (ENG., Illus.). 120p. (J). (gr. 4-8). pap. 10.95 (978-1-897187-08-1(4)) Second Story Pr. CAN. Dist: Orca Bk. Pubs. USA.

—Women Leaders Who Changed the World, 1 vol. 2011. (Great Women of Achievement Ser.). (ENG., Illus.). 112p. (YA). (gr. 5-6). lib. bdg. 39.80 (978-1-4488-6000-5(8), ee6c0b3d-bb96-4f88-83ea-f3ce1f735494) Rosen Publishing Group, Inc., The.

Bankston, John. Missy Elliott: Hip-Hop Superstar. l.t. ed. 2004. (Blue Banner Biography Ser.). (Illus.). 32p. (J). (gr. 3-8). lib. bdg. 25.70 (978-1-58415-219-4(2)) Mitchell Lane Pubs.

—Shirley Temple. l.t. ed. 2003. (Real-Life Reader Biography Ser.). (Illus.). 32p. (J). (gr. 3-8). lib. bdg. 25.70 (978-1-58415-172-2(2)) Mitchell Lane Pubs.

Bardoe, Cheryl. Nothing Stopped Sophie: The Story of Unshakable Mathematician Sophie Germain. McClintock, Barbara, illus. 2018. (ENG.). 40p. (J). (gr. -1-3). 18.99 (978-0-316-27820-1(3)) Little, Brown Bks. for Young Readers.

Bates, Marni. Marni: My True Story of Stress, Hair-Pulling, & Other Obsessions. 2009. (Louder Than Words Ser.). (ENG.). 168p. (YA). (gr. 7-18). pap. 7.95 (978-0-7573-1412-4(0), HCI Teens) Health Communications, Inc.

Bauer, Marion Dane. Harriet Tubman. Lyon, Tammie, illus. 2010. (My First Biography Ser.). (ENG.). 32p. (J). (gr. -1-3). 16.19 (978-0-545-23257-9(0)) Scholastic, Inc.

Baum, Margaux & Hopkins, Andrea. The Lives of Women, 1 vol. 2016. (Life in the Middle Ages Ser.). (ENG., Illus.). 64p. (J). (gr. 5-5). 36.13 (978-1-4994-6466-5(5), 362995aa-5630-4327-a5bc-c58924ad4f02, Rosen Central) Rosen Publishing Group, Inc., The.

Baxter-Wright, Emma. The Little Book of Chanel: New Edition. 3rd ed. 2013. (Little Books of Fashion Ser.: 3). (ENG., Illus.). 160p. 16.95 (978-1-78097-902-1(9)) Welbeck Publishing Group Ltd. GBR. Dist: Two Rivers Distribution.

Becker, Cynthia S. Chipeta: Ute Peacemaker. 2008. (Now You Know Bio Ser.: 11). (Illus.). 98p. (J). pap. 8.95 (978-0-86541-091-6(7)) Filter Pr., LLC.

Benatar, Raquel & Rubio, Adrian. Go, Milka, Go! The Life of Milka Duno. Benatar, Raquel & Rubio, Adrian, illus. 2008. Tr. of Corre, Milka, Corre! (SPA & ENG., Illus.). 32p. (J). 19.95 (978-1-56492-360-8(6)) Laredo Publishing Co., Inc.

Benavidez, Barbara. My School Years: Kindergarten Through Graduation. (Illus.). (J). (gr. 5-12). 24.95 (978-0-9619463-0-2(X)) Barmarie Pubns.

Benge, Janet & Benge, Geoff. Christian Heroes - Then & Now - Lillian Trasher: The Greatest Wonder in Egypt. 2003. (Christian Heroes Ser.). (ENG.). 189p. (YA). pap. 11.99 (978-1-57658-305-0(8)) YWAM Publishing.

Benjamin, Michelle & Mooney, Maggie. Nobel's Women of Peace, 1 vol. 2008. (Women's Hall of Fame Ser.: 13). (ENG., Illus.). 146p. (J). (gr. 4-8). pap. 10.95 (978-1-897187-38-8(6)) Second Story Pr. CAN. Dist: Orca Bk. Pubs. USA.

Benson, Michael. Gloria Estefan. 2005. (Biography Ser.). (Illus.). 112p. (gr. 6-12). lib. bdg. 27.93 (978-0-8225-4982-6(4)) Lerner Publishing Group.

Bertovich, Yvonne. The Untold Stories of Female Athletes. 2019. (ENG.). 279p. (YA). pap. 19.95 (978-1-62023-557-7(9), 920cbb03-5eb4-4f80-8415-6b53d89efece) Atlantic Publishing Group, Inc.

Bjorklund, Ruth. Aung San Suu Kyi, 1 vol. 2013. (Leading Women Ser.). (ENG.). 112p. (YA). (gr. 7-7). 42.64 (978-0-7614-4957-7(4), aaeb6ec8-3828-42f0-a34b-f07a093c2906) Cavendish Square Publishing LLC.

Bodden, Valerie. Rihanna. 2013. (Big Time Ser.). (ENG., Illus.). 24p. (J). (gr. 1-4). (978-1-60818-479-8(X), 21710, Creative Education) Creative Co., The.

Bohannon, Lisa Frederkisen. Failure Is Impossible: The Story of Susan B. Anthony. 2004. (Feminist Voices Ser.). (Illus.). 112p. (YA). (gr. 6-12). 23.95 (978-1-883846-77-0(3), First Biographies) Reynolds, Morgan Inc.

Boone, Mary. Ada Lovelace: A 4D Book. 2018. (STEM Scientists & Inventors Ser.). (ENG., Illus.). 24p. (J). (gr. 1-3). lib. bdg. 27.99 (978-1-5435-2772-8(8), 138222, Capstone Pr.) Capstone.

Borden, Louise & Kroeger, Mary Kay. Fly High! The Story of Bessie Coleman. Flavin, Teresa, illus. 2004. (ENG.). 40p. (J). (gr. 3-7). 8.99 (978-0-689-86462-9(0), Simon & Schuster/Paula Wiseman Bks.) Simon & Schuster/Paula Wiseman Bks.

Brackett, Virginia. A Home in the Heart: The Story of Sandra Cisneros. 2004. (World Writers Ser.). (Illus.). 112p. (J). (gr. 6-12). 23.95 (978-1-931798-42-6(7)) Reynolds, Morgan Inc.

—Restless Genius: The Story of Virginia Woolf. 2004. (World Writers Ser.). (Illus.). 144p. (YA). (gr. 6-12). 23.95 (978-1-931798-37-2(0)) Reynolds, Morgan Inc.

Bradley, Michael. Serena Williams, 1 vol. 2006. (All-Stars Ser.). (ENG., Illus.). 48p. (gr. 4-4). 34.07 (978-0-7614-1760-6(5), eaaed1f9-01fa-49a4-88ab-92b4e111e18f) Cavendish Square Publishing LLC.

Braun, Sandra. Women Inventors Who Changed the World, 1 vol. 2011. (Great Women of Achievement Ser.). (ENG., Illus.). 120p. (YA). (gr. 5-6). lib. bdg. 39.80 (978-1-4488-5996-2(4), 74a1163a-b33f-4640-aacc-883a75afabae, Rosen Reference) Rosen Publishing Group, Inc., The.

Bridges, Shirin Yim. Agrippina: "Atrocious & Ferocious" 2011. 18.95 (978-0-938425-65-6(X)); 18.95 (978-0-938425-61-8(7)) Goosebottom Bks. LLC.

Brooks, Ben. Stories for Kids Who Dare to Be Different: True Tales of Amazing People Who Stood up & Stood Out. Winter, Quinton, illus. 2019. (Dare to Be Different Ser.). (ENG.). 160p. (J). (gr. 3-7). 17.99 (978-0-7624-6855-3(6), Running Pr. Kids) Running Pr.

Brown, Don. Uncommon Traveler: Mary Kingsley in Africa. 2003. (ENG., Illus.). 32p. (J). (gr. -1-3). 7.99 (978-0-618-36916-4(3), 410064, Clarion Bks.) HarperCollins Pubs.

—A Voice from the Wilderness: The Story of Anna Howard Shaw. 2010. 32p. (J). (gr. k-3). pap. 5.95 (978-0-618-58544-1(3)) Houghton Mifflin Harcourt Trade & Reference Pubs.

Bruchac, Joseph & Locker, Thomas. Rachel Carson: Preserving a Sense of Wonder. 2009. (ENG., Illus.). 32p. (gr. 3-5). pap. 12.95 (978-1-55591-695-4(3)) Fulcrum Publishing.

Bryant, Jill. Dazzling Women Designers, 1 vol. 2010. (Women's Hall of Fame Ser.: 16). (ENG., Illus.). 128p. (J). (gr. 4-8). pap. 10.95 (978-1-897187-82-1(3)) Second Story Pr. CAN. Dist: Orca Bk. Pubs. USA.

—Phenomenal Female Entrepreneurs, 1 vol. 2013. (Women's Hall of Fame Ser.: 19). (ENG.). 152p. (J). (gr. 6-8). pap. 10.95 (978-1-927583-12-8(8)) Second Story Pr. CAN. Dist: Orca Bk. Pubs. USA.

Buckley, Carol. Travels with Tarra, 1 vol. 2005. (ENG., Illus.). 40p. (J). (gr. 3-7). 16.95 (978-0-88448-241-3(3)) Tilbury Hse. Pubs.

Burling, Alexis. Aung San Suu Kyi: Burmese Politician & Activist for Democracy. 2017. (Spotlight on Civic Courage: Heroes of Conscience Ser.). (Illus.). 48p. (J). (gr. 10-15). 70.50 (978-1-5383-8070-3(6)) Rosen Publishing Group, Inc., The.

Butler, Mary. Sojourner Truth: From Slave to Activist for Freedom. 2009. (Library of American Lives & Times Ser.). 112p. (gr. 5-5). 69.20 (978-1-60853-505-7(3)) Rosen Publishing Group, Inc., The.

Butts, Ed. She Dared: True Stories of Heroines, Scoundrels, & Renegades. Collins, Heather, illus. 2005. 128p. (J). (gr. 5-9). pap. 8.95 (978-0-88776-718-0(4), Tundra Bks.) Tundra Bks. CAN. Dist: Penguin Random Hse. LLC.

Büyüksahin, Mehmet, et al. Khadija Bint Khuwaylid. 2016. (Age of Bliss Ser.). (ENG.). 80p. (J). (gr. 4-8). pap. 5.95 (978-1-59784-375-1(X), Tughra Bks.) Blue Dome, Inc.

Byrne, Eva. Along Came Coco: A Story about Coco Chanel. 2019. (ENG., Illus.). 32p. (J). (gr. -1-3). 16.99 (978-1-4197-3425-0(3), 1264801, Abrams Bks. for Young Readers) Abrams, Inc.

Calkhoven, Laurie. Women Who Changed the World: 50 Amazing Americans. Castelao, Patricia, illus. 2016. 96p. (J). (978-1-5182-0923-9(8)) Scholastic, Inc.

Campbell, Cassie. H. E. A. R. T. 2007. (ENG., Illus.). 108p. (J). (gr. 2-9). pap. (978-1-55168-315-7(6)) Me to We.

Caravantes, Peggy. Daughters of Two Nations. Flores, Carolyn Dee, illus. 2013. 144p. (J). pap. 14.00 (978-0-87842-610-2(8)) Mountain Pr. Publishing Co., Inc.

Carey, Nicolette & Bryant, Jill. Women Athletes Who Changed the World, 1 vol. 2011. (Great Women of Achievement Ser.). (ENG., Illus.). 88p. (YA). (gr. 5-6). lib. bdg. 39.80 (978-1-4488-6001-2(6), ba333a43-e61c-4042-a75e-0d9703109f91) Rosen Publishing Group, Inc., The.

Carlson, Lisa, illus. Calamity Jane. 2007. (On My Own Folklore Ser.). 48p. (J). (gr. -1-3). per. 6.95 (978-0-8225-6480-5(7), First Avenue Editions) Lerner Publishing Group.

Cefrey, Holly. The Inventions of Amanda Jones: The Vacuum Method of Canning & Food Preservation. 2009. (19th Century American Inventors Ser.). 24p. (gr. 2-3). 42.50 (978-1-60854-950-4(X), PowerKids Pr.) Rosen Publishing Group, Inc., The.

Cheney, Lynne. A Is for Abigail: An Almanac of Amazing American Women. 2003. (ENG., Illus.). 48p. (J). (gr. 1-7). 19.99 (978-0-689-85819-2(1), Simon & Schuster Bks. For Young Readers) Simon & Schuster Bks. For Young Readers.

Chick, Chloe. Mighty Mira Based on the Story. 2016. (ENG., Illus.). 35p. (J). (978-981-320-254-2(8)) World Scientific Publishing Co. Pte Ltd.

Chin-Lee, Cynthia. Amelia to Zora: Twenty-Six Women Who Changed the World. Halsey, Megan & Addy, Sean, illus. 2008. (ENG.). 32p. (J). (gr. 3-7). pap. 7.95 (978-1-57091-523-9(7)) Charlesbridge Publishing, Inc.

Colbert, David. Anne Frank. 2008. (10 Days Ser.). (ENG., Illus.). 160p. (J). (gr. 3-8). pap. 8.99 *(978-1-4169-6445-2(2),* Aladdin) Simon & Schuster Children's Publishing.

Cole, Peter. Ben Fletcher: The Life & Times of a Black Wobbly: Including Fellow Worker Fletcher's Writings & Speeches. 10th annot. ed. 2006. (Labor Classics Ser.). (Illus.). 149p. per. 15.00 *(978-0-88286-311-5(8))* Kerr, Charles H. Publishing Co.

Collins, Ellen. A Biography: My Life As a Basset Hound (2005. 51p. pap. 16.95 *(978-1-4137-8776-4(2))* America Star Bks.

Collins, Kathleen. Sojourner Truth: Equal Rights Advocate. 2009. (Primary Sources of Famous People in American History Ser.). 32p. (gr. 2-3). 47.90 *(978-1-60851-727-5(6))* Rosen Publishing Group, Inc., The.

Collins, Lily. Unfiltered: No Shame, No Regrets, Just Me. 2017. (ENG., Illus.). 240p. (YA). (gr. 9). 18.99 *(978-0-06-247301-1(8),* HarperCollins) HarperCollins Pubs.

Conlan, Kathy & Canadian Museum of Nature Staff. Under the Ice: A Marine Biologist at Work. 2004. (Illus.). 56p. (J). (gr. 4-6). 11.95 *(978-1-55337-060-4(0))* Kids Can Pr., Ltd. CAN. Dist: Hachette Bk. Group.

Connors, Kathleen. The Life of Florence Nightingale, 1 vol., Vol. 1. 2013. (Famous Lives Ser.). (ENG., Illus.). 24p. (J). (gr. 1-2). 25.27 *(978-1-4824-0405-0(2),* a4ee7e1d-f389-4e59-acd6-f6658e980946) Stevens, Gareth Publishing LLLP.

Cooke, Tim. Explore with Gertrude Bell. 2017. (Travel with the Great Explorers Ser.). (Illus.). 32p. (J). (gr. 4-5). *(978-0-7787-3910-4(4));* pap. *(978-0-7787-3925-8(2))* Crabtree Publishing Co.

—Explore with Mary Kingsley. 2017. (Travel with the Great Explorers Ser.). (Illus.). 32p. (J). (gr. 4-5). *(978-0-7787-3920-3(1));* pap. *(978-0-7787-3926-5(0))* Crabtree Publishing Co.

—Malala Yousafzai, 1 vol. 2018. (Meet the Greats Ser.). (ENG.). 48p. (gr. 5-5). lib. bdg. 34.93 *(978-1-5382-2578-3(6),* 1ef298cb-6426-483f-a9fd-1dee8ea8f505) Stevens, Gareth Publishing LLLP.

Cooperman, Stephanie H. Chien-Shiung Wu: Pioneering Physicist & Atomic Researcher. 2009. (Women Hall of Famers in Mathematics & Science Ser.). 112p. (gr. 5-8). 63.90 *(978-1-60854-810-1(4),* Rosen Reference) Rosen Publishing Group, Inc., The.

Cregan, Elizabeth R. C. Marie Curie: Pioneering Physicist, 1 vol. rev. ed. 2007. (Science: Informational Text Ser.). (ENG., Illus.). 32p. (gr. 3-6). pap. 12.99 *(978-0-7439-0570-1(9))* Teacher Created Materials, Inc.

Croll, Jennifer. Bad Girls of Fashion: Style Rebels from Cleopatra to Lady Gaga. Buchholz, Ada, illus. 2016. (ENG.). 208p. (J). pap. 14.95 *(978-1-55451-785-5(0))* Annick Pr., Ltd. CAN. Dist: Publishers Group West (PGW).

Crysdale, Joy. Courageous Women Rebels, 1 vol. 2013. (Women's Hall of Fame Ser.: 18). (ENG.). 128p. (J). (gr. 6-8). pap. 10.95 *(978-1-926920-99-3(6))* Second Story Pr. CAN. Dist: Orca Bk. Pubs. USA.

Cullerton Johnson, Jen. Seeds of Change: Wangari's Gift to the World, 1 vol. Sadler, Sonia Lynn, illus. 2013. (ENG.). 32p. (J). (gr. 1-6). 19.95 *(978-1-60060-367-9(X),* leelowbooks) Lee & Low Bks., Inc.

D'Amelio, Charli. Essentially Charli: The Ultimate Guide to Keeping It Real. 2020. (ENG., Illus.). 192p. (YA). (gr. 7-9). 18.99 *(978-1-4197-5232-2(4),* 1723401) Abrams, Inc.

Darraj, Susan Muaddi. Mairead Corrigan & Betty Williams. 2006. (ENG., Illus.). 106p. (gr. 9-12). lib. bdg. 30.00 *(978-0-7910-9001-5(9),* P114508, Facts On File) Infobase Holdings, Inc.

Davis, Rebecca Henry. Fanny Crosby: Queen of Gospel Songs. 2003. (Illus.). 107p. (J). 6.49 *(978-1-57924-970-0(1))* BJU Pr.

DeFord, Diane. Sacagawea. 2009. pap. 13.25 *(978-1-60559-069-1(X))* Hameray Publishing Group, Inc.

Devera, Czeena. Frida Kahlo. Bane, Jeff, illus. 2017. (My Early Library: My Itty-Bitty Bio Ser.). (ENG.). 24p. (J). (gr. k-1). 30.64 *(978-1-63472-815-7(7),* 209686) Cherry Lake Publishing.

Ditchfield, Christin. Clara Barton: Founder of the American Red Cross. 2004. (Great Life Stories Ser.). (ENG., Illus.). 112p. (J). 30.50 *(978-0-531-12276-1(X),* Watts, Franklin) Scholastic Library Publishing.

DiVito, Anna. Annie Oakley Saves the Day: Ready-To-Read Level 2. DiVito, Anna, illus. 2004. (Ready-To-Read Childhood of Famous Americans Ser.). (ENG., Illus.). 32p. (J). (gr. k-2). pap. 4.99 *(978-0-689-86520-6(1),* Simon Spotlight) Simon Spotlight.

DK. DK Life Stories Jane Goodall. 2019. (ENG., Illus.). 128p. (J). *(978-0-241-37788-8(9))* Dorling Kindersley Publishing, Inc.

The Doctor with an Eye for Eyes: The Story of Dr. Patricia Bath. 2017. (Amazing Scientists Ser.: 2). (Illus.). 40p. (J). (gr. k-5). 17.99 *(978-1-943147-31-1(0),* 2f10b2c2-25f6-4146-a312-dab271416101) Innovation Pr., The.

Domenico, Kelly Di. Women Scientists Who Changed the World, 1 vol. 2011. (Great Women of Achievement Ser.). (ENG., Illus.). 112p. (YA). (gr. 5-6). lib. bdg. 39.80 *(978-1-4488-5999-3(9),* db33b50e-7497-43d0-8942-6b54062b5776) Rosen Publishing Group, Inc., The.

Donelly, Karen. Women Pilots of World War II, 1 vol. 2004. (American Women at War Ser.). (ENG., Illus.). 112p. (J). (gr. 8-8). lib. bdg. 39.80 *(978-0-8239-4453-8(0),* 8597215a-f8d8-446e-a757-5b97afa3e91a) Rosen Publishing Group, Inc., The.

Donohue, Moira Rose. Maggie L. Walker. 2012. (Illus.). 32p. (J). *(978-1-935884-62-0(X));* pap. *(978-1-935884-68-2(9))* State Standards Publishing, LLC.

Drimmer, Stephanie Warren. The Book of Heroines: Tales of History's Gutsiest Gals. 2016. (Illus.). 176p. (J). (gr. 3-7). 14.99 *(978-1-4263-2557-1(6),* National Geographic Kids) Disney Publishing Worldwide.

Dublin, Anne. Dynamic Women Dancers, 1 vol. 2009. (Women's Hall of Fame Ser.: 14). (ENG., Illus.). 130p. (J). (gr. 4-8). pap. 10.95 *(978-1-897187-56-2(4))* Second Story Pr. CAN. Dist: Orca Bk. Pubs. USA.

Dzidrums, Christine. Yuna Kim: Ice Queen. Rendon, Leah, ed. Dzidrums, Joseph et al, photos by. 2011. (Skate Stars Ser.: Vol. 2). (Illus.). 72p. (YA). pap. 10.99 *(978-0-9826435-9-4(4))* Creative Media Publishing.

Dzidrums, Christine & Rendon, Leah. Joannie Rochette: Canadian Ice Princess. Allison, Elizabeth, ed. Adeff, Jay & Mittan, J. Barry, photos by. 2nd exp. rev. ed. 2010. (Skate Stars Ser.: Vol. 1). (Illus.). 100p. (YA). pap. 12.99 *(978-0-9826435-0-1(0))* Creative Media Publishing.

Earl, C. F. Alicia Keys. 2012. (Superstars of Hip-Hop Ser.). (Illus.). 48p. (J). (gr. 3-4). 19.95 *(978-1-4222-2521-9(6))* Mason Crest.

Edison, Erin. Jane Goodall, 1 vol. 2013. (Great Women in History Ser.). (ENG.). 24p. (J). (gr. -1-2). pap. 6.29 *(978-1-4765-0144-4(0),* 122220); (gr. -1-2). lib. bdg. 24.65 *(978-1-4765-0143-7(2),* 122221); (gr. k-1). pap. 37.74 *(978-1-4765-0145-1(9),* 19587) Capstone. (Pebble).

Edwards, Laurie J. Rihanna, 1 vol. 2009. (People in the News Ser.). (ENG., Illus.). 104p. (gr. 7-7). lib. bdg. 41.03 *(978-1-4205-0129-2(1),* be21a8d6-e3ab-45f4-bc74-495b41cc71f5, Lucent Pr.) Greenhaven Publishing LLC.

Edwards, Roberta. Who Is Jane Goodall? 2012. (Who Is... ? Ser.). lib. bdg. 16.00 *(978-0-606-26651-2(8))* Turtleback.

Edwards, Roberta & Who HQ. Who Is Jane Goodall? O'Brien, John, illus. 2012. (Who Was? Ser.). 112p. (J). (gr. 3-7). 6.99 *(978-0-448-46192-2(7),* Penguin Workshop) Penguin Young Readers Group.

Egan, Tracie. Cynthia Ann Parker: Cautiva de los Comanches, 1 vol. Gonzalez, Tomas, tr. 2003. (Grandes Personajes en la Historia de Los Estados Unidos (Famous People in American History) Ser.). (SPA.). 32p. (gr. 3-4). pap. 10.00 *(978-0-8239-4225-1(2),* 5843e5b5-d80d-4f57-9417-a17007949bba); (Illus.). lib. bdg. 29.13 *(978-0-8239-4131-5(0),* 507592c3-ab4c-44d1-b4e0-abe5e02fb61a, Editorial Buenas Letras) Rosen Publishing Group, Inc., The.

—Francisca Alavez, the Angel of Goliad, 1 vol. 2003. (Primary Sources of Famous People in American History Ser.). (ENG., Illus.). 32p. (gr. 3-4). pap. 10.00 *(978-0-8239-4181-0(7),* 613c87ab-8793-466f-b2ba-e27df8520e76); (J). lib. bdg. 29.13 *(978-0-8239-4109-4(4),* 09802509-6753-48f4-b7e8-0bcf07c4aa8b, Rosen Reference) Rosen Publishing Group, Inc., The.

—Francisca Alvarez: El ángel de Goliad (Francisca Alvarez: the Angel of Goliad) 2009. (Grandes personajes en la historia de los Estados Unidos (Famous People in American History) Ser.). (SPA.). 32p. (gr. 2-3). 47.90 *(978-1-61512-798-6(4),* Editorial Buenas Letras) Rosen Publishing Group, Inc., The.

—Francisca Alvarez: The Angel of Goliad. 2009. (Primary Sources of Famous People in American History Ser.). 32p. (gr. 2-3). 47.90 *(978-1-60851-675-9(X))* Rosen Publishing Group, Inc., The.

—Francisca Alvarez: The Angel of Goliad / el ángel de Goliad. 2009. (Famous People in American History/Grandes personajes en la historia de los Estados Unidos Ser.). (ENG & SPA.). 32p. (gr. 2-3). 47.90 *(978-1-61512-544-9(2),* Editorial Buenas Letras) Rosen Publishing Group, Inc., The.

Emery, Joanna. Caring for a Colony: The Story of Jeanne Mance. 2005. (Stories of Canada Ser.: 8). (ENG., Illus.). 72p. (J). (gr. 4-7). 18.95 *(978-1-894917-07-0(3),* Napoleon & Co.) Dundurn Pr. CAN. Dist: Publishers Group West (PGW).

Engle, Margarita. Enchanted Air: Two Cultures, Two Wings: a Memoir. Rodriguez, Edel, illus. (ENG.). (YA). (gr. 7). 2016. 224p. pap. 11.99 *(978-1-4814-3523-9(X))* 2015. 208p. 19.99 *(978-1-4814-3522-2(1))* Simon & Schuster Children's Publishing.

Ernest, Brother. Angel of the Poor: A Story of Mother Emmelie Gamelin. Jagodits, Carolyn Lee, illus. 2011. 96p. 38.95 *(978-1-258-06652-9(1))* Literary Licensing, LLC.

Etingoff, Kim. Women Who Built Our Scientific Foundations. Lee-Karlon, Ann, ed. 2013. (Major Women in Science Ser.: 10). 64p. (J). (gr. 7-18). 22.95 *(978-1-4222-2933-0(5))* Mason Crest.

Favilli, Elena & Cavallo, Francesca. Good Night Stories for Rebel Girls: 50 Postcards of Women Creators, Leaders, Pioneers, Champions, & Warriors. 2018. (Good Night Stories for Rebel Girls Ser.). (ENG., Illus.). 50p. 20.00 *(978-0-525-57652-5(5),* Clarkson Potter) Potter/Ten Speed/Harmony/Rodale.

Favilli, Elena & Rebel Girls. Good Night Stories for Rebel Girls: 100 Immigrant Women Who Changed the World. 2020. (Good Night Stories for Rebel Girls Ser.: 3). (Illus.). 224p. (J). (gr. 2-12). 35.00 *(978-1-7333292-9-3(3))* Rebel Girls.

Favilli, Elena, et al. Good Night Stories for Rebel Girls: 100 Tales of Extraordinary Women. 2016. (Good Night Stories for Rebel Girls Ser.: 1). (Illus.). 224p. (J). (gr. 1-4). 35.00 *(978-0-9978958-1-0(0))* Rebel Girls.

—Good Night Stories for Rebel Girls 2. 2017. (Good Night Stories for Rebel Girls Ser.: 2). (Illus.). 224p. (J). (gr. 2-12). 35.00 *(978-0-9978958-2-7(9))* Rebel Girls.

Favor, Lesli J. Eva Perón, 1 vol. 2011. (Leading Women Ser.). (ENG.). 96p. (YA). (gr. 7-7). 42.64 *(978-0-7614-4962-1(0),* 45b3cf21-59b9-44ad-a63a-82c2334b62f3) Cavendish Square Publishing LLC.

Fearless Female Soldiers, Explorers, & Aviators, 12 vols. 2017. (Fearless Female Soldiers, Explorers, & Aviators Ser.). (ENG.). 128p. (gr. 9-9). lib. bdg. 284.16 *(978-1-5026-2680-6(2),* 188fac0a-713e-4f50-b32c-c3cba8b88786, Cavendish Square) Cavendish Square Publishing LLC.

Feldman, Heather. Valentina Tereshkova: The First Woman in Space. 2009. (Space Firsts Ser.). 24p. (gr. 3-4). 42.50 *(978-1-60853-114-1(7),* PowerKids Pr.) Rosen Publishing Group, Inc., The.

Ferris, Jeri Chase. Demanding Justice: A Story about Mary Ann Shadd Cary. Smith, Kimanne, illus. 2003. (Creative Minds Biographies Ser.). (ENG.). 64p. (gr. 4-8). 22.60 *(978-1-57505-177-2(X))* Lerner Publishing Group.

Fink, Nadia. Frida Kahlo para Niñas y Niños. Saa, Pitu, illus. 2016.Tr. of Frida Kalho for Girls & Boys. (SPA.). (gr. 2-12). pap. 12.99 *(978-0-9973280-0-4(2))* Bks. del Sur.

Fischer, Jean. 100 Extraordinary Stories for Courageous Girls: Unforgettable Tales of Women of Faith. 2018. (Courageous Girls Ser.). (ENG., Illus.). 208p. (J). 16.99 *(978-1-68322-748-9(4),* Shiloh Kidz) Barbour Publishing, Inc.

Fishman, Jon M. Soccer's G. O. A. T. Pelé, Lionel Messi, & More. 2019. (Sports' Greatest of All Time (Lerner (tm) Sports) Ser.). (ENG., Illus.). 32p. (J). (gr. 2-5). 30.65 *(978-1-5415-5600-3(3),* a986f891-88e2-4aef-b0fd-3b0dca613fd7); pap. 9.99 *(978-1-5415-7445-8(1),* 9364a458-bb62-4c70-9d40-23abef43f59c) Lerner Publishing Group. (Lerner Pubns.).

Fisk Pack, Mary. Cleopatra: "Serpent of the Nile" Malone, Peter, illus. 2011. (Thinking Girl's Treasury of Dastardly Dames Ser.). (ENG.). 32p. (J). (gr. 3-8). 18.95 *(978-0-9834256-0-1(4))* Goosebottom Bks. LLC.

Fitzpatrick, Anne. Mother Teresa. 2005. (Genius Ser.). (Illus.). 48p. (J). (gr. 5-9). lib. bdg. 21.95 *(978-1-58341-330-2(8),* Creative Education) Creative Co., The.

Flynn, Jean. Texas Women Who Dared to Be First. 2004. (Illus.). 144p. (gr. 4-7). 18.95 *(978-1-57168-232-1(5))* Eakin Pr.

Ford, Gabrielle. Gabe & Izzy: Standing up for America's Bullied. 2014. (Illus.). 192p. (J). (gr. 5). pap. 8.99 *(978-0-14-750994-9(7),* Viking Books for Young Readers) Penguin Young Readers Group.

Ford, Jeanne Marie. Adele: Music Sensation. 2017. (Superstar Stories Ser.). (ENG.). 24p. (J). (gr. 3-6). lib. bdg. 32.79 *(978-1-5038-1993-1(0),* 211869) Child's World, Inc, The.

Fournel, Kelly. Native Women of Courage, 1 vol. 2007. (Native Trailblazers Ser.: 1). (ENG., Illus.). 96p. (YA). (gr. 8-12). per. 9.95 *(978-0-9779183-2-4(7),* 7th Generation) BPC.

Frank, Mary Kate. Rihanna, 1 vol. 2009. (Today's Superstars Ser.). (ENG.). 48p. (J). (gr. 3-3). pap. 15.05 *(978-1-4339-2375-3(0),* 9003a7c0-c7fa-46a6-8607-d3ab01fb6ebf); lib. bdg. 34.60 *(978-1-4339-2379-1(3),* 55fa66cf-23c2-4bee-9d44-9a9a42c642d0) Stevens, Gareth Publishing LLLP.

Franklin, Virgil. The Story of Sacagawea. 2009. (Reading Room Collection 2 Ser.). 24p. (gr. 3-4). 42.50 *(978-1-60851-997-2(X),* PowerKids Pr.) Rosen Publishing Group, Inc., The.

Froggatt, Marilyn. Doña Gracia's Secret: The Adventures of an Extraordinary Jewish Woman in the Renaissance Who Was Almost an Unsung Hero. 2019. (ENG., Illus.). 56p. (J). pap. *(978-965-7023-08-2(4))* Gefen Publishing Hse., Ltd.

Fryar, Jane L. Hero of Faith - Katharina Von Bora. 2011. 64p. pap. 7.99 *(978-0-7586-2827-5(7))* Concordia Publishing Hse.

Fuller, Barbara. Great Britain, 1 vol. 2nd ed. 2005. (Cultures of the World (First Edition)(r) Ser.). (ENG., Illus.). 144p. (gr. 5-5). 49.79 *(978-0-7614-1845-0(8),* 802b64c1-df2d-4fc2-8fbf-b2dc4c280095) Cavendish Square Publishing LLC.

Gertner, Sheina Sachar. The Tree Stood Still. 2006. 96p. per. 9.95 *(978-1-58939-886-3(6))* Virtualbookworm.com Publishing, Inc.

Gilbert, Sara. Calamity Jane. 2005. (Legends of the West (Creative Education) Ser.). (Illus.). 48p. (J). (gr. 5-9). lib. bdg. 21.95 *(978-1-58341-337-1(5),* Creative Education) Creative Co., The.

Glavich, Mary Kathleen. Blessed Teresa of Calcutta: Missionary of Charity. Kiwak, Barbara, tr. Kiwak, Barbara, illus. 2003. (Encounter the Saints Ser.: Vol. 17). 136p. (J). pap. 7.95 *(978-0-8198-1160-8(2),* 332-024) Pauline Bks. & Media.

—Saint Therese of Lisieux: The Way of Love. Esquinaldo, Virginia, tr. Esquinaldo, Virginia, illus. 2003. (Encounter the Saints Ser.). 132p. (J). pap. 5.95 *(978-0-8198-7074-2(9),* 332-370) Pauline Bks. & Media.

Golden, Nancy. Life with the Comanches: The Kidnapping of Cynthia Ann Parker. 2009. (Great Moments in American History Ser.). 32p. (gr. 3-3). 47.90 *(978-1-61513-146-4(9))* Rosen Publishing Group, Inc., The.

Gorman, John. Queen Latifah, 1 vol. 2007. (Today's Superstars Ser.). (ENG., Illus.). 32p. (gr. 3-3). lib. bdg. 34.60 *(978-0-8368-7652-9(0),* 0b57b0a8-d1bf-477e-837e-f919da321c09) Stevens, Gareth Publishing LLLP.

Gosling, Maureen, et al. You Can Be a Woman Movie Maker. l.t ed. 2003. (Illus.). 80p. (J). 19.95 incl. DVD *(978-1-880599-64-8(3));* pap. 14.95 incl. DVD *(978-1-880599-63-1(5))* Cascade Pass, Inc.

Gueldenpfennig, Sonia. Women in Space Who Changed the World, 1 vol. 2011. (Great Women of Achievement Ser.). (ENG., Illus.). 120p. (YA). (gr. 5-6). lib. bdg. 39.80 *(978-1-4488-5998-6(0),* 23b11d1f-3a3c-46c7-a1c3-1af0f91d6e92, Rosen Reference) Rosen Publishing Group, Inc., The.

Gutowski, Eva. My Life As Eva: The Struggle Is Real. 2019. (ENG., Illus.). 208p. pap. 16.99 *(978-1-5011-4672-5(6),* Gallery Bks.) Gallery Bks.

Haldy, Emma E. Jane Goodall. Bane, Jeff, illus. 2016. (My Early Library: My Itty-Bitty Bio Ser.). (ENG.). 24p. (J). (gr. k-1). 30.64 *(978-1-63471-022-0(3),* 208168) Cherry Lake Publishing.

Halligan, Katherine. Herstory: 50 Women & Girls Who Shook up the World. Walsh, Sarah, illus. 2018. (Stories That Shook up the World Ser.). (ENG.). 112p. (J). (gr. 3). 19.99 *(978-1-5344-3664-0(2),* Simon & Schuster Bks. For Young Readers) Simon & Schuster Bks. For Young Readers.

Hally, Ashleigh. Lugenia Burns Hope. 2012. (Illus.). 24p. (J). lib. bdg. *(978-1-935884-76-7(X))* State Standards Publishing, LLC.

—Martha Berry. 2012. (Illus.). 24p. (J). *(978-1-935884-73-6(5));* pap. *(978-1-935884-79-8(4))* State Standards Publishing, LLC.

Hansen, Grace. Malala Yousafzai: Activista Por la Educación (Spanish Version) 2016. (Biografías: Personas Que Han Hecho Historia (History Maker Biographies) Ser.). (SPA., Illus.). 24p. (J). (gr. -1-2). lib. bdg. 32.79 *(978-1-68080-740-0(4),* 22642, Abdo Kids) ABDO Publishing Co.

Harkins, Susan Sales & Harkins, William H. Pochantas. 2008. (What's So Great About... ? Ser.). (Illus.). 32p. (J). (gr. 2-4). lib. bdg. 25.70 *(978-1-58415-682-6(1))* Mitchell Lane Pubs.

Harness, Cheryl. Remember the Ladies: 100 Great American Women. Harness, Cheryl, illus. 2003. (ENG., Illus.). 64p. (J). (gr. 3-18). pap. 8.99 *(978-0-06-443869-8(4),* HarperCollins) HarperCollins Pubs.

Harris, Laurie Lanzen. Biography for Beginners: Women Who Made a Difference. 2011. (J). lib. bdg. 49.00 *(978-1-931360-43-2(X))* Favorable Impressions.

Harrison, Vashti. Little Dreamers: Visionary Women Around the World. 2018. (Vashti Harrison Ser.). (ENG., Illus.). 96p. (J). (gr. 3-7). 17.99 *(978-0-316-47517-4(3))* Little, Brown Bks. for Young Readers.

Hart, Phillip S. Bessie Coleman. 2005. (Just the Facts Biographies Ser.). (ENG., Illus.). 112p. (gr. 5-12). 27.93 *(978-0-8225-2469-4(4))* Lerner Publishing Group.

Hartzog, Brooke. Ichthyosaurus & Little Mary Anning, 1 vol. 2004. (Dinosaurs & Their Discoverers Ser.). (ENG.). 24p. (J). (gr. 3-4). lib. bdg. 25.27 *(978-0-8239-5326-4(2),* f1091351-d265-456f-b824-a1a703ad899d, PowerKids Pr.) Rosen Publishing Group, Inc., The.

Havemeyer, Janie. Catherine de' Medici: "The Black Queen" Malone, Peter, illus. 2011. (Thinking Girl's Treasury of Dastardly Dames Ser.). (ENG.). 32p. (J). (gr. 3-8). 18.95 *(978-0-9834256-3-2(9))* Goosebottom Bks. LLC.

Heing, Bridey. ISIS Brides, 1 vol. 2017. (Crimes of ISIS Ser.). (ENG.). 104p. (gr. 8-8). pap. 20.95 *(978-0-7660-9582-3(7),* 47b8c129-0f0c-469b-a38f-7a6fe1852fdf) Enslow Publishing, LLC.

Heredia, David. Little Heroes of Color: 50 Who Made a BIG Difference. Heredia, David, illus. 2019. (ENG., Illus.). 24p. (J). (gr. -1 — 1). bds. 10.99 *(978-1-338-32642-0(2),* Scholastic Pr.) Scholastic, Inc.

Heroes of the Women's Suffrage Movement, 12 vols. 2016. (Heroes of the Women's Suffrage Movement Ser.). (ENG.). 128p. (gr. 6-6). lib. bdg. 233.58 *(978-0-7660-7507-8(9),* 1559d9d3-c207-45a2-a632-b3d10cd66cd2) Enslow Publishing, LLC.

Hill, Anne E. Michelle Kwan. 2004. (Sports Heroes & Legends Ser.). (ENG., Illus.). 112p. (J). (gr. 5-12). lib. bdg. 30.60 *(978-0-8225-1795-5(7))* Lerner Publishing Group.

Hilliam, David. Eleanor of Aquitaine: The Richest Queen in Medieval Europe. 2009. (Leaders of the Middle Ages Ser.). 112p. (gr. 5-8). 66.50 *(978-1-61513-897-5(8),* Rosen Reference) Rosen Publishing Group, Inc., The.

—Joan of Arc: Heroine of France, 1 vol. 2004. (Leaders of the Middle Ages Ser.). (ENG., Illus.). 112p. (J). (gr. 5-8). lib. bdg. 39.80 *(978-1-4042-0164-4(5),* 3da45756-c61b-4793-81ad-25b7cecbf6d5) Rosen Publishing Group, Inc., The.

Hockinson, Liz. Marie Antoinette "Madame Deficit" Malone, Peter, illus. 2011. (Thinking Girl's Treasury of Dastardly Dames Ser.). (ENG.). 32p. (J). (gr. 3-8). 18.95 *(978-0-9834256-4-9(7))* Goosebottom Bks. LLC.

Hollingsworth, Tamara. Helen Keller: A New Vision, 1 vol. 2nd rev. ed. 2013. (TIME for KIDS(r): Informational Text Ser.). (ENG., Illus.). 48p. (J). (gr. 4-5). lib. bdg. 29.96 *(978-1-4807-1115-0(2))* Teacher Created Materials, Inc.

Howat, Irene. Ten Girls Who Used Their Talents. rev. ed. 2006. (Lightkeepers Ser.). (ENG., Illus.). 160p. (J). (gr. 3-7). per. 8.99 *(978-1-84550-147-1(0),* 48f9a641-4ed8-4a03-be87-a6ef262de680) Christian Focus Pubns. GBR. Dist: Baker & Taylor Publisher Services (BTPS).

Hunsaker, Joyce Badgley. They Call Me Sacagawea. 2003. (ENG., Illus.). 48p. pap. 14.95 *(978-0-7627-2580-9(X),* TwoDot) Globe Pequot Pr., The.

Hunter, Ryan Ann. In Disguise! Stories of Real Women Spies. 2004. (Illus.). 133p. (J). (gr. 4-7). per. 9.95 *(978-1-58270-095-3(8))* Beyond Words Publishing, Inc.

Hurt, Avery Elizabeth. Ada Lovelace: Computer Programmer & Mathematician, 1 vol. 2017. (History Makers Ser.). (ENG.). 144p. (YA). (gr. 9-9). 47.36 *(978-1-5026-3295-1(0),* 147e5b8d-a96e-41a0-a052-0fc3ae0b6591) Cavendish Square Publishing LLC.

Ignotofsky, Rachel. Women in Science: 50 Fearless Pioneers Who Changed the World. 2016. (Women in Science Ser.). (Illus.). 128p. (YA). (gr. 5-12). 16.99 *(978-1-60774-976-9(9),* Ten Speed Pr.) Potter/Ten Speed/Harmony/Rodale.

—Women in Science: 100 Postcards. 2017. (Women in Science Ser.). (Illus.). 100p. 20.00 *(978-0-7-60774-981-3(5),* Clarkson Potter) Potter/Ten Speed/Harmony/Rodale.

—Women in Sports: 50 Fearless Athletes Who Played to Win. 2017. (Women in Science Ser.). (Illus.). 128p. (YA). (gr. 5-12). 16.99 *(978-1-60774-978-3(5),* Ten Speed Pr.) Potter/Ten Speed/Harmony/Rodale.

Indovino, Shaina. Women in Physics. Lee-Karlon, Ann, ed. 2013. (Major Women in Science Ser.: 10). 64p. (J). (gr. 7-18). 22.95 *(978-1-4222-2930-9(0))* Mason Crest.

—Women in the Environmental Sciences. Lee-Karlon, Ann, ed. 2013. (Major Women in Science Ser.: 10). 64p. (J). (gr. 7-18). 22.95 *(978-1-4222-2927-9(0))* Mason Crest.

Jenner, Caryn. Amazing Women. 2017. (Illus.). 96p. (J). *(978-1-5182-2593-2(4))* Dorling Kindersley Publishing, Inc.

Jökulsson, Illugi. Women's World Cup 2019. 2019. (World Soccer Legends Ser.: 0). (ENG., Illus.). 64p. (J). (gr. 1). 14.95 *(978-0-7892-1328-0(1),* 791328, Abbeville Kids) Abbeville Pr., Inc.

Jordan-Fenton, Christy & Pokiak-Fenton, Margaret. Not My Girl. Grimard, Gabrielle, illus. 2014. (ENG.). 36p. (J). (gr. 1-4). 21.95 *(978-1-55451-625-4(0),* 9781554516254); pap. 9.95 *(978-1-55451-624-7(2),* 9781554516247) Annick Pr., Ltd. CAN. Dist: Publishers Group West (PGW).

—A Stranger at Home: A True Story. Amini-Holmes, Liz, illus. 2011. (ENG.). 112p. (J). (gr. 3-7). 21.95 *(978-1-55451-362-8(6),* 9781554513628); 3rd ed. pap. 12.95 *(978-1-55451-361-1(8),* 9781554513611) Annick Pr., Ltd. CAN. Dist: Publishers Group West (PGW).

—When I Was Eight. Grimard, Gabrielle, illus. 2nd ed. 2013. (ENG.). 32p. (J). (gr. 1-4). pap. 9.95 *(978-1-55451-490-8(8),* 9781554514908);1. 21.95 *(978-1-55451-491-5(6),* 9781554514915) Annick Pr., Ltd. CAN. Dist: Publishers Group West (PGW).

Kalman, Bobbie & Aloian, Molly. Famous Native North Americans. 2003. (Native Nations of North America Ser.). (ENG., Illus.). 32p. (J). (gr. 5). pap. *(978-0-7787-0471-3(8));* lib. bdg. *(978-0-7787-0379-2(7))* Crabtree Publishing Co.

Kawa, Katie. Elena Delle Donne, 1 vol. 2018. (Young Sports Greats Ser.). (ENG.). 24p. (gr. 3-3). 25.27 *(978-1-5383-3039-5(3),* 11bf5c7f-0c38-4e97-94d3-ef7c427c78a9, PowerKids Pr.) Rosen Publishing Group, Inc., The.

ating, Susan K. Isadora Duncan: American Dancer. 2004. (Great Names Ser.). (Illus.). 32p. (J). (gr. 3-18). lib. bdg. 19.95 *(978-1-59084-144-0(1))* Mason Crest.

emeny, Esther. On the Shores of Darkness: The Memoir of Esther Kemeny Haller. Haller, Heather, ed. 2003. (Illus.). 144p. per. *(978-0-9743961-7-0(6))* Haller Company, The.

epnes, Caroline. Stephen Crane. 2004. (Classic Storytellers Ser.). (Illus.). 48p. (J). (gr. 4-8). lib. bdg. 29.95 *(978-1-58415-272-9(9))* Mitchell Lane Pubs.

eman, Elizabeth. Harriet Tubman: A Lesson in Bravery. 2009. (Reading Room Collection 2 Ser.). 24p. (gr. 3-4). 42.50 *(978-1-60851-966-8(X),* PowerKids Pr.) Rosen Publishing Group, Inc., The.

immel, Elizabeth Cody & Kimmel, Elizabeth. Ladies First (Direct Mail Edition) 40 Daring Woman Who Were Second to None. 2006. (ENG., Illus.). 192p. (J). (gr. 5-9). 18.95 *(978-0-7922-5393-8(0))* National Geographic Society.

ishel, Ann-Marie. Elizabeth Blackwell: A Life of Diligence. 2007. (Pull Ahead Bks.). (Illus.). 32p. (J). (gr. 3-7). lib. bdg. 22.60 *(978-0-8225-6459-1(9),* Lerner Pubns.) Lerner Publishing Group.

Kite, L. Patricia. Maya Angelou. 2006. (Just the Facts Biographies Ser.). (Illus.). 112p. (J). (gr. 3-7). pap. 9.95 *(978-0-8225-5997-9(8));* (ENG., (gr. 5-12). lib. bdg. 27.93 *(978-0-8225-3426-6(6))* Lerner Publishing Group. (Lerner Pubns.).

Kjelle, Marylou. Katherine Paterson. 2004. (Classic Storytellers Ser.). (Illus.). 48p. (J). (gr. 4-8). lib. bdg. 29.95 *(978-1-58415-268-2(0))* Mitchell Lane Pubs.

Kops, Deborah. Alice Paul & the Fight for Women's Rights: From the Vote to the Equal Rights Amendment. 2017. (ENG., Illus.). 216p. (J). (gr. 5-12). 17.95 *(978-1-62979-323-8(X),* Calkins Creek) Highlights Pr., c/o Highlights for Children, Inc.

Kortemeier, Todd. Greatest Moments in Women's Sports. 2017. (Women in Sports Ser.). (ENG., Illus.). 48p. (J). (gr. 4-8). lib. bdg. 34.21 *(978-1-5321-1155-6(X),* 25886, SportsZone) ABDO Publishing Co.

Kovatch, Sarah & Crumpler, Rebecca Lee. Rebecca Lee Crumpler. 2005. (Illus.). 16p. (J). *(978-0-7367-2891-1(0))* Zaner-Bloser, Inc.

Krasner, Barbara. Goldie Takes a Stand! Golda Meir's First Crusade. Garrity-Riley, Kelsey, illus. 2014. (ENG.). 32p. (J). (gr. k-4). 17.95 *(978-1-4677-1200-2(0))* Lerner Publishing Group.

—Goldie Takes a Stand: Golda Meir's First Crusade. Garrity-Riley, Kelsey, illus. 2014. (ENG.). 32p. (J). (gr. k-4). 7.95 *(978-1-4677-1201-9(9),* c426fcc0-d82b-4759-a9b0-3ae07363554b, Kar-Ben Publishing) Lerner Publishing Group.

Krensky, Stephen. Calamity Jane. Carlson, Lisa, illus. 2006. (On My Own Folklore Ser.). (ENG.). 48p. (gr. 2-4). lib. bdg. 25.26 *(978-1-57505-886-3(3),* Millbrook Pr.) Lerner Publishing Group.

Labrecque, Ellen. Maria Beasley & Life Rafts. 2017. (21st Century Junior Library: Women Innovators Ser.). (ENG., Illus.). 24p. (J). (gr. 2-5). lib. bdg. 29.21 *(978-1-63472-179-0(9),* 209288) Cherry Lake Publishing.

—Yvonne Brill & Satellite Propulsion. 2017. (21st Century Junior Library: Women Innovators Ser.). (ENG., Illus.). 24p. (J). (gr. 2-5). lib. bdg. 29.21 *(978-1-63472-184-4(5),* 209308) Cherry Lake Publishing.

Laidlaw, Jill A. Frida Kahlo. 2003. (Artists in Their Time Ser.). (ENG., Illus.). 48p. (J). (gr. 5-7). pap. 6.95 *(978-0-531-16642-0(2),* Watts, Franklin) Scholastic Library Publishing.

Lajiness, Katie. Adele. 2017. (Big Buddy Pop Biographies Set 2 Ser.). (ENG., Illus.). 32p. (J). (gr. 2-5). lib. bdg. 34.21 *(978-1-5321-1057-3(X),* 25690, Big Buddy Bks.) ABDO Publishing Co.

Lakin, Patricia. Amelia Earhart: More Than a Flier (Ready-To-Read Level 3) Daniel, Alan & Daniel, Lea, illus. 2003. (Ready-To-Read Stories of Famous Americans Ser.). (ENG.). 48p. (J). (gr. 1-3). pap. 4.99 *(978-0-689-85575-7(3),* Simon Spotlight) Simon Spotlight.

Larkin, Tanya. What Was Cooking in Abigail Adams' White House? 2009. (Cooking Throughout American History Ser.). 24p. (gr. 3-3). 42.50 *(978-1-61511-949-3(3),* PowerKids Pr.) Rosen Publishing Group, Inc., The.

—What Was Cooking in Dolley Madison's White House? 2009. (Cooking Throughout American History Ser.). 24p. (gr. 3-3). 42.50 *(978-1-61511-950-9(7),* PowerKids Pr.) Rosen Publishing Group, Inc., The.

—What Was Cooking in Edith Roosevelt's White House? 2009. (Cooking Throughout American History Ser.). 24p. (gr. 3-3). 42.50 *(978-1-61511-951-6(5),* PowerKids Pr.) Rosen Publishing Group, Inc., The.

—What Was Cooking in Martha Washington's Presidential Mansion? 2009. (Cooking Throughout American History Ser.). 24p. (gr. 3-3). 42.50 *(978-1-61511-953-0(1),* PowerKids Pr.) Rosen Publishing Group, Inc., The.

Lasky, Kathryn. A Voice of Her Own: A Story of Phillis Wheatley, Slave Poet. 2012. lib. bdg. 14.75 *(978-0-606-26940-7(1))* Turtleback.

Lassieur, Allison. 25 Mujeres Que Se Atrevieron. Aparicio Publishing LLC, Aparicio Publishing, tr. 2020. (Mujeres Valientes Ser.).Tr. of 25 Women Who Dared to Go. (SPA., Illus.). 64p. (J). (gr. 7-12). lib. bdg. 37.32 *(978-0-7565-6540-4(5),* 142070, Compass Point Bks.) Capstone.

—25 Women Who Dared to Go. 2018. (Daring Women Ser.). (ENG., Illus.). 64p. (J). (gr. 7-12). pap. 8.95 *(978-0-7565-5870-3(0),* 138485); lib. bdg. 35.32 *(978-0-7565-5853-6(0),* 138481) Capstone. (Compass Point Bks.).

Latta, Sara L. The Woman Who Invented Windshield Wipers: Mary Anderson & Her Wonderful Invention, 1 vol. 2014. (Inventors at Work! Ser.). (ENG.). 48p. (gr. 3-3). pap. 11.53 *(978-1-4644-0349-1(X),* 41ec4c09-d72a-41f1-b491-d3318309f5fe, Enslow Elementary) Enslow Publishing, LLC.

Lawlor, Laurie. Rachel Carson & Her Book That Changed the World. Beingessner, Laura, illus. 2014. (ENG.). 32p. (J). (gr. 1-4). 7.99 *(978-0-8234-3193-9(2))* Holiday Hse., Inc.

—Super Women: Six Scientists Who Changed the World. 2019. (Illus.). 64p. (J). (gr. 3-7). pap. 10.99 *(978-0-8234-4186-0(5))* Holiday Hse., Inc.

Leading Women (Group 3), 12 vols. 2014. (Leading Women Ser.). (ENG.). 112p. (YA). (gr. 7-7). 249.84 *(978-1-62713-138-4(8),* e825f03a-4971-497f-9526-426272494b41, Cavendish Square) Cavendish Square Publishing LLC.

Leading Women (Group 5), 12 vols. 2017. (Leading Women Ser.). (ENG.). 112p. (gr. 7-7). lib. bdg. 249.84 *(978-1-5026-2855-8(4),* 141b809c-ddb3-4a40-94d3-df279da98908, Cavendish Square) Cavendish Square Publishing LLC

Leading Women (Group 6), 12 vols. 2017. (Leading Women Ser.). (ENG.). (J). (gr. 7-7). lib. bdg. 249.84 *(978-1-5026-3219-7(5),* d5894f0f-c797-49c1-a4a1-467080103780) Cavendish Square Publishing LLC.

Leaf, Christina. Rachel Carson: Environmentalist. 2019. (Women Leading the Way Ser.). (ENG., Illus.). 24p. (J). (gr. k-3). lib. bdg. 26.95 *(978-1-62617-943-1(3),* Blastoff! Readers) Bellwether Media.

Leon, Georgina Lazaro. Conoce a Gabriela Mistral: Get to Know Gabriela Mistral. Palacios, Sara Helena, illus. 2014. (Personajes Del Mundo Hispnico Ser.). (ENG & SPA.). 32p. (J). (gr. -1-3). 15.95 *(978-1-61435-351-5(4),* Alfaguara) Santillana USA Publishing Co., Inc.

Leslie, Roger. Isak Dinesen: Gothic Storyteller. 2004. (World Writers Ser.). (Illus.). 128p. (YA). (gr. 6-12). 23.95 *(978-1-931798-17-4(6))* Reynolds, Morgan Inc.

Lew, Kristi. ADA Lovelace: Mathematician & First Programmer. 2017. (Britannica Beginner Bios Ser.). (Illus.). 32p. (J). (gr. 6-10). 77.40 *(978-1-5383-0022-0(2))* Rosen Publishing Group, Inc., The.

Lieneman, Danielle. Hidden in History: The Untold Stories of Female Revolutionaries & Activists. 2018. (ENG.). 172p. (YA). pap. 19.95 *(978-1-62023-554-6(4),* 5da5dd8a-43ed-460b-a120-b23796d17057) Atlantic Publishing Group, Inc.

Literature Connections English: So Far from the Bamboo Grove. 2004. (gr. 6-12). *(978-0-395-77138-9(2),* 2-70216) Holt McDougal.

Litmanovich, Ellina. Ronda Rousey: Champion Mixed Martial Arts Star, 1 vol. 2017. (Sports Star Champions Ser.). (ENG.). 48p. (gr. 5-6). lib. bdg. 29.60 *(978-0-7660-8696-8(8),* a7ddf10b-19f6-4e1c-863d-8ffc98f92aa1) Enslow Publishing, LLC.

Loh-Hagan, Virginia. Ada Lovelace. Bane, Jeff, illus. 2018. (Mi Mini Biografía (My Itty-Bitty Bio): My Early Library). (ENG.). 24p. (J). (gr. k-1). pap. 12.79 *(978-1-5341-0815-8(7),* 210624); lib. bdg. 30.64 *(978-1-5341-0716-8(9),* 210623) Cherry Lake Publishing.

—Girl Activists. 2019. (History's Yearbook Ser.). (ENG., Illus.). 32p. (J). (gr. 4-8). pap. 14.21 *(978-1-5341-5077-5(3),* 213615); lib. bdg. 32.07 *(978-1-5341-4791-1(8),* 213614) Cherry Lake Publishing. (45th Parallel Press).

—Girl Innovators. 2019. (History's Yearbook Ser.). (ENG., Illus.). 32p. (J). (gr. 4-8). pap. 14.21 *(978-1-5341-5076-8(5),* 213611); lib. bdg. 32.07 *(978-1-5341-4790-4(X),* 213610) Cherry Lake Publishing. (45th Parallel Press).

—Girl Spies. 2019. (History's Yearbook Ser.). (ENG.). 32p. (J). (gr. 4-8). pap. 14.21 *(978-1-5341-5080-5(3),* 213627); (Illus.). lib. bdg. 32.07 *(978-1-5341-4794-2(2),* 213626) Cherry Lake Publishing. (45th Parallel Press).

—Marie Curie. Bane, Jeff, illus. 2018. (Mi Mini Biografía (My Itty-Bitty Bio): My Early Library). (ENG.). 24p. (J). (gr. k-1). pap. 12.79 *(978-1-5341-0814-1(9),* 210620); lib. bdg. 30.64 *(978-1-5341-0715-1(0),* 210619) Cherry Lake Publishing.

—Rosalyn Sussman Yalow. Bane, Jeff, illus. 2018. (Mi Mini Biografía (My Itty-Bitty Bio): My Early Library). (ENG.). 24p. (J). (gr. k-1). pap. 12.79 *(978-1-5341-0813-4(0),* 210616); lib. bdg. 30.64 *(978-1-5341-0714-4(2),* 210615) Cherry Lake Publishing.

Lord, Michelle. A Girl Called Genghis Khan: The Story of Maria Toorpakai Wazir. Malik, Shehzil, illus. 2019. (People Who Shaped Our World Ser.: 5). 48p. (J). (gr. k). 16.95 *(978-1-4549-3136-2(1))* Sterling Publishing Co., Inc.

Lüsted, Marcia Amidon. The Most Influential Women in Business, 1 vol. 2018. (Breaking the Glass Ceiling: the Most Influential Women Ser.). (ENG., Illus.). 112p. (J). (gr. 8-8). 40.13 *(978-1-5081-7967-2(0),* aeb5ae19-8a78-4f9f-85be-5941a3cabdea) Rosen Publishing Group, Inc., The.

Lynette, Rachel. Sacagawea, 1 vol. 2013. (Pioneer Spirit: the Westward Expansion Ser.). (ENG.). 24p. (J). (ENG.). (gr. 2-3). 26.27 *(978-1-4777-0782-1(4),* 27f27716-d062-4a4c-b686-3e1f77b4d591); (gr. 3-6). pap. 49.50 *(978-1-4777-0898-9(7));* (ENG., Illus.). (gr. 2-3). pap. 9.25 *(978-1-4777-0897-2(9),* 313c432c-9263-492a-b9c8-e2314cd54659) Rosen Publishing Group, Inc., The. (PowerKids Pr.).

Lyon, George Ella. Mother to Tigers. Catalanotto, Peter, illus. 2003. (ENG.). 32p. (J). (gr. k-3). 18.99 *(978-0-689-84221-4(X),* Atheneum/Richard Jackson Bks.) Simon & Schuster Children's Publishing.

Macdonald, Maryann. Rosa's Animals: The Story of Rosa Bonheur & Her Painting Menagerie. 2018. (ENG., Illus.). 64p. (J). (gr. 3-7). 21.99 *(978-1-4197-2850-1(4),* 1162601, Abrams Bks. for Young Readers) Abrams, Inc.

Machajewski, David. Marta, 1 vol. 2018. (Soccer Stars Ser.). (ENG.). 24p. (J). (gr. 3-3). pap. 9.25 *(978-1-5383-4510-8(2),* e66b15cd-8c99-404b-a03e-2388970e3c36, PowerKids Pr.) Rosen Publishing Group, Inc., The.

Maclear, Kyo. Bloom: A Story of Fashion Designer Elsa Schiaparelli. Morstad, Julie, illus. 2018. (ENG.). 40p. (J). (gr. -1-3). 17.99 *(978-0-06-244761-6(0),* HarperCollins) HarperCollins Pubs.

MacLeod, Elizabeth. Marie Curie. Mantha, John, illus. 2009. (Kids Can Read Ser.). (ENG.). 32p. (J). (gr. 1-3). 11.99 *(978-1-55453-297-1(3))* Kids Can Pr., Ltd. CAN. Dist: Hachette Bk. Group.

MacMillan, Kathy & Bernardi, Manuela. She Spoke: 14 Women Who Raised Their Voices & Changed the World. Honesta, Kathrin, illus. 2019. (ENG.). 32p. (gr. k-2). 24.99 *(978-1-64170-131-0(5),* 550131) Familius LLC.

Majher, Patricia. Great Girls in Michigan History. 2015. (Great Lakes Books Ser.). (ENG., Illus.). 144p. pap. 14.99 *(978-0-8143-4073-8(3),* P454710) Wayne State Univ. Pr.

Marsh, Carole. Marie Curie, Nobel Prize Winning Scientist. 2004. 12p. (gr. k-4). 2.95 *(978-0-635-02374-2(1))* Gallopade International.

Marsh, Sarah Glenn. Alice Across America: The Story of the First Women's Cross-Country Road Trip. Ford, Gilbert, illus. 2020. (ENG.). 48p. (J). 18.99 *(978-1-250-29702-0(8),* 900195861, Holt, Henry & Co. Bks. For Young Readers) Holt, Henry & Co.

Martin, Carol. Catharine Parr Traill: Backwoods Pioneer. 2004. (ENG., Illus.). 128p. (YA). pap. *(978-0-88899-495-0(8),* Libros Tigrillo) Groundwood Bks. CAN. Dist: Publishers Group West (PGW).

Maslo, Lina. Free As a Bird: The Story of Malala. Maslo, Lina, illus. 2018. (ENG., Illus.). 40p. (J). (gr. -1-3). 17.99 *(978-0-06-256077-3(8),* Balzer & Bray) HarperCollins Pubs.

Mattern, Joanne. Elizabeth Cady Stanton & Susan B. Anthony: Fighting Together for Women's Rights. 2009. (Women Who Shaped History Ser.). 24p. (gr. 2-3). 42.50 *(978-1-60854-818-7(X),* PowerKids Pr.) Rosen Publishing Group, Inc., The.

Mattern, Joanne & Brandt, Keith. Marie Curie, Brave Scientist. Dugan, Karen, illus. 2005. 45p. (J). *(978-0-439-80153-9(2))* Scholastic, Inc.

McCann, Michelle Roehm. More Girls Who Rocked the World: Heroines from Ada Lovelace to Misty Copeland. Hahn, David, illus. 2017. (ENG.). 320p. (J). (gr. 3-7). 21.99 *(978-1-58270-640-5(9))* Aladdin/Beyond Words.

Mccann, Michelle Roehm & Welden, Amelie. Girls Who Rocked the World: From Anne Frank to Natalie Portman. 2012. lib. bdg. 22.10 *(978-0-606-26898-1(7))* Turtleback.

McCully, Emily Arnold. Caroline's Comets: A True Story. 2017. (ENG.). 40p. (J). (gr. 1-4). 16.95 *(978-0-8234-3664-4(0))* Holiday Hse., Inc.

McDonnell, Patrick. Me ... Jane (Caldecott Honor Book) 2011. (ENG., Illus.). 40p. (J). (gr. -1-3). 18.99 *(978-0-316-04546-9(2))* Little, Brown Bks. for Young Readers.

Mcdonnell, Patrick. Me... Jane. 2011. (CHI., Illus.). 40p. (J). (gr. -1-2). *(978-986-189-308-2(3))* Grimm Cultural Ent., Co., Ltd.

—Me... Jane. 2011. (J). *(978-1-4618-4349-8(9))* Recorded Bks., Inc.

McDonnell, Peter. The Last Princess. 2005. (Illus.). 16p. *(978-0-7367-2910-9(0))* Zaner-Bloser, Inc.

McIlroy, Michelle. Sophie Scholl: Student Resister & Anti-Nazi Political Activist. 2017. (Spotlight on Civic Courage: Heroes of Conscience Ser.). (Illus.). 48p. (J). (gr. 10-15). 70.50 *(978-1-5383-8108-3(7))* Rosen Publishing Group, Inc., The.

McKown, Robin. Marie Curie. Rethi, Lili, illus. 2012. 128p. 40.95 *(978-1-258-23532-1(3));* pap. 25.95 *(978-1-258-24675-4(9))* Literary Licensing, LLC.

McLean, Jacqueline. Victoria Woodhull: First Woman Presidential Candidate. 2004. (Feminist Voices Ser.). (Illus.). 112p. (J). (gr. 6-12). 23.95 *(978-1-883846-47-3(1),* First Biographies) Reynolds, Morgan Inc.

—Women of Adventure. 2003. (Profiles Ser.). (Illus.). 160p. (gr. 5-18). lib. bdg. 19.95 *(978-1-881508-73-1(0))* Oliver Pr., Inc.

McPherson, Stephanie Sammartino. My Dear Husband: Important Letters of Abigail Adams, 1 vol. 2003. (Great Moments in American History Ser.). (ENG., Illus.). 32p. (gr. 3-3). lib. bdg. 29.13 *(978-0-8239-4323-4(2),* 7378e0e7-c711-4f03-8d06-57a544602911, Rosen Reference) Rosen Publishing Group, Inc., The.

Meltzer, Milton. Emily Dickinson: A Biography. 2006. (Literary Greats Ser.). (ENG.). 128p. (gr. 7-12). lib. bdg. 33.26 *(978-0-7613-2949-7(8),* Millbrook Pr.) Lerner Publishing Group.

Menendez, Juliet. Latinitas: Celebrating 40 Big Dreamers. Menendez, Juliet, illus. 2021. (ENG., Illus.). 120p. (J). 18.99 *(978-1-250-23462-9(X),* 900210124, Holt, Henry & Co. Bks. For Young Readers) Holt, Henry & Co.

Miklowitz, Gloria. Anne Frank. 2009. pap. 13.25 *(978-1-60559-053-0(3))* Hameray Publishing Group, Inc.

Miklowitz, Gloria D. Jane Goodall. 2004. (ENG., Illus.). 28p. (J). (gr. 2-5). pap. 7.33 *(978-0-7685-1218-2(2),* Dominie Elementary) Savvas Learning Co.

Milani, Alice. Marie Curie: A Life of Discovery. Milani, Alice, illus. 2019. (ENG., Illus.). 208p. (YA). (gr. 9-12). pap. 14.99 *(978-1-5415-7286-7(6),* a623d3f9-7a12-4621-89ae-d0b1969b7646); lib. bdg. 33.32 *(978-1-5415-2817-8(4),* 0808a15c-bea9-462c-b2d4-e9601cf1155b) Lerner Publishing Group. (Graphic Universe™).

Miller, Calvin Craig. Spirit Like a Storm: The Story of Mary Shelley. 2nd rev. ed. 2004. (World Writers Ser.). (Illus.). 144p. (YA). (gr. 6-12). 23.95 *(978-1-931798-08-2(7))* Reynolds, Morgan Inc.

Mills, Cliff. Virginia Woolf. 2003. (Women in the Arts Ser.). (ENG., Illus.). 112p. (gr. 6-12). 30.00 *(978-0-7910-7459-6(5),* P113847, Facts On File) Infobase Holdings, Inc.

Mir, Saira. Muslim Girls Rise: Inspirational Champions of Our Time. Jaleel, Aaliya, illus. 2019. (ENG.). 48p. (J). (gr. 1). 19.99 *(978-1-5344-1888-2(1))* Simon & Schuster, Inc.

Mockingbird, Is That You? 2008. (ENG., Illus.). 48p. pap. 21.99 *(978-1-4343-1968-5(7))* AuthorHouse.

Moening, Kate. Angela Merkel: Chancellor of Germany. 2019. (Women Leading the Way Ser.). (ENG., Illus.). 24p. (J). (gr. k-3). lib. bdg. 26.95 *(978-1-64487-098-3(3),* Blastoff! Readers) Bellwether Media.

—Dolores Huerta. 2019. (Women Leading the Way Ser.). (ENG., Illus.). 24p. (J). (gr. k-3). lib. bdg. 26.95 *(978-1-64487-099-0(1),* Blastoff! Readers) Bellwether Media.

—Dolores Huerta: Labor Activist: Labor Activist. 2019. (Women Leading the Way Ser.). (ENG., Illus.). 24p. (J). (gr. k-3). pap. 7.99 *(978-1-61891-722-5(6),* 12303, Blastoff! Readers) Bellwether Media.

—Emma Watson: Women's Rights Activist. 2020. (Women Leading the Way Ser.). (ENG., Illus.). 24p. (J). (gr. k-3). pap. 7.99 *(978-1-61891-796-6(X),* 12581, Blastoff! Readers) Bellwether Media.

—Vera Wang: Fashion Designer. 2020. (Women Leading the Way Ser.). (ENG., Illus.). 24p. (J). (gr. k-3). pap. 7.99 *(978-1-61891-800-0(1),* 12585, Blastoff! Readers) Bellwether Media.

Morrison, John. Mathilde Krim & the Story of AIDS. 2004. (Women in Medicine Ser.). (ENG., Illus.). 112p. (gr. 6-12). 30.00 *(978-0-7910-8026-9(9),* P114103, Facts On File) Infobase Holdings, Inc.

Mosca, Julia Finley. The Girl Who Thought in Pictures: The Story of Dr. Temple Grandin. Rieley, Daniel, illus. 2017. (Amazing Scientists Ser.: 1). 40p. (J). (gr. k-5). 17.99 *(978-1-943147-30-4(2),* 5ae02658-cb15-4cd2-a907-670448522514) Innovation Pr., The.

Naden, Corinne J. & Blue, Rose. Mae Jeminson: Out of This World. 2003. (Gateway Biography Ser.: 4). (Illus.). 48p. lib. bdg. 23.90 *(978-0-7613-2570-3(0),* Millbrook Pr.) Lerner Publishing Group.

Nagle, Jeanne, ed. Top 101 Remarkable Women, 1 vol., 1. 2013. (People You Should Know Ser.). (ENG.). 176p. (YA). (gr. 8-8). 38.84 *(978-1-62275-126-6(4),* f2ac24dd-c5ee-4cb6-82b0-0acf8ea162ed) Rosen Publishing Group, Inc., The.

Nelson, Maria. The Life of Sacagawea, 1 vol. 2012. (Famous Lives Ser.). (ENG., Illus.). 24p. (J). (gr. 1-2). pap. 9.15 *(978-1-4339-6359-9(0),* 7d54f17b-b6a2-43d9-b239-7dc9a194049c); lib. bdg. 25.27 *(978-1-4339-6357-5(4),* 017bd324-2a9a-4cd4-b51c-3b2ba2208e5f) Stevens, Gareth Publishing LLLP.

Nelson, S. D. Buffalo Bird Girl: A Hidatsa Story. 2012. (ENG., Illus.). 56p. (J). (gr. 1-4). 21.95 *(978-1-4197-0355-3(2),* 698801, Abrams Bks. for Young Readers) Abrams, Inc.

Nichols, Catherine. Madam C.J. Walker. 2005. (Scholastic News Nonfiction Readers Ser.). (Illus.). 24p. (J). pap. 6.95 *(978-0-516-24784-7(0),* Children's Pr.) Scholastic Library Publishing.

Nicks, Erin. The Best of Team Canada. 2018. (ENG., Illus.). 32p. (J). *(978-1-63494-000-9(8))* Pr. Room Editions LLC.

Nivola, Claire A. Planting the Trees of Kenya: The Story of Wangari Maathai. Nivola, Claire A., illus. 2008. (ENG., Illus.). 32p. (J). (gr. k-3). 19.99 *(978-0-374-39918-4(2),* 900042039, Farrar, Straus & Giroux (BYR)) Farrar, Straus & Giroux.

Noland, Thelma. Annie Sweet Annie. 2004. 174p. (J). pap. 13.95 *(978-0-595-31138-5(5))* iUniverse, Inc.

O'Connell, Diane. People Person: The Story of Sociologist Marta Tienda. 2005. (Women's Adventures in Science Ser.). (ENG., Illus.). 120p. (YA). (gr. 5-9). lib. bdg. 31.50 *(978-0-531-16781-6(X))* Scholastic Library Publishing.

O'Keefe, Sherry. Aung San Suu Kyi. 2012. (Champion of Freedom Ser.). (J). (gr. 7-12). 28.95 *(978-1-59935-168-1(4))* Reynolds, Morgan Inc.

—From China to America: The Story of Amy Tan. 2011. (World Writers Ser.). 112p. (gr. 7-18). lib. bdg. 28.95 *(978-1-59935-138-4(2))* Reynolds, Morgan Inc.

Orgill, Roxane. Shout, Sister, Shout! Ten Girl Singers Who Shaped a Century. 2007. (ENG.). 160p. (YA). (gr. 7). pap. 12.95 *(978-1-4169-6391-2(X),* McElderry, Margaret K. Bks.) McElderry, Margaret K. Bks.

Orr, Tamra. Marie Curie. 2003. (World Was Never the Same Ser.). (J). pap. *(978-1-58417-263-5(0));* lib. bdg. *(978-1-58417-262-8(2))* Lake Street Pubs.

Ottaviani, Jim. Primates: The Fearless Science of Jane Goodall, Dian Fossey, & Biruté Galdikas. Wicks, Maris, illus. 2015. (ENG.). 144p. (YA). (gr. 7). pap. 14.99 *(978-1-250-06293-2(4),* 900142635) Square Fish.

The Padded Girdle: The Unbelievable True Story of Overcoming Adversity Again, & Again, & Again. . . 2003. (Illus.). 198p. pap. 19.95 *(978-0-9745860-0-7(5))* Eaglesquest Publishing.

Paige, Joy. Ellen Ochoa: The First Hispanic Woman in Space. 2009. (Library of Astronaut Biographies Ser.). 112p. (gr. 5-8). 63.90 *(978-1-60853-520-0(7),* Rosen Reference) Rosen Publishing Group, Inc., The.

Paprocki, Sherry Beck. Anita Roddick. 2010. (ENG., Illus.). 119p. (gr. 6-12). 35.00 *(978-1-60413-688-3(X),* P179330, Facts On File) Infobase Holdings, Inc.

Parish, James Robert. Gloria Estefan Singer: Singer. 2006. (Ferguson Career Biographies Ser.). (Illus.). 122p. (gr. 6-12). 25.00 *(978-0-8160-5833-4(4),* Ferguson Publishing Company) Infobase Holdings, Inc.

Parker-Rock, Michelle. Alma Flor Ada: An Author Kids Love, 1 vol. 2008. (Authors Kids Love Ser.). (ENG., Illus.). 48p. (gr. 3-3). lib. bdg. 27.93 *(978-0-7660-2760-2(0),* d2631633-ef15-4ebd-8cc5-ccf34b30f19f, Enslow Elementary) Enslow Publishing, LLC.

Patrick, Jean L. S. The Baseball Adventure of Jackie Mitchell, Girl Pitcher vs. Babe Ruth. Carbajal, Richard & Hammond, Ted, illus. 2011. (History's Kid Heroes Ser.). (ENG.). 32p. (J). (gr. 3-5). pap. 8.99 *(978-0-7613-7072-7(2),* 0eb1f305-1f7c-420f-894e-0428e7d89ce5, Graphic Universe™) Lerner Publishing Group.

—La Nina Que Poncho A Babe Ruth. Reeves, Jeni, illus. 2007. (Yo Solo - Historia (on My Own - History) Ser.). 48p. (J). (gr. 4-7). per. 6.95 *(978-0-8225-7788-1(7))* Lerner Publishing Group.

—La Niña Que Ponchó a Babe Ruth. Translations.com Staff, tr. from ENG. Reeves, Jeni, illus. 2007. (Yo Solo - Historia (on My Own - History) Ser.).Tr. of Girl Who Struck Out Babe Ruth. (SPA.). 48p. (gr. 2-4). lib. bdg. 25.26 *(978-0-8225-7785-0(2))* Lerner Publishing Group.

—La Nina Que Poncho a Babe Ruth; the Girl Who Struck Out Babe Ruth. 2008. pap. 40.95 *(978-0-8225-9725-4(X))* Lerner Publishing Group.

Patteson, Nelda. Adina de Zavala: "Angel of the Alamo" Her Life Story Presented Through the Clothes She Wore. Patteson, Nelda, illus. 2003. (Women of Texas Ser.: Vol. 3). Orig. Title: Angel of the Alamo. (Illus.). 32p. (J). (gr. 4-8). pap. 14.95 *(978-0-9629001-2-9(5))* Smiley Co.

Peels, H. G. L. True to Her Faith: A Story of France in the Time of the Huguenots. rev. ed. 2006. (ENG., Illus.). 224p. (J). per. 7.99 *(978-1-84550-220-1(5),* 272b90ce-5142-41a8-b954-38c8bfc6d007) Christian Focus Pubns. GBR. Dist: Baker & Taylor Publisher Services (BTPS).

Perry, Phyllis Jean. Bold Women in Colorado History. 2012. (Illus.). v, 153p. (J). pap. *(978-0-87842-584-6(5))* Mountain Pr. Publishing Co., Inc.

Peterson, Megan Cooley. Las Estrellas Del Fútbol Femenino. 2017. (En la Cancha Ser.). (SPA.). 32p. (J). (gr. 4-6). lib. bdg. *(978-1-68072-571-1(8),* 10603, Bolt) Black Rabbit Bks.

—Stars of Women's Soccer. 2017. (On the Pitch Ser.). (ENG., Illus.). 32p. (J). (gr. 4-6). lib. bdg. *(978-1-68072-172-0(0),* 10528, Bolt) Black Rabbit Bks.

Pferdehirt, Julia. Caroline Quarlls & the Underground Railroad. 2008. (Badger Biographies Ser.). (ENG., Illus.). 120p. (J). (gr. 3-7). per. 12.95 *(978-0-87020-388-6(6))* Wisconsin Historical Society.

Phillips, Larissa. Women Civil War Spies of the Confederacy, 1 vol. 2004. (American Women at War Ser.). (ENG., Illus.). 112p. (gr. 8-8). lib. bdg. 39.80 *(978-0-8239-4451-4(4),* 0e231b97-a361-4988-a631-9ba03b3bf6f3) Rosen Publishing Group, Inc., The.

Phillips, Robin. Who in the World Was the Acrobatic Empress? The Story of Theodora. unabr. ed. 2010. (Jim Weiss Audio Collection: 0). (ENG.). 1p. 12.95 *(978-1-933339-39-9(X),* 333939) Well-Trained Mind Pr.

Pimm, Nancy Roe. The Jerrie Mock Story: The First Woman to Fly Solo Around the World. 2016. (Biographies for Young Readers Ser.). (ENG., Illus.). 152p. (J). (gr. 1-6). 32.95 *(978-0-8214-2215-1(4))* Ohio Univ. Pr.

Polcovar, Jane. Rosalind Franklin & the Structure of Life. 2006. (Profiles in Science Ser.). (Illus.). 144p. (J). (gr. 3-7). lib. bdg. 27.95 *(978-1-59935-022-6(X))* Reynolds, Morgan Inc.

Polette, Nancy. Mae Jemison. 2003. (Rookie Biographies Ser.). (ENG., Illus.). 32p. (J). (gr. 1-2). 20.50 *(978-0-516-22856-3(0),* Children's Pr.) Scholastic Library Publishing.

Pomeroy, Sarah B. & Kathirithamby, Jeyaraney. Maria Sibylla Merian: Artist, Scientist, Adventurer. (J). 2018. (ENG., Illus.). 96p. (gr. 3-7). 21.95 *(978-1-947440-01-2(2),* 1317301) 2017. *(978-1-60606-555-6(6),* J. Paul Getty Museum) Getty Pubns.

Porterfield, Jason. Annie Oakley: Pistolera del Oeste Americano, 1 vol. 2003. (Grandes Personajes en la Historia de Los Estados Unidos (Famous People in American History) Ser.). (SPA., Illus.). 32p. (gr. 3-4). lib. bdg. 29.13 *(978-0-8239-4126-1(4),* 39142650-a87f-4054-81e2-0de1f5320e33, Editorial Buenas Letras) Rosen Publishing Group, Inc., The.

Proudfit, Benjamin. Bayley, 1 vol. 2018. (Superstars of Wrestling Ser.). (ENG.). 32p. (J). (gr. 1-2). 28.27 *(978-1-5382-2091-7(1),* aa77b5d0-c469-4b24-ba36-6e6631ae97c5) Stevens, Gareth Publishing LLLP.

Randolph, Ryan. Betsy Ross: The American Flag, & Life in a Young America. 2009. (Library of American Lives & Times Ser.). 112p. (gr. 5-5). 69.20 *(978-1-60853-473-9(1))* Rosen Publishing Group, Inc., The.

Raum, Elizabeth. The Life of Malala Yousafzai. 2019. (Sequence Change Maker Biographies Ser.). (ENG.). 32p. (J). (gr. 2-5). *(978-1-68151-677-6(2),* 10809) Amicus.

Rausch, Monica. Harriet Tubman, 1 vol. 2007. (Great Americans Ser.). (ENG.). 24p. (J). (gr. 2-4). pap. 9.15 *(978-0-8368-7693-2(8),* 4353d179-8f76-4e6a-a060-e37e98de4633); (Illus.). lib. bdg. 24.67 *(978-0-8368-7686-4(5),* 71172d49-c35b-42d9-9142-6c544f8c12fc) Stevens, Gareth Publishing LLLP. (Weekly Reader Leveled Readers).

Redmond, Shirley Raye. Courageous World Changers: 50 True Stories of Daring Women of God. 2020. (ENG., Illus.). 112p. (J). (gr. 2-6). 18.99 *(978-0-7369-7734-0(1),* 6977340) Harvest Hse. Pubs.

Reed, Jennifer. Computer Scientist Jean Bartik. 2016. (STEM Trailblazer Bios Ser.). (ENG., Illus.). 32p. (J). (gr. 2-5). 26.65 *(978-1-5124-0789-1(5),* 88b6a19d-1254-48db-ba2f-68fcdb02dcb3, Lerner Pubns.) Lerner Publishing Group.

Reid, Jamie. Diana Krall. 2004. 224p. pap. 17.95 *(978-1-894997-07-2(7))* Kingston Pr. CAN. Dist: SCB Distributors.

Rice, William B. Jane Goodall, 1 vol. 2nd rev. ed. 2012. (TIME for KIDS(r): Informational Text Ser.). (ENG.). 32p. (gr. 3-5). pap. 12.99 *(978-1-4333-3684-3(7))* Teacher Created Materials, Inc.

Rinaldo, Denise. Jane Goodall: With a Discussion of Responsibility. 2003. (Values in Action Ser.). (J). *(978-1-59203-062-0(9))* Learning Challenge, Inc.

Riner, Dax. Annika Sorenstam. 2007. (Sports Heroes & Legends Ser.). (YA). (gr. 7-12). lib. bdg. 30.60 *(978-0-8225-7160-5(9))* Twenty First Century Bks.

Rivera, Ursula. The Supremes. 2009. (Rock & Roll Hall of Famers Ser.). 112p. (gr. 5-8). 63.90 *(978-1-60852-479-2(5),* Rosen Reference) Rosen Publishing Group, Inc., The.

Robbins, Trina. Florence Nightingale: Lady with the Lamp, 1 vol. Timmons, Anne, illus. 2007. (Graphic Biographies Ser.). (ENG.). 32p. (J). (gr. 3-9). per. 8.10 *(978-0-7368-7902-6(1),* 93899, Capstone Pr.) Capstone.

Roberts, Russell. Sally Field. Lt. ed. 2003. (Billboard Biography Ser.). (Illus.). 32p. (J). (gr. 3-8). lib. bdg. 25.70 *(978-1-58415-183-8(8))* Mitchell Lane Pubs.

Robinson, Ella May. Stars in Her Heart. 2005. 127p. per. 10.95 *(978-1-57258-318-4(5))* TEACH Services, Inc.

Robinson, Fiona. Ada's Ideas: The Story of Ada Lovelace, the World's First Computer Programmer. 2016. (ENG., Illus.). 40p. (J). (gr. 1-4). 17.95 *(978-1-4197-1872-4(X),* 1103001, Abrams Bks. for Young Readers) Abrams, Inc.

Rockliff, Mara. Lights! Camera! Alice! The Thrilling True Adventures of the First Woman Filmmaker (Film Book for Kids, Non-Fiction Picture Book, Inspiring Children's Books) Ciraolo, Simona, illus. 2018. (ENG.). 60p. (J). (gr. k-3). 17.99 *(978-1-4521-4134-3(7))* Chronicle Bks. LLC.

Roehm McCann, Michelle. More Girls Who Rocked the World: Heroines from Ada Lovelace to Misty Copeland. Hahn, David, illus. 2017. (ENG.). 320p. (J). (gr. 3-7). pap. 11.99 *(978-1-58270-641-2(7))* Aladdin/Beyond Words.

Rolfe, Helen. Women Explorers (JR) 100 Years of Mountain Adventure. 2007. (Amazing Stories Ser.). (ENG., Illus.). 96p. (J). (gr. 4-5). pap. 9.95 *(978-1-55439-709-9(X),* 709) James Lorimer & Co. Ltd., Pubs. CAN. Dist: Formac Lorimer Bks. Ltd.

Romero, Libby. DK Life Stories: Jane Goodall. Ager, Charlotte, illus. 2019. (DK Life Stories Ser.). (ENG.). 128p. (J). (gr. 2). pap. 5.99 *(978-1-4654-8397-3(7),* DK Children) Dorling Kindersley Publishing, Inc.

Rooney, Frances. Exceptional Women Environmentalists, 1 vol. 2007. (Women's Hall of Fame Ser.: 11). (ENG., Illus.). 112p. (J). (gr. 4-8). pap. 10.95 *(978-1-897187-22-7(X))* Second Story Pr. CAN. Dist: Orca Bk. Pubs. USA.

—Extraordinary Women Explorers, 1 vol. 2005. (Women's Hall of Fame Ser.: 6). (ENG., Illus.). 120p. (J). (gr. 4-8). pap. 10.95 *(978-1-896764-98-6(3))* Second Story Pr. CAN. Dist: Orca Bk. Pubs. USA.

Rose, Mary Catherine. Clara Barton: Soldier of Mercy. Johnson, E. Harper, illus. 2011. 80p. 37.95 *(978-1-258-07364-0(1))* Literary Licensing, LLC.

Ross, Michael Elsohn. Fish Watching with Eugenie Clark. Smith, Wendy, illus. 2005. (Naturalist's Apprentice Biographies Ser.). 48p. (gr. 3-6). lib. bdg. 19.93 *(978-1-57505-384-4(5))* Lerner Publishing Group.

Ross, Nancy Wilson. Joan of Arc. 2003. vii, 182p. pap. 29.00 *(978-0-7581-5017-2(2))* Textbook Pubs.

Rubin, Susan Goldman. Coco Chanel: Pearls, Perfume, & the Little Black Dress. 2018. (ENG., Illus.). 144p. (J). (gr. 5-9). 19.99 *(978-1-4197-2544-9(0),* 1155101, Abrams Bks. for Young Readers) Abrams, Inc.

Ryan, Pam Muñoz. When Marian Sang: The True Recital of Marian Anderson. Selznick, Brian, illus. pap. 16.95 incl. audio *(978-1-59112-943-1(5));* pap. incl. audio *(978-1-59112-945-5(1));* pap. 18.95 incl. audio compact disk *(978-1-59112-947-9(8));* pap. incl. audio compact disk *(978-1-59112-949-3(4))* Live Oak Media.

Sabin, Francene & Macken, JoAnn Early. Elizabeth Blackwell, the First Woman Doctor. Toulmin-Rothe, Ann, illus. 2007. 53p. (J). *(978-0-439-66044-0(0))* Scholastic, Inc.

Sakany, Lois. Women Civil War Spies of the Union, 1 vol. 2004. (American Women at War Ser.). (ENG., Illus.). 112p. (gr. 8-8). lib. bdg. 39.80 *(978-0-8239-4450-7(6),* badfd22d-70f2-4115-bb75-98ffbe423da6) Rosen Publishing Group, Inc., The.

Sally Ride Science Editors, Sally Ride Science. What Do You Want to Be? Explore Earth Sciences. 2004. (J). 6.00 *(978-0-9753920-2-7(6))* Sally Ride Science.

—What Do You Want to Be? Explore Health Sciences. 2004. (J). 6.00 *(978-0-9753920-3-4(4))* Sally Ride Science.

Sanchez Vegara, Maria Isabel, concept. Little People, BIG DREAMS Matching Game: Put Your Brain to the Test with All the Girls of the Little People, BIG DREAMS Series!, Volume 25. 2018. (Little People, BIG DREAMS Ser.: 25). (ENG.). (J). (gr. -1-6). 19.99 *(978-1-63106-586-6(6),* 307748, Rock Point Gift & Stationery) Quarto Publishing Group USA.

Sanchez Vegara, Maria Isabel & Albero, Ana. Coco Chanel (Little People, Big Dreams) 2016. (Little People, Big Dreams Ser.). (ENG., Illus.). 32p. (J). 14.99 *(978-1-84780-771-7(2),* Frances Lincoln Children's Bks.) Quarto Publishing Group UK GBR. Dist: Littlehampton Bk Services, Ltd.

Sanchez Vegara, Maria Isabel & Fan, Eng Gee. Frida Kahlo (Little People Big Dreams) 2016. (Little People, Big Dreams Ser.). (ENG., Illus.). 32p. (J). 14.99 *(978-1-84780-770-0(4),* Frances Lincoln Children's Bks.) Quarto Publishing Group UK GBR. Dist: Littlehampton Bk Services, Ltd.

Sarantou, Katlin. Reshma Saujani. Bane, Jeff, illus. 2019. (My Early Library: My Itty-Bitty Bio Ser.). (ENG.). 24p. (J). (gr. k-1). pap. 12.79 *(978-1-5341-4985-4(6),* 213247); lib. bdg. 30.64 *(978-1-5341-4699-0(7),* 213246) Cherry Lake Publishing.

Sasso, Sandy Eisenberg. Regina Persisted. Lucas, Margeaux, illus. 2018. (ENG.). 32p. (J). 17.95 *(978-1-68115-540-1(0),* da407696-8acb-4483-8e12-4aed1ba27cfd, Apples & Honey Pr.) Behrman Hse., Inc.

Savage, Candace. Born to Be a Cowgirl: A Spirited Ride Through the Old West. 2004. (Illus.). *(978-1-55054-838-9(7),* Da Capo Pr. Inc.) Hachette Bks.

Sawyer, Sarah. Avril Lavigne, 1 vol. 2008. (Contemporary Musicians & Their Music Ser.). (ENG., Illus.). 48p. (gr. 6-6). (J). lib. bdg. 34.47 *(978-1-4042-1820-8(3),* b65c61a5-7e73-49d6-bae8-66d53e9c99d8); pap. 12.75 *(978-1-4358-5128-3(5),* a11e91be-e51e-4fb7-8873-76b0388b7fda, Rosen Classroom) Rosen Publishing Group, Inc., The.

Schatz, Kate. Rad Women Worldwide: Artists & Athletes, Pirates & Punks, & Other Revolutionaries Who Shaped History. Klein Stahl, Miriam, illus. 2016. (Rad Women Ser.). 112p. (gr. 5-12). 15.99 *(978-0-399-57886-1(2),* Ten Speed Pr.) Potter/Ten Speed/Harmony/Rodale.

Scheff, Matt. Aly Raisman. 2016. (Olympic Stars Ser.). (ENG., Illus.). 32p. (J). (gr. 3-9). lib. bdg. 32.79 *(978-1-68078-562-3(1),* 23807, SportsZone) ABDO Publishing Co.

Schott, Jane A. Dian Fossey & the Mountain Gorillas. Ramstad, Ralph L., illus. 2005. (On My Own Biographies Ser.). 48p. (gr. 2-5). lib. bdg. 23.93 *(978-1-57505-082-9(X))* Lerner Publishing Group.

Schwartz, Heather. Lizzie Johnson: Texan Cowgirl, 1 vol. rev. ed. 2012. (Social Studies: Informational Text Ser.). (ENG.). 32p. (gr. 3-5). pap. 11.99 *(978-1-4333-5051-1(3))* Teacher Created Materials, Inc.

Senker, Cath. J. K. Rowling: Creator of Harry Potter, 1 vol. 2011. (Famous Lives Ser.). (ENG., Illus.). 32p. (YA). (gr. 3-4). lib. bdg. 30.27 *(978-1-4488-3288-0(8),* 898cfb36-976b-437d-a19a-adc2303d6b29) Rosen Publishing Group, Inc., The.

Serrano, Francisco. La Malinche: The Princess Who Helped Cortés Conquer the Aztec Empire, 1 vol. Ouriou, Susan, tr. Serrano, Pablo, illus. 2012. (ENG.). 40p. (J). (gr. 4-7). 18.95 *(978-1-55498-111-3(5))* Groundwood Bks. CAN. Dist: Publishers Group West (PGW).

Sexton, Colleen. J. K. Rowling. 2008. pap. 52.95 *(978-1-57505-984-6(3))* Lerner Publishing Group.

Shannon, Chelsey. Chelsey: My True Story of Murder, Loss, & Starting Over. 2009. (Louder Than Words Ser.). (ENG.). 168p. (YA). (gr. 7-18). pap. 7.95 *(978-0-7573-1413-1(9),* HCI Teens) Health Communications, Inc.

Shapiro, Marc. J. K. Rowling: the Wizard Behind Harry Potter: The Wizard Behind Harry Potter. 4th ed. 2007. (ENG., Illus.). 288p. pap. 20.99 *(978-0-312-37697-0(9),* 900049029, St. Martin's Griffin) St. Martin's Pr.

Shaw, Maura D. Dorothy Day: A Catholic Life of Action. Marchesi, Stephen, illus. 2004. (Spiritual Biographies for Young Readers Ser.). (ENG.). 32p. (J). 12.99 *(978-1-59473-011-5(3),* 9135644c-888c-415d-a4b2-abbdcd24b83e, Skylight Paths Publishing) LongHill Partners, Inc.

Shecter, Vicky Alvear. Warrior Queens: True Stories of Six Ancient Rebels Who Slayed History. Mayer, Bill, illus. 2019. 160p. (J). (gr. 4-7). 17.99 *(978-1-62979-679-6(4),* Astra Young Readers) Astra Publishing Hse.

Sheen, Barbara. Danica Patrick, 1 vol. 2009. (People in the News Ser.). (ENG.). 104p. (gr. 7-7). 41.03 *(978-1-4205-0155-1(0),* bd91bdca-1a6a-408b-ab1c-b30dd0e930dc, Lucent Pr.) Greenhaven Publishing LLC.

Shepherd, Jodie. Jane Goodall. 2015. (Rookie Biographies(tm) Ser.). (ENG.). 32p. (J). lib. bdg. 25.00 *(978-0-531-21413-8(3),* Children's Pr.) Scholastic Library Publishing.

Sherman, Jill. Gal Gadot: Soldier, Model, Wonder Woman. 2018. (Gateway Biographies Ser.). (ENG., Illus.). 48p. (J). (gr. 4-8). 31.99 *(978-1-5415-2358-6(X),* d2d1310c-1b61-4586-9092-c59559e4db4f, Lerner Pubns.) Lerner Publishing Group.

—25 Mujeres Que Fueron Las Primeras en Pensar en Algo. Aparicio Publishing LLC, Aparicio Publishing, tr. 2020. (Mujeres Valientes Ser.).Tr. of 25 Women Who Thought of It First. (SPA., Illus.). 64p. (J). (gr. 7-12). lib. bdg. 37.32 *(978-0-7565-6539-8(1),* 142069, Compass Point Bks.) Capstone.

—25 Women Who Thought of It First. 2018. (Daring Women Ser.). (ENG., Illus.). 64p. (J). (gr. 7-12). lib. bdg. 35.32 *(978-0-7565-5852-9(2),* 138480, Compass Point Bks.) Capstone.

Shone, Rob. Harriet Tubman: The Life of an African-American Abolitionist. 2009. (Graphic Nonfiction Biographies Ser.). (ENG.). 48p. (YA). (gr. 4-5). 58.50 *(978-1-61513-018-4(7),* Rosen Reference) Rosen Publishing Group, Inc., The.

Shuemann, Bettina. 13 Women Artists Children Should Know. 2009. (13 Children Should Know Ser.). (ENG., Illus.). 48p. (J). (gr. 3-7). 14.95 *(978-3-7913-4333-4(5))* Prestel Verlag GmbH & Co KG. DEU. Dist: Penguin Random Hse. LLC.

Silate, Jennifer. Betsy Ross: Creadora de la bandera estadounidense (Betsy Ross: Creator of the American Flag) 2009. (Grandes personajes en la historia de los Estados Unidos (Famous People in American History) Ser.). (SPA.). 32p. (gr. 2-3). 47.90 *(978-1-61512-791-7(7),* Editorial Buenas Letras) Rosen Publishing Group, Inc., The.

—Betsy Ross: Creator of the American Flag. 2009. (Primary Sources of Famous People in American History Ser.). 32p. (gr. 2-3). 47.90 *(978-1-60851-657-5(1))* Rosen Publishing Group, Inc., The.

—Betsy Ross: Creator of the American Flag / Creadora de la bandera Estadounidense. 2009. (Famous People in American History/Grandes personajes en la historia de los Estados Unidos Ser.). (ENG & SPA.). 32p. (gr. 2-3). 47.90 *(978-1-61512-539-5(6),* Editorial Buenas Letras) Rosen Publishing Group, Inc., The.

—Little Sure Shot: Annie Oakley & Buffalo Bill's Wild West Show. 2009. (Great Moments in American History Ser.). 32p. (gr. 3-3). 47.90 *(978-1-61513-147-1(7))* Rosen Publishing Group, Inc., The.

Simons, Lisa M. Bolt. Marie Curie: Physicist & Chemist. 2018. (STEM Scientists & Inventors Ser.). (ENG., Illus.). 24p. (J). (gr. 1-3). pap. 7.95 *(978-1-5435-0649-5(6),* 137413, Capstone Pr.) Capstone.

Sita, Lisa. Pocahontas: The Powhatan Culture & the Jamestown Colony. (Library of American Lives & Times Ser.). 112p. (gr. 5-5). 2009. 69.20 *(978-1-60853-500-2(2))* 2004. (ENG., Illus.). (J). lib. bdg. 38.27 *(978-1-4042-2653-1(2),* 0630cc02-b680-457c-b3b0-922753babdca) Rosen Publishing Group, Inc., The.

Skeers, Linda. Women Who Dared: 52 Fearless Daredevils, Adventurers, & Rebels. Gosling, Livi, illus. 2017. 128p. (J). (gr. 3-8). 16.99 *(978-1-4926-5327-1(6))* Sourcebooks, Inc.

Skelton, Renee. A Woman of Courage. 2005. (Time for Kids Ser.). (ENG., Illus.). 48p. (J). (gr. 2-4). pap. 3.99 *(978-0-06-057607-3(3))* HarperCollins Pubs.

Skelton, Renee & Time for Kids Editors. Time for Kids: A Woman of Courage. 2005. (Time for Kids Ser.). (ENG., Illus.). 48p. (J). 16.99 *(978-0-06-057608-0(1))* HarperCollins Pubs.

Spiller, Sara. Lise Meitner. Bane, Jeff, illus. 2018. (My Early Library: My Itty-Bitty Bio Ser.). (ENG.). 24p. (J). (gr. k-1). lib. bdg. 30.64 *(978-1-5341-2883-5(2),* 211576) Cherry Lake Publishing.

—Tiera Fletcher. Bane, Jeff, illus. 2018. (My Early Library: My Itty-Bitty Bio Ser.). (ENG.). 24p. (J). (gr. k-1). lib. bdg. 30.64 *(978-1-5341-2881-1(6),* 211568) Cherry Lake Publishing.

St. George, Judith. Sacagawea. 2006. pap. 8.75 *(978-0-15-365175-5(X))* Harcourt Schl. Pubs.

Staley, Erin. The Most Influential Female Activists, 1 vol. 2018. (Breaking the Glass Ceiling: the Most Influential Women Ser.). (ENG., Illus.). 112p. (J). (gr. 8-8). 40.13 *(978-1-5081-7963-4(8),* 490411ad-d4e0-41c9-8383-d9585a665b8c) Rosen Publishing Group, Inc., The.

Stanborough, Rebecca. 25 Mujeres Que Gobernaron. Aparicio Publishing LLC, Aparicio Publishing, tr. 2020. (Mujeres Valientes Ser.).Tr. of 25 Women Who Ruled. (SPA., Illus.). 64p. (J). (gr. 7-12). lib. bdg. 37.32 *(978-0-7565-6538-1(3),* 142068, Compass Point Bks.) Capstone.

Stanborough, Rebecca J. 25 Women Who Ruled. 2018. (Daring Women Ser.). (ENG., Illus.). 64p. (J). (gr. 7-12). lib. bdg. 35.32 *(978-0-7565-5851-2(4),* 138479, Compass Point Bks.) Capstone.

Stanley, Phyllis M. Elizabeth Terwilliger - Someone Special: A Biography of the Celebrated Naturalist. 2003. (ENG., Illus.). 110p. (J). (gr. 4-10). pap. 17.95 *(978-1-878044-54-9(0))* Mayhaven Publishing, Inc.

Stanton, Sue. Great Women of Faith: Inspiration for Action. 2003. (Illus.). 128p. (J). 12.95 *(978-0-8091-4123-4(X),* 4123-x) Paulist Pr.

Stathis, Roberta & Blanch, Gregory. Women Who Ruled. 2003. (Explore the Ages Ser.). (Illus.). 79p. 17.00 *(978-1-55501-592-3(1))* Ballard & Tighe Pubs.

Sterling, Kristin. Jane Goodall: A Life of Loyalty. 2008. (Pull Ahead Bks.). (Illus.). 32p. (J). (gr. -1-3). lib. bdg. 22.60 *(978-0-8225-8727-9(0),* Lerner Pubns.) Lerner Publishing Group.

Stewart, Mark. Maria Sharapova, 1 vol. 2009. (Today's Superstars Ser.). (ENG.). 48p. (J). (gr. 3-3). pap. 15.05 *(978-1-4339-2160-5(X),* 24baefdc-301b-4986-bba8-d9089f3150cb); lib. bdg. 34.60 *(978-1-4339-1967-1(2),* 51b4d2c6-8be2-4fd4-961d-13284c76cb8e) Stevens, Gareth Publishing LLLP.

Stewart, Whitney. Aung San Suu Kyi Fearless Voice of Burma Second Edition. 2008. (ENG.). 150p. 24.95 *(978-0-595-62456-0(1));* pap. 14.95 *(978-0-595-48320-4(8))* iUniverse, Inc.

Stoltman, Joan. Rosa Parks, 1 vol. 2017. (Little Biographies of Big People Ser.). (ENG.). 24p. (J). (gr. 1-2). pap. 9.15 *(978-1-5382-0933-2(0),* aa3f53b1-426c-4f61-bf33-eb191f45a383) Stevens, Gareth Publishing LLLP.

—Rosa Parks, 1 vol. Garcia, Ana Maria, tr. 2017. (Pequeñas Biografías de Grandes Personajes (Little Biographies of Big People) Ser.). (SPA.). 24p. (J). (gr. 1-2). pap. 9.15 *(978-1-5382-1556-2(X),* 9be11b2b-c922-4bbc-b399-13cd29d27216); lib. bdg. 24.27 *(978-1-5382-1529-6(2),* 772b3554-c74d-4548-88b9-6c1c0c336571) Stevens, Gareth Publishing LLLP.

Strand, Jennifer. Great Women, 6 vols. 2016. (Great Women Ser.). (ENG.). 24p. (J). (gr. -1-2). 299.64 *(978-1-68079-387-1(X),* 23008, Abdo Zoom-Launch) ABDO Publishing Co.

Sullivan, Anne Marie. Mother Theresa: Religious Humanitarian. 2004. (Great Names Ser.). (Illus.). 32p. (J). (gr. 3-18). lib. bdg. 19.95 *(978-1-59084-142-6(5))* Mason Crest.

Sutcliffe, Jane. Amelia Earhart. 2003. (History Maker Bios Ser.). (Illus.). 48p. (J). (gr. 3-5). lib. bdg. 26.60 *(978-0-8225-0396-5(4))* Lerner Publishing Group.

Swanson, Jennifer. Environmental Activist Wangari Maathai. 2018. (STEM Trailblazer Bios Ser.). (ENG., Illus.). 32p. (J). (gr. 2-5). pap. 8.99 *(978-1-5415-1215-3(4),* f4632edc-ce4f-4012-b76a-c2d9b6afb0fd); lib. bdg. 26.65 *(978-1-5124-9982-7(X),* c99e835f-9a46-418c-9012-40ad8b652ff3, Lerner Pubns.) Lerner Publishing Group.

Terp, Gail. Demi Lovato. 2016. (Women Who Rock Ser.). (ENG., Illus.). 32p. (J). (gr. 4-6). 31.35 *(978-1-68072-066-2(X),* 10423, Bolt) Black Rabbit Bks.

Thatcher Murcia, Rebecca. What Its Like to Be Marta Vieira. de la Vega, Eida, tr. 2010. (What It's Like to Be/Que se Siente al Ser Ser.). (ENG & SPA., Illus.). 32p. (J). (gr. -1-2). lib. bdg. 25.70 *(978-1-58415-852-3(2))* Mitchell Lane Pubs.

—What It's Like to Be Shakira. de la Vega, Eida, tr. from SPA. 2010. (What It's Like to Be/Que se Siente al Ser Ser.). (ENG & SPA., Illus.). 32p. (J). (gr. -1-2). lib. bdg. 25.70 *(978-1-58415-851-6(4))* Mitchell Lane Pubs.

Thiel, Kristin. Joan of Arc, 1 vol. 2017. (Great Military Leaders Ser.). (ENG.). 128p. (YA). (gr. 9-9). 47.36 *(978-1-5026-2791-9(4),* 61492b8d-dfdd-49d4-9b3c-8b9f9c6129f2) Cavendish Square Publishing LLC.

Townsley, Janet Howe. Dakota Dreams: Fannie Sabra Howe's Own Story, 1881-1884. 2003. (Illus.). 77p. (J). 19.95 *(978-0-9715171-4-1(2))* South Dakota Historical Society Pr.

Tracy, Kathleen. Orianthi. 2010. (Blue Banner Biography Ser.). (Illus.). 32p. (YA). (gr. 4-7). lib. bdg. 25.70 *(978-1-58415-913-1(8))* Mitchell Lane Pubs.

Trouvé, Marianne Lorraine. Saint Catherine Labouré: And Our Lady of the Miraculous Medal. 2011. (ENG., Illus.). 119p. (J). pap. 7.95 *(978-0-8198-7224-1(5))* Pauline Bks. & Media.

Valdez, Patricia. Joan Procter, Dragon Doctor: The Woman Who Loved Reptiles. Sala, Felicita, illus. 2018. 40p. (J). (gr. -1-3). 18.99 *(978-0-399-55725-5(3),* Knopf Bks. for Young Readers) Random Hse. Children's Bks.

Valentine, Emily. Mother Teresa: With a Discussion of Compassion. 2004. (Values in Action Ser.). (J). *(978-1-59203-070-5(X))* Learning Challenge, Inc.

Van Allsburg, Chris. Queen of the Falls. Van Allsburg, Chris, illus. 2011. (ENG., Illus.). 40p. (J). (gr. 1-4). 18.99 *(978-0-547-31581-2(3),* 1415337, Clarion Bks.) HarperCollins Pubs.

Van Haeringen, Annemarie. Coco & the Little Black Dress. 2015. (ENG., Illus.). 32p. (J). (gr. -1-2). 16.95 *(978-0-7358-4239-7(6))* North-South Bks., Inc.

Vargas, Constanza Orozco. Coco Chanel: Una Mujer Salida del Molde. 2005. (100 Personajes Ser.). (SPA.). 152p. (YA). *(978-958-30-1765-0(5))* Panamericana Editorial.

Vegetarians of Washington. Vegetarian Pacific Northwest: A Guide to Restaurants & Shopping. 2008. (ENG., Illus.). 128p. (gr. 4-7). pap. 14.95 *(978-1-57067-211-8(3))* BPC.

Venezia, Mike. Getting to Know the World's Greatest Inventors & Scientists: Lise Meitner. Venezia, Mike, illus. 2010. (Getting to Know the World's Greatest Inventors & Scientists Ser.). (ENG., Illus.). 32p. (J). (gr. 3-4). pap. 6.95 *(978-0-531-20776-5(5),* Children's Pr.) Scholastic Library Publishing.

—Jane Goodall: Researcher Who Champions Chimps. 2010. (Getting to Know the World's Greatest Inventors & Scientists Ser.). 32p. (J). (gr. 3-4). pap. 6.95 *(978-0-531-22352-9(3),* Children's Pr.) Scholastic Library Publishing.

Vinberger, Naftali Yehiel ben Shelomoh Avraham, et al. The Story of Rebbetzin Kanievsky: A Biography for Young Readers. 2012. (Illus.). 204p. (J). *(978-1-4226-1333-7(X))* Mesorah Pubns., Ltd.

Volovar, Vivian. Lobster Lady. 2007. (Illus.). 32p. (J). pap. 14.95 *(978-0-9773725-8-4(8))* Flat Hammock Pr.

Walker, Sally M. Mary Anning: Fossil Hunter. Saroff, Phyllis V., illus. 2007. (On My Own Biographies Ser.). 48p. (J). (gr. 2-5). per. 6.95 *(978-1-57505-457-5(4),* First Avenue Editions) Lerner Publishing Group.

Waxman, Laura Hamilton. Marie Curie. 2003. (History Maker Biographies Ser.). (ENG., Illus.). 48p. (gr. 3-6). 27.93 *(978-0-8225-0300-2(X),* Lerner Pubns.) Lerner Publishing Group.

Webster, Christine. Sandra Cisneros: My Favorite Writer. 2008. (J). 29.05 *(978-1-59036-933-3(5))* Weigl Pubs., Inc.

Wein, Elizabeth. A Thousand Sisters: The Heroic Airwomen of the Soviet Union in World War II. 2019. (ENG., Illus.). 400p. (YA). (gr. 8). 19.99 *(978-0-06-245301-3(7),* Balzer & Bray) HarperCollins Pubs.

Weinberger, Kimberly. Let's Read About — Pocahontas. Marchesi, Stephen, illus. 2003. (Scholastic First Biographies Ser.). (J). pap. *(978-0-439-56148-8(5))* Scholastic, Inc.

White, Katherine. Sylvia Earle: Deep Sea Explorer & Ocean Activist. (Women Hall of Famers in Mathematics & Science

Ser.). 112p. (gr. 5-8). 2009. 63.90 *(978-1-60854-814-9(7))* 2003. (ENG., Illus.). lib. bdg. 39.80 *(978-0-8239-3879-7(4),* 605a1e36-bafd-4ce1-86f8-a6c460e534d4) Rosen Publishing Group, Inc., The. (Rosen Reference).
illen, Janet & Gann, Marjorie. Speak a Word for Freedom: Women Against Slavery. 2015. (Illus.). 216p. (YA). (gr. 7). 21.99 *(978-1-77049-651-4(3),* Tundra Bks.) Tundra Bks. CAN. Dist: Penguin Random Hse. LLC.
illiams, Alicia D. Jump at the Sun: The True Life Tale of Unstoppable Storycatcher Zora Neale Hurston. Alcántara, Jacqueline, illus. 2021. (ENG.). 48p. (J). (gr. -1-3). 17.99 *(978-1-5344-1913-1(6))* Simon & Schuster Children's Publishing.
illiams, Suzanne. China's Daughters. MacLean, Amber, illus. 2011. (J). *(978-1-881896-34-0(X))* Pacific View Pr.
ilson, Antoine. S. E. Hinton. 2009. (Library of Author Biographies Ser.). 112p. (gr. 5-8). 63.90 *(978-1-60853-553-8(3),* Rosen Reference) Rosen Publishing Group, Inc., The.
inegarten, Debra L. Katherine Stinson: The Flying Schoolgirl. 2004. (Illus.). 133p. (gr. 4-7). 26.95 *(978-1-57168-459-2(X))* Eakin Pr.
inter, Jeanette. My Name Is Georgia: A Portrait by Jeanette Winter. Winter, Jeanette, illus. 2003. (ENG., Illus.). 48p. (J). (gr. -1-3). pap. 9.99 *(978-0-15-204597-5(X),* 1193843, Clarion Bks.) HarperCollins Pubs.
—The Watcher: Jane Goodall's Life with the Chimps. Winter, Jeanette, illus. 2011. (ENG., Illus.). 48p. (J). (gr. -1-3). 18.99 *(978-0-375-86774-3(0),* Schwartz & Wade Bks.) Random Hse. Children's Bks.
Women Explorers. (J). pap. 4.95 *(978-0-88388-203-0(5))* Bellerophon Bks.
Women Who Changed History. 2017. (Women Who Changed History Ser.). 48p. (gr. 10-12). pap. 84.30 *(978-1-5081-0552-7(9));* (ENG.). (gr. 6-7). 170.46 *(978-1-5081-0550-3(2),* 3c844653-4d14-48db-8e0a-967a84fba9f1) Rosen Publishing Group, Inc., The. (Britannica Educational Publishing).
Wommack, Linda. Ann Bassett: Colorado's Cattle Queen. 2018. (Illus.). 247p. *(978-0-87004-619-3(5))* Caxton Pr.
Wood, S. Vaccine Innovators Pearl Kendrick & Grace Eldering. 2016. (STEM Trailblazer Bios Ser.). (ENG., Illus.). 32p. (J). (gr. 2-5). 26.65 *(978-1-5124-0790-7(9),* dc165329-e6c1-4b8e-bbaa-318d2c7a993c, Lerner Pubns.) Lerner Publishing Group.
Woods, Bob. Racer Girls. 2016. (Illus.). 32p. (J). *(978-1-4896-4781-8(3))* Weigl Pubs., Inc.
Yim Bridges, Shirin. Agrippina: "Atrocious & Ferocious" Malone, Peter, illus. 2011. (Thinking Girl's Treasury of Dastardly Dames Ser.). (ENG.). 32p. (J). (gr. 3-8). 18.95 *(978-0-9834256-1-8(2))* Goosebottom Bks. LLC.
—Qutlugh Terkan Khatun of Kirman. Nguyen, Albert, illus. 2010. (Thinking Girl's Treasury of Real Princesses Ser.). (ENG.). 24p. (J). (gr. 3-8). 18.95 *(978-0-9845098-3-6(6))* Goosebottom Bks. LLC.
Yolen, Jane. Sea Queens: Woman Pirates Around the World. Pratt, Christine Joy, illus. 2010. (ENG.). 112p. (J). (gr. 2-5). pap. 9.95 *(978-1-58089-132-5(2))* Charlesbridge Publishing, Inc.
Yolen, Jane & Stemple, Heidi E. Y. Bad Girls: Sirens, Jezebels, Murderesses, Thieves & Other Female Villains. 2015. lib. bdg. 20.80 *(978-0-606-37602-0(X))* Turtleback.
Zachry, Juanita Daniel. Katy O'Neil: She Found a Way or Made One. 2004. 224p. per. 14.95 *(978-0-9749725-1-0(7));* bds. 24.95 *(978-0-9749725-0-3(9))* LoneStar Abilene Publishing, LLC.
Zhang, Gui Jie. The Bamboo Forest: I Truly Love You, & God Loves You Too, 1 vol. 2009. 47p. pap. 24.95 *(978-1-60836-292-9(2))* America Star Bks.

WOMEN—CLOTHING

see Clothing and Dress

WOMEN—DRESS

see Clothing and Dress; Costume

WOMEN—EDUCATION

Abouraya, Karen Leggett. Malala Yousafzai: Guerrera con Palabras, 1 vol. Roth, Susan L., illus. 2019.Tr. of Malala Yousafzai: Warrior with Words. (SPA.). 40p. (J). (gr. k-3). pap. 11.95 *(978-1-62014-800-6(5),* leelowbooks) Lee & Low Bks., Inc.
Aretha, David. Malala Yousafzai & the Girls of Pakistan. 2014. (ENG.). (J). 27.45 *(978-1-59935-454-5(3))* Reynolds, Morgan Inc.
Barghoorn, Linda. Zuriel Oduwole: Filmmaker & Campaigner for Girls' Education. 2018. (Remarkable Lives Revealed Ser.). (ENG., Illus.). 32p. (J). (gr. 3-3). *(978-0-7787-4703-1(4));* pap. *(978-0-7787-4714-7(X))* Crabtree Publishing Co.
Brown, Dinah. Who Is Malala Yousafzai? Thomson, Andrew, illus. 2015. (Who Was-? Chapters Ser.). (ENG.). 112p. (J). (gr. 3-6). 18.69 *(978-1-4844-6131-0(2),* Penguin Workshop) Penguin Young Readers Group.
—Who Is Malala Yousafzai? 2015. (Who Is...? Ser.). lib. bdg. 16.00 *(978-0-606-37551-1(1))* Turtleback.
Catherman, Erica & Catherman, Jonathan. The Girls' Guide to Conquering Middle School: Do This, Not That Advice Every Girl Needs. 2018. (ENG., Illus.). 224p. pap. 13.99 *(978-0-8007-2981-3(1))* Revell.
Corey, Shana. Malala: a Hero for All. Sayles, Elizabeth, illus. 2016. (Step into Reading Ser.). 48p. (J). (gr. 2-4). pap. 4.99 *(978-0-553-53761-1(X),* Random Hse. Bks. for Young Readers) Random Hse. Children's Bks.
Doeden, Matt. Malala Yousafzai: Shot by the Taliban, Still Fighting for Equal Education. 2014. (Gateway Biographies Ser.). (ENG., Illus.). 48p. (J). (gr. 4-8). lib. bdg. 31.99 *(978-1-4677-4907-7(9),* 5a5d23db-df30-41a8-89a4-3bad4c20b3a9, Lerner Pubns.) Lerner Publishing Group.
Hansen, Grace. Malala Yousafzai: Activista Por la Educación (Spanish Version) 2016. (Biografías: Personas Que Han Hecho Historia (History Maker Biographies) Ser.). (SPA., Illus.). 24p. (J). (gr. -1-2). lib. bdg. 32.79 *(978-1-68080-740-0(4),* 22642, Abdo Kids) ABDO Publishing Co.
—Malala Yousafzai: Education Activist, 1 vol. 2015. (History Maker Biographies (Abdo Kids Jumbo) Ser.). (ENG.). 24p. (J). (gr. -1-2). lib. bdg. 32.79 *(978-1-62970-703-7(1),* 17013, Abdo Kids) ABDO Publishing Co.
—Malala Yousafzai: Education Activist. 2017. (History Maker Biographies Ser.). (ENG.). 24p. (J). (gr. -1-2). pap. 7.95 *(978-1-4966-1226-7(4),* 134990, Capstone Classroom) Capstone.
Langston-George, Rebecca. For the Right to Learn: Malala Yousafzai's Story. Bock, Janna Rose, illus. 2016. (Encounter: Narrative Nonfiction Picture Bks.). (ENG.). 40p. (J). (gr. 3-6). pap. 7.95 *(978-1-4914-6556-1(5),* 129041, Capstone Pr.) Capstone.
—For the Right to Learn: Malala Yousafzai's Story. Bock, Janna, illus. 2015. (Encounter: Narrative Nonfiction Picture Bks.). (ENG.). 40p. (J). (gr. 3-6). lib. bdg. 29.32 *(978-1-4914-6071-9(7),* 128971, Capstone Pr.) Capstone.
Leggett Abouraya, Karen & Roth, Susan L. Malala Yousafzai: Warrior with Words, 1 vol. 2019. (ENG., Illus.). 40p. (J). (gr. k-3). pap. 11.95 *(978-1-62014-799-3(8),* leelowbooks) Lee & Low Bks., Inc.
Lew, Kristi. Cool Biology Activities for Girls. 2012. (Girls Science Club Ser.). (ENG.). 32p. (gr. 3-4). pap. 47.70 *(978-1-4296-8517-7(4),* Capstone Pr.); (J). pap. 8.19 *(978-1-4296-8019-6(9),* 118351) Capstone.
Malala, a Brave Girl from Pakistan/Iqbal, a Brave Boy from Pakistan: Two Stories of Bravery. 2014. (ENG., Illus.). 40p. (J). (gr. 1-5). 17.99 *(978-1-4814-2294-9(4),* Beach Lane Bks.) Beach Lane Bks.
Manion, Jennifer. Safia AMA Jan. 2011. (J). lib. bdg. *(978-0-8225-9038-5(7))* Twenty First Century Bks.
McCarney, Rosemary. Every Day Is Malala Day, 1 vol. 2014. (ENG., Illus.). 32p. (J). (gr. 3-5). 18.95 *(978-1-927583-31-9(4))* Second Story Pr. CAN. Dist: Orca Bk. Pubs. USA.
Moening, Kate. Malala Yousafzai: Education Activist. 2019. (Women Leading the Way Ser.). (ENG., Illus.). 24p. (J). (gr. k-3). pap. 7.99 *(978-1-61891-724-9(2),* 12305); lib. bdg. 26.95 *(978-1-64487-101-0(7))* Bellwether Media. (Blastoff! Readers).
Montalbano, Julie Williams. Middle School. 2014. (Smart Girl's Guide Ser.). lib. bdg. 24.50 *(978-0-606-35213-0(9))* Turtleback.
Niver, Heather Moore. Malala Yousafzai, 1 vol., 1. 2015. (Britannica Beginner Bios Ser.). (ENG., Illus.). 32p. (J). (gr. 2-3). lib. bdg. 26.06 *(978-1-68048-253-9(X),* 6e887405-0ba1-49a1-944d-603e52a8a725, Britannica Educational Publishing) Rosen Publishing Group, Inc., The.
Peters, Elisa. Malala Yousafzai: Pakistani Activist for Female Education, 1 vol. 2017. (Spotlight on Civic Courage: Heroes of Conscience Ser.). (ENG., Illus.). 48p. (J). (gr. 6-6). 33.47 *(978-1-5081-7749-4(X),* 92731d4f-26f7-4da6-ae6b-19013b03ff01) Rosen Publishing Group, Inc., The.
Rice, Dona Herweck. Fantastic Kids: Malala Yousafzai (Level 5) 2017. (TIME for KIDS(r): Informational Text Ser.). (ENG., Illus.). 48p. (J). (gr. 4-8). pap. 13.99 *(978-1-4258-4988-7(1))* Teacher Created Materials, Inc.
Schwartz, Heather, et al. Girls Science Club. 2012. (Girls Science Club Ser.). (ENG.). 32p. (J). (gr. 3-9). pap., pap., pap. 31.80 *(978-1-4296-8521-4(2),* 17801) Capstone.
Schwartz, Heather E. Cool Engineering Activities for Girls. 2012. (Girls Science Club Ser.). (ENG.). 32p. (gr. 3-4). pap. 47.70 *(978-1-4296-8519-1(0),* Capstone Pr.); (Illus.). (J). pap. 8.19 *(978-1-4296-8021-9(0),* 118353) Capstone.
Slade, Suzanne. Cool Physics Activities for Girls. 2012. (Girls Science Club Ser.). (ENG.). 32p. (gr. 3-4). pap. 47.70 *(978-1-4296-8520-7(4),* Capstone Pr.); (J). pap. 8.19 *(978-1-4296-8022-6(9),* 118354) Capstone.
Speregen, Debra Newberger. Got Class? A GF's Guide to School Style. 2008. (Illus.). 48p. (J). *(978-0-545-04092-1(2))* Scholastic, Inc.
Stoltman, Joan. Malala Yousafzai, 1 vol. 2018. (Little Biographies of Big People Ser.). (ENG.). 24p. (gr. 1-2). 24.27 *(978-1-5382-2894-4(7),* e07fe2cf-0feb-42cd-b6b7-4a6037f33745) Stevens, Gareth Publishing LLLP.
Strand, Jennifer. Malala Yousafzai. 2016. (Great Women Ser.). (ENG.). 24p. (J). (gr. -1-2). 49.94 *(978-1-68079-390-1(X),* 23011, Abdo Zoom-Launch) ABDO Publishing Co.
Wang, Andrea. Malala Yousafzai: Nobel Peace Prize Winner & Education Activist, 1 vol. 2015. (Newsmakers Ser.). (ENG.). 48p. (J). (gr. 4-8). lib. bdg. 35.64 *(978-1-62403-646-0(5),* 17191) ABDO Publishing Co.
Wheeler-Toppen, Jodi. Cool Chemistry Activities for Girls. 2012. (Girls Science Club Ser.). (ENG.). 32p. (gr. 3-4). pap. 47.70 *(978-1-4296-8518-4(2),* Capstone Pr.); (Illus.). (J). pap. 8.19 *(978-1-4296-8020-2(2),* 118352) Capstone.
Wheeler-Toppen, Jodi, et al. Girls Science Club. 2012. (Girls Science Club Ser.). (ENG.). 32p. (gr. 3-4). pap. 190.80 *(978-1-4296-8522-1(0),* Capstone Pr.) Capstone.
Williams Montalbano, Julie. A Smart Girl's Guide: Middle School: Everything You Need to Know about Juggling More Homework, More Teachers, & More Friends! Mingus, Cathi, illus. 2014. (American Girl(r) Wellbeing Ser.). (ENG.). 96p. (J). pap. 12.99 *(978-1-60958-406-1(6))* American Girl Publishing, Inc.
Winter, Jeanette. Nasreen's Secret School: A True Story from Afghanistan. Winter, Jeanette, illus. 2009. (ENG., Illus.). 40p. (J). (gr. 1-4). 18.99 *(978-1-4169-9437-4(8),* Beach Lane Bks.) Beach Lane Bks.
Yousafzai, Malala. I Am Malala: How One Girl Stood up for Education & Changed the World (Young Readers Edition) (ENG., (J). (gr. 5-17). 2016. Illus.). 256p. pap. 10.99 *(978-0-316-32791-6(3))* 2014. (Illus.). 240p. 18.99 *(978-0-316-32793-0(X))* 2015. 240p. 17.00 *(978-0-316-31119-9(7))* Little, Brown Bks. for Young Readers.
—I Am Malala: The Girl Who Stood up for Education & Was Shot by the Taliban. 2016. (J). lib. bdg. 22.10 *(978-0-606-37164-3(8))* Turtleback.
—I Am Malala 9c Solid Floor Display: How One Girl Stood up for Education & Changed the World (Young Readers Edition) 2014. (ENG.). 256p. (J). (gr. 5-17). 153.00 *(978-0-316-33917-9(2))* Little, Brown Bks. for Young Readers.
—I Am Malala PB 9c Solid Floor Display: How One Girl Stood up for Education & Changed the World (Young Readers Edition) 2016. (ENG.). 256p. (J). (gr. 5-17). 98.91 *(978-0-316-30398-9(4))* Little, Brown Bks. for Young Readers.
—Malala's Magic Pencil. Kerascoët, illus. 2017. (ENG.). 48p. (J). (gr. -1-3). 17.99 *(978-0-316-31957-7(0))* Little, Brown Bks. for Young Readers.
Yousafzai, Malala & McCormick, Patricia. I Am Malala: The Girl Who Stood up for Education & Was Shot by the Taliban. Lt. ed. 2017. (ENG., Illus.). 302p. 22.99 *(978-1-4104-9916-5(2))* Cengage Gale.

WOMEN—EDUCATION—FICTION

Lyons, Wendy Ackerman. The Girl Who Reached for the Star. Sayles, John, illus. 2007. (J). *(978-0-696-23982-3(5))* Meredith Bks.

WOMEN—EMPLOYMENT

Berlatsky, Noah, ed. Working Women, 1 vol. 2015. (Opposing Viewpoints Ser.). (ENG.). 192p. (gr. 10-12). 50.43 *(978-0-7377-7302-6(2),* ad3e0b24-51c0-4643-a829-adb67b2bfbae, Greenhaven Publishing) Greenhaven Publishing LLC.
Campbell, Candy. My Mom Is A Nurse, 1 vol. 2010. (ENG.). 208p. pap., pap. 27.95 *(978-0-578-02360-1(1))* New Year Publishing.
—My Mom Is a Nurse. Imura, Toshiyoshi, tr. Fusco, Michael Vincent, illus. 2017. (JPN.). (J). pap. 14.95 *(978-0-9842385-4-5(9))* Peripatetic Productions, LLC.
Dorling Kindersley Publishing Staff. Feminism Is ... 2019. (ENG., Illus.). 160p. (YA). *(978-0-241-22802-9(6))* Dorling Kindersley.
Dorman, Jennifer, ed. Are Women Paid Fairly?, 1 vol. 2013. (At Issue Ser.). (ENG.). 104p. (gr. 10-12). pap. 28.80 *(978-0-7377-6154-2(7),* 829b5df8-04b2-4386-ba5d-91fa4d259df1); lib. bdg. 41.03 *(978-0-7377-6153-5(9),* 7cf1686a-2bb8-4a97-973c-a00a3ef6d40f) Greenhaven Publishing LLC. (Greenhaven Publishing).
Gagne, Tammy. Women in the Workplace. 2019. (Women & Society Ser.). (ENG.). 80p. (YA). (gr. 6-12). *(978-1-68282-553-2(1))* ReferencePoint Pr., Inc.
Isgro, Bailey Sisoy & Lapointe, Nicole. Rosie, a Detroit Herstory. 2018. (Great Lakes Books Ser.). (ENG., Illus.). 40p. 16.99 *(978-0-8143-4544-3(1),* P589729) Wayne State Univ. Pr.
Lanier, Wendy Hinote. Women in Literature. 2018. (Women in the Arts Ser.). (ENG.). 48p. (J). (gr. 4-8). lib. bdg. 35.64 *(978-1-5321-1476-2(1),* 29144) ABDO Publishing Co.
Lowery, Zoe & Freedman, Jeri. Women's Rights at Work, 1 vol. 2017. (Women in the World Ser.). (ENG., Illus.). 112p. (J). (gr. 6-6). 38.80 *(978-1-5081-7451-6(2),* 26fec6ce-e670-43cf-9cea-8d5470cbc887, Rosen Young Adult) Rosen Publishing Group, Inc., The.
MacDonald, Fiona. Equal Opportunities. (World Issues Ser.). (Illus.). 57p. (J). lib. bdg. 28.50 *(978-1-931983-30-3(5))* Chrysalis Education.
—Equal Opportunities, 1 vol. 2006. (Global Issues Ser.: 0). (ENG.). 57p. (YA). (gr. 6-10). pap. 12.95 *(978-1-55285-744-1(1),* 0766b7be-baee-4acd-9cfc-75eb7d603f58) Whitecap Bks., Ltd. CAN. Dist: Firefly Bks., Ltd.
Morkes, Andrew & McKenna, Amy. Nontraditional Careers for Women & Men: More Than 30 Great Jobs for Women & Men with Apprenticeships Through Phds. 2011. (ENG., Illus.). vii, 280p. (J). pap. 19.95 *(978-0-9745251-9-8(7))* College & Career Pr., LLC.
Petersen, Christine. Rosie the Riveter. 2008. (Cornerstones of Freedom Ser.). (ENG.). 48p. (J). pap. 5.95 *(978-0-531-20840-3(0),* Children's Pr.) Scholastic Library Publishing.
Pinede, Nadine. Women in Film. 2018. (Women in the Arts Ser.). (ENG., Illus.). 48p. (J). (gr. 4-8). lib. bdg. 35.64 *(978-1-5321-1475-5(3),* 29142) ABDO Publishing Co.
Shoup, Kate. Rosie the Riveter: A Cultural Icon, 1 vol. Landsberg, Bryan, illus. 2018. (American Legends & Folktales Ser.). (ENG.). 32p. (gr. 3-3). lib. bdg. 30.21 *(978-1-5026-3693-5(X),* 3efa2bf7-cf7c-4c59-b898-593c0b2accf4) Cavendish Square Publishing LLC.
Uhl, Xina M. Women in Television. 2018. (Women in the Arts Ser.). (ENG., Illus.). 48p. (J). (gr. 4-8). lib. bdg. 35.64 *(978-1-5321-1478-6(8),* 29148) ABDO Publishing Co.
Women in the World: Set 1, 12 vols. 2017. (Women in the World Ser.). (ENG.). 112p. (gr. 6-6). 232.80 *(978-1-4994-6639-3(0),* 98e36d95-09f3-48e7-ba4c-e6be54535927, Rosen Young Adult) Rosen Publishing Group, Inc., The.

WOMEN—EMPLOYMENT—FICTION

Finnan, Kristie. Mommy's High Heel Shoes. Achilles, Pat, illus. 2008. 32p. (J). 16.99 *(978-0-9817565-2-3(2))* Mommy Workshop Bks.

WOMEN—ENFRANCHISEMENT

see Women—Suffrage

WOMEN—FICTION

Anderson, Erin. Repulsive. 2008. 16p. pap. 24.95 *(978-1-4241-9429-2(6))* America Star Bks.
Anderson, Jessica Lee. Calli. 2011. (ENG.). 198p. (J). (gr. 6). 16.95 *(978-1-57131-702-5(3));* pap. 8.00 *(978-1-57131-699-8(X))* Milkweed Editions.
Anderson, William. Little Woman. Date not set. 32p. (J). (gr. 2-5). pap. 5.99 *(978-0-06-443574-1(1))* HarperCollins Pubs.
Arroyo, Madeline. Calie's Gift. Vavak, S. Dean, illus. 2003. 32p. (gr. 2-5). 16.95 *(978-0-9740061-0-9(6),* 1234106) Stairway Pubns.
Asai, Carrie. The Book of the Shadow. Alarcão, Renato, illus. 2013. (Samurai Girl Ser.: 2). (ENG.). 224p. (YA). (gr. 11). pap. 13.99 *(978-1-4814-1540-8(9),* Simon Pulse) Simon Pulse.
Barton, Bree. Heart of Thorns. 2019. (Heart of Thorns Ser.: 1). (ENG.). 480p. (YA). (gr. 8). pap. 11.99 *(978-0-06-244769-2(6))* 2018. (Heart of Thorns Ser.: 1). (ENG., Illus.). 464p. (YA). (gr. 8). 17.99 *(978-0-06-244768-5(8))* 2018. (Illus.). 464p. (J). *(978-0-06-288917-1(6))* HarperCollins Pubs. (Tegen, Katherine Bks).
Berry, Erick. Valiant Captive. 2011. 204p. 44.95 *(978-1-258-06194-4(5))* Literary Licensing, LLC.
Bertola, Ann Marie, et al, contrib. by. Four in the Afternoon. 2003. 118p. pap. 11.99 *(978-0-9743661-0-4(2))* Circle Pr.
Bloom, Deb-b. The Bird Who Could Fly. 2008. 24p. pap. 24.95 *(978-1-60441-383-0(2))* America Star Bks.
Burnett, Frances. A Lady of Quality. 2011. 190p. 26.95 *(978-1-4638-9631-7(X))* Rodgers, Alan Bks.
Chadwick, Katie. Meet Miss Molly. 2012. 44p. pap. *(978-1-84961-134-3(3))* RealTime Publishing.
Chopin, Kate. The Story of an Hour. (Illus.). 32p. 3.30 *(978-0-7891-5479-8(X))* Perfection Learning Corp.
Clark, K. M. Beautiful Disaster. 2013. 106p. 24.99 *(978-1-4797-6506-5(6));* pap. 15.99 *(978-1-4797-6505-8(8))* Xlibris Corp.
Colandro, Lucille. There Was an Old Lady Who Swallowed Some Leaves! Lee, Jared, illus. 2010. (ENG.). 32p. (J). (gr. -1-k). pap. 6.99 *(978-0-545-24198-4(7),* Cartwheel Bks.) Scholastic, Inc.
Davies, Kate, ed. Old Woman Who Swallowed a Fly. Horne, Sarah, illus. 2009. (First Reading Level 3 Ser.). 48p. (J). (gr. 2). 6.99 *(978-0-7945-2267-4(X),* Usborne) EDC Publishing.
Dee, Katya. Orna Puella, 1 vol. 2009. 194p. pap. 24.95 *(978-1-61582-195-2(3))* PublishAmerica, Inc.
Deracine, Anat. Driving by Starlight. 2019. (ENG.). 288p. (YA). pap. 21.99 *(978-1-250-30895-5(X),* 900177285) Square Fish.
d'Lacey, Chris. The Fire Eternal (the Last Dragon Chronicles #4) 2010. (Last Dragon Chronicles Ser.: 4). (ENG.). 512p. (J). (gr. 4-7). 9.99 *(978-0-545-05164-4(9),* Orchard Bks.) Scholastic, Inc.
Dokey, Cameron. Kissed: Belle; Sunlight & Shadow; Winter's Child. 2013. (ENG.). 624p. (YA). (gr. 7). pap. 9.99 *(978-1-4424-7220-4(0),* Simon Pulse) Simon Pulse.
Dolbeck, Andrew. Fever Jenny, Bk. 1. 2006. 120p. pap. 10.99 *(978-1-59092-324-5(3))* Blue Forge Pr.
Durkee, Noura. Yunus & the Whale. Durkee, Noura, illus. 2007. (ENG., Illus.). 28p. (J). (gr. k-5). 16.00 *(978-1-879402-60-7(2))* Tahrike Tarsile Quran, Inc.
Dyan, Penelope. Eve. Dyan, Penelope, illus. 2011. (Illus.). 34p. pap. 11.95 *(978-1-935630-95-1(4))* Bellissima Publishing, LLC.
Edwards, Jo. Go Figure. 2007. (ENG.). 288p. (YA). (gr. 9-12). pap. 13.99 *(978-1-4169-2492-0(2),* Simon Pulse) Simon Pulse.
Finley, Martha. Elsie Dinsmore, Vol. 1. 320p. (gr. 7-12). pap. 5.95 *(978-1-58182-064-5(X),* Cumberland Hse.) Sourcebooks, Inc.
—Elsie's Girlhood, Vol. 3. 320p. (gr. 7-12). pap. 5.95 *(978-1-58182-066-9(6),* Cumberland Hse.) Sourcebooks, Inc.
—Elsie's Holidays at Roselands, Vol. 2. 320p. (gr. 7-12). pap. 5.95 *(978-1-58182-065-2(8),* Cumberland Hse.) Sourcebooks, Inc.
—Elsie's Widowhood, Vol. 1. 320p. (gr. 7-12). pap. 5.95 *(978-1-58182-070-6(4),* Cumberland Hse.) Sourcebooks, Inc.
—Elsie's Womanhood, Vol. 4. 320p. (gr. 7-12). pap. 5.95 *(978-1-58182-067-6(4),* Cumberland Hse.) Sourcebooks, Inc.
—Grandmother Elsie. 2018. (ENG., Illus.). 196p. (YA). (gr. 7-12). pap. *(978-93-5297-362-0(3))* Alpha Editions.
—Grandmother Elsie, Vol. 8. 320p. (J). (gr. 7-12). pap. 5.95 *(978-1-58182-071-3(2),* Cumberland Hse.) Sourcebooks, Inc.
Follet, René. The Fascinating Madame Tussaud. Duchateau, illus. 2008. (Expresso Collection). 104p. pap. 19.95 *(978-1-905460-36-6(8))* CineBook GBR. Dist: National Bk. Network.
Fosberry, Jennifer. My Name Is Not Isabella. Litwin, Mike, illus. 2008. 32p. (J). (gr. -1-3). lib. bdg. 19.99 *(978-0-9802000-7-2(5))* Monkey Barrel Pr.
—My Name Is Not Isabella: Just How Big Can a Little Girl Dream? Litwin, Mike, illus. (ENG.). 32p. (J). 2020. (-3). 8.99 *(978-1-7282-2302-5(4))* 2010. (gr. -1-3). 16.99 *(978-1-4022-4395-0(2))* Sourcebooks, Inc. (Sourcebooks Jabberwocky).
Fraustino, Lisa Rowe, ed. Don't Cramp My Style: Stories about That Time of the Month. 2004. (ENG., Illus.). 304p. (YA). 15.95 *(978-0-689-85882-6(5),* Simon & Schuster Bks. For Young Readers) Simon & Schuster Bks. For Young Readers.
Frost, Helen. Crossing Stones. 2009. (ENG., Illus.). 192p. (YA). (gr. 7-18). 19.99 *(978-0-374-31653-2(8),* 900050356, Farrar, Straus & Giroux (BYR)) Farrar, Straus & Giroux.
Fuerst, Jeffrey B. The Old Woman Who Lived in a Shoe. Greenhead, Bill, illus. 2010. (Rising Readers Ser.). (J). 3.49 *(978-1-60719-703-4(0))* Newmark Learning LLC.
Gaudet, Cindy. Moon Time Prayer. Dorion, Leah, illus. 2nd ed. 2018. (ENG.). 80p. (J). pap. *(978-1-7752231-4-6(0))* MotherButterfly Bks.
Godbersen, Anna. Envy. (Luxe Ser.: 3). (ENG.). (YA). (gr. 9). 2018. 448p. pap. 9.99 *(978-0-06-285218-2(3),* HarperTeen) 2009. 432p. pap. 9.99 *(978-0-06-134574-6(1))* HarperCollins Pubs.
Guttentag, Devora. Saving Soraya. 236p. (YA). 18.99 *(978-1-56871-256-7(1))* Targum Pr., Inc.
Hattemer, Kate. The Feminist Agenda of Jemima Kincaid. 2020. (ENG.). 304p. (YA). (gr. 9). lib. bdg. 20.99 *(978-1-9848-4913-7(1),* Knopf Bks. for Young Readers) Random Hse. Children's Bks.
Hearn, Julie. Hazel: A Novel. 2010. (ENG.). 416p. (YA). (gr. 7). pap. 8.99 *(978-1-4169-2505-7(8),* Atheneum Bks. for Young Readers) Simon & Schuster Children's Publishing.
Hitchcock, Shannon. One True Way. (ENG.). 224p. (J). (gr. 4-7). 2019. pap. 8.99 *(978-1-338-18174-6(2))* 2018. (Illus.). 17.99 *(978-1-338-18172-2(6))* Scholastic, Inc. (Scholastic Pr.).
Hueller, Patrick. Archenemy. 2013. (Counterattack Ser.). (ENG.). 112p. (YA). (gr. 6-12). lib. bdg. 27.99 *(978-1-4677-0306-2(0),* 216dd675-0b23-439f-a7a1-9e1be6e375cf, Darby Creek) Lerner Publishing Group.
James, Henry. The Ambassadors. 1stWorld Library, ed. 2007. 516p. (YA). (gr. 12). pap. 20.95 *(978-1-4218-2714-8(X),* 1st World Library - Literary Society) 1st World Publishing, Inc.
—The Ambassadors. 312p. reprint ed. pap. 99.00 *(978-1-4047-3431-9(7))* Classic Textbooks.
—The Ambassadors. 2008. 368p. (YA). (gr. 13). pap. 20.99 *(978-1-59547-714-9(4))* NuVision Pubns., LLC.

W
X
Y
Z

—The Ambassadors. 2008. 376p. (YA). (gr. 12). 35.00 (978-1-4344-7145-1(4)); pap. 19.95 (978-1-4344-7144-4(6)) Wildside Pr., LLC.

Joyner, Andrew. The Pink Hat. (ENG.). 32p. (J). (gr. -1-3). 2019. pap. 7.99 (978-0-593-11896-2(0)) 2017. (Illus.). 17.99 (978-1-5247-7226-0(7)) Random Hse. Children's Bks. (Schwartz & Wade Bks.).

Keene, Carolyn. Dangerous Plays. 16th ed. 2006. (Nancy Drew (All New) Girl Detective Ser.: 16). (ENG.). 160p. (J). (gr. 3-7). pap. 7.99 (978-1-4169-0605-6(3), Aladdin) Simon & Schuster Children's Publishing.

—Wedding Day Disaster. Pamintuan, Macky, illus. 2008. (Nancy Drew & the Clue Crew Ser.: 17). (ENG.). 96p. (J). (gr. 1-4). pap. 5.99 (978-1-4169-6778-1(8), Aladdin) Simon & Schuster Children's Publishing.

Komada, Yoshihiro, et al. Flesh for the Beast. Pannone, Frank, ed. Ohtsuka, Tommy et al, illus. 2004. 132p. pap. 9.99 (978-1-58655-556-6(1), SSNOV-0419) Media Blasters, Inc.

Leslie, Emma. From Bondage to Freedom: A Tale of the Times of Mohammed. Symmons, Sheeres, illus. 2007. 308p. 24.95 (978-1-934671-10-8(X)) Salem Ridge Press LLC.

Llewellyn, Claire. Boudica: Band 15/Emerald (Collins Big Cat) 2016. (Collins Big Cat Ser.). (ENG.). 48p. (J). (gr. 3-4). pap. 12.99 (978-0-00-816391-4(X)) HarperCollins Pubs. Ltd. GBR. Dist: Independent Pubs. Group.

Marlo's Rainbow Pony. 2004.Tr. of Marlo'w Rainbow Pony. (Illus.). 12p. (J). 5.95 net. (978-0-9728871-0-6(5)) Rainbow Pony Publishing.

Martin, Ann M. Needle & Thread. Andreasen, Dan, illus. 2007. 205p. (J). pap. (978-0-545-03660-3(7)) Scholastic, Inc.

Martinez, Alejandro Cruz. La Mujer que Brillaba Aun Mas Que el Sol. 2004. (SPA.). (J). (gr. k-3). spiral bd. (978-0-616-07278-3(3)) Canadian National Institute for the Blind/Institut National Canadien pour les Aveugles.

McDougal-Littell Publishing Staff, creator. Picture Bride & Related Readings. 2006. (Literature Connections Ser.). 314p. (gr. 6-12). (978-0-395-77540-0(X), 2-80109) Holt McDougal.

McLaren, Clemence. Aphrodite's Blessing. 2008. (ENG.). 208p. (YA). (gr. 7). pap. 10.99 (978-1-4169-7860-2(7), Simon Pulse) Simon Pulse.

McOmber, Rachel B., ed. McOmber Phonics Storybooks: Miss Vie. rev. ed. (Illus.). (J). (978-0-944991-48-0(3)) Swift Learning Resources.

Montgomery, L. M. Rilla of Ingleside. 2014. (ENG.). 352p. (J). (gr. 4-7). 10.99 (978-0-349-00451-8(X), Virago Press) Little, Brown Book Group Ltd. GBR. Dist: Hachette Bk. Group.

—Rilla of Ingleside. 2018. (Anne of Green Gables: the Complete Collection: 8). (ENG.). 384p. (J). (gr. 6-12). 8.99 (978-1-78226-450-7(7), cfbc195c-e9b8-4a84-95ac-215863ae0828) Sweet Cherry Publishing GBR. Dist: Baker & Taylor Publisher Services (BTPS).

—Rilla of Ingleside. 2018. (ENG., Illus.). 318p. (J). (gr. 3-7). 24.99 (978-1-5287-0642-1(0), Classic Bks. Library) The Editorium, LLC.

—Rilla of Ingleside. (ENG.). (J). (gr. 3-7). 2019. 620p. pap. 35.99 (978-1-6968-0677-0(1)) 2019. 620p. pap. 24.99 (978-1-7000-5633-7(6)) 2019. 304p. pap. 13.99 (978-1-7020-8869-5(3)) 2019. 620p. pap. 35.99 (978-1-6916-0307-7(4)) 2019. 620p. pap. 35.99 (978-1-6949-8152-3(5)) 2019. 446p. pap. 25.99 (978-1-0899-1414-3(8)) 2019. 446p. pap. 25.99 (978-1-0774-0973-6(7)) 2019. 446p. pap. 25.99 (978-1-0807-2142-9(8)) 2019. 446p. pap. 25.99 (978-1-0830-1928-8(7)) 2019. 446p. pap. 25.99 (978-1-0726-9464-9(6)) 2019. 446p. pap. 25.99 (978-1-0708-8975-7(X)) 2019. 416p. pap. 24.99 (978-1-0705-2920-2(6)) 2019. 612p. pap. 35.99 (978-1-0989-2752-3(4)) 2019. 614p. pap. 35.99 (978-1-0917-8411-6(6)) 2019. 614p. pap. 39.99 (978-1-7965-5879-1(6)) 2018. (Illus.). 292p. pap. 17.99 (978-1-7919-2181-1(7)) 2018. (Illus.). 374p. pap. 18.00 (978-1-7312-9023-6(3)) Independently Published.

—Rilla of Ingleside. 2019. (ENG.). 292p. (J). (gr. 3-7). pap. 30.99 (978-1-7077-9463-8(4)) Independently Published.

Montgomery, Lucy M. Rilla of Ingleside. 2019. (ENG.). (J). 246p. 19.95 (978-1-61895-649-1(3)); 244p. pap. 12.95 (978-1-61895-648-4(5)) Bibliotech Pr.

Montgomery, Lucy Maud. Rilla of Ingleside. (ENG.). (J). 2020. 258p. pap. 11.99 (978-1-6599-5975-8(6)) 2019. 208p. pap. 8.99 (978-1-6719-9670-0(4)) 2019. 270p. pap. 18.99 (978-1-0895-3763-2(8)) 2019. 612p. pap. 35.99 (978-1-6937-2182-3(1)) 2019. 612p. pap. 37.99 (978-1-0812-6709-4(7)) 2018. (Illus.). 542p. pap. 32.99 (978-1-7916-5647-8(1)) Independently Published.

Mora, Pat. Dona Flor: A Tall Tale about a Giant Woman with a Great Big Heart. ón, Raul, illus. 2005. (ENG.). 40p. (J). (gr. -1-2). 16.99 (978-0-375-82337-4(9), Knopf Bks. for Young Readers) Random Hse. Children's Bks.

Munro, Alice. Runaway. 2011. 14.75 (978-0-7848-3510-4(1), Everbind) Marco Bk. Co.

Murphy, Claire Rudolf. Marching with Aunt Susan: Susan B. Anthony & the Fight for Women's Suffrage, 1 vol. Schuett, Stacey, illus. 2017. 36p. (J). (gr. 1-4). pap. 8.99 (978-1-56145-979-7(8)) Peachtree Publishing Co. Inc.

Murray, Victoria Christopher. Diamond. 2008. (Divas Ser.). (ENG.). 224p. (gr. 8-12). pap. 11.00 (978-1-4165-6216-0(8), Gallery Bks.) Gallery Bks.

Nicholls, Sally. Things a Bright Girl Can Do. (ENG.). 432p. (YA). (gr. 7). 2018. pap. 15.99 (978-1-78344-673-5(0)) 2017. 24.99 (978-1-78344-525-7(4)) Andersen Pr. GBR. Dist: Independent Pubs. Group.

Novel Units. Ellen Tebbits Novel Units Teacher Guide. 2019. (ENG.). (J). pap. 12.99 (978-1-56137-387-1(7), Novel Units, Inc.) Classroom Library Co.

—Pride & Prejudice Novel Units Student Packet. 2019. (ENG.). (YA). pap. 13.99 (978-1-56137-767-1(8), Novel Units, Inc.) Classroom Library Co.

O'Brien, Robert C. La Senora Frisby y las Ratas de NIMH. (Barco de Vapor). (SPA., Illus.). 200p. (J). (gr. 4-7). 6.36 (978-84-348-1601-5(6), SM2855) SM Ediciones ESP. Dist: Lectorum Pubns., Inc.

Ostow, Micol. Family. 2011. (ENG.). 384p. (YA). (gr. 9-12). 17.99 (978-1-60684-155-6(6), 3cf413e9-28d9-4423-89bd-f642128d3c03, Carolrhoda Lab™) Lerner Publishing Group.

Page, P. K. The Old Woman & the Hen. 2008. (ENG., Illus.). 32p. (J). pap. 10.95 (978-0-88984-309-7(0)) Porcupine's Quill, Inc. CAN. Dist: Univ. of Toronto Pr.

Peters, Julie Anne. Rage: a Love Story. 2010. 304p. (YA). (gr. 9). pap. 9.99 (978-0-375-84411-9(2), Knopf Bks. for Young Readers) Random Hse. Children's Bks.

Pinkney, Andrea. Sojourner Truth's Step-Stomp Stride. Pinkney, Brian, illus. 2009. (ENG.). 32p. (J). (gr. 1-3). 18.99 (978-0-7868-0767-3(9), Jump at the Sun) Hyperion Bks. for Children.

Posner-Sanchez, Andrea. I Am Belle (Disney Beauty & the Beast) Batson, Alan, illus. 2017. (Little Golden Book Ser.). (ENG.). 24p. (J). (-k). 5.99 (978-0-7364-3905-3(6), Golden/Disney) Random Hse. Children's Bks.

—I Am the Beast (Disney Beauty & the Beast) Batson, Alan, illus. 2017. (Little Golden Book Ser.). (ENG.). 24p. (J). (-k). 4.99 (978-0-7364-3907-7(2), Golden/Disney) Random Hse. Children's Bks.

Rigby Education Staff. Birdwoman Interview. (Sails Literacy Ser.). (Illus.). 16p. (gr. 2-3). 27.00 (978-0-7635-9953-9(0), 699530C99) Rigby Education.

Riley, Lehman & Austin, Megan. The Life of Babe Didrikson: "Greatness Is Never Forgotten" Wallace, Joshua, illus. 2005. 47p. (J). pap. (978-0-9760523-2-6(6)) Matter of Africa America Time.

Rohner, Dorothia, illus. Effie's Image. 2006. 32p. (J). (gr. -1-3). 17.95 (978-0-9759829-5-2(8)) Prairieland Pr.

Rueda, Claudia, illus. I Know an Old Lady Who Swallowed a Fly. 2005. 14p. (J). 12.95 (978-1-58117-267-6(2), Intervisual/Piggy Toes) Bendon, Inc.

San Souci, Robert D. Cut from the Same Cloth: American Women of Myth, Legend, & Tall Tale. Pinkney, Brian, illus. 2005. 140p. 17.00 (978-0-7569-6284-5(6)) Perfection Learning Corp.

Scandora, Julie. Rules Are Rules. 2008. (ENG., Illus.). 32p. (gr. -1). 17.95 (978-1-887542-64-7(7)) Scandora.

Siegel, R. V. The Son of Olympia. 2005. 20p. 7.43 (978-1-4116-2888-5(8)) Lulu Pr., Inc.

Silverberg, Selma Kritzer. Naomi's Song. 2009. (ENG.). 142p. (gr. 7-18). pap. 19.95 (978-0-8276-0886-3(1)) Jewish Pubn. Society.

Smith, Sherri L. Flygirl. 2010. 304p. (YA). (gr. 7-18). 11.99 (978-0-14-241725-6(4), Penguin Books) Penguin Young Readers Group.

—Flygirl. 2010. lib. bdg. 19.65 (978-0-606-14999-0(6)) Turtleback.

Solnit, Rebecca. Cinderella Liberator. Rackham, Arthur, illus. 2019. (Fairy Tale Revolution Ser.). (ENG.). 32p. 17.95 (978-1-60846-596-5(9)) Haymarket Bks.

Sorell, Traci. At the Mountain's Base. Alvitre, Weshoyot, illus. 2019. 32p. (J). (gr. -1-3). 18.99 (978-0-7352-3060-6(9), Kokila) Penguin Young Readers Group.

Stockton, Frank Richard. Kate Bonnet: The Romance of a Pirate's Daughter. reprint ed. pap. 28.00 (978-1-4047-8937-1(5)) Classic Textbooks.

—Kate Bonnet: The Romance of a Pirate's Daughter. 2007. 364p. (J). (gr. -1-7). 46.95 (978-0-548-02295-5(X)) Kessinger Publishing, LLC.

—Kate Bonnet: The Romance of a Pirate's Daughter. 2005. 29.95 (978-1-59818-254-5(4)) Wildside Pr., LLC.

Sutton, Margaret. The Yellow Phantom: A Judy Bolton Mystery. Doane, Pelagie, illus. 2011. 222p. 44.95 (978-1-258-10044-5(4)) Literary Licensing, LLC.

Thomas, Jacquelin. Divine Match-Up. 2008. (ENG., Illus.). 288p. (gr. 8-12). pap. 19.99 (978-1-4165-5145-4(X), Gallery Bks.) Gallery Bks.

Turner, Morrie. Super Sistahs: Featuring the Accomplishments of African-American Women. 2005. (Illus.). 112p. pap. 14.95 (978-0-9656739-5-2(2)) BYE Publishing Services.

Vanasse, Deb. Cold Spell. 2014. (Alaska Literary Ser.). (ENG.). 224p. pap. 17.95 (978-1-60223-242-6(3)) Univ. of Alaska Pr.

Vanderhoop, Jannette, illus. The Legend of Katama: The Creation Story of Dolphins, A Wampanoag Legend of Martha's Vineyard. 2004. 80p. (J). lib. bdg. 18.95 (978-0-9755605-0-1(6)) Island Moon Pr.

Webb, Holly. A Little Princess Finds Her Voice. 2018. (ENG.). 208p. (J). (gr. 3-7). pap. 7.99 (978-1-4926-3912-1(5)) Sourcebooks, Inc.

Whitney, A. D. T. The Other Girls. l.t. ed. 2007. (ENG.). 398p. pap. 26.99 (978-1-4346-0103-2(X)) Creative Media Partners, LLC.

Whitney, Adeline Dutton Train. The Other Girls. 2016. (ENG., Illus.). (J). 29.95 (978-1-358-75955-0(3)) Creative Media Partners, LLC.

WOMEN—HISTORY

Adiletta, Dawn. Elizabeth Cady Stanton: Women's Suffrage & the First Vote, 1 vol. 2004. (Library of American Lives & Times Ser.). (ENG., Illus.). 112p. (J). (gr. 5-5). lib. bdg. 38.27 (978-1-4042-2647-0(8), c7dcb355-12ad-4a2b-9bd6-5e815734870e) Rosen Publishing Group, Inc., The.

Baum, Margaux & Hopkins, Andrea. The Lives of Women, 1 vol. 2016. (Life in the Middle Ages Ser.). (ENG.). 64p. (J). (gr. 5-5). E-Book 36.13 (978-1-4994-6467-2(3), a36b64b6-1644-4a2f-8051-fc2036dc7847) Rosen Publishing Group, Inc., The.

Chambers, Veronica & The Staff of The New York Times, The Staff. Finish the Fight! The Brave & Revolutionary Women Who Fought for the Right to Vote. The Staff of The New York Times, The Staff, illus. 2020. (ENG., Illus.). 144p. (J). (gr. 3-7). 18.99 (978-0-358-40830-7(X), 1789830, Versify) HarperCollins Pubs.

Clinton, Chelsea. She Persisted Around the World: 13 Women Who Changed History. Boiger, Alexandra, illus. (She Persisted Ser.). (J). 2020. 30p. (— 1). bds. 9.99 (978-0-593-20414-6(X)) 2018. 32p. (gr. -1-3). 18.99 (978-0-525-51699-6(9)) Penguin Young Readers Group. (Philomel Bks.).

de la Cruz, Melissa. Because I Was a Girl: True Stories for Girls of All Ages. 2017. (ENG., Illus.). 256p. (YA). 18.99 (978-1-250-15446-0(4), 900184433, Holt, Henry & Co. Bks. For Young Readers) Holt, Henry & Co.

Eastwood, Kay. Women & Girls in the Middle Ages, 1 vol. 2003. (Medieval World Ser.). (ENG., Illus.). 32p. (J). (gr. 5). pap. (978-0-7787-1378-4(4)) Crabtree Publishing Co.

Fun Fact File: Women in History. 2015. (Fun Fact File: Women in History Ser.). (ENG.). 32p. (J). (gr. 2-3). pap., pap., pap. 63.00 (978-1-4824-3474-3(1)); lib. bdg. 167.58 (978-1-4824-2548-2(3), 690fc1fc-886a-449f-b2ab-1deacddd4315) Stevens, Gareth Publishing LLLP.

Furbee, Mary Rodd. Outrageous Women of Civil War Times. 2003. (Outrageous Women Ser.: 7). (ENG., Illus.). 132p. (J). (gr. 5-9). pap. 14.95 (978-0-471-22926-1(1), Jossey-Bass) Wiley, John & Sons, Inc.

Gillibrand, Kirsten. Bold & Brave: Ten Heroes Who Won Women the Right to Vote. Kalman, Maira, illus. 40p. (J). (gr. 1-4). 2020. pap. 8.99 (978-0-593-30266-8(4), Dragonfly Bks.) 2018. 18.99 (978-0-525-57901-4(X), Knopf Bks. for Young Readers) 2018. (ENG.). lib. bdg. 21.99 (978-0-525-57902-1(8), Knopf Bks. for Young Readers) Random Hse. Children's Bks.

Gordon, Sherri Mabry. Violence Against Women. 2019. (Women & Society Ser.). (ENG.). 80p. (YA). (gr. 6-12). (978-1-68282-545-7(0)) ReferencePoint Pr., Inc.

Hopkins, Andrea. Damsels Not in Distress: The Lives of Medieval Women, 1 vol. 2003. (Library of the Middle Ages Ser.). (ENG., Illus.). 64p. (YA). (gr. 5-8). lib. bdg. 37.13 (978-0-8239-3992-3(8), c64f320d-bfae-494a-972b-de632740c82e) Rosen Publishing Group, Inc., The.

—Damsels Not in Distress: The True Story of Women in Medieval Times. 2009. (Library of the Middle Ages Ser.). 64p. (gr. 5-8). 58.50 (978-1-60853-898-0(2), Rosen Reference) Rosen Publishing Group, Inc., The.

Hubbard, Ben, et al. Women's Stories from History. 2015. (Women's Stories from History Ser.). (ENG.). 112p. (J). (gr. 6-11). 138.60 (978-1-4846-0867-8(4), 22341, Heinemann) Capstone.

Huntley, Theresa. Women in the Renaissance. 2009. (ENG., Illus.). 32p. (J). (gr. 5-7). (978-0-7787-4598-3(8)); (gr. 6-9). pap. (978-0-7787-4618-8(6)) Crabtree Publishing Co.

Jenner, Caryn. Amazing Women. 2017. (Illus.). 96p. (J). (978-1-5182-2593-2(4)) Dorling Kindersley Publishing, Inc.

Kramer, Ann. Women & War. 2009. (J). 24.25 (978-1-59771-142-5(X)) Sea-To-Sea Pubns.

Langley, Andrew. Stories of Women in World War II: We Can Do It! 2015. (Women's Stories from History Ser.). (ENG., Illus.). 112p. (J). (gr. 6-11). 32.65 (978-1-4846-0865-4(8), 127948, Heinemann) Capstone.

Levy, Janey. 20 Fun Facts about Women of the Middle Ages, 1 vol. 2015. (Fun Fact File: Women in History Ser.). (ENG., Illus.). 32p. (J). (gr. 2-3). pap. 11.50 (978-1-4824-2824-7(5), 79ef435d-dc51-4e5b-8c2a-66b65f95d03f) Stevens, Gareth Publishing LLLP.

Libal, Autumn. Women in the World of Russia. 2006. (Women's Issues, Global Trends Ser.). (Illus.). 112p. (YA). lib. bdg. 22.95 (978-1-59084-866-1(7)) Mason Crest.

Lopez, Elizabeth Anderson. Mujeres Que Cambiaron el Mundo. rev. ed. 2019. (Social Studies: Informational Text Ser.). (SPA., Illus.). 32p. (J). (gr. 2-3). pap. 11.99 (978-1-64290-116-0(4)) Teacher Created Materials, Inc.

—Women Who Changed the World. rev. ed. 2018. (Social Studies: Informational Text Ser.). (ENG., Illus.). 32p. (J). (gr. 2-3). pap. 11.99 (978-1-4258-2517-1(6)) Teacher Created Materials, Inc.

Morrison, Jessica. Women's Issues. 2010. (Illus.). 48p. (978-1-55388-689-1(5)); pap. (978-1-55388-694-5(1)) Weigl Educational Pubs. Ltd.

Mundy, Liza. Code Girls: The True Story of the American Women Who Secretly Broke Codes in World War II (Young Readers Edition) (ENG., Illus.). 336p. (J). (gr. 3-7). 2019. pap. 8.99 (978-0-316-35377-9(9)) 2018. 17.99 (978-0-316-35373-1(6)) Little, Brown Bks. for Young Readers.

Perry, Phyllis Jean. Bold Women in Colorado History. 2012. (Illus.). v, 153p. (J). pap. (978-0-87842-584-6(5)) Mountain Pr. Publishing Co., Inc.

Pitman, Gayle E. Feminism from a to Z. Beith, Laura Huliska, illus. 2017. (ENG.). 254p. (J). E-Book (978-1-4338-2861-4(8), Magination Pr.) American Psychological Assn.

Rajczak Nelson, Kristen. 20 Fun Facts about Women in Ancient Greece & Rome, 1 vol. 2015. (Fun Fact File: Women in History Ser.). (ENG., Illus.). 32p. (J). (gr. 2-3). 27.93 (978-1-4824-2818-6(0), 4d434707-8ead-41ea-a037-4a8b7544ab7a) Stevens, Gareth Publishing LLLP.

Schatz, Kate. Rad Women Worldwide: Artists & Athletes, Pirates & Punks, & Other Revolutionaries Who Shaped History. Klein Stahl, Miriam, illus. 2016. (Rad Women Ser.). 112p. (gr. 5-12). 15.99 (978-0-399-57886-1(2), Ten Speed Pr.) Potter/Ten Speed/Harmony/Rodale.

Sharp, Anne Wallace. Women of Ancient Egypt. 2005. (Women in History Ser.). (ENG., Illus.). 112p. (YA). (gr. 7-10). lib. bdg. 33.45 (978-1-59018-361-8(4), Lucent Bks.) Cengage Gale.

Simpson, Kathleen. Women in the Renaissance: Set Of 6. 2011. (Navigators Ser.). (J). pap. 50.00 net. (978-1-4108-6266-2(6)) Benchmark Education Co.

—Women in the Renaissance: Text Pairs. 2008. (Bridges/Navigators Ser.). (J). (gr. 6). 89.00 (978-1-4108-8449-7(X)) Benchmark Education Co.

Swisher, Clarice. Women of Victorian England. 2004. (Women in History Ser.). (ENG., Illus.). 112p. (YA). (gr. 7-12). lib. bdg. 33.45 (978-1-59018-571-1(4), Lucent Bks.) Cengage Gale.

Thomson, Melissa & Dean, Ruth. Women of the Renaissance. 2004. (Women in History Ser.). (ENG., Illus.). 128p. (YA). (gr. 7-10). lib. bdg. 33.45 (978-1-59018-473-8(4), Lucent Bks.) Cengage Gale.

The Trail West. 2004. (Illus.). lib. bdg. 7.95 (978-0-8225-4283-4(8)) Lerner Publishing Group.

Women Groundbreakers. 2015. (Women Groundbreakers Ser.). (ENG.). 32p. (J). (gr. 4-5). pap., pap., pap. 360.00 (978-1-4994-1331-1(9), PowerKids Pr.) Rosen Publishing Group, Inc., The.

WOMEN—OCCUPATIONS

see Women—Employment

WOMEN—POLITICAL ACTIVITY

Aung San Suu Kyi, 1 vol. 2014. (Making a Difference: Leaders Who Are Changing the World Ser.). (ENG.). 48p. (J). (gr. 5-5). 28.41 (978-1-62275-430-4(1), 3b9d3618-deef-408a-8be8-7609435eb295) Rosen Publishing Group, Inc., The.

Bjorklund, Ruth. Aung San Suu Kyi, 1 vol. 2013. (Leading Women Ser.). (ENG.). 112p. (YA). (gr. 7-7). 42.64 (978-0-7614-4957-7(4), aaeb6ec8-3828-42f0-a34b-f07a093c2906); pap. 20.99 (978-1-62712-115-6(3), 2e888710-6001-4d60-82a9-ab8036eb7ebd) Cavendish Square Publishing LLC.

Cham, Stephanie. Tammy Duckworth. 2018. (Great Asian Americans Ser.). (ENG., Illus.). 24p. (J). (gr. -1-2). lib. bdg. 27.32 (978-1-5157-9955-9(7), 136953, Capstone Pr.) Capstone.

Coleman, Miriam. Mujeres en la Politica (Women in Politics), 1 vol. 2015. (Ellas Abrieron Camino (Women Groundbreakers Ser.). (SPA.). 32p. (J). (gr. 4-5). 27.93 (978-1-4994-0547-7(2), 87935073-2872-4247-a243-2d836045dfba, PowerKids Pr.) Rosen Publishing Group, Inc., The.

—Women in Politics, 1 vol. 2015. (Women Groundbreakers Ser.). (ENG., Illus.). 32p. (J). (gr. 4-5). 27.93 (978-1-4994-1084-6(0), 89a115f2-a431-4727-a06c-c8c479b222a9, PowerKids Pr.) Rosen Publishing Group, Inc., The.

Cooper, Meghan. The Women's Suffrage Movement, 1 vol. 2017. (Interwar Years Ser.). (ENG., Illus.). 128p. (YA). (gr. 9-9). 47.36 (978-1-5026-2711-7(6), 9fba2995-9bb5-4c20-8af0-ef0382acad3f) Cavendish Square Publishing LLC.

Crysdale, Joy. Courageous Women Rebels, 1 vol. 2013. (Women's Hall of Fame Ser.: 18). (ENG.). 128p. (J). (gr. 6-8). pap. 10.95 (978-1-926920-99-3(6)) Second Story Pr. CAN. Dist: Orca Bk. Pubs. USA.

Cunningham, Anne C. Women Political Leaders, 1 vol. 2016. (Defying Convention: Women Who Changed the Rules Ser.). (ENG., Illus.). 128p. (gr. 6-6). 38.93 (978-0-7660-8141-3(9), ece5a50d-0bf7-42a0-aedc-092002e7118c) Enslow Publishing, LLC.

Dillon, Molly, compiled by. Yes She Can: 10 Stories of Hope & Change from Young Female Staffers of the Obama White House. 2019. (Illus.). 288p. (YA). (gr. 7). 18.99 (978-1-9848-4845-1(3), Schwartz & Wade Bks.) Random Hse. Children's Bks.

Doak, Robin S. Hillary Clinton. 2013. (True Book: Biographies Ser.). (ENG., Illus.). 48p. (J). (gr. 3-5). lib. bdg. 21.19 (978-0-531-21906-5(2), Children's Pr.); pap. 6.95 (978-0-531-23877-6(6)) Scholastic Library Publishing.

Donohue, Caitlin. She Represents: 44 Women Who Are Changing Politics ... & the World. 2020. (ENG., Illus.). 216p. (YA). (gr. 8-12). pap. 16.99 (978-1-5415-7901-9(1), 211f4145-8df6-4719-b92d-3cba3a65ff9b, Zest Bks.) Lerner Publishing Group.

D'Orio, Wayner. Carol Moseley-Braun. 2003. (African American Leaders Ser.). (ENG., Illus.). 112p. (gr. 6-12). 30.00 (978-0-7910-7684-2(9), P113973, Facts On File) Infobase Holdings, Inc.

Friedman, Lita. Mary Robinson: Fighter for Human Rights. 2004. (Avisson Young Adult Ser.). (Illus.). 142p. (YA). pap. 19.95 (978-1-888105-65-0(8)) Avisson Pr., Inc.

Furstinger, Nancy. Women & Leadership, 1 vol. 2012. (Young Woman's Guide to Contemporary Issues Ser.). (ENG., Illus.). 112p. (YA). (gr. 8-9). lib. bdg. 39.80 (978-1-4488-8402-5(0), 54a004f4-ae4b-49b1-9c48-d0eb4f2eb510) Rosen Publishing Group, Inc., The.

Gottesfeld, Jeff. No Steps Behind: Beate Sirota Gordon's Battle for Women's Rights in Japan. Witanto, Shiella, illus. 2020. (ENG.). 44p. (J). (gr. 3-6). 18.99 (978-1-939547-55-2(5), 5357f810-90f0-4121-9d40-eb5fa01c8b11) Creston Bks.

Hanson-Harding, Alexandra. Activism: Taking on Women's Issues, 1 vol. 2012. (Young Woman's Guide to Contemporary Issues Ser.). (ENG., Illus.). 112p. (YA). (gr. 8-9). lib. bdg. 39.80 (978-1-4488-8401-8(2), f069fb3b-b51e-4963-9933-3115802d1b4f) Rosen Publishing Group, Inc., The.

Harris, Duchess & Head, Deirdre R. J. Barbara Jordan: Politician & Civil Rights Leader. 2018. (Freedom's Promise Ser.). (ENG., Illus.). 48p. (J). (gr. 4-8). lib. bdg. 35.64 (978-1-5321-1766-4(3), 30820) ABDO Publishing Co.

Henneberg, Susan, ed. Gender Politics, 1 vol. 2016. (At Issue Ser.). (ENG.). 120p. (YA). (gr. 10-12). pap. 28.80 (978-1-5345-0041-9(3), 52f77ffb-b619-480e-bc4e-71b562834b7b); lib. bdg. 41.03 (978-1-5345-0014-3(6), fcc4c713-c3f2-4b16-a860-e5fcf5126551) Greenhaven Publishing LLC. (Greenhaven Publishing).

Hinman, Bonnie. Ivanka Trump: Businesswoman & Political Activist. 2017. (Newsmakers Set 2 Ser.). (ENG., Illus.). 48p. (J). (gr. 4-8). lib. bdg. 35.64 (978-1-5321-1186-0(X), 25948) ABDO Publishing Co.

Hurt, Avery Elizabeth. Women in Politics, 1 vol. 2017. (Women in the World Ser.). (ENG., Illus.). 112p. (gr. 6-6). 38.80 (978-1-5081-7449-3(0), 284b23b4-63c7-4513-80eb-afa59e1e51e8, Rosen Young Adult) Rosen Publishing Group, Inc., The.

Hurt, Avery Elizabeth, ed. Gender Diversity in Government, 1 vol. 2019. (Global Viewpoints Ser.). (ENG.). 200p. (gr. 10-12). 47.83 (978-1-5345-0557-5(1), 66827825-8b20-438b-a00a-2fe38a76ce73) Greenhaven Publishing LLC.

Irma Rangel, 1 vol. 2014. (Great Women in History Ser.). (ENG., Illus.). 24p. (J). (gr. -1-2). lib. bdg. 24.65 (978-1-4914-0538-3(4), 125890, Pebble) Capstone.

Kaiser, Lisbeth. Emmeline Pankhurst, Volume 8. Sanfelippo, Ana, illus. 2017. (Little People, BIG DREAMS Ser.: 8). (ENG.). 32p. (J). (gr. k-3). 15.99 (978-1-78603-020-7(9), Frances Lincoln Children's Bks.) Quarto Publishing Group UK GBR. Dist: Hachette Bk. Group.

Kamps, Louisa, et al. Girl Activist. Rucker, Georgia, illus. 2019. (Generation Girl Ser.). (ENG.). 160p. (J). (gr. 4). pap. 12.99 (978-1-941367-64-3(X)) Downtown Bookworks.

Koya, Lena & Hanson-Harding, Alexandra. Female Activists, 1 vol. 2017. (Women in the World Ser.). (ENG., Illus.). 112p. (J). (gr. 6-6). 38.80 (978-1-5081-7720-3(1), 9b65c2f8-cabf-4233-ba96-02fa13e7d951); pap. 18.65 (978-1-5081-7883-5(6), 939d0056-a509-4316-8086-4a094b81a502) Rosen Publishing Group, Inc., The.

ull, Kathleen. A Woman for President: The Story of Victoria Woodhull. Dyer, Jane, illus. 2006. (J). (gr. 2-7). 14.60 *(978-0-7569-8179-2(4))* Perfection Learning Corp.
igh, Anna. Aly Raisman: Athlete & Activist. 2019. (Gateway Biographies Ser.). (ENG., Illus.). 48p. (J). (gr. 4-8). lib. bdg. 31.99 *(978-1-5415-4261-7(4),* 7f2fb359-a94f-4539-bd0f-586db1fb54fe, Lerner Pubns.) Lerner Publishing Group.
oh-Hagan, Virginia. Girl Activists. 2019. (History's Yearbook Ser.). (ENG., Illus.). 32p. (J). (gr. 4-8). pap. 14.21 *(978-1-5341-5077-5(3),* 213615); lib. bdg. 32.07 *(978-1-5341-4791-1(8),* 213614) Cherry Lake Publishing. (45th Parallel Press).
aathai, Wangari. How I Changed the World. 2018. (J). *(978-0-7166-2283-3(1))* World Bk., Inc.
lanion, Jennifer. Safia AMA Jan. 2011. (J). lib. bdg. *(978-0-8225-9038-5(7))* Twenty First Century Bks.
larcovitz, Hal. Eleanor Holmes Norton. 2003. (African American Leaders Ser.). (ENG., Illus.). 112p. (gr. 6-12). 30.00 *(978-0-7910-7682-8(2),* P113971, Facts On File) Infobase Holdings, Inc.
larsh, Carole. The First Woman President of the U. S. 2007. 48p. pap. 7.95 *(978-0-635-06404-2(9))* Gallopade International.
McElroy, Lisa Tucker. Nancy Pelosi. 2008. pap. 52.95 *(978-0-8225-9477-2(3))* Lerner Publishing Group.
Miller, Debra A., ed. Women in Politics, 1 vol. 2012. (Current Controversies Ser.). (ENG.). 168p. (gr. 10-12). pap. 33.00 *(978-0-7377-6250-1(0),* 0d6dc3f5-914a-46b7-b56b-495cf13532e8); lib. bdg. 48.03 *(978-0-7377-6249-5(7),* bfff8edf-097c-45bb-9133-1ebe9a2a4a7b) Greenhaven Publishing LLC. (Greenhaven Publishing).
Moening, Kate. Malala Yousafzai: Education Activist. 2019. (Women Leading the Way Ser.). (ENG., Illus.). 24p. (J). (gr. k-3). pap. 7.99 *(978-1-61891-724-9(2),* 12305); lib. bdg. 26.95 *(978-1-64487-101-0(7))* Bellwether Media. (Blastoff! Readers).
Naden, Corinne. Benazir Bhutto, 1 vol. 2011. (Leading Women Ser.). (ENG., Illus.). 96p. (J). (gr. 7-7). 42.64 *(978-0-7614-4952-2(3),* 4cb4dc26-f281-494e-b9ea-ec4657c25e37) Cavendish Square Publishing LLC.
Nivola, Claire A. Planting the Trees of Kenya: The Story of Wangari Maathai. Nivola, Claire A., illus. 2008. (ENG., Illus.). 32p. (J). (gr. k-3). 19.99 *(978-0-374-39918-4(2),* 900042039, Farrar, Straus & Giroux (BYR)) Farrar, Straus & Giroux.
Ohlin, Nancy. Women's Suffrage. Simó, Roger, illus. 2018. (Blast Back! Ser.). (ENG.). 112p. (J). (gr. 2-5). 16.99 *(978-1-4998-0619-9(1));* pap. 5.99 *(978-1-4998-0618-2(3))* Little Bee Books Inc.
Paulus, Rajdeep. The Most Influential Women in Politics, 1 vol. 2018. (Breaking the Glass Ceiling: the Most Influential Women Ser.). (ENG.). 112p. (gr. 8-8). 40.13 *(978-1-5081-7968-9(9),* 84b1d5fc-6861-43a5-9eed-63eddbecb077) Rosen Publishing Group, Inc., The.
Raatma, Lucia. Barbara Jordan, 1 vol. 2013. (Leading Women Ser.). (ENG.). 96p. (YA). (gr. 7-7). 42.64 *(978-0-7614-4956-0(6),* bbcd5f27-0fcc-47f5-88e7-57e8052fa895) Cavendish Square Publishing LLC.
Ross, Michael Elsohn. She Takes a Stand: 16 Fearless Activists Who Have Changed the World. (Women of Action Ser.). (ENG., Illus.). 208p. (YA). (gr. 7). 2019. pap. 14.99 *(978-1-64160-045-3(4))* 2015. 19.95 *(978-1-61373-026-3(8))* Chicago Review Pr., Inc.
Sarantou, Katlin. Tammy Duckworth. Bane, Jeff, illus. 2019. (My Early Library: My Itty-Bitty Bio Ser.). (ENG.). 24p. (J). (gr. k-1). pap. 12.79 *(978-1-5341-4990-8(2),* 213267); lib. bdg. 30.64 *(978-1-5341-4704-1(7),* 213266) Cherry Lake Publishing.
Shepherd, Jodie. Hillary Clinton. 2015. (Rookie Biographies(r) Ser.). (ENG., Illus.). 32p. (J). lib. bdg. 23.00 *(978-0-531-20592-1(4))* Scholastic Library Publishing.
Sherman, Jill. Donald Trump: Outspoken Personality & President. 2017. (Gateway Biographies Ser.). (ENG., Illus.). 48p. (J). (gr. 4-8). lib. bdg. 31.99 *(978-1-5124-2596-3(6),* 73ddd6e7-9543-41d2-9c95-2b6efefcc36c, Lerner Pubns.) Lerner Publishing Group.
—25 Mujeres Que Dieron Batalla. Aparicio Publishing LLC, Aparicio Publishing, tr. 2020. (Mujeres Valientes Ser.). Tr. of 25 Women Who Fought Back. (SPA., Illus.). 64p. (J). (gr. 7-12). lib. bdg. 37.32 *(978-0-7565-6537-4(5),* 142067, Compass Point Bks.) Capstone.
—25 Women Who Fought Back. 2018. (Daring Women Ser.). (ENG., Illus.). 64p. (J). (gr. 7-12). lib. bdg. 35.32 *(978-0-7565-5850-5(6),* 138478, Compass Point Bks.) Capstone.
Sherman, Patrice. Aung San Suu Kyi: Peaceful Resistance to the Burmese Military Junta, 1 vol. 2017. (Peaceful Protesters Ser.). (ENG.). 112p. (YA). (gr. 9-9). 44.50 *(978-1-5026-3110-7(5),* 14935aae-2a56-4bed-ab2b-1a6377bfad34); pap. 20.99 *(978-1-5026-3398-9(1),* 4a2f2457-bd6e-42b2-bafd-7a67db2018fd) Cavendish Square Publishing LLC.
Somervill, Barbara A. Votes for Women! The Story of Carrie Chapman Catt. 2004. (Feminist Voices Ser.). (Illus.). 128p. (YA). (gr. 6-12). 23.95 *(978-1-883846-96-1(X),* First Biographies) Reynolds, Morgan Inc.
Thimmesh, Catherine. Madam President: The Extraordinary, True (and Evolving) Story of Women in Politics. Jones, Douglas B., illus. 2008. (ENG.). 80p. (J). (gr. 1-4). pap. 9.99 *(978-0-618-97143-5(2),* 1023070, Clarion Bks.) HarperCollins Pubs.
Tracy, Kathleen. The Historic Fight for the 2008 Democratic Presidential Nomination: The Clinton View. 2009. (Monumental Milestones Ser.). (Illus.). 48p. (YA). (gr. 4-7). lib. bdg. 29.95 *(978-1-58415-731-1(3))* Mitchell Lane Pubs.
Ventura, Marne. Hillary Clinton: Historic Politician. 2017. (Newsmakers Set 2 Ser.). (ENG., Illus.). 48p. (J). (gr. 4-8). lib. bdg. 35.64 *(978-1-5321-1181-5(9),* 25938) ABDO Publishing Co.
Winter, Jeanette. Wangari's Trees of Peace: A True Story from Africa. Winter, Jeanette, illus. (ENG., Illus.). 32p. (J). (gr. -1-3). 2018. pap. 8.99 *(978-1-328-86921-0(0),* 1696685) 2008. 17.99 *(978-0-15-206545-4(8),* 1199505) HarperCollins Pubs. (Clarion Bks.).
Women in Politics. 2005. (Women in Politics Ser.). 112p. (gr. 6-12). 120.00 *(978-0-7910-7730-6(6),* Facts On File) Infobase Holdings, Inc.
Woodward, Kay. What Would She Do?: 25 True Stories of Trailblazing Rebel Women. 2018. (ENG.). 112p. (J). (gr. 3-7). 16.99 *(978-1-338-21640-0(6))* Scholastic, Inc.

WOMEN—SUFFRAGE

see also Suffragists

Adiletta, Dawn. Elizabeth Cady Stanton: Women's Suffrage & the First Vote. (Library of American Lives & Times Ser.). 112p. (gr. 5-5). 2009. 69.20 *(978-1-60853-479-1(0))* 2004. (ENG., Illus.). (J). lib. bdg. 38.27 *(978-1-4042-2647-0(8),* c7dcb355-12ad-4a2b-9bd6-5e815734870e) Rosen Publishing Group, Inc., The.
Barber, Lynn. Champions for Women's Rights: Matilda Joslyn Gage, Julia Ward Howe, Lucretia Mott, & Lucy Stone, 1 vol. 2016. (Heroes of the Women's Suffrage Movement Ser.). (ENG., Illus.). 128p. (gr. 6-6). 38.93 *(978-0-7660-7891-8(4),* eaa758a8-6dcc-4701-9fbb-ec0b9d1106c4) Enslow Publishing, LLC.
Bardhan-Quallen, Sudipta. Ballots for Belva: The True Story of a Woman's Race for the Presidency. Martin, Courtney A., illus. 2015. (ENG.). 32p. (J). (gr. k-2). pap. 12.99 *(978-1-4197-1627-0(1),* 650103) Abrams, Inc.
Bausum, Ann. With Courage & Cloth: More Than 100 Recipes & Foolproof Strategies to Help Your Kids Fall in Love. 2004. (Illus.). 112p. (J). (gr. 5-9). 21.95 *(978-0-7922-7647-0(7),* National Geographic Kids) Disney Publishing Worldwide.
Bjornlund, Lydia D. Women of the Suffrage Movement. 2003. (Women in History Ser.). (ENG., Illus.). 112p. (J). 33.45 *(978-1-59018-173-7(5),* Lucent Bks.) Cengage Gale.
Carson, Mary Kay. Who Was Susan B. Anthony Vote? And Other Questions about Women's Suffrage. 2015. (Good Question! Ser.). (ENG., Illus.). 32p. (J). (gr. 2). pap. 5.95 *(978-1-4549-1242-2(1))* Sterling Publishing Co., Inc.
Chambers, Veronica & The Staff of The New York Times, The Staff. Finish the Fight! The Brave & Revolutionary Women Who Fought for the Right to Vote. The Staff of The New York Times, The Staff, illus. 2020. (ENG., Illus.). 144p. (J). (gr. 3-7). 18.99 *(978-0-358-40830-7(X),* 1789830, Versify) HarperCollins Pubs.
Ching, Jacqueline. Abigail Adams: A Revolutionary Woman. 2009. (Library of American Lives & Times Ser.). 112p. (gr. 5-5). 69.20 *(978-1-60853-469-2(3))* Rosen Publishing Group, Inc., The.
Cooper, Meghan. The Women's Suffrage Movement, 1 vol. 2017. (Interwar Years Ser.). (ENG., Illus.). 128p. (YA). (gr. 9-9). 47.36 *(978-1-5026-2711-7(6),* 9fba2995-9bb5-4c20-8af0-ef0382acad3f) Cavendish Square Publishing LLC.
Day, Meredith & Adams, Colleen. A Primary Source Investigation of Women's Suffrage, 1 vol. 2015. (Uncovering American History Ser.). (ENG., Illus.). 64p. (J). (gr. 5-6). 36.13 *(978-1-4994-3519-1(3),* 660575d3-b2a5-4086-afca-025534c3c917, Rosen Central) Rosen Publishing Group, Inc., The.
DeAngelis, Therese. Women's Rights on the Frontier. 2012. (Illus.). 64p. (J). pap. *(978-1-4222-2369-7(8))* Mason Crest.
—Women's Rights on the Frontier. Harrington, A. Page, ed. 2012. (Finding a Voice: Women's Fight for Equality in U. S. Society Ser.). (Illus.). 64p. (J). (gr. 5). 22.95 *(978-1-4222-2359-8(0))* Mason Crest.
Frazer, Coral Celeste. Vote! Women's Fight for Access to the Ballot Box. 2019. (ENG., Illus.). 120p. (YA). (gr. 6-12). lib. bdg. 37.32 *(978-1-5415-2815-4(8),* a74c63c5-3458-47e1-8e30-cadd30fc7cec, Twenty-First Century Bks.) Lerner Publishing Group.
Fredericks, Carrie, ed. Amendment XIX: Granting Women the Right to Vote, 1 vol. 2009. (Constitutional Amendments: Beyond the Bill of Rights Ser.). (ENG., Illus.). 168p. (gr. 10-12). lib. bdg. 44.83 *(978-0-7377-4127-8(9),* 67e57581-d0bf-46db-8448-2e20baa77e48, Greenhaven Publishing) Greenhaven Publishing LLC.
Gelletly, LeeAnne. Seeking Th Right to Vote. 2012. (J). pap. *(978-1-4222-2364-2(7))* Mason Crest.
—Seeking Th Right to Vote. Harrington, A. Page, ed. 2012. (Finding a Voice: Women's Fight for Equality in U. S. Society Ser.). 64p. (J). (gr. 5). 22.95 *(978-1-4222-2354-3(X))* Mason Crest.
Gillibrand, Kirsten. Bold & Brave: Ten Heroes Who Won Women the Right to Vote. Kalman, Maira, illus. 40p. (J). (gr. 1-4). 2020. pap. 8.99 *(978-0-593-30266-8(4),* Dragonfly Bks.) 2018. 18.99 *(978-0-525-57901-4(X),* Knopf Bks. for Young Readers) 2018. (ENG.). lib. bdg. 21.99 *(978-0-525-57902-1(8),* Knopf Bks. for Young Readers) Random Hse. Children's Bks.
Goddu, Krystyna Poray. What's Your Story, Susan B. Anthony? 2016. (Cub Reporter Meets Famous Americans Ser.). (ENG., Illus.). 32p. (J). (gr. k-3). 26.65 *(978-1-4677-8785-7(X),* 199ae9d8-e2ff-4af1-8a22-f4579b2b7584, Lerner Pubns.) Lerner Publishing Group.
Guillain, Charlotte. Stories of Women's Suffrage: Votes for Women! 2015. (Women's Stories from History Ser.). (ENG., Illus.). 112p. (J). (gr. 6-11). 32.65 *(978-1-4846-0864-7(X),* 127947, Heinemann) Capstone.
Harris, Duchess. Women's Suffrage. 2017. (Protest Movements Ser.). (ENG.). 48p. (J). (gr. 4-8). lib. bdg. 35.64 *(978-1-5321-1399-4(4),* 27697) ABDO Publishing Co.
Hicks, Peter. Documenting Women's Suffrage, 1 vol. (Documenting History Ser.). (ENG., Illus.). 48p. (gr. 7-7). 2010. (YA). lib. bdg. 34.47 *(978-1-4358-9672-7(6),* 64e2f741-0196-4463-9572-81ba734a002c) 2009. (J). pap. 12.75 *(978-1-4358-9675-8(0),* 8051fc89-f56d-4c1d-93b0-cc7f216609cf, Rosen Reference) Rosen Publishing Group, Inc., The.
Hollihan, Kerrie Logan. Rightfully Ours: How Women Won the Vote, 21 Activities. 2012. (For Kids Ser.: 43). (ENG., Illus.). 144p. (J). (gr. 4). pap. 18.99 *(978-1-883052-89-8(0))* Chicago Review Pr., Inc.
Isecke, Harriet. Women's Suffrage: Fighting for Women's Rights. rev. ed. 2011. (Social Studies: Informational Text Ser.). (ENG.). 32p. (gr. 4-8). pap. 11.99 *(978-1-4333-1507-7(6))* Teacher Created Materials, Inc.
Kennedy, Nancy B. Women Win the Vote! 19 for the 19th Amendment. 2020. (ENG., Illus.). 128p. (J). (gr. 5-9). 19.95 *(978-1-324-00414-1(2),* 340414, Norton Young Readers) Norton, W. W. & Co., Inc.
Kent, Deborah. Elizabeth Cady Stanton: Founder of the Women's Suffrage Movement, 1 vol. 2016. (Heroes of the Women's Suffrage Movement Ser.). (ENG.). 128p. (gr. 6-6). 38.93 *(978-0-7660-7889-5(2),* 05025743-f964-4f6c-8e70-67989020d66a) Enslow Publishing, LLC.
Keppeler, Jill. Women's Suffrage Movement. 2017. (Civic Participation: Fighting for Rights Ser.). (ENG.). 32p. (J). (gr. 3-6). 21.80 *(978-1-5311-8872-6(9))* Perfection Learning Corp.
—Women's Suffrage Movement, 1 vol. 2016. (Civic Participation: Working for Civil Rights Ser.). (ENG.). 32p. (J). (gr. 5-5). pap. 11.00 *(978-1-4994-2685-4(2),* 26bc7299-33a3-49c0-91f8-52180b7ed231, PowerKids Pr.) Rosen Publishing Group, Inc., The.
Kops, Deborah. Alice Paul & the Fight for Women's Rights: From the Vote to the Equal Rights Amendment. 2017. (ENG., Illus.). 216p. (J). (gr. 5-12). 17.95 *(978-1-62979-323-8(X),* Calkins Creek) Highlights Pr., c/o Highlights for Children, Inc.
Koutras Bozonelis, Helen. A Look at the Nineteenth Amendment: Women Win the Right to Vote, 1 vol. 2009. (Constitution of the United States Ser.). (ENG., Illus.). 128p. (gr. 6-7). lib. bdg. 37.27 *(978-1-59845-067-5(0),* 9f5185c8-2fb9-494e-b9d5-673cfd539b25) Enslow Publishing, LLC.
Light, Kate. Questions & Answers about Women's Suffrage, 1 vol. 2018. (Eye on Historical Sources Ser.). (ENG.). 32p. (gr. 4-4). 27.93 *(978-1-5383-4135-3(2),* 4c7896f8-c1cc-40c8-bae7-f0586c7e95ce, PowerKids Pr.) Rosen Publishing Group, Inc., The.
Lynch, Seth. Women's Suffrage, 1 vol. 2018. (Look at U. S. History Ser.). (ENG.). 32p. (gr. 2-2). 28.27 *(978-1-5382-2135-8(7),* 325fee0c-fff5-468c-8535-021f02d59803) Stevens, Gareth Publishing LLLP.
Macbain-Stephens, Jennifer. Women's Suffrage: Giving the Right to Vote to All Americans, 1 vol. 2006. (Progressive Movement 1900 - 1920: Efforts to Reform America's New Industrial Society Ser.). (ENG., Illus.). 32p. (YA). (gr. 3-4). lib. bdg. 30.47 *(978-1-4042-0199-6(8),* 6bb8ef4c-2263-4ebe-bc6b-96b44ecb9683) Rosen Publishing Group, Inc., The.
MacBain-Stephens, Jennifer. Women's Suffrage: Giving the Right to Vote to All Americans. 2009. (Progressive Movement 1900-1920: Efforts to Reform America's New Industrial Society Ser.). 32p. (gr. 3-4). 47.90 *(978-1-60854-175-1(4))* Rosen Publishing Group, Inc., The.
MacDonald, Fiona. Be a Suffragist! A Protest Movement That's Rougher Than You Expected. Antram, David, illus. 2008. (You Wouldn't Want To... Ser.). (ENG.). 32p. (J). (gr. 4-6). 26.19 *(978-0-531-20701-7(3))* Scholastic Library Publishing.
—You Wouldn't Want to Be a Suffragist! A Protest Movement That's Rougher Than You Expected. Antram, David, illus. 2008. (You Wouldn't Want to...: History of the World Ser.). (ENG.). 32p. (J). (gr. 3-18). pap. 9.95 *(978-0-531-21911-9(9),* Watts, Franklin) Scholastic Library Publishing.
Malaspina, Ann. Heart on Fire: Susan B. Anthony Votes for President. James, Steve, illus. 2012. (ENG.). 32p. (J). (gr. 1-3). 17.99 *(978-0-8075-3188-4(X),* 080753188X) Whitman, Albert & Co.
McConnell, Robert L. & Baxter, Kathleen, contrib. by. The Split History of the Women's Suffrage Movement: A Perspectives Flip Book, 1 vol. 2014. (Perspectives Flip Bks.). (ENG., Illus.). 64p. (J). (gr. 5-9). lib. bdg. 34.65 *(978-0-7565-4735-6(0),* 124392, Compass Point Bks.) Capstone.
Metz, Lorijo. El Movimiento Por el Sufragio Femenino / the Women's Suffrage Movement, 1 vol., 1. Beullens-Maoui, Nathalie, ed. 2013. (¡Celebremos la Libertad! / Let's Celebrate Freedom! Ser.). (SPA & ENG.). 24p. (J). (gr. 3-3). 26.27 *(978-1-4777-3250-2(0),* b6e46375-61dd-4ef7-99ff-c96e2f52f0b4, PowerKids Pr.) Rosen Publishing Group, Inc., The.
—The Women's Suffrage Movement, 1 vol., 1. 2013. (Let's Celebrate Freedom! Ser.). (ENG., Illus.). 24p. (J). (gr. 3-3). 26.27 *(978-1-4777-2898-7(8),* 38e3511d-b727-4188-b743-c93ded4aae21, PowerKids Pr.) Rosen Publishing Group, Inc., The.
Mosley, Shelley & Charles, John. The Suffragists in Literature for Youth: The Fight for the Vote. annot. ed. 2006. (Literature for Youth Ser.: 10). (ENG.). 342p. (gr. 3-7). per. 87.00 *(978-0-8108-5372-0(8))* Scarecrow Pr., Inc.
National Geographic Learning. Language, Literacy & Vocabulary - Reading Expeditions (U. S. History & Life): Women Work for Change. 2006. (Avenues Ser.). (ENG., Illus.). 36p. (J). pap. 20.95 *(978-0-7922-5456-0(2))* CENGAGE Learning.
Ohlin, Nancy. Women's Suffrage. Simó, Roger, illus. 2018. (Blast Back! Ser.). (ENG.). 112p. (J). (gr. 2-5). 16.99 *(978-1-4998-0619-9(1));* pap. 5.99 *(978-1-4998-0618-2(3))* Little Bee Books Inc.
Peppas, Lynn. Women's Suffrage. 2015. (Uncovering the Past: Analyzing Primary Sources Ser.). (ENG., Illus.). 48p. (J). (gr. 5-6). *(978-0-7787-1720-1(8))* Crabtree Publishing Co.
Rice, Dona Herwick & Sugarman, Dorothy Alexander. Women's Suffrage, 1 vol. rev. ed. 2009. (Reader's Theater Ser.). (ENG., Illus.). 32p. (J). (gr. 3-8). pap. 11.99 *(978-1-4333-0550-4(X))* Teacher Created Materials, Inc.
Robbins, Dean. Miss Paul & the President: The Creative Campaign for Women's Right to Vote. Zhang, Nancy, illus. 2016. 40p. (J). (gr. -1-3). 18.99 *(978-1-101-93720-4(3),* Knopf Bks. for Young Readers) Random Hse. Children's Bks.
Roberts, David. Suffragette: the Battle for Equality. Roberts, David, illus. 2019. (ENG., Illus.). 128p. (J). (gr. 2-5). 25.00 *(978-1-5362-0841-2(8))* Candlewick Pr.
Rust Nash, Carol. Women Winning the Right to Vote in United States History, 1 vol. 2014. (In United States History Ser.). (ENG.). 96p. (gr. 5-6). 31.61 *(978-0-7660-6073-9(X),* c41fe8e8-30c2-4858-8d75-2ca289309c91); (Illus.). (J). pap. 13.88 *(978-0-7660-6074-6(8),* 43373f11-a8ff-4369-bd0d-e71e3f3270d4) Enslow Publishing, LLC.
Van Meter, Larry A. Votes for Women! The Fight for Women's Suffrage. 2019. (J). pap. *(978-1-9785-1527-7(8))* Enslow Publishing, LLC.
—Women Win the Vote: The Hard-Fought Battle for Women's Suffrage, 1 vol. 2008. (America's Living History Ser.). (ENG., Illus.). 128p. (gr. 5-6). lib. bdg. 35.93 *(978-0-7660-2940-8(9),* e2ef301e-36a7-40e3-aecf-b97a243931c4) Enslow Publishing, LLC.
Vink, Amanda. Suffragists & Those Who Opposed Them, 1 vol. 2019. (Opponents in American History Ser.). (ENG.). 32p. (gr. 4-5). 27.93 *(978-1-5383-4371-5(1),* 58d951df-193e-49d1-93ed-d1f796e00309, PowerKids Pr.) Rosen Publishing Group, Inc., The.
Weidt, Maryann N. Fighting for Equal Rights: A Story about Susan B. Anthony. Sartor, Amanda, tr. Sartor, Amanda, illus. 2004. (Creative Minds Biography Ser.). 64p. (J). 22.60 *(978-1-57505-181-9(8),* Carolrhoda Bks.) Lerner Publishing Group.
White, Linda Arms. I Could Do That! Esther Morris Gets Women the Vote. Carpenter, Nancy, illus. 2005. (ENG.). 40p. (J). (gr. 2-4). 18.99 *(978-0-374-33527-4(3),* 900022004, Farrar, Straus & Giroux (BYR)) Farrar, Straus & Giroux.
—I Could Do That! Esther Morris Gets Women the Vote. unabr. ed. 2006. (J). (gr. 2-4). 29.95 *(978-0-439-90582-4(6),* WHCD692) Weston Woods Studios, Inc.
Winter, Barbara. Fight for Rights. Kostic, Dimitri, illus. 2007. 48p. (J). lib. bdg. 23.08 *(978-1-4242-1636-9(2))* Fitzgerald Bks.
Women's Right to Vote, 1 vol. 2009. (Cartoon Nation Ser.). (ENG., Illus.). 32p. (J). (gr. 3-9). lib. bdg. 33.32 *(978-1-4296-2341-4(1),* 95069, Capstone Pr.) Capstone.
Women's Right to Vote. 2010. (J). *(978-0-7166-1508-8(8))* World Bk., Inc.
Zimet, Susan & Hasak-Lowy, Todd. Roses & Radicals: The Epic Story of How American Women Won the Right to Vote. 2020. 176p. (J). (gr. 5). pap. 9.99 *(978-0-425-29146-7(4),* Puffin Books) Penguin Young Readers Group.

WOMEN—UNITED STATES

see also Presidents' Spouses

Bausum, Ann. With Courage & Cloth: More Than 100 Recipes & Foolproof Strategies to Help Your Kids Fall in Love. 2004. (Illus.). 112p. (J). (gr. 5-9). 21.95 *(978-0-7922-7647-0(7),* National Geographic Kids) Disney Publishing Worldwide.
Bjornlund, Lydia D. Women in Colonial America. 2003. (Women in History Ser.). (ENG., Illus.). 112p. (J). 33.45 *(978-1-59018-470-7(X),* Lucent Bks.) Cengage Gale.
Brill, Marlene Targ. Annie Shapiro & the Clothing Workers' Strike. Akib, Jamel, illus. 2010. (History Speaks: Picture Books Plus Reader's Theater Ser.). (ENG.). 48p. (gr. 2-4). pap. 9.95 *(978-0-7613-6132-9(4))* Lerner Publishing Group.
Carosella, Melissa. Still Marching Strong: Women in Modern America. rev. ed. 2011. (Social Studies: Informational Text Ser.). (ENG.). 32p. (gr. 4-8). pap. 11.99 *(978-1-4333-1509-1(2))* Teacher Created Materials, Inc.
Casey, Susan. Women Heroes of the American Revolution: 20 Stories of Espionage, Sabotage, Defiance, & Rescue. 2017. (Women of Action Ser.). (ENG., Illus.). 240p. (YA). (gr. 7). pap. 14.99 *(978-1-61373-831-3(5))* Chicago Review Pr., Inc.
Clifford, Mary Louise & Clifford, J. Candace. Mind the Light, Katie: The History of Thirty-Three Female Lighthouse Keepers. 2006. (Illus.). iv, 136p. (J). per. 12.95 *(978-0-9636412-7-4(1))* Cypress Communications.
Cole, Peter. Ben Fletcher: The Life & Times of a Black Wobbly: Including Fellow Worker Fletcher's Writings & Speeches. 10th annot. ed. 2006. (Labor Classics Ser.). (Illus.). 149p. per. 15.00 *(978-0-88286-311-5(8))* Kerr, Charles H. Publishing Co.
Daily Life in America in the 1800s, 15 vols., Set. Incl. America at War: Military Conflicts, Home & Abroad in the 1800s. Strange, Matthew. pap. 9.95 *(978-1-4222-1851-8(1));* Bleeding, Blistering, & Purging: Health & Medicine in The 1800s. Strange, Matthew. pap. 9.95 *(978-1-4222-1848-8(1));* Buggies, Bicycles & Iron Horses: Transportation in the 1800s. McIntosh, Kenneth. pap. 9.95 *(978-1-4222-1849-5(X));* Cornmeal & Cider: Food & Drink in the 1800s. Chastain, Zachary. pap. 9.95 *(978-1-4222-1850-1(3));* From the Parlor to the Altar: Romance & Marriage in The 1800s. Chastain, Zachary. pap. 9.95 *(978-1-4222-1852-5(X));* Guardians of the Home: Women's Lives in The 1800s. Strange, Matthew. pap. 9.95 *(978-1-4222-1853-2(8));* Home Sweet Home: Around the House in the 1800s. Chastain, Zachary. pap. 9.95 *(978-1-4222-1854-9(6));* Jump Ropes, Jacks, & Endless Chores: Children's Lives in The 1800s. Strange, Matthew. pap. 9.95 *(978-1-4222-1855-6(4));* Outlaws & Lawmen: Crime & Punishment in the 1800s. McIntosh, Kenneth. pap. 9.95 *(978-1-4222-1857-0(0));* Passing the Time: Entertainment in The 1800s. Chastain, Zachary. pap. 9.95 *(978-1-4222-1858-7(9));* Reviving the Spirit, Reforming Society: Religion in The 1800s. McIntosh, Kenneth. pap. 9.95 *(978-1-4222-1856-3(2));* Rooting for the Home Team: Sports in The 1800s. Chastain, Zachary. pap. 9.95 *(978-1-4222-1859-4(7));* Saloons, Shootouts, & Spurs: The Wild West in The 1800's. McIntosh, Kenneth. pap. 9.95 *(978-1-4222-1862-4(7));* Scandals & Glory: Politics in The 1800s. Chastain, Zachary. pap. 9.95 *(978-1-4222-1860-0(0));* Sweat of Their Brow: Occupations in the 1800s. Chastain, Zachary. pap. 9.95 *(978-1-4222-1861-7(9));* (YA). (gr. 7-18). 2009. (Illus.). 64p. 2011. Set pap. 149.25 *(978-1-4222-1847-1(3),* 1317825); Set lib. bdg. 344.25 *(978-1-4222-1774-0(4),* 1317825) Mason Crest.
DeAngelis, Therese. Women's Rights on the Frontier. 2012. (Illus.). 64p. (J). pap. *(978-1-4222-2369-7(8))* Mason Crest.
—Women's Rights on the Frontier. Harrington, A. Page, ed. 2012. (Finding a Voice: Women's Fight for Equality in U. S. Society Ser.). (Illus.). 64p. (J). (gr. 5). 22.95 *(978-1-4222-2359-8(0))* Mason Crest.
Eboch, M. M. Living Through World War I. 2018. (American Culture & Conflict Ser.). (ENG., Illus.). 48p. (gr. 4-8). lib. bdg. 35.64 *(978-1-64156-416-8(4),* 9781641564168) Rourke Educational Media.
Florida's Women's Heritage Trail. (Heritage Trail Ser.). (J). (gr. -1-7). pap. 2.40 *(978-1-889030-19-7(8))* Florida Div. of Historical Resources.

WXYZ

Ford, Jeanne Marie. Eyewitness to the Role of Women in World War I. 2018. (Eyewitness to World War I Ser.). (ENG.). 32p. (J). (gr. 4-7). lib. bdg. 35.64 *(978-1-5038-1605-3(2),* 211163) Child's World, Inc, The.

Friedman, Michael & Friedman, Brett. Settlement Houses: Improving the Social Welfare of America's Immigrants, 1 vol. 2005. (Primary Sources of the Progressive Movement Ser.). (ENG., Illus.). 32p. (gr. 3-4). pap. 10.00 *(978-1-4042-0859-9(3),* e609beb3-5f0e-4e71-9ae6-522240de7366) Rosen Publishing Group, Inc., The.

Gelletly, LeeAnne. Seeking Th Right to Vote. 2012. (J). pap. *(978-1-4222-2364-2(7))* Mason Crest.

—Seeking Th Right to Vote. Harrington, A. Page, ed. 2012. (Finding a Voice: Women's Fight for Equality in U. S. Society Ser.). 64p. (J). (gr. 5). 22.95 *(978-1-4222-2354-3(X))* Mason Crest.

—A Woman's Place in Early America. 2012. (Illus.). 64p. (J). pap. *(978-1-4222-2365-9(5))* Mason Crest.

—A Woman's Place in Early America. Harrington, A. Page, ed. 2012. (Finding a Voice: Women's Fight for Equality in U. S. Society Ser.). (Illus.). 64p. (J). (gr. 5). 22.95 *(978-1-4222-2355-0(8))* Mason Crest.

Goldberg, Judy. Samantha's World: A Girl's-Eye View of the Turn of the 20th Century. Andreasen, Dan, illus. 2009. 30p. (YA). (gr. 3-18). 24.95 *(978-1-59369-554-5(3))* American Girl Publishing, Inc.

Gorman, Jacqueline Laks. The Modern Feminist Movement. 2011. (ENG., Illus.). 64p. (gr. 6-12). 35.00 *(978-1-60413-935-8(8),* P189949, Facts On File) Infobase Holdings, Inc.

Hall, Brianna. Great Women of the American Revolution. 2012. (Story of the American Revolution Ser.). (ENG.). 32p. (J). (gr. 3-4). pap. 48.60 *(978-1-4296-9285-4(5),* 18522, Capstone Pr.) Capstone.

Hamilton, Bailey & Hormel, Margaret. Virginia (Jennie) Claypool Meredith: An Amazing Woman, Ahead of Her Time. Taber, Melissa, illus. 2014. 25p. (J). *(978-0-9899472-5-1(4))* Kids At Heart Publishing, LLC.

Hicks, Peter. Documenting Women's Suffrage, 1 vol. (Documenting History Ser.). (ENG., Illus.). 48p. (gr. 7-7). 2010. (YA). lib. bdg. 34.47 *(978-1-4358-9672-7(6),* 64e2f741-0196-4463-9572-81ba734a002c) 2009. (J). pap. 12.75 *(978-1-4358-9675-8(0),* 8051fc89-f56d-4c1d-93b0-cc7f216609cf, Rosen Reference) Rosen Publishing Group, Inc., The.

Isecke, Harriet. Women's Suffrage: Fighting for Women's Rights. rev. ed. 2011. (Social Studies: Informational Text Ser.). (ENG.). 32p. (gr. 4-8). pap. 11.99 *(978-1-4333-1507-7(6))* Teacher Created Materials, Inc.

Jerome, Janice. A Dust of Flour. . . Beyond the Family Tree. 2003. spiral bd. 20.00 *(978-0-9729741-0-3(5))* Jerome, Janice.

Kent, Deborah. The Seneca Falls Convention: Working to Expand Women's Rights, 1 vol. 2016. (Heroes of the Women's Suffrage Movement Ser.). (ENG., Illus.). 128p. (gr. 6-6). 38.93 *(978-0-7660-7892-5(2),* 31bae9f2-5fb0-4b0c-b85c-a14646a95482) Enslow Publishing, LLC.

Kim, Carol. Women & the Family. 2019. (Women & Society Ser.). (ENG.). 80p. (J). (gr. 6-12). *(978-1-68282-551-8(5))* ReferencePoint Pr., Inc.

Loh-Hagan, Virginia. Rosalyn Sussman Yalow. Bane, Jeff, illus. 2018. (Mi Mini Biografía (My Itty-Bitty Bio): My Early Library). (ENG.). 24p. (J). (gr. k-1). pap. 12.79 *(978-1-5341-0813-4(0),* 210616); lib. bdg. 30.64 *(978-1-5341-0714-4(2),* 210615) Cherry Lake Publishing.

Lyman Schremmer, Patty. Women of the Green Mountain State: 25 Vermont Women You Should Know. Greenleaf, Lisa, illus. 2012. 136p. (J). pap. 16.00 *(978-0-9842549-5-8(1))* Apprentice Shop Bks., LLC.

Malaspina, Ann. Heart on Fire: Susan B. Anthony Votes for President. James, Steve, illus. 2012. (ENG.). 32p. (J). (gr. 1-3). 17.99 *(978-0-8075-3188-4(X),* 080753188X) Whitman, Albert & Co.

Mayr, Diane & Sisters, Write. Women of the Constitution State: 25 Connecticut Women You Should Know. Greenleaf, Lisa, illus. 2012. 136p. (J). pap. 16.00 *(978-0-9842549-1-0(9))* Apprentice Shop Bks., LLC.

McConnell, Robert L. & Baxter, Kathleen, contrib. by. The Split History of the Women's Suffrage Movement: A Perspectives Flip Book, 1 vol. 2014. (Perspectives Flip Bks.). (ENG., Illus.). 64p. (J). (gr. 5-9). lib. bdg. 34.65 *(978-0-7565-4735-6(0),* 124392, Compass Point Bks.) Capstone.

Metz, Lorijo. The Women's Suffrage Movement, 1 vol., 1. 2013. (Let's Celebrate Freedom! Ser.). (ENG., Illus.). 24p. (J). (gr. 3-3). 26.27 *(978-1-4777-2898-7(8),* 38e3511d-b727-4188-b743-c93cled4aae21, PowerKids Pr.) Rosen Publishing Group, Inc., The.

Micklos, John & Micklos, John, Jr. Courageous Children & Women of the American Revolution: Through Primary Sources, 1 vol. 2013. (American Revolution Through Primary Sources Ser.). (ENG., Illus.). 48p. (J). (gr. 4-6). 27.93 *(978-0-7660-4131-8(X),* 40dceef4-2d11-43ca-8481-3586da810fef) Enslow Publishing, LLC.

Miller, Brandon Marie. Good Women of a Well-Blessed Land: Women's Lives in Colonial America. 2003. (People's History Ser.). (Illus.). 96p. (J). 29.27 *(978-0-8225-0032-2(9))* Lerner Publishing Group.

Miller, Debra A., ed. Women in Politics, 1 vol. 2012. (Current Controversies Ser.). (ENG.). 168p. (gr. 10-12). pap. 33.00 *(978-0-7377-6250-1(0),* 0d6dc3f5-914a-46b7-b56b-495cf13532e8); lib. bdg. 48.03 *(978-0-7377-6249-5(7),* bfff8edf-097c-45bb-9133-1ebe9a2a4a7b) Greenhaven Publishing LLC. (Greenhaven Publishing).

Moening, Kate. Ann Bancroft: Explorer. 2020. (Women Leading the Way Ser.). (ENG., Illus.). 24p. (J). (gr. k-3). lib. bdg. 26.95 *(978-1-64487-119-5(X),* Blastoff! Readers) Bellwether Media.

Murray, Hallie. The Role of Women in the American Revolution, 1 vol. 2019. (Warrior Women in American History Ser.). (ENG.). 104p. (gr. 7-7). pap. 21.00 *(978-1-5026-5555-4(1),* 391d24c0-0d3e-4b52-8f48-fc26af3bab05); lib. bdg. 44.50 *(978-1-5026-5556-1(X),* 9e8a71d5-535d-4d0e-9216-705d6441800b) Cavendish Square Publishing LLC.

—The Role of Women in the American Revolution. 2019. (J). pap. *(978-1-9785-1419-5(0))* Enslow Publishing, LLC.

National Geographic Learning. Reading Expeditions (Social Studies: People Who Changed America): Votes for Women. 2007. (ENG., Illus.). 40p. (J). pap. 21.95 *(978-0-7922-8626-4(X))* CENGAGE Learning.

Nyman, Debbie & Wortzman, Ricki. The 10 Most Outstanding Women. 2007. 14.99 *(978-1-55448-468-3(5))* Scholastic Library Publishing.

Okamoto, Nadya. Period Power: A Manifesto for the Menstrual Movement. Elfast, Rebecca, illus. 2018. (ENG.). 368p. (YA). (gr. 7). 19.99 *(978-1-5344-3021-1(0));* pap. 12.99 *(978-1-5344-3020-4(2))* Simon & Schuster Bks. For Young Readers. (Simon & Schuster Bks. For Young Readers).

Roppelt, Donna. Women Go to Work, 1941-1945. 2012. (J). pap. *(978-1-4222-2367-3(1))* Mason Crest.

—Women Go to Work, 1941-1945. Harrington, A. Page, ed. 2012. (Finding a Voice: Women's Fight for Equality in U. S. Society Ser.). 64p. (J). (gr. 5). 22.95 *(978-1-4222-2357-4(4))* Mason Crest.

Rust Nash, Carol. Women Winning the Right to Vote in United States History, 1 vol. 2014. (In United States History Ser.). (ENG.). 96p. (gr. 5-6). 31.61 *(978-0-7660-6073-9(X),* c41fe8e8-30c2-4858-8d75-2ca289309c91) Enslow Publishing, LLC.

Sanford, William R. & Green, Carl R. Calamity Jane: Courageous Wild West Woman, 1 vol. 2013. (Courageous Heroes of the American West Ser.). (ENG., Illus.). 48p. (J). (gr. 5-7). pap. 11.53 *(978-1-4644-0093-3(8),* 3294d813-6625-4898-b0e3-ec98e86bcdec) Enslow Publishing, LLC.

Savage, Jeff. Pioneering Women: True Tales of the Wild West, 1 vol. 2012. (True Tales of the Wild West Ser.). (ENG., Illus.). 48p. (gr. 5-7). lib. bdg. 25.27 *(978-0-7660-4022-9(4),* ca454646-a36b-4509-8760-686725fe879c) Enslow Publishing, LLC.

Schmermund, Elizabeth. Do Women Have Equal Rights?, 1 vol. 2019. (Ask the Constitution Ser.). (ENG.). 48p. (gr. 5-5). pap. 12.70 *(978-1-9785-0345-3(X),* a4646b54-64e9-4ef3-96b9-447395aae94d) Enslow Publishing, LLC.

Spiller, Sara. Nellie Bly. Bane, Jeff, illus. 2019. (My Early Library: My Itty-Bitty Bio Ser.). (ENG.). 24p. (J). (gr. k-1). pap. 12.79 *(978-1-5341-3929-9(X),* 212545); lib. bdg. 30.64 *(978-1-5341-4273-2(8),* 212544) Cherry Lake Publishing.

Strange, Matthew. Guardians of the Home: Women's Lives in The 1800s. 2009. (Daily Life in America in the 1800s Ser.). 64p. (YA). (gr. 7-18). pap. 9.95 *(978-1-4222-1853-2(8));* lib. bdg. 22.95 *(978-1-4222-1780-1(9))* Mason Crest.

Swisher, Clarice. Women of the Roaring Twenties. 2005. (Women in History Ser.). (ENG., Illus.). 112p. (YA). (gr. 7-10). lib. bdg. 33.45 *(978-1-59018-363-2(0),* Lucent Bks.) Cengage Gale.

Walsh, Francis. Daring Women of the American Revolution. 2009. (American History Flashpoints! Ser.). 32p. (gr. 4-4). 47.90 *(978-1-61511-367-5(3),* PowerKids Pr.) Rosen Publishing Group, Inc., The.

WOMEN—UNITED STATES—BIOGRAPHY

Abrams, Dennis. Barbara Walters. 2010. (ENG., Illus.). 128p. (J). (gr. 6-12). 35.00 *(978-1-60413-686-9(3),* P179328, Facts On File) Infobase Holdings, Inc.

—Rachael Ray: Food Entrepreneur. 2009. (Women of Achievement Ser.). (ENG., Illus.). 136p. (gr. 7-12). 35.00 *(978-1-60413-078-2(4),* P161628, Facts On File) Infobase Holdings, Inc.

Acevedo, Sylvia. Path to the Stars: My Journey from Girl Scout to Rocket Scientist. 2018. (ENG., Illus.). 320p. (J). (gr. 5-7). 17.99 *(978-1-328-80956-8(0),* 1688046, Clarion Bks.) HarperCollins Pubs.

Adams, Colleen. The True Story of Pocahontas. 2009. (What Really Happened? Ser.). 24p. (gr. 2-3). 42.50 *(978-1-60854-765-4(5),* PowerKids Pr.) Rosen Publishing Group, Inc., The.

Adler, David A. A Picture Book of Amelia Earhart. Fisher, Jeff, illus. 2015. 32p. pap. 8.00 *(978-1-61003-403-6(1))* Center for the Collaborative Classroom.

—A Picture Book of Amelia Earhart. Fisher, Jeff, illus. 2018. (Picture Book Biography Ser.). 32p. (J). (gr. -1-3). pap. 7.99 *(978-0-8234-4056-6(7))* Holiday Hse., Inc.

—A Picture Book of Rosa Parks. Casilla, Robert, illus. 2004. (J). (gr. -1-2). 28.95 incl. audio compact disk *(978-1-59112-762-8(9))* Live Oak Media.

Allen, Audrey. Jennifer Lawrence, 1 vol. 2013. (Rising Stars Ser.). (ENG.). 32p. (J). (gr. 1-1). 27.93 *(978-1-4339-8977-3(8),* cb73c836-e458-480b-967b-22fb19378ad6); pap. 11.50 *(978-1-4339-8978-0(6),* 6157b18b-9bdf-4fde-b847-f16a776c809b) Stevens, Gareth Publishing LLLP.

Allen, Nancy. Barreling over Niagara Falls, 1 vol. 2013. (ENG., Illus.). 40p. (gr. k-3). 17.99 *(978-1-4556-1766-1(0),* Pelican Publishing) Arcadia Publishing.

Aller, Susan Bivin. Juliette Low. 2007. (History Maker Biographies Ser.). (Illus.). 48p. (J). (gr. 3-7). lib. bdg. 26.60 *(978-0-8225-6580-2(3),* Lerner Pubns.) Lerner Publishing Group.

—Madam C. J. Walker. 2007. (History Maker Biographies Ser.). (ENG., Illus.). 48p. (gr. 3-6). lib. bdg. 27.93 *(978-0-8225-6582-6(X),* Lerner Pubns.) Lerner Publishing Group.

Anderson, Jameson. Gabby Douglas, 1 vol. 2014. (Awesome Athletes Ser.). (ENG., Illus.). 32p. (J). (gr. 3-6). lib. bdg. 32.79 *(978-1-62403-338-4(5),* 1219, Checkerboard Library) ABDO Publishing Co.

Anderson, Jane. My Name Is Deborah Samson. 2005. (J). pap. *(978-1-4108-4225-1(8))* Benchmark Education Co.

Anderson, Laurie Halse. Independent Dames: What You Never Knew about the Women & Girls of the American Revolution. Faulkner, Matt, illus. 2008. (ENG.). 40p. (J). (gr. 1-5). 18.99 *(978-0-689-85808-6(6),* Simon & Schuster Bks. For Young Readers) Simon & Schuster Bks. For Young Readers.

—Shout. 2019. (ENG.). 304p. (YA). (gr. 9). 18.99 *(978-0-670-01210-7(6),* Viking Books for Young Readers) Penguin Young Readers Group.

Anema, Durlynn. Ynes Mexia: Botanist & Adventurer. 2005. (Women Adventurers Ser.). (Illus.). 144p. (J). (gr. 3-7). lib. bdg. 26.95 *(978-1-931798-67-9(2))* Reynolds, Morgan Inc.

Antal, Lara. Zora Neale Hurston: Author, 1 vol. 2016. (Artists of the Harlem Renaissance Ser.). (ENG.). 128p. (YA). (gr. 9-9). lib. bdg. 47.36 *(978-1-5026-1038-6(8),* ce7583d4-8db6-4e5c-bac4-7541d4941f79) Cavendish Square Publishing LLC.

Apel, Melanie Ann. Virginia Apgar: Innovative Female Physician & Inventor of the Apgar Score. 2009. (Women Hall of Famers in Mathematics & Science Ser.). 112p. (gr. 5-8). 63.90 *(978-1-60854-815-6(5),* Rosen Reference) Rosen Publishing Group, Inc., The.

Auch, Allison. Women Who Dared & Mujeres que se Atrevieron: 6 English, 6 Spanish Adaptations. 2011. (ENG & SPA.). (J). 97.00 net. *(978-1-4108-5692-0(5))* Benchmark Education Co.

Bailey, Diane. Venus & Serena Williams: Tennis Champions. 2010. (Sports Families Ser.). 48p. (YA). (gr. 5-8). lib. bdg., E-Book 53.00 *(978-1-4488-0124-4(9))* Rosen Publishing Group, Inc., The.

Bankston, John. Abby Wambach. 2013. (ENG.). 32p. (gr. 4-8). lib. bdg. 25.70 *(978-1-61228-465-1(5))* Mitchell Lane Pubs.

Banting, Erinn. Rosa Parks. 2005. (Great African American Women for Kids Ser.). (Illus.). 24p. (J). (gr. 2-3). lib. bdg. 26.00 *(978-1-59036-336-2(1));* (gr. 3-7). per. 8.95 *(978-1-59036-342-3(6))* Weigl Pubs., Inc.

Barasch, Lynne. Hiromi's Hands, 1 vol. Barasch, Lynne, illus. 2007. (ENG.). 40p. (J). (gr. 1-5). pap. 12.95 *(978-1-62014-251-6(1),* leelowbooks); (Illus.). (gr. k-6). 18.95 *(978-1-58430-275-9(5))* Lee & Low Bks., Inc.

Barbara Jordan. 2004. 12p. (gr. k-4). 2.95 *(978-0-635-02616-3(3))* Gallopade International.

Barghoorn, Linda. Dolores Huerta: Advocate for Women & Workers. 2017. (Remarkable Lives Revealed Ser.). (Illus.). 32p. (J). (gr. 3-3). *(978-0-7787-3418-5(8))* Crabtree Publishing Co.

—Mae Jemison: Trailblazing Astronaut, Doctor, & Teacher. 2016. (Remarkable Lives Revealed Ser.). (ENG., Illus.). 32p. (J). (gr. 2-5). *(978-0-7787-2693-7(2))* Crabtree Publishing Co.

—Temple Grandin: Pioneer for Animal Rights & Autism Awareness. 2016. (Remarkable Lives Revealed Ser.). (ENG., Illus.). 32p. (J). (gr. 2-5). *(978-0-7787-2688-3(6))* Crabtree Publishing Co.

Barrett, Hayley. What Miss Mitchell Saw. Sudyka, Diana, illus. 2019. (ENG.). 40p. (J). (gr. -1-3). 17.99 *(978-1-4814-8759-7(0),* Beach Lane Bks.) Beach Lane Bks.

Barron, Patricia. Meet Judge Patricia Barron. Barron, Robert, photos by. 2006. (Illus.). 40p. per. 14.95 *(978-1-59858-301-4(8))* Dog Ear Publishing, LLC.

Bates, Martine G. Heather Whitestone: Inspirational Miss America. 2007. (Illus.). 104p. (J). pap. *(978-1-59421-029-7(2))* Seacoast Publishing, Inc.

Baumann, Susan K. Harriet Tubman, 1 vol. 2013. (Jr. Graphic African American History Ser.). (ENG., Illus.). 24p. (J). (gr. 2-3). 28.93 *(978-1-4777-1312-9(3),* 5857a12b-5a9e-48cd-8def-0baf9168c30b); pap. 11.60 *(978-1-4777-1449-2(9),* 6d3e3e76-88e9-4073-a428-cdc6f9f55c07) Rosen Publishing Group, Inc., The. (PowerKids Pr.).

—Harriet Tubman: Conductor of the Underground Railroad. 2013. (Jr. Graphic African American History Ser.). (Illus.). 24p. (J). (gr. 3-6). pap. 63.60 *(978-1-4777-1450-8(2),* PowerKids Pr.) Rosen Publishing Group, Inc., The.

Benson, Michael. Gloria Estefan. 2003. (Biography Ser.). (Illus.). 112p. (YA). (gr. 6-18). pap. 7.95 *(978-0-8225-9692-9(X),* Carolrhoda Bks.) Lerner Publishing Group.

Bert, Ruth J. Everyone Called Her Sister Sarah. Westbeld, Kristine, illus. 2004. (ENG.). 32p. (J). (gr. -1-3). pap. 4.99 *(978-1-928915-62-1(0))* Evangel Publishing Hse.

Biery, Martha. Josephine Aspinwall Roche: Humanitarian. 2011. (ENG & SPA., Illus.). 66p. (J). pap. 8.95 *(978-0-86541-119-7(0))* Filter Pr., LLC.

Bindi, Paulo. Sally Ride: The Sky's the Limit. 2013. (InfoMax Readers Ser.). (ENG.). 24p. (J). (gr. 2-3). pap. 49.50 *(978-1-4777-2452-1(4));* (Illus.). pap. 8.25 *(978-1-4777-2451-4(6),* d70f7c7b-6573-44ec-b3ae-5dff30a650c8) Rosen Publishing Group, Inc., The. (Rosen Classroom).

Bisantz, Max & Bisantz, Kate. Who Was Selena? 2018. (Who Was... ? Ser.). lib. bdg. 16.00 *(978-0-606-41325-1(1))* Turtleback.

Black, Donnette. Madam C. J. Walker's Road to Success. 2010. 36p. pap. 17.50 *(978-1-4520-2443-1(X))* AuthorHouse.

Blashfield, Jean F. Hillary Clinton, 1 vol. 2011. (Leading Women Ser.). (ENG.). 96p. (YA). (gr. 7-7). 42.64 *(978-0-7614-4954-6(X),* e653b8cd-2fce-4ce2-be4a-065c33d4a87f) Cavendish Square Publishing LLC.

—Oprah Winfrey, 1 vol. 2004. (Trailblazers of the Modern World Ser.). (ENG., Illus.). 48p. (gr. 5-8). pap. 15.05 *(978-0-8368-5247-9(8),* a22221d7-89d8-49af-83a7-22a6b0cab35d, Gareth Stevens Secondary Library) Stevens, Gareth Publishing LLLP.

Bodden, Valerie. Hillary Clinton: Historic Leader. 2009. (Essential Lives Set 4 Ser.). (ENG., Illus.). 112p. (YA). (gr. 6-12). lib. bdg. 41.36 *(978-1-60453-699-7(3),* 6689, Essential Library) ABDO Publishing Co.

—Michelle Obama: First Lady & Role Model, 1 vol. 2009. (Essential Lives Set 4 Ser.). (ENG., Illus.). 112p. (YA). (gr. 6-12). lib. bdg. 41.36 *(978-1-60453-703-1(5),* 6697, Essential Library) ABDO Publishing Co.

—Nuclear Physicist Chien-Shiung Wu. 2016. (STEM Trailblazer Bios Ser.). (ENG., Illus.). 32p. (J). (gr. 2-5). 26.65 *(978-1-5124-0786-0(0),* bc397cd0-0220-433e-8b54-50739c954f80, Lerner Pubns.) Lerner Publishing Group.

Bodie, Idella. Heroines of the American Revolution. 2003. (Illus.). 99p. (J). pap. 6.95 *(978-0-87844-170-9(0))* Sandlapper Publishing Co., Inc.

Bohannon, Lisa Frederiksen. Woman's Work: The Story of Betty Friedan. 2004. (Illus.). 144p. (YA). (gr. 6-12). 23.95 *(978-1-931798-41-9(9))* Reynolds, Morgan Inc.

Bolden, Tonya. Searching for Sarah Rector: The Richest Blac Girl in America. 2014. (ENG., Illus.). 80p. (J). (gr. 3-7). 24.99 *(978-1-4197-0846-6(5),* 672501, Abrams Bks. for Young Readers) Abrams, Inc.

Borgert-Spaniol, Megan. Katherine Johnson: Guiding Spacecraft. 2017. (STEM Superstar Women Ser.). (ENG., Illus.). 32p. (J). (gr. 3-6). lib. bdg. 32.79 *(978-1-5321-1281-2(5),* 27605, Checkerboard Library) ABDO Publishing Co.

Bowdish, Lynea. With Courage: Seven Women Who Changec America. 2004. (Illus.). 48p. (J). 6.95 *(978-1-59336-280-5(3),* Mondo Publishing.

Bradley, Michael. Venus Williams, 1 vol. 2005. (All-Stars Ser.). (ENG., Illus.). 48p. (gr. 4-4). lib. bdg. 34.07 *(978-0-7614-1630-2(7),* aae35196-fb4a-4f79-9337-bc954d02fea4) Cavendish Square Publishing LLC.

Brainard, Cecilia Manguerra. Cecilia's Diary 1962-1969. 2003. (YA). per. 15.95 *(978-0-9719458-1-4(0))* PALH.

Braun, Eric. Loretta Lynch: First African American Woman Attorney General. 2016. (Gateway Biographies Ser.). (ENG., Illus.). 48p. (J). (gr. 4-8). E-Book 47.99 *(978-1-5124-0587-3(6),* Lerner Pubns.) Lerner Publishing Group.

Brean, Alta. Dear Grandchildren: Growing up on the Frontier. 2003. (Illus.). 144p. 18.95 *(978-0-9726360-0-1(5),* (408) 718-5654) Alta Omnimedia.

Bredeson, Carmen. The Chocolate Chip Cookie Queen: Ruth Wakefield & Her Yummy Invention, 1 vol. 2014. (Inventors at Work! Ser.). (ENG.). 48p. (gr. 3-3). lib. bdg. 27.93 *(978-0-7660-4242-1(1),* 3fda7dcb-b56a-456b-925d-0b3d37b78ada, Enslow Elementary) Enslow Publishing, LLC.

Bregoli, Jane. The Goat Lady. Bregoli, Jane, illus. 2008. (ENG., Illus.). 32p. (J). (gr. 2-6). pap. 8.95 *(978-0-88448-309-0(6),* 884309) Tilbury Hse. Pubs.

Brennan, Linda Crotta. Women of the Ocean State: 25 Rhode Island Women You Should Know. Greenleaf, Lisa, illus. 2012. 136p. (J). pap. 16.00 *(978-0-9842549-7-2(8))* Apprentice Shop Bks., LLC.

Brezina, Corona. Laura Ingalls Wilder: Children's Author. 2017. (Britannica Beginner Bios Ser.). 32p. (J). (gr. 6-10). 77.40 *(978-1-5383-0024-4(9),* Britannica Educational Publishing) Rosen Publishing Group, Inc., The.

Briere-Haquet, Alice. Nina. 2017. 40p. (J). (-2). 13.99 *(978-958-30-5461-7(5))* Panamericana Editorial COL. Dist: Lectorum Pubns., Inc.

Brière-Haquet, Alice. Nina: Jazz Legend & Civil-Rights Activist Nina Simone. Liance, Bruno, illus. 2017. (ENG.). 40p. (J). (gr. -1-3). lib. bdg. 16.99 *(978-1-58089-827-0(0))* Charlesbridge Publishing, Inc.

Brill, Marlene Targ. Dolores Huerta Stands Strong: The Woman Who Demanded Justice. 2018. (Biographies for Young Readers Ser.). (ENG.). 104p. pap. 15.95 *(978-0-8214-2330-1(4));* (Illus.). 32.95 *(978-0-8214-2329-5(0))* Ohio Univ. Pr.

Brooks, Riley. Taylor Swift: Fearless Star. 2010. (Illus.). 48p. (J). *(978-0-545-30382-8(6))* Scholastic, Inc.

Brown, Anne K. Gwen Stefani, 1 vol. 2009. (People in the News Ser.). (ENG., Illus.). 104p. (gr. 7-7). lib. bdg. 41.03 *(978-1-4205-0126-1(7),* b891cea2-1b2b-4f0c-bcde-ed3a11e1aeca, Lucent Pr.) Greenhaven Publishing LLC.

Brown, Elizabeth. Dancing Through Fields of Color: The Story of Helen Frankenthaler. Sicuro, Aimée, illus. 2019. (ENG.). 40p. (J). (gr. -1-3). 19.99 *(978-1-4197-3410-6(5),* 1190801, Abrams Bks. for Young Readers) Abrams, Inc.

Brown, Jonatha A. Eleanor Roosevelt, 1 vol. 2004. (People We Should Know Ser.). (ENG., Illus.). 24p. (gr. 2-4). lib. bdg. 24.67 *(978-0-8368-4468-9(8),* 7d17ffdd-908f-4bd8-81b7-cad97ccbf7c6, Weekly Reader Leveled Readers) Stevens, Gareth Publishing LLLP.

—Rosa Parks, 1 vol. (People We Should Know Ser.). (Illus.). 24p. (gr. 2-4). 2006. (ENG.). lib. bdg. 24.67 *(978-0-8368-4748-2(2),* 3fd2247d-ef71-4f76-8f9d-fe2565b41a2e, Weekly Reader Leveled Readers) 2005. (SPA., pap. 9.15 *(978-0-8368-4769-7(5),* dc6d6549-aadd-4a94-970a-bd4b21cb8052, Weekly Reader Leveled Readers) 2005. (ENG., pap. 9.15 *(978-0-8368-4755-0(5),* 04e24c04-67e0-444b-8563-13ff52afad09, Weekly Reader Leveled Readers) 2005. (SPA., lib. bdg. 24.67 *(978-0-8368-4762-8(8),* 8ef1c1f4-f871-42b6-b2cd-befae7e48778) Stevens, Gareth Publishing LLLP.

Bryan, Bethany. Melania Trump: Model & First Lady, 1 vol. 2017. (Leading Women Ser.). (ENG.). 112p. (YA). (gr. 7-7). 41.64 *(978-1-5026-3180-0(6),* ff5e7096-f03c-4465-bb2b-0a6a313da3e8) Cavendish Square Publishing LLC.

—Simone Biles: Dominant Gymnast, 1 vol. 2019. (At the Top of Their Game Ser.). (ENG.). 112p. (gr. 9-9). pap. 20.99 *(978-1-5026-5108-2(4),* c4783e1e-a488-4f8f-b54f-13357904ee95) Cavendish Square Publishing LLC.

Buckley, Annie. Ellen Ochoa. 2007. (21st Century Skills Library: Life Skills Biographies Ser.). (ENG., Illus.). 48p. (gr. 4-8). lib. bdg. 34.93 *(978-1-60279-075-9(2),* 200041) Cherry Lake Publishing.

Buckley, James. Katie Ledecky. 2017. (Amazing Americans: Olympians Ser.). (ENG.). 24p. (J). (gr. -1-3). 26.99 *(978-1-68402-240-3(1))* Bearport Publishing Co., Inc.

—Simone Biles. 2017. (Amazing Americans: Olympians Ser.). (ENG., Illus.). 24p. (J). (gr. -1-3). 26.99 *(978-1-68402-241-0(X))* Bearport Publishing Co., Inc.

Buell, Janet & Sisters, Write. Women of the Granite State: 25 New Hampshire Women You Should Know. Greenleaf, Lisa, illus. 2012. 136p. (J). pap. 16.00 *(978-0-9842549-8-9(6))* Apprentice Shop Bks., LLC.

Burke, John. Amelia Earhart: Flying Solo. 2017. (Great Leaders & Events Ser.). (ENG.). (J). (gr. 4-8). lib. bdg. 35.99 *(978-1-942875-45-1(2))* Quarto Publishing Group USA.

rlingame, Jeff. Taylor Swift: Music Superstar, 1 vol. 2012. (Hot Celebrity Biographies Ser.). (ENG., Illus.). 48p. (gr. 5-7). pap. 11.53 *(978-1-59845-286-0(X),* 30da60cc-4fd0-4672-97bc-a610677e8fb1) Enslow Publishing, LLC.

tler, Darren J. Helen Keller: Leader Without Sight or Sound. 2012. (Illus.). 108p. (J). pap. *(978-1-59421-083-9(7))* Seacoast Publishing, Inc.

zzeo, Toni. When Sue Found Sue: Sue Hendrickson Discovers Her T. Rex. Sudyka, Diana, illus. 2019. (ENG.). 32p. (J). (gr. 1-4). 18.99 *(978-1-4197-3163-1(7),* 1143101, Abrams Bks. for Young Readers) Abrams, Inc.

yers, Ann. Sacagawea, 1 vol. 2020. (Inside Guide: Famous Native Americans Ser.). (ENG.). 32p. (gr. 4-5). pap. 11.58 *(978-1-5026-5064-1(9),* 1a6f2658-afa0-4e6b-8867-726a692bb62f) Cavendish Square Publishing LLC.

yman, Jeremy. Madam Secretary: The Story of Madeleine Albright. rev. exp. ed. 2004. (Notable Americans Ser.). (Illus.). 128p. (YA). (gr. 6-12). 23.95 *(978-1-931798-34-1(6))* Reynolds, Morgan Inc.

alkhoven, Laurie. Ruth Bader Ginsburg: Ready-To-Read Level 3. Vukovic, Elizabet, illus. 2019. (You Should Meet Ser.). (ENG.). 48p. (J). (gr. 1-1). 17.99 *(978-1-5344-4858-2(6));* pap. 4.99 *(978-1-5344-4857-5(8))* Simon Spotlight. (Simon Spotlight).

—Women Who Launched the Computer Age: Ready-To-Read Level 3. Petersen, Alyssa, illus. 2016. (You Should Meet Ser.). (ENG.). 48p. (J). (gr. 1-3). pap. 4.99 *(978-1-4814-7046-9(9),* Simon Spotlight) Simon Spotlight.

Cameron, Charles. Why Lizzie Johnson Matters to Texas, 1 vol. 2013. (Texas Perspectives Ser.). (ENG., Illus.). 32p. (J). (gr. 4-4). lib. bdg. 28.93 *(978-1-4777-0908-5(8),* 3dbc605b-a618-4499-8ca8-04f4bd9c2864) Rosen Publishing Group, Inc., The.

Cantwell, Lois. Women Winners: Then & Now. 2009. (Sports Illustrated for Kids Bks). 176p. (gr. 7-12). 63.90 *(978-1-60853-157-8(0))* Rosen Publishing Group, Inc., The.

Cantwell, Lois & Smith, Pohla. Women Winners: Then & Now. (J). (gr. 3-9). pap. 3.99 *(978-1-930623-09-5(7))* Sports Illustrated For Kids.

Caravantes, Peggy. Petticoat Spies: Six Women Spies of the US Civil War. 2004. (Notable Americans Ser.). (Illus.). 112p. (YA). (gr. 6-12). 23.95 *(978-1-883846-88-6(9),* First Biographies) Reynolds, Morgan Inc.

—Waging Peace: The Story of Jane Addams. 2004. (Illus.). 144p. (YA). (gr. 6-12). 23.95 *(978-1-931798-40-2(0))* Reynolds, Morgan Inc.

—Zendaya: Star Performer. 2017. (Superstar Stories Ser.). (ENG.). 24p. (J). (gr. 3-6). lib. bdg. 32.79 *(978-1-5038-2000-5(9),* 211876) Child's World, Inc, The.

Carmen Harvey, Bonnie. Jane Addams: Social Worker & Nobel Peace Prize Winner, 1 vol. 2014. (Legendary American Biographies Ser.). (ENG.). 96p. (gr. 6-6). 29.60 *(978-0-7660-6460-7(3),* 12f6c2fd-a839-40b3-8a37-84081b36f8b4); pap. 13.88 *(978-0-7660-6461-4(1),* 7bc2ab23-d0db-4ad2-9f27-024f33c3847a) Enslow Publishing, LLC.

Carmon, Irin. Notorious RGB Young Readers' Edition: The Life & Times of Ruth Bader Ginsburg. 2017. (ENG., Illus.). 208p. (J). (gr. 3-7). 17.99 *(978-0-06-274853-9(X),* HarperCollins) HarperCollins Pubs.

Carosella, Melissa. Founding Mothers: Women Who Shaped America. rev. ed. 2011. (Social Studies: Informational Text Ser.). (ENG.). 32p. (gr. 4-8). pap. 11.99 *(978-1-4333-1505-3(X))* Teacher Created Materials, Inc.

Carson, Mary Kay. Who Was the Hair-Care Millionaire? Madam C. J. Walker, 1 vol. 2012. (I Like Inventors! Ser.). (ENG., Illus.). 24p. (gr. k-2). pap. 10.35 *(978-1-4644-0133-6(0),* 311e36ac-88bd-40d2-83a0-c0b0862b13e8, Enslow Elementary) Enslow Publishing, LLC.

Cartlidge, Cherese. Jennifer Lopez, 1 vol. 2012. (People in the News Ser.). (ENG., Illus.). 112p. (gr. 7-7). lib. bdg. 41.03 *(978-1-4205-0755-3(9),* a40e5be2-967b-44a9-9d2d-c72bade3b347, Lucent Pr.) Greenhaven Publishing LLC.

Castaldo, Nancy. The Race Around the World (Totally True Adventures) How Nellie Bly Chased an Impossible Dream... Lowe, Wesley, illus. 2015. (Totally True Adventures Ser.). (ENG.). 112p. (J). (gr. 2-5). 4.99 *(978-0-553-52278-5(7),* Random Hse. Bks. for Young Readers) Random Hse. Children's Bks.

Cefrey, Holly. The Inventions of Martha Coston: Signal Flares That Save Sailors' Lives. 2009. (19th Century American Inventors Ser.). 24p. (gr. 2-3). 42.50 *(978-1-60854-953-5(4),* PowerKids Pr.) Rosen Publishing Group, Inc., The.

—Taylor Swift, 1 vol. 2011. (Megastars Ser.). (ENG., Illus.). 48p. (YA). (gr. 5-5). 34.47 *(978-1-4358-3575-7(1),* 921b07f9-abfa-4faa-a863-86a1f80465d8); pap. 12.75 *(978-1-4488-2261-4(0),* e4a0ec47-97a8-4fd9-9147-9b1092b26f46) Rosen Publishing Group, Inc., The. (Rosen Reference).

Cham, Stephanie. Michelle Kwan. 2018. (Great Asian Americans Ser.). (ENG., Illus.). 24p. (J). (gr. -1-2). lib. bdg. 27.32 *(978-1-5157-9958-0(1),* 136956, Capstone Pr.) Capstone.

—Tammy Duckworth. 2018. (Great Asian Americans Ser.). (ENG., Illus.). 24p. (J). (gr. -1-2). lib. bdg. 27.32 *(978-1-5157-9955-9(7),* 136953, Capstone Pr.) Capstone.

Chambers, Veronica. Shirley Chisholm Is a Verb. Baker, Rachelle, illus. 2020. 40p. (J). (gr. -1-3). 18.99 *(978-0-8037-3089-2(6),* Dial Bks) Penguin Young Readers Group.

Charles, Tami. Fearless Mary: Mary Fields, American Stagecoach Driver. Almon, Claire, illus. 2019. (ENG.). 32p. (J). (gr. -1-3). 17.99 *(978-0-8075-2305-6(4),* 807523054) Whitman, Albert & Co.

Chen, Karen. Finding the Edge: My Life on the Ice. 2017. (ENG., Illus.). 224p. (J). (gr. 3-7). 17.99 *(978-0-06-282268-0(3),* HarperCollins) HarperCollins Pubs.

Cheney, Lynne. A Is for Abigail: An Almanac of Amazing American Women. 2003. (ENG., Illus.). 48p. (J). (gr. 1-7). 19.99 *(978-0-689-85819-2(1),* Simon & Schuster Bks. For Young Readers) Simon & Schuster Bks. For Young Readers.

Ching, Jacqueline. Abigail Adams: A Revolutionary Woman. 2009. (Library of American Lives & Times Ser.). 112p. (gr. 5-5). 69.20 *(978-1-60853-469-2(3))* Rosen Publishing Group, Inc., The.

Citro, Asia. Pigeon Math. Watson, Richard, illus. 2019. (ENG.). 40p. (J). (gr. k-5). 16.99 *(978-1-943147-62-5(0),* b0b01c77-c2cc-438d-bb9a-f16d4f6aa9eb) Innovation Pr., The.

Cline-Ransome, Lesa. Counting the Stars: The Story of Katherine Johnson, NASA Mathematician. ón, Raúl, illus. 2019. (ENG.). 32p. (J). (gr. -1-3). 17.99 *(978-1-5344-0475-5(9),* Simon & Schuster Bks. For Young Readers) Simon & Schuster Bks. For Young Readers.

Clinton, Chelsea. She Persisted: 13 American Women Who Changed the World. Boiger, Alexandra, illus. 2017. (She Persisted Ser.). 32p. (J). (gr. -1-3). 17.99 *(978-1-5247-4172-3(8),* Philomel Bks.) Penguin Young Readers Group.

—She Persisted in Sports: American Olympians Who Changed the Game. Boiger, Alexandra, illus. (She Persisted Ser.). (J). 2022. 30p. (— 1). bds. 9.99 *(978-0-593-35341-7(2))* 2020. 32p. (gr. -1-3). 17.99 *(978-0-593-11454-4(X))* Penguin Young Readers Group. (Philomel Bks.).

Cohen, Della. Eleanor Roosevelt: Proud & Tall. 2005. (Illus.). 16p. (J). pap. *(978-0-7367-2879-9(1))* Zaner-Bloser, Inc.

Cohen, Sheila & Terman Cohen, Sheila. Mai Ya's Long Journey. 2005. (Badger Biographies Ser.). (ENG., Illus.). 96p. (J). (gr. 3-7). per. 12.95 *(978-0-87020-365-7(7))* Wisconsin Historical Society.

Coleman, Miriam. Women in the Military, 1 vol. 2015. (Women Groundbreakers Ser.). (ENG.). 32p. (J). (gr. 4-5). pap. 11.00 *(978-1-4994-1052-5(2),* 03b6bd8a-34e7-4b3b-9ec4-f6f3fb5cfe5f, PowerKids Pr.) Rosen Publishing Group, Inc., The.

Collins, Kathleen. Sojourner Truth: Defensora de los derechos Civiles, 1 vol. 2003. (Grandes Personajes en la Historia de Los Estados Unidos (Famous People in American History) Ser.). (SPA.). 32p. (gr. 3-4). pap. 10.00 *(978-0-8239-4239-8(2),* 6f31c133-2276-4b5a-816a-e9203a1295c1, Rosen Classroom) Rosen Publishing Group, Inc., The.

—Sojourner Truth: Defensora de los derechos civiles (Sojourner Truth: Equal Rights Advocate) 2009. (Grandes personajes en la historia de los Estados Unidos (Famous People in American History) Ser.). (SPA.). 32p. (gr. 2-3). 47.90 *(978-1-61512-808-2(5),* Editorial Buenas Letras) Rosen Publishing Group, Inc., The.

—Sojourner Truth: Equal Rights Advocate, 1 vol. 2003. (Primary Sources of Famous People in American History Ser.). (ENG., Illus.). 32p. (gr. 3-4). pap. 10.00 *(978-0-8239-4193-3(0),* a3e0d003-2b16-455d-a83a-e5c1a3908d7c) Rosen Publishing Group, Inc., The.

—Sojourner Truth: Equal Rights Advocate / Defensora de los derechos Civiles. 2009. (Famous People in American History/Grandes personajes en la historia de los Estados Unidos Ser.). (ENG & SPA.). 32p. (gr. 2-3). 47.90 *(978-1-61512-556-2(6),* Editorial Buenas Letras) Rosen Publishing Group, Inc., The.

Conkling, Winifred. Heroism Begins with Her: Inspiring Stories of Bold, Brave, & Gutsy Women in the U. S. Military. Kuo, Julia, illus. 2019. (ENG.). 240p. (J). (gr. 3-7). 18.99 *(978-0-06-284741-6(4),* HarperCollins) HarperCollins Pubs.

Conrad, Vicki. Just Like Beverly: A Biography of Beverly Cleary. Hohn, David, illus. 2019. (Growing to Greatness Ser.). 48p. (J). (gr. k-4). 18.99 *(978-1-63217-222-8(4),* Little Bigfoot) Sasquatch Bks.

Cooper, Ilene. Eleanor Roosevelt, Fighter for Justice: Her Impact on the Civil Rights Movement, the White House, & the World. 2018. (ENG., Illus.). 192p. (J). (gr. 5-9). 17.99 *(978-1-4197-2295-0(6),* 1108501, Abrams Bks. for Young Readers) Abrams, Inc.

Crawford, Ann Fears. Rosa: A German Woman on the Texas Frontier. Fain, Cheryl, illus. l.t. ed. 2003. 60p. (J). (gr. 3-8). 16.95 *(978-1-931823-09-8(X))* Halcyon Pr.

Crowley Conn, Kathe. Juliette Kinzie: Frontier Storyteller. 2015. (Badger Biographies Ser.). (ENG., Illus.). 123p. (J). (gr. 4-6). pap. 12.95 *(978-0-87020-701-3(6))* Wisconsin Historical Society.

Curran, Abbey. The Courage to Compete: Living with Cerebral Palsy & Following My Dreams. 2015. (ENG., Illus.). 272p. (YA). (gr. 8-7). 17.99 *(978-0-06-236391-6(3),* HarperCollins) HarperCollins Pubs.

Currie-McGhee, Leanne K. Miley Cyrus, 1 vol. 2009. (People in the News Ser.). (ENG., Illus.). 96p. (gr. 7-7). lib. bdg. 41.03 *(978-1-4205-0127-8(5),* f0dfa9b2-ad1a-4d5c-b086-431d9f15c363, Lucent Pr.) Greenhaven Publishing LLC.

D'Addona, Dan & Sandeno, Kaitlin. Golden Glow: How Kaitlin Sandeno Achieved Gold in the Pool & in Life. 2019. (Illus.). 160p. 38.00 *(978-1-5381-1703-3(7))* Rowman & Littlefield Publishers, Inc.

Dakers, Diane. Vera Wang: A Passion for Bridal & Lifestyle Design. 2010. (Crabtree Groundbreaker Biographies Ser.). (ENG., Illus.). 112p. (J). pap. *(978-0-7787-2544-2(8));* (gr. 5-8). lib. bdg. *(978-0-7787-2535-0(9))* Crabtree Publishing Co.

Daly, Ruth. Rosa Parks. 2014. (Illus.). 24p. (J). *(978-1-4896-2452-9(X))* Weigl Pubs., Inc.

Daniel, Susanna. Paula Fox. 2009. (Library of Author Biographies Ser.). 112p. (gr. 5-8). 63.90 *(978-1-60853-550-7(9),* Rosen Reference) Rosen Publishing Group, Inc., The.

Darragh, Marty & Pitkin, Jo. Women of the Prairie State: 25 Illinois Women You Should Know. Greenleaf, Lisa, illus. 2012. 136p. (J). pap. 16.00 *(978-0-9842549-2-7(7))* Apprentice Shop Bks., LLC.

Darraj, Susan Muaddi. Anna Sui. 2009. (Asian Americans of Achievement Ser.). (ENG., Illus.). 120p. (gr. 7-12). 35.00 *(978-1-60413-570-1(0),* P171247, Facts On File) Infobase Holdings, Inc.

De Capua, Sarah. Sandra Day O'Connor, 1 vol. 2013. (Leading Women Ser.). (ENG.). 96p. (YA). (gr. 7-7). 42.64 *(978-0-7614-4961-4(2),* e5bd4eec-f5ac-4615-923a-b14ad1304d8e) Cavendish Square Publishing LLC.

DeFord, Diane. Harriet Tubman. 2009. pap. 13.25 *(978-1-60559-061-5(4))* Hameray Publishing Group, Inc.

Delle Donne, Elena. My Shot: Balancing It All & Standing Tall. (ENG.). 272p. (YA). (gr. 7). 2019. pap. 11.99 *(978-1-5344-1229-3(8))* 2018. (Illus.). 17.99 *(978-1-5344-1228-6(X))* Simon & Schuster Bks. For Young Readers. (Simon & Schuster Bks. For Young Readers).

Di Piazza, Domenica. Space Engineer & Scientist Margaret Hamilton. 2017. (STEM Trailblazer Bios Ser.). (ENG., Illus.). 32p. (J). (gr. 2-5). 26.65 *(978-1-5124-3450-7(7),* 00361086-11f1-4e7d-80a7-8140621d385a, Lerner Pubns.) Lerner Publishing Group.

Diamond, Cheryl. Model: A Memoir. 2008. (ENG., Illus.). 368p. (YA). (gr. 9-18). pap. 11.99 *(978-1-4169-5904-5(1),* Simon Pulse) Simon Pulse.

Dickmann, Nancy. Rachel Carson: Environmental Crusader, 1 vol. 2015. (Superheroes of Science Ser.). (ENG., Illus.). 48p. (J). (gr. 6-6). pap. 15.05 *(978-1-4824-3149-0(1),* cf89a6d9-d7b2-4292-8fe5-b6ecd6ec0962) Stevens, Gareth Publishing LLLP.

Dillon, Molly, compiled by. Yes She Can: 10 Stories of Hope & Change from Young Female Staffers of the Obama White House. 2019. (Illus.). 288p. (YA). (gr. 7). 18.99 *(978-1-9848-4845-1(3),* Schwartz & Wade Bks.) Random Hse. Children's Bks.

Ditchfield, Christin. Condoleezza Rice: America's Leading Stateswoman. 2006. (Great Life Stories Ser.). (ENG., Illus.). 112p. (J). (gr. 6-8). lib. bdg. 30.50 *(978-0-531-13874-8(7),* Watts, Franklin) Scholastic Library Publishing.

Doak, Robin S. Dian Fossey: Friend to Africa's Gorillas, 1 vol. 2014. (Women in Conservation Ser.). (ENG., Illus.). 48p. (J). (gr. 3-6). pap. 8.99 *(978-1-4846-0473-1(3),* 126605, Heinemann) Capstone.

Dodson Wade, Mary. Amazing Olympic Athlete Wilma Rudolph, 1 vol. 2009. (Amazing Americans Ser.). (ENG., Illus.). 24p. (gr. k-2). pap. 10.35 *(978-0-7660-5978-8(2),* d5d1fbaa-2c64-42f5-ac67-49964d2a9897, Enslow Elementary) Enslow Publishing, LLC.

Doeden, Matt. Ivanka Trump: A Brand of Her Own. 2017. (Gateway Biographies Ser.). (ENG., Illus.). 48p. (J). (gr. 4-8). lib. bdg. 31.99 *(978-1-5124-8624-7(8),* 464aeefc-51dd-4d37-9a2c-9fc1d4a7f19b, Lerner Pubns.) Lerner Publishing Group.

—Michele Bachmann: Tea Party Champion. 2011. (Gateway Biographies Ser.). (YA). (gr. 4-7). lib. bdg. 26.60 *(978-0-7613-9074-9(X))* Lerner Publishing Group.

Donaldson, Chelsea. Christine Sinclair, 1 vol. 2014. (Canadian Biographies Ser.). (ENG., Illus.). 24p. (J). (gr. -1-2). 27.32 *(978-1-4914-1959-5(8),* 127372, Capstone Pr.) Capstone.

Donaldson, Madeline. Venus & Serena Williams. (Amazing Athletes Ser.). 32p. 2005. (Illus.). (gr. 3-4). lib. bdg. 22.60 *(978-0-8225-3316-0(2))* 2nd rev. ed. 2011. (J). pap. 45.32 *(978-0-7613-7654-5(2))* Lerner Publishing Group.

Donelly, Karen. American Women Pilots of World War II, 1 vol. 2004. (American Women at War Ser.). (ENG.). 112p. (YA). (gr. 8-8). pap. 13.95 *(978-1-4358-3274-9(4),* 5d9f859d-ebd7-4c4b-9c01-4e9010f10a6f) Rosen Publishing Group, Inc., The.

Donohue, Caitlin. She Represents: 44 Women Who Are Changing Politics ... & the World. 2020. (ENG., Illus.). 216p. (YA). (gr. 8-12). pap. 16.99 *(978-1-5415-7901-9(1),* 211f4145-8df6-4719-b92d-3cba3a65ff9b, Zest Bks.) Lerner Publishing Group.

Dorrie, Roxanne. Venus & Serena Williams: The Smashing Sisters. 2003. (High Five Reading - Red Ser.). (ENG., Illus.). 48p. (gr. 3-4). per. 9.00 *(978-0-7368-2827-7(3))* Capstone.

Dubowski, Cathy East. Rosa Parks: Don't Give In! 2005. (Defining Moments Ser.). (Illus.). 32p. (J). (gr. 2-5). lib. bdg. 28.50 *(978-1-59716-078-0(4))* Bearport Publishing Co., Inc.

Dudley Gold, Susan. Sofia Coppola, 1 vol. 2014. (Great Filmmakers Ser.). (ENG.). 80p. (YA). (gr. 7-7). lib. bdg. 37.36 *(978-1-62712-945-9(6),* aef0b32c-6f48-413c-ab71-f389d1a6ac6e) Cavendish Square Publishing LLC.

—The Women's Rights Movement & Abolitionism, 1 vol. 2015. (Primary Sources of the Abolitionist Movement Ser.). (ENG., Illus.). 64p. (gr. 6-6). lib. bdg. 35.93 *(978-1-5026-0536-8(8),* e7cc3ec8-c0a6-456b-9f79-cb129c7788e2) Cavendish Square Publishing LLC.

Dunbar, Erica Armstrong & Van Cleve, Kathleen. Never Caught, the Story of Ona Judge: George & Martha Washington's Courageous Slave Who Dared to Run Away; Young Readers Edition. 2019. (ENG., Illus.). 272p. (J). (gr. 4-8). 19.99 *(978-1-5344-1617-8(X),* Aladdin) Simon & Schuster Children's Publishing.

Duncan, Alice Faye. A Song for Gwendolyn Brooks. Gordon, Xia, illus. 2019. (People Who Shaped Our World Ser.: 3). (ENG.). 48p. (J). (gr. k). 17.99 *(978-1-4549-3088-4(8))* Sterling Publishing Co., Inc.

Dunn, L. Kerr, et al. Dreaming with Animals: Anna Hyatt Huntington & Brookgreen Gardens. 2017. (Young Palmetto Bks.). (ENG., Illus.). 40p. 18.99 *(978-1-61117-820-3(7),* P544770) Univ. of South Carolina Pr.

Dunn, Mary R. & David, Rose. Michelle Wie. 2016. (Women in Sports Ser.). (ENG., Illus.). 24p. (J). (gr. -1-2). lib. bdg. 27.32 *(978-1-4914-7976-6(0),* 130472, Capstone Pr.) Capstone.

Dunn, Mary R. & Davin, Rose. Candace Parker. 2016. (Women in Sports Ser.). (ENG., Illus.). 24p. (J). (gr. -1-2). lib. bdg. 27.32 *(978-1-4914-7975-9(2),* 130471, Capstone Pr.) Capstone.

Dzidrums, Christine. Kelly Clarkson: Behind Her Hazel Eyes. 2013. 104p. pap. 9.99 *(978-1-938438-19-6(1))* Creative Media Publishing.

—Missy Franklin: Swimming Sensation. 2013. 72p. pap. 9.99 *(978-1-938438-23-3(X))* Creative Media Publishing.

Dzidrums, Christine & Rendon, Leah. Jennie Finch: Softball Superstar. Dzidrums, Joseph, photos by. 2013. (ENG., Illus.). 72p. (J). pap. 9.99 *(978-1-938438-13-4(2))* Creative Media Publishing.

Earl, C. F. Alicia Keys. 2012. (J). pap. *(978-1-4222-2547-9(X))* Mason Crest.

Earl, C. F. & Hill, Z. B. Rihanna. 2012. (Superstars of Hip-Hop Ser.). 48p. (J). (gr. 3-4). pap. 9.95 *(978-1-4222-2552-3(6));* (Illus.). 19.95 *(978-1-4222-2526-4(7))* Mason Crest.

Edgar, Susan E. & Edgar, Kathleen J. 50 American Women of Courage & Vision. 2007. (Illus.). 288p. (J). *(978-1-58865-391-8(9))* Kidsbooks, LLC.

Edgers, Geoff & Hempel, Carlene. Who Was Julia Child? Putra, Dede, illus. 2015. (Who Was-? Chapters Ser.). (ENG.). 112p. (J). (gr. 3-6). 21.19 *(978-1-4844-6776-3(0),* Penguin Workshop) Penguin Young Readers Group.

—Who Was Julia Child? Putra, Dede & Harrison, Nancy, illus. 2015. (Who Was? Ser.). 112p. (J). (gr. 3-7). 6.99 *(978-0-448-48297-2(5),* Penguin Workshop) Penguin Young Readers Group.

—Who Was Julia Child? 2015. (Who Was... ? Ser.). lib. bdg. 16.00 *(978-0-606-37555-9(4))* Turtleback.

Edison, Erin. Clara Barton, 1 vol. 2013. (Great Women in History Ser.). (ENG., Illus.). 24p. (J). (gr. -1-2). lib. bdg. 24.65 *(978-1-62065-076-9(2),* 120778, Pebble) Capstone.

—Helen Keller, 1 vol. 2014. (Great Women in History Ser.). (ENG., Illus.). 24p. (J). (gr. -1-2). lib. bdg. 24.65 *(978-1-4765-4217-1(1),* 124315, Pebble) Capstone.

—Rosa Parks, 1 vol. 2013. (Great Women in History Ser.). (ENG.). 24p. (J). (gr. -1-2). pap. 6.29 *(978-1-62065-863-5(1),* 121794); (gr. k-1). pap. 38.74 *(978-1-62065-864-2(X),* 19429) Capstone. (Pebble).

—Sally Ride, 1 vol. 2014. (Great Women in History Ser.). (ENG., Illus.). 24p. (J). (gr. -1-2). lib. bdg. 24.65 *(978-1-4765-4215-7(5),* 124313, Pebble) Capstone.

Edwards, Roberta. Michelle Obama: Primera Dama y Primera Mama. Call, Ken, illus. 2010. (SPA.). 48p. (gr. 3-5). pap. 9.99 *(978-1-60396-946-8(2))* Santillana USA Publishing Co., Inc.

Egan, Tracie. Cynthia Ann Parker: Cautiva de los comanches (Cynthia Ann Parker: Comanche Captive) 2009. (Grandes personajes en la historia de los Estados Unidos (Famous People in American History) Ser.). (SPA.). 32p. (gr. 2-3). 47.90 *(978-1-61512-796-2(8),* Editorial Buenas Letras) Rosen Publishing Group, Inc., The.

—Cynthia Ann Parker: Comanche Captive. 2009. (Primary Sources of Famous People in American History Ser.). 32p. (gr. 2-3). 47.90 *(978-1-60851-667-4(9))* Rosen Publishing Group, Inc., The.

—Cynthia Ann Parker: Comanche Captive = Cautiva de los Comanches, 1 vol. Gonzalez, Tomas, tr. 2003. (Famous People in American History / Grandes Personajes en la Historia de Los Estados Unidos Ser.). (SPA & ENG., Illus.). 32p. (J). (gr. 2-3). lib. bdg. 29.13 *(978-0-8239-4155-1(8),* 6e20de72-4518-4a36-8fe1-d1bde81121d9) Rosen Publishing Group, Inc., The.

—Cynthia Ann Parker: Comanche Captive / Cautiva de los Comanches. 2009. (Famous People in American History/Grandes personajes en la historia de los Estados Unidos Ser.). (ENG & SPA.). 32p. (gr. 2-3). 47.90 *(978-1-61512-542-5(6),* Editorial Buenas Letras) Rosen Publishing Group, Inc., The.

—Francisca Alvarez: El angel de Goliad, 1 vol. 2003. (Grandes Personajes en la Historia de Los Estados Unidos (Famous People in American History) Ser.). (SPA.). 32p. (gr. 3-4). pap. 10.00 *(978-0-8239-4227-5(9),* 9281ea04-af45-4d44-b992-87e389c837f6, Rosen Classroom) Rosen Publishing Group, Inc., The.

—Francisca Alvarez: The Angel of Goliad, 1 vol. 2003. (Famous People in American History / Grandes Personajes en la Historia de Los Estados Unidos Ser.). (ENG & SPA., Illus.). 32p. (gr. 2-3). lib. bdg. 29.13 *(978-0-8239-4157-5(4),* 8d646879-3215-45e0-97ba-5af78ef58304, Editorial Buenas Letras) Rosen Publishing Group, Inc., The.

Engle, Margarita. Soaring Earth: A Companion Memoir to Enchanted Air. 2019. (ENG., Illus.). 192p. (YA). (gr. 7). 18.99 *(978-1-5344-2953-6(0),* Atheneum Bks. for Young Readers) Simon & Schuster Children's Publishing.

Epstein, Dwayne. Hillary Clinton, 1 vol. 2009. (People in the News Ser.). (ENG., Illus.). 128p. (gr. 7-7). 41.03 *(978-1-4205-0268-8(9),* d39b223e-42d3-45d4-a896-84157b4a51bf, Lucent Pr.) Greenhaven Publishing LLC.

—Nancy Pelosi, 1 vol. 2008. (People in the News Ser.). (ENG., Illus.). 104p. (gr. 7-7). lib. bdg. 41.03 *(978-1-4205-0057-8(0),* 9eb2b367-5ac1-4f36-b140-7b3dc00bd1b1, Lucent Pr.) Greenhaven Publishing LLC.

Fabiny, Sarah. Who Is Gloria Steinem? 2014. (Who Is... ? Ser.). (Illus.). 105p. (J). lib. bdg. 16.00 *(978-0-606-36182-8(0))* Turtleback.

Fabiny, Sarah & Who HQ. Who Is Gloria Steinem? Hergenrother, Max, illus. 2014. (Who Was? Ser.). 112p. (J). (gr. 3-7). 5.99 *(978-0-448-48238-5(X),* Penguin Workshop) Penguin Young Readers Group.

Farrell, Mary Cronk. Standing up Against Hate: How Black Women in the Army Helped Change the Course of WWII. 2019. (ENG., Illus.). 208p. (J). (gr. 5-9). 17.99 *(978-1-4197-3160-0(2),* 1151301, Abrams Bks. for Young Readers) Abrams, Inc.

Faust, Daniel R. Ibtihaj Muhammad: Muslim American Champion Fencer & Olympian, 1 vol. 2017. (Breakout Biographies Ser.). (ENG., Illus.). 32p. (J). (gr. 4-5). 27.93 *(978-1-5081-6060-1(0),* edb48c2a-7335-4060-9e9d-88433e3aab1f, PowerKids Pr.) Rosen Publishing Group, Inc., The.

Favor, Lesli J. Women Doctors & Nurses of the Civil War. 2009. (American Women at War Ser.). 112p. (gr. 8-8). 63.90 *(978-1-61511-404-7(1))* Rosen Publishing Group, Inc., The.

Favor, Leslie. Women Doctors & Nurses of the Civil War, 1 vol. 2004. (American Women at War Ser.). (ENG.). 112p. (YA). (gr. 8-8). pap. 13.95 *(978-1-4358-3273-2(6),* d5d1a2e9-429e-42e8-b242-5f13ee7d9c16) Rosen Publishing Group, Inc., The.

Fedyszyn, Kirra. Molly Brown, 1 vol. 2014. (Jr. Graphic American Legends Ser.). (ENG., Illus.). 24p. (J). (gr. 2-3). pap. 11.60 *(978-1-4777-7201-0(4),* 388b9f70-8124-4905-b7df-40c49d57ed37, PowerKids Pr.) Rosen Publishing Group, Inc., The.

—Molly Pitcher, 1 vol. 2014. (Jr. Graphic American Legends Ser.). (ENG.). 24p. (J). (gr. 2-3). lib. bdg. 28.93 *(978-1-4777-7205-8(7),* 2ed331ae-074b-4148-a378-66f7467ec97b, PowerKids Pr.) Rosen Publishing Group, Inc., The.

Feinberg, Barbara Silberdick. Eleanor Roosevelt: Everything She Could Be. 2003. (Gateway Biography Ser.: 4). (Illus.). 48p. lib. bdg. 23.90 *(978-0-7613-2623-6(5),* Millbrook Pr.) Lerner Publishing Group.

Feldman, Heather. Marion Jones: Atleta de Categoría Internacional (World-Class Runner) 2009. (Superestrellas del Deporte (Superstars of Sports) Ser.). (SPA.). 24p. (gr.

1-2). 42.50 *(978-1-60853-227-8(5)*, Editorial Buenas Letras) Rosen Publishing Group, Inc., The.

—Marion Jones: World Class Runner. 2009. (Sports Superstars Ser.). 24p. (gr. 1-1). 42.50 *(978-1-60853-179-0(1)*, PowerKids Pr.) Rosen Publishing Group, Inc., The.

—Mia Hamm: Soccer Superstar. 2009. (Sports Superstars Ser.). 24p. (gr. 1-1). 42.50 *(978-1-60853-180-6(5)*, PowerKids Pr.) Rosen Publishing Group, Inc., The.

—Mia Hamm: Soccer/Soccer Superstar/Superestrella del Fútbol. 2009. (Superstars of Sports/Superestrellas del deporte Ser.). (ENG & SPA.). 24p. (gr. 1-2). 42.50 *(978-1-60853-240-7(2)*, Editorial Buenas Letras) Rosen Publishing Group, Inc., The.

—Mia Hamm: Superestrella del Fútbol Soccer (Soccer Superstar. 2009. (Superestrellas del Deporte (Superstars of Sports) Ser.). (SPA.). 24p. (gr. 1-2). 42.50 *(978-1-60853-228-5(3)*, Editorial Buenas Letras) Rosen Publishing Group, Inc., The.

—Venus Williams: Campeona de Tenis (Tennis Champion) 2009. (Superestrellas del Deporte (Superstars of Sports) Ser.). (SPA.). 24p. (gr. 1-2). 42.50 *(978-1-60853-229-2(1)*, Editorial Buenas Letras) Rosen Publishing Group, Inc., The.

—Venus Williams: Tennis Champion. 2009. (Sports Superstars Ser.). 24p. (gr. 1-1). 42.50 *(978-1-60853-183-7(X)*, PowerKids Pr.) Rosen Publishing Group, Inc., The.

—Venus Williams: Tennis Champion / Campeona de Tenis. 2009. (Superstars of Sports/Superestrellas del deporte Ser.). (ENG & SPA.). 24p. (gr. 1-2). 42.50 *(978-1-60853-241-4(0)*, Editorial Buenas Letras) Rosen Publishing Group, Inc., The.

Felix, Rebecca. Angie Bastian: Boomchickapop Boss. 2017. (Female Foodies Ser.). (ENG., Illus.). 32p. (J). (gr. 3-6). lib. bdg. 32.79 *(978-1-5321-1264-5(5)*, 27588, Checkerboard Library) ABDO Publishing Co.

—Debbi Fields: Mrs. Fields Founder. 2017. (Female Foodies Ser.). (ENG., Illus.). 32p. (J). (gr. 3-6). lib. bdg. 32.79 *(978-1-5321-1268-3(8)*, 27592, Checkerboard Library) ABDO Publishing Co.

—Marie Callender: Homemade Pie Maven. 2017. (Female Foodies Ser.). (ENG., Illus.). 32p. (J). (gr. 3-6). lib. bdg. 32.79 *(978-1-5321-1265-2(3)*, 27589, Checkerboard Library) ABDO Publishing Co.

—Peggy Cherng: Panda Express Empress. 2017. (Female Foodies Ser.). (ENG.). 32p. (J). (gr. 3-6). lib. bdg. 32.79 *(978-1-5321-1266-9(1)*, 27590, Checkerboard Library) ABDO Publishing Co.

—Rose Totino: Pizza Entrepreneur. 2017. (Female Foodies Ser.). (ENG., Illus.). 32p. (J). (gr. 3-6). lib. bdg. 32.79 *(978-1-5321-1269-0(6)*, 27593, Checkerboard Library) ABDO Publishing Co.

—Ruth Fertel: Ruth's Chris Steak House Creator. 2017. (Female Foodies Ser.). (ENG.). 32p. (J). (gr. 3-6). lib. bdg. 32.79 *(978-1-5321-1267-6(X)*, 27591, Checkerboard Library) ABDO Publishing Co.

Ferguson, Amanda. American Women of the Vietnam War. 2009. (American Women at War Ser.). 112p. (gr. 8-8). 63.90 *(978-1-61511-395-8(9))* Rosen Publishing Group, Inc., The.

Ferguson, Isabel & Frederick, Heather Vogel. A World More Bright: The Life of Mary Baker Eddy. 2013. (Illus.). vi, 279p. *(978-0-87510-494-2(0)*, Christian Science Publishing Society, The) Christian Science Publishing Society.

Fertig, Dennis. Sylvia Earle: Ocean Explorer, 1 vol. 2014. (Women in Conservation Ser.). (ENG., Illus.). 48p. (J). (gr. 3-6). 35.99 *(978-1-4846-0470-0(9)*, 126602); pap. 8.99 *(978-1-4846-0475-5(X)*, 126606) Capstone. (Heinemann).

Fiorelli, June Estep. Fannie Lou Hamer: A Voice for Freedom. 2004. (Avisson Young Adult Ser.). (Illus.). 117p. (J). pap. 19.95 *(978-1-888105-62-9(3))* Avisson Pr., Inc.

Fishman, Jon M. Danica Patrick. 2018. (Sports All-Stars (Lerner (tm) Sports) Ser.). (ENG., Illus.). 32p. (J). (gr. 2-5). pap. 9.99 *(978-1-5415-1200-9(6)*, e94a54a2-77d1-40f8-a0a9-985efa536e7b); lib. bdg. 29.32 *(978-1-5415-0849-1(1)*, 315a3240-be64-4007-9cd2-d838d09b3758, Lerner Pubns.) Lerner Publishing Group.

—Katie Ledecky. 2020. (Sports All-Stars (Lerner (tm) Sports) Ser.). (ENG., Illus.). 32p. (J). (gr. 2-5). 29.32 *(978-1-5415-9750-1(8)*, 32a444bc-57c0-49f9-8263-7f9d3d9a6721, Lerner Pubns.) Lerner Publishing Group.

—Simone Biles. 2017. (Sports All-Stars Ser.). (ENG.). 32p. (J). (gr. 2-5). 12.99 *(978-1-5124-4901-3(6))*; 39.99 *(978-1-5124-4900-6(8))*; (Illus.). lib. bdg. 29.32 *(978-1-5124-4897-9(4)*, f61f729f-7df7-4ed3-a2ac-28876fbf99fd); (Illus.). E-Book 42.65 *(978-1-5124-4899-3(0))* Lerner Publishing Group. (Lerner Pubns.).

—Sloane Stephens. 2020. (Sports All-Stars (Lerner (tm) Sports) Ser.). (ENG., Illus.). 32p. (J). (gr. 2-5). pap. 9.99 *(978-1-5415-8958-2(0)*, 5089db2c-4a39-4e4d-af4e-f67629a74600); lib. bdg. 29.32 *(978-1-5415-7728-2(0)*, e4bb1035-e696-4880-9223-7baf944cea1c) Lerner Publishing Group. (Lerner Pubns.).

Fleming, Candace. Amelia Lost: The Life & Disappearance of Amelia Earhart. 2011. (Illus.). 128p. (J). (gr. 3-7). 19.99 *(978-0-375-84198-9(9)*, Schwartz & Wade Bks.) Random Hse. Children's Bks.

—Cubs in the Tub: The True Story of the Bronx Zoo's First Woman Zookeeper. Downing, Julie, illus. 2020. (ENG.). 48p. (J). (gr. -1-3). 18.99 *(978-0-8234-4318-5(3)*, Neal Porter Bks) Holiday Hse., Inc.

Ford, Gilbert. How the Cookie Crumbled: The True (and Not-So-True) Stories of the Invention of the Chocolate Chip Cookie. Ford, Gilbert, illus. 2017. (ENG., Illus.). 40p. (J). (gr. -1-3). 18.99 *(978-1-4814-5067-6(0))* Simon & Schuster Children's Publishing.

Ford, Jeanne Marie. Rowan Blanchard: Teen Actress. 2017. (Superstar Stories Ser.). (ENG.). 24p. (J). (gr. 3-6). lib. bdg. 32.79 *(978-1-5038-1996-2(5)*, 211872) Child's World, Inc, The.

Fradin, Dennis Brindell & Fradin, Judith Bloom. Jane Addams: Champion of Democracy. 2006. (ENG., Illus.). 216p. (J). (gr. 5-7). 21.00 *(978-0-618-50436-7(2)*, 100801, Clarion Bks.) HarperCollins Pubs.

Frank, Mary Kate. Carrie Underwood, 1 vol. 2009. (Today's Superstars Ser.). (ENG.). 48p. (J). (gr. 3-3). pap. 15.05 *(978-1-4339-2377-7(7)*, 1096f238-965d-4a30-b64e-47509e74718f); lib. bdg. 34.60 *(978-1-4339-2381-4(5)*, 8aa7767b-bab4-4edc-9317-b88d5fefedba) Stevens, Gareth Publishing LLLP.

Franzen, Lenore. Venus Williams. 2003. (Ovations Ser.). (Illus.). 32p. (J). *(978-1-58341-249-7(2)*, Creative Education) Creative Co., The.

Freedman, Jeri. Elizabeth Warren: Democratic Senator from Massachusetts, 1 vol. 2017. (Leading Women Ser.). (ENG., Illus.). 112p. (YA). (gr. 7-7). 41.64 *(978-1-5026-2699-8(3)*, fd6cd751-fce0-41ed-92f6-f460528a8cbf) Cavendish Square Publishing LLC.

—Hillary Rodham Clinton: Profile of a Leading Democrat. 2009. (Career Profiles Ser.). 112p. (gr. 9-10). 63.90 *(978-1-61511-794-9(6))* Rosen Publishing Group, Inc., The.

Freedman, Lew. All about Amelia Earhart. 2015. (ENG., Illus.). 128p. (J). pap. 4.99 *(978-1-935628-44-6(5))* Blue River Pr.

Freedman, Russell. Babe Didrikson Zaharias: The Making of a Champion. 2014. (ENG., Illus.). 192p. (J). (gr. 5-7). pap. 11.99 *(978-0-544-10491-4(9)*, 1540799, Clarion Bks.) HarperCollins Pubs.

—The Voice That Challenged a Nation: A Newbery Honor Award Winner. 2011. (ENG., Illus.). 128p. (J). (gr. 5-7). pap. 11.99 *(978-0-547-48034-3(2)*, 1439385, Clarion Bks.) HarperCollins Pubs.

Freistadt, Margo. Kate Spade. 2011. (Profiles in Fashion Ser.). (Illus.). 112p. 28.95 *(978-1-59935-154-4(4))* Reynolds, Morgan Inc.

French, Martin, illus. Stompin' at the Savoy: The Story of Norma Miller. 2006. (ENG.). 64p. (J). (gr. 4-7). 17.99 *(978-0-7636-2244-2(3))* Candlewick Pr.

Frey, Wendy. Citizen Heroes. 2007. (Illus.). 68p. (J). *(978-1-4105-0888-1(9))*; *(978-1-4105-0887-4(0))* Building Wings LLC.

Friend, Robyn C. The Women of Apollo. Katz, David Arthur, illus. l.t. ed. 2006. 80p. (J). 17.95 *(978-1-880599-80-8(5))*; pap. 12.95 *(978-1-880599-79-2(1))* Cascade Pass, Inc.

Fry, Erin. The Power of Friendship. 2005. (Illus.). 16p. (J). pap. *(978-0-7367-2920-8(8))* Zaner-Bloser, Inc.

Furbee, Mary Rodd. Outrageous Women of Civil War Times. 2003. (Outrageous Women Ser.: 7). (ENG., Illus.). 132p. (J). (gr. 5-9). pap. 14.95 *(978-0-471-22926-1(1)*, Jossey-Bass) Wiley, John & Sons, Inc.

Furgang, Kathy. Bethany Mota, 1 vol. 2019. (Top YouTube Stars Ser.). (ENG.). 48p. (gr. 5-5). 33.47 *(978-1-7253-4619-2(2)*, 2ef430e5-c82b-4e26-8ed8-ec18670d1e0d, Rosen Reference) Rosen Publishing Group, Inc., The.

—Ruth Bader Ginsburg: Supreme Court Justice, 1 vol. 2019. (Junior Biographies Ser.). (ENG.). 24p. (gr. 3-4). 24.27 *(978-1-9785-0790-6(9)*, dbce21c1-e875-4a4c-861e-c30ec5685b1a) Enslow Publishing, LLC.

Garza, Carmen Lomas. Cuadros de Familia, 1 vol. Garza, Carmen Lomas, illus. 2nd anniv. ed. 2013. (Family Pictures Ser.).Tr. of Family Pictures. (ENG., Illus.). 32p. (J). (gr. 2-6). pap. 11.95 *(978-0-89239-207-0(X)*, leelowcbp) Lee & Low Bks., Inc.

Gaskill, Rachel. Agnes de Mille. 2009. (Library of American Choreographers Ser.). 48p. (gr. 5-8). 53.00 *(978-1-60853-454-8(5)*, Rosen Reference) Rosen Publishing Group, Inc., The.

Gateway Christian Academy (Fort Lauderdale, Fla.) Staff & Juvenile Collection Staff, contrib. by. Letters from Minty: An Imaginative Look into the Life & Thoughts of a Young Harriet Tubman. 2016. (Illus.). 31p. (J). *(978-1-338-13424-7(8))* Scholastic, Inc.

Gay, Kathlyn. Mother Jones. 2006. (American Workers Ser.). (Illus.). 144p. (J). (gr. 3-7). lib. bdg. 28.95 *(978-1-59935-016-5(5))* Reynolds, Morgan Inc.

Gayle, Sharon. Harriet Tubman & the Freedom Train: Ready-To-Read Level 3. Marshall, Felicia, illus. 2003. (Ready-To-Read Stories of Famous Americans Ser.). (ENG.). 32p. (J). (gr. 1-3). pap. 4.99 *(978-0-689-85480-4(3)*, Simon Spotlight) Simon Spotlight.

Gillibrand, Kirsten. Bold & Brave: Ten Heroes Who Won Women the Right to Vote. Kalman, Maira, illus. 40p. (J). (gr. 1-4). 2020. pap. 8.99 *(978-0-593-30266-8(4)*, Dragonfly Bks.) 2018. 18.99 *(978-0-525-57901-4(X)*, Knopf Bks. for Young Readers) 2018. (ENG.). lib. bdg. 21.99 *(978-0-525-57902-1(8)*, Knopf Bks. for Young Readers) Random Hse. Children's Bks.

Glaser, Jason. Danica Patrick, 1 vol. 2007. (Sports Idols Ser.). (ENG., Illus.). 24p. (J). (gr. 2-3). lib. bdg. 26.27 *(978-1-4042-4180-0(9)*, ba244585-5ae6-4721-bcf2-e7dfaa863d97) Rosen Publishing Group, Inc., The.

Glass, Maya. Abigail Adams: Destacada Primera Dama (Abigail Adams: Famous First Lady) 2009. (Grandes personajes en la historia de los Estados Unidos (Famous People in American History) Ser.). (SPA.). 32p. (gr. 2-3). 47.90 *(978-1-61512-787-0(9)*, Editorial Buenas Letras) Rosen Publishing Group, Inc., The.

—Abigail Adams: Famous First Lady / Destacada Primera Dama. 2009. (Famous People in American History/Grandes personajes en la historia de los Estados Unidos Ser.). (ENG & SPA.). 32p. (gr. 2-3). 47.90 *(978-1-61512-535-7(3)*, Editorial Buenas Letras) Rosen Publishing Group, Inc., The.

Glenn, Sharlee. Library on Wheels: Mary Lemist Titcomb & America's First Bookmobile. 2018. (ENG., Illus.). 56p. (J). (gr. 3-7). 18.99 *(978-1-4197-2875-4(X)*, 1127801, Abrams Bks. for Young Readers) Abrams, Inc.

Goddu, Krystyna Poray. A Girl Called Vincent: The Life of Poet Edna St. Vincent Millay. 2018. (ENG.). 224p. (J). (gr. 4). pap. 12.99 *(978-0-912777-85-6(0))* Chicago Review Pr., Inc.

Goldsmith, Connie. Women in the Military: From Drill Sergeants to Fighter Pilots. 2019. (ENG., Illus.). 120p. (YA). (gr. 6-12). 37.32 *(978-1-5415-2812-3(3)*, 926b05ea-eead-4685-b89f-468374efd7d4, Twenty-First Century Bks.) Lerner Publishing Group.

Goldstein, Margaret J. Astronaut & Physicist Sally Ride. 2018. (STEM Trailblazer Bios Ser.). (ENG., Illus.). 32p. (J). (gr. 2-5). 26.65 *(978-1-5415-0009-9(1)*, 0a678350-1fa6-471a-80d7-c4b325e81ef4, Lerner Pubns.) Lerner Publishing Group.

Goldsworthy, Steve. Sarah Palin. 2010. (Remarkable People Ser.). (Illus.). 24p. (J). (gr. 4-6). pap. 11.95 *(978-1-61690-167-7(5))*; lib. bdg. 25.70 *(978-1-61690-166-0(7))* Weigl Pubs., Inc.

Golio, Gary. Strange Fruit: Billie Holiday & the Power of a Protest Song. Riley-Webb, Charlotte, illus. 2017. (ENG.). 40p. (J). (gr. 3-6). E-Book 30.65 *(978-1-5124-2837-7(X)*, Millbrook Pr.) Lerner Publishing Group.

Golkar, Golriz. Meghan Markle. 2018. (Influential People Ser.). (ENG., Illus.). 32p. (J). (gr. 4-6). lib. bdg. 28.65 *(978-1-5435-4127-4(5)*, 139081, Capstone Pr.) Capstone.

Goodridge, Catherine. Michelle Kwan & Michelle Kwan (Spanish) 6 English, 6 Spanish Adaptations. 2011. (ENG & SPA.). (J). 79.00 net. *(978-1-4108-5659-3(3))* Benchmark Education Co.

—Michelle Kwan (Spanish) 2011. (SPA.). (J). pap. 40.00 net. *(978-1-4108-2428-8(4)*, A24284) Benchmark Education Co.

Gourley, Catherine. Who Is Maria Tallchief? Taylor, Val Paul, illus. 2003. (Who Was... ? Ser.). 103p. 15.00 *(978-0-7569-1592-6(9))* Perfection Learning Corp.

Graubart, Norman D. Laila Ali: Champion Boxer, 1 vol. 2015. (Exceptional African Americans Ser.). (ENG., Illus.). 24p. (gr. 3-4). 24.27 *(978-0-7660-6656-4(8)*, c766229a-246c-4942-a9e8-c07dcda2f088) Enslow Publishing, LLC.

Graves, Charles P. Annie Oakley: The Shooting Star. Cary, illus. 2011. 80p. (gr. 4-7). 37.95 *(978-1-258-01390-5(8))* Literary Licensing, LLC.

Graves, Jeseca, illus. Bessie Coleman: The Story of an Aviation Pioneer. 2007. 24p. (J). *(978-0-9745294-1-7(9))* San Diego County Regional Airport Authority.

Gray, Karlin. Serena: the Littlest Sister. Ahanonu, Monica, illus. 2019. (ENG.). 40p. (J). 18.99 *(978-1-62414-694-7(5)*, 900197962) Page Street Publishing Co.

Grayson, Robert. Estée Lauder: Businesswoman & Cosmetics Pioneer, 1 vol. 2013. (Essential Lives Set 8 Ser.). (ENG.). 112p. (YA). (gr. 6-12). lib. bdg. 41.36 *(978-1-61783-892-7(6)*, 6763, Essential Library) ABDO Publishing Co.

Green, Mary. Sarah Winnemucca: The Inspiring Life Story of the Activist & Educator. 2016. (Inspiring Stories Ser.). (ENG., Illus.). 112p. (J). (gr. 5-7). lib. bdg. 38.65 *(978-0-7565-5167-4(6)*, 128795, Compass Point Bks.) Capstone.

Greenberg, Michael. Sword of a Champion: The Sharon Monplaisir Story. 2003. (Anything You Can Do. . .Ser.: Vol. 2). (Illus.). 96p. (J). (gr. 2-5). pap. 9.95 *(978-1-930546-39-4(4))* Wish Publishing.

Greenberger, Robert. Christina Aguilera, 1 vol. 2008. (Contemporary Musicians & Their Music Ser.). (ENG., Illus.). 48p. (gr. 6-6). pap. 12.75 *(978-1-4358-5124-5(2)*, 5b5ddd5e-96c9-43cb-974f-fe04abea5bb7, Rosen Classroom) Rosen Publishing Group, Inc., The.

Griffin, Lydia. Susan Anderson: Colorado's Doc Susie. 2010. (ENG., Illus.). 72p. (J). pap. 8.95 *(978-0-86541-108-1(5))* Filter Pr., LLC.

Guglielmo, Amy & Tourville, Jacqueline. Pocket Full of Colors: The Magical World of Mary Blair, Disney Artist Extraordinaire. Barrager, Brigette, illus. 2017. (ENG.). 48p. (J). (gr. -1-3). 18.99 *(978-1-4814-6131-3(1))* Simon & Schuster Children's Publishing.

Haldy, Emma E. Helen Keller. Bane, Jeff, illus. 2016. (My Early Library: My Itty-Bitty Bio Ser.). (ENG.). 24p. (J). (gr. k-1). 30.64 *(978-1-63471-020-6(7)*, 208160) Cherry Lake Publishing.

—Sacagawea SP. Bane, Jeff, illus. 2018. (My Early Library: Mi Mini Biografía (My Itty-Bitty Bio) Ser.). (SPA.). 24p. (J). (gr. k-1). lib. bdg. 30.64 *(978-1-5341-3000-5(4)*, 212048) Cherry Lake Publishing.

Hall, Brianna. Great Women of the American Revolution, 1 vol. 2012. (Story of the American Revolution Ser.). (ENG., Illus.). 32p. (J). (gr. 3-6). pap. 8.10 *(978-1-4296-9284-7(7)*, 120343); lib. bdg. 27.99 *(978-1-4296-8451-4(8)*, 118514) Capstone. (Capstone Pr.).

Hally, Ashleigh. Jackie Cochran. 2012. (Illus.). 24p. (J). *(978-1-935884-75-0(1))*; pap. *(978-1-935884-81-1(6))* State Standards Publishing, LLC.

—Juliette Gordon Low. 2012. (Illus.). 24p. (J). *(978-1-935884-77-4(8))*; pap. *(978-1-935884-83-5(2))* State Standards Publishing, LLC.

—Rosalynn Carter. 2012. (Illus.). 24p. (J). *(978-1-935884-74-3(3))*; pap. *(978-1-935884-80-4(8))* State Standards Publishing, LLC.

Hansen, Grace. Aly Raisman. 2016. (Olympic Biographies Ser.). (ENG., Illus.). 24p. (J). (gr. -1-2). lib. bdg. 32.79 *(978-1-68080-944-2(X)*, 23353, Abdo Kids) ABDO Publishing Co.

—Michelle Obama: Former First Lady & Role Model. 2017. (History Maker Biographies (Abdo Kids Jumbo) Ser.). (ENG., Illus.). 24p. (J). (gr. -1-2). lib. bdg. 32.79 *(978-1-5321-0427-5(8)*, 26553, Abdo Kids) ABDO Publishing Co.

Harkins, Susan Sales & Harkins, William H. Betsy Ross. 2006. (Profiles in American History Ser.). (Illus.). 48p. (J). (gr. 3-7). lib. bdg. 29.95 *(978-1-58415-446-4(2))* Mitchell Lane Pubs.

Harmon, Daniel E. Amelia Earhart: Aviation Pioneer. 2017. (Britannica Beginner Bios Ser.). (Illus.). 32p. (J). (gr. 6-10). 77.40 *(978-1-5383-0020-6(6))* Rosen Publishing Group, Inc., The.

Harness, Cheryl. Remember the Ladies: 100 Great American Women. 2003. (J). (gr. 3-6). 19.65 *(978-0-613-61843-4(2))* Turtleback.

Harris, Kamala. The Truths We Hold: An American Journey (Young Readers Edition) (ENG., Illus.). 304p. (gr. 7). 2020. (J). pap. 10.99 *(978-0-593-11317-2(9)*, Penguin Books) 2019. (YA). 17.99 *(978-1-9848-3706-6(0)*, Philomel Bks.) Penguin Young Readers Group.

Harrison, Vashti. Little Leaders: Bold Women in Black History. 2017. (Vashti Harrison Ser.). (ENG., Illus.). 96p. (J). (gr. 3-7). 16.99 *(978-0-316-47511-2(4))* Little, Brown Bks. for Young Readers.

Heatley, Michael. Katy Perry. 2015. (Pop Icons Ser.). (Illus.). 64p. (J). (gr. 7). lib. bdg. 23.95 *(978-1-4222-3248-4(4))* Mason Crest.

Heatley, Michael & Gent, Mike. Taylor Swift. 2015. (Pop Icons Ser.). (Illus.). 64p. (J). (gr. 7). lib. bdg. 23.95 *(978-1-4222-3250-7(6))* Mason Crest.

Henderson, Leah. Mamie on the Mound: A Woman in Baseball's Negro Leagues. Doutsiopoulos, George, illus. 2020. (ENG.). 32p. (J). (gr. 3-5). 18.95 *(978-1-68446-023-6(9)*, 139306, Capstone Editions) Capstone.

Hernandez, Laurie. I Got This: To Gold & Beyond. (ENG., Illus.). 240p. (J). (gr. 3-7). 2018. pap. 8.99 *(978-0-06-267732-7(2))* 2017. 17.99 *(978-0-06-267731-0(4)*, HarperCollins) HarperCollins Pubs.

Herwick Rice, Dona & Greathouse, Lisa. Annie Oakley, 1 vol. rev. ed. 2009. (Reader's Theater Ser.). (ENG.). 24p. (gr. 2-4). pap. 8.99 *(978-1-4333-0997-7(1))* Teacher Created Materials, Inc.

Hewson, Anthony K. Alex Morgan. 2019. (Sports All-Stars (Lerner (tm) Sports) Ser.). (ENG., Illus.). 32p. (J). (gr. 2-5). pap. 9.99 *(978-1-5415-7446-5(X)*, bb6638ab-14b0-4d47-a638-847a373da994); lib. bdg. 29.32 *(978-1-5415-5611-9(9)*, 38419754-aadb-4b93-b503-58fa873928eb) Lerner Publishing Group. (Lerner Pubns.).

Hill, Z. B. Beyoncé. 2012. (J). pap. *(978-1-4222-2536-3(4))*; (Illus.). 48p. (gr. 3-4). 19.95 *(978-1-4222-2510-3(0))* Mason Crest.

Hillery, Louise. Bold Women in Indiana History. 2016. (Illus.). 212p. (J). pap. *(978-0-87842-655-3(8))* Mountain Pr. Publishing Co., Inc.

Hinman, Bonnie. Ivanka Trump: Businesswoman & Political Activist. 2017. (Newsmakers Set 2 Ser.). (ENG., Illus.). 48p. (J). (gr. 4-8). 55.65 *(978-1-68078-971-3(6)*, 26372) ABDO Publishing Co.

Hirsch, Jesse. Tina Fey, 1 vol., 1. 2015. (Giants of Comedy Ser.). (ENG.). 112p. (J). (gr. 7-7). 38.80 *(978-1-4994-6256-2(5)*, 8d07a78d-e54c-4b4a-819a-134d966b4db6, Rosen Young Adult) Rosen Publishing Group, Inc., The.

Hollihan, Kerrie Logan. Reporting under Fire: 16 Daring Women War Correspondents & Photojournalists. 2014. (Women of Action Ser.: 9). (ENG., Illus.). 256p. (YA). (gr. 7). 19.95 *(978-1-61374-710-0(1))* Chicago Review Pr., Inc.

Hoobler, Thomas & Hoobler, Dorothy. Real American Girls Tell Their Own Stories: Messages from the Heart & Heartland. 2012. (ENG.). 112p. (J). (gr. 5-9). pap. 6.99 *(978-1-4424-6043-0(1)*, Simon & Schuster Bks. For Young Readers) Simon & Schuster Bks. For Young Readers.

Hoose, Phillip. Claudette Colvin: Twice Toward Justice. 2010. (ENG., Illus.). 160p. (YA). (gr. 8-12). pap. 12.99 *(978-0-312-66105-2(3)*, 900070657) Square Fish.

Hopkins, H. Joseph. The Tree Lady: The True Story of How One Tree-Loving Woman Changed a City Forever. McElmurry, Jill, illus. 2013. (ENG.). 32p. (J). (gr. k-5). 18.99 *(978-1-4424-1402-0(2)*, Beach Lane Bks.) Beach Lane Bks.

Hopkinson, Deborah. Michelle. Ford, A. G., illus. 2009. 32p. (J). (gr. -1-2). 17.99 *(978-0-06-182739-6(8))* HarperCollins Pubs.

Hopping, Lorraine Jean. Women's Adventures in Science: Bone Detective. 2005. (Women's Adventures in Science Ser.). (ENG., Illus.). 128p. (YA). (gr. 5-9). 31.50 *(978-0-531-16776-2(3))* Scholastic Library Publishing.

Horn, Geoffrey M. Laila Ali, 1 vol. 2005. (Today's Superstars Ser.). (ENG., Illus.). 32p. (gr. 3-3). lib. bdg. 34.60 *(978-0-8368-6181-5(7)*, 5351e8c3-23ea-47a1-b65c-a542c98bbddc) Stevens, Gareth Publishing LLLP.

—Margaret Mead, 1 vol. 2004. (Trailblazers of the Modern World Ser.). (ENG., Illus.). 48p. (gr. 5-8). pap. 15.05 *(978-0-8368-5259-2(1)*, e27a92d6-8ea4-40ea-bdf4-0b7ba376e975); lib. bdg. 33.67 *(978-0-8368-5099-4(8)*, 1d9ac75a-4672-40d6-b6c8-da2ffda80202) Stevens, Gareth Publishing LLLP. (Gareth Stevens Secondary Library).

—Nancy Pelosi, 1 vol. 2009. (People We Should Know (Second Series) Ser.). (ENG.). 32p. (J). (gr. 3-5). pap. 11.50 *(978-1-4339-0162-1(5)*, cc982ed7-636a-43f2-8bf3-727da0c3c27f); lib. bdg. 33.67 *(978-1-4339-0021-1(1)*, 89210acd-7b88-4f6a-a1f2-f17328b75db2) Stevens, Gareth Publishing LLLP. (Gareth Stevens Learning Library).

Houts, Michelle. When Grandma Gatewood Took a Hike. 2016. (ENG., Illus.). 32p. (J). (gr. k-4). 17.95 *(978-0-8214-2235-9(9))* Ohio Univ. Pr.

Hughes, Sloane. Tig Notaro, 1 vol. 2019. (Giants of Comedy Ser.). (ENG.). 112p. (gr. 7-7). 38.80 *(978-1-5081-8870-4(X)*, a13bbbdf-3f17-4183-827e-9eb6e3122e14) Rosen Publishing Group, Inc., The.

Hull, Mary E. Mary Todd Lincoln: Civil War's First Lady, 1 vol. 2014. (Legendary American Biographies Ser.). (ENG.). 96p. (gr. 6-6). 29.60 *(978-0-7660-6480-5(8)*, 2334efaa-2847-413e-92a3-b06892d78510); pap. 13.88 *(978-0-7660-6481-2(6)*, 77e849a6-625a-4e25-a5bb-d16442ad7740) Enslow Publishing, LLC.

Isbell, Hannah. Rihanna: Pop Star, 1 vol. 2017. (Junior Biographies Ser.). (ENG.). 24p. (gr. 3-4). lib. bdg. 24.27 *(978-0-7660-8674-6(7)*, dcc2e073-c3db-4af0-818c-cead5e85845b) Enslow Publishing, LLC.

Jackson, Constance L. Over the River: Life of Lydia Maria Child, Abolitionist for Freedom, 1802-1880. 2008. (Illus.). 160p. pap. 18.95 *(978-0-9818204-0-8(9))* Permanent Productions Publishing.

Jackson, Garnet N. Shirley Chisholm, Congresswoman. 2012. (ENG., Illus.). (J). (gr. 1-4). pap. 7.47 net. *(978-0-8136-5247-4(2)*, Modern Curriculum Pr.) Savvas Learning Co.

Jarnow, Jesse. Phillis Wheatley: African American Poet / Poeta Afroamericana. 2009. (Famous People in American History/Grandes personajes en la historia de los Estados Unidos Ser.). (ENG & SPA.). 32p. (gr. 2-3). 47.90 *(978-1-61512-554-8(X)*, Editorial Buenas Letras) Rosen Publishing Group, Inc., The.

—Phillis Wheatley: Poeta afroamericana (Phillis Wheatley: African American Poet) 2009. (Grandes personajes en la historia de los Estados Unidos (Famous People in American History) Ser.). (SPA.). 32p. (gr. 2-3). 47.90 *(978-1-61512-807-5(7)*, Editorial Buenas Letras) Rosen Publishing Group, Inc., The.

-zynka, Kitson. National Geographic Readers: Helen Keller (Level 2) 2017. (Readers Bios Ser.). (Illus.). 32p. (J). (gr. 1-3). pap. 4.99 *(978-1-4263-2669-1(6),* National Geographic Kids) Disney Publishing Worldwide.
-nnifer Lawrence. 2013. (Rising Stars Ser.). 32p. (J). (gr. 3-6). pap. 63.00 *(978-1-4339-8979-7(4))* Stevens, Gareth Publishing LLLP.
-hnson, Robin. Kristen Stewart. 2010. (Superstars! Ser.). (ENG.). 32p. (J). pap. *(978-0-7787-7257-6(8))* Crabtree Publishing Co.
-Rihanna. 2013. (ENG., Illus.). 32p. (J). *(978-0-7787-1051-6(3))*; pap. *(978-0-7787-1055-4(6))* Crabtree Publishing Co.
-ones Donatelli, Jen. Oprah Winfrey: Celebrity with Heart, 1 vol. 2010. (Celebrities with Heart Ser.). (ENG., Illus.). 128p. (gr. 6-7). pap. 13.88 *(978-1-59845-206-8(1),* 69b2101f-ce1b-4592-83f6-0aeacdea60ab) Enslow Publishing, LLC.
-ones, Joyce Adams. Remembering the Marches in Selma, Alabama. 2006. 8.00 *(978-0-8059-7237-5(4))* Dorrance Publishing Co., Inc.
-opp, Kelsey. Kamala Harris. 2020. (Groundbreaking Women in Politics Ser.). (ENG., Illus.). 48p. (J). (gr. 5-6). pap. 11.95 *(978-1-64493-167-7(2),* 1644931672); lib. bdg. 34.21 *(978-1-64493-088-5(9),* 1644930889) North Star Editions. (Focus Readers).
—Tammy Duckworth. 2020. (Groundbreaking Women in Politics Ser.). (ENG., Illus.). 48p. (J). (gr. 5-6). pap. 11.95 *(978-1-64493-166-0(4),* 1644931664); lib. bdg. 34.21 *(978-1-64493-087-8(0),* 1644930870) North Star Editions. (Focus Readers).
Jordin Sparks. 2013. (Rising Stars Ser.). 32p. (J). (gr. 3-6). pap. 63.00 *(978-1-4339-8983-4(2))* Stevens, Gareth Publishing LLLP.
Juarez, Christine. Ellen Ochoa. 2016. (Great Hispanic & Latino Americans Ser.). (ENG., Illus.). 24p. (J). (gr. -1-2). lib. bdg. 24.65 *(978-1-5157-1888-8(3),* 132586, Pebble) Capstone.
Kaiser, Emma. Alexandria Ocasio-Cortez. 2020. (Groundbreaking Women in Politics Ser.). (ENG., Illus.). 48p. (J). (gr. 5-6). pap. 11.95 *(978-1-64493-168-4(0))*; lib. bdg. 34.21 *(978-1-64493-089-2(7),* 1644930897) North Star Editions. (Focus Readers).
Kamps, Louisa, et al. Girl Activist. Rucker, Georgia, illus. 2019. (Generation Girl Ser.). (ENG.). 160p. (J). (gr. 4). pap. 12.99 *(978-1-941367-64-3(X))* Downtown Bookworks.
Kanefield, Teri. The Girl from the Tar Paper School: Barbara Rose Johns & the Advent of the Civil Rights Movement. 2014. (ENG., Illus.). 56p. (J). (gr. 5-9). 19.95 *(978-1-4197-0796-4(5),* 1005601, Abrams Bks. for Young Readers) Abrams, Inc.
—Susan B. Anthony: The Making of America #4. 2019. (Making of America Ser.). (ENG., Illus.). 240p. (J). (gr. 5-9). 16.99 *(978-1-4197-3401-4(6),* 1263701, Abrams Bks. for Young Readers) Abrams, Inc.
Kann, Bob. Cordelia Harvey: Civil War Angel. 2011. (Badger Biographies Ser.). (ENG., Illus.). 128p. (J). pap. 12.95 *(978-0-87020-458-6(0))* Wisconsin Historical Society.
—A Recipe for Success: Lizzie Kander & Her Cookbook. 2006. (Badger Biographies Ser.). (ENG., Illus.). 144p. (J). (gr. 3-7). per. 12.95 *(978-0-87020-373-2(8))* Wisconsin Historical Society.
Katirgis, Jane. Celebrating First Lady Michelle Obama in Pictures, 1 vol. 2009. (Obama Family Photo Album Ser.). (ENG., Illus.). 32p. (gr. 3-3). lib. bdg. 26.60 *(978-0-7660-3652-9(9),* d9e0b307-d964-40e1-94b0-d84e91fa5515) Enslow Publishing, LLC.
Kelley, K. C. Taylor Swift. 2018. (Amazing Americans: Pop Music Stars Ser.). (ENG.). 24p. (J). (gr. -1-3). lib. bdg. 26.99 *(978-1-68402-456-8(0))* Bearport Publishing Co., Inc.
Kelly, David M. Jennifer Lawrence: Academy Award-Winning Actress, 1 vol. 2016. (Leading Women Ser.). (ENG.). 112p. (YA). (gr. 7-7). 41.64 *(978-1-5026-1985-3(7),* d51524df-8341-4b8a-8727-a6b8d9ad1edb) Cavendish Square Publishing LLC.
Kennon, Michou. Beyoncé, 1 vol. 2011. (Hip-Hop Headliners Ser.). (ENG., Illus.). 32p. (gr. 1-1). pap. 11.50 *(978-1-4339-4789-6(7),* ee1e7152-9d02-4fd4-bf05-4da3a1d5c0e1); (J). lib. bdg. 27.93 *(978-1-4339-4788-9(9),* 3f18dd4f-c807-4912-8fd6-6be85d5b19f8) Stevens, Gareth Publishing LLLP.
—Jordin Sparks, 1 vol. 2013. (Rising Stars Ser.). (ENG.). 32p. (J). (gr. 1-1). 27.93 *(978-1-4339-8981-0(6),* 288d8d95-0d9c-4550-ab47-07293d741549); pap. 11.50 *(978-1-4339-8982-7(4),* ce44b9e3-426b-408a-bebc-01d1b26f98bf) Stevens, Gareth Publishing LLLP.
Kent, Deborah. Elizabeth Cady Stanton: Woman Knows the Cost of Life, 1 vol. 2008. (Americans: the Spirit of a Nation Ser.). (ENG., Illus.). 128p. (gr. 5-6). lib. bdg. 35.93 *(978-0-7660-3357-3(0),* a08165a5-32e5-45ad-8cb3-d3e3ffca7805) Enslow Publishing, LLC.
Keppeler, Jill. Maya Angelou, 1 vol. 2018. (Heroes of Black History Ser.). (ENG.). 32p. (gr. 3-4). lib. bdg. 28.27 *(978-1-5382-3022-0(4),* 285d22b8-8db1-47e7-8e6d-7d577c9bd245) Stevens, Gareth Publishing LLLP.
Kessel, Kristin. Martha Graham. 2009. (Library of American Choreographers Ser.). 48p. (gr. 5-8). 53.00 *(978-1-60853-460-9(X),* Rosen Reference) Rosen Publishing Group, Inc., The.
King, David C. Dorothea Lange: Photographer of the People: Photographer of the People. 2009. (ENG., Illus.). 88p. (C). (gr. 6-18). lib. bdg. 180.00 *(978-0-7656-8154-6(4),* Y181941) Routledge.
Kinney, Dan. Hillary Clinton: Remarkable American Politician. 2017. (History Maker Biographies (Abdo Kids Jumbo) Ser.). (ENG., Illus.). 24p. (J). (gr. -1-2). lib. bdg. 32.79 *(978-1-5321-0426-8(X),* 26552, Abdo Kids) ABDO Publishing Co.
Kirkfield, Vivian. Sweet Dreams, Sarah. Ewald, Chris, illus. 2019. (ENG.). 36p. (J). (gr. 2-5). 17.99 *(978-1-939547-31-6(8),* 3d485949-2f4e-4940-82aa-fd4eaceb7367) Creston Bks.
Kirkpatrick, Rob. Mia Hamm: Soccer Star. 2009. (Great Record Breakers in Sports Ser.). 24p. (gr. 3-3). 42.50 *(978-1-61513-189-1(2),* PowerKids Pr.) Rosen Publishing Group, Inc., The.
—Tara Lipinski: Super Ice-Skater. 2009. (Great Record Breakers in Sports Ser.). 24p. (gr. 3-3). 42.50 *(978-1-61513-191-4(4),* PowerKids Pr.) Rosen Publishing Group, Inc., The.
Kishel, Ann-Marie. Jane Addams: A Life of Cooperation. 2006. (Pull Ahead Bks.). (Illus.). 32p. (J). (gr. 3-7). lib. bdg. 22.60 *(978-0-8225-6382-2(7),* Lerner Pubns.) Lerner Publishing Group.
—Rosa Parks: A Life of Courage. 2006. (Pull Ahead Books-Biographies Ser.). (ENG., Illus.). 32p. (gr. k-3). lib. bdg. 22.60 *(978-0-8225-3478-5(9),* Lerner Pubns.) Lerner Publishing Group.
Klepeis, Alicia Z. Calamity Jane: Frontierswoman, 1 vol. Lapegüe, Matías, illus. 2016. (American Legends & Folktales Ser.). (ENG.). 32p. (gr. 3-3). pap. 11.58 *(978-1-5026-2200-6(9),* c37a9dbf-ec06-4c83-9eab-a41507a4d866); lib. bdg. 30.21 *(978-1-5026-2202-0(5),* be2713c3-ecd7-41e4-bc29-d72b9e97a177) Cavendish Square Publishing LLC.
Kovatch, Sarah. Record Breaking Woman. 2005. (Voices Reading Ser.). (Illus.). 16p. (J). *(978-0-7367-2914-7(3))* Zaner-Bloser, Inc.
Kraft, Betsy Harvey. Mother Jones: One Woman's Fight for Labor. 2006. (Illus.). 116p. (YA). (gr. 6-10). reprint ed. 17.00 *(978-1-4223-5443-8(1))* DIANE Publishing Co.
Krass, Peter. Sojourner Truth: Antislavery Activist. 2004. (Black Americans of Achievement Legacy Edition Ser.). (ENG., Illus.). 112p. (gr. 6-12). 35.00 *(978-0-7910-8165-5(6),* P114169, Facts On File) Infobase Holdings, Inc.
Krebs, Laurie. A Day in the Life of a Colonial Indigo Planter. 2009. (Library of Living & Working in Colonial Times Ser.). 24p. (gr. 3-3). 42.50 *(978-1-60853-732-7(3),* PowerKids Pr.) Rosen Publishing Group, Inc., The.
Krensky, Stephen. Calamity Jane. 2008. pap. 40.95 *(978-0-8225-9291-4(6))* Lerner Publishing Group.
Krohn, Katherine E. Madam C. J. Walker & New Cosmetics, 1 vol. Dominguez, Richard et al, illus. 2006. (Inventions & Discovery Ser.). (ENG.). 32p. (J). (gr. 3-9). 8.10 *(978-0-7368-9647-4(3),* 93399, Capstone Pr.) Capstone.
—Oprah Winfrey. 2003. (Biography Ser.). (Illus.). 112p. (J). (gr. 6-18). pap. 7.95 *(978-0-8225-5000-6(8))* Lerner Publishing Group.
—Vera Wang. 2007. (Biography Ser.). (Illus.). 112p. (J). (gr. 3-7). lib. bdg. 29.27 *(978-0-8225-6612-0(5),* Twenty-First Century Bks.) Lerner Publishing Group.
—Women of the Wild West. 2003. (Biography Ser.). (Illus.). 112p. (YA). (gr. 6-18). pap. 7.95 *(978-0-8225-9690-5(3),* Carolrhoda Bks.) Lerner Publishing Group.
Krull, Kathleen. A Kids' Guide to America's First Ladies. DiVito, Anna, illus. 2017. (Kids' Guide to American History Ser.: 1). (ENG.). 256p. (J). (gr. 3-7). pap. 7.99 *(978-0-06-238106-4(7),* HarperCollins) HarperCollins Pubs.
—No Truth Without Ruth: The Life of Ruth Bader Ginsburg. Zhang, Nancy, illus. 2018. (ENG.). 48p. (J). (gr. -1-3). 17.99 *(978-0-06-256011-7(5),* Quill Tree Bks.) HarperCollins Pubs.
—A Woman for President: The Story of Victoria Woodhull. Dyer, Jane, illus. 2006. (J). (gr. 2-7). 14.60 *(978-0-7569-8179-2(4))* Perfection Learning Corp.
—Women Who Broke the Rules: Dolley Madison. Johnson, Steve & Fancher, Lou, illus. 2015. (Women Who Broke the Rules Ser.). (ENG.). 48p. (J). (gr. 1-4). 16.99 *(978-0-8027-3793-9(5),* 900139089, Bloomsbury USA Childrens) Bloomsbury Publishing USA.
Kudlinski, Kathleen. Sojourner Truth. Wooden, Lenny, illus. 2003. (Childhood of Famous Americans Ser.). (ENG.). 160p. (J). (gr. 3-7). mass mkt. 7.99 *(978-0-689-85274-9(6),* Simon & Schuster/Paula Wiseman Bks.) Simon & Schuster/Paula Wiseman Bks.
Kudlinski, Kathleen V. Rebel with a Cause: The Daring Adventure of Dicey Langston, Girl Spy of the American Revolution. Faber, Rudy, illus. 2015. (Encounter: Narrative Nonfiction Picture Bks.). (ENG.). 40p. (J). (gr. 3-6). lib. bdg. 29.32 *(978-1-4914-6073-3(3),* 128973, Capstone Young Readers) Capstone.
Kulling, Monica. Spic-And-Span! Lillian Gilbreth's Wonder Kitchen. Parkins, David, illus. 2016. (Great Idea Ser.: 6). 32p. (J). (gr. k-3). pap. 6.99 *(978-1-101-91843-2(8),* Tundra Bks.) Tundra Bks. CAN. Dist: Penguin Random Hse. LLC.
Labrecque, Ellen. Gertrude B. Elion & Pharmacology. 2017. (21st Century Junior Library: Women Innovators Ser.). (ENG., Illus.). 24p. (J). (gr. 2-5). lib. bdg. 29.21 *(978-1-63472-182-0(9),* 209300) Cherry Lake Publishing.
—Mary Anderson & Windshield Wipers. 2017. (21st Century Junior Library: Women Innovators Ser.). (ENG., Illus.). 24p. (J). (gr. 2-5). lib. bdg. 29.21 *(978-1-63472-178-3(0),* 209284) Cherry Lake Publishing.
Lajiness, Katie. Beyonce. 2017. (Big Buddy Pop Biographies Set 2 Ser.). (ENG., Illus.). 32p. (J). (gr. 2-5). lib. bdg. 34.21 *(978-1-5321-1058-0(8),* 25692, Big Buddy Bks.) ABDO Publishing Co.
—Rihanna. 2017. (Big Buddy Pop Biographies Set 2 Ser.). (ENG., Illus.). 32p. (J). (gr. 2-5). lib. bdg. 34.21 *(978-1-5321-1062-7(6),* 25700, Big Buddy Bks.) ABDO Publishing Co.
Lakin, Patricia. Abigail Adams: First Lady of the American Revolution. Bandelin, Debra & Dacey, Bob, illus. 2006. 48p. (J). lib. bdg. 15.00 *(978-1-4242-1560-7(9))* Fitzgerald Bks.
Lambert, Joseph. Annie Sullivan & the Trials of Helen Keller. Lambert, Joseph, illus. 2018. (Center for Cartoon Studies Presents Ser.). (ENG., Illus.). 96p. (J). (gr. 5-9). 17.99 *(978-1-368-02230-9(8))* Little, Brown Bks. for Young Readers.
Lang, Heather. Anybody's Game: Kathryn Johnston, the First Girl to Play Little League Baseball. Puglesi, Cecilia, illus. 2018. (She Made History Ser.). (ENG.). 32p. (J). (gr. -1-3). 16.99 *(978-0-8075-0379-9(7),* 807503797) Whitman, Albert & Co.
—Queen of the Track: Alice Coachman, Olympic High-Jump Champion. Cooper, Floyd, illus. 2012. (ENG.). 40p. (J). (gr. k-4). 18.99 *(978-1-59078-850-9(8),* Astra Young Readers) Astra Publishing Hse.
Lantier, Patricia. Harriet Tubman: Conductor on the Underground Railroad, 1 vol. 2009. (Voices for Freedom Ser.). (ENG., Illus.). 64p. (J). (gr. 5-8). pap. *(978-0-7787-4838-0(3))*; lib. bdg. *(978-0-7787-4822-9(7))* Crabtree Publishing Co.
Larkin, Tanya. What Was Cooking in Julia Grant's White House? 2009. (Cooking Throughout American History Ser.). 24p. (gr. 3-3). 42.50 *(978-1-61511-952-3(3),* PowerKids Pr.) Rosen Publishing Group, Inc., The.
Lasky, Kathryn. Vision of Beauty: Candlewick Biographies: The Story of Sarah Breedlove Walker. Bennett, Nneka, illus. 2012. (Candlewick Biographies Ser.). (ENG.). 56p. (J). (gr. 3-7). 14.99 *(978-0-7636-6428-2(6))*; pap. 5.99 *(978-0-7636-6092-5(2))* Candlewick Pr.
Lassieur, Allison. Eleanor Roosevelt: Activist for Social Change. 2006. (Great Life Stories Ser.). (ENG., Illus.). 112p. (J). (gr. 6-8). lib. bdg. 30.50 *(978-0-531-13871-7(2),* Watts, Franklin) Scholastic Library Publishing.
Latham, Donna. Norah Jones. (Sharing the American Dream Ser.). 64p. (YA). (gr. 7-12). 2009. 22.95 *(978-1-4222-0590-7(8))* 2007. pap. 9.95 *(978-1-4222-0751-2(X))* Mason Crest.
Lauber, Leah F. Soccer Dreams: My True Adventure Following the U. S. Women's National Soccer Team, As a Fan & 12-Year Old Junior Reporter for the St. Petersburg Times During the History-Making 1999 FIFA Women's World Cup! 2003. (Illus.). 96p. (YA). per. 19.99 *(978-0-9745480-0-5(6))* WCI Pr.
Leaf, Christina. Rachel Carson: Environmentalist. 2019. (Women Leading the Way Ser.). (ENG., Illus.). 24p. (J). (gr. k-3). pap. 7.99 *(978-1-61891-504-7(5),* 12154, Blastoff! Readers) Bellwether Media.
Leavitt, Amie Jane. Nancy Pelosi. 2007. (Blue Banner Biography Ser.). (Illus.). 32p. (YA). (gr. 4-7). lib. bdg. 25.70 *(978-1-58415-613-0(9))* Mitchell Lane Pubs.
—What It's Like to Be Miley Cyrus. Vega, Eida de la, tr. 2009. (What It's Like to Be/Que se Siente al Ser Ser.). (SPA & ENG., Illus.). 32p. (J). (gr. -1-2). lib. bdg. 25.70 *(978-1-58415-841-7(7))* Mitchell Lane Pubs.
Lee, Sally. Eleanor Roosevelt, 1 vol. 2010. (First Ladies Ser.). (ENG.). 24p. (J). (gr. -1-2). pap. 7.29 *(978-1-4296-5603-0(4),* 114106); (gr. k-1). pap. 43.74 *(978-1-4296-5604-7(2),* 15474, Capstone Pr.) Capstone.
—Hillary Clinton, 1 vol. 2010. (First Ladies Ser.). (ENG.). (J). (gr. -1-2). lib. bdg. 27.32 *(978-1-4296-5327-5(2),* 113736, Capstone Pr.) Capstone.
—Martha Washington, 1 vol. 2010. (First Ladies Ser.). (ENG.). 24p. (J). (gr. -1-2). pap. 7.29 *(978-1-4296-5605-4(0),* 114107, Capstone Pr.) Capstone.
Leed, Percy. Wilma Rudolph: Running for Gold. 2020. (Epic Sports Bios (Lerner (tm) Sports) Ser.). (ENG., Illus.). 32p. (J). (gr. 2-5). 30.65 *(978-1-5415-9744-0(3),* d02fb726-95e7-47ea-aa3b-c085bb381bd2, Lerner Pubns.) Lerner Publishing Group.
Leigh, Anna. Nancy Pelosi: Political Powerhouse. 2020. (Gateway Biographies Ser.). (ENG., Illus.). 48p. (J). (gr. 4-8). pap. 11.99 *(978-1-5415-8889-9(4),* 71ecdbfb-6ecb-45d4-817d-86bb18fb8795); lib. bdg. 31.99 *(978-1-5415-7746-6(9),* 3d6a23df-da43-4277-ab99-14602397f693) Lerner Publishing Group. (Lerner Pubns.).
Letters of a Woman Homesteader. 2003. (Our American Heritage Ser.). (J). pap. 62.00 incl. audio compact disk *(978-1-58472-527-5(3),* In Audio) Sound Room Pubs., Inc.
Levy, Debbie. Becoming RBG: Ruth Bader Ginsburg's Journey to Justice. Gardner, Whitney, illus. 2019. (ENG.). 208p. (J). (gr. 5). 19.99 *(978-1-5344-2456-2(3))*; pap. 12.99 *(978-1-5344-2455-5(5))* Simon & Schuster Bks. For Young Readers. (Simon & Schuster Bks. For Young Readers).
Lew, Kristi. Laurie Halse Anderson, 1 vol. 2013. (All about the Author Ser.). (ENG.). 112p. (YA). (gr. 7-7). 39.80 *(978-1-4777-1764-6(1),* fd7ef00b-e1d8-4df4-af98-449871d6f876) Rosen Publishing Group, Inc., The.
Lewis, Meharry H. Mary Lena Lewis Tate - Vision! The Woman Who Compassed a Man 2005. (Illus.). 484p. 74.95 *(978-0-910003-08-7(4))* New & Living Way Publishing Co.
Linde, Barbara M. Taylor Swift, 1 vol. 2010. (Today's Superstars Ser.). (ENG.). 48p. (J). (gr. 3-3). pap. 15.05 *(978-1-4339-4002-6(7),* 853b9cb5-e1e9-463b-8a39-ca65dff46301); lib. bdg. 34.60 *(978-1-4339-4001-9(9),* a1aef9a3-eda1-47da-8a35-4b06a9204418) Stevens, Gareth Publishing LLLP.
Lindin, Emily. UnSlut: A Diary & a Memoir. 2015. (ENG., Illus.). 272p. (YA). (gr. 9-12). 14.99 *(978-1-942186-00-7(2),* 5d5e5227-8b5d-4bd2-b66e-fbbc818a2dbe, Zest Bks.) Lerner Publishing Group.
Link, Theodore. Annie Oakley: Wild West Sharpshooter = Pistolera Del Lejano Oeste, 1 vol. 2003. (Famous People in American History / Grandes Personajes en la Historia de Los Estados Unidos Ser.). (SPA & ENG., Illus.). 32p. (J). (gr. 2-3). lib. bdg. 29.13 *(978-0-8239-4150-6(7),* c9bf44a4-8733-4b7d-9fe7-c08803ad5713) Rosen Publishing Group, Inc., The.
Lloyd, Carli & Coffey, Wayne. All Heart: My Dedication & Determination to Become One of Soccer's Best. (ENG., Illus.). 304p. (J). (gr. 5-7). 2018. pap. 9.99 *(978-1-328-74097-7(8),* 1677146) 2016. 16.99 *(978-0-544-97869-0(2),* 1663897) HarperCollins Pubs. (Clarion Bks.).
Lobb, Nancy. 16 Extraordinary Americans with Disabilities. 2nd ed. 2007. (16 Extraordinary Ser.). (Illus.). 139p. (J). (gr. 3-7). tchr. ed., per. 25.00 *(978-0-8251-6278-7(5))* Walch Education.
Loh-Hagan, Virginia. Abby Sunderland: Lost at Sea. 2019. (True Survival Ser.). (ENG., Illus.). 32p. (J). (gr. 4-8). pap. 14.21 *(978-1-5341-3988-6(5),* 212781); lib. bdg. 32.07 *(978-1-5341-4332-6(7),* 212780) Cherry Lake Publishing. (45th Parallel Press).
—Jane C. Wright & Chemotherapy. 2018. (21st Century Junior Library: Women Innovators Ser.). (ENG., Illus.). 24p. (J). (gr. 2-5). lib. bdg. 29.21 *(978-1-5341-2910-8(3),* 211684) Cherry Lake Publishing.
—Sally Ride. Bane, Jeff, illus. 2018. (Mi Mini Biografía (My Itty-Bitty Bio): My Early Library). (ENG.). 24p. (J). (gr. k-1). pap. 12.79 *(978-1-5341-0808-0(4),* 210596); lib. bdg. 30.64 *(978-1-5341-0709-0(6),* 210595) Cherry Lake Publishing.
—Shirley Ann Jackson. Bane, Jeff, illus. 2018. (Mi Mini Biografía (My Itty-Bitty Bio): My Early Library). (ENG.). 24p. (J). (gr. k-1). pap. 12.79 *(978-1-5341-0812-7(2),* 210612); lib. bdg. 30.64 *(978-1-5341-0713-7(4),* 210611) Cherry Lake Publishing.
Lohse, Joyce B. Unsinkable: The Molly Brown Story. 2006. (Now You Know Bio Ser.). (Illus.). 76p. (J). pap. 8.95 *(978-0-86541-081-7(X))* Filter Pr., LLC.
Lowery, Linda. Aunt Clara Brown: Official Pioneer. Porter, Janice Lee, illus. 2006. (On My Own Biographies Ser.). 48p. 16.95 *(978-0-7569-6699-7(X))* Perfection Learning Corp.
—Tía Clara Brown: Pionera Oficial. Porter, Janice Lee, illus. 2005. (Yo Solo Biografías Ser.). (SPA.). 48p. (J). (gr. 2-4). per. 6.95 *(978-0-8225-3129-6(1))* Lerner Publishing Group.
Lynette, Rachel. Julia Butterfly Hill: Saving the Ancient Redwoods, 1 vol. 2007. (Young Heroes Ser.). (ENG., Illus.). 48p. (gr. 4-8). lib. bdg. 37.33 *(978-0-7377-3628-1(3),* 564f9d9d-cbc9-4da5-9172-bd474925ca40, KidHaven Publishing) Greenhaven Publishing LLC.
MacBain, Jennifer. Gertrude Elion: Nobel Prize Winner in Physiology & Medicine. 2009. (Women Hall of Famers in Mathematics & Science Ser.). 112p. (gr. 5-8). 63.90 *(978-1-60854-811-8(2),* Rosen Reference) Rosen Publishing Group, Inc., The.
Mack, Lorna B. Lorna's Whale. 2011. 56p. pap. 26.12 *(978-1-4634-1610-2(5))* AuthorHouse.
Macy, Sue. Basketball Belles: How Stanford, Cal, & One Scrappy Player Put Women's Hoops on the Map. Collins, Matt, illus. 2019. 32p. (J). (gr. 1-4). pap. 7.99 *(978-0-8234-4175-4(X))* Holiday Hse., Inc.
—Bull's Eye: A Photobiography of Annie Oakley. 2015. (Photobiographies Ser.). 64p. (J). (gr. 5-9). pap. 7.99 *(978-1-4263-2218-1(6),* National Geographic Kids) Disney Publishing Worldwide.
—Bylines: A Photobiography of Nellie Bly. 2009. (Photobiographies Ser.). (Illus.). 64p. (J). (gr. 5-9). 19.95 *(978-1-4263-0513-9(3),* National Geographic Kids) Disney Publishing Worldwide.
—Miss Mary Reporting: The True Story of Sportswriter Mary Garber. Payne, C. F., illus. 2016. (ENG.). 40p. (J). (gr. k-3). 18.99 *(978-1-4814-0120-3(3),* Simon & Schuster Bks. For Young Readers) Simon & Schuster Bks. For Young Readers.
—Trudy's Big Swim: How Gertrude Ederle Swam the English Channel & Took the World by Storm. Collins, Matt, illus. 2019. 40p. (J). (gr. 1-4). pap. 8.99 *(978-0-8234-4189-1(X))* Holiday Hse., Inc.
Mah, Adeline Yen. Chinese Cinderella: The True Story of an Unwanted Daughter. 2010. (ENG.). 240p. (YA). (gr. 7). pap. 11.99 *(978-0-385-74007-4(7),* Ember) Random Hse. Children's Bks.
Maher, Jack. Animal Instincts. 2011. (J). pap. *(978-0-531-22560-8(7))* Scholastic, Inc.
Maimone, Sofia. Mary J. Blige, 1 vol. 2011. (Hip-Hop Headliners Ser.). (ENG., Illus.). 32p. (J). (gr. 1-1). 27.93 *(978-1-4339-4804-6(4),* 1391fd88-a999-445e-b3da-c7440c12e297); pap. 11.50 *(978-1-4339-4805-3(2),* 627330a9-d75d-4bb0-8f75-bf75fd56143a) Stevens, Gareth Publishing LLLP.
Mallory, Mark. Amelia Earhart: Queen of the Sky, 1 vol. 2008. (Real Life Readers Ser.). (ENG.). 16p. (gr. 2-3). pap. 7.05 *(978-1-4358-0053-3(2),* 113c4004-c2e4-4844-9b9d-1db3d2798793, Rosen Classroom) Rosen Publishing Group, Inc., The.
Maloof, Torrey. Mary Musgrove: Bringing People Together. rev. ed. 2016. (Social Studies: Informational Text Ser.). (ENG., Illus.). 32p. (gr. 2-4). pap. 10.99 *(978-1-4938-2557-8(7))* Teacher Created Materials, Inc.
Manzano, Sonia. Becoming Maria: Love & Chaos in the South Bronx. (ENG.). 272p. (YA). (gr. 7-7). 2017. pap. 10.99 *(978-0-545-62185-4(2))* 2015. 18.99 *(978-0-545-62184-7(4))* Scholastic, Inc. (Scholastic Pr.).
Mapua, Jeff. Hillary Clinton, 1 vol. 2014. (Britannica Beginner Bios Ser.). (ENG., Illus.). 32p. (J). (gr. 2-3). 26.06 *(978-1-62275-689-6(4),* c6a1ac5c-edfc-4d9f-8b71-fe87854a49f1, Britannica Educational Publishing) Rosen Publishing Group, Inc., The.
Mara, Wil. Laura Bush. 2003. (Rookie Biographies Ser.). (ENG., Illus.). 32p. (J). (gr. 1-2). 20.50 *(978-0-516-22854-9(4),* Children's Pr.) Scholastic Library Publishing.
—Laura Ingalls Wilder. 2003. (Rookie Biographies Ser.). (ENG., Illus.). 32p. (J). (gr. 1-2). 20.50 *(978-0-516-22855-6(2),* Children's Pr.) Scholastic Library Publishing.
—Rosa Parks. (Rookie Biographies Ser.). (ENG., Illus.). 32p. (J). (gr. 1-2). 2004. pap. 4.95 *(978-0-516-27916-9(5))* 2007. pap. 4.95 *(978-0-531-12592-2(0))* Scholastic Library Publishing. (Children's Pr.).
Marcovitz, Hal. Eleanor Holmes Norton. 2003. (African American Leaders Ser.). (ENG., Illus.). 112p. (gr. 6-12). 30.00 *(978-0-7910-7682-8(2),* P113971, Facts On File) Infobase Holdings, Inc.
—Venus & Serena Williams. 2012. (Role Model Athletes Ser.). 64p. (J). (gr. 7). 22.95 *(978-1-4222-2714-5(6))* Mason Crest.
Marie Ford, Jeanne. Ilhan Omar. 2020. (Groundbreaking Women in Politics Ser.). (ENG., Illus.). 48p. (J). (gr. 5-6). pap. 11.95 *(978-1-64493-169-1(9),* 1644931699); lib. bdg. 34.21 *(978-1-64493-090-8(0),* 1644930900) North Star Editions. (Focus Readers).
Markarian, Margie. Hilary Duff: Life in the Spotlight, 1 vol. 2009. (Hot Celebrity Biographies Ser.). (ENG., Illus.). 48p. (gr. 5-7). pap. 11.53 *(978-0-7660-3626-0(X),* 5f2f1040-458d-4bce-83b2-63037b5cbf42) Enslow Publishing, LLC.
Markel, Michelle. Hillary Rodham Clinton: Some Girls Are Born to Lead. Pham, LeUyen, illus. 2016. (ENG.). 40p. (J). (gr. -1-3). 17.99 *(978-0-06-238122-4(9),* Balzer & Bray) HarperCollins Pubs.
Marlgorz, Juliet. Elizabeth Cady Stanton & the Fight for Equal Rights, 1 vol. 2008. (Real Life Readers Ser.). (ENG.). 32p. (gr. 4-6). pap. 10.00 *(978-1-4358-0233-9(0),* c6a2072f-8727-488c-b3bd-4dfd47097ed8, Rosen Classroom) Rosen Publishing Group, Inc., The.

W X Y Z

Marsh, Carole. Abigail Adams. 2004. 12p. (gr. k-4). 2.95 *(978-0-635-02372-8(5))* Gallopade International.

—Amelia Earhart. 2003. 12p. (gr. k-4). 2.95 *(978-0-635-02131-1(5))* Gallopade International.

—Antonia C. Novello: First Female U. S. Surgeon General: First Female U. S. Surgeon General. 2003. 12p. (gr. k-4). 2.95 *(978-0-635-02139-7(0))* Gallopade International.

—Carol Moseley Braun. 2003. 12p. (gr. k-4). 2.95 *(978-0-635-02384-1(9))* Gallopade International.

—Clara Barton. 2003. 12p. (gr. k-4). 2.95 *(978-0-635-02353-7(9))* Gallopade International.

—Condoleezza Rice. 2003. 12p. (gr. k-4). 2.95 *(978-0-635-02385-8(7))* Gallopade International.

—Ellen Ochoa: First Hispanic American Woman in Space: First Hispanic American Woman in Space. 2003. 12p. (gr. k-4). 2.95 *(978-0-635-02138-0(2))* Gallopade International.

—Harriet Beecher Stowe. 2003. 12p. (gr. k-4). 2.95 *(978-0-635-02356-8(3))* Gallopade International.

—Meet Shirley Franklin, Mayor of Atlanta! 2003. 32p. (gr. 3-8). 21.95 *(978-0-635-01141-1(7))* Gallopade International.

—Molly Pitcher. 2004. 12p. (gr. k-4). 2.95 *(978-0-635-02375-9(X))* Gallopade International.

—Phillis Wheatley. 2003. 12p. (gr. k-4). 2.95 *(978-0-635-02371-1(7))* Gallopade International.

—Rachel Carson: Excellent Ecologist. 2004. (1000 Readers Ser.). (Illus.). 14p. (J). (gr. k-4). pap. 2.95 *(978-0-635-02524-1(8))* Gallopade International.

—Sacagawea: Native American Heroine: Native American Heroine. 2003. 12p. (gr. k-4). 2.95 *(978-0-635-02143-4(9))* Gallopade International.

—Sojourner Truth. 2003. 12p. (gr. k-4). 2.95 *(978-0-635-02355-1(5))* Gallopade International.

Marsico, Katie. Surviving a Shark Attack: Bethany Hamilton. 2019. (They Survived (Alternator Books (r)) Ser.). (ENG., Illus.). 32p. (J). (gr. 3-6). lib. bdg. 29.32 *(978-1-5415-2353-1(9),* 219854b2-a068-4315-bcbd-4a8a3f071a8e, Lerner Pubns.) Lerner Publishing Group.

—Sybil Ludington's Revolutionary War Story. Girard, Thomas, illus. 2018. (Narrative Nonfiction: Kids in War Ser.). (ENG.). 32p. (J). (gr. 2-4). pap. 9.99 *(978-1-5415-1194-1(8),* cec45b0f-080d-4da3-ab6d-0c870f19cc2b); lib. bdg. 27.99 *(978-1-5124-5676-9(4),* 5eb11b74-cf07-4032-890a-7cd3011602d0, Lerner Pubns.) Lerner Publishing Group.

Mattern, Joanne. Eleanor Roosevelt: More Than a First Lady. 2009. (Women Who Shaped History Ser.). 24p. (gr. 2-3). 42.50 *(978-1-60854-817-0(1),* PowerKids Pr.) Rosen Publishing Group, Inc., The.

—Sojourner Truth: Early Abolitionist. 2009. (Women Who Shaped History Ser.). 24p. (gr. 2-3). 42.50 *(978-1-60854-821-7(X),* PowerKids Pr.) Rosen Publishing Group, Inc., The.

—What's So Great about Michelle Obama. 2009. (What's So Great About...? Ser.). 32p. (J). (gr. 2-4). lib. bdg. 25.70 *(978-1-58415-833-2(6))* Mitchell Lane Pubs.

Mayo, Edith P., ed. The Smithsonian Book of the First Ladies. 2004. (J). 29.95 *(978-0-8050-7272-3(1),* Holt, Henry & Co. Bks. For Young Readers) Holt, Henry & Co.

McAneney, Caitie. Simone Biles: Greatest Gymnast of All Time, 1 vol. 2017. (Breakout Biographies Ser.). (ENG.). 32p. (J). (gr. 4-5). 27.93 *(978-1-5081-6072-4(4),* 8adaaead-b9fd-491b-81ff-90f0b3c72e6f); pap. 11.00 *(978-1-5081-6070-0(8),* ca8a14ef-16ed-45ca-920c-11a564023e31) Rosen Publishing Group, Inc., The. (PowerKids Pr.).

—20 Fun Facts about Native American Women, 1 vol. 2015. (Fun Fact File: Women in History Ser.). (ENG., Illus.). 32p. (J). (gr. 2-3). 27.93 *(978-1-4824-2810-0(5),* fb979223-2a85-450d-b5b3-83faeece1e46) Stevens, Gareth Publishing LLLP.

McCallum Staats, Ann. Women Heroes of the US Army: Remarkable Soldiers from the American Revolution to Today. 2019. (Women of Action Ser.: 23). (ENG., Illus.). 240p. (YA). (gr. 7). 19.99 *(978-0-914091-24-0(7))* Chicago Review Pr., Inc.

McCarthy, Meghan. Daredevil: The Daring Life of Betty Skelton. McCarthy, Meghan, illus. 2013. (ENG., Illus.). 48p. (J). (gr. -1-3). 17.99 *(978-1-4424-2262-9(9),* Simon & Schuster/Paula Wiseman Bks.) Simon & Schuster/Paula Wiseman Bks.

McDaniel, Jequita Potts. Mardy Murie Did! Grandmother of Conservation. Van Zyle, Jon, illus. 2011. (J). *(978-1-58979-525-9(3))* Taylor Trade Publishing.

McDaniel, Jequite Po & Van Zyle, Jon. Mardi Murie Did! Grandmother of Conservation. 2011. (ENG., Illus.). 32p. (J). (gr. -1-2). 15.95 *(978-1-58979-565-5(2))* Taylor Trade Publishing.

McDonough, Yona Zeldis. Who Was Harriet Tubman? 2004. (ENG., Illus.). 106p. (J). lib. bdg. 13.00 *(978-1-4242-2135-6(8))* Dingles & Co.

—Who Was Harriet Tubman? Harrison, Nancy, illus. 2003. (Who Was... ? Ser.). 106p. (gr. 4-7). 15.00 *(978-0-7569-1590-2(2))* Perfection Learning Corp.

McDonough, Yona Zeldis & Who HQ. Who Was Harriet Tubman? Harrison, Nancy, illus. 2019. (Who Was? Ser.). 112p. (J). (gr. 3-7). 5.99 *(978-0-593-09722-9(X))*; 15.99 *(978-0-593-09723-6(8))* Penguin Young Readers Group. (Penguin Workshop).

—Who Was Rosa Parks? Marchesi, Stephen, illus. 2010. (Who Was? Ser.). 112p. (J). (gr. 3-7). pap. 5.99 *(978-0-448-45442-9(4),* Penguin Workshop) Penguin Young Readers Group.

McGintry, Alice B. Cynthia Rylant. 2009. (Library of Author Biographies Ser.). 112p. (gr. 5-8). 63.90 *(978-1-60853-530-9(4),* Rosen Reference) Rosen Publishing Group, Inc., The.

Mcginty, Alice B. Meet Eve Bunting. 2009. (About the Author Ser.). 24p. (gr. 4-4). 42.50 *(978-1-61511-248-7(0),* PowerKids Pr.) Rosen Publishing Group, Inc., The.

—Meet Jane Yolen. 2009. (About the Author Ser.). 24p. (gr. 4-4). 42.50 *(978-1-61511-252-4(9),* PowerKids Pr.) Rosen Publishing Group, Inc., The.

—Sharon Creech. 2009. (Library of Author Biographies Ser.). 112p. (gr. 5-8). 63.90 *(978-1-60853-555-2(X),* Rosen Reference) Rosen Publishing Group, Inc., The.

McKay, C. R. Kate McKinnon, 1 vol. 2019. (Giants of Comedy Ser.). (ENG.). 112p. (J). (gr. 7-7). 38.80 *(978-1-5081-8867-4(X),* e1cb4503-b477-4c29-b68e-8f0ad72e9f57) Rosen Publishing Group, Inc., The.

McKissack, Patricia C. & McKissack, Fredrick, Jr. Sojourner Truth: Ain't I a Woman? 2003. (Illus.). 186p. (gr. 4-7). 17.20 *(978-0-7857-2515-2(6))* Turtleback.

McLendon, Jacquelyn. Phillis Wheatley: A Revolutionary Poet. 2009. (Library of American Lives & Times Ser.). 112p. (gr. 5-5). 69.20 *(978-1-60853-499-9(5))* Rosen Publishing Group, Inc., The.

McNamara, Margaret. Eliza: the Story of Elizabeth Schuyler Hamilton: With an Afterword by Phillipa Soo, the Original Eliza from Hamilton: an American Musical. Shapiro, Esmé, illus. 2018. 48p. (J). (gr. -1-3). 17.99 *(978-1-5247-6588-0(0),* Schwartz & Wade Bks.) Random Hse. Children's Bks.

Meade, Marion. Free Woman: The Life & Times of Victoria Woodhull. 2011. 176p. pap. 15.95 *(978-1-61756-052-1(9))* Open Road Integrated Media, Inc.

Medina, Melissa & Colting, Fredrik. What I Can Learn from the Incredible & Fantastic Life of Oprah Winfrey. Chen, Eszter, illus. 2017. (ENG.). 32p. (J). 14.95 *(978-0-9977145-8-6(1))* Moppet Bks.

Mello, Tara Baukus. Danica Patrick. 2007. (Race Car Legends Ser.). (Illus.). 71p. (YA). (gr. 5-9). lib. bdg. 25.00 *(978-0-7910-9126-5(0),* Facts On File) Infobase Holdings, Inc.

Meltzer, Brad. I Am Helen Keller. Eliopoulos, Christopher, illus. 2015. (Ordinary People Change the World Ser.). 40p. (J). (gr. k-4). 15.99 *(978-0-525-42851-0(8),* Dial Bks) Penguin Young Readers Group.

Meltzer, Brad. Soy Sonia Sotomayor. Eliopoulos, Christopher, illus. 2023.Tr. of I Am Sonia Sotomayor. (SPA.). 40p. (J). (gr. k-3). pap. 14.99 ***(978-1-5433-8606-6(7))*** Vista Higher Learning, Inc.

Messner, Kate & Powell, Margaret E. Only the Best: The Exceptional Life & Fashion of Ann Lowe. Robinson, Erin, illus. 2022. (ENG.). 56p. (J). (gr. k-3). 18.99 *(978-1-4521-6160-0(7))* Chronicle Bks. LLC.

Michelle Obama. 2009. (Political Profiles Ser.). 112p. (YA). (gr. 5-9). lib. bdg. 28.95 *(978-1-59935-090-5(4))* Reynolds, Morgan Inc.

Micklos Jr., John. Ruth Bader Ginsburg: Get to Know the Justice Who Speaks Her Mind. 2019. (People You Should Know Ser.). (ENG., Illus.). 32p. (J). (gr. 3-6). pap. 7.95 *(978-1-5435-5926-2(3),* 139904, Capstone Pr.) Capstone.

Miklowitz, Gloria D. Amelia Earhart. 2004. (ENG., Illus.). 31p. (J). (gr. 2-5). pap. 7.33 *(978-0-7685-1213-7(1),* Dominie Elementary) Savvas Learning Co.

Miller, Brandon Marie. Women of Colonial America: 13 Stories of Courage & Survival in the New World. 2016. (Women of Action Ser.: 14). (ENG., Illus.). 256p. (YA). (gr. 7). 19.95 *(978-1-55652-487-5(0))* Chicago Review Pr., Inc.

Miller, Connie Colwell. Mother Jones: Labor Leader, 1 vol. Erwin, Steve & Barnett, Charles, III, illus. 2006. (Graphic Biographies Ser.). (ENG.). 32p. (J). (gr. 3-9). per. 8.10 *(978-0-7368-9662-7(7),* 93447, Capstone Pr.) Capstone.

Miller, Debra A. Dolores Huerta: Labor Leader, 1 vol. 2006. (Twentieth Century's Most Influential Hispanics Ser.). (ENG., Illus.). 104p. (gr. 7-10). lib. bdg. 41.03 *(978-1-59018-971-9(X),* eadc6356-d2a2-4a4d-9e10-43e3a1586db7, Lucent Pr.) Greenhaven Publishing LLC.

Miller, Kat. I Love Taylor Swift, 1 vol. 2010. (Fan Club Ser.). (ENG.). 24p. (J). (gr. 2-3). lib. bdg. 27.27 *(978-1-61533-051-5(8),* 4b38f604-8508-4313-8545-8fefabce7c59); (Illus.). pap. 9.15 *(978-1-61533-052-2(6),* 6495b95f-37d2-49cd-b7a2-8f00c7268806) Rosen Publishing Group, Inc., The. (Windmill Bks.).

Mills Hoffman, Megan. Ivanka Trump: Entrepreneur & First Daughter, 1 vol. 2017. (Leading Women Ser.). (ENG.). 112p. (YA). (gr. 7-7). 41.64 *(978-1-5026-2701-8(9),* 07b0a821-6abe-4edf-b762-2d76a5de3781) Cavendish Square Publishing LLC.

Mills, Nathan & Peck, Audrey. Helen Keller: Miracle Child, 1 vol. 2012. (Rosen Readers Ser.). (ENG., Illus.). 24p. (J). (gr. 1-2). pap. 8.25 *(978-1-4488-8824-5(7),* 4870d10f-4237-4f28-bc91-622475a3a847, Rosen Classroom) Rosen Publishing Group, Inc., The.

Miriam Colon, Actriz y Fundadora de Teatro. 2003. 94.95 *(978-0-8136-9219-7(9))*; pap. 48.95 *(978-0-8136-9207-4(5))* Modern Curriculum Pr.

Moening, Kate. Melinda Gates: Philanthropist. 2020. (Women Leading the Way Ser.). (ENG., Illus.). 24p. (J). (gr. k-3). pap. 7.99 *(978-1-61891-797-3(8),* 12582, Blastoff! Readers) Bellwether Media.

—Michelle Howard: Four-Star Admiral. 2020. (Women Leading the Way Ser.). (ENG., Illus.). 24p. (J). (gr. k-3). pap. 7.99 *(978-1-61891-798-0(6),* 12583, Blastoff! Readers) Bellwether Media.

—Susan Wojcicki: CEO of YouTube. 2019. (Women Leading the Way Ser.). (ENG., Illus.). 24p. (J). (gr. k-3). pap. 7.99 *(978-1-61891-726-3(9),* 12307); lib. bdg. 26.95 *(978-1-64487-103-4(3))* Bellwether Media. (Blastoff! Readers).

Morgan, Terri. Venus & Serena Williams: Grand Slam Sisters. (Sports Achievers Biographies Ser.). (Illus.). 2005. 80p. (gr. 7-12). lib. bdg. 22.60 *(978-0-8225-3684-0(6))* 2003. 64p. (J). (gr. 4-9). pap. 5.95 *(978-0-8225-9866-4(3),* Carolrhoda Bks.) Lerner Publishing Group.

Morganelli, Adrianna. Wilma Rudolph: Track & Field Champion. 2016. (Remarkable Lives Revealed Ser.). (ENG.). 32p. (J). (gr. 2-5). *(978-0-7787-2689-0(4))* Crabtree Publishing Co.

Moriarty, J. T. Phillis Wheatley: African American Poet. 2009. (Primary Sources of Famous People in American History Ser.). 32p. (gr. 2-3). 47.90 *(978-1-60851-717-6(9))* Rosen Publishing Group, Inc., The.

Morretta, Alison. Ida B. Wells-Barnett & the Crusade Against Lynching, 1 vol. 2016. (Primary Sources of the Civil Rights Movement Ser.). (ENG., Illus.). 64p. (gr. 6-6). 35.93 *(978-1-5026-1874-0(5),* 44127a2f-3bba-4d97-985b-e0917805406e) Cavendish Square Publishing LLC.

Morris, Roz. Rosa Parks: Mother of the Civil Rights Movement. 2003. (Alabama Roots Biography Ser.). (ENG., Illus.). 109p. (J). *(978-1-878561-57-2(X))* Seacoast Publishing, Inc.

Mortensen, Lori. Maya Moore: Basketball Star. 2018. (Women Sports Stars Ser.). (ENG., Illus.). 32p. (J). (gr. 3-9). lib. bdg. 28.65 *(978-1-5157-9709-8(0),* 136857, Capstone Pr.) Capstone.

—Simone Biles: Gymnastics Star. 2018. (Women Sports Stars Ser.). (ENG., Illus.). 32p. (J). (gr. 3-9). lib. bdg. 28.65 *(978-1-5157-9708-1(2),* 136856, Capstone Pr.) Capstone.

Moss, Marissa. Brave Harriet. Payne, C. F., illus. 2015. 32p. pap. 8.00 *(978-1-61003-492-0(9))* Center for the Collaborative Classroom.

—Mighty Jackie: The Strike-Out Queen. Payne, C. F., illus. 2004. (ENG.). 32p. (J). (gr. k-3). 18.99 *(978-0-689-86329-5(2),* Simon & Schuster/Paula Wiseman Bks.) Simon & Schuster/Paula Wiseman Bks.

—Nurse, Soldier, Spy: The Story of Sarah Edmonds, a Civil War Hero. Hendrix, John, illus. 2011. (ENG.). 48p. (J). (gr. 3-7). 19.95 *(978-0-8109-9735-6(5),* 658701, Abrams Bks. for Young Readers) Abrams, Inc.

Mueller, Marilyn J. Thank You God for Everything! Gracias a Dios por Todo. 2007. pap. 11.00 *(978-0-8059-8648-8(0))* Dorrance Publishing Co., Inc.

Mueller, Pamela Bauer. Aloha Crossing. 2008. (Aloha Set Ser.: 2). (ENG., Illus.). 176p. (J). (gr. 3-7). pap. 8.99 *(978-0-9685097-9-1(7))* Pinata Publishing CAN. Dist: Independent Pubs. Group.

Murphy, Andrea & Ray, Joyce. Women of the Pine Tree State: 25 Maine Women You Should Know. Greenleaf, Lisa, illus. 2012. 136p. (J). pap. 16.00 *(978-0-9842549-6-5(X))* Apprentice Shop Bks., LLC.

Murphy, Claire Rudolf & Haigh, Jane G. Gold Rush Women. 12th ed. 2012. (Illus.). 128p. pap. 16.95 *(978-0-9627530-5-3(X))* Hillside Pr.

Murphy, Maggie. Taylor Swift: Country Music Star, 1 vol. 2010. (Young & Famous Ser.). (ENG., Illus.). 24p. (J). (gr. 1-2). pap. 9.85 *(978-1-4488-1803-7(6),* 899798c1-96d8-4871-a465-12883b3eb207, PowerKids Pr.) Rosen Publishing Group, Inc., The.

Murphy, Sage. Sally Ride: Female Astronaut, 1 vol. 2013. (Rosen Readers Ser.). (ENG.). 24p. (J). (gr. 2-2). pap. 8.25 *(978-1-4777-2306-7(4),* 314cafb2-a62a-41a4-afbf-0d09ace5ca3f); pap. 49.50 *(978-1-4777-2307-4(2))* Rosen Publishing Group, Inc., The. (Rosen Classroom).

Murray, Hallie. The Role of Female Confederate Spies in the Civil War, 1 vol. 2019. (Warrior Women in American History Ser.). (ENG.). 104p. (gr. 7-7). pap. 21.00 *(978-1-5026-5540-0(3),* eaa72ffe-9b57-4ea3-8b26-a98d4ac093e2); lib. bdg. 44.50 *(978-1-5026-5541-7(1),* 813ee375-f83d-4738-8a94-3357dd568210) Cavendish Square Publishing LLC.

—The Role of Female Confederate Spies in the Civil War. 2019. (J). pap. *(978-1-9785-1404-1(2))* Enslow Publishing, LLC.

—The Role of Female Doctors & Nurses in the Civil War, 1 vol. 2019. (Warrior Women in American History Ser.). (ENG.). 104p. (gr. 7-7). pap. 21.00 *(978-1-5026-5543-1(8),* 1d4603e4-36a5-404a-8032-14ce1cb0311f); lib. bdg. 44.50 *(978-1-5026-5544-8(6),* a5c3b949-3c8d-40e5-8e7a-8277fd0a565b) Cavendish Square Publishing LLC.

—The Role of Female Doctors & Nurses in the Civil War. 2019. pap. *(978-1-9785-1407-2(7))* Enslow Publishing, LLC.

Mussari, Mark & Bredeson, Carmen. Amy Tan, 1 vol. 2011. (Today's Writers & Their Works). (ENG.). 128p. (YA). (gr. 7-7). 45.50 *(978-0-7614-4127-4(1),* 3bef674b-0c07-4033-83c0-def5fa05edd6) Cavendish Square Publishing LLC.

Nagelhout, Ryan. Abby Wambach, 1 vol. 2016. (Sports MVPs Ser.). (ENG., Illus.). 24p. (J). (gr. 1-2). 24.27 *(978-1-4824-4639-5(1),* d9ec0017-f0e3-46f9-8aef-ac521cb9030f) Stevens, Gareth Publishing LLLP.

Nichols, Joan Kane. Civil War Heroines. 2005. (ENG., Illus.). 16p. (J). (gr. 5-5). pap. 9.97 net. *(978-0-328-14901-8(2),* Scott Foresman) Savvas Learning Co.

—The Civil War Sisterhood: Women Who Made a Difference. 2005. (ENG., Illus.). 16p. (J). (gr. 5-5). pap. 9.97 net. *(978-0-328-14902-5(0),* Scott Foresman) Savvas Learning Co.

—Women of the Civil War. 2005. (ENG., Illus.). 16p. (J). (gr. 5-5). pap. 9.97 net. *(978-0-328-14900-1(4),* Scott Foresman) Savvas Learning Co.

Nivola, Claire A. Life in the Ocean: The Story of Oceanographer Sylvia Earle, 1 vol. Nivola, Claire A., illus. 2012. (ENG., Illus.). 32p. (J). (gr. -1-3). 19.99 *(978-0-374-38068-7(6),* 900068269, Farrar, Straus & Giroux (BYR)) Farrar, Straus & Giroux.

Norgren, Jill. Belva Lockwood: The Woman Who Would Be President. 2007. (ENG., Illus.). 311p. 89.00 *(978-0-8147-5834-2(7),* 8431, NYU Pr.) New York Univ. Pr.

Norwich, Grace. I Am Harriet Tubman. Simon, Ute, illus. 2013. 127p. (J). *(978-0-545-61344-6(2))* Scholastic, Inc.

—I Am Harriet Tubman (I Am #6) Simon, Ute, illus. 2013. (I Am Ser.: 6). (ENG.). 128p. (J). (gr. 3-5). pap. 5.99 *(978-0-545-48436-7(7),* Scholastic Paperbacks) Scholastic, Inc.

Nothing Stood in Her Way, Captain Julie Clark. 2004. 232p. 24.95 *(978-0-9749190-0-3(4))* Women in Aviation, International.

Novesky, Amy. Mary Blair's Unique Flair: The Girl Who Became One of the Disney Legends. 2019. (ENG., Illus.). 40p. (J). (gr. 1-3). 17.99 *(978-1-4847-5720-8(3),* Disney Press Books) Disney Publishing Worldwide.

Noyes, Deborah. Ten Days a Madwoman: The Daring Life & Turbulent Times of the Original Girl Reporter, Nellie Bly. 2016. (Illus.). 144p. (J). (gr. 5). 18.99 *(978-0-8037-4017-4(4),* Viking Books for Young Readers) Penguin Young Readers Group.

Obama, Michelle. Becoming: Adapted for Young Readers. 2021. (ENG., Illus.). 432p. (J). (gr. 5). 18.99 *(978-0-593-30374-0(1))*; lib. bdg. 21.99 *(978-0-593-30375-7(X))* Random Hse. Children's Bks. (Delacorte Bks. for Young Readers).

O'Brien, John A. Who Was Helen Keller? Harrison, Nancy, illus. 2003. (Who Was... ? Ser.). 107p. (J). (gr. 3-7). 12.65 *(978-0-7569-1596-4(1))* Perfection Learning Corp.

O'Brien, Keith. Fly Girls Young Readers' Edition: How Five Daring Women Defied All Odds & Made Aviation History. 2019. (ENG., Illus.). 320p. (J). (gr. 5-7). 16.99 *(978-1-328-61842-9(0),* 1733755, Clarion Bks.) HarperCollins Pubs.

Omoth, Tyler. Taylor Swift: Music Icon. 2017. (Superstar Stories Ser.). (ENG.). 24p. (J). (gr. 3-6). lib. bdg. 32.79 *(978-1-5038-1999-3(X),* 211875) Child's World, Inc, The.

Orr, Tamra B. Abby Wambach. 2007. (No Hands Allowed Ser.). (Illus.). 32p. (J). (gr. 2-4). lib. bdg. 25.70 *(978-1-58415-601-7(5))* Mitchell Lane Pubs.

—Amelia Earhart. 2015. (ENG., Illus.). 48p. (J). pap. 6.95 *(978-0-531-21207-3(6),* Orchard Bks.) Scholastic Library Publishing.

O'Shaughnessy, Tam. Sally Ride: A Photobiography of America's Pioneering Woman in Space. 2015. (ENG., Illus.). 160p. (J). (gr. 5-8). 19.99 *(978-1-59643-994-8(7),* 900128935) Roaring Brook Pr.

Parks, Deborah A. Nature's Machines: The Story of Biomechanist Mimi Koehl. 2006. (ENG., Illus.). 128p. (gr. 7-9). per. 19.95 *(978-0-309-09559-4(X),* Joseph Henry Pr.) National Academies Pr.

Patterson, Marie. Pocahontas, 1 vol. rev. ed. 2004. (Social Studies: Informational Text Ser.). (ENG.). 24p. (J). (gr. 4-8). pap. 10.99 *(978-0-7439-8745-5(4))* Teacher Created Materials, Inc.

Payment, Simone. American Women Spies of World War II. 2009. (American Women at War Ser.). 112p. (gr. 8-8). 63.90 *(978-1-61511-399-6(1))* Rosen Publishing Group, Inc., The.

Peck, Audrey. Helen Keller: Miracle Child, 1 vol. 2012. (Beginning Biographies Ser.). (ENG., Illus.). 24p. (J). (gr. 1-2). 26.27 *(978-1-4488-8593-0(0),* 01d48232-e725-4281-a3eb-1235e4a32875, PowerKids Pr.) Rosen Publishing Group, Inc., The.

Pelleschi, Andrea. Mathematician & Computer Scientist Grace Hopper. 2016. (STEM Trailblazer Bios Ser.). (ENG., Illus.). 32p. (J). (gr. 2-5). 26.65 *(978-1-5124-0785-3(2),* e28f06e5-410e-42e5-a72b-f7bf211363ba, Lerner Pubns.) Lerner Publishing Group.

Peppas, Lynn. Miley Cyrus. 2010. (Superstars! Ser.). (ENG.). 32p. (J). pap. *(978-0-7787-7259-0(4))* Crabtree Publishing Co.

—Taylor Swift. 2010. (Superstars! Ser.). (ENG.). 32p. (J). pap. *(978-0-7787-7261-3(6))* Crabtree Publishing Co.

Perritano, John. Saving Private Lynch! a Rescue Story from Operation Iraqi Freedom, Vol. 8. 2018. (Special Forces Stories Ser.). 64p. (J). (gr. 7). lib. bdg. 31.93 *(978-1-4222-4081-6(9))* Mason Crest.

Petrick, Neila Skinner. Jane Wilkinson Long: Texas Pioneer, 1 vol. Haynes, Joyce, illus. 2004. (ENG.). 32p. (J). (gr. k-3). 16.99 *(978-1-58980-147-9(4),* Pelican Publishing) Arcadia Publishing.

Petrillo, Lisa. Vera Wang. 2011. (Profiles in Fashion Ser.). (Illus.). 112p. 28.95 *(978-1-59935-150-6(1))* Reynolds, Morgan Inc.

Pettinella, Amy. Queen Latifah: Award-Winning Actress & Hip-Hop Activist, 1 vol. 2014. (Leading Women Ser.). (ENG.). 112p. (YA). (gr. 7-7). lib. bdg. 41.64 *(978-1-62712-984-8(7),* 4969797f-1bd3-429a-8376-67f3f717b954) Cavendish Square Publishing LLC.

Phillips, Larissa. Women Civil War Spies of the Confederacy. 2009. (American Women at War Ser.). 112p. (gr. 8-8). 63.90 *(978-1-61511-402-3(5))* Rosen Publishing Group, Inc., The.

Ploscariu, Iemima. Mae Carol Jemison: Astronaut & Educator. 2017. (Women in Science Ser.). (ENG., Illus.). 112p. (J). (gr. 6-12). lib. bdg. 41.36 *(978-1-5321-1045-0(6),* 25666, Essential Library) ABDO Publishing Co.

Polacco, Patricia. Betty Doll. 2004. 18.00 *(978-0-7569-3208-4(4))* Perfection Learning Corp.

Polette, Nancy. Biography, by Golly! 2004. (J). pap. 7.50 *(978-1-931334-49-5(8))* Pieces of Learning.

Polinsky, Paige. Indra Nooyi: CEO of PepsiCo. 2019. (Women Leading the Way Ser.). (ENG., Illus.). 24p. (J). (gr. k-3). pap. 7.99 *(978-1-61891-503-0(7),* 12152, Blastoff! Readers) Bellwether Media.

Polinsky, Paige V. American Girl Entrepreneur: Pleasant Rowland. 2017. (Toy Trailblazers Set 2 Ser.). (ENG., Illus.). 32p. (J). (gr. 3-6). lib. bdg. 32.79 *(978-1-5321-1094-8(4),* 25764, Checkerboard Library) ABDO Publishing Co.

—Indra Nooyi: CEO of PepsiCo. 2019. (Women Leading the Way Ser.). (ENG., Illus.). 24p. (J). (gr. k-3). lib. bdg. 26.95 *(978-1-62617-941-7(7),* Blastoff! Readers) Bellwether Media.

Pollack, Pamela D. & Meg Belviso. Who Was Lucille Ball? 2017. (Who Was... ? Ser.). (Illus.). 107p. (J). lib. bdg. 16.00 *(978-0-606-39781-0(7))* Turtleback.

Porter, Esther. Abby Wambach. 2016. (Women in Sports Ser.). (ENG., Illus.). 24p. (J). (gr. -1-2). lib. bdg. 27.32 *(978-1-4914-7974-2(4),* 130470, Capstone Pr.) Capstone.

Porterfield, Jason. Annie Oakley: Tiradora del Lejano Oeste (Annie Oakley: Wild West Sharpshooter) 2009. (Grandes personajes en la historia de los Estados Unidos (Famous People in American History) Ser.). 32p. (gr. 2-3). 47.90 *(978-1-61512-789-4(5),* Editorial Buenas Letras) Rosen Publishing Group, Inc., The.

—Annie Oakley: Wild West Sharpshooter. 2009. (Primary Sources of Famous People in American History Ser.). 32p. (gr. 2-3). 47.90 *(978-1-60851-651-3(2))* Rosen Publishing Group, Inc., The.

—Annie Oakley: Wild West Sharpshooter / Tiradora del Lejano Oeste. 2009. (Famous People in American History/Grandes personajes en la historia de los Estados Unidos Ser.). 32p. (gr. 2-3). 47.90 *(978-1-61512-537-1(X),* Editorial Buenas Letras) Rosen Publishing Group, Inc., The.

Prentice, Andrew. Amelia Earhart (the First Names Series) Smith, Mike, illus. 2019. (First Names Ser.). (ENG.). 160p. (J). (gr. 3-7). 9.99 *(978-1-4197-3741-1(4),* 1279101, Abrams Bks. for Young Readers) Abrams, Inc.

PRESS, Celebration. Ellen Ochoa: Reaching for the Stars. 2003. (ENG.). (J). (gr. 2-5). pap., stu. ed. 34.95 *(978-0-673-62081-1(6),* Celebration Pr.) Savvas Learning Co.

Priscilla, Marie. L' il Bitty Book. 2007. 130p. (J). pap. 13.95 *(978-0-7414-4343-4(0))* Infinity Publishing.

uitt Stewart, Elinore & Zeinert, Karen. The Letters of Elinore Pruitt Stewart, Woman Homesteader, 1 vol. Kubinyi, Laszlo, illus. 2005. (In My Own Words Ser.). (ENG.). 64p. (J). (gr. 6-6). lib. bdg. 34.07 *(978-0-7614-1645-6(5),* 3264ed60-3195-4a15-b392-b3cd0d11054e) Cavendish Square Publishing LLC.
aatma, Lucia. Barbara Jordan, 1 vol. 2013. (Leading Women Ser.). (ENG.). 96p. (YA). (gr. 7-7). 42.64 *(978-0-7614-4956-0(6),* bbcd5f27-0fcc-47f5-88e7-57e8052fa895) Cavendish Square Publishing LLC.
—Shirley Chisholm, 1 vol. 2011. (Leading Women Ser.). (ENG., Illus.). 96p. (J). (gr. 7-7). 42.64 *(978-0-7614-4953-9(1),* 76e44034-3809-4585-b09c-6019d0e95e1c) Cavendish Square Publishing LLC.
and, Carol. Lydia Darragh: Quaker Patriot. Marshall, Dan, illus. (J). 15.95 *(978-0-945912-33-0(1))* Pippin Pr.
andolph, Jennifer & Benchmark Education Co. Staff. Women of the Civil War. 2014. (Text Connections Ser.). (J). (gr. 5). *(978-1-4900-1377-0(6))* Benchmark Education Co.
andolph, Joanne. The Angel of Goliad: Francisca Alvarez & the Texas War for Independence. 2009. (Great Moments in American History Ser.). 32p. (gr. 3-3). 47.90 *(978-1-61513-151-8(5))* Rosen Publishing Group, Inc., The.
andolph, Ryan P. Frontier Women Who Helped Shape the American West. 2009. (Library of the Westward Expansion Ser.). 24p. (gr. 3-4). 42.50 *(978-1-60853-936-9(9),* PowerKids Pr.) Rosen Publishing Group, Inc., The.
ansom, Candice. Maggie L. Walker: Pioneering Banker & Community Leader. 2008. (Trailblazer Biographies Ser.). (ENG.). 112p. (gr. 5-9). lib. bdg. 31.93 *(978-0-8225-6611-3(7))* Lerner Publishing Group.
appaport, Doreen. Eleanor, Quiet No More: The Life of Eleanor Roosevelt. Kelley, Gary, illus. 2009. (Big Words Book Ser.: 4). (ENG.). 48p. (J). (gr. -1-3). 16.99 *(978-0-7868-5141-6(4))* Little, Brown Bks. for Young Readers.
—Helen's Big World: The Life of Helen Keller. Tavares, Matt, illus. 2012. (Big Words Book Ser.: 6). (ENG.). 48p. (J). (gr. 1-3). 18.99 *(978-0-7868-0890-8(X))* Little, Brown Bks. for Young Readers.
Raum, Elizabeth. Carli Lloyd. 2017. (Pro Sports Biographies Ser.). (ENG.). 24p. (J). (gr. 1-4). 20.95 *(978-1-68151-132-0(0),* 14677) Amicus.
—Chloe Kim. 2017. (Pro Sports Biographies Ser.). (ENG., Illus.). 24p. (J). (gr. 1-4). lib. bdg. 20.95 *(978-1-68151-134-4(7),* 14678) Amicus.
—Pro Sports Biographies: Carli Lloyd. 2017. (Pro Sports Biographies Ser.). (ENG.). 24p. (J). (gr. 1-3). pap. 9.99 *(978-1-68152-163-3(6),* 14796) Amicus.
—Pro Sports Biographies: Chloe Kim. 2017. (Pro Sports Biographies Ser.). (ENG., Illus.). 24p. (J). (gr. 1-3). pap. 9.99 *(978-1-68152-165-7(2),* 14797) Amicus.
—Pro Sports Biographies: Maya Moore. 2017. (Pro Sports Biographies Ser.). (ENG., Illus.). 24p. (J). (gr. 1-3). pap. 10.99 *(978-1-68152-164-0(4),* 14800) Amicus.
Rausch, Monica. Sacagawea, 1 vol. 2007. (Grandes Personajes (Great Americans) Ser.). (SPA.). 24p. (gr. 2-4). pap. 9.15 *(978-0-8368-7991-9(0),* 867793cb-be46-4835-b2e0-95234bf0f2f2, Weekly Reader Leveled Readers); (Illus.). lib. bdg. 24.67 *(978-0-8368-7984-1(8),* f0398bb5-29a9-4689-829b-5a3f299c15cc) Stevens, Gareth Publishing LLLP.
Reed, Jennifer. Elizabeth Bloomer: Child Labor Activist, 1 vol. 2006. (Young Heroes Ser.). (ENG., Illus.). 48p. (gr. 4-8). lib. bdg. 34.08 *(978-0-7377-3615-1(1),* c18ec41d-dbe6-47a8-9a1f-bcadb3184183, KidHaven Publishing) Greenhaven Publishing LLC.
Reusser, Kayleen. Day by Day with Taylor Swift. 2010. (Randy's Corner Ser.). (Illus.). 32p. (J). (gr. -1-2). lib. bdg. 25.70 *(978-1-58415-857-8(3))* Mitchell Lane Pubs.
—Taylor Swift. 2008. (Blue Banner Biography Ser.). (Illus.). 32p. (YA). (gr. 4-7). lib. bdg. 25.70 *(978-1-58415-675-8(9))* Mitchell Lane Pubs.
Rhynes, Martha E. Gwendolyn Brooks: Poet from Chicago. 2004. (World Writers Ser.). (Illus.). 112p. (YA). (gr. 6-12). 23.95 *(978-1-931798-05-1(2))* Reynolds, Morgan Inc.
Rice, Dona Herweck. Laura Ingalls Wilder: Pioneer Woman (America in The 1800s) rev. ed. 2017. (Social Studies: Informational Text Ser.). (ENG., Illus.). 32p. (gr. 4-8). pap. 11.99 *(978-1-4938-3798-4(2))* Teacher Created Materials, Inc.
Riddolls, Tom. Sally Ride: The First American Woman in Space. 2010. (Crabtree Groundbreaker Biographies Ser.). (ENG., Illus.). 112p. (J). pap. *(978-0-7787-2550-3(2))*; (gr. 5-8). lib. bdg. *(978-0-7787-2541-1(3))* Crabtree Publishing Co.
Riddolls, Tom & Wearing, Judy. Hillary Clinton. 2009. (Remarkable People Ser.). (Illus.). 24p. (J). (gr. 4-6). pap. 8.95 *(978-1-60596-621-2(5))*; lib. bdg. 24.45 *(978-1-60596-620-5(7))* Weigl Pubs., Inc.
Rieken, Ethel Plaep. Growing Pains: A Childhood on Bear Creek. Zander, Julie McDonald, ed. Slavens, Rick, photos by. 2004. (Illus.). 140p. (YA). per. 23.00 *(978-0-9740348-2-9(7),* Special Editions — Customized Biographies) Slavens Enterprises, LLC.
Riley, John B. Jane Addams: A Photo Biography. I.t. ed. 2004. (First Biographies Ser.). (Illus.). 24p. (J). (gr. 5-18). 16.95 *(978-1-883846-61-9(7),* First Biographies) Reynolds, Morgan Inc.
Rinaldo, Denise. Amelia Earhart: With a Discussion of Courage. 2004. (Values in Action Ser.). (J). *(978-1-59203-068-2(8))* Learning Challenge, Inc.
—Eleanor Roosevelt: With a Discussion of Respect. 2003. (Values in Action Ser.). (J). *(978-1-59203-063-7(7))* Learning Challenge, Inc.
—Rosa Parks: With a Discussion of Courage. 2003. (Values in Action Ser.). (J). *(978-1-59203-061-3(0))* Learning Challenge, Inc.
Rinker, Jess. Gloria Takes a Stand: How Gloria Steinem Listened, Wrote, & Changed the World. Peoples-Riley, Daria, illus. 2019. (ENG.). 48p. (J). 17.99 *(978-1-68119-676-3(X),* 900180274, Bloomsbury Children's Bks.) Bloomsbury Publishing USA.
Rissman, Rebecca. Hidden Women: The African-American Mathematicians of NASA Who Helped America Win the Space Race. 2018. (Encounter: Narrative Nonfiction Stories Ser.). (ENG., Illus.). 112p. (J). (gr. 3-7). pap. 9.95 *(978-1-5157-9963-4(8),* 136958, Capstone Pr.) Capstone.
Rivera, Ursula. Aretha Franklin. 2009. (Rock & Roll Hall of Famers Ser.). 112p. (gr. 5-8). 63.90 *(978-1-60852-467-9(1),* Rosen Reference) Rosen Publishing Group, Inc., The.
Robbins, Dean. Miss Paul & the President: The Creative Campaign for Women's Right to Vote. Zhang, Nancy, illus. 2016. 40p. (J). (gr. -1-3). 18.99 *(978-1-101-93720-4(3),* Knopf Bks. for Young Readers) Random Hse. Children's Bks.
Robbins, Trina. Hedy Lamarr & a Secret Communication System, 1 vol. Martin, Cynthia, illus. 2006. (Inventions & Discovery Ser.). (ENG.). 32p. (J). (gr. 3-9). 8.10 *(978-0-7368-9641-2(4),* 93401, Capstone Pr.) Capstone.
Roberts, Cokie. Founding Mothers: Remembering the Ladies. Goode, Diane, illus. 2014. (ENG.). 40p. (J). (gr. 1-5). 17.99 *(978-0-06-078002-9(9),* HarperCollins) HarperCollins Pubs.
Roberts, Pauline. When I Was Just a Pea in a Pod: A True Story. 2012. 24p. pap. 13.50 *(978-1-4669-1401-8(7))* Trafford Publishing.
Robson, David. Soledad O'Brien. (Transcending Race in America: Biographies of Biracial Achievers Ser.). (Illus.). 64p. (J). (gr. 5-18). 2010. lib. bdg. 22.95 *(978-1-4222-1617-0(9))* 2009. pap. 9.95 *(978-1-4222-1631-6(4))* Mason Crest.
Rock, Meghan. Rachel Carson: Marine Biologist & Winner of the National Book Award, 1 vol. 2016. (Women in Science Ser.). (ENG., Illus.). 128p. (J). (gr. 9-9). 47.36 *(978-1-5026-2319-5(6),* 590270de-ea00-487a-b74f-e776c37c06f7) Cavendish Square Publishing LLC.
Rockliff, Mara. Billie Jean! How Tennis Star Billie Jean King Changed Women's Sports. Baddeley, Elizabeth, illus. 2019. 40p. (J). (gr. -1-3). 17.99 *(978-0-525-51779-5(0),* G.P. Putnam's Sons Books for Young Readers) Penguin Young Readers Group.
Rodriguez, Gaby. The Pregnancy Project: A Memoir. 2013. (ENG., Illus.). 240p. (YA). (gr. 9). pap. 12.99 *(978-1-4424-4623-6(4),* Simon & Schuster Bks. For Young Readers) Simon & Schuster Bks. For Young Readers.
Roland, James. Ruth Bader Ginsburg: Iconic Supreme Court Justice. 2016. (Gateway Biographies Ser.). (ENG., Illus.). 48p. (J). (gr. 4-8). E-Book 47.99 *(978-1-5124-0597-2(3),* Lerner Pubns.) Lerner Publishing Group.
Rose, Katherine. Annie Oakley: the Woman Who Never Missed a Shot, 1 vol. 2014. (American Legends & Folktales Ser.). (ENG., Illus.). 32p. (gr. 3-3). 31.21 *(978-1-62712-286-3(9),* 24b81b1d-1100-458e-bc67-2be07559c2f1); pap. 11.58 *(978-1-62712-287-0(7),* 2ea8bd50-5ade-44e7-ac8d-01ec12f139f7) Cavendish Square Publishing LLC.
Rosenstock, Barb. Dorothea's Eyes: Dorothea Lange Photographs the Truth. Dubois, Gerard, illus. 2016. (ENG.). 40p. (J). (gr. 2-5). 18.99 *(978-1-62979-208-8(X),* Calkins Creek) Highlights Pr., c/o Highlights for Children, Inc.
Ross, Michael Elsohn. Pond Watching with Ann Morgan. Smith, Wendy, illus. 2005. (Naturalist's Apprentice Biographies Ser.). 48p. (gr. 3-6). lib. bdg. 19.93 *(978-1-57505-385-1(3))* Lerner Publishing Group.
Roycroft, Mitch. Jennifer Harman. (Superstars of Poker Ser.). (Illus.). 64p. (YA). 2009. (gr. 3-7). lib. bdg. 22.95 *(978-1-4222-0227-2(5))* 2007. pap. 7.95 *(978-1-4222-0373-6(5))* Mason Crest.
Roza, Greg. Guide My Pen: The Poems of Phillis Wheatley. 2009. (Great Moments in American History Ser.). 32p. (gr. 3-3). 47.90 *(978-1-61513-133-4(7))* Rosen Publishing Group, Inc., The.
Rubini, Julie K. Eye to Eye: Sports Journalist Christine Brennan. 2019. (Biographies for Young Readers Ser.). (ENG., Illus.). 136p. (J). 32.95 *(978-0-8214-2374-5(6))*; pap. 15.95 *(978-0-8214-2375-2(4))* Ohio Univ. Pr.
Ruffin, Frances E. Annie Oakley. 2009. (American Legends Ser.). 24p. (gr. 3-3). 42.50 *(978-1-61511-378-1(9),* PowerKids Pr.) Rosen Publishing Group, Inc., The.
—Clara Barton. 2009. (American Legends Ser.). 24p. (gr. 3-3). 42.50 *(978-1-61511-379-8(7),* PowerKids Pr.) Rosen Publishing Group, Inc., The.
—Her Story, Her Words: The Narrative of Sojourner Truth. (Great Moments in American History Ser.). 32p. (gr. 3-3). 2009. 47.90 *(978-1-61513-144-0(2))* 2003. (ENG., Illus.). lib. bdg. 29.13 *(978-0-8239-4387-6(9),* b981b6e9-653c-4bc0-b07c-deb6aeab09a2, Rosen Reference) Rosen Publishing Group, Inc., The.
—Meet Patricia MacLachlan. 2009. (About the Author Ser.). 24p. (gr. 4-4). 42.50 *(978-1-61511-257-9(X),* PowerKids Pr.) Rosen Publishing Group, Inc., The.
—Molly Pitcher. 2009. (American Legends Ser.). 24p. (gr. 3-3). 42.50 *(978-1-61511-384-2(3),* PowerKids Pr.) Rosen Publishing Group, Inc., The.
—Sally Hemings. 2009. (American Legends Ser.). 24p. (gr. 3-3). 42.50 *(978-1-61511-386-6(X),* PowerKids Pr.) Rosen Publishing Group, Inc., The.
—Sojourner Truth: Early Abolitionist. 2009. (American Legends Ser.). 24p. (gr. 3-3). 42.50 *(978-1-61511-387-3(8),* PowerKids Pr.) Rosen Publishing Group, Inc., The.
—Unsinkable Molly Brown. 2009. (American Legends Ser.). 24p. (gr. 3-3). 42.50 *(978-1-61511-377-4(0),* PowerKids Pr.) Rosen Publishing Group, Inc., The.
Rule, Heather. Women in Sports Media. 2017. (Women in Sports Ser.). (ENG., Illus.). 48p. (J). (gr. 4-8). lib. bdg. 34.21 *(978-1-5321-1158-7(4),* 25892, SportsZone) ABDO Publishing Co.
Russell, Greta. Olive Boone: Frontier Woman. Hare, John, illus. 2014. (Notable Missourians Ser.). (ENG.). 48p. (J). lib. bdg. 24.00 *(978-1-61248-118-0(3))* Truman State Univ. Pr.
Sabin, Francene & Macken, JoAnn Early. Abigail Adams: Young Patriot. Miyake, Yoshi, illus. 2007. 55p. (J). pap. *(978-0-439-88003-9(3))* Scholastic, Inc.
Sabin, Francene & Mattern, Joanne. Helen Keller, Girl of Courage. Meyer, Jean, illus. 2006. 56p. (J). *(978-0-439-66043-3(2))* Scholastic, Inc.
Sakany, Lois. Women Civil War Spies of the Union. 2009. (American Women at War Ser.). 112p. (gr. 8-8). 63.90 *(978-1-61511-403-0(3))* Rosen Publishing Group, Inc., The.
Sanchez Vegara, Maria Isabel. Amelia Earhart, Volume 3. Mariadiamantes, illus. 2016. (Little People, BIG DREAMS Ser.: 3). (ENG.). 32p. (J). (gr. -1-2). 15.99 *(978-1-84780-888-2(3),* Frances Lincoln Children's Bks.) Quarto Publishing Group UK GBR. Dist: Hachette Bk. Group.
Santos, Rita. Alicia Keys: Singer-Songwriter, 1 vol. 2018. (Junior Biographies Ser.). (ENG.). 24p. (gr. 3-4). 24.27 *(978-1-9785-0205-5(2),* ee4a9889-71cf-487d-b124-44c8396e2be8) Enslow Publishing, LLC.
Sarantou, Katlin. Tammy Duckworth. Bane, Jeff, illus. 2019. (My Early Library: My Itty-Bitty Bio Ser.). (ENG.). 24p. (J). (gr. k-1). pap. 12.79 *(978-1-5341-4990-8(2),* 213267); lib. bdg. 30.64 *(978-1-5341-4704-1(7),* 213266) Cherry Lake Publishing.
Savage, Jeff. Danica Patrick. 2006. (Amazing Athletes Ser.). (Illus.). 32p. (J). (gr. 2-5). lib. bdg. 23.93 *(978-0-8225-5954-2(4),* Lerner Pubns.) Lerner Publishing Group.
—Danica Patrick, 2nd Edition. 2nd rev. ed. 2010. (Amazing Athletes Ser.). (ENG., Illus.). 32p. (J). (gr. 2-5). pap. 7.95 *(978-0-7613-5760-5(2),* bd187dc4-00d4-428d-b3b7-37b4db37ebad); lib. bdg. 26.65 *(978-0-7613-5750-6(5),* 69ade3af-bdb2-427f-9dc4-8bc6133293bd, Lerner Pubns.) Lerner Publishing Group.
—Marion Jones. 2005. (J). pap. 5.95 *(978-0-8225-2040-5(0),* First Avenue Editions); (Illus.). (gr. 3-4). lib. bdg. 22.60 *(978-0-8225-3657-4(9))* Lerner Publishing Group.
—Maya Moore. 2012. (Amazing Athletes Ser.). 32p. (J). (gr. 2-5). pap. 45.32 *(978-0-7613-9316-0(1))* Lerner Publishing Group.
Sawyer, Kem Knapp. Harriet Tubman. 2010. (DK Biography Ser.). (ENG., Illus.). 128p. (J). (gr. 5-8). 18.69 *(978-0-7566-5807-6(1))* Dorling Kindersley Publishing, Inc.
Schatz, Kate. Rad American Women A-Z: Rebels, Trailblazers, & Visionaries Who Shaped Our History ... & Our Future! Klein Stahl, Miriam, illus. 2015. (City Lights/Sister Spit Ser.). (ENG.). 64p. (J). (gr. 2-11). 16.95 *(978-0-87286-683-6(1))* City Lights Bks.
Scheff, Matt. Maya Moore: Basketball Star. 2019. (Biggest Names in Sports Set 4 Ser.). (ENG., Illus.). 32p. (J). (gr. 3-5). 31.35 *(978-1-64185-321-7(2),* 1641853212, Focus Readers) North Star Editions.
Schiffman, Jessica, illus. Sybil Ludington: Freedom's Brave Rider. 2005. 32p. (J). pap. *(978-0-7367-2931-4(3))* Zaner-Bloser, Inc.
Schoettler, Joan. Ruth Asawa: A Sculpting Life, 1 vol. Van Van Wagoner, Traci, illus. 2018. (ENG.). 32p. (gr. 1-4). 16.99 *(978-1-4556-2397-6(0),* Pelican Publishing) Arcadia Publishing.
Schulte, Mary. Helen Greiner: Cofounder of iRobot Corporation, 1 vol. 2009. (Innovators Ser.). (ENG., Illus.). 48p. (gr. 4-8). lib. bdg. 36.23 *(978-0-7377-4404-0(9),* 61d5b1e4-5645-4a6a-b53a-541c6c1a2815, KidHaven Publishing) Greenhaven Publishing LLC.
Schuman, Michael A. Tina Fey: TV Comedy Superstar, 1 vol. 2011. (People to Know Today Ser.). (ENG., Illus.). 112p. (gr. 6-7). lib. bdg. 35.93 *(978-0-7660-3557-7(3),* f10baa8a-662b-432c-8977-33c02cf0829f) Enslow Publishing, LLC.
Schwartz, Heather. Lizzie Johnson: Vaquera Texana. 2013. (Primary Source Readers Ser.). (SPA.). lib. bdg. 19.65 *(978-0-606-31871-6(2))* Turtleback.
Schwartz, Heather E. Carli Lloyd: Soccer Star. 2018. (Women Sports Stars Ser.). (ENG., Illus.). 32p. (J). (gr. 3-9). lib. bdg. 28.65 *(978-1-5157-9710-4(4),* 136858, Capstone Pr.) Capstone.
—Simone Manuel: Swimming Star. 2018. (Women Sports Stars Ser.). (ENG., Illus.). 32p. (J). (gr. 3-9). lib. bdg. 28.65 *(978-1-5157-9707-4(4),* 136855, Capstone Pr.) Capstone.
Schweitzer, Karen. Sheryl Swoopes. (Role Model Athletes Ser.). 64p. 2012. (J). (gr. 7). 22.95 *(978-1-4222-2712-1(X))* 2010. (Illus.). (YA). (gr. 7-12). 22.95 *(978-1-4222-0491-7(X))* 2007. (Illus.). (YA). pap. 9.95 *(978-1-4222-0778-9(1))* Mason Crest.
Seguin, Marilyn. Young & Courageous: American Girls Who Made History. 2012. (J). pap. *(978-0-8283-2463-2(8))* Branden Bks.
Shea, Mary Molly. Alicia Keys, 1 vol. 2011. (Hip-Hop Headliners Ser.). (ENG., Illus.). 32p. (gr. 1-1). pap. 11.50 *(978-1-4339-4785-8(4),* fd2058ad-7f71-4957-9395-180575e39eb2); (J). 27.93 *(978-1-4339-4784-1(6),* acb83c56-de2d-4634-b62d-0fc3f5992b68) Stevens, Gareth Publishing LLLP.
—Taylor Swift, 1 vol. 2010. (Country Music Stars Ser.). (ENG., Illus.). 32p. (J). (gr. 1-1). pap. 11.50 *(978-1-4339-3611-1(9),* aa8d0ab2-3397-4baa-bf59-d898a1fdb738); lib. bdg. 27.93 *(978-1-4339-3610-4(0),* a102993e-ed47-4b72-ad14-5f0f33e34f60) Stevens, Gareth Publishing LLLP.
Sheen, Barbara. Janet Guthrie: Indy Car Racing Pioneer, 1 vol. 2010. (Innovators Ser.). (ENG., Illus.). 48p. (gr. 4-8). 36.23 *(978-0-7377-5050-8(2),* f678dd09-a6ab-4eeb-8427-c19661cd050c, KidHaven Publishing) Greenhaven Publishing LLC.
—Natalie Coughlin, 1 vol. 2013. (People in the News Ser.). (ENG., Illus.). 96p. (gr. 7-7). lib. bdg. 41.03 *(978-1-4205-0998-4(5),* 9ee2b0d3-5fb0-4f71-8489-cf3a897d2d94, Lucent Pr.) Greenhaven Publishing LLC.
Shepherd, Jodie. Hillary Clinton. 2015. (Rookie Biographies(r) Ser.). (ENG., Illus.). 32p. (J). lib. bdg. 23.00 *(978-0-531-20592-1(4))* Scholastic Library Publishing.
Sherrard, Valerie. Vanessa Hudgens, 1 vol. 2010. (Superstars! Ser.). (ENG., Illus.). 32p. (J). pap. *(978-0-7787-7262-0(4))* Crabtree Publishing Co.
Shetterly, Margot Lee. Hidden Figures. 2016. (Illus.). 231p. (J). lib. bdg. 18.40 *(978-0-606-39623-3(3))* Turtleback.
—Hidden Figures: The True Story of Four Black Women & the Space Race. Freeman, Laura, illus. 2018. (ENG.). 40p. (J). (gr. -1-3). 18.99 *(978-0-06-274246-9(9),* HarperCollins) HarperCollins Pubs.
—Hidden Figures Young Readers' Edition. 2016. (ENG., Illus.). 240p. (J). (gr. 3-7). 16.99 *(978-0-06-266238-5(4))*; pap. 9.99 *(978-0-06-266237-8(6))* HarperCollins Pubs. (HarperCollins).
Shichtman, Sandra H. Nancy Pelosi. 2008. (Political Profiles Ser.). (Illus.). 112p. (YA). (gr. 5-9). lib. bdg. 27.95 *(978-1-59935-049-3(1))* Reynolds, Morgan Inc.
Shulman, Holly. Dolley Madison: Her Life, Letters, & Legacy. 2009. (Library of American Lives & Times Ser.). 112p. (gr. 5-5). 69.20 *(978-1-60853-477-7(4))* Rosen Publishing Group, Inc., The.
Silate, Jennifer. Betsy Ross: Creadora de la bandera Estadounidense, 1 vol. 2003. (Grandes Personajes en la Historia de Los Estados Unidos (Famous People in American History) Ser.). (SPA.). 32p. (gr. 3-4). pap. 10.00 *(978-0-8239-4222-0(8),* b34d9aab-1916-4ad0-86a3-3cbffcb1dc18, Rosen Classroom) Rosen Publishing Group, Inc., The.
Silva, Jesselyn. My Corner of the Ring. 2019. (ENG., Illus.). 256p. (J). (gr. 5). 17.99 *(978-0-525-51840-2(1),* G.P. Putnam's Sons Books for Young Readers) Penguin Young Readers Group.
Sjonger, Rebecca. Susan B. Anthony: On a Woman's Right to Vote. 2019. (Deconstructing Powerful Speeches Ser.). 48p. (J). (gr. 6-6). pap. *(978-0-7787-5255-4(0))* Crabtree Publishing Co.
Skinner, J. E. U. S. Women's National Soccer Team. 2018. (21st Century Skills Library: Sports Unite Us Ser.). (ENG., Illus.). 32p. (J). (gr. 3-6). lib. bdg. 32.07 *(978-1-5341-2964-1(2),* 211900) Cherry Lake Publishing.
Slade, Suzanne. A Computer Called Katherine: How Katherine Johnson Helped Put America on the Moon. Miller Jamison, Veronica, illus. 2019. (ENG.). 40p. (J). (gr. -1-3). 18.99 *(978-0-316-43517-8(1))* Little, Brown Bks. for Young Readers.
—Dangerous Jane: ?the Life & Times of Jane Addams, Crusader for Peace, 1 vol. Ratterree, Alice, illus. 2017. 40p. (J). (gr. 1-4). 17.95 *(978-1-56145-913-1(5))* Peachtree Publishing Co. Inc.
Small, Cathleen. Barbara Mcclintock: Cytogeneticist & Discoverer of Mobile Genetic Elements, 1 vol. 2016. (Women in Science Ser.). (ENG., Illus.). 128p. (J). (gr. 9-9). lib. bdg. 47.36 *(978-1-5026-2311-9(0),* 9a9e424b-2bc1-4eff-83ce-6de7ab66b444) Cavendish Square Publishing LLC.
—Bessie Coleman: First Female African American & Native American Pilot, 1 vol. 2017. (Fearless Female Soldiers, Explorers, & Aviators Ser.). (ENG.). 128p. (YA). (gr. 9-9). 47.36 *(978-1-5026-2753-7(1),* 540b86e0-0bdf-4647-bf98-ddfa43a6d928) Cavendish Square Publishing LLC.
Snow, Kevin. Ronda Rousey: Conquering New Ground, 1 vol. 2017. (At the Top of Their Game Ser.). (ENG., Illus.). 112p. (YA). (gr. 9-9). 44.50 *(978-1-5026-2832-9(5),* 200ad270-ab9f-4a63-89a5-a1de9d8892d8) Cavendish Square Publishing LLC.
Somervill, Barbara A. Votes for Women! The Story of Carrie Chapman Catt. 2004. (Feminist Voices Ser.). (Illus.). 128p. (YA). (gr. 6-12). 23.95 *(978-1-883846-96-1(X),* First Biographies) Reynolds, Morgan Inc.
Sonneborn, Liz. Wilma Mankiller, 1 vol. 2011. (Leading Women Ser.). (ENG., Illus.). 96p. (J). (gr. 7-7). 42.64 *(978-0-7614-4959-1(0),* 5204097f-b0a9-4759-bd7c-f2d49cc58607) Cavendish Square Publishing LLC.
Sotomayor, Sonia. The Beloved World of Sonia Sotomayor. 352p. (J). (gr. 5). 2019. (ENG.). 10.99 *(978-1-5247-7117-1(1),* Yearling) 2018. (Illus.). 17.99 *(978-1-5247-7114-0(7),* Delacorte Bks. for Young Readers) Random Hse. Children's Bks.
—Turning Pages: My Life Story. Delacre, Lulu, illus. 2018. 40p. (J). (gr. -1-3). 17.99 *(978-0-525-51408-4(2),* Philomel Bks.) Penguin Young Readers Group.
Spence, Kelly. Ellen Degeneres: Television Comedian & Gay Rights Activist, 1 vol. 2016. (Leading Women Ser.). (ENG., Illus.). 112p. (YA). (gr. 7-7). 41.64 *(978-1-5026-1989-1(X),* 58095109-7488-401a-96ca-42d5782be0ea) Cavendish Square Publishing LLC.
—Taylor Swift: Pop Music Superstar, 1 vol. 2016. (Leading Women Ser.). (ENG., Illus.). 112p. (J). (gr. 7-7). 41.64 *(978-1-5026-1991-4(1),* 7262e2c1-3b9b-4a88-9043-694d1e10493d) Cavendish Square Publishing LLC.
Spiller, Sara. Ruth Bader Ginsburg. Bane, Jeff, illus. 2019. (My Early Library: My Itty-Bitty Bio Ser.). (ENG.). 24p. (J). (gr. k-1). pap. 12.79 *(978-1-5341-3925-1(7),* 212529); lib. bdg. 30.64 *(978-1-5341-4269-5(X),* 212528) Cherry Lake Publishing.
—Susan B. Anthony. Bane, Jeff, illus. 2019. (My Early Library: My Itty-Bitty Bio Ser.). (ENG.). 24p. (J). (gr. k-1). pap. 12.79 *(978-1-5341-3923-7(0),* 212521); lib. bdg. 30.64 *(978-1-5341-4267-1(3),* 212520) Cherry Lake Publishing.
Spinner, Stephanie. Who Was Annie Oakley? Day, Larry, illus. 2003. (Who Was... ? Ser.). 109p. (gr. 4-7). 15.00 *(978-0-7569-1588-9(0))* Perfection Learning Corp.
—Who Was Clara Barton? 2014. (Who Was... ? Ser.). (Illus.). 103p. (J). lib. bdg. 16.00 *(978-0-606-35695-4(9))* Turtleback.
Staley, Erin. Maggie Stiefvater, 1 vol. 2013. (All about the Author Ser.). (ENG.). 112p. (YA). (gr. 7-7). 39.80 *(978-1-4777-1762-2(5),* e5c18288-1557-4598-9a8b-ae4c0dfca99c) Rosen Publishing Group, Inc., The.
Stein, R. Conrad. Harriet Tubman: On My Underground Railroad I Never Ran My Train off the Track, 1 vol. 2008. (Americans: the Spirit of a Nation Ser.). (ENG., Illus.). 128p. (J). (gr. 5-6). lib. bdg. 35.93 *(978-0-7660-3481-5(X),* f1675bad-1c07-4b76-adc6-eb89aa02c903) Enslow Publishing, LLC.
Stewart, Gail B. Maya Angelou, 1 vol. 2009. (People in the News Ser.). (ENG., Illus.). 104p. (gr. 7-7). lib. bdg. 41.03 *(978-1-4205-0092-9(9),* 5f651b45-e104-47a3-ac40-23df64948fc3, Lucent Pr.) Greenhaven Publishing LLC.
—Stephanie Kwolek: Creator of Kevlar, 1 vol. 2008. (Innovators Ser.). (ENG., Illus.). 48p. (gr. 4-8). lib. bdg. 36.23 *(978-0-7377-4040-0(X),* 1919a8c6-dc4f-4883-96d1-6a8388a4b8df, KidHaven Publishing) Greenhaven Publishing LLC.

W X Y Z

Stine, Megan. Who Is Michelle Obama? 2013. (Who Is... ? Ser.). lib. bdg. 14.75 (978-0-606-32131-0(4)) Turtleback.

Stock, Catherine. Vinnie & Abraham. unabr. ed. 2008. (J). (gr. 2-5). 27.95 incl. audio (978-0-8045-6967-5(3)); 29.95 incl. audio compact disk (978-0-8045-4190-9(6)) Spoken Arts, Inc.

Stoltman, Joan. Elizabeth Cady Stanton, 1 vol. 2018. (Little Biographies of Big People Ser.). (ENG.). 24p. (gr. 1-2). 24.27 (978-1-5382-1836-5(4), c624885d-3665-4dee-b5d7-777942743dfd) Stevens, Gareth Publishing LLLP.

—Michelle Obama, 1 vol. 2017. (Little Biographies of Big People Ser.). (ENG.). 24p. (J). (gr. 1-2). pap. 9.15 (978-1-5382-0929-5(2), fbc15435-d338-4ce0-8dfa-22308002b351) Stevens, Gareth Publishing LLLP.

—Michelle Obama, 1 vol. Garcia, Ana Maria, tr. 2017. (Pequeñas Biografías de Grandes Personajes (Little Biographies of Big People) Ser.). (SPA.). 24p. (J). (gr. 1-2). pap. 9.15 (978-1-5382-1555-5(1), 827c2c46-0ae9-4e2d-82a1-1ea660a36de8); lib. bdg. 24.27 (978-1-5382-1528-9(4), 72bafb7a-6a09-4f74-becc-105367d5c6c9) Stevens, Gareth Publishing LLLP.

Stone, Tanya Lee. Almost Astronauts: 13 Women Who Dared to Dream. 2009. (ENG., Illus.). 144p. (J). (gr. 5). 24.99 (978-0-7636-3611-1(8)) Candlewick Pr.

—The House That Jane Built: A Story about Jane Addams. Brown, Kathryn, illus. 2015. (ENG.). 32p. (J). (gr. 1-4). 19.99 (978-0-8050-9049-9(5), 900060591, Holt, Henry & Co. Bks. For Young Readers) Holt, Henry & Co.

Stout, Glenn. Baseball Heroes. 2010. (Good Sports Ser.). (ENG., Illus.). 128p. (J). (gr. 3-7). pap. 6.99 (978-0-547-41708-0(X), 1430003, Clarion Bks.) HarperCollins Pubs.

Strand, Jennifer. Barbara Bush. 2018. (First Ladies (Launch!) Ser.). (ENG., Illus.). 24p. (J). (gr. -1-2). lib. bdg. 31.36 (978-1-5321-2282-8(9), 28331, Abdo Zoom-Launch) ABDO Publishing Co.

—Hillary Clinton. 2018. (First Ladies (Launch!) Ser.). (ENG., Illus.). 24p. (J). (gr. -1-2). lib. bdg. 31.36 (978-1-5321-2283-5(7), 28333, Abdo Zoom-Launch) ABDO Publishing Co.

—Katy Perry. 2016. (Stars of Music Ser.). (ENG.). 24p. (J). (gr. -1-2). lib. bdg. 31.36 (978-1-68079-919-4(3), 24142, Abdo Zoom-Launch) ABDO Publishing Co.

—Lady Bird Johnson. 2018. (First Ladies (Launch!) Ser.). (ENG., Illus.). 24p. (J). (gr. -1-2). lib. bdg. 31.36 (978-1-5321-2284-2(5), 28335, Abdo Zoom-Launch) ABDO Publishing Co.

Streissguth, Tom. Wilma Rudolph. 2006. (Sports Heroes & Legends Ser.). (ENG., Illus.). 120p. (gr. 5-12). lib. bdg. 30.60 (978-0-8225-5958-0(7)) Lerner Publishing Group.

Stumpff, April D. & Messersmith, Patrick. Ann Richards: A Woman's Place Is in the Dome. 2006. (Stars of Texas Ser.: 6). (ENG., Illus.). 80p. (J). (gr. 4-7). 14.95 (978-1-933337-12-8(5), P148096) State Hse. Pr.

Sullivan, George. Berenice Abbott, Photographer: An Independent Vision. 2006. (ENG., Illus.). 176p. (J). (gr. 5-7). 20.00 (978-0-618-44026-9(7), 100362, Clarion Bks.) HarperCollins Pubs.

Summers, Kimberly Dillon. Miley Cyrus: A Biography, 1 vol. 2009. (Greenwood Biographies Ser.). (ENG.). 180p. 43.00 (978-0-313-37847-8(9), 900301084, Bloomsbury Academic) Bloomsbury Publishing Plc GBR. Dist: Macmillan.

Sutcliffe, Jane. Helen Keller. 2009. (History Maker Biographies Ser.). (gr. k-2). 27.93 (978-0-7613-4223-6(0), Lerner Pubns.) Lerner Publishing Group.

—Helen Keller. Verstraete, Elaine, illus. 2003. (On My Own Biographies Ser.). 48p. (J). (gr. 1-3). 6.95 (978-0-87614-903-4(4), Carolrhoda Bks.) Lerner Publishing Group.

—Sacagawea. 2009. (History Maker Biographies Ser.). (ENG.). 48p. (gr. 3-6). 27.93 (978-0-7613-4222-9(2), Lerner Pubns.) Lerner Publishing Group.

Sutton, A. Trevor. Dr. Bessie Rehwinkel. Pierce, Linda, illus. 2012. (Hero of Faith Ser.). (ENG.). 47p. (J). pap. 7.99 (978-0-7586-3078-0(6)) Concordia Publishing Hse.

Swain, Gwenyth. Sojourner Truth. Archambault, Matthew, illus. 2005. (On My Own Biography Ser.). 48p. (J). (gr. 1-3). pap. 6.95 (978-1-57505-827-6(8)) Lerner Publishing Group.

—Sojourner Truth. 2005. (On My Own Biography Ser.). (Illus.). 48p. (J). 25.26 (978-1-57505-651-7(8), Carolrhoda Bks.) Lerner Publishing Group.

Swanson, June. Venus & Serena Williams. Burke, Susan S., illus. 2003. (You Must Be Joking! Riddle Bks.). 32p. (J). (gr. 2-5). pap. 5.95 (978-0-8225-9842-8(6)) Lerner Publishing Group.

Tafolla, Carmen & Teneyuca, Sharyll. That's Not Fair! / No Es Justo! Emma Tenayuca's Struggle for Justice/la Lucha de Emma Tenayuca Por la Justicia. 2008. (ENG & SPA., Illus.). 40p. (J). (gr. k-2). 22.95 (978-0-916727-33-8(5), P459884) Wings Pr.

Terp, Gail. Misty Copeland. 2016. (Women Who Rock Ser.). (ENG., Illus.). 32p. (J). (gr. 4-6). 31.35 (978-1-68072-065-5(1), 10420, Bolt) Black Rabbit Bks.

—Taylor Swift. 2016. (Women Who Rock Ser.). (ENG., Illus.). 32p. (J). (gr. 4-6). 31.35 (978-1-68072-069-3(4), 10432, Bolt) Black Rabbit Bks.

Thermes, Jennifer. Grandma Gatewood Hikes the Appalachian Trail. 2018. (ENG., Illus.). 48p. (J). (gr. k-2). 18.99 (978-1-4197-2839-6(3), 1118001) Abrams, Inc.

Thiel, Kristin. Amelia Earhart: First Woman to Fly Solo Across the Atlantic, 1 vol. 2017. (Fearless Female Soldiers, Explorers, & Aviators Ser.). (ENG.). 128p. (YA). (gr. 9-9). 47.36 (978-1-5026-2749-0(3), f4ee7b7b-24c9-4aed-9fcc-73f5401b1c71) Cavendish Square Publishing LLC.

Thompson, Gare. Who Was Eleanor Roosevelt? Wolf, Elizabeth, illus. 2004. (Who Was... ? Ser.). 106p. (gr. 3-7). 15.00 (978-0-7569-2829-2(X)) Perfection Learning Corp.

Thornton, Jeremy. Famous Women of the American Revolution. 2009. (Building America's Democracy Ser.). 24p. (gr. 3-3). 42.50 (978-1-61511-763-5(6), PowerKids Pr.) Rosen Publishing Group, Inc., The.

Time for Kids Editors. Rosa Parks: Civil Rights Pioneer. 2007. (Time for Kids Biographies Ser.). (Illus.). 44p. (gr. 2-4). 14.00 (978-0-7569-8110-5(7)) Perfection Learning Corp.

Todd, Kim D. Jean Jennings Bartik: Computer Pioneer. 2015. (Notable Missourians Ser.). (ENG., Illus.). 48p. (J). pap. 24.00 (978-1-61248-145-6(0)) Truman State Univ. Pr.

Tol, Alex Van & National Geographic Learning Staff. Dolores Huerta: Voice for the Working Poor. 2010. (ENG., Illus.). 112p. (J). pap. (978-0-7787-2545-9(6)) Crabtree Publishing Co.

Turner, Ann. My Name Is Truth: The Life of Sojourner Truth. Ransome, James, illus. 2015. (ENG.). 40p. (J). (gr. 1-5). 18.99 (978-0-06-075898-1(8)); lib. bdg. 18.89 (978-0-06-075899-8(6)) HarperCollins Pubs. (HarperCollins).

Turner, Myra Faye. Hidden in History: The Untold Stories of Female Artists, Musicians, & Writers. 2018. (ENG.). 230p. (YA). pap. 19.95 (978-1-62023-563-8(3), 5260e7b3-2355-4b8a-91ee-e4e4a857abcd) Atlantic Publishing Group, Inc.

Uhl, Xina M. & Marx, Christy. Grace Hopper: Computer Pioneer, 1 vol. 2019. (Super Female Scientists Ser.). (ENG.). 104p. (gr. 7-7). pap. 18.65 (978-1-7253-4044-2(5), 9c26f5ec-5313-4436-8334-a03df741733b) Rosen Publishing Group, Inc., The.

Uschan, Michael V. Michelle Obama, 1 vol. 2010. (People in the News Ser.). (ENG., Illus.). 112p. (gr. 7-7). 41.03 (978-1-4205-0209-1(3), a36bfb24-c866-43d1-b0fe-08faaaaf913e, Lucent Pr.) Greenhaven Publishing LLC.

Valentin, Jean. The Bravery of Amelia Earhart, 1 vol. 2012. (InfoMax Readers Ser.). (ENG., Illus.). 24p. (J). (gr. 1-1). pap. 8.25 (978-1-4488-9067-5(5), 6a1c9295-dd60-4a1f-ac37-6fc0d547b7f3, Rosen Classroom) Rosen Publishing Group, Inc., The.

Van Tol, Alex. Dolores Huerta: Voice for the Working Poor. 2010. (Crabtree Groundbreaker Biographies Ser.). (ENG., Illus.). 112p. (J). (gr. 5-8). lib. bdg. (978-0-7787-2536-7(7)) Crabtree Publishing Co.

Van Vleet, Carmella & Sullivan, Kathy. To the Stars! The First American Woman to Walk in Space. Wong, Nicole, illus. 40p. (J). (gr. k-3). 2018. pap. 7.99 (978-1-58089-645-0(6)) 2016. lib. bdg. 16.95 (978-1-58089-644-3(8)) Charlesbridge Publishing, Inc.

Venezia, Mike. Georgia o'Keeffe (Revised Edition) (Getting to Know the World's Greatest Artists) Venezia, Mike, illus. 2015. (Getting to Know the World's Greatest Artists Ser.). (ENG., Illus.). 40p. (J). (gr. 3-4). pap. 7.95 (978-0-531-21291-2(2), Children's Pr.) Scholastic Library Publishing.

Ventura, Marne. Hillary Clinton: Historic Politician. 2017. (Newsmakers Set 2 Ser.). (ENG.). 48p. (J). (gr. 4-8). 55.65 (978-1-68078-966-9(X), 26367) ABDO Publishing Co.

Vescia, Monique. Kim Kardashian West & Kanye West, 1 vol. 2019. (Power Couples Ser.). (ENG.). 112p. (gr. 7-7). 38.80 (978-1-5081-8888-9(2), 0a000a04-2c84-4bf3-ba40-212fddaba8a0) Rosen Publishing Group, Inc., The.

Wade, Linda R. Condoleezza Rice. 2004. (Illus.). 32p. (J). lib. bdg. 25.70 (978-1-58415-332-0(6)) Mitchell Lane Pubs.

Wade, Mary Dodson. Condoleezza Rice. rev. ed. 2005. (Gateway Biography Ser.). (Illus.). 48p. (J). (gr. 4-7). pap. 8.95 (978-0-7613-9549-2(0), First Avenue Editions) Lerner Publishing Group.

—Condoleezza Rice: Being the Best. 2003. (Gateway Biography Ser.: 4). 48p. lib. bdg. 23.90 (978-0-7613-2619-9(7)); (Illus.). (gr. 2-4). pap. 8.95 (978-0-7613-1927-6(1)) Lerner Publishing Group. (Millbrook Pr.).

Wallace Sharp, Anne. Nancy Lopez: Golf Hall of Famer, 1 vol. 2008. (Twentieth Century's Most Influential Hispanics Ser.). (ENG., Illus.). 104p. (gr. 7-10). 41.03 (978-1-4205-0060-8(0), 35d00649-1a23-49d9-b3b3-e4d6809ea5ba, Lucent Pr.) Greenhaven Publishing LLC.

—Women Civil Rights Leaders, 1 vol. 2013. (Lucent Library of Black History Ser.). (ENG., Illus.). 120p. (gr. 7-7). 41.03 (978-1-4205-0880-2(6), 3604b1cb-3b3b-4e9d-94ef-2a661a00fc0b, Lucent Pr.) Greenhaven Publishing LLC.

Walsh, Barbara E. The Poppy Lady: Moina Belle Michael & Her Tribute to Veterans. Johnson, Layne, illus. 2012. (ENG.). 40p. (J). (gr. 2-5). 18.99 (978-1-59078-754-0(4), Calkins Creek) Highlights Pr., c/o Highlights for Children, Inc.

Walsh, Francis. Daring Women of the American Revolution, 1 vol. (American History Flashpoints! Ser.). (ENG.). 32p. (gr. 4-4). 2009. (J). lib. bdg. 28.93 (978-1-4358-2994-7(8), f170b92c-cc04-4a89-9f0b-79d32475f4d2, PowerKids Pr.) 2008. pap. 10.00 (978-1-4358-0177-6(6), 9279eae1-ee95-43d8-97ca-f35d83aceba0, Rosen Classroom) Rosen Publishing Group, Inc., The.

Wambach, Abby. Forward: My Story Young Readers' Edition. (ENG.). 224p. (J). (gr. 3-7). 2017. pap. 7.99 (978-0-06-245793-6(4)) 2016. 16.99 (978-0-06-245792-9(6)) HarperCollins Pubs. (HarperCollins).

Warner, Emily B. Dottie Lamm: A Friend to Families. 2007. (Now You Know Bio Ser.: 8). (J). pap. 8.95 (978-0-86541-085-5(2)) Filter Pr., LLC.

Warren, Sarah. Dolores Huerta: A Hero to Migrant Workers, 0 vols. Casilla, Robert, illus. 2012. (ENG.). 32p. (J). (gr. 1-4). 17.99 (978-0-7614-6107-4(8), 9780761461074, Two Lions) Amazon Publishing.

Washington, Shirley. A Gift for Girls: Words of Wisdom from Successful Women. 2005. (Illus.). 124p. (YA). (gr. 7). per. 12.95 (978-1-933285-06-1(0)) Brown Books Publishing Group.

Watson-Doost, Valeria. Phillis Wheatley. 2008. (ENG.). 35p. pap. 21.50 (978-0-557-03153-5(2)) Lulu Pr., Inc.

Watson, Marilyn Myrick. Rose Mofford: State Greats Arizona. 2007. (Acacia Biographies Ser.). (Illus.). 28p. (J). (gr. 3-7). lib. bdg. 16.95 (978-0-9788283-5-6(6)); (gr. 4-7). per. 6.95 (978-0-9790826-1-0(7)) Acacia Publishing, Inc.

Watson, Stephanie. Amy Poehler, 1 vol. 2013. (People in the News Ser.). (ENG., Illus.). 96p. (gr. 7-7). lib. bdg. 41.03 (978-1-4205-0883-3(0), 57b4f977-57f1-4fac-a2c4-27d9dd4d3c4e, Lucent Pr.) Greenhaven Publishing LLC.

Waxman, Laura Hamilton. Aerospace Engineer Aprille Ericsson. 2015. (STEM Trailblazer Bios Ser.). (ENG., Illus.). 32p. (J). (gr. 2-5). lib. bdg. 26.65 (978-1-4677-5793-5(4), 9fc3e93c-6fbb-4c6e-97f0-be8a0831d681, Lerner Pubns.) Lerner Publishing Group.

—Computer Engineer Ruchi Sanghvi. 2015. (STEM Trailblazer Bios Ser.). (ENG., Illus.). 32p. (J). (gr. 2-5). pap. 8.99 (978-1-4677-6119-2(2), 8bf6ae81-cba9-4efc-a1cb-75e2d8ecd73d); lib. bdg. 26.65 (978-1-4677-5794-2(2), 20104c02-02a9-4370-9e0e-e553857a507d, Lerner Pubns.) Lerner Publishing Group.

—Sojourner Truth. 2008. (History Maker Biographies Ser.). (ENG., Illus.). 48p. (gr. 3-6). lib. bdg. 27.93 (978-0-8225-7172-8(2), Lerner Pubns.) Lerner Publishing Group.

Weakland, Mark. When Amelia Earhart Built a Roller Coaster. Grivina, Oksana, illus. 2017. 31p. (J). (978-1-5158-0142-9(X), Picture Window Bks.) Capstone.

—When Bill Gates Memorized the Encyclopedia. Volpari, Daniela, illus. 2018. (Leaders Doing Headstands Ser.). (ENG.). 32p. (J). (gr. 1-4). pap. 7.95 (978-1-5158-3048-1(9), 138683, Picture Window Bks.) Capstone.

—When Ruth Bader Ginsburg - Chewed 100 Sticks of Gum. Volpari, Daniela, illus. 2018. (Leaders Doing Headstands Ser.). (ENG.). 32p. (J). (gr. 1-4). lib. bdg. 28.65 (978-1-5158-3039-9(X), 138676, Picture Window Bks.) Capstone.

—When Wilma Rudolph Played Basketball. Duncan, Daniel, illus. 2016. (Leaders Doing Headstands Ser.). (ENG.). 32p. (J). (gr. 1-4). lib. bdg. 28.65 (978-1-4795-9684-3(1), 132340, Picture Window Bks.) Capstone.

Wearing, Judy. Amelia Earhart. 2010. pap. 9.95 (978-1-61690-060-1(1)); 24p. (J). (gr. 2-4). lib. bdg. 25.70 (978-1-61690-059-5(8)) Weigl Pubs., Inc.

Weber, Rebecca. Ellen Ochoa. 2011. (Early Connections Ser.). (J). (978-1-61672-550-1(8)) Benchmark Education Co.

Weber, Terri Smith. Jennifer Lopez: Realizando Los Suenos. 2003. (SPA.). (J). pap. (978-0-9740180-4-1(X)); lib. bdg. (978-0-9740180-3-4(1)) Panda Publishing, L.L.C. (Bios for Kids).

Webster, Gayle. I Can Still Remember ..., 1 vol. 2010. 146p. pap. 24.95 (978-1-61546-175-2(2)) America Star Bks.

Weerts, Christine. Hero of Faith - Rosa Young. 2011. (Illus.). 64p. (J). pap. 7.99 (978-0-7586-2830-5(7)) Concordia Publishing Hse.

Weidt, Maryann N. Harriet Tubman. 2003. (History Maker Bios Ser.). (Illus.). 47p. (J). 26.60 (978-0-8225-4676-4(0), Lerner Pubns.) Lerner Publishing Group.

—Rosa Parks. (History Maker Bios Ser.). (Illus.). (J). 2004. 48p. pap. 8.95 (978-0-8225-4805-8(4)) 2003. 47p. 26.60 (978-0-8225-4673-3(6)) Lerner Publishing Group. (Lerner Pubns.).

Wells, Peggy Sue. Fergie. 2007. (Blue Banner Biography Ser.). (Illus.). 32p. (YA). (gr. 4-7). lib. bdg. 25.70 (978-1-58415-521-8(3)) Mitchell Lane Pubs.

Weston Woods Staff, creator. Ella Fitzgerald. 2011. 18.95 (978-0-545-02761-8(6)); 38.75 (978-0-545-02763-2(2)) Weston Woods Studios, Inc.

Wetzel, Dan. Epic Athletes: Alex Morgan. Thomas, Cory, illus. 2020. (Epic Athletes Ser.: 2). (ENG.). 176p. (J). pap. 8.99 (978-1-250-25071-1(4), 900195184) Square Fish.

Wheeler, Irvin, illus. Justina's Dream. 2005. 30p. (J). (978-1-887302-12-8(3)) Western Images Pubns., Inc.

Wheeler, Jill C. Ellen DeGeneres: Groundbreaking Entertainer. 2017. (Newsmakers Set 2 Ser.). (ENG., Illus.). 48p. (J). (gr. 4-8). lib. bdg. 35.64 (978-1-5321-1182-2(7), 25940) ABDO Publishing Co.

—Grace Hopper: Computer Scientist. 2017. (Women in Science Ser.). (ENG., Illus.). 112p. (J). (gr. 6-12). lib. bdg. 41.36 (978-1-5321-1044-3(8), 25664, Essential Library) ABDO Publishing Co.

—Harriet Tubman. 2003. (Breaking Barriers Ser.). (Illus.). 64p. (J). (gr. 3-8). 27.07 (978-1-57765-908-2(2), Abdo & Daughters) ABDO Publishing Co.

—Hillary Rodham Clinton. 2003. (Breaking Barriers Ser.). 64p. (gr. 3-8). lib. bdg. 27.07 (978-1-57765-741-5(1), Abdo & Daughters) ABDO Publishing Co.

—Rosa Parks, Set II. 2003. (Breaking Barriers Ser.). 64p. (gr. 3-8). lib. bdg. 27.07 (978-1-57765-640-1(7), Abdo & Daughters) ABDO Publishing Co.

Whiting, Jim. Annie Oakley. 2006. (What's So Great About... ? Ser.). (Illus.). 32p. (J). (gr. 2-4). lib. bdg. 25.70 (978-1-58415-477-8(2)) Mitchell Lane Pubs.

Winget, Mary. Eleanor Roosevelt. (Biography Ser.). (Illus.). 2005. 112p. (gr. 6-12). lib. bdg. 27.93 (978-0-8225-4985-7(9)) 2003. 48p. (J). pap. 8.95 (978-0-8225-4801-0(1), Lerner Pubns.) 2003. 48p. (J). (gr. 3-5). lib. bdg. 26.60 (978-0-8225-4675-7(2)) Lerner Publishing Group.

Winter, Jonah. Mother Jones & Her Army of Mill Children. Carpenter, Nancy, illus. 2020. (ENG.). 40p. (J). (gr. -1-3). 20.99 (978-0-449-81292-1(8), Schwartz & Wade Bks.) Random Hse. Children's Bks.

—Ruth Bader Ginsburg: The Case of R. B. G. vs. Inequality. Innerst, Stacy, illus. 2017. (ENG.). 48p. (J). (gr. 1-4). 18.95 (978-1-4197-2559-3(9), 1163401, Abrams Bks. for Young Readers) Abrams, Inc.

Wishinsky, Frieda. Freedom Heroines (Profiles #4) 2012. (Profiles Ser.: 4). (ENG., Illus.). 144p. (J). (gr. 4-7). pap. 6.99 (978-0-545-42518-6(2), Scholastic Paperbacks) Scholastic, Inc.

Wojahn, Rebecca Hogue & Wojahn, Rebecca. Dr. Kate: Angel on Snowshoes. 2009. (Badger Biographies Ser.). (ENG., Illus.). 104p. (J). (gr. 3-7). pap. 12.95 (978-0-87020-421-0(1)) Wisconsin Historical Society.

Wolff, Marion. Shedding Skins. 2004. pap. 12.00 (978-1-930401-27-3(2)) Central Coast Bks./Pr.

Wolny, Philip. Sylvia Mendez: Civil Rights Activist, 1 vol. 2019. (Our Voices: Spanish & Latino Figures of American History Ser.). (ENG.). 48p. (gr. 6-6). pap. 12.75 (978-1-5081-8531-4(X), a9bb9dfd-da70-4064-9b61-973e9b60e31c, Rosen Reference) Rosen Publishing Group, Inc., The.

Women in Science, 12 vols. 2016. (Women in Science Ser.). (ENG.). 128p. (YA). (gr. 9-9). lib. bdg. 284.16 (978-1-5026-2439-0(7), 0260eb06-1fea-40d6-9b9a-9413df0ea9c7, Cavendish Square) Cavendish Square Publishing LLC.

Women of the American Revolution (NCHS) Grades 5-8. 58p. (J). tchr. ed. 29.45 (978-0-382-40934-9(5)) Cobblestone Publishing Co.

Wood, Ramona. The Goat Woman of Smackover: An Arkansas Legend. Wood, Ramona, . 2006. (Illus.). 32p. (J). pap. 11.00 (978-0-9758622-1-6(9)) ABC Pr.

Wood, Susan. Elizabeth Warren: Nevertheless, She Persisted. Green, Sarah, illus. 2018. (ENG.). 48p. (J). (gr. 1-4). 18.99 (978-1-4197-3162-4(9), 1210001, Abrams Bks. for Young Readers) Abrams, Inc.

Woodward, Kay. What Would She Do?: 25 True Stories of Trailblazing Rebel Women. 2018. (ENG.). 112p. (J). (gr. 3-7). 16.99 (978-1-338-21640-0(6)) Scholastic, Inc.

Worth, Richard. Eva Longoria: Actress, Activist, & Entrepreneur, 1 vol. 2015. (Influential Latinos Ser.). (ENG., Illus.). 128p. (gr. 7-7). 38.93 (978-0-7660-6993-0(1), b5c7226a-a90f-40a0-ac51-66e4b9645f60) Enslow Publishing, LLC.

Wukovits, John F. Ellen Ochoa: First Female Hispanic Astronaut, 1 vol. 2006. (Twentieth Century's Most Influential Hispanics Ser.). (ENG., Illus.). 104p. (J). (gr. 7-10). lib. bdg. 41.03 (978-1-59018-976-4(0), 18130175-8284-4b98-bad3-c2d99e81fca4, Lucent Pr.) Greenhaven Publishing LLC.

Wyckoff, Edwin Brit. Hair-Care Millionaire: Madam C. J. Walker & Her Amazing Business, 1 vol. 2010. (Genius at Work! Great Inventor Biographies Ser.). (ENG.). 32p. (gr. 3-3). 26.60 (978-0-7660-3449-5(6), 428944d3-9333-4be6-9c5e-931e31820387) Enslow Publishing, LLC.

Yasuda, Anita. Lady Bird Johnson. 2010. (My Life Ser.). 24p. (J). (gr. 2-4). lib. bdg. 25.70 (978-1-61690-062-5(8)) Weigl Pubs., Inc.

—Lady Bird Johnson: My Life. 2010. pap. 9.95 (978-1-61690-063-2(6)) Weigl Pubs., Inc.

—Taylor Swift. 2010. (Remarkable People Ser.). (Illus.). 24p. (J). (gr. 4-6). pap. 11.95 (978-1-61690-158-5(6)); lib. bdg. 25.70 (978-1-61690-157-8(8)) Weigl Pubs., Inc.

—Women of the American West, 1 vol. 2016. (Wild West Ser.). (ENG., Illus.). 48p. (J). (gr. 4-8). lib. bdg. 35.64 (978-1-68078-262-2(2), 22125) ABDO Publishing Co.

Yim, Natasha. Sacajawea of the Shoshone. Nguyen, Albert, illus. 2012. (Thinking Girl's Treasury of Real Princesses Ser.). (ENG.). 32p. (J). (gr. 3-8). 18.95 (978-0-9845098-6-7(0)) Goosebottom Bks. LLC.

Yomtov, Nel. The Belles of Baseball: The All-American Girls Professional Baseball League. 2017. (Hidden Heroes Ser.). (ENG., Illus.). 112p. (J). (gr. 6-12). lib. bdg. 41.36 (978-1-68078-386-5(6), 23537, Essential Library) ABDO Publishing Co.

Young, Jeff C. Michelle Wie. 2012. (Xtreme Athletes Ser.). (Illus.). 112p. (YA). (gr. 7-12). 28.95 (978-1-59935-187-2(0)) Reynolds, Morgan Inc.

Younger, Barbara. Purple Mountain Majesties: The Story of Katharine Lee Bates & America the Beautiful. Schuett, Stacey, illus. 2005. 29p. (J). reprint ed. 16.00 (978-0-7567-8984-8(2)) DIANE Publishing Co.

WOMEN ARTISTS

Abirached, Zeina. I Remember Beirut. Abirached, Zeina, illus. 2014. (ENG., Illus.). 96p. (YA). (gr. 8-12). pap. 11.99 (978-1-4677-4458-4(1), 69b3f232-512a-4c66-8514-4517324523a0, Graphic Universe™) Lerner Publishing Group.

Amson-Bradshaw, Georgia. Amazing Artists & Designers. Petruccioli, Rita, illus. 2018. (ENG.). 48p. (J). (gr. 4-7). pap. 9.99 (978-1-4380-1217-9(9)) Sourcebooks, Inc.

Ball, Heather. Astonishing Women Artists, 1 vol. 2007. (Women's Hall of Fame Ser.: 10). (ENG., Illus.). 120p. (J). (gr. 4-8). pap. 10.95 (978-1-897187-23-4(8)) Second Story Pr. CAN. Dist: Orca Bk. Pubs. USA.

Baxter, Roberta. Women in Music. 2018. (Women in the Arts Ser.). (ENG., Illus.). 48p. (J). (gr. 4-8). lib. bdg. 35.64 (978-1-5321-1477-9(X), 29146) ABDO Publishing Co.

Bennett, Sophia. Women's Art Work: More Than 30 Female Artists Who Changed the World. Thapp, Manjit, illus. 2020. (ENG.). 112p. (J). (gr. 5-9). 19.99 (978-1-4197-4118-0(7), 1303801, Abrams Bks. for Young Readers) Abrams, Inc.

Doeden, Matt. Frida Kahlo: Artist & Activist. 2020. (Gateway Biographies Ser.). (ENG., Illus.). 48p. (J). (gr. 4-8). pap. 11.99 (978-1-5415-8888-2(6), 4e95bb11-576b-4bed-b211-32e60ca411e8); lib. bdg. 31.99 (978-1-5415-7745-9(0), 2a8ec86f-831c-4113-b8a2-fb3ac0b696ba) Lerner Publishing Group. (Lerner Pubns.).

Gruitrooy, Gerhard. Mary Cassatt: An American Impressionist, Vol. 8. 2018. (American Artists Ser.). 80p. (J). (gr. 7). 33.27 (978-1-4222-4162-2(9)) Mason Crest.

Harrison, Vashti. Little Dreamers: Visionary Women Around the World. 2018. (Vashti Harrison Ser.). (ENG., Illus.). 96p. (J). (gr. 3-7). 17.99 (978-0-316-47517-4(3)) Little, Brown Bks. for Young Readers.

Hurt, Avery Elizabeth. The Most Influential Women in the Arts, 1 vol. 2018. (Breaking the Glass Ceiling: the Most Influential Women Ser.). (ENG.). 112p. (gr. 8-8). 40.13 (978-1-5081-7964-1(6), 83cca142-f351-4921-8f48-9f897df951da) Rosen Publishing Group, Inc., The.

Hutchison, Patricia. Women in Dance. 2018. (Women in the Arts Ser.). (ENG., Illus.). 48p. (J). (gr. 4-8). lib. bdg. 35.64 (978-1-5321-1473-1(7), 29138) ABDO Publishing Co.

Manes, Cara & Ramos, Fatinha. Sonia Delaunay: A Life of Color. 2017. (ENG., Illus.). 40p. (J). 19.95 (978-1-63345-024-0(4), 1653401) Museum of Modern Art.

Markel, Michelle. Out of This World: The Surreal Art of Leonora Carrington. Hall, Amanda, illus. 2019. (ENG.). 40p. (J). (gr. -1-3). 17.99 (978-0-06-244109-6(4), Balzer & Bray) HarperCollins Pubs.

Meltzer, Brad. Soy Frida Kahlo. Eliopoulos, Christopher, illus. 2023.Tr. of I Am Frida Kahlo. (SPA.). (J). (gr. k-3). pap. 14.99 (978-1-5433-8604-2(0)) Vista Higher Learning, Inc.

Morlock, Rachael. Mary Cassatt: Famous Female Impressionist, 1 vol. 2018. (Eye on Art Ser.). (ENG.). 104p. (gr. 7-7). pap. 20.99 (978-1-5345-6609-5(0), 22dc5ed8-8d03-48e0-bdb6-7ae7c5e23115, Lucent Pr.) Greenhaven Publishing LLC.

O'Connor, Jane. Mary Cassatt: Family Pictures. Kalis, Jennifer, illus. 2003. (Smart about Art Ser.). (ENG.). 32p. (J). (gr. k-4).

nass mkt. 7.99 *(978-0-448-43152-9(1)*, Grosset & Dunlap) Penguin Young Readers Group.

mundson, Linda. How the West Was Drawn: Women's Art, 1 vol. 2014. (How the West Was Drawn Ser.). (ENG., Illus.). 32p. (J). (gr. k-7). 16.99 *(978-1-4556-1878-1(0)*, Pelican Publishing) Arcadia Publishing.

embert, Winfred, illus. Don't Hold Me Back: My Life & Art. 2003. (ENG.). 48p. (J). 19.95 *(978-0-8126-2703-9(2))* Cricket Bks.

uemann, Bettina. 13 Women Artists Children Should Know. 2009. (13 Children Should Know Ser.). (ENG., Illus.). 48p. (J). (gr. 3-7). 14.95 *(978-3-7913-4333-4(5))* Prestel Verlag GmbH & Co KG. DEU. Dist: Penguin Random Hse. LLC.

kander, Shahzia. Roots & Wings: How Shahzia Sikander Became an Artist. Barczyk, Hanna, illus. 2021. (ENG.). 40p. (J). (gr. -1-3). 19.95 *(978-1-63345-035-6(X)*, 1316801) Museum of Modern Art.

ingh, Rina. Pitseolak Ashoona: Une Artiste Inuite. 2004. (FRE., Illus.). (J). *(978-2-7650-0741-8(1))* Les Editions de la Cheneliere, Inc.

pinner, Stephanie. Who Was Annie Oakley? Day, Larry, illus. 2003. (Who Was... ? Ser.). 109p. (gr. 4-7). 15.00 *(978-0-7569-1588-9(0))* Perfection Learning Corp.

erp, Gail. Taylor Swift. 2016. (Women Who Rock Ser.). (ENG., Illus.). 32p. (J). (gr. 4-6). 31.35 *(978-1-68072-069-3(4)*, 10432, Bolt) Black Rabbit Bks.

Turner, Myra Faye. Hidden in History: The Untold Stories of Female Artists, Musicians, & Writers. 2018. (ENG.). 230p. (YA). pap. 19.95 *(978-1-62023-563-8(3)*, 5260e7b3-2355-4b8a-91ee-e4e4a857abcd) Atlantic Publishing Group, Inc.

Woodward, Kay. What Would She Do?: 25 True Stories of Trailblazing Rebel Women. 2018. (ENG.). 112p. (J). (gr. 3-7). 16.99 *(978-1-338-21640-0(6))* Scholastic, Inc.

WOMEN ATHLETES

Adler, David A. America's Champion Swimmer: Gertrude Ederle. Widener, Terry, illus. 2005. (ENG.). 32p. (J). (gr. -1-3). reprint ed. pap. 11.99 *(978-0-15-205251-5(8)*, 1195820, Clarion Bks.) HarperCollins Pubs.

Anderson, Jameson. Gabby Douglas, 1 vol. 2014. (Awesome Athletes Ser.). (ENG., Illus.). 32p. (J). (gr. 3-6). lib. bdg. 32.79 *(978-1-62403-338-4(5)*, 1219, Checkerboard Library) ABDO Publishing Co.

Axon, Rachel. Title IX Levels the Playing Field. 2017. (Women in Sports Ser.). (ENG., Illus.). 48p. (J). (gr. 4-8). lib. bdg. 34.21 *(978-1-5321-1157-0(6)*, 25890, SportsZone) ABDO Publishing Co.

Bertovich, Yvonne. The Untold Stories of Female Athletes. 2019. (ENG.). 279p. (YA). pap. 19.95 *(978-1-62023-557-7(9)*, 920cbb03-5eb4-4f80-8415-6b53d89efece) Atlantic Publishing Group, Inc.

Borth, Teddy. Charlotte Flair: Bow to Your Queen. 2017. (Wrestling Biographies Ser.). (ENG., Illus.). 24p. (J). (gr. 2-8). lib. bdg. 31.36 *(978-1-5321-2107-4(5)*, 26790, Abdo Zoom-Fly) ABDO Publishing Co.

Braun, Eric. Lindsey Vonn. 2017. (Sports All-Stars (Lerner (tm) Sports) Ser.). (ENG., Illus.). 32p. (J). (gr. 2-5). 29.32 *(978-1-5124-2580-2(X)*, 0c534438-90da-41c3-8f84-fabc1a245444); E-Book 6.99 *(978-1-5124-3786-7(7)*, 9781512437867); E-Book 42.65 *(978-1-5124-2825-4(6))*; E-Book 42.65 *(978-1-5124-3785-0(9)*, 9781512437850) Lerner Publishing Group. (Lerner Pubns.).

Buckey, A. W. Women in Basketball. 2020. (She's Got Game Ser.). (ENG., Illus.). 32p. (J). (gr. 3-5). pap. 9.95 *(978-1-64493-138-7(9)*, 1644931389); lib. bdg. 31.35 *(978-1-64493-059-5(5)*, 1644930595) North Star Editions. (Focus Readers).

—Women in Softball. 2020. (She's Got Game Ser.). (ENG., Illus.). 32p. (J). (gr. 3-5). pap. 9.95 *(978-1-64493-142-4(7)*, 1644931427); lib. bdg. 31.35 *(978-1-64493-063-2(3)*, 1644930633) North Star Editions. (Focus Readers).

—Women in Swimming. 2020. (She's Got Game Ser.). (ENG., Illus.). 32p. (J). (gr. 3-5). pap. 9.95 *(978-1-64493-143-1(5)*, 1644931435); lib. bdg. 31.35 *(978-1-64493-064-9(1)*, 1644930641) North Star Editions. (Focus Readers).

—Women in Volleyball. 2020. (She's Got Game Ser.). (ENG., Illus.). 32p. (J). (gr. 3-5). pap. 9.95 *(978-1-64493-145-5(1)*, 1644931451); lib. bdg. 31.35 *(978-1-64493-066-3(8)*, 1644930668) North Star Editions. (Focus Readers).

Buckley, James. Katie Ledecky. 2017. (Amazing Americans: Olympians Ser.). (ENG.). 24p. (J). (gr. -1-3). 26.99 *(978-1-68402-240-3(1))* Bearport Publishing Co., Inc.

—Simone Biles. 2017. (Amazing Americans: Olympians Ser.). (ENG., Illus.). 24p. (J). (gr. -1-3). 26.99 *(978-1-68402-241-0(X))* Bearport Publishing Co., Inc.

Bullaro, Angie. Breaking the Ice: The True Story of the First Woman to Play in the National Hockey League. Payne, C. F., illus. 2020. (ENG.). 40p. (J). (gr. -1-3). 19.99 *(978-1-5344-2557-6(8))* Simon & Schuster, Inc.

Burdett, Benjamin. Julie Ertz, 1 vol. 2018. (Soccer Stars Ser.). (ENG.). 24p. (J). (gr. 3-3). 25.27 *(978-1-5383-4349-4(5)*, e3255336-ded3-40ee-b590-e607c40d6324, PowerKids Pr.) Rosen Publishing Group, Inc., The.

Burns, Kylie. Simone Biles: Gold Medal Gymnast & Advocate for Healthy Living. 2018. (Remarkable Lives Revealed Ser.). (ENG., Illus.). 32p. (J). (gr. 3-3). *(978-0-7787-4701-7(8))*; pap. *(978-0-7787-4712-3(3))* Crabtree Publishing Co.

Cantwell, Lois. Women Winners: Then & Now. 2009. (Sports Illustrated for Kids Bks). 176p. (gr. 7-12). 63.90 *(978-1-60853-157-8(0))* Rosen Publishing Group, Inc., The.

Carey, Nicolette & Bryant, Jill. Women Athletes Who Changed the World, 1 vol. 2011. (Great Women of Achievement Ser.). (ENG., Illus.). 88p. (YA). (gr. 5-6). lib. bdg. 39.80 *(978-1-4488-6001-2(6)*, ba333a43-e61c-4042-a75e-0d9703109f91) Rosen Publishing Group, Inc., The.

Carroll, Myrna & Manley, Claudia B. Track & Field: Girls Rocking It, 1 vol., 1. 2015. (Title IX Rocks! Ser.). (ENG., Illus.). 64p. (J). (gr. 6-6). 36.13 *(978-1-5081-7043-3(6)*, 00e21e0c-43e5-45ad-93e9-ffc6648b847e, Rosen Young Adult) Rosen Publishing Group, Inc., The.

Chaffee, Kim. Her Fearless Run: Kathrine Switzer's Historic Boston Marathon. Rooney, Ellen, illus. 2019. (ENG.). 40p. (J). 17.99 *(978-1-62414-654-1(6)*, 900196525) Page Street Publishing Co.

Chick, Chloe. Mighty Mira Based on the Story. 2016. (ENG., Illus.). 35p. (J). *(978-981-320-254-2(8))* World Scientific Publishing Co. Pte Ltd.

Clinton, Chelsea. She Persisted in Sports: American Olympians Who Changed the Game. Boiger, Alexandra, illus. (She Persisted Ser.). (J). 2022. 30p. (— 1). bds. 9.99 *(978-0-593-35341-7(2))* 2020. 32p. (gr. -1-3). 17.99 *(978-0-593-11454-4(X))* Penguin Young Readers Group. (Philomel Bks.).

Davies, Monika. Spectacular Sports: Playing Like a Girl: Problem Solving (Grade 4) 2017. (Mathematics in the Real World Ser.). (ENG., Illus.). 32p. (J). (gr. 4-5). pap. 11.99 *(978-1-4258-5552-9(0))* Teacher Created Materials, Inc.

Dodson Wade, Mary. Amazing Olympic Athlete Wilma Rudolph, 1 vol. 2009. (Amazing Americans Ser.). (ENG., Illus.). 24p. (gr. k-2). pap. 10.35 *(978-0-7660-5978-8(2)*, d5d1fbaa-2c64-42f5-ac67-49964d2a9897, Enslow Elementary) Enslow Publishing, LLC.

Duling, Kaitlyn. Women in Hockey. 2020. (She's Got Game Ser.). (ENG., Illus.). 32p. (J). (gr. 3-5). pap. 9.95 *(978-1-64493-139-4(7)*, 1644931397); lib. bdg. 31.35 *(978-1-64493-060-1(9)*, 1644930609) North Star Editions. (Focus Readers).

Dzidrums, Christine. Missy Franklin: Swimming Sensation. 2013. 72p. pap. 9.99 *(978-1-938438-23-3(X))* Creative Media Publishing.

Dzidrums, Christine & Rendon, Leah. Jennie Finch: Softball Superstar. Dzidrums, Joseph, photos by. 2013. (ENG., Illus.). 72p. (J). pap. 9.99 *(978-1-938438-13-4(2))* Creative Media Publishing.

Faust, Daniel R. Ibtihaj Muhammad: Muslim American Champion Fencer & Olympian, 1 vol. 2017. (Breakout Biographies Ser.). (ENG., Illus.). 32p. (J). (gr. 4-5). 27.93 *(978-1-5081-6060-1(0)*, edb48c2a-7335-4060-9e9d-88433e3aab1f, PowerKids Pr.) Rosen Publishing Group, Inc., The.

Feldman, Heather. Marion Jones: Atleta de Categoría Internacional (World-Class Runner) 2009. (Superestrellas del Deporte (Superstars of Sports) Ser.). (SPA.). 24p. (gr. 1-2). 42.50 *(978-1-60853-227-8(5)*, Editorial Buenas Letras) Rosen Publishing Group, Inc., The.

—Marion Jones: World Class Runner. 2009. (Sports Superstars Ser.). 24p. (gr. 1-1). 42.50 *(978-1-60853-179-0(1)*, PowerKids Pr.) Rosen Publishing Group, Inc., The.

Fishman, Jon M. Breanna Stewart. 2018. (Sports All-Stars (Lerner (tm) Sports) Ser.). (ENG., Illus.). 32p. (J). (gr. 2-5). pap. 9.99 *(978-1-5415-2804-8(2)*, 0e3983a4-efc6-48af-b63e-8f4ff8e33737); lib. bdg. 29.32 *(978-1-5415-2458-3(6)*, e734d5f1-8010-4a48-bec4-23794e603c58, Lerner Pubns.) Lerner Publishing Group.

—Katie Ledecky. 2020. (Sports All-Stars (Lerner (tm) Sports) Ser.). (ENG., Illus.). 32p. (J). (gr. 2-5). 29.32 *(978-1-5415-9750-1(8)*, 32a444bc-57c0-49f9-8263-7f9d3d9a6721, Lerner Pubns.) Lerner Publishing Group.

—Simone Biles. 2017. (Sports All-Stars Ser.). (ENG.). 32p. (J). (gr. 2-5). 12.99 *(978-1-5124-4901-3(6))*; 39.99 *(978-1-5124-4900-6(8))*; (Illus.). lib. bdg. 29.32 *(978-1-5124-4897-9(4)*, f61f729f-7df7-4ed3-a2ac-28876fbf99fd); (Illus.). E-Book 42.65 *(978-1-5124-4899-3(0))* Lerner Publishing Group. (Lerner Pubns.).

—Soccer Superstar Alex Morgan. 2019. (Bumba Books (r) — Sports Superstars Ser.). (ENG., Illus.). 24p. (J). (gr. -1-1). 26.65 *(978-1-5415-5563-1(5)*, f7230529-e9de-4626-9c5a-87b8282d893b); pap. 8.99 *(978-1-5415-7364-2(1)*, 69c9753f-5320-439c-bbeb-6b200ade7bed) Lerner Publishing Group. (Lerner Pubns.).

Flynn, Brendan. Superstars of the WNBA Finals. 2018. (Sports' Greatest Superstars Ser.). (ENG., Illus.). 24p. (J). (gr. 1-1). pap. 8.95 *(978-1-63517-829-6(0)*, 1635178290) North Star Editions.

—Superstars of the WNBA Finals. 2018. (Sports' Greatest Superstars Ser.). (ENG., Illus.). 24p. (J). (gr. k-3). lib. bdg. 31.36 *(978-1-5321-6034-9(8)*, 28700, Pop! Cody Koala) Pop!

Freedman, Russell. Babe Didrikson Zaharias: The Making of a Champion. 2014. (ENG., Illus.). 192p. (J). (gr. 5-7). pap. 11.99 *(978-0-544-10491-4(9)*, 1540799, Clarion Bks.) HarperCollins Pubs.

Goddu, Krystyna Poray. Carli Lloyd. 2019. (Player Profiles Ser.). (ENG., Illus.). 32p. (J). (gr. 4-6). lib. bdg. *(978-1-68072-873-6(3)*, 12772, Bolt) Black Rabbit Bks.

Golkar, Golriz. Laurie Hernandez. 2018. (Influential People Ser.). (ENG., Illus.). 32p. (J). (gr. 4-6). lib. bdg. 28.65 *(978-1-5435-4134-2(8)*, 139088, Capstone Pr.) Capstone.

Gordon, Sherri Mabry. Women Athletes, 1 vol. 2016. (Defying Convention: Women Who Changed the Rules Ser.). (ENG., Illus.). 128p. (gr. 6-6). 38.93 *(978-0-7660-8147-5(8)*, 05e17a6e-6471-4408-a4dd-9ad04c15aec8) Enslow Publishing, LLC.

Green, Michelle Y. A Strong Right Arm: The Story of Mamie Peanut Johnson. Nelson, Kadir, illus. 2004. (ENG.). 128p. (J). (gr. 3-7). 7.99 *(978-0-14-240072-2(6)*, Puffin Books) Penguin Young Readers Group.

Guillemo-Newton, Judy. Competitive Tennis for Girls. 2009. (SportsGirl Ser.). 64p. (gr. 5-8). 58.50 *(978-1-60853-194-3(5)*, Rosen Reference) Rosen Publishing Group, Inc., The.

Hall, Brian. Pioneers in Women's Sports. 2017. (Women in Sports Ser.). (ENG., Illus.). 48p. (J). (gr. 4-8). lib. bdg. 34.21 *(978-1-5321-1156-3(8)*, 25888, SportsZone) ABDO Publishing Co.

Hansen, Grace. Chloe Kim. 2018. (Olympic Biographies Ser.). (ENG., Illus.). 24p. (J). (gr. -1-2). lib. bdg. 32.79 *(978-1-5321-8143-6(4)*, 29772, Abdo Kids) ABDO Publishing Co.

—Mikaela Shiffrin. 2018. (Olympic Biographies Ser.). (ENG., Illus.). 24p. (J). (gr. -1-2). lib. bdg. 32.79 *(978-1-5321-8144-3(2)*, 29774, Abdo Kids) ABDO Publishing Co.

—Red Gerard. 2018. (Olympic Biographies Ser.). (ENG., Illus.). 24p. (J). (gr. -1-2). lib. bdg. 32.79 *(978-1-5321-8145-0(0)*, 29776, Abdo Kids) ABDO Publishing Co.

Henderson, Leah. Mamie on the Mound: A Woman in Baseball's Negro Leagues. Doutsiopoulos, George, illus. 2020. (ENG.). 32p. (J). (gr. 3-5). 18.95 *(978-1-68446-023-6(9)*, 139306, Capstone Editions) Capstone.

Hernandez, Laurie. I Got This: To Gold & Beyond. (ENG., Illus.). 240p. (J). (gr. 3-7). 2018. pap. 8.99 *(978-0-06-267732-7(2))* 2017. 17.99 *(978-0-06-267731-0(4)*, HarperCollins) HarperCollins Pubs.

Hewson, Anthony K. Alex Morgan. 2019. (Sports All-Stars (Lerner (tm) Sports) Ser.). (ENG., Illus.). 32p. (J). (gr. 2-5). pap. 9.99 *(978-1-5415-7446-5(X)*, bb6638ab-14b0-4d47-a638-847a373da994); lib. bdg. 29.32 *(978-1-5415-5611-9(9)*, 38419754-aadb-4b93-b503-58fa873928eb) Lerner Publishing Group. (Lerner Pubns.).

—US Women's Hockey Team. 2018. (Olympic Stars Ser.). (ENG., Illus.). 32p. (J). (gr. 3-9). lib. bdg. 32.79 *(978-1-5321-1608-7(X)*, 29800, SportsZone) ABDO Publishing Co.

Hoena, Blake. Serena Williams: Athletes Who Made a Difference. LeDoyen, Sam, illus. 2020. (Athletes Who Made a Difference Ser.). (ENG.). 32p. (J). (gr. 3-6). 27.99 *(978-1-5415-7818-0(X)*, 004897ce-e80b-449f-bed7-0f55f0c5eaa1); pap. 8.99 *(978-1-7284-0296-3(4)*, e27a1a4d-c61a-46c5-b659-5555d51aab7f) Lerner Publishing Group. (Graphic Universe™).

Ignotofsky, Rachel. Women in Sports: 50 Fearless Athletes Who Played to Win. 2017. (Women in Science Ser.). (Illus.). 128p. (YA). (gr. 5-12). 16.99 *(978-1-60774-978-3(5)*, Ten Speed Pr.) Potter/Ten Speed/Harmony/Rodale.

Irwin, Sue. Breaking Through: Heroes in Canadian Women's Sport. 2018. (Lorimer Recordbooks Ser.). (ENG.). 144p. (YA). (gr. 4-4). pap. 12.95 *(978-1-4594-1372-6(5)*, 1372) James Lorimer & Co. Ltd., Pubs. CAN. Dist: Formac Lorimer Bks. Ltd.

Jökulsson, Illugi. Stars of Women's Soccer. 2nd ed. 2018. (ENG., Illus.). 64p. (J). (gr. 1-11). 14.95 *(978-0-7892-1305-1(2)*, 791305, Abbeville Kids) Abbeville Pr., Inc.

Jones, Emma. Girls Play Rugby, 1 vol. 2016. (Girls Join the Team Ser.). (ENG.). 24p. (J). (gr. 3-3). pap. 9.25 *(978-1-4994-2105-7(2)*, c7cc3f2a-c144-4018-87f4-9e3dee51f4b2, PowerKids Pr.) Rosen Publishing Group, Inc., The.

Kane, Bryce. Superstars of Women's Soccer. 2019. (J). *(978-1-4222-4212-4(9))*; Vol. 4. (Illus.). 80p. (gr. 12). lib. bdg. 33.27 *(978-1-4222-4213-1(7))* Mason Crest.

—Top Teams in Women's Soccer, Vol. 4. 2019. (Women's Soccer Today Ser.). (Illus.). 80p. (J). (gr. 12). lib. bdg. 33.27 *(978-1-4222-4214-8(5))* Mason Crest.

Kawa, Katie. Women in Sports, 1 vol. 2015. (Women Groundbreakers Ser.). (ENG., Illus.). 32p. (J). (gr. 4-5). pap. 11.00 *(978-1-4994-1051-8(4)*, c5574e83-3747-4e17-965c-d6b15b100252, PowerKids Pr.) Rosen Publishing Group, Inc., The.

Killion, Ann. Champions of Women's Soccer. 2019. 276p. (J). (gr. 3-7). 8.99 *(978-0-399-54903-8(X)*, Puffin Books) Penguin Young Readers Group.

Kirkpatrick, Rob. Florence Griffith Joyner: Olympic Runner. 2009. (Great Record Breakers in Sports Ser.). 24p. (gr. 3-3). 42.50 *(978-1-61513-187-7(6)*, PowerKids Pr.) Rosen Publishing Group, Inc., The.

Kortemeier, Todd. Greatest Female Athletes of All Time. 2017. (Women in Sports Ser.). (ENG., Illus.). 48p. (J). (gr. 4-8). lib. bdg. 34.21 *(978-1-5321-1154-9(1)*, 25884, SportsZone) ABDO Publishing Co.

—Greatest Moments in Women's Sports. 2017. (Women in Sports Ser.). (ENG., Illus.). 48p. (J). (gr. 4-8). lib. bdg. 34.21 *(978-1-5321-1155-6(X)*, 25886, SportsZone) ABDO Publishing Co.

Koya, Lena & La Bella, Laura. Female Athletes, 1 vol. 2017. (Women in the World Ser.). (ENG., Illus.). 112p. (J). (gr. 6-6). 38.80 *(978-1-5081-7718-0(X)*, c6f6606e-e453-42a4-a7e5-41d59a4abc07) Rosen Publishing Group, Inc., The.

La Bella, Laura. Women & Sports, 1 vol. 2012. (Young Woman's Guide to Contemporary Issues Ser.). (ENG., Illus.). 112p. (YA). (gr. 8-9). lib. bdg. 39.80 *(978-1-4488-8398-1(9)*, 3ada87d5-7266-4e3c-90d6-2aefb94a6e61) Rosen Publishing Group, Inc., The.

Labrecque, Ellen. Top 10 Women Athletes. 2018. (Top 10 in Sports Ser.). (ENG.). 24p. (J). (gr. 2-5). lib. bdg. 32.79 *(978-1-5038-2719-6(4)*, 212549) Child's World, Inc, The.

Lajiness, Katie. Ibtihaj Muhammad. 2016. (Big Buddy Olympic Biographies Ser.). (ENG.). 32p. (J). (gr. 2-5). lib. bdg. 34.21 *(978-1-68078-554-8(0)*, 23595, Big Buddy Bks.) ABDO Publishing Co.

—Katie Ledecky. 2016. (Big Buddy Olympic Biographies Ser.). (ENG., Illus.). 32p. (J). (gr. 2-5). lib. bdg. 34.21 *(978-1-68078-553-1(2)*, 23593, Big Buddy Bks.) ABDO Publishing Co.

—Laurie Hernandez. 2016. (Big Buddy Olympic Biographies Ser.). (ENG.). 32p. (J). (gr. 2-5). lib. bdg. 34.21 *(978-1-68078-552-4(4)*, 23591, Big Buddy Bks.) ABDO Publishing Co.

Lang, Heather. Queen of the Track: Alice Coachman, Olympic High-Jump Champion. Cooper, Floyd, illus. 2012. (ENG.). 40p. (J). (gr. k-4). 18.99 *(978-1-59078-850-9(8)*, Astra Young Readers) Astra Publishing Hse.

Leed, Percy. Wilma Rudolph: Running for Gold. 2020. (Epic Sports Bios (Lerner (tm) Sports) Ser.). (ENG., Illus.). 32p. (J). (gr. 2-5). 30.65 *(978-1-5415-9744-0(3)*, d02fb726-95e7-47ea-aa3b-c085bb381bd2, Lerner Pubns.) Lerner Publishing Group.

Leigh, Anna. Aly Raisman: Athlete & Activist. 2019. (Gateway Biographies Ser.). (ENG., Illus.). 48p. (J). (gr. 4-8). lib. bdg. 31.99 *(978-1-5415-4261-7(4)*, 7f2fb359-a94f-4539-bd0f-586db1fb54fe, Lerner Pubns.) Lerner Publishing Group.

Levit, Joe. Babe Didrikson Zaharias: Multisport Superstar. 2020. (Epic Sports Bios (Lerner (tm) Sports) Ser.). (ENG., Illus.). 32p. (J). (gr. 2-5). 30.65 *(978-1-5415-9745-7(1)*, 26f00417-b35c-4c98-b358-bebb5fbcf12f); pap. 9.99 *(978-1-7284-1338-9(9)*, ae0dd883-d71b-4725-9688-9c2ecc40270e) Lerner Publishing Group. (Lerner Pubns.).

Llanas, Sheila. Women in Track & Field. 2020. (She's Got Game Ser.). (ENG., Illus.). 32p. (J). (gr. 3-5). pap. 9.95 *(978-1-64493-144-8(3)*, 1644931443); lib. bdg. 31.35 *(978-1-64493-065-6(X)*, 164493065X) North Star Editions. (Focus Readers).

Lloyd, Carli & Coffey, Wayne. All Heart: My Dedication & Determination to Become One of Soccer's Best. (ENG., Illus.). 304p. (J). (gr. 5-7). 2018. pap. 9.99 *(978-1-328-74097-7(8)*, 1677146) 2016. 16.99 *(978-0-544-97869-0(2)*, 1663897) HarperCollins Pubs. (Clarion Bks.).

Lord, Michelle. A Girl Called Genghis Khan: The Story of Maria Toorpakai Wazir. Malik, Shehzil, illus. 2019. (People Who Shaped Our World Ser.: 5). 48p. (J). (gr. k). 16.95 *(978-1-4549-3136-2(1))* Sterling Publishing Co., Inc.

Lowell, Barbara. Maya Moore. 2019. (Player Profiles Ser.). (ENG.). 32p. (J). (gr. 4-6). pap. 9.99 *(978-1-64466-079-9(2)*, 12781); (Illus.). lib. bdg. *(978-1-68072-876-7(8)*, 12780) Black Rabbit Bks. (Bolt).

Luke, Andrew. U. S. Women's Team, Vol. 4. 2019. (Women's Soccer Today Ser.). (Illus.). 80p. (J). (gr. 12). lib. bdg. 33.27 *(978-1-4222-4215-5(3))* Mason Crest.

Macy, Sue. Roller Derby Rivals. Collins, Matt, illus. 2019. 40p. (J). (gr. 1-4). pap. 7.99 *(978-0-8234-4185-3(7))* Holiday Hse., Inc.

Manley, Claudia B. Competitive Track & Field for Girls. 2009. (SportsGirl Ser.). 64p. (gr. 5-8). 58.50 *(978-1-60853-195-0(3)*, Rosen Reference) Rosen Publishing Group, Inc., The.

Marquardt, Meg. Women in Lacrosse. 2020. (She's Got Game Ser.). (ENG., Illus.). 32p. (J). (gr. 3-5). pap. 9.95 *(978-1-64493-140-0(0)*, 1644931400); lib. bdg. 31.35 *(978-1-64493-061-8(7)*, 1644930617) North Star Editions. (Focus Readers).

Marsico, Katie. Surviving a Shark Attack: Bethany Hamilton. 2019. (They Survived (Alternator Books (r)) Ser.). (ENG., Illus.). 32p. (J). (gr. 3-6). lib. bdg. 29.32 *(978-1-5415-2353-1(9)*, 219854b2-a068-4315-bcbd-4a8a3f071a8e, Lerner Pubns.) Lerner Publishing Group.

McDougall, Chros. Girls Play to Win Figure Skating. 2010. (Girls Play to Win Ser.). 64p. (J). (gr. 3-6). lib. bdg. 27.93 *(978-1-59953-389-6(8))* Norwood Hse. Pr.

McKinney, Donna B. Women in Soccer. 2020. (She's Got Game Ser.). (ENG., Illus.). 32p. (J). (gr. 3-5). pap. 9.95 *(978-1-64493-141-7(9)*, 1644931419); lib. bdg. 31.35 *(978-1-64493-062-5(5)*, 1644930625) North Star Editions. (Focus Readers).

McMahon, Dave. Girls Play to Win Hockey. 2010. (Girls Play to Win Ser.). 64p. (J). (gr. 3-6). lib. bdg. 27.93 *(978-1-59953-390-2(1))* Norwood Hse. Pr.

Moening, Kate. Simone Biles: Olympic Gymnast. 2020. (Women Leading the Way Ser.). (ENG.). 24p. (J). (gr. k-3). lib. bdg. 26.95 *(978-1-64487-123-2(8)*, Blastoff! Readers) Bellwether Media.

Moon, Derek. Chloe Kim. 2018. (Olympic Stars Ser.). (ENG., Illus.). 32p. (J). (gr. 3-9). lib. bdg. 32.79 *(978-1-5321-1607-0(1)*, 29798, SportsZone) ABDO Publishing Co.

Mortensen, Lori & Schwartz, Heather. Women Sports Stars. 2018. (Women Sports Stars Ser.). (ENG.). 32p. (J). (gr. 3-9). 122.60 *(978-1-5157-9727-2(9)*, 27425, Capstone Pr.) Capstone.

Moss, Marissa. Mighty Jackie: The Strike-Out Queen. Payne, C. F., illus. 2004. (ENG.). 32p. (J). (gr. k-3). 18.99 *(978-0-689-86329-5(2)*, Simon & Schuster/Paula Wiseman Bks.) Simon & Schuster/Paula Wiseman Bks.

Muhammad, Ibtihaj. Proud (Young Readers Edition) Living My American Dream. (ENG., Illus.). (J). (gr. 3-7). 2019. 320p. pap. 9.99 *(978-0-316-47704-8(4))* 2018. 304p. 18.99 *(978-0-316-47700-0(1))* Little, Brown Bks. for Young Readers.

Nagelhout, Ryan. Beth Phoenix, 1 vol. 2013. (Superstars of Wrestling Ser.). (ENG., Illus.). 32p. (J). (gr. 1-1). pap. 11.50 *(978-1-4339-8513-3(6)*, bb046a5e-4ae5-4ec1-a0c8-503cef51bead); lib. bdg. 28.27 *(978-1-4339-8512-6(8)*, 43dc5b91-8b17-46e4-b1ab-a792fc7be356) Stevens, Gareth Publishing LLLP.

Offutt, Jason. Helen Stephens: The Fulton Flash. Hare, John, illus. 2014. (ENG.). 48p. (J). lib. bdg. 24.00 *(978-1-61248-114-2(0))* Truman State Univ. Pr.

Paul, Caroline. The Gutsy Girl: Escapades for Your Life of Epic Adventure. MacNaughton, Wendy, illus. 2016. (ENG.). 160p. (gr. 5-8). 18.00 *(978-1-63286-123-8(2)*, 900148432) Bloomsbury Publishing USA.

Pimentel, Annette Bay. Girl Running. Archer, Micha, illus. 2018. 32p. (J). (gr. k-3). 17.99 *(978-1-101-99668-3(4)*, Nancy Paulsen Books) Penguin Young Readers Group.

Poletti, Frances & Yee, Kristina. The Girl Who Ran: Bobbi Gibb, the First Woman to Run the Boston Marathon. Chapman, Susanna, illus. 2017. (J). *(978-1-943200-47-4(5))* Compendium, Inc., Publishing & Communications.

Rappoport, Ken. Ladies First: Women Athletes Who Made a Difference, 1 vol. 2010. (Illus.). 192p. (J). (gr. 3-7). pap. 8.95 *(978-1-56145-534-8(2))* Peachtree Publishing Co. Inc.

Riner, Dax & Savage, Jeff. Annika Sorenstam. 2008. (Sports Heroes & Legends Ser.). (ENG.). (gr. 5-12). pap. 56.72 *(978-0-8225-9397-3(1))* Lerner Publishing Group.

Robinson, Tom. Girls Play to Win Basketball. 2010. (Girls Play to Win Ser.). 64p. (J). (gr. 3-6). lib. bdg. 27.93 *(978-1-59953-388-9(X))* Norwood Hse. Pr.

Rockliff, Mara. Billie Jean! How Tennis Star Billie Jean King Changed Women's Sports. Baddeley, Elizabeth, illus. 2019. 40p. (J). (gr. -1-3). 17.99 *(978-0-525-51779-5(0)*, G.P. Putnam's Sons Books for Young Readers) Penguin Young Readers Group.

Roseborough, Elizabeth. Women's Soccer on the Rise, Vol. 4. 2019. (Women's Soccer Today Ser.). (Illus.). 80p. (J). (gr. 12). lib. bdg. 33.27 *(978-1-4222-4216-2(1))* Mason Crest.

Rubini, Julie K. Eye to Eye: Sports Journalist Christine Brennan. 2019. (Biographies for Young Readers Ser.). (ENG., Illus.). 136p. (J). 32.95 *(978-0-8214-2374-5(6))*; pap. 15.95 *(978-0-8214-2375-2(4))* Ohio Univ. Pr.

WXYZ

Rule, Heather. Women in the Olympics. 2017. (Women in Sports Ser.). (ENG., Illus.). 48p. (J) (gr. 4-8). lib. bdg. 34.21 *(978-1-5321-1159-4(2)*, 25894, SportsZone) ABDO Publishing Co.

Savage, Jeff. Maya Moore. 2012. (Amazing Athletes Ser.). (ENG., Illus.). 32p. (J). (gr. 2-5). pap. 7.95 *(978-0-7613-8666-7(1)*, da49541d-44f8-4b42-ba1c-b2594caa1038) Lerner Publishing Group.

Scheff, Matt. Alex Morgan: Soccer Star. 2019. (Biggest Names in Sports Set 4 Ser.). (ENG., Illus.). 32p. (J). (gr. 3-5). pap. 9.95 *(978-1-64185-380-4(8)*, 1641853808); lib. bdg. 31.35 *(978-1-64185-322-4(0)*, 1641853220) North Star Editions. (Focus Readers).

—Aly Raisman. 2016. (Olympic Stars Ser.). (ENG., Illus.). 32p. (J). (gr. 3-9). lib. bdg. 32.79 *(978-1-68078-562-3(1)*, 23807, SportsZone) ABDO Publishing Co.

—Katie Ledecky. 2016. (Olympic Stars Ser.). (ENG., Illus.). 32p. (J). (gr. 3-9). lib. bdg. 32.79 *(978-1-68078-559-3(1)*, 23801, SportsZone) ABDO Publishing Co.

—Simone Manuel. 2016. (Olympic Stars Ser.). (ENG., Illus.). 32p. (J). (gr. 3-9). lib. bdg. 32.79 *(978-1-68078-560-9(5)*, 23803, SportsZone) ABDO Publishing Co.

Schultz Nicholson, Lorna. Pink Power: The First Women's Hockey World Champions. 2007. (Lorimer Recordbooks Ser.). (ENG., Illus.). 128p. (gr. 3-8). (YA). 16.95 *(978-1-55028-989-3(6)*, 989); (J). 9.95 *(978-1-55028-987-9(X)*, 987) James Lorimer & Co. Ltd., Pubs. CAN. Dist: Formac Lorimer Bks. Ltd.

—Winning Gold: Canada's Incredible 2002 Olympic Victory in Women's Hockey, 1 vol. (Lorimer Recordbooks Ser.). (ENG., Illus.). 112p. 2010. (J). (gr. 8-12). 16.95 *(978-1-55277-473-1(2)*, 473) 2009. (YA). (gr. 7-12). pap. 8.99 *(978-1-55277-472-4(4)*, bde9609c-22c2-481e-9cc0-b14304a89986) James Lorimer & Co. Ltd., Pubs. CAN. Dist: Formac Lorimer Bks. Ltd., Lerner Publishing Group.

Schwartz, Heather. Sports for All: The Impact of Title IX (Level 5) 2017. (TIME for KIDS(r): Informational Text Ser.). (ENG., Illus.). 48p. (gr. 4-8). pap. 13.99 *(978-1-4258-4987-0(3))* Teacher Created Materials, Inc.

Segovia, Patty. Skate Girls. 2016. (Illus.). 32p. (J). *(978-1-4896-4783-2(X))* Weigl Pubs., Inc.

Seigerman, David. Becky Sauerbrunn. 2017. (Real Sports Content Network Presents Ser.). (ENG.). 128p. (J). (gr. 3-7). 17.99 *(978-1-4814-8217-2(3))*; (Illus.). pap. 7.99 *(978-1-4814-8216-5(5))* Simon & Schuster Children's Publishing. (Aladdin).

Sherman, Jill. Ronda Rousey. 2019. (Pro Sports Biographies Ser.). (ENG.). 24p. (J). (gr. 1-3). pap. 8.99 *(978-1-68152-451-1(1)*, 11037) Amicus.

—Simone Biles. 2019. (Pro Sports Biographies Ser.). (ENG.). 24p. (J). (gr. 1-3). pap. 10.99 *(978-1-68152-452-8(X)*, 11038) Amicus.

—Sylvia Fowles. 2019. (Pro Sports Biographies Ser.). (ENG.). 24p. (J). (gr. 1-3). pap. 8.99 *(978-1-68152-454-2(6)*, 11040) Amicus.

Spence, Kelly. Yusra Mardini: Refugee Hero & Olympic Swimmer. 2018. (Remarkable Lives Revealed Ser.). (ENG., Illus.). 32p. (J). (gr. 3-3). *(978-0-7787-4711-6(5))*; pap. *(978-0-7787-4726-0(3))* Crabtree Publishing Co.

Stanborough, Rebecca. 25 Mujeres Que Gobernaron. Aparicio Publishing LLC, Aparicio Publishing, tr. 2020. (Mujeres Valientes Ser.).Tr. of 25 Women Who Ruled. (SPA., Illus.). 64p. (J). (gr. 7-12). lib. bdg. 37.32 *(978-0-7565-6538-1(3)*, 142068, Compass Point Bks.) Capstone.

Stanborough, Rebecca J. 25 Women Who Ruled. 2018. (Daring Women Ser.). (ENG., Illus.). 64p. (J). (gr. 7-12). lib. bdg. 35.32 *(978-0-7565-5851-2(4)*, 138479, Compass Point Bks.) Capstone.

Swaby, Rachel & Fox, Kit. Mighty Moe: The True Story of a Thirteen-Year-Old Women's Running Revolutionary. 2019. (ENG., Illus.). 336p. (J). 22.99 *(978-0-374-31160-5(9)*, 900195713, Farrar, Straus & Giroux (BYR)) Farrar, Straus & Giroux.

Terrell, Brandon. Soccer Showdown: U. S. Women's Stunning 1999 World Cup Win. Garcia, Eduardo, illus. 2019. (Greatest Sports Moments Ser.). (ENG.). 32p. (J). (gr. 3-9). pap. 7.95 *(978-1-5435-4222-6(0)*, 139120); lib. bdg. 31.32 *(978-1-5435-4220-2(4)*, 139118) Capstone.

Wetzel, Dan. Epic Athletes: Alex Morgan. Thomas, Cory, illus. 2020. (Epic Athletes Ser.: 2). (ENG.). 176p. (J). pap. 8.99 *(978-1-250-25071-1(4)*, 900195184) Square Fish.

—Epic Athletes: Serena Williams. Leong, Sloane, illus. 2019. (Epic Athletes Ser.: 3). (ENG.). 176p. (J). 16.99 *(978-1-250-29578-1(5)*, 900195301, Holt, Henry & Co. Bks. For Young Readers) Holt, Henry & Co.

—Epic Athletes: Serena Williams. Leong, Sloane, illus. 2020. (Epic Athletes Ser.: 3). (ENG.). 192p. (J). pap. 7.99 *(978-1-250-25072-8(2)*, 900198023) Square Fish.

Young, Jeff C. Michelle Wie. 2012. (Xtreme Athletes Ser.). (Illus.). 112p. (YA). (gr. 7-12). 28.95 *(978-1-59935-187-2(0))* Reynolds, Morgan Inc.

Zuckerman, Gregory, et al. Rising above: Inspiring Women in Sports. 2018. (Illus.). 224p. (J). (gr. 5-9). 18.99 *(978-0-399-54747-8(9)*, Philomel Bks.) Penguin Young Readers Group.

WOMEN AUTHORS

Ball, Heather. Women Writers Who Changed the World, 1 vol. 2011. (Great Women of Achievement Ser.). (ENG., Illus.). 136p. (YA). (gr. 5-6). lib. bdg. 39.80 *(978-1-4488-5997-9(2)*, d5b4348f-c179-473e-959b-7d8c52859b5c, Rosen Reference) Rosen Publishing Group, Inc., The.

Barnett, Mac. The Important Thing about Margaret Wise Brown. Jacoby, Sarah, illus. 2019. (ENG.). 48p. (J). (gr. -1-3). 17.99 *(978-0-06-239344-9(8)*, Balzer & Bray) HarperCollins Pubs.

Butler, Erin. Writers. 2016. (Uncommon Women Ser.). (ENG., Illus.). 48p. (gr. 3-8). 27.99 *(978-1-62920-581-6(8))* Scobre Pr. Corp.

Cabose, Rachel Whitaker. Vision in the Storm. Mashburn, Marcus M., illus. 2018. 127p. (J). pap. *(978-0-8163-6421-3(4))* Pacific Pr. Publishing Assn.

Capaldi, Gina & Pearce, Q. L. Red Bird Sings: The Story of Zitkala-Sa, Native American Author, Musician, & Activist. Capaldi, Gina, illus. 2019. (ENG., Illus.). 32p. (J). (gr. 3-6). 9.99 *(978-1-5415-7836-4(8)*, 83dbf92b-8b47-42bc-a6c1-bc8ee2b3c024, Carolrhoda Bks.) Lerner Publishing Group.

Castor, Harriet. Charlotte Bronte: Band 18/Pearl (Collins Big Cat) Pinteño, Ismael, illus. 2016. (Collins Big Cat Ser.). (ENG.). 80p. (J). (gr. 5-6). pap. 12.99 *(978-0-00-816405-8(3))* HarperCollins Pubs. Ltd. GBR. Dist: Independent Pubs. Group.

Colbert, David. Maya Angelou. 2009. (10 Days Ser.). (ENG.). 160p. (J). pap. 6.99 *(978-1-4169-6804-7(0)*, Simon & Schuster/Paula Wiseman Bks.) Simon & Schuster/Paula Wiseman Bks.

Cunningham, Anne. The Most Influential Female Writers, 1 vol. 2018. (Breaking the Glass Ceiling: the Most Influential Women Ser.). (ENG.). 112p. (J). (gr. 8-8). 40.13 *(978-1-5081-7966-5(2)*, b968197e-e313-4236-808a-4f2222a3aed8); pap. 19.24 *(978-1-5081-7981-8(6)*, bbaa768f-9db7-4da5-898c-220ada364f27) Rosen Publishing Group, Inc., The. (Rosen Young Adult).

Demuth, Patricia Brennan. Who Was Laura Ingalls Wilder? 2013. (Who Was... ? Ser.). lib. bdg. 16.00 *(978-0-606-32134-1(9))* Turtleback.

Dubois, Muriel L. To My Countrywomen: The Life of Sarah Josepha Hale. 2006. 16.00 *(978-0-9723410-1-1(3))* Apprentice Shop Bks., LLC.

Engle, Margarita. Enchanted Air: Two Cultures, Two Wings: a Memoir. Rodriguez, Edel, illus. (ENG.). (YA). (gr. 7). 2016. 224p. pap. 11.99 *(978-1-4814-3523-9(X))* 2015. 208p. 19.99 *(978-1-4814-3522-2(1))* Simon & Schuster Children's Publishing.

—Enchanted Air: Two Cultures, Two Wings: A Memoir. 2016. lib. bdg. 20.85 *(978-0-606-38989-1(X))* Turtleback.

—Soaring Earth: A Companion Memoir to Enchanted Air. 2019. (ENG., Illus.). 192p. (YA). (gr. 7). 18.99 *(978-1-5344-2953-6(0)*, Atheneum Bks. for Young Readers) Simon & Schuster Children's Publishing.

Engsberg Cunningham, Meghan. Agatha Christie: Traveler, Archaeologist, & Author, 1 vol. 2017. (Fearless Female Soldiers, Explorers, & Aviators Ser.). (ENG.). 128p. (YA). (gr. 9-9). lib. bdg. 47.36 *(978-1-5026-2755-1(8)*, c8cfaa4a-9388-4020-98e1-292c51207ca9) Cavendish Square Publishing LLC.

Fabiny, Sarah & Who HQ. Who Was Beatrix Potter? Lacey, Mike, illus. 2015. (Who Was? Ser.). 112p. (J). (gr. 3-7). 5.99 *(978-0-448-48305-4(X)*, Penguin Workshop) Penguin Young Readers Group.

Ferguson, Isabel & Frederick, Heather Vogel. A World More Bright: The Life of Mary Baker Eddy. 2013. (Illus.). vi, 279p. *(978-0-87510-494-2(0)*, Christian Science Publishing Society, The) Christian Science Publishing Society.

Ferguson, Melissa. Suzanne Collins: Author of the Hunger Games Trilogy. 2016. (Famous Female Authors Ser.). (ENG., Illus.). 32p. (J). (gr. 3-9). lib. bdg. 28.65 *(978-1-5157-1326-5(1)*, 132359, Capstone Pr.) Capstone.

Freedman, Jeri. Arianna Huffington: Media Mogul & Internet News Pioneer, 1 vol. 2017. (Leading Women Ser.). (ENG.). 112p. (YA). (gr. 7-7). 41.64 *(978-1-5026-3170-1(9)*, 4293edd9-4229-4cb7-b4aa-99af895cb828); pap. 20.99 *(978-1-5026-3410-8(4)*, ad82ed50-e04a-4d2e-9f1c-b357faab5d2a) Cavendish Square Publishing LLC.

Fromowitz, Lori. Louisa May Alcott. 2013. (Great American Authors Ser.). (ENG.). 48p. (J). (gr. 4-8). pap. 18.50 *(978-1-61783-765-4(2)*, 10828) ABDO Publishing Co.

Griffiths, Katie. Harriet Beecher Stowe: Author & Abolitionist, 1 vol. 2016. (Great American Thinkers Ser.). (ENG., Illus.). 128p. (J). (gr. 9-9). 47.36 *(978-1-5026-1930-3(X)*, e0837d98-e85e-4f42-b472-bf45f0e02b37) Cavendish Square Publishing LLC.

Griskey, Michele. Beverly Cleary. 2006. (Classic Storytellers Ser.). (Illus.). 48p. (J). (gr. 4-7). lib. bdg. 29.95 *(978-1-58415-457-0(8)*, 1259543) Mitchell Lane Pubs.

Hagler, Gina. Sarah Dessen, 1 vol. 2013. (All about the Author Ser.). (ENG.). 112p. (YA). (gr. 7-7). 39.80 *(978-1-4777-1768-4(4)*, 9adc85b5-4526-4171-ad19-b0eccaa2524d) Rosen Publishing Group, Inc., The.

Haugen, Brenda. Harriet Beecher Stowe: The Inspiring Life Story of the Abolition Advocate. 2016. (Inspiring Stories Ser.). (ENG., Illus.). 112p. (J). (gr. 5-7). lib. bdg. 38.65 *(978-0-7565-5164-3(1)*, 128792, Compass Point Bks.) Capstone.

Haugrud Reiff, Raychel. Sandra Cisneros, 1 vol. 2013. (Today's Writers & Their Works). (ENG.). 144p. (YA). (gr. 7-7). pap. 23.34 *(978-1-62712-145-3(5)*, 00208a3c-ebe6-424e-8395-5f139564fc47) Cavendish Square Publishing LLC.

Hoover, Elizabeth. Suzanne Collins, 1 vol. 2012. (People in the News Ser.). (ENG., Illus.). 104p. (gr. 7-7). lib. bdg. 41.03 *(978-1-4205-0762-1(1)*, 6f72e596-ccf1-48ff-9492-287312efe398, Lucent Pr.) Greenhaven Publishing LLC.

Hunsicker, Jennifer, et al. Famous Female Authors. 2016. (Famous Female Authors Ser.). (ENG.). 32p. (J). (gr. 3-9). 122.60 *(978-1-5157-1351-7(2)*, 24851, Capstone Pr.) Capstone.

Johanson, Paula. Women Writers, 1 vol. 2016. (Defying Convention: Women Who Changed the Rules Ser.). (ENG., Illus.). 128p. (gr. 6-6). 38.93 *(978-0-7660-8145-1(1)*, fd312554-8829-4571-b170-8b66bc1a28f2) Enslow Publishing, LLC.

Kamberg, Mary-Lane. Margaret Peterson Haddix, 1 vol. 2013. (All about the Author Ser.). (ENG.). 112p. (YA). (gr. 7-7). 39.80 *(978-1-4777-1765-3(X)*, 9504214b-33e0-4167-ad37-2e1e7cc0e6a2) Rosen Publishing Group, Inc., The.

Kite, L. Patricia. Maya Angelou. 2006. (Just the Facts Biographies Ser.). (Illus.). 112p. (J). (gr. 3-7). pap. 9.95 *(978-0-8225-5997-9(8)*, Lerner Pubns.) Lerner Publishing Group.

Lasky, Kathryn. A Voice of Her Own: Candlewick Biographies: The Story of Phillis Wheatley, Slave Poet. Lee, Paul, illus. 2012. (Candlewick Biographies Ser.). (ENG.). 48p. (J). (gr. 3-7). 14.99 *(978-0-7636-6427-5(8))*; pap. 6.99 *(978-0-7636-6091-8(4))* Candlewick Pr.

Lazaro, Georgina. Juana Ines. Preza, Bruno Gonzalez, illus. 2007. (SPA.). 32p. (J). (gr. 3-5). 14.99 *(978-1-930332-57-7(2))* Lectorum Pubns., Inc.

Leaf, Christina. Laura Ingalls Wilder. 2015. (Children's Storytellers Ser.). (ENG., Illus.). 24p. (J). (gr. 2-5). lib. bdg. 26.95 *(978-1-62617-269-2(2)*, Blastoff! Readers) Bellwether Media.

Macy, Sue. Miss Mary Reporting: The True Story of Sportswriter Mary Garber. Payne, C. F., illus. 2016. (ENG.). 40p. (J). (gr. k-3). 18.99 *(978-1-4814-0120-3(3)*, Simon & Schuster Bks. For Young Readers) Simon & Schuster Bks. For Young Readers.

Marsh, Carole. Harriet Beecher Stowe. 2003. 12p. (gr. k-4). 2.95 *(978-0-635-02356-8(3))* Gallopade International.

Mora, Pat. Una Biblioteca para Juana: El Mundo de Sor Juana InésThe World of Sor Juana Inés, 1 vol. Vidal, Beatriz, illus. 2019. Orig. Title: A Library for Juana. (SPA.). 32p. (J). (gr. k-3). pap. 12.95 *(978-1-64379-059-6(5)*, leelowcbp) Lee & Low Bks., Inc.

—A Library for Juana: The World of Sor Juana Inés, 1 vol. Vidal, Beatriz, illus. 2019. (ENG.). 32p. (J). (gr. k-3). pap. 11.95 *(978-1-64379-058-9(7)*, leelowcbp) Lee & Low Bks., Inc.

O'Keefe, Sherry. From China to America: The Story of Amy Tan. 2011. (World Writers Ser.). 112p. (gr. 7-18). lib. bdg. 28.95 *(978-1-59935-138-4(2))* Reynolds, Morgan Inc.

Rau, Dana Meachen. Who Was Harriet Beecher Stowe? Copeland, Gregory, illus. 2015. (Who Was-? Chapters Ser.). (ENG.). 112p. (J). (gr. 3-6). 21.19 *(978-1-4844-5253-0(4)*, Penguin Workshop) Penguin Young Readers Group.

Rau, Dana Meachen & Who HQ. Who Was Harriet Beecher Stowe? Copeland, Gregory, illus. 2015. (Who Was? Ser.). 112p. (J). (gr. 3-7). 6.99 *(978-0-448-48301-6(7)*, Penguin Workshop) Penguin Young Readers Group.

Reef, Catherine. The Brontë Sisters: The Brief Lives of Charlotte, Emily, & Anne. 2015. (ENG., Illus.). 240p. (J). (gr. 5-7). pap. 9.99 *(978-0-544-45590-0(8)*, 1599315, Clarion Bks.) HarperCollins Pubs.

Rice, Dona Herweck. Stepping into Louisa May Alcott's World. 2017. (Time for Kids Nonfiction Readers Ser.). lib. bdg. 20.85 *(978-0-606-40262-0(4))* Turtleback.

—Stepping into Louisa May Alcott's World (Grade 7) 2nd rev. ed. 2017. (TIME(r): Informational Text Ser.). (ENG., Illus.). 48p. (J). (gr. 6-8). pap. 13.99 *(978-1-4938-3619-2(6))* Teacher Created Materials, Inc.

Rooney, Anne. Rachel Carson (Women in Science) Lundie, Isobel, illus. 2019. (Women in Science Ser.). (ENG.). 32p. (J). (gr. 2-3). pap. 9.95 *(978-0-531-23954-4(3)*, Watts, Franklin) Scholastic Library Publishing.

Sanderson, Caroline. Jane Austen: Novelist, 1 vol. 2016. (History Makers Ser.). (ENG., Illus.). 128p. (YA). (gr. 9-9). lib. bdg. 47.36 *(978-1-5026-2445-1(1)*, 40859400-eabe-4e19-a0c9-9b0ed1eef0eb) Cavendish Square Publishing LLC.

Sapet, Kerrily. Suzanne Collins. 2012. (Illus.). 112p. (J). *(978-1-59935-346-3(6))* Reynolds, Morgan Inc.

Sarantou, Katlin. Chimamanda Ngozi Adichie. Bane, Jeff, illus. 2019. (My Early Library: My Itty-Bitty Bio Ser.). (ENG.). 24p. (J). (gr. k-1). pap. 12.79 *(978-1-5341-4983-0(X)*, 213239); lib. bdg. 30.64 *(978-1-5341-4697-6(0)*, 213238) Cherry Lake Publishing.

Sexton, Colleen A. & Cosgrove, Martha. J. K. Rowling. 2006. (Just the Facts Biographies Ser.). (Illus.). 112p. (J). pap. 9.95 *(978-0-8225-5995-5(1)*, Lerner Pubns.) Lerner Publishing Group.

Staley, Erin. Maggie Stiefvater, 1 vol. 2013. (All about the Author Ser.). (ENG.). 112p. (YA). (gr. 7-7). 39.80 *(978-1-4777-1762-2(5)*, e5c18288-1557-4598-9a8b-ae4c0dfca99c) Rosen Publishing Group, Inc., The.

Sullivan, Laura. Jacqueline Woodson, 1 vol. 2014. (Spotlight on Children's Authors Ser.). (ENG., Illus.). 48p. (gr. 4-4). lib. bdg. 31.64 *(978-1-62712-855-1(7)*, 4ffab15e-3e31-4a5c-9981-b232d41c7a9a) Cavendish Square Publishing LLC.

Undset, Sigrid. Happy Times in Norway. 2013. (ENG., Illus.). 240p. pap. 16.95 *(978-0-8166-7827-3(8))* Univ. of Minnesota Pr.

Weldon, Christine. Reporter in Disguise: The Intrepid Vic Steinberg, 1 vol. 2013. (ENG.). 78p. (J). (gr. 3-5). pap. 11.95 *(978-1-55455-281-8(8)*, 9993a74e-9910-4d94-876e-7d61e331a2dc) Fitzhenry & Whiteside, Ltd. CAN. Dist: Firefly Bks., Ltd.

Wilson, Jacqueline & Carey, Joanna. Interview with Jacqueline Wilson. (Illus.). 96p. pap. 5.50 *(978-1-4052-0055-4(3))* Farshore GBR. Dist: Trafalgar Square Publishing.

WOMEN IN AERONAUTICS

Bissonette, Aimee. Aim for the Skies: Jerrie Mock & Joan Merriam Smith's Race to Complete Amelia Earhart's Quest. Ettlinger, Doris, illus. 2018. (ENG.). 32p. (J). (gr. 1-4). 16.99 *(978-1-58536-381-0(2)*, 204581) Sleeping Bear Pr.

Burke, John. Amelia Earhart: Flying Solo. 2017. (Great Leaders & Events Ser.). (ENG.). (J). (gr. 4-8). lib. bdg. 35.99 *(978-1-942875-45-1(2))* Quarto Publishing Group USA.

Dell, Pamela. The Soviet Night Witches: Brave Women Bomber Pilots of World War II. 2017. (Women & War Ser.). (ENG., Illus.). 32p. (J). (gr. 3-9). lib. bdg. 28.65 *(978-1-5157-7938-4(6)*, 136031, Capstone Pr.) Capstone.

Engle, Margarita. The Flying Girl: How Aida de Acosta Learned to Soar. Palacios, Sara, illus. 2018. (ENG.). 40p. (J). (gr. -1-3). 18.99 *(978-1-4814-4502-3(2))* Simon & Schuster Children's Publishing.

Friend, Robyn C. The Women of Apollo. Katz, David Arthur, illus. l.t. ed. 2006. 80p. (J). 17.95 *(978-1-880599-80-8(5))*; pap. 12.95 *(978-1-880599-79-2(1))* Cascade Pass, Inc.

Lakin, Patricia. Amelia Earhart: More Than a Flier (Ready-To-Read Level 3) Daniel, Alan & Daniel, Lea, illus. 2003. (Ready-To-Read Stories of Famous Americans Ser.). (ENG.). 48p. (J). (gr. 1-3). pap. 4.99 *(978-0-689-85575-7(3)*, Simon Spotlight) Simon Spotlight.

Langley, Wanda. Women of the Wind: Early Women Aviators. 2006. (Women Adventurers Ser.). (Illus.). 160p. (J). (gr. 6-12). lib. bdg. 26.95 *(978-1-931798-81-5(8))* Reynolds, Morgan Inc.

Lukesh, Jean A. Sky Rider: Story of Evelyn Sharp, World War II WASP. 2011. (Noteworthy Americans Young Readers Biography Book Ser.). (ENG., Illus.). 161p. (J). pap. 14.95 *(978-0-9647586-3-6(6))* Field Mouse Productions.

Montgomery, Christine. Marie Meyer Fower: Barnstormer. 2015. (ENG., Illus.). 48p. (J). 24.00 *(978-1-61248-149-4(3))* Truman State Univ. Pr.

Moore, Shannon Baker. Women with Wings: Women Pilots of World War II. 2017. (Hidden Heroes Ser.). (ENG., Illus.). 112p. (J). (gr. 6-12). lib. bdg. 41.36 *(978-1-68078-391-9(2)*, 23547, Essential Library) ABDO Publishing Co.

O'Brien, Keith. Fly Girls Young Readers' Edition: How Five Daring Women Defied All Odds & Made Aviation History. 2019. (ENG., Illus.). 320p. (J). (gr. 5-7). 16.99 *(978-1-328-61842-9(0)*, 1733755, Clarion Bks.) HarperCollins Pubs.

Pearson, P. O'Connell. Fly Girls: The Daring American Women Pilots Who Helped Win WWII. 2018. (ENG., Illus.). 208p. (J) (gr. 5). 18.99 *(978-1-5344-0410-6(4)*, Simon & Schuster Bks. For Young Readers) Simon & Schuster Bks. For Young Readers.

Prentice, Andrew. Amelia Earhart (the First Names Series) Smith, Mike, illus. 2019. (First Names Ser.). (ENG.). 160p. (J). (gr. 3-7). 9.99 *(978-1-4197-3741-1(4)*, 1279101, Abrams Bks. for Young Readers) Abrams, Inc.

Reyburn, Susan. Amelia Earhart. 2006. (Women Who Dare Ser.). (Illus.). 64p. 12.95 *(978-0-7649-3545-9(3)*, A111) Pomegranate Communications, Inc.

Rinaldo, Denise. Amelia Earhart: With a Discussion of Courage. 2004. (Values in Action Ser.). (J). *(978-1-59203-068-2(8))* Learning Challenge, Inc.

Simons, Lisa M. Bolt. The U. S. WASP: Trailblazing Women Pilots of World War II. 2017. (Women & War Ser.). (ENG., Illus.). 32p. (J). (gr. 3-9). pap. 8.19 *(978-1-5157-7944-5(0)*, 136039); lib. bdg. 28.65 *(978-1-5157-7937-7(8)*, 136030) Capstone. (Capstone Pr.).

Smith, Matthew Clark. Lighter Than Air: Sophie Blanchard, the First Woman Pilot. Tavares, Matt, illus. 2017. (ENG.). 32p. (J). (gr. 1-4). 16.99 *(978-0-7636-7732-9(9))* Candlewick Pr.

Weakland, Mark. When Amelia Earhart Built a Roller Coaster. Grivina, Oksana, illus. 2016. (Leaders Doing Headstands Ser.). (ENG.). 32p. (J). (gr. 1-4). pap. 7.95 *(978-1-5158-0138-2(1)*, 132346, Picture Window Bks.) Capstone.

WOMEN IN INDUSTRY

see Women—Employment

WOMEN IN POLITICS

see Women—Political Activity

WOMEN IN THE BIBLE

Bader, Joanne. The Widow's Offering. 2008. (Arch Bks.). 16p. (J). (gr. k-4). pap. 1.99 *(978-0-7586-1451-3(9))* Concordia Publishing Hse.

Fischer, Jean. 100 Extraordinary Stories for Courageous Girls: Unforgettable Tales of Women of Faith. 2018. (Courageous Girls Ser.). (ENG., Illus.). 208p. (J). 16.99 *(978-1-68322-748-9(4)*, Shiloh Kidz) Barbour Publishing, Inc.

Green, John. Women of the Bible. 2006. (Dover Classic Stories Coloring Book Ser.). (ENG., Illus.). 32p. (J). (gr. 3-8). 4.99 *(978-0-486-45193-0(3)*, 451933) Dover Pubns., Inc.

Krishna, McArthur & Spalding, Bethany Brady. Girls Who Choose God. Peterson, Kathleen, illus. 2014. (J). 17.99 *(978-1-60907-882-9(9)*, Ensign Peak) Shadow Mountain Publishing.

Larsen, Carolyn. Princess Stories: Real Bible Stories of God's Princesses. Eliseev, Sergey, illus. 2012. (ENG.). 128p. (J). 14.99 *(978-1-4143-4811-7(8)*, 4603801, Tyndale Kids) Tyndale Hse. Pubs.

Lo, Monica. Old Testament Heroines of the Faith. Diehl, Nichole, illus. 2007. 82p. per. 17.99 *(978-1-59879-224-9(5)*, Lifevest) Lifevest Publishing, Inc.

MacKenzie, Carine. Hannah: The Mother Who Prayed. rev. ed. 2013. (Bible Time Ser.). (ENG., Illus.). 32p. (J). (gr. -1-2). pap. 4.50 *(978-1-84550-163-1(2)*, 439d7b70-7d2d-42e8-9586-59d499ac64a2) Christian Focus Pubns. GBR. Dist: Baker & Taylor Publisher Services (BTPS).

—Rebekah: The Mother of Twins. rev. ed. 2012. (Bible Time Ser.). (ENG., Illus.). 32p. (J). (gr. -1-2). pap. 4.50 *(978-1-84550-172-3(1)*, fddcd45f-10f2-48ff-99fd-608192ccbc38) Christian Focus Pubns. GBR. Dist: Baker & Taylor Publisher Services (BTPS).

Rivadeneira, Caryn. Grit & Grace: Heroic Women of the Bible. Betz, Katy, illus. 2017. 144p. (J). (gr. 4-6). pap. 14.99 *(978-1-5064-2495-8(3)*, Sparkhouse Family) 1517 Media.

—Gritty & Graceful: 15 Inspiring Women of the Bible. Soekamto, Sonya Abby, illus. 2019. 32p. (J). (gr. k-3). 16.99 *(978-1-5064-5206-7(X)*, Beaming Books) 1517 Media.

Sasso, Sandy Eisenberg. But God Remembered: Stories of Women from Creation to the Promised Land. Andersen, Bethanne, illus. 2008. (ENG.). 32p. pap. 8.99 *(978-1-58023-372-9(4)*, 14658449-7565-40e4-9c7f-b0da8c2f75de, Jewish Lights Publishing) LongHill Partners, Inc.

Thomas Nelson Publishing Staff. Brave Girls Bible Stories, 1 vol. 2014. (Brave Girls Ser.). (ENG.). 224p. (J). 16.99 *(978-0-529-10898-2(4)*, Tommy Nelson) Nelson, Thomas Inc.

WOMEN JOURNALISTS

Bodden, Valerie. The Muckrakers: Ida Tarbell Takes on Big Business. 2017. (Hidden Heroes Ser.). (ENG., Illus.). 112p. (J). (gr. 6-12). lib. bdg. 41.36 *(978-1-68078-388-9(2)*, 23541, Essential Library) ABDO Publishing Co.

Crysdale, Joy. Fearless Female Journalists, 1 vol. 2010. (Women's Hall of Fame Ser.: 15). (ENG., Illus.). 128p. (J). (gr. 4-8). pap. 10.95 *(978-1-897187-71-5(8))* Second Story Pr. CAN. Dist: Orca Bk. Pubs. USA.

Freedman, Jeri. Arianna Huffington: Media Mogul & Internet News Pioneer, 1 vol. 2017. (Leading Women Ser.). (ENG.). 112p. (YA). (gr. 7-7). 41.64 *(978-1-5026-3170-1(9)*, 4293edd9-4229-4cb7-b4aa-99af895cb828); pap. 20.99 *(978-1-5026-3410-8(4)*, ad82ed50-e04a-4d2e-9f1c-b357faab5d2a) Cavendish Square Publishing LLC.

Hinman, Bonnie. Eternal Vigilance: The Story of Ida B. Wells-Barnett. 2011. (Civil Rights Leaders Ser.). 128p. (gr. 6-10). lib. bdg. 28.95 *(978-1-59935-111-7(0))* Reynolds, Morgan Inc.

llihan, Kerrie Logan. Reporting under Fire: 16 Daring Women War Correspondents & Photojournalists. 2014. (Women of Action Ser.: 9). (ENG., Illus.). 256p. (YA). (gr. 7). 19.95 *(978-1-61374-710-0(1))* Chicago Review Pr., Inc.

acy, Sue. Bylines: A Photobiography of Nellie Bly. 2009. (Photobiographies Ser.). (Illus.). 64p. (J). (gr. 5-9). 19.95 *(978-1-4263-0513-9(3))*, National Geographic Kids) Disney Publishing Worldwide.

yers, Walter Dean. Ida B. Wells: Let the Truth Be Told. Christensen, Bonnie, illus. 2008. (ENG.). 40p. (J). (gr. -1-3). 17.99 *(978-0-06-027705-5(X)*, Amistad) HarperCollins Pubs.

obson, David. Soledad O'Brien. 2010. (Transcending Race in America: Biographies of Biracial Achievers Ser.). (Illus.). 64p. (J). (gr. 5-18). lib. bdg. 22.95 *(978-1-4222-1617-0(9))* Mason Crest.

ule, Heather. Women in Sports Media. 2017. (Women in Sports Ser.). (ENG., Illus.). 48p. (J). (gr. 4-8). lib. bdg. 34.21 *(978-1-5321-1158-7(4)*, 25892, SportsZone) ABDO Publishing Co.

Spiller, Sara. Nellie Bly. Bane, Jeff, illus. 2019. (My Early Library: My Itty-Bitty Bio Ser.). (ENG.). 24p. (J). (gr. k-1). pap. 12.79 *(978-1-5341-3929-9(X)*, 212545); lib. bdg. 30.64 *(978-1-5341-4273-2(8)*, 212544) Cherry Lake Publishing.

WOMEN PHYSICIANS

Apel, Melanie Ann. Virginia Apgar: Innovative Female Physician & Inventor of the Apgar Score. (Women Hall of Famers in Mathematics & Science Ser.). 112p. (gr. 5-8). 2009. 63.90 *(978-1-60854-815-6(5))* 2003. (ENG., Illus.). lib. bdg. 39.80 *(978-0-8239-3880-3(8)*, ce7edbfa-c582-4033-985e-5cccc3ea2c50) Rosen Publishing Group, Inc., The. (Rosen Reference).

Bailey, Diane. Physics. 2017. (Illus.). 64p. (J). *(978-1-4222-3554-6(8))* Mason Crest.

Crayton, Lisa A. Elizabeth Blackwell: Doctor & Advocate for Women in Medicine, 1 vol. 2016. (Heroes of the Women's Suffrage Movement Ser.). (ENG., Illus.). 128p. (gr. 6-6). 38.93 *(978-0-7660-7890-1(6)*, 8a48dd6b-799b-440c-a49b-0ce996a37e86) Enslow Publishing, LLC.

Etingoff, Kim. Women in Medicine. Karlon, Ann Lee, ed. 2013. (Major Women in Science Ser.: 10). 64p. (J). (gr. 7-18). 22.95 *(978-1-4222-2929-3(7))* Mason Crest.

Favor, Lesli J. Women Doctors & Nurses of the Civil War. 2009. (American Women at War Ser.). 112p. (gr. 8-8). 63.90 *(978-1-61511-404-7(1))* Rosen Publishing Group, Inc., The.

Favor, Leslie. Women Doctors & Nurses of the Civil War, 1 vol. 2004. (American Women at War Ser.). (ENG.). 112p. (YA). (gr. 8-8). pap. 13.95 *(978-1-4358-3273-2(6)*, d5d1a2e9-429e-42e8-b242-5f13ee7d9c16) Rosen Publishing Group, Inc., The.

Gaines, Alison. Mary Edwards Walker: The Only Female Medal of Honor Recipient, 1 vol. 2017. (Fearless Female Soldiers, Explorers, & Aviators Ser.). (ENG.). 128p. (YA). (gr. 9-9). 47.36 *(978-1-5026-2745-2(0)*, 4f3af724-2a96-4315-a3da-8590d2a2d372) Cavendish Square Publishing LLC.

Kishel, Ann-Marie. Elizabeth Blackwell: A Life of Diligence. 2007. (Pull Ahead Bks.). (Illus.). 32p. (J). (gr. 3-7). lib. bdg. 22.60 *(978-0-8225-6459-1(9)*, Lerner Pubns.) Lerner Publishing Group.

Klobuchar, Lisa. Elizabeth Blackwell: With Profiles of Elizabeth Garrett Anderson & Susan la Flesche Picotte. 2006. (Biographical Connections Ser.). (Illus.). 112p. *(978-0-7166-1826-3(5))* World Bk., Inc.

Kovatch, Sarah & Crumpler, Rebecca Lee. Rebecca Lee Crumpler. 2005. (Illus.). 16p. (J). *(978-0-7367-2891-1(0))* Zaner-Bloser, Inc.

Leavitt, Amie Jane. Elizabeth Blackwell. 2007. (What's So Great About...? Ser.). (Illus.). 32p. (J). (gr. 1-5). lib. bdg. 25.70 *(978-1-58415-579-9(5))* Mitchell Lane Pubs.

Levy, Janey. Mae Jemison, 1 vol. 2018. (Heroes of Black History Ser.). (ENG.). 32p. (gr. 3-4). 28.27 *(978-1-5382-3020-6(8)*, b3b2ace8-1fbd-4542-956f-346352fbec0e) Stevens, Gareth Publishing LLLP.

Loh-Hagan, Virginia. Jane C. Wright & Chemotherapy. 2018. (21st Century Junior Library: Women Innovators Ser.). (ENG., Illus.). 24p. (J). (gr. 2-5). lib. bdg. 29.21 *(978-1-5341-2910-8(3)*, 211684) Cherry Lake Publishing.

Mah, Adeline Yen. Chinese Cinderella: The True Story of an Unwanted Daughter. 2010. (ENG.). 240p. (YA). (gr. 7). pap. 11.99 *(978-0-385-74007-4(7)*, Ember) Random Hse. Children's Bks.

Murray, Hallie. The Role of Female Doctors & Nurses in the Civil War, 1 vol. 2019. (Warrior Women in American History Ser.). (ENG.). 104p. (gr. 7-7). pap. 21.00 *(978-1-5026-5543-1(8)*, 1d4603e4-36a5-404a-8032-14ce1cb0311f); lib. bdg. 44.50 *(978-1-5026-5544-8(6)*, a5c3b949-3c8d-40e5-8e7a-8277fd0a565b) Cavendish Square Publishing LLC.

—The Role of Female Doctors & Nurses in the Civil War. 2019. pap. *(978-1-9785-1407-2(7))* Enslow Publishing, LLC.

Negley, Keith. Mary Wears What She Wants. Negley, Keith, illus. 2019. (ENG., Illus.). 48p. (J). (gr. -1-3). 18.99 *(978-0-06-284679-2(5)*, Balzer & Bray) HarperCollins Pubs.

Rich, Mari. Medicine, Vol. 10. Gilmore, Malinda & Pouson, Mel, eds. 2016. (Black Achievement in Science Ser.). (Illus.). 64p. (J). (gr. 7). 23.95 *(978-1-4222-3561-4(0))* Mason Crest.

Robbins, Trina. Elizabeth Blackwell: America's First Woman Doctor, 1 vol. Martin, Cynthia & Timmons, Anne, illus. 2006. (Graphic Biographies Ser.). (ENG.). 32p. (J). (gr. 3-9). per. 8.10 *(978-0-7368-9660-3(0)*, 93446, Capstone Pr.) Capstone.

Somervill, Barbara A. Elizabeth Blackwell: America's First Female Doctor, 1 vol. 2009. (Life Portraits Ser.). (ENG., Illus.). 112p. (YA). (gr. 6-8). lib. bdg. 38.67 *(978-1-4339-0055-6(6)*, 8ed3ef86-e654-4ea3-9358-51f729906c1e) Stevens, Gareth Publishing LLLP.

Sutton, A. Trevor. Dr. Bessie Rehwinkel. Pierce, Linda, illus. 2012. (Hero of Faith Ser.). (ENG.). 47p. (J). pap. 7.99 *(978-0-7586-3078-0(6))* Concordia Publishing Hse.

Thomas, Isabel. The World's First Women Doctors: Elizabeth Blackwell & Elizabeth Garrett Anderson: Band 16/Sapphire (Collins Big Cat) 2015. (Collins Big Cat Ser.). (ENG., Illus.). 56p. (J). (gr. 4-5). pap. 12.95 *(978-0-00-812789-3(1))* HarperCollins Pubs. Ltd. GBR. Dist: Independent Pubs. Group.

Uhl, Xina M. & Apel, Melanie Ann. Virginia Apgar, 1 vol. 2019. (Super Female Scientists Ser.). (ENG.). 104p. (gr. 7-7). pap. 18.65 *(978-1-7253-4053-4(4)*, 0c9c96a9-fc3d-4cfe-ba07-673ae12b97fa) Rosen Publishing Group, Inc., The.

Wojahn, Rebecca Hogue & Wojahn, Rebecca. Dr. Kate: Angel on Snowshoes. 2009. (Badger Biographies Ser.). (ENG., Illus.). 104p. (J). (gr. 3-7). pap. 12.95 *(978-0-87020-421-0(1))* Wisconsin Historical Society.

Women in Medicine. 2005. (Extraordinary Women Ser.). (Illus.). 112p. (gr. 6-12). 180.00 *(978-0-7910-8418-2(3)*, Facts On File) Infobase Holdings, Inc.

WOMEN PIRATES

Sharp, Anne Wallace. Daring Pirate Women. 2005. (Biography Ser.). (Illus.). 112p. (gr. 6-12). 27.93 *(978-0-8225-0031-5(0))* Lerner Publishing Group.

Yolen, Jane. Sea Queens: Woman Pirates Around the World. Pratt, Christine Joy, illus. 2010. (ENG.). 112p. (J). (gr. 2-5). pap. 9.95 *(978-1-58089-132-5(2))* Charlesbridge Publishing, Inc.

WOMEN SCIENTISTS

Allman, Barbara. The Most Influential Women in STEM, 1 vol. 2018. (Breaking the Glass Ceiling: the Most Influential Women Ser.). (ENG.). 112p. (gr. 8-8). 40.13 *(978-1-5081-7969-6(7)*, 31de5863-ef82-43d4-92b4-e273bda38fe9) Rosen Publishing Group, Inc., The.

Allman, Toney. Women Scientists & Inventors. 2016. (ENG.). 80p. (YA). (gr. 5-12). *(978-1-68282-032-2(7))* ReferencePoint Pr., Inc.

Anniss, Matt. Jane Goodall & Mary Leakey. 2014. (Dynamic Duos of Science Ser.). 48p. (YA). (gr. 5-8). pap. 84.30 *(978-1-4824-0822-5(8))* Stevens, Gareth Publishing LLLP.

Ardagh, Philip. Marie Curie. 7th ed. 2003. (ENG., Illus.). 64p. (J). pap. 6.99 *(978-0-330-37571-9(7)*, Pan) Pan Macmillan GBR. Dist: Trafalgar Square Publishing.

Barghoorn, Linda. Temple Grandin: Pioneer for Animal Rights & Autism Awareness. 2016. (Remarkable Lives Revealed Ser.). (ENG., Illus.). 32p. (J). (gr. 2-5). *(978-0-7787-2688-3(6))* Crabtree Publishing Co.

Bolden, Tonya. Changing the Equation: 50+ US Black Women in STEM. 2020. (ENG., Illus.). 208p. (J). (gr. 5-9). 19.99 *(978-1-4197-0734-6(5)*, 1056501, Abrams Bks. for Young Readers) Abrams, Inc.

Borgert-Spaniol, Megan. Jocelyn Bell Burnell: Discovering Pulsars. 2017. (STEM Superstar Women Ser.). (ENG., Illus.). 32p. (J). (gr. 3-6). lib. bdg. 32.79 *(978-1-5321-1278-2(5)*, 27602, Checkerboard Library) ABDO Publishing Co.

—Rosalind Franklin: Unlocking DNA. 2017. (STEM Superstar Women Ser.). (ENG., Illus.). 32p. (J). (gr. 3-6). lib. bdg. 32.79 *(978-1-5321-1279-9(3)*, 27603, Checkerboard Library) ABDO Publishing Co.

Brereton, Catherine. Women Scientists in Math & Coding, 1 vol. 2017. (Superwomen in STEM Ser.). (ENG.). 48p. (J). (gr. 5-5). pap. 15.05 *(978-1-5382-1469-5(5)*, 305dd367-2afe-4bd8-a764-f8575f1c4455); lib. bdg. 33.60 *(978-1-5382-1408-4(3)*, b0d0d1ca-dd3f-459e-ab30-fbf12c34f4fd) Stevens, Gareth Publishing LLLP.

—Women Scientists in Physics & Engineering, 1 vol. 2017. (Superwomen in STEM Ser.). (ENG.). 48p. (J). (gr. 5-5). pap. 15.05 *(978-1-5382-1465-7(2)*, 5c90b9f2-699b-47ac-940a-a3277790c90d); lib. bdg. 33.60 *(978-1-5382-1412-1(1)*, 57cdd5ff-fa4c-4183-9472-ff3b12375bf5) Stevens, Gareth Publishing LLLP.

Buzzeo, Toni. When Sue Found Sue: Sue Hendrickson Discovers Her T. Rex. Sudyka, Diana, illus. 2019. (ENG.). 32p. (J). (gr. 1-4). 18.99 *(978-1-4197-3163-1(7)*, 1143101, Abrams Bks. for Young Readers) Abrams, Inc.

Capek, Michael. Jane Goodall: Primatologist & Conservationist. 2017. (Women in Science Ser.). (ENG., Illus.). 112p. (J). (gr. 6-12). lib. bdg. 41.36 *(978-1-5321-1043-6(X)*, 25662, Essential Library) ABDO Publishing Co.

Carson, Mary Kay. The Tornado Scientist: Seeing Inside Severe Storms. Uhlman, Tom, illus. 2019. (Scientists in the Field Ser.). (ENG.). 80p. (J). (gr. 5-7). 18.99 *(978-0-544-96582-9(5)*, 1662355, Clarion Bks.) HarperCollins Pubs.

Coates, Eileen S. The Curies' Research with Radiation, 1 vol. 2018. (STEM Milestones: Historic Inventions & Discoveries Ser.). (ENG.). 24p. (gr. 3-3). 25.27 *(978-1-5383-4356-2(8)*, 71325f2e-1e93-474e-8b00-55a2d4904440, PowerKids Pr.) Rosen Publishing Group, Inc., The.

Coleman, Miriam. Women in Science, 1 vol. 2015. (Women Groundbreakers Ser.). (ENG., Illus.). 32p. (J). (gr. 4-5). pap. 11.00 *(978-1-4994-1047-1(6)*, 238f0b0d-cd19-486e-b8b7-497ecc92ffdf, PowerKids Pr.) Rosen Publishing Group, Inc., The.

Conkling, Winifred. Radioactive! How Irène Curie & Lise Meitner Revolutionized Science & Changed the World. 2018. (ENG., Illus.). 240p. (YA). (gr. 5-9). pap. 10.95 *(978-1-61620-641-3(1)*, 73641) Algonquin Young Readers.

Dickmann, Nancy. Rachel Carson: Environmental Crusader, 1 vol. 2015. (Superheroes of Science Ser.). (ENG., Illus.). 48p. (J). (gr. 6-6). pap. 15.05 *(978-1-4824-3149-0(1)*, cf89a6d9-d7b2-4292-8fe5-b6ecd6ec0962) Stevens, Gareth Publishing LLLP.

—Women Scientists in Astronomy & Space, 1 vol. 2017. (Superwomen in STEM Ser.). (ENG.). 48p. (J). (gr. 5-5). pap. 15.05 *(978-1-5382-1475-6(X)*, 0ef5c73e-6709-4183-8d90-34de842e956e); lib. bdg. 33.60 *(978-1-5382-1403-9(2)*, d8cb4f48-7fe3-4961-ac56-f9fbd8d6858a) Stevens, Gareth Publishing LLLP.

—Women Scientists in Life Science, 1 vol. 2017. (Superwomen in STEM Ser.). (ENG.). 48p. (J). (gr. 5-5). pap. 15.05 *(978-1-5382-1471-8(7)*, 803f9bb3-7a3a-4fe9-a1f3-220b2700693f); lib. bdg. 33.60 *(978-1-5382-1406-0(7)*, 895fc502-ec12-454d-90ae-f79e33e71b43) Stevens, Gareth Publishing LLLP.

—Women Scientists in Medicine, 1 vol. 2017. (Superwomen in STEM Ser.). (ENG.). 48p. (J). (gr. 5-5). pap. 15.05 *(978-1-5382-1467-1(9)*, 28c90262-7108-4eb1-b861-29093103892f); lib. bdg. 33.60 *(978-1-5382-1410-7(5)*, f755f0e7-d15d-424a-a0f0-31c34466a466) Stevens, Gareth Publishing LLLP.

Domenico, Kelly Di. Women Scientists Who Changed the World, 1 vol. 2011. (Great Women of Achievement Ser.). (ENG., Illus.). 112p. (YA). (gr. 5-6). lib. bdg. 39.80 *(978-1-4488-5999-3(9)*, db33b50e-7497-43d0-8942-6b54062b5776) Rosen Publishing Group, Inc., The.

Etingoff, Kim. Women Who Built Our Scientific Foundations. Lee-Karlon, Ann, ed. 2013. (Major Women in Science Ser.: 10). 64p. (J). (gr. 7-18). 22.95 *(978-1-4222-2933-0(5))* Mason Crest.

Faulkner, Nicholas, ed. 101 Women of STEM, 1 vol. 2016. (People You Should Know Ser.). (ENG., Illus.). 184p. (J). (gr. 8-8). lib. bdg. 38.84 *(978-1-68048-511-0(3)*, 315dc040-0784-49a3-80dd-a86ebb329319) Rosen Publishing Group, Inc., The.

Ferrie, Chris. Scientist, Scientist, Who Do You See? 2018. (Illus.). 32p. (J). (gr. -1-3). 17.99 *(978-1-4926-5618-0(6))* Sourcebooks, Inc.

Fertig, Dennis. Sylvia Earle: Ocean Explorer, 1 vol. 2014. (Women in Conservation Ser.). (ENG., Illus.). 48p. (J). (gr. 3-6). 35.99 *(978-1-4846-0470-0(9)*, 126602); pap. 8.99 *(978-1-4846-0475-5(X)*, 126606) Capstone. (Heinemann).

Freeman, Martha. Born Curious: 20 Girls Who Grew up to Be Awesome Scientists. Wu, Katy, illus. 2020. (ENG.). 128p. (J). (gr. 2-7). 19.99 *(978-1-5344-2153-0(X)*, Simon & Schuster Bks. For Young Readers) Simon & Schuster Bks. For Young Readers.

Green, Jen. DK Readers L3: Women in Science. 2018. (DK Readers Level 3 Ser.). (ENG., Illus.). 64p. (J). (gr. 2-4). pap. 4.99 *(978-1-4654-6859-8(5)*, DK Children) Dorling Kindersley Publishing, Inc.

—Women in Science. 2018. (Illus.). 64p. (J). *(978-0-7804-0038-2(0))* Dorling Kindersley Publishing, Inc.

Guidi, Victoria. Who on Earth Is Jane Goodall? Champion for the Chimpanzees, 1 vol. 2009. (Scientists Saving the Earth Ser.). (ENG., Illus.). 112p. (gr. 5-6). lib. bdg. 35.93 *(978-1-59845-119-1(7)*, 3bf4bd2e-0f8b-4d4f-91f8-096c6440187a) Enslow Publishing, LLC.

Haldy, Emma E. Jane Goodall. Bane, Jeff, illus. 2016. (My Early Library: My Itty-Bitty Bio Ser.). (ENG.). 24p. (J). (gr. k-1). 30.64 *(978-1-63471-022-0(3)*, 208168) Cherry Lake Publishing.

Hansen, Grace. Jane Goodall: Activista y Experta en Chimpancés (Spanish Version) 2016. (Biografías: Personas Que Han Hecho Historia (History Maker Biographies) Ser.). (SPA., Illus.). 24p. (J). (gr. -1-2). lib. bdg. 32.79 *(978-1-68080-739-4(0)*, 22640, Abdo Kids) ABDO Publishing Co.

Hustad, Douglas. Animal Scientist & Activist Jane Goodall. 2016. (STEM Trailblazer Bios Ser.). (ENG., Illus.). 32p. (J). (gr. 2-5). 26.65 *(978-1-5124-0788-4(7)*, 58f77d81-a91e-4461-82e6-f2bdc4755037, Lerner Pubns.) Lerner Publishing Group.

Ignotofsky, Rachel. I Love Science: A Journal for Self-Discovery & Big Ideas. 2017. (Women in Science Ser.). (Illus.). 192p. 14.99 *(978-1-60774-980-6(7)*, Ten Speed Pr.) Potter/Ten Speed/Harmony/Rodale.

—Mujeres de Ciencia. 2018. (ENG & SPA., Illus.). (J). (gr. 3-7). mass mkt. 19.99 *(978-607-01-3362-6(5))* Santillana USA Publishing Co., Inc.

Indovino, Shaina. Women in the Environmental Sciences. Lee-Karlon, Ann, ed. 2013. (Major Women in Science Ser.: 10). 64p. (J). (gr. 7-18). 22.95 *(978-1-4222-2927-9(0))* Mason Crest.

Juarez, Christine. Ellen Ochoa. 2016. (Great Hispanic & Latino Americans Ser.). (ENG., Illus.). 24p. (J). (gr. -1-2). lib. bdg. 24.65 *(978-1-5157-1888-8(3)*, 132586, Pebble) Capstone.

Keats Curtis, Jennifer & F. Angeli, Nicole. La Dama de Las Siguanas, 1 vol. Jones, Veronica, illus. 2018. (SPA.). 32p. (J). (gr. 2-3). pap. 11.95 *(978-1-60718-311-2(0)*, 04869b23-1f5d-45bd-8f9c-3c4143d9220a) Arbordale Publishing.

—The Lizard Lady, 1 vol. Jones, Veronica, illus. 2018. (ENG.). 32p. (J). (gr. k-3). 17.95 *(978-1-60718-066-1(9)*, 9781607180661); pap. 9.95 *(978-1-60718-091-3(X)*, 9781607180913) Arbordale Publishing.

Kelly, Tracey. Women Scientists in Chemistry, 1 vol. 2017. (Superwomen in STEM Ser.). (ENG.). 48p. (J). (gr. 5-5). pap. 15.05 *(978-1-5382-1473-2(3)*, bb9b2c06-954a-43ee-b7b5-a8cbefc3923a); lib. bdg. 33.60 *(978-1-5382-1405-3(9)*, a5297a5b-9c15-42a9-aad3-94b8efc15db3) Stevens, Gareth Publishing LLLP.

Kennon, Caroline. Hidden No More: African American Women in STEM Careers, 1 vol. 2017. (Lucent Library of Black History Ser.). (ENG., Illus.). 104p. (YA). (gr. 7-7). pap. 20.99 *(978-1-5345-6295-0(8)*, f6b36775-ace1-430c-ad0e-3da3b5b0d3f9); lib. bdg. 41.03 *(978-1-5345-6243-1(5)*, 32f7f915-4af2-498c-a26e-0e689563af1c) Greenhaven Publishing LLC. (Lucent Pr.).

Klein, Rebecca T. Careers for Tech Girls in Science, 1 vol. 2015. (Tech Girls Ser.). (ENG., Illus.). 80p. (J). (gr. 7-8). 37.47 *(978-1-4994-6103-9(8)*, e68f3614-3665-4ca7-a52b-04b2c080437f, Rosen Young Adult) Rosen Publishing Group, Inc., The.

Labrecque, Ellen. Gertrude B. Elion & Pharmacology. 2017. (21st Century Junior Library: Women Innovators Ser.). (ENG., Illus.). 24p. (J). (gr. 2-5). lib. bdg. 29.21 *(978-1-63472-182-0(9)*, 209300) Cherry Lake Publishing.

Lawlor, Laurie. Super Women: Six Scientists Who Changed the World. 2019. (Illus.). 64p. (J). (gr. 3-7). pap. 10.99 *(978-0-8234-4186-0(5))* Holiday Hse., Inc.

Loh-Hagan, Virginia. Girl Scientists. 2019. (History's Yearbook Ser.). (ENG., Illus.). 32p. (J). (gr. 4-8). pap. 14.21 *(978-1-5341-5079-9(X)*, 213623); lib. bdg. 32.07 *(978-1-5341-4793-5(4)*, 213622) Cherry Lake Publishing. (45th Parallel Press).

Maathai, Wangari. How I Changed the World. 2018. (J). *(978-0-7166-2283-3(1))* World Bk., Inc.

MacBain, Jennifer. Gertrude Elion: Nobel Prize Winner in Physiology & Medicine. 2009. (Women Hall of Famers in Mathematics & Science Ser.). 112p. (gr. 5-8). 63.90 *(978-1-60854-811-8(2)*, Rosen Reference) Rosen Publishing Group, Inc., The.

Marsh, Carole. Rachel Carson: Excellent Ecologist. 2004. (1000 Readers Ser.). (Illus.). 14p. (J). (gr. k-4). pap. 2.95 *(978-0-635-02524-1(8))* Gallopade International.

McAneney, Caitlin. Women in Space, 1 vol. 2015. (Women Groundbreakers Ser.). (ENG., Illus.). 32p. (J). (gr. 4-5). pap. 11.00 *(978-1-4994-1048-8(4)*, b71206d9-b318-467a-9769-3ca23c2f88cb, PowerKids Pr.) Rosen Publishing Group, Inc., The.

McDonnell, Patrick. Me ... Jane (Caldecott Honor Book) 2011. (ENG., Illus.). 40p. (J). (gr. -1-3). 18.99 *(978-0-316-04546-9(2))* Little, Brown Bks. for Young Readers.

Mcdonnell, Patrick. Me... Jane. 2011. (CHI., Illus.). 40p. (J). (gr. -1-2). *(978-986-189-308-2(3))* Grimm Cultural Ent., Co., Ltd.

—Me... Jane. 2011. (J). *(978-1-4618-4349-8(9))* Recorded Bks., Inc.

Nakamura, May. If You Love Dolphins, You Could Be... Ready-To-Read Level 2. Kwee, Natalie, illus. 2019. (If You Love Ser.). (ENG.). 32p. (J). (gr. k-2). 17.99 *(978-1-5344-4469-0(6))*; pap. 4.99 *(978-1-5344-4468-3(8))* Simon Spotlight. (Simon Spotlight).

Niver, Heather Moore. Careers for Tech Girls in Computer Science, 1 vol. 2015. (Tech Girls Ser.). (ENG., Illus.). 80p. (J). (gr. 7-8). 37.47 *(978-1-4994-6105-3(4)*, 45593414-5392-4983-87de-1332de536cf6, Rosen Young Adult) Rosen Publishing Group, Inc., The.

Nivola, Claire A. Life in the Ocean: The Story of Oceanographer Sylvia Earle, 1 vol. Nivola, Claire A., illus. 2012. (ENG., Illus.). 32p. (J). (gr. -1-3). 19.99 *(978-0-374-38068-7(6)*, 900068269, Farrar, Straus & Giroux (BYR)) Farrar, Straus & Giroux.

—Life in the Ocean: The Story of Oceanographer Sylvia Earle. 2012. (J). 38.75 *(978-1-4703-0113-2(X))* Recorded Bks., Inc.

Ottaviani, Jim. Primates: The Fearless Science of Jane Goodall, Dian Fossey, & Biruté Galdikas. Wicks, Maris, illus. 2015. (ENG.). 144p. (YA). (gr. 7). pap. 14.99 *(978-1-250-06293-2(4)*, 900142635) Square Fish.

Reichard, Susan E. Who on Earth Is Sylvia Earle? Undersea Explorer of the Ocean, 1 vol. 2009. (Scientists Saving the Earth Ser.). (ENG., Illus.). 112p. (J). (gr. 5-6). lib. bdg. 35.93 *(978-1-59845-118-4(9)*, dae42add-b697-4162-b665-6aa14bed4142) Enslow Publishing, LLC.

Robbins, Dean. Margaret & the Moon. Knisley, Lucy, illus. 2017. 40p. (J). (gr. -1-3). 18.99 *(978-0-399-55185-7(9)*, Knopf Bks. for Young Readers) Random Hse. Children's Bks.

Robeson, Teresa. Queen of Physics: How Wu Chien Shiung Helped Unlock the Secrets of the Atom. Huang, Rebecca, illus. 2019. (People Who Shaped Our World Ser.: 6). 48p. (J). (gr. k). 17.99 *(978-1-4549-3220-8(1))* Sterling Publishing Co., Inc.

Robinson, Fiona. The Bluest of Blues: Anna Atkins & the First Book of Photographs. 2019. (ENG., Illus.). 48p. (J). (gr. 1-4). 19.99 *(978-1-4197-2551-7(3)*, 1102901, Abrams Bks. for Young Readers) Abrams, Inc.

Rooney, Anne. Rachel Carson (Women in Science) Lundie, Isobel, illus. 2019. (Women in Science Ser.). (ENG.). 32p. (J). (gr. 2-3). pap. 9.95 *(978-0-531-23954-4(3)*, Watts, Franklin) Scholastic Library Publishing.

Rooney, Frances. Exceptional Women Environmentalists, 1 vol. 2007. (Women's Hall of Fame Ser.: 11). (ENG., Illus.). 112p. (J). (gr. 4-8). pap. 10.95 *(978-1-897187-22-7(X))* Second Story Pr. CAN. Dist: Orca Bk. Pubs. USA.

Saddleback Educational Publishing Staff, ed. Marie Curie, 1 vol. unabr. ed. 2007. (Graphic Biographies Ser.). (ENG., Illus.). 25p. (YA). (gr. 4-12). pap. 9.75 *(978-1-59905-226-7(1))* Saddleback Educational Publishing, Inc.

Sally Ride Science Editors, Sally Ride Science. What Do You Want to Be? Explore Earth Sciences. 2004. (J). 6.00 *(978-0-9753920-2-7(6))* Sally Ride Science.

Sammons, Sandra Wallus. The Three Marjories: Marjory Stoneman Douglas, Marjorie Kinnan Rawlings, Marjorie Harris Carr & Their Contributions to Florida. 2018. xvii, 128p. (J). *(978-1-68334-034-8(5))* Pineapple Pr., Inc.

Schwartz, Heather E. Astronaut Ellen Ochoa. 2017. (STEM Trailblazer Bios Ser.). (ENG., Illus.). 32p. (J). (gr. 2-5). 26.65 *(978-1-5124-3449-1(3)*, 77dea24e-dc77-43ae-9c9e-868ef497e527, Lerner Pubns.); pap. 8.99 *(978-1-5124-5627-1(6)*, 25ca4de8-6c4c-4b2e-809e-81b0ec07cf29) Lerner Publishing Group.

Silvey, Anita. Untamed: The Wild Life of Jane Goodall. 2015. (Illus.). 96p. (J). (gr. 3-7). 18.99 *(978-1-4263-1518-3(X)*, National Geographic Kids) Disney Publishing Worldwide.

Snedden, Robert. Mary Anning: Fossil Hunter, 1 vol. 2015. (Superheroes of Science Ser.). (ENG., Illus.). 48p. (J). (gr. 6-6). pap. 15.05 *(978-1-4824-3145-2(9)*, 2fd3d439-0630-4b2c-9e97-93982519151d) Stevens, Gareth Publishing LLLP.

Spiller, Sara. Mary Anning. Bane, Jeff, illus. 2018. (My Early Library: My Itty-Bitty Bio Ser.). (ENG.). 24p. (J). (gr. k-1). lib. bdg. 30.64 *(978-1-5341-2884-2(0)*, 211580) Cherry Lake Publishing.

Stoltman, Joan. Jane Goodall, 1 vol. 2018. (Little Biographies of Big People Ser.). (ENG.). 24p. (gr. 1-2). 24.27 *(978-1-5382-2895-1(5)*, 36fd3933-ef13-4e38-ba6f-089630b2e707) Stevens, Gareth Publishing LLLP.

Streissguth, Tom. Rosalind Franklin: DNA Discoverer. 2017. (Women in Science Ser.). (ENG., Illus.). 112p. (J). (gr. 6-12). lib. bdg. 41.36 *(978-1-5321-1042-9(1)*, 25660, Essential Library) ABDO Publishing Co.

Stux, Erica. The Achievers: Great Women in the Biological Sciences. 2005. (Avisson Young Adult Ser.). (Illus.). 148p. (J). *(978-1-888105-70-4(4))* Avisson Pr., Inc.

Swaby, Rachel. Trailblazers: 33 Women in Science Who Changed the World. 2017. 208p. (J). (gr. 5). 6.99

W X Y Z

(978-0-399-55418-6(1), Yearling) Random Hse. Children's Bks.

Thermes, Jennifer. Grandma Gatewood Hikes the Appalachian Trail. 2018. (ENG., Illus.). 48p. (J). (gr. k-2). 18.99 (978-1-4197-2839-6(3), 1118001) Abrams, Inc.

Thimmesh, Catherine. The Sky's the Limit: Stories of Discovery by Women & Girls. Sweet, Melissa, illus. 2005. 73p. (J). (gr. 4-8). reprint ed. 16.00 (978-0-7567-9631-0(8)) DIANE Publishing Co.

Van Vleet, Carmella & Sullivan, Kathy. To the Stars! The First American Woman to Walk in Space. Wong, Nicole, illus. 40p. (J). (gr. k-3). 2018. pap. 7.99 (978-1-58089-645-0(6)) 2016. lib. bdg. 16.95 (978-1-58089-644-3(8)) Charlesbridge Publishing, Inc.

Venezia, Mike. Lise Meitner: Had the Right Vision about Nuclear Fission. Venezia, Mike, illus. 2009. (Getting to Know the World's Greatest Inventors & Scientists Ser.). (ENG., Illus.). 32p. (J). (gr. 2-5). 28.00 (978-0-531-23702-1(8)) Scholastic Library Publishing.

Wallace, Elise. Unsung Heroes: Pioneers in Science. rev. ed. 2018. (TIME(r): Informational Text Ser.). (ENG.). 48p. (J). (gr. 6-8). pap. 13.99 (978-1-4258-5001-2(4)) Teacher Created Materials, Inc.

White, Katherine. Sylvia Earle: Deep Sea Explorer & Ocean Activist. (Women Hall of Famers in Mathematics & Science Ser.). 112p. (gr. 5-8). 2009. 63.90 (978-1-60854-814-9(7)) 2003. (ENG., Illus.). lib. bdg. 39.80 (978-0-8239-3879-7(4), 605a1e36-bafd-4ce1-86f8-a6c460e534d4) Rosen Publishing Group, Inc., The. (Rosen Reference).

Women in Science, 12 vols. 2016. (Women in Science Ser.). (ENG.). 128p. (YA). (gr. 9-9). lib. bdg. 284.16 (978-1-5026-2439-0(7), 0260eb06-1fea-40d6-9b9a-9413df0ea9c7, Cavendish Square) Cavendish Square Publishing LLC.

Wood, S. Vaccine Innovators Pearl Kendrick & Grace Eldering. 2016. (STEM Trailblazer Bios Ser.). (ENG., Illus.). 32p. (J). (gr. 2-5). 26.65 (978-1-5124-0790-7(9), dc165329-e6c1-4b8e-bbaa-318d2c7a993c, Lerner Pubns.) Lerner Publishing Group.

Woodward, Kay. What Would She Do?: 25 True Stories of Trailblazing Rebel Women. 2018. (ENG.). 112p. (J). (gr. 3-7). 16.99 (978-1-338-21640-0(6)) Scholastic, Inc.

Woolf, Alex. Jane Goodall (Women in Science) (Library Edition) Lundie, Isobel, illus. 2019. (Women in Science Ser.). (ENG.). 32p. (J). (gr. 2-3). lib. bdg. 29.00 (978-0-531-23535-5(1), Watts, Franklin) Scholastic Library Publishing.

Yasuda, Anita. Astronomy: Cool Women in Space. 2015. (Girls in Science Ser.). (ENG., Illus.). 112p. (J). (gr. 3-7). 19.95 (978-1-61930-326-3(4), 1abeb752-cabd-463c-89f0-e91be4b55e60) Nomad Pr.

Yount, Lisa. Rosalind Franklin. 2011. (ENG.). 152p. (gr. 6-12). 35.00 (978-1-60413-660-9(X), P210465, Facts On File) Infobase Holdings, Inc.

WOMEN'S CLOTHING

see Clothing and Dress

WOMEN'S RIGHTS

Adiletta, Dawn. Elizabeth Cady Stanton: Women's Suffrage & the First Vote. (Library of American Lives & Times Ser.). 112p. (gr. 5-5). 2009. 69.20 (978-1-60853-479-1(0)) 2004. (ENG., Illus.). (J). lib. bdg. 38.27 (978-1-4042-2647-0(8), c7dcb355-12ad-4a2b-9bd6-5e815734870e) Rosen Publishing Group, Inc., The.

Alter, Judy. Women's Rights. 2008. (21st Century Skills Library: Global Perspectives Ser.). (ENG., Illus.). 32p. (gr. 4-8). lib. bdg. 32.07 (978-1-60279-133-6(3), 200112) Cherry Lake Publishing.

Anderson, Dale. The Seneca Falls Women's Rights Convention, 1 vol. 2004. (Landmark Events in American History Ser.). (ENG., Illus.). 48p. (J). (gr. 5-8). pap. 15.05 (978-0-8368-5417-6(9), 14ca8a42-06df-4966-a508-cdfb939fbb1c); lib. bdg. 33.67 (978-0-8368-5389-6(X), 64629abc-e81e-4091-81b8-08c3b3728482) Stevens, Gareth Publishing LLLP. (Gareth Stevens Secondary Library).

Anderson, Dale & Crewe, Sabrina. The Seneca Falls Women's Rights Convention, 1 vol. 2004. (Events That Shaped America Ser.). (ENG., Illus.). 32p. (J). (gr. 3-5). lib. bdg. 28.67 (978-0-8368-3408-6(9), c4ccc77c-a091-449d-aa31-a0b003f98e5d, Gareth Stevens Learning Library) Stevens, Gareth Publishing LLLP.

The Antebellum Women's Movement, 1820-1860. (YA). (gr. 6-9). spiral bd., tchr.'s planning gde. ed. 12.00 (978-0-382-44465-4(5)) Cobblestone Publishing Co.

Bakshi, Kelly. Perspectives on the Women's Rights Movement. 2018. (Perspectives on US History Ser.). (ENG., Illus.). 32p. (J). (gr. 3-6). 32.80 (978-1-63235-405-1(5), 13727, 12-Story Library) Bookstaves, LLC.

Barber, Lynn. Champions for Women's Rights: Matilda Joslyn Gage, Julia Ward Howe, Lucretia Mott, & Lucy Stone, 1 vol. 2016. (Heroes of the Women's Suffrage Movement Ser.). (ENG., Illus.). 128p. (gr. 6-6). 38.93 (978-0-7660-7891-8(4), eaa758a8-6dcc-4701-9fbb-ec0b9d1106c4) Enslow Publishing, LLC.

Baskes Litwin, Laura. Susan B. Anthony: Social Reformer & Feminist, 1 vol. 2016. (Heroes of the Women's Suffrage Movement Ser.). (ENG., Illus.). 128p. (gr. 6-6). 38.93 (978-0-7660-7888-8(4), 9937aa3a-d7e8-460d-9069-21ceca68976f) Enslow Publishing, LLC.

Bjornlund, Lydia D. Women of the Suffrage Movement. 2003. (Women in History Ser.). (ENG., Illus.). 112p. (J). 33.45 (978-1-59018-173-7(5), Lucent Bks.) Cengage Gale.

Blumenthal, Karen. Jane Against the World: Roe V. Wade & the Fight for Reproductive Rights. 2020. (ENG., Illus.). 384p. (YA). 19.99 (978-1-62672-165-4(3), 900141057) Roaring Brook Pr.

Bohannon, Lisa Frederiksen. Women's Rights & Nothing Less: The Story of Elizabeth Cady Stanton. 2004. (Feminist Voices Ser.). (Illus.). 112p. (YA). (gr. 6-12). 23.95 (978-1-883846-66-4(8), First Biographies) Reynolds, Morgan Inc.

Bohannon, Lisa Frederkisen. Failure Is Impossible: The Story of Susan B. Anthony. 2004. (Feminist Voices Ser.). (Illus.). 112p. (YA). (gr. 6-12). 23.95 (978-1-883846-77-0(3), First Biographies) Reynolds, Morgan Inc.

Boothroyd, Jennifer. Susan B. Anthony: A Life of Fairness. 2006. (Pull Ahead Bks.). (Illus.). 32p. (J). (gr. 3-7). lib. bdg. 22.60 (978-0-8225-3479-2(7), Lerner Pubns.) Lerner Publishing Group.

—Susan B. Anthony: Una Vida de Igualdad. Translations.com Staff, tr. 2006. (Libros para Avanzar-Biografías (Pull Ahead Books-Biographies) Ser.). (ENG & SPA., Illus.). 32p. (gr. k-3). lib. bdg. 22.60 (978-0-8225-6234-4(0)) Lerner Publishing Group.

Braun, Eric. The Women's Rights Movement. 2018. (Movements That Matter (Alternator Books (r)) Ser.). (ENG., Illus.). 32p. (J). (gr. 3-6). 30.65 (978-1-5415-2332-6(6), 0459626b-8d38-4682-9f6d-0d146829f464, Lerner Pubns.) Lerner Publishing Group.

Bryan, Bethany. Great Exit Projects on the Women's Rights Movement, 1 vol. 2019. (Great Social Studies Exit Projects Ser.). (ENG.). 64p. (gr. 5-5). pap. 13.95 (978-1-4994-4054-6(5), 0c75f1a8-bbc5-40ff-9d6c-f53ef02c76d0) Rosen Publishing Group, Inc., The.

—Social Change in the Twenty-First Century. 2019. (Defining Events of the Twenty-First Century Ser.). (ENG.). 80p. (J). (gr. 6-12). 41.27 (978-1-68282-607-2(4)) ReferencePoint Pr., Inc.

Calkhoven, Laurie. Ruth Bader Ginsburg: Ready-To-Read Level 3. Vukovic, Elizabet, illus. 2019. (You Should Meet Ser.). (ENG.). 48p. (J). (gr. 1-1). 17.99 (978-1-5344-4858-2(6)); pap. 4.99 (978-1-5344-4857-5(8)) Simon Spotlight. (Simon Spotlight).

Carson, Mary Kay. Who Was Susan B. Anthony Vote? And Other Questions about Women's Suffrage. 2015. (Good Question! Ser.). (ENG., Illus.). 32p. (J). (gr. 2). pap. 5.95 (978-1-4549-1242-2(1)) Sterling Publishing Co., Inc.

Ching, Jacqueline. Women's Rights. 2009. (Individual Rights & Civic Responsibility Ser.). 128p. (gr. 7-12). 63.90 (978-1-61513-518-9(9)) Rosen Publishing Group, Inc., The.

Confronting Violence Against Women. 2015. (Confronting Violence Against Women Ser.). (ENG.). 64p. (J). (gr. 6-7). pap., pap., pap. 466.20 (978-1-4994-6148-0(8), Rosen Young Adult) Rosen Publishing Group, Inc., The.

Connors, Kathleen. Life of Susan B. Anthony. 2014. (Famous Lives (Gareth Stevens Paperback) Ser.). (ENG.). 24p. (J). (gr. 2-4). 18.95 (978-1-5311-8606-7(8)) Perfection Learning Corp.

—The Life of Susan B. Anthony, 1 vol., Vol. 1. 2013. (Famous Lives Ser.). (ENG.). 24p. (J). (gr. 1-2). 25.27 (978-1-4824-0425-8(7), acaba0c6-f2f2-4657-ad3c-0f0ca3e168d0) Stevens, Gareth Publishing LLLP.

Cullerton Johnson, Jen. Seeds of Change: Wangari's Gift to the World, 1 vol. Sadler, Sonia Lynn, illus. 2013. (ENG.). 32p. (J). (gr. 1-6). 19.95 (978-1-60060-367-9(X), leelowbooks) Lee & Low Bks., Inc.

DeAngelis, Therese. Women's Rights on the Frontier. 2012. (Illus.). 64p. (J). pap. (978-1-4222-2369-7(8)) Mason Crest.

—Women's Rights on the Frontier. Harrington, A. Page, ed. 2012. (Finding a Voice: Women's Fight for Equality in U. S. Society Ser.). (Illus.). 64p. (J). (gr. 5). 22.95 (978-1-4222-2359-8(0)) Mason Crest.

Donelly, Karen. American Women Pilots of World War II, 1 vol. 2004. (American Women at War Ser.). (ENG.). 112p. (YA). (gr. 8-8). pap. 13.95 (978-1-4358-3274-9(4), 5d9f859d-ebd7-4c4b-9c01-4e9010f10a6f) Rosen Publishing Group, Inc., The.

Dowdy, Penny. The Famous Five: Defining Moments in Canadian History/Graphic Novels. 2010. (Illus.). 32p. (978-1-77071-616-2(5)) Weigl Educational Pubs. Ltd.

Dudley Gold, Susan. Roberts V. Jaycees: Women's Rights, 1 vol. 2009. (Supreme Court Milestones Ser.). (ENG.). 128p. (YA). (gr. 8-8). lib. bdg. 45.50 (978-0-7614-2952-4(2), 04f9ffbc-33ce-4da1-a392-41abaff897a0) Cavendish Square Publishing LLC.

—The Women's Rights Movement & Abolitionism, 1 vol. 2015. (Primary Sources of the Abolitionist Movement Ser.). (ENG., Illus.). 64p. (gr. 6-6). lib. bdg. 35.93 (978-1-5026-0536-8(8), e7cc3ec8-c0a6-456b-9f79-cb129c7788e2) Cavendish Square Publishing LLC.

Frey, Wendy. Citizen Heroes. 2007. (Illus.). 68p. (J). (978-1-4105-0887-4(0)); (978-1-4105-0888-1(9)) Building Wings LLC.

Fry, Erin. The Power of Friendship. 2005. (Illus.). 16p. (J). pap. (978-0-7367-2920-8(8)) Zaner-Bloser, Inc.

Gelletly, LeeAnne. The Equal Rights Amendment. 2012. (J). pap. (978-1-4222-2361-1(2)) Mason Crest.

—The Equal Rights Amendment. Harrington, A. Page, ed. 2012. (Finding a Voice: Women's Fight for Equality in U. S. Society Ser.). 64p. (J). (gr. 5). 22.95 (978-1-4222-2351-2(5)) Mason Crest.

—Origins of the Women's Rights Movement. 2012. (Illus.). 64p. (J). pap. (978-1-4222-2363-5(9)) Mason Crest.

—Origins of the Women's Rights Movement. Harrington, A. Page, ed. 2012. (Finding a Voice: Women's Fight for Equality in U. S. Society Ser.). (Illus.). 64p. (J). (gr. 5). 22.95 (978-1-4222-2353-6(1)) Mason Crest.

—A Woman's Place in Early America. 2012. (Illus.). 64p. (J). pap. (978-1-4222-2365-9(5)) Mason Crest.

—A Woman's Place in Early America. Harrington, A. Page, ed. 2012. (Finding a Voice: Women's Fight for Equality in U. S. Society Ser.). (Illus.). 64p. (J). (gr. 5). 22.95 (978-1-4222-2355-0(8)) Mason Crest.

Goddu, Krystyna Poray. What's Your Story, Susan B. Anthony? 2016. (Cub Reporter Meets Famous Americans Ser.). (ENG., Illus.). 32p. (J). (gr. k-3). 26.65 (978-1-4677-8785-7(X), 199ae9d8-e2ff-4af1-8a22-f4579b2b7584, Lerner Pubns.) Lerner Publishing Group.

Gordon, Minette, et al. Understanding Women's Rights, 1 vol. 2011. (Personal Freedom & Civic Duty Ser.). (ENG.). 168p. (J). (gr. 7-7). lib. bdg. 39.80 (978-1-4488-4671-9(4), 81dd51a7-d7a7-43a8-b882-0d39b6f9f2f7) Rosen Publishing Group, Inc., The.

Gorman, Jacqueline Laks. The Modern Feminist Movement. 2011. (ENG., Illus.). 64p. (gr. 6-12). 35.00 (978-1-60413-935-8(8), P189949, Facts On File) Infobase Holdings, Inc.

Hanson-Harding, Alexandra. Activism: Taking on Women's Issues, 1 vol. 2012. (Young Woman's Guide to Contemporary Issues Ser.). (ENG., Illus.). 112p. (YA). (gr. 8-9). lib. bdg. 39.80 (978-1-4488-8401-8(2), f069fb3b-b51e-4963-9933-3115802d1b4f) Rosen Publishing Group, Inc., The.

Haughton, Emma. Equality of the Sexes? 2005. (Viewpoints (Sea to Sea) Ser.). (Illus.). 32p. (YA). (gr. 5-9). lib. bdg. 27.10 (978-1-932889-58-1(2)) Sea-To-Sea Pubns.

Hawker, Louise, ed. Women's Rights, 1 vol. 2010. (Global Viewpoints Ser.). (ENG., Illus.). 216p. (gr. 10-12). pap. 32.70 (978-0-7377-4475-0(8), fa77b707-4ce6-4953-b87c-ec83dc50697b); lib. bdg. 47.83 (978-0-7377-4474-3(X), 216e6af2-31d9-4e45-a684-372fb22388d4) Greenhaven Publishing LLC. (Greenhaven Publishing).

Herweck, Dona. Susan B. Anthony, 1 vol. 2nd rev. ed. 2014. (TIME for KIDS(r): Informational Text Ser.). (ENG., Illus.). 28p. (J). (gr. 2-3). lib. bdg. 23.96 (978-1-4807-1063-4(6)) Teacher Created Materials, Inc.

Hollihan, Kerrie Logan. Rightfully Ours: How Women Won the Vote, 21 Activities. 2012. (For Kids Ser.: 43). (ENG., Illus.). 144p. (J). (gr. 4). pap. 18.99 (978-1-883052-89-8(0)) Chicago Review Pr., Inc.

Hopkinson, Deborah. Susan B. Anthony: Fighter for Women's Rights. Bates, Amy, illus. 2005. 32p. (J). lib. bdg. 15.00 (978-1-4242-1563-8(3)) Fitzgerald Bks.

—Susan B. Anthony: Fighter for Women's Rights (Ready-To-Read Level 3) Bates, Amy June, illus. 2005. (Ready-To-Read Stories of Famous Americans Ser.). (ENG.). 32p. (J). (gr. 1-3). pap. 4.99 (978-0-689-86909-9(6), Simon Spotlight) Simon Spotlight.

—What Is the Women's Rights Movement? 2019. (Who HQ Ser.). (ENG.). 107p. (J). (gr. 2-3). 16.36 (978-1-64310-857-5(3)) Penworthy Co., LLC, The.

Hopkinson, Deborah & Who HQ. What Is the Women's Rights Movement? Conley, Laurie A., illus. 2018. (What Was? Ser.). 112p. (J). (gr. 3-7). 5.99 (978-1-5247-8629-8(2), Penguin Workshop) Penguin Young Readers Group.

Isecke, Harriet. Women's Suffrage: Fighting for Women's Rights. rev. ed. 2011. (Social Studies: Informational Text Ser.). (ENG.). 32p. (gr. 4-8). pap. 11.99 (978-1-4333-1507-7(6)) Teacher Created Materials, Inc.

Jennings, Terry Catasus. The Women's Liberation Movement, 1960-1990. 2012. (J). pap. (978-1-4222-2368-0(X)) Mason Crest.

—The Women's Liberation Movement, 1960-1990. Harrington, A. Page, ed. 2012. (Finding a Voice: Women's Fight for Equality in U. S. Society Ser.). 64p. (J). (gr. 5). 22.95 (978-1-4222-2358-1(2)) Mason Crest.

Kanefield, Teri. Susan B. Anthony: The Making of America #4. 2019. (Making of America Ser.). (ENG., Illus.). 240p. (J). (gr. 5-9). 16.99 (978-1-4197-3401-4(6), 1263701, Abrams Bks. for Young Readers) Abrams, Inc.

Kawa, Katie. What's Gender Equality?, 1 vol. 2017. (What's the Issue? Ser.). (ENG.). 24p. (J). (gr. 3-3). 26.23 (978-1-5345-2435-4(5), 6d301929-7fde-4386-9fe8-d360801d1c7f, KidHaven Publishing) Greenhaven Publishing LLC.

Kendall, Martha E. Failure Is Impossible! The History of American Women's Rights. 3rd ed. 2005. (People's History Ser.). (Illus.). 96p. (gr. 6-12). lib. bdg. 26.60 (978-0-8225-1744-3(2)) Lerner Publishing Group.

Kent, Deborah. The Seneca Falls Convention: Working to Expand Women's Rights, 1 vol. 2016. (Heroes of the Women's Suffrage Movement Ser.). (ENG., Illus.). 128p. (gr. 6-6). 38.93 (978-0-7660-7892-5(2), 31bae9f2-5fb0-4b0c-b85c-a14646a95482) Enslow Publishing, LLC.

Keppeler, Jill. Inside the Women's Rights Movement. 2017. (Eyewitness to History Ser.). 32p. (J). (gr. 4-5). 63.00 (978-1-5382-1170-0(X)); (ENG.). pap. 11.50 (978-1-5382-1169-4(6), 923a5efe-30ca-42b2-9031-35ce9e051895) Stevens, Gareth Publishing LLLP.

Kops, Deborah. Alice Paul & the Fight for Women's Rights: From the Vote to the Equal Rights Amendment. 2017. (ENG., Illus.). 216p. (J). (gr. 5-12). 17.95 (978-1-62979-323-8(X), Calkins Creek) Highlights Pr., c/o Highlights for Children, Inc.

Koya, Lena & Hanson-Harding, Alexandra. Female Activists, 1 vol. 2017. (Women in the World Ser.). (ENG., Illus.). 112p. (J). (gr. 6-6). 38.80 (978-1-5081-7720-3(1), 9b65c2f8-cabf-4233-ba96-02fa13e7d951); pap. 18.65 (978-1-5081-7883-5(6), 939d0056-a509-4316-8086-4a094b81a502) Rosen Publishing Group, Inc., The.

Kulling, Monica. Susan B. Anthony: Her Fight for Equal Rights. Plenzke, Maike, illus. 2020. (Step into Reading Ser.). 32p. (J). (gr. -1-1). pap. 4.99 (978-0-593-11982-2(7), Random Hse. Bks. for Young Readers) Random Hse. Children's Bks.

Langston-George, Rebecca. Women's Rights Movement: Then & Now. 2018. (America: 50 Years of Change Ser.). (ENG.). 64p. (J). (gr. 5-9). lib. bdg. 34.65 (978-1-5435-0386-9(1), 137211, Capstone Pr.) Capstone.

Levy, Janey. The Most Powerful Words about Women's Rights, 1 vol. 2019. (Words That Shaped America Ser.). (ENG.). 32p. (gr. 4-5). pap. 11.50 (978-1-5382-4807-2(7), 67040c36-d73c-4a25-a939-4f290cac0c77) Stevens, Gareth Publishing LLLP.

Lowery, Zoe & Bickerstaff, Linda. Gender-Based Violence & Women's Rights, 1 vol. 2017. (Women in the World Ser.). (ENG., Illus.). 112p. (J). (gr. 6-6). 38.80 (978-1-5081-7447-9(4), 56b06358-b22e-4f32-bdf5-ce0cc697bd2c, Rosen Young Adult) Rosen Publishing Group, Inc., The.

Lowery, Zoe & Bringle, Jennifer. Reproductive Health & Women's Rights, 1 vol. 2017. (Women in the World Ser.). (ENG., Illus.). 112p. (J). (gr. 6-6). 38.80 (978-1-5081-7445-5(8), 425946ed-f968-456b-877f-12a7c92c8e53, Rosen Young Adult) Rosen Publishing Group, Inc., The.

Lüsted, Marcia Amidon. The Fight for Women's Rights, 1 vol. 2019. (Activism in Action: a History Ser.). (ENG.). 112p. (gr. 8-8). pap. 18.65 (978-1-5081-8552-9(2), 0d2973da-0004-447c-be57-a7e61a77cd52) Rosen Publishing Group, Inc., The.

Margorz, Juliet. Elizabeth Cady Stanton & the Fight for Equal Rights, 1 vol. 2008. (Real Life Readers Ser.). (ENG.). 32p. (gr. 4-6). pap. 10.00 (978-1-4358-0233-9(0), c6a2072f-8727-488c-b3bd-4dfd47097ed8, Rosen Classroom) Rosen Publishing Group, Inc., The.

Mattern, Joanne. Elizabeth Cady Stanton & Susan B. Anthon Fighting Together for Women's Rights. 2009. (Women Whc Shaped History Ser.). 24p. (gr. 2-3). 42.50 (978-1-60854-818-7(X), PowerKids Pr.) Rosen Publishing Group, Inc., The.

McGraw Hill. American History Ink the Women's Rights Movement. 2007. (Jt Am Hist Graph Novel Ser.). (ENG., Illus.). 24p. (gr. 6-12). spiral bd. 15.08 (978-0-07-878025-7(X), 007878025X) McGraw-Hill Education.

McPherson, Stephanie Sammartino. Susan B. Anthony. 2006 (History Maker Bios Ser.). (Illus.). 48p. (J). (gr. 3-7). lib. bdg. 26.60 (978-0-8225-5938-2(2), Lerner Pubns.) Lerner Publishing Group.

Nardo, Don. The Women's Rights Movement. 2018. (Push for Social Change Ser.). (ENG.). 80p. (YA). (gr. 6-12). 39.93 (978-1-68282-425-2(X)) ReferencePoint Pr., Inc.

National Geographic Learning. Reading Expeditions (Social Studies: People Who Changed America): Votes for Women. 2007. (ENG., Illus.). 40p. (J). pap. 21.95 (978-0-7922-8626-4(X)) CENGAGE Learning.

Negley, Keith. Mary Wears What She Wants. Negley, Keith, illus. 2019. (ENG., Illus.). 48p. (J). (gr. -1-3). 18.99 (978-0-06-284679-2(5), Balzer & Bray) HarperCollins Pubs.

Paisley, Erinne. Can Your Conversations Change the World?, 1 vol. 2018. (PopActivism Ser.: 3). (ENG., Illus.). 160p. (YA). (gr. 8-12). pap. 14.95 (978-1-4598-1309-0(X)) Orca Bk. Pubs. USA.

Penguin Young Readers. The Little Book of Little Activists. 2017. (Illus.). 48p. (J). (gr. k-4). 10.99 (978-0-451-47854-2(1), Viking Books for Young Readers) Penguin Young Readers Group.

Pollack, Pam, et al. Who Was Susan B. Anthony? Lacey, Mike, illus. 2014. (Who Was? Ser.). (ENG.). 112p. (J). (gr. 3-7). 6.99 (978-0-448-47963-7(X), Penguin Workshop) Penguin Young Readers Group.

Rappaport, Doreen. Elizabeth Started All the Trouble. Faulkner, Matt, illus. 2016. (ENG.). 40p. (J). (gr. -1-3). 18.99 (978-0-7868-5142-3(2)) Disney Pr.

Raum, Elizabeth. The Life of Susan B. Anthony. 2019. (Sequence Change Maker Biographies Ser.). (ENG.). 32p. (J). (gr. 2-5). lib. bdg. (978-1-68151-681-3(0), 10813) Amicus.

Rich, KaeLyn. Girls Resist! A Guide to Activism, Leadership, & Starting a Revolution. Sagramola, Giulia, illus. 2018. 240p. (YA). (gr. 9). pap. 14.99 (978-1-68369-059-7(1)) Quirk Bks.

Robbins, Dean. Miss Paul & the President: The Creative Campaign for Women's Right to Vote. Zhang, Nancy, illus. 2016. 40p. (J). (gr. -1-3). 18.99 (978-1-101-93720-4(3), Knopf Bks. for Young Readers) Random Hse. Children's Bks.

Roberts, Kathryn, ed. Reproductive Rights, 1 vol. 2019. (Global Viewpoints Ser.). (ENG.). 176p. (gr. 10-12). pap. 32.70 (978-1-5345-0561-2(X), fde42a6d-3db1-42e7-bba2-0309339f197a) Greenhaven Publishing LLC.

Ross, Michael Elsohn. She Takes a Stand: 16 Fearless Activists Who Have Changed the World. (Women of Action Ser.). (ENG., Illus.). 208p. (YA). (gr. 7). 2019. pap. 14.99 (978-1-64160-045-3(4)) 2015. 19.95 (978-1-61373-026-3(8)) Chicago Review Pr., Inc.

Rossi, Ann. Created Equal (Direct Mail Edition) Women Campaign for the Right to Vote 1840 - 1920. 2005. (Crossroads America Ser.). (ENG., Illus.). 40p. (J). (gr. 5-9). 12.95 (978-0-7922-8275-4(2)) National Geographic Society.

Rust Nash, Carol. Women Winning the Right to Vote in United States History, 1 vol. 2014. (In United States History Ser.). (ENG.). 96p. (gr. 5-6). 31.61 (978-0-7660-6073-9(X), c41fe8e8-30c2-4858-8d75-2ca289309c91); (Illus.). (J). pap. 13.88 (978-0-7660-6074-6(8), 43373f11-a8ff-4369-bd0d-e71e3f3270d4) Enslow Publishing, LLC.

Sands, Crystal. Women & Feminism Today. 2019. (Women & Society Ser.). (ENG.). 80p. (J). (gr. 6-12). (978-1-68282-547-1(7)) ReferencePoint Pr., Inc.

Schmermund, Elizabeth. Do Women Have Equal Rights?, 1 vol. 2019. (Ask the Constitution Ser.). (ENG.). 48p. (gr. 5-5). pap. 12.70 (978-1-9785-0845-3(X), a4646b54-64e9-4ef3-96b9-447395aae94d) Enslow Publishing, LLC.

Schomp, Virginia. The Women's Movement, 1 vol. 2007. (American Voices From Ser.). (ENG., Illus.). 160p. (gr. 6-6). lib. bdg. 41.21 (978-0-7614-2171-9(8), 423501d2-b7a9-41e0-81d6-44c29393c44c) Cavendish Square Publishing LLC.

Sebree, Chet'la & Schomp, Virginia. Historical Sources on Women's Rights, 1 vol. 2019. (America's Story Ser.). (ENG.). 144p. (gr. 8-8). pap. 22.16 (978-1-5026-4098-7(8), 1bafb10e-fa36-4d23-b0f2-a2b36223dac6) Cavendish Square Publishing LLC.

Sherman, Jill. 25 Mujeres Que Dieron Batalla. Aparicio Publishing LLC, Aparicio Publishing, tr. 2020. (Mujeres Valientes Ser.).Tr. of 25 Women Who Fought Back. (SPA., Illus.). 64p. (J). (gr. 7-12). lib. bdg. 37.32 (978-0-7565-6537-4(5), 142067, Compass Point Bks.) Capstone.

—25 Women Who Fought Back. 2018. (Daring Women Ser.). (ENG., Illus.). 64p. (J). (gr. 7-12). lib. bdg. 35.32 (978-0-7565-5850-5(6), 138478, Compass Point Bks.) Capstone.

Singh, Rina. 111 Trees: How One Village Celebrates the Birth of Every Girl. Ferrer, Marianne, illus. 2020. (CitizenKid Ser.). (ENG.). 36p. (J). (gr. k-3). 18.99 (978-1-5253-0120-9(9)) Kids Can Pr., Ltd. CAN. Dist: Hachette Bk. Group.

Sjonger, Rebecca. Susan B. Anthony: On a Woman's Right to Vote. 2019. (Deconstructing Powerful Speeches Ser.). 48p. (J). (gr. 6-6). pap. (978-0-7787-5255-4(0)) Crabtree Publishing Co.

Spiller, Sara. Susan B. Anthony. Bane, Jeff, illus. 2019. (My Early Library: My Itty-Bitty Bio Ser.). (ENG.). 24p. (J). (gr. k-1). pap. 12.79 (978-1-5341-3923-7(0), 212521); lib. bdg. 30.64 (978-1-5341-4267-1(3), 212520) Cherry Lake Publishing.

oltman, Joan. Elizabeth Cady Stanton, 1 vol. 2018. (Little Biographies of Big People Ser.). (ENG.). 24p. (gr. 1-2). 24.27 (978-1-5382-1836-5(4), c624885d-3665-4dee-b5d7-777942743dfd) Stevens, Gareth Publishing LLLP.
eidt, Maryann N. Fighting for Equal Rights: A Story about Susan B. Anthony. Sartor, Amanda, tr. Sartor, Amanda, illus. 2004. (Creative Minds Biography Ser.). 64p. (J). 22.60 (978-1-57505-181-9(8), Carolrhoda Bks.) Lerner Publishing Group.
Women's Right to Vote. 2010. (J). (978-0-7166-1508-8(8)) World Bk., Inc.

WOMEN'S RIGHTS—FICTION

Banghart, Tracy. Grace & Fury. 2019. (Grace & Fury Ser.: 1). (ENG.). 336p. (YA). (gr. 9-17). pap. 10.99 (978-0-316-47142-8(9)) Little, Brown Bks. for Young Readers.
Deborah, Ellis. The Breadwinner. 2014. (ENG.). 176p. (J). 13.20 (978-1-63245-145-3(X)) Lectorum Pubns., Inc.
Dublin, Anne. 44 Hours or Strike!, 1 vol. 2015. (ENG., Illus.). 136p. (J). (gr. 5-9). pap. 11.95 (978-1-927583-76-0(4)) Second Story Pr. CAN. Dist: Orca Bk. Pubs. USA.
Ellis, Deborah. The Breadwinner. 2013. 164p. pap. (978-1-4596-6483-8(3)) ReadHowYouWant.com, Ltd.
—The Breadwinner (movie Tie-In Edition), 1 vol. 2017. (Breadwinner Ser.: 1). (ENG., Illus.). 160p. (J). (gr. 5-9). pap. 10.99 (978-1-77306-071-2(6)) Groundwood Bks. CAN. Dist: Publishers Group West (PGW).
Grimes, Nikki. Chasing Freedom: the Life Journeys of Harriet Tubman & Susan B. Anthony, Inspired by Historical Facts. Wood, Michele, illus. 2015. (ENG.). 56p. (J). (gr. 1-5). 21.99 (978-0-439-79338-4(6), Orchard Bks.) Scholastic, Inc.
Immel, Mary Blair. Giant Steps: Suffragettes & Soldiers. 2016. (Illus.). 227p. (J). pap. (978-0-87195-406-0(0)) Indiana Historical Society.
Mcdonald, Megan. Meet Julie 1974, 1. McAliley, Susan et al, illus. 2007. (American Girls Collection: Julie Stories Ser.). (ENG.). 104p. (J). (gr. 2-4). pap. 21.19 (978-1-59369-257-5(9)) American Girl Publishing, Inc.
Murphy, Claire Rudolf. Marching with Aunt Susan: Susan B. Anthony & the Fight for Women's Suffrage, 1 vol. Schuett, Stacey, illus. 2011. 36p. (J). (gr. 1-4). 17.99 (978-1-56145-593-5(8)) Peachtree Publishing Co. Inc.
Newbery, Linda. Polly's March. 2009. (Historical House Ser.). 192p. (YA). (gr. 5-18). pap. 5.99 (978-0-7945-2336-7(6), Usborne) EDC Publishing.
Robbins, Dean. Two Friends: Susan B. Anthony & Frederick Douglass. Qualls, Sean & Alko, Selina, illus. 2016. (ENG.). 32p. (J). (gr. -1-3). 17.99 (978-0-545-39996-8(3), Orchard Bks.) Scholastic, Inc.
Schwabach, Karen. The Hope Chest. 2010. 288p. (J). (gr. 3-7). 8.99 (978-0-375-84096-8(6), Yearling) Random Hse. Children's Bks.
Sheth, Kashmira. Keeping Corner. 2009. (ENG.). 304p. (J). (gr. 5-9). pap. 16.99 (978-0-7868-3860-8(4)) Hyperion Pr.
Watson, Renee & Hagan, Ellen. Watch Us Rise. (ENG.). 368p. (YA). 2020. pap. 11.99 (978-1-5476-0311-4(9), 900211274) 2019. 18.99 (978-1-5476-0008-3(X), 900194808) Bloomsbury Publishing USA. (Bloomsbury Young Adult).

WONDER WOMAN (FICTITIOUS CHARACTER)—FICTION

Aptekar, Devan. Darkseid's Revenge. Gordon, Eric A. & Gordon, Steven E., illus. 2012. (ENG.). 24p. (J). (gr. -1-3). pap. 3.99 (978-0-06-188533-4(9), HarperFestival) HarperCollins Pubs.
—Darkseid's Revenge. Gordon, Eric A. & Gordon, Steven E., illus. 2012. (Justice League Classic 8X8 Ser.). (J). lib. bdg. 13.55 (978-0-606-23566-2(3)) Turtleback.
Bardugo, Leigh. Wonder Woman: Warbringer. (DC Icons Ser.). (ENG.). (YA). (gr. 7). 2019. 464p. pap. 12.99 (978-0-399-54976-2(5), Ember) 2017. 384p. 18.99 (978-0-399-54973-1(0), Random Hse. Bks. for Young Readers) Random Hse. Children's Bks.
—Wonder Woman: Warbringer: Pelea Como una Guerrera (Spanish Edition) 2018. (Dc Icons Ser.: 1). (SPA.). 432p. (YA). (gr. 8-12). pap. 16.95 (978-607-31-5969-2(2), Montena) Penguin Random House Grupo Editorial ESP. Dist: Penguin Random Hse. LLC.
Carbone, Courtney. Butterfly Battle! Ørum, Pernille, illus. 2018. 29p. (J). (978-1-5444-0226-0(0)) Random Hse., Inc.
—Flower Power! (DC Super Friends) Schoening, Dan, illus. 2014. (Little Golden Book Ser.). (ENG.). 24p. (J). (-k). 4.99 (978-0-385-37396-8(1), Golden Bks.) Random Hse. Children's Bks.
—Wonder Woman to the Rescue! 2016. (Step into Reading Level 2 Ser.). lib. bdg. 14.75 (978-0-606-38476-6(6)) Turtleback.
—Wonder Woman to the Rescue! (DC Super Friends) Doescher, Erik, illus. 2016. (Step into Reading Ser.). (ENG.). 24p. (J). (gr. -1-1). 4.99 (978-1-101-93308-4(9), Random Hse. Bks. for Young Readers) Random Hse. Children's Bks.
Dahl, Michael. Be a Star, Wonder Woman! Lozano, Omar, illus. (DC Super Heroes Ser.). (ENG.). (J). (gr. -1-2). 2018. 30p. bds. 7.99 (978-1-68436-222-6(9), 138938) 2017. 32p. lib. bdg. 23.99 (978-1-5158-1402-3(5), 135195) 2017. 32p. 15.95 (978-1-62370-875-7(3), 135196) Capstone. (Stone Arch Bks.).
—Jet-Powered Justice. Lozano, Omar, illus. 2018. (Wonder Woman Tales of Paradise Island Ser.). (ENG.). 40p. (J). (gr. 4-8). lib. bdg. 24.65 (978-1-5158-3023-8(3), 138653, Stone Arch Bks.) Capstone.
—The Legendary Lasso. Lozano, Omar, illus. 2018. (Wonder Woman Tales of Paradise Island Ser.). (ENG.). 40p. (J). (gr. 4-8). lib. bdg. 24.65 (978-1-5158-3020-7(9), 138650, Stone Arch Bks.) Capstone.
—The Tiara & the Titan. Lozano, Omar, illus. 2018. (Wonder Woman Tales of Paradise Island Ser.). (ENG.). 40p. (J). (gr. 4-8). lib. bdg. 24.65 (978-1-5158-3021-4(7), 138651, Stone Arch Bks.) Capstone.
—The Unbreakable Bracelets. Lozano, Omar, illus. 2018. (Wonder Woman Tales of Paradise Island Ser.). (ENG.). 40p. (J). (gr. 4-8). lib. bdg. 24.65 (978-1-5158-3022-1(5), 138652, Stone Arch Bks.) Capstone.
—Wonder Woman Tales of Paradise Island. Lozano, Omar, illus. 2018. (Wonder Woman Tales of Paradise Island Ser.). (ENG.). 40p. (J). (gr. 4-8). 101.28 (978-1-5158-3024-5(1), 28531, Stone Arch Bks.) Capstone.
Fisch, Sholly & Kane, Bob. The Bride & the Bold. 2015. (All-New Batman: the Brave & the Bold Ser.). (ENG., Illus.). 32p. (J). (gr. 2-5). lib. bdg. 22.60 (978-1-4342-9661-0(X), 126962, Stone Arch Bks.) Capstone.
Katz, David Bar. My First Wonder Woman Book: Touch & Feel. 2011. (DC Super Heroes Ser.). (ENG.). 12p. (J). (gr. -1). bds. 11.99 (978-1-935703-13-6(7)) Downtown Bookworks.
Korté, Steve. Myth Monster Mayhem. Lozano, Omar, illus. 2019. (You Choose Stories: Wonder Woman Ser.). (ENG.). 112p. (J). (gr. 2-6). pap. 6.95 (978-1-4965-8439-7(2), 140964); lib. bdg. 32.65 (978-1-4965-8349-9(3), 140643) Capstone. (Stone Arch Bks.).
—Wonder Woman & the Heroes of Myth. Altmann, S., illus. 2017. (Wonder Woman Mythology Ser.). (ENG.). 32p. (J). (gr. 5-9). lib. bdg. 27.32 (978-1-5157-4585-3(6), 134282, Stone Arch Bks.) Capstone.
—Wonder Woman & the Monsters of Myth. Altmann, Scott, illus. 2017. (Wonder Woman Mythology Ser.). (ENG.). 32p. (J). (gr. 5-9). lib. bdg. 29.32 (978-1-5157-4583-9(X), 134279, Stone Arch Bks.) Capstone.
—Wonder Woman & the Villains of Myth. Altmann, Scott, illus. 2017. (Wonder Woman Mythology Ser.). (ENG.). 32p. (J). (gr. 5-9). lib. bdg. 27.32 (978-1-5157-4584-6(8), 134281, Stone Arch Bks.) Capstone.
—Wonder Woman & the World of Myth. Altmann, Scott, illus. 2017. (Wonder Woman Mythology Ser.). (ENG.). 32p. (J). (gr. 5-9). lib. bdg. 29.32 (978-1-5157-4582-2(1), 134280, Stone Arch Bks.) Capstone.
—Wonder Woman Mythology. Altmann, Scott, illus. 2017. (Wonder Woman Mythology Ser.). (ENG.). 32p. (J). (gr. 5-9). 117.28 (978-1-5157-4586-0(4), 25857, Stone Arch Bks.) Capstone.
Marsham, Liz. Wonder Woman: Maze of Magic. 2017. (I Can Read! Level 2 Ser.). (Illus.). 32p. (J). lib. bdg. 13.55 (978-0-606-40057-2(5)) Turtleback.
—Wonder Woman Classic: Maze of Magic. Ferguson, Lee, illus. 2017. (I Can Read Level 2 Ser.). 32p. (J). (gr. -1-3). pap. 3.99 (978-0-06-236093-9(0)) HarperCollins Pubs.
Marston, William Moulton. I Am an Amazon Warrior. Ferguson, Lee, illus. 2017. 31p. (J). (978-1-5182-4342-4(8)) Harper & Row Ltd.
Sazaklis, John. Wonder Woman: An Origin Story. Vecchio, Luciano, illus. 2015. (DC Super Heroes Origins Ser.). (ENG.). 48p. (J). (gr. k-2). lib. bdg. 23.99 (978-1-4342-9729-7(2), 127061, Stone Arch Bks.) Capstone.
Simonson, Louise. Ares' Underworld Army. Vecchio, Luciano, illus. 2018. (Wonder Woman the Amazing Amazon Ser.). (ENG.). 88p. (J). (gr. 2-7). lib. bdg. 24.65 (978-1-4965-6531-0(2), 138545, Stone Arch Bks.) Capstone.
—Giganta's Colossal Double-Cross. Vecchio, Luciano, illus. 2018. (Wonder Woman the Amazing Amazon Ser.). (ENG.). 88p. (J). (gr. 2-7). lib. bdg. 24.65 (978-1-4965-6532-7(0), 138546, Stone Arch Bks.) Capstone.
Snider, Brandon T. Cheetah Unleashed. Vecchio, Luciano, illus. 2018. (Wonder Woman the Amazing Amazon Ser.). (ENG.). 88p. (J). (gr. 2-7). lib. bdg. 24.65 (978-1-4965-6529-7(0), 138543, Stone Arch Bks.) Capstone.
—Circe's Dark Reign. Vecchio, Luciano, illus. 2018. (Wonder Woman the Amazing Amazon Ser.). (ENG.). 88p. (J). (gr. 2-7). lib. bdg. 24.65 (978-1-4965-6530-3(4), 138544, Stone Arch Bks.) Capstone.
—Wonder Woman the Amazing Amazon. Vecchio, Luciano, illus. 2018. (Wonder Woman the Amazing Amazon Ser.). (ENG.). 88p. (J). (gr. 2-7). 103.96 (978-1-4965-6545-7(2), 28454, Stone Arch Bks.) Capstone.
Steele, Michael Anthony. Movie Magic Madness. Lozano, Omar, illus. 2019. (You Choose Stories: Wonder Woman Ser.). (ENG.). 112p. (J). (gr. 2-6). pap. 6.95 (978-1-4965-8440-3(6), 140965); lib. bdg. 32.65 (978-1-4965-8350-5(7), 140644) Capstone. (Stone Arch Bks.).
Sutton, Laurie S. The Crystal Quest. Lozano, Omar, illus. 2019. (You Choose Stories: Wonder Woman Ser.). (ENG.). 112p. (J). (gr. 2-6). pap. 6.95 (978-1-4965-8441-0(4), 140966); lib. bdg. 32.65 (978-1-4965-8351-2(5), 140645) Capstone. (Stone Arch Bks.).
—The Heart of Hades. Lozano, Omar, illus. 2019. (You Choose Stories: Wonder Woman Ser.). (ENG.). 112p. (J). (gr. 2-6). pap. 6.95 (978-1-4965-8438-0(4), 140963); lib. bdg. 32.65 (978-1-4965-8348-2(5), 140642) Capstone. (Stone Arch Bks.).
—Wonder Woman vs. Circe, 1 vol. Vecchio, Luciano, illus. 2013. (DC Super Heroes Ser.). (ENG.). 56p. (J). (gr. 3-6). lib bdg. 26.65 (978-1-4342-6014-7(3), 123074, Stone Arch Bks.) Capstone.
Teitelbaum, Michael. Meet the Super Heroes. 2009. (Justice League Classic: I Can Read! Ser.). (J). lib. bdg. 13.55 (978-0-606-06941-0(0)) Turtleback.
Tillworth, Mary. Wonder Woman: an Amazing Hero! (DC Super Friends) Doescher, Erik, illus. 2017. (Big Golden Book Ser.). (ENG.). 32p. (J). (gr. -1-2). 9.99 (978-1-5247-1840-4(8), Golden Bks.) Random Hse. Children's Bks.
Yee, Lisa. Wonder Woman at Super Hero High (DC Super Hero Girls) Random House, illus. 2016. (ENG.). 240p. (J). (gr. 3-7). 13.99 (978-1-101-94059-4(X), Random Hse. Bks. for Young Readers) Random Hse. Children's Bks.

WOOD

see also Forests and Forestry; Lumber and Lumbering; Woodwork
also kinds of wood, e.g. Oak

Cardenas, Ernesto A. Wood or Paper? 2009. 23.95 (978-1-60698-059-0(9)); pap. 4.95 (978-1-60698-057-6(2)) Milo Educational Bks. & Resources.
Colich, Abby. Wood, 1 vol. 2013. (Exploring Materials Ser.). (ENG.). 24p. (J). (gr. -1-1). pap. 6.95 (978-1-4329-8028-3(9), 123183, Heinemann) Capstone.
Jennings, Terry. Wood. 2006. (Illus.). 32p. (YA). (gr. 1-18). lib. bdg. 27.10 (978-1-932333-00-8(2)) Chrysalis Education.
Langley, Andrew. Wood. 2008. (Everyday Materials Ser.). (ENG., Illus.). 24p. (J). (gr. k-3). pap. (978-0-7787-4137-4(0)) Crabtree Publishing Co.
Llewellyn, Claire. Wood. 2005. (I Know That! Ser.). (Illus.). 24p. (J). (gr. 1-3). lib. bdg. 22.80 (978-1-932889-51-2(5)) Sea-To-Sea Pubns.
Meachen Rau, Dana. Wood, 1 vol. 2012. (Use It! Reuse It! Ser.). (ENG.). 24p. (gr. 3-3). 25.50 (978-1-60870-519-1(6), b8aac278-5eab-4d2b-9b71-0c028aa8dc96) Cavendish Square Publishing LLC.
Meister, Cari. From Wood to Pencils. Pinilla, Albert, illus. 2019. (Who Made My Stuff? Ser.). (ENG.). 24p. (J). (gr. 1-3). pap. 9.99 (978-1-68152-485-6(6), 11071) Amicus.
Mitchell, Melanie S. Wood. 2003. (First Step Nonfiction - Materials Ser.). (ENG., Illus.). 24p. (gr. k-2). lib. bdg. 23.93 (978-0-8225-4618-4(3)) Lerner Publishing Group.
Morris, Neil. Wood. 2010. (Materials That Matter Ser.). (ENG.). 32p. (J). (gr. 4-6). lib. bdg. 28.50 (978-1-60753-070-1(8), 17219) Amicus.
Rae, Alison. Trees & Timber Products. 2010. (Development Without Damage Ser.). (YA). (gr. 5-9). 34.25 (978-1-59920-247-1(6)) Black Rabbit Bks.
Randolph, Joanne. Wedges in My World, 1 vol. 2006. (Journeys Ser.). (ENG.). 24p. (gr. k-2). pap. 7.05 (978-1-4042-8426-5(5), e5722743-6b08-4bcf-a8f8-bbf72ee84dae, Rosen Classroom) Rosen Publishing Group, Inc., The.
Ridley, Sarah. A Wooden Chair, 1 vol. 2005. (How It's Made Ser.). (ENG., Illus.). 32p. (gr. 2-4). lib. bdg. 28.67 (978-0-8368-6296-6(1), 8ed9a115-13b4-4372-a351-005e00de1441, Gareth Stevens Learning Library) Stevens, Gareth Publishing LLLP.
Rivera, Andrea. Wood. 2017. (Materials Ser.). (ENG., Illus.). 24p. (J). (gr. -1-2). lib. bdg. 31.36 (978-1-5321-2034-3(6), 25304, Abdo Zoom-Launch) ABDO Publishing Co.
Rooney, Anne. Infectious Diseases. 2011. (Mapping Global Issues Ser.). 48p. (J). (gr. 7-9). lib. bdg. 34.25 (978-1-59920-510-6(6)) Black Rabbit Bks.
Royston, Angela. Wood: Let's Look at a Sports Bat. 2005. (J). (978-1-4109-1819-2(X)); (ENG.). 24p. pap. (978-1-4109-1828-4(9)) Steck-Vaughn.
Shah, Nupur. In the Woods. Shah, Nupur, illus. rev. ed. 2010. (1-3Y Ecosystems Ser.). (ENG., Illus.). 12p. (J). (gr. k-1). pap. 8.00 (978-1-61541-458-1(4)) American Reading Co.
Tiner, John Hudson. Wood. 2003. (Matter & Materials Ser.). (J). (978-1-58417-160-7(X)); pap. (978-1-58417-166-9(9)) Lake Street Pubs.
Wallace, Holly. Wood. 2007. (How We Use Materials/Watts Ser.). (Illus.). 30p. (J). (gr. 4-7). lib. bdg. 28.50 (978-1-59920-007-1(4)) Black Rabbit Bks.

WOOD-CARVING

Dorling Kindersley Publishing Staff. Woodcarving. 2009. 72p. (J). (gr. 5-18). 12.99 (978-0-7566-3507-7(1)) Dorling Kindersley Publishing, Inc.
Egholm, Frank. Easy Wood Carving for Children: Fun Whittling Projects for Adventurous Kids, 36 vols. Cardwell, Anna, tr. 2018. Orig. Title: Das Große Buch Vom Schnitzen. (ENG., Illus.). 128p. pap. 14.95 (978-1-78250-515-0(6)) Floris Bks. GBR. Dist: Consortium Bk. Sales & Distribution.
Tiede, Karen. Carve Smart. 2004. 189p. (YA). pap. 19.95 (978-0-7414-2093-0(7)) Infinity Publishing.
Trudel, Robin Edward. Carving for Kids: An Introduction to Woodcarving. 2006. (ENG., Illus.). 95p. pap. 16.95 (978-1-933502-02-1(9)) Linden Publishing Co., Inc.
Waltner, Elma. Carving Animal Caricatures. 2012. (Dover Woodworking Ser.). (ENG., Illus.). 104p. (gr. 7-12). pap. 22.95 (978-0-486-22813-6(4), 228134) Dover Pubns., Inc.

WOOD-ENGRAVING

Noble, Marty. Color Your Own Japanese Woodblock Prints. 2011. (Dover Art Masterpieces to Color Ser.). (ENG., Illus.). 32p. (gr. 3-8). pap. 4.99 (978-0-486-47651-3(0), 476510) Dover Pubns., Inc.

WOOD WIND INSTRUMENTS

see Wind Instruments

WOODCHUCK

Beer, Amy-Jane. Woodchucks. 2008. (Nature's Children Ser.). (Illus.). 52p. (J). (978-0-7172-6267-0(7)) Grolier, Ltd.
Gibbons, Gail. Groundhog Day! 2007. (ENG., Illus.). 32p. (J). (gr. -1-3). pap. 8.99 (978-0-8234-2116-9(3)) Holiday Hse., Inc.
Lindeen, Mary. Groundhog Day. 2015. (Beginning-To-Read Ser.). (ENG.). 32p. (J). (gr. k-2). pap. 13.26 (978-1-60357-748-9(3)) Norwood Hse. Pr.
McNeil, Niki, et al. HOCPP 1146 Mr. Groundhog. 2007. spiral bd. 15.50 (978-1-60308-146-7(1)) In the Hands of a Child.
Meister, Cari. Groundhogs. 2015. (J). lib. bdg. 25.65 (978-1-62031-167-7(4), Bullfrog Bks.) Jump! Inc.
Peppas, Lynn. Groundhog Day. 2010. (Celebrations in My World Ser.). (ENG., Illus.). 32p. (J). (gr. k-3). (978-0-7787-4926-4(6)); pap. (978-0-7787-4933-2(9)) Crabtree Publishing Co.
Phillips, Dee. Groundhog's Burrow. (Science Slam: the Hole Truth Ser.). 24p. (J). (gr. -1-3). 2018. (ENG.). 7.99 (978-1-64280-088-3(0)) 2012. (Illus.). lib. bdg. 26.99 (978-1-61772-410-7(6), 1338903) Bearport Publishing Co., Inc.
Schuetz, Kari. Groundhogs. 2014. (Backyard Wildlife Ser.). (ENG., Illus.). 24p. (J). (gr. k-3). lib. bdg. 26.95 (978-1-62617-057-5(6), Blastoff! Readers) Bellwether Media.

WOODCHUCK—FICTION

Balian, Lorna. A Garden for a Groundhog, 1 vol. (ENG., Illus.). 32p. (J). 2011. pap. 6.95 (978-1-59572-296-6(3)) 2004. 15.95 (978-1-932065-38-1(5)) Star Bright Bks., Inc.
Bang, Molly. Goose. 2018. (ENG., Illus.). 36p. (J). 14.95 (978-1-930900-95-0(3)) Purple Hse. Pr.
Bell, Cece. Chuck & Woodchuck. Bell, Cece, illus. 2016. (ENG., Illus.). 32p. (J). (gr. -1-3). 15.99 (978-0-7636-7524-0(5)) Candlewick Pr.
Biedrzycki, David. Groundhog's Runaway Shadow. Biedrzycki, David, illus. (Illus.). 32p. (J). (gr. -1-3). 2019. pap. 8.99 (978-1-62354-112-5(3)) 2016. 17.99 (978-1-58089-734-1(7)) Charlesbridge Publishing, Inc.
Canady, Mary Monica. Why Is My Name Sam? Papeo, Maria Eugenia & Saumell, Marina, illus. 2008. 24p. pap. 24.95 (978-1-60474-028-8(0)) America Star Bks.
Clover. Groundhogs & Golfers. 2011. 24p. pap. 11.50 (978-1-4634-2909-6(6)) AuthorHouse.
Dalton, Kippy. Groundhog & the Sun. Czernichowska, Joanna, illus. 2016. (Spring Forward Ser.). (J). (gr. 1). (978-1-4900-9369-7(9)) Benchmark Education Co.
Debowski, Sharon. The Snowman, the Owl, & the Groundhog. 2007. (J). lib. bdg. 15.95 (978-1-60227-468-6(1)); (Illus.). 32p. (gr. -1-4). 14.95 (978-1-60227-470-9(3)) Above the Clouds Publishing.
Elish, Dan. The Attack of the Frozen Woodchucks. Call, Greg, illus. 2008. (ENG.). 256p. (J). (gr. 3-7). 16.99 (978-0-06-113870-6(3), Geringer, Laura Book) HarperCollins Pubs.
Freeman, Don. Gregory's Shadow. Freeman, Don, illus. 2003. (Illus.). pap. 39.95 incl. audio compact disk (978-1-59112-536-5(7)) Live Oak Media.
Graffius, Richard. The Great Groundhog Caper. 2007. pap. 9.00 (978-0-8059-8423-1(2)) Dorrance Publishing Co., Inc.
Hillert, Margaret. It's Ground Hog Day Dear Dragon. Schimmell, David, illus. 2012. (BeginningtoRead Ser.). 32p. (J). (-2). lib. bdg. 22.60 (978-1-59953-504-3(1)) Norwood Hse. Pr.
—It's Groundhog Day, Dear Dragon. David Schimmell, illus. 2012. (Beginning-To-Read Ser.). (ENG.). 32p. (J). (gr. k-2). pap. 13.26 (978-1-60357-384-9(4)) Norwood Hse. Pr.
Hondel, Gary. Pudgee Woodchuck. Hondel, Gary, illus. 2007. (Illus.). 36p. per. 14.95 (978-1-59858-323-6(9)) Dog Ear Publishing, LLC.
Jenkins, Emily. A Greyhound, a Groundhog. Appelhans, Chris, illus. 2017. 32p. (J). (gr. -1-2). 17.99 (978-0-553-49805-9(3), Schwartz & Wade Bks.) Random Hse. Children's Bks.
Johnson, Crockett. Will Spring Be Early? or Will Spring Be Late? Johnson, Crockett, illus. 2016. (ENG., Illus.). 48p. (J). (gr. -1-3). 14.99 (978-0-06-243037-3(8), HarperCollins) HarperCollins Pubs.
Korman, Susan. Groundhog at Evergreen Road. 2005. (Smithsonian's Backyard Ser.). (ENG., Illus.). 32p. (J). (gr. -1-2). 9.95 (978-1-59249-028-8(X), PB5074) Soundprints.
—Groundhog at Evergreen Road. Bond, Higgins, illus. (Smithsonian's Backyard Ser.). (ENG.). 32p. (J). (gr. -1-2). 2005. 15.95 (978-1-59249-022-6(0), B5024) 2003. 19.95 (978-1-59249-025-7(5), BC5024) 2003. 8.95 (978-1-59249-061-5(1), SC5024) 2003. 6.95 (978-1-59249-024-0(7), S5024) 2003. 4.95 (978-1-59249-023-3(9), B5074) Soundprints.
Lamm, C. Drew. Woodchuck at Blackberry Road. Davis, Allen, illus. 2011. (Smithsonian's Backyard Ser.). (ENG.). 32p. (J). (gr. -1-3). 19.95 (978-1-60727-644-9(5)) Soundprints.
Landry, Leo. What's up, Chuck? Landry, Leo, illus. 2016. (Illus.). 48p. (J). (gr. k-3). lib. bdg. 12.95 (978-1-58089-698-6(7)) Charlesbridge Publishing, Inc.
McArthur, Cathy E. The Adventures of Elvis the Groundhog: The Golden Glow. 2005. 9.00 (978-0-8059-8154-4(3)) Dorrance Publishing Co., Inc.
Mean Margaret. 2014. (ENG., Illus.). 176p. (J). (gr. 2-7). 16.99 (978-1-4814-1014-4(8), Atheneum Bks. for Young Readers) Simon & Schuster Children's Publishing.
Menear, Linda. The Little Groundhog Discovers the True Meaning of Christmas. 2011. 24p. pap. 24.95 (978-1-4626-3288-6(2)) America Star Bks.
Miller, Jean. Curious Chucky. 2013. 32p. pap. 16.00 (978-1-939615-05-3(4)) Perfect Bound Marketing.
Miller, Pat. Substitute Groundhog. Ember, Kathi, illus. 2012. (J). (978-1-61913-133-0(1)) Weigl Pubs., Inc.
—Substitute Groundhog, 1 vol. Ember, Kathi, illus. 2010. (ENG.). 32p. (J). (gr. -1-3). pap. 7.99 (978-0-8075-7644-1(1), 807576441) Whitman, Albert & Co.
Pace, Anne Marie. Groundhug Day. Denise, Christopher, illus. 2017. (ENG.). 48p. (J). (gr. -1-k). 18.99 (978-1-4847-5356-9(9)) Little, Brown Bks. for Young Readers.
Pearlman, Robb. Groundhog's Day Off. Helquist, Brett, illus. 2015. (ENG.). 40p. (J). (gr. -1-1). 16.99 (978-1-61963-289-9(6), 900131859, Bloomsbury USA Childrens) Bloomsbury Publishing USA.
Remenar, Kristen. Groundhog's Dilemma. Faulkner, Matt, illus. 2015. (ENG.). 32p. (J). (gr. -1-2). lib. bdg. 18.99 (978-1-58089-600-9(6)) Charlesbridge Publishing, Inc.
Sargent, Dave & Sargent, Pat. Greta Groundhog: I'm Special!, 20 vols., Vol. 20. Huff, Jeane, illus. 2nd rev. ed. 2003. (Animal Pride Ser.: 20). 42p. (J). pap. 10.95 (978-1-56763-798-4(1)); lib. bdg. 20.95 (978-1-56763-797-7(3)) Ozark Publishing.
Schertle, Alice. Little Blue Truck Makes a Friend: A Friendship Book for Kids. McElmurry, Jill, illus. 2022. (Little Blue Truck Ser.). (ENG.). 40p. (J). (gr. -1-3). 18.99 (978-0-358-72282-3(9), Clarion Bks.) HarperCollins Pubs.
Swallow, Pamela C. Groundhog Gets a Say. Bunkus, Denise, illus. 2007. (ENG.). 40p. (J). (gr. k-3). pap. 8.99 (978-0-14-240896-4(4), Puffin Books) Penguin Young Readers Group.
Thaler, Mike. Groundhog Day from the Black Lagoon. Lee, Jared, illus. 2016. (Black Lagoon Adventures Set 4 Ser.). (ENG.). 64p. (J). (gr. 2-6). lib. bdg. 31.36 (978-1-61479-605-3(X), 24338, Chapter Bks.) Spotlight.
Vogel, Rob & Azarov, Max. Garry the Groundhog. l.t. ed. 2005. (Illus.). 10p. (J). spiral bd. 19.95 incl. DVD (978-0-9768455-0-8(4), N/A) Vogel, Robert.
Waggoner, Tom. Danger in the Hills. 2017. (ENG., Illus.). (J). pap. 12.95 (978-1-946746-18-4(5)) ASA Publishing Corp.

WOODPECKERS

Caez, Joshua, illus. To Find an Ivory-billed Woodpecker. l.t. ed. 2005. 21p. (YA). 9.95 net. (978-0-9771752-0-8(0)) Harrison, Bobby.
Carr, Aaron. Woodpeckers. 2014. (J). (978-1-4896-2950-0(5)) Weigl Pubs., Inc.
Colby, Jennifer. Woodpeckers to Helmets. 2019. (21st Century Junior Library: Tech from Nature Ser.). (ENG.). 24p. (J). (gr. 2-5). pap. 12.79 (978-1-5341-3950-3(8), 212629); (Illus.). lib. bdg. 30.64 (978-1-5341-4294-7(0), 212628) Cherry Lake Publishing.
Elora, Grace. A Bird Watcher's Guide to Woodpeckers, 1 vol. 2017. (Backyard Bird Watchers Ser.). (ENG.). 32p. (J). (gr. 2-3). pap. 11.50 (978-1-5382-0331-6(6), f788f293-ac6e-4f31-8b2e-4e3f15276465) Stevens, Gareth Publishing LLLP.
Gish, Melissa. Woodpeckers. (Living Wild Ser.). (Illus.). 48p. (J). 2013. (ENG.). (gr. 4-7). pap. 12.00 (978-0-89812-779-9(3), 21906, Creative Paperbacks) 2012. (gr. 5-12). 23.95 (978-1-60818-172-8(3), Creative Education) Creative Co., The.
Gregory, Josh. From Woodpeckers to... Helmets. 2012. (21st Century Skills Innovation Library: Innovations from Nature Ser.). (ENG.). 32p. (gr. 4-8). pap. 14.21

WXYZ

(978-1-61080-669-5(7), 202279); (Illus.). 32.07 (978-1-61080-495-0(3), 202105) Cherry Lake Publishing.
Kalz, Jill. Woodpeckers. 2003. (Birds Ser.). (Illus.). 24p. (J). lib. bdg. 21.35 (978-1-58340-132-3(6)) Black Rabbit Bks.
Mara, Wil. Woodpeckers, 1 vol. 2014. (Backyard Safari Ser.). (ENG.). 32p. (gr. 3-3). 30.21 (978-1-62712-837-7(9), 5a9d54dd-bd31-41e6-a84e-7484984e3859) Cavendish Square Publishing LLC.
Murray, Julie. Woodpeckers. 2019. (Animal Kingdom Ser.). (ENG.). 32p. (J). (gr. 2-5). lib. bdg. 34.21 (978-1-5321-1659-9(4), 32429, Big Buddy Bks.) ABDO Publishing Co.
Phillips, Dee. Woodpecker. 2013. (Science Slam: Treed-Animal Life in the Trees Ser.). 24p. (J). (gr. -1-3). lib. bdg. 26.99 (978-1-61772-913-3(2)) Bearport Publishing Co., Inc.
Riggs, Kate. Woodpeckers. 2014. (Amazing Animals Ser.). 24p. (J). (ENG.). (gr. 1-4). pap. 8.99 (978-0-89812-931-1(1), 23068, Creative Paperbacks); (Illus.). 25.65 (978-1-60818-352-4(1), Creative Education) Creative Co., The.
Sabelko, Rebecca. Pileated Woodpeckers. 2018. (North American Animals Ser.). (ENG., Illus.). 24p. (J). (gr. k-3). lib. bdg. 26.95 (978-1-62617-799-4(6), Blastoff! Readers) Bellwether Media.
Schuetz, Kari. Woodpeckers. 2011. (Backyard Wildlife Ser.). (ENG., Illus.). 24p. (J). (gr. k-3). lib. bdg. 26.95 (978-1-60014-599-5(X), Blastoff! Readers) Bellwether Media.
Sill, Cathryn. About Woodpeckers: A Guide for Children. Sill, John, illus. 2018. (About... Ser.: 23). 48p. (J). (gr. -1-2). 16.95 (978-1-68263-004-4(8)) Peachtree Publishing Co. Inc.
Statts, Leo. Woodpeckers. 2017. (Awesome Birds Ser.). (ENG., Illus.). 24p. (J). (gr. -1-2). lib. bdg. 31.36 (978-1-5321-2062-6(1), 26745, Abdo Zoom-Launch) ABDO Publishing Co.
Waxman, Laura Hamilton. Pileated Woodpeckers: Insect-Hunting Birds. 2016. (Comparing Animal Traits Ser.). (ENG., Illus.). 32p. (J). (gr. 2-4). E-Book 39.99 (978-1-4677-9638-5(7), Lerner Pubns.) Lerner Publishing Group.

WOODS, TIGER, 1975-

Brown, Jonatha A. Tiger Woods, 1 vol. 2004. (Gente Que Hay Que Conocer (People We Should Know) Ser.). 24p. (gr. 2-4). (SPA.). pap. 9.15 (978-0-8368-4362-0(2), 1565d36b-2fdd-44d1-a2b6-cdea92ee2f73); (SPA.). lib. bdg. 24.67 (978-0-8368-4355-2(X), 84120c8c-19c4-46cb-aeba-7b181e42f291); (ENG., Illus.). pap. 9.15 (978-0-8368-4320-0(7), 7b2c36d1-ed6b-4d9f-a6b1-5f013e007c67); (ENG., Illus.). lib. bdg. 24.67 (978-0-8368-4313-2(4), 2668eccd-5bb3-4d38-a77f-1fb75a2db23c) Stevens, Gareth Publishing LLLP. (Weekly Reader Leveled Readers).
Doeden, Matt. Tiger Woods. 2005. (Sports Heroes & Legends Ser.). (ENG., Illus.). 112p. (gr. 5-12). lib. bdg. 30.60 (978-0-8225-3082-4(1)) Lerner Publishing Group.
Gallagher, Jim. Tiger Woods. 2008. (Pop Culture Ser.). (Illus.). 64p. (YA). (gr. 3-7). lib. bdg. 22.95 (978-1-4222-0211-1(9)) Mason Crest.
Glaser, Jason. Tiger Woods. (Sports Idols Ser.). 24p. (gr. 2-3). 2009. 42.50 (978-1-60853-143-1(0), PowerKids Pr.) 2007. (ENG., Illus.). (J). lib. bdg. 26.27 (978-1-4042-4179-4(5), e4fe1467-4721-41fa-b504-555a45b60164) Rosen Publishing Group, Inc., The.
Glave, Tom. Tiger Woods vs. Jack Nicklaus. 2017. (Versus Ser.). (ENG., Illus.). 32p. (J). (gr. 3-6). lib. bdg. 32.79 (978-1-5321-1359-8(5), 27657, SportsZone) ABDO Publishing Co.
Goodman, Michael E. Tiger Woods. 2003. (Ovations Ser.). (Illus.). 32p. (J). (978-1-58341-246-6(8), Creative Education) Creative Co., The.
Goodridge, Catherine. Tiger Woods. 2004. (SPA.). (J). pap. 5.00 (978-1-4108-2427-1(6), A24276) Benchmark Education Co.
—Tiger Woods & Tiger Woods (Spanish) 6 English, 6 Spanish Adaptations. 2011. (ENG & SPA.). (J). 76.00 net. (978-1-4108-5660-9(7)) Benchmark Education Co.
Hasday, Judy L. Tiger Woods. 2008. (Black Americans of Achievment Ser.). (ENG., Illus.). 112p. (gr. 6-12). pap. 11.95 (978-1-60413-327-1(9), P158538, Checkmark Bks.) Infobase Holdings, Inc.
Raatma, Lucia. Tiger Woods. 2007. (21st Century Skills Library: Life Skills Biographies Ser.). (ENG., Illus.). 48p. (gr. 4-8). lib. bdg. 34.93 (978-1-60279-076-6(0), 200048) Cherry Lake Publishing.
Riddolls, Tom & Wearing, Judy. Tiger Woods. 2009. (Remarkable People Ser.). (Illus.). 24p. (J). (gr. 4-6). pap. 8.95 (978-1-60596-623-6(1)); lib. bdg. 24.45 (978-1-60596-622-9(3)) Weigl Pubs., Inc.
Roberts, Jeremy. Tiger Woods. 2008. pap. 52.95 (978-0-8225-5238-3(8)) 2007. (Illus.). 112p. (J). (gr. 4-7). per. 7.95 (978-0-8225-8563-3(4), First Avenue Editions) Lerner Publishing Group.
Savage, Jeff. Tiger Woods. (Amazing Athletes Ser.). (Illus.). 32p. 2005. (gr. 3-4). lib. bdg. 22.60 (978-0-8225-1337-7(4)) 2007. (ENG., (gr. 2-5). per. 7.95 (978-0-8225-6890-2(X), First Avenue Editions) Lerner Publishing Group.
Tiger Woods Foundation & Woods, Earl. Start Something: You Can Make a Difference. 2006. (ENG., Illus.). 144p. (gr. 4-7). pap. 14.00 (978-1-4165-3704-5(X)) Simon & Schuster.

WOODS

see Forests and Forestry

WOODSON, CARTER GODWIN, 1875-1950

Durden, Robert F. The Life of Carter G. Woodson: Father of African-American History, 1 vol. 2014. (Legendary African Americans Ser.). (ENG.). 96p. (gr. 6-7). 31.61 (978-0-7660-6122-4(1), 6a37ced8-3884-4795-a224-ad55f9cf5476); (Illus.). (J). pap. 13.88 (978-0-7660-6123-1(X), 86dff0c7-dc36-4f2e-a43e-8fc47e6cee73) Enslow Publishing, LLC.
Hopkinson, Deborah. Carter Reads the Newspaper. Tate, Don, illus. 2019. 36p. (J). (gr. 1-4). 17.99 (978-1-56145-934-6(8)) Peachtree Publishing Co. Inc.
Mckissack, Patricia & Mckissack, Fredrick. Carter G. Woodson: Black History Pioneer, 1 vol. 2013. (Famous African Americans Ser.). (ENG.). 24p. (gr. k-2). pap. 10.35 (978-1-4644-0195-4(0), 95b9c3c7-6c85-48b9-8055-2bd45d164715); (Illus.). lib. bdg. 25.27 (978-0-7660-4109-7(3), 3ca3fb9f-df18-4e8d-aa1d-0ffff11fbaf7) Enslow Publishing, LLC. (Enslow Elementary).

WOODWORK

see also Cabinetwork; Carpentry; Furniture; Wood-Carving

Beeby, Betty. Great Granny's Sturdy Stable Picnic Tables. 2004. (Illus.). 32p. (J). (978-0-9674525-2-4(X)) Pearl Pr.
Braithwaite, Jill. From Tree to Table. 2003. (Start to Finish Ser.). (ENG., Illus.). 24p. (gr. k-3). 19.93 (978-0-8225-0947-9(4), Lerner Pubns.) Lerner Publishing Group.
Dorling Kindersley Publishing Staff. Woodworking. 2009. 72p. (J). (gr. 5-18). 12.99 (978-0-7566-3506-0(3)) Dorling Kindersley Publishing, Inc.
LaBerge, Armand J. Speed Toys for Boys: (and for Girls, Too)_. 2008. (Woodworking Classics Ser.). (ENG., Illus.). 96p. (J). (gr. 3-7). pap. 12.95 (978-1-933502-18-2(5)) Linden Publishing Co., Inc.
Larson, Margaret. Wood Shop: Handy Skills & Creative Building Projects for Kids. 2018. (ENG., Illus.). 216p. (J). (gr. 3-7). pap. 19.99 (978-1-61212-942-6(0), 622942) Storey Publishing, LLC.
Levete, Sarah. Maker Projects for Kids Who Love Woodworking. 2016. (Be a Maker! Ser.). (ENG., Illus.). 32p. (J). (gr. 5-9). (978-0-7787-2579-4(0)) Crabtree Publishing Co.
Llimós, Anna. Earth-Friendly Wood Crafts in 5 Easy Steps, 1 vol. 2013. (Earth-Friendly Crafts in 5 Easy Steps Ser.). (ENG., Illus.). 32p. (gr. 3-3). lib. bdg. 26.61 (978-0-7660-4193-6(X), 4bb0ab2e-d011-48f9-8a7f-0cf400322bac) Enslow Publishing, LLC.
—¡VAMOS a CREAR! MADERA y CORCHO. 2003. (Coleccion Ivamos a Crear!). (SPA., Illus.). 32p. (J). (gr. k-2). 12.00 (978-84-342-2344-8(9)) Parramon Ediciones S.A. ESP. Dist: Lectorum Pubns., Inc.
Llimós, Anna & Llimós, Anna. Earth-Friendly Wood Crafts in 5 Easy Steps, 1 vol. 2013. (Earth-Friendly Crafts in 5 Easy Steps Ser.). (ENG.). 32p. (gr. 3-3). pap. 10.35 (978-1-4644-0317-0(1), ed1e90f4-3b80-407e-810f-60e1cdfc8550, Enslow Elementary) Enslow Publishing, LLC.
Riley, Margaret. Awesome Woodlets: Wooden Cut-Out Projects for Every Season. 2012. (ENG., Illus.). 16p. pap. 8.99 (978-1-57421-354-6(7), DO3477, Design Originals) Fox Chapel Publishing Co., Inc.
Robertson, Barbara, et al. The Kids' Building Workshop: 15 Woodworking Projects for Kids & Parents to Build Together. 2004. (ENG., Illus.). 144p. (J). (gr. 3-7). pap. 16.95 (978-1-58017-488-6(4), 67488) Storey Publishing, LLC.
Staff, Gareth Editorial Staff. Wood & Cork, 1 vol. 2003. (Let's Create! Ser.). (ENG., Illus.). 32p. (gr. 2-4). lib. bdg. 28.67 (978-0-8368-3749-0(5), ae98e55b-e2e7-482b-8c19-6461def9f0bc, Gareth Stevens Learning Library) Stevens, Gareth Publishing LLLP.
Sullivan, Laura. The Colonial Woodworker, 1 vol. 2015. (Colonial People Ser.). (ENG.). 48p. (gr. 4-4). 34.07 (978-1-5026-0484-2(1), 386ffcf4-89db-431c-95a0-e161e8b61c6a) Cavendish Square Publishing LLC.

WOOL

see also Dyes and Dyeing

Blaxland, Wendy. Sweaters, 1 vol. 2010. (How Are They Made? Ser.). (ENG., Illus.). 32p. (J). (gr. 4-4). lib. bdg. 21.27 (978-0-7614-4756-6(3), 77807708-6bb9-41b4-892f-6620e65770e9) Cavendish Square Publishing LLC.
Gibbons, Gail. From Sheep to Sweater. Date not set. (J). (978-0-8234-1885-5(5)) Holiday Hse., Inc.
Gleason, Carrie. The Biography of Wool. 2007. (How Did That Get Here? Ser.). (ENG., Illus.). 32p. (J). (gr. 3-7). lib. bdg. (978-0-7787-2496-4(4)); (gr. 2-9). pap. (978-0-7787-2532-9(4)) Crabtree Publishing Co.
Langley, Andrew. Wool. 2008. (Everyday Materials Ser.). (ENG., Illus.). 24p. (J). (gr. k-3). pap. (978-0-7787-4138-1(9)) Crabtree Publishing Co.
Levete, Sarah. Wool. 2006. (Material Matters Ser.). (J). (978-1-59389-274-6(8)) Chrysalis Education.
Nelson, Robin. From Sheep to Sweater. 2003. (Start to Finish Ser.). (Illus.). 24p. (J). 18.60 (978-0-8225-0716-1(1), Lerner Pubns.) Lerner Publishing Group.
Weston Woods Staff, creator. Charlie Needs a Cloak. 2004. 18.95 (978-1-55592-382-2(8)); 38.75 (978-1-55592-383-9(6)) Weston Woods Studios, Inc.

WORD GAMES

Amery, Heather & Cartwright, Stephen. First One Hundred Words Sticker Book. 2004. (First Hundred Words Ser.). (ENG., Illus.). 1p. (J). pap. 8.95 (978-0-7945-0190-7(7), Usborne) EDC Publishing.
Andrews McMeel Publishing, Andrews McMeel. Go Fun! Big Book of Word Search. 2014. (Go Fun! Ser.: 4). (ENG.). 144p. (J). pap. 8.99 (978-1-4494-6487-5(4)) Andrews McMeel Publishing.
—Go Fun! Big Book of Word Search 2. 2015. (Go Fun! Ser.: 10). (ENG.). 128p. (J). pap. 8.99 (978-1-4494-7232-0(X)) Andrews McMeel Publishing.
Barbara Jordan. 2004. 12p. (gr. k-4). 2.95 (978-0-635-02616-3(3)) Gallopade International.
Berthel, Alice H. Power Puzzles: John. 2007. (J). per. 12.95 (978-1-59352-193-6(6)) Christian Services Publishing.
—Power Puzzles: Luke. 2007. (J). per. 12.95 (978-1-59352-192-9(8)) Christian Services Publishing.
—Power Puzzles: Mark. 2007. (J). per. 12.95 (978-1-59352-191-2(X)) Christian Services Publishing.
—Power Puzzles: Matthew. 2006. (J). per. 12.95 (978-1-59352-174-5(X)) Christian Services Publishing.
Beth, Georgia. World's Best (and Worst) Puns. 2018. (Laugh Your Socks Off! Ser.). (ENG., Illus.). 24p. (J). (gr. 1-4). pap. 6.99 (978-1-5415-1173-6(5), 977ce5b3-e6eb-43f6-880b-72364933d32b); 26.65 (978-1-5124-8350-5(8), 0fa76756-fd06-454b-a8d4-b447a908d348, Lerner Pubns.) Lerner Publishing Group.
Black, Howard & Parks, Sandra. Dr. Funster's Word Benders B1: Thinking & Vocabulary Fun! 2003. (Dr. Funster's Ser.). 30p. (gr. 5-6). pap. 4.99 (978-0-89455-813-9(7)) Critical Thinking Co., The.
—Dr. Funster's Word Benders C1: Thinking & Vocabulary Fun! 2003. (Dr. Funster's Ser.). 30p. (gr. 7-12). pap. 4.99 (978-0-89455-814-6(5)) Critical Thinking Co., The.
Blair, Beth L. & Ericsson, Jennifer A. The Everything Kids' Word Search Puzzle & Activity Book: Solve Clever Clues & Hunt for Hidden Words in 100 Mind-Bending Puzzles. 2008. (Everything(r) Kids Ser.). (ENG., Illus.). 144p. (gr. 4-7). pap., act. bk. ed. 9.99 (978-1-59869-545-8(2), Everything) Adams Media Corp.
Booth, Karon. Aslan Is on the Move: Romp in Narnia with Study Helps, Art & Play. 2003. (Illus.). 196p. (J). per. (978-0-941367-13-4(4)) Peach Blossom Pubns.
Carole Marsh. California Indians. 2004. (California Experienc Ser.). 36p. (gr. 3-8). pap. 7.95 (978-0-635-02254-7(0)) Gallopade International.
Chamberlain, Kim. The Five-Minute Brain Workout for Kids: 365 Amazing, Fabulous, & Fun Word Puzzles. Chamberlain, Jon, illus. 2015. (ENG.). 416p. (J). (gr. 1-1). pap. 14.99 (978-1-63450-159-0(4), Sky Pony Pr.) Skyhorse Publishing Co., Inc.
Charlip, Remy. Arm in Arm: A Collection of Connections, Endless Tales, Reiterations, & Other Echolalia. 2019. (ENG., Illus.). 40p. (J). (gr. -1-2). 19.95 (978-1-68137-373-7(4), NYR Children's Collection) New York Review of Bks., Inc., The.
Chronicle Books Staff. 75 Word Puzzles. 2005. (Genius Decks Ser.: GENI). (ENG., Illus.). (gr. 8-17). 13.95 (978-0-8118-5196-1(6)) Chronicle Bks. LLC.
Cleary, Brian P. Madam & Nun And 1001: What Is a Palindrome? Gable, Brian, illus. 2014. (Words Are CATegorical (r) Ser.). (ENG.). 32p. (J). (gr. 2-5). pap. 7.99 (978-1-4677-2628-3(1), 05e9a968-02fe-47dd-a9c8-47678052de06, Millbrook Pr.) Lerner Publishing Group.
DeNinno, Joanne & Gill, Kim. The Question Challenge Card Game Fun Sheets. 2012. 34.95 net. (978-1-60723-023-6(2)) Super Duper Pubns.
Dompierre, Judith. Read It Whichever Direction You Want. 2012. 50p. 29.95 (978-1-4626-3524-5(5)) America Star Bks.
Dompierre, Judith E. Read It Whichever Direction You Want. 2012. 38p. pap. 24.95 (978-1-4626-9324-5(5)) America Star Bks.
DynaNotes Lab Measurement & Equipment Workbook. 2007. (J). pap. (978-1-933854-72-4(3)) DynaStudy, Inc.
Frantz, Jennifer & Stern, Leonard. Animals, Animals, Animals! Mad Libs Junior: World's Greatest Word Game. 2004. (Mad Libs Junior Ser.). 48p. (J). (gr. k-3). 6.99 (978-0-8431-0951-1(3), Mad Libs) Penguin Young Readers Group.
Gardner, Martin. Mind-Boggling Word Puzzles. Myers, V. G., illus. 2010. (Dover Kids Activity Bks.). (ENG.). 96p. (J). (gr. 3-5). pap. 4.99 (978-0-486-47496-0(8), 474968) Dover Pubns., Inc.
Geatches, Hazel, ed. At the Beach. 2012. (ENG., Illus.). 32p. 11.00 (978-0-19-464628-4(9)) Oxford Univ. Pr., Inc.
—Cities. 2012. (ENG., Illus.). 40p. pap. 11.00 (978-0-19-464682-6(3)) Oxford Univ. Pr., Inc.
—Earth. 2012. (ENG., Illus.). 40p. pap., act. bk. ed. 11.00 (978-0-19-464679-6(3)) Oxford Univ. Pr., Inc.
Grimes, Nikki. Words with Wings. 2013. (ENG., Illus.). 96p. (J). (gr. 3-7). 16.99 (978-1-59078-985-8(7), Wordsong) Highlights Pr., c/o Highlights for Children, Inc.
Harpster, Steve, illus. First Word Search: Easy First Words. 2011. (First Word Search Ser.). 64p. (J). (gr. -1-1). pap. 4.95 (978-1-4027-7808-7(2)) Sterling Publishing Co., Inc.
—First Word Search: Fun First Words. 2011. (First Word Search Ser.). (ENG.). 64p. pap. 4.95 (978-1-4027-7807-0(4)) Sterling Publishing Co., Inc.
Highlights Learning, creator. Write-On Wipe-off Let's Write Words. 2018. (Highlights Write-On Wipe-off Fun to Learn Activity Bks.). 56p. (J). (-k). 12.99 (978-1-62979-923-0(8), Highlights) Highlights Pr., c/o Highlights for Children, Inc.
Hoffman, Joan. Word Search People & Places. 2004. (ENG.). 32p. (J). pap. 2.99 (978-1-58947-388-1(4), 02193) School Zone Publishing Co.
HOP, LLC. Hooked on Phonics Word Games. 2006. 64p. 3.79 (978-1-933863-93-1(5)) HOP, LLC.
Keeley, Shannon. Sight Words Puzzles & Games. 2018. (Illus.). 576p. (J). (gr. -1-3). pap. 19.95 (978-1-4114-7904-3(1), Spark Publishing Group) Sterling Publishing Co., Inc.
Kellaher, Karen. Grammar Games & Activities Kids Can't Resist! 40 Super-Cool Crosswords, Codes, Mazes & More That Teach the Essential Rules of Grammar. 2003. (ENG., Illus.). 64p. (J). pap. 10.95 (978-0-439-07756-9(7)) Scholastic, Inc.
Kurchan, Rodolfo, et al. Giant Book of Hard-to-Solve Word Puzzles/Giant Book of Hard-to-Solve Mind Puzzles: Flip Book. Sterling Publishing Company Staff, ed. (Illus.). 512p. pap. 9.98 (978-1-4027-0285-3(X)) Sterling Publishing Co., Inc.
Kurtz, John. SPARK Amazing America! Word Search. 2017. (Dover Kids Activity Books: U. S. A. Ser.). (ENG.). 64p. (J). (gr. 1-4). pap. 6.99 (978-0-486-81609-8(5), 816095) Dover Pubns., Inc.
Levin, Freddie. Outer Space Activity Book. 2009. (Dover Little Activity Bks.). (ENG.). 64p. (J). (gr. k-3). pap. 2.99 (978-0-486-47389-5(9), 473899) Dover Pubns., Inc.
Mad Libs. History of the World Mad Libs: World's Greatest Word Game. 2015. (Mad Libs Ser.). 48p. (J). (gr. 3-7). bds. 5.99 (978-0-8431-8075-6(7), Mad Libs) Penguin Young Readers Group.
—I Love Seattle Mad Libs: World's Greatest Word Game. 2015. (Mad Libs Ser.). 48p. (J). (gr. 3-7). bds. 5.99 (978-0-8431-8268-2(7), Mad Libs) Penguin Young Readers Group.
—Letters from Camp Mad Libs: Stationery to Fill Out & Send! 2006. (Mad Libs Ser.). (ENG., Illus.). 48p. (J). (gr. 3-7). 6.99 (978-0-8431-1827-8(X), Mad Libs) Penguin Young Readers Group.
—Mad Scientist Mad Libs: World's Greatest Word Game. 2014. (Mad Libs Ser.). 48p. (J). (gr. 3-7). 5.99 (978-0-8431-8057-2(9), Mad Libs) Penguin Young Readers Group.
Marsh, Carole. Abigail Adams. 2004. 12p. (gr. k-4). 2.95 (978-0-635-02372-8(5)) Gallopade International.
—Albert Einstein. 2003. 12p. (gr. k-4). 2.95 (978-0-635-02352-0(0)) Gallopade International.
—Alexander Graham Bell. 2003. 12p. (gr. k-4). 2.95 (978-0-635-02354-4(7)) Gallopade International.
—Alvar Nunez Cabeza de Vaca:Explorer & Survivor: Explorer & Survivor. 2003. 12p. (gr. k-4). 2.95 (978-0-635-02135-9(8)) Gallopade International.
—Amelia Earhart. 2003. 12p. (gr. k-4). 2.95 (978-0-635-02131-1(5)) Gallopade International.
—Andrew Jackson. 2003. 12p. (gr. k-4). 2.95 (978-0-635-02360-5(1)) Gallopade International.
—Anne Hutchinson. 2004. 12p. (gr. k-4). 2.95 (978-0-635-02370-4(9)) Gallopade International.
—Antonia C. Novello: First Female U. S. Surgeon General: First Female U. S. Surgeon General. 2003. 12p. (gr. k-4). 2.95 (978-0-635-02139-7(0)) Gallopade International.
—Ben Nighthorse Campbell. 2003. 12p. (gr. k-4). 2.95 (978-0-635-02383-4(0)) Gallopade International.
—Benjamin Banneker. 2003. 12p. (gr. k-4). 2.95 (978-0-635-02129-8(3)) Gallopade International.
—Carol Moseley Braun. 2003. 12p. (gr. k-4). 2.95 (978-0-635-02384-1(9)) Gallopade International.
—Charles Drew: Dedicated Doctor. 2004. (1000 Readers Ser.). (Illus.). 12p. (J). (gr. k-4). per. 2.95 (978-0-635-02528-9(0)) Gallopade International.
—Charles Kettering: Patent Giant. 2004. (1000 Readers Ser.). (Illus.). 14p. (J). (gr. k-4). pap. 2.95 (978-0-635-02525-8(6)) Gallopade International.
—Charles Lindbergh. 2003. 12p. (gr. k-4). 2.95 (978-0-635-02130-4(7)) Gallopade International.
—Charles W. Dryden: Tuskegee Airman. 2004. (1000 Readers Ser.). (Illus.). 12p. (J). (gr. k-4). pap. 2.95 (978-0-635-02493-0(4)) Gallopade International.
—Clara Barton. 2003. 12p. (gr. k-4). 2.95 (978-0-635-02353-7(9)) Gallopade International.
—Crazy Horse. 2003. 12p. (gr. k-4). 2.95 (978-0-635-02382-7(2)) Gallopade International.
—Dick Cheney: U. S. Vice President. 2004. (1000 Readers Ser.). (Illus.). 14p. (J). (gr. k-4). pap. 2.95 (978-0-635-02670-5(8)) Gallopade International.
—Diego Rivera: Acclaimed Mural Painter: Acclaimed Mural Painter. 2003. 12p. (gr. k-4). 2.95 (978-0-635-02137-3(4)) Gallopade International.
—Ellen Ochoa: First Hispanic American Woman in Space: First Hispanic American Woman in Space. 2003. 12p. (gr. k-4). 2.95 (978-0-635-02138-0(2)) Gallopade International.
—Father Junipero Serra: California Missions Founder: California Missions Founder. 2003. 12p. (gr. k-4). 2.95 (978-0-635-02136-6(6)) Gallopade International.
—Ferdinand Magellan, World Voyager. 2004. 12p. (gr. k-4). 2.95 (978-0-635-02373-5(3)) Gallopade International.
—Frederick Douglass. 2003. 12p. (gr. k-4). 2.95 (978-0-635-02125-0(0)) Gallopade International.
—Garrett Morgan, Innovative Inventor. 2004. 12p. (gr. k-4). 2.95 (978-0-635-02526-5(4)) Gallopade International.
—General Colin Powell. 2003. 12p. (gr. k-4). 2.95 (978-0-635-02359-9(8)) Gallopade International.
—Geronimo. 2003. 12p. (gr. k-4). 2.95 (978-0-635-02381-0(4)) Gallopade International.
—Granville Woods: Excellent Inventor. 2004. (1000 Readers Ser.). (Illus.). 14p. (J). (gr. k-4). pap. 2.95 (978-0-635-02527-2(2)) Gallopade International.
—Harriet Beecher Stowe. 2003. 12p. (gr. k-4). 2.95 (978-0-635-02356-8(3)) Gallopade International.
—John C. Fremont. 2004. 12p. (gr. k-4). 2.95 (978-0-635-02380-3(6)) Gallopade International.
—John Edwards: Vice Presidential Hopeful. 2004. (Did You Know... ? Ser.). (Illus.). 12p. (J). (gr. k-4). pap. 2.95 (978-0-635-02671-2(6)) Gallopade International.
—King George III. 2004. 12p. (gr. k-4). 2.95 (978-0-635-02364-3(4)) Gallopade International.
—Marco Polo. 2004. 12p. (gr. k-4). 2.95 (978-0-635-02376-6(8)) Gallopade International.
—Meriwether Lewis & William Clark: Explorers of the Uncharted West: Explorers of the Uncharted West. 2003. 12p. (gr. k-4). 2.95 (978-0-635-02133-5(1)) Gallopade International.
—Roberto Clemente: Baseball Hero & Humanitarian: Baseball Hero & Humanitarian. 2003. 12p. (gr. k-4). 2.95 (978-0-635-02140-3(4)) Gallopade International.
—Sacagawea: Native American Heroine: Native American Heroine. 2003. 12p. (gr. k-4). 2.95 (978-0-635-02143-4(9)) Gallopade International.
—Sequoyah. 2003. 12p. (gr. k-4). 2.95 (978-0-635-02363-6(6)) Gallopade International.
—Sitting Bull. 2003. 12p. (gr. k-4). 2.95 (978-0-635-02378-0(4)) Gallopade International.
—Theodore Roosevelt. 2004. 12p. (gr. k-4). 2.95 (978-0-635-02362-9(8)) Gallopade International.
—Thomas Paine. 2004. 12p. (gr. k-4). 2.95 (978-0-635-02369-8(5)) Gallopade International.
—William Penn. 2003. 12p. (gr. k-4). 2.95 (978-0-635-02358-2(X)) Gallopade International.
Martorana, Cherie. Made You Laugh for Kids: Wacky Word Searches. 2005. (Kids Made You Laugh Ser.). (ENG., Illus.). pap. 5.95 (978-1-57528-926-7(1)) Univ. Games.
Matheis, Mickie. Peanuts Mad Libs: World's Greatest Word Game. 2015. (Peanuts Ser.). (ENG.). 48p. (J). (gr. 3-7). pap. 4.99 (978-0-8431-8331-3(4), Mad Libs) Penguin Young Readers Group.
McCowan Nevills, Jennifer. Have You Ever? Part 2. 2008. (Illus.). 31p. (YA). pap. 17.99 (978-0-9655792-4-7(7)) Don Paul Publishing, LLC.
—Have You Ever? Part 3. 2008. (Illus.). 31p. (YA). pap. 17.99 (978-0-9655792-5-4(5)) Don Paul Publishing, LLC.
—Have You Ever? Part 4. 2008. (Illus.). 33p. (YA). pap. 17.99 (978-0-9655792-6-1(3)) Don Paul Publishing, LLC.
Nicholas, Mother Andrea, compiled by. My Little Orthodox Christian Feast Days Activity Book. 2005. (J). spiral bd. 6.95 (978-0-9773579-0-1(2)) St. Nicholas Monastery.
Nye, Mark Aaron. Scriptureabble Game Book - Bible King James Version. 2003. 88p. (YA). spiral bd. 13.95 (978-0-9746665-1-8(3)) Nye Products.
—Scriptureabble Game Book - LDS Version. 2003. 194p. (YA). spiral bd. 17.95 (978-0-9746665-0-1(5)) Nye Products.

rker, Sherri. God's Word Ages 4-10, Bk. 2. 2004. (J). spiral bd. 5.18 net. (978-1-56870-554-5(9)) Hewell Publishing.
ant, Cherie A. Word Roots A1: Learning the Building Blocks of Better Spelling & Vocabulary. 2013. (Word Roots Ser.). 72p. (gr. 5-12). pap. 15.99 (978-0-89455-804-7(8)) Critical Thinking Co., The.
-Word Roots B1: Learning the Building Blocks of Better Spelling & Vocabulary. 2012. (Word Roots Ser.). 112p. (gr. 7-12). pap. 15.99 (978-0-89455-805-4(6)) Critical Thinking Co., The.
rice, Roger & Stern, Leonard. Best of Mad Libs: World's Greatest Word Game. 2008. (Mad Libs Ser.). (ENG.). 288p. (J). (gr. 3-7). pap. 6.99 (978-0-8431-2698-3(1), Mad Libs) Penguin Young Readers Group.
-Diva Girl Mad Libs: World's Greatest Word Game. 2004. (Mad Libs Ser.). 48p. (J). (gr. 3-7). mass mkt. 5.99 (978-0-8431-0837-8(1), Mad Libs) Penguin Young Readers Group.
—Family Tree Mad Libs: World's Greatest Word Game. 2007. (Mad Libs Ser.). (Illus.). 48p. (J). (gr. 3-7). 5.99 (978-0-8431-1643-4(9), Mad Libs) Penguin Young Readers Group.
—Gobble Gobble Mad Libs: World's Greatest Word Game. 2013. (Mad Libs Ser.). 48p. (J). (gr. 3-7). 4.99 (978-0-8431-7292-8(4), Mad Libs) Penguin Young Readers Group.
—Happily Ever Mad Libs: World's Greatest Word Game. 2010. (Mad Libs Ser.). 48p. (J). (gr. 3-7). 5.99 (978-0-8431-9962-8(8), Mad Libs) Penguin Young Readers Group.
—More Best of Mad Libs: World's Greatest Word Game. 2009. (Mad Libs Ser.). 288p. (J). (gr. 3-7). 6.99 (978-0-8431-2549-8(7), Mad Libs) Penguin Young Readers Group.
—Sleepover Party Mad Libs: World's Greatest Word Game. 2008. (Mad Libs Ser.). 48p. (J). (gr. 3-7). 5.99 (978-0-8431-2699-0(X), Mad Libs) Penguin Young Readers Group.
Puzzler's Giant Book of Word Games. 2003. (YA). Vol. 10. per. 9.45 (978-1-55956-870-8(4)) Vol. 11. per. 9.45 (978-1-55956-873-9(9)) Penny Pubns., LLC. (Penny Pr.).
Puzzler's Giant Book of Word Seeks. 2003. (YA). 10. per. 9.45 (978-1-55956-871-5(2))11. per. 9.45 (978-1-55956-874-6(7)) Penny Pubns., LLC. (Penny Pr.).
Rosenthal, Amy Krouse. Wumbers. 2015. (J). lib. bdg. 18.40 (978-0-606-36988-6(0)) Turtleback.
Rubins, Diane Teitel & Daste, Larry. Nature Search-a-Words. 2005. (Dover Kids Activity Books: Nature Ser.). (ENG., Illus.). 48p. (J). (gr. 1-3). per. 4.99 (978-0-486-44291-4(8), 442918) Dover Pubns., Inc.
Sastrías, Martha. Lecto-Juego-Acertijos: Para Motivar a los Niños a Leer el Mundo Natural. 2005. (ENG., Illus.). 200p. (gr. 4-7). per. 12.99 (978-968-860-725-1(8)) Editorial Pax MEX. Dist: Independent Pubs. Group.
School Zone Publishing. Spelling Puzzles. 2003. (Language Arts Ser.). (ENG.). cd-rom 19.99 (978-1-58947-914-2(9)) School Zone Publishing Co.
—Vocabulary Puzzles. 2003. (ENG.). cd-rom 19.99 (978-1-58947-931-9(9)) School Zone Publishing Co.
—Word Search Challenges. 2006. (ENG.). 32p. (J). pap. 2.99 (978-1-58947-392-8(2), 02194) School Zone Publishing Co.
School Zone Publishing Company Staff. Three-Letter Words, 56 vols. rev. ed. 2019. (ENG.). 55p. (J). (gr. -1-1). 3.49 (978-0-88743-277-4(8), b50358b0-3e20-4da5-99f3-1f99e97baf25) School Zone Publishing Co.
Schujer, Silvia. Palabras para Jugar (Word Play) (SPA.). (J). pap. (978-950-07-0664-3(4)) Editorial Sudamericana S.A.
Schulz, Charles. The Peanuts Guide to the Seasons: A Jumbo Activity Book. Bennett, Elizabeth, illus. 2003. (Peanuts Club with Charlie Brown & Friends Ser.). 144p. (J). (978-0-439-46826-8(4)) Scholastic, Inc.
Schulz, Charles & Bennett, Elizabeth. The Peanuts Guide to Sports: A Jumbo Activity Book. 2003. (Peanuts Club with Charlie Brown & Friends Ser.). (Illus.). 144p. (J). (978-0-439-46824-4(8)) Scholastic, Inc.
Simpson, Dana. Rainy Day Unicorn Fun: A Phoebe & Her Unicorn Activity Book. 2017. (ENG.). 144p. (J). pap., act. bk. ed. 11.99 (978-1-4494-8725-6(4)) Andrews McMeel Publishing.
Skeete, D. C., creator. Hip Hop Wordsearch. 2005. (YA). pap. 3.99 (978-0-9769012-0-4(X), 0-9769012) Skeete, D.
So, Patty. So Simple Sightwords At-Home: 31 Fun Sightword Activities. 2007. 36p. (J). spiral bd. (978-0-9772158-3-6(0)) So Simple Learning.
—So Simple Sightwords at-Home Volume 1. 2007. (Illus.). 124p. (J). spiral bd. (978-0-9772158-1-2(4)) So Simple Learning.
—So Simple Sightwords at-Home Volume 2. 2007. (Illus.). 132p. (J). spiral bd. (978-0-9772158-2-9(2)) So Simple Learning.
—So Simple Sightwords at-Home Volume 3. So, Patty, illus. 2008. (Illus.). 117p. (J). spiral bd. (978-0-9772158-4-3(9)) So Simple Learning.
Steig, William. C d C ? 2008. (ENG., Illus.). 64p. (J). (gr. 1-4). pap. 10.99 (978-0-312-38012-0(7), 900050537) Square Fish.
—Cdb! Steig, William, illus. 2003. (ENG., Illus.). 48p. (J). (gr. k-3). pap. 8.99 (978-0-689-85706-5(3), Aladdin) Simon & Schuster Children's Publishing.
Stern, Leonard. School Rules! Mad Libs Junior: World's Greatest Word Game. 2004. (Mad Libs Junior Ser.). (Illus.). 48p. (J). (gr. k-3). 5.99 (978-0-8431-0853-8(3), Mad Libs) Penguin Young Readers Group.
—You've Got Mad Libs: World's Greatest Word Game. 2004. (Mad Libs Ser.). (Illus.). 48p. (J). (gr. 3-7). pap. 5.99 (978-0-8431-0855-2(X), Mad Libs) Penguin Young Readers Group.
Stern, Leonard & Price, Roger. Luck of the Mad Libs: World's Greatest Word Game. 2014. (Mad Libs Ser.). 48p. (J). (gr. 3-7). 4.99 (978-0-8431-8005-3(6), Mad Libs) Penguin Young Readers Group.
Sullivan, Alesha. Wacky Word Games to Play with Your Friends. 2018. (Jokes, Tricks, & Other Funny Stuff Ser.). (ENG., Illus.). 32p. (J). (gr. 3-9). lib. bdg. 27.32 (978-1-5435-0338-8(1), 137190, Capstone Pr.) Capstone.
Tallarico, Tony J., Jr. Eco-Logical Brain Games. 2009. (Dover Kids Activity Books: Nature Ser.). (ENG., Illus.). 48p. (J). (gr. 3-8). pap. 4.99 (978-0-486-46840-2(2), 468402) Dover Pubns., Inc.
The Puzzle Society, The Puzzle. Pocket Posh Girl Hangman 2: 100 Puzzles. 2011. (ENG.). 112p. pap. 7.99 (978-1-4494-0733-9(1)) Andrews McMeel Publishing.
The Sun & The Sun Brain Teasers, The Sun. The Sun Wordsearch Book 1: 300 Fun Puzzles from Britain's Favourite Newspaper, Bk. 1. 2015. (ENG.). 360p. 10.95 (978-0-00-812767-1(0)) HarperCollins Pubs. Ltd. GBR. Dist: Independent Pubs. Group.
Vigla, Vincent, illus. My Magnetic Word Puzzles: Let's Make Words. 2006. (Magnix Learning Fun Ser.). 12p. (J). (gr. -1-3). 9.95 (978-1-932915-19-8(2)) Sandvik Innovations, LLC.
Word Games. 2004. (Play & Learn Pads Ser.). 48p. (J). 3.99 (978-1-85997-719-4(7)) Byeway Bks.
Word Puzzles. Date not set. (Illus.). 96p. (J). 2.98 (978-0-7525-7520-9(1)) Parragon, Inc.
Words are Fun. 2004. (Play & Learn Pads Ser.). 48p. (J). 3.99 (978-1-85997-722-4(7)) Byeway Bks.
Wordsearch. 2004. (Play & Learn Pads Ser.). 48p. (J). 3.99 (978-1-85997-716-3(2)) Byeway Bks.
Wordsearch Fun. 2004. (Play & Learn Pads Ser.). 48p. (J). 3.99 (978-1-85997-723-1(5)) Byeway Bks.
Xu, Bing. Look! What Do You See? An Art Puzzle Book of American & Chinese Songs. Stadtlander, Becca, illus. 2017. 48p. (J). (gr. 2-5). 18.99 (978-0-451-47377-6(9), Viking Books for Young Readers) Penguin Young Readers Group.
Zamazing, Cherie. ComicQuest Adventure Island. 2010. (Dover Kids Activity Books: Fantasy Ser.). (ENG., Illus.). 48p. (J). (gr. 2-5). pap. 4.99 (978-0-486-47829-6(7), 478297) Dover Pubns., Inc.

WORD GAMES—FICTION

Banks, Kate. Max's Words. Kulikov, Boris, illus. 2006. (Max's Words Ser.: 1). (ENG.). 32p. (J). (gr. -1-3). 21.99 (978-0-374-39949-8(2), 900028396, Farrar, Straus & Giroux (BYR)) Farrar, Straus & Giroux.
Brown, J. Darrell. I Play with Words! 2009. 24p. pap. 14.95 (978-1-60844-050-4(8)) Dog Ear Publishing, LLC.
Handford, Martin. Where's Waldo? the Search for the Lost Things. Handford, Martin, illus. 2012. (Where's Waldo? Ser.). (ENG., Illus.). 104p. (J). (gr. 2-5). pap. 12.99 (978-0-7636-5832-8(4)) Candlewick Pr.
Lezin, Katya. Knight Swam. 2010. 138p. pap. 14.99 (978-0-557-20384-0(8)) Lulu Pr., Inc.
Lubar, David. Punished! (ENG.). 96p. (J). (gr. 2-5). 2007. per. 7.99 (978-1-58196-063-1(8), a8f270fb-e08a-4c39-ae88-1b652fca8362, Millbrook Pr.) 2006. 15.95 (978-1-58196-042-6(5), Darby Creek) Lerner Publishing Group.
Mathis, Pamela. Sound Town the Story of Words. 2010. 32p. pap. 15.99 (978-1-4389-9194-8(0)) AuthorHouse.
Parish, Peggy. Good Work, Amelia Bedelia. Sweat, Lynn, illus. 2003. (I Can Read Level 2 Ser.). (ENG.). 64p. (J). (gr. k-3). pap. 4.99 (978-0-06-051115-9(X), Greenwillow Bks.) HarperCollins Pubs.
—Good Work, Amelia Bedelia. 2003. (Amelia Bedelia: I Can Read! Ser.: 6). (J). (gr. k-3). lib. bdg. 13.55 (978-0-613-68343-2(9)) Turtleback.
Perlman, Rhea. Born to Drive. Santat, Dan, illus. 2006. (Otto Undercover Ser.). 127p. (J). (gr. 4-7). 14.99 (978-0-06-075496-9(6), Tegen, Katherine Bks) HarperCollins Pubs.
—Canyon Catastrophe. Santat, Dan, illus. 2006. (Otto Undercover Ser.). 128p. (J). (gr. 4-7). 14.99 (978-0-06-075498-3(2)) HarperCollins Pubs.
Petrey, Ashley. The Abc's Game. 2013. 36p. pap. 24.95 (978-1-62709-707-9(4)) America Star Bks.

WORD PROCESSING

Dalton, James. The Computer Classroom: Word Processing. (Illus.). (J). (gr. 5-6). pap. (978-1-876973-01-8(3)) Wizard Bks.
Gilpin, Rebecca. An Introduction to Word Processing: Using Microsoft Word 2000 or Microsoft Office 2000. 2004. (Computer Guides Ser.). (SPA., Illus.). 64p. (J). (gr. 5-18). lib. bdg. 18.95 (978-1-58086-310-0(8)) EDC Publishing.
Greek, Joseph. Writing Term Papers with Cool New Digital Tools, 1 vol. 2013. (Way Beyond PowerPoint: Making 21st Century Presentations Ser.). (ENG., Illus.). 48p. (J). (gr. 6-6). 34.41 (978-1-4777-1835-3(4), 11e05faf-7156-4e40-9a7d-36b819904331); pap. 12.75 (978-1-4777-1853-7(2), d34f6a1c-6ef5-49e7-b6b2-3c53ea31a554) Rosen Publishing Group, Inc., The. (Rosen Reference).
Howell, Sara. How to Plan, Revise, & Edit Your Text, 1 vol., 1. 2013. (Core Writing Skills Ser.). (ENG.). 24p. (J). (gr. 3-3). 26.27 (978-1-4777-2910-6(0), 402ce120-0894-4ef9-8108-b7945a10007a, PowerKids Pr.) Rosen Publishing Group, Inc., The.
—How to Use Technology to Write & Publish, 1 vol., 1. 2013. (Core Writing Skills Ser.). (ENG.). 24p. (J). (gr. 3-3). 26.27 (978-1-4777-2911-3(9), dc380e55-1b0d-40ba-b7cd-b87a223fb319, PowerKids Pr.) Rosen Publishing Group, Inc., The.
Oleck, Joan. Graphic Design & Desktop Publishing, 1 vol. 2010. (Digital & Information Literacy Ser.). (ENG.). 48p. (YA). (gr. 6-6). pap. 12.75 (978-1-4488-0593-8(7), 2782ed62-1dc7-4215-aa5b-90cb681f4648); lib. bdg. 33.47 (978-1-4358-9425-9(1), ff05d17a-450d-4466-beaf-eeba8be0cfae) Rosen Publishing Group, Inc., The. (Rosen Reference).
Ross, Allison J. Choosing a Career in Desktop Publishing. 2009. (World of Work Ser.). 64p. (gr. 5-5). 58.50 (978-1-60854-331-1(5)) Rosen Publishing Group, Inc., The.
Wanniarachchi, Ruwan. Early Childhood Computer Learning Workbook - Level 1. 2007. (ENG.). 79p. pap. 18.50 (978-0-615-17026-8(9)) Wanniarachchige, Somiruwan.
Writing Term Papers with Cool New Digital Tools. 2013. (Way Beyond PowerPoint: Making 21st Century Presentations Ser.). (Illus.). 48p. (J). (gr. 5-8). pap. 70.50 (978-1-4777-1854-4(0), Rosen Reference) Rosen Publishing Group, Inc., The.
Zocchi, Judy. Dear Principal Petunia: Word Processing. Bird, Nikolai, illus. 2005. (Click & Squeak Ser.). 32p. (J). pap. 9.95 (978-1-59646-111-6(X)) Dingles & Co.

WORDS

see Vocabulary

WORK

Here are entered works on the physical or mental exertion of individuals to produce or accomplish something. Works on the collective human activities involved in the production and distribution of goods and services are entered under Labor.

see also Labor

Ancona, George. Mis Quehaceres - My Chores. 2005. (Somos Latinos (We Are Latinos) Ser.). (SPA., Illus.). 32p. (J). (gr. 1-3). lib. bdg. 21.00 (978-0-516-25291-9(7), Children's Pr.) Scholastic Library Publishing.
Boothroyd, Jennifer. From Assembly Lines to Home Offices: How Work Has Changed. 2011. (Comparing Past & Present Ser.). pap. 7.95 (978-0-7613-7842-6(1)); pap. 45.32 (978-0-7613-8389-5(1)); (ENG., Illus.). 32p. lib. bdg. 26.60 (978-0-7613-6748-2(9)) Lerner Publishing Group.
Bullard, Lisa. Ella Earns Her Own Money. Moran, Mike, illus. 2013. (Cloverleaf Books (tm) — Money Basics Ser.). (ENG.). 24p. (J). (gr. k-2). pap. 8.99 (978-1-4677-1511-9(5), b168e408-3e49-4a15-844f-da1cd1a4830f, Millbrook Pr.) Lerner Publishing Group.
Feldmann, Roseann & Walker, Sally M. Trabajo (Work) King, Andy, photos by. 2005. (Libros de Física para Madrugadores (Early Bird Physics) Ser.). (SPA., Illus.). 48p. (J). (gr. 3-6). lib. bdg. 26.65 (978-0-8225-2984-2(X), 3d141b04-f130-4bc9-8f29-316c0a288cbe, Ediciones Lerner) Lerner Publishing Group.
Fischer, James. Earning Money: Jobs. 2010. (Junior Library of Money). 64p. (YA). (gr. 7-18). pap. 9.95 (978-1-4222-1882-2(1)); lib. bdg. 22.95 (978-1-4222-1763-4(9)) Mason Crest.
Harcourt School Publishers Staff. People & Work Big Book No. 6. 2nd ed. 2003. (Illus.). pap. 139.70 (978-0-15-337571-2(X)) Harcourt Schl. Pubs.
Harper, Reggie. Honeybees Work Together: Working As a Team, 1 vol. 2017. (Computer Science for the Real World Ser.). (ENG.). 12p. (gr. 1-2). pap. (978-1-5383-5156-7(0), c6ef6aa3-0792-402c-a3a7-f604a10b46ba, Rosen Classroom) Rosen Publishing Group, Inc., The.
Hinman, Bonnie. The Scoop on School & Work in Colonial America, 1 vol. 2012. (Life in the American Colonies Ser.). (ENG.). 32p. (J). (gr. 3-6). pap. 8.10 (978-1-4296-7986-2(7), 118318) Capstone.
La Plante, Clare. A Teen's Guide to Working. 2003. (Illus.). 60p. (J). 11.60 net. (978-0-7398-5171-5(3)) Steck-Vaughn.
Murphy, Patricia J. Earning Money. 2005. (How Economics Works). (Illus.). 48p. (J). (gr. 3-7). lib. bdg. 25.26 (978-0-8225-2149-5(0), Lerner Pubns.) Lerner Publishing Group.
Nelson, Robin. Jobs. 2004. (First Step Nonfiction — Basic Human Needs Ser.). (ENG., Illus.). 8p. (J). (gr. k-2). pap. 5.99 (978-0-8225-3929-2(2), 1e0dc3ad-f246-4c33-8f26-757a0f0575e2) Lerner Publishing Group.
—Working Then & Now. 2008. pap. 34.95 (978-0-8225-9486-4(2)) Lerner Publishing Group.
Whittaker, Helen. How Toys Slide. 2012. (Toys & Forces Ser.). 32p. (gr. 1-4). lib. bdg. 28.50 (978-1-59920-466-6(5)) Black Rabbit Bks.

WORK—FICTION

Banks, Kate. The Night Worker. Hallensleben, Georg, illus. 2007. (ENG.). 40p. (J). (gr. -1-1). 9.99 (978-0-374-40000-2(8), 900038843) Square Fish.
—Night Worker. 2014. 19.00 (978-1-63419-674-1(0)) Perfection Learning Corp.
Barkley, Brad & Hepler, Heather. Dream Factory. 2009. 272p. (YA). (gr. 7-18). 8.99 (978-0-14-241298-5(8), Speak) Penguin Young Readers Group.
Beresford, Elisabeth. The Wombles at Work. Price, Nick, illus. 2011. (ENG.). 256p. (J). (gr. 3-5). pap. (978-1-4088-0836-8(6), 30801, Bloomsbury Children's Bks.) Bloomsbury Publishing Plc.
Bilan Hochenberg, Nerissa. Mommy Works. Bilan, Edgar, illus. 2013. 24p. pap. (978-1-4602-2602-5(X)) FriesenPress.
Brunel, Aude. Let's Go to Work. Mancek, Marjan, illus. 2007. 32p. (J). (ARA & ENG.). pap. 16.95 (978-1-60195-089-5(6)); (POL & ENG.). pap. 16.95 (978-1-60195-101-4(9)) International Step by Step Assn.
Capucilli, Alyssa Satin. Katy Duck Goes to Work. 2014. (Simon & Schuster Ready-To-Read Level 1 Ser.). lib. bdg. 13.55 (978-0-606-35455-4(7)) Turtleback.
—Katy Duck Goes to Work: Ready-To-Read Level 1. Cole, Henry, illus. 2014. (Katy Duck Ser.). (ENG.). 24p. (J). (gr. -1-1). pap. 4.99 (978-1-4424-7281-5(2), Simon Spotlight) Simon Spotlight.
Carlson, Nancy. Loudmouth George Earns His Allowance. Carlson, Nancy, illus. 2007. (ENG., Illus.). 32p. (J). (gr. k-2). 15.95 (978-0-8225-6560-4(9), Carolrhoda Bks.) Lerner Publishing Group.
Clark, Eleanor. Eleanor Jo: The Farmer's Daughter. 2007. (Eleanor Ser.: Bk. 5). (Illus.). 193p. (J). 14.99 (978-0-9788726-1-8(4)) HonorNet.
Clark, Ruth. Airport Mouse Works the Nightshift. 2008. (ENG.). 32p. (J). 15.95 (978-0-9792963-3-8(1)) Hibiscus Publishing.
Cushman, Jean, et al. Little Golden Book Mommy Stories. Wilkin, Eloise & Meisel, Paul, illus. 2015. 80p. (J). (-k). 7.99 (978-0-385-39273-0(7), Golden Bks.) Random Hse. Children's Bks.
Dalrymple, Marilyn. Bartholomew's Buttons. 2006. 18p. (J). 9.73 (978-1-4116-9200-8(4)) Lulu Pr., Inc.
De Jong, Riet M. W. I. Little Freebie & All His Friends. 2011. 124p. pap. 42.75 (978-1-4269-5243-2(0)) Trafford Publishing.
DeSpain, Christine. And Please Take the Banana off Your Head. 2003. (Illus.). 34p. (J). (gr. 1-3). pap. 6.95 (978-0-9678030-1-2(2)) Caribbean Scene.
Douglas, Ryke. Tock a Tick. 2007. 32p. per. 11.95 (978-1-59800-756-5(4)) Outskirts Pr., Inc.
Floyd, Gina. Can Daddy Stay Home & Play? Scott, Judy, illus. 2011. 28p. pap. 12.99 (978-1-4567-1373-7(6)) AuthorHouse.
Gallagher, Diana G. Advice about Work & Play: Claudia Cristina Cortez Uncomplicates Your Life. Garvey, Brann, illus. 2010. (Claudia Cristina Cortez Ser.). (ENG.). 80p. (J). (gr. 4-8). pap. 6.10 (978-1-4342-2253-4(5), 103116, Stone Arch Bks.) Capstone.
Gardner, Lindsey, et al. Pan Fydd Popi a Macs yn Fawr. 2005. (WEL., Illus.). 20p. (978-1-902416-45-8(7)) Cymdeithas Lyfrau Ceredigion.
Goldman, Leslie. On the Job. 2004. 138p. (J). lib. bdg. 16.92 (978-1-4242-0674-2(X)) Fitzgerald Bks.
Goodrich, C. C. Barnabee: Goes to Work. 2009. (Illus.). 32p. pap. 13.99 (978-1-4389-8461-2(8)) AuthorHouse.
Green, Melissa J. & G., Melissa J. Mona Whine'ona: (the List) G., Ashley R., illus. 2007. 20p. per. 24.95 (978-1-4241-8451-4(7)) PublishAmerica, Inc.
Greene, Stephanie. Owen Foote, Money Man. Weston, Martha, illus. 2003. 88p. (gr. 2-4). 14.95 (978-0-7569-1559-9(7)) Perfection Learning Corp.
Heim, Robert. The Squeaking Earl. 2009. 32p. pap. 16.50 (978-1-60693-711-2(1), Strategic Bk. Publishing) Strategic Book Publishing & Rights Agency (SBPRA).
Jordan, Terry W. Carson Goes to Work with Dad. 2012. 28p. pap. 24.95 (978-1-4626-8892-0(6)) America Star Bks.
Katherine, Paterson. Lyddie. 2014. (Puffin Modern Classics Ser.). (ENG.). 192p. (J). (gr. 1-4). 11.24 (978-1-63245-222-1(7)) Lectorum Pubns., Inc.
Keilbart, L. S. One. Benson, Barbara, illus. 2007. (ENG.). 76p. (J). (gr. k-k). per. (978-1-85756-610-9(6)) Janus Publishing Co.
Kiernan, Tim. Liams Luck & Finnegans Fortune. 2009. (ENG.). 144p. pap. 10.95 (978-1-933916-48-4(6), Ferne Pr.) Nelson Publishing & Marketing.
Liwska, Renata. Red Wagon. Liwska, Renata, illus. 2013. (Illus.). 34p. (J). (gr. -1 — 1). bds. 8.99 (978-0-399-16239-8(9), Philomel Bks.) Penguin Young Readers Group.
Lovett, Darrell F. Darrell's Lake Franklin. 2007. 13.00 (978-0-8059-8807-9(6)) Dorrance Publishing Co., Inc.
Montes, Marisa. Juan Bobo Busca Trabajo: Juan Bobo Goes to Work (Spanish Edition), 1 vol. Cepeda, Joe, illus. 2006. (SPA.). 32p. (J). (gr. -1-3). pap. 7.99 (978-0-06-113681-8(6)) HarperCollins Español.
Naoshi. Ice Cream Work. Naoshi, illus. 2015. (ENG., Illus.). 40p. (J). (gr. -1-k). 14.95 (978-0-9834917-3-6(9)) Overcup Pr.
Patrick, B. Blob's Odd Jobs. Torre, Attilio, illus. 2006. (ENG.). 48p. (J). (gr. -1-3). 16.95 (978-0-9741319-3-1(8)) 4N Publishing LLC.
Pearson, Betty Jean. Learn with Ladee: A Service Dog. 2008. 30p. pap. 24.95 (978-1-4241-9507-7(1)) America Star Bks.
Petty, Colin, illus. The Three Little Pigs: A Tale about Working Hard. 2006. (J). 6.99 (978-1-59939-016-1(7)) Cornerstone Pr.
Pittar, Gill. Milly, Molly & Aunt Maude. 2004. 28p. (978-1-86972-014-8(8)) Milly Molly Bks.
Reichert, Amy. Take Your Mama to Work Today. Boiger, Alexandra, illus. 2012. (ENG.). 40p. (J). (gr. -1-8). 16.99 (978-1-4169-7095-8(9), Atheneum Bks. for Young Readers) Simon & Schuster Children's Publishing.
Reynolds, Peter H. So Few of Me. Reynolds, Peter H., illus. 2006. (ENG., Illus.). 32p. (J). (gr. k-4). 15.00 (978-0-7636-2623-5(6)) Candlewick Pr.
Roth, Carol. Here Comes the Choo Choo! Cushman, Doug, illus. 2007. (J). 7.95 (978-0-15-205582-0(7)) Harcourt Trade Pubs.
Santillo, LuAnn. Rags. Santillo, LuAnn, ed. 2003. (Half-Pint Kids Readers Ser.). (Illus.). 7p. (J). (gr. -1-1). pap. 1.00 (978-1-59256-073-8(3)) Half-Pint Kids, Inc.
—Ted's Job. Santillo, LuAnn, ed. 2003. (Half-Pint Kids Readers Ser.). (Illus.). 7p. (J). (gr. -1-1). pap. 1.00 (978-1-59256-060-8(1)) Half-Pint Kids, Inc.
Sommer, Carl. No Longer a Dilly Dally. James, Kennon, illus. 2014. (J). pap. (978-1-57537-961-6(9)) Advance Publishing, Inc.
—No Longer a Dilly Dally, 1 bk. 2003. (Another Sommer-Time Story Ser.). (Illus.). 48p. (J). 16.95 incl. audio (978-1-57537-550-2(8)) Advance Publishing, Inc.
—No Longer a Dilly Dally, 11 vols. James, Kennon, illus. 2003. (Another Sommer-Time Story Ser.). (ENG.). 48p. (J). (gr. 1-4). 16.95 incl. audio compact disk (978-1-57537-501-4(X)) Advance Publishing, Inc.
—No Longer a Dilly Dally(Nunca Mas a Troche y Moche) James, Kennon, illus. 2009. (Another Sommer-Time Story Bilingual Ser.). (SPA & ENG.). 48p. (J). lib. bdg. 16.95 (978-1-57537-162-7(6)) Advance Publishing, Inc.
—Your Job Is Easy. James, Kennon, illus. (J). 2014. pap. (978-1-57537-973-9(2)) 2003. (ENG.). 48p. (gr. -1-4). 9.95 (978-1-57537-018-7(2)) 2003. (ENG.). 48p. (J). (gr. -1-4). 16.95 incl. audio compact disk (978-1-57537-517-5(6)) 2003. (ENG.). 48p. (gr. 2-4). lib. bdg. 16.95 (978-1-57537-067-5(0)) Advance Publishing, Inc.
—Your Job Is Easy. 2003. (Another Sommer-Time Story Ser.). (Illus.). 48p. (J). (gr. 1-4). 16.95 incl. audio (978-1-57537-566-3(4)) Advance Publishing, Inc.
—Your Job Is Easy(Tu Trabajo Es Facil) James, Kennon, illus. 2009. (Another Sommer-Time Story Bilingual Ser.). (SPA & ENG.). 48p. (J). lib. bdg. 16.95 (978-1-57537-173-3(1)) Advance Publishing, Inc.
Stanek, Robert, pseud. Visit Dad & Mom at Work. 2008. (ENG., Illus.). 28p. (J). pap. 5.29 (978-1-57545-187-9(5)) RP Media.
Staunton, Ted. Morgan Makes a Deal. Slavin, Bill, illus. 2005. 60p. (J). lib. bdg. 12.00 (978-1-4242-1205-7(7)) Fitzgerald Bks.
Steers, Billy. Tractor Mac Builds a Barn. 2015. (Tractor Mac Ser.). (ENG., Illus.). 32p. (J). (gr. -1-2). 8.99 (978-0-374-30105-7(0), 900138383, Farrar, Straus & Giroux (BYR)) Farrar, Straus & Giroux.
Studio Mouse Staff. Sesame Street Bert & Ernie Work Together. rev. ed. 2008. (ENG.). 24p. 4.99 (978-1-59069-620-0(4)) Studio Mouse LLC.
Sweeney, Kathleen. Matty Monster Truck. 2008. 14p. pap. 24.95 (978-1-60672-865-9(2)) America Star Bks.
Swerling, Lisa & Lazar, Ralph. Flying Memos & Other Office Antics. 2004. (Illus.). 64p. 9.95 (978-1-84072-605-3(9)) M Q Pubns.
Tarver, Whitney B. When Mommy Went Back to Work. 2011. 20p. (gr. 1-2). pap. 13.95 (978-1-4269-6833-4(7)) Trafford Publishing.
Tucker, Krista. Disney Junior Fancy Nancy: Nancy Goes to Work. Disney Storybook Art Team, Disney Storybook, illus. 2019. (Disney Junior Fancy Nancy Ser.). (ENG.). 24p. (J).

W X Y Z

(gr. -1-3). pap. 6.99 (978-0-06-284382-1(6), HarperFestival) HarperCollins Pubs.

Wagler, Elizabeth. Sojourn in Africa. 2003. (Travels with Aunt Laura Ser.: Vol. 1). (Illus.). v, 256p. (J). (978-0-87813-607-0(X)) Christian Light Pubns., Inc.

WORKING CLASS

Here are entered works on the social class composed of persons who work for wages, generally excluding managers, professionals, and those not at the lower end of the educational and economic scale.

see also Labor

Bair, Sheila. The Bullies of Wall Street: This Is How Greed Messed up Our Economy. (ENG.). (YA). (gr. 7). 2016. 288p. pap. 12.99 (978-1-4814-0086-2(X)) 2015. (Illus.). 272p. 17.99 (978-1-4814-0085-5(1)) Simon & Schuster Bks. For Young Readers. (Simon & Schuster Bks. For Young Readers).

Barber, Nicola. Ancient Roman Jobs, 1 vol. 2010. (Ancient Communities: Roman Life Ser.). (ENG., Illus.). 32p. (J). (gr. 4-4). pap. 11.60 (978-1-61532-317-3(1), ef772b05-c222-4fcc-9411-cc42272ebd3d); lib. bdg. 30.27 (978-1-61532-307-4(4), d0ccd0fd-8bd5-4d66-b590-b7da4e773aef) Rosen Publishing Group, Inc., The. (PowerKids Pr.).

Gunderson, Jessica. The Triangle Shirtwaist Factory Fire. Miller, Phil & Barnett III, Charles, illus. 2006. (Disasters in History Ser.). (ENG.). 32p. (J). (gr. 3-9). per. 8.10 (978-0-7368-6878-5(X), 91581); pap. 48.60 (978-0-7368-6999-7(9), 5667) Capstone. (Capstone Pr.).

Michele, Tracey. People Who Work for the City. 2011. (Learn-Abouts Ser.). (Illus.). 16p. (J). pap. 7.95 (978-1-59920-640-0(4)) Black Rabbit Bks.

Skurzynski, Gloria. Sweat & Blood: A History of U. S. Labor Unions. 2008. (People's History Ser.). (ENG.). 112p. (gr. 5-12). lib. bdg. 33.26 (978-0-8225-7594-8(9)) Lerner Publishing Group.

WORKING CLASS—FICTION

Almond, David. The Tightrope Walkers. 2016. (ENG.). 336p. (YA). (gr. 9). pap. 9.99 (978-0-7636-9104-2(6)) Candlewick Pr.

Kurstedt, Rosanne. And I Thought about You. Carletta-Vietes, Lisa, illus. 2012. (J). 14.95 (978-1-937406-65-3(2)) Amplify Publishing Group.

WORKING CLASSES

see Working Class

WORKING GIRLS

see Child Labor

WORKING WOMEN

see Women—Employment

WORKINGMEN'S INSURANCE

see Social Security

WORKSHOP COUNCILS

see Management—Employee Participation

WORLD

see Earth (Planet)

WORLD ECONOMICS

see Economic Geography; Economic History; Economic Policy

WORLD, END OF THE

see end of the World

WORLD GOVERNMENT

see International Organization

WORLD HEALTH ORGANIZATION

Connolly, Sean. The World Health Organization. 2009. (Global Organizations Ser.). (ENG., Illus.). 48p. (J). (gr. 4-7). pap. (978-1-897563-39-7(6)) Saunders Bk. Co.

Marsico, Katie. The World Health Organization. 2014. (Community Connections: How Do They Help? Ser.). (ENG., Illus.). 24p. (J). (gr. 2-5). 29.21 (978-1-63188-030-8(6), 205527) Cherry Lake Publishing.

WORLD HISTORY

see also Geography; History, Ancient; History, Modern

Abraham, Henry & Pfeffer, Irwin. Enjoying Global History. rev. ed. 2005. 600p. (gr. 10-12). pap. (978-0-87720-890-7(5), R625P) AMSCO Schl. Pubns., Inc.

Adams, Simon. The Kingfisher Atlas of World History: A Pictoral Guide to the World's People & Events, 10000BCE-Present. 2016. (ENG.). 192p. (J). 24.99 (978-0-7534-7294-1(5), 900161418, Kingfisher) Roaring Brook Pr.

Adamson, Lynda G. Literature Links to World History, K-12: Resources to Enhance & Entice, 1 vol. 2010. (Children's & Young Adult Literature Reference Ser.). (ENG.). 700p. 90.00 (978-1-59158-470-4(1), 900316570, Libraries Unlimited) ABC-CLIO, LLC.

Aftermath of History, 8 vols., Set. Incl. Aftermath of the Anglo-Zulu War. Weltig, Matthew Scott. (Illus.). (gr. 9-12). 2008. lib. bdg. 38.60 (978-0-8225-7599-3(X)); Aftermath of the Chinese Nationalist Revolution. Gay, Kathlyn. (Illus.). (J). (gr. 9-12). 2008. lib. bdg. 38.60 (978-0-8225-7601-3(5)); Aftermath of the French Defeat in Vietnam. Cunningham, Mark E. & Zwier, Lawrence. (gr. 9-12). 2009. 38.60 (978-0-8225-9093-4(X)); Aftermath of the French Revolution. Arnold, James R. (gr. 9-12). 2008. lib. bdg. 38.60 (978-0-8225-7598-6(1)); Aftermath of the Mexican Revolution. Beller, Susan Provost. (gr. 9-12). 2008. lib. bdg. 38.60 (978-0-8225-7600-6(7)); Aftermath of the Russian Revolution. Gay, Kathlyn. (gr. 9-12). 2009. 38.60 (978-0-8225-9092-7(1)); Aftermath of the Sandinista Revolution. Kallen, Stuart A. (YA). (gr. 7-12). 2009. 38.60 (978-0-8225-9091-0(3)); Aftermath of the Wars Against the Barbary Pirates. January, Brendan. (gr. 9-12). 2009. 38.60 (978-0-8225-9094-1(8)); 160p. (Aftermath of History Ser.). (ENG.). 2008. Set lib. bdg. 47.26 (978-0-8225-7597-9(3), Twenty-First Century Bks.) Lerner Publishing Group.

All about My World, 12 vols. 2016. (All about My World Ser.). (ENG.). 24p. (J). (gr. k-1). lib. bdg. 145.62 (978-0-7660-8361-5(6), e1323a8a-be99-4581-9e32-8add15b3e060) Enslow Publishing, LLC.

Allen, Mark, ed. New Tales of Euterpe: The Star of India as a British Emigrant Ship. unabr. ed. 2003. (Mains'L Haul Special Publications). (Illus.). 68p. (J). pap. (978-0-944580-13-4(0)) Maritime Museum Assn. of San Diego.

Ancient World History: Patterns of Interaction. 2005. (gr. 6-12). tchr. ed. (978-0-618-37681-0(X), 2-00462) Holt McDougal.

Ancient World History: Patterns of Interaction: EEdition Plus Online. (gr. 6-12). 2005. (978-0-618-42268-5(4), 2-00681) 2003. (978-0-618-19413-1(4), 2-70055) Holt McDougal.

Ancient World History: Patterns of Interaction: EEdition Plus Online with purchase of print Pupil's Edition-1 Year. 2005. (gr. 6-12). (978-0-618-42278-4(1), 2-00683) Holt McDougal.

Anon. The Great Men & Women That Shaped Our World - a Selection of Articles from a Classic Children's Encyclopedi. 2012. 504p. pap. 32.95 (978-1-4474-6903-2(8)) Audubon Pr. & Christian Bk. Service.

Aronson, Marc & Bartoletti, Susan Campbell, eds. 1968: Today's Authors Explore a Year of Rebellion, Revolution, & Change. (ENG.). 208p. (J). (gr. 7). 2019. pap. 8.99 (978-1-5362-0887-0(6)) 2018. (Illus.). 18.99 (978-0-7636-8993-3(9)) Candlewick Pr.

Around the World In..., 10 vols., Set. 2003. (Around the World In... Ser.). (ENG.). (gr. 6-6). 184.65 (978-0-7614-1083-6(X), d894e6cc-b5af-4b0b-9c5b-a3db1d453782, Cavendish Square) Cavendish Square Publishing LLC.

Atlas de los Animales. (Coleccion Atlas del Saber). (SPA., Illus.). (YA). (gr. 4-18). 20.95 (978-950-11-0886-6(4), SGM64) Sigmar ARG. Dist: Continental Bk. Co., Inc.

Bauer, Susan Wise. Ancient Times Vol. 1: From the Earliest Nomads to the Last Roman Emperor. 2003. (Story of the World: Vol. 1). (ENG., Illus.). 1p. (J). 21.95 (978-0-9714129-6-5(0)) Well-Trained Mind Pr.

—The Story of the World: History for the Classical Child, Volume 4 Vol. 4: The Modern Age — from Victoria's Empire to the End of the USSR (Tests & Answer Key) 2007. (Story of the World Ser.: 0). (ENG., Illus.). 176p. per. 14.95 (978-1-933339-02-3(0), 333902) Well-Trained Mind Pr.

Bauer, Susan Wise & Johnson, Barbara Allen. The Story of the World: History for the Classical Child. unabr. ed. 2005. (ENG.). 1p. 55.95 (978-0-9742391-2-5(7)) Open Texture.

Beck, Roger B. Modern World History: Patterns of Interaction: Pupil's Edition. I.t. ed. 2005. (YA). (gr. 9-12). 83.76 (978-0-618-37711-4(5), 2-00492) Holt McDougal.

Beck, Roger B., et al. Modern World History: Patterns of Interaction. 2006. (Illus.). 716p. (gr. 6-12). (978-0-618-10820-6(3), 2-81212) Holt McDougal.

—World History: Patterns of Interaction. 2006. (Illus.). 1082p. (gr. 6-12). (978-0-395-87274-1(X), 2-80400) Holt McDougal.

Benchmark Education Co., LLC. Becoming a World Power: 1890-1918. 2014. (PRIME Ser.). (J). (gr. 6-8). pap. (978-1-4509-9497-2(0)) Benchmark Education Co.

Benchmark Education Company, LLC Staff, compiled by. Eve Bunting's World of Stories & Citizenship. 2005. spiral bd. 225.00 (978-1-4108-5807-8(3)) Benchmark Education Co.

—20th Century History: Theme Set. 2006. (J). 183.00 (978-1-4108-7144-2(4)) Benchmark Education Co.

Berlatsky, Noah, ed. Stalin's Great Purge, 1 vol. 2012. (Perspectives on Modern World History Ser.). (ENG., Illus.). 200p. (gr. 10-12). lib. bdg. 49.43 (978-0-7377-6371-3(X), 83452ca5-c80b-41f6-b1b3-4427ec08a0c2, Greenhaven Publishing) Greenhaven Publishing LLC.

Berndl, Klaus & Hattstein, Markus. The Contemporary World: From 1945 to the 21st Century, 1 vol. 2012. (Witness to History: a Visual Chronicle of the World Ser.). (ENG., Illus.). 144p. (J). (gr. 7-7). 51.80 (978-1-4488-7225-1(1), 6689e371-a3af-4288-a326-f94740872739) Rosen Publishing Group, Inc., The.

Billings. History of Our World 2003. 2003. (Steck-Vaughn History of Our World Ser.). (ENG., Illus.). 592p. (gr. 6-12). 72.15 (978-0-7398-6087-8(9)) Houghton Mifflin Harcourt Publishing Co.

Bingham, Jane. Encyclopedia of World History: Prehistoric, Ancient, Medieval, Last 500 Years. 2004. (World History Ser.). (Illus.). 415p. (J). pap. 19.99 (978-0-7945-0332-1(2), Usborne) EDC Publishing.

Bingham, Jane, et al. Encyclopedia of World History: Prehistoric, Ancient, Medieval, Last 500 Years. 2004. (World History Ser.). (Illus.). 415p. (J). (gr. 3-18). lib. bdg. 47.95 (978-1-58086-336-0(1)) EDC Publishing.

—The Usborne Internet-Linked Encyclopedia of World History: Prehistoric, Ancient, Medieval, Last 500 Years. 2004. (World History Ser.). (ENG., Illus.). 1p. (J). (gr. 3-18). 39.95 (978-0-7460-4168-0(3)) EDC Publishing.

Biography from Ancient Civilizations: Legends, Folklore, & Stories of Ancient Worlds, 20 vols., Set. Incl. Life & Times of Alexander the Great. Bankston, John. (gr. 4-8). 2005. lib. bdg. 29.95 (978-1-58415-283-5(4)); Life & Times of Archimedes. Zannos, Susan. (gr. 4-8). 2004. lib. bdg. 29.95 (978-1-58415-242-2(7)); Life & Times of Augustus Caesar. Whiting, Jim. (gr. -1-7). 2005. lib. bdg. 29.95 (978-1-58415-336-8(9)); Life & Times of Buddha. Gedney, Mona K. (gr. -1-7). 2005. lib. bdg. 29.95 (978-1-58415-342-9(3)); Life & Times of Catherine the Great. Gibson, Karen Bush. (gr. 4-7). 2005. lib. bdg. 29.95 (978-1-58415-347-4(4)); Life & Times of Charlemagne. Whiting, Jim. (gr. 4-8). 2005. lib. bdg. 29.95 (978-1-58415-346-7(6)); Life & Times of Cleopatra. Adams, Michelle Medlock. (gr. 4-8). 2005. lib. bdg. 29.95 (978-1-58415-335-1(0)); Life & Times of Confucius. Tracy, Kathleen. (gr. 4-8). 2004. lib. bdg. 29.95 (978-1-58415-246-0(X)); Life & Times of Constantine. Tracy, Kathleen. (gr. 4-8). 2005. lib. bdg. 29.95 (978-1-58415-343-6(1)); Life & Times of Genghis Khan. Whiting, Jim. (gr. 4-8). 2005. lib. bdg. 29.95 (978-1-58415-348-1(2)); Life & Times of Hammurabi. Bryant, Tamera. (gr. -1-7). 2005. lib. bdg. 29.95 (978-1-58415-338-2(5), 1244807); Life & Times of Homer. Tracy, Kathleen. (gr. 4-8). 2004. lib. bdg. 29.95 (978-1-58415-260-6(5)); Life & Times of Joan of Arc. Whiting, Jim. (gr. 4-8). 2005. lib. bdg. 29.95 (978-1-58415-345-0(8)); Life & Times of Julius Caesar. Whiting, Jim. (gr. -1-7). 2005. lib. bdg. 29.95 (978-1-58415-337-5(7)); Life & Times of Marco Polo. Zannos, Susan. (gr. 4-8). 2004. lib. bdg. 29.95 (978-1-58415-264-4(8)); Life & Times of Moses. Whiting, Jim. (gr. -1-7). 2005. lib. bdg. 29.95 (978-1-58415-340-5(7)); Life & Times of Nero. Whiting, Jim. (gr. 5-8). 2005. lib. bdg. 29.95 (978-1-58415-349-8(0)); Life & Times of Pericles. Whiting, Jim. (gr. -1-7). 2005. lib. bdg. 29.95 (978-1-58415-339-9(3)); Life & Times of Rameses the Great. Whiting, Jim. (gr. 5-8). 2005. lib. bdg. 29.95 (978-1-58415-341-2(5)); Life & Times of Socrates. Zannos, Susan. (gr. 4-8). 2004. lib. bdg. 29.95 (978-1-58415-282-8(6)); (Illus.). 48p. (J). 2005. lib. bdg. (978-1-58415-407-5(1)) Mitchell Lane Pubs.

Boardworks Learning Centers: Where in the World? 2006. (J). bds. (978-0-9755252-6-5(3)) Evergreen Pr. of Brainerd, LLC.

Body, Robert J. Bob. I Survived the Bataan Death March. 2003. 2003p. per. 14.95 net. (978-1-931934-21-3(5)) Back Yard Pub.

Brasier, Michael. The World Through A Child's Eyes: A View of Various Countries & Global Cultures from a Child's Perspective. 2005. 110p. (J). per. 29.95 (978-0-9772591-0-6(2)) Around The World Pubns., LLC.

Brookes, Olivia. Uncover History, 1 vol. Kent, Peter, illus. 2009. (Hide-And-Seek Visual Adventures Ser.). (ENG.). 24p. (J). (gr. 2-2). lib. bdg. 27.27 (978-1-60754-653-5(1), 95b8ab39-24d3-48fb-b12d-7e1139c7df0b, Windmill Bks.) Rosen Publishing Group, Inc., The.

Burns Knight, Margy. Talking Walls: Discover Your World, 1 vol. Sibley O'Brien, Anne, illus. 2014. (ENG.). 64p. (J). (gr. 2-7). 18.95 (978-0-88448-356-4(8), 884356) Tilbury Hse. Pubs.

Capstone Classroom & Stead, Tony. Where Does Your Time Machine Go? 2017. (What's the Point? Reading & Writing Expository Text Ser.). (ENG., Illus.). 32p. (J). (gr. 5-5). pap. 7.95 (978-1-4966-0732-4(5), 132367, Capstone Classroom) Capstone.

Capstone Press. Disgusting History. 2010. (Disgusting History Ser.). (ENG.). 32p. lib. bdg. 155.94 (978-1-4296-5932-1(7), Capstone Pr.) Capstone.

—Unusual Histories. 2010. (Unusual Histories Ser.). (ENG.). 32p. lib. bdg. 122.60 (978-1-4296-5899-7(1)) Capstone.

Carnagie, Julie. U-X-L World Eras, 10 vols. 2016. (U-X-L World Eras Ser.). (ENG., Illus.). 2400p. (gr. 5-8). 995.00 (978-1-57302-967-4(X)) Cengage Gale.

Celebrate! Set 8 Volumes - China, France, Germany, India, Italy, Japan, Mexico, United States. 2009. (Celebrate! (Chelsea Clubhouse) Ser.). (ENG.). (gr. 4-6). 224.00 (978-1-60413-600-5(6), P169972, Chelsea Clubhse.) Infobase Holdings, Inc.

Chandler, F. First Encyclopedia of History. 2004. (First Encyclopedias Ser.). (Illus.). 64p. (J). lib. bdg. 17.99 (978-1-58086-518-0(6)) EDC Publishing.

Chandler, Fiona. Ancient world - internet Linked. McCaffrey, Susie, illus. rev. ed. 2004. 96p. (J). pap. 14.95 (978-0-7945-0816-6(2), Usborne) EDC Publishing.

—Encyclopedia of World History. rev. ed. 2011. (World History Ser.). 416p. (J). ring bd. 39.99 (978-0-7945-2688-7(8), Usborne) EDC Publishing.

Chin-Lee, Cynthia. Akira to Zoltan: Twenty-Six Men Who Changed the World. Halsey, Megan & Addy, Sean, illus. 2008. 32p. (J). (gr. 3-7). pap. 7.95 (978-1-57091-580-2(6)) Charlesbridge Publishing, Inc.

Chinese Kites: Level A, 6 vols. 8p. 20.95 (978-0-322-00627-0(9)) Wright Group/McGraw-Hill.

Chisholm, Jane. Timelines of World History. 2004. (World History Ser.). (Illus.). (J). 128p. 7.95 (978-0-7945-0358-1(6), Usborne); (ENG., 1p. (gr. 3-18). 19.95 (978-0-7460-4103-1(9)); 128p. (gr. 3-18). lib. bdg. 27.95 (978-1-58086-329-2(9)) EDC Publishing.

Clarke, Evelyn. Crisis. 2007. (Steck-Vaughn BOLDPRINT Anthologies Ser.). (ENG., Illus.). 48p. (gr. 9-12). pap. 16.90 (978-1-4190-4034-4(0)) Houghton Mifflin Harcourt Publishing Co.

Class, Michael S. Anthony & the Magic Picture Frame: The Story of the Boy Who Traveled into the Past by Stepping into the Picture Frame on His Bedroom Wall & Returned to See His Own Time in A New Light. 2005. (Illus.). 225p. (YA). (gr. 6-12). 35.00 (978-0-9749269-0-2(6)) Magic Picture Frame Studio, LLC.

Cole, Sonja. Booktalking Around the World: Great Global Reads for Ages 9-14. 2010. (ENG.). 178p. E-Book 50.00 (978-1-59884-614-0(0), A3138E, Libraries Unlimited) ABC-CLIO, LLC.

Countries of the World Set 2, 15 vols. 2013. (Countries of the World Set 2 Ser.: 16). (ENG.). 144p. (YA). (gr. 6-12). lib. bdg. 641.85 (978-1-61783-624-4(9), 4872, Essential Library) ABDO Publishing Co.

Cribb, John T. E., Jr., et al. The Human Odyssey, 2 vols. 2004. (Illus.). (978-1-931728-53-9(4)); (978-1-931728-56-0(9)); (978-1-60153-018-9(8)) K12.

Cultures of the World Group 11, 12 vols., Set. 2nd ed. Incl. Afghanistan. Enayat Ali, Sharifah. lib. bdg. 49.79 (978-0-7614-2064-4(9), 129d1203-dc94-4876-992b-8e433d02fe7b); Belgium. Pateman, Robert & Elliott, Mark. lib. bdg. 49.79 (978-0-7614-2059-0(2), 0727f0e7-726e-4079-ba8d-a0c3b559a499); Bolivia. Pateman, Robert & Cramer, Marcus. lib. bdg. 49.79 (978-0-7614-2066-8(5), 6d842c98-642e-47a4-8cc2-ef9dd3f8131e); Norway. Kagda, Sakina & Cooke, Barbara. lib. bdg. 49.79 (978-0-7614-2067-5(3), 83c806b9-8a5a-444a-a789-31a3f4ec077c); Peru. Falconer, Kieran & Quek, Lynette. lib. bdg. 49.79 (978-0-7614-2068-2(1), 13434fe9-7cfe-45ec-9de2-834ec5e9804f); Taiwan. Moiz, Azra & Wu, Janice. lib. bdg. 49.79 (978-0-7614-2069-9(X), e2b6e016-acdc-4d9d-9580-d24874bb9c96); (Illus.). 144p. (gr. 5-5). (Cultures of the World (Second Edition)(r) Ser.). (ENG.). 2007. Set lib. bdg. 298.74 (978-0-7614-2057-6(6), 5de08dd2-e45d-422c-b470-60a3aba364e2, Cavendish Square) Cavendish Square Publishing LLC.

Cultures of the World Group 12, 12 vols., Set. 2nd rev. ed. Incl. Cambodia. Sheehan, Sean & Cooke, Barbara. lib. bdg. 49.79 (978-0-7614-2071-2(1), 7ba35484-2dec-4d68-ba50-3c19b4e3f47d); Ethiopia. Gish, Steven. lib. bdg. 49.79 (978-0-7614-2025-5(8), b7d9fbbb-ffc7-41ca-a2ca-347a37982056); Finland. Tan, Chung Lee. lib. bdg. 49.79 (978-0-7614-2073-6(8), d9eb692c-cea6-4e83-b312-21ad748c50e2); Iceland. Wilcox, Jonathan & Latif, Zawiah Abdul. lib. bdg. 49.79 (978-0-7614-2074-3(6), 076819e3-d615-4a18-b2f6-5fc2d1b76ec0); Panama. Hassig, Susan M. & Quek, Lynette. lib. bdg. 49.79 (978-0-7614-2028-6(2), ba52c295-3c5e-4f11-849f-68a1ffe4430a); Tibet. Levy, Patricia & Bosco, Don. lib. bdg. 49.79 (978-0-7614-2076-7(2), 51f93797-12fa-4845-acc7-43f8e465ee0a); (Illus.). 144p. (gr. 5-5). (Cultures of the World (Second Edition)(r) Ser.). (ENG. 2007. Set lib. bdg. 298.74 (978-0-7614-2070-5(3), 37a95fd8-fa4d-43e3-8f59-5e28c7d8fba6, Cavendish Square) Cavendish Square Publishing LLC.

Cultures of the World Group 25, 12 vols., Set. Incl. Benin. Kneib, Martha. lib. bdg. 49.79 (978-0-7614-2328-7(1), 7abe4d4a-7a39-4b74-b750-211ad5343868); Botswana. LeVert, Suzanne. lib. bdg. 49.79 (978-0-7614-2330-0(3), 104473a2-6675-476e-92a6-c682771a817b); Chad. Kneib, Martha. lib. bdg. 49.79 (978-0-7614-2327-0(3), fc8333b0-994c-4c95-92be-078377156245); Mozambique. King, David C. lib. bdg. 49.79 (978-0-7614-2331-7(1), 6b9aa739-973e-4d2c-9080-fdc0b7e32977); Rwanda. King, David C. lib. bdg. 49.79 (978-0-7614-2333-1(8), 7ec6212e-9ba8-4fd8-852f-66244b51265c); Sierra Leone. LeVert, Suzanne. lib. bdg. 49.79 (978-0-7614-2334-8(6), 1dd7a85e-482a-4f1c-867e-77daa1383351); (Illus.). 144p. (gr. 5-5). (Cultures of the World (First Edition)(r) Ser.). (ENG.). 2007. Set lib. bdg. 298.74 (978-0-7614-2326-3(5), a7c735b5-862b-4f46-bb81-5c6d55f8b2ee, Cavendish Square) Cavendish Square Publishing LLC.

Dalby, Elizabeth. World History Sticker Atlas. Larkum, Adam, illus. 2006. (Sticker Atlases Ser.). 24p. (J). (gr. 1-4). pap. 8.99 (978-0-7945-1244-6(5), Usborne) EDC Publishing.

Dawson, Ian. SHP History Year 7 Student Book. 2006. (ENG., Illus.). 228p. (YA). pap., stu. ed. (978-0-340-90733-7(9)) Hodder & Stoughton.

Dawson, Ian, et al. SHP History Elearning Activities. 2006. (ENG.). (YA). cd-rom (978-0-340-90735-1(5)) Hodder & Stoughton.

DBQ Practice: World History. 2003. spiral bd. 19.95 (978-1-56004-145-0(5)) Social Studies Schl. Service.

Deary, Terry. Blood-Curdling Box, 20 vols. Brown, Martin, illus. 2008. 2880p. pap. (978-1-4071-0815-5(8), Scholastic) Scholastic, Inc.

Decades of the 20th & 21st Centuries, 22 vols. 2015. (Decades of the 20th & 21st Centuries Ser.). (ENG.). 96p. (J). (gr. 7-7). lib. bdg. 398.97 (978-0-7660-6693-9(2), 5b504d34-75bf-43c6-860c-14903758b242) Enslow Publishing, LLC.

Dickmann, Nancy & Throp, Claire. Deadly History. 2017. (Deadly History Ser.). (ENG.). 48p. (J). (gr. 3-6). 143.96 (978-1-4846-4186-6(8), 27044, Heinemann) Capstone.

Discovering Cultures - Group 5, 12 vols., Set. 2006. (Discovering Cultures Ser.). (ENG.). (J). (gr. 4-4). 187.26 (978-0-7614-1790-3(7), 082c7e68-8501-44a8-a451-5c32a623cd5e, Cavendish Square) Cavendish Square Publishing LLC.

Discovering Cultures Group 6, 12 vols., Set. Incl. Austria. Grahame, Deborah A. lib. bdg. 31.21 (978-0-7614-1984-6(5), de63d051-8675-42ea-888d-637a3af45d0d); Chile. Meachen Rau, Dana. lib. bdg. 31.21 (978-0-7614-1988-4(8), 3932aacc-0dfb-45c6-b9fc-83901b4945c6); Haiti. Mara, Wil. lib. bdg. 31.21 (978-0-7614-1987-7(X), 92e81c51-d220-4181-ad40-40b2aa736c13); Iran. Mara, Wil. lib. bdg. 31.21 (978-0-7614-1986-0(1), 54d2e6eb-ff6f-4706-a2fc-fe6c86518ec0); Sweden. Grahame, Deborah. lib. bdg. 31.21 (978-0-7614-1985-3(3), 44b1f1a0-b948-4bb4-976a-0f5dc6b887ec); Thailand. Meachen Rau, Dana. lib. bdg. 31.21 (978-0-7614-1989-1(6), cae376d1-2a07-4372-a85f-dc412c842884); (Illus.). 48p. (gr. 3-4). (Discovering Cultures Ser.). (ENG.). 2007. Set lib. bdg. 187.26 (978-0-7614-1983-9(7), 523dd2c2-ee0b-4bea-b684-756f10049937, Cavendish Square) Cavendish Square Publishing LLC.

Disgusting History. 2010. (Disgusting History Ser.). (ENG.). 32p. (gr. 3-4). (J). pap., pap., pap. 32.40 (978-1-4296-6355-7(3), 171190); lib. bdg. 55.98 (978-1-4296-5407-4(4)); lib. bdg. 83.97 (978-1-4296-5408-1(2)); lib. bdg. 83.97 (978-1-4296-4735-9(3)) Capstone. (Capstone Pr.).

Disgusting History Classroom Collection. 2010. (Disgusting History Ser.). (ENG.). 32p. (J). (gr. 3-4). 198.40 (978-1-4296-6481-3(9), 171230, Capstone Pr.) Capstone.

Diwrnod i'r Brenin: Chwaraeon, Hamdden a Thwristiaeth Er 1900. 2005. (978-1-902346-01-4(7)) Addysg Y Cyfryngau Cymru.

Documenting History, 8 vols., Set. Incl. Documenting Slavery & Civil Rights. Steele, Philip. lib. bdg. 34.47 (978-1-4358-9671-0(8), de590d5b-def7-4fb6-b704-1413dd3454bb); Documenting the Industrial Revolution. Hicks, Peter. lib. bdg. 34.47 (978-1-4358-9670-3(X), 14e523cb-06fc-4506-9179-f47b8febe350); Documenting Women's Suffrage. Hicks, Peter. lib. bdg. 34.47 (978-1-4358-9672-7(6), 64e2f741-0196-4463-9572-81ba734a002c); Documenting World War I. Steele, Philip. lib. bdg. 34.47 (978-1-4358-9673-4(4), da32ef22-9691-4291-a4bd-371917b0ab2c); (YA). (gr. 7-7). 2010. (Documenting History Ser.). (ENG., Illus.). 48p. 2009. Set lib. bdg. 137.88 (978-1-4358-9705-2(6), 1d2277fe-a203-499b-94c6-35274e29cf9b, Rosen Reference) Rosen Publishing Group, Inc., The.

Drimmer, Stephanie Warren. The Book of Heroines: Tales of History's Gutsiest Gals. 2016. (Illus.). 176p. (J). (gr. 3-7). 14.99 (978-1-4263-2557-1(6), National Geographic Kids) Disney Publishing Worldwide.

Dupré, Judith. De las pirámides a los Rascacielos. 2011. (SPA.). 32p. (J). pap. 49.00 net. (978-1-4108-2338-0(5), A23385) Benchmark Education Co.

Eaton, Gale. A History of Civilization in 50 Disasters, 1 vol. Hoose, Phillip, ed. 2015. (History In 50 Ser.: 0). (ENG., Illus.). (YA). (gr. 6-12). 224p. 24.95 (978-0-88448-383-0(5), 884383); 240p. pap. 16.95 (978-0-88448-489-9(0), 884489) Tilbury Hse. Pubs.

Editors of Kingfisher. The Kingfisher History Encyclopedia. 3rd ed. 2012. (Kingfisher Encyclopedias Ser.). (ENG., Illus.). 496p. (J). (gr. 4-9). 34.99 (978-0-7534-6875-3(1), 900085068, Kingfisher) Roaring Brook Pr.

Enchantment of the World & Trade 2013, Set. 2013. (Enchantment of the World™, Second Ser.). (J). 240.00

(978-0-531-26700-4(8), Children's Pr.) Scholastic Library Publishing.
Enchantment of the World, Second Series, 6 vols., Set. Incl. Enchantment of the World: Afghanistan. Willis, Terri. 39.00 (978-0-531-18483-7(8)); Enchantment of the World: Iran. Milivojevic, JoAnn. 39.00 (978-0-531-18484-4(6), Children's Pr.); (Illus.). 144p. (J). (gr. 5-9). 2008. Set lib. bdg. 222.00 o.p. (978-0-531-20409-2(X)); 216.00 o.p. (978-0-516-25407-4(3)) Scholastic Library Publishing. (Children's Pr.).
Enchantment of the World, Second Series Spring 2012 Set Of 6. 2012. (Enchantment of the World, Second Ser.). 234.00 (978-0-531-25818-7(1), Children's Pr.) Scholastic Library Publishing.
Encyclopedia of World History. (Children's Reference Ser.). (Illus.). 256p. (J). (978-1-4054-1702-0(1)) Parragon, Inc.
Essential Histories: War & Conflict in Modern Times, 8 vols., Set. Incl. Arab-Israeli Conflict: The 1948 War. Karsh, Efraim. lib. bdg. 38.47 (978-1-4042-1842-0(4), 83253158-6ad2-4a5c-b3cb-ef330d170f20); Korean War. Malkasian, Carter. lib. bdg. 38.47 (978-1-4042-1834-5(3), 5db45bbf-3e65-40c9-8e60-f54806e8b5d1); (Illus.). 96p. (YA). (gr. 10-10). (Essential Histories: War & Conflict in Modern Times Ser.). (ENG.). 2008. Set lib. bdg. 153.88 (978-1-4042-1894-9(7), 99b8f345-b0b7-4dcc-a7ef-c286314a825c) Rosen Publishing Group, Inc., The.
Evans, Charlotte. Historia (Enciclopedias Everst Internacional) (SPA.). 804p. (YA). (gr. 5-8). 39.99 (978-84-241-9403-1(9)) Everest Editora ESP. Dist: Lectorum Pubns., Inc.
Eyewitness to History: Sets 1-2. 2014. (Eyewitness to History Ser.). 32p. (J). (gr. 4-6). pap. 126.00 (978-1-4824-1601-5(8)) Stevens, Gareth Publishing LLLP.
Farman, John. Shockingly Short History Of Absolutely Everything. (ENG., Illus.). 110p. (J). pap. 8.99 (978-0-330-34904-8(X)) Pan Macmillan GBR. Dist: Trafalgar Square Publishing.
Farndon, John. A History of Civilization Illustrated History Encyclopedia: The Great Landmarks in the Development of Mankind. 2006. (Illus.). 256p. (gr. 7-10). reprint ed. pap. 22.00 (978-1-4223-5514-5(4)) DIANE Publishing Co.
Fisher, Douglas & McGraw-Hill - Jamestown Education Staff. World History. 2nd ed. 2004. (Human Experience - Modern Era Ser.). (ENG., Illus.). 432p. (gr. 6-9). stu. ed., pap. 13.08 (978-0-07-867561-4(8), 0078675618) McGraw-Hill Higher Education.
Fisher, Douglas & McGraw-Hill Staff. Glencoe World History. 2nd ed. 2004. (World History (hs) Ser.). (ENG., Illus.). 568p. (gr. 6-9). stu. ed., per. 13.60 (978-0-07-867553-9(7), 0078675537) McGraw-Hill Education.
Fleming, F. & Dowswell, P. Shock Horror History! 2004. (Illus.). 128p. (YA). (gr. 5-18). 22.95 (978-0-7460-3369-2(9)) EDC Publishing.
Frankopan, Peter. The Silk Roads: The Extraordinary History That Created Your World - Illustrated Edition. Packer, Neil, illus. 2018. (ENG.). 128p. (J). 26.99 (978-1-5476-0021-2(7), 900195170, Bloomsbury Children's Bks.) Bloomsbury Publishing USA.
Gale Research Inc Staff, contrib. by. Global Events: Milestone Events Throughout History. 2014. (Illus.). (J). (978-1-4144-9133-2(6)) Gale Research International, Ltd.
Ganeri, Anita. The Top Ten Events That Changed the World, 1 vol. 2009. (Top Ten Ser.). (ENG.). 32p. (gr. 4-5). (J). pap. 11.00 (978-1-4358-9162-3(7), ae4efe6f-4d90-413d-9e2b-7eb0679e97d5, PowerKids Pr.); (Illus.). (YA). 30.27 (978-1-4358-9161-6(9), 4512d307-dee5-4398-bf88-aa93c32ae681) Rosen Publishing Group, Inc., The.
—The Top Ten Leaders That Changed the World. 2009. (J). 60.00 (978-1-4358-9166-1(X), PowerKids Pr.); (ENG., Illus.). 32p. (J). (gr. 4-5). pap. 11.00 (978-1-4358-9165-4(1), 3b811668-8509-412a-9644-35bfef082751, PowerKids Pr.); (ENG., Illus.). 32p. (YA). (gr. 4-5). 30.27 (978-1-4358-9164-7(3), 2ce1f0bb-e00f-44c3-8ff3-31056aced95f) Rosen Publishing Group, Inc., The.
George, Enzo. The Modern Age, 1 vol. 2016. (Primary Sources in World History Ser.). (ENG.). 48p. (gr. 6-6). 33.07 (978-1-5026-1828-3(1), 8a27b5d6-923c-4933-969a-632ec09a04e4) Cavendish Square Publishing LLC.
Gibbons, David, ed. Timechart History of the World: 6000 Years of World History Unfolded. 2004. (ENG., Illus.). 34p. 14.98 (978-0-7607-6534-0(0)) Barnes & Noble, Inc.
Gifford, Clive. Killer History: A Gruesome & Grisly Trip Through the Past. 2012. 143p. (J). (978-1-62145-031-3(7)) Reader's Digest Assn., Ltd.
Glencoe McGraw-Hill Staff. World History. 2007. (World History (hs) Ser.). (ENG., Illus.). 64p. (gr. 6-9). pap., stu. ed. 4.28 (978-0-07-878230-5(9), 0078782309) McGraw-Hill Education.
Glencoe McGraw-Hill Staff, creator. Glencoe world history StudentWorks Plus. 2nd ed. 2005. (World History (hs) Ser.). (ENG.). (gr. 6-9). stu. ed. 86.88 (978-0-07-865380-3(0), 0078653800) McGraw-Hill Higher Education.
Glencoe Staff. Beginnings '83, Level 17. (J). (gr. 3). (978-0-02-132050-9(0)) Macmillan Publishing Co., Inc.
—Rainbow World '83: Level 9-10. (J). (gr. 1). (978-0-02-131720-2(8)) Macmillan Publishing Co., Inc.
Global Hotspots, 12 vols., Set. Incl. Afghanistan. Downing, David. (Illus.). (J). lib. bdg. 21.27 (978-0-7614-3177-0(2), 133e9d9a-f4ce-420f-8b81-20c4cb3bb67d); Indian Subcontinent. Mason, Paul. lib. bdg. 21.27 (978-0-7614-3178-7(0), b4d0ca0a-284c-4fd3-a4ae-4ef69259727c); Iran. Downing, David. lib. bdg. 21.27 (978-0-7614-3179-4(9), 4ec1ec8f-235f-4acd-843f-aa915d799997); Iraq. Mason, Paul. lib. bdg. 21.27 (978-0-7614-3180-0(2), 7668a935-7646-46b8-895c-c028c2b5791b); Israel & Palestine. Mason, Paul. lib. bdg. 21.27 (978-0-7614-3181-7(0), 934277a6-9922-4bda-bb3e-f52728915c35); Sudan. Barker, Geoff. lib. bdg. 21.27 (978-0-7614-3182-4(9), 6baf70c8-b2e8-49d2-9ea1-2457e7b53943); 32p. (gr. 5-5). (Global Hotspots Ser.). (ENG.). 2009. Set lib. bdg. 127.62 (978-0-7614-3175-6(6), a3611918-f376-42b9-a807-d8ea62a374d6, Cavendish Square) Cavendish Square Publishing LLC.
Goes, Peter. Timeline: A Visual History of Our World. Goes, Peter, illus. 2016. (ENG., Illus.). 80p. (J). (gr. 5-12). 29.99 (978-1-77657-069-0(3), 7fbfd890-3e90-43a9-9317-766edad484d9) Gecko Pr. NZL. Dist: Lerner Publishing Group.
Goldman, Phyllis, ed. Monkeyshines on Mysteries in History. 2003. (Illus.). 92p. per. 32.95 (978-1-888325-20-1(8)) Allosaurus Pubs.
Gombrich, E. H. A Little History of the World. Harper, Clifford, illus. (Little Histories Ser.). (ENG.). 304p. 2008. pap. 15.00 (978-0-300-14332-4(X)) 2005. 25.00 (978-0-300-10883-5(4)) Yale Univ. Pr.
—A Little History of the World: Illustrated Edition. 2013. (Little Histories Ser.). (ENG., Illus.). 364p. pap. 25.00 (978-0-300-19718-1(7)) Yale Univ. Pr.
Gorman, Joe & Trammell, Jack. Conversations in History: 9 Important Historical Events & the People Who Starred in Them. 2004. (Illus.). 80p. (J). pap. 6.50 (978-1-931334-30-3(7)) Pieces of Learning.
Gray, Dee. Po Cats (9 Lives) Cultural Adventure Series: 2 Low-Income Felines Share Their Musings on Travel, Colonialism, & Geopolitics, 4 bks., Set. 2003. (Illus.). per. 200.00 (978-0-9742007-0-5(0)) Poor Magazine.
Green, Janessa. Perimeters of the Ancient World: Recognize Perimeter, 1 vol. 2014. (InfoMax Math Readers Ser.). (ENG.). 24p. (J). (gr. 3-3). pap. 8.25 (978-1-4777-4585-4(8), 668970c6-0412-43f8-b600-4f839032277f, Rosen Classroom) Rosen Publishing Group, Inc., The.
Gritzner, Charles F., ed. Modern World Nations. (Illus.). (J). 848.30 (978-0-7910-7272-1(X), Facts On File) Infobase Holdings, Inc.
Hands-On History, 10 vols., Group 2. Incl. Projects about Nineteenth-Century Chinese Immigrants. Broida, Marian. lib. bdg. 34.07 (978-0-7614-1978-5(0), b08f1fd7-21d5-46c5-8de6-13bf50870de3); Projects about Nineteenth-Century European Immigrants. Broida, Marian. lib. bdg. 34.07 (978-0-7614-1980-8(2), d27dec08-f4be-42aa-a850-1c326d5708f6); Projects about the American Revolution. Broida, Marian. lib. bdg. 34.07 (978-0-7614-1981-5(0), 9accd3af-7002-4ce8-8212-853be6e77e08); Projects about the Spanish West. King, David C. lib. bdg. 34.07 (978-0-7614-1982-2(9), a52eb496-efaf-4d41-8b47-36b641d7e99d); Projects about the Woodland Indians. King, David C. lib. bdg. 34.07 (978-0-7614-1979-2(9), 43069906-e0f5-4c16-9808-35832224f2b0); (Illus.). 48p. (gr. 3-3). (Hands-On History Ser.). (ENG.). 2007. 170.35 (978-0-7614-1977-8(2), 63195346-bfe1-4b69-aef2-e0a18a23abcf, Cavendish Square) Cavendish Square Publishing LLC.
Hands-On History Group 3, 5 bks., Set. Incl. Projects about Ancient China. Bjorklund, Ruth. lib. bdg. 34.07 (978-0-7614-2257-0(9), 71b20aa7-5123-4613-92cf-d725af9dd9aa); Projects about Ancient Egypt. King, David C. lib. bdg. 34.07 (978-0-7614-2258-7(7), 3b65b462-50f5-490b-a814-a515f3fc5752); Projects about Ancient Greece. Broida, Marian. lib. bdg. 34.07 (978-0-7614-2259-4(5), e29c90d2-89d8-49a2-a447-fd0e46182995); Projects about Ancient Rome. Frankel, Karen. lib. bdg. 34.07 (978-0-7614-2260-0(9), c50ab922-409b-4a0d-8841-a5a2b9e547c0); Projects about the Ancient Aztecs. King, David C. lib. bdg. 34.07 (978-0-7614-2256-3(0), b0e5e12c-d7d3-4713-95cd-6922d265908a); (Illus.). 48p. (gr. 3-3). 2007. lib. bdg. (978-0-7614-2255-6(2), Cavendish Square) Cavendish Square Publishing LLC.
Harcourt School Publishers Staff. Beginnings 1877. 3rd ed. 2003. (Harcourt School Publishers Horizons Ser.). (ENG.). 728p. (gr. 4-5). stu. ed., pupil's gde. ed. 85.65 (978-0-15-321349-6(3)) Harcourt Schl. Pubs.
—World History, 5 Packs. 3rd ed. (Horizons Ser.). 2004. pap. 7.30 (978-0-15-338611-4(8)) 2003. pap. 38.10 (978-0-15-338635-0(5))Bk. 2. 2004. pap. 7.30 (978-0-15-338612-1(6))Bk. 2. 2003. pap. 38.10 (978-0-15-338636-7(3))Bk. 3. 2004. pap. 7.30 (978-0-15-338613-8(4))Bk. 3. 2003. pap. 38.10 (978-0-15-338637-4(1))Bk. 4. 2004. pap. 7.30 (978-0-15-338614-5(2))Bk. 5. 2004. pap. 7.30 (978-0-15-338615-2(0))Bk. 5. 2003. pap. 38.10 (978-0-15-338639-8(8))Bk. 6. 2004. pap. 7.30 (978-0-15-338616-9(9))Bk. 6. 2003. pap. 38.10 (978-0-15-338640-4(1))Bk. 7. 2004. pap. 7.30 (978-0-15-338617-6(7))Bk. 7. 2003. pap. 38.10 (978-0-15-338641-1(X))Bk. 8. 2004. pap. 7.30 (978-0-15-338618-3(5))Bk. 8. 2003. pap. 38.10 (978-0-15-338642-8(8))Bk. 9. 2004. pap. 7.30 (978-0-15-338619-0(3))Bk. 9. 2003. pap. 38.10 (978-0-15-338643-5(6))Bk. 10. 2004. pap. 7.30 (978-0-15-338620-6(7))Bk. 10. 2003. pap. 38.10 (978-0-15-338644-2(4))Bk. 11. 2004. pap. 7.30 (978-0-15-338621-3(5))Bk. 11. 2003. pap. 38.10 (978-0-15-338645-9(2))Bk. 12. 2004. pap. 7.30 (978-0-15-338622-0(3))Bk. 12. 2003. pap. 38.10 (978-0-15-338646-6(0))Bk. 13. 2004. pap. 7.30 (978-0-15-338623-7(1))Bk. 13. 2003. pap. 38.10 (978-0-15-338647-3(9))Bk. 14. 2004. pap. 7.30 (978-0-15-338624-4(X))Bk. 14. 2003. pap. 38.10 (978-0-15-338648-0(7))Bk. 15. 2004. pap. 7.30 (978-0-15-338625-1(8))Bk. 15. 2003. pap. 38.10 (978-0-15-338649-7(5))Bk. 16. 2004. pap. 7.30 (978-0-15-338626-8(6))Bk. 16. 2003. pap. 38.10 (978-0-15-338650-3(9))Bk. 17. 2004. pap. 7.30 (978-0-15-338627-5(4))Bk. 17. 2003. pap. 38.10 (978-0-15-338651-0(7))Bk. 18. 2004. pap. 7.30 (978-0-15-338628-2(2))Bk. 18. 2003. pap. 38.10 (978-0-15-338652-7(5))Bk. 19. 2004. pap. 7.30 (978-0-15-338629-9(0))Bk. 19. 2003. pap. 38.10 (978-0-15-338653-4(3))Bk. 20. 2004. pap. 7.30 (978-0-15-338630-5(4))Bk. 20. 2003. pap. 38.10 (978-0-15-338654-1(1))Bk. 21. 2004. pap. 7.30 (978-0-15-338631-2(2))Bk. 21. 2003. pap. 38.10 (978-0-15-338655-8(X))Bk. 22. 2004. pap. 7.30 (978-0-15-338632-9(0))Bk. 22. 2004. pap. 7.30 (978-0-15-338632-9(0))Bk. 22. 2003. pap. 38.10 (978-0-15-338656-5(8))Bk. 23. 2004. pap. 7.30 (978-0-15-338633-6(9))Bk. 23. 2003. pap. 38.10 (978-0-15-338657-2(6))Bk. 24. 2004. pap. 7.30 (978-0-15-338634-3(7))Bk. 24. 2003. pap. 38.10 (978-0-15-338658-9(4)) Harcourt Schl. Pubs.
—World History: The Civil War to the Present. 3rd ed. 2003. (Harcourt Horizons Ser.). (ENG., Illus.). 680p. (gr. 5-6). stu. ed. 89.15 (978-0-15-339621-2(0)) Harcourt Schl. Pubs.
—World History: Time for Kids Reader 5-Pack, Bk. 4. 3rd ed. 2003. (Horizons Ser.). pap. 38.10 (978-0-15-338638-1(X)) Harcourt Schl. Pubs.
Hardyman, Robyn. Lost Kings & Kingdoms, 1 vol. 2016. (Mystery Hunters Ser.). (ENG.). 48p. (J). (gr. 5-5). lib. bdg. 33.60 (978-1-4824-6009-4(2), 46ec4985-6b7e-48a0-aa19-88d8f02e4bb0) Stevens, Gareth Publishing LLLP.
—Tombs & Cursed Treasure, 1 vol. 2016. (Mystery Hunters Ser.). (ENG.). 48p. (J). (gr. 5-5). pap. 15.05 (978-1-4824-6011-7(4), 1934c3ec-a244-4342-a09a-69766f83d514) Stevens, Gareth Publishing LLLP.
Healey, Tim. The 1960s. 2005. (Picture History of the 20th Century Ser.). (Illus.). 48p. (YA). (gr. 7-12). lib. bdg. 29.95 (978-1-932889-74-1(4)) Sea-To-Sea Pubns.
Hibbert, Clare. Moments in History That Changed the World. 2017. (Revolutions Ser.). (ENG., Illus.). 64p. (J). (gr. 3-6). 19.99 (978-0-7123-5670-1(3)) British Library, The GBR. Dist: Independent Pubs. Group.
Hirschmann, Kris & Herndon, Ryan. Test Your Smarts! 2009. (Illus.). 80p. (J). (978-0-545-12042-5(X)) Scholastic, Inc.
Historia y Geografía del Mundo: Del Renacimiento al Siglo XX. (SPA., Illus.). (J). 40.00 (978-958-04-3807-6(2)) Norma S.A. COL. Dist: Distribuidora Norma, Inc.
History & Geography. 2004. (Switched on Schoolhouse Ser.). (YA). (gr. 7). cd-rom 69.95 (978-0-7403-0587-0(5));Set. (Illus.). (gr. 5). tchr. ed., stu. ed. 47.95 (978-1-58095-651-2(3), HIS05015, Lifepac) Alpha Omega Pubns., Inc.
History & Geography: Government & Economics. 2004. (Illus.). (gr. 12). tchr. ed., stu. ed. 47.95 (978-1-58095-672-7(6), HIS1215, Lifepac) Alpha Omega Pubns., Inc.
History & Geography: U. S. History, 12 vols., Set. 2004. (Illus.). (gr. 11-12). tchr. ed., stu. ed. 47.95 (978-1-58095-669-7(6), HIS1115, Lifepac) Alpha Omega Pubns., Inc.
History of the World 8-Book Set. 2014. (Book Collection). (ENG., Illus.). 32p. (gr. 4-5). 71.92 (978-1-4938-0840-3(0)) Teacher Created Materials, Inc.
History's Fearless Fighters. 2015. (History's Fearless Fighters Ser.). (ENG.). 48p. (J). (gr. 5-6). pap., pap., pap. 505.80 (978-1-4824-3480-4(6)) Stevens, Gareth Publishing LLLP.
Hogan, Maggie S. Student History Notebook of America. 2007. (Illus.). 111p. per. 12.95 (978-0-9663722-3-6(9)) Coffee Hse. Ink.
HOLT, RINEHART AND WINSTON. World History: People & Nations. 2003. (Holt World History: People & a Nation Ser.). (ENG.). 1040p. (gr. 9-9). 187.85 (978-0-03-053359-4(7)) Houghton Mifflin Harcourt Publishing Co.
Holt, Rinehart and Winston Staff. The Human Journey: Online Edition. 3rd ed. 2003. 77.13 (978-0-03-072542-5(9)) Holt McDougal.
—The Human Journey: The Modern World: Online Edition. 3rd ed. 2003. 75.93 (978-0-03-072541-8(0)) Holt McDougal.
—World History: The Human Journey: Online Edition. 5th ed. 2004. (gr. 1). 17.26 (978-0-03-038134-8(7)); (gr. 6). 78.60 (978-0-03-038136-2(3)) Holt McDougal.
—World History: The Human Journey: Online Edition Plus. 3rd ed. 2003. 17.26 (978-0-03-037426-5(X)); 17.26 (978-0-03-037423-4(5)); 17.26 (978-0-03-037424-1(3)) Holt McDougal.
—World History & Doc-B's Questions: New York Edition. 3rd ed. 2003. (Holt World History Ser.). (J). pap. 8.40 (978-0-03-070236-5(4)) Holt, Rinehart & Winston of Canada, Ltd. CAN. Dist: Harcourt Canada, Ltd.
Hyde, Natalie. History Mysteries Revealed. 2010. (ENG., Illus.). 32p. (J). pap. (978-0-7787-7429-7(5)); (gr. 4-7). lib. bdg. (978-0-7787-7414-3(7)) Crabtree Publishing Co.
Images of War. (Illus.). 192p. (J). (978-0-7835-0153-6(6)) Time-Life Education, Inc.
Incas Mayas Aztecs: Mr Donn & Maxie's World History Series. 2006. spiral bd. 29.95 net. (978-1-56004-244-0(3)) Social Studies Schl. Service.
Johnson, Terri, creator. Blackline Maps of World History: The Complete Set - Revised, 4 sets. 2nd rev. ed. 2004. (Illus.). 250p. (J). ring bd. 39.95 (978-1-932786-16-3(3)) Knowledge Quest.
—Wonders of Old: A Blank Timeline Book of World History. 2007. (Illus.). 96p. 21.95 (978-1-932786-10-1(4)) Knowledge Quest.
Kemp, Ellwood W. Streams of History. 2008. 64p. pap. 7.95 (978-1-59915-260-8(6)) Yesterday's Classics.
Knapp-Fisher, H. C. Outline of World History: For Boys & Girls. (J). 25.00 (978-0-8196-2798-8(4)) Biblo & Tannen Booksellers & Pubs., Inc.
Knebel, Arthur & Udelhoven, Hermann-Josef. The Modern Era through World War II: From the 18th Century To 1945, 1 vol. 2012. (Witness to History: a Visual Chronicle of the World Ser.). (ENG., Illus.). 192p. (J). (gr. 7-7). 51.80 (978-1-4488-7224-4(3), efd6028a-5206-438b-b52e-0e340411ddd4) Rosen Publishing Group, Inc., The.
Leaders of the Ancient World: Set 1, 16 vols. 2016. (Leaders of the Ancient World Ser.). (ENG.). 00112p. (J). (gr. 6-6). 310.40 (978-1-5081-7358-8(3), 02bc3b13-b65e-45d1-a013-7410cadb08d5, Rosen Young Adult) Rosen Publishing Group, Inc., The.
Leaders of the Ancient World: Set 2, 16 vols. 2017. (Leaders of the Ancient World Ser.). (ENG.). 112p. (gr. 6-6). 310.40 (978-1-4994-6629-4(3), c39b9aab-d13e-4f63-bca8-e772ecf462b1, Rosen Young Adult) Rosen Publishing Group, Inc., The.
LernerClassroom Editors. Count Your Way Teaching Guide. 2009. pap. 7.95 (978-0-8225-6886-5(1)) Lerner Publishing Group.
El Libro de los Acertijos Historicos. (Coleccion Acertijos). (SPA.). (YA). (gr. 5-8). pap. (978-950-724-249-6(X), LMA8235) Lumen ARG. Dist: Lectorum Pubns., Inc.
Looking at Countries, 6 vols., Set. Incl. Looking at Canada. Pohl, Kathleen. lib. bdg. 28.67 (978-0-8368-8168-4(0), e078449b-5f70-48a5-95c1-e420f38550f4); Looking at Japan. Powell, Jillian. lib. bdg. 28.67 (978-0-8368-8171-4(0), e07764ae-bb1f-4f0d-9280-688362417ec9); Looking at Mexico. Pohl, Kathleen. lib. bdg. 28.67 (978-0-8368-8172-1(9), e92d071d-4761-46c6-978b-2684617b265e); Looking at Russia. Powell, Jillian. lib. bdg. 28.67 (978-0-8368-8173-8(7), 1b1c43c1-b323-4421-a9dd-77138aea4843); (Illus.). 32p. (gr. 2-4). 2007., Gareth Stevens Learning Library 2007. Set lib. bdg. 151.62 o.p. (978-0-8368-8167-7(2)) Stevens, Gareth Publishing LLLP.
Lubawy, Susan. World View: A Global Study of Geography, History & Culture, Bk. 1. (J). stu. ed. 8.95 (978-0-916591-30-4(1)) Linmore Publishing, Inc.
Macdonald, Fiona. The World in the Time Of ... 2005. (World in the Time of... Ser.). 48p. (gr. 5-8). 137.70 (978-0-7910-8407-6(8), Facts On File) Infobase Holdings, Inc.
MacMillan, Kathy & Bernardi, Manuela. She Spoke: 14 Women Who Raised Their Voices & Changed the World. Honesta, Kathrin, illus. 2019. (ENG.). 32p. (gr. k-2). 24.99 (978-1-64170-131-0(5), 550131) Familius LLC.
Mad Libs. History of the World Mad Libs: World's Greatest Word Game. 2015. (Mad Libs Ser.). 48p. (J). (gr. 3-7). bds. 5.99 (978-0-8431-8075-6(7), Mad Libs) Penguin Young Readers Group.
McDougal-Littell Publishing Staff. Modern World History: Patterns of Interaction - Reading Study Guide. 2004. (McDougal Littell World History: Patterns of Interaction Ser.). (SPA.). 240p. (gr. 9-12). pap. 4.90 (978-0-618-40992-1(0), 2-00648) Great Source Education Group, Inc.
—World History: Patterns of Interaction. 2004. (World History: Patterns of Interaction Ser.). (ENG.). 160p. (gr. 9-12). pap., wbk. ed. 7.40 (978-0-618-40938-9(6), 2-00619) Great Source Education Group, Inc.
—World History - Patterns of Interaction. 2004. (World History: Patterns of Interaction Ser.). (ENG.). 384p. (gr. 9-12). pap. 7.40 (978-0-618-40933-4(5), 2-00614) Great Source Education Group, Inc.
—World History - Patterns of Interaction: Reading Study Guide. 2004. (McDougal Littell World History: Patterns of Interaction Ser.). (SPA.). 384p. (gr. 9-12). pap. 7.40 (978-0-618-40934-1(3), 2-00615) Great Source Education Group, Inc.
McGraw Hill. Exploring Our World, Reading Essentials & Note-Taking Guide Workbook. 2007. (WORLD & ITS PEOPLE EASTERN Ser.). (ENG., Illus.). 224p. (gr. 6-8). per. 26.16 (978-0-07-877602-1(3), 0078776023) McGraw-Hill Education.
—Exploring Our World, Standardized Test Practice Workbook. 2007. (WORLD & ITS PEOPLE EASTERN Ser.). (ENG., Illus.). 128p. (gr. 6-8). spiral bd., wbk. ed. 7.56 (978-0-07-877605-2(8), 0078776058) McGraw-Hill Education.
—Glencoe World History, Modern Times, Student Edition. 2007. (World History (hs) Ser.). (ENG., Illus.). 992p. (gr. 6-9). stu. ed. 140.60 (978-0-07-874527-0(6), 0078745276) McGraw-Hill Education.
—Glencoe World History: Modern Times, Student Edition. 2nd ed. 2004. (Human Experience - Modern Era Ser.). (ENG., Illus.). 912p. (gr. 6-9). stu. ed. 68.48 (978-0-07-860705-9(1), 0078607051) McGraw-Hill Education.
—Glencoe World History, Modern Times, StudentWorks Plus CD-ROM. 2nd ed. 2005. (Human Experience - Modern Era Ser.). (ENG.). (gr. 6-9). stu. ed. 170.20 (978-0-07-865302-5(9), 0078653029) McGraw-Hill Education.
—Glencoe World History, Student Edition. (World History (hs) Ser.). (ENG., Illus.). (gr. 6-9). 2007. 1248p. stu. ed. 149.96 (978-0-07-874525-6(X), 007874525X) 2nd ed. 2004. 1136p. pap., stu. ed. 144.20 (978-0-07-860702-8(7), 0078607027) McGraw-Hill Education.
—Human Heritage, StudentWorks. 3rd ed. 2005. (Merrill Human Heritage Ser.). (ENG.). (gr. 6-9). cd-rom 160.00 (978-0-07-873136-5(4), 0078731364) McGraw-Hill Education.
—Journey Across Time, Active Reading & Note-Taking Guide. 2nd ed. 2007. (MS Wh Jat Full Survey Ser.). (ENG., Illus.). 480p. (gr. 6-9). per. 13.24 (978-0-07-878949-6(4), 0078789494) McGraw-Hill Education.
—Journey Across Time, Activity Workbook, Student Edition. 2nd ed. 2007. (MS Wh Jat Full Survey Ser.). (ENG., Illus.). 56p. (gr. 6-9). stu. ed., spiral bd., act. bk. ed. 7.92 (978-0-07-878954-0(0), 0078789540) McGraw-Hill Education.
—Journey Across Time, Early Ages, Active Reading & Note-Taking Guide. 2nd ed. 2007. (MS Wh Jat Full Survey Ser.). (ENG.). 384p. (gr. 6-9). pap. 13.24 (978-0-07-878926-7(5), 0078789265) McGraw-Hill Education.
—Journey Across Time, Early Ages, Active Reading Note-Taking Strategies, Student Edition. 2004. (MS World History Ser.). (ENG.). 384p. (gr. 6-9). pap., stu. ed. 13.48 (978-0-07-868132-5(4), 0078681324) McGraw-Hill Education.
—Journey Across Time, Early Ages, Activity Workbook, Student Edition. 2nd ed. 2007. (MS Wh Jat Full Survey Ser.). (ENG.). 48p. (gr. 6-9). spiral bd. 7.92 (978-0-07-878931-1(1), 0078789311) McGraw-Hill Education.
—Journey Across Time, Early Ages, Interactive Tutor: Self-Assessment CD. 2nd ed. 2007. (MS Wh Jat Full Survey Ser.). (ENG.). (gr. 6-9). cd-rom 120.64 (978-0-07-878941-0(9), 0078789419) McGraw-Hill Education.
—Journey Across Time, Early Ages, Reading Essentials & Study Guide, Workbook. 2nd ed. 2007. (MS Wh Jat Full Survey Ser.). (ENG.). 400p. (gr. 6-9). pap. 13.24 (978-0-07-878923-6(0), 0078789230) McGraw-Hill Education.
—Journey Across Time, Early Ages, Reading Essentials & Study Guide, Workbook. 2004. (MS World History Ser.).

W X Y Z

(ENG., Illus.). 400p. (gr. 6-9). stu. ed., per., wbk. ed. 6.96 *(978-0-07-860318-1(8)*, 0078603188) McGraw-Hill Higher Education.

—Journey Across Time, Early Ages, Spanish Reading Essentials & Study Guide, Workbook. 2004. (MS World History Ser.). (SPA., Illus.). 400p. (gr. 6-9). stu. ed., per., wbk. ed. 14.60 *(978-0-07-868194-3(4)*, 0078681944) McGraw-Hill Education.

—Journey Across Time, Early Ages, Standardized Test Practice, Student Edition. 2004. (MS World History Ser.). (ENG., Illus.). 48p. (gr. 6-9). stu. ed., spiral bd. 3.80 *(978-0-07-868191-2(X)*, 007868191X) McGraw-Hill Education.

—Journey Across Time, Early Ages, StudentWorks Plus CD-ROM. 2005. (MS World History Ser.). (ENG.). (gr. 6-9). stu. ed. 155.52 *(978-0-07-867415-0(8)*, 0078674158) McGraw-Hill Education.

—Journey Across Time, Early Ages, StudentWorks Plus DVD. 2007. (MS Wh Jat Full Survey Ser.). (ENG.). (gr. 6-9). cd-rom 166.28 *(978-0-07-878150-6(7)*, 0078781507) McGraw-Hill Education.

—Journey Across Time, StudentWorks Plus DVD. 2nd ed. 2007. (MS Wh Jat Full Survey Ser.). (ENG.). (gr. 6-9). cd-rom 175.20 *(978-0-07-878158-2(2)*, 0078781582) McGraw-Hill Education.

—The World & Its People: Western Hemisphere, Europe, & Russia, Standardized Test Practice Workbook, Student Edition. 2004. (GEOGRAPHY: WORLD & ITS PEOPLE Ser.). (ENG., Illus.). 59p. (gr. 6-9). pap., stu. ed., wbk. ed. 3.96 *(978-0-07-865523-4(4)*, 0078655234) McGraw-Hill Education.

McGraw Hill, creator. The World & Its People, Activity Workbook, Student Edition. 2004. (GEOGRAPHY: WORLD & ITS PEOPLE Ser.). (ENG., Illus.). 59p. (gr. 6-9). pap., stu. ed., wbk. ed. 4.44 *(978-0-07-865502-9(1)*, 0078655021) McGraw-Hill Education.

McGraw-Hill Education Editors. World History: Modern Times: Spanish Reading Essentials & Note-Taking Guide. 2007. (World History (hs) Ser.). (SPA., Illus.). 264p. (gr. 6-9). per. 6.16 *(978-0-07-878270-1(8)*, 0078782708) McGraw-Hill Education.

McGraw-Hill Education Staff. Glencoe World History. 2007. (World History (hs) Ser.). (ENG.). (gr. 6-9). cd-rom 113.68 *(978-0-07-878250-3(3)*, 0078782503) McGraw-Hill Education.

McGraw-Hill Staff. Human Heritage, Spanish Reading Essentials & Study Guide, Student Edition. 2005. pap. 18.00 *(978-0-07-869627-5(5))* Glencoe/McGraw-Hill.

McGraw-Hill Staff, creator. World History: Modern Times. 2007. (World History (hs) Ser.). (ENG., Illus.). 50p. (gr. 6-9). stu. ed., per., wbk. ed. 8.24 *(978-0-07-878261-9(9)*, 0078782619) McGraw-Hill Education.

McNeese, Tim, ed. Rivers in World History. 2005. (Rivers in World History Ser.). (Illus.). 120p. (C). (gr. 9-13). 195.00 *(978-0-7910-8473-1(6)*, Facts On File) Infobase Holdings, Inc.

Mcneill, William H., et al, eds. Berkshire Encyclopedia of World History, 5 vols. 2005. (Illus.). 2500p. lib. bdg. 575.00 *(978-0-9743091-0-1(9))* Berkshire Publishing Group.

Millard, A. World History. 2009. (World History Ser.). 192p. (YA). (gr. 3-18). 24.99 *(978-0-7945-2478-4(8)*, Usborne) EDC Publishing.

Miller, D. L. BigFoot Goes Back in Time: A Spectacular Seek & Find Challenge for All Ages! 2018. (BigFoot Search & Find Ser.). (ENG., Illus.). 48p. (J). 14.99 *(978-1-64124-003-1(2)*, 0031B) Fox Chapel Publishing Co., Inc.

Miller, Olive Beaupre & Baum, Harry Neal. A Picturesque Tale of Progress. 2009. (J). *(978-1-59731-394-0(7))*; *(978-1-59731-364-3(5))*; *(978-1-59731-374-2(2))*; *(978-1-59731-398-8(X))*; *(978-1-59731-397-1(1))*; *(978-1-59731-396-4(3))*; *(978-1-59731-395-7(5))*; *(978-1-59731-399-5(8))* Perennis, Sophia.

—A Picturesque Tale of Progress: Beginnings I. 2009. (Illus.). 282p. (J). pap. 14.95 *(978-1-59731-365-0(3)*, Dawn Chorus Pr.) Perennis, Sophia.

—A Picturesque Tale of Progress: Beginnings I-II. 2009. (Illus.). 540p. (J). pap. 19.95 *(978-1-59731-389-6(0)*, Dawn Chorus Pr.) Perennis, Sophia.

—A Picturesque Tale of Progress: Beginnings II. 2009. (Illus.). 304p. (J). pap. 14.95 *(978-1-59731-366-7(1)*, Dawn Chorus Pr.) Perennis, Sophia.

—A Picturesque Tale of Progress: Conquests III. 2009. (Illus.). 348p. (J). pap. 15.95 *(978-1-59731-367-4(X)*, Dawn Chorus Pr.) Perennis, Sophia.

—A Picturesque Tale of Progress: Conquests III-IV. 2009. (Illus.). 544p. (J). pap. 19.95 *(978-1-59731-390-2(4)*, Dawn Chorus Pr.) Perennis, Sophia.

—A Picturesque Tale of Progress: Conquests IV. 2009. (Illus.). 264p. (J). pap. 14.95 *(978-1-59731-368-1(8)*, Dawn Chorus Pr.) Perennis, Sophia.

—A Picturesque Tale of Progress: Explorations VII. 2009. (Illus.). 340p. (J). pap. 15.95 *(978-1-59731-371-1(8)*, Dawn Chorus Pr.) Perennis, Sophia.

—A Picturesque Tale of Progress: Explorations VII-VIII. 2009. 568p. (J). pap. 19.95 *(978-1-59731-392-6(0)*, Dawn Chorus Pr.) Perennis, Sophia.

—A Picturesque Tale of Progress: Explorations VIII. 2009. (Illus.). 292p. (J). pap. 14.00 *(978-1-59731-372-8(6)*, Dawn Chorus Pr.) Perennis, Sophia.

—A Picturesque Tale of Progress: Index. 2009. 238p. (J). pap. 13.95 *(978-1-59731-393-3(9)*, Dawn Chorus Pr.) Perennis, Sophia.

—A Picturesque Tale of Progress: Index IX. 2009. 238p. (J). pap. 12.95 *(978-1-59731-373-5(4)*, Dawn Chorus Pr.) Perennis, Sophia.

—A Picturesque Tale of Progress: New Nations V. 2009. (Illus.). 296p. (J). pap. 14.95 *(978-1-59731-369-8(6)*, Dawn Chorus Pr.) Perennis, Sophia.

—A Picturesque Tale of Progress: New Nations V-VI. 2009. (Illus.). 540p. (J). pap. 19.95 *(978-1-59731-391-9(2))* Perennis, Sophia.

—A Picturesque Tale of Progress: New Nations VI. 2009. (Illus.). 308p. (J). pap. 14.95 *(978-1-59731-370-4(X)*, Dawn Chorus Pr.) Perennis, Sophia.

Modern World History: Patterns of Interaction: EEdition Plus Online. (gr. 6-12). 2005. *(978-0-618-41039-2(2)*, 2-00657) 2003. *(978-0-618-19414-8(2)*, 2-70056) Holt McDougal.

Modern World History: Patterns of Interaction: EEdition Plus Online with purchase of print Pupil's Edition-1 Year. (gr. 6-12). 2005. *(978-0-618-41042-2(2)*, 2-00660) 2003. *(978-0-618-25845-1(0)*, 2-10037) Holt McDougal.

Modern World History: Patterns of Interaction: Reading Study Guide Answer Key. 2005. (gr. 6-12). *(978-0-618-40994-5(7)*, 2-00649) Holt McDougal.

Morter, Peter. Atlas Visual de los Descubrimientos. (SPA., Illus.). 412p. (YA). (gr. 5-8). *(978-84-216-1814-1(8)*, BU4892) Bruño, Editorial ESP. Dist: Lectorum Pubns., Inc.

Nardo, Don. The Inquisition, 1 vol. 2007. (World History Ser.). (ENG., Illus.). 104p. (gr. 7-7). lib. bdg. 41.53 *(978-1-59018-653-4(2)*, 3252a331-2bab-47aa-a0d2-0f8d0e214101, Lucent Pr.) Greenhaven Publishing LLC.

National Geographic Learning. World Windows 3 (Social Studies): Famous Landmarks: Content Literacy, Nonfiction Reading, Language & Literacy. 2011. (World Windows Ser.). (ENG.). 16p. stu. ed. 10.95 *(978-1-133-56616-8(2))* Cengage Heinle.

Nineteen Sixty-Eight (World History) (Illus.). 192p. (J). *(978-0-7835-0152-9(8))* Time-Life Education, Inc.

Notgrass, Ray. Exploring World History. 2014. (Illus.). *(978-1-60999-061-9(7))* Notgrass Co.

Olson, Tod. A Wicked History, 4 vols., Set. Incl. Wicked History: Leopold II. (Illus.). 128p. (J). (gr. 8-12). 2008. 18.69 *(978-0-531-18552-0(4)*, Watts, Franklin); 2008. Set lib. bdg. 120.00 o.p. *(978-0-531-20417-7(0)*, Watts, Franklin) Scholastic Library Publishing.

O'Neill, Elizabeth. The World's Story. 2013. 394p. 39.95 *(978-0-9885106-3-0(4))* Hillside Education.

Otfinoski, Steven. World War II (Library Edition) 2017. (Step into History(tm) Ser.). (ENG., Illus.). 144p. (J). lib. bdg. 36.00 *(978-0-531-22572-1(0))* Scholastic Library Publishing.

Pak, Amy. History Through the Ages - Napoleon to Now: Historical Timeline Figures (1750 AD - Present) Pak, Amy, illus. 2003. (Illus.). (J). pap. 22.95 *(978-0-9720265-3-6(3))* Home Schl. in the Woods.

Phan, Sandy. Imperialism: Expanding Empires, 1 vol. rev. ed. 2012. (Social Studies: Informational Text Ser.). (ENG.). 32p. (gr. 4-8). pap. 11.99 *(978-1-4333-5015-3(7))* Teacher Created Materials, Inc.

A Political & Diplomatic History of the Modern World, 8 vols. 2016. (Political & Diplomatic History of the Modern World Ser.). (ENG.). 224p. (gr. 10-10). 190.36 *(978-1-5081-0228-1(7)*, c16444f4-8abe-4557-be1f-3bfb4fec72c2, Britannica Educational Publishing) Rosen Publishing Group, Inc., The.

Price, Sean. Truth & Rumors, 4 vols., Set. Doty, Eldon, illus. Incl. U. S. Presidents: Truth & Rumors. (ENG., Illus.). 32p. (J). (gr. 3-9). 2010. lib. bdg. 30.65 *(978-1-4296-3952-1(0)*, 102562, Capstone Pr.); (Truth & Rumors Ser.). (ENG.). 32p. 2010. Set lib. bdg. 85.95 *(978-1-4296-4444-0(3)*, Capstone Pr.) Capstone.

Primary Sources in World History, 12 vols. 2016. (Primary Sources in World History Ser.). (ENG.). 48p. (gr. 6-6). lib. bdg. 198.42 *(978-1-5026-1825-2(7)*, b949fdd7-bf72-45af-a72d-6ac746a8f3b3, Cavendish Square) Cavendish Square Publishing LLC.

Primary Sources of Countries of the World: Set 1, 8 vols., Set. 2003. (Countries of the World: a Primary Source Journey Ser.). (ENG., Illus.). (J). (gr. 2-3). 105.08 *(978-0-8239-8487-9(7)*, e4da4237-3576-4fc8-88b4-444d7ab92079, PowerKids Pr.) Rosen Publishing Group, Inc., The.

Quick Revision KS3 History Staff. Quick Revision KS3 History. 2007. (ENG.). pap. 9.95 *(978-0-340-94309-0(2)*, Hodder Education) Hodder Education Group GBR. Dist: Trans-Atlantic Pubns., Inc.

Raum, Elizabeth & Collins, Terry. You Choose: Historical Eras. 2012. (You Choose: Historical Eras Ser.). (ENG.). 112p. (gr. 3-4). pap. 333.60 *(978-1-4296-9477-3(7)*, Capstone Pr.) Capstone.

Reformation: PowerPoint Presentation in World History. 2005. cd-rom 49.95 net. *(978-1-56004-216-7(8))* Social Studies Schl. Service.

Reid, Scott, ed. The Great Society, 1 vol. 2015. (Perspectives on Modern World History Ser.). (ENG., Illus.). 200p. (gr. 10-12). lib. bdg. 49.43 *(978-0-7377-7308-8(1)*, f4d03204-318e-4bcd-9463-2e96bc8a7a8f, Greenhaven Publishing) Greenhaven Publishing LLC.

Rigby Education Staff. Discovery World. (Illus.). 68.00 *(978-0-7635-8444-3(4))* Rigby Education.

—Discovery World Orange Encyclopedia: Tiny Big Book. (Discovery World Ser.). 12p. (gr. 1-2). 27.00 *(978-0-7635-2702-0(5))* Rigby Education.

Road to War: Causes of Conflict, 5 vols., Set. Incl. Causes of the American Revolution. Strum, Richard M. 64p. (J). lib. bdg. 22.95 *(978-1-59556-001-8(7))*; Causes of the Civil War. Epperson, James F. 64p. (J). lib. bdg. 22.95 *(978-1-59556-002-5(5))*; Causes of the Iraq War. Gallagher, Jim. 72p. (J). lib. bdg. 22.95 *(978-1-59556-009-4(2))*; Causes of World War I. Ziff, John. 72p. (J). lib. bdg. 22.95 *(978-1-59556-003-2(3))*; Causes of World War II. Corrigan, Jim. 64p. lib. bdg. 22.95 *(978-1-59556-004-9(1))*; (gr. 4-18). 2005. (Road to War Ser.). (Illus.). 64p. 2005. Set lib. bdg. 114.75 *(978-1-59556-000-1(9))* OTTN Publishing.

Rupert, Matthews. Visual Factfinder HIST Timelines. 2008. 512p. pap. *(978-1-84810-077-0(9))* Miles Kelly Publishing, Ltd.

Scholastic Library Publishing. Enchantment of the World. 2012. (Second Ser.). (J). 240.00 *(978-0-531-23525-6(4)*, Children's Pr.) Scholastic Library Publishing.

Schwartz, Heather E. & Salzano, Tammi. Around the World: An Amazing World. 2009. (Illus.). 48p. (J). pap. *(978-0-545-17229-5(2))* Scholastic, Inc.

Scientific Revolution: PowerPoints in World History. 2005. cd-rom 49.95 net. *(978-1-56004-215-0(X))* Social Studies Schl. Service.

Shukin, Barbara. Modern History Portfolio: A History of America & the World from the 17th to the 21st Centuries. 2004. (J). ring bd. 29.95 *(978-0-9762918-3-1(5))* Homeschool Journey.

Smith, David J. If: A Mind-Bending New Way of Looking at Big Ideas & Numbers. Adams, Steve, illus. 2014. (ENG.). 40p. (J). (gr. 3-7). 19.99 *(978-1-894786-34-8(3))* Kids Can Pr., Ltd. CAN. Dist: Hachette Bk. Group.

Steck-Vaughn Staff. History of Our World. 2003. (Steck-Vaughn History of Our World Ser.). (ENG.). 624p. (gr. 6-12). pap., tchr. ed. 120.80 *(978-0-7398-6088-5(7))* Houghton Mifflin Harcourt Publishing Co.

Steele, Philip, et al. Weird & Wacky History Book Box: Find Out What Is Fact or Fantasy in 8 Amazing Books, 8 vols. 2012. (Illus.). 200p. (J). (gr. -1-12). pap. 20.00 *(978-1-84322-797-7(5)*, Armadillo) Anness Publishing GBR. Dist: National Bk. Network.

Stewart, David. World of Wonder, 3 vols., Set. Incl. Dinosaurs. Hewetson, Nick, illus. 29.00 *(978-0-531-20450-4(2))*; Ocean Life. Franklin, Carolyn. Franklin, Carolyn, illus. 29.00 *(978-0-531-20451-1(0))*; Rain Forest Animals. Franklin, Carolyn. Franklin, Carolyn, illus. 29.00 *(978-0-531-20452-8(9))*; (Illus.). 32p. (J). (gr. 1-4). 2008. Set lib. bdg. 203.00 *(978-0-531-21004-8(9)*, Children's Pr.) Scholastic Library Publishing.

Synge, M. B. The Discovery of New Worlds, Book II of the Story of the World. 2007. 224p. 21.99 *(978-1-60206-621-2(3))*; per. 14.99 *(978-1-60206-620-5(5))* Cosimo, Inc.

—The Discovery of New Worlds (Yesterday's Classics) Synge, E. M., illus. l.t. ed. 2006. 252p. (J). per. *(978-1-59915-014-7(X))* Yesterday's Classics.

—The Struggle for Sea Power, Book Iv of the Story of the World. 2007. 248p. 21.99 *(978-1-60206-625-0(6))*; per. 14.99 *(978-1-60206-624-3(8))* Cosimo, Inc.

—The Struggle for Sea Power (Yesterday's Classics) Synge, E. M., illus. l.t. ed. 2006. 276p. (J). per. 11.95 *(978-1-59915-016-1(6))* Yesterday's Classics.

Tames, Richard. Tell Me Why Didn't Mummies Have Brains? And More about History. 2004. (Illus.). 32p. (J). pap. *(978-1-84458-059-0(8)*, Pavilion Children's Books) Pavilion Bks.

Taylor, Trace. One World Single Copy Set. 2010. pap. 46.22 *(978-0-7613-7046-8(3))* American Reading Co.

Thornton, Brian. The Everything Kids' States Book: Wind Your Way Across Our Great Nation. 2007. (Everything(r) Kids Ser.). (ENG., Illus.). 144p. per. 16.99 *(978-1-59869-263-1(1))* Adams Media Corp.

Thunder from Above. (Illus.). 192p. (J). *(978-0-7835-0155-0(2))* Time-Life Education, Inc.

Timelines of World History. 2017. (World History Ser.). (ENG.). (J). 19.99 *(978-0-7945-3921-4(1)*, Usborne) EDC Publishing.

Trembinski, Donna. Medieval Myths, Legends & Songs, 1 vol. 2005. (Medieval World Ser.). (ENG., Illus.). 32p. (J). (gr. 4-9). pap. *(978-0-7787-1391-3(1))* Crabtree Publishing Co.

Truth & Rumor [Capstone Sole Source]. 2010. (Truth & Rumors Ser.). 32p. lib. bdg. 106.60 *(978-1-4296-5886-7(X)*, Capstone Pr.) Capstone.

Turner, Tracey & Lenman, Jamie. Hard As Nails Kings & Queens. 2015. (Hard As Nails in History Ser.). (ENG., Illus.). 64p. (J). (gr. 4-5). lib. bdg. *(978-0-7787-1519-1(1))* Crabtree Publishing Co.

Turning Points in History, 8 vols., Set. Incl. Britannica Guide to Explorers & Explorations That Changed the Modern World. Pletcher, Kenneth. 352p. lib. bdg. 48.59 *(978-1-61530-028-0(7)*, 79cb531e-1d74-4c92-b4ad-ad724030f85f); Britannica Guide to Inventions That Changed the Modern World. Curley, Robert, ed. 392p. lib. bdg. 48.59 *(978-1-61530-020-4(1)*, bba4d0b9-7e2d-4177-831f-805bf7bf43f6); (YA). (gr. 10-10). (Turning Points in History Ser.). (ENG., Illus.). 392p. 2010. Set lib. bdg. 194.36 *(978-1-61530-034-1(1)*, 268cedcd-6aa1-4252-b38b-d7180145ee35) Rosen Publishing Group, Inc., The.

Understanding History: Concepts & Skills. 2006. 19.50 net. *(978-1-56004-263-1(X))* Social Studies Schl. Service.

Understanding People in the Past, 5 bks., Set 1. (J). (gr. 4-6). lib. bdg. 135.35 *(978-1-57572-891-9(5))* Heinemann-Raintree.

Unusual Histories, 1 vol. 2010. (Unusual Histories Ser.). (ENG.). 48p. (gr. 3-4). lib. bdg. 65.30 *(978-1-4296-4793-9(0))* Capstone.

Van Loon, Hendrik Willem. The Story of Mankind. 2006. 31.95 *(978-1-59605-956-6(7)*, Cosimo Classics) Cosimo, Inc.

—The Story of Mankind. 2007. 382p. pap. 25.99 *(978-1-4346-3848-9(0))* Creative Media Partners, LLC.

—The Story of Mankind. 2003. xxiv, 548p. pap. 29.00 *(978-0-7581-9568-5(0))* Textbook Pubs.

Vanloon, Hendrik Willem & Sullivan, Robert. The Story of Mankind. 2013. (Liveright Classics Ser.: 0). (ENG., Illus.). 736p. (gr. 5-9). 35.00 *(978-0-87140-715-3(9)*, 40715) Liveright Publishing Corp.

Visions of History SPICE. 115p. (YA). (gr. 5-9). spiral bd., tchr.'s planning gde. ed. 39.95 *(978-0-382-40952-3(3))* Cobblestone Publishing Co.

Visions of History SPICE: Grades 5-9. 115p. (YA). (gr. 5-9). tchr. ed. 48.95 *(978-0-382-40953-0(1))* Cobblestone Publishing Co.

A Visual History of the World, 14 vols. 2016. (Visual History of the World Ser.). (ENG.). 00096p. (YA). (gr. 8-8). 271.60 *(978-1-4994-6561-7(0)*, f38621e7-6e5e-4685-baa0-062bc15fae4f, Rosen Young Adult) Rosen Publishing Group, Inc., The.

Welch, Laura & Hodge, Bodie, eds. Big Book of History: A 15' Fold-Out Time-Line from Creation to Modern Computers. 2011. 21p. (J). (gr. 4-6). lib. bdg. 24.99 *(978-0-89051-623-2(5)*, Master Books) New Leaf Publishing Group.

Wijesinha, Rajiva. Foundations of Modern Society. 2004. 75p. pap. *(978-81-7596-244-6(5))* Cambridge Univ. Pr. India Pvt. Ltd.

Williams, Brian. History. 2010. (What About... Ser.). (Illus.). 40p. (J). (gr. 6-8). lib. bdg. 19.95 *(978-1-4222-1559-3(8))* Mason Crest.

—History: Biggest & Best. 2004. (Biggest & Best Ser.). (Illus.). 40p. (J). pap. 7.95 *(978-1-84236-065-1(5))* Miles Kelly Publishing, Ltd. GBR. Dist: Independent Pubs. Group.

—Natural World: Biggest & Best. 2004. (Biggest & Best Ser.). (Illus.). 40p. (J). pap. 7.95 *(978-1-84236-061-3(2))* Miles Kelly Publishing, Ltd. GBR. Dist: Independent Pubs. Group.

—What about HIST. 2008. 40p. pap. *(978-1-84810-068-8(X))* Miles Kelly Publishing, Ltd.

—What about People & Places. 2008. 40p. pap. *(978-1-84810-072-5(8))* Miles Kelly Publishing, Ltd.

Williams, Rozanne. Long Ago & Today. 2017. (Learn-To-Rea[d] Ser.). (ENG., Illus.). (J). pap. 3.49 *(978-1-68310-255-7(X))* Pacific Learning, Inc.

World Book, Inc. Staff, contrib. by. Explore & Learn — People in Place & Time. 2008. (J). *(978-0-7166-3020-3(6))* World Bk., Inc.

World History - Patterns of Interaction: Reading Study Guide. 2003. (SPA.). (gr. 6-12). *(978-0-618-18291-6(8)*, 2-01372) Holt McDougal.

World History: Patterns of Interaction. 2005. (gr. 6-12). tchr. ed *(978-0-618-37774-9(3)*, 2-00552) Holt McDougal.

World History: Patterns of Interaction: EEdition Plus Online. (gr 6-12). 2005. *(978-0-618-40923-5(8)*, 2-00604) 2003. *(978-0-618-19415-5(0)*, 2-70057) Holt McDougal.

World History: Patterns of Interaction: EEdition Plus Online with purchase of print Pupil's Edition-1 Year. 2005. (gr. 6-12). *(978-0-618-40925-9(4)*, 2-00606) Holt McDougal.

World History: Patterns of Interaction: EEdition Plus Online with Purchase of Print Pupil's Edition-1 Year. 2003. (gr. 6-12). *(978-0-618-25863-5(9)*, 2-01416) Holt McDougal.

World History: Patterns of Interaction: Electronic Library of Primary Sources. (gr. 6-12). 2005. cd-rom *(978-0-618-42871-7(2)*, 2-00770) 2003. cd-rom *(978-0-618-18619-8(0)*, 2-01392) Holt McDougal.

World History: Patterns of Interaction: Reading Study Guide Answer Key. (gr. 6-12). 2005. *(978-0-618-40932-7(7)*, 2-00613) 2003. *(978-0-618-18288-6(8)*, 2-01370) Holt McDougal.

World History: Patterns of Interaction: World History: Patterns of Interaction Workbook Answer Key. 2005. (gr. 6-12). *(978-0-618-40939-6(4)*, 2-00620) Holt McDougal.

World History: Patterns of Interaction: World History Workbook Answer Key. 2003. (gr. 6-12). *(978-0-395-95208-5(5)*, 2-81094) Holt McDougal.

World View: A Global Study of Geography, History & Culture, Bk. 2. stu. ed. 21.95 *(978-0-916591-45-8(X))* Linmore Publishing, Inc.

Wukovits, John F. Internment of Japanese Americans, 1 vol. 2012. (World History Ser.). (ENG., Illus.). 120p. (gr. 7-7). lib. bdg. 41.53 *(978-1-4205-0824-6(5)*, 2e07a3d0-03bf-4a0b-8e29-021ac7be5902, Lucent Pr.) Greenhaven Publishing LLC.

Ylla-Somers, Christophe. All of Us: a Young People's History of the World. Lehmann, Anna, tr. Pommaux, Yvan, illus. 2019. (ENG.). 88p. (J). (gr. 3-6). 29.95 *(978-1-68137-321-8(1)*, NYR Children's Collection) New York Review of Bks., Inc., The.

You Choose: History. 2011. (You Choose: History Ser.). (ENG.). 112p. (gr. 3-4). pap. 1000.80 *(978-1-4296-6442-4(8)*, Capstone Pr.) Capstone.

You Choose Assortment [Levy]. 2010. (You Choose Bks.). 37.56 *(978-1-4296-5882-9(7)*, Capstone Pr.) Capstone.

You Choose Books [Capstone Sole Source]. 2010. (You Choose Bks.). 112p. 858.20 *(978-1-4296-5892-8(4)*, Capstone Pr.) Capstone.

You Choose: Historical Eras Classroom Collection. 2011. (You Choose: Historical Eras Ser.). (ENG.). 112p. (gr. 3-4). pap. 250.20 *(978-1-4296-6443-1(6)*, Capstone Pr.) Capstone.

You Choose History Assortment [Levy]. 2010. (You Choose Bks.). pap. 6.95 *(978-1-4296-5182-0(2)*, Capstone Pr.) Capstone.

You Choose Pack 1 [Levy]. 2010. (You Choose Bks.). pap. 3.13 *(978-1-4296-5830-0(4)*, Capstone Pr.) Capstone.

You Choose Pack 2 [Levy]. 2010. (You Choose Bks.). pap. 3.13 *(978-1-4296-5831-7(2)*, Capstone Pr.) Capstone.

You Choose Pack 3 [Levy]. 2010. (You Choose Bks.). pap. 3.13 *(978-1-4296-5832-4(0)*, Capstone Pr.) Capstone.

You Choose Pack 4 [Levy]. 2010. (You Choose Bks.). pap. 3.13 *(978-1-4296-5833-1(9)*, Capstone Pr.) Capstone.

You Choose Pack 5 [Levy]. 2010. (You Choose Bks.). pap. 3.13 *(978-1-4296-5834-8(7)*, Capstone Pr.) Capstone.

You Choose Pack 6 [Levy]. 2010. (You Choose Bks.). pap. 3.13 *(978-1-4296-5835-5(5)*, Capstone Pr.) Capstone.

Zacharias, Gary. Events That Changed the World - 1900-1920. 2003. (Illus.). 224p. pap. 22.45 *(978-0-7377-1753-2(X))* Cengage Gale.

19th Century Nationalism. 2003. spiral bd. 16.95 *(978-1-56004-171-9(4))* Social Studies Schl. Service.

20 Questions: History, 4 vols., Set. 2007. (20 Questions: History Ser.). (ENG.). (J). (gr. 2-3). lib. bdg. 52.54 *(978-1-4042-4242-5(2)*, 70a1330d-c12a-4ea7-a907-8f38a7130fd9) Rosen Publishing Group, Inc., The.

21st Century Issues, 4 vols. 2004. (21st Century Issues Ser.). (ENG.). 48p. (gr. 5-8). lib. bdg. 67.34 *(978-0-8368-5640-8(6)*, 1e79c3a1-f105-4508-9c55-962d8d781d37, Gareth Stevens Secondary Library) Stevens, Gareth Publishing LLLP.

WORLD ORGANIZATION

see International Organization

WORLD POLITICS

see also International Organization; International Relations; World War, 1939-1945

also names of countries with the subdivisions Foreign Relations and Politics and Government, e.g. United States—Foreign Relations; United States—Politics and Government

Aronson, Marc. The Real Revolution: The Global Story of American Independence. 2005. (ENG., Illus.). 256p. (YA). (gr. 7-12). 22.00 *(978-0-618-18179-7(2)*, 111143, Clarion Bks.) HarperCollins Pubs.

Baker, Lawrence W. Cold War Reference Library Cumulative Index. 2003. (Cold War Reference Library). (ENG.). 85p. (J). 5.00 *(978-0-7876-7667-4(5)*, UXL) Cengage Gale.

—Immigration & Migration Reference. 2004. (US Immigration & Migration Reference Library). (ENG.). (J). 5.00 *(978-0-7876-7734-3(5)*, UXL) Cengage Gale.

Beyer, Mark. Nuclear Weapons & the Cold War. (Library of Weapons of Mass Destruction Ser.). 64p. (gr. 5-5). 2009. 58.50 *(978-1-60853-953-6(9))* 2004. (ENG., Illus.). (J). lib. bdg. 37.13 *(978-1-4042-0290-0(0)*, 0a80bba8-6f1b-4ad3-a8af-407d12a0d36d) Rosen Publishing Group, Inc., The.

Brown Bear Books. Cold War. 2010. (Modern Military History Ser.). (ENG.). 64p. (J). (gr. 8-11). 39.95 *(978-1-933834-52-8(8)*, 16526) Brown Bear Bks.

Byers, Ann. The Legacy of the Cold War, 1 vol. 2017. (Cold War Chronicles Ser.). (ENG., Illus.). 112p. (YA). (gr. 9-9).

44.50 (978-1-5026-2865-7(1), 94a0da2e-2d0f-4240-8fb1-c3b2dcb81268) Cavendish Square Publishing LLC.

ay, Meredith, ed. The Cold War, 1 vol. 2016. (Political & Diplomatic History of the Modern World Ser.). (ENG.). 224p. (J). (gr. 10-10). 47.59 (978-1-68048-358-1(7), ca58086b-d005-41e7-9f47-e22aa3ba5457) Rosen Publishing Group, Inc., The.

uling, Kaitlyn. Nuclear Proliferation, the Military-Industrial Complex, & the Arms Race, 1 vol. 2017. (Cold War Chronicles Ser.). (ENG.). 112p. (YA). (gr. 9-9). 44.50 (978-1-5026-2730-8(2), 63bb416f-313e-4f0c-82a7-dcb9de3df1a7) Cavendish Square Publishing LLC.

gan, Tracie. Weapons of Mass Destruction & North Korea. (Library of Weapons of Mass Destruction Ser.). 64p. (gr. 5-5). 2009. 58.50 (978-1-60853-961-1(X)) 2004. (ENG., Illus.). (J). lib. bdg. 37.13 (978-1-4042-0296-2(X), 92b49345-de0d-4fe7-9fdc-4f194164ad58) Rosen Publishing Group, Inc., The.

Fleischman, Paul. Dateline: Troy. Morrow, Glenn & Frankfeldt, Gwen, illus. 2006. (ENG.). 80p. (J). (gr. 7-10). pap. 8.99 (978-0-7636-3084-3(5)) Candlewick Pr.

Gale Editors, ed. Worldmark Conflict & Diplomacy: 2 Volume Set, 2 vols. 2014. (Worldmark Conflict & Diplomacy Ser.). (ENG.). 1000p. 399.00 (978-1-57302-726-7(X)) Cengage Gale.

George, Enzo. The Cold War, 1 vol. 2015. (Primary Sources in U. S. History Ser.). (ENG., Illus.). 48p. (gr. 4-4). 33.07 (978-1-5026-0498-9(1), ad38b917-1676-4972-b8e9-ea15e825a072) Cavendish Square Publishing LLC.

Gitlin, Martin, ed. Citizenship in the 21st Century, 1 vol. 2019. (Global Viewpoints Ser.). (ENG.). 176p. (gr. 10-12). 47.83 (978-1-5345-0551-3(2), eeefe166-5300-44d5-8e9c-7c58818a7cb5) Greenhaven Publishing LLC.

Gottfried, Ted. The Cold War. Reim, Melanie, illus. 2003. (Rise & Fall of the Soviet Union Ser.). (ENG.). 160p. (gr. 7-12). lib. bdg. 29.20 (978-0-7613-2560-4(3), Twenty-First Century Bks.) Lerner Publishing Group.

Grant, R. G. The Great Depression, 1 vol. 2005. (How Did It Happen? Ser.). (ENG., Illus.). 48p. (gr. 4-8). lib. bdg. 38.33 (978-1-59018-606-0(0), b0781d0e-ddeb-475e-a2ae-da9e894e3a0b, Lucent Pr.) Greenhaven Publishing LLC.

Grapes, Bryan J. Events That Changed the World - 1980-2000. 2003. (EVENTS THAT CHANGED the WRLD Ser.). (ENG., Illus.). 187p. lib. bdg. 38.45 (978-0-7377-1760-0(2)) Cengage Gale.

Gunderson, Cory Gideon. The Need for Oil. 2003. (World in Conflict-the Middle East Ser.). 32p. (gr. 4-8). 27.07 (978-1-59197-417-8(8), Abdo & Daughters) ABDO Publishing Co.

Hanes, Sharon M., et al. Cold War: Almanac, 2 vols. 2003. (U-X-L Cold War Reference Library). (Illus.). (J). (978-0-7876-9087-8(2)); 200p. 55.00 (978-0-7876-7662-9(4)); (ENG., 376p. lib. bdg. 233.00 (978-0-7876-9089-2(9)) Cengage Gale. (UXL).

—Cold War - Primary Sources. 2003. (Cold War Reference Library). (ENG., Illus.). 400p. (J). 129.00 (978-0-7876-7666-7(7), UXL) Cengage Gale.

—Cold War Reference Library: Includes Cumulative Index, 6 vols. Incl. Cold War: Almanac. 200p. 55.00 (978-0-7876-7662-9(4)); Cold War: Biographies. 474p. 233.00 (978-0-7876-7663-6(2)); Cold War - Primary Sources. 400p. 129.00 (978-0-7876-7666-7(7)); (J). (Cold War Reference Library). (ENG., Illus.). 1205p. 2003. Set lib. bdg. 557.00 (978-0-7876-7609-4(8), UXL) Cengage Gale.

Harrison, Paul. The Cold War. 2005. (How Did It Happen? Ser.). (ENG., Illus.). 48p. (YA). (gr. 7-10). lib. bdg. 32.10 (978-1-59018-603-9(6), Lucent Bks.) Cengage Gale.

—Why Did the Cold War Happen?, 1 vol. 2010. (Moments in History Ser.). (ENG.). 48p. (gr. 6-8). (J). pap. 15.05 (978-1-4339-4167-2(8), aad632c8-c029-458d-b7f9-b25990910bc2, Gareth Stevens Secondary Library); (Illus.). (YA). lib. bdg. 34.60 (978-1-4339-4166-5(X), eae20eee-654b-480c-9bb2-4b4e7dcf1173) Stevens, Gareth Publishing LLLP.

Hasan, Tahara. Anthrax Attacks Around the World. 2009. (Terrorist Attacks Ser.). 64p. (gr. 5-5). 58.50 (978-1-60853-307-7(7)) Rosen Publishing Group, Inc., The.

Johnson, Cynthia. Worldmark Conflict & Diplomacy. 2014. (J). (978-1-57302-727-4(8)) Cengage Gale.

Levering, Ralph B. The Cold War, 1945-1991. Eisenstadt, Abraham S. & Franklin, John Hope, eds. 2003. (American History Ser.). (Illus.). 200p. (J). (gr. 11-12). pap. 13.95 (978-0-88295-912-2(3)) Davidson, Harlan Inc.

Link, Theodore. Communism: A Primary Source Analysis. 2009. (Primary Sources of Political Systems Ser.). 64p. (gr. 5-8). 58.50 (978-1-60851-835-7(3)) Rosen Publishing Group, Inc., The.

MacDonald, Fiona & Weaver, Clare. Human Rights. 2003. (World Issues Ser.). (Illus.). 57p. (J). (gr. 5-18). lib. bdg. 29.95 (978-1-931983-82-2(8)) Chrysalis Education.

Mason, Paul. Did Anything Good Come Out of the Cold War?, 1 vol., 1. 2015. (Innovation Through Adversity Ser.). (ENG.). 48p. (J). (gr. 6-7). 33.47 (978-1-5081-7066-2(5), b071e82a-3543-4dd8-9ee4-301f921cd25a, Rosen Young Adult) Rosen Publishing Group, Inc., The.

Maybury, Richard J. World War II: The Rest of the Story & How It Affects You Today, 1930 to September 11 2001. Williams, Jane A., ed. rev. ed. 2003. ("Uncle Eric" Bk.: 11). (ENG., Illus.). 349p. pap. 19.95 (978-0-942617-43-6(6)) Bluestocking Pr.

McCarthy, Rose. Dictatorship: A Primary Source Analysis. 2009. (Primary Sources of Political Systems Ser.). 64p. (gr. 5-8). 58.50 (978-1-60851-837-1(X)) Rosen Publishing Group, Inc., The.

Nelson, Sheila. The Birth of the un, Decolonization & Building Strong Nations, Vol. 10. Russett, Bruce, ed. 2015. (United Nations: Leadership & Challenges in a Global World Ser.). (Illus.). 88p. (J). (gr. 7). lib. bdg. 24.95 (978-1-4222-3430-3(4)) Mason Crest.

—Decolonization: Dismantling Empires & Building Independence. 2008. (United Nations Ser.). (Illus.). 88p. (YA). (gr. 5-18). lib. bdg. 21.95 (978-1-4222-0066-7(3)) Mason Crest.

Olson, Steven P. The International Atomic Energy Agency. 2009. (Library of Weapons of Mass Destruction Ser.). 64p. (gr. 5-5). 58.50 (978-1-60853-957-4(1)) Rosen Publishing Group, Inc., The.

Otfinoski, Steven. A Step into History: the Cold War (Library Edition) 2018. (Step into History Ser.). (ENG., Illus.). 144p. (J). lib. bdg. 36.00 (978-0-531-22691-9(3), Children's Pr.) Scholastic Library Publishing.

Perritano, John. Education, Poverty, & Inequality. 2017. (Illus.). 64p. (J). (978-1-4222-3634-5(X)) Mason Crest.

Piddock, Charles. The Cold War. 2016. (Illus.). 48p. (J). (978-1-5105-1282-5(9)) SmartBook Media, Inc.

Porterfield, Jason. Communism: A Primary Source Analysis, 1 vol. 2004. (Primary Sources of Political Systems Ser.). (ENG., Illus.). 64p. (YA). (gr. 5-8). 37.13 (978-0-8239-4517-7(0), 31b490a6-8e6e-48f7-97b9-91019d1414da) Rosen Publishing Group, Inc., The.

Richardson, Erik. NATO, the Warsaw Pact, & the Iron Curtain, 1 vol. 2017. (Cold War Chronicles Ser.). (ENG., Illus.). 112p. (YA). (gr. 9-9). 44.50 (978-1-5026-2727-8(2), 37fd8157-5916-41d7-9852-9f26364cd4c6) Cavendish Square Publishing LLC.

Riggs, Kate. The End of the Cold War. 2016. (Turning Points Ser.). (ENG., Illus.). 48p. (J). (gr. 4-7). (978-1-60818-748-5(9), 20810, Creative Education) Creative Co., The.

Rivera, Sheila. Weapons of Mass Destruction. 2003. (World in Conflict-the Middle East Ser.). 32p. (gr. 4-8). 27.07 (978-1-59197-421-5(6), Abdo & Daughters) ABDO Publishing Co.

Roxburgh, Ellis. John F. Kennedy vs. Nikita Khrushchev: Cold War Adversaries, 1 vol. 2014. (History's Greatest Rivals Ser.). (ENG., Illus.). 48p. (J). (gr. 6-8). lib. bdg. 33.60 (978-1-4824-2221-4(2), bfc1cb51-8eeb-416d-af93-4cb9dbc51ac4) Stevens, Gareth Publishing LLLP.

Seward, Pat. Countdown to Catastrophe, 1 vol. 2011. (World War II Ser.). (ENG.). 128p. (gr. 6-6). 38.36 (978-0-7614-4944-7(2), 388ef178-cef9-4c94-abcf-8e4c674c146c) Cavendish Square Publishing LLC.

Sheehan, Sean. The Cold War. 2003. (Questioning History Ser.). (Illus.). 64p. (J). (gr. 5). lib. bdg. 28.50 (978-1-58340-266-5(7)) Black Rabbit Bks.

Sherman, Josepha. The Cold War. 2004. (Chronicle of America's Wars Ser.). (Illus.). 96p. (J). (gr. 5-12). 27.93 (978-0-8225-0150-3(3)) Lerner Publishing Group.

Sirimarco, Elizabeth. The Cold War, 1 vol. 2006. (American Voices From Ser.). (ENG., Illus.). 160p. (gr. 6-6). 41.21 (978-0-7614-1694-4(3), b9c0d0fe-4d12-4bf9-8b70-5c75a3b56140) Cavendish Square Publishing LLC.

Spalding, Frank. Nuclear Annihilation. 2010. (Doomsday Scenarios: Separating Fact from Fiction Ser.). 64p. (YA). (gr. 5-8). E-Book 58.50 (978-1-4488-1208-0(9)); (ENG.). (gr. 7-7). pap. 13.95 (978-1-4358-8522-6(8), cdd04e17-bb4e-47ca-9b69-ab27f237dd09, Rosen Reference); (ENG., Illus.). (gr. 7-7). lib. bdg. 37.13 (978-1-4358-3560-3(3), 26e39103-8f17-433b-9c0b-5cee1e78350f, Rosen Reference) Rosen Publishing Group, Inc., The.

Stanley, George E. An Emerging World Power (1900-1929), 1 vol. 2004. (Primary Source History of the United States Ser.). (ENG., Illus.). 48p. (gr. 5-8). pap. 15.05 (978-0-8368-5837-2(9), 324523d2-5e90-424c-bfff-97e703f50d4c); lib. bdg. 33.67 (978-0-8368-5828-0(X), 1d569960-8f8b-4d2e-81b1-983ee7fe4527) Stevens, Gareth Publishing LLLP. (Gareth Stevens Secondary Library).

Stites, Bill. Democracy: A Primary Source Analysis. (Primary Sources of Political Systems Ser.). 64p. (gr. 5-8). 2009. 58.50 (978-1-60851-836-4(1)) 2004. (ENG., Illus.). (YA). lib. bdg. 37.13 (978-0-8239-4518-4(9), 8434ef5f-7a20-4e91-9d32-c046d6203e48) Rosen Publishing Group, Inc., The.

Strum, Richard M. Causes of the American Revolution. 2005. (Road to War Ser.). (Illus.). 64p. (J). pap. 12.95 (978-1-59556-005-6(X)); (gr. 4-18). lib. bdg. 22.95 (978-1-59556-001-8(7)) OTTN Publishing.

Van Dijk, Ruud. The Making of the Modern World: 1945 to the Present: Governance & the Quest for Security, Vol. 9. 2016. (Making of the Modern World: 1945 to the Present Ser.: Vol. 9). (ENG., Illus.). 64p. (J). (gr. 7-12). 23.95 (978-1-4222-3638-3(2)) Mason Crest.

Wilson, John. Failed Hope: The Story of the Lost Peace (Large Print 16pt) 2013. 180p. pap. (978-1-4596-6314-5(4)) ReadHowYouWant.com, Ltd.

WORLD POLITICS—FICTION

Levithan, David. Love Is the Higher Law. 2010. 176p. (YA). (gr. 7). pap. 9.99 (978-0-375-83469-1(9), Knopf Bks. for Young Readers) Random Hse. Children's Bks.

O'Donnell, Liam. Power Play: A Graphic Guide Adventure, 1 vol. Deas, Mike, illus. 2011. (Graphic Guides: 6). (ENG.). 64p. (J). (gr. 4-7). pap. 9.95 (978-1-55469-069-5(2)) Orca Bk. Pubs. USA.

WORLD RECORDS

Brill, Calista. Guinness World Records: Wacky & Wild! 2016. (J). lib. bdg. 24.50 (978-0-606-38194-9(5)) Turtleback.

Burnham, Molly B. Almost a World Record Breaker. 2016. (Teddy Mars Ser.: 1). (J). lib. bdg. 17.20 (978-0-606-38132-1(5)) Turtleback.

Gilpin, Daniel. Record Breakers, 1 vol. Pang, Alex, illus. 2011. (Machines Close-Up Ser.). (ENG.). 32p. (gr. 4-4). 31.21 (978-1-60870-113-1(1), 4582474e-2edb-4155-a62a-6f9144194f4c) Cavendish Square Publishing LLC.

—Record-Breaking Buildings, 1 vol. 2011. (Record Breakers Ser.). (ENG.). 32p. (J). (gr. 2-3). lib. bdg. 30.27 (978-1-4488-5288-8(9), 9e36e3b7-9a34-457a-b709-c6dcc28ab21b, PowerKids Pr.) Rosen Publishing Group, Inc., The.

—Record-Breaking Cars, 1 vol. 2011. (Record Breakers Ser.). (ENG., Illus.). 32p. (J). (gr. 2-3). lib. bdg. 30.27 (978-1-4488-5289-5(7), fe859679-f59e-4d3e-afc6-79dde7f83592, PowerKids Pr.) Rosen Publishing Group, Inc., The.

Glass, Calliope. Guinness World Records: Wacky & Wild! 2016. (Guinness World Records Ser.). (ENG., Illus.). 176p. (J). (gr. 3-7). pap. 13.99 (978-0-06-234176-1(6)) HarperCollins Pubs.

Grove, Tim & National Air and Space Museum. First Flight Around the World: The Adventures of the American Fliers Who Won the Race. 2015. (ENG., Illus.). 96p. (J). (gr. 3-9). 21.95 (978-1-4197-1482-5(1), 1087101) Abrams, Inc.

Guinness Editors. Guinness World Records 2016, Gamers Edition. 2015. lib. bdg. 26.95 (978-0-606-38494-0(4)) Turtleback.

Hansen, Grace. Records Mundiales Insolitos! (World Records to Wow You!) 2016. (Ver para Creer (Seeing Is Believing) Ser.). (SPA., Illus.). 24p. (J). (gr. -1-2). lib. bdg. 32.79 (978-1-68080-773-8(0), 22708, Abdo Kids) ABDO Publishing Co.

—World Records to Wow You!, 1 vol. 2015. (Seeing Is Believing Ser.). (ENG., Illus.). 24p. (J). (gr. -1-2). lib. bdg. 32.79 (978-1-62970-736-5(8), 17289, Abdo Kids) ABDO Publishing Co.

—World Records to Wow You! 2017. (Seeing Is Believing Ser.). (ENG.). 24p. (J). (gr. -1-2). pap. 7.95 (978-1-4966-1321-9(X), 135033, Capstone Classroom) Capstone.

Harris, Michelle. National Geographic Kids Extreme Records. 2018. (Illus.). 208p. (J). (gr. 3-7). pap. 14.99 (978-1-4263-3021-6(9)); (ENG., lib. bdg. 23.90 (978-1-4263-3022-3(7)) Disney Publishing Worldwide. (National Geographic Kids).

Herndon, Ryan, compiled by. 3-D Extreme! 2006. (Illus.). 31p. (J). pap. (978-0-439-79190-8(1)) Scholastic, Inc.

Hirschmann, Kris & Herndon, Ryan, compiled by. Guinness World Records. 2011. (Illus.). 80p. (J). (978-0-545-30851-9(8)) Scholastic, Inc.

—Guinness World Records: Records of Overwhelming Size. 2007. (Illus.). 90p. (J). pap. (978-0-439-89829-4(3)) Scholastic, Inc.

—Guinness World Records, up Close. 2007. (Illus.). 47p. (978-0-439-89828-7(5)) Scholastic, Inc.

Lemke, Donald. Guinness World Records: Super Humans! 2016. (J). lib. bdg. 24.50 (978-0-606-38193-2(7)) Turtleback.

—Guinness World Records: Man-Made Marvels! 2016. (Guinness World Records Ser.). (ENG., Illus.). 176p. (J). (gr. 3-7). pap. 12.99 (978-0-06-234180-8(4), HarperCollins) HarperCollins Pubs.

Mattern, Joanne & Herndon, Ryan, compiled by. Guinness World Records: Extraordinary Records of Unusual Facts & Feats. 2005. (Illus.). 90p. (J). pap. (978-0-439-79192-2(8)) Scholastic, Inc.

McCollum, Sean. The World's Most Daring Stunts. 2016. (World Record Breakers Ser.). (ENG., Illus.). 32p. (J). (gr. 3-9). lib. bdg. 28.65 (978-1-4914-8179-0(X), 130655, Capstone Pr.) Capstone.

McCollum, Sean, et al. World Record Breakers. 2016. (World Record Breakers Ser.). (ENG., Illus.). 32p. (J). (gr. 3-9). 122.60 (978-1-4914-8192-9(7), 23998, Capstone Pr.) Capstone.

Mitchell, Susan. The Longest Bridges, 1 vol. 2007. (Megastructures Ser.). (ENG., Illus.). 32p. (gr. 3-3). lib. bdg. 28.67 (978-0-8368-8364-0(0), 80084532-0cae-4209-84be-718bb51457c2) Stevens, Gareth Publishing LLLP.

Morse, Jenifer Corr. Scholastic Book of World Records. 2008. (Scholastic Book of World Records Ser.). (Illus.). 304p. (J). (gr. 4-7). 17.65 (978-0-7569-8839-5(X)) Perfection Learning Corp.

—Scholastic Book of World Records, 2008. 2007. (Illus.). 304p. (J). (978-1-4287-5691-5(4), Scholastic Reference) Scholastic, Inc.

—Scholastic Book of World Records 2016. 2015. lib. bdg. 22.10 (978-0-606-37751-5(4)) Turtleback.

Ripley Entertainment. Life in the Fast Lane. 2010. (Ripley's Believe It or Not Ser.). 36p. (YA). (gr. 3-18). lib. bdg. 19.95 (978-1-4222-1538-8(5)) Mason Crest.

Ripley's Believe It Or Not! Staff. Awesome Feats. 2012. (Ripley's Disbelief & Shock Ser.). 36p. (J). (gr. 3-4). 19.95 (978-1-4222-2562-2(3)) Mason Crest.

—World Wonders. 2012. (Ripley's Disbelief & Shock Ser.). 36p. (J). (gr. 3-4). 19.95 (978-1-4222-2576-9(3)) Mason Crest.

Roberts, Christa. Guinness World Records: Amazing Body Records! 100 Mind-Blowing Body Records from Around the World! 2016. (J). lib. bdg. 16.00 (978-0-606-38192-5(9)) Turtleback.

—Guinness World Records: Incredible Animals: Amazing Animals & Their Awesome Feats! 2016. (J). lib. bdg. 16.00 (978-0-606-38191-8(0)) Turtleback.

—Guinness World Records: Incredible Animals! 2016. (Guinness World Records Ser.). (ENG., Illus.). 112p. (J). (gr. 1-5). pap. 5.99 (978-0-06-234167-9(7)) HarperCollins Pubs.

Wallace, Elise. Amazing Animals: World Record Wildlife: Adding & Subtracting Fractions (Grade 5) 2018. (Mathematics in the Real World Ser.). (ENG., Illus.). 32p. (J). (gr. 4-8). pap. 11.99 (978-1-4258-5813-1(9)) Teacher Created Materials, Inc.

Webster, Christy. Guinness World Records: Biggest & Smallest! 2016. (J). lib. bdg. 24.50 (978-0-606-38195-6(3)) Turtleback.

—Guinness World Records: Biggest & Smallest! 2016. (Guinness World Records Ser.). (ENG., Illus.). 176p. (J). (gr. 3-7). pap. 12.99 (978-0-06-234178-5(2)) HarperCollins Pubs.

WORLD SERIES (BASEBALL)

Cho, Alan. World Series. (We Are the Champions Ser.). (J). 2019. (ENG.). 32p. (gr. 4-7). pap. 13.95 (978-1-7911-0584-6(X)) 2018. (Illus.). 32p. (978-1-7911-0053-7(8), AV2 by Weigl) 2012. (978-1-61913-063-0(7)) 2012. pap. (978-1-61913-625-0(2)) 2007. (Illus.). 32p. (gr. 4-6). lib. bdg. 26.00 (978-1-59036-699-8(9)) 2007. (Illus.). 32p. (gr. 4-7). per. 9.95 (978-1-59036-700-1(6)) Weigl Pubs., Inc.

Doeden, Matt. The World Series: Baseball's Biggest Stage. 2014. (Spectacular Sports Ser.). (ENG., Illus.). 64p. (J). (gr. 5-8). lib. bdg. 34.65 (978-1-4677-1896-7(3), 1fd36ffb-1548-4f01-8583-0b105567a991, Millbrook Pr.) Lerner Publishing Group.

Garcia, Tom & Naga, Karun. Daddy's Heroes: Gibby's Homer: the 1988 World Series. Donnelly, Jenifer, illus. 2007. (1988 World Ser.). 32p. (J). (gr. -1-3). pap. 9.95 (978-0-9792111-0-2(7)) Daddy's Heroes, Inc.

Herman, Gail & Who HQ. What Is the World Series? Kenyon, David Grayson, illus. 2015. (What Was? Ser.). 112p. (J). (gr. 3-7). 5.99 (978-0-448-48406-8(4), Penguin Workshop) Penguin Young Readers Group.

Sandler, Michael. David Eckstein & the St. Louis Cardinals: 2006 World Series. 2008. (World Series Superstars). (Illus.). 24p. (J). (gr. 1-4). lib. bdg. 26.99 (978-1-59716-636-2(7)) Bearport Publishing Co., Inc.

—Mike Lowell & the Boston Red Sox: 2007 World Series. 2008. (World Series Superstars). (Illus.). 24p. (J). (gr. 1-4). lib. bdg. 26.99 (978-1-59716-739-0(8), 1284374) Bearport Publishing Co., Inc.

—Randy Johnson & the Arizona Diamondbacks: 2001 World Series. 2008. (World Series Superstars). (Illus.). 24p. (J). (gr. 1-4). lib. bdg. 26.99 (978-1-59716-638-6(3)) Bearport Publishing Co., Inc.

—Troy Glaus & the Anaheim Angels: 2002 World Series. 2008. (World Series Superstars). (Illus.). 24p. (J). (gr. 1-4). lib. bdg. 26.99 (978-1-59716-640-9(5)) Bearport Publishing Co., Inc.

Scheff, Matt. The World Series: Baseball's Fall Classic. 2020. (Big Game (Lerner (tm) Sports) Ser.). (ENG., Illus.). 32p. (J). (gr. 2-5). 30.65 (978-1-5415-9754-9(0), f1f2d0bb-80cc-4d46-b56b-4bb6e5f6da91, Lerner Pubns.) Lerner Publishing Group.

Terrell, Brandon. Calling His Shot: Babe Ruth's Legendary Home Run. Garcia, Eduardo, illus. 2018. (Greatest Sports Moments Ser.). (ENG.). 32p. (J). (gr. 3-9). lib. bdg. 31.32 (978-1-5435-2868-8(6), 138371, Capstone Pr.) Capstone.

Winters, Jaime. For the Win: The World Series. 2015. (Baseball Source Ser.). (ENG., Illus.). 32p. (J). (gr. 3-4). (978-0-7787-1477-4(2)) Crabtree Publishing Co.

WORLD WAR, 1914-1918

Adams, Simon. Eyewitness World War I: Witness the Horror & Heroism of the Great War — From the Assassination of an Arc. 2014. (DK Eyewitness Ser.). (ENG.). 72p. (J). (gr. 3-7). pap. 9.99 (978-1-4654-2058-9(4), DK Children) Dorling Kindersley Publishing, Inc.

Baldwin, Douglas & Kissock, Heather. World War I. 2010. (Illus.). 48p. (978-1-55388-719-5(0)); pap. (978-1-55388-723-2(9)) Weigl Educational Pubs. Ltd.

Barton, Chris. Dazzle Ships: World War I & the Art of Confusion. Ngai, Victo, illus. 2017. (ENG.). 36p. (J). (gr. 2-5). lib. bdg. 19.99 (978-1-5124-1014-3(4), f606e87d-56aa-4cff-b87c-c59ad06e0b83, Millbrook Pr.) Lerner Publishing Group.

Batten, Jack. The War to End All Wars: The Story of World War I. 2009. (Illus.). 160p. (J). (gr. 5-18). 22.95 (978-0-88776-879-8(2), Tundra Bks.) Tundra Bks. CAN. Dist: Penguin Random Hse. LLC.

Bausum, Ann. Stubby the War Dog: The True Story of World War I's Bravest Dog. 80p. (J). (gr. 5-9). 2014. (Illus.). 17.99 (978-1-4263-1486-5(8)) 2018. pap. 8.99 (978-1-4263-3266-1(1)) Disney Publishing Worldwide. (National Geographic Kids).

Beller, Susan Provost. The Doughboys over There: Soldiering in World War I. 2007. (Soldiers on the Battlefront Ser.). (ENG., Illus.). 112p. (J). (gr. 6-8). lib. bdg. 33.26 (978-0-8225-6295-5(2)) Lerner Publishing Group.

Benjamin, Andrew. World War I: The War to End All Wars. 2014. (J). pap. (978-1-62712-862-9(X)) Cavendish Square Publishing LLC.

Brocklehurst, Ruth & Brook, Henry. First World War. Chisholm, Jane, ed. 2007. (World Wars Ser.). (Illus.). 128p. (J). (gr. 4-7). 19.99 (978-0-7945-1455-6(3), Usborne) EDC Publishing.

—The Usborne Introduction to the First World War. 2007. (Illus.). 128p. (J). pap. (978-0-545-03901-7(0)) Scholastic, Inc.

Brouwer, Sigmund. Innocent Heroes: Stories of Animals in the First World War. 2017. (ENG., Illus.). 208p. (J). (gr. 4-7). 16.99 (978-1-101-91846-3(2), Tundra Bks.) Tundra Bks. CAN. Dist: Penguin Random Hse. LLC.

Brown Bear Books. The Early 20th Century. 2010. (Technology Through the Ages Ser.). (ENG.). 112p. (J). (gr. 9-12). 42.80 (978-1-933834-87-0(0), 16806) Brown Bear Bks.

—World War I. 2010. (Modern Military History Ser.). (ENG.). 64p. (J). (gr. 8-11). 39.95 (978-1-933834-49-8(8), 16529) Brown Bear Bks.

Budgen, David. British Children's Literature & the First World War: Representations Since 1914. 2018. (ENG.). 256p. (C). (978-1-4742-5685-8(6), 291239, Bloomsbury Academic) Bloomsbury Publishing Plc.

Burgan, Michael. Split History of World War I. 2013. (Perspectives Flip Bks.). (ENG.). 64p. (J). (gr. 5-9). 34.65 (978-0-7565-4694-6(X), 123111); pap. 8.95 (978-0-7565-4700-4(8), 123617) Capstone. (Compass Point Bks.).

Clarke, Gordon. Canada in World War I: Outstanding Victories Create a Nation. 2014. (World War I: Remembering the Great War Ser.). (ENG., Illus.). 48p. (J). (gr. 5-5). (978-0-7787-0327-3(4)) Crabtree Publishing Co.

Cox Cannons, Helen. The Remembrance Day & the Poppy. 2016. (Important Events in History Ser.). (ENG., Illus.). 24p. (J). (gr. 1-3). lib. bdg. 25.99 (978-1-4846-2707-5(5), 131159, Heinemann) Capstone.

Davis, Kenneth C. More Deadly Than War: The Hidden History of the Spanish Flu & the First World War. 2018. (ENG., Illus.). 304p. (YA). 19.99 (978-1-250-14512-3(0), 900180782, Holt, Henry & Co. Bks. For Young Readers) Holt, Henry & Co.

Dell, Pamela. A World War I Timeline, 1 vol. 2014. (War Timelines Ser.). (ENG., Illus.). 48p. (J). (gr. 4-7). lib. bdg. 35.32 (978-1-4765-4159-4(0), 124264, Capstone Pr.) Capstone.

Dennis, Elizabeth. Fearless Flyers, Dazzle Painters, & Code Talkers! World War I (Ready-To-Read Level 3) Fabbretti, Valerio, illus. 2018. (Secrets of American History Ser.). (ENG.). 48p. (J). (gr. 1-3). 16.99 (978-1-5344-1052-7(X)); pap. 4.99 (978-1-5344-1051-0(1)) Simon Spotlight. (Simon Spotlight).

WXYZ

Dickmann, Nancy. The Horror of World War I. 2017. (Deadly History Ser.). (ENG., Illus.). 48p. (J). (gr. 3-6). lib. bdg. 35.99 *(978-1-4846-4168-2(X)*, 136218, Heinemann) Capstone.

Doeden, Matt. Weapons of World War I. rev. ed. 2017. (Weapons of War Ser.). (ENG., Illus.). 32p. (J). (gr. 3-9). lib. bdg. 27.32 *(978-1-5157-7907-0(6)*, 136022, Capstone Pr.) Capstone.

Dowswell, Paul. First World War - Internet Referenced. rev. ed. 2007. (True Stories Ser.). 137p. (J). pap. 4.99 *(978-0-7945-1979-7(2)*, Usborne) EDC Publishing.

—The Story of the First World War. 2014. (ENG., Illus.). 95p. (J). (gr. 4-7). pap. 10.99 *(978-0-7945-2974-1(7)*, Usborne) EDC Publishing.

—True Stories of the First World War. (True Adventure Stories Ser.). (Illus.). (J). 2004. 137p. (gr. 5). lib. bdg. 12.95 *(978-1-58086-652-1(2))* 2011. 144p. pap. 4.99 *(978-0-7945-0721-3(2))* EDC Publishing. (Usborne).

—War Stories. rev. ed. 2012. (True Stories Ser.). 432p. (J). pap. 12.99 *(978-0-7945-3221-5(7)*, Usborne) EDC Publishing.

Dowswell, Paul, et al. The World Wars: An Introduction to the First & Second World Wars. Chisholm, Jane, ed. 2007. (World Wars Ser.). (Illus.). 256p. (J). (gr. 4-7). 25.99 *(978-0-7945-1971-1(7)*, Usborne) EDC Publishing.

Endrulat, Harry & Innes, Stephanie. A Bear in War. Deines, Brian, illus. 2009. (ENG.). 40p. (J). (gr. k-3). *(978-1-55470-097-4(3))* Me to We.

Essential Library of World War I, 9 vols. 2015. (Essential Library of World War I Ser.: 10). (ENG.). 112p. (J). (gr. 6-12). lib. bdg. 372.24 *(978-1-62403-920-1(0)*, 19130, Essential Library) ABDO Publishing Co.

Etinde-Crompton, Charlotte & Crompton, Samuel Willard. Horace Pippin: Painter & Decorated Soldier, 1 vol. 2019. (Celebrating Black Artists Ser.). (ENG.). 104p. (gr. 7-7). 38.93 *(978-1-9785-0360-1(1)*, f4497f18-7ea9-485e-9743-077c011da8ee) Enslow Publishing, LLC.

Feldman, Ruth Tenzer. World War I. 2004. (Chronicle of America's Wars Ser.). (Illus.). 88p. (gr. 5-12). lib. bdg. 27.93 *(978-0-8225-0148-0(1))* Lerner Publishing Group.

Ford, Jeanne Marie. Code Breakers & Spies of World War I, 1 vol. 2018. (Code Breakers & Spies Ser.). (ENG.). 80p. (YA). (gr. 8-8). 38.79 *(978-1-5026-3850-2(9)*, f8938ee1-8a7c-4260-b9b9-74c7d69b6c0a) Cavendish Square Publishing LLC.

—Eyewitness to the Role of Women in World War I. 2018. (Eyewitness to World War I Ser.). (ENG.). 32p. (J). (gr. 4-7). lib. bdg. 35.64 *(978-1-5038-1605-3(2)*, 211163) Child's World, Inc, The.

Freedman, Russell. The War to End All Wars: World War I. 2013. (ENG., Illus.). 192p. (YA). (gr. 7). pap. 11.99 *(978-0-544-02171-6(1)*, 1528505, Clarion Bks.) HarperCollins Pubs.

Gagne, Tammy. World War I Technology. 2017. (War Technology Ser.). (ENG., Illus.). 48p. (J). (gr. 4-8). lib. bdg. 35.64 *(978-1-5321-1192-1(4)*, 25960) ABDO Publishing Co.

Gail, Margaret. Moggie Grows up, 1939-1945. 2006. (ENG., Illus.). 74p. pap. *(978-0-7552-0227-0(9))* Authors OnLine, Ltd.

Garstecki, Julia. Harlem Hellfighters. 2016. (All-American Fighting Forces Ser.). (ENG.). 32p. (J). (gr. 4-6). pap. 9.99 *(978-1-64466-153-6(5)*, 10314); (Illus.). 31.35 *(978-1-68072-002-0(3)*, 10313) Black Rabbit Bks. (Bolt).

George, Enzo. World War I. 2015. (J). lib. bdg. *(978-1-62713-493-4(X))* 2014. (ENG.). 48p. (gr. 4-4). lib. bdg. 33.07 *(978-1-5026-0252-7(0)*, b87e410c-3a78-4a6e-bb4a-f0e1186700b9) Cavendish Square Publishing LLC.

—World War I: The War to End All Wars, 1 vol. 2014. (Voices of War Ser.). (ENG.). 48p. (gr. 4-4). lib. bdg. 33.07 *(978-1-62712-861-2(1)*, af1f5ca5-d857-4234-8744-06e8ee6c83b4) Cavendish Square Publishing LLC.

Goodman, Michael. World War I Spies. 2015. (Wartime Spies Ser.). (ENG., Illus.). 48p. (J). (gr. 4-7). *(978-1-60818-602-0(4)*, 21090, Creative Education) Creative Co., The.

Goodman, Michael E. World War I Spies. 2016. (Wartime Spies Ser.). (Illus.). 48p. (J). (gr. 4-7). pap. 12.00 *(978-1-62832-207-1(1)*, 21091, Creative Paperbacks) Creative Co., The.

Gould, Jane. World War I: 1914-1916 - A Terrible New Warfare Begins. 2014. (World War I: Remembering the Great War Ser.). (ENG., Illus.). 48p. (J). (gr. 5-5). *(978-0-7787-0325-9(8))* Crabtree Publishing Co.

Grant, R. G. Why Did World War I Happen?, 1 vol. 2010. (Moments in History Ser.). (ENG.). 48p. (gr. 6-8). (J). pap. 15.05 *(978-1-4339-4182-5(1)*, 93ab282f-f7fc-4044-bf86-b9373c5db742, Gareth Stevens Secondary Library); (Illus.). (YA). lib. bdg. 34.60 *(978-1-4339-4181-8(3)*, dbc68180-7d50-4924-bbf4-621b4712124b) Stevens, Gareth Publishing LLLP.

—World War I, 1 vol. 2005. (How Did It Happen? Ser.). (ENG., Illus.). 48p. (gr. 4-8). lib. bdg. 38.33 *(978-1-59018-605-3(2)*, ff93fc6d-c950-48f8-a569-b4ca7d8055ac, Lucent Pr.) Greenhaven Publishing LLC.

Green, Robert. World War I, 1 vol. 2007. (World History Ser.). (ENG., Illus.). 104p. (J). (gr. 7-7). lib. bdg. 41.53 *(978-1-4205-0025-7(2)*, c128c266-3b55-48e9-8432-fe9cb60c6054, Lucent Pr.) Greenhaven Publishing LLC.

Gregory, Josh. Cornerstones of Freedom, Third Series: World War I. 2012. (Cornerstones of Freedom, Third Ser.). (ENG., Illus.). 64p. (J). (gr. 4-6). lib. bdg. 30.00 *(978-0-531-23068-8(6)*, Children's Pr.) Scholastic Library Publishing.

Hale, Nathan. Treaties, Trenches, Mud, & Blood. 2017. (Nathan Hale's Hazardous Tales Ser.). (J). lib. bdg. 24.45 *(978-0-606-40707-6(3))* Turtleback.

—Treaties, Trenches, Mud, & Blood (Nathan Hale's Hazardous Tales #4) A World War I Tale. 2014. (Nathan Hale's Hazardous Tales Ser.). (ENG., Illus.). 128p. (J). (gr. 3-7). 14.99 *(978-1-4197-0808-4(2)*, 1047901, Amulet Bks.) Abrams, Inc.

Hamilton, John. Battles of World War I. 2017. (World War I Ser.). (ENG., Illus.). 48p. (J). (gr. 5-9). lib. bdg. 34.21 *(978-1-5321-1286-7(6)*, 27494, Abdo & Daughters) ABDO Publishing Co.

Hamilton, John, contrib. by. Aircraft of World War I. 2017. (World War I Ser.). (ENG., Illus.). 48p. (J). (gr. 5-9). lib. bdg. 34.21 *(978-1-5321-1285-0(8)*, 27493, Abdo & Daughters) ABDO Publishing Co.

—Weapons of World War I. 2017. (World War I Ser.). (ENG.). 48p. (J). (gr. 5-9). lib. bdg. 34.21 *(978-1-5321-1290-4(4)*, 27498, Abdo & Daughters) ABDO Publishing Co.

Hardyman, Robyn. What Caused World War I?, 1 vol. 2016. (Why War Happened Ser.). (ENG.). 48p. (gr. 6-8). lib. bdg. 33.60 *(978-1-4824-5182-5(4)*, 7f077ec1-fd2d-402e-9f69-da799c96339d) Stevens, Gareth Publishing LLLP.

Heinrichs, Ann. Voices of World War I: Stories from the Trenches. 2010. (Voices of War Ser.). (ENG.). 32p. (J). (gr. 3-4). pap. 49.74 *(978-1-4296-5701-3(4)*, 15490); (Illus.). pap. 8.29 *(978-1-4296-5626-9(3)*, 114117) Capstone. (Capstone Pr.).

Hinman, Bonnie. World War I: 12 Things to Know. 2017. (America at War Ser.). (ENG., Illus.). 32p. (J). (gr. 3-6). 32.80 *(978-1-63235-270-5(2)*, 11709, 12-Story Library) Bookstaves, LLC.

Hoena, Blake. Stubby the Dog Soldier: World War I Hero, 1 vol. 2014. (Animal Heroes Ser.). (ENG., Illus.). 32p. (J). (gr. k-2). 29.32 *(978-1-4795-5461-4(8)*, 126110, Picture Window Bks.) Capstone.

Hosch, William L. World War I: People, Politics, & Power, 4 vols. 2010. (America at War Ser.). (ENG.). 240p. (YA). (gr. 10-10). 105.18 *(978-1-61530-092-1(9)*, 9abc8394-f956-4ae2-8d48-e3e10c1d4950) Rosen Publishing Group, Inc., The.

Hosch, William L., ed. World War I: People, Politics, & Power, 1 vol. 2010. (America at War Ser.). (ENG., Illus.). 240p. (YA). (gr. 10-10). lib. bdg. 52.59 *(978-1-61530-013-6(9)*, 2a9225aa-addc-419c-b6e7-c1a9f093d455) Rosen Publishing Group, Inc., The.

Hosein, Ann, ed. Key Figures of World War I, 4 vols. 2015. (Biographies of War Ser.). (ENG.). 112p. (YA). (gr. 7-8). 70.94 *(978-1-68048-055-9(3)*, 3e431d1d-a298-4fd9-920b-e8d3e6223504, Britannica Educational Publishing) Rosen Publishing Group, Inc., The.

Hunter, Nick. The National Archives: World War I: The Story Behind the War That Shook the World. 2014. (ENG., Illus.). 64p. (J). (gr. 2-4). *(978-1-4729-0525-3(3)*, 246405, A&C Black Childrens & Educational) Bloomsbury Publishing Plc.

—World War I: Frontline Soldiers & Their Families, 1 vol. 2015. (Frontline Families Ser.). (ENG., Illus.). 48p. (J). (gr. 5-6). pap. 15.05 *(978-1-4824-3065-3(7)*, d7e60e0b-7549-43df-8c2f-ca8f6e762b6e) Stevens, Gareth Publishing LLLP.

Hyde, Natalie. World War I: The Cause for War. 2014. (World War I: Remembering the Great War Ser.). (ENG., Illus.). 48p. (J). (gr. 5-5). *(978-0-7787-0387-7(8))* Crabtree Publishing Co.

Innes, Stephanie & Endrulat, Harry. A Bear in War. Deines, Brian, illus. 2019. (ENG.). 40p. (J). (gr. k-4). pap. 14.95 *(978-1-77278-086-4(3))* Pajama Pr. CAN. Dist: Publishers Group West (PGW).

Kenney, Karen L. National Geographic Kids Everything World War I: Dig in with Thrilling Photos & Fascinating Facts. 2014. (National Geographic Kids Everything Ser.). (Illus.). 64p. (J). (gr. 3-7). pap. 12.99 *(978-1-4263-1715-6(8)*, National Geographic Kids) Disney Publishing Worldwide.

Ladybird, Ladybird. First World War. 2013. (Ladybird Histories Ser.). (Illus.). 64p. (J). (gr. 2-4). pap. 13.99 *(978-0-7232-7085-0(6))* Penguin Bks., Ltd. GBR. Dist: Independent Pubs. Group.

Lanser, Amanda. World War I by the Numbers. 2015. (America at War by the Numbers Ser.). (ENG., Illus.). 32p. (J). (gr. 3-9). lib. bdg. 28.65 *(978-1-4914-4296-8(4)*, 128691, Capstone Pr.) Capstone.

Lassieur, Allison. At Battle in World War I: An Interactive Battlefield Adventure. 2015 (You Choose: Battlefields Ser.). (ENG., Illus.). 112p. (J). (gr. 3-7). lib. bdg. 32.65 *(978-1-4914-2151-2(7)*, 127632, Capstone Pr.) Capstone.

—Courageous Spies & International Intrigue of World War I. 2017. (Spies! Ser.). (ENG., Illus.). 64p. (J). (gr. 4-8). lib. bdg. 34.65 *(978-0-7565-5499-6(3)*, 134228, Compass Point Bks.) Capstone.

Lassieur, Allison, et al. You Choose: Battlefields. 2015. (You Choose: Battlefields Ser.). (ENG.). 112p. (J). (gr. 3-7). 138.60 *(978-1-4914-2630-2(6)*, 22630, Capstone Pr.) Capstone.

Lawson, J. C. The Litany of the Elves. 2013. (ENG.). 36p. pap. 17.99 *(978-1-107-68397-6(1))* Cambridge Univ. Pr.

Lewis, J. Patrick. And the Soldiers Sang. Kelley, Gary, illus. 2012. (ENG.). 32p. (J). (gr. 3-6). pap. 9.99 *(978-0-89812-975-5(3)*, 22034, Creative Paperbacks) Creative Co., The.

—Harlem Hellfighters. Kelley, Gary, illus. 2014. (ENG.). 32p. (J). (gr. 4-7). 27.99 *(978-1-56846-246-2(8)*, 21309, Creative Editions) Creative Co., The.

Long, David. War School for Dogs: Band 16/Sapphire. 2017. (Collins Big Cat Ser.). (ENG., Illus.). 56p. (J). pap. 12.99 *(978-0-00-820891-2(3))* HarperCollins Pubs. Ltd. GBR. Dist: Independent Pubs. Group.

Malam, John. World War I: Armistice Day. 2003. 45p. (J). lib. bdg. 28.50 *(978-1-58340-410-2(4))* Black Rabbit Bks.

Mason, Conrad. The First World War. 2014. (Usborne Young Reading: Series Three Ser.). (ENG., Illus.). 63p. (J). (gr. 4-7). 6.99 *(978-0-7945-2092-2(8)*, Usborne) EDC Publishing.

Matthews, Rupert. The World Wars. 2008. (Timelines Ser.). (Illus.). 96p. (J). pap. *(978-1-84236-809-1(5))* Miles Kelly Publishing, Ltd.

Maybury, Richard J. World War I: The Rest of the Story & How It Affects You Today, 1870 To 1935. Williams, Jane A., ed. rev. ed. 2003. ("Uncle Eric" Bk.: 10). (ENG., Illus.). 253p. pap. 17.95 *(978-0-942617-42-9(8))* Bluestocking Pr.

McCollum, Sean. Secrets of World War I. 2017. (Top Secret Files Ser.). (ENG., Illus.). 32p. (J). (gr. 3-9). lib. bdg. 28.65 *(978-1-5157-4139-8(7)*, 133947, Capstone Pr.) Capstone.

McNeil, Niki, et al. HOCPP 1086 World War I. 2006. spiral bd. 19.50 *(978-1-60308-086-6(4))* In the Hands of a Child.

Messier, Mireille. Sergeant Billy: The True Story of the Goat Who Went to War. Reich, Kass, illus. 2019. (ENG.). 40p. (J). (gr. -1-3). 17.99 *(978-0-7352-6442-7(2)*, Tundra Bks.) Tundra Bks. CAN. Dist: Penguin Random Hse. LLC.

Miller, Derek. Minority Soldiers Fighting in World War I, 1 vol. 2017. (Fighting for Their Country: Minorities at War Ser.). (ENG.). 112p. (YA). (gr. 8-8). 44.50 *(978-1-5026-2663-9(2)*, e056128f-8dc0-44bd-8c57-ca1ed35a1b58) Cavendish Square Publishing LLC.

Morgan, Elizabeth & Green, Robert. World War I & the Rise of Global Conflict, 1 vol. 2016. (World History Ser.). (ENG.). 104p. (J). (gr. 7-7). lib. bdg. 41.53 *(978-1-5345-6058-1(0)*, 0af22495-d2e9-4344-a26e-4868fe0dce96, Lucent Pr.) Greenhaven Publishing LLC.

Myers, Walter Dean & Miles, Bill. The Harlem Hellfighters: When Pride Met Courage. 2014. (ENG.). 160p. (J). (gr. 3-7). pap. 9.99 *(978-0-06-001138-3(6)*, Amistad) HarperCollins Pubs.

Myers, Walter Dean & William Miles. The Harlem Hellfighters: When Pride Met Courage. 2014. (J). lib. bdg. 20.85 *(978-0-606-35507-0(3))* Turtleback.

Nardo, Don. Cause & Effect: World War I. 2017. (ENG.). 80p. (YA). (gr. 5-12). *(978-1-68282-172-5(2))* ReferencePoint Pr., Inc.

Nelson, Sheila. A Nation Is Born: World War I & Independence, 1910-1929. 2007. (How Canada Became Canada Ser.). (Illus.). 87p. (YA). (gr. 3-7). lib. bdg. 21.95 *(978-1-4222-0006-3(X)*, 1247972) Mason Crest.

Niver, Heather Moore. Real-World Projects to Explore World War I & the Roaring '20s, 1 vol. 2018. (Project-Based Learning in Social Studies). (ENG., Illus.). 64p. (J). (gr. 5-5). 37.47 *(978-1-5081-8225-2(6)*, 2271897a-73bd-4150-a216-d87b9d43c70a) Rosen Publishing Group, Inc., The.

Oakes, John. Kitchener's Lost Boys: From the Playing Fields to the Killing Fields. 2009. (ENG., Illus.). 256p. 38.95 *(978-0-7524-4930-2(3))* History Pr. Ltd.,The GBR. Dist: Independent Pubs. Group.

O'Keefe, Emily. Eyewitness to World War I Medicine. 2018. (Eyewitness to World War I Ser.). (ENG.). 32p. (J). (gr. 4-7). lib. bdg. 35.64 *(978-1-5038-1610-7(9)*, 211168) Child's World, Inc, The.

Otfinoski, Steven. World War I (a Step into History) (Library Edition) 2017. (Step into History Ser.). (ENG., Illus.). 144p. (J). (gr. 5-8). lib. bdg. 36.00 *(978-0-531-22571-4(2)*, Children's Pr.) Scholastic Library Publishing.

Perritano, John. World War I. 2010. (America at War Ser.). 32p. (J). pap. 8.95 *(978-0-531-24912-3(3)*, Watts, Franklin) Scholastic Library Publishing.

Powell, Jillian. The First World War: Band 11 Lime/Band 16 Sapphire (Collins Big Cat Progress) 2014. (Collins Big Cat Progress Ser.). (ENG., Illus.). 32p. (J). (gr. 4-5). pap. 11.99 *(978-0-00-751936-1(2))* HarperCollins Pubs. Ltd. GBR. Dist: Independent Pubs. Group.

—War Art: Band 10 White/Band 17 Diamond (Collins Big Cat Progress) 2014. (Collins Big Cat Progress Ser.). (ENG., Illus.). 32p. (J). (gr. 5-6). pap. 9.99 *(978-0-00-751930-9(3))* HarperCollins Pubs. Ltd. GBR. Dist: Independent Pubs. Group.

Pratt, Mary K. World War I, 1 vol. 2013. (Essential Library of American Wars Ser.). (ENG.). 112p. (YA). (gr. 6-12). lib. bdg. 41.36 *(978-1-61783-881-1(0)*, 6611, Essential Library) ABDO Publishing Co.

Prince, Jennifer S. The Life & Times of Asheville's Thomas Wolfe. 2016. (True Tales for Young Readers Ser.). (ENG., Illus.). 116p. (YA). pap. 17.00 *(978-0-86526-484-7(8)*, 01OSPS) Univ. of North Carolina Pr.

Rasmussen, R. Kent. World War I for Kids: A History with 21 Activities. 2014. (For Kids Ser.: 50). (ENG., Illus.). 192p. (J). (gr. 4). pap. 19.99 *(978-1-61374-556-4(7))* Chicago Review Pr., Inc.

Ridley, Sarah. Remembering the Fallen of the First World War. 2019. (ENG., Illus.). 48p. (J). (gr. 6-12). pap. 10.99 *(978-1-4451-4834-2(X)*, Franklin Watts) Hachette Children's Group GBR. Dist: Hachette Bk. Group.

Roberts, Steven & Gould, Jane H. The United States in World War I: America's Entry Ensures Victory. 2014. (World War I: Remembering the Great War Ser.). (ENG., Illus.). 48p. (J). (gr. 5-5). *(978-0-7787-0389-1(4))* Crabtree Publishing Co.

Robson, Pam. The First World War. 2nd ed. 2003. (All about Ser.). (ENG., Illus.). 48p. pap. *(978-0-7500-1936-1(0)*, Wayland) Hachette Children's Group.

Roby, Cynthia A. Strategic Inventions of World War I, 1 vol. 2015. (Tech in the Trenches Ser.). (ENG., Illus.). 112p. (YA). (gr. 9-9). lib. bdg. 44.50 *(978-1-5026-1024-9(8)*, 1b749332-332f-49b6-ba53-8d49e7f27ffa) Cavendish Square Publishing LLC.

Ross, Stewart. World War I, 1 vol. 2004. (Atlas of Conflicts Ser.). (ENG., Illus.). 64p. (gr. 6-8). pap. 15.05 *(978-0-8368-5675-0(9)*, e9f7e218-082c-478c-bea9-752962b2a6c2); lib. bdg. 36.67 *(978-0-8368-5668-2(6)*, eff73d95-c809-488d-a4f3-c4c487c7ae7a) Stevens, Gareth Publishing LLLP. (Gareth Stevens Secondary Library).

Rothstein, Evelyn. Clara's Great War. Uhlig, Elizabeth, illus. 2011. 88p. (J). pap. 12.95 *(978-0-9815345-9-6(7))* Marble Hse. Editions.

Royce, Ruth. The Children of France. 2007. 88p. per. *(978-1-4068-4064-3(5))* Echo Library.

Ruggiero, Adriane. World War I, 1 vol. Kubinyi, Laszlo, illus. 2003. (American Voices From Ser.). (ENG.). 160p. (gr. 6-6). 41.21 *(978-0-7614-1203-8(4)*, 028d71aa-58cd-4650-9831-c22bb6820eb6) Cavendish Square Publishing LLC.

Samuels, Charlie. Machines & Weaponry of World War I, 1 vol. 2013. (Machines That Won the War Ser.). (ENG., Illus.). 48p. (J). (gr. 5-6). pap. 15.05 *(978-1-4339-8604-8(3)*, def5d1aa-6819-4514-ae97-a3ec6ee02951); lib. bdg. 34.60 *(978-1-4339-8603-1(5)*, 1622fcc1-73e4-4789-9d45-744b4ace99a4) Stevens, Gareth Publishing LLLP.

Schaub, Michelle. Vehicles of World War I, 1 vol. 2013. (War Vehicles Ser.). (ENG.). 32p. (J). (gr. 3-9). 28.65 *(978-1-4296-9911-2(6)*, 120624, Capstone Pr.) Capstone.

Scott, Janine. The Two Great Wars. 2007. (Shockwave: History & Politics Ser.). (ENG., Illus.). 36p. (J). (gr. 4-6). lib. bdg. 25.00 *(978-0-531-17756-3(4)*, Children's Pr.) Scholastic Library Publishing.

Sebree, Chet'la. Historical Sources on World War I, 1 vol. 2019. (America's Story Ser.). (ENG.). 144p. (gr. 8-8). pap. 22.16 *(978-1-5026-5219-5(6)*, dead47d4-4df1-4687-a8b0-d15119679ca1) Cavendish Square Publishing LLC.

Seward, Pat. Countdown to Catastrophe, 1 vol. 2011. (World War II Ser.). (ENG.). 128p. (gr. 6-6). 38.36 *(978-0-7614-4944-7(2)*, 388ef178-cef9-4c94-abcf-8e4c674c146c) Cavendish Square Publishing LLC.

Sheffield, Gary. World War I Told Through 100 Artifacts, 1 vol. 2018. (War Told Through Artifacts Ser.). (ENG.). 256p. (gr. 8-8). pap. 24.52 *(978-1-5026-4463-3(0)*, af109bc4-3a44-4a4a-9baa-325cee9c792e) Cavendish Square Publishing LLC.

Sherman, Jill. Eyewitness to the Harlem Hellfighters. 2018. (Eyewitness to World War I Ser.). (ENG.). 32p. (J). (gr. 4-7). lib. bdg. 35.64 *(978-1-5038-1604-6(4)*, 211162) Child's World, Inc, The.

Steele, Philip. Did Anything Good Come Out of World War I?, 1 vol., 1. 2015. (Innovation Through Adversity Ser.). (ENG.). 48p. (J). (gr. 6-7). 33.47 *(978-1-5081-7068-6(1)*, 7a91b17a-851f-4b6a-9d35-8d2fb28a937c, Rosen Young Adult) Rosen Publishing Group, Inc., The.

Sullivan, Laura L. Life As an Ambulance Driver in World War I, 1 vol. 2017. (Life As... Ser.). (ENG.). 32p. (gr. 3-3). pap. 11.58 *(978-1-5026-3055-1(9)*, a1609210-1da1-4a95-a6ef-af704127826e) Cavendish Square Publishing LLC.

Summers, Elizabeth. Weapons & Vehicles of World War I. 2015. (Tools of War Ser.). (ENG., Illus.). 32p. (J). (gr. 3-9). lib. bdg. 27.32 *(978-1-4914-4095-7(3)*, 128653, Capstone Pr.) Capstone.

Swain, Gwenyth. World War I: An Interactive History Adventure. 2012. (You Choose: History Ser.). (ENG.). 112p. (gr. 3-4). pap. 41.70 *(978-1-4296-8484-2(4)*, Capstone Pr.) Capstone.

Swayze, Alan. The End of World War I: The Treaty of Versailles & Its Tragic Legacy. 2014. (World War I: Remembering the Great War Ser.). (ENG., Illus.). 48p. (J). (gr. 5-5). *(978-0-7787-0388-4(6))* Crabtree Publishing Co.

Tonatiuh, Duncan. Soldier for Equality: José de la Luz Sáenz & the Great War. 2019. (ENG., Illus.). 40p. (J). (gr. 1-3). 19.99 *(978-1-4197-3682-7(5)*, 1193001, Abrams Bks. for Young Readers) Abrams, Inc.

Torres, Jennifer. Alan Jackson. 2006. (Blue Banner Biography Ser.). (Illus.). 32p. (YA). (gr. 4-7). lib. bdg. 25.70 *(978-1-58415-504-1(3)*, 1259609) Mitchell Lane Pubs.

Turner, Jason. World War I. 2008. (Wars Day by Day Ser.). 48p. (gr. 5-9). 37.10 *(978-1-933834-40-5(4))* Brown Bear Bks.

Walker, Robert. World War I: 1917-1918 - The Turning of the Tide. 2014. (World War I: Remembering the Great War Ser.). (ENG., Illus.). 48p. (J). (gr. 5-5). *(978-0-7787-0326-6(6))* Crabtree Publishing Co.

Whiting, Jim. An Overview of World War I. 2006. (Monumental Milestones Ser.). (Illus.). 48p. (YA). (gr. 4-7). lib. bdg. 29.95 *(978-1-58415-471-6(3))* Mitchell Lane Pubs.

Wiest, Andrew. World War I, 1 vol. 2016. (Primary Sources in World Warfare Ser.). (ENG.). 256p. (YA). (gr. 9-9). lib. bdg. 56.71 *(978-1-5026-2470-3(2)*, d8b31e87-4304-4f52-a37a-9f14628bdcca) Cavendish Square Publishing LLC.

Williams, Brian. DKfindout! World War I. 2018. (DK Findout! Ser.). (ENG., Illus.). 64p. (J). (gr. 1-4). 16.99 *(978-1-4654-7317-2(3)*, DK Children) Dorling Kindersley Publishing, Inc.

Williams, Brian & Adams, Simon. World War I. 2018. (Illus.). 64p. (J). *(978-1-5182-5423-9(3))* Dorling Kindersley Publishing, Inc.

World War I: PowerPoint Presentations in World History. 2005. cd-rom 49.95 net. *(978-1-56004-208-2(7))* Social Studies Schl. Service.

Zaboly, Gary. Story of World War I. 2013. (Dover American History Coloring Bks.). (ENG.). 48p. (gr. 3-12). pap. 4.99 *(978-0-486-49791-4(7)*, 497917) Dover Pubns., Inc.

Zamosky, Lisa. World War I, 1 vol. rev. ed. 2007. (Social Studies: Informational Text Ser.). (ENG.). 32p. (gr. 4-8). pap. 11.99 *(978-0-7439-0664-7(0))* Teacher Created Materials, Inc.

Ziff, John. The American Revolution. 2015. (Illus.). 64p. (J). *(978-1-4222-3352-8(9))* Mason Crest.

—World War I, Vol. 11. Musteen, Jason R., ed. 2015. (Major U. S. Historical Wars Ser.). (Illus.). 64p. (J). (gr. 7). lib. bdg. 23.95 *(978-1-4222-3362-7(6))* Mason Crest.

Zullo, Allan. World War I Heroes. 2014. 162p. (J). pap. *(978-0-545-67533-8(2))* Scholastic, Inc.

WORLD WAR, 1914-1918—AERIAL OPERATIONS

Adams, Simon. Warplanes. 2009. (J). 28.50 *(978-1-59920-223-5(9))* Black Rabbit Bks.

Claasen, A. Fearless Untold Story of NZs Great Airma. 2017. (Chp Ser.). (ENG., Illus.). 496p. 50.00 *(978-0-9941407-8-4(9))* Massey University Press NZL. Dist: Independent Pubs. Group.

Jeffrey, Gary. War in the Air. 2013. (ENG., Illus.). 48p. (J). *(978-0-7787-0914-5(0))*; pap. *(978-0-7787-0924-4(8))* Crabtree Publishing Co.

Myhra, David. The Horten Ho 9/Ho 229 Vol. 1: Vol 1: Retrospective, 1 vol. 2003. (ENG., Illus.). 224p. (gr. 10-13). 49.95 *(978-0-7643-1666-1(4)*, 3108, Schiffer Military History) Schiffer Publishing, Ltd.

Orr, Tamra. What's So Great about the Tuskegee Airmen. 2009. (What's So Great About... ? Ser.). 32p. (J). (gr. 2-4). lib. bdg. 25.70 *(978-1-58415-832-5(8))* Mitchell Lane Pubs.

Purcell, Martha Sias. Pioneer Pilots & Flying Aces of World War I. 2003. (Reading Essentials in Social Studies). (Illus.). 48p. (J). 9.00 *(978-0-7891-5881-9(7))* Perfection Learning Corp.

Vansant, Wayne. The Red Baron: The Graphic History of Richthofen's Flying Circus & the Air War in WWI. Vansant, Wayne, illus. 2015. (Graphic Histories Ser.). (ENG., Illus.). 104p. (YA). (gr. 8-12). 34.65 *(978-1-939581-80-8(X)*, 0a637c45-08f0-49f9-82e8-d7c7fca3fad3, Zenith Pr.) Quarto Publishing Group USA.

—The Red Baron: The Graphic History of Richthofen's Flying Circus & the Air War in WWI. 2014. (Zenith Graphic Histories Ser.). (ENG., Illus.). 104p. pap. 19.99 *(978-0-7603-4602-0(X)*, 076034602X, Zenith Pr.) Quarto Publishing Group USA.

atson, Marilyn Myrick. Frank Luke, the Arizona Balloon Buster. 2007. (978-0-9790826-3-4(3)); (978-0-9790826-4-1(1)) Acacia Publishing, Inc.

ORLD WAR, 1914-1918—BIOGRAPHY

cton, Vanessa. Momcilo Gavric's World War I Story. Kronheimer, Ann, illus. 2018. (Narrative Nonfiction: Kids in War Ser.). (ENG.). 32p. (J). (gr. 2-4). 27.99 (978-1-5124-5679-0(9), 5300603e-3906-4416-9734-1ea47dd1a084, Lerner Pubns.); pap. 9.99 (978-1-5415-1193-4(X), 95ef1b3c-5db0-4edb-8ae0-fb702f810dc6) Lerner Publishing Group.

rooker, Marion Fargey. Hold the Oxo! A Teenage Soldier Writes Home. 2011. (Canadians at War Ser.: 6). (ENG., Illus.). 144p. (YA). pap. 14.99 (978-1-55488-870-2(0)) Dundurn Pr. CAN. Dist: Publishers Group West (PGW).

ollins, Terry, et al. Stories of War. 2012. (Stories of War Ser.). (ENG.). 32p. (J). (gr. 3-9). 133.28 (978-1-4296-9164-2(6), 18453, Capstone Pr.) Capstone.

osein, Ann. Key Figures of World War I, 1 vol. 2015. (Biographies of War Ser.). (ENG., Illus.). 112p. (J). (gr. 7-8). 35.47 (978-1-68048-054-2(5), f7ca3f72-69df-415b-a69e-36c7cc493083, Britannica Educational Publishing) Rosen Publishing Group, Inc., The.

Purcell, Martha Sias. Pioneer Pilots & Flying Aces of World War I. 2003. (Reading Essentials in Social Studies). (Illus.). 48p. (J). 9.00 (978-0-7891-5881-9(7)) Perfection Learning Corp.

Raum, Elizabeth, et al. Stories of War Classroom Collection. 2012. (Stories of War Ser.). (ENG.). 32p. (J). (gr. 3-4). pap., pap. 195.40 (978-1-4296-9349-3(5), 18568, Capstone Pr.) Capstone.

Williams, Brian. Heroes of the Battlefield. 2015. (Heroes of World War II Ser.). (ENG., Illus.). 48p. (J). (gr. 4-6). 35.32 (978-1-4109-8048-9(0), 130127, Raintree) Capstone.

Yomtov, Nel. True Stories of World War I, 1 vol. Proctor, Jon & Proctor, Jon, illus. 2012. (Stories of War Ser.). (ENG.). 32p. (J). (gr. 3-9). pap. 8.10 (978-1-4296-9344-8(4), 120379); lib. bdg. 31.32 (978-1-4296-8625-9(1), 118646) Capstone. (Capstone Pr.).

—True Stories of World War I. Proctor, Jon, illus. 2012. (Stories of War Ser.). (ENG.). 32p. (J). (gr. 3-4). pap. 48.60 (978-1-4296-9345-5(2), 18565, Capstone Pr.) Capstone.

Yomtov, Nel, et al. Stories of War. 2012. (Stories of War Ser.). (ENG.). 32p. (J). (gr. 3-9). pap., pap., pap. 31.80 (978-1-4296-9348-6(7), 18567, Capstone Pr.) Capstone.

WORLD WAR, 1914-1918—CAMPAIGNS

Burnett, Allan. World War I: Scottish Tales of Adventure. 2014. (ENG., Illus.). 112p. (J). (gr. 4-7). pap. 8.00 (978-1-84158-932-9(2)) Birlinn, Ltd. GBR. Dist: Casemate Pubs. & Bk. Distributors, LLC.

Feldman, Ruth Tenzer. World War I. 2004. (Chronicle of America's Wars Ser.). (Illus.). 88p. (gr. 5-12). lib. bdg. 27.93 (978-0-8225-0148-0(1)) Lerner Publishing Group.

George, Enzo. World War II in Europe & North Africa: Preserving Democracy, 1 vol. 2014. (Voices of War Ser.). (ENG.). 48p. (gr. 4-4). lib. bdg. 33.07 (978-1-62712-864-3(6), 4dbc917e-fb5c-4704-92c7-e0e7479d9512) Cavendish Square Publishing LLC.

Greenwood, Mark. The Donkey of Gallipoli: A True Story of Courage in World War I. Lessac, Frane, illus. 2008. (ENG.). 32p. (J). (gr. 1-4). 17.99 (978-0-7636-3913-6(3)) Candlewick Pr.

Hamilton, John, contrib. by. Final Years of World War I. 2017. (World War I Ser.). (ENG.). 48p. (J). (gr. 5-9). lib. bdg. 34.21 (978-1-5321-1288-1(2), 27496, Abdo & Daughters) ABDO Publishing Co.

—Trench Fighting of World War I. 2017. (World War I Ser.). (ENG., Illus.). 48p. (J). (gr. 5-9). lib. bdg. 34.21 (978-1-5321-1289-8(0), 27497, Abdo & Daughters) ABDO Publishing Co.

Henzel, Cynthia Kennedy. Eyewitness to the Western Front. 2018. (Eyewitness to World War I Ser.). (ENG.). 32p. (J). (gr. 4-7). lib. bdg. 35.64 (978-1-5038-1609-1(5), 211167) Child's World, Inc, The.

Jeffrey, Gary. Gallipoli & the Southern Theaters, 1 vol. 2013. (ENG., Illus.). 48p. (J). pap. (978-0-7787-0917-6(5)) Crabtree Publishing Co.

—Lawrence of Arabia & the Middle East & Africa. 2013. (ENG., Illus.). 48p. (J). (978-0-7787-0912-1(4)); pap. (978-0-7787-0918-3(3)) Crabtree Publishing Co.

—On the Eastern Front. 2013. (ENG., Illus.). 48p. (J). (978-0-7787-0910-7(8)); pap. (978-0-7787-0916-9(7)) Crabtree Publishing Co.

—On the Western Front. 2013. (ENG., Illus.). 48p. (J). (978-0-7787-0909-1(4)); pap. (978-0-7787-0915-2(9)) Crabtree Publishing Co.

—War in the Air. 2013. (ENG., Illus.). 48p. (J). (978-0-7787-0914-5(0)); pap. (978-0-7787-0924-4(8)) Crabtree Publishing Co.

Kalman, Bobbie & Jeffrey, Gary. Gallipoli & the Southern Theaters. 2013. (ENG.). 48p. (J). (978-0-7787-0911-4(6)) Crabtree Publishing Co.

Samuels, Charlie. Timeline of World War I, 1 vol. 2011. (Americans at War: a Gareth Stevens Timeline Ser.). (ENG.). 48p. (J). (gr. 6-8). pap. 15.05 (978-1-4339-5928-8(3), 43163fdb-49cf-403d-b0a4-957036586410); lib. bdg. 34.60 (978-1-4339-5926-4(7), a3c760fd-f6d0-488f-8719-f005ab1fa356) Stevens, Gareth Publishing LLLP. (Gareth Stevens Secondary Library).

WORLD WAR, 1914-1918—CAUSES

Bodden, Valerie. The Assassination of Archduke Ferdinand. 2009. (Days of Change Ser.). (ENG.). 48p. (J). (gr. 5-8). 22.95 (978-1-58341-731-7(1), 22143) Creative Co., The.

Feldman, Ruth Tenzer. World War I. 2004. (Chronicle of America's Wars Ser.). (Illus.). 88p. (gr. 5-12). lib. bdg. 27.93 (978-0-8225-0148-0(1)) Lerner Publishing Group.

Hamilton, John, contrib. by. Events Leading to World War I. 2017. (World War I Ser.). (ENG., Illus.). 48p. (J). (gr. 5-9). lib. bdg. 34.21 (978-1-5321-1287-4(4), 27495, Abdo & Daughters) ABDO Publishing Co.

Maybury, Richard J. World War I: The Rest of the Story & How It Affects You Today, 1870 To 1935. Williams, Jane A., ed. rev. ed. 2003. ("Uncle Eric" Bk.: 10). (ENG., Illus.). 253p. pap. 17.95 (978-0-942617-42-9(8)) Bluestocking Pr.

O'Keefe, Emily. Eyewitness to the Assassination of Archduke Francis Ferdinand. 2018. (Eyewitness to World War I Ser.). (ENG.). 32p. (J). (gr. 4-7). lib. bdg. 35.64 (978-1-5038-1603-9(6), 211161) Child's World, Inc, The.

WORLD WAR, 1914-1918—FICTION

Aaron, Chester. Alex, Who Won His War. 2014. 225p. (YA). (978-1-936144-26-6(3)) Zumaya Pubns. LLC.

Altsheler, Joseph A. The Complete 'Great War' Series: The Guns of Europe, the Forest of Swords & the Hosts of the Air. 2010. (Great War Ser.). 576p. (J). (gr. 4-7). reprint ed. (978-0-85706-344-1(8)); pap. (978-0-85706-343-4(X)) Leonaur Ltd.

—The Forest of Swords: A Story of Paris & the Marne. 2006. (World War I Ser.: Vol. 3). 284p. (J). reprint ed. 28.95 (978-1-4218-1772-9(1)); pap. 13.95 (978-1-4218-1872-6(8)) 1st World Publishing, Inc. (1st World Library - Literary Society).

—The Forest of Swords: A Story of Paris & the Marne. 2004. (World War I Ser.: Vol. 3). (J). reprint ed. 32.95 (978-0-8488-3005-2(9)) Amereon Ltd.

—The Forest of Swords: A Story of Paris & the Marne. 2006. (World War I Ser.: Vol. 3). (J). reprint ed. pap. (978-1-4065-0809-3(8)) Dodo Pr.

—The Forest of Swords: A Story of Paris & the Marne. 2006. (World War I Ser.: Vol. 3). (J). reprint ed. pap. (978-1-4068-0742-4(7)) Echo Library.

—The Forest of Swords: A Story of Paris & the Marne. 2010. (World War I Ser.: Vol. 3). (Illus.). 150p. (J). (gr. 4-7). reprint ed. pap. 19.99 (978-1-153-70289-8(4)) General Bks. LLC.

—The Forest of Swords: A Story of Paris & the Marne. 2010. (World War I Ser.: Vol. 3). 216p. (J). reprint ed. pap. (978-1-4076-1521-9(1)) HardPr.

—The Forest of Swords: A Story of Paris & the Marne. 2011. (World War I Ser.: Vol. 3). 252p. (J). (gr. 4-7). reprint ed. pap. (978-3-8424-7930-2(1)) tredition Verlag.

—The Guns of Europe. Date not set. reprint ed. lib. bdg. 39.95 (978-0-8488-1860-9(1), 204) Amereon Ltd.

—The Guns of Europe. 2009. 174p. (J). pap. (978-1-150-78710-2(4)) Books LLC.

—The Guns of Europe. 2010. (World War I Ser.: Vol. 1). 342p. pap. 31.75 (978-1-148-38046-9(9), Nabu Pr.) 2009. 339p. pap. 23.99 (978-1-113-15368-5(7), BiblioLife) 2009. (World War I Ser.: Vol. 1). 340p. (J). (gr. 3-7). 32.99 (978-1-113-15374-6(1)) 2009. (World War I Ser.: Vol. 1). 340p. (J). (gr. 3-7). pap. 30.75 (978-1-113-15371-5(7)) 2009. (World War I Ser.: Vol. 1). 339p. (J). (gr. 3-7). pap. 24.99 (978-1-113-15369-2(5), BiblioLife) 2010. (World War I Ser.: Vol. 1). (ENG.). 346p. (J). (gr. 4-7). reprint ed. pap. 32.75 (978-1-176-64128-0(X)) 2009. (ENG.). 330p. (J). reprint ed. 36.99 (978-1-117-70555-2(2)) 2009. 332p. (J). reprint ed. pap. 30.75 (978-1-117-70556-9(0)) 2009. (World War I Ser.: Vol. 1). 330p. (J). (gr. 4-7). reprint ed. pap. 23.99 (978-1-117-70557-6(9), BiblioLife) Creative Media Partners, LLC.

—The Guns of Europe. 2010. (World War I Ser.: Vol. 1). (J). reprint ed. 144p. (gr. 4-7). pap. 19.99 (978-1-153-65770-9(8)); (gr. 5-7). 15.89 (978-1-154-98722-5(1)); (gr. 5-7). 19.99 (978-1-154-72171-3(X)) General Bks. LLC.

—The Guns of Europe. 2012. (World War I Ser.: Vol. 1). 352p. (J). reprint ed. pap. (978-1-290-02432-7(4)) HardPr.

—The Guns of Europe. Wrenn, Charles, illus. (World War I Ser.: Vol. 1). (J). reprint ed. 2010. 338p. (gr. 4-7). 36.76 (978-1-164-35775-9(1)) 2010. 338p. (gr. 4-7). pap. 24.76 (978-1-163-97980-8(5)) 2008. 336p. 45.95 (978-0-548-98692-9(4)) 2007. 340p. per. 30.95 (978-0-548-66038-6(7)) Kessinger Publishing, LLC.

—The Hosts of the Air: The Story of a Quest in the Great War. 2006. (World War I Ser.: Vol. 2). 288p. (J). reprint ed. 28.95 (978-1-4218-1773-6(X)); pap. 13.95 (978-1-4218-1873-3(6)) 1st World Publishing, Inc. (1st World Library - Literary Society).

—The Hosts of the Air: The Story of a Quest in the Great War. (World War I Ser.: Vol. 2). 327p. (J). reprint ed. lib. bdg. 25.95 (978-0-88411-947-0(5)) Amereon Ltd.

—The Hosts of the Air: The Story of a Quest in the Great War. 2010. 352p. pap. 32.75 (978-1-142-69983-3(8)); (World War I Ser.: Vol. 2). 356p. (J). (gr. 3-7). reprint ed. pap. 32.75 (978-1-149-41015-8(9), Nabu Pr.) Creative Media Partners, LLC.

—The Hosts of the Air: The Story of a Quest in the Great War. 2006. (World War I Ser.: Vol. 2). (Illus.). (J). reprint ed. pap. (978-1-4065-0814-7(4)) Dodo Pr.

—The Hosts of the Air: The Story of a Quest in the Great War. 2007. (World War I Ser.: Vol. 2). 168p. (J). reprint ed. per. (978-1-4068-1679-2(5)) Echo Library.

—The Hosts of the Air: The Story of a Quest in the Great War. (World War I Ser.: Vol. 2). (J). reprint ed. 2010. 152p. (gr. 4-7). pap. 19.99 (978-1-4432-1323-3(3)) 2009. 170p. pap. 9.39 (978-1-150-51448-7(5)) General Bks. LLC.

—The Hosts of the Air: The Story of a Quest in the Great War. Wrenn, Charles, illus. (World War I Ser.: Vol. 2). (J). reprint ed. 2010. 346p. (gr. 4-7). 37.56 (978-1-164-36346-0(8)) 2010. 346p. (gr. 4-7). pap. 25.56 (978-1-163-98051-4(X)) 2008. 344p. 46.95 (978-0-548-98763-6(7)) 2007. 348p. per. 31.95 (978-0-548-65961-8(3)) Kessinger Publishing, LLC.

—The Hosts of the Air: The Story of a Quest in the Great War. 2011. (World War I Ser.: Vol. 2). 252p. (J). (gr. 4-7). reprint ed. pap. (978-3-8424-7804-6(6)) tredition Verlag.

Angus, Sam. Soldier Dog. 2014. (ENG.). 272p. (J). (gr. 4-7). pap. 8.99 (978-1-250-04417-4(0), 900128304) Square Fish.

Autio, Karen. Sabotage, 1 vol. 2014. (ENG.). 293p. (J). (gr. 4-7). pap. 10.95 (978-1-55039-208-1(5)) Sono Nis Pr. CAN. Dist: Orca Bk. Pubs. USA.

Avi. The Button War: A Tale of the Great War. 2018. (ENG.). 240p. (J). (gr. 5-9). 17.99 (978-0-7636-9053-3(8)) Candlewick Pr.

Black, Robert. Liberty Girl. (YA). pap. 9.99 (978-0-88092-488-7(8)) Royal Fireworks Publishing Co.

Brown, Teri. Velvet Undercover. 2015. (ENG.). 336p. (YA). (gr. 8). 17.99 (978-0-06-232127-5(7), Balzer & Bray) HarperCollins Pubs.

Burnett, Frances. Robin. 2008. 236p. pap. 15.95 (978-1-60664-143-9(3)) Aegypan.

Carradice, Phil. The Black Chair. 2009. (ENG.). 128p. (J). pap. 10.50 (978-1-84323-978-9(7)) Gomer Pr. GBR. Dist: Casemate Pubs. & Bk. Distributors, LLC.

Carroll, Emma. In Darkling Wood. 2018. (ENG.). 256p. (J). (gr. 5). 6.99 (978-0-399-55604-3(4), Yearling) Random Hse. Children's Bks.

Cary, Kate. Bloodline. 2006. 352p. (YA). (gr. 7-12). 9.99 (978-1-59514-078-4(6), Razorbill) Penguin Young Readers Group.

Cowsill, Alan. World War One: 1914-1918. Sharma, Lalit Kumar, illus. 2014. (Campfire Graphic Novels Ser.). (ENG.). 114p. (YA). (gr. 8-12). pap. 15.99 (978-93-80741-85-7(5), Campfire) Steerforth Pr.

Crew, Gary. Memorial. Tan, Shaun, illus. 32p. (978-0-85091-983-7(5), Lothian Children's Bks.) Hachette Australia.

Daviess, Maria Thompson. The Golden Bird. 2007. 92p. per. (978-1-4068-1853-6(4)) Echo Library.

Drake, Ensign Robert L. The Boy Allies with Uncle Sams Cruisers. 2004. reprint ed. pap. 21.95 (978-1-4191-5495-9(8)) Kessinger Publishing, LLC.

Drake, Robert L. The Boy Allies at Jutland. 2005. 28.95 (978-1-4218-0384-5(4)); 264p. pap. 13.95 (978-1-4218-0484-2(0)) 1st World Publishing, Inc. (1st World Library - Literary Society).

—The Boy Allies at Jutland. 2004. reprint ed. pap. 22.95 (978-1-4191-5492-8(3)); pap. 1.99 (978-1-4192-5492-5(8)) Kessinger Publishing, LLC.

—The Boy Allies under the Sea. 2005. 27.95 (978-1-4218-1083-6(2)); 244p. pap. 12.95 (978-1-4218-1183-3(9)) 1st World Publishing, Inc. (1st World Library - Literary Society).

—The Boy Allies under the Sea. 2018. (ENG., Illus.). 188p. (YA). (gr. 7-12). pap. (978-93-5297-244-9(9)) Alpha Editions.

—The Boy Allies under the Sea. 2017. (ENG., Illus.). (J). 23.95 (978-1-374-95915-6(4)) Capital Communications, Inc.

—The Boy Allies under Two Flags. 2005. 28.95 (978-1-4218-0383-8(6)); 256p. pap. 13.95 (978-1-4218-0483-5(2)) 1st World Publishing, Inc. (1st World Library - Literary Society).

—The Boy Allies under Two Flags. 2018. (ENG., Illus.). 182p. (YA). (gr. 7-12). pap. (978-93-5297-245-6(7)) Alpha Editions.

—The Boy Allies under Two Flags. 2004. reprint ed. pap. 1.99 (978-1-4192-5493-2(6)) Kessinger Publishing, LLC.

—The Boy Allies with the Victorious Fleet. 2005. 236p. pap. 12.95 (978-1-4218-1182-6(0), 1st World Library - Literary Society) 1st World Publishing, Inc.

—The Boy Allies with the Victorious Fleet. 2018. (ENG., Illus.). 186p. (YA). (gr. 7-12). pap. (978-93-5297-246-3(5)) Alpha Editions.

—The Boy Allies with the Victorious Fleets. 2005. 27.95 (978-1-4218-1082-9(4), 1st World Library - Literary Society) 1st World Publishing, Inc.

—The Boy Allies with Uncle Sams Cruisers. 2005. 27.95 (978-1-4218-1081-2(6)); 212p. pap. 12.95 (978-1-4218-1181-9(2)) 1st World Publishing, Inc. (1st World Library - Literary Society).

—The Boy Allies with Uncle Sam's Cruisers. 2018. (ENG., Illus.). 162p. (YA). (gr. 7-12). pap. (978-93-5297-247-0(3)) Alpha Editions.

—The Boy Allies with Uncle Sam's Cruisers. 2017. (ENG., Illus.). (J). 23.95 (978-1-374-85558-8(8)) Capital Communications, Inc.

—The Boy Allies with Uncle Sams Cruisers. 2004. reprint ed. pap. 1.99 (978-1-4192-5495-6(2)) Kessinger Publishing, LLC.

Driscoll, James R. The Brighton Boys with the Flying Corps. 2005. 26.95 (978-1-59540-818-1(5), 1st World Library - Literary Society) 1st World Publishing, Inc.

—The Brighton Boys with the Submarine Fleet. 2005. 26.95 (978-1-59540-819-8(3), 1st World Library - Literary Society) 1st World Publishing, Inc.

Dumbleton, Mike. Digger. Cowcher, Robin, illus. 2018. (ENG.). 32p. (J). (gr. k-3). 19.99 (978-1-76029-673-5(2)) Allen & Unwin AUS. Dist: Independent Pubs. Group.

Dunn, Joeming. Armistice Day. Dunn, Ben, illus. 2015. (Graphic Warfare Ser.). (ENG.). 32p. (J). (gr. 3-8). 32.79 (978-1-61641-978-3(4), 19202, Graphic Planet - Fiction) Magic Wagon.

Durston, George. Boy Scouts' Victory. 2005. pap. 26.95 (978-1-885529-58-9(9)) Stevens Publishing.

Emerson, Alice B. Ruth Fielding at the War Front. 2007. 148p. per. (978-1-4065-2538-0(3)) Dodo Pr.

Farenhorst, Christine. A Cup of Cold Water: The Compassion of Nurse Edith Cavell. 2007. 222p. (J). (gr. 3-7). per. 11.99 (978-1-59638-026-4(8)) P & R Publishing.

Fitzhugh, Percy K. Tom Slade: Motorcycle Dispatch Bearer. 2005. pap. 26.95 (978-1-4191-6253-4(5)) Kessinger Publishing, LLC.

—Tom Slade with the Boys over There. 2005. (Illus.). pap. 24.95 (978-1-885529-89-3(9)) Stevens Publishing.

—Tom Slade with the Flying Corps. 2005. (Illus.). pap. 27.95 (978-1-885529-87-9(2)) Stevens Publishing.

French, Jackie. A Rose for the Anzac Boys. 2008. (ENG., Illus.). 304p. pap. (978-0-7322-8540-1(2)) HarperCollins Pubs. Australia.

French, Moira. The Swingewood Stories. 2009. 36p. pap. 16.99 (978-1-4490-4777-1(7)) AuthorHouse.

Frost, Helen. Crossing Stones. 2009. (ENG., Illus.). 192p. (YA). (gr. 7-18). 19.99 (978-0-374-31653-2(8), 900050356, Farrar, Straus & Giroux (BYR)) Farrar, Straus & Giroux.

Hagar, Erin. Doing Her Bit: A Story about the Women's Land Army of America. Hill, Jen, illus. 2016. 32p. (J). (gr. 1-4). lib. bdg. 16.95 (978-1-58089-646-7(4)) Charlesbridge Publishing, Inc.

Hahn, Mary Downing. One for Sorrow: A Ghost Story. 2017. (ENG.). 304p. (J). (gr. 5-7). 16.99 (978-0-544-81809-5(1), 1642968, Clarion Bks.) HarperCollins Pubs.

Hancock, H. Irving. Uncle Sam's Boys with Pershing's Troops. 2006. 27.95 (978-1-4218-2944-9(4)); pap. 12.95 (978-1-4218-3044-5(2)) 1st World Publishing, Inc.

Harrison, Charles Yale. Generals Die in Bed: 100th Anniversary of World War I Special Edition. 100th ed. 2014. (ENG., Illus.). 168p. (YA). (gr. 9-18). pap. 11.95 (978-1-55451-692-6(7), 9781554516926) Annick Pr., Ltd. CAN. Dist: Publishers Group West (PGW).

Hart, Alison. Darling, Mercy Dog of World War I, 1 vol. Montgomery, Michael G., illus. (Dog Chronicles Ser.: 5). 160p. (J). (gr. 2-5). 2017. pap. 7.95 (978-1-56145-981-0(X)) 2013. 12.95 (978-1-56145-705-2(1)) Peachtree Publishing Co. Inc.

Hartnett, Sonya. The Silver Donkey. Spudvilas, Anne, illus. 2004. viii, 193p. (J). (978-0-670-04240-1(4), Viking Adult) Penguin Publishing Group.

Hayes, Clair W. The Boy Allies at Verdun. 2005. 28.95 (978-1-4218-0324-1(0)); 264p. pap. 13.95 (978-1-4218-0424-8(7)) 1st World Publishing, Inc. (1st World Library - Literary Society).

—The Boy Allies at Verdun. 2018. (ENG., Illus.). 184p. (YA). (gr. 7-12). pap. (978-93-5297-249-4(X)) Alpha Editions.

—The Boy Allies at Verdun. 2007. 200p. per. (978-1-4065-4393-3(4)) Dodo Pr.

—The Boy Allies at Verdun or Saving France from the Enemy. 2007. 124p. (gr. -1-7). per. (978-1-4068-1712-6(0)) Echo Library.

—The Boy Allies in Great Peril. 2018. (ENG., Illus.). 188p. (YA). (gr. 7-12). pap. (978-93-5297-250-0(3)) Alpha Editions.

—The Boy Allies in Great Peril. 2017. (ENG., Illus.). (J). pap. 13.95 (978-1-374-94474-9(2)) Capital Communications, Inc.

—The Boy Allies in Great Peril. 2007. 200p. per. (978-1-4065-4394-0(2)) Dodo Pr.

—The Boy Allies in the Balkan Campaign. 2007. 208p. per. (978-1-4065-4395-7(0)) Dodo Pr.

—The Boy Allies in the Balkan Campaign or the Struggle to Save a Nation. 2007. 128p. per. (978-1-4068-1714-0(7)) Echo Library.

—The Boy Allies in the Trenches. 2007. 192p. per. (978-1-4065-4396-4(9)) Dodo Pr.

—The Boy Allies on the Firing Line. 2007. 188p. per. (978-1-4065-4397-1(7)) Dodo Pr.

—The Boy Allies on the Firing Line or Twelve Days Battle along the Marne. 2007. 120p. per. (978-1-4068-1716-4(3)) Echo Library.

—The Boy Allies with Haig in Flanders. 2018. (ENG., Illus.). 158p. (YA). (gr. 7-12). pap. (978-93-5297-254-8(6)) Alpha Editions.

—The Boy Allies with Haig in Flanders. 2007. 172p. per. (978-1-4065-4398-8(5)) Dodo Pr.

—The Boy Allies with Haig in Flanders. 2004. reprint ed. pap. 21.95 (978-1-4191-5494-2(X)); pap. 1.99 (978-1-4192-5494-9(4)) Kessinger Publishing, LLC.

Hayes, Clair Wallace. The Boy Allies at Verdun: Saving France from the Enemy. 2017. (ENG., Illus.). (J). 23.95 (978-1-374-95591-2(4)); pap. 13.95 (978-1-374-95590-5(6)) Capital Communications, Inc.

Hendrix, John, illus. Shooting at the Stars. 2014. (ENG.). 40p. (J). (gr. 3-7). 19.99 (978-1-4197-1175-6(X), 697001, Abrams Bks. for Young Readers) Abrams, Inc.

Herwick Rice, Dona & Sugarman, Dorothy Alexander. World War I: In Flanders Fields, 1 vol. rev. ed. 2009. (Reader's Theater Ser.). (ENG.). 32p. (gr. 4-8). pap. 11.99 (978-1-4333-0551-1(8)) Teacher Created Materials, Inc.

Hutton, Keely. Secret Soldiers: A Novel of World War I. 2019. (ENG.). 320p. (J). 17.99 (978-0-374-30903-9(5), 900188381, Farrar, Straus & Giroux (BYR)) Farrar, Straus & Giroux.

Jorgenson, Norman. In Flanders Fields. Harrison-Lever, Brian, illus. 2010. (ENG.). 32p. (J). (gr. -1-3). pap. 9.95 (978-1-894965-83-5(3)) Simply Read Bks. CAN. Dist: Ingram Publisher Services.

Kacer, Kathy. The Night Spies, 1 vol. 2003. (Holocaust Remembrance Series for Young Readers Ser.: 4). (ENG., Illus.). 200p. (J). (gr. 4-8). pap. 12.95 (978-1-896764-70-2(3)) Second Story Pr. CAN. Dist: Orca Bk. Pubs. USA.

Kassel, Roger de. Mr P & the Red Poppy. 2013. (ENG., Illus.). 22p. pap. 8.75 (978-1-78035-707-2(9), Fastprint Publishing) Upfront Publishing Ltd. GBR. Dist: Printondemand-worldwide.com.

Keenan, Sheila. Dogs of War: a Graphic Novel. Fox, Nathan, illus. 2013. (ENG.). 208p. (J). (gr. 3-7). pap. 14.99 (978-0-545-12888-9(9), Graphix) Scholastic, Inc.

Killgore, James. Soldier's Game, 32 vols. 2011. (Illus.). 160p. (J). 9.95 (978-0-86315-838-4(2), Kelpies) Floris Bks. GBR. Dist: Consortium Bk. Sales & Distribution.

Lalana, Fernando & Almarcegui, Jose Maria. La Bomba. 2003. (SPA.). 144p. (978-84-216-1540-9(8), BU5058) Bruño, Editorial ESP. Dist: Lectorum Pubns., Inc.

Landsberry, Belinda. Anzac Ted. 2016. (ENG., Illus.). 32p. (J). (gr. -1-5). 17.99 (978-1-921966-56-9(4), EK Bks.) Exisle Publishing Pty Ltd. AUS. Dist: Two Rivers Distribution.

Larson, Kirby. Hattie Big Sky. (Hattie Ser.: 1). (YA). (gr. 7-7). 2008. (ENG.). 304p. 8.99 (978-0-385-73595-7(2), Yearling) 2007. 336p. pap. 9.99 (978-0-440-23941-3(9), Ember) Random Hse. Children's Bks.

—Hattie Big Sky. l.t. ed. 2007. (Literacy Bridge Young Adult Ser.). 381p. (YA). (gr. 7-12). 23.95 (978-0-7862-9697-2(6)) Thorndike Pr.

Lewis, J. Patrick. And the Soldiers Sang. Kelley, Gary, illus. 2011. (ENG.). 32p. (J). (gr. 4-7). 19.99 (978-1-56846-220-2(4), 22033, Creative Editions) Creative Co., The.

Lough, Amber. Open Fire. 2020. (ENG.). 264p. (YA). (gr. 6-12). 18.99 (978-1-5415-7289-8(0), 26390117-2d45-4720-a977-2ce45d9ddfb3, Carolrhoda Lab™) Lerner Publishing Group.

Mattick, Lindsay & Greenhut, Josh. Winnie's Great War. Blackall, Sophie, illus. (ENG.). 256p. (J). (gr. 3-7). 2019. pap. 7.99 (978-0-316-44709-6(9)) 2018. 16.99 (978-0-316-44712-6(9)) Little, Brown Bks. for Young Readers.

McCutcheon, John. Christmas in the Trenches, 1 vol. Sorensen, Henri, illus. 2006. 32p. (J). (gr. 2-5). 22.99 (978-1-56145-374-0(9)) Peachtree Publishing Co. Inc.

McDonough, Yona Zeldis. The Doll Shop Downstairs. Maione, Heather, illus. 2011. 144p. (J). (gr. 2-5). 5.99 (978-0-14-241691-4(6), Puffin Books) Penguin Young Readers Group.

McKay, Hilary. Love to Everyone. 2018. (ENG., Illus.). 336p. (J). (gr. 5-9). 17.99 (978-1-5344-2710-5(4), McElderry, Margaret K. Bks.) McElderry, Margaret K. Bks.

Miller, Sarah. The Lost Crown. (ENG., Illus.). 448p. (YA). (gr. 7). 2012. pap. 12.99 (978-1-4169-8341-5(4)) 2011. 17.99 (978-1-4169-8340-8(6)) Simon & Schuster Children's Publishing. (Atheneum Bks. for Young Readers).

W X Y Z

Montgomery, L. M. Rilla of Ingleside. l.t. ed. 2007. (ENG.). 314p. pap. 24.99 *(978-1-4346-5286-7(6))* Creative Media Partners, LLC.
—Rilla of Ingleside. 2004. 224p. (YA). pap. 10.95 *(978-1-57646-891-3(7))* Quiet Vision Publishing.
—Rilla of Ingleside. 2006. 384p. pap. 25.45 *(978-1-59462-427-8(5)*, Bk. Jungle) Standard Publications, Inc.
Morpurgo, Michael. Private Peaceful. 2006. 18.00 *(978-0-7569-6630-0(2))* Perfection Learning Corp.
—Private Peaceful. 2006. (YA). 1.25 *(978-1-4193-2976-0(6))* Recorded Bks., Inc.
—Private Peaceful. 2006. (ENG., Illus.). 224p. (J). (gr. 7-12). per. 8.99 *(978-0-439-63653-7(1)*, Scholastic Paperbacks) Scholastic, Inc.
—War Horse. 2016. (CHI.). 176p. (J). *(978-7-5442-7926-0(X))* Nanhai Publishing Co.
—War Horse. 2nd ed. 2013. (ENG., Illus.). 72p. pap. 11.00 *(978-0-19-424982-9(4))* Oxford Univ. Pr., Inc.
—War Horse. 2010. (ENG.). 176p. (J). (gr. 4-7). pap. 7.99 *(978-0-439-79664-4(4)*, Scholastic Pr.) Scholastic, Inc.
Myers, Walter Dean. Invasion. 2015. (ENG.). 224p. (YA). (gr. 7). pap. 12.99 *(978-0-545-38429-2(X)*, Scholastic Pr.) Scholastic, Inc.
Nielsen, Jennifer A. Lines of Courage, 1 vol. 2022. (ENG.). 400p. (J). (gr. 3-7). 17.99 *(978-1-338-62093-1(2)*, Scholastic Pr.) Scholastic, Inc.
Ober, Pierre-Jacques. The Good Son: a Story from the First World War, Told in Miniature. Ober, Jules & Coonan, Felicity, illus. 2019. (ENG.). 104p. (J). (gr. 9). 22.00 *(978-1-5362-0482-7(X))* Candlewick Pr.
O'Brien, Johnny. Day of the Assassins: A Jack Christie Adventure. Hardcastle, Nick, illus. 2010. (Jack Christie Adventure Ser.: 1). (ENG.). 224p. (J). (gr. 4-7). pap. 6.99 *(978-0-7636-4995-1(3)*, Templar) Candlewick Pr.
—Day of the Assassins: A Jack Christie Adventure, 1. Hardcastle, Nick, illus. 2009. (Jack Christie Adventure Ser.: 1). (ENG.). 224p. (J). (gr. 4-7). 15.99 *(978-0-7636-4595-3(8)*, Templar) Candlewick Pr.
Palmer, Tony. The Soldier's Gift. Tanner, Jane, illus. 2017. 44p. (J). (gr. 3-7). 16.99 *(978-0-14-350716-1(8))* Penguin Random Hse. AUS. Dist: Independent Pubs. Group.
Pickett, Anola. Callahan Crossroads. 2015. (ENG.). 192p. (J). pap. 12.99 *(978-1-4621-1715-4(5)*, Sweetwater Bks.) Cedar Fort, Inc./CFI Distribution.
Presley, Daniel & Polders, Claire. A Whale in Paris. McGuire, Erin, illus. 2019. (ENG.). 256p. (J). (gr. 5). pap. 7.99 *(978-1-5344-1916-2(0)*, Atheneum Bks. for Young Readers) Simon & Schuster Children's Publishing.
Reid, Charles. Ghost of Heroes Past. 2010. (ENG., Illus.). 170p. pap. 10.95 *(978-1-55380-102-3(4))* Ronsdale Pr. CAN. Dist: SPD-Small Pr. Distribution.
Remarque, Erich-Maria. All Quiet on the Western Front: With Related Readings. Wheen, A. W., tr. from GER. 2003. (EMC Masterpiece Series Access Editions). (Illus.). xxv, 249p. (YA). 13.99 *(978-0-8219-2420-4(6))* EMC/Paradigm Publishing.
Remarque, Erich Marie. All Quiet on the Western Front. Wimperis, Sarah, illus. 2014. (World War I Ser.). (ENG.). 64p. pap. 7.95 *(978-1-906230-66-1(8))* Real Reads Ltd. GBR. Dist: Casemate Pubs. & Bk. Distributors, LLC.
Rix, Megan. The Runaways, Bk. 6. 2015. (Illus.). 272p. (J). (gr. 3-5). pap. 11.99 *(978-0-14-135764-5(9)*, Puffin) Penguin Bks., Ltd. GBR. Dist: Independent Pubs. Group.
—A Soldier's Friend. 2014. (Illus.). 336p. (J). (gr. 2-4). pap. 11.99 *(978-0-14-135190-2(X)*, Puffin) Penguin Bks., Ltd. GBR. Dist: Independent Pubs. Group.
Salten, Felix. Renni the Rescuer. Kaufman, Kenneth C., tr. 2013. (Bambi's Classic Animal Tales Ser.). (ENG., Illus.). 384p. (J). (gr. 3-7). pap. 6.99 *(978-1-4424-8273-9(7)*, Aladdin) Simon & Schuster Children's Publishing.
—Renni the Rescuer. Kaufman, Kenneth C., tr. 2013. (Bambi's Classic Animal Tales Ser.). (ENG., Illus.). 384p. (J). (gr. 3-7). 16.99 *(978-1-4424-8274-6(5)*, Simon & Schuster/Paula Wiseman Bks.) Simon & Schuster/Paula Wiseman Bks.
Saunders, Kate. Five Children on the Western Front. 2015. (ENG.). 336p. (J). pap. 10.00 *(978-0-571-32318-0(9)*, Faber & Faber Children's Bks.) Faber & Faber, Inc.
Saunders, Kate & Nesbit, E. Five Children on the Western Front. 2016. (J). *(978-0-553-49785-4(5)*, Delacorte Pr) Random House Publishing Group.
Searching for Silverheels. 2014. (ENG., Illus.). 304p. (J). (gr. 5-9). 16.99 *(978-1-4814-0029-9(0)*, McElderry, Margaret K. Bks.) McElderry, Margaret K. Bks.
Skrypuch, Marsha Forchuk. Silver Threads, 1 vol. Martchenko, Michael, illus. 2004. (ENG.). 32p. (J). (gr. 4-6). pap. 8.95 *(978-1-55041-903-0(X)*, 46dd6d4a-dd98-446a-9908-c50f5ee0fd58) Fitzhenry & Whiteside, Ltd. CAN. Dist: Firefly Bks., Ltd.
Skurzynski, Gloria. Good-Bye, Billy Radish. 2013. (ENG., Illus.). 152p. (J). (gr. 3-7). pap. 13.99 *(978-1-4814-0158-6(0)*, Simon & Schuster Bks. For Young Readers) Simon & Schuster Bks. For Young Readers.
Spillebeen, Geert. Kipling's Choice. 2007. (ENG.). 160p. (YA). (gr. 7-9). pap. 12.95 *(978-0-618-80035-3(2)*, 496440, Clarion Bks.) HarperCollins Pubs.
—Kipling's Choice. Edelstein, Terese, tr. 2007. 147p. (YA). (gr. 7-9). 15.65 *(978-0-7569-8061-0(5))* Perfection Learning Corp.
Swindells, Robert. Roger's War. 2017. (ENG., Illus.). 96p. (J). pap. 7.99 *(978-1-78270-163-7(X))* Parkwest Pubns., Inc.
Trottier, Maxine. Forget-Me-Not, 1 vol. Keating, Nancy, illus. 2008. (ENG.). 32p. (J). (gr. 1-8). pap. *(978-1-897174-24-1(1))* Breakwater Bks., Ltd.
Valder, Hayim. Di Vunderlikhe Ertseylung Fun Motl. Heler, Moti, illus. 2017. (YID.). 57p. (J). *(978-1-68091-169-5(4))* Kinder Shpiel USA, Inc.
Van Dyne, Edith. Aunt Jane's Nieces in the Red Cross. rev. ed. 2006. 180p. 26.95 *(978-1-4218-1724-8(1))*; pap. 11.95 *(978-1-4218-1824-5(8))* 1st World Publishing, Inc. (1st World Library - Literary Society).
—Aunt Jane's Nieces in the Red Cross. 2017. (ENG., Illus.). (J). 22.95 *(978-1-374-81524-7(1))* Capital Communications, Inc.
—Aunt Jane's Nieces in the Red Cross. 2018. (ENG.). 294p. (J). pap. 12.25 *(978-1-63391-657-9(X))* Westphalia Press.
Watts, Julia. Secret City. 2013. (ENG.). 264p. (gr. 7). pap. 13.95 *(978-1-59493-390-5(1))* Bella Bks., Inc.
Wilson, John. And in the Morning. 2010. (ENG.). 200p. (YA). (gr. 7-18). pap. *(978-1-55470-264-0(X))* Me to We.
—And in the Morning: The Somme 1916. 2015. (Fields of Conflict Ser.: 1). (ENG.). 224p. (YA). (gr. 8-12). pap. 12.95 *(978-1-77203-014-3(7)*, Wandering Fox) Heritage Hse. CAN. Dist: Orca Bk. Pubs. USA.
Zajonc, Taylor. The Iron Island. Rodriguez, Geraldine, illus. 2018. (Adventures of Samuel Oliver Ser.). (ENG.). 48p. (J). (gr. 3-7). lib. bdg. 34.21 *(978-1-5321-3373-2(1)*, 31169, Spellbound) Magic Wagon.

WORLD WAR, 1914-1918—NAVAL OPERATIONS

Hopkinson, Deborah. Dive! World War II Stories of Sailors & Submarines in the Pacific (Scholastic Focus) The Incredible Story of U. S. Submarines in WWII. 2018. (ENG.). 384p. (J). (gr. 3-7). pap. 7.99 *(978-0-545-42559-9(X))* Scholastic, Inc.
Jeffrey, Gary. War at Sea. 2013. (ENG., Illus.). 48p. (J). *(978-0-7787-0913-8(2))*; pap. *(978-0-7787-0923-7(X))* Crabtree Publishing Co.
Otfinoski, Steven. The Sinking of the Lusitania: An Interactive History Adventure, 1 vol. 2014. (You Choose: History Ser.). (ENG., Illus.). 112p. (J). (gr. 3-7). 32.65 *(978-1-4765-4186-0(8)*, 124291, Capstone Pr.) Capstone.
Preston, Diana. Remember the Lusitania! 2004. (Illus.). 112p. (J). (gr. 3-7). 21.85 *(978-0-8027-8847-4(5))* Walker & Co.

WORLD WAR, 1914-1918—PERSONAL NARRATIVES

Allan, Robert Marshall, et al. War Diaries. 2014. (Text Connections Ser.). (J). (gr. 5). *(978-1-4900-1386-2(5))* Benchmark Education Co.
Brooker, Marion Fargey. Hold the Oxo! A Teenage Soldier Writes Home. 2011. (Canadians at War Ser.: 6). (ENG., Illus.). 144p. (YA). pap. 14.99 *(978-1-55488-870-2(0))* Dundurn Pr. CAN. Dist: Publishers Group West (PGW).
Schomp, Virginia. World War I, 1 vol. 2005. (Letters from the Battlefront Ser.). (ENG., Illus.). 96p. (gr. 6-6). lib. bdg. 36.93 *(978-0-7614-1661-6(7)*, cc375b73-7593-4712-8ae5-828673427107) Cavendish Square Publishing LLC.
Zullo, Allan. World War I Heroes. 2015. (Ten True Tales Ser.). (ENG.). 176p. (J). (gr. 3-7). pap. 5.99 *(978-0-545-83751-4(0))* Scholastic, Inc.

WORLD WAR, 1914-1918—REGIMENTAL HISTORIES

Dowdy, Penny. The Battle of Vimy Ridge: Defining Moments in Canadian History/Graphic Novels. 2010. (Illus.). 32p. *(978-1-77071-615-5(7))* Weigl Educational Pubs. Ltd.
Raven, Margot Theis. Rags: Hero Dog of WWI: A True Story. Brown, Petra, illus. 2014. (ENG.). 32p. (J). (gr. 2-5). 18.99 *(978-1-58536-258-5(1)*, 203672) Sleeping Bear Pr.

WORLD WAR, 1914-1918—UNITED STATES

Adamson, Thomas K. World War One. 2017. (J). *(978-1-5105-3504-6(7))* SmartBook Media, Inc.
Bosco, Peter I. World War I: Revised Edition. 2nd rev. ed. 2010. (America at War Ser.). (ENG.). 200p. (gr. 6-12). 45.00 *(978-0-8160-8188-2(3)*, P459478, Facts On File) Infobase Holdings, Inc.
Crompton, Samuel Willard. How Woodrow Wilson Fought World War I, 1 vol. 2017. (Presidents at War Ser.). (ENG.). 128p. (gr. 8-8). lib. bdg. 38.93 *(978-0-7660-8529-9(5)*, 64acc819-1e5c-4ab3-bc93-b627f6f32da0) Enslow Publishing, LLC.
Dunn, Joeming & Dunn, Ben. Cher Ami: WWI Homing Pigeon, 1 vol. 2011. (Famous Firsts: Animals Making History Ser.). (ENG., Illus.). 32p. (J). (gr. 3-8). 32.79 *(978-1-61641-639-3(4)*, 7208, Graphic Planet - Fiction) Magic Wagon.
Eboch, M. M. Living Through World War I. 2018. (American Culture & Conflict Ser.). (ENG., Illus.). 48p. (gr. 4-8). lib. bdg. 35.64 *(978-1-64156-416-8(4)*, 9781641564168) Rourke Educational Media.
Feldman, Ruth Tenzer. World War I. 2004. (Chronicle of America's Wars Ser.). (Illus.). 88p. (gr. 5-12). lib. bdg. 27.93 *(978-0-8225-0148-0(1))* Lerner Publishing Group.
Gitlin, Marty. World War I. 2016. (Illus.). 48p. (J). *(978-1-5105-1294-8(2))* SmartBook Media, Inc.
Goldsworthy, Steve. World War I: 1914-1918. 2014. (Illus.). 48p. (J). *(978-1-62127-657-9(0))* Weigl Pubs., Inc.
Hamilton, John, contrib. by. Final Years of World War I. 2017. (World War I Ser.). (ENG.). 48p. (J). (gr. 5-9). lib. bdg. 34.21 *(978-1-5321-1288-1(2)*, 27496, Abdo & Daughters) ABDO Publishing Co.
Haugen, David M. & Musser, Susan, eds. War in Ernest Hemingway's a Farewell to Arms, 1 vol. 2014. (Social Issues in Literature Ser.). (ENG., Illus.). 208p. (gr. 10-12). lib. bdg. 48.03 *(978-0-7377-6395-9(7)*, c9428654-5c4c-4691-ab6d-08a3cc0d4574, Greenhaven Publishing) Greenhaven Publishing LLC.
Kent, Zachary A. World War I: From the Lusitania to Versailles, 1 vol. 2011. (United States at War Ser.). (ENG., Illus.). 128p. (gr. 5-6). lib. bdg. 35.93 *(978-0-7660-3641-3(3)*, f2834449-d726-445e-94b6-51ef5ea5f96f) Enslow Publishing, LLC.
McGraw Hill. The American Journey to World War 1, Reading Essentials & Study Guide, Workbook. 2005. (MS Wh Jat Building America Ser.). (ENG.). 312p. (gr. 6-9). pap., stu. ed., wbk. ed. 7.12 *(978-0-07-873198-3(4)*, 0078731984) McGraw-Hill Education.
—The American Journey to World War I, Active Reading Note-Taking Guide, Student Workbook. 2005. (MS Wh Jat Building America Ser.). (ENG., Illus.). 350p. (gr. 6-8). per. 7.32 *(978-0-07-870384-3(0)*, 0078703840) McGraw-Hill Education.
McGraw-Hill Education Staff. The American Journey to World War 1, StudentWorks Plus! 2005. (MS Wh Jat Building America Ser.). (ENG.). (gr. 6-9). cd-rom 79.24 *(978-0-07-873445-8(2)*, 0078734452) McGraw-Hill Higher Education.
Micklos, John, Jr. Harlem Hellfighters: African-American Heroes of World War I. 2017. (Military Heroes Ser.). (ENG., Illus.). 32p. (J). (gr. 3-6). lib. bdg. 27.99 *(978-1-5157-3348-5(3)*, 133345, Capstone Pr.) Capstone.
Osborne, Linda Barrett. Come on in, America: The United States in World War I. 2017. (ENG., Illus.). 176p. (J). (gr. 5-17). 17.95 *(978-1-4197-2378-0(2)*, 1166001, Abrams Bks. for Young Readers) Abrams, Inc.
Raven, Margot Theis. Rags: Hero Dog of WWI: A True Story. Brown, Petra, illus. 2014. (ENG.). 32p. (J). (gr. 2-5). 18.99 *(978-1-58536-258-5(1)*, 203672) Sleeping Bear Pr.
Vander Hook, Sue. The United States Enters World War I. 2010. (Essential Events Set 4 Ser.). (ENG.). 112p. (YA). (gr. 6-12). lib. bdg. 41.36 *(978-1-60453-947-9(X)*, 6397, Essential Library) ABDO Publishing Co.
Worth, Richard. America in World War I, 1 vol. 2006. (Wars That Changed American History Ser.). (ENG., Illus.). 48p. (gr. 5-8). lib. bdg. 33.67 *(978-0-8368-7292-7(4)*, 3471b7ea-23b3-4e05-a209-af04cc00ddc9, Gareth Stevens Secondary Library) Stevens, Gareth Publishing LLLP.

WORLD WAR, 1939-1945

Adamson, Thomas K. World War Two. 2017. (J). *(978-1-5105-3506-0(3))* SmartBook Media, Inc.
Allen, John. Cause & Effect World War II: World War II. 2015. (ENG., Illus.). 80p. (J). lib. bdg. *(978-1-60152-798-1(5))* ReferencePoint Pr., Inc.
Anderson, M. T. Symphony for the City of the Dead: Dmitri Shostakovich & the Siege of Leningrad. 2015. (ENG., Illus.). 464p. (YA). (gr. 9). 25.99 *(978-0-7636-6818-1(4))* Candlewick Pr.
Atwood, Kathryn J. Women Heroes of World War II-The Pacific Theater: 15 Stories of Resistance, Rescue, Sabotage, & Survival. 2016. (Women of Action Ser.: 18). (ENG., Illus.). 240p. (YA). (gr. 9). 19.99 *(978-1-61373-168-0(X))* Chicago Review Pr., Inc.
Baier, Bret & Whitney, Catherine. Three Days at the Brink: Young Readers' Edition: FDR's Daring Gamble to Win World War II. 2019. (ENG., Illus.). 272p. (J). (gr. 3-7). 17.99 *(978-0-06-291537-5(1)*, HarperCollins) HarperCollins Pubs.
Bailey, Rachel A. The Japanese Internment Camps: A History Perspectives Book. 2014. (Perspectives Library). (ENG., Illus.). 32p. (J). (gr. 4-8). 32.07 *(978-1-62431-666-1(2)*, 203228) Cherry Lake Publishing.
Bains, Alisha, ed. World War II, 1 vol. 2016. (Political & Diplomatic History of the Modern World Ser.). (ENG.). 224p. (J). (gr. 10-10). 47.59 *(978-1-68048-360-4(9)*, 44e87af0-33ac-4c71-8f99-5cc288c3ba16) Rosen Publishing Group, Inc., The.
Baldwin, Douglas & Baldwin, Patricia. World War II. 2010. (Illus.). 48p. *(978-1-55388-720-1(4))* Weigl Educational Pubs. Ltd.
Baldwin, Douglas & Baldwin, Patricia L. World War II. 2010. (Illus.). 48p. pap. *(978-1-55388-724-9(7))* Weigl Educational Pubs. Ltd.
Bascomb, Neal. The Nazi Hunters: How a Team of Spies & Survivors Captured the World's Most Notorious Nazi, 1 vol. (ENG., Illus.). (YA). (gr. 7-7). 2018. 272p. pap. 9.99 *(978-0-545-43100-2(X))* 2013. 256p. 17.99 *(978-0-545-43099-9(2))* Scholastic, Inc. (Levine, Arthur A. Bks.).
Bell-Rehwoldt, Sheri. Great World War II Projects: You Can Build Yourself. 2006. (Build It Yourself Ser.). (ENG., Illus.). 128p. (J). (gr. 3-7). pap. 15.95 *(978-0-9771294-1-6(1)*, 12c745e8-acf5-45e6-877e-dce152689a4b) Nomad Pr.
Benchmark Education Co., LLC. The Aftermath of World War II. 2014. (PRIME Ser.). (J). (gr. 6-8). pap. *(978-1-4509-9501-6(2))* Benchmark Education Co.
Benchmark Education Company. World War II (Teacher Guide) By the Numbers. 2004. *(978-1-4108-2589-6(2))* Benchmark Education Co.
Bingham, Jane. Explore!: World War Two. 2017. (Explore! Ser.). (ENG., Illus.). 32p. (J). (gr. 4-6). pap. 11.99 *(978-0-7502-8883-5(3)*, Wayland) Hachette Children's Group GBR. Dist: Hachette Bk. Group.
Black, Hermann. World War II. 2008. (Wars Day by Day Ser.). 48p. (gr. 5-9). 37.10 *(978-1-933834-41-2(2))* Brown Bear Bks.
Blohm, Craig E. Holocaust Camps & Killing Centers. 2015. (ENG., Illus.). 80p. (J). lib. bdg. *(978-1-60152-842-1(6))* ReferencePoint Pr., Inc.
—Holocaust Resistance. 2015. (ENG., Illus.). 80p. (J). lib. bdg. *(978-1-60152-846-9(9))* ReferencePoint Pr., Inc.
Booth, Owen & Walton, John. World War II, 1 vol. 2016. (Primary Sources in World Warfare Ser.). (ENG.). 256p. (YA). (gr. 9-9). lib. bdg. 56.71 *(978-1-5026-2472-7(9)*, ed43b3ab-7e5f-4faa-afdd-1d13d94179c0) Cavendish Square Publishing LLC.
Braun, Eric. Trapped Behind Enemy Lines: The Story of the U. S. Army Air Force 807th Medical Evacuation Squadron. 2016. (Encounter: Narrative Nonfiction Stories Ser.). (ENG., Illus.). 224p. (J). (gr. 4-5). lib. bdg. 33.32 *(978-1-4914-8042-7(4)*, 130545, Capstone Young Readers) Capstone.
Braun, Eric Mark & Dickmann, Nancy. Fighting to Survive World War II: Terrifying True Stories. 2019. (Fighting to Survive Ser.). (ENG., Illus.). 64p. (J). (gr. 4-9). pap. 8.95 *(978-0-7565-6235-9(X)*, 140936); lib. bdg. 35.32 *(978-0-7565-6188-8(4)*, 140666) Capstone. (Compass Point Bks.).
Brook, Henry. D-Day. rev. ed. 2008. (True Stories Ser.). 160p. (J). pap. 4.99 *(978-0-7945-1840-0(0)*, Usborne) EDC Publishing.
Brown Bear Books. The Early 20th Century. 2010. (Technology Through the Ages Ser.). (ENG.). 112p. (J). (gr. 9-12). 42.80 *(978-1-933834-87-0(0)*, 16806) Brown Bear Bks.
Burgan, Michael. The Attack on Pearl Harbor: U. S. Entry into World War II, 1 vol. 2012. (Perspectives On Ser.). (ENG., Illus.). 112p. (YA). (gr. 8-8). 42.64 *(978-1-60870-448-4(3)*, 8295e9d5-7add-4634-94de-b5f45c295476) Cavendish Square Publishing LLC.
Burian, Boris & Zhizhenko, V. A. Nekogda Ne Zabudem: Rasskazy Belorusskikh Rebiat o Dniakh Velikoi Otechestvennoi Voiny. 2010. (RUS., Illus.). 330p. (J). *(978-985-02-1082-1(6))* Mastackaja literatura, Vydavectva.
Burrell, Bill. The Path to Glory. 2011. 24p. pap. *(978-1-4269-9427-2(3))* Trafford Publishing (UK) Ltd.
Byers, Ann. Auschwitz, Bergen-Belsen, Treblinka: The Holocaust Camps, 1 vol. 2014. (Remembering the Holocaust Ser.). (ENG.). 96p. (gr. 6-7). (J). pap. 13.88 *(978-0-7660-6213-9(9)*, 67eeeb0b-a0e0-494c-a751-d169be1b2071); 31.61 *(978-0-7660-6212-2(0)*, 7f4c46a5-f83d-469d-8552-fe364379c05f) Enslow Publishing, LLC.
Capek, Michael. The Wilhelm Gustloff Story. 2017. (Famous Ships Ser.). (ENG., Illus.). 112p. (J). (gr. 6-12). lib. bdg. 41.36 *(978-1-5321-1323-9(4)*, 27531, Essential Library) ABDO Publishing Co.
Chandler, Matt. Behind Enemy Lines: The Escape of Robert Grimes with the Comet Line Ginevra, Dante, illus. 2017. (Great Escapes of World War II Ser.). (ENG.). 32p. (J). (gr. 3-9). lib. bdg. 31.32 *(978-1-5157-3530-4(3)*, 133505, Capstone Pr.) Capstone.
Chant, Christopher. The Allied Powers Fight Back. 2017. (World War II Ser.: Vol. 5). (ENG., Illus.). 79p. (YA). (gr. 7-12). 24.95 *(978-1-4222-3895-0(4))* Mason Crest.
Clare, John D. Vietnam, 1939-75. 2nd rev. ed. 2004. (Hodder 20th Century History Ser.). (ENG., Illus.). 48p. (YA). pap. 26.50 *(978-0-340-81476-5(4)*, Hodder Education) Hodder Education Group GBR. Dist: Trans-Atlantic Pubns., Inc.
Connolly, Kieron. America's Bloody History from World War II to the Civil Rights Movement, 1 vol. 2017. (Bloody History of America Ser.). (ENG.). 88p. (gr. 8-8). 37.60 *(978-0-7660-9179-5(1)*, ce7f5754-d0d1-49f5-8ebd-935f815267bb) Enslow Publishing, LLC.
Cooke, Tim. Behind the Lines. 2015. (World War II: the Full Story Ser.). (ENG., Illus.). 48p. (J). (gr. 6-9). 37.10 *(978-1-78121-234-9(1)*, 16837) Brown Bear Bks.
—Causes & Outbreak. 2015. (World War II: the Full Story Ser.). (ENG., Illus.). 48p. (J). (gr. 6-9). 37.10 *(978-1-78121-229-5(5)*, 16838) Brown Bear Bks.
—Home Fronts. 2015. (World War II: the Full Story Ser.). (ENG., Illus.). 48p. (J). (gr. 6-9). 37.10 *(978-1-78121-232-5(5)*, 16839) Brown Bear Bks.
—Life in the War. 2015. (World War II: the Full Story Ser.). (ENG., Illus.). 48p. (J). (gr. 6-9). 37.10 *(978-1-78121-233-2(3)*, 16840) Brown Bear Bks.
—War in the Pacific (1941-1945) 2015. (World War II: the Full Story Ser.). (ENG., Illus.). 48p. (J). (gr. 6-9). 37.10 *(978-1-78121-231-8(7)*, 16842) Brown Bear Bks.
Copeland, Peter F. Story of World War II. 2004. (Dover American History Coloring Bks.). (ENG., Illus.). 48p. (gr. 3-8). pap. 5.99 *(978-0-486-43695-1(0)*, 436950) Dover Pubns., Inc.
Corrigan, Jim. World War II, Vol. 11. Musteen, Jason R., ed. 2015. (Major U. S. Historical Wars Ser.). (Illus.). 64p. (J). (gr. 7). lib. bdg. 23.95 *(978-1-4222-3363-4(4))* Mason Crest.
Darman, Peter, ed. The Home Fronts: Allied & Axis Life During World War II, 1 vol. 2012. (World War II Ser.). (ENG., Illus.). 64p. (J). (gr. 6-6). lib. bdg. 37.13 *(978-1-4488-9236-5(8)*, abece658-d7f4-498e-8fbe-ab6536120860) Rosen Publishing Group, Inc., The.
Deem, James M. The Prisoners of Breendonk: Personal Histories from a World War II Concentration Camp. 2015. (ENG., Illus.). 352p. (YA). (gr. 9). 18.99 *(978-0-544-09664-6(9)*, 1539223, Clarion Bks.) HarperCollins Pubs.
DeLibero, Nicholas & Benchmark Education Co. Staff. The Cadence of War. 2014. (Text Connections Ser.). (J). (gr. 5). *(978-1-4900-1379-4(2))* Benchmark Education Co.
Dickmann, Nancy. The Horror of World War II. 2017. (Deadly History Ser.). (ENG., Illus.). 48p. (J). (gr. 3-6). lib. bdg. 35.99 *(978-1-4846-4165-1(5)*, 136215, Heinemann) Capstone.
DK. World War II: Visual Encyclopedia. 2015. (DK Children's Visual Encyclopedias Ser.). (ENG., Illus.). 208p. (J). (gr. 4-7). 16.99 *(978-1-4654-4027-3(5)*, DK Children) Dorling Kindersley Publishing, Inc.
Doeden, Matt. At Battle in World War II: An Interactive Battlefield Adventure. 2015. (You Choose: Battlefields Ser.). (ENG., Illus.). 112p. (J). (gr. 3-7). lib. bdg. 32.65 *(978-1-4914-2152-9(5)*, 127633, Capstone Pr.) Capstone.
—The Manhattan Project. 2018. (Heroes of World War II (Alternator Books (r)) Ser.). (ENG., Illus.). 32p. (J). (gr. 3-6). 30.65 *(978-1-5415-2150-6(1)*, e2e6a5d2-827b-4c5a-80ad-3897eb71e2bc, Lerner Pubns.) Lerner Publishing Group.
—Weapons of World War II. rev. ed. 2017. (Weapons of War Ser.). (ENG., Illus.). 32p. (J). (gr. 3-9). lib. bdg. 27.32 *(978-1-5157-7906-3(8)*, 136021, Capstone Pr.) Capstone.
Dooling, Sandra. Japanese Internment: Defining Moments in Canadian History. 2011. (Illus.). 32p. (gr. 5-8). *(978-1-77071-688-9(2))* Weigl Educational Pubs. Ltd.
Dougherty, Martin J. Tanks of World War II up Close, 1 vol., 1. Pearson, Colin, illus. 2015. (Military Technology: Top Secret Clearance Ser.). (ENG.). 224p. (YA). (gr. 7-8). 46.80 *(978-1-5081-7086-0(X)*, ba99d0bc-7c0f-4334-913a-da6201606697, Rosen Young Adult) Rosen Publishing Group, Inc., The.
Dowswell, Paul. The Second World War. rev. ed. 2007. (True Stories Ser.). (Illus.). 169p. (YA). pap. 4.99 *(978-0-7945-1841-7(9)*, Usborne) EDC Publishing.
—Second world war - internet Linked. Le, Leonard Rolland, illus. 2005. 128p. (J). 19.99 *(978-0-7945-1044-2(2)*, Usborne) EDC Publishing.
—Story of Second World War. 2012. (Science Stories Ser.). 96p. (J). pap. 10.99 *(978-0-7945-3247-5(0)*, Usborne) EDC Publishing.
—True Stories of the Second World War. 2004. (True Adventure Stories Ser.). 144p. (J). pap. 4.95 *(978-0-7945-0599-8(6))* EDC Publishing.
—True Stories of the Secong World War. 2004. (True Adventure Stories Ser.). (Illus.). 169p. (J). (gr. 5). lib. bdg. 12.95 *(978-1-58086-615-6(8)*, Usborne) EDC Publishing.
—War Stories. rev. ed. 2012. (True Stories Ser.). 432p. (J). pap. 12.99 *(978-0-7945-3221-5(7)*, Usborne) EDC Publishing.
Dowswell, Paul, et al. The World Wars: An Introduction to the First & Second World Wars. Chisholm, Jane, ed. 2007. (World Wars Ser.). (Illus.). 256p. (J). (gr. 4-7). 25.99 *(978-0-7945-1971-1(7)*, Usborne) EDC Publishing.
Duling, Kaitlyn. The Order to Drop the Atomic Bomb 1945, 1 vol. 2018. (America's Most Important Documents: Inquiry into Historical Sources Ser.). (ENG.). 64p. (gr. 6-6). lib. bdg. 37.36 *(978-1-5026-3619-5(0)*, d7ccedcb-4d67-4f2b-96c2-f5700f00e95b) Cavendish Square Publishing LLC.
Edsel, Robert M. The Greatest Treasure Hunt in History: the Story of the Monuments Men (Scholastic Focus) 2019. (ENG., Illus.). 368p. (YA). (gr. 4-7). 18.99 *(978-1-338-25119-7(8)*, Scholastic Nonfiction) Scholastic, Inc.
Ellis, Catherine, ed. Key Figures of World War II, 4 vols. 2015. (Biographies of War Ser.). (ENG.). 112p. (YA). (gr. 7-8). 70.94 *(978-1-68048-058-0(8)*,

d2a0302f-a837-4e93-945e-b90d84273215, Britannica Educational Publishing) Rosen Publishing Group, Inc., The.

ssential Library of World War II, 6 vols. 2015. (Essential Library of World War II Ser.: Vol. 10). (ENG.). 112p. (YA). (gr. 6-12). 289.52 (978-1-62403-789-4(5), 17776, Essential Library) ABDO Publishing Co.

ein, Eric. Vehicles of World War II, 1 vol. 2013. (War Vehicles Ser.). (ENG.). 32p. (J). (gr. 3-9). 28.65 (978-1-4296-9915-0(9), 120628, Capstone Pr.) Capstone.

letcher, Robert A. Jeeps at War. Naples, Thomas R. et al, eds. Fletcher, Robert A., illus. 2008. (Illus.). 36p. (J). 19.95 (978-0-9722961-1-3(5)) Iron Mountain Pr.

reedman, Jeri. Strategic Inventions of World War II, 1 vol. 2015. (Tech in the Trenches Ser.). (ENG., Illus.). 112p. (YA). (gr. 9-9). lib. bdg. 44.50 (978-1-5026-1026-3(4), 56d8e5a6-deb5-44f5-bfc5-9c75c0877db1) Cavendish Square Publishing LLC.

Garstecki, Julia. American Indian Code Talkers. 2016. (All-American Fighting Forces Ser.). (ENG.). 32p. (J). (gr. 4-6). pap. 9.99 (978-1-64466-150-5(0), 10302); (Illus.). 31.35 (978-1-68072-003-7(1), 10301) Black Rabbit Bks. (Bolt).

George, Enzo. World War II, 1 vol. 2015. (Primary Sources in U. S. History Ser.). (ENG., Illus.). 48p. (gr. 4-4). 33.07 (978-1-5026-0492-7(2), c1e2a0f8-aaa3-48cd-8c1e-94be41dcaf5f) Cavendish Square Publishing LLC.

Gerdes, Louise I. World War II. 2004. (gr. 10-12). 17.45 (978-0-7377-2536-0(2), Greenhaven Pr., Inc.) Cengage Gale.

Gitlin, Martin. World War II on the Home Front: An Interactive History Adventure. 2012. (You Choose: History Ser.). (ENG.). 112p. (gr. 3-4). pap. 41.70 (978-1-4296-8483-5(6), Capstone Pr.) Capstone.

Goldstein, Margaret J. World War II: Europe. 2004. (Chronicle of America's Wars Ser.). (Illus.). 96p. (J). (gr. 5-12). 27.93 (978-0-8225-0139-8(2)) Lerner Publishing Group.

Graphic Battles of World War II, 6 vols., Set. Incl. Battle of Guadalcanal: Land & Sea Warfare in the South Pacific. Hama, Larry. lib. bdg. 37.13 (978-1-4042-0784-4(8), b4f5a2ed-2d0d-4d09-9691-70197b96a3ce); Battle of Iwo Jima: Guerilla Warfare in the Pacific. Hama, Larry. Williams, Anthony, illus. lib. bdg. 37.13 (978-1-4042-0781-3(3), f30f6ecb-9a55-43d5-adb9-7d1eab4429b4); Battle of Midway: The Destruction of the Japanese Fleet. Abnett, Dan. Elson, Richard, illus. lib. bdg. 37.13 (978-1-4042-0783-7(X), 504f9af2-4160-40ae-8de9-6d3ee0f78eca); Battle of the Bulge. Cain, Bill. lib. bdg. 37.13 (978-1-4042-0782-0(1), c8c8efc3-cd37-4e69-b9c4-e6967fa65d69); D-Day. Murray, Doug. lib. bdg. 37.13 (978-1-4042-0786-8(4), 84fc88c9-7171-4a70-aeea-23ee0767a2d2); Pearl Harbor: A Day of Infamy. White, Steve D. Spahn, Jerrold, illus. lib. bdg. 37.13 (978-1-4042-0785-1(6), 30d5dd6e-eba7-4615-992a-9714f1d9620e); (YA). (gr. 5-5). 2007. (Graphic Battles of World War II Ser.). (ENG.). 48p. 2006. Set lib. bdg. 111.39 (978-1-4042-1052-3(0), f6c178dc-0413-49f2-ab67-3e5eb86e6fcc) Rosen Publishing Group, Inc., The.

Group/McGraw-Hill, Wright. History: World War II, 6 vols. (Book2WebTM Ser.). (gr. 4-8). 36.50 (978-0-322-04455-5(3)) Wright Group/McGraw-Hill.

Gutner, Howard. America's Secret Weapon: The Navajo Code Talkers of World War II. 2003. (ENG., Illus.). 32p. (J). (gr. 6-8). pap. 7.97 net. (978-0-7652-3266-3(9), Celebration Pr.) Savvas Learning Co.

Hamen, Susan E. World War II, 1 vol. 2013. (Essential Library of American Wars Ser.). (ENG., Illus.). 112p. (YA). (gr. 6-12). lib. bdg. 41.36 (978-1-61783-882-8(9), 6613, Essential Library) ABDO Publishing Co.

Heinrichs, Ann. The Japanese American Internment: Innocence, Guilt, & Wartime Justice, 1 vol. 2011. (Perspectives On Ser.). (ENG., Illus.). 112p. (J). (gr. 8-8). 42.64 (978-0-7614-4983-6(3), 134471b9-944f-4a56-99ea-d911466205eb) Cavendish Square Publishing LLC.

Hoena, Blake. Navajo Code Talkers: Top Secret Messengers of World War II. Massegu, Marcel P., illus. 2019. (Amazing World War II Stories Ser.). (ENG.). 32p. (J). (gr. 3-9). pap. 7.95 (978-1-5435-7549-1(8), 141081); lib. bdg. 34.65 (978-1-5435-7314-5(2), 140619) Capstone.

Hosch, William L. World War II: People, Politics, & Power, 1 vol. 2010. (America at War Ser.). (ENG., Illus.). 264p. (YA). (gr. 10-10). lib. bdg. 52.59 (978-1-61530-008-2(2), 6f99d295-8a87-4a02-be51-5ac1aca6dec4) Rosen Publishing Group, Inc., The.

Hosch, William L., ed. World War II: People, Politics, & Power, 4 vols. 2010. (America at War Ser.). (ENG.). 264p. (YA). (gr. 10-10). 105.18 (978-1-61530-093-8(7), 5bd9ca2a-5880-4b0d-914d-85153c1392c9) Rosen Publishing Group, Inc., The.

Hunter, Nick. World War II: Frontline Soldiers & Their Families, 1 vol. 2015. (Frontline Families Ser.). (ENG., Illus.). 48p. (J). (gr. 5-6). pap. 15.05 (978-1-4824-3069-1(X), 9e2358e2-d852-4f43-9a2c-4f3ca1935a94) Stevens, Gareth Publishing LLLP.

Hutchison, Patricia. World War II: 12 Things to Know. 2017. (America at War Ser.). (ENG., Illus.). 32p. (J). (gr. 3-6). 32.80 (978-1-63235-271-2(0), 11710, 12-Story Library) Bookstaves, LLC.

Jacobs Altman, Linda. Warsaw, Lodz, Vilna: The Holocaust Ghettos, 1 vol. 2014. (Remembering the Holocaust Ser.). (ENG.). 96p. (J). (gr. 6-7). pap. 13.88 (978-0-7660-6208-5(2), ec751daf-6e53-4560-947e-0e7831cc2b92) Enslow Publishing, LLC.

Jones, Rob Lloyd. See Inside the Second World War. Pritelli, Maria Cristina, illus. 2012. (See Inside Board Bks). 16p. (J). ring bd. 13.99 (978-0-7945-3085-3(0), Usborne) EDC Publishing.

Kaelberer, Angie Peterson. Eyewitness to World War II. 2017. (Eyewitness to World War II Ser.). (ENG.). 112p. (J). (gr. 5-9). 154.60 (978-0-7565-5606-8(6), 26647, Compass Point Bks.) Capstone.

Kallen, Stuart A. Navajo Code Talkers. 2018. (Heroes of World War II (Alternator Books (r)) Ser.). (ENG., Illus.). 32p. (J). (gr. 3-6). 30.65 (978-1-5124-8644-5(2), b22bb522-0710-477b-9a82-187c62ea0db1, Lerner Pubns.) Lerner Publishing Group.

Keyes, Anna. World War II: 6 English, 6 Spanish Adaptations: by the Numbers & Los números de la Segunda Guerra Mundial. 2011. (ENG & SPA.). (J). 101.00 net. (978-1-4108-5736-1(0)) Benchmark Education Co.

—World War II by the Numbers: Set Of 6. 2011. (Navigators Ser.). (J). pap. 50.00 net. (978-1-4108-2574-2(4)) Benchmark Education Co.

Klar, Jeremy & Lily, Henrietta M. Josef Mengele, 1 vol., 1. 2015. (Holocaust Ser.). (ENG., Illus.). 112p. (J). (gr. 7-7). 38.80 (978-1-5081-7047-1(9), 235b5638-0a52-4682-847f-b5852fc56307, Rosen Young Adult) Rosen Publishing Group, Inc., The.

Kramer, Ann. Women & War. 2009. (J). 24.25 (978-1-59771-142-5(X)) Sea-To-Sea Pubns.

Langley, Andrew. Stories of Women in World War II: We Can Do It! 2015. (Women's Stories from History Ser.). (ENG., Illus.). 112p. (J). (gr. 6-11). 32.65 (978-1-4846-0865-4(8), 127948, Heinemann) Capstone.

Lanier, Wendy H. Life During World War II, 1 vol. 2015. (Daily Life in US History Ser.). (ENG., Illus.). 48p. (J). (gr. 4-8). lib. bdg. 35.64 (978-1-62403-629-3(5), 16898) ABDO Publishing Co.

Lanser, Amanda. World War II by the Numbers. 2015. (America at War by the Numbers Ser.). (ENG., Illus.). 32p. (J). (gr. 3-9). lib. bdg. 28.65 (978-1-4914-4297-5(2), 128692, Capstone Pr.) Capstone.

Lombardo, Jennifer & Robson, David. The Horrors of Auschwitz, 1 vol. 2016. (World History Ser.). (ENG.). 104p. (YA). (gr. 7-7). 41.53 (978-1-5345-6054-3(8), 9060cc72-3515-4ea6-a50a-71ab4a51a5cc, Lucent Pr.) Greenhaven Publishing LLC.

Lowry, Lois. On the Horizon. Pak, Kenard, illus. 2020. (ENG.). 80p. (J). (gr. 5-7). 16.99 (978-0-358-12940-0(0), 1752988, Clarion Bks.) HarperCollins Pubs.

Lukesh, Jean A. Sky Rider: Story of Evelyn Sharp, World War II WASP. 2011. (Noteworthy Americans Young Readers Biography Book Ser.). (ENG., Illus.). 161p. (J). pap. 14.95 (978-0-9647586-3-6(6)) Field Mouse Productions.

Malam, John. You Wouldn't Want to Be a Secret Agent During World War II! A Perilous Mission Behind Enemy Lines. 2010. (You Wouldn't Want to... Ser.). 32p. (J). 29.00 (978-0-531-20474-0(X), Watts, Franklin) Scholastic Library Publishing.

Marchione, Margherita. Pope Pius XII: Bilingual Coloring Book. Elliott, John, illus. 2004. (SPA & ENG.). 32p. 1.00 (978-0-8091-6721-0(2), 6721-2) Paulist Pr.

Marcovitz, Hal. Cause & Effect: World War II. 2017. (ENG.). 80p. (YA). (gr. 5-12). (978-1-68282-174-9(9)) ReferencePoint Pr., Inc.

Marrin, Albert. FDR & the American Crisis. 2016. (Illus.). 336p. (YA). (gr. 7). pap. 15.99 (978-0-385-75362-3(4), Ember) Random Hse. Children's Bks.

—Uprooted: The Japanese American Experience During World War II. 2016. (Illus.). 256p. (YA). (gr. 7). 32.99 (978-0-553-50936-6(5), Knopf Bks. for Young Readers) Random Hse. Children's Bks.

Marriott, Emma. Did Anything Good Come Out of World War II?, 1 vol., 1. 2015. (Innovation Through Adversity Ser.). (ENG.). 48p. (J). (gr. 6-7). 33.47 (978-1-5081-7070-9(3), dfe63667-8846-4c37-b431-a4283f731809, Rosen Young Adult) Rosen Publishing Group, Inc., The.

Marsh, Carole. World War II: Reproducible Activity Book. 2004. (Illus.). 28p. (J). (gr. 4-12). pap. 5.95 (978-0-635-02678-1(3)) Gallopade International.

—World War II Reproducible Activity Book (HC) 2004. 28p. (gr. 4-12). 29.95 (978-0-635-02679-8(1)) Gallopade International.

Mason, Paul. Reports from the Front in WWII. 2010. (ENG.). 32p. (J). (978-0-7787-9905-4(0)); pap. (978-0-7787-9926-9(3)) Crabtree Publishing Co.

Maybury, Richard J. World War II: The Rest of the Story & How It Affects You Today, 1930 to September 11 2001. Williams, Jane A., ed. rev. ed. 2003. ("Uncle Eric" Bk.: 11). (ENG., Illus.). 349p. pap. 19.95 (978-0-942617-43-6(6)) Bluestocking Pr.

Mazzeo, Tilar J. Irena's Children: Young Readers Edition; a True Story of Courage. 2017. (ENG., Illus.). 288p. (J). (gr. 5). pap. 8.99 (978-1-4814-4992-2(3), McElderry, Margaret K. Bks.) McElderry, Margaret K. Bks.

McGowen, Tom. D-Day. 2017. (J). (978-0-531-22093-1(1), Orchard Bks.) Scholastic, Inc.

McNeil, Niki, et al. HOCPP 1089 World War II. 2006. spiral bd. 24.50 (978-1-60308-089-7(9)) In the Hands of a Child.

Meyer, Susan. Nazi Concentration Camps: A Policy of Genocide, 1 vol. 2014. (Documentary History of the Holocaust Ser.). (ENG., Illus.). 80p. (J). (gr. 7-7). 37.47 (978-1-4777-7603-2(6), a90d81d4-bdf8-4f25-8211-ac3d311d6855) Rosen Publishing Group, Inc., The.

Miles, John C. Fighting Forces of World War II on Land. 2019. (Fighting Forces of World War II Ser.). (ENG., Illus.). 32p. (J). (gr. 3-9). lib. bdg. 28.65 (978-1-5435-7483-8(1), 141004) Capstone.

Miller, Terry. D-Day at Omaha Beach: Turning the Tide of World War II. 2011. (J). (978-0-545-32945-3(0)) Scholastic, Inc.

Modern Eras Uncovered: From Jesse Owens to Hiroshima. 2005. (Modern Eras Uncovered Ser.). (ENG., Illus.). 56p. (J). (978-1-84443-952-2(6)) Steck-Vaughn.

Moss, Marissa. Barbed Wire Baseball. Shimizu, Yuko, illus. 2013. (ENG.). 48p. (J). (gr. 1-5). 19.95 (978-1-4197-0521-2(0), 671701, Abrams Bks. for Young Readers) Abrams, Inc.

Murray, Laura K. World War II Technology. 2017. (War Technology Ser.). (ENG.). 48p. (J). (gr. 4-8). lib. bdg. 35.64 (978-1-5321-1193-8(2), 25962) ABDO Publishing Co.

Murray, Stuart. World War II. 2009. (FACT ATLAS Ser.). 72p. (J). (gr. 3-7). pap. 13.99 (978-0-8416-1093-4(2)) Hammond World Atlas Corp.

Murray, Stuart A. P. World War II: Step into the Action & Behind Enemy Lines from Hitler's Rise to Japan's Surrender. 2015. (Fact Atlas Ser.). (ENG., Illus.). 72p. (J). (gr. 2-7). 14.99 (978-1-63220-433-2(9), Sky Pony Pr.) Skyhorse Publishing Co., Inc.

Nardo, Don. Nazi War Criminals. 2015. (Illus.). 80p. (J). (978-1-60152-850-6(7)) ReferencePoint Pr., Inc.

Nelson, Peter. Left for Dead: A Young Man's Search for Justice for the USS Indianapolis. 2003. 224p. (YA). (gr. 7-7). pap. 10.99 (978-0-385-73091-4(8), Delacorte Bks. for Young Readers) Random Hse. Children's Bks.

Norton, James. The Holocaust: Jews, Germany, & the National Socialists. 2009. (Genocide in Modern Times Ser.). 64p. (gr. 6-6). 58.50 (978-1-61512-677-4(5)) Rosen Publishing Group, Inc., The.

Norton, James R. The Holocaust: Jews, Germany, & the National Socialists, 1 vol. 2008. (Genocide in Modern Times Ser.). (ENG., Illus.). 64p. (YA). (gr. 6-6). lib. bdg. 37.13 (978-1-4042-1821-5(1), 6ee55512-c4b4-41da-9e1e-f65f491bb9ba) Rosen Publishing Group, Inc., The.

O'Neill, Robert John. World War II: Essential Histories, 12 vols., Set. Incl. World War II: Europe, 1944-1945. Havers, R. P. W. lib. bdg. 38.47 (978-1-4358-9130-2(9), 55bd8326-7dd6-4127-b88d-28c6ebdb906a); World War II: Northwest Europe, 1944-1945. Hart, R. & Hart, S. lib. bdg. 38.47 (978-1-4358-9129-6(5), 32f43014-5156-4018-8e2f-f94f19d3bdb2); World War II: The Eastern Front 1941-1945. Jukes, Geoffrey. lib. bdg. 38.47 (978-1-4358-9134-0(1), 364c546d-4d20-4553-90dc-f1789407d04f); World War II: The Mediterranean 1940-1945. Collier, Paul H. lib. bdg. 38.47 (978-1-4358-9132-6(5), 1b1b7b2b-a34e-4801-8751-2f315236ed09); World War II: The Pacific. Horner, D. M. lib. bdg. 38.47 (978-1-4358-9133-3(3), 4abac419-bc3c-4d85-bbbd-8a9445be0639); World War II: The War at Sea. Grove, Philip D. & Grove, Mark J. lib. bdg. 38.47 (978-1-4358-9131-9(7), 3d0cdabb-69b1-42d1-80fc-600a57da9181); (YA). (gr. 10-10). 2010. (World War II: Essential Histories Ser.). (ENG., Illus.). 96p. 2009. Set lib. bdg. 230.82 (978-1-4358-9135-7(X), 5e627fc8-bafe-443e-b116-be6a4aa18d00) Rosen Publishing Group, Inc., The.

Oppenheim, Joanne. Dear Miss Breed: True Stories of the Japanese American Incarceration During World War II & a Librarian Who Made a Difference. 2006. (ENG., Illus.). 288p. (J). (gr. 7-7). 27.99 (978-0-439-56992-7(3)) Scholastic, Inc.

Osborne, Mary Pope & Boyce, Natalie Pope. World War II: A Nonfiction Companion to Magic Tree House Super Edition #1: World at War 1944. Molinari, Carlo, illus. 2017. (Magic Tree House (R) Fact Tracker Ser.: 36). 144p. (J). (gr. 4-7). 6.99 (978-1-101-93639-9(8), Random Hse. Bks. for Young Readers) Random Hse. Children's Bks.

Osborne, Mary Pope & Natalie Pope Boyce. World War II: A Nonfiction Companion to Magic Tree House Super Edition #1 World at War 1944. 2017. (Magic Tree House Fact Trackers Ser.). lib. bdg. 17.20 (978-0-606-39849-7(X)) Turtleback.

Oshiro, Beverly & Sachs, Ruth. Adolf Eichmann, 1 vol., 1. 2015. (Holocaust Ser.). (ENG., Illus.). 112p. (J). (gr. 7-7). 38.80 (978-1-4994-6246-3(8), 72e969a8-1c46-4180-b92c-fc9636f96ca3, Rosen Young Adult) Rosen Publishing Group, Inc., The.

Otfinoski, Steven. Japanese American Internment: Prisoners in Their Own Land. 2019. (Tangled History Ser.). (ENG., Illus.). 112p. (J). (gr. 3-9). pap. 6.95 (978-1-5435-7557-6(9), 141089); lib. bdg. 32.65 (978-1-5435-7257-5(X), 140593) Capstone.

Owens, Lisa L. World War II Code Breakers. 2018. (Heroes of World War II (Alternator Books (r)) Ser.). (ENG., Illus.). 32p. (J). (gr. 3-6). lib. bdg. 30.65 (978-1-5415-2151-3(X), 65a6b607-14f2-49c3-98bd-70f5ab825dc9, Lerner Pubns.) Lerner Publishing Group.

Page, Andrea. The Sioux Code Talkers of World War II, 1 vol. 2017. (ENG., Illus.). 136p. (J). (gr. 3-7). 14.95 (978-1-4556-2243-6(5), Pelican Publishing) Arcadia Publishing.

Parsons, Martin. Women's War. (ENG., Illus.). 31p. (YA). pap. (978-0-7502-2845-9(8), Wayland) Hachette Children's Group.

Perritano, John. Health & Medicine, Vol. 9. van Dijk, Ruud, ed. 2016. (Making of the Modern World: 1945 to the Present Ser.). (Illus.). 64p. (J). (gr. 7). 23.95 (978-1-4222-3639-0(0)) Mason Crest.

—The Making of the Modern World: 1945 to the Present: Migration & Refugees, Vol. 9. van Dijk, Ruud, ed. 2016. (Making of the Modern World: 1945 to the Present Ser.: Vol. 9). (ENG.). 64p. (J). (gr. 7-12). 23.95 (978-1-4222-3640-6(4)) Mason Crest.

PRESS, Celebration. America's Secret Weapon: The Navajo Code Talkers of World War II. 2003. (ENG.). (J). (gr. 6-8). pap. 37.95 (978-0-7652-3246-5(4), Celebration Pr.) Savvas Learning Co.

Ramen, Fred. Hermann Goring: Hitler's Second-in-Command. 2009. (Holocaust Biographies Ser.). 112p. (gr. 7-12). 63.90 (978-1-61513-387-1(9)) Rosen Publishing Group, Inc., The.

Raum, Elizabeth. Stealing Nazi Secrets in World War II: An Interactive Espionage Adventure. 2015. (You Choose: Spies Ser.). (ENG., Illus.). 112p. (J). (gr. 3-7). pap. 6.95 (978-1-4914-5934-8(4), 128854, Capstone Pr.) Capstone.

—World War II: An Interactive History Adventure, 1 vol. 2009. (You Choose: History Ser.). (ENG.). 112p. (J). (gr. 3-7). pap. 6.95 (978-1-4296-3457-1(X), 96000, Capstone Pr.) Capstone.

—A World War II Timeline, 1 vol. 2014. (War Timelines Ser.). (ENG., Illus.). 48p. (J). (gr. 4-7). lib. bdg. 35.32 (978-1-4765-4158-7(2), 124263, Capstone Pr.) Capstone.

Renaud, Anne. A Bloom of Friendship: The Story of the Canadian Tulip Festival, 1 vol. 2014. (ENG., Illus.). 32p. (J). (gr. 5-8). pap. 9.95 (978-1-77050-215-4(7), 022a1f0d-8833-4962-9b73-97ebfe93e74f) Whitecap Bks., Ltd. CAN. Dist: Firefly Bks., Ltd.

Reynoldson, Fiona. The Home Front. (ENG., Illus.). 48p. (J). pap. (978-0-7502-2696-7(X), Wayland) Hachette Children's Group.

Robertson, David A. The Scout: Tommy Prince. Henderson, Scott B., illus. 2014. (Tales from Big Spirit Ser.: 3). (ENG.). 30p. (J). (gr. 4-6). pap. (978-1-55379-478-3(8), 78912685-2d85-4153-9f88-b7d8feb31ffe, HighWater Pr.) Portage & Main Pr.

Rosenberg, Aaron. World War II (Profiles #2) 2011. (Profiles Ser.: 2). (ENG.). 160p. (J). (gr. 4-8). pap. 6.99 (978-0-545-31655-2(3), Scholastic Paperbacks) Scholastic, Inc.

Ross, Stewart. The Home Front in World War II. (ENG., Illus.). 32p. 22.99 (978-0-7502-4184-7(5)) Hodder & Stoughton GBR. Dist: Trafalgar Square Publishing.

Roxburgh, Ellis. Adolf Hitler vs. Winston Churchill: Foes of World War II, 1 vol. 2014. (History's Greatest Rivals Ser.). (ENG.). 48p. (J). (gr. 6-8). lib. bdg. 33.60 (978-1-4824-2205-4(0), c5134eae-5010-4fa0-84b3-e4c1e9ff2158) Stevens, Gareth Publishing LLLP.

Rubin, Susan Goldman. The Flag with Fifty-Six Stars: A Gift from the Survivors of Mauthausen. Farnsworth, Bill, illus. 2005. (ENG.). 40p. (J). (gr. 1-5). 17.95 (978-0-8234-1653-0(4)) Holiday Hse., Inc.

Ruelle, Karen Gray. Surprising Spies: Unexpected Heroes of World War II. 2020. (Illus.). 160p. (J). (gr. 3-7). 19.99 (978-0-8234-3757-3(4)) Holiday Hse., Inc.

Ruggiero, Adriane. World War II, 1 vol. 2003. (American Voices From Ser.). (ENG., Illus.). 160p. (J). (gr. 6-6). 41.21 (978-0-7614-1206-9(9), fdea97f5-91c3-478b-8640-d66ec601d883) Cavendish Square Publishing LLC.

Sachs, Ruth. Adolf Eichmann: Engineer of Death. 2009. (Holocaust Biographies Ser.). 112p. (gr. 7-12). 63.90 (978-1-61513-380-2(1)) Rosen Publishing Group, Inc., The.

Samuels, Charles. Home Front. 2012. (World War II: Sourcebook Ser.). (ENG., Illus.). 48p. (J). (gr. 5-8). lib. bdg. 37.10 (978-1-936333-22-6(8), 16832) Brown Bear Bks.

—Propaganda. 2012. (World War II: Sourcebook Ser.). (ENG., Illus.). 48p. (J). (gr. 5-8). lib. bdg. 37.10 (978-1-936333-23-3(6), 16834) Brown Bear Bks.

—Soldiers. 2012. (World War II: Sourcebook Ser.). (ENG., Illus.). 48p. (J). (gr. 5-8). lib. bdg. 37.10 (978-1-936333-24-0(4), 16835) Brown Bear Bks.

Samuels, Charlie. Machines & Weaponry of World War II, 1 vol. 2013. (Machines That Won the War Ser.). (ENG., Illus.). 48p. (J). (gr. 5-6). pap. 15.05 (978-1-4339-8608-6(6), 97164ac8-6562-4407-aacd-bcf84d741d8d); lib. bdg. 34.60 (978-1-4339-8607-9(8), 08005b31-3a63-49db-93b2-5c260d4ab83f) Stevens, Gareth Publishing LLLP.

Schomp, Virginia. World War II, 1 vol. 2005. (Letters from the Battlefront Ser.). (ENG., Illus.). 96p. (gr. 6-6). lib. bdg. 36.93 (978-0-7614-1662-3(5), 2ef22db5-a487-414b-9d38-8a7ab9b6be67) Cavendish Square Publishing LLC.

Scott, Janine. The Two Great Wars. 2007. (Shockwave: History & Politics Ser.). (ENG., Illus.). 36p. (J). (gr. 4-6). lib. bdg. 25.00 (978-0-531-17756-3(4), Children's Pr.) Scholastic Library Publishing.

Seidlitz, Lauri. The Legacy of World War II. 2015. (World War II: History's Deadliest Conflict Ser.). (ENG., Illus.). 48p. (J). (gr. 5-5). (978-0-7787-2117-8(5)) Crabtree Publishing Co.

Senker, Cath. Why Did World War II Happen?, 1 vol. 2010. (Moments in History Ser.). (ENG.). 48p. (gr. 6-8). (J). pap. 15.05 (978-1-4339-4185-6(6), b128f537-7929-479a-93e4-2fd4ddff14cd, Gareth Stevens Secondary Library); (Illus.). (YA). lib. bdg. 34.60 (978-1-4339-4184-9(8), 8cebe7d6-0af0-46bd-ab47-a1890c7ffe55) Stevens, Gareth Publishing LLLP.

—World War II, 1 vol. 2005. (How Did It Happen? Ser.). (ENG., Illus.). 48p. (gr. 4-8). lib. bdg. 38.33 (978-1-59018-604-6(4), cc9be58e-f6aa-41b0-bddc-383d66b40efe, Lucent Pr.) Greenhaven Publishing LLC.

Setterington, Ken. Branded by the Pink Triangle, 1 vol. 2013. (ENG.). 196p. (YA). (gr. 7-13). pap. 18.95 (978-1-926920-96-2(1)) Second Story Pr. CAN. Dist: Orca Bk. Pubs. USA.

Shaw, Antony. World War II. 2010. (Facts at Your Fingertips: Modern Military History Ser.). 64p. (YA). (gr. 9-12). 35.65 (978-1-933834-50-4(1)) Brown Bear Bks.

Sheehan, Sean. From Jessie Owens to Hiroshima: The Mid 1930s to 1945. 2005. (Modern Eras Uncovered Ser.). (Illus.). 56p. (J). pap. (978-1-4109-1795-9(9)) Steck-Vaughn.

—Modern Eras Uncovered: From Jesse Owens to Hiroshima. 2005. (Modern Eras Uncovered Ser.). (Illus.). 56p. (J). (978-1-84443-962-1(3)) Steck-Vaughn.

Shoup, Kate. Life As a Navajo Code Talker in World War II, 1 vol. 2017. (Life As... Ser.). (ENG.). 32p. (gr. 3-3). pap. 11.58 (978-1-5026-3051-3(6), 8c5232e5-8cb4-44af-b319-3a757917e174) Cavendish Square Publishing LLC.

Simons, Lisa M. Bolt. The U. S. WASP: Trailblazing Women Pilots of World War II. 2017. (Women & War Ser.). (ENG., Illus.). 32p. (J). (gr. 3-9). pap. 8.19 (978-1-5157-7944-5(0), 136039, Capstone Pr.) Capstone.

Smith, Sherri L. Who Were the Tuskegee Airmen? 2019. (Who HQ Ser.). (ENG.). 108p. (J). (gr. 2-3). 16.36 (978-1-64310-860-5(3)) Penworthy Co., LLC, The.

Smith, Sherri L. & Who HQ. Who Were the Tuskegee Airmen? Murray, Jake, illus. 2018. (Who Was? Ser.). 112p. (J). (gr. 3-7). 5.99 (978-0-399-54194-0(2), Penguin Workshop) Penguin Young Readers Group.

Spilsbury, Richard & Spilsbury, Louise. WWII Survival Tips. 2010. (ENG.). 32p. (J). (978-0-7787-9898-9(4)); pap. (978-0-7787-9919-1(0)) Crabtree Publishing Co.

Stalcup, Ann. America's Secret Weapon: Navajo Code Talkers of World War II. 2017. (Illus.). 59p. (J). pap. (978-1-63293-176-4(1)) Sunstone Pr.

Stein, R. Conrad. Cornerstones of Freedom, Third Series: World War II. 2012. (Cornerstones of Freedom, Third Ser.). (ENG., Illus.). 64p. (J). (gr. 4-6). lib. bdg. 30.00 (978-0-531-23069-5(4), Children's Pr.) Scholastic Library Publishing.

Stephens, Chris S. A Wartime Scrapbook. 2004. (ENG., Illus.). 32p. pap. 14.95 (978-1-84323-285-8(5)) Beekman Bks., Inc.

Summers, Elizabeth. Weapons & Vehicles of World War II. 2015. (Tools of War Ser.). (ENG., Illus.). 32p. (J). (gr. 3-9). lib. bdg. 27.32 (978-1-4914-4080-3(5), 128651, Capstone Pr.) Capstone.

Thompson, Ben. Guts & Glory: World War II. 2016. (ENG., Illus.). 384p. (J). E-Book (978-0-316-32199-0(0)) Little Brown & Co.

Thompson, Julian & Millett, Allan R. World War II Told Through 100 Artifacts, 1 vol. 2018. (War Told Through Artifacts Ser.). (ENG.). 256p. (gr. 8-8). pap. 24.52 *(978-1-5026-4464-0(9),* 15b70f26-a166-487d-a664-c5de8b9c1d2e) Cavendish Square Publishing LLC.

Timmons, Angie. Real-World Projects to Explore World War II, 1 vol. 2018. (Project-Based Learning in Social Studies). (ENG.). 64p. (gr. 5-5). lib. bdg. 37.47 *(978-1-5081-8228-3(0),* c28cd080-f3a8-4b7b-86aa-d54f4a7e8d51) Rosen Publishing Group, Inc., The.

Townsend, John. Army. 2016. (Action Force: World War II Ser.). 32p. (gr. 3-7). 31.35 *(978-1-59920-982-1(9),* Smart Apple Media) Black Rabbit Bks.

—Special Operations. 2016. (Action Force: World War II Ser.). 32p. (gr. 3-7). 31.35 *(978-1-59920-983-8(7),* Smart Apple Media) Black Rabbit Bks.

Troupe, Thomas Kingsley. The Tuskegee Airmen's Mission to Berlin: A Fly on the Wall History. Tejido, Jomike, illus. 2018. (Fly on the Wall History Ser.). (ENG.). 32p. (J). (gr. 1-3). lib. bdg. 27.99 *(978-1-5158-1600-3(1),* 136253, Picture Window Bks.) Capstone.

A True Book(tm) — World at War (Set Of 5) 2014. (True Book — World War II Ser.). (J). lib. bdg. 145.00 *(978-0-531-24356-5(7))* Scholastic Library Publishing.

Tucker, Spencer C. & Roberts, Priscilla, eds. World War II Set, Vol. 1: 5 Volumes [5 Volumes]. 5 vols. 2005. (ENG., Illus.). 2008p. (C). 461.00 *(978-1-85109-857-6(7),* 900301928) ABC-CLIO, LLC.

Watts, Ana Dearborn & Dearborn, Dorothy. The Pony Princess. Taylor, Carol, illus. 2008. (ENG.). 32p. pap. 6.00 *(978-1-896543-32-1(4))* DreamCatcher Publishing CAN. Dist: Univ. of Toronto Pr.

Wehrertuchtigungslager der Hitler-Jugend, 1942-1945. (GER.). *(978-3-928379-00-7(3))* Verein zur Fordenrung der Umweltforschung.

Welky, Ali, ed. A Captive Audience: Voices of Japanese American Youth in World War II Arkansas. 2015. (ENG., Illus.). 124p. (J). pap. 21.95 *(978-1-935106-86-9(4),* P483240) Butler Ctr. for Arkansas Studies.

Williams, Brenda & Williams, Brian. Saving the Persecuted. 2015. (Heroes of World War II Ser.). (ENG., Illus.). 48p. (J). (gr. 4-6). 35.32 *(978-1-4109-8046-5(4),* 130125, Raintree) Capstone.

Williams, Brian. DKfindout! World War II. 2017. (DK Findout! Ser.). (ENG., Illus.). 64p. (J). (gr. 1-4). pap. 10.99 *(978-1-4654-6311-1(9),* DK Children) Dorling Kindersley Publishing, Inc.

Wood, Douglas. Franklin & Winston: A Christmas That Changed the World. Moser, Barry, illus. 2011. (ENG.). 40p. (J). (gr. 1-4). 16.99 *(978-0-7636-3383-7(6))* Candlewick Pr.

World War II: PowerPoint Presentations in World History. 2005. cd-rom 49.95 net. *(978-1-56004-209-9(5))* Social Studies Schl. Service.

World War II Instructional Guide. 2009. (Grade 8: Social Studies Exit Project Kits Ser.). spiral bd. *(978-1-4042-4039-1(X),* Rosen Classroom) Rosen Publishing Group, Inc., The.

Wukovits, John F. World War II in Europe. 2004. (World History Ser.). (ENG., Illus.). 112p. (gr. 7-10). 34.95 *(978-1-59018-185-0(9),* Lucent Bks.) Cengage Gale.

WWII Airplanes. (Color & Learn Ser.). 36p. (J). (gr. 1-5). pap. *(978-1-882210-01-5(8))* Action Publishing, Inc.

Yomtov, Nel. Great Escapes of World War II. Tortosa, Wilson & Bartolo, Michael, illus. 2017. (Great Escapes of World War II Ser.). (ENG.). 32p. (J). (gr. 3-9). 133.28 *(978-1-5157-3533-5(8),* 25399, Capstone Pr.) Capstone.

Zamosky, Lisa & Conklin, Wendy. World War II, 1 vol. rev. ed. 2007. (Social Studies: Informational Text Ser.). (ENG.). 32p. (gr. 4-8). pap. 11.99 *(978-0-7439-0668-5(3))* Teacher Created Materials, Inc.

WORLD WAR, 1939-1945—AERIAL OPERATIONS

Adams, Simon. Warplanes. 2009. (J). 28.50 *(978-1-59920-223-5(9))* Black Rabbit Bks.

Asso, B. & Bergese, F. Cinebook Recounts: Battle of Britain. movie tie-in ed. 2010. (Cinebook Recounts Ser.). (Illus.). 48p. pap. 11.95 *(978-1-84918-025-2(3))* CineBook GBR. Dist: National Bk. Network.

Asso, Bernard & Bergèse, Francis. Battle of Britain. 2008. (ENG., Illus.). 48p. pap. 11.95 *(978-1-905460-39-7(2))* CineBook GBR. Dist: National Bk. Network.

Baker, Brynn. Tuskegee Airmen: Freedom Flyers of World War II. 2015. (Military Heroes Ser.). (ENG., Illus.). 32p. (J). (gr. 3-6). lib. bdg. 27.99 *(978-1-4914-4839-7(3),* 128724, Capstone Pr.) Capstone.

Barnes, Pete. Richard Bong: World War II Flying Ace. 2009. (Badger Biographies Ser.). (ENG., Illus.). 128p. (J). (gr. 2-7). pap. 12.95 *(978-0-87020-434-0(3))* Wisconsin Historical Society.

Benge, Janet & Benge, Geoff. Jacob Deshazer: Forgive Your Enemies. 2009. (ENG.). 224p. (YA). pap. 11.99 *(978-1-57658-475-0(5))* YWAM Publishing.

Brook, Henry. True Stories of the Blitz. McNee, Ian, illus. 2006. (True Adventure Stories Ser.). 160p. (J). (gr. 4-7). per. 4.99 *(978-0-7945-1245-3(3),* Usborne) EDC Publishing.

Burgan, Michael. World War II Pilots, 1 vol. 2013. (You Choose: World War II Ser.). (ENG., Illus.). 112p. (J). (gr. 3-7). pap. 6.95 *(978-1-62065-718-8(X),* 121704, Capstone Pr.) Capstone.

—World War II Pilots: An Interactive History Adventure. 2013. (You Choose: World War II Ser.). (ENG.). 112p. (J). (gr. 3-4). pap. 41.70 *(978-1-62065-719-5(8),* 19311); (Illus.). lib. bdg. 32.65 *(978-1-4296-9899-3(3),* 120615) Capstone. (Capstone Pr.).

Burgan, Michael, et al. You Choose: World War II Classroom Collection. 2013. (You Choose: World War II Ser.). (ENG.). 112p. (J). (gr. 3-4). pap., pap., pap. 132.05 *(978-1-62065-725-6(2),* 19315, Capstone Pr.) Capstone.

Dell, Pamela. The Soviet Night Witches: Brave Women Bomber Pilots of World War II. 2017. (Women & War Ser.). (ENG., Illus.). 32p. (J). (gr. 3-9). lib. bdg. 28.65 *(978-1-5157-7938-4(6),* 136031, Capstone Pr.) Capstone.

Doeden, Matt. Tuskegee Airmen. 2018. (Heroes of World War II (Alternator Books (r)) Ser.). (ENG., Illus.). 32p. (J). (gr. 3-6). 30.65 *(978-1-5415-2149-0(8),* f1f7cb2d-9a30-4d6e-9751-c268493b806e, Lerner Pubns.) Lerner Publishing Group.

Donelly, Karen. American Women Pilots of World War II, 1 vol. 2004. (American Women at War Ser.). (ENG.). 112p. (YA). (gr. 8-8). pap. 13.95 *(978-1-4358-3274-9(4),* 5d9f859d-ebd7-4c4b-9c01-4e9010f10a6f) Rosen Publishing Group, Inc., The.

Garstecki, Julia. Tuskegee Airmen. 2016. (All-American Fighting Forces Ser.). (ENG., Illus.). 32p. (J). (gr. 4-6). 31.35 *(978-1-68072-004-4(X),* 10317, Bolt) Black Rabbit Bks.

—WASPs. 2016. (All-American Fighting Forces Ser.). (ENG.). 32p. (J). (gr. 4-6). pap. 9.99 *(978-1-64466-155-0(1),* 10322); (Illus.). 31.35 *(978-1-68072-005-1(8),* 10321) Black Rabbit Bks. (Bolt).

Graham, Ian. You Wouldn't Want to Be a World War II Pilot! Air Battles You Might Not Survive. Antram, David, illus. 2009. (You Wouldn't Want to Ser.). (ENG.). 32p. (J). 29.00 *(978-0-531-21326-1(9))* Scholastic Library Publishing.

Group/McGraw-Hill, Wright. Al Ataque!, 6 vols. (First Explorers, Primeros Exploradores Nonfiction Sets Ser.). (SPA.). (gr. 1-2). 29.95 *(978-0-7699-1477-0(2))* Shortland Pubns. (U. S. A.) Inc.

Hale, Nathan. Raid of No Return (Nathan Hale's Hazardous Tales #7) A World War II Tale of the Doolittle Raid. 2017. (Nathan Hale's Hazardous Tales Ser.). (ENG., Illus.). 128p. (J). (gr. 3-7). 14.99 *(978-1-4197-2556-2(4),* 1128101) Abrams, Inc.

Hillenbrand, Laura. Unbroken (the Young Adult Adaptation) An Olympian's Journey from Airman to Castaway to Captive. 2014. (ENG., Illus.). 320p. (YA). (gr. 7). 21.99 *(978-0-385-74251-1(7),* Delacorte Pr.) Random Hse. Children's Bks.

Horn, Bernd. Men of Steel: Canadian Paratroopers in Normandy 1944. 2010. (Canadians at War Ser.: 2). (ENG., Illus.). 120p. (YA). (gr. 6). pap. 19.99 *(978-1-55488-708-8(9))* Dundurn Pr. CAN. Dist: Publishers Group West (PGW).

Jackson, Robert. Warplanes of World War II up Close, 1 vol., 1. Pearson, Colin, illus. 2015. (Military Technology: Top Secret Clearance Ser.). (ENG.). 224p. (YA). (gr. 7-8). 46.80 *(978-1-5081-7078-5(9),* 9f3f6b2f-2e4f-4cff-86b5-774ba8a01736, Rosen Young Adult) Rosen Publishing Group, Inc., The.

Mullaney, Patricia E. Documentary of an Airman' Tour with the Eighth 1944-1945. 2003. (Illus.). 355p. cd-rom 34.99 *(978-1-893767-02-7(7))* E-Booksgen.

Murray, Aaron R. Aircraft of World War II. 2014. (Illus.). 48p. (J). *(978-1-4351-5366-0(9))* Barnes & Noble, Inc.

—Aircraft of World War II, 1 vol., 1. 2015. (What's Inside? Ser.). (ENG.). 48p. (J). (gr. 3-4). pap. 12.75 *(978-1-5081-4599-8(7),* ef3580fb-22cc-4044-bbf0-7891f2db0452, PowerKids Pr.) Rosen Publishing Group, Inc., The.

Murray, Hallie. The Role of Female Pilots in World War II, 1 vol. 2019. (Warrior Women in American History Ser.). (ENG.). 104p. (gr. 7-7). pap. 21.00 *(978-1-5026-5546-2(2),* 5ce2a824-5325-4026-8c46-b6a66b58437b); lib. bdg. 44.50 *(978-1-5026-5547-9(0),* 5fac20a9-dca4-42c2-8144-f62db67f6cb3) Cavendish Square Publishing LLC.

—The Role of Female Pilots in World War II. 2020. pap. *(978-1-9785-1410-2(7))* Enslow Publishing, LLC.

Nicholson, Dorinda Makanaonalani. The School the Aztec Eagle Built, 1 vol. 2016. (ENG., Illus.). 40p. (J). (gr. 3-7). 18.95 *(978-1-60060-440-9(4),* leelowbooks) Lee & Low Bks., Inc.

Nobleman, Marc Tyler. Thirty Minutes over Oregon: A Japanese Pilot's World War II Story. Iwai, Melissa, illus. 2018. (ENG.). 40p. (J). (gr. 1-4). 17.99 *(978-0-544-43076-1(X),* 1595751, Clarion Bks.) HarperCollins Pubs.

Olson, Tod. Lost in the Pacific, 1942: Not a Drop to Drink (Lost #1) 2016. (Lost Ser.: 1). (ENG., Illus.). 176p. (J). (gr. 5-9). 14.99 *(978-0-545-92811-3(7),* Scholastic Nonfiction) Scholastic, Inc.

Otfinoski, Steven. Pilots in Peril! The Untold Story of U. S. Pilots Who Braved the Hump in World War II. 2016. (Encounter: Narrative Nonfiction Stories Ser.). (ENG., Illus.). 232p. (J). (gr. 3-6). pap. 9.95 *(978-1-4914-5166-3(1),* 128780, Capstone Pr.) Capstone.

Pearson, P. O'Connell. Fly Girls: The Daring American Women Pilots Who Helped Win WWII. 2018. (ENG., Illus.). 208p. (J). (gr. 5). 18.99 *(978-1-5344-0410-6(4),* Simon & Schuster Bks. For Young Readers) Simon & Schuster Bks. For Young Readers.

Prien, Jochen. Jagdgeschwader 3 Udet in World War II: II. /JG 3 in Action with the Messerschmitt Bf 109, 1 vol. 2003. (ENG., Illus.). 464p. (gr. 10-13). 69.95 *(978-0-7643-1774-3(1),* 491, Schiffer Military History) Schiffer Publishing, Ltd.

Rice, Earle. Claire Chennault. 2003. (Famous Flyers Ser.). (ENG., Illus.). 112p. (gr. 6-12). 30.00 *(978-0-7910-7217-2(7),* P113746, Facts On File) Infobase Holdings, Inc.

Sears, Stephen W. Air War Against Hitler's Germany. 2007. (ENG., Illus.). 124p. pap. 9.95 *(978-1-59687-004-8(4))* IBks., Inc.

Shea, John M. The Tuskegee Airmen, 1 vol. 2015. (Heroes of Black History Ser.). (ENG., Illus.). 32p. (J). (gr. 3-4). 28.27 *(978-1-4824-2918-3(7),* 32dec262-dcb5-454b-80bd-9bab13a8f86c) Stevens, Gareth Publishing LLLP.

Simons, Lisa M. Bolt. The U. S. WASP: Trailblazing Women Pilots of World War II. 2017. (Women & War Ser.). (ENG., Illus.). 32p. (J). (gr. 3-9). lib. bdg. 28.65 *(978-1-5157-7937-7(8),* 136030, Capstone Pr.) Capstone.

Townsend, John. Air Force. 2016. (Action Force: World War II Ser.). 32p. (gr. 3-7). 31.35 *(978-1-59920-985-2(3),* Smart Apple Media) Black Rabbit Bks.

Wein, Elizabeth. A Thousand Sisters: The Heroic Airwomen of the Soviet Union in World War II. 2019. (ENG., Illus.). 400p. (YA). (gr. 8). 19.99 *(978-0-06-245301-3(7),* Balzer & Bray) HarperCollins Pubs.

Yomtov, Nel. The Unbreakable Zamperini: A World War II Survivor's Brave Story. Szlapa, Rafal, illus. 2019. (Amazing World War II Stories Ser.). (ENG.). 32p. (J). (gr. 3-9). pap. 7.95 *(978-1-5435-7548-4(X),* 141080); lib. bdg. 34.65 *(978-1-5435-7313-8(4),* 140618) Capstone.

WORLD WAR, 1939-1945—AFRICAN AMERICANS

Baker, Brynn. Tuskegee Airmen: Freedom Flyers of World War II. 2015. (Military Heroes Ser.). (ENG., Illus.). 32p. (J). (gr. 3-6). lib. bdg. 27.99 *(978-1-4914-4839-7(3),* 128724, Capstone Pr.) Capstone.

Doeden, Matt. Tuskegee Airmen. 2018. (Heroes of World War II (Alternator Books (r)) Ser.). (ENG., Illus.). 32p. (J). (gr. 3-6). 30.65 *(978-1-5415-2149-0(8),* f1f7cb2d-9a30-4d6e-9751-c268493b806e, Lerner Pubns.) Lerner Publishing Group.

Fleischman, John. Black & White Airmen: Their True History. 2007. (ENG., Illus.). 160p. (gr. 5-12). 28.80 *(978-1-4287-3953-6(X),* Follettbound) Follett School Solutions.

—Black & White Airmen: Their True History. 2007. (ENG., Illus.). 160p. (J). (gr. 3-7). 20.00 *(978-0-618-56297-8(4),* 585704, Clarion Bks.) HarperCollins Pubs.

Lang, Matt. Minority Soldiers Fighting in World War II, 1 vol. 2017. (Fighting for Their Country: Minorities at War Ser.). (ENG.). 112p. (YA). (gr. 8-8). 44.50 *(978-1-5026-2664-6(0),* 5dbd85b9-c68b-40fe-abe8-b04e62c95406) Cavendish Square Publishing LLC.

Orr, Tamra. What's So Great about the Tuskegee Airmen. 2009. (What's So Great About... ? Ser.). 32p. (J). (gr. 2-4). lib. bdg. 25.70 *(978-1-58415-832-5(8))* Mitchell Lane Pubs.

Ruggiero, Adriane. World War II, 1 vol. 2003. (American Voices From Ser.). (ENG., Illus.). 160p. (J). (gr. 6-6). 41.21 *(978-0-7614-1206-9(9),* fdea97f5-91c3-478b-8640-d66ec601d883) Cavendish Square Publishing LLC.

Sheinkin, Steve. The Port Chicago 50: Disaster, Mutiny, & the Fight for Civil Rights. 2014. (ENG., Illus.). 208p. (J). (gr. 5-9). 21.99 *(978-1-59643-796-8(0),* 900083654) Roaring Brook Pr.

WORLD WAR, 1939-1945—BATTLES

see World War, 1939-1945—Campaigns

WORLD WAR, 1939-1945—BIOGRAPHY

Atwood, Kathryn J. Women Heroes of World War II: 32 Stories of Espionage, Sabotage, Resistance, & Rescue. 2nd ed. 2019. (Women of Action Ser.: 24). (Illus.). 352p. (YA). (gr. 7). 21.99 *(978-1-64160-006-4(3))* Chicago Review Pr., Inc.

Boomhower, Ray E. The Soldier's Friend: A Life of Ernie Pyle. 2006. (Illus.). 134p. 17.95 *(978-0-87195-200-4(9))* Indiana Historical Society.

Borden, Louise. Ski Soldier: A World War II Biography. 2018. (ENG., Illus.). 176p. (J). (gr. 5-9). 17.95 *(978-1-62979-674-1(3),* Calkins Creek) Highlights Pr., c/o Highlights for Children, Inc.

Bozuwa, Titia. In the Shadow of the Cathedral: Growing up in Holland During WW II. 2004. (ENG & DUT., Illus.). 199p. 22.95 *(978-0-9754825-0-6(5));* 212p. per. 15.95 *(978-0-9754825-1-3(3))* Triple Tulip Pr.

Bryant, Jen. Music for the End of Time. Peck, Beth, illus. 2005. 32p. (J). (gr. 4-5). 17.00 *(978-0-8028-5229-8(7))* Eerdmans, William B. Publishing Co.

Byers, Ann. Saving Children from the Holocaust: The Kindertransport, 1 vol. 2012. (Holocaust Through Primary Sources Ser.). (ENG., Illus.). 128p. (gr. 6-7). pap. 13.88 *(978-1-59845-344-7(0),* ef006a13-f6f9-49ac-963c-c8b6cf01445b); lib. bdg. 35.93 *(978-0-7660-3323-8(6),* 5b209fcd-5b79-4241-b064-3d26a7fc54c7) Enslow Publishing, LLC.

Collins, Terry. True Stories of World War II, 1 vol. Kinsella, Patrick & Kinsella, Patrick, illus. 2012. (Stories of War Ser.). (ENG.). 32p. (J). (gr. 3-9). pap. 8.10 *(978-1-4296-9346-2(0),* 120380); lib. bdg. 31.32 *(978-1-4296-8623-5(5),* 118644) Capstone. (Capstone Pr.).

—True Stories of World War II. Kinsella, Patrick, illus. 2012. (Stories of War Ser.). (ENG.). 32p. (J). (gr. 3-4). pap. 48.60 *(978-1-4296-9347-9(9),* 18566, Capstone Pr.) Capstone.

Collins, Terry, et al. Stories of War. 2012. (Stories of War Ser.). (ENG.). 32p. (J). (gr. 3-9). 133.28 *(978-1-4296-9164-2(6),* 18453, Capstone Pr.) Capstone.

Ellis, Catherine. Key Figures of World War II, 1 vol. 2015. (Biographies of War Ser.). (ENG., Illus.). 112p. (J). (gr. 7-8). 35.47 *(978-1-68048-057-3(X),* c8c002e4-32fc-4c81-8999-15657ed1eb7a, Britannica Educational Publishing) Rosen Publishing Group, Inc., The.

Gifford, Clive. World War II: True Stories. (ENG., Illus.). 128p. (J). pap. *(978-0-340-80497-1(1),* Hodder Children's Books) Hachette Children's Group.

Hardin, Travis. Called to Serve. 2007. (Young Writers Ser.). 95p. (YA). (gr. 8-14). per. 5.99 *(978-1-58158-108-9(4))* McDougal Publishing Co.

Hawes, Alison. Who's Who in WWII. 2010. (ENG.). 32p. (J). *(978-0-7787-9912-2(3));* (gr. 3-6). pap. *(978-0-7787-9933-7(6))* Crabtree Publishing Co.

Huey, Lois Miner. Voices of World War II: Stories from the Front Lines, 1 vol. 2010. (Voices of War Ser.). (ENG.). 32p. (J). (gr. 3-9). lib. bdg. 28.65 *(978-1-4296-4738-0(8),* 103279, Capstone Pr.) Capstone.

Hyde, Natalie. Significant People of World War II. 2015. (World War II: History's Deadliest Conflict Ser.). (ENG., Illus.). 48p. (J). (gr. 5-5). *(978-0-7787-2115-4(9))* Crabtree Publishing Co.

Jones, Tina C. Mothballs, Mothballs All in the Hall: Memories of a Great World War II Hero. Jones, Tina C. & Balogh, Jared, illus. 2012. 48p. pap. 24.95 *(978-1-4560-7483-8(0))* America Star Bks.

Kamei, Susan H. When Can We Go Back to America? Voices of Japanese American Incarceration During WWII. 2021. (ENG., Illus.). 736p. (YA). (gr. 7). 22.99 *(978-1-4814-0144-9(0),* Simon & Schuster Bks. For Young Readers) Simon & Schuster Bks. For Young Readers.

Knapp, Ron. Fighting U. S. Generals of World War II, 1 vol. 2013. (Inspiring Collective Biographies Ser.). (ENG.). 112p. (gr. 5-6). 35.93 *(978-0-7660-4164-6(6),* d509e7a7-1d86-408e-91fd-74f28a8d5305); pap. 13.88 *(978-1-4644-0249-4(3),* 57e9f019-1c57-4cd8-9d85-c53e736bef72) Enslow Publishing, LLC.

Lukesh, Jean A. Lucky Ears: The True Story of Ben Kuroki, World War II Hero. 2010. (Noteworthy Americans Young Readers Biography Book Ser.). (ENG., Illus.). 140p. (J). pap. 9.99 *(978-0-9647586-2-9(8))* Field Mouse Productions.

Raum, Elizabeth, et al. Stories of War Classroom Collection. 2012. (Stories of War Ser.). (ENG.). 32p. (J). (gr. 3-4). pap., pap. 195.40 *(978-1-4296-9349-3(5),* 18568, Capstone Pr.) Capstone.

—The World War II Soldiers' Experience. 2014. (You Choose: World War II Ser.). (ENG., Illus.). 328p. (J). (gr. 3-7). pap., pap., pap. 14.95 *(978-1-4914-1514-6(2),* 126767, Capstone Pr.) Capstone.

Ruelle, Karen Gray. Hidden on the Mountain: Stories of Children Sheltered from the Nazis in le Chambon. DeSaix, Deborah Durland, illus. 2007. (ENG.). 272p. (J). (gr. 5-18). 24.95 *(978-0-8234-1928-9(2))* Holiday Hse., Inc.

Welter, Anni. Child of War: How We Lived & Survived under the Third Reich. 2nd ed. 2003. Orig. Title: Child of the Third Reich: How We Lived & Survived. 160p. (YA). per. 14.95 *(978-0-9741434-0-8(5))* A H W Publishing.

Wills, Charles, et al. World War II Battles & Leaders. 2004. (Battles & Leaders Ser.). (ENG., Illus.). 96p. (J). (gr. 5-8). 26.19 *(978-0-7566-0259-8(9))* Dorling Kindersley Publishing, Inc.

Yomtov, Nel. The Unbreakable Zamperini: A World War II Survivor's Brave Story. Szlapa, Rafal, illus. 2019. (Amazing World War II Stories Ser.). (ENG.). 32p. (J). (gr. 3-9). pap. 7.95 *(978-1-5435-7548-4(X),* 141080); lib. bdg. 34.65 *(978-1-5435-7313-8(4),* 140618) Capstone.

Yomtov, Nel, et al. Stories of War. 2012. (Stories of War Ser.). (ENG.). 32p. (J). (gr. 3-9). pap., pap., pap. 31.80 *(978-1-4296-9348-6(7),* 18567, Capstone Pr.) Capstone.

WORLD WAR, 1939-1945—CAMPAIGNS

see also Ardennes, Battle Of The, 1944-1945; Britain, Battle of, Great Britain, 1940; Guadalcanal, Battle of, Solomon Islands, 1942-1943; Iwo Jima, Battle of, Japan, 1945; Leyte Gulf, Battle of, Philippines, 1944; Midway, Battle Of, 1942; Stalingrad, Battle of, Volgograd, Russia, 1942-1943

Alberti, Enigma. Spy on History: Victor Dowd & the World War II Ghost Army. Wegener, Scott, illus. 2018. (Spy on History Ser.). (ENG.). 96p. (J). (gr. 3-9). 12.95 *(978-0-7611-9326-5(X),* 19326) Workman Publishing Co., Inc.

Archer, Jules. Jungle Fighters: A Firsthand Account of the Forgotten New Guinea Campaign. 2016. (Jules Archer History for Young Readers Ser.). (ENG., Illus.). 224p. (J). (gr. 6-6). 16.99 *(978-1-63450-175-0(6),* Sky Pony Pr.) Skyhorse Publishing Co., Inc.

Barber, Nicola. The Western Front. 2003. (Questioning History Ser.). (J). lib. bdg. 28.50 *(978-1-58340-268-9(3))* Black Rabbit Bks.

Benchmark Education Co., LLC. The Battles of World War II. 2014. (PRIME Ser.). (J). (gr. 6-8). pap. *(978-1-4509-9500-9(4))* Benchmark Education Co.

Benge, Janet & Benge, Geoff. Jacob Deshazer: Forgive Your Enemies. 2009. (ENG.). 224p. (YA). pap. 11.99 *(978-1-57658-475-0(5))* YWAM Publishing.

Big Battles of World War II. 2014. (ENG.). 48p. (J). lib. bdg. 29.00 *(978-0-531-20494-8(4))* Scholastic Library Publishing.

Burgan, Michael. The Split History of the d-Day Invasion: A Perspectives Flip Book. 2018. (Perspectives Flip Books: Famous Battles Ser.). (ENG., Illus.). 64p. (J). (gr. 5-9). lib. bdg. 34.65 *(978-0-7565-5690-7(2),* 137035, Compass Point Bks.) Capstone.

Cochrane, Kelly. Significant Battles of World War II. 2015. (World War II: History's Deadliest Conflict Ser.). (ENG., Illus.). 48p. (J). (gr. 5-5). *(978-0-7787-2114-7(0))* Crabtree Publishing Co.

Collier, Paul H. & O'Neill, Robert John. World War II: The Mediterranean 1940-1945, 1 vol. 2010. (World War II: Essential Histories Ser.). (ENG., Illus.). 96p. (YA). (gr. 10-10). lib. bdg. 38.47 *(978-1-4358-9132-6(5),* 1b1b7b2b-a34e-4801-8751-2f315236ed09) Rosen Publishing Group, Inc., The.

D-DAY & the LIBERATION of FRANCE. 2010. (ENG., Illus.). 136p. (gr. 9-18). 35.00 *(978-1-60413-280-9(9),* P179262, Facts On File) Infobase Holdings, Inc.

Darman, Peter, ed. The Battle of the Atlantic: Naval Warfare From 1939-1945, 1 vol. 2012. (World War II Ser.). (ENG., Illus.). 64p. (YA). (gr. 6-6). 37.13 *(978-1-4488-9237-2(6),* fd437575-acdc-45c2-9e27-aa8317799a38) Rosen Publishing Group, Inc., The.

Demuth, Patricia Brennan & Who HQ. What Was D-Day? Kenyon, David Grayson, illus. 2015. (What Was? Ser.). 112p. (J). (gr. 3-7). 5.99 *(978-0-448-48407-5(2),* Penguin Workshop) Penguin Young Readers Group.

dePaola, Tomie. I'm Still Scared. 2007. (26 Fairmount Avenue Bks.). (Illus.). 83p. (gr. 2-5). 17.00 *(978-0-7569-8150-1(6))* Perfection Learning Corp.

Doeden, Matt. D-Day Invasion. 2018. (Heroes of World War II (Alternator Books (r)) Ser.). (ENG., Illus.). 32p. (J). (gr. 3-6). 30.65 *(978-1-5124-8640-7(X),* 1b60cc63-6a45-409e-aaf9-f213c81e0976, Lerner Pubns.) Lerner Publishing Group.

George, Enzo. World War II in the Pacific: War with Japan, 1 vol. 2014. (Voices of War Ser.). (ENG., Illus.). 48p. (gr. 4-4). lib. bdg. 33.07 *(978-1-62712-867-4(0),* c8c2345e-1193-4d13-9160-520cfd5f7f26) Cavendish Square Publishing LLC.

Grant, R. G. World War II: Europe, 1 vol. 2004. (Atlas of Conflicts Ser.). (ENG., Illus.). 64p. (gr. 6-8). lib. bdg. 36.67 *(978-0-8368-5669-9(4),* 9e62f175-cd42-4d16-a8f7-3f388602cc2f, Gareth Stevens Secondary Library) Stevens, Gareth Publishing LLLP.

Hachette Children's Group. The Western Front in World War I. (ENG., Illus.). 32p. *(978-0-7502-4183-0(7),* Wayland) Hachette Children's Group.

Havers, R. P. W. & O'Neill, Robert John. World War II: Europe, 1944-1945, 1 vol. 2010. (World War II: Essential Histories Ser.). (ENG., Illus.). 96p. (YA). (gr. 10-10). lib. bdg. 38.47 *(978-1-4358-9130-2(9),* 55bd8326-7dd6-4127-b88d-28c6ebdb906a) Rosen Publishing Group, Inc., The.

Horn, Bernd. Men of Steel: Canadian Paratroopers in Normandy 1944. 2010. (Canadians at War Ser.: 2). (ENG., Illus.). 120p. (YA). (gr. 6). pap. 19.99 *(978-1-55488-708-8(9))* Dundurn Pr. CAN. Dist: Publishers Group West (PGW).

Horner, D. M. & O'Neill, Robert John. World War II: The Pacific, 1 vol. 2010. (World War II: Essential Histories Ser.). (ENG., Illus.). 96p. (YA). (gr. 10-10). lib. bdg. 38.47 *(978-1-4358-9133-3(3),* 4abac419-bc3c-4d85-bbbd-8a9445be0639) Rosen Publishing Group, Inc., The.

ffrey, Gary. Battle for the Atlantic. 2012. (ENG., Illus.). 48p. (J). (978-0-7787-4192-3(3)); pap. (978-0-7787-4199-2(0)) Crabtree Publishing Co.
The Eastern Front. 2012. (ENG., Illus.). 48p. (J). (978-0-7787-4194-7(X)); pap. (978-0-7787-4201-2(6)) Crabtree Publishing Co.
North Africa & the Mediterranean. 2012. (ENG., Illus.). 48p. (J). (978-0-7787-4193-0(1)); pap. (978-0-7787-4200-5(8)) Crabtree Publishing Co.
-War in the Pacific. 2012. (ENG., Illus.). 48p. (J). (978-0-7787-4197-8(4)); pap. (978-0-7787-4204-3(0)) Crabtree Publishing Co.
ukes, Geoffrey & O'Neill, Robert John. World War II: The Eastern Front 1941-1945. 1 vol. 2010. (World War II: Essential Histories Ser.). (ENG., Illus.). 96p. (YA). (gr. 10-10). lib. bdg. 38.47 (978-1-4358-9134-0(1), 364c546d-4d20-4553-90dc-f1789407d04f) Rosen Publishing Group, Inc., The.
essman, Steve. D-Day: American Character. 2010. (Illus.). 32p. (J). lib. bdg. 15.95 (978-1-58107-181-8(7)) New Forums Pr.
Marsico, Katie. Calvin Graham's World War II Story. Hill, Dave, illus. 2018. (Narrative Nonfiction: Kids in War Ser.). (ENG.). 32p. (J). (gr. 2-4). lib. bdg. 27.99 (978-1-5124-5681-3(0), 804aec63-24d9-46d5-80b8-cfeb552b88d1, Lerner Pubns.) Lerner Publishing Group.
McGowen, Tom. Cornerstones of Freedom: D-Day. 2008. (Cornerstones of Freedom Ser.). (ENG.). 48p. (J). (gr. 4-6). pap. 5.95 (978-0-531-20831-1(1), Children's Pr.) Scholastic Library Publishing.
Nicholson, Dorinda Makanaonalani. The School the Aztec Eagle Built. 1 vol. 2016. (ENG., Illus.). 40p. (J). (gr. 3-7). 18.95 (978-1-60060-440-9(4), leelowbooks) Lee & Low Bks., Inc.
O'Neill, Robert John, et al. World War II: Northwest Europe, 1944-1945. 1 vol. 2010. (World War II: Essential Histories Ser.). (ENG., Illus.). 96p. (YA). (gr. 10-10). lib. bdg. 38.47 (978-1-4358-9129-6(5), 32f43014-5156-4018-8e2f-f94f19d3bdb2) Rosen Publishing Group, Inc., The.
O'Reilly, Bill. Hitler's Last Days. 2015. (ENG., Illus.). 320p. (J). pap. (978-1-62779-455-8(7)) Holt, Henry & Co.
—Hitler's Last Days: The Death of the Nazi Regime & the World's Most Notorious Dictator. 2017. (ENG.). 336p. (J). pap. 14.99 (978-1-250-08859-8(3), 900158402) Square Fish.
Orr, Tamra. What's So Great about the Tuskegee Airmen. 2009. (What's So Great About...? Ser.). 32p. (J). (gr. 2-4). lib. bdg. 25.70 (978-1-58415-832-5(8)) Mitchell Lane Pubs.
Platt, Richard. DK Readers L4: d-Day Landings: the Story of the Allied Invasion: The Story of the Allied Invasion. 2004. (DK Readers Level 4 Ser.). (ENG., Illus.). 32p. (J). (gr. 3-7). pap. 4.99 (978-0-7566-0275-8(0), DK Children) Dorling Kindersley Publishing, Inc.
Rice, Earle, Jr. Blitzrieg! Hitler's Lightning War. 2007. (Monumental Milestones Ser.). (Illus.). 48p. (YA). (gr. 4-7). lib. bdg. 29.95 (978-1-58415-542-3(6)) Mitchell Lane Pubs.
Samuels, Charlie. Timeline of World War II: Europe & North Africa. 1 vol. 2011. (Americans at War: a Gareth Stevens Timeline Ser.). (ENG.). 48p. (J). (gr. 6-8). pap. 15.05 (978-1-4339-5932-5(1), ce073631-9ff2-45d8-96f4-4afe8c47d1da); lib. bdg. 34.60 (978-1-4339-5930-1(5), fdf653c1-af49-4a07-8970-d5138ea76081) Stevens, Gareth Publishing LLLP. (Gareth Stevens Secondary Library).
—Timeline of World War II: Pacific. 1 vol. 2011. (Americans at War: a Gareth Stevens Timeline Ser.). (ENG.). 48p. (J). (gr. 6-8). pap. 15.05 (978-1-4339-5935-6(6), e418b037-7987-47be-a970-f4f073de9976); lib. bdg. 34.60 (978-1-4339-5934-9(8), 6a480c37-243f-4eec-b142-ce8d7ec50e84) Stevens, Gareth Publishing LLLP. (Gareth Stevens Secondary Library).
Seward, Pat. The Final Victories. 1 vol. 2011. (World War II Ser.). (ENG.). 128p. (gr. 6-6). lib. bdg. 38.36 (978-0-7614-4950-8(7), 6dc8d90b-9f00-4e10-a066-78458bf275ee) Cavendish Square Publishing LLC.
—The First Bloody Battles. 1 vol. 2011. (World War II Ser.). (ENG.). 128p. (gr. 6-6). 38.36 (978-0-7614-4946-1(9), bb66888a-4814-44d7-97f5-85d0bd08ba1a) Cavendish Square Publishing LLC.
—Global Chaos. 1 vol. 2011. (World War II Ser.). (ENG.). 128p. (gr. 6-6). lib. bdg. 38.36 (978-0-7614-4948-5(5), b3e092f8-fef4-4431-bd5e-e935c7888250) Cavendish Square Publishing LLC.
—Horrific Invasions. 1 vol. 2011. (World War II Ser.). (ENG.). 128p. (gr. 6-6). 38.36 (978-0-7614-4947-8(7), 37840d0e-4730-4492-a810-a76836210e62) Cavendish Square Publishing LLC.
—Terror & Triumph. 1 vol. 2011. (World War II Ser.). (ENG.). 128p. (gr. 6-6). lib. bdg. 38.36 (978-0-7614-4949-2(3), f1faa5b7-fc9f-4309-ac14-2dbb0dfcaa31) Cavendish Square Publishing LLC.
Sheehan, Sean. World War II: the Pacific. 1 vol. 2004. (Atlas of Conflicts Ser.). (ENG., Illus.). 64p. (gr. 6-8). lib. bdg. 36.67 (978-0-8368-5670-5(8), 1201675c-d6eb-4e81-a822-8485e3f6f6df, Gareth Stevens Secondary Library) Stevens, Gareth Publishing LLLP.
Stanley, George E. George S. Patton: War Hero. Henderson, Meryl, illus. 2007. (Childhood of Famous Americans Ser.). (ENG.). 192p. (J). (gr. 3-7). pap. 7.99 (978-1-4169-1547-8(8), Simon & Schuster/Paula Wiseman Bks.) Simon & Schuster/Paula Wiseman Bks.
Stein, R. Conrad. World War II in the Pacific: From Pearl Harbor to Nagasaki. 1 vol. 2011. (United States at War Ser.). (ENG., Illus.). 128p. (gr. 5-6). lib. bdg. 35.93 (978-0-7660-3640-6(5), 471c3ce0-e74c-439d-bf93-7548fa85145e) Enslow Publishing, LLC.
Stone, Tanya Lee. Courage Has No Color, the True Story of the Triple Nickles: America's First Black Paratroopers. 2013. (ENG., Illus.). 160p. (J). (gr. 5). pap. 17.99 (978-0-7636-6548-7(7)); 24.99 (978-0-7636-5117-6(6)) Candlewick Pr.
Williams, Brian. The Normandy Beaches. 2011. (Place in History Ser.). 48p. (YA). (gr. 5-9). lib. bdg. 34.25 (978-1-84837-675-5(8)) Arcturus Publishing GBR. Dist: Black Rabbit Bks.
Wills, Charles, et al. World War II Battles & Leaders. 2004. (Battles & Leaders Ser.). (ENG., Illus.). 96p. (J). (gr. 5-8). 26.19 (978-0-7566-0259-8(9)) Dorling Kindersley Publishing, Inc.
Yomtov, Nel. U. S. Ghost Army: The Master Illusionists of World War II. Valdrighi, Alessandro, illus. 2019. (Amazing World War II Stories Ser.). (ENG.). 32p. (J). (gr. 3-9). pap. 7.95 (978-1-5435-7551-4(X), 141083); lib. bdg. 34.65 (978-1-5435-7316-9(9), 140621) Capstone.

WORLD WAR, 1939-1945—CAMPAIGNS—FRANCE—NORMANDY

Benoit, Peter. A True Book: d-Day (Library Edition) 2014. (ENG.). 48p. (J). lib. bdg. 29.00 (978-0-531-20498-6(7)) Scholastic Library Publishing.
Biskup, Agnieszka. D-Day: June 6 1944. 1 vol. Pleece, Warren, illus. 2014. (24-Hour History Ser.). (ENG.). 48p. (J). (gr. 3-9). pap. 8.95 (978-1-4329-9301-6(1), 124617, Heinemann) Capstone.
Burgan, Michael. Turning Point: The Story of the d-Day Landings. 2017. (Tangled History Ser.). (ENG., Illus.). 112p. (J). (gr. 3-9). lib. bdg. 32.65 (978-1-5157-3607-3(5), 133597, Capstone Pr.) Capstone.
Challen, Paul C. Surviving D-Day. 1 vol. 2015. (Surviving Disaster Ser.). (ENG., Illus.). 48p. (J). (gr. 5-6). 33.47 (978-1-4994-3653-2(X), 684042bb-9744-4528-8bde-eac9ed85ebb3, Rosen Central) Rosen Publishing Group, Inc., The.
Darman, Peter, ed. The Allied Invasion of Europe. 1 vol. 2012. (World War II Ser.). (ENG., Illus.). 64p. (YA). (gr. 6-6). 37.13 (978-1-4488-9234-1(1), b7222421-19b1-4443-832a-2f6b12ec8cb2) Rosen Publishing Group, Inc., The.
Donohue, Moira Rose. The Invasion of Normandy: Epic Battle of World War II. 2017. (Major Battles in US History Ser.). (ENG., Illus.). 32p. (J). (gr. 3-5). pap. 9.95 (978-1-63517-080-1(X), 163517080X, Focus Readers) North Star Editions.
Drez, Ronald J. Remember D-Day: The Plan, the Invasion, Survivor Stories. 2015. (Remember Ser.). (Illus.). 64p. (J). (gr. 5-9). pap. 7.99 (978-1-4263-2245-7(3), National Geographic Kids) Disney Publishing Worldwide.
Otfinoski, Steven. World War II Infantrymen: An Interactive History Adventure. 2013. (You Choose: World War II Ser.). (ENG.). 112p. (J). (gr. 3-4). pap. 41.70 (978-1-62065-717-1(1), 19310); (Illus.). pap. 6.95 (978-1-62065-716-4(3), 121702) Capstone. (Capstone Pr.).
Samuels, Charlie. D-Day. 1 vol., Vol. 1. 2013. (Turning Points in U. S. Military History Ser.). (ENG.). 48p. (J). (gr. 5-6). 34.61 (978-1-4824-0432-6(X), b8a3884b-e2cd-4cd6-af2a-ec5dbbb5e138) Stevens, Gareth Publishing LLLP.
Sepahban, Lois. 12 Incredible Facts about the d-Day Invasion. (Turning Points in US History Ser.). (ENG., Illus.). 32p. (J). (gr. 3-6). 2016. 32.80 (978-1-63235-128-9(5), 12000) 2015. pap. (978-1-63235-171-5(4)) Bookstaves, LLC. (12-Story Library).
Zaloga, Steven J. The Most Daring Raid of World War II: D-Day — Pointe-Du-Hoc. 1 vol. 2011. (Most Daring Raids in History Ser.). (ENG., Illus.). 64p. (YA). (gr. 7-7). lib. bdg. 37.13 (978-1-4488-1867-9(2), 3ef3ba30-ecb1-412b-bdd2-8540d49e07d0) Rosen Publishing Group, Inc., The.

WORLD WAR, 1939-1945—CAUSES

Benchmark Education Co., LLC. The Causes of World War II. 2014. (PRIME Ser.). (J). (gr. 6-8). pap. (978-1-4509-9499-6(7)) Benchmark Education Co.
Corrigan, Jim. Causes of World War II. 2005. (Road to War Ser.). (Illus.). 64p. (J). (gr. 4-18). lib. bdg. 22.95 (978-1-59556-004-9(1)) OTTN Publishing.
Darman, Peter, ed. Attack on Pearl Harbor: America Enters World War II. 1 vol. 2012. (World War II Ser.). (ENG., Illus.). 64p. (J). (gr. 6-6). lib. bdg. 37.13 (978-1-4488-9233-4(3), 09fbfaf9-e84a-4d0a-ba41-bb3c08bf4f91, Rosen Reference) Rosen Publishing Group, Inc., The.
—World War II Begins. 1 vol. 2012. (World War II Ser.). (ENG., Illus.). 64p. (J). (gr. 6-6). lib. bdg. 37.13 (978-1-4488-9232-7(5), 09d9bc7c-f2ef-4864-9a09-6a6eef62c38e) Rosen Publishing Group, Inc., The.
Dougherty, Steve. Attack on Pearl Harbor: World War II Strikes Home in the USA. 2011. (J). pap. (978-0-545-32930-9(2)) Scholastic, Inc.
Freed, Kira. Surviving Pearl Harbor. 1 vol. 2015. (Surviving Disaster Ser.). (ENG., Illus.). 48p. (J). (gr. 5-6). 33.47 (978-1-4994-3649-5(1), 9dfc7861-bc93-4beb-839d-969f107fd9bc, Rosen Central) Rosen Publishing Group, Inc., The.
Johnson, Robin. Pearl Harbor. 2014. (Crabtree Chrome Ser.). (ENG., Illus.). 48p. (J). (gr. 2-2). (978-0-7787-1367-8(9)) Crabtree Publishing Co.
Lassieur, Allison. The Attack on Pearl Harbor [Scholastic]: An Interactive History Adventure. 2009. (You Choose: History Ser.). 112p. (gr. 3-4). pap. 0.86 (978-1-4296-4046-6(4), Capstone Pr.) Capstone.
Marcovitz, Hal. Cause & Effect: World War II. 2017. (ENG.). 80p. (YA). (gr. 5-12). (978-1-68282-174-9(9)) ReferencePoint Pr., Inc.
Offord, Alexander. The Causes of World War II. 2015. (World War II: History's Deadliest Conflict Ser.). (ENG., Illus.). 48p. (J). (gr. 5-5). (978-0-7787-2116-1(7)) Crabtree Publishing Co.
Otfinoski, Steven. The Split History of the Attack on Pearl Harbor: A Perspectives Flip Book. 2018. (Perspectives Flip Books: Famous Battles Ser.). (ENG., Illus.). 64p. (J). (gr. 5-9). lib. bdg. 34.65 (978-0-7565-5691-4(0), 137036, Compass Point Bks.) Capstone.
Ross, Stewart & Woodward, Joe. Pearl Harbor. 2011. (Place in History Ser.). (Illus.). 48p. (YA). (gr. 5-9). lib. bdg. 34.25 (978-1-84837-676-2(6)) Arcturus Publishing GBR. Dist: Black Rabbit Bks.
Samuels, Charlie. The Attack on Pearl Harbor. 1 vol., Vol. 1. 2013. (Turning Points in U. S. Military History Ser.). (ENG.). 48p. (J). (gr. 5-6). 34.61 (978-1-4824-0409-8(5), 24a85a65-96ca-4173-b00a-66c7a0e08511) Stevens, Gareth Publishing LLLP.
Seward, Pat. Countdown to Catastrophe. 1 vol. 2011. (World War II Ser.). (ENG.). 128p. (gr. 6-6). 38.36 (978-0-7614-4944-7(2), 388ef178-cef9-4c94-abcf-8e4c674c146c) Cavendish Square Publishing LLC.
Uschan, Michael V. The Bombing of Pearl Harbor. 1 vol. 2003. (Landmark Events in American History Ser.). (ENG., Illus.). 48p. (gr. 5-8). lib. bdg. 33.67 (978-0-8368-5373-5(3), 520a4ee3-bdeb-4540-b404-a7b2fa061bcc, Gareth Stevens Secondary Library) Stevens, Gareth Publishing LLLP.
Woog, Adam. Pearl Harbor. 2013. (Illus.). 96p. (J). lib. bdg. (978-1-60152-486-7(2)) ReferencePoint Pr., Inc.
Wukovits, John F. The Bombing of Pearl Harbor. 1 vol. 2011. (World History Ser.). (ENG.). 112p. (gr. 7-7). lib. bdg. 41.53 (978-1-4205-0330-2(8), d539e821-6330-440d-8f7f-a38ff5ca6493, Lucent Pr.) Greenhaven Publishing LLC.
Yomtov, Nel. The Attack on Pearl Harbor: December 7 1941. 1 vol. Campidelli, Maurizio, illus. 2014. (24-Hour History Ser.). (ENG.). 48p. (J). (gr. 3-9). pap. 8.95 (978-1-4329-9299-6(6), 124615); lib. bdg. 33.99 (978-1-4329-9293-4(7), 124610) Capstone. (Heinemann).

WORLD WAR, 1939-1945—CHILDREN

Byers, Ann. Courageous Teen Resisters: Primary Sources from the Holocaust. 1 vol. 2010. (True Stories of Teens in the Holocaust Ser.). (ENG., Illus.). 128p. (gr. 9-10). 35.93 (978-0-7660-3269-9(8), a34fdb7f-26c5-49d1-9d7d-2d7a5ef33d86) Enslow Publishing, LLC.
—Trapped: Youth in the Nazi Ghettos: Primary Sources from the Holocaust. 1 vol. 2010. (True Stories of Teens in the Holocaust Ser.). (ENG., Illus.). 128p. (gr. 9-10). 35.93 (978-0-7660-3272-9(8), 9afa1134-8341-4789-8f4b-36170c40f22d) Enslow Publishing, LLC.
—Youth Destroyed: the Nazi Camps: Primary Sources from the Holocaust. 1 vol. 2010. (True Stories of Teens in the Holocaust Ser.). (ENG., Illus.). 128p. (gr. 9-10). 35.93 (978-0-7660-3273-6(6), 0fb7eb94-913c-4a19-b319-711d17fa21ff) Enslow Publishing, LLC.
Chase, Odette. This Child's War: A World War II Memoir. unabr. ed. 2004. (ENG., Illus.). 122p. per. 15.00 (978-0-9759421-0-9(7)) Red Bud Publishing.
Garner, Eleanor Ramrath. Eleanor's Story: An American Girl in Hitler's Germany. 1 vol. 2003. (Illus.). 224p. (YA). (gr. 7-18). pap. 9.95 (978-1-56145-296-5(3), Q19196) Peachtree Publishing Co. Inc.
Grady, Cynthia. Write to Me: Letters from Japanese American Children to the Librarian They Left Behind. Hirao, Amiko, illus. 32p. (J). (gr. -1-3). 2019. (ENG.). pap. 7.99 (978-1-62354-111-8(5)) 2018. 16.99 (978-1-58089-688-7(X)) Charlesbridge Publishing, Inc.
Heiligman, Deborah. Torpedoed: The True Story of the World War II Sinking of the Children's Ship. 2019. (ENG., Illus.). 288p. (J). 19.99 (978-1-62779-554-8(5), 900155418, Holt, Henry & Co. Bks. For Young Readers) Holt, Henry & Co.
Innes, Stephanie & Endrulat, Harry. Bear on the Homefront. 1 vol. Deines, Brian, illus. 2014. (ENG.). 32p. (J). (gr. k-3). 17.95 (978-1-927485-13-2(4)) Pajama Pr. CAN. Dist: Publishers Group West (PGW).
Jacobs Altman, Linda. Escape: Teens on the Run: Primary Sources from the Holocaust. 1 vol. 2010. (True Stories of Teens in the Holocaust Ser.). (ENG., Illus.). 128p. (gr. 9-10). 35.93 (978-0-7660-3270-5(1), 16a24f0b-cc62-468e-842c-5aa7c9118ea4) Enslow Publishing, LLC.
—Hidden Teens, Hidden Lives: Primary Sources from the Holocaust. 1 vol. 2010. (True Stories of Teens in the Holocaust Ser.). (ENG., Illus.). 128p. (gr. 9-10). 35.93 (978-0-7660-3271-2(X), 4a632054-a5be-4132-9757-692c215d3f24) Enslow Publishing, LLC.
Josephson, Judith P. Growing up in World War II, 1941-1945. 2003. (Our America Ser.). (Illus.). 64p. (J). (gr. 4-7). lib. bdg. 26.60 (978-0-8225-0660-7(2)) Lerner Publishing Group.
Kamei, Susan H. When Can We Go Back to America? Voices of Japanese American Incarceration During WWII. (ENG.). 736p. (YA). 2022. pap. 15.99 (978-1-4814-0145-6(9)) 2021. (Illus.). (gr. 7). 22.99 (978-1-4814-0144-9(0)) Simon & Schuster Bks. For Young Readers. (Simon & Schuster Bks. For Young Readers).
MacCarald, Clara. Children in Japanese American Confinement Camps. 2018. (Children in History Ser.). (ENG., Illus.). 48p. (J). (gr. 5-6). pap. 11.95 (978-1-63517-976-7(9), 1635179769); lib. bdg. 34.21 (978-1-63517-875-3(4), 1635178754) North Star Editions. (Focus Readers).
Oppenheim, Joanne. Dear Miss Breed: True Stories of the Japanese American Incarceration During World War II & a Librarian Who Made a Difference. 2006. (ENG., Illus.). 288p. (J). (gr. 7-7). 27.99 (978-0-439-56992-7(3)) Scholastic, Inc.
Ruelle, Karen Gray. Peter's War: A Boy's True Story of Survival in World War II Europe. Durland DeSaix, Deborah, illus. 2020. 40p. (J). (gr. 2). 18.99 (978-0-8234-2416-0(2)) Holiday Hse., Inc.
Sís, Peter. Nicky & Vera. 2021. (ENG., Illus.). 64p. (J). (gr. 1-4). 19.95 (978-1-324-01574-1(8), 341574, Norton Young Readers) Norton, W. W. & Co., Inc.
Thomas, Isabel. Little Guides to Great Lives: Anne Frank. Escobar, Paola, illus. 2019. (Little Guides to Great Lives Ser.). (ENG.). 64p. (J). (gr. 2-6). 11.99 (978-1-78627-398-7(5), King, Laurence Publishing) Orion Publishing Group, Ltd. GBR. Dist: Hachette Bk. Group.
Tunnell, Michael O. Desert Diary: Japanese American Kids Behind Barbed Wire. 2020. 144p. (J). (gr. 4-7). lib. bdg. 19.99 (978-1-58089-789-1(4)) Charlesbridge Publishing, Inc.
Vander Zee, Ruth. Erika's Story. Innocenti, Roberto, illus. 2003. (ENG.). 24p. (J). (gr. 2-5). 19.99 (978-1-56846-176-2(3), 22044) Creative Co., The.
Welch, Catherine A. Children of the Relocation Camps. 2005. (Picture the American Past Ser.). (Illus.). 48p. (J). (gr. 2-5). lib. bdg. 22.60 (978-1-57505-350-9(0)) Lerner Publishing Group.
Whitman, Sylvia. Children of the World War II Home Front. 2005. (Picture the American Past Ser.). (Illus.). 48p. (J). (gr. 2-5). lib. bdg. 22.60 (978-1-57505-484-1(1)) Lerner Publishing Group.
Wintrob, Kitty. I'm Not Going Back: Wartime Memoir of a Child Evacuee. 2009. (978-0-9784435-1-1(9)) Now & Then Bks.
Ziemian, Joseph. The Cigarette Sellers of Three Crosses Square. 2005. (Library of Holocaust Testimonies Ser.). (ENG., Illus.). 168p. pap. 19.95 (978-0-85303-686-9(1)) Vallentine Mitchell Pubs. GBR. Dist: Independent Pubs. Group.

WORLD WAR, 1939-1945—CHINA

Himsl, Sharon M. Events That Changed the World - 1940-1960. 2003. (EVENTS THAT CHANGED THE WRLD Ser.). (ENG., Illus.). lib. bdg. 38.45 (978-0-7377-1756-3(4)) Cengage Gale.
Otfinoski, Steven. Pilots in Peril! The Untold Story of U. S. Pilots Who Braved the Hump in World War II. 2016. (Encounter: Narrative Nonfiction Stories Ser.). (ENG., Illus.). 232p. (J). (gr. 3-6). pap. 9.95 (978-1-4914-5166-3(1), 128780, Capstone Pr.) Capstone.

WORLD WAR, 1939-1945—EUROPE

Boas, Jacob. We Are Witnesses: Five Diaries of Teenagers Who Died in the Holocaust. 2009. (ENG.). 208p. (YA). (gr. 6-10). pap. 10.99 (978-0-312-53567-4(8), 900054746) Square Fish.
Buckley, James, Jr. Adolf Hitler. 2017. (History's Worst Ser.). (ENG., Illus.). 208p. (J). (gr. 3-7). pap. 8.99 (978-1-4814-7942-4(3), Aladdin) Simon & Schuster Children's Publishing.
Byers, Ann. Rescuing the Danish Jews: A Heroic Story from the Holocaust. 1 vol. 2012. (Holocaust Through Primary Sources Ser.). (ENG., Illus.). 128p. (gr. 6-7). lib. bdg. 35.93 (978-0-7660-3321-4(X), 82ad2f9d-f92e-4294-81a4-3a2bd64d9ad3) Enslow Publishing, LLC.
Chant, Christopher. The Defeat of the Nazis: The Allied Victory in Europe. 2017. (World War II Ser.: Vol. 5). (ENG., Illus.). 79p. (J). (gr. 7-12). 24.95 (978-1-4222-3897-4(0)) Mason Crest.
George, Enzo. World War II in Europe & North Africa: Preserving Democracy. 1 vol. 2014. (Voices of War Ser.). (ENG.). 48p. (gr. 4-4). lib. bdg. 33.07 (978-1-62712-864-3(6), 4dbc917e-fb5c-4704-92c7-e0e7479d9512) Cavendish Square Publishing LLC.
Havers, R. P. W. & O'Neill, Robert John. World War II: Europe, 1944-1945. 1 vol. 2010. (World War II: Essential Histories Ser.). (ENG., Illus.). 96p. (YA). (gr. 10-10). lib. bdg. 38.47 (978-1-4358-9130-2(9), 55bd8326-7dd6-4127-b88d-28c6ebdb906a) Rosen Publishing Group, Inc., The.
Hoffman, Betty N. Liberation: Stories of Survival from the Holocaust. 1 vol. 2012. (Holocaust Through Primary Sources Ser.). (ENG., Illus.). 128p. (gr. 6-7). pap. 13.88 (978-1-59845-348-5(3), ae8d4f43-e1b6-42c2-badb-93a219f2338f); lib. bdg. 35.93 (978-0-7660-3319-1(8), 5d444e32-dbd3-48fb-83c2-fefb3e94148c) Enslow Publishing, LLC.
Jeffrey, Gary. The Western Front. 2012. (ENG., Illus.). 48p. (J). (978-0-7787-4196-1(6)); pap. (978-0-7787-4203-6(2)) Crabtree Publishing Co.
Rice, Earle, Jr. Blitzrieg! Hitler's Lightning War. 2007. (Monumental Milestones Ser.). (Illus.). 48p. (YA). (gr. 4-7). lib. bdg. 29.95 (978-1-58415-542-3(6)) Mitchell Lane Pubs.
Rodgers, Kelly. World War II in Europe. rev. ed. 2019. (Social Studies: Informational Text Ser.). (ENG., Illus.). 32p. (J). (gr. 4-8). pap. 11.99 (978-1-4258-5070-8(7)) Teacher Created Materials, Inc.
Ruelle, Karen Gray. Peter's War: A Boy's True Story of Survival in World War II Europe. Durland DeSaix, Deborah, illus. 2020. 40p. (J). (gr. 2). 18.99 (978-0-8234-2416-0(2)) Holiday Hse., Inc.
Samuels, Charles. Life under Occupation. 2012. (World War II: Sourcebook Ser.). (ENG., Illus.). 48p. (J). (gr. 5-8). lib. bdg. 37.10 (978-1-936333-26-4(0), 16833) Brown Bear Bks.
Samuels, Charlie. Timeline of World War II: Europe & North Africa. 1 vol. 2011. (Americans at War: a Gareth Stevens Timeline Ser.). (ENG.). 48p. (J). (gr. 6-8). pap. 15.05 (978-1-4339-5932-5(1), ce073631-9ff2-45d8-96f4-4afe8c47d1da); lib. bdg. 34.60 (978-1-4339-5930-1(5), fdf653c1-af49-4a07-8970-d5138ea76081) Stevens, Gareth Publishing LLLP. (Gareth Stevens Secondary Library).
—Timeline of World War II: Pacific. 1 vol. 2011. (Americans at War: a Gareth Stevens Timeline Ser.). (ENG.). 48p. (J). (gr. 6-8). pap. 15.05 (978-1-4339-5935-6(6), e418b037-7987-47be-a970-f4f073de9976); lib. bdg. 34.60 (978-1-4339-5934-9(8), 6a480c37-243f-4eec-b142-ce8d7ec50e84) Stevens, Gareth Publishing LLLP. (Gareth Stevens Secondary Library).
Seward, Pat. Global Chaos. 1 vol. 2011. (World War II Ser.). (ENG.). 128p. (gr. 6-6). lib. bdg. 38.36 (978-0-7614-4948-5(5), b3e092f8-fef4-4431-bd5e-e935c7888250) Cavendish Square Publishing LLC.
—Terror & Triumph. 1 vol. 2011. (World War II Ser.). (ENG.). 128p. (gr. 6-6). lib. bdg. 38.36 (978-0-7614-4949-2(3), f1faa5b7-fc9f-4309-ac14-2dbb0dfcaa31) Cavendish Square Publishing LLC.
Stein, R. Conrad. World War II in Europe: From Normandy to Berlin. 1 vol. 2011. (United States at War Ser.). (ENG., Illus.). 128p. (gr. 5-6). lib. bdg. 35.93 (978-0-7660-3639-0(1), 5e076b81-a50e-457a-9023-4b28d9d18303) Enslow Publishing, LLC.
Toll, Nelly S. Behind the Secret Window. 2003. 176p. (J). (gr. 3-7). 5.99 (978-0-14-230241-5(4), Puffin Books) Penguin Young Readers Group.
World Book, Inc. Staff, contrib. by. World War II in Europe. 2010. (J). (978-0-7166-1509-5(6)) World Bk., Inc.

WORLD WAR, 1939-1945—FICTION

Adlington, Lucy. The Red Ribbon. 2018. (ENG.). 288p. (J). (gr. 7). 17.99 (978-1-5362-0104-8(9)) Candlewick Pr.
Alexander, Carol. When My Name Was Keoko. Friedland, Joyce & Kessler, Rikki, eds. 2008. (Novel-Ties Ser.). 29p. pap. 16.95 (978-0-7675-1520-7(X)) Learning Links Inc.
Allen, Nancy. Amazing Grace: A Kentucky Girl with Gumption During World War II. Shapiro, Meryl R. B., illus. 2014. Orig.

WXYZ

Title: Amazing Grace: a Kentucky Girl with Gumption During World War II. (ENG.). 160p. (gr. 4-7). 29.99 (978-1-62619-405-2(X), History Pr., The) Arcadia Publishing.

Appelfeld, Aharon. Adam & Thomas. Green, Jeffrey M., tr. Dumas, Philippe, illus. 2017. 160p. (J). (gr. 3-7). pap. 14.95 (978-1-60980-744-3(8), Triangle Square) Seven Stories Pr.

Arvidson, Douglas. Brothers of the Fire Star. Scarborough, Rob, illus. 2012. 207p. (YA). pap. 15.95 (978-1-890109-91-2(6), Cross Time) Crossquarter Publishing Group.

Avery, Al. A Yankee Flier in the Far East. Laune, Paul, illus. 2011. 224p. 44.95 (978-1-258-06349-8(2)) Literary Licensing, LLC.

Avi. Don't You Know There's a War On? 2003. 208p. (J). (ENG.). (gr. 3-7). pap. 7.99 (978-0-380-81544-9(3)); 2nd ed. pap. (978-0-439-53096-5(2)) HarperCollins Pubs. (HarperCollins).

—Don't You Know There's a War On? 2003. 193p. (gr. 3-7). 18.00 (978-0-7569-1383-0(7)) Perfection Learning Corp.

Banks, Lynne Reid. Uprooted - a Canadian War Story. 2014. (ENG.). 336p. (J). 8.99 (978-0-00-758943-2(3), HarperCollins Children's Bks.) HarperCollins Pubs. Ltd. GBR. Dist: HarperCollins Pubs.

Barker, Michelle. A Year of Borrowed Men. Benoit, Renne, illus. 2016. (ENG.). 40p. (J). (gr. 1-4). 18.95 (978-1-927485-83-5(5)) Pajama Pr. CAN. Dist: Publishers Group West (PGW).

Barry, Rick. Gunner's Run: A World War II Novel. 2007. 215p. (YA). (gr. 8-12). per. 8.99 (978-1-59166-761-2(5)) BJU Pr.

Bee, Harry. Printer Street's War. 2008. (ENG.). 140p. pap. 10.99 (978-1-4196-5700-9(3)) CreateSpace Independent Publishing Platform.

Bertman, Jennifer Chambliss. The Unbreakable Code. 2018. (Book Scavenger Ser.: 2). (J). lib. bdg. 18.40 (978-0-606-41092-2(9)) Turtleback.

Bishop, Claire Huchet. Twenty & Ten. 76p. (J). (gr. 3-5). pap. 4.99 (978-0-8072-1418-3(3), Listening Library) Random Hse. Audio Publishing Group.

Blackford, Cheryl. Lizzie & the Lost Baby. 2017. (ENG.). 192p. (J). (gr. 5-7). pap. 6.99 (978-0-544-93525-9(X), 1658134, Clarion Bks.) HarperCollins Pubs.

Bloor, Edward. London Calling. 2008. (Illus.). 304p. (YA). (gr. 7-9). per. 8.99 (978-0-375-84363-1(9), Ember) Random Hse. Children's Bks.

Boland, Shalini. A Shirtful of Frogs. 2012. 244p. pap. (978-0-9569985-4-5(2)) Adrenalin Bks.

Booth, Martin. War Dog. 2012. (ENG.). 144p. (YA). (gr. 7). pap. 8.99 (978-1-4424-7297-6(9), McElderry, Margaret K. Bks.) McElderry, Margaret K. Bks.

Borden, Louise. Across the Blue Pacific: A World War II Story. Parker, Robert Andrew, illus. 2015. (ENG.). 48p. (J). (gr. -1-3). 7.99 (978-0-544-55552-5(X), 1610459, Clarion Bks.) HarperCollins Pubs.

—The Greatest Skating Race: A World War II Story from the Netherlands. Daly, Niki, illus. 2004. (ENG.). 48p. (J). (gr. 4-7). 19.99 (978-0-689-84502-4(2), McElderry, Margaret K. Bks.) McElderry, Margaret K. Bks.

—The Little Ships: The Heroic Rescue at Dunkirk in World War II. Foreman, Michael, illus. 2003. (ENG.). 32p. (J). (gr. 4-7). 8.99 (978-0-689-85396-8(3), McElderry, Margaret K. Bks.) McElderry, Margaret K. Bks.

Bowen, Robert Sidney. Dave Dawson at Guadalcanal. 2011. 242p. 46.95 (978-1-258-01956-3(6)) Literary Licensing, LLC.

—Dave Dawson, Flight Lieutenant. 2011. 248p. 46.95 (978-1-258-01820-7(9)) Literary Licensing, LLC.

Boyne, John. The Boy at the Top of the Mountain. 2017. (J). lib. bdg. 18.40 (978-0-606-39937-1(2)) Turtleback.

—The Boy in the Striped Pajamas. 2023. (ENG.). lib. bdg. 24.99 Cengage Gale.

—The Boy in the Striped Pajamas. 2006. (ENG.). 224p. (YA). (gr. 7). 17.99 (978-0-385-75106-3(0)) Fickling, David Bks. GBR. Dist: Penguin Random Hse. LLC.

—The Boy in the Striped Pajamas. 2011. 10.54 (978-0-7848-3514-2(4), Everbind) Marco Bk. Co.

—The Boy in the Striped Pajamas. 2008. 215p. (gr. 7-12). 20.00 (978-0-7569-8943-9(4)) Perfection Learning Corp.

—The Boy in the Striped Pajamas. 2007. (ENG.). 224p. (YA). (gr. 7-18). pap. 12.99 (978-0-385-75153-7(2), Ember) Random Hse. Children's Bks.

—The Boy in the Striped Pajamas. rev. l.t. ed. 2007. (Thorndike Literacy Bridge Ser.). (ENG.). 247p. (YA). (gr. 7-12). 23.95 (978-0-7862-9425-1(6)) Thorndike Pr.

—The Boy in the Striped Pajamas. 2007. 215p. (YA). (gr. 7-12). 20.85 (978-1-4178-1823-5(9)) Turtleback.

—The Boy in the Striped Pajamas (Movie Tie-In Edition) movie tie-in ed. 2008. (ENG.). 240p. (YA). (gr. 7). pap. 12.99 (978-0-385-75189-6(3)) Fickling, David Bks. GBR. Dist: Penguin Random Hse. LLC.

Bradley, Kimberly Brubaker. For Freedom: The Story of a French Spy. 2005. 181p. 16.00 (978-0-7569-5091-0(0)) Perfection Learning Corp.

—For Freedom: The Story of a French Spy. 2005. (ENG.). 192p. (YA). (gr. 7-9). mass mkt. 8.99 (978-0-440-41831-3(3), Laurel Leaf) Random Hse. Children's Bks.

—The War I Finally Won. (ENG.). (J). (gr. 4-7). 2018. 416p. 9.99 (978-0-14-751681-7(1), Puffin Books) 2017. 400p. 18.99 (978-0-525-42920-3(4), Dial Bks) Penguin Young Readers Group.

—The War That Saved My Life. (ENG.). (J). (gr. 4-7). 2016. 352p. 9.99 (978-0-14-751048-8(1), Puffin Books) 2015. 320p. 17.99 (978-0-8037-4081-5(6), Dial Bks) Penguin Young Readers Group.

—The War That Saved My Life. 2016. (J). lib. bdg. 19.65 (978-0-606-38843-6(5)) Turtleback.

Brigham, Anthea. Henrietta, World War II Hen: This Is a True Story. Brigham, Anthea, illus. 2003. (ENG., Illus.). 28p. (J). 7.00 (978-0-9740778-2-6(8)) Whale's Jaw Publishing.

Brooks, Kaarina. Boy from Karelia. 2017. (ENG., Illus.). 248p. pap. 14.95 (978-1-988763-09-5(6)) Villa Wisteria Pubns.

Bruchac, Joseph. Code Talker: A Novel about the Navajo Marines of World War Two. 2006. 240p. (YA). (gr. 7-18). 10.99 (978-0-14-240596-3(5), Speak) Penguin Young Readers Group.

Buckey, Sarah Masters. The Light in the Cellar: A Molly Mystery. 2003. (American Girl Mysteries Ser.). (ENG., Illus.). 176p. (gr. 4-7). 10.95 (978-1-59369-159-2(9)) American Girl Publishing, Inc.

Burg, Ann E. Rebekkah's Journey: A World War II Refugee Story. Iskowitz, Joel, illus. 2006. (Tales of Young Americans Ser.). (ENG.). 48p. (J). (gr. 1-4). 17.95 (978-1-58536-275-2(1), 202086) Sleeping Bear Pr.

Burkinshaw, Kathleen. The Last Cherry Blossom. 2016. (ENG.). 240p. (J). (gr. 5-8). 16.99 (978-1-63450-693-9(6), Sky Pony Pr.) Skyhorse Publishing Co., Inc.

Bylsma, Dan & Bylsma, Jay M. Slam Dunks Not Allowed! 2003. (Illus.). 238p. (YA). (978-0-938682-72-1(5)); pap. (978-0-938682-77-6(6)) River Road Pubns., Inc.

Calkhoven, Laurie. G. I. Dogs: Judy, Prisoner of War (G. I. Dogs #1) 2018. (ENG., Illus.). 128p. (J). (gr. 2-5). pap. 5.99 (978-1-338-18523-2(3)) Scholastic, Inc.

—Judy, Prisoner of War. 2018. (G. I. Dogs Ser.: 1). lib. bdg. 16.00 (978-0-606-41055-7(4)) Turtleback.

Campbell, Isaiah. AbrakaPOW. Perillo, Dave, illus. 2016. (ENG.). 400p. (J). (gr. 3-7). 16.99 (978-1-4814-2634-3(6), Simon & Schuster Bks. For Young Readers) Simon & Schuster Bks. For Young Readers.

Candlewick Press. Voices from the Second World War: Stories of War As Told to Children of Today. (ENG., Illus.). 320p. (J). (gr. 5-9). 2019. pap. 17.99 (978-1-5362-0885-6(X)) 2018. 24.99 (978-0-7636-9492-0(4)) Candlewick Pr.

Carelli, Anne O'Brien. Skylark & Wallcreeper. 2018. (ENG., Illus.). 416p. (J). (gr. 3-7). 17.99 (978-1-4998-0745-5(7), Yellow Jacket) Bonnier Publishing USA.

Carradice, Phil & Thomas, Frances. Hannah Goes to War. 2005. (ENG.). 144p. pap. 12.95 (978-1-84323-461-6(0)) Beekman Bks., Inc.

Carroll, Emma. Letters from the Lighthouse: 'the QUEEN of HISTORICAL FICTION' Guardian. 2017. (ENG.). 288p. (J). pap. 9.95 (978-0-571-32758-4(3), Faber & Faber Children's Bks.) Faber & Faber, Inc.

Casanova, Mary. The Klipfish Code. 2012. (ENG.). 240p. (J). (gr. 5-7). pap. 7.99 (978-0-547-74447-6(1), 1485490, Clarion Bks.) HarperCollins Pubs.

Center for Learning Network Staff. Slaughterhouse-Five: Curriculum Unit. 2005. (Novel Ser.). 76p. (YA). tchr. ed., spiral bd. 19.95 (978-1-56077-789-2(3)) Center for Learning, The.

Cerrito, Angela. The Safest Lie. 2018. 192p. (J). (gr. 3-7). pap. 7.99 (978-0-8234-4046-7(X)) Holiday Hse., Inc.

Chaconas, Dori. Pennies in a Jar, 1 vol. Lewin, Ted, illus. 2007. 36p. (J). (gr. 1-4). 16.95 (978-1-56145-422-8(2)) Peachtree Publishing Co. Inc.

Chambers, Aidan. Postcards from No Man's Land. 2004. (ENG.). 320p. (YA). (gr. 9-18). reprint ed. 8.99 (978-0-14-240145-3(5), Speak) Penguin Young Readers Group.

Chang, Pei-Yu. Mr. Benjamin's Suitcase of Secrets. 2017. (ENG., Illus.). 48p. (J). (gr. -1-3). 18.95 (978-0-7358-4280-9(9)) North-South Bks., Inc.

Cheaney, J. B. My Friend the Enemy. 2007. 266p. (gr. 4-7). 16.50 (978-0-7569-7946-1(3)) Perfection Learning Corp.

Clark, Kathy. Guardian Angel House, 1 vol. 2009. (Holocaust Remembrance Series for Young Readers Ser.: 10). (ENG., Illus.). 228p. (J). (gr. 4-8). pap. 14.95 (978-1-897187-58-6(0)) Second Story Pr. CAN. Dist: Orca Bk. Pubs. USA.

Coker, Rachel. Interrupted: A Life Beyond Words, 1 vol. 2013. (ENG.). 256p. (YA). pap. 9.99 (978-0-310-72810-8(X)) Zondervan.

Cooper, Michelle. The FitzOsbornes at War. 2013. (Montmaray Journals: 3). (ENG.). 560p. (YA). (gr. 7). pap. 12.99 (978-0-307-93058-3(0), Ember) Random Hse. Children's Bks.

Cooper, Susan. Dawn of Fear. 2007. (ENG., Illus.). 176p. (J). (gr. 5-7). pap. 7.99 (978-0-15-206106-7(1), 1198341, Clarion Bks.) HarperCollins Pubs.

Copeland, Cynthia L. Elin's Island. 2003. (Single Titles Ser.: up). (ENG.). 144p. (YA). (gr. 6-12). lib. bdg. 22.60 (978-0-7613-2522-2(0), Millbrook Pr.) Lerner Publishing Group.

Cormier, Robert. Heroes. 2006. (York Notes Ser.). (ENG., Illus.). 112p. pap. (978-1-4058-3559-6(1)) Pearson Education, Ltd.

Couloumbis, Audrey & Couloumbis, Akila. War Games. 2011. (ENG.). 240p. (J). (gr. 3-7). pap. 6.99 (978-0-375-85629-7(3), Yearling) Random Hse. Children's Bks.

Cram-Donahue, Marilyn. When the Crickets Stopped Singing. 2018. (ENG.). 288p. (J). (gr. 5-9). 18.95 (978-1-62979-723-6(5), Calkins Creek) Highlights Pr., c/o Highlights for Children, Inc.

Cronin, Bernie. We're Coming Home. 2004. 56p. pap. (978-1-84401-253-4(0)) Athena Pr.

Cummings, Mary. And the Baker's Boy Went to Sea. 2006. (Illus.). 195p. (YA). 16.95 (978-0-9774855-0-5(1)) Sparkling Pr.

Cutler, Jane. My Wartime Summers. 2011. 160p. (gr. 4-6). pap. 12.95 (978-1-4502-5419-9(5)) iUniverse, Inc.

Dalager, Stig. David's Story. 2010. (ENG., Illus.). 280p. (J). (gr. 10). pap. 16.99 (978-1-906582-04-3(1)) Aurora Metro Pubns. Ltd. GBR. Dist: Publishers Group West (PGW).

Dallas, Sandra. Red Berries, White Clouds, Blue Sky. (ENG., Illus.). 216p. (J). (gr. 3-6). 2015. pap. 9.99 (978-1-58536-907-2(1), 203820) 2014. 15.95 (978-1-58536-906-5(3), 203673) Sleeping Bear Pr.

Davis, Alexandra. Lumber Jills: The Unsung Heroines of World War II. Hickey, Katie, illus. 2019. (ENG.). 32p. (J). (gr. -1-3). 16.99 (978-0-8075-4795-3(6), 807547956) Whitman, Albert & Co.

Davis, Tanita S. Mare's War. 2011. (ENG.). 352p. (YA). (gr. 7). pap. 12.99 (978-0-375-85077-6(5), Knopf Bks. for Young Readers) Random Hse. Children's Bks.

De Vries, Maggie. Hunger Journeys: A Novel. 2012. (ENG.). 288p. (J). mass mkt. 7.99 (978-1-55468-580-6(X), Harper Trophy) HarperCollins Pubs.

Deborah Strandberg, Rebecca Reynolds and. Trammler Triplet Tales #2 - HIDDEN in TIME. 2007. 116p. pap. 8.94 (978-1-4303-2097-5(4)) Lulu Pr., Inc.

di Vries, Maggie. Hunger Journeys. 2014. 240p. (YA). (gr. 8). pap. 8.99 (978-0-06-231351-5(7)) HarperCollins Pubs.

Doyle, Brian. Boy O'Boy, 1 vol. 2005. (ENG.). 176p. (J). (gr. 6-8). pap. 6.95 (978-0-88899-654-1(3)) Groundwood Bks. CAN. Dist: Publishers Group West (PGW).

Dudley, David L. Caleb's Wars. 2011. (ENG.). 272p. (YA). (gr. 9). 17.99 (978-0-547-23997-2(1), 1098585, Clarion Bks.) HarperCollins Pubs.

Dunlop, Ed. The Incredible Rescues. Halverson, Tom, illus. 2003. 166p. (J). (gr. 4-7). 7.49 (978-1-59166-012-5(2)) BJU Pr.

—The Search for the Silver Eagle. Halverson, Tom, illus. 2003. 159p. (J). (gr. 4-7). 7.49 (978-1-59166-014-9(9)) BJU Pr.

Dunn, Joeming W. & Dunn, Ben. D-Day. Dunn, Joeming W. & Dunn, Ben, illus. 2015. (Graphic Warfare Ser.). (ENG., Illus.). 32p. (J). (gr. 3-8). 32.79 (978-1-61641-979-0(2), 19204, Graphic Planet - Fiction) Magic Wagon.

Duras, Marguerite. Hiroshima Mon Amour, Level B.Tr. of Hiroshima My Love. (FRE.). (YA). (gr. 7-12). 9.95 (978-0-88436-998-1(6), 40308) EMC/Paradigm Publishing.

Elliott, L. M. Under a War-Torn Sky. 2003. (ENG.). 288p. (J). (gr. 5-9). pap. 6.99 (978-0-7868-1753-5(4)) Little, Brown Bks. for Young Readers.

—Under a War-Torn Sky. 2003. (J). (gr. 7-12). lib. bdg. 17.20 (978-0-613-69092-8(3)) Turtleback.

Elvgren, Jennifer. The Whispering Town. Santomauro, Fabio, illus. 2014. (ENG.). 32p. (J). (gr. 2-5). 8.99 (978-1-4677-1195-1(0), ea7ed36f-d609-41ba-9b7b-1f284ebcad1d, Kar-Ben Publishing) Lerner Publishing Group.

Engle, Margarita. Jazz Owls: A Novel of the Zoot Suit Riots. Gutierrez, Rudy, illus. 2018. (ENG.). 192p. (YA). (gr. 7). 17.99 (978-1-5344-0943-9(2)) Simon & Schuster Children's Publishing.

Falkner, Brian. The Project. 2012. (ENG.). 288p. (J). (gr. 7-12). lib. bdg. 24.94 (978-0-375-96945-4(4)) Random Hse. Bks. for Young Readers.

Falligant, Erin. Prints in the Sand. 2017. 183p. (J). (978-1-5182-5318-8(0), American Girl) American Girl Publishing, Inc.

Farrant, Natasha. What We Did for Love: Resistance, Heartbreak, Betrayal, 1 vol. 2014. (Scarlet Voyage Ser.). (ENG., Illus.). 208p. (YA). (gr. 6-7). pap. 13.88 (978-1-62324-029-5(8), 10e6a221-1c2f-4eae-8d7f-a72204b5de2f) Enslow Publishing, LLC.

Faulkner, Matt. Gaijin: American Prisoner of War. 2014. (ENG., Illus.). 144p. (J). (gr. 3-7). 19.99 (978-1-4231-3735-1(3)) Little, Brown Bks. for Young Readers.

Ferrari, Michael. Born to Fly. 2011. 224p. (J). (ENG.). (gr. 4-6). lib. bdg. 21.19 (978-0-385-90649-4(8), Delacorte Pr.); (gr. 3-7). 7.99 (978-0-375-84607-6(7), Yearling) Random Hse. Children's Bks.

Fisher, Rick. Unknown Heroes. 2007. (ENG., Illus.). 32p. (J). per. 14.95 (978-1-59800-899-9(4)) Outskirts Pr., Inc.

Fleming, Candace. Boxes for Katje. Dressen-McQueen, Stacey, illus. 2003. (ENG.). 40p. (J). (gr. -1-3). 19.99 (978-0-374-30922-0(1), 900021221, Farrar, Straus & Giroux (BYR)) Farrar, Straus & Giroux.

—Boxes for Katje. Dressen-McQueen, Stacey, illus. 2004. (YA). 27.95 incl. audio (978-0-8045-6930-9(4), SAC6930) Spoken Arts, Inc.

Florida-James, Mark. Berlin Wolf. 2013. (ENG.). 336p. pap. (978-1-78306-005-4(0)) Troubador Publishing Ltd.

Fox, Janet. The Charmed Children of Rookskill Castle. 2017. 400p. (J). (gr. 5). 9.99 (978-0-14-751713-5(3), Puffin Books) Penguin Young Readers Group.

French, Jackie. Goodbye, Mr Hitler. 2021. 208p. 8.99 (978-1-4607-5129-9(9), HarperCollins) HarperCollins Pubs.

Friedman, D. Dina. Escaping into the Night. 2009. (ENG.). 208p. (J). (gr. 5-9). pap. 9.99 (978-1-4169-8648-5(0), Simon & Schuster Bks. For Young Readers) Simon & Schuster Bks. For Young Readers.

—Escaping into the Night. 2006. (ENG., Illus.). 208p. (J). (gr. 6-8). 22.44 (978-1-4169-0258-4(9)) Simon & Schuster, Inc.

Frische, Muffet. Moon Tears. 2014. (ENG.). 256p. (J). pap. 11.99 (978-0-9916348-1-1(0)) Ten Story Bks., LLC.

Gadsby, Maggie. Owl Be Home for Christmas. 2012. (J). 14.95 (978-1-62086-064-9(3)) Amplify Publishing Group.

Gallaz, Christophe. ROSA BLANCA. 2nd ed. 2003. (Rosa y Manzana Ser.). (SPA., Illus.). 32p. (978-84-85334-52-0(3), LG2811) Lóguez Ediciones ESP. Dist: Lectorum Pubns., Inc.

—Rose Blanche. 2011. (ENG., Illus.). 32p. (gr. 5-17). pap. 11.99 (978-0-89812-385-2(2), 22057, Creative Paperbacks) Creative Co., The.

Geras, Adèle, et al. War Girls: A Collection of First World War Stories Through the Eyes of Young Women. 2014. (ENG.). 288p. (YA). (gr. 7). pap. 15.99 (978-1-78344-060-3(0)) Andersen Pr. GBR. Dist: Independent Pubs. Group.

Giff, Patricia Reilly. Genevieve's War. 2019. (ENG.). 240p. (J). (gr. 3-7). pap. 7.99 (978-0-8234-4178-5(4)) Holiday Hse., Inc.

—Gingersnap. 2014. (ENG.). 160p. (J). (gr. 3-7). 6.99 (978-0-440-42178-8(0), Yearling) Random Hse. Children's Bks.

—Island War. 208p. (J). (gr. 3-7). 2020. pap. 7.99 (978-0-8234-4540-0(2)) 2018. 16.99 (978-0-8234-3954-6(2)) Holiday Hse., Inc.

—Willow Run. 2007. 149p. (J). 13.65 (978-0-7569-7769-6(X)) Perfection Learning Corp.

—Willow Run. 2007. (ENG.). 160p. (J). (gr. 3-7). per. 6.99 (978-0-440-23801-0(3), Yearling) Random Hse. Children's Bks.

Glatshteyn, Yankev. Emil & Karl: A Novel. Shandler, Jeffrey, tr. 2008. (ENG.). 208p. (J). (gr. 4-9). per. 18.99 (978-0-312-37387-0(2), 900045531) Square Fish.

Gleitzman, Morris. Once. 2005. 160p. (J). pap. (978-0-14-330195-0(0), Puffin) Penguin Publishing Group.

—Once. 2013. (Once Ser.: 1). (ENG.). 192p. (YA). (gr. 7). pap. 10.99 (978-0-312-65304-0(2), 900069444) Square Fish.

—Soon. 2015. (Once/Now/Then/after Ser.). (ENG.). 192p. (J). (gr. 4). pap. 11.99 (978-0-14-136279-3(0)) Penguin Bks., Ltd. GBR. Dist: Independent Pubs. Group.

—Then. 2013. (Once Ser.: 2). (ENG.). 224p. (YA). (gr. 7). pap. 11.99 (978-1-250-00341-6(5), 900079882) Square Fish.

—Then. 2013. (YA). lib. bdg. 20.85 (978-0-606-31904-1(2)) Turtleback.

Graber, Janet. Resistance. 2005. 144p. (YA). 15.95 (978-0-7614-5214-0(1)) Marshall Cavendish Corp.

Grant, Michael. Purple Hearts. (Front Lines Ser.: 3). (ENG.). 576p. (YA). (gr. 9). 2019. pap. 9.99 (978-0-06-234222-5(3)) 2018. 18.99 (978-0-06-234221-8(5)) HarperCollins Pubs. (Tegen, Katherine Bks).

—Silver Stars. (Front Lines Ser.: 2). (ENG.). (YA). (gr. 9). 2018. 592p. pap. 9.99 (978-0-06-234219-5(3)) 2017. (Illus.). 576p. 18.99 (978-0-06-234218-8(5)) HarperCollins Pubs. (Tegen, Katherine Bks).

—Silver Stars: A Front Lines Novel, Volume 2. 2017. (ENG., Illus.). 496p. (YA). pap. (978-1-4052-8786-9(1)) HarperCollins Pubs.

Gratz, Alan. Allies. 2019. (ENG., Illus.). 336p. (J). (gr. 4-7). 17.99 (978-1-338-24572-1(4), Scholastic Pr.) Scholastic, Inc.

—Grenade. (ENG.). 288p. E-Book 17.99 (978-1-338-24571-4(6)); 2018. (Illus.). (J). (gr. 4-7). 17.99 (978-1-338-24569-1(4)) Scholastic, Inc. (Scholastic Pr.).

—Grenade. l.t. ed. 2020. (ENG.). lib. bdg. 22.99 (978-1-4328-7747-7(X)) Thorndike Pr.

—Projekt 1065: a Novel of World War II. 2016. (ENG.). 320p. (J). (gr. 4-7). 17.99 (978-0-545-88016-9(5), Scholastic Pr.) Scholastic, Inc.

Graziani, E. War in My Town, 1 vol. 2015. (ENG., Illus.). 192p. (YA). (gr. 7-10). pap. 11.95 (978-1-927583-71-5(3)) Second Story Pr. CAN. Dist: Orca Bk. Pubs. USA.

Green, Connie Jordan. The War at Home. 2nd ed. 2003. 144p. (J). pap. 15.00 (978-0-916078-75-1(2)) Iris Publishing Group, Inc., The.

Greene, Bette. Summer of My German Soldier (Puffin Modern Classics) 2006. (Puffin Modern Classics Ser.). (ENG.). 240p. (J). (gr. 5-18). 8.99 (978-0-14-240651-9(1), Puffin Books) Penguin Young Readers Group.

Greenwood, Mark. Diamond Jack. 2017. (History Mysteries Ser.). 96p. (J). (gr. 3-7). 9.99 (978-0-14-330926-0(9)) Random Hse. Australia AUS. Dist: Independent Pubs. Group.

Griffis, Molly Levite. The Rachel Resistance. 224p. 8.95 (978-1-57168-553-7(7)) Eakin Pr.

—Simon Says. 2004. vi, 263p. (J). 22.95 (978-1-57168-836-1(6)); pap. (978-1-57168-847-7(1)) Eakin Pr. (Eakin Pr.).

Grindley, Sally. Feather Wars. 2003. (J). pap. 12.99 (978-0-7475-6338-9(1)) Bloomsbury Publishing Plc GBR. Dist: Independent Pubs. Group.

Gutman, Dan. Ted & Me. 2012. (Baseball Card Adventures Ser.). (ENG., Illus.). 208p. (J). (gr. 5-9). 15.99 (978-0-06-123487-3(7), HarperCollins) HarperCollins Pubs.

Haar, Jaap Ter & Mearns, Martha. Boris. Poortvliet, Rien, illus. 2009. (J). pap. (978-0-921100-72-0(8)) Inheritance Pubns.

Hahn, Mary Downing. Stepping on the Cracks. 2009. (ENG., Illus.). 224p. (J). (gr. 5-7). pap. 7.99 (978-0-547-07660-7(6), 1041958, Clarion Bks.) HarperCollins Pubs.

Halahmy, Miriam. Rip to the Rescue. 2020. (ENG.). 208p. (J). (gr. 3-7). 16.99 (978-0-8234-4441-0(4)) Holiday Hse., Inc.

—Saving Hanno: The Story of a Refugee Dog. 2019. (ENG.). 112p. (J). (gr. 3-7). 17.99 (978-0-8234-4165-5(2)) Holiday Hse., Inc.

Hamley, Dennis. Divided Loyalties. 2010. (J). (978-0-7636-3418-6(2)) Candlewick Pr.

Hannigan, Kate. Cape. Spaziante, Patrick, illus. 2019. (League of Secret Heroes Ser.: 1). (ENG.). 336p. (J). (gr. 3-7). 17.99 (978-1-5344-3911-5(0), Simon & Schuster/Paula Wiseman Bks.) Simon & Schuster/Paula Wiseman Bks.

Harlow, Joan Hiatt. Shadows on the Sea. (ENG., Illus.). (J). (gr. 3-7). 2005. 272p. pap. 7.99 (978-0-689-84927-5(3)) 2003. 256p. 17.99 (978-0-689-84926-8(5)) McElderry, Margaret K. Bks. (McElderry, Margaret K. Bks.).

—The Watcher. 2015. (ENG.). 304p. (J). (gr. 3-7). pap. 8.99 (978-1-4424-2912-3(7), McElderry, Margaret K. Bks.) McElderry, Margaret K. Bks.

Hart, Derek. Secret of the Dragon's Eye. 2007. 264p. per. 16.95 (978-0-595-42967-7(X)) iUniverse, Inc.

Hartnett, Sonya. The Midnight Zoo. Offermann, Andrea, illus. 2018. (ENG.). 224p. (J). (gr. 5-9). pap. 8.99 (978-0-7636-6462-6(6)) Candlewick Pr.

—The Midnight Zoo. 2018. lib. bdg. 18.40 (978-0-606-40915-5(7)) Turtleback.

Hayes, Clair W. The Boy Allies in the Trenches Midst Shot & Shell along the Aisne. 2018. (ENG., Illus.). 188p. (YA). (gr. 7-12). pap. (978-93-5297-252-4(X)) Alpha Editions.

Haywood, Carolyn. Primrose Day. Haywood, Carolyn, illus. 2005. (ENG., Illus.). 176p. (J). (gr. 1-4). pap. 10.95 (978-0-15-205229-4(1), 1195756, Clarion Bks.) HarperCollins Pubs.

Helmer, Marilyn. One Splendid Tree. Eastman, Dianne, illus. 2007. 32p. (J). (gr. -1-3). 6.95 (978-1-55453-166-0(7)) Kids Can Pr., Ltd. CAN. Dist: Hachette Bk. Group.

Henderson's Boys: Scorched Earth: Book 7, Bk. 7. 2013. (Henderson's Boys Ser.). (ENG., Illus.). 368p. (YA). (gr. 7-17). pap. 10.99 (978-1-4449-0233-4(4)) Hachette Children's Group GBR. Dist: Hachette Bk. Group.

Herman, Charlotte. My Chocolate Year: A Novel with 12 Recipes. Pham, LeUyen, illus. 2008. (ENG.). 176p. (J). (gr. 3-7). 15.99 (978-1-4169-3341-0(7), Simon & Schuster Bks. For Young Readers) Simon & Schuster Bks. For Young Readers.

Hesse, Karen. Aleutian Sparrow. Zerbetz, Evon, illus. 2005. (ENG.). 160p. (J). (gr. 4-9). reprint ed. pap. 8.99 (978-1-4169-0327-7(5), McElderry, Margaret K. Bks.) McElderry, Margaret K. Bks.

—Aleutian Sparrow. Zerbetz, Evon, illus. 2005. 156p. (J). (gr. 5-9). 13.65 (978-0-7569-5589-2(0)) Perfection Learning Corp.

Hesse, Monica. Girl in the Blue Coat. (ENG.). 320p. (YA). (gr. 7-17). 2017. pap. 11.99 (978-0-316-26063-3(0)) 2016. E-Book 45.00 (978-0-316-26064-0(9)) Little, Brown Bks. for Young Readers.

—Girl in the Blue Coat. 2017. (YA). lib. bdg. 20.85 (978-0-606-39918-0(6)) Turtleback.

—The War Outside. (ENG.). (YA). (gr. 7-17). 2019. 352p. pap. 10.99 (978-0-316-31671-2(7)) 2018. (Illus.). 336p. 34.99 (978-0-316-31669-9(5)) Little, Brown Bks. for Young Readers.

Heuvel, Eric. A Family Secret. Miller, Lorraine T., tr. Heuvel, Eric, illus. 2009. (ENG., Illus.). 64p. (J). (gr. 5-8). pap. 11.99 (978-0-374-42265-3(6), 900057558) Square Fish.

Hoffman, Emily Allen. A Friend of the Enemy. 2003. 108p. (J). pap. 7.95 (978-1-57249-312-4(7), White Mane Kids) White Mane Publishing Co., Inc.

ood, Susan. Lifeboat 12. 2018. (ENG., Illus.). 336p. (J). (gr. 3-8). 17.99 (978-1-4814-6883-1(9), Simon & Schuster Bks. For Young Readers) Simon & Schuster Bks. For Young Readers.

orvath, Polly. The Night Garden. 2019. (ENG.). 304p. (J). pap. 12.99 (978-1-250-29414-2(2), 900159362) Square Fish.

oward, Ellen. Different Kind of Courage. 2007. (ENG.). 184p. (J). (gr. 3-7). pap. 10.95 (978-1-4169-6730-9(3), Simon & Schuster/Paula Wiseman Bks.) Simon & Schuster/Paula Wiseman Bks.

ughes, Dean. Four-Four-Two. 2016. (ENG., Illus.). 272p. (YA). (gr. 7). 18.99 (978-1-4814-6252-5(0), Atheneum Bks. for Young Readers) Simon & Schuster Children's Publishing.

—Soldier Boys. 2004. 230p. (gr. 7-12). 17.00 (978-0-7569-4566-4(6)) Perfection Learning Corp.

—Soldier Boys. 2003. (ENG.). 240p. (YA). (gr. 7-12). mass mkt. 8.99 (978-0-689-86021-8(8), Simon Pulse) Simon Pulse.

—Soldier Boys. 2015. (ENG., Illus.). 240p. (YA). (gr. 7). pap. 11.99 (978-1-4814-2704-3(0), Atheneum Bks. for Young Readers) Simon & Schuster Children's Publishing.

Hughes, Monica. Blaine's Way, 1 vol. 2006. (ENG.). 240p. (YA). (gr. 7-12). per. 9.95 (978-1-55041-934-4(X), b91073ce-06f9-44cf-ae69-ee5e4d20c5be) Trifolium Bks., Inc. CAN. Dist: Firefly Bks., Ltd.

Hughes, Shirley. Hero on a Bicycle. 2017. (ENG.). 224p. (J). (gr. 5). pap. 8.99 (978-0-7636-9778-5(8)) Candlewick Pr.

—Ruby in the Ruins. Hughes, Shirley, illus. 2018. (ENG., Illus.). 32p. (J). (gr. k-4). 15.99 (978-0-7636-9237-7(9)) Candlewick Pr.

—Whistling in the Dark. 2017. (ENG., Illus.). 240p. (J). (gr. 5). 16.99 (978-0-7636-9072-4(4)) Candlewick Pr.

Hunter, Sara Hoagland. The Unbreakable Code. Miner, Julia, illus. 2007. (ENG.). 32p. (J). (gr. 1-3). per. 7.95 (978-0-87358-917-8(3)) Cooper Square Publishing Llc.

Ibbotson, Eva. The Dragonfly Pool. 2008. (YA). 1.25 (978-1-4361-5202-0(X)); 122.75 (978-1-4361-5209-9(7)); 256.75 (978-1-4361-5206-8(2)); 90.75 (978-1-4361-5207-5(0)); 92.75 (978-1-4361-5205-1(4)); 120.75 (978-1-4361-5211-2(9)) Recorded Bks., Inc.

Jablonski, Carla. Resistance: Book 1, Bk. 1. Purvis, Leland, illus. 2010. (Resistance Ser.: 1). (ENG.). 128p. (YA). (gr. 7-12). pap. 19.99 (978-1-59643-291-8(8), 900044619, First Second Bks.) Roaring Brook Pr.

James, Brian. Dangerous Skies. 2016. (ENG., Illus.). 186p. (J). (gr. 5-7). pap. 9.99 (978-1-910461-27-3(X)) Claret Pr. GBR. Dist: Lightning Source UK, Ltd.

Joffo, Joseph. A Bag of Marbles: The Graphic Novel. Bailly, Vincent, illus. 2013. (ENG.). 128p. (YA). (gr. 7-12). pap. 12.99 (978-1-4677-1516-4(6), 3cb490f5-e7ac-4c1a-8900-02f6f003202d); E-Book 43.99 (978-1-4677-1651-2(0)) Lerner Publishing Group. (Graphic Universe™).

Johns, Eric. Home Front. 2012. 146p. pap. (978-1-4716-5390-2(0)) Lulu.com.

Johnston, Julie. Little Red Lies. 2015. (Illus.). 352p. (YA). (gr. 7). pap. 8.99 (978-1-77049-807-5(9), Tundra Bks.) Tundra Bks. CAN. Dist: Penguin Random Hse. LLC.

Johnston, Tony. The Harmonica. Mazellan, Ron, illus. 2004. (ENG.). 32p. (J). (gr. 2-4). 22.44 (978-1-57091-547-5(4)) Charlesbridge Publishing, Inc.

Jones, Marcia Thornton. Woodford Brave. Whipple, Kevin, illus. 2015. (ENG.). 200p. (J). (gr. 4-7). 16.95 (978-1-62979-305-4(1), Calkins Creek) Highlights Pr., c/o Highlights for Children, Inc.

Kacer, Kathy. Masters of Silence. 2019. (Heroes Quartet Ser.: 2). (Illus.). 272p. (J). (gr. 4-7). 18.95 (978-1-77321-262-3(1)); (ENG., pap. 9.95 (978-1-77321-261-6(3)) Annick Pr., Ltd. CAN. Dist: Publishers Group West (PGW).

—Shanghai Escape, 1 vol. 2013. (Holocaust Remembrance Series for Young Readers Ser.: 14). (ENG.). 240p. (J). (gr. 6-8). pap. 14.95 (978-1-927583-10-4(1)) Second Story Pr. CAN. Dist: Orca Bk. Pubs. USA.

Kadohata, Cynthia. Weedflower. 2009. (ENG.). 272p. (J). (gr. 5-9). pap. 7.99 (978-1-4169-7566-3(7), Atheneum Bks. for Young Readers) Simon & Schuster Children's Publishing.

—Weedflower. 2006. (ENG., Illus.). 272p. (J). (gr. 5-9). 22.99 (978-0-689-86574-9(0)) Simon & Schuster, Inc.

Katz, Gwen C. Among the Red Stars. (ENG.). 384p. (YA). (gr. 8). 2018. pap. 9.99 (978-0-06-264275-2(8)) 2017. 17.99 (978-0-06-264274-5(X)) HarperCollins Pubs. (HarperTeen).

Katz, Jennifer A. The Era of Courting. 2006. 119p. pap. 19.95 (978-1-4241-3321-5(1)) PublishAmerica, Inc.

Keenan, Sheila. Dogs of War: a Graphic Novel. Fox, Nathan, illus. 2013. (ENG.). 208p. (J). (gr. 3-7). pap. 14.99 (978-0-545-12888-9(9), Graphix) Scholastic, Inc.

Kemp, Kristin. The Boy in the Striped Pajamas: An Instructional Guide for Literature. rev. ed. 2015. (Great Works). (ENG., Illus.). 72p. (gr. 4-8). pap. 9.99 (978-1-4807-8507-6(5)) Shell Educational Publishing.

Kendall, Jane. Horse Diaries #4: Maestoso Petra. Sanderson, Ruth, illus. 2010. (Horse Diaries: 4). 160p. (J). (gr. 3-7). pap. 7.99 (978-0-375-85842-0(3), Random Hse. Bks. for Young Readers) Random Hse. Children's Bks.

Kerkow, Larry. Angel Goes to Sea. 2010. 24p. 12.56 (978-1-4269-3490-2(4)) Trafford Publishing.

Kerr, Judith. En la Batalla de Inglaterra. (SPA.). 304p. (YA). (gr. 5-8). (978-84-204-3221-2(0), AF0691) Ediciones Alfaguara ESP. Dist: Lectorum Pubns., Inc.

—En la Batalla de Inglaterra. (SPA.). (YA). (gr. 5-8). pap. (978-84-345-8580-5(4), AF0691) Salvat Editores, S.A. ESP. Dist: Lectorum Pubns., Inc.

Kerr, M. E., pseud. Slap Your Sides. 2003. 198p. (YA). 13.65 (978-0-7569-4240-3(3)) Perfection Learning Corp.

Kezar, Wanda. It's a Scamp's Life! Derby, Sarah, illus. 2013. 186p. pap. 14.99 (978-1-62839-371-2(8)) Salem Author Services.

Kimpton, Paul & Kimpton, Ann Kaczkowski. Dog Tags: A Young Musician's Sacrifice During WWII. 2012. (Adventures with Music Ser.: 2). (ENG.). 120p. (J). (gr. 4-7). pap. 8.95 (978-1-57999-882-0(8)) G I A Pubns., Inc.

—Starting Early: A Boy & His Bugle in America During WWII. 2011. (Adventures with Music Ser.: 1). (ENG., Illus.). 204p. (J). (gr. 4-7). pap. 8.95 (978-1-57999-805-9(4)) G I A Pubns., Inc.

King-Smith, Dick. Spider Sparrow. unabr. ed. 2004. 176p. (J). (gr. 5-9). pap. 36.00 incl. audio (978-0-8072-8407-0(6), Listening Library) Random Hse. Audio Publishing Group.

Knight, Clayton & Royce, Ralph. We Were There at the Normandy Invasion. 2011. 192p. 42.95 (978-1-258-10198-5(X)) Literary Licensing, LLC.

Korman, Gordon. War Stories. 2021. (ENG.). 240p. (J). (gr. 3-7). pap. 8.99 (978-1-338-29022-6(3)) Scholastic, Inc.

Kositsky, Lynne. The Thought of High Windows. 2004. 176p. (J). (gr. 7-9). 6.95 (978-1-55337-622-4(6)) Kids Can Pr., Ltd. CAN. Dist: Hachette Bk. Group.

Krishnaswami, Uma. Step up to the Plate, Maria Singh, 1 vol. 2017. (ENG.). 288p. (J). (gr. 3-7). 21.95 (978-1-60060-261-0(4), leelowtu, Tu Bks.) Lee & Low Bks., Inc.

Landsberry, Belinda. Anzac Ted. 2016. (ENG., Illus.). 32p. (J). (gr. -1-5). 17.99 (978-1-921966-56-9(4), EK Bks.) Exisle Publishing Pty Ltd. AUS. Dist: Two Rivers Distribution.

Larson, Kirby. Dash (Dogs of World War II) 2016. (Dogs of World War II Ser.). (ENG.). 256p. (J). (gr. 3-7). pap. 8.99 (978-0-545-41636-8(1), Scholastic Paperbacks) Scholastic, Inc.

—Duke (Dogs of World War II) 2015. (Dogs of World War II Ser.). (ENG.). 240p. (J). (gr. 3-7). pap. 8.99 (978-0-545-41638-2(8), Scholastic Paperbacks) Scholastic, Inc.

—The Fences Between Us: The Diary of Piper Davis. 2010. (Illus.). 313p. (J). pap. (978-0-545-27094-6(4)) Scholastic, Inc.

—Growing up with Aloha. 2017. 208p. (J). (978-1-5182-5294-5(X), American Girl) American Girl Publishing, Inc.

—Hula for the Home Front. 2017. 176p. (J). (978-1-5182-5295-2(8), American Girl) American Girl Publishing, Inc.

—Liberty. 2018. (Dogs of World War II Ser.). lib. bdg. 18.40 (978-0-606-41133-2(X)) Turtleback.

Lasky, Kathryn. Night Witches: A Novel of World War II. 2017. 211p. (J). (978-1-338-15866-3(X), Scholastic Pr.) Scholastic, Inc.

Lehman, Theodore H. Defying Odds. 2014. (YA). pap. (978-1-935604-63-1(5)) Gaon Bks.

LeSourd, Nancy. Attack at Pearl Harbor, 1 vol. 2008. (Liberty Letters Ser.). (ENG.). 224p. (J). pap. 7.99 (978-0-310-71389-0(7)) Zonderkidz.

Lewis, Floyd. The Foundered Mule. 2006. (YA). 9.95 (978-0-9788283-2-5(1)) Acacia Publishing, Inc.

Lieurance, Suzanne. The Lucky Baseball: My Story in a Japanese-American Internment Camp, 1 vol. 2010. (Historical Fiction Adventures Ser.). (ENG., Illus.). 160p. (J). (gr. 3-5). lib. bdg. 31.93 (978-0-7660-3311-5(2), de535228-7abe-4f5d-92ff-dfd0e351cb79) Enslow Publishing, LLC.

Locke, Katherine. The Spy with the Red Balloon. 2019. (Balloonmakers Ser.: 2). (ENG.). 368p. (YA). (gr. 8-12). pap. 9.99 (978-0-8075-2938-6(9), 807529389) Whitman, Albert & Co.

Lois, Lowry. Compte les Etoiles. pap. 16.95 (978-2-211-03436-4(5)) Archimede Editions FRA. Dist: Distribooks, Inc.

—Number the Stars. 2004. 144p. (J). (gr. 5-9). pap. 29.00 incl. audio (978-1-4000-8637-5(X), Listening Library) Random Hse. Audio Publishing Group.

Lowry, Lois. Number the Stars. l.t. ed. 2019. (ENG.). 282p. (J). (gr. 5-7). pap. 12.99 (978-1-4328-6393-7(2), Large Print Pr.) Thorndike Pr.

—Number the Stars: A Newbery Award Winner. 2011. (ENG.). 160p. (J). (gr. 5-7). pap. 9.99 (978-0-547-57709-8(5), 1458457, Clarion Bks.) HarperCollins Pubs.

—Number the Stars 25th Anniversary Edition: A Newbery Award Winner. 25th anniv. ed. 2014. (ENG.). 160p. (J). (gr. 5-7). 17.99 (978-0-544-34000-8(0), 1584700, Clarion Bks.) HarperCollins Pubs.

Lynch, Chris. Alive & Kicking. 2015. 182p. (J). (978-0-545-78940-0(0), Scholastic Pr.) Scholastic, Inc.

—The Right Fight. 2014. 189p. (YA). (978-0-545-63728-2(7), Scholastic Pr.) Scholastic, Inc.

MacDonald, Jerry. Red Eyes & Crazy Jake. 2009. 24p. pap. 15.95 (978-1-4389-2706-0(1)) AuthorHouse.

MacKay, Andrew. Young Lions Roar. 2012. 316p. pap. (978-1-909395-27-5(7)) Legend Pr.

MacPherson, M. j. The Magic Thread: Overcoming challenges during World War II, a young girl discovers secrets that change adversity into Adventure. 2009. 208p. pap. 17.95 (978-0-595-52812-7(0)) iUniverse, Inc.

Mah, Adeline Yen. Chinese Cinderella & the Secret Dragon Society. 2006. (ENG., Illus.). 256p. (J). (gr. 5-9). pap. 7.99 (978-0-06-056736-1(8), HarperCollins) HarperCollins Pubs.

Maruno, Jennifer. Kid Soldier. 2013. (ENG., Illus.). 208p. (YA). pap. 10.99 (978-1-4597-0677-4(3), 9781459706774) Dundurn Pr. CAN. Dist: Publishers Group West (PGW).

Mason, Caroline. The Blacksmith's Cottage: A Pastoral War. 2009. 150p. pap. 13.95 (978-1-4327-4969-9(2)); 120p. pap. 33.95 (978-1-4327-2987-5(X)) Outskirts Pr., Inc.

Matas, Carol. Code Name Kris. 2007. (ENG.). 164p. (J). (gr. 3-7). pap. 12.95 (978-1-4169-6162-8(3), Aladdin) Simon & Schuster Children's Publishing.

—Dear Canada: Turned Away. 2005. (Dear Canada Ser.). (ENG., Illus.). 208p. (J). (978-0-439-96946-8(8)) Scholastic Canada, Ltd.

—Lisa's War. 2007. (ENG.). 128p. (J). (gr. 2-7). pap. 11.95 (978-1-4169-6163-5(1), Aladdin) Simon & Schuster Children's Publishing.

Mazer, Harry. A Boy at War: A Novel of Pearl Harbor. 2004. (Illus.). 104p. (gr. 5-9). 16.00 (978-0-7569-4088-1(5)) Perfection Learning Corp.

—A Boy No More. 2007. 136p. (gr. 5-9). 16.00 (978-0-7569-8112-9(3)) Perfection Learning Corp.

—Heroes Don't Run. 2007. (Aladdin Historical Fiction Ser.). 113p. (gr. 3-7). 16.00 (978-0-7569-8111-2(5)) Perfection Learning Corp.

—Heroes Don't Run, 3. 2005. (Boy at War Ser.). (ENG., Illus.). 113p. (J). (gr. 6-8). 18.69 (978-0-689-85534-4(6)) Simon & Schuster, Inc.

—The Last Mission. 192p. (YA). (gr. 7-18). pap. 4.99 (978-0-8072-1366-7(7), Listening Library) Random Hse. Audio Publishing Group.

McDonough, Yona Zeldis. The Bicycle Spy. 2016. (ENG.). 208p. (J). (gr. 3-7). 17.99 (978-0-545-85095-7(9), Scholastic Pr.) Scholastic, Inc.

McSwigan, Marie. Snow Treasure. 2006. (Illus.). 208p. (J). (gr. 3-7). 7.99 (978-0-14-240224-5(9), Puffin Books) Penguin Young Readers Group.

Meir, Tamar. Francesco Tirelli's Ice Cream Shop. Albert, Yael, illus. 2019. (ENG.). 32p. (J). (gr. 3-6). 9.99 (978-1-5415-3465-0(4), 3436a1ef-0e38-40bc-bf54-16acb9a854ee, Kar-Ben Publishing) Lerner Publishing Group.

Mercer, Christa Blum. German War Child: Growing Up in World War II. 2004. (Illus.). 176p. pap. 14.95 (978-1-893597-07-5(5)) A. Borough Bks.

Merkel, Ruth Vitrano. Ann: 1833-1897. 2006. (Hannah's Girls Ser.). (Illus.). 112p. (J). (gr. 4-7). per. 9.99 (978-0-8280-1951-4(7)) Review & Herald Publishing Assn.

—Grace: 1890-1973, 6. 2006. (Hannah's Girls Ser.). (Illus.). 128p. (J). (gr. 4-7). per. 9.99 (978-0-8280-1953-8(3)) Review & Herald Publishing Assn.

—Marilla 1851-1916, 6 bks. 2006. (Hannah's Girls Ser.). (Illus.). 144p. (J). (gr. 4-7). per. 9.99 (978-0-8280-1952-1(5)) Review & Herald Publishing Assn.

—Ruthie: Born 1931. 2007. (Hannah's Girls Ser.). (Illus.). 144p. (J). (gr. 4-7). per. 9.99 (978-0-8280-1954-5(1)) Review & Herald Publishing Assn.

Messner, Kate. D-Day: Battle on the Beach (Ranger in Time #7) McMorris, Kelley, illus. 2018. (Ranger in Time Ser.: 7). (ENG.). 160p. (J). (gr. 2-5). pap. 6.99 (978-1-338-13390-5(X), Scholastic Pr.) Scholastic, Inc.

Miller, Peggy Reiff. The Seagoing Cowboy. Ewart, Claire, illus. 2016. 39p. (J). (978-0-87178-212-0(X)) Brethren Pr.

Mochizuki, Ken. Baseball Saved Us. 97th rev. ed. 2014. (ENG.). 30p. (J). (gr. k-12). 15.65 (978-1-63245-249-8(9)) Lectorum Pubns., Inc.

—Baseball Saved Us, 1 vol. Lee, Dom, illus. 2018. (ENG.). 32p. (J). (gr. k-3). pap. 10.95 (978-1-880000-19-9(9), leelowbooks) Lee & Low Bks., Inc.

—Baseball Saved Us. Lee, Dom, illus. (Picture Book Readalong Ser.). pap. 39.95 incl. audio compact disk (978-1-59112-917-2(6)); 2004. (J). (gr. -1-2). 25.95 incl. audio (978-1-59112-456-6(5)) Live Oak Media.

Moller, Sharon Chickering. Jeep: The Coyote Who Flew in World War II. Cranford, Darren, illus. 2014. 59p. (J). pap. 9.95 (978-0-9860799-0-0(1)) Chickering-Moller Project.

Morpurgo, Michael. An Elephant in the Garden: Inspired by a True Story. 2013. (ENG.). 224p. (J). (gr. 5-9). pap. 8.99 (978-1-250-03414-4(0), 900120584) Square Fish.

—Half a Man. O'Callaghan, Gemma, illus. 2015. (ENG.). 64p. (J). (gr. 5). 16.99 (978-0-7636-7747-3(7)) Candlewick Pr.

Morrill, Stephanie. Within These Lines, 1 vol. 2019. (ENG.). 352p. (YA). 17.99 (978-0-310-76523-3(4)) Blink.

Moskowitz-Sweet, Gloria & Smith, Hope Anita. It Rained Warm Bread: Moishe Moskowitz's Story of Hope. Lyon, Lea, illus. 2019. (ENG.). 160p. (J). 16.99 (978-1-250-16572-5(5), 900187113, Holt, Henry & Co. Bks. For Young Readers) Holt, Henry & Co.

Moulder, Holly. Crystal City Lights. 2013. (ENG.). 190p. (J). pap. 8.99 (978-0-9885295-0-2(5)) Blue Marlin Pubns.

Muchamore, Robert. Henderson's Boys: Eagle Day: Book 2. 2009. (Henderson's Boys Ser.). (ENG., Illus.). 432p. (J). (gr. 7-17). 11.99 (978-0-340-95649-6(6)) Hachette Children's Group GBR. Dist: Hachette Bk. Group.

—Henderson's Boys: Secret Army: Book 3. 2010. (Henderson's Boys Ser.). (ENG., Illus.). 384p. (YA). (gr. 7-17). pap. 11.99 (978-0-340-95650-2(X)) Hachette Children's Group GBR. Dist: Hachette Bk. Group.

Myers, Walter Dean. Invasion. 2013. (ENG.). 224p. (YA). E-Book (978-0-545-57659-8(8), Scholastic Pr.) Scholastic, Inc.

Nagai, Mariko. Dust of Eden. 2018. (ENG.). 144p. (J). (gr. 3-7). pap. 9.99 (978-0-8075-1738-3(0), 807517380) Whitman, Albert & Co.

—Under the Broken Sky. 2019. (ENG., Illus.). 304p. (J). 17.99 (978-1-250-15921-2(0), 900185614, Holt, Henry & Co. Bks. For Young Readers) Holt, Henry & Co.

Napoli, Donna Jo. Fire in the Hills. 2008. (ENG.). 240p. (YA). (gr. 7-18). 7.99 (978-0-14-241200-8(7), Speak) Penguin Young Readers Group.

Nesher, A. A Shrek Inmitn Yam. 2017. (YID., Illus.). 82p. (J). (978-1-63587-090-9(9)) Double Bridge Publishing.

Nielsen, Jennifer A. Behind Enemy Lines. 2016. (Infinity Ring Ser.: 6). lib. bdg. 17.20 (978-0-606-38623-4(8)) Turtleback.

—Behind Enemy Lines (Infinity Ring, Book 6), 1 vol. (Infinity Ring Ser.: 6). (ENG., 192p. (J). (gr. 3-7). 2013. Illus.). 12.99 (978-0-545-38701-9(9)) 6th ed. 2016. pap. 6.99 (978-0-545-90121-5(9), Scholastic Pr.) Scholastic, Inc.

—Resistance (Scholastic Gold) 2018. (ENG.). 400p. (J). (gr. 3-7). 17.99 (978-1-338-14847-3(8), Scholastic Pr.) Scholastic, Inc.

Novel Units. Lily's Crossing Novel Units Student Packet. 2019. (ENG.). (J). pap. 13.99 (978-1-58130-645-3(8), Novel Units, Inc.) Classroom Library Co.

—Lily's Crossing Novel Units Teacher Guide. 2019. (ENG.). (J). pap. 12.99 (978-1-58130-644-6(X), Novel Units, Inc.) Classroom Library Co.

—Summer of My German Soldier Novel Units Teacher Guide. 2019. (ENG.). (YA). pap. 12.99 (978-1-56137-113-6(0), Novel Units, Inc.) Classroom Library Co.

Orlev, Uri. Lidia, Reina de Palestina. (SPA.). 158p. (YA). (gr. 5-8). (978-84-279-3237-1(5), NG8035) Noguer y Caralt Editores, S. A. ESP. Dist: Lectorum Pubns., Inc.

Orme, David. Blitz. 2007. (Sharp Shades Ser.). (ENG., Illus.). 64p. (J). (gr. 6-8). pap. 8.99 (978-0-237-53444-8(4)) Evans Brothers, Ltd. GBR. Dist: Independent Pubs. Group.

Osborne, Mary Pope. My Secret War: The World War II Diary of Madeline Beck, Long Island, New York 1941. 2008. (Dear America Ser.). (J). (gr. 3-7). 39.95 incl. audio compact disk (978-1-4301-0359-2(0)) Live Oak Media.

Osborne, William. Hitler's Secret. 2013. (Illus.). 333p. (YA). (978-0-545-51533-7(5), Chicken Hse., The) Scholastic, Inc.

Owen, James A. The Shadow Dragons. Owen, James A., illus. 2009. (Chronicles of the Imaginarium Geographica Ser.: 4). (ENG., Illus.). 432p. (YA). (gr. 7-18). 21.99 (978-1-4169-5879-6(7), Simon & Schuster Bks. For Young Readers) Simon & Schuster Bks. For Young Readers.

Palacio, R. J. White Bird: a Wonder Story (a Graphic Novel) 2019. (Wonder Ser.). (ENG., Illus.). 224p. (J). (gr. 3-7). 24.99 (978-0-525-64553-5(5)); lib. bdg. 27.99 (978-0-525-64554-2(3)) Random Hse. Children's Bks. (Knopf Bks. for Young Readers).

Parenteau, Shirley. Dolls of War. (Friendship Dolls Ser.: 3). 320p. (J). (gr. 3-7). 2019. (ENG.). pap. 7.99 (978-1-5362-0889-4(2)) 2017. 16.99 (978-0-7636-9069-4(4)) Candlewick Pr.

Park, Linda Sue. When My Name Was Keoko. 2004. 199p. (J). (gr. 5). 14.65 (978-0-7569-2928-2(8)) Perfection Learning Corp.

—When My Name Was Keoko. 2012. lib. bdg. 18.40 (978-0-606-24716-0(5)) Turtleback.

Parkhurst, Liz S. Under One Flag: A Year at Rohwer. Clifton, Tom, illus. 2006. (ENG.). 32p. (J). (gr. 3-7). 16.95 (978-0-87483-759-9(6), 1241971) August Hse. Pubs., Inc.

Patneaude, David. Thin Wood Walls. 2008. (ENG., Illus.). 240p. (J). (gr. 5-7). pap. 7.99 (978-0-618-80915-8(5), 492685, Clarion Bks.) HarperCollins Pubs.

Paulsen, Gary. The Quilt. 2005. 83p. (gr. 3-7). 16.00 (978-0-7569-4781-1(2)) Perfection Learning Corp.

—The Quilt. 2005. (Alida Ser.). (ENG., Illus.). 96p. (J). (gr. 3-7). 6.99 (978-0-440-22936-0(7), Yearling) Random Hse. Children's Bks.

Pausewang, Gudrun. Traitor. 2006. (Illus.). 220p. (J). (gr. -1-7). 16.95 (978-0-8225-6195-8(6), Carolrhoda Bks.) Lerner Publishing Group.

Pearsall, Shelley. Jump into the Sky. 2013. 352p. (J). (gr. 4-7). pap. 8.99 (978-0-440-42140-5(3), Yearling) Random Hse. Children's Bks.

Pearson, Kit. The Lights Go on Again: Puffin Classics Edition. 2014. (Canada Puffin Classics Ser.). (ENG.). 240p. (J). (gr. 3-7). 10.99 (978-0-14-319232-9(9), Puffin Canada) PRH Canada Young Readers CAN. Dist: Penguin Random Hse. LLC.

—Looking at the Moon: Puffin Classics Edition. 2014. (Canada Puffin Classics Ser.). (ENG., Illus.). 248p. (J). (gr. 3-7). 10.99 (978-0-14-319231-2(0), Puffin Canada) PRH Canada Young Readers CAN. Dist: Penguin Random Hse. LLC.

—The Sky Is Falling: Puffin Classics Edition. 2014. (Canada Puffin Classics Ser.). (ENG.). 296p. (J). (gr. 3-7). 12.99 (978-0-14-319233-6(7), Puffin Canada) PRH Canada Young Readers CAN. Dist: Penguin Random Hse. LLC.

Peck, Richard. On the Wings of Heroes. 2008. (ENG.). 160p. (J). (gr. 3-7). 8.99 (978-0-14-241204-6(X), Puffin Books) Penguin Young Readers Group.

—On the Wings of Heroes. rev. l.t. ed. 2007. (Literacy Bridge Middle Reader Ser.). 171p. (J). (gr. 4-7). 23.95 (978-0-7862-9703-0(4)) Thorndike Pr.

Peet, Mal. Tamar: A Novel of Espionage, Passion, & Betrayal. (ENG.). 432p. (YA). (gr. 9). 2018. pap. 10.99 (978-1-5362-0030-0(1)) 2007. (Illus.). 17.99 (978-0-7636-3488-9(3)) Candlewick Pr.

Perl, Lila. Isabel's War. 2014. (ENG.). 224p. (J). (gr. 2-7). pap. 12.95 (978-1-939601-27-8(4)) Ig Publishing, Inc.

—Lilli's Quest. 2015. (ENG.). 224p. (J). (-9). pap. 12.95 (978-1-939601-53-7(3)) Ig Publishing, Inc.

Phillips, Dee. Over the Top. 2014. (Yesterday's Voices Ser.). (YA). lib. bdg. 19.60 (978-0-606-35582-7(0)) Turtleback.

—Tail Gunner. 2014. (Yesterday's Voices Ser.). (YA). lib. bdg. 19.60 (978-0-606-35579-7(0)) Turtleback.

Platt, Randall. The Girl Who Wouldn't Die. 2017. (ENG.). 368p. (J). (gr. 8-8). 16.99 (978-1-5107-0809-9(X), Sky Pony Pr.) Skyhorse Publishing Co., Inc.

—Incommunicado. 2017. (ENG.). 352p. (J). (gr. 5-8). pap. 9.99 (978-1-5107-0991-1(6), Sky Pony Pr.) Skyhorse Publishing Co., Inc.

Polacco, Patricia. The Butterfly. 2009. 48p. (J). (gr. k-3). pap. 8.99 (978-0-14-241306-7(2), Puffin Books) Penguin Young Readers Group.

—Tucky Jo & Little Heart. Polacco, Patricia, illus. 2015. (ENG., Illus.). 48p. (J). (gr. -1-3). 19.99 (978-1-4814-1584-2(0), Simon & Schuster Bks. For Young Readers) Simon & Schuster Bks. For Young Readers.

Presley, Daniel & Polders, Claire. A Whale in Paris. McGuire, Erin, illus. 2018. (ENG.). 256p. (J). (gr. 5). 17.99 (978-1-5344-1915-5(2), Atheneum Bks. for Young Readers) Simon & Schuster Children's Publishing.

Preus, Margi. Shadow on the Mountain. 2014. (ENG., Illus.). 320p. (YA). (gr. 3-7). pap. 9.99 (978-1-4197-1159-6(8), 1006603) Abrams, Inc.

Prins, Piet. Hideout in the Swamp. 2006. (Illus.). 136p. (J). pap. (978-1-894666-73-2(9)) Inheritance Pubns.

—The Lonely Sentinel. 2006. (Illus.). 140p. (J). pap. (978-1-894666-72-5(0)) Inheritance Pubns.

Pryor, Bonnie. Simon's Escape: A Story of the Holocaust, 1 vol. 2011. (Historical Fiction Adventures Ser.). (ENG., Illus.). 160p. (J). (gr. 3-5). 31.93 (978-0-7660-3388-7(0), 77eae799-a832-47e4-96ef-4e05fa560d75); pap. 13.88 (978-1-59845-216-7(9), 5304890e-e1fa-4a41-9faf-e8971ad9e71f) Enslow Publishing, LLC.

Razzell, Mary. White Wave. (J). pap. 7.95 (978-0-88899-161-4(4)) Groundwood Bks. CAN. Dist: Publishers Group West (PGW).

Redmond, Shirley Raye. Pigeon Hero! Ettlinger, Doris, illus. 2005. (Ready-to-Read Ser.). 31p. (gr. k-2). 14.00 (978-0-7569-5560-1(2)) Perfection Learning Corp.

—Pigeon Hero! Ettlinger, Doris, illus. 2003. (Ready-To-Reads Ser.). (ENG.). 32p. (J). lib. bdg. 11.89 (978-0-689-85487-3(0), Aladdin Library) Simon & Schuster Children's Publishing.

—Pigeon Hero! Ready-To-Read Level 2. Ettlinger, Doris, illus. 2003. (Ready-To-Read Ser.). (ENG.). 32p. (J). (gr. k-2). pap. 4.99 (978-0-689-85486-6(2), Simon Spotlight) Simon Spotlight.

Reece, Colleen L. Last Page in the Diary. 2011. 94p. pap. 8.95 (978-1-61633-179-5(8)) Guardian Angel Publishing, Inc.

Reid, Charles. Ghost of Heroes Past. 2010. (ENG., Illus.). 170p. pap. 10.95 (978-1-55380-102-3(4)) Ronsdale Pr. CAN. Dist: SPD-Small Pr. Distribution.

—Hurricanes over London. 2005. (ENG., Illus.). 152p. (J). (gr. 3-9). pap., tchr. ed. 8.95 (978-0-921870-82-1(5)) Ronsdale Pr. CAN. Dist: Literary Pr. Group of Canada.

Rice, Dona Herwick & Sugarman, Dorothy Alexander. World War II: Battle of Normandy, 1 vol. rev. ed. 2009. (Reader's

Theater Ser.). (ENG., Illus.). 32p. (gr. 3-8). pap. 11.99 *(978-1-4333-0553-5(4))* Teacher Created Materials, Inc.
Richmond, Caroline Tung. The Darkest Hour. 2016. (ENG.). 320p. (YA). (gr. 7). 17.99 *(978-0-545-80127-0(3),* Scholastic Pr.) Scholastic, Inc.
Rinaldi, Ann. Keep Smiling Through. 2005. (ENG.). 208p. (J). (gr. 3-7). pap. 13.95 *(978-0-15-205399-4(9),* 1196254, Clarion Bks.) HarperCollins Pubs.
RollasonJane. Freddie's War Level 6 Advanced. 2010. (Cambridge Experience Readers Ser.). (ENG.). 128p. pap. 14.75 *(978-84-8323-909-4(4))* Cambridge Univ. Pr.
Romero, R. M. The Dollmaker of Krakow. 2017. (ENG.). 336p. (J). (gr. 3-7). lib. bdg. 19.99 *(978-1-5247-1540-3(9),* Delacorte Bks. for Young Readers) Random Hse. Children's Bks.
Ross, Stewart. Dear Mum, I Miss You! Clark, Linda, illus. 54p. (J). *(978-0-237-52318-3(3))* Evans Brothers, Ltd.
Rothstein, Evelyn. Evelyn & the Two Evas. Uhlig, Elizabeth, illus. 2013. 63p. (YA). pap. 12.95 *(978-0-9834030-5-0(8))* Marble Hse. Editions.
Roy, James. Billy Mack's War. 2004. 245p. (J). pap. *(978-0-7022-3479-8(6))* Univ. of Queensland Pr.
Ruby, Lois. Shanghai Shadows. 2006. (ENG.). 256p. (YA). 16.95 *(978-0-8234-1960-9(6))* Holiday Hse., Inc.
Rushby, Allison. The Turnkey of Highgate Cemetery. 2018. (ENG.). 256p. (J). (gr. 3-7). 15.99 *(978-0-7636-9685-6(4))* Candlewick Pr.
Rylant, Cynthia. I Had Seen Castles. 2004. (ENG.). 128p. (YA). (gr. 7-12). reprint ed. pap. 7.99 *(978-0-15-205312-3(3),* 1196003, Clarion Bks.) HarperCollins Pubs.
—I Had Seen Castles. 2005. 97p. 15.95 *(978-0-7569-5834-3(2))* Perfection Learning Corp.
Sales, Leila. Once Was a Time. 2016. (ENG., Illus.). 272p. (J). (gr. 5-17). 16.99 *(978-1-4521-4009-4(X))* Chronicle Bks. LLC.
—Once Was a Time: (Middle Grade Fiction Books, Friendship Stories for Young Adults, Middle Grade Novels in Verse) 2017. (ENG.). 340p. (J). (gr. 5-9). pap. 7.99 *(978-1-4521-6139-6(9))* Chronicle Bks. LLC.
Salisbury, Graham. Under the Blood Red Sun. 246p. (YA). 22.00 *(978-0-8446-7322-6(6))* Smith, Peter Pub., Inc.
Sanderson, Whitney. Horse Diaries #15: Lily. Sanderson, Ruth, illus. 2018. (Horse Diaries: 15). 160p. (J). (gr. 3-7). pap. 7.99 *(978-1-5247-6654-2(2),* Random Hse. Bks. for Young Readers) Random Hse. Children's Bks.
Sands, Monty. King of Nine Mile Canyon. 2008. 124p. 11.99 *(978-0-615-25788-4(7))* Sands, Monty.
Savit, Gavriel. Anna & the Swallow Man. 2016. (CHI.). 272p. (YA). (gr. 7). pap. *(978-957-33-3251-0(5))* Crown Publishing Co., Ltd.
—Anna & the Swallow Man. 2017. (ENG.). 256p. (YA). (gr. 7). pap. 9.99 *(978-0-553-52208-2(6),* Ember) Random Hse. Children's Bks.
—Anna & the Swallow Man. 2017. lib. bdg. 20.85 *(978-0-606-39876-3(7))* Turtleback.
Schott, Elizabeth, illus. Jake & Sam at the Empty Abbey. 2006. 96p. (J). per. 9.95 *(978-0-9724421-1-4(1))* Fountain Square Publishing.
Schroder, Jack. Dugout. 2004. 190p. (YA). per. 12.95 *(978-0-9745665-6-6(X))* Catalpa Pr.
Schröder, Monika. The Dog in the Wood. 2019. 176p. (J). (gr. 5). pap. 8.95 *(978-1-68437-277-5(1),* Astra Young Readers) Astra Publishing Hse.
Schwartz, Ellen. Heart of a Champion. 2017. 272p. (J). (gr. 4-7). pap. 10.99 *(978-1-77049-881-5(8),* Tundra Bks.) Tundra Bks. CAN. Dist: Penguin Random Hse. LLC.
Sepahban, Lois. Paper Wishes. 2017. (ENG.). 192p. (J). pap. 8.99 *(978-1-250-10414-4(9),* 900163680) Square Fish.
—Paper Wishes. 2017. (J). lib. bdg. 18.40 *(978-0-606-39942-5(9))* Turtleback.
Sepetys, Ruta. Salt to the Sea. l.t. ed. 2016. 500p. 24.95 *(978-1-4104-9287-6(7))* Cengage Gale.
—Salt to the Sea. (ENG.). (YA). (gr. 7). 2017. 448p. pap. 12.99 *(978-0-14-242362-2(9),* Penguin Books) 2016. (Illus.). 400p. 19.99 *(978-0-399-16030-1(2),* Philomel Bks.) Penguin Young Readers Group.
—Salt to the Sea. 2017. lib. bdg. 22.10 *(978-0-606-40492-1(9))* Turtleback.
Seredy, Kate. The Chestry Oak. 2015. (Illus.). 253p. (J). pap. 12.95 *(978-1-930900-81-3(3))* Purple Hse. Pr.
Shepherd, Megan. The Secret Horses of Briar Hill. 2018. (ENG.). 240p. (J). (gr. 5). 9.99 *(978-1-101-93978-9(8),* Yearling) Random Hse. Children's Bks.
Sherman, M. Zachary. A Time for War, 1 vol. Casas, Fritz, illus. 2011. (Bloodlines Ser.). (ENG.). 88p. (J). (gr. 4-8). 27.32 *(978-1-4342-2558-0(5),* 113616, Stone Arch Bks.) Capstone.
Skrypuch, Marsha Forchuk. Making Bombs for Hitler. 2019. (ENG.). 240p. (J). (gr. 3-7). pap. 8.99 *(978-1-338-31283-6(9))* Scholastic, Inc.
—Stolen Girl. 2019. (ENG.). 208p. (J). (gr. 3-7). 17.99 *(978-1-338-23304-9(1),* Scholastic Pr.) Scholastic, Inc.
—The War Below. 2018. (ENG.). 256p. (J). (gr. 3-7). 17.99 *(978-1-338-23302-5(5),* Scholastic Pr.) Scholastic, Inc.
Smelcer, John. Kiska. 2017. (ENG.). 192p. (YA). (gr. 6-11). pap. 12.95 *(978-1-935248-93-4(6))* Leapfrog Pr.
Smith, Annie Laura. The Legacy of Bletchley Park. 2004. (YA). mass mkt. 6.99 *(978-0-9753367-1-7(1))* Onstage Publishing, LLC.
Smith, Icy. Three Years & Eight Months. Kindert, Jennifer C., illus. 2013. (J). *(978-0-9856237-8-4(0))* East West Discovery Pr.
Smith, Roland. Elephant Run. 2009. (ENG.). 336p. (J). (gr. 5-9). pap. 8.99 *(978-1-4231-0401-8(3))* Hyperion Pr.
Smith, Sherri L. Flygirl. 2010. 304p. (YA). (gr. 7-18). 11.99 *(978-0-14-241725-6(4),* Penguin Books) Penguin Young Readers Group.
—Flygirl. 2010. lib. bdg. 19.65 *(978-0-606-14999-0(6))* Turtleback.
Smith, William D. Becoming a Superhero: Adventures of an American Superhero. 2008. 128p. per. 13.95 *(978-1-4327-2071-1(6))* Outskirts Pr., Inc.
Snell, Roy Judson. Sparky Ames of the Ferry Command. Darwin, Erwin L., illus. 2012. 246p. 46.95 *(978-1-258-25306-6(2));* pap. 31.95 *(978-1-258-25572-5(3))* Literary Licensing, LLC.
Sorell, Traci. At the Mountain's Base. Alvitre, Weshoyot, illus. 2019. 32p. (J). (gr. -1-3). 18.99 *(978-0-7352-3060-6(9),* Kokila) Penguin Young Readers Group.
Spinelli, Jerry. Milkweed. 2010. (ENG.). 240p. (YA). (gr. 7). pap. 10.99 *(978-0-375-86147-5(5),* Ember) Random Hse. Children's Bks.
Spradlin, Michael P. Into the Killing Seas. 2015. (J). (ENG.). 224p. (gr. 3-7). 16.99 *(978-0-545-72602-3(6),* Scholastic Pr.); 185p. *(978-0-545-83764-4(2))* Scholastic, Inc.
Spring, Debbie. The Righteous Smuggler, 1 vol. 2005. (Holocaust Remembrance Series for Young Readers Ser.: 6). (ENG., Illus.). 162p. (J). (gr. 4-7). pap. 9.95 *(978-1-896764-97-9(5))* Second Story Pr. CAN. Dist: Orca Bk. Pubs. USA.
Stein, R. Conrad. Someone Talked! 2011. (ENG.). 146p. (J). pap. 8.95 *(978-1-935178-17-0(2),* ChironBooks) Coleman/Perrin.
Stevens, Mitchell. The Village of Lights. Pritchett, Emily, illus. 2018. (ENG.). 32p. (J). (gr. 2-5). 14.99 *(978-1-4621-2275-2(2))* Cedar Fort, Inc./CFI Distribution.
Stier, Catherine. Welcome to America, Champ. Ettlinger, Doris, illus. 2013. (Tales of the World Ser.). (ENG.). 32p. (J). (gr. 1-4). 17.95 *(978-1-58536-606-4(4),* 202360) Sleeping Bear Pr.
Stoltzfus, Donna J. Captive, 1 vol. 2018. (ENG.). 128p. (gr. 3-6). 12.99 *(978-0-7643-5551-6(1),* 9859) Schiffer Publishing, Ltd.
Stone, Phoebe. Romeo Blue. 2013. (ENG.). 352p. (J). (gr. 3-7). 16.99 *(978-0-545-44360-9(1),* Levine, Arthur A. Bks.) Scholastic, Inc.
Sullivan, Jacqueline Levering. Annie's War. 2007. (Illus.). 183p. (J). (gr. 3-7). 15.00 *(978-0-8028-5325-7(0),* Eerdmans Bks For Young Readers) Eerdmans, William B. Publishing Co.
Sullivan, Laura L. Delusion. 2014. (ENG.). 352p. (YA). (gr. 7). pap. 18.99 *(978-0-544-10478-5(1),* 1540787, Clarion Bks.) HarperCollins Pubs.
Sutherland, Robert. Survivor's Leave. 2010. (ENG., Illus.). 176p. pap. 10.95 *(978-1-55380-097-2(4))* Ronsdale Pr. CAN. Dist: SPD-Small Pr. Distribution.
Sutter, Marcus. Soldier Dogs #1: Air Raid Search & Rescue. Kinsella, Pat, illus. 2018. (Soldier Dogs Ser.: 1). (ENG.). 224p. (J). (gr. 3-7). pap. 7.99 *(978-0-06-284403-3(2),* HarperFestival) HarperCollins Pubs.
Swindells, Robert. Doodlebug Alley. (ENG., Illus.). 56p. (J). pap. 6.99 *(978-0-7497-3860-0(X))* Farshore GBR. Dist: Trafalgar Square Publishing.
Tak, Bibi Dumon. Soldier Bear. Philip Hopman, illus. 2011. (ENG.). 158p. (J). 13.00 *(978-0-8028-5375-2(7),* Eerdmans Bks For Young Readers) Eerdmans, William B. Publishing Co.
Tarshis, Lauren. I Survived the Bombing of Pearl Harbor 1941. 2011. (I Survived Ser.: No. 4). lib. bdg. 14.75 *(978-0-606-23744-4(5))* Turtleback.
—I Survived the Bombing of Pearl Harbor, 1941 (I Survived #4), 1 vol. Dawson, Scott, illus. 2011. (I Survived Ser.: 4). (ENG.). 112p. (J). (gr. 2-5). pap. 5.99 *(978-0-545-20698-3(7),* 49b44782-3a49-4716-a4c4-75402e52d8fb, Scholastic Paperbacks) Scholastic, Inc.
—I Survived the Nazi Invasion 1944. 2014. (I Survived Ser.: No. 9). lib. bdg. 14.75 *(978-0-606-35397-7(6))* Turtleback.
—I Survived the Nazi Invasion, 1944 (I Survived #9) 2014. (I Survived Ser.: 9). (ENG., Illus.). 112p. (J). (gr. 3-7). pap. 5.99 *(978-0-545-45938-9(9))* Scholastic, Inc.
Taylor, Mary Ann. Traitors: A Gander's Cove Mystery. Casteel, Kay, illus. 2006. (J). mass mkt. 5.99 *(978-0-9753367-9-3(7))* Onstage Publishing, LLC.
Ter Haar, Jaap. The Ice Road. Mearns, Martha, tr. from DUT. 2005. 157p. (J). (gr. k-9). pap. 5.95 *(978-1-903015-38-4(3))* Barn Owl Bks, London GBR. Dist: Independent Pubs. Group.
Theobald, John Owen. A Kingdom Falls. 2018. (Ravenmaster Trilogy Ser.: 3). (ENG., Illus.). (gr. 7). 320p. (J). 9.99 *(978-1-78497-444-2(7),* 667192, Zephyr); 368p. (YA). 22.95 *(978-1-78497-442-8(0))* Head of Zeus GBR. Dist: Bloomsbury Publishing Plc. Independent Pubs. Group.
Thor, Annika. A Faraway Island. Schenck, Linda, tr. 2011. (Faraway Island Ser.: 1). 256p. (J). (gr. 3-7). 7.99 *(978-0-375-84495-9(3),* Yearling) Random Hse. Children's Bks.
—The Lily Pond. Schenck, Linda, tr. (Faraway Island Ser.). 224p. (J). (gr. 4-7). 2012. 7.99 *(978-0-385-74040-1(9),* Yearling)2. 2013. (ENG.). lib. bdg. 21.19 *(978-0-385-90838-2(5),* Delacorte Pr.) Random Hse. Children's Bks.
Travers, P. L. I Go by Sea, I Go by Land. 2016. (Vmc Ser.). (ENG., Illus.). 208p. (J). (gr. 4-17). 11.99 *(978-0-349-00574-4(5),* Virago Press) Little, Brown Book Group Ltd. GBR. Dist: Hachette Bk. Group.
Tripp, Valerie. Molly Story Collection. Backes, Nick, illus. 2004. (ENG.). 388p. 29.95 *(978-1-59369-458-6(X))* American Girl Publishing, Inc.
Turnbull, Ann. Josie under Fire. 2009. (Historical House Ser.). 176p. (YA). (gr. 5-18). pap. 5.99 *(978-0-7945-2335-0(8),* Usborne) EDC Publishing.
Upjohn, Rebecca. The Secret of Village Fool, 1 vol. Benoit, Renné, illus. 2012. (ENG.). 32p. (J). (gr. 2-4). lib. bdg. 18.95 *(978-1-926920-75-7(9))* Second Story Pr. CAN. Dist: Orca Bk. Pubs. USA.
Van Stockum, Hilda. The Borrowed House. 2016. 203p. (J). pap. *(978-1-930900-89-9(9))* Purple Hse. Pr.
Venkatraman, Padma. Climbing the Stairs. 2010. (ENG., Illus.). 254p. (YA). (gr. 7-18). 10.99 *(978-0-14-241490-3(5),* Speak) Penguin Young Readers Group.
Walters, Eric. Camp 30. 2005. (ENG.). 224p. (J). (gr. 3-7). 6.99 *(978-0-14-301678-6(4),* Penguin Canada) Penguin Canada CAN. Dist: Penguin Random Hse. LLC.
Wang, Gabrielle. The Pearlie Stories: 4 books in one. 2018. (Our Australian Girl Ser.). 496p. (J). (gr. 3-6). 19.99 *(978-0-14-378870-6(1))* Random Hse. Australia AUS. Dist: Independent Pubs. Group.
Watkins, Steve. Sink or Swim: a Novel of World War II. 2017. (ENG.). 272p. (J). (gr. 3-7). 16.99 *(978-1-338-05790-4(1),* Scholastic Pr.) Scholastic, Inc.
Watkins, Yoko Kawashima. So Far from the Bamboo Grove. 2008. (ENG., Illus.). 192p. (J). (gr. 3-7). reprint ed. pap. 9.99 *(978-0-688-13115-9(8),* HarperCollins) HarperCollins Pubs.
Watts, Irene N. Escape from Berlin. 2013. (Illus.). 432p. (J). (gr. 3-7). pap. 17.95 *(978-1-77049-611-8(4),* Tundra Bks.) Tundra Bks. CAN. Dist: Penguin Random Hse. LLC.
—Seeking Refuge, 1 vol. Shoemaker, Kathryn E., illus. 2017. (ENG.). 128p. (J). (gr. 4-7). pap. 15.95 *(978-1-926890-02-9(7))* Tradewind Bks. CAN. Dist: Orca Bk. Pubs. USA.
Webb, Holly. Return to the Secret Garden. (ENG.). (J). (gr. 3-7). 2019. 240p. pap. 11.99 *(978-1-4926-8424-4(4))* 2016. 224p. 16.99 *(978-1-4926-3909-1(5),* 9781492639091) Sourcebooks, Inc.
Weber, Judith Eichler. Seeking Safety. Martin, John F., illus. 2006. (Adventures in America Ser.). (J). *(978-1-893110-46-5(X))* Silver Moon Pr.
Wein, Elizabeth. Code Name Verity. l.t. ed. 2018. (ENG.). (J). pap. 12.99 *(978-1-4328-5038-8(5))* Cengage Gale.
—Code Name Verity. 2012. (ENG.). 352p. (YA). (gr. 9-12). 16.99 *(978-1-4231-5219-4(0))* Little, Brown Bks. for Young Readers.
—Code Name Verity. 2013. (YA). lib. bdg. 20.85 *(978-0-606-31760-3(0))* Turtleback.
—The Pearl Thief. (ENG.). (YA). (gr. 7-12). 2018. 352p. pap. 10.99 *(978-1-4847-2370-8(8))* 2017. 336p. 18.99 *(978-1-4847-1716-5(3))* Hyperion Bks. for Children.
—The Pearl Thief. 2018. (YA). lib. bdg. 20.85 *(978-0-606-40964-3(5))* Turtleback.
—Rose under Fire. 2014. (ENG.). 384p. (YA). (gr. 9-17). pap. 10.99 *(978-1-4231-8469-0(6))* Little, Brown Bks. for Young Readers.
Wells, Helen. Cherry Ames, Army Nurse. 2005. (Cherry Ames Nurse Stories Ser.: Bk. 3). 224p. (J). (gr. 4-7). 14.95 *(978-0-9771597-2-7(8))* Springer Publishing Co., Inc.
—Cherry Ames, Chief Nurse. 2005. (Cherry Ames Nurse Stories Ser.: Bk. 4). 224p. (YA). (gr. 8-12). 14.95 *(978-0-9771597-3-4(6))* Springer Publishing Co., Inc.
—Cherry Ames, Flight Nurse. 2006. (Cherry Ames Nurse Stories Ser.). 224p. (J). (gr. 3-7). 14.95 *(978-0-8261-0397-0(9))* Springer Publishing Co., Inc.
—Cherry Ames, Senior Nurse. 2005. (Cherry Ames Nurse Stories Ser.: Bk. 2). 224p. (J). (gr. 4-7). 14.95 *(978-0-9771597-1-0(X))* Springer Publishing Co., Inc.
West, Nancy. Chips - the War Dog: Based on the True-Life Adventures of the World War II K-9 Hero. 2nd ed. 2004. 183p. (J). per. 8.95 *(978-0-9743659-1-6(2))* Hero Dog Pubns.
Weymouth, Laura E. The Light Between Worlds. (ENG.). (YA). (gr. 8). 2019. 384p. pap. 10.99 *(978-0-06-269688-5(2))* 2018. 368p. 17.99 *(978-0-06-269687-8(4))* HarperCollins Pubs. (HarperTeen).
Whelan, Gloria. Burying the Sun. 2004. 224p. (J). (gr. 5-18). (ENG.). 15.99 *(978-0-06-054112-5(1));* lib. bdg. 16.89 *(978-0-06-054113-2(X))* HarperCollins Pubs.
—Summer of the War. 2006. 163p. (J). (gr. 5-9). lib. bdg. 16.89 *(978-0-06-008073-0(6)); (978-1-4287-0030-7(7))* HarperCollins Pubs.
Wilbur, Helen L. Lily's Victory Garden. Steele, Robert Gantt, illus. 2010. (Tales of Young Americans Ser.). (ENG.). 32p. (J). (gr. 1-4). 16.95 *(978-1-58536-450-3(9),* 202175) Sleeping Bear Pr.
Wilson, John. Flames of the Tiger. 2003. (Illus.). 176p. (J). (gr. 13-18). 6.95 *(978-1-55337-619-4(6))* Kids Can Pr., Ltd. CAN. Dist: Hachette Bk. Group.
—Flames of the Tiger: Germany 1945. 2015. (Fields of Conflict Ser.: 2). (ENG.). 224p. (YA). (gr. 8-12). pap. 12.95 *(978-1-77203-039-6(2),* Wandering Fox) Heritage Hse. CAN. Dist: Orca Bk. Pubs. USA.
Wilson, Kip. White Rose. 2019. (ENG.). 368p. (YA). (gr. 7). 17.99 *(978-1-328-59443-3(2),* 1730256, Versify) HarperCollins Pubs.
Wolf, Joan M. Someone Named Eva. 2009. (ENG., Illus.). 208p. (J). (gr. 5-7). pap. 7.99 *(978-0-547-23766-4(9),* 1083877, Clarion Bks.) HarperCollins Pubs.
Wolfer, Dianne & Harrison-Lever, Brian. Photographs in the Mud. 2007. (Illus.). 32p. pap. 15.50 *(978-1-921361-04-3(2))* Fremantle Pr. AUS. Dist: Independent Pubs. Group.
Wolff, Virginia Euwer. Bat 6. 256p. (J). (gr. 4-6). pap. 4.99 *(978-0-8072-8223-6(5));* 2004. (gr. 5-9). pap. 36.00 incl. audio *(978-0-8072-8222-9(7),* YYA144SP) Random Hse. Audio Publishing Group. (Listening Library).
Woodson, Jacqueline. Coming on Home Soon. Lewis, E. B., illus. 2004. (ENG.). 32p. (J). (gr. k-3). 18.99 *(978-0-399-23748-5(8),* G.P. Putnam's Sons Books for Young Readers) Penguin Young Readers Group.
Wulffson, Don L. Soldier X. 2003. 240p. (YA). (gr. 7-18). 6.99 *(978-0-14-250073-6(9),* Puffin Books) Penguin Young Readers Group.
Wynne-Jones, Tim. The Emperor of Any Place. 2015. 336p. (YA). (gr. 9). 17.99 *(978-0-7636-6973-7(3))* Candlewick Pr.
Yelchin, Eugene. Spy Runner. Yelchin, Eugene, illus. 2019. (ENG., Illus.). 352p. (J). 21.99 *(978-1-250-12081-6(0),* 900173090, Holt, Henry & Co. Bks. For Young Readers) Holt, Henry & Co.
Zindel, Paul. The Gadget. 2003. (ENG., Illus.). 192p. (YA). (gr. 7). mass mkt. 7.99 *(978-0-440-22951-3(0),* Laurel Leaf) Random Hse. Children's Bks.
Zusak, Markus. The Book Thief. 2014. (ENG.). 576p. (YA). 17.24 *(978-1-63245-052-4(6))* Lectorum Pubns., Inc.
—The Book Thief. 2009. 12.64 *(978-0-7848-1941-8(6),* Everbind) Marco Bk. Co.
—The Book Thief. 2008. 552p. (gr. 7-12). 23.00 *(978-0-7569-8440-3(8))* Perfection Learning Corp.
—The Book Thief. (ENG., Illus.). (YA). (gr. 7-12). 2007. 608p. pap. 14.99 *(978-0-375-84220-7(9))* 2013. 592p. pap. 14.99 *(978-0-385-75472-9(8))* Random Hse. Children's Bks. (Knopf Bks. for Young Readers).
—The Book Thief. l.t. ed. 2006. (ENG.). 552p. 23.99 *(978-1-4104-6806-2(2));* 757p. (YA). (gr. 7-12). 24.95 *(978-0-7862-9021-5(8))* Thorndike Pr.
—The Book Thief. 2008. (ENG., Illus.). 560p. pap. *(978-0-552-77389-8(1),* Black Swan) Transworld Publishers Ltd.
—The Book Thief. 2007. 552p. lib. bdg. 24.50 *(978-1-4177-9738-7(X))* 2013. lib. bdg. 24.50 *(978-0-606-34656-6(2))* Turtleback.
—The Book Thief (Anniversary Edition) anniv. ed. 2016. (ENG., Illus.). 592p. (YA). (gr. 7-12). 22.99 *(978-1-101-93418-0(2),* Knopf Bks. for Young Readers) Random Hse. Children's Bks.

WORLD WAR, 1939-1945—FRANCE

D-DAY & the LIBERATION of FRANCE. 2010. (ENG., Illus.). 136p. (gr. 9-18). 35.00 *(978-1-60413-280-9(9),* P179262, Facts On File) Infobase Holdings, Inc.
Draper, Allison Stark. Pastor André Trocmé: Spiritual Leader o the French Village le Chambon. 2009. (Holocaust Biographies Ser.). 112p. (gr. 7-12). 63.90 *(978-1-61513-390-1(9))* Rosen Publishing Group, Inc., The.
Drez, Ronald J. Remember D-Day: The Plan, the Invasion, Survivor Stories. 2015. (Remember Ser.). (Illus.). 64p. (J). (gr. 5-9). pap. 7.99 *(978-1-4263-2245-7(3),* National Geographic Kids) Disney Publishing Worldwide.
Murray, Doug. D-Day, 1 vol. 2007. (Graphic Battles of World War II Ser.). (ENG., Illus.). 48p. (YA). (gr. 5-5). lib. bdg. 37.13 *(978-1-4042-0786-8(4),* 84fc88c9-7171-4a70-aeea-23ee0767a2d2) Rosen Publishing Group, Inc., The.
Platt, Richard. DK Readers L4: d-Day Landings: the Story of the Allied Invasion: The Story of the Allied Invasion. 2004. (DK Readers Level 4 Ser.). (ENG., Illus.). 32p. (J). (gr. 3-7). pap. 4.99 *(978-0-7566-0275-8(0),* DK Children) Dorling Kindersley Publishing, Inc.
Ruelle, Karen Gray & Desaix, Deborah Durland. The Grand Mosque of Paris: A Story of How Muslims Rescued Jews During the Holocaust. 2010. (ENG., Illus.). 40p. (J). (gr. 2-18). pap. 8.99 *(978-0-8234-2304-0(2))* Holiday Hse., Inc.
Williams, Brian. The Normandy Beaches. 2011. (Place in History Ser.). 48p. (YA). (gr. 5-9). lib. bdg. 34.25 *(978-1-84837-675-5(8))* Arcturus Publishing GBR. Dist: Black Rabbit Bks.

WORLD WAR, 1939-1945—GERMANY

Cain, Bill. Battle of the Bulge, 1 vol. 2007. (Graphic Battles of World War II Ser.). (ENG., Illus.). 48p. (YA). (gr. 5-5). lib. bdg. 37.13 *(978-1-4042-0782-0(1),* c8c8efc3-cd37-4e69-b9c4-e6967fa65d69) Rosen Publishing Group, Inc., The.
Chant, Christopher. The Start of World War II: The Flood of the German Tide. 2017. (World War II Ser.: Vol. 5). (ENG., Illus.). 79p. (YA). (gr. 7-12). 24.95 *(978-1-4222-3894-3(6))* Mason Crest.
Davenport, John. The Nuremberg Trials, 1 vol. 2006. (World History Ser.). (ENG., Illus.). 96p. (gr. 7-7). lib. bdg. 41.53 *(978-1-59018-634-3(6),* bfc67b00-10ad-434c-9b50-1b33d7f9a9a6, Lucent Pr.) Greenhaven Publishing LLC.
Drez, Ronald J. Remember D-Day: The Plan, the Invasion, Survivor Stories. 2015. (Remember Ser.). (Illus.). 64p. (J). (gr. 5-9). pap. 7.99 *(978-1-4263-2245-7(3),* National Geographic Kids) Disney Publishing Worldwide.
McIlroy, Michelle. Sophie Scholl: Student Resister & Anti-Nazi Political Activist. 2017. (Spotlight on Civic Courage: Heroes of Conscience Ser.). (Illus.). 48p. (J). (gr. 10-15). 70.50 *(978-1-5383-8108-3(7));* (ENG., (gr. 6-6). pap. 12.75 *(978-1-5383-8107-6(9),* cf78e72c-2428-4e72-8c6c-b30196101a64) Rosen Publishing Group, Inc., The.
O'Reilly, Bill. Hitler's Last Days. 2015. (ENG., Illus.). 320p. (J). pap. *(978-1-62779-455-8(7))* Holt, Henry & Co.
—Hitler's Last Days: The Death of the Nazi Regime & the World's Most Notorious Dictator. 2017. (ENG.). 336p. (J). pap. 14.99 *(978-1-250-08859-8(3),* 900158402) Square Fish.
Rice, Earle, Jr. Blitzrieg! Hitler's Lightning War. 2007. (Monumental Milestones Ser.). (Illus.). 48p. (YA). (gr. 4-7). lib. bdg. 29.95 *(978-1-58415-542-3(6))* Mitchell Lane Pubs.
Saltzwedel, Hans H. Hans' Journal: A Young German's Memories of His Family's Survival During Germany's Darkest Days. 2003. (Illus.). 234p. per. 19.95 net. *(978-1-931934-17-6(7))* Back Yard Pub.
Schloss, Eva & Powers, Barbara. The Promise: The Moving Story of a Family in the Holocaust. Yaron, Sophie, illus. 2006. 160p. (J). (gr. 13-18). 12.99 *(978-0-14-132081-6(8))* Penguin Bks., Ltd. GBR. Dist: Independent Pubs. Group.
Sears, Stephen W. Air War Against Hitler's Germany. 2007. (ENG., Illus.). 124p. pap. 9.95 *(978-1-59687-004-8(4))* IBks., Inc.
Welter, Anni. Child of War: How We Lived & Survived under the Third Reich. 2nd ed. 2003. Orig. Title: Child of the Third Reich: How We Lived & Survived. 160p. (YA). per. 14.95 *(978-0-9741434-0-8(5))* A H W Publishing.
Zaugg, Sandra L. Escape. 2007. (Illus.). 95p. (J). *(978-0-8163-2140-7(X))* Pacific Pr. Pubns.

WORLD WAR, 1939-1945—GREAT BRITAIN

Allport, Allan. The Battle of Britain. 2012. (ENG.). 128p. 35.00 *(978-1-60413-920-4(X),* P218002, Facts On File) Infobase Holdings, Inc.
Byers, Ann. Saving Children from the Holocaust: The Kindertransport, 1 vol. 2012. (Holocaust Through Primary Sources Ser.). (ENG., Illus.). 128p. (gr. 6-7). pap. 13.88 *(978-1-59845-344-7(0),* ef006a13-f6f9-49ac-963c-c8b6cf01445b); lib. bdg. 35.93 *(978-0-7660-3323-8(6),* 5b209fcd-5b79-4241-b064-3d26a7fc54c7) Enslow Publishing, LLC.
Gardner, Faye, et al. A Wartime Childhood, 1 vol. 2011. (When I Was Young Ser.). (ENG., Illus.). 32p. (J). pap. 10.99 *(978-0-237-54384-6(2))* Evans Brothers, Ltd. GBR. Dist: Independent Pubs. Group.
Innes, Stephanie & Endrulat, Harry. Bear on the Homefront, 1 vol. Deines, Brian, illus. 2014. (ENG.). 32p. (J). (gr. k-3). 17.95 *(978-1-927485-13-2(4))* Pajama Pr. CAN. Dist: Publishers Group West (PGW).
Owens, Lisa L. Heroes of Dunkirk. 2018. (Heroes of World War II (Alternator Books (r)) Ser.). (ENG., Illus.). 32p. (J). (gr. 3-6). 30.65 *(978-1-5415-2703-4(8),* 10bb2fd0-86e1-488e-80ee-24f3b134ae11, Lerner Pubns.) Lerner Publishing Group.
Ridley, Sarah. Winston Churchill: ...And World War II. 2013. (History Makers Ser.). (ENG., Illus.). 24p. (J). (gr. 2-4). lib. bdg. 25.65 *(978-1-59771-393-1(7))* Sea-To-Sea Pubns.
Stephens, Chris S. A Wartime Scrapbook. Pack. 2004. (ENG., Illus.). 48p. pap. 42.95 *(978-1-84323-329-9(0))* Beekman Bks., Inc.

ınder Hook, Sue. Winston Churchill: British Prime Minister & Statesman, 1 vol. 2009. (Essential Lives Set 3 Ser.). (ENG., Illus.). 112p. (YA). (gr. 6-12). lib. bdg. 41.36 (978-1-60453-523-5(7), 6675, Essential Library) ABDO Publishing Co.
ıntrob, Kitty. I'm Not Going Back: Wartime Memoir of a Child Evacuee. 2009. (978-0-9784435-1-1(9)) Now & Then Bks.

ORLD WAR, 1939-1945—GUERRILLAS

ee World War, 1939-1945—Underground Movements

ORLD WAR, 1939-1945—HOSPITALS

ee World War, 1939-1945—Medical Care

VORLD WAR, 1939-1945—JAPAN

urgan, Michael. Japanese American Internment. 2017. (Eyewitness to World War II Ser.). (ENG., Illus.). 112p. (J). (gr. 5-9). lib. bdg. 38.65 (978-0-7565-5581-8(7), 135466, Compass Point Bks.) Capstone.
hant, Christopher. The End of World War II: The Japanese Surrender. 2017. (World War II Ser.: Vol. 5). (ENG., Illus.). 79p. (YA). (gr. 7-12). 24.95 (978-1-4222-3898-1(9)) Mason Crest.
—Japanese Aggression in the Pacific. 2017. (World War II Ser.: Vol. 5). (ENG., Illus.). 80p. (YA). (gr. 7-12). 24.95 (978-1-4222-3896-7(2)) Mason Crest.
Grant, R. G. Why Did Hiroshima Happen?, 1 vol. 2010. (Moments in History Ser.). (ENG., Illus.). 48p. (YA). (gr. 6-8). pap. 15.05 (978-1-4339-4164-1(3), 4285aa00-25dc-4d29-8457-40bedebcfee9, Gareth Stevens Secondary Library); lib. bdg. 34.60 (978-1-4339-4163-4(5), 2b6ea7b6-a641-4b5e-86c9-252c57d25795) Stevens, Gareth Publishing LLLP.
Hyde, Natalie. Internment Camps. 2016. (Uncovering the Past: Analyzing Primary Sources Ser.). (ENG., Illus.). 48p. (J). (gr. 5-9). (978-0-7787-2860-3(9)) Crabtree Publishing Co.
King, Margaret. World War II in the Pacific. rev. ed. 2019. (Social Studies: Informational Text Ser.). (ENG., Illus.). 32p. (J). (gr. 4-8). pap. 11.99 (978-1-4258-5071-5(5)) Teacher Created Materials, Inc.
Literature Connections English: So Far from the Bamboo Grove. 2004. (gr. 6-12). (978-0-395-77138-9(2), 2-70216) Holt McDougal.
Lowry, Lois. On the Horizon. Pak, Kenard, illus. 2020. (ENG.). 80p. (J). (gr. 5-7). 16.99 (978-0-358-12940-0(0), 1752988, Clarion Bks.) HarperCollins Pubs.
Ohlenroth, Patricia. Up from the Ashes: Rebuilding Japan after World War II, 1 vol. 2007. (Lucent Library of Historical Eras Ser.). (ENG., Illus.). 104p. (gr. 7-10). lib. bdg. 39.08 (978-1-4205-0028-8(7), 83b6d240-f9e9-4c1b-bd5e-09ab0840e6c3, Lucent Pr.) Greenhaven Publishing LLC.
Peppas, Lynn. Hiroshima & Nagasaki. 2013. (ENG., Illus.). 48p. (J). (978-0-7787-1171-1(4)); pap. (978-0-7787-1179-7(X)) Crabtree Publishing Co.
Sandler, Martin W. Imprisoned: The Betrayal of Japanese Americans During World War II. 2013. (ENG., Illus.). 176p. (J). (gr. 5-8). 24.99 (978-0-8027-2277-5(6), 900074397, Bloomsbury USA Childrens) Bloomsbury Publishing USA.
Smibert, Angie. 12 Incredible Facts about the Dropping of the Atomic Bombs. 2015. (Turning Points in US History Ser.). (ENG., Illus.). 32p. (J). (gr. 3-5). 32.80 (978-1-63235-129-6(3), 12-Story Library) Bookstaves, LLC.
Stein, R. Conrad. World War II in the Pacific: From Pearl Harbor to Nagasaki, 1 vol. 2011. (United States at War Ser.). (ENG., Illus.). 128p. (gr. 5-6). lib. bdg. 35.93 (978-0-7660-3640-6(5), 471c3ce0-e74c-439d-bf93-7548fa85145e) Enslow Publishing, LLC.
Stelson, Caren. A Bowl Full of Peace: A True Story. Kusaka, Akira, illus. 2020. (ENG.). 40p. (J). (gr. 1-5). 18.99 (978-1-5415-2148-3(X), 6e68f323-73fa-4b42-adb2-47050749fd75, Carolrhoda Bks.) Lerner Publishing Group.
—Sachiko: A Nagasaki Bomb Survivor's Story. 2016. (ENG., Illus.). 144p. (J). (gr. 5-12). E-Book 30.65 (978-1-5124-0893-5(X)); E-Book 9.99 (978-1-5124-1884-2(6), 9781512418842); E-Book 30.65 (978-1-5124-1885-9(4), 9781512418859) Lerner Publishing Group. (Carolrhoda Bks.).
Whiting, Jim. The Story of the Attack on Pearl Harbor. 2005. (Monumental Milestones Ser.). (Illus.). 48p. (YA). (gr. 4-7). lib. bdg. 29.95 (978-1-58415-397-9(0)) Mitchell Lane Pubs.

WORLD WAR, 1939-1945—JEWS

Batalion, Judy. The Light of Days Young Readers' Edition: The Untold Story of Women Resistance Fighters in Hitler's Ghettos. (ENG.). 288p. (J). (gr. 5). 2022. pap. 8.99 (978-0-06-303770-0(X)) 2021. (Illus.). 17.99 (978-0-06-303769-4(6)) HarperCollins Pubs. (HarperCollins).
Bernay, Emma & Berne, Emma Carlson. Escaping the Nazis on the Kindertransport. 2017. (Encounter: Narrative Nonfiction Stories Ser.). (ENG., Illus.). 112p. (J). (gr. 3-6). lib. bdg. 30.65 (978-1-5157-4545-7(7), 134269, Capstone Pr.) Capstone.
Blohm, Craig E. Holocaust Rescue & Liberation. 2015. (ENG., Illus.). 80p. (J). lib. bdg. (978-1-60152-844-5(2)) ReferencePoint Pr., Inc.
Brophy Down, Susan. Irena Sendler: Bringing Life to Children of the Holocaust. 2012. (ENG.). 112p. (J). pap. (978-0-7787-2556-5(1)); (Illus.). (978-0-7787-2553-4(7)) Crabtree Publishing Co.
Byers, Ann. Courageous Teen Resisters: Primary Sources from the Holocaust, 1 vol. 2010. (True Stories of Teens in the Holocaust Ser.). (ENG., Illus.). 128p. (gr. 9-10). 35.93 (978-0-7660-3269-9(8), a34fdb7f-26c5-49d1-9d7d-2d7a5ef33d86) Enslow Publishing, LLC.
—Rescuing the Danish Jews: A Heroic Story from the Holocaust, 1 vol. 2012. (Holocaust Through Primary Sources Ser.). (ENG., Illus.). 128p. (gr. 6-7). pap. 13.88 (978-1-59845-343-0(2), 92e1f854-298d-4272-889c-57646367b2ed); lib. bdg. 35.93 (978-0-7660-3321-4(X), 82ad2f9d-f92e-4294-81a4-3a2bd64d9ad3) Enslow Publishing, LLC.
—Saving Children from the Holocaust: The Kindertransport, 1 vol. 2012. (Holocaust Through Primary Sources Ser.). (ENG., Illus.). 128p. (gr. 6-7). pap. 13.88 (978-1-59845-344-7(0), ef006a13-f6f9-49ac-963c-c8b6cf01445b); lib. bdg. 35.93 (978-0-7660-3323-8(6), 5b209fcd-5b79-4241-b064-3d26a7fc54c7) Enslow Publishing, LLC.
Cohen, Robert Z. Jewish Resistance Against the Holocaust, 1 vol. 2014. (Documentary History of the Holocaust Ser.). (ENG., Illus.). 80p. (YA). (gr. 7-7). 37.47 (978-1-4777-7601-8(X), a7fa1035-6c1f-4975-9d7c-d859a532a552) Rosen Publishing Group, Inc., The.
Darman, Peter, ed. The Holocaust & Life under Nazi Occupation, 1 vol. 2012. (World War II Ser.). (ENG., Illus.). 64p. (YA). (gr. 6-6). lib. bdg. 37.13 (978-1-4488-9235-8(X), ccc8b3e4-86a1-4236-9e10-27c64e09e64a) Rosen Publishing Group, Inc., The.
Draper, Allison Stark. Pastor André Trocmé: Spiritual Leader of the French Village le Chambon. 2009. (Holocaust Biographies Ser.). 112p. (gr. 7-12). 63.90 (978-1-61513-390-1(9)) Rosen Publishing Group, Inc., The.
Finkelstein, Norman H. Remember Not to Forget: A Memory of the Holocaust. 2004. (ENG., Illus.). 32p. pap. 16.95 (978-0-8276-0770-5(9)) Jewish Pubn. Society.
Freedman, Jeri. The Warsaw Ghetto & Uprising, 1 vol. 2014. (Documentary History of the Holocaust Ser.). (ENG.). 80p. (YA). (gr. 7-7). 37.47 (978-1-4777-7605-6(2), 0d8ae687-16a1-4b29-bdca-8131f389d9f6) Rosen Publishing Group, Inc., The.
Fremon, David K. Schindler, Wallenberg, Miep Gies: The Holocaust Heroes, 1 vol. 2014. (Remembering the Holocaust Ser.). (ENG.). 96p. (gr. 6-7). 31.61 (978-0-7660-6217-7(1), f93e050f-44cc-4e9f-8dbc-cda3e2be1c4a) Enslow Publishing, LLC.
Gottfried, Ted. Heroes of the Holocaust. Alcorn, Stephen, illus. (Holocaust History Ser.). 112p. (YA). (gr. 7-12). 22.95 (978-1-58013-222-0(7), Kar-Ben Publishing) Lerner Publishing Group.
Greek, Joe. Righteous Gentiles: Non-Jews Who Fought Against Genocide, 1 vol. 2014. (Documentary History of the Holocaust Ser.). (ENG.). 80p. (YA). (gr. 7-7). 37.47 (978-1-4777-7611-7(7), eeeb3c62-d63a-41ef-9a17-b56ccc0151fc) Rosen Publishing Group, Inc., The.
Greenspan, Judy. Irena Sendler: Get to Know the World War II Rescuer. 2019. (People You Should Know Ser.). (ENG., Illus.). 32p. (J). (gr. 3-6). pap. 7.95 (978-1-5435-7465-4(3), 140905); lib. bdg. 29.99 (978-1-5435-7183-7(2), 140434) Capstone.
Hodge, Deborah. Rescuing the Children: The Story of the Kindertransport. 2012. (Illus.). 64p. (J). (gr. 5). 17.95 (978-1-77049-256-1(9), Tundra Bks.) Tundra Bks. CAN. Dist: Penguin Random Hse. LLC.
Hoffman, Amalia. The Brave Cyclist: The True Story of A Holocaust Hero. Fedele, Chiara, illus. 2019. (ENG.). 40p. (J). (gr. 3-4). lib. bdg. 17.95 (978-1-68446-063-2(8), 140522, Capstone Editions) Capstone.
Idzikowski, Lisa. Raoul Wallenberg: Rescuer of Hungarian Jews During the Holocaust. 2017. (Spotlight on Civic Courage: Heroes of Conscience Ser.). (Illus.). 48p. (J). (gr. 10-15). 70.50 (978-1-5383-8118-2(4)); (ENG., (gr. 6-6). pap. 12.75 (978-1-5383-8117-5(6), ea8d7ac5-a3fc-4a6d-9d1d-32106a23dec7) Rosen Publishing Group, Inc., The.
Leyson, Leon. The Boy on the Wooden Box: How the Impossible Became Possible ... on Schindler's List. (ENG., Illus.). (J). (gr. 4-9). 2015. 256p. pap. 9.99 (978-1-4424-9782-5(3)) 2013. 240p. 19.99 (978-1-4424-9781-8(5)) Simon & Schuster Children's Publishing. (Atheneum Bks. for Young Readers).
—The Boy on the Wooden Box: How the Impossible Became Possible ... on Schindler's List. 2015. lib. bdg. 19.65 (978-0-606-36097-5(2)) Turtleback.
Lowery, Zoe & Roberts, Jeremy. Oscar Schindler, 1 vol., 1. 2015. (Holocaust Ser.). (ENG., Illus.). 112p. (J). (gr. 7-7). 38.80 (978-1-4994-6252-4(2), f7cbda7f-67d9-4bd1-88b5-b1c8a4cc01d6, Rosen Young Adult) Rosen Publishing Group, Inc., The.
Mazzeo, Tilar J. Irena's Children: Young Readers Edition; a True Story of Courage. 2016. (ENG., Illus.). 272p. (J). (gr. 5-7). 17.99 (978-1-4814-4991-5(5), McElderry, Margaret K. Bks.) McElderry, Margaret K. Bks.
Mochizuki, Ken. Pasajea la Libertad. 2004. (SPA., Illus.). (J). (gr. k-4). spiral bd. (978-0-616-03091-2(6)) Canadian National Institute for the Blind/Institut National Canadien pour les Aveugles.
—Passage to Freedom: The Sugihara Story. 2005. 19.45 (978-0-7569-4773-6(1)) Perfection Learning Corp.
Murray, Hallie & Jacobs Altman, Linda. Escaping Nazi Atrocities, 1 vol. 2018. (Tales of Atrocity & Resistance: First-Person Stories of Teens in the Holocaust Ser.). (ENG.). 128p. (gr. 7-7). 40.27 (978-0-7660-9827-5(3), c3f61e0d-f5b6-417e-ac43-17c38121a1f2) Enslow Publishing, LLC.
—Hiding from the Nazis, 1 vol. 2018. (Tales of Atrocity & Resistance: First-Person Stories of Teens in the Holocaust Ser.). (ENG.). 128p. (gr. 7-7). 40.27 (978-0-7660-9830-5(3), c3dfeaf2-034f-49aa-b58e-19ee982d1ab0) Enslow Publishing, LLC.
Opdyke, Irene Gut. In My Hands: Memories of a Holocaust Rescuer. 2016. (ENG., Illus.). 288p. (YA). (gr. 9). pap. 10.99 (978-0-553-53884-7(5), Ember) Random Hse. Children's Bks.
Opdyke, Irene Gut & Armstrong, Jennifer. In My Hands: Memories of a Holocaust Rescuer. pap. (978-0-385-72870-6(0)) Knopf Doubleday Publishing Group.
—In My Hands: Memories of a Holocaust Rescuer. 2009. 9.14 (978-0-7848-2512-9(2)); 14.72 (978-0-7848-2511-2(4)) Marco Bk. Co. (Everbind).
Rappaport, Doreen. Beyond Courage: The Untold Story of Jewish Resistance During the Holocaust. 2012. (ENG., Illus.). 240p. (J). (gr. 5). 22.99 (978-0-7636-2976-2(6)) Candlewick Pr.
Rogow, Sally M. Faces of Courage: Young Heroes of World War II. 2008. (ENG., Illus.). 162p. (J). pap. (978-1-894694-67-4(8)) Granville Island Publishing.
Ruelle, Karen Gray. Hidden on the Mountain: Stories of Children Sheltered from the Nazis in le Chambon. DeSaix, Deborah Durland, illus. 2007. (ENG.). 272p. (J). (gr. 5-18). 24.95 (978-0-8234-1928-9(2)) Holiday Hse., Inc.
Ruelle, Karen Gray & Desaix, Deborah Durland. The Grand Mosque of Paris: A Story of How Muslims Rescued Jews During the Holocaust. 2010. (ENG., Illus.). 40p. (J). (gr. 2-18). pap. 8.99 (978-0-8234-2304-0(2)) Holiday Hse., Inc.
Selzer, Anita. I Am Sasha. 2019. 336p. (YA). (gr. 7). 14.99 (978-0-14-378574-3(5)) Penguin Random Hse. AUS. Dist: Independent Pubs. Group.
Simon, Emma & Streissguth, Thomas. Raoul Wallenberg, 1 vol., 1. 2015. (Holocaust Ser.). (ENG., Illus.). 112p. (J). (gr. 7-7). 38.80 (978-1-4994-6242-5(5), 80ac7adc-988d-44a6-975f-71ad0b70e651, Rosen Young Adult) Rosen Publishing Group, Inc., The.
Sís, Peter. Nicky & Vera. 2021. (ENG., Illus.). 64p. (J). (gr. 1-4). 19.95 (978-1-324-01574-1(8), 341574, Norton Young Readers) Norton, W. W. & Co., Inc.
Vaughan, Marcia. Irena's Jars of Secrets, 1 vol. Mazellan, Ron, illus. 2011. (ENG.). 40p. (J). 18.95 (978-1-60060-439-3(0)) Lee & Low Bks., Inc.
—The Story of World War II Hero Irena Sendler, 1 vol. Mazellan, Ron, illus. 2018. (Story Of Ser.). (ENG.). 64p. (J). (gr. 4-8). pap. 8.95 (978-1-62014-791-7(2), leelowbooks) Lee & Low Bks., Inc.
Vaughan, Marcia & Mazellan, Ron. Irena's Jars of Secrets, 1 vol. 2011. (ENG.). 40p. (J). (gr. 2-7). pap. 10.95 (978-1-62014-252-3(X), leelowbooks) Lee & Low Bks., Inc.
Ziemian, Joseph. The Cigarette Sellers of Three Crosses Square. 2005. (Library of Holocaust Testimonies Ser.). (ENG., Illus.). 168p. pap. 19.95 (978-0-85303-686-9(1)) Vallentine Mitchell Pubs. GBR. Dist: Independent Pubs. Group.
Zullo, Allan & Bovsun, Mara. Heroes of the Holocaust: True Stories of Rescues by Teens. 2005. (Illus.). 183p. (J). (978-0-439-67608-3(8)) Scholastic, Inc.

WORLD WAR, 1939-1945—MEDICAL CARE

Lensky, Mordechai. A Physician Inside the Warswa Ghetto. 2009. 257p. (YA). pap. 27.50 (978-0-9814686-3-1(2)) Yad Vashem Pubns. ISR. Dist: Coronet Bks.
Saxby, Claire. Meet... Weary Dunlop. Lord, Jeremy, illus. 2016. 36p. (J). (gr. k-2). 15.99 (978-0-85798-587-3(6)) Random Hse. Australia AUS. Dist: Independent Pubs. Group.

WORLD WAR, 1939-1945—NAVAL OPERATIONS

Grove, Philip D., et al. World War II: The War at Sea, 1 vol. 2010. (World War II: Essential Histories Ser.). (ENG., Illus.). 96p. (YA). (gr. 10-10). lib. bdg. 38.47 (978-1-4358-9131-9(7), 3d0cdabb-69b1-42d1-80fc-600a57da9181) Rosen Publishing Group, Inc., The.
Kevin, McDonald. Tin Can Sailors Save the Day. 2015. (Illus.). 86p. (J). pap. 10.95 (978-1-55571-786-5(1), Paloma Bks.) L & R Publishing, LLC.
Miles, John C. Fighting Forces of World War II at Sea. 2019. (Fighting Forces of World War II Ser.). (ENG., Illus.). 32p. (J). (gr. 3-9). lib. bdg. 28.65 (978-1-5435-7481-4(5), 141002) Capstone.
Mullenbach, Cheryl. Torpedoed! A World War II Story of a Sinking Passenger Ship & Two Children's Survival at Sea. 2017. (ENG., Illus.). 176p. (J). (gr. 5). 17.99 (978-1-61373-824-5(2)) Chicago Review Pr., Inc.
Raum, Elizabeth. World War II Naval Forces, 1 vol. 2013. (You Choose: World War II Ser.). (ENG., Illus.). 112p. (J). (gr. 3-7). pap. 6.95 (978-1-62065-720-1(1), 121705, Capstone Pr.) Capstone.
—World War II Naval Forces: An Interactive History Adventure. 2013. (You Choose: World War II Ser.). (ENG.). 112p. (J). (gr. 3-4). pap. 41.70 (978-1-62065-721-8(X), 19312); (Illus.). lib. bdg. 32.65 (978-1-4296-4780-9(9), 103305) Capstone. (Capstone Pr.).
Sutcliffe, Jane & Kodera, Craig. Chester Nimitz & the Sea, 1 vol. 2013. (ENG., Illus.). 32p. (J). (gr. k-3). 16.99 (978-1-4556-1796-8(2), Pelican Publishing) Arcadia Publishing.
Townsend, John. Navy. 2016. (Action Force: World War II Ser.). 32p. (gr. 3-7). 31.35 (978-1-59920-984-5(5), Smart Apple Media) Black Rabbit Bks.
A True Book: the U. S. Navy in World War II (Library Edition) 2014. (True Book, a — World at War Ser.). (ENG.). 48p. (J). lib. bdg. 31.00 (978-0-531-20497-9(9)) Scholastic Library Publishing.

WORLD WAR, 1939-1945—PACIFIC OCEAN

Beller, Susan Provost. Battling in the Pacific: Soldiering in World War II. 2007. (Soldiers on the Battlefront Ser.). (ENG., Illus.). 112p. (gr. 6-8). lib. bdg. 33.26 (978-0-8225-6381-5(9)) Lerner Publishing Group.
George, Enzo. World War II in the Pacific: War with Japan, 1 vol. 2014. (Voices of War Ser.). (ENG., Illus.). 48p. (gr. 4-4). lib. bdg. 33.07 (978-1-62712-867-4(0), c8c2345e-1193-4d13-9160-520cfd5f7f26) Cavendish Square Publishing LLC.
Horner, D. M. & O'Neill, Robert John. World War II: The Pacific, 1 vol. 2010. (World War II: Essential Histories Ser.). (ENG., Illus.). 96p. (YA). (gr. 10-10). lib. bdg. 38.47 (978-1-4358-9133-3(3), 4abac419-bc3c-4d85-bbbd-8a9445be0639) Rosen Publishing Group, Inc., The.
King, Margaret. World War II in the Pacific. rev. ed. 2019. (Social Studies: Informational Text Ser.). (ENG., Illus.). 32p. (J). (gr. 4-8). pap. 11.99 (978-1-4258-5071-5(5)) Teacher Created Materials, Inc.
Samuels, Charles. Life under Occupation. 2012. (World War II: Sourcebook Ser.). (ENG., Illus.). 48p. (J). (gr. 5-8). lib. bdg. 37.10 (978-1-936333-26-4(0), 16833) Brown Bear Bks.
World Book, Inc. Staff, contrib. by. World War II: Asian & Pacific Fronts. 2019. (Illus.). 128p. (YA). (978-0-7166-3809-4(6)) World Bk., Inc.
—World War II in the Pacific. 2010. (J). (978-0-7166-1510-1(X)) World Bk., Inc.

WORLD WAR, 1939-1945—PERSONAL NARRATIVES

Allen, Thomas B. Remember Pearl Harbor: American & Japanese Survivors Tell Their Stories. 2015. (Remember Ser.). (Illus.). 64p. (J). (gr. 5-9). pap. 7.99 (978-1-4263-2248-8(8), National Geographic Kids) Disney Publishing Worldwide.
Byers, Ann. Trapped: Youth in the Nazi Ghettos: Primary Sources from the Holocaust, 1 vol. 2010. (True Stories of Teens in the Holocaust Ser.). (ENG., Illus.). 128p. (gr. 9-10). 35.93 (978-0-7660-3272-9(8), 9afa1134-8341-4789-8f4b-36170c40f22d) Enslow Publishing, LLC.
Grady, Cynthia. Write to Me: Letters from Japanese American Children to the Librarian They Left Behind. Hirao, Amiko, illus. 32p. (J). (gr. -1-3). 2019. (ENG.). pap. 7.99 (978-1-62354-111-8(5)) 2018. 16.99 (978-1-58089-688-7(X)) Charlesbridge Publishing, Inc.
Jacobs Altman, Linda. Hidden Teens, Hidden Lives: Primary Sources from the Holocaust, 1 vol. 2010. (True Stories of Teens in the Holocaust Ser.). (ENG., Illus.). 128p. (gr. 9-10). 35.93 (978-0-7660-3271-2(X), 4a632054-a5be-4132-9757-692c215d3f24) Enslow Publishing, LLC.
Mihulka, Krystyna & Goddu, Krystyna Poray. Krysia: A Polish Girl's Stolen Childhood During World War II. 2017. (ENG., Illus.). 192p. (J). (gr. 5). 17.99 (978-1-61373-441-4(7)) Chicago Review Pr., Inc.
Nicholson, Dorinda. Remember World War II: Kids Who Survived Tell Their Stories. 2015. (Remember Ser.). (Illus.). 64p. (J). (gr. 5-9). pap. 7.99 (978-1-4263-2251-8(8), National Geographic Kids) Disney Publishing Worldwide.
Opdyke, Irene Gut. In My Hands: Memories of a Holocaust Rescuer. 2016. (ENG., Illus.). 288p. (YA). (gr. 9). pap. 10.99 (978-0-553-53884-7(5), Ember) Random Hse. Children's Bks.
Opdyke, Irene Gut & Armstrong, Jennifer. In My Hands: Memories of a Holocaust Rescuer. pap. (978-0-385-72870-6(0)) Knopf Doubleday Publishing Group.
—In My Hands: Memories of a Holocaust Rescuer. 2009. 9.14 (978-0-7848-2512-9(2)); 14.72 (978-0-7848-2511-2(4)) Marco Bk. Co. (Everbind).
Oppenheim, Joanne. Dear Miss Breed: True Stories of the Japanese American Incarceration During World War II & a Librarian Who Made a Difference. 2006. (ENG., Illus.). 288p. (J). (gr. 7-7). 27.99 (978-0-439-56992-7(3)) Scholastic, Inc.
Reiss, Johanna. The Upstairs Room. 2019. (ENG.). 208p. (J). (gr. 3-7). pap. 9.99 (978-0-06-284980-9(8), HarperCollins) HarperCollins Pubs.
Schomp, Virginia. World War II, 1 vol. 2005. (Letters from the Battlefront Ser.). (ENG., Illus.). 96p. (gr. 6-6). lib. bdg. 36.93 (978-0-7614-1662-3(5), 2ef22db5-a487-414b-9d38-8a7ab9b6be67) Cavendish Square Publishing LLC.
Tunnell, Michael O. Desert Diary: Japanese American Kids Behind Barbed Wire. 2020. (Illus.). 144p. (J). (gr. 4-7). lib. bdg. 19.99 (978-1-58089-789-1(4)) Charlesbridge Publishing, Inc.

WORLD WAR, 1939-1945—PHILIPPINES

Gigliotti, Jim. World War II Prison Breakout! Army Rangers Make Their Mark, Vol. 8. 2018. (Special Forces Stories Ser.). 64p. (J). (gr. 7). 31.93 (978-1-4222-4085-4(1)) Mason Crest.
Otfinoski, Steven. World War II Infantrymen: An Interactive History Adventure. 2013. (You Choose: World War II Ser.). (ENG.). 112p. (J). (gr. 3-4). pap. 41.70 (978-1-62065-717-1(1), 19310, Capstone Pr.) Capstone.

WORLD WAR, 1939-1945—PICTORIAL WORKS

Bradley, James & Powers, Ron. Flags of Our Fathers: A Young People's Edition. 2005. (Illus.). 224p. (YA). (gr. 4-7). mass mkt. 7.99 (978-0-440-22920-9(0), Laurel Leaf) Random Hse. Children's Bks.
—Flags of Our Fathers: Heroes of Iwo Jima. 2003. (ENG., Illus.). 240p. (YA). (gr. 4-7). reprint ed. pap. 8.99 (978-0-385-73064-8(0), Delacorte Bks. for Young Readers) Random Hse. Children's Bks.

WORLD WAR, 1939-1945—POLAND

Brophy Down, Susan. Irena Sendler: Bringing Life to Children of the Holocaust. 2012. (ENG.). 112p. (J). pap. (978-0-7787-2556-5(1)); (Illus.). (978-0-7787-2553-4(7)) Crabtree Publishing Co.
Lensky, Mordechai. A Physician Inside the Warswa Ghetto. 2009. 257p. (YA). pap. 27.50 (978-0-9814686-3-1(2)) Yad Vashem Pubns. ISR. Dist: Coronet Bks.
Selzer, Anita. I Am Sasha. 2019. 336p. (YA). (gr. 7). 14.99 (978-0-14-378574-3(5)) Penguin Random Hse. AUS. Dist: Independent Pubs. Group.
Vaughan, Marcia. Irena's Jars of Secrets, 1 vol. Mazellan, Ron, illus. 2011. (ENG.). 40p. (J). 18.95 (978-1-60060-439-3(0)) Lee & Low Bks., Inc.
Ziemian, Joseph. The Cigarette Sellers of Three Crosses Square. 2005. (Library of Holocaust Testimonies Ser.). (ENG., Illus.). 168p. pap. 19.95 (978-0-85303-686-9(1)) Vallentine Mitchell Pubs. GBR. Dist: Independent Pubs. Group.

WORLD WAR, 1939-1945—PRISONERS AND PRISONS

Benge, Janet & Benge, Geoff. Heroes of History - Louis Zamperini: Redemption. 2014. (ENG.). 218p. (J). pap. 11.99 (978-1-62486-049-2(4)) Emerald Bks.
—Jacob Deshazer: Forgive Your Enemies. 2009. (ENG.). 224p. (YA). pap. 11.99 (978-1-57658-475-0(5)) YWAM Publishing.
Bryant, Jen. Music for the End of Time. Peck, Beth, illus. 2005. 32p. (J). (gr. 4-5). 17.00 (978-0-8028-5229-8(7)) Eerdmans, William B. Publishing Co.
Burgan, Michael. Great Escapes #1: Nazi Prison Camp Escape. Bernardin, James, illus. 2020. (Great Escapes Ser.: 1). (ENG.). 128p. (J). (gr. 3-7). 16.99 (978-0-06-286036-1(4)); pap. 4.99 (978-0-06-286035-4(6)) HarperCollins Pubs. (HarperCollins).
Deem, James M. The Prisoners of Breendonk: Personal Histories from a World War II Concentration Camp. 2015. (ENG., Illus.). 352p. (YA). (gr. 9). 18.99 (978-0-544-09664-6(9), 1539223, Clarion Bks.) HarperCollins Pubs.
Doeden, Matt. Surviving a World War II Prison Camp: Louis Zamperini. 2019. (They Survived (Alternator Books (r)) Ser.). (ENG., Illus.). 32p. (J). (gr. 3-6). 29.32 (978-1-5415-2354-8(7), 7bdb1ea4-c7dc-400a-952c-f0e87a35174b, Lerner Pubns.) Lerner Publishing Group.
—World War II Escapes & Rescues. 2018. (Heroes of World War II (Alternator Books (r)) Ser.). (ENG., Illus.). 32p. (J). (gr. 3-6). lib. bdg. 30.65 (978-1-5415-2152-0(8),

W X Y Z

05db5389-d4bd-4cf8-b332-576519f5e983, Lerner Pubns.) Lerner Publishing Group.

Hickman, Pamela & Cavalluzzo, Jean Smith. Righting Canada's Wrongs: Italian Canadian Internment in the Second World War. 2012. (Righting Canada's Wrongs Ser.). (ENG., illus.). 112p. (gr. 8-12). 34.95 *(978-1-4594-0095-5(X),* 0095) James Lorimer & Co. Ltd., Pubs. CAN. Dist: Formac Lorimer Bks. Ltd.

Hillenbrand, Laura. Unbroken: An Olympian's Journey from Airman to Castaway to Captive (Young Readers Edition) 2017. lib. bdg. 22.10 *(978-0-606-39867-1(8))* Turtleback.

—Unbroken (the Young Adult Adaptation) An Olympian's Journey from Airman to Castaway to Captive. 2017. (ENG.). 320p. (YA). (gr. 7). pap. 14.99 *(978-0-385-74252-8(5),* Ember) Random Hse. Children's Bks.

—Unbroken (the Young Adult Adaptation) An Olympian's Journey from Airman to Castaway to Captive. 2014. (ENG., illus.). 320p. (YA). (gr. 7). 21.99 *(978-0-385-74251-1(7),* Delacorte Pr.) Random Hse. Children's Bks.

Perl, Lila. Behind Barbed Wire: The Story of Japanese-American Internment During World War II, 1 vol. 2003. (Great Journeys Ser.). (ENG., illus.). 112p. (J). (gr. 6-6). 39.79 *(978-0-7614-1321-9(9),* df488a39-ae2b-4b65-97d6-f35a181fcf6a) Cavendish Square Publishing LLC.

Saxby, Claire. Meet Weary Dunlop. Lord, Jeremy, illus. 2015. (Meet... Ser.). (ENG.). 32p. (J). (gr. -1-k). 21.99 *(978-0-85798-536-1(1))* Random Hse. Australia AUS. Dist: Independent Pubs. Group.

—Meet... Weary Dunlop. Lord, Jeremy, illus. 2016. 36p. (J). (gr. k-2). 15.99 *(978-0-85798-587-3(6))* Random Hse. Australia AUS. Dist: Independent Pubs. Group.

Schloss, Eva & Powers, Barbara. The Promise: The Moving Story of a Family in the Holocaust. Yaron, Sophie, illus. 2006. 160p. (J). (gr. 13-18). 12.99 *(978-0-14-132081-6(8))* Penguin Bks., Ltd. GBR. Dist: Independent Pubs. Group.

Weintraub, Robert. No Better Friend: Young Readers Edition: A Man, a Dog, & Their Incredible True Story of Friendship & Survival in World War II. 2018. (ENG., illus.). 304p. (J). (gr. 5-17). pap. 9.99 *(978-0-316-34465-4(6))* Little, Brown Bks. for Young Readers.

Yomtov, Nel. Tunnelling to Freedom: The Great Escape from Stalag Luft III. Valdrighi, Alessandro, illus. 2017. (Great Escapes of World War II Ser.). (ENG.). 32p. (J). (gr. 3-9). lib. bdg. 31.32 *(978-1-5157-3531-1(1),* 133506, Capstone Pr.) Capstone.

WORLD WAR, 1939-1945—REFUGEES

Hoffman, Betty N. Liberation: Stories of Survival from the Holocaust, 1 vol. 2012. (Holocaust Through Primary Sources Ser.). (ENG., illus.). 128p. (gr. 6-7). pap. 13.88 *(978-1-59845-348-5(3),* ae8d4f43-e1b6-42c2-badb-93a219f2338f); lib. bdg. 35.93 *(978-0-7660-3319-1(8),* 5d444e32-dbd3-48fb-83c2-fefb3e94148c) Enslow Publishing, LLC.

Jacobs Altman, Linda. Escape: Teens on the Run: Primary Sources from the Holocaust, 1 vol. 2010. (True Stories of Teens in the Holocaust Ser.). (ENG., illus.). 128p. (gr. 9-10). 35.93 *(978-0-7660-3270-5(1),* 16a24f0b-cc62-468e-842c-5aa7c9118ea4) Enslow Publishing, LLC.

Murray, Hallie & Jacobs Altman, Linda. Escaping Nazi Atrocities, 1 vol. 2018. (Tales of Atrocity & Resistance: First-Person Stories of Teens in the Holocaust Ser.). (ENG.). 128p. (gr. 7-7). 40.27 *(978-0-7660-9827-5(3),* c3f61e0d-f5b6-417e-ac43-17c38121a1f2) Enslow Publishing, LLC.

Williams, Brenda & Williams, Brian. Saving the Persecuted. 2015. (Heroes of World War II Ser.). (ENG., illus.). 48p. (J). (gr. 4-6). 35.32 *(978-1-4109-8046-5(4),* 130125, Raintree) Capstone.

Zaugg, Sandra L. Escape. 2007. (illus.). 95p. (J). *(978-0-8163-2140-7(X))* Pacific Pr. Pubns.

WORLD WAR, 1939-1945—SECRET SERVICE

Burgan, Michael. World War II Spies, 1 vol. 2013. (You Choose: World War II Ser.). (ENG., illus.). 112p. (J). (gr. 3-7). pap. 6.95 *(978-1-62065-722-5(8),* 121706, Capstone Pr.) Capstone.

—World War II Spies: An Interactive History Adventure. 2013. (You Choose: World War II Ser.). (ENG.). 112p. (J). (gr. 3-4). pap. 41.70 *(978-1-62065-723-2(6),* 19313, Capstone Pr.) Capstone.

—World War II Spies: An Interactive History Adventure, 1 vol. 2013. (You Choose: World War II Ser.). (ENG., illus.). 112p. (J). (gr. 3-7). lib. bdg. 32.65 *(978-1-4296-9898-6(5),* 120614, Capstone Pr.) Capstone.

Caravantes, Peggy. The Many Faces of Josephine Baker: Dancer, Singer, Activist, Spy. (Women of Action Ser.). (ENG.). 208p. (YA). (gr. 7). 2018. pap. 14.99 *(978-1-61373-832-0(3))* 2015. (illus.). 19.95 *(978-1-61373-034-8(9))* Chicago Review Pr., Inc.

Cipriano, Jeri. Moe Berg: Spy Catcher. Brooks, Scott R., illus. 2018. (Hidden History — Spies Ser.). (ENG.). 32p. (J). (gr. 2-5). pap. 8.99 *(978-1-63440-294-1(4),* ef609875-eac4-4c2b-890c-414d134f3af7) Red Chair Pr.

Goodman, Michael E. World War II Spies. (Wartime Spies Ser.). (illus.). 48p. (J). (gr. 4-7). 2016. pap. 12.00 *(978-1-62832-208-8(X),* 21094, Creative Paperbacks) 2015. (ENG., *(978-1-60818-603-7(2),* 21093, Creative Education) Creative Co., The.

Jeffrey, Gary. The Secret War. 2012. (ENG., illus.). 48p. (J). *(978-0-7787-4195-4(8))*; pap. *(978-0-7787-4202-9(4))* Crabtree Publishing Co.

McCollum, Sean. Secrets of World War II. 2017. (Top Secret Files Ser.). (ENG., illus.). 32p. (J). (gr. 3-9). lib. bdg. 28.65 *(978-1-5157-4140-4(0),* 133948, Capstone Pr.) Capstone.

Mitchell, Don. The Lady Is a Spy: Virginia Hall, World War II Hero of the French Resistance (Scholastic Focus) 2019. (ENG., illus.). 288p. (YA). (gr. 7-7). 18.99 *(978-0-545-93612-5(8),* Scholastic Nonfiction) Scholastic, Inc.

Payment, Simone. American Women Spies of World War II. 2009. (American Women at War Ser.). 112p. (gr. 8-8). 63.90 *(978-1-61511-399-6(1))* Rosen Publishing Group, Inc., The.

Samuels, Charles. Spying & Security. 2012. (World War II: Sourcebook Ser.). (ENG.). 48p. (J). (gr. 5-8). lib. bdg. 37.10 *(978-1-936333-25-7(2),* 16836) Brown Bear Bks.

Seiple, Samantha. Nazi Saboteurs: Hitler's Secret Attack on America. 2019. (illus.). 206p. (J). pap. *(978-1-338-25919-3(9))* Scholastic, Inc.

—Nazi Saboteurs: Hitler's Secret Attack on America (Scholastic Focus) 2019. (ENG., illus.). 224p. (YA). (gr. 7-7). 17.99 *(978-1-338-25914-8(8),* Scholastic Nonfiction) Scholastic, Inc.

Sheinkin, Steve. Bomb: The Race to Build — And Steal — the World's Most Dangerous Weapon. 2012. (ENG., illus.). 272p. (J). (gr. 5-9). 24.99 *(978-1-59643-487-5(2),* 900056075) Roaring Brook Pr.

—Bomb: The Race to Build — And Steal — the World's Most Dangerous Weapon. 2018. (ENG., illus.). 304p. (J). (gr. 5-9). pap. 16.99 *(978-1-250-05064-9(2),* 900134132) Square Fish.

Small, Cathleen. Code Breakers & Spies of World War II, 1 vol. 2018. (Code Breakers & Spies Ser.). (ENG.). 80p. (J). (gr. 8-8). lib. bdg. 38.79 *(978-1-5026-3853-3(3),* 8e8ea6af-5a7a-4270-a993-896000b0f30a) Cavendish Square Publishing LLC.

WORLD WAR, 1939-1945—SOVIET UNION

Dell, Pamela. The Soviet Night Witches: Brave Women Bomber Pilots of World War II. 2017. (Women & War Ser.). (ENG., illus.). 32p. (J). (gr. 3-9). lib. bdg. 28.65 *(978-1-5157-7938-4(6),* 136031, Capstone Pr.) Capstone.

Gottfried, Ted. The Great Fatherland War: The Soviet Union in World War II. Reim, Melanie K., illus. 2003. (Rise & Fall of the Soviet Union Ser.). 160p. (gr. 7-18). lib. bdg. 28.90 *(978-0-7613-2559-8(X),* Twenty-First Century Bks.) Lerner Publishing Group.

WORLD WAR, 1939-1945—UNDERGROUND MOVEMENTS

Batalion, Judy. The Light of Days Young Readers' Edition: The Untold Story of Women Resistance Fighters in Hitler's Ghettos. (ENG.). 288p. (J). (gr. 5). 2022. pap. 8.99 *(978-0-06-303770-0(X))* 2021. (illus.). 17.99 *(978-0-06-303769-4(6))* HarperCollins Pubs. (HarperCollins).

Chaline, Eric. Secret Heroes of World War II: Tales of Courage from the Worlds of Espionage & Resistance. 2016. (illus.). 224p. (YA). *(978-1-4351-6251-8(X))* Metro Bks.

Hoose, Phillip. The Boys Who Challenged Hitler: Knud Pedersen & the Churchill Club. 2015. (ENG., illus.). 208p. (YA). (gr. 7-12). 19.99 *(978-0-374-30022-7(4),* 900129106, Farrar, Straus & Giroux (BYR)) Farrar, Straus & Giroux.

Hopkinson, Deborah. Courage & Defiance: Stories of Spies, Saboteurs, & Survivors in World War II Denmark. 2015. *(978-0-545-91597-7(X))* Scholastic, Inc.

—Courage & Defiance: Stories of Spies, Saboteurs, & Survivors in World War II Denmark (Scholastic Focus) (ENG.). 352p. (J). (gr. 3-7). 2016. pap. 7.99 *(978-0-545-59221-5(6))* 2015. (illus.). 17.99 *(978-0-545-59220-8(8),* Scholastic Pr.) Scholastic, Inc.

Miles, John C. Fighting Forces of World War II on the Home Front. 2019. (Fighting Forces of World War II Ser.). (ENG., illus.). 32p. (J). (gr. 3-9). lib. bdg. 28.65 *(978-1-5435-7484-5(X),* 141005) Capstone.

Murray, Hallie & Byers, Ann. Teenage Resistance to the Nazi Regime, 1 vol. 2018. (Tales of Atrocity & Resistance: First-Person Stories of Teens in the Holocaust Ser.). (ENG.). 128p. (J). (gr. 7-7). 40.27 *(978-0-7660-9842-8(7),* b9f6cafd-478c-425e-a00a-c0707535672e) Enslow Publishing, LLC.

Sahgal, Lara & Axelrod, Toby. Hans & Sophie Scholl, 1 vol., 1. 2015. (Holocaust Ser.). (ENG., illus.). 112p. (J). (gr. 7-7). 38.80 *(978-1-4994-6244-9(1),* d62f6a9f-fda2-48c5-9508-bfd454fe78f0, Rosen Young Adult) Rosen Publishing Group, Inc., The.

Walsh, Alison. Hugh O'Flaherty: His Wartime Adventures. 2011. (ENG., illus.). 114p. (J). pap. 4.99 *(978-1-84889-058-9(3),* Collins Pr., The) M.H. Gill & Co. U. C. IRL. Dist: Vearsa.

WORLD WAR, 1939-1945—UNITED STATES

Bjorklund, Ruth. Internment: Japanese Americans in World War II, 1 vol. 2016. (Public Persecutions Ser.). (ENG., illus.). 128p. (J). (gr. 9-9). 47.36 *(978-1-5026-2323-2(4),* 8ba43ff0-9098-489a-a112-40427750d362) Cavendish Square Publishing LLC.

Burgan, Michael. America in World War II, 1 vol. 2006. (Wars That Changed American History Ser.). (ENG.). 48p. (gr. 5-8). pap. 15.05 *(978-0-8368-7302-3(5),* 3c7c7b65-4d09-4e9e-b736-d5a5ae7f7da9); (illus.). lib. bdg. 33.67 *(978-0-8368-7293-4(2),* 146d02e3-54e1-4273-bbfe-d7aac9260076) Stevens, Gareth Publishing LLLP. (Gareth Stevens Secondary Library).

Center for Learning Staff. World War II: 1935-1945 — Elementary U. S. History Series, 10 bks. 2003. (Social Studies Ser.). (illus.). vi, 147p. (J). tchr. ed., spiral bd. 29.95 *(978-1-56077-737-3(0))* Center for Learning, The.

Donohue, Moira Rose. The Invasion of Normandy: Epic Battle of World War II. 2017. (Major Battles in US History Ser.). (ENG., illus.). 32p. (J). (gr. 3-5). pap. 9.95 *(978-1-63517-080-1(X),* 163517080X, Focus Readers) North Star Editions.

Dougherty, Steve. Pearl Harbor: The U. S. Enters World War II. 2009. (24/7 Goes to War Ser.). (ENG.). 64p. (J). (gr. 5-8). lib. bdg. 22.44 *(978-0-531-25525-4(5))* Scholastic Library Publishing.

—Pearl Harbor: the U. S. Enters World War II (24/7: Goes to War) 2009. (24/7: Goes to War Ser.). (ENG.). 64p. (J). (gr. 6-12). pap. 7.95 *(978-0-531-25450-9(X),* Watts, Franklin) Scholastic Library Publishing.

Garstecki, Julia. Go for Broke Regiment. 2016. (All-American Fighting Forces Ser.). (ENG.). 32p. (J). (gr. 4-6). pap. 9.99 *(978-1-64466-152-9(7),* 10310); (illus.). 31.35 *(978-1-68072-001-3(5),* 10309) Black Rabbit Bks. (Bolt).

Gitlin, Martin. The Great Depression & World War II: 1929-1945. 2007. (Presidents of the United States Ser.). (illus.). 48p. (J). (gr. 4-7). lib. bdg. 29.05 *(978-1-59036-749-0(9))*; per. 10.95 *(978-1-59036-750-6(2))* Weigl Pubs., Inc.

—World War II U. S. Homefront: A History Perspectives Book. 2014. (Perspectives Library). (ENG., illus.). 32p. (J). (gr. 4-8). 32.07 *(978-1-63137-621-4(7),* 205267) Cherry Lake Publishing.

Gitlin, Marty. World War II. 2016. (illus.). 48p. (J). *(978-1-5105-1296-2(9))* SmartBook Media, Inc.

Grant, R. G. Why Did Hiroshima Happen?, 1 vol. 2010. (Moments in History Ser.). (ENG., illus.). 48p. (YA). (gr. 6-8). pap. 15.05 *(978-1-4339-4164-1(3),* 4285aa00-25dc-4d29-8457-40bedebcfee9, Gareth Stevens Secondary Library); lib. bdg. 34.60 *(978-1-4339-4163-4(5),* 2b6ea7b6-a641-4b5e-86c9-252c57d25795) Stevens, Gareth Publishing LLLP.

Henzel, Cynthia Kennedy. The USS Arizona Story. 2017. (Famous Ships Ser.). (ENG., illus.). 112p. (J). (gr. 6-12). lib. bdg. 41.36 *(978-1-5321-1322-2(6),* 27530, Essential Library) ABDO Publishing Co.

Isgro, Bailey Sisoy & Lapointe, Nicole. Rosie, a Detroit Herstory. 2018. (Great Lakes Books Ser.). (ENG., illus.). 40p. 16.99 *(978-0-8143-4544-3(1),* P589729) Wayne State Univ. Pr.

Jones, Tina C. Mothballs, Mothballs All in the Hall: Memories of a Great World War II Hero. Jones, Tina C. & Balogh, Jared, illus. 2012. 48p. pap. 24.95 *(978-1-4560-7483-8(0))* America Star Bks.

Künstler, Mort, illus. World War II: 1939-1945. 2016. (ENG.). 48p. (J). (gr. 2-5). 13.95 *(978-0-7892-1261-0(7),* 791261, Abbeville Kids) Abbeville Pr., Inc.

Marcovitz, Hal. Cause & Effect: World War II. 2017. (ENG.). 80p. (YA). (gr. 5-12). *(978-1-68282-174-9(9))* ReferencePoint Pr., Inc.

Marrin, Albert. FDR & the American Crisis. 2015. (illus.). 336p. (YA). (gr. 7). 24.99 *(978-0-385-75359-3(4),* Knopf Bks. for Young Readers) Random Hse. Children's Bks.

McNeill, Allison & Hanes, Richard Clay. American Home Front in World War II Reference Library Cumulative Index. 2004. (American Homefront in World War II Reference Library). (ENG.). 32p. 5.00 *(978-0-7876-9125-7(9),* UXL) Cengage Gale.

Mundy, Liza. Code Girls: The True Story of the American Women Who Secretly Broke Codes in World War II (Young Readers Edition) (ENG., illus.). 336p. (J). (gr. 3-7). 2019. pap. 8.99 *(978-0-316-35377-9(9))* 2018. 17.99 *(978-0-316-35373-1(6))* Little, Brown Bks. for Young Readers.

National Geographic Learning. Reading Expeditions (Social Studies: Seeds of Change in American History): the Home Front During World War II. 2007. (Nonfiction Reading & Writing Workshops Ser.). (ENG., illus.). 40p. pap. 21.95 *(978-0-7922-4558-2(X))* CENGAGE Learning.

Oppenheim, Joanne. Dear Miss Breed: True Stories of the Japanese American Incarceration During World War II & a Librarian Who Made a Difference. 2006. (ENG., illus.). 288p. (J). (gr. 7-7). 27.99 *(978-0-439-56992-7(3))* Scholastic, Inc.

Petersen, Christine. Rosie the Riveter. 2008. (Cornerstones of Freedom Ser.). (ENG.). 48p. (J). pap. 5.95 *(978-0-531-20840-3(0),* Children's Pr.) Scholastic Library Publishing.

Peterson, Sheryl. The Great Depression & World War II. 2011. (Explorer Library: Language Arts Explorer Ser.). (ENG.). 32p. (gr. 4-8). pap. 14.21 *(978-1-61080-287-1(X),* 201210); (illus.). lib. bdg. 32.07 *(978-1-61080-199-7(7),* 201174) Cherry Lake Publishing.

Rice, Earle, Jr. How Franklin D. Roosevelt Fought World War II, 1 vol. 2017. (Presidents at War Ser.). (ENG.). 128p. (gr. 8-8). lib. bdg. 38.93 *(978-0-7660-8527-5(9),* 90068e3a-c02b-490c-960b-c2d1bf00735c) Enslow Publishing, LLC.

Rodgers, Kelly. World War II in Europe. rev. ed. 2019. (Social Studies: Informational Text Ser.). (ENG., illus.). 32p. (J). (gr. 4-8). pap. 11.99 *(978-1-4258-5070-8(7))* Teacher Created Materials, Inc.

Roppelt, Donna. Women Go to Work, 1941-1945. 2012. (J). pap. *(978-1-4222-2367-3(1))* Mason Crest.

—Women Go to Work, 1941-1945. Harrington, A. Page, ed. 2012. (Finding a Voice: Women's Fight for Equality in U. S. Society Ser.). 64p. (J). (gr. 5). 22.95 *(978-1-4222-2357-4(4))* Mason Crest.

Rose, Simon. World War II: 1939-1945. 2014. (illus.). 48p. (J). *(978-1-62127-659-3(7))* Weigl Pubs., Inc.

Rubin, Susan Goldman. The Flag with Fifty-Six Stars: A Gift from the Survivors of Mauthausen. Farnsworth, Bill, illus. 2006. (ENG.). 40p. (J). (gr. 1-5). reprint ed. 6.95 *(978-0-8234-2019-3(1))* Holiday Hse., Inc.

Shoup, Kate. Rosie the Riveter: A Cultural Icon, 1 vol. Landsberg, Bryan, illus. 2018. (American Legends & Folktales Ser.). (ENG.). 32p. (gr. 3-3). lib. bdg. 30.21 *(978-1-5026-3693-5(X),* 3efa2bf7-cf7c-4c59-b898-593c0b2accf4) Cavendish Square Publishing LLC.

Stein, R. Conrad. World War II in the Pacific: From Pearl Harbor to Nagasaki, 1 vol. 2011. (United States at War Ser.). (ENG., illus.). 128p. (gr. 5-6). lib. bdg. 35.93 *(978-0-7660-3640-6(5),* 471c3ce0-e74c-439d-bf93-7548fa85145e) Enslow Publishing, LLC.

Stone, Tanya Lee. Courage Has No Color, the True Story of the Triple Nickles: America's First Black Paratroopers. 2013. (ENG., illus.). 160p. (J). (gr. 5). pap. 17.99 *(978-0-7636-6548-7(7))*; 24.99 *(978-0-7636-5117-6(6))* Candlewick Pr.

Taylor, Charlotte & Kent, Deborah. The Internment of Japanese Americans, 1 vol. 2015. (Our Shared History Ser.). (ENG., illus.). 128p. (J). (gr. 7-7). lib. bdg. 38.93 *(978-0-7660-7008-0(5),* 2cb03d49-bd3c-43a8-aa2c-98c8dbbae5af) Enslow Publishing, LLC.

A True Book: the U. S Army in World War II (Library Edition) 2014. (ENG.). 48p. (J). lib. bdg. 29.00 *(978-0-531-20496-2(0))* Scholastic Library Publishing.

Wallenfeldt, Jeff, ed. A New World Power: America from 1920 To 1945, 4 vols. 2012. (Documenting America: the Primary Source Documents of a Nation Ser.). (ENG., illus.). 168p. (YA). (gr. 10-10). 89.42 *(978-1-61530-784-5(2),* 06045b1f-3f45-492d-a2c0-1e7c79a7221d) Rosen Publishing Group, Inc., The.

Wallenfeldt, Jeffrey H. A New World Power: America from 1920 to 1945, 1 vol. 2012. (Documenting America: the Primary Source Documents of a Nation Ser.). (ENG., illus.). 168p. (J). (gr. 10-10). lib. bdg. 44.71 *(978-1-61530-694-7(3),* 464203e0-e791-4a10-b121-3bocef65d268) Rosen Publishing Group, Inc., The.

Whiting, Jim. The Story of the Attack on Pearl Harbor. 2005. (Monumental Milestones Ser.). (illus.). 48p. (YA). (gr. 4-7). lib. bdg. 29.95 *(978-1-58415-397-9(0))* Mitchell Lane Pubs.

Whitman Publishing, creator. Discover World War II: History Project Toolkit. 2011. pap. 19.95 *(978-0-7948-3588-0(0))* Whitman Publishing LLC.

WORLD WIDE WEB

see also Internet

Doyle, Eamon, ed. The Dark Web, 1 vol. 2019. (Current Controversies Ser.). (ENG.). 200p. (gr. 10-12). pap. 33.00 *(978-1-5345-0606-0(3),* a29a3da6-93cc-45bd-af18-b159560ea9ba, Greenhaven Publishing) Greenhaven Publishing LLC.

Green, Sara. Sergey Brin. 2014. (Tech Icons Ser.). (ENG., illus.). 24p. (J). (gr. 3-8). lib. bdg. 27.95 *(978-1-60014-993-1(6),* Pilot Bks.) Bellwether Media.

Hamilton, John. Internet, 1 vol. 2005. (Straight to the Source Ser.). (ENG., illus.). 32p. (gr. k-6). 27.07 *(978-1-59197-544-1(1),* Checkerboard Library) ABDO Publishing Co.

Hixson, Bryce. The Original World Wide Web. Hixson, Bryce, illus. 2003. (illus.). (J). per. 12.95 *(978-1-931801-07-2(X))* Loose In The Lab.

Minton, Eric. Spam & Scams: Using Email Safely, 1 vol., 1. 2014. (Stay Safe Online Ser.). (ENG.). 32p. (J). (gr. 4-5). 28.93 *(978-1-4777-2934-2(8),* 6591d669-16fb-4e43-a439-ce46dbd1e7ba, PowerKids Pr.) Rosen Publishing Group, Inc., The.

Owings, Lisa. Stay Safe Online. 2013. (Library Smarts Ser.). (ENG., illus.). 24p. (J). (gr. -1-2). lib. bdg. 23.99 *(978-1-4677-1505-8(0),* b6683641-9e17-4ae4-a386-f9e1305366fd, Lerner Pubns.) Lerner Publishing Group.

Popek, Emily. Understanding the World of User-Generated Content, 1 vol. 2010. (Digital & Information Literacy Ser.). (ENG.). 48p. (YA). (gr. 6-6). pap. 12.75 *(978-1-4488-0598-3(8),* 7f64d7e5-de62-433d-8f83-3d262f95b277); lib. bdg. 33.47 *(978-1-4358-9431-0(6),* 7bf81bc7-128e-4177-84b3-187fe2455167) Rosen Publishing Group, Inc., The. (Rosen Reference).

Porterfield, Jason. Tim Berners-Lee, 1 vol., 1. 2015. (Tech Pioneers Ser.). (ENG.). 112p. (J). (gr. 7-7). 38.80 *(978-1-4994-6290-6(5),* 634d8e95-2000-46a6-a1a2-aec3f6879496, Rosen Young Adult) Rosen Publishing Group, Inc., The.

Randolph, Ryan P. New Research Techniques: Getting the Most Out of Search Engine Tools, 1 vol. 2011. (Digital & Information Literacy Ser.). (ENG., illus.). 48p. (J). (gr. 6-6). pap. 12.75 *(978-1-4488-2292-8(0),* 3d79a5df-3c56-4c8a-8e18-dc596f889809); lib. bdg. 33.47 *(978-1-4488-1321-6(2),* b78b8bdc-252c-46c9-b581-6a449eeaea08) Rosen Publishing Group, Inc., The. (Rosen Reference).

Scientific American Staff. The Future of the Web. 2009. (Scientific American Cutting-Edge Science Ser.). 118p. (gr. 9-9). 63.90 *(978-1-60853-081-6(7))* Rosen Publishing Group, Inc., The.

Vanden-Heuvel, John C., Sr. & Ostrovsky, Andrey. ABCs of the Web. Holmes, Tom, illus. 2016. (ENG.). 28p. (J). (gr. -1-3). bds. 8.99 *(978-1-4998-0312-9(5))* Little Bee Books Inc.

Web Wisdom, 12 vols. 2014. (Web Wisdom Ser.). (ENG.). 48p. (J). (gr. 5-5). lib. bdg. 198.42 *(978-1-5026-0316-6(0),* 38c1304a-e8be-4c69-b2c4-bcd0e964b77b, Cavendish Square) Cavendish Square Publishing LLC.

Yearling, Tricia. The Internet: What It Is & How to Use It, 1 vol. 2015. (Zoom in on Technology Ser.). (ENG., illus.). 24p. (gr. 2-2). lib. bdg. 25.60 *(978-0-7660-7382-1(3),* 41e06e3f-14f8-405a-b447-b2c001dbe7f4) Enslow Publishing, LLC.

—The World Wide Web: What It Is & How to Use It, 1 vol. 2015. (Zoom in on Technology Ser.). (ENG., illus.). 24p. (gr. 2-2). pap. 10.95 *(978-0-7660-7386-9(6),* 45bcbc73-d195-4841-9729-b6fdfe576990) Enslow Publishing, LLC.

WORLD'S FAIRS

see Exhibitions; Fairs

WORMS

Alessi, Jolene. Zombie Fish, 1 vol. 2015. (Zombie Animals: Parasites Take Control! Ser.). (ENG., illus.). 24p. (J). (gr. 2-3). pap. 9.15 *(978-1-4824-2840-7(7),* 14471fc0-e230-4025-9308-ce45a1bb2975) Stevens, Gareth Publishing LLLP.

Bergeron, Alain M. & Quintin, Michel. Do You Know Leeches?, 1 vol. Sampar, illus. 2013. (Do You Know? Ser.). (ENG.). 64p. (J). (gr. 2-4). pap. 9.95 *(978-1-55455-318-1(0),* 39b99820-62ee-4051-a87f-4d06b5fa244d) Trifolium Bks., Inc. CAN. Dist: Firefly Bks., Ltd.

Black, Nessa. Worms. (Spot Creepy Crawlies Ser.). (ENG.). 16p. (J). (gr. -1-2). 2018. pap. 7.99 *(978-1-68152-230-2(6),* 14761) 2017. 17.95 *(978-1-68151-111-5(8),* 14642) Amicus.

Bodden, Valerie. Creepy Creatures: Worms. 2011. (Creepy Creatures Ser.). (ENG.). 24p. (J). (gr. 1-3). pap. 9.99 *(978-0-89812-570-2(7),* 22141, Creative Paperbacks) Creative Co., The.

—Worms. 2011. (Creepy Creatures Ser.). (ENG.). 24p. (J). (gr. 1-4). 24.25 *(978-1-58341-997-7(7),* 22136, Creative Education) Creative Co., The.

—Worms. 2010. (ENG., illus.). 24p. (J). pap. 8.95 *(978-1-926853-77-2(6))* Saunders Bk. Co. CAN. Dist: Creative Co., The.

Cheek, Diane. Wiggly Workers. 2011. 28p. pap. 12.03 *(978-1-4634-0022-4(5))* AuthorHouse.

Ciletti, Barbara. Roundworms. 2016. (Awful, Disgusting Parasites Ser.). (ENG.). 32p. (J). (gr. 4-6). pap. 9.99 *(978-1-64466-139-0(X),* 10258); (illus.). 31.35 *(978-1-68072-009-9(0),* 10257) Black Rabbit Bks. (Bolt).

—Tapeworms. 2016. (Awful, Disgusting Parasites Ser.). (ENG.). 32p. (J). (gr. 4-6). pap. 9.99 *(978-1-64466-140-6(3),* 10262); (illus.). 31.35 *(978-1-68072-010-5(4),* 10261) Black Rabbit Bks. (Bolt).

Clark, Willow & Rockwood, Leigh. Worms Are Gross!, 1 vol. 2010. (Creepy Crawlies Ser.). (ENG., illus.). 24p. (gr. 2-3). (J). pap. 9.25 *(978-1-4488-1361-2(1),* 5da9a814-43d8-4a8d-a90c-6a50d23f3416, PowerKids Pr.); (YA). lib. bdg. 26.27 *(978-1-4488-0700-0(X),*

96faee34-cae4-4e0d-92ed-13b94be7bfe5) Rosen Publishing Group, Inc., The.

Coleman, Miriam. Leeches Eat Blood!, 1 vol., 1. 2013. (Disgusting Animal Dinners Ser.). (ENG.). 24p. (J). (gr. 2-3). 26.27 (978-1-4777-2881-9(3), 6c42d353-617c-4341-be32-5fdc806d94ab, PowerKids Pr.) Rosen Publishing Group, Inc., The.

vans, Arthur V. Grzimek's Student Animal Life Resource: Crustaceans, Mollusks & Segmented Worms. Harris, Madeline S. et al, eds. 2005. (Grzimek's Student Animal Life Resource Ser.). (ENG., Illus.). 384p. (J). (gr. 3-7). 129.00 (978-0-7876-9411-1(8), UXL) Cengage Gale.

Gravel, Elise. The Worm: The Disgusting Critters Series. (Disgusting Critters Ser.). (ENG., Illus.). 32p. (J). (gr. 1-4). 2016. pap. 5.99 (978-1-101-91841-8(1)) 2014. 10.99 (978-1-77049-633-0(5)) Tundra Bks. CAN. (Tundra Bks.). Dist: Penguin Random Hse. LLC.

Gray, Susan H. Junior Scientists: Experiment with Bugs. 2010. (Explorer Junior Library: Science Explorer Junior Ser.). (ENG., Illus.). 32p. (gr. 3-6). lib. bdg. 32.07 (978-1-60279-842-7(7), 200550) Cherry Lake Publishing.

Green, Jen. Worms. 2009. (Illus.). 52p. (J). (978-0-7172-8078-0(0)) Grolier, Ltd.

Gregson, Agatha. I See a Worm, 1 vol. 2018. (In My Backyard Ser.). (ENG.). 24p. (gr. k-k). 25.27 (978-1-5382-2876-0(9), 9ec74d12-df04-4e6e-af5e-c0e63203207b) Stevens, Gareth Publishing LLLP.

Hanson, Lynne. Worm World: Clue Books. 2008. (Illus.). 32p. (J). pap. 4.00 (978-1-58793-226-7(1)) Creekside Publishing.

Inserra, Rose. Worms, 1 vol. 2010. (Weird, Wild, & Wonderful Ser.). (ENG., Illus.). 24p. (J). (gr. 2-3). lib. bdg. 24.67 (978-1-4339-3577-0(5), 8513f8cc-a119-4a93-b087-c9660b9d9575, Gareth Stevens Learning Library) Stevens, Gareth Publishing LLLP.

Kalman, Bobbie. The Life Cycle of an Earthworm. 2003. (Life Cycle Ser.). (ENG., Illus.). 32p. (J). pap. (978-0-7787-0696-0(6)) Crabtree Publishing Co.

—Les Vers de Terre. 2009. (Petit Monde Vivant Ser.). (FRE., Illus.). 32p. (J). pap. 9.95 (978-2-89579-228-4(3)) Bayard Canada Livres CAN. Dist: Crabtree Publishing Co.

Kawa, Katie. Tapeworms, 1 vol. 2015. (Freaky Freeloaders: Bugs That Feed on People Ser.). (ENG.). 24p. (J). (gr. 2-3). 25.27 (978-1-4994-0765-5(3), 770e19ad-9b96-4236-b145-6b8fc0d033b5, PowerKids Pr.) Rosen Publishing Group, Inc., The.

Kelly, Joni. 250-Year-Old Tube Worms!, 1 vol. 2018. (World's Longest-Living Animals Ser.). (ENG.). 24p. (gr. 1-2). 24.27 (978-1-5382-1689-7(2), f403b158-8ee8-4927-827f-c34665f8570b) Stevens, Gareth Publishing LLLP.

Kite, L. Patricia. Leeches. 2004. (Early Bird Nature Bks.). (ENG., Illus.). 48p. (gr. 2-5). 26.60 (978-0-8225-3054-1(6), Lerner Pubns.) Lerner Publishing Group.

Lane, Bonnie. Bob the Inchworm & the Four Seasons. 2009. 20p. pap. 11.00 (978-1-4389-9833-6(3)) AuthorHouse.

Lehman, Julie. Kyle in His Compost Pile: The Story of a Red Wiggler. 2010. 28p. pap. 14.99 (978-1-4490-9112-5(1)) AuthorHouse.

Mitchell, Susan K. Biggest vs. Smallest Creepy, Crawly Creatures, 1 vol. 2010. (Biggest vs. Smallest Animals Ser.). (ENG., Illus.). 24p. (gr. k-2). 25.27 (978-0-7660-3581-2(6), 4e77b2a2-6e9d-4810-a5ff-98770a3c0885, Enslow Elementary) Enslow Publishing, LLC.

Murray, Laura K. Worms. (Seedlings Ser.). (ENG.). 24p. (J). (gr. -1-k). 2016. pap. 7.99 (978-1-62832-190-6(3), 21039, Creative Paperbacks) 2015. (Illus.). (978-1-60818-585-6(0), 21038, Creative Education) Creative Co., The.

Nelson, Robin. Worms. 2009. pap. 34.95 (978-0-7613-4111-6(0)) Lerner Publishing Group.

Neuman, Pearl. Bloodsucking Leeches. 2009. (No Backbone! Ser.). (Illus.). 24p. (J). (gr. k-3). lib. bdg. 26.99 (978-1-59716-755-0(X)) Bearport Publishing Co., Inc.

Patterson, Jack K. Worms, 1 vol. 2018. (Creepy Crawlers Ser.). (ENG.). 24p. (gr. 1-1). lib. bdg. 25.93 (978-1-5026-4272-1(7), cf1b067f-babe-4163-bc39-73ca01a661aa) Cavendish Square Publishing LLC.

Peters, Polly. The Wim Wom from the Mustard Mill. Angeletti, Roberta, illus. 2008. (Child's Play Library). (ENG.). 32p. (J). (gr. -1-3). pap. (978-1-84643-253-8(7)) Child's Play International Ltd.

Schuetz, Kari. Mealworms. 2015. (Creepy Crawlies Ser.). (ENG., Illus.). 24p. (J). (gr. k-3). lib. bdg. 26.95 (978-1-62617-224-1(2), Blastoff! Readers) Bellwether Media.

Smalley, Carol. A Project Guide to Sponges, Worms, & Mollusks. 2010. (Life Science Projects for Kids Ser.). (Illus.). 48p. (J). (gr. 4-8). lib. bdg. 29.95 (978-1-58415-876-9(X)) Mitchell Lane Pubs.

Sobol, Richard. The Story of Silk: From Worm Spit to Woven Scarves. Sobol, Richard, illus. 2012. (Traveling Photographer Ser.). (ENG., Illus.). 40p. (J). (gr. 1-4). 17.99 (978-0-7636-4165-8(0)) Candlewick Pr.

Somervill, Barbara A. Leeches: Waiting in the Water. 2009. (Bloodsuckers Ser.). 24p. (gr. 2-3). 42.50 (978-1-61511-633-1(8), PowerKids Pr.) Rosen Publishing Group, Inc., The.

Sroda, George. Facts about Nightcrawlers: Redworms & Garden Worms. (Illus.). 157p. (J). reprint ed. 10.95 (978-0-9604486-0-9(8)) Sroda, George.

Strain Trueit, Trudi. Slugs, Snails, & Worms, 1 vol. 2013. (Backyard Safari Ser.). (ENG.). 32p. (gr. 3-3). 31.21 (978-1-60870-247-3(2), 8efd9e6f-7a42-4131-8c18-b405c5b18cd2); pap. 11.58 (978-1-62712-030-2(0), 19a27dfb-191e-4634-a652-c7279b71561f) Cavendish Square Publishing LLC.

—Worms, 1 vol. 2010. (Creepy Critters Ser.). (ENG.). 24p. (gr. k-1). 25.50 (978-0-7614-3966-0(8), 9ef289a9-910d-4934-9eb2-73e8defd5d0a) Cavendish Square Publishing LLC.

Tilden, Thomasine E. Lewis. Worms! Parasites Plague a Village. 2011. (J). pap. (978-0-545-32804-3(7)) Scholastic, Inc.

Veitch, Catherine. Bug Babies. 2013. (Animal Babies Ser.). (ENG.). 24p. (J). (gr. -1-1). pap. 6.95 (978-1-4329-8420-5(9), 124402); pap. 41.70 (978-1-4329-8427-4(6), 20519) Capstone. (Heinemann).

Waters, Kate. Curious about Worms. 2017. (Smithsonian Ser.). (Illus.). 32p. (J). (gr. 1-3). pap. 5.99 (978-0-451-53369-2(0), Grosset & Dunlap) Penguin Young Readers Group.

Williams, Susie. Worms. Tolson, Hannah, illus. 2020. 32p. (J). (978-0-7787-7389-4(2)) Crabtree Publishing Co.

WORMS—FICTION

Amato, Mary. The Word Eater. Ryniak, Christopher, illus. 2005. (ENG.). 151p. (J). (gr. 3-7). reprint ed. pap. 7.99 (978-0-8234-1940-1(1)) Holiday Hse., Inc.

Arnold, Caroline. Wiggle & Waggle. Peterson, Mary, illus. 2009. (ENG.). 48p. (J). (gr. k-3). pap. 6.99 (978-1-58089-307-7(4)) Charlesbridge Publishing, Inc.

Austrian, J. J. Worm Loves Worm. Curato, Mike, illus. 2016. (ENG.). 32p. (J). (gr. -1-3). 17.99 (978-0-06-238633-5(6), Balzer & Bray) HarperCollins Pubs.

Balash, Sue Beth. Mimi the Inchworm. 2009. (ENG.). 32p. pap. 10.95 (978-1-933916-44-6(3), Ferne Pr.) Nelson Publishing & Marketing.

Barber, Alison. The Little Green Pea. Keiser, Paige, illus. 2009. (ENG.). 28p. (J). (gr. 1-4). 15.95 (978-1-58536-448-0(7), 202173) Sleeping Bear Pr.

Barnes, Brenda J. Calvin Compost in Organic City: The Story of an Earthworm. Williams, Nancy E., ed. 2012. 28p. (J). (-18). pap. 10.98 (978-1-938526-21-3(X)) Laurus Co., Inc., The.

Bartolome, Teresita Africano. Where Is Warren D. Worm?, 1 vol. 2010. 28p. 24.95 (978-1-4489-5869-6(5)) PublishAmerica, Inc.

Batten, Scott A. Johnny the Phoenix. 2008. 64p. pap. 23.95 (978-1-4343-7297-0(9)) AuthorHouse.

Becton, Sarah Walker, et al. Wormy Worm. Becton, Daniel Walker, illus. 2007. 88p. (J). 19.95 (978-1-878398-59-8(8), Blue Note Bks.) Blue Note Pubns.

Bedford, William. The Glowworm Who Lost Her Glow. Joyce, Sophie, illus. 2005. (Blue Go Bananas Ser.). (ENG.). 48p. (J). (gr. 1-2). (978-0-7787-2652-4(5)) Crabtree Publishing Co.

Beitler, Stacey Ann. Willy Goes to School. 2011. 28p. pap. 14.50 (978-1-61204-397-5(6), Strategic Bk. Publishing) Strategic Book Publishing & Rights Agency (SBPRA).

Bennett, Bonnie. Howard the Worm. 2011. 28p. pap. 16.95 (978-1-4626-0004-5(2)) America Star Bks.

Bill, Poppa. The Adventures of Huggyman & Wiggly Worm: The Explorers meet Mr. Moley. 2011. (Illus.). 28p. pap. 14.09 (978-1-4567-7295-6(3)) AuthorHouse.

Blackbird. Mr. Hookworm. Blackbird, illus. 2006. (Illus.). (J). per. 18.00 (978-0-9789798-6-7(9), 978-0-9789798-6-7) Blackbird's World Publishing Co.

Brody, Lazer. The Worry Worm. Shapiro, Rebecca, illus. 2007. 26p. (J). 26.95 (978-0-9797530-1-5(5)) Kalcom Publishing.

Brown, Adam. The Adventures of Wormie Wormington Book Three: Wormie & the Snowball. Smart, Andy, illus. 2013. 48p. pap. (978-0-9919196-3-5(7)) Beckon Creative.

—The Adventures of Wormie Wormington Book Two: Wormie & the Kite. Smart, Andy, illus. 2013. 48p. pap. (978-0-9919196-2-8(9)) Beckon Creative.

Brown, Adam & Smart, Andy. The Adventures of Wormie Wormington Book One: Wormie & the Fish. Smart, Andy, illus. 2013. (Illus.). 50p. pap. (978-0-9919196-0-4(2)) Beckon Creative.

Carpenter, Cindy. The Little Inchworm. 2008. 16p. per. 24.95 (978-1-4241-9681-4(7)) America Star Bks.

Carr, Heather. The Jiggleworm. Carr, Greg, illus. 2005. 18p. (J). 21.95 incl. audio compact disk (978-0-9768450-0-3(8), Giggletins) Le Bk. Moderne, LLC.

Clinton, Ann M. Stevie Inchworm. Canavan, Jean, illus. 2009. 24p. (J). 31.99 (978-1-4363-9471-0(6)) Xlibris Corp.

Coccia, Mina. Mother Nature & Mz Bee. 2012. 36p. pap. 14.95 (978-1-4575-0709-0(9)) Dog Ear Publishing, LLC.

Coldwell, Lamar. The Worm Hunt, 1 vol. 2016. (Rosen REAL Readers: STEM & STEAM Collection). (ENG.). 8p. (gr. k-1). pap. 5.46 (978-1-5081-2628-7(3), d523eca2-a528-4083-8405-3077b540077f, Rosen Classroom) Rosen Publishing Group, Inc., The.

Cook, Sherry & Johnson, Terri. Watery William, 26. Kuhn, Jesse, illus. l.t. ed. 2006. (Quirkles — Exploring Phonics through Science Ser.: 23). 32p. (J). 7.99 (978-1-933815-22-0(1), Quirkles, The) Creative 3, LLC.

Coulton, Mia. Danny & the Little Worm. Coulton, Mia, photos by. 2004. (ENG., Illus.). pap. 5.35 (978-0-9746475-6-2(X)) Maryruth Bks., Inc.

Cronin, Doreen. Diary of a Worm. 2003. (Illus.). (J). 127.92 (978-0-06-056900-6(X)); 127.92 (978-0-06-056901-3(8)) HarperCollins Pubs.

—Diary of a Worm. Bliss, Harry, illus. 2003. (ENG.). 40p. (J). (gr. -1-3). 18.99 (978-0-06-000150-6(X)); lib. bdg. 18.89 (978-0-06-000151-3(8)) HarperCollins Pubs. (HarperCollins).

—Diary of a Worm. Bliss, Harry, illus. pap. 16.95 incl. audio (978-1-59112-867-0(6)); pap. incl. audio compact disk (978-1-59112-873-1(0)); pap. 18.95 incl. audio compact disk (978-1-59112-871-7(4)); pap. incl. audio (978-1-59112-869-4(2)) Live Oak Media.

—Diary of a Worm. 2004. (Illus.). (J). 28.95 incl. audio compact disk (978-1-59112-872-4(2)) Live Oak Media.

—Diary of a Worm. 2013. (Diary of a Worm: I Can Read Level 1 Ser.). (J). lib. bdg. 13.55 (978-0-606-31819-8(4)) Turtleback.

—Diary of a Worm: Nat the Gnat. 2014. (I Can Read Level 1 Ser.). (ENG., Illus.). 32p. (J). (gr. -1-3). pap. 4.99 (978-0-06-208707-2(X), HarperCollins) HarperCollins Pubs.

—Diary of a Worm: Teacher's Pet. Bliss, Harry, illus. 2013. (I Can Read Level 1 Ser.). (ENG.). 32p. (J). (gr. -1-3). 16.99 (978-0-06-208705-8(3), HarperCollins) HarperCollins Pubs.

—Nat the Gnat. 2014. (Diary of a Worm: I Can Read Level 1 Ser.). (J). lib. bdg. 13.55 (978-0-606-35494-3(8)) Turtleback.

Cronin, Doreen & Bliss, Harry. Diary of a Worm: Teacher's Pet. 2013. (I Can Read Level 1 Ser.). (ENG., Illus.). 32p. (J). (gr. -1-3). pap. 4.99 (978-0-06-208704-1(5), HarperCollins) HarperCollins Pubs.

Cueva, Susana & Shibaja, Calixto. Lita the Hardworking Worm/Lita la Trabajadora. 2012. (ENG & SPA.). 26p. pap. 9.99 (978-0-9883927-1-7(2)) Carsume.

Cummings, Troy. Day of the Night Crawlers. 2013. (Notebook of Doom Ser.: 2). (ENG.). 96p. (J). (gr. 1-3). 15.99 (978-0-545-49324-6(2)) Scholastic, Inc.

—Day of the Night Crawlers. 2013. (Notebook of Doom Ser.: 2). lib. bdg. 14.75 (978-0-606-32368-0(6)) Turtleback.

—Day of the Night Crawlers: a Branches Book (the Notebook of Doom #2) Cummings, Troy, illus. 2013. (Notebook of Doom Ser.: 2). (ENG.). 96p. (J). (gr. 1-3). pap. 6.99 (978-0-545-49325-3(0)) Scholastic, Inc.

—Day of the Night Crawlers: a Branches Book (the Notebook of Doom #2) A Branches Book. Cummings, Troy, illus. 2013. (Notebook of Doom Ser.: 2). (ENG.). 96p. (J). (gr. 1-3). E-Book (978-0-545-49327-7(7)) Scholastic, Inc.

Dale, Jay. Up & Down. Bailey, Martin, illus. 2012. (Engage Literacy Magenta Ser.). (ENG.). 16p. (J). (gr. k-2). pap. 36.94 (978-1-4296-8879-6(3), 18335, Capstone Pr.) Capstone.

Defreitas, Henrietta. Henratty Mortimer Presents: Poppy the Most Beautiful Worm. 2012. (Illus.). 28p. pap. 21.35 (978-1-4772-3890-5(5)) AuthorHouse.

Donaldson, Julia. Superworm. Scheffler, Axel, illus. 2014. (ENG.). 32p. (J). (gr. -1-3). 16.99 (978-0-545-59176-8(7), Levine, Arthur A. Bks.) Scholastic, Inc.

Dozier, Mike. The Little Inchworm with the Big Dream. 2009. (J). pap. 12.50 (978-1-61623-365-5(6)) Independent Pub.

Duncan-Goetz, Betty. Squiggle the Wiggle Worm. 2011. (Illus.). 20p. (gr. -1). pap. 13.77 (978-1-4269-5585-3(5)) Trafford Publishing.

Eastabrooks, Linda. Willie's New Home. 2008. 24p. per. 24.95 (978-1-4241-8931-1(4)) America Star Bks.

Eldridge, VonDa. Wiggles the Worm, 1 vol. 2010. 26p. pap. 24.95 (978-1-4489-2547-6(9)) PublishAmerica, Inc.

Ellefson, D. R. Willie Woolly Wiggle Worm. 2011. 20p. pap. 24.95 (978-1-4626-2624-3(6)) America Star Bks.

Fettig, Pamela. Leelah at the Lake. Strecker, Darren, illus. 2010. 28p. pap. 9.99 (978-1-60844-697-1(2)) Dog Ear Publishing, LLC.

French, Vivian. Yucky Worms. 2012. (Read & Wonder Ser.). lib. bdg. 17.20 (978-0-606-23803-8(4)) Turtleback.

—Yucky Worms: Read & Wonder. Ahlberg, Jessica, illus. 2012. (Read & Wonder Ser.). (ENG.). 32p. (J). (gr. -1-3). pap. 8.99 (978-0-7636-5817-5(0)) Candlewick Pr.

Friedman, Joe. Boobela & the Belching Giant. Childs, Sam, illus. 2010. (ENG.). 128p. 12.99 (978-1-4440-0046-7(2)) Orion Publishing Group, Ltd. GBR. Dist: Hachette Bk. Group.

—Boobela, Worm & Potion Power. Childs, Sam, illus. 2010. (ENG.). 128p. 12.99 (978-1-4440-0045-0(4)) Orion Publishing Group, Ltd. GBR. Dist: Hachette Bk. Group.

A Friend with No Name. 2006. (ENG., Illus.). 28p. per. 11.95 (978-1-59800-476-2(X)) Outskirts Pr., Inc.

Gentry, J. B. Lily the Worm. 2011. 32p. pap. 15.99 (978-1-4568-2926-1(2)) Xlibris Corp.

Georgieva, Zoia. Herman the Earth Worm: Illustrated by Emma C. Van Dyke. 2008. pap. 18.00 (978-0-8059-8630-3(8)) Dorrance Publishing Co., Inc.

Gibson, James E. Rico, the Mysterious Worm, 1 vol. 2009. 17p. pap. 24.95 (978-1-60749-148-4(6)) America Star Bks.

Gibson, Sylvia Scott. Ricky the Skating Worm & Friends, 1 vol. Gibson, Gregory V., illus. 2009. 21p. pap. 24.95 (978-1-60836-473-2(9)) America Star Bks.

Gilbert, Scott W. The Adventures of Willie the Worm: Willie's Big Adventure. 2012. 28p. pap. 19.99 (978-1-4772-5407-3(2)) AuthorHouse.

Gleitzman, Morris. Worm Story. 2016. 160p. (J). (gr. 1-3). 14.99 (978-0-14-330893-5(9)) Random Hse. Australia AUS. Dist: Independent Pubs. Group.

Green, Brandon. This Wriggler Is a Giggler a Review of Diary of a Worm. 2017. (Text Connections Guided Close Reading Ser.). (J). (gr. 2). (978-1-4900-1836-2(0)) Benchmark Education Co.

Hart, Janice. Henry & the Oranges: Henry's Wild Adventures. McDonald, Suzi, illus. 2010. 32p. pap. 13.00 (978-1-60860-911-6(1), Eloquent Bks.) Strategic Book Publishing & Rights Agency (SBPRA).

Hicks, Betty. The Worm Whisperer. Hatke, Ben, illus. 2017. (ENG.). 192p. (J). pap. 9.99 (978-1-250-14820-9(0), 900181893) Square Fish.

How To Eat Fried Worms. 116p. (J). (gr. 3-5). pap. 5.50 (978-0-8072-1382-7(9), Listening Library) Random Hse. Audio Publishing Group.

How To Eat Fried Worms. 2005. (J). (978-1-59564-950-8(6)) Steps To Literacy, LLC.

Huber, Mike. Bree Finds a Friend. Cowman, Joseph, illus. 2014. (ENG.). 32p. (gr. -1). 15.95 (978-1-60554-211-9(3)) Redleaf Pr.

Hunter, Lee Hargus. Welby the Worm Who Lost His Wiggle. Thompson, Lydia, illus. 2004. 32p. (J). (gr. -1-1). (978-1-930093-04-1(7)) Brookfield Reader, Inc., The.

Huston, Donna. Inch by Inch. 2006. (J). spiral bd. 19.95 (978-0-9771192-3-3(8)) Shayne Publishing.

Ingle, L. G. Little Willy Wiggle & Johnny Amigo. 2012. 40p. pap. (978-1-77097-479-1(2)) FriesenPress.

Karen, Frantz. Children's Parables: Earthly Stories with Heavenly Lessons for Children. 2013. 162p. pap. 13.95 (978-1-4908-1675-3(5), WestBow Pr.) Author Solutions, LLC.

Kayaalp, Suzan. Inch Worm Inch Worm. Merrifield, Monarca, illus. 2013. 20p. pap. 12.95 (978-1-62838-072-9(1)) Page Publishing Inc.

Knudsen, Michelle. A Slimy Story. Billin-Frye, Paige, illus. 2004. 32p. (J). lib. bdg. 20.00 (978-1-4242-1150-0(6)) Fitzgerald Bks.

Krulik, Nancy. Revenge of the Killer Worms #16. Blecha, Aaron, illus. 2015. (George Brown, Class Clown Ser.: 16). 128p. (J). (gr. 1-3). bds. 6.99 (978-0-448-48284-2(3), Grosset & Dunlap) Penguin Young Readers Group.

Kügler, Tina. Snail & Worm: Three Stories about Two Friends. (Snail & Worm Ser.). (ENG., Illus.). 32p. (J). (gr. -1-3). 2019. pap. 6.99 (978-1-328-59645-1(1), 1730707) 2016. 16.99 (978-0-544-49412-1(1), 1604088) HarperCollins Pubs. (Clarion Bks.).

—Snail & Worm Again: Three Stories about Two Friends. 2017. (Snail & Worm Ser.). (ENG., Illus.). 32p. (J). (gr. -1-3). 16.99 (978-0-544-79249-4(1), 1639349, Clarion Bks.) HarperCollins Pubs.

Lansky, Bruce. Early Birdy Gets the Worm. Wummer, Amy, illus. 2010. 10p. (J). bds. 6.99 (978-1-4169-9316-2(9)) Meadowbrook Pr.

Lever, Jill. The Worm Who Knew Karate! Denton, Terry, illus. 2019. 32p. (J). (gr. k-3). 15.99 (978-0-14-350602-7(1), Puffin) Penguin Bks., Ltd. GBR. Dist: Independent Pubs. Group.

Lionni, Leo. Inch by Inch. 2018. lib. bdg. 18.40 (978-0-606-40949-0(1)) Turtleback.

Mabbitt, Will. I Can Only Draw Worms. 2019. (ENG., Illus.). 32p. (J). (-k). 15.99 (978-1-5247-8822-3(8), Penguin Workshop) Penguin Young Readers Group.

Macdonald, Alan. Dirty Bertie: Worms! Roberts, David, illus. 2008. 96p. (J). (gr. 4-7). 3.99 (978-1-56148-645-8(0), Good Bks.) Skyhorse Publishing Co., Inc.

Mammano, Meredith. The Electronic Adventures of Diga Byte: Wrong Turn, the First of His Adventures. Cesarski, Thomas, photos by. 2008. (ENG.). 50p. pap. 22.49 (978-1-4343-9636-5(3)) AuthorHouse.

Marie, Jacqueline. Felix the Wannabe Firefly. 2017. (ENG., Illus.). (J). (gr. -1-3). pap. 9.95 (978-1-946977-97-7(7)) Yorkshire Publishing Group.

Martin, Jayme. Skinny Little Tree. 2013. (ENG.). 28p. (J). 18.95 (978-1-4787-0813-1(1)); pap. 13.95 (978-1-4787-0870-4(0)) Outskirts Pr., Inc.

Masterson, Josephine. Worm's World, 1 vol. 2015. (Rosen REAL Readers: STEM & STEAM Collection). (ENG.). 8p. (gr. k-1). pap. 5.46 (978-1-4994-9564-5(1), 31e83cc1-930d-4de6-9b30-664889ab145c, Rosen Classroom) Rosen Publishing Group, Inc., The.

Mathews, Leslie. Edgar Wants to Be Alone. Dumont, Jean-François, illus. 2015. (ENG.). 26p. (J). 16.00 (978-0-8028-5457-5(5), Eerdmans Bks For Young Readers) Eerdmans, William B. Publishing Co.

Matt and Dave, Matt and. Yuck's Pet Worm. Baines, Nigel, illus. 2013. (Yuck Ser.). (ENG.). 112p. (J). (gr. 2-5). pap. 6.99 (978-1-4424-8149-7(8), Simon & Schuster/Paula Wiseman Bks.) Simon & Schuster/Paula Wiseman Bks.

McBrier, Page. The Chicken & the Worm. Peterson, Rick, illus. 2008. 36p. (J). (978-0-9798439-2-1(8)) Heifer Project International.

Messner, Kate. Marty McGuire Digs Worms! Floca, Brian, illus. 2012. (ENG.). 176p. (J). (gr. -1-3). pap. 5.99 (978-0-545-14247-2(4), Scholastic Pr.) Scholastic, Inc.

Mickiewicz, Ricky. The Adventure of Wormee the Worm. 2011. 36p. (gr. 4-6). pap. 16.86 (978-1-4634-0007-1(1)) AuthorHouse.

Miller, H. James. Willy the Worm Gets Lost. Sy, Jan Michael Vincent, illus. 2011. (ENG.). 24p. pap. 15.99 (978-1-4568-9801-4(9)) Xlibris Corp.

Morris, Ann. Surprise in Auntie's Garden! Varkarotas, Heather, illus. 2013. (ENG.). (J). (gr. -1-3). 14.95 (978-1-62086-224-7(7)) Amplify Publishing Group.

Mr. Worm. 2008. (ENG & SPA., Illus.). 64p. (J). 14.95 (978-0-9787462-6-1(0)) Heritage Publishing Co.

Myrl, Melanie. Why Some Birds Don't Eat Worms. 2011. 16p. 8.99 (978-1-4490-4092-5(6)) AuthorHouse.

Nelsen, Sissy. Wiggly & Giggly. 2012. 24p. pap. 17.99 (978-1-4772-6721-9(2)) AuthorHouse.

Newman, Jeff. The Greedy Worm. Newman, Jeff, illus. 2023. (ENG., Illus.). 32p. (J). (gr. -1-3). 18.99 (978-1-4424-7195-5(6), Simon & Schuster Bks. For Young Readers) Simon & Schuster Bks. For Young Readers.

Noyes, Deborah. Red Butterfly: How a Princess Smuggled the Secret of Silk Out of China. Blackall, Sophie, illus. 2019. (ENG.). 32p. (J). (gr. 1-4). 7.99 (978-1-5362-0376-9(9)) Candlewick Pr.

Oberlin, Linda. Eco in the Garden. Oberlin, Linda, illus. 2013. (Illus.). 26p. pap. 10.00 (978-0-9911382-0-3(1)) Little Worm Publishing.

Oliver, Charlene. The Life & Tails of Herman the Worm. 2010. 20p. pap. 10.49 (978-1-4490-9357-0(4)) AuthorHouse.

Park, Linda Sue. Project Mulberry. 2007. 225p. (gr. 4-7). 17.00 (978-0-7569-7921-8(8)) Perfection Learning Corp.

Pauli, Gunter. Shiitake Love Caffeine. 2007. (Zeri Fables Ser.). (ENG & SPA., Illus.). 32p. (J). (gr. k-3). pap. 9.95 (978-958-692-833-5(0)) Fondo Editorial Grania, Fundacion Hogares Juveniles Campesinos COL. Dist: Chelsea Green Publishing.

Pilkey, Dav. Ricky Ricotta's Mighty Robot vs. the Naughty Nightcrawlers from Neptune (Ricky Ricotta's Mighty Robot #8) Santat, Dan, illus. 2016. (Ricky Ricotta's Mighty Robot Ser.: 8). (ENG.). 128p. (J). (gr. -1-3). pap. 5.99 (978-0-439-37709-6(9)) Scholastic, Inc.

Pinczes, Elinor J. Inchworm & a Half. Enos, Randall, illus. 2003. (ENG.). 32p. (J). pap. 7.99 (978-0-618-31101-9(7), 493403, Clarion Bks.) HarperCollins Pubs.

Pisella, Donna. The Blue Goblin. 2013. (ENG.). 30p. (J). 22.95 (978-1-4787-1269-5(4)) Outskirts Pr., Inc.

Ray, Angela M. Herbie the Worm's Journey for Apples. 2008. 23p. pap. 24.95 (978-1-60672-698-3(6)) America Star Bks.

Rinaldo, Jim. Wally the Worm's Adventures on the Farm. 2011. 28p. pap. 15.99 (978-1-4568-9102-2(2)) Xlibris Corp.

Rockwell, Thomas. How to Eat Fried Worms. (J). (gr. 3-5). 179p. pap. 4.99 (978-0-8072-1395-7(0)); 2004. 116p. pap. 29.00 incl. audio (978-0-8072-8797-2(0)) Random Hse. Audio Publishing Group. (Listening Library).

—How to Eat Fried Worms (Scholastic Gold) McCully, Emily Arnold, illus. 2019. (ENG.). 144p. (J). (gr. 3-7). pap. 6.99 (978-1-338-56589-8(3)) Scholastic, Inc.

Rodriguez, Raul. Mamma's Worm House. 2011. 28p. pap. 15.99 (978-1-4568-8498-7(0)) Xlibris Corp.

Rogers, Martha. Bernie's Journey. 2012. 24p. pap. 13.99 (978-1-4497-5185-2(7), WestBow Pr.) Author Solutions, LLC.

Rosen, Robert. Hungry for Worms. Curzon, Brett, illus. 2017. (Seasons Around Me Ser.). (ENG.). 24p. (gr. -1-2). pap. 9.95 (978-1-68342-776-6(9), 9781683427766) Rourke Educational Media.

Rosno, Connie. This Is My Lucky Day. 2011. 16p. pap. 9.49 (978-1-4567-5534-8(X)) AuthorHouse.

Runton, Andy. Owly & Wormy, Bright Lights & Starry Nights. Runton, Andy, illus. 2012. (ENG., Illus.). 40p. (J). (gr. -1-3). 19.99 (978-1-4169-5775-1(8), Atheneum Bks. for Young Readers) Simon & Schuster Children's Publishing.

—Owly & Wormy, Friends All Aflutter! Runton, Andy, illus. 2011. (ENG., Illus.). 40p. (J). (gr. -1-2). 17.99 (978-1-4169-5774-4(X), Atheneum Bks. for Young Readers) Simon & Schuster Children's Publishing.

Ryan, Nancy. The Bookworm & His New Book. 2012. 32p. pap. 24.95 (978-1-4626-6492-4(X)) America Star Bks.

Saveley, Barb. Curse of Moonstone Island. 2009. (Illus.). 36p. pap. 16.99 (978-1-4389-4938-3(3)) AuthorHouse.

W
X
Y
Z

Scanlon, Liz Garton. Noodle & Lou. Howard, Arthur, illus. 2011. (ENG.). 32p. (J). (gr. -1-1). 15.99 *(978-1-4424-0288-1(1)*, Beach Lane Bks.) Beach Lane Bks.

Scarry, Richard. Best Lowly Worm Book Ever! 2014. (ENG., Illus.). 32p. (J). (gr. -1-2). 17.99 *(978-0-385-38782-8(2)*, Random Hse. Bks. for Young Readers) Random Hse. Children's Bks.

Schaub, Barbara Miller. Charlie Worm & Harley Dragonfly. 2005. (ENG.). 24p. pap. 12.99 *(978-1-4134-7922-5(7))* Xlibris Corp.

Schlunke, Eva, illus. Little Worm's Big Question, 1 vol. 2016. (ENG.). 36p. (J). (gr. -1-3). pap. 9.95 *(978-1-78026-261-1(2))* New Internationalist Pubns., Ltd. GBR. Dist: Consortium Bk. Sales & Distribution.

Sheppard, Hazel A. The Inchy Books: Inch Worm Goes a Mile; Inchy Goes the Extra Mile; Inchy Goes the Distance, 3bks. 2005. (Illus.). (J). 28.85 *(978-0-9725286-3-4(6))* Sheppard Publishing.

—Inchy Goes the Distance. 2005. (Illus.). (J). 9.95 *(978-0-9725286-2-7(8))* Sheppard Publishing.

Sprouse, Jackie. Orry & Izzy's Perfect Worm. 2010. (ENG.). 32p. pap. 15.95 *(978-0-557-39078-5(8))* Lulu Pr., Inc.

Sroda, George. The Life Story of TV Star Herman the Worm. Hughes, Janet, illus. 199p. (Orig.). (J). (gr. 3-18). 10.95 *(978-0-9604486-2-3(4))* Sroda, George.

Taft, Jean. Worm Weather. Hunt, Matt, illus. 2015. 32p. (J). (-k). bds. 5.99 *(978-0-448-48740-3(3)*, Grosset & Dunlap) Penguin Young Readers Group.

Terry, Jill. Jack & a Worm, 1 vol. 2010. 42p. pap. 24.95 *(978-1-4489-7069-8(5))* PublishAmerica, Inc.

Tomos, Angharad. Jam Poeth. 2005. (WEL., Illus.). 48p. pap. *(978-0-86243-145-7(X))* Y Lolfa.

Vento, Anthony. Holes Are Us: A Worm's Tale about Friendship & Trust. 2009. 40p. pap. 21.99 *(978-1-4415-3446-0(6))* Xlibris Corp.

Wiley, Melissa. Inch & Roly & the Sunny Day Scare: Ready-To-Read Level 1. Jatkowska, Ag, illus. 2014. (Inch & Roly Ser.). (ENG.). 24p. (J). (gr. -1-1). 17.99 *(978-1-4424-9072-7(1)*, Simon Spotlight) Simon Spotlight.

—Inch & Roly & the Very Small Hiding Place: Ready-To-Read Level 1. Jatkowska, Ag, illus. 2013. (Inch & Roly Ser.). (ENG.). 24p. (J). (gr. -1-1). 17.99 *(978-1-4424-5281-7(1))*; pap. 4.99 *(978-1-4424-5279-4(X))* Simon Spotlight. (Simon Spotlight).

—Inch & Roly Make a Wish: Ready-To-Read Level 1. Jatkowska, Ag, illus. 2012. (Inch & Roly Ser.). (ENG.). 24p. (J). (gr. -1-1). 15.99 *(978-1-4424-5277-0(3))*; pap. 3.99 *(978-1-4424-5276-3(5))* Simon Spotlight. (Simon Spotlight).

Williams, Dawn. Winston J. Worm Hunts for a New Name. Chou, Joey, illus. 2010. 52p. (J). 15.00 *(978-0-9770783-5-6(3))* SunriseHouse Pubs.

Williams, Greg. Wilberton the Worm. 2011. 34p. pap. 19.00 *(978-1-60746-344-3(X))* FastPrncil, Inc.

Ziefert, Harriet & Kreloff, Elliot. Found an Apple. 2007. (I'm Going to Read! Level 1 Ser.). (ENG., Illus.). 28p. (J). (gr. -1-1). 16.19 *(978-1-4027-4295-8(9))* Sterling Publishing Co., Inc.

WORSHIP

see also Prayer

Al-Ghazali. Al-Ghazali: The Mysteries of Prayer for Children. 2018. (Illus.). 312p. (J). *(978-1-941610-38-1(2))* Fons Vitae of Kentucky, Inc.

Barnhill, Carla. The One Year Devotions for Preschoolers 2. Kucharik, Elena, illus. 2010. (Little Blessings Ser.). (ENG.). 384p. (J). 17.99 *(978-1-4143-3445-5(1)*, 4602435, Tyndale Kids) Tyndale Hse. Pubs.

Bernard, M. My First Mass Book. Date not set. (J). (gr. -1-3). pap. 1.95 *(978-0-88271-165-2(2))* Regina Pr., Malhame & Co.

Bissell, Sybil A. God & Me: A Journey of Divine Encounters. 2004. (ENG.). 118p. pap. 13.95 *(978-0-9747516-4-1(2)*, 1005) Heart Communications.

Brown, Barbara J. The Many Different Ways to Worship: Is apart of everyday Life. 2009. 48p. pap. 11.99 *(978-1-4490-3275-3(3))* AuthorHouse.

Brown, Carolyn A. My Worship Book Student Book. 2nd ed. 2004. (J). spiral bd. 14.99 *(978-0-9752605-3-1(7))* LOGOS System Assocs.

Bytheway, John. The Sacrament. Pinnock, Nathan, illus. 2013. 18.99 *(978-1-60907-790-7(3))* Deseret Bk. Co.

Elkins, Stephen. Tell Me about Praise & Worship. 2014. (Train 'Em Up Ser.). (ENG.). 24p. (J). pap. 4.99 *(978-1-4143-9676-7(7)*, 4608666) Tyndale Hse. Pubs.

Fears, Melissa. Thank God It's Sunday. 2004. (J). per. 6.95 *(978-0-89315-413-4(X))* Lambert Bk. Hse., Inc.

God & Me! Devotions for Girls. 2004. (Illus.). 248p. (J). (gr. 5-7). spiral bd. 12.99 *(978-1-885358-85-1(7)*, Legacy Pr.) Rainbow Pubs. & Legacy Pr.

God Is a Promise Keeper. 2.99 *(978-0-7847-0857-6(6))* Standard Publishing.

Guest, John. Collective Worship Unwrapped: 33 Tried & Tested Story-Based Assemblies for Primary Schools. 2nd ed. 2013. (ENG.). 132p. pap. *(978-1-84101-618-4(7)*, Barnabas in Schools) Bible Reading Fellowship.

Hitchen, Danielle. Psalms of Praise: A Movement Primer. 2018. (Baby Believer Ser.). (ENG., Illus.). 20p. (J). (— 1). bds. 12.99 *(978-0-7369-7234-5(X)*, 6972345) Harvest Hse. Pubs.

Jeanne Grieser & Pearson, Mary Rose. Worship Bulletins for Kids: Fall & Winter. 2004. (Illus.). 128p. (J). (gr. -1-7). pap. 13.95 *(978-1-58411-014-9(7))* Rainbow Pubs. & Legacy Pr.

—Worship Bulletins for Kids: Spring & Summer. 2004. 128p. (J). (gr. -1-7). pap. 13.95 *(978-1-58411-015-6(5))* Rainbow Pubs. & Legacy Pr.

Kinnaman, Scott A. Worshiping with Angels & Archangels: An Introduction to the Divine Service. Kirchhoff, Arthur, illus. 2005. 48p. 7.99 *(978-0-7586-1206-9(0))* Concordia Publishing Hse.

Kitch, Anne E. What We Do in Church: An Anglican Child's Activity Book. Perez, Dorothy Thompson, illus. 2004. (ENG.). 48p. (J). pap. 11.95 *(978-0-8192-2105-6(8)*, e4a75c07-f9c3-4a14-a65c-6fbe0bed347c) Church Publishing, Inc.

Krueger, Naomi Joy. I Can Praise God. Jones, Anna, illus. 2017. (Frolic First Faith Ser.). 22p. (J). 6.99 *(978-1-5064-2190-2(3)*, Sparkhouse Family) 1517 Media.

Lee, Witness. The Holy Word for Morning Revival: Ephesians 4:1-6:24, Vol. 2. (J). (gr. 6). *(978-0-7363-1593-7(4))* Living Stream Ministry.

Let's Go to Mass. 2003. (Illus.). *(978-2-89507-087-0(3))* Novalis Publishing.

Lutz, A. Fowler. Stories of the Child Jesus from Many Lands. 2003. (Illus.). viii, 175p. (J). pap. 10.95 *(978-1-928832-96-6(2))* Sophia Institute Pr.

Mortimer, F. L. Lines Left Out. 176p. (J). pap. 7.99 *(978-1-85792-593-7(9))* Christian Focus Pubns. GBR. Dist: Riverside.

My Precious Moments with God: Quiet Time Devotionals for Girls & Boys, White. (Precious Moments Ser.). (J). 19.95 *(978-1-55976-449-0(X))* CEF Pr.

Perkins, Nicole. I Believe God Will: Book of Devotion & Prayer for Children. Perkins, Nicole & Frisk, Maria, illus. 2008. 32p. (J). 7.00 *(978-0-9755566-1-0(4))* Azreal Publishing Co.

Savary, Louis M. Rosary for Children. Date not set. (J). (gr. -1-3). pap. 1.25 *(978-0-88271-158-4(X))* Regina Pr., Malhame & Co.

—Way of the Cross. Date not set. (J). (gr. -1-3). pap. 1.95 *(978-0-88271-160-7(1))* Regina Pr., Malhame & Co.

SPCK. I Can Join in Common Worship: A Children's Communion Book. 2003. (Illus.). 24p. 5.00 *(978-0-281-05568-5(8))* SPCK Publishing GBR. Dist: Pilgrim Pr., The/United Church Pr.

St. James, Rebecca. 40 Days with God: A Devotional Journey. rev. ed. 2006. 112p. pap. 12.99 *(978-0-7847-1274-0(3)*, 23338) Standard Publishing.

Stiegemeyer, Julie. Things I Hear in Church. Mitter, Kathy, illus. 2003. 20p. (J). bds. 5.49 *(978-0-7586-0125-4(5))* Concordia Publishing Hse.

Stohs, Anita. Here Is the Church. Mitter, Kathy, illus. 2009. 32p. (J). (gr. -1). 8.99 *(978-0-7586-1633-3(3))* Concordia Publishing Hse.

Waller, Steven H. My Child: What Every Parent... - Girl Edition. 2008. (ENG., Illus.). 48p. 9.95 *(978-0-88271-173-7(3)*, RG13010) Regina Pr., Malhame & Co.

—My Child:what Every Parent... - Boy Edition. 2008. (ENG., Illus.). 48p. 9.95 *(978-0-88271-172-0(5)*, RG13009) Regina Pr., Malhame & Co.

We Worship. 2004. (gr. 5). suppl. ed. 1.75 *(978-0-8294-0853-9(3))* Loyola Pr.

Wood, Alix. Human Sacrifice, 1 vol. Wood, Alix, illus. 2013. (Why'd They Do That? Strange Customs of the Past Ser.). (Illus.). 32p. (J). (gr. 4-5). (ENG.). pap. 11.50 *(978-1-4339-9585-9(9)*, 119d8337-4b39-4d26-a607-feceaa213bc5); (ENG., lib. bdg. 29.27 *(978-1-4339-9584-2(0)*, 85628a83-85b7-4e1b-bda0-e5e00918aa94); pap. 63.00 *(978-1-4339-9586-6(7))* Stevens, Gareth Publishing LLLP.

5 Minute Interactive Worship Devotions for Kids Vol. 1: Names & Games. 2003. (J). per. 12.95 *(978-0-9746161-0-0(9))* Vision Pubns.

WOUNDED, FIRST AID TO

see First Aid

WRECKS

see Shipwrecks

WRENS—FICTION

Crew, Gary. The Cat on the Island. Warden, Gillian, illus. 2008. 32p. *(978-0-207-20070-0(X))* HarperCollins Pubs. Australia.

Lloyd-Jones, Sally. Baby Wren & the Great Gift, 1 vol. Corace, Jen, illus. 2016. (ENG.). 32p. (J). 16.99 *(978-0-310-73389-8(8))* Zonderkidz.

WRESTLING

see also Judo

Abdo, Kenny. Alexa Bliss: Five Feet of Fury. 2019. (Wrestling Biographies Ser.). (ENG., Illus.). 24p. (J). (gr. 2-8). lib. bdg. 31.36 *(978-1-5321-2751-9(0)*, 31709, Abdo Zoom-Fly) ABDO Publishing Co.

—Braun Strowman: Monster among Men. 2019. (Wrestling Biographies Ser.). (ENG., Illus.). 24p. (J). (gr. 2-8). lib. bdg. 31.36 *(978-1-5321-2752-6(9)*, 31711, Abdo Zoom-Fly) ABDO Publishing Co.

—Dwayne Johnson. 2018. (Star Biographies Ser.). (ENG., Illus.). 24p. (J). (gr. 2-8). lib. bdg. 31.36 *(978-1-5321-2544-7(5)*, 30097, Abdo Zoom-Fly) ABDO Publishing Co.

—Pro Wrestling. 2018. (Arena Events Ser.). (ENG., Illus.). 24p. (J). (gr. 2-8). lib. bdg. 31.36 *(978-1-5321-2537-9(2)*, 30083, Abdo Zoom-Fly) ABDO Publishing Co.

—Randy Orton: the Viper. 2019. (Wrestling Biographies Ser.). (ENG., Illus.). 24p. (J). (gr. 2-8). lib. bdg. 31.36 *(978-1-5321-2753-3(7)*, 31713, Abdo Zoom-Fly) ABDO Publishing Co.

—Ronda Rousey: Baddest Woman on the Planet. 2019. (Wrestling Biographies Ser.). (ENG., Illus.). 24p. (J). (gr. 2-8). lib. bdg. 31.36 *(978-1-5321-2754-0(5)*, 31715, Abdo Zoom-Fly) ABDO Publishing Co.

—Seth Rollins: the Architect. 2019. (Wrestling Biographies Ser.). (ENG., Illus.). 24p. (J). (gr. 2-8). lib. bdg. 31.36 *(978-1-5321-2755-7(3)*, 31717, Abdo Zoom-Fly) ABDO Publishing Co.

—The Undertaker: Rest in Peace. 2019. (Wrestling Biographies Ser.). (ENG., Illus.). 24p. (J). (gr. 2-8). lib. bdg. 31.36 *(978-1-5321-2756-4(1)*, 31719, Abdo Zoom-Fly) ABDO Publishing Co.

Armstrong, Jesse. Big Show. 2015. (Wrestling Superstars Ser.). (ENG., Illus.). 24p. (J). (gr. 3-7). lib. bdg. 26.95 *(978-1-62617-178-7(5)*, Epic Bks.) Bellwether Media.

—Dolph Ziggler. 2015. (Wrestling Superstars Ser.). (ENG., Illus.). 24p. (J). (gr. 3-7). lib. bdg. 26.95 *(978-1-62617-179-4(3)*, Epic Bks.) Bellwether Media.

—Mark Henry. 2015. (Wrestling Superstars Ser.). (ENG., Illus.). 24p. (J). (gr. 3-7). lib. bdg. 26.95 *(978-1-62617-181-7(5)*, Epic Bks.) Bellwether Media.

Bell, Samantha S. Dwayne Johnson. 2019. (Influential People Ser.). (ENG., Illus.). 32p. (J). (gr. 4-6). pap. 7.95 *(978-1-5435-6039-8(3)*, 140085); lib. bdg. 28.65 *(978-1-5435-5794-7(5)*, 139750) Capstone.

Black, Jake. WWE Ultimate Superstar Guide, 2nd Edition. 2nd ed. 2018. (ENG., Illus.). 208p. (J). (gr. 4-7). 18.99 *(978-1-4654-6783-6(1)*, DK Children) Dorling Kindersley Publishing, Inc.

Brickweg, Jason. Santino Marella. 2013. (Illus.). 24p. (J). *(978-0-531-26807-0(1))* Bellwether Media.

Brownell, Richard. Wrestling, 1 vol. 2014. (Science Behind Sports Ser.). (ENG., Illus.). 104p. (gr. 7-7). lib. bdg. 41.03 *(978-1-4205-1022-5(3)*, 3cd2d949-263c-45d2-bfd0-b4555ea8a7c3, Lucent Pr.) Greenhaven Publishing LLC.

Chapman, Mike. The Sport of Lincoln 2003. (Illus.). 48p. (YA). pap. 5.95 *(978-0-9676080-6-8(6))* Culture Hse.

Chiu, David & Regis, Natalie. An Insider's Guide to Wrestling, 1 vol. 2014. (Sports Tips, Techniques, & Strategies Ser.). (ENG.). 48p. (YA). (gr. 6-6). pap. 12.75 *(978-1-4777-8090-9(4)*, ed163ce2-9732-4b93-b89d-4ed11cfab036, Rosen Central) Rosen Publishing Group, Inc., The.

Crabtree Staff & Johnson, Robin. Takedown Wrestling, 1 vol. 2012. (ENG., Illus.). 32p. (J). pap. *(978-0-7787-3182-5(0))* Crabtree Publishing Co.

Crossingham, John & Rouse, Bonna. Wrestling in Action. 2003. (Sports in Action Ser.). (ENG., Illus.). 32p. (J). (gr. 1-4). pap. *(978-0-7787-0356-3(8))*; lib. bdg. *(978-0-7787-0336-5(3))* Crabtree Publishing Co.

Davids, Tom & Davids, Veronica. Wrestling the ABCs: Creating Character & Fostering Fitness. 2009. (ENG.). 32p. (J). 17.95 *(978-1-933916-33-0(8))*; pap. 11.95 *(978-1-933916-34-7(6))* Nelson Publishing & Marketing.

Davies, Ross. Andre the Giant. 2009. (Wrestling Greats Ser.). 112p. (gr. 5-5). 63.90 *(978-1-60854-861-3(9))* Rosen Publishing Group, Inc., The.

—Wrestling Greats, 8 bks. Incl. Bobo Brazil. (Illus.). 112p. (YA). (gr. 5-5). 2000. lib. bdg. 39.80 *(978-0-8239-3431-7(4)*, ada58d73-bf25-46af-9240-6fe9fe93897c); (Illus.). 2005. Set lib. bdg. 38.10 o.p. *(978-0-8239-9446-5(5))* Rosen Publishing Group, Inc., The.

DK. DK Readers L2: WWE: How to Be a WWE Superstar. 2017. (DK Readers Level 2 Ser.). (ENG., Illus.). 48p. (J). (gr. k-2). pap. 4.99 *(978-1-4654-6287-9(2)*, DK Children) Dorling Kindersley Publishing, Inc.

—DK Readers Level 2: WWE Meet the Champions. 2019. (DK Readers Level 2 Ser.). (ENG., Illus.). 96p. (J). (gr. -1-1). pap. 8.99 *(978-1-4654-9037-7(X)*, DK Children) Dorling Kindersley Publishing, Inc.

Doeden, Matt. Combat Sports. 2015. (Summer Olympic Sports Ser.). (ENG., Illus.). 32p. (J). (gr. 2-4). 19.95 *(978-1-60753-807-3(5))* Amicus Learning.

—The Miz: Pro Wrestling Superstar, 1 vol. 2014. (Pro Wrestling Superstars Ser.). (ENG., Illus.). 24p. (J). (gr. 1-3). lib. bdg. 27.99 *(978-1-4765-4208-9(2)*, 124309, Capstone Pr.) Capstone.

Dorling Kindersley Publishing Staff. WWE Greatest Rivalries. 2019. (Illus.). 200p. *(978-0-241-36141-2(9))* Dorling Kindersley Publishing, Inc.

—WWE Tag-Teams & Team-Ups DK Reader Level 2. 2019. (ENG., Illus.). 48p. (J). *(978-0-241-36136-8(2))* Dorling Kindersley Publishing, Inc.

Douglas, Peter. Wrestling: Contending on the Mat. 2017. (Preparing for Game Day Ser.: Vol. 10). (ENG., Illus.). 79p. (J). (gr. 7-12). 24.95 *(978-1-4222-3922-3(5))* Mason Crest.

Ellis, Carol & Bredeson, Carmen. Wrestling, 1 vol. 2011. (Martial Arts in Action Ser.). (ENG.). 48p. (gr. 5-5). lib. bdg. 32.64 *(978-0-7614-4941-6(8)*, 458b9d95-76a1-4156-aeff-0810ac843366) Cavendish Square Publishing LLC.

Fishman, Jon M. Pro-Wrestling Superstar John Cena. 2019. (Bumba Books (r) — Sports Superstars Ser.). (ENG., Illus.). 24p. (J). (gr. -1-1). pap. 8.99 *(978-1-5415-7363-5(3)*, 83506c01-9579-4696-9da6-5c2a9cfd3694); lib. bdg. 26.65 *(978-1-5415-5565-5(1)*, 50cbd44f-7328-4555-a59c-31a9d4a57581) Lerner Publishing Group. (Lerner Pubns.).

Frazel, Ellen. Wrestling. 2011. (Illus.). 24p. (J). *(978-0-531-20637-9(8))*; (ENG., (gr. 2-5). lib. bdg. 26.95 *(978-1-60014-571-1(X)*, Blastoff! Readers) Bellwether Media.

Freedman, Jeri. Professional Wrestling: Steroids in & Out of the Ring, 1 vol. 2009. (Disgraced! the Dirty History of Performance-Enhancing Drugs in Sports Ser.). (ENG., Illus.). 48p. (YA). (gr. 5-6). 34.47 *(978-1-4358-5305-8(9)*, 52b87a15-470d-4647-bf8b-be68f153dd1c) Rosen Publishing Group, Inc., The.

Gifford, Clive. Wrestling. 2010. (Combat Sports Ser.). 32p. (J). (gr. 2-5). lib. bdg. 28.50 *(978-1-59771-278-1(7))* Sea-To-Sea Pubns.

Gordon, Nick. Alberto Del Rio. 2012. (Pro Wrestling Champions Ser.). (ENG., Illus.). 24p. (J). (gr. 3-7). lib. bdg. 26.95 *(978-1-60014-782-1(8)*, Torque Bks.) Bellwether Media.

—Kofi Kingston. 2012. (Pro Wrestling Champions Ser.). (ENG., Illus.). 24p. (J). (gr. 3-7). lib. bdg. 26.95 *(978-1-60014-784-5(4)*, Torque Bks.) Bellwether Media.

—Mark Henry. 2012. (Pro Wrestling Champions Ser.). (ENG., Illus.). 24p. (J). (gr. 3-7). lib. bdg. 26.95 *(978-1-60014-785-2(2)*, Torque Bks.) Bellwether Media.

Greenberg, Keith Elliot. Pro Wrestling: From Carnivals to Cable TV. (Sports Legacy Ser.). (Illus.). (J). (gr. 7-12). 2005. 144p. 26.63 *(978-0-8225-3332-0(4))* 2003. 128p. pap. 9.95 *(978-0-8225-9864-0(7))* Lerner Publishing Group.

Hamilton, John. Steer Wrestling. 2013. (Xtreme Rodeo Ser.). (ENG., Illus.). 32p. (J). (gr. 3-9). lib. bdg. 32.79 *(978-1-61783-981-8(7)*, 15760, Abdo & Daughters) ABDO Publishing Co.

Johnson, Robin. Takedown Wrestling. 2012. (ENG., Illus.). 32p. (J). lib. bdg. *(978-0-7787-3155-9(3))* Crabtree Publishing Co.

Jones, Jen. Dwayne Johnson. 2016. (Hollywood Action Heroes Ser.). (ENG., Illus.). 32p. (J). (gr. 3-9). lib. bdg. 28.65 *(978-1-5157-1096-7(3)*, 132312) Capstone.

Kaelberer, Angie Peterson. The Big Show: Pro Wrestling Superstar. 2015. (Pro Wrestling Superstars Ser.). (ENG., Illus.). 24p. (J). (gr. 1-3). lib. bdg. 27.99 *(978-1-4914-2058-4(8)*, 127536, Capstone Pr.) Capstone.

Kortemeier, Todd. Superstars of WWE. 2016. (Pro Sports Superstars Ser.). (ENG., Illus.). 24p. (J). (gr. 1-4). pap. 8.99 *(978-1-68152-108-4(3)*, 15679); lib. bdg. 20.95 *(978-1-60753-943-8(8)*, 15673) Amicus.

Lebell, Gene. The Toughest Man Alive. 2003. (Illus.). 256p. 24.95 *(978-0-9531766-7-0(3))* New Awareness Network, Inc.

Linde, Barbara. Olympic Wrestling. 2009. (Great Moments in Olympic History Ser.). 48p. (gr. 5-6). 53.00 *(978-1-61513-166-2(3)*, Rosen Reference) Rosen Publishing Group, Inc., The.

Linde, Barbara M. Olympic Wrestling, 1 vol. 2007. (Great Moments in Olympic History Ser.). (ENG., Illus.). 48p. (YA). (gr. 5-6). lib. bdg. 34.47 *(978-1-4042-0972-5(7)*, ee6cb8eb-6a82-4f4b-98eb-35a4a88d2322) Rosen Publishing Group, Inc., The.

Luke, Andrew. Wrestling, Vol. 13. 2016. (Inside the World of Sports Ser.: Vol. 13). (ENG., Illus.). 80p. (J). (gr. 7-12). 24.95 *(978-1-4222-3468-6(1))* Mason Crest.

Markegard, Blake. Alberto Del Rio. 2014. (Wrestling Superstars Ser.). (ENG., Illus.). 24p. (J). (gr. 3-7). 26.95 *(978-1-62617-139-8(4)*, Epic Bks.) Bellwether Media.

—John Cena. 2014. (Wrestling Superstars Ser.). (ENG.). 24p. (J). (gr. 3-7). 26.95 *(978-1-62617-141-1(6)*, Epic Bks.) Bellwether Media.

—The Miz. 2014. (Wrestling Superstars Ser.). (ENG., Illus.). 24p. (J). (gr. 3-7). 26.95 *(978-1-62617-146-6(7)*, Epic Bks.) Bellwether Media.

—Rey Mysterio. 2014. (Wrestling Superstars Ser.). (ENG., Illus.). 24p. (J). (gr. 3-7). 26.95 *(978-1-62617-143-5(2)*, Epic Bks.) Bellwether Media.

—Santino Marella. 2014. (Wrestling Superstars Ser.). (ENG., Illus.). 24p. (J). (gr. 3-7). 26.95 *(978-1-62617-144-2(0)*, Epic Bks.) Bellwether Media.

—Sheamus. 2014. (Wrestling Superstars Ser.). (ENG., Illus.). 24p. (J). (gr. 3-7). 26.95 *(978-1-62617-145-9(9)*, Epic Bks.) Bellwether Media.

—Zack Ryder. 2014. (Wrestling Superstars Ser.). (ENG., Illus.). 24p. (J). (gr. 3-7). 26.95 *(978-1-62617-148-0(3)*, Epic Bks.) Bellwether Media.

Marx, Mandy R. Stars of Pro Wrestling, 1 vol. 2014. (Sports Stars Ser.). (ENG.). 24p. (J). (gr. -1-2). 27.32 *(978-1-4914-0594-9(5)*, 125932, Capstone Pr.) Capstone.

Mattern, Joanne. Wrestling. 2008. (Illus.). 24p. (J). (gr. 3-8). lib. bdg. *(978-1-60472-399-1(8))* Rourke Educational Media.

McClellan, Ray. Chris Jericho. 2014. (Wrestling Superstars Ser.). (ENG., Illus.). 24p. (J). (gr. 3-7). 26.95 *(978-1-62617-140-4(8)*, Epic Bks.) Bellwether Media.

—Undertaker. 2014. (Wrestling Superstars Ser.). (ENG., Illus.). 24p. (J). (gr. 3-7). 26.95 *(978-1-62617-147-3(5)*, Epic Bks.) Bellwether Media.

McIntosh, J. S. Wrestling. 2010. (Getting the Edge Ser.). 96p. (YA). lib. bdg. 24.95 *(978-1-4222-1743-6(4))* Mason Crest.

McNab, Chris. Wrestling. 2005. (Sports Injuries Ser.). (Illus.). 64p. (YA). lib. bdg. 19.95 *(978-1-59084-642-1(7))* Mason Crest.

Nelson, Kristen. The Greatest Wrestlers of All Time, 1 vol. 2019. (Greatest of All Time: Sports Stars Ser.). (ENG.). 32p. (gr. 3-4). pap. 11.50 *(978-1-5382-4791-4(7)*, 6637d669-c224-45dd-8ee6-c931be9787bf) Stevens, Gareth Publishing LLLP.

Orr, Tamra. Day by Day with Dwayne the Rock Johnson. 2011. (Day by Day with... Ser.). (Illus.). 32p. (J). (gr. -1-2). lib. bdg. 25.70 *(978-1-58415-982-7(0))* Mitchell Lane Pubs.

Pantaleo, Steve. DK Reader Level 2: WWE the Rock. 2014. (DK Readers Level 2 Ser.). (ENG., Illus.). 32p. (J). (gr. 1-3). pap. 4.99 *(978-1-4654-2295-8(1)*, DK) DK Games.

—Meet the Champions. 2019. (Illus.). 96p. (J). *(978-1-5444-3793-4(5))* Dorling Kindersley Publishing, Inc.

—WWE Tag Teams & Team-Ups. 2019. (DK Readers Level 2 Ser.). (Illus.). (J). (gr. k-2). (ENG.). 48p. pap. 4.99 *(978-1-4654-7972-3(4)*, DK Children); 46p. *(978-1-5444-3012-6(4))* Dorling Kindersley Publishing, Inc.

Proudfit, Benjamin. Brock Lesnar, 1 vol. 2018. (Superstars of Wrestling Ser.). (ENG.). 32p. (J). (gr. 1-2). 28.27 *(978-1-5382-2095-5(4)*, 74c624c1-1df9-47bf-8c16-252a7acb08fd) Stevens, Gareth Publishing LLLP.

—Daniel Bryan, 1 vol. 2018. (Superstars of Wrestling Ser.). (ENG.). 32p. (J). (gr. 1-2). 28.27 *(978-1-5382-2103-7(9)*, 340ff903-f44f-414d-8602-8668140c5a5e) Stevens, Gareth Publishing LLLP.

—The Miz, 1 vol. 2018. (Superstars of Wrestling Ser.). (ENG.). 32p. (J). (gr. 1-2). 28.27 *(978-1-5382-2111-2(X)*, fb54b7a8-7b6f-4cbb-a64e-c96980c0aea0) Stevens, Gareth Publishing LLLP.

—Roman Reigns, 1 vol. 2018. (Superstars of Wrestling Ser.). (ENG.). 32p. (J). (gr. 1-2). pap. 11.50 *(978-1-5382-2109-9(8)*, 1ff3ad67-c28d-4b6e-82b9-35befa3aa985) Stevens, Gareth Publishing LLLP.

Rebman, Nick. Wrestling. 2018. (Sports Ser.). (ENG., Illus.). 16p. (J). (gr. k-1). pap. 7.95 *(978-1-64185-026-1(4)*, 1641850264); lib. bdg. 25.64 *(978-1-63517-924-8(6)*, 1635179246) North Star Editions. (Focus Readers).

Regis, Natalie & Chiu, David. An Insider's Guide to Wrestling, 1 vol. 2014. (Sports Tips, Techniques, & Strategies Ser.). (ENG.). 48p. (YA). (gr. 6-6). 33.47 *(978-1-4777-8089-3(0)*, 919c5fb5-d543-4e0c-8cb2-913b2971f79d, Rosen Reference) Rosen Publishing Group, Inc., The.

Sandler, Michael. The Rock. 2012. (Wrestling's Tough Guys Ser.). 24p. (J). (gr. 1-6). lib. bdg. 26.99 *(978-1-61772-574-6(9))* Bearport Publishing Co., Inc.

Sauver, Dennis St. Dwayne Johnson. 2018. (Big Buddy Pop Biographies Ser.). (ENG., Illus.). 32p. (J). (gr. 2-5). lib. bdg. 34.21 *(978-1-5321-1800-5(7)*, 30646, Big Buddy Bks.) ABDO Publishing Co.

Scheff, Matt. Pro Wrestling's Greatest Faces. 2016. (Pro Wrestling's Greatest Ser.). (ENG., Illus.). 32p. (J). (gr. 3-9). lib. bdg. 32.79 *(978-1-68078-494-7(3)*, 23811, SportsZone) ABDO Publishing Co.

—Pro Wrestling's Greatest Heels. 2016. (Pro Wrestling's Greatest Ser.). (ENG., Illus.). 32p. (J). (gr. 3-9). lib. bdg. 32.79 *(978-1-68078-495-4(1)*, 23813, SportsZone) ABDO Publishing Co.

—Pro Wrestling's Greatest Matches. 2016. (Pro Wrestling's Greatest Ser.). (ENG., Illus.). 32p. (J). (gr. 3-9). lib. bdg. 32.79 *(978-1-68078-496-1(X)*, 23815, SportsZone) ABDO Publishing Co.

—Pro Wrestling's Greatest Rivalries. 2016. (Pro Wrestling's Greatest Ser.). (ENG., Illus.). 32p. (J). (gr. 3-9). lib. bdg. 32.79 *(978-1-68078-497-8(8)*, 23817, SportsZone) ABDO Publishing Co.

—Pro Wrestling's Greatest Secrets Exposed. 2016. (Pro Wrestling's Greatest Ser.). (ENG., Illus.). 32p. (J). (gr. 3-9). lib. bdg. 32.79 *(978-1-68078-498-5(6)*, 23819, SportsZone) ABDO Publishing Co.

Pro Wrestling's Greatest Tag Teams. 2016. (Pro Wrestling's Greatest Ser.). (ENG., Illus.). 32p. (J). (gr. 3-9). lib. bdg. 32.79 *(978-1-68078-499-2(4)*, 23821, SportsZone) ABDO Publishing Co.
ıerman, Jill. Ronda Rousey. 2019. (Pro Sports Biographies Ser.). (ENG.). 24p. (J). (gr. 1-3). pap. 8.99 *(978-1-68152-451-1(1)*, 11037) Amicus.
-Wrestling. 2019. (Let's Play Sports! Ser.). (ENG., Illus.). 24p. (J). (gr. k-3). lib. bdg. 26.95 *(978-1-64487-003-7(7)*, Blastoff! Readers) Bellwether Media.
t. John, Chris. Wrestling, 1 vol. 2011. (Master This! Ser.). (ENG., Illus.). 32p. (J). (gr. 4-4). lib. bdg. 28.93 *(978-1-4488-5286-4(2)*, 2f8d7150-8837-45b1-b1db-25a7541229d6, PowerKids Pr.) Rosen Publishing Group, Inc., The.
Stars of Pro Wrestling [Capstone Sole Source]. 2010. (Stars of Pro Wrestling Ser.). 32p. lib. bdg. 266.50 *(978-1-4296-5884-3(3)*, Capstone Pr.) Capstone.
Stone, Adam. Edge. 2011. (Pro Wrestling Champions Ser.). (ENG., Illus.). 24p. (J). (gr. 3-7). lib. bdg. 26.95 *(978-1-60014-635-0(X)*, Torque Bks.) Bellwether Media.
—Randy Orton. 2011. (Pro Wrestling Champions Ser.). (ENG., Illus.). 24p. (J). (gr. 3-7). lib. bdg. 26.95 *(978-1-60014-638-1(4)*, Torque Bks.) Bellwether Media.
—Triple H. 2011. (Pro Wrestling Champions Ser.). (ENG., Illus.). 24p. (J). (gr. 3-7). lib. bdg. 26.95 *(978-1-60014-641-1(4)*, Torque Bks.) Bellwether Media.
—The Undertaker. 2011. (Pro Wrestling Champions Ser.). (ENG., Illus.). 24p. (J). (gr. 3-7). lib. bdg. 26.95 *(978-1-60014-640-4(6)*, Torque Bks.) Bellwether Media.
Sullivan, Kevin & DK. DK Reader Level 2: WWE John Cena Second Edition. 2nd rev. ed. 2014. (DK Readers Level 2 Ser.). (ENG.). 32p. (J). (gr. 1-3). pap. 4.99 *(978-1-4654-2088-6(6)*, DK) DK Games.
Wrestling Greats. 2005. (Illus.). 112p. (gr. 7-12). lib. bdg. 265.30 *(978-0-8239-3911-4(1))* Rosen Publishing Group, Inc., The.
Wyborny, Sheila. Dwayne Johnson, 1 vol. 2009. (People in the News Ser.). (ENG., Illus.). 104p. (gr. 7-7). lib. bdg. 41.03 *(978-1-4205-0125-4(9)*, 18135982-5f23-4e70-b56f-cfc848218d5b, Lucent Pr.) Greenhaven Publishing LLC.

WRESTLING—FICTION

Biedrzycki, David. SumoKitty. Biedrzycki, David, illus. 2019. (Illus.). 48p. (J). (gr. k-3). lib. bdg. 18.99 *(978-1-58089-682-5(0))* Charlesbridge Publishing, Inc.
Cazet, Denys. Rumors. 2017. (ENG., Illus.). 212p. (J). (gr. 1-5). 16.99 *(978-1-939547-32-3(6)*, 091db7fb-6140-480f-b98d-5e831ea61f79) Creston Bks.
Eldridge, Jim. The Final Showdown: Match Six. Bielecki, Jan, illus. 2016. (Wrestling Trolls Ser.: 6). (ENG.). 176p. (J). (gr. k-3). pap. 9.99 *(978-1-4714-0269-2(X))* Bonnier Publishing GBR. Dist: Independent Pubs. Group.
Garza, Xavier. The Great & Mighty Nikko! �el Gran y Poderoso Nikko!, 1 vol. Garza, Xavier, illus. 2015. (ENG., Illus.). 32p. (J). (gr. k-3). pap. 11.95 *(978-1-935955-83-2(7)*, 23353382, Cinco Puntos Press) Lee & Low Bks., Inc.
—Lucha Libre: The Man in the Silver Mask - A Bilingual Cuento, 1 vol. 2007. (SPA., Illus.). 40p. (J). (gr. 2-7). pap. 12.95 *(978-1-933693-10-1(X)*, 23353382, Cinco Puntos Press) Lee & Low Bks., Inc.
—Maximilian - The Bingo Rematch: A Bilingual Lucha Libre Thriller, 1 vol. Garza, Xavier, illus. 2013. (Max's Lucha Libre Adventures Ser.: 2).Tr. of Maximilian (Max's Lucha Libre Adventures #2). (ENG., Illus.). 224p. (J). (gr. 3-7). pap. 18.95 *(978-1-935955-46-7(2)*, 23353382, Cinco Puntos Press) Lee & Low Bks., Inc.
—Maximilian & the Mystery of the Guardian Angel, 1 vol. Garza, Xavier, illus. 2011. (Max's Lucha Libre Adventures Ser.: 1). (ENG., Illus.). 208p. (J). (gr. 3-7). pap. 18.95 *(978-1-933693-98-9(3)*, 23353382, Cinco Puntos Press) Lee & Low Bks., Inc.
Gottesfeld, Jeff & Bennett, Cherie. SuperFan. 2011. (WWE Chapter Bks.). (ENG.). 144p. (J). (gr. 3-6). 17.44 *(978-0-448-45611-9(7))* Penguin Young Readers Group.
Lemke, Donald & Lemke, Donald B. Lucha Lizards: Chameleon Cage Match! Eliopoulos, Chris, illus. 2013. (Lucha Lizards Ser.). (ENG.). 48p. (J). (gr. 3-5). pap. 5.95 *(978-1-4342-3874-0(1)*, 118055); lib. bdg. 23.99 *(978-1-4342-3285-4(9)*, 116244) Capstone. (Stone Arch Bks.).
Lynch, Janet Nichols. Addicted to Her. 2010. (ENG.). 256p. (YA). (gr. 7-18). pap. 17.95 *(978-0-8234-2186-2(4))* Holiday Hse., Inc.
Maddox, Jake. Heavyweight Takedown. 2015. (Jake Maddox JV Ser.). (ENG., Illus.). 96p. (J). (gr. 4-6). lib. bdg. 26.65 *(978-1-4342-9638-2(5)*, 126917, Stone Arch Bks.) Capstone.
—Takedown, 1 vol. Tiffany, Sean, illus. 2008. (Jake Maddox Sports Stories Ser.). (ENG.). 72p. (J). (gr. 3-6). pap. 5.95 *(978-1-4342-0870-5(2)*, 95231, Stone Arch Bks.) Capstone.
Martino, Alfred C. Pinned. 2006. (ENG., Illus.). 320p. (YA). (gr. 7-12). reprint ed. pap. 8.99 *(978-0-15-205631-5(9)*, 1196935, Clarion Bks.) HarperCollins Pubs.
Morales, Yuyi. Niño Wrestles the World. Morales, Yuyi, illus. 2013. (ENG., Illus.). 40p. (J). (gr. -1-3). 19.99 *(978-1-59643-604-6(2)*, 900065749) Roaring Brook Pr.
—Rudas: niño's Horrendous Hermanitas. 2018. (ENG., Illus.). 40p. (J). pap. 9.99 *(978-1-250-14336-5(5)*, 900180500) Square Fish.
Morgan, Allen. Matthew & the Midnight Wrestlers, 1 vol. Martchenko, Michael, illus. 2005. (First Flight Level 3 Ser.). (ENG.). 40p. (J). (gr. k-3). lib. bdg. 11.95 *(978-1-55041-915-3(3)*, 354c9091-1e9a-482b-86c0-bbd1228f8727) Trifolium Bks., Inc. CAN. Dist: Firefly Bks., Ltd.
Mulhall, M. B. Heavyweight. 2014. (ENG.). 230p. (YA). pap. 14.99 *(978-1-62798-712-7(6)*, Harmony Ink Pr.) Dreamspinner Pr.
Mulhall, MB. Heavyweight. 2016. (ENG., Illus.). (J). 24.99 *(978-1-63533-026-7(2)*, Harmony Ink Pr.) Dreamspinner Pr.
Nicoll, Maxwell & Smith, Matthew. Slamdown Town. 2020. (ENG., Illus.). 320p. (YA). (gr. 3-7). 14.99 *(978-1-4197-3885-2(2)*, 1291701, Amulet Bks.) Abrams, Inc.
Rayo, Alberto. Thumbelina, Wrestling Champ: A Graphic Novel. López, Álex, illus. 2019. (Far Out Fairy Tales Ser.). (ENG.). 40p. (J). (gr. 3-6). pap. 5.95 *(978-1-4965-8445-8(7)*, 140970); lib. bdg. 26.65 *(978-1-4965-8396-3(5)*, 140687) Capstone. (Stone Arch Bks.).
Richardson, William K. The Grappler. 2011. 184p. (J). (gr. 10-12). pap. 14.50 *(978-1-4269-6035-2(2))* Trafford Publishing.
Schaffter, Ehren. Through the Curtain. 2009. 239p. pap. 20.00 *(978-0-557-20001-6(6))* Lulu Pr., Inc.
Scieszka, Jon. See You Later, Gladiator. McCauley, Adam, illus. 2004. (Time Warp Trio Ser.: No. 9). 87p. (J). (gr. 4-7). 12.65 *(978-0-7569-5986-9(1))* Perfection Learning Corp.
—See You Later, Gladiator #9. McCauley, Adam, illus. 2004. (Time Warp Trio Ser.: 9). 96p. (J). (gr. 2-4). pap. 5.99 *(978-0-14-240117-0(X)*, Puffin Books) Penguin Young Readers Group.
Spinelli, Jerry. There's a Girl in My Hammerlock. 2008. 199p. (gr. 4-8). 16.00 *(978-0-7569-8465-6(3))* Perfection Learning Corp.
—There's a Girl in My Hammerlock. 2007. (ENG.). 208p. (J). (gr. 4-8). pap. 7.99 *(978-1-4169-3937-5(7)*, Aladdin) Simon & Schuster Children's Publishing.
Sterner, Nathan. Onami: The Great Wave. Dutchak, Shelly, illus. 2007. (J). per. *(978-0-9795529-0-8(7))* 716 Productions.
Thomson, Melissa. Tito the Bonecrusher. 2020. (ENG.). 240p. (J). pap. 10.99 *(978-1-250-23331-8(3)*, 900156462) Square Fish.
Villareal, Ray. Body Slammed! 2012. (YA). pap. 11.95 *(978-1-55885-749-0(4)*, Piñata Books) Arte Publico Pr.
Weis, Lyle Percy. Let's Wrestle. (J). 5.95 *(978-0-9686899-4-3(9))* Hodgepog Bks. CAN. Dist: Coteau Bks.
Wenjen, Mia. Sumo Joe, 1 vol. Iwata, Nat, illus. 2019. (ENG.). 40p. (J). (gr. k-3). 20.95 *(978-1-62014-802-0(1)*, leelowbooks) Lee & Low Bks., Inc.
West, Tracey. Night of Champions, 2 vols. 2011. (WWE Chapter Bks.: 2). (ENG.). 96p. (J). (gr. 3-6). 17.44 *(978-0-448-45706-2(7))* Penguin Young Readers Group.
—Race to the Rumble, No. 1. 2011. (WWE Chapter Bks.: 1). (ENG.). 96p. (J). (gr. 3-6). 17.44 *(978-0-448-45555-6(2))* Penguin Young Readers Group.
Wheeler, Lisa. Dino-Wrestling. Gott, Barry, illus. 2013. (Dino-Sports Ser.). (ENG.). 32p. (J). (YA). (gr. k-3). 18.99 *(978-1-4677-0212-6(9)*, 2e5de2ee-280b-4cac-95fb-12593f921942, Carolrhoda Bks.) Lerner Publishing Group.

WRIGHT, FRANK LLOYD, 1869-1959

Adkins, Jan. Frank Lloyd Wright: A Twentieth-Century Life. 2008. (Up Close Ser.). (ENG.). 304p. (YA). (gr. 7-18). 8.99 *(978-0-14-241244-2(9)*, Puffin Books) Penguin Young Readers Group.
Atlantic Publishing Group. People That Changed the Course of History: The Story of Frank Lloyd Wright 150 Years after His Birth. 2017. (ENG.). 180p. (YA). lib. bdg. 34.95 *(978-1-62023-225-5(1)*, 54d8c914-cc51-4c1b-b9f9-19d84d64a41d) Atlantic Publishing Group, Inc.
Fandel, Jennifer. Frank Lloyd Wright. (Odysseys in Artistry Ser.). (Illus.). (J). 2016. (ENG.). 80p. (gr. 7-10). *(978-1-60818-718-8(7)*, 20656) 2005. 48p. (gr. 5-9). lib. bdg. 21.95 *(978-1-58341-378-4(2))* Creative Co., The. (Creative Education).
Going, K. L. The Shape of the World: A Portrait of Frank Lloyd Wright. Stringer, Lauren, illus. 2017. (ENG.). 40p. (J). (gr. k-5). 18.99 *(978-1-4424-7821-3(7))* Beach Lane Bks.
Harshman, Marc & Egan Smucker, Anna. Fallingwater: the Building of Frank Lloyd Wright's Masterpiece. Pham, LeUyen, illus. 2017. (ENG.). 40p. (J). 21.99 *(978-1-59643-718-0(9)*, 900075229) Roaring Brook Pr.
Labrecque, Ellen. Who Was Frank Lloyd Wright? 2015. (Who Was...? Ser.). lib. bdg. 16.00 *(978-0-606-37558-0(9))* Turtleback.
Labrecque, Ellen & Who HQ. Who Was Frank Lloyd Wright? Copeland, Gregory, illus. 2015. (Who Was? Ser.). 112p. (J). (gr. 3-7). 6.99 *(978-0-448-48313-9(0)*, Penguin Workshop) Penguin Young Readers Group.
Levy, Janey. The Architecture of Frank Lloyd Wright: Understanding the Concepts of Parallel & Perpendicular, 1 vol. (Math for the REAL World Ser.). 32p. 2010. (ENG., Illus.). (gr. 5-6). pap. 10.00 *(978-1-4042-5144-1(8)*, 93db5db0-fa1c-44cb-8c39-b3df2728a5e6, PowerKids Pr.) 2009. (gr. 4-5). 47.90 *(978-1-60851-418-2(8)*, PowerKids Pr.) 2004. (ENG., Illus.). (YA). (gr. 5-6). lib. bdg. 28.93 *(978-1-4042-2940-2(X)*, 43c84d13-4667-4fa2-be38-e60c95ffce9b) Rosen Publishing Group, Inc., The.
Nardo, Don. Frank Lloyd Wright, 1 vol. 2012. (Eye on Art Ser.). (ENG., Illus.). 112p. (gr. 7-7). lib. bdg. 41.03 *(978-1-4205-0813-0(X)*, 8d2b8810-18f2-4fdb-a86f-a7cfbe7d56a8, Lucent Pr.) Greenhaven Publishing LLC.
Nash, Eric Peter. Frank Lloyd Wright: Force of Nature, Vol. 8. 2018. (American Artists Ser.). 80p. (J). (gr. 7). 33.27 *(978-1-4222-4158-5(0))* Mason Crest.
Simply Wright: A Journey into the Ideas of Frank Lloyd Wright's Architecture. 2004. (J). spiral bd. 17.95 *(978-0-9677348-3-5(5))* Castleconal Pr.
Teegarden, Catherine. How to Think Like Frank Lloyd Wright: Insights, Inspiration, & Activities for Future Architects. Frank Lloyd Wright Foundation, The, ed. 2021. (ENG., Illus.). 144p. (gr. 5). pap. 17.99 *(978-1-941367-47-6(X))* Downtown Bookworks.
Thorne-Thomsen, Kathleen. Frank Lloyd Wright for Kids: His Life & Ideas. 2nd ed. 2014. (For Kids Ser.: 47). (Illus.). 144p. (J). (gr. 4). pap. 18.99 *(978-1-61374-474-1(9))* Chicago Review Pr., Inc.
Will Mayo, Gretchen. Frank Lloyd Wright, 1 vol. 2004. (Trailblazers of the Modern World Ser.). (ENG., Illus.). 48p. (gr. 5-8). pap. 15.05 *(978-0-8368-5261-5(3)*, 45f3ebcf-b375-4780-9b64-64207084e0e8); lib. bdg. 33.67 *(978-0-8368-5101-4(3)*, cac22d00-d471-4739-bc1c-0356d95e9ea2) Stevens, Gareth Publishing LLLP. (Gareth Stevens Secondary Library).

WRIGHT, ORVILLE, 1871-1948

Arrathoon, Leigh A. Men Who Changed the World Vol. II: The First Birdmen: Wilbur & Orville Wright. Davio, John, ed. Hajdyla, Ken, illus. 56p. (J). (gr. 5-6). pap. 5.95 *(978-0-9648564-6-2(8))* Archus Pr., LLC.
Berger, Melvin & Berger, Gilda. Can You Fly High, Wright Brothers? (Scholastic Science Supergiants) Dorman, Brandon, illus. 2007. (ENG.). 48p. (J). (gr. 2-5). pap. 4.99 *(978-0-439-83378-3(7)*, Scholastic Nonfiction) Scholastic, Inc.
Borden, Louise & Marx, Trish. Touching the Sky: The Flying Adventures of Wilbur & Orville Wright. Fiore, Peter M., illus. 2003. (ENG.). 64p. (J). (gr. k-3). 24.99 *(978-0-689-84876-6(5)*, McElderry, Margaret K. Bks.) McElderry, Margaret K. Bks.
Brown, Jonatha A. Los Hermanos Wright (the Wright Brothers), 1 vol. 2004. (Gente Que Hay Que Conocer (People We Should Know) Ser.).Tr. of Wright Brothers. (SPA., Illus.). 24p. (gr. 2-4). lib. bdg. 24.67 *(978-0-8368-4356-9(8)*, 4fe494ac-7534-44de-9528-4e9ba0eeaaf4, Weekly Reader Leveled Readers) Stevens, Gareth Publishing LLLP.
—The Wright Brothers, 1 vol. 2004. (People We Should Know Ser.). (ENG., Illus.). 24p. (gr. 2-4). lib. bdg. 24.67 *(978-0-8368-4314-9(2)*, e7cdd458-a4dd-426f-b07c-25ff618aa2b6, Weekly Reader Leveled Readers) Stevens, Gareth Publishing LLLP.
Buckley, James, Jr. & Who HQ. Who Were the Wright Brothers? Foley, Tim, illus. 2014. (Who Was? Ser.). (ENG.). 112p. (J). (gr. 3-7). 5.99 *(978-0-448-47951-4(6)*, Penguin Workshop) Penguin Young Readers Group.
Buckley, James. Who Were the Wright Brothers? Foley, Tim, illus. 2014. 106p. (J). *(978-1-101-99527-3(0))* Penguin Publishing Group.
Carson, Mary Kay. The Wright Brothers for Kids: How They Invented the Airplane, 21 Activities Exploring the Science & History of Flight. 2003. (For Kids Ser.: 1). (ENG., Illus.). 160p. (J). (gr. 4). pap. 19.99 *(978-1-55652-477-6(3))* Chicago Review Pr., Inc.
Collins, Mary. Airborne: A Photobiography of Wilbur & Orville Wright. 2015. (Photobiographies Ser.). (Illus.). 64p. (J). (gr. 5-9). pap. 7.99 *(978-1-4263-2221-1(6)*, National Geographic Kids) Disney Publishing Worldwide.
—Airborne (Direct Mail Edition) A Photobiography of Wilbur & Orville Wright. 2003. (Photobiographies Ser.). (ENG., Illus.). 64p. (J). (gr. 5-9). 18.95 *(978-0-7922-6957-1(8)*, 53238483) National Geographic Society.
Crompton, Samuel Willard. The Wright Brothers: First in Flight. 2007. (Milestones in American History Ser.). (ENG., Illus.). 128p. (gr. 7-12). lib. bdg. 35.00 *(978-0-7910-9356-6(5)*, P125501, Facts On File) Infobase Holdings, Inc.
Cudeyro, Erica M. American History for Young Minds - Volume 1, Looking Towards the Sky, Book 1, the First Airplane. Butler, Lindsay L., illus. 2008. 20p. pap. 11.95 *(978-1-934925-34-8(9)*, Eloquent Bks.) Strategic Book Publishing & Rights Agency (SBPRA).
Dakers, Diane. Orville & Wilbur Wright: Pioneers of the Age of Flight. 2016. (Crabtree Groundbreaker Biographies Ser.). (ENG., Illus.). 112p. (J). (gr. 5-9). *(978-0-7787-2609-8(6))* Crabtree Publishing Co.
Davis, Lynn. The Wright Brothers. 2015. (Amazing Inventors & Innovators Ser.). (ENG., Illus.). 24p. (J). (gr. k-3). 32.79 *(978-1-62403-726-9(7)*, 17958, Super SandCastle) ABDO Publishing Co.
Deines, Ann, ed. Wilbur & Orville Wright: A Handbook of Facts. 2007. (Illus.). 64p. per. 5.95 *(978-1-888213-75-1(2))* Eastern National.
Dorfman, Janet. The Wright Brothers. Adams, Alison, ed. 2011. (Early Connections Ser.). (ENG.). (J). (gr. 1). 7.17 net. *(978-1-61672-564-8(8))* Benchmark Education Co.
Graham, Ian. You Wouldn't Want to Be on the First Flying Machine! A High-Soaring Ride You'd Rather Not Take. 2013. (You Wouldn't Want To Ser.). lib. bdg. 20.80 *(978-0-606-31631-6(0))* Turtleback.
Hagler, Gina. Orville & Wilbur Wright: The Brothers Who Invented the Airplane. 2019. (YA). pap. *(978-1-9785-1458-4(1))* Enslow Publishing, LLC.
Hamen, Susan E. The Wright Brothers, 1 vol. 2007. (Essential Lives Set 1 Ser.). (ENG., Illus.). 112p. (YA). (gr. 6-12). lib. bdg. 41.36 *(978-1-59928-846-8(X)*, 6645, Essential Library) ABDO Publishing Co.
Hernandez, Marissa. The Wright Brothers (Grade 3) rev. ed. 2018. (Smithsonian: Informational Text Ser.). (ENG., Illus.). 32p. (J). (gr. 3-4). pap. 12.99 *(978-1-4938-6684-7(2))* Teacher Created Materials, Inc.
Hill, Lee Sullivan. The Flyer Flew! The Invention of the Airplane. Orback, Craig, illus. 2006. (On My Own Science Ser.). 48p. (J). (gr. 3-7). per. 6.95 *(978-1-57505-855-9(3))*; (gr. k-3). lib. bdg. 25.26 *(978-1-57505-758-3(1)*, Millbrook Pr.) Lerner Publishing Group.
James, Emily. The Wright Brothers. 2017. (Great Scientists & Inventors Ser.). (ENG., Illus.). 24p. (J). (gr. -1-2). lib. bdg. 27.32 *(978-1-5157-3885-5(X)*, 133788, Capstone Pr.) Capstone.
Jenner, Caryn. First Flight Vol. 4: The Story of the Wright Brothers. 2004. (DK Readers Ser.). (Illus.). 48p. (J). (gr. -1-3). 14.00 *(978-0-7569-3361-6(7))* Perfection Learning Corp.
Kenney, Karen Latchana. Who Invented the Airplane? Wright Brothers vs. Whitehead. 2018. (STEM Smackdown (Alternator Books (r)) Ser.). (ENG., Illus.). 32p. (J). (gr. 3-6). 29.32 *(978-1-5124-8318-5(4)*, daf638d4-934a-4166-819c-14d2eda7d582, Lerner Pubns.) Lerner Publishing Group.
Lefèvre-Garros, J. P. The Wright Brothers, Vol. 3. Uderzo, M., illus. 2012. (Cinebook Recounts Ser.: 3). 48p. (YA). (gr. 6-17). pap. 11.95 *(978-1-84918-100-6(4))* CineBook GBR. Dist: National Bk. Network.
MacLeod, Elizabeth. The Wright Brothers. Krystoforski, Andrej, illus. 2008. (Kids Can Read Ser.). 32p. (J). (gr. 1-3). 14.95 *(978-1-55453-053-3(9))* Kids Can Pr., Ltd. CAN. Dist: Hachette Bk. Group.
McCormick, Lisa Wade. Wright Brothers. 2005. (Scholastic News Nonfiction Readers Ser.). (Illus.). 24p. (J). pap. *(978-0-516-24786-1(7))* Children's Pr., Ltd.
McLaughlin, Kari Massie. My Adventure with the Wright Brothers. 2007. 44p. (J). 8.99 *(978-1-59092-471-6(1))* Blue Forge Pr.
McPherson, Stephanie Sammartino & Gardner, Joseph Sammartino. Wilbur & Orville Wright: Taking Flight. 2004. (Trailblazer Biography Ser.). (Illus.). 120p. (J). 30.60 *(978-1-57505-443-8(4)*, Carolrhoda Bks.) Lerner Publishing Group.
Mills, Nathan & Weir, William. The Wright Brothers: The First to Fly, 1 vol. 2012. (Rosen Readers Ser.). (ENG., Illus.). 24p. (J). (gr. 1-2). pap. 8.25 *(978-1-4488-8863-4(8)*, 4fd8a307-5a9a-4533-b6f4-5f440a65381e, Rosen Classroom) Rosen Publishing Group, Inc., The.
Niz, Xavier W. & Barnett, Charles, III. The Wright Brothers & the Airplane, 1 vol. Erwin, Steve, illus. 2007. (Inventions & Discovery Ser.). (ENG.). 32p. (J). (gr. 3-9). per. 8.10 *(978-0-7368-7897-5(1)*, 93894, Capstone Pr.) Capstone.
Old, Wendie C. The Wright Brothers: Aviation Pioneers & Inventors, 1 vol. 2014. (Legendary American Biographies Ser.). (ENG.). 96p. (J). (gr. 6-6). 29.60 *(978-0-7660-6505-5(7)*, ed65a615-dab7-421f-9cf1-6600a1927377); pap. 13.88 *(978-0-7660-6506-2(5)*, d1a22648-6bca-407f-9867-731dac5e8607) Enslow Publishing, LLC.
Orr, Tamra B. The Dawn of Aviation: The Story of the Wright Brothers. 2005. (Monumental Milestones Ser.). (Illus.). 48p. (YA). (gr. 4-7). lib. bdg. 29.95 *(978-1-58415-396-2(2)*, 1244922) Mitchell Lane Pubs.
Perkis, Andrea. The Wright Brothers Make History!, 1 vol. 2012. (InfoMax Readers Ser.). (ENG., Illus.). 24p. (J). (gr. 1-1). pap. 8.25 *(978-1-4488-9076-7(4)*, d5c44b82-df89-41d1-a1d6-6311f4eaf96c, Rosen Classroom) Rosen Publishing Group, Inc., The.
Prince, Jennifer S. The Life & Times of Asheville's Thomas Wolfe. 2016. (True Tales for Young Readers Ser.). (ENG., Illus.). 116p. (YA). pap. 17.00 *(978-0-86526-484-7(8)*, 01OSPS) Univ. of North Carolina Pr.
Rausch, Monica. Los Hermanos Wright y el Avión (the Wright Brothers & the Airplane), 1 vol. 2007. (Inventores y Sus Descubrimientos (Inventors & Their Discoveries) Ser.). (SPA., Illus.). 24p. (gr. 2-4). pap. 9.15 *(978-0-8368-8001-4(3)*, 0089d5b8-895b-4339-9379-2bb018ad6d59); lib. bdg. 24.67 *(978-0-8368-7996-4(1)*, e778d04d-e2ba-44ac-ac53-08c1d2a75ffc) Stevens, Gareth Publishing LLLP. (Weekly Reader Leveled Readers).
—The Wright Brothers & the Airplane, 1 vol. 2007. (Inventors & Their Discoveries Ser.). (ENG., Illus.). 24p. (gr. 2-4). pap. 9.15 *(978-0-8368-7733-5(0)*, ecc95362-9b04-4b1e-abf9-784c24e3d859); lib. bdg. 24.67 *(978-0-8368-7502-7(8)*, 60ccdd65-0f4b-4610-a9b6-44cc776f23a6) Stevens, Gareth Publishing LLLP. (Weekly Reader Leveled Readers).
Roop, Peter & Roop, Connie. Let's Fly Wilbur & Orville! 2003. (Before I Made History Ser.). (Illus.). 60p. (J). *(978-0-439-55441-1(1))* Scholastic, Inc.
Schulz, Walter A. Johnny Moore & the Wright Brothers' Flying Machine. Bowles, Doug, illus. 2011. (History Speaks: Picture Books Plus Reader's Theater Ser.). 48p. pap. 56.72 *(978-0-7613-7633-0(X))* Lerner Publishing Group.
—Will y Orv. Translations.com Staff, tr. from ENG. Schulz, Janet, illus. 2006. (Yo Solo - Historia (on My Own - History) Ser.). (SPA.). 48p. (gr. 2-4). lib. bdg. 25.26 *(978-0-8225-6263-4(4))* Lerner Publishing Group.
Schulz, Walter A. & Schultz, Walter A. Johnny Moore & the Wright Brothers' Flying Machine. Bowles, Doug, illus. 2011. (History Speaks: Picture Books Plus Reader's Theater Ser.). (ENG.). 48p. (gr. 2-4). pap. 9.95 *(978-0-7613-7117-5(6))* Lerner Publishing Group.
Spilsbury, Louise. The Wright Brothers & the Airplane, 1 vol., 1. 2015. (Inventions That Changed the World Ser.). (ENG.). 32p. (J). (gr. 4-5). pap. 11.00 *(978-1-5081-4643-8(8)*, 4c56e57e-fc15-45c7-9dd2-ab3e8e4a3563, PowerKids Pr.) Rosen Publishing Group, Inc., The.
Sproule, Anna. The Wright Brothers. 2005. (Giants of Science Bilingual Ser.). (J). 9.95 *(978-1-4103-0507-7(4)*, Blackbirch Pr., Inc.) Cengage Gale.
Stevenson, Augusta. Wilbur & Orville Wright: Boys with Wings. Laune, Paul, illus. 2011. 192p. (gr. 2-5). 42.95 *(978-1-258-07857-7(0))* Literary Licensing, LLC.
Stolfo, Paul. The Wright Brothers, 1 vol. 2008. (Real Life Readers Ser.). (ENG.). 12p. (gr. 2-3). pap. 5.90 *(978-1-4042-7955-1(5)*, 882138b3-3b29-4426-9d58-e09d9db8a5be, Rosen Classroom) Rosen Publishing Group, Inc., The.
Strand, Jennifer. The Wright Brothers. 2016. (Incredible Inventors Ser.). (ENG., Illus.). 24p. (J). (gr. -1-2). 49.94 *(978-1-68079-400-7(0)*, 23021, Abdo Zoom-Launch) ABDO Publishing Co.
Tate, Suzanne. Flyer: A Tale of the Wright Dog. Melvin, James, illus. 2003. (Suzanne Tate's History Ser.). (J). pap. 4.95 *(978-1-878405-42-5(X))* Nags Head Art, Inc.
Troupe, Thomas Kingsley. The Wright Brothers' First Flight: a Fly on the Wall History. Tejido, Jomike, illus. 2017. (Fly on the Wall History Ser.). (ENG.). 32p. (J). (gr. 1-3). pap. 7.95 *(978-1-4795-9791-8(0)*, 133420); lib. bdg. 27.99 *(978-1-4795-9787-1(2)*, 133416) Capstone. (Picture Window Bks.).
Van Steenwyk, Elizabeth. One Fine Day: A Radio Play. Farnsworth, Bill, illus. 2004. 32p. (J). (gr. 3-5). 16.00 *(978-0-8028-5234-2(3))* Eerdmans, William B. Publishing Co.
Venezia, Mike. The Wright Brothers: Inventors Whose Ideas Really Took Flight. Venezia, Mike, illus. 2010. (Getting to Know the World's Greatest Inventors & Scientists Ser.). (ENG., Illus.). 32p. (J). (gr. 3-4). 28.00 *(978-0-531-23732-8(X)*, Scholastic Library Publishing.
Wadsworth, Ginger. The Wright Brothers. 2004. (History Maker Bios Ser.). (Illus.). 47p. (J). 26.60 *(978-0-8225-0199-2(6)*, Lerner Pubns.) Lerner Publishing Group.
Weir, William. The Wright Brothers: The First to Fly, 1 vol. 2012. (Beginning Biographies Ser.). (ENG., Illus.). 24p. (J). (gr. 1-2). 26.27 *(978-1-4488-8597-8(3)*, a6eae507-3701-4923-b334-43588179a232, PowerKids Pr.) Rosen Publishing Group, Inc., The.
Will Mayo, Gretchen & O'Hern, Kerri. Los Hermanos Wright (the Wright Brothers), 1 vol. 2007. (Biografías Gráficas (Graphic Biographies) Ser.). (SPA.). 32p. (gr. 3-3). pap. 11.50 *(978-0-8368-7890-5(6)*, 58ce27aa-c072-4dfb-9f5c-978015396e91); (Illus.). lib. bdg. 29.67 *(978-0-8368-7883-7(3)*, e33df689-3e46-453f-903d-d79f662e8c62) Stevens, Gareth Publishing LLLP.
—The Wright Brothers, 1 vol. 2005. (Graphic Biographies Ser.). (ENG., Illus.). 32p. (gr. 3-3). pap. 11.50

W X Y Z

(978-0-8368-6251-5(1), 72802697-9fe2-437e-b5ff-dcb42d5e3a38); lib. bdg. 29.67 *(978-0-8368-6199-0(X),* 75c92bb1-cfee-4542-bb08-9ad55ba5532a) Stevens, Gareth Publishing LLLP.

Will y Orv (Will & Orv) 2006. (J). pap. 6.95 *(978-0-8225-6615-1(X),* Ediciones Lerner) Lerner Publishing Group.

WRIGHT, RICHARD, 1908-1960

Harris, Duchess & Gagne, Tammy. Richard Wright: Author & World Traveler. 2019. (Freedom's Promise Ser.). (ENG., Illus.). 48p. (J). (gr. 4-8). lib. bdg. 35.64 *(978-1-5321-1878-4(3),* 32625) ABDO Publishing Co.

Levy, Debbie. Richard Wright: A Biography. 2007. (Literary Greats Ser.). (ENG., Illus.). 160p. (gr. 7-12). lib. bdg. 33.26 *(978-0-8225-6793-6(8),* Twenty-First Century Bks.) Lerner Publishing Group.

Novel Units. Native Son Novel Units Student Packet. 2019. (ENG.). (YA). pap. 13.99 *(978-1-56137-624-7(8),* Novel Units, Inc.) Classroom Library Co.

—Native Son Novel Units Teacher Guide. 2019. (ENG.). (YA). pap. 12.99 *(978-1-56137-623-0(X),* Novel Units, Inc.) Classroom Library Co.

Wright, Richard & Crews, Nina. Seeing into Tomorrow: Haiku by Richard Wright. Crews, Nina, illus. 2018. (ENG., Illus.). 32p. (J). (gr. k-4). 19.99 *(978-1-5124-1865-1(X),* 483d0e30-7138-4aed-b08c-f9eaa1a926fd, Millbrook Pr.) Lerner Publishing Group.

WRIGHT, WILBUR, 1867-1912

Arrathoon, Leigh A. Men Who Changed the World Vol. II: The First Birdmen: Wilbur & Orville Wright. Davio, John, ed. Hajdyla, Ken, illus. 56p. (J). (gr. 5-6). pap. 5.95 *(978-0-9648564-6-2(8))* Archus Pr., LLC.

Berger, Melvin & Berger, Gilda. Can You Fly High, Wright Brothers? (Scholastic Science Supergiants) Dorman, Brandon, illus. 2007. (ENG.). 48p. (J). (gr. 2-5). pap. 4.99 *(978-0-439-83378-3(7),* Scholastic Nonfiction) Scholastic, Inc.

Borden, Louise & Marx, Trish. Touching the Sky: The Flying Adventures of Wilbur & Orville Wright. Fiore, Peter M., illus. 2003. (ENG.). 64p. (J). (gr. k-3). 24.99 *(978-0-689-84876-6(5),* McElderry, Margaret K. Bks.) McElderry, Margaret K. Bks.

Brown, Jonatha A. Los Hermanos Wright (the Wright Brothers), 1 vol. 2004. (Gente Que Hay Que Conocer (People We Should Know) Ser.).Tr. of Wright Brothers. (SPA., Illus.). 24p. (gr. 2-4). lib. bdg. 24.67 *(978-0-8368-4356-9(8),* 4fe494ac-7534-44de-9528-4e9ba0eeaaf4, Weekly Reader Leveled Readers) Stevens, Gareth Publishing LLLP.

—The Wright Brothers, 1 vol. 2004. (People We Should Know Ser.). (ENG., Illus.). 24p. (gr. 2-4). lib. bdg. 24.67 *(978-0-8368-4314-9(2),* e7cdd458-a4dd-426f-b07c-25ff618aa2b6, Weekly Reader Leveled Readers) Stevens, Gareth Publishing LLLP.

Buckley, James, Jr. & Who HQ. Who Were the Wright Brothers? Foley, Tim, illus. 2014. (Who Was? Ser.). (ENG.). 112p. (J). (gr. 3-7). 5.99 *(978-0-448-47951-4(6),* Penguin Workshop) Penguin Young Readers Group.

Buckley, James. Who Were the Wright Brothers? Foley, Tim, illus. 2014. 106p. (J). *(978-1-101-99527-3(0))* Penguin Publishing Group.

Carson, Mary Kay. The Wright Brothers for Kids: How They Invented the Airplane, 21 Activities Exploring the Science & History of Flight. 2003. (For Kids Ser.: 1). (ENG., Illus.). 160p. (J). (gr. 4). pap. 19.99 *(978-1-55652-477-6(3))* Chicago Review Pr., Inc.

Collins, Mary. Airborne: A Photobiography of Wilbur & Orville Wright. 2015. (Photobiographies Ser.). (Illus.). 64p. (J). (gr. 5-9). pap. 7.99 *(978-1-4263-2221-1(5),* National Geographic Kids) Disney Publishing Worldwide.

—Airborne (Direct Mail Edition) A Photobiography of Wilbur & Orville Wright. 2003. (Photobiographies Ser.). (ENG., Illus.). 64p. (J). (gr. 5-9). 18.95 *(978-0-7922-6957-1(8),* 53238483) National Geographic Society.

Crompton, Samuel Willard. The Wright Brothers: First in Flight. 2007. (Milestones in American History Ser.). (ENG., Illus.). 128p. (gr. 7-12). lib. bdg. 35.00 *(978-0-7910-9356-6(5),* P125501, Facts On File) Infobase Holdings, Inc.

Cudeyro, Erica M. American History for Young Minds - Volume 1, Looking Towards the Sky, Book 1, the First Airplane. Butler, Lindsay L., illus. 2008. 20p. pap. 11.95 *(978-1-934925-34-8(9),* Eloquent Bks.) Strategic Book Publishing & Rights Agency (SBPRA).

Dakers, Diane. Orville & Wilbur Wright: Pioneers of the Age of Flight. 2016. (Crabtree Groundbreaker Biographies Ser.). (ENG., Illus.). 112p. (J). (gr. 5-9). *(978-0-7787-2609-8(6))* Crabtree Publishing Co.

Davis, Lynn. The Wright Brothers. 2015. (Amazing Inventors & Innovators Ser.). (ENG., Illus.). 24p. (J). (gr. k-3). 32.79 *(978-1-62403-726-9(7),* 17958, Super SandCastle) ABDO Publishing Co.

Deines, Ann, ed. Wilbur & Orville Wright: A Handbook of Facts. 2007. (Illus.). 64p. per. 5.95 *(978-1-888213-75-1(2))* Eastern National.

Dorfman, Janet. The Wright Brothers. Adams, Alison, ed. 2011. (Early Connections Ser.). (ENG.). (J). (gr. 1). 7.17 net. *(978-1-61672-564-8(8))* Benchmark Education Co.

Graham, Ian. You Wouldn't Want to Be on the First Flying Machine! A High-Soaring Ride You'd Rather Not Take. 2013. (You Wouldn't Want To Ser.). lib. bdg. 20.80 *(978-0-606-31631-6(0))* Turtleback.

Hagler, Gina. Orville & Wilbur Wright: The Brothers Who Invented the Airplane. 2019. (YA). pap. *(978-1-9785-1458-4(1))* Enslow Publishing, LLC.

Hamen, Susan E. The Wright Brothers, 1 vol. 2007. (Essential Lives Set 1 Ser.). (ENG., Illus.). 112p. (YA). (gr. 6-12). lib. bdg. 41.36 *(978-1-59928-846-8(X),* 6645, Essential Library) ABDO Publishing Co.

Hill, Lee Sullivan. The Flyer Flew! The Invention of the Airplane. Orback, Craig, illus. 2006. (On My Own Science Ser.). 48p. (J). (gr. 3-7). per. 6.95 *(978-1-57505-855-9(3));* (gr. k-3). lib. bdg. 25.26 *(978-1-57505-758-3(1),* Millbrook Pr.) Lerner Publishing Group.

James, Emily. The Wright Brothers. 2017. (Great Scientists & Inventors Ser.). (ENG., Illus.). 24p. (J). (gr. -1-2). lib. bdg. 27.32 *(978-1-5157-3885-5(X),* 133788, Capstone Pr.) Capstone.

Jenner, Caryn. First Flight Vol. 4: The Story of the Wright Brothers. 2004. (DK Readers Ser.). (Illus.). 48p. (gr. -1-3). 14.00 *(978-0-7569-3361-6(7))* Perfection Learning Corp.

Kenney, Karen Latchana. Who Invented the Airplane? Wright Brothers vs. Whitehead. 2018. (STEM Smackdown (Alternator Books (r)) Ser.). (ENG., Illus.). 32p. (J). (gr. 3-6). 29.32 *(978-1-5124-8318-5(4),* daf638d4-934a-4166-819c-14d2eda7d582, Lerner Pubns.) Lerner Publishing Group.

Lefèvre-Garros, J. P. The Wright Brothers, Vol. 3. Uderzo, M., illus. 2012. (Cinebook Recounts Ser.: 3). 48p. (YA). (gr. 6-17). pap. 11.95 *(978-1-84918-100-6(4))* CineBook GBR. Dist: National Bk. Network.

MacLeod, Elizabeth. The Wright Brothers. Krystoforski, Andrej, illus. 2008. (Kids Can Read Ser.). 32p. (J). (gr. 1-3). 14.95 *(978-1-55453-053-3(9))* Kids Can Pr., Ltd. CAN. Dist: Hachette Bk. Group.

McCormick, Lisa Wade. Wright Brothers. 2005. (Scholastic News Nonfiction Readers Ser.). (Illus.). 24p. (J). pap. *(978-0-516-24786-1(7))* Children's Pr., Ltd.

McLaughlin, Kari Massie. My Adventure with the Wright Brothers. 2007. 44p. (J). 8.99 *(978-1-59092-471-6(1))* Blue Forge Pr.

McPherson, Stephanie Sammartino & Gardner, Joseph Sammartino. Wilbur & Orville Wright: Taking Flight. 2004. (Trailblazer Biography Ser.). (Illus.). 120p. (J). 30.60 *(978-1-57505-443-8(4),* Carolrhoda Bks.) Lerner Publishing Group.

Mills, Nathan & Weir, William. The Wright Brothers: The First to Fly, 1 vol. 2012. (Rosen Readers Ser.). (ENG., Illus.). 24p. (J). (gr. 1-2). pap. 8.25 *(978-1-4488-8863-4(8),* 4fd8a307-5a9a-4533-b6f4-5f440a65381e, Rosen Classroom) Rosen Publishing Group, Inc., The.

Niz, Xavier W. & Barnett, Charles, III. The Wright Brothers & the Airplane, 1 vol. Erwin, Steve, illus. 2007. (Inventions & Discovery Ser.). (ENG.). 32p. (J). (gr. 3-9). per. 8.10 *(978-0-7368-7897-5(1),* 93894, Capstone Pr.) Capstone.

Old, Wendie C. The Wright Brothers: Aviation Pioneers & Inventors, 1 vol. 2014. (Legendary American Biographies Ser.). (ENG.). 96p. (gr. 6-6). 29.60 *(978-0-7660-6505-5(7),* ed65a615-dab7-421f-9cf1-6600a1927377); pap. 13.88 *(978-0-7660-6506-2(5),* d1a22648-6bca-407f-9867-731dac5e8607) Enslow Publishing, LLC.

Orr, Tamra B. The Dawn of Aviation: The Story of the Wright Brothers. 2005. (Monumental Milestones Ser.). (Illus.). 48p. (YA). (gr. 4-7). lib. bdg. 29.95 *(978-1-58415-396-2(2),* 1244922) Mitchell Lane Pubs.

Perkis, Andrea. The Wright Brothers Make History!, 1 vol. 2012. (InfoMax Readers Ser.). (ENG., Illus.). 24p. (J). (gr. 1-1). pap. 8.25 *(978-1-4488-9076-7(4),* d5c44b82-df89-41d1-a1d6-6311f4eaf96c, Rosen Classroom) Rosen Publishing Group, Inc., The.

Prince, Jennifer S. The Life & Times of Asheville's Thomas Wolfe. 2016. (True Tales for Young Readers Ser.). (ENG., Illus.). 116p. (YA). pap. 17.00 *(978-0-86526-484-7(8),* 01OSPS) Univ. of North Carolina Pr.

Rausch, Monica. Los Hermanos Wright y el Avión (the Wright Brothers & the Airplane), 1 vol. 2007. (Inventores y Sus Descubrimientos (Inventors & Their Discoveries) Ser.). (SPA., Illus.). 24p. (gr. 2-4). pap. 9.15 *(978-0-8368-8001-4(3),* 0089d5b8-895b-4339-9379-2bb018ad6d59); lib. bdg. 24.67 *(978-0-8368-7996-4(1),* e778d04d-e2ba-44ac-ac53-08c1d2a75ffc) Stevens, Gareth Publishing LLLP. (Weekly Reader Leveled Readers).

—The Wright Brothers & the Airplane, 1 vol. 2007. (Inventors & Their Discoveries Ser.). (ENG., Illus.). 24p. (gr. 2-4). pap. 9.15 *(978-0-8368-7733-5(0),* ecc95362-9b04-4b1e-abf9-784c24e3d859); lib. bdg. 24.67 *(978-0-8368-7502-7(8),* 60ccdd65-0f4b-4610-a9b6-44cc776f23a6) Stevens, Gareth Publishing LLLP. (Weekly Reader Leveled Readers).

Roop, Peter & Roop, Connie. Let's Fly Wilbur & Orville! 2003. (Before I Made History Ser.). (Illus.). 60p. (J). *(978-0-439-55441-1(1))* Scholastic, Inc.

Schulz, Walter A. Johnny Moore & the Wright Brothers' Flying Machine. Bowles, Doug, illus. 2011. (History Speaks: Picture Books Plus Reader's Theater Ser.). 48p. pap. 56.72 *(978-0-7613-7633-0(X))* Lerner Publishing Group.

—Will y Orv. Translations.com Staff, tr. from ENG. Schulz, Janet, illus. 2006. (Yo Solo - Historia (on My Own - History) Ser.). (SPA.). 48p. (gr. 2-4). lib. bdg. 25.26 *(978-0-8225-6263-4(4))* Lerner Publishing Group.

Schulz, Walter A. & Schultz, Walter A. Johnny Moore & the Wright Brothers' Flying Machine. Bowles, Doug, illus. 2011. (History Speaks: Picture Books Plus Reader's Theater Ser.). (ENG.). 48p. (gr. 2-4). pap. 9.95 *(978-0-7613-7117-5(6))* Lerner Publishing Group.

Spilsbury, Louise. The Wright Brothers & the Airplane, 1 vol., 1. 2015. (Inventions That Changed the World Ser.). (ENG.). 32p. (J). (gr. 4-5). pap. 11.00 *(978-1-5081-4643-8(8),* 4c56e57e-fc15-45c7-9dd2-ab3e8e4a3563, PowerKids Pr.) Rosen Publishing Group, Inc., The.

Sproule, Anna. The Wright Brothers. 2005. (Giants of Science Bilingual Ser.). (J). 9.95 *(978-1-4103-0507-7(4),* Blackbirch Pr., Inc.) Cengage Gale.

Stevenson, Augusta. Wilbur & Orville Wright: Boys with Wings. Laune, Paul, illus. 2011. 192p. (gr. 2-5). 42.95 *(978-1-258-07857-7(0))* Literary Licensing, LLC.

Stolfo, Paul. The Wright Brothers, 1 vol. 2008. (Real Life Readers Ser.). (ENG.). 12p. (gr. 2-3). pap. 5.90 *(978-1-4042-7955-1(5),* 882138b3-3b29-4426-9d58-e09d9db8a5be, Rosen Classroom) Rosen Publishing Group, Inc., The.

Strand, Jennifer. The Wright Brothers. 2016. (Incredible Inventors Ser.). (ENG., Illus.). 24p. (J). (gr. -1-2). 49.94 *(978-1-68079-400-7(0),* 23021, Abdo Zoom-Launch) ABDO Publishing Co.

Tate, Suzanne. Flyer: A Tale of the Wright Dog. Melvin, James, illus. 2003. (Suzanne Tate's History Ser.). (J). pap. 4.95 *(978-1-878405-42-5(X))* Nags Head Art, Inc.

Thompson, Ben & Slader, Erik. The Wright Brothers: Nose-Diving into History (Epic Fails #1) Foley, Tim, illus. 2018. (Epic Fails Ser.: 1). (ENG.). 128p. (J). pap. 7.99 *(978-1-250-15056-1(6),* 900182545) Roaring Brook Pr.

Troupe, Thomas Kingsley. The Wright Brothers' First Flight: a Fly on the Wall History. Tejido, Jomike, illus. 2017. (Fly on the Wall History Ser.). (ENG.). 32p. (J). (gr. 1-3). pap. 7.95 *(978-1-4795-9791-8(0),* 133420); lib. bdg. 27.99 *(978-1-4795-9787-1(2),* 133416) Capstone. (Picture Window Bks.).

Van Steenwyk, Elizabeth. One Fine Day: A Radio Play. Farnsworth, Bill, illus. 2004. 32p. (J). (gr. 3-5). 16.00 *(978-0-8028-5234-2(3))* Eerdmans, William B. Publishing Co.

Venezia, Mike. The Wright Brothers: Inventors Whose Ideas Really Took Flight. Venezia, Mike, illus. 2010. (Getting to Know the World's Greatest Inventors & Scientists Ser.). (ENG., Illus.). 32p. (J). (gr. 3-4). 28.00 *(978-0-531-23732-8(X))* Scholastic Library Publishing.

Weir, William. The Wright Brothers: The First to Fly, 1 vol. 2012. (Beginning Biographies Ser.). (ENG., Illus.). 24p. (J). (gr. 1-2). 26.27 *(978-1-4488-8597-8(3),* a6eae507-3701-4923-b334-43588179a232, PowerKids Pr.) Rosen Publishing Group, Inc., The.

Wilgus, Alison. Science Comics: Flying Machines: How the Wright Brothers Soared. 2017. (Science Comics Ser.). (ENG., Illus.). 128p. (J). pap. 12.99 *(978-1-62672-139-5(4),* 900140349, First Second Bks.) Roaring Brook Pr.

Will Mayo, Gretchen & O'Hern, Kerri. Los Hermanos Wright (the Wright Brothers), 1 vol. 2007. (Biografías Gráficas (Graphic Biographies) Ser.). (SPA.). 32p. (gr. 3-3). pap. 11.50 *(978-0-8368-7890-5(6),* 58ce27aa-c072-4dfb-9f5c-978015396e91); (Illus.). lib. bdg. 29.67 *(978-0-8368-7883-7(3),* e33df689-3e46-453f-903d-d79f662e8c62) Stevens, Gareth Publishing LLLP.

—The Wright Brothers, 1 vol. 2005. (Graphic Biographies Ser.). (ENG., Illus.). 32p. (gr. 3-3). pap. 11.50 *(978-0-8368-6251-5(1),* 72802697-9fe2-437e-b5ff-dcb42d5e3a38); lib. bdg. 29.67 *(978-0-8368-6199-0(X),* 75c92bb1-cfee-4542-bb08-9ad55ba5532a) Stevens, Gareth Publishing LLLP.

Will y Orv (Will & Orv) 2006. (J). pap. 6.95 *(978-0-8225-6615-1(X),* Ediciones Lerner) Lerner Publishing Group.

WRIGHT, WILBUR, 1867-1912—FICTION

Bailey, Gerry & Foster, Karen. The Wright Brothers' Glider. Radford, Karen & Noyes, Leighton, illus. 2008. (Stories of Great People Ser.). (ENG.). 40p. (J). (gr. 3-8). pap. *(978-0-7787-3715-5(2));* lib. bdg. *(978-0-7787-3693-6(8))* Crabtree Publishing Co.

Glass, Andrew. The Wondrous Whirligig: The Wright Brothers¿ First Flying Machine. Glass, Andrew, illus. 2007. (Illus.). 30p. (J). reprint ed. 17.00 *(978-1-4223-6765-0(7))* DIANE Publishing Co.

Gutman, Dan. Race for the Sky: The Kitty Hawk Diaries of Johnny Moore. 2003. (ENG., Illus.). 192p. (J). (gr. 5-9). 19.99 *(978-0-689-84554-3(5),* Simon & Schuster Bks. For Young Readers) Simon & Schuster Bks. For Young Readers.

Herodotus. The Wright Brothers Adventure. 2005. (Illus.). (J). *(978-0-9762509-1-3(8))* Society For The Understanding Of Early Child Development.

Rigsby, Annelle & Raffa, Edwina. Race to Kitty Hawk. 2003. (Adventures in America Ser.). (Illus.). 84p. (gr. 4). 14.95 *(978-1-893110-33-5(8))* Silver Moon Pr.

Sutton, Felix. We Were There at the First Airplane Flight. Matulay, Laszlo, illus. 2013. (ENG.). 192p. (J). (gr. 3-8). pap. 6.99 *(978-0-486-49258-2(3),* 492583) Dover Pubns., Inc.

Sutton, Felix & Loening, Grover. We Were There at the First Airplane Flight. Matulay, Laszlo, illus. 2011. 194p. 42.95 *(978-1-258-09600-7(5))* Literary Licensing, LLC.

WRITERS

see Authors

WRITING

see also Alphabet; Calligraphy; Ciphers; Cryptography; Hieroglyphics; Picture-Writing; Typewriting

Activity Worksheets. 2004. (J). spiral bd. 29.95 *(978-1-886441-64-4(2))* Zoo-phonics, Inc.

Amaze Us!, 6 vols. (Wildcats Ser.). 32p. (gr. 2-8). *(978-0-322-02442-7(0))* Wright Group/McGraw-Hill.

Amazing Maps: Level Q, 6 vols. (Wonder Worldtm Ser.). 48p. 39.95 *(978-0-7802-2945-7(2))* Wright Group/McGraw-Hill.

Analogies 1: Grade 7-8. 2004. (Analogies Ser.). pap. 7.25 *(978-0-8388-2225-8(8))* Educators Publishing Service, Inc.

Analogies 2: Grade 9-10. 2004. (Analogies Ser.). pap. 7.25 *(978-0-8388-2227-2(4))* Educators Publishing Service, Inc.

Analogies 3: Grade 11-12. 2004. (Analogies Ser.). pap. 7.25 *(978-0-8388-2229-6(0))* Educators Publishing Service, Inc.

Analogies 3: Grade11-12 Quiz Book. 2004. (Analogies Ser.). pap. 8.20 *(978-0-8388-2230-2(4))* Educators Publishing Service, Inc.

Anorak Press Staff. Anorak: Writing. 2013. (ENG., Illus.). 68p. (J). pap. 9.99 *(978-1-4236-3390-7(3),* Anorak Pr.) Gibbs Smith, Publisher.

Aprende a Escribir. 2003. (SPA.). 22p. (J). (gr. -1-1). *(978-968-5308-89-2(6),* Silver Dolphin en Español) Advanced Marketing, S. de R. L. de C. V.

Arnold, Clareen. Handwriting - Modern Manuscript. 2003. (Skill Builders Ser.). 80p. 2.95 *(978-1-932210-26-2(1))* Rainbow Bridge Publishing.

The Art of Calligraphy. 2004. (Classic Craft Cases Ser.). (ENG., Illus.). 64p. *(978-1-84229-800-8(3))* Top That! Publishing PLC.

Ashton, Christine. The Genie of the Bike Lamp: Level P, 6 vols. (Mountain Peaks Ser.). 128p. (gr. 6-18). 36.95 *(978-0-322-05892-7(9))* Wright Group/McGraw-Hill.

Beyond the Beyond, 6 vols. (Wildcats Ser.). 32p. (gr. 2-8). *(978-0-322-02444-1(7))* Wright Group/McGraw-Hill.

BJU Staff. Handwriting Worktext Grd 2. 2004. pap. 11.50 *(978-1-57924-103-2(4))* BJU Pr.

—Handwriting Worktext Grd 3. 2004. pap. 11.50 *(978-1-57924-215-2(4))* BJU Pr.

—Handwriting Worktext Grd 4. 2004. pap. 11.50 *(978-1-57924-263-3(4))* BJU Pr.

—Handwriting Worktext Grd 5. 2004. pap. 11.50 *(978-1-57924-298-5(7))* BJU Pr.

—Handwriting Worktext Grd 6. 2004. pap. 11.50 *(978-1-57924-352-4(5))* BJU Pr.

Bradshaw, Georgine & Wrighton, Charlene. Basic Kit - Kindergarten. Clark, Irene, illus. 2005. Orig. Title: Basic Kit I (J). 249.95 *(978-1-886441-31-6(6))* Zoo-phonics, Inc.

—Kindergarten Zoo-per Kit. Clark, Irene, illus. 2005. (J). 499.95 *(978-1-886441-34-7(0),* ZOP4219) Zoo-phonics, Inc.

—Preschool Zoo-per Kit. Clark, Irene, illus. 2005. (J). 449.95 *(978-1-886441-32-3(4),* ZOP4218) Zoo-phonics, Inc.

Bright & Beyond - Writing. 2004. (J). *(978-0-9726170-9-3(4))* Pal Toys, LLC.

Brown Conroy, Erin. Writing Skillbuilders Bk. 1: A Fun-Filled Book of Prewriting Skills for Beginning Writers. 2004. (J). spiral bd. 14.95 *(978-0-9740981-6-6(7))* Celtic Cross Communications.

—Writing Skillbuilders Bk. 2: A Fun-Filled Activity Book to Build Strong Handwriting Skills. 2004. (J). spiral bd. 14.95 *(978-0-9740981-7-3(5))* Celtic Cross Communications.

—Writing Skillbuilders Bk. 3: A Fun-Filled Activity Book for Beautiful Cursive Handwriting. 2004. (J). spiral bd. 14.95 *(978-0-9740981-8-0(3))* Celtic Cross Communications.

Budgell, Gill & Ruttle, Kate. Penpals for Handwriting Year 2 Practice Book. 2nd rev. ed. 2015. (Penpals for Handwriting Ser.). (ENG., Illus.). 32p. pap. 15.35 *(978-1-316-50137-5(X))* Cambridge Univ. Pr.

—Penpals for Handwriting Year 3 Practice Book. 2nd rev. ed. 2015. (Penpals for Handwriting Ser.). (ENG., Illus.). 32p. pap. 15.35 *(978-1-316-50141-2(8))* Cambridge Univ. Pr.

Bukiet, Suzanne. Scripts of the World. 2nd ed. (Illus.). 91p. (YA). reprint ed. 19.95 *(978-0-9656274-1-2(1))* Another Language Pr.

Burke, Mary F. Four Square: The Personal Writing Coach, Grades 1-3. Radtke, Becky, illus. 2005. 112p. (J). pap. 12.95 *(978-1-57310-446-3(9))* Teaching & Learning Co.

Callella, Trisha. Daily Writing Warm-Ups: Grades 3-4. 2006. (Illus.). 128p. (J). (gr. 5-6). per. 13.99 *(978-1-59198-306-4(1))* Creative Teaching Pr., Inc.

—Daily Writing Warm-Ups: Grades 5-6. 2006. (SAM., Illus.). 128p. (J). (gr. 5-6). per. 13.99 *(978-1-59198-307-1(X))* Creative Teaching Pr., Inc.

Canavan, Roger. You Wouldn't Want to Live Without Writing! 2015. (You Wouldn't Want to Live Without Ser.). lib. bdg. 20.80 *(978-0-606-37474-3(4))* Turtleback.

Cheaney, Janie B. Wordsmith Craftsman Grd 10 + 2004. pap. 16.00 *(978-1-929683-20-8(0))* Colbert Hse., LLC, The.

—Wordsmith Grd 7-9. 2004. pap. 16.00 *(978-1-929683-18-5(9))* Colbert Hse., LLC, The.

Citylit Kids. Write On! 2012. 68p. pap. 10.00 *(978-1-936328-10-9(0))* CityLit Pr.

Claire, Elizabeth. Hi! (Illus.). (J). wbk. ed. *(978-0-8056-0122-0(8))* Minerva Bks., Ltd.

Collins Easy Learning. Pen Control Age 3-5 Wipe Clean Activity Book: Ideal for Home Learning. 2017. (Collins Easy Learning Preschool Ser.). (ENG.). 24p. (J). (gr. -1-k). 7.99 *(978-0-00-821290-2(2))* HarperCollins Pubs. Ltd. GBR. Dist: Independent Pubs. Group.

Coon, Nora. Teen Dream Jobs: How to Find the Job You Really Want Now! 2004. (Illus.). 132p. (YA). (gr. 8-12). per. 9.95 *(978-1-58270-093-9(1))* Beyond Words Publishing, Inc.

Cyberspace, 6 vols. (Wildcats Ser.). 32p. (gr. 2-8). *(978-0-322-00600-3(7))* Wright Group/McGraw-Hill.

David, Juliet. Learn & Play: Chalkboard Activities. Prole, Helen, illus. 2007. (Candle Bible for Toddlers Ser.). 12p. (J). (gr. -1-k). bds. 11.99 *(978-0-8254-7331-9(4),* Candle Bks.) Lion Hudson PLC GBR. Dist: Kregel Pubns.

Davidson, Kay. Writing the Simple 6: A Writing Rubic for Kids. 2004. pap. 28.95 *(978-1-931334-38-9(2))* Pieces of Learning.

de Diaz, Rosario Ahumada. Juguemos con Letras: Ejercicios de Iniciación a la Escritura. (SPA.). (J). pap. 9.95 *(978-968-24-0919-6(5),* TRM40) Trillas Editorial, S. A. MEX. Dist: Continental Bk. Co., Inc.

Dinosaur Detective: 6 Each of 1 Anthology, 6 vols. (Wildcats Ser.). 32p. (gr. 2-8). *(978-0-322-00586-0(8))* Wright Group/McGraw-Hill.

Dwyer, Carol. Cursive Writing 3-4. 2019. (ENG.). 64p. (Orig.). (J). (gr. 3-4). pap. 4.49 *(978-1-58947-398-0(1),* 17b019d0-f3ed-4a47-9e85-38e7c57275dc) School Zone Publishing Co.

Early Stage 2 Models for Writing. 2003. 135.95 *(978-0-673-77820-8(7))* Celebration Pr.

Early Stage 2 Shared Writing Templates. 2003. 135.95 *(978-0-673-77821-5(5))* Celebration Pr.

Emergent Stage 1 Models for Writing. 2003. 135.95 *(978-0-673-77818-5(5))* Celebration Pr.

Emergent Stage 1 Shared Writing Templates. 2003. 135.95 *(978-0-673-77819-2(3))* Celebration Pr.

English I: Language Skills, Chapter 3 Activities. 2005. (Illus.). 54p. (YA). pap. 5.00 *(978-1-59476-139-3(6))* Paradigm Accelerated Curriculum.

Erickson, Karen. MEville to WEville Unit 1: Unit 1 ME, 2 Bks., manual and children's Bk. 2004. 292p. 75.00 *(978-0-9666667-5-5(5))* AbleNet, Inc.

Evan-Moor Educational Publishers. Text Based Writing Nonfiction, Grade 2. 2014. (Text Based Writing Ser.). (ENG., Illus.). 132p. (J). (gr. 2-2). pap., tchr. ed. 23.99 *(978-1-61368-995-0(0))* Evan-Moor Educational Pubs.

Everett, Reese. Reciting the Pledge, Yes or No. 2016. (Seeing Both Sides Ser.). (ENG.). 32p. (gr. 3-6). 32.79 *(978-1-68191-381-0(X),* 9781681913810) Rourke Educational Media.

Feldgus, Eileen G. & Cardonick, Isabell. Kid Writing: A Systematic Approach to Phonics, Journals, & Writing Workshop. 2nd rev. ed. 192p. (J). (gr. k-2). pap. 26.50 *(978-0-322-06435-5(X))* Wright Group/McGraw-Hill.

Festival Fun: 6 Each of 1 Anthology, 6 vols. (Wildcats Ser.). 32p. (gr. 2-8). *(978-0-322-02424-3(2))* Wright Group/McGraw-Hill.

Findley, Violet. Cursive Writing Practice: Wacky Facts. 2016. (ENG., Illus.). 48p. (J). (gr. 2-5). pap. 10.99 *(978-0-545-94317-8(5),* 594317) Scholastic, Inc.

—Handwriting Practice: Wacky Facts. 2016. (ENG., Illus.). 48p. (J). (gr. k-3). pap. 10.99 *(978-1-338-03061-7(2),* 803061) Scholastic, Inc.

Fire! Fire! 6 Each of 1 Anthology, 6 vols. (Wildcats Ser.). 32p. (gr. 2-8). *(978-0-322-00581-5(7))* Wright Group/McGraw-Hill.

tzGerald, Elizabeth. Cursive First: An Introduction to Cursive Penmanship. 2nd ed. 2003. (Illus.). pap. 14.95 *(978-0-9744920-1-8(9))* LITHBTH Educational Services.
ash Kids Editors, ed. Print Writing: A Creepy-Crawly Alphabet. Reese, Brandon, illus. 2012. (ENG.). 112p. (J). (gr. k-2). pap. 5.95 *(978-1-4114-6344-8(7)*, Spark Publishing Group) Sterling Publishing Co., Inc.
ash Kids Editors, Flash Kids & Christoph, Jamey, illus. Cursive Writing: Around the World in 26 Letters. 2012. 112p. (J). (gr. 2-4). pap. 5.95 *(978-1-4114-6345-5(5)*, Spark Publishing Group) Sterling Publishing Co., Inc.
lath, Camden. Freelance & Technical Writers: Words for Sale. 2010. (New Careers for the 21st Century Ser.). (Illus.). 64p. (YA). (gr. 7-18). lib. bdg. 22.95 *(978-1-4222-1814-3(7))* Mason Crest.
luency Stage 3 Shared Writing Templates. 2003. 125.50 *(978-0-673-77822-2(3))* Celebration Pr.
redericks, Anthony D. & Lynott, Vicky. Write to Comprehend: Using Writing as a Tool to Build Reading Comprehension. 2007. (Illus.). 138p. per. 19.95 *(978-1-59647-120-7(4))* Good Year Bks.
redrich, Volker, illus. Rechtschreibtraining fuer die 1. Klasse. (Duden-Lernminuten Ser.). (GER.). 32p. (J). wbk. ed. *(978-3-411-70831-4(X))* Bibliographisches Institut & F. A. Brockhaus AG DEU. Dist: International Bk. Import Service, Inc.
—Rechtschreibtraining fuer die 1. und 2. Klasse. (Duden-Lernminuten Ser.). (GER.). 32p. (J). wbk. ed. *(978-3-411-70841-3(7))* Bibliographisches Institut & F. A. Brockhaus AG DEU. Dist: International Bk. Import Service, Inc.
Get Smart Skills Staff. PSSA Writing: Pennsylvania System of School Assessment. 2004. 192p. (gr. 11-18). pap. 14.95 *(978-1-932635-29-4(7))* Webster House Publishing LLC.
Gibbons, Casey Hartley. A Girl's Life with God. 2006. 160p. pap. 8.99 *(978-1-56309-757-7(5)*, N034115, New Hope Pubs.) Iron Stream Media.
Gould, Judith S. & Burke, Mary F. Four Square: The Personal Writing Coach, Grades 4-6. Ginger Illustration, illus. 2005. 112p. (J). pap. 12.95 *(978-1-57310-447-0(7))* Teaching & Learning Co.
—Four Square: The Personal Writing Coach, Grades 7-9. Wheeler, Ron, illus. 2005. 112p. (J). pap. 12.95 *(978-1-57310-448-7(5))* Teaching & Learning Co.
Gould, Judith S. & Gould, Evan Jay. Four Square: A Companion to the Four Square Writing Method: Writing in the Content Areas for Grades 1-4. Mitchell, Judy, ed. Radtke, Becky J., illus. 2004. 112p. (J). pap. 11.95 *(978-1-57310-421-0(3))* Teaching & Learning Co.
—Four Square: A Companion to the Four Square Writing Method: Writing in the Content Areas for Grades 5-9. Mitchell, Judy, ed. Wheeler, Ron, illus. 2004. 112p. (J). pap. 11.95 *(978-1-57310-422-7(1))* Teaching & Learning Co.
Greeley, August. Mayan Writing in Mesoamerica. 2009. (Writing in the Ancient World Ser.). 24p. (gr. 3-3). 42.50 *(978-1-60854-903-0(8)*, PowerKids Pr.) Rosen Publishing Group, Inc., The.
Green, Lyric & Meachen Rau, Dana. Future Ready Creative Writing Projects, 1 vol. 2017. (Future Ready Project Skills Ser.). (ENG.). 48p. (gr. 3-4). pap. 12.70 *(978-0-7660-8767-5(0)*, c88bc4a1-b814-4602-ba06-6c9da2e1812b) Enslow Publishing, LLC.
Group/McGraw-Hill, Wright. Babies: Collection 1. (Storyteller Interactive Writing Cards Ser.). (gr. k-3). *(978-0-322-09361-4(9))* Wright Group/McGraw-Hill.
—Bad News Good News: Level N, 6 vols. (Autumn Leaves Ser.). 128p. (gr. 3-6). 36.95 *(978-0-322-06733-2(2))* Wright Group/McGraw-Hill.
—The Butterfly: Collection 2. (Storyteller Interactive Writing Cards Ser.). (gr. k-3). *(978-0-322-09335-5(X))* Wright Group/McGraw-Hill.
—Cats: Collection 4. (Storyteller Interactive Writing Cards Ser.). (gr. k-3). *(978-0-322-09323-2(6))* Wright Group/McGraw-Hill.
—Early Fluency-Fluency Writing Kit. 2004. (Wright Group Literacy Ser.). (gr. k-3). 132.50 *(978-0-322-07021-9(X))* Wright Group/McGraw-Hill.
—Emergent Writing Kit. 2004. (Wright Group Literacy Ser.). (gr. k-3). 79.50 *(978-0-322-06615-1(8))* Wright Group/McGraw-Hill.
—Five Little Frogs: Collection 1. (Storyteller Interactive Writing Cards Ser.). (J). (gr. k-3). *(978-0-322-09363-8(5))* Wright Group/McGraw-Hill.
—In the Rain Forest, 6 vols. (Wildcats Ser.). 32p. (gr. 2-8). *(978-0-322-00599-0(X))* Wright Group/McGraw-Hill.
—Mischief & Mayhem: Level O, 6 vols. (Autumn Leaves Ser.). 128p. (gr. 3-6). 36.95 *(978-0-322-06727-1(8))* Wright Group/McGraw-Hill.
—Move It & Shake It! 6 Each of 1 Anthology, 6 vols. (Wildcats Ser.). 32p. (gr. 2-8). *(978-0-322-05621-3(7))* Wright Group/McGraw-Hill.
—Movie Magic, 6 vols. (Wildcats Ser.). 32p. (gr. 2-8). *(978-0-322-05630-5(6))* Wright Group/McGraw-Hill.
—The Music Scene, 6 vols. (Wildcats Ser.). 32p. (gr. 2-8). *(978-0-322-05631-2(4))* Wright Group/McGraw-Hill.
—On the Prowl: 6 Each of 1 Anthology, 6 vols. (Wildcats Ser.). 32p. (gr. 2-8). *(978-0-322-05852-1(X))* Wright Group/McGraw-Hill.
—The Party: Collection 1. (Storyteller Interactive Writing Cards Ser.). (gr. k-3). *(978-0-322-09364-5(3))* Wright Group/McGraw-Hill.
—Pigeon Princess: Level O, 6 vols. (Autumn Leaves Ser.). 128p. (gr. 3-6). 36.95 *(978-0-322-06729-5(4))* Wright Group/McGraw-Hill.
—Pixels & Paint, 6 vols. (Wildcats Ser.). 32p. (gr. 2-8). *(978-0-322-05625-1(X))* Wright Group/McGraw-Hill.
—Ready, Set, Pop! Collection 3. (Storyteller Interactive Writing Cards Ser.). (gr. k-3). *(978-0-322-09348-5(1))* Wright Group/McGraw-Hill.
—River Wild: 6 Each of 1 Anthology, 6 vols. (Wildcats Ser.). 32p. (gr. 2-8). *(978-0-322-05857-6(0))* Wright Group/McGraw-Hill.
—Sand: Collection 3. (Storyteller Interactive Writing Cards Ser.). (gr. k-3). *(978-0-322-09349-2(X))* Wright Group/McGraw-Hill.
—Slimed! 6 Each of 1 Anthology, 6 vols. (Wildcats Ser.). 32p. (gr. 2-8). *(978-0-322-05853-8(8))* Wright Group/McGraw-Hill.
—Tiger Level: Adventure Journal Set. (Wildcats Ser.). (gr. 2-8). 31.95 *(978-0-322-05790-6(6))* Wright Group/McGraw-Hill.
—Tiger Level: Lesson Plan Set. (Wildcats Ser.). (gr. 2-8). 96.50 *(978-0-322-06677-9(8))* Wright Group/McGraw-Hill.
—Tiger Level: Wildcats Tiger Complete Kit. (Wildcats Ser.). (gr. 2-8). 599.95 *(978-0-322-06483-6(X))* Wright Group/McGraw-Hill.
—What Sport Is It? Collection 3. (Storyteller Interactive Writing Cards Ser.). (gr. k-3). *(978-0-322-09352-2(X))* Wright Group/McGraw-Hill.
—Working Like a Dog: 6 Each of 1 Anthology, 6 vols. (Wildcats Ser.). 32p. (gr. 2-8). *(978-0-322-05854-5(6))* Wright Group/McGraw-Hill.
—Young & Wild: 6 Each of 1 Anthology, 6 vols. (Wildcats Ser.). 32p. (gr. 2-8). *(978-0-322-05851-4(1))* Wright Group/McGraw-Hill.
—Zoo Tales: 6 Each of 1 Anthology, 6 vols. (Wildcats Ser.). 32p. (gr. 2-8). *(978-0-322-05856-9(2))* Wright Group/McGraw-Hill.
—The 13th Floor: Level O, 6 vols. (Autumn Leaves Ser.). 128p. (gr. 3-6). 36.95 *(978-0-322-06731-8(6))* Wright Group/McGraw-Hill.
Hazan, Maurice, creator. Escrivons: Introduction to Writing in French. (FRE.). (J). 199.95 *(978-1-932770-66-7(6)*, FG11) Symtalk, Inc.
Headley, Shannon. Writing Organizers. 2004. 120p. (J). per. 14.95 *(978-0-9760534-1-5(1))* MK Publishing.
Healy, Nick. Image & Imagination: Ideas & Inspiration for Teen Writers. 2016. (ENG., Illus.). 256p. (YA). (gr. 8-8). pap. 16.95 *(978-1-63079-044-8(3)*, 131435, Switch Pr.) Capstone.
Hoffman, Joan. Tracing Trails Pre-Writing Skills. 2019. (ENG.). 32p. (J). (gr. -1-k). pap. 4.49 *(978-1-60159-117-3(9)*, a6d13a4f-fa3a-48b4-b0ad-a64b6f93add0) School Zone Publishing Co.
Hohenthal, K. D., creator. The Reading & Writing Connection Journal with Herman the Crab No. 1: What Is the Story About? 2003. 70p. (J). spiral bd. 15.95 *(978-0-9716907-5-2(8)*, Ridgewood Publishing) Ridgewood Group, The.
HOP, LLC. Hooked on Handwriting Learn to Print. 2006. 24.99 *(978-1-933863-15-3(3))* HOP, LLC.
—Hooked on Learning Handwriting. 2006. 64p. 3.79 *(978-1-933863-91-7(9))* HOP, LLC.
Howard, Ian T. One Love, Two Worlds. Bishop, Tracey, illus. 2010. 36p. pap. 14.75 *(978-1-60911-771-9(9)*, Eloquent Bks.) Strategic Book Publishing & Rights Agency (SBPRA).
I Can Write Streetland. 2003. (J). Bk. 1. mass mkt., wbk. ed. 6.95 *(978-0-9743971-0-8(5))*Bk. 2. mass mkt., wbk. ed. 9.95 *(978-0-9743971-1-5(3))*Bk. 3. mass mkt., wbk. ed. 9.95 *(978-0-9743971-2-2(1))* Deziner Media International.
I Can Write Waterworld, Bk. 1. 2003. (J). mass mkt., wbk. ed. 6.95 *(978-0-9743971-4-6(8))* Deziner Media International.
Improving Student Writing: Paragraphs. 2004. (J). per. 12.95 *(978-1-56911-528-2(1))* Learning Resources, Inc.
Improving Student Writing: Sentences. 2004. (J). per. 12.95 *(978-1-56911-526-8(5))* Learning Resources, Inc.
In the News, 6 vols. (Wildcats Ser.). 32p. (gr. 2-8). *(978-0-322-02437-3(4))* Wright Group/McGraw-Hill.
In the News, 10 vols., Set 2. Incl. Climate Change. Brezina, Corona. lib. bdg. 37.13 *(978-1-4042-1913-7(7)*, ce033f3b-9ebc-4b4f-bd33-927192731467); Darfur: African Genocide. Xavier, John. lib. bdg. 37.13 *(978-1-4042-1912-0(9)*, c1460c9a-534c-4c82-b437-8f2e8043133d); Green Technology: Earth-Friendly Innovations. Sobha, Geeta. lib. bdg. 37.13 *(978-1-4042-1914-4(5)*, cdb65425-01f2-4ef2-8139-bb82aaace90a); Nukes: The Spread of Nuclear Weapons. Minneus, Steve. lib. bdg. 37.13 *(978-1-4042-1916-8(1)*, ba946ed1-9ee7-406e-b6ca-7ffd9b6ca863); Oil: The Economics of Fuel. Jovinelly, Joann. lib. bdg. 37.13 *(978-1-4042-1915-1(3)*, a88f9a66-8373-458c-9781-2ad0f1d76ce7); (Illus.). 64p. (YA). (gr. 6-6). 2007. (In the News Ser.). (ENG.). 2007. Set lib. bdg. 185.65 *(978-1-4042-1112-4(8)*, 14a575df-1acb-45cf-a0fc-1aaf534c7153) Rosen Publishing Group, Inc., The.
Incredible Places: 6 Each of 1 Anthology, 6 vols. (Wildcats Ser.). 32p. (gr. 2-8). *(978-0-322-00587-7(6))* Wright Group/McGraw-Hill.
Kalman, Bobbie. What Will I Write? 2017. (My World Ser.). (Illus.). 24p. (J). (gr. 1-1). *(978-0-7787-9600-8(0))*; pap. *(978-0-7787-9608-4(6))* Crabtree Publishing Co.
Keats, Felicity. Dancing Pencils. 2007. (Illus.). 168p. pap. *(978-1-86900-163-6(X))* UmSinsi Pr. ZAF. Dist: Michigan State Univ. Pr.
Kelly, Richard. Learn to Write Horses. 2017. (ENG., Illus.). 14p. (J). pap. 5.95 *(978-1-78209-706-8(6))* Miles Kelly Publishing, Ltd. GBR. Dist: Parkwest Pubns., Inc.
Kids Can Learn Franklin Staff, ed. Printing. 2004. (Kids Can Learn with Franklin Ser.). (Illus.). 32p. (J). (gr. k-2). 3.95 *(978-1-55337-602-6(1))* Kids Can Pr., Ltd. CAN. Dist: Hachette Bk. Group.
Lamb, Stacey, illus. Wipe Clean Ready for Writing. 2011. (Wipe-Clean Bks). 20p. (J). pap. 7.99 *(978-0-7945-3076-1(1)*, Usborne) EDC Publishing.
Laufer, Liora. Callirobics: Advanced Handwriting Exercises with Music from Around the World. (J). (gr. 2-9). pap. 19.95 incl. audio *(978-0-9630478-3-0(3)*, CL550) Callirobics.
Learning Company Books Staff, ed. Reader Rabbit: Writing Mechanics. 2003. (Illus.). 32p. (J). pap., wbk. ed. *(978-0-7630-7642-9(2))* Magma.
Learning to Write: 1-Year Personal Use Version. 2003. E-Book incl. cd-rom *(978-0-9726808-5-1(3))* MEIER Enterprises Inc.
Learning to Write: 12-Month Academic Access Version. 2003. (C). E-Book incl. cd-rom *(978-0-9726808-6-8(2))* MEIER Enterprises Inc.
Learning to Write (Gr. K-1) 2003. (J). *(978-1-58232-034-2(9))* ECS Learning Systems, Inc.
Libby, Kathryn. Cursive Connections: Modern Style. 2003. 84p. (J). (gr. 2-6). 10.99 *(978-0-9666572-2-7(5))* Acacia Publishing, Inc.
Licker, Lori. Writing-Right with Professor Pendleton Pencil. 2006. spiral bd. 21.95 *(978-0-9772196-0-5(7))* Writing-Right.
Lindsay, Sarah. Cambridge Grammar & Writing Skills, Bk. 1. 2019. (Cambridge Grammar & Writing Skills Ser.). (ENG., Illus.). 88p. pap. 13.75 *(978-1-108-73058-7(2))* Cambridge Univ. Pr.
Loewen, Nancy. Writer's Toolbox, 4 vols., Set. Lyles, Christopher, illus. Incl. Show Me a Story: Writing Your Own Picture Book. (ENG., Illus.). 32p. (J). (gr. 2-4). 2009. lib. bdg. 27.99 *(978-1-4048-5341-6(3)*, 95562, Picture Window Bks.); (Writer's Toolbox Ser.). (ENG.). 32p. 2009. 83.97 o.p. *(978-1-4048-5402-4(9)*, 168049, Picture Window Bks.) Capstone.
Longman Publishing Staff. My Second Handwriting. Date not set. (ENG., Illus.). 32p. (J). pap. 61.25 *(978-0-582-51113-2(5))* Addison-Wesley Longman, Ltd. GBR. Dist: Trans-Atlantic Pubns., Inc.
Longman Publishing Staff & Dallas, Donald. My First Handwriting. Date not set. (ENG., Illus.). 32p. (J). pap. 61.25 *(978-0-582-51112-5(7))* Addison-Wesley Longman, Ltd. GBR. Dist: Trans-Atlantic Pubns., Inc.
Maps & Codes: 6 Each of 1 Anthology, 6 vols. (Wildcats Ser.). 32p. (gr. 2-8). *(978-0-322-00588-4(4))* Wright Group/McGraw-Hill.
Mayer, Mercer. Scholastic Success with Writing. 2003. (Success with Workbooks Ser.). (ENG.). 48p. (J). pap. 5.95 *(978-0-439-44496-5(9))* Scholastic, Inc.
McCain, Murray. Writing! Alcorn, John, illus. 2016. (ENG.). 48p. 17.95 *(978-1-62326-075-0(2))* AMMO Bks., LLC.
McOmber, Rachel B., ed. McOmber Phonics Storybooks Vol. 1: Writing Book. rev. ed. (Illus.). (J). *(978-0-944991-93-0(9))* Swift Learning Resources.
—McOmber Phonics Storybooks Vol. 2: Writing Book. rev. ed. (Illus.). (J). *(978-0-944991-94-7(7))* Swift Learning Resources.
Meachen Rau, Dana. Ace Your Creative Writing Project, 1 vol. 2009. (Ace It! Information Literacy Ser.). (ENG., Illus.). 48p. (gr. 3-3). lib. bdg. 27.93 *(978-0-7660-3395-5(3)*, 713bb4eb-ca6e-4188-bb51-14fa85658e5d) Enslow Publishing, LLC.
Meyer-Hullmann, Kerstin, illus. Rechtschreibtraining fuer die 3. Klasse. (Duden-Lernminuten Ser.). (GER.). 44p. (J). wbk. ed. *(978-3-411-70801-7(8))* Bibliographisches Institut & F. A. Brockhaus AG DEU. Dist: International Bk. Import Service, Inc.
—Rechtschreibtraining fuer die 3. und 4. Klasse. (Duden-Lernminuten Ser.). (GER.). 44p. (J). wbk. ed. *(978-3-411-70811-6(5))* Bibliographisches Institut & F. A. Brockhaus AG DEU. Dist: International Bk. Import Service, Inc.
Meyer, Stephanie H., et al. Teen Ink: What Matters. 2003. (Teen Ink Ser.). (ENG., Illus.). 400p. (YA). pap. 17.95 *(978-0-7573-0063-9(4)*, HCI Teens) Health Communications, Inc.
Minden, Cecilia & Roth, Kate. Language Arts Explorer Junior (Set), 10 vols., Set. Incl. How to Write a Journal. lib. bdg. 29.21 *(978-1-60279-994-3(6)*, 200988); How to Write a Letter. lib. bdg. 29.21 *(978-1-60279-991-2(1)*, 200982); How to Write a Poem. lib. bdg. 29.21 *(978-1-60279-995-0(4)*, 200990); How to Write a Report. lib. bdg. 29.21 *(978-1-61080-105-8(9)*, 201112); How to Write about Your Adventure. lib. bdg. 29.21 *(978-1-61080-106-5(7)*, 201114); How to Write an Ad. lib. bdg. 29.21 *(978-1-61080-107-2(5)*, 201116); How to Write an E-Mail. lib. bdg. 29.21 *(978-1-60279-993-6(8)*, 200986); How to Write an Interview. lib. bdg. 29.21 *(978-1-60279-996-7(2)*, 200992); How to Write & Give a Speech. lib. bdg. 29.21 *(978-1-61080-108-9(3)*, 201118); 24p. (gr. 1-4). (Explorer Junior Library: Language Arts Explorer Junior Ser.). (ENG., Illus.). 2011. 256.40 *(978-1-61080-153-9(9)*, 201024) Cherry Lake Publishing.
Miss Conner'S Class. Look How We've Grown! A Collection of First Grade Writing. 2009. 52p. pap. 21.27 *(978-1-4389-6438-6(2))* AuthorHouse.
Mitchell, George. My handwriting & colouring Book. 2009. 64p. pap. 13.95 *(978-1-4452-3485-4(8))* Lulu Pr., Inc.
Moshel, Eluzer. Learn to Write. 2004. pap. 12.00 *(978-0-9728849-2-1(0))*; Vol. 1. pap. 8.50 *(978-0-9728849-0-7(4))*; Vol. 2. pap. 8.50 *(978-0-9728849-4-5(7))*; Vol. 3. pap. 8.50 *(978-0-9728849-7-6(1))* Cong Bais Tziporah.
Olien, Rebecca. Kids Write: Fantasy & Sci Fi, Mystery, Autobiography, Adventure & More! Kline, Michael, illus. 2005. (Kids Can Ser.). (ENG.). 128p. (YA). (gr. 7-14). 14.95 *(978-0-8249-6775-8(5)*, Ideals Pubns.) Worthy Publishing.
On & off the Road: 6 Each of 1 Anthology, 6 vols. (Wildcats Ser.). 32p. (gr. 2-8). *(978-0-322-02421-2(8))* Wright Group/McGraw-Hill.
Ottaway, Jacqueline. Riddle of the Seaplanes (Level S), 6 vols. (Mountain Peaks Ser.). 128p. (gr. 6-18). 36.95 *(978-0-322-05891-0(0))* Wright Group/McGraw-Hill.
Penmanship 1, 2 vols., Set. 2004. (gr. 1). 25.50 *(978-0-7403-0207-7(8)*, JSP115); (Illus.). tchr. ed., stu. ed. 34.95 *(978-0-7403-0215-2(9)*, JSC100) Alpha Omega Pubns., Inc. (Horizons).
Penmanship 2, 2 vols., Set. 2004. (Illus.). (J). (gr. 2-3). tchr. ed., stu. ed. 25.50 *(978-0-7403-0211-4(6)*, JSP215) Alpha Omega Pubns., Inc.
Peter Pauper Press, Inc., creator. Handwriting: Learn to Print! 2015. (Handwriting Ser.). (ENG., Illus.). 96p. (J). pap. 5.99 *(978-1-4413-1816-9(X)*, 8e03afa1-f5b9-4bf5-812e-15c27734e1b9) Peter Pauper Pr. Inc.
Priddy, Roger. Wipe Clean Workbook: Cursive Handwriting: Ages 5-7; Wipe-Clean with Pen. 2017. (Wipe Clean Learning Bks.). (ENG., Illus.). 48p. (J). spiral bd. 8.99 *(978-0-312-52202-5(9)*, 900171743) St. Martin's Pr.
Pulse- Fun with Reading & Writing. 2006. cd-rom 4.99 *(978-1-60245-040-0(4))* GDL Multimedia, LLC.
Read, Write & Publish. (J). (gr. 5). 125.25 *(978-0-669-17767-1(9))* Houghton Mifflin Harcourt School Pubs.
Reading & Writing. 2004. (Help with Homework Ser.). 32p. (J). (gr. k-2). wbk. ed. 3.99 *(978-1-904586-24-1(4))*; (gr. 1-4). wbk. ed. 3.99 *(978-1-904586-20-3(1))* Byeway Bks.
Rechtschreibung 1. (Duden-Schuelerhilfen Ser.). (GER.). 80p. (J). (gr. 2-3). *(978-3-411-06312-3(2))* Bibliographisches Institut & F. A. Brockhaus AG DEU. Dist: International Bk. Import Service, Inc.
Rechtschreibung 2. (Duden-Schuelerhilfen Ser.). (GER.). 96p. (J). (gr. 3-4). *(978-3-411-06322-2(X))* Bibliographisches Institut & F. A. Brockhaus AG DEU. Dist: International Bk. Import Service, Inc.
Rechtschreibung 3. (Duden-Schuelerhilfen Ser.). (GER.). 96p. (J). (gr. 4-5). *(978-3-411-06332-1(7))* Bibliographisches Institut & F. A. Brockhaus AG DEU. Dist: International Bk. Import Service, Inc.
Rechtschreibung 4. (Duden-Schuelerhilfen Ser.). (GER.). 112p. (J). (gr. 5-6). *(978-3-411-05681-1(9))* Bibliographisches Institut & F. A. Brockhaus AG DEU. Dist: International Bk. Import Service, Inc.
Rechtschreibung 5. (Duden-Schuelerhilfen Ser.). (GER.). 112p. (YA). (gr. 7-8). *(978-3-411-05691-0(6))* Bibliographisches Institut & F. A. Brockhaus AG DEU. Dist: International Bk. Import Service, Inc.
Rechtschreibung und Wortkunde. (Duden-Schuelerduden Ser.). (GER.). 384p. (YA). (gr. 4-18). *(978-3-411-04215-9(X))* Bibliographisches Institut & F. A. Brockhaus AG DEU. Dist: International Bk. Import Service, Inc.
Rhodes, Immacula A. Write-N-Seek: Sight Words. 2017. (Write-N-Seek: Ser.). (ENG.). 64p. (gr. -1-2). pap. 10.99 *(978-1-338-18022-0(3))* Scholastic, Inc.
—Write-N-Seek: Word Families. 2017. (ENG.). 64p. (J). (gr. -1-2). pap. 10.99 *(978-1-338-18023-7(1))* Scholastic, Inc.
Ridgewood Analogies. 2004. Bk. 1. pap., tchr. ed. 2.65 *(978-0-8388-2292-0(4))*Bk. 3. pap., tchr. ed. 2.65 *(978-0-8388-2294-4(0))* Educators Publishing Service, Inc.
Ridgewood Analogies Grade 4, Bk. 1. 2004. (Ridgewood Analogies Ser.). pap. 6.65 *(978-0-8388-2289-0(4))* Educators Publishing Service, Inc.
Ridgewood Analogies Grade 5, Bk. 2. 2004. (Ridgewood Analogies Ser.). pap. 6.65 *(978-0-8388-2290-6(8))* Educators Publishing Service, Inc.
Ridgewood Analogies Grade 6, Bk. 3. 2004. (Ridgewood Analogies Ser.). 6.65 *(978-0-8388-2291-3(6))* Educators Publishing Service, Inc.
Right or Wrong? 6 Each of 1 Anthology, 6 vols. (Wildcats Ser.). 32p. (gr. 2-8). *(978-0-322-00598-3(1))* Wright Group/McGraw-Hill.
Rossi, Renzo. A Gift from the Gods, 1 vol. 2009. (Reading & Writing Ser.). (ENG., Illus.). 32p. (gr. 4-4). 31.21 *(978-0-7614-4318-6(5)*, f215cdb2-1dbf-4062-b50c-21af8a277813) Cavendish Square Publishing LLC.
—The Revolution of the Alphabet, 1 vol. 2009. (Reading & Writing Ser.). (ENG., Illus.). 32p. (gr. 4-4). 31.21 *(978-0-7614-4320-9(7)*, 867337c4-757d-44a6-b8a1-fa774b98fd00) Cavendish Square Publishing LLC.
Rossi, Renzo. & Pauli, Erika. The Age of the Book, 1 vol. Baldanzi, Alessandro, illus. 2009. (Reading & Writing Ser.). (ENG.). 32p. (gr. 4-4). 31.21 *(978-0-7614-4321-6(5)*, 0bf4e344-1411-43bb-b7b4-eeda2e17f646) Cavendish Square Publishing LLC.
—How Writing Began, 1 vol. 2009. (Reading & Writing Ser.). (ENG., Illus.). 32p. (gr. 4-4). 31.21 *(978-0-7614-4317-9(7)*, 8eba249a-f8b7-405b-a203-35cccc58ef7c) Cavendish Square Publishing LLC.
Ruff, Karen S. Cooney. The Sensory Pen: Unique Writing Prompts for Journalism Students & Other Writers. 2004. (Illus.). 94p. (J). spiral bd. *(978-0-9761186-0-2(2))* Scribbler's Sword.
Ruffenach, Jessie E., et al. Learn along with Ashkii: First Grade Level 2. Whitethorne, Bahe, Jr., illus. 2003. (NAV & ENG.). (Illus.). 16p. (J). (gr. -1-3). pap. 7.95 *(978-1-893354-42-5(3))* Salina Bookshelf Inc.
—Learn along with Ashkii: Second Grade Level 1. Whitethorne, Bahe, Jr., illus. 2003. (ENG & NAV.). 16p. (J). (gr. -1-3). pap. 7.95 *(978-1-893354-43-2(1))* Salina Bookshelf Inc.
—Learn along with Ashkii: Second Grade Level 2. Whitethorne, Bahe, Jr., illus. 2003. (NAV & ENG.). 16p. (J). (gr. -1-3). pap. 7.95 *(978-1-893354-44-9(X))* Salina Bookshelf Inc.
—Learn along with Ashkii: Third Grade Level 1. Whitethorne, Bahe, Jr., illus. 2003. (NAV & ENG.). 16p. (J). (gr. 4-7). pap. 7.95 *(978-1-893354-45-6(8))* Salina Bookshelf Inc.
Sanseri, Wanda. SWR Chart Pack. 2003. (J). pap. 9.95 *(978-1-880045-30-5(3))* Back Home Industries.
School Zone Publishing Company Staff. Bilingual Cursive Writing 3-4. 2007. (ENG.). 64p. (J). pap., wbk. ed. 3.99 *(978-1-58947-962-3(9))* School Zone Publishing Co.
—Bilingual Manuscript Writing K-2. 2007. (ENG.). 64p. (J). (gr. k-1). pap. 3.99 *(978-1-58947-961-6(0))* School Zone Publishing Co.
Service, Regina. The Ginger Family. 2006. 24p. per. 12.00 *(978-1-58961-391-1(0))* PageFree Publishing, Inc.
Shannon, Rosemarie, et al, adapted by. Printing Practice. 2003. (Kids Can Learn with Franklin Ser.). (ENG., Illus.). 32p. (J). (gr. k-1). 3.95 *(978-1-55337-590-6(4))* Kids Can Pr., Ltd. CAN. Dist: Hachette Bk. Group.
—Ready for Printing. 2004. (Kids Can Learn with Franklin Ser.). (ENG., Illus.). 32p. (J). (gr. -1-1). 3.95 *(978-1-55337-603-3(X))* Kids Can Pr., Ltd. CAN. Dist: Hachette Bk. Group.
Shulte, Sharon. Sandy's Aunt. Shulte, Sara, illus. 2004. (J). per. 12.00 *(978-0-9747147-5-2(5))* MK Publishing.
Sicinski-Skeans, Sharon & Baron, Lindamichelle. Skills for Super Writers Softcover: Grade 3. 2003. (Writing Program Ser.). (J). tchr.'s training gde. ed. 19.95 *(978-0-7652-0759-3(1))* Modern Curriculum Pr.
—Transparencies. 2003. (J). (gr. 3). 23.50 *(978-0-7652-1045-6(2))*; (gr. 5). 23.50 *(978-0-7652-1047-0(9))* Modern Curriculum Pr.
—The Write Direction: Hardcover Student Book. 2003. (Illus.). (J). (gr. 4). stu. ed. 18.95 *(978-0-7652-0751-7(6))*; (gr. 5). stu. ed. 18.95 *(978-0-7652-0752-4(4))* Modern Curriculum Pr.
Silva, Patricia. Reading & Writing Today, 1 vol. 2009. (Reading & Writing Ser.). (ENG., Illus.). 32p. (J). (gr. 4-4). 31.21 *(978-0-7614-4324-7(X)*, 9e246e7a-bfe2-4bad-8e04-4642e18d92fe) Cavendish Square Publishing LLC.
Sleeping Bear Press. Diary of a Pennsylvania Kid. Moore, Cyd, illus. 2011. (State Journal Ser.). (ENG.). 128p. (J). (gr. 4-8). pap. 9.95 *(978-1-58536-610-1(2)*, 202226) Sleeping Bear Pr.

W
X
Y
Z

—Diary of a Texas Kid. Moore, Cyd, illus. 2011. (State Journal Ser.). (ENG.). 128p. (J). (gr. 4-8). pap. 9.95 *(978-1-58536-608-8(0),* 202225) Sleeping Bear Pr.

Soper, Sandra. Reading & Writing, Bk. 3. rev. ed. (ENG., Illus.). 32p. (J). pap. 5.99 *(978-0-330-32075-7(0),* Pan) Pan Macmillan GBR. Dist: Trafalgar Square Publishing.

Squiggles & Strokes, 6 vols., Pack. (Bookweb Ser.). 32p. (gr. 5-18). 34.00 *(978-0-7635-3795-1(0))* Rigby Education.

The Standard Pocket Chart. (Professional Resources Ser.). 29.95 *(978-0-7802-4243-2(2))* Wright Group/McGraw-Hill.

Steck-Vaughn Staff. Head for Home: Handwriting - Cursive. 2004. (Illus.). pap. 5.99 *(978-0-7398-8556-7(1))* Steck-Vaughn.

—Head for Home: Handwriting - Manuscript. 2004. (Illus.). pap. *(978-0-7398-8555-0(3))* Steck-Vaughn.

Stella, Heather. Get Ready for School: Handwriting. 2017. (Get Ready for School Ser.). (ENG., Illus.). 128p. (J). (gr. -1-3). spiral bd. 13.99 *(978-0-316-50254-2(5),* Black Dog & Leventhal Pubs. Inc.) Running Pr.

Stott, Jon C. Gerald Mcdermott & YOU, 1 vol. 2004. (ENG., Illus.). 128p. pap. 40.00 *(978-1-59158-175-8(3),* 900322223, Libraries Unlimited) ABC-CLIO, LLC.

Tell Me No Lies, 6 vols. (Ragged Island Mysteriestm Ser.). 161p. (gr. 5-7). 42.50 *(978-0-322-01654-5(1))* Wright Group/McGraw-Hill.

Thomas, Vernada. Pre-Handwriting Book. 2008. 200p. 29.99 *(978-1-4363-8001-0(4));* pap. 19.99 *(978-1-4363-8000-3(6))* Xlibris Corp.

Trimmer, Joseph F. Writing Without a Purpose: AP Version. 14th ed. 2003. (YA). (gr. 6-12). 86.76 *(978-0-618-31848-3(8),* 356312) CENGAGE Learning.

Tuszynski, Kathy Cromwell & Yarber, Angela. The Write Answer. 2003. (Illus.). 96p. (J). pap. 11.95 *(978-1-57310-407-4(8))* Teaching & Learning Co.

Vaughan, Marcia. Story Teller Quilts: Level S, 6 vols. (Raging Rivers Ser.). 128p. (gr. 3-6). 36.95 *(978-0-322-05899-6(6))* Wright Group/McGraw-Hill.

Veinje, Marie. Manuscript Writing K-2. Boyer, Robin, illus. 2019. (ENG.). 64p. (J). (gr. k-2). pap. 4.49 *(978-1-58947-397-3(3),* 0d117dbf-0d21-4ec1-ad45-4005f86b43d0) School Zone Publishing Co.

Voyages in English: Writing & Grammar. 2004. (gr. 4-18). *(978-0-8294-1305-2(7));* (gr. 5-18). *(978-0-8294-1307-6(3));* (gr. 5-18). tchr. ed. *(978-0-8294-0989-5(0));* (gr. 5-18). tchr. ed., wbk. ed. *(978-0-8294-1323-6(5));* (gr. 5-18). stu. ed. *(978-0-8294-0990-1(4));* (gr. 5-18). stu. ed., wbk. ed. *(978-0-8294-1322-9(7));* (gr. 6-18). *(978-0-8294-1310-6(3));* (gr. 6-18). tchr. ed. *(978-0-8294-0991-8(2));* (gr. 6-18). tchr. ed., wbk. ed. *(978-0-8294-1325-0(1));* (gr. 6-18). stu. ed. *(978-0-8294-0992-5(0));* (gr. 6-18). stu. ed., wbk. ed. *(978-0-8294-1324-3(3));* (gr. 7-18). *(978-0-8294-1313-7(8));* (gr. 7-18). tchr. ed. *(978-0-8294-0993-2(9));* (gr. 7-18). tchr. ed., wbk. ed. *(978-0-8294-1328-1(6));* (gr. 7-18). stu. ed. *(978-0-8294-0994-9(7));* (gr. 7-18). stu. ed., wbk. ed. *(978-0-8294-1327-4(8));* (gr. 8-18). *(978-0-8294-1315-1(4));* (gr. 8-18). tchr. ed. *(978-0-8294-0995-6(5));* (gr. 8-18). tchr. ed., wbk. ed. *(978-0-8294-1330-4(6));* (gr. 8-18). stu. ed. *(978-0-8294-0996-3(3));* (gr. 8-18). stu. ed., wbk. ed. *(978-0-8294-1329-8(4))* Loyola Pr.

Walton, Ruth. Let's Read a Book: Find Out about Books & How They Are Made. 2013. (Let's Find Out Ser.). (ENG., Illus.). 32p. (J). (gr. k-5). 28.50 *(978-1-59771-387-0(2))* Sea-To-Sea Pubns.

Watson, Joy. The Birthday Flood: Level O, 6 vols. (Raging Rivers Ser.). 128p. (gr. 3-6). 36.95 *(978-0-322-05896-5(1))* Wright Group/McGraw-Hill.

Webber, Diane. Do You Read Me? Famous Cases Solved by Handwriting Analysis! 2007. (24/7: Science Behind the Scenes Ser.). (ENG., Illus.). 64p. (YA). (gr. 9-12). 29.00 *(978-0-531-12066-8(X),* Watts, Franklin) Scholastic Library Publishing.

What Is That Smell? S-Family Blends: Level B, 6 vols. (Wright Skills Ser.). 16p. (gr. k-3). 17.95 *(978-0-322-01461-9(1))* Wright Group/McGraw-Hill.

What's in the Woods? Consonant digraph review: Level C, 6 vols. (Wright Skills Ser.). 16p. (gr. k-3). 26.50 *(978-0-322-01497-8(2))* Wright Group/McGraw-Hill.

Willever, Lisa. Exciting Writing. 2004. 64p. pap., instr.'s hndbk. ed. 5.95 *(978-0-9760469-1-2(1),* 329-003) Franklin Mason Pr.

Williams, Lynette Gain. Handwriting Begins with Art: The Partner Book to ArbeZ ZebrA Teaches A to Z. 2007. 165p. (J). spiral bd. 19.99 *(978-0-9779063-1-4(0))* Gain Literacy Skills / Lynette Gain Williams.

Williams, Rozanne Lanczak & Faulkner, Stacey. Learn to Write Resource Guide: Grades K-2. 2006. (Illus.). 104p. (J). (gr. k-2). per. 13.99 *(978-1-59198-314-9(2))* Creative Teaching Pr., Inc.

Wise Owl Printing Plus Inc, creator. I Can Write Streetland, PreK-2: Integrated learning Workbook. 2006. (I Can Write Ser.). (Illus.). 78p. (J). (gr. -1-3). pap. 99.95 incl. audio compact disk *(978-0-9743971-3-9(X))* Deziner Media International.

Wolfe, Hillary. Common Core Writing Strategies PD Pack. 2015. (Maupin House Ser.). (ENG.). pap., pap. 59.90 *(978-1-4966-0602-0(7),* 23898) Capstone.

Wood, Kevin. Create Your Own Story with Scratch. McBeth, Glen, illus. 2018. (Project Code Ser.). (ENG.). 32p. (J). (gr. 4-7). pap. 9.99 *(978-1-5415-2512-2(4),* bdfeaf49-0705-4a0d-bdd4-203c469320ea); lib. bdg. 29.32 *(978-1-5415-2438-5(1),* 12ab94ea-485d-4dd5-bb34-8b22827818b6, Lerner Pubns.) Lerner Publishing Group.

Woods, Irons, & Greens: 6 Each of 1 Anthology, 6 vols. (Wildcats Ser.). 32p. (gr. 2-8). *(978-0-322-00589-1(2))* Wright Group/McGraw-Hill.

World Book, Inc. Staff, contrib. by. Hieroglyphics to Hypertext: A Timeline of the Written Word. 2016. (Illus.). 40p. (J). *(978-0-7166-3546-8(1))* World Bk.-Childcraft International.

Wrighton, Charlene & Bradshaw, Georgine. Basic Kit - Preschool. Clark, Irene, illus. 2005. Orig. Title: Basis Kit I. (J). 249.95 *(978-1-886441-30-9(8))* Zoo-phonics, Inc.

Write Right! Set 2, 12 vols. 2014. (Write Right! Ser.). (ENG.). 24p. (J). (gr. 2-3). 151.62 *(978-1-4824-1140-9(7),* 6179045e-8a2d-4d07-940b-a295b1d3d1ac) Stevens, Gareth Publishing LLLP.

Write Right! Sets 1-2, 24 vols. 2014. (Write Right! Ser.). (ENG.). 24p. (J). (gr. 2-3). 303.24 *(978-1-4824-1179-9(2),* a76e6033-700e-4227-b021-b932a051323d) Stevens, Gareth Publishing LLLP.

Writer's Solution. Bronze Level. (YA). (gr. 7). stu. ed. 23.47 *(978-0-13-828781-8(3))*Copper Level. (J). (gr. 6). stu. ed. 23.47 *(978-0-13-828773-3(2))*Copper Level. (J). (gr. 6). pap. 1.97 *(978-0-13-434758-5(7))*Diamond Level. (YA). (gr. 12). stu. ed. 25.47 *(978-0-13-828831-0(3))*Gold Level. (YA). (gr. 9). stu. ed. 25.47 *(978-0-13-828807-5(0))*Platinum Level. (YA). (gr. 10). stu. ed. 25.47 *(978-0-13-828815-0(1))*Ruby Level. (YA). (gr. 11). stu. ed. 25.47 *(978-0-13-828823-5(2))*Silver Level. (YA). (gr. 8). stu. ed. 23.47 *(978-0-13-828799-3(6))* Prentice Hall PTR.

Writing Skills 3. 2004. (Writing Skills Ser.). pap. 12.00 *(978-0-8388-2052-0(2))* Educators Publishing Service, Inc.

Writing with Grace. 2nd ed. 2003. (Academy Handwriting Program Ser.: Vol. 4). (J). pap. 5.50 *(978-1-930367-88-3(0))* Christian Liberty Pr.

Zeros And Ones, 6 vols. (Wildcats Ser.). 32p. (gr. 2-8). *(978-0-322-02438-0(2))* Wright Group/McGraw-Hill.

Zoo-phonics Quick Tests for the Classroom. 2004. cd-rom *(978-1-886441-41-5(3))* Zoo-phonics, Inc.

WRITING—MATERIALS AND INSTRUMENTS

Besel, Tucker. Build Your Own Scribble Bot. Gould, Grant, illus. 2018. (Bot Maker Ser.). (ENG.). 24p. (J). (gr. 4-6). lib. bdg. *(978-1-68072-324-3(3),* 12080, Hi Jinx) Black Rabbit Bks.

—Build Your Own Scribble Bot. 2018. (Bot Maker Ser.). (ENG.). (J). (gr. 3-7). pap. 8.95 *(978-1-68072-648-0(X))* Hi Jinx Pr.

Blaxland, Wendy. Pencils, 1 vol. 2009. (How Are They Made? Ser.). (ENG.). 32p. (gr. 4-4). lib. bdg. 21.27 *(978-0-7614-4750-6(6),* 99891504-99f3-4677-9886-cd40671dde6d) Cavendish Square Publishing LLC.

Fejto, Raphael & Fejto, Raphael. The Pen. 2016. (Little Inventions Ser.). (ENG., Illus.). 32p. (J). (gr. 3-5). 9.95 *(978-1-77085-748-3(6),* 7e82e334-cb60-4f09-b640-a1760df47b9f) Firefly Bks., Ltd.

Hansen, Grace. How Is a Pencil Made? 2018. (How Is It Made? Ser.). (ENG., Illus.). 24p. (J). (gr. -1-2). lib. bdg. 32.79 *(978-1-5321-8192-4(2),* 29899, Abdo Kids) ABDO Publishing Co.

Hayward, Linda. I Am a Pencil. Nicklaus, Carol, illus. 2003. (Silly Millies Ser.). 32p. lib. bdg. 17.90 *(978-0-7613-2904-6(8),* Millbrook Pr.) Lerner Publishing Group.

Lynette, Rachel. Pencils. 2016. (J). *(978-1-4896-4539-5(X))* Weigl Pubs., Inc.

Miller, Derek. Pencils, 1 vol. 2019. (Making of Everyday Things Ser.). (ENG.). 24p. (gr. 1-1). pap. 9.22 *(978-1-5026-4698-9(6),* d8d3a7ee-3c99-43eb-a13e-451908cf2180) Cavendish Square Publishing LLC.

Silva, Patricia & Pauli, Erika. Modern Times, 1 vol. Baldanzi, Alessandro, illus. 2009. (Reading & Writing Ser.). (ENG.). 32p. (gr. 4-4). 31.21 *(978-0-7614-4322-3(3),* 7dbe8905-aa51-4531-b174-ecbd61167701) Cavendish Square Publishing LLC.

WRITING (AUTHORSHIP)

see Authorship; Journalism

WYOMING

Baldwin, Guy & Hart, Joyce. Wyoming, 1 vol. 2nd rev. ed. 2008. (Celebrate the States (Second Edition) Ser.). (ENG.). 144p. (gr. 6-6). lib. bdg. 39.79 *(978-0-7614-2563-2(2),* db5b7f01-ec60-4570-b18a-9fe0aa702a14) Cavendish Square Publishing LLC.

Britton, Tamara L. Devil's Tower. 2005. (Symbols, Landmarks, & Monuments Set 3 Ser.). (Illus.). 32p. (gr. k-6). 27.07 *(978-1-59197-833-6(5),* Checkerboard Library) ABDO Publishing Co.

Brown, Vanessa. Wyoming. 2009. (Bilingual Library of the United States of America Ser.). (ENG & SPA.). 32p. (gr. 2-2). 47.90 *(978-1-60853-394-7(3),* Editorial Buenas Letras) Rosen Publishing Group, Inc., The.

Fontes, Justine & Fontes, Ron. Wyoming, 1 vol. 2003. (World Almanac(r) Library of the States Ser.). (ENG., Illus.). 48p. (gr. 4-6). pap. 15.05 *(978-0-8368-5335-3(0),* 5bfb64ff-33f9-41e1-a622-07762a5635c9); lib. bdg. 33.67 *(978-0-8368-5164-9(1),* cc5ccd40-12d2-4c20-9aa6-62fb3a76fc11) Stevens, Gareth Publishing LLLP. (Gareth Stevens Learning Library).

Frisch, Carlienne. Wyoming. 2012. (J). lib. bdg. 25.26 *(978-0-7613-4519-0(1),* Lerner Pubns.) Lerner Publishing Group.

Gagliano, Eugene. C Is for Cowboy: A Wyoming Alphabet. Guy, Susan, illus. 2003. (Discover America State by State Ser.). (ENG.). 40p. (J). (gr. 1-3). 18.99 *(978-1-58536-097-0(X),* 201977) Sleeping Bear Pr.

Galiano, Dean. Wyoming, 1 vol. Brusca, Maria Cristina, tr. 2005. (Bilingual Library of the United States of America Ser.: Set 2). (ENG & SPA., Illus.). 32p. (J). (gr. 2-2). lib. bdg. 28.93 *(978-1-4042-3116-0(1),* 39eb3ac8-bfe6-4991-9f34-9f49d759db06) Rosen Publishing Group, Inc., The.

Hansen, Grace. Grand Teton National Park. 2018. (National Parks (Abdo Kids Jumbo) Ser.). (ENG., Illus.). 24p. (J). (gr. -1-2). lib. bdg. 32.79 *(978-1-5321-8207-5(4),* 29873, Abdo Kids) ABDO Publishing Co.

Hanson-Harding, Alexandra. From Sea to Shining Sea: Wyoming. 2008. (From Sea to Shining Sea Ser.). (ENG.). 80p. (J). (gr. 3-5). pap. 22.44 *(978-0-531-20819-9(2),* Children's Pr.) Scholastic Library Publishing.

Hanson-Harding, Alexandra L. Wyoming. 2003. (From Sea to Shining Sea Ser.: 2). (ENG., Illus.). 80p. (J). 30.50 *(978-0-516-22490-9(5),* Children's Pr.) Scholastic Library Publishing.

Harasymiw, Roman. Devils Tower, 1 vol. 2014. (Scariest Places on Earth Ser.). (ENG., Illus.). 24p. (J). (gr. 2-3). 24.27 *(978-1-4824-1151-5(2),* 22628fd1-e9b8-4ec5-8742-91f329915433) Stevens, Gareth Publishing LLLP.

Heinrichs, Ann. Wyoming. Kania, Matt, illus. 2017. (U. S. A. Travel Guides). (ENG.). 40p. (J). (gr. 2-5). lib. bdg. 38.50 *(978-1-5038-1990-0(6),* 211628) Child's World, Inc, The.

Lusted, Marcia Amidon. Wyoming: The Equality State, 1 vol. 2010. (Our Amazing States Ser.). (ENG.). 24p. (J). (gr. 3-3). pap. 9.25 *(978-1-4488-0762-8(X),* c0424029-3a90-4efe-b153-bf9c861b8ee7); lib. bdg. 26.27 *(978-1-4488-0663-8(1),* aa2b5626-fa72-4647-8879-2a5b6972a9d8) Rosen Publishing Group, Inc., The. (PowerKids Pr.).

Marsh, Carole. Wyoming Current Events Projects: 30 Cool, Activities, Crafts, Experiments & More for Kids to Do to Learn about Your State! 2003. (Wyoming Experience Ser.). 32p. (gr. k-5). pap. 5.95 *(978-0-635-02069-7(6),* Marsh, Carole Bks.) Gallopade International.

—Wyoming Geography Projects: 30 Cool, Activities, Crafts, Experiments & More for Kids to Do to Learn about Your State! 2003. (Wyoming Experience Ser.). 32p. (gr. k-5). pap. 5.95 *(978-0-635-01868-7(3),* Marsh, Carole Bks.) Gallopade International.

—Wyoming Government Projects: 30 Cool, Activities, Crafts, Experiments & More for Kids to Do to Learn about Your State! 2003. (Wyoming Experience Ser.). 32p. (gr. k-5). pap. 5.95 *(978-0-635-01969-1(8),* Marsh, Carole Bks.) Gallopade International.

—Wyoming People Projects: 30 Cool, Activities, Crafts, Experiments & More for Kids to Do to Learn about Your State! 2003. (Wyoming Experience Ser.). 32p. (gr. k-5). pap. 5.95 *(978-0-635-02019-2(X),* Marsh, Carole Bks.) Gallopade International.

—Wyoming Symbols & Facts Projects: 30 Cool, Activities, Crafts, Experiments & More for Kids to Do to Learn about Your State! 2003. (Wyoming Experience Ser.). 32p. (gr. k-5). pap. 5.95 *(978-0-635-01919-6(1),* Marsh, Carole Bks.) Gallopade International.

Mis, M. S. How to Draw Wyoming's Sights & Symbols. 2009. (Kid's Guide to Drawing America Ser.). 32p. (gr. k-k). 50.50 *(978-1-61511-106-0(9),* PowerKids Pr.) Rosen Publishing Group, Inc., The.

Murray, Julie. Wyoming, 1 vol. 2006. (Buddy Book Ser.). (ENG., Illus.). 32p. (gr. 2-4). 27.07 *(978-1-59197-709-4(6),* Buddy Bks.) ABDO Publishing Co.

Parker, Bridget. Wyoming. 2016. (States Ser.). (ENG., Illus.). 32p. (J). (gr. 3-6). lib. bdg. 27.99 *(978-1-5157-0439-3(4),* 132050, Capstone Pr.) Capstone.

Petreycik, Rick. Wyoming, 1 vol. Santoro, Christopher, illus. 2007. (It's My State! (First Edition)(r) Ser.). (ENG.). 80p. (gr. 4-4). lib. bdg. 34.07 *(978-0-7614-1930-3(6),* 25ee087a-c9a1-4c2f-ac20-ddadacc99001) Cavendish Square Publishing LLC.

Thomas, William David. Wyoming, 1 vol. 2006. (Portraits of the States Ser.). (ENG.). 32p. (gr. 3-5). pap. 11.50 *(978-0-8368-4729-1(6),* 527fc64c-9b10-48c5-8c96-c09a2f78e781, Gareth Stevens Learning Library) Stevens, Gareth Publishing LLLP.

—Wyoming, 1 vol. 2006. (Portraits of the States Ser.). (ENG., Illus.). 32p. (gr. 3-5). lib. bdg. 28.67 *(978-0-8368-4712-3(1),* aef34818-106f-4316-b068-48bec30cba08, Gareth Stevens Learning Library) Stevens, Gareth Publishing LLLP.

2006-2007 Tongue River Elementary 3rd Graders, text. Sheridan County History ABC Coloring & Activity Book - 2007. 2006-2007 Tongue River Elementary 3rd Graders, . 2007. (Illus.). 32p. (J). 3.95 *(978-0-9792871-1-4(1))* Sherian County Historical Society Pr.

WYOMING—FICTION

Ahlman, Larry. Terror in the Tetons. Larsen, Chuck, ed. Hanson, Dana, illus. 2005. (YA). (gr. 9-12). pap. 9.95 *(978-0-9712906-2-4(8))* Ahlman Publishing.

Alphin, Elaine Marie. Dinosaur Hunter. Bolognese, Don, illus. 2004. (I Can Read Bks.). 48p. (gr. 2-4). 14.00 *(978-0-7569-3241-1(6))* Perfection Learning Corp.

Banks, Radine. Nochi Come Back. 2006. 112p. per. 12.20 *(978-1-4120-8803-9(8))* Trafford Publishing.

Bjornson, Nancy. Llamas, Ponies & Pyrite. 2007. (J). *(978-1-930596-82-5(0))* Amherst Pr.

Black Hills Summer. 2003. (YA). per. *(978-0-9740718-0-0(3))* Strathmoor Pr.

Brezenoff, Steve. Field Trip Mysteries: the Yellowstone Kidnapping That Wasn't. Canga, Chris & Calo, Marcos, illus. 2012. (Field Trip Mysteries Ser.). (ENG.). 88p. (J). (gr. 3-6). pap. 5.95 *(978-1-4342-4200-6(5),* 120258); lib. bdg. 25.32 *(978-1-4342-3789-7(3),* 117088) Capstone. (Stone Arch Bks.).

Burkhart, Jessica. Wild Hearts. 2015. (If Only... Ser.). (ENG.). 368p. (YA). (gr. 7). 17.99 *(978-1-61963-258-5(6),* 9781619632585, Bloomsbury USA Childrens) Bloomsbury Publishing USA.

Clark, Joan. Ann Drew Jackson. Clark, Nathan, illus. 2007. 122p. per. 17.95 *(978-1-931282-45-1(5))* Autism Asperger Publishing Co.

—Jackson Whole Wyoming. 2005. 16.00 *(978-1-931282-72-7(2),* 9945) Autism Asperger Publishing Co.

Curtin, Ann. Dreamcatcher. 2015. 201p. (YA). *(978-1-61271-246-8(0))* Zumaya Pubns. LLC.

Farnsworth, Frances Joyce. Tike & Tiny in the Tetons. 2007. (Illus.). 172p. (J). pap. 14.95 *(978-0-943972-79-4(5))* Homestead Publishing.

Gebhart, Ryan. There Will Be Bears. 2016. (ENG.). 224p. (J). (gr. 5). pap. 8.99 *(978-0-7636-8765-6(0))* Candlewick Pr.

George, Jean Craighead. Snowboard Twist. Minor, Wendell, illus. 2004. (Outdoor Adventures Ser.). (ENG.). 32p. (J). 15.99 *(978-0-06-050595-0(8))* HarperCollins Pubs.

Hand, Cynthia. Boundless. 2013. (Unearthly Ser.: 3). (ENG.). 448p. (YA). (gr. 8). pap. 9.99 *(978-0-06-199621-4(1),* HarperTeen) HarperCollins Pubs.

—Hallowed: An Unearthly Novel. 2012. (Unearthly Ser.: 2). (ENG.). 432p. (YA). (gr. 8). pap. 10.99 *(978-0-06-199619-1(X),* HarperTeen) HarperCollins Pubs.

—Unearthly. 2011. (Unearthly Ser.: 1). (ENG.). 464p. (YA). (gr. 8). pap. 9.99 *(978-0-06-199617-7(3),* HarperTeen) HarperCollins Pubs.

Hawley, Jim. Homer & Friends. 2012. 50p. pap. *(978-1-77097-709-9(0))* FriesenPress.

Hays, Sharon. The Tumbleweed Family. 2011. 28p. pap. 15.99 *(978-1-4568-6825-3(X))* Xlibris Corp.

Jacobs, Lily. The Littlest Bunny in Wyoming: An Easter Adventure. Dunn, Robert, illus. 2015. (Littlest Bunny Ser.). (ENG.). 32p. (J). (gr. -1-3). 9.99 *(978-1-4926-1243-8(X),* Hometown World) Sourcebooks, Inc.

James, Eric. Santa's Sleigh Is on Its Way to Wyoming: A Christmas Adventure. Dunn, Robert, illus. 2016. (Santa's Sleigh Is on Its Way Ser.). (ENG.). 32p. (J). (gr. k-2). 12.99 *(978-1-4926-4365-4(3),* 9781492643654, Hometown World) Sourcebooks, Inc.

—The Spooky Express Wyoming. Piwowarski, Marcin, illus. 2017. (Spooky Express Ser.). (ENG.). 32p. (J). (gr. k-6). 9.99 *(978-1-4926-5413-1(2),* Hometown World) Sourcebooks, Inc.

Jensen, Brandi Ann & Courtright, Jordan K. The Hilarious & Brave Adventures of Hog & Dog. 2011. 40p. pap. 16.95 *(978-1-4560-3955-4(5))* America Star Bks.

Kares, P. S. Hole-in-the-Wall with the Prairie Orphans. 2009. 32p. pap. 24.95 *(978-1-60813-521-9(7))* America Star Bks.

Law, Ingrid. Scumble. 2011. 432p. (J). (gr. 3-7). 9.99 *(978-0-14-241962-5(1),* Puffin Books) Penguin Young Readers Group.

—Scumble. Lt. ed. 2011. (Companion to the Newberry Honor Winner Savvy Ser.). (ENG.). 575p. 23.99 *(978-1-4104-3531-6(8))* Thorndike Pr.

London, Jonathan. Desolation Canyon. London, Sean, illus. 2015. (Aaron's Wilderness Ser.: 1). (ENG.). 168p. (J). (gr. 3-5). pap. 12.99 *(978-1-941821-29-9(4),* West Winds Pr.) West Margin Pr.

Mackall, Dandi Daley. Horse Gentler in Training. 2018. (Winnie: the Early Years Ser.: 1). (ENG., Illus.). 112p. (J). pap. 5.99 *(978-1-4964-3280-3(0),* 20_31611, Tyndale Kids) Tyndale Hse. Pubs.

—A Horse's Best Friend. 2018. (Winnie: the Early Years Ser.: 2). (ENG., Illus.). 112p. (J). pap. 6.99 *(978-1-4964-3284-1(3),* 20_31613, Tyndale Kids) Tyndale Hse. Pubs.

Marsh, Carole. The Case of the Crybaby Cowboy. 2006. (3 Amigos Ser.). (Illus.). 54p. (J). (gr. 4-7). 14.95 *(978-0-635-06199-7(6))* Gallopade International.

—The Mystery at Grizzly Graveyard. 2014. (Real Kids, Real Places Ser.: Vol. 3). (ENG., Illus.). 158p. (J). (gr. 3-5). pap. 7.99 *(978-0-635-11187-6(X),* Marsh, Carole Mysteries) Gallopade International.

—The Riddle of the Oogli Boogli. 2006. (Illus.). 54p. (J). (gr. 4-7). 14.95 *(978-0-635-06200-0(3))* Gallopade International.

Minich, Eric. Digger & the Search for Home. 2006. 48p. pap. 16.95 *(978-1-4241-0321-8(5))* PublishAmerica, Inc.

Neil, Deanna. Lost in Yellowstone: The Land of Curiosities, 1872-1873, vol. 2. 2nd rev. ed. 2015. (J). reprint ed. 19.99 *(978-0-9798800-9-4(2))* EcoSeekers, The.

Oneill, Elizabeth. Alfred Visits Wyoming. 2008. 24p. (J). pap. 12.00 *(978-0-9822288-1-4(3))* Funny Bone Bks.

Ryan, Pam Muñoz. Pinta el Viento (Paint the Wind) 2008. (SPA.). 320p. (J). (gr. 4-7). pap. 7.99 *(978-0-545-07789-7(3),* Scholastic en Espanol) Scholastic, Inc.

Sanchez, Mary Louise, illus. The Wind Called My Name, 1 vol. 2018. (ENG.). 288p. (J). (gr. 3-7). 20.95 *(978-1-62014-780-1(7),* leelowtu, Tu Bks.) Lee & Low Bks., Inc.

Sargent, Dave & Sargent, Pat. Hondo: (Silver Dun) Look for Good in Others, 30 vols., Vol. 34. Lenoir, Jane, illus. 2003. (Saddle up Ser.: Vol. 34). 42p. (J). pap. 10.95 *(978-1-56763-802-8(3));* lib. bdg. 23.60 *(978-1-56763-801-1(5))* Ozark Publishing.

Sully, Katherine. Night-Night Wyoming. Poole, Helen, illus. 2017. (Night-Night Ser.). (ENG.). 20p. (J). (gr. -1-1). bds. 9.99 *(978-1-4926-5489-6(2),* Hometown World) Sourcebooks, Inc.

Sutherland, Tui T. & Sutherland, Kari H. The Menagerie. 2013. (Menagerie Ser.: 1). (ENG., Illus.). 288p. (J). (gr. 3-7). 16.99 *(978-0-06-078064-7(9),* HarperCollins) HarperCollins Pubs.

Yep, Laurence. The Traitor. 2004. (Golden Mountain Chronicles). 310p. (J). (gr. 5). 14.65 *(978-0-7569-3457-6(5))* Perfection Learning Corp.

WYOMING—HISTORY

Byers, Ann. Wyoming: Past & Present, 1 vol. 2010. (United States: Past & Present Ser.). (ENG.). 48p. (YA). (gr. 5-5). pap. 12.75 *(978-1-4358-9527-0(4),* d2770a77-bbb8-4251-a954-8c9649a18df6); lib. bdg. 34.47 *(978-1-4358-9500-3(2),* df268d65-6954-49ff-a75c-eee743d0f98d) Rosen Publishing Group, Inc., The. (Rosen Reference).

Carole Marsh. Wyoming Indians. 2004. (Wyoming Experience Ser.). 36p. (gr. 3-8). pap. 7.95 *(978-0-635-02344-5(X))* Gallopade International.

Felix, Rebecca. What's Great about Wyoming? 2015. (Our Great States Ser.). (ENG., Illus.). 32p. (J). (gr. 2-5). 26.65 *(978-1-4677-3882-8(4),* d3249e27-4502-4751-9034-656508ae16ad, Lerner Pubns.) Lerner Publishing Group.

Gagliano, Eugene. Four Wheels West: A Wyoming Number Book. Guy, Susan, illus. 2006. (America by the Numbers Ser.). (ENG.). 40p. (J). (gr. 1-3). 17.95 *(978-1-58536-210-3(7),* 202041) Sleeping Bear Pr.

—Little Wyoming. Urban, Helle, illus. 2010. (Little State Ser.). (ENG.). 20p. (J). (gr. -1-1). bds. 9.95 *(978-1-58536-544-9(0),* 202251) Sleeping Bear Pr.

Hamilton, John. Wyoming, 1 vol. 2016. (United States of America Ser.). (ENG., Illus.). 48p. (J). (gr. 5-9). 34.21 *(978-1-68078-354-4(8),* 21693, Abdo & Daughters) ABDO Publishing Co.

Hanel, Rachael. Wyoming. 2009. (This Land Called America Ser.). 32p. (YA). (gr. 3-6). 19.95 *(978-1-58341-803-1(2))* Creative Co., The.

Harvey, Dan. Rocky Mountain: Colorado, Utah, Wyoming, Vol. 19. 2015. (Let's Explore the States Ser.). (Illus.). 64p. (J). (gr. 5). 23.95 *(978-1-4222-3332-0(4))* Mason Crest.

Marsh, Carole. Exploring Wyoming Through Project-Based Learning: Geography, History, Government, Economics & More. 2016. (Wyoming Experience Ser.). (ENG.). (J). pap. 9.99 *(978-0-635-12374-9(6))* Gallopade International.

—I'm Reading about Wyoming. 2014. (Wyoming Experience Ser.). (ENG., Illus.). (J). pap., pap. 8.99 *(978-0-635-11325-2(2))* Gallopade International.

—Wyoming History Projects: 30 Cool, Activities, Crafts, Experiments & More for Kids to Do to Learn about Your State! 2003. (Wyoming Experience Ser.). 32p. (gr. k-5). pap. 5.95 *(978-0-635-01819-9(5),* Marsh, Carole Bks.) Gallopade International.

—Wyoming Native Americans: A Kid's Look at Our State's Chiefs, Tribes, Reservations, Powwows, Lore & More from the Past to the Present. 2004. (Wyoming Experience Ser.).

(Illus.). 36p. (J). (gr. 3-8). 29.95 *(978-0-635-02345-2(8))* Gallopade International.

aynard, Charles W. Fort Laramie. 2009. (Famous Forts Throughout American History Ser.). 24p. (gr. 3-4). 42.50 *(978-1-61512-516-6(7)*, PowerKids Pr.) Rosen Publishing Group, Inc., The.

arker, Janice. Wyoming. 2011. (Guide to American States Ser.). (Illus.). 48p. (YA). (gr. 3-6). 29.99 *(978-1-61690-824-9(6))*; (J). *(978-1-61690-499-9(2))* Weigl Pubs., Inc.

-Wyoming: The Equality State. 2016. *(978-1-4896-4968-3(9))* Weigl Pubs., Inc.

etreycik, Rick. Wyoming, 1 vol. 2nd rev. ed. 2014. (It's My State! (Second Edition)(r) Ser.). (ENG.). 80p. (gr. 4-4). pap. 18.64 *(978-1-62712-489-8(6)*, dcad8b33-2b3e-4c29-bf9f-71d88c235096); (Illus.). 35.93 *(978-1-62712-225-2(7)*, 7ed1add4-0499-4851-bfaa-b69ab8e11876) Cavendish Square Publishing LLC.

'etreycik, Rick & Klepeis, Alicia Z. Wyoming, 1 vol. 3rd rev. ed. 2015. (It's My State! (Third Edition)(r) Ser.). (ENG., Illus.). 80p. (gr. 4-4). 35.93 *(978-1-62713-259-6(7)*, 856de934-88ff-47d8-b919-59101ed734e1) Cavendish Square Publishing LLC.

'ratt, Laura. Wyoming: The Cowboy State. 2012. (J). *(978-1-61913-421-8(7))* Weigl Pubs., Inc.

'rentzas, G. S. America the Beautiful: Wyoming (Revised Edition) 2014. (America the Beautiful, Third Ser. (Revised Edition) Ser.). (ENG.). 144p. (J). lib. bdg. 40.00 *(978-0-531-28300-4(3))* Scholastic Library Publishing.

Sniffin, Bill. High Altitudes, Low Multitudes: More Stories about Wyoming, the Best Part of America, 1. 2003. (Illus.). 252p. per. 14.95 *(978-0-9639350-2-1(X)*, 2000) WCS Corp.

Wallace, Audra. Wyoming (a True Book: My United States) (Library Edition) 2018. (True Book (Relaunch) Ser.). (ENG., Illus.). 48p. (J). (gr. 3-5). 31.00 *(978-0-531-23586-7(6)*, Children's Pr.) Scholastic Library Publishing.

X

X, MALCOLM, 1925-1965

Archer, Jules. They Had a Dream: The Struggles of Four of the Most Influential Leaders of the Civil Rights Movement, from Frederick Douglass to Marcus Garvey to Martin Luther King Jr. & Malcolm X. 2016. (Jules Archer History for Young Readers Ser.). (ENG., Illus.). 272p. (J). (gr. 6-6). 16.99 *(978-1-63450-194-1(2)*, Sky Pony Pr.) Skyhorse Publishing Co., Inc.

Aretha, David. A Time for Martyrs: The Life of Malcolm X. 2012. (YA). 28.95 *(978-1-59935-328-9(8))* Reynolds, Morgan Inc.

Benson, Michael. Malcolm X. 2005. (Just the Facts Biographies Ser.). (ENG., Illus.). 112p. (gr. 5-12). 27.93 *(978-0-8225-2444-1(9))* Lerner Publishing Group.

Bourcier, Cammy S. Carlos Mencia. 2007. (Sharing the American Dream Ser.). 64p. (YA). (gr. 7-18). pap. 9.95 *(978-1-4222-0756-7(0))* Mason Crest.

—Malcolm X. 2009. (Sharing the American Dream Ser.). (Illus.). 64p. (YA). (gr. 7-12). 22.95 *(978-1-4222-0577-8(0))* Mason Crest.

Burlingame, Jeff. Malcolm X: Fighting for Human Rights, 1 vol. 2017. (Rebels with a Cause Ser.). (ENG., Illus.). 128p. (gr. 8-8). lib. bdg. 38.93 *(978-0-7660-8519-0(8)*, 134a6980-d408-4fd9-b9fb-02c1f2e2a05c) Enslow Publishing, LLC.

—Malcolm X: I Believe in the Brotherhood of Man, All Men, 1 vol. 2010. (American Rebels Ser.). (ENG.). 160p. (gr. 9-10). 38.60 *(978-0-7660-3384-9(8)*, eb5e0065-c688-4ee6-a24b-d4a63dae6600) Enslow Publishing, LLC.

Draper, Allison Stark. The Assassination of Malcolm X. 2009. (Library of Political Assassinations Ser.). 64p. (gr. 5-5). 58.50 *(978-1-60853-827-0(3))* Rosen Publishing Group, Inc., The.

Graves, Renee. Cornerstones of Freedom: Malcolm X. 2003. (Cornerstones of Freedom Ser.). (ENG., Illus.). 48p. (J). 26.00 *(978-0-516-24224-8(5)*, Children's Pr.) Scholastic Library Publishing.

Gunderson, Jessica. X: a Biography of Malcolm X. Hayden, William, illus. 2010. (American Graphic Ser.). (ENG.). 32p. (J). (gr. 3-9). pap. 8.10 *(978-1-4296-6267-3(0)*, 115414, Capstone Pr.) Capstone.

—X: a Biography of Malcolm X. Hayden, William, illus. 2010. (American Graphic Ser.). (ENG.). 32p. (J). (gr. 3-4). pap. 48.60 *(978-1-4296-6438-7(X)*, 16179, Capstone Pr.) Capstone.

Jeffrey, Gary. Malcolm X & the Fight for African American Unity, 1 vol. 2012. (Graphic History of the Civil Rights Movement Ser.). (ENG., Illus.). 24p. (J). (gr. 3-3). pap. 9.15 *(978-1-4339-7488-5(6)*, ac449642-0f3b-44cf-8131-02b10109e51c); lib. bdg. 26.60 *(978-1-4339-7487-8(8)*, 0cddf17f-cab8-4844-8920-287b54b1b8d7) Stevens, Gareth Publishing LLLP.

Linde, Barbara M. Malcolm X, 1 vol. 2011. (Civil Rights Crusaders Ser.). (ENG.). 24p. (J). (gr. 2-3). pap. 9.15 *(978-1-4339-5688-1(8)*, cb5e9f55-51aa-41c2-9adf-993f87a5c71f, Gareth Stevens Learning Library); lib. bdg. 25.27 *(978-1-4339-5686-7(1)*, 4e87775e-6f64-4b5f-95d2-f3d8eb576963) Stevens, Gareth Publishing LLLP.

Machajewski, Sarah. Malcolm X in His Own Words. 2014. (Eyewitness to History Ser.). 32p. (J). (gr. 4-6). pap. 63.00 *(978-1-4824-1220-8(9))* Stevens, Gareth Publishing LLLP.

Mancini, Candice L., ed. Racism in the Autobiography of Malcolm X, 1 vol. 2008. (Social Issues in Literature Ser.). (ENG., Illus.). 176p. (gr. 10-12). pap. 33.00 *(978-0-7377-4261-9(5)*, c11e206d-a850-44b5-b6cc-7956a1b11178); lib. bdg. 48.03 *(978-0-7377-4260-2(7)*, b9cdb352-b77e-4921-abad-b6f5038b9070) Greenhaven Publishing LLC. (Greenhaven Publishing).

Mis, Melody S. Meet Malcolm X. (Civil Rights Leaders Ser.). 24p. (gr. 2-3). 2009. 42.50 *(978-1-61511-853-3(5)*, PowerKids Pr.) 2007. (ENG., Illus.). (YA). lib. bdg. 26.27 *(978-1-4042-4214-2(7)*, 46796c58-721e-437d-97d9-595c2e45b237) Rosen Publishing Group, Inc., The.

Myers, Walter Dean. Malcolm X: A Fire Burning Brightly. Jenkins, Leonard, illus. 2003. (ENG.). 40p. (J). (gr. k-3). pap. 8.99 *(978-0-06-056201-4(3)*, Amistad) HarperCollins Pubs.

—Malcolm X: A Fire Burning Brightly. 2004. (J). 14.65 *(978-0-7569-3199-5(1))* Perfection Learning Corp.

Redmond, Jillian. Malcolm X, Vol. 9. 2018. (Civil Rights Leaders Ser.). 128p. (J). (gr. 7). lib. bdg. 35.93 *(978-1-4222-4007-6(X))* Mason Crest.

Robinson, Tom. Malcolm X: Rights Activist & Nation of Islam Leader, 1 vol. 2013. (Essential Lives Set 8 Ser.). (ENG.). 112p. (YA). (gr. 6-12). lib. bdg. 41.36 *(978-1-61783-893-4(4)*, 6765, Essential Library) ABDO Publishing Co.

Shabazz, Ilyasah. Malcolm Little: The Boy Who Grew up to Become Malcolm X. Ford, A. G., illus. 2014. (ENG.). 48p. (J). (gr. 1-5). 19.99 *(978-1-4424-1216-3(X))* Simon & Schuster Children's Publishing.

Shabazz, Ilyasah & Magoon, Kekla. X: A Novel. 2016. (ENG.). 384p. (YA). (gr. 9). 19.65 *(978-0-606-39098-9(7))* Turtleback.

Stoltman, Joan. Malcolm X, 1 vol. 2018. (Heroes of Black History Ser.). (ENG.). 32p. (gr. 3-4). 28.27 *(978-1-5382-3019-0(4)*, 5baf4fe1-a895-43e9-b752-d7fe2d35f552) Stevens, Gareth Publishing LLLP.

Vietze, Andrew. The Life & Death of Malcolm X. 2017. (Spotlight on the Civil Rights Movement Ser.). 48p. (J). (gr. 10-15). 70.50 *(978-1-5383-8032-1(3))*; (ENG.). (gr. 6-6). pap. 12.75 *(978-1-5383-8031-4(5)*, 482e1ecb-a26d-4a6b-8991-514724ac5e84) Rosen Publishing Group, Inc., The. (Rosen Young Adult).

Wallace Sharp, Anne. Malcolm X & Black Pride, 1 vol. 2010. (Lucent Library of Black History Ser.). (ENG.). 104p. (gr. 7-7). 37.73 *(978-1-4205-0123-0(2)*, 774055c3-4b23-4f81-9f73-7272320b2f83, Lucent Pr.) Greenhaven Publishing LLC.

X-MEN (FICTITIOUS CHARACTERS)—FICTION

Black, Lee. Cyclops. Haspiel, Dean, illus. 2011. (X-Men: First Class Ser.: No. 2). (ENG.). 24p. (J). (gr. 2-6). 31.36 *(978-1-59961-947-7(4)*, 15634, Marvel Age) Spotlight.

Chaykin, Howard. Magneto. Chaykin, Howard, illus. 2011. (X-Men: First Class Ser.: No. 2). (ENG., Illus.). 24p. (J). (gr. 2-6). 31.36 *(978-1-59961-949-1(0)*, 15636, Marvel Age) Spotlight.

Clevinger, Brian. Ice Man & Angel. Doe, Juan, illus. 2011. (X-Men: First Class Ser.: No. 2). (ENG.). 24p. (J). (gr. 2-6). 31.36 *(978-1-59961-948-4(2)*, 15635, Marvel Age) Spotlight.

Fialkov, Joshua Hale. Marvel Girl. Plati, Nuno, illus. 2011. (X-Men: First Class Ser.: No. 2). (ENG.). 24p. (J). (gr. 2-6). 31.36 *(978-1-59961-950-7(4)*, 15637, Marvel Age) Spotlight.

Gallagher, Michael. X-Men, Magneto's Master Plan. Severin, Marie, illus. 24p. (YA). (gr. k-18). 12.95 *(978-0-9627001-6-3(9))* Futech Educational Products, Inc.

—X-Men, Scourge of the Savage Land. Severin, Marie, illus. 24p. (YA). (gr. k-18). 12.95 *(978-0-9627001-7-0(7))* Futech Educational Products, Inc.

Jensen, Jeff. X-Factor. Ranson, Arthur, illus. 2003. (X-Men Ser.: Vol. 1). 96p. (YA). pap. 9.99 *(978-0-7851-1016-3(X))* Marvel Worldwide, Inc.

Macri, Thomas. The Story of the X-Men. 2013. (Marvel World of Reading Level 2 Ser.). (J). lib. bdg. 13.55 *(978-0-606-32300-0(7))* Turtleback.

Marvel, Saga, et al. Marvel Saga. 2009. (Astonishing X-Men Ser.). (Illus.). 152p. pap. 14.99 *(978-0-7851-3846-4(3))* Marvel Worldwide, Inc.

McDonnell, David, ed. Spiderman & Other Amazing Heroes. 2004. (Starlog Movie Magic Ser.). (YA). pap. *(978-0-88013-065-3(2))* Profile Entertainment, Inc.

Millar, Mark. Ultimate X-Men, 3 vols., Vol. 3. 2003. (Ultimate X-Men Ser.). (Illus.). 312p. 29.99 *(978-0-7851-1131-3(X))* Marvel Worldwide, Inc.

Millar, Mark & Austen, Chuck. Ultimate X-Men, 2 vols., Vol. 2. Kubert, Adam et al, illus. 2003. (Ultimate X-Men Ser.). 336p. (YA). 29.99 *(978-0-7851-1130-6(1))* Marvel Worldwide, Inc.

Milligan, Peter. Good Omens, Vol. 1. Allred, Mike, illus. 2003. (X-Statix Ser.). 128p. (YA). pap. 11.99 *(978-0-7851-1059-0(3))* Marvel Worldwide, Inc.

—X-Force: Famous, Mutant & Mortal. Allred, Mike, illus. 2003. (X-Statix Ser.). 352p. (YA). 29.99 *(978-0-7851-1023-1(2))* Marvel Worldwide, Inc.

Nicieza, Fabián. X-Force: Big Guns. Liefeld, Rob, illus. 2004. (X-Force Ser.). 136p. pap. 15.99 *(978-0-7851-1483-3(1))* Marvel Worldwide, Inc.

Parker, Jeff. A Life of the Mind. Paniccia, Mark, ed. Cruz, Roger, illus. 2007. (X-Men: First Class Ser.: No. 1). (ENG.). 24p. (J). (gr. 2-6). lib. bdg. 31.36 *(978-1-59961-399-4(9)*, 15630, Marvel Age) Spotlight.

—Seeing Red. Paniccia, Mark, ed. Cruz, Roger, illus. 2007. (X-Men: First Class Ser.: No. 1). (ENG.). 24p. (J). (gr. 2-6). 31.36 *(978-1-59961-400-7(6)*, 15631, Marvel Age) Spotlight.

Publications International Ltd. Staff, ed. Look & Find Wolverine & X Men. 2009. 24p. (J). 7.98 *(978-1-4127-3592-6(0)*, PIL Kids) Publications International, Ltd.

Rodi, Robert & Richards, Cliff. Rogue: Going Rogue. 2005. (X-Men Ser.). (Illus.). 144p. pap. 14.99 *(978-0-7851-1336-2(3))* Marvel Worldwide, Inc.

Sumerak, Marc. Big Trouble at the Big Top! Gurihiru Staff, illus. 2006. (X-Men Power Pack - 4 Titles Ser.). 24p. lib. bdg. 22.78 *(978-1-59961-219-5(4))* Spotlight.

—Costumes On! Gurihiru Staff, illus. 2006. (X-Men Power Pack - 4 Titles Ser.). 24p. lib. bdg. 22.78 *(978-1-59961-220-1(8))* Spotlight.

—Mind over Matter. Gurihiru Staff, illus. 2006. (X-Men Power Pack - 4 Titles Ser.). 24p. lib. bdg. 22.78 *(978-1-59961-222-5(4))* Spotlight.

Thomas, Rich. The Uncanny X-Men. Disney Storybook Artists Staff, illus. 2012. (Marvel Origins Ser.). (ENG.). 48p. (J). (gr. k-5). lib. bdg. 31.36 *(978-1-61479-012-9(4)*, 11340, Marvel Age) Spotlight.

Van Lente, Fred. Substitute. Koblish, Scott, illus. 2013. (Wolverine: First Class Ser.). (ENG.). 24p. (J). (gr. 2-6). lib. bdg. 31.36 *(978-1-61479-181-2(3)*, 15329, Marvel Age) Spotlight.

X-Men. 2003. (J). *(978-1-57657-859-9(3))* Paradise Pr., Inc.

X-Men - First Class: Set, 4 vols. Incl. Cyclops. Black, Lee. Haspiel, Dean, illus. 31.36 *(978-1-59961-947-7(4)*, 15634); Ice Man & Angel. Clevinger, Brian. Doe, Juan, illus. 31.36 *(978-1-59961-948-4(2)*, 15635); Magneto. Chaykin, Howard. Chaykin, Howard, illus. 31.36 *(978-1-59961-949-1(0)*, 15636); Marvel Girl. Fialkov, Joshua Hale. Plati, Nuno, illus. 31.36 *(978-1-59961-950-7(4)*, 15637); (J). (gr. 2-6). (X-Men: First Class Ser.: 4). (ENG.). 24p. 2011. Set lib. bdg. 125.44 *(978-1-59961-946-0(6)*, 15633, Marvel Age) Spotlight.

X-Men Power Pack. 2006. (X-Men Power Pack Ser.). (ENG.). (J). 45.56 *(978-1-59961-218-8(6))* Spotlight.

X-RAYS

Horstschafer, Felicitas. X-Ray Me! Look Inside Your Body. Vogt, Johannes, illus. 2019. (ENG.). 22p. (J). (gr. 1-5). bds. 12.99 *(978-0-06-288996-6(6)*, Greenwillow Bks.) HarperCollins Pubs.

National Geographic Learning. Reading Expeditions (Science: Everyday Science): Science at the Airport. 2007. (ENG., Illus.). 24p. (J). pap. 15.95 *(978-0-7922-4568-1(7))* CENGAGE Learning.

Olson, Karen. Cooper Gets a Cast. Pritchett and Hull Associates, Inc., illus. 2003. (J). 4.50 *(978-0-939838-86-8(9))* Pritchett & Hull Assocs., Inc.

Porterfield, Jason. Jump-Starting a Career in Radiology, 1 vol. 2018. (Health Care Careers in 2 Years Ser.). (ENG.). 80p. (gr. 7-7). pap. 16.30 *(978-1-5081-8507-9(7)*, 81494c42-5a45-4a77-8a73-9d3dcf0a10bc, Rosen Young Adult) Rosen Publishing Group, Inc., The.

Rubio, Elizabeth. Understanding & Using X-Rays, 1 vol. 2021. (Electromagnetic Spectrum Ser.). (ENG.). 64p. (J). (gr. 7-7). pap. 16.24 *(978-1-9785-1500-0(6)*, 8ad136a0-9afa-44f5-adec-fe8876f2230c) Enslow Publishing, LLC.

Scirri, Kaitlin. The Science of Invisibility & X-Ray Vision, 1 vol. 2018. (Science of Superpowers Ser.). (ENG.). 48p. (gr. 4-4). 33.07 *(978-1-5026-3790-1(1)*, 55b850c3-c1f1-4248-89dd-6134f201f18d) Cavendish Square Publishing LLC.

Thiel, Kristin. Dorothy Hodgkin: Biochemist & Developer of Protein Crystallography, 1 vol. 2016. (Women in Science Ser.). (ENG., Illus.). 128p. (J). (gr. 9-9). lib. bdg. 47.36 *(978-1-5026-2313-3(7)*, becac5ab-b36b-4864-bd8e-0d71d6e8829e) Cavendish Square Publishing LLC.

Wojton, Nick. Oops! They're X-Rays! 2019. (Accidental Scientific Discoveries That Changed the World Ser.). (ENG.). 32p. (gr. 3-4). 63.00 *(978-1-5382-4003-8(3))* Stevens, Gareth Publishing LLLP.

Y

YACHTS AND YACHTING

see also Sailing

Hopping, Lorraine Jean. Crossing the Atlantic: One Family's Story. 2004. (ENG., Illus.). 16p. (J). (gr. 2-2). pap. 11.00 net. *(978-0-7652-5186-2(8))* Celebration Pr.

Loh-Hagan, Virginia. Steven Callahan: Adrift in the Atlantic. 2018. (True Survival Ser.). (ENG., Illus.). 32p. (J). (gr. 4-8). pap. 14.21 *(978-1-5341-0874-5(2)*, 210860); lib. bdg. 32.07 *(978-1-5341-0775-5(4)*, 210859) Cherry Lake Publishing. (45th Parallel Press).

YANGTZE RIVER AND VALLEY

Manning, Paul. The Yangtze. (River Adventures Ser.). 2014. (J). lib. bdg. 31.35 *(978-1-59920-919-7(5))* 2013. 48p. (gr. 5-11). lib. bdg. 37.10 *(978-1-59920-925-8(X))* Black Rabbit Bks.

Rice Jr., Earle. The Yangtze River. 2012. (Illus.). 47p. (J). lib. bdg. 29.95 *(978-1-61228-299-2(7))* Mitchell Lane Pubs.

The Yangtzee. 2011. (River Journey Ser.). (ENG.). 48p. (YA). (gr. 5-8). 27.95 *(978-1-4488-6014-2(8)*, Rosen Reference) Rosen Publishing Group, Inc., The.

YANGTZE RIVER AND VALLEY—FICTION

Sedgwick, Julian. Ghosts of Shanghai: Return to the City of Ghosts: Book 3, Bk. 3. 2019. (Ghosts of Shanghai Ser.). (ENG., Illus.). 360p. (J). (gr. 3-7). pap. 9.99 *(978-1-4449-2451-0(6))* Hachette Children's Group GBR. Dist: Hachette Bk. Group.

YEARBOOKS

see also Almanacs; Calendars

Cohn, Scotti. One Wolf Howls, 1 vol. Detwiler, Susan, illus. 2009. (ENG.). 32p. (J). (gr. -1-3). 16.95 *(978-1-934359-92-1(0))* Arbordale Publishing.

YELLOW FEVER

Cefrey, Holly. Yellow Fever. 2009. (Epidemics Ser.). 64p. (gr. 5-5). 58.50 *(978-1-61512-309-4(1))* Rosen Publishing Group, Inc., The.

Hamen, Susan E. The 12 Worst Health Disasters of All Time. 2019. (All-Time Worst Disasters Ser.). (ENG., Illus.). 32p. (J). (gr. 3-6). 14.25 *(978-1-63235-602-4(3)*, 13919); 32.80 *(978-1-63235-537-9(X)*, 13911) Bookstaves, LLC. (12-Story Library).

Jurmain, Suzanne. Secret of the Yellow Death: A True Story of Medical Sleuthing. 2013. (ENG., Illus.). 112p. (J). (gr. 5-7). pap. 10.99 *(978-0-547-74624-1(5)*, 1486407, Clarion Bks.) HarperCollins Pubs.

Murphy, Jim. An American Plague: A Newbery Honor Award Winner. 2003. (ENG., Illus.). 176p. (J). (gr. 5-7). tchr. ed. 21.99 *(978-0-395-77608-7(2)*, 111936, Clarion Bks.) HarperCollins Pubs.

YELLOWSTONE NATIONAL PARK

Apel, Melanie Ann. The Yellowstone Park Fire Of 1988. 2009. (Tragic Fires Throughout History Ser.). 48p. (gr. 5-8). 53.00 *(978-1-60854-585-8(7)*, Rosen Reference) Rosen Publishing Group, Inc., The.

Aretha, David. Yellowstone National Park: Adventure, Explore, Discover, 1 vol. 2008. (America's National Parks Ser.). (ENG., Illus.). 128p. (gr. 6-7). lib. bdg. 37.27 *(978-1-59845-087-3(5)*, 02db7824-af76-4042-b576-e5aad31bd0cd) Enslow Publishing, LLC.

Bauer, Marion Dane. Yellowstone. Wallace, John, illus. 2008. (Ready-To-Read Level 1 Ser.). (ENG.). 32p. (J). (gr. -1-1). lib. bdg. 16.19 *(978-1-4169-5405-7(8)*, Aladdin) Simon & Schuster Children's Publishing.

—Yellowstone: Ready-To-Read Level 1. Wallace, John, illus. 2008. (Wonders of America Ser.). (ENG.). 32p. (J). (gr. -1-1). pap. 4.99 *(978-1-4169-5404-0(X)*, Simon Spotlight) Simon Spotlight.

Craighead, Shirley A. Bugling Elk & Sleeping Grizzlies: The Who, What, & When of Yellowstone & Grand Teton National Parks. 2004. (ENG., Illus.). 48p. pap. 9.95 *(978-0-7627-2864-0(7)*, Falcon Guides) Globe Pequot Pr., The.

Francis, Michael H. Yellowstone Memories: 30 Years of Photographs & Stories. 2005. (Illus.). 95p. 22.95 *(978-1-931832-59-5(5)*, 8667872363) Riverbend Publishing.

Frisch, Nate. Yellowstone National Park. 2013. (Illus.). 48p. (J). 35.65 *(978-1-60818-198-8(7)*, Creative Education) Creative Co., The.

Gamble, Adam & Jasper, Mark. Good Night Yellowstone. Kelly, Cooper, illus. 2013. (Good Night Our World Ser.). (ENG.). 20p. (J). (— 1). bds. 9.95 *(978-1-60219-079-5(8))* Good Night Bks.

George, Jean Craighead. The Wolves Are Back. Minor, Wendell, illus. 2008. (ENG.). 32p. (J). (gr. -1-3). 17.99 *(978-0-525-47947-5(3)*, Dutton Books for Young Readers) Penguin Young Readers Group.

Gilbert, Sara. Yellowstone. 2016. (National Park Explorers Ser.). (ENG., Illus.). 24p. (J). (gr. 1-4). *(978-1-60818-634-1(2)*, 20510, Creative Education) Creative Co., The.

Glastetter, KC & Holiman, Jeremie, photos by. Yellowstone Natl Park Abc Adv. 2010. (Illus.). 64p. (J). pap. 12.00 *(978-0-87842-572-3(1))* Mountain Pr. Publishing Co., Inc.

Godkin, Celia. The Wolves Return. Godkin, Celia, illus. 2017. (ENG., Illus.). 32p. (J). (gr. 1-3). 17.95 *(978-1-77278-011-6(1))* Pajama Pr. CAN. Dist: Publishers Group West (PGW).

Goldish, Meish. Gray Wolves: Return to Yellowstone. 2016. (America's Animal Comebacks Ser.). (ENG., Illus.). 32p. (J). (gr. 2-7). pap. 7.99 *(978-1-944998-72-1(1))* Bearport Publishing Co., Inc.

Halfpenny, James C. Yellowstone Wolves in the Wild. 2003. (ENG., Illus.). 104p. per. 19.95 *(978-1-931832-26-7(9)*, 8667872363) Riverbend Publishing.

Hansen, Grace. Parque Nacional de Yellowstone (Yellowstone National Park) 2018. (Parques Nacionales (National Parks) Ser.). (SPA., Illus.). 24p. (J). (gr. -1-2). lib. bdg. 32.79 *(978-1-5321-8047-7(0)*, 28309, Abdo Kids) ABDO Publishing Co.

—Yellowstone National Park. 2017. (National Parks (Abdo Kids Jumbo) Ser.). (ENG., Illus.). 24p. (J). (gr. -1-2). lib. bdg. 32.79 *(978-1-5321-0436-7(7)*, 26562, Abdo Kids) ABDO Publishing Co.

Holland, Ilona E. & National Geographic Kids. Buddy Bison's Yellowstone Adventure. 2016. (Illus.). 32p. (J). (gr. -1-k). pap. 9.99 *(978-1-4263-2297-6(6)*, National Geographic Kids) Disney Publishing Worldwide.

Johanek, Durrae. What I Saw! in Yellowstone: A Kid's Guide to Wonderland. Cauble, Christopher, photos by. 2012. (ENG., Illus.). 40p. (J). (gr. 3-7). pap. 12.95 *(978-1-60639-035-1(X))* Riverbend Publishing.

Kalman, Bobbie. Yellowstone National Park. 2009. (Introducing Habitats Ser.). (ENG., Illus.). 32p. (J). (gr. k-3). pap. *(978-0-7787-2989-1(3))* Crabtree Publishing Co.

Marsh, Carole. I'm Reading about Yellowstone. 2016. (I'm Reading about Mount Rushmore Ser.). (ENG., Illus.). (J). pap. 7.99 *(978-0-635-12184-4(0))* Gallopade International.

Mattern, Joanne. Yellowstone: America's First National Park. 2017. (Core Content Social Studies — Let's Celebrate America Ser.). (ENG., Illus.). 32p. (J). (gr. 2-5). pap. 8.99 *(978-1-63440-230-9(8)*, 3077318d-5875-4e19-ba46-59213a673162); lib. bdg. 26.65 *(978-1-63440-220-0(0)*, 3d7224e3-a051-4680-a699-1518b838e480) Red Chair Pr.

McCarthy, Cecilia Pinto. Yellowstone National Park. 2016. (National Parks (Core Library) Ser.). (ENG., Illus.). 48p. (J). (gr. 4-8). lib. bdg. 35.64 *(978-1-68078-475-6(7)*, 23887) ABDO Publishing Co.

Nussbaum, Ben. Travel Adventures: Yellowstone. 2018. (Mathematics in the Real World Ser.). (ENG., Illus.). 32p. (J). (gr. 4-8). pap. 11.99 *(978-1-4258-5809-4(0))* Teacher Created Materials, Inc.

Ogden, Charlie. Surviving the Yellowstone Supervolcano, 1 vol. 2017. (Surviving the Impossible Ser.). (ENG.). 32p. (J). (gr. 4-5). pap. 11.50 *(978-1-5382-1455-8(5)*, 276510a3-dc80-4a05-9a0a-86ee47d954b7); lib. bdg. 28.27 *(978-1-5382-1426-8(1)*, c9deeb4b-5194-49e9-8841-ca52ee35aeff) Stevens, Gareth Publishing LLLP.

Patent, Dorothy Hinshaw. When the Wolves Returned: Restoring Nature's Balance in Yellowstone. Hartman, Dan, illus. Hartman, Dan, photos by. 2008. (ENG.). 40p. (J). (gr. 1-4). 19.99 *(978-0-8027-9686-8(9)*, 900045639, Bloomsbury USA Childrens) Bloomsbury Publishing USA.

Pecorella, Jane. Yellowstone: Our First National Park. 2009. (Reading Room Collection 2 Ser.). 24p. (gr. 3-4). 42.50 *(978-1-60852-004-6(8)*, PowerKids Pr.) Rosen Publishing Group, Inc., The.

Piehl, Janet. Yellowstone National Park. 2010. (Lightning Bolt Books (r) — Famous Places Ser.). (ENG., Illus.). 32p. (J). (gr. 1-3). pap. 9.99 *(978-0-7613-5588-5(X)*, 876598db-3a7c-4336-bce8-cac969a8b87a); lib. bdg. 30.65 *(978-0-7613-4455-1(1)*, 46efe48e-7059-41ba-bc38-c619b757a09b, Lerner Pubns.) Lerner Publishing Group.

Robson, Gary D. Who Pooped in the Park? Yellowstone. 2004. (Illus.). 48p. (J). pap. 11.95 *(978-1-56037-273-8(7))* Farcountry Pr.

Swirnow, Linda. Take on Yellowstone! 2011. 32p. pap. 12.99 *(978-1-4490-2219-8(7))* AuthorHouse.

Teri, Bob & Temple, Teri. Welcome to Yellowstone National Park. 2018. (National Parks Ser.). (ENG.). 32p. (J). (gr. 2-5). lib. bdg. 35.64 *(978-1-5038-2346-4(6)*, 212181) Child's World, Inc, The.

Wallace, Audra. Yellowstone (a True Book: National Parks) (Library Edition) 2017. (True Book (Relaunch) Ser.). (ENG., Illus.). 48p. (J). (gr. 3-5). lib. bdg. 31.00 (978-0-531-23396-2(0), Children's Pr.) Scholastic Library Publishing.

—Yellowstone National Park (Rookie National Parks) (Library Edition) 2017. (Rookie National Parks Ser.). (ENG., Illus.). 32p. (J). (gr. 1-2). lib. bdg. 25.00 (978-0-531-23335-1(9), Children's Pr.) Scholastic Library Publishing.

Webster, Dawn & Yost, Emily. Yellowstone for Kids: A Kid's Guide to Yellowstone National Park. 2016. (Illus.). (J). pap. (978-0-934948-40-1(2)) Yellowstone Forever.

White, Kelly Anne. Yellowstone National Park. 2018. (Natural Wonders of the World Ser.). (ENG., Illus.). 32p. (J). (gr. 3-5). lib. bdg. 31.35 (978-1-63517-518-9(6), 1635175186, Focus Readers) North Star Editions.

Zschock, Martha. Hello, Yellowstone! 2012. (Hello Ser.). (ENG., Illus.). 16p. (J). (gr. -1-k). bds. 9.99 (978-1-933212-61-6(6), Commonwealth Editions) Applewood Bks.

YETI

Anderson, Jennifer Joline. Bigfoot & Yeti, 1 vol. 2014. (Creatures of Legend Ser.). (ENG., Illus.). 48p. (J). (gr. 4-8). lib. bdg. 35.64 (978-1-62403-150-2(1), 4934) ABDO Publishing Co.

Colson, Mary. Bigfoot & Yeti: Myth or Reality? 2018. (Investigating Unsolved Mysteries Ser.). (ENG., Illus.). 32p. (J). (gr. 3-9). lib. bdg. 28.65 (978-1-5435-3569-3(0), 138910, Capstone Pr.) Capstone.

Dennett, Preston. Bigfoot, Yeti, & Other Ape-Men. 2008. (Mysteries, Legends, & Unexplained Phenomena Ser.). (ENG., Illus.). 152p. (gr. 7-12). 29.95 (978-0-7910-9386-3(7), P159098, Facts On File) Infobase Holdings, Inc.

McClellan, Ray. Bigfoot. 2014. (Unexplained Mysteries Ser.). (ENG., Illus.). 24p. (J). (gr. 3-7). lib. bdg. 26.95 (978-1-62617-103-9(3), Epic Bks.) Bellwether Media.

Nagle, Jeanne. Investigating the Abominable Snowman & Other Legendary Beasts, 1 vol. 2014. (Understanding the Paranormal Ser.). (ENG.). 48p. (J). (gr. 5-5). 28.41 (978-1-62275-853-1(6), 92010f80-11ef-454f-ad16-67fdc566426e, Britannica Educational Publishing) Rosen Publishing Group, Inc., The.

Rivkin, Jennifer. Searching for the Yeti, 1 vol. 2014. (Mysterious Monsters Ser.). (ENG., Illus.). 32p. (J). (gr. 4-5). 27.93 (978-1-4777-7097-9(6), 6b68b0d2-258a-4f85-8562-5f5aaea1cab3, PowerKids Pr.) Rosen Publishing Group, Inc., The.

Roberts, Steven. The Yeti!, 1 vol. 2012. (Jr. Graphic Monster Stories Ser.). (ENG., Illus.). 24p. (J). (gr. 2-3). 28.93 (978-1-4488-7905-2(1), 433a7b27-6d4f-43e4-8ffe-9bad699534a5); pap. 11.60 (978-1-4488-8005-8(X), 6e248ef2-5e1a-4233-a33d-14c914efc816) Rosen Publishing Group, Inc., The. (PowerKids Pr.).

Shone, Rob. Bigfoot & Other Strange Beasts. 2009. (Graphic Mysteries Ser.). (ENG.). 48p. (YA). (gr. 5-5). 58.50 (978-1-61512-961-4(8), Rosen Reference) Rosen Publishing Group, Inc., The.

—Bigfoot & Other Strange Beasts, 1 vol. Spender, Nik, illus. 2006. (Graphic Mysteries Ser.). (ENG.). 48p. (gr. 5-5). pap. 14.05 (978-1-4042-0804-9(6), c20454f9-d03a-4d79-8ded-553c3791d531) Rosen Publishing Group, Inc., The.

—Bigfoot & Other Strange Beasts, 1 vol. Spender, Nick, illus. 2006. (Graphic Mysteries Ser.). (ENG.). 48p. (YA). (gr. 5-5). lib. bdg. 37.13 (978-1-4042-0793-6(7), 63bbb09b-1918-4cff-a780-95b413b15bca) Rosen Publishing Group, Inc., The.

Teitelbaum, Michael. Bigfoot Caught on Film: And Other Monster Sightings! 2008. (24/7: Science Behind the Scenes Ser.). (ENG., Illus.). 64p. (J). (gr. 9-12). 29.00 (978-0-531-12078-1(3), Watts, Franklin) Scholastic Library Publishing.

Truet, Turin & Gilman, Laura Anne. Searching for Yeti: The Abominable Snowman. 2011. (Illus.). 64p. (J). 77.70 (978-1-4488-4781-5(8)); (ENG., (gr. 5-5). 37.13 (978-1-4488-4764-8(8), 88a94ec2-4603-4f4f-82af-5f86ddd1d7fb); (ENG., (gr. 5-5). pap. 13.95 (978-1-4488-4773-0(7), 76e4a1f8-9529-48e0-8c05-544da1e11b5f) Rosen Publishing Group, Inc., The.

Vale, Jenna & Gilman, Laura Anne. Tracking the Yeti, 1 vol. 2018. (Paranormal Seekers Ser.). (ENG., Illus.). 64p. (J). (gr. 5-8). 36.13 (978-1-4994-6726-0(5), a44c19b5-0847-4983-b600-c97fc85bf70f) Rosen Publishing Group, Inc., The.

Walker, Kathryn. Mysteries of Giant Humanlike Creatures. 2008. (ENG., Illus.). 32p. (J). (gr. 3-7). pap. (978-0-7787-4156-5(7)); lib. bdg. (978-0-7787-4143-5(5)) Crabtree Publishing Co.

YOGA

Baptiste, Baron. My Daddy Is a Pretzel. Fatus, Sophie, illus. 2012. (ENG.). 48p. (J). (gr. k-2). pap. 10.99 (978-1-84686-899-3(8)) Barefoot Bks., Inc.

—My Daddy Is a Pretzel: Yoga for Parents & Kids. Fatus, Sophie, illus. 2004. (ENG.). 48p. (J). (gr. -1-2). 16.99 (978-1-84148-151-7(3)) Barefoot Bks., Inc.

Bauer, Joy. Yummy Yoga: Playful Poses & Tasty Treats. Stephens, Bonnie, illus. 2019. (ENG.). 24p. (J). (gr. -1-17). 14.99 (978-1-4197-3824-1(0), 1284101, Abrams Bks. for Young Readers) Abrams, Inc.

Beliveau, Kathy. The Yoga Game. 2012. (Illus.). 42p. (J). (gr. -1-2). pap. 9.95 (978-1-897476-72-7(8)) Simply Read Bks. CAN. Dist: Ingram Publisher Services.

—The Yoga Game by the Sea. Holmes, Denise, illus. 2015. (Yoga Game Ser.: 1). (ENG.). 32p. (J). 16.95 (978-1-927018-49-1(8)) Simply Read Bks. CAN. Dist: Ingram Publisher Services.

—The Yoga Game in the Garden. Holmes, Denise, illus. 2016. (Yoga Game Ser.: 2). (ENG.). 32p. (J). (gr. -1-3). 16.95 (978-1-927018-71-2(4)) Simply Read Bks. CAN. Dist: Ingram Publisher Services.

Bersma, Danielle & Visscher, Marjoke. Yoga Games for Children: Fun & Fitness with Postures, Movements & Breath. Kooistra, Alex, illus. 2003. (SmartFun Activity Bks.). (ENG.). 160p. (J). pap. 21.99 (978-0-89793-389-6(3), Hunter Hse.) Turner Publishing Co.

Brukner, Lauren. Stay Cool & in Control with the Keep-Calm Guru: Wise Ways for Children to Regulate Their Emotions & Senses. Apsley, illus. 2016. 136p. 21.95 (978-1-78592-714-0(0), 694029) Kingsley, Jessica Pubs. GBR. Dist: Hachette UK Distribution.

Buckley, Annie. The Breathing Bridge. (Illus.). 2012. (978-1-927004-14-2(4)) 2011. pap. (978-1-927004-13-5(6)) Brighter Bks. Publishing Hse.

—The Kids' Yoga Deck: 50 Poses & Games. 2003. (ENG., Illus.). 50p. (gr. 8-17). 14.95 (978-0-8118-3698-2(3)) Chronicle Bks. LLC.

Burrill, Jenny. Yoga. Kushnir, Hilli, illus. 2020. (Baby's Big World Ser.). 18p. (J). bds. 8.99 (978-1-946000-03-3(5), Starry Forest Bks.) Starry Forest Bks., Inc.

Capucilli, Alyssa Satin. My First Yoga Class: Ready-To-Read Pre-Level 1. Wachter, Jill, photos by. 2017. (My First Ser.). (ENG., Illus.). 32p. (J). (gr. -1-k). 16.99 (978-1-5344-0485-4(6)); pap. 4.99 (978-1-5344-0484-7(8)) Simon Spotlight. (Simon Spotlight).

Carpenter, Nora Shalaway. Yoga Frog. Chambers, Mark, illus. 2018. (ENG.). 40p. (J). (gr. -1-3). 14.99 (978-0-7624-6467-8(4), Running Pr. Kids) Running Pr.

Chissick, Michael. Ladybird's Remarkable Relaxation: How Children (And Frogs, Dogs, Flamingos & Dragons) Can Use Yoga Relaxation to Help Deal with Stress, Grief, Bullying & Lack of Confidence. 2013. (Illus.). 48p. 21.95 (978-1-84819-146-4(4), 694213, Singing Dragon) Kingsley, Jessica Pubs. GBR. Dist: Hachette UK Distribution.

Crabtree Editors & Wilson, Kyla. Stretch It Yoga. 2012. (Sports Starters Ser.). (ENG., Illus.). 32p. (J). (gr. 1-4). lib. bdg. (978-0-7787-3153-5(7)) Crabtree Publishing Co.

Dezé, Ulrika. Anytime Yoga: Fun & Easy Exercises for Concentration & Calm. Kroug, Simon, illus. 2019. 64p. (J). (gr. -1-2). 16.95 (978-1-61180-439-3(6), Bala Kids) Shambhala Pubns., Inc.

Duch, Mamen. Relaxations: Big Tools for Little Warriors. Nieto Guridi, Raúl, illus. 2018. 40p. (J). (978-1-4338-2904-8(5), Magination Pr.) American Psychological Assn.

Engel, Christiane. ABC for Me: ABC Yoga, Volume 1. 2016. (ABC for Me Ser.: 1). (ENG., Illus.). 36p. (J). (gr. -1-1). 16.95 (978-1-63322-146-8(6), 224014, Walter Foster Jr) Quarto Publishing Group USA.

Galjasevic, Marko & Wood, Deborah. Power down for Fitness: Yoga for Flexible Mind & Body. 2018. (Let's Move Ser.). (ENG., Illus.). 32p. (J). (gr. 1-3). lib. bdg. 19.99 (978-1-63440-410-5(6), 9bb9ee3f-28ba-44cf-ad19-a76987cdcdcf) Red Chair Pr.

Gates, Mariam. Good Morning Yoga: A Pose-By-Pose Wake up Story, 1 vol. 2016. (Good Night Yoga Ser.: 2). (ENG., Illus.). 36p. (J). 17.95 (978-1-62203-602-8(6), 900220700) Sounds True, Inc.

—Good Night Yoga: A Pose-By-Pose Bedtime Story. (Good Night Yoga Ser.: 4). (ENG., Illus.). (J). 2018. 22p. bds. 9.99 (978-1-68364-107-0(8), 900220873) 2015. 36p. 17.95 (978-1-62203-466-6(X), 900220589) Sounds True, Inc.

—This Moment Is Your Life (and So Is This One) A Fun & Easy Guide to Mindfulness, Meditation, & Yoga. VanderPloeg, Libby, illus. 2018. 248p. (J). (gr. 5-9). 18.99 (978-0-399-18662-2(X), Dial Bks) Penguin Young Readers Group.

Gates, Mariam & Gates, Rolf. Yoga Friends: A Pose-By-Pose Partner Adventure for Kids. 2018. (Good Night Yoga Ser.: 3). (ENG., Illus.). 32p. (J). 17.95 (978-1-62203-816-9(9), 900220772) Sounds True, Inc.

Gillen, Lynea & Gillen, Jim. Yoga Calm for Children: Educating Heart, Mind, & Body. 2008. (ENG., Illus.). 181p. (J). per. 19.95 (978-0-9799289-0-1(7)) Three Pebble Pr., LLC.

Guber, Tara & Kalish, Leah. Yoga Pretzels. Fatus, Sophie, illus. 2005. (Barefoot Books Activity Decks Ser.). (ENG.). 58p. (J). (gr. k-5). 16.99 (978-1-905236-04-6(2)) Barefoot Bks., Inc.

Hinder, Sarah Jane. Yoga Bear: Simple Animal Poses for Little Ones. 2018. (Yoga Kids & Animal Friends Board Bks.: 2). (ENG., Illus.). 24p. (J). bds. 9.99 (978-1-68364-075-2(6), 900220862) Sounds True, Inc.

—Yoga Bug: Simple Poses for Little Ones. 2017. (Yoga Kids & Animal Friends Board Bks.: 1). (ENG., Illus.). 24p. (J). bds. 9.99 (978-1-62203-979-1(3), 900220837) Sounds True, Inc.

Hughes, Emma. The Go Yogi! Card Set: 50 Everyday Yoga Poses for Calm, Happy, Healthy Kids. Smisson, John, illus. 2017. 50p. 25.00 (978-1-84819-370-3(X), 700615, Singing Dragon) Kingsley, Jessica Pubs. GBR. Dist: Hachette UK Distribution.

Humphrey, Mary. The Kids' Yoga Book of Feelings, 1 vol. Hamlin, Janet, illus. Frost, Michael, photos by. 2008. (ENG.). 40p. (J). (gr. 3-7). 15.99 (978-0-7614-5424-3(1)) Marshall Cavendish Corp.

James, Sara. Yoga & Pilates. Hart, Diane H., ed. 2014. (Integrated Life of Fitness Ser.). (Illus.). 64p. (J). (gr. 7-18). pap. 11.95 (978-1-4222-3204-0(2)); 23.95 (978-1-4222-3166-1(6)) Mason Crest.

Jordan, Apple. Meddy Teddy: A Mindful Journey. Hong, Nicholas, illus. 2018. 32p. (J). (gr. -1-3). 17.99 (978-1-63565-046-4(1), 9781635650464, Rodale Kids) Random Hse. Children's Bks.

Kacev, Glenda. Bal Yoga for Kids. 2012. (ENG.). (J). spiral bd. (978-1-4675-4626-7(X)) Independent Pub.

Kalish, Leah & Fatus, Sophie. Yoga Planet: 50 Fun Activities for a Greener World. 2008. (ENG., Illus.). (J). 14.99 (978-1-84686-181-9(0)) Barefoot Bks., Inc.

Kramer, Susan. Yoga for all Kids, Preschoolers to Teens. 2010. 96p. pap. 14.95 (978-0-557-42836-6(X)) Lulu Pr., Inc.

Lark, Liz. Yoga for Kids. Park, Clare, photos by. 2005. (Illus.). 127p. (J). reprint ed. pap. 20.00 (978-0-7567-9410-1(2)) DIANE Publishing Co.

Leavitt, Amy. Yoga Fitness. 2014. (ENG.). 48p. (gr. 4-8). 29.95 (978-1-61228-551-1(1)) Mitchell Lane Pubs.

MacAulay, Kelley. Yoga in Action. 2008. (FRE.). 32p. (J). pap. 9.95 (978-2-89579-205-5(4)) Bayard Canada Livres CAN. Dist: Crabtree Publishing Co.

MacAulay, Kelley & Kalman, Bobbie. Yoga in Action, 1 vol. Crabtree, Marc, photos by. 2005. (Sports in Action Ser.). (ENG., Illus.). 32p. (J). (gr. 2-3). pap. (978-0-7787-0364-8(9)) Crabtree Publishing Co.

MacLean, Kerry Lee. Peaceful Piggy Yoga. MacLean, Kerry Lee, illus. (ENG., Illus.). 32p. (J). (gr. -1-3). 2016. 12.99 (978-0-8075-6388-5(9), 807563889) 2014. 7.99 (978-0-8075-6383-0(8), 807563838) Whitman, Albert & Co.

Marek, Susan. A Children's Guide to Chakras. 2009. 32p. pap. 14.95 (978-0-578-00741-0(X)) Angelworks Pr.

Modi, Narendra. Exam Warriors. 2019. (ENG., Illus.). 208p. pap. 14.95 (978-0-14-344150-2(7), Penguin Enterprise) Penguin Bks. India PVT, Ltd IND. Dist: Independent Pubs. Group.

Pajalunga, Lorena V. Yoga for Kids: Simple Animal Poses for Any Age. Forlati, Anna, illus. 2015. (ENG.). 32p. (J). (gr. -1-3). 16.99 (978-0-8075-9172-7(6), 807591726) Whitman, Albert & Co.

Pegrum, Juliet. Yoga Fun for Toddlers, Children & You. 2010. (ENG., Illus.). 128p. pap. (978-1-907030-14-7(X)) www.clickok.co.uk.

Pierce, Karen F. Yoga Bear: Yoga for Youngsters. Brinkman, Paula, illus. 2004. (ENG.). 48p. (J). (gr. -1-1). 15.95 (978-1-55971-897-4(8)) Cooper Square Publishing Llc.

Power, Teresa. The ABCs of Yoga for Kids. Rietz, Kathleen, illus. 2009. (ENG.). 32p. (J). (gr. -1-3). 19.95 (978-0-9822587-0-5(4), 4e17cd6f-1cd3-4995-a291-23f8e9041df7) Stafford House.

Power, Teresa Anne. The ABCs of Yoga for Kids 56 Learning Cards. Rietz, Kathleen, illus. 2011. (ENG.). 57p. (J). 19.95 (978-0-9822587-3-6(9)) Stafford House.

—ABECÉ de Yoga para Ninos. Rietz, Kathleen, illus. 2011. (ENG & SPA.). 32p. (J). pap. 8.95 (978-0-9822587-4-3(7)) Stafford House.

Purperhart, Helen. The Yoga Adventure for Children: Playing, Dancing, Moving, Breathing, Relaxing. Von Amelsfort, Barbara, illus. 2007. (ENG.). 144p. (gr. -1-6). spiral bd. 19.95 (978-0-89793-471-8(7)); per. 14.95 (978-0-89793-470-1(9)) Turner Publishing Co. (Hunter Hse.).

—Yoga Exercises for Teens: Developing a Calmer Mind & a Stronger Body. Marix Evans, Amina, tr. van Amelsfort, Barbara, illus. 2008. (SmartFun Activity Bks.). (ENG.). 160p. (J). (gr. 4). spiral bd. 19.95 (978-0-89793-504-3(7)); pap. 16.95 (978-0-89793-503-6(9)) Turner Publishing Co. (Hunter Hse.).

Randall, Kat. Yoga for Youngsters: Playful Poses for Little People. 2004. (Illus.). 24p. pap. 8.95 (978-0-9749516-0-7(9)) Kat's Kids Kreation, A.

Rissman, Rebecca. Calm Girl: Yoga for Stress Relief. 2015. (Yoga for You Ser.). (ENG.). 64p. (J). (gr. 4-8). lib. bdg. 35.32 (978-1-4914-2121-5(5), 127604) Capstone.

—Fit Girl: Yoga for Fitness & Flexibility. 2015. (Yoga for You Ser.). (ENG.). 64p. (J). (gr. 4-8). lib. bdg. 35.32 (978-1-4914-2120-8(7), 127603) Capstone.

—Smart Girl: Yoga for Brain Power. 2015. (Yoga for You Ser.). (ENG.). 64p. (J). (gr. 4-8). lib. bdg. 35.32 (978-1-4914-2119-2(3), 127602) Capstone.

—Strong Girl: Yoga for Building Strength. 2015. (Yoga for You Ser.). (ENG.). 64p. (J). (gr. 4-8). lib. bdg. 35.32 (978-1-4914-2122-2(3), 127605) Capstone.

—Yoga for You. 2015. (Yoga for You Ser.). (ENG.). 64p. (J). (gr. 4-8). 149.28 (978-1-4914-2558-9(X), 22550) Capstone.

—Yoga for Your Mind & Body: A Teenage Practice for a Healthy, Balanced Life. 2015. (ENG., Illus.). 208p. (YA). (gr. 4-8). pap., pap., pap. 14.95 (978-1-63079-013-4(3), 128134, Switch Pr.) Capstone.

Ryzewski, Deborah. The Yoga ABC's with Alvin, Beatrice & Conner. 2005. (Illus.). (J). ring bd. 12.95 net. (978-0-9765302-0-6(1)) Ryzewski, Deborah.

Sheen, Barbara. Yoga, 1 vol. 2014. (Science Behind Sports Ser.). (ENG.). 104p. (gr. 7-7). 41.03 (978-1-4205-1229-8(3), 626b05a3-c278-4f3c-9de8-aa80d33795b8, Lucent Pr.) Greenhaven Publishing LLC.

Silas, Elizabeth & Goodney, Diane. Yoga. (Life Balance Ser.). (ENG.). 80p. (gr. 5-8). 2004. (YA). pap. 6.95 (978-0-531-15577-6(3)) 2003. (Illus.). (J). 20.50 (978-0-531-12258-7(1)) Scholastic Library Publishing. (Watts, Franklin).

Sumner, Christine. I Can Be: A Child's Whimsical Introduction to Yoga. Salopek, Kirk, illus. 2008. 32p. (J). 8.95 (978-0-615-16566-0(4)) Q & J Bird Pr., LLC.

Teddy, Meddy. Meddy Teddy: Mindful Poses for Little Yogis. 2018. (Illus.). 24p. (J). (— 1). bds. 7.99 (978-1-63565-129-4(8), 9781635651294, Rodale Kids) Random Hse. Children's Bks.

Verde, Susan. I Am Yoga. 2017. (I Am Bks.). (ENG., Illus.). 24p. (J). (gr. -1 — 1). bds. 8.95 (978-1-4197-2697-2(8), 1191610, Abrams Appleseed) Abrams, Inc.

Whitford, Rebecca. Little Yoga: A Toddler's First Book of Yoga. Selway, Martina, illus. 2005. (ENG.). 32p. (J). (gr. -1 — 1). 13.99 (978-0-8050-7879-4(7), 900030787, Holt, Henry & Co. Bks. For Young Readers) Holt, Henry & Co.

Wilson, Kyla. Stretch It Yoga. 2012. (ENG., Illus.). 32p. (J). pap. (978-0-7787-3164-1(2)) Crabtree Publishing Co.

Winters, Jaime. Get into Yoga. 2017. (Get-Into-It Guides). (Illus.). 32p. (J). (gr. 4-5). (978-0-7787-3644-8(X)) Crabtree Publishing Co.

YOM KIPPUR

Hashanah, Rosh & Kippur, Yom. Rosh Hashanah & Yom Kippur Coloring Book. 2.99 (978-1-58330-168-5(2)) Feldheim Pubs.

Head, Honor. Celebrating Yom Kippur: The Jewish New Year, 1 vol. (We Love Holidays (2008-2009) Ser.). (ENG., 24p. (J). (gr. 2-2). 2009. Illus.). pap. 9.25 (978-1-4358-2906-0(9), ba45fb90-3bb8-401a-a578-511932207233) 2008. lib. bdg. 26.27 (978-1-4358-2846-9(1), 093657ba-5efd-4c4a-b3f7-543e5dc1d20e) Rosen Publishing Group, Inc., The.

Richardson, Betsy. Lent, Yom Kippur & Days of Repentance, Vol. 10. 2018. (Celebrating Holidays & Festivals Around the World Ser.). (Illus.). 112p. (J). (gr. 7). lib. bdg. 34.60 (978-1-4222-4149-3(1)) Mason Crest.

Zimmerman, Noam. Yom Kippur Children's Machzor. 2006. (ENG.). 64p. 15.95 (978-965-229-362-6(8)) Gefen Publishing Hse., Ltd ISR. Dist: Gefen Bks.

YOM KIPPUR—FICTION

Adler, David. Yom Kippur Shortstop. Ceolin, Andre, illus. 2017. (ENG.). 32p. (J). 17.95 (978-1-68115-521-0(4), 49f3280f-23c8-4bfb-b3e9-53590244a34b) Behrman Hse., Inc.

Rouss, Sylvia A. Sammy Spider's First Yom Kippur. Kahn, Katherine Janus, illus. 2013. (ENG.). 32p. (J). (gr. -1-3). 7.99 (978-0-7613-9196-8(7), 583af9d7-d61d-4ca1-ae6b-8befc99b7c80); E-Book 27.99 (978-1-4677-1639-0(1)) Lerner Publishing Group. (Kar-Ben Publishing).

YORKTOWN (VA.)

Rudolph, Ellen K. Willi Gets a History Lesson: In Virginia's Historic Triangle. Rudolph, Ellen K., photos by. 2007. (ENG., Illus.). 80p. pap. 24.00 (978-0-9791348-0-7(3)) EKR Pubns.

YORKTOWN (VA.)—HISTORY—SIEGE, 1781

Anderson, Dale. The Battle of Yorktown, 1 vol. 2004. (Landmark Events in American History Ser.). (ENG., Illus.). 48p. (gr. 5-8). lib. bdg. 33.67 (978-0-8368-5393-3(8), 0db045af-952f-4a0b-9a9a-475f92040a9a, Gareth Stevens Secondary Library) Stevens, Gareth Publishing LLLP.

Anderson, Dale & Crewe, Sabrina. The Battle of Yorktown, 1 vol. 2004. (Events That Shaped America Ser.). (ENG.). 32p. (gr. 3-5). lib. bdg. 28.67 (978-0-8368-3412-3(7), bf6cff83-7094-4cc1-b8c5-9d5e89928070, Gareth Stevens Learning Library) Stevens, Gareth Publishing LLLP.

Braun, Eric. At the Battle of Yorktown: An Interactive Battlefield Adventure. 2018. (You Choose: American Battles Ser.). (ENG., Illus.). 112p. (J). (gr. 3-7). pap. 6.95 (978-1-5435-0293-0(8), 137162); lib. bdg. 32.65 (978-1-5435-0289-3(X), 137157) Capstone. (Capstone Pr.).

Brindell Fradin, Dennis. The Battle of Yorktown, 1 vol. 2009. (Turning Points in U. S. History Ser.). (ENG.). 48p. (gr. 4-4). lib. bdg. 34.07 (978-0-7614-3008-7(3), 4430d16e-dea9-44f7-8f10-3baa94868afb) Cavendish Square Publishing LLC.

Keppeler, Jill. Team Time Machine Witnesses the Siege at Yorktown, 1 vol. 2019. (Team Time Machine: American Revolution Ser.). (ENG.). 32p. (J). (gr. 2-3). pap. 11.50 (978-1-5382-4694-8(5), 1d1a42e3-7e0c-4b8a-8014-c297568851d3) Stevens, Gareth Publishing LLLP.

Randolph, Joanne. The Call of Liberty: Marquis de Lafayette & the American Revolution. 2009. (Great Moments in American History Ser.). 32p. (gr. 3-3). 47.90 (978-1-61513-152-5(3)) Rosen Publishing Group, Inc., The.

Roberts, Russell. Battle of Yorktown. 2011. (Technologies & Strategies in Battle Ser.). (Illus.). 48p. (J). (gr. 4-7). lib. bdg. 29.95 (978-1-61228-074-5(9)) Mitchell Lane Pubs.

Vierow, Wendy. The Battle of Yorktown. 2009. (Atlas of Famous Battles of the American Revolution Ser.). 24p. (gr. 3-3). 42.50 (978-1-60853-332-9(8), PowerKids Pr.) Rosen Publishing Group, Inc., The.

YOSEMITE NATIONAL PARK (CALIF.)

Dell, Pamela. Welcome to Yosemite National Park. 2018. (National Parks Ser.). (ENG.). 32p. (J). (gr. 2-5). lib. bdg. 35.64 (978-1-5038-2347-1(4), 212182) Child's World, Inc, The.

Ellis, Paula. Yosemite Activity Book, 1 vol. Nitzsche, Shane, illus. 2013. (Color & Learn Ser.). 64p. (J). (gr. 2-3). pap. 5.95 (978-1-59193-299-4(8), Adventure Pubns.) AdventureKEEN.

Frisch, Nate. Yosemite National Park. (Preserving America Ser.). (ENG.). 48p. (J). (gr. 4-7). 2014. pap. 12.00 (978-0-89812-882-6(X), 21663, Creative Paperbacks) 2013. (Illus.). 35.65 (978-1-60818-199-5(5), 21662, Creative Education) Creative Co., The.

Gilbert, Sara. Yosemite. 2016. (National Park Explorers Ser.). (ENG.). 24p. (J). (gr. 1-4). (978-1-60818-635-8(0), 20513, Creative Education) Creative Co., The.

Graf, Mike. My Yosemite: A Guide for Young Adventurers. Filice, Annette, illus. 2012. (J). (978-1-59714-170-3(4)) Heyday.

—My Yosemite: A Guide for Young Adventurers. Filice, Annette, illus. 2012. (ENG.). 176p. (gr. 4). pap. 12.95 (978-1-930238-30-5(4)) Yosemite Conservancy.

Hansen, Grace. Yosemite National Park. 2017. (National Parks (Abdo Kids Jumbo) Ser.). (ENG.). 24p. (J). (gr. -1-2). lib. bdg. 32.79 (978-1-5321-0437-4(5), 26563, Abdo Kids) ABDO Publishing Co.

Perritano, John. Yosemite. 2019. (J). (978-1-7911-1062-8(2), AV2 by Weigl) Weigl Pubs., Inc.

Rice, Dona Herweck. Travel Adventures: Yosemite: Perimeter & Area (Grade 4) 2017. (Mathematics in the Real World Ser.). (ENG., Illus.). 32p. (gr. 4-5). pap. 11.99 (978-1-4258-5560-4(1)) Teacher Created Materials, Inc.

Rosenstock, Barb. The Camping Trip That Changed America: Theodore Roosevelt, John Muir, & Our National Parks. Gerstein, Mordecai, illus. 2012. 32p. (J). (gr. 1-3). 18.99 (978-0-8037-3710-5(6), Dial Bks) Penguin Young Readers Group.

Spalding, Maddie. Yosemite National Park. 2016. (National Parks (Core Library) Ser.). (ENG., Illus.). 48p. (J). (gr. 4-8). lib. bdg. 35.64 (978-1-68078-476-3(5), 23889) ABDO Publishing Co.

Wadsworth, Ginger. Camping with the President. Dugan, Karen, illus. 2009. (ENG.). 32p. (J). (gr. 2-5). 16.99 (978-1-59078-497-6(9), Calkins Creek) Highlights Pr., c/o Highlights for Children, Inc.

Wallace, Audra. Yosemite (a True Book: National Parks) (Library Edition) 2017. (True Book (Relaunch) Ser.). (ENG., Illus.). 48p. (J). (gr. 3-5). lib. bdg. 31.00 (978-0-531-23395-5(2), Children's Pr.) Scholastic Library Publishing.

YOSEMITE NATIONAL PARK (CALIF.)—FICTION

Bethune, Helen. A Road Trip to Yosemite, 1 vol. rev. ed. 2013. (Literary Text Ser.). (ENG., Illus.). 28p. (J). (gr. 2-3). pap. 9.99 (978-1-4333-5569-1(8)) Teacher Created Materials, Inc.

Lemon, Sarah Nicole. Valley Girls. 2018. (ENG., Illus.). 400p. (gr. 7-17). 18.99 (978-1-4197-2964-5(0), 1218701, Amulet Bks.) Abrams, Inc.

Wadsworth, Ginger. Yosemite's Songster: One Coyote's Story. San Souci, Daniel, illus. 2013. (ENG.). 32p. (J). (gr. -1-2). 15.95 (978-1-930238-34-3(7)) Yosemite Conservancy.

YOSEMITE VALLEY (CALIF.)

Danneberg, Julie. John Muir Wrestles a Waterfall. Hogan, Jamie, illus. 2015. (ENG.). 32p. (J). (gr. -1-3). lib. bdg. 17.99 (978-1-58089-586-6(7)) Charlesbridge Publishing, Inc.

Gamble, Adam & Jasper, Mark. Good Night Yosemite. Chan, Suwin, illus. 2016. (Good Night Our World Ser.). (ENG.). 20p. (J). (— 1). bds. 9.95 (978-1-60219-389-5(4)) Good Night Bks.

OUNG, BRIGHAM, 1801-1877

ncyclopaedia Britannica, Inc. Staff, compiled by. Brigham Young. 2008. 49.95 *(978-1-59339-525-4(6))* Encyclopaedia Britannica, Inc.

anford, William R. & Green, Carl R. Brigham Young: Courageous Mormon Leader, 1 vol. 2013. (Courageous Heroes of the American West Ser.). (ENG., Illus.). 48p. (J). (gr. 5-7). 25.27 *(978-0-7660-4004-5(6),* 1af10d1c-95b1-437f-899f-75c721185f12); pap. 11.53 *(978-1-4644-0089-6(X),* 739c4ab8-19fe-43ed-9eb1-b1824bf5d05b) Enslow Publishing, LLC.

OUNG ADULTS

ere are entered works on people in the general age range of eighteen through twenty-five years.

ee also Youth

oersma, Heather. Dream Big: 30 Days to Life Beyond All You Could Ask or Imagine. 2012. ix, 119p. *(978-1-77069-453-8(6))* Word Alive Pr.

urkhart, Jessica, et al. Life Inside My Mind: 31 Authors Share Their Personal Struggles. Burkhart, Jessica, ed. 2018. (ENG., Illus.). 320p. (YA). (gr. 9). 17.99 *(978-1-4814-9464-9(3),* Simon Pulse) Simon Pulse.

Dunagan, Cindy. Journaling Toward Moral Excellence Volume Four for Young Adults: A Character Building Workbook of 100 Thought-Provoking Questions to Help the Young Discover the Value of Moral Strength. 2004. (Journaling Toward Moral Excellence Ser.: Vol. 4). 107p. (YA). (gr. 11-18). 11.95 *(978-0-9759871-3-1(5))* Straight Paths Pr.

Epstein, Alex. The Circle Cast: The Lost Years of Morgan le Fey, 1 vol. 2011. (ENG., Illus.). 240p. (YA). (gr. 8-12). pap. 12.95 *(978-1-896580-63-0(7))* Tradewind Bks. CAN. Dist: Orca Bk. Pubs. USA.

Lee, Darrien. Denim Diaries 1: 16 Going On 21. 2008. (Denim Diaries: 1). (ENG., Illus.). 181p. (YA). (gr. 9). 17.00 *(978-1-933967-71-4(4),* Urban Renaissance) Kensington Publishing Corp.

McGuinness, Denis E. & Thomson, Sarah L. Gary Paulsen, 1 vol., 1. 2015. (All about the Author Ser.). (ENG., Illus.). 112p. (J). (gr. 7-7). 39.80 *(978-1-4994-6268-5(9),* e4dcf753-f057-4597-a283-c72ffc5bd2c0, Rosen Young Adult) Rosen Publishing Group, Inc., The.

Meyer, Susan. Gayle Forman, 1 vol., 1. 2015. (All about the Author Ser.). (ENG., Illus.). 112p. (J). (gr. 7-7). 39.80 *(978-1-4994-6272-2(7),* 068a8c00-bcac-4ee3-a265-8d5f8a135a8e, Rosen Young Adult) Rosen Publishing Group, Inc., The.

Peterson, Judy Monroe. First Budget Smarts. 2009. (J). 77.70 *(978-1-4358-5553-3(1));* (ENG.). 64p. (gr. 6-6). pap. 13.95 *(978-1-4358-5552-6(3),* d0a890d8-1fc2-4d2c-a2e4-2a0a072267b9); (ENG., Illus.). 64p. (gr. 6-6). lib. bdg. 37.13 *(978-1-4358-5273-0(7),* 1c4bd3f3-55f0-43ee-9378-09e23f41f773) Rosen Publishing Group, Inc., The.

YOUTH

Here are entered works on the time of life between thirteen and twenty-five years, as well as on people in this general age range, including teenagers and young adults.

see also Adolescence; Boys; Dropouts; Girls

Aggarwal, Shelley, et al. No Weigh! A Teen's Guide to Positive Body Image, Food, & Emotional Wisdom. 2018. 192p. pap. 20.95 *(978-1-78592-825-3(2),* 696872) Kingsley, Jessica Pubs. GBR. Dist: Hachette UK Distribution.

Allen, John. Growing up in China. 2017. (Growing up Around the World Ser.). (ENG.). 80p. (YA). (gr. 5-12). *(978-1-68282-209-8(5))* ReferencePoint Pr., Inc.

Allman, Toney. Living a Healthy Lifestyle. 2019. (Teen Life Skills Ser.). (ENG.). 64p. (YA). (gr. 6-12). 41.27 *(978-1-68282-745-1(3))* ReferencePoint Pr., Inc.

American Medical Association & Pfeifer, Kate Gruenwald. American Medical Association Boy's Guide to Becoming a Teen. Middleman, Amy B., ed. 2006. (ENG., Illus.). 128p. (gr. 4-7). per. 14.95 *(978-0-7879-8343-7(8),* Jossey-Bass) Wiley, John & Sons, Inc.

Anderson, Judith. Know the Facts about Personal Safety. 2009. (Illus.). 48p. (J). 70.50 *(978-1-4358-5465-9(9),* 1300674); (ENG.). (J). (gr. 5-6). lib. bdg. 34.47 *(978-1-4358-5340-9(7),* acf0c876-aa9b-4c8f-aeaf-705c75a2db4b); (ENG., (YA). (gr. 5-6). pap. 12.75 *(978-1-4358-5464-2(0),* dc0649f7-6d19-43e1-ab73-1163788657fa) Rosen Publishing Group, Inc., The. (Rosen Reference).

Anniss, Matt. Music, Fashion, & Style. 2015. (Music Scene Ser.). (J). lib. bdg. 37.10 *(978-1-59920-912-8(8))* Black Rabbit Bks.

Aretha, David. On the Rocks: Teens & Alcohol. 2006. (ENG., Illus.). 144p. (J). (gr. 9-13). 30.50 *(978-0-531-16792-2(5),* Watts, Franklin) Scholastic Library Publishing.

Ashabranner, Brent. Gavriel & Jemal: Two Boys of Jerusalem. Conklin, Paul, photos by. 2005. (Illus.). 94p. (J). (gr. 4-10). reprint ed. 12.00 *(978-0-7567-9758-4(6))* DIANE Publishing Co.

Baden-Powell, Robert. Scouting for Boys. 2013. pap. 16.99 *(978-1-4621-1233-3(1),* Horizon Pubs.) Cedar Fort, Inc./CFI Distribution.

Bailey, Diane. Cyber Ethics. 2009. (Cyber Citizenship & Cyber Safety Ser.). 48p. (gr. 5-5). 53.00 *(978-1-61512-102-1(1),* Rosen Reference) Rosen Publishing Group, Inc., The.

—Our Teenage Life in the Navajo Nation. 2017. (Customs & Cultures of the World Ser.). (Illus.). 128p. (J). *(978-1-4222-3908-7(X))* Mason Crest.

Bailey, Lorilyn. The Original Dating Questionnaire for Teens: A Great Way to Get to Know Each Other. (Illus.). 128p. (Orig.). (YA). (gr. 7-12). pap. *(978-0-9641239-7-7(5))* Lormax Communications.

Banigan, Melissa. Coping with Teen Pregnancy, 1 vol. 2018. (Coping Ser.). (ENG.). 112p. (gr. 7-7). pap. 19.24 *(978-1-5081-8324-2(4),* f29cb6b3-7df7-40f1-9e7a-103e1bad70bf) Rosen Publishing Group, Inc., The.

Barakat, Ibtisam. Balcony on the Moon: Coming of Age in Palestine. 2018. (ENG.). 256p. (YA). pap. 11.99 *(978-1-250-14429-4(9),* 900180629) Square Fish.

—Balcony on the Moon: Coming of Age in Palestine. 2018. (YA). lib. bdg. 20.85 *(978-0-606-41085-4(6))* Turtleback.

Baruch-Feldman, Caren. The Grit Guide for Teens: A Workbook to Help You Build Perseverance, Self-Control, & a Growth Mindset. 2017. (ENG.). 152p. (YA). (gr. 6-12). pap. 18.95 *(978-1-62625-856-3(2),* 38563) New Harbinger Pubns.

Bauchner, Elizabeth. Teen Minorities in Rural North America: Growing up Different. 2009. (Youth in Rural North America Ser.). (Illus.). 96p. (YA). (gr. 3-7). lib. bdg. 22.95 *(978-1-4222-0014-8(0))* Mason Crest.

BeaverSimon. YOUNG AND AMAZING: TEENS AT THE TOP HIGH BEGINNING BOOK WITH ONLINE ACCESS, 1 vol. 2014. (ENG., Illus.). 24p. pap., E-Book 9.50 *(978-1-107-62252-4(2))* Cambridge Univ. Pr.

Bender, Alexandra Sabina. Alana's Advice... When There's a Clique, You've Got to Think Quick. 2007. (ENG., Illus.). 152p. (C). (gr. 4-10). per. 14.95 *(978-1-84590-075-5(8))* Crown Hse. Publishing LLC.

Berman, Ron. Who's Got Next? Future Leaders of America. 2013. (Av2 Audio Chapter Bks.). (ENG., Illus.). 92p. (J). (gr. 4-7). lib. bdg. 27.13 *(978-1-62127-998-3(7),* AV2 by Weigl) Weigl Pubs., Inc.

Bernstein, Ben. Stressed Out! for Teens: How to Be Calm, Confident & Focused. 2014. (ENG., Illus.). 270p. (gr. 8-12). pap. 18.95 *(978-1-939629-38-8(1),* 552938) Familius LLC.

Bireda, Martha R. & Cummings, Jaha F. Omowali: The Child Returns Home - Reconnecting Our Children with Their True Culture. 2008. 232p. pap. *(978-4-902837-10-0(2))* Aoishima Kenkyusha.

Boersma, Heather. Dream Big: 30 Days to Life Beyond All You Could Ask or Imagine. 2012. ix, 119p. *(978-1-77069-453-8(6))* Word Alive Pr.

Borgenicht, David, et al. The Worst-Case Scenario Survival Handbook: Middle School. 2009. (Worst Case Scenario Ser.). (ENG., Illus.). 128p. (J). (gr. 6-8). pap. 10.99 *(978-0-8118-6864-8(8))* Chronicle Bks. LLC.

Bow, James. Binge Drinking. 2015. (Straight Talk About... Ser.). (ENG., Illus.). 48p. (J). (gr. 5-5). *(978-0-7787-2200-7(7))* Crabtree Publishing Co.

Brancato, Robin F. Food Choices: The Ultimate Teen Guide. 2010. (It Happened to Me Ser.: 28). (ENG., Illus.). 240p. (gr. 7-10). 62.00 *(978-0-8108-6109-1(7))* Scarecrow Pr., Inc.

Braun, Eric. Never Again: The Parkland Shooting & the Teen Activists Leading a Movement. 2019. (Gateway Biographies Ser.). (ENG., Illus.). 48p. (J). (gr. 4-8). lib. bdg. 31.99 *(978-1-5415-5270-8(9),* 1d67ab4e-63d9-4275-93c9-da0dd22e15c6, Lerner Pubns.) Lerner Publishing Group.

—Taking Action to Improve People's Health. 2016. (Who's Changing the World? Ser.). (ENG., Illus.). 48p. (J). (gr. 4-6). E-Book 4.99 *(978-1-5124-2521-5(4),* 9781512425215); E-Book 50.65 *(978-1-4677-9668-2(9))* Lerner Publishing Group. (Lerner Pubns.).

Bryfonski, Dedria, ed. Street Teens, 1 vol. 2011. (Opposing Viewpoints Ser.). (ENG., Illus.). 224p. (gr. 10-12). 50.43 *(978-0-7377-5761-3(2),* 586d14ae-665f-4f8c-8012-c378487e5821); pap. 34.80 *(978-0-7377-5762-0(0),* 0c0a19cb-c896-4850-a471-75c786dce71c) Greenhaven Publishing LLC. (Greenhaven Publishing).

Buckley, James. My Teenage Life in Greece. 2017. (Customs & Cultures of the World Ser.). (ENG., Illus.). 64p. (J). (gr. 7-12). 23.95 *(978-1-4222-3904-9(7))* Mason Crest.

Bure, Natasha. Let's Be Real: Living Life As an Open & Honest You, 1 vol. 2018. (ENG.). 224p. (YA). pap. 14.99 *(978-0-310-76308-6(8))* Zondervan.

Campbell, Carol P. & Orr, Tamra. Frequently Asked Questions about Teen Pregnancy, 1 vol. 2011. (FAQ: Teen Life Ser.). (ENG.). 64p. (J). (gr. 5-6). lib. bdg. 37.13 *(978-1-4488-4627-6(7),* 9a2b4b13-04ad-47a8-ba3e-25c407cf0820) Rosen Publishing Group, Inc., The.

Campolo, Tony. You Can Make a Difference, 1 vol. 2008. (ENG.). 144p. (gr. 8-12). per. 10.98 *(978-0-8499-1885-8(5))* Nelson, Thomas Inc.

Canwell, Nancy. He's Got Your Back: A Daily Devotional for Juniors. 2014. (J). *(978-0-8280-2804-2(4))* Review & Herald Publishing Assn.

Carlson, Dale, et al. Out of Order: Young Adult Manual of Mental Illness & Recovery. 2014. (ENG., Illus.). 256p. (YA). pap. 14.95 *(978-1-884158-37-7(4))* Bick Publishing Hse.

Cartlidge, Cherese. Homeless Youth. 2016. (ENG., Illus.). 80p. (J). (gr. 5-12). *(978-1-60152-978-7(3))* ReferencePoint Pr., Inc.

—Teens & Suicide. 2017. (Teen Mental Health Ser.). (ENG., Illus.). 80p. (J). (gr. 5-12). *(978-1-68282-131-2(5))* ReferencePoint Pr., Inc.

Cassriel, Betsy. My Teenage Life in Mexico. 2017. (Customs & Cultures of the World Ser.). (ENG., Illus.). 64p. (J). (gr. 7-12). 23.95 *(978-1-4222-3907-0(1))* Mason Crest.

Catherman, Erica & Catherman, Jonathan. The Girls' Guide to Conquering Middle School: Do This, Not That Advice Every Girl Needs. 2018. (ENG., Illus.). 224p. pap. 13.99 *(978-0-8007-2981-3(1))* Revell.

Centore, Michael. My Teenage Life in India. 2017. (Customs & Cultures of the World Ser.). (ENG., Illus.). 64p. (J). (gr. 7-12). 23.95 *(978-1-4222-3905-6(5))* Mason Crest.

Centore, Michael & Lebeko, Tshwarelo. My Teenage Life in South Africa. 2017. (Illus.). 128p. (J). *(978-1-4222-3911-7(X))* Mason Crest.

Chandler, Matt. Understanding Suicide. 2019. (21st Century Skills Library: Upfront Health Ser.). (ENG., Illus.). 32p. (J). (gr. 4-8). pap. 14.21 *(978-1-5341-5086-7(2),* 213651); lib. bdg. 32.07 *(978-1-5341-4800-0(0),* 213650) Cherry Lake Publishing.

—Understanding Tobacco. 2019. (21st Century Skills Library: Upfront Health Ser.). (ENG., Illus.). 32p. (J). (gr. 4-8). pap. 14.21 *(978-1-5341-5087-4(0),* 213655); lib. bdg. 32.07 *(978-1-5341-4801-7(9),* 213654) Cherry Lake Publishing.

Chopra, Deepak. Fire in the Heart: A Spiritual Guide for Teens. 2006. (ENG., Illus.). 208p. (YA). (gr. 7-12). pap. 15.99 *(978-0-689-86217-5(2),* Simon & Schuster Bks. For Young Readers) Simon & Schuster Bks. For Young Readers.

Compiled by Barbour Staff, Compiled by. The Prayer Map for Teens: A Creative Journal. 2018. (Faith Maps Ser.). (ENG.). 176p. (YA). spiral bd. 7.99 *(978-1-68322-556-0(2),* Barbour Bks.) Barbour Publishing, Inc.

Conley, Erin Elisabeth, et al. Crap: How to Deal with Annoying Teachers, Bosses, Backstabbers, & Other Stuff That Stinks. 2009. (Illus.). 96p. (YA). (gr. 7-17). pap. 22.44 *(978-0-9790173-5-3(1),* Zest Bks.) Lerner Publishing Group.

Connolly, Michael & Goolbis, Brie. Young Enough to Change the World: Stories of Kids & Teens Who Turned Their Dreams into Action, 750 vols. 2015. (ENG., Illus.). 144p. pap. 21.95 *(978-1-935826-38-5(7))* Kalindi Pr.

Covey, Sean. The 6 Most Important Decisions You'll Ever Make: A Guide for Teens: Updated for the Digital Age. 2017. (ENG., Illus.). 336p. pap. 18.99 *(978-1-5011-5713-4(2),* Touchstone) Touchstone.

Crooks, Claire V. Engagement et Responsabilisation des Jeunes Autochtones: Trousse D'Outils DestinéE Aux Fournisseurs des Services. 2010. (FRE.). 168p. pap. 45.99 *(978-1-4269-1299-3(4))* Trafford Publishing.

Culp, Jennifer. I Have Been Sexually Abused. Now What?, 1 vol. 2014. (Teen Life 411 Ser.). (ENG.). 112p. (J). (gr. 7-7). 38.80 *(978-1-4777-7976-7(0),* c978461e-f112-4cc7-b145-307f4d1aaaa6, Rosen Young Adult) Rosen Publishing Group, Inc., The.

currie-mcghee, leanne. Teenage Alcoholism. 2011. (Compact Research Ser.). 96p. (YA). (gr. 7-12). lib. bdg. 43.93 *(978-1-60152-164-4(2))* ReferencePoint Pr., Inc.

Currie-McGhee, Leanne. Teenage Drug Abuse. 2011. (Compact Research Ser.). 96p. (YA). (gr. 7-12). lib. bdg. 43.93 *(978-1-60152-165-1(0))* ReferencePoint Pr., Inc.

De la Bédoyère, Camilla. Balancing Work & Play. 2010. (Healthy Lifestyles Ser.). 48p. (J). lib. bdg. 35.65 *(978-1-60753-083-1(X))* Amicus Learning.

—Personal Hygiene & Sexual Health. 2010. (Healthy Lifestyles Ser.). 48p. (J). 35.65 *(978-1-60753-087-9(2))* Amicus Learning.

Dennis, Rainey. Passport 2 Purity. 2004. 29.99 *(978-1-57229-656-5(9))* FamilyLife.

Desetta, Al & Wolin, Sybil, eds. The Struggle to Be Strong: True Stories by Teens about Overcoming Tough Times (Updated Edition) 2nd ed. 2019. (ENG.). 192p. (YA). pap. 18.99 *(978-1-63198-460-0(8),* 84600) Free Spirit Publishing Inc.

Dobosz, Ann Marie. The Perfectionism Workbook for Teens: Activities to Help You Reduce Anxiety & Get Things Done. 2016. (ENG., Illus.). 200p. (YA). (gr. 6-12). pap. 21.95 *(978-1-62625-454-1(0),* 34541) New Harbinger Pubns.

Donahue, Mary P. Surviving Bullies & Mean Teens, 1 vol. 2017. (Teen Survival Guide Ser.). (ENG.). 48p. (gr. 6-6). pap. 12.70 *(978-0-7660-9368-3(9),* c441be89-638c-491a-88f6-b4839adcfd45); lib. bdg. 29.60 *(978-0-7660-9194-8(5),* 3971d482-ac2d-4e8c-8c37-2b2468f7fcb5) Enslow Publishing, LLC.

Dunagan, Cindy. Journaling Toward Moral Excellence Volume Three for Teenagers: A Character Building Workbook of 100 Thought-Provoking Questions to Help the Young Discover the Value of Moral Strength. 2004. (Journaling Toward Moral Excellence Ser.: Vol. 3). 107p. (YA). (gr. 8-10). 11.95 *(978-0-9759871-2-4(7))* Straight Paths Pr.

Eagen, Rachel. Suicide. 2010. (ENG.). 48p. (J). pap. *(978-0-7787-2138-3(8));* lib. bdg. *(978-0-7787-2131-4(0))* Crabtree Publishing Co.

Edelfield, Bruce & Moosa, Tracey J. Drug Abuse, 1 vol. 2011. (Teen Mental Health Ser.). (ENG., Illus.). 48p. (YA). (gr. 5-6). lib. bdg. 34.47 *(978-1-4488-4590-3(4),* cf95815c-8b99-43da-9083-5dfad148bb21) Rosen Publishing Group, Inc., The.

Edge, Laura B. & Edge, Laura Bufano. From Jazz Babies to Generation Next: The History of the American Teenager. 2011. (People's History Ser.). (ENG., Illus.). 112p. (J). (gr. 5-12). 33.26 *(978-0-7613-5868-8(4))* Lerner Publishing Group.

Emanuele, Patricia. Coping with Aggression. 2009. (Coping Ser.). 192p. (gr. 7-12). 63.90 *(978-1-61511-989-9(2))* Rosen Publishing Group, Inc., The.

Esherick, Joan. Dying for Acceptance: A Teen's Guide to Drug- & Alcohol-Related Health Issues. 2006. (Science of Health Ser.). (Illus.). 128p. (YA). lib. bdg. 24.95 *(978-1-59084-847-0(0))* Mason Crest.

—The Laws That Protect Youth with Special Needs. Albers, Lisa et al, eds. 2014. (Living with a Special Need Ser.: 16). 128p. (J). (gr. 7-18). 25.95 *(978-1-4222-3039-8(2))* Mason Crest.

—Physical Challenges. Albers, Lisa et al, eds. 2014. (Living with a Special Need Ser.: 16). 128p. (J). (gr. 7-18). 25.95 *(978-1-4222-3041-1(4))* Mason Crest.

—Smoking-Related Health Issues. 2014. (Illus.). 128p. (J). *(978-1-4222-2803-6(7))* Mason Crest.

—Suicide & Self-Destructive Behaviors. McDonnell, Mary Ann & Forman, Sara, eds. 2013. (Young Adult's Guide to the Science of Health Ser.: 15). 128p. (J). (gr. 7-18). 24.95 *(978-1-4222-2817-3(7))* Mason Crest.

Espejo, Roman, ed. Custody & Divorce, 1 vol. 2013. (Teen Rights & Freedoms Ser.). (ENG., Illus.). 144p. (gr. 10-12). lib. bdg. 43.63 *(978-0-7377-6400-0(7),* dd89d64e-09b7-46d6-b577-8fa8024548df, Greenhaven Publishing) Greenhaven Publishing LLC.

—How Does Advertising Impact Teen Behavior?, 1 vol. 2011. (At Issue Ser.). (ENG.). 104p. (gr. 10-12). 41.03 *(978-0-7377-5578-7(4),* 33145f8c-79b1-41fd-9c15-392bdd8cf18e); pap. 28.80 *(978-0-7377-5579-4(2),* 0e3fcc1e-52ec-45b9-9e6f-718823ac05bc) Greenhaven Publishing LLC. (Greenhaven Publishing).

—Sexting, 1 vol. 2015. (At Issue Ser.). (ENG.). 88p. (gr. 10-12). pap. 28.80 *(978-0-7377-7186-2(0),* da6766c2-e11e-43b1-85d7-5f96343c02f2, Greenhaven Publishing) Greenhaven Publishing LLC.

Etler, Cyndy. The Dead Inside: A True Story. 2017. (ENG.). 304p. (YA). (gr. 8-12). 17.99 *(978-1-4926-3573-4(1),* 9781492635734) Sourcebooks, Inc.

—Dead Inside: They Tried to Break Me. This Is the True Story of How I Survived. 2018. (ENG.). 320p. (YA). (gr. 8-12). pap. 16.99 *(978-1-4926-5279-3(2))* Sourcebooks, Inc.

Evans, Tony. Kingdom Quest - A Strategy Guide for Teens & Their Parents/Mentors: Taking Faith & Character to the Next Level, Ages 14+ 2015. (ENG., Illus.). 144p. (YA). pap. 13.99 *(978-1-58997-809-6(9),* 4622363) Focus on the Family Publishing.

Faerber, Jessie. More Than Just Pretty: Discover Your True Value, Beauty & Purpose. 2018. (ENG.). 144p. pap. 16.99 *(978-0-281-07786-1(X),* e7e12ae8-cd02-4ddd-ac1f-9c4e1fbad751) SPCK Publishing GBR. Dist: Baker & Taylor Publisher Services (BTPS).

FAQ: Teen Life: Set 8, 16 vols. Incl. Frequently Asked Questions about Antidepressants. Peterson, Judy Monroe. (YA). lib. bdg. 37.13 *(978-1-4358-3547-4(6),* 00bfd2b1-e7cc-4b66-a618-565341dcb701); Frequently Asked Questions about Concussions. Bickerstaff, Linda. (YA). lib. bdg. 37.13 *(978-1-4358-3513-9(1),* 10ee3c6e-afa1-4c24-80fa-be187d044181); Frequently Asked Questions about Driving & the Law. Roza, Greg. (YA). lib. bdg. 37.13 *(978-1-4358-3544-3(1),* 1eedd4ec-f967-4c8d-856f-e85e817f7b25); Frequently Asked Questions about Foster Care. Sommers, Annie Leah. (YA). lib. bdg. 37.13 *(978-1-4358-3546-7(8),* 29977fc8-fd1f-4280-b227-ae97b3798d76); Frequently Asked Questions about Online Gaming Addiction. Cefrey, Holly. (J). lib. bdg. 37.13 *(978-1-4358-3548-1(4),* 1306964); Frequently Asked Questions about Overscheduling & Stress. Harmon, Daniel E. (YA). lib. bdg. 37.13 *(978-1-4358-3514-6(X),* 68e79d1c-1987-42f4-bfab-2896e1c7a538); Frequently Asked Questions about Sleep & Sleep Deprivation. Peterson, Judy Monroe. (YA). lib. bdg. 37.13 *(978-1-4358-3512-2(3),* 3b6e314f-2528-452d-ac35-f7cb5b69fe54); Frequently Asked Questions about Tanning & Skin Care. Brezina, Corona. (YA). lib. bdg. 37.13 *(978-1-4358-3545-0(X),* 0b7ef74b-6c06-441d-939f-6d0562df3d03); (gr. 5-6). 2010. (FAQ: Teen Life Ser.). (ENG., Illus.). 64p. 2009. Set lib. bdg. 297.04 *(978-1-4358-3608-2(1),* fe4b88d1-eec7-47b7-bbfb-430e34b41143) Rosen Publishing Group, Inc., The.

Federman, Carolyn. New Favorites for New Cooks: 50 Delicious Recipes for Kids to Make [a Cookbook]. 2018. (Illus.). 176p. 19.99 *(978-0-399-57945-5(1),* Ten Speed Pr.) Potter/Ten Speed/Harmony/Rodale.

Ferguson, Olivia, ed. Teen Sex, 1 vol. 2010. (At Issue Ser.). (ENG.). 112p. (gr. 10-12). 41.03 *(978-0-7377-5095-9(2),* 68d489f6-2f30-47bc-ba17-e4a1eefc6e8c); pap. 28.80 *(978-0-7377-5096-6(0),* 5afc66e6-636a-4022-abd6-fa1b1ff74fb1) Greenhaven Publishing LLC. (Greenhaven Publishing).

Fighting the Monster. 2004. (YA). ring bd. 59.95 *(978-0-9661256-2-7(2))* Youth Communication - New York Center.

Financial Security & Life Success for Teens. 2014. (Financial Security & Life Success for Teens Ser.). 80p. (YA). (gr. 7-12). pap. 84.90 *(978-1-4777-8110-4(2))* Rosen Publishing Group, Inc., The.

Foster, Joanne. Bust Your BUTS: Tips for Teens Who Procrastinate. 2017. (ENG.). 168p. pap. 18.95 *(978-1-935067-33-7(8))* Gifted UnLtd., LLC.

Gasklins, Pearl Fuyo. I Believe In... Christian, Jewish, & Muslim Young People Speak about Their Faiths. 2004. (ENG., Illus.). 160p. (J). 18.95 *(978-0-8126-2713-8(X))* Cricket Bks.

Gay, Kathlyn. Activism: The Ultimate Teen Guide. 2016. (It Happened to Me Ser.: 47). (Illus.). 234p. 59.00 *(978-1-4422-4293-7(0))* Rowman & Littlefield Publishers, Inc.

—Are You Fat? The Obesity Issue for Teens, 1 vol. 2014. (Got Issues? Ser.). (ENG., Illus.). 112p. (gr. 6-7). lib. bdg. 38.93 *(978-0-7660-4322-0(3),* da651fb9-b91a-4747-89b1-2e7ad5a905e9) Enslow Publishing, LLC.

Gilbert, Laura. Everything You Need to Know about Compulsive Sexual Behavior. 2009. (Need to Know Library). 64p. (gr. 5-5). 58.50 *(978-1-60854-059-4(6))* Rosen Publishing Group, Inc., The.

Gillard, Arthur, ed. Drug Abuse, 1 vol. 2013. (Issues That Concern You Ser.). (ENG., Illus.). 208p. (gr. 7-10). lib. bdg. 43.63 *(978-0-7377-6290-7(X),* 656a8762-bd56-4a74-b751-14c75666d155, Greenhaven Publishing) Greenhaven Publishing LLC.

Gilles, Renae. Understanding Alcohol. 2019. (21st Century Skills Library: Upfront Health Ser.). (ENG., Illus.). 32p. (J). (gr. 4-8). pap. 14.21 *(978-1-5341-5081-2(1),* 213631); lib. bdg. 32.07 *(978-1-5341-4795-9(0),* 213630) Cherry Lake Publishing.

—Understanding Drugs. 2019. (21st Century Skills Library: Upfront Health Ser.). (ENG., Illus.). 32p. (J). (gr. 4-8). pap. 14.21 *(978-1-5341-5084-3(6),* 213643); lib. bdg. 32.07 *(978-1-5341-4798-0(5),* 213642) Cherry Lake Publishing.

Gitlin, Marty. Helping a Friend in an Abusive Relationship, 1 vol. 2016. (How Can I Help? Friends Helping Friends Ser.). (ENG., Illus.). 64p. (J). (gr. 6-6). pap. 13.95 *(978-1-4994-6436-8(3),* 51f7c56f-6c2d-447f-b926-9c6212f4b749) Rosen Publishing Group, Inc., The.

Gootman, Marilyn E. When a Friend Dies: A Book for Teens about Grieving & Healing. 3rd ed. 2019. (ENG., Illus.). 136p. (YA). pap. 12.99 *(978-1-63198-422-8(5),* 84228) Free Spirit Publishing Inc.

Gordon, Sherri Mabry. Beyond Bruises: The Truth about Teens & Abuse, 1 vol. 2009. (Issues in Focus Today Ser.). (ENG., Illus.). 128p. (gr. 6-7). lib. bdg. 35.93 *(978-0-7660-3064-0(4),* 5822eb56-2aec-4498-acba-f6743849a612) Enslow Publishing, LLC.

—Everything You Need to Know about Smoking, Vaping, & Your Health, 1 vol. 2018. (Need to Know Library). (ENG.). 64p. (gr. 6-6). pap. 13.95 *(978-1-5081-8351-8(1),* 012a7052-942c-425c-9de7-01bc82a54666, Rosen Young Adult) Rosen Publishing Group, Inc., The.

—Teens & Addiction. 2018. (Teen Health & Safety Ser.). (ENG.). 80p. (YA). (gr. 6-12). 39.93 *(978-1-68282-503-7(5))* ReferencePoint Pr., Inc.

Grayson, Robert. Managing Your Digital Footprint, 1 vol. 2011. (Digital & Information Literacy Ser.). (ENG., Illus.). 48p. (YA). (gr. 6-6). pap. 12.75 *(978-1-4488-2290-4(4),* 92da1fac-6980-42e2-9157-3a0ce49c42a4); lib. bdg. 33.47 *(978-1-4488-1319-3(0),* 92774e04-b8f9-4fb1-865f-13a57e1d60d7) Rosen Publishing Group, Inc., The. (Rosen Reference).

Gutowski, Eva. My Life As Eva: The Struggle Is Real. 2019. (ENG., Illus.). 208p. pap. 16.99 *(978-1-5011-4672-5(6),* Gallery Bks.) Gallery Bks.

WXYZ

Hagler, Gina. Money-Making Opportunities for Teens Who Are Artistic, 1 vol. 2013. (Make Money Now! Ser.). (ENG., Illus.). 80p. (YA). (gr. 7-7). lib. bdg. 38.41 *(978-1-4488-9387-4(9),* c4f51914-1559-4110-b282-9142951b13c5) Rosen Publishing Group, Inc., The.

Hall, LaMarcus J. I Refuse to Let You Give Up: To My Teens Who Feel All Hope Is Gone... 2009. 52p. pap. 15.95 *(978-1-4327-3417-6(2))* Outskirts Pr., Inc.

Hamilton, Jill, ed. Activism, 1 vol. 2009. (Issues That Concern You Ser.). (ENG., Illus.). 120p. (gr. 7-10). 43.63 *(978-0-7377-4493-4(6),* e7775855-2254-456c-9806-1d5bc59f717f, Greenhaven Publishing) Greenhaven Publishing LLC.

Hansen, Mark & Ferber, Kevin S. Success 101 for Teens: Dollars & Sense for a Winning Financial Life. 2012. (ENG.). 176p. pap. 12.95 *(978-1-55778-901-3(0),* 5e304a18-9516-4718-a318-b52a07c05a38) Paragon Hse. Pubs.

Hare, Eric B. Skyscrapers: 365 Stories That Build You up: Daily Devotions for Juniors. 2009. (J). *(978-0-8280-2466-2(9))* Review & Herald Publishing Assn.

Harmon, Daniel E. First Job Smarts. 2009. (J). 77.70 *(978-1-4358-5543-4(4));* (ENG.). 64p. (gr. 6-6). pap. 13.95 *(978-1-4358-5542-7(6),* 2fd3582e-6c48-488b-b781-dfd682b216b6); (ENG., Illus.). 64p. (gr. 6-6). lib. bdg. 37.13 *(978-1-4358-5268-6(0),* 390533b6-a78f-46c6-8c78-5cca0a666058) Rosen Publishing Group, Inc., The.

Haugen, David M. & Musser, Susan, eds. The Millennial Generation, 1 vol. 2012. (Opposing Viewpoints Ser.). (ENG., Illus.). 216p. (gr. 10-12). pap. 34.80 *(978-0-7377-6327-0(2),* b112c8dc-9cb2-48f8-9c88-6d6cc693e634); lib. bdg. 50.43 *(978-0-7377-6326-3(4),* 87215dc6-fe20-42a0-a98a-dee82786f067) Greenhaven Publishing LLC. (Greenhaven Publishing).

—Sex, 1 vol. 2013. (Teen Rights & Freedoms Ser.). (ENG., Illus.). 160p. (gr. 10-12). lib. bdg. 43.63 *(978-0-7377-6404-8(X),* bc95c851-279b-4758-b7df-e0e4f736cd1d, Greenhaven Publishing) Greenhaven Publishing LLC.

Hawke, Rosanne. The Truth about Peacock Blue. 2016. (ENG.). 272p. (YA). (gr. 8-11). pap. 11.99 *(978-1-74331-994-9(0))* Allen & Unwin AUS. Dist: Independent Pubs. Group.

Heiman, Diane & Suneby, Liz. See What You Can Be: Explore Careers That Could Be for You! Wood, Tracey, illus. 2009. (ENG.). 108p. (gr. 4-7). spiral bd. 9.95 *(978-1-59369-277-3(3))* American Girl Publishing, Inc.

Heing, Bridey. Critical Perspectives on Millennials, 1 vol. 2017. (Analyzing the Issues Ser.). (ENG.). 208p. (gr. 8-8). lib. bdg. 50.93 *(978-0-7660-8485-8(X),* 94fbe924-cf2c-4155-9f99-61cbc26c2e72) Enslow Publishing, LLC.

Henneberg, Susan. Money-Making Opportunities for Teens Who Like Working with Kids, 1 vol. 2013. (Make Money Now! Ser.). (ENG., Illus.). 80p. (YA). (gr. 7-7). lib. bdg. 38.41 *(978-1-4488-9385-0(2),* c76f2e72-638b-4924-91fd-5ee4d977b4e9) Rosen Publishing Group, Inc., The.

Hill, Katie Rain. Rethinking Normal: A Memoir in Transition. 2014. (ENG., Illus.). 272p. (YA). (gr. 8). 17.99 *(978-1-4814-1823-2(8),* Simon & Schuster Bks. For Young Readers) Simon & Schuster Bks. For Young Readers.

Hilton, John & Sweat, Anthony. How? Essential Skills for Living the Gospel. 2010. (Illus.). xii, 251p. (YA). 34.99 *(978-1-60641-789-8(4))* Deseret Bk. Co.

Hinds, Maurene. Do You Know Your Rights?, 1 vol. 2015. (Got Issues? Ser.). (ENG., Illus.). 112p. (gr. 7-8). 38.93 *(978-0-7660-7193-3(6),* 7430fc35-2512-4a3f-b039-c15d73db11dd) Enslow Publishing, LLC.

Hipp, Earl. Fighting Invisible Tigers: Stress Management for Teens. 4th ed. 2019. (ENG., Illus.). 144p. (J). pap. 14.99 *(978-1-63198-435-8(7),* 84358) Free Spirit Publishing Inc.

Hood, Korey K. Type 1 Teens: A Guide to Managing Your Life with Diabetes. Ische, Bryan, illus. 2010. 150p. (YA). (gr. 7-18). pap. 14.95 *(978-1-4338-0798-6(2),* Magination Pr.) American Psychological Assn.

Huddle, Lorena & Schleifer, Jay. Teen Suicide, 1 vol. 2011. (Teen Mental Health Ser.). (ENG., Illus.). 48p. (YA). (gr. 5-6). lib. bdg. 34.47 *(978-1-4488-4586-6(6),* d95d7194-8901-4ee2-925c-400d4de402c1) Rosen Publishing Group, Inc., The.

Hunter, David. Teen Life among the Amish & Other Alternative Communities: Choosing a Lifestyle. 2009. (Youth in Rural North America Ser.). 96p. (J). (gr. 7-18). lib. bdg. 22.95 *(978-1-4222-0017-9(5))* Mason Crest.

Hunter, Miranda & Hunter, William. Sexually Transmitted Infections. McDonnell, Mary Ann & Forman, Sara, eds. 2013. (Young Adult's Guide to the Science of Health Ser.: 15). 128p. (J). (gr. 7-18). 24.95 *(978-1-4222-2814-2(2))* Mason Crest.

—Sexually Transmitted Infections. Forman, Sara & McDonnell, Mary Ann, eds. 2013. (Young Adult's Guide to the Science of Health Ser.). (Illus.). 128p. (J). (gr. 7-18). pap. 14.95 *(978-1-4222-3007-7(4))* Mason Crest.

Hurt, Avery Elizabeth. I Am a Teen Caregiver. Now What?, 1 vol. 2016. (Teen Life 411 Ser.). (ENG., Illus.). 112p. (J). (gr. 7-7). 38.80 *(978-1-5081-7204-8(6),* 8dd26442-78b8-4214-b38e-eb70a43859a9, Rosen Young Adult) Rosen Publishing Group, Inc., The.

Jackson, J. S. Bye-Bye, Bully: A Kid's Guide for Dealing with Bullies. Alley, R. W., tr. Alley, R. W., illus. 2003. (J). per. 6.95 *(978-0-87029-369-6(9))* Abbey Pr.

Jacobs, Thomas A. What Are My Rights? Q&a about Teens & the Law. 4th rev. ed. 2019. (Teens & the Law Ser.). (ENG., Illus.). 240p. (J). (gr. 7). pap. 16.99 *(978-1-63198-311-5(3),* 83115) Free Spirit Publishing Inc.

Jaime, Everett. Baby Don't Smoke. Brown, Eliot R., illus. 2012. (ENG.). 40p. (YA). pap. 9.95 *(978-1-935826-20-0(4))* Kalindi Pr.

Jamiolkowski, Raymond M. A Baby Doesn't Make the Man: Alternative Sources of Power & Manhood for Young Men. 2009. (Teen Pregnancy Prevention Library). 64p. (gr. 5-5). 58.50 *(978-1-60854-244-4(0))* Rosen Publishing Group, Inc., The.

Jana, Rosalind. Notes on Being Teenage. 2018. (ENG.). 272p. (J). (gr. 7-12). pap. 9.99 *(978-0-7502-8732-6(2),* Wayland) Hachette Children's Group GBR. Dist: Hachette Bk. Group.

Johanson, Paula. Money-Making Opportunities for Teens Who Like Pets & Animals, 1 vol. 2013. (Make Money Now! Ser.). (ENG.). 80p. (YA). (gr. 7-7). 38.41 *(978-1-4488-9384-3(4),* ebfa8e7f-92af-432e-83fa-1219a75b6a18) Rosen Publishing Group, Inc., The.

Johnson, Jason. How We See Things. 2012. 20p. pap. 17.99 *(978-1-4685-5832-6(3))* AuthorHouse.

Johnson, Kevin, et al. Find Your Fit: Unlock God's Unique Design for Your Talents, Spiritual Gifts, & Personality. rev. ed. 2018. (ENG., Illus.). 256p. (YA). pap. 14.99 *(978-0-7642-3135-3(9))* Bethany Hse. Pubs.

—Find Your Fit Discovery Workbook: Discover Your Unique Design. rev. ed. 2018. (ENG., Illus.). 48p. (YA). pap. 7.99 *(978-0-7642-3136-0(7))* Bethany Hse. Pubs.

Johnson, Nerissa & Parra, Angelo. Teen Reflections, Then & Now. 2011. (Readers' & Writers' Genre Workshop Ser.). (YA). pap. *(978-1-4509-3025-3(5))* Benchmark Education Co.

Jovinelly, Joann. Coping with Bipolar Disorder & Manic-Depressive Illness. 2009. (Coping Ser.). 192p. (gr. 7-12). 63.90 *(978-1-61511-992-9(2))* Rosen Publishing Group, Inc., The.

Kahaner, Ellen. Everything You Need to Know about Growing up Female. 2009. (Need to Know Library). 64p. (gr. 5-5). 58.50 *(978-1-60854-070-9(7))* Rosen Publishing Group, Inc., The.

Kaplan, Arie. Dating & Relationships: Navigating the Social Scene, 1 vol. 2011. (Young Man's Guide to Contemporary Issues Ser.). (ENG.). 104p. (YA). (gr. 8-9). lib. bdg. 39.80 *(978-1-4488-5523-0(3),* 8fa7d52b-b1da-4d38-b261-06a2999a31f0) Rosen Publishing Group, Inc., The.

Karpan, Andrew, ed. Vaping, 1 vol. 2019. (At Issue Ser.). (ENG.). 128p. (gr. 10-12). pap. 28.80 *(978-1-5345-0513-1(X),* d1861875-05c1-4727-ba76-83209a6fa943) Greenhaven Publishing LLC.

Katz, Naomi. Beautiful-Being an Empowered Young Woman. 2016. (ENG., Illus.). 154p. (J). pap. 16.95 *(978-1-59687-441-1(4),* ipicturebooks) ibooks, Inc.

Keen, Lisa. Out Law: What LGBT Youth Should Know about Their Legal Rights. 2007. (Queer Ideas/Queer Action Ser.: 2). 176p. (gr. 3-7). per. 13.00 *(978-0-8070-7966-9(9),* Beacon Pr.) Beacon Pr.

Kendi, Ibram X. & Stone, Nic. How to Be a (Young) Antiracist. 2023. 208p. (YA). (gr. 7). (ENG.). pap. 14.99 ***(978-0-593-46161-7(4));*** (Illus.). 19.99 *(978-0-593-46160-0(6))* Penguin Young Readers Group. (Kokila).

Keyishian, Elizabeth. Todo lo que necesitas saber sobre el cigarillo (Everything You Need to Know about Smoking) 2009. (Todo lo que necesitas (the Need to Know Library) Ser.). (SPA.). 64p. (gr. 6-6). 58.50 *(978-1-60854-407-3(9),* Editorial Buenas Letras) Rosen Publishing Group, Inc., The.

Keyishian, Elizabeth. Everything You Need to Know about Smoking. 2009. (Need to Know Library). 64p. (gr. 5-5). 58.50 *(978-1-60854-086-0(3))* Rosen Publishing Group, Inc., The.

—Smoking, 1 vol. rev. ed. 2003. (Need to Know Library (1994-2004) Ser.). (ENG., Illus.). 64p. (J). (gr. 5-5). lib. bdg. 37.13 *(978-0-8239-4092-9(6),* 99252132-b6f2-4c6d-bf79-63a05e89f907) Rosen Publishing Group, Inc., The.

Kiesbye, Stefan, ed. Can Busy Teens Succeed Academically?, 1 vol. 2009. (At Issue Ser.). (ENG.). 96p. (gr. 10-12). 41.03 *(978-0-7377-4286-2(0),* 5bc92631-14f7-4b5c-8360-9d0bd655338d, Greenhaven Publishing) Greenhaven Publishing LLC.

Kimlan, Lanie & Alvergue, Anne. The Truth about Ecstasy, 1 vol. 2011. (Drugs & Consequences Ser.). (ENG.). 64p. (YA). (gr. 5-5). lib. bdg. 37.13 *(978-1-4488-4643-6(9),* e437d314-81c7-4dc7-8a90-de0e00e2e3e3) Rosen Publishing Group, Inc., The.

Koya, Lena & Kamberg, Mary-Lane. Teen Pregnancy & What Comes Next, 1 vol. 2017. (Women in the World Ser.). (ENG.). 112p. (J). (gr. 6-6). 38.80 *(978-1-5081-7722-7(8),* 827b8adc-abcb-4dfd-9242-6087e380ed8d) Rosen Publishing Group, Inc., The.

Krueger, Lisa, ed. Teen Pregnancy & Parenting, 1 vol. 2010. (Current Controversies Ser.). (ENG.). 184p. (gr. 10-12). 48.03 *(978-0-7377-4923-6(7),* 36060e2a-f79b-4808-8f6a-2b78ba2d24ec); pap. 33.00 *(978-0-7377-4924-3(5),* 854ee047-98b8-498e-8cde-a8df636255d7) Greenhaven Publishing LLC. (Greenhaven Publishing).

Krumsiek, Allison. Teens & Alcohol: A Dangerous Combination, 1 vol. 2018. (Hot Topics Ser.). (ENG.). 104p. (J). (gr. 7-7). pap. 20.99 *(978-1-5345-6497-8(7),* 319958d9-2eb2-463c-84aa-db2087086f47, Lucent Pr.) Greenhaven Publishing LLC.

Kyi, Tanya Lloyd. Canadian Boys Who Rocked the World, 1 vol. Bagley, Tom, illus. 2007. (ENG.). 126p. (J). (gr. 3-2). pap. 12.95 *(978-1-55285-799-1(9),* cdd5bd07-9efa-44a5-b2bd-f3a752998b15) Whitecap Bks., Ltd. CAN. Dist: Firefly Bks., Ltd.

Lambillion, Paul. Staying Cool. 2004. (Illus.). 196p. pap. 13.95 *(978-0-7171-3598-1(5))* M.H. Gill & Co. U. C. IRL. Dist: Hushion Hse. Publishing, Ltd.

Landau, Jennifer. Bipolar Disorder, 1 vol. 2013. (Teen Mental Health Ser.). (ENG., Illus.). 48p. (J). (gr. 5-6). 34.47 *(978-1-4777-1747-9(1),* 92a40807-f79f-4d73-ac03-b2c12b2b77a8) Rosen Publishing Group, Inc., The.

—Helping a Friend with an Alcohol Problem, 1 vol. 2016. (How Can I Help? Friends Helping Friends Ser.). (ENG., Illus.). 64p. (J). (gr. 6-6). pap. 13.95 *(978-1-4994-6448-1(7),* 696c2194-d18f-4ca3-bc24-7205df47f286) Rosen Publishing Group, Inc., The.

Landau, Jennifer, ed. Teens Talk about Anxiety & Depression. 2017. (Teen Voices: Real Teens Discuss Real Problems Ser.). 64p. (J). (gr. 12-17). 77.70 *(978-1-5081-7631-2(0))* Rosen Publishing Group, Inc., The.

—Teens Talk about Drugs & Alcohol. 2017. (Teen Voices: Real Teens Discuss Real Problems Ser.). (Illus.). 64p. (J). (gr. 12-17). 77.70 *(978-1-5081-7634-3(5))* Rosen Publishing Group, Inc., The.

—Teens Talk about Leadership & Activism. 2017. (Teen Voices: Real Teens Discuss Real Problems Ser.). (Illus.). 64p. (J). (gr. 12-17). 77.70 *(978-1-5081-7635-0(3))* Rosen Publishing Group, Inc., The.

—Teens Talk about Self-Esteem & Self-Confidence. 2017. (Teen Voices: Real Teens Discuss Real Problems Ser.). (Illus.). 64p. (J). (gr. 12-17). 77.70 *(978-1-5081-7637-4(X))* Rosen Publishing Group, Inc., The.

Latchana Kenney, Karen. The Hidden Story of Drugs, 1 vol., 1. 2013. (Undercover Story Ser.). (ENG.). 48p. (J). (gr. 5-5). 34.41 *(978-1-4777-2803-1(1),* 6a39043e-82f2-42c8-b8ca-d7a9c4c1938f, Rosen Reference) Rosen Publishing Group, Inc., The.

Lee, Helen. Where in the World? Stories from Everywhere: Daily Devotions for Juniors. 2006. 373p. (J). *(978-0-8280-1874-6(X))* Review & Herald Publishing Assn.

Libal, Autumn. Fats, Sugars, & Empty Calories: The Fast Food Habit. 2007. (Obesity Ser.). (Illus.). 104p. (YA). (gr. 4-7). lib. bdg. 23.95 *(978-1-59084-943-9(4))* Mason Crest.

—Health Implications of Cosmetic Surgery, Makeovers, & Body Alterations. McDonnell, Mary Ann & Forman, Sara, eds. 2013. (Young Adult's Guide to the Science of Health Ser.: 15). 128p. (J). (gr. 7-18). 24.95 *(978-1-4222-2811-1(8))* Mason Crest.

—Runaway Train: Youth with Emotional Disturbance. 2003. (Youth with Special Needs Ser.). (Illus.). 127p. (YA). (gr. 7). pap. 14.95 *(978-1-4222-0429-0(4))* Mason Crest.

Lily, Henrietta M. & Harmon, Daniel E. Frequently Asked Questions about Alcohol Abuse & Binge Drinking, 1 vol. 2011. (FAQ: Teen Life Ser.). (ENG.). 64p. (J). (gr. 5-6). lib. bdg. 37.13 *(978-1-4488-4629-0(3),* 12892c05-6dbc-46a6-8e7a-4295a8713306) Rosen Publishing Group, Inc., The.

Lindsey, Brooklyn. Confessions of a Not-So-Supermodel: Faith, Friends, & Festival Queens, 1 vol. 2008. (Invert Ser.). (ENG., Illus.). 176p. (YA). (gr. 7-14). pap. 9.99 *(978-0-310-27753-8(1))* Zondervan.

Lishak, Antony. Drugs. 2007. (What's That Got to Do with Me?/Watts Ser.). (Illus.). 32p. (YA). (gr. 4-7). lib. bdg. 28.50 *(978-1-59920-035-4(X))* Black Rabbit Bks.

Lucado, Max. Every Day Deserves a Chance: Wake up & Live!, 1 vol. 2007. (ENG., Illus.). 164p. (YA). (gr. 7-12). pap. 14.99 *(978-1-4003-1077-7(6),* Tommy Nelson) Nelson, Thomas Inc.

Lüsted, Marcia Amidon. Coping with Homelessness, 1 vol. 2017. (Coping Ser.). (ENG., Illus.). 112p. (J). (gr. 7-7). pap. 19.24 *(978-1-5081-7851-4(8),* 999306f7-5940-40a1-b98f-5355ef80bf08) Rosen Publishing Group, Inc., The.

Mack, Cassandra. Cool, Confident & Strong: 52 Power Moves for Girls. 2007. 100p. per. 11.95 *(978-0-595-47560-5(4),* Authors Choice Pr.) iUniverse, Inc.

Madsen, Susan Arrington. I Walked to Zion: True Stories of Young Pioneers on the Mormon Trail. 2008. 192p. pap. 9.95 *(978-1-59038-930-0(1))* Deseret Bk. Co.

Marcovitz, Hal. Teens & Career Choices. Developed in Association with the Gallup Organization Staff, ed. 2013. (Gallup Youth Survey: Major Issues & Trends Ser.: 14). 112p. (J). (gr. 7-18). 24.95 *(978-1-4222-2950-7(5))* Mason Crest.

—Teens & Family Issues. Developed in Association with the Gallup Organization Staff, ed. 2013. (Gallup Youth Survey: Major Issues & Trends Ser.: 14). 112p. (J). (gr. 7-18). 24.95 *(978-1-4222-2952-1(1))* Mason Crest.

—Teens & Race. Developed in Association with the Gallup Organization Staff, ed. 2013. (Gallup Youth Survey: Major Issues & Trends Ser.: 14). 112p. (J). (gr. 7-18). 24.95 *(978-1-4222-2955-2(6))* Mason Crest.

—Teens & Sex. Developed in Association with the Gallup Organization Staff, ed. 2013. (Gallup Youth Survey: Major Issues & Trends Ser.: 14). 112p. (J). (gr. 7-18). 24.95 *(978-1-4222-2957-6(2))* Mason Crest.

—Teens & Suicide. Developed in Association with the Gallup Organization Staff, ed. 2013. (Gallup Youth Survey: Major Issues & Trends Ser.: 14). 112p. (J). (gr. 7-18). 24.95 *(978-1-4222-2958-3(0))* Mason Crest.

—Teens & the Supernatural & Paranormal. Developed in Association with the Gallup Organization Staff, ed. 2013. (Gallup Youth Survey: Major Issues & Trends Ser.: 14). (Illus.). 112p. (J). (gr. 7-18). 24.95 *(978-1-4222-2959-0(9))* Mason Crest.

—Teens & the Supernatural & Paranormal. 2008. (Gallup Youth Survey, Major Issues & Trends Ser.). (Illus.). 112,128p. (J). (gr. 7-9). lib. bdg. 22.95 *(978-1-59084-876-0(4))* Mason Crest.

—Teens, Religion & Values. Developed in Association with the Gallup Organization Staff, ed. 2013. (Gallup Youth Survey: Major Issues & Trends Ser.: 14). 112p. (J). (gr. 7-18). 24.95 *(978-1-4222-2962-0(9))* Mason Crest.

Marsico, Katie. Alcohol Abuse, 1 vol. 2013. (Real Teens... Real Issues Ser.). (ENG.). 80p. (YA). (gr. 7-7). 36.93 *(978-1-60870-848-2(9),* 6b352248-469d-4bbc-84a2-e1d946365ac2); pap. 18.64 *(978-1-62712-125-5(0),* 4b62f134-9958-4b2d-9412-3b48fa32646f) Cavendish Square Publishing LLC.

—Drug Abuse, 1 vol. 2013. (Real Teens... Real Issues Ser.). (ENG.). 80p. (YA). (gr. 7-7). 36.93 *(978-1-60870-852-9(7),* ff3e6194-4aaa-49fb-a39a-0403336142f8) Cavendish Square Publishing LLC.

Mason, Paul. Know the Facts about Drinking & Smoking. 2009. (J). 70.50 *(978-1-4358-5463-5(2),* Rosen Reference); (ENG.). 48p. (YA). (gr. 5-6). pap. 12.75 *(978-1-4358-5462-8(4),* 9f74385e-5423-4c2a-ad5b-60043b320a85, Rosen Reference); (ENG., Illus.). 48p. (YA). (gr. 5-6). lib. bdg. 34.47 *(978-1-4358-5339-3(3),* ac847bdd-b18b-4c77-a0e0-bf83a0a39684) Rosen Publishing Group, Inc., The.

Matlock, Mark. Wisdom On... Making Good Decisions, 1 vol. 2008. (Invert Ser.). (ENG.). 144p. (YA). (gr. 7-14). pap. 9.99 *(978-0-310-27926-6(7))* Zondervan.

McDowell, Pamela. Teen Pregnancy, 1 vol. 2010. (ENG.). 48p. (J). pap. *(978-0-7787-2139-0(6));* lib. bdg. *(978-0-7787-2132-1(9))* Crabtree Publishing Co.

McGraw, Sally. Living Simply: A Teen Guide to Minimalism. 2019. (ENG., Illus.). 112p. (YA). (gr. 6-12). lib. bdg. 37.32 *(978-1-5415-0054-9(7),* f14874b1-c7c8-4fdf-bd1f-79639c62e48f, Twenty-First Century Bks.) Lerner Publishing Group.

McGuire, Kara. Cover Your Assets: The Teens' Guide to Protecting Their Money, Their Stuff, & Themselves, 1 vol. 2014. (Financial Literacy for Teens Ser.). (ENG.). 64p. (J). (gr. 5-9). lib. bdg. 34.65 *(978-0-7565-4921-3(3),* 126059, Compass Point Bks.) Capstone.

—Making Money Work: A Teen's Guide to Saving, Investing, & Building Wealth, 1 vol. 2014. (Financial Literacy for Teens Ser.). (ENG.). 64p. (J). (gr. 5-9). lib. bdg. 34.65 *(978-0-7565-4922-0(1),* 126060, Compass Point Bks.) Capstone.

—Smart Spending: The Teens' Guide to Cash, Credit, & Life's Costs, 1 vol. 2014. (Financial Literacy for Teens Ser.). (ENG.). 64p. (J). (gr. 5-9). lib. bdg. 34.65 *(978-0-7565-4923-7(X),* 126061, Compass Point Bks.) Capstone.

McIntosh, Kenneth & Livingston, Phyllis. Youth with Alcohol & Drug Addiction: Escape from Bondage. 2009. (Helping Youth with Mental, Physical, & Social Challenges Ser.). (Illus.). 128p. (YA). (gr. 7-18). lib. bdg. 24.95 *(978-1-4222-0143-5(0))* Mason Crest.

McIntosh, Kenneth & Walker, Ida. Youth with Cultural/Language Differences: Interpreting an Alien World. 2009. (Helping Youth with Mental, Physical, & Social Challenges Ser.). (Illus.). 128p. (YA). (gr. 7-18). lib. bdg. 24.95 *(978-1-4222-0141-1(4))* Mason Crest.

McKay, Jenny. Children of the Holocaust. 2015. (ENG., Illus.). 80p. (J). (gr. 5-12). lib. bdg. *(978-1-60152-838-4(8))* ReferencePoint Pr., Inc.

Medina, Sarah. Know the Facts about Drugs. 2009. 48p. (J). 70.50 *(978-1-4358-5459-8(4));* (ENG.). (YA). (gr. 5-6). pap. 12.75 *(978-1-4358-5458-1(6),* 3bb1dcc6-8dd2-4faa-a143-007560729278) Rosen Publishing Group, Inc., The. (Rosen Reference).

Mercadante, Frank. Positively Dangerous: Live Loud, Be Real, Change the World. 2003. (ENG.). 117p. (YA). pap. 12.50 *(978-0-88489-790-3(7))* Saint Mary's Press of Minnesota.

Merino, Noël, ed. Emancipation, 1 vol. 2014. (Teen Rights & Freedoms Ser.). (ENG., Illus.). 152p. (gr. 10-12). lib. bdg. 43.63 *(978-0-7377-6999-9(8),* 9582398a-302d-495a-9116-ad93053f1a2d, Greenhaven Publishing) Greenhaven Publishing LLC.

Metzger, Julie & Lehman, Robert. Will Puberty Last My Whole Life? REAL Answers to REAL Questions from Preteens about Body Changes, Sex, & Other Growing-Up Stuff. Cerizo, Lia, illus. 2018. 224p. (J). (gr. 4-7). pap. 18.99 *(978-1-63217-179-5(1),* Little Bigfoot) Sasquatch Bks.

Meyers Jugendlexikon. (GER., Illus.). 672p. *(978-3-411-07804-2(9))* Bibliographisches Institut & F. A. Brockhaus AG DEU. Dist: i. b. d., Ltd.

Miles, Lisa & Chown, Xanna Eve. How to Survive Being Dumped, 1 vol. 2013. (Girl Talk Ser.). (Illus.). 48p. (J). (gr. 5-5). (ENG.). pap. 12.75 *(978-1-4777-0716-6(6),* 2dfa00da-a728-4f0e-ba1f-1566aea435a4, Rosen Classroom); (ENG., lib. bdg. 34.41 *(978-1-4777-0704-3(2),* 1307468d-3216-4ad4-9cc7-e86faa8debf6, Rosen Reference); pap. 70.50 *(978-1-4777-0717-3(4),* Rosen Reference) Rosen Publishing Group, Inc., The.

Mincher, Kevin. The Ultimate Youth Lifestyle: 7 Steps Any Teenager Can Use to Achieve More Success & Happiness. 2017. 64p. (C). pap. 14.95 *(978-0-9956079-0-3(7))* Unstoppable Teen, Ltd. GBR. Dist: Crown Hse. Publishing LLC.

Mirk, Sarah. You Do You: Figuring Out Your Body, Dating, & Sexuality. 2019. (ENG., Illus.). 120p. (YA). (gr. 6-12). 37.32 *(978-1-5415-4022-4(0),* aef64119-3944-4b93-8221-7ad043de9e05, Twenty-First Century Bks.) Lerner Publishing Group.

Monckeberg, Paulina. Artilugia 2007 English. 2006. (Pascualina Family of Products Ser.). 274p. (J). spiral bd. 14.99 *(978-956-8222-49-9(9))* Pascualina Producciones S.A.

Moore, Andrew. Meditation, 1 vol. 2008. (Teen Mental Health Ser.). (ENG., Illus.). 48p. (YA). (gr. 5-6). lib. bdg. 34.47 *(978-1-4042-1799-7(1),* 09f7d881-47e4-49fc-a994-bcb5ecbad3f2) Rosen Publishing Group, Inc., The.

Morgan, Nicola. Blame My Brain. 2007. (Illus.). 192p. (YA). pap. *(978-1-4063-1116-7(2))* Walker Bks., Ltd.

Murray, Hallie & Byers, Ann. Teenage Resistance to the Nazi Regime, 1 vol. 2018. (Tales of Atrocity & Resistance: First-Person Stories of Teens in the Holocaust Ser.). (ENG.). 128p. (J). (gr. 7-7). 40.27 *(978-0-7660-9842-8(7),* b9f6cafd-476c-425e-a00a-c0707535672e) Enslow Publishing, LLC.

Murray, Hallie & Jacobs Altman, Linda. Teen Victims of the Nazi Regime, 1 vol. 2018. (Tales of Atrocity & Resistance: First-Person Stories of Teens in the Holocaust Ser.). (ENG.). 128p. (gr. 7-7). 40.27 *(978-0-7660-9839-8(7),* 77a4cc23-278d-4d98-a977-50ce39ef3f40) Enslow Publishing, LLC.

My Parents are Divorcing. Now What? Set 2, 16 vols. 2014. (Teen Life 411 Ser.). (ENG.). 112p. (YA). (gr. 7-7). lib. bdg. 310.40 *(978-1-4777-7988-0(4),* aeb867a6-869c-4b5e-af95-2c640f78b305, Rosen Young Adult) Rosen Publishing Group, Inc., The.

Nagle, Jeanne. Great Lifelong Learning Skills. 2009. (Work Readiness Ser.). 64p. (gr. 6-6). 58.50 *(978-1-60854-825-5(2))* Rosen Publishing Group, Inc., The.

Nagle, Jeanne M. Great Lifelong Learning Skills, 1 vol. 2008. (Work Readiness Ser.). (ENG., Illus.). 64p. (YA). (gr. 6-6). lib. bdg. 37.13 *(978-1-4042-1424-8(0),* 177e38f6-1fe1-4d52-ae61-03fa7988d1f3) Rosen Publishing Group, Inc., The.

Nardo, Don. Teen Guide to Mental Health. 2019. (ENG.). 80p. (J). (gr. 6-12). 41.27 *(978-1-68282-753-6(4))* ReferencePoint Pr., Inc.

Nelson, David Erik, ed. Teen Drug Abuse, 1 vol. 2010. (Opposing Viewpoints Ser.). (ENG.). 240p. (gr. 10-12). 50.43 *(978-0-7377-4992-2(X),* 80de8aed-6664-406c-8141-c73822843513); pap. 34.80 *(978-0-7377-4993-9(8),*

8356e8e8-84c5-4f4c-9a52-dd6e29dae7cf) Greenhaven Publishing LLC. (Greenhaven Publishing).
etzley, Patricia D. Teens & Sexting. 2015. (Illus.). 80p. (J). 28.95 *(978-1-60152-916-9(3))* ReferencePoint Pr., Inc.
oble, Alan R. Foundations of the Christian Faith. 2008. 160p. pap. 13.99 *(978-1-60477-694-2(3))* Salem Author Services.
aks, Robert C. Believe! Helping Youth Learn to Trust in the Lord. 2003. (Illus.). xiii, 126p. (J). pap. 14.95 *(978-1-59038-203-5(X))* Deseret Bk. Co.
besity: Modern-Day Epidemic, 10 vols., Set. Incl. Diet & Your Emotions: The Comfort Food Falsehood. Esherick, Joan. (J). 2004. lib. bdg. 23.95 *(978-1-59084-950-7(7))*; Fats, Sugars, & Empty Calories: The Fast Food Habit. Libal, Autumn. (YA). 2007. lib. bdg. 23.95 *(978-1-59084-943-9(4))*; Medications & Surgeries for Weight Loss: When Dieting Isn't Enough. Hunter, William. (YA). 2007. lib. bdg. 23.95 *(978-1-59084-947-7(7))*; (gr. 4-7). (Illus.). 104p. 2005. Set lib. bdg. 239.50 *(978-1-59084-941-5(8))* Mason Crest.
Orr, Tamra. Coping with Racial Inequality, 1 vol. 2017. (Coping (2017-2020) Ser.). (ENG., Illus.). 112p. (J). (gr. 7-7). 40.13 *(978-1-5081-7396-0(6),* dd44a0c7-946c-4929-a399-f55a8518494e, Rosen Young Adult) Rosen Publishing Group, Inc., The.
—Home & Family Relationships, 1 vol. 2010. (Teens: Being Gay, Lesbian, Bisexual, or Transgender Ser.). (ENG., Illus.). 80p. (YA). (gr. 6-6). lib. bdg. 38.47 *(978-1-4358-3579-5(4),* 201cec76-f0db-4e89-94af-cbb94ee32ee4) Rosen Publishing Group, Inc., The.
Orr, Tamra B. Money-Making Opportunities for Teens Who Like Working Outside, 1 vol. 2013. (Make Money Now! Ser.). (ENG., Illus.). 80p. (YA). (gr. 7-7). lib. bdg. 38.41 *(978-1-4488-9383-6(6),* b870f6ad-bdc8-44e9-9b23-0389cffe871e) Rosen Publishing Group, Inc., The.
Owens, Peter. Teens, Health & Obesity. Developed in Association with the Gallup Organization Staff, ed. 2013. (Gallup Youth Survey: Major Issues & Trends Ser.: 14). (Illus.). 112p. (J). (gr. 7-18). 24.95 *(978-1-4222-2961-3(0))* Mason Crest.
Pack-Jordan, Erin. Everything You Need to Know about Suicide & Self-Harm, 1 vol. 2018. (Need to Know Library). (ENG.). 64p. (J). (gr. 6-6). pap. 13.95 *(978-1-5081-8354-9(6),* c914db63-ccba-4ec3-89d0-cc54af2859b1, Rosen Young Adult) Rosen Publishing Group, Inc., The.
Paonessa, Mary. Growth & Development: Understanding Yourself, 8 vols. 3rd ed. 2003. (Human Growth & Development Ser.). (Illus.). 82p. (J). (gr. 8-18). pap. 11.00 *(978-0-9711721-6-6(1),* 394) Paon Pubns.
Pardes, Bronwen. Doing It Right: Making Smart, Safe, & Satisfying Choices about Sex. 2013. (ENG., Illus.). (YA). (gr. 9). 160p. 18.99 *(978-1-4424-8370-5(9))*; 146p. pap. 12.99 *(978-1-4424-8371-2(7))* Simon Pulse. (Simon Pulse).
Parks, Peggy J. The Dangers of E-Cigarettes. 2016. (ENG.). 80p. (J). (gr. 5-12). *(978-1-68282-014-8(9))* ReferencePoint Pr., Inc.
parks, peggy j. Teenage Sex & Pregnancy. 2011. (Compact Research Ser.). 96p. (YA). (gr. 7-12). lib. bdg. 43.93 *(978-1-60152-168-2(5))* ReferencePoint Pr., Inc.
Parks, Peggy J. Teenage Suicide. 2011. (Compact Research Ser.). 96p. (YA). (gr. 7-12). lib. bdg. 43.93 *(978-1-60152-156-9(1))* ReferencePoint Pr., Inc.
—Teens & Stress. 2015. (ENG., Illus.). 96p. (J). lib. bdg. *(978-1-60152-768-4(3))* ReferencePoint Pr., Inc.
—Teens & Substance Abuse. 2015. (ENG., Illus.). 80p. (J). lib. bdg. *(978-1-60152-832-2(9))* ReferencePoint Pr., Inc.
Payment, Simone. Friendship, Dating, & Relationships, 1 vol. 2010. (Teens: Being Gay, Lesbian, Bisexual, or Transgender Ser.). (ENG., Illus.). 80p. (YA). (gr. 6-6). lib. bdg. 38.47 *(978-1-4358-3578-8(6),* b2430111-4a34-4bda-bf17-4ec9a99f5c6b) Rosen Publishing Group, Inc., The.
Penne, Barbra & Renehan, Patrick. Your Rights As an LGBTQ+ Teen, 1 vol. 2017. (LGBTQ+ Guide to Beating Bullying Ser.). (ENG., Illus.). 64p. (J). (gr. 6-6). 36.13 *(978-1-5081-7439-4(3),* 7f5511ac-a4e9-4874-9f82-82d288f98fbf, Rosen Young Adult) Rosen Publishing Group, Inc., The.
Peter, Val J. & Dowd, Tom. Boundaries: A Guide for Teens. 2004. 113p. (gr. 8-12). pap. 8.95 *(978-1-889322-37-7(7),* 25-014) Boys Town Pr.
Peters, Jennifer. Alcohol Abuse, 1 vol. 2018. (Overcoming Addiction Ser.). (ENG.). 64p. (gr. 7-7). 36.13 *(978-1-5081-7938-2(7),* dca1f579-ab5a-4072-9882-d6252c498361) Rosen Publishing Group, Inc., The.
Phillips, Sherre Florence. The Teen Brain. 2007. (Gray Matter Ser.). (Illus.). 130p. (YA). (gr. 9-12). lib. bdg. 35.00 *(978-0-7910-9415-0(4),* Facts On File) Infobase Holdings, Inc.
Piehl, Norah, ed. Underage Drinking, 1 vol. 2010. (Social Issues Firsthand Ser.). (ENG., Illus.). 120p. (gr. 10-12). 39.93 *(978-0-7377-4799-7(4),* c72efb66-2ddd-443e-94ac-083885a0a299, Greenhaven Publishing) Greenhaven Publishing LLC.
Poole, H. W. Teen Parents, Vol. 12. 2016. (Families Today Ser.). (Illus.). 48p. (J). (gr. 5). 20.95 *(978-1-4222-3624-6(2))* Mason Crest.
Rauf, Don. Social Network-Powered Investing & Saving Opportunities, 1 vol. 2013. (Teen's Guide to the Power of Social Networking Ser.). (ENG.). 80p. (YA). (gr. 7-7). 38.41 *(978-1-4777-1684-7(X),* d9da7601-f48d-4d81-a4c5-ceaad8855b82); pap. 15.15 *(978-1-4777-1917-6(2),* 84c45237-7b64-4bf0-9e9b-fc1ada0c6078) Rosen Publishing Group, Inc., The.
Regan Gregson, Susan. Cyber Literacy: Evaluating the Reliability of Data. 2009. (Cyber Citizenship & Cyber Safety Ser.). 48p. (gr. 5-5). 53.00 *(978-1-61512-103-8(X),* Rosen Reference) Rosen Publishing Group, Inc., The.
Reino, Jessica. Food Allergies: The Ultimate Teen Guide. 2015. (It Happened to Me Ser.: 45). (Illus.). 182p. 59.00 *(978-1-4422-3573-1(X))* Rowman & Littlefield Publishers, Inc.
Reynolds, Luke, ed. Break These Rules: 35 YA Authors on Speaking up, Standing Out, & Being Yourself. 2013. (ENG.). 224p. (YA). (gr. 7). pap. 14.99 *(978-1-61374-784-1(5))* Chicago Review Pr., Inc.
Rich, Mari. My Teenage Life in Japan. 2017. (Customs & Cultures of the World Ser.). (ENG., Illus.). 64p. (J). (gr. 7-12). 23.95 *(978-1-4222-3906-3(3))* Mason Crest.
Robertson, Sadie. Live Fearless: A Call to Power, Passion, & Purpose, 1 vol. 2018. (ENG.). 224p. (YA). 19.99 *(978-1-4003-0939-9(5),* Tommy Nelson) Nelson, Thomas Inc.
Robinson, Sharon. Child of the Dream (a Memoir Of 1963) 2019. (ENG., Illus.). 240p. (J). (gr. 3-7). 16.99 *(978-1-338-28280-1(8),* Scholastic Pr.) Scholastic, Inc.
Rodger, Ellen. Jazz Jennings: Voice for LGBTQ Youth. 2017. (Remarkable Lives Revealed Ser.). (Illus.). 32p. (J). (gr. 3-3). *(978-0-7787-3419-2(6))* Crabtree Publishing Co.
Rooke, Margaret. You Can Change the World! Everyday Teen Heroes Making a Difference Everywhere. McHale, Kara, illus. 2019. 320p. (J). 18.95 *(978-1-78592-502-3(4),* 696801) Kingsley, Jessica Pubs. GBR. Dist: Hachette UK Distribution.
Rosenberg, Carol & Rosenberg, Gary. Jon & Jayne's Guide to Throwing, Going To, & Surviving Parties: Advice & More from Your Average but Xtraordinary Friends. 2008. (Jon & Jayne Doe Ser.). (ENG., Illus.). 128p. (YA). (gr. 7-11). pap. 9.95 *(978-0-7573-0726-3(4))* Health Communications, Inc.
Ross, Michael & Ross, Christopher. A Kid's Game Plan for Great Choices: An All-Sports Devotional. 2019. (ENG., Illus.). 208p. (J). (gr. 2-7). pap. 12.99 *(978-0-7369-7524-7(1),* 6975247) Harvest Hse. Pubs.
Rusch, Elizabeth. You Call This Democracy? How to Fix Our Government & Deliver Power to the People. 2020. (ENG., Illus.). 288p. (YA). (gr. 7). 19.99 *(978-0-358-17692-3(1),* 1758901); pap. 9.99 *(978-0-358-38742-8(6),* 1787374) HarperCollins Pubs. (Greenwillow Bks.).
Sanders, Angela. 100 Days: The Glory Experiment. 2018. 224p. (J). pap. *(978-1-4627-9942-8(6))* Lifeway Christian Resources.
Saul, Laya. Ways to Help Disadvantaged Youth: A Guide to Giving Back. 2010. (How to Help Ser.). (Illus.). 48p. (J). (gr. 4-8). lib. bdg. 29.95 *(978-1-58415-918-6(9))* Mitchell Lane Pubs.
Scarlet, Janina. Superhero Therapy: Mindfulness Skills to Help Teens & Young Adults Deal with Anxiety, Depression, & Trauma. Alves, Wellinton, illus. 2017. (ENG.). 112p. (YA). (gr. 6-12). pap. 21.95 *(978-1-68403-033-0(1),* 40330) New Harbinger Pubns.
Scherer, Lauri S., ed. Dating, 1 vol. 2014. (Issues That Concern You Ser.). (ENG., Illus.). 128p. (gr. 7-10). lib. bdg. 43.63 *(978-0-7377-6288-4(8),* 6fb98a4a-45b4-409a-92b8-63f558047940, Greenhaven Publishing) Greenhaven Publishing LLC.
Scott, Jerry & Borgman, Jim. Extra Cheesy Zits: A Zits Treasury. 2016. (Zits Ser.: 33). (ENG., Illus.). 208p. pap. 18.99 *(978-1-4494-7982-4(0))* Andrews McMeel Publishing.
Seguin, Marilyn. No Ordinary Lives: Four 19th Century Teenage Diaries. 2009. (J). pap. *(978-0-8283-2158-7(2))* Branden Bks.
Shames, Stephen. Transforming Lives: Turning Uganda's Forgotten Children into Leaders. Shames, Stephen, photos by. 2009. (Illus.). 40p. (YA). pap. 12.95 *(978-1-59572-213-3(0))* Star Bright Bks., Inc.
Shea, John M. Self-Injury & Cutting: Stopping the Pain, 1 vol. 2013. (Helpline: Teen Issues & Answers Ser.). (ENG., Illus.). 80p. (YA). (gr. 5-6). lib. bdg. 38.41 *(978-1-4488-9448-2(4),* 6ad61855-2f3d-4de8-93cc-633919557690, Rosen Classroom) Rosen Publishing Group, Inc., The.
Sheen, Barbara. Growing up in Mexico. 2017. (Growing up Around the World Ser.). (ENG.). 80p. (YA). (gr. 5-12). *(978-1-68282-221-0(4))* ReferencePoint Pr., Inc.
Simms, Jennifer. Teens & Distracting Driving. 2018. (Teen Health & Safety Ser.). (ENG.). 80p. (YA). (gr. 6-12). 39.93 *(978-1-68282-507-5(8))* ReferencePoint Pr., Inc.
Simons, Rae. A Guide to Teaching Young Adults about Money. 2010. (Junior Library of Money). 64p. (YA). (gr. 7-18). pap. 9.95 *(978-1-4222-1884-6(8))*; lib. bdg. 22.95 *(978-1-4222-1765-8(5))* Mason Crest.
Siuda Jacques, Michele, ed. Teen Driving, 1 vol. 2012. (At Issue Ser.). (ENG.). 88p. (gr. 10-12). pap. 28.80 *(978-0-7377-6419-2(8),* 58328b70-fded-41a4-9796-8143e3609ca7, Greenhaven Publishing) Greenhaven Publishing LLC.
Skeen, Michelle & Skeen, Kelly. Just As You Are: A Teen's Guide to Self-Acceptance & Lasting Self-Esteem. 2018. (Instant Help Solutions Ser.). (ENG.). 176p. (YA). pap. 17.95 *(978-1-62625-590-6(3),* 35906) New Harbinger Pubns.
Snyder, Gail. Growing up in Canada. 2017. (Growing up Around the World Ser.). (ENG.). 80p. (YA). (gr. 5-12). *(978-1-68282-207-4(9))* ReferencePoint Pr., Inc.
—Teens & Alcohol. Developed in Association with the Gallup Organization Staff, ed. 2013. (Gallup Youth Survey: Major Issues & Trends Ser.: 14). 112p. (J). (gr. 7-18). 24.95 *(978-1-4222-2949-1(1))* Mason Crest.
Social Network-Powered Investing & Saving Opportunities. 2013. (Teen's Guide to the Power of Social Networking Ser.). 80p. (YA). (gr. 7-12). pap. 84.90 *(978-1-4777-1918-3(0))* Rosen Publishing Group, Inc., The.
Sokol, Leslie & Fox, Marci G. The Think Confident, Be Confident Workbook for Teens: Activities to Help You Create Unshakable Self-Confidence & Reach Your Goals. 2016. (ENG.). 224p. (YA). (gr. 6-12). pap. 19.95 *(978-1-62625-483-1(4),* 34831) New Harbinger Pubns.
Some Assembly Required: The Not-So-Secret Life of a Transgender Teen. 2014. (ENG., Illus.). 256p. (YA). (gr. 8). 17.99 *(978-1-4814-1675-7(8),* Simon & Schuster Bks. For Young Readers) Simon & Schuster Bks. For Young Readers.
Spencer, Lauren. Everything You Need to Know about Falling in Love. 2009. (Need to Know Library). 64p. (gr. 5-5). 58.50 *(978-1-60854-067-9(7))* Rosen Publishing Group, Inc., The.
Staley, Erin. I'm an Undocumented Immigrant, Now What?, 1 vol. 2016. (Teen Life 411 Ser.). (ENG.). 112p. (J). (gr. 7-7). 38.80 *(978-1-5081-7193-5(9),* 6e0f878d-ab84-4f7c-bba7-586fa312bc13) Rosen Publishing Group, Inc., The.
Stenquist, Anjali. Teens & Dieting. 2018. (Teen Health & Safety Ser.). (ENG.). 80p. (YA). (gr. 6-12). 39.93 *(978-1-68282-505-1(1))* ReferencePoint Pr., Inc.
Stephens, Aarti D., ed. Teenage Sexuality, 1 vol. 2012. (Opposing Viewpoints Ser.). (ENG., Illus.). 248p. (gr. 10-12). 50.43 *(978-0-7377-5763-7(9),* 307560b7-00df-48ef-941e-79a5e41e31a8); pap. 34.80 *(978-0-7377-5764-4(7),* ceda39ee-52a0-4f6c-a423-82dfe2fbd20e) Greenhaven Publishing LLC. (Greenhaven Publishing).
Stewart, Faith. Teens & Rural Education: Opportunities & Challenges. 2009. (Youth in Rural North America Ser.). (Illus.). 96p. (YA). (gr. 3-7). lib. bdg. 22.95 *(978-1-4222-0015-5(9))* Mason Crest.
Stollers, Veronica & Keyishian, Elizabeth. Frequently Asked Questions about Smoking, 1 vol. 2011. (FAQ: Teen Life Ser.). (ENG.). 64p. (J). (gr. 5-6). lib. bdg. 37.13 *(978-1-4488-4631-3(5),* 4007b9e8-1579-4c56-8ba1-730efad04c56) Rosen Publishing Group, Inc., The.
Strehle Hartman, Ashley. Teens & STDs. 2018. (Teen Health & Safety Ser.). (ENG.). 80p. (YA). (gr. 6-12). 39.93 *(978-1-68282-513-6(2))* ReferencePoint Pr., Inc.
Synder, Gail. Teens & Smoking. 2015. (Illus.). 80p. (J). *(978-1-60152-918-3(X))* ReferencePoint Pr., Inc.
Tabone, Francis. The ASD Independence Workbook: Transition Skills for Teens & Young Adults with Autism. 2018. (ENG.). 192p. (YA). (gr. 8-12). pap. 24.95 *(978-1-68403-064-4(1),* 40644) New Harbinger Pubns.
Taylor, Julia V. The Body Image Workbook for Teens: Activities to Help Girls Develop a Healthy Body Image in an Image-Obsessed World. 2014. (ENG.). 200p. (YA). (gr. 6-12). pap. 21.95 *(978-1-62625-018-5(9),* 30185) New Harbinger Pubns.
Tecco, Betsy Dru. Food for Fuel: The Connection Between Food & Physical Activity, 1 vol. (Science Instructional Targets (SIT) Ser.). (Illus.). 48p. 2007. (ENG.). (gr. 5-8). per. 12.75 *(978-1-4042-1635-8(9),* 030297f5-d816-480a-aa89-080d24465e77) 2004. (J). lib. bdg. 26.50 *(978-1-4042-0303-7(6))* Rosen Publishing Group, Inc., The.
Teen Issues, 26 bks., Set. (Illus.). (YA). (gr. 6-12). lib. bdg. 344.10 *(978-0-89490-887-3(1))* Enslow Publishing, LLC.
Teen Life 411: Set 3, 12 vols. 2015. (Teen Life 411 Ser.). (ENG.). 112p. (J). (gr. 7-7). lib. bdg. 232.80 *(978-1-4994-6190-9(9),* 2cad72a2-2c80-40f6-8b5b-dc53fcb0e884, Rosen Young Adult) Rosen Publishing Group, Inc., The.
Teen Life 411: Set 4, 16 vols. 2016. (Teen Life 411 Ser.). (ENG.). 00112p. (J). (gr. 7-7). 310.40 *(978-1-5081-7354-0(0),* 9e9705ea-a49c-4688-b4ed-1124317d79e9, Rosen Young Adult) Rosen Publishing Group, Inc., The.
Teen Mental Health, 10 vols., Set. Incl. Addictive Personality. Juzwiak, Richard. lib. bdg. 34.47 *(978-1-4042-1802-4(5),* 38d603c5-5160-43e4-87b6-a4b63c7c74ad); Anxiety & Panic Attacks. Levin, Judith. lib. bdg. 34.47 *(978-1-4042-1797-3(5),* 90c85477-8a2e-43de-8061-1bb0c027f8e5); Depression & Mood Disorders. Levin, Judith. lib. bdg. 34.47 *(978-1-4042-1798-0(3),* 9c40e589-e64e-4404-b343-55eb231f226a); Meditation. Moore, Andrew. lib. bdg. 34.47 *(978-1-4042-1799-7(1),* 09f7d881-47e4-49fc-a994-bcb5ecbad3f2); (Illus.). 48p. (YA). (gr. 5-6). 2008. (Teen Mental Health Ser.). (ENG.). 2008. Set lib. bdg. 172.35 *(978-1-4042-1888-8(2),* 54036480-a68c-4627-bdf3-e012a25e8456) Rosen Publishing Group, Inc., The.
Teen Mental Health: Set 2, 12 vols. 2011. (Teen Mental Health Ser.). (ENG., Illus.). 48p. (J). (gr. 5-6). 206.82 *(978-1-4488-4873-7(3),* 2c86fe20-8343-4ec8-a443-3bbb661d5466) Rosen Publishing Group, Inc., The.
Teen Mental Health: Set 4, 12 vols. 2013. (Teen Mental Health Ser.). (ENG.). 48p. (YA). (gr. 5-6). 206.82 *(978-1-4777-1761-5(7),* f23c20a6-fddc-4b9b-ac32-fffc3a1486b6) Rosen Publishing Group, Inc., The.
Teenage Refugees Speak Out. 2005. (Illus.). (gr. 7-12). lib. bdg. 106.35 *(978-0-8239-9331-4(0))* Rosen Publishing Group, Inc., The.
A Teen's Guide to the Power of Social Networking. 2013. (Teen's Guide to the Power of Social Networking Ser.). 80p. (YA). (gr. 7-12). pap. 56.60 *(978-1-4777-7809-8(8))*; pap. 339.60 *(978-1-4777-7808-1(X))*; (ENG.). 153.64 *(978-1-4777-1689-2(0),* 6b87d0b2-0b1b-47ef-b044-07ace0e1be89) Rosen Publishing Group, Inc., The.
Telgemeier, Raina. Smile. 2010. 21.00 *(978-1-60686-896-6(9))* Perfection Learning Corp.
—Smile. Telgemeier, Raina, illus. 2010. (ENG., Illus.). 224p. (J). (gr. 3-7). pap. 10.99 *(978-0-545-13206-0(1),* Graphix) Scholastic, Inc.
—Smile. 2010. lib. bdg. 22.10 *(978-0-606-14082-9(4))* Turtleback.
—Smile: a Graphic Novel. Telgemeier, Raina, illus. 2010. (ENG.). 224p. (J). (gr. 3-7). 24.99 *(978-0-545-13205-3(3),* Graphix) Scholastic, Inc.
Thiel, Kristin. True Stories of Teen Soldiers, 1 vol. 2017. (True Teen Stories Ser.). (ENG.). 112p. (YA). (gr. 9-9). 44.50 *(978-1-5026-3164-0(4),* b47c7b3a-ccce-4ba4-a7ae-e212f0331e28); pap. 20.99 *(978-1-5026-3401-6(5),* cb95eec0-6fc6-42bd-8453-6ee3f6caf87b) Cavendish Square Publishing LLC.
—True Teen Stories from Syria: Surviving Civil War, 1 vol. 2018. (Surviving Terror: True Teen Stories from Around the World Ser.). (ENG.). 112p. (YA). (gr. 8-8). 45.93 *(978-1-5026-3541-9(0),* 2eeee78a-55f8-4749-8b4f-bf490be5c502) Cavendish Square Publishing LLC.
Turck, Mary C. Freedom Song: Young Voices & the Struggle for Civil Rights. 2008. (ENG., Illus.). 160p. (J). (gr. 4). pap. 18.95 *(978-1-55652-773-9(X))* Chicago Review Pr., Inc.
Turnbull, Stephanie. Fun with Friends: Style Secrets for Girls. 2014. (Girl Talk Ser.). (ENG., Illus.). 32p. (J). (gr. 4-8). pap. 9.95 *(978-1-77092-203-7(2))* Saunders Bk. Co. CAN. Dist: RiverStream Publishing.
Vink, Amanda. Online Activism: Social Change Through Social Media, 1 vol. 2018. (Hot Topics Ser.). (ENG.). 104p. (gr. 7-7). 41.03 *(978-1-5345-6356-8(3),* 2c771fb2-893f-4926-855b-85f609d31d54, Lucent Pr.) Greenhaven Publishing LLC.
Vizzini, Ned. Teen Angst? Naaah ... 2010. 272p. (YA). (gr. 7-12). 9.99 *(978-0-385-73945-0(1),* Delacorte Pr.) Random Hse. Children's Bks.
von Holleben, Jan & Helms, Antje. Does This Happen to Everyone? A Budding Adult's Guide to Puberty. 2014. (ENG.). 160p. (gr. 5-12). 24.95 *(978-3-89955-521-9(X))* Die Gestalten Verlag DEU. Dist: Ingram Publisher Services.
Wallace, L. Jean & Cypert, Christopher F. What Every Teen Should Know about Texas Law. 2018. (ENG.). 254p. (gr. 9-14). pap. 19.95 *(978-1-4773-1563-7(2))* Univ. of Texas Pr.
Walsch, Neale Donald. Conversations with God for Teens. unabr. ed. 2004. 244p. (J). (gr. 7-18). pap. 38.00 incl. audio *(978-0-8072-0856-4(6),* LYA 368 SP, Listening Library) Random Hse. Audio Publishing Group.
Watkins, Christine, ed. Age of Consent, 1 vol. 2013. (At Issue Ser.). (ENG.). 120p. (gr. 10-12). pap. 28.80 *(978-0-7377-6817-6(7),* 6242ed52-8f1e-4fa5-9260-fa90bdffce85); lib. bdg. 41.03 *(978-0-7377-6816-9(9),* e7003f78-206f-46d6-87c7-fb96fafcfc42) Greenhaven Publishing LLC. (Greenhaven Publishing).
Webber, Diane. The Skin You're In: Staying Healthy Inside & Out. 2008. (Scholastic Choices Ser.). (ENG.). 112p. (J). (gr. 7-18). pap. 8.95 *(978-0-531-20527-3(4),* Watts, Franklin) Scholastic Library Publishing.
Weierbach, Jane & Phillips-Hershey, Elizabeth. Mind over Basketball: Coach Yourself to Handle Stress. Beyl, Charles, illus. 2007. (Coach Yourself to Handle Stress Ser.). 48p. (J). (gr. 3-7). 14.95 *(978-1-4338-0135-8(3),* 4418006); per. 9.95 *(978-1-4338-0136-5(1),* 4418007) American Psychological Assn. (Magination Pr.).
Wheeler, Christine. The Tapping Solution for Teenage Girls: How to Stop Freaking Out & Keep Being Awesome. 2016. 296p. (gr. 5-12). pap. 26.99 *(978-1-4019-4892-4(8))* Hay Hse., Inc.
Whiting, Jim & Li, Shi Yu. My Teenage Life in China. 2017. (Customs & Cultures of the World Ser.). (Illus.). 128p. (J). *(978-1-4222-3902-5(0))* Mason Crest.
Whiting, Jim & Nabil, Muhammad. My Teenage Life in Egypt. 2017. (Illus.). 64p. (J). *(978-1-4222-3899-8(7))* Mason Crest.
Whitney, Brooks. How to Master the School Universe: Homework, Teachers, Tests, Bullies, & Other Ways to Survive the Classroom. Kennedy, Kelly, illus. 2004. 80p. (J). pap. *(978-0-439-57902-5(3))* Scholastic, Inc.
Whittaker, Helen. How Toys Roll. 2012. (Toys & Forces Ser.). 32p. (gr. 1-4). lib. bdg. 27.10 *(978-1-59920-468-0(1))* Black Rabbit Bks.
Wilcox, Christine. Teens & Body Image. 2015. (ENG., Illus.). 80p. (J). lib. bdg. *(978-1-60152-828-5(0))* ReferencePoint Pr., Inc.
—Teens, Nutrition, & Dieting. 2015. (ENG., Illus.). 80p. (J). lib. bdg. *(978-1-60152-834-6(5))* ReferencePoint Pr., Inc.
The Winners. 2005. (YA). 14.95 *(978-0-9661256-4-1(9))* Youth Communication - New York Center.
Wolny, Philip. Abusing Prescription Drugs, 1 vol. 2007. (Incredibly Disgusting Drugs Ser.). (ENG., Illus.). 48p. (YA). (gr. 5-8). lib. bdg. 34.47 *(978-1-4042-1955-7(2),* 5bfb0cb6-77e0-42a2-aff6-94557036e265) Rosen Publishing Group, Inc., The.
Wroble, Lisa A. Dealing with Stress: A How-To Guide, 1 vol. 2011. (Life: a How-To Guide Ser.). (ENG., Illus.). 128p. (gr. 6-7). pap. 13.88 *(978-1-59845-309-6(2),* 63e7ab87-ee86-43c4-9146-1a5cda9c93c1) Enslow Publishing, LLC.
Zarate, Gustavo Azgad. Youth Law: A Practical Guide to Legal Issues That Affect Young Adults. 2nd ed. 2005. (YA). per. 25.00 *(978-0-9763167-9-4(X))* Living Ministry, Inc.

YOUTH—FICTION

A Pastor. The Pearl Box: Containing One Hundred Beautiful Stories for Young People. 2017. (ENG., Illus.). (J). 22.95 *(978-1-374-84170-3(6))*; pap. 12.95 *(978-1-374-84169-7(2))* Capital Communications, Inc.
Abrahams, Peter, et al. Up All Night: A Short Story Collection. 2008. (Illus.). 240p. (J). (gr. 7). lib. bdg. 17.89 *(978-0-06-137077-9(0))*; 16.99 *(978-0-06-137076-2(2))* HarperCollins Pubs. (Geringer, Laura Book).
Adkins, Jan. A Storm Without Rain. 2004. (ENG., Illus.). 179p. (YA). (gr. 7). 14.95 *(978-0-937822-80-7(9))* WoodenBoat Pubns.
Aker, Don. The First Stone. 2004. (ENG.). 304p. (J). mass mkt. 6.50 *(978-0-00-639286-6(5),* Harper Trophy) HarperCollins Pubs.
Alcott, Louisa. A Garland for Girls. Lt. ed. 2005. 376p. pap. *(978-1-84637-049-6(3))* Echo Library.
Alsaid, Adi. Let's Get Lost. 2015. (ENG.). 384p. (YA). pap. 11.99 *(978-0-373-21149-4(X),* Harlequin Teen) Harlequin Enterprises ULC CAN. Dist: HarperCollins Pubs.
Ando, Yuma. Sherlock Bones 1, Vol. 1. Sato, Yuki, illus. 2013. (Sherlock Bones Ser.: 1). 200p. (gr. 8-12). pap. 10.99 *(978-1-61262-444-0(8))* Kodansha America, Inc.
Anonymous. Lucy in the Sky. 2012. (Anonymous Diaries). (ENG.). 288p. (YA). (gr. 9). 19.99 *(978-1-4424-5187-2(4))*; pap. 11.99 *(978-1-4424-5185-8(8))* Simon Pulse. (Simon Pulse).
Aspin, Diana. Ordinary Miracles, 1 vol. 2003. (Northern Lights Young Novels Ser.). (ENG.). 192p. (YA). (gr. 13-16). pap. 4.95 *(978-0-88995-277-5(9),* 9455532e-8f00-4265-870f-e491fc35ff85) Red Deer Pr. CAN. Dist: Firefly Bks., Ltd.
Attema, Martha. A Time to Choose. braille ed. 2003. (J). (gr. 2). spiral bd. *(978-0-616-15262-1(0))* Canadian National Institute for the Blind/Institut National Canadien pour les Aveugles.
Baker, Samuel White. Cast up by the Sea by Sir Samuel W Baker Complete with Ten Illustrations by Huard. 2006. 408p. per. 26.99 *(978-1-4255-4629-8(3))* Michigan Publishing.
Banting, Celia. I only said I couldn't Cope. 2006. (Illus.). 240p. (YA). per. 14.99 *(978-0-9786648-2-4(5))* Wighita Pr.
—I Only Said I Didn't Want You Because I Was Terrified. 2006. (I Only Said Ser.: 4). 240p. (YA). pap. 14.99 *(978-0-9786648-3-1(3))* Wighita Pr.
—I Only Said I Had No Choice. 2006. (I Only Said Ser.). (Illus.). 202p. (YA). pap. 14.99 *(978-0-9786648-0-0(9))* Wighita Pr.
—I only said I was telling the Truth. 2006. 240p. (YA). per. 14.99 *(978-0-9786648-4-8(1))* Wighita Pr.

W
X
Y
Z

—I Only Said Yes So That They'd Like Me. 2006. (Illus.). 224p. (YA). per. 14.99 *(978-0-9786648-1-7(7))* Wighita Pr.

Baratz-Logsted, Lauren. Secrets of My Suburban Life. 2008. (ENG.). 240p. (YA). (gr. 9-18). pap. 7.99 *(978-1-4169-2525-5(2)*, Simon Pulse) Simon Pulse.

Barnard, Sara. A Quiet Kind of Thunder. (ENG.). (YA). (gr. 9). 2019. 416p. pap. 12.99 *(978-1-5344-0242-3(X))* 2018. 400p. 19.99 *(978-1-5344-0241-6(1))* Simon Pulse. (Simon Pulse).

Barnum, P. T. Dick Broadhead: A Story of Perilous Adve. 2006. pap. 30.95 *(978-1-4286-1959-3(3))* Kessinger Publishing, LLC.

Batchelor, Rhonda. She Loves You. 2008. (ENG.). 136p. (YA). (gr. 7-8). pap. 11.99 *(978-1-55002-789-1(1))* Dundurn Pr. CAN. Dist: Publishers Group West (PGW).

Batista, Joaquin. Westward Eden. 2003. 196p. (YA). 28.95 *(978-1-59113-371-1(8))*; pap. 15.95 *(978-1-59113-316-2(5))* Booklocker.com, Inc.

Beck, B. E. Who Are You, Trudy Herman? A Novel. 2018. (ENG.). 294p. (YA). pap. 16.95 *(978-1-63152-377-9(5))* She Writes Pr.

Beechwood, Beth, adapted by. Hannah Montana - Keeping Secrets. 2006. (Hannah Montana Ser.). (Illus.). 124p. (J). (gr. 3-7). 12.65 *(978-0-7569-8317-8(7))* Perfection Learning Corp.

Beede, John. Climb On! Success Strategies for Teens. 2005. (YA). per. 14.95 *(978-0-9765697-0-1(1))* Sierra Nevada Publishing Hse.

Birle, Pete. Locals Only. 2013. (Av2 Audio Chapter Bks.). (ENG.). 121p. (J). 27.13 *(978-1-62127-985-3(5)*, AV2 by Weigl) Weigl Pubs., Inc.

Black, Jenna. Replica. 2013. (Replica Ser.: 1). (ENG.). 368p. (YA). (gr. 8-12). pap. 18.99 *(978-0-7653-3371-1(6)*, 900086439, Tor Teen) Doherty, Tom Assocs., LLC.

Blume, Judy. Are You There God? It's Me, Margaret. 149p. (J). (gr. 4-6). pap. 3.50 *(978-0-8072-1421-3(3))*; (YA). (gr. 5-18). pap. 4.99 *(978-0-8072-1508-1(2))* Random Hse. Audio Publishing Group. (Listening Library).

Boggess, Eileen. Mia the Meek. 2006. (ENG.). 166p. (J). (gr. 6-9). per. 14.95 *(978-1-890862-47-3(9)*, 19189455-bd03-4ce0-bb2b-b2fc6ec8ccd7) Bancroft Pr.

Bolden-Thompson, Angela. When Company Comes. 2007. 254p. pap. 19.99 *(978-0-615-14774-1(7))* Thompson, Angela Bolden.

Bond, Gwenda. Triple Threat. (Lois Lane Ser.). (ENG.). 360p. (YA). (gr. 9-12). 2018. pap. 9.95 *(978-1-63079-084-4(2)*, 134777) 2017. 16.95 *(978-1-63079-082-0(6)*, 134776) Capstone. (Switch Pr.).

Bone, Ian. Fat Boy Saves World. 2011. (ENG.). 240p. (YA). (gr. 9). pap. 11.99 *(978-1-4424-3105-8(9)*, Simon Pulse) Simon Pulse.

Booth, Coe. Bronxwood. 2013. (ENG.). 336p. (YA). (gr. 9). pap. 12.99 *(978-0-439-92535-8(5)*, PUSH) Scholastic, Inc.

Bossley, Michele Martin. Tampered, 1 vol. 2013. (Orca Currents Ser.). (ENG.). 136p. (J). (gr. 4-7). pap. 9.95 *(978-1-4598-0356-5(6))* Orca Bk. Pubs. USA.

Boudreau, Bobby A. Inspirational Stories for Spiritual Youth. 2010. 124p. 29.99 *(978-1-4490-8105-8(3))*; pap. 18.99 *(978-1-4490-8106-5(1))* AuthorHouse.

Bowen, L. A. One Too Many Lies, 1 vol. 2018. (YA Verse Ser.). (ENG.). 200p. (YA). (gr. 3-4). 25.80 *(978-1-5383-8250-9(4)*, b5978d52-c5e7-4ca0-902e-3af9c871b80c); pap. 16.35 *(978-1-5383-8249-3(0)*, 602014c4-3603-4eb4-a045-851fb6bfd803) Enslow Publishing, LLC.

Bremer, Terry. Dandylion: The Most Misunderstood Flower. Pierce, M. Deborah, illus. 2003. 32p. (J). lib. bdg. 15.00 *(978-1-931646-90-1(2))* Beaver's Pond Pr., Inc.

Brenna, Beverley. Something to Hang on To. 2009. (ENG.). 176p. (J). pap. 12.95 *(978-1-897235-57-7(7))* Thistledown Pr., Ltd. CAN. Dist: Univ. of Toronto Pr.

Brian, Kate, pseud. Invitation Only. 2009. (Private Ser.: No. 2). (ENG.). 272p. (YA). pap. 9.99 *(978-1-4169-9947-8(7)*, Simon & Schuster Bks. For Young Readers) Simon & Schuster Bks. For Young Readers.

Brody, Jessica. Boys of Summer. 2016. (ENG., Illus.). 352p. (J). (gr. 9). 17.99 *(978-1-4814-6349-2(7)*, Simon Pulse) Simon Pulse.

Burk, Josh. The Summer of Saint Nick. 2007. (ENG.). 152p. (YA). per. 12.95 *(978-0-9768042-2-0(0))* Maven Of Memory Publishing.

Burkhart, Jessica. Jealousy. 2013. (Canterwood Crest Ser.: 17). (ENG.). 208p. (J). (gr. 4-7). pap. 7.99 *(978-1-4424-3657-2(3)*, Aladdin) Simon & Schuster Children's Publishing.

Burns, T. R. The Bad Apple. 2013. (Merits of Mischief Ser.: 1). (ENG.). 368p. (J). (gr. 3-7). pap. 7.99 *(978-1-4424-4030-2(9)*, Aladdin) Simon & Schuster Children's Publishing.

Cabot, Meg. Code Name Cassandra. 2007. (1-800-Where-R-You Ser.: No. 2). (ENG., Illus.). 272p. (YA). (gr. 9-12). mass mkt. 6.99 *(978-1-4169-2704-4(2)*, Simon Pulse) Simon Pulse.

Carey, Anna. Deadfall. 2015. 256p. (J). pap. *(978-0-06-242788-5(1))* HarperCollins Pubs.

Carlson, Melody. Bad Connection. 2006. (Secret Life of Samantha Mcgregor Ser.: 1). (ENG.). 256p. (J). (gr. 7-12). per. 12.99 *(978-1-59052-692-7(9)*, Multnomah) Crown Publishing Group, The.

—Meant to Be: Kim: Book 2. 2005. (Diary of a Teenage Girl Ser.: 11). (ENG.). 272p. (J). (gr. 7-7). pap. 15.99 *(978-1-59052-322-3(9)*, Multnomah Bks.) Crown Publishing Group, The.

Carter, Brooke. Learning Seventeen, 1 vol. 2018. (Orca Soundings Ser.). (ENG.). 144p. (YA). (gr. 8-12). pap. 9.95 *(978-1-4598-1553-7(X))* Orca Bk. Pubs. USA.

Cartwheel: A Sequel to Double Eagle. 2013. (ENG.). 252p. (YA). 17.00 *(978-0-9844460-3-2(6))* Bucking Horse Bks.

Castlemon, Harry. No Moss; or, the Career of a Rolling Stone, by Harry Castlemon [Pseud.]. 2006. 328p. per. 23.99 *(978-1-4255-3290-1(X))* Michigan Publishing.

Chan, Queenie. The Dreaming Collection. 2010. (ENG., Illus.). 576p. pap. 19.99 *(978-1-4278-1871-3(1))* TOKYOPOP, Inc.

Chandler, Elizabeth. Dark Secrets 2 No. 2: No Time to Die; the Deep End of Fear. 2010. (Dark Secrets Ser.: 2). (ENG.). 624p. (YA). (gr. 7). pap. 9.99 *(978-1-4169-9462-6(9)*, Simon Pulse) Simon Pulse.

Chapman, Patricia. Beth. 2011. 20p. pap. 16.95 *(978-1-4626-1060-0(9))* America Star Bks.

Chase, Barbara. The Silent Killer. 2005. (ENG.). 121p. pap. 9.95 *(978-976-637-179-1(2)*, P474185) Randle, Ian Pubs. JAM. Dist: Eurospan Group, The.

Chbosky, Stephen & Perez-Sauquillo, Vanesa. Las Ventajas de Ser Invisible. 2013. (SPA.). 272p. (YA). (gr. 7). pap. 15.99 *(978-1-4767-3245-9(0)*, MTV Bks.) MTV Books.

Choyce, Lesley. Plank's Law, 1 vol. 2017. (ENG.). 192p. (YA). (gr. 8-12). pap. 14.95 *(978-1-4598-1249-9(2))* Orca Bk. Pubs. USA.

Clark, K. M. Beautiful Disaster. 2013. 106p. 24.99 *(978-1-4797-6506-5(6))*; pap. 15.99 *(978-1-4797-6505-8(8))* Xlibris Corp.

Clarke, Judith. My Lovely Frankie. 2018. (ENG.). 224p. (YA). (gr. 7). pap. 12.99 *(978-1-76029-633-9(3))* Allen & Unwin AUS. Dist: Independent Pubs. Group.

Coates-Smith, Renee. Bobby's Secret Is Out. 2007. (Illus.). 43p. (J). 12.95 *(978-0-615-14325-5(3))* Imani Productions.

Condon, Bill. No Worries. 2005. 216p. (YA). pap. *(978-0-7022-3491-0(5))* Univ. of Queensland Pr.

Connor, Naomi. I Am. 2011. 52p. pap. 22.49 *(978-1-4634-3673-5(4))* AuthorHouse.

Cormier, Robert. The Chocolate War. 191p. (YA). (gr. 7-18). pap. 4.99 *(978-0-8072-1428-2(0)*, Listening Library) Random Hse. Audio Publishing Group.

—The Chocolate War. 30th ed. 2004. (Chocolate War Ser.: 1). (ENG.). 272p. (YA). (gr. 7-12). pap. 10.99 *(978-0-375-82987-1(3)*, Ember) Random Hse. Children's Bks.

Cotugno, Katie. Top Ten. 2017. 357p. (J). *(978-0-06-269403-4(0)*, Balzer & Bray) HarperCollins Pubs.

—99 Days. 2019. (ENG.). 400p. (YA). (gr. 8). pap. 11.99 *(978-0-06-221639-7(2)*, Balzer & Bray) HarperCollins Pubs.

Crane, Cheri J. Moment of Truth: A Novel. 2005. 238p. (YA). *(978-1-59156-727-1(0))* Covenant Communications.

Crouch, Katie. The White Glove War. 2013. (Magnolia League Ser.: 2). (ENG.). 320p. (YA). (gr. 10-17). pap. 17.99 *(978-0-316-18749-7(6)*, Poppy) Little, Brown Bks. for Young Readers.

Crutcher, Chris. Losers Bracket. (ENG.). 256p. (YA). (gr. 9). 2019. pap. 10.99 *(978-0-06-222008-0(X))* 2018. 17.99 *(978-0-06-222006-6(3))* HarperCollins Pubs. (Greenwillow Bks.).

Dakers, Diane. Bad Business, 1 vol. 2015. (Orca Currents Ser.). (ENG.). 128p. (J). (gr. 4-7). pap. 9.95 *(978-1-4598-0969-7(6))* Orca Bk. Pubs. USA.

Dance, Jennifer. Hawk. 2016. (ENG.). 264p. (YA). pap. 12.99 *(978-1-4597-3184-4(0))* Dundurn Pr. CAN. Dist: Publishers Group West (PGW).

Darling, Angela. Lauren's Beach Crush. 2013. (Crush Ser.: 1). (ENG., Illus.). 176p. (J). (gr. 3-7). 15.99 *(978-1-4424-8038-4(6))*; pap. 5.99 *(978-1-4424-8036-0(X))* Simon Spotlight. (Simon Spotlight).

De Los Santos, Elizabeth G. The Secret House. 2011. 18p. pap. 16.95 *(978-1-4626-4409-4(0))* America Star Bks.

De Palma, Toni. The Devil's Triangle. 2013. 216p. pap. 14.99 *(978-1-939173-03-4(5))* Crescent Moon Pr.

Delaney, Joseph. The Last Apprentice: Slither (Book 11), Bk. 11. 2014. (Last Apprentice Ser.). (ENG.). 432p. (YA). (gr. 8). pap. 11.99 *(978-0-06-219235-6(3)*, Greenwillow Bks.) HarperCollins Pubs.

Denis, Erik & LeBlanc, Natalie. The Bubble. 2005. 16p. 10.10 *(978-1-4116-6424-1(8))* Lulu Pr., Inc.

Devine, Eric. Look Past. 2016. (ENG.). 288p. (YA). (gr. 8-17). 17.99 *(978-0-7624-5921-6(2)*, Running Pr. Kids) Running Pr.

DeVita, James. The Silenced. 2007. 512p. (J). (gr. 8-12). lib. bdg. 18.89 *(978-0-06-078464-5(4)*, HarperTeen) HarperCollins Pubs.

DeVita, James & Devita, James. The Silenced. 2007. (ENG.). 368p. (J). (gr. 8-12). 17.99 *(978-0-06-078462-1(8)*, HarperTeen) HarperCollins Pubs.

Dower, Laura. On the Case. 2004. 170p. (J). lib. bdg. 16.92 *(978-1-4242-0648-3(0))* Fitzgerald Bks.

Doyle, Brian. Angel Square, 1 vol. 2nd ed. 2003. (ENG.). 144p. (J). (gr. 4-6). pap. 9.95 *(978-0-88899-609-1(8))* Groundwood Bks. CAN. Dist: Publishers Group West (PGW).

—Covered Bridge. Date not set. (J). (gr. 4-6). pap. *(978-0-88899-190-4(8))* Groundwood Bks. CAN. Dist: Publishers Group West (PGW).

—Covered Bridge, 1 vol. 2004. (ENG., Illus.). 128p. (J). (gr. 4-7). pap. 6.95 *(978-0-88899-603-9(9))* Groundwood Bks. CAN. Dist: Publishers Group West (PGW).

—Up to Low, 1 vol. 3rd ed. 2004. (ENG.). 112p. (J). (gr. 6-8). pap. 11.99 *(978-0-88899-622-0(5))* Groundwood Bks. CAN. Dist: Publishers Group West (PGW).

—You Can Pick Me up at Peggy's Cove. Date not set. (J). (gr. 4-6). reprint ed. pap. 5.95 *(978-0-88899-231-4(9))* Groundwood Bks. CAN. Dist: Publishers Group West (PGW).

Drown, Merle. Lighting the World. 2015. (ENG.). 278p. pap. 18.00 *(978-0-9898971-4-3(1))* Whitepoint Pr.

Duval, Alex. Vampire Beach 2: Ritual; Legacy. 2011. (Vampire Beach Ser.: 2). (ENG.). 448p. (YA). (gr. 9). pap. 9.99 *(978-1-4424-0694-0(1)*, Simon Pulse) Simon Pulse.

Dwinell, Kim. Surfside Girls: the Mystery at the Old Rancho. 2019. (Surfside Girls Ser.: 2). (Illus.). 208p. (J). (gr. 4-7). pap. 14.99 *(978-1-60309-447-4(4))* Top Shelf Productions.

Eaton, Anthony. Fireshadow. 2004. 320p. (YA). *(978-0-7022-3381-4(1))* Univ. of Queensland Pr.

Echo of Hooves. 2005. (J). *(978-1-933343-10-5(9)*, PONY) Stabenfeldt Inc.

Echols, Jennifer & Hapka, Catherine. Winter's Kiss: The Ex Games; the Twelve Dates of Christmas. 2012. (ENG.). 496p. (YA). (gr. 7). pap. 9.99 *(978-1-4424-5040-0(1)*, Simon Pulse) Simon Pulse.

Edwards, Hazel. Stalker. 2003. 176p. pap. *(978-0-7344-0103-8(5)*, Lothian Children's Bks.) Hachette Australia.

Edwards, Mark. The Gang Book 1 the Saint's Bones. 2004. (YA). per. 10.95 *(978-0-9755704-0-1(4))* New Classics Pr.

Ellis, Deborah. No Safe Place. 2013. 224p. pap. *(978-1-4596-6447-0(7))* ReadHowYouWant.com, Ltd.

Elwell, Sharon. Caught in the Middle: Reflections of a Middle School Teacher. 2007. 112p. per. 10.95 *(978-1-4327-0621-0(7))* Outskirts Pr., Inc.

Emery, Airin. Dance Divas: The Dance Series (Book #2) 2013. 128p. pap. *(978-1-927794-01-2(3))* Lechner Syndications.

—Tap In: The Dance Series (Book #3) 2013. 118p. pap. *(978-1-927794-02-9(1))* Lechner Syndications.

Evangelista, Kate. No Second Chances. 2017. (Dodge Cove Trilogy Ser.: 3). (ENG.). 224p. (YA). pap. 18.99 *(978-1-250-10067-2(4)*, 900162482) Feiwel & Friends.

Evans, Mari. I'm Late: The Story of Laneese & Moonlight & Alisha Who Didn't Have Anyone of Her Own. 2006. (Illus.). 86p. (J). (gr. 7-18). 14.95 *(978-1-933491-00-4(0))* Just Us Bks., Inc.

Evans, Richard Paul. Michael Vey: The Prisoner of Cell 25. (Michael Vey Ser.: 1). (ENG., Illus.). (YA). (gr. 7). 2012. 352p. pap. 12.99 *(978-1-4424-6812-2(2))* 2011. 336p. 19.99 *(978-1-4516-5650-3(5))* Simon Pulse/Mercury Ink. (Simon Pulse/Mercury Ink).

—Michael Vey 6: Fall of Hades. (Michael Vey Ser.: 6). (ENG., Illus.). 352p. (YA). (gr. 7). 2017. pap. 12.99 *(978-1-4814-6983-8(5))* 2016. 19.99 *(978-1-4814-6982-1(7))* Simon Pulse/Mercury Ink. (Simon Pulse/Mercury Ink).

—Michael Vey 7: The Final Spark. 2017. (Michael Vey Ser.: 7). (ENG., Illus.). 336p. (YA). (gr. 7). 19.99 *(978-1-4814-9703-9(0)*, Simon Pulse/Mercury Ink) Simon Pulse/Mercury Ink.

Forney, Lane. The Super Power Teens 2: A Blast from the Past. 2009. (ENG.). 137p. pap. 14.99 *(978-0-557-09707-4(X))* Lulu Pr., Inc.

Francis, Brian. Fruit: A Novel about a Boy & His Nipples. 2004. (ENG., Illus.). 278p. pap. 18.95 *(978-1-55022-620-1(7)*, a3500f08-fb52-4324-8d46-72c04800704d) ECW Pr. CAN. Dist: Baker & Taylor Publisher Services (BTPS).

Freeman, Lisa. Honey Girl. 2015. 288p. (J). (gr. 6-6). 16.99 *(978-1-63220-425-7(8)*, Sky Pony Pr.) Skyhorse Publishing Co., Inc.

Gaetz, Dayle Campbell. No Problem. 2004. (Orca Soundings Ser.). 87p. 19.95 *(978-0-7569-4317-2(5))* Perfection Learning Corp.

Gardam, Jane. Bilgewater. 2016. (ENG.). 208p. pap. 17.00 *(978-1-60945-331-2(X))* Europa Editions, Inc.

Garisch, Dawn. Babyshoes. 2004. (ENG.). 288p. (J). pap. 9.99 *(978-0-689-83778-4(X))* Simon & Schuster, Ltd. GBR. Dist: Simon & Schuster, Inc.

Garner, Paula. Phantom Limbs. 2016. 368p. (YA). (gr. 9). 16.99 *(978-0-7636-8205-7(5))* Candlewick Pr.

Gliori, Debi. No Matter What Padded Board Book. Gliori, Debi, illus. 2017. (ENG., Illus.). 24p. (J). (— 1). bds. 8.99 *(978-0-544-91584-8(4)*, 1655572, Clarion Bks.) HarperCollins Pubs.

Godbersen, Anna. Rumors. 2008. (Luxe Ser.: No. 2). (YA). (gr. 9-12). (ENG.). 304p. 17.99 *(978-0-06-134569-2(5))*; 423p. lib. bdg. 18.89 *(978-0-06-134570-8(9))* HarperCollins Pubs. (HarperTeen).

Goobie, Beth. Who Owns Kelly Paddik? 2004. (Orca Soundings Ser.). 89p. 19.95 *(978-0-7569-4358-5(2))* Perfection Learning Corp.

Gottesfeld, Jeff. Xo Ronette. 2013. (Campus Confessions Ser.). (ENG.). 160p. (YA). (gr. 9-12). pap. 11.95 *(978-1-62250-701-6(0))* Saddleback Educational Publishing, Inc.

Gough, Erin. Get It Together, Delilah! (Young Adult Novels for Teens, Books about Female Friendship, Funny Books) 2017. (ENG., Illus.). 336p. (YA). 16.99 *(978-1-4521-5187-8(3))* Chronicle Bks. LLC.

Graves, Judith. Infiltrate, 1 vol. 2017. (Orca Soundings Ser.: 5). (ENG.). 160p. (YA). (gr. 8-12). pap. 9.95 *(978-1-4598-0723-5(5))* Orca Bk. Pubs. USA.

—Second Skin. 2011. 280p. (J). pap. 16.99 *(978-1-61603-006-3(2))* Leap Bks.

—Under My Skin. Cox, Val, illus. 2010. 328p. (YA). (gr. 8-18). pap. 16.99 *(978-1-61603-000-1(3))* Leap Bks.

Gray, Amy. How to Be a Vampire: A Fangs-On Guide for the Newly Undead. Erwert, Scott, illus. 2009. (ENG.). 144p. (YA). (gr. 7-18). 14.99 *(978-0-7636-4915-9(5))* Candlewick Pr.

Gray, Keith. The Chain. 2013. (ENG.). 80p. (YA). (gr. 6-12). pap. 6.95 *(978-1-78112-173-3(7))*; lib. bdg. 22.60 *(978-1-78112-172-6(9))* Lerner Publishing Group.

Griffin, Paul. Adrift. 2015. 228p. (YA). *(978-0-545-87195-2(6)*, Scholastic Pr.) Scholastic, Inc.

Griffiths, Emma. After I Wake. 2016. (ENG., Illus.). (J). 24.99 *(978-1-63477-931-9(2)*, Harmony Ink Pr.) Dreamspinner Pr.

Groth, Darren. Are You Seeing Me?, 1 vol. 2015. (ENG., Illus.). 288p. (YA). (gr. 8-12). 19.95 *(978-1-4598-1079-2(1))* Orca Bk. Pubs. USA.

Hall, S.C. Turns of Fortune & Other Tales. 2007. (ENG.). 116p. per. *(978-1-4065-1586-2(8))* Dodo Pr.

Hand, Cynthia. Unearthly. 2011. (Unearthly Ser.: 1). (ENG.). 464p. (YA). (gr. 8). pap. 9.99 *(978-0-06-199617-7(3)*, HarperTeen) HarperCollins Pubs.

Hardy, Melissa. The Geomancer's Compass. 2012. 256p. (YA). (gr. 7). 17.95 *(978-1-77049-292-9(5)*, Tundra Bks.) Tundra Bks. CAN. Dist: Penguin Random Hse. LLC.

Harley, Rex. Baby, Now That I've Found You. 2003. (ENG.). 200p. pap. 12.95 *(978-1-84323-107-3(7))* Beekman Bks., Inc.

Harris, Patrick. Where the Day Takes You volume One. 2010. 172p. pap. 10.00 *(978-0-557-04401-6(4))* Lulu Pr., Inc.

Harrop, Isobel. The Isobel Journal, 1 vol. 2014. (ENG.). 208p. (YA). (gr. 10-12). 16.95 *(978-1-63079-003-5(6)*, 126769, Switch Pr.) Capstone.

Hasiuk, Brenda. Where the Rocks Say Your Name. 2006. (ENG.). 296p. per. 19.95 *(978-1-897235-11-9(9))* Thistledown Pr., Ltd. CAN. Dist: Univ. of Toronto Pr.

Heneghan, James & Charles, Norma. Bank Job, 1 vol. 2009. (ENG.). 176p. (J). (gr. 4-7). pap. 14.95 *(978-1-55143-855-9(0))* Orca Bk. Pubs. USA.

Henson, S. F. Devils Within. 2017. (ENG.). 404p. (J). (gr. 8-8). 17.99 *(978-1-5107-1456-4(1)*, Sky Pony Pr.) Skyhorse Publishing Co., Inc.

Herron, Edward A. The Return of the Alaskan: Mailboat in the Outpost. Langley, Gene, illus. 2011. 190p. 42.95 *(978-1-258-09093-7(7))* Literary Licensing, LLC.

Highley, Kendra C. Defying Gravity. 2016. (ENG., Illus.). 210p. (J). pap. 14.99 *(978-1-68281-253-2(7))* Entangled Publishing, LLC.

Hill, David. Coming Back. 2007. (ENG.). 200p. (gr. 10-17). per. 16.99 *(978-0-9542330-2-0(6))* Aurora Metro Pubns. Ltd. GBR. Dist: Publishers Group West (PGW).

Hinton, Susan E. LA LEY DE LA CALLE. 2nd ed. 2003. (SPA., Illus.). 128p. (YA). (gr. 8-12). pap. 13.95 *(978-84-204-4858-9(3))* Santillana USA Publishing Co., Inc.

Hodgson, Miriam. Love from Dad: Stories about Fathers & Daughters. (ENG.). 160p. (J). pap. 8.99 *(978-0-7497-4330-7(1))* Farshore GBR. Dist: Trafalgar Square Publishing.

Hogan, Edward. The Messengers. 2015. (ENG.). 224p. (YA). (gr. 9). 16.99 *(978-0-7636-7112-9(6))* Candlewick Pr.

Hook. Wrinkled Crinkled Grapes: A Purple Monster. 2007. 52p. per. 8.95 *(978-0-595-42310-1(8))* iUniverse, Inc.

Hope, Laura Lee. Outdoor Girls in Florida. 2006. 26.95 *(978-1-4218-2982-1(7))*; pap. 11.95 *(978-1-4218-3082-7(5))* 1st World Publishing, Inc.

—Outdoor Girls in the Saddle. 2006. 26.95 *(978-1-4218-2983-8(5))*; pap. 11.95 *(978-1-4218-3083-4(3))* 1st World Publishing, Inc.

Hopkins, Cathy. Mates, Dates, & Diamond Destiny. 2011. (Mates, Dates Ser.). (ENG.). 272p. (YA). (gr. 7). pap. 12.99 *(978-1-4424-3082-2(6)*, Simon Pulse) Simon Pulse.

Hopkins, Ellen. Crank. 2013. lib. bdg. 24.50 *(978-0-606-35118-8(3))* Turtleback.

Howe, Tina Field. Alysa of the Fields: Book One in the Tellings of Xunar-kun. 2006. (Illus.). 320p. (YA). pap. 16.95 *(978-0-9768585-1-5(7)*, 002) Howe, Tina Field.

Ice Water Press Staff. Secrets of the Deep. 2010. (J). pap. *(978-1-921639-95-1(4))* Ripley Entertainment, Inc.

Ireland, Justina. Devils' Pass, 6 vols. Champion, Tyler, illus. 2018. (Devils' Pass Ser.). (ENG.). 128p. (J). (gr. 4-8). 159.90 *(978-1-4965-6528-0(2)*, 28445, Stone Arch Bks.) Capstone.

Jackson, Melanie. Medusa's Scream, 1 vol. 2017. (Orca Currents Ser.). (ENG.). 144p. (J). (gr. 4-7). pap. 9.95 *(978-1-4598-1441-7(X))* Orca Bk. Pubs. USA.

Jacobs, Evan. Varsity 170, 1 vol., Bk. 10. 2015. (Gravel Road Ser.). (ENG.). 184p. (YA). (gr. 9-12). pap. 11.95 *(978-1-62250-889-1(0))* Saddleback Educational Publishing, Inc.

Johnson, Angela. All This & Heaven Too: Heaven; the First Part Last; Sweet, Hereafter. 2013. (ENG., Illus.). 400p. (YA). (gr. 7). pap. 11.99 *(978-1-4424-8719-2(4)*, Simon & Schuster Bks. For Young Readers) Simon & Schuster Bks. For Young Readers.

Johnston, Jeffry W. Fragments. 2007. (ENG.). 208p. (YA). (gr. 7). per. 9.99 *(978-1-4169-2486-9(8)*, Simon Pulse) Simon Pulse.

Jones, Don. When the Firewood Comes. 2009. 86p. pap. 19.95 *(978-1-4489-9667-4(8))* America Star Bks.

Jones, Frewin. The Faerie Path #3: the Seventh Daughter. 2009. (Faerie Path Ser.: 3). (ENG.). 352p. (YA). (gr. 8). pap. 9.99 *(978-0-06-087110-9(5)*, HarperTeen) HarperCollins Pubs.

Jones, Kari. At the Edge of the World, 1 vol. 2016. (ENG.). 256p. (YA). (gr. 8-12). pap. 14.95 *(978-1-4598-1062-4(7))* Orca Bk. Pubs. USA.

—Shimmy, 1 vol. 2015. (Orca Limelights Ser.). (ENG.). 144p. (J). (gr. 4-7). pap. 9.95 *(978-1-4598-0764-8(2))* Orca Bk. Pubs. USA.

Judge, Emma. Ink Stained Hands. 2010. (ENG.). 96p. pap. *(978-1-907629-12-9(2))* ShieldCrest.

Karasyov, Carrie & Kargman, Jill. Jet Set. 2008. 256p. (J). (gr. 7-18). 16.99 *(978-0-06-143177-7(X))* HarperCollins Pubs.

Karp, Ruby. Earth Hates Me: True Confessions from a Teenage Girl. 2017. (ENG., Illus.). 288p. (YA). (gr. 8-17). 15.99 *(978-0-7624-6260-5(4)*, Running Pr. Kids) Running Pr.

Kaye, Marilyn. Speak No Evil, 6. 2011. (Gifted Ser.). (ENG.). 208p. (YA). (gr. 6-8). pap. 22.44 *(978-0-7534-6564-6(7)*, 9780753465646) Kingfisher Publications, plc GBR. Dist: Children's Plus, Inc.

Keane, Danni. No Big Deal. 2016. (ENG., Illus.). (J). 24.99 *(978-1-63533-051-9(3)*, Harmony Ink Pr.) Dreamspinner Pr.

Kearns, Ann. Dell's Discovery. 2006. 108p. (YA). per. 9.95 *(978-0-9710696-6-4(2))* Jorlan Publishing, Inc.

Kellogg, Elijah. The Young Shipbuilders of Elm Island by Rev Elijah Kellogg. 2006. 316p. per. 23.99 *(978-1-4255-3063-1(X))* Michigan Publishing.

Keswick, Kitty. Freaksville. Cox, Val, illus. 2010. 328p. (YA). (gr. 8-12). pap. 16.99 *(978-1-61603-001-8(1))* Leap Bks.

Kijinski, Paul. Camp Limestone. 2006. (Illus.). 104p. (YA). per. 7.99 *(978-1-59958-016-6(0))* Journey Stone Creations, LLC.

King, Katina. Ride Wit' Me: A Young Adult Urban Tale. 2006. 144p. (J). per. 12.00 *(978-0-9724003-8-1(9))* Power Play Media.

Kiyuduki, Satoko, creator. GA: Geijutsuka Art Design Class, Vol. 7, Vol. 7. 2016. (GA: Geijutsuka Art Design Class Ser.: 7). (ENG., Illus.). 128p. (J). (gr. 8-17). pap. 17.00 *(978-0-316-54536-5(8))* Yen Pr. LLC.

Komorn, Julie, adapted by. Out of the Dark. 2004. (W. I. T. C. H. Ser.: Bk. 8). (Illus.). 128p. (J). lib. bdg. 16.92 *(978-1-4242-0789-3(4))* Fitzgerald Bks.

Komorn, Julie & Lenhard, Elizabeth, adapted by. The Light of Meridian. 2004. (W. I. T. C. H. Ser.: Bk. 7). (Illus.). 144p. (J). lib. bdg. 16.92 *(978-1-4242-0794-7(0))* Fitzgerald Bks.

Kopple, Deborah, ed. Heads in the Ground: Short Stories by Norwalk High School Honor's English Students. 2008. 188p. pap. 13.95 *(978-0-595-50775-7(1))* iUniverse, Inc.

Lake, Nick. Satellite. (ENG.). 464p. (YA). (gr. 7). 2019. pap. 10.99 *(978-1-5247-1356-0(2)*, Ember) 2017. 17.99 *(978-1-5247-1353-9(8)*, Knopf Bks. for Young Readers) Random Hse. Children's Bks.

Langston, Laura. Hot New Thing, 1 vol. 2014. (Orca Limelights Ser.). (ENG.). 136p. (J). (gr. 4-7). pap. 9.95 *(978-1-4598-0431-9(7))* Orca Bk. Pubs. USA.

Laughton, Geoff. Under the Stars. (ENG., Illus.). 2016. (J). 24.99 *(978-1-63477-986-9(X))* 2014. 180p. (YA). pap. 14.99 *(978-1-63216-306-6(3))* Dreamspinner Pr. (Harmony Ink Pr.).

Laybourne, Emmy. Monument 14. 2013. (Monument 14 Ser.: 1). (ENG., Illus.). 352p. (YA). (gr. 8-13). pap. 11.99 *(978-1-250-02738-2(1)*, 900098310) Square Fish.

—Sky on Fire. 2013. (Monument 14 Ser.: Bk. 2). (ENG.). vi, 217p. (YA). *(978-1-4449-1765-9(X))* Feiwel & Friends.

Lee, J. A. The Trials of Edward Finlay. 2010. 223p. pap. 15.99 *(978-0-557-36757-3(3))* Lulu Pr., Inc.

enhard, Elizabeth. A Bridge Between Worlds. 2004. (W. I. T. C. H. Ser.: Bk. 10). 158p. (J). lib. bdg. 16.92 *(978-1-4242-0796-1(7))* Fitzgerald Bks.
The Disappearance. (W. I. T. C. H. Ser.: Bk. 2). 158p. (J). lib. bdg. 16.92 *(978-1-4242-0799-2(1))* Fitzgerald Bks.
Finding Meridian. 2004. (W. I. T. C. H. Ser.: Bk. 3). 158p. (J). lib. bdg. 16.92 *(978-1-4242-0801-2(7))* Fitzgerald Bks.
Power of Five. 2004. 158p. (J). lib. bdg. 16.92 *(978-1-4242-0795-4(9))* Fitzgerald Bks.
enhard, Elizabeth, adapted by. The Disappearance. 2004. (W. I. T. C. H. Ser.). (Illus.). 144p. (J). 12.65 *(978-0-7569-4620-3(4))* Perfection Learning Corp.
-The Return of a Queen. 2004. (W. I. T. C. H. Ser.: Bk. 12). 152p. (J). lib. bdg. 16.92 *(978-1-4242-0797-8(5))* Fitzgerald Bks.
eno, Katrina. Everything All at Once. 2017. (ENG.). 368p. (YA). (gr. 8). 17.99 *(978-0-06-249309-5(4)*, HarperTeen) HarperCollins Pubs.
evithan, David. Boy Meets Boy. 2005. (ENG.). 240p. (YA). (gr. 7-12). reprint ed. per. 11.99 *(978-0-375-83299-4(8)*, Ember) Random Hse. Children's Bks.
.ewis, Linda. All for the Love of That Boy. 2007. (ENG.). 224p. (YA). (gr. 7). pap. 12.95 *(978-1-4169-6142-0(9)*, Simon Pulse) Simon Pulse.
.eznoff, Glenda. Heartache & Other Natural Shocks. 2015. (Illus.). 384p. (YA). (gr. 9). 19.99 *(978-1-77049-836-5(2)*, Tundra Bks.) Tundra Bks. CAN. Dist: Penguin Random Hse. LLC.
.indquist, N. J. A Friend in Need. 2016. (Circle of Friends Ser.: Vol. 3). (ENG., Illus.). (YA). pap. *(978-1-927692-06-6(7))* That's Life! Communications.
—More Than a Friend. 2016. (Circle of Friends Ser.: Vol. 4). (ENG., Illus.). (YA). pap. *(978-1-927692-07-3(5))* That's Life! Communications.
—With Friends Like These. 2016. (Circle of Friends Ser.: Vol. 2). (ENG., Illus.). (YA). pap. *(978-1-927692-05-9(9))* That's Life! Communications.
Litrel, Suzanne M. Jackie Tempo & the Emperor's Seal. 2007. 172p. (YA). per. 13.95 *(978-0-595-46822-5(5))* iUniverse, Inc.
Lobdell, Scott. The Opposite Numbers. Rendon, Daniel et al, illus. 2006. 111p. (J). *(978-1-4156-9815-0(5))* Papercutz.
Lohans, Alison. Laws of Emotion. 2006. (ENG.). 207p. mass mkt. 9.95 *(978-1-895449-07-5(3))* Thistledown Pr., Ltd. CAN. Dist: Univ. of Toronto Pr.
Lovelace, Eloise. I Was a Boy Just Like You. 2011. 36p. pap. 15.14 *(978-1-4634-4378-8(1))* AuthorHouse.
Lynch, Chris. I Pledge Allegiance. 2011. (Vietnam Ser.: 1). (ENG.). 192p. (J). (gr. 5-9). 16.99 *(978-0-545-27029-8(4)*, Scholastic Pr.) Scholastic, Inc.
Maberry, Jonathan. Broken Lands. 2018. (Broken Lands Ser.: 1). (ENG., Illus.). 544p. (YA). (gr. 9). 19.99 *(978-1-5344-0637-7(9)*, Simon & Schuster Bks. For Young Readers) Simon & Schuster Bks. For Young Readers.
MacKay, Andrew. Young Lions Roar. 2012. 316p. pap. *(978-1-909395-27-5(7))* Legend Pr.
Maracle, Lee. Will's Garden. 2nd rev. ed. 2008. (ENG.). 194p. pap. 16.95 *(978-1-894778-59-6(6))* Theytus Bks., Ltd. CAN. Dist: Univ. of Toronto Pr.
Marchetta, Melina. Jellicoe Road. 2008. (ENG.). 432p. (YA). (gr. 8-18). 17.99 *(978-0-06-143183-8(4)*, HarperTeen) HarperCollins Pubs.
Marks, Rachel A. Darkness Savage. 2016. (Dark Cycle Ser.: 3). (ENG.). 380p. (YA). (gr. 8-13). pap. 9.99 *(978-1-5039-5030-6(1)*, 9781503950306, Skyscape) Amazon Publishing.
Marriott, Zoë. The Name of the Blade. 2014. (Name of the Blade Ser.: 1). (ENG.). 368p. (YA). (gr. 7). 16.99 *(978-0-7636-6957-7(1))* Candlewick Pr.
Martens, J. D. Days of Anarchy: Book 2. 2017. (Meteor Ser.). (ENG.). 184p. (YA). (gr. 5-12). 31.42 *(978-1-68076-828-2(X)*, 27431, Epic Escape) EPIC Pr.
—Defeat Judgment Day: Book 3. 2017. (Meteor Ser.). (ENG.). 184p. (YA). (gr. 5-12). 31.42 *(978-1-68076-829-9(8)*, 27432, Epic Escape) EPIC Pr.
—A New World Order: Book 6. 2017. (Meteor Ser.). (ENG.). 184p. (YA). (gr. 5-12). 31.42 *(978-1-68076-832-9(8)*, 27435, Epic Escape) EPIC Pr.
—The Sky Is Falling: Book 1. 2017. (Meteor Ser.). (ENG.). 184p. (YA). (gr. 5-12). 31.42 *(978-1-68076-827-5(1)*, 27430, Epic Escape) EPIC Pr.
Maskame, Estelle. Did I Mention I Miss You? 2016. (Did I Mention I Love You (DIMILY) Ser.: 3). (ENG.). 352p. (YA). (gr. 8-12). pap. 10.99 *(978-1-4926-3221-4(X)*, 9781492632214) Sourcebooks, Inc.
Mass, Wendy. 13 Gifts: a Wish Novel. 2013. (ENG.). 352p. (J). (gr. 3-7). pap. 7.99 *(978-0-545-31004-8(0))* Scholastic, Inc.
Matagrano, Joseph F. Forever Brothers. 2007. 396p. 26.95 *(978-1-4327-0963-1(1))*; per. 16.95 *(978-1-4327-1524-3(0))* Outskirts Pr., Inc.
Mbuyazi, Phiwayinkosi G. The Wiby Kids - How It All Began. 2011. 204p. pap. 12.99 *(978-1-61667-337-6(0))* Raider Publishing International.
McCaffrey, Kate. Destroying Avalon. 2006. (ENG.). 264p. (J). pap. 13.00 *(978-1-921064-57-9(9))* Fremantle Pr. AUS. Dist: Independent Pubs. Group.
McCorkle, Mark & Schooley, Bob. Grudge Match. 2005. (Illus.). 80p. (J). *(978-1-4155-9100-0(8))* Disney Pr.
McCormick, Patricia. Sold (National Book Award Finalist) 2008. (ENG.). 272p. (J). (gr. 5-9). pap. 11.99 *(978-0-7868-5172-0(4))* Little, Brown Bks. for Young Readers.
McCormick, Wilfred. Quick Kick: A Bronc Burnett Story. 2011. 192p. 42.95 *(978-1-258-10149-7(1))* Literary Licensing, LLC.
—The Three-Two Pitch: A Bronc Burnett Story. 2011. 192p. 42.95 *(978-1-258-10008-7(8))* Literary Licensing, LLC.
McCreight, Kimberly. The Outliers. (Outliers Ser.: 1). (ENG.). (YA). (gr. 9). 2017. 368p. pap. 10.99 *(978-0-06-235910-0(X))* 2016. 352p. 18.99 *(978-0-06-235909-4(6))* HarperCollins Pubs. (HarperCollins).
McDonald, Abby. Sophomore Switch. 2010. (ENG., Illus.). 304p. (YA). (gr. 9). pap. 8.99 *(978-0-7636-4774-2(8))* Candlewick Pr.
Mcgill, Leslie. Gearhead. 2015. (Cap Central Ser.: 4). (YA). lib. bdg. 20.80 *(978-0-606-36839-1(6))* Turtleback.
McPhee, Peter. Every Move, 1 vol. 2004. (Lorimer SideStreets Ser.). (ENG.). 184p. (YA). (gr. 9-12). 8.99 *(978-1-55028-850-6(4)*, d1a22e47-4203-474a-b8c4-db6f6606818d) James Lorimer & Co. Ltd., Pubs. CAN. Dist: Lerner Publishing Group.
Mechling, Lauren & Moser, Laura. Foreign Exposure: The Social Climber Abroad. 2007. (ENG.). 320p. (YA). (gr. 7-18). pap. 18.95 *(978-0-618-66379-8(7)*, 441918, Clarion Bks.) HarperCollins Pubs.
Meyer, Marissa. Cress. 2014. 552p. (YA). *(978-1-250-05632-0(2))* Feiwel & Friends.
Meyer, Stephanie H. & Meyer, John. Teen Ink: Written in the Dirt: A Collection of Short Stories, Poetry, Art & Photography. 2004. (ENG., Illus.). 360p. (YA). pap. 12.95 *(978-0-7573-0050-9(2)*, HCI Teens) Health Communications, Inc.
MIA the Meek. 2006. (ENG.). 166p. (J). (gr. 6-11). 16.95 *(978-1-890862-46-6(0)*, 008ac6fb-e1b7-42f2-948d-8297dcf6bc97) Bancroft Pr.
Millard, Glenda. The Stars at Oktober Bend. 2018. (ENG.). 288p. (J). (gr. 7). 16.99 *(978-0-7636-9272-8(7))* Candlewick Pr.
Mitchell, Randall. Teenership: Leadership for Teens. 2013. 112p. 29.99 *(978-1-4797-7767-9(6))*; pap. 19.99 *(978-1-4797-7766-2(8))* Xlibris Corp.
Moore, Lisa. Flannery, 1 vol. 2016. (ENG.). 256p. (YA). (gr. 8). 16.95 *(978-1-55498-076-5(3))* Groundwood Bks. CAN. Dist: Publishers Group West (PGW).
Morgan, Mario. Making the Message Mine. Grimme, Jeannette, ed. Garrison, Carri, illus. Date not set. 115p. (Orig.). (YA). pap. *(978-1-883473-01-3(2))* MM Co.
Myers, Sharon A. Slumber Party. 2009. 73p. 24.99 *(978-1-4415-9854-7(5))*; pap. 15.99 *(978-1-4415-9853-0(7))* Xlibris Corp.
Nagatsuki, Tappei. Re:ZERO -Starting Life in Another World-Ex, Vol. 1 (light Novel) The Dream of the Lion King. 2017. (Re:ZERO Ex (light Novel) Ser.: 1). (ENG., Illus.). 224p. (YA). (gr. 8-17). pap. 14.00 *(978-0-316-41290-2(2)*, Yen Pr.) Yen Pr. LLC.
Nazemian, Abdi. The Authentics. 2017. (ENG.). 288p. (YA). (gr. 8). 17.99 *(978-0-06-248646-2(2)*, Balzer & Bray) HarperCollins Pubs.
Nelson, Colleen. Sadia. 2018. (ENG.). 240p. (YA). pap. 12.99 *(978-1-4597-4029-7(7))* Dundurn Pr. CAN. Dist: Publishers Group West (PGW).
Ness, Patrick. The Rest of Us Just Live Here. (YA). 2016. (ENG.). 336p. (gr. 9). pap. 12.99 *(978-0-06-240317-9(6)*, Quill Tree Bks.) 2015. (ENG.). 336p. (gr. 9-12). 17.99 *(978-0-06-240316-2(8)*, Quill Tree Bks.) 2015. 352p. *(978-1-4063-3116-5(3))* HarperCollins Pubs.
Nichols, Michael. Beating the Air. 2007. 176p. per. 24.95 *(978-1-4241-7795-0(2))* America Star Bks.
Novel Units. Night Novel Units Student Packet. 2019. (ENG.). (YA). pap. 13.99 *(978-1-56137-805-0(4)*, NU8054SP, Novel Units, Inc.) Classroom Library Co.
Nyman, Mary. High School Stories: Short Takes from the Writers' Club. 2010. 64p. pap. 8.95 *(978-1-4502-1585-5(8))* iUniverse, Inc.
Odentz, Howard. Wicked Dead. 2016. (ENG., Illus.). (YA). pap. 15.95 *(978-1-61194-712-0(X))* BelleBks., Inc.
On Thin Ice. 2005. per. *(978-0-9772505-2-3(0))* Adibooks.com.
Optic, Oliver, pseud. Outward Bound. 2007. 180p. (gr. 4-7). per. *(978-1-4068-4343-9(1))* Echo Library.
—Outward Bound: Or Young America Afloat. l.t. ed. 2007. (ENG.). 274p. pap. 23.99 *(978-1-4264-9153-5(0))* Creative Media Partners, LLC.
O'Shea, M.J. Blood Moon. 2016. (ENG., Illus.). (J). 24.99 *(978-1-63477-941-8(X)*, Harmony Ink Pr.) Dreamspinner Pr.
Parker, Mike. Break-In. 208p. pap. 6.95 *(978-0-86327-898-3(1))* Wolfhound Pr. IRL. Dist: Interlink Publishing Group, Inc.
Paul & Juliana: A Novel. 2003. (ENG.). 188p. (J). 19.95 *(978-1-890862-33-6(9)*, 3a4b7b92-f233-4386-9bd5-6fb939e47eb8) Bancroft Pr.
Paulson, Ingrid. Why I Loathe Sterling Lane. 2017. (ENG.). 150p. (YA). pap. 9.99 *(978-1-63375-700-4(5)*, 9781633757004) Entangled Publishing, LLC.
Payne, Mary Jennifer. Darkness Rising: Daughters of Light. 2019. (Daughters of Light Ser.: 3). (ENG.). 312p. (YA). (gr. 7-10). pap. 12.99 *(978-1-4597-4103-4(X))* Dundurn Pr. CAN. Dist: Publishers Group West (PGW).
Penn, Astor. All the Devils Here. 2016. (ENG., Illus.). (YA). (gr. 8-12). 24.99 *(978-1-63477-933-3(9)*, Harmony Ink Pr.) Dreamspinner Pr.
Peymani, Christine. Super Starz Masquerade. 2007. (Illus.). 94p. (J). pap. *(978-0-439-91952-4(5))* Scholastic, Inc.
Pfitzenmaier, Audrey. Cheating Fate, 1 vol. 2008. (ENG.). 240p. (J). (gr. 8-18). pap. 12.95 *(978-1-897235-41-6(0))* Thistledown Pr., Ltd. CAN. Dist: Univ. of Toronto Pr.
Phelan, James. The Last Thirteen Book Six: 8. 2014. (ENG., Illus.). 192p. (J). pap. *(978-1-4431-3352-4(3))* Kane Miller.
Philips, A. If You Believe in Mermaids Don't Tell. 2007. 160p. per. 12.95 *(978-1-59858-359-5(X))* Dog Ear Publishing, LLC.
Pipkin, Bonnie. Aftercare Instructions: A Novel. 2018. (ENG.). 368p. (YA). pap. 27.00 *(978-1-250-11485-3(3)*, 900171581) Flatiron Bks.
Plotkin, Andy. The Black Block Legend. 2007. 64p. per. 19.95 *(978-1-4241-9190-1(4))* America Star Bks.
Plum, Amy. Dreamfall. (Dreamfall Ser.: 1). (ENG.). (YA). (gr. 9). 2018. 304p. pap. 10.99 *(978-0-06-242988-9(4))* 2017. 288p. 17.99 *(978-0-06-242987-2(6))* HarperCollins Pubs. (HarperTeen).
Polak, Monique. Planet Grief, 1 vol. 2018. (ENG.). 208p. (J). (gr. 4-7). pap. 10.95 *(978-1-4598-1568-1(8))* Orca Bk. Pubs. USA.
—121 Express, 1 vol. 2008. (Orca Currents Ser.). (ENG.). 144p. (J). (gr. 4-7). pap. 9.95 *(978-1-55143-976-1(X))* Orca Bk. Pubs. USA.
Poole-Carter, Rosemary. Juliette Ascending. 2007. (YA). pap. 14.00 *(978-1-929976-41-6(0)*, TOP) Top Pubns., Ltd.
Poulsen, David A. Last Sam's Cage. rev. ed. 2008. (ENG.). 222p. (YA). (gr. 9-18). per. *(978-1-55263-953-5(3))* Me to We.
—Last Sam's Cage. 2018. (ENG., Illus.). 232p. (J). pap. 11.99 *(978-0-9959708-0-9(7))* Red Hawk Bks.
Quince, Lia. Abby & Jules. 2009. *(978-1-933791-14-2(4))* Finial Publishing.
Ramsey, Jo. Blue Jeans & Sweatshirts. 2016. (ENG., Illus.). (J). 24.99 *(978-1-63477-942-5(8)*, Harmony Ink Pr.) Dreamspinner Pr.
Raymond, Jeanpaul. The Kids That Could. 2009. 40p. pap. 17.99 *(978-1-4389-5585-8(5))* AuthorHouse.
Reisfeld, Randi. Everyone Who's Anyone. 2007. (ENG.). 304p. (gr. 7-12). pap. 8.99 *(978-1-4231-0502-2(8))* Hyperion Pr.
Ricci, Caitlin. Weathering the Storm. 2016. (ENG., Illus.). (J). 24.99 *(978-1-63477-992-0(4))* Dreamspinner Pr.
Rich, Juliann. Taking the Stand. 2015. (ENG.). 264p. (J). (gr. 7). pap. 11.95 *(978-1-62639-408-7(3))* Bold Strokes Bks.
Richards, Elizabeth. Wings. 2015. (Black City Novel Ser.: 3). 416p. (YA). (gr. 9). pap. 9.99 *(978-0-14-751140-9(2)*, Speak) Penguin Young Readers Group.
Riffe, Ruth. Survival Guide for the Teenage Life. Smith, Geoff & Aretha, David, eds. 2016. (ENG., Illus.). 124p. (J). pap. 12.49 *(978-1-61984-511-4(3)*, Gatekeeper Pr.) Gatekeeper Pr.
Ripley's Believe It Or Not! Ripley's Bureau of Investigation 2: Dragon's Triangle. 2010. (Rbi Ser.: 2). (ENG.). 128p. (J). pap. 4.99 *(978-1-893951-53-2(7))* Ripley Entertainment, Inc.
—Ripley's Bureau of Investigation 3: Running Wild. 2010. (Rbi Ser.: 3). (ENG.). 128p. (J). pap. 4.99 *(978-1-893951-55-6(3))* Ripley Entertainment, Inc.
—Ripley's Bureau of Investigation 4: Secrets of the Deep. 2010. (Rbi Ser.: 4). (ENG.). 128p. (J). pap. 4.99 *(978-1-893951-54-9(5))* Ripley Entertainment, Inc.
Robins, Eleanor. Boy of Their Dreams, 1 vol. unabr. ed. 2010. (Carter High Chronicles Ser.). (ENG.). 52p. (YA). (gr. 9-12). pap. 9.75 *(978-1-61651-305-4(5))* Saddleback Educational Publishing, Inc.
—Double-Cross, 1 vol. unabr. ed. 2011. (Choices Ser.). (ENG.). 52p. (YA). (gr. 5-12). 9.75 *(978-1-61651-595-9(3))* Saddleback Educational Publishing, Inc.
—Friend or Foe?, 1 vol. unabr. ed. 2011. (Choices Ser.). (ENG.). 52p. (YA). (gr. 5-12). 9.75 *(978-1-61651-593-5(7))* Saddleback Educational Publishing, Inc.
—It Does Matter, 1 vol. unabr. ed. 2010. (Carter High Senior Year Ser.). (ENG.). 52p. (YA). (gr. 9-12). pap. 9.75 *(978-1-61651-324-5(1))* Saddleback Educational Publishing, Inc.
—It Is Not a Date, 1 vol. unabr. ed. 2010. (Carter High Chronicles Ser.). (ENG.). 52p. (YA). (gr. 9-12). pap. 9.75 *(978-1-61651-309-2(8))* Saddleback Educational Publishing, Inc.
—Just Be Yourself, 1 vol. unabr. ed. 2010. (Carter High Senior Year Ser.). (ENG.). 52p. (YA). (gr. 9-12). pap. 9.75 *(978-1-61651-325-2(X))* Saddleback Educational Publishing, Inc.
—The Last Time, 1 vol. unabr. ed. 2010. (Carter High Senior Year Ser.). (ENG.). 52p. (YA). (gr. 9-12). pap. 9.75 *(978-1-61651-326-9(8))* Saddleback Educational Publishing, Inc.
—No Exceptions, 1 vol. unabr. ed. 2011. (Choices Ser.). (ENG.). 52p. (YA). (gr. 5-12). 9.75 *(978-1-61651-597-3(X))* Saddleback Educational Publishing, Inc.
—No Limits, 1 vol. unabr. ed. 2011. (Choices Ser.). (ENG.). 52p. (YA). (gr. 5-12). 9.75 *(978-1-61651-598-0(8))* Saddleback Educational Publishing, Inc.
—One Date Too Many, 1 vol. unabr. ed. 2010. (Carter High Chronicles Ser.). (ENG.). 52p. (YA). (gr. 9-12). pap. 9.75 *(978-1-61651-310-8(1))* Saddleback Educational Publishing, Inc.
—One More Chance, 1 vol. unabr. ed. 2010. (Carter High Senior Year Ser.). (ENG.). 52p. (YA). (gr. 9-12). pap. 9.75 *(978-1-61651-327-6(6))* Saddleback Educational Publishing, Inc.
—The Secret Admirer Mystery, 1 vol. unabr. ed. 2011. (Carter High Mysteries Ser.). (ENG.). 48p. (YA). (gr. 9-12). 9.75 *(978-1-61651-567-6(8))* Saddleback Educational Publishing, Inc.
—Someone to Count, 1 vol. unabr. ed. 2010. (Carter High Senior Year Ser.). (ENG.). 52p. (YA). (gr. 9-12). pap. 9.75 *(978-1-61651-328-3(4))* Saddleback Educational Publishing, Inc.
—Time to Move On, 1 vol. unabr. ed. 2010. (Carter High Senior Year Ser.). (ENG.). 52p. (YA). (gr. 9-12). pap. 9.75 *(978-1-61651-329-0(2))* Saddleback Educational Publishing, Inc.
—Too Late, 1 vol. unabr. ed. 2010. (Carter High Chronicles Ser.). (ENG.). 52p. (YA). (gr. 9-12). pap. 9.75 *(978-1-61651-312-2(8))* Saddleback Educational Publishing, Inc.
—The Worst Year Ever, 1 vol. unabr. ed. 2010. (Carter High Senior Year Ser.). (ENG.). 52p. (YA). (gr. 9-12). pap. 9.75 *(978-1-61651-330-6(6))* Saddleback Educational Publishing, Inc.
—The Wrong Way, 1 vol. unabr. ed. 2010. (Carter High Senior Year Ser.). (ENG.). 52p. (YA). (gr. 9-12). pap. 9.75 *(978-1-61651-331-3(4))* Saddleback Educational Publishing, Inc.
Robinson, Gwen G. The Jensen Case. 2010. (Illus.). 228p. pap. *(978-0-7552-0496-0(4))* Authors OnLine, Ltd.
Roman, Annette. 1 World Manga, Vol. 5. Ng, Leandro, illus. 2007. (1 World Manga Ser.). (ENG.). 240p. pap. 3.99 *(978-1-4215-1169-6(X))* Viz Media.
Russell, Kristin. A Sky for Us Alone. 2019. (ENG.). 336p. (YA). (gr. 8). 17.99 *(978-0-06-269702-8(1)*, Tegen, Katherine Bks) HarperCollins Pubs.
Ryan, Ann. The Little Wannabee. Ryan, Ann, illus. 2006. (ENG., Illus.). 24p. (J). 16.95 *(978-1-933660-31-8(7)*, Tadpole Pr. 4 Kids) Mystic Harbor Pr., LLC.
Ryan, Tom. Totally Unrelated, 1 vol. 2013. (Orca Limelights Ser.). (J). (ENG.). 128p. (gr. 4-7). pap. 9.95 *(978-1-4598-0458-6(9))*; 120p. *(978-1-4598-0648-1(4))* Orca Bk. Pubs. USA.
Sadd, Kenn. Crazy Cracked Pots. 2009. 144p. pap. 24.95 *(978-1-61546-673-3(8))* America Star Bks.
Saddleback Educational Publishing Staff, ed. Twister, 1 vol. unabr. ed. 2011. (Heights Ser.). (ENG.). 52p. (gr. 4-8). 9.75 *(978-1-61651-626-0(7))* Saddleback Educational Publishing, Inc.
Saunders, Harry M. Teenagers on an Adventure: Journey of Two Boys & a Girl. 2013. 168p. pap. 19.95 *(978-1-62709-466-5(0))* America Star Bks.
Sawyer, Kim Vogel. Katy's Debate, 1 vol. 2015. (Katy Lambright Ser.). (ENG.). 208p. (YA). pap. 9.99 *(978-0-310-74755-0(4))* Zondervan.
—Katy's Decision, 1 vol. 2015. (Katy Lambright Ser.). (ENG.). 208p. (YA). pap. 9.99 *(978-0-310-74850-2(X))* Zondervan.
—Katy's Homecoming, 1 vol. 2015. (Katy Lambright Ser.). (ENG.). 208p. (YA). pap. 9.99 *(978-0-310-74835-9(6))* Zondervan.
—Katy's New World, 1 vol. 2015. (Katy Lambright Ser.). (ENG.). 208p. (YA). pap. 9.99 *(978-0-310-74782-6(1))* Zondervan.
Scheidies, Carolyn R. My Summer Journal: the Rescue. 2007. (ENG.). 96p. pap. 14.99 *(978-0-615-16029-0(8))* C R Pubns.
Schraff, Anne. Leap of Faith, 1 vol. unabr. ed. 2011. (Urban Underground Ser.). (ENG.). 201p. (YA). (gr. 9-12). pap. 11.95 *(978-1-61651-588-1(0))* Saddleback Educational Publishing, Inc.
—The Lost, 1 vol. unabr. ed. 2011. (Urban Underground Ser.). (ENG.). 198p. (YA). (gr. 9-12). pap. 11.95 *(978-1-61651-585-0(6))* Saddleback Educational Publishing, Inc.
—The Quality of Mercy, 1 vol. unabr. ed. 2010. (Urban Underground Ser.). (ENG.). 183p. (YA). (gr. 9-12). pap. 11.95 *(978-1-61651-006-0(4))* Saddleback Educational Publishing, Inc.
—The Unforgiven, 1 vol. unabr. ed. 2011. (Urban Underground Ser.). (ENG.). 198p. (YA). (gr. 9-12). pap. 11.95 *(978-1-61651-586-7(4))* Saddleback Educational Publishing, Inc.
—The Water's Edge. unabr. ed. 2011. (Urban Underground Ser.). (ENG.). 197p. (YA). (gr. 9-12). pap. 11.95 *(978-1-61651-589-8(9))* Saddleback Educational Publishing, Inc.
—Wildflower, 1 vol. unabr. ed. 2010. (Urban Underground Ser.). (ENG.). 183p. (YA). (gr. 9-12). pap. 11.95 *(978-1-61651-009-1(9))* Saddleback Educational Publishing, Inc.
Scott, Jerry. Zits: Shredded. Borgman, Jim, illus. 2014. (Zits Ser.: 2). (ENG.). 224p. (YA). (gr. 8). pap. 9.99 *(978-0-06-222853-6(6)*, HarperTeen) HarperCollins Pubs.
Seib, Anke & Cameron, Emma. Out of This Place. 2013. (ENG.). 416p. (YA). (gr. 9). 17.99 *(978-0-7636-6404-6(9))* Candlewick Pr.
Self, Jeffery. Drag Teen. 2016. (ENG.). 272p. (YA). (gr. 9). 17.99 *(978-0-545-82993-9(3)*, PUSH) Scholastic, Inc.
Shaw, Esther. The Winter Mare. 2005. (ENG., Illus.). 198p. pap. *(978-1-84401-447-7(9))* Athena Pr.
Shepard, Sara. Pretty Little Liars: Ali's Pretty Little Lies. 2013. (Pretty Little Liars Companion Novel Ser.). (ENG.). 320p. (YA). (gr. 9). pap. 10.99 *(978-0-06-223337-0(8)*, HarperTeen) HarperCollins Pubs.
Sherrard, Valerie. Sam's Light. 2004. (ENG.). 200p. (YA). pap. 8.99 *(978-1-55002-535-4(X))* Dundurn Pr. CAN. Dist: Publishers Group West (PGW).
Siegert, Mia. Jerkbait. 2016. (ENG.). 350p. (YA). (gr. 9-12). pap. 14.99 *(978-1-63163-066-8(0)*, 1631630660, Jolly Fish Pr.) North Star Editions.
Sim, Tara. Firestarter. 2019. (Timekeeper Ser.: 3). (ENG., Illus.). 528p. (YA). (gr. 9-9). 26.99 *(978-1-5107-0620-0(8)*, Sky Pony Pr.) Skyhorse Publishing Co., Inc.
Sividious Stark & the Stadium Between Worlds. 2013. (ENG.). 236p. (YA). pap. 12.99 *(978-1-62108-273-6(3))* Covenant Communications, Inc.
Smith, Mary P. Wells. The Young Puritans in King Philip's War. Bridgman, L. J., illus. 2011. 396p. 54.95 *(978-1-258-05550-9(3))* Literary Licensing, LLC.
Smith, Naiya. Pinky Swear: The Heart Wants What the Heart Wants. 2012. 120p. (gr. 10-12). 23.99 *(978-1-4772-6552-9(X))*; pap. 14.95 *(978-1-4772-6554-3(6))* AuthorHouse.
Squires, Megan. The Rules of Regret, 0 vols. 2014. (ENG.). 290p. (YA). (gr. 9-12). pap. 9.99 *(978-1-4778-2488-7(X)*, 9781477824887, Skyscape) Amazon Publishing.
Stevens, Jessica. Within Reach: A Novel. 2016. (ENG.). 248p. (YA). pap. 17.00 *(978-1-940716-69-5(1))* SparkPr. (a Bks.parks Imprint).
Stevenson, Robert Louis. Kidnapped & Catriona. 2007. 480p. per. 15.00 *(978-1-84697-033-7(4))* Birlinn, Ltd. GBR. Dist: Casemate Pubs. & Bk. Distributors, LLC.
Stevenson, Robin. The World Without Us. 2014. (ENG.). 240p. E-Book *(978-1-4598-0681-8(6))* Orca Bk. Pubs.
Stinson, Kathy. 101 Ways to Dance, 1 vol. 2006. (ENG.). 152p. (YA). (gr. 8-12). pap. 9.95 *(978-1-897187-10-4(6))* Second Story Pr. CAN. Dist: Orca Bk. Pubs. USA.
Stone, Vicki L. Why Should I Stay A Virgin? 2004. 74p. (YA). per. *(978-1-59196-850-4(X))* Instant Pub.
The Strange & Beautiful Sorrows of Ava Lavender. 2014. (ENG.). 320p. (YA). (gr. 9). E-Book 12.99 *(978-0-7636-7034-4(0)*, 28917) Candlewick Pr.
Strasser, Todd & Thacker, Nola. The Shore: Shirt & Shoes Not Required; LB (Laguna Beach) 2011. (ENG.). 480p. (YA). (gr. 9). pap. 9.99 *(978-1-4424-1970-4(9)*, Simon Pulse) Simon Pulse.
Suarez, Maria. Mr Giggles. 2011. 20p. pap. 24.95 *(978-1-4626-3617-4(9))* America Star Bks.
Sullivan, Jenny. Nowhere Again. 2004. (ENG.). 230p. pap. 13.95 *(978-1-84323-297-1(9))* Beekman Bks., Inc.
Summer, Mary Elizabeth. Trust Me, I'm Lying. 2015. (Trust Me Ser.). (ENG.). 352p. (YA). (gr. 7). pap. 9.99 *(978-0-385-74413-3(7)*, Ember) Random Hse. Children's Bks.
Swindells, Pat. Junk Food Hero. 2010. (ENG., Illus.). 280p. (J). (gr. 6-12). pap. 18.95 *(978-1-906582-02-9(5))* Aurora Metro Pubns. Ltd. GBR. Dist: Publishers Group West (PGW).
Taylor, Drew Hayden. The Night Wanderer: A Native Gothic Novel. 5th ed. 2007. (ENG., Illus.). 228p. (YA). (gr. 7-12). pap. 12.95 *(978-1-55451-099-3(6)*, 9781554510993) Annick Pr., Ltd. CAN. Dist: Publishers Group West (PGW).
Terrell, Brandon. Second Chance Delivery. 2016. (Tartan House Ser.). (ENG., Illus.). 96p. (J). (gr. 3-6). pap. 9.95 *(978-1-63235-205-7(2)*, 11905, 12-Story Library) Bookstaves, LLC.
Thornley, Rebecca Gundersen. I Know He Is There: A Lift-A-Flap Book about Faith. Dorman, Brandon, illus. 2006. (J). *(978-1-59038-550-0(0))* Deseret Bk. Co.

Tibbets, Albert B. Youth, Youth, Youth: Stories of Challenge, Confidence & Comradeship. Tibbets, Albert B., ed. 2011. 256p. 47.95 *(978-1-258-05880-7(4))* Literary Licensing, LLC.

Tiernan, Cate. Sweep: Book of Shadows, the Coven, & Blood Witch: Volume 1. 2010. (Sweep Ser.: 1). (ENG.). 592p. (YA). (gr. 7-18). 12.99 *(978-0-14-241717-1(3),* Speak) Penguin Young Readers Group.

Torres, J. Degrassi the Next Generation Extra Credit Suddenly, Last Summer. Northcott, Ed, illus. 2nd ed. 2006. (Degrassi the Next Generation Ser.). (ENG.). 128p. (J). pap. *(978-1-55168-320-1(2))* Fenn, H. B. & Co., Ltd.

—In My House. Rolston, Steve, illus. 4th ed. 2007. (Degrassi the Next Generation Ser.). (ENG.). 120p. (J). pap. *(978-1-55168-303-4(2))* Fenn, H. B. & Co., Ltd.

Torres, J. & Kim, Eric. Missing You. 3rd ed. 2007. (Degrassi the Next Generation Ser.). (ENG., Illus.). 120p. (J). pap. *(978-1-55168-301-0(6))* Fenn, H. B. & Co., Ltd.

Tracey, Rhian. Isla & Luke: Make or Break? 2004. (J). pap. 12.95 *(978-0-7475-6649-6(6))* Bloomsbury Publishing Plc GBR. Dist: Independent Pubs. Group.

Tullson, Diane. Edge, 1 vol. 2009. (ENG.). 214p. (YA). (gr. 6-10). pap. 11.95 *(978-1-55005-142-1(3),* 31aaba7e-4ef1-425e-9483-2fe49ffe6534) Trifolium Bks., Inc. CAN. Dist: Firefly Bks., Ltd.

Ure, Jean. Gone Missing. 2007. (ENG., Illus.). 192p. (gr. 4-7). pap. 8.99 *(978-0-00-722459-3(1),* HarperCollins Children's Bks.) HarperCollins Pubs. Ltd. GBR. Dist: HarperCollins Pubs.

Van Draanen, Wendelin. Wild Bird. 2019. (ENG.). 336p. (YA). (gr. 7). pap. 10.99 *(978-1-101-94047-1(6),* Ember) Random Hse. Children's Bks.

Van Dyne, Edith. Mary Louise. 2007. (ENG.). 148p. pap. 18.99 *(978-1-4264-1952-2(X));* 144p. pap. 19.99 *(978-1-4264-2063-4(3))* Creative Media Partners, LLC.

Van Syckle, A. & Schwartz, Josh. The OC: 'twas the Night Before Chrismukkah. 2005. 206p. (YA). *(978-1-4156-3915-3(9))* Scholastic, Inc.

Varrato, Tony. Outrage. Doherty, Catherine, illus. 2007. (HIP Edge Ser.). 112p. (YA). (gr. 7-18). pap. *(978-1-897039-28-1(X))* High Interest Publishing (HIP).

Walmsley, Tom. Kid Stuff: A Novel. 2004. (ENG.). 288p. pap. 17.95 *(978-1-55152-153-4(9),* 187) Arsenal Pulp Pr. CAN. Dist: Consortium Bk. Sales & Distribution.

Walters, Eric. Alexandria of Africa. 2008. (ENG.). 208p. (YA). (gr. 7). pap. 12.95 *(978-0-385-66639-8(X))* Doubleday Canada, Ltd. CAN. Dist: Penguin Random Hse. LLC.

Walton, Leslye. The Strange & Beautiful Sorrows of Ava Lavender. (ENG.). 320p. (YA). (gr. 9). 2015. pap. 12.99 *(978-0-7636-8027-5(3))* 2014. 17.99 *(978-0-7636-6566-1(5))* Candlewick Pr.

—The Strange & Beautiful Sorrows of Ava Lavender. 2015. lib. bdg. 19.65 *(978-0-606-36879-7(5))* Turtleback.

Warren, Bertie. Sammie's Journey to Freedom. 2006. (ENG.). 52p. per. 16.95 *(978-1-4241-5142-4(2))* America Star Bks.

Welford, Sue. Nowhere to Run. l.t. ed. 2006. 180p. per. *(978-1-905665-15-0(6))* Pollinger In Print.

—Secret Love. l.t. ed. 2006. pap. *(978-1-905665-10-5(5))* Pollinger In Print.

West, Kasie. Love, Life, & the List. 2018. (ENG.). 400p. (YA). (gr. 8). pap. 10.99 *(978-0-06-274045-8(8))* 2018. 375p. (J). *(978-0-06-283569-7(6))* 2017. (ENG.). 384p. (YA). (gr. 8). 17.99 *(978-0-06-267577-4(X))* HarperCollins Pubs. (HarperTeen).

West Lewis, Amanda. The Pact, 1 vol. 2016. (ENG., Illus.). 352p. (YA). (gr. 7-12). pap. 14.95 *(978-0-88995-544-8(1),* 996a5f80-c8eb-4176-9d48-0345fa4f947d) Trifolium Bks., Inc. CAN. Dist: Firefly Bks., Ltd.

Westerfeld, Scott. Bogus to Bubbly: An Insider's Guide to the World of Uglies. Phillips, Craig, illus. 2008. (Uglies Ser.). (ENG.). 224p. (YA). (gr. 7). pap. 11.99 *(978-1-4169-7436-9(9),* Simon Pulse) Simon Pulse.

Westergard, Tim. A Penny for Your Thoughts. 2008. 28p. pap. 24.95 *(978-1-60441-417-2(0))* America Star Bks.

Whitaker, Alecia. The Queen of Kentucky. 2013. (ENG.). 384p. (J). (gr. 7-17). pap. 19.99 *(978-0-316-12494-2(X),* Poppy) Little, Brown Bks. for Young Readers.

Whitney, Adeline Dutton Train. The Other Girls. 2016. (ENG., Illus.). (J). 29.95 *(978-1-358-75955-0(3))* Creative Media Partners, LLC.

Whitney, Daisy. The Rivals. 2013. (ENG.). 352p. (J). (gr. 10-17). pap. 18.99 *(978-0-316-09056-8(5))* Little, Brown Bks. for Young Readers.

Wignall, Kevin. When We Were Lost. 2019. (ENG.). 320p. (YA). (gr. 9-17). 17.99 *(978-0-316-41779-2(3),* Jimmy Patterson) Little Brown & Co.

Wilson, Jacqueline. Kiss: A Novel. 2010. (ENG., Illus.). 256p. (YA). (gr. 7-12). 33.99 *(978-1-59643-242-0(X),* 900042189) Roaring Brook Pr.

Winfrey, Kerry. Things Jolie Needs to Do Before She Bites It. 2019. (ENG.). 288p. (YA). pap. 18.99 *(978-1-250-30890-0(9),* 900198411) Square Fish.

Yansky, Brian. Utopia, Iowa. 2015. (ENG.). 336p. (YA). (gr. 9). 17.99 *(978-0-7636-6533-3(9))* Candlewick Pr.

Yee, Paul. What Happened This Summer, 1 vol. 2006. (ENG., Illus.). 128p. (YA). (gr. 8-12). per. 10.95 *(978-1-896580-88-3(2))* Tradewind Bks. CAN. Dist: Orca Bk. Pubs. USA.

Zindel, Paul. The Pigman's Legacy. 2005. 168p. (YA). (gr. 7-12). 13.65 *(978-0-7569-4962-4(9))* Perfection Learning Corp.

YOUTH MOVEMENT

Cruden, Alexander, ed. Student Movements of The 1960s, 1 vol. 2012. (Perspectives on Modern World History Ser.). (ENG., Illus.). 192p. (gr. 10-12). lib. bdg. 49.43 *(978-0-7377-6372-0(8),* 14651fb4-c263-4b44-9e48-b6532700ad96, Greenhaven Publishing) Greenhaven Publishing LLC.

Gitlin, Martin, ed. Student Protests, 1 vol. 2019. (Introducing Issues with Opposing Viewpoints Ser.). (ENG.). 120p. (gr. 7-10). 43.63 *(978-1-5345-0574-2(1),* 448b618d-b505-4f53-8a10-6e797143b3f3) Greenhaven Publishing LLC.

Halpin, Mikki. It's Your World — If You Don't Like It, Change It. 2014. 19.00 *(978-1-63419-713-7(5))* Perfection Learning Corp.

YUCATAN PENINSULA

Hayes, Amy. Ancient Maya Geography, 1 vol. 2016. (Spotlight on the Maya, Aztec, & Inca Civilizations Ser.). (ENG.). 32p. (J). (gr. 4-6). pap. 12.75 *(978-1-4994-1971-9(6),* 2894b284-fc58-4634-9e53-777ff2e45923, PowerKids Pr.) Rosen Publishing Group, Inc., The.

Sauri, Trudy. Gift of Yucatan Nouns A-Z. 2008. (ENG & SPA., Illus.). 64p. (J). per. 18.00 *(978-0-9797637-3-1(8))* Your Culture Gifts.

YUCATAN PENINSULA—FICTION

Maartman, Ben. The Lost Treasures of Yucatan: A Belizean Saga. 2004. (Illus.). 106p. (YA). pap. 14.50 *(978-1-4120-1487-8(5))* Trafford Publishing.

Marsh, Carole. The Mystery at the Mayan Ruins: Mexico. 2014. (Around the World in 80 Mysteries Ser.: Vol. 16). (ENG., Illus.). 133p. (J). (gr. 3-5). pap. 7.99 *(978-0-635-11163-0(2),* Marsh, Carole Bks.) Gallopade International.

Sauri, Trudy. Gift of Yucatan Pancho's Quest. 2007. (ENG & SPA., Illus.). 64p. (J). per. 18.00 *(978-0-9797637-0-0(3))* Your Culture Gifts.

YUGOSLAVIA

Hughes, Christopher. Yugoslavia. 2003. (Nations in Conflict Ser.). 48p. (YA). 26.19 *(978-1-56711-549-9(7),* Blackbirch Pr., Inc.) Cengage Gale.

YUGOSLAVIA—HISTORY

Behnke, Alison. Serbia & Montenegro in Pictures. 2006. (Visual Geography Ser.). (Illus.). 80p. (YA). (gr. 7-12). lib. bdg. 27.93 *(978-0-8225-2679-7(4))* Lerner Publishing Group.

Ching, Jacqueline. Genocide & the Bosnian War. 2009. (Genocide in Modern Times Ser.). 64p. (gr. 6-6). 58.50 *(978-1-61512-672-9(4))* Rosen Publishing Group, Inc., The.

Flotz, Katherine Haeger. A Pebble in My Shoe: A Memoir. 2004. (Illus.). 185p. lib. bdg. 29.95 *(978-0-9657793-2-6(7))* Pannonia Pr.

Honovich, Nancy. Immigration from the Former Yugoslavia. 2005. (Changing Face of North America Ser.). (Illus.). 112p. (YA). lib. bdg. 24.95 *(978-1-59084-690-2(7))* Mason Crest.

Sullivan, Kimberly L. Slobodan Milosevic's Yugoslavia. 2009. (Dictatorships Ser.). (ENG., Illus.). 144p. (J). (gr. 9-12). 38.60 *(978-0-8225-9098-9(0),* 1299571) Lerner Publishing Group.

Transchel, Kate. The Breakup of Yugoslavia. Matray, James I., ed. 2006. (Arbitrary Borders Ser.). (ENG., Illus.). 134p. (gr. 9). lib. bdg. 35.00 *(978-0-7910-8651-3(8),* P114364, Facts On File) Infobase Holdings, Inc.

YUKON—FICTION

Appel, Benjamin & Clark, Henry W. We Were There in the Klondike Gold Rush. Docktor, Irv, illus. 2011. 188p. 42.95 *(978-1-258-05908-8(8))* Literary Licensing, LLC.

Hobbs, William. Jason's Gold. unabr. ed. 2004. 240p. (J). (gr. 5-9). pap. 38.00 incl. audio *(978-0-8072-8229-8(4),* Listening Library) Random Hse. Audio Publishing Group.

London, Jack. The Call of the Wild, 1 vol. VanArsdale, Anthony, illus. 2010. (Calico Illustrated Classics Ser.). (ENG.). 112p. (J). (gr. 2-5). 38.50 *(978-1-60270-742-9(1),* 3985, Calico Chapter Bks.) ABDO Publishing Co.

—The Call of the Wild. 2014. iv, 96p. (J). pap. *(978-1-4677-4602-1(9),* First Avenue Editions) Lerner Publishing Group.

—The Call of the Wild. Moser, Barry, illus. 2011. (ENG.). 144p. (J). (gr. 4-9). pap. 8.99 *(978-1-4424-3411-0(2),* Simon & Schuster Bks. For Young Readers) Simon & Schuster Bks. For Young Readers.

—The Call of the Wild. 2003. (Aladdin Classics Ser.). (ENG.). 160p. (J). (gr. 4-7). mass mkt. 6.99 *(978-0-689-85674-7(1),* Aladdin) Simon & Schuster Children's Publishing.

—The Call of the Wild. Clift, Eva, tr. Clift, Eva, illus. 2003. (Values in Action Illustrated Classics Ser.). (J). *(978-1-59203-047-7(5))* Learning Challenge, Inc.

—La Llamada de la Naturaleza. 2003. (Historias de Siempre Ser.).Tr. of Call of the Wild. (SPA., Illus.). 92p. (J). (gr. 5-8). pap. 10.95 *(978-84-204-5731-4(0))* Santillana USA Publishing Co., Inc.

—White Fang, 1 vol. VanArsdale, Anthony, illus. 2011. (Calico Illustrated Classics Ser.: No. 3). (ENG.). 112p. (J). (gr. 2-5). 38.50 *(978-1-61641-112-1(0),* 4031, Calico Chapter Bks.) ABDO Publishing Co.

Wallace, Ian. The True Story of Trapper Jack's Left Big Toe. (Illus.). 32p. (J). 18.95 *(978-0-88899-415-8(X))* Groundwood Bks. CAN. Dist: Publishers Group West (PGW).

Z

ZACCHAEUS (BIBLICAL FIGURE)

Lashbrook, Marilyn. Out on a Limb. Britt, Stephanie McFetridge, illus. 2012. 32p. (J). pap. 8.00 *(978-1-935014-37-9(4))* Hutchings, John Pubs.

Zacchaeus: Physically Small but Spiritually Tall! (Illus.). 16p. (J). pap. 1.50 *(978-0-87162-871-8(6),* E6038) Warner Pr., Inc.

ZAHARIAS, BABE DIDRIKSON, 1911-1956

Brocker, Susan. Sports Legends & Leyendas del Deporte: 6 English, 6 Spanish Adaptations. 2011. (ENG & SPA.). (J). 89.00 net. *(978-1-4108-5678-4(X))* Benchmark Education Co.

Ferrara, Cos. Babe Didrikson Zaharias: Outcast & Hero. 2004. (Girls Explore, Reach for the Stars Ser.). (Illus.). 109p. (J). 20.00 *(978-0-9749456-2-0(5),* Girls Explore) Girls Explore LLC.

Levit, Joe. Babe Didrikson Zaharias: Multisport Superstar. 2020. (Epic Sports Bios (Lerner (tm) Sports) Ser.). (ENG., Illus.). 32p. (J). (gr. 2-5). 30.65 *(978-1-5415-9745-7(1),* 26f00417-b35c-4c98-b358-bebb5fbcf12f); pap. 9.99 *(978-1-7284-1338-9(9),* ae0dd883-d71b-4725-9688-9c2ecc40270e) Lerner Publishing Group. (Lerner Pubns.).

Strand, Jennifer. Babe Didrikson Zaharias. 2016. (Trailblazing Athletes Ser.). (ENG.). 24p. (J). (gr. -1-2). 49.94 *(978-1-68079-417-5(5),* 23038, Abdo Zoom-Launch) ABDO Publishing Co.

ZAIRE

see Congo (Democratic Republic)

ZAMBIA

Holmes, Timothy & Wong, Winnie. Zambia, 1 vol. 2nd rev. ed. 2009. (Cultures of the World (Second Edition)(r) Ser.). (ENG.). 144p. (gr. 5-5). lib. bdg. 49.79 *(978-0-7614-3039-1(3),* c4e2008c-26e5-412e-9409-29fa5010b9bb) Cavendish Square Publishing LLC.

Holmes, Timothy, et al. Zambia, 1 vol. 2017. (Cultures of the World (Third Edition)(r) Ser.). (ENG.). 144p. (gr. 5-5). 48.79 *(978-1-5026-3243-2(8),* 073a0096-0e0b-42ff-ad25-8f5f15f0189b) Cavendish Square Publishing LLC.

Kalz, Jill. Victoria Falls. 2004. (Natural Wonders of the World Ser.). (Illus.). 32p. (J). lib. bdg. 18.95 *(978-1-58341-327-2(8),* Creative Education) Creative Co., The.

Pearce, Q. L. Given Kachepa: Advocate for Human Trafficking Victims, 1 vol. 2007. (Young Heroes Ser.). (ENG., Illus.). 48p. (gr. 4-8). lib. bdg. 37.33 *(978-0-7377-3668-7(2),* dfb81306-01be-4abb-b38b-3ab790d1a238, KidHaven Publishing) Greenhaven Publishing LLC.

Torres, John Albert. Meet Our New Student from Zambia. 2010. (Meet Our New Student Ser.). 48p. (J). (gr. 2-5). 29.95 *(978-1-58415-735-9(6))* Mitchell Lane Pubs.

Waters, Bella. Zambia in Pictures. 2009. (J). lib. bdg. 31.93 *(978-1-57505-955-6(X))* Twenty First Century Bks.

ZEBRAS

Anderson, Jill. Zebras. 2005. (Wild Ones Ser.). (ENG., Illus.). 24p. (J). (gr. -1-1). 12.95 *(978-1-55971-926-1(5));* pap. 6.95 *(978-1-55971-927-8(3))* Cooper Square Publishing Llc.

Andrus, Aubre. National Geographic Readers: a Zebra's Day (Prereader) 2020. (Readers Ser.). (Illus.). 24p. (J). (gr. -1-k). pap. 4.99 *(978-1-4263-3717-8(5));* (ENG., lib. bdg. 14.90 *(978-1-4263-3718-5(3))* Disney Publishing Worldwide. (National Geographic Kids).

Borgert-Spaniol, Megan. Baby Zebras. 2017. (Super Cute! Ser.). (ENG., Illus.). 24p. (J). (gr. k-3). lib. bdg. 26.95 *(978-1-62617-548-8(9),* Blastoff! Readers) Bellwether Media.

Caswell, Deanna. Baby Zebras. 2020. (J). pap. *(978-1-62310-069-8(0))* Black Rabbit Bks.

Cunningham, Kevin. Zebras & Ostriches. 2016. (21st Century Junior Library: Better Together Ser.). (ENG., Illus.). 24p. (J). (gr. 2-5). 29.21 *(978-1-63471-082-4(7),* 208407) Cherry Lake Publishing.

Duling, Kaitlyn. Zebras. 2019. (Animals of the Grasslands Ser.). (ENG., Illus.). 24p. (J). (gr. k-3). lib. bdg. 26.95 *(978-1-64487-059-4(2),* Blastoff! Readers) Bellwether Media.

Feldman, Thea. Milia's Big Day. 2006. (Illus.). (J). *(978-0-696-23290-9(1))* Meredith Bks.

Gagne, Tammy. Zebras. 2017. (Animals of Africa Ser.). (ENG., Illus.). 32p. (J). (gr. 2-3). pap. 9.95 *(978-1-63517-334-5(5),* 1635173345); lib. bdg. 31.35 *(978-1-63517-269-0(1),* 1635172691) North Star Editions. (Focus Readers).

Gillespie, Katie. Meet the Zebra. 2017. (Illus.). 24p. (J). *(978-1-5105-0557-5(1))* SmartBook Media, Inc.

Gish, Melissa. Living Wild: Zebras. 2013. (Living Wild Ser.). (ENG., Illus.). 48p. (J). (gr. 4-7). pap. 12.00 *(978-0-89812-780-5(7),* 21907, Creative Paperbacks) Creative Co., The.

—Zebra. 2019. (Spotlight on Nature Ser.). (ENG.). 32p. (J). (gr. 4-7). pap. 9.99 *(978-1-62832-750-2(2),* 19201, Creative Paperbacks) Creative Co., The.

—Zebras. 2012. (Living Wild Ser.). (ENG., Illus.). 48p. (J). (gr. 4-7). 23.95 *(978-1-60818-173-5(1),* 21899, Creative Education) Creative Co., The.

Gray, Susan H. Zebras Have Stripes. 2015. (Tell Me Why Library). (ENG., Illus.). 24p. (gr. 2-5). 29.21 *(978-1-63362-001-8(8),* 205916) Cherry Lake Publishing.

Hansen, Grace. Zebra. 2017. (African Animals (Abdo Kids Jumbo) Ser.). (ENG., Illus.). 24p. (J). (gr. -1-2). lib. bdg. 32.79 *(978-1-5321-0423-7(5),* 26549, Abdo Kids) ABDO Publishing Co.

Ipcizade, Catherine. Zebras. 2010. (African Animals Ser.). (ENG.). 24p. (gr. k-1). pap. 41.70 *(978-1-4296-5085-4(0),* Capstone Pr.) Capstone.

—Zebras [Scholastic]. 2010. (African Animals Ser.). 24p. pap. 0.49 *(978-1-4296-5789-1(8),* Capstone Pr.) Capstone.

Klukow, Mary Ellen. Las Cebras. 2019. (Animales Africanos Ser.). (SPA.). 16p. (J). (gr. -1-2). *(978-1-68151-882-4(1),* 10827) Amicus.

—Zebras. 2019. (Spot African Animals Ser.). (ENG.). 16p. (J). (gr. -1-2). lib. bdg. *(978-1-68151-643-1(8),* 10775) Amicus.

MacAulay, Kelley. Les Zebres. 2008. (FRE.). 32p. (J). pap. 9.95 *(978-2-89579-203-1(8))* Bayard Canada Livres CAN. Dist: Crabtree Publishing Co.

MacAulay, Kelley & Kalman, Bobbie. Endangered Zebras. 2007. (Earth's Endangered Animals Ser.). (ENG., Illus.). 32p. (J). (gr. 1-5). lib. bdg. *(978-0-7787-1864-2(6));* pap. *(978-0-7787-1910-6(3))* Crabtree Publishing Co.

Markle, Sandra. Follow Those Zebras: Solving a Migration Mystery. 2020. (Sandra Markle's Science Discoveries Ser.). (ENG., Illus.). 40p. (J). (gr. 4-6). 33.32 *(978-1-5415-3837-5(4),* 2245696f-689a-4a9f-90b1-e178a59cb64c, Millbrook Pr.) Lerner Publishing Group.

—Zebras. (Animal Prey Ser.). 2008. (Illus.). 39p. (J). (gr. 3-7). per. 7.95 *(978-0-8225-6065-4(8),* First Avenue Editions) 2008. pap. 46.95 *(978-0-8225-9325-6(4))* 2007. (ENG., Illus.). 40p. (J). (gr. 3-6). lib. bdg. 25.26 *(978-0-8225-6062-3(3))* Lerner Publishing Group.

Meister, Cari. Zebras. 2015. (J). lib. bdg. 25.65 *(978-1-62031-171-4(2),* Bullfrog Bks.) Jump! Inc.

Moldovo, Eustacia. Baby Zebras at the Zoo. 2015. (J). *(978-0-7660-6617-5(7));* (ENG., Illus.). 24p. (gr. -1-1). pap. 10.35 *(978-0-7660-7093-6(X),* 6799f403-4959-4041-ab19-4ff336ec13fe) Enslow Publishing, LLC.

Murray, Julie. Zebras. 2019. (Animal Kingdom Ser.). (ENG.). 32p. (J). (gr. 2-5). lib. bdg. 34.21 *(978-1-5321-1660-5(8),* 32431, Big Buddy Bks.) ABDO Publishing Co.

Noble-Goodman, Katherine. Zebras, 1 vol. 2007. (Animals, Animals Ser.). (ENG., Illus.). 48p. (gr. 5-5). lib. bdg. 32.64 *(978-0-7614-1871-9(7),* 2de3cbfe-bd15-467a-b208-22e43bd8408f) Cavendish Square Publishing LLC.

Pelusey, Michael & Pelusey, Jane. Giraffes & Zebras, 1 vol. 2009. (Zoo Animals Ser.). (ENG.). 32p. (gr. 2-2). lib. bdg. 21.27 *(978-0-7614-3149-7(7),* 9b52e0ca-ec5a-4fb9-a857-2d5beb65d130) Cavendish Square Publishing LLC.

Raatma, Lucia. Plains Zebras. 2014. (Nature's Children Ser.). (ENG.). 48p. (J). lib. bdg. 28.00 *(978-0-531-21226-4(2))* Scholastic Library Publishing.

Reade, Clara. Zebras, 1 vol. 2012. (PowerKids Readers: Safari Animals Ser.). (ENG., Illus.). 24p. (J). (gr. k-k). pap. 9.25 *(978-1-4488-7535-1(8),* 774a1116-255b-4d8f-b5f5-7b89e5fe7100); lib. bdg. 26.27 *(978-1-4488-7395-1(9),* bb195b6c-0114-4f48-93bf-495adab0072e) Rosen Publishing Group, Inc., The. (PowerKids Pr.).

Riggs, Kate. Amazing Animals: Zebras. 2014. (Amazing Animals Ser.). (ENG.). 24p. (J). (gr. 1-3). pap. 9.99 *(978-0-89812-932-8(X),* 23069, Creative Paperbacks) Creative Co., The.

—Seedlings: Zebras. 2015. (Seedlings Ser.). (ENG.). 24p. (J). (gr. -1-1). pap. 10.99 *(978-1-62832-118-0(0),* 21266, Creative Paperbacks) Creative Co., The.

—Zebras. (Seedlings Ser.). 24p. (J). 2015. (ENG.). (gr. -1-k). *(978-1-60818-518-4(4),* 21265) 2014. (Illus.). 25.65 *(978-1-60818-353-1(X))* Creative Co., The. (Creative Education).

Rustad, Martha E. H. Zebras & Oxpeckers Work Together. 2011. (Animals Working Together Ser.). (ENG.). 24p. (gr. k-1). pap. 41.70 *(978-1-4296-6369-4(3),* Capstone Pr.) Capstone.

Schuh, Mari. Zebras. 2017. (Black & White Animals Ser.). (ENG., Illus.). 24p. (J). (gr. -1-2). lib. bdg. 22.65 *(978-1-5157-3374-4(2),* 133370, Pebble) Capstone.

Staff, Gareth Editorial Staff. Zebras, 1 vol. 2004. (All about Wild Animals Ser.). (ENG., Illus.). 32p. (gr. 2-4). lib. bdg. 28.67 *(978-0-8368-4190-9(5),* 5d5191b4-3b69-4a19-967c-01229fd6223e, Gareth Stevens Learning Library) Stevens, Gareth Publishing LLLP.

Statts, Leo. Zebras. 2016. (Savanna Animals Ser.). (ENG.). 24p. (J). (gr. -1-2). 49.94 *(978-1-68079-372-7(1),* 22993, Abdo Zoom-Launch) ABDO Publishing Co.

Stone, Lynn M. Zebras. 2008. (Nature Watch Ser.). (ENG., Illus.). 48p. (gr. 4-8). lib. bdg. 27.93 *(978-0-8225-7511-5(6),* Lerner Pubns.) Lerner Publishing Group.

Taylor, Trace. You Think You Know Zebras. 2009. (1-3Y Wild Animals Ser.). (ENG.). 24p. (J). (gr. k-2). pap. 8.00 *(978-1-59301-062-1(1))* American Reading Co.

Ticktock Media, Ltd. Staff. What Do Zebras Do? 2008. (What Do Animals Do? Ser.). (ENG.). 10p. (J). (gr. k — 1). bds. 4.95 *(978-1-84696-795-5(3),* TickTock Books) Octopus Publishing Group GBR. Dist: Independent Pubs. Group.

Von Zumbusch, Amelie. Zebras, 1 vol. 2007. (Safari Animals Ser.). (ENG., Illus.). 24p. (J). (gr. 1-1). lib. bdg. 26.27 *(978-1-4042-3613-4(9),* c5541b6c-b16c-4692-bb54-0c36dff0a7d6, PowerKids Pr.) Rosen Publishing Group, Inc., The.

von Zumbusch, Amelie. Zebras. 2009. (Safari Animals Ser.). 24p. (gr. 1-1). 42.50 *(978-1-60852-969-8(X),* PowerKids Pr.) Rosen Publishing Group, Inc., The.

Von Zumbusch, Amelie. Zebras/Cebras, 1 vol. 2006. (Safari Animals / Animales de Safari Ser.). (SPA & ENG., Illus.). 24p. (J). (gr. 1-1). lib. bdg. 26.27 *(978-1-4042-7609-3(2),* e00a787e-9900-45e4-a410-7d2bfd0f8735) Rosen Publishing Group, Inc., The.

von Zumbusch, Amelie. Zebras/Cebras. 2009. (Safari Animals/Animales de safari Ser.). (ENG & SPA.). 24p. (gr. 1-1). 42.50 *(978-1-60852-979-7(7),* Editorial Buenas Letras) Rosen Publishing Group, Inc., The.

Wilsdon, Christina. Zebras. 2006. (J). 7.99 *(978-1-59939-033-8(7))* Cornerstone Pr.

—Zebras, 1 vol. 2009. (Amazing Animals Ser.). (ENG.). 48p. (J). (gr. 3-5). pap. 11.50 *(978-1-4339-2030-1(1),* 8b6ae613-1376-44b6-aca4-76f635ec8748, Gareth Stevens Learning Library); lib. bdg. 30.67 *(978-0-8368-9113-3(9),* a4d14fa4-ff9e-4624-9d3b-7880db765a74) Stevens, Gareth Publishing LLLP.

Zebras. 2006. (Zootles Ser.). (J). 4.95 *(978-1-932396-23-2(3))* National Wildlife Federation.

Zebra's Stripes. Date not set. (Touch & Feel Ser.). (Illus.). (J). 4.98 *(978-0-7525-9571-9(7))* Parragon, Inc.

Zobel, Derek. Zebras. 2011. (Animal Safari Ser.). (ENG., Illus.). 24p. (J). (gr. k-3). lib. bdg. 26.95 *(978-1-60014-611-4(2),* Blastoff! Readers) Bellwether Media.

ZEBRAS—FICTION

Anderson, Doug. Too Big to Dance (Paperback) Anderson, Sara, illus. 2015. (ENG.). 32p. (J). (gr. -1-2). pap. 10.95 *(978-0-9702784-9-4(7))* Sara Anderson Children's Bks.

Arnold, Vickie. The Baby Zebra Adventure. 2009. 20p. pap. 12.49 *(978-1-4389-5818-7(8))* AuthorHouse.

Arrhenius, Ingela P., illus. Where's the Zebra? 2018. (Where's The Ser.). (ENG.). 10p. (J). (— 1). bds. 8.99 *(978-0-7636-9914-7(4))* Candlewick Pr.

Austin, Cassie Rita. Peppermint. Austin, Cassie Rita, illus. 2011. (Illus.). 53p. 15.95 *(978-0-9846151-1-7(3))* Paintbrush Tales Publishing, LLC.

Beeson, Paul & Beeson, Lady Jan. Zeela the Zebra of a Different Color. Beeson, Jan, illus. 2013. 38p. pap. 12.99 *(978-0-9890482-5-5(X))* Beeson, Jan.

Bingham, Kelly. Circle, Square, Moose. Zelinsky, Paul O., illus. 2014. (ENG.). 48p. (J). (gr. -1-3). 17.99 *(978-0-06-229003-8(7),* Greenwillow Bks.) HarperCollins Pubs.

—Z Is for Moose. Zelinsky, Paul O., illus. 2012. (ENG.). 32p. (J). (gr. -1-2). 17.99 *(978-0-06-079984-7(6));* lib. bdg. 17.89 *(978-0-06-079985-4(4))* HarperCollins Pubs. (Greenwillow Bks.).

Cabatingan, Erin. A Is for Musk Ox. Myers, Matthew, illus. 2012. (Musk Ox Ser.: 1). (ENG.). 40p. (J). (gr. k-2). 19.99 *(978-1-59643-676-3(X),* 900071112) Roaring Brook Pr.

Castleton, Chaffee. Runty's Adventure: A Story of Love. Queen, Dana, illus. 2010. (ENG.). 97p. (J). pap. 17.95 *(978-0-578-06109-2(0))* Castleton, Julia J.

Chambers, Willie. The Painted Zebra. 2007. (ENG.). 36p. per. 19.95 *(978-1-4343-3997-3(1))* AuthorHouse.

Childs, Simon. Snowy the Zebra. 2018. (ENG., Illus.). 44p. (J). *(978-1-5289-2520-4(3));* pap. *(978-1-5289-2521-1(1))* Austin Macauley Pubs. Ltd.

-ronicle Books & ImageBooks. Little Zebra: Finger Puppet Book: (Finger Puppet Book for Toddlers & Babies, Baby Books for First Year, Animal Finger Puppets) 2013. (Little Finger Puppet Board Bks.). (ENG., Illus.). 12p. (J). (gr. -1 — 1). bds. 6.99 *(978-1-4521-1252-7(5))* Chronicle Bks. LLC.

-ook, Sherry & Johnson, Terri. Zany Science Zeke. 26. Kuhn, Jesse, illus. I.t. ed. 2006. (Quirkies — Exploring Phonics through Science Ser.: 26). 32p. (J). 7.99 *(978-1-933815-25-1(6),* Quirkles, The) Creative 3, LLC.

-raig, Bobby & Manifold, Delwyn. The Learning Adventures of Spot. 2011. 28p. pap. 24.95 *(978-1-4560-3110-7(4))* America Star Bks.

-reek, Silent. All the Ice of Afric. 2009. 160p. 22.95 *(978-1-4401-2118-0(4))* iUniverse, Inc.

-ahl, Michael. Bye-Bye Bottles, Zebra. Vidal, Oriol, illus. 2015. (Hello Genius Ser.). (ENG.). 20p. (J). (gr. -1 — 1). bds. 7.99 *(978-1-4795-5792-9(7),* 126822, Picture Window Bks.) Capstone.

-ale, Jay. Little Zebra. East, Jacqueline, illus. 2012. (Wonder Words Ser.). (ENG.). 16p. (J). (gr. k-2). pap. 36.94 *(978-1-4296-8907-6(2),* 18350, Capstone Pr.) Capstone.

-ale, Jay & Scott, Kay. Little Zebra, 1 vol. East, Jacqueline, illus. 2012. (Wonder Words Ser.). (ENG.). 16p. (J). (gr. k-2). pap. 6.99 *(978-1-4296-8906-9(4),* 119956, Capstone Pr.) Capstone.

Derubertis, Barbara. Zachary Zebra's Zippity Zooming. Alley, R. W., illus. 2011. (Animal Antics A to Z Set III Ser.). pap. 45.32 *(978-0-7613-8435-9(9))* Astra Publishing Hse.

deRubertis, Barbara. Zachary Zebra's Zippity Zooming. Alley, R. W., illus. 2011. (Animal Antics A to Z Ser.). 32p. (J). (gr. -1-3). pap. 7.95 *(978-1-57565-351-8(6),* c1ec6b17-d95a-42d6-8f11-06c8d8f9765c, Kane Press) Astra Publishing Hse.

deRubertis, Barbara & DeRubertis, Barbara. Zachary Zebra's Zippity Zooming. Alley, R. W., illus. 2012. (Animal Antics A to Z Ser.). 32p. (J). (gr. 2 — 1). cd-rom 7.95 *(978-1-57565-419-5(9))* Astra Publishing Hse.

Dorner, V. K. The Little Lambs & the Rainbow Zebra. 2011. 36p. 13.95 *(978-1-4497-0889-4(7),* WestBow Pr.) Author Solutions, LLC.

Douglas-Hobbs, Kathy. Kobe & the Rescue Adventure. 2012. 16p. pap. 15.99 *(978-1-4772-0326-2(5))* AuthorHouse.

Eburne, Tim. Zebra Stripes: A Tail of Personal Branding. 2012. (Illus.). 48p. pap. 31.99 *(978-1-4691-4536-5(7))* Xlibris Corp.

Ellis, Libby. Ziggy the Zebra. Yoon, Salina, illus. 2005. 14p. (J). (gr. k-3). 9.95 *(978-1-58117-104-4(8),* Intervisual/Piggy Toes) Bendon, Inc.

Grey, Chelsea Gillian. Leperit the Zebra. Denman, Michael & Huiett, William, illus. 2005. (Internet Interactive Ser.). (ENG.). 36p. (J). (gr. -1-3). 8.95 *(978-1-59249-440-8(4),* SD6505); (gr. 2-2). 14.95 *(978-1-59249-438-5(2),* H6505); (gr. 2-2). pap. 6.95 *(978-1-59249-439-2(0),* S6505) Soundprints.

—Leperit the Zebra: African Wildlife Foundation. Denman, Michael L. & Huiett, William J., illus. 2005. (Meet Africa's Animals Ser.). (ENG.). 36p. (J). (gr. -1-2). 2.95 *(978-1-59249-441-5(2),* S6555) Soundprints.

Harrington, Jenna. Katie Mcginty Wants a Pet! Simpson, Finn, illus. 2015. (ENG.). 32p. (J). (gr. -1-2). 16.99 *(978-1-58925-192-2(X))* Tiger Tales.

Henkes, Kevin. The Zebra Wall. 2005. (ENG., Illus.). 160p. (J). (gr. 3-7). pap. 7.99 *(978-0-06-073303-2(9),* Greenwillow Bks.) HarperCollins Pubs.

Jacobs, Nadine. Zefir, la Cebrita en Peligro. Vicens, Paula, tr. Jacobs, Nadine, illus. 2004. (SPA., Illus.). 32p. (J). 15.99 *(978-84-8470-108-8(5))* Corimbo, Editorial S.L. ESP. Dist: Lectorum Pubns., Inc.

Kim, JiYu. Zippy the Runner. Seon, JeongHyeon, illus. rev. ed. 2014. (MySELF Bookshelf Ser.). (ENG.). 32p. (J). (gr. k-2). pap. 11.94 *(978-1-60357-656-7(8));* lib. bdg. 25.27 *(978-1-59953-647-7(1))* Norwood Hse. Pr.

Kim, YoeongAh. The Shooting Stars Soccer Team. Lee, Hyeongjin, illus. rev. ed. 2014. (MySELF Bookshelf Ser.). (ENG.). 32p. (J). (gr. k-2). lib. bdg. 25.27 *(978-1-59953-648-4(X))* Norwood Hse. Pr.

Kompelien, Tracy. Zebra Stripes. Nobens, C. A., illus. 2006. (Fact & Fiction Ser.). 24p. (J). pap. 48.42 *(978-1-59679-972-1(2))* ABDO Publishing Co.

Kuenzler, Lou. Not yet Zebra. Woolf, Julia, illus. 2018. (ENG.). 32p. (J). (gr. -1-1). 16.95 *(978-0-571-34288-4(4),* Faber & Faber Children's Bks.) Faber & Faber, Inc.

Law, Felicia. Zanzibar the Zebra: A Tale of Individuality, 1 vol. Messina, Lilli, illus. 2009. (Animal Fair Values Ser.). (ENG.). 32p. (J). (gr. 2-2). pap. 11.55 *(978-1-60754-807-2(0),* c79a910b-d360-4a57-87b3-42c4d35ebebe); lib. bdg. 27.27 *(978-1-60754-803-4(8),* 48824c77-8566-4a74-b1c5-dd01393714cf) Rosen Publishing Group, Inc., The. (Windmill Bks.).

Madden, Gloria. Grandmothers Bedtime Stories. 2008. 68p. (gr. -1-7). pap. 10.49 *(978-1-4343-9201-5(5))* AuthorHouse.

Mallory, Nicole. I Wish I Was an Alligator. 2013. (ENG.). 29p. (J). pap. 15.95 *(978-1-4787-1066-0(7))* Outskirts Pr., Inc.

Meadows, Daisy. Savannah the Zebra Fairy. 2015. (Rainbow Magic — Baby Animal Rescue Fairies Ser.: 4). lib. bdg. 14.75 *(978-0-606-37052-3(8))* Turtleback.

Mello, Craig. Difference: the Rainbow Zebra: An African Tale of Diversity. 2007. 40p. per. 24.95 *(978-1-4241-8269-5(7))* PublishAmerica, Inc.

Miller, Kathryn L. Abc's with Sadie: Sadie Goes to the Zoo. 2011. 32p. pap. 17.25 *(978-1-4269-5940-0(0))* Trafford Publishing.

Neiman, Jahcolyn Russell. Kekula. 2011. 32p. pap. 13.99 *(978-1-4520-8086-4(0))* AuthorHouse.

Nelson, M. R. The Zebra Said Shhh. Sheldon, Tamia, illus. 2013. (ENG.). 32p. (J). (gr. -1-k). pap. 9.99 *(978-1-62395-440-6(1))* Xist Publishing.

Northfield, Gary. Julius Zebra: Battle with the Britons! Northfield, Gary, illus. (Julius Zebra Ser.: 2). (ENG., Illus.). 288p. (J). (gr. 2-5). 2019. pap. 7.99 *(978-1-5362-0636-4(9))* 2018. 15.99 *(978-0-7636-7854-8(6))* Candlewick Pr.

—Julius Zebra: Rumble with the Romans! Northfield, Gary, illus. 2018. (Julius Zebra Ser.: 1). (ENG., Illus.). 288p. (J). (gr. 2-5). pap. 7.99 *(978-0-7636-9846-1(6))* Candlewick Pr.

Nunez, Marisa. Camilla the Zebra. Villan, Oscar, illus. 2003. 32p. (J). 14.95 *(978-84-95730-39-8(1))* Kalandraka Catalunya, Edicions, S.L. ESP. Dist: Independent Pubs. Group.

Núñez, Marisa. La cebra Camila. 2005. (SPA., Illus.). 216p. (J). (gr. k-2). 16.95 *(978-84-95123-60-2(6),* KA8243) Kalandraka Editora, S.L. ESP. Dist: Lectorum Pubns., Inc., Iaconi, Marisco/Mariuccia Bk. Imports.

Pastis, Stephan. Beginning Pearls. 2013. lib. bdg. 20.85 *(978-0-606-31764-1(3))* Turtleback.

Paterson, Brian. Zigby - the Picnic. Paterson, Brian, illus. 2006. (ENG., Illus.). 16p. (J). (gr. -1). bds. 6.99 *(978-0-00-717421-8(7),* HarperCollins Children's Bks.) HarperCollins Pubs. Ltd. GBR. Dist: Trafalgar Square Publishing.

—Zigby Camps Out. Paterson, Brian, illus. 2003. (Zigby Ser.). (ENG., Illus.). 32p. (J). (gr. -1-2). pap. 8.99 *(978-0-00-713180-8(1),* HarperCollins Children's Bks.) HarperCollins Pubs. Ltd. GBR. Dist: Independent Pubs. Group.

Plant, Marilyn. Trinka's Magic Bracelet. 2012. 40p. pap. *(978-1-77067-956-6(1))* FriesenPress.

Rizvi, Sobia. Zebra Stripes. 2011. 24p. pap. 15.99 *(978-1-4653-4618-6(X))* Xlibris Corp.

Robaard, Jedda. The Little Zebra Who Lost His Stripes. 2013. (Illus.). (J). *(978-1-4351-5392-9(8))* Barnes & Noble, Inc.

Rudolph, Shaina & Royer, Danielle. All My Stripes: A Story for Children with Autism. Zivoin, Jennifer, illus. 2014. (J). pap. *(978-1-4338-1917-9(1),* Magination Pr.) American Psychological Assn.

Sims, Lesley. How Zebras Got Their Stripes. 2009. (Young Reading Ser.). 64p. (J). 6.99 *(978-0-7945-2525-5(3),* Usborne) EDC Publishing.

Sullivan, Candida. Zippy & the Stripes of Courage. 2011. (J). pap. 13.99 *(978-1-937331-08-5(3))* ShadeTree Publishing, LLC.

Uvezian, Verne. The Day Benny Stuck His Neck Out. 2011. 12p. (gr. 1-2). 9.95 *(978-1-4567-3119-9(X))* AuthorHouse.

Volker, Kerstin. Emma Goes Shopping. 2003. (Funny Friends Lift-and-Learn Bks.). 14p. (J). 5.99 *(978-1-59384-021-1(7))* Parklane Publishing.

—Suzie Goes to Sleep. 2003. (Funny Friends Lift-and-Learn Bks.). (Illus.). 14p. (J). 5.99 *(978-1-59384-024-2(1))* Parklane Publishing.

Walker, Anna. I Love Christmas. Walker, Anna, illus. 2009. (ENG., Illus.). 32p. (J). (gr. -1-1). 9.99 *(978-1-4169-8317-0(1),* Simon & Schuster Bks. For Young Readers) Simon & Schuster Bks. For Young Readers.

—I Love My Dad. Walker, Anna, illus. 2010. (ENG., Illus.). 32p. (J). (gr. -1-1). 9.99 *(978-1-4169-8319-4(8),* Simon & Schuster Bks. For Young Readers) Simon & Schuster Bks. For Young Readers.

—I Love My Mom. Walker, Anna, illus. 2010. (ENG., Illus.). 32p. (J). (gr. -1-1). 9.99 *(978-1-4169-8318-7(X),* Simon & Schuster Bks. For Young Readers) Simon & Schuster Bks. For Young Readers.

—I Love to Dance. Walker, Anna, illus. 2011. (ENG., Illus.). 32p. (J). (gr. -1-1). 9.99 *(978-1-4169-8323-1(6),* Simon & Schuster Bks. For Young Readers) Simon & Schuster Bks. For Young Readers.

—I Love to Sing. Walker, Anna, illus. 2011. (ENG., Illus.). 32p. (J). (gr. -1-1). 9.99 *(978-1-4169-8322-4(8),* Simon & Schuster Bks. For Young Readers) Simon & Schuster Bks. For Young Readers.

—I Love Vacations. Walker, Anna, illus. 2011. (ENG., Illus.). 32p. (J). (gr. -1-1). 9.99 *(978-1-4169-8321-7(X),* Simon & Schuster Bks. For Young Readers) Simon & Schuster Bks. For Young Readers.

Waller, Alesha. The Spotted Zebr. 2011. 20p. pap. 13.99 *(978-1-4634-7456-0(3))* AuthorHouse.

Weaver, Amy Garrett. Zoe the Zebra. Schneider, Robin, illus. 2009. 33p. pap. 24.95 *(978-1-60749-552-9(X))* PublishAmerica, Inc.

ZENGER, JOHN PETER, 1697-1746

Gibson, Karen Bush. John Peter Zenger. 2006. (Profiles in American History Ser.). (Illus.). 48p. (J). (gr. 3-7). lib. bdg. 29.95 *(978-1-58415-437-2(3))* Mitchell Lane Pubs.

ZEPPELINS

see Airships

ZIMBABWE

Baughan, Michael Gray. Zimbabwe. Rotberg, Robert I., ed. 2012. (Evolution of Africa's Major Nations Ser.). (Illus.). 80p. (J). (gr. 7). 22.95 *(978-1-4222-2188-4(1))* Mason Crest.

—Zimbabwe. 2011. (J). pap. *(978-1-4222-2216-4(0))* Mason Crest.

Chifamba-Barnes, Sarudzayi Elizabeth. The Village Story-Teller: Zimbabwean Folktales. 2009. (Illus.). 100p. (gr. 3-7). pap. *(978-0-9558082-1-0(9))* Lion Pr. Ltd., The.

Di Piazza, Francesca. Zimbabwe in Pictures. 2005. (Visual Geography Series, Second Ser.). (ENG., Illus.). 80p. (gr. 5-12). 31.93 *(978-0-8225-2399-4(X))* Lerner Publishing Group.

Glynne, Andy. Juliane's Story: A Real-Life Account of Her Journey from Zimbabwe. 2017. (Seeking Refuge Ser.). (ENG., Illus.). 32p. (J). (gr. k-5). 27.99 *(978-1-5158-1414-6(9),* 135356, Picture Window Bks.) Capstone.

Haskins, Jim & Benson, Kathleen. Count Your Way Through Zimbabwe. Park, Janie Jaehyun, illus. 2006. (Count Your Way Ser.). (ENG.). 24p. (gr. 2-5). lib. bdg. 19.93 *(978-1-57505-885-6(5),* Millbrook Pr.) Lerner Publishing Group.

Kalz, Jill. Victoria Falls. 2004. (Natural Wonders of the World Ser.). (Illus.). 32p. (J). lib. bdg. 18.95 *(978-1-58341-327-2(8),* Creative Education) Creative Co., The.

Klepeis, Alicia Z. Zimbabwe, 1 vol. 2017. (Exploring World Cultures (First Edition) Ser.). (ENG., Illus.). 32p. (gr. 3-3). pap. 12.16 *(978-1-5026-2496-3(6),* 5ffc1521-462f-4241-a0f1-e083a8409357) Cavendish Square Publishing LLC.

Korky Paul: Biography of an Illustrator: Individual Title Six-Packs. (Discovery World Ser.). 24p. (gr. 1-2). 33.00 *(978-0-7635-8471-9(1))* Rigby Education.

Sheehan, Sean. Zimbabwe, 1 vol. 2nd rev. ed. 2004. (Cultures of the World (Second Edition)(r) Ser.). (ENG., Illus.). 144p. (gr. 5-5). lib. bdg. 49.79 *(978-0-7614-1706-4(0),* 77a98452-0091-4e11-b3a1-2aed2995b1d7) Cavendish Square Publishing LLC.

Sheehan, Sean & Spilling, Michael. Zimbabwe, 1 vol. 3rd rev. ed. 2014. (Cultures of the World (Third Edition)(r) Ser.). (ENG., Illus.). 144p. (gr. 5-5). lib. bdg. 48.79 *(978-0-7614-8017-4(X),* afae48b4-7d8f-4704-a6d4-7a33a2d85734) Cavendish Square Publishing LLC.

Thorpe, Yvonne. Zimbabwe, 1 vol. 2010. (Global Hotspots Ser.). (ENG.). 32p. (gr. 5-5). lib. bdg. 21.27 *(978-0-7614-4763-4(6),* a9bcae51-7437-4072-afa9-1037ea12b618) Cavendish Square Publishing LLC.

Trent, Tererai. The Girl Who Buried Her Dreams in a Can: A True Story. Gilchrist, Jan Spivey, illus. 2015. 40p. (J). (gr. 1-3). 18.99 *(978-0-670-01654-9(3),* Viking Books for Young Readers) Penguin Young Readers Group.

ZIMBABWE—FICTION

Chikuhwa, Jacob. From the Cradle to the Bonfire. 2012. 78p. pap. 16.95 *(978-1-4626-9859-2(X))* America Star Bks.

Chinodya, Shimmer. Tale of Tamari. 2003. (Illus.). 76p. pap. *(978-1-77922-026-4(X))* Weaver Pr.

Cooper, Ross Gordon. Clarence the Catfish. 2010. (ENG.). 32p. pap. 21.95 *(978-0-557-30913-9(1))* Lulu Pr., Inc.

Deogratias Simba. The Mystery Door. 2005. (Illus.). 22p. pap. *(978-9987-417-21-6(3))* Mkuki na Nyoka Pubs. TZA. Dist: Michigan State Univ. Pr.

Farmer, Nancy. The Ear, the Eye, & the Arm. 2012. (ENG.). 336p. (J). (gr. 4-7). pap. 8.99 *(978-0-545-35661-9(X),* Scholastic Paperbacks) Scholastic, Inc.

—The Ear, the Eye, & the Arm. 2012. lib. bdg. 18.40 *(978-0-606-23944-8(8))* Turtleback.

Kandimba, V. T. Folktales from Zimbabwe: Short Stores. 2009. (Illus.). 56p. 24.99 *(978-1-4415-4281-6(7))* Xlibris Corp.

Kandimba, Vt. Folk Tales from Zimbabwe. 2009. 58p. pap. 15.99 *(978-1-4415-4280-9(9))* Xlibris Corp.

Knight, Deborah Janet. A Puzzling Picnic. Hauvette, Marion, illus. 2010. 32p. pap. 13.00 *(978-1-60860-963-5(4),* Eloquent Bks.) Strategic Book Publishing & Rights Agency (SBPRA).

Lide, Emily. Zimbabwe. 2006. per. 11.95 *(978-1-59094-120-1(9))* Jawbone Publishing Corp.

Literature Connections English: Nervous Conditions. 2004. (gr. 6-12). *(978-0-395-77560-8(4),* 2-80129) Holt McDougal.

Rundell, Katherine. Cartwheeling in Thunderstorms. Castrillón, Melissa & Castrillón, Melissa, illus. 2014. (ENG.). 256p. (J). (gr. 3-7). 18.99 *(978-1-4424-9061-1(6),* Simon & Schuster Bks. For Young Readers) Simon & Schuster Bks. For Young Readers.

St. John, Lauren. The Last Leopard. 2010. (ENG.). 224p. (J). (gr. 3-7). 6.99 *(978-0-14-241515-3(4),* Puffin Books) Penguin Young Readers Group.

Wallace, Jason. Encounters. 2018. (ENG.). 320p. (YA). (gr. 7). 13.99 *(978-1-84939-621-9(3))* Andersen Pr. GBR. Dist: Independent Pubs. Group.

Williams, Michael. Diamond Boy. 2014. (ENG., Illus.). 400p. (YA). (gr. 7-17). 18.00 *(978-0-316-32069-6(2))* Little, Brown Bks. for Young Readers.

—Now Is the Time for Running. 2013. (ENG.). 240p. (YA). (gr. 7-17). pap. 10.99 *(978-0-316-07788-0(7))* Little, Brown Bks. for Young Readers.

Wolfson, Steve. Elephants at the Airport. Brulot, Heleen, illus. 2013. 32p. pap. 11.95 *(978-0-9798324-5-1(4))* Argami Productions, LLC.

ZIONISM

Hurt, Avery Elizabeth. Arab Nationalism & Zionism, 1 vol. 2017. (Interwar Years Ser.). (ENG.). 128p. (YA). (gr. 9-9). 47.36 *(978-1-5026-2720-9(5),* cd67c366-202b-4374-a021-510cf0b6d9eb) Cavendish Square Publishing LLC.

Whiting, Jim. The Creation of Isreal. 2007. (Monumental Milestones Ser.). (Illus.). 48p. (YA). (gr. 4-7). lib. bdg. 29.95 *(978-1-58415-538-6(8))* Mitchell Lane Pubs.

ZIONISM—FICTION

Shapiro, David L. Sara's Journey. 2005. (ENG.). 224p. (gr. 7-12). per. 16.95 *(978-0-8276-0776-7(8))* Jewish Pubn. Society.

ZODIAC

Lee, Jen Sookfong. The Animals of Chinese New Year / 中国农历新年动物生肖, 1 vol. Wong, Kileasa Che Wan, tr. 2019. (ENG & CHI., Illus.). 28p. (J). (gr. -1 — 1). bds. 9.95 *(978-1-4598-1902-3(0))* Orca Bk. Pubs. USA.

Peters, Stephanie True. Gemini. 2009. (Library of Constellations Ser.). 24p. (gr. 3-4). 45.00 *(978-1-60853-574-3(6),* PowerKids Pr.) Rosen Publishing Group, Inc., The.

—Pisces. 2009. (Library of Constellations Ser.). 24p. (gr. 3-4). 45.00 *(978-1-60853-576-7(2),* PowerKids Pr.) Rosen Publishing Group, Inc., The.

Stewart, Pat. Learning about the Zodiac. 2003. (Dover Little Activity Bks.). (ENG., Illus.). 16p. (J). (gr. 3-5). pap. 1.50 *(978-0-486-43024-9(3))* Dover Pubns., Inc.

Tang, Sanmu. Chinese Zodiac Animals. Jingwen, Zhu, tr. 2011. (Illus.). 56p. (gr. 4-6). pap. 8.95 *(978-1-60220-977-0(4))* Shanghai Pr.

Zodiac Fun [Capstone Sole Source]. 2010. (Zodiac Fun Ser.). 32p. lib. bdg. 106.60 *(978-1-4296-5895-9(9),* Capstone Pr.) Capstone.

ZOMO, THE RABBIT (FICTITIOUS CHARACTER)—FICTION

Ralles, H. J. Keeper of the Empire, Vol. 3. 2004. (Illus.). 235p. (J). pap. 9.95 *(978-1-929976-25-6(9))* Top Pubns., Ltd.

ZOO ANIMALS

Accord Publishing, Accord. Zoo Babies. 2010. (ENG., Illus.). 12p. (J). (gr. -1). 9.99 *(978-0-7407-9201-4(6))* Andrews McMeel Publishing.

Alkire, Jessie. Captive Animal Welfare. 2017. (Animal Rights Ser.). (ENG., Illus.). 32p. (J). (gr. 3-6). lib. bdg. 32.79 *(978-1-5321-1258-4(0),* 27575, Checkerboard Library) ABDO Publishing Co.

All about Baby Zoo Animals. 2015. (All about Baby Zoo Animals Ser.). (ENG.). 24p. (J). (gr. -1-1). pap., pap., pap. 336.60 *(978-0-7660-6690-8(8))* Enslow Publishing, LLC.

All about Baby Zoo Animals: Set 3, 12 vols. 2016. (All about Baby Zoo Animals Ser.). 24p. (ENG.). (gr. k-1). lib. bdg. 145.62 *(978-0-7660-7489-7(7),* 3303150c-5c3b-4f59-8cef-fe99a206712d); (gr. 1-k). pap. 56.10 *(978-0-7660-7961-8(9))* Enslow Publishing, LLC.

All about Baby Zoo Animals: Set 1, 12 vols. 2015. (All about Baby Zoo Animals Ser.). (ENG.). 24p. (J). (gr. -1-1). lib. bdg. 145.62 *(978-0-7660-7131-5(6),* 52a5b678-3d07-4f17-94c7-a094e1f5ca23) Enslow Publishing, LLC.

Amery, Heather. Zoo Talkabout Board Book. Cartwright, Stephen, illus. 2008. (Talkabout Board Bks). 12p. (J). bds. 8.99 *(978-0-7945-1793-9(5),* Usborne) EDC Publishing.

Andrews McMeel Publishing, LLC Staff. Zoo Babies. 2015. (ENG.). 12p. (J). bds. 5.99 *(978-1-4494-6058-7(5))* Andrews McMeel Publishing.

Animales Del Zoológico / Zoo Animals, 12 vols. 2015. (Animales Del Zoológico / Zoo Animals Ser.). (ENG & SPA.). 24p. (J). (gr. k-k). lib. bdg. 145.62 *(978-1-4824-2975-6(6),* 3b5f7089-1822-4a73-899b-cc2a8c97c14d) Stevens, Gareth Publishing LLLP.

Appleby, Alex. Dinosaurs at the Zoo, 1 vol. 2013. (Dinosaur School Ser.). 24p. (J). (gr. k-k). (ENG.). pap. 9.15 *(978-1-4339-9046-5(6),* f582a76e-f6d7-431c-aec5-1ec19181cf1b); pap. 48.90 *(978-1-4339-9047-2(4));* (ENG., Illus.). lib. bdg. 25.27 *(978-1-4339-9045-8(8),* 91280a3c-0c38-4e6a-8e2c-60d72437329a) Stevens, Gareth Publishing LLLP.

At the Zoo. (Boxset Small Ser.). 32p. *(978-1-4054-7068-1(2))* Parragon, Inc.

Ayers, Chris. MY Daily Zoo: A Drawing Activity Book for All Ages. 2011. (ENG., Illus.). 96p. pap. 9.95 *(978-1-933492-63-6(5))* Design Studio Pr.

AZ Books Staff. Noisy Zoo. Tulup, Natalia, ed. 2012. (How We Speak Ser.). (ENG.). 12p. (J). (gr. -1-k). bds. 10.95 *(978-1-61889-094-8(8))* AZ Bks. LLC.

Beylon, Cathy. At the Zoo/en el Zoologico: Bilingual Coloring Book. Gongora, Oscar, tr. 2011. (Dover Bilingual Books for Kids Ser.). (ENG., Illus.). 32p. (J). (gr. k-6). pap. 3.99 *(978-0-486-47814-2(9),* 478149) Dover Pubns., Inc.

Bishop, Celeste. A Visit to the Zoo, 1 vol. 2016. (Places in My Community Ser.). (ENG.). 24p. (J). (gr. 1-1). pap. 9.25 *(978-1-4994-2772-1(7),* 68cc7326-ad11-4d83-8c12-c04b9cb4620b, PowerKids Pr.) Rosen Publishing Group, Inc., The.

Bleiman, Andrew & Eastland, Chris. ABC ZooBorns! 2013. (ZooBorns Ser.). (ENG., Illus.). 40p. (J). (gr. -1 — 1). bds. 8.99 *(978-1-4424-7376-8(2),* Little Simon) Little Simon.

—Hello, Mommy ZooBorns! Ready-To-Read Level 1. 2013. (ZooBorns Ser.). (ENG., Illus.). 24p. (J). (gr. -1-1). 16.99 *(978-1-4424-4382-2(0),* Simon Spotlight) Simon & Schuster Children's Publishing.

—Hello, Mommy ZooBorns! Ready-To-Read Level 1. 2013. (ZooBorns Ser.). (ENG., Illus.). 24p. (J). (gr. -1-1). pap. 4.99 *(978-1-4424-4383-9(9),* Simon Spotlight) Simon Spotlight.

—I Love You, ZooBorns! Ready-To-Read Level 1. 2012. (ZooBorns Ser.). (ENG., Illus.). 24p. (J). (gr. -1-1). 15.99 *(978-1-4424-4379-2(0));* pap. 4.99 *(978-1-4424-4380-8(4))* Simon Spotlight. (Simon Spotlight).

—Nighty Night, ZooBorns: Ready-To-Read Level 1. 2013. (ZooBorns Ser.). (ENG., Illus.). 24p. (J). (gr. -1-1). 16.99 *(978-1-4424-4385-3(5));* pap. 4.99 *(978-1-4424-4386-0(3))* Simon Spotlight. (Simon Spotlight).

—Snuggle up, ZooBorns! 2015. (J). *(978-1-4806-9333-3(2),* Simon Spotlight) Simon Spotlight.

—Snuggle up, ZooBorns! Ready-To-Read Level 1. 2015. (ZooBorns Ser.). (ENG., Illus.). 24p. (J). (gr. -1-1). pap. 4.99 *(978-1-4814-3100-2(5),* Simon Spotlight) Simon Spotlight.

—Welcome to the World, Zooborns! Ready-To-Read Level 1. 2012. (ZooBorns Ser.). (ENG., Illus.). 24p. (J). (gr. -1-1). 17.99 *(978-1-4424-4376-1(6));* pap. 4.99 *(978-1-4424-4377-8(4))* Simon Spotlight. (Simon Spotlight).

—ZigZag ZooBorns! Zoo Baby Colors & Patterns. 2018. (ZooBorns Ser.). (ENG., Illus.). 40p. (J). (gr. -1-3). pap. 7.99 *(978-1-5344-2119-6(X),* Beach Lane Bks.) Beach Lane Bks.

—ZooBorns! Zoo Babies from Around the World. 2010. (ZooBorns Ser.). (ENG.). 40p. (J). (gr. -1-1). 14.99 *(978-1-4424-1272-9(0),* Beach Lane Bks.) Beach Lane Bks.

—ZooBorns! Zoo Babies from Around the World. 2012. (ZooBorns Ser.). (ENG.). 40p. (J). (gr. -1 — 1). bds. 7.99 *(978-1-4424-4329-7(4),* Little Simon) Little Simon.

—1-2-3 ZooBorns! (ZooBorns Ser.). (ENG.). 32p. (J). (gr. -1-3). 2017. pap. 8.99 *(978-1-4814-9174-7(1))* 2015. (Illus.). 14.99 *(978-1-4814-3103-3(X))* Beach Lane Bks. (Beach Lane Bks.).

Bossù, Rossana. How Big Is an Elephant? 2018. (ENG., Illus.). 24p. (J). (gr. -1-k). 18.95 *(978-1-55451-998-9(5))* Annick Pr., Ltd. CAN. Dist: Publishers Group West (PGW).

—How Big Is an Elephant? 2018. (ENG., Illus.). 24p. (J). (gr. -1-k). 9.95 *(978-1-55451-997-2(7))* Annick Pr., Ltd. CAN. Dist: Publishers Group West (PGW).

Boughton, Samantha. Day at the Zoo Adventure Coloring Book. 2014. (Dover Animal Coloring Bks.). (ENG., Illus.). 48p. (J). (gr. k-3). pap. 4.99 *(978-0-486-49154-7(4),* 491544) Dover Pubns., Inc.

Brannon, Cecelia H. Baby Flamingos at the Zoo. 2016. (All about Baby Zoo Animals Ser.). 24p. (J). (gr. k-1). pap. 56.10 *(978-0-7660-7525-2(7))* Enslow Publishing, LLC.

—Baby Gorillas at the Zoo, 1 vol. 2015. (All about Baby Zoo Animals Ser.). (ENG.). 24p. (gr. k-1). pap. 10.35 *(978-0-7660-7141-4(3),* a7ba5ff1-e2a2-4efe-bfaf-556ef3651c5f); (Illus.). 24.27 *(978-0-7660-7143-8(X),* 724fb4b9-7b1d-40be-926c-27cb88449b84) Enslow Publishing, LLC.

—Baby Hippos at the Zoo, 1 vol. 2015. (All about Baby Zoo Animals Ser.). (ENG.). 24p. (gr. k-1). pap. 10.35 *(978-0-7660-7145-2(6),* 332fafb9-857f-46d9-973c-9ad6a8238d5d); (Illus.). lib. bdg. 24.27 *(978-0-7660-7148-3(0),* 9858544c-5bf4-4217-89a3-4a911e1b5596) Enslow Publishing, LLC.

—Baby Penguins at the Zoo, 1 vol. 2015. (All about Baby Zoo Animals Ser.). (ENG., Illus.). 24p. (gr. k-1). lib. bdg. 24.27 *(978-0-7660-7152-0(9),* 675fbde3-4243-422a-bbee-59b870c91993) Enslow Publishing, LLC.

—Baby Polar Bears at the Zoo, 1 vol. 2015. (All about Baby Zoo Animals Ser.). (ENG.). 24p. (gr. k-1). pap. 10.35 *(978-0-7660-7154-4(5),* 67d2174d-2fa3-49e9-ad88-0c3365d2d272); (Illus.). lib. bdg. 24.27 *(978-0-7660-7156-8(1),*

WXYZ

c16345b9-41b4-4d27-a721-3f03af690b13) Enslow Publishing, LLC.
—Baby Seals at the Zoo. 2016. (All about Baby Zoo Animals Ser.). 24p. (J). (gr. k-1). pap. 56.10 *(978-0-7660-7520-7(6)*, Enslow Publishing) Enslow Publishing, LLC.
—Baby Turtles at the Zoo, 1 vol. 2015. (All about Baby Zoo Animals Ser.). (ENG.). 24p. (gr. k-1). pap. 10.35 *(978-0-7660-7158-2(8)*, 4ed21be0-12c3-4927-b0a5-0e5de4d3d259); (Illus.). lib. bdg. 24.27 *(978-0-7660-7160-5(X)*, 9e85e27e-7cbb-4acb-9d32-a2521d1441bb) Enslow Publishing, LLC.
—Baby Whales at the Zoo, 1 vol. 2016. (All about Baby Zoo Animals Ser.). (ENG.). 24p. (gr. k-1). 24.27 *(978-0-7660-7563-4(X)*, 697d132b-f6a3-4b73-95d9-a25e2f958fc9) Enslow Publishing, LLC.
Brinker, Spencer. At the Zoo. 2019. (I Spy Ser.). (ENG., Illus.). 16p. (J). (gr. -1-1). 6.99 *(978-1-64280-391-4(X))* Bearport Publishing Co., Inc.
Brown, Heather. Chomp! Zoo: A Pull-Tab Book. 2012. (ENG.). 12p. (J). (gr. -1-k). bds. 7.99 *(978-1-4494-2312-4(4))* Andrews McMeel Publishing.
Calver, Paul & Reynolds, Toby. First Sticker Art: Zoo Animals: Use Stickers to Create 20 Cute Zoo Animals. Savva, Ksenya, illus. 2019. (First Sticker Art Ser.). (ENG.). 64p. (J). (gr. -1-2). pap. 9.99 *(978-1-4380-1248-3(9))* Sourcebooks, Inc.
Capstone Press. Zoo Animal Mysteries. 2010. (Zoo Animal Mysteries Ser.). (ENG.). 32p. lib. bdg. 143.94 *(978-1-4296-5901-7(7)*, Capstone Pr.) Capstone.
Chilek, Laurie. Counting at the Zoo: Learning to Add 1 to One-Digit Numbers, 1 vol. (Math for the REAL World Ser.). (ENG., Illus.). 8p. (gr. k-1). 2010. pap. 5.15 *(978-0-8239-8909-6(7)*, 22b91f7d-d712-4e42-b958-eb07d568866a) 2004. 29.95 *(978-0-8239-7628-7(9))* Rosen Publishing Group, Inc., The.
Christopher, Nick. Should We Keep Animals in Zoos?, 1 vol. 2017. (Points of View Ser.). (ENG.). 24p. (gr. 3-3). pap. 9.25 *(978-1-5345-2325-8(1)*, cd0b997d-0b2c-4284-b43f-87057086a3b2); lib. bdg. 26.23 *(978-1-5345-2327-2(8)*, 2f1ca732-0d28-4c01-b78c-cda23407fbd7) Greenhaven Publishing LLC.
Clark, Rosalyn. A Visit to the Zoo. 2017. (Bumba Books (r) — Places We Go Ser.). (ENG., Illus.). 24p. (J). (gr. -1-1). 26.65 *(978-1-5124-3373-9(X)*, 10cc16dd-3250-4d9b-899e-5e914788a0fe, Lerner Pubns.) Lerner Publishing Group.
Clarke, Phillip, ed. 100 Animals to Spot at the Zoo. McGregor, Malcolm, illus. 2009. (Spotter's Cards Ser.). 52p. (J). 9.99 *(978-0-7945-2254-4(8)*, Usborne) EDC Publishing.
Clemson, David & Clemson, Wendy. Zookeeper for a Day, 1 vol. 2007. (Math Adventures Ser.). (ENG., Illus.). 32p. (gr. 2-4). pap. 11.50 *(978-0-8368-8142-4(7)*, 8fca5a6f-8ceb-434a-ad91-3563fc5b103d, Gareth Stevens Learning Library) Stevens, Gareth Publishing LLLP.
Dawson, Emily C. The Zoo. 2010. (My Community Ser.). (ENG.). 24p. (J). (gr. k-2). lib. bdg. 25.65 *(978-1-60753-024-4(4)*, 17152) Amicus.
Dee, Nora. Spanish Words at the Zoo, 1 vol., Vol. 1. 2013. (Learn My Language! Spanish Ser.). (ENG.). 24p. (J). (gr. 1-2). 25.27 *(978-1-4824-0355-8(2)*, d63433d1-6aec-4924-af1b-ee016c0578fc); pap. 9.15 *(978-1-4824-0358-9(7)*, 2d22ae17-b141-49ba-ac74-7b9351482ec2) Stevens, Gareth Publishing LLLP.
Devera, Czeena. At the Zoo. 2019. (I Can See Ser.). (ENG.). 16p. (J). (gr. -1-2). pap. 11.36 *(978-1-5341-3914-5(1)*, 212492, Cherry Blossom Press) Cherry Lake Publishing.
DiCicco, Sue. 1, 2 at the Zoo. DiCicco, Sue, illus. 2012. (ENG., Illus.). 12p. (J). (— 1). bds. 6.99 *(978-0-545-43239-9(1))* Scholastic, Inc.
DK. Tabbed Board Books: My First Zoo: Let's Meet the Animals! 2016. (My First Tabbed Board Book Ser.). (ENG., Illus.). 28p. (J). (— 1). bds. 12.99 *(978-1-4654-4883-5(7)*, DK Children) Dorling Kindersley Publishing, Inc.
Drews, Judith. The Zoo's Grand Opening: An ABC & Counting Book. 2014. (ENG., Illus.). 64p. (J). 16.95 *(978-3-89955-714-5(X))* Die Gestalten Verlag DEU. Dist: Ingram Publisher Services.
Earhart, Kristin, ed. Life-Size Zoo: From Tiny Rodents to Gigantic Elephants, an Actual Size Animal Encyclopedia. 2009. (ENG., Illus.). 48p. (gr. -1). 17.95 *(978-1-934734-20-9(9))* Seven Footer Pr.
Early Macken, JoAnn. Monkeys / Los Monos, 1 vol. 2004. (Animals I See at the Zoo / Animales Que Veo en el Zoológico Ser.). (SPA & ENG., Illus.). 24p. (gr. k-2). pap. 9.15 *(978-0-8368-4388-0(6)*, 587ba187-efee-4c04-8038-7a341b6c3e63); lib. bdg. 24.67 *(978-0-8368-4383-5(5)*, 71140c8e-67d7-41b2-b060-7530fa6b1ef5) Stevens, Gareth Publishing LLLP. (Weekly Reader Leveled Readers).
—Penguins / Los Pinguinos, 1 vol. 2004. (Animals I See at the Zoo / Animales Que Veo en el Zoológico Ser.). (ENG & SPA., Illus.). 24p. (J). (gr. k-2). pap. 9.15 *(978-0-8368-4006-3(2)*, 74d6e910-2d98-4e43-adf6-203bc5265399, Weekly Reader Leveled Readers) Stevens, Gareth Publishing LLLP.
Encyclopaedia Britannica, Inc. Staff, compiled by. Discover English with Ben & Bella: Series 4: at the Zoo. 2010. 180.00 *(978-1-61535-351-4(8))* Encyclopaedia Britannica, Inc.
Feeding time at the Zoo: Individual Title Six-Packs. (gr. 1-2). 22.00 *(978-0-7635-9178-6(5))* Rigby Education.
Felix, Rebecca. Patterns at the Zoo. 2015. (21st Century Basic Skills Library: Patterns All Around Ser.). (ENG., Illus.). 24p. (J). (gr. k-3). pap. 12.79 *(978-1-63188-935-6(4)*, 206001) Cherry Lake Publishing.
Franks, Katie. Elephants, 1 vol. 2014. (Zoo's Who's Who Ser.). (ENG.). 24p. (J). (gr. 1-2). pap. 9.25 *(978-1-4777-6568-5(9)*, 26263ff1-4406-4736-a672-41970fea7473, PowerKids Pr.) Rosen Publishing Group, Inc., The.
—Lions, 1 vol. 2014. (Zoo's Who's Who Ser.). (ENG., Illus.). 24p. (J). (gr. 1-2). 25.27 *(978-1-4777-6475-6(5)*, 914772d6-403b-42d1-b74b-31fda4861ec8, PowerKids Pr.) Rosen Publishing Group, Inc., The.
—Sea Lions, 1 vol. 2014. (Zoo's Who's Who Ser.). (ENG., Illus.). 24p. (J). (gr. 1-2). pap. 9.25 *(978-1-4777-6585-2(9)*, 11037f1f-ded6-40a8-be18-4ff734d26aa1, PowerKids Pr.) Rosen Publishing Group, Inc., The.
Fuerst, Jeffrey B. Feeding Time at the Zoo: Lap Book. 2009. (My First Reader's Theater Set B Ser.). (J). 28.00 *(978-1-4108-8541-8(0))* Benchmark Education Co.
Gallagher, Debbie. Penguins, 1 vol. 2010. (Zoo Animals Ser.). (ENG.). 32p. (gr. 2-2). lib. bdg. 21.27 *(978-0-7614-4747-4(4)*, 875ea76c-72cd-45dd-927c-58f786a873c1) Cavendish Square Publishing LLC.
—Seals & Sea Lions, 1 vol. 2010. (Zoo Animals Ser.). (ENG.). 32p. (gr. 2-2). lib. bdg. 21.27 *(978-0-7614-4748-1(2)*, 9f05e3ae-e51a-4bdb-b382-e17cad3799e8) Cavendish Square Publishing LLC.
—Snakes, 1 vol. 2010. (Zoo Animals Ser.). (ENG.). 32p. (gr. 2-2). lib. bdg. 21.27 *(978-0-7614-4749-8(0)*, 5cd43b20-2cda-4486-b087-4ba770fe0ef9) Cavendish Square Publishing LLC.
Galvin, Laura Gates. First Look at Zoo Animals. Fulcher, Roz, illus. 2009. (ENG.). 16p. (J). bds. 6.95 *(978-1-59249-998-4(8))* Studio Mouse LLC.
Gardner, Robert. How Heavy Is Heavy? Science Projects with Weight, 1 vol. 2014. (Hot Science Experiments Ser.). (ENG.). 48p. (gr. 3-4). pap. 11.53 *(978-0-7660-6601-4(0)*, 00044fdd-2a98-406e-bafa-21046483ad3f, Enslow Elementary) Enslow Publishing, LLC.
—How Hot Is Hot? Science Projects with Temperature, 1 vol. 2014. (Hot Science Experiments Ser.). (ENG.). 48p. (gr. 3-4). E-Book 26.93 *(978-0-7660-6609-0(6)*, e836d299-7fe9-40ce-bafd-789cdb29acbd) Enslow Publishing, LLC.
Gilders, Michelle. A Kids' Guide to Zoo Animals, 1 vol. 2004. (ENG., Illus.). 264p. (J). (gr. 2-3). pap. 12.95 *(978-0-88995-301-7(5)*, c12a8b0a-1926-4cde-9dc3-bf3fdd1e3921) Trifolium Bks., Inc. CAN. Dist: Firefly Bks., Ltd.
Gregory, Josh. Elephants. 2012. (21st Century Basic Skills Library: Baby Zoo Animals Ser.). (ENG.). 24p. (gr. k-3). pap. 12.79 *(978-1-61080-626-8(3)*, 202236); (Illus.). 26.35 *(978-1-61080-452-3(X)*, 202062) Cherry Lake Publishing.
—Giraffes. 2012. (21st Century Basic Skills Library: Baby Zoo Animals Ser.). (ENG.). 24p. (gr. k-3). pap. 12.79 *(978-1-61080-630-5(1)*, 202240); (Illus.). 26.35 *(978-1-61080-456-1(2)*, 202066) Cherry Lake Publishing.
—Polar Bears. 2012. (21st Century Basic Skills Library: Baby Zoo Animals Ser.). (ENG.). 24p. (gr. k-3). pap. 12.79 *(978-1-61080-633-6(6)*, 202243); (Illus.). 26.35 *(978-1-61080-459-2(7)*, 202069) Cherry Lake Publishing.
Gunzi, Christiane. Zoo. Zwemmer, Dominic, ed. 2015. (ENG., Illus.). 34p. (J). bds. 7.95 *(978-1-906572-30-3(5))* Award Pubns. Ltd. GBR. Dist: Parkwest Pubns., Inc.
Halls, Kelly Milner & Sumner, William. Saving the Baghdad Zoo: A True Story of Hope & Heroes. Sumner, William, illus. 2010. (ENG., Illus.). 64p. (J). (gr. 3-18). pap. 17.99 *(978-0-06-177202-3(X)*, Greenwillow Bks.) HarperCollins Pubs.
Harrison, Sarah. A Day at a Zoo. 2008. (Time Goes By Ser.). (ENG.). (gr. k-3). pap. 39.62 *(978-0-7613-4710-1(0))*; (Illus.). 24p. (J). lib. bdg. 22.60 *(978-1-58013-554-2(4)*, 1c1a6444-1558-46fb-a710-1875244d8dbe, Millbrook Pr.) Lerner Publishing Group.
Hatkoff, Craig. Knut: How One Little Polar Bear Captivated the World. 2007. (Illus.). (J). pap. 16.99 *(978-0-545-04717-3(X)*, Scholastic Pr.) Scholastic, Inc.
Hemming, Alice. The Black & White Club. Scott, Kimberley, illus. 2019. (Early Bird Readers — Orange (Early Bird Stories (tm)) Ser.). (ENG.). 32p. (J). (gr. k-3). pap. 9.99 *(978-1-5415-7411-3(7)*, 51725c5e-a9dc-4055-b2d8-99f108a48329, Lerner Pubns.) Lerner Publishing Group.
Hewett, Richard, illus. & photos by. A Monkey Baby Grows Up. Hewett, Richard, photos by. Hewett, Joan, photos by. 2004. (Baby Animals Ser.). 32p. (J). (gr. k-3). lib. bdg. 21.27 *(978-1-57505-199-4(0))* Lerner Publishing Group.
Hoena, Blake A. The Zoo: A 4D Book. rev. ed. 2018. (Visit To... Ser.). (ENG., Illus.). 24p. (J). (gr. -1-2). lib. bdg. 29.32 *(978-1-5435-0832-1(4)*, 137595, Capstone Pr.) Capstone.
Holden, Pam. Come to the Zoo, 1 vol. 2017. (ENG., Illus.). 21p. (J). pap. *(978-1-77654-220-8(7)*, Red Rocket Readers) Flying Start Bks.
—King of the Zoo, 1 vol. Cammell, Sandra, illus. 2009. (Red Rocket Readers Ser.). (ENG.). 16p. (gr. -1-1). pap. *(978-1-877363-13-9(8)*, Red Rocket Readers) Flying Start Bks.
Holtz, Monica Stauber. Behind the Zoo: Find Out What the Animals Eat & Do at Irvine Park Zoo, Chippewa Falls, Wisconsin. Opatz, Shane, illus. Opatz, Shane, photos by. 2011. (J). *(978-0-9837617-1-6(X))* Holtz Creative Enterprises.
Hullabaloo at the Zoo, 3 vols., Pack. (Sails Literacy Ser.). 24p. (gr. 1-18). 57.00 *(978-0-7578-3208-6(3))* Rigby Education.
Irvine, Georgeanne. Fabulous Floyd: The True Story of a Flamingo Who Never Gave Up. 2018. (Illus.). (J). *(978-1-943198-05-4(5))* Southwestern Publishing Hse., Inc.
—Karen's Heart: The True Story of a Brave Baby Orangutan. 2018. (Illus.). (J). *(978-1-943198-04-7(7))* Southwestern Publishing Hse., Inc.
Johnson, Bruce & McKay, Sindy. We Both Read-Zoo Day. Johnson, Meredith, illus. 2015. (We Both Read - Level 1 (Quality) Ser.). (ENG.). 44p. (J). (gr. k-2). pap. 5.99 *(978-1-60115-274-9(4))* Treasure Bay, Inc.
—Zoo Day/Dia Del Zoologico: Spanish/English Bilingual Edition (We Both Read - Level 1) Johnson, Meredith, illus. 2016. (We Both Read - Level 1 Ser.). (ENG & SPA.). 41p. (J). pap. 5.99 *(978-1-60115-078-3(4))* Treasure Bay, Inc.
Jones, Kimberly & Jones, Laura. Morning Zoo. 2009. 24p. pap. 11.99 *(978-1-4389-4086-1(6))* AuthorHouse.
Katirgis, Jane. Baby Zoo Animals, 1 vol. 2010. (All about Baby Animals Ser.). (ENG., Illus.). 24p. (-1). pap. 10.35 *(978-1-59845-159-7(6)*, 288acfbf-146a-4285-835d-2a0a954f8353); (gr. -1-1). 25.27 *(978-0-7660-3796-0(7)*, 70bb05ee-72b2-4500-a931-38c3cbc8b404) Enslow Publishing, LLC. (Enslow Publishing).
Keats Curtis, Jennifer. La Historia de Kali: El Rescate de un Oso Polar Hu�rfano (Spanish Edition) Gomes, John, illus. 2014.Tr. of Kali's Story: an Orphaned Polar Bear Rescue. (SPA.). 32p. (J). (gr. 1-4). pap. 9.95 *(978-1-62855-226-3(3)*, 11a0ca79-a95c-4be8-9369-86515af3f55b) Arbordale Publishing.
—Kali's Story: an Orphaned Polar Bear Rescue, 1 vol. Gomes, John, illus. 2014. (ENG.). 32p. (J). (gr. 1-4). 17.95 *(978-1-62855-208-9(5))* Arbordale Publishing.
—The Lucky Litter: Wolf Pups Rescued from Wildfire, 1 vol. Gomes, John, photos by. 2015. (Illus.). 32p. (J). (gr. 2-3). (SPA.). pap. 11.95 *(978-1-62855-720-6(6)*, 5e9c3f2f-0e65-4218-b81c-fded60a85f87); (ENG., 17.95 *(978-1-62855-718-3(4))* Arbordale Publishing.
—Maggie: Alaska's Last Elephant, 1 vol. Saroff, Phyllis, illus. 2018. (ENG.). 32p. (J). (gr. k-3). 17.95 *(978-1-60718-450-8(8)*, 9781607184508); pap. 9.95 *(978-1-60718-461-4(3)*, 9781607184614) Arbordale Publishing.
—Maggie, el último Elefante en Alaska, 1 vol. Saroff, Phyllis, illus. 2018.Tr. of Maggie: Alaska's Last Elephant. (SPA.). 32p. (J). (gr. k-3). pap. 11.95 *(978-1-60718-466-9(4)*, 9781607184669) Arbordale Publishing.
—Primate School, 1 vol. 2015. (ENG., Illus.). 32p. (J). (gr. 2-5). 17.95 *(978-1-62855-555-4(6))* Arbordale Publishing.
Kobasa, Paul A. Zoo Animals. 2018. (J). *(978-0-7166-3577-2(1))* World Bk., Inc.
Komiya, Teruyuki. More Life-Size Zoo: An All-New Actual-Size Animal Encyclopedia. Miyakoshi, Junko, tr. 2010. (ENG., Illus.). 48p. (gr. -1). 18.95 *(978-1-934734-19-3(5))* Seven Footer Pr.
Lacey, Saskia. Creating a Habitat. rev. ed. 2019. (Smithsonian: Informational Text Ser.). (ENG.). 32p. (J). (gr. 2-3). pap. 10.99 *(978-1-4938-6663-2(X))* Teacher Created Materials, Inc.
Lluch, Alex A. I Like to Learn Alphabet: Zoo Clues. 2011. 32p. (J). (gr. -1-k). bds. 4.95 *(978-1-934386-00-2(6))* WS Publishing.
Lynch, Seth. Monkeys at the Zoo, 1 vol. 2019. (Zoo Animals Ser.). (ENG.). 24p. (gr. k-k). pap. 9.15 *(978-1-5382-3934-6(5)*, ec789337-943e-41e7-a823-e49e40a35c41) Stevens, Gareth Publishing LLLP.
—Otters at the Zoo, 1 vol. 2019. (Zoo Animals Ser.). (ENG.). 24p. (gr. k-k). pap. 9.15 *(978-1-5382-3938-4(8)*, fe6db6bb-df1e-4b34-84f5-b9e582544d23) Stevens, Gareth Publishing LLLP.
—Reindeer at the Zoo, 1 vol. 2019. (Zoo Animals Ser.). (ENG.). 24p. (gr. k-k). pap. 9.15 *(978-1-5382-3942-1(6)*, 2b4a0934-6d3a-429b-a4f8-48c6f9fa9f68) Stevens, Gareth Publishing LLLP.
—Snakes at the Zoo, 1 vol. 2019. (Zoo Animals Ser.). (ENG.). 24p. (gr. k-k). pap. 9.15 *(978-1-5382-3946-9(9)*, e761849a-de6b-44ea-a255-292b30a3a695) Stevens, Gareth Publishing LLLP.
—Tigers at the Zoo, 1 vol. 2019. (Zoo Animals Ser.). (ENG.). 24p. (gr. k-k). pap. 9.15 *(978-1-5382-3950-6(7)*, b5de3383-c42c-4d07-b0bb-0ecf82daf56a) Stevens, Gareth Publishing LLLP.
—Toucans at the Zoo, 1 vol. 2019. (Zoo Animals Ser.). (ENG.). 24p. (gr. k-k). pap. 9.15 *(978-1-5382-3954-4(X)*, e302b288-bd3a-4249-9fcd-971502a6e929) Stevens, Gareth Publishing LLLP.
Markovics, Joyce. Mi Cuerpo Es Duro y Gris (Armadillo) 2016. (Pistas de Animales 2/Zoo Clues 2 Ser.). (SPA.). 24p. (J). (gr. -1-3). 26.99 *(978-1-944102-81-4(7))* Bearport Publishing Co., Inc.
—MIS Patas Son Palmeadas y Anaranjadas (Puffin) 2016. (Pistas de Animales 2/Zoo Clues 2 Ser.). (SPA.). 24p. (J). (gr. -1-3). 26.99 *(978-1-944102-80-7(9))* Bearport Publishing Co., Inc.
Markovics, Joyce L. My Body Is Tough & Gray. 2016. (Zoo Clues 2 Ser.). (ENG., Illus.). 24p. (J). (gr. -1-3). 26.99 *(978-1-944102-63-0(9))* Bearport Publishing Co., Inc.
—My Feet Are Webbed & Orange. 2016. (Zoo Clues 2 Ser.). (ENG., Illus.). 24p. (J). (gr. -1-3). 26.99 *(978-1-944102-62-3(0))* Bearport Publishing Co., Inc.
Marsico, Katie. Cheetahs. 2012. (21st Century Basic Skills Library: Baby Zoo Animals Ser.). (ENG.). 24p. (gr. k-3). pap. 12.79 *(978-1-61080-627-5(1)*, 202237); (Illus.). 26.35 *(978-1-61080-453-0(8)*, 202063) Cherry Lake Publishing.
—Chimpanzees. 2012. (21st Century Basic Skills Library: Baby Zoo Animals Ser.). (ENG.). 24p. (gr. k-3). pap. 12.79 *(978-1-61080-629-9(8)*, 202239); (Illus.). 26.35 *(978-1-61080-455-4(4)*, 202065) Cherry Lake Publishing.
—Hippopotamuses. 2012. (21st Century Basic Skills Library: Baby Zoo Animals Ser.). (ENG.). 24p. (gr. k-3). pap. 12.79 *(978-1-61080-632-9(8)*, 202242); (Illus.). 26.35 *(978-1-61080-458-5(9)*, 202068) Cherry Lake Publishing.
—Jaguars. 2012. (21st Century Basic Skills Library: Baby Zoo Animals Ser.). (ENG.). 24p. (gr. k-3). pap. 12.79 *(978-1-61080-628-2(X)*, 202238); (Illus.). 26.35 *(978-1-61080-454-7(6)*, 202064) Cherry Lake Publishing.
—Koala Bears. 2012. (21st Century Basic Skills Library: Baby Zoo Animals Ser.). (ENG.). 24p. (gr. k-3). pap. 12.79 *(978-1-61080-631-2(X)*, 202241); (Illus.). 26.35 *(978-1-61080-457-8(0)*, 202067) Cherry Lake Publishing.
Martin, Isabel. A Zoo Field Trip. 2015. (Let's Take a Field Trip Ser.). (ENG., Illus.). 24p. (J). (gr. -1-2). pap. 6.95 *(978-1-4914-2316-5(1)*, 127774, Capstone Pr.) Capstone.
Marx, David F. Doc Block. 2006. (Reader's Clubhouse Level 1 Reader Ser.). (Illus.). 24p. (J). (gr. k-1). pap. 3.99 *(978-0-7641-3288-9(1))* Sourcebooks, Inc.
Mellark, Kat. Our Zoo Adventure: Compare Numbers. 2013. (Rosen Math Readers Ser.). (ENG.). 16p. (J). (gr. k-1). pap. 42.00 *(978-1-4777-1600-7(9))*; (Illus.). pap. 7.00 *(978-1-4777-1599-4(1)*, 2e157cf4-efa5-4119-a42d-2d440a89a8c4) Rosen Publishing Group, Inc., The. (Rosen Classroom).
Moldovo, Eustacia. Baby Elephants at the Zoo. 2015. (J). *(978-0-7660-6613-7(4))*; (ENG., Illus.). 24p. (gr. -1-1). pap. 10.35 *(978-0-7660-7089-9(1)*, b4a6bbea-3463-4f9c-ac3a-934b9a7ece9a) Enslow Publishing, LLC.
—Baby Lions at the Zoo, 1 vol. 2015. (All about Baby Zoo Animals Ser.). (ENG., Illus.). 24p. (gr. -1-1). pap. 10.35 *(978-0-7660-7085-1(9)*, 70694cd4-a76e-49e8-95e8-e0b2b8473381) Enslow Publishing, LLC.
—Baby Monkeys at the Zoo. 2015. (J). *(978-0-7660-6597-0(9))*; (ENG., Illus.). 24p. (gr. -1-1). pap. 10.35 *(978-0-7660-7073-8(5)*, 3495e041-ffce-45a2-bd51-720b3822052e) Enslow Publishing, LLC.
—Baby Pandas at the Zoo, 1 vol. 2015. (All about Baby Zoo Animals Ser.). (ENG., Illus.). 24p. (gr. -1-1). 24.27 *(978-0-7660-7079-0(4)*, 780286b2-899a-4146-a601-b98b84fa95fd); pap. 10.35 *(978-0-7660-7077-6(8)*, 5063e83a-2870-452f-a74f-ad2c3b725759) Enslow Publishing, LLC.
—Baby Zebras at the Zoo. 2015. (J). *(978-0-7660-6617-5(7))*; (ENG., Illus.). 24p. (gr. -1-1). pap. 10.35 *(978-0-7660-7093-6(X)*, 6799f403-4959-4041-ab19-4ff336ec13fe) Enslow Publishing, LLC.
Moore, Katharine & Sonne, Lisa T. E., texts. Zoo Animals. 2010. (Illus.). (J). *(978-1-4351-2492-9(8))* Barnes & Noble, Inc.
Nault, Jennifer. Project Polar Bear. Kissock, Heather & Marshall, Diana, eds. 2003. (Zoo Life Ser.). (Illus.). 24p. (J). pap. 8.95 *(978-1-59036-060-6(5))* Weigl Pubs., Inc.
Newman, Patricia. Zoo Scientists to the Rescue. Crawley, Annie, photos by. 2017. (ENG., Illus.). 64p. (J). (gr. 4-8). lib. bdg. 33.32 *(978-1-5124-1571-1(5)*, 85e5e5e1-e4d4-40b1-a39a-cfa8a6664d14, Millbrook Pr.) Lerner Publishing Group.
Novick, Mary & Hale, Jenny. Farm & Zoo. 2006. (Illus.). 32p. *(978-1-921049-26-2(X))* Little Hare Bks. AUS. Dist: HarperCollins Pubs. Australia.
Olmedillas, Cathy, compiled by. Anorak. 2013. (ENG., Illus.). 64p. (J). pap. 9.99 *(978-1-4236-3340-2(7)*, Anorak Pr.) Gibbs Smith, Publisher.
Orr, Tamra. The National Zoo. 2017. (Smithsonian Field Trips Ser.). (ENG., Illus.). 32p. (J). (gr. 2-5). pap. 7.95 *(978-1-5157-7990-2(4)*, 136053); lib. bdg. 28.65 *(978-1-5157-7980-3(7)*, 136049) Capstone. (Capstone Pr.).
Orr, Tamra B. Working at the Zoo. 2011. (21st Century Junior Library: Careers Ser.). (ENG., Illus.). 24p. (gr. 2-5). lib. bdg. 29.21 *(978-1-60279-978-3(4)*, 200946) Cherry Lake Publishing.
Owen, Ruth. The Wild World of a Zoo Vet. 2015. (Get to Work with Science & Technology Ser.). (ENG., Illus.). 32p. (J). (gr. 2-7). lib. bdg. 29.32 *(978-1-910549-34-6(7)*, 9ec15f5b-6d49-4a71-bbfa-bd7cefe46953) Ruby Tuesday Books Limited GBR. Dist: Lerner Publishing Group.
Paiva, Johannah Gilman, ed. Zoo Friends. 2013. (Illus.). 20p. (J). bds. 8.99 *(978-1-77093-629-4(7))* Flowerpot Children's Pr. Inc. CAN. Dist: Cardinal Pubs. Group.
Pajalunga, Lorena V. Yoga for Kids: Simple Animal Poses for Any Age. Forlati, Anna, illus. 2015. (ENG.). 32p. (J). (gr. -1-3). 16.99 *(978-0-8075-9172-7(6)*, 807591726) Whitman, Albert & Co.
Parker, Gary & Parker, Mary. The Complete Zoo Adventure: A Field Trip in a Book. 2008. (Illus.). 160p. (J). (gr. -1-6). 22.99 *(978-0-89051-500-6(X)*, Master Books) New Leaf Publishing Group.
Pelusey, Michael & Pelusey, Jane. Bears, 1 vol. 2009. (Zoo Animals Ser.). (ENG.). 32p. (gr. 2-2). lib. bdg. 21.27 *(978-0-7614-3147-3(0)*, d5e20841-20c7-4772-96e6-bdbb636c365c) Cavendish Square Publishing LLC.
—Elephants, 1 vol. 2009. (Zoo Animals Ser.). (ENG.). 32p. (gr. 2-2). lib. bdg. 21.27 *(978-0-7614-3148-0(9)*, 32a39138-78f4-40a1-a467-529a295fb033) Cavendish Square Publishing LLC.
—Giraffes & Zebras, 1 vol. 2009. (Zoo Animals Ser.). (ENG.). 32p. (gr. 2-2). lib. bdg. 21.27 *(978-0-7614-3149-7(7)*, 9b52e0ca-ec5a-4fb9-a857-2d5beb65d130) Cavendish Square Publishing LLC.
—Lions & Tigers, 1 vol. 2009. (Zoo Animals Ser.). (ENG.). 32p. (gr. 2-2). lib. bdg. 21.27 *(978-0-7614-3151-0(9)*, 0b10e42f-c952-460e-8738-7ecf87a74c11) Cavendish Square Publishing LLC.
—Rhinoceroses & Hippopotamuses, 1 vol. 2009. (Zoo Animals Ser.). (ENG.). 32p. (gr. 2-2). lib. bdg. 21.27 *(978-0-7614-3150-3(0)*, a49e31d3-2cc9-4284-8ad9-ff4719f536d1) Cavendish Square Publishing LLC.
—Zoo Animals, 6 bks., Set. Incl. Apes & Monkeys. lib. bdg. 21.27 *(978-0-7614-3144-2(6)*, 8eac7eab-e7d7-4293-ab33-2f7fe1c3fe18); Bears. lib. bdg. 21.27 *(978-0-7614-3147-3(0)*, d5e20841-20c7-4772-96e6-bdbb636c365c); Elephants. lib. bdg. 21.27 *(978-0-7614-3148-0(9)*, 32a39138-78f4-40a1-a467-529a295fb033); Giraffes & Zebras. lib. bdg. 21.27 *(978-0-7614-3149-7(7)*, 9b52e0ca-ec5a-4fb9-a857-2d5beb65d130); Lions & Tigers. lib. bdg. 21.27 *(978-0-7614-3151-0(9)*, 0b10e42f-c952-460e-8738-7ecf87a74c11); Rhinoceroses & Hippopotamuses. lib. bdg. 21.27 *(978-0-7614-3150-3(0)*, a49e31d3-2cc9-4284-8ad9-ff4719f536d1); 32p. (gr. 2-2). 2009. (Zoo Animals Ser.). 2008. Set lib. bdg. 119.70 net. *(978-0-7614-3143-5(8)*, Cavendish Square) Cavendish Square Publishing LLC.
Peters, Chris. A New Home for Lolo: Moving into the Omaha Zoo's African Grasslands. 2016. (ENG., Illus.). 32p. (J). 14.95 *(978-0-692-74658-5(7))* Omaha World-Herald.
Pettiford, Rebecca. Zoo. Fretland VanVoorst, Jenny, ed. 2016. (First Field Trips). (Illus.). 24p. (J). (gr. k-2). lib. bdg. 25.65 *(978-1-62031-299-5(9)*, Bullfrog Bks.) Jump! Inc.
—El Zoológico. 2016. (Los Primeros Viajes Escolares (First Field Trips)).Tr. of Zoo. (SPA., Illus.). 24p. (J). (gr. k-2). lib. bdg. 25.65 *(978-1-62031-333-6(2)*, Bullfrog Bks.) Jump! Inc.
Picthall, Chez. Flip Flaps Zoo. 2015. (Illus.). 18p. (J). bds. 9.99 *(978-1-907604-53-9(7))* Award Pubns. Ltd. GBR. Dist: Parkwest Pubns., Inc.
—Zoo Animals. 2015. (Illus.). 10p. (J). bds. 7.99 *(978-1-906572-06-8(2))* Award Pubns. Ltd. GBR. Dist: Parkwest Pubns., Inc.
Powell, Janet. St. Louis Zoo. 2009. (Great Zoos of the United States Ser.). 24p. (gr. 3-4). 42.50 *(978-1-61513-226-3(0)*, PowerKids Pr.) Rosen Publishing Group, Inc., The.

ddy, Roger. Busy Babies Zoo Animals. 2010. 8p. (J). bds. 4.99 (978-0-312-50856-2(5), Priddy Bks.) St. Martin's Pr.

rperhart, Helen. The Yoga Zoo Adventure: Animal Poses & Games for Little Kids. van Amelsfort, Barbara, illus. 2008. SmartFun Activity Bks.). (ENG.). 160p. (gr. k-2). pap. 16.95 (978-0-89793-505-0(5), Hunter Hse.) Turner Publishing Co.

eilly, Pamela. My Day at the Zoo. 2011. 24p. pap. 12.95 (978-1-935268-72-7(4)) Halo Publishing International.

ng, Susan. Elok. 2009. (J). (978-1-60596-659-5(2)); (978-1-60596-660-1(6)) Weigl Pubs., Inc.

-Herbie. 2009. (J). (978-1-60596-661-8(4)); (978-1-60596-662-5(2)) Weigl Pubs., Inc.

-Project Elephant. Kissock, Heather & Marshall, Diana, eds. 2003. (Zoo Life Ser.). 24p. (J). pap. 8.95 (978-1-59036-056-9(7)) Weigl Pubs., Inc.

-Project Hippopotamus. Kissock, Heather & Marshall, Diana, eds. 2003. (Zoo Life Ser.). (Illus.). 24p. (J). pap. 8.95 (978-1-59036-057-6(5)) Weigl Pubs., Inc.

-Project Hippopotamus. 2003. (Zoo Babies Ser.). (Illus.). 24p. (J). (gr. 2-4). lib. bdg. 24.45 (978-1-59036-013-2(3)) Weigl Pubs., Inc.

-Project Orangutan. Marshall, Diana & Nault, Jennifer, eds. 2003. (Zoo Life Ser.). (Illus.). 24p. (J). pap. 8.95 (978-1-59036-058-3(3)) Weigl Pubs., Inc.

—Project Otter. Kissock, Heather & Marshall, Diana, eds. 2003. (Zoo Life Ser.). (Illus.). 24p. (J). pap. 8.95 (978-1-59036-059-0(1)) Weigl Pubs., Inc.

—Project Tiger. Marshall, Diana & Nault, Jennifer, eds. 2003. (Zoo Life Ser.). (Illus.). 24p. (J). pap. 8.95 (978-1-59036-061-3(3)) Weigl Pubs., Inc.

Rivers-Moore, Debbie & Davis, Caroline. In the Zoo. 2017. (ENG.). 8p. (J). (gr. -1 — 1). 4.99 (978-1-4380-7829-8(3)) Sourcebooks, Inc.

Robinson, Joanna Jarc. Andrew & Allen Learn about Adverbs. Boyer, Robin, illus. 2014. (Language Builders Ser.). (ENG.). 32p. (J). (gr. 2-4). pap. 11.94 (978-1-60357-704-5(1)); lib. bdg. 25.27 (978-1-59953-669-9(2)) Norwood Hse. Pr.

Rudolph, Jessica. MIS Orejas Son Enormes y Peludas (Fennec Fox) 2016. (Pistas de Animales 2/Zoo Clues 2 Ser.). (SPA.). 24p. (J). (gr. -1-3). 26.99 (978-1-944102-75-3(2)) Bearport Publishing Co., Inc.

—My Ears Are Huge & Fuzzy. 2016. (Zoo Clues 2 Ser.). (ENG., Illus.). 24p. (J). (gr. -1-3). 26.99 (978-1-944102-57-9(4)) Bearport Publishing Co., Inc.

Ruggieri, Linda. Amazing Animals: Critter Camp: Division (Grade 3) 2017. (Mathematics in the Real World Ser.). (ENG., Illus.). 32p. (J). (gr. 3-4). pap. 11.99 (978-1-4807-5800-1(0)) Teacher Created Materials, Inc.

Santa Maria, Christa, des. Zoo Animal Crafts, 1 vol., 1. 2015. (Creating Creature Crafts Ser.). (ENG., Illus.). 24p. (J). (gr. 2-3). pap. 11.60 (978-1-5081-9121-6(2), 54b94926-17a9-4d87-883f-630641ca9f6a, Windmill Bks.) Rosen Publishing Group, Inc., The.

Slade, Suzanne. What's New at the Zoo? an Animal Adding Adventure, 1 vol. Waites, Joan, illus. 2009. (Basic Math Operations Ser.). (ENG.). 32p. (J). (gr. -1-3). 16.95 (978-1-934359-93-8(9)); (gr. k-1). pap. 10.95 (978-1-60718-038-8(3), 479761a6-5614-411c-aa10-e3fb2bbac00c) Arbordale Publishing.

Small & Big Animals at the Zoo, 1 vol. 2015. (Our Wonderful World Ser.). 8p. (J). (gr. -1-1). pap. 9.35 (978-1-5081-1237-2(1), 872abaa8-e561-46f1-8670-4ef49376a5c6); pap. 9.35 (978-1-5081-1225-9(8), 8681c99e-ccea-4a38-bff8-6169957bdd2f); pap. 9.35 (978-1-5081-1243-3(6), 2620656d-93f0-4e81-a6a5-d43f7f67560e); pap. 9.35 (978-1-5081-1261-7(4), d72a16dd-14f3-4e45-a4cd-ea80ca0e4aa6); (ENG & SPA.). pap. 9.35 (978-1-5081-1255-6(X), fb73b15b-829a-4aa3-86df-2c5abc0fdac4); pap. 9.35 (978-1-5081-1249-5(5), 79c99280-5743-405d-adba-b7a40f7d301b) Rosen Publishing Group, Inc., The. (Rosen Classroom).

Sohn, Emily & Foster, Barbara J. Animal Needs. 2019. (IScience Ser.). (ENG., Illus.). 24p. (J). (gr. k-2). 23.94 (978-1-68450-973-7(4)) Norwood Hse. Pr.

Stead, Tony. Should There Be Zoos? A Persuasive Text. 2011. (ENG., Illus.). 32p. (J). (gr. 3-7). pap. 29.99 (978-1-57255-817-5(2)) Mondo Publishing.

Stillerman, Robbie. Color Your Own Zoo Animals Stickers. 2006. (Dover Sticker Bks.). (ENG., Illus.). 2p. (J). (gr. k-3). 2.95 (978-0-486-44887-9(8)) Dover Pubns., Inc.

Taylor, Trace & Sanchez, Lucia M. En el zoológico (at the Zoo) 2011. (Animales Ser.). (SPA.). 16p. pap. 39.62 (978-1-61541-419-2(3)) American Reading Co.

Wallace, Karen. DK Readers L1: a Trip to the Zoo. 2003. (DK Readers Level 1 Ser.). (ENG., Illus.). 32p. (J). (gr. k-2). pap. 4.99 (978-0-7894-9219-7(9), DK Children) Dorling Kindersley Publishing, Inc.

Walter Foster Jr. Creative Team, Walter. Learn to Draw Zoo Animals: Step-By-step Instructions for More Than 25 Popular Animals. Cuddy, Robbin, illus. 2016. (Learn to Draw: Expanded Edition Ser.). (ENG.). 64p. (J). (gr. 3-5). lib. bdg. 33.32 (978-1-939581-99-0(0), adefab0d-1c47-4380-beb5-52b66ccfebea, Walter Foster Jr) Quarto Publishing Group USA.

Ward, Finn. Elephants at the Zoo, 1 vol. 2015. (Zoo Animals Ser.). (ENG., Illus.). 24p. (J). (gr. k-k). pap. 9.15 (978-1-4824-2589-5(0), 7aab0005-38c4-4a56-8aef-8f4f1d58b887) Stevens, Gareth Publishing LLLP.

—Giraffes at the Zoo, 1 vol. 2015. (Zoo Animals Ser.). (ENG., Illus.). 24p. (J). (gr. k-k). pap. 9.15 (978-1-4824-2593-2(9), 52772889-2dc6-48a4-99e9-d019572b3482) Stevens, Gareth Publishing LLLP.

—Gorillas at the Zoo, 1 vol. 2015. (Zoo Animals Ser.). (ENG., Illus.). 24p. (J). (gr. k-k). pap. 9.15 (978-1-4824-2597-0(1), 965809b2-0086-4301-ad33-3a8feb5d4973) Stevens, Gareth Publishing LLLP.

—Ostriches at the Zoo, 1 vol. 2015. (Zoo Animals Ser.). (ENG., Illus.). 24p. (J). (gr. k-k). pap. 9.15 (978-1-4824-2601-4(3), c10efd1c-803c-4945-89ee-c9ddf9b8b6c0) Stevens, Gareth Publishing LLLP.

—Penguins at the Zoo, 1 vol. 2015. (Zoo Animals Ser.). (ENG., Illus.). 24p. (J). (gr. k-k). pap. 9.15 (978-1-4824-2605-2(6), d20682ad-7406-4fc5-bbb2-c957e6fabd87) Stevens, Gareth Publishing LLLP.

—Polar Bears at the Zoo, 1 vol. 2015. (Zoo Animals Ser.). (ENG., Illus.). 24p. (J). (gr. k-k). pap. 9.15 (978-1-4824-2609-0(9), 08c7d29d-e3bc-40cf-b2bb-a09aaa9d718a) Stevens, Gareth Publishing LLLP.

Wexo, John Bonnett. Focas y Leones Marinos. Rountree, Monica, tr. 2003. (Zoobooks Ser.). Orig. Title: Seals & Sea Lions. (SPA., Illus.). 24p. (J). (gr. k-6). lib. bdg. 15.95 (978-1-888153-79-8(2)) National Wildlife Federation.

Wilson, Phyllis M. My Two Friends. 2010. 24p. pap. 12.99 (978-1-4520-7959-2(5)) AuthorHouse.

Wong, Angi Ma, illus. My Story: Reggie: The L.A. Gator. 2007. 25p. (978-1-928753-12-4(4)) Pacific Heritage Bks.

Working with Animals: Individual Title Six-Packs. (gr. k-1). 23.00 (978-0-7635-9035-2(5)) Rigby Education.

Yanofsky, Tsivia. Take Me to the Zoo: Lions, Elephants & Snakes in the Midrash & Nature (ArtScroll Youth) 2003. (ArtScroll Youth Ser.). (ENG.). 95p. 19.99 (978-1-57819-099-7(1), ZOOH) Mesorah Pubns., Ltd.

A Zoo, 6 Packs. (Literatura 2000 Ser.). (gr. -1-1). 28.00 (978-0-7635-0044-3(5)) Rigby Education.

Zoo Animals. 2015. (Zoo Animals Ser.). (ENG.). 24p. (J). (gr. k-k). pap., pap., pap. 293.40 (978-1-4824-3502-3(0)); pap., pap., pap. 48.90 (978-1-4824-3503-0(9)); lib. bdg. 145.62 (978-1-4824-2539-0(4), 306f9fb3-f8a7-4968-bbbc-a39e052e3aef) Stevens, Gareth Publishing LLLP.

Zoo Animals for Kids: Amazing Pictures & Fun Fact Children Book. 2013. 32p. pap. 9.97 (978-1-63022-042-6(6)) Speedy Publishing LLC.

The Zoo's Who's Who. 2014. (Zoo's Who's Who Ser.). 24p. (J). (gr. k-2). pap. 49.50 (978-1-4777-7254-6(5)); (ENG.). (gr. 1-2). 151.62 (978-1-4777-6899-0(8), 137aa13c-6cec-4776-b94a-0f6348cd720a) Rosen Publishing Group, Inc., The. (PowerKids Pr.).

ZOO ANIMALS—FICTION

Anderson, Amanda. The Story of Larry the Hamster. 2008. 24p. pap. 24.95 (978-1-60703-125-3(6)) America Star Bks.

AZ Books Staff. My Zoo. Yaroshevich, Angelica, ed. 2012. (Open the Book-I Am Alive Ser.). (ENG.). 8p. (J). (— 1). bds. 5.95 (978-1-61889-044-3(1)) AZ Bks. LLC.

Babb, Gina. Zain & Zoe's Zoo Adventures: Numbers & Colors. 2011. 16p. 9.36 (978-1-4520-5578-7(5)) AuthorHouse.

Barretta, Gene. Dear Deer: A Book of Homophones. 2007. (J). (gr. k-3). 29.95 incl. audio compact disk (978-0-8045-4181-7(7)); 27.95 incl. audio (978-0-8045-6958-3(4)) Spoken Arts, Inc.

—Dear Deer: A Book of Homophones. Barretta, Gene, illus. 2010. (ENG., Illus.). 40p. (J). (gr. -1-2). pap. 7.99 (978-0-312-62899-4(4), 900066866) Square Fish.

Beaumont, Karen. Wild about Us! Stevens, Janet, illus. 2015. (ENG.). 40p. (J). (gr. -1-3). 17.99 (978-0-15-206294-1(7), 1198860, Clarion Bks.) HarperCollins Pubs.

Beilenson, Evelyn. The Zoo Is Closed Today! Kennedy, Anne, illus. 2014. (ENG.). 32p. (J). 16.99 (978-1-4413-1526-7(8), bafefaaa-3ed9-4f39-af87-f94b55eddd8d) Peter Pauper Pr. Inc.

Berthiaume, Donna M. Our Cool School Zoo Revue. Jirak, Tracey, illus. 2008. 36p. pap. 24.95 (978-1-60672-672-3(2)) America Star Bks.

Bianchi, John. Is the Spaghetti Ready?, 1 vol. Edwards, Frank, illus. 2008. (New Reader Ser.). (ENG.). 32p. (J). (978-1-894323-35-2(1)) Bungalo Bks.

Boland, Gerry. Marco Moves In. McGuinness, Āine, illus. 2012. (Rather Remarkable Grizzly Be Ser.). (ENG.). 64p. (J). 12.95 (978-1-84717-229-7(6)) O'Brien Pr., Ltd., The IRL. Dist: Dufour Editions, Inc.

Bolden-Fournier, Laura. An Orangutan's Night Before Christmas, 1 vol. Jaskiel, Stan, illus. 2016. (Night Before Christmas Ser.). (ENG.). 32p. (J). (gr. k-3). 16.99 (978-1-4556-2154-5(4), Pelican Publishing) Arcadia Publishing.

Bostrom, Kathleen Long. The View at the Zoo. Francis, Guy, illus. 2019. (ENG.). 26p. (J). (gr. -1-1). bds. 7.99 (978-0-8249-1690-9(5), Worthy Kids/Ideals) Worthy Publishing.

—The View at the Zoo. 2015. (ENG., Illus.). 32p. (J). pap. 7.99 (978-0-8249-5669-1(9), Ideals Pubns.) Worthy Publishing.

Brannon, Pat. Quirky Kids Zoo. Jimena Pinto-Krowjiline, illus. 2011. 32p. pap. 11.99 (978-1-933300-83-2(3)) Wandering Sage Pubns., LLC.

Bratcher, Shirley Kay. Tudy Goes to the Zoo. 2013. 24p. pap. 24.95 (978-1-4626-9560-7(4)) America Star Bks.

Brennan-Nelson, Denise. Maestro Stu Saves the Zoo. Bowers, Tim, illus. 2012. (ENG.). 32p. (J). (gr. -1-3). 15.95 (978-1-58536-802-0(4), 202340) Sleeping Bear Pr.

Brown, Joe. Race to the Rescue. Marchesi, Stephen, illus. 2009. (J). (978-0-545-13473-6(0)) Scholastic, Inc.

Bryant, Jen. Call Me Marianne. Johnson, David, illus. 2006. 32p. (J). (gr. 1-4). 16.00 (978-0-8028-5242-7(4), Eerdmans Bks For Young Readers) Eerdmans, William B. Publishing Co.

Burton, Jeffrey. Jingle Bells at the Zoo. Trithart, Emma, illus. 2018. (ENG.). 14p. (J). (gr. -1 — 1). bds. 8.99 (978-1-5344-2034-2(7), Little Simon) Little Simon.

Çaglar, Atife. Sayabiliyorum. 2011. 16p. pap. (978-1-4269-9408-1(7)) Trafford Publishing (UK) Ltd.

Campbell, Rod. Dear Zoo. 2005. (Dear Zoo & Friends Ser.). (ENG., Illus.). 20p. (J). (gr. -1-k). 15.99 (978-0-689-87751-3(X), Little Simon) Little Simon.

—Dear Zoo. Campbell, Rod, illus. 2004. (Illus.). 16p. (J). (RUS & ENG.). bds. (978-1-84444-178-5(4)); (VIE & ENG., bds. (978-1-84444-183-9(0)); (CHI & ENG., bds. (978-1-84444-171-6(7)) Mantra Lingua.

—Dear Zoo. 2004. (BEN & ENG., Illus.). 16p. (J). bds. (978-1-84444-169-3(5)) Mantra Lingua.

—Dear Zoo. Campbell, Rod, illus. 2004. (Illus.). 16p. (J). (ENG & POR.). bds. (978-1-84444-177-8(6)); (ENG & PAN., bds. (978-1-84444-176-1(8)); (ENG & HIN., bds. (978-1-84444-175-4(X)); (ENG & GUJ., bds. (978-1-84444-174-7(1)); (ENG & FRE., bds. (978-1-84444-173-0(3)); (ENG & PER., bds. (978-1-84444-172-3(5)); (CHI & ENG., bds. (978-1-84444-170-9(9)); (ENG & ARA., bds. (978-1-84444-168-6(7)); (ENG & ALB., bds. (978-1-84444-167-9(9)); (ENG & TUR., bds. (978-1-84444-181-5(4)); (ENG & SOM., bds. (978-1-84444-180-8(6)); (URD & ENG., bds. (978-1-84444-182-2(2)); (ENG & SPA., bds. (978-1-84444-179-2(2)) Mantra Lingua.

—Dear Zoo. Campbell, Rod, illus. 2019. (Dear Zoo & Friends Ser.). (ENG., Illus.). 24p. (J). (— 1). 17.99 (978-1-5344-6012-6(8), Little Simon) Little Simon.

—Dear Zoo: A Lift-The-Flap Book. Campbell, Rod, illus. 25th ed. 2007. (Dear Zoo & Friends Ser.). (ENG., Illus.). 18p. (J). (gr. -1 — 1). bds. 7.99 (978-1-4169-4737-0(X), Little Simon) Little Simon.

—Dear Zoo Animal Shapes. Campbell, Rod, illus. 2016. (Dear Zoo & Friends Ser.). (ENG., Illus.). 20p. (J). (gr. -1 — 1). bds. 6.99 (978-1-4814-8069-7(3), Little Simon) Little Simon.

Carter, Stephanie. The Great Zoo Breakout That Never Happened. 2012. 24p. pap. 11.50 (978-1-62212-043-7(4), Strategic Bk. Publishing) Strategic Book Publishing & Rights Agency (SBPRA).

A Change for Zoe: Individual Title Six-Packs. (gr. k-1). 23.00 (978-0-7635-8840-3(7)) Rigby Education.

Chick, Bryan. Riddles & Danger. 2011. (Secret Zoo Ser.: 3). (ENG.). 288p. (J). (gr. 3-7). 16.99 (978-0-06-198927-8(4), Greenwillow Bks.) HarperCollins Pubs.

—The Secret Zoo: Raids & Rescues. (Secret Zoo Ser.: 5). (ENG.). 272p. (J). (gr. 3-7). 2014. pap. 9.99 (978-0-06-219229-5(9)) 2013. 16.99 (978-0-06-219228-8(0)) HarperCollins Pubs. (Greenwillow Bks.).

—The Secret Zoo: Secrets & Shadows. 2011. (Secret Zoo Ser.: 2). (ENG.). 272p. (J). (gr. 3-7). pap. 7.99 (978-0-06-198926-1(6)); 16.99 (978-0-06-198925-4(8)) HarperCollins Pubs. (Greenwillow Bks.).

—The Secret Zoo: Traps & Specters. 2013. (Secret Zoo Ser.: 4). (ENG.). 320p. (J). (gr. 3-7). pap. 7.99 (978-0-06-219223-3(X), Greenwillow Bks.) HarperCollins Pubs.

Cochran, Jean M. If a Monkey Jumps onto Your School Bus. Morris, Jennifer & Morris, Jennifer E., illus. 2008. (ENG.). 32p. (J). (gr. -1-k). 16.95 (978-0-9792035-2-7(X)) Pleasant St. Pr.

Cole, Babette. Tarzana. 2nd ed. 2003. (Babette Cole Ser.).Tr. of Tarzanna! (SPA., Illus.). 34p. (J). 12.95 (978-84-233-2274-9(2)) Ediciones Destino ESP. Dist: Planeta Publishing Corp.

Coy Manier, Julie. Grant the Jigsaw Giraffe: Different Is More. Manier, Grant, illus. 2017. (J). 16.95 (978-1-941515-83-9(5)) LongTale Publishing, LLC.

Craig, Sherryn. Midnight Madness at the Zoo, 1 vol. Jones, Karen, illus. 2016. (J). (gr. k-1). (SPA.). 39p. pap. 11.95 (978-1-62855-744-2(3), 9f8858c6-8461-4bd2-8a81-65b1c9987029); (ENG.). 32p. 17.95 (978-1-62855-730-5(3)) Arbordale Publishing.

Crispin, Barbara. City Zoo Blizzard Revue. Houghton, Roswitha, illus. 2003. 40p. 14.95 (978-0-9716346-1-9(0)) Dancing Words Pr., Inc.

Crubel, Thomas K. Kyanna's Trip to the Zoo, 1 vol. 2010. 24p. pap. 24.95 (978-1-4489-2926-9(1)) PublishAmerica, Inc.

Cuartas, Jennifer M. So Many Things. 2012. 28p. 24.95 (978-1-4626-6328-6(1)) America Star Bks.

Curious George at the Zoo (Touch & Feel Board Book) 2007. (Curious George Ser.). (ENG., Illus.). 10p. (J). (gr. -1-k). bds. 7.99 (978-0-618-80042-1(5), 415594, Clarion Bks.) HarperCollins Pubs.

DeAngelo, Jeremy. The Out Crowd. 2006. (J). pap. (978-0-88092-613-3(9)); lib. bdg. (978-0-88092-612-6(0)) Royal Fireworks Publishing Co.

Degman, Lori. 1 Zany Zoo. Jack, Colin, illus. 2010. (ENG.). 32p. (J). (gr. -1-2). 19.99 (978-1-4169-8990-5(0), Simon & Schuster Bks. For Young Readers) Simon & Schuster Bks. For Young Readers.

Deich, Cheri Bivin. The Messy Monkey Tea Party. Genth, Christina, illus. 2007. 32p. (J). (gr. -1-3). 15.95 (978-1-60108-006-6(9)) Red Cygnet Pr.

Donnelly, Liza. A Hippo in Our Yard. 2017. (I Like to Read Ser.). (ENG.). 32p. (J). (gr. -1-3). 7.99 (978-0-8234-3844-0(9)) Holiday Hse., Inc.

Dyer, Heather. Tina & the Penguin. Levert, Mireille, illus. 2004. 32p. (J). (gr. k-3). pap. 5.95 (978-1-55337-767-2(2)) Kids Can Pr., Ltd. CAN. Dist: Hachette Bk. Group.

Ebie, Mora. Going to the Zoo in Hawaii. 2006. (Illus.). 28p. (J). 10.95 (978-1-56647-790-1(5)) Mutual Publishing LLC.

Ferron, Joanne. Luis Saves the Llama. 2012. (ENG.). 35p. (J). pap. 17.95 (978-1-4327-7623-7(1)) Outskirts Pr., Inc.

Ferry, Beth. Sealed with a Kiss. Tallec, Olivier, illus. 2019. (ENG.). 32p. (J). (gr. -1-3). 19.99 (978-0-06-247577-0(0), HarperCollins) HarperCollins Pubs.

Fields, Jan. Lions, Tiger & Bears, Oh My!, Bk. 24. Shephard, Dave, illus. 2017. (Ghost Detectors Ser.: 24). (ENG.). 80p. (J). (gr. 2-5). lib. bdg. 35.64 (978-1-5321-3156-1(9), 27053, Calico Chapter Bks.) ABDO Publishing Co.

Fischer, Kristen. Zoo Zen: A Yoga Story for Kids. 2017. (ENG., Illus.). 32p. (J). (gr. -1-2). 17.95 (978-1-62203-891-6(6), 900220816) Sounds True, Inc.

Fletcher, Donna. Sweet Baby Heather: Day at the Zoo. 2010. 24p. pap. 14.99 (978-1-4520-2444-8(8)) AuthorHouse.

Freeman, Laura. Natalie's Hair Was Wild! Freeman, Laura, illus. 2018. (ENG., Illus.). 32p. (J). (gr. -1-3). 19.99 (978-1-328-66195-1(4), 1667517, Clarion Bks.) HarperCollins Pubs.

Gabretti, Tisa. The Number Zoo, 1 vol. 2009. (ENG.). 15p. 24.95 (978-1-60813-941-5(7)) America Star Bks.

Geer-Drummond, Vanessa T. Olivia's Trip to the Zoo. 2011. 32p. (gr. -1). pap. 12.77 (978-1-4567-4558-5(1)) AuthorHouse.

Gibbs, Stuart. Belly Up. 2011. (ENG.). (J). (gr. 4-7). lib. bdg. 18.60 (978-1-61383-640-8(6)) Perfection Learning Corp.

—Belly Up. (FunJungle Ser.). (ENG.). (J). (gr. 3-7). 2011. 320p. pap. 8.99 (978-1-4169-8732-1(0)) 2010. (Illus.). 304p. 18.99 (978-1-4169-8731-4(2)) Simon & Schuster Bks. For Young Readers. (Simon & Schuster Bks. For Young Readers).

—Big Game. 2015. (FunJungle Ser.). (ENG., Illus.). 352p. (J). (gr. 3-7). 18.99 (978-1-4814-2333-5(9), Simon & Schuster Bks. For Young Readers) Simon & Schuster Bks. For Young Readers.

—Even More FunJungle: Panda-Monium; Lion down; Tyrannosaurus Wrecks. 2020. (FunJungle Ser.). (ENG., Illus.). 1040p. (J). (gr. 3-7). 53.99 (978-1-5344-6783-5(1), Simon & Schuster Bks. For Young Readers) Simon & Schuster Bks. For Young Readers.

—The FunJungle Mystery Madness Collection: Panda-Monium; Lion down; Tyrannosaurus Wrecks. 2021. (FunJungle Ser.). (ENG., Illus.). 1120p. (J). (gr. 3-7). pap. 26.99 (978-1-6659-0048-5(2), Simon & Schuster Bks. For Young Readers) Simon & Schuster Bks. For Young Readers.

—The FunJungle Paperback Collection (Boxed Set) Belly up; Poached; Big Game. 2021. (FunJungle Ser.). (ENG., Illus.). 1040p. (J). (gr. 3-7). pap. 26.99 (978-1-6659-0042-3(3), Simon & Schuster Bks. For Young Readers) Simon & Schuster Bks. For Young Readers.

—Lion Down. 2019. (FunJungle Ser.). (ENG., Illus.). 352p. (J). (gr. 3-7). 18.99 (978-1-5344-2473-9(3), Simon & Schuster Bks. For Young Readers) Simon & Schuster Bks. For Young Readers.

—Panda-Monium. (FunJungle Ser.). (ENG.). (J). (gr. 3-7). 2018. 384p. pap. 8.99 (978-1-4814-4568-9(5)) 2017. (Illus.). 352p. 18.99 (978-1-4814-4567-2(7)) Simon & Schuster Bks. For Young Readers. (Simon & Schuster Bks. For Young Readers).

—Panda-Monium. 2018. (Funjungle (Teddy Fitzroy) Ser.: 4). lib. bdg. 18.40 (978-0-606-40849-3(5)) Turtleback.

—Poached. (FunJungle Ser.). (ENG., Illus.). 352p. (J). (gr. 3-7). 2015. pap. 8.99 (978-1-4424-6778-1(9)) 2014. 18.99 (978-1-4424-6777-4(0)) Simon & Schuster Bks. For Young Readers. (Simon & Schuster Bks. For Young Readers).

Giff, Patricia Reilly. Meet the Crew at the Zoo. Carter, Abby, illus. 2020. (Mysteries on Zoo Lane Ser.: 1). 112p. (J). (gr. 2-5). 16.99 (978-0-8234-4666-7(2)) Holiday Hse., Inc.

Glassman, Bruce. Zoolidays. Klaulevicius, Rolandas, illus. 2006. 32p. (J). (gr. -1-3). 15.95 (978-1-60108-011-0(5)) Red Cygnet Pr.

Hall, Michael. My Heart Is Like a Zoo. 2009. (ENG., Illus.). 32p. (J). (gr. -1-3). 16.99 (978-0-06-191510-9(6), Greenwillow Bks.) HarperCollins Pubs.

—My Heart Is Like a Zoo Board Book. 2013. (ENG., Illus.). 34p. (J). (gr. -1-k). bds. 7.99 (978-0-06-191512-3(2), Greenwillow Bks.) HarperCollins Pubs.

Hartnett, Sonya. The Midnight Zoo. Offermann, Andrea, illus. 2018. (ENG.). 224p. (J). (gr. 5-9). pap. 8.99 (978-0-7636-6462-6(6)) Candlewick Pr.

—The Midnight Zoo. 2018. lib. bdg. 18.40 (978-0-606-40915-5(7)) Turtleback.

Heap, Sue. Danny's Drawing Book. Heap, Sue, illus. 2008. (ENG., Illus.). 32p. (J). (gr. -1-3). 9.99 (978-0-7636-3654-8(1)) Candlewick Pr.

Heder, Thyra. Fraidyzoo. 2013. (ENG., Illus.). 48p. (J). (gr. k-2). 18.99 (978-1-4197-0776-6(0), 1059101, Abrams Bks. for Young Readers) Abrams, Inc.

Hemming, Alice. A Gold Star for George. Scott, Kimberley, illus. 2019. (Early Bird Readers — Orange (Early Bird Stories (tm)) Ser.). (ENG.). 32p. (J). (gr. k-3). pap. 9.99 (978-1-5415-7413-7(3), f3a42b56-6413-4cc5-a0a4-c95f60c2e3ef, Lerner Pubns.) Lerner Publishing Group.

Hensel, Boots. The Zoopendous Surprise! Gabriel, Andrea, illus. 2009. (ENG.). 32p. (J). (gr. -1-k). 16.95 (978-0-9792035-5-8(4)) Pleasant St. Pr.

Hinchcliffe, L. T. For the Love of Prudence Possum. 2008. 76p. pap. 15.50 (978-1-60693-136-3(9), Eloquent Bks.) Strategic Book Publishing & Rights Agency (SBPRA).

Hogg, Gary. Beautiful Buehla & the Zany Zoo Makeover. Chess, Victoria, illus. 2006. 32p. (J). (gr. -1-2). 15.99 (978-0-06-009420-1(6), Tegen, Katherine Bks) HarperCollins Pubs.

Ide, Laurie Shimizu. Okazu at the Zoo. Kanekuni, Daniel, illus. 2006. (J). (978-1-56647-776-5(X)) Mutual Publishing LLC.

Ipcizade, Catherine. 'Twas the Day Before Zoo Day, 1 vol. Hodson, Ben, illus. 2008. (Basic Math Operations Ser.). (ENG.). 32p. (J). (gr. -1-2). 17.95 (978-1-60718-585-7(7)) Arbordale Publishing.

Irwin, Bindi & Kunz, Chris. Trouble at the Zoo. 2011. (Bindi's Wildlife Adventures Ser.: 1). (ENG.). 112p. (J). (gr. 3-6). pap. 5.99 (978-1-4022-5514-4(4), Sourcebooks Jabberwocky) Sourcebooks, Inc.

Jones, Gareth P. Ninja Meerkats (#1): the Clan of the Scorpion, 1. Finlayson, Luke, illus. 2013. (Ninja Meerkats Ser.: 1). (ENG.). 128p. (J). (gr. 2-4). pap. 16.99 (978-1-250-01664-5(9), 900087078) Square Fish.

Jones, Julie. The Problem at Pepperpine Zoo. Jones, Julie., illus. l.t. ed. 2004. (Illus.). 24p. (J). pap. 7.95 (978-0-9745553-0-0(4)) Greenwood Street Publishing. GSP.

Katz, Karen. Roar, Roar, Baby! A Karen Katz Lift-The-Flap Book. Katz, Karen, illus. 2015. (ENG., Illus.). 14p. (J). (gr. -1 — 1). bds. 6.99 (978-1-4814-1788-4(6), Little Simon) Little Simon.

Kaufman, Seufert. Wee Wilhelmina & Her Magic Marbles. 2012. (ENG.). pap. (978-1-4675-4364-4(0)) Independent Pub.

Ketteman, Helen. If Beaver Had a Fever, 0 vols. O'Malley, Kevin, illus. 2012. (ENG.). 32p. (J). (gr. -1-3). 16.99 (978-0-7614-5951-4(0), 9780761459514, Two Lions) Amazon Publishing.

Klein, Adria F. Max Goes to the Zoo. Gallagher-Cole, Mernie, illus. 2007. (Read-It! Readers: the Life of Max Ser.). (ENG.). 24p. (J). (gr. -1-2). per. 3.95 (978-1-4048-3683-9(7), 94291, Picture Window Bks.) Capstone.

Kline, Trish & Donev, Mary. A Day at the Zoo: KA Reader 3. 2007. (Illus.). 32p. (J). per. 20.00 (978-0-9717234-5-0(1)) Ghost Hunter Productions.

Landry, Barbara. A Day at the Zoo. 2012. 28p. pap. 24.95 (978-1-4626-6684-3(1)) America Star Bks.

Latham, Irene. Don't Feed the Boy. Graegin, Stephanie, illus. 2014. (ENG.). 304p. (J). (gr. 3-7). pap. 13.99 (978-1-250-04428-0(6), 900128320) Square Fish.

Lendler, Ian. The Stratford Zoo Midnight Revue Presents Macbeth. Giallongo, Zack, illus. 2014. (Stratford Zoo Ser.). (ENG.). 80p. (J). (gr. 2-5). pap. 13.99 (978-1-59643-915-3(7), 900121316, First Second Bks.) Roaring Brook Pr.

—The Stratford Zoo Midnight Revue Presents Romeo & Juliet. 2015. (Stratford Zoo Midnight Revue Presents Ser.). (J). lib. bdg. 25.75 (978-0-606-38215-1(1)) Turtleback.

Lunablau, Jani. Little Snowflake. 2006. (ENG., Illus.). 32p. (J). (gr. -1-k). *(978-1-59692-139-9(0))* MacAdam/Cage Publishing, Inc.

Malone, D. L. 52 Purple Monkeys. 2009. 24p. pap. 24.95 *(978-1-60749-085-2(4))* America Star Bks.

Mamma Macs. Mick Mac Adoo's Australian Zoo. 2013. 30p. (J). pap. *(978-0-9923379-9-5(2))* Karen Mc Dermott.

Marie, Jill Jana. Zoo Rendezvous. Zamboni, David, illus. 2008. 24p. pap. 12.95 *(978-0-9817572-9-2(4))* Peppertree Pr., The.

Marsh, Carole. The Zany Zoo Mystery. 2008. (Carole Marsh Mysteries: Awesome Mysteries Ser.). (ENG.). 128p. (J). (gr. 2-4). 18.69 *(978-0-635-06332-8(8))* Gallopade International.

Martin, Bill, Jr. Polar Bear, Polar Bear, What Do You Hear? Carle, Eric, illus. (Brown Bear & Friends Ser.). (J). 2012. (ENG.). 28p. (gr. -1-k). bds. 14.99 *(978-0-8050-9095-6(9),* 900062022) 2007. 32p. 7.95 *(978-0-8050-8798-7(2))* Holt, Henry & Co. (Holt, Henry & Co. Bks. For Young Readers).

—Polar Bear, Polar Bear, What Do You Hear? 20th Anniversary Edition with CD. Carle, Eric, illus. 20th anniv. ed. 2011. (Brown Bear & Friends Ser.). (ENG.). 32p. (J). (gr. -1-k). 19.99 *(978-0-8050-9066-6(5),* 900061041, Holt, Henry & Co. Bks. For Young Readers) Holt, Henry & Co.

—Polar Bear, Polar Bear, What Do You Hear? My First Reader. Carle, Eric, illus. 2010. (My First Reader Ser.). (ENG.). 40p. (J). (gr. -1-2). 8.99 *(978-0-8050-9245-5(5),* 900066985, Holt, Henry & Co. Bks. For Young Readers) Holt, Henry & Co.

—Polar Bear, Polar Bear What Do You Hear? Sound Book. Carle, Eric, illus. 2011. (Brown Bear & Friends Ser.). (ENG.). 24p. (J). (gr. -1-k). bds. 14.95 *(978-0-312-51346-7(1),* 900079163) St. Martin's Pr.

Martin-Duttmann, Robin. Zoo on the Moon. 2013. 24p. pap. 12.97 *(978-1-62212-735-1(8),* Strategic Bk. Publishing) Strategic Book Publishing & Rights Agency (SBPRA).

Massie, Diane Redfield. The Baby Beebee Bird. Kellogg, Steven, illus. 2003. (ENG.). 32p. (J). (gr. -1-1). pap. 7.99 *(978-0-06-051784-7(0),* HarperCollins) HarperCollins Pubs.

Matthias, Catherine. Rookie Ready to Learn en Español: Demasiados Globos. Sharp, Gene, illus. 2011. (Rookie Ready to Learn Español Ser.). Orig. Title: Rookie Ready to Learn: Too Many Balloons. (SPA.). 40p. (J). pap. 5.95 *(978-0-531-26792-9(X),* Children's Pr.) Scholastic Library Publishing.

—Too Many Balloons. Sharp, Gene, illus. 2011. (Rookie Ready to Learn Ser.). 40p. (J). (gr. -1-k). pap. 5.95 *(978-0-531-26749-3(0));* lib. bdg. 23.00 *(978-0-531-26449-2(1))* Scholastic Library Publishing. (Children's Pr.).

McClatchy, Lisa. Eloise Visits the Zoo: Ready-To-Read Level 1. Lyon, Tammie, illus. (Eloise Ser.). (ENG.). 32p. (J). (gr. -1-1). 2018. 17.99 *(978-1-5344-2039-7(3))* 2009. pap. 4.99 *(978-1-4169-8642-3(1))* Simon Spotlight. (Simon Spotlight).

McDonald, Regina. Friday Night at the Zoo, 1 vol. McDonald, Amanda, illus. 2010. 16p. 24.95 *(978-1-4489-4090-5(7))* PublishAmerica, Inc.

McMahon, Michael. The Zoo & You: A Guidebook, 1 vol. rev. ed. 2013. (Literary Text Ser.). (ENG., Illus.). 28p. (J). (gr. 2-3). pap. 10.99 *(978-1-4333-5606-3(6));* lib. bdg. 19.96 *(978-1-4807-1728-2(2))* Teacher Created Materials, Inc.

Meachen Rau, Dana. At the Zoo, 1 vol. 2008. (Fun Time Ser.). (ENG., Illus.). 24p. (gr. k-1). lib. bdg. 25.50 *(978-0-7614-2610-3(8),* 6d7f5074-b11c-44a6-b918-579799b16eca) Cavendish Square Publishing LLC.

—En el Zoológico (at the Zoo), 1 vol. 2009. (Tiempo de la Diversión (Fun Time) Ser.). (SPA., Illus.). 24p. (gr. k-1). lib. bdg. 25.50 *(978-0-7614-2777-3(5),* b63f8050-3988-480a-9027-3d00fc989b66) Cavendish Square Publishing LLC.

Meldrum, Margaret. Peter Panda & His Friends. 2009. (Illus.). 24p. pap. 11.49 *(978-1-4343-7826-2(8))* AuthorHouse.

Metzger, Steve. Dancing Clock. Nez, John Abbott, illus. 2011. (ENG.). 32p. 12.95 *(978-1-58925-100-7(8));* (J). pap. 7.95 *(978-1-58925-429-9(5))* Tiger Tales.

Munsch, Robert. Alligator Baby. Martchenko, Michael, illus. 2021. (ENG.). 32p. (J). (gr. -1-3). pap. 8.99 *(978-0-590-12387-7(4))* Scholastic Canada, Ltd. CAN. Dist: Publishers Group West (PGW).

Nelson, M. R. The Zebra Said Shhh. Sheldon, Tamia, illus. 2013. (ENG.). 32p. (J). (gr. -1-k). pap. 9.99 *(978-1-62395-440-6(1))* Xist Publishing.

Normand, James G. My Funny Little Zoo. 2008. 48p. pap. 17.49 *(978-1-4389-2322-2(8))* AuthorHouse.

Oddo, Jennifer M. Asim the Awesome Possum: Asim Gets His Awesome. Lamb, T. S., illus. 2012. 36p. 16.95 *(978-0-9855906-2-8(9))* Pie Plate Publishing Co.

Park, Linda Sue. Xander's Panda Party. Phelan, Matt, illus. (ENG.). 40p. (J). (gr. -1-3). 2017. pap. 8.99 *(978-1-328-74058-8(7),* 1677033) 2013. 16.99 *(978-0-547-55865-3(1),* 1453620) HarperCollins Pubs. (Clarion Bks.).

Parker, Emma. What a Hullabaloo. 2010. 20p. pap. *(978-1-877561-32-0(0))* First Edition Ltd.

Pauline, Christi. Hullabaloo at the Zoo. 2008. 28p. pap. 14.95 *(978-1-4389-1204-2(8))* AuthorHouse.

Pitt, Sarah. Peek a Boo! Zoo. 2009. (Little Peek a Boo Bks.). (Illus.). (J). bds. 9.99 *(978-1-934650-57-8(9))* Just For Kids Pr., LLC.

Portis, Michael. Pinky Got Out! Richmond, Lori, illus. 2019. (ENG.). 40p. (J). (gr. -1-2). lib. bdg. 20.99 *(978-1-101-93299-5(6),* Crown Books For Young Readers) Random Hse. Children's Bks.

Prince, Daniel. Zoe the Zookeeper. 2007. (Illus.). 48p. per. *(978-1-84748-047-7(0))* Athena Pr.

Purton, Marie. Josh's Day at the Zoo. 2006. (Illus.). 48p. pap. *(978-1-84401-606-8(4))* Athena Pr.

Ramoutar, Tagore. Brownie the Monkey Visits the Zoo. Cline, Ian, photos by. 2012. (Illus.). 38p. pap. *(978-1-907837-48-7(5))* Longshot Ventures, Ltd.

Rathmann, Peggy. Good Night, Gorilla (oversized Board Book) Rathmann, Peggy, illus. 2004. (Illus.). 34p. (J). (gr. -1 — 1). bds. 15.99 *(978-0-399-24260-1(0),* G.P. Putnam's Sons Books for Young Readers) Penguin Young Readers Group.

Ray, Keri. Dancing in the Rain: At the Zoo. 2009. 32p. pap. 12.99 *(978-1-4490-0673-0(6))* AuthorHouse.

Ray, Sandra. Grandma & Me Oh What Do We See When We Go to the Zoo? Bailey, Sidney, illus. 2011. 32p. 14.99 *(978-1-4520-8133-5(6))* AuthorHouse.

Reid, A. Elaine Holt. Who Did Mr. Stork Bring to the Zoo? 2010. 28p. 15.00 *(978-1-4520-0419-8(6))* AuthorHouse.

Richards, Dan. Can One Balloon Make an Elephant Fly? Newman, Jeff, illus. 2016. (ENG.). 40p. (J). (gr. -1-3). 17.99 *(978-1-4424-5215-2(3))* Simon & Schuster Bks. For Young Readers.

Richardson, Justin & Parnell, Peter. And Tango Makes Three. Cole, Henry, illus. 2005. (ENG.). 32p. (J). (gr. -1-3). 18.99 *(978-0-689-87845-9(1),* Simon & Schuster Bks. For Young Readers) Simon & Schuster Bks. For Young Readers.

Robbins, Karen S. Think Zoo Animals: A Lift-The-Flap Guessing Book, 1 vol. Brunson, Rachael, illus. 2018. (ENG.). 24p. (J). bds. 12.99 *(978-0-7643-5583-7(X),* 9908) Schiffer Publishing, Ltd.

Rockwell, Anne. Zoo Day. Rockwell, Lizzy, illus. 2018. (My First Experience Book Ser.). (ENG.). 32p. (J). (gr. -1-3). 7.99 *(978-1-4814-2735-7(0),* Aladdin) Simon & Schuster Children's Publishing.

—Zoo Day. Rockwell, Lizzy, illus. 2017. (My First Experience Book Ser.). (ENG.). 32p. (J). (gr. -1-3). 17.99 *(978-1-4814-2734-0(2),* Simon & Schuster/Paula Wiseman Bks.) Simon & Schuster/Paula Wiseman Bks.

Roskifte, Kristin. Animal Beauty. 2015. (ENG., Illus.). 50p. (J). 17.00 *(978-0-8028-5454-4(0),* Eerdmans Bks For Young Readers) Eerdmans, William B. Publishing Co.

Ruiz-Flores, Lupe. The Woodcutter's Gift/el Regalo del Lenador. Ventura, Gabriela Baeza, tr. from ENG. Jerome, Elaine, illus. 2007. (SPA & ENG.). 32p. (J). (gr. -1-2). 16.95 *(978-1-55885-489-5(4),* Piñata Books) Arte Publico Pr.

Russell, David. Who'z Who at the Zoo. 2012. (Illus.). 26p. pap. 12.95 *(978-1-4575-1395-4(1))* Dog Ear Publishing, LLC.

Ryan, Candace. Zoo Zoom! Pamintuan, Macky, illus. 2015. (ENG.). 32p. (J). (gr. -1-1). 16.99 *(978-1-61963-357-5(4),* 900134207, Bloomsbury USA Childrens) Bloomsbury Publishing USA.

Sansone, V. K. A Strange Day at the Zoo. 2009. 32p. pap. 14.98 *(978-0-557-06519-6(4))* Lulu Pr., Inc.

Scanlon, Jack. Rainbow Zoo, 1 vol. 2006. (Neighborhood Readers Ser.). (ENG., Illus.). 8p. (gr. k-1). pap. 5.15 *(978-1-4042-6686-5(0),* 59a8fa80-4f08-4c73-85b0-e625d32b9002, Rosen Classroom) Rosen Publishing Group, Inc., The.

Schultz, Lucy & Shultz, Lucy. Zoo Faces. Larranaga, Ana, illus. 2007. (ENG.). 12p. (J). (gr. -1 — 1). bds. 6.99 *(978-1-58476-556-1(9),* IKIDS) Innovative Kids.

Scollon, Bill, adapted by. Zootopia. 2016. (Illus.). 60p. (J). *(978-1-4806-9793-5(1),* Golden Bks.) Random Hse. Children's Bks.

Scotton, Rob. Splat & the Cool School Trip. Scotton, Rob, illus. 2013. (Splat the Cat Ser.). (ENG., Illus.). 40p. (J). (gr. -1-3). 17.99 *(978-0-06-213386-1(1),* HarperCollins) HarperCollins Pubs.

Shannon, Carol. Dusky Langurs at the Zoo. 2013. 40p. pap. 16.95 *(978-1-4525-1014-9(8),* Balboa Pr.) Author Solutions, LLC.

Sierra, Judy. Wild about Books. Brown, Marc, illus. 2004. (ENG.). 40p. (J). (gr. -1-2). 18.99 *(978-0-375-82538-5(X),* Knopf Bks. for Young Readers) Random Hse. Children's Bks.

Sklar, David. A Day at the Zoo with My Daddy. 2013. 24p. pap. 17.99 *(978-1-4817-0152-5(5))* AuthorHouse.

Smith, Danna. Two at the Zoo/Dos en el Zoologico Board Book: Bilingual English-Spanish. Petrone, Valeria, illus. 2011.Tr. of Two at the Zoo - A Counting Book. (ENG.). 30p. (J). (gr. -1-k). bds. 5.99 *(978-0-547-58137-8(8),* 1459824, Clarion Bks.) HarperCollins Pubs.

Snyder, Marilyn. A Second Chance for Tina. Shiffman, Lena, illus. 2003. (Hello Reader! Ser.). (J). *(978-0-439-44154-4(4))* Scholastic, Inc.

Stead, Philip C. A Sick Day for Amos McGee. Stead, Erin E., illus. 2010. (JPN.). 32p. (J). (gr. -1-1). *(978-4-89572-814-0(5))* Hisakata-Child.

—A Sick Day for Amos McGee. 2012. (CHI.). (J). (gr. -1-1). *(978-986-211-314-1(6))* Hsaio Lu Publishing Co., Ltd.

—A Sick Day for Amos Mcgee. Stead, Erin E., illus. (ENG.). (J). 2018. 34p. bds. 9.99 *(978-1-250-17110-8(5),* 900188204) 2010. 32p. (gr. -1-1). 18.99 *(978-1-59643-402-8(3),* 900051603) Roaring Brook Pr.

—A Sick Day for Amos Mcgee: 10th Anniversary Edition. Stead, Erin E., illus. 10th ed. 2019. (ENG.). 40p. (J). 29.99 *(978-1-62672-105-0(X),* 900136450) Roaring Brook Pr.

—A Sick Day for Amos Mcgee: Book & CD Storytime Set: Book & CD Storytime Set. Stead, Erin E., illus. 2017. (Macmillan Young Listeners Story Time Sets Ser.). (ENG.). 32p. (J). 12.99 *(978-1-4272-8722-9(8),* 900178665) Macmillan Audio.

Swain, Cynthia. Wishing with Pennies. 2006. (Early Explorers Ser.). (J). pap. *(978-1-4108-6041-5(8))* Benchmark Education Co.

Tait, Barbara. Timothy Toot... Goes to the Zoo. 2011. (Illus.). 28p. (J). 24.95 *(978-1-58909-961-6(3))* Bookstand Publishing.

Taplin, Sam. Noisy Zoo. Wildish, Lee, illus. 2009. (Busy Sounds Board Book Ser.). 10p. (J). (gr. -1). bds. 18.99 *(978-0-7945-2517-0(2),* Usborne) EDC Publishing.

Taylor, Michael. Going to the Zoo. Curzon, Brett, illus. 2017. (Field Trip Fun Ser.). (ENG.). 24p. (gr. -1-2). pap. 9.95 *(978-1-68342-765-0(3),* 9781683427650) Rourke Educational Media.

Taylor, Qiana. Jordyen & Lionnel the Seal. 2013. 24p. pap. 24.95 *(978-1-62709-057-5(6))* America Star Bks.

Tinsley, Jillian. Wally the Warthog. Wood, Douglas, illus. 2012. 24p. (J). pap. 10.99 *(978-1-61254-782-4(6))* Small Pr., The.

Tnt. God's Zoo. 2005. (On the Way Ser.). (ENG., Illus.). 96p. (J). per. 17.99 *(978-1-84550-069-6(5),* 9f2c21ba-f254-4919-a2e2-f25087a3997b) Christian Focus Pubns. GBR. Dist: Baker & Taylor Publisher Services (BTPS).

Trapani, Iza. Old MacDonald Had a ... Zoo? Trapani, Iza, illus. 2017. (Iza Trapani's Extended Nursery Rhymes Ser.). (Illus.). 32p. (J). (-k). lib. bdg. 16.99 *(978-1-58089-729-7(0))* Charlesbridge Publishing, Inc.

Valentine, Sophie. Zoo Hullabaloo, 1 vol. rev. ed. 2013. (Literary Text Ser.). (ENG., Illus.). 12p. (gr. k-2). (J). lib. bdg. 12.96 *(978-1-4807-1137-2(3));* 6.99 *(978-1-4333-5458-8(6))* Teacher Created Materials, Inc.

Vassallo, Theresa. Day at the Zoo Sing-along. 2011. 20p. pap. 24.95 *(978-1-4560-6832-5(6))* America Star Bks.

Wallace, Adam. How to Catch a Unicorn. Elkerton, Andy, illus. 2019. (How to Catch Ser.: 0). (ENG.). 40p. (J). (gr. k-6). 10.99 *(978-1-4926-6973-9(3))* Sourcebooks, Inc.

Wan, Joyce. Peek-A-Boo Zoo. Wan, Joyce, illus. 2015. (ENG., Illus.). 14p. (J). (— 1). bds. 6.99 *(978-0-545-75042-4(3),* Cartwheel Bks.) Scholastic, Inc.

Weston Woods Staff, creator. Wild about Books. 2011. 29.95 *(978-0-439-80485-1(X))* Weston Woods Studios, Inc.

Weston Woods Studios Inc. Staff, creator. Good Night, Gorilla. 2004. (J). 18.95 *(978-1-55592-419-5(0));* 38.75 *(978-1-55592-421-8(2))* Weston Woods Studios, Inc.

White, George. Halloween at the Zoo: A Pop-up Trick of Treat Experience. 2007. (Illus.). 16p. (J). 16.99 *(978-0-9795441-0-1(6))* Jumping Jack Pr.

Wilson, Karma. Animal Strike at the Zoo. It's True! Spengler, Margaret, illus. 2006. (ENG.). 32p. (J). (gr. -1-1). 16.99 *(978-0-06-057502-1(6),* HarperCollins) HarperCollins Pubs.

Winthrop, Elizabeth. Dancing Granny, 1 vol. Murdocca, Sal, illus. 2003. (ENG.). 32p. (J). 16.95 *(978-0-7614-5141-9(2))* Marshall Cavendish Corp.

Woodcock, Fiona. Look! 2018. (ENG., Illus.). 40p. (J). (gr. -1-3). 17.99 *(978-0-06-264455-8(6),* Greenwillow Bks.) HarperCollins Pubs.

Young, Judy. Digger & Daisy Go to the Zoo. Sullivan, Dana, illus. 2013. (Digger & Daisy Ser.). (ENG.). 32p. (J). (gr. k-1). 9.99 *(978-1-58536-841-9(5),* 202897) Sleeping Bear Pr.

—Digger y Daisy Van Al Zoológico (Digger & Daisy Go to the Zoo) Sullivan, Dana, illus. 2016. (Digger & Daisy Ser.). (SPA.). 32p. (J). (gr. k-2). 9.99 *(978-1-62753-951-7(4),* 204174) Sleeping Bear Pr.

The Zany Zanimal Zoo. 2005. (Illus.). 40p. (J). 14.95 *(978-0-9769738-0-5(4))* Redel, Nicole.

ZOOGEOGRAPHY

see Animal Distribution

ZOOLOGICAL GARDENS

see Zoos

ZOOLOGY

see also Anatomy, Comparative; Animals; Embryology; Evolution; Fossils; Natural History; Physiology, Comparative; Psychology, Comparative

also names of divisions, classes, etc. of the animal kingdom (e.g. Invertebrates; Vertebrates; birds; Mammals; etc.)

Abbott, Henry. Hormigueros (Inside Anthills), 1 vol. 2015. (Las Casas de Los Animales (Inside Animal Homes) Ser.). (SPA.). 24p. (J). (gr. 2-3). 25.27 *(978-1-4994-0593-4(6),* 2c009ff1-a9a4-401c-a53e-25930c0fee41, PowerKids Pr.) Rosen Publishing Group, Inc., The.

Anderson, Holly Lynn. Unexplained Monsters & Cryptids. 2015. (J). *(978-1-61900-071-1(7))* Eldorado Ink.

Animal Watch. 2003. (ENG., Illus.). 32p. (gr. 2-4). 23.00 *(978-0-7910-7409-1(9),* P179933, Facts On File) Infobase Holdings, Inc.

Artell, Mike. Pee-Yew! The Stinkiest, Smelliest Animals, Insects, & Plants on Earth! 2006. (Illus.). 96p. (YA). per. 14.95 *(978-1-59647-054-5(2))* Good Year Bks.

AZ Books, creator. Walk Around Africa. 2012. (Put Together Ser.). (ENG., Illus.). 16p. (J). (gr. -1-k). spiral bd. 6.95 *(978-1-61889-191-4(X))* AZ Bks. LLC.

Bedoyere, Camilla & Bedoyere, Camilla. Fastest & Slowest. 2010. (Animal Opposites Ser.). (ENG., Illus.). 32p. (J). (gr. -1-3). pap. 5.95 *(978-1-55407-809-7(1),* 59ccdcef-29bb-4aa0-ae05-48ce7fe86876) Firefly Bks., Ltd.

Belton, Blair. Be a Zoologist, 1 vol. 2014. (Be a Scientist! Ser.). (ENG.). 32p. (J). (gr. 3-4). pap. 11.50 *(978-1-4824-1286-4(1),* 089f14d6-6a23-4624-beeb-b63a31d359b3) Stevens, Gareth Publishing LLLP.

Berne, Emma Carlson. Coyotes, 1 vol. 2014. (Scavengers: Eating Nature's Trash Ser.). (ENG., Illus.). 24p. (J). (gr. 2-3). lib. bdg. 25.27 *(978-1-4777-6607-1(3),* 25075873-62c4-4e4d-9031-f1e7a6910807, PowerKids Pr.) Rosen Publishing Group, Inc., The.

—Flesh Flies, 1 vol. 2014. (Scavengers: Eating Nature's Trash Ser.). (ENG., Illus.). 24p. (J). (gr. 2-3). lib. bdg. 25.27 *(978-1-4777-6588-3(3),* 0f00a895-c69a-4983-990e-03dd28a96c4d, PowerKids Pr.) Rosen Publishing Group, Inc., The.

Blough, Glenn O. After the Sun Goes Down: The Story of Animals at Night. Bendick, Jeanne, illus. 2011. 50p. (gr. 1). 35.95 *(978-1-258-09913-8(6))* Literary Licensing, LLC.

Borgert-Spaniol, Megan. Cryptozoology: Could Unexplained Creatures Be Real? 2018. (Science Fact or Science Fiction? Ser.). (ENG., Illus.). 32p. (gr. 3-6). lib. bdg. 32.79 *(978-1-5321-1539-4(3),* 28932, Checkerboard Library) ABDO Publishing Co.

Broderip, W. J. Zoological Recreations. 2006. pap. 36.95 *(978-1-4286-3565-4(3))* Kessinger Publishing, LLC.

Brown, Jonatha A. Las Cabezas y Los Cuellos de Los Animales (Animal Heads & Necks), 1 vol. 2006. (En Qué Se Diferencian Los Animales (Why Animals Look Different) Ser.). (SPA., Illus.). 24p. (J). (gr. 2-4). lib. bdg. 24.67 *(978-0-8368-7412-9(9),* 26e9bf06-59e9-4fa5-85e2-b127f607f0c8, Weekly Reader Leveled Readers) Stevens, Gareth Publishing LLLP.

—Las Colas de Los Animales (Animal Tails), 1 vol. 2006. (En Qué Se Diferencian Los Animales (Why Animals Look Different) Ser.). (SPA., Illus.). 24p. (J). (gr. 2-4). lib. bdg. 24.67 *(978-0-8368-7413-6(7),* 2622b524-93d6-4ced-9f07-b86020f82e31, Weekly Reader Leveled Readers) Stevens, Gareth Publishing LLLP.

Brown, Martin. Lesser Spotted Animals. Brown, Martin, illus. 2016. (ENG., Illus.). 56p. (J). (gr. 2-5). 18.99 *(978-1-338-08934-9(X))* Scholastic, Inc.

Buckland, Francis Trevelyan. Log-Book of a Fisherman & Zoologist. 2011. 422p. pap. 32.95 *(978-1-4460-5845-9(X),* Kent Pr.) Kent Communications, Ltd.

Bull, Mary P. It's Cool! Early Inhabitants of Santa Cruz Valley. 2003. (ENG., Illus.). 54p. pap. 28.50 *(978-1-4120-0178-6(1))* Trafford Publishing.

Burgan, Michael. Bat Researcher, 1 vol. 2011. (Dirty & Dangerous Jobs Ser.). (ENG.). 32p. (gr. 3-3). 31.21 *(978-1-60870-170-4(0),* d2d4bbb4-cd0f-4719-96d8-f4136440b305) Cavendish Square Publishing LLC.

Burgess, Thornton W. The Burgess Animal Book for Children. 2005. 29.95 *(978-1-4218-0996-0(6));* 304p. pap. 14.95 *(978-1-59540-696-5(4))* 1st World Publishing, Inc. (1st World Library - Literary Society).

—The Burgess Animal Book for Children. 2009. 248p. 26.99 *(978-1-60512-323-3(4));* (Illus.). pap. 13.99 *(978-1-60512-423-0(0))* Akasha Publishing, LLC. (Akasha Classics).

—The Burgess Animal Book for Children. (J). 28.95 *(978-0-8488-0716-0(2))* Amereon Ltd.

—The Burgess Animal Book for Children. Fuertes, Louis Agassiz, illus. 2008. 284p. (gr. 4-7). pap. *(978-1-4099-2052-6(6))* Dodo Pr.

—The Burgess Animal Book for Children. 2004. (Dover Children's Classics Ser.). (ENG., Illus.). 288p. (gr. 1-5). pap. 9.99 *(978-0-486-43745-3(0),* 437450) Dover Pubns., Inc.

—The Burgess Animal Book for Children. 2010. (Illus.). 130p. (gr. 4-7). pap. 19.99 *(978-1-153-69658-6(4));* 146p. pap. 21.89 *(978-1-152-50810-1(5))* General Bks. LLC.

—The Burgess Animal Book for Children. Fuertes, Louis Agassiz, illus. 2011. 478p. 52.95 *(978-1-169-84273-1(9))* 2010. 478p. 42.36 *(978-1-163-21392-6(6))* 2010. 478p. pap. 30.36 *(978-1-162-64734-0(5))* 2004. 476p. (gr. 4-7). 52.95 *(978-1-4326-2165-0(3))* Kessinger Publishing, LLC.

—The Burgess Animal Book for Children. 2004. reprint ed. pap. 1.99 *(978-1-4192-5555-7(X))* Kessinger Publishing, LLC.

—The Burgess Animal Book for Children. Fuertes, Louis Agassiz, illus. 2004. reprint ed. pap. 37.95 *(978-1-4179-2978-8(2))* Kessinger Publishing, LLC.

—The Burgess Animal Book for Children (Yesterday's Classics) Fuertes, Louis Agassiz, illus. 2006. (J). per. 13.95 *(978-1-59915-171-7(5))* Yesterday's Classics.

Burgess, Thornton W. & Fuertes, Louis Agassiz. The Burgess Animal Book for Children. 2010. (ENG.). 484p. pap. 38.75 *(978-1-171-73852-7(8));* 486p. pap. 38.75 *(978-1-176-23716-2(0))* Creative Media Partners, LLC.

Canetti, Yanitzia. Adivina, Adivinador: ¿Quién está Escondido? 2010. (SPA.). 24p. (J). pap. *(978-1-59835-126-2(5),* BrickHouse Education) Cambridge BrickHouse, Inc.

—Guess Who? Who Crosses Here? 2010. (ENG.). 24p. (J). pap. 8.99 *(978-1-59835-136-1(2),* BrickHouse Education) Cambridge BrickHouse, Inc.

—Guess Who? Who's Hiding? 2010. (ENG.). 24p. (J). pap. 8.99 *(978-1-59835-137-8(0),* BrickHouse Education) Cambridge BrickHouse, Inc.

—Guess Who? Who's Looking at Me? 2010. (ENG.). (J). pap. 8.99 *(978-1-59835-138-5(9),* BrickHouse Education) Cambridge BrickHouse, Inc.

—Guess Who? Who's Shadow Is This? 2010. (ENG.). 24p. (J). pap. 8.99 *(978-1-59835-140-8(0))* Cambridge BrickHouse, Inc.

—Guess Who? Whose Skin Is This? 2010. (ENG.). (J). pap. 8.99 *(978-1-59835-142-2(7),* BrickHouse Education) Cambridge BrickHouse, Inc.

—Guess Who? Whose Tracks Are These? 2010. (ENG.). 24p. (J). pap. 8.99 *(978-1-59835-141-5(9),* BrickHouse Education) Cambridge BrickHouse, Inc.

—Quien cruza por Aqui? Adivina, Adivinador. 2010. (SPA.). 24p. (J). pap. 8.99 *(978-1-59835-125-5(7),* BrickHouse Education) Cambridge BrickHouse, Inc.

—Quien deja esta Huella? Adivina, Adivinador. 2010. (SPA.). 24p. (J). pap. 8.99 *(978-1-59835-130-9(3),* BrickHouse Education) Cambridge BrickHouse, Inc.

—¿Quién se oculta tras la Luz? 2010. (SPA.). 24p. (J). pap. 8.99 *(978-1-59835-128-6(1),* BrickHouse Education) Cambridge BrickHouse, Inc.

—¿Quién tiene esta Piel? 2010. (SPA.). 24p. (J). pap. 8.99 *(978-1-59835-131-6(1),* BrickHouse Education) Cambridge BrickHouse, Inc.

—Rhyming Tongue Twisters Animals. 2010. 32p. (J). 6.99 *(978-1-59835-269-6(5),* BrickHouse Education) Cambridge BrickHouse, Inc.

—Trabalenguas Zoológicos. 2010. (SPA.). 32p. (J). pap. 6.99 *(978-1-59835-159-0(1),* BrickHouse Education) Cambridge BrickHouse, Inc.

Catala, Ellen. Snakes & Lizards, 6 vols. 2003. (Yellow Umbrella Early Level Ser.). (ENG.). 16p. (gr. k-1). pap. 35.70 *(978-0-7368-3017-1(0),* Capstone Pr.) Capstone.

Clarke, Ginjer L. Maxed Out! Gigantic Creatures from the Past. Mueller, Pete, illus. 2010. (Penguin Young Readers, Level 3 Ser.). 48p. (J). (gr. 1-3). mass mkt. 4.99 *(978-0-448-44827-5(0),* Penguin Young Readers) Penguin Young Readers Group.

Cook, Gladys Emerson. Zoo Animals. 2011. 54p. 36.95 *(978-1-258-10530-3(6))* Literary Licensing, LLC.

Dale, Kim. What Am I? (Illus.). 32p. pap. *(978-0-7344-0125-0(6),* Lothian Children's Bks.) Hachette Australia.

Dorling Kindersley Publishing Staff & Ring, Susan. Mammals, 6 vols., Set. 2003. (Yellow Umbrella Early Level Ser.). (ENG.). 16p. (gr. k-1). pap. 35.70 *(978-0-7368-2996-0(2),* Capstone Pr.) Capstone.

Drimmer, Stephanie Warren. National Geographic Readers: Roar! 100 Facts about African Animals (L3) 2018. (Readers Ser.). (Illus.). 48p. (J). (gr. 3-7). pap. 4.99 *(978-1-4263-3241-8(6));* (ENG., lib. bdg. 14.90 *(978-1-4263-3242-5(4))* Disney Publishing Worldwide. (National Geographic Kids).

Duhig, Holly. Bones & Bodies. 2020. (Animals Eat What? Ser.). (ENG., Illus.). 24p. (J). (gr. 1-4). pap. 8.99 *(978-1-5415-8704-5(9),* 22ac964d-ac8e-450c-b1f0-c31cdca14f94); lib. bdg. 26.65 *(978-1-5415-7932-3(1),* e4231000f-971e-4337-bc4d-990b414fffb1) Lerner Publishing Group. (Lerner Pubns.).

Evans, Hubert R. Forest Friends: Stories of Animals, Fish, & Birds, West of the Rockies. 2012. 260p. 47.95 *(978-1-258-23041-8(0));* pap. 32.95 *(978-1-258-24397-5(0))* Literary Licensing, LLC.

Facts on File, Inc. Staff. Animals. 2010. (New Discovering Careers for Your Future Ser.). (Illus.). 128p. (gr. 4-9). 24.95 *(978-0-8160-8044-1(5),* Ferguson Publishing Company) Infobase Holdings, Inc.

lbright, Jeannie. Exploring Creation with Zoology 1: The Flying Creatures of Day Five. Wile, Jay L., ed. 2005. (Illus.). xvi, 240p. (J). 35.00 (978-1-932012-61-3(3)) Apologia Educational Ministries, Inc.
ardner, Jane. Animal Science, Vol. 11. Lewin, Russ, ed. 2015. (Science 24/7 Ser.). (Illus.). 48p. (J). (gr. 5). lib. bdg. 20.95 (978-1-4222-3405-1(3)) Mason Crest.
illespie, Katie. Meet the Impala. 2017. (Illus.). 24p. (J). (978-1-5105-0551-3(2)) SmartBook Media, Inc.
–Meet the Warthog. 2017. (Illus.). 24p. (J). (978-1-5105-0554-4(7)) SmartBook Media, Inc.
reen, Ivah E. Animals under Your Feet. Reece, Maynard, illus. 2011. 140p. 40.95 (978-1-258-06244-6(5)) Literary Licensing, LLC.
resham, Jennifer. Arctic Animals. 2013. (Illus.). (J). (978-1-58865-837-1(6)) Kidsbooks, LLC.
alls, Kelly Milner. Cryptid Creatures: A Field Guide to 50 Fascinating Beasts. Spears, Rick, illus. 2019. 224p. (J). (gr. 2). pap. 16.99 (978-1-63217-210-5(0), Little Bigfoot) Sasquatch Bks.
–Death Eaters: Meet Nature's Scavengers. 2018. (ENG., Illus.). 40p. (J). (gr. 4-8). 33.32 (978-1-5124-8200-3(5), 7fcb3d03-0833-4503-a7ee-89defc0d2e2b, Millbrook Pr.) Lerner Publishing Group.
Hestermann, Josh & Hestermann, Bethanie. Zoology for Kids: Understanding & Working with Animals, with 21 Activities. 2015. (For Kids Ser.: 54). (Illus.). 144p. (J). (gr. 4). pap. 19.99 (978-1-61374-961-6(9)) Chicago Review Pr., Inc.
Holden, Pam. Hoppity Hop, 1 vol. Morris, Sandra, illus. 2009. (Red Rocket Readers Ser.). (ENG.). 16p. (gr. -1-1). pap. (978-1-877363-19-1(7), Red Rocket Readers) Flying Start Bks.
Holland, Mary. Animal Mouths, 1 vol. 2015. (Animal Adaptations Ser.). (ENG.). 32p. (J). (gr. 1-4). 17.95 (978-1-62855-552-3(1)) Arbordale Publishing.
Hyde, Natalie. Glow-In-the-Dark Creatures, 1 vol. 2014. (ENG., Illus.). 32p. (J). (gr. 1-2). 19.95 (978-1-55455-330-3(X), 213f23a7-6893-422a-adf8-97fec34c8c10) Trifolium Bks., Inc. CAN. Dist: Firefly Bks., Ltd.
Jackie, Glassman. Amazing Arctic Animals, Vol. 2. 2014. (Penguin Young Readers, L3 Ser.). (ENG.). 48p. (J). (gr. 2-12). 8.24 (978-1-63245-253-5(7)) Lectorum Pubns., Inc.
Jenkins, Steve & Page, Robin. What Do You Do with a Tail Like This? A Caldecott Honor Award Winner. Calvo, Carlos, tr. Jenkins, Steve, illus. 2008. (ENG., Illus.). 32p. (J). (gr. -1-3). pap. 7.95 (978-0-618-99713-8(X), 1028080, Clarion Bks.) HarperCollins Pubs.
Jolivet, Joëlle. Zoo - Ology. Jolivet, Joëlle, illus. rev. ed. 2003. (ENG., Illus.). 40p. (J). (gr. -1-3). 36.99 (978-0-7613-1894-1(1), 900029495) Roaring Brook Pr.
Kalman, Bobbie. Big Science Ideas. 2008. (J). pap. (978-0-7787-3292-1(4)) Crabtree Publishing Co.
—How Does It Move? 2008. (Looking at Nature Ser.). (ENG., Illus.). 24p. (J). (gr. -1-2). pap. (978-0-7787-3342-3(4)); lib. bdg. (978-0-7787-3322-5(X)) Crabtree Publishing Co.
—Nature's Cleaners. 2008. (Big Science Ideas Ser.). (ENG., Illus.). 32p. (J). (gr. 1-4). pap. (978-0-7787-3300-3(9)); lib. bdg. (978-0-7787-3280-8(0)) Crabtree Publishing Co.
—Le Regne Animal. 2004. (Petit Monde Vivant Ser.). (FRE., Illus.). 32p. (J). pap. 10.95 (978-2-89579-025-9(6)) Bayard Canada Livres CAN. Dist: Crabtree Publishing Co.
Kelly, Joni. 1,000-Year-Old Sponges!, 1 vol. 2018. (World's Longest-Living Animals Ser.). (ENG.). 24p. (gr. 1-2). 24.27 (978-1-5382-1697-2(3), f5ee0f77-ebc2-457d-b697-30bbfe9f3fba) Stevens, Gareth Publishing LLLP.
Kessel, Quinta Cattell. Mama Is A Mammal. Kessel, Margaret May, illus. 2005. 80p. (J). 16.95 (978-0-9725027-3-3(4)) Vernissage Pr., LLC.
Kite, Lorien. Anteaters. 2009. (Illus.). 52p. (J). (978-0-7172-8058-2(6)) Grolier, Ltd.
Kratt, Chris & Kratt, Martin. Wild Animal Babies! (Wild Kratts) 2016. (Step into Reading Ser.). (Illus.). 24p. (J). (gr. -1-1). 5.99 (978-1-101-93171-4(X), Random Hse. Bks. for Young Readers) Random Hse. Children's Bks.
Kravetz, Jonathan. Locusts, 1 vol. 2005. (Gross Bugs Ser.). (ENG., Illus.). 24p. (J). (gr. 3-4). lib. bdg. 26.27 (978-1-4042-3042-2(4), ffb7192c-a4ed-4cb1-9193-f65ad61be782, PowerKids Pr.) Rosen Publishing Group, Inc., The.
—Ticks. 2009. (Gross Bugs Ser.). 24p. (gr. 3-4). 42.50 (978-1-61513-233-1(3), PowerKids Pr.) Rosen Publishing Group, Inc., The.
Lee, Justin. How to Draw African Animals. 2009. (Kid's Guide to Drawing Ser.). 24p. (gr. 3-3). 47.90 (978-1-61511-008-7(9), PowerKids Pr.) Rosen Publishing Group, Inc., The.
Lewin, Ted & Lewin, Betsy. Elephant Quest, 1 vol. 2014. (Adventures Around the World Ser.). (ENG., Illus.). 48p. (J). (gr. 1-6). pap. 13.95 (978-1-62014-183-0(3), leelowbooks) Lee & Low Bks., Inc.
El Libro de los Acertijos Zoologicos. (Coleccion Acertijos). (SPA.). (YA). (gr. 5-8). pap. (978-950-724-261-8(9), LMA8236) Lumen ARG. Dist: Lectorum Pubns., Inc.
Litton, Jonathan. Baby 101: Zoology for Babies. Elliott, Thomas, illus. 2018. (Baby 101 Ser.). (ENG.). 22p. (J). (— 1). bds. 8.99 (978-0-525-64879-6(8), Doubleday Bks. for Young Readers) Random Hse. Children's Bks.
Long, William. Secrets of the Woods. 2007. 148p. 19.99 (978-1-59986-710-6(9)) Filiquarian Publishing, LLC.
Long, William Joseph. Wilderness Ways. 2017. (ENG., Illus.). (J). pap. 12.95 (978-1-374-82075-3(X)) Capital Communications, Inc.
Markle, Sandra. What If You Had an Animal Nose!? McWilliam, Howard, illus. 2017. 32p. (J). (978-1-338-20647-0(8)) Scholastic, Inc.
Martin, Ruth. Little Explorers: the Animal World. Sanders, Allan, illus. 2016. (Little Explorers Ser.). (ENG.). 18p. (J). (gr. -1-3). 10.99 (978-1-4998-0249-8(8)) Little Bee Books Inc.
Mattern, Joanne. Animals of the Savannah. 2009. (Reading Room Collection 2 Ser.). 24p. (gr. 3-4). 42.50 (978-1-60851-957-6(0), PowerKids Pr.) Rosen Publishing Group, Inc., The.
McDonald, Joe. African Wildlife, Vol. 12. 2018. (Animals in the Wild Ser.). (Illus.). 72p. (J). (gr. 7). 33.27 (978-1-4222-4164-6(5)) Mason Crest.
McDonnell, Julia . Being a Sloth, 1 vol. 2013. (Can You Imagine? Ser.). (ENG.). 32p. (gr. 2-3). pap. 11.50 (978-1-4824-3274-9(9), b108051a-34fd-4d15-ba0e-ab633b330413) Rosen Publishing Group, Inc., The.
Miller, Debbie S. Arctic Lights, Arctic Nights. Van Zyle, Jon, illus. 2007. (ENG.). 32p. (J). (gr. k-4). pap. 8.99 (978-0-8027-9636-3(2), 900042471, Bloomsbury USA Childrens) Bloomsbury Publishing USA.
—Survival at 40 Below. Van Zyle, Jon, illus. 2012. (ENG.). 40p. (J). (gr. 2-5). lib. bdg. 24.94 (978-0-8027-9816-9(0), 9780802798169) Walker & Co.
Miller, Janet. Cut, Color & Paste: God's Creatures. 2004. (Illus.). 96p. (J). (gr. -1-2). 11.95 (978-1-885358-81-3(4)) Rainbow Pubs. & Legacy Pr.
Mitchell, Melanie. Wings. 2004. (First Step Nonfiction — Animal Traits Ser.). (ENG., Illus.). 8p. (J). (gr. k-2). pap. 5.99 (978-0-8225-3916-2(0), 15e38c7a-775d-4f6c-9cc4-3e73495b14bc) Lerner Publishing Group.
Morgan, Sally. Insect Eaters. 2004. (J). lib. bdg. 27.10 (978-1-59389-174-9(1)) Chrysalis Education.
Nagelhout, Ryan. Clownfish, 1 vol. 2013. (Underwater World Ser.). (ENG., Illus.). 24p. (J). (gr. k-k). pap. 9.15 (978-1-4339-8564-5(0), 9b10bd49-edb4-4b8d-8b2c-b5c196bb79f0); lib. bdg. 25.27 (978-1-4339-8563-8(2), 66aea018-8e9f-4d20-9f7b-938aa658642e) Stevens, Gareth Publishing LLLP.
Nichols, Catherine. An Arctic Year, 1 vol. 2003. (We Can Read about Nature! Ser.). (ENG., Illus.). 32p. (gr. 1-2). 25.50 (978-0-7614-1430-8(4), a925ab7a-2859-4ad6-99f8-5a230ceb9cda) Cavendish Square Publishing LLC.
Nsrc. Science & Technology for Children BOOKS: Plant Growth & Development. 2007. (Illus.). 64p. (J). (978-1-933008-39-4(3), Science and Technology Concepts (STC)) Smithsonian Science Education Ctr. (SSEC).
Orr, Tamra. Camouflage & Mimicry in the Wild. 2003. (Extreme Animals Ser.). (J). pap. (978-1-58417-257-4(6)) Lake Street Pubs.
Owen, Ruth. Zoologists & Ecologists, 1 vol. 2013. (Out of the Lab: Extreme Jobs in Science Ser.). (ENG.). 32p. (J). (gr. 4-5). 28.93 (978-1-4777-1293-1(3), 8b0be3ac-b02c-43da-93c6-5c0a436af047); pap. 11.00 (978-1-4777-1384-6(0), bb1ee34a-d032-4e5e-b472-4626a81bd4d9) Rosen Publishing Group, Inc., The. (PowerKids Pr.).
Pierson, Clara Dillingham. Among the Forest People (Yesterday's Classics) 2005. (Illus.). 148p. (J). per. 8.95 (978-1-59915-018-5(2)) Yesterday's Classics.
—Among the Pond People (Yesterday's Classics) 2005. (Illus.). 160p. (J). per. 8.95 (978-1-59915-021-5(2)) Yesterday's Classics.
Pipe, Jim. Swarms. 2009. (Scary Creatures Ser.). (ENG., Illus.). 32p. (J). (gr. 3-5). 27.00 (978-0-531-21674-3(8), Children's Pr.); pap. 8.95 (978-0-531-21045-1(6), Watts, Franklin) Scholastic Library Publishing.
Pruetz, Jill. You Can Be a Primatologist: Studying Primates with Dr. Pruetz. 2020. (You Can Be A ... Ser.). (Illus.). 32p. (J). (gr. -1-k). 16.99 (978-1-4263-3754-3(X), National Geographic Kids) Disney Publishing Worldwide.
Rake, Jody Sullivan. Spines, Horns, & Armor: Animal Weapons & Defenses. 2012. (Animal Weapons & Defenses Ser.). (ENG.). 32p. (gr. 1-2). pap. 47.70 (978-1-4296-8502-3(6), Capstone Pr.) Capstone.
Redfern, Nick. True Stories of Real-Life Monsters, 1 vol. 2014. (Off the Record! Ser.). (ENG., Illus.). 288p. (J). (gr. 7-7). 41.47 (978-1-4777-7835-7(7), e1d95ece-f289-4e9c-b377-d548f82d928b) Rosen Publishing Group, Inc., The.
Riggs, Kate. Vultures. 2015. (Amazing Animals Ser.). (ENG., Illus.). 24p. (J). (gr. 1-4). (978-1-60818-492-7(7), 21148, Creative Education) Creative Co., The.
Rodríguez, Ana María. The Secret of the Deceiving Striped Lizard... & More!, 1 vol. 2017. (Animal Secrets Revealed! Ser.). (ENG.). 48p. (gr. 4-4). pap. 12.70 (978-0-7660-8853-5(7), 9cd3f1d4-9945-414d-9e1d-102f2dfd26b7); lib. bdg. 29.60 (978-0-7660-8625-8(9), 78339ad2-1847-433e-b425-e9b332bc4a79) Enslow Publishing, LLC.
Rooney, Anne. A Math Journey Through the Animal Kingdom. 2014. (Go Figure! Ser.). (ENG., Illus.). 32p. (J). (gr. 4-4). (978-0-7787-0732-5(6)) Crabtree Publishing Co.
Rose, Simon. Taxidermist. 2014. (J). (978-1-4896-1006-5(5)) Weigl Pubs., Inc.
Royston, Angela. What Do You Know about Human & Animal Bodies?, 1 vol. 2017. (Test Your Science Skills Ser.). (ENG.). 32p. (J). (gr. 5-5). 29.27 (978-1-5383-2213-0(7), 8db546ad-7725-450d-9370-eabff5026844); pap. 12.75 (978-1-5383-2306-9(0), 017fe1bc-681f-4fe0-9245-3473a4949623) Rosen Publishing Group, Inc., The. (PowerKids Pr.).
Rushworth, Gary. What Makes an Animal an Animal? Set Of 6. 2011. (Navigators Ser.). (J). pap. 48.00 net. (978-1-4108-6230-3(5)) Benchmark Education Co.
Salariya, David, creator. Scary Creatures, 6 vols., Set. Incl. Arctic. Clarke, Penny. 27.00 (978-0-531-20449-8(9), Children's Pr.); Jellyfish - Scary Creatures. Cheshire, Gerard. 27.00 (978-0-531-20446-7(4), Children's Pr.); Killer Whales. Malam, John. 27.00 (978-0-531-20447-4(2)); Lizards - Scary Creatures. Cheshire, Gerard. 27.00 (978-0-531-20448-1(0), Children's Pr.); Of the Night. Malam, John. 27.00 (978-0-531-20424-5(3), Children's Pr.); Scary Creatures of the Rain Forest. Clarke, Penny. 27.00 (978-0-531-20544-0(4), Children's Pr.); (Illus.). 32p. (J). (gr. 2-7). 2008. Set lib. bdg. 156.00 o.p. (978-0-531-20416-0(2), Watts, Franklin) Scholastic Library Publishing.
Schulte, Mary. The Dover Demon, 1 vol. 2009. (Mysterious Encounters Ser.). (ENG., Illus.). 48p. (gr. 4-8). 35.23 (978-0-7377-4570-2(3), 662c62b6-291d-489d-861b-7a8c091f651f, KidHaven Publishing) Greenhaven Publishing LLC.
Shields, Mary & Grace, Susan. What's a Shrew to You? Van Zyle, Jon, illus. 2008. (J). (978-0-9618348-7-6(0)) Pyrola Publishing.
Silvey, Anita. Untamed: The Wild Life of Jane Goodall. 2015. (Illus.). 96p. (J). (gr. 3-7). 18.99 (978-1-4263-1518-3(X), National Geographic Kids) Disney Publishing Worldwide.
Somervill, Barbara A. Ticks: Digging for Blood. 2009. (Bloodsuckers Ser.). 24p. (gr. 2-3). 42.50 (978-1-61511-636-2(2), PowerKids Pr.) Rosen Publishing Group, Inc., The.
Spilsbury, Louise. Zoologists in the Field. 2010. (Big Picture: People & Culture Ser.). (ENG.). 24p. (gr. 1-2). pap. 41.70 (978-1-4296-5822-5(3), Capstone Pr.) Capstone.
Suen, Anastasia. Polar Bears. 2020. (Spot Arctic Animals Ser.). (ENG.). 16p. (J). (gr. -1-2). lib. bdg. (978-1-68151-797-1(3), 10671) Amicus.
—Reindeer. 2020. (Spot Arctic Animals Ser.). (ENG.). 16p. (J). (gr. -1-1). pap. 7.99 (978-1-68152-526-6(7), 10725) Amicus.
—Sea Otters. 2020. (Spot Arctic Animals Ser.). (ENG.). 16p. (J). (gr. -1-2). lib. bdg. (978-1-68151-799-5(X), 10673) Amicus.
—Snowy Owls. 2020. (Spot Arctic Animals Ser.). (ENG.). 16p. (J). (gr. -1-2). lib. bdg. (978-1-68151-800-8(7), 10674) Amicus.
Swanson, Jennifer. Zoology: Cool Women Who Work with Animals. Chandhok, Lena, illus. 2017. (Girls in Science Ser.). (ENG.). 112p. (J). (gr. 3-7). 19.95 (978-1-61930-501-4(1), a9292fbc-33d3-4ab8-98ba-2200c6e68e1f) Nomad Pr.
Tagliaferro, Linda. Galapagos Islands: Nature's Delicate Balance at Risk. 2005. (Discovery! Ser.). (Illus.). 120p. (gr. 5-12). lib. bdg. 27.93 (978-0-8225-0648-5(3)) Lerner Publishing Group.
Time Living Wonders: The Marvels & Mysteries of Life on Earth. 2009. (Time Inc. Home Entertainment Library-Bound Titles Ser.). (ENG.). 128p. (gr. 5-12). 39.93 (978-0-7613-4229-8(X), Twenty-First Century Bks.) Lerner Publishing Group.
Uncover a T. Rex. 2004. (J). bds. 22.95 (978-1-932855-10-4(6)) becker&mayer! books.
Vaughan, Marcia. I Howl, I Growl: Southwest Animal Antics. Powell, Polly, illus. 2003. (ENG.). 26p. (J). (gr. -1-k). bds. 7.95 (978-0-87358-835-5(5)) Cooper Square Publishing Llc.
Wadsworth, Pamela. Golwg Gyntaf Ar Bethau Byw. Owen, Ken & Owen, Siân, illus. 2005. (WEL.). 24p. pap. (978-1-85596-250-7(0)) Dref Wen.
Wood, J. g. Illustrated Natural History: Arranged Fo. 2006. pap. 27.95 (978-1-4286-0489-6(8)) Kessinger Publishing, LLC.
World Book, Inc. Staff, contrib. by. Encyclopedia of Animals. 2013. (Illus.). (J). (978-0-7166-7518-1(8)) World Bk., Inc.
El Zoologico, 2 Packs. (Chiquilibros Ser.). (SPA.). (gr. -1-1). 12.00 (978-0-7635-8556-3(4)) Rigby Education.
Zoologists & Ecologists. 2013. (Out of the Lab: Extreme Jobs in Science Ser.). 32p. (J). (gr. 3-6). pap. 60.00 (978-1-4777-1385-3(9), PowerKids Pr.) Rosen Publishing Group, Inc., The.

ZOOLOGY—ANATOMY

see Anatomy, Comparative

ZOOLOGY, ECONOMIC

see also Domestic Animals; Insect Pests

Ridley, Sarah. In the Home. 2010. (J). 28.50 (978-1-59920-328-7(6)) Black Rabbit Bks.
Sherman, Jill. Animals & Fish, 1 vol. 2017. (Let's Learn about Natural Resources Ser.). (ENG.). 24p. (gr. 1-2). 24.27 (978-0-7660-9238-9(0), 564bedf6-42b7-4f24-a7fc-a9150bf0a9bf) Enslow Publishing, LLC.

ZOOLOGY OF THE BIBLE

see Bible—Natural History

ZOOS

Allan, John. Be a Zookeeper. 2019. (Math Adventures (Step 1) Ser.). (ENG., Illus.). 32p. (J). (gr. 1-3). lib. bdg. 29.32 (978-1-912108-25-1(9), 65f34c20-4ce3-4e9f-8a56-8a426e62e5a4, Hungry Tomato (r)) Lerner Publishing Group.
Appleby, Alex. Dinosaurs at the Zoo, 1 vol. 2013. (Dinosaur School Ser.). 24p. (J). (gr. k-k). (ENG.). pap. 9.15 (978-1-4339-9046-5(6), f582a76e-f6d7-431c-aec5-1ec19181cf1b); pap. 48.90 (978-1-4339-9047-2(4)); (ENG., Illus.). lib. bdg. 25.27 (978-1-4339-9045-8(8), 91280a3c-0c38-4e6a-8e2c-60d72437329a) Stevens, Gareth Publishing LLLP.
Avery, Sherrie. Miami Metrozoo. 2009. (Great Zoos of the United States Ser.). 24p. (gr. 3-4). 42.50 (978-1-61513-222-5(8), PowerKids Pr.) Rosen Publishing Group, Inc., The.
Ayers, Amy. Contado en el Zoológico (Counting at the Zoo), 1 vol. 2007. (Las Matemáticas en Nuestro Mundo - Nivel 1 (Math in Our World - Level 1) Ser.). (SPA.). 24p. (gr. 1-1). pap. 9.15 (978-0-8368-8496-8(5), 3520a786-480e-4a8a-8bbe-1d77a334020a, Weekly Reader Leveled Readers) Stevens, Gareth Publishing LLLP.
—Counting at the Zoo, 1 vol. 2007. (Math in Our World - Level 1 Ser.). (ENG., Illus.). 24p. (gr. 1-1). pap. 9.15 (978-0-8368-8478-4(7), 6e4f87c1-ee5f-4598-8368-a96eba98b28f); lib. bdg. 24.67 (978-0-8368-8469-2(8), 36c9139b-11a9-47fe-9b3a-5067032a5db5) Stevens, Gareth Publishing LLLP. (Weekly Reader Leveled Readers).
AZ Books Staff & Evans, Olivia. Making the Zoo. Sisoj, Natalja, ed. 2012. (Modeling Clay Bk Ser.). (ENG., Illus.). 12p. (J). (gr. -1-2). bds. 10.95 (978-1-61889-196-9(0)) AZ Bks. LLC.
Baby's Very First Slide & See Zoo. 2017. (Baby's Very First Slide & See BDs Ser.). (ENG.). (J). bds. 14.99 (978-0-7945-3878-1(9), Usborne) EDC Publishing.
Battistoni, I. At the Zoo: Learning the Z Sound. 2009. (PowerPhonics Ser.). 24p. (gr. 1-1). 39.90 (978-1-60851-433-5(1), PowerKids Pr.) Rosen Publishing Group, Inc., The.
Bishop, Celeste. A Visit to the Zoo, 1 vol. 2016. (Places in My Community Ser.). (ENG.). 24p. (J). (gr. 1-1). pap. 9.25 (978-1-4994-2772-1(7), 68cc7326-ad11-4d83-8c12-c04b9cb4620b, PowerKids Pr.) Rosen Publishing Group, Inc., The.
Christopher, Nick. Should We Keep Animals in Zoos?, 1 vol. 2017. (Points of View Ser.). (ENG.). 24p. (gr. 3-3). pap. 9.25 (978-1-5345-2325-8(1), cd0b997d-0b2c-4284-b43f-87057086a3b2); lib. bdg. 26.23 (978-1-5345-2327-2(8), 2f1ca732-0d28-4c01-b78c-cda23407fbd7) Greenhaven Publishing LLC.
Clark, Rosalyn. A Visit to the Zoo. 2017. (Bumba Books (r) — Places We Go Ser.). (ENG., Illus.). 24p. (J). (gr. -1-1). 26.65 (978-1-5124-3373-9(X), 10cc16dd-3250-4d9b-899e-5e914788a0fe, Lerner Pubns.) Lerner Publishing Group.
Colby, Jennifer. Zoo. 2016. (21st Century Junior Library: Explore a Workplace Ser.). (ENG., Illus.). 24p. (J). (gr. 2-5). 29.21 (978-1-63471-080-0(0), 208399) Cherry Lake Publishing.
Color All About: The Zoo: A Coloring Book about Going to the Zoo. 2004. (Illus.). (J). (978-0-9763307-2-1(5)) Food Marketing Consultants, Inc.
Dale, Jay. The Zookeeper, 1 vol. 2012. (Engage Literacy Magenta Ser.). (ENG.). 16p. (J). (gr. k-2). pap. 6.99 (978-1-4296-8864-2(5), 119934); pap. 36.94 (978-1-4296-8865-9(3), 18328) Capstone. (Capstone Pr.).
Davis, Bela. Patterns at the Zoo. 2018. (Patterns Are Fun! Ser.). (ENG., Illus.). 24p. (J). (gr. -1-2). lib. bdg. 31.36 (978-1-5321-0795-5(1), 28151, Abdo Kids) ABDO Publishing Co.
Dawson, Emily C. The Zoo. 2010. (My Community Ser.). (ENG.). 24p. (J). (gr. k-2). lib. bdg. 25.65 (978-1-60753-024-4(4), 17152) Amicus.
Dee, Nora. Spanish Words at the Zoo, 1 vol., Vol. 1. 2013. (Learn My Language! Spanish Ser.). (ENG.). 24p. (J). (gr. 1-2). pap. 9.15 (978-1-4824-0358-9(7), 2d22ae17-b141-49ba-ac74-7b9351482ec2) Stevens, Gareth Publishing LLLP.
Devera, Czeena. At the Zoo. 2019. (I Can See Ser.). (ENG.). 16p. (J). (gr. -1-2). pap. 11.36 (978-1-5341-3914-5(1), 212492, Cherry Blossom Press) Cherry Lake Publishing.
Dorling Kindersley Publishing Staff & Baker, Nick. Bug Zoo. 2010. (ENG., Illus.). 64p. (J). (gr. k-3). 12.99 (978-0-7566-6166-3(8)) Dorling Kindersley Publishing, Inc.
Early Macken, JoAnn. Animals I See at the Zoo/Animales Que Veo en el Zoológico, 4 bks. Incl. Bears / Los Osos. 2002. pap. 9.15 (978-0-8368-4003-2(8), f749894c-c2a6-4393-a62c-c99d95295df5); Elephants / Los Elefantes. 2002. pap. 9.15 (978-0-8368-4004-9(6), 4f0213e6-b7df-4581-99ff-495a7f31bf60); Penguins / Los Pinguinos. (J). 2004. pap. 9.15 (978-0-8368-4006-3(2), 74d6e910-2d98-4e43-adf6-203bc5265399); 24p. (gr. k-2)., Weekly Reader Leveled Readers (SPA & ENG., Illus.). 2003. pap. o.p. (978-0-8368-4002-5(X), Weekly Reader) Stevens, Gareth Publishing LLLP.
Estigarribia, Diana. Smithsonian National Zoological Park. 2009. (Great Zoos of the United States Ser.). 24p. (gr. 3-4). 42.50 (978-1-61513-225-6(2), PowerKids Pr.) Rosen Publishing Group, Inc., The.
Fleming, Candace. Cubs in the Tub: The True Story of the Bronx Zoo's First Woman Zookeeper. Downing, Julie, illus. 2020. (ENG.). 48p. (J). (gr. -1-3). 18.99 (978-0-8234-4318-5(3), Neal Porter Bks) Holiday Hse., Inc.
Friedman, Sharon. Grin & Bear It: Zoo Jokes to Make You Roar. Gable, Brian, illus. 2005. (Make Me Laugh! Ser.). 32p. (J). (gr. k-3). lib. bdg. 19.93 (978-1-57505-660-9(7)) Lerner Publishing Group.
Gale Research Inc. Animal Rights: Zoos & Aquariums. 2018. (Animal Rights & Welfare Ser.). (ENG., Illus.). 224p. 51.00 (978-1-4103-8114-9(5)) Cengage Gale.
Galvin, Laura Gates. Tamarin's Mealtime. Cohen, Jessie, illus. 2005. (Let's Go to the Zoo! Ser.). (ENG.). 16p. (J). (gr. -1-k). 5.95 (978-1-56899-858-9(9)) Soundprints.
Gangelhoff, Jeanne M. & Belk, Bradford. A Walk Through the Minnesota Zoo. Gangelhoff, Gene, illus. 32p. (J). 9.95 (978-0-9635006-1-8(9)) G J & B Publishing.
Garnett, Jaye. Zoo. Cottage Door Press, ed. Nowowiejska, Kasia, illus. 2016. (Peek-A-Flap Ser.). (ENG.). 12p. (J). (gr. -1-1). bds. 9.99 (978-1-68052-126-9(8), 1001190) Cottage Door Pr.
Guidone, Lisa M. What Happens at a Zoo?, 1 vol. 2008. (Where People Work Ser.). (ENG.). 24p. (gr. k-2). (J). lib. bdg. 24.67 (978-0-8368-9272-7(0), f9e6189e-f60d-4e95-aa81-5e3123525583); pap. 9.15 (978-0-8368-9371-7(9), 81f70f7a-0e05-41fb-8c9d-50d9843c78c7) Stevens, Gareth Publishing LLLP. (Weekly Reader Leveled Readers).
—What Happens at a Zoo? / ¿Qué Pasa en un Zoológico?, 1 vol. 2008. (Where People Work / ¿dónde Trabaja la Gente? Ser.). (SPA & ENG.). 24p. (gr. k-2). (J). lib. bdg. 24.67 (978-0-8368-9278-9(X), 2c3b7f0e-7905-4e34-aaf3-4f47bdd5f6e6); pap. 9.15 (978-0-8368-9377-9(8), 077ea83c-4ad5-47fc-b4aa-0f852e14ee97) Stevens, Gareth Publishing LLLP. (Weekly Reader Leveled Readers).
Halls, Kelly Milner & Sumner, William. Saving the Baghdad Zoo: A True Story of Hope & Heroes. Sumner, William, illus. 2010. (ENG., Illus.). 64p. (J). (gr. 3-18). pap. 17.99 (978-0-06-177202-3(X), Greenwillow Bks.) HarperCollins Pubs.
Harrison, Sarah. A Day at a Zoo. 2008. (Time Goes By Ser.). (ENG.). (gr. k-3). pap. 39.62 (978-0-7613-4710-1(0)) Lerner Publishing Group.
Hoena, Blake A. The Zoo: A 4D Book. rev. ed. 2018. (Visit To... Ser.). (ENG., Illus.). 24p. (J). (gr. -1-2). lib. bdg. 29.32 (978-1-5435-0832-1(4), 137595, Capstone Pr.) Capstone.
Holden, Pam. Come to the Zoo, 1 vol. 2017. (ENG., Illus.). 21p. (J). pap. (978-1-77654-220-8(7), Red Rocket Readers) Flying Start Bks.
Johnson, Bruce. We Read Phonics-A Day at the Zoo. Johnson, Meredith, illus. 2012. 32p. (J). 9.95 (978-1-60115-349-4(X)); pap. 4.99 (978-1-60115-350-0(3)) Treasure Bay, Inc.
Johnson, Bruce & Johnson, Meredith, illus. A Day at the Zoo. 2012. 27p. (J). (978-1-60115-595-5(6)) Treasure Bay, Inc.
Johnson, Bruce & McKay, Sindy. We Both Read-Zoo Day. Johnson, Meredith, illus. 2015. (We Both Read - Level 1 (Quality) Ser.). (ENG.). 44p. (J). (gr. k-2). pap. 5.99 (978-1-60115-274-9(4)) Treasure Bay, Inc.
Kawa, Katie. My First Trip to the Zoo, 1 vol. Livingston, Jessica, illus. 2012. (My First Adventures Ser.). (ENG.). 24p. (J). (gr. k-k). pap. 9.15 (978-1-4339-6259-2(4), b036a57f-83a7-48ca-9d01-31c814db9444); lib. bdg. 25.27 (978-1-4339-6257-8(8),

61fbaff9-169d-44f0-8a46-1438b877923d) Stevens, Gareth Publishing LLLP.
—My First Trip to the Zoo / Mi Primera Visita Al Zoológico, 1 vol. Livingston, Jessica, illus. 2012. (My First Adventures / Mis Primeras Aventuras Ser.). (ENG & SPA.). 24p. (J). (gr. k-k). lib. bdg. 25.27 *(978-1-4339-6635-4(2)*, fb89ec94-36fa-4f54-a815-7e2cfa5d9201) Stevens, Gareth Publishing LLLP.
Keats Curtis, Jennifer. Animal Helpers: Zoos, 1 vol. 2013. (Animal Helpers Ser.). (ENG.). 32p. (J). (gr. 2-5). pap. 9.95 *(978-1-60718-850-6(3))* Arbordale Publishing.
Kent, Lorna, illus. At the Zoo. 2004. 8p. (J). bds. 3.99 *(978-1-85854-084-9(4))* Brimax Books Ltd. GBR. Dist: Byeway Bks.
Kirsten, A. We Bring the Zoo to You. 2005. 32p. pap. 9.95 *(978-0-9704876-5-0(7))* First Mom's Club, The.
Kumon Publishing North America, creator. My Book of Coloring at the Zoo. Kumon Publishing North America, . 2007. (Kumon Workbooks Ser.). (ENG., Illus.). 80p. per. 7.95 *(978-1-933241-39-5(X))* Kumon Publishing North America, Inc.
Laks Gorman, Jacqueline. The Zoo, 1 vol. 2004. (I Like to Visit Ser.). (ENG., Illus.). 24p. (gr. k-2). pap. 9.15 *(978-0-8368-4463-4(7)*, abbe7a73-bac8-47f5-b08f-eea7765dc077); lib. bdg. 24.67 *(978-0-8368-4456-6(4)*, c721a9a4-f071-454f-a12e-4526447895b3) Stevens, Gareth Publishing LLLP. (Weekly Reader Leveled Readers).
—The Zoo / el Zoológico, 1 vol. 2004. (I Like to Visit / Me Gusta Visitar Ser.). (ENG & SPA., Illus.). 24p. (gr. k-2). pap. 9.15 *(978-0-8368-4607-2(9)*, 34433e5a-d50f-4f8c-9425-6eceb1966000); lib. bdg. 24.67 *(978-0-8368-4600-3(1)*, 7b67d300-7961-4ebf-b536-39e928d21f61) Stevens, Gareth Publishing LLLP. (Weekly Reader Leveled Readers).
Liebman, Dan & Liebman, Dan. I Want to Be a Zookeeper. 2003. (I Want to Be Ser.). (ENG., Illus.). 24p. (J). (gr. -1-2). 14.95 *(978-1-55297-699-9(8)*, deb3c20e-084d-43a7-a555-8900051a89cb); pap. 3.99 *(978-1-55297-697-5(1)*, d8ac208f-0508-42b4-b99f-689b5f3ff9c7) Firefly Bks., Ltd.
—Quiero Ser Guardian de Zoologico. 2003. (Quiero Ser.). Tr. of I Want to Be a Zookeeper. (SPA., Illus.). 24p. (J). (gr. -1-2). pap. 5.99 *(978-1-55297-730-9(7)*, 5484bd85-1d9d-4f9f-b47a-e715b86f5738) Firefly Bks., Ltd.
Lyon, George Ella. Mother to Tigers. Catalanotto, Peter, illus. 2003. (ENG.). 32p. (J). (gr. k-3). 18.99 *(978-0-689-84221-4(X)*, Atheneum/Richard Jackson Bks.) Simon & Schuster Children's Publishing.
Macaulay, David. How Machines Work: Zoo Break! 2015. (DK First Reference Ser.). (ENG., Illus.). 32p. (J). (gr. 2-5). 19.99 *(978-1-4654-4012-9(7)*, DK Children) Dorling Kindersley Publishing, Inc.
Martin, Emmett. Exploring the Zoo, 1 vol. 2018. (So into Science! Ser.). (ENG.). 24p. (gr. k-k). 24.27 *(978-1-5382-2890-6(4)*, d284f215-4fd7-4ce2-98ea-137a03676fb9) Stevens, Gareth Publishing LLLP.
Martin, Isabel. A Zoo Field Trip. 2015. (Let's Take a Field Trip Ser.). (ENG., Illus.). 24p. (J). (gr. -1-2). pap. 6.95 *(978-1-4914-2316-5(1)*, 127774, Capstone Pr.) Capstone.
Maxwell, Cassandre. Fur, Fins, & Feathers: Abraham Dee Bartlett & the Invention of the Modern Zoo. 2015. (ENG., Illus.). 34p. (J). 17.00 *(978-0-8028-5432-2(X)*, Eerdmans Bks For Young Readers) Eerdmans, William B. Publishing Co.
McCullough, Ana L. The Zoo at the End of My Book. 2009. 32p. pap. 16.49 *(978-1-4389-0535-8(1))* AuthorHouse.
McReynolds, Stacy. San Antonio Zoo. 2009. (Great Zoos of the United States Ser.). 24p. (gr. 3-4). 42.50 *(978-1-61513-223-2(6)*, PowerKids Pr.) Rosen Publishing Group, Inc., The.
Murray, Julie. Cuidadores Del Zoológico. 2018. (Trabajos en Mi Comunidad (My Community: Jobs) Ser.).Tr. of Zookeepers. (SPA.). 24p. (J). (gr. -1-2). lib. bdg. 31.36 *(978-1-5321-8371-3(2)*, 29935, Abdo Kids) ABDO Publishing Co.
—Zookeepers. 2018. (My Community: Jobs Ser.). (ENG., Illus.). 24p. (J). (gr. -1-2). lib. bdg. 31.36 *(978-1-5321-0791-7(9)*, 28143, Abdo Kids) ABDO Publishing Co.
Newman, Patricia. Zoo Scientists to the Rescue. Crawley, Annie, photos by. 2017. (ENG., Illus.). 64p. (J). (gr. 4-8). lib. bdg. 33.32 *(978-1-5124-1571-1(5)*, 85e5e5e1-e4d4-40b1-a39a-cfa8a6664d14, Millbrook Pr.) Lerner Publishing Group.
O'Connell, Caitlin. Bridge to the Wild: Behind the Scenes at the Zoo. 2016. (ENG., Illus.). 208p. (J). (gr. 5-7). 18.99 *(978-0-544-27739-7(2)*, 1570273, Clarion Bks.) HarperCollins Pubs.
Olmedillas, Cathy, compiled by. Anorak. 2013. (ENG., Illus.). 64p. (J). pap. 9.99 *(978-1-4236-3340-2(7)*, Anorak Pr.) Gibbs Smith, Publisher.
Orr, Tamra. The National Zoo. 2017. (Smithsonian Field Trips Ser.). (ENG., Illus.). 32p. (J). (gr. 2-5). pap. 7.95 *(978-1-5157-7990-2(4)*, 136053, Capstone Pr.) Capstone.
Orr, Tamra B. How Did They Build That? Zoo. 2011. (Community Connections: How Did They Build That? Ser.). (ENG., Illus.). 24p. (gr. 2-5). lib. bdg. 29.21 *(978-1-61080-113-3(X)*, 201120) Cherry Lake Publishing.
—Working at the Zoo. 2011. (21st Century Junior Library: Careers Ser.). (ENG., Illus.). 24p. (gr. 2-5). lib. bdg. 29.21 *(978-1-60279-978-3(4)*, 200946) Cherry Lake Publishing.
Osburn, Mary Rose. Using Money at the Zoo, 1 vol. 2017. (Animal Math Ser.). (ENG.). 24p. (J). (gr. 1-2). pap. 9.15 *(978-1-5382-0864-9(4)*, 3594b480-5db0-4a15-9494-60d282d7776e) Stevens, Gareth Publishing LLLP.
Pearce, Claudia. San Diego Zoo. 2009. (Great Zoos of the United States Ser.). 24p. (gr. 3-4). 42.50 *(978-1-61513-224-9(4)*, PowerKids Pr.) Rosen Publishing Group, Inc., The.
Pettiford, Rebecca. Zoo. Fretland VanVoorst, Jenny, ed. 2016. (First Field Trips). (Illus.). 24p. (J). (gr. k-2). lib. bdg. 25.65 *(978-1-62031-299-5(9)*, Bullfrog Bks.) Jump! Inc.
—El Zoológico. 2016. (Los Primeros Viajes Escolares (First Field Trips)).Tr. of Zoo. (SPA., Illus.). 24p. (J). (gr. k-2). lib. bdg. 25.65 *(978-1-62031-333-6(2)*, Bullfrog Bks.) Jump! Inc.
Powell, Elizabeth. Math at the Zoo, 1 vol. 2016. (Math Is Everywhere! Ser.). (ENG., Illus.). 24p. (J). (gr. k-k). pap. 9.15 *(978-1-4824-5500-7(5)*, 42bfa1a9-7ff9-4694-b31a-0cb71ccae1f4) Stevens, Gareth Publishing LLLP.
Powell, Janet. St. Louis Zoo. 2009. (Great Zoos of the United States Ser.). 24p. (gr. 3-4). 42.50 *(978-1-61513-226-3(0)*, PowerKids Pr.) Rosen Publishing Group, Inc., The.
Priddy, Roger. Bright Baby Touch & Feel at the Zoo. 2006. (Bright Baby Touch & Feel Ser.). (ENG., Illus.). 10p. (J). (gr. -1 — 1). bds. 5.99 *(978-0-312-49857-3(8)*, 900041828) St. Martin's Pr.
Rice, Dona & Wilder, Nellie. Solving Problems as the Zoo. rev. ed. 2019. (Smithsonian: Informational Text Ser.). (ENG., Illus.). 24p. (J). (gr. 1-2). pap. 8.99 *(978-1-4938-6657-1(5))* Teacher Created Materials, Inc.
Ring, Susan. Project Otter. Kissock, Heather & Marshall, Diana, eds. 2003. (Zoo Life Ser.). (Illus.). 24p. (J). pap. 8.95 *(978-1-59036-059-0(1))* Weigl Pubs., Inc.
Ritchey, Kate. Lion, Tiger, & Bear. 2015. (Penguin Young Readers, Level 4 Ser.). (ENG., Illus.). 48p. (J). (gr. 3-4). pap. 4.99 *(978-0-448-48336-8(X)*, Penguin Young Readers) Penguin Young Readers Group.
Roe-Pimm, Nancy. Colo's Story. 2011. (ENG.). 80p. (gr. 4-8). 18.95 *(978-0-9841554-4-6(9))*; pap. 8.95 *(978-0-9841554-5-3(7))* Columbus Zoo & Aquarium, The.
Rolle, Elvy P. Five Little Children at the Zoo. Stasuyk, Max, illus. 2016. (ENG.). 26p. (J). pap. 13.95 *(978-1-4796-0534-7(4)*, Aspect) Grand Central Publishing.
Rosa-Mendoza, Gladys. Let's Go to the Zoo!/Vamos Al Zoolgico! Elkerton, Andy, illus. 2007. (English Spanish Foundations Ser.). (ENG & SPA.). 20p. (J). (gr. -1-k). bds. 6.95 *(978-1-931398-20-6(8))* Me+Mi Publishing.
Ruggieri, Linda. Amazing Animals: Critter Camp: Division (Grade 3) 2017. (Mathematics in the Real World Ser.). (ENG., Illus.). 32p. (J). (gr. 3-4). pap. 11.99 *(978-1-4807-5800-1(0))* Teacher Created Materials, Inc.
Shaw, Gina. Curious about Zoo Vets. 2015. (Smithsonian: Curious About Ser.). (ENG., Illus.). 32p. (J). (gr. 1-3). 17.44 *(978-1-4844-6359-8(5))* Penguin Publishing Group.
Shea, Therese. Discovering STEM at the Zoo, 1 vol. 2015. (STEM in the Real World Ser.). (ENG., Illus.). 24p. (J). (gr. 2-3). pap. 9.25 *(978-1-4994-0928-4(1)*, f51373b9-d1eb-41db-be95-b08d6f436aeb, PowerKids Pr.) Rosen Publishing Group, Inc., The.
Smith, Roland & Smith, Marie. Z Is for Zookeeper: A Zoo Alphabet. Cole, Henry, illus. (Sleeping Bear Alphabet Ser.). (ENG.). 40p. (J). (gr. 1-4). 2005. 16.95 *(978-1-58536-158-8(5)*, 202018) 2007. pap. 7.95 *(978-1-58536-329-2(4)*, 202292) Sleeping Bear Pr.
Soundprints, creator. Tiger Cub See-and-Do. 2011. (Let's Go to the Zoo! Ser.). (ENG., Illus.). 16p. (gr. -1). 5.95 *(978-1-60727-460-5(4))* Soundprints.
Stead, Tony. Should There Be Zoos? A Persuasive Text. 2011. (ENG., Illus.). 32p. (J). (gr. 3-7). pap. 29.99 *(978-1-57255-817-5(2))* Mondo Publishing.
Toufexis, George. At the Zoo Stickers. 2011. (Dover Little Activity Books Stickers Ser.). (ENG.). 8p. (J). (gr. k-3). 1.99 *(978-0-486-48181-4(6))* Dover Pubns., Inc.
Valdez, Patricia. Joan Procter, Dragon Doctor: The Woman Who Loved Reptiles. Sala, Felicita, illus. 2018. 40p. (J). (gr. -1-3). 18.99 *(978-0-399-55725-5(3)*, Knopf Bks. for Young Readers) Random Hse. Children's Bks.
Ventura, Marne. Zookeeper. 2019. (Jobs with Animals Ser.). (ENG., Illus.). 32p. (J). (gr. 4-6). pap. 7.95 *(978-1-5435-6045-9(8)*, 140089); lib. bdg. 28.65 *(978-1-5435-5783-1(X)*, 139739) Capstone.
Wagner, Jeff. My Day... at the Zoo. Alvarado, Paulo, illus. 2004. 20p. (J). bds. *(978-0-9754515-0-2(2))* Wagner Entertainment.
Who Lives at the Zoo? 2004. (Who Lives... Ser.). 12p. (J). bds. 4.99 *(978-1-85854-645-2(1))* Brimax Books Ltd. GBR. Dist: Byeway Bks.
The Zoo, 2 Packs. (Chiquilibros Ser.). (gr. -1-1). 12.00 *(978-0-7635-8536-5(X))* Rigby Education.
Zoo (Gr. PreK-5) 2003. (J). *(978-1-58232-027-4(6))* ECS Learning Systems, Inc.

ZOOS—FICTION

Adams, William J. Goin' to the Zoo / Vamos Al Zoologico. Stiglich, Tom, illus. 2007. (ENG & SPA.). 58p. (J). pap. 10.95 *(978-0-9772757-2-4(8))* Mandy & Andy Bks., Inc.
—Goin' to the Zoo Coloring Book: Vamos Al Zoologico. Stiglich, Tom, illus. 2007. (ENG & SPA.). (J). pap. 3.95 *(978-0-9772757-3-1(6))* Mandy & Andy Bks., Inc.
Adler, David A. Young Cam Jansen & the Lions' Lunch Mystery, No. 13. Natti, Susanna, illus. 2008. (Young Cam Jansen Ser.: 13). (ENG.). 32p. (J). (gr. 1-3). mass mkt. 4.99 *(978-0-14-241176-6(0)*, Penguin Young Readers) Penguin Young Readers Group.
Ahlberg, Allan. Funnybones: the Black Cat: A Funnybones Story. 2018. (Funnybones Ser.: 3). (Illus.). 32p. (J). (gr. -1-k). pap. 12.99 *(978-0-14-137871-8(9))* Penguin Bks., Ltd. GBR. Dist: Independent Pubs. Group.
Alexander, Carmen. Zoo 1000 Miles. Henderson, Cecil, illus. 2005. 42p. (J). (gr. -1-5). pap. 9.99 *(978-1-886383-57-9(X))* Blue Forge Pr.
Alien at the Zoo, 6 vols. (Sunshinetm Ser.). 16p. (gr. k-18). 29.50 *(978-0-7802-5429-9(5))* Wright Group/McGraw-Hill.
Anderson, Amanda. The Story of Larry the Hamster. 2008. 24p. pap. 24.95 *(978-1-60703-125-3(6))* America Star Bks.
Anderson, Dawn. Chimpanzee, Como Yo ! 2006. (Illus.). (J). 15.95 *(978-0-9786570-1-7(2))* Opposable Thumb Pr.
—Chimpanzee, Like Me! 2006. (Illus.). (J). 15.95 *(978-0-9786570-0-0(4))* Opposable Thumb Pr.
Arnold, Vickie. The Baby Zebra Adventure. 2009. 20p. pap. 12.49 *(978-1-4389-5818-7(8))* AuthorHouse.
Asch, Frank. The Lending Zoo. Asch, Frank, illus. 2016. (ENG., Illus.). 32p. (J). (gr. -1-3). 16.99 *(978-1-4424-6678-4(2)*, Aladdin) Simon & Schuster Children's Publishing.
Avila, Nelson Moreno. The Boy & the Zoo. 2012. 32p. pap. 16.95 *(978-1-4497-7474-5(1)*, WestBow Pr.) Author Solutions, LLC.
AZ Books. Big Zoo Book. 2013. (Smart Pad Ser.). (ENG.). 14p. (J). (gr. -1-k). bds. 19.95 *(978-1-61889-418-2(8))* AZ Bks. LLC.
AZ Books, creator. Magic Zoo. 2012. (Baby Book Ser.). (ENG., Illus.). 10p. (J). (gr. -1 — 1). bds. 4.95 *(978-1-61889-284-3(3))* AZ Bks. LLC.
Bamboo Zoo Set: Meet Lester Panda & his Friends. 2006. (J). 17.95 *(978-0-9774493-1-6(9))* Bamboo Zoo, LLC.
Battle, Cleaton D. A Saturday Surprise. Cooper, Emmanuel, illus. 2006. 68p. (J). pap. 11.95 *(978-1-59663-504-3(5)*, Castle Keep Pr.) Rock, James A. & Co. Pubs.
Bauer, Marion Dane. A Bear Named Trouble. 2006. (ENG.). 128p. (J). (gr. 4-6). 18.69 *(978-0-440-42132-0(2))* Random House Publishing Group.
Bercowetz, Cynthia. Grandpa Herman's Petting Zoo. 2007. (Illus.). 48p. (J). per. 14.95 *(978-0-9708430-9-8(7))* Uitti, Daniel.
Bhadresa, G. N. Tymrose a Fantasy. 2012. (Illus.). 120p. *(978-1-4602-0561-7(8))*; pap. *(978-1-4602-0560-0(X))* FriesenPress.
Bhakta, Sanjini. The Chocolate Pony. 2010. 28p. pap. 12.99 *(978-1-4490-9761-5(8))* AuthorHouse.
Bixley, Donovan. My First Board Book: a Day at the Zoo. 2022. (My First Board Book Ser.). (ENG., Illus.). 20p. (J). (gr. -1-k). bds. 13.99 *(978-1-86971-366-9(4))* Hachette New Zealand NZL. Dist: Hachette Bk. Group.
Blance, Ellen & Cook, Tony. Monster Goes to the Zoo. Date not set. (Illus.). 24p. pap. 129.15 *(978-0-582-18599-9(8))* Addison-Wesley Longman, Ltd. GBR. Dist: Trans-Atlantic Pubns., Inc.
BookSource Staff, compiled by. Petting Zoo. 2013. (DK Reader Pre Level Ser.). lib. bdg. 13.55 *(978-0-606-32439-7(9))* Turtleback.
Bowie, Sarah. We're Going to the Zoo! 2018. (ENG., Illus.). 32p. (J). 20.00 *(978-1-84717-949-4(5))* O'Brien Pr., Ltd., The IRL. Dist: Casemate Pubs. & Bk. Distributors, LLC.
Bratcher, Shirley Kay. Tudy Goes to the Zoo. 2013. 24p. pap. 24.95 *(978-1-4626-9560-7(4))* America Star Bks.
Brennan-Nelson, Denise. Maestro Stu Saves the Zoo. Bowers, Tim, illus. 2012. (ENG.). 32p. (J). (gr. -1-3). 15.95 *(978-1-58536-802-0(4)*, 202340) Sleeping Bear Pr.
Brezenoff, Steven. The Missing Bully: An Interactive Mystery Adventure. Calo, Marcos, illus. 2017. (You Choose Stories: Field Trip Mysteries Ser.). (ENG.). 112p. (J). (gr. 3-7). lib. bdg. 32.65 *(978-1-4965-2642-7(2)*, 131205, Stone Arch Bks.) Capstone.
Britner, Scott & Britner, Melissa. Tyler & Destiny Tales: Lunch at the Zoo. 2004. 17p. (J). pap. 8.33 *(978-1-4116-0919-8(0))* Lulu Pr., Inc.
Broach, Elise. The Wolf Keepers. Ratterree, Alice, illus. 2018. (ENG.). 368p. (J). pap. 15.99 *(978-1-250-16501-5(6)*, 900186931) Square Fish.
Brooks, Heather. Running Horse Ridge #2: Hercules: a Matter of Trust. 2nd ed. 2009. (Running Horse Ridge Ser.: 2). (ENG.). 224p. (J). (gr. 5-18). pap. 6.99 *(978-0-06-142981-1(3)*, HarperCollins) HarperCollins Pubs.
Brown, Joe. Race to the Rescue. Marchesi, Stephen, illus. 2009. (J). *(978-0-545-13473-6(0))* Scholastic, Inc.
Browne, Anthony. Little Beauty. Browne, Anthony, illus. 2010. (ENG., Illus.). 32p. (J). (gr. -1-2). pap. 8.99 *(978-0-7636-4967-8(8))* Candlewick Pr.
—Little Beauty. 2010. lib. bdg. 17.20 *(978-0-606-14714-9(4))* Turtleback.
Bryant, Jen. Call Me Marianne. Johnson, David, illus. 2006. 32p. (J). (gr. -1-4). 16.00 *(978-0-8028-5242-7(4)*, Eerdmans Bks For Young Readers) Eerdmans, William B. Publishing Co.
Burkhart, Lorene. Raccoon Tales: Hip, Flip, Skip & Boo go to the Zoo. 2007. (Illus.). (J). 8.95 *(978-0-9790975-2-2(5))* Burkhart Bks.
Burson, Ronda Pfohl. Monk-Monk the Monkey. 2010. 20p. 10.49 *(978-1-4520-0351-1(3))* AuthorHouse.
Button, Joshua & Wells, Robyn. Steve Goes to Carnival. Button, Joshua, illus. 2019. (ENG., Illus.). 56p. (J). (gr. k-3). 17.99 *(978-1-5362-0034-8(4))* Candlewick Pr.
Caletti, Deb. The Nature of Jade. 2008. (ENG.). 320p. (YA). (gr. 7-12). pap. 10.99 *(978-1-4169-1006-0(9)*, Simon Pulse) Simon Pulse.
Campbell, Susan. Little Jimmy: The Itty Bitty Fifty Foot Tall Giraffe. 2011. 24p. pap. 24.95 *(978-1-4626-2929-9(6))* America Star Bks.
Carney, Larry, adapted by. Silly Book/CD - Silly Zoo. 2010. (Illus.). 24p. (J). pap. 6.95 incl. cd-rom *(978-1-60072-155-7(9))* PC Treasures, Inc.
Carolan, Dr. Where Are My Slippers? A Book of Colors. Carolan, Joanna F., illus. 2007. 32p. 17.95 *(978-0-9715333-7-0(7))* Banana Patch Pr.
Castellucci, Cecil. The Queen of Cool. 2007. (ENG., Illus.). 176p. (YA). (gr. 9-18). pap. 7.99 *(978-0-7636-3413-1(1))* Candlewick Pr.
Chambers, Whittaker, tr. The City Jungle. 2014. (Bambi's Classic Animal Tales Ser.). (ENG., Illus.). 288p. (J). (gr. 3-7). pap. 7.99 *(978-1-4424-8751-2(8)*, Aladdin) Simon & Schuster Children's Publishing.
Chartier, Doris E. Ben's Desert Journey. 2009. 32p. pap. 14.49 *(978-1-4389-7756-0(5))* AuthorHouse.
Chick, Bryan. Riddles & Danger. 2011. (Secret Zoo Ser.: 3). (ENG.). 288p. (J). (gr. 3-7). 16.99 *(978-0-06-198927-8(4)*, Greenwillow Bks.) HarperCollins Pubs.
—The Secret Zoo. 2010. (Secret Zoo Ser.: 1). (ENG.). 304p. (J). (gr. 3-7). 18.99 *(978-0-06-198750-2(6)*, Greenwillow Bks.) HarperCollins Pubs.
—The Secret Zoo: Traps & Specters. 2012. (Secret Zoo Ser.: 4). (ENG.). 320p. (J). (gr. 3-7). 16.99 *(978-0-06-219222-6(1)*, Greenwillow Bks.) HarperCollins Pubs.
—The Secret Zoo: Raids & Rescues. (Secret Zoo Ser.: 5). (ENG.). 272p. (J). (gr. 3-7). 2014. pap. 9.99 *(978-0-06-219229-5(9))* 2013. 16.99 *(978-0-06-219228-8(0))* HarperCollins Pubs. (Greenwillow Bks.).
—The Secret Zoo: Secrets & Shadows. 2011. (Secret Zoo Ser.: 2). (ENG.). 272p. (J). (gr. 3-7). pap. 7.99 *(978-0-06-198926-1(6))*; 16.99 *(978-0-06-198925-4(8))* HarperCollins Pubs. (Greenwillow Bks.).
—The Secret Zoo: Traps & Specters. 2013. (Secret Zoo Ser.: 4). (ENG.). 320p. (J). (gr. 3-7). pap. 7.99 *(978-0-06-219223-3(X)*, Greenwillow Bks.) HarperCollins Pubs.
Choldenko, Gennifer. Notes from a Liar & Her Dog. 2003. (ENG.). 240p. (J). (gr. 3-7). pap. 7.99 *(978-0-14-250068-2(2)*, Puffin Books) Penguin Young Readers Group.
—Notes from a Liar & Her Dog. 2004. 224p. (J). (gr. 4-7). pap. 38.00 incl. audio *(978-0-8072-2097-9(3)*, Listening Library) Random Hse. Audio Publishing Group.
Clark, Seneca & Giardi, Sandy. Lily & the Imaginary Zoo, 1. Decedue, Julie, illus. 2005. (ENG.). 30p. (J). 15.95 *(978-0-9767276-1-3(7))* Three Bean Pr.
Clarkson, Kelly. River Rose & the Magical Lullaby. Hughes, Laura, illus. 2016. (ENG.). 32p. (J). (gr. -1-3). 18.99 *(978-0-06-242756-4(3)*, HarperCollins) HarperCollins Pubs.
Cobb, Amelia. The Silky Seal Pup (Zoe's Rescue Zoo #3) 2016. (Zoe's Rescue Zoo Ser.: 3). (ENG., Illus.). 128p. (J). (gr. 2-5). pap. 4.99 *(978-0-545-84224-2(7)*, Scholastic Paperbacks) Scholastic, Inc.
Cole, Babette. Tarzana. 2nd ed. 2003. (Babette Cole Ser.).Tr. of Tarzanna! (SPA., Illus.). 34p. (J). 12.95 *(978-84-233-2274-9(2))* Ediciones Destino ESP. Dist: Planeta Publishing Corp.
Colhoun, Sheelah. Elric's Florida Holiday. Cotton, Sue Lynn, illus. 2012. 20p. pap. 13.95 *(978-1-61493-110-2(0))* Peppertree Pr., The.
Conn, Marla. At the Zoo with Dear Dragon, 10 vols. David Schimmell, illus. 2019. (Dear Dragon Developing Readers Ser.). (ENG.). 24p. (J). (gr. k-k). pap. 11.94 *(978-1-68404-318-7(2))* Norwood Hse. Pr.
Cook, Melissa. Anna & the Garden Fairy: Anna's Little Black Bear. 2009. (ENG., Illus.). 20p. (J). 14.95 *(978-1-57197-501-0(2)*, Ivy House Publishing Group) Pentland Pr., Inc.
Cottrell, Kim. Jimmy Has the Bugaloo Zoo Flu. 2009. 32p. pap. 12.99 *(978-1-4389-5209-3(0))* AuthorHouse.
Cowdrey, Richard. Fiona the Hippo, 1 vol. 2018. (Fiona the Hippo Book Ser.). (ENG., Illus.). (J). 32p. 18.99 *(978-0-310-76639-1(7))*; 30p. bds. 8.99 *(978-0-310-76636-0(2))* Zonderkidz.
Craig, Sherryn. Midnight Madness at the Zoo, 1 vol. Jones, Karen, illus. 2016. (J). (gr. k-1). (SPA.). 39p. pap. 11.95 *(978-1-62855-744-2(3)*, 9f8858c6-8461-4bd2-8a81-65b1c9987029); (ENG.). 32p. 17.95 *(978-1-62855-730-5(3))* Arbordale Publishing.
Cressey, Roger. The Talking Giraffe. Cressey, Roger, illus. 2013. (Illus.). 118p. pap. *(978-1-78222-143-2(3))* Paragon Publishing, Rothersthorpe.
Crispin, Barbara. City Zoo Blizzard Revue. Houghton, Roswitha, illus. 2003. 40p. 14.95 *(978-0-9716346-1-9(0))* Dancing Words Pr., Inc.
Crofoot, Nancy. Sandy & Mitzi: Off to the Zoo. Rawal, Ishita, illus. 2013. 48p. pap. 24.95 *(978-1-62709-868-7(2))* America Star Bks.
Cunningham, Sheila S. Willow's Walkabout: A Children's Guide to Boston. Kelleher, Kathie, illus. 2012. (ENG.). 32p. (J). (gr. 1-3). 17.95 *(978-1-59373-096-3(9))* Bunker Hill Publishing, Inc.
Curious George Goes to the Zoo. 2014. (Curious George Ser.). (ENG., Illus.). 24p. (J). (gr. -1-3). 4.99 *(978-0-544-11000-7(5)*, 1541240, Clarion Bks.) HarperCollins Pubs.
Curry, Don, ed. The Crate Escape No. 2. 2008. (I Can Find It Ser.). 22p. (J). 7.99 *(978-0-696-23490-3(4))* Meredith Bks.
—Esape Africa. 2008. 22p. (J). 15.95 *(978-0-696-23488-0(2))* Meredith Bks.
Dakota, Heather. Emma's Very Busy Week. Panaccione, Nancy, illus. 2009. 31p. (J). *(978-0-545-17227-1(6))* Scholastic, Inc.
Danneberg, Julie. Field-Trip Fiasco. Love, Judy, illus. 2015. (Jitters Ser.: 5). 32p. (J). (gr. k-3). 16.95 *(978-1-58089-671-9(5))* Charlesbridge Publishing, Inc.
Davies, Benji, illus. Bizzy Bear: Zookeeper. 2015. (Bizzy Bear Ser.). (ENG.). 8p. (J). (— 1). bds. 7.99 *(978-0-7636-7603-2(9))* Candlewick Pr.
Daykin, Chloe. The Boy Who Hit Play, Bk. 2. 2018. (ENG.). 336p. (J). pap. 9.95 *(978-0-571-32678-5(1)*, Faber & Faber Children's Bks.) Faber & Faber, Inc.
DiGuardo, Maggie & Leventis, Kelly. Celly. 2012. (J). 14.95 *(978-1-937406-17-2(2))* Amplify Publishing Group.
Dill, Mark. Maddie & Me: Go to the Zoo. 2012. 40p. pap. 20.99 *(978-1-4685-7481-4(7))* AuthorHouse.
Dixon, Franklin. The Great Pumpkin Smash. Gutierrez, Santy, illus. 2019. (Hardy Boys Clue Book Ser.: 10). (ENG.). 96p. (J). (gr. 1-4). pap. 5.99 *(978-1-5344-3123-2(3)*, Simon & Schuster/Paula Wiseman Bks.) Simon & Schuster/Paula Wiseman Bks.
Douglas-Hobbs, Kathy. Kobe & the Rescue Adventure. 2012. 16p. pap. 15.99 *(978-1-4772-0326-2(5))* AuthorHouse.
Eberhart, Nancy. The Adventures of Granny: Granny Goes to the Zoo. Pyers, Kelsey, illus. 2007. (J). 24p. per. 10.99 *(978-1-59879-372-7(1))*; (gr. -1-3). 13.99 *(978-1-59879-373-4(X))* Lifevest Publishing, Inc.
Ebie, Mora. Going to the Zoo in Hawaii. 2006. (Illus.). 28p. (J). 10.95 *(978-1-56647-790-1(5))* Mutual Publishing LLC.
Elliott, George. The Boy Who Loved Bananas. Krystoforski, Andrej, illus. 2005. 32p. (J). (gr. -1-2). 15.95 *(978-1-55337-744-3(3))* Kids Can Pr., Ltd. CAN. Dist: Hachette Bk. Group.
Everyday Signs of Zoo Animals. 2007. (J). bds. *(978-0-9791059-1-3(9))* Dakitab, Inc.
Feiffer, Jules. A Room with a Zoo. Feiffer, Jules, illus. 2005. (ENG., Illus.). 192p. (gr. 2-17). 16.95 *(978-0-7868-3702-1(0)*, di Capua, Michael Bks.) Hyperion Bks. for Children.
Fields, Jan. Lions, Tiger & Bears, Oh My!, Bk. 24. Shephard, Dave, illus. 2017. (Ghost Detectors Ser.: 24). (ENG.). 80p. (J). (gr. 2-5). lib. bdg. 35.64 *(978-1-5321-3156-1(9)*, 27053, Calico Chapter Bks.) ABDO Publishing Co.
Finnegan, Evelyn M. My Little Friend Goes to the Zoo. Bruno, Margaret Farrell, illus. 2006. 32p. (J). (gr. -1-3). reprint ed. pap. 7.00 *(978-1-4223-5402-5(4))* DIANE Publishing Co.
Foster, Evelyn. Alan & the Animals. 2011. (Tadpoles Ser.). (ENG., Illus.). 24p. (J). (gr. k-2). *(978-0-7787-0573-4(0))*; pap. *(978-0-7787-0584-0(6))* Crabtree Publishing Co.
French, Jackie. My Pa the Polar Bear. King, Stephen Michael, illus. 2015. (Wacky Families Ser.: 08). 130p. 5.99 *(978-0-207-20078-6(5)*, HarperCollins) HarperCollins Pubs.
Fretz, Denette. I Want Your Smile, Crocodile, 1 vol. Urbanovic, Jackie, illus. 2018. (ENG.). 32p. (J). 17.99 *(978-0-310-75890-7(4))* Zonderkidz.

edlander, Tim. The I Like Me Dance! Edwards, W M, illus. 2007. (Playdate Kids Musical Ser.). 27p. (J). (gr. -1-3). 14.95 incl. audio compact disk *(978-1-933721-07-1(3))* Playdate Kids Publishing.

abretti, Tisa. The Number Zoo, 1 vol. 2009. (ENG.). 15p. 24.95 *(978-1-60813-941-5(7))* America Star Bks.

ale, Eric Kahn. The Zoo at the Edge of the World. Nielson, Sam, illus. 2015. (ENG.). 240p. (J). (gr. 3-7). pap. 7.99 *(978-0-06-212517-0(6)*, Balzer & Bray) HarperCollins Pubs.

amble, Adam. Good Night Zoo. Stevenson, Harvey, illus. 2007. (Good Night Our World Ser.). (ENG.). 26p. (J). (gr. k — 1). bds. 9.95 *(978-1-60219-018-4(6))* Good Night Bks.

amble, Adam & Jasper, Mark. Good Night Central Park. Palmer, Ruth, illus. 2013. (Good Night Our World Ser.). (ENG.). 20p. (J). (— 1). bds. 9.95 *(978-1-60219-082-5(8))* Good Night Bks.

ibbs, Stuart. Belly Up. 2011. (ENG.). (J). (gr. 4-7). lib. bdg. 18.60 *(978-1-61383-640-8(6))* Perfection Learning Corp.

—Belly Up. (FunJungle Ser.). (ENG.). (J). (gr. 3-7). 2011. 320p. pap. 8.99 *(978-1-4169-8732-1(0))* 2010. (Illus.). 304p. 18.99 *(978-1-4169-8731-4(2))* Simon & Schuster Bks. For Young Readers. (Simon & Schuster Bks. For Young Readers).

—Big Game. 2015. (FunJungle Ser.). (ENG., Illus.). 352p. (J). (gr. 3-7). 18.99 *(978-1-4814-2333-5(9)*, Simon & Schuster Bks. For Young Readers) Simon & Schuster Bks. For Young Readers.

—Even More FunJungle: Panda-Monium; Lion down; Tyrannosaurus Wrecks. 2020. (FunJungle Ser.). (ENG., Illus.). 1040p. (J). (gr. 3-7). 53.99 *(978-1-5344-6783-5(1)*, Simon & Schuster Bks. For Young Readers) Simon & Schuster Bks. For Young Readers.

—The FunJungle Mystery Madness Collection: Panda-Monium; Lion down; Tyrannosaurus Wrecks. 2021. (FunJungle Ser.). (ENG., Illus.). 1120p. (J). (gr. 3-7). pap. 26.99 *(978-1-6659-0048-5(2)*, Simon & Schuster Bks. For Young Readers) Simon & Schuster Bks. For Young Readers.

—The FunJungle Paperback Collection (Boxed Set) Belly up; Poached; Big Game. 2021. (FunJungle Ser.). (ENG., Illus.). 1040p. (J). (gr. 3-7). pap. 26.99 *(978-1-6659-0042-3(3)*, Simon & Schuster Bks. For Young Readers) Simon & Schuster Bks. For Young Readers.

—Lion Down. 2019. (FunJungle Ser.). (ENG., Illus.). 352p. (J). (gr. 3-7). 18.99 *(978-1-5344-2473-9(3)*, Simon & Schuster Bks. For Young Readers) Simon & Schuster Bks. For Young Readers.

—Panda-Monium. (FunJungle Ser.). (ENG.). (J). (gr. 3-7). 2018. 384p. pap. 8.99 *(978-1-4814-4568-9(5))* 2017. (Illus.). 352p. 18.99 *(978-1-4814-4567-2(7))* Simon & Schuster Bks. For Young Readers. (Simon & Schuster Bks. For Young Readers).

—Panda-Monium. 2018. (Funjungle (Teddy Fitzroy) Ser.: 4). lib. bdg. 18.40 *(978-0-606-40849-3(5))* Turtleback.

—Poached. (FunJungle Ser.). (ENG., Illus.). 352p. (J). (gr. 3-7). 2015. pap. 8.99 *(978-1-4424-6778-1(9))* 2014. 18.99 *(978-1-4424-6777-4(0))* Simon & Schuster Bks. For Young Readers. (Simon & Schuster Bks. For Young Readers).

Giff, Patricia Reilly. Animal at Large. Carter, Abby, illus. 2020. (Mysteries on Zoo Lane Ser.: 2). 128p. (J). (gr. 2-5). 16.99 *(978-0-8234-4667-4(0))* Holiday Hse., Inc.

—Meet the Crew at the Zoo. Carter, Abby, illus. 2020. (Mysteries on Zoo Lane Ser.: 1). 112p. (J). (gr. 2-5). 16.99 *(978-0-8234-4666-7(2))* Holiday Hse., Inc.

Goode, Teresa. Jayhawk Adventures, a Day at the Zoo. Kotrous, Chad, illus. 2006. 29p. (J). (gr. 1-3). pap. 5.95 *(978-0-9646898-5-5(5))* Leathers Publishing.

Goulbourne, Nathaniel. The Aliens Zoo. 2013. (Illus.). 28p. pap. 21.35 *(978-1-4817-8198-5(7))* AuthorHouse.

Gutman, Dan. My Weirder School #1: Miss Child Has Gone Wild! Paillot, Jim, illus. 2011. (My Weirder School Ser.: 1). (ENG.). 112p. (J). (gr. 1-5). pap. 5.99 *(978-0-06-196916-4(8)*, HarperCollins) HarperCollins Pubs.

Hamilton, Kersten. In the Forests of the Night, 2. 2013. (Goblin Wars Ser.). (ENG.). 288p. (YA). (gr. 7-12). 24.94 *(978-0-547-43560-2(6)*, Clarion Bks.) HarperCollins Pubs.

Hand, Renne. What Would You Do If You Were Left at the Zoo? Mathieu, Middy, illus. 2012. 24p. pap. 8.99 *(978-1-938768-06-4(X))* Gypsy Pubns.

Harkrader, Lisa. Snoozy Zoo. 2016. (Spring Forward Ser.). (J). (gr. 2). *(978-1-4900-9424-3(5))* Benchmark Education Co.

Harris, Robie H. Who's in My Family? All about Our Families. Westcott, Nadine Bernard, illus. 2012. (Let's Talk about You & Me Ser.). (ENG.). 40p. (J). (gr. -1-2). 17.99 *(978-0-7636-3631-9(2))* Candlewick Pr.

Harrison, Sarah. A Day at a Zoo. 2009. (Time Goes By Ser.). (ENG., Illus.). 24p. (J). (gr. k-3). pap. 8.99 *(978-1-58013-800-0(4)*, 2b433973-c801-4a80-a12b-394dee0b7649, First Avenue Editions) Lerner Publishing Group.

Hartnett, Sonya. The Midnight Zoo. Offermann, Andrea, illus. 2018. (ENG.). 224p. (J). (gr. 5-9). pap. 8.99 *(978-0-7636-6462-6(6))* Candlewick Pr.

Hasany, Syed M. Stop the Train, Monkey! 2013. 28p. pap. 16.09 *(978-1-4669-7792-1(2))* Trafford Publishing.

Heder, Thyra. Fraidyzoo. 2013. (ENG., Illus.). 48p. (J). (gr. k-2). 18.99 *(978-1-4197-0776-6(0)*, 1059101, Abrams Bks. for Young Readers) Abrams, Inc.

Higgins, Jim. The Enchanted Nursery: Heather & Hamish, Fun in Florida, Reggie Rabbit at the Seaside, Percy Penguin's Friends. 2009. (Illus.). 36p. pap. 15.49 *(978-1-4389-9904-3(6))* AuthorHouse.

Highlights, creator. That's Silly!(TM) at the Zoo: A Very Silly Lift-The-Flap Book. 2019. (Highlights Lift-The-Flap Bks.). (Illus.). 10p. (J). (-k). bds. 9.99 *(978-1-68437-255-3(0)*, Highlights) Highlights Pr., c/o Highlights for Children, Inc.

Hillert, Margaret. Dear Dragon Goes to the Zoo. Schimmell, David, illus. 2010. (BeginningtoRead Ser.). 32p. (J). (gr. k-2). lib. bdg. 22.60 *(978-1-59953-348-3(0))* Norwood Hse. Pr.

—Little Puff. Dammer, Mike, illus. 2016. (BeginningtoRead Ser.). (ENG.). 32p. (J). (gr. k-2). 22.60 *(978-1-59953-800-6(8))* Norwood Hse. Pr.

—Little Puff. Mike Dammer, illus. 2016. (Beginning-To-Read Ser.). (ENG.). 32p. (J). (gr. k-2). pap. 13.26 *(978-1-60357-941-4(9))* Norwood Hse. Pr.

Hilliard, Michael. Butter Bee Grows up Too Fast! 2010. 20p. pap. 12.49 *(978-1-4490-7300-8(X))* AuthorHouse.

Howell, Heather. Emanuele Goes to the Zoo. 2010. 20p. 10.49 *(978-1-4490-4816-7(1))* AuthorHouse.

Hudson, Marilyn A. Elephant Hips Are Expensive! A Tale of the Sooner State. Fulco, Haley, illus. 2007. 50p. (J). per. *(978-0-9778850-2-2(X)*, WhorlBooks Thumbprints) Whorl Bks.

Ide, Laurie Shimizu. Okazu at the Zoo. Kanekuni, Daniel, illus. 2006. (J). *(978-1-56647-776-5(X))* Mutual Publishing LLC.

The Imaginary Zoo. 2007. (J). 16.95 *(978-0-9789880-0-5(0))* Wild About Learning, Inc.

Ipcizade, Catherine. 'Twas the Day Before Zoo Day, 1 vol. Hodson, Ben, illus. 2008. (Basic Math Operations Ser.). (ENG.). 32p. (J). (gr. -1-2). 17.95 *(978-1-60718-585-7(7))* Arbordale Publishing.

It's a Zoo! Individual Title, 6 Packs. (gr. -1-2). 27.00 *(978-0-7635-9454-1(7))* Rigby Education.

Jacques, Brian. The Tale of Urso Brunov: Little Father of All Bears. Natchev, Alexi, illus. 2003. (ENG.). 48p. (J). (gr. -1-1). 21.19 *(978-0-399-23762-1(3))* Penguin Young Readers Group.

Jantzen, Doug. Henry Hyena, Why Won't You Laugh? Claude, Jean, illus. 2015. (ENG.). 32p. (J). (gr. -1-2). 17.99 *(978-1-4814-2822-4(5)*, Aladdin) Simon & Schuster Children's Publishing.

Jarman, Julia. Class Two at the Zoo. Chapman, Lynne, illus. 2007. (Carolrhoda Picture Bks.). (ENG.). 32p. (J). (gr. k-2). 16.95 *(978-0-8225-7132-2(3)*, Carolrhoda Bks.) Lerner Publishing Group.

Jerome, Kate Boehm. The Chef down at the Zoo. 2005. (J). 15.95 *(978-0-9769087-2-2(7)*, Grand Kidz, The) Vertical Connect Pr.

Judybee. The Zoo Crew Play Ball. LittlePinkPebble, illus. 2011. 40p. pap. *(978-1-78092-000-9(8))* MX Publishing, Ltd.

Kangaroo at the Zoo IR. 2017. (Phonics Readers Ser.). (ENG.). (J). pap. 6.99 *(978-0-7945-3716-6(2)*, Usborne) EDC Publishing.

Kann, Victoria. Pinkalicious & the Pinkatastic Zoo Day. Kann, Victoria, illus. 2012. (I Can Read Level 1 Ser.). (ENG., Illus.). 32p. (J). (gr. -1-3). 16.99 *(978-0-06-218780-2(5))*; pap. 5.99 *(978-0-06-218779-6(1))* HarperCollins Pubs. (HarperCollins).

—Pinkalicious & the Pinkatastic Zoo Day. 2012. (Pinkalicious I Can Read Ser.). (J). lib. bdg. 13.55 *(978-0-606-26527-0(9))* Turtleback.

Katz, Karen. Roar, Roar, Baby! A Karen Katz Lift-The-Flap Book. Katz, Karen, illus. 2015. (ENG., Illus.). 14p. (J). (gr. -1 — 1). bds. 6.99 *(978-1-4814-1788-4(6)*, Little Simon) Little Simon.

Keating, Jess. How to Outfox Your Friends When You Don't Have a Clue. 2015. (My Life Is a Zoo Ser.: 3). 304p. (J). (gr. 4-7). pap. 11.99 *(978-1-4926-1794-5(6)*, 9781492617945) Sourcebooks, Inc.

—How to Outrun a Crocodile When Your Shoes Are Untied. 2014. (My Life Is a Zoo Ser.: 1). 288p. (J). (gr. 4-7). pap. 11.99 *(978-1-4022-9755-7(6)*, 9781402297557) Sourcebooks, Inc.

—How to Outswim a Shark Without a Snorkel. 2015. (My Life Is a Zoo Ser.: 2). 304p. (J). (gr. 4-7). pap. 11.99 *(978-1-4022-9758-8(0)*, 9781402297588) Sourcebooks, Inc.

Keene, Carolyn. The Zoo Crew. Pamintuan, Macky, illus. 14th ed. 2008. (Nancy Drew & the Clue Crew Ser.: 14). (ENG.). 96p. (J). (gr. 1-4). pap. 5.99 *(978-1-4169-5899-4(1)*, Aladdin) Simon & Schuster Children's Publishing.

Ken Lindstrom To Ken Lindstrom. Ollie & Grampa Go to the Zoo: How the Polar Bear Got to the Zoo. Jones., Amber, illus. 2011. 28p. pap. 12.49 *(978-1-4520-1529-3(5))* AuthorHouse.

Keret, Etgar. Long-Haired Cat-Boy Cub. Silverston, Sondra, tr. Basil, Aviel, illus. 2020. (ENG.). 32p. (J). (gr. -1-1). 18.95 *(978-1-60980-931-7(9)*, Triangle Square) Seven Stories Pr.

Kertell, Lynn Maslen. My School Trip. 2012. (BOB Books: Scholastic Readers Level 1 Ser.: 3). lib. bdg. 13.55 *(978-0-606-26232-3(6))* Turtleback.

Kirby, Stan. Captain Awesome & the Missing Elephants. O'Connor, George, illus. 2014. (Captain Awesome Ser.: 10). (ENG.). 128p. (J). (gr. k-4). 17.99 *(978-1-4424-8995-0(2))*; pap. 6.99 *(978-1-4424-8994-3(4))* Little Simon. (Little Simon).

Klein, Adria F. Max Goes to the Zoo. Gallagher-Cole, Mernie, illus. 2007. (Read-It! Readers: the Life of Max Ser.). (ENG.). 24p. (J). (gr. -1-2). per. 3.95 *(978-1-4048-3683-9(7)*, 94291, Picture Window Bks.) Capstone.

Kline, Trish & Donev, Mary. A Day at the Zoo: KA Reader 3. 2007. (Illus.). 32p. (J). per. 20.00 *(978-0-9717234-5-0(1))* Ghost Hunter Productions.

Korman, Gordon. Zoobreak. 2009. 230p. (J). *(978-0-545-20027-1(X)*, Scholastic Pr.) Scholastic, Inc.

—Zoobreak (Swindle #2) 2010. (Swindle Ser.: 2). (ENG.). 240p. (J). (gr. 4-7). pap. 8.99 *(978-0-545-12500-0(6)*, Scholastic Paperbacks) Scholastic, Inc.

Ladybird. Topsy & Tim: Go to the Zoo Ladybird Readers Level 1. 2016. (Ladybird Readers Ser.). (Illus.). 48p. (J). (gr. 2-4). pap. 9.99 *(978-0-241-25414-1(0))* Penguin Bks., Ltd. GBR. Dist: Independent Pubs. Group.

Larson, Angela. Anthony Smoochiano: First Loves. 2012. pap. *(978-1-4507-7998-2(0))* Independent Pub.

—Harry Hiccers: Friends of A Feether. 2012. pap. *(978-1-4507-7996-8(4))* Independent Pub.

Latham, Irene. Don't Feed the Boy. Graegin, Stephanie, illus. 2014. (ENG.). 304p. (J). (gr. 3-7). pap. 13.99 *(978-1-250-04428-0(6)*, 900128320) Square Fish.

Latimer, Alex. Wild Violet! Latimer, Patrick, illus. 2018. (ENG.). 32p. (J). (gr. -1-k). pap. 9.99 *(978-1-84365-382-0(6)*, Pavilion) Pavilion Bks. GBR. Dist: Independent Pubs. Group.

Lawson, Jennifer. The Secret Tea Party at the Zoo. 2010. (Illus.). 34p. pap. 19.95 *(978-0-557-13707-7(1))* Lulu Pr., Inc.

Lee, Howard. A Day at the Zoo. Reasoner, Charles, illus. 2009. (Inside Outside Board Bks.). 10p. (J). bds. 10.99 *(978-1-934650-55-4(2))* Just For Kids Pr., LLC.

Lee, Steven. TruthQuest: In the Beginning. 2009. 72p. (J). pap. 6.95 *(978-1-4327-3473-2(3))* Outskirts Pr., Inc.

LeMae, Katie. The Color Bunch Goes to the Zoo. 2010. 48p. pap. 17.89 *(978-1-4520-1223-0(7))* AuthorHouse.

Lilienstein, Jennel. Trip to the Zoo. 2003. (J). 8.99 *(978-0-9741215-3-6(3))* Stories of My Life, The.

Lubratt, Mark. Buffy Meets the Zoonicorns. Weingartner, Sara, illus. 2015. 32p. (J). 16.95 *(978-1-59298-893-8(8))* Beaver's Pond Pr., Inc.

Mack, Paulette. Cookout at Grandma's House: The Adventures of Mielle & Cheeky. 2006. (ENG., Illus.). 24p. per. 10.95 *(978-1-59800-998-9(2))* Outskirts Pr., Inc.

MacPherson, Dwight L. Lil' Hellions. O'Reilly, Sean Patrick, ed. 2011. (Illus.). 82p. (YA). pap., pap. 14.95 *(978-1-926914-37-4(6))* Arcana Studio, Inc.

Mademann Vaughan, Kathryn. My Day at the Zoo. Martin, Don, illus. 2004. (J). per. 19.95 *(978-0-9747447-1-1(9))* Chaser Media LLC.

Mae, Darcie. Sammy & Robert. 2008. 24p. pap. 24.95 *(978-1-60474-811-6(7))* America Star Bks.

Malone, Cheryl Lawton. Elephants Walk Together. 2018. (2019 Av2 Fiction Ser.). (ENG.). 32p. (J). lib. bdg. 34.28 *(978-1-4896-8261-1(9)*, AV2 by Weigl) Weigl Pubs., Inc.

—Elephants Walk Together. Masseva, Bistra, illus. 2017. (ENG.). 32p. (J). (gr. -1-3). 16.99 *(978-0-8075-1960-8(X)*, 080751960X) Whitman, Albert & Co.

Marciano, John Bemelmans. Madeline Loves Animals. 2005. (Madeline Ser.). (Illus.). 16p. (J). (gr. -1 — 1). bds. 9.99 *(978-0-670-06021-4(6)*, Viking Books for Young Readers) Penguin Young Readers Group.

Marinaro, Stacy. Treasure Monkey. 2008. 32p. pap. 15.95 *(978-1-4357-2840-0(8))* Lulu Pr., Inc.

Marlow, Herb. The Tiger's Den. Head, Pat, illus. 2003. 22p. (J). 19.95 *(978-1-893595-37-8(4))* Four Seasons Bks., Inc.

Marsalis, Dustin S. The Alligator Astronauts Go to the Zipper Zoo. 2013. 36p. pap. 15.99 *(978-1-4624-0678-4(5)*, Inspiring Voices) Author Solutions, LLC.

Marsh, Carole. The Zany Zoo Mystery. 2008. (Carole Marsh Mysteries: Awesome Mysteries Ser.). (ENG.). 128p. (J). (gr. 2-4). 18.69 *(978-0-635-06332-8(8))* Gallopade International.

Marsoli, Lisa Ann. Let's Go to the Zoo. Smitherton, Jeb, illus. 2005. (J). bds. 14.99 *(978-0-9767325-4-9(8))* Toy Quest.

—Let's Go to the Zoo & Leaping Lilly. Smitherton, Jeb, illus. 2005. (J). bds. 19.99 *(978-0-9767325-6-3(4))* Toy Quest.

Martin, Kentrell. Shelly Goes to the Zoo. Rodriguez, Marc, illus. 2013. 32p. pap. 8.50 *(978-0-9851845-1-3(5))* Shelly's Adventures LLC.

Mason, Albert. Ooshu the Monkey Escapes from the Zoo. 2009. 40p. pap. 16.99 *(978-1-4389-0974-5(8))* AuthorHouse.

Massie, Diane Redfield. The Baby Beebee Bird. Kellogg, Steven, illus. 2003. (ENG.). 32p. (J). (gr. -1-1). pap. 7.99 *(978-0-06-051784-7(0)*, HarperCollins) HarperCollins Pubs.

Mayer, Mercer. Professor Wormbog in Search for the Zipperump-a-Zoo. 2011. (Classic Collectible Ser.: 1). (ENG.). 42p. (J). (gr. -1-3). pap. 12.95 *(978-1-60746-765-6(8)*, Premiere) FastPrncil, Inc.

McAdams, Susan. Shubert. McAdams, Caleb, illus. 2008. 16p. per. 24.95 *(978-1-4241-9756-9(2))* America Star Bks.

McClatchy, Lisa. Eloise Visits the Zoo: Ready-To-Read Level 1. Lyon, Tammie, illus. (Eloise Ser.). (ENG.). 32p. (J). (gr. -1-1). 2018. 17.99 *(978-1-5344-2039-7(8))* 2009. pap. 4.99 *(978-1-4169-8642-3(1))* Simon Spotlight. (Simon Spotlight).

McNeal, Cari. What Would I Do If I Had a Zoo? Balogh, Jared, illus. 2012. 36p. 24.95 *(978-1-4560-4006-2(5))* America Star Bks.

Meachen Rau, Dana. En el Zoológico (at the Zoo), 1 vol. 2009. (Tiempo de la Diversión (Fun Time) Ser.). (SPA., Illus.). 24p. (gr. k-1). lib. bdg. 25.50 *(978-0-7614-2777-3(5)*, b63f8050-3988-480a-9027-3d00fc989b66) Cavendish Square Publishing LLC.

Meldrum, Margaret. Peter Panda & His Friends. 2009. (Illus.). 24p. pap. 11.49 *(978-1-4343-7826-2(8))* AuthorHouse.

Merrick, Gabriel. It's Time for a Field Trip, 1 vol. 2017. (Let's Tell Time Ser.). (ENG.). 24p. (J). (gr. 1-1). 25.27 *(978-1-5081-5724-3(3)*, e1a3d030-a3c6-4ea8-a462-f5492daf5c91, PowerKids Pr.) Rosen Publishing Group, Inc., The.

Merveille, David. Hello Mr. Hulot. 2013. (ENG., Illus.). 32p. (J). (gr. -1-3). 17.95 *(978-0-7358-4135-2(7))* North-South Bks., Inc.

Metzger, Steve. Dancing Clock. Nez, John Abbott, illus. 2011. (ENG.). 32p. 12.95 *(978-1-58925-100-7(8))*; (J). pap. 7.95 *(978-1-58925-429-9(5))* Tiger Tales.

Meyers, Haily & Meyers, Kevin. All Aboard! Washington DC: A Capitol Primer, 1 vol. 2016. (Lucy Darling Ser.). (ENG., Illus.). 22p. (J). (— 1). bds. 9.99 *(978-1-4236-4245-9(7))* Gibbs Smith, Publisher.

Michaels, Evan. Tressa & Dan's Picnic at the Zoo. 2010. (Illus.). 34p. (J). pap. 19.95 *(978-0-9826865-0-8(1))* Win Enterprises LLC.

Michaels, Rune. Fix Me. 2011. (ENG., Illus.). 160p. (YA). (gr. 9). 16.99 *(978-1-4169-5772-0(3)*, Atheneum Bks. for Young Readers) Simon & Schuster Children's Publishing.

Michalak, Jamie. Joe & Sparky Get New Wheels: Candlewick Sparks. Remkiewicz, Frank, illus. 2013. (Candlewick Sparks Ser.). (ENG.). 48p. (J). (gr. k-4). pap. 5.99 *(978-0-7636-6641-5(6))* Candlewick Pr.

Middleton, Nancy. The Zookeeper's Christmas Eve. 2009. 36p. pap. 16.50 *(978-1-60693-302-2(7)*, Eloquent Bks.) Strategic Book Publishing & Rights Agency (SBPRA).

Miedoso, Andres. Night of the Zombie Zookeeper. Rivas, Victor, illus. 2018. (Desmond Cole Ghost Patrol Ser.: 4). (ENG.). 128p. (J). (gr. k-4). 16.99 *(978-1-5344-1805-9(9))*; pap. 6.99 *(978-1-5344-1804-2(0))* Little Simon. (Little Simon).

Miller, Kathryn L. Abc's with Sadie: Sadie Goes to the Zoo. 2011. 32p. pap. 17.25 *(978-1-4269-5940-0(0))* Trafford Publishing.

Mitchell, Rae. Anna's Wish. 2009. 24p. pap. 13.50 *(978-1-60860-441-8(1)*, Eloquent Bks.) Strategic Book Publishing & Rights Agency (SBPRA).

Morrison, Cathy. I Want a Pet. 2012. (ENG., Illus.). 32p. (J). *(978-1-58925-113-7(X))* Tiger Tales.

Mothergoose-Zany Zoo. 2003. (J). per. *(978-1-57657-167-5(X))* Paradise Pr., Inc.

Mucklow, Hope. Rojo the Baby Red Panda at the Zoo: An Allegory about Self-Worth Through a Red Panda & Giant Panda Comparison. 2014. (ENG., Illus.). 32p. (J). (gr. -1-3). 14.95 *(978-1-62086-593-4(9))* Amplify Publishing Group.

Munns, Skye. Who's at the Zoo. 2011. 24p. pap. 28.03 *(978-1-4568-5447-8(X))* Xlibris Corp.

Murray, Laura. The Gingerbread Man Loose at the Zoo. Lowery, Mike, illus. 2016. (Gingerbread Man Is Loose Ser.: 4). 32p. (J). (gr. k-3). 18.99 *(978-0-399-16867-3(2)*, G.P. Putnam's Sons Books for Young Readers) Penguin Young Readers Group.

My Big Book of Beginner Books about Me. 2011. (Beginner Books(R) Ser.). (ENG., Illus.). 208p. (J). (gr. -1-2). 16.99 *(978-0-307-93183-2(8)*, Random Hse. Bks. for Young Readers) Random Hse. Children's Bks.

My Uncle Has Wheels. 2005. (J). 8.00 *(978-0-9767077-1-4(3))* Carson, Tracy.

Neely, M. W. Saving the Kilda Street Zoo. 2012. 218p. 29.99 *(978-1-4771-0179-7(9))*; pap. 19.99 *(978-1-4771-0178-0(0))* Xlibris Corp.

Nesquens, Daniel. A Good Day. Lora, Miren Asiain, illus. 2019. (ENG.). 32p. (J). *(978-0-8028-5530-5(X)*, Eerdmans Bks For Young Readers) Eerdmans, William B. Publishing Co.

Nguyen, Taohuu. Mighty Mite 2: Zoo Gone Wild. Nguyen, Taohuu, illus. 2007. (Illus.). (J). 14.95 *(978-0-9788469-2-3(3))* Amazing Factory, The.

Noble, Kate. Pamela's Plan. Bass, Rachel, illus. (Zoo Stories Ser.). 32p. (J). (gr. -1-4). 15.95 *(978-0-9631798-4-5(5))* Salmon Run Pr.

O'Hely, Eileen. Penny on Safari. Phelan, Nicky, illus. 2010. (ENG.). 192p. (J). pap. 15.95 *(978-1-85635-572-8(1))* Mercier Pr., Ltd., The IRL. Dist: Dufour Editions, Inc.

Olson, Kevin Noel. Eerey Tocsin in the Cryptoid Zoo. Hammack, Debi, illus. 2006. (ENG.). 176p. (YA). per. 15.95 *(978-1-887560-17-7(3)*, Cornerstone Bk. Publishers) Cornerstone Bk. Pubs.

One for Me, Zoo for You. 2003. (J). per. *(978-1-57657-855-1(0))* Paradise Pr., Inc.

Oxford-White, Bly. Mr. Woo's Zoo. l.t. ed. 2003. (Illus.). 16p. (J). *(978-0-9740833-2-2(1))* Port Town Publishing.

Paling, Chris. The Adventures of Rumble, Tumble, & Titch: Uncertain Times. 2010. 62p. pap. 9.99 *(978-1-60911-263-9(6)*, Eloquent Bks.) Strategic Book Publishing & Rights Agency (SBPRA).

Papp, Robert, illus. Monkey Trouble. 2011. (Boxcar Children Mysteries Ser.: 127). (ENG.). 128p. (J). (gr. 2-5). pap. 7.99 *(978-0-8075-5240-7(2)*, 807552402); lib. bdg. 14.99 *(978-0-8075-5239-1(9)*, 807552399) Random Hse. Children's Bks. (Random Hse. Bks. for Young Readers).

Parish, Herman. Amelia Bedelia Chapter Book #4: Amelia Bedelia Goes Wild! (Special Edition) 2014. (ENG.). 160p. (J). *(978-0-06-227058-0(3)*, Harper Design) HarperCollins Pubs.

—Amelia Bedelia Chapter Book #4: Amelia Bedelia Goes Wild! Avril, Lynne, illus. 2014. (Amelia Bedelia Ser.: No. 4). (ENG.). 160p. (J). (gr. 1-5). 15.99 *(978-0-06-209507-7(2))*; pap. 6.99 *(978-0-06-209506-0(4))* HarperCollins Pubs. (Greenwillow Bks.).

Pauline, Christi. Hullabaloo at the Zoo. 2008. 28p. pap. 14.95 *(978-1-4389-1204-2(8))* AuthorHouse.

Peck, J. L. Mr Crabby Pants & the Zoo. 2012. 24p. pap. 17.99 *(978-1-4685-7953-6(3))* AuthorHouse.

Peeler, Penny. The Adventures of Spike & Sally. 2011. 52p. pap. 15.99 *(978-1-4568-9981-3(3))* Xlibris Corp.

Peterka, Edward S. Zoe Isabella Goes to the Zoo. 2011. 32p. pap. 12.77 *(978-1-4520-0305-4(X))* AuthorHouse.

Phillips, Dee. Baby's Day. 2009. (Flip Flap Fun Bks.). (ENG.). 5p. (J). (gr. -1-k). bds. 5.95 *(978-1-84696-087-1(8)*, TickTock Books) Octopus Publishing Group GBR. Dist: Independent Pubs. Group.

Piano, Maureen. When Flamingos Fly: Discovering the Wonders of the World. 2006. (Illus.). 44p. (J). (gr. -1-3). pap. 12.99 incl. audio compact disk *(978-1-59092-362-7(6))* Blue Forge Pr.

Pichon, Liz. Penguins. 2008. (J). *(978-0-545-08292-1(7)*, Orchard Bks.) Scholastic, Inc.

Pilkey, Dav. The Dumb Bunnies Go to the Zoo. Pilkey, Dav, illus. 2009. (ENG., Illus.). 32p. (J). (gr. -1-3). 16.99 *(978-0-545-03937-6(1)*, Blue Sky Pr., The) Scholastic, Inc.

—The Dumb Bunnies Go to the Zoo. 2007. (ENG.). 32p. pap. 5.99 *(978-0-439-93049-9(9))* Scholastic, Inc.

Pittman, Samuel, II. Alligator Jazz, 1 vol. Bailey, Sheila, illus. 2018. (ENG.). 32p. (J). (gr. -1-3). 16.99 *(978-1-4556-2422-5(5)*, Pelican Publishing) Arcadia Publishing.

Plant, David J. Hungry Roscoe. 2015. (ENG., Illus.). 40p. (J). (gr. -1-2). 17.95 *(978-1-909263-53-6(2))* Flying Eye Bks. GBR. Dist: Penguin Random Hse. LLC.

Portis, Michael. Pinky Got Out! Richmond, Lori, illus. 2019. (ENG.). 40p. (J). (gr. -1-2). lib. bdg. 20.99 *(978-1-101-93299-5(6)*, Crown Books For Young Readers) Random Hse. Children's Bks.

Potter, Tracy. Charlie the Chimp's Day Out. 2013. 24p. pap. 24.95 *(978-1-63000-036-3(1))* America Star Bks.

Power, Michael. The Zoo. 2009. 201p. pap. 13.75 *(978-1-60695-075-3(4))* Cacoethes Publishing Hse., LLC.

Priddy, Roger. Giraffe Is Lost: An Animal Search-And-find Book. 2019. (Search & Find Ser.). (ENG., Illus.). 10p. (J). bds. 9.99 *(978-0-312-52789-1(6)*, 900194735) St. Martin's Pr.

Prince, Daniel. Zoe the Zookeeper. 2007. (Illus.). 48p. per. *(978-1-84748-047-7(0))* Athena Pr.

Rathmann, Peggy. Good Night, Gorilla (oversized Board Book) Rathmann, Peggy, illus. 2004. (Illus.). 34p. (J). (gr. -1 — 1). bds. 15.99 *(978-0-399-24260-1(0)*, G.P. Putnam's Sons Books for Young Readers) Penguin Young Readers Group.

Redmond, E. S. Felicity Floo Visits the Zoo. Redmond, E. S., illus. 2010. (ENG., Illus.). 32p. (J). (-k). pap. 7.99 *(978-0-7636-4975-3(9))* Candlewick Pr.

Reilly, Carmel & Young, Karen. Anna Goes to the Zoo. 2008. (Rigby Focus Forward: Level D Ser.). (Illus.). 24p. (J). (gr. 4-7). pap. *(978-1-4190-3663-7(7)*, Rigby) Pearson Education Australia.

Rey, H. A. Curious George Goes to the Zoo. 2014. (Curious George 8x8 Ser.). lib. bdg. 14.75 *(978-0-606-23335-4(0))* Turtleback.

Rey, H. A. & Rey, Margret. Curious George Feeds the Animals Book & Cd, 1 vol. 2005. (Curious George Ser.). (ENG., Illus.). 24p. (J). (gr. -1-3). audio compact disk 10.99 *(978-0-618-60387-9(5)*, 495928, Clarion Bks.) HarperCollins Pubs.

Rim, Sujean. Zoogie Boogie Fever!: an Animal Dance Book. Rim, Sujean, illus. 2018. (ENG., Illus.). 40p. (J). (gr. -1-k). 17.99 *(978-0-545-90005-8(0)*, Orchard Bks.) Scholastic, Inc.

Rippin, Sally. The Extra-Special Helper. 2014. (ENG., Illus.). 48p. (J). pap. 4.99 *(978-1-61067-099-9(X))* Kane Miller.

WXYZ

Rissi, Anica Mrose. Anna, Banana, & the Monkey in the Middle. Park, Meg, illus. 2015. (Anna, Banana Ser.: 2). (ENG.). 128p. (J). (gr. 1-5). 17.99 *(978-1-4814-1608-5(1),* Simon & Schuster Bks. For Young Readers) Simon & Schuster Bks. For Young Readers.

Robinson, Tom. Fibonacci Zoo, 1 vol. 2015. (ENG., Illus.). 32p. (J). (gr. 1-4). 17.95 *(978-1-62855-553-0(X))* Arbordale Publishing.

Rockwell, Anne. Zoo Day. Rockwell, Lizzy, illus. 2018. (My First Experience Book Ser.). (ENG.). 32p. (J). (gr. -1-3). 7.99 *(978-1-4814-2735-7(0),* Aladdin) Simon & Schuster Children's Publishing.

—Zoo Day. Rockwell, Lizzy, illus. 2017. (My First Experience Book Ser.). (ENG.). 32p. (J). (gr. -1-3). 17.99 *(978-1-4814-2734-0(2),* Simon & Schuster/Paula Wiseman Bks.) Simon & Schuster/Paula Wiseman Bks.

Rosen, Kymberlee S. Do You Have Better Manners Than the Monkeys at the Zoo? 2010. (Illus.). 32p. pap. 13.00 *(978-1-60911-179-3(6),* Eloquent Bks.) Strategic Book Publishing & Rights Agency (SBPRA).

Rosenthal, Pamela. My Trip to the Zoo. 2005. (Illus.). 48p. (J). lib. bdg. 24.95 *(978-1-932762-28-0(0))* Elderberry Press, Inc.

Roy, Ron. Capital Mysteries #9: a Thief at the National Zoo. Bush, Timothy, illus. 2007. (Capital Mysteries Ser.: 9). 96p. (J). (gr. 1-4). per. 5.99 *(978-0-375-84804-9(5),* Random Hse. Bks. for Young Readers) Random Hse. Children's Bks.

—A Thief at the National Zoo. Bush, Timothy, illus. 2008. (Capital Mysteries Ser.: No. 9). 87p. (gr. k-3). 15.00 *(978-0-7569-8329-1(0))* Perfection Learning Corp.

—A Thief at the National Zoo, 9. Bush, Timothy, illus. 2007. (Capital Mysteries Ser.: No. 9). (ENG.). 87p. (J). (gr. 2-4). lib. bdg. 17.44 *(978-0-375-94804-6(X))* Random House Publishing Group.

Ruiz, Rachel. The Wild Field Trip. May, Steve, illus. 2017. (Superhero Harry Ser.). (ENG.). 48p. (J). (gr. k-2). pap. 8.95 *(978-1-4795-9861-8(5),* 135318); lib. bdg. 23.32 *(978-1-4795-9857-1(7),* 135310) Capstone. (Picture Window Bks.).

Russell, David. Who'z Who at the Zoo. 2012. (Illus.). 26p. pap. 12.95 *(978-1-4575-1395-4(1))* Dog Ear Publishing, LLC.

Rutley, Erika L. Adventures in Pup-A-Dupping. 2012. 36p. pap. 24.95 *(978-1-62709-710-9(4))* America Star Bks.

Sampson, Brent. One Wacky Wasp: The Perfect Children's Book for Kids Ages 3-6 Who Are Learning to Read. 2010. 24p. (J). 14.95 *(978-1-4327-6217-9(6));* pap. 9.95 *(978-1-4327-0465-0(6))* Outskirts Pr., Inc.

Sansone, V. K. A Strange Day at the Zoo. 2009. 32p. pap. 14.98 *(978-0-557-06519-6(4))* Lulu Pr., Inc.

Sava, Scott Christian. Animal Crackers. 2011. (Illus.). 152p. pap. 11.99 *(978-1-60010-619-4(6))* Idea & Design Works, LLC.

Sax, Anita. Oscar & the Zoo. Jasuna, Aija, illus. 2013. 32p. (J). 14.95 *(978-1-60131-174-0(5))* Big Tent Bks.

Scanlon, Jack. Rainbow Zoo, 1 vol. 2006. (Neighborhood Readers Ser.). (ENG., Illus.). 8p. (gr. k-1). pap. 5.15 *(978-1-4042-6686-5(0),* 59a8fa80-4f08-4c73-85b0-e625d32b9002, Rosen Classroom) Rosen Publishing Group, Inc., The.

Shalev, Michal. How to Be Famous. Shalev, Michal, illus. 2016. (ENG., Illus.). 32p. (J). (gr. -1-1). E-Book 26.65 *(978-1-77657-057-7(X),* 9781776570577); E-Book 26.65 *(978-1-77657-047-8(2));* E-Book 9.99 *(978-1-77657-045-4(6),* 9781776570454) Gecko Pr. NZL. Dist: Lerner Publishing Group.

Shannon, Carol. Dusky Langurs at the Zoo. 2013. 40p. pap. 16.95 *(978-1-4525-1014-9(8),* Balboa Pr.) Author Solutions, LLC.

Shepherd, Kat. The Gemini Mysteries: the Cat's Paw (the Gemini Mysteries Book 2) 2021. (Gemini Mysteries Ser.: 2). (ENG., Illus.). 304p. (J). (gr. 3-7). 16.99 *(978-1-4998-0810-0(0),* Yellow Jacket) Bonnier Publishing USA.

Shoopman, Jim. Cowboy Zack & the Monkey from the Muggletown Zoo. 2013. 50p. pap. 13.98 *(978-0-9887836-2-1(2))* Taylor and Seale Publishing.

Shrode, Donna. Fun with Nana: A Trip to the Zoo. Olds, Irene, illus. 2012. (ENG.). 28p. pap. 12.03 *(978-1-4685-4598-2(1))* AuthorHouse.

Sierra, Judy. Everyone Counts. Brown, Marc, illus. 2019. 40p. (J). (gr. -1-2). 17.99 *(978-0-525-64620-4(5),* Knopf Bks. for Young Readers) Random Hse. Children's Bks.

Sklar, David. A Day at the Zoo with My Daddy. 2013. 24p. pap. 17.99 *(978-1-4817-0152-5(5))* AuthorHouse.

Smith, Danna. Two at the Zoo/Dos en el Zoologico Board Book: Bilingual English-Spanish. Petrone, Valeria, illus. 2011.Tr. of Two at the Zoo - A Counting Book. (ENG.). 30p. (J). (gr. -1-k). bds. 5.99 *(978-0-547-58137-8(8),* 1459824, Clarion Bks.) HarperCollins Pubs.

Smith M.Ed TVI, Kristie. Dottie & Dots See Animal Spots: Learning Braille with Dots & Dottie. Knorr, Kandice, illus. 2007. (ENG.). 48p. per. 8.95 *(978-0-595-47130-0(7))* iUniverse, Inc.

Snow, Peggy. My Favorite Places from a to Z. Barber, Brian, illus. 2007. (My Favorites Ser.). (ENG.). 32p. (J). (gr. -1). lib. bdg. 15.99 *(978-1-934277-03-4(7))* Mam Green Publishing, Inc.

Snyder, Marilyn. A Second Chance for Tina. Shiffman, Lena, illus. 2003. (Hello Reader! Ser.). (J). *(978-0-439-44154-4(4))* Scholastic, Inc.

Sobel, Deane. Philip the Sea Lion. 2012. (ENG.). (J). pap. *(978-1-4675-2347-9(X))* Independent Pub.

Sparks, David. Flat-Top Sam & the Junkyard Elephant. Sparks, David, illus. 2008. (Illus.). 36p. pap. 12.95 *(978-1-59858-587-2(8))* Dog Ear Publishing, LLC.

Spooner, Joe. The Elephant Walk. McCann, Michelle, ed. Spooner, Joe, illus. 2005. (ENG., Illus.). 36p. (J). (gr. -1-3). 15.00 *(978-0-9745686-3-8(5))* ACS, LLC Amica Creative Services.

Stead, Philip C. A Sick Day for Amos McGee. Stead, Erin E., illus. 2010. (JPN.). 32p. (J). (gr. -1-1). *(978-4-89572-814-0(5))* Hisakata-Child.

—A Sick Day for Amos McGee. 2012. (CHI.). (J). (gr. -1-1). *(978-986-211-314-1(6))* Hsaio Lu Publishing Co., Ltd.

—A Sick Day for Amos Mcgee. Stead, Erin E., illus. (ENG.). (J). 2018. 34p. bds. 9.99 *(978-1-250-17110-8(5),* 900188204) 2010. 32p. (gr. -1-1). 18.99 *(978-1-59643-402-8(3),* 900051603) Roaring Brook Pr.

—A Sick Day for Amos Mcgee: 10th Anniversary Edition. Stead, Erin E., illus. 10th ed. 2019. (ENG.). 40p. (J). 29.99 *(978-1-62672-105-0(X),* 900136450) Roaring Brook Pr.

Steele, Michael Anthony. Vampire Zoo Hullabaloo. Jeralds, Scott, illus. 2017. (Scooby-Doo! Beginner Mysteries Ser.). (ENG.). 112p. (J). (gr. 1-3). lib. bdg. 22.65 *(978-1-4965-4770-5(5),* 135307, Stone Arch Bks.) Capstone.

Stofko, Michael D. A Visit from the Zoo. 2011. 32p. pap. 12.77 *(978-1-4567-2968-4(3))* AuthorHouse.

Stone, Jessica J. Picnic at the Zoo. 2011. 24p. 11.32 *(978-1-4567-4386-4(4))* AuthorHouse.

Stossel, Sage. On the Loose in Washington, D. C. 2013. (Find the Animals Ser.). (ENG., Illus.). 28p. (J). (gr. -1-3). 14.95 *(978-1-938700-14-9(7),* Commonwealth Editions) Applewood Bks.

Sutherland, Tui T. The Menagerie: Krakens & Lies. 2016. (Menagerie Ser.: 3). (ENG.). 368p. (J). (gr. 3-7). pap. 9.99 *(978-0-06-078069-2(X),* HarperCollins) HarperCollins Pubs.

Sutherland, Tui T. & Sutherland, Kari. The Menagerie #2: Dragon on Trial. 2015. (Menagerie Ser.: 2). (ENG.). 320p. (J). (gr. 3-7). pap. 7.99 *(978-0-06-085145-3(7),* HarperCollins) HarperCollins Pubs.

Sutherland, Tui T. & Sutherland, Kari H. The Menagerie. 2013. (Menagerie Ser.: 1). (ENG., Illus.). 288p. (J). (gr. 3-7). 16.99 *(978-0-06-078064-7(9),* HarperCollins) HarperCollins Pubs.

—The Menagerie #3: Krakens & Lies. 2015. (Menagerie Ser.: 3). (ENG., Illus.). 368p. (J). (gr. 3-7). 16.99 *(978-0-06-078067-8(3),* HarperCollins) HarperCollins Pubs.

Sutton, Laurie S. Going Ape. Gordon, Eric A. & Gordon, Steven E., illus. 2012. (I Can Read Level 2 Ser.). (ENG.). 32p. (J). (gr. -1-3). pap. 3.99 *(978-0-06-188522-8(3))* HarperCollins Pubs.

—Going Ape. 2012. (Justice League Classic: I Can Read! Ser.). (J). lib. bdg. 13.55 *(978-0-606-26260-6(1))* Turtleback.

Swartz, Patricia. Pig-A-Poo Moves to the Zoo. 2009. (Illus.). 28p. pap. 14.99 *(978-1-4490-4616-3(9))* AuthorHouse.

Taber-Montgomery, Kathy. We Live in a Zoo. 2012. 24p. pap. *(978-1-4602-0028-5(4))* FriesenPress.

Thompson, Berine. Tedi the Bear & His Pals Adventure at the Zoo! 2005. 44p. per. 21.99 *(978-1-4208-1007-3(3))* AuthorHouse.

Thompson, Kay & Knight, Hilary. Eloise Ready-To-Read Value Pack: Eloise's Summer Vacation; Eloise at the Wedding; Eloise & the Very Secret Room; Eloise Visits the Zoo; Eloise Throws a Party!; Eloise's Pirate Adventure, Pack. 2012. (Eloise Ser.). (ENG.). 192p. (J). (gr. -1-1). pap. 17.96 *(978-1-4424-4949-7(7),* Simon Spotlight) Simon Spotlight.

Tinsley, Jillian. Wally the Warthog. Wood, Douglas, illus. 2012. 24p. (J). pap. 10.99 *(978-1-61254-782-4(6))* Small Pr., The.

Toral, Miguel A. Babu Goes Back to the Zoo. 2009. 32p. pap. 15.70 *(978-1-4389-6330-3(0))* AuthorHouse.

Tsong, Jing Jing & BeachHouse Publishing. Aloha Zoo. 2010. (ENG.). 16p. (J). (gr. -1-1). bds. 7.95 *(978-1-933067-32-2(2))* Beachhouse Publishing, LLC.

Vicuña, Claudio Orrego. The Surprising Adventures of Balthazar. 2011. (Peace, Justice, Human Rights, & Freedom in Latin America Ser.). (ENG.). 160p. 15.00 *(978-1-58966-218-6(0))* Univ. of Scranton Pr.

Waldron, Kevin. Panda-Monium at Peek Zoo. Waldron, Kevin, illus. 2014. (ENG., Illus.). 40p. (J). (gr. -1-2). 16.99 *(978-0-7636-6658-3(0),* Templar) Candlewick Pr.

Wall, Laura. Goose Goes to the Zoo. Wall, Laura, illus. 2016. (ENG., Illus.). 48p. (J). (gr. -1-3). 12.99 *(978-0-06-232441-2(1),* HarperCollins) HarperCollins Pubs.

Wallace, Adam. How to Catch a Unicorn. Elkerton, Andy, illus. 2019. (How to Catch Ser.: 0). (ENG.). 40p. (J). (gr. k-6). 10.99 *(978-1-4926-6973-9(3))* Sourcebooks, Inc.

Weatherstone, Hollie. When the Pandas Came to Scotland. Cochrane, Claire, illus. 2012. (ENG.). 24p. pap. 19.82 *(978-1-4772-3528-7(0))* AuthorHouse.

Weston Woods Studios Inc. Staff, creator. Good Night, Gorilla. 2004. (J). 18.95 *(978-1-55592-419-5(0));* 38.75 *(978-1-55592-421-8(2))* Weston Woods Studios, Inc.

What Would I Do If I Lived at the Zoo? 2004. (Illus.). 12p. (J). 5.95 *(978-0-9759321-2-4(8))* Rascal Treehouse Publishing.

Williams, Emma. The Story of Hurry. Quraishi, Ibrahim, illus. 2014. 36p. (J). (gr. -1-2). 16.95 *(978-1-60980-589-0(5),* Triangle Square) Seven Stories Pr.

Winkler, Henry & Oliver, Lin. How to Hug an Elephant #6. Garrett, Scott, illus. 2015. (Here's Hank Ser.: 6). 128p. (J). (gr. 1-3). bds. 6.99 *(978-0-448-48656-7(3),* Grosset & Dunlap) Penguin Young Readers Group.

Winnard, Rebecca Victoria & Winnard, Linda. Giraffe Liberation: An Act of Freedom. 2006. 53p. pap. 16.95 *(978-1-4241-0552-6(8))* PublishAmerica, Inc.

Winthrop, Elizabeth. Dancing Granny, 1 vol. Murdocca, Sal, illus. 2003. (ENG.). 32p. (J). 16.95 *(978-0-7614-5141-9(2))* Marshall Cavendish Corp.

Woodcock, Fiona. Look! 2018. (ENG., Illus.). 40p. (J). (gr. -1-3). 17.99 *(978-0-06-264455-8(6),* Greenwillow Bks.) HarperCollins Pubs.

Zaring, Laurie. Who Could You Be at the Zoo? Barlup, Jessica, illus. 2013. 24p. pap. 12.95 *(978-1-61244-175-7(0))* Halo Publishing International.

Zschock, Martha. Hello, Rhode Island! 2011. (Hello Ser.). (ENG., Illus.). 16p. (J). (gr. -1-k). bds. 9.99 *(978-1-933212-62-3(4),* Commonwealth Editions) Applewood Bks.

ZULU (AFRICAN PEOPLE)

Gleimius, Nita, et al. The Zulu of Africa. 2005. (First Peoples Ser.). (Illus.). 48p. (J). (gr. 4-8). 23.95 *(978-0-8225-0661-4(0))* Lerner Publishing Group.

Spilsbury, Richard. Shaka Zulu, 1 vol. 2013. (Hero Journals). (ENG., Illus.). 48p. (J). (gr. 4-6). pap. 9.95 *(978-1-4109-5368-1(8),* 123252, Raintree) Capstone.

ZULU (AFRICAN PEOPLE)—FICTION

Powers, J. L. This Thing Called the Future, 1 vol. 2011. (ENG.). 208p. (YA). (gr. 9-12). 16.95 *(978-1-933693-95-8(9),* 23353382, Cinco Puntos Press) Lee & Low Bks., Inc.

ZULUS

see Zulu (African People)

PUBLISHER NAME INDEX

1 Lone Crow Media, *(978-1-7333609)* 22430 82nd Ave W, Edmonds, WA 98026 USA Tel 425-775-8494
E-mail: mtmartzke@gmail.com.

10 Finger Pr., *(978-0-9728131; 978-1-933174)* 8435 Belize Pl., Wellington, FL 33414 USA Tel 561-434-9044; Toll Free: 866-7-author
E-mail: mahesh@10fingerspress.com
Web site: http://www.10fingerspress.com
Dist(s): **Independent Pubs. Group**
Midpoint Trade Bks., Inc.

10 To 2 Children's Bks., *(978-0-9849487; 978-0-615-74608-1; 978-0-615-74627-2; 978-0-615-79610-9; 978-0-615-79632-1; 978-0-615-84753-5; 978-0-615-87923-9)* P.O. Box 5173, Clinton, NJ 08809 USA Tel 610-570-4196
E-mail: darylkcobb@yahoo.com
Web site: http://www.darylcobb.com
Dist(s): **CreateSpace Independent Publishing Platform.**

100 Book Challenge *See* **American Reading Co.**

101 Bk. *Imprint of* **Michaelson Entertainment**

1021 Pr., *(978-0-9854151)* P.O. Box 11232, Detroit, MI 48211 USA Tel 313-701-6708
E-mail: 1021press@gmail.com; novaceks@att.net.

1072 Studio *See* **1072 Studio**

1072 Studio, *(978-0-578-42806-2; 978-0-578-61389-5; 978-0-578-87918-5; 979-8-218-05608-7; 979-8-218-10746-8)* 6001 Main Street, No. 1701, Zachary, LA 70791 USA Tel 225-803-8082
E-mail: 1072studio@gmail.com.

1105 West House, *(978-0-9976172)* P.O. Box 1835, McKinney, TX 75070 USA Tel 214-606-7735
E-mail: hello@knookerdoodle.com.

114th Aviation Co. Assn., *(978-0-9742465)* 15151 Berry Trail, Suite 403, Dallas, TX 75248-6319 USA
E-mail: steve@stibbens.com.

11th Hour Productions *See* **Twilight Tales, Inc.**

1212 Pr., *(978-0-9764985)* 1212 Beverley Rd., Brooklyn, NY 11218 USA Tel 718-462-4004
E-mail: rgistudio@earthlink.net.

12-Story Library *Imprint of* **Bookstaves, LLC**

12th Media Services, *(978-1-68092)* 3651 Peachtree Pkwy. Suite E275, Suwanee, GA 30024 USA
E-mail: tony.darnell@12thmedia.com.

13 Hands Pubns., *(978-0-9767260)* Div. Crooked Roads Productions, LLC, Orders Addr.: 914 Westwood Blvd., #518, Los Angeles, CA 90024 USA Fax: 310-388-6012
E-mail: mnaughton@earthlink.net
Web site: http://www.13handsonline.com; http://www.gildedhearse.com.

1-315-820-1714 *See* **Liber Publishing Hse.**

138 In Progress Publishing, *(978-0-692-55798-3; 978-0-9982768; 978-0-578-32802-7; 979-8-218-05928-6)* 160 Holsapple Rd. # 107, Dover Plains, NY 12522 USA Tel 845-797-9536
Dist(s): **CreateSpace Independent Publishing Platform.**

13th & Joan, *(978-0-9916015; 978-0-9985210; 978-0-9989702; 978-1-7322479; 978-1-7324712; 978-1-7326464; 978-1-7335154; 978-1-7331313; 978-1-7342346; 978-1-953156; 978-1-961863)* 205 N. Michigan Ave. Suite No. 810, Chicago, IL 60601 USA Tel 770-609-9833
E-mail: info@13thandjoan.com
Web site: www.13thandjoan.com.

15 Minutes to Shift LLC, *(978-1-7348787)* 12029 Stanwood Dr., LA, CA 90066 USA Tel 310-800-0440
E-mail: barbaraligeti@mac.com
Web site: www.shiftpoetry.com.

†1517 Media, *(978-0-8006; 978-0-8066; 978-1-4514; 978-1-5064; 979-8-88983)* Orders Addr.: 411 Washington Ave N, FL 3, Minneapolis, MN 55401-1301 USA (SAN 169-4081) Toll Free Fax: 800-722-7766; Toll Free: 800-328-4648 (orders only); Edit Addr.: 411 Washington Ave N, FL 3, Minneapolis, MN 55401-1301 USA Tel 800-328-4648 800-722-7766; *Imprints:* Fortress Press (Fortress Pr); Augsburg Books (Augsburg Bks); Augsburg Fortress (Augs Fortress); Sparkhouse Family (Sparkhse); Beaming Books (Beaming Bks)
E-mail: customerservice@augsburgfortress.org; info@augsburgfortress.org; subscriptions@augsburgfortress.org; copyright@augsburgfortress.org; international@augsburgfortress.org
Web site: http://www.augsburgfortress.org
Dist(s): **JSTOR**
National Bk. Network
ebrary, Inc.; *CIP.*

1517 Publishing *See* **New Reformation Pubns.**

153 Fish Publishing, *(978-0-9747918)* 230 SW Railroad St., Sheridan, OR 97378-1745 USA.

1537 Pr., *(978-0-692-81624-0; 978-0-578-50588-6)* 1537 1/2 N Commonwealth Ave, Los Angeles, CA 90027 USA Tel 559-991-6031
E-mail: beckmedina@gmail.com
Web site: http://beckmedina.com.

1610 Media, LLC *See* **Appointed Media Group, LLC**

16th Avenue Pr., *(978-0-9742854)* P.O. Box 166, Portage, MI 49081 USA Fax: 269-372-6970
E-mail: theawrites@sbcglobal.net
Web site: http://www.fearnoflame.com.

16th Place Publishing, *(978-0-9745152)* 171 S. 16th Pl., Pocatello, ID 83201 USA
E-mail: brobergbook@yahoo.com
Web site: http://www.stoleninnocencebook.com.

1776 Pr., *(978-0-9825243)* 19 Coleman Rd., Wethersfield, CT 06109 USA.

1-800 ProColor, Incorporated *See* **Robertson Publishing**

1948, *(978-1-7325027)* 21605 Quail Springs Rd., Tehachapi, CA 93561 USA Tel 661-972-2442; Fax: 661-823-4612
E-mail: iwuvmts@live.com.

1948, *(978-0-692-73934-1; 978-0-692-74533-5; 978-0-692-75287-6; 978-0-692-77028-3)* 333 jones Lester Rd., ROXBORO, NC 27574 USA Tel 336-599-8006.

1985Poet LLC, *(978-0-578-67988-4; 978-0-578-78481-6; 978-0-578-78483-0; 979-8-218-04239-4; 979-8-218-04240-0)* 1525 Somerset pl, Marrero, LA 70072 USA Tel 504-232-4404
E-mail: 1985poet@gmail.com
Web site: www.1985poet.com.

1988 *See* **Sofija Zlatanova**

1989, *(978-0-578-45545-7)* 3333 Port Royale Dr. S., Ft. Lauderdale, FL 33308 USA Tel 954-591-6614
E-mail: bunnytrailseries@gmail.com.

1992 *See* **Morgan, Briana**

1996, *(978-0-9998071)* Miramar RWay, BLDG 5112, San Diego, CA 92145 USA Tel 619-813-1254; Fax: 619-813-1254
E-mail: carloocaya15@yahoo.com.

1Ellipsis Press *See* **Ellipsis Pr.**

1st Impression Publishing, *(978-0-9763365)* P.O. Box 10339, Burbank, CA 91510-0339 USA Tel 818-843-1300; Fax: 818-846-5657
E-mail: sahysen@earthlink.net
Web site: http://www.1stimpressionpublishing.com.

1st Word Pr., *(978-0-578-85573-8)* 100 Georgianna Ln., Greenville, SC 29605 USA Tel 864-270-9109
E-mail: seldonpeden@gmail.com.

1st World Library *See* **Groundbreaking Pr.**

1st World Library - Literary Society *Imprint of* **1st World Publishing, Inc.**

1st World Publishing *Imprint of* **1st World Publishing, Inc.**

1st World Publishing, Inc., *(978-0-9638502; 978-1-887472; 978-1-59540; 978-1-4218)* Orders Addr.: 1100 N. 4th St., Suite 9, Fairfield, IA 52556-2169 USA Toll Free: 877-209-5004; *Imprints:* 1st World Publishing (Frst Wrld Pub); 1st World Library - Literary Society (1st Wrld); Sunstar Publishing (SunstarPub)
E-mail: ed@1stworldpublishing.com; order@1stworldpublishing.com; info@1stworldpublishing.com; rodney@1stworldlibrary.org
Web site: http://www.1stworldpublishing.com
Dist(s): **Follett School Solutions**
Ingram Content Group
New Leaf Distributing Co., Inc.

1stBooks Library *See* **AuthorHouse**

1stWorld Library, Limited *See* **1st World Publishing, Inc.**

2 Donn Bks., *(978-0-9770893)* 11354 Links Dr., Reston, VA 20190-4807 USA (SAN 256-7407)
Web site: http://www.2donnbooks.com.

2018, *(978-1-7328064)* 4642 Rowell Point, Colorado Springs, CO 80923 USA Tel 719-491-0963
E-mail: batprime3986@gmail.com.

20/20 Publishing *See* **iLearn.vip**

2020 Vision Pr., *(978-0-9710675)* 2744 Crown Point, Las Cruces, NM 88011 USA Tel 505-532-9693; Fax: 505-532-9694
E-mail: josh@joshhunt.com
Web site: http://www.joshhunt.com.

20th Maine, Inc., *(978-0-9704408)* 859 Lawrence Rd., Pownal, ME 04069-6118 USA
E-mail: pat@20thmaine.com
Web site: http://www.20thmaine.com.

21st Century Pr., *(978-0-9660906; 978-0-9700639; 978-0-9717009; 978-0-9725719; 978-0-9728899; 978-0-9749811; 978-0-9766243; 978-0-9771964; 978-0-9779535; 978-0-9817769; 978-0-9824428; 978-0-9827616; 978-0-9838359; 978-0-9894317; 978-0-9911004; 978-0-9863864; 978-0-9981392; 978-1-951774; 978-1-961167) 3308 S. Meadowlark Ave., Springfield, MO 65807 USA Tel 417-889-4803; Fax: 417-889-2210; Toll Free: 800-658-0284; Imprints:* Sonship Press (Sonship Pr) Do not confuse with 21st Century Press in Southlake, TX
E-mail: lee@21stcenturypress.com
Web site: https://www.21stcenturypress.com
Dist(s): **Anchor Distributors**
CreateSpace Independent Publishing Platform
Send The Light Distribution LLC
Two Rivers Distribution.

21st Century Pubs., *(978-0-9607298)* 1320 Curt Gowdy Dr., Cheyenne, WY 82009 USA (SAN 239-1740) Tel 307-638-2254
E-mail: chismaturi@prodigy.net
Web site: http://www.triplecrownwinnerearlsande.com
Dist(s): **Emery-Pratt Co.**
Blackwell.

21st Century Publishing Hse. (CHN) *(978-7-5391; 978-7-88861; 978-7-900386; 978-7-5568) Dist. by* **Chinasprout.**

22 West Bks., *(978-0-9767788)* Orders Addr.: P.O. Box 155, Sheldonville, MA 02070-0155 USA
E-mail: chris@22wb.com
Web site: http://www.22wb.com.

23rd St. Publishing, *(978-0-9800821)* Orders Addr.: P.O. Box 863734, Plano, TX 75086-3734 USA (SAN 855-1421) Tel 214-717-7244
E-mail: stacy@23rdstpublishing.com
Web site: http://23rdStPublishing.com
Dist(s): **Follett School Solutions.**

25 Dreams Educational Media, *(978-0-9768019)* 8622 Bellanca Ave., Suite J, Los Angeles, CA 90045 USA.

2B Pr., *(978-0-9765430)* 206 Clear Springs, Peachtree City, GA 30269 USA Tel 770-487-1348
E-mail: tami@2bpress.com
Web site: http://www.2bpress.com.

2DHse. Publishing, *(978-0-615-75181-8; 978-0-615-76647-8; 978-0-9895256)* 2075 Clover Dr., Monterey Park, CA 91735 USA Tel 818-793-9252
E-mail: 2dhouse@earthlink.net.

2Giggles, *(978-0-9801020)* 25811 Mill Pond Ln., Spring, TX 77373 USA
E-mail: vineandfig@gmail.com.

2Lakes Publishing, *(978-0-9722400; 978-0-578-52353-8)* Orders Addr.: 3661 Natalie Way, Bandon, OR 97411 USA
E-mail: heidi2lakes@2lakespublishing.com
Web site: http://www.2lakespublishing.com.

2MPower, *(978-0-9767046)* 25231 Grissom Rd., Laguna Hills, CA 92653-5237 USA Tel 949-837-1268; Fax: 949-470-0659
E-mail: amovigen@yahoo.com
Web site: http://www.2mpwr.com.

2Nimble, *(978-1-7324371; 978-1-970109)* P.O. Box 5958, Philadelphia, PA 19137 USA; *Imprints:* AnewPress, Inc. (MYID_K_ANEWPRE)
E-mail: operations@2nimble.com
Web site: www.2nimble.com.

2Nimble, Inc. *See* **2Nimble**

3 Fates Pr., *(978-1-940938)* 2025 Bell Rd., Morgantown, IN 46160 USA Tel 269-235-4737; *Imprints:* Line By Lion Publications (LineByLion)
E-mail: admin@3fatespress.com
Web site: www.3fatespress.com.

3 Pals Media, LLC, *(978-0-9770960)* 424 Greenleaf Ave., Burlington, WA 98233 USA Tel 360-755-2299; Fax: 360-755-8010
Web site: http://www.pumpkinpatchpals.com.

3,000 Letters, *(978-0-9983577)* 240 e. Connecticut Ave., southern pines, NC 28387 USA Tel 910-690-3190
E-mail: gayvinpowers07@gmail.com
Web site: www.gayvinpowers.com.

302 Publishing, *(978-0-9790165)* 9139 SW Excalibur Pl., Portland, OR 97219-9721 USA Tel 503-246-2499 (phone/fax).

333 Publishing, *(978-0-578-23196-9)* 2020, 412 Vista Cove, Victoria, TX 77904 USA.

336Love *See* **Quinnova Pr.**

341 Enterprise, *(978-0-578-62340-5; 978-0-578-65661-8; 978-1-7353435; 978-1-7370688; 979-8-9891268)* 130 Alton Terr. 0, ROSSVILLE, GA 30741 USA Tel 4236539305
E-mail: 341enterprise@gmail.com
Dist(s): **Ingram Content Group.**

353rd Regimental History Project, *(978-0-9748916)* 2650 N. 64th, Wavnatusa, WI 53213-1407 USA Tel 414-444-7120
E-mail: suzannb@wyoming.com.

35th Parallel Concepts LLC, *(978-0-9747615)* 301 Hollyhock Dr, Matthews, NC 28104 USA
Dist(s): **Unique Bks., Inc.**

360 Degrees *Imprint of* **Tiger Tales**

360 Marketing, LLC, *(978-0-9702654)* 6 Trumbull St., Saintnington, CT 06378 USA Tel 860-535-2240; Fax: 860-535-3243 (call first)
E-mail: three60mrk@aol.com; claudia@chasem2.com.

360 Size Up, *(978-1-7368886)* 318 walker brow ridge rd nw, CLEVELAND, TN 37312 USA Tel 423-504-6995
E-mail: danking120@aol.com
Web site: www.danfireman.com.

3BL Publishing LLC, *(978-1-7355914)* 101 glouchester Rd. apt 9, Lafayette, LA 70506 USA Tel 985-248-2765
E-mail: Brandi.3BLPublishing@yahoo.com
Web site: 3blPublish.com.

3-C Institute for Social Development, *(978-0-9779290; 978-0-9789871; 978-1-934409)* 1903 N. Harrison Ave., Suite 101, Cary, NC 27513 USA Tel 919-677-0101; Fax: 919-677-0112
E-mail: info@3cisd.com
Web site: http://www.3cisd.com.

3cs Publishing, The, *(978-0-9773341)* P.O. Box 8096, Silver Spring, MD 20907 USA
Web site: http://www.the3cs.com.

3D Alley, Inc., *(978-0-9776845)* 4525 Harding Rd., Suite 317, Nashville, TN 37205 USA.

3DLegacy, *(978-1-7361002)* 1100 S. Raven Rd. 0, SHOREWOOD, IL 60404 USA Tel 2144053697
E-mail: katie@3dlegacy.org
Dist(s): **Ingram Content Group.**

3DTotal.com (GBR) *(978-0-9551530) Dist. by* **Consort Bk Sales.**

3G Publishing, (*978-0-692-55052-6; 978-0-578-68341-6; 978-0-578-84360-5; 978-1-7365353*) 4415 S. Gary Ave., Tulsa, OK 74105 USA
Dist(s): **CreateSpace Independent Publishing Platform.**

3G Publishing, Inc., (*978-0-9833544; 978-0-9854968; 978-1-941247; 978-1-956382*) 3508 Pk. Lake Ln., Norcross, GA 30092 USA Tel 404-553-1566; Fax: 770-676-0626 Do not confuse with 3G Publishing, Inc in New Berlin, WI
E-mail: myrna.gale@gmail.com
Web site: 3gpublishinginc.com.

3H Dowsing International LLC, (*978-0-9656653; 978-1-932229*) W10160 Cty. Rd. C, Wautoma, WI 54982 USA Tel 920-787-4747; Fax: 920-787-2006
E-mail: ilovedowsing@hotmail.com
Web site: http://store.yahoo.com/dowsing.

3N Media Group, (*978-0-9741686*) P.O. Box 705, Morris Plains, NJ 07950 USA Fax: 240-220-0500
E-mail: 3nmediagrp@optonline.net.

3perfections, (*978-0-9759909*) 833 Great Oaks Trail, Eagan, MN 55123 USA Tel 651-905-1098
E-mail: perfections3@aol.com
Web site: http://www.3perfections.com.

3rd Coast Bks., (*978-1-946743*) 11111 W. Little York Rd., No. 222, houston, TX 77041 USA Tel 713-937-9184
E-mail: rita.mills@comcast.net
Web site: http://www.3rdCoastBooks.com.

4 Childrens Sake Pubns., (*978-0-9752982*) Orders Addr.: P.O. Box 594, Moosup, CT 06354 USA; Edit Addr.: 357 N. Main St., Moosup, CT 06354 USA.

4 Sonkist Angels *See* **Four Sonkist Angels**

4000 Years of Writing History, (*978-0-9748786*) P.O. Box 484, Redondo Beach, CA 90277-0484 USA
Web site: http://www.lmlk.com.

405 Pubns., (*978-0-9790832; 978-0-692-91923-1; 978-0-692-08339-0*) Orders Addr.: 10026 S. Linn Ave, Oklahoma City, OK 73159 USA (SAN 852-3754); *Imprints:* Three Ring Circus Publishing House, Inc. (MYID_I_THREE R)
E-mail: quimbysneet@gmail.com
Web site: http://www.quimbysneet.com
Dist(s): **Ingram Content Group.**

423-508-9642 *See* **Noble Success Publishing**

43 Degrees North LLC, (*978-0-9744444*) P.O. Box 781, Wilson, NY 14172 USA Tel 716-751-3604; Fax: 716-751-0105
E-mail: jeff@tailgatetrivia.com
Web site: http://www.tailgatetrivia.com.

4336 Pr., LLC, (*978-1-7335606*) 316 Ladson Rd., Silver Spring, MD 20901 USA
E-mail: 4336press@gmail.com
Web site: 4336press.com.

44 Enterprises, (*978-0-615-22510-4; 978-0-615-24951-3*) 820A W. 47th St., Savannah, GA 31405 USA.

45th Parallel Press *Imprint of* **Cherry Lake Publishing**

47North *Imprint of* **Amazon Publishing**

499, (*978-1-7335569; 978-1-7379693*) 500 Westover Dr., No. 13616, Sanford, NC 27330 USA Tel 336-917-9783; *Imprints:* Evolved Teacher Press (MYID_D_EVOLVED)
E-mail: gahmya@evolvedteacher.com
Web site: www.evolvedteacher.com.

49th Avenue Productions, (*978-0-578-87791-4; 978-0-578-87792-1*) 15 Joseph St., Manalapan, NJ 07726 USA Tel 845-304-6701
E-mail: chris.curti@yahoo.com.

4All Ages LLC, (*978-0-9787986*) 5 Murdock Rd., Suite 100, East Rockaway, NY 11518 USA (SAN 851-643X) Tel 516-561-3146
E-mail: laws123@aol.com
Web site: http://www.colorpets.com.

4Elliott Publishing, Inc., (*978-0-9846963*) 6829 NW 15th Ave., Miami, FL 33142 USA Tel 786-277-2693
E-mail: sxye320@yahoo.comtees.

4Him Publishing, LLC, (*978-0-692-58199-5; 978-0-692-71223-8; 978-0-578-99183-2; 978-0-578-31111-1; 978-0-578-35703-4*) 4442 Buckfield Terr., TREVOSE, PA 19053 USA Tel 215-245-1380.

4N Publishing LLC, (*978-0-9741319; 978-0-9798841*) Orders Addr.: 44-73 21st St., D-6, Long Island City, NY 11101 USA Tel 718-482-1135
E-mail: brendan@4npublishing.com; erin@4npublishing.com; lj@4npublishing.com
Web site: http://www.4npublishing.com.

4RV Pub, (*978-0-9797513; 978-0-9818685; 978-0-9840708; 978-0-9825886; 978-0-9826423; 978-0-9826594; 978-0-9828346; 978-0-9832740; 978-0-9838018; 978-0-9852661; 978-0-9889617; 978-1-940310; 978-1-950074*) 2912 Rankin Terr., Edmond, OK 73013 USA Tel 405-225-6851
E-mail: president@4rvpublishingllc.com
Web site: http://www.4rvpublishingllc.com
Dist(s): **Follett School Solutions.**

4th Dimension Enterprises, Inc., (*978-0-9819088*) 40 Memorial Hwy. Apt. 27N, New Rochelle, NY 10801-8340 USA
E-mail: info@4thdimensionpublishing.com
Web site: http://www.4thdimensionpublishing.com.

4th Division Pr. *Imprint of* **Kurdyla, E L Publishing LLC**

4themasses LLC, (*978-1-7371332*) 410 N oakhurst Dr., Beverly Hills, CA 90210 USA Tel 347-680-2646
E-mail: ricardo@efftwelve.world
Web site: www.efftwelve.world.

4U2B Bks. & Media *Imprint of* **Loyola Pr.**

5 Fold Media LLC *See* **Andy Sanders**

5 Muses Publishing, (*978-0-9786180*) 100 Andover Pk. Ste 150-108, TUKWILA, WA 98188 USA
E-mail: rlpolhill@5musespublishing.com
Web site: http://www.5MusesPublishing.com.

5 Prince Publishing, (*978-0-615-46134-2; 978-0-615-52891-5; 978-0-9848529; 978-0-9853345; 978-0-615-64941-2; 978-0-615-65268-9; 978-0-615-65747-9; 978-0-615-66869-7; 978-0-615-68734-6; 978-0-615-68919-7; 978-1-939217; 978-1-63112*) P.O. Box 865, Arvada, CO 80001 USA Tel 303-257-0389
E-mail: books@5princebooks.com
Web site: www.5princebooks.com
Dist(s): **CreateSpace Independent Publishing Platform**
Ingram Content Group
Smashwords.

5 Star Pubns., LLC, (*978-0-9843881; 978-0-9832473; 978-0-9854386*) c/o Tlj Bookstore, Llc, 9134 Piscataway Rd. No. 805, Clinton, MD 20735 USA
E-mail: shawn5star@yahoo.com; shawncvalentine@yahoo.com
Web site: http://www.5starpublications.net
Dist(s): **Icon Distribution.**

5 Star Stories, Inc., (*978-0-9659470*) Orders Addr.: 14625 Greenville St., Houston, TX 77015-4711 USA Tel 713-455-1073; Fax: 713-583-7017
E-mail: isellfantasy@hotmail.com
Web site: http://www.TexasSecedes.com.

50/50 Publishing *See* **Soulo Communications**

5,6 Pickup Sticks Publishing, (*978-0-9762145*) 2493 Sunridge Ave., SE, Atlanta, GA 30315 USA Tel 404-627-9132
E-mail: tcmac1@bellsouth.net.

5am Pr., LLC, (*978-0-692-81057-6*) 27034 Glenside Ln., OLMSTED TWP, OH 44138 USA Tel 216-262-7725
E-mail: keith@messypopup.com
Web site: http://www.messypopup.com.

5m Publishing (GBR) (*978-0-9530150; 978-0-9555011; 978-1-910455; 978-1-78918*) *Dist. by* **IPG Chicago.**

5SailPublishing, (*978-1-7341248*) 14045 Hazelwood Ct, Jacksonville, FL 32224 USA Tel 828-514-3139
E-mail: evensen_marie@yahoo.com.

64Square Publishing, (*978-1-943748*) 701 Ideal Way, Charlotte, NC 28203 USA Tel 704-460-6767
E-mail: darinkennedy@mac.com.

671 Press *See* **Octane Pr.**

6-mile Roots, (*978-0-9771255*) 1469 260th, Marion, KS 66861 USA Tel 620-924-5254
E-mail: joel@hillsborofreepress.com.

7 Cats Press *Imprint of* **Gibbs Smith, Publisher**

7 Robots, Inc., (*978-0-9778454*) 714 Washington Ave., Suite No. 9, New York, NY 11238 USA
Web site: http://www.7robots.com
Dist(s): **Diamond Comic Distributors, Inc.**

711Press *Imprint of* **Vendera Publishing**

716 Productions, (*978-0-9795529*) 3200 Airport Ave., Suite 16, Santa Monica, CA 90405 USA
Web site: http://learningwhoweare.com.

7Seven Spark Publishing, (*978-0-9797699; 978-0-578-32373-2; 979-8-218-00179-7; 979-8-218-23138-5; 979-8-218-23540-6; 979-8-218-24658-7; 979-8-218-25244-1; 979-8-218-27393-4*)
E-mail: lesleynu@yahoo.com
Web site: www.lesleynurse.com
Dist(s): **Lulu Pr., Inc.**

7th Generation *Imprint of* **BPC**

7th Seal Advantage, LLC, (*978-1-7377864*) 417 Glenshire, Glenview, IL 60025 USA Tel 312-244-0201
E-mail: 7thsealadvantage@gmail.com
Web site: 7thsealadvantage.com.

7th Sign Publishing, (*978-0-9890767; 978-0-692-20201-2; 978-0-692-30458-7; 978-0-692-36761-2; 978-0-692-36762-9; 978-0-692-36763-6; 978-0-692-40896-4; 978-0-692-53681-0; 978-0-692-79646-7; 978-0-692-82683-6; 978-0-692-82923-3; 978-0-692-85528-7; 978-0-692-85589-8; 978-0-692-87668-8; 978-0-692-96681-5; 978-0-692-97358-5; 978-0-692-16351-1; 978-0-578-41335-8; 978-0-578-45880-9; 978-0-578-49867-6; 978-0-578-60101-4; 978-0-578-60102-1; 978-0-578-65283-2; 978-0-578-72252-8; 978-0-578-72255-9; 978-0-578-74107-9; 978-) 4331 Rosemeade Nr. 528, Dallas, TX 75287 USA Tel 281-217-5479*
E-mail: Carlos.Harleaux@gmail.com.

80 West Publishing, Inc., (*978-0-9763417*) 2222 Ponce de Leon Blvd., 6th Flr., Coral Gables, FL 33134 USA Tel 305-448-8117; Fax: 305-448-8453
E-mail: joellen@adkinsadv.com.

826 National *See* **826 Valencia**

826 Valencia, (*978-0-9768457; 978-0-9770844; 978-0-9779289; 978-0-9790073; 978-1-934750; 978-1-948644; 979-8-88694*) 44 Gough St., San Francisco, CA 94103 USA
E-mail: field.ops@826national.org
Web site: www.826national.org
Dist(s): **Publishers Group West (PGW).**

826michigan, (*978-0-9779289; 978-0-9827293; 978-0-9966315*) 115 E. Liberty St., Ann Arbor, MI 48104-2109 USA
Web site: http://www.826michigan.org.

8-Ball Express, Inc., (*978-0-9747273*) 316 California, Suite 529, Reno, NV 89509-1650 USA Tel 415-776-1596 (for wholesale orders); Toll Free: 877-368-2255 (for retail sales only)
E-mail: rgivens@toast.net
Web site: http://www.8-ballbible.com.

8N Publishing, LLC, (*978-0-9992523; 979-8-9879774*) P.O. Box 972364, Ypsilanti, MI 48197 USA Tel 734-985-8519
E-mail: SJLomas9@gmail.com.

90-Minute Bks., (*978-0-692-41259-6; 978-0-692-41598-6; 978-0-692-41924-3; 978-0-692-42187-1; 978-0-692-42276-2; 978-0-692-42488-9; 978-0-692-42529-9; 978-0-692-42642-5; 978-0-692-42958-7; 978-0-692-43030-9; 978-0-692-43715-5; 978-0-692-44217-3; 978-0-692-44229-6; 978-0-692-44461-0; 978-0-692-44481-8; 978-0-692-44558-7; 978-0-692-44887-8; 978-0-692-44901-1; 978-0-692-44976-9; 978-0-692-45175-5; 978-0-692-45521-0; 978-0-692-45834-1; 978-0-692-46013-9; 978-0-692-46499-1; 978-0-692-46808-1; 978-0-692-47243-9;) 302 Martinique Dr., Winter Haven, FL 33884 USA Tel 863-318-0464*
E-mail: production@90minutebooks.com
Web site: http://www.90minutebooks.com/
Dist(s): **CreateSpace Independent Publishing Platform.**

978-0-8283Branden Books *See* **Branden Bks.**

A & B Books *See* **A & B Distributors & Pubs. Group**

A & B Distributors & Pubs. Group, (*978-1-881316; 978-1-886433*) Div. of A&B Distributors, 1000 Atlantic Ave., Brooklyn, NY 11238 USA (SAN 630-9216) Tel 718-783-7808; Fax: 718-783-7267; Toll Free: 877-542-6657; 146 Lawrence St., Brooklyn, NY 11201 (SAN 631-385X)
E-mail: maxtay@webspan.net
Dist(s): **D & J Bk. Distributors**
Red Sea Pr.

A & D Bks., (*978-0-9743294*) 3708 E. 45th St., Tulsa, OK 74135 USA Tel 918-748-4348 (phone/fax)
E-mail: a_dbooks@live.com.

A & E Children's Pr., (*978-0-9728134*) 6107 S. Jericho Way, Centennial, CO 80016 USA
E-mail: maked4@aol.com.

A & E Sivells Pubns. *Imprint of* **Word For Word Publishing Co.**

A & L Communications, Inc., (*978-0-9714320*) 1946 Magnolia Crest Ln., Sugar Land, TX 77478 USA
E-mail: allysoncward@yahoo.com
Web site: http://www.algiershistory.com
Dist(s): **Forest Sales & Distributing Co.**

A & M Writing and Publishing,, (*978-0-9764824; 978-0-9861841; 978-1-7330228*) 141 Saratoga Avenue, No. 1317, Santa Clara, CA 95051 USA Tel 408-244-8053; Fax: 408-244-8098
E-mail: ctillson@amwriting.com
Web site: http://www.amwriting.com
Dist(s): **Partners Bk. Distributing, Inc.**

A & P Publishing and Games, LLC, (*978-0-578-41366-2; 978-0-578-46505-0; 978-0-578-46506-7*) 1714 Ave. C, Danbury, TX 77534 USA Tel 713-817-1267
E-mail: willabel01@yahoo.com
Dist(s): **Independent Pub.**

A & W Enterprises, (*978-0-9617896*) P.O. Box 8133, Roanoke, VA 24014 USA (SAN 665-603X) Tel 540-427-1154; Toll Free: 800-484-1492 (ext. 4267)
E-mail: gwalker@interlink.com.

A B C-123 Publishing *See* **Dewey Does Corp, A**

A B C-Clio Information Services *See* **ABC-CLIO, LLC**

A B Publishing, (*978-1-881545; 978-1-59765*) P.O. Box 83, North Star, MI 48862-0083 USA Toll Free: 800-882-6443
E-mail: abpub@hotmail.com; joabpub@hotmail.com
Web site: http://www.abpub.com
Dist(s): **Send The Light Distribution LLC**
Spring Arbor Distributors, Inc.

A Beautiful, Wonderful Me LLC, (*978-0-9986624*) 1503 Main St No. 172, Grandview, MO 64030 USA Tel 816-277-7467
E-mail: abeautifulwonderfulme@gmail.com.

A Blessed Heritage Educational Resources, (*978-0-9759320; 978-0-9767866; 978-1-7326022*) 10602 Redwood Dr., Baytown, TX 77520 USA
E-mail: belinda.bullard@blessedheritage.com
Web site: http://www.blessedheritage.com.

A+ Bk. Publishing, (*978-1-929819*) Orders Addr.: P.O. Box 250165, Franklin, MI 48025-0165 USA Tel 248-223-9322; Fax: 248-223-9161; Edit Addr.: 29233 Wellington Ct., No. 61, Southfield, MI 48034 USA
E-mail: kpcartwright@ameritech.net
Dist(s): **Capstone.**

A Book's Mind, (*978-0-9828751; 978-0-9883288; 978-1-939828; 978-1-944255; 978-1-949563; 978-1-953284; 978-1-961194*) P.O. Box 272847, Fort Collins, CO 80527 USA Tel 877-839-9984 (phone/fax)
E-mail: info@abooksmind.com
Web site: http://abooksmind.com
Dist(s): **Ingram Content Group.**

A. Borough Bks., (*978-0-9640606; 978-1-893597*) Orders Addr.: 3901 Silver Bell Dr., Charlotte, NC 28211 USA Tel 704-364-1788; Fax: 704-366-9079; Toll Free: 800-843-8490
E-mail: humorbooks@aol.com
Dist(s): **Parnassus Bk. Distributors.**

A Boy Named Jack, (*978-0-9987153*) 6383 W Conestoga St, Beverly Hills, FL 34465 USA Tel 813-727-5551
E-mail: aboynamedjack@yahoo.com
Web site: aboynamedjack.us.

A Buen Paso S.C.P. (ESP) (*978-84-937211; 978-84-938036; 978-84-939414; 978-84-940533; 978-84-941579; 978-84-942854*) *Dist. by* **Lectorum Pubns.**

A Cappela Publishing, (*978-0-9656309; 978-0-9724979; 978-0-9779139; 978-0-9818933; 978-0-9846177; 978-0-9850202*) P.O. Box 3691, Sarasota, FL 34230-3691 USA (SAN 253-567X) Tel 941-351-2050; Fax: 941-351-4735; *Imprints:* Advocate House (Advoca Hse) Do not confuse with A Cappella Publishing, Los Angeles, CA
E-mail: acappub@aol.com
Web site: http://www.acappela.com; http://www.lillythelash.com.

A Cappella Bks., (*978-1-55652*) 814 N. Franklin, Chicago, IL 60610 USA Tel 312-337-0747; Fax: 312-640-0542; Toll Free: 800-888-4741
E-mail: publish@ipgbook.com; orders@ipgbook.com
Web site: http://www.ipgbook.com.

Caribbean Experience Con Amor, LLC, A, (*978-0-9797641*) P.O. Box 1155, Avondale, PA 19311 USA Tel 610-806-2013 Alternate #610-806-2013
Web site: http://www.marisadejesus.com.

A Cupcake & Giggles Publishing, (*978-0-9963847*) 902 Greenhouse Patio Dr. NW, Kennesaw, GA 30144 USA Tel 4047881379
Dist(s): **CreateSpace Independent Publishing Platform.**

Dewey Does Corp, A, (*978-0-9711474; 978-0-578-16435-9; 978-0-578-25558-3*) Orders Addr.: P.O. Box 30096, Staten Island, NY 10303 USA Fax: 718-980-4416; 718-351-4863; Toll Free: 866-339-3936; Edit Addr.: P.O. Box 30096, Staten Island, NY 10303 USA; P.O. Box 30096, Staten Island, NY 30096
E-mail: thomas@deweydoes.com; contact@deweydoes.com
Web site: http://www.deweydoes.com; www.deweydoes.org.

A Different Kind of Safari LLC, (*978-0-9890134; 978-1-7350061*) 39 Skunk Hollow Rd., Jericho, VT 05495 USA Tel 802-238-0822
E-mail: hchipp@comcast.net
Web site: www.adifferentkindofsafari.com.

AEVAC, Inc., (*978-0-913356*) 7 Silver Lake Dr., Summit, NJ 07901-3233 USA (SAN 204-5567).

A H W Publishing, (*978-0-9741434*) 1124 W. 19th Ave., Spokane, WA 99203 USA (SAN 255-4070)
E-mail: annifrommainz@dc4pc.net.

AIMS International Bks., Inc., (*978-0-922852*) 7709 Hamilton Ave., Cincinnati, OH 45231-3103 USA (SAN 630-270X) Tel 513-521-5590; Fax: 513-521-5592; Toll Free: 800-733-2067
E-mail: aimsbooks@fuse.net
Web site: http://www.aimsbooks.com
Dist(s): **Shen's Bks.**

A i T/Planet Lar, (*978-0-9676847; 978-0-9709360; 978-1-932051*) 2034 47th Ave., San Francisco, CA 94116 USA Tel 415-504-7516 (phone/fax)
E-mail: larry@ait-planetlar.com
Web site: http://www.ait-planetlar.com
Dist(s): **Diamond Comic Distributors, Inc.**
Diamond Bk. Distributors
L P C Group.

A JuneOne Production *Imprint of* **JuneOne Publishing Hub**

AK Peters, Ltd., (*978-1-56881; 978-1-138-05124-9*) 5 Commonwealth Rd. Suite 2c, Natick, MA 01760 USA (SAN 299-1810) Tel 508-651-0887 All inquiries; Fax: 508-651-0889; 7625 Empire Dr., Florence, KY 41042
E-mail: service@akpeters.com
Web site: http://www.akpeters.com
Dist(s): **Follett School Solutions**
MyiLibrary
Taylor & Francis Group.

A K Peters/CRC Pr. *Imprint of* **CRC Pr. LLC**

A Kidz World *Imprint of* **ABUAA, Inc.**

ALPI International, Ltd., (*978-1-886647*) 1685 34th St., Oakland, CA 94608 USA Tel 510-655-6456; Fax: 510-655-2093; Toll Free: 800-678-2574
E-mail: becky@alpi.net.

AMG Pubs., (*978-0-89957; 978-1-61715; 978-1-63070*) Subs. of AMG Publishing Inc., Orders Addr.: P.O. Box 22000, Chattanooga, TN 37422 USA Tel 423-894-6060; Fax: 423-894-9511; Toll Free Fax: 800-265-6690; Toll Free: 800-266-4977; Edit Addr.: 6815 Shallowford Rd., Chattanooga, TN 37421 USA (SAN 211-3074) Toll Free Fax: 800-266-4577; 800-265-6690; *Imprints:* Living Ink Books (Liv Ink Bks)
E-mail: trevor@amgpublishers.com; sales@AMGpublishers.com
Web site: http://www.amgpublishers.com; http://www.livinginkbooks.com
Dist(s): **Anchor Distributors**
Spring Arbor Distributors, Inc.

AMICA Publishing Hse., (*978-1-884187*) Div. of AMICA International, 844 Industry Dr., No. 20, Seattle, WA 98188-3410 USA Tel 206-467-1035; Fax: 206-467-1522
E-mail: amica@ix.netcom.com
Web site: http://www.amicaint.com.

AMSC, Adventures in Math & Social Studies for Children, (*978-1-889639*) Orders Addr.: 818 W. Grover St., Lynden, WA 98264 USA Tel 360-354-4412; Toll Free: 800-306-1772
E-mail: math1@earthlink.net.

Matter of Rhyme, A, (*978-1-7330943; 978-1-958741*) 335 Schrader Rd., Killeen, TX 76542 USA Tel 254-554-8774
E-mail: sheri@amatterofrhyme.com
Web site: amatterofrhyme.com.

A N A D E M, Incorporated *See* **Anadem Publishing, Inc.**

A N R Publications *See* **Univ. of California, Agriculture and Natural Resources**

A Neat Read Publishing LLC, (*978-0-578-19321-2; 978-0-692-93443-2; 978-1-7321596; 978-1-7330555; 978-1-7357612; 978-1-956576*) 3018 Brush St NE, Canton, OH 44705 USA Tel 330-452-1522
E-mail: clarknoveltysign@aol.com
Web site: http://aneatreadpublishing.com.

A New Day..A New Way!, (*978-0-9749177*) 5525B Via La Mesa, Laguna Woods, CA 92637 USA Tel 949-340-0615; Fax: 949-723-0030
E-mail: kathleenscott@anewday-anewway.com; kathleen_scott@sbcglobal.net
Web site: http://www.anewday-anewway.com
Dist(s): **New Leaf Distributing Co., Inc.**

APTE, Inc., (*978-1-889651; 978-1-931872; 978-1-932736; 978-1-933229*) 820 Church St., Suite 300, Evanston, IL 60201 USA Toll Free: 800-494-1112
E-mail: pierred@apte.com; sally@apte.com
Web site: http://www.apte.com
Dist(s): **Brodart Co.**
Educational Resources
Follett School Solutions
Learning Services.

A PAR Educational, LLC, (*978-0-578-12712-5; 978-0-9973365*) 300 Adams Dr. Apt 301, McKees Rocks , PA 15136 USA.

ARO Publishing Co., (*978-0-89868*) Box 193, 398 S. 1100 W., Provo, UT 84601 USA (SAN 212-6370) Tel 801-377-8218; Fax: 801-818-0616
E-mail: arobook@yahoo.com
Dist(s): **Forest Hse. Publishing Co., Inc.**

A Road to Discovery Series Guide *Imprint of* **Perry Heights Pr.**

A. Rose *See* **Rose, A.**

SDA Publishing, Inc., *(978-0-9632319)* 904 Forest Lake Dr., Lakeland, FL 33809 USA Tel 841-859-2194.

SM International, *(978-0-87170; 978-1-61503; 978-1-62708)* 9639 Kinsman Rd., Materials Park, OH 44073-0002 USA (SAN 204-7586) Tel 440-338-5151; Fax: 440-338-4634; Toll Free: 800-336-5152 Do not confuse with ASM International, Inc., Fort Lauderdale, FL
E-mail: karen.marken@asminternational.org; madrid.tramble@asminternational.org; scott.henry@asminternational.org; sue.sellers@asminternational.org; memberservicecenter@asminternational.org
Web site: http://www.asminternational.org
Dist(s): **ebrary, Inc.**

alty Rim Publishing, A, *(978-1-7352763)* 20 ELLEN AVE, MOUNT PLEASANT, SC 29464 USA Tel 704-517-4500
E-mail: julieweldon123@yahoo.com.

Story Plus Children Bks., *(978-0-9778477)* Div. of Top Award, Inc., P.O. Box 1174, Pine Lake, GA 30072-1174 USA (SAN 850-3907) Tel 404-667-2619
E-mail: astoryplu@comcast.net
Web site: http://www.astoryplus.com.

A StoryPlus *See* **A Story Plus Children Bks.**

A to Z Publishing, LLC *See* **Summer Storm Publishing, LLC**

Trio of Mermaids Publishing, A, *(978-0-9893075; 979-8-9850207)* 2873 SW 85th Ave., Miramar, FL 33025 USA Tel 954-391-7520
E-mail: Crimpy79@hotmail.com.

A. V. P., Incorporated *See* **IBE, Inc.**

A. W. Ink, Inc., *(978-0-9820932)* P.O. Box 1184, Kamas, UT 84036-1184 USA
E-mail: lesliesaunders@kw.com.

A2Z Bks. Publishing, *(978-1-943284; 978-1-955148)* 1990 Young Rd, Lithonia, GA 30058 USA Tel 770-808-4478
E-mail: sdoverharris@gmail.com
Web site: www.A2ZBooksPublishing.com.

A3 Publishing *See* **Burnett Young Books**

A3D Impressions, *(978-0-578-19392-2; 978-0-578-19453-0; 978-0-578-20193-1; 978-0-578-20194-8; 978-1-7320677; 978-1-7327285; 978-1-7344724; 978-1-7371922; 979-8-9864049; 979-8-9890817)* 4335 E Whitman St., Tucson, AZ 85711 USA
Web site: www.a3dimpressions.com.

A4J Publishing, *(978-0-9831372)* P.O. Box 1101, Orlando, FL 32802 USA Tel 678-358-9820; Fax: 407-237-0135
E-mail: vikki@a4jpublishing.com
Web site: www.a4jpublishing.com.

AAA POP, *(978-0-9762282)* 4147 S. Tenmile Lake, Lakeside, OR 97449 USA
Web site: http://www.aaapop.com.

AAA Reality Games LLC, *(978-0-9837264)* 11693 San Vicente Blvd. Suite 380, Los Angeles, CA 90049 USA Tel 310-696-1045
E-mail: hartgetzen@hotmail.com
Dist(s): **Smashwords.**

Aaduna, *(978-0-9768626)* 2021 Del Norte Ave., Saint Louis, MO 63117 USA Tel 314-647-3437
E-mail: mroach@thecollegeschool.org
Web site: http://www.senecorps.com.

Aakenbaaken & Kent, *(978-1-938436; 978-1-958022)* 2206 White Oak Dr., Valdosta, GA 31602 USA Tel 917-607-8263
E-mail: akeditor@inbox.com.

Açedrex Publishing *See* **Acedrex Publishing**

A&D Xtreme *Imprint of* **ABDO Publishing Co.**

A&J Publishing LLC, *(978-1-943346)* 3266 Hartwell St., Johns Island, SC 29455 USA Tel 843-670-2642
E-mail: geoffcollins66@hotmail.com
Web site: theajadventures.com
Dist(s): **INscribe Digital**
Independent Pubs. Group.

A&M Moonlight Creations, *(978-1-938783)* 5848 Birchwood Dr, Mentor, OH 44060 USA Tel 440-257-5008
E-mail: comboj2@yahoo.com
Web site: www.mortalrealmwitch.com.

AAO Publishing, *(978-0-9786431)* a/o Melody Farloe, P.O. Box 6208, Beverly Hills, CA 90212 USA
E-mail: puffybuffy1@yahoo.com
Web site: http://www.puffybuffy.com.

Aardvark Global Publishing, *(978-0-9770328; 978-1-933570; 978-1-59971; 978-1-4276)* 9587 S. Grandview Dr., Sandy, UT 84092 USA Do not confuse with Aardvark Global Publishing, Atlanta, GA
E-mail: info@eckohousepublishing.com
Web site: http://eckohousepublishing.com/; http://aardvarkglobalpublishing.com/; http://eckobooks.com
Dist(s): **AK Pr. Distribution**
Follett School Solutions
Lulu Pr., Inc.
SPD-Small Pr. Distribution.

Aardvark Publishing, *(978-0-615-13532-8; 978-0-615-13673-8; 978-0-615-14219-7; 978-0-615-17808-0)* 1615 Shannon Rd., Girard, OH 44420 USA
E-mail: info@aardvarkpublishers.com
Web site: http://www.aardvarkpublishers.com
Dist(s): **Lulu Pr., Inc.**

Aardvark's Weedpatch Pr., *(978-0-9755567)* P.O. Box 1841, Rogue River, OR 97537-1841 USA
Web site: http://www.aardvarksweedpatch.com.

AARO Publishing, *(978-1-893563)* Orders Addr.: P.O. Box 1281, Palisade, CO 81526 USA; Edit Addr.: P.O. Box 1281 Palisade, Co 81526, Palisade, CO 81526 USA (SAN 255-7185) Tel 970-314-7690 (phone/fax)970 985 4018
E-mail: carwe@earthlink.net
Web site: http://www.snowff.com
Dist(s): **Follett School Solutions.**

Aaron Bk. Publishing, *(978-0-9819195)* 1093 Bristol Caverns Hwy., Bristol, TN 37620 USA (SAN 856-924X) Tel 423-212-1208
E-mail: info@aaronbookpublishing.com
Web site: http://www.aaronbookpublishing.com.

Aaron C Ministries, *(978-1-933519)* 1005 Pine Oak Dr., Edmond, OK 73034-5139 USA Tel 405-348-3410
E-mail: bible@jpdawson.com
Web site: http://www.jpdawson.com.

Aaron Levy Pubns., LLC, *(978-1-931463)* 1760 Stumpf Blvd., Gretna, LA 70056 USA Tel 504-258-4332
E-mail: aaronlevy1@aol.com; kelleylevy12@gmail.com
Web site: http://www.goodlifemediallc.com.

Aaron Press *See* **Publishing Assocs., Inc.**

Aaron-Barrada, Inc., *(978-0-9768671; 978-0-615-12767-5)* 79 Valley High, Ruffs Dale, PA 15679 USA Tel 724-696-4332; Fax: 612-545-3210
E-mail: aaronbarradainc@aol.com
Web site: http://www.pottiestickers.com.

Aarow Pr., *(978-0-9749046)* 3215 Buckingham Ave., Lakeland, FL 33803 USA (SAN 255-8653) Tel 863-709-8882 (phone/fax)
E-mail: aarowpress@yahoo.com.

Aawat LLC dba Epoch Publishing, *(978-1-7357970)* 1260 Cleveland Ave, San Diego, CA 92103 USA Tel 858-229-9180
E-mail: kurt@kurtfrancis.com
Web site: kurtfrancis.com.

AB Film Publishing, *(978-0-9897068)* 290 W. 12 Street, Apt. A, New York, NY 10014 USA Tel 212-741-1441
E-mail: abaxter@ramapo.edu
Web site: http://abfilmpublishing9.wordpress.com
Dist(s): **Lulu Pr., Inc.**

AB Rolle Publications *See* **ABR Pubns.**

A-BA-BA HAUS, *(978-0-9965606)* 227 W. 149th Street, Apt. No. 6F, NEW YORK, NY 10039 USA Tel 347-951-6263
E-mail: tmalkovych@gmail.com.

A-BA-BA-HA-LA-MA-HA Pubs. *Imprint of* **Windy Press International Publishing Hse., LLC**

Abacus Bks., Inc., *(978-0-9716292)* Div. of Abacus Bks.com, 1420 58th Ave. N, Saint Petersburg, FL 33703 USA Tel 727-742-3889; Fax: 727-522-0606
E-mail: necole@abacusbooks.com; info@abacusbooks.com
Web site: http://www.abacusbooks.com.

Abadaba Reading LLC, *(978-0-9789473)* P.O. Box 80, Charlottesville, VA 22902-5335 USA (SAN 852-0240)
Web site: http://www.adabadaalphabet.com.

aBASK Publishing, *(978-0-9843855; 978-0-9962399)* 320 National Pl., Apt 5, Longmont, CO 80501-3326 USA
E-mail: Publisher@AbaskPublishing.com; kathygode@yahoo.com
Web site: http://abaskpublishing.com.

Abba's Hse. International Publishing, *(978-0-692-37641-6; 978-0-692-39156-3; 978-0-9971037)* 3015 W. Maplewood Ave, Bellingham, WA 98225 USA Tel 360-201-5574
E-mail: gatheringtheharvest@yahoo.com
Web site: www.anthonyecclesiastes.com.

†ABBE Pubs. Assn. of Washington, D.C., *(978-0-7883; 978-0-88164; 978-0-941864; 978-1-55914)* Orders Addr.: 4111 Gallows Rd., Virginia Div., Annandale, VA 22003 USA (SAN 239-1430)
E-mail: abbe.publishers@verizon.net; vze3hcqz@verizon.net; *CIP.*

Abbeville Kids *Imprint of* **Abbeville Pr., Inc.**

†Abbeville Pr., Inc., *(978-0-7892; 978-0-89659; 978-1-55859)* 137 Varick St., 5th Flr., New York, NY 10013 USA (SAN 211-4755) Tel 212-366-5585; Fax: 212-366-6966; Toll Free: 800-278-2665; 1094 Flex Dr., Jackson, TN 38301; *Imprints:* Abbeville Kids (Abbeville Kids)
E-mail: abbeville@abbeville.com
Web site: http://www.abbeville.com
Dist(s): **Follett School Solutions**
MyiLibrary
Norton, W. W. & Co., Inc.
Penguin Random Hse. Distribution
Penguin Random Hse. LLC
Two Rivers Distribution
ebrary, Inc.; *CIP.*

Abbey Pr., *(978-0-87029)* 1 Hill Dr., Saint Meinrad, IN 47577-0128 USA (SAN 201-2057) Tel 812-357-8215; Fax: 812-357-8388; Toll Free: 800-325-2511
E-mail: customerservice@abbeypress.com
Web site: http://www.abbeypress.com/
Dist(s): **Open Road Integrated Media, Inc.**
Open Road Distribution.

Abbott Avenue Pr., *(978-0-9767514)* 859 Hollywood Way, Suite 258, Burbank, CA 91505 USA
E-mail: info@abbottavenuepress.com
Web site: http://www.abbottavenuepress.com.

Abbott Pr. *Imprint of* **Author Solutions, LLC**

Abby Invents, *(978-1-7321975)* 2250 NW Thorncroft Dr, Apt 332, Hillsboro, OR 97124 USA Tel 404-713-5605
E-mail: arlynesimonphd@gmail.com
Web site: www.arlynesimon.com.

Abby Invents, LLC *See* **Abby Invents**

ABC *Imprint of* **DC Comics**

ABC Bk. *Imprint of* **Michaelson Entertainment**

ABC Bks. (AUS) *(978-0-7333; 978-1-74086; 978-1-921534; 978-0-646-51687-5) Dist. by* **HarperCollins Pubs.**

ABC Bks., *(978-0-9785108)* P.O. Box 2246, Sunnyvale, CA 94087-2246 USA Do not confuse with ABC Books in Plano, TX.

ABC Children's Bks. (AUS) *(978-0-9577218) Dist. by* **HarperCollins Pubs.**

ABC Development, Inc., *(978-0-9767179)* 6869 Stapoint Ct., Suite 107, Winter Park, FL 32792 USA Tel 407-671-6000; Fax: 407-671-6602; Toll Free: 800-222-3053
E-mail: sales@abc-development.com
Web site: http://www.abc-development.com.

ABC for Girls Like Me, *(978-0-692-14101-4; 978-0-692-14664-4; 978-0-692-14714-6; 978-0-692-16271-2; 978-0-578-45811-3; 978-1-7336910)* 530 W Stocker St Apt 206, GLENDALE, CA 91202 USA Tel 404-345-1312
E-mail: goolsbymelanie@gmail.com
Dist(s): **Ingram Content Group.**

ABC Pr., *(978-0-9758622)* 550 Iron Mountain Rd., El Dorado, AR 71730 USA Tel 870-863-5779 Do not confuse with ABC Pr. in Walnut Creek, CA
E-mail: srwood@suddenlink.net
Web site: http://RamonaWoodBooks.com.

ABC Pubs., *(978-0-9772685)* 32 Meadowlark Ln., Willingboro, NJ 08046-2108 USA Tel 609-880-0897
E-mail: fg@abc-advantage.com
Web site: http://www.abc-advantage.com.

ABC Schermerhorn Walters Company *See* **Schermerhorn, Walters Co.**

†ABC-CLIO, LLC, *(978-0-275; 978-0-313; 978-0-8371; 978-0-86569; 978-0-87287; 978-0-87436; 978-0-89789; 978-0-89930; 978-0-903450; 978-0-938865; 978-1-56308; 978-1-56720; 978-1-57607; 978-1-85109; 978-1-58683; 978-1-59158; 978-0-9742537; 978-1-59884; 978-1-4408; 978-1-61069; 979-8-4006; 979-8-216) 147 Castilian Dr., Santa Barbara, CA 93117 USA (SAN 301-5467) Tel 805-968-1911; Fax: 805-685-9685; Toll Free: 800-368-6868; P.O. Box 93116, Goleta, CA 93116 (SAN 857-7099); Imprints:* Praeger (Praeger Pubs); Greenwood (GreenWABC); Libraries Unlimited (LibdUnltd); Linworth Publishing, Incorporated (Linworth)
E-mail: customerservice@abc-clio.com; service@abc-clio.com; salesuk@abc-clio.com
Web site: http://www.abc-clio.com
Dist(s): **Casemate Academic**
Ebsco Publishing
Follett School Solutions
Cengage Gale
Macmillan
MyiLibrary
ebrary, Inc.; *CIP.*

Abccurate Business Ventures, *(978-0-9755341)* P.O. Box 2236, Smyrna, TN 37167 USA Tel 615-831-7100
E-mail: editor@abccurate.com
Web site: http://www.abccurate.com.

ABCDE Academic Bks. for Children's Development Through Education, *(978-0-9754006)* P.O. Box 374, Shrub Oak, NY 10588 USA.

ABCDMoon *See* **ABCDMoon Publishing**

ABCDMoon Publishing, *(978-0-9729216)* P.O. Box 910732, Lexington, KY 40591-0732 USA Tel 859-873-5031
E-mail: tex@charliethemonkey.com; amy@charliethemonkey.com
Web site: http://www.charliethemonkey.com.

ABCs Connection, Inc., *(978-0-9755475)* 1209 Caribou Crossing, Suite 101, Durham, NC 27713 USA Tel 919-451-4991; Fax: 919-484-1980
E-mail: casey_wallace@yahoo.com
Web site: http://www.abcsconnection.com.

ABCS OF GOD, *(978-0-578-44895-4)* 704 Blossom Ln., Lincoln, CA 95648 USA Tel 916-203-8112
E-mail: 704@att.net
Dist(s): **Ingram Content Group.**

ABC's Unlimited *See* **See abc's LC**

Abdelsalam Corp., *(978-0-9755975)* 2499 Trewigtown Rd., Colmar, PA 18915 USA.

Abdiel Productions, *(978-0-9768088)* 4802 Nassau Ave., NE, No. 31, Tacoma, WA 98422-4632 USA.

Abdo & Daughters *Imprint of* **ABDO Publishing Co.**

Abdo & Daughters Publishing *See* **ABDO Publishing Co.**

Abdo Kids *Imprint of* **ABDO Publishing Co.**

Abdo Kids-Jumbo *Imprint of* **ABDO Publishing Co.**

Abdo Kids-Junior *Imprint of* **ABDO Publishing Co.**

†ABDO Publishing Co., *(978-0-939179; 978-1-56239; 978-1-57765; 978-1-59197; 978-1-59679; 978-1-59928; 978-1-59961; 978-1-60270; 978-1-60453; 978-1-61613; 978-1-61714; 978-1-61758; 978-1-61783; 978-1-61784; 978-1-61785; 978-1-61786; 978-1-61787; 978-1-61478; 978-1-61479; 978-1-61480; 978-1-62401; 978-1-62402; 978-1-62403; 978-1-62968; 978-1-62969; 978-1-62970; 978-1-68076; 978-1-68077; 978-1-68078; 978-1-68079; 978-1-68080; 978-1-5321; 978-1-0982; 979-8-3849) Div. of ABDO Publishing Group, Orders Addr.: 8000 W. 78th St. Suite 310, Edina, MN 55439 USA (SAN 662-9172) Tel 952-831-2120; Fax: 952-831-1632; Toll Free Fax: 800-862-3480; Toll Free: 800-800-1312; Edit Addr.: P.O. Box 398166, Minneapolis, MN 55439 USA Tel 800-800-1312; Imprints:* Abdo & Daughters (Abdo & Dghtrs); Checkerboard Library (Checkerboard Library); SandCastle (SndCastle); Buddy Books (Buddy Bks); Abdo Kids-Junior (AbdoKidsJr); Abdo Kids-Jumbo (AKJumbo); Abdo Zoom-Launch (AbdoZLaunch); Abdo Zoom-Dash (AbdoZDash); Calico Kid (CalicoKid); Kids Core (Kids Core); Claw (Claw); Early Encyclopedias (Early Ency); Super SandCastle (SuperSandcastle); Essential Library (EssentialLibrary); A&D Xtreme (A&DXtreme); SportsZone (SportsZone); Big Buddy Books (BigBuddy); Graphic Planet (GraphicPlanet); Core Library (CoreLibrary); Calico Chapter Books (CalicoChapter); Abdo Kids (AbdoKids); EPIC Press (EPICPress); Spellbound (MYID_U_SPELLBO); Abdo Zoom-Fly (AbdoZFly)
E-mail: info@abdopublishing.com
Web site: http://www.abdopublishing.com
Dist(s): **Blackstone Audio, Inc.**
Carson-Dellosa Publishing, LLC
Ebsco Publishing
Follett School Solutions
Cengage Gale
MyiLibrary
North Star Editions; *CIP.*

Abdo Zoom-Dash *Imprint of* **ABDO Publishing Co.**

Abdo Zoom-Fly *Imprint of* **ABDO Publishing Co.**

Abdo Zoom-Launch *Imprint of* **ABDO Publishing Co.**

Abdullah, Mary, *(978-1-7324576)* 131 Purchase Street, Apt. No. C24, Rye, NY 10580 USA Tel 917-355-6467
E-mail: gremi5@icloud.com.

Abecedarian Bks., *(978-0-9763106; 978-0-9791401; 978-0-9822985; 978-0-9915275)* 2817 Forest Glen Dr., Baldwin, MD 21013-9574 USA Tel 410-692-6777; 877-782-2221; Fax: 410-692-9125 Do not confuse with Abecedarian Books in Portland, OR
E-mail: books@abeced.com
Web site: http://www.abeced.com
Dist(s): **Book Clearing Hse.**

Abedus Pr., *(978-0-9763091)* P.O. Box 8018, La Crescenta, CA 91224-0018 USA (SAN 256-2936)
E-mail: jadams@usc.edu.

Abegg Press *See* **Milner Crest Publishing, LLC**

Abelard Bks. (GBR) *(978-0-9558483) Dist. by* **LuluCom.**

Abelson Pr., *(978-0-9830421)* Orders Addr.: 8334 E. 133rd St., GRANDVIEW, MO 64030 USA Tel 816-398-5859
E-mail: jabelson27@gmail.com.

Abernathy Hse. Publishing, *(978-0-9741940)* Orders Addr.: P.O. Box 1109, Yarmouth, ME 04096-1109 USA (SAN 255-4380) Tel 207-838-6170
E-mail: info@abernathyhousepub.com; abernathyhp@aol.com
Web site: http://www.abernathyhousepub.com
Dist(s): **Brodart Co.**
Follett School Solutions.

Aberon Pubns., *(978-0-9641959; 978-0-9963210)* 549 W. 123rd St., Suite 2b, New York, NY 10027 USA Tel 212-663-9228; Fax: 212-961-9515
E-mail: aberonp@aol.com.

Abidenme Bks., *(978-0-9714515)* P.O. Box 144, Island Heights, NJ 08732-0144 USA (SAN 254-1203) Fax: 732-573-0551; Toll Free: 888-540-8022
E-mail: angela@booksformilitarykids.com
Web site: http://booksformilitarykids.com.

Abiding Life Ministries International, *(978-0-9670843; 978-0-9819546)* Orders Addr.: P.O. Box 620998, Littleton, CO 80162-0998 USA (SAN 299-8629) Tel 303-972-0859; 719-485-5558; Fax: 303-973-2682; Edit Addr.: 8191 Southpark Ln. Unit 102, Littleton, CO 80120-4639 USA; *Imprints:* Abiding Life Press (Abiding Life Pr)
E-mail: AbideLife@aol.com
Web site: http://www.abidinglife.com.

Abiding Life Pr. *Imprint of* **Abiding Life Ministries International**

Abiding Life Press *See* **Abiding Life Ministries International**

Abilene Bks., *(978-0-578-99784-1)* 30 Whitford St., Roslindale, MA 02131 USA Tel 781-492-7360
E-mail: soleildete12@yahoo.com
Web site: www.abilenebooks.com.

Abilene Christian Univ. Pr., *(978-0-89112; 978-0-915547; 978-1-68426)* ACU Box 29138, Abilene, TX 79699-9138 USA (SAN 207-1681) Tel 325-674-2720; Fax: 325-674-6471; Toll Free: 800-444-4228; *Imprints:* Leafwood Publishers (LeafwoodPubs)
E-mail: lettie.morrow@acu.edu
Web site: http://www.acupressbooks.com/; http://www.leafwoodpublishers.com
Dist(s): **Anchor Distributors**
INscribe Digital
Independent Pubs. Group
JSTOR
Send The Light Distribution LLC
ebrary, Inc.

†Abingdon Pr., *(978-0-687; 978-1-4267; 978-1-63088; 978-1-5018; 978-1-7910)* Div. of United Methodist Publishing House, Orders Addr.: 810 12th Ave. S., Nashville, TN 37203 USA Tel 615-749-6409; 615-749-6000; Fax: 615-749-6056; Toll Free: 800-627-1789; Edit Addr.: 810 12th Ave. S., Nashville, TN 37203 USA (SAN 699-9956) Tel 615-749-6000; Toll Free Fax: 800-445-8189; Toll Free: 800-672-1789; *Imprints:* Cokesbury (Cokesbury)
E-mail: rburgoyne@umpublishing.org; cokes_serv@cokesbury.com
Web site: http://www.abingdonpress.com/; http://www.umph.org
Dist(s): **Church Publishing, Inc.**
Follett School Solutions
Simon & Schuster, Inc.
United Methodist Publishing Hse.
ebrary, Inc.; *CIP.*

Abingdon Square Publishing, Ltd., *(978-0-9823480; 978-0-9830762; 978-1-7349849)* 463 W. St., Suite G-122, New York, NY 10014-2029 USA Tel 212-691-2543
Web site: http://www.abingdonsquarepublishing.com.

Abique, Incorporated *See* **Abique Pub**

Abique Pub, *(978-1-892298)* Orders Addr.: 50 Haystack Pl., Pagosa Springs, CO 81147 USA Tel 970-731-2513 during spring and summer; 214-466-1074 during winter; Edit Addr.: 1512 Country Ln., Allen, TX 75002 USA Tel 972-359-0136 Fall and winter
E-mail: abique@gmail.com.

Able Journey Pr., *(978-1-934249)* P.O. Box 5517, Trenton, NJ 08638-9998 USA Toll Free Fax: 877-650-3610; Toll Free: 877-650-3610
E-mail: ivanwright@ablejourneypress.com
Web site: http://ablejourneypress.com.

AbleNet, Inc., *(978-0-9666667; 978-0-9764246; 978-0-9819934; 978-0-9825180; 978-1-935696; 978-1-62744)* 2625 Patton Rd., Roseville, MN 55113 USA Tel 651-294-2200; Toll Free: 800-322-0956; 1081 Tenth Ave./Southeast, Minneapolis, MN 55414
E-mail: kbrown@ablenetinc.com; customerservice@ablenetinc.com
Web site: http://www.ablenetinc.com
Dist(s): **Follett School Solutions.**

Abligio Bks., *(978-1-934437)* 1330 E Scorpio Pl, Chandler, AZ 85249-2136 USA (SAN 853-2362) Tel 480-272-6063
E-mail: publisher@abligio.com
Web site: http://abligio.com.

ABM Enterprises, Inc., *(978-0-9656688)* Orders Addr.: P.O. Box 123, Amelia Court House, VA 23002-0123 USA Tel 804-561-3655; Fax: 804-561-2065; Edit Addr.: 16311 Goodesbridge Rd., Amelia Court House, VA 23002 USA
E-mail: LarryDavies@SowingSeedsofFaith.com
Web site: http://www.SowingSeedsofFaith.com.

ABM Pubns. Inc., *(978-0-578-50209-0; 978-0-578-67091-1; 978-0-578-68061-3; 978-0-578-80375-3; 978-0-578-80376-0; 978-1-7366698; 979-8-9858514; 979-8-9881725)* 350 S Cypress Rd. 521, Pompano Beach, FL 33060 USA Tel 510-504-7466
E-mail: markabm123@gmail.com
Dist(s): **Ingram Content Group.**

Abolet Publishing, *(978-0-9774555; 978-0-9818984)* 1348 East Capitol St., NE, Washington, DC 20003 USA (SAN 856-8618)
Web site: http://www.ronkoshes.com.

Abounding Love Ministries, Inc., *(978-0-9678519)* Orders Addr.: P.O. Box 425, Jackson, CA 95642 USA Tel 209-296-7264 (phone/fax); Edit Addr.: 225 Endicott Ave., Jackson, CA 95642-2512 USA
E-mail: alms@aboundinglove.org
Web site: http://www.aboundinglove.org.

About Comics, *(978-0-9716338; 978-0-9753958; 978-0-9790750; 978-0-9819563; 978-1-936404; 978-1-949996)* 1569 Edgemont Dr., Camarillo, CA 93010-3130 USA
E-mail: questions@aboutcomics.com
Web site: http://www.Combustoica.com; http://www.aboutcomics.com
Dist(s): **Diamond Comic Distributors, Inc.**
Diamond Bk. Distributors.

About Time Publishing, *(978-0-9791550; 978-0-9821214; 978-0-9847928; 978-0-9983133; 978-1-7349133)* 29792 Harper Rd., Junction City, OR 97448 USA Tel 541-954-6724
E-mail: mfaris1950@gmail.com
Web site: http://www.abouttimepublishing.com; http://www.judeco.net.

About Your Time LLC, *(978-0-9744768; 978-0-9799737; 978-0-9844266)* P.O. Box 582, S. Orange, NJ 07079 USA Tel 646-232-3212; Fax: 973-766-1019
E-mail: ayt1@busybodybook.com
Web site: http://www.busybodybook.com
Dist(s): **Publishers Storage & Shipping.**

Above Any Odds Enterainment, *(978-0-578-40081-5; 978-0-578-67440-7; 978-0-578-97541-2)* 20 Blum St., Newark, NJ 07103 USA Tel 917-573-9236
E-mail: vineldaa85@gmail.com

Above the Clouds Publishing, *(978-1-60227)* P.O. Box 313, Stanhope, NJ 07874 USA (SAN 852-1328) Fax: 973-448-7789; Toll Free: 800-936-2319
E-mail: publisher@abovethecloudspublishing.com
Web site: http://abovethecloudspublishing.com
Dist(s): **Follett School Solutions.**

Abovo Publishing, *(978-0-9762007)* P.O. Box 1231, Bonita, CA 91908 USA
E-mail: abovo@cox.net
Dist(s): **Quality Bks., Inc.**

ABR Pubns., *(978-0-9742367)* Orders Addr.: 1945 Cliff Valley Way, Ste. 250b, Atlanta, GA 30329 USA Tel 404-510-3131; Fax: 404-371-1838
E-mail: roll6128@bellsouth.net
Web site: http://www.drboydpublications.com
Dist(s): **Follett School Solutions.**

Abrams & Co. Pubs., Inc.,
Dist(s): **Abrams Learning Trends.**

Abrams Appleseed *Imprint of* **Abrams, Inc.**

Abrams Bks. for Young Readers *Imprint of* **Abrams, Inc.**

Abrams ComicArts *Imprint of* **Abrams, Inc.**

Abrams, Harry N. Incorporated *See* **Abrams, Inc.**

Abrams Image *Imprint of* **Abrams, Inc.**

Abrams, Inc., *(978-0-8109; 978-1-4197; 978-1-61769; 978-1-61312; 978-1-68335)* A Subsidiary of La Martinière Groupe, Orders Addr.: The Market Building Third Floor, 72-82 Rosebery Ave., London, EC1R 4RW GBR Tel 020 7713 2060; Fax: 020 7713 2061; Edit Addr.: 115 West 18th St., New York, NY 10011 USA (SAN 200-2434) Tel 212-206-7715; Fax: 212-519-1210; *Imprints:* Amulet Books (Amulet Bks); Abrams Books for Young Readers (ABYR); Abrams Press (Abrams Pr); Overlook Press, The (OvrlkPr); Abrams Image (Abrams Image); Abrams ComicArts (Abram ComicArts); Abrams Appleseed (AbramsAppleseed); Abrams Noterie (Abrams Noterie)
E-mail: webmaster@abramsbooks.com
Web site: http://www.abramsbooks.com
Dist(s): **Andrews McMeel Publishing**
Atlas Bks.
Children's Plus, Inc.
Ediciones Universal
Follett School Solutions
Hachette Bk. Group
Norton, W. W. & Co., Inc.
Open Road Integrated Media, Inc.

Abrams Noterie *Imprint of* **Abrams, Inc.**

Abrams Pr. *Imprint of* **Abrams, Inc.**

ABREN (A Bk. to Read Empowers Nicaraguans), *(978-1-937314)* 1310 Mercy St., Mountain View, CA 94041 USA Tel 415-637-4243
E-mail: kmundera@yahoo.com.

Abril BookStore & Publishing, *(978-0-9704131; 978-0-9772265; 978-0-9796842; 978-1-949618)* 415 E. Broadway, Suite 102, Glendale, CA 91205 USA Tel 818-243-4112; Fax: 818-243-4158
E-mail: noor@abrilbooks.com; abrilbooks@earthlink.net
Web site: http://www.abrilbooks.com
Dist(s): **Follett School Solutions.**

Absalon Pr., *(978-0-9846687)* 34192 Capistrano by the Sea, Dana Point, CA 92629 USA (SAN 920-1335) Tel 949-493-6953 (phone/fax)
E-mail: jody.payne@cox.net
Web site: www.absalonpress.com.

Absecon Lighthouse, *(978-0-9779988)* 31 S. Rhode Island Ave., Atlantic City, NJ 08401 USA Tel 609-441-1360; Fax: 609-449-1919
E-mail: abseconlighthouse@verizon.net
Web site: http://www.abseconlighthouse.org.

Absey & Co., *(978-1-888842)* 23011 Northcrest, Spring, TX 77389 USA Tel 281-257-2340; Fax: 281-251-4676; Toll Free: 888-412-2739
E-mail: Abseyandco@aol.com
Web site: http://www.absey.biz
Dist(s): **Bibliotech, Inc.**
Brodart Co.
Follett School Solutions.

Absolutely Perfect!, *(978-0-9970546)* 139 Summer St., Kennebunk, ME 04043 USA Tel 207-985-8888
E-mail: danie.connolly@yahoo.com.

ABTA Pubns. & Products, *(978-0-9761517; 978-0-9844660)* P.O. Box 492123, Redding, CA 96049 USA Fax: 530-221-0917
E-mail: info@abtaproducts.com
Web site: http://www.autismandbehavior.com.

ABUAA, Inc., *(978-0-9760406)* Orders Addr.: P.O. Box 1542, Whitefish, MT 59937 USA Fax: 406-362-3407; Edit Addr.: 7347 Farm to Market Rd., Whitefish, MT 59937 USA; *Imprints:* A Kidz World (Kidz Wrld)
Web site: http://www.akidzworld.com.

Abundant Harvest Publishing, *(978-1-7327173; 978-1-7349949; 978-1-7377261; 978-1-958137)* 35145 Oak Glen Rd, Yucaipa, CA 92399 USA Tel 909-222-5338
E-mail: eriksahakian@gmail.com
Web site: www.abundantharvestpublishing.com.

Abundant Living Artwork, *(978-0-9786898)* P.O. Box 6973, Tallahassee, FL 32314 USA.

Abuzz Bks., *(978-0-9715865)* P.O. Box 15753, Scottsdale, AZ 85267 USA
E-mail: author@20umbrellas.com
Dist(s): **Quality Bks., Inc.**

Abuzz Press *Imprint of* **Booklocker.com, Inc.**

Abysso Bks., *(978-0-9747228)* 817 E. Mackinac Ave., Oak Creek, WI 53154 USA
E-mail: asala@mac.com
Web site: http://www.pottersfield.posthaven.com; pottersfield.posthaven.com.

AC Pubns. Group LLC, *(978-1-933302)* P.O. Box 260543, Lakewood, CO 80226 USA
E-mail: dksimoneau@acpublicationsgroup.com
Web site: http://www.acpublicationsgroup.com.

AC Writings, *(978-0-9796780; 978-0-578-50055-3; 978-0-578-68252-5)* 322 PUNTA BAJA Dr., Solana Beach, CA 92075 USA (SAN 854-0896).

Acacia Publishing, Inc., *(978-0-9666572; 978-0-9671187; 978-0-9762224; 978-0-9774306; 978-0-9788283; 978-0-9790826; 978-0-9792531; 978-0-9793273; 978-0-9814629; 978-1-935089)* 770 N. Monterey St. Ste. C, Gilbert, AZ 85233-3821 USA Toll Free: 866-265-4553
E-mail: jason@hiredpen.com; editor@acaiapublishing.com; kgray@acaciapublishing.com
Web site: http://www.acaciapublishing.com
Dist(s): **Book Clearing Hse.**
Follett School Solutions.

Academia Pr. Publishing, *(978-1-7354007)* 1715 Rolling Water Dr. No. 4, Chula Vista, CA 91915 USA Tel 619-871-3595
E-mail: pulecreations@gmail.com.

Academic Edge, Inc., *(978-0-9754754; 978-0-9814537)* Orders Addr.: P.O. Box 23605, Lexington, KY 40523-3605 USA Tel 859-224-3000; Fax: 812-331-8021; Edit Addr.: 216 E. Allen St., Suite 143, Bloomington, IN 47402 USA
E-mail: george@academicedge.com
Web site: http://www.academicedge.com.

Academic Internet Publishers Incorporated *See* **Cram101 Inc.**

Academic Media Solutions *See* **Putnam Productions**

Academic Solutions, Inc., *(978-0-9635364; 978-0-9740200)* Orders Addr.: P.O. Box 102, Harvard, MA 01451 USA Tel 978-456-6829; Fax: 978-456-3053; Toll Free: 877-222-3765 (877-ACADSOL)
E-mail: asibooks@acadsol.com
Web site: http://www.acadsol.com.

Academic Systems Corp., *(978-1-928962)* 2933 Bunker Hill Ln. Ste. 107, Santa Clara, CA 95054-1124 USA Toll Free: 800-694-6830
E-mail: info@academic.com
Web site: http://www.academic.com.

Academic Therapy Pubns., Inc., *(978-0-87879; 978-1-57128; 978-1-63402)* 20 Leveroni Ct., Novato, CA 94949-5746 USA (SAN 201-2111) Tel 415-883-3314; Fax: 415-883-3720; Toll Free: 800-422-7249
E-mail: sales@academictherapy.com; customerservice@academictherapy.com
Web site: http://www.academictherapy.com; http://www.highnoonbooks.com
Dist(s): **Cambium Education, Inc.**
Follett School Solutions
P C I Education
PRO-ED, Inc.

Academy Chicago Pubs., Ltd. *Imprint of* **Chicago Review Pr., Inc.**

†**Academy of American Franciscan History**, *(978-0-88382)* 4050 Mission Ave., Oceanside, CA 92057 USA (SAN 201-1964) Tel 510-484-3561; Fax: 510-549-9466
E-mail: acadafh@fst.edu
Web site: http://www.aafh.org
Dist(s): **Catholic Univ. of America Pr.**
Univ. Pr. of Florida; *CIP.*

Academy Park Pr. *Imprint of* **Williamson County Public Library**

Acadian Hse. Publishing, *(978-0-925417; 978-0-9995884; 978-1-7352641; 979-8-9864600)* Orders Addr.: P.O. Box 52247, Lafayette, LA 70505 USA Tel 337-235-8851; Fax: 337-235-9925; Toll Free: 800-850-8851; Edit Addr.: 100 Asma Blvd., Suite 395, Lafayette, LA 70508 USA (SAN 253-1305)
E-mail: info@acadianhouse.com
Web site: http://www.acadianhouse.com
Dist(s): **Baker & Taylor Bks.**
Follett School Solutions
Forest Sales & Distributing Co.

ACC Children's Classics (GBR) *(978-1-85149)* *Dist. by* **Natl Bk Netwk.**

Accelarated Christian Education, Incorporated *See* **Accelerated Christian Education, Inc.**

Accelerated Christian Education, Inc., *(978-1-56265)* P.O. Box 1438, Lewisville, TX 75067-1438 USA Tel 972-315-1776; Fax: 972-315-8681
Web site: aceministries.com; schooloftomorrow.com/store.

Accelerator Bks., *(978-0-9815245; 978-0-9841399; 978-0-9838940; 978-0-9848966; 978-0-692-79234-6; 978-0-578-91189-2)* P.O. Box 1241, Princeton, NJ 08542 USA Tel 732-642-9721
E-mail: gemma@acceleratorbooks.com
Web site: http://www.acceleratorbooks.com.

Accend Pr., *(978-0-692-09336-8; 978-0-578-43344-8)* 39 Evergreen St., Mount Holly, NJ 08060 USA Tel 609-744-5078
E-mail: kristlokan@gmail.com.

Accent On Success, *(978-0-9743700)* 29 Benton Pl., Saint Louis, MO 63104 USA Tel 314-664-6110; Fax: 314-664-6577
E-mail: jbishop@accentonsuccess.com
Web site: http://www.TeachingMoments.com.

Accent Pubns. *Imprint of* **Ajoyin Publishing, Inc.**

Access for Disabled Americans, *(978-1-928616)* 301 Village Sq., Orinda, CA 94563-2505 USA
E-mail: PSmither@aol.com
Web site: http://maxpages.com/disabledaccess; http://www.accessfordisabled.com.

Access Media Group, *(978-1-948828; 978-1-952182)* 4152 Barnett St., Philadelphia, PA 19135 USA Tel 323-522-4624
E-mail: management@quillspace.com; admin@accessmedia-group.com
Web site: www.quillspace.com; http://www.accessmedia-group.com.

Access-4-All, Inc., *(978-0-9744908)* P.O. Box 220751, Sain Louis, MO 63122-0751 USA Tel 314-821-7011; Fax: 314-909-8086
E-mail: steve@access-4-all.com
Web site: http://www.access-4-all.com.

Accessibilities, *(978-0-9774546)* 1131 E. Spruce St., Sault Ste. Marie, MI 49783 USA
E-mail: geri.taeckens@isahealthfund.org
Web site: http://www.isahealthfund.org.

Accessible Bks. For Children, LLC, *(978-0-692-63717-3; 978-0-578-48996-4)* 1125 Charming St., Maitland, FL 32751 USA Tel 407-319-3704
E-mail: Rios.kimberly@gmail.com.

Acclaim Pr., Inc., *(978-0-9773198; 978-0-9790025; 978-0-9798802; 978-1-935001; 978-1-938905; 978-1-942613; 978-1-948901; 978-1-956027)* Orders Addr.: P.O. Box 238, Morley, MO 63767 USA (SAN 991-0980) Tel 573-472-9800; Fax: 573-472-1608; Toll Free: 877-427-2665; Edit Addr.: 171 Co. Hwy. 430, Oran, MO 63771 USA; *Imprints:* Joey Books (Joey Bks)
Web site: http://www.acclaimpress.com
Dist(s): **Follett School Solutions**
Partners Bk. Distributing, Inc.

Acclimated Spooks, Light, & Power, *(978-0-615-25755-6)* 1106 W. 2nd, Tahlequah, OK 74464 USA
E-mail: graciandwest@gmail.com
Web site: http://www.acclimatedspooks.com
Dist(s): **Lulu Pr., Inc.**

Accordian Bks., *(978-0-9754098)* Orders Addr.: P.O. Box 69912, West Hollywood, CA 90069 USA (SAN 256-0046); Edit Addr.: 69912 W. Hollywood, Hollywood, CA 90069 USA
E-mail: crystalilluminations@msn.com.

Ace *Imprint of* **Penguin Publishing Group**

Ace Academics, Inc., *(978-1-57633; 978-1-881374)* 69 Tulip St., Bergenfield, NJ 07621 USA Tel 201-784-0001; Fax: 201-784-7704; *Imprints:* Exambusters (Exambusters)
E-mail: highself@aol.com; info@exambusters.com; exambusters@aol.com
Web site: http://www.exambusters.com
Dist(s): **INscribe Digital**
Independent Pubs. Group
eBookit.com

Ace Reid Enterprises *See* **Cowpokes Cartoon Bks.**

Acedrex Publishing, *(978-1-937291)* 550 N. Harrison Rd. No. 5101, Tucson, AZ 85748 USA Tel 401-743-0052
E-mail: acedrexpublishing@yahoo.com
Web site: acedrex.com.

AceMZ, *(978-1-7368747)* 7252 Esfera St, Carlsbad, CA 92009 USA Tel 626-808-8192
E-mail: AmandaMZ2187@gmail.com.

Acen Press *See* **DNA Pr.**

Acey, Mary J., *(978-0-9771920)* 178-39 147th Ave., Springfield Gardens, NY 11434 USA Tel 718-949-2670; Fax: 718-949-7464
E-mail: jestac1@aol.com.

Aceybee Publishing, *(978-0-9763958)* 285 W. Kootenai, No. 7, Richfield, ID 23349-5344 USA.

Achiev *See* **Achieve Pubns.**

Achieve Pubns., *(978-0-9727762; 978-0-615-12053-9)* Orders Addr.: 1216 Scobee Dr., Lansdale, PA 19446 USA Fax: 215-368-1431 (fax orders)
E-mail: achievepub@verizon.net
Web site: http://www.achievepublications.com
Dist(s): **Book Clearing Hse.**
Follett School Solutions.

Achieve3000, *(978-1-932166; 978-0-615-12027-0; 978-1-935675; 978-1-938916; 978-1-63256)* 1091 River Ave., Lakewood, NJ 08701 USA Tel 732-367-5505; Fax: 732-367-2313; Toll Free: 877-803-6505
E-mail: kelly.tanko@achieve3000.com
Web site: http://www.achieve3000.com.

Achievers Technology Resource, Inc., *(978-0-9716113)* PMB No. 455, 442 Rte. 202-206 N., Bedminster, NJ 07921-1522 USA (SAN 254-2811)
Web site: http://www.achieversrus.com.

Achieving Corporate Excellence, Inc., *(978-0-9746262)* Orders Addr.: P.O. Box 651119, Vero Beach, FL 32965-1119 USA Toll Free: 877-656-8313; Edit Addr.: 8003 Kenwood Rd., Fort Pierce, FL 34951 USA
Web site: http://www.acespeaks.com.

ACME Pr., *(978-0-9629880)* Orders Addr.: P.O. Box 1702, Westminster, MD 21158 USA Tel 410-848-7577; Edit Addr.: 1116 E. Deep Run Rd., Westminster, MD 21158 USA
Dist(s): **Follett School Solutions.**

Acmon Blue Publishing, *(978-0-9744792)* P.O. Box 475, Tujunga, CA 91043-0475 USA (SAN 255-5638) Tel 818-352-2551 (phone/fax)
E-mail: info@acmonblue.com
Web site: http://www.acmonblue.com.

Acorn *Imprint of* **Oak Tree Publishing**

Acorn Bks., *(978-0-9648957; 978-0-9837299)* P.O. Box 7348, Springfield, IL 62791-7348 USA Tel 217-525-8202; Fax: 217-525-8212 Do not confuse with companies iwth the same or similar name in Kansas, MO, Bloomington, IN, St. Albans, VT
E-mail: amy@afterabortion.org; elliotinstitute@gmail.com
Web site: http://www.afterabortion.org
Dist(s): **Ingram Content Group**
MyiLibrary.

Acorn Bks., *(978-0-9664470; 978-1-930472)* 7337 Terrace, Kansas City, MO 64114-1256 USA Tel 816-523-8321; Fax: 816-333-3843; Toll Free: 888-422-0320 Do not confuse with companies with the same or similar name in Springfield, IL, Bloomington, IN, St. Albans, VT
E-mail: jami.parkison@micro.com
Web site: http://www.acornbks.com.

Acorn Hill Pr., *(978-0-9788889)* 155 Parkhurst Dr., Jackson, MS 39202 USA Tel 601-668-3533.

Acorn Pr., The (CAN) *(978-0-9698606; 978-1-894838; 978-1-77366)* *Dist. by* **BTPS.**

Acorn Publishing, *(978-0-937921)* Div. of Vitesse Pr., PMB 367, 45 State St., Montpelier, VT 05601 USA (SAN 659-4840) Tel 802-229-4243; Fax: 802-229-6939 Do not confuse with companies with the same or similar name in Midvale, UT, Broomfield, CO, Battle Creek, MI, Sisters, OR, Suffern, NY,Saltlake City, UT, Portland, OR, Sping Lake, MI
E-mail: dick@vitessepress.com
Web site: http://www.vitessepress.com
Dist(s): **Hood, Alan C. & Co., Inc.**

Acorn Publishing, *(978-0-9678801; 978-0-9710988; 978-0-9728969; 978-0-9774449)* Div. of Development Initiatives, 186 N. 23rd St., Battle Creek, MI 49015-1711 USA (SAN 854-6258) Tel 269-962-8184 (phone\fax); Toll Free: 877-700-2219 (phone\fax) Do not confuse with companies with the same or similar name in Broomfield, CO, Midvale, UT, Montpelier, VT, Sisters, OR, Suffern, NY, Salt Lake City, UT, Portland, OR, Sping Lake, MI
E-mail: editor@acornpublishing.com
Web site: http://www.acornpublishing.com.

Acoustic Learning Inc., *(978-0-9761435; 978-0-9800581; 978-1-936412)* 215 Prospect Ave., Highland Park, IL 60035-3357 USA
E-mail: eartraining@aruffo.com
Web site: http://www.acousticlearning.com.

Acres Publishing, *(978-0-9741081)* 311 Prospect St., Alton, IL 62002 USA.

Across Ocean Bks., *(978-0-944176)* 1309 Redwood Ln., Davis, CA 95616 USA (SAN 242-8741) Tel 530-304-9927 Do not confuse with Terra Nova Press in Pacifica, CA.

ACS, LLC Amica Creative Services, *(978-0-9726535; 978-0-9745686; 978-0-9794771; 978-0-9801942; 978-0-9816822; 978-0-9822482; 978-0-9826401)* 41206 wood Haven Dr., Palm Desert, CA 92211 USA (SAN 255-0091) Tel 503-593-2618
E-mail: ross@ideasbyacs.com
Web site: http://www.ideasbyacs.com
Dist(s): **American West Bks.**

ACSkye, *(978-1-954200)* P.O. Box 957, Castle Rock, CO 80104 USA Tel 970-310-7311
E-mail: tarynsemail@gmail.com.

ACTA Pubns., *(978-0-87946; 978-0-914070; 978-0-915388)* 5559 Howard St., Skokie, IL 60077-2621 USA (SAN 204-7489) Toll Free Fax: 800-397-0079; Toll Free: 800-397-2282; 4848 N. Clark St., Chicago, IL 60640
E-mail: actapublications@aol.com
Web site: http://www.actapublications.com
Dist(s): **BookMobile**
INscribe Digital
Independent Pubs. Group
Spring Arbor Distributors, Inc.

Actar D, *(978-0-9893317; 978-1-940291; 978-1-945150; 978-1-948765; 978-1-63840)* 440 Pk. Ave. South, 17th FL, New York, NY 10016 USA Tel 212-966-2207; Fax: 212-966-2214
E-mail: brian@actar-d.com; ricardo.devesa@actar-d.com
Web site: www.actar-d.com
Dist(s): **Consortium Bk. Sales & Distribution**
Ingram Publisher Services.

Action Bks., *(978-0-900575; 978-0-9765692; 978-0-9799755; 978-0-9831480; 978-0-9898048)* Dept Of English, U. Of Notre Dame 356 O'shaughnessy Hall, Notre Dame, IN 46556 USA
Web site: http://www.actionbooks.org
Dist(s): **SPD-Small Pr. Distribution.**

Action Factor, Inc., *(978-0-9720763; 978-0-9754618)* PMB 218, 3195 Dayton-Xenia Rd., Suite 900, Beavercreek, OH 45434-6390 USA Tel 937-426-4364 (phone/fax)
E-mail: cgifford@actionfactor.com
Web site: http://www.actionfactor.com.

Action Lab Entertainment, *(978-0-9854952; 978-0-9859652; 978-1-939352; 978-1-63229)* 306 Bridlewood Ct., Canonsburg, PA 15317 USA Tel 513-313-7612
E-mail: spryor@actionlabcomics.com
Web site: http://www.actionlabcomics.com
Dist(s): **Children's Plus, Inc.**
Diamond Comic Distributors, Inc.
Diamond Bk. Distributors
MyiLibrary.

For full information on wholesalers and distributors, refer to the Wholesaler and Distributor Name Index

...tion Organizing, *(978-0-9721964)* Div. of Successful Organizing Solutions, Orders Addr.: 406 Shato Ln., Madison, WI 53716 USA Tel 608-441-6767; Edit Addr.: P.O. Box 202, Milton, WI 53563 USA Tel 608-868-4079; Toll Free: 888-577-6655
E-mail: info@SOSorganize.net; sales@SOSorganize.net
Web site: http://www.actionorganizing.com.

...tion Publishing, Inc., *(978-1-882210)* Div. of Action Products International, Inc., 344 Cypress Rd., Ocala, FL 34472-3108 USA Tel 352-687-2202; Fax: 352-687-4961; Toll Free: 800-772-2846 Do not confuse with companies with the same or similar name in Newport Beach, CA, Burlingame, CA, West Los Angeles, CA, Houstin, TX, Chicago, IL, Glendale, CA, Austin, TX.

...ctionopolis *Imprint of* **Komikwerks, LLC**

...ctive Images, *(978-0-9740567; 978-0-9766761)* Orders Addr.: 8910 Rayford Dr., Los Angeles, CA 90045 USA Tel 310-215-0362; Fax: 775-890-5787 do not confuse with Active Images, Incorporated in Sterling, VA
E-mail: richard@comicraft.com
Web site: http://www.activeimages.com
Dist(s): **Ingram Content Group**
Partners Pubs. Group, Inc.

Active Learning Corp., *(978-0-912813)* P.O. Box 254, New Paltz, NY 12561 USA (SAN 282-7794) Tel 845-255-0844; Fax: 845-255-8796
E-mail: panmans@newpaltz.edu; info@activelearning.com
Web site: http://www.activelearningcorp.com.

Active Learning Systems, LLC, *(978-1-57652)* P.O. Box 254, Epping, NH 03042 USA Tel 603-679-3332; Fax: 603-679-2611; Toll Free: 800-644-5059
E-mail: info@iimresearch.com
Web site: http://www.iimresearch.com.

Active Media Publishing, LLC, *(978-0-9745645; 978-0-9848808; 978-1-940367)* Orders Addr.: 614 E. Hwy 50 No. 235, Clermont, FL 34711 USA (SAN 255-6545); 614 E. Hwy 50 No. 235, Clermont, FL 34711 (SAN 255-6545); *Imprints:* Red Giant Entertainment (RedGiant)
E-mail: wizbenny@aol.com
Web site: http://redgiantentertainment.com
Dist(s): **Diamond Comic Distributors, Inc.**
Diamond Bk. Distributors
Elsevier.

Active Parenting Pubs., *(978-0-9618020; 978-1-880283; 978-1-59723)* 1955 Vaughn Rd. NW, Suite 108, Kennesaw, GA 30144-7808 USA (SAN 666-301X) Tel 770-429-0565; Fax: 770-429-0334; Toll Free: 800-825-0060
E-mail: cservice@activeparenting.com; ckeller@activeparenting.com
Web site: http://www.activeparenting.com
Dist(s): **Follett School Solutions**
National Bk. Network.

Active Spud Pr., *(978-0-9845388)* 324 E. 13th St., No. 3, New York, NY 10003 USA Tel 818-518-7381
E-mail: steve@activespudpress.com
Web site: http://www.activespudpress.com.

Active Synapse, *(978-0-9677255)* Orders Addr.: 5336 Park Lane Dr., Columbus, OH 43231-4072 USA
E-mail: Daryn@ActiveSynapse.com
Web site: http://www.activesynapse.com
Dist(s): **Brodart Co.**
Cold Cut Comics Distribution
Diamond Distributors, Inc.
Emery-Pratt Co.
Follett School Solutions
Midwest Library Service.

Activity Resources Co., Inc., *(978-0-918932; 978-1-882293)* Orders Addr.: P.O. Box 4875, Hayward, CA 94540 USA (SAN 209-0201) Tel 510-782-1300; Fax: 510-782-8172; Edit Addr.: 20655 Hathaway Ave., Hayward, CA 94541 USA
E-mail: info@activityresources.com
Web site: http://www.activityresources.com
Dist(s): **Delta Education, LLC**
Follett School Solutions
Seymour, Dale Pubns.

ACTNew Bks., *(978-0-9762326)* 12687 Blue Star Memorial Hwy., South Haven, MI 49090 USA
E-mail: actnewbooks@yahoo.com
Web site: http://www.actnewbooks.com.

Acts of Kindness, *(978-1-7333535)* 3103 S. 115th E. Ave., Tulsa, OK 74146 USA Tel 918-812-5181
E-mail: godwinchishala@yahoo.com
Web site: HEAVENSHEARTEDT.COM.

ACTS Pr., *(978-0-9721698; 978-0-9800065; 978-1-940661)* Div. of Coptic Orthodox Church - Diocese of Los Angeles, 1617 W. La Palma Ave., Anaheim, CA 92801 USA
E-mail: office@actslibrary.org
Web site: www.actslibrary.org.

Actual Magic Enterprises, LLC, *(978-0-9891807; 978-1-7353558)* 17606 N. 17th Pl., Unit 1106, Phoenix, AZ 85022 USA Tel 602-992-5552
E-mail: debmctiernan@centurylink.net
Web site: www.deborahmctiernan.com.

Ad Center, The *See* **Leathers Publishing**

Ad Stellae Bks., *(978-0-615-31487-7; 978-0-615-31488-4; 978-0-615-34834-6; 978-0-615-62523-2; 978-0-615-64517-9; 978-0-615-80434-7; 978-0-692-29376-8; 979-8-9858532)* 2811 Bailey Ln Rm 52, Eugene, OR 97401 USA Fax: 866-302-3827
Web site: http://www.sylviaengdahl.com
Dist(s): **CreateSpace Independent Publishing Platform**
Draft2Digital
Smashwords.

Adam Enterprises *See* **Amberwood Pr.**

Adam Hill Pubns., *(978-0-9769360)* Orders Addr.: 9001 SW 55 Ct., Fort Lauderdale, FL 33328 USA
E-mail: adamhilldesign@gmail.com
Web site: http://www.adamhilldesign.us
Dist(s): **BWI**
Follett School Solutions.

Adams & Perkins *See* **Rocket City Publishing**

Adams, Anne Marie Rea, *(978-0-9742782)* 9 Terraza Dr., Newport Coast, CA 92657-1510 USA.

Adams, Carl M, *(978-0-9899710)* 1207 Honu Loop, Aiea, HI 96701 USA Tel 309-696-7636
E-mail: cmadams6@yahoo.com.

Adams, Clint *See* **Credo Italia**

Adam's Creations Publishing, LLC, *(978-0-9785695)* Div. of JAH Innovations, Inc., 550 Fossett Rd., Zebulon, GA 30295 USA (SAN 851-0091) Tel 404-909-1025
E-mail: info@adamscreationspublishing.com
Web site: http://www.adamscreationspublishing.com
Dist(s): **BCH Fulfillment & Distribution.**

Adams, Evelyn, *(978-0-9761102)* 727 Virginia Ave., Midland, PA 15059-1429 USA Tel 724-643-9968; Fax: 724-775-8648
E-mail: rjb@timesnet.net
Web site: http://www.storiesfromvic.com.

Adams, Jeanette *See* **Camelot Tales**

†Adams Media Corp., *(978-0-937860; 978-1-55850; 978-1-58062; 978-1-59337; 978-1-59869; 978-1-60550; 978-1-4405; 978-1-5072)* Div.of Simon & Schuster, Inc., Orders Addr.: Simon and Schuster, Inc. Ordering Processing Dept. 100 Front St., Riverside, NJ 08075-1197 USA (SAN 215-2886) Toll Free Fax: 800-943-9831; Toll Free: 800-223-2336; Edit Addr.: Adams Media 57 Littlefield St., Avon, MA 02322 USA Tel 508-427-7100; *Imprints:* Everything (EverythingUSA)
E-mail: Khelsea.Purvis@simonandschuster.com; Purchaseorders@simonandschuster.com
Web site: http://www.simonandschuster.com
Dist(s): **Cranbury International**
CreateSpace Independent Publishing Platform
Ebsco Publishing
Follett School Solutions
Curreri, Michelle Morrow
MyiLibrary
Simon & Schuster, Inc.
Univ. Pr. of Kentucky
ebrary, Inc.; *CIP.*

Adams Publishing *See* **Adams Media Corp.**

Adams Publishing, *(978-0-9729189)* 320 Lincoln Rd., Branchland, WV 25506 USA Tel 304-824-2504 (phone/fax) Do not confuse with companies with the same or similar name in Topanga, CA, Rainier, WA, Boston, MA
E-mail: Adamspublisher@zoominternet.net
Web site: http://www.geocities.com/daycarebook/index.html.

Adamson, Bruce Campbell, *(978-1-892501; 979-8-9850150; 978-0-578-99885-5; 978-0-578-99886-2; 978-0-578-99887-9; 978-0-578-99888-6)* Div. of Bruce Campbell Adamson Bks. & Videos, P. O. Box 3511, Santa Cruz, CA, 95063, Santa Cruz, CA 95063-3511 USA Tel 831-465-9272
E-mail: bca@ciajfk.com; bca@got.net
Web site: http://www.ciajfk.com; http://barrymorefamily.com.

Adamson, Bruce Campbell Books *See* **Adamson, Bruce Campbell**

Adamson, Mac, *(978-0-9779369)* P.O. Box 690, Midway, UT 84049 USA Tel 801-318-8544
E-mail: madamson@kids4fitkids.org
Web site: http://kids4fitkids.org.

Adams-Pomeroy Pr., *(978-0-9661009; 978-0-9967921)* Orders Addr.: P.O. Box 189, Albany, WI 53502 USA Tel 608-862-3645; Fax: 608-862-3647; Toll Free: 877-862-3645; Edit Addr.: 103 N. Jackson St., Albany, WI 53502 USA
E-mail: adamspomeroy@ckhnet.com
Dist(s): **Follett School Solutions.**

Adaptive Studios, *(978-0-9960666; 978-0-9864484; 978-0-9964887; 978-1-945293)* 3733 Motor Ave 3rd Flr., Los Angeles, CA 90034 USA Tel 310-876-1675
E-mail: tj@adaptivestudios.com
Web site: adaptivestudios.com
Dist(s): **Ingram Publisher Services**
MyiLibrary.

Adazing, *(978-0-9977331)* Deer Watch Rd, Bridgeville, PA 15017 USA Tel 412-221-0813
E-mail: cj@adazing.com
Web site: www.adazing.com.

ADB Artist Publishing, *(978-0-9798580)* Div. of Fusion Group, Inc., Orders Addr.: P.O. Box 490965, Lawrenceville, GA 30049 USA (SAN 854-5774).

Addassa Prendergast Pubs., *(978-0-9715016; 978-0-9716264; 978-0-9722239; 978-0-9723202)* Div. of Dawkins Project, The, 1531 Palmer Dr., Fayetteville, NC 28303 USA Tel 910-488-3953 (phone/fax); 910 488 3953
E-mail: bookman1531@yahoo.com; paulandrewdawkins@yahoo.com
Web site: http://www.thedawkinsproject.com.

Added Upon, Inc., *(978-0-9740319)* Orders Addr.: P.O. Box 65327, Vancouver, WA 98665 USA
E-mail: dunnjessel@msn.com.

Addi-Boo Bks., *(978-0-9911410)* 78 Ryerson St., Brooklyn, NY 11205 USA Tel 347-512-7862
E-mail: stephen.epps@eppsscholars.org.

Addison Wesley, *(978-0-06; 978-0-13; 978-0-201; 978-0-321; 978-0-582; 978-0-673; 978-0-8053)* 75 Arlington St., Suite 300, Boston, MA 02116 USA Tel 617-848-7500
Web site: http://www.aw-bc.com
Dist(s): **InterVarsity Pr.**
Pearson Education
Pearson Technology Group.

Addison Wesley Schl., Orders Addr.: a/o Order Dept., 200 Old Tappan Rd., Old Tappan, NJ 07675 USA Toll Free Fax: 800-445-6991; Toll Free: 800-922-0579; Edit Addr.: 75 Arlington St., Boston, MA 02116 USA Tel 617-848-7500; *Imprints:* Scott Foresman (S-Foresman)
Web site: http://www.aw-bc.com.

Addison-Wesley Educational Pubs., Inc., *(978-0-321; 978-0-328; 978-0-673)* Div. of Addison Wesley Longman, Inc., 75 Arlington St., Boston, MA 02116 USA Tel 617-848-7500; Toll Free: 800-447-2226; *Imprints:* Scott Foresman (Scott Frsmn); Scott Foresman (S-Foresman)
Web site: http://www.awl.com.

†Addison-Wesley Longman, Inc., *(978-0-201; 978-0-321; 978-0-582; 978-0-673; 978-0-8013; 978-0-8053; 978-0-9654123)* Orders Addr.: 200 Old Tappan Rd., Old Tappan, NJ 07675 USA (SAN 299-4739) Toll Free: 800-922-0579; Edit Addr.: 75 Arlington St., Suite 300, Boston, MA 02116 USA (SAN 200-2000) Tel 617-848-7500; Toll Free: 800-447-2226
E-mail: pearsoned@eds.com; orderdeptnj@pearsoned.com
Web site: http://www.awl.com
Dist(s): **Continental Bk. Co., Inc.**
MyiLibrary
Pearson Education
Trans-Atlantic Pubns., Inc.; *CIP.*

Addison-Wesley Longman, Ltd. (GBR) *(978-0-582) Dist. by* **Trans-Atl Phila.**

Addison-Wesley Publishing Company, Incorporated *See* **Addison-Wesley Longman, Inc.**

Addwin Publishing & Media, LLC, *(978-0-578-21220-3; 978-1-7345164)* 6253 Cates Ave., University City, MO 63130 USA Tel 404-542-2018
E-mail: addwinpm@gmail.com
Dist(s): **Independent Pub.**

Addy's Rescue Fund, *(978-0-692-75867-0; 978-0-692-87784-5; 978-0-692-90384-1; 978-0-692-10251-0)* 642 Tamarack Ln, LEMOORE, CA 93245 USA Tel 559-904-1705.

Adelante Productions, Inc., *(978-0-9748017)* 600 Columbus Ave., 8G, New York, NY 10024 USA
E-mail: info@adelantepro.com
Web site: http://www.adelantepro.com.

Adelphi Pr., *(978-0-9610796)* 324 Hammonton Pl., Silver Spring, MD 20904-6344 USA (SAN 265-0541) Do not confuse with Adelphi Pr., Wyomissing, PA.

Adhemar Pr. USA, *(978-0-578-06275-4)* 7440 S. Black Hawk, No. 15-102, Englewood, CO 80112 USA
E-mail: jtbeiser@gmail.com.

AdHouse Bks., *(978-0-9721794; 978-0-9770304; 978-1-935233)* 3905 Brook Road., Richmond, VA 23227 USA
Dist(s): **Diamond Comic Distributors, Inc.**
Diamond Bk. Distributors.

Adibooks.com, *(978-0-9728909; 978-0-9743872; 978-0-9748753; 978-0-9758993; 978-0-9760575; 978-0-9763465; 978-0-9764322; 978-0-9767424; 978-0-9772505; 978-0-9776044; 978-0-9778606; 978-0-9779682; 978-0-9787515; 978-0-9789741; 978-0-9791289; 978-0-9794769; 978-0-9797885; 978-0-9801635; 978-0-9815594; 978-0-9817447; 978-0-9821073; 978-0-9823972; 978-0-9841294; 978-0-9843390; 978-0-9845852; 978-0-9846346; 978-0-9852824; 978-0-9887395; 978-0-9899978; 978-0-9914043; 978-0-9960318; 978-0-9904151; 978-0-9908554;) 181 Industrial Ave., Lowell, MA 01852 USA Fax: 978-458-3026*
E-mail: tcampbell@kingprinting.com
Web site: http://www.adibooks.com
Dist(s): **Cardinal Pubs. Group.**

Adirondack Kids Pr., *(978-0-9707044; 978-0-9826250; 978-1-7346509)* 39 Second St., Camden, NY 13316 USA Tel 315-245-2437
E-mail: info@adirondackkids.com
Web site: http://www.adirondackkids.com.

†Adirondack Mountain Club, Inc., *(978-0-935272; 978-1-931951; 978-0-9896073; 978-0-9961168; 978-0-9986371; 978-1-7332240)* 4833 Cascade Rd., Lake Placid, NY 12946 USA (SAN 204-7691) Tel 518-668-4447 (customer service); 518-637-7310 (orders only); Fax: 518-668-3746
E-mail: pubs@adk.org; ann@adk.org
Web site: http://www.adk.org
Dist(s): **Alpenbooks Pr. LLC**
Equinox, Ltd.
North Country Bks., Inc.
Peregrine Outfitters; *CIP.*

Adisoft, Inc., *(978-0-9674897)* Orders Addr.: P.O. Box 2094, San Leandro, CA 94577-2094 USA Tel 510-483-3556; Fax: 510-483-3885; Edit Addr.: 664 Joaquin Ave., San Leandro, CA 94577 USA; *Imprints:* Wawa Press (Wawa)
E-mail: information@adisoft-inc.com
Web site: http://www.adisoft-inc.com.

Adiva, Incorporated *See* **TEG Publishing**

Adjunct Professor, ARC *See* **Retired Professor**

Adjust Communications, *(978-0-9765973)* 905 Hwy. 321 NW, Suite No. 364, Hickory, NC 28601 USA Tel 828-850-3237; Fax: 866-334-4360
Web site: http://www.victoryafterhighschool.com.

Adler, Karen, *(978-0-9679772)* 34738 McDaniel Dr., Northfork, CA 93643 USA Tel 559-877-2033.

Adler, Sigal, *(978-0-9989065; 978-1-947417)* 6805 Del Monte ave, RICHMOND, CA 94805 USA Tel 510-453-4845
E-mail: sigalingramspark@gmail.com.

Admirable Publishing LLC, *(978-0-9986891)* P.O. Box 881821, Port St. Lucie, FL 34988 USA Tel 772-332-5822
E-mail: debrasweeting@icloud.com.

Adonoke Inc., *(978-0-9773180)* 8354 Craine Dr., Manlius, NY 13104-9421 USA
E-mail: info@adonokebooks.com
Web site: http://www.adonokebooks.com.

Adoption Tribe Publishing *See* **MMB Enterprises, LLC**

ADR BookPrint *See* **ADR Inc.**

ADR Inc., *(978-0-9742743; 978-0-9761513; 978-0-9795033; 978-0-9802452; 978-0-9819864; 978-0-9908488; 978-0-578-76765-9)* 2012 Northern Ave., Wichita, KS 67216 USA Tel 316-522-5599; Fax: 316-522-5445; Toll Free: 800-767-6066
E-mail: bcatron@adr.biz
Web site: http://www.adr.biz.

Adrema Pr., *(978-0-9717290; 978-1-59611)* Orders Addr.: P.O. Box 14592, North Palm Beach, FL 33408 USA; Edit Addr.: P.O. Box 14157, Palm Beach Gardens, FL 33418 USA
E-mail: media@melissaa.com; melissaalvarez2121@outlook.com
Dist(s): **Ingram Content Group.**

ad-shot LLC, *(978-1-7366247)* 815 Ponce de Leon Blvd. Suite 209, Coral Gables, FL 33134 USA Tel 646-812-2383
E-mail: f.sommerfeld@ad-shot.net.

ADV Manga, *(978-1-57813)* Div. of A. D. Vision, Inc., 5750 Bintliff, Suite 200, Houston, TX 77036 USA
Web site: http://www.ADVFilms.com
Dist(s): **Diamond Comic Distributors, Inc.**
Diamond Bk. Distributors.

Advance Cal Tech, Inc., *(978-0-943759)* 210 Clary Ave., San Gabriel, CA 91776-1375 USA (SAN 242-2603).

Advance Materials Ltd. (GBR) *(978-0-9532440; 978-0-9559265; 978-0-9547695; 978-0-9565431; 978-0-9576012; 978-0-9927056) Dist. by* **Cambridge U Pr.**

Advance Publishers, Incorporated *See* **Advance Pubs. LLC**

Advance Pubs. LLC, *(978-0-9619525; 978-1-57973; 978-1-885222)* 1060 Maitland Center Cmns Blvd. Ste. 365, Maitland, FL 32751-7499 USA (SAN 244-9226) Toll Free: 800-777-2041
E-mail: advpublish@aol.com; questions@adv-pub.com
Web site: http://www.advancepublishers.com.

Advance Publishing, Inc., *(978-0-9610810; 978-1-57537; 978-1-64206)* 6950 Fulton St., Houston, TX 77022 USA (SAN 263-9572) Tel 713-695-0600; Fax: 713-695-8585; Toll Free: 800-917-9630; *Imprints:* Another Sommer-Time Story (Another Sommer) Do not confuse with Advance Publishing, Brownburg, IN
E-mail: info@advancepublishing.com
Web site: http://www.advancepublishing.com
Dist(s): **Follett School Solutions.**

Advanced Marketing, S. de R. L. de C. V. (MEX) *(978-970-718) Dist. by* **Bilingual Pubns.**

Advanced Publishing LLC, *(978-0-9857367; 978-1-63132)* 3200 A Danville Blvd. Suite 204, Alamo, CA 94507 USA Tel 925-837-7303
E-mail: eric@aliveeastbay.com
Web site: www.alivebookpublishing.com.

Advantage BibleStudy *Imprint of* **Advantage Bks.**

Advantage Books *See* **Advantage Bks., LLC**

Advantage Bks., *(978-0-9754332; 978-1-59755)* Div. of Advantage Pr., Inc., Orders Addr.: P.O. Box 160847, Altamonte Springs, FL 32716 USA; *Imprints:* Advantage Childrens (Advan Childrens); Advantage BibleStudy (Adv BibleStudy) Do not confuse with companies with the same or similar name in Newport Beach, CA, Silver Spring, MD
E-mail: mike@advbooks.com
Web site: http://advbookstore.com
Dist(s): **National Bk. Network.**

Advantage Bks., LLC, *(978-0-9660366; 978-0-9714609; 978-0-9823326)* 3268 Arcadia Pl.NW, Washington, DC 20015-2330 USA (SAN 253-8237) Tel 202-966-4044; Fax: 2002-966-1561; Toll Free: 888-238-8588 Do not confuse with companies with the same or similar name in New Port Beach, CA, Longwood, FL
E-mail: advantagebooksdc@aol.com
Web site: http://www.addvance.com
Dist(s): **National Bk. Network.**

Advantage Childrens *Imprint of* **Advantage Bks.**

Advantage World Pr., *(978-1-932450)* Div. of TheMoneyCoach.net, LLC, 19015 Parkland View Dr., Cypress, TX 77433 USA (SAN 255-7452) Fax: 866-494-2461; Toll Free: 866-494-2461
Web site: http://www.themoneycoach.net
Dist(s): **Ingram Content Group**
Smashwords.

Advent Truth Ministries, *(978-0-9749490)* P.O. Box 307, Forsyth, GA 31029 USA Tel 404-322-5683
E-mail: adventtruth@yahoo.com
Web site: www.adventtruth.org; www.thesabbathtruth.org.

Adventure Ahead Pubn., *(978-0-692-15189-1)* P.O. Box 842, Shaw Island, WA 98286 USA Tel 360-317-6238
E-mail: adventureahead@outlook.com
Dist(s): **CreateSpace Independent Publishing Platform.**

Adventure & Discovery Pr., *(978-0-9744672)* P.O. Box 11631, Syracuse, NY 13218 USA Toll Free: 800-682-2662.

Adventure Beyond The Horizon *See* **Omega Pr.**

Adventure Bks. of Seattle, *(978-0-9823271; 978-0-692-32193-5)* 2415 I St. NE, No. D, Auburn, WA 98002 USA (SAN 857-8664) Tel 253-929-6259
Web site: http://www.adventurebooksofseattle.com
Dist(s): **Ingram Content Group.**

Adventure Boys Inc., *(978-0-9791922; 978-0-9791952; 978-0-9796392)* 11005 35th Ave. NE, Seattle, WA 98119-6809 USA (SAN 852-727X) 11/20/06: Do not be confused with Madison Park Greetings & Front Porch Classics, Inc.
Web site: http://www.adventureboys.com.

Adventure Experience *See* **Adventure Experience Pr.**

Adventure Experience Pr., *(978-1-7322694)* 7010 Streamwood Pt, Colorado Springs, CO 80922 USA Tel 719-322-6992
E-mail: eric@adventureexperience.net
Web site: www.AdventureExperience.net; www.AdventureDevos.com; 40DayPrayerGuides.com.

Adventure Hse., *(978-1-886937; 978-1-59798)* 914 Laredo Rd., Silver Spring, MD 20901-1867 USA Tel 301-754-1589; Fax: 978-215-7412
E-mail: sales@adventurehouse.com
Web site: http://www.adventurehouse.com
Dist(s): **Diamond Comic Distributors, Inc.**
Diamond Bk. Distributors.

Publisher Name Index

Adventure in Discovery, (978-0-9743414; 978-0-578-62668-0) 18011 N. Hwy. A1A, Jupiter, FL 33477 USA Tel 561-746-8410
E-mail: info@adventureindiscovery.com
Web site: http://adventureindiscovery.com/
Dist(s): **Follett School Solutions**
Southern Bk. Service
Sunburst Bks., Inc., Distributor of Florida Bks.

Adventure Pr., (978-0-9758654) Orders Addr.: P.O. Box 1778, Canon City, CO 81215 USA Tel 208-880-7899; P.O. Box 1778, Canon City, CO 81215 Tel 208-880-7899
E-mail: antelope85@hotmail.com
Web site: http://www.kingsventures.com.

Adventure Productions, Inc., (978-0-9614904) 3404 Terry Lake Rd., Fort Collins, CO 80524 USA (SAN 693-3955) Tel 970-493-8776; Fax: 970-484-5825 Do not confuse with Adventure Productions, Reno, NV.
E-mail: cjansen@wild-west.com.

Adventure Pubns. *Imprint of* **AdventureKEEN**

AdventureKEEN, (978-0-89732; 978-0-89997; 978-0-911824; 978-0-934860; 978-0-9617367; 978-0-9647083; 978-1-57860; 978-1-878208; 978-1-885061; 978-1-59193; 978-0-9777651; 978-1-939324; 978-1-62809; 978-0-9903716; 978-1-63404; 978-1-64359; 978-1-64755; 978-1-64901) 2204 First Ave. S. Suite 102, Birmingham, AL 35233 USA Tel 205-322-0439; Fax: 205-326-1012; Imprints: Adventure Publications (AdvntrPubns); Wilderness Press (WildrnssPr); Clerisy Press (ClerisyPress)
E-mail: molly@adventurewithkeen.com
Web site: www.theunofficialguides.com; www.adventurewithkeen.com; www.adventurepublications.net; www.clerisypress.com; www.wildernesspress.com; www.menasharidge.com
Dist(s): **MyiLibrary**
Publishers Group West (PGW).

Adventures Galore, (978-0-9759542) Orders Addr.: P.O. Box 748, Lake George, CO 80827 USA Tel 719-748-8458; Fax: 719-748-8459; Edit Addr.: 35100 Hwy. 24, Lake George, CO 80827 USA
Web site: http://www.adventuresgalore.com.

Adventures in Print, (978-0-615-37286-0; 978-0-9908487; 978-0-9972665; 978-0-9974036) 55 Greenview Dr. Apt 6, Manchester, NH 03102 USA Tel 603-728-7701
E-mail: i.message99@live.com.

Adventures Into The Heart *See* **Playful Mind Pr.**

Adventures of Everyday Geniuses, The *Imprint of* **Mainstream Connections Publishing**

Adventures of Henry, LLC, (978-1-936813) 627 Evans St., Oshkosh, WI 54901 USA Tel 920-252-3578
E-mail: Darrin.Anderson@gmail.com
Web site: Www.adventuresofhenry.com.

Adventures of Hillary, The *Imprint of* **Nelson Publishing, LLC**

Adventures of Lady LLC, The, (978-0-9789984) 4907 White Bud Ct., Windermere, FL 34786 USA (SAN 852-1360).

Adventures of Pookie, The, (978-0-692-16062-6; 978-0-578-58257-3) 86027 Albermarle Ct., Fernandina Beach, FL 32034 USA Tel 330-844-7602
E-mail: theadventuresofpookie@gmail.com
Dist(s): **Ingram Content Group.**

Adventures Unlimited Pr., (978-0-932813; 978-1-931882; 978-1-935487; 978-1-939149; 978-1-948803) Orders Addr.: P.O. Box 74, Kempton, IL 60946 USA (SAN 630-1126) Tel 815-253-6390; Fax: 815-253-6300; Edit Addr.: 303 Main St., Kempton, IL 60946 USA (SAN 250-3484)
E-mail: auphq@frontiernet.net
Web site: http://www.adventuresunlimitedpress.com
Dist(s): **Hancock Hse. Pubs.**
New Leaf Distributing Co., Inc.
SCB Distributors.

Advocate Hse. *Imprint of* **A Cappela Publishing**

Aea Media, LLC, (978-0-9862908) 500 Umstead Dr., Chapel Hill, NC 27516 USA Tel 919-357-6948
E-mail: atkinsae@gmail.com
Web site: terrowintrilogy.com.

Aegaeon Publishing, (978-1-934810) Div. of Aegaeon Group International, One Penn Plaza 250 W. 34th St., 36th Flr., New York, NY 10119 USA Tel 212-835-1629
Web site: http://www.aegaeonpublishing.com.

Aegean Design, (978-0-9758803) 5009 20th Ave., NW, Seattle, WA 98107 USA Tel 206-612-9698
E-mail: bdarling@handofzeus.com
Web site: http://www.aegeandesign.net.

Aegypan, (978-1-59818; 978-1-60312) Div. of Alan Rodgers Bks., 4750 Lincoln Blvd., No. 360, Marina del Rey, CA 90292-9303 USA.

Aenor Trust, The, (978-0-9724251; 978-0-9766401; 978-0-9768128) Orders Addr.: P.O. Box 1410, Silverton, OR 97381 USA; Edit Addr.: 1286 Pressler Court S., Salem, OR 97306 USA
Web site: http://www.aenortrust.org; http://www.stellarlane.org.

Aeon Publishing Inc., (978-0-9713099; 978-0-9718509; 978-1-932047; 978-1-932303; 978-1-932560; 978-1-59526; 978-1-933626; 978-1-60594) Orders Addr.: 7580 NW 5th St. #16535, Fort Lauderdale, FL 33318 USA Tel 954-726-0902; Fax: 954-726-0903; Toll Free: 866-229-9244; Imprints: Llumina Christian Books (LluminaChrist); Llumina Press (Llumina Pr); Llumina Kids (Llumina Kids)
E-mail: diane@llumina.com
Web site: http://www.llumina.com.

Aeon Publishing, Incorporated *See* **Breezeway Books**

AequiLibris Publishing LLC, (978-0-9816446) Orders Addr.: P.O. Box 1542, New London, NH 03257 USA
Web site: http://www.AequiLibrisPublishing.com.

Aerial Photography Services, Inc., (978-0-936672; 978-1-880970; 978-0-9789603; 978-0-9815804; 978-0-9836193; 978-0-9916287) 2511 S. Tryon St., Charlotte, NC 28203 USA (SAN 214-2791) Tel 704-333-5143; Fax: 704-333-4911
E-mail: aps@aps-1.com; gregg@aps-1.com
Web site: http://www.aps-1.com.

Aerospace 1 Pubns., (978-0-9705150) 8 Brookstone Ct., Streamwood, IL 60107 USA
E-mail: aerospace1@aol.com.

Aesop Pubs., LLC, (978-0-9725218) 11153 Powder Horn Dr., Potomac, MD 20854 USA
E-mail: plastcfgs@aol.com.

AFCHRON, (978-1-892824; 978-1-938976) Orders Addr.: 1692 Golf Link Dr., Atlanta, GA 30088 USA
E-mail: satbantv@gmail.com
Web site: http://www.afchron.com
Dist(s): **Copyright Clearance Ctr., Inc.**
EBSCO Media.

Afewerki, Wegahta, (978-0-578-83778-9) 4465 Oakdale Crescent Ct., Fairfax, VA 22030 USA Tel 703-485-6256
E-mail: afewerki.wegahta@gmail.com.

Affirming Faith, (978-0-9798627; 978-0-9897373; 978-1-7335517) 1181 Whispering Knoll Ln., Rochester Hills, MI 48306 USA (SAN 854-591X) Tel 248-909-5735; Fax: 248-608-1756
E-mail: loriwagner@affirmingfaith.com
Web site: http://www.affirmingfaith.com
Dist(s): **Pentecostal Publishing Hse.**

Affordable Pub, (978-0-9778348; 978-0-9819688; 978-0-9836378; 978-0-578-46531-9; 978-0-578-51978-4; 978-0-578-73139-1; 978-0-578-73141-4; 978-0-578-73272-5; 978-0-578-27424-9) P.O. Box 720952, San Diego, CA 92129 USA Tel 866-661-8821; P.O. Box 185, Julian, CA 92036
E-mail: BLSSDASSR1@aol.com
Web site: http://www.affordablepublishing.org.

Africa World Pr., (978-0-86543; 978-1-59221) 541 W. Ingham Ave., Suite B, Trenton, NJ 08638 USA (SAN 692-3925) Tel 609-695-3200; Fax: 609-695-6466
E-mail: customerservice@africaworldpressbooks.com
Web site: http://www.africaworldpressbooks.com.

African American Chronicle Software Publishing Corporation *See* **AFCHRON**

African American Images, (978-0-913543; 978-0-9749000; 978-1-934155) P.O. Box 1799, Chicago Hts, IL 60412-1799 USA Toll Free: 800-552-1991
E-mail: aai@africanamericanimages.com; customer@africanamericanimages.com
Web site: http://AfricanAmericanImages.com
Dist(s): **Ebsco Publishing**
Follett School Solutions
Independent Pubs. Group
MyiLibrary
ebrary, Inc.

African Christian Pr. (GHA) (978-9964-87) *Dist. by* **Mich St U Pr.**

Africana Homestead Legacy Pubs., Inc., (978-0-9653308; 978-0-9770904; 978-0-9799537; 978-0-9818939; 978-0-9825842; 978-0-9831151; 978-1-937622) Orders Addr.: 926 Haddonfield Rd., Suite E. #329, Cherry Hill, NJ 08002 USA (SAN 914-4811) Tel 856-673-0363; Imprints: Nefu Books (Nefu Bks)
E-mail: sales@ahlpub.com; customer-service@ahlpub.com
Web site: http://www.ahlpub.com.

Afro Princess Publishing Co., (978-0-692-65060-8; 978-0-692-77536-3; 978-0-692-19672-4) 1511 Colorado Ave, Grand Rapids, MI 49507 USA Tel 616-375-4233; Toll Free: 616-375-4233
Dist(s): **CreateSpace Independent Publishing Platform.**

Afrolez Productions, LLC, (978-0-615-16123-5) P.O. Box 58085, Philadelphia, PA 19102-8085 USA Tel 215-701-6150
E-mail: contact@notherapedocumentary.org
Web site: http://www.notherapedocumentary.org.

AfterShock Comics, (978-0-9795939; 978-0-9801479; 978-1-935002; 978-0-692-94590-2; 978-1-949028; 978-1-956731) 15300 Ventura Blvd Suite 507, Sherman Oaks, CA 91403 USA
E-mail: christinaharrington@aftershock.ninja; mikemarts@aftershock.ninja; katherinejamison@aftershock.ninja; JoePruett@aftershock.ninja
Web site: www.aftershockcomics.com
Dist(s): **Diamond Comic Distributors, Inc.**

Afton, Brian, (978-0-9985693) 1234 Burnt Hill Rd, Olean, NY 14760 USA Tel 716-372-5850; Fax: 716-372-5850
E-mail: bafton@attglobal.net.

Afton Historical Society Pr., (978-0-9639338; 978-1-890434; 978-0-9976296; 978-1-7361021; 979-8-9880255) 6800 France Ave. S. Suite 370, Edina, MN 55435 USA Tel 651-436-8443
E-mail: aftonpress@gmail.com
Web site: http://www.aftonpress.com
Dist(s): **Bookmen, Inc.**
Brodart Co.
Coutts Information Services
Eastern Bk. Co.
Follett School Solutions
Galda Library Services, Inc.

Afton Publishing, (978-0-39359) Orders Addr.: P.O. Box 1399, Andover, NJ 07821-1399 USA (SAN 692-2570) Tel 973-579-2442; Fax: 973-579-2842; Toll Free: 888-238-6665
E-mail: info3@aftonpublishing.com
Web site: http://www.aftonpublishing.com.

Against All Oddz Publishing, (978-0-9913040; 978-0-9961916) 2500 Chamberlayne Ave., Richmond, VA 23222 USA Tel 804-347-2590
E-mail: lbking73@gmail.com.

Agape Inc, The Lighthouse Books *See* **LightHse. Bks., The**

Agapy LLC *See* **Agapy Publishing**

Agapy Publishing, (978-0-9721328; 978-1-938522) a/o Agapy Publishing, 1608 Sun Prairie Dr., St. Joseph, MI 49085 USA Tel 321-345-8297
E-mail: info@agapy.com; president@agapy.com
Web site: http://www.agapy.com
Dist(s): **Ingram Content Group.**

Agate Publishing, Inc., (978-0-940625; 978-0-9609516; 978-1-57284; 978-0-9724562; 978-1-932841) 1501 Madison St., Evanston, IL 60202 USA
Web site: http://www.agatepublishing.com
Dist(s): **MyiLibrary**
Open Road Integrated Media, Inc.
Publishers Group West (PGW)
ebrary, Inc.

A-Gator Publishing,

AGB Publishing, (978-1-930908) Div. of Mini Enterprises - M.E., 19425 Bankers House Dr., Katy, TX 77449-0243 USA; Imprints: AGB/me (AGB-me)
E-mail: minienterprises@msn.com; minitaylr@msn.com.

AGB/me *Imprint of* **AGB Publishing**

AGC Outreach Ministry, (978-0-9774115) 801 WHITEHEAD RD, GREENSBURG, PA 15658 USA Tel 724-219-3858
E-mail: stevenjsmith799@gmail.com
Web site: www.hisgreatworks.com.

AGD Publishing *See* **AGD Publishing Services, LLC**

AGD Publishing Services, LLC, (978-1-7346758; 978-1-7372867; 979-8-9864864; 979-8-9888162) 10904 Hollaway Dr., Upper Marlboro, MD 20772 USA Tel 202-258-4987
E-mail: allisongdaniels@verizon.net
Web site: www.agdpublishing.com.

Ageless Treasures, (978-0-9705726) Orders Addr.: 3536 Saint Andrews Village Cir., Louisville, KY 40241-2664 USA (SAN 253-794X) Tel 502-412-5940; Fax: 502-327-6233
E-mail: dcw0810@insightbb.com; carlawebb@agelesstreasures.net.

Agent of Danger *Imprint of* **Komikwerks, LLC**

Agents of Change, (978-1-928992) Div. of Granite Publishing, LLC, P.O. Box 1429, Columbus, NC 28722-1429 USA Tel 828-894-3088; Fax: 828-894-8454; Toll Free: 800-366-0264
E-mail: brian@5thworld.com
Web site: http://5thworld.com
Dist(s): **New Leaf Distributing Co., Inc.**

Age-Trotters Press *See* **Cameltrotters Publishing**

Agile Pig, (978-1-7333925) 1442 E Parkview Dr, Gilbert, AZ 85295 USA Tel 602-708-7467
E-mail: edouano@gmail.com.

Agile Pr., (978-0-9718239) P.O. Box 1939, Chicago, IL 60690-1939 USA
E-mail: agilepress@agileresearch.com.

AGL Editions, (978-0-9745629) 1000 Bay Dr., No. 524, Niceville, FL 32578 USA.

Aglob Publishing, (978-0-9708560; 978-1-59427) P.O. Box 4036, Hallandale, FL 33008 USA Tel 954-456-1476; Fax: 954-456-3903
E-mail: info@aglobpublishing.com; info@aglob.com
Web site: http://www.aglobpublishing.com.

AGM Communications, (978-0-9985807) P.O. Box 52772, Baton Rouge, LA 70892 USA; Imprints: Muscle Books (MYID_A_MUSCLE)
E-mail: mvgray2000@yahoo.com.

Agnello-Sylvester, Susanne, (978-0-578-69875-5; 978-1-7361592) 372 Wildwood Rd. 0, RONKONKOMA, NY 11779 USA Tel 5168852257
E-mail: ms.susanne2020@gmail.com.

Agnes & Aubrey (GBR) (978-1-9164745) *Dist. by* **Consort Bk Sales.**

Agora *Imprint of* **Polis Bks.**

Agora Pubns., Inc., (978-1-887250; 978-0-9904599) 17 Dean St., Millis, MA 02054 USA (SAN 851-8521) Tel 508-376-1073 (phone/fax)
E-mail: agorapub@verizon.net; info@agorapublication.com
Web site: http://www.agorapublications.com
Dist(s): **Philosophy Documentation Ctr.**

Agreka Bks., LLC, (978-1-888106; 978-0-9777072; 978-1-934243) P.O. Box 14405, Scottsdale, AZ 85267-14405 USA Tel 480-767-1774; Toll Free Fax: 888-771-7758; Toll Free: 800-360-5284
E-mail: info@agreka.com
Web site: http://www.agreka.com; http://www.utahbooks.com; http://www.historypreserved.com
Dist(s): **Ingram Content Group**
Quality Bks., Inc.

AGS Secondary *Imprint of* **Savvas Learning Co.**

Agua Caliente Pr., (978-0-9768275) 4352 Riley Rd., Gladwin, MI 48624 USA Tel 989-426-8400
E-mail: maryhansen4@hotmail.com.

Aguilar *Imprint of* **Penguin Random Hse. Grupo Editorial (USA) LLC**

Aguilar, Altea, Taurus, Alfaguara, S.A. de C.V (MEX) (978-968-19) *Dist. by* **Santillana.**

Aguilar Chilena de Ediciones, Ltd. (CHL) (978-956-239; 978-956-347) *Dist. by* **Ediciones.**

Aguilar Chilena de Ediciones, Ltd. (CHL) (978-956-239; 978-956-347) *Dist. by* **Santillana.**

Aguilar Editorial (MEX) *Dist. by* **Santillana.**

Aguirre Cox, Vicki & Ernest, (978-0-9767994) 10810 Lake Path Dr., San Antonio, TX 78217 USA Tel 210-364-8590; Fax: 210-653-3089
E-mail: vacernas@aol.com.

Aha! Elora Danan Productions, (978-0-9786729) P.O. Box 428, Estero, FL 33928 USA
Dist(s): **Follett School Solutions.**

aha! Process, Inc., (978-0-9647437; 978-1-929229; 978-1-934583; 978-1-938248; 978-1-948244) P.O. Box 727, Highlands, TX 77562-0727 USA Tel 281-426-5300; Fax: 281-426-5600; Toll Free: 800-424-9484
Web site: http://www.ahaprocess.com
Dist(s): **Follett School Solutions**
Greenleaf Book Group.

Aharon, Sara *See* **Enterprise Leaf Pr.**

A-Head Publishing, (978-0-9816283) 41 Via Del Sol, Nicasio, CA 94946 USA (SAN 856-0862)
E-mail: aheadpublishing@gmail.com
Web site: http://www.a-headpublishing.com.

Ahlman Publishing, (978-0-9712906) Div. of KODIAK Publishing, 9525 W. 230 St., Morristown, MN 55052 USA Tel 507-685-4247; Fax: 507-685-4280
E-mail: larryahlman@hotmail.com
Web site: http://www.ahlmans.com/mittens.html
Dist(s): **Partners Bk. Distributing, Inc.**

Ahmed, (978-0-692-69940-9) 2600 Gramercy St apt 447, houston, TX 77030 USA Tel 713-470-8000.

Ahonen, Melissa *See* **Melissa Ahonen LLC**

Ahoy Comics, (978-0-9980442; 978-1-952090) 101 Enderberry Cir., Syracuse, NY 13224 USA Tel 410-683-7080
E-mail: info@comicsahoy.com
Web site: www.comicsahoy.com
Dist(s): **Diamond Comic Distributors, Inc.**
Simon & Schuster, Inc.

Ahrendt, Evan, (978-1-7366086) 2885 Sw. 122nd Ave., Beaverton, OR 97005 USA Tel 503-349-0996
E-mail: evanahrendt@gmail.com.

Ahzar's Bk. Co. Publishing, (978-0-9746130) 3675 So. Rainbow Blvd No. 107, Las Vegas, NV 89103 USA Tel 702-391-1914; Fax: 702-871-8777
E-mail: croesus@joimail.com.

AIC Publications, (978-0-9799464) P.O. Box 152672, Arlington, TX 76015-8672 USA
E-mail: president@aicpublications.com.

Aidan's Butterfly Pubns., (978-0-9787341) 4946 W. Laurie Ln., Glendale, AZ 85302 USA Fax: 623-776-9921
E-mail: eetagt@aol.com.

Ailam Publishing LLC, (978-0-9837759) 12900 S. May, Calumet Park, IL 60827 USA (SAN 860-2859)
E-mail: ailampublishing@aol.com.

A.I.M. Enterprises, (978-0-9772303) 507 Grace - Stockham, Aurora, NE 68818-7019 USA
Web site: http://www.aim4theheart.com.

Aim Higher Bks., (978-0-9713292) 10556 Combie Rd., Suite 6242, Auburn, CA 95602 USA
E-mail: sales@aimhigherbooks.com
Web site: http://www.AimHigherBooks.com.

Aim Higher Publishing *See* **Aim Higher Bks.**

AIMS Education Foundation, (978-1-881431; 978-1-932093; 978-1-60519) Orders Addr.: 1595 S. Chestnut Ave., Fresno, CA 93702-4706 USA Tel 559-255-4094; Fax: 559-255-6396; Toll Free: 888-733-2467
E-mail: aimsed@aimsedu.org
Web site: http://www.aimsedu.org.

AIMS Multimedia, (978-0-8068) 1 Discovery Pl., Silver Spring, MD 20910-3354 USA (SAN 687-3464) Toll Free: 800-367-2467
Web site: http://www.aimsmultimedia.com/
Dist(s): **Follett School Solutions**
Weston Woods Studios, Inc.

Ain't No Joke Bks., (978-0-9778342) 118 Lyman Pl., West Palm Beach, FL 33409 USA Tel 305-399-3596
E-mail: keithgwright@yahoo.com
Web site: AintNoJoke.com
Dist(s): **BookBaby.**

Aint No Jokes Books Incorporated *See* **Ain't No Joke Bks.**

Air & Nothingness Pr., (978-0-9679429; 978-0-9991953; 978-1-7358356; 979-8-9868195) 2224 Delaware Ave., Pittsburgh, PA 15218 USA
E-mail: info@aanpress.com
Web site: http://www.aanpress.com.

airjam.com, (978-0-9786478) 3379 C1/2 Road, Palisade, CO 81526 USA.

Airplane Reader Publishing, (978-0-9702405; 978-0-9765485) Div. of Pro Leisure Tour, Inc., 9260 E. Lake Pl., Greenwood Village, CO 80111 USA (SAN 253-6935) Fax: 303-221-2766 24-hour dedicated fax line; Toll Free: 877-611-6222 voice mail, 24 hours
E-mail: theo@12milestoparadise.com; tedsimendinger@comcast.net; ted@funnyted.com
Web site: http://www.proleisuretour.com; http://www.piggychurch.com; http://www.12milestoparadise.com; http://www.richwithoutmoney.org; http://www.jurassictrout.com; http://www.tukibanjo.com.

Airship *Imprint of* **Seven Seas Entertainment, LLC**

Airways International, Inc., (978-0-9653993) Orders Addr.: P.O. Box 1109, Sandpoint, ID 83864 USA Tel 208-263-2098; Fax: 208-263-5906; Edit Addr.: P.O. Box 1109, Sandpoint, ID 83864 USA
E-mail: airways@airwaysmag.com
Web site: http://www.airwaysmag.com.

AJ Publishing, (978-0-578-46066-6) 268 Armstrong Ave., Jersey City, NJ 07305 USA Tel 201-920-5881
E-mail: lspears@kismetofkings.org.

AJL Publishers, (978-0-9794618) 25 Auvergne, Newport Coast, CA 92657 USA (SAN 853-5116) Tel 949-887-9073; Fax: 949-640-0339
E-mail: bachas@cox.net.

AJM Bks., (978-0-9896211) 11121 W. Amelia Ave, Avondale, AZ 85392 USA Tel 623-877-9114
E-mail: ajohnsonmccurdy@yahoo.com.

Ajoyin Publishing, Inc., (978-0-9787472; 978-0-9792739; 978-0-9818488; 978-1-60920) Orders Addr.: P.O. Box 342, Three Rivers, MI 49093 USA; Edit Addr.: 55919 Buckhorn Rd., Three Rivers, MI 49093 USA (SAN 852-9817) Toll Free: 888-273-4569; Imprints: Accent Publications (Acent)
E-mail: pam@ajoyin.com
Web site: http://www.ajoyin.com.

AJS Pubns., Inc., (978-0-931298; 978-1-892291; 978-0-9904772) 229 Brier Ct., Island Lake, IL 60042 USA (SAN 223-5846) Tel 847-526-5027; Fax: 847-487-5229 Do not confuse with AJS Publishing, Inc., Los Angeles, CA
Web site: http://www.ajspublications.com.

AK Classics, LLC, (978-0-9814945; 978-0-692-92223-1; 978-1-7320482; 978-1-7357964; 978-1-7378648;

979-8-9878326) P.O. Box 77023, Charlotte, NC 28271-7003 USA
E-mail: marcuskimbrough@aol.com
Web site: www.akclassicstories.com.

K Pr. (GBR) *(978-1-873176; 978-1-902593; 978-1-904859; 978-1-84935) Dist. by* **Consort Bk Sales.**

K Pr. Distribution, *(978-1-873176; 978-1-902593; 978-0-9830597; 978-1-939202)* 370 Ryan Ave, Unit 100, Chico, CA 95973 USA (SAN 298-2234) Tel 510-208-1708; Fax: 510-208-1701
E-mail: akpress@akpress.org
Web site: http://www.akpress.org
Dist(s): **Consortium Bk. Sales & Distribution.**

KA Wendy Wonder, *(978-0-9967904)* 3020 SW 15th Ct, Gresham, OR 97080 USA Tel 541-771-3711
E-mail: mssveen@aol.com.

Akasha Classics *Imprint of* **Akasha Publishing, LLC**

Akasha Publishing, LLC, *(978-1-60512)* Orders Addr.: 2050 Emerald Ln., Fairfield, IA 52556 USA Fax: 866-485-5727; Toll Free: 877-745-7317; *Imprints:* Akasha Classics (Akasha Classics)
E-mail: registrar@akashapublishing.com
Web site: http://www.akashapublishing.com
Dist(s): **Follett School Solutions**
Ingram Content Group.

Akashic Bks., *(978-1-888451; 978-0-9719206; 978-1-933354; 978-1-936070; 978-1-61775)* 232 Third St., No. B404, Brooklyn, NY 11215 USA Tel 718-643-9193; Fax: 718-643-9195; *Imprints:* Black Sheep (BlckSheep); Jones, Kaylie Books (KJones Bks)
E-mail: info@akashicbooks.com
Web site: http://www.akashicbooks.com
Dist(s): **Blackstone Audio, Inc.**
Children's Plus, Inc.
Consortium Bk. Sales & Distribution
Follett School Solutions
MyiLibrary
Open Road Integrated Media, Inc.
SPD-Small Pr. Distribution
ebrary, Inc.

AKA:yoLa, *(978-0-9842288; 978-1-936688; 978-1-942168; 978-1-951960)* 315 Bernadette Dr. Ste 3, Columbia, MO 65203 USA Tel 573-864-1479; *Imprints:* Compass Flower Press (CompassFlower)
Web site: http://www.akayola.com; www.compassflowerpress.com; www.aka-publishing.com
Dist(s): **eBookit.com.**

AKB Design, *(978-0-9748702)* Orders Addr.: 17640 Corkill Rd., #27, Desert Hot Springs, CA 92241 USA Tel 760-329-3233; 760-895-5646
Web site: www.akbdesign.com.

Aker Pr., *(978-0-578-41124-8)* 3701 S. Flagler Dr. a-206, West Palm Beach, FL 33405 USA Tel 323-309-1077
E-mail: ldwphotog@gmail.com
Dist(s): **Independent Pub.**

Akiara Bks. (ESP) *(978-84-17440) Dist. by* **IPG Chicago.**

Akimbo Bks., *(978-0-9990787)* P.O. Box 944, New York, NY 10002 USA Tel 917-530-6611
E-mail: adjowii@yahoo.com.

Akinleye, Titilope, *(978-0-9983312)* 3410 whispering hills Pl., Laurel, MD 20724 USA Tel 301-317-3924
E-mail: Titiakinleye@yahoo.com.

Akins, Brittany, *(978-1-7369882)* 108 Tiburon Ct. 0, GOLDSBORO, NC 27534 USA Tel (757)608-8491
E-mail: brittanyakins1989@gmail.com.

Akins, ShaKera, *(978-0-692-98411-6; 978-0-578-47467-0; 978-0-578-34743-1)* P.O. Box 616815, Orlando, FL 32861 USA Tel 407-970-7480
E-mail: shakera.akins@gmail.com.

Akinyemi, Philip, *(978-0-9979238; 978-1-7342603; 978-1-7351099)*
E-mail: akinspo88@gmail.com
Web site: www.philipakinyemi.com.

Akmaeon Publishing, LLC, *(978-0-9850410; 978-0-9988827)* 309 Pirkle Ferry Rd. Suite C200, Cumming, GA 30040 USA Tel 404-402-3793
E-mail: free3055@bellsouth.net.

AKMO Pubs., *(978-0-9745952)* P.O. Box 669, Odessa, FL 33556-9998 USA.

Aknowingspirit LLC, *(978-1-7333675; 978-1-7377860)* P.O. Box 3324, Washington, DC 20010 USA Tel 202-567-7434
E-mail: cpaul@aknowingspirit.com
Web site: www.aknowingspirit.com.

Akom Publishing Hse., *(978-0-9799134)* 244 Madison Ave., No. 745, New York, NY 10016 USA
E-mail: Akom2000@aol.com
Web site: http://www.akompublishinghouse.com.

AKP Holdings, LLC, *(978-1-7366518; 978-1-7378585; 979-8-9861567)* 3773 Howard Hughes Pkwy., Las Vegas, NV 89169 USA Tel 407-575-9625
E-mail: 1000akpholdings@gmail.com.

Al Ghuriar Print, *(978-1-941940; 978-1-946026; 978-1-950926; 978-1-953724; 978-1-954328; 978-1-956213)* Masafi Compound 5613, Dubai, AL 75210 USA Tel 504-427-4110
E-mail: go2farhan@gmail.com.

Alaafia Kids Co., *(978-0-9788737)* 1020 Stonebrook Rd. Unit B, Sykesville, MD 21784-6173 USA.

Alabama Folklife Assn., *(978-0-9672672; 978-0-9772132)* Orders Addr.: c/o Alabama Center for Traditional Culture, 410 N. Hull St, Montgomery, AL 36104 USA Tel 334-242-3601; Fax: 334-269-9098
E-mail: joycecauthen@bellsouth.net
Web site: http://www.alabamafolklife.org.

Alabaster Bk. Pub., *(978-0-9725031; 978-0-9768108; 978-0-9790949; 978-0-9796866; 978-0-9815763; 978-0-9823005; 978-0-9846137; 978-0-9846320; 978-0-9840004; 978-0-9860300; 978-0-9912660; 978-0-9861790; 978-0-9982352; 978-1-7346763)* Orders Addr.: P.O. Box 401, Kernersville, NC 27285 USA Tel 336-295-4322; Fax: 336-996-2011; P.O. Box 401, Kernersville, NC 27285 Fax: 336-996-2011; Edit Addr.: 324 Lakeside Dr., Kernersville, NC 27284 USA
E-mail: pblshralabaster@aol.com; ljdixle@aol.com
Web site: http://www.publisheralabaster.org; http://www.PublisherAlabaster.biz.

Alabaster Books *See* **Alabaster Bk. Pub.**

Aladdin *Imprint of* **Simon & Schuster Children's Publishing**

Aladdin Library *Imprint of* **Simon & Schuster Children's Publishing**

Aladdin Paperbacks *Imprint of* **Simon & Schuster Children's Publishing**

Aladdin/Beyond Words,
Dist(s): **Children's Plus, Inc.**
Simon & Schuster, Inc.

Alarie, Shirley, *(978-0-9968087; 978-1-7334983)* 10423 Hallmark Blvd, Riverview, FL 33578 USA Tel 413-441-9769
E-mail: shirleyalarie@gmail.com
Web site: https://findinggodamongus.com.

Alaska Avenue Pr., *(978-0-9748091)* 5770 Alaska Ave., Alto, MI 49302-9714 USA Tel 616-868-0308
E-mail: stonehills47657@aol.com.

Alaska Geographic Assn., *(978-0-930931; 978-0-9602876; 978-0-9825765; 978-1-938494)* 241 N. C St., Anchorage, AK 99501 USA (SAN 223-5269) Tel 907-274-8440; Fax: 907-274-8343
E-mail: dwhitecar@alaskageographic.org
Web site: http://www.alaskageographic.org.

Alaska Independent Pubs., *(978-0-9743369; 978-0-9797442; 978-0-9883390)* Orders Addr.: P.O. Box 1125, Homer, AK 99603 USA Toll Free: 877-210-2665
E-mail: wizardworksak@gmail.com
Dist(s): **Wizard Works.**

Alaska Native Language Ctr., *(978-0-933769; 978-1-55500)* Univ. of Alaska, P.O. Box 757680, Fairbanks, AK 99775-7680 USA (SAN 692-9796) Tel 907-474-7874; Fax: 907-474-6586
E-mail: fntla@uaf.edu
Web site: http://www.uaf.edu/anlc
Dist(s): **Chicago Distribution Ctr.**
Todd Communications
Wizard Works.

Alaska Natural History Association *See* **Alaska Geographic Assn.**

Alaska Northwest Bks. *Imprint of* **West Margin Pr.**

Alaska Zoo, The, *(978-0-9673915)* 4731 O'Malley Rd., Anchorage, AK 99516 USA.

Alazar Pr. *Imprint of* **Royal Swan Enterprises, Inc.**

Alba House *See* **St Pauls/Alba Hse. Pubs.**

Alban Lake Publishing, *(978-0-9915767; 978-0-578-43514-5; 978-0-578-50253-3; 978-0-578-52502-0)* P.O. Box 782, Cedar Rapids, IA 52406-0782 USA Tel 319-431-5206
E-mail: albanlake@yahoo.com
Web site: www.albanlake.com.

Albatros (ARG) *(978-950-24) Dist. by* **Lectorum Pubns.**

Albatros, Nakladatelstvi pro deti mladez, a.s. (CZE) *(978-80-00) Dist. by* **Consort Bk Sales.**

Albatross FunnyBks., *(978-0-9983792; 978-1-949889)* PO Box 60627, Nashville, TN 37206 USA Tel 615-430-1647
E-mail: ericpwl@icloud.com
Web site: www.albatrossfunnybooks.com
Dist(s): **Diamond Comic Distributors, Inc.**
Penguin Random Hse. LLC.

Albatross Pubs., *(978-0-615-45506-8; 978-1-946963)* Orders Addr.: Corso Europa 382, Villaricca Napoli , 80010 ITA Tel 406-219-4006; Edit Addr.: 54-3853 Akoni Pule Hwy, Kapaau, HI 96755 USA
E-mail: albatrosspublishers@gmail.com.

Albee, Michael, *(978-0-9745405)* 1575 W. Mable, Anaheim, CA 92802 USA Tel 714-863-2149
E-mail: malbee@fairmontschools.net.

Albers, Christine, *(978-0-615-19666-4)* 6924 Brookview Dr., Urbandale, IA 50322 USA Tel 515-270-4606
E-mail: albears5@msn.com.

Albin-Michel, Editions (FRA) *(978-2-226) Dist. by* **Distribks Inc.**

Albright Creative, LLC, *(978-0-578-44332-4; 978-0-578-45680-5; 978-0-578-45681-2; 978-0-578-68069-9)* P.O. Box 2381, Lee's Summit, MO 64063 USA Tel 816-875-6416
E-mail: erin@albrightcreative.us
Web site: albrightcreative.us.

Album Publishing Company, Incorporated *See* **RJI Publishing**

ALCAPS, LLC, *(978-0-9769769)* 4004 Cibola Village Dr., NE, Albuquerque, NM 87111 USA
Web site: http://www.heartstohearts.net.

Alchemist's Almanac *See* **Pseudepigrapha Publishing**

Alchemy, *(978-1-7336622)* 3733 S. 34th St., Greenfield, WI 53221 USA Tel 414-331-8280
E-mail: mark@bradfordweb.com
Web site: markbradford.org.

Alchemy Bks., *(978-0-931290)* 1029 Solano Ave., No. E, Albany, CA 94706-1680 USA (SAN 111-3119).

Alchemy Creative, Inc., *(978-0-9675901)* 4650 Cardinal Dr., Beaumont, TX 77705 USA Tel 409-842-5240 ext 18
Web site: http://www.ecpadventures.com; http://www.adventuresoftheelements.com/.

Alchemy Hero Publishing, *(978-0-9975433)* 10442 s artesian, Chicago, IL 60655 USA Tel 773-732-7722
E-mail: luisr124@gmail.com
Web site: www.themagicinourmess.com.

ALCHEMY RANCH STUDIOS LLC, *(978-0-9881814; 978-0-9909461)* Orders Addr.: 655 Orville Rd. E., Eatonville, WA 98328 USA
E-mail: cb@cbwilliams.us; cammywilliams@me.com
Web site: www.cbwilliams.us.

ALCJR Enterprises, *(978-0-9752760; 978-0-692-60956-9)* P.O. Box 4067, Midlothian, VA 23112-0001 USA Tel 804-677-4557; Fax: 804-744-0100
E-mail: alcjr@verizon.net
Web site: http://www.alcjr.com.

Aldelo Systems Inc., *(978-0-9765992)* 4641 Spyres Way Ste. 4, Modesto, CA 95356-9802 USA
E-mail: sales@aldelo.com
Web site: http://www.aldelo.com.

Alderac Entertainment Group, *(978-1-887953; 978-1-59472)* 4045 Guasti Rd., No. 210, Ontario, CA 91761 USA
E-mail: kcarpenter@alderac.com; dlepore@alderac.com
Web site: http://www.alderac.com
Dist(s): **PSI (Publisher Services, Inc.).**

Aldine de Gruyter *See* **Aldine Transaction**

Aldine Transaction, *(978-0-202)* Div. of Transaction Publishers, 390 Campus Dr., Somerset, NJ 08873 USA (SAN 212-4726) Fax: 732 748 9801; Toll Free: 888 999 6778; c/o Rutgers — The State University of New Jersey, 35 Berrue Cir., Piscataway, NJ 08854
E-mail: orders@transactionpub.com
Web site: http://www.transactionpub.com
Dist(s): **MyiLibrary**
Transaction Pubs.
ebrary, Inc.

Alef Design Group, *(978-1-881283)* 4423 Fruitland Ave., Los Angeles, CA 90058 USA Tel 323-582-1200; Fax: 323-585-0327; Toll Free: 800-845-0662
E-mail: jane@torahaura.com
Web site: http://www.torahaura.com
Dist(s): **Follett School Solutions.**

Alegria Hispana Pubns., *(978-0-944356)* Orders Addr.: P.O. Box 3765, Ventura, CA 93003 USA (SAN 243-4695) Tel 805-642-3969; Edit Addr.: 958 Scenic Way Dr., Ventura, CA 93003-1435 USA (SAN 243-4709).

Alegro Publishing, *(978-0-9799740; 978-0-615-63638-2; 978-0-578-43831-3; 978-0-578-43833-7)* 10644 Marine View Dr. SW, Seattle, WA 98146 USA Tel 206-999-8824
E-mail: joycemajor1@hotmail.com; info@alegropublishing.com
Web site: http://www.alegropublishing.com; http://www.smilingattheworld.com
Dist(s): **Partners/West Book Distributors.**

Aleixo, James, *(978-0-692-19030-2; 978-0-578-41294-8)* 196 Galloping Hill Rd., Roselle Park, NJ 07204 USA Tel 908-380-3903
E-mail: anna_aleixo@yahoo.com.

Alenick, Chaya, *(978-0-692-05225-9; 978-0-692-06592-1)* 3347 Forrest Dr., Hollywood, FL 33021 USA Tel 786-426-8611
E-mail: chaya.alenick@yahoo.com
Dist(s): **Ingram Content Group.**

Alerksousi, *(978-1-959482)* Lindenstr.13, Wuerselen, AE 52146 USA Tel 170-824-9619
E-mail: nalerksousi@gmail.com.

Alethea In Heart, *(978-0-9719805; 978-1-932370)* PO Box 127, Charlotte, MI 48813 USA
E-mail: truthinheart@hotmail.com
Web site: http://www.truthinheart.com.

Alex Joseph Publishing, *(978-0-9988744)* 2120 N Pass Ave, Burbank, CA 91505 USA
E-mail: leadintoink@gmail.com.

Alexander Art L.P., *(978-1-883576)* P.O. Box 1417, Beaverton, OR 97075-1417 USA Tel 503-362-7939; Fax: 503-361-7401; Toll Free: 800-896-4630
E-mail: sales@alexanderart.com
Web site: http://www.alexanderart.com.

Alexander, John, *(978-0-692-15209-6; 978-0-692-15211-9; 978-0-578-40682-4; 978-1-959815)* 8548 Markham Dr., FRISCO, TX 75035 USA Tel 214-762-5945
E-mail: john@alexandernovels.com
Dist(s): **Ingram Content Group.**

Alexander, Lorraine *See* **Alexander, Raine**

Alexander, Preshes, *(978-1-7368098)* P.O. Box 190107, Roxbury, MA 02119 USA Tel 774-712-5283
E-mail: Preshesalexander@gmail.com.

Alexander Pubns., *(978-0-9623078)* Orders Addr.: P.O. Box 518, Forney, TX 75126 USA Tel 972-552-9519; Edit Addr.: 806 E. Buffalo St., Forney, TX 75126 USA.

Alexander, Raine, *(978-0-9816301)* 2356 Peeler Rd., Dunwoody, GA 30338 USA
E-mail: 2raine@gmail.com
Web site: www.EdoSchool.org.

Alexander Stoll Templeton, *(978-0-9982464)* 3513 W. Howe St., Seattle, WA 98199 USA Tel 206-669-9536
E-mail: templetonas@gmail.com.

Alexander-Marcus Publishing, *(978-0-9760944)* 1115 Tunnel Rd., Santa Barbara, CA 93105 USA
E-mail: andreamarcuslaw@cox.net.

Alexie Bks., *(978-0-9679416)* Div. of Alexie Enterprises, Inc., P.O. Box 3843, Carmel, IN 46082 USA Tel 317-844-5638; Fax: 317-846-0788
E-mail: BusJobs@aol.com; alexie8@aol.com; sales@alexiebooks.com
Web site: http://www.alexieenterprises.com
Dist(s): **Distributors, The.**

AlexMax Publishing Inc., *(978-0-9796643)* Orders Addr.: 4919 Flat Shoals Pkwy Suite 107B-137, Decatur, GA 30034 USA Tel 404-981-4442
E-mail: isbninfo@alexmaxpublishing.com
Web site: http://www.alexmaxpublishing.com.

ALEXZUS Bks., *(978-0-9724733)* 244 Fifth Ave., Suite B260, New York, NY 10001 USA
E-mail: jenbvic@aol.com.

Alfaguara *Imprint of* **Santillana USA Publishing Co., Inc.**

Alfaguara S.A. de Ediciones (ARG) *(978-950-511; 978-987-04) Dist. by* **Santillana.**

Alfranpedoc, *(978-1-930502)* 4100 W. Coyote Ridge Tr., Tucson, AZ 85746 USA Tel 213-926-0762
E-mail: Waylandhi@aol.com
Web site: http://www.books-by-doc.com.

Alfred Music,

Alfred Publishing Co., Inc., *(978-0-7390; 978-0-87487; 978-0-88284; 978-1-58951; 978-1-4574; 978-1-4706)* Orders Addr.: P.O. Box 10003, Van Nuys, CA 91410-0003 USA; Edit Addr.: 123 Dry Rd., Oriskany, NY 13424 USA Tel 315-736-1572; Fax: 315-736-7281; *Imprints:* Warner Bros. Publications (Warner Bro); Suzuki (Suzuki)
E-mail: customerservice@alfred.com; permissions@alfred.com; submissions@alfred.com
Web site: http://www.alfred.com
Dist(s): **Follett School Solutions**
Leonard, Hal Corp.

Algar Editorial, Feditres, S.L. (ESP) *(978-84-923853; 978-84-931382; 978-84-95722; 978-84-96514) Dist. by* **Lectorum Pubns.**

†Algonquin Bks. of Chapel Hill, *(978-0-7611; 978-0-912697; 978-0-945575; 978-1-56512; 978-1-61620; 978-1-64375; 978-1-64904)* Div. of Workman Publishing Co., Inc., Orders Addr.: 225 Varick St. Flr. 9, New York, NY 10014-4381 USA Toll Free Fax: 800-521-1832 (fax orders, customer service); Toll Free: 800-722-7202 (orders, customer service); Edit Addr.: P.O. Box 2225, Chapel Hill, NC 27515-2225 USA (SAN 282-7506) Tel 919-967-0108 (editorial, publicity, marketing); Fax: 919-933-0272 (editorial, publicity, marketing)
E-mail: dialogue@algonquin.com; inquiring@algonquin.com; brunson@algonquin.com
Web site: http://www.algonquin.com; http://www.booksellerscorner.com
Dist(s): **Blackstone Audio, Inc.**
Hachette Bk. Group
Open Road Integrated Media, Inc.
Workman Publishing Co., Inc.; *CIP.*

Algonquin Young Readers, *(978-1-61620)* Div. of Algonquin Books of Chapel Hill, Orders Addr.: P.O. Box 2225, Chapel Hill, NC 27515 USA; Edit Addr.: 225 Varick St., 9th Flr., New York, NY 10014 USA
Web site: http://algonquinyoungreaders.com/
Dist(s): **Blackstone Audio, Inc.**
Children's Plus, Inc.
Hachette Bk. Group
Open Road Integrated Media, Inc.

ALHsiccesslines, *(978-0-615-62527-0)* 13737 Dunbar Terr., Germantown, MD 20874 USA Tel 301-540-2928
E-mail: ALHpromo@aol.com.

Ali Gator (AUS) *(978-1-921772) Dist. by* **Consort Bk Sales.**

ALI Pictures *See* **Bks. That Will Enhance Your Life**

Alianza Editorial, S. A. (ESP) *(978-84-206; 978-84-605; 978-84-9104; 978-84-9181; 978-84-1362) Dist. by* **Distribks Inc.**

Alianza Editorial, S. A. (ESP) *(978-84-206; 978-84-605; 978-84-9104; 978-84-9181; 978-84-1362) Dist. by* **Continental Bk.**

Alianza Editorial, S. A. (ESP) *(978-84-206; 978-84-605; 978-84-9104; 978-84-9181; 978-84-1362) Dist. by* **AIMS Intl.**

Alianza Editorial, S. A. (ESP) *(978-84-206; 978-84-605; 978-84-9104; 978-84-9181; 978-84-1362) Dist. by* **Lectorum Pubns.**

Alianza Editorial, S. A. (ESP) *(978-84-206; 978-84-605; 978-84-9104; 978-84-9181; 978-84-1362) Dist. by* **Libros in Spanish, LLC.**

Alias Enterprises LLC *See* **Lamp Post Inc.**

Alice Bell Books *See* **Dark Ink Media**

Alicia, *(978-0-578-90103-9; 979-8-218-21299-5)* 998 meridian Ave., San Jose, CA 95126 USA Tel 408-292-9359
E-mail: Aliciasmith526@gmail.com.

Alicia R. Jeremiah, *(978-0-578-75351-5)* 352 Midwood St Apt.3R, Brooklyn, NY 11225 USA Tel 646-943-2916
E-mail: Aliciajerimi@gmail.com.

Alien Time Treasure, *(978-0-9727309)* P.O. Box 2665, Newport, RI 02840 USA
E-mail: webmaster@alientimetreasure.com
Web site: http://alientimetreasure.com.

ALife Media, LLC, *(978-1-7321425)* 65 W. 73rd St., New York, NY 10023 USA Tel 347-721-0479
E-mail: alfie.writes@gmail.com.

Alisa Hope Wagner *See* **Marked Writers Publishing**

Aliso Street Productions, *(978-0-9840120)* P.O. Box 36422, Albuquerque, NM 87176 USA Tel 505-414-6366
E-mail: AlisoStreet@aol.com.

Al-Kitaab & As-Sunnah Publishing, *(978-1-891229)* P.O. Box 2542, Arlington, TX 76004 USA Tel 817-801-6933
E-mail: al_jibaly@juno.com.

All About Kids Publishing, *(978-0-9700863; 978-0-9710278; 978-0-9744446; 978-0-9801468; 978-0-615-11427-9; 978-0-9963756; 978-1-7330468; 979-8-9889084)* Orders Addr.: P.O. Box 159, Gilroy, CA 95021 USA (SAN 253-8601) Tel 408-337-1152
E-mail: lguevara@allaboutkidspub.com
Web site: www.oliverbrightside.com; www.allaboutkidspub.com
Dist(s): **Ingram Content Group**
Pathway Bk. Service.

All About Learning Pr., *(978-1-935197; 978-1-959954)* 615 Commerce Loop, Eagle River, WI 54521 USA (SAN 856-8812) Tel 715-477-1976
E-mail: marie@allaboutlearningpress.com
Web site: http://https://www.allaboutlearningpress.com.

All Around Our World Publishing Co., Inc., *(978-0-9799050)* 629 Park Ave., Beloit, WI 53511 USA Tel 608-207-9777; Fax: 608-207-9888
E-mail: brendaaaow@charter.net.

All For One Pr., *(978-0-9745951)* 29193 Northwestern Hwy, No. 658, Southfield, MI 48034 USA (SAN 255-6804) Tel 313-617-4012
E-mail: allforonepress@hotmail.com.

All Gold Publishing Co., *(978-0-9701519)* Orders Addr.: P.O. Box 13504, Dayton, OH 45413-0504 USA Tel 937-586-9804; Edit Addr.: 907 Reist, Dayton, OH 45408-1350 USA
E-mail: allgoldceo@netzero.net
Web site: http://www.allgoldpublishing.com.

All Hallows Eve Press *See* **HallowStyle, LLC**

All Health Chiropractic Ctrs. Inc., *(978-0-9770527)* 567 Church St., Royersford, PA 19468 USA (SAN 256-6443) Tel 610-948-4161
E-mail: susiequsie6@aol.com
Web site: http://www.drsnappy.com.

Publisher Name Index

All Heart Pr., *(978-1-7350877)* 5853 Hartford Way, Brighton, MI 48116-7809 USA Tel 517-927-6419
E-mail: aoginsky@gmail.com
Web site: www.annaoginsky.com.

All Kidding Aside, *(978-0-9794317)* 2829 S. Cypress, Sioux City, IA 51106 USA Tel 712-276-4315
E-mail: bestma34@cableone.net
Web site: http://www.allkiddingaside.biz.

All Nations Pr., *(978-0-9725110; 978-0-9777954; 978-0-9912721)* P.O. Box 10821, Tallahassee, FL 32302 USA Do not confuse with companies with the same or similar name in Colorado Springs, CO, Southlake, TX
E-mail: rcamp427@gmail.com; allnationseditors@gmail.com
Web site: http://http:/allnationseditors.wix.com/books-seller
Dist(s): **Follett School Solutions**
Itasca Bks.

All Over Creation, *(978-0-9788950)* P.O. Box 382, Madera, CA 93639 USA
E-mail: astorybytory@yahoo.com.

All Points Pr., *(978-0-9850827; 978-1-7339161; 979-8-218-16713-4)* 103 Chestnut Ridge Rd., Latrobe, PA 15650 USA (SAN 920-2501) Tel 724-539-4591; Fax: 724-539-3417
E-mail: edward.t62@gmail.com.

All Star Pr., *(978-0-9767816; 978-1-937376)* 944 Oakview Rd., Tarpon Springs, FL 34689 USA Tel 502-713-3149
E-mail: allstarpress@verizon.net
Web site: www.allstarpress.com
Dist(s): **Smashwords.**

All Systems Grow, *(978-0-578-41284-9)* 6721 SW 64th Ave., Miami, FL 33143 USA Tel 305-298-8026
E-mail: patdonovanauthor@yahoo.com
Dist(s): **Ingram Content Group.**

All That Productions, Inc., *(978-0-9679441; 978-0-9903422; 978-1-7339510)* Orders Addr.: P.O. Box 1594, Humble, TX 77347 USA Tel 281-878-2062
E-mail: allthat3@peoplepc.com.

All Things Liz Loves, *(978-1-949142)*
E-mail: allthingslizloves@gmail.com
Web site: www.allthingslizloves.com.

All Things That Matter Pr., *(978-0-9822056; 978-0-9822722; 978-0-9840984; 978-0-9842594; 978-0-9844219; 978-0-9846154; 978-0-9846216; 978-0-9846297; 978-0-9846392; 978-0-9846517; 978-0-9847215; 978-0-9850066; 978-0-9857789; 978-0-9885427; 978-0-9894032; 978-0-9960413; 978-0-9907158; 978-0-9966634; 978-0-9980717; 978-0-9995243; 978-1-7327237; 978-1-7334448; 978-1-7346855; 978-1-7367318; 978-1-7377671; 979-8-9862885; 979-8-9871296; 979-8-9883353) 79 Jones Rd., Somerville, ME 04348 USA*
E-mail: allthingsthatmatterpress@gmail.com
Web site: http://www.allthingsthatmatterpress.com.

Allaf, Mashhad Al, *(978-0-9722722)* P.O. Box 2063, Chester, VA 23831-8440 USA.

Allbaugh, Dan *See* **Green Meeple Bks.**

Allecram Publishing, *(978-0-9764198)* P.O. Box 6003, Dayton, OH 45405 USA Tel 937-278-6630
E-mail: marcellaashe@sbcglobal.net
Web site: http://www.allecrampublishing.com.

Allegheny Pr., *(978-0-910042)* 19323 Elgin Rd., Corry, PA 16407 USA (SAN 201-2456) Tel 814-664-8504
E-mail: hjohn@tbscc.com
Dist(s): **Follett School Solutions.**

Allegiant Publishing Group, *(978-1-945737)* 171 Durham Rd., Dover, NH 03820 USA Tel 603-343-8107
E-mail: info@allegiantpublishing.com
Web site: www.allegiantpublishing.com.

Allen & Unwin (AUS) *(978-0-04; 978-0-86861; 978-1-86373; 978-1-86448; 978-1-875680; 978-0-7299; 978-1-86508; 978-1-74114; 978-1-74175; 978-1-74176; 978-1-74237; 978-1-74269; 978-1-877505; 978-0-646-24696-3; 978-1-74331; 978-1-74343; 978-1-76029; 978-1-925395; 978-1-925575; 978-1-925576; 978-1-925577; 978-1-76063; 978-1-76087; 978-1-922351; 978-1-76106; 978-1-76118; 978-1-922616; 978-1-988547; 978-1-922928; 978-1-76147; 978-1-76150; 978-1-74115; 978-0-7316-7153-3; 978-1-76011; 978-1-925393; 978-1-925394; 978-1-) Dist. by* **IPG Chicago.**

Allen, Edward Publishing, LLC *See* **Leah St. James Bks.**

Allen Publishing, USA *See* **ALEXZUS Bks.**

Allen, Toi Operations, *(978-0-9753787)* 11300 E. 85th Terr., Raytown, MO 64138 USA Tel 816-737-5293; Fax: 816-923-2634
E-mail: itasca2001@aol.com.

Allen-Ayers Bks., *(978-0-9658702)* 4621 S. Atlantic Ave., No. 7603, Ponce Inlet, PA 32127 USA Tel 386-761-3956
E-mail: allen-ayers@cfl.rr.com.

AllensRusk Pr., *(978-0-9672246)* P.O. Box 100213, Nashville, TN 37224 USA Tel 615-365-0993
E-mail: dmt209@aol.com.

Allergic Child Publishing Group, *(978-1-58628)* 6660 Delmonico Dr., Suite D249, Colorado Springs, CO 80919 USA Tel 719-338-0202; Fax: 719-633-0375
E-mail: nicole@allergicchild.com
Web site: http://www.allergicchild.com
Dist(s): **Follett School Solutions.**

Alli Kat Publishing, *(978-0-9788725)* 2353 Alexandria Dr., Suite 201, Lexington, KY 40504 USA Tel 859-264-7700; Fax: 859-264-7744
E-mail: eyemanjlh@aol.com.

Alliance Publishing & Media, LLC, *(978-1-7320596)* 7 Whittier Dr., Friendswood, TX 77546 USA Tel 713-501-1515
E-mail: bobdeluca66@gmail.com.

Allied Publishing *See* **Flying Frog Publishing, Inc.**

Alligator Boogaloo, *(978-0-9721416)* 2531 San Jose Ave, Alameda, CA 94501 USA
E-mail: jerroldconnors@gmail.com; business@alligatorboogaloo.com
Web site: http://www.alligatorboogaloo.com.

Alligator Pr., *(978-0-9675658; 978-0-9884057; 978-0-9914334)* Orders Addr.: P.O. Box 526368, Salt Lake City, UT 84152 USA Tel 512-762-5427 Do not confuse with Alligator Press, Carson City, NV
E-mail: k.kimball333@gmail.com
Web site: http://www.alligatorpress.com
Dist(s): **BookBaby.**

Allison & Busby, Ltd. (GBR) *(978-0-7490; 978-0-85031; 978-1-902809) Dist. by* **BTPS.**

Allison's Infant & Toddler Ctr., *(979-8-9869149; 978-1-960446)* 234 E 115th St, Chicago, IL 60628 USA Tel 773-840-4502; Fax: 773-840-4504
E-mail: allison@allisonschildcare.org
Web site: www.allisonschildcare.org.

Allocca Biotechnology, LLC, *(978-0-9659987; 978-0-9769213)* 19 Lorraine Ct., Northport, NY 11768 USA Tel 631-757-3919; Fax: 631-757-3918
E-mail: john@allocca.com
Web site: http://www.allocca.com.

Allocca, Christine A., *(978-0-615-21480-1)* 3940 Laurel Canyon Blvd., No. 399, Studio City, CA 91604 USA Tel 818-486-2730
Web site: http://www.little-green-giants.com.

Allocca Technology & Healthcare Research *See* **Allocca Biotechnology, LLC**

Allosaurus Pubs., *(978-0-9620900; 978-1-888325)* Div. of North Carolina Learning Institute for Fitness & Education, Orders Addr.: P.O. Box 10245, Greensboro, NC 27404 USA (SAN 250-0906) Tel 336-292-6999
E-mail: ally@infionline.net
Web site: http://www.allosauruspublishers.com
Dist(s): **Follett School Solutions.**

Allpony, *(978-1-7323871)* 106 Laurel Hill Rd, Chapel Hill, NC 27514 USA Tel 919-818-3734
E-mail: susan@allpony.com.

Allured Business Media, *(978-0-931710; 978-1-932633)* 336 Gundersen Dr. Ste. A, Carol Stream, IL 60188-2403 USA (SAN 222-4933)
Web site: http://www.alluredbooks.com/
Dist(s): **ebrary, Inc.**

Allured Publishing Corporation *See* **Allured Business Media**

Allworth Pr. *Imprint of* **Skyhorse Publishing Co., Inc.**

AllWrite Advertising & Publishing *See* **Allwrite Publishing**

Allwrite Publishing, *(978-0-9744935; 978-0-9844931; 978-0-9887332; 978-1-941716)* Orders Addr.: 3300 Buckeye Rd. Suite 264, Atlanta, GA 30341 USA Tel 770-284-8983; Fax: 770-284-8986; Edit Addr.: P.O. Box 1071, Atlanta, GA 30301 USA Tel 404-221-0703
E-mail: info@allwritepublishing.com; annette@allwritepublishing.com
Web site: http://www.allwritepublishing.com; http://www.e-allwrite.com
Dist(s): **Ingram Content Group.**

Alma Bks. (GBR) *(978-0-9517497; 978-1-84688; 978-1-84749) Dist. by* **Macmillan.**

Alma Classics *Imprint of* **Bloomsbury Publishing USA**

Alma Little *Imprint of* **Elva Resa Publishing, LLC**

Alma Pr., *(978-0-9746333)* 1204 Abbot Kinney Blvd., Venice, CA 90291 USA (SAN 255-6723) Fax: 310-314-3883
E-mail: info@almapress.com
Web site: http://www.almapress.com.

Almadraba Infantil y Juvenil (ESP) *(978-84-92702; 978-84-15207) Dist. by* **Lectorum Pubns.**

Almanac Publishing Co., *(978-1-928720)* Mt. Hope Ave., Lewiston, ME 04240 USA Tel 207-755-2246; Fax: 207-755-2422
Web site: http://www.farmersalmanac.com
Dist(s): **Sterling Publishing Co., Inc.**

Almond Publishing, *(978-0-9777314)* P.O. Box 573, Petaluma, CA 94953 USA (SAN 850-0673)
E-mail: contact@almondpublishing.com
Web site: http://www.almondpublishing.com.

Almuzara, Editorial (ESP) *(978-84-607; 978-84-933378; 978-84-933901; 978-84-96416; 978-84-88586; 978-84-96968) Dist. by* **Spanish.**

ALNI Publishing, *(978-1-7356895)* 4822 S 133 St, Ste 200, Omaha, NE 68137 USA Tel 402-884-5995
E-mail: alni@conciergemarketing.com.

Aloha Publications *See* **catBOX Entertainment, Inc.**

Aloha Wellness Pubs., *(978-0-9727548)* 2333 Kapiolani Blvd., Suite 2108, Honolulu, HI 96826 USA (SAN 255-0539) Tel 808-941-8253; Fax: 808-925-4233; Toll Free: 866-233-6941
E-mail: crites@hawaii.rr.com
Web site: http://www.alohawellnesstravel.com
Dist(s): **Booklines Hawaii, Ltd.**

Alouette Enterprises, Inc., *(978-0-9797577; 978-0-9799922; 978-0-578-34779-0)* 7307 E. Solano Dr., Scottsdale, AZ 85250 USA
E-mail: DonnaFridrych@aol.com.

Alpenrose Pr., *(978-0-9603624; 978-1-889385)* Orders Addr.: P.O. Box 4245, Frisco, CO 80443 USA (SAN 222-2612) Tel 970-409-1479
E-mail: alpenrosepress@msn.com
Web site: http://www.alpenrosepress.com
Dist(s): **Alpenbooks Pr. LLC.**

Alpha *Imprint of* **Dorling Kindersley Publishing, Inc.**

Alpha Academic Pr., *(978-0-9660943)* 321 College Dr., Edison, NJ 08817 USA Tel 732-248-6582
E-mail: alpha-academic@usa.net
Web site: http://www.alpha-academic.com.

Alpha & Omega Publishing, *(978-0-9767778)* 3409 Daniel Place Dr., Charlotte, NC 28213 USA Tel 704-724-1683; Fax: 270-721-6019 Do not confuse iwth companies with the same name in Fremont, NE, Springfield, OR
E-mail: alphaomega@carolina.rr.com.

Alpha Behavior Consultants, *(978-0-9758755)* 12740 NW 11th St., Miami, FL 33172 USA
E-mail: info@alphbehc.com
Web site: http://www.alphabehc.com.

Alpha Bible Pubns., *(978-1-877917)* P.O. Box 155, Hood River, OR 97031 USA; P.O. Box 157, Morton, WA 98356 Tel 541-386-6634
Dist(s): **Pentecostal Publishing Hse.**
eBookit.com.

Alpha Buddies Inc., *(978-0-692-68521-1; 978-0-578-46331-5; 978-0-578-48867-7; 978-0-578-33380-9; 979-8-218-10520-4)* 711 Linda Terr., Wheeling, IL 60090 USA Tel 847-971-3788
E-mail: donnarink@alphabuddies.com.

Alpha Connections, *(978-0-9715779; 978-0-9747610; 978-1-936933)* 530 W. Idaho Blvd., Emmett, ID 83617 USA
E-mail: contact@dragonsfuryseries.com
Web site: http://www.dragonsfuryseries.com
Dist(s): **Ingram Content Group**
Smashwords.

Alpha Heartland Press *See* **Heartland Foundation, Inc.**

Alpha Ink, LLC, The, *(978-1-7334090)* 1603 Capitol Ave., No. 310 A247, Cheyenne, WY 82001 USA Tel 307-222-2976
E-mail: marketing@thealphaink.com
Web site: www.thealphaink.com.

Alpha Learning World, Inc., *(978-0-9791680)* 1064 Mohegan Rd., Venice, FL 34293 USA (SAN 852-6362)
E-mail: trisley1@verizon.net
Web site: http://alphalearningworld.com.

Alpha Media & Publishing - AM & P, LLC, 2851 S. Ocean Blvd. Ste 6-V, BOCA RATON, FL 33432 USA Tel 561-613-7770
E-mail: Editor@AlphaMediaAndPublishing.com
Dist(s): **Ingram Content Group.**

Alpha Omega Pubns., Inc., *(978-0-7403; 978-0-86717; 978-1-58095)* 300 N. McKemy Ave., Chandler, AZ 85226-2618 USA Tel 602-438-2717; Fax: 480-785-8034; Toll Free: 800-682-7391; 804 N. 2nd Ave. E., Rock Rapids, IA 51246 (SAN 853-2826) Tel 800-622-3070; Fax: 712-472-4856; *Imprints:* Lifepac (Lifepac); Horizons (Hrnzns AZ); Weaver (Weaver)
E-mail: cpatterson@aop.com
Web site: http://www.aop.com
Dist(s): **Follett School Solutions**
Send The Light Distribution LLC
Spring Arbor Distributors, Inc.

Alpha OmeGa Publishing, *(978-0-9658073)* 1217 Cape Coral Pkwy., Cape Coral, FL 33904 USA Tel 941-542-3666; Fax: 941-945-7963; Toll Free: 800-542-3666; 4219 SE First Ct., Cape Coral, FL 33904
E-mail: GPMueller@aol.com
Web site: http://www.Floridawest.com/Liestorm.

Alpha Run Pr., LLC, *(978-0-9761182; 978-1-933289)* Orders Addr.: P.O. Box 15079, Silver Spring, MD 20914-5079 USA Tel 202-508-3392; Edit Addr.: 1717 K St. NW, Suite 600, Washington, DC 20036 USA
E-mail: alpharp@aol.com
Web site: http://www.alpharunpress.com.

Alpha Shade, Inc., *(978-0-9768705)* 11850 85th Pl., N., Maple Grove, MN 55369 USA Tel 763-424-9316
E-mail: alphashade1@aol.com
Web site: http://www.alpha-shade.com.

Alpha Writers Ltd., *(978-0-9772018)* Orders Addr.: P.O. Box 561262, The Colony, TX 75056 USA (SAN 256-9256) Fax: 425-955-0859; Toll Free: 866-751-4340 Outside of Dallas
E-mail: source@alphawritersltd.com
Web site: http://www.alphawritersltd.com.

Alpha-kidZ, *(978-0-9749220; 978-0-9823534)* P.O. Box 1552, West Monroe, LA 71294-1552 USA Tel 318-651-0833; Fax: 318-396-4073
Web site: http://www.alphakidz.com.

AlphaLove Publishing, *(978-0-9764307)* P.O. Box 248, South Orange, NJ 07079 USA Fax: 973-275-3973.

Alpine Archaeological Consultants, Inc., *(978-0-9743137)* P.O. Box 2075, Montrose, CO 81402-2075 USA Tel 970-249-6761; Fax: 970-249-8482
E-mail: susan_chandler@alpinearchaeology.com
Web site: http://www.alpinearchaeology.com.

†Alpine Pubns., Inc., *(978-0-931866; 978-1-57779)* Orders Addr.: 38262 Linman Rd., Crawford, CO 81415 USA (SAN 255-2094) Tel 970-921-5005; Fax: 970-921-5081; Toll Free: 800-777-7257
E-mail: customerservice@alpinepub.com; alpinepublishing@aol.com
Web site: http://www.alpinepub.com
Dist(s): **Follett School Solutions;** *CIP.*

Alpine River Pr., *(978-0-9891471)* 660 Haley LN, Red Bluff, CA 96080 USA Tel 530-200-2745
E-mail: alpineriverpress@gmail.com.

Alta Omnimedia, *(978-0-9726360)* 2 Valley View Ave., Ste. 116, San Jose, CA 95127 USA
Web site: http://www.altaomnimedia.com.

Alta Publishing LLC, *(978-0-9767120)* P.O. Box 108, Bellvue, CO 80512 USA (SAN 256-4874) Do not confuse with companies with the same name in Sandy, UT, Midvale, UT.

Alta Retreat Ctr., *(978-0-9746151)* 20 Alta School Rd., Alta, WY 83414 USA Tel 307-353-8200; Fax: 208-354-4002
E-mail: altacp@ida.net.

Altar of Influence, 370 E Silver Hawk Ct, Washington, UT 84780 USA Tel 619.884.9718
E-mail: Jacob@circleofreign.com.

Altea, Ediciones, S.A. - Grupo Santillana (ESP) *(978-84-372) Dist. by* **Lectorum Pubns.**

Altea, Ediciones, S.A. - Grupo Santillana (ESP) *(978-84-372) Dist. by* **Santillana.**

Alterna Comics, *(978-0-9797874; 978-1-934985; 978-1-945762)* Div. of Alterna Comics, Inc., P.O. Box PO Box 282, Newfields, NH 03856 USA Tel 516-304-6733
E-mail: publisher@alternacomics.com
Web site: http://www.alternacomics.com
Dist(s): **Diamond Comic Distributors, Inc.**
Independent Pubs. Group
MyiLibrary.

Alternative Comics, *(978-1-891867; 978-1-934460; 978-1-68148)* 21607B Stevens Creek Blvd., Cupertino, CA 95014 USA Do not confuse with companies with the same or similar name in Goleta, GA, Billerica, MA
E-mail: marc@wowcool.com
Web site: http://www.indyworld.com
Dist(s): **Consortium Bk. Sales & Distribution**
Diamond Comic Distributors, Inc.
Diamond Bk. Distributors
Last Gasp of San Francisco.

Alternative Press, Incorporated *See* **Alternative Comics**

AlterNet Bks., *(978-0-9633687; 978-0-9752724)* 77 Federal St., 2nd Flr., San Francisco, CA 94107 USA Tel 415-284-1420; Fax: 415-284-1414
E-mail: valrie@alternet.org
Web site: http://www.alternet.org.

Althos *See* **DiscoverNet**

Altrusa Club of Baton /Rouge, Inc., *(978-0-692-04117-8; 978-0-578-55199-9)* 16246 Shenandoah Dr., Baton Rouge, LA 70817 USA Tel 225-753-9307
E-mail: carmels@cox.net
Dist(s): **Ingram Content Group.**

Altschuler, Richard & Assocs., Inc., *(978-1-884092)* 100 W. 57th St., No. 2M, New York, NY 10019 USA (SAN 299-2949) Tel 212-397-7233; Fax: 212-397-6090; *Imprints:* Chaucer Press (Chaucer Pr)
E-mail: icra@aol.com; raltschuler@rcn.com
Web site: http://www.richardaltschuler.com
Dist(s): **BookBaby**
Ingram Content Group
Longleaf Services
Syracuse Univ. Pr.
Univ. Pr. of New England.

A-Lu Publishing, *(978-0-9817092)* 4257 Holiday Rd., Traverse City, MI 49686 USA
Dist(s): **BookBaby.**

Alvarado, Rudolph *See* **Caballo Pr. of Ann Arbor**

ALVARADOPLUS, *(978-0-9791782)* 315 Luna St., Apt 1B, San Juan, PR 00901-1488 USA (SAN 852-6710)
E-mail: ALVARADOPlus@aol.com.

Alvarez, Jesus, *(978-0-9792507)* 254 San Diego Ave., Brownsville, TX 78526 USA Tel 956-542-2722
E-mail: alvarcorp@msn.com.

Alway, Bruce, *(978-0-692-93718-1; 978-0-692-94868-2; 978-0-692-06155-8)* 2714 Regway Ave., Long Beach, CA 90810 USA Tel 540-877-7482
E-mail: BruceAlway23@gmail.com.

Always Devoted LLC, *(978-1-7357565)* 2776 Joyce Ave., Decatur, GA 30032 USA Tel 404-447-1388
E-mail: latoyamarie.farmer@gmail.com
Web site: alwaysdevoted.com.

A.M. Green Publishing, *(978-1-935479)* P.O. Box 1085, Amston, CT 06231 USA Tel 617-391-7350
E-mail: JSmith@amgreenpublishing.com
Web site: http://www.amgreenpublishing.com.

AM Ink Publishing, *(978-0-9845801; 978-0-9852146; 978-0-9884468; 978-0-9910330; 978-1-943201; 978-1-958842)* PO Box 194, Southwick, MA 01077 USA (SAN 859-8142) Tel 413-222-1143
E-mail: Mike@AuthorMike.com
Web site: http://www.AMInkPublishing.com; https://aminkpublishing.com/dark-ink.

Ama Deus Energy Pr., *(978-0-9962780; 978-0-9987414; 978-0-9998412; 978-1-7348359)* 1065 Alden Nash, Lowell, MI 49331 USA Tel 616-340-7892
E-mail: bcomos@sbcglobal.net
Web site: www.ama-deus-international.com.

AMA Verlag GmbH (DEU) *(978-3-89922; 978-3-927190; 978-3-932587) Dist. by* **Mel Bay.**

†AMACOM, *(978-0-7612; 978-0-8144)* Div. of Harpercollins Leadership, P.O. Box 141000, Nashville, TN 37214 USA (SAN 201-1670) Toll Free: 800-250-5308
E-mail: pubservice@amanet.org
Web site: http://www.amacombooks.org
Dist(s): **Ebsco Publishing**
Follett School Solutions
Cengage Gale
HarperCollins Christian Publishing
HarperCollins Pubs.
JSTOR
MyiLibrary
Nelson, Thomas Inc.
Productivity Pr.
Wybel Marketing Group
ebrary, Inc.; *CIP.*

Amadeus Press *Imprint of* **Leonard, Hal Corp.**

Amagi Bks. *Imprint of* **Liberty Fund, Inc.**

Amalgamated Story *Imprint of* **Santore, Marcia**

Amalgamated Widgets Unlimited, *(978-0-615-54280-5; 978-0-692-74884-8; 978-0-692-76379-7)* 2995 Woodside Rd., Suite 400-166, Woodside, CA 94062 USA Tel 650-780-9288; 425-298-6552
E-mail: ng@awun.net
Web site: dandelom.com
Dist(s): **CreateSpace Independent Publishing Platform**
Dummy Record Do Not USE!!!!.

Amalia Pr., *(978-1-7322453)* 7427 Hillside Dr, Houghton, NY 14744 USA Tel 630-440-0732
E-mail: jeffwies@yahoo.com.

amana pubns., *(978-0-915957; 978-1-59008)* Div. of amana corp., 8599 Trail View Dr., Ellicott City, MD 21043 USA (SAN 630-9798) Tel 301-595-5999; Fax: 301-595-5888; Toll Free: 800-660-1777
E-mail: amana@igprinting.com
Web site: http://www.amana-publications.com.

Amanda Lowney Bks. LLC, *(978-0-578-47290-4; 978-0-578-47451-9; 978-1-7348460)* 2729 W Woodfield Dr, Mequon, WI 53092 USA Tel 414-467-3456
E-mail: amandalowneybooks@gmail.com
Web site: www.amandalowneybooks.com.

Amani Publishing, LLC, *(978-0-9752851; 978-0-9788937; 978-0-9815847; 978-0-9833666)* P.O. Box 12045, Tallahassee, FL 32317 USA Tel 850-264-3341 Do not confuse with Amani Publishing in Pineville, LA
E-mail: amanipublishing@aol.com
Web site: http://www.barbarajoewilliams.com
Dist(s): **Ingram Content Group.**

Amaquemecan, Editorial (MEX) *(978-968-7205) Dist. by* **Continental Bk.**

Amaquemecan, Editorial (MEX) *(978-968-7205) Dist. by* **AIMS Intl.**

MARA Entertainment, *(978-0-9760745)* 1024 Frans Rd., Westfield, NC 27053 USA Tel 336-351-3437 (phone/fax)
E-mail: rpitt@charliesthechef.com
Web site: http://www.charlesthechef.com.

nato, G. J., *(978-0-615-38545-7; 978-0-9829962; 978-0-9894561; 978-1-7338936)* 5 Westview Ct., Avon, CT 06001-4540 USA Tel 860-675-6712
E-mail: gaetanoja@aol.com
Web site: getkidsmovingnow.com.

mazeBk. Pr., *(978-0-9986360)* 5729 SE 50th Ave, Portland, OR 97206 USA Tel 503-961-2656
E-mail: clubchris@gmail.com.

mazement Square, *(978-0-9815308)* 27 Ninth St., Lynchburg, VA 24504 USA
Web site: http://www.amazementsquare.org.

mazing Dreams Publishing, *(978-0-9719628)* P.O. Box 1811, Asheville, NC 28802 USA
E-mail: contact@amazingdreamspublishing.com
Web site: http://www.amazingdreamspublishing.com
Dist(s): **ASP Wholesale**
CreateSpace Independent Publishing Platform.

Amazing Factory, The, *(978-0-9776282; 978-0-9788469; 978-0-9790302)* 5527 San Gabriel Way, Orlando, FL 32837 USA
E-mail: theamazingfactory@hotmail.com
Web site: http://www.theamazingfactory.com.

Amazing Herbs Pr., *(978-0-9742962)* 545 8th Ave., Suite 401, New York, NY 10018 USA Tel 770-982-0107; Fax: 770-982-0273; Toll Free: 800-241-9138 (orders)
E-mail: tnc100@bellsouth.net
Web site: http://www.amazingherbspress.com.

AMazing Pubns., *(978-0-9763434)* 337 W. Napa St., Sonoma, CA 95476 USA.

Amazing Publishing Company, A *See* **Rhymeglow LLC**

Amazon Children's Publishing *Imprint of* **Amazon Publishing**

Amazon Creations, *(978-1-7336818)* 14107 Chartley Falls Dr, Houston, TX 77044 USA Tel 214-455-3808
E-mail: gyw1954@gmail.com.

Amazon Encore *Imprint of* **Amazon Publishing**

Amazon Kindle Direct Publishing, *(978-1-943914)* 551 Boren Ave., Seattle, WA 98109 USA Tel 206-740-4926
E-mail: pritadas@amazon.com
Web site: https://kdp.amazon.com.

Amazon Publishing, *(978-0-8034; 978-1-61109; 978-1-4778; 978-1-5039; 978-1-5420; 978-1-6625)* 2021 7th Ave., Seattle, WA 98121 USA; *Imprints:* AmazonCrossing (AmazonCross); Amazon Children's Publishing (AmazonChldns); Thomas & Mercer (Thomas&MercerA); Montlake Romance (Montlake); 47North (FortySevN); Amazon Encore (Amazon Encore); Little A (LittleA); Jet City Comics (JetCityComics); Two Lions (TwoLions); Skyscape (Skyscape); AmazonClassics (AmazonClass)
E-mail: Customerservice@brilliancepublishing.com
Web site: http://www.amazon.com/amazoncrossing; http://www.apub.com/; http://www.amazon.com/amazonpublishing
Dist(s): **Brilliance Publishing, Inc.**
Children's Plus, Inc.
CreateSpace Independent Publishing Platform
MyiLibrary.

AmazonClassics *Imprint of* **Amazon Publishing**

AmazonCrossing *See* **Amazon Publishing**

AmazonCrossing *Imprint of* **Amazon Publishing**

Ambassador Bks. *Imprint of* **Paulist Pr.**

Ambassador Bks., Inc., *(978-0-9646439; 978-1-929039; 978-1-64960)* 446 Main St. Ste. 19, Worcester, MA 01608-2368 USA Toll Free: 800-577-0909
E-mail: info@ambassadorbooks.com
Web site: http://www.ambassadorbooks.com
Dist(s): **Christian Bk. Distributors**
Spring Arbor Distributors, Inc.

Ambassador International *Imprint of* **Emerald Hse. Group, Inc.**

Ambassador Pubns., *(978-1-58572)* 3110 E. Medicine Lake Blvd., Plymouth, MN 55441 USA Tel 763-545-5631; Fax: 763-545-0079
E-mail: parished@aflc.org
Web site: http://www.aflc.org.

Ambassador-Emerald, International *Imprint of* **Emerald Hse. Group, Inc.**

Amber Bks. (GBR) *(978-1-904687; 978-0-9544356; 978-1-905704; 978-1-906626; 978-1-909160; 978-1-908696; 978-1-907446; 978-1-78274; 978-1-83886) Dist. by* **Sterling.**

Amber Bks., *(978-0-9655064; 978-0-9702224; 978-0-9727519; 978-0-9749779; 978-0-9767735; 978-0-9790976; 978-0-9824922; 978-1-937269)* Div. of Amber Communications Group, Inc., Orders Addr.: 1334 E. Chandler Blvd., Suite 5-D67, Phoenix, AZ 85048 USA Tel 602-743-7211; 602-743-7426; Fax: 480-283-0991; *Imprints:* Colossus Books (Colossus)
E-mail: amberbks@aol.com
Web site: http://www.amberbooks.com
Dist(s): **A & B Distributors & Pubs. Group**
African World Bks.
Book Wholesalers, Inc.
Brodart Co.
D & J Bk. Distributors
Follett School Solutions
Independent Pubs. Group
Midwest Library Service
Quality Bks., Inc.
Unique Bks., Inc.

Amber Communications Group, Inc., 1334 East Chandler Blvd., Suite 5-D67, Phoenix, AZ 85048 USA.

Amber Marie Publishing, *(978-0-9771981)* 10413 Coffee Grinder Ct., Las Vegas, NV 89129 USA (SAN 256-9744) Tel 702-238-3846.

Amber Skye Publishing LLC, *(978-0-9819860; 978-0-9831839; 978-0-9894003; 978-0-692-47081-7; 978-0-9977266)* 1935 Berkshire Dr., Eagan, MN 55122 USA
E-mail: publisher@amberskyepublishing.com
Web site: http://www.amberskyepublishing.com; www.itascabooks.com
Dist(s): **CreateSpace Independent Publishing Platform**
Itasca Bks.

Amber Trust, The *See* **Aenor Trust, The**

Amber Victoria LLC, *(978-1-7335285)* 18436 N. 92 St., Scottsdale, AZ 85255 USA Tel 480-430-7777
E-mail: ambervictoria360@gmail.com.

Amber Woods Publishing, *(978-0-9743717)* P.O. Box 280, Excelsior, MN 55331 USA Tel 952-476-1670
Web site: http://www.amberwoodspublishing.com.

Amberjack Publishing Co., *(978-0-692-30068-8; 978-0-692-30154-8; 978-0-692-33339-6; 978-0-692-33341-9; 978-0-692-39045-0; 978-0-692-40203-0; 978-0-692-42948-8; 978-0-692-42951-8; 978-0-692-44642-3; 978-0-692-44646-1; 978-0-692-46743-5; 978-0-692-48712-9; 978-0-692-50148-1; 978-0-692-51719-2; 978-0-692-51720-8; 978-0-692-53639-1; 978-0-692-53640-7; 978-0-692-58289-3; 978-0-692-58297-8; 978-0-692-58721-8; 978-0-9972377; 978-1-944995; 978-1-948705; 978-1-950064) P.O. Box 4668 #89611, New York, NY 10163 USA; Imprints:* Little Adventures (Little Advent)
Dist(s): **Independent Pubs. Group**
Midpoint Trade Bks., Inc.

Amberley Publishing (GBR) *(978-1-84868; 978-1-4456) Dist. by* **IPG Chicago.**

Amberlot, *(978-1-7346030)* 124 Lincoln Ave, Purchase, NY 10577 USA Tel 646-944-0155
E-mail: alextkelleher@gmail.com.

Amberlot Books *See* **Amberlot**

Amberock Pubns., *(978-0-9754636)* P.O. Box 491, Dallas, NC 28034 USA
Web site: http://www.meandmybassguitar.com.

Amberwaves, *(978-0-9708913)* P.O. Box 487, Becket, MA 01223 USA (SAN 256-4254) Tel 413-623-0012; 413-623-6042 (phone/fax); 305 Brooker Hill Rd., Becket, MA 01223 Tel 413-623-0012; Fax: 413-623-6042
E-mail: shenwa@bcn.net
Web site: http://www.amberwaves.org.

Amberwood Pr., *(978-0-9630243; 978-0-9776445; 978-0-615-95885-9)* 509 Albany Post Rd., New Paltz, NY 12561-3629 USA Do not confuse with Amberwood Pr., in Ventura, CA
E-mail: nava@vegkitchen.com
Web site: http://www.vegkitchen.com
Dist(s): **CreateSpace Independent Publishing Platform.**

Ambitious Abbey, LLC, *(978-0-692-10005-9; 978-0-578-95482-0; 979-8-218-03088-9; 979-8-218-27380-4; 979-8-218-29250-8)* 1105 Howard St., Bridgeport, OH 43219 USA Tel 304-951-0221
E-mail: ambitiousabbeybooks@gmail.com
Web site: www.AmbitiousAbbey.com.

Ambrosia Press LLC, *(978-0-9729346; 978-0-9778656; 978-0-9525344; 978-0-9862590)* 2 Waban Rd., Timberlake, OH 44095 USA Tel 440-951-7780; Fax: 440-951-0565
E-mail: willowhse@yahoo.com
Web site: http://www.ruthfawcettbooks.com.

Ameeramac Bks. *Imprint of* **Ameeramac Bks. Inc.**

Ameeramac Bks. Inc., *(978-0-9762911)* Div. of Ameeramac Reporting, Inc., 168 Putnam Ave., Brooklyn, NY 11216-1606 USA Tel 917-353-1644; Fax: 718-636-8210; *Imprints:* Ameeramac Books (AmeeraBks)
E-mail: ameeramac@optonline.com.

Ameeramac Reporting, Incorporated *See* **Ameeramac Bks. Inc.**

Amelia Street Press *See* **Prytania Pr.**

Amereon Ltd., *(978-0-8488; 978-0-88411; 978-0-89190; 978-1-59683)* Orders Addr.: P.O. Box 1200, Mattituck, NY 11952 USA (SAN 201-2413) Tel 631-298-5100; Fax: 631-298-5631; *Imprints:* Rivercity Press (Rivercity Pr); American Reprint Company (Am Repr)
E-mail: info@amereon.net
Dist(s): **Follett School Solutions**
Ingram Publisher Services.

America Hispanic Consulting Group Inc., P.O. Box 1709, Fresno, CA 93717 USA Tel 559-392-3710
E-mail: susan@cottoncandybooks.com
Web site: www.cottoncandybooks.com.

America Sports Publishing, *(978-0-9721199)* Orders Addr.: P.O. Box 132, Brookfield, OH 44403 USA Tel 330-448-0866; Toll Free: 866-255-2267; Edit Addr.: 6881 Stewart Rd., Brookfield, OH 44403 USA Fax: 330-448-0936
E-mail: Info@AthleticScholarshipBook.com
Web site: http://www.AthleticScholarshipBook.com
Dist(s): **Cardinal Pubs. Group**
Quality Bks., Inc.
Unique Bks., Inc.

America Star Bks., *(978-1-61102; 978-1-63249; 978-1-63382; 978-1-63448; 978-1-68090; 978-1-68122; 978-1-68176; 978-1-68229; 978-1-63508; 978-1-68290; 978-1-68394)* 550 Highland St. Ste 105, Frederick, MD 21701 USA Tel 301-228-2595; Fax: 301-228-2596; P.O. Box 151, Frederick, MD 21705
Web site: www.americastarbooks.pub
Dist(s): **Independent Pubs. Group.**

American Academy of Pediatrics, *(978-0-910761; 978-1-58110; 978-0-578-04930-4; 978-0-578-05484-1; 978-1-61002)* 141 NW Point Blvd., Elk Grove Village, IL 60007-1098 USA (SAN 265-3540) Tel 847-434-4000; Fax: 847-434-8000; Toll Free: 888-227-1770; 387 Park Ave., S., New York, NY 10016
E-mail: pubs@aap.org
Web site: http://www.aap.org/bookstore
Dist(s): **Caldwell Letter Service**
Ebsco Publishing
Follett School Solutions
Independent Pubs. Group
Majors, J. A. Co.
MyiLibrary
Rittenhouse Bk. Distributors
Two Rivers Distribution
ebrary, Inc.

American Animal Hospital Assn. Pr., *(978-0-941451; 978-0-9616498; 978-1-58326)* Orders Addr.: 12575 W. Bayaud Ave., Lakewood, CO 80228 USA (SAN 224-4799) Tel 303-986-2800; Fax: 303-986-1700; Toll Free: 800-252-2242
E-mail: msc@aahanet.org
Web site: http://press.aahanet.org
Dist(s): **Matthews Medical Bk. Co.**

American Antiquarian Society, *(978-0-912296; 978-0-944026; 978-1-929545)* 185 Salisbury St., Worcester, MA 01609 USA (SAN 206-474X) Tel 508-752-5221; Fax: 508-754-9069
E-mail: library@mwa.org
Web site: http://www.americanantiquarian.org
Dist(s): **Oak Knoll Pr.**

American Assn. of Veterinary Parasitologists, *(978-0-9770942)* 3915 S. 48th St. Terr., Saint Joseph, MO 64503 USA
Web site: http://www.aavp.org.

American Atheist Pr., *(978-0-910309; 978-0-911826; 978-1-57884; 978-0-9981819)* Subs. of Charles E. Stevens, P.O. Box 5733, Parsippany, NJ 07054-6733 USA (SAN 206-7188) Tel 908-276-7300; Fax: 908-276-7402
E-mail: editor@atheists.org; info@atheists.org
Web site: http://www.atheists.org.

American Bar Assn., *(978-0-89707; 978-1-57073; 978-1-59031; 978-1-60442; 978-1-61632; 978-0-615-36849-8; 978-0-615-36850-4; 978-1-61438; 978-1-62722; 978-1-63425; 978-0-578-55688-8)* 321 N Clark St, 20th FL, Chicago, IL 60654 USA (SAN 211-4798) Tel 312-988-6011 Toll Free: 800-285-2221
E-mail: natalie.cirar@americanbar.org
Web site: http://www.americanbar.org
Dist(s): **MyiLibrary**
National Bk. Network
Two Rivers Distribution.

American Bible Society, *(978-0-8267; 978-1-58516; 978-1-937628; 978-1-941448; 978-1-941449)* Orders Addr.: 6201 E. 43rd St., Tulsa, OK 74135-6562 USA (SAN 662-7129) Toll Free Fax: 866-570-2877; Edit Addr.: 1865 Broadway, New York, NY 10023-9980 USA (SAN 203-5189) Tel 212-408-1200; Fax: 212-408-1305; 700 Plaza Dr., 2nd Flr., Secaucus, NJ 07094
E-mail: info@americanbible.org
Web site: http://www.bibles.org; http://www.americanbible.org
Dist(s): **Anchor Distributors.**

American Bk. Co., *(978-1-932410; 978-1-59807; 978-1-62800; 978-1-64117)* 103 Executive Dr., Woodstock, GA 30188 USA Tel 770-928-2834 Toll Free: 888-254-5877 Do not confuse with companies with the same name in Chesterfield, VA, Knoxville, TN, Florence, AL
E-mail: dpintozzi@americanbookcompany.com
Web site: http://www.americanbookcompany.com.

American Book Publishing *See* **American Bk. Publishing Group**

American Bk. Publishing Group, *(978-1-930586; 978-1-58982; 978-0-615-54716-9)* P.O. Box 65624, Salt Lake City, UT 84165 USA (SAN 254-4725) Fax: 801-382-0881; Toll Free: 888-288-7413; *Imprints:* Bedside Books (Bedside Bks); Millennial Mind Publishing (Millennial Mind)
E-mail: orders@american-book.com; info@american-book.com; operations@american-book.com
Web site: http://www.american-book.com
Dist(s): **Seven Locks Pr.**

American Bookworks Corp., *(978-0-9622813; 978-1-884965)* 309 Florida Hill Rd., Ridgefield, CT 06877 USA Tel 203-438-0345; Fax: 203-438-0379
E-mail: info@abwcorporation.com
Web site: http://www.abwcorporation.com.

†American Camping Assn., *(978-0-87603)* 5000 State Rd. 67, N., Martinsville, IN 46151-7902 USA (SAN 201-2596) Tel 765-342-8456 (General Info.); Fax: 765-349-6357 (orders); Toll Free: 800-428-2267 (orders)
E-mail: bookstore@aca-camps.org
Web site: http://www.acacamps.org; *CIP.*

American Cancer Society, Inc., *(978-0-944235; 978-1-60443)* 250 Williams St., Atlanta, GA 30303-1002 USA (SAN 227-6941) Tel 404-320-3333; Fax: 404-325-9341; Toll Free: 800-ACS-2345
Web site: http://www.cancer.org
Dist(s): **Independent Pubs. Group**
McGraw-Hill Cos., The
McGraw-Hill Professional Publishing
MyiLibrary
Wiley-Blackwell.

American Carriage Hse. Publishing, *(978-0-9705734; 978-1-935176)* P.O. Box 1778, Penn Valley, CA 95946 USA Tel 530-432-8860; Fax: 530-265-9650 Do not confuse with Carriage House Publishing in Middleton, CA
E-mail: info@americancarriagehousepublishing.com; editor@americancarriagehousepublishing.com; research@americancarriagehousepublishing.com; assistant@americancarriagehousepublishing.com
Web site: http://www.americancarriagehousepublishing.com
Dist(s): **Send The Light Distribution LLC**
Smashwords.

†American Chemical Society, *(978-0-8412; 978-0-692-96437-8; 978-0-692-96439-2; 978-0-578-62767-0; 978-0-578-62768-7)* 1155 16th St., NW, Washington, DC 20036 USA (SAN 201-2626) Tel 202-872-4600; Toll Free: 800-227-5558; 2001 Evans Rd., Cary, NC 27513
E-mail: service@acs.org; help@acs.org
Web site: http://www.acs.org; http://www.ChemCenter.org
Dist(s): **Follett School Solutions**
Oxford Univ. Pr., Inc.; *CIP.*

American Classical League, The, *(978-0-939507)* Orders Addr.: 860 NW Washington Blvd. Suite A, Hamilton, OH 45013 USA (SAN 225-8358) Tel 513-529-7741; Fax: 513-529-7742
E-mail: info@aclclassics.org
Web site: http://www.aclclassics.org.

American Correctional Assn., *(978-0-929310; 978-0-942974; 978-1-56991)* 206 N. Washington St. Ste. 200, Alexandria, VA 22314-2528 USA (SAN 204-8051) Toll Free: 800-222-5646 (ext. 1860)
Web site: http://www.aca.org.

American Dental Assn., *(978-0-910074; 978-1-932305; 978-1-60122; 978-1-935201; 978-0-9860279; 978-1-941807; 978-1-68447)* 211 E. Chicago Ave., Chicago, IL 60611 USA (SAN 202-4519) Tel 312-440-2568; 312-440-2500; Fax: 312-440-7461
E-mail: survey@ada.org
Web site: http://www.ada.org.

American Diabetes Assn., *(978-0-945448; 978-1-58040)* Orders Addr.: 1701 N. Beauregard St., Alexandria, VA 22311 USA Toll Free Fax: 800-998-3103 (orders); Toll Free: 800-323-4900 (orders)
E-mail: lboswell@diabetes.org
Web site: http://www.diabetes.org
Dist(s): **McGraw-Hill Cos., The**
McGraw-Hill Professional Publishing
McGraw-Hill Trade
MyiLibrary
Publishers Group West (PGW).

American Dog *Imprint of* **Ideate Prairie**

American Driving Society, *(978-0-9727292)* P.O. Box 278, Cross Plains, WI 53528-0278 USA Do not confuse with American Driving Society in Lakeville, CT
E-mail: ann@americandrivingsociety.org
Web site: http://www.americandrivingsociety.org.

American Fisheries Society, *(978-0-913235; 978-1-888569; 978-1-934874)* 5410 Grosvenor Ln., Suite 110, Bethesda, MD 20814-2199 USA (SAN 284-964X) Tel 301-897-8616; Fax: 301-897-5080
E-mail: main@fisheries.org; afspubs@pbd.com
Web site: http://www.fisheries.org
Dist(s): **PBD, Inc.**

American French Genealogical Society, *(978-1-929920; 978-1-932749; 978-1-60305)* Orders Addr.: P.O. Box 830, Woonsocket, RI 02895 USA; Edit Addr.: 78 Earle St., Woonsocket, RI 02895 USA
E-mail: RDBeaudry@afgs.org
Web site: http://www.afgs.org.

American Girl *Imprint of* **American Girl Publishing, Inc.**

†American Girl Publishing, Inc., *(978-0-937295; 978-1-56247; 978-1-58485; 978-1-59369; 978-1-60958; 978-1-68337)* Subs. of Mattel, Inc., Orders Addr.: P.O. Box 620991, Middleton, WI 53562-0991 USA Tel 608-836-4848; Toll Free Fax: 800-257-3865; Toll Free: 800-233-0264; Edit Addr.: 8400 Fairway Pl., Middleton, WI 53562 USA (SAN 298-6337) Tel 608-836-4848; Fax: 608-831-7089; *Imprints:* American Girl (Amer Girl)
E-mail: pub.orders@americangirl.com
Web site: http://www.americangirlpublishing.com
Dist(s): **Children's Plus, Inc.**
Follett School Solutions
Simon & Schuster, Inc.; *CIP.*

American Gramaphone LLC *See* **Mannheim Steamroller L.L.C.**

American Ground Water Trust, *(978-0-9641186)* Orders Addr.: 16 Centre St., Concord, NH 03301 USA Tel 603-228-5444; Fax: 603-228-6557
E-mail: trustinfo@agwt.org
Web site: http://www.agwt.org.

American Health Publishing, *(978-0-9754443)* Orders Addr.: P.O. Box 282, Clarence, NY 14031 USA Tel 716-741-0177 Do not confuse with Americanhealth Publishing Company in Dallas, TX
E-mail: americahealthpub@aol.com
Web site: http://www.growingahealthyfamily.com.

American Heritage *See* **Forbes Custom Publishing**

American Heritage Publishing, *(978-0-9754859; 978-0-578-12953-2; 978-1-7362423)* 5710 Mt. Repose Ln. NW, Peachtree Corners, GA 30092-1428 USA Tel 404-495-3720 (phone/fax)
E-mail: tomross01@gmail.com
Web site: http://www.privilegesofwar.com
Dist(s): **BookBaby.**

American Historical Pr., *(978-0-9654754; 978-1-892724)* 10755 Sherman Way, Suite 2, Sun Valley, CA 91352 USA Tel 818-503-0133; Fax: 818-503-9081; Toll Free: 800-550-5750
E-mail: ahp@amhistpress.com
Web site: http://www.amhistpress.com/
Dist(s): **Chicago Distribution Ctr.**

American Home-School Publishing, LLC, *(978-0-9667067; 978-0-9779000)* Orders Addr.: 6102 SE. State Rte. C, Cameron, MO 64429 USA (SAN 254-7244) Tel 816-632-1503; Fax: 816-632-1448; Toll Free Fax: 800-557-0234; Toll Free: 800-684-2121
E-mail: booklovers@ahsp.com
Web site: http://www.ahsp.com.

American Humanist Assn., *(978-0-931779)* 1821 Jefferson Pl. NW, Washington, 20036 SUN (SAN 266-9412) Tel 202-238-9088; Fax: 202-238-9047; Toll Free: 800-837-3792; *Imprints:* Humanist Press (Humanist Press)
E-mail: publishing@americanhumanist.org
Web site: http://www.thehumanist.org; http://www.americanhumanist.org; http://humanistpress.com
Dist(s): **Ingram Content Group.**

American Institute For CPCU, *(978-0-89462; 978-0-89463)* 720 Providence Rd., Malvern, PA 19355 USA (SAN

210-1629) Tel 610-644-2100; Fax: 610-640-9576; Toll Free: 800-644-2101
E-mail: cserv@cpcuiia.org
Web site: http://www.aicpcu.org.

American Institute for Property & Liability Underwriters, Incorporated *See* **American Institute For CPCU**

American International Distribution Corp., Orders Addr.: 82 Winter Sport Ln., Williston, VT 05495 USA (SAN 631-1083) Tel 802-488-2665; Edit Addr.: 82 Winter Sport Ln., Williston, VT 05495 USA (SAN 630-2238) Toll Free: 800-488-2665
E-mail: jmacon@aidcvt.com
Web site: http://www.aidcvt.com/Specialty/Home.asp.

American International Printing & Marketing *See* **Graphix Network**

American LaserTechnic, *(978-0-9741805)* 1300 NE Miami Gardens Dr. Apt. 407, Miami, FL 33179-4731 USA
E-mail: dan-gregory@attbi.com
Web site: http://www.americanlasertechnic.com.

American Law Institute, *(978-0-8318)* 4025 Chestnut St., Philadelphia, PA 19104-3099 USA (SAN 204-756X) Tel 215-243-1656 Director of Books; 215-245-1654 (Library); 215-243-1700 (Customer Service); Fax: 215-243-0319; Toll Free: 800-253-6397
E-mail: mcarroll@ali-cle.org; namster@ali.org
Web site: http://www.ali-cle.org; http://www.ali.org.

†**American Library Assn.,** *(978-0-8389; 978-1-937589)* 225 N. Michigan Ave. Suite 1300, chicago, IL 60601 USA (SAN 201-0062) Tel 312-280-2425; 312-944-8085; Fax: 770-280-4155 (Orders); Toll Free: 800-545-2433; 866-746-7252 (Orders)
E-mail: agwizdala@ala.org
Web site: http://www.ala.org; http://www.alastore.ala.org
Dist(s): **Chicago Distribution Ctr.**
Ebsco Publishing
Follett School Solutions
Independent Pubs. Group
MyiLibrary
ebrary, Inc.; *CIP.*

American Literary Pr., *(978-1-56167; 978-1-934696)* Orders Addr.: 8019 Belair Rd., Suite 10, Baltimore, MD 21236 USA Tel 410-882-7700; Fax: 410-882-7703; Toll Free: 800-873-2003; *Imprints:* Shooting Star Edition (SSE)
E-mail: americanliterarypress@comcast.net
Web site: http://www.my-new-publisher.com
Dist(s): **MyiLibrary.**

American Literary Publishing *Imprint of* **LifeReloaded Specialty Publishing LLC**

American Map Corp., *(978-0-8416)* Div. of Langenscheidt Pubs., Inc., P.O. Box 780010, Maspeth, NY 11378-0010 USA (SAN 202-4624) Toll Free: 800-432-6277
E-mail: customerservice@americanmap.com
Web site: http://www.americanmap.com
Dist(s): **Fujii Assocs.**
Langenscheidt Publishing Group.

†**American Mathematical Society,** *(978-0-8218; 978-0-8284; 978-0-88385; 978-0-9835005; 978-1-61444; 978-1-4704; 978-1-939512)* Orders Addr.: 201 Charles St., Providence, RI 02904 USA (SAN 250-3263) Tel 401-455-4000; Fax: 401-331-3842; Toll Free: 800-321-4267; *Imprints:* Chelsea Publishing Company, Incorporated (Chelsea Pub Co); MAA Press (MAAPress)
E-mail: las@ams.org
Web site: http://www.ams.org
Dist(s): **Cambridge Univ. Pr.**
Ebsco Publishing
ProQuest LLC; *CIP.*

American Meteorological Society, *(978-0-933876; 978-1-878220; 978-1-935704; 978-1-940033; 978-1-944970; 978-0-578-59598-6; 978-1-960459)* 45 Beacon St, Boston, MA 02108-3693 USA (SAN 225-2139) Tel 617-227-2425; Fax: 617-742-8718
E-mail: mfriedman@ametsoc.org
Web site: http://www.ametsoc.org/ams
Dist(s): **Chicago Distribution Ctr.**
MyiLibrary
Springer
Univ. of Chicago Pr. Distribution Clients
ebrary, Inc.

American Mythology Productions, *(978-1-945205)* P.O. Box 325, Bel Air, MD 21014 USA Tel 410-652-7008
E-mail: james.kuhoric@americanmythology.net
Web site: www.americanmythology.net
Dist(s): **Diamond Comic Distributors, Inc.**
Diamond Bk. Distributors.

American Poets Society *Imprint of* **Gem Printing**

†**American Psychological Assn.,** *(978-0-912704; 978-0-945354; 978-1-55798; 978-1-59147; 978-0-9792125; 978-1-4338)* Orders Addr.: P.O. Box 92984, Washington, DC 20090-2984 USA (SAN 685-3137) Tel 202-336-6123; 202-336-5510 202-336-5502 (orders); Toll Free: 800-374-2721; Edit Addr.: 750 First St., NE, Washington, DC 20002-4242 USA (SAN 255-5921) Tel 202-336-5500; P.O. Box 77318, Washington, DC 20013-8318 Toll Free: 800-374-2721; *Imprints:* Magination Press (Magination Press)
E-mail: ghughes@spa.org; jmacomber@apa.org; books@apa.org
Web site: http://www.apa.org
Dist(s): **Follett School Solutions**
JSTOR
Oxford Univ. Pr., Inc.; *CIP.*

American Quilter's Society *Imprint of* **Collector Bks.**

American Reading Co., *(978-1-59301; 978-1-61541; 978-1-61406; 978-1-63437; 978-1-64053; 978-1-64851)* Orders Addr.: 480 Norristown Rd., Blue Bell, PA 19422 USA (SAN 992-0315); Edit Addr.: 201 S. Gulph Rd., King Of Prussia, PA 19406 USA (SAN 930-3553) Tel 610-992-4150; Toll Free: 866-810-2665; *Imprints:* ARC Press Books (MYID_M_ARC PRE); ARC Press Comics (MYID_J_ARC PRE); Bird, Bunny & Bear (MYID_H_BIRD, B); Pajarito, Conjeo y Oso (MYID_K_PAJARIT)
E-mail: EDI@americanreading.com; IT@americanreading.com
Web site: http://www.americanreading.com.

American Reprint Co. *Imprint of* **Amereon Ltd.**

American Retrospects, LLC, *(978-0-9747666)* Orders Addr.: P.O. Box 352576, Toledo, OH 43635-2576 USA Tel 419-824-4500; Fax: 419-885-4255
E-mail: jkw@americanretro.net; jkw@bex.net; mds@bex.net; mds@americanretro.net
Web site: http://www.americanretro.net.

American Revolution Publishing, *(978-0-9760948)* 12514 Mustang Dr., Poway, CA 92064 USA Tel 858-513-7864
E-mail: marc-m@cox.net; marciceman@cox.net; amrevpub@cox.net
Web site: http://www.amrevpub.com
Dist(s): **Book Clearing Hse.**
Quality Bks., Inc.

American Schl. of Classical Studies at Athens, *(978-0-87661; 978-1-62139)* 6-8 Charlton St., Princeton, NJ 08540-5232 USA (SAN 201-1697) Tel 609-683-0800; Fax: 609-924-0578
E-mail: castein@ascsa.org
Web site: http://www.ascsa.edu.gr/publications
Dist(s): **Firebrand Technologies**
ISD
JSTOR
MyiLibrary
ebrary, Inc.

American Society for Microbiology *See* **ASM Pr.**

American Society of Mechanical Engineers, The, *(978-0-7918)* 22 Law Dr.,, Fairfield, NJ 07007-2300 USA (SAN 201-1379) Tel 973-882-1176; Fax: 973-882-1717; Toll Free: 800-843-2763
E-mail: pruskil@asme.org
Web site: http://www.asme.org.

American Society of Plant BIOLOGISTS, *(978-0-943088)* 15501 Monona Dr., Rockville, MD 20855-2768 USA (SAN 240-3366) Tel 301-251-0560; Fax: 301-279-2996
E-mail: education@aspb.org
Web site: http://aspp.org.

American Society of Plant Physiologists *See* **American Society of Plant BIOLOGISTS**

American Stars *See* **American Stars Publishing Hse.**

American Stars Publishing Hse., *(978-1-936999)* 8545 NE 110th st., Kansas City, MO 64157 USA Tel 816-905-6923
E-mail: daisytaylor223@gmail.com
Web site: americanstarspublishinghouse.com.

American Success Institute, Inc., *(978-1-884864)* 31 Central St. #5, Wellesley, MA 02482 USA Tel 781-237-7368
E-mail: info@Success.org
Web site: http://www.success.org
Dist(s): **BookBaby.**

American Swedish Historical Museum, *(978-0-9800761)* 1900 Pattison Ave., Philadelphia, PA 19145-5901 USA Tel 215-389-1776; Fax: 215-389-9901
E-mail: info@americanswedish.org
Web site: http://www.americanswedish.org.

American Technical Pubs., Inc., *(978-0-8269)* 10100 Orland Pkwy., Orland Park, IL 60467-5756 USA (SAN 206-8141) Toll Free: 800-323-3471
E-mail: service@americantech.net
Web site: http://www.americantech.net
Dist(s): **Follett School Solutions.**

American Traveler Pr., *(978-0-914846; 978-0-935810; 978-0-939650; 978-1-55838; 978-1-885590; 978-1-58581; 978-1-55838-153-7)* Orders Addr.: 5738 N. Central Ave., Phoenix, AZ 85012 USA (SAN 220-0864) Tel 602-234-1574; Fax: 602-234-3062; Toll Free: 800-521-9221; *Imprints:* Golden West Publishers (GoldenWest)
E-mail: info@AmericanTravelerPress.com
Web site: http://www.PrimerPublishers.com; http://www.RenaissanceHousePublishers.com; http://www.AmericanTravelerPress.com; http://www.ClayThompsonBooks.com; http://www.GoldenWestPublishers.com; www.GoldenWestCookbooks.com
Dist(s): **Chicago Distribution Ctr.**
Follett School Solutions
INscribe Digital.

American Trek Bks., *(978-0-9815221; 978-0-9821178)* 1371 Morley Ave., Rochester Hills, MI 48307 USA (SAN 855-7748).

American Trust Pubns., *(978-0-89259)* 745 Mcclintock Dr., Suite 314, Burr Ridge, IL 60527 USA (SAN 664-6158)
Dist(s): **Halalco Bks.**
Meta Co., LLC.

American Water Works Assn., *(978-0-89867; 978-1-58321; 978-1-61300; 978-1-62576; 978-1-64717)* 6666 W. Quincy Ave., Denver, CO 80235-3098 USA (SAN 212-8241) Tel 303-347-6266; Fax: 303-794-7310; Toll Free: 800-926-7337 (customer service/orders)
E-mail: mramey@awwa.org
Web site: http://www.awwa.org
Dist(s): **Follett School Solutions**
ebrary, Inc.

American Wind Power Ctr., *(978-0-9679480)* Div. of National Windmill Project, Inc., 1501 Canyon Lake Dr., Lubbock, TX 79403 USA Tel 806-747-8734; Fax: 806-740-0668
E-mail: charris@windmill.com
Web site: http://www.windmill.com.

American World Publishing, *(978-0-615-16443-4; 978-0-615-16444-1; 978-0-615-16701-5)* P.O. Box 534, Union City, GA 30291 USA
E-mail: andrewhitmore@yahoo.com
Dist(s): **Lulu Pr., Inc.**

Americana Souvenirs & Gifts, *(978-1-890541)* 206 Hanover St., Gettysburg, PA 17325-1911 USA (SAN 169-7366) Toll Free: 800-692-7436.

America's Great Stories, *(978-0-615-34265-8; 979-8-9854296)* 6809 Northridge Rd. 6809 Northridge Rd., Lincoln, NE 68516 USA
E-mail: terrificteam@aol.com
Web site: AmericasGreatStories.org; HuggingHistory.org.

Americas Group, The, *(978-0-935047)* Subs. of Harris/Ragan Management Group, 654 N. Sepulveda Blvd. Ste. 1, Los Angeles, CA 90049-2170 USA (SAN 694-4698) Toll Free: 800-966-7716
E-mail: hrmg@aol.com
Web site: http://www.americasgroup.com
Dist(s): **Penton Overseas, Inc.**

America's Test Kitchen, *(978-0-936184; 978-1-933615; 978-1-936493; 978-1-940352; 978-1-945256; 978-1-948703; 978-1-954210)* 21 Drydock Ave Suite 210 E, Boston, MA 02210 USA (SAN 221-1939) Tel 617-232-1000; Fax: 617-232-1572; *Imprints:* America's Test Kitchen Kids (Am Test Kit Kids) Do not confuse with Cook's Illustrated, Lubbock, TX
E-mail: taylor.argenzio@americastestkitchen.com; lauren.robbins@americastestkitchen.com
Web site: http://www.cooksillustrated.com; http://www.americastestkitchentv.com; http://www.cookscountrytv.com; http://www.cookscountry.com; http://www.americastestkitchen.com
Dist(s): **Penguin Random Hse. Distribution**
Penguin Random Hse. LLC
Random Hse., Inc.

America's Test Ktichen Kids *Imprint of* **America's Test Kitchen**

Amerisearch, Inc., *(978-0-9653557; 978-0-9753455; 978-0-9778085; 978-0-9827101; 978-0-9896491; 978-1-7369590)* Orders Addr.: 12621 Stone Valley Loop, Fort Myers, FL 33913 USA (SAN 254-6426) Tel 314-502-8924; 314-326-9652; Toll Free: 888-872-9673 (888-USA-WORD); Edit Addr.: P.O. Box 60442, Fort Myers, FL 33906 USA Tel 314-326-9652
E-mail: wjfederer@gmail.com; smfederer@gmail.com
Web site: http://www.amerisearch.net; https://americanminute.com/.

Amerissis Pr., *(978-0-578-85096-2; 978-0-578-91341-4; 978-0-578-93320-7; 978-0-578-94965-9)* 275 S. Bryn Mawr Ave., Bryn Mawr, PA 19010 USA Tel 610-284-9266
E-mail: saraleelangsam@aol.com.

AmeriTales Entertainment, LLC, *(978-0-9798739)* 3525 Del Mar Heights Rd., Suite 623, San Diego, CA 92130 USA Tel 858-449-6900; Fax: 425-795-6026
E-mail: tcarter@ameritales.com
Dist(s): **Follett School Solutions.**

Amerotica *Imprint of* **NBM Publishing Co.**

Amethyst Moon *See* **Amethyst Moon Publishing and Services**

Amethyst Moon Publishing and Services, *(978-0-9792426; 978-1-935354; 978-1-938714)* Orders Addr.: P.O. Box 87885, Tucson, AZ 85754 USA
Web site: http://www.ampubbooks.com.

Amharic Kids, *(978-0-9797481)* 7201 88th Ave., Brooklyn Park, MN 55445 USA Tel 612-636-7878
E-mail: hamish@bellward.com
Web site: http://www.amharickids.com
Dist(s): **Follett School Solutions.**

Amherst Pr., *(978-0-910122; 978-0-942495; 978-1-930596)* Div. of The Guest Cottage, Inc., Orders Addr.: P.O. Box 774, Saint Germain, WI 54558 USA (SAN 213-9820) Tel 715-477-0424; Fax: 715-477-0405; Toll Free: 800-333-8122; Edit Addr.: P.O. Box 774, Saint Germain, WI 54558 USA (SAN 666-6450) Do not confuse with companies with the same name in Amherst, NY, North Hampton, NH
E-mail: sales@theguestcottage.com
Web site: http://www.theguestcottage.com
Dist(s): **Partners Bk. Distributing, Inc.**

Amiaya Entertainment, *(978-0-9745075; 978-0-9777544)* 1154 E. 229 St., Apt. 12C, Bronx, NY 10466 USA.

Amichai Chamoff, *(978-0-692-81729-2; 978-0-692-82098-8)* 11812 Smoketree Rd., POTOMAC, MD 20854 USA Tel 301-706-7385
E-mail: amichamoff@gmail.com; amichamoff@gmail.com
Dist(s): **CreateSpace Independent Publishing Platform.**

Amicus, *(978-1-68152; 978-1-64549; 979-8-88988)* P.O. Box 227, Mankato, MN 56002 USA Tel 507-388-9357
E-mail: rglaser@amicuspublishing.us; anna.erickson@amicuspublishing.us; info@amicuspublishing.us
Web site: www.amicuspublishing.us
Dist(s): **Chronicle Bks. LLC**
Creative Co., The
Hachette Bk. Group.

Amicus High Interest *Imprint of* **Amicus Learning**

Amicus Illustrated *Imprint of* **Amicus Learning**

Amicus Learning, *(978-1-60753; 978-1-68151; 978-1-64549; 979-8-89200)* P.O. Box 227, Mankato, MN 56002 USA Tel 507-388-9357; Fax: 507-388-2746; *Imprints:* Amicus High Interest (High Interest); Amicus Illustrated (Illustrate); Amicus Readers (Readers)
E-mail: anna.erickson@amicuspublishing.us; rglaser@amicuspublishing.us; info@amicuspublishing.us
Web site: http://www.amicuspublishing.us
Dist(s): **Creative Co., The**
Follett School Solutions
MyiLibrary.

Amicus Pr., *(978-0-914861)* 4201 Underwood Rd., Baltimore, MD 21218 USA (SAN 289-0518) Tel 301-889-5056.

Amicus Publishing *See* **Amicus Learning**

Amicus Readers *Imprint of* **Amicus Learning**

AMIDEAST, *(978-0-913957)* 1730 M. St. NW, Suite 1100, Washington, DC 20036-4505 USA (SAN 286-7184) Tel 202-776-9600; Fax: 202-776-7000
E-mail: inquiries@amideast.org
Web site: http://www.amideast.org.

Amigo Pubns., Inc., *(978-0-9658533)* Orders Addr.: P.O. Box 666, Los Olivos, CA 93441-0666 USA Tel 805-686-4616; Fax: 805-688-3427; Toll Free: 888-502-6446; Edit Addr.: 3029 W. Hwy. 154, Los Olivos, CA 93441-0666 USA
E-mail: Amigo@Conquistador.com
Web site: http://www.conquistador.com; http://www.equibooks.com.

Aminov, Iskander, *(978-0-692-11432-2)* 7055 Forest Glen D K, Rockford, IL 61114 USA Tel 217-721-8483
E-mail: iskander.aminov@gmail.com
Dist(s): **Ingram Content Group.**

Amira Rock Publishing, *(978-0-9821075; 978-0-9828007; 978-0-9833354)* 31 High St., Felton, PA 17322 USA (SAN 857-2844).

Amistad *Imprint of* **HarperCollins Pubs.**

AMMO Bks., LLC, *(978-0-9786076; 978-1-934429; 978-1-62326; 978-0-9976536; 978-1-7364783)* P.O. Box PO Box 412402, Los Angeles, CA 90041 USA (SAN 851-1128) Tel 323-223-2666; Fax: 323-978-4200; 1 Ingram Blvd., La Vergne, TN 37086
E-mail: contact@ammobooks.com; paul@ammobooks.com
Web site: http://www.ammobooks.com
Dist(s): **Consortium Bk. Sales & Distribution**
Follett School Solutions
Ingram Publisher Services.

Ammons Communications, Ltd., *(978-0-9651232; 978-0-9753023; 978-0-9815702; 978-0-9824099; 978-0-9827611; 978-0-9837382; 978-0-9853728; 978-0-9892169; 978-0-9895694; 978-0-9913803; 978-0-9908766; 978-0-9965199; 978-0-9971647; 978-0-9987359; 978-1-7338640; 978-1-7351316; 978-1-7376908; 979-8-9876120) 1025 Milford Church Rd., Taylors,, SC 29687 USA (SAN 851-0881) Tel 828-226-0640; Imprints:* Catch the Spirit of Appalachia (CSA)
E-mail: amyammonsgarza@gmail.com; violetamyammons@gmail.com
Web site: http://www.spiritofappalachia.org; http://www.catchthespiritofappalachia.com; http://www.storiesofmountainfolk.com; http://www.csabooks.com; http://www.sharingspokenstories.com.

Ammons, Terry, *(978-0-578-78102-0)* 620 Trinity Ave. No. C7, Bronx, NY 10455 USA Tel 917-922-5357
E-mail: TerryAmmons30@gmail.com.

AMN Publishing, *(978-0-9728129)* P.O. Box 323, Massapequa, NY 11758 USA
E-mail: AMNPub@aol.com
Web site: http://amnpub.tripod.com.

Amoeba Bks., *(978-0-9786473)* 5260 Rogers Rd., G-6, Hamburg, NY 14075 USA
E-mail: marketing@amoebabooks.com
Web site: http://www.amoebabooks.com
Dist(s): **Follett School Solutions.**

Amory, Jenny, *(978-1-7329500)* 8 Andrews Hollow, Rockport, MA 02130 USA Tel 781-248-0706
E-mail: jamory@alum.mit.edu
Dist(s): **CreateSpace Independent Publishing Platform.**

Amos Media Co., *(978-0-89487)* Orders Addr.: P.O. Box 4129, Sidney, OH 45365 USA (SAN 205-9770) Tel 937-498-2111; Toll Free Fax: 888-304-8388; Toll Free: 800-572-6885 (800-327-1259 in Ohio); 800-327-1259 In Ohio; Edit Addr.: 911 Vandemark Rd., Sidney, OH 45365 USA (SAN 658-1579) Do not confuse with companies with the same or similar name in Kalispell, MT, Houston, TX, Edmonds, WA
Web site: http://www.amosadvantage.com.

Ampdzine, *(978-0-9980332)* 435 N. Andrews Ave., Loft 404, Fort Lauderdale, FL 33301 USA Tel 954-525-2624; Fax: 954-525-2634
E-mail: info@ampdzine.com
Web site: ampdzine.com.

Amped Media, *(978-0-9742287)* 22 Shaw Pl., Walla Walla, WA 99362 USA.

Ampelon Publishing, LLC, *(978-0-9748825; 978-0-9786394; 978-0-9798104; 978-0-9817705; 978-0-9823286; 978-0-9840095; 978-0-9893419; 978-0-9982617; 978-0-9990527; 978-1-7323117; 978-1-7336206)* P.O. Box 140675, Boise, ID 83714 USA
E-mail: info@ampelonpublishing.com
Web site: http://www.ampelonpublishing.com
Dist(s): **Smashwords.**

Ampersand, Inc., *(978-0-9745932; 978-0-9761235; 978-0-9818126; 978-0-9905603; 978-0-9962525; 978-0-9974493; 978-0-9985222; 978-0-9994775; 978-1-7340708)* Orders Addr.: 515 Madison St., New Orleans, LA 70116 USA
Web site: http://www.ampersandworks.com
Dist(s): **Follett School Solutions.**

Ampersand Media LLC, *(978-1-950107)* 34 Buckingham Dr, Colchester, VT 05446 USA Tel 802-249-4983
E-mail: danielholtz802@gmail.com; katrina@ampersandmedia.rocks
Web site: http://stinkleberrypie.com; http://danielmholtz.com; http://ampersandmedia.rocks.

Amphorae Publishing Group,; *Imprints:* Goldminds Publishing (MYID_F_GOLDMIN)
E-mail: info@amphoraepublishing.com
Web site: www.amphoraepublishing.com
Dist(s): **Independent Pubs. Group**
Midpoint Trade Bks., Inc.

Amplify Church Group, Inc., *(978-0-9772047)* 2951 SW 186th Ave., Miramar, FL 33029 USA Tel 305-822-7000
E-mail: bob@calvarywired.com
Web site: http://www.amplifychurchgroup.com.

Amplify Publishing Group, *(978-0-9743442; 978-1-932888; 978-1-934878; 978-1-936319; 978-1-937406; 978-1-62086; 978-1-63177; 978-1-68401; 978-1-64307; 978-1-64543; 978-1-63755; 979-8-89138)* Orders Addr.: 620 Herndon Pkwy. Suite 220, Herndon, VA 20170 USA Tel 703-437-3584; Fax: 703-437-3554; Toll Free:

877-862-7568; *Imprints:* Mascot Kids (MascotKids); Mascot Books (MascotBks)
E-mail: debbie@mascotbooks.com; naren@mascotbooks.com; kristin@mascotbooks.com; nina@mascotbooks.com
Web site: http://www.mascotbooks.com
Dist(s): **Partners Bk. Distributing, Inc.**

msco Music *Imprint of* **Music Sales Corp.**

MSCO Schl. Pubns., Inc., *(978-0-87720; 978-1-56765)* 315 Hudson St., Suite 501, New York, NY 10013-1085 USA (SAN 201-1751) Toll Free: 866-902-6726 all orders
Web site: http://www.amscopub.com
Dist(s): **Bolchazy-Carducci Pubs.**

MSI Venture, Incorporated *See* **Sleep Garden, Inc.**

mulet Bks. *Imprint of* **Abrams, Inc.**

muzed Art, *(978-0-9996978)* 4389 S. Carson St., Carson City, NV 89701 USA Tel 775-232-1282; Fax: 775-232-1282
E-mail: amuzedart@yahoo.com
Web site: amuzedart.com.

Amy, Mary, *(978-0-578-54081-8; 978-0-578-66753-9)* 377 Midland Ave., No. 2, Rye, NY 10580 USA Tel 914-329-5870
E-mail: maryamyintuitive@gmail.com
Web site: maryamyofficial.com.

Amy Misch, *(978-0-692-92249-1)* 21522A Marine Dr, Stanwood, WA 98292 USA Tel 937-308-1345; Fax: 937-308-1345
E-mail: amymisch27@gmail.com
Web site: www.amymisch.com.

An Encouraging Thought Pubs., *(978-1-7378809)* 104 Victoria Sta., Alabaster, AL 35114 USA Tel 334-430-9294
E-mail: amk1208@live.com
Web site: angelamorse.com.

An Ice Wine Bk. *Imprint of* **Ice Wine Productions, Inc.**

Anachel Communications, *(978-0-615-62081-7)* 2008 Waterstone Dr., Franklin, TN 37069 USA Tel 615-370-8450
E-mail: carrie@anachel.com
Web site: www.carriegerlachcecil.com.

Anadem Publishing, Inc., *(978-0-9646891; 978-1-890018)* 3620 N. High St., Suite 201, Columbus, OH 43214 USA Tel 614-262-2539; Fax: 614-262-6630; Toll Free: 800-633-0055
E-mail: anadem@erinet.com
Web site: http://www.anadem.com.

Anaiah, Ruth, *(978-0-9769675)* P.O. Box 2142, Brandon, FL 33509-2142 USA
E-mail: dozministry2001@yahoo.com.

Anamchara Bks. *Imprint of* **Harding Hse. Publishing Sebice Inc.**

Anana Pr., *(978-1-957400)* 920 19th St., Snohomish, WA 98290 USA Tel 360-348-7078
E-mail: christylynn.anana@gmail.com
Web site: christylynnanana.com.

Anancy Bks. LLC, *(978-0-9753297; 978-1-941553)* Div. of Anancy Enterprise LLC, P.O. Box 28677, San Jose, CA 95159-8677 USA Tel 408-286-0726 Call Anytime; Fax: 408-947-0668 Fax Anytime
Web site: http://www.Anancybooks.com.

Anancybooks.com *See* **Anancy Bks. LLC**

Ananda Publications *See* **Crystal Clarity Pubs.**

Ananse Pr., *(978-0-9605670; 978-0-9749437)* Orders Addr.: P.O. Box 22565, Seattle, WA 98122-0565 USA (SAN 216-3292) Tel 206-325-8205; Fax: 206-328-4371; 1504 32nd Ave. S., Seattle, WA 98144-3918 (SAN 241-6123)
E-mail: gumbomedia@earthlink.net; gumbomedia@yahoo.com
Web site: http://home.usaa.net/~gumbomedia/ananse/index.htm.

AnaPlinaPub-Dallas *See* **Phebe Phillips, Inc.**

Anar Bks. LLC, *(978-0-9748285)* 10266 Virginia Swan Pl., Cupertino, CA 95014-2025 USA
E-mail: anoopbusiness@yahoo.com
Web site: http://www.anarbooks.com.

Anat Tour, *(978-0-9978432; 978-1-7341648)* 6340 Raydel Ct., San Diego, CA 92120 USA Tel 619-920-1213
Dist(s): **CreateSpace Independent Publishing Platform.**

Anaya Multimedia, S.A. (ESP) *(978-84-415; 978-84-7614)* *Dist. by* **Continental Bk.**

Anbeyond Pr., *(978-0-9744014)* 10420 NE 190th St., Bothell, WA 98011 USA (SAN 255-7886) Tel 425-483-9943; 22833 Bothell Everett Hwy. No. 102, PMB 1227, Bothell, WA 98021
E-mail: rm@anbeyond.com
Web site: http://www.anbeyond.com.

Ancestor Anderson Publishing, *(978-0-9845303)* P.O. Box 341, Lorain, OH 44052 USA
E-mail: cynthiadrlnj@aol.com.

Ancestral Light Publishing, *(978-0-9718530)* 1969 S. Alafaya Trail, No. 322, Orlando, FL 32828 USA Tel 407-382-1707; Fax: 509-356-6971
E-mail: gigante@uaia.org.

Ancestral Tracks, *(978-0-9701266; 978-0-9754161)* P.O. Box 1064, Hillsboro, OR 97123-1064 USA
E-mail: books@ancestraltracks.com; cbeattie@ancestraltracks.com; ginger@ancestraltracks.com
Web site: http://www.ancestraltracks.com.

Anchor *Imprint of* **Knopf Doubleday Publishing Group**

Anchor Group, *(978-0-9852663; 978-0-9855385; 978-0-9882707; 978-0-615-71893-4; 978-0-9886334; 978-0-9888476; 978-0-9891753; 978-0-9897073; 978-0-615-91474-9; 978-0-9915174)* 225 Brookside Dr., FLUSHING, MI 48433 USA Tel 810-964-3767 (Tel/Fax)
E-mail: rourkewrites@gmail.com
Dist(s): **CreateSpace Independent Publishing Platform.**

Anchor Shine Productions, *(978-1-7376838)* 3700 Pacific Ave No. 11, Marina del Rey, CA 90292 USA Tel 818-424-3660
E-mail: christimartinelli@gmail.com.

Anchorage Foundation Pr., *(978-0-9795266)* 1518 Mohle Dr., Austin, TX 78703 USA
Dist(s): **Greenleaf Book Group.**

Anchored Anew Publishing, LLC, *(978-1-7347310)* P.O. Box 1031, Cordova, TN 38088 USA Tel 901-258-1712
E-mail: anchoredredemption@gmail.com
Web site: www.anchoredredemption.com.

Anchored Redemption *See* **Anchored Anew Publishing, LLC**

Ancient Days Pubs., *(978-0-9741405)* P.O. Box 356, Landisville, PA 17538 USA
E-mail: abrdl@ptd.net.

Ancient Faith Publishing, *(978-0-9622713; 978-1-888212; 978-0-9822770; 978-1-936270; 978-1-944967; 978-1-955890)* Orders Addr.: P.O. Box 748, Chesterton, IN 46304 USA Tel 831-336-5118; Fax: 831-336-8882; Toll Free: 800-967-7377; Edit Addr.: 1550 Birdie Way, Chesterton, IN 46304 USA (SAN 175-8624) Tel 831-336-5118; Fax: 831-336-8682; Toll Free: 800-967-7377
Web site: store.ancientfaith.com
Dist(s): **Midpoint Trade Bks., Inc.**
Spring Arbor Distributors, Inc.

Ancient Golf Publishing *See* **LuckySports**

Ancient Studios, *(978-0-9744216; 978-0-692-95854-4; 979-8-218-19940-1; 979-8-218-19942-5; 979-8-218-21585-9)* 13 Pine St., Winooski, VT 05404 USA Tel 8023389293
E-mail: janivescampbell@aol.com
Dist(s): **CreateSpace Independent Publishing Platform.**

Ancker Haply & the Amazing Vasa ship *See* **Grecia Saavedra Pinto**

& P PUBLISHING & GAMES, A *See* **A & P Publishing and Games, LLC**

Andana Editorial (ESP) *(978-84-17497; 978-84-18762)* *Dist. by* **Lectorum Pubns.**

Andehem Publishing, LLC, *(978-1-946813)* 1643 Heatherwood Trail, Xenia, OH 45385 USA Tel 937-912-9063
E-mail: dawn30fl@hotmail.com.

Andersen Pr. (GBR) *(978-0-86264; 978-0-905478; 978-1-84270; 978-1-84939; 978-1-78344)* *Dist. by* **Trafalgar.**

Andersen Pr. (GBR) *(978-0-86264; 978-0-905478; 978-1-84270; 978-1-84939; 978-1-78344)* *Dist. by* **IPG Chicago.**

Andersen Pr. (GBR) *(978-0-86264; 978-0-905478; 978-1-84270; 978-1-84939; 978-1-78344)* *Dist. by* **Lerner Pub.**

Anderson, Christine F. Publishing & Media, *(978-0-692-21124-3; 978-0-692-22045-0; 978-0-692-23961-2; 978-0-692-24772-3; 978-0-692-26421-8; 978-0-692-26422-5; 978-0-692-26423-2; 978-0-692-26424-9; 978-0-692-27096-7; 978-0-692-27363-0; 978-0-692-27912-0; 978-0-692-27914-4; 978-0-692-28210-6; 978-0-692-28212-0; 978-0-692-28750-7; 978-0-692-29483-3; 978-0-692-29484-0; 978-0-692-29949-4; 978-0-692-30398-6; 978-0-692-30399-3; 978-0-692-30415-0; 978-0-692-30814-1; 978-0-692-31267-4; 978-0-692-32217-8; 978-0-692-32992-4; 978-0-692-33385-3)* *P.O. Box 1492, Madison, VA 22727 USA Tel 5409484973*
Dist(s): **CreateSpace Independent Publishing Platform.**

Anderson, Frost, *(978-0-692-85913-1)* 733 Ash St., Twin Falls, ID 83301 USA Tel 208-360-6707
E-mail: jeffwcrawford5+LVP0003482@gmail.com; jeffwcrawford5+LVP0003482@gmail.com.

Anderson, George, *(978-0-9743682; 978-0-9819004)* 12301 Wilshire Blvd., Suite 418, Los Angeles, CA 90025 USA Tel 310-207-3591; Fax: 310-207-6234
E-mail: georgeandereson@aol.com
Web site: http://www.andersonservices.com.

Anderson House Foundation *See* **Windy Press International Publishing Hse., LLC**

Anderson Law Group, *(978-0-9728128; 978-0-9797860)* 3225 Mcleod Dr., Las Vegas, NV 89121 USA; 3225 Mcleod Dr., Las Vegas, NV 89121
E-mail: tmathis@algiaw.com
Web site: http://www.andersonadvisors.com.

Anderson, Mariya, *(978-0-692-07564-7; 978-0-692-08373-4; 978-0-578-66904-5; 978-0-578-67012-6; 978-0-578-70551-4; 978-0-578-75159-7; 978-0-578-76132-9)* 2 Camino Por Los Arboles, ATHERTON, CA 94027 USA Tel 650-276-5368
E-mail: mariyanikiforova@gmail.com
Dist(s): **Ingram Content Group.**

Anderson, Marshall, *(978-0-578-43586-2)* 23916 S Stoney Path Dr, Sun Lakes, AZ 85248 USA Tel 602-622-9696
E-mail: marshalla17@hotmail.com.

Anderson Publishing, *(978-0-9718249)* Orders Addr.: P.O. Box 5544, Douglasville, GA 30154 USA Toll Free: 866-942-0790 (phone/fax); Edit Addr.: 5178 Holly Springs Dr., Douglasville, GA 30135 USA Do not confuse with companies with the same or similar name in Navato, CA, Saginawi, MI, Burley, ID, Cincinnati, MO, Anacortes, WA, Indio, CA
E-mail: canderson@andersonpub.com
Web site: http://www.andersonpub.com
Dist(s): **ACW Pr.**

Anderson, Sara *See* **Sara Anderson Children's Bks.**

ANDInternational, *(978-0-9762291)* 74 Woodcleft Ave., Freeport, NY 11520 USA Tel 516-546-2025; Fax: 516-546-6010; Toll Free: 800-229-2634
E-mail: orders@andihq.com; andihq@aol.com
Web site: http://www.andihq.com.

Andre Deutsch (GBR) *(978-0-233; 978-1-78097)* *Dist. by* **Trafalgar.**

Andre Deutsch (GBR) *(978-0-233; 978-1-78097)* *Dist. by* **Trans-Atl Phila.**

Andre' Largent, *(978-0-578-37676-9)* 105 Hunters Glen Dr., Warner Robins, GA 31093 USA Tel 910-797-7355
E-mail: andre.l.largent@gmail.com.

Andrea Miles, *(978-0-578-54047-4; 978-0-578-32397-8)* 3003 River Vista Way, Mount Pleasant, SC 29466 USA Tel 804-787-4677
E-mail: andrea@andreamiles.com
Dist(s): **Independent Pub.**

AndreCitroen Pubns., *(978-0-578-86624-6)* 141 Chapmans Ave., Warwick, RI 02886 USA Tel 401-737-5398
E-mail: jmorganbooks@hotmail.com.

andreoni, stephen, *(978-1-7367113)* 3 Hope Ct., HUNTINGTON, NY 11743 USA Tel 631-553-5703
E-mail: sandreoni@yahoo.com.

Andres & Blanton, *(978-0-9830318; 978-0-9966721)* 42 Corey Ln., Niantic, CT 06357 USA Tel 860-941-9258
E-mail: sscheyder@sbcglobal.net.

†Andrews McMeel Publishing, *(978-0-8362; 978-0-939251; 978-1-57939; 978-0-7407; 978-1-4494; 978-1-5248)* Orders Addr.: c/o Simon & Schuster, Inc., 100 Front St., Riverside, NJ 08075 USA Toll Free Fax: 800-943-9831; Toll Free: 800-943-9839 (Customer Service); 800-897-7650 (Credit Dept.); Edit Addr.: 1130 Walnut St., Kansas City, MO 64106-2109 USA (SAN 202-540X) Toll Free: 800-851-8923
Web site: http://www.AndrewsMcMeel.com
Dist(s): **Atlas Bks.**
Blackstone Audio, Inc.
Children's Plus, Inc.
Follett School Solutions
Open Road Integrated Media, Inc.
Simon & Schuster, Inc.; *CIP.*

Andromeda Pr. *Imprint of* **Oyebanji, Adam**

Andromeda Press, Incorporated *See* **Andromeda Pr**

Andromeda Pr, *(978-0-9820649; 978-1-938503)* Andromedia Multimeda & Scientific INC, 2600 Birdie Thompson Dr., Pocatello, ID 83201 USA Tel 208-406-1220
E-mail: Andromedapress@gmail.com; awstrickland2600@gmail.com.

Androscoggin Pr., *(978-1-7329471; 979-8-9866181)* 60 Warrens Way, Kennebunk, ME 04094 USA Tel 207-216-3438
E-mail: pleasant13@icloud.com
Web site: androscoppinpres.com.

Andrus, Ashley, *(978-0-9772000)* 104 Kempton Dr., Lafayette, LA 70508-6547 USA
E-mail: ala@andrus.com.

Andy Sanders, *(978-0-9825775; 978-0-9827980; 978-1-936578; 978-1-942056)* 5701 East Cir. Dr. No. 338, Cicero, NY 13039 USA
E-mail: cathysanders.design@gmail.com
Dist(s): **Whitaker Hse.**

ANEKO Pr. *Imprint of* **Life Sentence Publishing, Inc.**

Anela Publishing *See* **Abidenme Bks.**

Anemone Publishing, *(978-0-9759264)* 16 Rope Ferry Rd, Hanover, NH 03755 USA Tel 603-643-0922
E-mail: carolynne.krusi.99@alum.dartmouth.org.

AnewPr., Inc. *Imprint of* **2Nimble**

AnEx Pubns., *(978-0-9711774)* 9 Bartlet St., Suite 131, Andover, MA 01810 USA Toll Free: 866-616-4400
E-mail: rich_hewett@yahoo.com
Web site: http://www.anexx.com.

Angel Applications, *(978-0-615-18904-8)* 1624 Yorktown Dr., Charlottesville, VA 22901 USA Tel 434-293-2819 (phone/fax)
E-mail: kgarstang@cstone.net
Dist(s): **Not So Plain Jane Publishing.**

Angel Avenue Press *See* **Candlelight Bay Publishing**

Angel Eyes Publishing, *(978-0-9755346)* 1914 Hollywood Rd., Atlanta, GA 30318 USA (SAN 256-0542) Tel 404-566-0598
E-mail: dawnettelounds@yahoo.com
Web site: http://www.angeleyespublishing.com.

Angel Fingers Foundation *See* **Mullins Pubns. & Apparel, LLC**

Angel Heart Children's Pr., *(978-0-9712124)* Orders Addr.: P.O. Box 63, East Enterprise, IN 47019 USA Tel 812-594-2438; Fax: 812-594-2438
E-mail: dianemccarty@hotmail.com
Web site: http://www.geocities.com/hs_mom2000.

Angel Insights Press *See* **Stop N Go Fitness**

Angel Island Assoc., *(978-0-9667352)* P.O. Box 866, Tiburon, CA 94920 USA Tel 415-435-3522; Fax: 415-435-2950
E-mail: valaia@att.net
Web site: http://www.angelisland.org
Dist(s): **Follett School Solutions.**

Angel Island Productions, *(978-0-578-19637-4; 978-0-578-19799-9)* 28 Great Hill Dr, Bethel, CT 06801 USA.

Angel Mind, *(978-0-9792866)* 5776-D Lindero Canyon Dr. #123, Westlake Village, CA 91362 USA Tel 818-424-2619; Fax: 818-780-8880
E-mail: bill@angelmind.net
Web site: http://www.angelmind.net.

Angel Pr., *(978-0-9716590)* Div. of The Angelic Light Research Institute, Orders Addr.: P.O. Box 1375, Sedona, AZ 86339 USA Tel 928-451-1222; 928-853-5753 Do not confuse with companies with the same or similar names in Tiburon, CA, Pell City, AL, Concord, NC, Rancho Santa Margarita, CA, St. Thomas, VI, TraversAFB, CA, Monterey, CA
E-mail: angelpress@angelsangelsangels.org; angels@angelsangelsangels.org
Web site: http://www.angelsangelsangels.org; http://www.angelsangelsangels.com; http://www.angelsangelsangels.net; http://www.angellightfeather.com.

Angela J. Ford, LLC, *(978-0-692-16876-9; 978-0-578-98060-7; 978-0-578-34519-2; 979-8-9858488; 979-8-9878276)*
Web site: https://angelajford.com.

Angela Ritacca-Lovenguth, *(978-0-692-97659-3)* 4660 NE Belknap Ct. Suite No. 101 G, HILLSBORO, OR 97124 USA Tel 503-539-7459
E-mail: ImpressionsbyACRL@gmail.com
Dist(s): **Ingram Content Group.**

AngelaCstyles Holdngs LLC, *(978-0-9974495)* 13055 Moorpark, Studio City, CA 91604 USA Tel 312-927-5786
E-mail: angelacstyles@me.com
Web site: www.prettycurlsclub.com.

Angela's Bookshelf *See* **A B Publishing**

AngelBooks, *(978-0-9771749)* 1486 N Woodrow Ave, Wichita, KS 67203 USA
Web site: http://www.thesecretofpink.com.

Angelic Matters, *(978-1-7354453)* 2043 Switzer ave., St. Louis, MO 63136 USA Tel 314-320-3913
E-mail: Mommie.mihungry@gmail.com.

Angelique, Jhala, *(978-1-7338202)* 10801 Lemon Ave, Rancho Cucamonga, CA 91737 USA Tel 323-445-5361
E-mail: akluvgod@yahoo.com.

Angel's BBQ, *(978-0-578-16633-9)* 21 W. Oglethorpe Ln, Savannah, GA 314019 USA.

Angel's Boy Enterprises, *(978-0-9755352)* 8306 Wilshire Blvd., No. 3004, Beverly Hills, CA 90211 USA
Web site: http://www.angelboi.com.

Angel's Diary, *(978-0-615-31217-0; 978-0-9860041)* 6321 Thunder Blitz Ave., Las Vegas, NV 89131 USA.

Angels Landing, *(978-0-9899141)* 347 Butterfly Ln., Hermitage, PA 16148 USA Tel 724-977-0847
E-mail: trpags@roadrunner.com
Web site: https://sites.google.com/site/littlelambs20/.

Angels of Agape, *(978-0-615-25466-1)* 211 Shawnee Valley, East Stroudsburg, PA 18302 USA Tel 973-460-3882
E-mail: angelsofagape@yahoo.com
Web site: http://www.angelsofagape.com.

Angelus Pr., *(978-0-935952; 978-0-9639032; 978-1-892331; 978-1-930959; 978-1-937843; 978-1-949124; 978-1-68529)* Div. of Society of Saint Pius X, Orders Addr.: P.O. Box 217, Saint Marys, KS 66536 USA Tel 816-753-3150; Edit Addr.: P.O. Box 217, Saint Marys, KS 66536 USA (SAN 222-769X) Tel 816-753-3150; Fax: 816-753-3557; Toll Free Fax: 888-855-9022; Toll Free: 800-966-7337 (orders)
E-mail: info@angeluspress.org; stownshend@angeluspress.org; bklaske@angeluspress.org; vtan@angeluspress.org
Web site: http://www.angeluspress.org.

Angelworks Pr., *(978-0-578-00741-0; 978-0-578-12854-2)* 901 Brutscher St., No.D144, Newberg, OR 97132 USA Tel 503-830-0741; 17884 Kelok Rd., Lake Oswego, OR 97034
E-mail: susan@susanmarek.com
Dist(s): **Lulu Pr., Inc.**

ANGI PERRETTI *Imprint of* **MCrc Industries, LLC — A Publishing Hse.**

Angie Blue Bks., LLC, *(978-0-9677547)* 376 County Road 2740., Mico, TX 78056-5353 USA
E-mail: info@AngieBlue.com
Web site: http://www.AngieBlue.com.

AngiesInk, *(978-0-615-17415-0)* P.O. Box 323, Tuskegee Institute, AL 36087 USA
E-mail: angiesink@bellsouth.net
Dist(s): **Lulu Pr., Inc.**

Angle Press *See* **Angle Valley Pr.**

Angle Valley Pr., *(978-0-9711950)* P.O. Box 4098, Winchester, VA 22604 USA (SAN 255-8629) Tel 540-539-1260
E-mail: anglevalleypress@yahoo.com
Web site: http://www.AngleValleyPress.com
Dist(s): **Ingram Content Group.**

Anglican Bk. Ctr. (CAN) *(978-0-919030; 978-0-919891; 978-0-921846; 978-1-55126)* *Dist. by* **Forward Movement.**

Anglo-American Book Company, Limited (UK) *See* **Crown Hse. Publishing LLC**

Angry Bicycle *Imprint of* **Walter, Wendy D.**

Angry Eagle Publishing, *(978-1-7326212; 978-1-7350071; 978-1-7366043; 979-8-9856502; 979-8-9869231)* P.O. Box PO Box 683, Alstead, NH 03602 USA Tel 603-293-3323
E-mail: angryeaglepublishing@gmail.com
Web site: http://angryeaglepublishing.com.

Animal Band Productions, Inc., The, *(978-0-9752619)* P.O. Box 392, Mount Juliet, TN 37121 USA Tel 615-754-8701
E-mail: info@theanimalband.com
Web site: http://www.theanimalband.com.

Animal Crackers Publishing, LLC, *(978-0-9798343)* 1143 Auraria Pkwy. No. A-201, Denver, CO 80204 USA (SAN 854-5170)
Web site: www.animalcrackerspublishing.com.

Animal Hero Kids, *(978-0-615-99522-9; 978-0-578-67171-0; 978-1-7357399; 978-0-578-29472-8)* 13782 151 Ln. N., Jupiter, FL 33478 USA Tel 561-236-8843
E-mail: Susanh@animalherokids.org
Web site: AnimalHeroKids.org; SusanHargreaves.com; BEanAnimalHero.org.

Animal Teachers Enterprises, *(978-0-9788858)* 5902G Queenston St., Springfield, VA 22152 USA
E-mail: snork5902g@yahoo.com
Web site: http://funkman.org/animal/services/catalog.html.

Animal Tracks Pr., *(978-0-9760342)* P.O. Box 432, Cotah, CA 94931 USA (SAN 256-1808) Tel 707-776-8019; Fax: 707-795-2919
Web site: http://www.animaltrackspress.com.

Animalations, *(978-0-9776628; 978-1-933818)* 4186 Melodia Songo Ct., Las Vegas, NV 89135 USA (SAN 257-9111) Fax: 702-804-4220; Toll Free Fax: 866-670-8337; Toll Free: 866-670-8337
E-mail: info@animalations.com
Web site: http://Animalations.com.

AnimeVillage.com *See* **Bandai Entertainment, Inc.**

Animus Ferrum Publishing, *(978-0-692-49790-6; 978-0-9974906; 978-0-578-67684-5; 978-0-578-83084-1; 978-1-954843)* 1525 BENNINGTON DR, MISHAWAKA, IN 46544 USA Tel 574-261-8317
E-mail: tracykorn@comcast.net.

Publisher Name Index

Anita, (*978-0-615-52716-1*) 6639 E. Broadway 165, Tucson, AZ 85710 USA Tel 520-370-8993
E-mail: its4u@aneattook.com
Web site: www.yourstoryyourtalent.com.

Anita S. Faherty, (*978-1-7372131*) 140 W. 74th Street, 5C, New York, NY 10023 USA Tel 212-875-8590
E-mail: anitasfaherty@hotmail.com.

Anjana Publishing (HKG) (*978-988-12394; 978-988-12395; 978-988-15028*) *Dist. by* **BTPS.**

ANKA, (*978-0-615-73378-4*) 3165 Nostrand Ave., 6B, Brooklyn, NY 11229 USA Tel 917-294-2939
E-mail: anna.kaplun@gmail.com.

Ankh Bks. (CAN) (*978-0-9738036*) *Dist. by* **Mtn Bk Co.**

Ann Arbor District Library, (*978-0-9749589; 978-1-947989; 978-1-956697*) 343 S. 5th Ave., Ann Arbor, MI 48104 USA Tel 734-327-4200; Fax: 734-327-8324; *Imprints:* Fifth Avenue Press (FifthAvePr)
E-mail: PURCHASING@AADL.ORG
Web site: http://www.aadl.org.

Ann Arbor Editions LLC, (*978-1-58726*) 2500 S. State St., Ann Arbor, MI 48104 USA Tel 734-913-1302; Fax: 734-913-1249; 1094 Flex Dr., Jackson, TN 38301; *Imprints:* Mitten Press (Mitten Pr)
E-mail: ljohnson@aaeditions.com
Web site: http://www.annarbormediagroup.com; http://www.mittenpress.com; http://www.aaeditions.com
Dist(s): **Follett School Solutions**
Independent Pubs. Group
Two Rivers Distribution.

Ann Arbor Media Group, LLC *See* **Ann Arbor Editions LLC**

Anna Stilianessis, (*978-0-692-18047-1*) 54 Chandler Dr., Wayne, NJ 07470 USA Tel 973-879-9320
E-mail: astilly1208@gmail.com
Web site: www.themomof4.com.

Annadale Comics, (*978-0-9972562; 978-1-945582*) 72 Lorrain Avenu, Staten Island, NY 10312 USA Tel 718-967-1470
E-mail: johnrap316@gmail.com.

Annade Publishing, (*978-0-9761740*) 18964 Lauder, Detroit, MI 48235 USA
Web site: www.annade.com.

Annapolis Publishing Co., (*978-1-884878*) 55 West St., Annapolis, MD 21401 USA (SAN 631-4414) Toll Free: 800-536-1414
E-mail: Katherine@AnnapolisCollection.com
Web site: http://www.mewarren.com; http://www.AnnapolisBooks.com; http://www.AnnapolisCollection.com.

AnnArt Pr., (*978-0-9769719*) R R 1, Box 621, Richards, MO 64778 USA.

Anna's Friends, (*978-0-692-63196-6; 978-0-692-63197-3; 978-0-692-63198-0; 978-0-692-65763-8; 978-0-692-65851-2; 978-0-692-69324-7; 978-0-692-71370-9; 978-0-692-74368-3; 978-1-7325002*) 243 E. Savoy St., Lecanto, FL 34461 USA Tel 615-815-7068
E-mail: yvonne@annasfriends.com
Web site: www.annasfriends.com
Dist(s): **CreateSpace Independent Publishing Platform.**

Annedawn Publishing, (*978-0-9632793; 978-0-9755153; 978-1-7342967*)
E-mail: annedawn@aol.com.

AnnEmma, (*978-1-7327094*) 266 Florence Way, State College, PA 16801 USA Tel 347-282-8006
E-mail: ann_eneh2000@yahoo.co.uk.

Anness Publishing (GBR) (*978-1-85967; 978-1-86147; 978-1-901289; 978-1-901688; 978-1-84038; 978-0-7548; 978-1-84090; 978-1-903141; 978-1-84215; 978-1-84309; 978-1-84322; 978-1-84476; 978-1-84477; 978-0-85723; 978-1-78019; 978-1-84681*) *Dist. by* **Natl Bk Netwk.**

Anness Publishing, Inc., (*978-1-886890*) 39 Sandy Ln., Eatontown, NJ 07724-2445 USA (SAN 299-0563) Toll Free: 800-354-9657
E-mail: AFioravanti@anness.com
Dist(s): **National Bk. Network.**

Annick Pr., Ltd. (CAN) (*978-0-920236; 978-0-920303; 978-1-55037; 978-1-55451*) *Dist. by* **PerseuPGW.**

Annick Pr., Ltd. (CAN) (*978-0-920236; 978-0-920303; 978-1-55037; 978-1-55451*) *Dist. by* **Children Plus.**

Annie Mouse Bks., (*978-0-9793379; 978-0-9914094*) 286 Donation Rd, Greenville, PA 16125 USA (SAN 853-1676)
E-mail: anniemousebooks@gmail.com; anniemousebooks@yahoo.com
Web site: http://www.anniemousebooks.com.

annie tillery mysteries, (*978-0-692-85719-9; 978-0-9989714*) 283 Grand Blvd., Massapequa Park, NY 11762 USA Tel 516-798-0341; Fax: 516-798-0341
E-mail: lmf217@hotmail.com
Web site: lindamariafrank.com.

Annie's *Imprint of* **Annie's Publishing, LLC**

Annie's Media, LLC *See* **Annie's Publishing, LLC**

Annie's Publishing, LLC, (*978-0-88195; 978-0-9638031; 978-0-9655269; 978-1-57367; 978-1-882138; 978-1-931171; 978-1-59012; 978-1-59217; 978-0-9748217; 978-1-59635; 978-1-933802; 978-1-64025*) 111 Corporate Dr., Big Sandy, TX 75755 USA Fax: 260-589-8093 (Clothilde); *Imprints:* Annie's (Annies)
E-mail: Michelle_Harger@annies-publishing.com
Web site: http://www.drgnetwork.com; https://anniesfiction.com; https://www.anniescatalog.com
Dist(s): **Follett School Solutions**
Independent Pubs. Group
MyiLibrary
ebrary, Inc.

Annika Pubns., (*978-0-9670516*) Orders Addr.: P.O. Box 264, Fergus Falls, MN 56537 USA Tel 218-736-7735; Edit Addr.: R.R. 4, Box 50, Fergus Falls, MN 56537 USA.

Anno Domini, (*978-0-9792145; 978-1-939689*) 14541 Livesay Rd., Oregon City, OR 97045 USA (SAN 852-7946) Tel 971-226-4356.

†Annual Reviews, Inc., (*978-0-8243*) 4139 El Camino Way, P.O. Box 10139, Palo Alto, CA 94303-0139 USA (SAN 201-1816) Tel 650-493-4400; Fax: 650-424-0910; Toll Free: 800-523-8635 (including California, Alaska, Hawaii & Canada)
E-mail: service@annualreviews.org
Web site: http://www.AnnualReviews.org; *CIP.*

Anointed Pubs., (*978-0-9763841*) Orders Addr.: 1227-40 Seaton Rd., Durham, NC 27713 USA Tel 919-806-0651; Edit Addr.: 1227-40 seaton Rd., Durham, NC 27713 USA
E-mail: jainjie@msn.com
Web site: http://www.joanjai.com
Dist(s): **Brown Enterprises, Inc.**

Anointed Publishing Co., (*978-0-615-19205-5; 978-0-615-25069-4; 978-0-615-36490-2; 978-0-615-37865-7; 978-0-615-78457-1*) 8123 Winter Blue Ct., Springfield, VA 22153 USA Tel 321-947-0706
Web site: http://www.cheniselytrelle.com.

Anointed Word Pubns., (*978-0-9744024*) 611 N. Pennsylvania Ave., Lansing, MI 48912 USA Tel 517-372-3407.

Anomaly Publishing, (*978-0-9800123*) 3700 Ceres Dr., Salt Lake City, UT 84124 USA Tel 801-278-3245
Dist(s): **Smashwords.**

Anorak Pr. *Imprint of* **Gibbs Smith, Publisher**

Another Chance Media, (*978-1-7325205*) P.O. Box 78, Mullins, SC 29574 USA Tel 843-879-8361
E-mail: wehavethesolution@outlook.com
Web site: www.anotherchancemedia.org.

Another Ep Publishing, (*978-0-9740685; 978-0-615-11795-9*) Div. of Episodes By Wroe, P.O. Box 300, Walnut, CA 91788-0300 USA (SAN 253-2530) Tel 909-448-5356.

Another Language Pr., (*978-0-922852*) 7709 Hamilton Ave., Cincinnati, OH 45231-3103 USA Tel 513-521-5590; Fax: 513-521-5592; Toll Free: 800-733-2067
E-mail: aimsbooks@juno.com
Dist(s): **AIMS International Bks., Inc.**

Another Sommer-Time Story *Imprint of* **Advance Publishing, Inc.**

Another World Pr., (*978-0-615-98065-2*) 326 W. Liberty St., Reno, NV 89501 USA Tel 775-324-3333
E-mail: rbl@robertbrucelindsay.com.

AnotherThinkComing Pr., (*978-0-692-82443-6; 978-0-9987767*) 19830 WALLFLOWER LN, APPLE VALLEY, CA 92308-3643 USA Tel 760-553-1644
E-mail: d_thompson@hotmail.com; d_thompson@hotmail.com; d_thompson@hotmail.com
Dist(s): **CreateSpace Independent Publishing Platform.**

Ansel Adams *Imprint of* **Little Brown & Co.**

Answers In Genesis, (*978-1-893345; 978-1-60092; 978-1-62691; 978-1-9844*) Orders Addr.: P.O. Box 510, Hebron, KY 41048 USA Fax: 859-727-2299; Toll Free: 800-778-3390
E-mail: dzordel@answersingenesis.org
Web site: http://www.answersingenesis.org
Dist(s): **Master Bks.**
New Leaf Publishing Group
Send The Light Distribution LLC.

Answers in Genesis Ministries *See* **Answers In Genesis**

ANT Bank$ *See* **VIP INK Publishing Group, Inc.**

Antarctic Pr., Inc., (*978-0-930655; 978-0-9663588; 978-0-9728978; 978-1-932453; 978-0-9768043; 978-0-9776424; 978-0-9787725; 978-0-9792723; 978-0-9797719; 978-0-9801255; 978-0-9816647; 978-0-9822253; 978-0-9823742; 978-0-9841107; 978-0-9843375; 978-0-9844879; 978-0-9831823; 978-0-9837934; 978-0-9850925; 978-1-939364; 978-1-955929) Div. of Ben Dunn Corp., 4334 Parkwood Dr, San Antonio, TX 78218 USA Tel 210-614-0396; Fax: 210-614-5029 Do not confuse with Antarctic Pr., Bellevue, WA*
E-mail: apcog1@gmail.com
Web site: http://www.antarctic-press.com
Dist(s): **Diamond Comic Distributors, Inc.**
Diamond Bk. Distributors
MyiLibrary.

Anthem Pr. (GBR) (*978-1-898855; 978-1-84331; 978-0-85728; 978-1-78308; 978-1-83998; 978-1-78527*) *Dist. by* **Bolchazy-Carducci.**

Anthem Pr. (GBR) (*978-1-898855; 978-1-84331; 978-0-85728; 978-1-78308; 978-1-83998; 978-1-78527*) *Dist. by* **Bks Intl VA.**

Anthem Pr. (GBR) (*978-1-898855; 978-1-84331; 978-0-85728; 978-1-78308; 978-1-83998; 978-1-78527*) *Dist. by* **TwoRivers.**

AntHill Publishing, (*978-0-9718544*) 5315 Clarendon Rd., Brooklyn, NY 11203 USA Tel 718-629-0294 (phone/fax) Do not confuse with Ant Hill Publishing in Gorman, TX
E-mail: anthillpublishing@hotmail.com.

Anthology of Poetry, Inc., (*978-1-883931*) Orders Addr.: P.O. Box 698, Asheboro, NC 27204-0698 USA Tel 336-626-7762; Fax: 336-626-2622; Edit Addr.: 307 E. Salisbury St., Asheboro, NC 27203 USA
E-mail: poetry@anthologyofpoetry.com
Web site: http://www.anthologyofpoetry.com.

Anthro Co., The, (*978-1-878464*) 200 Carroll St., No. 21, Susanville, CA 96130 USA Tel 530-251-5712
E-mail: devajan@earthlink.net
Web site: http://www.ishifacts.com
Dist(s): **Social Studies Schl. Service.**

Anthropology Major Publishing, (*978-1-7373255*) 15951 Parkview Loop, San Diego, CA 92127 USA Tel 619-993-6714
E-mail: jasontorbert@gmail.com
Web site: www.kidsbooksrule.com.

Anthroposophic Press, Incorporated *See* **SteinerBooks, Inc.**

Anticipation Pr., (*978-0-9754046*) 3563 Sueldo St. Ste. Q, Sn Luis Obisp, CA 93401-7332 USA Do not confuse with Anticipation Press in Cheyenne, WY
E-mail: doingbigbiz@aol.com
Web site: http://www.anticipationpress.com; http://www.zacacreekdevelopment.com.

Antioch Publishing Co., (*978-0-7824; 978-0-89954; 978-1-4017*) Div. of Trends International, 5188 W. 74th St., Indianapolis, IN 46268 USA Tel 317-388-4060; 317-388-1414; Toll Free: 800-315-2110 Do not confuse with Antioch Publishing Co., Torrance, CA
Web site: http://www.antioch.com.

Antipodes Bks. & Beyond, 9707 Fairway Ave., Silver Spring, MD 20901-3001 USA Tel 301-602-9519; Fax: 301-565-0160
E-mail: Antipode@antipodesbooks.com
Web site: http://www.antipodesbooks.com.

Antique Collectors' Club, (*978-0-902028; 978-0-907462; 978-1-85149*) Orders Addr.: Eastworks, 116 Pleasant St., Easthampton, MA 01027 USA (SAN 630-7787) Tel 413-529-0861; Fax: 413-529-0862; Toll Free: 800-252-5231 (orders)
E-mail: info@antiquecc.com; sales@antiquecc.com
Web site: http://www.antiquecollectorsclub.com
Dist(s): **National Bk. Network.**

Antiques, Incorporated *See* **Kovels Antiques, Inc.**

Antiquity Publishing, (*978-0-9793284*) 4127 McLaughlin Ave., No. 15, Los Angeles, CA 90066-5445 USA Tel 310-390-9093 (phone/fax)
E-mail: Randwulf@humnet.ucla.edu.

Antlers & Fins LLC, (*978-0-9800643*) P.O. Box 82, Henefer, UT 84033 USA
E-mail: info@billygoeshunting.com
Web site: http://www.BillyGoesHunting.com.

Anton Berkshire Publishing, (*978-0-9746330*) Orders Addr.: P.O. Box 372, Markle, IN 46770 USA (SAN 255-6618); Edit Addr.: 9374 N. Marzane Rd., Markle, IN 46770 USA
Web site: http://www.antonberkshirepublishing.com.

Antoniades, Basil, (*978-0-615-24661-1*) 9 Belden Ct., Timonium, MD 21093 USA Tel 410-560-9911
E-mail: basilantoniades@earthlink.net
Web site: http://www.havingfunwithgreekmythology.com
Dist(s): **Lulu Pr., Inc.**

Antonucci, Jason, (*978-0-692-11302-8; 978-0-578-66897-0*) 126 JOSIAH NORTON RD, CAPE NEDDICK, ME 03902 USA Tel 603-988-4935
E-mail: jasonm.antonucci@gmail.com
Dist(s): **Ingram Content Group.**

Antrim Hse., (*978-0-9662783; 978-0-9762091; 978-0-9770633; 978-0-9792226; 978-0-9798451; 978-0-9817883; 978-0-9823970; 978-0-9843418; 978-1-936482; 978-1-943826; 979-8-9855621; 979-8-9865522*) 400 Seabury Dr. 5196, Bloomfield, CT 06002 USA; P.O. Box 111, Tariffville, CT 06081
Web site: http://www.antrimhousebooks.com
Dist(s): **BookBaby**
Distributors, The.

Antroll Publishing Co., (*978-1-877656*) 2616 Elmont St., Wheaton, MD 20902 USA Tel 301-942-0492.

Anyone Can Write bks., (*978-0-9771470*) 2890 N. Hills Dr., NE, Atlanta, GA 30305-3210 USA Tel 404-261-1616
Web site: http://www.anyonecanwrite.com.

Anystar Publishing *See* **Nolia Crown Prods.**

Anythings Possible, Inc., (*978-1-892186*) Orders Addr.: 1863 N. Farwell Ave., Milwaukee, WI 53202 USA Fax: 414-226-4901; Toll Free: 800-543-7153
E-mail: info@special-kids.com
Web site: http://www.special-kids.com.

Anzalone, Alex Hadassah, (*978-0-692-92593-5; 978-0-692-97448-3*) 55 Stockbridge Terr., Lee, MA 01238 USA Tel 646-712-0722
E-mail: alexanzalone@gmail.com.

Anzalone, Frank, (*978-0-9770786*) P.O. Box 110422, Campbell, CA 95011 USA Tel 408-247-7572; Fax: 408-984-1519
E-mail: info@mckyfoto.com
Web site: http://www.mckyfoto.com.

AoPS Inc., (*978-0-9773045; 978-1-934124*) 15330 Ave. of Science, San Diego, CA 92128 USA Tel 858-675-4555; Fax: 855-430-9531; Toll Free Fax: 855-430-9531
E-mail: purchasing@aops.com
Web site: http://www.artofproblemsolving.com; http://www.beastacademy.com.

Aoyama Publishing *See* **Marble Hse. Editions**

AP Bks., (*978-0-9841927*) P.O. Box 799, Pennington, NJ 08534 USA Fax: 609-730-1286
Dist(s): **Cardinal Pubs. Group.**

AP Publishing, (*978-0-9722906*) Orders Addr.: P.O. Box 160, Merrimac, WI 53561 USA
Web site: http://www.wildlife-trails.com
Dist(s): **Ingram Content Group.**

Apage4You Bk. Publishing, (*978-0-9723616*) 2025 Balla Way, Suite 200, Grand Prairie, TX 75051-3907 USA Tel 972-264-2892; Fax: 214-722-1254; Toll Free: 800-519-7323
E-mail: apage4you@starband.net
Web site: http://www.publishfast.com; http://www.apage4youpublishing.com.

APCWriter & Pub. *Imprint of* **Cox, Audrey Phillips**

Ape Entertainment, (*978-0-9741398; 978-0-9791050; 978-0-9801314; 978-1-934944; 978-1-936340; 978-1-937676; 978-1-62782*) P.O. Box 7100, San Diego, CA 92167 USA
Dist(s): **Diamond Comic Distributors, Inc.**
Diamond Bk. Distributors.

Ape Pen Publishing *See* **Ballard, Donald W.**

Aperturas Foundation, (*978-0-9745220*) P.O. Box 25163, Chicago, IL 60625 USA Tel 773-478-7973
E-mail: aperturas@yahoo.com
Web site: http://www.aperturas.info.

Aperture *Imprint of* **Aperture Foundation, Inc.**

†Aperture Foundation, Inc., (*978-0-89381; 978-0-912334; 978-0-900406; 978-1-931788; 978-1-59711; 978-1-68395*) 547 West 27th St., 4th Flr., New York, NY 10001 USA (SAN 201-1832); *Imprints:* Aperture (Aper)
E-mail: alang@aperture.org
Dist(s): **D.A.P./Distributed Art Pubs.**
Farrar, Straus & Giroux
Ingram Publisher Services
Two Rivers Distribution; *CIP.*

Aperture Pr., LLC, (*978-0-615-40395-3; 978-0-615-41313-6; 978-0-615-41888-9; 978-0-9833310; 978-0-9836878; 978-0-9850026; 978-0-9889351; 978-0-9910962; 978-0-9909302; 978-0-9973020; 978-0-9995158; 978-1-7329329*) PO Box 6485, Reading, PA 19610 USA
E-mail: steve@aperturepress.net
Web site: http://www.aperturepress.net
Dist(s): **Lulu Pr., Inc.**

Apex *Imprint of* **North Star Editions**

Apex Performance Solutions, LLC, (*978-0-9824519*) 467 Springdale Rd., Westfield, MA 01085 USA Tel 413-562-2299; Fax: 413-562-2289; 113 Ne Carleston Oaks Dr., Port St.Lucie, FL 34983
E-mail: jwojcik@apexperformancesolutions.com
Web site: http://www.apexperformancesolutions.com
Dist(s): **Follett School Solutions**
Partners Pubs. Group, Inc.

APG Sales & Distribution Services, Div. of Warehousing and Fulfillment Specialists, LLC (WFS, LLC), 7344 Cockrill Bend Blvd., Nashville, TN 37209-1043 USA (SAN 630-818X) Toll Free: 800-327-5113
E-mail: sswift@agpbooks.com
Web site: http://www.apgbooks.com.

APG Sales & Fulfillment *See* **APG Sales & Distribution Services**

Aplastic Anemia + MDS International Foundation, (*978-0-9755572*) Orders Addr.: P.O. Box 613, Annapolis, MD 21404-0613 USA Tel 410-867-0242; Fax: 410-867-0240; Toll Free: 800-747-2820; Edit Addr.: P.O. Box 310, Churchton, MD 20733-0310 USA
E-mail: help@aamds.org
Web site: http://www.aamds.org.

Apni Heritage LLC, (*978-1-7377740*) 3475 Naamans Dr, Claymont, DE 19703 USA Tel 240-678-2178
E-mail: apniheritage@gmail.com.

Apocalyptic Tangerine Pr., (*978-0-9821138; 978-0-9897496*) Orders Addr.: 1969 Laurel Ave., No. 5, Saint Paul, MN 55104-5820 USA Tel 304-942-4912.

Apodixis Press *See* **Read Well Publishing Inc.**

Apollo Computer Systems, Inc., (*978-0-9610582*) 616 14th St., Arcata, CA 95521 USA (SAN 264-651X) Tel 707-822-0318.

Apollo Pubs., (*978-0-9718532; 978-0-9721368; 978-1-932832; 978-1-946599; 978-1-960333*) 1963 Catalina Dr, Santa Cruz, CA 95062 USA Tel 831 479 9626 (phone/fax); 800-881-0181
E-mail: michael@apollopub.com
Web site: http://www.apollopub.com
Dist(s): **TNT Media Group, Inc.**

Apollo Publishing L.L.C. *See* **Carpe Diem Pubs.**

Apollo Science Pubs., LLC, (*978-0-9814551*) P.O. Box 26671, San Diego, CA 92196 USA Tel 858-635-6558
E-mail: zhibo.zhang@ieee.org
Web site: http://www.aspublishers.com.

Apologetics Pr., Inc., (*978-0-932859; 978-1-60063*) 230 Landmark Dr., Montgomery, AL 36117-2752 USA (SAN 688-9190) Tel 334-272-8558; Fax: 334-270-2002; Toll Free: 800-234-8558 (orders only)
E-mail: mail@apologeticspress.org
Web site: http://www.apologeticspress.org
Dist(s): **Send The Light Distribution LLC.**

Apologia Educational Ministries, Inc., (*978-0-9656294; 978-1-932012; 978-1-935495; 978-1-940110; 978-1-946506; 978-1-960929*) 5808 Valley Stream Trail, Waxhaw, NC 28173 USA Tel 765-608-3280
E-mail: khulsizer@apologia.com
Web site: http://www.apologia.com.

Apologue Entertainment, LLC, (*978-0-9819825*) Orders Addr.: 1075 Meghan Ave., Algonquin, IL 60102 USA
E-mail: gary.mack@apologueentertainment.com
Web site: http://www.apologueentertainment.com.

Appalachian Bible Co., (*978-1-889049*) Orders Addr.: 522 Princeton Rd., Johnson City, TN 37605 USA (SAN 169-7889) Tel 423-282-9475; Fax: 423-282-9110; Toll Free: 800-289-2772; Edit Addr.: P.O. Box 1573, Johnson City, TN 37601 USA
E-mail: appainc@aol.com.

Appalachian Hse., (*978-0-9662800*) Orders Addr.: P.O. Box 627, Boiling Springs, PA 17007 USA (SAN 299-5328) Tel 717-609-6234
E-mail: apphouse@pa.net.

Appalachian, Incorporated *See* **Appalachian Bible Co.**

Appalachian Log Publishing Co., The, (*978-1-885935*) Orders Addr.: P.O. Box 20297, Charleston, WV 25362-1297 USA Tel 304-342-5789; Edit Addr.: 878 Anaconda Ave., Charleston, WV 25302 USA
E-mail: gregory@newwave.net.

†Appalachian Mountain Club Bks., (*978-0-910146; 978-1-878239; 978-1-929173; 978-1-934028; 978-1-62842*) 5 Joy St., Boston, MA 02108 USA (SAN 203-4808) Tel 617-523-0655; Fax: 617-523-0722; Toll Free: 800-262-4455
E-mail: kbreunig@outdoors.org; alakri@outdoors.org
Web site: http://www.outdoors.org
Dist(s): **Globe Pequot Pr., The**
National Bk. Network; *CIP.*

Applause Theatre & Cinema *Imprint of* **Leonard, Hal Corp.**

Apple Corps Pubs., (*978-0-9619484; 978-1-934397*) 1600 Sunset Ln., Oklahoma City, OK 73127 USA (SAN 245-0461) Fax: 888-375-7017; Toll Free: 800-335-9208
E-mail: tom@tomquaid.com
Dist(s): **Univ. of Oklahoma Pr.**

Apple Cover Books *See* **New Monic Bks.**

Apple House Publishing, (*978-0-9966954*) 8 Orchard Blossom Rd, Windham, NH 03087 USA Tel 301-717-3034
E-mail: jennifersmithwriter@outlook.com
Web site: www.jenniferwsmith.com.

Apple of the Eye Publishing, (*978-0-615-38892-2; 978-0-9829289*) 2800 Neilson Way, No. 614, Santa Monica, CA 90405 USA Tel 818-486-0904
Web site: http://www.thealmightybible.com
Dist(s): **Casscom Media.**

Apple Pie Pubs., (*978-0-9675123*) 5745 SW 75th St., PMB 325, Gainesville, FL 32608 USA Tel 352-472-2833 (phone/fax); Fax: 352-335-9080
E-mail: applepienow@aol.com
Web site: http://www.applepienow.com.

pleby, Linda *See* **Seeds of Imagination**
pleNobb Books *See* **Happy Apple Bks.**
ples & Honey Pr. *Imprint of* **Behrman Hse., Inc.**
plesauce Pr. *Imprint of* **Cider Mill Pr. Bk. Pubs., LLC**
pleseed Pr. Bk. Pub. LLC, *(978-1-60464)* Orders Addr.: 12 Port Farm Rd., Kennebunkport, ME 04046-0404 USA (SAN 854-5405) Tel 207-641-3489; Fax: 207-967-8233
E-mail: appleseedgiftbooks@mac.com
Web site: http://www.appleseedpress.com.
pleton, Brian H., *(978-0-692-84690-2; 978-0-692-86873-7; 978-0-692-86890-4; 978-0-692-87342-7; 978-0-692-88335-8; 978-0-692-90690-3; 978-0-692-97720-0; 978-0-692-98035-4; 978-0-692-99289-0; 978-0-692-19972-5; 978-0-692-04293-9; 978-0-578-40299-4; 978-0-578-57697-8; 978-0-578-57839-2; 978-0-578-83337-8; 978-0-578-89525-3; 978-0-578-90474-0; 978-0-578-94013-7; 978-0-578-34321-1; 979-8-218-09356-3; 979-8-218-10608-9) 5669 Snell Ave # 126, SAN JOSE, CA 95123 USA Tel 408 363 1721*
E-mail: iranianb@sbcglobal.net; iranianb@sbcglobal.net.
Applewood Bks., *(978-0-918222; 978-1-55709; 978-1-889833; 978-1-933212; 978-1-4290; 978-0-9819430; 978-1-60889; 978-0-9844156; 978-0-9836416; 978-1-938700; 978-0-9882885; 978-1-941216; 978-1-5162; 978-1-944038; 978-1-945187; 978-1-64194)* 1 River Rd., Carlisle, MA 01741-1820 USA (SAN 210-3419) Toll Free: 800-277-5312; 1 Ingram Blvd., La Vergne, TN 37086; *Imprints:* Commonwealth Editions (CommonwealthEd)
E-mail: applewood@awb.com; svec@awb.com
Web site: http://www.awb.com
Dist(s): **Arcadia Publishing**
Children's Plus, Inc.
Follett School Solutions
Ingram Publisher Services
Two Rivers Distribution; *CIP.*
Applied Database Technology, Inc., *(978-0-9742610)* 715 E. Sprague Ave. Suite 125, Spokane, WA 99202 USA
Web site: http://www.applieddatabase.com.
Appointed Media Group, LLC, *(978-0-9984148)* 1425 Battlefield Blvd. No. 1934, Chesapeake, VA 23327 USA Tel 757-935-7180
E-mail: roy@appointedpictures.org.
Apprentice Hse., *(978-1-934074; 978-1-62720)* Dept. Communication/Loyola College in MD, 4501 N. Charles St., Baltimore, MD 21210 USA.
Apprentice Shop Bks., LLC, *(978-0-9723410; 978-0-9842549; 978-0-9850144)* P.O. Box 375, Amherst, NH 03031 USA Fax: 603-472-2588
E-mail: apprenticeshpbks@aol.com
Web site: http://www.apprenticeshopbooks.com
Dist(s): **Follett School Solutions.**
Apricot and Bee, LLC, *(978-0-578-16418-2; 978-0-9987264)* 2626 Tunnel Blvd Apt. 153, Pittsburgh, PA 15203 USA Tel 540-840-2137
E-mail: hello@apricotandbee.com.
Apricot Pr., *(978-1-885027)* P.O. Box 98, Nephi, UT 84648 USA Toll Free: 800-731-6145
E-mail: books@apricotpress.com
Web site: http://www.apricotpress.com.
April Arts Press & Productions, *(978-0-9650918)* P.O. Box 64, Morgan Hill, CA 95038-0064 USA
E-mail: books@aprilartspress.com
Web site: http://www.aprilartspress.com
Dist(s): **Follett School Solutions.**
April Fool Publishing, *(978-0-692-16938-4; 978-0-578-52314-9; 978-0-578-53203-5; 978-0-578-66786-7; 978-0-578-78502-8; 978-0-578-97357-9; 978-0-578-38602-7; 979-8-218-07989-5; 979-8-218-09018-0; 979-8-218-14666-5; 979-8-218-17087-5)* 352 Home Pl. Dr., Easley, SC 29640 USA Tel 864-770-5986
E-mail: mattpelicano@icloud.com
Dist(s): **Ingram Content Group.**
April Joy Manger, *(978-1-7343786)* 10 De Sabla Rd., No. Apt. 309, San Mateo, CA 94402 USA Tel 650-347-5530
E-mail: april@projectgardengate.com.
April Press *See* **April Arts Press & Productions**
April Tale, *(978-1-957093)* Olenivska 8 app.12, Kyiv, 04080 UKR
E-mail: april4tale@gmail.com.
April Tale Books *See* **April Tale**
APS Publishing, *(978-0-9906361; 978-1-945145)* 5739 S. Calumet Ave Unit 1s, Chicago, IL 60637 USA Tel 773-440-2004; 847-942-6135
E-mail: authorspromotingsuccess@gmail.com
Web site: www.weareaps.com.
AP's Travels *See* **Aunt Patty's Travels-London**
Apte, Stu, *(978-0-615-20409-3; 978-0-9821227)* 133 Plantation Dr., Tavernier, FL 33070 USA Tel 305-852-7440 (phone/fax)
E-mail: stuwho@bellsouth.net
Dist(s): **Emerald Bk. Co.**
Apthorp, Bretworth B., *(978-0-692-83004-8; 978-0-578-30515-8)* P.O. Box 1301, NANTUCKET, MA 02554 USA Tel 508-292-3755
E-mail: jeffwcrawford5+LVP0003237@gmail.com; jeffwcrawford5+LVP0003237@gmail.com.
Aquafire Sulis, *(978-0-9826321)* 216 Seventh Ave., 5E, New York, NY 10011 USA Tel 212-691-7288
E-mail: info@aquafiresulis.com.
Aquarian Age Publishing, Inc., *(978-0-9767530)* 250, 56th St., Fort Lauderdale, FL 33334 USA
E-mail: info@aquarianagepublishing.com
Web site: http://www.lawsofhealing.com; http://www.aquarianagepublishing.com.
Aquarius Pr., *(978-0-9718214; 978-0-9819208; 978-0-9846212; 978-0-9852877; 978-0-9897357; 978-0-9961390; 978-0-9971996; 978-0-9985278; 978-0-9992232; 978-1-7322091; 978-1-7330898; 978-1-7348273; 978-1-7357408; 978-1-7367677; 978-1-7379676; 979-8-9881655)* Orders Addr.: P.O. Box 23096, Detroit, MI 48223 USA Tel 313-515-8122; Toll Free Fax: 877-979-3639 Do not confuse with companies with the same or similar names in Santa Fe, NM, Baltimore, MD, Watchung, NJ
E-mail: aquariuspress@sbcglobal.net; aquariuspress@gmail.com
Web site: http://www.AUXmedia.studio; http://www.AquariusPress.net; http://www.WillowLit.net
Dist(s): **SPD-Small Pr. Distribution.**
AquaZebra, *(978-0-9905827; 978-0-9972085; 978-1-7324567; 978-1-954604)* 35070 Maria Rd., Cathedral City, CA 92234 USA Tel 760-880-5174
E-mail: mark@aquazebra.com
Web site: www.aquazebra.com.
AquaZebra Book Publishing *See* **AquaZebra**
Aqueduct Pr., *(978-0-9746559; 978-1-933500; 978-1-61976)* P.O. Box 95787, Seattle, WA 98145-2787 USA (SAN 256-131X); 4 White Brook Rd., Gilsum, NH 6448
Web site: http://www.aqueductpress.com
Dist(s): **Follett School Solutions**
Pathway Bk. Service.
Aquila Ink Publishing, *(978-0-9760789)* P.O. Box 160, Rio Nido, CA 95471 USA (SAN 850-9050) Tel 707-799-5981; 707-887-9090; Fax: 707-869-2973
E-mail: aquila@aquilaink.com
Web site: http://www.aquilaink.com.
Aquinas & Krone Publishing, LLC, *(978-0-9800448; 978-0-9843526; 978-0-9849505)* P.O. Box 1304, Merchantville, NJ 08109 USA (SAN 855-0751) Tel 856-665-3999.
A.R. Harding Publishing Co., *(978-0-936622)* 2878 E. Main St., Columbus, OH 43209 USA (SAN 206-4936) Tel 614-231-9585
E-mail: erics@furfishgame.com.
AR Thomas Publishing, *(978-0-692-12809-1)* 25222 NW Fwy 141, Cypress, TX 77429 USA Tel 832-914-7510
E-mail: ibhawi@yahoo.com.
Aradiance Publishing, *(978-0-9715737)* P.O. Box 13855, Mill Creek, WA 98082 USA.
Arago Publishing, LLC, *(978-0-9742698; 978-0-9788457)* 90087 Cape Arago Hwy., Coos Bay, OR 97420 USA (SAN 255-4607)
E-mail: surfdance@iceinternet.com.
Arango-Duque, J. F. *See* **Arango's Publishing**
Arango's Publishing, *(978-0-9655750)* 1776 Polk St., No. 3K-032, Hollywood, FL 33020 USA (SAN 299-2078)
E-mail: arangoduke@aol.com
Dist(s): **Hispanic Bks. Distributors & Pubs., Inc.**
Lectorum Pubns., Inc.
Libros Sin Fronteras
Quality Bks., Inc.
Aranjo, Karl, *(978-0-9770667)* 16 Greenwood, Irvine, CA 92604 USA Tel 949-786-8765
E-mail: karlaranjo@yahoo.com
Web site: http://guitaru.com.
Arbiter Pr., *(978-0-9621385; 978-0-615-35216-9; 978-0-615-35859-8)* 1732 N. Lakemont Ave., Winter Park, FL 32792 USA (SAN 251-1282); 1732 Arbor Pk. Dr., Winter Park, FL 32789 Tel 407-647-2606
E-mail: chsblackwell@gmail.com
Dist(s): **Bookazine Co., Inc.**
Arbor Bks., *(978-0-9771870; 978-0-9777764; 978-0-9786107; 978-0-9790469; 978-0-9794118; 978-0-9800582; 978-0-9818658; 978-0-9841992)* 244 Madison Ave., No. 254, New York, NY 10016 USA; 19 Apero Rd., Suite 301, Ramsey, NJ 7446 Do not confuse with Arbor Books in Media, PA
Web site: http://www.arborbooks.com
Dist(s): **Follett School Solutions.**
Arbor Center for Teaching, *(978-0-9821363)* 4201 SW Borland Rd., Arbor School of Arts & Sciences, Tualatin, OR 97062-6779 USA (SAN 857-3573)
E-mail: publications@arborcenterforteaching.org; will@arborschool.org
Web site: http://www.arborcenterforteaching.org/books.
Arbordale Publishing, *(978-0-9764943; 978-0-9768823; 978-0-9777423; 978-1-934359; 978-1-60718; 978-1-62855; 978-1-64351; 978-1-63817)* 612 Johnnie Dodds Blvd., Suite A2, Mount Pleasant, SC 29464 USA (SAN 256-6109) Tel 843-971-6722; Fax: 843-216-3804
E-mail: leegerman@arbordalepublishing.com; donna@arbordalepublishing.com
Web site: https://www.arbordalepublishing.com
Dist(s): **BWI**
Baker & Taylor Bks.
Brodart Co.
Children's Plus, Inc.
Ediciones Enlace de PR, Inc.
Follett School Solutions
Ingram Publisher Services.
Arborville Bks., *(978-0-9886988)* 2115 Nature Cove Ct. No. 203, Ann Arbor, MI 48104 USA Tel 734-663-8175
E-mail: arborvillebooks@gmail.com
Dist(s): **Lulu Pr., Inc.**
Arborwoodgen LLC, *(978-0-9973686)* 23500 Cristo Rey Dr. Unit 107D, Cupertino, CA 95014-6520 USA Tel 650-967-3008
E-mail: wualan@labmed2.ucsf.edu.
Arbutus Pr., *(978-0-9665316; 978-0-9766104; 978-1-933926)* Orders Addr.: 2364 Pinehurst Trail, Traverse City, MI 49686 USA Tel 231-946-7240
E-mail: editor@arbutuspress.com
Web site: http://www.arbutuspress.com
Dist(s): **Follett School Solutions.**
Arc Manor, *(978-0-9786536; 978-0-9794154; 978-1-60450; 978-1-61242; 978-1-64710; 978-1-64973)* P.O. Box 10339, Rockville, MD 20849 USA Tel 240-645-2214; Fax: 310-388-8449; *Imprints:* TARK Classic Fiction (TARK Classic Fiction); Serenity Publishers (Serentiy Pubs)
E-mail: admin@arcmanor.com
Web site: http://www.HeartsKiss.com; http://www.ArcManor.com; http://www.PhoenixPick.com; http://www.PhoenixRider.com; http://http://www.ManorWodehouse.com; http://www.galaxysedge.com/
Dist(s): **Consortium Bk. Sales & Distribution**
Follett School Solutions
Smashwords.
ARC Pr. Bks. *Imprint of* **American Reading Co.**
ARC Pr. Comics *Imprint of* **American Reading Co.**
ARC Pr., Div. of American Reading Co., 201 S. Gulph Rd., King of Prussia, PA 19406 USA.
Arcade Publishing *Imprint of* **Skyhorse Publishing Co., Inc.**
Arcadia Publications *See* **Linden Hill Publishing**
Arcadia Publishing, *(978-0-88289; 978-0-910462; 978-0-911116; 978-1-56554; 978-0-7385; 978-1-58973; 978-1-58980; 978-1-59629; 978-1-4396; 978-1-60949; 978-1-4556; 978-1-61423; 978-1-4671; 978-0-578-11080-6; 978-1-62584; 978-1-62585; 978-1-62619; 978-0-578-12310-3; 0-615-91258-5; 978-0-9903765; 978-1-944313; 978-1-5316; 978-1-5402; 978-0-578-19068-6; 978-0-578-59417-0; 978-0-578-59418-7) Orders Addr.: 420 Wando Pk. Blvd., Mount Pleasant, SC 29464 USA (SAN 255-268X) Tel 843-853-2070; Fax: 843-853-0044; Toll Free: 888-313-2665;* *Imprints:* History Press, The (HistoryPress); Pelican Publishing (PelicanPub) Do not confuse with Arcadia Publishing in Greenwood Village, CO
E-mail: sales@arcadiapublishing.com
Web site: http://www.arcadiapublishing.com
Dist(s): **INscribe Digital**
Independent Pubs. Group
MyiLibrary
Open Road Integrated Media, Inc.
Arcadiam Games, *(978-0-9769951)* 3106 NE 83rd Ave., Portland, OR 97220 USA
E-mail: travisbrown@crossroads-rpg.com
Web site: http://www.crossroads-rpg.com.
Arcadian Hse., *(978-0-9766666)* 3040 Rightmire Blvd., Columbus, OH 43221 USA
E-mail: lyn@arcadianhouse.com
Web site: http://www.arcadianhouse.com.
Arcana Studio, Inc., *(978-0-9763095; 978-0-9809204; 978-1-926914; 978-1-927424; 978-1-927421)* 930 Winthrop Ln., Rockford, IL 61107 USA
Web site: http://www.arcanastudio.com
Dist(s): **Diamond Comic Distributors, Inc.**
Diamond Bk. Distributors.
Archaeopress (GBR) *(978-0-9539923; 978-1-905739; 978-1-78491; 978-1-78969; 978-1-80327) Dist. by* **ISD USA.**
Archaia Entertainment *Imprint of* **BOOM! Studios**
Archangel Studios, LLC, *(978-0-9714714)* 507 S. Parish Pl., Burbank, CA 91506-2951 USA
E-mail: thredstar_hq@hotmail.com
Web site: http://www.theredstar.com
Dist(s): **Diamond Comic Distributors, Inc.**
Diamond Bk. Distributors.
Archbury Pr., *(978-0-615-44224-2; 978-0-615-56552-1; 978-0-615-60617-0; 978-0-615-81067-6; 978-0-615-90212-8; 978-0-692-23243-9; 978-0-578-97027-1)* P.O. Box 20668, Boulder, CO 80308 USA Tel 303-516-9694
E-mail: archburypress@aol.com.
Archdeacon Bks., *(978-0-692-20966-0; 978-0-692-24065-6; 978-0-692-43443-7; 978-0-692-53166-2; 978-0-692-55279-7; 978-0-692-75684-3; 978-0-692-91562-2; 978-0-692-96824-6; 978-0-692-07939-3; 978-1-949422)* 1713 Strawberry Ln, Birmingham, AL 35244 USA Tel 205-424-2255
E-mail: woody.norman@gmail.com
Dist(s): **CreateSpace Independent Publishing Platform**
Ingram Bk. Co.
ArcheBooks *Imprint of* **ArcheBooks Publishing, Inc.**
ArcheBooks Publishing, Inc., *(978-1-59507)* 6081 Silver King Blvd. Unit 903, Cape Coral, FL 33914 USA Tel 239-542-7595; 9101 W. Sahara Ave., Las Vegas, NV 89117; *Imprints:* ArcheBooks (ArchBks)
E-mail: publisher@archebooks.com
Web site: http://www.archebooks.com
Dist(s): **Follett School Solutions**
ISD.
Archelon Press, LLC *See* **Akasha Publishing, LLC**
Archeological Assessments, Inc., *(978-0-9638956; 978-0-9794044)* P.O. Box 1631, Nashville, AR 71852 USA
E-mail: aaimjb@aol.com
Web site: http://www.arkansasstories.com.
Archer & Rose Pr., LLC, *(978-1-954143)* P.O. Box P.O. Box 140111, Lakewood, CO 80214 USA Tel 520-303-2203
E-mail: monicamccayne@gmail.com.
Archer Fields, Inc., *(978-0-9627767; 978-1-56466)* 155 Sixth Ave., New York, NY 10013 USA Tel 212-627-1999; Fax: 212-627-9484; Toll Free: 800-338-2665
Dist(s): **D.A.P./Distributed Art Pubs.**
Archer's Pr., *(978-0-615-68449-9; 978-0-615-70040-3; 978-0-615-70731-0; 978-0-9894749; 978-0-692-23029-9; 978-0-692-41131-5; 978-0-692-47473-0; 978-0-692-61477-8; 978-0-692-62625-2)* 2795 Parker Rd., Florissant, MO 63033 USA Tel 3146168101
Web site: www.archerspress.com
Dist(s): **CreateSpace Independent Publishing Platform.**
Archeworks, *(978-0-9753405)* 625 N. Kingsbury St., Chicago, IL 60610 USA Tel 312-867-7254; Fax: 312-867-7260
E-mail: info@archeworks.org
Web site: http://www.archeworks.org.
Archie Comic Pubns., Inc., *(978-1-879794; 978-1-936975; 978-1-61988; 978-1-62738; 978-1-68183; 978-1-68255; 978-1-64576; 979-8-88967)* 629 Fifth Ave, Suite 100, Pelham, NY 10803-1242 USA Tel 914-381-5155; Fax: 914-381-2335; *Imprints:* Dark Circle Comics (Dark Circle)
E-mail: stevem@archiecomics.com
Web site: http://www.archiecomics.com
Dist(s): **Children's Plus, Inc.**
Diamond Comic Distributors, Inc.
Diamond Bk. Distributors
Follett School Solutions
Independent Pubs. Group
Penguin Random Hse. Distribution
Penguin Random Hse. LLC
Random Hse., Inc.
Archie Publishing, *(978-0-9779064)* P.O. Box 521732, Salt Lake City, UT 84152-1732 USA (SAN 850-5616) Tel 801-232-3840
E-mail: mcf@archiepublishing.com
Web site: http://www.archiepublishing.com
Dist(s): **American West Bks.**
Archimede Editions (FRA) *(978-2-211) Dist. by* **Distribks Inc.**
Archipelago Pr., *(978-1-893335)* Orders Addr.: P.O. Box 1540, Los Gatos, CA 95031 USA (SAN 299-7541) Tel 408-354-5587 (phone/fax) Do not confuse with companies with the same name in Saint Thomas, VI, Friday Harbor, WA
E-mail: pelago2000@aol.com
Web site: http://www.rosswell.com.
ArchiTanvi, *(978-1-7372658)* 110 Livorno Way, REDWOOD CITY, CA 94065 USA Tel 650-350-0188
E-mail: avanti@gmail.com.
Archival Services, Incorporated *See* **Red River Pr.**
Archives Pr. *Imprint of* **Media Assocs.**
Archives Press, The *See* **Media Assocs.**
Archus Pr., LLC, *(978-0-9648564; 978-1-893047; 978-0-9852248)* 620 Miller St., Rochester, MI 48307 USA Tel 248-218-0356; Toll Free: 888-275-5639
E-mail: leigharrathoon@gmail.com.
Archway Publishing, *(978-1-4808; 978-1-6657)* Div. of Author Solutions, Inc., 1663 Liberty Dr., Bloomington, IN 47403 USA Fax: 317-454-0544 Toll Free: 888-242-5904
E-mail: sfurr@authorsolutions.com
Web site: http://www.archwaypublishing.com
Dist(s): **Author Solutions, LLC**
Baker & Taylor Publisher Services (BTPS).
Arco *Imprint of* **Peterson's**
Arcoiris Records, Inc., *(978-1-57417)* P.O. Box 7428, Berkeley, CA 94707 USA Tel 510-527-5539
Dist(s): **Follett School Solutions**
Lectorum Pubns., Inc.
Arctos Pr., *(978-0-9657015; 978-0-9725384; 978-0-9897847)* 116 Cloud View Rd., Sausalito, CA 94965 USA Tel 415 331 2503
Web site: http://www.members.aol.com/runes/index.html
Dist(s): **Quality Bks., Inc.**
SPD-Small Pr. Distribution.
Arcturus Pubs., Inc., *(978-0-916877)* P.O. Box 606, Cherry Hill, NJ 08003 USA (SAN 653-9718) Tel 609-428-3863
Dist(s): **Children's Plus, Inc.**
Arcturus Publishing (GBR) *(978-1-900032; 978-1-84193; 978-1-84837; 978-1-84858; 978-1-78404; 978-1-78428; 978-1-78828; 978-1-78888; 978-1-78950; 978-1-83857; 978-1-83940; 978-1-78599; 978-1-78212) Dist. by* **Black Rab.**
Arcturus Publishing (GBR) *(978-1-900032; 978-1-84193; 978-1-84837; 978-1-84858; 978-1-78212; 978-1-78404; 978-1-78428; 978-1-78599; 978-1-78828; 978-1-78888; 978-1-78950; 978-1-83857; 978-1-83940) Dist. by* **BTPS.**
Ardden Entertainment (GBR) *(978-0-9561259) Dist. by* **Diamond Book Dists.**
Arden, Alys LLC *See* **fortheARTofit Publishing**
Arden Pr., Inc., *(978-0-912869)* Orders Addr.: P.O. Box 418, Denver, CO 80201 USA (SAN 277-6553) Tel 303-697-6766; Fax: 303-697-3443; Edit Addr.: 20723 Seminole Rd., Indian Hills, CO 80454 USA Do not confuse with Arden Pr. Inc., Cleveland, OH
E-mail: ardenpress@msn.com
Dist(s): **Follett School Solutions.**
Ardent Writer Pr., LLC, The, *(978-1-938667; 978-1-64066)* 1014 Stone Dr., Brownsboro, AL 35741 USA Tel 256-694-6744
E-mail: gierhartsteve@att.net.
ARDI Research Pr., *(978-0-9640600)* 13571 Millpond Way, San Diego, CA 92129 USA (SAN 298-1866) Fax: 619-484-0377
E-mail: roger@rdooley.com.
Area Fifty One Productions *See* **Media Blasters, Inc.**
Areteem Institute, *(978-1-944863)* 15707 Rockfield Blvd, Irvine, CA 92618 USA Tel 949-679-8989
E-mail: kren@areteem.org
Web site: www.areteem.org.
Argami Productions, LLC, *(978-0-9798324)* 774 Verona Lake Dr., Weston, FL 33326 USA; 4501 Forbes Blvd, Lanham, MD 20706
E-mail: ellenwv@aol.com
Dist(s): **Follett School Solutions**
National Bk. Network
New Leaf Publishing Group.
Argee Pubs., *(978-0-917961)* 4453 Manitou, Okemos, MI 48864 USA (SAN 247-7858) Tel 517-349-1254.
Argo Brothers INC., *(978-0-692-52501-2; 978-0-692-68528-0; 978-0-692-68683-6; 978-0-692-73658-6; 978-0-692-74741-4; 978-0-692-75597-6; 978-0-692-76107-6; 978-0-692-77283-6; 978-0-9979948; 978-1-946755; 978-0-692-93635-1; 978-0-692-93636-8; 978-0-692-99867-0; 978-1-951048) 900 LENOX RD, BROOKLYN, NY 11374 USA Tel 347-927-2711*
Web site: www.argobrothers.com
Dist(s): **CreateSpace Independent Publishing Platform.**
Argon Pr., *(978-0-9910554; 978-0-9908831; 978-1-944815)* 3442 Pigeon Hill, Muskegon, MI 49441 USA Tel 231-224-6468
E-mail: steve@argonpress.com
Web site: http://www.argonpress.com.
Argonaut Publishing Co., *(978-0-9635118)* 284 Clearview Rd., Chuluota, FL 32766 USA (SAN 297-8199) Tel 407-977-5207 (phone) Do not confuse with companies

Publisher Name Index

with the same or similar name in Los Angeles, CA, Santa Barbara, CA
E-mail: spottedtail@spottedtail.com
Web site: http://www.spottedtail.com.

Argonauts, The, *(978-0-615-23045-0; 978-0-615-33914-6; 978-0-9827842)* Orders Addr.: 929 Canterbury Ln., Waukesha, WI 53188 USA
E-mail: smkstoll@yahoo.com
Web site: http://www.theArgonauts.com.

Argonne Bks. LLC, *(978-0-692-18264-0; 978-0-578-60012-3)* 542 Argonne Dr. NW, Atlanta, GA 30305 USA Tel 404-852-7919
E-mail: lissa.webber@gmail.com
Dist(s): **Ingram Content Group.**

Argos Gameware *See* **H&M Systems Software, Inc.**

Argot Pr., *(978-1-64489)* 206 Cherry St., Muscatine, IA 52761 USA Tel 563-299-3362
E-mail: spostr@gmail.com.

Argus Enterprises International, Inc., *(978-0-9801555; 978-0-9819075; 978-0-9823050; 978-0-9841342; 978-0-9842596; 978-0-9845142; 978-0-9846195; 978-0-9846348; 978-0-9846439; 978-0-615-50768-2; 978-0-615-50816-0; 978-0-615-50820-7; 978-0-615-51728-5; 978-0-615-51733-9; 978-0-615-51734-6; 978-0-615-52229-6; 978-0-615-52387-3; 978-0-615-52392-7; 978-0-615-52688-1; 978-0-615-53228-8; 978-0-615-53320-9; 978-0-615-53503-6; 978-0-615-53629-3; 978-0-615-54552-3; 978-0-615-55032-9; 978-0-615-55098-5; 978-0-615-55127-2; 978-0-615-55238-5) Orders Addr.: P.O. Box 914, Kernersville, NC 27285 USA Tel 336-354-7173; Fax: 336-993-2497; Edit Addr.: 9001 Ridge Hill St., Kernersville, NC 27284 USA*
Web site: http://www.a-argusbooks.com; http://www.abetterbewrite.com; http://abook4you.com
Dist(s): **CreateSpace Independent Publishing Platform**
Follett School Solutions.

Ariella Publishing, *(978-0-9861106)* 320 Kearney Dr., Owings Mills, MD 21117 USA Tel 410-654-3822
E-mail: izya50@yahoo.com.

Aries Diamond Publishing, *(978-1-952804)* 7230 McClean Blvd, Baltimore, MD 21234 USA Tel 410-905-4287
E-mail: Ariesdiamondpublishing@gmail.com
Web site: Ariesdiamondpublishing.com.

AriJ Publishing *See* **AJ Publishing**

Arise Foundation, *(978-1-58614)* P.O. Box 2147, Jupiter, FL 33468-2147 USA (SAN 253-4835) Toll Free: 888-680-6100
E-mail: yisaacs@ariselife-skills.org
Web site: http://www.ariseife-skills.org
Dist(s): **Follett School Solutions.**

Aristata Publishing, *(978-0-9754912)* 16429 Lost Canyon Rd., Santa Clarita, CA 91387 USA (SAN 256-6508) Tel 661-299-9478 (phone/fax)
E-mail: aristata@craigelliottgallery.com; celliottl@socal.rr.com
Web site: http://www.craigelliottgallery.com
Dist(s): **APG Sales & Distribution Services.**

ARIVA Publishing, *(978-0-9822952; 978-1-938056)* 244 Madison Ave, Suite 7100, New York, NY 10016-2817 USA Tel 646-706-7129
E-mail: info@arivapublishing.com
Dist(s): **Greenleaf Book Group.**

Arizona Blueberry Studios, *(978-0-9727894)* P.O. Box 5, Pasadena, CA 91102 USA Toll Free: 800-767-7186
E-mail: books@rossanthony.com
Web site: http://www.rossanthony.com/books.

Arizona Elk Society, *(978-0-9825181)* P.O. Box 190, Peoria, AZ 85380 USA.

Arizona Highways, *(978-0-916179; 978-1-893860; 978-1-932082; 978-0-9822788; 978-0-9845709; 978-0-9837132; 978-0-9887875; 978-0-9916228; 978-0-9971247; 978-0-9987893; 978-0-9989812; 978-0-9989813; 978-1-7366632; 978-1-7366633)* Div. of Arizona Dept. of Transportation, 2039 W. Lewis Ave., Phoenix, AZ 85009 USA (SAN 294-8974)
E-mail: mbianchi@azdot.gov; aphares@azdot.gov; kmero@azdot.gov; kfarugia@azdot.gov
Web site: http://www.arizonahighways.com.

†Arizona Historical Society, *(978-0-910037)* 949 E. Second St., Tucson, AZ 85719 USA (SAN 201-6982) Tel 520-628-5774; Fax: 520-628-5695
Dist(s): **University of Arizona Pr.**; *CIP.*

Arizona Sonora Desert Museum Pr., *(978-1-886679)* Arizona Sonora Desert Museum, 2021 N. Kinney Rd., Tucson, AZ 85743 USA Tel 520-883-3061; Fax: 520-883-3048
E-mail: asdmpress@desertmuseum.org; info@desertmuseum.org
Web site: http://www.desertmuseum.org
Dist(s): **Rio Nuevo Pubs.**

Ark Hse. Pr. (AUS) *(978-0-9752044; 978-0-9757986; 978-0-9775671; 978-0-9803458; 978-0-9804523; 978-0-9805414; 978-1-921589; 978-0-9873888; 978-0-9875839; 978-0-9922699; 978-0-9925192; 978-0-9941941; 978-0-9942832; 978-0-9943675; 978-0-9944299; 978-0-9953917; 978-0-9954215; 978-0-6480451; 978-0-6480508; 978-0-6480845; 978-0-6481016; 978-0-6481734; 978-0-6482639; 978-0-6482914; 978-0-6483719; 978-0-6483905; 978-0-6484410; 978-0-6484585; 978-0-6485077; 978-0-6485780; 978-0-6486703; 978-0-6487150; 978-0-6487607;) Dist. by* **STL Dist.**

Ark Watch Holdings LLC, *(978-0-9765358; 978-0-615-25019-9; 978-0-615-25020-5; 978-0-615-25021-2; 978-0-578-05938-9; 978-0-615-99015-6; 978-0-692-39260-7; 978-0-692-57098-2; 978-0-692-57589-5; 978-0-692-58048-6; 978-0-692-59038-6; 978-0-692-59199-4)* Div. of Serpentauria Media LLC, 4766 E. Eden Dr., Cave Creek, AZ 85331-3870 USA
E-mail: erikauthor@aol.com; arkwatchholdingsllc@hotmail.com
Web site: http://www.arkwatch.com
Dist(s): **CreateSpace Independent Publishing Platform.**

ARK7EVEN Entertainment, *(978-0-9771154)* Div. of ThunderHouse Entertainment, 5805 W 8th St. No. 306, Los Angeles , CA 90036 USA
E-mail: reggiecook@yahoo.com
Web site: http://www.reggiethewriter.com; ARK7EVEN.com.

Arlen Hse. (IRL) *(978-1-903631) Dist. by* **LongleafServ.**

Arlene, Carmen Hibbs, *(978-0-9762567)* 584 Choctaw Dr., Madisonville, KY 42431 USA Tel 270-821-1968
E-mail: arlenehibbs@yahoo.com
Web site: http://www.heavenlyharborbooks.com.

Arlington & Ameilia, *(978-1-886541)* Orders Addr.: 1830 Lee Rd., Winter Park, FL 32789 USA Tel 407-293-1132; Toll Free Fax: 1-866-618-0540 Do not confuse with Priority Press in Dallas, TX & Yardley, PA
E-mail: nbaa@cfl.rr.com
Web site: http://www.weddingsurvivalguide.net
Dist(s): **Southern Bk. Service.**

Arlington Pubns., *(978-0-9753611)* 2205 Manera St., Odessa, TX 79763 USA Tel 432-582-0272; Fax: 432-332-2499 Do not confuse with Arlington Publications Incorporated in Arlington, TX
E-mail: tommwhite@cableone.net.

Armadillo Bks., *(978-0-9786132)* 4735 NE 24th Ave., Portland, OR 97211 USA (SAN 851-0865) Do not confuse with Armadillo Books in Houston, TX
E-mail: phtdoyle@yahoo.com
Web site: http://www.edgarfont.com; http://www.nextreststopearth.com
Dist(s): **Follett School Solutions.**

Armchair Pr., LLC, *(978-0-9744627)* P.O. Box 215, Ross, CA 94957-0215 USA Tel 415-460-9750; Fax: 415-460-0850
E-mail: ozzie@armchairpress.com.

Armen, Rose Maiolo, *(978-0-692-06994-3)* 12 N. Ledge Rock Rd., Niantic, CT 06357 USA Tel 860-514-3027
E-mail: rarmen@sbcglobal.net.

Arment Biological Press *See* **Coachwhip Pubns.**

Armina Pr. *Imprint of* **Polis Bks.**

Armon Bks., *(978-0-615-54188-4; 978-0-615-57469-1; 978-0-692-27843-7; 978-0-692-28275-5; 978-0-692-28316-5; 978-0-692-28354-7; 978-0-692-53664-3; 978-0-692-54844-8; 978-0-692-60545-5; 978-0-692-72321-0; 978-0-9984257)* 945 Taraval St. No. 130, San Francisco, CA 94116 USA Tel 916-501-8083
Dist(s): **CreateSpace Independent Publishing Platform**
Smashwords.

Armor of Hope Writing & Publishing Services, LLC, *(978-0-692-05841-1; 978-0-692-16932-2; 978-1-7336134)*
E-mail: armorofhope121@gmail.com
Web site: www.armorofhopewritingservices.com.

Armour of Light Publishing, *(978-0-9620604; 978-0-9788590; 978-0-9817120; 978-0-9825476; 978-0-9857539)* P.O. Box 778, Chapel Hill, NC 27514 USA (SAN 249-4337)
E-mail: publisher@armourofiight.org
Web site: http://www.armourofiight.org.

Armstrong, Greg, *(978-0-578-11703-4; 978-0-578-12191-8; 978-0-578-12368-4)* 27082 O Neill Dr., Unit 325, Ladera Ranch, CA 92694 USA Tel 949-701-7190.

Armstrong Valley Publishing Co., *(978-1-928798)* Orders Addr.: P.O. Box 1275, Murfreesboro, TN 37133-1275 USA Tel 615-895-5445; Fax: 615-893-2688; Edit Addr.: 2568 Armstrong Valley Rd., Murfreesboro, TN 37128 USA
E-mail: rsanders@raider.net.

Arnett & Rugby Publishing *See* **Positively Black Publishing**

Arnica Publishing, *(978-0-9728538)* Orders Addr.: P.O. Box 543, Choteau, MT 59422 USA; Edit Addr.: 3961 Hwy 89 S., Choteau, MT 59422 USA
E-mail: arnica@3rivers.net; pbechtold1@gmail.com.

Arnica Publishing, Incorporated *See* **ACS, LLC Arnica Creative Services**

Arnold, Cyrena, *(978-1-7350791)* 984 Bible Hill Rd, Francestown, NH 03043 USA Tel 603-915-3369
E-mail: wxcyrena@gmail.com.

Arnold, Patricia *See* **www.margaretmouse.com publishing co.**

Arnstein, Bennett, *(978-0-9620058)* 3049 W. Eighth St., No. 535, Los Angeles, CA 90005 USA (SAN 247-5162) Tel 213-388-3517
E-mail: b_arnstein@hotmail.com.

ARose Bks. *Imprint of* **ARose Books Publishing, LLC**

ARose Books Publishing, LLC, *(978-0-9723970; 978-0-9740636; 978-0-9819298; 978-0-9846081; 978-0-692-37550-1; 978-1-945986)* 310 Fox Rd., Havre De Grace, MD 21078 USA Fax: 888-889-6945 (phone/fax); *Imprints:* ARose Books (ARoseBks)
Web site: http://www.arosebooks.com
Dist(s): **CreateSpace Independent Publishing Platform.**

Around The Globe Pr., *(978-0-9760573)* 11505 E. Calle Javelina, Tucson, AZ 85748-6339 USA Tel 520-290-8915
E-mail: aroundtheglobepress@earthlink.net
Web site: http://www.aroundtheglobepress.com.

Around the Way Book Publishers *See* **Around the Way Books**

Around the Way Books, *(978-0-9755342)* P.O. Box 1497, Waterbury, CT 06721 USA Toll Free: 888-610-5969
E-mail: htaylor@AroundTheWayBooks.com; info@aroundthewaybooks.com
Web site: http://www.AroundTheWayBooks.com
Dist(s): **Lushena Bks.**

Around The World Pubns., LLC, *(978-0-9772591)* P.O. Box 1024, Franktown, CO 80116-1024 USA Do not confuse with Around The World Publications in Seattle, WA
E-mail: bbrasier@etsgroup.com
Web site: http://www.worldthroughchildseyes.com.

Around the World Publishing LLC, *(978-0-615-61881-4; 978-0-615-61897-5; 978-0-615-62185-2; 978-0-615-62193-7; 978-0-615-62428-0; 978-0-615-62677-2; 978-0-615-67742-2; 978-0-615-75932-6; 978-1-68223)* 4919 Cooper Rd., Suite 145, Cincinnati, OH 45242 USA Tel 513-500-4274
E-mail: remwriter95@gmail.com
Dist(s): **CreateSpace Independent Publishing Platform**
Smashwords.

Arquilla Pr., *(978-0-692-14751-1)* 1801 Paddington Ave., Naperville, IL 60563 USA Tel 630-369-2169
E-mail: carmelamartino@gmail.com
Dist(s): **Ingram Content Group.**

Arreboles, *(978-1-954548)* 83 Hall St. 0, NEW HAVEN, CT 06512 USA Tel 2038231879
E-mail: nohrambl@yahoo.com
Web site: nohrabernal.com
Dist(s): **Ingram Content Group.**

Arrest Me Not Publishing *See* **As Seen on the Internet / Arrest Me Not**

Arrinton Pubns., *(978-0-9754540)* Orders Addr.: P.O. Box 2573, Chesapeake, VA 23327 USA Tel 757-450-6068; Fax: 757-410-4215; Edit Addr.: 1601 Orchard Grove Dr., Chesapeake, VA 23320-1411 USA
E-mail: gobooks@cox.net.

Arrow Pubns., *(978-0-9715514; 978-0-9765849)* Orders Addr.: 16653 E. Kingstree Blvd., Fountain Hills, AZ 85268-5439 USA Do not confuse with companies with the same or similar names in Cedar Rapids, IA, Kensington, MD
E-mail: arrowpublications@cox.net
Web site: http://www.arrowpublications.net.

Arrowhead Publishing, *(978-0-9640056)* 1238 Riva Rose Cir., Castle Rock, CO 80104-9650 USA Tel 303-663-9415 Do not confuse with companies with the same name in Lake Arrowhead, CA, Carlsbad, CA.

Arruzza, Richard *See* **Three Spots Productions**

Arsenal Pulp Pr. (CAN) *(978-0-88978; 978-1-55152) Dist. by* **Consort Bk Sales.**

Arseya, LLC, *(978-0-9745185; 978-1-935093)* 10 Pleasantville Rd., New Vernon, NJ 07976 USA (SAN 255-6588) Tel 973-993-1504; Fax: 973-993-9182; *Imprints:* Arseya Publishing (Arseya Pub)
E-mail: arseya@arseya.com
Web site: http://www.arseya.com.

Arseya Publishing *Imprint of* **Arseya, LLC**

Art & Creativity For Healing, Inc., *(978-0-9748462)* 26079 Getty Dr., Laguna Niguel, CA 92677 USA Tel 949-367-1902; Fax: 949-367-1904
E-mail: laurie@art4healing.org
Web site: http://www.art4healing.org.

Art & Soul Expressions, *(978-0-9729192)* P.O. Box 957, Mount Shasta, CA 96067 USA.

ART AS RESPONSA *See* **Art as Responsa**

Art as Responsa, *(978-0-578-05270-0; 978-0-9845456)* 5290 Southbrook Ct. Condo 45, Hudsonville, MI 49426 USA (SAN 859-631X) Tel 310-650-1990 (phone/fax)
E-mail: marsha@art-responsa.com
Web site: http://www.artasresponsa.com; http://www.art-responsa.com; https://artresponsa.wordpress.com.

A.R.T Bks. 4Kids, *(978-0-9968775)* 6256 Hillandale Dr. Apt 106, Lithonia, GA 30058 USA Tel 404-821-1726
E-mail: Reading_Is_Golden@yahoo.com.

Art Deco Dog Publishing, *(978-1-7323827)* P.O. Box 193, Moss Beach, CA 94038 USA Tel 650-728-8400; Fax: 650-728-5400
E-mail: artdecodog@gmail.com
Web site: https://longnoselegacy.com; houndbeautiful.com; artdecodog.com.

Art In The Heartland, *(978-0-9725461; 978-0-9752839; 978-0-9762103; 978-0-9766587; 978-0-9778450)* P.O. Box 1785, Columbus, IN 47202-1785 USA
E-mail: sbreeding@artintheheartland.com
Web site: http://www.breedingbooks.com; http://www.artintheheartlandbooks.com.

Art Night Bks., *(978-0-9794004)* 3348 N. Dousman St., Milwaukee, WI 53212 USA Tel 414-213-7443
E-mail: devintrudell@mac.com; angievasquez13@sbcglobal.net
Web site: http://artnightbooks.com.

Art Of Essex Fine Art, The, *(978-0-615-31464-8)* 3007 Lakewood Ct., Jefferson City, MO 65109 USA
Web site: www.essexgamer.com.

Art of War Plus Bks. *Imprint of* **Clearbridge Publishing**

Art Official Media LLC, *(978-0-9768061; 978-0-9834874; 978-0-9883825)* Orders Addr.: P.O. Box 532532, Baltimore, MD 21212 SUN Tel 443-693-7622; Edit Addr.: 1044 Radnor Ave., Indianapolis, IN 46253-2532 USA
Web site: http://www.artofficialmedia.com; http://www.UrbaniaMag.com
Dist(s): **Afrikan World Bk. Distributor.**

Art With Heart, *(978-0-9715240; 978-0-9841365; 978-1-7375888)* Div. of Art with Heart, 316 Broadway, Seattle, WA 98122 USA (SAN 850-2676)
E-mail: info@artwithheart.org
Web site: http://www.artwithheart.org
Dist(s): **Partners/West Book Distributors.**

Art With Heart Press *See* **Art With Heart**

Art&Media Communications LLC, *(978-0-9778932)* P.O. Box 7743, Bloomfield Hills, MI 48302-4830 USA (SAN 850-4520)
E-mail: lrtucci@artemediacomm.com
Web site: http://www.artineraries.com; http://www.touringtracks.com.

ArtAnswer, *(978-0-9755413; 978-0-9771520)* P.O. Box 50387, Billings, MT 59105 USA Tel 406-672-8482
E-mail: artanswer@artanswer.com
Web site: http://www.artanswer.com.

†Arte Publico Pr., *(978-0-934770; 978-1-55885; 978-1-6119…; 978-1-5185)* Univ. of Houston 4902 Gulf Fwy, Bldg. 19, Rm. 100, Houston, TX 77204-2004 USA (SAN 213-4594) Tel 713-743-2998; 713-743-3080; Fax: 713-743-2847; Toll Free: 800-633-2783; Univ. of Housto… 4902 Gulf Freeway, Rm. 100, Houston, TX 77023; *Imprints:* Piñata Books (Piñata Bks)
E-mail: bkorders@uh.edu; appinfo@uh.edu
Web site: http://www.artepublicopress.com
Dist(s): **Book Wholesalers, Inc.**
Booksource, The
Bound to Stay Bound Bks.
Brodart Co.
Children's Plus, Inc.
Follett School Solutions
Keystone Bks. & Media LLC
Lectorum Pubns., Inc.
Mackin Educational Resources
Midwest Library Service
Perfection Learning Corp.
Perma-Bound Bks.
Quality Bks., Inc.
Rainbow Bk. Co.
Unique Bks., Inc.
Yankee Bk. Peddler, Inc.
ebrary, Inc.; *CIP.*

Artemesia Publishing, LLC, *(978-1-932926; 978-1-951122)* Orders Addr.: 9 Mockingbird Hill Rd., Tijeras, NM 87059 USA Tel 505-286-0892; *Imprints:* Kinkajou Press (Kinkajou Pr)
E-mail: info@artemesiapublishing.com; g.habiger@artemesiapublishing.com
Web site: http://www.apbooks.net; http://www.artemesiapublishing.com; http://www.tangent-games.com; http://www.kinkajoupress.com/
Dist(s): **Bks. West**
Follett School Solutions
Hachette Bk. Group
Independent Pubs. Group
Midpoint Trade Bks., Inc.

Artemisia Enterprises, *(978-0-9755416)* P.O. Box 3106 Mosshall Way, San Jose, CA 95135 USA
E-mail: sales@amazonheart.org
Web site: http://www.amazonheart.org.

Artesian Pr., *(978-1-58659)* 372 South 900 W., Provo, UT 84601 USA (SAN 253-1259) Tel 801-375-0800; Fax: 801-222-9199; Toll Free Fax: 888-326-3125; Toll Free: 888-734-9355; 20 Commercial Blvd., Novato, CA 94949
E-mail: info@artesianpress.com
Web site: http://www.artesianpress.com
Dist(s): **Follett School Solutions.**

Artful Options, LLC, *(978-1-7348596; 979-8-218-09941-1; 979-8-218-09942-8)* 2060 Shore Dr., Edgewater, MD 21037 USA Tel 730-728-2900
E-mail: heiket@outlook.com.

Arthritis Foundation, *(978-0-912423; 978-0-692-63011-2)* 1330 W. Peachtree St., Atlanta, GA 30309 USA (SAN 267-677X) Tel 404-965-7622; Fax: 404-872-9559; Toll Free: 800-283-7800 Do not confuse with Arthritis Foundation, Southfield, MI
E-mail: sbernstein@arthritis.org
Web site: http://www.arthritis.org.

ARTiCHOKE presents, *(978-0-9823778)* 664 Manhattan Ave., 4L, Brooklyn, NY 11222 USA
Web site: http://www.artichokepresents.com.

Article One *See* **Marsh Creek Pr.**

ARTIFEX SOUL PUBLISHING, *(978-0-9977395)* 914 164th ST SE APT 231, Mill Creek, WA 98012 USA Tel 425-314-1685
E-mail: thompsondietrich3@yahoo.com.

Artisan, *(978-1-57965; 978-1-885183; 978-1-64829)* Div. of Workman Publishing Co., Inc., 225 Varick St. Flr. 9, New York, NY 10014-4381 USA Toll Free: 800-967-5630 Do not confuse with Artisan, Wheaton, IL
E-mail: artisan@workman.com
Dist(s): **Blackstone Audio, Inc.**
Hachette Bk. Group
Open Road Integrated Media, Inc.
Workman Publishing Co., Inc.

Artisan Bookworks, *(978-0-9898692; 978-0-9911747; 978-0-9979578; 978-0-9991200; 978-1-7357891; 979-8-9869695)*
E-mail: books@artisanbookworks.com
Web site: http://www.artisanbookworks.com.

Artisan House *See* **Artisan**

Artisan Pubs., *(978-0-934666)* P.O. Box 1529, Muskogee, OK 74402 USA (SAN 211-8408) Tel 918-682-8341; Fax: 918-682-1263.

Artisan Sales *See* **Artisan Pubs.**

Artist Designs, *(978-0-9760409)* P.O. Box 548, Webster, WI 54893 USA Tel 715-222-2362.

Artist Studios, Ltd., *(978-1-931037; 978-1-59487; 978-1-61562)* 444 Spear St. Ste. 101, San Francisco, CA 94105-1693 USA.

Artistic Angels Corp., *(978-0-9890410)* 535 Valley View Rd. Apt. D301, Branson, MO 65616 USA Tel 417-544-1766; Fax: 417-544-1766
E-mail: artisticangels4you@yahoo.com.

Artistic Creations Bk. Publishing, *(978-0-9796843; 978-0-692-76837-2; 978-0-9982826)* 2215 6th Ave., Apt. D, Moline, IL 61265 USA
E-mail: bookwoman1110@hotmail.com
Web site: http://beserrashomebasedbiz.blogspot; http://artisticcreationsbookpublishing.books.officelive.com/default.aspx; http:///site/discoveryourtalentshow/; http:///site/fairytalekidssite/
Dist(s): **Partners Bk. Distributing, Inc.**

Artistic Endeavors, *(978-0-692-57650-2; 978-0-578-85432-8; 978-0-578-88728-9; 978-0-578-89201-6; 979-8-9857617)* P.O. Box 95, Placitas, NM 87043-0095 USA Tel (505) 867-2939
Dist(s): **CreateSpace Independent Publishing Platform.**

rtistic Ventures LLC, *(978-0-9771495)* Orders Addr.: 3 Glade Mallow Rd., Malta, NY 12020 USA; Edit Addr.: 3 Glade Mallow Rd., Malta, NY 12020-4326 USA; *Imprints:* Artistic Ventures Publishing (Artistic Ventures)
E-mail: dawn@artistic-ventures.com
Web site: http://www.artistic-ventures.com
Dist(s): **Follett School Solutions.**

rtistic Ventures Publishing *Imprint of* **Artistic Ventures LLC**

rtists On Video, LLC / (d/b/a) MN Productions, *(978-0-9799440; 978-1-937106)* 84 Chaumont Sq. NW, Atlanta, GA 30327 USA.

rtists' Orchard, LLC, The, *(978-0-9843166; 978-0-9857014; 978-0-9964592)* P.O. Box 113317, Pittsburgh, PA 15241 USA (SAN 859-0389) Tel 724-255-6408
E-mail: sales@theartistsorchard.com; publish@theartistsorchard.com
Web site: http://theartistsorchard.com.

rtist's Pr., *(978-0-924556)* P.O. Box 16087, Minneapolis, MN 55416-0087 USA Tel 952-486-8353
E-mail: artistspress@aim.com
Web site: http://www.artistspress.com.

ArtMar Productions, *(978-0-9799089)* 60 W. 71st St., No. 1B, New York, NY 10023 USA (SAN 854-7416)
E-mail: mihorowitz@aol.com
Web site: http://www.marlynhorowitz.com.

Art-Medium, *(978-0-9817971)* P.O. Box 390739, Mountain View, CA 94039-0739 USA (SAN 856-5848)
E-mail: tangobelly@yahoo.com
Web site: http://www.AKPhotography.net.

Artos Press Enterprises *See* **Creative Cranium Concept, The**

Artpacks, *(978-0-9790247; 978-0-9834637)* 535 22nd St., NE, Rochester, MN 55906 USA (SAN 852-2227) Tel 507-273-2529
E-mail: storymatters@charter.net.

Artpress Publishing, Inc. *See* **Cheesy Bread Publishing**

Artrum Media, *(978-0-9840574; 978-0-9841957; 978-0-9845352; 978-0-9837050; 978-1-938107)* 302 Maple Grove Ln, Apison, TN 37302 USA (SAN 858-3080)
E-mail: info@artrummedia.com
Web site: http://www.artrummedia.com
Dist(s): **New Tradition Bks.**

Arts and Minds Studio Inc., *(978-0-9767048)* Div. of Brian Alan Lane & Donna Cohen Lane, 19655 NW Stavis Bay Rd., Seabeck, WA 98380-9797 USA Tel 360-830-2614 (phonefax)
E-mail: bal@brianalanlane.com; dc@donnacohen.com
Web site: http://www.artsandminds.studio/; http://www.atinytale.com/; http://www.mindgameswithaserialkiller.com/.

Arts Love Expression, *(978-0-9998515)* 11319 Palisades Dr., Pacific Palisades, CA 90272 USA Tel 310-461-8647; *Imprints:* Bahoo Tide, LLC (Bahoo Tide)
E-mail: ajahd@bahootide.com.

Arts Pubns., *(978-0-9766590)* P.O. Box 3006, Evansdale, IA 50707-0006 USA (SAN 256-4963) Tel 319-287-5901 (phone/fax) Do not confuse with Arts Publications in Corte Madera, CA
E-mail: ceremonypress@mchsi.com; infoartspublications@mchsi.com
Web site: http://www.artspublicationsbooks.com.

ArtScroll Series *Imprint of* **Mesorah Pubns., Ltd.**

ArtsKindred, *(978-1-7321862; 978-1-951183)* 11 4th Ave., East Northport, NY 11731 USA Tel 347-615-0784
E-mail: anetta4music@gmail.com.

Artstreet LLC, *(978-0-9758971)* 10 Crestmont Rd. Apt. 7P, Montclair, NJ 07042-1936 USA Toll Free: 866-543-7878
E-mail: sjimenez@brandstreetllc.com
Web site: http://www.brandstreetllc.com.

Artsy Bee, LLC, *(978-0-615-75521-2; 978-0-692-48443-2; 978-0-692-58845-1)* 133 Naperville Dr., Cary, NC 27519-5409 USA Tel 919-274-6155
E-mail: rtbliss@gmail.com.

Artust Nasus Publishing, *(978-0-9763260)* 500 Rosita Ave., PO Box 1515, Westcliffe, CO 81252 USA
Web site: http://www.naturallybalancedhealth.com.

Artworks International, *(978-1-57938)* Orders Addr.: 3101 Clairmont Rd., Suite C, Atlanta, GA 30329 USA (SAN 255-6456) Tel 404-214-4331; Fax: 404-214-4390
E-mail: derek.adams@andersonpress.com
Web site: http://www.andersonpress.com.

ArtWrite Productions, *(978-0-9777693; 978-1-939846)* 1555 Gardena Ave. NE, Fridley, MN 55432-5848 USA (SAN 850-1432) Tel 612-803-0436
E-mail: artwrite@bitstream.net
Web site: http://artwriteproductions.com; http://adaptedclassics.com
Dist(s): **Follett School Solutions.**

Arundel Press *See* **Arundel Publishing**

Arundel Publishing, *(978-1-933608)* 10 Weeping Willow Cir., Hendersonville , NC 28739-8406 USA Do not confuse with Arundel Press in Seattle, WA
E-mail: Sharon@SharonLinnea.com
Dist(s): **Follett School Solutions**
Ingram Publisher Services.

Arutam Pr., *(978-0-9745477)* 62 Ave Maria, Monterey, CA 93940 USA Tel 831-375-6005
E-mail: emurray@sacredsite.com
Web site: http://www.elizabethmurray.com.

Arzana, Inc., *(978-0-9770475)* Orders Addr.: P.O. Box 60473, Potomac, MD 20859 USA Tel 301-437-0017
E-mail: balance@arzanaworld.com
Web site: http://www.arzanaworld.com.

As Sabr Pubns. *Imprint of* **Imago Pr.**

As Seen on the Internet / Arrest Me Not, *(978-0-9640336)* P.O. Box 608685, Cleveland, OH 44108-0685 USA Tel 440-487-8413; Fax: 425-963-3821
Web site: http://www.asseenontheinternet.tv.

As Simple As That Publishing, *(978-0-9728666)* Orders Addr.: P.O. Box 25 Fern Road, Southampton, NY 11968 USA
Web site: http://www.simpleasthat.com.

As Sparkle Speaks & Informs/ASSI, *(978-0-9706187)* Orders Addr.: P.O. Box 1313, Madison, TN 37116-1313 USA Tel 615-860-9762; Fax: 615-870-0959; Edit Addr.: 1672 Liberty Hill Dr., Madison, TN 37115 USA
E-mail: searlessparkle@aol.com.

ASA Publishing Company *See* **ASA Publishing Corp.**

ASA Publishing Corp., *(978-1-886528; 978-0-615-13671-4; 978-0-615-14056-8; 978-0-615-14611-9; 978-0-615-15185-4; 978-0-615-15682-8; 978-0-615-17383-2; 978-0-615-18613-9; 978-0-615-18894-2; 978-0-615-21769-7; 978-0-615-21856-4; 978-0-615-25705-1; 978-0-615-26064-8; 978-0-615-26127-0; 978-0-615-27139-2; 978-0-615-27323-5; 978-0-9819570; 978-0-9841442; 978-0-9826490; 978-0-9828135; 978-0-615-44821-3; 978-0-615-46081-9; 978-0-615-46083-3; 978-0-615-46622-4; 978-0-615-46780-1; 978-0-615-47496-0; 978-0-615-47775-6; 97) 105 E. Front St., Suite 101, Monroe, MI 48161 USA Tel 734-230-7174; Fax: 734-230-7176*
E-mail: asapublishingcorporation@gmail.com; asapublisher@gmail.com
Web site: http://www.asapublishingcorporation.com/
Dist(s): **CreateSpace Independent Publishing Platform**
Ingram Content Group.

ASA-CSSA-SSSA, *(978-0-89118)* 5585 Guilford Rd., Madison, WI 53711 USA (SAN 206-2879) Tel 608-268-4960; Fax: 608-273-2021
E-mail: books@agronomy.org; books@crops.org; books@soils.org
Web site: http://www.soils.org; http://www.crops.org; http://www.agronomy.org.

Asbury Heritage Publishing, *(978-0-9859132)* 4601 Abercorne Terr., Louisville, KY 40241 USA Tel 502-897-3241; Fax: 502-897-3241
E-mail: bakerbutterfly@gmail.com.

Ascend Bks., LLC, *(978-0-9817166; 978-0-9841130; 978-0-9830619; 978-0-9836952; 978-0-9856314; 978-0-9889964; 978-0-9893095; 978-0-9912756; 978-0-9904375; 978-0-9961944; 978-0-9966742; 978-0-9989224; 978-1-7323447; 978-1-7344637; 978-1-7369431; 979-8-9863584)* 11722 W 91st St., Overland Park, KS 66214 USA (SAN 856-3454) Tel 913-948-5500
E-mail: bsnodgrass@ascendbooks.com; mgore@ascendbooks.com
Web site: http://www.ascendbooks.com
Dist(s): **Cardinal Publishing Group.**

Ascend Media, LLC *See* **Ascend Bks., LLC**

Ascend Pr., *(978-0-9998571)* 67 Magnolia Farms Dr., Asheville, NC 28806 USA Tel 828-260-2645
E-mail: richardaab@gmail.com.

Ascend Pubns. (InJoy IT, LLC), *(978-1-7328463)* 805 S. Glynn St. S., Fayetteville, GA 30214 USA Tel 678-478-8028
E-mail: justgetitwrite@gmail.com.

Ascended Ideas, *(978-0-9795103; 978-0-692-00063-2; 978-0-9823969)* P.O. Box 120, Coldiron, KY 40819-0120 USA
Web site: http://www.ascendedideas.com.

Ascending Realm Publishing, *(978-0-9762135)* P.O. Box 2223, Centennial, CO 80161-2223 USA
E-mail: brandon@ascendingrealm.com
Web site: http://www.ascendingrealm.com.

Ascension Education, *(978-0-9640837)* Orders Addr.: P.O. Box 504, Venice, CA 90294 USA Tel 310-254-4092; Edit Addr.: 1814 Pacific Ave., No. 17, Venice, CA 90291 USA
E-mail: ascension2020@comcast.net
Web site: http://www.ascension-education.com.

Ascension Lutheran Church, *(978-0-9715472)* 314 W. Main St., Danville, VA 24541 USA Tel 434-792-5795; Fax: 434-799-3900
E-mail: chrismonsministry@gmail.com
Web site: http://www.chrismon.org.

Ascension Pr., *(978-0-9659228; 978-0-9742238; 978-0-9744451; 978-1-932631; 978-1-932645; 978-1-932927; 978-1-934217; 978-1-935940; 978-1-945179; 978-1-950784; 978-1-954881; 978-1-954882)* Orders Addr.: W5180 Jefferson St., Necedah, WI 54646 USA (SAN 256-0224) Tel 608-565-2024; Fax: 608-565-2025; Toll Free: 800-376-0520; Edit Addr.: P.O. Box 1990, West Chester, PA 19341 USA Tel 610-696-7795; Fax: 610-696-7796; Toll Free: 800-376-0520; 20 Hagerty Blvd., Suite 3, West Chester, PA 19341
E-mail: mflickinger@ascensionpress.com
Web site: http://www.ascensionpress.com
Dist(s): **Follett School Solutions.**

Ascent Pubns., *(978-0-9815302)* P.O. Box 928, Warrenton, MO 63383 USA
E-mail: michael@ascentpublications.com; info@ascentpublications.com
Web site: http://www.ascentpublications.com.

Ascribed *Imprint of* **dg ink**

ASD Publishing, *(978-0-9836049; 978-0-9853441; 978-0-9961029)* 102 Arlington Ave., Hawthorne, NJ 07506 USA Tel 973-280-0145
E-mail: goldstongregory@gmail.com
Web site: asdmedia.co
Dist(s): **BookBaby.**

ASE Media, *(978-0-9768890)* 5777 Crowntree Ln. Apt 208, ORLANDO, FL 32829 USA
E-mail: anne@easterlingfamily.com
Web site: http://www.asemedia.com.

Ashanti Royalty Publishing, *(978-1-7362246)* 39 Dion St, West Springfield, MA 01089 USA Tel 413-682-4745
E-mail: Crystalboat2010@gmail.com.

Ashay by the Bay, *(978-0-9704048)* Orders Addr.: P.O. Box 2394, Union City, CA 94587 USA Tel 510-477-0967; Edit Addr.: P.O. Box 2394, Union City, CA 94587-7394 USA
E-mail: poetashay@aol.com
Web site: http://www.ashaybythebay.com.

Ashberry Lane, *(978-0-9893967; 978-1-941720)* 13607 Bedford Rd NE, Cumberland, MD 21502 USA Tel 301-876-4876
E-mail: d.white@whitefire-publishing.com
Web site: www.ashberrylane.com.

Ashcroft, Yoko, *(978-0-9993077)* 9946 Clyde Cir., LITTLETON, CO 80129 USA Tel 720-308-8172
E-mail: yokoashcroft@yahoo.com.

Ashland Creek Pr. *Imprint of* **Byte Level Research**

Ashley *Imprint of* **Music Sales Corp.**

Ashley & Taylor Publishing, Co., *(978-0-9745469)* P.O. Box 2793, Huntsville, AL 35804 USA Tel 256-430-1889
E-mail: AshleyTaylor4God@comcast.net.

AshleyAlan Enterprises, *(978-0-9702171; 978-0-9710145)* Orders Addr.: P.O. Box 1510, Kyle, TX 78640-1510 USA Tel 512-405-3065; Fax: 512-405-3066; Edit Addr.: 115 Hogan, Kyle, TX 78640 USA
E-mail: celestem@kyle-tx.com
Web site: http://www.ashleyanlan.com.

Ashlye V. Enterprises, LLC, *(978-0-9792934)* P.O. Box 3301, Columbia, SC 29230 USA Tel 803-361-1161; Fax: 803-772-2878; Toll Free: 866-382-3558
E-mail: ashlyev@gmail.com
Web site: http://www.ashlyev.com.

Ashmolean Museum (GBR) *(978-0-900090; 978-0-907849; 978-1-85444) Dist. by* **Natl Bk Netwk.**

Ashtabula County Genealogical Society, *(978-1-888851)* 860 Sherman St., Geneva, OH 44041-9101 USA Tel 440-466-4521; Fax: 440-466-0162
E-mail: acgs@ashtabulagen.org
Web site: http://www.ashtabulagen.org.

Ashtastical *See* **Strange Jane Creations**

Ashway Pr., *(978-0-9754575; 978-1-7365830)* Div. of Ashway, 5624 Double Tree Cir., Birmingham, AL 35242 USA Tel 205-995-8482
E-mail: janetpeine@aol.com
Web site: http://www.givingmeaway.com.

ASI, *(978-0-9759271)* 12 Brandywine Dr., Warwick, NY 10990 USA
Web site: www.asipublishing.com.

Asia for Kids *Imprint of* **Infini Pr., LLC**

Asiana Media, *(978-0-9778994)* Orders Addr.: P.O. Box 13693, Tempe, AZ 85284-0062 USA Tel 602-743-7155; *Imprints:* Juice & Berries(r), The (The Juice & Ber)
E-mail: info@asianamedia.com; info@thejuiceandberries.com
Web site: http://www.asianamedia.com; http://www.thejuiceandberries.com; http://www.faithittomakeit.com.

Asia's Closet, *(978-1-7358095)* 100 N. Point Ctr. E, Alpharetta, GA 30022 USA Tel 248-470-8049
E-mail: rhonda@asiascloset.com
Web site: www.asiascloset.com.

Asimow, Dyanne, *(978-0-9859522)* 8071 Willow Glen Rd., Los Angeles, CA 90046 USA Tel 323-654-3075
E-mail: dyanne8071@sbcglobal.net.

AS/IS Pr., *(978-0-578-31933-9; 978-0-578-33709-8; 979-8-218-16727-1)* 111 Eastfield Dr., Madison, AL 35758 USA Tel 256-683-0967
E-mail: bamawriter2002@yahoo.com
Web site: irenejsteele.com.

ASJA Pr. *Imprint of* **iUniverse, Inc.**

ASK Publishing, L.L.C., *(978-0-9742967)* 34046 Jefferson Ave., St Clr Shores, MI 48082-1162 USA (SAN 255-4976)
E-mail: admin@askpublishingllc.net
Web site: http://www.askpublishingllc.net
Dist(s): **Quality Bks., Inc.**

ASL Tales, *(978-0-9818139)* Orders Addr.: P.O. Box 80354, Portland, OR 97210 USA
E-mail: info@asltales.net
Web site: http://www.asltales.net
Dist(s): **Follett School Solutions.**

Aslan Publishing, *(978-0-944031)* Owned by Renaissance Book Services Corp., 2490 Black Rock Tpke., No. 342, Fairfield, CT 06432 USA (SAN 242-6129) Fax: 203-374-4766; Toll Free: 800-786-5427
E-mail: information@AslanPublishing.com; harold@aslanpublishing.com; aslan@sevenlive.net
Web site: http://www.AslanPublishing.com
Dist(s): **APG Sales & Distribution Services.**

ASM Pr., *(978-0-914826; 978-1-55581; 978-1-68367; 978-0-578-19314-4)* Div. of American Society For Microbiology, 1752 N St., NW, Washington, DC 20036 USA (SAN 202-1153) Toll Free Fax: 1-800-546-1503; P.O. Box 605, Herndon, VA 20172
E-mail: books@asmusa.org
Web site: http://www.asmpress.org; www.asmscience.org
Dist(s): **Follett School Solutions**
MyiLibrary
Rittenhouse Bk. Distributors
Wiley, John & Sons, Inc.
ebrary, Inc.

ASMedia Publishing, *(978-0-9743407)* 299 Swanville Rd., Frankfort, ME 04438 USA Fax: 207-223-5241
E-mail: asmedia2002@aol.com.

Asmodee North America, Inc., *(978-1-887911; 978-1-58994; 978-1-61661; 978-1-63344)* 1995 Cty. Rd. B2 W, Roseville, MN 55113-2725 USA
Web site: http://www.asmodeena.com
Dist(s): **Diamond Comic Distributors, Inc.**
Diamond Bk. Distributors.

ASP Corp. Entertainment Group, Inc., *(978-0-9754147)* 3695 F Cascade Rd., Suite 229, Atlanta, GA 30331 USA Tel 404-344-7700; Fax: 404-344-7700
Web site: http://www.hannibaltrilogy.com.

Aspect *Imprint of* **Grand Central Publishing**

Aspect Bk. *Imprint of* **TEACH Services, Inc.**

Aspen Bks., *(978-1-56236)* Div. of Worldwide Pubs., Inc., P.O. Box 1271, Bountiful, UT 84011-1271 USA Toll Free: 800-748-4850
E-mail: jasay@qwest.net; prawlins@aspenbook.com
Dist(s): **Cedar Fort, Inc./CFI Distribution**
Independent Pubs. Group
Origin Bk. Sales, Inc.

Aspen Light Publishing, *(978-0-9743620; 978-0-9834896; 978-0-9913920)* Orders Addr.: 13506 Summerport Village Pkwy. Suite #155, Windermere, FL 34786 USA Fax: 407-910-2453; Toll Free: 800-437-1695
E-mail: orders@aspenlightpublishing.com
Dist(s): **DeVorss & Co.**

Aspen MLT, Inc., *(978-0-9774821; 978-0-9823628; 978-0-9854473; 978-1-941511; 978-1-944902; 978-1-946960)* 5855 Green Valley Cir. Suite 111, Culver City, CA 90230-9023 USA (SAN 257-6260) Fax: 310-348-9731
Web site: www.aspencomics.com
Dist(s): **Diamond Comic Distributors, Inc.**
Diamond Bk. Distributors.

AspenSpree Publishing, *(978-0-578-44906-7; 978-0-578-73090-5; 978-0-578-73094-3; 978-1-7356818)* 1021 NW Summercrest Blvd, Apt A, Burleson, TX 76028 USA Tel 480-258-4961
E-mail: aspenspree.author@gmail.com
Web site: aspenspree.com.

Aspirations Media, Inc., *(978-0-9776043; 978-0-9800034)* 7755 Lakeview Ln., Spring Lake Park, MN 55432 USA (SAN 257-7305)
Web site: http://www.aspirationsmediainc.com.

Aspire Publishing, *(978-0-9799021)* 30081 Canyon Creek, Trabuco Canyon, CA 92679 USA
Web site: 4aspirebooks.com.

Aspiring Author's Ink. *See* **MTE Publishing**

Aspiring Families Press, *(978-0-9961941)* 12625 High Bluff Drive, Suite 104, Dan Diego, CA 92130 USA Tel 858-531-1122
E-mail: azmairamaker@gmail.com; j@monkeycmedia.com
Web site: www.aspiringfamiliespress.com.

ASQ Quality Press *See* **Quality Pr.**

Associated Arts Pub., *(978-0-9840358)* 536 Tiara Dr., Grand Junction, CO 81507 USA Tel 970-241-8024
E-mail: suehughey@optimum.net
Web site: http://SCStrange.com; HerbysSecretFormula.com
Dist(s): **CreateSpace Independent Publishing Platform**
Follett School Solutions.

Association for Supervision & Curriculum Development, *(978-0-87120; 978-1-4166)* 1703 N. Beauregaurd St., Alexandria, VA 22311 USA (SAN 201-1352) Tel 703-578-9600; Fax: 703-575-5400; Toll Free: 800-933-2723
E-mail: member@ascd.org; books@ascd.org; acquisitions@ascd.org
Web site: http://www.ascd.org
Dist(s): **Ebsco Publishing**
Follett School Solutions
Cengage Gale
Ingram Content Group
MyiLibrary
ebrary, Inc.

Assn. of Asthma Educators, *(978-0-9821228)* 1215 Anthony Ave., Columbia, SC 29201-1701 USA Tel 803-540-7530; Fax: 803-254-3773; Toll Free: 888-988-7747
E-mail: marie.queen@queencommunicationsllc.com
Web site: http://www.asthmaeducators.org.

Assn. of Christian Schls. International, *(978-1-58331)* Orders Addr.: P.O. Box 65130, Colorado Springs, CO 80962-5130 USA; Edit Addr.: 731 Chapel Hills Dr., Colorado Springs, CO 80920 USA (SAN 689-5751) Tel 719-528-6906; Fax: 719-531-0631; Toll Free: 800-367-0798 (orders only)
E-mail: webmaster@acsi.org; info@acsi.org
Web site: http://www.acsi.org.

Association of Jewish Libraries, *(978-0-929262)* P.O. Box 1118, Teaneck, NJ 07666 USA
E-mail: ajlibs@osu.edu; publications@jewishlibraries.org
Web site: http://www.jewishlibraries.org.

Assouline (FRA) *(978-2-84323; 978-2-908228; 978-2-7594) Dist. by* **TwoRivers.**

AS-Sunnah Foundation of America *See* **Islamic Supreme Council of America**

Asta Publications, LLC, *(978-0-9777060; 978-1-934947)* Orders Addr.: 112 Black Oak Ct., Saintckbridge, GA 30281 USA Fax: 678-814-1370; Toll Free: 800-482-4190
E-mail: acollins@astapublications.com; astapubl@gmail.com; ahoward@astapublications.com
Web site: http://www.astapublications.com
Dist(s): **A & B Distributors & Pubs. Group.**

Astakos Publishing, *(978-0-9792991)* P.O. Box 227, Roscoe, IL 61073-9330 USA Tel 815-623-6616
E-mail: astakospublishing@charter.net
Web site: http://www.astakospublishing.com
Dist(s): **Follett School Solutions**
Quality Bks., Inc.

A-Star*, *(978-0-9858935)* 13 W. St. Apt. 2, Greenfield, MA 01301 USA Tel 415-505-5873
E-mail: info@adriennenunez.net
Web site: www.adriennenunez.net.

Asteroid Publishing, *(978-0-9841187)* 251 Middle Rd., Boxborough, MA 01719 USA Tel 978-549-0464
Dist(s): **Smashwords.**

Aston & James Publications *See* **Aston & James Publishing, LLC**

Aston & James Publishing, LLC, *(978-1-946745)* 500 N. Michigan Ave., Chicago, IL 60611 USA Tel 773-412-6212
Dist(s): **CreateSpace Independent Publishing Platform.**

Astonish Comics, *(978-0-9721259)* 10061 Riverside Dr., Suite No. 785, Toluca Lake, CA 91602 USA
Web site: http://www.theastonishfactory.com
Dist(s): **Diamond Comic Distributors, Inc.**
Diamond Bk. Distributors.

Astor Pr., *(978-0-9764119; 978-0-615-14497-9; 978-0-615-18601-6; 978-0-615-21360-6; 978-0-615-26465-3; 978-0-578-00527-0; 978-0-578-01799-0; 978-0-578-02611-4;*

Publisher Name Index

978-0-578-02667-1; 978-0-9899257; 978-1-949464) 6 Prospect St., Maynard, MA 01754 USA
E-mail: mail@shanddaramon.com; klangerdude@gmail.com
Web site: http://www.astorpress.com; http://brassbellbooks.com
Dist(s): **Lulu Pr., Inc.**
Smashwords.

Astor-Honor, Inc., (*978-0-8392*) 16 E. 40th St., Third Flr., New York, NY 10016 USA (SAN 203-5022) Tel 212-840-8800; Fax: 212-840-7246.

Astra Publishing Hse., ., New York City, NY 000000 USA; *Imprints:* Front Street (FrtSt); Toon Books (Toon Bks); Kane Press (Kane Pr EBC); TOON Books (TOON APH); Astra Young Readers (Astra Yng Read); Hippo Park (Hippo Park)
E-mail: hello@astrapublishinghouse.com
Web site: https://www.astrapublishinghouse.com/
Dist(s): **Children's Plus, Inc.**
Penguin Random Hse. Distribution
Penguin Random Hse. LLC.

Astra Publishing Hse., (*978-1-57565; 978-0-9819697; 978-1-940947; 978-1-63592; 978-1-6626*) 19 W 21st St, New York, NY 10177 USA
E-mail: tgonzalez@astrapublishinghouse.com; atrager@astrapublishinghouse.com; odontsov@astrapublishinghouse.com
Web site: https://boydsmillsandkane.com/
Dist(s): **Children's Plus, Inc.**
Follett School Solutions
Lerner Publishing Group
MyiLibrary
Penguin Random Hse. Distribution
Penguin Random Hse. LLC.

Astra Young Readers *Imprint of* **Astra Publishing Hse.**

Astral Publishing Co., (*978-0-9645367*) Orders Addr.: P.O. Box 3955, Santa Barbara, CA 93130-3955 USA (SAN 298-5705) Tel 805-967-7667; Edit Addr.: 333 Old Mill Rd., No. 324, Santa Barbara, CA 93110 USA
E-mail: wveigele@aol.com
Web site: http://www.astralpublishing.com
Dist(s): **Quality Bks., Inc.**

Astri My Astri Publishing, (*978-0-9760541; 978-0-9859712*) 602 3rd Ave. SW, Waukon, IA 52172 USA Tel 563-568-6229; Fax: 563-568-5377
E-mail: gourleyd@mchsi.com; deb@astrimyastri.com; gourleydeb@gmail.com
Web site: http://www.astrimyastri.com.

Astronaut Ink, (*978-0-9772727*) Orders Addr.: 180 Newbury St. 4106, Danvers, MA 01923 USA
E-mail: joe@popartproperties.com
Web site: http://www.popartproperties.com.

ASunnyDay Publishing, (*978-0-9818366*) 17 Hillside Ave., Suite 102, Rockville Centre, NY 11570 USA Tel 516-884-7661
E-mail: dariarosebooks@gmail.com
Web site: http://www.dariarosebooks.com.

Asura Pr., (*978-1-929928*) 2341 San Juan Ct., Portales, NM 88130 USA
E-mail: author@paulbspence.com
Web site: http://www.paulbspence.com.

Asura Publishing *See* **Asura Pr.**

At Ease Pr., (*978-0-917921*) Div. of Be at Ease School of Etiquette, 1212 W. Ben White Blvd., #214, Austin, TX 78704-7197 USA (SAN 656-9900)
E-mail: haroldalmon@gmail.com; schoolofetiquette@ateasepress.com
Web site: http://ateasepress.com; http://baeschoolofetiquette.blogspot.com/; http://baesoe.com
Dist(s): **Lulu Pr., Inc.**

At Home With Cristin *Imprint of* **Mill Creek Pr.**

At Peace Media, LLC, (*978-0-9742002*) 1117 E. Putnam Ave., No. 345, Riverside, CT 06878 USA Tel 203-698-2688; Fax: 203-698-3441; Toll Free: 800-575-7715
E-mail: john@atpeacemedia.com
Web site: http://www.atpeacemedia.com.

At Your Service of St. Louis County, LLC, (*978-0-9856611*) 73 Clermont Ln., St. Louis, MO 63124 USA Tel 314-994-1382; Fax: 314-997-6227
E-mail: katec1112@gmail.com
Web site: www.atyourservicestlcounty.com.

Ategbole, Charles, (*978-0-578-63571-2; 978-1-7366002*) 455 Claridge Trace SW 0, ATLANTA, GA 30331 USA Tel 4044546236
E-mail: Categbole@gmail.com
Dist(s): **Ingram Content Group.**

Atelier Finwhale, (*978-0-9882561*) P.O. Box 60608, Palo Alto, CA 94306-9991 USA Tel 650-787-2198
E-mail: 3marjorie14@gmail.com.

Atelier Mythologie, (*978-0-9899905; 978-1-945308*) 3815 E Pike, Seattle, WA 98122 USA Tel 206-724-4144
E-mail: publisher@ateliermythologie.com.

Atelier19, (*978-1-7325495*) 1570 26th Ave., San Francisco, CA 94122 USA Tel 415-205-4994
E-mail: info@bizibots.com
Web site: www.bizibots.com.

ATF Pr. (AUS) (*978-0-9586399; 978-1-920691; 978-1-921511; 978-1-921816; 978-0-646-29485-8; 978-0-646-35334-0; 978-1-922239; 978-1-925232; 978-1-925309; 978-1-925371; 978-1-925438; 978-1-925486; 978-1-925612; 978-1-925643; 978-1-925679; 978-1-925872; 978-1-922582; 978-1-922737; 978-1-923006*) *Dist. by* **ISD USA.**

Athanata Arts, Ltd., (*978-0-9727993*) P.O. Box 321, Garden City, NY 11530 USA (SAN 255-5018) Tel 516-742-8735
E-mail: info@athanata.com
Web site: http://www.athanata.com.

Athanatos Publishing Group, (*978-0-9791276; 978-0-9822776; 978-1-936830; 978-1-947844; 978-1-64594*) Orders Addr.: PO Box 57, Greenwood, WI 54437 USA; Edit Addr.: PO Box 57, Greenwood, WI 54437 USA (SAN 852-5234); *Imprints:* Suzeteo Enterprises (SuzeteoEnt)
E-mail: publisher@suzeteo.com
Web site: http://www.suzeteo.com.

Athenaeum Music & Arts Library *Imprint of* **Library Assn. of La Jolla**

Atheneum Bks. for Young Readers *Imprint of* **Simon & Schuster Children's Publishing**

Atheneum/Caitlyn Dlouhy Books *Imprint of* **Simon & Schuster Children's Publishing**

Atheneum/Richard Jackson Bks. *Imprint of* **Simon & Schuster Children's Publishing**

Atherstone, Pamela, (*978-0-9979271*) 828 Grimes Ave, MODESTO, CA 95358 USA Tel 209-605-4746.

Atherton Haight, (*978-0-9840678*) 2021 NW 65th St., No. 3, Seattle, WA 09117 USA (SAN 858-3358)
E-mail: info@athertonhaight.com
Web site: http://www.athertonhaight.com.

AthertonCustoms, (*978-0-578-00865-3; 978-0-615-33485-1; 978-0-9827167*) 6536 Aldergate Ln., Las Vegas, NV 89110 USA Tel 702-438-6596
E-mail: jim@athertoncustoms.com
Web site: http://www.athertoncustoms.com
Dist(s): **Lulu Pr., Inc.**

ATInternational Pubs., (*978-0-9773816*) 227 Sunflower Ln., West Windsor, NJ 08550-2439 USA
E-mail: atinetus@yahoo.com.

ATKINS ARTHse., (*978-0-9969215; 978-1-7379591*) 2029 Lake Trail Dr., Heartland, TX 75126 USA Tel 214-356-3963
E-mail: gregtkns@yahoo.com
Web site: WWW.ATKINSARTHOUSE.COM
Dist(s): **Ingram Content Group.**

Atkinson, Janet Irene *See* **Irene, Jan Pubns.**

Atlantic Bks. *Imprint of* **Tabby Hse. Bks.**

Atlantic Bks., Ltd. (GBR) (*978-1-903809; 978-1-84354; 978-1-84887; 978-0-85789; 978-0-85740; 978-1-78239; 978-1-78649*) *Dist. by* **IPG Chicago.**

Atlantic Bridge Publishing, (*978-0-9700930; 978-0-9706913; 978-1-931761; 978-1-59578; 978-1-62210*) 10509 Sedgegrass Dr., Indianapolis, IN 46235 USA Tel 317-826-8059 Do not confuse with Bridge Works Publishing Company, Inc. in Bridgehampton, NY
E-mail: linda@atlanticbridge.net
Web site: http://www.liquidsilverbooks.com; http://www.atlanticbridge.net
Dist(s): **INscribe Digital**
Independent Pubs. Group.

Atlantic Publishing Company *See* **Atlantic Publishing Group, Inc.**

Atlantic Publishing Group, Inc., (*978-0-910627; 978-1-60138; 978-1-62023*) 1210 SW 23rd PL, Ocala, FL 34471-0640 USA (SAN 268-1250) Tel 352-622-1825 Do not confuse with companies with the same or similar name in Tabor City, NC , Aurora, IL , Lakeland, FL , Combs, KY , Neosho, MO
E-mail: info@atlantic-pub.com; sales@atlantic-pub.com
Web site: http://www.atlantic-pub.com
Dist(s): **MyiLibrary.**

Atlantida (ARG) (*978-950-08*) *Dist. by* **AIMS Intl.**

Atlas Bks., 2541 Ashland Rd., Ashland, OH 44905 USA.

Atlas Games *Imprint of* **Trident, Inc.**

Atlas Publishing *Imprint of* **Atlas Publishing LLC**

Atlas Publishing LLC, (*978-0-9969679; 978-1-945033*) 42072 5th St Suite 103, Temecula, CA 92590 USA Tel 858-222-3747; *Imprints:* Atlas Publishing (AtlasP)
E-mail: permissions@atlaspublishing.biz; brent@atlaspublishing.biz
Web site: http://www.atlaspublishing.biz.

Atma Global Knowledge Media, Inc., (*978-0-9905459; 978-1-943967*) 41 W. 25th St., New York, NY 10010 USA Tel 212-254-0083; *Imprints:* Full Circle Media, Inc. (FullCircleMedia)
E-mail: spdunung@msn.com; sdunung@atmaglobal.com; sarora@atmaglobal.com
Web site: www.maddieandsayara.com; www.fcmediainc.com; www.atmaglobal.com.

Atmen Pr., (*978-1-7330545*) 847 Lovers Ln., Houston, TX 77091 USA Tel 713-502-0102
E-mail: arianeroesch@gmail.com
Web site: www.atmenpress.com
Dist(s): **Ingram Bk. Co.**

Atom Pr., 926 Flemington St., Pittsburgh, PA 15217 USA Tel 951-801-0391
E-mail: atomtitan@hotmail.com.

Atombank Bks., (*978-0-9905160*) 111 Pheasant Walk, Guilderland, NY 12303 USA Tel 518-421-5962
E-mail: atombankbooks@gmail.com
Web site: atombankbooks.com.

Atomic Basement, 1222 N. Commonwealth Ave. Apt. No. 4, Los Angeles, CA 90029-2058 USA Tel 386-679-9106
E-mail: oilerhggns@aol.com.

Atomic Fruit Pr., (*978-0-9753225*) 404 13th Ave., Huntington, WV 25701 USA
Web site: http://www.apocalyptictangerine.com.

Atria Bks. *Imprint of* **Simon & Schuster**

Atria Bks *Imprint of* **Atria Bks.**

Atria Bks., (*978-1-6680*) Div. of Simon & Schuster, 1230 Avenue of the Americas, 13th Flr., New York, NY 10020 USA; *Imprints:* Beyond Words/Atria Books (AtriaBks); Atria Books (AtriBksimp); Keywords Press (Keywords Press)
Dist(s): **Children's Plus, Inc.**
Follett School Solutions
MyiLibrary
Simon & Schuster, Inc.

Atria/Emily Bestler Bks. *Imprint of* **Atria/Emily Bestler Bks.**

Atria/Emily Bestler Bks., 1230 Avenue of the Americas, New York, NY 10020 USA; *Imprints:* Atria/Emily Bestler Books (AEBB)
Dist(s): **Simon & Schuster, Inc.**

Atrium Publishing, Incorporated *See* **mTrellis Publishing, Inc.**

ATS Publish, (*978-1-956555*) 95 E. Pioneer Ave, Sandy, UT 84070 USA Tel 801-472-3421
E-mail: vlascu77@yahoo.com.

Attack The Text / Magedo Publishing *See* **Attack The Text Publishing**

Attack The Text Publishing, (*978-0-9755923; 978-0-9842882*) 905 N. Pacific St., No. C, Oceanside, CA 92831 USA
Web site: http://www.attackthetext.com; http://www.magedo.com.

Attainment Co., Inc., (*978-0-934731; 978-1-57861; 978-1-943148; 978-1-944315; 978-1-64856*) Orders Addr.: P.O. Box 930160, Verona, WI 53593 USA (SAN 694-1656) Tel 608-845-7880; Fax: 608-845-8040; Toll Free: 800-327-4269; Edit Addr.: 1158 Clarity St., Verona, WI 53953 USA (SAN 631-6174); *Imprints:* IEP Resources (IEP Res)
E-mail: info@attainmentcompany.com; ameyer@attainmentcompany.com
Web site: http://www.attainmentcompany.com/.

Attic Studio Pr. *Imprint of* **Attic Studio Publishing Hse.**

Attic Studio Publishing Hse., (*978-1-883551*) Orders Addr.: P.O. Box 75, Clinton Corners, NY 12514 USA (SAN 298-2838) Tel 845-266-8100; P.O. Box 75, Clinton Corners, NY 12514 (SAN 298-2846); *Imprints:* Attic Studio Press (Attic Studio); Maple Corners Press (Maple Corners Pr)
E-mail: collegeavepress@aol.com; atticstudiopress@aol.com; jubileestudio33@aol.com
Dist(s): **BookBaby**
Emerald Bk. Co.
Spring Arbor Distributors, Inc.

Atticus, C. J., (*978-0-9887780*) 41 Radford Ct. Sw, Marietta, GA 30060 USA Tel 770-805-9422
E-mail: atticus@cjatticus.com.

Attitude Pie Publishing, (*978-0-692-01275-8; 978-0-692-90265-3*) 2100 NE 214th St., North Miami Beach, FL 33179 USA Tel 305-725-0446; 419-281-5100 (x 1151)
E-mail: MPYANOWSKI@BOOKMASTERS.COM
Dist(s): **Baker & Taylor Publisher Services (BTPS).**

Attitude Pr. Inc.,

Attitudes in Dressing, Inc., (*978-0-9766640*) 1350 Broadway, New York, NY 10018 USA Tel 212-279-3492; Fax: 212-564-3426; Toll Free: 800-899-0503
Web site: http://www.bodywrappers.com.

ATU Golden Pubns., (*978-0-9753119*) 8283 Main St., Bokeelia, FL 33922 USA
E-mail: chrissydl@aol.com
Web site: http://www.pgaa.com.

Aubey, LLC, (*978-0-9962260; 978-0-9964234*) P.O. Box 31011, Washington, DC 20030 USA Tel 202-316-7972
E-mail: dj@aubeyllc.com
Web site: www.aubeyllc.com.

Auckland Univ. Pr. (NZL) (*978-1-86940; 978-1-77558; 978-0-9941465-0-2; 978-1-77671*) *Dist. by* **IPG Chicago.**

Auctus Pubs., (*978-0-9979607; 978-1-7327882; 978-1-7334456; 978-1-7368278; 979-8-9868429*) 606 Merion Avenue, First Flr., Havertown, PA 19083 USA Tel 267-844-0733
E-mail: info@auctuspublishers.com
Web site: Auctuspublishers.com.

Audible Studios on Brilliance Audio *Imprint of* **Brilliance Publishing, Inc.**

Audio Bookshelf, (*978-1-883332; 978-0-9741711; 978-0-9761932; 978-0-9814890; 978-1-935430*) Orders Addr.: 44 Ocean View Dr., Middletown, RI 02842 USA Tel 401-849-2333; Fax: 401-842-0440; Toll Free: 800-234-1713; Edit Addr.: P.O. Box 83, Belfast, ME 04915-0083 USA
E-mail: dd@audiobookshelf.com
Web site: http://www.audiobookshelf.com
Dist(s): **AudioGO**
Follett School Solutions
Landmark Audiobooks
Professional Media Service Corp.

Audio Craft Press *See* **AudioCraft Publishing, Inc.**

Audio Holdings, LLC, (*978-1-60136*) P.O. Box 119, Franklin Park, NJ 08823 USA (SAN 851-0776) Tel 732-940-4286; Fax: 732-940-0534
E-mail: mgladishev@gmail.com
Dist(s): **Ebsco Publishing.**

Audio Partners, Incorporated *See* **Audio Partners Publishing Corp.**

Audio Partners Publishing Corp., (*978-0-88690; 978-0-945353; 978-1-57270*) 42 Whitecap Dr., North Kingstown, RI 02852-7445 USA (SAN 253-4622) Toll Free Fax: 877-492-0873; Toll Free: 800-621-0182
E-mail: info@audiopartners.com
Dist(s): **Follett School Solutions**
Landmark Audiobooks.

Audio Renaissance *See* **Macmillan Audio**

AudioCraft Publishing, Inc., (*978-1-893699; 978-1-942950*) Orders Addr.: P.O. Box 281, Topinabee, MI 49791 USA Tel 231-238-0338; Fax: 231-238-0339; Toll Free: 888-420-4244; Edit Addr.: P.O. Box 281, Topinabee, MI 49791 USA
E-mail: ck@americanchillers.com; store@americanchillers.com; shawn@americanchillers.com
Web site: http://www.audiocraftpublishing.com; http://www.michiganchillers.com; http://www.americanchillers.com
Dist(s): **Follett School Solutions**
Partners Bk. Distributing, Inc.

†AudioGO, (*978-0-563; 978-0-7540; 978-0-7927; 978-0-89340; 978-1-55504; 978-1-60283; 978-1-60998; 978-1-62064; 978-1-62460; 978-1-4815; 978-1-4821*) Orders Addr.: c/o Perseus, 1094 Flex Dr., Jackson, TN 38301 USA; Edit Addr.: 42 Whitecap Dr., North Kingstown, RI 02852-7445 USA (SAN 858-7701) Toll Free: 800-621-0182; *Imprints:* Sound Library (SoundLib)
E-mail: laura.almeida@audiogo.com
Web site: http://www.audiogo.com/us/
Dist(s): **Blackstone Audio, Inc.**
Ebsco Publishing
Findaway World, LLC
Follett School Solutions
INscribe Digital; *CIP.*

Audioscope, (*978-1-57375*) Div. of K-tel International (USA), Inc., 2605 Fernbrook Ln., N., No. H-O, Plymouth, MN 55447 USA Tel 612-559-6888; Fax: 612-559-6848; Toll Free: 800-328-6640
Web site: http://www.ktel.com
Dist(s): **Follett School Solutions.**

AUDISEE Media, (*978-0-9666910; 978-1-930827; 978-0-9980365*) PO Box 193 PO Box 193, BICKLETON, WA 99322-0193 USA Tel 206-499-1401
E-mail: audisee@audisee.com
Web site: https://peterbstories.com/.

Audisee Sound & Music *See* **AUDISEE Media**

Auditors of God, The (GBR) (*978-0-9561587; 978-0-9572919*) *Dist. by* **LuluCom.**

Audrey Pr., (*978-1-936426*) P.O. Box 6113, Maryville, TN 37802 USA Tel 865-254-4463
E-mail: valarie@audreypress.com
Web site: www.audreypress.com.

Audrey Productions, (*978-0-9722673*) 7809 Paper Flower Ct., Las Vegas, NV 89128 USA Tel 702-228-4803 (phone/fax)
Dist(s): **Follett School Solutions.**

Audubon Pr. & Christian Bk. Service, (*978-0-9652883; 978-0-9742365; 978-0-9820731*) Orders Addr.: P.O. Box 8055, Laurel, MS 39441 USA Tel 601-649-8572; Fax: 601-649-8571; Toll Free: 800-405-3788; Edit Addr.: 2601 Audubon Dr., Laurel, MS 39440 USA
E-mail: buybooks@audubonpress.com
Web site: http://www.audubonpress.com.

Augsburg Bks. *Imprint of* **1517 Media**

Augsburg Fortress *Imprint of* **1517 Media**

Augsburg Fortress, Publishers *See* **1517 Media**

†August Hse. Pubs., Inc., (*978-0-87483; 978-0-935304; 978-1-939160; 978-1-941459; 978-1-941460; 978-1-947301*) 3500 Piedmont Rd. NE, Suite 310, Atlanta, GA 30305 USA (SAN 223-7288) Tel 404-442-4425; Fax: 404-442-4435; Toll Free: 800-284-8784; 3500 Piedmont Rd. Suite 310, Atlanta, GA 30305; *Imprints:* August House Story Cove (August Hse Story Cove)
E-mail: ahinfo@augusthouse.com; order@augusthouse.com
Web site: http://www.augusthouse.com
Dist(s): **Children's Plus, Inc.**
Findaway World, LLC
Follett School Solutions; *CIP.*

August House Story Cove *Imprint of* **August Hse. Pubs., Inc.**

August in Au Train Press, (*978-0-9904124*) P.O. Box 6, Au Train, MI 49806 USA Tel 810-516-1434
E-mail: kwujciak@stadiumadventureseries.com
Web site: stadiumadventureseries.com.

August Publishing Company, The *See* **August Publishing Co., The**

August Too Publishing, (*978-0-9767103*) 1346 E. Poinsettia St., Long Beach, CA 90805-3128 USA
E-mail: writeme@paulcarhart.com.

Augusta Win Publishing, (*978-0-9766597*) Orders Addr.: P.O. Box 53, Turin, NY 13473 USA; Edit Addr.: 6159 W. Main, Turin, NY 13473 USA
E-mail: augustawinpub@yahoo.com
Web site: http://www.augustawinpublishing.com.

Augustana College Geology Dept. Pr., (*978-0-9797015*) 639 38th St., Rock Island, IL 61201-2296 USA Tel 309-794-7318; Fax: 309-794-7564
Web site: http://www.augustana.edu.

Augustine Pr., (*978-0-9626431*) 900 Old Koenig Ln., No. 135, Austin, TX 78756 USA Tel 512-459-5194; Fax: 512-451-0755
E-mail: morganp@flash.net.

Augustinians of the Assumption *See* **Ambassador Bks., Inc.**

Augustus Publishing, (*978-0-9759453; 978-0-9792816; 978-0-9825415; 978-1-935883; 978-0-578-50932-7; 978-0-578-58774-5*) Div. of Augustus Productions, 600 W. 218 St., Suite 3K, New York, NY 10034 USA Tel 646-526-7998
E-mail: jc@augustuspublishing.com; gfhood1@aol.com; aw@augustuspublishing.com
Web site: http://www.augustuspublishing.com
Dist(s): **A & B Distributors & Pubs. Group**
Follett School Solutions
MyiLibrary
Publishers Group West (PGW).

Aukema, Karen George, (*978-0-9992832*) 355 Hwy 90, Chipley, FL 32428 USA Tel 850-326-2658; Fax: 850-326-2658
E-mail: karengaukema@gmail.com.

Aunt Patty's Travels-London, (*978-0-9659668*) 4811 Wesleyan Woods Dr., Macon, GA 31210 USA.

Aunt Strawberry Bks., (*978-0-9669988*) Orders Addr.: P.O. Box 819, Boulder, CO 80306-0819 USA (SAN 299-9811) Tel 303-449-3574; Fax: 303-444-9221
E-mail: readasbs@hotmail.com
Dist(s): **Brodart Co.**
Follett School Solutions.

Auntielynny Publications *See* **Chanticlair Publishing**

Aunty Ems Boutique, (*978-0-9742122*) P.O. Box 1963, Havasu Lake Landing, CA 92363 USA.

Aura Printing, Inc., (*978-0-911643*) 88 Parkville Ave., Brooklyn, NY 11230 USA (SAN 237-9317) Tel 718-435-9103; Fax: 718-871-9488
Dist(s): **Bookazine Co., Inc.**

Aura Productions LLC *See* **Simple Ink, LLC**

Aurandt, Paul H II, *(978-0-9887774)* 1035 Pk. Ave., River Forest, IL 60305 USA Tel 708-366-5371; Fax: 708-366-9184
E-mail: paul@paulharvey.com
Web site: http://www.paulharvey.com.

Auricle Ink Pubs., *(978-0-9661826; 978-0-9825785)* P.O. Box 20607, Sedona, AZ 86341 USA Tel 928-284-0860
E-mail: rcarmen27@yahoo.com
Web site: http://www.hearingproblems.com
Dist(s): **Academic Bk. Ctr., Inc.**
Bk. Hse., Inc., The
Brodart Co.
Coutts Information Services
Emery-Pratt Co.
Follett School Solutions
Franklin Bk. Co., Inc.
Majors, J. A. Co.
Matthews Medical Bk. Co.
Midwest Library Service
Yankee Bk. Peddler, Inc.

Auriga, Ediciones S.A. (ESP) *(978-84-7281) Dist. by* **Continental Bk.**

Aurora Books *Imprint of* **Eco-Justice Pr., LLC**

Aurora Bks., *(978-0-9753508)* 512 Willow Branch Rd., Norman, OK 73072 USA
E-mail: aurorabooks@netzero.net.

Aurora Libris Corp., *(978-1-932233)* 40 E. 83rd St., Apt. 35, New York, NY 10028 USA Toll Free: 866-763-8411
E-mail: lavinia@laviniasworld.com
Web site: http://www.laviniasworld.com.

Aurora Metro Pubns. Ltd. (GBR) *(978-0-9515877; 978-0-9536757; 978-0-9542330; 978-0-9546912; 978-0-9551566; 978-1-906582; 978-0-9566329) Dist. by* **PerseuPGW.**

Aurora Publishing, Incor[porated *See* **Aurora Publishing, Inc.**

Aurora Publishing, Inc., *(978-1-934496)* 3655 Torrance Blvd., Suite 430, Torrance, CA 90503 USA; *Imprints:* Deux (Deux); LuvLuv (LuvLuv) Do not confuse with companies with the same or similar name in Arligton, VA, College Grove, TN,, West Palm Beach, FL, Eagle River, AK, West Hartford, CT, Fort Lauderdale, FL
E-mail: info@aurora-publishing.com
Web site: http://www.aurora-publishing.com; http://www.deux-press.com; http://www.luvluv-press.com
Dist(s): **Diamond Comic Distributors, Inc.**
Diamond Bk. Distributors.

Austin & Charlie Adventures *Imprint of* **Paw Print Pubns.**

Austin & Company, Inc., *(978-0-9657153)* 104 S. Union St., Suite 202, Traverse City, MI 49684 USA (SAN 631-1466) Tel 231-933-4649; Fax: 231-933-4659
E-mail: aandn@aol.com
Web site: http://www.austinandcompanyinc.com.

Austin & Nelson Publishing *See* **Austin & Company, Inc.**

Austin Christopher Swift, *(978-0-9764208)* 154 Golden Autumn Pl., Woodlands, TX 77384 USA Tel 956-421-5750; Fax: 956-421-5721
E-mail: john@toppmarketing.com.

Austin, Dorothy, *(978-0-578-40192-8)* 4948 S. Forrestville Garden unit, Chicago, IL 60615 USA Tel 312-835-0403
E-mail: DorithyAustin4948@gmail.com
Dist(s): **Independent Pub.**

Austin Energy Green Building Program, *(978-0-9679069)* Orders Addr.: P.O. Box 1088, Austin, TX 78767 USA Tel 512-322-6172; Fax: 512-505-3711; Edit Addr.: 721 Barton Springs Rd., Austin, TX 78704 USA
E-mail: dick.peterson@austinenergy.com
Web site: http://www.austinenergy.com.

Austin, Laurie , *(978-0-578-18226-1)* 15627 158th Ave SE, Renton, WA 98058 USA.

Austin Macauley Pubs. Ltd. (GBR) *(978-1-905609; 978-1-84963; 978-1-78455; 978-1-78554; 978-1-78629; 978-1-78612; 978-1-78823; 978-1-78693; 978-1-78710; 978-1-78848; 978-1-78878; 978-1-5289) Dist. by* **LightSource CS.**

Austin, Nanette, *(978-0-9600409)* 540 Strathaven Ct., Turlock, CA 95382 USA Tel 209-613-1622
E-mail: nan@nanaustinink.com
Web site: www.nanaustinink.com.

Austin, Phoenyx, *(978-0-9848630)* 3016 Red Lion Ln., Silver Spring, MD 20904 USA Tel 352-279-1433
E-mail: dr.phoenyx@gmail.com.

Austin, Stephen F. State Univ. Pr., *(978-1-936205; 978-1-62288)* Orders Addr.: P.O. Box 13002, Nacogdoches, TX 75962 USA Tel 936-468-1078; Fax: 936-468-2614; Edit Addr.: 1936 North St. Liberal Arts N., 203 English, Nacogdoches, TX 75962 USA
Dist(s): **MyiLibrary**
Texas A&M Univ. Pr.
ebrary, Inc.

Australian Fishing Network (AUS) *(978-0-9587143; 978-1-86513; 978-1-86252-412-5; 978-0-646-00117-3; 978-0-646-15871-6; 978-0-646-19310-6; 978-0-646-20528-1; 978-0-646-20908-1; 978-0-646-21731-4; 978-0-646-24873-8; 978-0-646-25433-3; 978-0-646-25434-0; 978-0-646-30130-3; 978-0-646-31918-6) Dist. by* **Cardinal.**

Authentic Media (GBR) *(978-0-8499; 978-0-85009; 978-1-86024; 978-1-78078) Dist. by* **EMI CMG Dist.**

Authentic Media, *(978-0-85364; 978-0-9630908; 978-1-884543; 978-0-903843; 978-0-948902; 978-1-85078; 978-1-86024; 978-1-932805; 978-1-934068; 978-1-60657)* Div. of Send The Light Distribution LLC, Orders Addr.: 129 Mobilization Dr., Waynesboro, GA 30830-2047 USA Tel 706-554-5827; Fax: 706-554-7444; Toll Free: 866-732-6657; P.O. Box 1047, Waynesboro, GA 30830; Edit Addr.: 9 Holdom Ave. Bletchley, Milton Keynes, Buckinghamshire MK1 1QR GBR Tel 01908 364200; Fax: 01908 648592; 1820 Jet Stream Dr., Colorado Springs, CO 80921 Tel 719-488-9200
E-mail: angela@omlit.om.org; info@authenticmedia.co.uk
Web site: http://www.authenticbooks.com
Dist(s): **EMI CMG Distribution**
Send The Light Distribution LLC
Wipf & Stock Pubs.

Autherine Publishing, *(978-0-9912000)* PO Box 1528, Windermere, FL 34786 USA Tel 407-542-5002
E-mail: JanetAutherine@GrowintoGreatness.com; Autherine@aol.com
Web site: www.GrowintoGreatness.com; www.janetautherine.com.

Author Academy Elite, *(978-0-692-31830-0; 978-1-943526; 978-1-946114; 978-0-692-85391-7; 978-1-64085; 978-0-692-88922-0; 978-0-578-57522-3; 978-1-64746; 978-0-578-80646-4; 979-8-88583)* P.O. Box 43, Powell, OH 43065 USA Tel 740-272-0093
Dist(s): **CreateSpace Independent Publishing Platform.**

Author at Work *Imprint of* **Owen, Richard C. Pubs., Inc.**

Author Pubns., *(978-0-9724987)* P.O. Box 927, Turlock, CA 95381-0927 USA
E-mail: ochoa_f@msn.com
Web site: http://www.gonzostation.org.

Author Solutions, Incorporated *See* **Author Solutions, LLC**

Author Solutions, LLC, *(978-1-5043; 978-1-9822; 979-8-7652)* Div. of Penguin Group (USA) Inc., 1663 Liberty Dr., Bloomington, IN 47403 USA Tel 812-334-5223; Toll Free: 877-655-1722; *Imprints:* WestBow Press (WestBowPr); Balboa Press (BalboaPr); Inspiring Voices (InspVoices); Wordclay (Wrdclay); Abbott Press (AbbottPr); PartridgeIndia (PARTRIDGEINDIA)
E-mail: sfurr@authorsolutions.com
Web site: http://www.authorsolutions.com
Dist(s): **Baker & Taylor Publisher Services (BTPS)**
CreateSpace Independent Publishing Platform
Xlibris Corp.
Zondervan.

AuthorHouse, *(978-1-58500; 978-0-9675669; 978-1-58721; 978-1-58820; 978-0-7596; 978-1-4033; 978-1-4107; 978-1-4140; 978-1-4184; 978-1-4208; 978-1-4259; 978-1-4343; 978-1-4389; 978-1-4490; 978-1-4520; 978-1-61764; 978-1-4567; 978-1-4582; 978-1-4624; 978-1-4633; 978-1-4634; 978-0-9846457; 978-1-4670; 978-1-4678; 978-1-4685; 978-1-4772; 978-1-4817; 978-1-4918; 978-1-4969; 978-1-5049; 978-1-5065; 978-1-5246; 978-1-5462; 978-1-7283; 978-1-6655; 979-8-8230) Div. of Author Solutions, Inc., 1663 Liberty Dr., Suite 200, Bloomington, IN 47403 USA (SAN 253-7605) Fax: 812-336-5449; Toll Free: 888-519-5121; Imprints:* Life Rich Publishing (Life Rich Pub)
E-mail: authorsupport@authorhouse.com; sfurr@authorsolutions.com
Web site: http://www.authorhouse.com
Dist(s): **Author Solutions, LLC**
Baker & Taylor Publisher Services (BTPS)
BookBaby
CreateSpace Independent Publishing Platform
Follett School Solutions
Ingram Publisher Services
Lulu Pr., Inc.
MyiLibrary
Smashwords.

AuthorMike Ink *See* **AM Ink Publishing**

Authors & Artists Publishers of New York, Inc., *(978-0-9708053; 978-0-9724922; 978-0-9740683; 978-0-9754298; 978-0-9763993; 978-0-9766716; 978-0-9771482; 978-0-9786211; 978-0-9787113; 978-0-9819746; 978-0-9825971; 978-0-9839121; 978-0-9850947)* 21 Sta. Rd. Suite 211, Wilton, CT 06897 USA; *Imprints:* Ithaca Press (IthacaPress)
Web site: http://www.ithacapress.com
Dist(s): **Follett School Solutions.**

Authors Choice Pr. *Imprint of* **iUniverse, Inc.**

Author's Connection Pr., *(978-0-927206)* 777 College Pk. Dr., SW No. 60, Albany, OR 97322-8430 USA
Web site: http://www.acpublish.com.

Authors' Discovery Cooperation, Inc., *(978-0-9794443; 978-0-9800854; 978-0-9844730)* 165 Cherry Ln., Robert Lee, TX 76945 USA (SAN 853-4276) Tel 325-453-4595
E-mail: ldudney@nwol.net
Web site: http://www.authorsdiscovery.com.

Authors Guild Back in Print Distribution, *(978-1-62536)* 31 E 32nd St. 7th Flr., New York, NY 10016 USA Tel 212-563-5904; Fax: 212-564-5363
E-mail: cbarila@authorsguild.org
Web site: www.authorsguild.org
Dist(s): **INscribe Digital**
Independent Pubs. Group.

Authors Guild, Incorporated, The *See* **Authors Guild Back in Print Distribution**

Author's Herald *See* **Cadmus Publishing**

Authors Pen, LLC, The, *(978-0-9906711; 978-1-948248; 978-0-578-35464-4)* P.O. Box 16314, Fort Worth, TX 76162 USA Tel 904-613-6299
E-mail: info@tapwriting.com
Web site: www.tapwriting.com.

Authors Pr., *(978-1-947995; 978-1-948653; 978-1-64314)* Orders Addr.: 1321 Buchanan Rd, Pittsburg, 94565 SUN; Edit Addr.: 1321 Buchanan Rd, Pittsburg, CA 94565 USA Tel 925-698-2619.

Authors' Press, The *See* **Quantum Manifestations Publishing**

Author's Publishing, LLC, *(978-0-9728902; 978-1-60415)* 104 Lake June Rd. NW, Lake Placid, FL 33852 USA
E-mail: debono@strato.net
Web site: http://www.fantasyreaders.com.

Authorunit, *(978-1-7349645)*
E-mail: citynetforlife@gmail.com
Web site: authorunit.com.

Autism & Behavior Training Associates *See* **ABTA Pubns. & Products**

Autism Asperger Publishing Co., *(978-0-9672514; 978-1-931282; 978-1-934575; 978-1-937473; 978-1-942197)* Orders Addr.: P.O. Box 23173, Overland Park, KS 66283-0173 USA Tel 913-599-3311; Fax: 913-492-2546; 11209 Strang Line Rd, Lenexa, KS 66215 (SAN 920-9220); Edit Addr.: 15490 Qunvira, Overland Park, KS 66221 USA
E-mail: kmcbr41457@aol.com
Web site: http://www.asperger.net
Dist(s): **Follett School Solutions**
Independent Pubs. Group.

Autism Research Institute, *(978-0-9740360)* 4182 Adams Ave., San Diego, CA 92116 USA Fax: 619-563-6840
E-mail: sait97302@yahoo.com
Web site: http://www.autismresearchinstitute.com.

Automatic Pictures Publishing, *(978-0-9818737; 978-0-9892221; 978-0-9912729)* 5721 Valley Oak Dr., Los Angeles, CA 90068 USA Tel 323-935-1800; Fax: 323-935-8040
E-mail: automaticstudio@gmail.com
Web site: http://www.lookingglasswars.com
Dist(s): **Diamond Comic Distributors, Inc.**
Diamond Bk. Distributors
Publishers Group West (PGW).

Automatic Publishing *See* **Automatic Pictures Publishing**

Automobile Assn. (GBR) *(978-0-7495; 978-0-86145; 978-0-901088; 978-1-872163) Dist. by* **Trafalgar.**

Automobile Assn. (GBR) *(978-0-7495; 978-0-86145; 978-0-901088; 978-1-872163) Dist. by* **IPG Chicago.**

Automobiles-Memory Lane Publishing, *(978-0-9746667)* Orders Addr.: P.O. Box 228, Vicksburg, MI 49097 USA (SAN 255-7118) Tel 269-649-3614 (phone/fax); Edit Addr.: 2294 E. VW Ave., Vicksburg, MI 49097 USA.

Autonomedia, *(978-0-936756; 978-1-57027)* Orders Addr.: P.O. Box 568, Brooklyn, NY 11211-0568 USA; Edit Addr.: 55 S. Eleventh St., #4b, Brooklyn, NY 11211-0568 USA (SAN 221-3869) Tel 718-963-2603
E-mail: info@autonomedia.org
Web site: http://www.autonomedia.org
Dist(s): **AK Pr. Distribution**
Lulu Pr., Inc.
SPD-Small Pr. Distribution.

Autumn Arch Publishing, *(978-0-9904504; 978-0-9992026; 978-1-7338095)* 3115 Blue Ridge Ct NE, Cedar Rapids, IA 52402 USA Tel 319-200-6398
E-mail: bunceaaron@gmail.com
Web site: autumnarchpublishing.com.

Autumn Gold Pr., *(978-0-9972158)* 5374 Dunwoody Club Creek, ATLANTA, GA 30360 USA Tel 770-396-7001
E-mail: geliad@bellsouth.net
Web site: geliawrites.com.

Autumn Hill Bks., Inc., *(978-0-9754444; 978-0-9843036; 978-0-9827466; 978-0-9987400; 978-1-7362682)* P.O. Box 22, BLOOMINGTON, IN 47401 USA; 814 N. Franklin St., Chicago, IL 60610
E-mail: info@autumnhillbooks.com
Web site: http://www.autumnhillbooks.com
Dist(s): **Ebsco Publishing**
Follett School Solutions
Independent Pubs. Group
MyiLibrary.

Autumn Hse. Publishing, *(978-0-9637825)* Orders Addr.: P.O. Box 763833, Dallas, TX 75376 USA; Edit Addr.: 1535 Acapulco Dr., Dallas, TX 75232 USA Tel 214-376-8959 Do not confuse with the same or similar name in Lexington, KY, Hagerstown, MD
E-mail: millijp@earthlink.net.

Autumn Hse. Publishing Co., *(978-0-8127; 978-1-878951)* Div. of Review & Herald Publishing Assn., 55 W. Oakridge Dr., Hagerstown, MD 21740 USA Do not confuse with companies with the same name in Lexington, KY, Dallas, TX.

Autumn Publishing Group, LLC, *(978-1-890877)* Orders Addr.: P.O. Box 71604, Madison Heights, MI 48071 USA Tel 248-589-5249; Fax: 248-585-5715; Toll Free: 888-876-4114; Edit Addr.: 30755 Barrington Ave., Madison Heights, MI 48071 USA
Web site: http://www.wiredin.net/childcare
Dist(s): **Unique Bks., Inc.**

Autumn's End Pr., *(978-0-9984076)* P.O. Box 999, Tacoma, WA 98401 USA Tel 253-225-0702
E-mail: contact@byjenn.com
Web site: www.byjenn.com.

AV2 by Weigl *Imprint of* **Weigl Pubs., Inc.**

Avalerion Bks., Inc., *(978-0-9834119; 978-1-954551)* 190 Beagle Rd., Bethel, PA 19507 USA Tel 717-933-9999
E-mail: avalerionbooks@yahoo.com.

Avalon Publishing, *(978-0-7867; 978-0-912528; 978-0-918373; 978-0-929654; 978-0-931188; 978-0-935701; 978-0-941423; 978-0-945465; 978-0-9603322; 978-1-56025; 978-1-56201; 978-1-56261; 978-1-56691; 978-1-56858; 978-1-56924; 978-1-57354; 978-1-58005; 978-1-878067; 978-1-59880; 978-1-60094; 978-1-61237; 978-1-61238; 978-1-63121; 978-1-64049; 978-1-64171; 979-8-88647) Div. of Perseus Books Group, 1700 4th St., Berkeley, CA 94710-1711 USA (SAN 221-7406); Imprints:* Westview Press (WstvwPr)
Web site: http://www.avalonpub.com
Dist(s): **Bilingual Pubns. Co., The**
CreateSpace Independent Publishing Platform
Ebsco Publishing
Follett School Solutions
Hachette Bk. Group
MyiLibrary
Publishers Group West (PGW)
ebrary, Inc.

Avant Garde Publishing *See* **The Publishing Place LLC**

Avant-garde Bks., *(978-0-9743676; 978-0-9908992; 978-0-9977566; 978-1-946753)* Orders Addr.: P.O. Box 566, Mableton, GA 30126 USA Tel 770-739-4039 Do not confuse with Avant garde Publishing in Norman, OK
E-mail: brightsmile.hardy@live.com
Web site: www.avantgardebooks.net.

Avant-garde Publishing Company *See* **Avant-garde Bks.**

Avari Pr., *(978-1-933770)* 2198 Old Philadelphia Pk., Lancaster, PA 17602 USA (SAN 257-9413)
E-mail: av42@antham.net.

Avatar Pr., Inc., *(978-0-9706784; 978-1-59291)* 9 Triumph Dr., Urbana, IL 61802 USA Tel 217-384-2211; Fax: 217-384-2216 Do not confuse with companies with the same or similar name in Sunnyside, NY, Atlanta, GA, Brick, NJ
E-mail: william@avatarpress.net
Web site: http://www.avatarpress.com
Dist(s): **Diamond Comic Distributors, Inc.**
Diamond Bk. Distributors
Simon & Schuster
Simon & Schuster, Inc.

Avatar Pubns., Inc. (CAN) *(978-0-9735379; 978-0-9738442; 978-0-9737401; 978-0-9738555; 978-1-897455) Dist. by* **indiCo.**

Ave Maria Pr., *(978-0-87061; 978-0-87793; 978-0-88347; 978-0-939516; 978-1-893732; 978-1-932057; 978-1-59471; 978-1-933495; 978-0-9972710; 978-1-64680)* P.O. Box 428, Notre Dame, IN 46556-0428 USA (SAN 201-1255) Tel 574-287-2831; Fax: 574-239-2904; Toll Free Fax: 800-282-5681; Toll Free: 800-282-1865
E-mail: avemariapress.1@nd.edu
Web site: http://www.forestofpeace.com; http://www.avemariapress.com; http://www.sorinbooks.com
Dist(s): **MyiLibrary.**

Aventine Pr, *(978-0-9719382; 978-0-9722932; 978-1-59330; 978-1-955162)* 750 State St. Unit 319, San Diego, CA 92101-6073 USA Toll Free: 866-246-6142
E-mail: info@aventinepress.com
Web site: http://www.aventinepress.com
Dist(s): **Ingram Publisher Services.**

Average Dog Publishing, *(978-1-7337590)* 802 N Kaufman Dr, Deer Park, TX 77536 USA Tel 281-785-1572
E-mail: lhcattle@yahoo.com.

AverHill Pr., *(978-0-9766107)* 2545 SW Terwilliger Blvd., No. 807, Portland, OR 97201 USA.

Avery *Imprint of* **Penguin Publishing Group**

Avery Color Studios, Inc., *(978-0-932212; 978-1-892384)* 511 D Ave., Gwinn, MI 49841 USA (SAN 211-1470) Tel 906-346-3908; Fax: 906-346-3015; Toll Free: 800-722-9925
E-mail: avery@portup.com
Dist(s): **Partners Bk. Distributing, Inc.**
Hale, Robert & Co., Inc.

Avery Goode-Reid Pubs., *(978-0-9766620)* P.O. Box 702, Ormond Beach, FL 32175-0702 USA Tel 386-615-0493
E-mail: mariánstomblin@aol.com
Web site: http://www.mariantomblin.com.

Avery's, Tom Totally Tennis, *(978-0-9727444)* 5771 12th Ave., NW, Naples, FL 34119 USA
Web site: http://tomavery.com.

AveryToday, Inc., *(978-0-692-84145-7; 978-0-692-89846-8; 978-0-692-91908-8)* P.O. Box 1516, ENGLEWOOD, CO 80150 USA Tel 409-200-4774
E-mail: jeffwcrawford5+LVP0003232@gmail.com; jeffwcrawford5+LVP0003232@gmail.com.

Avian Welfare Coalition, Inc., *(978-0-615-19395-3)* 1923 Ashland Ave., Saint Paul, MN 55104 USA
E-mail: info@avianwelfare.org
Web site: http://www.avianwelfare.org.

Aviation Supplies & Academics, Inc., *(978-0-940732; 978-1-56027; 978-1-61954; 978-1-63134; 978-1-64425)* 7005 132nd Pl., SE, Newcastle, WA 98059-3153 USA (SAN 219-709X) Tel 425-235-1500; Fax: 425-235-0128
E-mail: asa@asa2fly.com
Web site: http://www.asa2fly.com
Dist(s): **Aviation Bk. Co.**
Baker & Taylor Publisher Services (BTPS)
Follett School Solutions
Legato Pubs. Group
MyiLibrary
Publishers Group West (PGW)
Wing Aero
ebrary, Inc.

Avid Readers Publishing Group, *(978-0-9797106; 978-0-9801438; 978-1-935105; 978-1-61286)* 2802 Belshire Ave., Lakewood, CA 90715 USA Tel 562-243-5918; Toll Free: 888-966-6835
E-mail: arpg@ericpatterson.name
Web site: http://www.avidreaderspg.com.

Avisson Pr., Inc., *(978-1-888105)* Orders Addr.: P.O. Box 38816, Greensboro, NC 27438-8816 USA (SAN 298-8127) Tel 336-288-6989; Fax: 336-288-6989; Edit Addr.: 3007 Taliaferro Rd., Greensboro, NC 27408 USA (SAN 298-8097)
Dist(s): **Follett School Solutions.**

Avista Products, *(978-0-9798741)* 2411 NE Loop 410. Ste. 108, San Antonio, TX 78217-6600 USA
E-mail: cbooker@avistaproducts.com
Web site: http://www.avistaproducts.com.

Avitable Publisher *See* **Avitable Pub.**

Aviva Gittle Publishing, *(978-0-692-35568-8; 978-1-942736)* 330 Rayford Rd. 177, Spring, TX 77386 USA Tel 619-577-0126
Web site: http://gotogittle.com/
Dist(s): **CreateSpace Independent Publishing Platform.**

Aviva Publishing *See* **Aviva Publishing**

Aviva Publishing, *(978-1-890427; 978-0-9841497; 978-1-935586; 978-1-938686; 978-1-940984; 978-0-692-40228-3; 978-1-943164; 978-1-944335; 978-1-947937; 978-0-692-06101-5; 978-0-578-43916-7; 978-1-950241; 978-0-578-66763-8; 978-1-63618;*

978-0-578-93808-0) 2301 Saranac Ave., Suite 101, Lake Placid, NY 12946-1139 USA Tel 518-523-1320
E-mail: susan@avivapubs.com
Web site: http://www.avivapubs.com
Dist(s): **BookBaby**
Lulu Pr., Inc.
Midpoint Trade Bks., Inc.

Avocus Publishing, Inc., (*978-0-9627671; 978-1-890765*) 4 White Brook Rd., Gilsum, NH 03448 USA (SAN 248-2223) Tel 603-357-0236; Fax: 603-357-2073; Toll Free: 800-345-6665
E-mail: info@avocus.com
Web site: http://www.avocus.com
Dist(s): **Pathway Bk. Service.**

Avon Bks. *Imprint of* **HarperCollins Pubs.**

Avon Impulse *Imprint of* **HarperCollins Pubs.**

AW Teen *Imprint of* **Whitman, Albert & Co.**

AW2 Visions, (*978-0-615-41407-2; 978-0-692-29349-2; 978-0-692-50071-2*) 15323 Ensenada Dr., Houston, TX 77083 USA Tel 281-561-7714; Fax: 281-561-7070
E-mail: awashington88@comcast.net.

A.W.A. Gang *Imprint of* **Journey Stone Creations, LLC**

Awa Pr. (NZL) (*978-0-9582509; 978-0-9582538; 978-0-9582629; 978-0-9582750; 978-0-9582916; 978-1-877551; 978-1-927249; 978-1-927249-13-0; 978-1-927249-14-7*) *Dist. by* **IPG Chicago.**

Awaken Publishing *See* **Now Age Knowledge**

Awaken Specialty Pr., (*978-0-9794713*) P.O. Box 491, Centerton, AR 72719 USA (SAN 853-5248) Tel 479-586-2574
E-mail: celeste@awakenspecialtypress.com
Web site: http://www.awakenspecialtypress.com
Dist(s): **Follett School Solutions.**

Awakened Path Bks., LLC, (*978-0-578-21111-4; 978-1-7329486*) 18 Maple Ave., No. 279, Barrington, RI 02806 USA
Dist(s): **Ingram Content Group.**

Award Pubns. Ltd. (GBR) (*978-0-86163; 978-1-84135; 978-0-9537785; 978-1-904618; 978-1-905503; 978-1-907604; 978-1-906572; 978-1-78270; 978-1-909763*) *Dist. by* **Parkwest Pubns.**

Awareness Pubns., (*978-0-9744163*) 310-A S. Alu Rd., Wailuku, HI 96793 USA Tel 808-244-3782 Do not confuse with companies with the same name in Greenfield, WI, Santa Maria, CA, Houston, TX, Pocomoke City, MD
E-mail: awarep@mauigateway.com
Web site: http://www.awarenesspublications.org
Dist(s): **New Leaf Distributing Co., Inc.**

Awen Hse. Publishing, (*978-0-9826670*) 8949 Bellcove Cir., Colorado Springs, CO 80920 USA Tel 719-287-7074
E-mail: dunning.rebecca@gmail.com
Web site: http://www.rebeccadunning.com.

Awesome Bk. Publishing, (*978-0-9840538; 978-0-9895194*) P.O. Box 1157, Roseland, FL 32957 USA Tel 321-632-0177.

Awesome Guides, Inc., (*978-0-9703694; 978-0-9723218*) 127 W. Fairbanks Ave., Suite No. 421, Winter Park, FL 32789 USA Fax: 407-678-4337
E-mail: sales@awesomeguides.com; cl@awesomeguides.com
Web site: http://www.awesomeguides.com.

Awe-Struck E-Books, Incorporated *See* **Awe-Struck Publishing**

Awe-Struck Publishing, (*978-1-928670; 978-1-58749*) Div. of Mundania Pr., LLC, 6470a Glenway Ave. #109, Cincinnati, OH 45211 USA (SAN 854-4980); *Imprints:* Byte/Me Teen Book (Byte Me Teen); Earthling Press (Earthling Prss)
E-mail: dan@mundania.com
Web site: http://www.awe-struck.net.

Awkward Labs, (*978-0-615-79808-0; 978-0-578-97371-5*) P.O. Box 398, Felton, DE 19943 USA Tel 302-430-6077
E-mail: wjwalton@yahoo.com.

AWOC.COM, (*978-0-9707507; 978-1-62016*) P.O. Box 2819, Denton, TX 76202 USA
E-mail: editor@awoc.com
Web site: http://www.awoc.com.

A-Works New York, Incorporated *See* **One Peace Bks., Inc.**

Axiom Hse., (*978-0-9760237*) P.O. Box 2901, Fairfax, VA 22031 USA
E-mail: orders@axiomhouse.com
Web site: http://www.axiomhouse.com/index.htm
Dist(s): **Follett School Solutions.**

Axiom Pr. *Imprint of* **Genesis Communications, Inc.**

Axios Pr., (*978-0-9661908; 978-0-9753662; 978-1-60419*) P.O. Box 118, Mount Jackson, VA 22842 USA Tel 540-984-3829; Fax: 540-984-3843; Toll Free: 888-542-9467 (orders only); 4501 Forbes Blvd., Lanham, MD 20706 Do not confuse with Axios Publishing Corporation, Seattle, WA
E-mail: info@axiosinstitute.org
Web site: http://www.axiosinstitute.org
Dist(s): **Follett School Solutions**
MyiLibrary
National Bk. Network.

Axle Publishing Co., Inc., (*978-0-9755895*) Orders Addr.: P.O. Box 269, Rockdale, TX 76567 USA (SAN 256-3746) Tel 800-866-2685 (Toll-Free); 512-446-0644 (Jody"s Direct Line); Fax: 512-446-2686 Fax Line; Edit Addr.: 1506 O'Kelley Rd., Rockdale, TX 76567 USA Tel 512-446-0644; Toll Free: 800-866-2685
E-mail: jody@axlegalench.com; jody@laid-back.com; roosterrdz@aol.com
Web site: http://www.axlegalench.com; http://www.laid-back.com; http://www.roostermorris.com
Dist(s): **Follett School Solutions.**

AY Chen Illustration & Design, (*978-0-692-23349-8; 978-0-692-33306-8; 978-0-692-84099-3; 978-0-692-88976-3; 978-0-578-35199-5; 979-8-9861147*) 145 Ike Dr., ALEXANDRIA, VA 22314 USA Tel 703-975-0993
Dist(s): **CreateSpace Independent Publishing Platform.**

Aylen Publishing, (*978-0-9708623; 978-0-9765040; 978-0-9857708; 978-0-9910084; 978-0-9862848*) Subs. of Master Planning Group International, 7830 E. Camelback Re No. 711, Scottsdale, AZ 85251 USA Toll Free: 800-443-1976
Web site: http://www.masterplanninggroup.com; http://www.Aylen.com.

AZ Bks. LLC, (*978-1-61889*) 9330 LBJ Freeway, Dallas, TX 74243 USA Tel 214-438-3922; Fax: 214-561-6795; 245 8Th Ave., #180, New York, NY 10011
E-mail: anastasia.lobynko@az-books.com; support@booksonix.com
Dist(s): **Follett School Solutions.**

AZ Group Publishing House *See* **AZ Bks. LLC**

AZ I AM Bks., (*978-0-9884449; 978-0-9898077; 978-0-9862075*) P.O. Box 267, Santa Monica, CA 90406 USA Tel 310-913-1315
E-mail: info@aziam.com.

Azaida Media, LLC, (*978-0-9864405*) 7726 Gunston Plaza No. 1648, Lorton, VA 22199 USA Tel 571-375-8500
E-mail: info@azaidamedia.com
Web site: http://www.azaidamedia.com.

Azalea Creek Publishing, (*978-0-9677934; 978-1-7363643*) c/o Tom Kendrick, 308 Bloomfield Rd., Sebastopol, CA 95472 USA Tel 707-823-2911 (phone/fax)
E-mail: azalea@sonic.net
Web site: http://www.sonic.net/dragonfly/azaleaforth.html; http://www.sonic.net/dragonfly/adhtml.html; http://southwestdragonflies.net/Order_Form.html; http://southwestdragonflies.net/ColoringBook.html
Dist(s): **American West Bks.**
Bored Feet Pr.
Rio Nuevo Pubs.

AZIAM Books *See* **AZ I AM Bks.**

Azimuth Media *Imprint of* **Hopkins Publishing**

Azimuth Pr., (*978-0-9632074; 978-1-886218*) 4041 Bowman Blvd., Suite 211, Macon, GA 31210 USA Tel 770-994-9449; Fax: 770-996-6928 Do not confuse with companies with the same or similar name in Alexander, NC, Arnold, MD.

Azmy, Lois, (*978-1-7370402*) 909 Rte. 103 E, Warner, NH 03278 USA Tel 603-369-9899
E-mail: happyazmy@gmail.com.

Azoka Co., The, (*978-0-9745560*) P.O. Box Box 323, Greenland, NH 03885 USA Tel 603-772-0181; Fax: 603-772-0550
Web site: http://www.seacoastcenter.com.

Azreal Publishing Co., (*978-0-9755566*) Orders Addr.: P.O. Box 21139, Tallahassee, FL 32312 USA; Edit Addr.: 1937 Saxon St., Tallahassee, FL 32310 USA
Web site: http://.

Azrec Book Publishing *See* **Aztec Bk. Publishing**

Azro Pr., Inc., (*978-0-9660239; 978-1-929115*) Orders Addr.: 1704 Llano St., Suite B, PMB 342, Sante Fe, NM 87505 USA Tel 505-989-3272; Fax: 505-989-3832
E-mail: books@azropress.com
Web site: http://www.azropress.com
Dist(s): **Follett School Solutions**
SCB Distributors.

Aztec 5 Publishing, (*978-0-9769478*) Orders Addr.: P.O. Box 11693, Glendale, AZ 85318 USA Tel 623-537-4567 (phone/fax)
E-mail: aztec5publishing@aol.com.

Aztec Bk. Publishing, (*978-0-9787674; 978-0-9801258; 978-0-9838916; 978-0-9905293*) 1606 Delaware Ave., Wilmington, DE 19806 USA Tel 302-575-1993; Fax: 302-575-1977
Web site: http://www.azteccopies.com.

Aztex Corp., (*978-0-89404*) P.O. Box 50046, Tucson, AZ 85703-1046 USA (SAN 210-0371) Tel 520-882-4656; Fax: 520-792-8501
E-mail: ac@aztexcorp.com
Web site: http://www.aztexcorp.com.

AZTexts Publishing, Inc., (*978-0-9677292*) P.O. Box 93487, Phoenix, AZ 85070-3487 USA Tel 480-283-0994 (phone/fax); 1043 E. Amberwood Dr., Phoenix, AZ 85048
E-mail: aztexts@cox.net
Web site: http://FrecklesFriends.org; http://www.aztexts.com
Dist(s): **Quality Bks., Inc.**

Azul Publishing, (*978-0-9995299*) 110 E. Houston St 7th Flr., SAN ANTONIO, TX 78261 USA Tel 210-910-7789
E-mail: ladiazs2@yahoo.com
Dist(s): **Ingram Content Group.**

Azure Coast Pr., (*978-0-578-42189-6; 978-0-578-85407-6*) 1600 Ctr. Ave. Suite 1A, Fort Lee, NJ 07024 USA Tel 201-486-1377
E-mail: rarrechea@aol.com
Dist(s): **Independent Pub.**

Azure Communications, (*978-0-9618741*) Orders Addr.: P.O. Box 23387, New Orleans, LA 70183 USA (SAN 668-7695); Edit Addr.: 37383 Overland Trail, Prairieville, LA 70769 USA (SAN 668-7709) Tel 225-744-4094
E-mail: gszczurek@eatel.net.

Azuria Bks., (*978-0-9796444*) P.O. Box 535, Clyde, NC 28721 USA Tel 828-627-9685
E-mail: timbramlett@charter.net.

Azz1 Productions, (*978-0-9827110*) 150 W. Columbia St., Apt.3B, Hempstead, NY 11550 USA Tel 516-234-3568.

Azzurri Publishing, (*978-0-692-30257-6; 978-0-692-42035-5; 978-0-9967298*) 2355 Westwood Blvd. No. 647, Los Angeles, CA 90064 USA Tel 206-683-1718
E-mail: peterawick@gmail.com
Web site: www.peter-wick.com.

B & B Educational Advancement & Pubns., Inc., (*978-1-937065*) 1407 Ford St., Golden, CO 80401 USA (SAN 860-1801) Tel 303-279-8659; Fax: 303-648-5135
E-mail: lmrpc@aol.com.

B&B Publishing, (*978-1-885813*) 63418 Everett Rd., Coos Bay, OR 97420 USA Tel 541-269-9277 Do not confuse with companies with the same or similar name in Fort Collins, CO, Westminster, CO, Walworth, WI, Greenfield, IN
Dist(s): **Partners/West Book Distributors.**

B B Y Publications *See* **bby Publications at The University of West Alabama**

B. Craig Jones, (*978-1-7331853; 978-1-955664*) P.O. Box 6991, Sherwood, AR 72124 USA Tel 501-448-6613
E-mail: doozybird@icloud.com; craig@doozybird.com
Web site: Doozybird.com.

BF Publishing, (*978-0-9653327*) 17503 Brushy River Ct., Houston, TX 77095-6905 USA Tel 281-256-1213 Do not confuse with B.F. Publishing, Huntington Beach, CA
E-mail: BFPub1@aol.com
Dist(s): **Origin Bk. Sales, Inc.**

B F Q Press, Incorporated *See* **TotalRecall Pubns.**

B G R Publishing *See* **EMG Networks**

B. L. Moore, (*978-0-578-43796-5*) 310 N. Broad St. S7, Carneys Point, NJ 08069 USA Tel 609-805-7330
E-mail: BLMooreAuthor@gmail.com
Dist(s): **Ingram Content Group.**

B.R. Publishing Co., (*978-0-9625593; 978-1-884538*) 1725 Pinebrook Dr., Knoxville, TN 37909 USA Tel 423-691-1990.

B Small Publishing (GBR) (*978-1-874735; 978-1-902915; 978-1-905710; 978-1-908164; 978-1-911509; 978-1-909767*) *Dist. by* **IPG Chicago.**

B. T. Brooks, (*978-0-9772282*) Orders Addr.: 7015 Crabapple Ln., Kansas City, MO 64129 USA Tel 816-810-1277; 7015 Crabapple Ln., Kansas City, MO 64129 Tel 816-810-1277
E-mail: btbrookspublish@aol.com.

B The Inspired, (*978-1-7339943*) 10246 Gate Dr., Indianapolis, IN 46239 USA Tel 317-213-6555
E-mail: bwarren1553@yahoo.com
Web site: btheinspired.com.

B V Wespat, (*978-0-9713342; 978-0-9788934; 978-0-9819699*) 1641 N. Memorial Dr., Lancaster, OH 43130 USA
Dist(s): **Brodart Co.**
Partners Bk. Distributing, Inc.

B2Z Publishing, Inc., (*978-0-9712070*) Orders Addr.: P.O. Box 307, Severna Park, MD 21146 USA (SAN 254-1068) Tel 410-431-8890; Fax: 410-431-5236
E-mail: towardcure@aol.com
Web site: http://www.mabcie.com.

B3 Publishing, (*978-0-9767849*) Div. of Dream Believer Factory, Inc., Orders Addr.: P.O. Box 360170, Strongsville, OH 44136 USA; Edit Addr.: 19428 Bennington Dr., Strongsville, OH 44136 USA
E-mail: dbfiest@roadrunner.com.

BABAIAN, Edward, (*978-1-7331068*) 2386 E. Del Mar Blvd. No. 104, Pasadena, CA 91107 USA Tel 909-208-5182
E-mail: Eddiewritescopy@gmail.com
Dist(s): **Ingram Content Group.**

Babb, James, (*978-0-9914921*) P.O. Box 547, De Queen, AR 71832 USA Tel 870-584-6131
E-mail: JASUB1017@YAHOO.COM.

Babbling Bks., (*978-0-9798609*) 3849 Prado Dr., Sarasota, FL 34235-3528 USA
E-mail: babblingbooks@yahoo.com.

Babel Books, Inc *See* **Pintos, Yoselem G.**

Babel Corp., (*978-0-9836402; 978-0-9892326; 978-0-9914789; 978-1-7377083*) Pacific Business News Bldg .No. 208 1833 Kalakaua Ave., Honolulu, HI 96815 USA Tel 808-946-3773; Fax: 808-946-3993; *Imprints:* Babel Press U.S.A. (Babel Pr)
E-mail: contact-world@bookandright.com; trans@babel.edu
Web site: http://www.babel.co.jp/usa/; http://www.bookandright.com.

Babel Libros (COL) (*978-958-8445; 978-958-97602; 978-958-98273*) *Dist. by* **Lectorum Pubns.**

Babel Pr. U.S.A. *Imprint of* **Babel Corp.**

Babl Books, Incorporated, (*978-1-68304*) 510 Crestwood Rd, Kaysville, UT 84606 USA Toll Free: 844-311-9649
E-mail: contact@bablbooks.com
Web site: http://www.bablbooks.com.

BaBk.y, (*978-0-9982323; 978-1-952199*) 14595 S. 1515 W., Bluffdale, UT 84065 USA Tel 801-898-2263; *Imprints:* Imagine Creatively (ImagineCreat)
E-mail: andersrosebergbooks@gmail.com; info@babooky.com
Web site: www.andersroseberg.com; https://www.facebook.com/AndersRoseberg/; copycats.andersroseberg.com; babooky.com.

Baboosic Enterprises, LLC, (*978-0-9787660*) P.O. Box 6102, Bloomington, IN 47408-9990 USA
Web site: http://www.bunnyrabbitonthemoon.com.

Babulinka Libros (ESP) *Dist. by* **Lectorum Pubns.**

Baby Abuelita Productions, Inc., (*978-0-9788379; 978-0-615-19145-4*) 6619 S. Dixie Hwy. No. 139, Miami, FL 33143 USA (SAN 851-7207) Toll Free: 877-722-8352
E-mail: cfenster@babyabuelita.com
Web site: http://www.babyabuelita.com.

Baby Einstein Co., LLC, The, (*978-1-892309; 978-1-931580*) Subs. of Walt Disney Productions, 1233 Flower St., Glendale, CA 91201 USA Tel 818-544-4842
E-mail: ellen.portantino@disney.com
Web site: http://www.babyeinstein.com
Dist(s): **Disney Publishing Worldwide**
Penton Overseas, Inc.
Right Start, Inc.
Rounder Kids Music Distribution.

Baby Faye Bks. *Imprint of* **Northstar Entertainment Group, LLC**

Baby Music Boom, Inc., (*978-0-9647786*) Orders Addr.: P.O. Box 62188, Minneapolis, MN 55426 USA Tel 612-470-1667; Fax: 612-474-1297; Toll Free: 888-470-1667; Edit Addr.: 19000 Maple Ln., Deephaven, MN 55331 USA
E-mail: babyboomms@aol.com
Web site: http://www.babymusicboom.com.

Baby Professor (Education Kids) *Imprint of* **Speedy Publishing LLC**

Baby Shadows, (*978-0-9744928*) 150 W. 56th St., Suite 4410, New York, NY 10019 USA (SAN 255-6367)
Web site: http://www.babyshadows.com.

Baby Shark Productions, (*978-0-9765125*) 15338 Roberts Ave., Jacksonville, FL 32218-1833 USA Tel 904-751-1564
E-mail: jackbradford90@aol.com
Web site: http://www.gregmoutafis.com.

Baby Tattoo Bks., (*978-0-9729388; 978-0-9778949; 978-0-9793307; 978-0-9845210; 978-1-61404*) 6045 Longridge Ave., Van Nuys, CA 91401 USA (SAN 255-2159) Tel 818-416-5314
E-mail: info@babytatto.com
Web site: http://www.babytattoo.com
Dist(s): **SCB Distributors.**

Babypie Publishing, (*978-0-9753668; 978-0-9884471; 978-1-945446; 978-1-957972*) 151 Mansfield Rd., Waitsfield, VT 05673 USA Tel 310-823-2661
E-mail: info@relationship-masters.com
Web site: http://www.babypiepublishing.com.

Bacchus Bks., (*978-0-9717952*) Div. of Petmida, Incorporated, P.O. Box 1801, Pacific Palisades, CA 90272 USA Fax: 310-459-4233; Toll Free: 877-604-6522
E-mail: customerservice@domdeluise.com
Web site: http://www.domdeluise.com.

Back Bay Bks. *Imprint of* **Little Brown & Co.**

Back Channel Pr., (*978-0-9767590; 978-0-9789546; 978-1-934582*) 170 Mechanic St., Portsmouth, NH 03801 USA Tel 603-436-9485
E-mail: ngstudio@comcast.net
Web site: http://www.nancygrossmanbooks.com
Dist(s): **Ingram Content Group.**

Back Home Industries, (*978-1-880045*) Orders Addr.: P.O. Box 22495, Milwaukie, OR 97269 USA Tel 503-654-2300; Fax: 503-659-9351; Edit Addr.: 8431 SE 36th Ave., Portland, OR 97222 USA
E-mail: backhome@integrity.com
Web site: http://webs.integrity.com/backhome.

Back In THE BRONX, (*978-0-9657221*) Orders Addr.: P.O. Box 141H, Scarsdale, NY 10583 USA Tel 914-592-1647; Fax: 914-592-4893; Toll Free: 800-727-6695; Edit Addr.: 40 Herkimer Rd., Scarsdale, NY 10583 USA
E-mail: info@backinthebronx.com
Web site: http://www.backinthebronx.com.

Back of the Yards Publishing, (*978-1-7349968*) 126 Cir. Ridge Dr., Burr Ridge, IL 60527 USA Tel 312-520-3694
E-mail: dimucci66@gmail.com
Web site: www.backofyards.com.

Back River Company, The, LLC, (*978-0-9672882*) 238 Robinson St. # 13, Wakefield, RI 02879-3549 USA.

Back Yard Pub., (*978-0-9707560; 978-1-931934*) Div. of Wensel Enterprises, 7720 N. Moonwind Terr., Dunnellon, FL 34433 USA Tel 352-795-0844; Fax: 352-795-0813
E-mail: wwensel@backyardpublisher.com; wwensel@hughes.net; wensel@hughes.net
Web site: http://www.backyardpublisher.com.

Back2Life, Inc., (*978-0-9760151*) 8608 N. Richmond Ave., 1st Flr., Kansas City, MO 64157 USA Tel 816-835-4477; Fax: 816-891-7789
E-mail: ckehoe@back2life.us
Web site: http://www.back2life.us.

Back2Life Ministries *See* **Back2Life, Inc.**

Backinprint.com *Imprint of* **iUniverse, Inc.**

Backintyme *Imprint of* **Backintyme Publishing**

Backintyme Publishing, (*978-0-939479*) 1341 Grapevine Rd., Crofton, KY 42217 USA (SAN 663-2726) Tel 270-985-8568; *Imprints:* Backintyme (Backintyme FL)
E-mail: backintyme@mehrapublishing.com
Web site: http://www.backintyme.biz.

Backpack Bowie *See* **Educational Expertise, LLC**

Backpack Pubs., (*978-0-9854439*) Orders Addr.: P.O. Box 31, South Webster, OH 45682 USA Tel 740-778-3110
E-mail: itsthedoc@yahoo.com
Web site: http://www.backpackpublishers.com.

Backroads Pr., (*978-0-9642371; 978-0-9724033*) Orders Addr.: P.O. Box 651, Mooresville, IN 46158 USA Tel 317-831-2815 (phone/fax); Edit Addr.: 452 Tulip Dr., Mooresville, IN 46158 USA
E-mail: wend@iquest.net
Web site: http://www.publishershomepages.com/php/Backroads_Press.

Backwaters Pr., The, (*978-0-9677149; 978-0-9726187; 978-0-9765231; 978-0-9785782; 978-0-9793934; 978-0-9816936; 978-1-935218*) 3502 N. 52nd St., Omaha, NE 68104-3506 USA Tel 402-451-4052
E-mail: thebackwaterspress@gmail.com
Web site: http://www.thebackwaterspress.org
Dist(s): **SPD-Small Pr. Distribution**
Univ. of Nebraska Pr.

Backwoods Publishing Co., (*978-0-9722501*) Rte. 1, Box 270, Boswell, OK 74727 USA Do not confuse with Backwoods Publishing in Logan, OH.

Backyard Ambassador Reader Publishing Co., (*978-0-9793808*) 2 New Grant Ct., Columbia, SC 29209 USA
E-mail: caroline.bennett@att.com
Web site: http://www.bareader.com.

Backyard Scientist, Inc., (*978-0-9618663; 978-1-888427*) P.O. Box 16966, Irvine, CA 92623 USA (SAN 219-1725) Tel 714-551-2392; Fax: 714-552-5351
E-mail: backyrdsci@aol.com.

Bad Choices Media *See* **One Foot in the Grave Media**

Bad Frog Art/SMG Bks, (*978-0-9795361*) Orders Addr.: 14931 251st Pl. SE, Issaquah, WA 98027 USA
E-mail: steve@stevegritton.info
Web site: www.stevegritton.info.

B.A.D Mouse Publishing, (*978-0-615-40313-7; 978-0-9905353*) 234 Ryder Rd., Manhasset, NY 11030 USA
E-mail: charlotte.lee@lhh.com
Web site: http://www.bringadeadmouse.com.

Bad Publishing, (*978-0-9765414*) 21522 5th Pl. S., DeMoines, WA 98198 USA Tel 206-824-6106
E-mail: edwardhl@hsd401.org.

Badalamenti, Andrew, (*978-0-615-25180-6*) 206 Franklin Rd., Denville, NJ 07834 USA
Dist(s): **Lulu Pr., Inc.**

For full information on wholesalers and distributors, refer to the Wholesaler and Distributor Name Index

dalato, *(978-0-692-80076-8)*
Dist(s): **CreateSpace Independent Publishing Platform.**

adCoaches, Incorporated *See* **Tony Franklin Cos., The**

adgerland Bks. LLC, *(978-0-9765510)* Orders Addr.: 5407 Marsh Woods Dr., McFarland, WI 53558 USA
E-mail: sales@badgerlandbooks.com; joe_martino@uwbucky.com
Web site: http://www.badgerlandbooks.com; http://www.uwbucky.com
Dist(s): **Follett School Solutions.**

adgley Publishing Co., *(978-0-615-16452-6; 978-0-615-18086-1; 978-0-615-22382-7; 978-0-615-48336-8; 978-0-615-48533-1; 978-0-615-49470-8; 978-0-615-50189-5; 978-0-615-51007-1; 978-0-615-52884-7; 978-0-615-53929-4; 978-0-615-55272-9; 978-0-615-56181-3; 978-0-615-56748-8; 978-0-615-58055-5; 978-0-615-60373-5; 978-0-615-62091-6; 978-0-9854403; 978-0-615-75840-4; 978-0-615-76440-5; 978-0-615-78594-3; 978-0-615-80762-1; 978-0-615-80981-6; 978-0-615-81198-7; 978-0-615-84531-9; 978-0-615-86207-1; 978-0-615-88046-4; 978-) 5570 Sherrick Dr., Canal Winchester, OH 43110 USA Tel 614-893-1612*
Web site: http://www.badgleypublishingcompany.com/
Dist(s): **CreateSpace Independent Publishing Platform**
Ingram Content Group
Lulu Pr., Inc.
Dummy Record Do Not USE!!!!.

Badi Publishing Corporation *See* **Changing-Times.net**

Badiru, Adedeji, *(978-0-9768100)* P.O. Box 341441, Beavercreek, OH 45434 USA
E-mail: deji@badiru.com
Web site: abicspublications.com.

Baen Bks., *(978-0-671; 978-1-55594; 978-0-7434)* Orders Addr.: c/o Simon & Schuster, 200 Old Tappan Rd., Old Tappan, NJ 07675 USA Fax: 800-445-6991; Toll Free: 800-223-2336; Edit Addr.: c/o Simon & Schuster, 1230 Ave. of the Americas, New York, NY 10020 USA (SAN 658-8417) Tel 212-698-7000; Toll Free: 800-223-2348 (customer service)
Web site: http://www.simonsays.com/
Dist(s): **Children's Plus, Inc.**
Diamond Comic Distributors, Inc.
Diamond Bk. Distributors
Simon & Schuster
Simon & Schuster, Inc.

Baetzel, Jeff, *(978-0-692-97869-6)* 4531 N. Krueger Rd., Long Grove, IL 60047 USA Tel 847-438-3370
E-mail: jjbaetzel@hotmail.com
Dist(s): **Ingram Content Group.**

BAF Designs, *(978-1-7364012)* 210 Johnson St. 0, GLENVILLE, WV 26351 USA Tel 3047777101
E-mail: baf.designs.contact@gmail.com
Dist(s): **Ingram Content Group.**

Baha'i Publishing, *(978-1-931847; 978-1-61851)* Orders Addr.: 2427 Bond St., University Park, IL 60466-3101 USA Toll Free Fax: 800-705-4923; Toll Free: 800-705-4925; Edit Addr.: 415 Linden Ave., Wilmete, IL 60091-2886 USA Tel 847-425-7950; Fax: 847-425-7951
Web site: http://www.bahaibooksusa.com/
Dist(s): **Follett School Solutions**
Independent Pubs. Group.

Baha'i Publishing Trust, U.S., *(978-0-87743)* 415 Linden Ave., Wilmette, IL 60091 USA
Dist(s): **Baha'i Distribution Service.**

BaHar Publishing, L.C., *(978-0-9718939; 978-0-9818219; 978-0-9837742)* 1429 Commercial St., Waterloo, IA 50702 USA Toll Free: 888-600-6033
E-mail: chaveevahdread@yahoo.com
Web site: http://www.baharpublishing.com.

BaHart Publications / Eight Legs Publishing *See* **Bh Pubns.**

Bahoo Tide, LLC *Imprint of* **Arts Love Expression**

Bailey, Martha, *(978-0-9786448)* 6882 S. Peaceful Hills Rd., Morrison, CO 80465 USA Tel 303-697-4591 (phone/fax)
E-mail: nebjr@earthlink.net

Bailie, Julene, *(978-0-692-81857-2; 978-0-692-90946-1; 978-0-692-13157-2; 978-0-578-59084-4)*
E-mail: juleneba@yahoo.com; juleneba@yahoo.com; juleneba@yahoo.com
Dist(s): **CreateSpace Independent Publishing Platform.**

Bailiwick Pr., *(978-1-934649)* 3836 Tradition St., Fort Collins, CO 80526-3107 USA; 250 W. 57Th St. 15Th Flr., New York, NY 10016
Web site: http://bailiwickpress.com
Dist(s): **Follett School Solutions**
Legato Pubs. Group
MyiLibrary
Publishers Group West (PGW)
ebrary, Inc.

Baird, Jeri, *(978-0-692-07599-9)* 1120 Phillips Ct., Apt D, Montrose, CO 81401 USA Tel 217-512-9074
E-mail: jeribaird11@gmail.com
Dist(s): **Ingram Content Group.**

Baird, Robert Kade, *(978-0-692-99142-8; 978-0-692-99542-6)* 6453 Amanda Michelle Ln., NORTH LAS VEGAS, NV 89086 USA Tel 702-498-7275
E-mail: rafaandthemistbook@gmail.com
Dist(s): **Ingram Content Group.**

Baker Academic, *(978-0-8010)* Div. of Baker Publishing Group, Orders Addr.: P.O. Box 6287, Grand Rapids, MI 49516-6287 USA Toll Free Fax: 800-398-3111 (orders only); Toll Free: 800-877-2665 (orders only); Edit Addr.: 6030 Fulton Ave., Ada, MI 49301 USA Tel 616-676-9185; Fax: 616-676-9573
Web site: http://www.bakerpublishinggroup.com
Dist(s): **Baker Publishing Group**
ebrary, Inc.

Baker, Adam, *(978-0-9967190)* 604 E Colgate, Tempe, AZ 85283 USA Tel 480-695-2731; *Imprints:* Stapled By Mom Publishing (Stapled By Mom)
E-mail: abaker237@yahoo.com.

Baker & Taylor Bks., *(978-0-8480; 978-1-222; 978-1-223)* A Follett Company, Orders Addr.: Commerce Service Ctr., 251 Mt. Olive Church Rd., Commerce, GA 30599 USA (SAN 169-1503) Tel 404-335-5000; Toll Free: 800-775-1200 (customer service); 800-775-1800 (orders); Reno Service Ctr., 1160 Trademark Dr., Suite 111, Reno, NV 89511 (SAN 169-4464) Tel 775-850-3800; Fax: 775-850-3826 (customer service); Toll Free Fax: 800-775-1700 (orders); Edit Addr.: Bridgewater Service Ctr. 1120 US Hwy. 22, E., Bridgewater, NJ 08807 USA (SAN 169-4901) Toll Free: 800-775-1500 (customer service); Momence Service Ctr., 501W. Gladiolus St., Momence, IL 60954-1799 (SAN 169-2100) Tel 815-472-2444 (international customers); Fax: 815-472-9886 (international customers); Toll Free: 800-775-2300 (customer service, academic libraries)
E-mail: btinfo@btol.com
Web site: http://www.btol.com.

Baker & Taylor, CATS, *(978-1-4352; 978-1-4395; 978-1-4420; 978-1-4487; 978-1-4517; 978-1-4806; 978-1-5182)* 1120 Rte. 22 E., Bridgewater, NJ 08807 USA Toll Free: 800-775-1500; *Imprints:* Paw Prints (Paw Prints USA)
Web site: http://www.baker-taylor.com/pawprints
Dist(s): **Baker & Taylor Publisher Services (BTPS)**
Baker & Taylor Bks.
Follett School Solutions.

Baker & Taylor Publisher Services (BTPS), A Follett Company, Orders Addr.: 30 Amberwood Pkwy., Ashland, OH 44805 USA (SAN 631-936X) Fax: 419-281-6883; Toll Free: 800-537-6727; 30 Amberwood Pkwy., Ashland, OH 44805 (SAN 760-9264) Fax: 419-281-6883; Toll Free: 800-537-6727
E-mail: orders@atlasbooks.com; MMG@btpubservices.com; eBooks@btpubservices.com
Web site: http://www.bookmasters.com/.

Baker & Taylor Publishing Group *See* **Readerlink Distribution Services, LLC**

Baker Book House, Incorporated *See* **Baker Publishing Group**

Baker Bks., *(978-0-8010; 978-0-913686; 978-0-8010-9491-0)* Div. of Baker Publishing Group, Orders Addr.: P.O. Box 6287, Grand Rapids, MI 49516-6287 USA (SAN 299-1500) Toll Free Fax: 800-398-3111 (orders only); Toll Free: 800-877-2665 (orders only); Edit Addr.: 6030 E. Fulton, Ada, MI 49301 USA (SAN 201-4041) Tel 616-676-9185; Fax: 616-676-9573
Web site: http://www.bakerpublishinggroup.com
Dist(s): **Baker Publishing Group**
Faith Alive Christian Resources
Follett School Solutions
Twentieth Century Christian Bks.
ebrary, Inc.

Baker, Carol Robinson, *(978-0-692-07947-8; 978-0-692-07962-1; 978-0-692-07967-6)* 9009 Buckingham Ct., Woodway, TX 76712 USA Tel 254-644-6123
E-mail: carolsbaker@gmail.com
Dist(s): **Ingram Content Group.**

Baker College Publishing Co., *(978-1-885545)* Div. of Baker College, 1050 W. Bristol Rd., Flint, MI 48507 USA Toll Free: 800-339-9879
Dist(s): **Follett School Solutions.**

Baker, Debbie, *(978-0-692-04498-8; 978-0-578-91976-8)* 611 N Johnson St., Tallassee, AL 36078 USA Tel 334-415-3553
E-mail: debbiebaker095@gmail.com
Dist(s): **Ingram Content Group.**

Baker, Elizabeth, *(978-0-578-45052-0)* 7091 Webster Rd., Creston, CA 93432 USA Tel 805-400-4357
E-mail: Ed@biochem3d.com
Dist(s): **Ingram Content Group.**

Baker, Helen Interiors, Inc., *(978-0-9743511)* Orders Addr.: P.O. Box 367, West Harwich, MA 02671 USA Tel 508-432-0287; Fax: 508-430-7744; Edit Addr.: 94 Main St., West Harwich, MA 02671 USA
E-mail: hbunce@attbi.com
Web site: http://www.shoppingthecape.com.

Baker Publishing Group, *(978-0-8007; 978-0-8010; 978-1-58743; 978-1-4412; 978-1-4934; 978-1-68196; 978-1-5409)* Orders Addr.: P.O. Box 6287, Grand Rapids, MI 49516-6287 USA Tel 616-676-9573; Toll Free Fax: 800-398-3111 (orders only); Toll Free: 800-877-2665 (orders only); Edit Addr.: 6030 E. Fulton, Ada, MI 49301 USA Tel 616-676-9185; Fax: 616-676-9573; Toll Free Fax: 800-398-3111; Toll Free: 800-877-2665
E-mail: webmaster@bakerpublishinggroup.com
Web site: http://www.bakerbooks.com; http://www.bakerpublishinggroup.com
Dist(s): **Follett School Solutions**
Twentieth Century Christian Bks.
christianaudio
ebrary, Inc.

Baker Trittin Concepts *See* **Baker Trittin Pr.**

Baker Trittin Pr., *(978-0-9729256; 978-0-9752880; 978-0-9787316; 978-0-9814893)* P.O. Box 277, Winona Lake, IN 46590-0277 USA Fax: 574-269-6100; Toll Free: 1-888-741-4386; *Imprints:* Innovative Christian Publications (Innov Chris Pubns); Tweener Press (Tweener Pr)
E-mail: paul@btconcepts.com
Web site: http://www.bakertrittinpress.com; http://www.gospelstoryteller.com.

Baker, Walter H. Company *See* **Baker's Plays**

Baker's Plays, *(978-0-87440)* Div. of Samuel French, Inc., 45 W. 25th St., New York, NY 10010 USA (SAN 202-3717) Tel 212-255-8085; Fax: 212-627-7754
E-mail: info@bakersplays.com
Web site: http://www.bakersplays.com.

Bala Kids *Imprint of* **Shambhala Pubns., Inc.**

Balaam Books LLC, *(978-0-9785585)* 1825 W. Ave., Unit 11, Miami Beach, FL 33139-1441 USA (SAN 850-9972) Tel 305-531-9351; Fax: 305-531-9348
E-mail: Info@BalaamBooks.com
Web site: http://www.BalaamBooks.com.

Balance Bks., Inc., *(978-0-9743908)* P.O. Box 86, Des Plaines, IL 60016-0086 USA
Web site: http://www.balance-books.com
Dist(s): **Distributors, The.**

Balanced Families, *(978-0-9759468)* 432 N. 750 E., Lindon, UT 84042 USA Tel 801-380-3247; Fax: 801-785-3938
E-mail: info@starsofthesky.com.

Balanced Systems, Inc., *(978-0-9760037)* 995 Artdale, White Lake, MI 48383 USA.

Balboa Pr *Imprint of* **Author Solutions, LLC**

Balboa Pr., *(978-1-5043-2314-7)* Div. of Hay House, Inc., 1663 Liberty Dr., Bloomington, IN 47403 USA Tel 877-407-4847
E-mail: customersupport@balboapress.com
Web site: http://www.balboapress.com
Dist(s): **Author Solutions, LLC**
Baker & Taylor Publisher Services (BTPS)
Zondervan.

Balcony Bks., *(978-0-615-46893-8; 978-0-9879732-4-5)* 1606 Willow Ln., McKinney, TX 75070 USA Tel 214-790-4686; 469-879-8696
Dist(s): **CreateSpace Independent Publishing Platform**
Dummy Record Do Not USE!!!!.

Bald Eagle Books *See* **Who Would Win?**

Baldner, Jean V., *(978-0-9615317)* 1618 Burnett Ave., Ames, IA 50010-5337 USA (SAN 694-6526).

Baldwin, Christopher John, *(978-1-938384)* P.O. Box 1141, Northhampton, MA 01061 USA Tel 360-705-2742
E-mail: chrisjohnbaldwin@gmail.com.

Balhund Entertainment, LLC, *(978-0-9743277)* 3018 Paulcrest Dr., Los Angeles, CA 90046 USA Tel 323-848-8778
Web site: http://www.magusgame.com.

Bali Bliss Pr., *(978-0-578-08580-7)* 3017 Riverdale Ave. 3G, Riverdale, NY 10463 USA Tel 609-406-1860
E-mail: bartdavidoff@verizon.net.

Baliko, Janelle A., *(978-0-9799012)* 45486 Locust Grove Dr., Valley Lee, MD 20692-3217 USA
E-mail: itdoesnthavetobepink@yahoo.com
Web site: http://www.itdoesnthavetobepink.com.

Ball, Jennifer, *(978-0-692-35516-9; 978-0-692-35517-6; 978-0-692-56522-3; 978-0-692-13935-6)* 15170 Copeland Way, SPRING HILL, FL 34604 USA Tel 352-650-2717.

Ball, Michael, *(978-0-9765750)* 2000 Bradley Ln., Russellville, AR 72801-4627 USA.

Ball, Rulon Jay *See* **JBall Publishing**

Ballad Productions, *(978-0-9753663)* Orders Addr.: P.O. Box 4, North Miami Beach, FL 33164 USA Tel 786-285-3619; Edit Addr.: 163rd St., Suite No. 4, North Miami Beach, FL 33164 USA
E-mail: drlaz770@aol.com
Web site: http://www.drlaz.com.

Ballantine Bks. *Imprint of* **Random House Publishing Group**

Ballantine, Robert *See* **P.F.B. Publishing**

Ballard & Tighe Pubs., *(978-0-937270; 978-1-55501; 978-1-59989)* Div. of Educational Ideas, Inc., 471 Atlas St., Brea, CA 92821 USA (SAN 200-7991) Tel 714-990-4332; Fax: 714-255-9828; Toll Free: 800-321-4332
Web site: http://www.ballard-tighe.com.

Ballard, Donald W., *(978-0-9768779)* Orders Addr.: 37823 Menard Ct., Fremont, CA 94536 USA Toll Free: 800-506-7401
E-mail: donballard@comcast.net
Web site: http://www.magicalhotel.com.

Ballard Publishing Group, LLC, *(978-1-7324067; 978-1-7332980)* 434 NW 20 Ave., Fort Lauderdale, FL 33311 USA Tel 954-303-8789
E-mail: ballardpublishinggroup@gmail.com.

BalletMet Dance Centre, *(978-0-692-01667-1)* 322 Mount Vernon Ave., Columbus, OH 43235 USA Tel 614-586-8635
E-mail: education@balletmet.org
Web site: http://www.balletmet.org
Dist(s): **BookMasters.**

Ballinger Printing & Graphics, *(978-0-9754957; 978-0-615-20730-8)* 906 Hutchings Ave., Ballinger, TX 76821 USA Tel 325-365-8206; Fax: 325-365-2209; Toll Free: 888-915-8206
E-mail: michael.o.white@att.net; ballingerprinting@verizon.net
Dist(s): **Publishers Services.**

Balloon Bks. *Imprint of* **Sterling Publishing Co., Inc.**

Balloon Magic, *(978-1-931084)* 928 W. 20 N., Orem, UT 84057-1918 USA; *Imprints:* Penny's Publishing (Pennys Pubng)
E-mail: mlh@balloonmagic.com
Web site: http://www.balloonmagic.com.

Ballybunnion Bks., *(978-0-9726340)* Orders Addr.: P.O. Box 6357, Virginia Beach, VA 23456 USA; Edit Addr.: 833 Maitland Dr., Virginia Beach, VA 23454 USA
E-mail: brian@wbrianmurphy.com
Web site: http://www.warrenmurphy.com.

Ballyhoo Books *See* **Ballyhoo BookWorks, Inc.**

Ballyhoo BookWorks, Inc., *(978-0-936335)* Orders Addr.: P.O. Box 534, Shoreham, NY 11786 USA (SAN 697-8487); Edit Addr.: 1 Sylvan Dr., Wading River, NY 11792 USA (SAN 698-2239) Tel 631-929-8148
E-mail: ballyhoo@optonline.net.

Ballyhoo Printing, *(978-0-9742792; 978-0-9800580; 978-0-9976224; 979-8-9855091)* 187 W. Frontage Rd., Lewistown, MT 59457 USA Tel 406-538-7988
E-mail: ballyhoo@ballyhooprinting.com
Web site: http://www.ballyhooprinting.com.

Ballylongford Bks., *(978-0-9753612; 978-0-9961943)* 2588 Welsford Rd., Suite 100, Columbus, OH 43221 USA Tel 614-774-0300.

Balm and Blade Publishing, *(978-0-615-23584-4; 978-0-9841386; 978-1-961261)* 1927 Mountain Rd., Hamburg, PA 19526 USA; *Imprints:* Chrysalis (ChrysalisUSA)
E-mail: balmandblade@gmail.com
Dist(s): **CreateSpace Independent Publishing Platform**
Independently Published.

Balona Bks., *(978-0-9765479; 978-1-934376)* P.O. Box 690106, Stockton, CA 95269-0106 USA
E-mail: author@balona.com; jonathan@balona.com
Web site: http://www.balona.com.

Balticbard Publishing *Imprint of* **Leyva, Barbara**

Baltov, Deanna, *(978-0-692-78706-9)* 909 Agate St, San Diego, CA 92109 USA Tel 973-296-7331
E-mail: dpost24@gmail.com.

Balue Fox Publishing Company *See* **McWilliams Mediation Group Ltd.**

Balzer & Bray *Imprint of* **HarperCollins Pubs.**

Bamboo River Pr., *(978-0-9798173)* 12565 SE Callahan Rd., Portland, OR 97086-9708 USA (SAN 854-4484) Tel 503-761-4360
Web site: http://www.bambooriverpress.com.

Bamboo Zoo, LLC, *(978-0-9774493)* 1637 Dahlia St., Denver, CO 80220 USA (SAN 257-5965) Tel 720-323-4955
E-mail: kim@bamboo-zoo.com
Web site: http://www.bamboo-zoo.com.

Banana Bunch Publishing, *(978-0-9761763)* 2260 Banana St., Saint James City, FL 33956 USA Tel 239-283-9306.

Banana Luna Bks., *(978-0-692-52556-2; 978-0-578-40270-3)* 18400 SW Boones Ferry Rd. G206, TIGARD, OR 97224 USA Tel 503-443-5638.

Banana Oil Bks. *Imprint of* **Cyberwizard Productions**

Banana Patch Pr., *(978-0-9715333; 978-0-9800063)* Orders Addr.: P.O. Box 950, Hanapepe, HI 96716 USA (SAN 254-3087) Tel 808-335-5944; Fax: 808-335-3830; Toll Free: 800-914-5944
E-mail: carolan@aloha.net
Web site: http://www.bananapatchpress.com
Dist(s): **Booklines Hawaii, Ltd.**
Islander Group.

Banana Pr., *(978-0-9799065)* 2935 S. Fish Hatchery Rd., No. 3, Suite 254, Fitchburg, WI 53711 USA Tel 608-658-0023
E-mail: info@bananalady.com
Web site: http://www.bananalady.com.

Banana Tree Publishing, *(978-1-7327484)* 4936 SE 114th Ave, Portland, OR 97266 USA Tel 971-865-6415
E-mail: melinda.m.tran@outlook.com
Web site: www.bananatreepublishing.com.

Bancroft Pr., *(978-0-9631246; 978-0-9635376; 978-1-890862; 978-1-61088)* P.O. Box 65360, Baltimore, MD 21209-9945 USA Tel 410-358-0658; Fax: 410-764-1967; Toll Free: 800-637-7377 Do not confuse with Bancroft Pr., San Rafael, CA
E-mail: bruceb@bancroftpress.com
Web site: http://www.bancroftpress.com
Dist(s): **Academic Bk. Ctr., Inc.**
Baker & Taylor Publisher Services (BTPS)
Book Wholesalers, Inc.
Bk. Hse., Inc., The
Brodart Co.
Coutts Information Services
Emery-Pratt Co.
Follett School Solutions
Mackin Library Media
Midwest Library Service
Smashwords
Yankee Bk. Peddler, Inc.

Band of Brothers Bks., *(978-1-7321278; 978-1-7376576; 979-8-9877626)* 13000 Green Valley Dr., Oklahoma City, OK 73120 USA Tel 405-210-5336
E-mail: bhale1978@gmail.com.

Banda Pr. International, Inc., *(978-0-9773175)* 6050 Stetson Hills Blvd., No. 313, Colorado Springs, CO 80922 USA
Web site: http://www.bandapress.com.

Bandai Entertainment, Inc., *(978-1-58354; 978-1-59409; 978-1-60496)* Div. of Bandai Entertainment, Inc., 5551 Katella Ave., Cypress, CA 90630 USA Tel 714-816-9760; Fax: 714-816-6708; Toll Free: 877-772-6463
Web site: http://www.bandai-ent.com
Dist(s): **Diamond Comic Distributors, Inc.**
Diamond Bk. Distributors
Follett School Solutions.

B&B Publishing, *(978-0-9894693; 978-0-9907476)* 1970 N. Leslie St. No. 560, Pahrump, NV 89060 USA Tel 641-424-0367
E-mail: bvos98@gmail.com.

B&H Bks. *Imprint of* **B&H Publishing Group**

B&H Kids *Imprint of* **B&H Publishing Group**

B&H Publishing Group *See* **B&H Publishing Group**

†B&H Publishing Group, *(978-0-8054; 978-0-87981; 978-1-55819; 978-1-58640; 978-0-8400; 978-1-4336)* Div. of LifeWay Christian Resources of the Southern Baptist Convention, One LifeWay Plaza MSN 114, Nashville, TN 37234-0114 USA (SAN 201-937X) Tel 615-251-2520; Fax: 615-251-5026 (Books Only); 615-251-2036 (Bibles Only); 615-251-2413 (Gifts/Supplies Only); Toll Free: 800-725-5416; 800-251-3225 (retailers); 800-296-4036 (orders/returns); 800-448-8032 (consumers); 800-458-2772 (churches); *Imprints:* Holman Bible Publishers (Holman Bible); B&H Books (B&H Bks.); B&H Kids (B&H Kids)
E-mail: broadmanholman@lifeway.com; heather.counsellor@bhpublishinggroup.com; laurene.martin@lifeway.com; tom.gilbert@lifeway.com
Web site: http://www.bhpublishinggroup.com; http://www.lifeway.com
Dist(s): **Follett School Solutions**
Simon & Schuster, Inc.
christianaudio; *CIP.*

B&J Marketing LLC, *(978-0-9774606)* 17 Robbins Wilks Rd., Bassfield, MS 39421 USA Tel 601-731-2447
E-mail: wastvedt@bellsouth.net.

Bangzoom Pubs., *(978-0-9728646; 978-0-9772927; 978-0-9779099)* Div. of Bangzoom Software, Inc., 14

Storrs Ave., Braintree, MA 02184 USA (SAN 256-6923) Toll Free: 800-589-7333
Web site: http://www.bangzoom.com
Dist(s): **Partners Pubs. Group, Inc.**

Bangzoom Software, Incorporated *See* **Bangzoom Pubs.**

Banis & Associates *See* **Science & Humanities Pr.**

Banks, A J & Associates, Incorporated *See* **BaHar Publishing, L.C.**

Banner of Truth, The, *(978-0-85151)* Orders Addr.: P.O. Box 621, Carlisle, PA 17013 USA Tel 717-249-5747; Fax: 717-249-0604; Toll Free: 800-263-8085; Edit Addr.: 63 E. Louther St., Carlisle, PA 17013 USA (SAN 112-1553)
E-mail: info@banneroftruth.org
Web site: http://www.banneroftruth.co.uk
Dist(s): **Spring Arbor Distributors, Inc.**

Banta, Sandra, *(978-0-9799729)* 16849A Willow Glen Rd., Brownsville, CA 95919 USA Tel 530-675-2010
E-mail: sfbanta@aol.com
Web site: http://www.lilionesbooks.com.

Bantam *Imprint of* **Random House Publishing Group**

Bantam Doubleday Dell Large Print Group, Inc., *(978-0-385)* Orders Addr.: 2451 S. Wolf Rd., Des Plaines, IL 60018 USA Toll Free: 800-323-9872 (orders); 800-258-4233 (EDI ordering); Edit Addr.: 1540 Broadway, New York, NY 10036-4094 USA
Dist(s): **Penguin Random Hse. Distribution**
Penguin Random Hse. LLC
Beeler, Thomas T. Pub.

Banyan Bks., *(978-0-615-63108-0)* 251 Bethany Farms Dr., Ball Ground, GA 30107 USA Tel 770-315-1244 Do not confuse with Banyan Books in Miami, FL, Santa Barbara, CA
Web site: www.juliekorzenko.com
Dist(s): **CreateSpace Independent Publishing Platform.**

Banyan Hypnosis Center for Training & Services, Inc., *(978-0-9712290)* 1431 Warner Ave. Ste. E, Tustin, CA 92780-6444 USA (SAN 253-9381)
E-mail: Maureen@hypnosiscenter.com.

Banyan Publishing, Incorporated *See* **Banyan Hypnosis Center for Training & Services, Inc.**

Banyon Publishing, Inc., *(978-0-9747960)* 235 W Brandon Blvd., Suite 223, Brandon, FL 33511 USA Fax: 813-243-0701
E-mail: banyonpublishing@aol.com
Web site: http://www.banyonpublishing.com.

Baobab Pr., *(978-1-936097)* 121 California Ave., Reno, NV 89509 USA (SAN 858-298X) Tel 775-786-1188
Dist(s): **Publishers Group West (PGW).**

Baobab Publishing, *(978-0-692-52890-7; 978-0-692-52959-1; 978-0-692-52981-2; 978-0-692-52993-5; 978-0-692-54987-2; 978-0-692-55392-3; 978-0-692-59517-6; 978-0-692-59520-6; 978-0-692-63252-9; 978-0-692-66153-6; 978-0-692-68957-8; 978-0-692-72627-3; 978-0-9982231; 978-1-947045) 7421 Penland Dr., Riverdale, GA 30296 USA Tel 770-376-5243*
Dist(s): **CreateSpace Independent Publishing Platform.**

Baptist Publishing Hse., *(978-0-89114)* Div. of Baptist Missionary Assn. of America, P.O. Box 7270, Texarkana, TX 75505-7270 USA (SAN 183-6544) Tel 870-772-4550; Fax: 870-772-5451; Toll Free: 800-333-1442
E-mail: info@bph.org; pathway@bph.org
Web site: http://www.bph.org.

Baptist Spanish Publishing Hse./Casa Bavtista de Publicaciones: Mundo Hispano, *(978-0-311)* 7000 Alabama St., El Paso, TX 79914 USA (SAN 299-920X) Tel 916-566-9656; Fax: 916-562-6502; Toll Free: 800-755-5958
E-mail: cbpsales1@juno.com
Web site: http://casabautista.org.

Bar charts Publishing, Inc. *See* **BarCharts Publishing, Inc.**

Bara Publishing, *(978-0-9842517)* 131 Gilbert Dr., Beaufort, NC 28516 USA Tel 252-838-1803
Dist(s): **Follett School Solutions**
ebrary, Inc.

Barabara Pr., *(978-0-9719097)* 5929 S. Kolmar Ave., Chicago, IL 60629 USA Tel 773-735-1176 (phone/fax)
E-mail: captsma@comcast.net
Web site: http://www.barabarapress.com.

Barach Publishing, *(978-0-9767453)* 900 N. Walnut Creek, Suite 100, No. 280, Mansfield, TX 76063 USA
E-mail: lgonzalez@barachpublishing.com
Web site: http://www.barachpublishing.com.

Barany Publishing, *(978-0-9832960; 978-0-9895004; 978-1-944841)* 771 Kingston Ave. No. 108, Oakland, CA 94611 USA Tel 510-333-7320
E-mail: BETH@BETHBARANY.COM
Web site: http://www.bethbarany.com
Dist(s): **Smashwords.**

Barbara, *(978-1-7362610)* 204 Elmont Dr., Columbia, SC 29203 USA Tel 803-754-4569
E-mail: bcmdawhorn@gmail.com.

Barbara Browning, *(978-0-578-50827-6; 978-0-578-50828-3)* 1207 Danbury Rd., Houston, TX 77055 USA Tel 832-549-6339
E-mail: barbbrowning1207@yahoo.com.

Barbary Coast Books *See* **Gold Street Pr.**

Barber, *(978-0-578-89567-3)* 16835 E Lake Ave, Centennial, CO 80016 USA Tel 720-226-5498
E-mail: jlexbarber@outlook.com.

Barbour & Company, Incorporated *See* **Barbour Publishing, Inc.**

Barbour Bibles *Imprint of* **Barbour Publishing, Inc.**

Barbour Bks. *Imprint of* **Barbour Publishing, Inc.**

Barbour Espanol *Imprint of* **Barbour Publishing, Inc.**

Barbour Publishing, Inc., *(978-0-916441; 978-1-55748; 978-1-57748; 978-1-58660; 978-1-59310; 978-1-59789; 978-1-60260; 978-1-60742; 978-1-61626; 978-1-62029; 978-1-62416; 978-1-62836; 978-1-63058; 978-1-63409; 978-1-944836; 978-1-68322; 978-1-64352; 978-1-63609; 979-8-89151) Orders Addr.: P.O. Box 719, Uhrichsville, OH 44683 USA (SAN 295-7094) Fax: 740-922-5948; Toll Free Fax: 800-220-5948; Toll Free: 800-852-8010; Imprints:* Barbour Books (Barbour Bks); Barbour Espanol (BarbEspanol); Casa Promesa (Casa Promesa); Shiloh Run Studios (Shiloh Run); Barbour Bibles (Barb Bibles); Shiloh Kidz (Shiloh Kidz)
E-mail: info@barbourbooks.com
Web site: http://www.barbourbooks.com
Dist(s): **Anchor Distributors**
Firebrand Technologies
Follett School Solutions
Spring Arbor Distributors, Inc.

Barcelona Pubs., *(978-0-9624080; 978-1-891278; 978-1-937440; 978-1-945411)* 135 Glen Ave, Glen Rock, PA 17327 USA (SAN 298-6299) Tel 717-781-4972; Toll Free: 866-620-6943
E-mail: warehouse@barcelonapublishers.com; stevens@barcelonapublishers.com
Web site: http://www.barcelonapublishers.com
Dist(s): **MyiLibrary**
Ware-Pak, Inc.
ebrary, Inc.

BarCharts Publishing, Inc., *(978-1-57222; 978-1-4232)* 6000 Pk. of Commerce Blvd. Suite D, Boca Raton, FL 33487-8230 USA (SAN 299-5026) Tel 561-989-3666 ext.3054; Fax: 561-989-3722; Toll Free: 800-226-7799
E-mail: jmijares@barcharts.com
Web site: http://www.quickstudy.com; http://www.barcharts.com
Dist(s): **Firebrand Technologies**
Follett School Solutions.

Bard College Pubns. Office, *(978-0-941276; 978-1-931493; 978-1-936192)* P.O. Box 5000, Annandale-on-Hudson, NY 12504-5000 USA Tel 845-758-7872 (7418); Fax: 845-758-7554; *Imprints:* Center for Curatorial Studies (Ctr Curatorial Studies)
E-mail: admission@bard.edu; info@levy.org
Web site: http://www.levy.org; http://www.bard.edu
Dist(s): **D.A.P./Distributed Art Pubs.**

Bard, Frank, *(978-0-9767098)* Orders Addr.: 3801 Corbett Rd., North Lewisburg, OH 43060-9616 USA Tel 937-869-0235
E-mail: fbard@ctcn.net
Web site: http://www.ctcn.net/~febard.

Bardic Pr., *(978-0-9745667)* P.O. Box 761, Oregon House, CA 95962-0761 USA Tel 539-692-1180
E-mail: info@bardic-press.com; andrew@bardic-press.com
Web site: http://www.bardic-press.com.

Bardin & Marsee Publishing, *(978-0-9770169; 978-0-9792394; 978-0-9840857; 978-1-60969)* po box 190351, Birmingham, AL 35219 USA (SAN 854-6215) Toll Free: 866-846-4338
E-mail: bobby@bardinmarsee.com
Web site: http://www.bardinmarsee.com.

Bare Bones Training & Consulting Company *See* **Straus, Jane**

BareBones Publishing *See* **Neighborhood Pubs.**

Barefoot Bks., Ltd. (GBR) *(978-1-84148; 978-1-898000; 978-1-901223; 978-1-902283; 978-1-905236; 978-1-84686; 978-1-78285) Dist. by* **Children Plus.**

Barefoot Bks., Inc., *(978-1-84148; 978-1-898000; 978-1-901223; 978-1-902283; 978-1-905236; 978-1-84686; 978-1-64686; 979-8-88859)* Orders Addr.: 2067 Massachusetts Ave., 5th Fl., Cambridge, MA 02140 USA Tel 866-417-2369; Fax: 888-346-9138
E-mail: ussales@barefootbooks.com
Web site: http://www.barefootbooks.com
Dist(s): **Banta Packaging & Fulfillment.**

Barefoot Pr., *(978-1-882133)* Orders Addr.: P.O. Box 28514, Raleigh, NC 27611 USA (SAN 248-5656) Tel 919-834-1164; Edit Addr.: 700 W. Morgan St., Raleigh, NC 27603 USA (SAN 248-5664).

Barefoot Seeker: Art by Emily Brunner, *(978-1-7361272)* 11455 Cumpston St., North Hollywood, CA 91601 USA Tel 360-244-0311
E-mail: barefootseekerart@gmail.com
Web site: www.barefootseeker.com.

Barker, Lesley, *(978-0-9763211)* 1630 Rathford Dr., Saint Louis, MO 63146-3911 USA
E-mail: asklesley@teamlesley.com
Web site: http://www.teamlesley.com.

Barker, Thomas Bks., Photography, & Films, 1223 Lake Point Dr., Webster, NY 14580 USA Tel 585-265-4015
E-mail: tbbeqa@mac.com
Web site: tombarker.net.

Barker, William J. , Jr., *(978-1-7343242)* 410 Roundhill Rd., St. Davids, PA 19087 USA Tel 610-859-7300
E-mail: bbarker@visitvisual.com.

Barksdale, Colleen, *(978-0-578-50447-6)* 21155 Fondant Ave. N., Forest Lake, MN 55025 USA Tel 651-464-0094
E-mail: 2019authoroflife@gmail.com.

Barlow Bk. Publishing (CAN) *(978-0-9917411; 978-0-9937656; 978-1-988025) Dist. by* **IPG Chicago.**

Barmarie Pubns., *(978-0-9619463)* 735 Nardo Rd., Encinitas, CA 92024 USA (SAN 245-0070) Tel 760-753-6950.

Barnaby & Co., *(978-0-9642836; 978-0-615-74648-7; 979-8-9877544)* 30 W. Chester St., Nantucket, MA 02554 USA Tel 508-901-1793.

Barnaby Bks., Inc., *(978-0-940350)* 3290 Pacific Heights Rd., Honolulu, HI 96813 USA (SAN 217-5010) Fax: 808-531-0089
E-mail: barnaby@lava.net; publisher@barnabybooks.com
Web site: http://www.barnabybooks.com
Dist(s): **Bess Pr., Inc.**

Barner, Oren , *(978-0-578-19413-4)* 5534 Charlotte Dr., New Orleans, LA 70122 USA.

Barnes & Noble Bks.-Imports, *(978-0-389)* 4720 Boston Way, Lanham, MD 20706 USA (SAN 206-7803) Tel 301-459-3366; Toll Free: 800-462-6420
Dist(s): **Rowman & Littlefield Publishers, Inc.**

Barnes & Noble, Inc., *(978-0-7607; 978-0-88029; 978-1-4028; 978-1-4114; 978-1-4351; 978-1-61551; 978-1-61552; 978-1-61553; 978-1-61554; 978-1-61555; 978-1-61556; 978-1-61557; 978-1-61558; 978-1-61559; 978-1-61560; 978-1-61679; 978-1-61680; 978-1-61681; 978-1-61682; 978-1-61683; 978-1-61684; 978-1-61685; 978-1-61686; 978-1-61687; 978-1-61688; 978-1-970008) 76 Ninth Ave., 9th Flr., New York, NY 10011 USA (SAN 141-3651) Tel 212-414-6385; 122 Fifth Ave., New York, NY 10011; Imprints:* Blackbirch Press, Incorporated (Blackbirch Pr); SparkNotes (SparkNotes)
E-mail: smcculloch@bn.com
Dist(s): **Bookazine Co., Inc.**
Dover Pubns., Inc.
Sterling Publishing Co., Inc.

Barnes & Noble Pr., *(978-1-68101; 978-1-5380; 978-1-9870; 978-1-0787; 978-1-6635; 978-1-6662; 978-0-578-90031-5; 978-1-6685; 979-8-7655; 979-8-218-02565-6; 979-8-8231; 979-8-3692; 979-8-8556)* 76 Ninth Ave., New York, NY 10011 USA; 1166 Avenue of the Americas 18th Flr., New York, NY 10036
Web site: print.nookpress.com; press.barnesandnobel.com.

BARNES, DONNA, *(978-1-7337993)* 122 Nelson St., Durham, NC 27707 USA Tel 919-680-0805
E-mail: quasifree@msn.com
Dist(s): **Ingram Content Group.**

Barnes Printing, *(978-0-9658838; 978-0-9863483; 978-1-948254)* 1076 Klopman Mill Rd., Denton, NC 27239-7305 USA Tel 336-859-1964; Fax: 336-859-4923
E-mail: elizabeth@barnesprinting.com
Web site: www.barnesprinting.com.

Barnesyard Bks., *(978-0-9764681)* P.O. Box 254, Sergeantsville, NJ 08557 USA Tel 609-397-6600; Fax: 609-397-3262
E-mail: info@barnesyardbooks.com
Web site: http://www.barnesyardbooks.com
Dist(s): **Follett School Solutions.**

Barnette, Donald, *(978-0-9747816)* 591 Mira Vista Ave., Oakland, CA 94610-1928 USA.

Barnhardt & Ashe Publishing, Inc., *(978-0-9715402; 978-0-9801744)* 444 Brickell Ave., Suite 51, PMB 432, Miami, FL 33131 USA Toll Free: 800-283-6360
E-mail: barnhardtashe@aol.com
Web site: http://www.barnhardtashepublishing.com.

Barnsley Ink *Imprint of* **Write Way Publishing Co. LLC**

Baron Ridge Productions, *(978-0-692-02990-9; 978-0-692-03128-5)* 7703 W. Shady Ln., Wichita, KS 67205 USA Tel 316-409-6498
E-mail: mindycook@cox.net; mindy@baronridgeproductions.com
Web site: http://www.baronridgeproductions.org.

Barr, Tricia, *(978-0-9989777; 978-1-7337494)* P.O. Box 1224, SAHUARITA, AZ 85629 USA Tel 520-954-4422
Dist(s): **Ingram Content Group.**

Barranca Pr., *(978-1-939604)* 1450 Couse St. (No. 10), Taos, NM 87571 USA Tel 575-613-1026
E-mail: lisa@barrancapress.com
Web site: www.barrancapress.com.

Barre Chord Pr., *(978-1-7369445)* 547 Roslyn Rd., East Williston, NY 11596 USA Tel 516-642-9426
E-mail: lisa.czarina.michaud@gmail.com.

Barren Hill Bks., *(978-0-9769896)* 646 Highland Ave., South Portland, ME 04106 USA Tel 207-767-3268
E-mail: info@BarrenHillBooks.com
Web site: http://www.barrenhillbooks.com/.

Barrera, Elizabeth Paige, *(978-0-9984620; 978-0-578-51830-5; 979-8-9861598)* 4025 Burke Rd., Pasadena, TX 77504 USA Tel 713-550-7220; *Imprints:* Infinity Flower Publishing, LLC (MYiD_A_INFINIT)
E-mail: epaigeburks.book@gmail.com
Web site: http://www.epaigeburks.com/.

Barrett, Dave, *(978-0-578-21461-0; 978-0-578-21462-7; 978-0-578-60756-6; 978-0-578-60757-3)* 5 Independence Ave., Hampden, ME 04444 USA.

Barrett's Bookshelf, *(978-0-9728731)* 16165 SW Inverurie Rd., Lake Oswego, OR 97035 USA Tel 503-697-4208.

†Barricade Bks., Inc., *(978-0-934878; 978-0-942637; 978-0-9623032; 978-1-56980)* 2037 Lemoine Ave., Suite 362, Fort Lee, NJ 07024 USA (SAN 299-1780) Tel 201-944-7600; Toll Free: 800-592-6657; 4501 Forbes Blvd., Lanham, MD 20706
E-mail: customerservice@barricadebooks.com
Web site: http://www.barricadebooks.com
Dist(s): **Follett School Solutions**
MyiLibrary
National Bk. Network
Partners Bk. Distributing, Inc.
ebrary, Inc.; *CIP.*

Barricks, Jeri Ministry, *(978-0-9743512)* P.O. Box 347, Buffalo, NY 14225 USA Fax: 716-685-6839
E-mail: jeribar37@hotmail.com
Web site: http://www.jeribarricks.net.

Barrier Breaker Publishing Inc., *(978-0-9823078)*
E-mail: ave@barrierbreakeronline.com
Web site: http://www.barrierbreakeronline.com.

Barringer Publishing, *(978-0-9825109; 978-0-9828425; 978-0-9831989; 978-0-9833088; 978-0-9839050; 978-0-9851184; 978-0-9882034; 978-0-9891694; 978-0-9896338; 978-0-9903935; 978-0-9908209; 978-0-9961973; 978-0-9989069; 978-1-7339837; 978-1-7352525; 978-1-954396)* 2317 Harrier Run, Naples, FL 34105 USA
Web site: barringerpublishing.com
Dist(s): **Follett School Solutions.**

Barron's Educational Series, Inc. *Imprint of* **Kaplan Publishing**

Barrow, Shelley *See* **Mikenzi's Kardz & Bks. Llc.**

Barsotti Bks., *(978-0-9642112; 978-0-9818188)* 2239 Hidden Valley Ln., Camino, CA 95709-9722 USA Tel 530-642-8341; Fax: 530-642-9703
E-mail: jb@barsottibooks.com
Web site: http://www.barsottibooks.com.

Bartleby Pr., *(978-0-910155; 978-0-935437)* 8600 Foundry St. Savage Mill Box 2043, Savage, MD 20763 USA (SAN 241-2098) Tel 301-949-2443; Fax: 301-949-2205; Toll Free: 800-953-9929
E-mail: Inquiries@bartlebythepublisher.com
Web site: http://www.BartlebythePublisher.com
Dist(s): **Casemate Pubs. & Bk. Distributors, LLC**
Independent Pubs. Group
MyiLibrary.

Barton Bks., *(978-0-615-69695-9; 978-0-615-78343-7)* Orders Addr.: 4505 Sentinel Ct., Rocklin, CA 95677 USA Tel 916-787-0962; *Imprints:* Flickerfawn (Flickerfawn)
E-mail: dredsovm@me.com; dredsovm@wavecable.com
Web site: www.flickerfawn.com; www.FionaThornBook.com; www.jbartonbooks.com.

Barton, Carol, *(978-1-7330134)* 165 Lost River Ln., Bowling Green, KY 42104 USA Tel 270-779-5563
E-mail: noel10new2@twc.com.

Barton, D.C. Publishing, *(978-0-9759426)* P.O. Box 3057, Lakeland, FL 33801-6602 USA Tel 863-665-5986
E-mail: dfcbible@aol.com.

Barton Publications, *(978-0-9778455)* Orders Addr.: 1613 Sunrise Ln., Eau Claire, WI 54703-2574 USA
E-mail: bartonpub@ymail.com
Web site: http://www.westmusic.com/1002410-print-music-books/m1090-music-therapy-books/m1090i-texts/biomedical-foundations-of-music-as-therapy-838708.htm
Dist(s): **West Music Co.**

Barton-Veerman Co., *(978-0-9724616; 978-0-9978516)* 205 N Washington St, Wheaton, IL 60187 USA Tel 630-871-1212
E-mail: accounting@livingstonecorp.com
Web site: http://www.livingstonecorp.com
Dist(s): **BookBaby.**

Bartram Team, The, *(978-0-615-31220-0)* 1251 Pine Valley Dr., New Bern , NC 28562 USA.

Bas Relief, LLC, *(978-0-9657472)* Orders Addr.: P.O. Box 645, Union, WV 24983 USA Tel 304-832-6647
E-mail: Barea@basrelief.org
Web site: http://www.basrelief.org
Dist(s): **Follett School Solutions.**

Bas Relief Publishing *See* **Bas Relief, LLC**

Basement Monster Productions, The, *(978-0-692-98462-8; 978-1-7359041)* 140-10 84th Dr. Apt. 3E, Jamaica, NY 11435 USA Tel 917-440-0714; Fax: 917-440-0714
E-mail: daniel.obrienis@gmail.com
Web site: www.danielostudios.com.

Bases Loaded Bks. *Imprint of* **ChildrenzBks.**

Basic Black Publishing, *(978-0-9801320)* Orders Addr.: 8584 W. Appleton Ave., Unit X, Milwaukee, WI 53225 USA.

†Basic Bks., *(978-0-201; 978-0-465; 978-0-7382; 978-0-7867; 978-0-8133; 978-0-86531; 978-0-931188; 978-0-938410; 978-0-941423; 978-1-56025; 978-1-56858; 978-1-56924; 978-1-58005; 978-1-58243; 978-1-878067; 978-1-887178; 978-1-4789; 978-1-5416)* A Member of Perseus Books Group, Orders Addr.: 5500 Central Ave., Boulder, CO 80301-2877 USA Fax: 303-449-3356 (customer service); Toll Free: 800-371-1669 (customer service); Edit Addr.: 387 Park Ave., S., New York, NY 10016 USA (SAN 201-4521) Tel 212-340-8100; Fax: 212-340-8135; 1290 Avenue of the Americas, New York, NY 10104; *Imprints:* Seal Press (SealPrHBG)
E-mail: perseus.orders@perseusbooks.com
Web site: http://www.perseusbooksgroup.com; http://www.perseusbooksgroup.com/basic/home.jsp
Dist(s): **Blackstone Audio, Inc.**
Follett School Solutions
Hachette Bk. Group
MyiLibrary
ebrary, Inc.; *CIP.*

Basic Distribution, Inc., 360 Hurst St., Linden, NJ 07036 USA Tel 908-523-0555; Fax: 908-523-0373
E-mail: ssullivan@basicdistributioninc.com
Web site: http://www.basicdistributioninc.com.

Basic ESL *Imprint of* **Bilingual Dictionaries, Inc.**

Basic Health Pubns., Inc., *(978-1-59120)* 28812 Top of the World Dr., Laguna Beach, CA 92651 USA (SAN 858-4893) Tel 949-715-7327; Fax: 949-415-7328; Toll Free: 800-575-8890 (orders only)
E-mail: ngoldfind@basicmediagroup.com
Web site: http://www.basichealthpub.com
Dist(s): **Follett School Solutions**
Ingram Publisher Services
Two Rivers Distribution.

Basic Knowledge Publishing Co., *(978-1-885501)* 1024 Debbie Ln., Maryville, MO 64468 USA Tel 816-562-2665.

Basic Skills Assessment & Educational Services, *(978-1-888786)* 19146 S. Molalla Ave., Oregon City, OR 97045-8975 USA Tel 503-650-5282; Fax: 503-557-2953
E-mail: basicsk@MSN.COM
Web site: http://www.basicskills.net.

Basketball Fundamentals *See* **SportAmerica**

Basm Bks., *(978-1-7322337; 979-8-218-23590-1)* 4610 Chattahoochee Xing SE, Marietta, GA 30067 USA Tel 770-547-5215
E-mail: bailabooks@gmail.com.

Basone, Pina *See* **Pina Bird Bks. LLC**

Bass Cove Bks., *(978-0-9630074)* 57 North St., Kennebunkport, ME 04046 USA Tel 207-967-4152
E-mail: amabee@adelphia.net.

Bass, Robert Enterprises, *(978-0-692-09813-4; 978-0-578-52952-3)* 67 Stratford Dr., Penrose, NC 28766 USA Tel 828-553-8741
E-mail: adalynelliott@gmail.com
Dist(s): **Ingram Content Group.**

Bass, Sheila, *(978-0-9766366)* 23 Conn. St., Woodsville, NH 03785 USA
E-mail: a_15bass@yahoo.com.

Bassan, Malca, *(978-0-9744039; 978-0-692-25535-3; 979-8-218-15472-1; 979-8-218-26389-8)* 9801 Collins Ave., Apt. 15Q, Bal Harbor, FL 33154 USA Tel 305-868-0365; Fax: 305-865-6992
E-mail: mabassan27@gmail.com.

Bassett, Maurice, *(978-0-9760402; 978-0-9762653; 978-1-60025)* Orders Addr.: P.O. Box 839, Anna Maria, FL 34216-0839 USA Tel 919-423-2460
E-mail: reinventingyourself@gmail.com
Web site: http://www.abrahammaslow.com; http://www.stevechandler.com; http://www.mauricebassett.com.

Bastion Pr., Inc., *(978-0-9714392; 978-1-59263)* Orders Addr.: P.O. Box 46753, Seattle, WA 98146 USA; Edit Addr.: 8405 16th Ave., SW., Seattle, WA 98106-2365 USA Tel 206-763-3368; Fax: 206-763-3370 Do not confuse with Bastion Pr., Los Angeles, CA
E-mail: jim@bastionpress.com
Web site: http://www.bastionpress.com
Dist(s): **Studio 2 Publishing, Inc.**

Bat Wing Pr *Imprint of* **Harbor Hse.**

Batchelor, Leyetta, *(978-0-578-44012-5)* 6193 Aurelian Springs Rd, Halifax, NC 27839 USA Tel 252-326-3341
E-mail: leyetta13@gmail.com.

Bat-El Publishing, *(978-0-9832025)* 3400 Colville Pl., Encino, CA 91436 USA Tel 818-461-9294
E-mail: talyanai7@gmail.com.

Batelier Publishing, *(978-0-9789429)* 3140 Bourbon St. Cir., Rockwall, TX 75032 USA
E-mail: batelierpublishing@yahoo.com
Web site: http://www.batelier.bravehost.com.

Bates, Carol *See* **Jolly Journey Publishing**

Bates Jackson Engraving Co., Inc., *(978-1-932583; 978-0-9831157; 978-0-9885895)* 17-21 Elm St., Buffalo, NY 14203 USA Tel 716-854-3000; Fax: 716-847-1965
E-mail: ed@batesjackson.com
Web site: http://www.batesjackson.com.

Batfish Bks., *(978-0-9728653)* Div. of O'Neill, Michael P. Photography, Inc., P.O. Box 32909, Palm Beach Gardens, FL 33420-2909 USA (SAN 255-1780) Tel 305-333-7166; Fax: 561-840-1939
E-mail: mpo@msn.com
Web site: http://www.batfishbooks.com
Dist(s): **Follett School Solutions**
Southern Bk. Service.

†**Bathtub Row Pr.,** *(978-0-941232)* Orders Addr.: P.O. Box 43, Los Alamos, NM 87544 USA (SAN 276-9603) Tel 505-662-2660; Fax: 505-662-6312; Edit Addr.: 1050 Bathtub Row, Los Alamos, NM 87544 USA (SAN 241-9025)
E-mail: shar5992@gmail.com
Web site: http://losalamoshistory.org; *CIP.*

Battat, Inc., *(978-0-9794542; 978-0-9843722; 978-0-9844904; 978-0-9883165; 978-0-9891839; 978-0-9963272; 978-0-692-81454-3; 978-0-692-82334-7; 978-0-692-82578-5; 978-0-692-82579-2; 978-0-692-89111-7; 978-0-692-96027-1; 978-0-692-98872-5; 978-0-692-04479-7; 978-0-692-07793-1; 978-0-692-08323-9; 978-0-692-10296-1; 978-0-692-13583-9; 978-0-578-40814-9; 978-0-578-46375-9; 978-0-578-50767-5; 978-0-578-50822-1; 978-0-578-51878-7; 978-0-578-53553-1; 978-0-578-54717-6; 978-0-578-62758-8; 978-0-578-63262-9; 978-0) 1560 Military Tpke., Plattsburgh, NY 12901-7458 USA (SAN 853-4683).*

Battle Creek Area Mathematics & Science Ctr., *(978-1-933281)* 765 Upton Ave., Battle Creek, MI 49015 USA Tel 269-965-9440
Web site: http://bcmsc.k12.mi.us.

Batyah & Assocs. Publishing, *(978-0-9749571)* 141 California St, Highland Park, MI 48203 USA
E-mail: baroberts07@yahoo.com
Web site: http://www.batasspub.com.

Batyah Productions, Inc., *(978-0-9649608)* 6434 Saxet St., Houston, TX 77055-5317 USA.

BAU Publishing Group, *(978-0-9766770)* 1808 Strawberry Dr NE, Rio Rancho, NM 87144 USA
E-mail: tizeclark2000@yahoo.com; admin@baupublishing.com
Web site: http://www.baupublishing.com.

Bauer, Linda, *(978-0-9798146)* Orders Addr.: P.O. Box 308, Eastford, CT 06242 USA
Dist(s): **CreateSpace Independent Publishing Platform.**

Bauer Media Bks. (AUS) *(978-0-949126; 978-0-949892; 978-1-86396; 978-1-74245; 978-0-646-36336-3; 978-1-906312) Dist. by* **HachBkGrp.**

Bauer, Tina, *(978-1-7375675)* 2640 211th St., Bayside, NY 11360 USA Tel 347-848-8482
E-mail: Traverstina@yahoo.com.

Baum & Baum, LLC, *(978-0-9839373)* 14196 Cranston St., Livonia, MI 48154-4251 USA Tel 734-422-0546
E-mail: lbaum@mi.rr.com.

Bauman, Chris *See* **Blynbeek Publishing**

Baumbach, Laura *See* **MLR Pr., LLC**

Baxter Pr., *(978-1-888237; 978-0-9907879; 978-0-9973372; 978-1-947505; 979-8-218-20675-8; 979-8-218-22545-2)* 700 S. Friendswood Dr., Suite C, Friendswood, TX 77546 USA Tel 281-992-0628; Fax: 815-572-5115
E-mail: baxter2@flash.net
Web site: http://baxterpress.com
Dist(s): **Greenleaf Book Group**
Spirit Rising
Whitaker Hse.

Baxter The Dog Bks., *(978-1-7321588; 978-1-7344749)* 9850 S. Maryland Pkwy. Ste A-5 336, Las Vegas, NV 89183 USA Tel 702-518-9213
E-mail: hi@baxterthedogbooks.com
Web site: baxterthedogbooks.com.

Bay Company Books, Inc. *See* **Bay Co. Bks., Inc.**

Bay Co. Bks., Inc., *(978-1-7324647; 978-0-692-15964-4)* 825 Front St., Santa Cruz, CA 95060 USA Tel 831-460-3258.

Bay Horse Creations LLC, *(978-0-9749320)* 508 W. Irvine Rd., Phoenix, AZ 85086 USA Tel 602-818-7879
Web site: http://www.bayhorsecreations.com.

Bay Light Publishing, *(978-0-9670280; 978-0-9741817)* P.O. Box 3032, Mooresville, NC 28117 USA (SAN 299-9196) Tel 704-664-7541; Fax: 704-664-2712; Toll Free: 866-541-3895
E-mail: baylightpub@compuserve.com
Web site: http://www.baylightpub.com.

Bay Media, Inc., *(978-0-9665239; 978-0-9717047; 978-0-9823354)* Orders Addr.: 550m Ritchie Hwy., #271 Severna Pk., Severna Park, MD 21146 USA Tel 410-647-8402; Fax: 410-544-4640
Web site: http://www.baymed.com.

Bay Mills Indian Community, *(978-0-9758801)* 12140 W. Lakeshore Dr., Brimley, MI 49715 USA
Web site: http://www.bmic.net.

Bay Oak Pubs., Ltd., *(978-0-9704692; 978-0-9741713; 978-0-9800874)* 34 Wimbledon Dr., Dover, DE 19904 USA
E-mail: bayoakpublishers@aol.com
Web site: http://www.bayoakpublishers.com
Dist(s): **Follett School Solutions**
Washington Bk. Distributors.

Bay Publishing, *(978-0-9822046)* P.O. Box 4569, Santa Rosa, CA 95402-4569 USA (SAN 857-5401)
E-mail: ron@bayyellow.com.

Bay Villager, The, *(978-0-9769742)* 4923 43rd. St., Dickinson, TX 77539 USA
E-mail: lindalou36@hotmail.com.

Bay, William Music, *(978-0-9859227; 978-0-9888327; 978-0-9983842; 978-0-9996980; 978-1-7327088; 978-1-7337169; 978-1-7363630; 978-1-7377953; 979-8-9856504)* 4 Denny Ln., St. Louis, MO 63131 USA Tel 314-707-7366
E-mail: bill@melbay.com
Dist(s): **Mel Bay Pubns., Inc.**

BAYADA Publishing Hse., LLC, *(978-0-692-92260-6)* 9012 Kinsale Cir., Richmond, VA 23228 USA Tel 804-218-3110; Fax: 804-218-3110
E-mail: jackiehunter.11@juno.com.

Bayard Editions (FRA) *(978-2-227; 978-2-7009; 978-2-7470; 978-2-915480; 978-2-9518356) Dist. by* **Distribks Inc.**

Bayberry Cottage Gallery, *(978-0-615-61021-4; 978-0-615-89363-1)* 9074 Highland St., Mauricetown, NJ 08329 USA Tel 856-785-9927
E-mail: nanptidy@yahoo.com
Web site: http://nancy-patterson.artistwebsites.com.

Bayeux Arts, Inc. (CAN) *(978-1-896209; 978-1-897411; 978-1-988440) Dist. by* **Chicago Distribution Ctr.**

Bayliss, Erin, *(978-0-9778471)* 320 Roan Dr., Grants Pass, OR 97526 USA
E-mail: rise4him@q.com.

Baylor College of Medicine, *(978-1-888997; 978-1-944035)* Div. of Center for Educational Outreach, Orders Addr.: Center For Educational Outreach Baylor College Of Medicine One Baylor Plaza, Bcm411, Houston, TX 77030 USA Tel 713-798-8200; Fax: 713-798-8201; Toll Free: 800-798-8244; *Imprints:* BioEd (BioEd)
E-mail: edoutreach@bcm.edu; nmoreno@bcm.edu; marthay@bcm.edu; mslopez@bcm.edu; takelleh@bcm.edu
Web site: http://www.bcm.edu/edoutreach; http://www.bioedonline.org; http://www.bcm.edu.

Baylor Univ. Pr., *(978-0-918954; 978-1-878804; 978-1-932792; 978-1-60258; 978-1-4813)* 1920 S. Fourth St., Waco, TX 76706 USA Tel 254-710-3164; Fax: 254-710-3440
E-mail: David_Aycock@baylor.edu; Michelle_McCaig@baylor.edu; Jenny_Hunt@baylor.edu; Dave_Nelson@baylor.edu; BUP_Production@baylor.edu
Web site: http://www.baylorpress.com
Dist(s): **Longleaf Services**
MyiLibrary
ebrary, Inc.

Bayou Publishing, *(978-1-886298)* Div. of Bayou Publishing, LLC, Orders Addr.: 2524 Nottingham, Houston, TX 77005 USA (SAN 859-2810) Tel 713-526-4558; Fax: 713-526-4342; Toll Free: 800-340-2034 Do not confuse with Bayou Publishing, Longboat Key, FL
E-mail: info@bayoupublishing.com; orders@bayoupublishing.com; vloos@bayoupublishing.com
Web site: http://www.bayoupublishing.com
Dist(s): **Baker & Taylor Publisher Services (BTPS)**
Quality Bks., Inc.
Unique Bks., Inc.

Bayou Publishing, *(978-0-9643441)* 700 John Ringling Blvd., No. T1810, Sarasota, FL 34236-1542 USA Do not confuse with Bayou Publishing, Houston, TX
E-mail: mnecht7725@aol.com
Web site: http://members.aol.com/mnecht7725/FORDVCE/index.html
Dist(s): **Distributors, The**
North Country Bks., Inc.

Bayport Pr. *Imprint of* **Wellness Pubn.**

Baysh Learns to Read *See* **Once Upon A Page Pr.**

BaySidePr., *(978-0-9988034; 978-0-578-24300-9)* 330 Mission Bay Blvd. N. Unit 302, San Francisco, CA 94158 USA Tel 415-621-8937
Web site: www.jacksonfahnestock.com.

Baysmore Bks., *(978-0-9857160; 978-0-692-78985-8)* P.O. Box 21402, Long Beach, CA 90801 USA Tel 562-208-3646
E-mail: baysmorebooks@gmail.com.

Bazow, Thomas, *(978-0-9777725)* 4845 Romaine Spring Dr., Fenton, MO 63026-5840 USA
Web site: http://www.inhistimepublishing.com.

Bazuji Publishing LLC, *(978-0-9761555)* 3843 53rd St., SE, Tappen, ND 58487 USA (SAN 256-2626) Toll Free: 800-615-7606
Web site: http://www.bazuji.com.

BB International Productions, Incorporated *See* **Bibi Art Media Inc.**

BBC Audiobooks America *See* **AudioGO**

BBI Incorporated *See* **Bush Brothers & Co.**

BBM Bks., *(978-1-938504)* 21 Harbor Pointe Dr., Corona del Mar, CA 92625 USA Tel 949-302-5849
E-mail: inspiredcreationsca@gmail.com.

BBR *Imprint of* **BBR: Books for Brilliance & Resilience**

BBR: Books for Brilliance & Resilience, *(978-0-9753245)* P.O. Box 5236, Takoma Park, MD 20913-5236 USA Toll Free: 888-898-2322; *Imprints:* BBR (B B R)
Web site: http://www.letscommunicate.com.

BBRACK Productions, Inc., *(978-0-9726837)* 1345-B Triad Ctr. Dr., No. 181, Saint Peters, MO 63376 USA Tel 636-936-2311
E-mail: 1stB@bbrack.com
Web site: http://www.bbrack.com.

B-Bright publishing, *(978-1-943417)* 16210 tahoe dr, Jersey Village, TX 77040 USA Tel 281-606-5820
E-mail: gdbanks@gmail.com.

bby Publications at The University of West Alabama, *(978-1-885775)* Div. of College of Education, Orders Addr.: UWA Station 60, Livingston, AL 35470 USA Tel 205-652-5406; Fax: 205-652-5400
E-mail: tpartridge@uwa.edu; dknight@uwa.edu
Web site: http://www.bbypublications.com.

BC Publishing, *(978-0-9740511)* 633-1 Elk Ct., Fayetteville, NC 28301 USA Tel 910-578-2621; *Imprints:* Kids1st Books (Kids1st Bks) Do not confuse with BC Publishing in Tampa, FL
E-mail: dbradleyclarke@yahoo.com.

BCB Productions, 180 church st, whitinsville, MA 01588 USA Tel 508-372-9151
Dist(s): **CreateSpace Independent Publishing Platform.**

BCM International Inc., *(978-0-86508)* 201 Granite Run Dr., Suite 260, Lancaster, PA 17601 USA (SAN 211-7762) Tel 717-560-9601 Main Phone Number; Toll Free: 888-226-4685
E-mail: info@bcmintl.org
Web site: https://www.bcmintl.org; instepmasterteacher.com
Dist(s): **CLC Pubns.**
Send The Light Distribution LLC.

BCM Publications, Incorporated *See* **BCM International Inc.**

BCP Pubns., *(978-0-615-20692-9; 978-0-615-21056-8; 978-0-578-02129-4)* 3215 E. 17th St., Vancouver, WA 98661 USA
E-mail: bcpwriter2000@yahoo.com
Web site: http://www.authortree.com/bcpwriter2000
Dist(s): **AuthorHouse.**

BCZ Pubs. LLC, *(978-1-7367153; 979-8-9889822)* 3365 E Miraloma Ave STE 205, Anaheim, CA 92806 USA Tel 714-392-2189
E-mail: bczpublishers@gmail.com
Web site: bczpublishers.com.

BDA Publishing, *(978-0-9794716)* P.O. Box 541715, Dallas, TX 75354-1715 USA Tel 972-532-8805; Fax: 214-350-9275; 3163 Citation Dr., Dallas, TX 75229-5840
E-mail: bbd@sbcglobal.net
Web site: http://www.evanbrain.com; http://barrybdoyle.com/.

Be Bold About It, *(978-1-7325964)* 493 Landmark Way, Austell, GA 30168 USA Tel 404-906-6433
E-mail: praisedancingbeth@yahoo.com
Web site: www.beboldaboutit.com.

Be Heard Publishing, *(978-0-692-93977-2; 978-1-7342949)* 939 Dalkeith, St Louis, MO 63132 USA Tel 314-323-2737
E-mail: rebeccatclark@yahoo.com
Web site: www.wittykidsclub.com.

Be Naturally Curious, *(978-1-942403)* 160 W 85th St., New York, NY 10024 USA Tel 347-229-5559
E-mail: valerie@benaturallycurious.com
Web site: www.benaturallycurious.com.

Be There Bedtime Stories LLC, *(978-0-692-74330-0)* 35 Giovanni Aisle, IRVINE, CA 92614 USA Tel 949-394-1714.

Be You Bks., *(978-1-952637)* 2003 Costa Del Mar No. 680, Carlsbad, CA 92009 USA Tel 619-992-5115
E-mail: edesio@usa.net.

Bea is for Business, *(978-0-9893403)* P.O. Box 3009, Charlotte, NC 28230 USA Tel 704-325-9232
E-mail: jamieabrown@hotmail.com
Web site: www.beaisforbusiness.com.

Beach Bks., *(978-0-9763052; 978-0-615-57831-6)* 430 Noe St., San Francisco, CA 94114 USA Tel 415-251-3845
E-mail: gyaltsen@yahoo.com
Web site: http://www.jefferybeach.com
Dist(s): **CreateSpace Independent Publishing Platform.**

Beach Front Bks., *(978-0-9651281)* P.O. Box 545, East Bridgewater, MA 02333 USA Tel 508-378-9319; Fax: 508-378-7621 Do not confuse with Beach Front Books in East Bridgewater, MA
E-mail: beachfrontbooks@aol.com.

Beach Lane Bks. *Imprint of* **Beach Lane Bks.**

Beach Lane Bks., Div. of Simon & Schuster Children's Publishing, 1230 Ave. of the Americas, New York, NY 10020 USA; *Imprints:* Beach Lane Books (BeachLane)
Dist(s): **Children's Plus, Inc.**
Follett School Solutions
Simon & Schuster, Inc.

Beach Lloyd Pubs., LLC, *(978-0-9743158; 978-0-9792778; 978-0-9819417)* Orders Addr.: P.O. Box 2183, Southeastern, PA 19399-2183 USA (SAN 255-4992) Tel 610-407-0130; Fax: 775-254-0633; Toll Free: 866-218-3253; Edit Addr.: 40 Cabot Dr., Wayne, PA 19087-5619 USA
E-mail: beachlloyd@erols.com
Web site: http://www.beachlloyd.com
Dist(s): **MBS Textbook Exchange, Inc.**

Beachcomber Press.com, *(978-0-9800630)* 33021 Adelante St., Temecula, CA 92592 USA Tel 951-699-2932
E-mail: ashleyludwig@verizon.net.

Beachfront Bks., *(978-0-9768816)* Orders Addr.: P.O. Box 16-287, Seattle, WA 98116 USA; Edit Addr.: 5641 Beach Dr. SW, Seattle, WA 98116 USA
Web site: http://www.beachfront books.org
Dist(s): **Follett School Solutions.**

Beachfront Productions, *(978-0-692-70896-5)* 1815 Farmington Dr., Franklin, TN 37069 USA Tel 615-400-0152
E-mail: lesliedowns@gmail.com.

Beachfront Publishing, *(978-1-892339)* Div. of Words, Words, Words, Inc., Orders Addr.: P.O. Box 811922, Boca Raton, FL 33481 USA; 4705 Brook Top Ct., Raleigh, NC 27606
E-mail: info@beachfrontentertainment.com
Web site: http://www.beachfrontentertainment.com
Dist(s): **Follett School Solutions.**

BeachHouse Bks. *Imprint of* **Science & Humanities Pr.**

Beachhouse Publishing, LLC, *(978-0-9729905; 978-1-933067; 978-1-949000)* P.O. Box 5464, Kaneohe, HI 96744 USA
E-mail: info@beachhousepublishing.com
Web site: www.beachhousepublishing.com
Dist(s): **Booklines Hawaii, Ltd.**
Islander Group.

BeachWalk Bks. Inc., *(978-0-9770158)* P.O. Box 446, Glenview, IL 60025 USA Tel 847-729-2222; Fax: 847-729-5215; Toll Free Fax: 866-720-3222; 2136 Fir St., Glenview, IL 60025
E-mail: amcdonald@beachwalkbooks.com
Web site: http://www.beachwalkbooks.com.

Beachwalker Pr., *(978-0-9727639)* 5557 SW Village Pl., Beaverton, OR 97007 USA Tel 503-799-6061; Fax: 503-644-9335
E-mail: beachwalkerpress@aol.com
Web site: http://www.beachwalkerpress.com.

Beacon Hill Press of Kansas City *See* **Beacon Hill Pr. of Kansas City**

Beacon Pr. *Imprint of* **Beacon Pr.**

Beacon Pr., *(978-0-8070)* Orders Addr.: 25 Beacon St., Boston, MA 02108-2892 USA (SAN 201-4483) Tel 617-742-2110; Fax: 617-723-3097; *Imprints:* Beacon Press (BeaconPress)
E-mail: marketing@beacon.org
Web site: http://www.beacon.org
Dist(s): **Ebsco Publishing**
Houghton Mifflin Harcourt Publishing Co.
Houghton Mifflin Harcourt Trade & Reference Pubs.
MyiLibrary
Penguin Random Hse. Distribution
Penguin Random Hse. LLC
Random Hse., Inc.
Simon & Schuster, Inc.

Beacon Street Girls *Imprint of* **B*tween Productions, Inc.**

BeActive Publishing Co., *(978-0-9722714)* 29834 N. Cave Creek Rd., S118, PMB 142, Cave Creek, AZ 85331-7831 USA Tel 480-563-0315; Fax: 480-502-0664
Web site: http://www.beactivesportsmarketing.com.

Beagle Bay Bks., *(978-0-9679591; 978-0-9749610)* Div. of Beagle Bay, Inc., 2325 Homestead Pl., Reno, NV 89509-3657 USA
E-mail: info@beaglebay.com
Web site: http://www.beaglebay.com
Dist(s): **Brodart Co.**

Beagle Bks. Publishing, LLC, *(978-0-9841813)* 43 Highridge Rd., Westport, MA 02790 USA (SAN 858-6519).

Beak Star Bks., *(978-1-944724)* 10620 Belmont Pl., Powell, OH 43065 USA Tel 614-307-2663
E-mail: jdmilligan@columbus.rr.com
Web site: beakstarbooks.com.

BeaLu Bks., *(978-0-9990924; 978-1-7333092; 978-1-7341065; 978-1-7353641; 978-1-7356455)* 10401 N Oregon Ave, Tampa, FL 33612 USA Tel 813-390-5467
E-mail: luana@bealubooks.com
Web site: www.bealubooks.com.

Beaming Books *Imprint of* **1517 Media**

Bean Bk. Publishing, *(978-0-9761990)* 9246 E. Havasupai Dr., Scottsdale, AZ 85255 USA Tel 480-502-1257 (phone/fax)
E-mail: dawn.crichton@dcranch.com; Juliecrichton@cox.net
Web site: http://www.stringbeansorjellybeans.com; http://www.bean-books.com.

Bean Bks., *(978-0-9825601)* 416 W. Ave. B, Newberry, MI 49868 USA.

Bean Sprouts *Imprint of* **Standard Publishing**

Beaner Bks., *(978-0-9849293)* 541 Redford Pl. Dr., Rolesville, NC 27571 USA Tel 855-286-9687
E-mail: alphabetownusa@gmail.com
Web site: http://www.alphabetownusa.com.

BeanPole Bks. *Imprint of* **OH Industries**

BeanSprout Bks., *(978-0-692-25923-8; 978-1-7322049; 978-1-950471)* 6151 White Tip Rd., Jacksonville, FL 32258 USA Tel 407-234-1837
E-mail: thesecretartgallery@gmail.com; tgrant5625@gmail.com
Dist(s): **Ingram Content Group.**

Beanstalk Pubns, *(978-0-9785302)* 4762 Camino del Rey, Santa Barbara, CA 93110 USA Tel 805-448-0898
E-mail: mjmckechnie@beanstalkpublications.com
Web site: http://www.beanstalkpublications.com.

Beantown Bks., *(978-1-7364689)* 3 Frost Cir., Wellesley, MA 02482 USA Tel 617-851-9685
E-mail: Julielee.bbm@gmail.com.

Bear & Company *See* **Boyds Collection Ltd., The**

†**Bear & Co.,** *(978-0-939680; 978-1-879181; 978-1-59143)* Orders Addr.: P.O. Box 388, Rochester, VT 05767-0388 USA; Edit Addr.: One Park St., Rochester, VT 05767 USA (SAN 216-7174) Tel 802-767-3174; Fax: 802-767-3726; Toll Free: 800-246-8648; *Imprints:* Bear Cub Books (Bear Cub Books)
E-mail: customerservice@innertraditions.com; info@innertraditions.com
Web site: http://www.innertraditions.com
Dist(s): **Book Wholesalers, Inc.**
Bookazine Co., Inc.
Brodart Co.
Inner Traditions International, Ltd.
Integral Yoga Pubns.
MyiLibrary

New Leaf Distributing Co., Inc.
Nutri-Bks. Corp.
Partners Bk. Distributing, Inc.
Partners/West Book Distributors
Phoenix Distributors
Quality Bks., Inc.
Simon & Schuster
Simon & Schuster, Inc.; *CIP.*

Bear Claw Bks. *Imprint of* **Bearport Publishing Co., Inc.**

Bear Cub Bks. *Imprint of* **Bear & Co.**

Bear Foot Printing *See* **Artistic Endeavors**

Bear State Bks., *(978-1-892622)* Orders Addr.: P.O. Box 96, Exeter, CA 93221 USA Tel 559-280-8547; Fax: 559-594-5383; Edit Addr.: 199 E. Pine St., Exeter, CA 93221 USA Tel 559-280-8547
E-mail: cdbrewer@gmx.com
Web site: bearstatebooks.com.

Bearcub Bks. *Imprint of* **Bearport Publishing Co., Inc.**

Bearhead Bks., *(978-1-7347669)* 1145 Camp Carolwood Rd., Lenoir, NC 28645 USA Tel 954-445-5931
E-mail: belinda@belindagrimbeek.com
Web site: www.belindagrimbeek.com.

Bearhead Publishing, LLC, *(978-0-9776260; 978-0-9799153; 978-0-9824373; 978-0-9829307; 978-1-937508)* P.O. Box 16539, Louisville, KY 40256 USA (SAN 257-7798); 2217 Mary Catherine Dr., Louisville, KY 40216
E-mail: garyd@sissymarlyn.com; garydbhp@insightbb.com
Web site: http://www.sissymarlyn.com; http://www.bearheadpublishing.com.

Bearly Cooking *Imprint of* **Mountain n' Air Bks.**

BearManor Media, *(978-0-9714570; 978-1-59393; 978-1-62933; 979-8-88771)* 1317 Edgewater Dr No. 110, Orlando, FL 32804 USA Tel 760-709-9696
E-mail: benohmart@gmail.com
Web site: http://www.bearmanormedia.com.

Bearport Publishing Co., Inc., *(978-1-59716; 978-1-936087; 978-1-936088; 978-1-936089; 978-1-936090; 978-0-9824758; 978-0-9824759; 978-0-9824760; 978-0-9824761; 978-0-9824762; 978-0-9824763; 978-0-9824764; 978-1-61772; 978-1-62724; 978-1-943074; 978-1-943553; 978-1-944102; 978-1-944997; 978-1-944998; 978-1-68402; 978-1-64280; 978-1-64747; 978-1-63691; 979-8-88509; 979-8-88822; 979-8-88916; 979-8-89232)* 5357 Penn Ave S, Minneapolis, MN 55419 USA (SAN 256-2103) Toll Free: 877-337-8577 (and fax); 5357 Penn Ave. S., Minneapolis, MN 55419 Tel 877-337-8577; Fax: 866-337-8557; *Imprints:* Bearcub Books (BearcubBks); Fusion Books (FusionBks); Bear Claw Books (BearClawBk); Create! Books (CreateBooks); SilverTip Books (SilverTip Books)
E-mail: marketing@bearportpublishing.com; info@bearportpublishing.com; jen@bearportpublishing.com
Web site: http://www.bearportpublishing.com
Dist(s): **Follett School Solutions**
Independent Pubs. Group
MyiLibrary.

Bear's Designs Unlimited, *(978-0-9638473)* 7505 320th St., W., Northfield, MN 55057 USA Tel 507-645-9050; Toll Free: 800-497-8757.

Bear's Place Publishing, *(978-1-7328112; 978-1-7342675)* 584 Horse Ferry Rd, Lawrenceville, GA 30044 USA Tel 770-845-8130
E-mail: doctorsdl@yahoo.com
Web site: doctordlane.com.

Bearwallow Blessings Ministries, *(978-0-9768514)* HC 63 Box 77A-1 Rte. 637, Jewell Ridge, VA 24622 USA
Web site: http://www.bearwallowblessings.com.

Beascoa, Ediciones S.A. (ESP) *(978-84-488; 978-84-7546) Dist. by* **Distribks Inc.**

Beascoa, Ediciones S.A. (ESP) *(978-84-488; 978-84-7546) Dist. by* **Lectorum Pubns.**

Beatin' Path Pubns., LLC, *(978-0-9795470; 978-0-9797522; 978-0-9825839; 978-0-9832648; 978-0-9882814; 978-0-9894773; 978-0-9861795; 978-0-9963591; 978-1-7333455; 978-1-7360891; 979-8-9856510; 979-8-9891279)* Orders Addr.: 302 E. College St., Bridgewater, VA 22812-1509 USA (SAN 853-7003) Tel 540-478-4833; Fax: 540-237-4684
E-mail: beatinpath@mac.com
Web site: http://www.beatinpathpublications.com
Dist(s): **Music is Elementary**
Plank Road Publishing
Music in Motion
West Music Co.

Beatto, Sabat, *(978-1-7337532)* 550 W. 125th St., New York, NY 10472 USA Tel 347-641-5754
Dist(s): **CreateSpace Independent Publishing Platform.**

Beau Francis Pr., *(978-0-9792147)* 4100 Newport Pl., Suite 400, Newport Beach, CA 92660 USA Tel 949-499-0679.

BeauDesigns, *(978-0-9841395; 978-0-9968870)* P.O. Box 496, Youngstown, NY 14174 USA Tel 716-745-7328
Dist(s): **Niagara Collectibles.**

Beaufort Bks., Inc., *(978-0-8253; 978-0-9852135)* 27 W. 20th St., Suite 1102, New York, NY 10011 USA (SAN 215-2304) Tel 212-727-0190; Fax: 212-727-0195
E-mail: midpointny@aol.com
Dist(s): **Follett School Solutions**
Independent Pubs. Group
Midpoint Trade Bks., Inc.

Beautiful America Publishing Co., *(978-0-89802)* Orders Addr.: P.O. Box 244, Woodburn, OR 97071-0244 USA (SAN 251-2548) Tel 503-982-4616; Fax: 503-982-2825; Toll Free: 800-874-1233; Edit Addr.: 2600 Progress Way, Woodburn, OR 97071 USA (SAN 211-4623)
E-mail: bapco@beautifulamericapub.com
Web site: http://www.beautifulamericapub.com
Dist(s): **Follett School Solutions**
Koen Pacific
Partners/West Book Distributors.

Beautiful Feet Bks., *(978-0-9643803; 978-1-893103)* 1306 Mill St., San Luis Obispo, CA 93401-2817 USA Toll Free: 800-889-1978
E-mail: russell@bfbooks.com
Web site: http://www.bfbooks.com
Dist(s): **Follett School Solutions.**

Beautiful Zion Baptist Church *See* **A & L Communications, Inc.**

Beauty Beneath the Rubble, *(978-0-692-11094-2; 978-0-578-46205-9; 978-0-578-46226-4)* 256 W. Pebble Creek Ln., Orange, CA 92865 USA Tel 909-702-4052
E-mail: nushinalloo@gmail.com.

Beaver Island Arts, *(978-0-9708575)* P.O. Box 40, Bay City, MI 49708-0040 USA (SAN 253-8385) Tel 517-894-5925
E-mail: mblocksma@yahoo.com
Web site: http://beaverislandarts.com
Dist(s): **Follett School Solutions**
Indiana Univ. Pr.
Partners Bk. Distributing, Inc.
Two Rivers Distribution.

Beaver Meadow Publishing, *(978-0-9742085)* 11 Clarence Russell Rd., Thurman, NY 12885 USA Tel 518-623-9305; 352-463-3089
E-mail: PerkinFL@aol.com
Web site: http://www.persisgranger.com.

Beaver's Pond Pr., Inc., *(978-1-890676; 978-1-931646; 978-1-59298; 978-1-64343)* 939 Seventh St. W., Saint Paul, MN 55102 USA Tel 952-829-8818
E-mail: mack@beaverspondpress.com
Web site: http://www.beaverspondpress.com
Dist(s): **Itasca Bks.**

Because Time Flies, Inc., *(978-0-9652652; 978-0-9754073)* 155 N. Harbor Dr., Concourse Suite 2, Chicago, IL 60601-7364 USA Tel 312-938-0938; Fax: 312-938-0029; Toll Free: 800-694-4786
E-mail: journals@covad.net
Web site: http://www.becausetimeflies.com.

Becca J. Camp, LLC, *(978-1-7366938)* 418 Forest St, MARION, OH 43302 USA Tel 740-971-3577
E-mail: beccajcamp@icloud.com.

Beck Global Publishing, *(978-0-9816942)* 712 Wildwood Dr., COLUMBIA, MO 65203 USA
E-mail: nancy@nursenancybeck.com
Web site: http://nursenancybeck.com.

Beck Publishing *See* **Beck Global Publishing**

Becker, Christie, *(978-0-9728116)* 7 Whispering Pines Ct., Hilton Head, SC 29926-2542 USA
E-mail: beachbeckers@msn.com
Web site: http://www.cbeckerbooks.com.

Becker, Curtis Bks., *(978-0-692-15677-3; 978-0-578-44617-2; 978-0-578-52760-4; 978-0-578-55942-1; 978-0-578-57489-9; 978-0-578-61100-6; 978-0-578-61304-8; 978-0-578-62706-9; 978-0-578-63152-3; 978-0-578-63365-7; 978-0-578-70865-2; 978-0-578-90109-1; 978-0-578-92245-4; 978-0-578-96487-4; 978-0-578-99049-1) 1114 Commercial No. 304, Emporia, KS 66801 USA Tel 620-757-2455*
E-mail: curtis@curtisbeckerbooks.com
Dist(s): **Ingram Content Group.**

Becker Doyle & Associates *See* **BDA Publishing**

Becker, Frank *See* **Greenbush Pr.**

Becker, Savan C., *(978-0-615-23554-7)* 1521 Farlow Ave., Crofton, MD 21114 USA Tel 443-292-8098; Fax: 443-603-2998
E-mail: savan@psinerspace.net
Dist(s): **Lulu Pr., Inc.**

becker&mayer! books, *(978-0-9700346; 978-0-9748486; 978-1-932855; 978-1-60380)* 11120 NE 33rd Pl. No. 101, Bellevue, WA 98004-1448 USA (SAN 760-7792) Toll Free: 866-319-5900; *Imprints:* SmartLab (SmartLab)
E-mail: cindyd@beckermayer.com; info@beckermayer.com
Web site: http://www.beckermayer.com; http://www.everydaywisdom.net
Dist(s): **Bks. Are Fun, Ltd.**
Chronicle Bks. LLC
Hachette Bk. Group
INscribe Digital
Independent Pubs. Group
Midpoint Trade Bks., Inc.
Open Road Integrated Media, Inc.
Quarto Publishing Group USA.

Becket, *(978-0-9898785; 978-1-941240)* 78665 Villeta Dr, La Quinta, CA 92253 USA Tel 760-413-0031
E-mail: ibecket7@gmail.com.

Beckham Pubns. Co, *(978-0-931761; 978-0-9802380; 978-0-9816505; 978-0-9823876; 978-0-9841991; 978-0-9827943; 978-0-9833402; 978-0-9848243; 978-0-9905904; 978-0-9984870)* Orders Addr.: 13619 Cedar Creek Ln., SILVER SPRING, MD 20904 USA (SAN 683-2237) Tel 240-643-9284; Fax: 866-659-3306; Toll Free Fax: 866-659-3306; Edit Addr.: 13619 Cedar Creek Ln., Silver Spring, MD 20904-5308 USA
E-mail: barry@beckhamhouse.com
Web site: http://www.beckhamhouse.com
Dist(s): **BCH Fulfillment & Distribution.**

Beckham Publications Group, Incorporated *See* **Beckham Pubns. Co**

Becklyns, LLC, *(978-0-9860222)* 23 Bob White Way, Weatogue, CT 06089 USA.

Beckon Bks. *Imprint of* **Southwestern Publishing Hse., Inc.**

Become a Millionaire *See* **Grampa Jones's Publishing Co.**

Becoming Hero, *(978-0-9990022; 979-8-9877667)* Urb. Los Caobos, Ponce, PR 00716 USA Tel 540-287-7629; Fax: 540-287-7629
E-mail: jen.finelli.veldhuyzen@gmail.com
Web site: byjenfinelli.com.

Bed Bks., *(978-1-933652)* 101 Westgate Dr., Trinidad, CA 95570 USA
Web site: http://www.readinginbed.com; http://www.bedbooks.NET.

Bed of Angels, Inc., *(978-0-9909751)* 9663 Santa Monica Blvd. Suite 559, Beverly Hills, CA 90210 USA Tel 310-734-8542
E-mail: h@eworldmedia.com
Web site: www.eworldmedia.com.

Bedazzled Ink Publishing Co., *(978-0-9759555; 978-1-934452; 978-1-939562; 978-1-943837; 978-1-945805; 978-1-949290; 978-1-960373)* 2137 Pennsylvania Ave., Fairfield, CA 94533 USA
E-mail: publisher@bedazzledink.com
Web site: http://www.bedazzledink.com
Dist(s): **Follett School Solutions**
Independent Pubs. Group.

Bedbug Bks., *(978-0-692-04504-6)* 4044 Carmel Brooks Way, SAN DIEGO, CA 92130 USA Tel 858-922-9554
E-mail: rachelmarie.rm@gmail.com
Dist(s): **Ingram Content Group.**

Bedell, Barbara F., *(978-0-9743731)* 74 Hidden Bay Dr., S Dartmouth, MA 02748-3089 USA
E-mail: bb280z@yahoo.com.

Bedell, Lashundra, *(978-0-615-58737-0; 978-0-9896672)* P.O. Box 33552, Decatur, GA 30033 USA Tel 678-755-3270
E-mail: lashundrabedell@yahoo.com.

Bedford Hse. Bks., *(978-0-9960916)* 93 hancock St., brooklyn, NY 11216 USA Tel 917-815-5969
E-mail: dave@bedfordhousebooks.com.

Bedford/Saint Martin's, *(978-0-312; 978-1-4576)* Div. of Holtzbrinck Publishers, Orders Addr.: 16365 James Madison Hwy., Gordonsville, VA 22942 USA Tel 540-672-7600; Toll Free Fax: 800-672-2054; Toll Free: 888-330-8477; Edit Addr.: 33 Irving Pl., New York, NY 10003 USA Tel 212-375-7000; Fax: 212-614-1885; Toll Free: 800-223-1715; 75 Arlington St., Boston, MA 02116 Tel 617-399-4000; Fax: 617-426-8582; Toll Free: 800-779-7440
E-mail: permissionsdept@bedfordstmartins.com; communication@bedfordstmartins.com
Web site: http://www.bfwpub.com
Dist(s): **Follett School Solutions**
MacMillan Learning USA 1
MacMillan Learning USA 2
MacMillan Learning USA 3
Macmillan
Springer.

Bednarczyk, Casey, *(978-0-578-44523-6; 978-0-578-58146-0)* 310 Tiger Way, Boonsboro, MD 21713 USA Tel 240-385-6289
E-mail: caseybednarczyk@gmail.com.

Bednark, Sara, *(978-0-615-18545-3)* 10013 SE Eastmont Dr., Damascus, OR 97089 USA
E-mail: rbednark@gmail.com
Web site: http://www.sara.bednark.com
Dist(s): **Lulu Pr., Inc.**

Bedrock Books, Incorporated *See* **Dry, Paul Bks., Inc.**

Bedside Bks. *Imprint of* **American Bk. Publishing Group**

Bedside Pr. (CAN) *(978-0-9939970; 978-1-988715) Dist. by* **D C D.**

Bee at Ease Press *See* **At Ease Pr.**

Bee Creative, LLC, *(978-0-615-75686-8; 978-0-615-94698-6; 978-0-615-98240-3; 978-0-9975745)* 2704 NW 119th, Oklahoma City, OK 73120 USA Tel 405-924-9265
E-mail: callie.belinda@gmail.com
Web site: www.beecreativeinc.com.

Bee Instinctive, *(978-0-692-17262-9)* 547 Blue Hill Ave., BOSTON, MA 02121 USA Tel 617-861-7520
E-mail: ssenat2@gmail.com
Dist(s): **Ingram Content Group.**

Beech, Michael, *(978-0-9817741)* 8603 W. 84th Cir., Arvada, CO 80005 USA Tel 303-456-5350
Web site: http://www.ebookselfpublishing.com; http://www.digital3dstereo.com.

Beech River Bks., *(978-1-930149; 978-0-9776514; 978-0-9793778; 978-0-9825214; 978-0-9839367; 978-0-9905814)* P.O. Box 62, Center Ossipee, NH 03814 USA Tel 603-539-3537; *Imprints:* Writer's Publishing Cooperative (Writ Pub Coop)
E-mail: banddmarion@roadrunner.com
Web site: http://www.beechriverbooks.com
Dist(s): **Enfield Publishing & Distribution Co., Inc.**

Beecher Scott, *(978-0-9763077)* 1925 Westchester Rd. Apt. 214, Waterloo, IA 50701-4522 USA.

Beecroft Publishing (GBR) *(978-0-9546186) Dist. by* **LightSource CS.**

BeeHappi, *(978-0-9993343)* P.O. Box 81042, Austin, TX 78728 USA Tel 855-445-9556
E-mail: Maribel.Valls@beehappi.com
Web site: www.beehappi.com.

Beehive Bks., *(978-1-948886)* 4701 Chester Ave suite 1B, Philadelphia, PA 19143 USA Tel 609-468-8659
E-mail: joshuaon@gmail.com
Web site: beehivebooks.com
Dist(s): **Consortium Bk. Sales & Distribution.**

Beehive Inc., *(978-0-692-77210-2)* 9213 camptown Ct., MECHANICSVILLE, VA 23116 USA Tel 804-299-3772.

Beekman & Hathaway, *(978-0-9758970)* P.O. Box 2355, Amherst, MA 01004-2355 USA
E-mail: cdc@beekmanandhathaway.com
Web site: http://www.beekmanandhathaway.com.

Beekman Bks., Inc., *(978-0-8464)* 300 Old All Angels Hill Rd., Wappingers Falls, NY 12590 USA (SAN 170-1622) Tel 845-297-2690; Fax: 845-297-1002
E-mail: manager@beekmanbooks.com
Web site: http://www.beekmanbooks.com
Dist(s): **Follett School Solutions.**

BeeLine Bks., *(978-0-9903368)* 2 Fallgreen Ct., Santa Rosa, CA 95409 USA Tel 414-686-4777
E-mail: bonjourdwd@comcast.net.

Beeman Jorgensen, Inc., *(978-0-929758)* 7510 Allisonville Rd., Indianapolis, IN 46250 USA (SAN 250-1279) Tel 317-841-7677; Fax: 317-849-2001; Toll Free: 800-553-5319
Dist(s): **Hachette Bk. Group**
MBI Distribution Services/Quayside Distribution
Practice Ring.

BeerBooks.com, *(978-0-9662084; 978-0-9819282; 978-0-9904513)* P.O. Box 771012, Cleveland, OH 44107 USA
E-mail: email@beerbooks.com
Web site: http://www.beerbooks.com.

Bee's Ink Publishing, *(978-0-615-57799-9; 978-0-615-63296-4)* 15800 Hwy. 3 No. 113, Webster, TX 77598 USA Tel 713-876-3222
E-mail: bwilsonent@aol.com.

Beeson, Jan, *(978-0-9890482)* 232 E. 52nd St., San Bernardino, CA 92404 USA Tel 714-936-1390
E-mail: rotcmpj@charter.net.

Beetle Bug Bks., *(978-0-9658365)* Orders Addr.: P.O. Box 4636, San Clemente, CA 92674 USA (SAN 299-3864) Tel 949-498-0162; Fax: 949-498-2531; Edit Addr.: 1504 Avenida Hacienda, San Clemente, CA 92672 USA (SAN 299-3872)
E-mail: BookOrders@BeetleBugBooks.com
Web site: http://www.BeetleBugBooks.com
Dist(s): **Follett School Solutions**
Unique Bks., Inc.

Beevinwood, Inc., *(978-0-9652902)* Orders Addr.: 5748 Clark Rd., West Manchester, OH 45382 USA Tel 937-678-9910; Fax: 937-678-7715
E-mail: C1C2C3@aol.com.

Beex Art Bks., *(978-0-9724358)* P.O. Box 9143, Fountain Valley, CA 92728-9143 USA.

Before Christmas Pr., *(978-0-9759902)* Orders Addr.: 15170 State Rte. 550, Athens, OH 45701 USA
Web site: http://www.beforechristmaspress.com.

Before Someday Publishing, *(978-0-9850659; 978-1-943598)* P.O. Box 371, Apex, NC 27502-9998 USA
E-mail: beforesomeday@gmail.com.

Beggs, Christina, *(978-0-692-18086-0)* 4824 Washington St., Lake Wales, FL 33859 USA Tel 863-241-1632
E-mail: christinab1589@gmail.com
Dist(s): **Ingram Content Group.**

Begin Smart LLC, *(978-1-934618; 978-1-60906)* 515 Valley St., Suite 180, Maplewood, NJ 07040 USA (SAN 854-0497) Tel 973-763-8191; Fax: 973-763-5944
E-mail: info@beginsmartbooks.com
Dist(s): **Sterling Publishing Co., Inc.**

Beginner Method Series *Imprint of* **Songburd Music**

Begoo Bks., LLC, *(978-0-9884922)* 40 N. Clover Dr., Great Neck, NY 11021 USA Tel 516-314-4808
E-mail: cullly@aol.com.

Beguile Media, *(978-1-953787)* 2 Elisabeth Ln., Collegeville, PA 19426 USA Tel 484-358-7571
E-mail: triviatownbooks@gmail.com.

Behave'n Kids Pr., *(978-0-9714405)* 8922 Cuming St., Omaha, NE 68114 USA Tel 402-926-4373; Fax: 402-926-3898
E-mail: janiep@behavenkids.com
Web site: http://www.behavenkids.com/
Dist(s): **Book Clearing Hse.**

Behavenkids Press *See* **Behave'n Kids Pr.**

Behavioral Health & Human Development Ctr., *(978-0-9777672)* 4517 Lorino St., Suite 1, Metairie, LA 70006 USA Tel 504-454-3015
E-mail: carlos@littleduckyjr.com
Web site: http://littleduckyjr.com.

Behind the Scenes Bks., *(978-0-9770879)* 90 Windsor Dr., Pine Brook, NJ 07058 USA Tel 973-274-9472; Fax: 973-274-9272
E-mail: ma@behindthescenesmarketing.com.

Behrman Hse., Inc., *(978-0-87441; 978-1-68115)* 11 Edison Pl., Springfield, NJ 07081 USA (SAN 201-4459) Tel 973-379-7200; Fax: 973-379-7280; Toll Free: 800-221-2755; *Imprints:* Apples & Honey Press (ApplesandHoney)
E-mail: webmaster@behrmanhouse.com; orders@behrmanhouse.com; customersupport@behrmanhouse.com
Web site: http://www.behrmanhouse.com; http://www.arepublish.com
Dist(s): **Follett School Solutions**
Ingram Publisher Services
Two Rivers Distribution.

Beijing Language & Culture Univ. Pr., China (CHN) *(978-7-5619) Dist. by* **China Bks.**

Beil, Frederic C. Pub., Inc., *(978-0-913720; 978-1-929490)* Orders Addr.: 609 Whitaker St., Savannah, GA 31401 USA (SAN 240-9909) Tel 912-233-2446
Web site: http://www.beil.com.

Belgrave Hse., *(978-0-9660643; 978-0-9741068; 978-0-9801778; 978-0-9821717; 978-0-9844144; 978-1-61084; 978-1-947812)* 190 Belgrave Ave., San Francisco, CA 94117-4228 USA Tel 415-661-5025; Fax: 415-661-5703
E-mail: neff@belgravehouse.com
Web site: http://www.belgravehouse.com.

Belice, Wendy, *(978-0-578-74711-8)* 2 Raleigh Pl., BROOKLYN, NY 11226 USA Tel 347-792-1964
E-mail: wbelice@yahoo.com.

Believe In Your Bk., *(978-1-7342191; 978-1-953194)* 7381 NW 35 St., Apt. 3, Hollywood, FL 33024 USA Tel 954-908-9946
E-mail: chanellfair@gmail.com.

Believer's Dream Publishing, *(978-0-9832273; 978-0-9905951)* 9650 Strickland Rd. Suite 103 - 255, Raleigh, NC 27615 USA Tel 919-847-3884
E-mail: believersdreampublishing@gmail.com
Web site: believersdreampublishing.com.

Believers Publishing, *(978-0-9795680)* 2245 N. Green Valley Pkwy., Suite 282, Henderson, NV 89014 USA
E-mail: believerspublishing@gmail.com
Web site: http://believerspublishing.com
Dist(s): **Send The Light Distribution LLC.**

Belisarian Bks., *(978-0-9658481)* Div. of Iconoclast, 6513 NW 30th Terr., Bethany, OK 73008 USA Tel 405-789-1030
E-mail: belisarianbooks@yahoo.com
Web site: http://www.belisarianbooks.tk/.

Belknap Digital Archives, *(978-0-9747471)* Orders Addr.: P.O. Box 1487, Meredith, NH 03253 USA Tel 603-279-8358; Edit Addr.: 20 True Rd., Unit No. 86, Meredith, NH 03253 USA
E-mail: apollock@worldpath.net
Web site: http://www.belknapdigital.com.

Belknap Pr. *Imprint of* **Harvard Univ. Pr.**

Belknap Publishing & Design, *(978-0-9723420; 978-0-9816403)* P.O. Box 22387, Honolulu, HI 96823-2387 USA; *Imprints:* Calabash Books (Calabash Bks)
Web site: http://belknappublishing.com
Dist(s): **Booklines Hawaii, Ltd.**
Follett School Solutions.

Bell, Albert, *(978-0-9979288)* 22 W. 12th St., Holland, MI 49423 USA Tel 616-395-7558
E-mail: bell@hope.edu
Web site: www.albertbell.com.

Bell & Murry, *(978-0-9987995)* P.O. Box 164, Walnut Creek, CA 94597 USA Tel 925-708-2350
E-mail: Dot@bellandmurry.com
Web site: bellandmurry.com.

Bell Bridge Bks. *Imprint of* **BelleBks., Inc.**

Bell, Danny, *(978-0-692-99739-0)* 11853 Lindblade St., Culver City, CA 90230 USA Tel 310-896-6904
E-mail: elanaruthblack@gmail.com
Dist(s): **Ingram Content Group.**

Bell, Jay Bks., *(978-1-7338597)* 2307 S. 60th Ct., Cicero, IL 60804 USA Tel 773-425-1408
E-mail: foolsbones@hotmail.com.

Bell, Keith, *(978-0-9995720)* 1613 N. Federal Hwy., LAKE WORTH, FL 33460 USA Tel 561-582-1881
E-mail: kbellrpi@gmail.com
Dist(s): **Ingram Content Group.**

Bell, Megan, *(978-0-9889775)*
E-mail: msbgoldens@gmail.com
Web site: www.msbgoldens.com.

Bell Pond Bks. *Imprint of* **SteinerBooks, Inc.**

Bella & Bruno Bks., *(978-0-9894402)* 34-08 30th St. Apt A22, Astoria, NY 11106 USA Tel 585-746-2696
E-mail: aneeck@rochester.rr.com
Web site: bellaandbrunobooks.com.

Bella Bks., Inc., *(978-0-930044; 978-0-941483; 978-1-56280; 978-0-9677753; 978-1-931513; 978-1-59493; 978-1-64247)* Orders Addr.: P.O. Box 10543, Tallahassee, FL 32302 USA Tel 850-576-2370; Fax: 850-576-3498; Toll Free: 800-729-4992
E-mail: Linda@BellaBooks.com
Web site: http://www.bellabooks.com
Dist(s): **Bella Distribution**
Ingram Publisher Services
Two Rivers Distribution.

Bella International, Limited *See* **Wanderlust Publishing**

Bella Lucia Books *See* **Curiously Created Bks.**

Bella Publishing *See* **Bellissima Publishing, LLC**

Bella Rosa Bks., *(978-0-9747685; 978-1-933523; 978-1-62268)* P.O. Box 4251, Rock Hill, SC 29732 USA
E-mail: info@bellarosabooks.com
Web site: http://www.bellarosabooks.com
Dist(s): **Follett School Solutions.**

Bellaboozle Books, Inc., *(978-0-9765398)* 104 Lariat Dr., Canonsburg, PA 15317-3284 USA
E-mail: lkravec@adelphia.net.

Bellagio Pr. *Imprint of* **Taj Bks. International LLC**

Bellamy, Christopher Daniel, *(978-0-9979039)* 301 Cassidy Rd. Ext., Thomasville, GA 31792 USA Tel 254-498-1559
E-mail: danbellamy@yahoo.com
Web site: www.inflatablestories.com.

Bellamy, Kaitlin, *(978-0-692-19572-7; 978-0-578-44576-2; 978-0-578-59663-1; 978-0-578-77205-9)* 8741 McCormack McRae Way, Orlando, FL 32836 USA Tel 540-570-0727
E-mail: ExecutiveGeekVO@gmail.com
Dist(s): **Ingram Content Group.**

Bellassai, Anna, *(978-0-578-80002-8)* 1020 N. Orlando Ave, MAITLAND, FL 32751 USA Tel 407-622-4673
E-mail: sgoble@cnfl.wish.org.

Bellastoria Pr., *(978-0-615-40644-2; 978-0-9910861; 978-1-942209; 978-1-959102)* 100 Hilltop Rd., Longmeadow, MA 01106 USA Tel 413-567-3278
E-mail: lcardillopiatzer@hotmail.com
Web site: http://www.lindacardillo.com/.

Belle, Alec John, *(978-0-692-94771-5)* 1175 Airport Rd., CARSON CITY, NV 89701 USA Tel 775-430-3186
E-mail: bellealec@gmail.com
Dist(s): **Ingram Content Group.**

Belle Isle Bks. *Imprint of* **Brandylane Pubs., Inc.**

Belle Isle Bks., LLC, *(978-0-578-29787-3)* 4117 Bishops Pl, Portsmouth, VA 23703 USA Tel 757-632-8690
E-mail: Toysosa@hotmail.com.

Belle Lumiere True News, 2525 Squaw Ct., Antioch, CA 94531-8003 USA Toll Free: 888-473-1555; *Imprints:* Holmes Bookshop (Holmes Bkshop).

Belle Media International, Incorporated *See* **Belle Media International, Inc. Div of True News**

Belle Media International, Inc. Div of True News, *(978-0-9703419; 978-1-60361)* Div. of Belle Lumiere True News, Orders Addr.: P.O. Box 191024, San Francisco, CA 94119 USA Tel 949-813-5343
E-mail: holmesbookshop@yahoo.com; BelleBusiness@yahoo.com; dr.miawhite@yahoo.com.

Belle Publishing, *(978-0-578-11303-6; 978-0-578-11304-3; 978-0-9909986)* 18000 S. Park Blvd., Shaker Heights, OH 44120 USA Tel 216-543-7671
E-mail: lleya1@yahoo.com
Web site: www.thecupcakejones.com
Dist(s): **Independent Pubs. Group.**

BelleAire Pr., *(978-0-9640138; 978-0-9765234)* 5707 NW 50th Pl., Gainesville, FL 32653-4079 USA Tel 352-377-1870
E-mail: belleairepress@earthlink.net
Dist(s): **Atlas Bks.**
Follett School Solutions
MyiLibrary.

BelleBks., Inc., *(978-1-893896; 978-0-9673035; 978-0-9759653; 978-1-933417; 978-0-9768760; 978-0-9802453; 978-0-9821756; 978-0-9841258; 978-0-9843256; 978-1-935661; 978-1-61026; 978-1-61194)* 4513 Ernie Dr., Memphis, TN 38116 USA Tel 901-344-9024; Fax: 901-344-9068; *Imprints:* Bell Bridge Books (Bell Bridge); ImaJinn Books (ImaJinnBooks)
E-mail: bellebooks@bellebooks.com; debbsmith@aol.com; production@bellebooks.com
Web site: http://www.BelleBooks.com; http://www.BellBridgeBooks.com
Dist(s): **MyiLibrary.**

Bellerophon Bks., *(978-0-88388)* Orders Addr.: P.O. Box 21307, Santa Barbara, CA 93121-1307 USA (SAN 254-7856) Tel 805-965-7034; Fax: 805-965-8286; Toll Free: 800-253-9943
E-mail: bellerophonbooks@bellerophonbooks.com
Web site: http://www.bellerophonbooks.com
Dist(s): **Follett School Solutions.**

Bellissima Publishing, LLC, *(978-0-9768417; 978-0-9771916; 978-0-9776993; 978-0-9790449; 978-0-9793358; 978-0-9794006; 978-0-9794815; 978-1-935118; 978-1-935630; 978-1-61477)* Orders Addr.: P.O. Box 60, Jamul, CA 91935 USA
E-mail: pdweigandjd@aol.com; admin@bellissimapublishing.com
Web site: http://www.bellissimapublishing.com; http://www.surfergirlsummer.com; http://bellissimapublishing.viewwork.com/bellissima_publishing_llc/sellfolio.html.

Bello, Andres (CHL) *(978-956-13) Dist. by* **Continental Bk.**

Bellreh Publishing, *(978-0-9966102)* 2501 Ohio Dr, No. 214, Plano, TX 75093 USA Tel 716-946-7308
E-mail: sheriabell@gmail.com
Web site: www.sheriabell.com.

Bellwether Media, *(978-1-60014; 978-1-61211; 978-1-61891; 978-1-62617; 978-1-68103; 978-1-64487; 978-1-64834; 979-8-88687)* Orders Addr.: 6012 Blue Circle Dr., Minnetonka, MN 55343 USA (SAN 920-8135) Tel 612-825-2545; Fax: 612-825-2544; Toll Free Fax: 800-675-6679; Toll Free: 800-679-8068; Edit Addr.: 6012 Blue Circle Dr., Minnetonka, MN 55343 USA; *Imprints:* Blastoff! Readers (Blastoff Rdrs); Torque Books (Torque Bks); Pilot Books (PilotBks); Epic Books (EpicBks); Express Books (Express Bks); Blastoff! Discovery (MYID_O_BLASTOF); Black Sheep (BlackSheepUSA)
E-mail: marketing@bellwethermedia.com; tom@bellwethermedia.com; dzobel@bellwethermedia.com; kayla@bellwethermedia.com
Web site: http://www.bellwethermedia.com
Dist(s): **Follett Media Distribution**
Follett School Solutions
Independent Pubs. Group.

Belmar Pubns., *(978-0-9746366; 978-1-7335191)* 504 - 17th Ave., South Belmar, NJ 07719 USA Fax: 212-737-5211
E-mail: arthurpaone@aol.com.

Beloved World LLC, *(978-0-9883592)* 232 Saint Paul St., Westfield, NJ 08904 USA Tel 908-232-6233
E-mail: Predtree@gmail.com.

BelovedworldLLC *See* **Beloved World LLC**

Belshe, Judy *See* **Snuggle Up Bks.**

Beluga-Duga Pr., *(978-1-932176)* Orders Addr.: P.O. Box 893, Rio Vista, CA 94571 USA.

BeMana LLC, *(978-0-9844041)* 292 Keelson Dr., Detroit, MI 48215 USA Tel 313-529-6989
E-mail: mario.beasley@gmail.com
Web site: http://www.laugh-a-bets.com.

Ben Franklin Pr., *(978-0-9772447; 978-0-615-64586-5)* 910 S. Hohokam Dr., Suite 104, Tempe, AZ 85281 USA Tel 480-968-7959; Fax: 480-966-3694
E-mail: rickburress@benfranklinpress.net.

Benavides, Griselda, *(978-0-692-77556-1; 978-0-692-15691-9)* 13063 Magnolia Ave, Chino, CA 91710 USA Tel 917-473-5144
E-mail: g_benavides@aol.com
Web site: griseldabenavides.com.

BenBella Bks., *(978-1-932100; 978-1-933771; 978-0-9792331; 978-1-935251; 978-1-935618; 978-1-936661; 978-1-937856; 978-1-939529; 978-1-940363; 978-1-941631; 978-1-942952; 978-1-944648; 978-1-946885; 978-1-948836; 978-1-950665; 978-1-953295; 978-1-63774)* 10300 N Central Expy Suite 400, Dallas, TX 75231 USA Tel 214-750-3600; Fax: 214-750-3645; 387 Park Ave. St., New York, NY 10016; *Imprints:* SmartPop (SmartPop)
E-mail: brittney@benbellabooks.com
Web site: http://www.benbellabooks.com
Dist(s): **Follett School Solutions**
MyiLibrary
Open Road Integrated Media, Inc.
Penguin Random House Publisher Services
Penguin Random Hse. Distribution
Penguin Random Hse. LLC
ebrary, Inc.

Bench Press *See* **Gallant Hse. Publishing**

Benchland Publishing, *(978-0-615-89563-5; 978-0-615-99890-9; 978-0-692-33103-3; 978-0-692-50463-5; 978-0-692-74329-4; 978-1-7321915)* 1525 Treehouse Ln S, Keller, TX 76262 USA Tel 8174319899
E-mail: jay.hosler@gmail.com; paul@treent.com
Dist(s): **CreateSpace Independent Publishing Platform.**

Benchmark Book Craft, *(978-0-9744015)* P.O. Box 19583, Colorado City, CO 81019 USA Tel 719-676-3009.

Benchmark Education Co., *(978-1-58344; 978-1-892393; 978-1-59000; 978-1-4108; 978-1-60437; 978-1-60634; 978-1-935440; 978-1-935441; 978-1-60859; 978-1-935469; 978-1-935470; 978-1-935471; 978-1-935472; 978-1-935473; 978-1-61672; 978-1-936254; 978-1-936255; 978-1-936256;-1-936257; 978-1-936258; 978-1-4509; 978-1-4900; 978-1-5021; 978-1-5125; 978-1-5322; 978-1-9873; 978-1-0786; 978-1-6677; 979-8-3853)* 145 Huguenot St 8th Flr, New Rochelle, NY 10801 USA Tel 914-637-7200; Toll Free Fax: 877-732-8273; Toll Free: 877-236-2465
E-mail: bhaggerty@benchmarkeducation.com
Web site: http://www.benchmarkeducation.com.

Bendon, Inc., *(978-1-57759; 978-1-58117; 978-1-888443; 978-1-888567; 978-1-4037; 978-1-932209; 978-1-59394; 978-1-60139; 978-1-61568; 978-1-4530; 978-1-61405; 978-1-62191; 978-1-62615; 978-1-63109; 978-1-63346; 978-1-5050; 978-1-6902)* 1840 Baney Rd. South, Ashland, OH 44805 USA (SAN 803-317X); *Imprints:* Spirit Press (SpiritPr); Intervisual/Piggy Toes (IntervisPiggy)
Web site: http://www.bendonpub.com.

Bendon Publishing International *See* **Bendon, Inc.**

Bendt Family Ministries *See* **Valerie Bendt**

Bene Factum Publishing, Ltd. (GBR) *(978-0-9522754; 978-1-903071; 978-1-909657) Dist. by* **IPG Chicago.**

Benedetti, Jef, *(978-0-9801372)* 4242 Johnstown Rd., Gahanna, OH 43230 USA (SAN 855-2991).

Benedict, James, *(978-1-955419)* 804 Edwin Dr., Virginia Beach, VA 23464 USA Tel 757-264-0520
E-mail: jamesbenedict@gmail.com
Web site: emmanuelliteracy.com.

Benefactory, Inc., The, *(978-1-58021; 978-1-882728)* 3 Baneberry Ln., Riverwoods, IL 60015-3534 USA Toll Free: 800-729-7251
E-mail: benefactry@aol.com.

Benicia Literary Arts, *(978-0-9703737; 978-0-578-43134-5; 979-8-218-10589-1)* P.O. Box 763, Benicia, CA 94510 USA Tel 707-745-5540 (phone/fax)
E-mail: editor@carquinezreview.com
Web site: http://www.carquinezreview.com.

Benitez Productions, *(978-0-9966030; 978-1-949328)* P.O. Box 16101, Encino, CA 91416 USA Tel 818-343-5159
E-mail: art@joebenitez.com
Web site: joebenitez.com
Dist(s): **Diamond Comic Distributors, Inc.**

Benjamin Franklin Pr., *(978-0-9789827; 978-0-9795257; 978-0-9799941; 978-0-692-98402-4; 978-0-692-06064-3; 978-0-578-43090-4; 978-0-578-50901-3; 978-0-578-50902-0)* P.O. Box 51936, Pacific Grove, CA 93950 USA Fax: 831-626-3734; *Imprints:* Osanto University Press (OsantoUniv)
E-mail: loye@benjaminfranklinpress.com
Web site: http://www.benjaminfranklinpress.com
Dist(s): **BookBaby.**

Benjamin Pr., *(978-0-9663478; 978-0-9793431; 978-0-9836106; 978-1-7334047)* Div. of Elmwood Inn Fine Teas, 135 N. 2nd St., Danville, KY 40422 USA Tel 859-236-6641; Toll Free Fax: 888-879-0467; Toll Free: 800-765-2139 Do not confuse with Benjamin Pr., Northampton, MA
E-mail: BR@benjaminpress.com
Web site: http://www.benjaminpress.com
Dist(s): **Independent Pubs. Group**
Midpoint Trade Bks., Inc.
Partners Pubs. Group, Inc.

Benjey Media *See* **Tuxedo Pr.**

Bennett Day Schl., Inc., *(978-0-578-47162-4; 978-1-7333606)* 955 W Grand Ave, Chicago, IL 60642 USA Tel 312-870-0286
E-mail: cameron.smith@bennettday.org
Web site: www.bennettday.org.

Bennett, Kathryn, *(978-0-578-82401-7; 978-0-578-90592-1)* 5221 S Cloverdale Ln, Battlefield, MO 65619 USA Tel 417-872-9156
E-mail: KatieMBennett@outlook.com
Web site: www.ThatKatieLady.com.

Bennett, Krista, *(978-1-7347045)* 3271 E Sweetwater Springs Dr, Washington, UT 84780 USA Tel 4357604258
E-mail: bennett.krista.l@gmail.com
Dist(s): **Ingram Content Group.**

Bennett, Margot *See* **Fetch Pr. Publishing**

Bennett Media & Marketing, *(978-1-957114)* 1603 Capitol Ave., Suite 310 A233, Cheyenne, WY 82001 USA Tel 307-459-1333
E-mail: fulfillment@bennettmarketingteam.com
Web site: https://thebennettmediaandmarketing.com.

Bennett, Robert *See* **Archeological Assessments, Inc.**

Bennett/Novak & Co., Inc., *(978-0-9713454)* 8500 Holloway Dr., Los Angeles, CA 90069 USA Tel 310-657-2975; Fax: 310-657-4006
Dist(s): **National Bk. Network.**

Bennovations Publishing Services, *(978-0-9721066)* P.O. Box 28906, San Diego, CA 92198 USA Tel 858-663-5302; Fax: 858-777-5779
E-mail: info@bennovations.com
Web site: http://www.bennovations.com.

Benny's Bks., *(978-0-692-13602-7; 978-0-692-13997-4; 978-0-578-33142-3)* 9116 Jason Dr., FORT WORTH, TX 76108 USA Tel 940-765-1818
E-mail: jose.a.robles@hotmail.com
Dist(s): **Ingram Content Group.**

Benoit-Elkaoui, Brooke, *(978-0-9988260)* 9141 Peck Ave No. 300, Anchorage, AK 99504 USA Tel 907-770-0300
E-mail: brookebenoit@hotmail.com
Web site: brookebenoit.com.

Benoy Publishing, *(978-0-9720809; 978-1-932162)* 735 Bragg Dr., Unit H, Wilmington, NC 28412 USA Tel 910-796-0424 (phone/fax)
E-mail: bbppdodo@aol.com
Web site: http://www.benoypublishing.com.

Bensley, Ann-Mari, *(978-0-9995242)* 12307 NE 68th Pl, Kirkland, WA 98033 USA Tel 425-443-6940
E-mail: sbens@outlook.com.

Bensley, Lis, *(978-1-7334228)* 235 Surfside Ave., Santa Cruz, CA 95060-2150 USA Tel 831-471-2542
E-mail: lrbensley@gmail.com.

Benson, Lyn, *(978-0-615-13524-3)* 7063 E. Briarwood Dr., Centennial, CO 80112 USA Fax: 303-736-4075
E-mail: lynbenson@msn.com.

Benson, Queen M., *(978-0-615-12716-3)* 106 James River Dr., Newport News, VA 23601 USA
E-mail: dbbenson@verizon.net
Web site: http://www.lactose-limited.com.

Bent Branch Press, *(978-0-9990363)* 108 Crestwood Dr., Tullahoma, TN 37388 USA Tel 615-517-0545
E-mail: ibprayin@hotmail.com.

Bent Castle Workshops, *(978-0-9768848)* P.O. Box 10551, Rochester, NY 14610-0551 USA
E-mail: knot@enchantedglyph.com
Web site: http://www.bentcastle.com.

BentDaiSha, *(978-0-9749465)* 11020 E. Indigo Bush Pl., Tucson, AZ 85748-3558 USA Tel 520-591-3371 (phone/fax)
E-mail: nickpintozzi7@gmail.com.

BentDaiSha, LLC *See* **BentDaiSha**

Bentivegna, Fred, *(978-0-9766228)* 445 W. 27th St., Chicago, IL 60616 USA Tel 312-225-5514 (phone/fax)
E-mail: fbentivegna@sbcglobal.net.

Bentle Bks., *(978-0-9746904)* Orders Addr.: P.O. Box 2274, Oakhurst, CA 93644 USA Fax: 559-683-6206; Edit Addr.: 42564 Buckeye Rd., Oakhurst, CA 93644 USA
E-mail: terrahulse@sierratel.com
Web site: http://www.bentlebooks.com
Dist(s): **Follett School Solutions.**

Bentley, Trish, *(978-0-9774752)* 347 E. 6th St., Apt. 2B, New York, NY 10002 USA.

Benton, John Bks., *(978-0-9635411)* 127 S. El Molino Ave., Pasadena, CA 91101-2510 USA Tel 626-405-0950; Fax: 818-564-0952
Dist(s): **Spring Arbor Distributors, Inc.**

Benzie, Andrew Bks., *(978-0-9852229; 978-0-9897584; 978-1-941713; 978-1-950562)* 2982 Santos Ln. APT No. 306, Walnut Creek, CA 94597 USA Tel 925-253-7790
E-mail: andrew@andrewbenzie.com
Web site: http://www.andrewbenziebooks.com.

Berbay Publishing (AUS) *(978-0-9806711; 978-0-9942895; 978-0-9943841; 978-0-6483973; 978-0-6485291; 978-0-6487851; 978-0-6489533; 978-0-6450696; 978-1-922610) Dist. by* **Consort Bk Sales.**

Bercovici, Elizabeth, *(978-0-578-81597-8; 978-0-578-81598-5)* 140 Pine St., Hackensack, NJ 07601 USA Tel 201-575-2844
E-mail: elizabethdylanbercovici@gmail.com.

Berens, David F., *(978-0-692-07272-1; 978-0-692-09037-4; 978-0-578-51034-7)* 1013 Cross Meadow Rd., KNOXVILLE, TN 37934 USA Tel 865-382-7773
E-mail: david.f.berens@gmail.com
Dist(s): **Ingram Content Group.**

Beres, Nancy, *(978-0-9752801)* 2025 Willow Glen Ln., Columbus, OH 43229-1550 USA.

Berg, Jeremy, *(978-0-9791700; 978-0-9837422; 978-1-939790)* 2204 E. Grand Ave., Everett, WA 98201-3339 USA
Web site: http://www.lorian.org.

Berger, Susan J, *(978-1-7370751)* 7123 Allott Ave. 0, VAN NUYS, CA 91405 USA Tel 8186872613
E-mail: sueberger3@gmail.com
Dist(s): **Ingram Content Group.**

Bergida, Dr. Robert, *(978-1-7328036)* 116-14 Metropolitan Ave., Richmond Hill, NY 11418 USA Tel 718-441-8685
E-mail: drbergidadds@aol.com.

Berglund, Sheila M, *(978-1-7369358)* 2998 W COUNTRY FAIR DR, TUCSON, AZ 85742 USA Tel 520-248-3146
E-mail: sheilamnster@aol.com.

Bergner, Bobby, *(978-0-615-21301-9; 978-0-615-22670-9)* 237 Sycamore Ln., Phoenixville, PA 19460 USA
Web site: http://www.moofax.com.

Bergstrom Bks., *(978-0-9787648)* 521 12th Ave. NE., Devils Lake, ND 58301 USA Tel 701-662-3320
E-mail: Candace@lakechevy.com.

Berkeley Major Publishing, *(978-0-9720691)* 8282 Skyline Cir., Oakland, CA 94605-4230 USA Fax: 419-791-7109
E-mail: dailon@progidy.net; BMP@berkeleymp.com
Web site: http://www.berkeleymp.com.

Berkeley Science Bks., *(978-0-9764138)* 529 Bonnie Dr., El Cerrito, CA 94530 USA Tel 510-524-8094
E-mail: wdflannery@aol.com.

Berkley *Imprint of* **Penguin Publishing Group**

Berkshire Publishing Group, *(978-0-9743091; 978-0-9770159; 978-1-933782; 978-1-61472)*
E-mail: cservice@berkshirepublishing.com
Web site: http://www.berkshirepublishing.com
Dist(s): **Follett School Solutions**
Cengage Gale
JSTOR
MyiLibrary.

Berlin, Stuart, *(978-0-615-22518-0; 978-0-615-48240-8; 978-0-9914128)* 1910 Larch St., Simi Valley, CA 93065 USA
E-mail: westwing1910@yahoo.com.

Berlinda Wall, *(978-1-7359858)* 1441 Southland Vista Ct. NE, Atlanta, GA 30329 USA Tel 404-234-9379
E-mail: berlindawall@gmail.com.

Berlitz Languages, Inc. *Imprint of* **Berlitz Publishing**

Berlitz Publishing, 46-35 54th Rd., Maspeth, NY 11378 USA; *Imprints:* Berlitz Languages, Incorporated (Berlitz Lang)
E-mail: customerservice@langenscheidt.com
Web site: http://www.berlitzbooks.com
Dist(s): **Ingram Publisher Services**
Langenscheidt Publishing Group.

Bernal, Nohra *See* **Arreboles**

Bernie's Bks., *(978-0-692-19119-4; 978-0-692-19120-0; 978-0-578-40480-6)* 5452 Trumpet Vine Trl. SE, Mableton, GA 30126-5650 USA Tel 443-825-5954
E-mail: karimi.faith@gmail.com.

Bernson Pr., *(978-0-9720509)* Orders Addr.: P.O. Box 55563, Sherman Oaks, CA 91413 USA Tel 818-268-3660; Edit Addr.: 5530 Allot Ave., Sherman Oaks, CA 91401 USA
E-mail: janet.bernson@gmail.com; thehealingartist@mac.com
Web site: http://www.thehealingartist.com; www.janetbernson.com.

Bernstein, Susan, *(978-0-9706596)* 31100 Northwestern Hwy., Farmington Hills, MI 48344-2519 USA Tel

Publisher Name Index

248-737-8400; Fax: 248-737-4392; Toll Free: 800-225-5726
E-mail: les380414744@aol.com
Web site: http://www.epominonousepstein.com.

Berry, Alicia J, *(978-1-7343660)* 4597 Main St., Jasper, TN 37347 USA Tel 423-942-3030
E-mail: Davidberry0070@yahoo.com.

Berry, Howard A., *(978-1-7335376)* 8003 Walker Ave, Kansas City, KS 66112 USA Tel 913-334-0352
E-mail: hberry6936@aol.com.

Berry, Joy Enterprises, *(978-1-60577)* 146 W. 29th St., Suite 11RW, New York, NY 10001 USA Tel 212-868-8282; Fax: 212-868-4110
Web site: http://www.joyberrymedia.com
Dist(s): **Children's Plus, Inc.**

Bertelsman, Verlagsgruppe C. GmbH (DEU) *(978-3-570) Dist. by* **Distribks Inc.**

Bertrand Brasil Editora SA (BRA) *(978-85-286) Dist. by* **Distribks Inc.**

Berube, Stacey, *(978-0-578-41461-4; 978-1-7334109)* 14 Howard Ave., Bourne, MA 02532 USA Tel 508-265-6717
E-mail: TaylynSenec@gmail.com
Dist(s): **Ingram Content Group.**

Berwick Court Publishing, *(978-0-615-34122-4; 978-0-615-35191-9; 978-0-9838846; 978-0-9889540; 978-0-9909515; 978-1-944376)* 9510 Kilbourn Ave., Skokie, IL 60076 USA Tel 312-772-3799
E-mail: matt@berwickcourt.com
Web site: https://www.berwickcourt.com.

Beryl Bks., *(978-1-7321747)* 7412 Madison St., Forest Park, IL 60130 USA Tel 216-403-8561
E-mail: jaymontville@gmail.com.

Bes Pr., *(978-0-9987236)* 3437 Airport Rd., Portage, IN 46368 USA Tel 219-762-7787; Fax: 219-763-9752
E-mail: shortpowerpress@gmail.com
Web site: www.storyofbes.com.

B.E.S. Publishing *Imprint of* **Peterson's**

Beshqoy, Nisreen, *(978-0-9759181)* P.O. Box 3846, Costa Mesa, CA 92628-3846 USA
E-mail: nisreenbeshqoy@hotmail.com
Web site: http://www.arabicandislamicbooksbynisreen.com.

Bess Pr., Inc., *(978-0-935848; 978-1-57306; 978-1-880188; 978-0-615-50460-5; 978-0-615-56510-1)* 3565 Harding Ave., Honolulu, HI 96816 USA (SAN 239-4111) Tel 808-734-7159; Fax: 808-732-3627
E-mail: kelly@besspress.com
Web site: http://www.besspress.com
Dist(s): **China Books & Periodicals, Inc.**
Follett School Solutions
Univ. of Hawaii Pr.

Best Books *See* **Library Reprints, Inc.**

Best eWay Pubns., Inc., *(978-0-9910062; 978-1-944084)* 3233 NE 34th St., Fort Lauderdale, FL 33308 USA Tel 847-612-7866
E-mail: barbaragoodheart@hotmail.com; cgoodheart847@hotmail.com
Web site: BesteWay.com.

Best Fairy Bks., *(978-0-9632524; 978-0-9786791; 978-1-7365459; 979-8-9868490)* 739 San Joaquin Rd, Poinciana, FL 34759 USA (SAN 851-2930) Tel 410-371-1855
E-mail: fairybooklady@gmail.com
Web site: http://bestfairybooks.com
Dist(s): **Follett School Solutions.**

Best Family Publishing *See* **Damon Strom**

Best Friends Books *See* **Children's Kindness Network**

Best Friends Productions, *(978-0-9765140)* 131 Bank St., New York, NY 10014-2177 USA
Web site: http://www.bestfriendsproductions.com.

Best of East Texas Pubs., *(978-1-878096)* Div. of Bob Bowman & Assocs., 515 S. First, Lufkin, TX 75901 USA Tel 409-634-7444; Fax: 409-634-7750.

Best Publishing Co., *(978-0-941332; 978-1-930536; 978-1-947239)* Div. of WCHMedia Group, Orders Addr.: 631 U.S. Hwy. 1, Ste 307, North Palm Beach, FL 33408 USA (SAN 238-9509) Tel 561-776-6066; Fax: 561-776-7476
E-mail: lorraine@bestpub.com
Web site: http://www.bestpub.com
Dist(s): **Rittenhouse Bk. Distributors.**

BEST VARIETY SHOP *See* **FASTLANE LLC**

Beth Bks., *(978-0-578-72453-9; 978-1-7353862; 979-8-218-11013-0; 979-8-218-11014-7)* 1261Lakeview Dr., Blackshear, GA 31516 USA Tel 321-900-0048
E-mail: authorbethclark@gmail.com.

Beth Detjens, Author, *(978-0-578-44327-0; 978-0-578-49724-2; 978-1-7340742)* 1134 Collinsville Crossing Boulevard, Suite 111, Collinsville, IL 62234 USA Tel 618-975-3141
E-mail: beth.detjens@gmail.com.

Bethany Claire Bks., *(978-0-9899502; 978-0-9960037; 978-0-9961136; 978-0-9978610; 978-1-947731; 978-1-970110)* P.O. Box 278, Clarendon, TX 79226 USA Tel 806-662-7201
E-mail: bclaire@bethanyclaire.com
Web site: www.bethanyclaire.com
Dist(s): **BookBaby.**

†Bethany Hse. Pubs., *(978-0-7642; 978-0-87123; 978-1-55661; 978-1-56179; 978-1-57778; 978-1-880089; 978-1-59066)* Div. of Baker Publishing Group, Orders Addr.: P.O. Box 6287, Grand Rapids, MI 49516-6287 USA Toll Free Fax: 800-398-3111 (orders); Toll Free: 800-877-2665 (orders); Edit Addr.: 11400 Hampshire Ave., S., Bloomington, MN 55438-2455 USA (SAN 201-4416) Tel 952-829-2500; Fax: 952-996-1393
E-mail: orders@bakerbooks.com
Web site: http://www.bethanyhouse.com
Dist(s): **Anchor Distributors**
Appalachian Bible Co.
Baker Publishing Group
Brodart Co.
Cambridge Univ. Pr.
Faith Alive Christian Resources
Follett School Solutions
Send The Light Distribution LLC
Spring Arbor Distributors, Inc.
Beeler, Thomas T. Pub.; *CIP.*

Bethany Stahl, *(978-1-7323951; 978-1-951987)* 2921 Windsock Ln, KNOXVILLE, TN 37924 USA Tel 727-400-1972
E-mail: bethanydstahl@gmail.com.

BethBirdBks., *(978-1-950603)* 2229 Crystal Spring Ave. SW No. 8584, Roanoke, VA 24014-9998 USA Tel 540-287-4621
E-mail: maryvogelsongwriter@gmail.com
Web site: MaryVogelsong.com.

Bethlehem Bks., *(978-1-883937; 978-1-932350; 978-1-954443; 978-1-958095)* Div. of Bethlehem Community, Orders Addr.: 10194 Garfield St. S., Bathgate, ND 58216-4031 USA Tel 701-265-3725; Fax: 701-265-3716; Toll Free: 800-757-6831 Do not confuse with bethlehem Books in Richmond, VA
E-mail: contact@bethlehembooks.com
Web site: http://www.bethlehembooks.com
Dist(s): **Follett School Solutions**
Ignatius Pr.
Spring Arbor Distributors, Inc.

Bethstewartministries, *(978-0-9909447)* 510 Knob hill ct, Ft Wright, KY 41011 USA Tel 859-391-6656
E-mail: Bethstewartky@gmail.com
Web site: Www.bethstewartministries.com.

Betrock Information Systems, Inc., *(978-0-9629761)* 7770 Davie Rd. Ext., Hollywood, FL 33024 USA Tel 954-981-2821; Fax: 954-981-2823
E-mail: Lori@betrock.com
Web site: http://www.hortworld.com.

Betsy Quinn *See* **Willow Glen Pubns.**

Bettenhausen, Jo Anne *See* **CBM Publishing**

Better Be Write Publisher, A *See* **W & B Pubs.**

Better Bound Hse., *(978-1-955963)* 1500 E Tropicana Ave. Ste 151, Las Vegas, NV 89119, Las Vegas, NV 89119 USA Tel 888-224-8399
E-mail: donvenanciolii@gmail.com.

Better Chinese LLC, *(978-1-60603; 978-1-68194)* P.O. Box 695, Palo Alto, CA 94303 USA Tel 650-384-0902; 2479 E Bayshore Rd., Suite 110, Palo Alto, CA 94303 Tel 650-384-0902; Fax: 702-442-7968
E-mail: usa@betterchinese.com
Web site: http://www.BetterChinese.com.

Better Comics, *(978-0-9728070)* P.O. Box 541924, Dallas, TX 75354-1924 USA
E-mail: JESmith@bettercomics.com
Web site: http://www.bettercomics.com.

Better Homes & Gardens Books *See* **Meredith Bks.**

Better Karma, LLC, *(978-0-9824329; 978-0-9828426; 978-0-9847753; 978-0-9962897)* 6018 Goldenrod Ct., Alexandria, VA 22310 USA (SAN 858-1495) Tel 703-971-1072
E-mail: publisher@betterkarmapublishing.com
Web site: http://www.BetterKarmaPublishing.com
Dist(s): **Smashwords.**

Better Me Bks., Inc., *(978-0-9770294)* P.O. Box 834, Marlton, NJ 08053 USA Tel 609-206-6318; Fax: 856-489-0234
E-mail: bettermebooks@aol.Com
Web site: http://www.bettermebooks.com.

Better Non Sequitur, *(978-0-9743235)* 11925 Via Zapata, El Cajon, CA 92019 USA Tel 619-246-5190
E-mail: steven@betternonsequitur.com
Web site: http://www.betternonsequitur.com.

Better Than One Publishing, *(978-0-9758958)* 27582 120th St., Staples, MN 56479 USA
Web site: http://www.creatingedumaterials.com.

Better Tomorrow Publishing, A, *(978-0-9795768)* P.O. Box 2975, Upper Marlboro, MD 20773-2975 USA Fax: 301-576-8070
E-mail: andy@abettertomorrowpublishing.net; sandy@abtpub.com
Web site: http://abettertomorrowpublishing.net.

BetterLink Pr., Inc., *(978-1-60220)* 99 Pk. Ave., R.R. Donnelley, New York, NY 10016 USA
Dist(s): **Penguin Publishing Group**
Simon & Schuster, Inc.
Tuttle Publishing
Univ. of Hawaii Pr.

BetterNot Enterprises, *(978-0-692-47105-0; 978-0-692-69079-6; 978-0-692-93150-9)* 200 E Del Mar Blvd Suite 304, PASADENA, CA 91105 USA Tel 661-287-9995.

Bettino, Teresa Adele, *(978-0-9742842)* 8403 Cosby Ln., Mechanicsville, VA 23116 USA Tel 804-779-2672
E-mail: tbettino@msn.com.

Betts, Linda, *(978-0-9767802)* Orders Addr.: 6050 Pagenkopf Rd., Maple Plain, MN 55359 USA Tel 763-479-2789; Fax: 763-476-6508
E-mail: lynrae@hotmail.com.

Between the Lakes Group, LLC, *(978-0-9727403; 978-0-9766342; 978-0-9791000; 978-0-9826073)* Orders Addr.: P.O. Box 13, Taconic, CT 06079-0013 USA Tel 860-824-0640
E-mail: geoff@betweenthelakes.com
Web site: http://www.betweenthelakes.com.

Between the Lines (CAN) *(978-0-919946; 978-0-921284; 978-1-896357; 978-1-897071; 978-1-926662; 978-1-77113) Dist. by* **AK Pr Dist.**

Between the Lines Publishing, *(978-0-9979395; 978-0-9996556; 978-1-7321723; 978-1-950502; 978-1-958901)* 410 caribou trail, lutsen, MN 55612 USA (SAN 990-6533) Tel 910-331-8171; *Imprints:* Willow River Press (MYID_N_WILLOW)
E-mail: inquiries@btwnthelines.com
Web site: www.btwnthelines.com.

Beverly Hills Publishing, *(978-0-9758870; 978-0-9777074; 978-0-9791967)* 291 S. La Cienega Blvd., Suites 107/108, Beverly Hills, CA 90211-3325 USA (SAN 850-0029) Tel 310-854-0705; Fax: 310-854-1840; Toll Free: 800-521-5669
E-mail: silvers@bevhillspub.com
Web site: http://www.bevhillspub.com.

Beyer, Jenna, *(978-0-692-99946-2; 978-1-7320529; 978-0-692-12203-7; 978-0-692-19882-7; 979-8-9884373)* 218 N Madison St., Monroe, WA 98272 USA Tel 425-870-7179
E-mail: GoldenBeyer@gmail.com
Dist(s): **Ingram Content Group.**

Beyond Bks., *(978-0-615-63333-6; 978-0-615-73882-6; 978-0-615-76677-5; 978-0-615-87076-2; 978-0-615-95841-5; 978-0-692-65694-5; 978-0-692-07536-4; 978-0-692-07573-9; 978-0-692-14044-4; 978-0-692-14045-1; 978-0-692-14046-8; 978-0-692-14060-4; 978-0-692-14090-1; 978-1-7364573)*
E-mail: leo.ramirez7@icloud.com.

BEYOND PUBLISHING, *(978-0-9961486; 978-0-692-82269-2; 978-0-9987292; 978-1-947256; 978-1-7326299; 978-1-949873; 978-1-952884; 978-1-63792)* 7722 Liberty Dr. Suite C, Huntington Beach, CA 92647 USA Tel 918-955-3227
E-mail: michael@beyondpublishing.net
Web site: www.Beyondpublishing.net.

Beyond the Stars, Incorporated *See* **Beyond the Stars Pubns.**

Beyond the Stars Pubns., *(978-0-9763635)* 14902 Preston Rd., Suite 404-764, Dallas, TX 75254 USA
E-mail: rjohnson@beyondthestarsbooks.com
Web site: http://www.beyondthestarsbooks.com.

Beyond Words *Imprint of* **Simon & Schuster**

Beyond Words Publishing, Inc., *(978-0-941831; 978-1-58270; 978-1-885223; 979-8-88681)* 1750 S.W. Skyline Blvd., Suite 20, Portland, OR 97221-2543 USA (SAN 666-4210) Tel 503-531-8700; Fax: 503-531-8773; Toll Free: 800-284-9673
E-mail: info@beyondword.com; sales@beyondword.com; editorial@beyondword.com
Web site: http://www.beyondword.com
Dist(s): **Follett School Solutions**
Simon & Schuster, Inc.

Beyond Words/Atria Bks. *Imprint of* **Atria Bks.**

Beyond Your Words, *(978-0-9788789)* P.O. Box 5842, Newport Beach, CA 92662-9266 USA
Web site: http://www.beyondyourwords.com.

Bezalel Bks., *(978-0-9792258; 978-0-9794976; 978-0-9800483; 978-0-9818854; 978-0-9821222; 978-0-9823388; 978-0-9844864; 978-1-936453)* P.O. Box 300427, Waterford, MI 48330 USA
E-mail: bezalelbooks@gmail.com
Web site: http://www.bezalelbooks.com.

BFG Pr., LLC, *(978-0-9820307)* Div. of The PIE Group, P.O. Box 2269, Ewa Beach, HI 96706 USA (SAN 857-0590) Tel 808-428-0733
Web site: http://www.bfgpress.com/.

BFI Publishing (GBR) *(978-0-85170; 978-0-900212; 978-1-903786; 978-1-84457; 978-1-911239) Dist. by* **Macmillan.**

BGA Stories, *(978-0-9724806)* 3414 Forest Hills Cir., Garland, TX 75044-2000 USA (SAN 254-878X) Tel 972-496-0416
E-mail: bga@bgastories.com
Web site: http://www.bgastories.com.

BGS Productions, Inc., *(978-0-9972861)* 17798 SW 36th St., MIRAMAR, FL 33029 USA Tel 404-594-4962
E-mail: info.blackgirlspeaks@gmail.com; tanyabwele@gmail.com
Web site: www.blackgirlspeaks.com.

Bh Pubns., *(978-0-9760348)*
Web site: http://www.octopusrex.com; www.iammyhair.com.

Bhakta Program Institute *See* **Rupanuga Vedic College**

Bharat Babies, *(978-0-692-96283-1)* 31 Perry St., Somerville, MA 02143 USA Tel 508-369-6853
E-mail: namaste@bharatbabies.com
Web site: www.bharatbabies.com.

BHB International, Incorporated *See* **Continental Enterprises Group, Inc. (CEG)**

BHC Pr., *(978-0-692-56880-4; 978-0-692-59166-6; 978-1-946006; 978-1-946848; 978-1-947727; 978-1-948540; 978-1-64397)* 36056 Ann Arbor Trail No. 403, Livonia, MI 48150 USA Tel 248-982-9068
E-mail: books@bhcpress.com
Web site: http://www.bhcpress.com/
Dist(s): **CreateSpace Independent Publishing Platform.**

BHF Publishing, *(978-0-9801913; 978-0-615-13143-6)* 7139 Hwy. 85, Suite 274, Riverdale, GA 30274 USA Tel 678-925-4175
E-mail: melissabowan@hotmail.com; stdennis@highly-favored.net
Web site: http://www.highly-favored.net.

BHHR Energies Group, *(978-1-935684)* 689 Amador St., Richmond, CA 94805 USA.

Biabe Publishing, *(978-0-9825944; 978-0-9984926; 978-1-63740)* 401 E Las Olas Blvd. Ste 130 Box 412, Fort Lauderdale, FL 33301 USA
E-mail: lissee@gmail.com.

Bibi Art Media Inc., *(978-0-9754329)* 7133 Bay Dr. 706, Miami Beach, FL 33141 USA
Web site: http://www.theadventuresofbibiandfriends.com.

Bibia, LLC, *(978-0-9826276; 978-0-615-74924-2; 978-1-940760)* PMB206 2880 Bicentennial Pkwy., Suite 100, Henderson, NV 89044 USA Tel 702-896-0967; *Imprints:* Bibia Publishing (Bibia)
E-mail: bibiapublishing@gmail.com
Web site: www.bibiapublishing.com.

Bibia Publishing *Imprint of* **Bibia, LLC**

Bible Based Studies, *(978-0-9797786)* 1134 SE 3rd St., Crystal River, FL 34429 USA Tel 352-795-5128
E-mail: info@biblebasedstudies.org
Web site: http://www.biblebasedstudies.org.

Bible Facts Pr., *(978-0-9762892; 978-0-9772942)* 631 Martin Ave. Suite 1, Rohnert Park, CA 94928 USA
Web site: http://www.biblefactspress.com.

Bible Game *Imprint of* **IMAGINEX, LLC**

Bible League, *(978-1-882536; 978-1-61825; 978-1-61870; 978-1-62826; 979-8-88788)*
E-mail: info@bibleleagueusa.com
Web site: http://www.bibleleagueusa.com.

Bible Pathway Ministries, *(978-1-879595)* Orders Addr.: P.O Box 20123, Murfreesboro, TN 37133 USA Tel 615-896-4243; Fax: 615-893-1744; Toll Free: 800-598-7884; Edit Addr.: P.O. Box 20123, Murfreesboro TN 37129-0123 USA
E-mail: mail@biblepathway.org
Web site: http://www.biblepathway.org
Dist(s): **Send The Light Distribution LLC.**

Bible Visuals International, Inc., *(978-1-932381; 978-1-933206; 978-1-64104)* Orders Addr.: P.O. Box 153 Akron, PA 17501-0153 USA
Web site: http://www.biblevisuals.org.

Bible-4-Life.com *See* **SundaySchoolNetwork.com**

BibleByte Books *See* **Kidware Software, LLC**

Bibleco, Inc., *(978-0-9746058; 978-0-9754978)* 153 Pinehurst Dr., Easton, PA 18042 USA (SAN 256-0801) Fax: 610-438-3964; *Imprints:* Biblemania (Bibleman)
E-mail: biblemania@aol.com
Web site: http://www.biblemania.com.

Biblemania *Imprint of* **Bibleco, Inc.**

BibleRhymes *Imprint of* **BibleRhymes Publishing, L.L.C.**

BibleRhymes Publishing, L.L.C., *(978-0-9790605; 978-1-947049)* Orders Addr.: 54211 Horizon Dr., Shelby Township, MI 48316 USA (SAN 852-3207); *Imprints:* BibleRhymes (BibleRhymes USA)
E-mail: CustomerService@BibleRhymes.com
Web site: http://www.BibleRhymes.com.

Biblesoft, Inc., *(978-1-56514)* 22030 Seventh Ave., S., Suite 204, Seattle, WA 98198-6235 USA (SAN 298-7473) Tel 206-824-0547; Fax: 206-824-2729
Web site: http://www.biblesoft.com
Dist(s): **Anchor Distributors**
Spring Arbor Distributors, Inc.

BiblesPlus, *(978-0-9769109)* 13741 Annandale Dr., No. 20D, Seal Beach, CA 90740 USA Toll Free: 866-924-2537
E-mail: biblesplus7@yahoo.com
Web site: http://www.biblesplus.com.

Biblical Counseling Institute *See* **Skinner, Kerry L.**

Biblical Standards Pubns., *(978-0-9678798)* 287 Caldwell Dr., Maggie Valley, NC 28751 USA Tel 828-926-0606
E-mail: waltdot@primeline.com.

Biblio Bks. International, *(978-0-9729545; 978-0-9741190; 978-0-9748524; 978-0-9766681; 978-0-9785565; 978-0-9833352)* Kendall Tamiami Executive Airport 14005 SW 127th St., Miami, FL 33186 USA Tel 786 573 3999; Fax: 786 573 2090
E-mail: info@bibliobooks.com
Web site: http://www.bibliobooks.com.

Biblio Graficas *Imprint of* **Biblio Services, Inc.**

Biblio Resource Pubns., Inc., *(978-1-934185)* 108 1/2 S. Moore St., Bessemer, MI 49911 USA Tel 906-364-2190
E-mail: info@BiblioResource.com
Web site: http://www.BiblioResource.com
Dist(s): **Follett School Solutions.**

Biblio Services, Inc., *(978-1-59608; 978-1-61887; 978-1-64131)* 399 Ave. Munoz Rivera, San Juan, PR 00918 USA Tel 787-753-1231; Fax: 787-753-1222; *Imprints:* Biblio Graficas (BiblioGraficas)
E-mail: ventas@biblioservices.com; vale@biblioservices.com; anthony@biblioservices.com
Web site: http://www.biblioservices.com.

Biblioasis (CAN) *(978-0-9735881; 978-0-9735971; 978-1-897231; 978-0-9738184; 978-1-926845) Dist. by* **Consort Bk Sales.**

BiblioBazaar *See* **Creative Media Partners, LLC**

BiblioCrunch, *(978-1-938321)* 175 E. 96th St. Apt. 9K, NY, NY 10128 USA Tel 732-713-1996
E-mail: miral@bibliocrunch.com.

Bibliograf, S.A. (ESP) *(978-84-7153; 978-84-8332) Dist. by* **Distribks Inc.**

Bibliograf, S.A. (ESP) *(978-84-7153; 978-84-8332) Dist. by* **Continental Bk.**

Bibliographisches Institut & F. A. Brockhaus AG (DEU) *(978-3-411) Dist. by* **Intl Bk Import.**

Bibliographisches Institut & F. A. Brockhaus AG (DEU) *(978-3-411) Dist. by* **Distribks Inc.**

Bibliographisches Institut & F. A. Brockhaus AG (DEU) *(978-3-411) Dist. by* **Continental Bk.**

Bibliographisches Institut & F. A. Brockhaus AG (DEU) *(978-3-411) Dist. by* **IBD Ltd.**

BiblioLife *Imprint of* **Creative Media Partners, LLC**

BibliotecaLatinx, *(978-1-959040)* 3041 S. Gilpin St., Denver, CO 80210 USA Tel 303-503-8983
E-mail: osomoza@du.edu
Web site: www.bibliotecalatinx.com.

Bibliotech Pr., *(978-1-61895; 978-1-64799; 978-1-63637; 979-8-88830)* 8559 GLEN CREST DR, SUN VALLEY, CA 91352 USA Tel 818-546-1554
E-mail: BibliotechPress@gmail.com.

Biblo & Tannen Booksellers & Pubs., Inc., *(978-0-8196)* P.O. Box 302, Cheshire, CT 06410 USA (SAN 202-4071) Tel 203-250-1647 (phone/fax); Toll Free: 800-272-8778
E-mail: biblo.moser@gte.net.

BIC Alliance, *(978-0-9768310)* Orders Addr.: P.O. Box 40166, Baton Rouge, LA 70835 USA Fax: 225-751-9993; Toll Free: 800-460-4242; Edit Addr.: 6378 Quinn Dr., Baton Rouge, LA 70817 USA
E-mail: brady@bicalliance.com
Web site: http://www.bicpublishing.com.

Bicast, Inc., *(978-0-9638258; 978-0-9701008; 978-0-9766753)* Orders Addr.: P.O. Box 2676, Williamsburg, VA 23187 USA Tel 757-229-3276; Fax: 757-253-2273; Toll Free: 800-767-8273; Edit Addr.: 231 K Parkway Dr., Williamsburg, VA 23185 USA
E-mail: bicastpub@aol.com; jogaertner@hughes.net
Web site: http://www.lighthousesusa.com.

Bicep Bks., *(978-1-7341546; 978-1-7344730; 978-1-7347816; 978-1-953221)* 1004 Corralito Rd., Roswell, NM 88201 USA Tel 575-626-7456
E-mail: jplemay@plateautel.net.

ck Publishing Hse., *(978-1-884158)* 307 Neck Rd., Madison, CT 06443 USA Tel 203-245-0073; 203 245 0073; Fax: 203-245-5990; 30 Amberwood Pkwy., Ashland, OH 44805
E-mail: bickpubhse@aol.com
Web site: http://www.bickpubhouse.com
Dist(s): **Follett School Solutions**
Quality Bks., Inc.

ickering Owls Publishing *Imprint of* **Maracle, Derek**

ickico Enterprises, Inc., *(978-0-9746508; 978-0-9834081)* 19W042 Ave. Normandy E., Oak Brook, IL 60523 USA
E-mail: bickico@aol.com.

ICs Pr., *(978-0-9764253)* 1866 John F. Kennedy Blvd., No. B1, Jersey City, NJ 07305 USA.

icycle Bell Bks., *(978-0-9981468; 978-1-7358172)* 10808 NW 75th St., KANSAS CITY, MO 64152 USA Tel 816-659-5268
E-mail: j.ballou@sbcglobal.net
Web site: BicycleBellBooks.com.

ide Ahwee Publishing & Mulitmedia, *(978-1-7325270)* 201 Jasmine Rd. W., Lehigh Acres, FL 33936 USA Tel 239-247-1262
E-mail: naomijacksonwrites@gmail.com
Web site: naomijacksonwrites.com; https://www.naomireidwrites.com/.

Bienna Bks., *(978-0-9815075)* 21310 Poplar Way, Brier, WA 98036 USA Tel 206-774-3649.

Bienvenue Pr., *(978-0-692-08164-8; 978-0-692-11737-8; 978-0-692-12191-7; 978-0-692-14427-5; 978-0-692-15533-2; 978-0-692-18524-7; 978-0-578-41249-8; 978-0-578-42335-7; 978-0-578-43970-9; 978-0-578-46164-9; 978-0-578-47234-8; 978-0-578-49555-2; 978-0-578-52069-8; 978-0-578-57088-4; 978-0-578-60544-9; 978-0-578-61817-3; 978-0-578-67611-1; 978-1-7350454) 112 Sapphire Springs Rd., Youngsville, LA 70592 USA Tel 337-230-4097*
E-mail: alvincent@bienvenuepress.com
Web site: www.bienvenuepress.com
Dist(s): **CreateSpace Independent Publishing Platform.**

Bier Brothers, Inc., *(978-0-9677238)* 147 Wild Dunes Way, Jackson, NJ 08527-4050 USA (SAN) Fax: 810-815-2979; *Imprints:* Sweet Dreams Press (Sweet Press)
E-mail: Dsb342@aol.com; contactus@nightsprytes.com
Web site: http://www.newbreedcomics.com; http://www.nightsprytes.com.

BiG *Imprint of* **Humanoids, Inc.**

Big Bear Publishing U.S., *(978-0-9801215)* P.O. Box 191, Ronks, PA 17572-9611 USA (SAN 855-2517) Tel 717-768-4644
E-mail: lonniebrinkley@yahoo.com
Web site: http://www.ibelievesanta.com.

Big Belly Bks., *(978-0-9749554; 978-0-692-37003-2; 978-0-9961792)* Orders Addr.: 2778 W. Schuss Mtn. Dr., Bellaire, MI 49615 USA; Edit Addr.: 2778 W. Schuss Mtn. Dr., Bellaire, MI 49615 USA
E-mail: sc@bigbellybooks.com
Web site: http://www.bigbellybooks.com.

Big Bks. for Little People *Imprint of* **Friendly Planet**

Big Blue World Bks. *Imprint of* **Gumdrop Pr.**

Big Book Pr., LLC, *(978-0-9793219; 978-0-9848920)* Orders Addr.: 47774 Scots Borough Sq., Potomac Falls, VA 20165 USA Tel 240-355-3465
E-mail: frankchawkins@gmail.com; books@boysguidebooks.com; books@bigbookpress.com; books@girlsguidebooks.net; books@boysandgirlsguidebooks.com
Web site: http://www.boysguidebooks.blogspot.com; http://www.boysguidebooks.com; http://www.girlsguidebooks.net; http://www.bigbookpress.com; http://www.boysandgirlsguidebooks.com
Dist(s): **Independent Pubs. Group**
MyiLibrary
Small Pr. United.

Big Bk. Pubns., *(978-0-615-17074-9; 978-0-615-21065-0)* P.O. Box 7867, Largo, MD 20792 USA
E-mail: nicole@bigbookpublications.com
Web site: http://www.nigbookpublications.com.

Big Books, by George!, *(978-1-59246)* Orders Addr.: P.O. Box 1018, Keller, TX 76244 USA; Edit Addr.: 901 Briar Ridge Dr., Keller, TX 76244 USA
Dist(s): **Follett School Solutions.**

Big Brown Box, Inc., The, *(978-0-9764647)* 443 Hill Rd., Douglassville, PA 19518-9530 USA Tel 610-385-7587
Web site: http://www.thebigbrownbox.com
Dist(s): **Book Clearing Hse.**

Big Buddy Bks. *Imprint of* **ABDO Publishing Co.**

Big City Publishing, *(978-0-9762071; 978-0-9845873)* 230 Central St., Auburndale, MA 02492 USA Fax: 617-795-1650
E-mail: mellisa@bigcitypublishing.com
Web site: http://www.anglesfromtheattic.com.

Big Company, LLC, The, *(978-0-9800752)* 4790 Irvine Blvd., Suite 105-176, Irvine, CA 92620 USA (SAN 855-1383)
E-mail: info@thebigcompanyllc.com.

Big Country Publishing, LLC, *(978-0-9845088; 978-0-9847831; 978-1-938487)* 7691 Shaffer Pkwy., Suite C, Littleton, CO 80127 USA.

Big Creek Publishing, *(978-0-9742021)* Orders Addr.: P.O. Box 884, Sunberry, OH 43074 USA Tel 740-965-4127; Fax: 740-965-9541; Edit Addr.: 930 Joe Walker Rd., Sunbury, OH 43074 USA (SAN 255-4054) Tel 740-965-4127
E-mail: bigcreekpublishing@msn.com.

Big Dreams Publishing, *(978-0-9771868)* 8180 S. Allison Ct., Littleton, CO 80128 USA.

Big Earth Publishing *See* **Bower Hse.**

Big Entertainment, Inc., *(978-0-9645175; 978-1-57780)* 2255 Glades Rd., Suite 237W, Boca Raton, FL 33431-7395 USA Tel 407-998-8000; Fax: 407-998-2974
Dist(s): **Kable Media Services.**

Big Eyes Publishing, *(978-1-943574)* 1221 Inverness Ct., Schererville, IN 46375 USA Tel 219-515-2565
E-mail: Thomasconti@yahoo.com.

Big Guy Bks., Inc, *(978-1-929945)* 6866 Embarcadero Ln., Carlsbad, CA 92011 USA (SAN 253-0392) Toll Free: 800-536-3030
E-mail: robert@bigguybooks.com
Web site: http://www.timesoldiers.com; http://www.bigguybooks.com; http://www.freedinosaurbook.com; https://GreatBooksForBoys.com
Dist(s): **Follett School Solutions.**

Big Guy Books, Incorporated *See* **Big Guy Bks., Inc**

Big H Bks. *Imprint of* **Harvey, Alan**

Big Head Pr., *(978-0-9743814; 978-0-9853167)* P.O. Box 1853, Round Rock, TX 78680 USA
E-mail: contact@bigheadpress.com
Web site: http://www.bigheadpress.com
Dist(s): **Diamond Comic Distributors, Inc.**

Big Hoops Production LLC, *(978-1-7356492)* 5139 Lister Ave., Kansas City, MO 64130 USA Tel 816-616-7672
E-mail: cheryl.hampton47@gmail.com.

Big Idea Productions, P.O. Box 189, Lombard, IL 60148 USA Tel 630-652-6000; Fax: 630-652-6001
Dist(s): **Vision Video**
Word Entertainment.

Big Ideas Learning, LLC, *(978-1-60840; 978-1-68033; 978-1-63598; 978-1-64208; 978-1-64245; 978-1-64312; 978-1-64432; 978-1-64727; 978-1-63708; 978-1-63736; 978-1-63896; 979-8-88632; 979-8-88698; 979-8-88802; 979-8-88803; 979-8-89028; 979-8-89223)* 1762 Norcross Rd., Erie, PA 16510 USA (SAN 857-751X) Tel 814-824-6365; 814-824-6370; Fax: 814-824-6377; Toll Free Fax: 888-432-9245; Toll Free: 877-552-7766
E-mail: BIL_products@larsontexts.com
Web site: http://bigideaslearning.com
Dist(s): **Houghton Mifflin Harcourt Publishing Co.**
Macmillan
National Geographic School Publishing, Inc.

Big Kid Bks., *(978-0-9771990)* 6671 Sunset Blvd., No. 1585-101, Los Angeles, CA 90028 USA.

Big Kid Science, *(978-0-9721819; 978-1-937548; 978-1-944161)* 680 Iris Ave., Boulder, CO 80304 USA; 814 N. Franklin St., Chicago, IL 60610
E-mail: jeff@bigkidscience.com
Web site: http://www.jeffreybennett.com
Dist(s): **Follett School Solutions**
Independent Pubs. Group
MyiLibrary
ebrary, Inc.

Big Kids Productions (Publishing) *See* **LL Cameron Group, LLC**

Big Lil' Bks., *(978-0-9749041)* Div. of ShadeTree Publishing, 3625 Tallman SE, Grand Rapids, MI 49508 USA
E-mail: janiceintheshade@msn.com.

Big Little Pr., *(978-0-578-52313-2; 978-1-7333217; 978-1-7372214; 978-1-959140)* 2274 Cottle Ave, San Jose, CA 95125 USA Tel 408-809-1001
E-mail: linda@lherron.com
Web site: www.lherron.com.

Big Mouth Hse. *Imprint of* **Small Beer Pr.**

Big Picture Press *Imprint of* **Candlewick Pr.**

Big Picture, The, *(978-0-9794304; 978-0-9882125; 978-0-9996724)* 5976 Leland, Ann Arbor, MI 48105-9309 USA Tel 734-223-4933
E-mail: kmaclean@kjmaclean.com
Web site: http://www.kjmaclean.com/.

Big Ransom Studio, *(978-0-9754728; 978-1-933732)* P.O. Box 489, Georgetown, TX 78627-0489 USA
E-mail: sales@bigransom.com
Web site: http://www.mindtrippress.com
Dist(s): **Mind Trip Pr.**

Big Rig LLC, *(978-0-692-79625-2; 978-0-9997696)* 2820 Selwyn Ave Suite 847, Charlotte, NC 28209 USA Tel 704-585-7609
E-mail: thebigrigkids@gmail.com
Web site: www.thebigrigkids.org.

Big River Distribution, *(978-0-9795944; 978-0-9823575; 978-0-9845519)* Orders Addr.: 8214 Exchange Way, Saint Louis, MO 63144 USA (SAN 631-9114) Tel 314-918-9800; Fax: 314-918-9804
E-mail: info@bigriverdist.com; randy@bigriverdist.com
Web site: http://www.bigriverdist.com
Dist(s): **Follett School Solutions.**

Big Secret, The, *(978-0-9724924)* P.O. Box 1994, Slidell, LA 70459 USA Tel 985-781-8704 (phone/fax)
Web site: http://www.thebigsecret.org.

Big Sil LLC., *(978-0-9967352; 978-0-9983357)* P.O. Box 1755, Hoboken, NJ 07030 USA Tel 201-615-9601
E-mail: bigsiladventures@gmail.com.

Big Sky Stories Publishing *See* **Amica Publishing**

Big Smile, Inc., *(978-0-9761891)* P.O. Box 1042, Stroudsburg, PA 18360 USA Fax: 646-542-5319
E-mail: marcjohnjefferies@yahoo.com
Web site: http://www.marcjohnonline.com.

Big Smile Pr., LLC, *(978-0-9888462)* 180 Hollow Way, Ingleside, IL 60041 USA Tel 847-973-9084
E-mail: kellyp123@comcast.net

Big Table Publishing Co., *(978-0-9753211; 978-0-9824955; 978-0-9842473; 978-0-9845733; 978-0-9830666; 978-0-9849567; 978-0-9886191; 978-0-9904872; 978-0-9908413; 978-0-9965405; 978-0-9969887; 978-1-945917)* 289 Elliot St., Newton Upper Falls, MA 02464 USA Tel 617-592-5805
Web site: http://www.bigtablepublishing.com.

Big Tent Bks., *(978-1-60131; 978-0-578-47138-9; 978-0-578-66280-0)* 115 Bluebill Dr., Savannah, GA 31419 USA (SAN 851-1136); *Imprints:* Parents Publishing Group (Parents Pub); Castlebridge Books (Castlebridge Bks)
E-mail: admin@dragonpencil.com; admin@bigtentbooks.com
Web site: http://www.bigtentbooks.com
Dist(s): **Castlebridge Distribution**
Music, Bks. & Business, Inc.

Big Tent Entertainment, Inc., *(978-1-59226)* 216 W. 18th St., New York, NY 10011 USA Tel 212-604-0064
Dist(s): **Independent Pubs. Group**
Midpoint Trade Bks., Inc.

Big Tomato Pr., *(978-0-9791233)* Orders Addr.: 1480 Sutterville Rd., Sacramento, CA 95822 USA Tel 916-798-2125
E-mail: jocelyn@bigtomatopress.com
Web site: http://www.bigtomatopress.com
Dist(s): **Follett School Solutions.**

Big Valley Pr., *(978-0-9765372)* 401 E. Holum St, Deforest, WI 53532 USA Tel 608-513-0724
E-mail: stuart@stotts.com
Web site: http://www.bigvalleypress.com
Dist(s): **Follett School Solutions.**

Big Valley Publishing, *(978-0-9726004)* 516 N. Chinowth, Visalia, CA 93291 USA Do not confuse with company with similar name in Northridge, CA
E-mail: erkna@aol.com.

Big Wave Bks., *(978-0-9754979)* P.O. Box 108, Charlestown, RI 02813 USA Tel 401-322-8711
Web site: http://www.bigwavebooks.com.

Big Wonderworld of Books *See* **Children's Bible Project, The**

Big World Little Om *See* **Sahtva**

Bigfoot Bks. (GBR) *(978-0-9554555) Dist. by* **NStarEdit.**

Biggaloo Bks., *(978-0-9818145)* 660 Fairway Terr., Naples, FL 34103 USA (SAN 856-6267)
Dist(s): **Music, Bks. & Business, Inc.**

Biggie, Kat Press *See* **WritePublishSell**

Big-head fish, *(978-0-9765007)*
E-mail: info@bigheadfish.com/.

BigKids Bilingual Bks., *(978-0-9844310)* P.O. Box 537, Glendale, CA 91209 USA (SAN 859-385X) Tel 626-407-8886
E-mail: jalexan@alumni.usc.edu
Web site: http://www.bigkidsbilingualbooks.com.

Bikhazi, Karen, *(978-1-7342358)* 689 Windsor Ln., Kaysville, UT 84037 USA Tel 801-510-2734
E-mail: karenkostiuk@yahoo.com.

Bilal, Nabeeh, *(978-0-615-95158-4; 978-0-692-57311-2; 978-0-692-62252-0; 978-0-692-75743-7; 978-0-692-81373-7; 978-0-692-91555-4; 978-0-692-08756-5; 978-0-692-13045-2)* Orders Addr.: 1888 Savannah Pl SE, washington, DC 20020 USA Tel 202-421-8241; 700 S. Berendo St. Apt. 403, Los Angeles, CA 90005
E-mail: mtcanady@gmail.com; nabeeh_bilal@hotmail.com
Web site: http://www.callalootbook.com.

Bilbo Bks., *(978-0-9800108; 978-0-9981627; 978-1-7326180; 978-1-7364596; 979-8-9867043)* 1384 W. Peachtree St., NW, No. C-4, Atlanta, GA 30309-2913 USA
E-mail: bilbobookspublishing@gmail.com.

Bilingual Dictionaries, Inc., *(978-0-933146; 978-1-946986)* Orders Addr.: P.O. Box 1154, Murrieta, CA 92564 USA (SAN 221-9697) Tel 951-296-2445; Fax: 951-296-9911; 42225 Remington Ave, A4, Temecula, CA 92590 (SAN 990-4972) Tel 951-296-2445; Fax: 951-296-9911; *Imprints:* Basic ESL (MYID_H_BASIC E)
E-mail: manager@bilingualdictionaries.com; support@bilingualdictionaries.com
Web site: http://www.bilingualdictionaries.com
Dist(s): **Booksource, The**
Follett School Solutions.

Bilingual Educational Services, Inc., *(978-0-86624; 978-0-89075)* 2514 S. Grand Ave., Los Angeles, CA 90007 USA (SAN 218-4680) Tel 213-749-6213; Fax: 213-749-1820; Toll Free: 800-448-6032
E-mail: sales@besbooks.com
Web site: http://www.besbooks.com
Dist(s): **Follett School Solutions.**

Bilingual Language Materials *See* **MAAT Resources, Inc.**

Bilingual Language Materials *Imprint of* **MAAT Resources, Inc.**

Bilingual Pr./Editorial Bilingue, *(978-0-916950; 978-0-927534; 978-1-931010; 978-1-939743)* Orders Addr.: Hispanic Research Ctr. Arizona State Univ. P.O. Box 875303, Tempe, AZ 85287-5303 USA (SAN 208-5526) Fax: 480-965-8309; Toll Free: 800-965-2280; Edit Addr.: Bilingual Review Pr. Administration Bldg. Rm. B-255 Arizona State Univ., Tempe, AZ 85281 USA
E-mail: brp@asu.edu
Web site: http://www.asu.edu/brp
Dist(s): **Libros Sin Fronteras**
SPD-Small Pr. Distribution.

Bilingual Pubns., *(978-0-9644678)* P.O. Box 12678, Denver, CO 80212 USA Tel 303-433-0979 Do not confuse with Bilingual Pubns. Co., New York, NY.

Bilingual Pubns. Co., The, 270 Lafayette St., New York, NY 10012 USA (SAN 164-8993) Tel 212-431-3500; Fax: 212-431-3567 Do not confuse with Bilingual Pubns., in Denver, CO
E-mail: lindagoodman@juno.com; spanishbks@aol.com.

Bill of Rights Institute, The, *(978-1-932785; 978-0-692-23022-0; 978-0-692-89225-1)* 200 N. Glebe Rd. Ste. 200, Arlington, VA 22203-3756 USA Toll Free: 800-838-7870
E-mail: sales@billofrightsinstitute.org; mwong@billofrightsinstitute.org; wneal@billofrightsinstitute.org
Web site: http://www.billofrightsinstitute.org
Dist(s): **CLEARVUE/eav, Inc.**
Social Studies Schl. Service
Teacher's Discovery.

Billiard Congress of America, *(978-1-878493)* 5 Piedmont Ctr NE Ste. 435, Atlanta, GA 30305-1509 USA
E-mail: amy@bca-pool.com; marketing@bca-pool.com
Web site: http://www.bca-pool.com.

Billie Holladay Skelley, *(978-1-947847)* 3780 W. 26th St., Joplin, MO 64804 USA Tel 417-782-7145; *Imprints:* LawMux Press (Lawmux Pr)
E-mail: bhskelley24@gmail.com.

Billings, David J., *(978-0-9789036)* 12441 SE Lusted Rd., Sandy, OR 97055-7556 USA
E-mail: david@davidjbillings.com; david@roadtripbook.com
Web site: http://www.roadtripbook.com.

Billings Worldwide Brain, *(978-0-9654169)* P.O. Box 701, Addison, TX 75001 USA (SAN 299-2426)
E-mail: dave@hamr.com
Web site: http://www.hamr.com
Dist(s): **Distributors, The.**

Billion $ Baby Pubns., *(978-0-9707945)* 22817 Ventura Blvd., Suite 408, Woodland Hills, CA 91364 USA (SAN 254-3265) Toll Free Fax: 888-232-9022; Toll Free: 800-499-2771
E-mail: Diedra@BabyPublications.com; dottie@babypublications.com
Web site: http://www.BabyPublication.com.

Billionaire Butterfly, LLC, *(978-0-9852262; 978-0-692-81697-4; 978-0-692-81764-3)* 109-15 Queens Blvd. Apt. 2C, Forest Hills, NY 11375 USA Tel 718-810-8700
E-mail: lenaure@gmail.com.

Billiot, Wendy Wilson, *(978-0-9762592)* 2715 Bayou DuLarge Rd., Theriot, LA 70397 USA
E-mail: wwbilliot@gmail.com
Web site: http://www.wetlandbooks.com.

Billy Jo Bks., *(978-0-9765088)* 9111 Oat Ave., Gerber, CA 96035-9723 USA Tel 530-385-1820
E-mail: biljoho@earthlink.net.

Billy the Bear & His Friends, Inc., *(978-0-9641338)* 1909 Munster Ave., Saint Paul, MN 55116 USA Tel 651-699-7636; Fax: 651-690-4815.

BillyFish Bks. LLC, *(978-0-9849155)* 518 E. Datura Ct., Pueblo West, CO 81007 USA Tel 719-464-1126
E-mail: jason@expedition360.com
Dist(s): **Ingram Content Group.**

Bimini Bks., *(978-0-9753118)* 9553 SW 189 Terr., Suite 200, Miami, FL 33157 USA Tel 305-256-0638
E-mail: biminibooks@aol.com.

Binary Pubns., *(978-0-9854807; 978-0-9860578)* 44114 Parkside, Canton, MI 48187 USA Tel 734-812-8733
E-mail: reedgar@gmail.com.

Bindlestick Bks., *(978-0-578-16673-5; 978-0-578-16732-9; 978-0-692-59737-8; 978-0-692-70921-4; 978-0-692-70929-0; 978-0-692-77061-0; 978-0-578-42172-8; 978-0-578-43023-2; 978-0-578-44968-5; 979-8-218-10816-8)* 616 1/2 Canyon Rd., Santa Fe, NM 87501 USA Tel 917-679-8080
E-mail: jeffreyschweitzer01@gmail.com
Web site: www.bindlestickbooks.com.

Bindu Bks. *Imprint of* **Inner Traditions International, Ltd.**

Binet International, *(978-0-942787)* P.O. Box 1429, Carlsbad, CA 92008 USA (SAN 667-7088) Tel 760-941-7929.

Bing Note, Inc., *(978-0-9794323)* 300 Caldecott Ln., No. 215, Oakland, CA 94618 USA
E-mail: lisa@bingnote.com
Web site: http://www.bingnote.com.

Bingham Putnam Publishing, *(978-0-9760504)* 326 Newport Dr., No. 1710, Naples, FL 34114 USA.

Bingo Bks., Inc., *(978-1-933530)* P.O. Box 3355, Austin, TX 78763-3355 USA Toll Free: 877-246-4644
Web site: http://www.bingobooks.com.

Binney & Smith, Inc., *(978-0-86696)* P.O. Box 431, Easton, PA 18042 USA (SAN 216-5899).

Binx Bks., *(978-0-9801796)* 33 W. Delaware Pl. Apt. 9F, Chicago, IL 60610-7361 USA.

Bio Rx, *(978-0-9772977)* 10828 Kenwood Rd., Cincinnati, OH 45242-2812 USA
E-mail: info@biorx.net
Web site: http://www.biorx.net.

Bio-Dynamic Farming & Gardening Assn., Inc., *(978-0-938250)* 25844 Butler Rd., Junction City, OR 97448 USA (SAN 224-9871) Tel 541-998-0105; Fax: 541-998-0406; Toll Free: 888-516-7797
E-mail: info@biodynamics.com
Web site: http://www.biodynamics.com
Dist(s): **New Leaf Distributing Co., Inc.**
Small Changes, Inc.
SteinerBooks, Inc.

BioEd *Imprint of* **Baylor College of Medicine**

Biographical Publishing Co., *(978-0-9637240; 978-1-929882; 978-0-9913521; 978-0-9976028; 978-1-7338120; 978-1-7369019)* 95 Sycamore Dr., Prospect, CT 06712-1493 USA (SAN 298-2692) Tel 203-758-3661; Fax: 253-793-2618
E-mail: biopub@aol.com
Web site: http://www.biopub.us
Dist(s): **Pathway Bk. Service.**

BIONIC Pr., *(978-0-9892448)* 8612 S. Terra Pointe Way, West Jordan, UT 84088 USA Tel 801-231-1969
E-mail: r.harkness@hsc.utah.edu
Web site: www.bionicpressbooks.com.

Bios for Kids *Imprint of* **Panda Publishing, L.L.C.**

Birch Bark Pr., *(978-0-692-66213-7; 978-0-692-88842-1; 978-0-578-58964-0; 978-0-578-76776-5; 978-0-578-86986-5; 978-0-578-98986-0)* 3405 Clemson Ave, Sartell, MN 56377 USA Tel 320-252-6764
Dist(s): **CreateSpace Independent Publishing Platform.**

Birch Brook Pr., *(978-0-913559; 978-0-9789974; 978-0-9842003; 978-0-9915777)* P.O. Box 81, Delhi, NY 13753 USA (SAN 631-5321) Fax: 607-746-7453 (phone/fax)
E-mail: birchbrook@copper.net
Web site: http://www.birchbrookpress.info.

Birch Island, *(978-0-9772692; 978-0-9818668; 978-0-615-96113-2)* P.O. Box 988 27 Dillingham Rd., Manchester, VT 05254 USA (SAN 257-1625) Tel 802-362-0074; 802-342-7844
E-mail: historicalpages@yahoo.com
Web site: http://www.historicalpages.com
Dist(s): **CreateSpace Independent Publishing Platform**
Independent Pubs. Group.

Publisher Name Index

Birch Tree Publishing, *(978-0-615-60274-5; 978-0-9894487)* 3830 Valley Centre Dr. Suite 705-432, San Diego, CA 92130 USA Tel 858-212-6111 Do not confuse with Birch Tree Publishing in Miami, FL, Southbury, CT
E-mail: nimpentoad@gmail.com
Dist(s): **CreateSpace Independent Publishing Platform.**

Birchall Publishing, *(978-0-9857816)* P.O. Box 92054, Oceanside, CA 92054 USA Tel 720-347-0771
E-mail: lorrielbirchall@gmail.com.

Bird, Bunny & Bear *Imprint of* **American Reading Co.**

Bird Tree Press *See* **Birdtree Pr., LLC**

Bird Upstairs *Imprint of* **Girl Friday Bks.**

Birdcage Books *See* **Birdcage Pr.**

Birdcage Pr., *(978-0-9889613; 978-1-59960)* 853 Alma St., Palo Alto, CA 94301 USA Tel 650-462-6300; Fax: 650-462-6305; Toll Free: 800-247-6553
E-mail: info@birdcagepress.com
Web site: http://www.birdcagepress.com.

Birdhouse Kids Media (CAN) *Dist. by* **Orca Bk Pub.**

Birdland Media Works, *(978-0-615-49781-5; 978-0-578-12427-8)* 11509 Village Brook Dr., Riverview, FL 33579 USA Tel 941-526-6789
E-mail: dhhier@gmail.com
Web site: http://www.birdlandmediaworks.com.

Birdsall, Bonnie Thomas, *(978-0-9762679)* 3421 Lacewood Rd., Tampa, FL 33618 USA
E-mail: swimtaichibon@juno.com.

Birdseed Bks., *(978-0-9774142)* 520 17th St., Dallas, WI 54733 USA; *Imprints:* Birdseed Books for Kids (Birdseed Books for Kids)
Web site: http://www.birdseedbooksforkids.com.

Birdseed Books for Kids *Imprint of* **Birdseed Bks.**

Birdtree Pr., LLC, *(978-1-7340854)* 4065 Venetian Rd, WestColumbia, SC 29169 USA Tel 803-727-3775
E-mail: birdtreepress@gmail.com; annecatharineblake@gmail.com
Web site: www.birdtreepress.com.

Birkhauser Boston *See* **Birkhäuser Boston**

Birkhäuser *Imprint of* **Birkhäuser Boston**

Birkhäuser Boston, *(978-0-8176)* Div. of Springer-Verlag GmbH & Co. KG, Orders Addr.: P.O. Box 2485, Secaucus, NJ 07094 USA (SAN 241-6344) Tel 201-348-4033; Edit Addr.: 675 Massachusetts Ave., Cambridge, MA 02139 USA (SAN 213-2869) Tel 617-876-2333; Toll Free: 800-777-4643 (customer service); *Imprints:* Birkhäuser (BirkBos2)
Web site: http://www.birkhauser.com
Dist(s): **Follett School Solutions**
Metapress
MyiLibrary
Palgrave Macmillan
Springer
ebrary, Inc.

Birks, Alison, *(978-0-9997208)* 100 Blueberry Hill Rd., Bridgewater, CT 06752 USA Tel 860-733-5191
E-mail: Alison.Birks@gmail.com.

Birlinn, Ltd. (GBR) *(978-1-874744; 978-1-84158; 978-1-84341; 978-1-84697; 978-0-85790; 978-1-78027; 978-1-912476; 978-1-78885; 978-1-78886; 978-1-83983)* *Dist. by* **Casemate Pubs.**

Birt Hse. Publishing, *(978-0-578-11306-7; 978-0-578-11315-9)* 100 Bluebonnet St., Apt. 108, Stephenville, TX 76401 USA.

Bis B.V., Uitgeverij (BIS Publishers) (NLD) *(978-90-72007; 978-90-6369)* *Dist. by* **HachBkGrp.**

Bis B.V., Uitgeverij (BIS Publishers) (NLD) *(978-90-72007; 978-90-6369)* *Dist. by* **Consort Bk Sales.**

Bisham Hill Books *See* **Design to Spec LLC**

Bishop Museum Pr., *(978-0-910240; 978-0-930897; 978-1-58178)* Orders Addr.: 1525 Bernice St., Honolulu, HI 96817-2704 USA (SAN 202-408X) Tel 808-847-8260; 808-848-4135; *Imprints:* Kamehoi Press (Kamahoi Pr)
E-mail: press@bishopmuseum.org
Web site: http://www.bishopmuseum.org
Dist(s): **Booklines Hawaii, Ltd.**
Islander Group.

Bishop, Susan Lynn, *(978-0-9772878)* Orders Addr.: P.O. Box 13, Onley, IL 62450 USA Tel 618-392-4011; Edit Addr.: P.O. Box 13, Olney, IL 62450-0013 USA
E-mail: suzyb@wabash.net.

Bisiar Music Publishing, *(978-0-9753091)* Orders Addr.: P.O. Box 424, Evergreen, CO 80437-0424 USA (SAN 256-0356) Tel 303-670-0752 (phone/fax); Edit Addr.: 3661- A Joyful Way, Evergreen, CO 80437-0424 USA
E-mail: bisiar@earthlink.net
Web site: http://www.eddiespaghettiusa.com.

Bison Bks. *Imprint of* **Univ. of Nebraska Pr.**

Bit of Boston Bks., A, *(978-0-9788637)* Orders Addr.: 208 Commonwealth Ave., Boston, MA 02116 USA; Edit Addr.: P.O. Box 990208, Boston, MA 02116 USA
E-mail: jamesrholland@mindspring.com.

Bitingduck Pr., *(978-1-938463; 978-1-68553)* 1262 Sunnyoaks Cir., Altadena, CA 91001 USA Tel 626-507-8033
E-mail: jay@bitingduckpress.com
Web site: http://www.bitingduckpress.com
Dist(s): **Follett School Solutions**
Independent Pubs. Group
Midpoint Trade Bks., Inc.
SPD-Small Pr. Distribution.

Bitter Oleander Pr., The, *(978-0-9664358; 978-0-9786335; 978-0-9883525; 978-0-9862049; 978-0-9993279; 978-1-7346535)* 4983 Tall Oaks Dr., Fayetteville, NY 13066-9776 USA (SAN 855-9686)
E-mail: info@bitteroleander.com
Web site: http://www.bitteroleander.com
Dist(s): **SPD-Small Pr. Distribution.**

Bitterroot Mountain Publishing, *(978-0-9817874; 978-0-9852784; 978-1-940025)* P.O. Box 3508, Hayden, ID 83835-3508 USA
E-mail: jargoodwin@gmail.com; info@bmphmedia.com
Web site: bmphmedia.com.

Bitty Book Pr., *(978-1-887270)* 851 Mt. Vernon Ct., Naperville, IL 60563 USA Tel 630-420-1887; Fax: 630-963-0341; Toll Free: 800-750-6649; 2736 Maple Ave., Downers Grove, IL 60515
E-mail: maryannako@aol.com
Web site: http://www.namepower101.com.

Bixie Gate Publishing, *(978-0-9773433)* 22694 SW Lincoln St., Sherwood, OR 97140 USA (SAN 257-3474)
E-mail: shannonk23@comcast.net
Web site: http://www.bixiegatepublishing.com; http://www.shannonkeegan.com.

Biz Hub (Business & Investing) *Imprint of* **Speedy Publishing LLC**

Biz4Kids *Imprint of* **Round Cow Media Group**

BizyBks., *(978-0-578-26917-7; 978-0-578-27059-3; 978-0-578-27089-0; 978-0-578-27090-6)* 2862 Burning Log St., San Antonio, TX 78247 USA
Web site: www.jackandmilo.com.

Bizzy Girls Publishing, *(978-0-9833532)* 1508 Veteran Ave. No. 205, Los Angeles, CA 90024 USA Tel 310-467-7300
E-mail: dekanafani@yahoo.com
Web site: Www.bizzygirls.com.

Bjelkier Pr., *(978-0-9828217)* 1620 Louis Ln., Hastings, MN 55033 USA (SAN 859-9025) Tel 651-437-8244
E-mail: toysammy@embarqmail.com.

Bjelopetrovich, Beba Foundation, *(978-0-9745724)* 5555 W. Howard St., Skokie, IL 60077-2621 USA Tel 847-679-6710; Fax: 847-679-6717.

Bjork Print, *(978-0-578-41420-1; 978-0-578-71739-5; 978-0-578-74325-7)* 320 W 1675 N, Cedar City, UT 84721 USA Tel 480-766-6527
E-mail: maddie_janes@hotmail.com
Dist(s): **Ingram Content Group.**

†BJU Pr., *(978-0-89084; 978-1-57924; 978-1-59166; 978-1-60682; 978-1-62856; 978-1-64626)* 1430 Wade Hampton Blvd., Greenville, SC 29609 USA (SAN 223-7512) Tel 800-845-5731 Customer Service; Fax: 800-258-5853 Corporate Accounts; Toll Free: 864-370-1800 ext 3707, 4363 Content Development/Operations; 888-262-9914 Corporate Accounts-Pam Schaedel; *Imprints:* JourneyForth (JmyForth); Bloomsbury Visual Arts (BloomsVisual)
E-mail: bjup@bjup.com
Web site: http://www.bjupress.com
Dist(s): **Follett School Solutions**; *CIP.*

Bk. Jungle *Imprint of* **Standard Publications, Inc.**

BK Royston Publishing, *(978-0-9818135; 978-0-9859439; 978-0-615-90819-9; 978-0-615-93714-4; 978-0-615-94453-1; 978-0-615-98076-8; 978-0-615-98476-6; 978-0-615-99864-0; 978-0-692-20210-4; 978-0-692-20225-8; 978-0-692-20417-7; 978-0-692-20556-3; 978-0-692-22593-6; 978-0-692-24242-1; 978-0-692-29253-2; 978-0-692-31099-1; 978-0-692-31145-5; 978-0-692-32344-1; 978-0-692-32527-8; 978-0-692-37169-5; 978-0-692-39673-5; 978-0-692-39674-2; 978-0-692-40254-2; 978-0-692-44865-6; 978-0-692-49804-0; 978-0-692-49927-6; 978-0-69) 3117 Wooded Way, Jeffersonville, IN 47130 USA Tel 502-802-5385; Fax: 812-288-4654*
E-mail: bkroystonpublishing@gmail.com
Web site: http://www.bkroystonpublishing.com
Dist(s): **CreateSpace Independent Publishing Platform.**

BKB Group, Inc., The, *(978-0-9747628)* Orders Addr.: 11146 Harbour Springs Cr., Boca Raton, FL 33428 USA Tel 561-218-1215; Fax: 561-218-1214; Toll Free: 888-321-7664; Edit Addr.: 11146 HARBOUR SPRINGS CR., 11146 HARBOUR SPRINGS CR., BOCA RATON, FL 33428 USA
E-mail: rfproductions@adelphia.net
Web site: http://www.billybutterfly.com.

Bk.barn Publishing *Imprint of* **Compass Productions Inc.**

Bk.ify by Sanitaryum *Imprint of* **Sanitaryum**

Bks. for Young Learners *Imprint of* **Owen, Richard C. Pubs., Inc.**

Black Academy Pr., Inc., *(978-0-87831)* Orders Addr.: 4011 Old Court Rd., Pikesville, MD 21208-2808 USA (SAN 218-6489)
E-mail: bapress@aol.com; info@blackacademypress.com
Web site: http://www.blackacademypress.com.

Black, Amy Jackson, *(978-0-615-16743-5)* 107 Southglen, Terre Haute, IN 47802 USA
E-mail: godzgrl4evr@msn.com
Dist(s): **Lulu Pr., Inc.**

Black and White Publishing Ltd. (GBR) *(978-1-873631; 978-0-9515151; 978-1-902927; 978-1-903265; 978-1-84502; 978-1-910230; 978-1-78530)* *Dist. by* **IPG Chicago.**

Black Bart Bks., *(978-0-615-20238-9; 978-0-615-23723-7; 978-0-578-01524-8; 978-0-578-02511-7; 978-0-578-08320-9)* 3447 Little Carpenter Creek Rd., Fernwood, ID 83830 USA
Web site: http://www.blackbaradventures.com
Dist(s): **Lulu Pr., Inc.**

Black Bed Sheet Bks., *(978-0-9822530; 978-0-9842136; 978-0-9833773; 978-0-9858829; 978-0-9886590; 978-0-615-88139-3; 978-0-615-90327-9; 978-0-615-90623-2; 978-0-615-90684-3; 978-0-615-94207-0; 978-0-615-94575-0; 978-0-615-94689-4; 978-0-615-94893-5; 978-0-615-99827-5; 978-0-692-21851-8; 978-0-692-23039-8; 978-0-692-23974-2; 978-0-692-24044-1; 978-0-692-24087-8; 978-0-692-25565-0; 978-0-692-25829-3; 978-0-692-26626-7; 978-0-692-26983-1; 978-0-692-27830-7; 978-0-692-31231-5; 978-0-692-31456-2; 978-0-692-31673-3; 9) 7865 Valley Quail Ct., Antelope, CA 95843-2031 USA (SAN 857-6785)*
E-mail: bbsadmin@downwarden.com
Web site: http://www.downwarden.com/blackbedsheet; https://www.downwarden.com/blackbedsheetdigital
Dist(s): **CreateSpace Independent Publishing Platform.**

Black Belt Training, *(978-0-9759744)* 9109 Cochran Heights, Dallas, TX 75220 USA Tel 214-351-2234 (phone/fax)
E-mail: drted@wwwin.com
Web site: http://www.wwwin.com.

Black Bird Bks., *(978-0-9763238)* Orders Addr.: P.O. Box 901, Ankeny, IA 50021 USA; Edit Addr.: P.O. Box 901, Ankeny, IA 50021-0901 USA
E-mail: lizzie3blackbird@hotmail.com.

Black Butterfly Way *See* **Richale R. Reed**

Black Cat *Imprint of* **Grove/Atlantic, Inc.**

Black Chook Bks. (NZL) *(978-0-473-40332-4)* *Dist. by* **IPG Chicago.**

Black, Clinton L., *(978-0-9620180)* Orders Addr.: P.O. Box 9096, Fort Lauderdale, FL 33310 USA Tel 954-722-0415; Fax: 954-720-7674
E-mail: thepurposeofhumanlife@yahoo.com
Dist(s): **Southern Bk. Service.**

Black Coat Pr. *Imprint of* **HollywoodComics.com, LLC**

Black Coffee Publishing, *(978-0-9745238)* Orders Addr.: 5543 Edmondson Pike, No. 213, Nashville, TN 37211-5808 USA Tel 615-969-5516
E-mail: Jenniferwiseblack@gmail.com; bcpubl@aol.com
Web site: Http://www.MediaTrauma.com; http://www.blackcoffeepublishing.com.

Black Creek Publishing Group, *(978-0-9895323; 978-0-9904596; 978-0-9962919; 978-0-9978983)* 2102 Kimberton Rd. No. 266, Kimberton, PA 19460 USA Tel 832-350-3029
E-mail: jchenry@blackcreekpublishinggroup.com
Web site: www.blackcreekpublishinggroup.com.

Black Diamond Publishing, *(978-0-9715139)* 415 E. 32nd St., Indianapolis, IN 46205 USA Do not confuse with Black Diamond Publishing in Brooklyn,NY
E-mail: LWatk82805@aol.com; BDPub@aol.com; Linda@lindawatkins.org
Web site: http://www.lindawatkins.org.

Black Dog & Leventhal Pubs. Inc. *Imprint of* **Running Pr.**

Black Dog & Leventhal Pubs. Inc. *Imprint of* **Hachette Bks.**

Black Dog Books, *(978-1-884449; 978-1-928619)* 1115 Pine Meadows Ct., Normal, IL 61761 USA Tel 309-310-6984
E-mail: info@blackdogbooks.net; blackdogbooks_tomroberts@yahoo.com
Web site: http://www.blackdogbooks.net.

Black Dog Publishing Ltd. (GBR) *(978-0-9521773; 978-1-901033; 978-1-904772; 978-1-906155; 978-1-907317; 978-1-908966; 978-1-910433)* *Dist. by* **Consort Bk Sales.**

Black Dog Publishing/Tuscany Bay Books *See* **Tuscany Bay Bks.**

Black Dolphin Diving, *(978-0-9646281)* 5022 Two Harbors, Avalon, CA 90704-5022 USA Tel 310-510-2109
E-mail: bkdolphin@aol.com
Web site: http://www.divecatalina.com.

Black Dome Pr. Corp., *(978-0-9628523; 978-1-883789; 979-8-9856921)* 1011 Rte. 296, Hensonville, NY 12439 USA (SAN 257-6996) Tel 518-734-6357; Fax: 518-734-5802; Toll Free: 800-513-9013; 649 Delaware Ave., Delmar, NY 12054
E-mail: blackdomep@aol.com
Web site: http://www.blackdomepress.com
Dist(s): **Follett School Solutions**
North Country Bks., Inc.

Black Dot Pubns., *(978-0-9649740)* Orders Addr.: P.O. Box 1068, Ojai, CA 93024 USA Tel 805-640-8825; Edit Addr.: 1208 Gregory St., Ojai, CA 93023 USA
E-mail: blackdotpubs@yahoo.com
Web site: http://www.backdotpubs.com; http://www.chuckhillig.com
Dist(s): **New Leaf Distributing Co., Inc.**

Black Eagle Bks., *(978-1-64560)* 7464 Wisdom Ln., Dublin, OH 43016 USA Tel 614-602-7021
E-mail: satyapatnaik11@gmail.com.

Black Falcon Publications *See* **LMW Works**

Black Forest Pr., *(978-1-58275; 978-1-881116)* Div. of Black Forest Enterprises, Orders Addr.: P.O. Box 6342, Chula Vista, CA 91909-6342 USA Fax: 619-482-8704; Toll Free: 800-451-9404 (General Information, Submission Inquiries and Acquisitions); 888-808-5440 (Book Sales, Marketing and Promotion); Edit Addr.: 1075 Hayuco Plz., Chula Vista, CA 91910-7006 USA (SAN 298-8445); *Imprints:* Sonnenschein Books (Sonnenschein Bks)
E-mail: bfp@blackforestpress.com
Web site: http://www.blackforestpress.com.

Black Forge, *(978-0-615-55725-0; 978-0-615-58405-8; 978-1-938083)* 304 S. Jones Blvd. No. 3593, Las Vegas, NV 89107 USA
E-mail: aya@ayaknight.com
Web site: http://www.ayaknight.com
Dist(s): **CreateSpace Independent Publishing Platform**
Independently Published.

Black Garnet Pr., *(978-0-9832383; 978-0-9911790)* 1313 St. Helena Ave., Santa Rosa, CA 95404 USA Tel 707-526-3331
E-mail: sandybaker131@gmail.com
Web site: sandybakerwriter.com.

Black Girl Speaks *See* **BGS Productions, Inc.**

Black Hat Pr., *(978-0-9614462; 978-1-887649)* Orders Addr.: P.O. Box 12, Goodhue, MN 55027-0012 USA (SAN 689-4259) Tel 651-923-4590; Edit Addr.: 508 Second Ave., Goodhue, MN 55027-0012 USA
E-mail: blackhatpress@yahoo.com.

Black Hawk Pr., Inc., The, *(978-0-9778731; 978-0-9817613)* 803 Charter Pl., Charlotte, NC 28211 USA Tel 704-364-1164
E-mail: info@blackhawkpress.com
Web site: http://www.blackhawkpress.com
Dist(s): **Blu Sky Media Group.**

Black Heart, Inc., *(978-0-9701879)* Orders Addr.: P.O. Box 3856, Rock Island, IL 61201 USA Tel 319-355-8223; Fax: 801-991-6950; Toll Free: 877-839-5115; Edit Addr.: 935 17th St., Bettendorf, IA 52722 USA
E-mail: jbryson@black-heart.net
Web site: http://www.black-heart.net.

Black Hearts Publishing, *(978-0-9988921)* 934 Wickerleaf Way, Garner, NC 27529 USA Tel 919-662-8009
E-mail: BFurney@ymail.com
Web site: www.billfurney.com.

Black Heron Pr., *(978-0-930773; 978-1-936364)* Orders Addr.: P.O. Box 13396, Mill Creek, WA 98145 USA (SAN 677-623X) Fax: 425-355-4929; Edit Addr.: 27 West 20Th St., New York, NY 10011 USA
E-mail: Jgoldberon@aol.com
Web site: http://www.blackheronpress.com
Dist(s): **Follett School Solutions**
Independent Pubs. Group
Midpoint Trade Bks., Inc.
ebrary, Inc.

Black Jasmine, *(978-0-9788802)* 46 Pleasant St., Sharon, MA 02067 USA
E-mail: deemajoan@yahoo.com
Web site: http://www.deemasglass.com.

Black, Judith Storyteller, *(978-0-9701073)* 33 Prospect St., Marblehead, MA 01945 USA Tel 781-631-4417
E-mail: jb@storiesalive.com
Web site: http://www.storiesalive.com.

Black Kite Publishing, *(978-0-9906795; 978-0-9957215-3-1)* 3 Buckeye, Galena, IL 61036 USA Tel 815-776-0285
E-mail: kathleen@ewtravel.com
Dist(s): **Lulu Pr., Inc.**

Black Lab Publishing LLC, *(978-0-9742815; 979-8-9868264)* Orders Addr.: P.O. Box 6244, Laconia, NH 03247 USA Tel 603-714-8023; 606-524-1114
E-mail: loni@bearandkatie.com
Web site: http://www.bearandkatie.com; http://www.blacklabpublishing.com.

BLACK LACQUER Pr. & MARKETING INC., *(978-1-948288; 978-1-951313)* 3225 McLEOD Dr. SUITE100, LAS VEGAS, NV 89121 USA Tel 855-505-5640
E-mail: gulia.alba@blacklacquerpress.com
Web site: www.blacklacquerpress.com.

Black Literary, Inc., *(978-0-615-22609-5; 978-0-615-30323-9; 978-0-615-37753-7)* P.O. Box 492, Catlett, VA 20119 USA Tel 540-788-4992
E-mail: CHancasky@aol.com.

Black Mask Studios, ., Los Angeles, CA 90232 USA
E-mail: hitusup@blackmaskstudios.com
Web site: http://www.http://blackmaskstudios.com
Dist(s): **Simon & Schuster, Inc.**

Black, MeKael, *(978-0-578-83194-7; 978-0-578-91400-8)* 172 Bridgewater Dr., Hattiesburg, MS 39402 USA Tel 601-466-6275
E-mail: mekaelblack@gmail.com
Web site: http://www.mekaelblack.com.

Black Oak Media, Incorporated *See* **Lake Ridge Pr.**

Black Orb *See* **Angie Blue Bks., LLC**

Black Pearl Bks., *(978-0-9728005; 978-0-9766007; 978-0-9773438)* Orders Addr.: 3653-F Flakes Mill Road, PMB 306, Atlanta, GA 30034 USA Do not
E-mail: hurst@blackpearlbooks.com
Web site: http://www.blackpearlbooks.com
Dist(s): **African World Bks.**
American Wholesale Bk. Co.
Bookazine Co., Inc.
Brodart Co.
Quality Bks., Inc.

Black Plum Bks., *(978-0-9785317)* Orders Addr.: 1302 Abby Ct., Juneau, AK 99801-9599 USA
Web site: http://www.blackplumebooks.com
Dist(s): **Follett School Solutions.**

Black Rabbit Bks., *(978-1-58340; 978-1-887068; 978-1-59920; 978-1-77092; 978-1-62310; 978-1-62588; 978-1-68071; 978-1-68072; 978-1-64466)* Orders Addr.: P.O. Box 227, Mankato, MN 56002 USA (SAN 925-4862); Edit Addr.: 2140 Howard Dr. W., North Mankato, MN 56003 USA (SAN 858-902X) Tel 507-388-6273; *Imprints:* Smart Apple Media (SmartAppleMed); Bolt (Bolt); Hi Jinx (HiJinx); Bolt Jr. (MYID_K_BOLT JR)
E-mail: info@blackrabbitbooks.com; info@thecreativecompany.us; rglaser@thecreativecompany.us
Web site: http://www.blackrabbitbooks.com
Dist(s): **Creative Co., The**
Follett School Solutions
Hachette Bk. Group
INscribe Digital
Independent Pubs. Group
RiverStream Publishing
Scholastic, Inc.
myON.

Black River Trading Co., *(978-0-9649083; 978-0-9797492)* P.O. Box 7, Oxford, MI 48371 USA (SAN 854-2724) Tel 248-628-5150; Fax: 248-628-6422
E-mail: jane@whoopforjoy.com
Web site: http://www.whoopforjoy.com
Dist(s): **Bookmen, Inc.**

Black Rose Writing, *(978-0-615-20158-0; 978-0-615-20274-7; 978-0-615-20494-9; 978-0-615-20616-5; 978-0-9821012; 978-0-9819742; 978-0-9825542; 978-0-9825823; 978-1-935605; 978-1-61296; 978-1-944715; 978-1-68433; 978-1-68513)* P.O. Box 1540, Castroville, TX 78009 USA
E-mail: creator@blackrosewriting.com; sales@blackrosewriting.com
Web site: http://www.blackrosewritiing.com; http://www.blackrosewriting.com/books
Dist(s): **Ingram Content Group**
Lulu Pr., Inc.

Black Sheep *Imprint of* **Akashic Bks.**

Black Sheep *Imprint of* **Bellwether Media**

Black Ship Publishing, *(978-0-9851969; 978-0-9914484; 978-0-9905469)* 1767 12th St. Suite 378, Hood River, OR 97031 USA Tel 310-696-9515
E-mail: smartcookie1@mac.com
Dist(s): **BookBaby**
Legato Pubs. Group
Ingram Content Group

MyiLibrary
Publishers Group West (PGW).

Black Society Pages, Inc., *(978-0-9758611)* 228 S. Washington St., Alexandria, VA 22314 USA.

Black Squirrel Bks. *Imprint of* **Kent State Univ. Pr.**

Black Sugar Pr., *(978-0-9976010)* 13518 L St., Omaha, NE 68137 USA Tel 402-884-5995
E-mail: blacksugar@conciergemarketing.com.

Black Threads Pr., *(978-0-9824796)* 3037 S. Buchanan St., Arlington, VA 22206-1512 USA
Web site: http://www.BlackThreads.com
Dist(s): **CreateSpace Independent Publishing Platform**
Ingram Content Group.

Blackberry Bks., *(978-1-7340342)* 1170 Pinecroft Rd., Colfax, CA 95713 USA Tel 530-774-3027
E-mail: dehanosh@yahoo.com.

Blackberry Hill Pr., *(978-0-9792947)* Orders Addr.: 2860 Mohawk St., Sauquoit, NY 13456-3322 USA Tel 315-737-5147
Web site: http://www.dorothystacy.com
Dist(s): **North Country Bks., Inc.**

Blackberry Maine, *(978-0-942396; 978-0-615-15951-5; 978-0-9824389)* 617 E. Neck Rd., Nobleboro, ME 04555 USA (SAN 207-7949) Tel 207-729-5083; Fax: 207-729-6783
E-mail: chimfarm@gwi.net
Web site: http://www.blackberrybooksme.com
Dist(s): **SPD-Small Pr. Distribution.**

Blackberry Pubns., *(978-0-9776987; 978-0-9972260)* 3915 11th Street, Ecorse, MI 48229 USA Tel 313-297-7809; 313-627-1520
E-mail: blackberrybooks@yahoo.com.

Blackberry Pubs., *(978-0-615-12702-6)* 2545 Hwy. 76, Portland, TN 37148 USA Tel 615-325-3970
E-mail: fussellb@comcast.net
Web site: http://www.blackberrypublishers.com
Dist(s): **Sadler, Dale.**

Blackberry: Salted in the Shell *See* **Blackberry Maine**

Blackbirch Pr., Inc. *Imprint of* **Barnes & Noble, Inc.**

Blackbirch Pr., Inc. *Imprint of* **Peel Productions, Inc.**

Blackbirch Pr., Inc. *Imprint of* **Cengage Gale**

Blackbirch Pr., Inc. *Imprint of* **Soundprints**

Blackbirch Pr., Inc. *Imprint of* **Seacoast Publishing, Inc.**

Blackbirch Pr., Inc. *Imprint of* **Sunstone Pr.**

Blackbirch Pr., Inc. *Imprint of* **Cherry Lake Publishing**

Blackbirch Pr., Inc. *Imprint of* **Mardick Pr.**

Blackbird Bks., *(978-1-61053)* 17693 Cir. Pond Ct., Boca Raton, FL 33496-1002 USA Tel 310-422-7098
E-mail: editor@bbirdbooks.com
Web site: http://www.bbirdbooks.com.

Blackbird's World Publishing Co., *(978-0-9789798)* Orders Addr.: P.O. Box 475, Clyde, TX 79510 USA Tel 325-201-2495; Edit Addr.: Box 475 212 Hunt St., Clyde, TX 79510 USA
E-mail: blackbird@blackbirdsworldpublishingcompany.net
Web site: http://blackbirdsworldpublishingcompany.net.

Blackcurrant Press Company *See* **Blackcurrant Pr.**

Blackcurrant Pr., *(978-0-9817111; 978-0-9840379; 978-0-9903781; 979-8-9882754)* 116-35 194th St., Saint Albans, NY 11412 USA (SAN 856-3128)
E-mail: beverlybcp9@gmail.com
Web site: http://www.blackcurrantpress.com
Dist(s): **Ingram Content Group.**

Blackfoot Burkino Cherokee Publishing, *(978-0-9722724)* Orders Addr.: P.O. Box 58074, Houston, TX 77258 USA Tel 832-504-1331; Edit Addr.: 1912 Trentwood Pl., Charlotte, NC 28216 USA
E-mail: bbcpublishin80@gmail.com.

Blackie Bks. (ESP) *(978-84-941409; 978-84-17552) Dist. by* **Peng Rand Hse.**

BlacknBlue Pr. UK *Imprint of* **Blacknblue Pr.**

Blacknblue Pr., *(978-0-9677652; 978-0-9840718)* 108 Benarr Ave., Fort Walton Beach, FL 32548 USA Tel 850-862-2874 (phone/fax); 13 Dellands Overton, Basingstoke, RG25 3LD Tel 1256 770736 (phone/fax); *Imprints:* BlacknBlue Press UK (BlacknBlue Pr UK)
E-mail: edddwicke@hotmail.com
Web site: http://www.blacknbluepress.info
Dist(s): **Ingram Content Group.**

Blackside Publishing, *(978-1-943630; 978-1-68355)* 5209 Del Paz Dr., Colorado Springs, CO 80918 USA
E-mail: publishing@blacksideconcepts.com; blacksidepublishing@gmail.com
Web site: www.blacksidepublishing.com.

Blacksmith Bks. (HKG) *(978-962-86732; 978-988-17742; 978-988-99799; 978-988-19003; 978-988-16139; 978-988-13765) Dist. by* **Natl Bk Netwk.**

Blacksmith Books, LLC *See* **Mark Boone**

Black-Smith Enterprises, *(978-0-9762720)* 31536 Avondale, Westland, MI 48186 USA
E-mail: blacksmithenterprises@yahoo.com; janaya_black@yahoo.com
Web site: http://www.black-smithenterprises.com
Dist(s): **Ingram Content Group.**

Blackstaff Pr., Ltd. (GBR) *(978-0-85640) Dist. by* **Casemate Pubs.**

Blackstone Audio Books, Incorporated *See* **Blackstone Audio, Inc.**

Blackstone Audio, Inc., *(978-0-7861; 978-1-4332; 978-1-4417; 978-1-4551; 978-1-4708; 978-1-4829; 978-1-4830; 978-1-5046; 978-1-5047; 978-1-5384; 978-1-5385; 978-1-9824; 978-1-9825; 978-1-9826; 978-1-7999; 978-1-0940; 978-1-0941; 978-1-6644; 978-1-6645; 978-1-6646; 978-1-6647; 978-1-6650; 978-1-6651; 978-1-6652; 979-8-200; 979-8-212)* 31 *Mistletoe Rd., Ashland, OR 97520 USA (SAN 173-2811) Fax: 800-482-9294; Toll Free Fax: 800-482-9294; Toll Free: 800-729-2665*
E-mail: Orders@blackstoneaudio.com; megan.wahrenbrock@blackstoneaudio.com; heather.johnson@blackstoneaudio.com
Web site: http://www.blackstoneaudio.com
Dist(s): **Ebsco Publishing**
Findaway World, LLC
Follett School Solutions
Hachette Bk. Group
INscribe Digital
Independent Pubs. Group
Listen & Live Audio, Inc.
MyiLibrary
OverDrive, Inc.
Penguin Publishing Group
Simon & Schuster, Inc.
Zondervan.

Blackstone Editions, *(978-0-9725017; 978-0-9816402)* 312-24 Wellesley St. W., Toronto, ON M4Y 2X6 CAN Tel 647-344-2206
Web site: http://www.blackstoneeditions.com.

Blacktastic.net, *(978-0-9834275; 978-0-9961146)* 7945 Fincastle Ct., Sacramento, CA 95829 USA Tel 916-525-1703
E-mail: brotherhypnotic@hotmail.com.

Blacktypewriter Pr. *Imprint of* **Pittsburgh Literary Arts Network LLC**

BlackWords Press *See* **KA Productions, LLC**

Blade Publishing, *(978-1-929409)* 110 W. C St. Ste. 1300, San Diego, CA 92101-3978 USA (SAN 254-7678)
E-mail: bladeinternational@yahoo.com.

BladeRunner Publishing, *(978-0-9785477)* P.O. Box 4298, Greenville, SC 29608 USA Tel 864-313-6182
E-mail: bladerunnerpublishing@charter.net.

Bladestar Publishing, *(978-0-9787931)* Orders Addr.: 1499 N. 950 W., Orem, UT 84057 USA Fax: 484-414-1674
E-mail: Promotion@BladestarPublishing.com
Web site: http://www.bladestarpublishing.com
Dist(s): **Brodart Co.**

Blaft Pubns., , , , CA 1 USA
Web site: http://www.blaft.com/
Dist(s): **SPD-Small Pr. Distribution**
Smashwords.

Blair *Imprint of* **Carolina Wren Pr.**

Blair, Rebecca E, *(978-0-692-17683-2)* 214 SW 9th St., Ogden, IA 50212 USA Tel 515-230-0014
E-mail: rebl@netins.net
Dist(s): **Ingram Content Group.**

Blaisdell, George W, *(978-1-942720)* P.O. Box 644, Hampton Falls, NH 03844 USA Tel 603-926-9998
E-mail: george@blaisdellinsurance.com
Web site: thegovernorsmansion.org
Dist(s): **Lulu Pr., Inc.**

Blake, Edna, *(978-0-9668906)* 7 Babble Creek Ct., O Fallon, MO 63368-8321 USA.

Blake, John Publishing, Ltd. (GBR) *(978-0-905846; 978-1-85782; 978-1-903402; 978-1-904034; 978-1-84358; 978-1-84454; 978-1-78219; 978-1-78418; 978-1-78606; 978-1-78946) Dist. by* **IPG Chicago.**

Blake, Monica, *(978-0-9764155)* P.O. Box 475233, San Francisco, CA 94147 USA Tel 415-995-2515; Fax: 415-876-1002
E-mail: blakesfo@yahoo.com.

Blake, Nyron, *(978-0-578-52946-2)* 2132 Houston st, Norman, OK 73073 USA Tel 718-687-7541
E-mail: nyronblake@yahoo.com.

Blake-Virostko, Pamela, *(978-0-9801975)* 7546 S. Virostko Rd., Rockville, IN 47872 USA Tel 765-548-2635
E-mail: PVirostko@aol.com.

Blanchard, Graham, *(978-0-9854090; 978-0-9897949; 978-0-692-85033-6)* P.O. Box 300235, Austin, TX 78703 USA Tel 512-647-2099
E-mail: callie@grahamblanchard.com
Web site: http://www.grahamblanchard.com
Dist(s): **Ingram Publisher Services**
Send The Light Distribution LLC.

Blancmange Publishing LLC, *(978-0-9779488)* P.O. Box 17184, Memphis, TN 38187-7184 USA (SAN 850-7023).

Blanket Street Publishing, *(978-0-9760929)* 17278 Summit Hills Dr., Santa Clarita, CA 91387 USA
E-mail: kstrauss@socal.rr.com.

Blast Books *See* **Scramjet Bks.**

Blast Cafe, *(978-1-948750)* 21381 Pinetree Ln, Huntington Beach, CA 92646 USA Tel 310-625-9141
E-mail: stephenhcook@gmail.com
Web site: www.BlastCafe.com.

Blast Off to Learning, LLC, *(978-0-9831996; 978-0-692-03729-4; 979-8-9871599)* 208A Oxhead Rd., Centereach, NY 11720 USA Tel 631-780-4206
E-mail: cheryl_orlassino@live.com
Web site: www.blastofftolearning.com.

Blast Off to Learning Press *See* **Blast Off to Learning, LLC**

Blastoff! Discovery *Imprint of* **Bellwether Media**

Blastoff! Readers *Imprint of* **Bellwether Media**

Blatant Times, *(978-0-9744376)* 608 Patton Rd., Great Bend, KS 67530 USA
Web site: http://www.cpcis.net.

Blaumond Pr., *(978-0-9789031)* 740 SE. Greenville Blvd., Suite 400, Box 283, Greenville, NC 27858 USA (SAN 851-9021) Tel 252-754-4837; Fax: 252-353-0732
E-mail: info@blaumondpress.com
Web site: http://www.blaumondpress.com.

Blaze Publishing, LLC, *(978-0-9970104; 978-1-945519)* 64 Melvin Dr., Fredericksburg, VA 22406 USA Tel 703-470-8323
E-mail: kdehaba@blazepub.com; etilton@blazepub.com
Web site: www.blazepub.com.

Blaze, Ronan *See* **Medal Bks.**

Blazing Ideas Ltd., *(978-0-9801243; 978-0-9856029; 978-0-9992828; 978-0-9997030; 978-1-948518)* 11141 Blackforest way, Gaithersburg, MD 20879 USA Tel 301-476-0778
E-mail: lotit2000@yahoo.com; ookubena@gmail.com; ololade@blazing-ideas.com; olayemi@blazing-ideas.com
Web site: www.blazing-ideas.com.

B.L.Blocher *See* **Emerald City Pr., The**

BLD Enterprises *See* **Innovo Publishing, LLC**

Blessed and Highly Favored *See* **BHF Publishing**

Blessed Beginnings Publishing, *(978-0-9727201)* P.O. Box 241282, Milwaukee, WI 53223 USA Tel 414-351-6467
E-mail: pinksolitaire97@yahoo.com.

Blessed Bk. Publishing, *(978-0-692-90686-6; 978-0-692-94964-1; 978-1-7350881)* 936 B 7th St. PMB 180, Novato, CA 94945 USA Tel 415-612-0401
E-mail: laurie@beatingtheoddsnow.com
Dist(s): **Independent Pub.**

Blessings Unlimited, LLC *See* **CMD UnLtd., LLC**

Blessitt, Arthur Evangelistic Assn., *(978-0-692-27983-0)* P.O. Box 632246, Littleton, CO 80163 USA Tel 303-355-2234
E-mail: irjablessitt@me.com
Web site: www.blessitt.com.

Blind Ferret Entertainment (CAN) *(978-0-9736946) Dist. by* **Diamond Book Dists.**

Blind Wolf Studios, *(978-0-9749941)* P.O. Box 465, Cross River, NY 10518 USA
Web site: http://www.blindwolfstudios.com.

Blink,
Dist(s): **Zondervan.**

Bliss Group, *(978-0-9885359; 978-1-940021)* 725 River Rd. No. 32-215, Edgewater, NJ 07020 USA Tel 551-333-9409
E-mail: alansrbradshaw@gmail.com
Dist(s): **Ingram Content Group**
MyiLibrary.

Bliss on Tap, *(978-0-9763768; 978-0-9825098; 978-0-9896143)* 28326 Wellfleet Ln., Saugus, CA 91350 USA
E-mail: pephillipson@aol.com
Web site: http://www.godthedyslexicdog.com
Dist(s): **MyiLibrary.**

Bliss Publishing, *(978-0-9910996)* 3127 176th St., Lansing, IL 60438 USA Tel 708-474-6702
E-mail: blisswoods@comcast.net.

Blissful Light Pr., *(978-0-692-89247-3; 978-0-578-49714-3)* 1334 W. 21st. St., Houston, TX 77008 USA Tel 832-654-4831
E-mail: sandirhea@yahoo.com.

Blister Books LLC *See* **Mother Lode Pr. LLC**

BLLE Creative, *(978-0-692-96918-2)* 1453 NW Davenport Ave, BEND, OR 97703 USA Tel 206-947-0576
E-mail: kayla@jetstarpublishing.com
Dist(s): **Ingram Content Group.**

Bloated Toe Publishing, *(978-0-9795741; 978-0-9836925; 978-1-939216)* P.O. Box 324, Peru, NY 12972 USA Tel 518-563-9469 (phone/fax)
E-mail: sales@bloatedtoe.com; jcj@bloatedtoe.com
Web site: http://www.bloatedtoe.com.

Bloch Publishing Co., *(978-0-8197)* 5875 Mining Ter. Ste. 104, Jacksonville, FL 32257-3225 USA (SAN 214-204X)
E-mail: BlochPub@worldnet.att.net
Web site: http://www.blochpub.com/
Dist(s): **Follett School Solutions.**

Block Publishing, *(978-0-9761625)* 1120 Forest Ave., No. 306, Pacific Grove, CA 93950 USA Fax: 831-655-4830
E-mail: blockpub@sbcglobal.net
Web site: http://www.blockpublishing.com
Dist(s): **Follett School Solutions.**

Block System, The *See* **Block System, The**

Block System, The, *(978-0-9665545; 978-0-9800875)* 3824 Brookhaven Cir., Fort Worth, TX 76109 USA Tel 817-732-2633; Fax: 817-732-0836
E-mail: andblock@gmail.com
Web site: http://www.blockcenter.com.

Blockstar Publishing, *(978-1-7349493)* 13 Wakefield Ave., Port Washington, NY 11050 USA Tel 917-209-6553
E-mail: coronaviruschildrensbook@gmail.com.

BlogIntoBook.com *Imprint of* **Gatekeeper Pr.**

Blom Pubns., *(978-0-9906871; 978-0-692-18818-7; 978-0-578-40953-5; 978-0-578-41236-8; 978-1-7336349; 978-1-7345901; 979-8-9854691; 979-8-9873783)* 2280 Braumiller Rd., Delaware, OH 43015 USA Tel 503-939-7627
E-mail: TracyBlom@hotmail.com
Web site: theblomdotcom.com.

Blondvic Enterprises, *(978-0-692-81633-2)* 141 E. 4th St., # 420, Saint Paul, MN 55101 USA Tel 651-295-4033
E-mail: stacybecker@comcast.net; stacybecker@comcast.net.

Blood-Horse, Inc., The, *(978-0-936032; 978-0-939049; 978-1-58150)* Div. of The Blood-Horse, Inc., 3101 Beaumont Centre Cir., Lexington, KY 40513 USA (SAN 203-5294) Tel 859-278-2361 (Retailers); Fax: 859-276-6868; Toll Free: 800-866-2361 (Retailers); *Imprints:* Eclipse Press (Eclip Press)
E-mail: info@eclipsepress.com
Web site: http://www.eclipsepress.com
Dist(s): **Rowman & Littlefield Publishers, Inc.**
Rowman & Littlefield Unlimited Model
Smashwords
Western International, Inc.

Bloodletting Pr., *(978-0-9720859; 978-0-9768531; 978-1-935006)* 25222 E Welches Rd Unit 29 USA, Welches, OR 97067 USA Tel 503-298-4811
Web site: http://www.miskatonicbooks.com.

Bloom & Grow Bks., *(978-1-931969)* Div. of Bloom & Grow, Inc., Orders Addr.: 149 S. Barrington Ave., #363, Los Angeles, CA 90049 USA Tel 310-472-0505
E-mail: stephanie@bloomandogrow.com; info@bloomandgrow.com
Web site: http://www.bloomandgrow.com; http://www.placetogrow.com
Dist(s): **Beyda for Bks., LLC.**

Bloom & Grow, Incorporated *See* **Bloom & Grow Bks.**

Bloom, Barbara, *(978-0-615-64982-5; 978-0-9883351)* 11907 Oakcroft Dr., Houston, TX 77070 USA Tel 832-717-7818
Web site: www.smartscarlet.com
Dist(s): **CreateSpace Independent Publishing Platform.**

Bloom Bks. *Imprint of* **Sourcebooks, Inc.**

Bloomer's Bks. Llc., *(978-0-9840295; 978-0-692-24835-5; 978-0-9997244)* 272 Prospect St., Willimantic, CT 06226 USA Tel 860-423-0901
E-mail: rhbloomer@pobox.com
Web site: Bloomer'sBooks.com.

Blooming Tree Pr., *(978-0-9718348; 978-0-9769417; 978-1-933831)* Div. of Hees Enterprises, LLC, Orders Addr.: P.O. Box 140934, Austin, TX 78714-0934 USA Tel 512-921-8846; Fax: 512-873-7710; Edit Addr.: 10703 Jonwood Way, Austin, TX 78753 USA Tel 512-921-8846; Fax: 512-873-7710; *Imprints:* Ready Blade (Ready Blade)
E-mail: email@bloomingtreepress.com; bloomingtree@gmail.com
Web site: http://www.bloomingtreepress.com.

Blooming Twig Books LLC, *(978-0-9777736; 978-1-933918; 978-1-61343; 978-1-937753)* Orders Addr.: 228 Pk. Ave S Num 66675, NEW YORK, NY 10003 USA Tel 212-464-7507; Edit Addr.: 228 Pk. Ave S Num 66675, NEW YORK, NY 10003 USA (SAN 991-1693) Tel 212-464-7507
Web site: http://www.bloomingtwig.com
Dist(s): **Cardinal Pubs. Group.**

BloomingFields, *(978-0-9645971)* 44 Voyagers Ln., Ashland, MA 01721 USA; *Imprints:* Wisdom Audio-Books (Wisdom Aud-Bks)
E-mail: markpoetry@hotmail.com.

BloominThyme Pr., *(978-0-9832464; 978-0-9884871; 978-0-9911182; 978-0-9964391; 978-0-9977738)* P.O. Box 491345, Leesburg, FL 34749 USA Tel 352-638-3121
E-mail: dsvenetta@aol.com
Dist(s): **Follett School Solutions.**

Bloom's Literary Criticism *Imprint of* **Infobase Holdings, Inc.**

Bloomsbury Academic & Professional *See* **Bloomsbury Academic & Professional**

Bloomsbury Academic & Professional, *(978-1-4411; 978-1-62892)* 175 Fifth Ave., New York, NY 10010 USA; *Imprints:* Continuum (Continu); Fairchild Books (Fairchild Bks)
E-mail: AskAcademic@BloomsburyUSA.com
Web site: https://www.bloomsbury.com/us/academic/
Dist(s): **Bloomsbury Publishing US Textbook 2**
Bloomsbury Publishing USA
Casemate Academic
Independent Pubs. Group
Macmillan
MyiLibrary
National Bk. Network.

Bloomsbury Activity Bks. *Imprint of* **Bloomsbury Publishing USA**

Bloomsbury Children's Bks. *Imprint of* **Bloomsbury Publishing USA**

Bloomsbury Pr., *(978-0-9667039)* 4340 Anza St., No. 6, San Francisco, CA 94121 USA Do not confuse with Bloomsberry Pr., New York, NY
Dist(s): **Macmillan.**

Bloomsbury Publishing Plc (GBR) *(978-0-225; 978-0-245; 978-0-264; 978-0-333; 978-0-485; 978-0-510; 978-0-540; 978-0-567; 978-0-7136; 978-0-7470; 978-0-7475; 978-0-7478; 978-0-85045; 978-0-85177; 978-0-85263; 978-0-85314; 978-0-85496; 978-0-86292; 978-0-906515; 978-0-907582; 978-0-948230; 978-1-85399; 978-1-85532; 978-1-85973; 978-1-899791; 978-1-901362; 978-0-212; 978-0-85146; 978-0-85147; 978-0-85317; 978-0-86019; 978-0-946716; 978-0-9507160; 978-1-902579; 978-1-84113; 978-1-85691; 978-1-897737; 978-0-9506785; 978-1-8735) Dist. by* **Natl Bk Netwk.**

Bloomsbury Publishing Plc (GBR) *(978-0-225; 978-0-245; 978-0-264; 978-0-333; 978-0-485; 978-0-510; 978-0-540; 978-0-567; 978-0-7136; 978-0-7470; 978-0-7475; 978-0-7478; 978-0-85045; 978-0-85177; 978-0-85263; 978-0-85314; 978-0-85496; 978-0-86292; 978-0-906515; 978-0-907582; 978-0-948230; 978-1-85399; 978-1-85532; 978-1-85973; 978-1-899791; 978-1-901362; 978-0-212; 978-0-85146; 978-0-85147; 978-0-85317; 978-0-86019; 978-0-946716; 978-0-9507160; 978-1-902579; 978-1-84113; 978-1-85691; 978-1-897737; 978-0-9506785; 978-1-8735) Dist. by* **Trafalgar.**

Bloomsbury Publishing Plc (GBR) *(978-0-225; 978-0-245; 978-0-264; 978-0-333; 978-0-485; 978-0-510; 978-0-540; 978-0-567; 978-0-7136; 978-0-7470; 978-0-7475; 978-0-7478; 978-0-85045; 978-0-85177; 978-0-85263; 978-0-85314; 978-0-85496; 978-0-86292; 978-0-906515; 978-0-907582; 978-0-948230; 978-1-85399; 978-1-85532; 978-1-85973; 978-1-899791; 978-1-901362; 978-0-212; 978-0-85146; 978-0-85147; 978-0-85317; 978-0-86019; 978-0-946716; 978-0-9507160; 978-1-902579; 978-1-84113; 978-1-85691; 978-1-897737; 978-0-9506785; 978-1-8735) Dist. by* **Macmillan.**

Bloomsbury Publishing Plc (GBR) *(978-0-225; 978-0-245; 978-0-264; 978-0-333; 978-0-485; 978-0-510; 978-0-540; 978-0-567; 978-0-7136; 978-0-7470; 978-0-7475; 978-0-7478; 978-0-85045; 978-0-85177; 978-0-85263; 978-0-85314; 978-0-85496; 978-0-86292; 978-0-906515; 978-0-907582; 978-0-948230; 978-1-85399; 978-1-85532; 978-1-85973; 978-1-899791; 978-1-901362; 978-0-212; 978-0-85146; 978-0-85147; 978-0-85317; 978-0-86019; 978-0-946716; 978-0-9507160; 978-1-902579; 978-1-84113; 978-1-85691; 978-1-897737; 978-0-9506785; 978-1-8735) Dist. by* **IPG Chicago.**

Bloomsbury Publishing Plc (GBR) *(978-0-225; 978-0-245; 978-0-264; 978-0-333; 978-0-485; 978-0-510; 978-0-540; 978-0-567; 978-0-7136; 978-0-7470; 978-0-7475; 978-0-7478; 978-0-85045; 978-0-85177; 978-0-85263; 978-0-85314; 978-0-85496; 978-0-86292; 978-0-906515; 978-0-907582; 978-0-948230; 978-1-85399; 978-1-85532; 978-1-85973; 978-1-899791; 978-1-901362; 978-0-212; 978-0-85146; 978-0-85147; 978-0-85317; 978-0-86019; 978-0-946716; 978-0-9507160; 978-1-902579; 978-1-84113; 978-1-85691; 978-1-897737; 978-0-9506785; 978-1-8735) Dist. by* **Players Pr.**

Bloomsbury Publishing Plc (GBR) *(978-0-225; 978-0-245; 978-0-264; 978-0-333; 978-0-485; 978-0-510; 978-0-540; 978-0-567; 978-0-7136; 978-0-7470; 978-0-7475;*

Publisher Name Index

978-0-7478; 978-0-85045; 978-0-85177; 978-0-85263; 978-0-85314; 978-0-85496; 978-0-86292; 978-0-906515; 978-0-907582; 978-0-94230; 978-1-85399; 978-1-85532; 978-1-85973; 978-1-899791; 978-1-901362; 978-0-212; 978-0-85146; 978-0-85147; 978-0-85317; 978-0-86019; 978-0-946716; 978-0-9507160; 978-1-902579; 978-1-84113; 978-1-85691; 978-1-897737; 978-0-9506785; 978-1-8735) Dist. by **Consort Bk Sales.**

Bloomsbury Publishing USA, *(978-1-58234; 978-1-59691; 978-1-59990; 978-1-60819; 978-1-84706; 978-1-61963; 978-1-62040; 978-1-62356; 978-1-62892; 978-1-63286; 978-1-5013; 978-1-68119; 978-1-63557; 978-1-5476; 978-1-63973; 979-8-7651)* Orders Addr.: 16365 James Madison Hwy., Gordonsville, VA 22942-8501 USA Tel 888-330-8477; Toll Free: 888-330-8477; Edit Addr.: 175 Fifth Ave., Suite 300, New York, NY 10010 USA Toll Free: 888-330-8477; 1385 Broadway, New York, NY 10018 Tel 212-419-5300; *Imprints:* Bloomsbury USA Childrens (Bloom Child); Greenwood (GreenWABC); Libraries Unlimited (LibdUnltd); Bloomsbury USA (BloomsburyUSA); Bloomsbury Sigma (BloomsSigma); Alma Classics (AlmaClassics); Osprey (OspreyUSA); Bloomsbury Sport (BloomSport); Bloomsbury Activity Books (BloomActivity); The Arden Shakespeare (ArdenUSA); Bloomsbury Children's Books (BloomsChildren); Bloomsbury Young Adult (BlmsburyYA)
E-mail: bloomsbury.kids@bloomsburyusa.com; nathaniel.knaebel@bloomsbury.com; mike.o'connor@bloomsbury.com
Web site: https://www.bloomsbury.com/us/
Dist(s): **Bloomsbury Publishing US Textbook 1
Bloomsbury Publishing US Textbook 2
Bloomsbury Publishing US Trade
Casemate Academic
Children's Plus, Inc.
INscribe Digital
Macmillan
MyiLibrary
Penguin Random Hse. Distribution
Penguin Random Hse. LLC
St. Martin's Pr.
Sterling Publishing Co., Inc.**

Bloomsbury Sigma *Imprint of* **Bloomsbury Publishing USA**

Bloomsbury Sport *Imprint of* **Bloomsbury Publishing USA**

Bloomsbury USA *Imprint of* **Bloomsbury Publishing USA**

Bloomsbury USA Childrens *Imprint of* **Bloomsbury Publishing USA**

Bloomsbury Visual Arts *Imprint of* **BJU Pr.**

Bloomsbury Young Adult *Imprint of* **Bloomsbury Publishing USA**

Blow's Innovation to Art - (BIA), *(978-0-9820772)* 8090 Atlantic Blvd, E-160, Jacksonville, FL 32211 USA Tel 904-469-1169 business number
E-mail: biabizz@aol.com; blows.art@gmail.com
Web site: http://www.myspace.com/biabizz1
Dist(s): **Ingram Content Group.**

BLPH, Inc., *(978-0-9759158; 978-0-9772425; 978-0-9791099)* P.O. Box 764, Springfield, OR 97477-0132 USA
E-mail: printing@bestlittleprinthouse.com
Web site: http://www.bestlittleprinthouse.com.

BLR Bks., *(978-0-9721839)* 94 Circle Dr., Waltham, MA 02452 USA
Dist(s): **Pathway Bk. Service.**

BLTJ Creations LLC, *(978-1-7335422)* 304 Springtown Rd., New Paltz, NY 12561 USA Tel 917-881-4345
E-mail: bltjcreations@gmail.com.

Blu Phi'er Publishing, LLC, *(978-0-9772034; 978-0-9799884; 978-0-9823845; 978-0-9858378)* 2400 W. Grand Ave., Marshall, TX 75670 USA Tel 903-935-4223
E-mail: phierstarter@bluphier.com
Web site: http://www.bluphier.com.

Blue Apple Bks., *(978-1-934706; 978-1-60905)* 515 Valley St., Suite 180, Maplewood, NJ 07040 USA (SAN 854-4727) Fax: 973-763-5944
E-mail: info@blueapplebooks.com
Web site: http://www.blueapplebooks.com
Dist(s): **Children's Plus, Inc.
Chronicle Bks. LLC
Consortium Bk. Sales & Distribution
Hachette Bk. Group
Learning Connection, The
Penguin Random Hse. Distribution
Penguin Random Hse. LLC
Random Hse., Inc.**

Blue Bark Pr., *(978-0-615-18110-3)* 7 View South Ave., Jamaica Plain, MA 02130 USA Tel 617-840-3418.

Blue Barn, Inc., *(978-0-692-84662-9; 978-0-692-84810-4; 978-0-692-84855-5)* 4313 Bluebell Ave., STUDIO CITY, CA 91604 USA Tel 310-625-2837
E-mail: jeffwcrawford5+LVP0003368@gmail.com; jeffwcrawford5+LVP0003368@gmail.com.

Blue Bear Publishing *See* **Beach Front Bks.**

Blue Begonia Pr., *(978-0-911287)* 311 Hillcrest Dr, Selah, WA 98942 USA (SAN 268-3652) Tel 509-452-9748
E-mail: adpeters@charter.net
Web site: http://bluebegoniapress.com
Dist(s): **Partners/West Book Distributors.**

Blue Bike Bks. (CAN) *(978-0-9739116; 978-1-897278; 978-1-926700) Dist. by* **Lone Pine.**

Blue Blanket Publishing, *(978-0-9903623)* 16 Poland Spring Rd., Auburn, ME 04210 USA Tel 207-402-0954
E-mail: cjiadonisi@gmail.com.

Blue Bk. Pubns., Inc., *(978-0-9625943; 978-1-886768; 978-1-936120; 978-1-947314)* 8009 34th Ave. S., Suite 250, Minneapolis, MN 55425 USA (SAN 860-4452) Tel 952-854-5229; Fax: 952-853-1486; Toll Free: 800-877-4867 Do not confuse with Blue Book Pubs., Inc. in La Jolla, CA
E-mail: bluebook@bluebookinc.com; clints@bluebookinc.com; support@bluebookinc.com
Web site: bluebookofgunvalues.com; bluebookofguitarvalues.com
Dist(s): **Alfred Publishing Co., Inc.
Follett School Solutions
Music Sales Corp.
Omnibus Pr.**

Blue Botte, *(978-0-9896257)* 14907 W. Autumn Ln., Nine Mile Falls, WA 99026 USA Tel 509-465-4534
E-mail: willarda2z@msn.com.

Blue Boy Publishing Co., *(978-0-9742632)* P.O. Box 691, Camillus, NY 13031-0691 USA.

Blue Brush Media, *(978-0-9777382)* 851 Monroe Ave., NE, Renton, WA 98056 USA (SAN 850-0878) Tel 425-818-8850 Do not confuse with Dolphin Media LLC in Huntsville, AL
E-mail: kunle@mamaAfricana.com
Web site: http://www.bluebrushmedia.com
Dist(s): **Follett School Solutions
NewLife Bk. Distributors.**

Blue Cat (GBR) *(978-0-9559351) Dist. by* **LuluCom.**

Blue Cat Bks, *(978-0-9779763)* P.O. Box 2818, Covina, CA 91722 USA Tel 626-339-1223
E-mail: info@bluecatpublishers.com
Web site: http://bluecatpublishers.com.

Blue Chip Publishing, *(978-0-9673970)* Orders Addr.: P.O. Box 26657, Austin, TX 78755 USA Tel 512-345-3021; Fax: 512-345-0181; Edit Addr.: 4119 Circletree Loop, Austin, TX 78731 USA Do not confuse with Blue Chip Publishing Corp., Keizer, OR
E-mail: MAMA19@aol.com.

Blue Cove Publishing, *(978-1-945595)* P.O. Box 1828, Dunnellon, FL 34430 USA Tel 352-489-0436
E-mail: mbatesd@aol.com
Web site: www.bluecovepublishing.com.

Blue Creek Publishing LLC, *(978-0-692-51298-2)* 226 Douglas Fir Ave, Castle Rock, CO 80104 USA Tel 720-394-9037
Web site: www.bluecreekpublishing.com
Dist(s): **CreateSpace Independent Publishing Platform.**

Blue Crown Pr., *(978-0-615-52468-9; 978-0-9839308; 978-0-9855874)* P.O. Box 871826, Canton, MI 48187 USA Tel 734-905-0068
E-mail: author@emlynchand.com
Web site: www.novelpublicity.com.

Blue Cubicle Pr., LLC, *(978-0-9745900; 978-0-9827136; 978-1-938583)* P.O. Box 250382, Plano, TX 75025-0382 USA Tel 972-824-0646; *Imprints:* Castle Builder Press (Castle Builder)
Web site: http://www.bluecubiclepress.com.

Blue Devil Games, *(978-0-9763795)* P.O. Box 19359, Plantation, FL 33318 USA Tel 954-315-0920
Web site: http://www.bluedevilgames.com.

Blue Dog Pr., *(978-0-615-70122-6; 978-0-615-70260-5; 978-0-615-75677-6; 978-0-9893053; 978-0-692-29258-7; 978-0-692-30477-8; 978-0-692-35353-0; 978-0-692-37687-4; 978-0-692-39537-0; 978-0-692-50934-0; 978-0-692-53397-0; 978-1-7353218)* 324 Martin Ave, Maple Shade, NJ 08056 USA Tel 8567184621
E-mail: accounts@ebbrown.net
Dist(s): **Ingram Bk. Co.**

Blue Dolphin Publishing, Inc., *(978-0-931892; 978-1-57733)* Orders Addr.: P.O. Box 8, Nevada City, CA 95959 USA (SAN 223-2480) Tel 530-477-1503; Fax: 530-477-8342; Toll Free: 800-643-0765; Edit Addr.: 13340-d Grass Valley Ave., Grass Valley, CA 95945 USA (SAN 696-009X); *Imprints:* Papillon Publishing (Papillon Pubng)
E-mail: bdolphin@bluedolphinpublishing.com; clemens@bluedolphinpublishing.com
Web site: http://www.bluedolphinpublishing.com
Dist(s): **Follett School Solutions
New Leaf Distributing Co., Inc.**

Blue Dome, Inc., *(978-0-9720654; 978-1-932099; 978-1-59784; 978-1-935295; 978-1-68206; 978-1-68236)* 335 Clifton Ave, Clifton, NJ 07011 USA Tel 646-415-9331; Fax: 646-827-6228; *Imprints:* Tughra Books (TughraBks)
E-mail: info@bluedomepress.com
Web site: http://www.tughrabooks.com; http://www.bluedomepress.com
Dist(s): **National Bk. Network.**

Blue Dome Press *See* **Blue Dome, Inc.**

Blue Dot Pubns. LLC, *(978-1-7331212; 978-1-7350005; 978-1-7362264; 978-1-7376032; 979-8-9858494)* 819 Greenberry Ln., San Rafael, CA 94903 USA Tel 415-205-4884
E-mail: hello@bluedotkidspress.com
Web site: https://www.bluedotkidspress.com/
Dist(s): **Consortium Bk. Sales & Distribution.**

Blue Dragon Publishing, *(978-0-9832454; 978-1-939696)* P.O. Box 247, Lightfoot, VA 23090 USA Tel 757-941-5007
E-mail: BlueDragonPub@cox.net
Web site: http://www.blue-dragon-publishing.com
Dist(s): **Ingram Bk. Co.**

Blue Dream Studios, *(978-0-9789168)* 1133 Cedarview Ln., Franklin, TN 37067-4075 USA
Web site: http://www.bluedreamstudios.com
Dist(s): **Diamond Comic Distributors, Inc.
Diamond Bk. Distributors
Diamond Distributors, Inc.**

Blue Drop, *(978-0-578-75649-3; 978-0-578-99770-4; 979-8-218-05166-2)* 1385 Canal St SE, Washington, DC 20003 USA Tel 202-792-4793
E-mail: fran@bluedrop.co
Web site: bluedrop.co.

Blue Eagle Bks., Inc., *(978-0-9794655)* 5773 Woodway, PMB 190, Houston, TX 77057 USA Tel 713-789-1516 (phone/fax)
E-mail: sjones@blueeaglebooks.com
Web site: http://blueeaglebooks.com.

Blue Eyed Mayhem Publishing, *(978-0-9794545)* 6 Hopemont Dr., Mount Laurel, NJ 08054 USA Tel 609-781-0291
Dist(s): **Smashwords.**

Blue Forge Pr., *(978-1-883573; 978-1-886383; 978-1-59092)* Div. of Blue Forge Group, 7419 Ebbert Dr., SE, Port Orchard, WA 98367 USA (SAN 299-1330) Tel 360-550-2071 phone
E-mail: blueforgepress@gmail.com
Web site: http://www.blueforgepress.com.

Blue Fox Pr., *(978-0-9763119)* Pierce Arrow Bldg., 1685 Elmwood Ave., Suite 315, Buffalo, NY 14207-2407 USA Tel 716-447-1590; Fax: 716-837-7066
E-mail: bluefoxpress@yahoo.com
Web site: http://www.bluefoxpress.com.

Blue Fuji Pubs., *(978-0-9843647)* 14 Cambridge Rd., East Hanover, NJ 07936 USA
E-mail: kevin@kevinkato.com
Web site: http://www.kevinkato.com
Dist(s): **Smashwords.**

Blue Fyre Pr., *(978-1-7327701; 978-1-951009)* 6172 S Crestview St, Littleton, CO 80120 USA Tel 720-235-2087
E-mail: kendramerritt85@gmail.com.

Blue Gate Bks., *(978-0-9792612)* P.O. Box 2137, Nevada City, CA 95959 USA (SAN 852-923X) Tel 530-263-4501
E-mail: babette@babettedonaldson.com; info@emmaleabooks.com
Web site: http://www.bluegatebooks.com; http://www.sidecarscooter.com; http://www.emmaleabooks.com; http://www.Fun-With-Tea.com.

Blue Horizon Publishing Co., *(978-0-9658786; 978-0-9955738-0-2)* 25012 S. Harmony Rd., Cheney, WA 99004-9798 USA Tel 509-235-8547.

Blue Horse Books *Imprint of* **Great Lakes Literary, LLC**

Blue Ink Press *See* **Blue Ink Pr.**

Blue Ink Pr., *(978-0-9817234)* 1246 Heart Ave., Amherst, OH 44001 USA Tel 440-823-8320
E-mail: dougk@icehorseadventures.com
Web site: http://www.icehorseadventures.com
Dist(s): **Blu Sky Media Group.**

Blue Ink Pr., *(978-0-692-35368-4; 978-0-9968673; 978-0-692-63512-4; 978-0-692-71762-2; 978-0-692-72745-4; 978-1-948449)* 2621 Hiking Trail, Raleigh, NC 27615 USA Tel 919-418-8746 Do not confuse with Blue Ink Press in Amherst, OH
Web site: www.blueinkpress.com; www.sherrytorgent.com
Dist(s): **CreateSpace Independent Publishing Platform
Ingram Content Group.**

Blue Jay Bks. *Imprint of* **Crooked River Pr.**

Blue Jay Pr., *(978-0-9913000)* 1020 se 22 ave, Portland, OR 97214 USA Tel 503-679-7652
E-mail: ktboyer@spiretech.com.

Blue Kitty, The, *(978-0-9796814)* P.O. Box 254, Syracuse, NY 13214 USA
E-mail: info@thebluekitty.com.

Blue Lantern Books *See* **Laughing Elephant**

Blue Lion Productions, Ltd, *(978-0-9761132)* 302 Smith St., Freeport, NY 11520 USA Tel 516-546-4611
E-mail: info@bluelionproductions.com
Web site: http://www.bluelionproductions.com.

Blue Lobster Pr., *(978-0-9709569)* Orders Addr.: 3919 Union St., Levant, ME 04456-4358 USA
E-mail: books@bluelobsterpress.com; poet@robertpottle.com
Web site: http://www.bluelobsterpress.com.

Blue Logic Publishing, *(978-0-9860669)* P.O. Box 797492, Dallas, TX 75379 USA Tel 972-380-1467
E-mail: contact@bluelogicpublishing.com
Web site: www.bluelogicpublishing.com.

Blue Lotus Wave, *(978-0-9789624)* Orders Addr.: 15 Surrey Dr., Riverside, CT 06878-1516 USA (SAN 852-0631) Tel 203-344-1344 Do not confuse with Blue Lotus Press in Palmyra, MA.

blue manatee children's Bookstore *See* **Blue Manatee Press**

Blue Manatee Press, *(978-1-936669; 979-8-218-13755-7; 979-8-9886382)* 6222 Wiehe Rd. Suite 2, Cincinnati, OH 45237 USA (SAN 920-4601) Tel 513-703-9968
E-mail: press@bluemanateebooks.com; johnh@bluemanateebooks.com
Web site: www.bluemanateepress.com
Dist(s): **Children's Plus, Inc.
Independent Pubs. Group.**

Blue Marble Bks. *Imprint of* **Sphinx Publishing**

Blue Marlin Pubns., *(978-0-9674602; 978-0-9792918; 978-0-9885295; 978-1-7321097; 978-1-7345734)* 823 Aberdeen Rd., West Bay Shore, NY 11706 USA Tel 631-666-0353 (phone/fax)
E-mail: jude@bluemarlinpubs.com
Web site: http://www.BlueMarlinPubs.com
Dist(s): **Follett School Solutions.**

Blue Morpho Bks., *(978-1-7321165; 978-1-960457)* 455 Pernello Rd., Ferrum, VA 24088 USA Tel 540-365-2151
E-mail: janefenton.books@gmail.com.

Blue Moth Press, The *See* **Blue Moth Pr., The LLC**

Blue Moth Pr., The LLC, *(978-1-7359483)* 1075 Broad Ripple Ave suit 133, Indianapolis, IN 46220 USA Tel 708-209-8203
E-mail: thebluemothpress@gmail.com.

Blue Mountain Arts Inc., *(978-0-88396; 978-1-58786; 978-1-59842; 978-1-68088)* Orders Addr.: P.O. Box 4549, Boulder, CO 80306 USA (SAN 299-9609) Tel 303-449-0536; Fax: 303-417-6434; 303-417-6496; Toll Free Fax: 800-943-6666; 800-545-8573; Toll Free: 800-525-0642; *Imprints:* Blue Mountain Press (Blue Mntn Pr); Rabbit's Foot Press (Rabb Ft Pr)
Web site: http://www.sps.com/.

Blue Mountain Arts (R) by SPS Studios, Incorporated *See* **Blue Mountain Arts Inc.**

Blue Mountain Pr. *Imprint of* **Blue Mountain Arts Inc.**

Blue Mustang Pr., *(978-0-9759737; 978-1-935199)* 175B Mansfield Ave., Suite 240, Norton, MA 02766 USA Tel 206-350-2823 (phone/fax)
E-mail: info@bluemustangpress.com
Web site: http://www.bluemustangpress.com.

Blue Note Bks. *Imprint of* **Blue Note Pubns.**

Blue Note Pubns., *(978-1-878398; 978-0-9830758; 978-0-9855562; 978-0-9895563; 978-0-9903068; 978-0-9963066; 978-0-9977638; 978-1-7338019)* P.O. Box 237483, Cocoa, FL 32923-7483 USA; *Imprints:* Blue Note Books (Blue Note Bks)
E-mail: bluenotepress@gmail.com
Web site: http://www.bluenotepublications.com.

Blue Oink Bks., *(978-1-7343321)* 4205 South Cty. Rd. 7, Fort Collins, CO 80525 USA Tel 970-685-8569
E-mail: lisarbruce@hotmail.com.

Blue Owl Editions, *(978-0-9672793)* 6254 Girvin Dr., Oakland, CA 94611 USA Tel 510-482-3038 (phone/fax)
E-mail: edanti@ispwest.com; enricoanti@yahoo.com
Dist(s): **Independent Pubs. Group
Smashwords.**

Blue Peach Publishing, *(978-0-615-15922-5)* 2 Wyeth Cir., Southborough, MA 01772 USA
Dist(s): **Lulu Pr., Inc.**

Blue Pig Productions, *(978-1-932545)* P.O. Box 691779, Orlando, FL 32869-1779 USA (SAN 255-4763) Tel 407-854-5679 (phone/fax)
E-mail: bluepigprod@aol.com
Web site: http://www.repunzal.com.

Blue Planet Press *See* **Ninth Planet Pr.**

Blue Portal Pr. LLC, *(978-0-9893963)* 2400 Wilderness Way, Marietta, GA 30066 USA Tel 404-372-1530
E-mail: red170@yahoo.com
Web site: http://blueportalpressllc.weebly.com/.

Blue Reamker, *(978-0-9795620)* 13725 Hawk Lake Dr., Orlando, FL 32837 USA.

Blue River Pr., *(978-0-9718959; 978-0-9763361; 978-0-9799240; 978-0-9819289; 978-1-935628; 978-1-68157; 978-0-9963247)* Orders Addr.: 2402 N. Shadeland Ave., Suite A, Indianapolis, IN 46219 USA Tel 317-352-8200; Fax: 317-352-8202; Toll Free: 800-296-0481 Do not confuse with Blue River Press in Bloomingdale, IL
E-mail: tdoherty@cardinalpub.com
Web site: http://www.cardinalpub.com; www.brpressbooks.com; www.rubberduckypress.com
Dist(s): **Cardinal Pubs. Group
Children's Plus, Inc.
MyiLibrary
Login Canada.**

Blue Room Bks. *Imprint of* **WRITER for HIRE!**

Blue Scarab Pr., *(978-0-937179)* Orders Addr.: 811 Normandie Blvd., Bowling Green, OH 43402 USA (SAN 658-4640) Tel 419-819-4506
E-mail: haraldwyndham@gmail.com.

Blue Scribbles Publishing, *(978-0-615-24897-4)* P.O. Box 2054, Centreville, VA 20120 USA
E-mail: bluescribbles@gmail.com
Web site: http://www.bluescribbles.com.

Blue Shoe Publishing, *(978-0-9725552)* c/o Christine Merser, 38 W. 74th St., 3A, New York, NY 10023 USA Tel 212-579-0310
E-mail: inquiry@blueshoestrategy.com; inquiry@blueshoepublishing.com; LLim@BlueShoeStrategy.com
Web site: http://www.blueshoepublishing.com.

Blue Shutter Bks., *(978-0-9729379)* Orders Addr.: 5125 Schultz Bridge Rd., Zionsville, PA 18092-2543 USA Tel 215-541-3362; Fax: 425-491-4282
E-mail: rworthington@blueshutterbooks.com
Web site: http://www.blueshutterbooks.com.

Blue Skies Above Texas Co., *(978-0-9800019)* 14781 Memorial Dr., No. 399, Houston, TX 77079 USA Tel 281-920-0043
E-mail: BlueSkiesAboveTexas@yahoo.com.

Blue Sky at Night Publishing, *(978-0-9768623)* 601 W River St, Monticello, MN 55362 USA
E-mail: Jill@JournalBuddies.com
Web site: http://www.JournalBuddies.com.

Blue Sky Daisies, *(978-0-9905529; 978-1-944435)* 1907 N. Valleyview, Wichita, KS 67212 USA Tel 316-573-9733
E-mail: blueskydaisies@gmail.com
Web site: www.blueskydaisies.wordpress.com.

Blue Sky Ink, *(978-1-59475)* P.O. Box 1067, Brentwood, TN 37024-1067 USA (SAN 255-7401) Tel 805-677-6815
Dist(s): **Send The Light Distribution LLC.**

Blue Sky Pr., The *Imprint of* **Scholastic, Inc.**

Blue Sky Pr., *(978-0-9746896)* P.O. Box 6192, Malibu, CA 90264-6192 USA Tel 818-706-9814; 557 Broadway., New York, NY 10012 Do not confuse with Blue Sky Press in San Jose CA, Placerville CO, Silver Spring MD, Berkeley CA, Dallas TX
E-mail: laura@lauralarsen.com
Web site: http://www.lauralarsen.com
Dist(s): **Follett School Solutions.**

Blue Socks Media LLC, *(978-0-692-80162-8; 978-0-692-80714-9)* 2108 S. Boulevard, Suite 108, Charlotte, NC 28203 USA Tel 704-562-4502
E-mail: tsteedman@raggs.com
Web site: http://www.raggs.com.

Blue Sparrow Books *See* **Viident Co.**

Blue Star Pr., *(978-1-941325; 978-1-944515; 978-1-950968; 978-1-958803)* 2843 NW Lolo Dr. Suite 200, Bend, OR 97703 USA Tel 505-306-5494; *Imprints:* Paige Tate & Co. (PaigeTate)
E-mail: contact@bluestarcoloring.com
Dist(s): **Ingram Publisher Services
Penguin Random Hse. Distribution
Penguin Random Hse. LLC.**

Blue State Pr., *(978-0-9773674)* 17771 Plumtree Ln., Yorba Linda, CA 92886 USA.

Blue Suit Bks., *(978-0-9748563)* P.O. Box 840057, New Orleans, LA 70184 USA (SAN 255-8998) Tel 504-450-4334
E-mail: bluesuit@imaginationmovers.com
Web site: http://www.imaginationmovers.com.

Blue Thistle Pr., *(978-0-9760505; 978-0-9786302)* 6187 FM 314, Ben Wheeler, TX 75754-4030 USA Tel 903-539-2500
E-mail: lkayers@hotmail.com
Web site: http://www.lindaayersbooks.com.

Blue Thunder Bks., *(978-0-9673000; 978-0-9839454; 978-1-958387)* 5070 Vegas Valley Dr. Unit 621833, Las Vegas, NV 89142 USA //Do not confuse with Blue Thunder Bks in Grand Rapids, MI
E-mail: dereksavage7@yahoo.com
Web site: http://SAVAGE1.com; http://www.CoolCatLovesYou.com.

Blue Thunder One, Inc., *(978-0-9719284)* P.O. Box 2435, Riverview, MI 48192 USA.

Blue Tide Pr., *(978-0-9987537)* 1701 Hwy. A1A, Suite 212, Vero Beach, FL 32963 USA Tel 586-322-3109
E-mail: kristenheaney@yahoo.com
Web site: www.inthreegenerations.com.

Blue Tie Publishing, *(978-0-9777972)* 1 Hale Rd., East Hampton, CT 06424 USA Tel 860-267-0432
E-mail: tanner@sbcglobal.net.

Blue Tiger Publishing, *(978-0-9759903)* P.O. Box 3776, Glendale, CA 91221-0776 USA Tel 310-497-9291
E-mail: travis_english@charter.net.

Blue Tree LLC, *(978-0-9711321; 978-0-9792014; 978-0-9802245; 978-0-9893088)* Orders Addr.: P.O. Box 148, Portsmouth, NH 03802 USA Tel 603-436-0831; Fax: 603-686-5054
E-mail: contact@thebluetree.com
Web site: http://www.thebluetree.com.

Blue Unicorn Edition, LLC, *(978-1-891355; 978-1-58396)* 12300 NW 56th Ave., Gainesville, FL 32653 USA Toll Free Fax: 866-334-1497 (orders)
E-mail: tienda1@instabook.net
Web site: http://www.instabookpublisher.com.

Blue Vase Productions, *(978-0-9770125)* 2455 Otay Ctr. Dr. Apt 118 Ste 252, San Diego, CA 92154 USA (SAN 257-4454) Fax: 619-819-6311
E-mail: legal@eljarronazul.com; ventas@eljarronazul.com
Web site: http://www.eljarronazul.com.

Blue Water Pr., LLC, *(978-0-9796046)* 8814 Sir Barton Ln., Waxhaw, NC 28173 USA Tel 704-551-9051
E-mail: Tonibranner@aol.com; jmacgregor@cadencemarketinggroup.com.

Blue Water Publishing, *(978-0-9796160)* 805 N. Orange Ave., Fallbrook, CA 92028-1525 USA
E-mail: bluewaterpub@sbcglobal.net.

Blue Whale Pr., *(978-0-9814938; 978-1-7328935)* 102 S Swenson St., Stamford, TX 79553 USA (SAN 855-7004) Tel 325-773-5550
E-mail: sales@bluewhalepress.com
Web site: https://www.bluewhalepress.com; https://www.clearforkpublishing.com/
Dist(s): **Follett School Solutions**
Ingram Content Group Inc.

Blue Whale Press. LLC *See* **Blue Whale Pr.**

Blue Willow Pr., *(978-0-9767473)* 197 Lamplight Ln., Bozeman, MT 59718 USA Tel 406-388-0272; Fax: 423-318-2329
E-mail: bluewillowpress@yahoo.com; obachs@juno.com
Web site: http://www.bluewillowpress.com
Dist(s): **Canyonlands Pubns.**

Blue Wing Pubns., Workshops & Lectures, *(978-0-9795663; 978-0-692-73942-6)* 11985 N. Cayce Ln, Casa Grande, AZ 85194 USA Toll Free: 877-591-4156
E-mail: sdk@bluewingworkshops.com
Web site: http://www.bluewingworkshops.com
Dist(s): **CreateSpace Independent Publishing Platform.**

Blue Zebra Entertainment, Incorporated *See* **Murphey, Hiromi**

Blueberry Illustrations *See* **Sherry Chakrabarti**

Blueberry Illustrations, *(978-0-692-75274-6)* 104 Overlook Bend, Kingsland, GA 31548 USA Tel 912-409-7343
E-mail: SLCarrollauthor@gmail.com.

Bluebonnets, Boots & Bks. Pr., *(978-0-9645493; 978-0-9800061)* 11010 Hanning Ln., Houston, TX 77041-5006 USA; P.O. Box 19632, Houston, TX 77224-9632
E-mail: rita@bookconnectiononline.com
Web site: http://www.ABCsPress.com
Dist(s): **Complete Book & Media Supply**
Follett School Solutions
News Group
Partners Pubs. Group, Inc.

BlueBoreas Press *See* **PM Moon Pub., LLC**

BlueBoyImprints, *(978-1-7373781)* 2309 Wagon Rd., Knoxville, TN 37920-2895 USA Tel 865-382-4226
E-mail: pepintm@gmail.com.

Bluechip Publishers *See* **BlueChip Pubs.**

BlueChip Pubs., *(978-0-930251)* Orders Addr.: P.O. Box 4204, Jackson, WY 83001 USA
E-mail: info@bluechippublishers.com
Dist(s): **Ingram Content Group.**

BlueCougar Studios, *(978-0-615-16770-1; 978-0-615-17434-1)* 3805 Grandview Ave., NW No. 4, Roanoke, VA 24012 USA
E-mail: info@bluecougarsrufios.com
Dist(s): **Lulu Pr., Inc.**

Bluedoor, llc, *(978-1-59984; 978-1-68135; 978-1-64386)* 10949 Bren Rd., E., Minneapolis, MN 55343 USA Tel 952-934-1624; Fax: 952-934-4269; Toll Free: 800-979-1624
E-mail: mary@bluedoorpublishing.com
Web site: http://bluedoorpublishing.com.

Blue-Eyed Star Creations, LLC, *(978-0-9994409)* 2 Old Forest St., Middleton, MA 01949 USA Tel 617-592-9958
E-mail: blueeyedstarcreations@gmail.com
Web site: blue-eyedstarcreations.com.

Bluefire *Imprint of* **Random Hse. Children's Bks.**

Bluefish River Pr., *(978-0-9714701)* P.O. Box 1398, Duxbury, MA 02332 USA
E-mail: dpallai@bluefishriverpress.com
Web site: http://www.bluefishriverpress.com.

BlueInk Scribbe, *(978-1-7358263; 978-1-7363082; 978-1-7366722; 978-1-7371714; 978-1-7376097; 979-8-9858173; 979-8-9871406; 979-8-9875819; 979-8-9883724; 979-8-9888051; 979-8-9892304)* 711 E. Ascension St No. 648, Gonzales, LA 70737 USA Tel 225-317-7420
E-mail: blueinkscribbleservices@gmail.com
Web site: blueinkscribble.com.

BlueLine Book Publishers *See* **Great American Pubs.**

Blueline Publishing, *(978-0-9776906)* P.O. Box 11569, Denver, CO 80211 USA (SAN 856-2539) Tel 303-477-5272; Fax: 866-876-2915
Web site: http://www.bluelinepub.com
Dist(s): **Follett School Solutions.**

BlueMoonGreenLake, *(978-0-9968237)* 700 N. Colorado Blvd, Denver, CO 80206 USA Tel 303-548-8507
E-mail: Kellymcondon66@gmail.com
Web site: www.BlueMoonGreenLake.com.

BlueSky Publishing, *(978-0-9724386)* Div. of BlueSky Medical Group, Inc., 6965 El Camino Real Suite 105-602, Carlsbad, CA 92009 USA Tel 760-603-8130; 760-603-8331 (phone/fax)
E-mail: publishingdivision@blueskymedical.com
Web site: http://www.boypresident.com.

Bluestar Communications Corp., *(978-1-885394)* c/o Words Distributing Company, 7900 Edgewater Dr., Oakland, CA 94621 USA; Edit Addr.: 7080 Norfolk Rd., Berkeley, CA 94705 USA.

Bluestocking Pr., *(978-0-942617)* Orders Addr.: P.O. Box 1134, Eagle, ID 83616 USA (SAN 667-2981) Tel 800-959-8586; Fax: 800-959-8586; Edit Addr.: P.O. Box 1134, Eagle, ID 83616 USA (SAN 667-299X)
E-mail: annmarie@bluestockingpress.com
Web site: http://www.bluestockingpress.com.

Bluestone Bks., *(978-0-9720046)* P.O. Box 761, Edmonds, WA 98020 USA
Web site: http://www.cmc.net/~jwrig.

Bluestreak Books *Imprint of* **Weldon Owen, Inc.**

Bluewater Productions, Inc., *(978-0-9792751)* 2950 Newmarket Pl., Suite 101, Bellingham, WA 98226 USA Tel 360-778-1033
Web site: http://www.bluewaterprod.com/
Dist(s): **Diamond Comic Distributors, Inc.**
Diamond Bk. Distributors
MyiLibrary
SCB Distributors.

Bluewater Pubns., *(978-0-9719946; 978-1-934610; 978-1-949711; 978-1-958273)* 1812 Cty. Rd. 111, Killen, AL 35645 USA Tel 256-762-7153 Do not confuse with Heart Of Dixie Publishing Corporation in Foley, AL
E-mail: angela.broyles@gmail.com; malcolm.broyles@gmail.com
Web site: http://www.bwpublications.com
Dist(s): **Follett School Solutions.**

Bluewood Bks., *(978-0-912517)* Div. of The Siyeh Group, Inc., P.O. Box 689, San Mateo, CA 94010 USA (SAN 265-3214) Tel 650-548-0754; Fax: 650-548-0654
E-mail: Bluewoodb@aol.com
Dist(s): **Follett School Solutions**
L P C Group
SCB Distributors.

Bluffton Bks., *(978-0-89986; 978-0-9702635)* Orders Addr.: 714b Kodiak Trail, Cedar Park, TX 78613 USA
E-mail: ethno777@mac.com.

Blume (ESP) *(978-84-89396; 978-84-932442; 978-84-95939; 978-84-9801) Dist. by* **IPG Chicago.**

Blumenberg Bks. Publishing Co., *(978-0-9997925)* 7843 Pk. N. Bend, Indianapolis, IN 46260 USA Tel 317-731-8349
E-mail: BlumenbergBooks@gmail.com.

Blumont Company, The, *(978-0-9776024)* 161 Great Rd., Littleton, MA 01460 USA (SAN 257-702X) Tel 781-899-6468
E-mail: slblu@netway.com.

Blurb, Inc., *(978-0-464; 978-1-4579; 978-1-320; 978-1-5184; 978-1-364; 978-1-366; 978-1-367; 978-1-388; 978-1-389; 978-0-368; 978-0-578-46536-4; 978-1-714; 978-1-715; 978-1-006; 978-1-034; 979-8-210; 979-8-211)* Orders Addr.: 580 California St. #300, San Francisco, CA 94104 USA (SAN 860-0813)
Web site: http://www.blurb.com
Dist(s): **Lulu Pr., Inc.**

Blushing Rose Publishing, *(978-1-884807)* Orders Addr.: P.O. Box 2238, San Anselmo, CA 94979-2238 USA Tel 415-407-0170 Toll Free: 800-898-2263
E-mail: nancya555@yahoo.com
Web site: http://www.blushingrose.com.

Blynbeek Publishing, *(978-0-9996633)* 1117 Phyllis Ave., Mountain View, CA 94040 USA Tel 408-431-9467
E-mail: jchristianb@gmail.com.

Blysster Pr., *(978-0-9826818; 978-0-9840151; 978-0-9883734; 978-1-940247)* P.O. Box 1242, Port Orchard, WA 98366 USA Tel 360-286-5256
Web site: http://www.blysster.com
Dist(s): **Smashwords.**

BMC Advertising, Incorporated *See* **BMCFerrell**

BMCFerrell, *(978-0-9764460; 978-0-9788242)* 6450 S. Lewis Ave. Ste. 300, Tulsa, OK 74136-1068 USA
Web site: http://www.bmcferrell.com.

BMI Educational Services, *(978-0-922443; 978-1-60884; 978-1-60933; 978-1-63071; 978-1-5367)* Orders Addr.: 26 Hayprees Rd., Cranbury, NJ 08512 USA (SAN 760-7032); Edit Addr.: P.O. Box 800, Dayton, NJ 08810-0800 USA (SAN 169-4669) Tel 732-329-6991; Fax: 732-329-6994; Toll Free Fax: 800-986-9393 (orders only); Toll Free: 800-222-8100 (orders only)
E-mail: info@bmionline.com
Web site: http://www.bmionline.com/.

BN Publishing, *(978-1-68411; 978-1-63823; 978-0-578-31197-5; 978-0-578-31695-6)* 3503 Jack Northrup Ave., Ste. # Z2741, Hawthorne, CA 90250 USA
E-mail: info@bnpublishing.com
Web site: http://www.bnpublishing.com.

Boarding House Publishing, *(978-0-9725365; 978-0-9774432)* 3896 Miramonte Ave., Loveland, CO 80538 USA
Web site: http://www.rdeducation.home.att.net.

Boardwalk Bks., LLC *Imprint of* **Boardwalk Bks.**

Boardwalk Bks., *(978-0-9976078)* 5 Sweetwater Ave., Bedford, MA 01730 USA Tel 781-910-9129; *Imprints:* Boardwalk Books, LLC (MYID_W_BOARDWA)
E-mail: Jimpetipas@me.com
Web site: www.boardwalkbooks.net.

Boathouse Press *See* **BoathouseBooks**

BoathouseBooks, *(978-0-9776469)* P.O. Box 244, Tiburon, CA 94920 USA
Web site: http://boathousebooks.com
Dist(s): **Follett School Solutions.**

Boatman Pr., LLC, *(978-0-9909025; 978-0-578-59915-1; 978-1-7355514)* 545 Tucker Hill Rd., Thetford Center, VT 05075 USA Tel 802-785-2012
E-mail: boatman@deanwhitlock.com
Web site: deanwhitlock.com.

Bob Thomas Bks., *(978-0-9717682)* Orders Addr.: P.O. Box 853, Black Mountain, NC 28711 USA; Edit Addr.: P.O. Box 815, Kure Beach, NC 28449 USA Toll Free Fax: 866-615-0417.

Bobcat Publishing, *(978-0-9776419)* 5105 Cascabel Rd., Atascadero, CA 93422 USA (SAN 852-9051)
E-mail: llyn@llynsplace.com; llyntroy@sbcglobal.net
Web site: http://www.llynsplace.com.

Bobola, Frederick, *(978-0-692-16136-4; 978-1-7331094)* 22521, Santa Clarita, CA 91350 USA Tel 661-860-0818
E-mail: flbobola@gmail.com.

Bobos babes, Ltd., *(978-1-7374375; 979-8-9859822; 979-8-9871807)* 222 E Chestnut St. Unit 11A, Chicago, IL 60611 USA Tel 312-735-6979
E-mail: karen@bobosbabes.com
Web site: www.BobosBabes.com.

Bobrich Publishing *See* **Wollaston Pr.**

Boca Raton Museum of Art, *(978-0-936859)* 501 Plaza Real, Mizner Park, Boca Raton, FL 33432 USA (SAN 278-2251) Tel 561-392-2500; Fax: 561-391-6410
E-mail: amodine@bocamuseum.org
Web site: http://www.bocamuseum.org
Dist(s): **Antique Collectors' Club**
RAM Pubns. & Distribution
Univ. Pr. of Florida.

Bocelli Production, *(978-0-9908444)* 3924 Song Sparrow Dr., Wake Forest, NC 27587 USA Tel 919-247-6198
E-mail: bocelliproduction@gmail.com.

BOCH Publishing, L.L.C., *(978-1-949350)* 41620 Pheasant Creek Dr., Canton, MI 48188 USA Tel 734-718-2973
E-mail: BOCHpublishing@gmail.com
Web site: www.bochpub.com.

BoCook Publishing, *(978-0-9848791)* 12702 SE 222nd Dr., Damascus, OR 97089 USA Tel 503-853-1362
E-mail: janet_l_carlson@yahoo.com.

Bodkin Pointe Pr., *(978-0-9752684)* Orders Addr.: P.O. Box 654, Gibson Island, MD 21056 USA; 116 Tim Mara Dr., Jupiter, FL 33477 Tel 561-629-2528
E-mail: cathy@bodkinpointepress.com
Web site: http://www.bodkinpointepress.com.

Bodleian Library (GBR) *(978-1-85124; 978-0-900177) Dist. by* **Chicago Distribution Ctr.**

Body & Mind Productions, Inc., *(978-0-9742569; 978-0-9752648; 978-0-9771609; 978-0-9792177; 978-0-9820889; 978-0-9828370; 978-0-9830885; 978-0-9855550; 978-0-9904468)* 9429 Cedar Heights Ave., Las Vegas, NV 89134-0194 USA Tel 949-263-4676
E-mail: bodymindheal@aol.com
Web site: http://www.healingreiki.com
Dist(s): **Follett School Solutions**
New Leaf Distributing Co., Inc.
Quality Bks., Inc.

Body by Bella, LLC, *(978-0-9993882; 978-0-578-26832-3)* 3400 Duveneck Dr, Raleigh, NC 27616 USA Tel 919-561-3111; 9020 Albatross Ct., Raleigh, NC 27613 Tel 919-561-3111
E-mail: bodybybelladotcom@gmail.com; jacqui1718@yahoo.com
Dist(s): **Ingram Content Group.**

Body Tone Multimedia, *(978-0-9760650)* P.O. Box 580691, Elk Grove, CA 95758-0012 USA
E-mail: body_tone_multimedia@mac.com
Web site: http://www.bodytonemultimedia.com.

Bodycrafting Systems, Inc., *(978-0-9745265)* Orders Addr.: P.O. Box 1512, Nokomis, FL 34274 USA Fax: 941-484-9650
Web site: http://www.kidpowerfitness.com.

BodyLife Publishers *See* **Windblown Media**

Boettcher, Ashley L., *(978-0-9768123)* Orders Addr.: P.O. Box 997, Southwick, MA 01077-0997 USA (SAN 256-5811) Tel 413-569-9492 available from 10am to 5pm m-f and 11am to 4pm sat; Edit Addr.: 45 Powder Mill Rd., Southwick, MA 01077 USA
E-mail: ljabphil413@juno.com
Web site: http://www.ALBbooks.com.

Boggs Publishing, *(978-1-7332353)* 962 Lillies Way, Beaumont, CA 92223 USA Tel 909-557-3503
E-mail: steviboggs@yahoo.com.

Boggs-Johnson, SteFanie *See* **Stefanie Boggs-Johnson**

Bohemian Trash Studios, *(978-0-9767540)* 3322 Clearview, San Angelo, TX 76904 USA Tel 325-944-3282; *Imprints:* Star Cross'd Destiny (Star Cross)
Web site: http://www.bohemiantrash.com.

Boho Bks., *(978-0-9814709; 978-0-9891181; 978-0-9907073; 978-0-9988455)* 36179 S. Sawtell Rd, Molalla, OR 97038 USA Tel 503-807-8908; 503-829-3630
E-mail: leeglbeagl@bohobooks.com
Web site: http://www.bohobooks.com.

Bohobza Music, *(978-0-9744943)* P.O. Box 745, Teaneck, NJ 07666-0745 USA Tel 201-862-1692 (phone/fax)
E-mail: wetalkjazz@aol.com
Web site: http://www.ronibenhur.com.

Bohutskyy, Andriy, *(978-1-7371602; 978-1-957457)* 27 Merry Ln. NP000351397, East Hanover, NJ 07936 USA Tel 973-947-6185
E-mail: a.bohutskyi@gmail.com.

Bois Pubns., *(978-0-9727967; 978-0-9971403)* 5411 Colfax Pl., Oklahoma City, OK 73112 USA Tel 405-510-4071 Evening; 405-510-4071 Daytime
E-mail: au444@cox.net; athomas14@cox.net.

Boland, Janie M., *(978-0-692-78147-0; 978-0-692-83475-6; 978-0-692-86491-3; 978-0-692-93936-9)* 4128 Abbott Dr., BAKERSFIELD, CA 93312 USA Tel 559-936-9838.

†Bolchazy-Carducci Pubs., *(978-0-86516; 978-1-61041)* 1570 Baskin Rd., Mundelein, IL 60060-4474 USA (SAN 219-7685) Toll Free: 800-392-6453
E-mail: jcull@bolchazy.com
Web site: http://www.bolchazy.com
Dist(s): **Follett School Solutions**
MyiLibrary; *CIP.*

Bold Illustrations *Imprint of* **FASTLANE LLC**

Bold Strokes Bks., *(978-1-933110; 978-1-60282; 978-1-62639; 978-1-63555; 978-1-63679)* 648 S Cambridge Rd, Johnsonville, NY 12094 USA Tel 518-753-6642; Fax: 518-753-6648
E-mail: bsb@boldstrokesbooks.com; publisher@boldstrokesbooks.com
Web site: http://www.boldstrokesbooks.com
Dist(s): **Abraham Assocs. Inc.**
Bella Distribution
Bookazine Co., Inc.
Two Rivers Distribution.

Bold Venture Pr., *(978-0-9712246)* 2726 NW 104th Avenue, No. 105, Sunrise, FL 33322 USA Tel 609-346-4184
E-mail: boldventurepress@aol.com
Web site: http://www.boldventurepress.com.

Bold Vision Bks., *(978-0-9853563; 978-0-615-66644-0; 978-0-615-83824-3; 978-0-615-89134-7; 978-0-615-90206-7; 978-0-9892842; 978-0-692-29107-8; 978-0-692-29972-2; 978-0-692-33303-7; 978-0-692-33924-4; 978-0-692-36096-5; 978-0-692-38991-1; 978-0-692-42912-9; 978-0-692-43536-6; 978-0-692-43641-7; 978-0-692-43701-8; 978-0-692-43876-3; 978-0-692-43904-3; 978-0-692-65630-3; 978-0-692-65946-5; 978-0-692-65959-5; 978-0-692-68050-6; 978-0-692-74301-0; 978-0-692-74695-0; 978-0-9978514; 978-1-946708) P.O. Box 2011, Friendswood, TX 77549 USA Tel 281-797-3920 (Tel/Fax)*
E-mail: kaeporter@gmail.com
Web site: www.boldvisionbooks.com
Dist(s): **CreateSpace Independent Publishing Platform.**

Bold Visions Consulting, LLC, *(978-0-692-73996-9; 978-1-7330563)* 2350 W. Galbraith, Apt 8, Cincinnati, OH 45239 USA Tel 513-317-9553
Web site: www.boldvisionsconsulting.com
Dist(s): **CreateSpace Independent Publishing Platform.**

Bolden, Christian, *(978-0-692-96171-1)* 70 I St. ST APT 130, Washington, DC 20003 USA Tel 202-294-2747; Fax: 202-294-2747
E-mail: chris93047@yahoo.com.

Boll Weevil Pr., *(978-0-9889568; 978-0-692-93440-1; 978-0-692-96596-2; 978-0-578-46887-7; 978-1-7334670)* 2 Camphor Dr., Newnan, GA 30265 USA Tel 404-594-6278
E-mail: wjeffbishop@yahoo.com
Web site: www.bollweevilpress.com.

Bollix Bks., *(978-1-932188)* 1609 W. Callender Ave., Peoria, IL 61606 USA
E-mail: staley.krause@insightbb.com
Web site: http://www.bollixbooks.com
Dist(s): **Follett School Solutions**
PSI (Publisher Services, Inc.).

Bollywood Groove, *(978-1-945792)* 1304 N Wood St., Unit 1, Chicago, IL 60622 USA Tel 312-772-6559
E-mail: info@bollygroove.com.

Bolt *Imprint of* **Black Rabbit Bks.**

Bolt Jr. *Imprint of* **Black Rabbit Bks.**

Bolton Publishing LLC, *(978-0-9855312)* Orders Addr.: 7255 N. US Hwy. 377, Rochelle, TX 76872-3019 USA
E-mail: ghbolton51@gmail.com.

Bon Tiki Bks., *(978-0-9747072)* 8100 Thomas Dr., Panama City Beach, FL 32408 USA
E-mail: bontiki@knology.net
Web site: http://www.sparkythome.com.

Bond, Shannon, *(978-1-7365204)* 807 Blackberry Cir., Kearney, MO 64060 USA Tel 816-678-1537
E-mail: shannonpaulbond@gmail.com
Web site: www.shannonbond.com.

Bond, Troy, *(978-0-615-45092-6; 978-0-692-68481-8)* 800 45Th St, West Des Moines, IA 50265 USA Tel 515-326-4025
E-mail: troydonovanbond@yahoo.com
Dist(s): **Lulu Pr., Inc.**

Bondcliff Bks., *(978-0-9657475; 978-1-931271)* Orders Addr.: P.O. Box 385, Littleton, NH 03561 USA Toll Free: 800-859-7581; Edit Addr.: 8 Bluejay Ln., Littleton, NH 03561 USA
E-mail: bondcliff@ncia.net
Dist(s): **Peregrine Outfitters.**

Publisher Name Index

Bongiorno Bks., *(978-0-9715819)* P.O. Box 83-2345, Richardson, TX 75083 USA Tel 972-671-6117; Fax: 972-671-0601
E-mail: info@bongiornobooks.com
Web site: http://www.tangledhearts.com; http://www.bongiornobooks.com
Dist(s): **Nonetheless Pr.**

Bongo Comics Group *Imprint of* **Bongo Entertainment, Inc.**

Bongo Entertainment, Inc., *(978-0-9642999; 978-1-892849; 978-1-940293)* 1440 S. Sepulveda, 3rd Flr., Los Angeles, CA 90025 USA Tel 310-966-6168; Fax: 310-966-6181; *Imprints:* Bongo Comics Group (Bongo Comics Grp).

Bonita and Hodge Publishing Group, *(978-0-9838935; 978-1-7355432; 979-8-9867834)* 1553 Emporia St. Bldg 21 Unit 101, Aurora, CO 80010 USA; *Imprints:* Seraphina (Seraphina)
E-mail: bandhpublishing@gmail.com; booknerd436@gmail.com; sheliawritesbooks@yahoo.com
Web site: http://www.sheliawritesbooks.com; http://www.sheliaebell.net.

Bonita & Hodge Publishing Group *See* **Bonita and Hodge Publishing Group**

Bonjour Publishing, *(978-0-9789747; 978-0-9834750; 978-0-9972274; 978-1-7370962)* 33 Willow Ln., Oostburg, WI 53070 USA
Web site: http://cherieburbach.com/.

Bonne Amie Publishing *See* **Chantilly Books**

Bonne Terre, *(978-1-7348682)* 808 Hazeltine Ave SE, SALEM, OR 97306 USA Tel 925-209-9681
E-mail: westhavenacademy@gmail.com.

Bonner, Larry, *(978-0-9747855)* 305 Chapwith Rd., Garner, NC 27529-4882 USA
Web site: http://www.bigrawhidebutte.com.

Bonneville Bks. *Imprint of* **Cedar Fort, Inc./CFI Distribution**

Bonneville B.V. (NLD) *(978-90-73304) Dist. by* **CFI Dist.**

Bonnier Publishing (GBR) *(978-1-78576) Dist. by* **IPG Chicago.**

Bonnier Publishing USA, Div. of Bonnier Publishing, 251 Park Ave. S., 12th Flr., New York, NY 10010 USA; *Imprints:* Yellow Jacket (YellowJack)
Web site: http://bonnierpublishingusa.com/
Dist(s): **Simon & Schuster, Inc.**

Bonnier Zaffre (GBR) *(978-1-78576; 978-1-78696; 978-1-83877) Dist. by* **IPG Chicago.**

Bonsai Bks., *(978-0-9998338)* 3595 Canton Rd. Ste. 116-141, Marietta, GA 30066 USA Tel 678-358-5182
E-mail: MuCompAd@gmail.com.

Bonus Bks., Inc., *(978-0-929387; 978-0-931028; 978-0-933893; 978-1-56625)* 875 N. Michigan Ave., Suite 1416, Chicago, IL 60611 USA (SAN 630-0804) Tel 312-467-0580; Fax: 312-467-9271
E-mail: amanda@bonusbooks.com
Web site: http://www.bonusbooks.com
Dist(s): **National Bk. Network**
Send The Light Distribution LLC.

Boo Bks., Inc., *(978-1-887864)* 7628 S. Paulina, Chicago, IL 60620 USA Tel 312-873-1584; Toll Free: 800-205-1140.

Booger Red's Bks., Inc., *(978-0-9650751)* P.O. Drawer G, Clifton, CO 81520 USA Tel 970-434-4140
E-mail: booger-gj@att.net.

Bk. Bench, The, *(978-1-891142)* 617 Herschler Ave., Evanston, WY 82930 USA Tel 307-789-3642
E-mail: atterol@allwest.net.

Bk. Buddies, *(978-1-7375153)* 1122 TEBO RD, New Bern, NC 28562 USA Tel 405-696-2034
E-mail: madisonnoelle753@gmail.com.

Bk. Bunny Publishing, *(978-1-7357838)* 11632 Davenport Rd., Los Alamitos, CA 90720-3834 USA Tel 562-280-4028
E-mail: samimp03@gmail.com.

Bk. Club of America, *(978-1-59384)* 1812 Front St., Scotch Plains, NJ 07076-1103 USA (SAN 255-3279) Do not confuse with Book Club of America in Mechanicsburg, PA
E-mail: dcarey@bookclubusa.com.

Bk. Club of California, The, *(978-0-9819597; 978-0-692-05342-3; 978-0-692-06779-6; 978-1-7325482)* 312 Sutter St., Suite 500, San Francisco, CA 94108 USA.

Book Co. Publishing Pty, Ltd., The (AUS) *(978-1-74047; 978-1-86309; 978-1-74202) Dist. by* **Penton Overseas.**

Book Couple LLC, The, *(978-0-9908458; 978-1-7331571)* 21161 Via Ventura, BOCA RATON, FL 33433 USA Tel 561-218-4237
E-mail: gary@thebookcouple.com
Web site: www.thebookcouple.com.

Bk. Cravers Publishing, LLC, *(978-1-945375)* 1750 Delta Waters Rd. No 102-263, Medford, OR 97504 USA Tel 541-944-8982
E-mail: john.bcpublishing@gmail.com.

Bk. Ends, *(978-0-9677817)* 2001 N. Halsted St. Ste. 201, Chicago, IL 60614-4365 USA
E-mail: sacredflight@yahoo.com
Web site: http://www.sacredflight.com.

Bk. Experts, The, *(978-1-951561; 978-1-956365)* 9644 Saddlebrook Dr. S., Mobile, AL 36695 USA Tel 251-767-7102
E-mail: brian@evergreen777.com.

Bk. Garden Publishing, *(978-0-9818614)* Orders Addr.: 147 Roesch Ave., Oreland, PA 19075 USA
E-mail: JDHoliday51@gmail.com; JDHoliday51@outlook.com; jangen51@verizon.net
Web site: http://jdholiday.blogspot.com; https://www.barnesandnoble.com/s/%22J.D.+Holiday%22?_requestid=793356; http://jdswritersblog.blogspot.com.

Book Guild, Ltd. (GBR) *(978-1-85776; 978-0-86332; 978-1-84624; 978-1-909716; 978-1-910878; 978-1-912083; 978-1-911320; 978-1-910508; 978-1-910298; 978-1-909984; 978-1-912362; 978-1-912575; 978-1-912881; 978-1-913551; 978-1-915122) Dist. by* **Trans-Atl Phila.**

Book Her Publications *Imprint of* **Bk. Her Publishing**

Bk. Her Publishing, *(978-0-9727776)* 5402 Belle Vista Ave., Baltimore, MD 21206 USA; *Imprints:* Book Her Publications (Bk Hr Pubns)
Web site: http://www.sheribooker.com.

Book Hse. (GBR) *(978-1-904194; 978-1-904642; 978-1-905087; 978-1-906714; 978-1-907184; 978-1-910184; 978-1-911242; 978-1-913971) Dist. by* **Black Rab.**

Book Hse. (GBR) *(978-1-904194; 978-1-904642; 978-1-905087; 978-1-906714; 978-1-907184; 978-1-910184; 978-1-911242; 978-1-913971) Dist. by* **Sterling.**

Book M Publishing, *(978-0-9829502; 978-0-9913761)* 10925 Briar Forest No. 2016, Houston, TX 77042 USA Tel 713-962-0754
E-mail: bmeg@sbcglobal.net.

Bk. Nook Productions, *(978-0-9748990)* P.O. Box 101, Richmond, TX 77406 USA Tel 832-721-7655
E-mail: stephiemara@aol.com
Dist(s): **Follett School Solutions.**

Bk. of Signs Foundation, *(978-0-9773009; 978-1-952115)* 444 E. Roosevelt Rd., Suite 173, Lombard, IL 60148 USA Tel 630-914-5015.

Book Peddlers, *(978-0-916773; 978-1-931863)* 2828 Hedberg Dr., Hopkins, MN 55305-3403 USA (SAN 653-9548) Toll Free: 800-255-3379
E-mail: vlansky@bookpeddlers.com
Web site: http://www.practicalparenting.com; http://www.bookpeddlers.com
Dist(s): **Gryphon Hse., Inc.**
MyiLibrary
Publishers Group West (PGW)
Skandisk, Inc.

Bk. Plug LLC, The, *(978-1-946221)* 2025 Lakewood trl, Atlanta, GA 30315 USA Tel 404-396-7366
E-mail: corneliasmith14@yahoo.com.

Bk. Pubs. Network, *(978-1-887542; 978-0-9755407; 978-1-935359; 978-1-937454; 978-1-940598; 978-1-945271; 978-1-948963)* P.O. Box 2256, Bothell, WA 98041 USA Tel 425-483-3040; Fax: 425-483-3098
E-mail: sherynhara@earthlink.net
Web site: http://www.bookpublishersnetwork.com
Dist(s): **BookBaby**
Danforth Bk. Distribution
Epicenter Pr., Inc.
Follett School Solutions
Greenleaf Book Group
Independent Pubs. Group
Midpoint Trade Bks., Inc.
MyiLibrary
Partners Bk. Distributing, Inc.
Smashwords.

Bk. Pubs. of El Paso, *(978-0-944551; 978-0-9836455; 978-0-9916296; 978-0-9979247; 978-0-9992117; 978-1-7345223; 978-1-7373972)* a/o Book Publishers of El Paso, 2200 San Jose Ave., El Paso, TX 79930 USA Tel 915-778-6670 (phone/fax) Do not confuse with Sundance Pr., Glen Carbon, IL
E-mail: bpep2@sbcglobal.net
Web site: bookpublishersofelpaso.com.

Book Publishing Company *See* **BPC**

Book Publishing Co., *(978-0-939737)* 701 E. Water St., Charlottesvle, VA 22902-5389 USA (SAN 663-7175) Toll Free: 800-537-7881; *Imprints:* Westlake Press (Westlake Pr) Do not confuse with The Book Publishing Co., Summertown, TN
Dist(s): **Orca Bk. Pubs. USA.**

Book Sales, Inc., *(978-0-7628; 978-0-7858; 978-0-89009; 978-1-55521; 978-1-57715; 978-1-4161)* Orders Addr.: 400 1st Ave N. Ste. 300, Minneapolis, MN 55401-1721 USA (SAN 169-488X) Toll Free: 800-526-7257; Edit Addr.: 276 Fifth Ave., Suite 206, New York, NY 10001 USA (SAN 299-4062) Tel 212-779-4972; Fax: 212-779-6058; *Imprints:* Chartwell (Chrtwell)
E-mail: sales@booksalesusa.com
Web site: http://www.booksalesusa.com/
Dist(s): **Continental Bk. Co., Inc.**
Hachette Bk. Group
MyiLibrary
Quarto Publishing Group USA.

Bk. Shelf, *(978-0-9714160; 978-0-9913845)* Orders Addr.: P.O. Box 320804, Fairfield, CT 06825 USA Tel 203-257-0158
E-mail: service@bookshelf123.com; michellespraybooks@gmail.com
Web site: http://www.bookshelf123.com; http://www.myabcsbook.com/; http://www.havingscoliosis.com.

Book Shop, Ltd., The, *(978-1-936199)* 35 E. 9th St., No. 74, New York, NY 10003 USA Tel 917-388-2493; Fax: 917-534-1304
E-mail: nancy@thebookshopltd.com
Web site: http://thebookshopltd.com.

Book Smugglers Publishing, *(978-1-942302)* 99 Kingsland Ave. No. 302, Brooklyn, NY 11222 USA Tel 310-795-7394
E-mail: contact@thebooksmugglers.com
Web site: www.thebooksmugglers.com.

Book Star Pub., *(978-0-615-21005-6; 978-0-578-02827-9; 978-0-615-30612-4; 978-0-692-00622-1; 978-0-9843033)* 3748 S.em Light Dr., Las Vegas, NV 89115 USA (SAN 924-5243) Fax: 702-644-2909
Web site: http://www.bookstarpublisher.com.

Bk. Stops Here, *(978-0-9631612)* 1108 Rocky Point Ct., NE, Albuquerque, NM 87123 USA Tel 505-296-9047 (phone/fax)
E-mail: gldjvb@home.com
Web site: http://www.bookstopshere.com.

Book Tree, The, *(978-1-885395; 978-1-58509)* Orders Addr.: P.O. Box 16476, San Diego, CA 92176 USA Tel 619-280-1263; Fax: 619-280-1285; Toll Free: 800-700-8733
E-mail: orders@thebooktree.com
Web site: http://www.thebooktree.com
Dist(s): **New Leaf Distributing Co., Inc.**

Bk. Vine Pr., *(978-1-949574; 978-1-950955; 978-1-951886; 978-1-952835; 978-1-953699; 978-1-954941; 978-1-955885; 978-1-956896; 978-1-957781; 978-1-958128; 978-1-958678; 978-1-959450; 978-1-960063)* 505 W. Lancaster Ct., Inverness, IL 60010 USA Tel 847-382-9090
E-mail: admin@bookvinepress.com
Web site: www.bookvinepress.com.

Book Web Publishing, Limited, *(978-0-9716567; 978-0-9795733)* P.O. Box 81, Bellmore, NY 11710 USA
E-mail: jeri@jerifink.com; donna@bookwebpublishing.com
Web site: http://www.bookwebpublishing.com.

Book Wholesalers, Inc., *(978-0-7587; 978-1-4046; 978-1-4131; 978-1-4155; 978-1-4156; 978-1-4287)* 1847 Mercer Rd., Lexington, KY 40511-1001 USA (SAN 135-5449) Toll Free: 800-888-4478
E-mail: jcarrico@bwibooks.com; lison@bwibooks.com
Web site: http://www.bwibooks.com
Dist(s): **Follett School Solutions.**

Bk. Woman & Friends, *(978-1-7361053)* 2204 Makarios Dr, St. Augustine, FL 32080 USA Tel 904-599-0413
E-mail: yohannatheresa@aol.com.

Bk. Writing Inc, *(978-0-9994657; 978-1-950088; 978-1-951630; 978-1-952263)* 1111 Wilshire Blvd, Los Angeles, CA 90017 USA Tel 888-588-5175
E-mail: irene.pearson@bookwritinginc.com
Web site: https://www.bookwritinginc.com/.

Bookaroos Publishing, Inc., *(978-0-9678167)* Orders Addr.: P.O. Box 8518, Fayetteville, AR 72703 USA Tel 479-443-0339; Fax: 479-443-0339; Edit Addr.: 484 E. Pharris Dr., Fayetteville, AR 72703 USA
E-mail: books@bookaroos.com; tammybronson@bookaroos.com
Web site: http://www.bookaroos.com; http://www.seahorserun.com; http://www.tammybronson.com; http://www.tinysnail.com
Dist(s): **Follett School Solutions.**

Book-Art Press Solutions LLC *See* **INFORMA INC**

Bookateer Publishing, *(978-0-9819368; 978-1-936476)* 4 Park Ave., Uncasville, CT 06382 USA
E-mail: mj@denicalisdragonchronicles.com; grizlegirl@sbcglobal.net
Web site: www.grizlegirlproductions.com; www.bookateerpublishing.com; www.denicalisdragonchronicles.com
Dist(s): **Smashwords.**

BookBaby, *(978-1-60984; 978-1-61792; 978-1-61842; 978-1-61927; 978-1-62095; 978-1-62309; 978-1-62488; 978-1-62675; 978-1-4835; 978-1-63192; 978-1-943612; 978-1-68222; 978-1-5439; 978-0-692-95466-9; 978-0-692-11235-9; 978-0-692-11236-6; 978-0-578-41517-8; 978-1-0983; 978-1-6678; 978-0-578-94766-2; 979-8-3509)* 7905 N. Rt 130, Pennsauken, NJ 08110 USA Toll Free: 877-961-6878; *7905 N Crescent Blvd, Pennsauken, NJ 08110 Toll Free: 877-961-6878*
E-mail: info@bookbaby.com; support@bookbaby.com; jburton@bookbaby.com; jfoley@bookbaby.com
Web site: http://www.bookbaby.com
Dist(s): **Amazon Digital Services Inc.**
Independent Pubs. Group.

BookBar, Inc., *(978-1-7339887)* 4280 Tennyson St., Denver, CO 80212 USA (SAN 920-4784) Tel 303-908-9620
E-mail: welcome@bookbardenver.com
Web site: www.bookbardenver.com.

BookBound Publishing, *(978-1-932367)* Orders Addr.: 26500 W. Agoura Rd., Suite 102-593, Calabasas, CA 91302 USA (SAN 256-3177) Toll Free: 866-985-2665
E-mail: stacyquest@bookbound.net
Web site: http://www.bookbound.net; http://bookboundpublishing.com.

BookChamp LLC., *(978-0-9760111)* c/o Winter & Company P.C, 605 King Georges Post Rd., Fords, NJ 08863 USA
E-mail: info@bookchamp.net
Web site: http://www.bookchamp.net
Dist(s): **Chicago Review Pr., Inc.**

Bookcraft, Inc. *Imprint of* **Deseret Bk. Co.**

BookCrafters, *(978-0-9845194; 978-0-9832819; 978-0-9837470; 978-1-937862; 978-1-943650; 978-1-950647; 978-1-957077; 979-8-218-02590-8)* Orders Addr.: 12056 Ridgeview Ln., Parker, CO 80138-7141 USA (SAN 859-6352) Tel 720-851-0397; *Imprints:* Philip M. Hudson (MYID_O_PHILIP)
E-mail: bookcrafterscolorado@gmail.com
Web site: http://bookcrafters.net
Dist(s): **Advocate Distribution Solutions**
BookPartners, Inc.
Ingram Content Group
Send The Light Distribution LLC
Smashwords.

Bookends Press *See* **Bk.ends Pr./Renaissance Printing**

Bk.ends Pr./Renaissance Printing, *(978-0-9724926; 978-0-9740922; 978-1-932667; 978-1-938315; 978-1-950125; 978-1-953166)* 4130 NW 16th Blvd., Gainesville, FL 32605 USA Tel 352-375-2129; Fax: 352-375-0522
E-mail: copyright@renaissance-printing.com
Dist(s): **Freeman Family Ministries**
Rosewood Foundation, The
StarCrossed Productions
Truth Pubns.

Booker Lane Press *See* **Punta Gorda Pr.**

Booker, Thomishia *See* **Hey Carter!**

BOOKGEMSFORKIDS, *(978-0-9763596)* 111 Primrose Ln., Wyomissing, PA 19610 USA
E-mail: sukumar@idreampublications.com
Web site: http://www.idreampublications.com.

Bk.lantropy, *(978-1-7336743)* 4877 Knox Ct., Denver, CO 80221 USA Tel 303-477-6278
E-mail: marcia@booklanthropy.com.

BookLife Publishing Ltd. (GBR) *(978-1-78637; 978-1-910512; 978-1-78998; 978-1-83927) Dist. by* **IPG Chicago.**

BookLight Pr., *(978-0-9841307; 978-0-615-73688-4)* Orders Addr.: 5994 S. Holly St. #118, Greenwood Village, CO 80111 USA (SAN 858-5164) Tel 303-916-8124; Edit Addr.: P.O. Box 380161, Cambridge, MA 02139-0161 USA
E-mail: jmarsh@booklightpress.com
Web site: www.booklightpress.com
Dist(s): **Follett School Solutions.**

Booklight Publishing, *(978-1-7337407)* 12429 Madrone Forest Dr., Nevada City, CA 95959 USA Tel 530-913-9608
E-mail: lila@lilareyna.com.

Booklines Hawaii, Ltd., *(978-1-929844; 978-1-58849; 978-1-60274)* Div. of Islander Group, 269 Pali'i St., Mililani, HI 96789 USA (SAN 630-6624) Tel 808-676-0116; Fax: 808-676-0634
E-mail: customerservice@booklines.com
Web site: http://www.booklineshawaii.com
Dist(s): **Follett School Solutions**
Islander Group.

Booklocker.com, Inc., *(978-1-929072; 978-1-931391; 978-1-59113; 978-1-60145; 978-1-60910; 978-1-61434; 978-1-62141; 978-1-62646; 978-1-63263; 978-1-63490; 978-1-63491; 978-1-63492; 978-1-64438; 978-1-64718; 978-1-64719; 979-8-88531; 979-8-88532; 979-8-88533; 978-1-958877; 978-1-958878; 978-1-958889; 978-1-958890; 978-1-958891; 978-1-958892; 978-1-959620; 978-1-959621; 978-1-959622; 978-1-959623; 978-1-959624; 978-1-961265; 978-1-961266; 978-1-961267; 978-1-961268; 978-1-961269; 978-1-961270; 978-1-961271; 978-1-) 12441 N. Main St., No. 38, Trenton, GA 30752 USA (SAN 254-363X) Fax: 305-768-0261;* *Imprints:* Abuzz Press (AbuzzPr)
E-mail: booklocker@booklocker.com; angela@writersweekly.com; angela@booklocker.com; richard@booklocker.com
Web site: http://www.booklocker.com; http://www.writersweekly.com.

BookLogix, *(978-0-615-18278-0; 978-0-615-18390-9; 978-0-615-25890-4; 978-1-61005; 978-0-9894848; 978-1-63183; 978-0-9978038; 978-1-6653)* 1264 Old Alpharetta Rd., Alpharetta, GA 30005 USA (SAN 860-0376) Tel 470-239-8547; Fax: 888-564-7890; *Imprints:* Lanier Press (LanierPr)
E-mail: Angela@booklogix.com; Ahmad@booklogix.com
Web site: http://www.booklogix.com.

Booklogix Publishing Services *See* **BookLogix**

BookMann Pr. *Imprint of* **Mann Publishing Group**

Bookmark Bks., LLC, *(978-0-9764163)* P.O. Box 2996, Chester, VA 23831 USA Tel 804-706-6399 (phone/fax)
E-mail: bookmarkbooks@verizon.net.

Bookmark, The, *(978-0-930227)* Orders Addr.: 29021 Ave. Sherman, Unit 109, Santa Clarita, CA 91355 USA (SAN 694-6410) Tel 661-294-8022; Fax: 661-294-8027; Toll Free: 800-220-7767 Do not confuse with other companies with the same name in Marietta, GA, Knightstown, IN
E-mail: thebookmark@earthlink.net
Web site: http://www.thebookmark.com.

Bk.marked Pr., *(978-0-578-63767-9)* 7491 Bethel Rd., Dora, AL 35062 USA Tel 205-541-7106
E-mail: muddysmurf@gmail.com
Web site: www.bookmarkedpress.com.

Bookmasters Distribution *See* **Baker & Taylor Publisher Services (BTPS)**

Bookmates *Imprint of* **Penny Laine Papers, Inc.**

BookMobile *See* **Syren Bk. Co.**

BookPartners, LLC, *(978-1-936495)* 725 3rd St. P.O. Box 790, Cedar Key, FL 32625-0790 USA Tel 352-543-9307; Fax: 407-287-6002
E-mail: jpdwyer@dwyerogrady.com
Web site: www.bookpartners.org.

BookPatch LLC, The, *(978-1-62030; 978-1-63318; 978-1-68273; 978-1-946447; 978-1-946634; 978-1-946812; 978-1-946982; 978-1-947136; 978-1-947289; 978-1-947519; 978-1-947778; 978-1-947962; 978-1-948186; 978-1-948339; 978-1-64254; 978-1-64550; 978-1-64858; 978-0-578-68064-4; 978-1-63790; 978-0-578-84218-9; 978-0-578-99682-0; 978-0-578-99683-7; 978-0-578-30346-8; 979-8-88567; 978-0-578-38925-7; 979-8-218-09384-6; 979-8-218-18657-9; 979-8-89090) 4400 N. Scottsdale Rd., Scottsdale, AZ 85251 USA Tel 602-403-5600*
E-mail: victor@thebookpatch.com
Web site: http://www.thebookpatch.com
Dist(s): **BookBaby**
Ingram Content Group
Lulu Pr., Inc.

BookPatch.com, The *See* **BookPatch LLC, The**

Bk.places Publishing, *(978-0-578-43935-8; 978-0-578-43936-5)* 500 Westover Dr. Unit 12852, Sanford, NC 27330 USA Tel 317-737-6993
E-mail: kay@whiteriverwriters.com
Web site: https://bookplaces.blog
Dist(s): **Ingram Content Group.**

BookPress Publishing, *(978-0-9855133; 978-0-9862416; 978-0-9964428; 978-0-9967616; 978-1-947305; 978-1-960259)* P.O. Box 71532, Des Moines, IA 50325 USA Tel 515-554-8900
E-mail: info@bookpresspublishing.com
Dist(s): **Baker & Taylor Publisher Services (BTPS).**

Bookpublisher.com *See* **Wheatmark, Inc.**

Bks. Are Fun, Ltd., *(978-0-9649777; 978-1-58209; 978-1-890409; 978-1-59795; 978-1-60626)* 1 Readers Digest Rd., Pleasantville, NY 10570-7000 USA
E-mail: msmall@booksarefun.com
Web site: http://www.booksarefun.com
Dist(s): **Sandvik Publishing.**

Bks. By Aleena, *(978-0-692-12283-9)* 4163 Bowen Way, VALDOSTA, GA 31605 USA Tel 912-398-0365
E-mail: hector.m.rodriguezortiz@gmail.com
Dist(s): **Ingram Content Group.**

Books by Bookends *See* **Long Dash Publishing**

ks. by Bree, *(978-0-578-22068-0)* 1368 Hiatt St., Indianapolis, IN 46221 USA Tel 317-249-7708
E-mail: briannareshae17@yahoo.com.

ks. by Elle, Inc., *(978-0-692-72108-7; 978-0-692-78400-6; 978-0-9982709; 978-0-9992504; 978-1-951017)* 225 College Dr. #65504, Orange Park, FL 32065 USA Tel 904-962-8587
Web site: www.elleklass.weebly.com
Dist(s): **CreateSpace Independent Publishing Platform.**

ooks by Kids LLC, *(978-0-615-19963-4; 978-0-9830954)* 1021 Oak St., Jacksonville, FL 32204 USA Tel 904-376-7029; Fax: 904-355-1832
Web site: http://www.booksbykids.com
Dist(s): **Chicago Distribution Ctr.**

ks. by Matt, *(978-0-9727660)* 33 Stoddard Way, Berkeley, CA 94708 USA Tel 510-849-2986; Fax: 510-849-1012
E-mail: mylamby@hotmail.com.

Bks. by Tillie, *(978-0-578-63484-5)* 10009 Preakness Dr., Upper Marlboro, MD 20772 USA Tel 240-682-4247
E-mail: tillieave@gmail.com.

Bks. del Sur, *(978-0-9973280; 978-1-7339785; 978-1-7362001)* 1375 Heron Dr., Antioch, IL 60002 USA Tel 608-217-0758
E-mail: heather@booksdelsur.org
Web site: www.booksdelsurstore.org.

Books for Brats *Imprint of* **Little Redhaired Girl Publishing, Inc.**

Bks. for Children of the World, *(978-0-9661186; 978-0-9762078)* 6701 N. Bryant Ave., Oklahoma City, OK 73121 USA Tel 405-721-7417; Fax: 405-478-4352; Toll Free: 888-838-0003.

Books for Children Publishing *See* **Guiffre Bk. Publishing**

Bks. for the Culture LLC, *(978-0-9845572; 979-8-218-01877-1)* 3530 Central Pk. Dr., Loganville, GA 30052 USA Tel 718-415-3401
E-mail: kevinwrites4u@gmail.com.

Books International, Inc., *(978-1-891078)* Orders Addr.: P.O. Box 605, Herndon, VA 20172-0605 USA (SAN 131-761X) Tel 703-661-1500; Fax: 703-661-1501
E-mail: bimail@presswarehouse.com.

Bks. Leaving Footprints, *(978-0-9765432; 978-0-9908172; 978-1-948910)* 861 W. US 10, Scottville, MI 49454 USA Tel 231-757-2205
E-mail: info@booksleavingfootprints.com
Web site: http://www.booksleavingfootprints.com
Dist(s): **Smashwords.**

Bks. on Demand, *(978-0-608; 978-0-7837; 978-0-8357; 978-0-598; 978-3-7494)* Div. of UMI, 300 N. Zeeb Rd., Ann Arbor, MI 48106-1346 USA.

Bks. on the Path, *(978-0-9743390)* P.O. Box 436, Barker, TX 77413-0436 USA Tel 281-492-6050; Fax: 832-201-7620; Toll Free: 866-875-7284
E-mail: info@patriarchspath.org
Web site: http://www.booksonthepath.com.

Bks. Scribe, LLC, *(978-1-956135)* 645 E Fir St, SEQUIM, WA 98382 USA Tel 253-693-0015
E-mail: publishingfulfillment@gmail.com
Web site: https://booksscribe.com/.

Bks. That Will Enhance Your Life, *(978-0-615-20297-6; 978-0-615-38405-4; 978-0-9831419; 978-0-9838457; 978-0-9848980; 978-0-692-68079-7)* Div. of Andrews Leadership International, 8816 Ave. M New St., Brooklyn, NY 11236 USA Tel 917-327-1029; *Imprints:* BTWEYL (BTWEYL)
E-mail: production@alipictures.com; john@johnaandrews.com
Web site: http://www.alipictures.com.

Books To Believe In *Imprint of* **Thornton Publishing, Inc.**

Books To Remember *Imprint of* **Flyleaf Publishing**

Books to UPLIFT, *(978-0-9991492; 978-0-692-07336-0)* 332 S. Gretna Green Way, Los Angeles, CA 90049 USA Tel 310-472-6700
E-mail: garyarosenberg@aol.com; ssj4health@earthlink.net
Web site: http://susansmithjones.com/.

Bks. Unbound E-Publishing Co., *(978-1-59201)* 1110 Kerwin St., Piscataway, NJ 08854-3323 USA
Web site: http://www.booksunbound.com.

Bks. with a Porpoise, LLC, *(978-1-7327454)* 1807 Doris Dr., Menlo Park, CA 94025 USA Tel 312-622-4593
E-mail: rglass2222@gmail.com.

Bks. With Purpose LLC., *(978-1-7326422; 978-1-7330313)* 989 Riverpoint Ct., POWELL, OH 43065 USA Tel 614-595-2045
E-mail: laurenkelleybooks@gmail.com.

Bks. With Soul, *(978-1-949325)* 12653 N 17th Pl., Phoenix, AZ 85022 USA Tel 602-758-9189
E-mail: aksmithbook@gmail.com
Web site: www.bookswithsoul.com.

Books2Go, *(978-1-59590)* 780 Reservoir Ave., Suite 243, Cranston, RI 02910 USA Tel 401-537-9175
E-mail: books2go@writerscollective.net
Web site: http://www.mybooks2go.com.

Books-A-Million, Inc., *(978-1-63111; 978-1-5325)* 402 Industrial Dr., Birmingham, AL 35211 USA Tel 205-942-3737
E-mail: Publishing@BooksAMillion.com
Web site: www.booksamillion.com.

BooksbyDave Inc., *(978-0-9768867)* Orders Addr.: 5010 James loop, Killeen, TX 76542 USA Tel 254-628-1961
E-mail: project17us@yahoo.com
Web site: http://www.geocities.com/oilsbydave.

Booksforboys, *(978-0-9761440)* 8 Marigold Ct., Holtsville, NY 11742 USA
Web site: http://booksforboys.com.

Bookshelf Global Publishing, *(978-0-9755395; 978-0-9766954; 978-0-9779012; 978-0-9800430; 978-0-9850656)* 503 Second Ave., Destin, FL 32541 USA (SAN 850-4652) Tel 770-560-8016
E-mail: office@bookshelfglobal.com
Web site: http://www.bookshelfglobal.com.

Bookshelf, The *See* **Open Door Publishers, Inc.**

Booksmart Pubns., *(978-0-9790896)* Orders Addr.: P.O. Box 4774, Mission Viejo, CA 92690 USA (SAN 852-4211) Tel 949-462-0076; Edit Addr.: 19 Bolero, Mission Viejo, CA 92692 USA
E-mail: b_smart@cox.net
Web site: http://www.booksmartpublications.com.

booksonnet.com, *(978-1-888562; 978-0-9675540)* Div. of Shoestring Productions, P.O. Box 36, Saint Augustine, FL 32085 USA Tel 904-829-3812 Do not confuse with companies with the same name in Prather CA, Santa Barbara CA, Aptos CA, Belvedere CA, Albion CA, Pensacola, FL
E-mail: billbooks@bellsouth.net
Dist(s): **Ingram Content Group.**

Booksource, The, *(978-0-7383; 978-0-8335; 978-0-911891; 978-0-9641084; 978-1-886379; 978-1-890760; 978-0-7568; 978-1-4117; 978-1-4178; 978-0-606; 978-1-60446; 978-1-4364; 979-8-3685)* Div. of GL group, Inc., Orders Addr.: 1230 Macklind Ave., Saint Louis, MO 63110-1432 USA (SAN 169-4324) Tel 314-647-0600 Toll Free Fax: 800-647-1923; Toll Free: 800-444-0435
E-mail: khostman@booksource.com; shankins@glgrp.com; shankins@booksource.com
Web site: http://www.booksource.com; http://www.goodluckgroup.com/.

Bookstand Publishing, *(978-1-58909; 978-1-61863; 978-1-63498; 978-1-953710; 978-1-956785)* Orders Addr.: 530 S Lake Ave. No. 473, Pasadena, CA 91101 USA; Edit Addr.: 530 S Lake Avenue, No. 473, Pasadena, CA 91101 USA Tel 408-852-1832; Fax: 408-852-1832
E-mail: orders@bookstandpublishing.com
Web site: http://www.BookstandPublishing.com.

Bookstaves, LLC, *(978-1-63235; 978-1-64582)* P.O. Box 727, Mankato, MN 56002 USA Tel 651-242-3066; *Imprints:* 12-Story Library (12StryLib)
E-mail: rglaser@thecreativecompany.us
Web site: http://www.12storylibrary.com
Dist(s): **Creative Co., The.**

Bookstock Press *See* **Finding Forward Bks.**

Bookstrand-Siren Publishing, Incorporated *See* **Siren-BookStrand, Inc.**

Booksville, U.S.A., *(978-0-9630887; 978-0-9720041)* P.O. Box 710352, Houston, TX 77271-0352 USA Tel 713-726-8115 (phone/fax); *Imprints:* Circle of Friends (CirFriends)
E-mail: elkewat@aol.com; lindawatersbooks@aol.com; ethnicbooks@aol.com
Web site: http://lindawaters.com.

BooktiMookti Pr., *(978-0-9800952)* P.O. Box 17520, Seattle, WA 98127 USA
E-mail: helen@booktimookti.com
Web site: http://www.BooktiMookti.com; http://www.RuntFarm.com
Dist(s): **Itasca Bks.**

Bk.Trail Agency, *(978-1-7328704; 978-1-951505; 978-1-953731; 978-1-63767; 978-1-959082; 979-8-9887523; 978-1-962225; 978-1-962256)* 8838 Sleepy Hollow Rd., Kansas, MO 64114 USA Tel 888-446-3094
E-mail: booktrailsalesandmarketing@gmail.com
Web site: https://booktrailagency.com/.

Booktrope, *(978-0-9841786; 978-1-935961; 978-1-62015; 978-1-5137)* Div. of Libertary Co., 1219 Sixteenth Ave East, Seattle, WA 98112 USA (SAN 858-639X) Tel 206-235-3384; *Imprints:* Booktrope Editions (Booktrope Edtns); Vox Dei (VoxDei)
E-mail: publisher@booktrope.com; production@booktrope.com; info@booktrope.com; accounting@booktrope.com
Web site: http://www.booktrope.com.

Booktrope Editions *Imprint of* **Booktrope**

Bookwhip, *(978-1-948801; 978-1-949723; 978-1-950580; 978-1-951469; 978-1-953537; 978-0-578-90857-1; 978-0-578-90858-8; 978-1-956998; 978-1-960204)* Orders Addr.: 1545 S Harbor Blvd No. 2100, FULLERTON, CA 92832 USA Tel 855-339-3589; Edit Addr.: 1545 S Harbor Blvd No. 2100, FULLERTON, CA 92832 USA Tel 855-339-3589
E-mail: brandon@bookwhip.com
Web site: www.bookwhip.com.

BookWise Publishing, *(978-1-60645; 978-0-615-15370-4; 978-0-578-42434-7)* Orders Addr.: 12707 S. City Pk. Way, Riverton, UT 84065 USA Tel 801-635-4821
E-mail: chrisbizzz@comcast.net; karenkchristoffersen@gmail.com
Web site: http://www.bookwisepublishing.com
Dist(s): **CreateSpace Independent Publishing Platform.**

Bookworks, LLC, *(978-0-615-98953-2; 978-0-692-21126-7; 978-0-9906156; 978-1-942407; 978-0-9993556)* 78 Beech St., Trumbull, CT 06611 USA
E-mail: w.thorpe@bookworksllc.com.

Bk.worm, *(978-1-949808)* P.O. Box 90101, Alexandria, VA 22309 USA Tel 703-799-6666
E-mail: peacedrama@gmail.com.

Bookworm Books *See* **Kingdom Come Pr.**

Boom Entertainment, Inc., 5670 Wilshire Blvd., Ste 450, Los Angeles, CA 90036 USA
Dist(s): **Diamond Comic Distributors, Inc.**
Diamond Bk. Distributors
Follett School Solutions
Simon & Schuster, Inc.

Boom! Studios *See* **BOOM! Studios**

BOOM! Studios, *(978-1-932386; 978-1-934506; 978-1-60886; 978-1-936393; 978-1-61398; 978-1-939867; 978-1-68159; 978-1-68415; 978-1-64144; 978-1-64668; 978-1-63796; 979-8-89215)* 1800 Century Pk. E., Suite 200, Los Angeles, CA 90067 USA Tel 310-895-7746; 5670 Wilshire Blvd., Suite No. 400, Los Angeles, CA 90036; *Imprints:* Archaia Entertainment (ArchaiaEnt)
E-mail: slazarski@boom-studios.com; mchristopher@boom-studios.com
Web site: http://www.boom-studios.com
Dist(s): **Children's Plus, Inc.**
INscribe Digital
Independent Pubs. Group
MyiLibrary
Simon & Schuster, Inc.
Simon & Schuster Children's Publishing.

Boomer Bks. *Imprint of* **The Editorium, LLC**

Boone Bks., *(978-0-9765294)* P.O. Box 262147, Plano, TX 75026-2147 USA Toll Free: 800-755-6628
E-mail: cadprof@boonebooks.com
Web site: http://www.boonebooks.com.

Boosey & Hawkes, Inc., 229 W. 28th St. Flr. 11, New York, NY 10001-5915 USA
E-mail: bhsales@ny.boosey.com
Web site: http://www.boosey.com
Dist(s): **Leonard, Hal Corp.**

Boot in the Door Pubns., *(978-0-9788183; 978-1-7340231)* P.O. Box 132031, Spring, TX 77393 USA
E-mail: lesaboutin@gmail.com; lesakhoward@gmail.com
Web site: https://www.bootinthedoor.com/.

Boot Top Bks., *(978-1-7333697; 979-8-9856556)* 4942 Orcas Pl. NE, Lacey, WA 98516 USA Tel 360-338-0584
E-mail: Copalisbelle@yahoo.com
Web site: kb-taylor.com.

Booth, Jesse, *(978-0-692-19470-6; 978-0-578-48160-9)* 294 W. 680 N., Centerville, UT 84014 USA Tel 385-290-2081
E-mail: jtulkas2@hotmail.com
Dist(s): **Ingram Content Group.**

Booth, John Harvey, *(978-0-9754291)* 246 Schilling St., West Lafayette, IN 47906 USA Tel 765-743-8728
E-mail: jhbooth2003@yahoo.com.

Boothroyd & Allnut, *(978-0-578-11204-6; 978-0-9904207)* 5115 68th Ave. NE, Marysville, WA 98270 USA.

Bootstrap Publishing, *(978-0-9846502; 978-0-692-20844-1)* 54 Forest Ave., Rochester, NY 14622 USA Tel 480-560-4933
Web site: http://www.bookstrappublishing.net
Dist(s): **CreateSpace Independent Publishing Platform.**

Borah Pr., *(978-0-9657879)* 1100 Rd. M, Redwood Valley, CA 95470 USA Tel 707-485-0922; Fax: 707-485-7071
E-mail: JPack@pacific.net.

Border Pr., *(978-0-9650977; 978-0-9843150; 978-0-9848915; 978-0-9898641; 978-0-9862801; 978-0-9968737; 978-0-9997804; 978-1-7346802)* Orders Addr.: P.O. Box 3124, Sewanee, TN 37375 USA Tel 337-577-1762; Toll Free Fax: 866-669-3207
E-mail: borderpress@gmail.com
Web site: http://borderpressbooks.com.

Borders Group, Inc., *(978-0-681)* 100 Phoenix Dr., Ann Arbor, MI 48108 USA Tel 734-477-1100
Web site: http://www.borders.com.

Borders Personal Publishing, *(978-1-4134)* a/o Pam Durant, 2 International Plaza, Suite 340, Philadelphia, PA 19113 USA Tel 610-915-5214; Fax: 610-915-0294; Toll Free: 888-795-4274
E-mail: dave@xlibris.com
Dist(s): **Xlibris Corp.**

Borders Pr., *(978-0-681)* Div. of Borders Group, Inc., 100 Phoenix Dr., Ann Arbor, MI 48108 USA; *Imprints:* State Street Press (State St Pr)
Web site: http://www.bordersstores.com; http://www.bordersgroupinc.com; http://www.borders.com.

BorderStone Pr., LLC, *(978-0-9842284; 978-1-936670)* Orders Addr.: P.O. Box 1383, Mountain Home, AR 72653 USA Tel 870-405-1146; 436 Olympic Dr., MOUNTAIN HOME, 72654 Tel 870-405-1146
E-mail: borderstonepress@gmail.com
Web site: http://www.borderstonepress.com; http://www.facebook.com/pages/BorderStone-Press-LLC/137970880138?ref=ts.

Bordighera Incorporated, *(978-1-884419; 978-1-59954)* Orders Addr.: P.O. Box 1374, Lafayette, IN 47902-1374 USA; Edit Addr.: John D. Calandra Italian American Institute 25 W. 43rd St., 17th Flr., New York, NY 10036 USA Tel 212-642-2005
E-mail: dstarewich@verizon.net; anthony.tamburri@qc.cuny.edu
Dist(s): **SPD-Small Pr. Distribution.**

Borealis Bk. *Imprint of* **Minnesota Historical Society Pr.**

Borealis Pr., *(978-0-9632651; 978-0-9819950)* P.O. Box 230, Surry, ME 04684 USA Tel 207-667-3700; Fax: 207-667-9649; Toll Free: 800-669-6845.

Bored Games Publishing, *(978-1-7375419)* 11615 Timberline Cir, Fort Myers, FL 33966 USA Tel 239-357-8995
E-mail: penelopestrong@hotmail.com.

Borghesi & Adam Pubs. Pty Ltd (AUS) *(978-0-9577403; 978-1-877035; 978-0-9775720; 978-0-9802892; 978-1-921346; 978-0-9806308; 978-0-9807307; 978-1-921756; 978-0-9871404; 978-0-9871986; 978-0-9872735; 978-0-9873068; 978-0-9873895; 978-0-9925668; 978-1-925386; 978-0-6484095; 978-0-6484571; 978-0-6485557; 978-0-6486918; 978-1-922418; 978-0-9942634)* *Dist. by* **IPG Chicago.**

Borgo Press *See* **Borgo Publishing**

Borgo Publishing, *(978-0-9843979; 978-0-9883893; 978-0-9905431; 978-0-9968783; 978-0-9984606; 978-0-9993830; 978-1-7339165; 978-1-7345730; 979-8-9852286)* 15 Guildswood, TUSCALOOSA, AL 35401 USA Tel 205-454-4256
E-mail: borgogirl@bellsouth.net.

BoriBoricha INC *See* **Starry Forest Bks., Inc.**

Born to Blaze Ministries, *(978-0-9762910)* 130 Yancey Ct., Apple Valley, MN 55124 USA Tel 612-207-5682
E-mail: info@borntoblaze.com
Web site: http://www.borntoblaze.com.

borntalking.com, *(978-0-9720892)* 34116 Blue Heron Dr., Solon, OH 44139-5641 USA
E-mail: david@borntalking.com
Web site: http://www.borntalking.com.

Borromeo Bks., *(978-0-9763098)* Orders Addr.: P.O. Box 7273, Saint Paul, MN 55107 USA.

Borucki, Rebekah *See* **Wheat Penny Pr.**

Boshu Pr., *(978-0-9755624)* 3 Dogwood Ct., Greenville, NC 27858 USA
E-mail: boshucell@earthlink.net.

Bosque Ecosystem Monitoring Program (BEMP), *(978-1-7336661)* 4000 Bosque School Rd NW, Albuquerque, NM 87120 USA Tel 505-573-1464
E-mail: bemp.job@bosqueschool.org
Web site: bosqueschool.org.

BOSS Business Services *See* **Anderson Law Group**

Boss Paws Publishing, *(978-0-9769058)* 2536 Ridgewood Ave., Louisville, KY 40217 USA Tel 502-649-6864
E-mail: ag@animalgambill.org.

Bosse, Andre Ctr., *(978-0-9786128)* 302 Hanson St., Hart, MI 49420-1385 USA Tel 231-873-1707; Fax: 231-873-1456
E-mail: maltbie7@charter.net
Web site: http://www.andrebossecenter.org.

BossLady Terrie Publications *See* **Branch & Brooks Publishing & Consulting Solutions LLC**

Boston Common Press *See* **America's Test Kitchen**

BOT Publishing, LLC, *(978-0-9759493)* P.O. Box 62, Mount Pleasant, SC 29465 USA
Web site: http://thebeautyoftruth.com.

BotDM, *(978-0-692-15315-4; 978-1-7327353)* 14895 W. 54th Ave, Golden, CO 80403 USA Tel 303-808-5881
E-mail: kate.b.marshall@gmail.com.

Botero de Borrero, Beatriz & Martha Olga Botero de Gomez (COL) *(978-958-33)* *Dist. by* **Lectorum Pubns.**

Bothwell Pr., *(978-0-9855353)* 664 H St., Salt Lake City, UT 84103 USA (SAN 920-3397) Tel 801-532-2204 Do not confuse with Bothwell Pr. in Athens, GA
E-mail: Bothwellpress@gmail.com.

Bo-Tree Hse., *(978-0-9832227; 978-0-9968516)* 1749 Del Mar Dr., Idaho Falls, ID 83404 USA Tel 650-701-4645 (cell)
E-mail: Debu.majumdar@botreehouse.com
Web site: http://www. botreehouse.com
Dist(s): **CreateSpace Independent Publishing Platform**
Follett School Solutions
Ingram Content Group
Smashwords.

Bottom Line Media, *(978-0-9759997; 978-0-9852192; 978-0-9899545; 978-1-7352345)* 10123 William Carey Dr., Orlando, FL 32832 USA Tel 407-382-6000; Fax: 407-382-1008
E-mail: bottomline@orlandoteam.com
Web site: www.pioneers.org/books.

Bottom of the Hill Publishing, *(978-1-935785; 978-1-61203; 978-1-4837)* 200 Terry Rd., Somerville, TN 38068 USA Tel 901-465-8497
E-mail: info@bottomofthehillpublishing.com
Web site: bottomofthehillpublishing.com
Dist(s): **MyiLibrary.**

Bottom-Up Media, *(978-0-9765337)* 5413 Nueces Bay Dr., Rowlett, TX 75089 USA (SAN 854-7440) Tel 214-550-2563
E-mail: steve@bottomupmedia.com
Web site: http://www.bottomupmedia.com
Dist(s): **Ingram Content Group.**

Bouje Publishing, LLC, *(978-0-9779265)* Orders Addr.: 17659 Montebello Rd, Cupertino, CA 95014 USA.

Boulden Publishing, *(978-1-878076; 978-1-892421)* Div. of Turtle Pine, Inc., Orders Addr.: P.O. Box 1186, Weaverville, CA 96093-1186 USA Tel 530-623-5399; Fax: 530-623-5525; Toll Free: 800-238-8433
E-mail: ken@bouldenpublishing.com
Web site: http://www.bouldenpublishing.com
Dist(s): **Follett School Solutions**
MAR*CO Products, Inc.
Social Studies Schl. Service
Sunburst Communications, Inc.

Boulder Bks. (CAN) *(978-0-9730271; 978-0-9738501; 978-0-9809144; 978-0-9783381; 978-0-9865376; 978-1-927099; 978-1-7752345; 978-1-989417; 978-1-9994910)* *Dist. by* **Firefly Bks Limited.**

Boulder Street Bks. LLC, *(978-0-578-06778-0)* P.O. Box 380, Green Mountain Falls, CO 80819 USA
E-mail: editor@boulderstreetbooks.com
Web site: http://www.boulderstreetbooks.com
Dist(s): **Outskirts Pr., Inc.**

Bouncing Ball Bks., Inc., *(978-1-934138)* P.O. Box 6509, Spring Hill, FL 34611-6509 USA (SAN 851-6073)
E-mail: bouncingballbooks@yahoo.com
Web site: http://www.bouncingballbooks.com.

Bouncing Ball Media, *(978-1-7326684; 978-1-7365044)* 5324 Timber Ridge Dr., Mount Vernon, WA 98273 USA Tel 206-715-3101
E-mail: georgia@bouncingballmedia.com
Web site: http://bouncingballmedia.com.

Bound & Determined Pubs., *(978-0-9704006)* Orders Addr.: 18116 Woodrow Rd., Brainerd, MN 56401 USA
E-mail: adammarcotte@yahoo.com
Web site: http://www.sover.net/~niliacus/a&h/; http://www.adamandheidi.net.

Bound by Grace Pr., LLC, *(978-0-9787087)* Orders Addr.: 924 Campbell St., Batavia, IL 60510 USA Tel 630-772-7172
E-mail: denise@boundbygracepress.com
Web site: http://www.boundbygracepress.com
Dist(s): **Theological Bk. Service.**

Bound Publishing *See* **Spellbound River Pr.**

Bounty Project, The, *(978-0-9665861)* 6310 Georgetown Pike, McLean, VA 22101 USA Tel 703-442-7557
E-mail: kjackson@1771.org.

Bourg, Cameron, *(978-1-7360818)* 8816 Indigo Sky Trl SW, Albuquerque, NM 87121 USA Tel 505-314-3355
E-mail: Bourgconsulting@gmail.com.

Bourgeois Media & Consulting, *(978-0-9796288; 978-0-9827877; 978-0-9830355; 978-0-9831971; 978-0-9834868; 978-0-9840281; 978-0-9854244; 978-0-9967348; 978-1-7323679; 978-1-7375239)* 1712 E. Riverside Dr. 124, Austin, TX 78741 USA; *Imprints:* Creative House Kids Press (CreatHseKids)
E-mail: chpress@live.com
Web site: http://bourgeoismedia.com.

Publisher Name Index

Boutin, Lesa *See* **Boot in the Door Pubns.**
Boutique Natural Health Solutions, LLC, *(978-0-9982234)* 4410 Wood Creek Dr, Marietta, GA 30062 USA Tel 404-200-6851; Fax: 404-200-6851
E-mail: birgit@birgitscoaching.com.
Boutique of Quality Books Publishing Co., Inc., *(978-1-60808; 978-0-9828689; 978-0-9831699; 978-1-937084; 978-1-939371; 978-1-945448; 978-1-952782; 979-8-88633)* 960 Oaktree Blvd., Christiansburg, VA 24073 USA Tel 678-316-4150; Fax: 678-999-3738; *Imprints:* BQB Publishing (BQBPubng); WriteLife Publishing (WriteLifePub)
E-mail: writelife@boutiqueofqualitybooks.com
Web site: http://www.bqbpublishing.com
Dist(s): **Independent Pubs. Group**
New Leaf Distributing Co., Inc.
StreetLib USA, Inc.
Boutte, Sarah, *(978-0-692-96434-7; 978-0-578-52568-6)* 300 Copperfield Way, YOUNGSVILLE, LA 70592 USA Tel 858-699-5437
E-mail: sneels_44@yahoo.com
Dist(s): **Ingram Content Group.**
Bow Historical Bks.,
Dist(s): **Oxford Univ. Pr., Inc.**
Bowden Music Co., *(978-0-9702219)* 1511 Grand Ave., Fort Worth, TX 76106 USA Tel 817-624-1547 (phone/fax)
E-mail: essieb@mindspring.com.
Bowen, Kyana, *(978-1-7352545)* WEB 4631, Miami, FL 33192-2147 USA Tel 246-850-7055
E-mail: kyana.bowen@gmail.com.
Bower Bks. *Imprint of* **Storybook Meadow Publishing**
†**Bower Hse.,** *(978-0-915024; 978-0-917895; 978-0-929969; 978-0-933472; 978-0-942394; 978-0-9634607; 978-0-9643161; 978-0-9653751; 978-0-9657159; 978-1-55566; 978-1-56579; 978-1-879483; 978-1-889593; 978-1-890768; 978-0-9704098; 978-1-931599; 978-0-9713678; 978-0-9718378; 978-1-932557; 978-1-934553; 978-1-60648; 978-1-942280; 978-1-917895) P.O. Box 7459, Denver, CO 80207 USA (SAN 209-2425) Toll Free Fax: 800-217-7104; Toll Free: 800-217-7104; Imprints:* Trails Books (Trails Bks); Johnson Books (JohnsonBks); Westcliffe Publishers (WestcliffePubs)
E-mail: books@bowerhousebooks.com; margaret@bowerhousebooks.com
Web site: http://www.bowerhousebooks.com
Dist(s): **Consortium Bk. Sales & Distribution**
National Bk. Network; *CIP.*
Bower, Theresa *See* **Raina Nightingale**
Bowers, Renata *See* **Frieda B.**
Bowles, Sharon, *(978-0-692-67659-2)* 9 Wellington Ct., Little Rock, AR 72227 USA Tel 501-517-6084
E-mail: sharon@aristotle.net.
Bowman, Rosanne, *(978-0-578-41245-0; 979-8-9861861)* 1612 Karen Ave., Lima, OH 45801 USA Tel 419-516-6149
E-mail: writer@rosannebowman.com
Dist(s): **Ingram Content Group.**
Bowman's Pr., LLC, *(978-1-933142)* 9321 226th St. SE, Woodinville, WA 98077 USA
E-mail: info@bowmanspress.com
Web site: http://www.bowmanspress.com.
Bowmar/Noble Pubs., *(978-0-8107; 978-0-8372)* 220 E. Danieldale Dr., De Soto, TX 75115-2490 USA (SAN 201-4157).
Bowrider Pr., *(978-0-9825663)* 1451 Fairbanks Pl., Los Angeles, CA 90026 USA Tel 310-497-1789
Dist(s): **Follett School Solutions.**
Box Girls, The, *(978-0-9769908)* 149 S. Barrington Ave. No. 126, Los Angeles, CA 90049 USA Fax: 310-440-0145
Web site: http://www.theboxgirls.com.
Boxer Bks., Ltd. (GBR) *(978-0-9547373; 978-1-905417; 978-1-910126; 978-1-912757; 978-1-914912) Dist. by* **Sterling.**
Boxes & Arrows, Incorporated *See* **Backintyme Publishing**
Boyars, Marion Pubs., Inc., *(978-0-7145; 978-0-905223)* 237 E. 39th St., No. 1A, New York, NY 10016-2110 USA (SAN 284-981X) Tel 212-697-1599; Fax: 212-808-0664; Toll Free: 800-283-3572 (orders only)
Dist(s): **Consortium Bk. Sales & Distribution**
MyiLibrary.
Boyars, Marion Pubs., Ltd. (GBR) *(978-0-7145; 978-0-907325; 978-1-903018; 978-1-84230; 978-1-909248) Dist. by* **Consort Bk Sales.**
Boyce, S. M. *See* **Wispvine Publishing**
Boyce, Tami Design, *(978-0-692-78511-9; 978-0-692-97044-7; 978-0-692-99539-6; 978-1-7361586; 978-1-7376115)* 1772 Orange Grove Shores Dr., Charleston, SC 29407 USA Tel 843-814-4664
Web site: http://www.tamiboyce.com
Dist(s): **CreateSpace Independent Publishing Platform.**
Boyd Books *See* **Melissa Boyd**
Boyd, Charlisa Dunning, *(978-0-692-96963-2)* 1421 Beacon Valley Dr., Raleigh, NC 27604 USA Tel 919-890-5773
E-mail: Charlisa.boyd@outlook.com.
Boyds Collection Ltd., The, *(978-0-9712840; 978-0-9713174)* 75 Cunningham Rd., Gettysburg, PA 17325-7142 USA
E-mail: alana@boydsstuff.com
Web site: http://www.boydsstuff.com.
Boyds Mills & Kane *See* **Astra Publishing Hse.**
Boyds Mills Press *See* **Highlights Pr., c/o Highlights for Children, Inc.**
Boyes, Sandra, *(978-1-7344214)* P.O. Box 325, Moneta, VA 24121 USA Tel 804-836-3489
E-mail: sandraperiwinkle@gmail.com.
Boyle & Dalton *Imprint of* **Columbus Pr.**
Boynton, Colin (GBR) *(978-0-9559931) Dist. by* **LuluCom.**
Boys Read Bks., *(978-0-9801224)* 3211 NW 75th St., Seattle, WA 98117 USA Tel 206-321-5500
E-mail: john@boysread.org.
Boys Town, Nebraska Center, Public Service Division *See* **Boys Town Pr.**
Boys Town Pr. *Imprint of* **Boys Town Pr.**
Boys Town Pr., *(978-0-938510; 978-1-889322; 978-1-934490; 978-1-935734; 978-1-944882; 979-8-88907)* Div. of Father Flanagan's Boys' Home, 13603 Flanagan Blvd, Boys Town, NE 68010 USA (SAN 215-8477) Tel 531-355-1320; Fax: 531-355-1310; Toll Free: 800-282-6657; *Imprints:* Boys Town Press (MYID_B_BOYS TO)
E-mail: btpress@boystown.org
Web site: http://www.boystownpress.org
Dist(s): **Brodart Co.**
Children's Plus, Inc.
Quality Bks., Inc.
†**BPC,** *(978-0-913990; 978-1-57067; 978-0-9669317; 978-0-9673108; 978-0-9779183; 978-1-939053)* P.O. Box 99, Summertown, TN 38483 USA (SAN 202-439X) Tel 931-964-3571; Fax: 931-964-3518; Toll Free: 888-260-8458; *Imprints:* Native Voices (Native Voices); 7th Generation (SeventhGen); GroundSwell Books (MYID_A_GROUNDS)
E-mail: info@bookpubco.com
Web site: http://www.bookpubco.com
Dist(s): **Children's Plus, Inc.**
CreateSpace Independent Publishing Platform
Follett School Solutions
Four Winds Trading Co.
Integral Yoga Pubns.
New Leaf Distributing Co., Inc.
Nutri-Bks. Corp.
Orca Bk. Pubs. USA
Partners Bk. Distributing, Inc.
Rio Nuevo Pubs.
Smashwords; *CIP.*
bPlus Bks. *Imprint of* **Bumble Bee Publishing**
BPM Research LLC, *(978-0-9829224)* 939 Bloomfield St., Hoboken, NJ 07030 USA Tel 551-226-9372
E-mail: michael@bpm-research.com
Web site: http://www.bpm-research.com.
BPT Media, *(978-0-9772126)* P.O. Box 28663, Philadelphia, PA 19151-0663 USA
E-mail: vharris52@gmail.com.
BQB Publishing *Imprint of* **Boutique of Quality Books Publishing Co., Inc.**
Bradbury, Heidi, *(978-0-692-90149-6; 978-0-692-98968-5; 978-0-692-19591-8; 978-0-578-94660-3; 979-8-218-10193-0; 979-8-218-17276-3)* 2244 E. Ojai Ave., OJAI, CA 93023 USA Tel 805-701-4945
E-mail: heidi@heidibradburyfineart.com
Dist(s): **Ingram Content Group.**
Braddom, Diana V. *See* **Magnolia**
Bradford, Elizabeth, *(978-0-692-18388-5)* 36 Bird Ln., Garrison, NY 10524 USA Tel 845-736-4029
E-mail: bradford.eliz11@gmail.com
Dist(s): **Ingram Content Group.**
Bradford Pr., Inc., *(978-0-9705618; 978-0-9801563)* Orders Addr.: P.O. Box 6802, South Bend, IN 46660-6802 USA Tel 574-876-3601; Fax: 574-255-9358 Do not confuse with companies with same name in Bradford, MA, Palm Beach, FL, Chicago, IL
E-mail: BradfordPress@comcast.net; Info@Bradford-Press.com
Web site: http://www.Bradford-Press.com.
Bradford-Franklin, *(978-0-9767676)* P.O. Box 495, Hartsville, TN 37074 USA Tel 615-374-3712; Fax: 615-374-4649
E-mail: bradfordfranklin@bellsouth.net
Web site: http://www.jackmccall.com.
Bradley, Andrea W., *(978-0-692-14988-1; 978-0-692-14989-8)* P.O. Box 550, MARION, IL 62959 USA Tel 618-751-3093
E-mail: andrea@inshouse.com
Dist(s): **Ingram Content Group.**
Bradley, Judy & Assocs., LLC, *(978-0-615-57032-7)* 230 E. 45th St., Savannah, GA 31405 USA Tel 912-232-7636
E-mail: judybee58@gmail.com.
Brady, Hanna, *(978-1-7324001)* P.O. Box 13481, Fairlawn, OH 44334 USA Tel 330-281-7390
E-mail: newsletter@arcananovels.com
Web site: www.arcananovels.com.
BradyBooks *See* **Nature Works Press**
Bradybooks.biz, *(978-0-9754169)* 1888 County Road 72., Bailey, CO 80421-2175 USA
E-mail: readbradybooks@aol.com
Web site: http://bradybooks.biz.
Brae, Caroline, *(978-0-9978300)* 1256 Maple View Dr., Charlottesville, VA 22902 USA Tel 540-335-6996
E-mail: Caroline.Brae@gmail.com.
Braided Image, *(978-0-9725170)* 3064 Old New Cut Rd., Springfield, TN 37172 USA
E-mail: masterbraider@mindspring.com
Web site: http://www.braidedimage.com.
BrailleInk, *(978-0-9769313)* 1704 Holly St., Austin, TX 78702-5424 USA Toll Free: 800-324-2919
E-mail: info@brailleink.org
Web site: http://www.brailleink.org.
Brainbow Pr., *(978-0-9796715; 978-0-9825867)* 7914 N. Roundstone Dr., Tucson, AZ 85741 USA (SAN 854-0594) Tel 520-481-1919
E-mail: 19@19.org; eclipyuksel@gmail.com; brainbowpress@gmail.com
Web site: http://www.brainbowpress.com; http://www.islamicreform.org; http://www.yuksel.org; http://www.19.org
Dist(s): **Ingram Content Group.**
BrainBox, Limited *See* **Gray Jay Bks.**
Brainchild Publishing *See* **Mindfull Publishing**
Brainerd Enterprises, *(978-0-9747441)* 419 Old Clyde Pk. Rd., Livingston, MT 59047 USA Tel 406-222-8273; Fax: 406-222-3769
E-mail: sally@heirofkingmeldh.com
Web site: http://www.heirofkingmeldh.com.
BrainFriendly Learning, *(978-0-9759226)* 6801 6th St., NW, Washington, DC 20012-1911 USA Tel 202-723-7337; Fax: 202-726-6117
E-mail: stevecarroll@speakeasy.net
Web site: http://www.kathleencarroll.com.
Brainiac Bloomers, LLC, *(978-1-948123)* 7155 Country Oaks Dr, Memphis, TN 38125 USA Tel 901-273-4202
E-mail: la@brainiacbloomers.com
Web site: brainiacbloomers.com.
Brainstorm Pubns., Inc., *(978-0-9723429)* 24 NE 24th Ave., Pompano Beach, FL 33062 USA Tel 954-941-3329; Fax: 954-943-7708 Do not confuse with Brainstorm Publications in Lake Oswego, OR
E-mail: tditocco@brainstormpublications.com
Web site: http://www.brainstormpublications.com.
BrainStorm 3000, *(978-0-9651174)* P.O. Box 80513, Goleta, CA 93118 USA Tel 805-448-7149; 805-448-7149
Dist(s): **Educational Bk. Distributors.**
BrainStream, *(978-0-9785892)* 21307 Park Valley Dr., Katy, TX 77450-4811 USA
E-mail: bvogt@brainstream.com.
Braintext, Inc., *(978-0-9816270)* 3660 Wilshire Blvd. Ste. 400, Los Angeles, CA 90010-2753 USA
E-mail: info@braintext.com
Web site: http://www.braintext.com.
BrainX, Inc., *(978-0-9741604)* 45 Rincon Dr. Unit 1033B, Camarillo, CA 93012-8424 USA
E-mail: info@brainx.com
Web site: http://www.brainx.com
Dist(s): **Majors, J. A. Co.**
Rittenhouse Bk. Distributors.
Braley & Thompson, Inc., *(978-1-883239)* P.O. Box 1396, Saint Albans, WV 25177-1396 USA Tel 304-722-1704; Fax: 304-722-1709; Toll Free: 800-258-5453.
Bran Nue Productions, *(978-0-615-44662-2; 978-0-9851574)* 7878 LaSalle Ave. No. 231, Baton Rouge, LA 70806 USA Tel 225-678-6631
E-mail: brannuepro@gmail.com.
Branch & Brooks Publishing & Consulting Solutions LLC, *(978-0-692-61412-9; 978-0-578-25389-3; 978-0-578-26121-8; 979-8-218-03824-3; 979-8-9879073)* 1 Red Oak Pl., Hampton, VA 23666 USA Tel 757-660-1547; 700 Tech Ctr. Pkwy. Suite 200, Newport News, VA 23606
E-mail: BBConsultingSolutions@gmail.com
Web site: BranchandBrooks.com
Dist(s): **CreateSpace Independent Publishing Platform.**
Branch Springs Publishing, *(978-0-9727622)* Orders Addr.: 500 Watts Dr., Huntsville, AL 35801 USA Tel 256 539 1064; Edit Addr.: 500 Watts Dr., Huntsville, AL 35801 USA
E-mail: fchap10220@aol.com.
Branching Plot Bks., *(978-0-9860166; 978-0-9891840; 978-1-7363392)* 5900 Balcones Dr Ste 5650, Austin, TX 78731 USA
E-mail: arthur@branchingplotbooks.com
Web site: http://www.branchingplotbooks.com.
Brand New Happy moon Pub., *(978-0-692-19898-8; 979-8-9877528)* 154 Ctr. St., WEST HAVEN, CT 06516 USA Tel 475-449-3971
E-mail: weread@brandnewhappymoonpublishing.com; justA.S.K.publishing@gmail.com
Web site: brandnewhappymoonpublishing.com.
Brand X Bks., *(978-0-9903936; 979-8-218-11807-5)* 168-10 127 Ave. Apt. 6g, Jamaica, NY 11434 USA Tel 718-528-7942
E-mail: the-deeman@webtv.net
Dist(s): **Ingram Content Group.**
Branded Black Publishing, *(978-0-9746913)* P.O. Box 950781, Oklahoma City, OK 73195 USA
Web site: http://www.ebonymarshal.com; http://www.brandedblackpublishing.com; http://www.gospelofthegun.com; http://www.seanchandler.com.
Branded Pros., *(978-0-578-19793-7; 978-0-578-57190-4)* 2040 S. Alma School Rd. #1-171, Chandler, AZ 85286 USA.
Branden Bks., *(978-0-8283)* Div. of Branden Publishing Co., P.O. Box 812094, Wellesley, MA 02482 USA (SAN 201-4106) Tel 781-235-3634; Fax: 781-790-1056
E-mail: branden@brandenbooks.com; danteu@danteuniversity.org
Web site: http://www.brandenbooks.com; http://www.danteuniversity.org; http://www.adolphcaso.com
Dist(s): **Brodart Co.**
Follett School Solutions
eBookit.com.
Brandrock Creative Co., The, *(978-0-692-13056-8; 978-0-578-59049-3)* 1034 Grider Dr., Gallatin, TN 37066 USA Tel 281-818-8188
E-mail: jwhit243@gmail.com.
Brandylane Pubs., Inc., *(978-0-9627635; 978-1-883911; 978-0-9838264; 978-0-9849588; 978-0-9859358; 978-1-939930; 978-1-947860; 978-1-951565; 978-1-953021; 978-1-958754; 978-1-962416)* Orders Addr.: 5 S. 1st St., Richmond, VA 23219-3716 USA; *Imprints:* Belle Isle Books (BelleIsle)
E-mail: robert@brandylanepublishers.com
Web site: http://www.brandylanepublishers.com
Dist(s): **Baker & Taylor International**
Follett School Solutions
Ingram Content Group
Smashwords.
Brasher, Joan, *(978-0-578-43072-0; 978-0-578-29968-6)* 2100 Acklen Ave. Unit 311, Nashville, TN 37212 USA Tel 615-438-8475
E-mail: joan.brasher@gmail.com.
Brass in Color *See* **Songburd Music**
BrassHeart Music, *(978-0-9673762; 978-0-9721478; 978-0-9826278)* 256 S. Robertson Blvd., Suite 2288, Beverly Hills, CA 90211 USA Tel 323-932-0534; Fax: 323-937-6884; 323-933-4209; *Imprints:* Kid's Creative Classics (Kids Creative Classics); Dream A World (Dream A World)
E-mail: bunny@dreamaworld.com; brassheartmusic@aol.com
Web site: http://www.brassheartmusic.com; http://www.dreamaworld.com
Dist(s): **DeVorss & Co.**
Music Design, Inc.
New Leaf Distributing Co., Inc.
Bratcher Publishing *Imprint of* **Write Place**
Brattle Publishing Group, *(978-0-9854295; 978-0-9905872; 978-0-9908706; 978-0-9972902)* 5304 Running Brook Ln., McKinney , TX 75071 USA (SAN 920-7104) Tel 214-773-0792
E-mail: richard@brattlepublishing.com
Dist(s): **Greenleaf Book Group.**
Braughler Bks. LLC, *(978-0-9822187; 978-0-9971375; 978-1-945091; 978-1-970063; 978-1-955791)* 251 W Central Ave No. 163, Springboro, OH 45066 USA Tel 937-582-6657
E-mail: david.braughler@braughlerbooks.com
Web site: http://www.braughlerbooks.com.
Braun Pubns., *(978-0-9774302)* 150 Clinton Ln., Spring Valley, NY 10977 USA.
Brave Knight Media, LLC, *(978-0-9997141)* 13451 Columbine Cir, Thornton, CO 80241 USA Tel 508-667-0367
E-mail: peter@braveknightmedia.com
Web site: braveknightmedia.com.
Brave Ulysses Bks., *(978-0-9700125; 978-0-615-16272-0; 978-0-615-18969-7; 978-0-615-22032-1; 978-0-615-26030-3)* P.O. Box 1877, Asheville, NC 28802 USA
E-mail: cecil@braveulysses.com; info@braveulysses.com
Dist(s): **Lulu Pr., Inc.**
Parnassus Bk. Distributors.
Braveheart Pr., LLC, *(978-0-9763935)* 23852 Pacific Coast Hwy., Suite 572, Malibu, CA 90265 USA Tel 310-770-7831; Fax: 310-456-5109 do not confuse with BraveHeart Press in Woodland Park, CO
E-mail: showrunnerbrv@aol.com
Web site: http://www.braveheartpresslc.com.
Braxton, Theresa, *(978-0-692-95780-6)* 1 Gloucester ct, GLYNDON, MD 21136 USA Tel 443-240-5948
E-mail: lilbraxton23@gmail.com
Dist(s): **Ingram Content Group.**
Braziller, George Inc., *(978-0-8076)* 171 Madison Ave., Suite 1103, New York, NY 10016 USA (SAN 201-9310) Tel 212-889-0909; Fax: 212-689-5405
Dist(s): **Norton, W. W. & Co., Inc.**
Penguin Random Hse. Distribution
Penguin Random Hse. LLC.
Brazos Valley Pr., *(978-0-9726822)* Orders Addr.: P.O. Box 215, Calvert, TX 77837-0215 USA Tel 979-364-2439; Fax: 800-881-2032; Edit Addr.: 508 E. Texas, Calvert, TX 77837 USA (SAN 858-2947)
E-mail: jkennedy@brazosvalleypress.com
Web site: http://www.brazosvalleypress.com.
BRAZZLE, *(978-0-692-93528-6; 978-1-7324015)* 1777 LARIMER ST, Denver, CO 80202 USA Tel 303-888-6288; Fax: 303-888-6288
E-mail: jensalimi@yahoo.com.
Brda, Tracy, *(978-0-9742355)* P.O. Box 510065, Saint Louis, MO 63129 USA Tel 314-293-0015; Fax: 636-343-0564
E-mail: info@power-twins.com.
Bread & Butter Bks., *(978-0-9800816)* 229 E. Ct. St., Cincinnati, OH 45202 USA Tel 513-884-0468
E-mail: jkiddielit@cinci.rr.com.
Bread of Life, *(978-0-578-31941-4; 979-8-218-10884-7)* P.O. Box 692, Burson, CA 95225 USA Tel 209-518-2435
E-mail: amurray95225@yahoo.com.
Breadcrumbs LLC, *(978-0-692-85182-1; 978-0-692-94143-0; 978-0-692-14348-3; 978-0-578-64399-1)* 862 Longmeadow St., Longmeadow, MA 01106 USA Tel 413-567-8019
E-mail: cropsey@comcast.net.
Breahte Art Calm LLC, *(978-1-7373667)* 12100 NW 42nd Ave, Vancouver, WA 98685 USA Tel 415-309-3578
E-mail: jocefitz@gmail.com
Web site: www.breatheartcalm.com.
Break-A-Leg Bks., *(978-0-9668522)* 12332 Laurel Terr., Studio City, CA 91604 USA Tel 818-508-5585; Fax: 818-752-0682.
Breakaway Bks., *(978-1-55821; 978-1-891369; 978-1-62124)* P.O. Box 24, Halcottsville, NY 12438 USA Tel 607-326-4805; Fax: 212-898-0408; Toll Free: 800-548-4348 (voicemail) Do not confuse with Breakaway Bks., Albany, TX
E-mail: breakawaybooks@gmail.com
Web site: http://www.breakawaybooks.com
Dist(s): **Consortium Bk. Sales & Distribution.**
Breaking Cycles Bks., *(978-0-9741202)* Orders Addr.: P.O. Box 402, Severn, MD 21144-0402 USA Tel 410-519-6787
E-mail: BrCyBks@msn.com
Web site: http://www.breaking-cycles-visions-of-hope.com.
Breaking the Barrier, Inc., *(978-0-9712817; 978-0-9728570; 978-0-9758573; 978-0-9777987; 978-0-9817961; 978-0-9846477; 978-0-9846490; 978-0-9903122; 978-0-9963192; 978-0-9976527; 978-1-955306)* 63 Shirley Rd., Groton, MA 01450 USA Fax: 978-448-1237; Toll Free: 866-862-7325 Do not confuse with Breaking the Barrier Ministry, Inc. in Pennsauken, NJ
E-mail: info@tobreak.com; john@tobreak.com
Web site: http://www.tobreak.com.
Breaklight Pubns., *(978-0-9974421)* 380 Red Bay Ln., Marco Island, FL 34145 USA Tel 516-680-4494
E-mail: dr.dolores.burton@gmail.com
Web site: www.breaklightpublications.com.
Breakneck Bks. *Imprint of* **Variance Author Services**
Breakneck Books *See* **Breakneck Media**
Breakneck Media, *(978-0-9786551; 978-0-9796929; 978-0-9836017; 978-0-9840423; 978-0-9886725;*

978-1-941539) 20 Sampson Rd., Rochester, NH 03867 USA
E-mail: jrobinsonauthor@gmail.com
Web site: http://www.bewareofmonsters.com.

Healey, Nicholas Publishing, *(978-0-9839558; 978-1-941176)* 20 Park Plaza, Suite 1115A, Boston, MA 02116 USA
Dist(s): **Consortium Bk. Sales & Distribution**
Hachette Bk. Group
MyiLibrary.

Breath & Shadows Productions, *(978-0-9720176; 978-0-9821029)* P.O. Box 10557, Tampa, FL 33679 USA Tel 813-251-8187
Web site: http://www.breathandshadows.com.

Breathe Art Calm, *(978-0-578-81922-8)* 12100 NW 42nd Ave, Vancouver, WA 98685 USA Tel 415-309-3578
E-mail: hello@breatheartcalm.com
Web site: www.breatheartcalm.com.

Breathless Vintage Enterprises, *(978-0-9842053)* Orders Addr.: PO Box 28168, Portland, OR 97228 USA (SAN 858-7221)
E-mail: morgan@breathlessvintage.com.

Breault, Shalini, *(978-0-692-19652-6; 978-1-7331172)* 192 Carlton Ave., Marlton, NJ 08053 USA Tel 856-797-1423
E-mail: shalini_chandini@yahoo.com.

Breckling Pr., *(978-0-9721218; 978-1-933308)* 283 Michigan Ave., Elmhurst, IL 60126 USA
Web site: http://www.brecklingpress.com
Dist(s): **Independent Pubs. Group.**

Breely Crush Publishing, *(978-1-61433; 979-8-89006)* 10808 River Front Pkwy STE 3013 Suite 3013, South Jordan, UT 84095 USA (SAN 860-1941) Tel 888-621-3730
E-mail: info@breelycrush.com.

Bree's Gift Publishing, *(978-0-9748512)* 3840 Listerman Rd., Howell, MI 48855 USA Tel 517-552-9184
E-mail: kimmie67@sbcglobal.net.

Breezeway Books, *(978-1-62550)* 7101 W. Commercial Blvd. No. 4E, Tamarac, FL 33319 USA Tel 954-726-0902; Fax: 954-726-0903
E-mail: dgreenspan@llumina.com
Web site: www.llumina.com.

Breezy Reads, *(978-0-9759784; 978-1-938327)* Orders Addr.: 2800 N Bogus Basin Rd APT C103, Boise, ID 83702 USA (SAN 256-3762)
E-mail: breezyreads@gmail.com
Web site: http://www.breezyreads.com.

Breezy Way Publishing *Imprint of* **Gatekeeper Pr.**

Bremer Press *See* **Zachmeyer, Mary L.**

Brenden, Sally, *(978-0-9898918; 978-0-9972957)* 831 2nd Ave. N., Sauk Rapids, MN 56379 USA Tel 320-250-5245
E-mail: brendenbooks@gmail.com
Web site: brendenbooks.com.

BrenMar Communications, *(978-0-9903034)* 17313 Hialeah Dr., Odessa, FL 33556 USA Tel 813-920-9761
E-mail: authorbrendamartin@gmail.com
Web site: http://www.brendamartin.net.

Brennan, Laura, *(978-1-7323846)* P.O. Box 4956, West Hills, CA 91308 USA Tel 818-264-8379
E-mail: Laura@LauraBrennanWrites.com.

Brennan, Matt, *(978-0-692-12587-8; 978-0-578-72366-2)* 1719 Grismer Ave. Apt. 11, BURBANK, CA 91504 USA Tel 818-469-5661
E-mail: mattarama.mb@gmail.com
Dist(s): **Ingram Content Group.**

Brenneman, Lynette, *(978-0-9859737)* 260 Brenneman Rd., Lancaster, PA 17603 USA Tel 717-872-4815
E-mail: lleaman@verizon.net.

Brenner Publishing, LLC, *(978-0-9777203)* P.O. Box 584, Hicksville, NY 11802-0584 USA Tel 516-433-0804.

Brent Darnell International, *(978-0-9799258; 978-0-9836709; 978-0-9889330; 978-0-9862965; 978-0-9962646; 978-0-9970445; 978-1-946637)* 1940 The Exchange Suite 100, Atlanta, GA 30339 USA.

Brenton, Lindsey, *(978-1-7351858)* 3013 NE 132nd Terr, Smithville, MO 64089 USA Tel 816-896-3001
E-mail: lindsey@lindseybrenton.com.

Brentwood Christian Pr. *Imprint of* **Brentwood Communications Group**

Brentwood Communications Group, *(978-0-916573; 978-1-55630; 978-1-59581)* P.O. Box 4773, Columbus, GA 31914-4773 USA (SAN 297-1895) Tel 706-576-5787; Toll Free: 800-334-8861; *Imprints:* Brentwood Christian Press (BrtwdChrist Pr) Do not confuse with Brentwood Communications Group in Vista, CA
E-mail: brentwood@knology.net
Web site: http://www.brentwoodbooks.com; http://www.brentwoodreview.com; http://www.newchristianbooks.com
Dist(s): **Ingram Publisher Services.**

Brentwood Home Video, *(978-0-7378; 978-0-924739; 978-1-57119; 978-1-879902)* Div. of Brentwood Communications, Inc., 810 Lawrence Dr., Suite 100, Newbury Park, CA 91320 USA Toll Free: 888-335-0528
E-mail: brentcom@earthlink.net
Web site: http://www.ssetsites.com/e-bol/default.htm
Dist(s): **Follett School Solutions.**

Brentwood Kids Co. *Imprint of* **Brentwood Music, Inc.**

Brentwood Music, Inc., *(978-0-7601; 978-1-55897)* 2555 Meridian Blvd. Ste. 100, Franklin, TN 37067-6364 USA Toll Free: 800-333-9000 (audio & video orders); 800-846-7664 (book orders); *Imprints:* Brentwood Kids Company (Brentwood Kids)
Web site: http://www.providentmusic.com
Dist(s): **Appalachian Bible Co.**
Central South Christian Distribution
Leonard, Hal Corp.
New Day Christian Distributors Gifts, Inc.
Provident Music Distribution
Spring Arbor Distributors, Inc.

Brentwood Publishing Group *See* **Writing for the Lord Ministries**

Brentwood-Benson Music Publishing, *(978-1-59802; 978-0-9830602)* Orders Addr.: 101 Winners Cir., Brentwood, TN 37027 USA (SAN 256-9574) Toll Free: 800-846-7664
E-mail: sales@brentwoodbenson.com; jroher@brentwoodbenson.com
Web site: http://www.brentwoodbenson.com
Dist(s): **Leonard, Hal Corp.**

†Brethren Pr., *(978-0-87178)* Div. of Church of the Brethren, 1451 Dundee Ave., Elgin, IL 60120-1694 USA (SAN 201-9329) Tel 847-742-5100; 800-441-3712; Fax: 847-742-1407; Toll Free: 800-441-3712
E-mail: brethren_press_gb@brethren.org
Web site: http://www.brethrenpress.com
Dist(s): **Follett School Solutions**; *CIP.*

Brethren Revival Fellowship, *(978-0-9745027; 978-0-9777766; 978-0-9828895; 978-1-946688)* 26 United Zion Cir., Lititz, PA 17543-7956 USA Fax: 717-625-0511
E-mail: harpri@dejazzd.com; brf@brfwitness.org
Web site: http://www.brfwitness.org.

Brewer Bear Bks., *(978-0-692-19549-9; 978-0-9600441)* 10416 SW 17 Pl., Gainesville, FL 32607 USA Tel 352-514-1351
E-mail: caseyh181@gmail.com
Dist(s): **CreateSpace Independent Publishing Platform.**

Brewer, Neil, *(978-0-9771807)* 5290 Cedar Way Dr., NE, Corydon, IN 47112 USA Tel 812-952-3482
E-mail: 8oclock@aye.net
Web site: http://www.booksbybrewer.com
Dist(s): **BookBaby.**

Brewer Technologies, *(978-0-9774748)* P.O. Box 141, Cornwall, PA 17016 USA Tel 717-228-1708; Fax: 717-228-1709; Toll Free: 877-449-2556
E-mail: nicholelmoore@comcast.net
Web site: http://www.tonybrewer.com.

Brewer's Historical Publications *See* **Bear State Bks.**

Brewster Moon, *(978-0-9854423)* 13940 Cedar Rd. Suite 386, University Heights, OH 44118 USA Tel 216-408-1616
E-mail: tbrown@brewstermoon.com.

Brewster, Robert, *(978-0-615-37153-5)* 185 NE 4th Ave. Apt 317, Delray Beach, FL 33483 USA Tel 561-400-7799
Dist(s): **Outskirts Pr., Inc.**

Brian A. Griffen, *(978-0-578-42024-0)* 4021 Jefferson Woods Dr., Powhatan, VA 23139 USA Tel 804-598-3092
E-mail: brianagriffen@gmail.com
Dist(s): **Ingram Content Group.**

Brian J. Publishing, Incorporated *See* **Holography Sells**

Brianna Rae Quinn, *(978-1-7356362)* 8814 Pk. Heights Ave., Garfield Heights, OH 44125 USA Tel 216-337-8909
E-mail: miss.briannaquinn@gmail.com.

Briarcliffe Press *See* **Sunny Palms Pr.**

Brickey E-Publishing, *(978-0-9758964)* 1029E Salisbury St., Kernersville, NC 27284-3063 USA
E-mail: mainoffice@brickey-epublishing.com
Web site: http://www.brickey-epublishing.com.

BrickHouse Bks., Inc., *(978-0-932616; 978-1-935916; 978-1-938144)* 306 Suffolk Rd., Baltimore, MD 21218 USA (SAN 209-4622) Tel 410-235 7690
E-mail: charriss@towson.edu; clarindaharriss13@gmail.com
Web site: http://www.brickhousebooks.com
Dist(s): **INscribe Digital**
Itasca Bks.

BrickHouse Education *Imprint of* **Cambridge BrickHouse, Inc.**

Bridge Ink, *(978-0-9641963)* 32580 SW Arbor Lake Dr., Wilsonville, OR 97070-8471 USA
E-mail: bob@bridgeink.com
Web site: http://www.bridgeink.com
Dist(s): **Far West Bk. Service**
Follett School Solutions
Partners/West Book Distributors.

Bridge Pubns., Inc., *(978-0-88404; 978-1-57318; 978-1-4031; 978-1-61177; 978-1-4572; 978-1-0789)* Orders Addr.: 5600 E. Olympic Blvd., Commerce, CA 90022 USA (SAN 208-3884) Tel 323-888-6200; Fax: 323-888-6210; Toll Free: 800-722-1733; 800-334-5433; Edit Addr.: 4751_Fountain Ave., Los Angeles, CA 90029 USA
E-mail: annarnow@bridgepub.com; daniellem@bridgepub.com; donarnow@bridgepub.com; purchaser@bridgepub.com
Web site: http://www.bridgepub.com; http://www.clearbodyclearmind.com; http://www.scientology.org; http://www.dianetics.org
Dist(s): **Bookazine Co., Inc.**
Brodart Co.
Follett School Solutions
Landmark Audiobooks.

Bridge Publishing Group, *(978-0-9728439)* P.O. Box 1673, Walnut, CA 91788-1673 USA Tel 909-444-9088; Fax: 909-595-9526
E-mail: dafangzeng@yahoo.com.

Bridge To Life Ministries, Incorporated *See* **Advent Truth Ministries**

Bridge2Worlds Bks., *(978-0-692-09033-6; 978-1-7328802)* 5942 Harvest Point Cir., Mountain Green, UT 84050 USA Tel 801-294-3554
E-mail: tchristensen77@gmail.com
Dist(s): **CreateSpace Independent Publishing Platform.**

Bridge-Logos Foundation *See* **Bridge-Logos, Inc.**

Bridge-Logos, Inc., *(978-0-88270; 978-0-912106; 978-0-9841034; 978-1-61036)* Orders Addr.: 14260 W. Newberry Rd, Newberry, FL 32669 USA (SAN 253-5254) Tel 352-727-9324; Toll Free: 800-935-6467 (orders only); 800-631-5802 (orders only)
E-mail: SWooldridge@bridgelogos.com
Web site: http://www.bridgelogos.com
Dist(s): **Anchor Distributors**
Destiny Image Pubs.
Send The Light Distribution LLC
Spring Arbor Distributors, Inc.
Whitaker Hse.

Bridges, Joseph (AUS) *(978-0-646-19404-2)* *Dist. by* **Carson Dellos.**

Bridges to Better Learning, *(978-0-9970558)* 3201 NE 183 St. Apt. 508, Aventura, FL 33160 USA Tel 954-849-1157; Fax: 305-682-0032
E-mail: dwander6@gmail.com.

Bridget Maloy Steber, *(978-0-578-45211-1)* 7790 Lake Blvd., Spanish Fort, AL 36527 USA Tel 251-979-5622
E-mail: steberb1@gmail.com
Dist(s): **Ingram Content Group.**

Bridgeway Bks., *(978-1-933538; 978-1-934454)* Div. of BookPros, LLC, 2100 Kramer Ln., Suite 300, Austin, TX 78758 USA Tel 512-478-2028
Web site: http://www.bridgewaybooks.net.

BR:IEFing Assocs. of New England, *(978-0-9706105)* Orders Addr.: P.O. Box 3159, Kingston, NY 12402-3159 USA Tel 845-339-0998; Edit Addr.: 289 Fair St., Suite 2A, Kingston, NY 12401-3844 USA.

Briggs & Schuster, *(978-0-9835120; 978-1-7321916; 978-1-956567)* 520 Ashford Dr., Coppell, TX 75019 USA Tel 214-810-2443; Fax: 443-797-1909
E-mail: douglas@donascimento.com; nicoledonascimento@gmail.com
Web site: http://www.bsa.im.

Briggs, Don Film & Video, *(978-1-892502)* 520 Marin Ave., Mill Valley, CA 94941 USA Tel 415-383-9702.

Briggs, Jae, *(978-0-578-24808-0; 978-0-578-34466-9)* 19387 E. Eastman Pl., Aurora, CO 80013 USA
E-mail: EMAIL.

Briggs, Mark, *(978-1-7343345)* 10303 E.150th Ave, Brighton, CO 80602 USA Tel 817-798-4893
E-mail: mbriggswriting@gmail.com.

Briggs, Sharon, *(978-0-615-13051-4)* 109 Hope Way, Auburn, KY 42206 USA
E-mail: sharondeneice109@yahoo.com.

Brigham Young Univ., *(978-0-8425)* 205 UPB, Provo, UT 84602 USA (SAN 201-9337) Tel 801-422-2809; Fax: 801-422-0591; *Imprints:* BYU Creative Works (BYUCreative)
E-mail: diane_foerster@byu.edu
Web site: http://www.upb.byu.edu
Dist(s): **Brigham Young Univ. Print Services**
Chicago Distribution Ctr.
Follett School Solutions
Indiana Univ. Pr.
Univ. of Chicago Pr.

Brighid Publishing, *(978-0-9965974)* 20735 SW 90th Ave, Tualatin, OR 97062 USA Tel 503-691-0349
E-mail: abuenzli_pdx@hotmail.com
Web site: http://skyegenaro.com.

Bright & Morning Star Bks., *(978-0-9986879)* 19506 Whitewood Dr., Spring, TX 77373 USA
E-mail: sharon47@embarqmail.com.

Bright Cloud Publishing, *(978-0-9770727)*
E-mail: brightcloud@verizon.net
Web site: http://www.brightcloudpublishing.com.

Bright Connections Media, *(978-1-62267)* 233 N. Michigan Ave. Suite 2000, Chicago, IL 60601 USA Tel 312-729-5800
E-mail: orders@innlog.net
Web site: www.brightconnectionsmedia.com
Dist(s): **Continental Sales.**

Bright Eyes Pr., *(978-0-9728019)* 862 Congressional Rd., Simi Valley, CA 93065 USA Tel 805-579-0027
E-mail: kassie@kgraves.com
Web site: http://www.brighteyespress.com.

Bright Hse. Publishing, LLC, *(978-0-9981891)* 1303 Clover Valley Way, Edgewood, MD 21040 USA Tel 443-819-8919
E-mail: yvannabright@gmail.com.

Bright Ideas! Educational Resources, *(978-1-892427)* P.O. Box 333, Cheswold, DE 19936 USA Toll Free: 877-492-8081
E-mail: hogan@inet.net.

BRIGHT IDEAS GRAPHICS, *(978-0-692-79823-2; 978-0-692-83463-3; 978-0-692-87847-7; 978-0-692-93004-5; 978-0-692-93084-7; 978-0-692-04911-2; 978-0-692-14946-1; 978-0-692-15729-9; 978-0-578-98706-4; 978-0-578-35402-6)* 1105 S. OLMSTED PARKWAY, MIDDLETOWN, DE 19709 USA Tel 609-481-7089.

Bright Matter Books *Imprint of* **Random Hse. Children's Bks.**

Bright of America, *(978-1-930355)* 300 Greenbrier Rd., Summersville, WV 26651 USA Tel 304-872-3000; Fax: 304-872-3033; Toll Free: 800-917-2368.

Bright Pittman, Portia, *(978-1-7349356)* P.O. Box 60, Winterville, NC 28590 USA Tel 252-717-7491
E-mail: portiabright@yahoo.com.

Bright Sky Publishing *See* **Night Heron Media**

Bright Solutions for Dyslexia, LLC, *(978-0-9744343; 978-0-9755871)* 2059 Camden Ave., Suite 186, San Jose, CA 95124-2024 USA Tel 408-559-3652; Fax: 408-377-0503
E-mail: susan@brightsolutions.us
Web site: http://www.brightsolutions.us.

Bright Spots, *(978-0-9769150)* P.O. Box 3868, Rancho Santa Fe, CA 92067 USA Toll Free: 888-301-8880
E-mail: lmameson@msn.com
Web site: http://www.brightspotsgames.com.

Bright Tyke Creations LLC, *(978-0-615-33119-5; 978-0-615-63721-1)* 217 Sassafras St., New Florence, PA 15944 USA
Web site: http://www.brighttykecreations.info.

Bright Wish Bks., *(978-1-7377277)* 5 Candlewood Dr., Pittsford, NY 14534 USA Tel 716-984-0666
E-mail: Brightwishbooks@gmail.com
Web site: Www.brightwishbooks.com.

BrightBerry Pr., *(978-0-9720924)* 4262 Kennebec Rd., Dixmont, ME 04932 USA Tel 207-234-4225
E-mail: jeanhay@brightberrypress.com; dbright@brightberrypress.com
Web site: http://www.brightberrypress.com
Dist(s): **CreateSpace Independent Publishing Platform.**

Bright-Brights Media Co., The, *(978-0-9752553)* 1059 Briar Ave., Provo, UT 84604 USA Tel 801-375-3455.

Brighter Child *Imprint of* **Carson-Dellosa Publishing, LLC**

Brighter Day Publishing, *(978-0-615-26080-8; 978-0-9841855)* P.O. Box 505, Washington Township, MI 48094 USA
Web site: http://www.publishinganswers.com.

Brighter Horizons Publishing, *(978-1-929662)* P.O. Box 448, Littleton, CO 80160 USA Tel 303-347-2904; Fax: 303-795-5951
E-mail: brighterhorizons@earthlink.net
Web site: http://home.earthlink.net/~brighterhorizons
Dist(s): **Book Wholesalers, Inc.**

Brighter Minds Children's Publishing, *(978-1-57791)* Div. of Brighter Child Interactive, LLC, 600 D Lakeview Plaza Blvd., Worthington, OH 43085 USA Tel 614-430-3021; Fax: 614-430-3152; *Imprints:* Little Melody Press (Little Melody Pr); Penny Candy Press (Penny Candy Pr)
E-mail: ranf@brightermindsmedia.com; books@Brightermindspublishing.com
Web site: http://www.brightermindspublishing.com.

Brightline Publishing *See* **Rainbow Reach**

Brightlings, *(978-1-953507)* 31 strand beach Dr., dana point, CA 92629 USA Tel 949-463-5233
E-mail: Bookcamp@brightlings.co
Web site: Brightlings.co.

Brighton Publishing LLC, *(978-1-936587; 978-1-62183)* 501 W. Ray Rd. Suite No. 4, Chandler, AZ 85225 USA Tel 602-487-2964
E-mail: donald@brightonpublishing.com
Web site: http://www.brightonpublishing.com.

BrightPoint Pr. *Imprint of* **ReferencePoint Pr., Inc.**

BrightShadow Publishing, *(978-0-9914513)* 2131 Five Mile Line Rd., Penfield, NY 14526 USA Tel 585-764-3493
E-mail: penfieldartscenter@gmail.com.

Brightside Co., *(978-0-9743720)* 5040 S. Elmira St., Greenwood Village, CO 80111-3608 USA (SAN 255-5573) Tel 303-694-6065; Fax: 303-694-1009
E-mail: cynthiadormer@msn.com.

Brightspark, *(978-0-9839339)* 1600 Fillmore St. Apt. 247, Denver, CO 80206 USA Tel 720-226-1375
E-mail: jodie@jodiebrownlee.com.

Brightwell Publishing, LLC, *(978-0-9776033)* 7151 Delmar Blvd., Saint Louis, MO 63130-4304 USA (SAN 257-7046) Tel 314-662-2736
E-mail: publisher@brightwellpublishing.net
Web site: http://www.brightwellpublishing.net; http://maryedwardswertsch.net.

Brikwoo Creative Group, *(978-0-615-77571-5; 978-0-615-88374-8; 978-0-692-46476-2; 978-0-692-93834-8; 978-0-692-04738-5; 978-1-7368412; 978-0-578-33810-1)* 224 Poplar Ave., Trenton, GA 30752 USA Tel 423-618-9178
E-mail: brian@brikwoo.com
Web site: www.brikwoo.com.

Briley & Baxter Publications, *(978-1-7331536; 978-1-7350168; 978-1-954819; 978-1-961978)* 1 Chapel Hill Dr., Plymouth, MA 02360 USA Tel 781-389-7299
E-mail: stacy.ohalloran@brileybaxterbooks.com
Web site: brileybaxterbooks.com.

Brilliance Publishing *See* **Brilliance Publishing, Inc.**

Brilliance Publishing, Inc., *(978-0-930435; 978-1-56100; 978-1-56740; 978-1-58788; 978-1-59086; 978-1-59355; 978-1-59600; 978-1-59710; 978-1-59737; 978-1-4233; 978-1-4418; 978-1-61106; 978-1-4558; 978-1-4692; 978-1-4805; 978-1-4915; 978-1-5012; 978-1-5113; 978-1-5226; 978-1-5318; 978-1-5366; 978-1-5436; 978-1-9786; 978-1-7213; 978-1-7997; 978-1-7135; 978-1-7136; 979-8-9850001; 979-8-4001) Orders Addr.: P.O. Box 887, Grand Haven, MI 49417 USA (SAN 690-1395) Tel 616-846-5256; Fax: 616-846-0630; Toll Free: 800-648-2312 x330 (phone/fax, retail & library orders); Edit Addr.: 1704 Eaton Dr., Grand Haven, MI 49417 USA (SAN 858-138X) Toll Free: 800-648-2312 x330; Imprints:* Audible Studios on Brilliance Audio (AudibleStudios); Candlewick on Brilliance Audio (Candlewick)
E-mail: sales@brillianceaudio.com; customerservice@brillianceaudio.com; jcraig@brilliancepublishing.com
Web site: http://www.brilliancepublishing.com
Dist(s): **Bolinda Publishing, Inc.**
Bookazine Co., Inc.
Diamond Bk. Distributors
Findaway World, LLC
Follett School Solutions
Readerlink Distribution Services, LLC.

Brimax Books Ltd. (GBR) *(978-0-86112; 978-0-900195; 978-0-904494; 978-1-85854; 978-1-904952; 978-1-84656; 978-1-905279)* *Dist. by* **Byeway Bks.**

Brimming Cup, The, *(978-0-9991525)* 2266 Broadwater Dr., Jacksonville, FL 32225 USA Tel 904-707-7914
E-mail: brimmingcup@gmail.com
Web site: www.thebrimmingcup.com.

BriMoral Stories, *(978-0-578-41528-4; 978-0-578-43173-4; 978-0-578-43530-5; 978-0-578-45825-0; 978-1-7332425; 978-1-953581)* 1977 S. Saint Michael Dr., Tucson, AZ 85713 USA Tel 520-891-1149
E-mail: brian.determined.morales.8@gmail.com
Dist(s): **Ingram Content Group.**

Brimstone Fiction *Imprint of* **LPC**

BrimWood Pr., *(978-0-9770704)* 1941 Larsen Dr., Camino, CA 95709 USA Tel 530-644-7538; Fax: 530-647-9208; *Imprints:* Tools For Young Historians (Tools YngHist)
E-mail: marcia@brimwoodpress.com
Web site: http://www.brimwoodpress.com.

Brindle Pr., *(978-0-9749080; 978-0-692-99148-0)* 14121 Cardinal Ln., Houston, TX 77079 USA
Web site: http://www.brindlepress.com.

Brinkley Bks., Inc., *(978-0-9793288)* P.O. Box 1753, Healdsburg, CA 95448 USA
E-mail: laura@brinkleybooks.com
Web site: http://www.brinkleybooks.com
Dist(s): **BCH Fulfillment & Distribution.**

Brinsights, LLC, *(978-0-9799454; 978-0-615-31228-6; 978-0-615-36380-6)* 141 E. 88th St., New York, NY 10128-2248 USA (SAN 854-848X)
E-mail: geri@brinsights.net; linaperl@gmail.com
Web site: http://www.mygreensanta.com.

BRIO Pr., *(978-0-9817830; 978-0-9819290; 978-0-9826687; 978-1-937061)* 12 S. Sixth St., No.1250, Minneapolis, MN 55402 USA (SAN 856-5376) Tel 612-746-8800; Fax: 612-746-8811; Toll Free: 888-333-7979
E-mail: tmiller@briobooks.com
Web site: http://www.briobooks.com.

BRIO Publishing *See* **BRIO Pr.**

Brisance Bks. Group, *(978-1-944194)* 21001 N. Tatum Blvd, Phoenix, AZ 85050 USA Tel 480-390-2574; Fax: 480-419-9087
E-mail: mgambetta@monagambetta.com
Dist(s): **Ingram Publisher Services**
Ingram Academic
Two Rivers Distribution.

Briscoe, Nicole , *(978-0-578-17838-7)* 8302 Widgeon Place, Laurel, MD 20724 USA.

Brisk Pr., *(978-0-9770885; 978-0-9799254; 978-0-9832758; 978-0-9899895; 978-0-9966774; 978-0-9987907; 978-1-7343038; 979-8-9884113)* 10 Denim Dr, Wappingers Falls, NY 12590 USA
E-mail: brisk.press@gmail.com
Web site: http://www.briskpress.com
Dist(s): **Bella Distribution**
Two Rivers Distribution.

Bristol Hse., Ltd., *(978-0-917851; 978-1-885224)* P.O. Box 4020, Anderson, IN 46013 USA (SAN 225-4638) Tel 765-644-0856; Fax: 765-622-1045; Toll Free: 800-451-7323.

Bristol Park Bks., *(978-0-88486)* 252 W. 38th St. Suite 206, New York, NY 10018-5806 USA (SAN 859-533X)
Dist(s): **National Bk. Network**
Sterling Publishing Co., Inc.

Bristol Publishing Co., *(978-0-9755667)* P.O. Box 3103, San Angelo, TX 76902-3103 USA Do not confuse with Bristal Publishing Company in San Jacinto, CA
E-mail: bristolpublishing@sbcglobal.net
Dist(s): **Alliance Bk. Co.**

Britannica Bks. *Imprint of* **What on Earth Books**

Britannica Educational Publishing *Imprint of* **Rosen Publishing Group, Inc., The**

Brite Bks., *(978-0-9726363)* Orders Addr.: P.O. Box 801, Ortonville, MI 48462 USA; Edit Addr.: 1580 Duck Creek Ln., Ortonville, MI 48462 USA
E-mail: twebb@britebooks.org; twebb@tawglobal.com
Web site: http://www.britebooks.org; http://www.tawglobal.com; http://www.promises-for-life.com.

Brite International *See* **Brite Music, Inc.**

Brite Music, Inc., *(978-0-944803)* Orders Addr.: P.O. Box 65688-0688, Salt Lake City, UT 84165 USA (SAN 244-948X) Tel 801-263-9191; Fax: 801-263-9198; Edit Addr.: P.O. Box 171076, Salt Lake City, UT 84117-1076 USA (SAN 244-9498)
Web site: http://www.britemusic.com.

Brite Pr., *(978-0-9743185)* 3447 Countyline Rd., Chalfont, PA 18914-3625 USA Tel 215-822-1659; Fax: 305-402-8163
E-mail: tntdns@aol.com.

Britfield *Imprint of* **Devonfield**

British Library, Historical Print Editions *Imprint of* **Creative Media Partners, LLC**

British Library, The (GBR) *(978-0-7123) Dist. by* **IPG Chicago.**

Britt Allcroft Productions, *(978-0-9743690; 978-0-9767139; 978-0-9793343)* 133 Wadsworth Ave., Santa Monica, CA 90405 USA Tel 310-428-4033; Fax: 310 392 9769
E-mail: holly_wright@verizon.net
Web site: http://www.brittallcroftproductions.com.

Brittany's Bks, *(978-0-9778796)* 1736 Crest Pl., Colorado Spgs, CO 80911-1110 USA
E-mail: admin@brittanysbooks.com
Web site: http://www.brittanysbooks.com.

Britton & Case Prs., *(978-0-9980056)* 10871 S. Durand Rd, Durand, MI 48429 USA.

Broad Creek Pr., *(978-0-9837148; 978-0-9904662)* P.O. Box 43, Mount Airy, NC 27030 USA Tel 336-473-7256
Dist(s): **BookBaby.**

Broad View Publishing, *(978-0-9815384)* P.O. Box 2726, Bristol, CT 06011-2726 USA Tel 860-793-7618
E-mail: info@broadviewpublishing.com; publicity@painisnotadisease.com
Web site: http://www.broadviewpublishing.com; http://www.painisnotadisease.com.

Broadcast Quality Productions, Inc., *(978-0-9716136)* 3199 Nottaway Ct., Atlanta, GA 30341 USA Tel 404-292-7777 (phone/fax)
Web site: http://www.bqproductions.com.

Broader Horizon Books *See* **Littletonhouse Publishing**

Broadnax, Cassandra A.L., *(978-0-9771608)* 295 Pannel Rd., Reidsville, NC 27320 USA.

BroadStreet Publishing, *(978-1-4245)* Orders Addr.: 2745 Chicory Rd., Racine, WI 53403 USA (SAN 990-2635); Edit Addr.: 8646 Eagle Creek Cir. Suite 210, Savage, MN 55378 USA (SAN 256-8535) Tel 952-300-6250
E-mail: michelle.winger@broadstreetpublishing.com
Web site: http://www.BROADSTREETPUBLISHING.COM.

BroadSword Comics/ Jim Balent Studios, *(978-0-9745367)* P.O. Box 596, Brodheadsville, PA 18322 USA
E-mail: tarot@jimbalent.com
Web site: http://www.jimbalent.com.

Broadway Bks. *Imprint of* **Crown Publishing Group, The**

Broadway Cares, *(978-0-9754840)* 165 W. 46th St., 13th Flr., New York, NY 10036 USA Tel 212-840-0770; Fax: 212-840-0551
E-mail: viola@bcefa.org.

Broadway Play Publishing Inc, *(978-0-88145; 979-8-88856)* 148 W. 80th St., New York, NY 10024 USA (SAN 260-1699)
E-mail: cwdg@broadwayplaypublishing.com; info@broadwayplaypublishing.com; michael@broadwayplaypublishing.com
Web site: https://www.broadwayplaypublishing.com
Dist(s): **Follett School Solutions**
MyiLibrary.

Broadway Play Publishing, Incorporated *See* **Broadway Play Publishing Inc**

Broccoli Bks. *Imprint of* **Broccoli International USA, Inc.**

Broccoli International USA, Inc., *(978-1-932480; 978-1-59741)* Orders Addr.: P.O. Box 66078, Los Angeles, CA 90066 USA Tel 310-815-0600; Fax: 310-815-0660; Edit Addr.: 11806 Gorham Ave. Apt. 4, Los Angeles, CA 90049-5446 USA; *Imprints:* Broccoli Books (Broccoli Bks)
E-mail: info@broccolibooks.com; ardith@bro-usa.com; wholesale@broccolibooks.com; books@animegamers.com; wholesale@bro-usa.com
Web site: http://www.bro-usa.com; http://www.broccolibooks.com; http://www.synch-point.com; http://www.boysenberrybooks.com
Dist(s): **Diamond Bk. Distributors**
Simon & Schuster, Inc.

Brockhaus, F. A., GmbH (DEU) *(978-3-325; 978-3-7653) Dist. by* **Intl Bk Import.**

Brodie, Richard *See* **Firebreak Publishing Co.**

Brogan, Kelly MD, *(978-0-692-17060-1)* 3975 Crawford Ave., Miami, FL 33133 USA Tel 646-418-4934
E-mail: drbrogan@kellybroganmd.com.

Broken Bread Publishing, *(978-0-9769464)* 6417 S. Iris Way, Littleton, CO 80123-3135 USA
E-mail: books@brokenbreadpublishing.com
Web site: http://www.brokenbreadpublishing.com
Dist(s): **Spring Arbor Distributors, Inc.**

Broken Leg Bks., *(978-0-692-45627-9)* 10021 Briley Way, Villa Park, CA 92861 USA Tel 1-714-872-7969
Dist(s): **CreateSpace Independent Publishing Platform.**

Broken Oak Publishing, *(978-0-9795020)* P.O. Box 255, Ridgetop, TN 37152 USA.

Broken Shackle Publishing, International, *(978-0-9759908)* P.O. Box 20312, Piedmont, CA 94620 USA
E-mail: jstickmon@msn.com.

Bromell Inc, *(978-0-692-86950-5)* 22406 Friar St., WOODLAND HILLS, CA 91367 USA Tel 714-363-2666
E-mail: jeffwcrawford5+LVP0003580@gmail.com; jeffwcrawford5+LVP0003580@gmail.com.

Bromwell Bks., *(978-0-9753345)* 2500 E. Fourth Ave., Denver, CO 80206 USA Tel 303-388-5969; Fax: 303-764-7544
E-mail: steven_replogle@dpsk12.org
Web site: http://bromwell.dpsk12.org.

Bronwen Publishing, *(978-0-9779267)* 4 Colchester Pl., Suite 4A, Newtown, PA 18940 USA (SAN 850-6426) Tel 215-968-2204
Web site: http://www.bronwenpublishing.com
Dist(s): **Follett School Solutions.**

Bronwynn Pr., LLC, *(978-0-9821404; 978-0-9848487)* P.O. Box 297, Troy, NY 12182 USA Tel 518-328-7891
E-mail: bell@bronwynnpress.com
Web site: http://www.bronwynnpress.com; http://www.gappy.tv.

BronwynToffelson *See* **BronwynTollefson**

BronwynTollefson, *(978-1-7348886)* 4857 Jersey Ave N, Crystal, MN 55428 USA Tel 612-260-5944
E-mail: haudelevesque@hotmail.com.

Bronx Originals Books *See* **Daylight Bks.**

Brook Farm Bks., *(978-0-919761)* 479 U.S. Hwy. 1, P.O. Box 246, Bridgewater, ME 04735 USA (SAN 133-9095) Tel 506-375-4680 (phone/fax); Toll Free: 877-375-4680
E-mail: jean@brookfarmbook.com; jean@brookfarmbooks.com
Dist(s): **Brodart Co.**
ebrary, Inc.

Brooke, Karen L., *(978-0-692-35518-3; 978-0-692-35520-6; 978-0-692-38746-7; 978-0-692-57377-8; 978-0-692-59152-9; 978-0-692-62381-7; 978-0-692-81452-9; 978-0-692-94837-8; 978-0-692-95735-6; 978-0-578-45818-2; 978-0-578-53755-9; 978-0-578-87615-3; 979-8-9861612)* 214 Waterloo St., Warrenton, VA 20186 USA Tel 5402167969
Web site: http://katlynnbrooke.com/
Dist(s): **CreateSpace Independent Publishing Platform.**

BrookeBubble, *(978-0-692-11628-9)* 1310 W. Huron St., Ann Arbor, MI 48103 USA Tel 219-508-0352
E-mail: i.am.brandon.patterson@gmail.com
Web site: www.BrookeBubble.com.

Brookehaven Publishing, *(978-0-9844867; 978-1-940905)* P.O. Box 352, Rocklin, CA 95677 USA
E-mail: info@brookehavenpublishing.com
Web site: http://www.brookehavenpublishing.com
Dist(s): **Lulu Pr., Inc.**
Smashwords.

Brookes, Paul H. Publishing Company Incorporated *See* **Brookes Publishing**

Brookes Publishing, *(978-0-933716; 978-1-55766; 978-1-59857; 978-1-68125)* Orders Addr.: P.O. Box 10624, Baltimore, MD 21285-0624 USA (SAN 212-730X) Tel 410-337-9580; Fax: 410-337-8539; Toll Free: 800-638-3775 (customer service/ordering/billing/fulfillment); Edit Addr.: 409 Washington Ave., Suite 500, Baltimore, MD 21204 USA (SAN 666-6485)
E-mail: custserv@brookespublishing.com
Web site: http://www.brookespublishing.com
Dist(s): **Firebrand Technologies**
Follett School Solutions.

Brookfield Reader, Inc., The, *(978-0-9660172; 978-1-930093)* 137 Peyton Rd., Sterling, VA 20165-5605 USA (SAN 299-4445)
Dist(s): **Book Wholesalers, Inc.**
Brodart Co.
Quality Bks., Inc.

Brooklyn Botanic Garden, *(978-0-945352; 978-1-889538)* 1000 Washington Ave., Brooklyn, NY 11225-1099 USA (SAN 203-1094) Tel 718-623-7200; 718-625-5838; Fax: 718-622-7839; 718-857-2430
E-mail: ripodell@bbg.org
Web site: http://www.bbg.org
Dist(s): **Sterling Publishing Co., Inc.**

Brooklyn Girl Bks., *(978-1-7320936)* 49 Orchardhill Rd, Boston, MA 02130 USA Tel 617-524-5367
E-mail: randysusanmeyers@gmail.com
Web site: www.randysusanmeyers.com.

Brooklyn Pubs., *(978-1-930961; 978-1-931000; 978-1-931805; 978-1-932404; 978-1-60003; 978-1-64479)* Orders Addr.: P.O. Box 248, Cedar Rapids, IA 52406 USA
E-mail: orders@brookpub.com; customerservice@brookpub.com
Web site: http://https://www.brookpub.com
Dist(s): **Follett School Solutions.**

Brooklyn Publishing, *(978-0-692-96601-3; 978-0-692-12500-7; 978-0-578-49099-1; 978-0-578-60438-1; 978-0-578-69347-7; 978-0-578-84462-6; 978-0-578-84464-0; 978-0-578-90608-9; 979-8-218-02825-1)* 11627 Dublin Grafton Dr, Riverview, FL 33647 USA Tel 646-529-9300
E-mail: karlin@brooklynpublishing.com
Dist(s): **Ingram Content Group.**

Brooklyn Publishing Company *See* **Brooklyn Pubs.**

Brooks & Brooks, *(978-0-9682530)* 5510 Owensmouth Ave. Apt. 102, Woodland Hls, CA 91367-7011 USA
E-mail: runningbrooks@hotmail.com.

Brooks, Andree Aelion, *(978-0-9702700)* 15 Hitchcock Rd., Westport, CT 06880 USA Tel 203-226-9834; Fax: 203-226-0814
E-mail: andreebrooks@hotmail.com.

†**Brooks/Cole,** *(978-0-12; 978-0-15; 978-0-314; 978-0-534; 978-0-8185; 978-1-56527; 978-0-495)* Div. of Thomson Learning, Orders Addr.: 7625 Empire Dr., Florence, KY 41042-2978 USA Tel 606-525-2230; Toll Free: 800-354-9706 (orders); Edit Addr.: 511 Forest Lodge Rd., Pacific Grove, CA 93950 USA (SAN 202-3369) Tel 831-373-0728; Fax: 831-375-6414; 10 Davis Dr., Belmont, CA 94002 Tel 650-595-2350
E-mail: info@brookscole.com
Web site: http://www.brookscole.com; http://www.duxbury.com
Dist(s): **CENGAGE Learning**
Houghton Mifflin Harcourt Trade & Reference Pubs.; *CIP.*

Brooks/Cole Publishing Company *See* **Brooks/Cole**

Brookshire Pubns., Inc., *(978-1-880976)* 200 Hazel St., Lancaster, PA 17603 USA Tel 717-392-1321; Fax: 717-392-2078
E-mail: carla@brookshireprinting.com.

Brookstone Pr., *(978-0-578-76410-8; 979-8-9892102)* 1461 Brookstone Rd., Charleston, WV 25314 USA Tel 304-543-3359
E-mail: rachelm19@yahoo.com.

Brookstone Publishing Group, *(978-1-949856; 978-1-960814)* 10289 Colonial Hwy, Evington, VA 24550 USA Tel 434-851-2801
E-mail: andrew@brookstonecreativegroup.com; suzanne@suzyq4u.com; vincent@brookstonecreativegroup.com
Dist(s): **Iron Stream Media**
Whitaker Hse.

Brookteam Corp., *(978-0-9745864)* P.O. Box 276225, Boca Raton, FL 33427 USA Fax: 561-367-9976; Toll Free: 866-571-7878; *Imprints:* Shirt Tales (Shirt Tales)
E-mail: brookteam@worldnet.att.net
Web site: http://www.brookteam.com.

Broomstick Engine LLC, *(978-0-692-82451-1)* 850 Morning Sun Dr., Encinitas, CA 92024 USA Tel 604-671-5252
E-mail: spencer@broomstickengine.com
Web site: www.alittleradical.com.

Brophy, Doris Anne, *(978-0-9745232)* 90 Bingham Ave., Rumson, NJ 07760 USA Tel 732-345-7276
E-mail: dambrophy@yahoo.com.

Broqueville Publishing, Inc., *(978-0-9669024; 978-0-9719413)* 1260 Logan Ave., Suite B3, Costa Mesa, CA 92626 USA (SAN 255-0083) Tel 714-624-6441; Fax: 714-668-9972
E-mail: bookorders@broqueville.com
Web site: http://www.broqueville.com.

Brosen Bks., *(978-0-9830359)* 124 Wave, Laguna Beach, CA 92651 USA Tel 949-374-4127
E-mail: bryan@brosencreative.com
Web site: www.brosenbooks.com
Dist(s): **Follett School Solutions.**

Brosquil Edicions, S.L. (ESP) *(978-84-95620; 978-84-96154; 978-84-9795) Dist. by* **Lectorum Pubns.**

Bross Publishing, *(978-0-9763561)* 168 Island Pond Rd., No. 1, Manchester, NH 03109 USA (SAN 256-355X) Tel 603-623-2503 (phone/fax)
E-mail: brosspublishing@sunnyfla.us.

Brother Maynard Publishing, *(978-0-615-55017-6; 978-0-578-40603-9)* 6879 Blue Ridge Dr., Belmont, MI 49306 USA Do not confuse with Brother Maynard Publishing in Crystal River, FL
Dist(s): **CreateSpace Independent Publishing Platform**
Dummy Record Do Not USE!!!!.

BrotherBiz Publishing, *(978-0-615-47658-2)* 96 School St., Lexington, MA 02421 USA Tel 781-862-3962
E-mail: BrotherBiz@earthlink.net.

Brothers Epps, The *See* **Unified Future**

Brothers N Publishing Corp., *(978-0-9886272)* 565 S. Mason Rd. No. 204, Katy, TX 77450 USA Tel 832-472-8200
E-mail: brothersnbooks@gmail.com.

Brotman-Marshfield Curriculums, *(978-0-9762568)* 22 Howard St., Newton, MA 02458 USA Tel 617-332-5616; Fax: 617-332-9679
E-mail: brotmanco@aol.com.

Broviak Publishing, *(978-0-9897522)* 10203 holly berry Cir., fishers, IN 46038 USA Tel 317-776-0421
E-mail: broviak@evilteacher.com.

Brown, Ana, *(978-0-692-84467-0; 978-0-692-07004-8; 978-1-7320214)* 868 Pk. View No. 5, Mountain view, CA 95054 USA Tel 305-772-0671; Fax: 305-772-0671
E-mail: anadvbrown@gmail.com.

Brown & Duncan Brand *See* **ELOHAI International Publishing & Media**

Brown & Lowe Bks., *(978-1-7322303; 978-1-7355048)* 6564 Loisdale Ct No. 600, Springfield, VA 22150 USA (SAN 991-4943) Tel 703-408-0485
E-mail: denise@brownlowebooks.com; info@brownlowebooks.com
Web site: www.brownlowebooks.com.

Brown Barn Bks., *(978-0-9746481; 978-0-9768126; 978-0-9798824)* Div. of Pictures of Record, Inc., Orders Addr.: Editorial@brownbarnbooks.com 119 Kettle Creek Rd., Weston, CT 06883 USA Tel 203-227-3387; Fax: 203-222-9673
E-mail: editorial@brownbarnbooks.com
Web site: http://www.brownbarnbooks.com
Dist(s): **BookBaby**
Follett School Solutions.

Brown Bear Books, *(978-0-9670861)* 325 High St., Santa Cruz, CA 95060 USA Tel 831-457-1135
E-mail: brwnbear@sasquatch.com.

Brown Bear Bks., *(978-1-933834; 978-1-936333)* PMB 20, 6890 E. Sunrise Dr., Suite 120, Tucson, AZ 85750-0739 USA
E-mail: info@brownreference.com
Dist(s): **Black Rabbit Bks.**
Creative Co., The.

Brown, Beatrice W, *(978-0-9983360)* 4664 Clifden Ave, Grovetown, GA 30813 USA Tel 706-350-5400
E-mail: beabrown2580@gmail.com.

Brown, Beth *See* **Divot & Swish Publishing**

Brown Bks. *Imprint of* **Olivo, Andy**

Brown Bks. Kids *Imprint of* **Brown Books Publishing Group**

Brown, Bonnie M., *(978-0-9624705)* 548 Saint Johns Pl., Franklin, TN 37064-8901 USA
E-mail: bonnibear@aol.com.

Brown Books Publishing Group, *(978-0-9713265; 978-0-9744597; 978-0-9753907; 978-1-933285; 978-1-934812; 978-1-61254; 978-1-948307)* 16250 Knoll Trail Dr. Ste 205, Dallas, TX 75248 USA Tel 972-381-0009; Fax: 972-248-4336; *Imprints:* Brown Books Kids (MYID_D_BROWN B)
E-mail: brittany.griffith@brownbooks.com
Web site: https://www.brownbookskids.com; https://www.brownbooks.com; https://www.thep3press.com
Dist(s): **BookBaby**
Brown Books Publishing Group
Follett School Solutions
Itasca Bks.
Ingram Content Group
Open Road Integrated Media, Inc.

Brown Books Small Press *See* **Small Pr., The**

Brown Brainy Brilliant Bks. *Imprint of* **InkDrops Publishing**

Brown County Historical Society, *(978-0-9641499)* Orders Addr.: P.O. Box 1411, Green Bay, WI 54305-1411 USA Tel 920-437-1840; Fax: 920-455-4518; Edit Addr.: 1008 S. Monroe Ave., Green Bay, WI 54301-3206 USA Do not confuse with Brown County Historical Society, Nashville, IN, New Ulm, MN
E-mail: bchs@netnet.net
Web site: http://www.browncohistoricalsoc.org.

Brown County Historical Society, *(978-0-9765095; 978-0-9964029)* 2 N. Broadway, New Ulm, MN 56073 USA Fax: 507-354-1068 Do not confuse with Brown County Historical Society in Green Bay, WI
E-mail: director@browncountyhistorymn.org.

Brown, Darin, *(978-0-9995031)* 81 Daniel Ward Rd, PO Box 459, Madison, NH 03849 USA Tel 603-367-9266; Fax: 603-367-9266
E-mail: darin@darincbrown.com
Web site: darincbrown.com.

Brown, David Book Company, The *See* **Casemate Academic**

Brown Dog Bks., *(978-0-9721967)* P.O. Box 2196, Flemington, NJ 08822 USA
E-mail: darhosta@mac.com
Web site: http://www.browndogbooks.com
Dist(s): **Book Wholesalers, Inc.**
Brodart Co.
Follett Media Distribution
Follett School Solutions.

Brown, Donald R., *(978-1-7326542)* 2345 185th Ct. Apt. 17, Lansing, IL 60438 USA Tel 708-953-2815
E-mail: Donnieb1087@gmail.com.

Brown Girls Bks., LLC, *(978-1-944359)* 107 Terrell Dr., Rolesville, NC 27571 USA Tel 919-909-8038
E-mail: jacquelinthomas@gmail.com
Dist(s): **INscribe Digital.**

Brown Girls Publishing *Imprint of* **INscribe Digital**

Brown, Harold *See* **Brown&Matthews**

Brown, Kathleen, *(978-0-9796063)* P.O. Box 1920, Clemmons, NC 27012 USA (SAN 853-8719) Tel 336-778-0699
E-mail: rbrown20221@bellsouth.net.

Brown, Kawani, *(978-0-9971763)* 1017 Chestnut ave., Long Beach, CA 90813 USA Tel 909-913-0260
E-mail: nahbexpo@gmail.com.

Brown, Keith, *(978-0-578-47285-0; 978-0-578-47852-4; 978-0-578-48877-6; 978-0-578-69989-9;*

978-0-578-69990-5) 24196 Andover, Dearborn Heights, MI 48125 USA Tel 313-418-6932
E-mail: keith@keithperrybrown.com
Dist(s): **Ingram Content Group.**

Brown, Linda P., *(978-0-9989128)* 481 Guilford Ave, Claremont CA, CA 91711 USA Tel 310-701-7409
E-mail: info@lindapbrown.com
Web site: lindapbrown.com.

Brown, Nielsen, *(978-0-9725581)* Orders Addr.: P.O. Box 4174 , Estes Park, CO 80517 USA
E-mail: kristinnielsen@msn.com.

Brown, Pat Dr, *(978-0-9859551)* 1507 E. 53rd St. No. 443, Chicago, IL 60615 USA Tel 312-371-7949
E-mail: drpatbrown@live.com.

Brown, P.C., *(978-0-578-52176-3; 978-0-578-23087-0)* 30 N Gould St Suite R, Sheridan, WY 82801 USA Tel 757-618-0712
E-mail: moonrisingauthor@gmail.com
Web site: http://pcbrownauthor.com.

Brown, Samuel E., *(978-0-9770372)* P.O. Box 7009, Jackson, MS 39282 USA Tel 601-540-5470
E-mail: pcsandc@hotmail.com.

Brown Spotted Dog Publishing, *(978-1-7321250)* 6327 N. 126th St., Enid, OK 73701 USA Tel 580-554-5995
E-mail: lbenkendorf@gmail.com.

Brown Tones Publishing, *(978-0-9840050)* PO Box. 97322, Tacoma, WA 98497 USA Tel 253-238-3642
E-mail: browntonesproductions@gmail.com
Web site: www.browntonespublishing.com.

Brown, William N. Jr., *(978-0-692-96477-4; 979-8-218-25746-0; 979-8-9890577)* 8728 Potomac Blvd, Charlotte, NC 28216 USA Tel 704-779-8342; Fax: 704-779-8342
E-mail: wnbcreative@yahoo.com.

Brown&Matthews, *(978-0-9759370)* 2923 E. Michigan St., Orlando, FL 32806 USA (SAN 256-2030)
E-mail: jkmatthews@cfl.rr.com
Web site: http://www.cafepress.com/sitm; http://www.janetmatthews.com.

Brownell, F. & Son, Pubs., *(978-0-9767409; 978-0-9789127)* P.O. Box 76, Montezuma, IA 50171 USA
Web site: http://www.brownells.com.

Brownian Bee Pr., *(978-0-9789688)* 37574 Dew Drop Rd., Lanesboro, MN 55949 USA
E-mail: info@brownianbee.com
Web site: http://www.brownianbee.com
Dist(s): **Unique Bks., Inc.**

Brownlee, Jodie *See* **Brightspark**

Brownstone Monkey Productions, Inc., *(978-0-9785773)* 55 W. 84th St., No. 9, New York, NY 10024-1002 USA Tel 212-933-4168; Fax: 212-228-6149
E-mail: nicole@brownstonemonkey.com; kflore@nyc.rr.com
Web site: http://brownstonemonkey.com; http://lenithepug.com.

BRP Publishing Group, *(978-0-9801506; 978-1-935460; 978-1-941295)* P.O. Box 822674, Vancouver, WA 98682 USA
E-mail: publisher@nitisbooks.com; publisher@barkingrainpress.org
Web site: http://www.nitisbooks.com; http://www.barkingrainpress.org
Dist(s): **CreateSpace Independent Publishing Platform**
Ingram Content Group
Mackin Educational Resources
OverDrive, Inc.

Brujo Film Production *See* **Pascualina Producciones S.A.**

Brumby Kids, *(978-1-63998)* 30 N Gould St STE, Sheridan, WY 82801 USA Tel 631-268-0532
E-mail: max.osterhagen11@gmail.com; arganesciuc.mihai@yahoo.com.

Bruno & Brown Pr., *(978-1-7321238)* 8949 Clairton Ct., Las Vegas, NV 89117 USA Tel 702-504-6354
E-mail: sunshinegbruno@gmail.com.

Bruno, Elizabeth *See* **Uitti, Daniel**

Brunson Publishing, *(978-0-9758614)* Orders Addr.: P.O. Box 1133, Alamogordo, NM 88310 USA Tel 706-367-1334
E-mail: oldmaid4jesus@yahoo.com; tim@teenpact.com
Web site: http://www.oldmaidministries.com; http://www.teenpact.com.

Brunswick Publishing Corp., *(978-0-931494; 978-1-55618)* 593 Southlake Blvd., Richmond, VA 23236-3092 USA (SAN 211-6332)
E-mail: brunswickbooks@verizon.net; info@brunswickbooks.com
Web site: http://www.brunswickbooks.com/.

Bruño, Editorial (ESP) *(978-84-216) Dist. by* **Lectorum Pubns.**

Bruño, Editorial (ESP) *(978-84-216) Dist. by* **Dist Plaza Mayor.**

Brush Creek Publishing, *(978-0-692-75888-5)* 6690 Little Galilee Rd., CLINTON, IL 61727 USA Tel 217-219-0323.

Bryan House Publishers, Incorporated *See* **ECS Learning Systems, Inc.**

Bryan, Tracy Publishing, *(978-0-692-70088-4; 978-0-692-70091-4; 978-0-692-71069-2; 978-0-692-81614-1; 978-0-692-83014-7; 978-0-692-83153-3; 978-0-578-41015-9; 978-0-578-41016-6; 978-0-578-41017-3)* 2886 rickenbacker trail, PORT ORANGE, FL 32128 USA Tel 386-299-5310.

Bryan-Kennedy Entertainment, LLC, *(978-0-615-34098-2; 978-0-615-34699-1; 978-0-9885358)* PO Box 1561, Santa Rosa Beach, FL 32459 USA Tel 615-405-9939
E-mail: mackennedy@mac.com
Web site: http://www.Bryan-Kennedy.com.

Bryant, Makayla, *(978-0-578-66751-5; 978-0-578-67667-8; 978-1-7352421)* 103 Fallow Way, Bastrop, TX 78602 USA Tel 512-988-7078
E-mail: makbryant88@gmail.com.

Bryars, Bart, *(978-0-692-82963-9)* 2521 Piedmont Rd. NE #2432, ATLANTA, GA 30324 USA Tel 917-251-0463
E-mail: jeffwcrawford5+LVP0003234@gmail.com; jeffwcrawford5+LVP0003234@gmail.com.

Bryce Cullen Publishing, *(978-1-935752)* 510 MONROE ST STE 201, HOBOKEN, NJ 07030 USA Tel 201-888-8570
E-mail: davidgettis@brycecullen.com
Web site: http://www.brycecullen.com
Dist(s): **Ingram Content Group.**

BRYN WILLIAMS LLC *See* **ALCHEMY RANCH STUDIOS LLC**

Brynestad, Lea, *(978-0-692-10001-1)* 906 Sawyer Pl., Stillwater, MN 55082 USA Tel 651-275-1345
E-mail: dlbrynestad@gmail.com
Dist(s): **Ingram Content Group.**

Bryson Taylor Press *See* **Bryson Taylor Publishing**

Bryson Taylor Publishing, *(978-0-9773738; 978-0-9841934; 978-0-9882940; 978-0-9963867; 979-8-9855398)* Div. of Bryson Taylor Inc., 199 New County Rd., Saco, ME 04072 USA (SAN 257-4403) Tel 207-838-2146
E-mail: deb@brysontaylor.com
Web site: http://www.brysontaylor.com.

Brzamo Publishing, *(978-0-9743580)* 887 Richart Ln., Greenwood, IN 46142 USA.

Bsimps Productions LLC, *(978-0-578-48467-9)* 3415 Lilac Ln., Rowlett, TX 75089 USA Tel 214-448-7927
E-mail: emailbillysimpson@gmail.com.

B'Squeak Productions, *(978-0-9746782)* P.O. Box 151, Menlo Park, CA 94026-0151 USA
E-mail: rights@bsqueak.com
Web site: http://www.bsqueak.com.

btb, *(978-1-63652)* 600 broadway, Ste 200 No. 2036, albany, NY 12207 USA Tel 516-402-3325
E-mail: bthebookcase@gmail.com.

BTH CREATIONS, LLC, *(978-0-9995736)* 3539 MULBERRY WAY, Duluth, GA 30096 USA Tel 678-665-2225
E-mail: drkelahenry@gmail.com.

BTSena Pubns., *(978-0-692-20521-1; 978-0-692-78537-9; 978-0-692-79943-7; 978-0-692-90381-0; 978-0-692-91765-7)* 2703 N Northacres Dr., Hobbs, NM 88240 USA Tel 5754411649
Dist(s): **CreateSpace Independent Publishing Platform.**

B*tween Productions, Inc., *(978-0-9746587; 978-0-9758511; 978-1-933566)* 1666 Massachusetts Ave., Suite 17, Lexington, MA 02420 USA Tel 781-863-8228; Fax: 781-863-8338; *Imprints:* Beacon Street Girls (B Street Girls)
E-mail: kblais@btweenproductions.com
Web site: http://www.beaconstreetgirls.com.

BTWEYL *Imprint of* **Bks. That Will Enhance Your Life**

Bubble Gum Pr., *(978-0-9729833; 978-0-9839907)* 1420 N. State St., Aberdeen, SD 57401-2167 USA
E-mail: bmehrmantraut@msn.com
Web site: http://www.bubblegumpress.com
Dist(s): **Follett School Solutions.**

Buchbinder, Leonardo, *(978-0-9774044; 978-0-615-34717-2)* 8001 NW 84 Terr., Tamarac, FL 33321 USA Tel 954-261-9488
E-mail: mstenn5031@aol.com.

Bucher, Maryleigh, *(978-0-9908752)* 149 Whites Point Dr., Cookeville, TN 38506 USA Tel 931-349-0808
E-mail: mlkbucher@hotmail.com.

Buchmann, Jana, *(978-1-7354586; 978-1-954835)* 1 Spring Garden Dr., Madison, NJ 07940 USA Tel 201-400-8162
E-mail: buchmannjana@yahoo.com.

Buchonia Publishing, *(978-0-9635416)* Orders Addr.: P.O. Box 42492, Portland, OR 97242-0492 USA; Edit Addr.: 3714 SE 11th, Portland, OR 97202 USA
Dist(s): **Lulu Pr., Inc.**

BuchWyrm, LLC, *(978-1-7358371)* 341 Forest Cove Rd, Anderson, SC 29626 USA Tel 443-789-7578
E-mail: phoenix@buchwyrm.com
Web site: buchwyrm.com.

Buck Engineering Company, Incorporated, Lab-Volt Systems Division *See* **Lab-Volt Systems, Inc.**

Buck Publishing, *(978-0-9725912)* Orders Addr.: P.O. Box 12231, Roanoke, VA 24023-2231 USA Tel 540-985-0618 (phone/fax); Edit Addr.: 710 Ferdinand Ave., No. 9, Roanoke, VA 24016 USA Do not confuse with companies with the same or similar name in Birmingham, AL, Fairbanks, AK.

Buck Stop Publishing, *(978-1-7326890)* 3562 COLLONADE Dr., WELLINGTON, FL 33449 USA Tel 954-270-8771
E-mail: loriegivens@gmail.com
Web site: loriegivens.com.

Buckbeech Studios, *(978-0-9771494)* Orders Addr.: P.O. Box 430, Stanford, IN 47463-0430 USA Tel 812-369-6061; Edit Addr.: 30 Amberwood Pkwy., Ashland, OH 44805 USA
E-mail: publisher@buckbeech.com
Web site: http://www.buckbeech.com
Dist(s): **Follett School Solutions.**

Bucket Fillers, Inc. *See* **Cardinal Rule Pr.**

Bucket Fillosophy *Imprint of* **Cardinal Rule Pr.**

Bucket of Books *See* **Bimini Bks.**

Bucking Horse Bks., *(978-0-9844460; 978-1-7328753)* P.O. Box 8507, Missoula, MT 59807 USA
E-mail: collard@bigsky.net
Web site: http://www.buckinghorsebooks.com
Dist(s): **Mountain Pr. Publishing Co., Inc.**

Buckley, Barbara, *(978-0-692-89591-7; 978-0-578-74166-6)* 3416 Pebble Beach Dr., LAKE WORTH, FL 33467 USA Tel 561-868-5699
E-mail: babfla@aol.com
Dist(s): **Ingram Content Group.**

Buckley, Lakisha, *(978-1-7365288)* 29 Van Cott Ave, Hempstead, NY 11550 USA Tel 516-263-1245
E-mail: Praymrpraise@gmail.com.

Bucknell Univ. Pr., *(978-0-8387; 978-1-68448)* 6 Taylor Hall, Lewisburg, PA 17837 USA
E-mail: esm102@rutgers.edu
Web site: http://www.bucknell.edu/UniversityPress
Dist(s): **Associated Univ. Presses**
Baker & Taylor International
Chicago Distribution Ctr.
JSTOR
MyiLibrary
Rowman & Littlefield Publishers, Inc.
Rowman & Littlefield Unlimited Model
Rutgers Univ. Pr.
TextStream
Univ. of Chicago Pr. Distribution Clients
ebrary, Inc.

Bucks Enterprises — Services and Training Inc., *(978-0-692-62430-2; 978-0-692-70595-7; 978-0-692-82321-7; 978-0-692-88137-8; 978-0-692-88658-8; 978-0-692-92634-5; 978-0-578-51066-8)* 90444 Cty. Rd. H, Mitchell, NE 69357 USA Tel 308-641-4835; Toll Free: 308-641-4835
Dist(s): **CreateSpace Independent Publishing Platform.**

Buddha Baby Bks., *(978-0-9968660)* 113 Norfolk Ave SW No. 8, Roanoke, VA 24011 USA Tel 919-536-8715
E-mail: buddhababybooks@gmail.com.

Buddhapuss Ink LLC, *(978-0-9842035; 978-1-941523)* 4923 Mandavilla Way, Apex, NC 27539 USA; *Imprints:* Writer's Coffee Bar Press (MYID_L_WRITERS)
E-mail: MaryChris@TheBookTeam.com.

Buddha's Light Publications USA Corp, *(978-0-9715612; 978-0-9717495; 978-1-932293; 978-1-939596)* 3456 S. Glenmark Dr., Hacienda Heights, CA 91745 USA Tel 626-961-9697; 84 Margaret St., London, w1w 8td Tel 020-7636-8394; Fax: 020-7580-6220
E-mail: blpusacorp@gmail.com
Web site: http://www.blpusa.com
Dist(s): **Follett School Solutions.**

Buddha's Light Publishing *See* **Buddha's Light Publications USA Corp**

Buddhi Pubns., *(978-0-9644226)* Orders Addr.: P.O. Box 208, Canyon, CA 94516 USA Tel 510-376-7796; Fax: 510-376-3503; Edit Addr.: 35 Pinehurst Rd., Canyon, CA 94516 USA.

Buddhist Text Translation Society, *(978-0-88139; 978-0-917512; 978-1-60103; 978-0-88139-767-3; 978-1-64217)* Affil. of Dharma Realm Buddhist Assoc., Orders Addr.: 4951 Bodhi Way, Ukiah, CA 95482 USA Tel 707-462-0939; Fax: 707-462-0949; Edit Addr.: 4951 Bodhi Way, Ukiah, CA 95482 USA (SAN 281-3556) Tel 707-463-4977 (phone/fax)
E-mail: vajrawheel@gmail.com; heng.yin@drbu.edu; bttsonline@snetworking.com; jinjingshih@gmail.com; katherine.lam-hansard@drba.org
Web site: http://www.bttsonline.org; http://buddhisttexts.org
Dist(s): **Follett School Solutions.**

Buddies Publishing, LLC, *(978-1-946719)* 37263 Charter Oaks Blvd., Clinton Township, MI 48036 USA Tel 586-855-6400
E-mail: philpirkola@gmail.com
Web site: http://www.buddiespublishing.com.

Budding Artists, Inc., *(978-1-888108)* 222 Palisades Ave., Santa Monica, CA 90402-2734 USA.

Budding Family Publishing, *(978-0-9741882)* P.O. Box 2078, Manhattan Beach, CA 90267-2078 USA Fax: 310-374-1030
E-mail: renee@buddingfamily.com
Web site: http://www.buddingfamily.com.

BuddingRose Pubns., *(978-0-9915556; 978-1-7378094)* 15061 Calle Verano, Chino Hills, CA 91709 USA Tel 909-636-3448
E-mail: buddingrose.publications@gmail.com.

Buddy Bks. *Imprint of* **ABDO Publishing Co.**

Buddy Bks. Publishing, *(978-0-9799980; 978-1-934887)* P.O. Box 3354, Pinehurst, NC 28374 USA Tel 910-295-2876
E-mail: admin@buddybookspublishing.com
Web site: http://www.buddybookspublishing.com.

Buenaventura Pr., *(978-0-9766848; 978-0-9800039; 978-1-935443)* P.O. Box 23661, Oakland, CA 94623 USA
Web site: http://www.buenaventurapress.com
Dist(s): **D.A.P./Distributed Art Pubs.**

Buffalo Arts Publishing, *(978-0-9839170; 978-0-615-93179-1; 978-0-692-38985-0; 978-0-692-43404-8; 978-0-692-46782-4; 978-0-692-53862-3; 978-0-692-72347-0; 978-0-9978741; 978-1-950006)* 179 Greenfield Dr., Tonawanda, NY 14150 USA Tel 716-692-1042
E-mail: lkagelmacher@gmail.com; sales@buffaloartspublishing.com
Web site: http://www.buffaloartspublishing.com.

Buffalo Fine Arts Academy *See* **Buffalo Fine Arts/Albright-Knox Art Gallery**

†Buffalo Fine Arts/Albright-Knox Art Gallery, *(978-0-914782; 978-1-887457)* Albright-Knox Art Gallery, 1285 Elmwood Ave., Buffalo, NY 14222 USA (SAN 202-4845) Tel 716-882-8700; Fax: 716-882-1958
Dist(s): **D.A.P./Distributed Art Pubs.**; *CIP.*

Bug Bot Pr., *(978-0-9840740)* Orders Addr.: P.O. Box 1335 N. La Brea #2233, Hollywood, CA 90028 USA Fax: 323-908-4101
E-mail: bugbotpress@yahoo.com; taracontact@yahoo.com
Web site: http://www.bugbotpress.com
Dist(s): **Emerald Bk. Co.**

Bug Boy Bks., *(978-0-615-19036-5)* 2085 Kenneth St., Burton, MI 48529 USA
E-mail: nativeamericanandrew@yahoo.com; andrew@bugboyandy.com
Dist(s): **Lulu Pr., Inc.**

Bug Boy Publishing *See* **Bug Boy Bks.**

Bug Rhymes Bks., *(978-0-9845687)* P.O. Box 211, East Olympia, WA 98540 USA
E-mail: bugrhymesbooks@comcast.net
Web site: http://bugrhymesbooks.com
Dist(s): **Partners/West Book Distributors.**

BugaBk. llc, *(978-0-9888974)* 7667 Cahill Rd. Suite 100, Edina, MN 55439 USA Tel 952-943-1441
E-mail: dustinh@bugabook.com
Web site: www.bugabook.com.

BugBear Bks., *(978-0-9978669)* 2203 E 51st Ln, Spokane, WA 99223 USA Tel 206-240-9961
E-mail: guypace@me.com
Web site: guypace.com.

Bugeye Bks., *(978-0-9722249)* 10645 N. Tatum Blvd., Suite 200-246, Phoenix, AZ 85028 USA Tel 602-980-7101; Fax: 480-483-3460
E-mail: insightstudios@cox.net
Web site: http://www.bugeyebooks.com.

Buggs Books *See* **Mogul Comics**

Buhman, Ron, *(978-0-9747961)* Orders Addr.: , Aransas Pass, TX 78335 USA; Edit Addr.: P.O. Box P O Box 634, Aransas Pass, TX 78335 USA Tel 361-944-0671; Fax: 361-944-0671
E-mail: rkb919@juno.com
Web site: http://jam-packed-action.com.

Buie, Alphonso, *(978-0-692-09788-5; 978-1-7342183)* 42426 S. Marsuerite Way, Lancaster, CA 93536 USA Tel 573-353-0279
E-mail: alphonsoabuie@gmail.com.

Build Your Story, *(978-0-9748416)* Orders Addr.: P.O. Box 6003, Midlothian, VA 23112 USA Fax: 810-592-2479; Toll Free: 866-807-8679; Edit Addr.: 2212 Water Horse Ct., Midlothian, VA 23112 USA
E-mail: oscar@buildyourstory.com
Web site: http://www.buildyourstory.com.

Builders' Stone Publishing, LLC, *(978-0-9791504)* 6932 Sylvan Woods Dr., Sanford, FL 32771 USA (SAN 852-5994) Tel 407-549-5066
E-mail: pschoemann@broadandcassel.com
Web site: http://www.buildersstonepublishing.com.

Building Authors Publishing, *(978-0-578-56280-3; 978-0-578-77994-2)* 5114 Radnor Ct., Mayslanding, NJ 08330 USA Tel 443-819-9803
E-mail: info@nateevansjr.com.

Building Blocks, LLC, *(978-0-943452)* 38 W. 567 Brindlewood Ln., Elgin, IL 60123 USA (SAN 240-6063) Tel 847-742-1013; Fax: 847-742-1054 (orders); Toll Free: 800-233-2448 Do not confuse with companies with similar and same name in Madison,NJ, Westbury NY
E-mail: dick@bblocksonline.com
Web site: http://www.bblocksonline.com
Dist(s): **Gryphon Hse., Inc.**

Building Readers First, LLC, *(978-1-7372447)* 180 Kelli Ln. NW, Milledgeville, GA 31061 USA Tel 478-251-7779
E-mail: jemeria@buildingreadersfirst.com
Web site: www.buildingreadersfirst.com.

Building Wings LLC *See* **Building Wings LLC**

Building Wings LLC, *(978-1-893376; 978-1-58702; 978-1-4105)* 26799 W. Commerce Dr., Volo, IL 60073 USA Tel 847-238-8889; Fax: 847-740-7349
Web site: http://www.buildingwings.com.

Bukowski, Katie Lynn, *(978-0-692-97225-0; 978-0-692-98878-7; 978-0-692-07032-1; 978-0-692-15675-9)* 261 S Walnut St, Manteno, IL 60950 USA Tel 815-953-5073
E-mail: katie_bukowski@yahoo.com
Dist(s): **Ingram Content Group.**

Bulkeley, Amy, *(978-1-7344258)* 40 Tierney St, Cambridge, MA 02138 USA Tel 508-717-7187
E-mail: amytarb@gmail.com.

Bull & Brain Creative, *(978-1-7341119)* P.O. Box 507, Erie, CO 80516 USA Tel 206-779-6957
E-mail: seancarney@gmail.com
Web site: wedivided.us.

Bull, David Publishing, Inc., *(978-0-9649722; 978-1-893618; 978-1-935007)* 4250 E. Camelback Rd., Suite K150, Phoenix, AZ 85018 USA Tel 602-852-9500; Fax: 602-852-9503; Toll Free: 800-831-1758
E-mail: dbull@bullpublishing.com; info@bullpublishing.com; tmoore@bullpublishing.com
Web site: http://www.bullpublishing.com.

Bullard, Belinda *See* **A Blessed Heritage Educational Resources**

Bulldog Pr., *(978-0-9672710)* P.O. Box 620358, Woodside, CA 94062-0358 USA Tel 650-851-8218; Fax: 650-851-1753 Do not confuse with companies with the same name in Frankfort, IN, Whittier, CA
E-mail: dputnam555@aol.com
Web site: http://www.americanbuildogger.com.

Bullfrog Bks. *Imprint of* **Jump! Inc.**

BullsEye, LLC *See* **Hargrave Pr.**

Bull'sEye Publishing Co., *(978-1-890181)* Orders Addr.: P.O. Box 24024, Saint Simons Island, GA 31522 USA (SAN 299-3546) Tel 912-638-0110; Fax: 912-634-7974; Edit Addr.: 103 Driftwood Place, Saint Simons Island, GA 31522 USA
E-mail: revenson@bullseyepublishing.com
Web site: http://www.bullseyepublishing.com
Dist(s): **Brodart Co.**

Bumble Bee Bks., *(978-0-9914701)* 1804 Benodot St., Champaign, IL 61822 USA Tel 217-898-7835
E-mail: storytym@comcast.net.

Bumble Bee Publishing, *(978-0-9754342; 978-1-933982)* Div. of Bumble Bee Productions, Inc., Orders Addr.: 725 Watch Island Reach, Chesapeake, VA 23320 USA (SAN 256-1611) Tel 757-410-9409 (phone/fax); Toll Free: 866-782-9533 (phone/fax); Edit Addr.: P.O. Box 1757, Chesapeake, VA 23327-1757 USA (SAN 256-162X) Tel 747-410-9409; 5721 M St., Lincoln, NE 68510 USA (SAN 256-1638); *Imprints:* bPlus Books (bPlus Bks)
E-mail: buzz707@bbpmail.com
Web site: http://www.yesterdaywehadahurricane.com; http://www.bumblebeepublishing.com; http://www.rubyleethebumblebee.com; http://www.bumblebeeproductions.com; http://www.bplusbooks.com.

Bumples, *(978-0-9700952; 978-0-578-83575-4; 978-0-578-83751-2; 978-0-578-25468-5; 978-0-578-25649-8; 978-0-578-25661-0; 978-0-578-25848-5; 979-8-218-95241-9;*

Publisher Name Index

979-8-218-95309-6; 979-8-218-96314-9) 676 Post Rd., Darien, CT 06820-4717 USA; 61 Portrait Ln., Pawleys Island, SC 29585
E-mail: bumples2020@gmail.com
Web site: bumples.com.

Bumpy Pumpkin, (*978-0-9754696*) 3405 Heather Dr., Augusta, GA 30909 USA
Web site: http://www.bumpypumpkin.com.

Bundoran Pr. (CAN) (*978-0-9782052; 978-0-9877352; 978-1-927881; 978-0-9880674*) *Dist. by* **D C D.**

Bunim and Bannigan Ltd., (*978-1-933480*) PMB 157, 111 E. 14th St., New York, NY 10003-4103 USA
Web site: http://www.bunim&bannigan.com; http://www.bunimbannigan.com
Dist(s): **Itasca Bks.**

Bunker Hill Publishing, Inc., (*978-1-59373*) 285 River Rd., Piermont, NH 03779-3009 USA; 27 W. 20th St., New York, NY 10011
E-mail: mail@bunkerhillpublishing.com
Web site: http://www.bunkerhillpublishing.com
Dist(s): **Follett School Solutions**
Independent Pubs. Group
Midpoint Trade Bks., Inc.

Bunny & The Crocodile Pr., The, (*978-0-938572*) 1821 Glade Ct., Annapolis, MD 21403-1945 USA Tel 410-267-7432 (phone/fax); *Imprints*: Forest Woods Media Productions (Forest Woods Media)
E-mail: gracecav@comcast.net
Web site: http://www.members.aol.com/grace7623/grace.htm.

Bunnyfly's Big Bk. Machine, (*978-0-692-59823-8*) 77 So Lake Ave, Albany, NY 12203 USA Tel 518-426-8277
Web site: www.hellobunnyfly.com
Dist(s): **CreateSpace Independent Publishing Platform.**

Bunnyone Bks., (*978-0-692-11454-4; 978-0-578-41518-5*) 48 Boclair rd, Grenada, MS 38901 USA Tel 662-614-0309
E-mail: Janiehouston51@gmail.com.

Bunster, Alejandra, (*978-0-692-40506-2; 978-0-692-73515-2; 978-0-692-19115-6*) 254 San Sebastian Ave., Coral Gables, FL 33134 USA Tel 305-446-5673
E-mail: abunster@carrollton.org.

Bunt, Stephanie, (*978-0-692-08504-2; 978-1-948863*) 4454 Vista Del Monte No. 5, Sherman Oaks, CA 91403 USA Tel 310-592-9844
E-mail: stephanie_bunt@yahoo.com
Dist(s): **Ingram Content Group.**

Burbank, Claire, (*978-0-9975647; 978-1-949701*) 10 Francesca Way, Nottingham, NH 03290 USA Tel 603-418-4121; Fax: 603-734-2381
E-mail: billandmaura@aol.com

Burbank Publishing, (*978-0-9841950*) 421 N. Catalina St., Burbank, CA 91505 USA.

Burden-Evans, Patricia, (*978-0-615-15120-5*) 1814 Palmyra Dr., Greenville, MS 38701 USA
E-mail: pevan6@aol.com
Dist(s): **Lulu Pr., Inc.**

BurgYoung Publishing, (*978-0-9716511*) 4105 E. Florida Ave., No. 300, Denver, CO 80222 USA Tel 303-757-5406
E-mail: tmcco@msn.com; infoby@burgyoungpublishing.com
Web site: http://www.burgyoungpublishing.com; http://www.gettingtoknowgod.com.

Buried Treasure Publishing, (*978-0-9800993; 978-0-615-14018-6*) 6061 Utopia Dr, Zephyrhills, FL 33540 USA
E-mail: sales@buriedtreasurepublishing.com; duaneporter@yahoo.com
Web site: http://buriedtreasurepublishing.com
Dist(s): **Lulu Pr., Inc.**

Burkhardt The Artist, (*978-0-9762996*) P.O. Box 35, Alexandria, KY 41001 USA Tel 859-694-6000
E-mail: rockyburk@hotmail.com
Web site: http://www.rockyburkhardt.com.

Burkhart Bks. *Imprint of* **Burkhart Bks.**

Burkhart Bks., (*978-0-9790975*) 4000 N. Meridian St., Suite 17G, Indianapolis, IN 46208 USA (SAN 852-4270)
E-mail: l.burkhart@sbcglobal.net
Web site: http://www.burkhartnetwork.com
Dist(s): **Distributors, The**
Partners Bk. Distributing, Inc.

Burkhart Bks., (*978-0-615-40779-1; 978-0-9830980; 978-0-9859908; 978-0-9890006; 978-1-940359; 978-1-959464*) 2444 Bedford Cir., Bedford, TX 76021 USA Tel 817-313-4508; *Imprints*: Burkhart Books (BuckhartBks)
E-mail: Revtt007@gmail.com; burkhartbks@gmail.com
Web site: www.burkhartbooks.com
Dist(s): **Amazon Digital Services Inc.**
Whitaker Hse.

Burleigh Dodds Science Publishing Ltd. (GBR) (*978-1-78676*) *Dist. by* **IngramPubServ.**

Burley Creek Studio *See* **White Dog Studio**

Burlington, David, (*978-0-9772136*) 16723 Basin Oak., San Antonio, TX 78247-6220 USA
E-mail: dave@bassfishingaskdave.com
Web site: http://www.bassfishingaskdave.com.

Burlington National, Inc., (*978-1-57706*) Orders Addr.: P.O. Box 841, Mandeville, LA 70470 USA Tel 504-250-7228; Edit Addr.: 6301 Perrier, New Orleans, LA 70118 USA
E-mail: books@burlingtonnational.com.

Burman Books, Inc. (CAN) (*978-0-9736632; 978-0-9737166; 978-0-9739097; 978-1-897404; 978-0-9781380; 978-1-927005*) *Dist. by* **InnovativeLog.**

Burnett Young Books, (*978-1-64071*) P.O. Box 1, Clarklake, MI 49234 USA Tel 330-651-1604
E-mail: cyleyoung61@yahoo.com
Web site: www.burnettyoungbooks.com.

Burnette Fowler Communications, LLC, (*978-0-578-26202-4*) 8478 Gleneagle Way, Naples, FL 34120 USA
E-mail: fowler.nancy@gmail.com
Web site: burnettefowler.com
Dist(s): **Outskirts Pr., Inc.**

Burney Enterprises Unlimited, (*978-0-9745360*) P.O. Box 401402, Redford, MI 48240-9402 USA.

BurnhillWolf, (*978-0-9645655*) 321 Prospect St., NW, Lenoir, NC 28645 USA Tel 704-754-0287
E-mail: Burnwolf@charter.net
Web site: http://www.burnhillwolf.com
Dist(s): **CreateSpace Independent Publishing Platform.**

Burning Bush Creation, (*978-0-9768680; 978-1-60390*) 2114 Queen Ave. N., Minneapolis, MN 55411-2435 USA Tel 612-529-0198; Fax: 612-529-0199
E-mail: ron@mcconico.com
Web site: http://www.burningbushcreation.com.

Burns, Hazlette H., (*978-0-692-10725-6; 979-8-218-03942-4*) 5 WHITE BIRCH Ln., Pinehurst, NC 28374 USA Tel 704-322-0969
E-mail: hazburns@yahoo.com
Dist(s): **Ingram Content Group.**

Burns, Phillys, (*978-0-9620065*) 7450 Olivetas Ave., No. 230, La Jolla, CA 92037 USA (SAN 247-526X).

BurnsBooks, (*978-0-9726099*) 50 Joe's Hill Rd., Danbury, CT 06811 USA Tel 203-744-0232
E-mail: burnsbookspub@aol.com
Web site: http://www.burnsbookspublishing.com.

Burres Bks. *Imprint of* **Youngs, Bettie Bks.**

Burris, Tamar, (*978-0-578-75990-6*) 227 Beverly Ct, Arcata, CA 95521 USA Tel 707-599-3485
E-mail: tabwriters@gmail.com
Web site: www.tamarburris.com.

Burro Bks., (*978-0-615-84637-8; 978-1-7377548*) P.O. Box 304, Cotopaxi, CO 81223 USA Tel 719-942-4361
Web site: www.nancyoswald.com
Dist(s): **CreateSpace Independent Publishing Platform.**

Burt Creations *See* **Burt, Steven E.**

Burt, Steven E., (*978-0-9649283; 978-0-9741407; 978-0-9856188; 979-8-9877213*) Orders Addr.: 17101 SE. 94th Berrien Ct., The Villages, FL 32162 USA (SAN 253-925X) Tel 352-391-8293
E-mail: passtev@aol.com
Web site: http://www.SteveBurtBooks.com.

Burton, Kenneth Hugh, (*978-0-9747043*) Orders Addr.: P.O. Box 38142, Atlanta, GA 30334 USA Tel 404-799-1908; Edit Addr.: 406 Collier Ridge Dr. NW, Atlanta, GA 30318-7312 USA
E-mail: notrub18@bellsouth.net.

Bury Your Inner Weapons Publishing Co., (*978-0-692-13367-5; 978-0-692-13810-6*) 5355 Tartan Hill Ave, LAS VEGAS, NV 89141 USA Tel 321-298-2212
E-mail: stewartmarriott@gmail.com
Web site: www.buryyourinnerweapons4peace.com
Dist(s): **CreateSpace Independent Publishing Platform**
Ingram Content Group.

Busch, Melinda K., (*978-0-692-99192-3*) 8724 Avalon St., Rancho Cucamonga, CA 91701 USA Tel 909-319-0962
E-mail: melikay.busch@gmail.com
Dist(s): **Ingram Content Group.**

Buscher, Julie W., (*978-0-9786352*) Orders Addr.: P.O. Box 627, Brighton, CO 80601-0627 USA (SAN 851-1802) Tel 303-659-7354
E-mail: julobush2@q.com
Web site: http://www.homerthehelicopter.com.

Bush, Bill *See* **Bush Publishing Inc.**

Bush Brothers & Co., (*978-0-9779308*) 1016 E. Weisgarber Rd., Knoxville, TN 37909-2683 USA.

Bush Publishing Inc., (*978-0-9723102; 978-0-9778728; 978-0-9798113; 978-0-9824391; 978-0-9836109*) 5427 S. 94th E. Ave., Tulsa, OK 74104 USA
Web site: http://www.bushpublishing.com.

Bush, Vicki-Ann *See* **Faccia Brutta**

Bushel & Peck Bks., (*978-1-7336335; 978-1-952239; 978-1-63819*) 7675 N First St, Apt 206, Fresno, CA 93720 USA Tel 717-318-5003; *Imprints*: You Are Here Books (URHereBks)
E-mail: bushelandpeckbooks@gmail.com
Web site: https://bushelandpeckbooks.com/
Dist(s): **Baker & Taylor Publisher Services (BTPS).**

Bushweller, Ellie, (*978-0-615-24478-5*) 9 Worth St., South Burlington, VT 05403 USA
Dist(s): **Lulu Pr., Inc.**

Business Angel Pr., (*978-0-9798909*) 174 W. Foothill Blvd., No. 327, Monrovia, CA 91016 USA (SAN 854-6738) Tel 626-357-1922; Fax: 818-475-1474; Toll Free: 800-705-6545
E-mail: contact@businessangelpress.com
Web site: http://www.businessangelpress.com.

Business Bks. International, (*978-0-916673*) P.O. Box 1587, New Canaan, CT 06840 USA (SAN 297-1860) Tel 203-966-9645; Fax: 203-966-6018
E-mail: lesdv@businessbooksusa.com
Web site: http://www.businessbooksusa.com.

Business Bks., LLC, (*978-0-9723714*) 2709 Washington Ave., 21A, Evansville, IN 47714 USA
E-mail: mbussingbu@aol.com
Web site: http://www.bussinessbooksllc.com.

Business Jobs *See* **Alexie Bks.**

Business Plus *Imprint of* **Grand Central Publishing**

Business Word, The *See* **Sterling Investments I, LLC DBA Twins Magazine**

Buster B.B. Publishing, (*978-0-9726691*) 1530 Indian Springs Rd., Pine Beach, NY 12566 USA
E-mail: mirror38@aol.com
Web site: http://www.reflectionsseminars.com.

Busy Bee Bks., (*978-0-9759281*) 2160 110th St., SE, Delano, MN 55328 USA Tel 952-237-7218
E-mail: debbyanderson@juno.com.

Busy Publishing, (*978-1-7356874*) 747 NE 4 Ave, Fort Lauderdale, FL 33304 USA Tel 305-283-7778
E-mail: Amanda.werner@ymail.com.

Butler Book Publishing *See* **Butler Bks.**

Butler Bks., (*978-0-9627459; 978-1-884532; 978-1-935497; 978-1-941953; 978-1-953058*) Orders Addr.: 608 Briar Hill Rd., Louisville, KY 40206 USA (SAN 990-0667) Tel 502-897-9393; Fax: 502-897-9797
E-mail: ckbutler@aol.com; eric@butlerbooks.com; billy@butlerbooks.com
Web site: https://www.butlerbooks.com
Dist(s): **Follett School Solutions.**

Butler Ctr. for Arkansas Studies, (*978-0-9708574; 978-0-9800897; 978-1-935106; 978-1-945624*) c/o Central Arkansas Library System, 100 Rock St., Little Rock, AR 72201 USA
Web site: http://www.cals.org; http://www.butlercenter.org
Dist(s): **Chicago Distribution Ctr.**
JSTOR
MyiLibrary
Univ. of Arkansas Pr.
Univ. of Chicago Pr. Distribution Clients.

Butler, Kate Bks., (*978-0-9993600; 978-1-948927; 978-1-952725; 978-1-957124; 978-1-962407*) 157 Bridgeton Pike, Mullica Hill, NJ 08062 USA Tel 714-401-1371
E-mail: katebutlerbooks@gmail.com
Web site: www.katebutlerbooks.com.

Butler, Reggie, (*978-0-578-59766-9*) 30137 S Meadowridge, Farmington Hills, MI 48334 USA Tel 248-860-1326
E-mail: fullcourtvision@gmail.com.

BuTo, Ltd. Co., (*978-0-9729569*) P.O. Box 9018, Austin, TX 78766 USA (SAN 255-4321) Fax: 512-450-0372
E-mail: butoltdco@aol.com
Web site: http://www.buto.biz.

Buttar, Deborah *See* **GMEC Publishing**

Buttercup Media, (*978-0-9768152*) Orders Addr.: P.O. Box 222003, Dallas, TX 75222 USA Tel 214-890-6833
E-mail: michael.p.collins1@gmail.com
Dist(s): **BookBaby.**

Butterfly Bk. Makers, (*978-0-9754117*) 1450 W. 800 N., Orem, UT 84057 USA
E-mail: hatfiron@aol.com.

Butterfly Books *See* **Black Garnet Pr.**

Butterfly Bks. Publishing, (*978-1-7360444*) 14825 Larsen Ave, Gowen, MI 49326 USA Tel 616-263-0444
E-mail: alicia.kelley@Valpo.edu
Web site: butterflybookspublishing.com.

Butterfly Garden Bks., (*978-0-692-26847-6; 978-0-692-29926-5; 978-1-7321166*) 723 Euel Dr., McDonough, GA 30252 USA Tel 770-713-9735
E-mail: sabrina30054@yahoo.com
Web site: www.sabrinasargent.com.

Butterfly Ink Publishing, (*978-0-9745423*) 20637 Skouras Dr., Winnetka, CA 91306 USA
E-mail: butterflyinkpub@aol.com; kim@butterflyinkpublishing.com
Web site: http://www.butterflyinkpublishing.com.

Butterfly Park Educational Materials, Inc., (*978-0-9744575*) 3126 Elmira Ct., Denver, CO 80238-2929 USA
E-mail: butterflypark@comcast.net
Web site: http://www.butterflyparkphonics.com.

Butterfly Pavilion, (*978-0-9729000*) 6252 W. 104th Ave., Westminster, CO 80020 USA Tel 303-469-5441; Fax: 303-657-5944
E-mail: ptennyson@butterflies.org
Web site: http://www.butterflies.org.

Butterfly Press *See* **Butterfly Productions, LLC**

Butterfly Productions, LLC, (*978-0-9752936*) 165 Shadow Rock Dr., Sedona, AZ 86336 USA Tel 928-204-2811; Fax: 928-204-9118 Do not confuse with companies with the same or similar name in New York, NY, Worcester, MA, Houston, TX, Old Town, ME, Dayton, OH, Cochranville, PA, Princeton, NJ , Amherst, MA, Charston, WV, Pheonix, AZ
E-mail: butterfly@sedona.net
Web site: http://www.butterflyproductions.info.

Butterfly Typeface, The, (*978-1-942022; 978-0-9909919; 978-0-692-48438-8; 978-1-947656; 978-1-951883; 978-1-962446*) 8509 W Markham St No. 56193, Little Rock, AR 72215 USA Tel 501-681-0080
E-mail: butterflytypeface.imw@gmail.com; butterflypublisher@gmail.com
Web site: www.butterflytypeface.com.

Butterfly Voice, (*978-0-578-94233-9*) 15 Barnard Pl., Manhasset, NY 11030 USA Tel 516-526-4557
E-mail: tarakb@optonline.net.

Butterhouse Publishing, (*978-0-9763971*) 12251 N. 32nd St., Suite 4, Phoenix, AZ 85032 USA
E-mail: financialstories@juno.com.

Buttermilk Bks., (*978-0-9978909; 978-1-7331576; 978-1-7365555; 979-8-9873669*) 1482 Highland Cir., Myrtle Beach, SC 29575 USA Tel 843-655-5377
E-mail: tomwinn@sc.rr.com.

Buttermoth Pr. (AUS) (*978-0-9803367*) *Dist. by* **LuluCom.**

Butters Pr., (*978-0-9754960*) 2047 Gale Rd., Eaton Rapids, MI 48827 USA
Web site: http://www.throughtheears.com.

Button Bks. (GBR) (*978-1-908985*) *Dist. by* **PerseuPGW.**

Button Bucket Bks., (*978-0-615-91505-0; 978-0-615-95000-6; 978-0-692-11232-8*) 2715 N. Ocean Boulevard, 14-F, Fort Lauderdale, FL 33308 USA Tel 954554-3153
Dist(s): **CreateSpace Independent Publishing Platform.**

Button Flower Pr., (*978-0-9747836*) 7422 Westview Dr., Boardman, OH 44512 USA.

Button Poetry, (*978-0-9896415; 978-1-943735; 978-1-63834*) 2855 Anthony Ln. S., St. Anthony, MN 55418 USA
E-mail: sam@buttonpoetry.com
Web site: ButtonPoetry.com
Dist(s): **SCB Distributors.**

Button Pr., (*978-1-7333932; 978-1-955286*) 10200 E 150th Ave, Brighton, CO 80602 USA Tel 720-579-6609
E-mail: Cindygauthor@gmail.com.

Buttonberry Bks., (*978-0-9768227*) 29 Sawmill Rd., Lebanon, NJ 08833 USA
Web site: http://www.buttonberrybooks.com
Dist(s): **Follett School Solutions.**

Buttonweed Pr., L.L.C., (*978-0-9755675*) 204 7th St W. # 125, Northfield, MN 55057-2419 USA (SAN 256-1700)
E-mail: info@buttonweedpress.com
Web site: http://www.buttonweedpress.com
Dist(s): **Follett School Solutions**
Partners Bk. Distributing, Inc.

Buttonwood Pr., (*978-0-9660685; 978-0-9742920; 978-0-9823351; 978-0-9891462; 978-0-9965562; 978-0-9972464; 978-0-9998096*) Orders Addr.: P.O. Box 716, Haslett, MI 48840 USA Tel 517-339-9871; Fax: 517-339-5908; Edit Addr.: 5951 Buttonwood Dr., Haslett, MI 48840 USA Do not confuse with companies with the same name Champaign, IL, Potomac, MD, New York, NY, Solvang, CA
E-mail: rlbald@aol.com
Web site: http://www.buttonwoodpress.com
Dist(s): **Partners Bk. Distributing, Inc.**

Buy Books on the Web.Com *See* **Infinity Publishing**

Buy Rite, (*978-0-9723744; 978-1-60421*) 88 Vanderveer Rd., Freehold, NJ 07728 USA Tel 732-294-9000; Fax: 732-294-9363; Toll Free: 888-777-7952
Web site: http://www.buyriteinc.com.

Buz-Land Presentations, Inc., (*978-0-9766990*) 73 Harding Rd., Wyckoff, NJ 07481 USA Tel 201-848-0595; 73 Harding Rd., Wyckoff, NJ 07481-2730 (SAN 256-5692)
E-mail: buzi.bee@verizon.net
Web site: http://www.buz-land.com; www.WWRT.org.

Buzzard Pr. International, (*978-0-9648488*) 506 W. Donna Dr., Merced, CA 95348 USA Tel 209-723-6738; Fax: 209-723-6253
E-mail: buzzard@buzzardpress.com
Dist(s): **Sunbelt Pubns., Inc.**

BuzzPop *Imprint of* **Little Bee Books Inc.**

Buzzy's Bks., (*978-0-9719054*) P.O. Box 566, Grafton, MA 01519 USA Tel 508-839-2442; Fax: 508-839-7396
E-mail: buzzy@buzzysbooks.org
Web site: http://www.buzzysbooks.org.

B.W. Van Alstyne, (*978-0-692-94898-9; 978-0-692-97327-1; 978-0-578-42650-1; 978-0-578-42651-8*) 602 W 28th St., Bryan, TX 77803 USA Tel 979-777-6094
E-mail: b.w.vanalstyne@gmail.com
Dist(s): **Ingram Content Group.**

By Grace Enterprises, (*978-0-9663629; 978-1-940591*) 9515 Twin Oaks Dr., Manvel, TX 77578-5307 USA
E-mail: hulettepl@aol.com; pamlv@aol.com
Web site: http://www.bygraceent.com
Dist(s): **Follett School Solutions.**

By His Grace Publishing, (*978-0-9991835*) 1189 East Hwy. C, Lamar, MO 64759 USA Tel 417-214-1847; Fax: 417-214-1847
E-mail: rebecca.emery@gmail.com
Web site: byhisgracepublishing.com.

by shayne, (*978-0-9725593*) P.O. Box 221474, Santa Clarita, CA 91322 USA
Web site: http://www.byshayne.com.

By the Bk. Writing, (*978-0-578-66378-4*) 337 William St., Huntington, IN 46750 USA Tel 434-882-4742
E-mail: bbevca@gmail.com.

By The Creek Pubns., (*978-0-9974810*) 238 Shore Brook Ln., Commerce Twp., MI 48390 USA Tel 248-390-3906
E-mail: lindakmclean@yahoo.com.

By the Light of the Moon Pr., (*978-0-9992614*) 27071 Catamaran Dr., Tega Cay, SC 29708 USA Tel 720-326-2502
E-mail: maryjane.capps@gmail.com.

ByD Pr., (*978-0-9721035*) 1424 33rd St., NW, Washington, DC 20007 USA Tel 202-342-9189 (phone/fax)
E-mail: bydpress@erols.com
Dist(s): **Independent Pubs. Group.**

BYE Publishing Services, (*978-0-9656739*) Orders Addr.: PO. BOX 582016, Elk Grove, CA 95758 USA Tel 916-529-3119 Corporate Hq; Fax: 916-683-1476; Edit Addr.: PO BOX 582016, Elk Grove, CA 95758 USA Tel 916-529-3119
E-mail: byepublishing@comcast.net
Web site: http://www.byepublishing.com; http://www.nationalbyesociety.org.

Byeway *Imprint of* **Byeway Bks.**

Byeway Bks., (*978-1-85997; 978-1-904586; 978-1-933581; 978-1-934004; 978-1-60176*) 15941 W. 65th St., Shawnee, KS 66217-9342 USA Toll Free Fax: 866-426-3929; Toll Free: 866-429-3929; *Imprints*: Byeway (Byeway)
E-mail: customerservice@byewaybooks.com
Web site: http://www.byewaybooks.com/how_to_order.html.

Byrd, Fay T., (*978-0-9776805*) 9325 Pan Ridge Rd., Baltimore, MD 21234 USA (SAN 257-9898) Tel 410-661-0295
E-mail: faysangelharp@aol.com
Web site: www.faysangelharp.com.

Byrd, Jesse Jr, (*978-0-692-90925-6; 978-0-692-90926-3; 978-0-9997050; 979-8-9854099*) 1630 Kabel Dr., New Orleans, LA 70131 USA Tel 510-290-9490
E-mail: marybmorrison@aol.com; 87byrd@gmail.com
Web site: www.MaryMorrison.com; www.JesseBCreative.com
Dist(s): **Ingram Content Group.**

Byrne, Robert, (*978-0-692-14366-7; 979-8-218-29655-1*) 1854 Ringsted Dr., Solvang, CA 93463 USA Tel 805-886-9321
E-mail: robert@robertbyrne.com
Web site: www.robertbyrne.com.

Byte Level Research, (*978-0-9796475; 978-1-61822*) 2305 Ashland St. No. C417, Ashland, OR 97520 USA (SAN 853-9847); *Imprints*: Ashland Creek Press (AshlandCreek)
Web site: https://www.bytelevelbooks.com; https://www.ashlandcreekpress.com
Dist(s): **Follett School Solutions**
INscribe Digital.

Byte Me! Inc., (*978-0-9798611; 978-0-615-14953-0*) P.O. Box 60705, Reno, NV 89506 USA (SAN 854-5863) Tel

775-772-6378; 775-972-3322; Fax: 775-972-3323 Never after 5p.m. pst
E-mail: saraw1@clearwire.net; alma_corazon12@yahoo.com
Web site: http://www.cdebooksbyteme.org; http://www.stores.lulu.com/georgiahedrick; http://www.stores.lulu.com/georgiahedrick; http://www.stores.lulu.com/georgiahedrick
Dist(s): **Lulu Pr., Inc.**

yte/Me Teen Bk. *Imprint of* **Awe-Struck Publishing**

YU Creative Works *Imprint of* **Brigham Young Univ.**

ywater Bks., *(978-0-9653017)* P.O. Box 133, Honaunau, HI 96726-0133 USA; 387 Pk. Ave. S., New York, NY 10016 Do not confuse with Bywater Books in Ann Arbor, MI
Dist(s): **Consortium Bk. Sales & Distribution.**

ywater Bks., *(978-1-932859; 978-1-61294)* P.O. Box 3671, Ann Arbor, MI 48106-3671 USA Tel 734-662-8815 Do not confuse with Bywater Books in Honaunau, HI
E-mail: salemwestbywater@gmail.com; ann.mcman@gmail.com
Web site: http://www.bywaterbooks.com
Dist(s): **Consortium Bk. Sales & Distribution**
MyiLibrary.

Bywater Pr., *(978-1-7330675)* 2824 Kulshan St, Bellingham, WA 98225 USA Tel 425-213-0450
E-mail: jeff@bywaterpress.com
Web site: bywaterpress.com.

C A Filius *See* **Charwood Pubns.**

C & C Educational Materials, LLC, *(978-0-9640524; 978-0-9747205; 978-0-9963509)* 12514 Dermott Dr., Houston, TX 77065 USA
E-mail: barbara.cobaugh@att.net
Web site: www.strategiesforstaar.com.

C & C Productions, *(978-0-9753273)* PMB 254, 330 SW 43rd St., No. K, Renton, WA 98055 USA.

C&D Enterprises, *(978-0-9633231; 978-0-9765938)* P.O. Box 7201, Arlington, VA 22207-7201 USA Fax: 703-276-3033
E-mail: harryfp@comcast.net.

C&D International, *(978-0-937347)* 111 Ferguson Ct., Suite 105, Irving, TX 75062-7014 USA (SAN 659-1523) Toll Free: 800-231-0442.

C & H Pubns., *(978-0-9740882)* 31201 S. 596 Ln., Grove, OK 74344 USA.

C & N Publishing *See* **C&N Publishing**

†C & T Publishing, *(978-0-914881; 978-1-57120; 978-1-60705; 978-1-61745; 978-1-64403)* Orders Addr.: 1651 Challenge Dr., Concord, CA 94520 USA (SAN 289-0720) Tel 925-677-0377; Fax: 925-617-0374; Toll Free: 800-284-1114; *Imprints*: Stash Books (StashBks); FunStitch Studio (FunStitch Stu)
E-mail: ctinfo@ctpub.com
Web site: http://www.ctpub.com
Dist(s): **Follett School Solutions**
MyiLibrary
National Bk. Network
Open Road Integrated Media, Inc.
ebrary, Inc.; *CIP*.

CBI Pr., *(978-0-9705812)* 6 Jeffrey Cir., Bedford, MA 01730 USA Do not confuse with C B I Press, Arlington, VA
E-mail: nancy_nugent@comcast.net
Web site: http://www.cbipress.com.

C B P Press *See* **Chalice Pr.**

C. B. Publishing House, Incorporated *See* **Cubbie Blue Publishing**

C C L S Publishing Hse., *(978-1-928882; 978-0-7428)* 3191 Coral Way, Suite 114, Miami, FL 33145-3209 USA (SAN 254-4695) Tel 305-529-2257
E-mail: info@cclscorp.com; cpinho@cclscorp.com
Web site: http://www.cclsmiami.edu
Dist(s): **Continental Bk. Co., Inc.**

CEF Pr., *(978-1-55976)* Div.of Child Evangelism Fellowship, Orders Addr.: P.O. Box 348, Warrenton, MO 63383 USA Tel 636-456-4321; Fax: 636-456-2078; Toll Free: 800-748-7710; Edit Addr.: 2300 E. Hwy. M, Warrenton, MO 63383 USA (SAN 211-7789)
E-mail: custserv@cefonline.com
Web site: http://www.cefonline.com; http://www.cefpress.com.

CES Industries, Inc., *(978-0-86711)* 2023 New Hwy., Farmingdale, NY 11735-1103 USA (SAN 237-9864)
E-mail: m.nesenoff@cesindustries.com
Web site: http://www.cesindustries.com.

C. F. E. Black, *(978-1-7379425; 978-1-962066)* 811 Telephone Tower Rd., Laceys Spring, AL 35754 USA Tel 205-792-8692
E-mail: cfeblack@gmail.com.

CFKR Career Materials, Inc., *(978-0-934783; 978-1-887481)* P.O. Box 99, Meadow Vista, CA 95722-0099 USA (SAN 694-2547) Toll Free Fax: 800-770-0433; Toll Free: 800-525-5626
E-mail: requestinfo@cfkr.com; cfkr@cfkr.com; order@cfkr.com
Web site: http://www.cfkr.com.

C I S Communications, Inc., *(978-0-935063; 978-1-56062)* 180 Park Ave., Lakewood, NJ 08701 USA (SAN 694-5953) Tel 732-905-3000; Fax: 732-367-6666.

C. LaVielle, *(978-0-9983260)* 2313 NE Alameda St., Portland, OR 97212 USA Tel 503-287-0511; Fax: 503-287-0511
E-mail: clavielle@hotmail.com
Web site: www.clavielle.com.

C. Lee McKenzie *Imprint of* **McKenzie, Cheryl**

CMSP Projects, *(978-0-942851)* School of Engineering, 51 Astor Pl., New York, NY 10003 USA (SAN 667-6731) Tel 212-228-0950.

C P GLOBAL WELLNESS LLC, *(978-1-7359524)* 430 E Packwood Ave, Maitland, FL 32751 USA Tel 407-780-0380
E-mail: simscori15@gmail.com.

CPI Pubs., *(978-0-9648363)* Div. of Christopher Productions, Inc., 1115 David Ave., Pacific Grove, CA 93950 USA Tel 818-831-9268; Fax: 818-845-2128
Dist(s): **Austin & Company, Inc.**

CPI Publishing, Inc., 311 E. 51st St., New York, NY 10022 USA (SAN 218-6896) Tel 212-753-3800
Dist(s): **Modern Curriculum Pr.**

CPM Educational Program, *(978-1-885145; 978-1-931287; 978-1-60328)* 1233 Noonan Dr., Sacramento, CA 95822 USA Tel 916-446-9936; Fax: 916-444-5263
E-mail: cpm@cpm.org; bradley@cpm.org
Web site: http://www.cpm.org.

C R C Publications *See* **Faith Alive Christian Resources**

C R C World Literature Ministries *See* **C R C World Literature Ministries/Libros Desafio**

C R C World Literature Ministries/Libros Desafio, *(978-0-939125; 978-1-55883; 978-1-55955)* Subs. of CRC Pubns., 2850 Kalamazoo Ave., SE, Grand Rapids, MI 49560 USA (SAN 251-3269) Tel 616-224-0785 (customer service); Fax: 616-224-0834; Toll Free: 800-333-8300
E-mail: info@worldliterature.org
Web site: http://www.worldliterature.org/
Dist(s): **Faith Alive Christian Resources.**

CRM, *(978-0-9713534; 978-1-933341)* Orders Addr.: P.O. Box 2124, Hendersonville, NC 28793 USA Tel 828-877-3356; Fax: 828-890-1511; Edit Addr.: 1916 Reasonover Rd., Cedar Mountain, NC 28218 USA
E-mail: crm@ciridmus.com
Web site: http://www.ciridmus.com
Dist(s): **Send The Light Distribution LLC.**

C R Pubns., *(978-0-615-15964-5; 978-0-615-15981-2; 978-0-615-16029-0; 978-0-615-16673-5)* 415 E. 15th, Kearny, NE 68847-6959 USA
Web site: http://www.IDealinHope.com/author
Dist(s): **Lulu Pr., Inc.**

†CSS Publishing Co., *(978-0-7880; 978-0-89536; 978-1-55673; 978-0-615-84860-0)* Orders Addr.: 5450 N. Dixie Hwy., Lima, OH 45807-9559 USA Tel 800-241-4056; 419-227-1818; Fax: 419-228-9184; Toll Free: 800-241-4056 Customer Service; 800-537-1030 Orders; Edit Addr.: P.O. Box 4503, Lima, OH 45802-4503 USA (SAN 207-0707) Tel 419-227-1818; Fax: 419-228-9184; Toll Free: 800-537-1030 (Orders); 800-241-4056 (Customer Service); *Imprints*: Fairway Press (Fairway Pr) Do not confuse with CSS Publishing in Tularosa, NM
E-mail: editor@csspub.com; csr@csspub.com; info@csspub.com; orders@csspub.com
Web site: http://www.csspub.com
Dist(s): **Spring Arbor Distributors, Inc.**; *CIP*.

C T A, Inc., *(978-0-9712618; 978-0-9718985; 978-0-9728816; 978-0-9744640; 978-0-9747923; 978-0-9754499; 978-0-9759330; 978-1-933234; 978-1-935404; 978-1-943216; 978-1-947699; 978-1-951094; 978-1-955246; 978-1-961346)* P.O. Box 1205, Fenton, MO 63026-1205 USA Tel 636-305-3100; Toll Free: 800-999-1874
Web site: http://www.ctainc.com.

C Turtle Publishing, *(978-0-9979656)* 30 N. Gould St. Suite 5467, Sheridan, WY 82801 USA Tel 812-786-5594
E-mail: kylelbmorey@gmail.com
Web site: www.cturtlepublishing.com.

C. W. Historicals, LLC, *(978-0-9637745)* Orders Addr.: P.O. Box 113, Collingswood, NJ 08108 USA Tel 856-854-1290; Fax: 856-854-1290 (*69); Edit Addr.: 901 Lakeshore Dr., Westmont, NJ 08108 USA
E-mail: cwhist@erols.com.

C Z M Press *See* **Touchstones Discussion Project**

C2 (C squared) Publishing, *(978-0-9773115)* P.O. Box 5269, Vienna, WV 26105 USA
E-mail: noelclntn@yahoo.com; princeofwarwood@gmail.com.

Caballito Children's Bks. *Imprint of* **Caballo Pr. of Ann Arbor**

Caballo Pr. of Ann Arbor, *(978-0-615-18757-0; 978-0-9824766; 978-0-615-44366-9; 978-0-9840418; 978-0-692-39908-8; 978-0-692-50604-2; 978-0-692-82464-1)* Orders Addr.: 24 Frank Lloyd Wright Dr. P.O. Box 415, Ann Arbor, MI 48106-0445 USA Tel 734-972-5790; *Imprints*: Caballito Children's Books (Caballito)
E-mail: admin@caballopress.com
Web site: http://www.caballopress.com
Dist(s): **CreateSpace Independent Publishing Platform**
Ingram Content Group.

Cabat Studio Pubns., *(978-0-913521)* 627 N. Fourth Ave., Tucson, AZ 85705 USA (SAN 285-1539) Tel 520-622-6362
E-mail: junecabat@hotmail.com.

Cabbage Patch Pr., *(978-0-9729044)* 2255 Orange Grove Rd. No. 23205, Tucson, AZ 85741 USA Tel 520-241-2680
E-mail: cabbagepatchpress@hotmail.com
Web site: http://www.cabbagepatchpress.com.

CABI (GBR) *(978-0-85198; 978-0-85199)* *Dist. by* **Stylus Pub VA.**

Cabin Bks., *(978-0-578-47477-9; 978-0-578-93912-4; 978-0-578-37998-2)* P.O. Box 5522, San Angelo, TX 76902 USA Tel 325-277-9689
E-mail: brushandplume@gmail.com
Web site: www.sherryscabin.com.

Cable Creek Publishing, *(978-1-954064)* 120 N. Pitt St, Carlisle, PA 17013 USA Tel 717-706-5562
E-mail: laura@cablecreekpublishing.com
Web site: https://www.cablecreekpublishing.com/.

Cable Publishing, *(978-0-9799494; 978-1-934980)* 14090 E. Keinenen Rd., Brule, WI 54820 USA Tel 715-372-8497; Fax: 715-372-8448
Web site: http://www.cablepublishing.com
Dist(s): **Follett School Solutions.**

Caboandcoral.com, *(978-0-615-17598-0; 978-0-692-00269-8; 978-0-692-01170-6; 978-0-9833841)* 1227 Stratford Ct., Del Mar, CA 92014 USA
E-mail: udo@caboandcoral.com
Web site: http://www.caboandcoral.com.

Cackleberry Creek Publishing *See* **Cackleberry Creek Publishing LLC**

Cackleberry Creek Publishing LLC, *(978-0-692-83961-4; 978-0-692-97274-8; 978-0-692-06142-8; 978-0-692-07060-4; 978-0-692-11030-0; 978-0-578-88695-4; 978-0-578-89784-4; 979-8-9876235)*
E-mail: kristyjovolchko@gmail.com; kristyjovolchko@gmail.com; kristyjovolchko@gmail.com
Web site: www.kristyjovolchko.com
Dist(s): **CreateSpace Independent Publishing Platform.**

Cacoethes Publishing Hse., LLC, *(978-0-9799015; 978-0-9802447; 978-0-9816190; 978-0-9817733; 978-0-9818208; 978-1-60695)* 14715 Pacific Ave. S., Suite 604, Tacoma, WA 98444 USA (SAN 854-7122) Tel 253-536-3747; Fax: 253-537-3117
E-mail: cacoethespublishing@comcast.net
Web site: http://www.cacoethespublishing.com; http://www.loticmagazine.com
Dist(s): **Ingram Content Group.**

Cactus Publishing, LLC, *(978-0-9766674)* 1235 S. Gilbert Rd., Suite 3-62, Mesa, AZ 85204 USA Do not confuse with companies iwht the same or similar name in East Perth, WA, Atlanta, GA, Peoria, AZ
E-mail: glsweetaz@msn.com.

CaDaVa Publishing, *(978-0-9997814)* 906 Oscar Cross Ave., PADUCAH, KY 42003 USA Tel 270-845-1304
E-mail: cadavapublishing@gmail.com
Dist(s): **Ingram Content Group.**

Cadcim Technologies, *(978-0-9663537; 978-1-932709; 978-1-936646; 978-1-942689; 978-1-64057)* 525 St. Andrews Dr., Schererville, IN 46375 USA Tel 219-614-7235; 219-228-4908; Fax: 270-717-0185
E-mail: cadcim@yahoo.com; sales@cadcim.com
Web site: https://www.cadcim.com.

Cadence Group, The *See* **New Shelves Bks.**

Cadmus Publishing, *(978-0-9998590; 978-1-7343644; 978-1-63751)* P.O. Box 2146, Port Angeles, WA 98362 USA Tel 651-302-2539
E-mail: frank@cadmuspublishing.com
Dist(s): **Ingram Content Group.**

Cadogan Guides (GBR) *(978-0-946313; 978-0-947754; 978-1-85744; 978-1-86011; 978-1-78194)* *Dist. by* **Globe Pequot.**

Cady, Kristen Bks., *(978-1-7337974)* 2121 Jay St., Slidell, LA 70460 USA Tel 504-491-8131
E-mail: pianogoddess101@yahoo.com.

Cafe Lango *See* **Pavilion Pubs.**

Caged Dragon Publishing, *(978-1-7321659)* 2036 E. Cuming St., Fremont, NE 68025 USA Tel 530-315-8144
E-mail: j.d.campbell.author@gmail.com.

Cahill Publishing, *(978-0-9744027)* 1016-F Brentwood Way, Atlanta, GA 30350 USA
E-mail: e-diane@hotmail.com.

Cahill Publishing Company *See* **Advance Publishing, Inc.**

Cahokia Mounds Museum Society, *(978-1-881563)* 30 Ramey St., Collinsville, IL 62234 USA Tel 618-344-7316; Fax: 618-346-5162
E-mail: cmms@ezl.com; giftshop@ezl.com
Web site: http://www.cahokiamounds.com.

CAI Publishing, *(978-0-9787766; 978-0-9971381)* Orders Addr.: 807 Black Duck Dr., Port Orange, FL 32127-4726 USA (SAN 851-6006) Tel 386-383-5198
E-mail: wacumminspub@gmail.com
Web site: http://www.calpublishing.net
Dist(s): **Ingram Content Group.**

Caillouet, Gerry, *(978-0-578-05418-6; 978-2-89718)* 8193 Emerick Rd., West Milton, OH 45383 USA Tel 937-698-3656
E-mail: ggoutdoors@aol.com
Web site: http://www.godsgreatoutdoors.org
Dist(s): **Publishers Group West (PGW)**
Perseus Bks. Group.

Cairns, Mary C., *(978-0-692-98477-2)* P.O. Box 34, Altenburg, MO 63732 USA Tel 573-768-4814
E-mail: mchriscairns@gmail.com
Dist(s): **Ingram Content Group.**

Caitboo LLC, *(978-0-9818717)* 2474 Walnut St., No. 260, Cary, NC 27518-9212 USA (SAN 856-7948) Tel 919-851-8646
E-mail: caitboo@gmail.com
Web site: http://www.caitboo.com.

Caitlin Pr., Inc. (CAN) *(978-0-920576; 978-1-894759; 978-1-927575; 978-1-987915)* *Dist. by* **IPG Chicago.**

Calabash Bks. *Imprint of* **Belknap Publishing & Design**

Calabrese, Christine, *(978-0-9995220; 978-1-960669)* 10 Marlboro Dr., Huntington, NY 11743 USA Tel 516-312-2078
E-mail: chrissykcalabrese@gmail.com
Web site: www.christinecalabrese.com.

Calaca Pr., *(978-0-9660773; 978-0-9717035; 978-0-9843359)* Orders Addr.: P.O. Box 2309, National City, CA 91951 USA Tel 619-434-9036 (phone/fax); Edit Addr.: 502 Rose Dr., National City, CA 91950 USA; *Imprints*: Red CalacArts Publications (Red CalacArts)
E-mail: calacapress@cox.net
Web site: http://calacapress.com; http://redcalacartscollective.org; http://www.myspace.com/calacalandia
Dist(s): **BookMobile**
SPD-Small Pr. Distribution.

Calaida Ecaterina, *(978-1-7342530)* 612 N Colonial Ave ste F, Wilmington, DE 19805 USA Tel 736-093-6000
E-mail: ecaterina.calaida@gmail.com.

Calaroga Publishing, *(978-0-9815793)* 619 Madison St., Suite 110, Oregon City, OR 97045 USA
Web site: www.slimsaneandsexy.com.

Calcano, David *See* **Fantoons, LLC**

Caldwell, Judy, *(978-0-9774463)* 11216 Windy Peak Rdg., Sandy, UT 84094 USA Fax: 801-571-1422
E-mail: jlynncaldwell@msn.com.

Caleb's Pr., *(978-0-9729568)* 421 Seminole Ct., High Point, NC 27265-8631 USA Tel 336-887-6846; Fax: 888-726-9304
E-mail: calebspress@aol.com
Web site: http://www.calebspress.com.

Caledonia Pr., LLC, *(978-0-9890975)* P.O. Box 436166, Louisville, KY 40253 USA Tel 502-773-5874
E-mail: gbgodby@insightbb.com
Web site: http://giovannagodby.com.

Calfee, Susan S. *See* **Wordwhittler Bks.**

Cali Publishing, *(978-0-9793004)* 2875 NE 191st St., Suite 511, Aventua, FL 33180 USA Tel 786-200-9374; Fax: 305-937-4161
E-mail: lallouz@glmace.com
Web site: http://www.calipublishing.com.

Caliber Comics, *(978-0-941613; 978-0-9826549; 978-0-9836307; 978-0-9857493; 978-0-9960306; 978-1-942351; 978-1-63529)* P.O. Box 44114 Parkside, Canton, MI 48187 USA (SAN 666-1777) Tel 734-453-8346; 734-812-8733
E-mail: calcomic@aol.com
Web site: http://www.calibercomics.com
Dist(s): **Diamond Comic Distributors, Inc.**
MyiLibrary.

Caliber Pubns., *(978-0-9673696; 978-93-88448)* 1295 Lincoln Dr., Marion, IA 52302 USA Tel 319-294-9468; Fax: 319-373-1370; Toll Free: 877-480-5790
E-mail: larson1965@aol.com
Web site: http://www.calpubs.com.

Caliburn Bks. *Imprint of* **MQuills Publishing**

Calico Chapter Bks. *Imprint of* **ABDO Publishing Co.**

Calico Chapter Bks *Imprint of* **Magic Wagon**

Calico Connection, Inc., The, *(978-0-9767658)* 300 N. David Ln., Muskogee, OK 74403 USA Tel 918-687-6577 Do not confuse with Calico Publishing in Seabrook, TX
E-mail: calicoasay@cox.net.

Calico Kid *Imprint of* **ABDO Publishing Co.**

Calico Publishing *See* **Calico Connection, Inc., The**

California Foundation for Agriculture in the Classroom, *(978-0-615-26927-6; 978-0-615-34893-3; 978-0-615-44052-1; 978-0-9850855)* 2300 River Plaza Dr., Sacramento, CA 95833 USA
Web site: LearnAboutAg.org.

California Is Me, *(978-0-9742010)* P.O. Box 23841, Alexandria, VA 22304 USA Tel 202-321-1425
E-mail: QueenC@callisme.com
Web site: http://www.callisme.com.

California Street *Imprint of* **Firefall Editions**

Calkins Creek *Imprint of* **Highlights Pr., c/o Highlights for Children, Inc.**

Callaham, Sheila, *(978-1-936934)* 901 Iystra Ln., Chapel Hill, NC 27517 USA Tel 919-968-8909
E-mail: sheilacallaham@gmail.com
Web site: sheilacallaham.com.

Callaway Editions, Inc., *(978-0-935112; 978-1-7345377; 978-1-7372051; 979-8-9874124)* Div. of Callaway Arts & Entertainment, 41 Union Sq. West, Suite 1101, New York, NY 10003 USA (SAN 213-2931) Tel 646-465-4667
E-mail: ivan@callaway.com
Web site: http://www.callaway.com
Dist(s): **Abrams, Inc.**
Holt, Henry & Co.
Hachette Bk. Group
National Bk. Network
Penguin Random Hse. Distribution
Penguin Random Hse. LLC
Penguin Publishing Group
Simon & Schuster Children's Publishing.

Calliope Publications *See* **Sounds Devine**

Callirobics, *(978-0-9630478)* Orders Addr.: P.O. Box 6634, Charlottesville, VA 22906 USA Tel 804-293-7055; Fax: 804-293-9008; Toll Free: 800-769-2891; Edit Addr.: 1616 King Mountain Rd., Charlottesville, VA 22901 USA
E-mail: cal-avir@cfw.com
Web site: http://www.callirobics.com.

Callis Editora Ltda (BRA) *(978-85-7416; 978-85-85642)* *Dist. by* **IPG Chicago.**

Callison, J.L., *(978-0-9987771)* 407 Hinman St, Aurora, IL 60505 USA Tel 630-978-2093; Fax: 630-978-2093
E-mail: authorjlcallison@gmail.com
Web site: www.jlcallison.com.

Callisto Media Inc., *(978-0-615-59880-2; 978-1-62315; 978-1-939754; 978-1-64152; 978-1-64611; 978-1-64739; 978-1-64876; 978-1-63807; 978-1-63878; 978-1-68539; 979-8-88608; 979-8-88650)* 918 Parker St #A-12, Berkeley, CA 94710 USA; *Imprints*: Rockridge Press (RockridgePr)
E-mail: production@callistopublishing.com; metadata@callistopublishing.com
Web site: www.rockridgeuniversity.com; http://www.callistomedia.com
Dist(s): **CreateSpace Independent Publishing Platform**
Ingram Publisher Services
Ingram Content Group
Simon & Schuster, Inc.
Sourcebooks, Inc.

Callout Pr., *(978-0-9971911)* PO Box 250, Olalla, WA 98359 USA Tel 844-344-4374
E-mail: robert@calloutpress.com.

Cally Pr., *(978-0-9766199)* 3964 Loftlands Dr., Earlysville, VA 22936 USA
E-mail: callypress@aol.com.

Calm & Colorful, *(978-1-7321831)* 2224 Wetstone Dr., Thousand Oaks, CA 91362 USA Tel 805-657-1884
E-mail: accounts@calmandcolorful.com
Web site: www.calmandcolorful.com.

Calm Flame Publishing Co., *(978-0-9745263)* 10745 Gilespie St., Las Vegas, NV 89123 USA.

Calm Unity Books *See* **Calm Unity Pr.**

Calm Unity Pr., *(978-1-882260)* 3922 23rd St., San Francisco, CA 94114-3303 USA Fax: 415-821-5389 (Call before faxing); *Imprints*: Pelagia Press (Pelagia Pr)
E-mail: rabar@mindspring.com.

Calvary Chapel Church, Inc., *(978-0-9708600; 978-1-932283)* 2401 W. Cypress Creek Rd., Fort Lauderdale, FL 33309 USA
E-mail: snt@thecalebgroup.com; kirk@calvaryftl.org
Dist(s): **Send The Light Distribution LLC.**

Publisher Name Index

Calvary Chapel Pasadena, *(978-0-9773829; 978-0-9796332; 978-0-9898616; 978-0-9975110; 978-1-7333057)* 2200 E. Colorado Blvd., Pasadena, CA 91107 USA Tel 626-584-9992; Fax: 626-584-0728; *Imprints:* Simple Truths (SimpleTruths)
E-mail: ccp@ccpas.com
Web site: http://www.calvarychapelpasadena.com.

Calvin Partnership, LLC, *(978-1-891533)* 40 Ardmore Rd., Ho-Ho-Kus, NJ 07443-1008 USA Tel 201-670-8412; Fax: 201-670-0464
E-mail: jahelka@attglobal.net.

Calychio Publishing, *(978-0-9649156; 978-0-9964126)* 4138 Kildare St., Eugene, OR 97404 USA Tel 501-653-8990
E-mail: tshionyim@yahoo.com.

Camahort, Nuria, *(978-1-7347967)* 1570 Merryweather Dr, Bethlehem, PA 18015 USA Tel 484-515-9160
E-mail: nuria.camahort@gmail.com.

Camas Pr., *(978-0-9856698)* 2219 240th Ave. SE, Sammamish, WA 98075 USA Tel 425-922-5064
E-mail: info@camaspress.com.

Camber Pr., *(978-0-9727455)* 807 Central Ave. # 2, Peekskill, NY 10566-2039 USA
Web site: http://www.camberpress.com.

Cambium Education, Inc., *(978-0-944584; 978-1-57035; 978-1-59318; 978-1-932282; 978-1-4168; 978-1-60218; 978-1-60697)* 4093 Specialty Pl., Longmont, CO 80504 USA (SAN 243-945X) Tel 303-651-2829; Fax: 303-907-8694; Toll Free: 800-547-6747 (orders only)
E-mail: publishing@sopriswest.com; customerservice@cambiumlearning.com
Web site: http://www.sopriswest.com.

Cambria Creations, LLC, *(978-0-9770916)* 515 Main St., Johnston, PA 15901 USA Tel 814-535-5571; Fax: 814-535-1079
E-mail: djwlaw@wvdsl.net.

Cambridge Bks. *Imprint of* **Write Words, Inc.**

Cambridge Bk. Co., *(978-0-8428)* Div. of Simon & Schuster, Inc., 4350 Equity Dr., Box 249, Columbus, OH 43216 USA (SAN 169-5703) Toll Free: 800-238-5833
Web site: http://www.simonsays.com/.

Cambridge BrickHouse, Inc., *(978-1-58018; 978-1-59835)* 60 Island St. Suite 102 E., Lawrence, MA 01844 USA; *Imprints:* CBH Books (CBH Bks); BrickHouse Education (BrickHse)
E-mail: edelgado@cambridgebh.com; ycanetti@cambridgebh.com; mkamelle@cambridgebh.com
Web site: http://www.cambridgebh.com; http://www.brickhouseeducation.com
Dist(s): **Ediciones Universal**
Follett School Solutions
Lectorum Pubns., Inc.

Cambridge Educational Services, Inc., *(978-1-58894)* 2860 S River Rd, Des Plaines, IL 60018 USA Tel 847-299-2930; Fax: 847-299-2933 Do not confuse with Cambridge Educational in Charleston, WV
Web site: http://www.cambridgeed.com.

Cambridge House Pr. *Imprint of* **Sterling & Ross Pubs.**

Cambridge Hse. Publishing Co., LLC, *(978-0-9711359)* P.O. Box 383, Saddle River, NJ 07458 USA Fax: 973-777-8075
E-mail: cambridgehouse@verizon.net
Web site: http://www.cezanneismissing.com; http://www.cambridgehousepublishing.com.

Cambridge Univ. Pr. (GBR) *(978-0-521; 978-1-108; 978-1-107; 978-1-139; 978-1-009; 978-1-316) Dist. by* **Cambridge U Pr.**

Cambridge Univ. Pr. (SGP) *(978-0-521) Dist. by* **Cambridge U Pr.**

†**Cambridge Univ. Pr.,** *(978-0-521; 978-0-511)* Orders Addr.: 100 Brook Hill Dr., West Nyack, NY 10994-2133 USA (SAN 281-3769) Tel 845-353-7500; Fax: 845-353-4141; Toll Free: 800-872-7423 (orders, returns, credit & accounting); 800-937-9600; Edit Addr.: 32 Avenue of the Americas, New York, NY 10013-2473 USA (SAN 200-206X) Tel 212-924-3900; Fax: 212-691-3239
E-mail: customer_service@cup.org; orders@cup.org; information@cup.org
Web site: http://www.cambridge.org/
Dist(s): **Baker Bks.**
Boydell & Brewer, Inc.
Casemate Academic
Chicago Distribution Ctr.
CreateSpace Independent Publishing Platform
Ebsco Publishing
Cengage Gale
ISD
Ingram Publisher Services
Ingram Content Group
Rittenhouse Bk. Distributors
Savvas Learning Co.
Two Rivers Distribution
ebrary, Inc.; *CIP.*

Cambridge Way Publishing, *(978-0-9746976)* 149 Cambridge Way, Macon, GA 31220-8736 USA (SAN 255-8041) Tel 478-475-1763
E-mail: whwatson2@cox.net.

CamCat Publishing, *(978-1-929017; 978-0-7443; 978-0-9702385; 978-1-931540)* Orders Addr.: 101 Creekside Crossing Ste 280, Brentwood, TN 37027 USA (SAN 254-4962) Tel 833-782-5747; Edit Addr.: 101 Creekside Crossing Ste 280, Brentwood, TN 37027 USA Tel 833-782-5747
E-mail: sue@camcatpublishing.com; staff@camcatpublishing.com; dayna@camcatpublishing.com
Web site: http://www.synergebooks.com; https://camcatpublishing.com/; http://camcatbooks.com/
Dist(s): **Independent Pubs. Group.**

Camelot Publishing, *(978-0-9754063)* Orders Addr.: P.O. Box 500057, Lake Los Angeles, CA 93535 USA (SAN 256-0666)
E-mail: camelotpublishing@hotmail.com
Web site: http://www.camelotpublishing.com.

Camelot Tales, *(978-0-9672375)*
E-mail: jeanette.adams@hotmail.com
Web site: http://www.bellowinghills.com.

Cameltrotters Publishing, *(978-0-9666110; 978-0-9764475)* Orders Addr.: P.O. Box 3026, Pinedale, CA 93650-3526 USA Tel 559-447-9393 (phone/fax)
E-mail: ted@atborgeas.com
Web site: http://www.atborgeas.com.

Cameo Pubns., LLC, *(978-0-9715739; 978-0-9744149; 978-0-9744966; 978-0-9774659)* Orders Addr.: 2175 Deer Run Trl., Jacksonville, FL 32246-1068 USA
E-mail: info@cameopublications.com; publisher@cameopublications.com
Web site: http://www.cameopublications.com
Dist(s): **Bookazine Co., Inc.**
CreateSpace Independent Publishing Platform
Distributors, The
New Leaf Publishing Group
Scholastic, Inc.
Shenanigan Bks.

Cameo Renae Bks., *(978-1-7350467)* 9693 Marcelline Ave, Las Vegas, NV 89148 USA Tel 901-414-0231
E-mail: cameo.renae@gmail.com
Web site: www.cameorenae.com.

Cameron + Co., *(978-0-918684; 978-1-937359; 978-1-944903; 978-1-949480; 978-1-951836)* 149 Kentucky St., Suite 7, Petaluma, CA 94952 USA Tel 707-769-1617; Fax: 415-223-8520; *Imprints:* Cameron Kids (CameronKids); Cameron Books (Cameron Bks)
E-mail: orders@cameronbooks.com; info@cameronbooks.com
Web site: http://www.cameronbooks.com
Dist(s): **Abrams, Inc.**
Abrams & Co. Pubs., Inc.
Andrews McMeel Publishing
Follett School Solutions
Hachette Bk. Group
Ingram Publisher Services
MyiLibrary
Open Road Integrated Media, Inc.
Publishers Group West (PGW).

Cameron Books *Imprint of* **Cameron + Co.**

Cameron Kids *Imprint of* **Cameron + Co.**

Camino Bks., Inc., *(978-0-940159; 978-1-933822; 978-1-68098)* P.O. Box 59026, Philadelphia, PA 19102 USA (SAN 664-225X) Tel 215-413-1917; Fax: 215-413-3255
E-mail: camino@caminobooks.com
Web site: http://www.caminobooks.com
Dist(s): **Follett School Solutions**
INscribe Digital
Independent Pubs. Group
Partners Pubs. Group, Inc.

Camino E.E. & Bk. Co., *(978-0-940808; 978-1-55893)* Orders Addr.: a/o Jan Linzy, P.O. Box 6400, Incline Village, NV 89450 USA (SAN 219-841X) Tel 775-831-3078 (phone/fax); Fax: 775-831-3078 (phone/fax)
E-mail: info@camino-books.com
Web site: http://www.camino-books.com.

Camino Real Calendar LLC, *(978-0-9743501)* P.O. Box 17667, Anaheim, CA 92817 USA Toll Free: 800-200-6331
E-mail: support@caminosports.com
Web site: http://www.caminosports.com.

Camino Real Sports Marketing *See* **Camino Real Calendar LLC**

Cammilleri Productions, *(978-0-615-25933-8)* 2565 San Clemente Dr., Unit 206, Corta Mesa, CA 92626 USA (SAN 857-507X) Tel 714-486-1318
E-mail: jcammilleri@ca.rr.com.

Camozzi, Victor, *(978-0-692-58132-2; 978-0-692-75176-3)* 7220 Lapin Cove, AUSTIN, TX 78739 USA Tel 512-468-7188.

Camp Pope Publishing, *(978-0-9628936; 978-1-929919)* Orders Addr.: P.O. Box 2232, Iowa City, IA 52244 USA Tel 319-351-2407; Fax: 319-339-5964; Toll Free: 800-204-2407; Edit Addr.: 1117 E. Davenport, Iowa City, IA 52245 USA
E-mail: mail@camppope.com
Web site: http://www.camppope.com
Dist(s): **Ingram Content Group.**

Campanita Bks. *Imprint of* **Editorial Campana**

Campbell, Ruth, *(978-0-9839798; 978-1-952049)* 1611 Highland Ave., Glendale, CA 91202 USA Tel 818-371-5238
E-mail: lzglotz@pacbell.net.

Campbell, Sherrel, *(978-1-7353760)* 52 Dunlap St, New Providence, NJ 07974 USA Tel 973-534-2210
E-mail: tytajurel@verizon.net.

CampCrest Publishing, *(978-0-9763257)* 385 Hidden Hollow Ln., Chickamauga, GA 30707 USA
E-mail: sallyworland@mindspring.com.

Campfire *Imprint of* **Steerforth Pr.**

Campfire Technology LLC, *(978-1-7360406)* 172 Ethan Dr, Windsor, CT 06095 USA Tel 413-308-0312
E-mail: jlouro@campfiretechnology.com
Web site: https://www.campfiretechnology.com.

Camping Guideposts *See* **Wordshed**

Campus Crusade for Christ, *(978-1-56399)* Affil. of Campus Crusade for Christ International, Orders Addr.: 375 Hwy. 74 S., Suite A, Peachtree City, GA 30269 USA Tel 770-631-9940; Fax: 770-631-9916; Toll Free: 800-827-2788
E-mail: customerservice@campuscrusade.org
Web site: http://www.campuscrusade.com.

Can Do Duck Publishing, *(978-0-9768384)* P.O. Box 1045, Voorhees, NJ 08043 USA Tel 856-816-5255; Fax: 856-429-0094
E-mail: ducktormorty@thecandoduck.com
Web site: http://www.thecandoduck.com.

Canadian Geographic Enterprises (CAN) *(978-0-9685821; 978-1-894524; 978-0-9867516; 978-1-989227) Dist. by* **HachBkGrp.**

Canal History & Technology Pr. *Imprint of* **Delaware &Lehigh National Heritage Corridor, Inc.**

Canary Connect Pubns., *(978-0-9643462)* Div. of SOBOLE, Inc., 605 Holiday Rd., Coralville, IA 52241-1016 USA Tel 319-338-3827; Fax: 612-435-3340; *Imprints:* Just Think Books (Just Think Bks)
E-mail: sondrak@canaryconnect.com
Web site: http://www.canaryconnect.com; http://www.justthinkbooks.com; http://www.simplechoicesforhealthiereating.com; http://www.transitionstobetterliving.com
Dist(s): **Follett School Solutions**
Integral Yoga Pubns.
Nutri-Bks. Corp.

Candalyse Publishing, *(978-0-9798217; 978-0-9802275; 978-0-9817112)* Orders Addr.: P.O. Box 783, Smallwood, NY 12778 USA; Edit Addr.: 57 Karl Ave., Smallwood, NY 12778-0783 USA; *Imprints:* Chaklet Coffee Books (ChakletCoffee)
E-mail: candalysepublishing@gmail.com; chakletcoffee@gmail.com
Web site: http://www.candalysepublishing.com; http://www.chakletbooks.com
Dist(s): **Ingram Content Group.**

C&C Educational Materials, LLC *See* **C & C Educational Materials, LLC**

Candid Liv, *(978-0-9600373; 978-0-578-91684-2)* P.O. Box 335690, North Las Vegas, NV 89033 USA
Web site: www.candidliv.com.

C&K Publishing Co., *(978-0-9844342)* Orders Addr.: P.O. Box 291162, Columbia, SC 29229 USA Tel 803-414-0180; Fax: 803-462-1188; Edit Addr.: 320 Whitehurst Way, Columbia, SC 29229 USA
E-mail: candkpub@bellsouth.net.

Candle Light Pr., *(978-0-9743147; 978-0-9766053; 978-0-9895371; 978-0-9966176)* 1470 Walker Way, Coralville, IA 52242 USA Do not confuse with Candle Light Press in Martinez, CA.
E-mail: ding@candlelightpress.com
Web site: http://www.candlelightpress.com
Dist(s): **Follett School Solutions.**

CandleHill Publishing Co., *(978-1-945383)* 40 Pinehurst Ln., Half Moon Bay, CA 94019 USA Tel 415-350-6020
E-mail: tkirkhillyard@gmail.com.

Candlelight Bay Publishing, *(978-1-7326633)* 351 Riverview Dr., Grafton, WI 53024 USA Tel 414-573-7899
E-mail: Kidsdorool@gmail.com.

Candlelight Stories, Inc., *(978-0-615-14024-7)* 9909 Topanga Canyon Blvd., Chatsworth, CA 91311 USA
E-mail: orders@candlelightstories.com
Web site: http://www.candlelightstories.com
Dist(s): **Lulu Pr., Inc.**

Candleshoe Bks., *(978-0-9825089)* 3122 N. California Ave., Suite 3L, Chicago, IL 60618 USA
E-mail: info@candleshoebooks.com
Web site: http://www.candleshoebooks.com
Dist(s): **Music, Bks. & Business, Inc.**

Candleshoe Press, Inc. *See* **Candleshoe Bks.**

Candlewick Entertainment *Imprint of* **Candlewick Pr.**

Candlewick on Brilliance Audio *Imprint of* **Brilliance Publishing, Inc.**

†**Candlewick Pr.,** *(978-0-7636; 978-1-56402; 978-1-5362)* Div. of Walker Bks., London, England, 99 Dover St., Somerville, MA 02144 USA Tel 617-661-3330; Fax: 617-661-0565; *Imprints:* Templar (Templar); Nosy Crow (NosyCrow); Big Picture Press (Big Picture Pr); Toon Books (Toon Bks); MIT Kids Press (MIT Kids); MITeen Press (MITEEN); Candlewick Entertainment (Candlewick Entmt) Do not confuse with Candlewick Pr., Crystal Lake, IL
E-mail: bigbear@candlewick.com; salesinfo@candlewick.com
Web site: http://www.candlewick.com/
Dist(s): **Chicago Distribution Ctr.**
Children's Plus, Inc.
Follett School Solutions
Penguin Random Hse. Distribution
Penguin Random Hse. LLC
Perfection Learning Corp.
Random Hse., Inc.; *CIP.*

Candlewood Pr. *Imprint of* **Harding Hse. Publishing Sebice Inc.**

C&N Publishing, *(978-0-578-94385-5; 978-0-578-95650-3)* 5560 Franklin Pike Cir Suite 202, Nashville, TN 37221 USA Tel 615-428-3082
Dist(s): **CreateSpace Independent Publishing Platform.**

C&V 4 Seasons Publishing, *(978-0-692-26548-2; 978-0-9864036; 978-1-7358388)* P.O. Box 683, Mayflower, AR 72106 USA Tel 501-336-4726
E-mail: mariahoskins50@yahoo.com
Web site: www.seasons2dream.com.

Candy Cane Bks. *Imprint of* **Sunlight Publishing**

Candy Wrapper, *(978-1-940556)* 1520 Belle View Blvd, Alexandria, VA 22307 USA
E-mail: hello@candywrapper.co
Web site: candywrapper.co.

Candy Wrapper Inc. *See* **Candy Wrapper**

Candy's Creations *See* **Fruitbearer Publishing, LLC**

Cane Creek Productions, *(978-0-578-22728-3)* 325 County Rd. 519, Moulton, AL 35650 USA Tel 256-214-3710
E-mail: icemancoolwater@yahoo.com.

Cane River Trading Co., Inc., *(978-0-9744189)* 1473 Cty. Rte. 26, Climax, NY 12042-2211 USA Tel 518-731-8598
E-mail: ny5kmagi@aol.com
Web site: http://members.aol.com/CaneR71456/.

Canh Nam Pubs., *(978-0-9749097; 978-0-9772129; 978-0-9799345; 978-0-9883504)* 2607 Military Rd., Arlington, VA 22207 USA
E-mail: canhnam@dc.net.

Canis Lupus Productions, *(978-0-9661789)* Orders Addr.: P.O. Box 128262, San Diego, CA 92102-8262 USA; Edit Addr.: 1940 Third Ave., Unit 406, San Diego, CA 92101-2622 USA Tel 310-873-3232 (phone/fax)
E-mail: jlbrooks@email.com.

Canmore Pr., *(978-1-887774)* Orders Addr.: P.O. Box 510794 Melbourne Beach, FL 32951-0794 USA Tel 321-729-0078; Fax: 321-724-1162; *Imprints:* Wynden (Wynden)
E-mail: publish@canmorepress.com
Web site: http://www.canmorepress.com.

Cannady, John, *(978-0-9754345)* 6126 Dunwoody Ct., Montgomery, AL 36117-5012 USA
E-mail: katphishe@starband.net
Web site: http://www.hopetkd.com.

Cannon, K. L., *(978-0-9675594)* 9412 Meadow Vale, Austin, TX 78758 USA Tel 512-837-6281; Fax: 512-837-7205
E-mail: cankl@msn.com.

Cannon Publishing Group, *(978-0-9766291)* 230 Merrill Rd., Walla Walla, WA 99362 USA
Web site: http://www.cannonpublishinggroup.com.

Canoed Sun Publishing, LLC, *(978-0-9836081)* 902 Franklin Ave., Council Bluffs, IA 51503 USA Tel 402-541-6452.

Canon Pr., *(978-1-885767; 978-1-930443; 978-1-59128; 978-1-935000; 978-1-944503; 978-1-947644; 978-1-952410; 978-1-954887; 978-1-957905)* Div. of Credenda Agenda, Orders Addr.: P.O. Box 8729, Moscow, ID 83843 USA (SAN 257-3792); 207 N Main St, Moscow, ID 83843 (SAN 990-1671) Tel 208-596-3867; *Imprints:* Canonball Books (Canonball) Do not confuse with companies with the same or similar names in Grand Rapids, MI, Centerville, UT
E-mail: brian@canonpress.org
Web site: http://www.canonpress.com; http://www.canonballbooks.com; http://www.logospressonline.com
Dist(s): **Follett School Solutions.**

Canonball Bks. *Imprint of* **Canon Pr.**

Cantab Publishing, *(978-0-9745150)* P.O. Box 381591, Cambridge, MA 02238-1591 USA.

Cantata Learning, *(978-1-63290; 978-1-68410)* 1710 Roe Crest Dr., North Mankato, MN 56003 USA Tel 952-224-0518
E-mail: info@cantatalearning.com
Web site: cantatalearning.com
Dist(s): **Capstone.**

Cantemos-bilingual bks. and music, *(978-0-9623930; 978-1-892306)* Orders Addr.: 15696 Altamira Dr., Chino Hills, CA 91709 USA Tel 909-239-2735
E-mail: jarjetb@writeme.com; bakergeorgette@yahoo.com
Web site: http://www.cantemosco.com; http://www.simplespanishsongs.com
Dist(s): **Continental Bk. Co., Inc.**
Follett School Solutions
Midwest Library Service.

Canterbury & York Society (GBR) *(978-0-907239; 978-0-903491) Dist. by* **TwoRivers.**

Canterbury Classics *Imprint of* **Printers Row Publishing Group**

Canterbury Hse. Publishing, Ltd., *(978-0-9825396; 978-0-9829054; 978-0-9881897; 978-0-9908416; 978-0-9970119; 978-1-945401)* P.O. Box 102, Sonoita, AZ 85637 USA Tel 520-329-2729
Web site: www.canterburyhousepublishing.com
Dist(s): **Ingram Content Group Inc.**
Smashwords.

Canterwine Pr., *(978-0-9764184)* 608 Longview Ave., Anacortes, WA 98221 USA Tel 360-941-4692
E-mail: jordanmcmakin@hotmail.com
Web site: http://www.canterwinepress.com.

Cantrell, Wendy, *(978-1-7325057)* 45 Allison Rd., Mills River, NC 28759 USA Tel 828-891-2750
E-mail: cantrellfarm@yahoo.com.

Cantu, Ricardo, *(978-0-615-14898-4; 978-0-615-15149-6; 978-0-615-18600-9)* 2389 Tobello Blvd., Indianapolis, IN 46234 USA
E-mail: ricardocantu6908@sbcglobal.net
Dist(s): **Lulu Pr., Inc.**

Canyada Publishing, LLC, *(978-1-7346220)* 2613 W Stuart St., Fort Collins, CO 80526 USA Tel 818-427-3986
E-mail: kchew@alumni.nd.edu.

Canyon Beach Visual Communications, *(978-0-9754221)* PMB 108, 10 St. Francis Way, Unit 9, Cranberry Township, PA 16066 USA Tel 724-612-5784
E-mail: info@canyonbeach.com
Web site: http://www.canyonbeach.com.

Canyon Hawk Bks., *(978-0-578-10507-9)* 1750 El Paso Real, La Jolla, CA 92037 USA Tel 858-454-2475
E-mail: hobbes@san.rr.com.

Cap & Compass, LLC, *(978-0-9717366)* 132 Chestnut St., Branford, CT 06405 USA Tel 203-483-7005
E-mail: jesse@capandcompass.com
Web site: http://www.capandcompass.com
Dist(s): **Baker & Taylor Publisher Services (BTPS).**

Capercaillie Bks., Ltd (GBR) *(978-0-9542905; 978-0-9545206; 978-0-9549625; 978-0-9551246; 978-1-909305) Dist. by* **MYID_F_GATEWOO.**

Capital Apple Pr., *(978-0-9830686)* 742 Front St. No. 1, Catasauqua, PA 18032 USA Tel 610-596-0266.

Capital City Bks. LLC, *(978-0-9842881; 978-0-9835788)* c/o Hartwood Publishing, 1 N. 5th St., Suite 511, Richmond, VA 23219 USA Tel 804-836-6870; Fax: 804-644-3092
E-mail: capitalcitybooks@gmail.com
Web site: http://www.capitalcitybooks.com.

Capital Communications, Inc., *(978-0-9647700)* P.O. Box 10338, Sarasota, FL 34278-0338 USA Tel 941-342-9088; Fax: 941-377-3120; Toll Free: 800-546-8378
E-mail: capital@investors.org
Web site: http://www.investors.org.

Capital Publishing, *(978-0-9773016)* 6311 10th Ave., Brooklyn, NY 11219 USA Tel 718-921-6400; Fax: 718-921-0160
E-mail: pommedia@pommedia.com.

Capital Station Bks., LLC, *(978-0-9980452; 978-1-7334428; 978-1-7347587; 978-1-7369899; 978-1-7379416; 978-1-957613)* 5115 Hildreth Ln., Stockton, CA 95212 USA
E-mail: s.adelle.s@gmail.com.

For full information on wholesalers and distributors, refer to the Wholesaler and Distributor Name Index

apitol Advantage Publishing *See* **Congress At Your Fingertips**
appella Publishing, A, *(978-0-9760271)* 20505 Yorba Linda Blvd., Suite 505, Yorba Linda, CA 92886 USA Tel 714-336-2350; Fax: 714-685-7773
E-mail: cgriffiths@acappellapublishing.com
Web site: http://www.acappellapublishing.com.
apri Publishing, *(978-0-9769132; 978-0-9788612)* 4401 NW 39th St., #518, Midwest City, OK 73112 USA Tel 405-623-7619
E-mail: capripub@aol.com
Web site: http://www.capripublishing.net.
apriccio Publishing, *(978-0-9770076)* 11100 SW 93rd Ct. Rd., Suite 10-405, Ocala, FL 34481 USA Tel 352-873-1403.
apricorn Hse. Publishing, *(978-0-9791702; 978-1-60466)* 5122 Annesway Dr., Nashville, TN 37205 USA
E-mail: pclif@comcast.net.
apricorn Publishing, *(978-0-9753970; 978-0-9774757)* 706 E. Brewster St., Appleton, WI 54911 USA Tel 920-475-0674; Fax: 920-954-9533
E-mail: getovd@yahoo.com
Web site: http://www.CapricornPublishing.com.
Capricorn Publishing, Incorporated *See* **Capricorn Publishing**
CAPS, LLC *See* **ALCAPS, LLC**
Capstone *Imprint of* **Wiley, John & Sons, Inc.**
Capstone, *(978-0-7368; 978-0-929895; 978-1-56065; 978-0-7565; 978-1-4048; 978-1-59889; 978-1-4296; 978-1-934338; 978-1-4342; 978-1-936700; 978-1-937412; 978-1-62065; 978-1-4765; 978-1-62370; 978-1-4795; 978-1-62521; 978-1-4914; 978-1-63079; 978-1-4965; 978-1-4966; 978-1-5157; 978-1-5158; 978-1-68436; 978-1-5435; 978-1-9771; 978-1-68446; 978-1-6639; 978-1-6663; 978-1-6690) Div. of Coughlan Companies, LLC, 1905 Lookout Dr., North Mankato, MN 55003 USA Tel 507-385-8215; Fax: 507-388-3752; Orders Addr.: 1710 Roe Crest Dr., North Mankato, MN 56003 USA (SAN 254-1815) Toll Free Fax: 888-262-0705; Toll Free: 800-747-4992; Edit Addr.: 5050 Lincoln Dr Suite 200, Edina, MN 55436 USA Fax: 952-933-2410; Toll Free: 888-517-8977;* *Imprints:* Pebble (Pebble Bks); Capstone Press (Capstone); Capstone Classroom (Cpstone Class); Capstone Editions (Caps Editions); Capstone Young Readers (Cap Young Rea); Compass Point Books (Compass Pt); Heinemann (Heinem); Maupin House Publishing (Maupin Pub); NA-r (NA-r); Picture Window Books (Pic Window); Raintree (RaintreeCap); Red Brick Learning (Red BrickL); Switch Press (Switch Pr); Stone Arch Books (Stone Arch) Do not confuse with Capstone Pr., Inc. in Decatur, IL
E-mail: customerservice@capstonepub.com
Web site: http://www.capstone-press.com; http://www.capstonepub.com; http://www.capstoneclassroom.com
Dist(s): **Casemate Pubs. & Bk. Distributors, LLC**
Continental Bk. Co., Inc.
Ebsco Publishing
Follett School Solutions
Lectorum Pubns., Inc.
MyiLibrary
SPD-Small Pr. Distribution.
Capstone Academics LLC, *(978-1-933557)* 3815 N. Brookfield Rd., Suite No. 104-122, Brookfield, WI 53045 USA (SAN 256-6761) Tel 262-754-4699; Toll Free: 888-922-7786
E-mail: contact@capstoneacademics.com
Web site: http://www.capstoneacademics.com.
Capstone Bks., *(978-0-9752843)* P.O. Box 7025, Greenwood, IN 46142 USA Tel 317-414-4770; 1710 Roe Crest Drive, N. Mankato, MN 56003
Web site: http://www.capstonebooks.com
Dist(s): **Follett School Solutions.**
Capstone Classroom *Imprint of* **Capstone**
Capstone Editions *Imprint of* **Capstone**
Capstone Media Services, *(978-0-578-42014-1; 978-0-578-42394-4; 978-0-578-42414-9; 978-0-578-42644-0; 978-0-578-43104-8; 978-0-578-43108-6; 978-0-578-43109-3; 978-0-578-43110-9; 978-0-578-43112-3; 978-0-578-43113-0; 978-0-578-43115-4; 978-0-578-43176-5; 978-0-578-43350-9; 978-0-578-43399-8; 978-0-578-43400-1; 978-0-578-43522-0; 978-0-578-43529-9; 978-0-578-43630-2; 978-0-578-43738-5; 978-0-578-43894-8; 978-0-578-43896-2; 978-0-578-43950-1; 978-0-578-43951-8; 978-0-578-43952-5; 978-0-578-43988-4; 978-0-578-44038-5;) 14 Wall St., NEW YORK, NY 10005 USA Tel 347-748-1480*
E-mail: Support@capstonemediaservice.com
Dist(s): **Ingram Content Group.**
Capstone Pr. *Imprint of* **Capstone**
Capstone Press, Incorporated *See* **Capstone**
Capstone Pr., Inc., *(978-0-9667204)* 172 Dipper Ln., No. 6, Decatur, IL 62522 USA Tel 217-422-6033 Do not confuse with Capstone Pr., Inc., Mankato, MN
E-mail: jsjcjj@fgi.net.
Capstone Young Readers *Imprint of* **Capstone**
Captain & Harry LLC, The, *(978-0-9724777)* 8875 Section Line Rd., Harbor Beach, MI 48441-9616 USA
E-mail: janlangley5@gmail.com
Web site: http://www.michiganghoststories.net; http://www.thecaptainandharry.com.
Captain Caleb Communications, *(978-0-9703021)* 1250 Cynder Ct., Annapolis, MD 21401-7504 USA Tel 410 626 8904; 410-626-8904
E-mail: jcurtis@toad.net
Web site: http://www.oysterbook.com.
Captain Fiddle Pubns., *(978-0-931877)* 4 Elm Ct., Newmarket, NH 03857 USA (SAN 686-0508) Tel 603-659-2658
E-mail: cFiddle@tiac.net
Web site: http://www.captainfiddle.com.
Captain McFinn and Friends LLC, McFinn Pr., *(978-0-9799283; 978-0-9859482)* 2445 Belmont Ave., Youngstown, OH 44504-0186 USA Tel 330-747-2661; Fax: 330-743-2719
E-mail: kbaker@cafarocompany.com.
Captain, Tamira R. *See* **Stories From Four Publishing Co.**
Captain the Big Dog Pr., *(978-0-9995096)* P.O. Box 1135, Pentwater, MI 49449 USA Tel 231-869-5896
E-mail: ordoobadifamily@gmail.com.
Captio Corp., *(978-0-9766614)* 2230 Tioga Dr., Menlo Park, CA 94025-6640 USA
Web site: http://www.captio.com.
Capture Bks., *(978-0-9798664)* 12331 Checkerboard Cir., Norman, OK 73026 USA (SAN 854-6207) Tel 405-485-8131
Web site: http://capturebooks.com.
Capturing Memories, *(978-0-9727759)* 9228 SW 209th St, Vashon, WA 98070 USA Tel 206-463-5652
E-mail: roger@capturingmemories.com; stories@capturingmemories.com
Web site: http://www.capturingmemories.com.
Captus, LLC, *(978-0-9776627)* 32725 Ledge Hill Dr., Solon, OH 44139 USA Tel 440-498-9178; Fax: 440-238-2967
E-mail: cziance@yahoo.com
Web site: http://www.babyalmamater.com.
Capybara Madness, *(978-0-9899847)* 700 Jerrys Ln., Buda, TX 78610 USA Tel 512-751-6667
E-mail: typaldos@gmail.com
Web site: www.capybaramadness.com.
Carapetian, Chris, *(978-1-7324264)* 44509 Palo Verde st, Lancaster, CA 93536 USA Tel 818-216-3302
E-mail: hirisedesign@gmail.com.
Caravan of Dreams Productions, *(978-0-929856)* Div. of Caravan of Dreams, 512 Main St. Ste. 1500, Fort Worth, TX 76102-3922 USA (SAN 250-4855).
Carazona Creations LLC, *(978-0-9753724)* PO Box 635, Clarkdale, AZ 86324 USA Toll Free: 888-328-3300
E-mail: carazona@carazonacreations.com
Web site: http://www.carazonacreations.com.
Carbon Publishing *See* **Parallel Vortex**
Carden Jennings Publishing Co., Ltd., *(978-1-891524)* 375 Greenbrier Dr., Suite 100, Charlottesvle, VA 22901-1618 USA
Web site: http://www.cjp.com.
Cardigras.com *See* **airjam.com**
Cardinal Brands, Inc., *(978-1-932435)* 1251 SW Arrowhead Rd. Ste. A, Topeka, KS 66604-4061 USA Toll Free: 800-444-0038
Web site: http://www.witty-one.com; http://www.cardinalbrands.com.
Cardinal Pr., *(978-0-9779518)* 19 W. 76th St. Suite 1be, New York, NY 10023 USA
Web site: http://www.cardinal-press.com.
Cardinal Pubs. Group, 2402 N. Shadeland Ave. Ste. A, Indianapolis, IN 46219-1746 USA (SAN 631-7936)
E-mail: tdoherty@in.net.
Cardinal Rule Pr. *Imprint of* **Dismondy, Maria Inc.**
Cardinal Rule Pr., *(978-0-9960999; 978-0-9974864; 978-1-945369)* 1181 W. Lake Dr., Novi, MI 48377 USA; *Imprints:* Bucket Fillosophy (BucketFillosoph)
E-mail: info@cardinalrulepress.com
Web site: http://www.cardinalrulepress.com
Dist(s): **Independent Pubs. Group.**
Cardlings, *(978-0-9760108)* Orders Addr.: P.O. Box 931, Pueblo, CO 81002 USA; Edit Addr.: 815 W. 14th St., Pueblo, CO 81003 USA
E-mail: gnome@cardlings.com
Web site: http://www.cardlings.com.
Cardwell, Robert K, *(978-1-7323433; 978-1-7338348; 978-1-7377407)* 1 Warwick Rd., Ocean City, NJ 08226 USA Tel 609-334-3777
E-mail: kdrc4@aol.com.
Career Pr. *Imprint of* **Red Wheel/Weiser**
Carefree Publishing *Imprint of* **Milano, Jacque & Assocs.**
Carello, John, *(978-1-7348516)* 11 North Ave., New Rochelle, NY 10805 USA Tel 914-349-7226
E-mail: inhumanesoc@optonline.net
Web site: Theinhumanesociety.com.
Carey III, John, *(978-0-9799876)* 5510 NE. Antioch Suite 133, Gladstone, MO 64118 USA (SAN 854-9222)
E-mail: ecarey1222@yahoo.com.
Carey, Nicole, *(978-0-578-46245-5; 978-1-7331945; 978-1-7354788)* 3801 14th Ave., Kearney, NE 68845 USA Tel 308-240-0142
E-mail: ronicki@yahoo.com.
Carey, Rebecca, *(978-0-9791331)* 1035 S. 43rd St., Wilmington, NC 28403-4369 USA
E-mail: because@aol.com
Web site: http://www.bigarthouse.com.
Carey, William Library Publishers *See* **Carey, William Publishing**
Carey, William Publishing, *(978-0-87808; 978-1-64508)* 10 W. Dry Creek Cir., Littleton, CO 80120 USA (SAN 208-2101)
E-mail: publishing@wclbooks.com
Web site: https://missionbooks.org/
Dist(s): **Anchor Distributors**
Ingram Content Group
Whitaker Hse.
Cargill Consulting, Inc., *(978-0-9743780; 978-1-7333428)* P.O. Box PO Box 160, Harrah, OK 73045-9351 USA
Web site: http://www.chadcargill.com.
Caribbean Publishing *See* **Coconut Pr., LLC**
Caribbean Scene, *(978-0-9678030)* 5 Walnut Ave., East Norwich, NY 11732 USA.
CaribbeanReads, *(978-0-615-22865-5; 978-0-9832978; 978-0-9899305; 978-0-9908659; 978-0-9964358; 978-0-9978900; 978-0-9992372; 978-1-7338299; 978-1-953747)* 10314 Collingham Dr., Fairfax, VA 22032 USA Tel 202-683-0611
E-mail: carol.mitchell@caribbeanreads.com
Web site: www.caribbeanreads.com.
Caritas Communications, *(978-0-9668228; 978-0-9753259; 978-0-9799390; 978-0-615-76666-9; 978-0-615-87196-7)* 216 N. Green Bay Road, No. 208, Thiensville, WI 53092-2010 USA Tel 414-531-0503; Fax: 262-238-9039 Do not confuse with Caritas Communications Incorporated in New York, NY, Rhinebeck, NY
E-mail: dgawlik@wi.rr.com
Dist(s): **CreateSpace Independent Publishing Platform.**
Carleton Bks., *(978-0-9759738)* 335 N. Main Ave., Tucson, AZ 85701 USA.
Carlisle Pr.- Walnut Creek, *(978-0-9642548; 978-1-890050; 978-1-933753; 978-1-957814)* 2673 Township Rd., No. 421, Sugarcreek, OH 44681 USA Tel 330-852-1900; Fax: 330-852-3285; Toll Free: 800-852-4482 Do not confuse with companies with the same name in Mechanicsburg, PA, Sedona, AZ, Benbrook, TX.
CarLou Interactive Media & Publishing, *(978-0-9759325)* 12439 Magnolia Blvd., No. 170, Valley Village, CA 91607 USA
E-mail: tess@worldtrust.org
Web site: http://www.carloumedia.com.
Carlsbad Caverns Guadalupe Mountains Assn., *(978-0-916907)* P.O. Box 1417, Carlsbad, NM 88221-1417 USA (SAN 268-6627) Tel 505-785-2485.
Carlsbad Caverns Natural History Association *See* **Carlsbad Caverns Guadalupe Mountains Assn.**
Carlsen Verlag (DEU) *(978-3-551) Dist. by* **Distribks Inc.**
Carlson, Aimee, *(978-1-7374457)* 15464 Hunting Ridge Trail, Granger, IN 46530 USA Tel 574-344-6915
E-mail: acarlson128@gmail.com.
Carlson, Debra R., *(978-0-9765950)* 1705 N. 160th St., Omaha, NE 68118-2408 USA
Web site: http://www.cozykidspress.com.
Carlson Pr., *(978-0-9972220)* 614 BRADBURY RD, MONROVIA, CA 91016 USA Tel 951-541-7944
E-mail: carlsonlighthouse@hotmail.com.
Carlton Bks., Ltd. (GBR) *(978-1-85868; 978-1-84222; 978-1-84442; 978-1-84732; 978-1-78097; 978-1-78739; 978-1-911610) Dist. by* **TwoRivers.**
Carlton Kids (GBR) *(978-1-78312) Dist. by* **TwoRivers.**
Carmean Productions LLC, *(978-0-9839799)* 1905 NW 37th Blvd., Gainesville, FL 32605 USA Tel 352-514-5625
E-mail: John@johncarmean.com
Web site: www.carmeanproductions.com.
Carmel Concepts, Ltd., *(978-0-9646285)* 50 Mt. Tiburon Rd., Tiburon, CA 94920 USA Tel 415-435-8066; Fax: 415-435-3750.
Carnaval Editorial, *(978-1-7377170)* 3441 S Decker Ln. Dr, West Valley City, UT 84119 USA Tel 916-308-3840
E-mail: carnavaleditorial@gmail.com.
Carnegie Learning Incorporated *See* **Carnegie Learning Inc.**
Carnegie Learning Inc., *(978-1-930804; 978-1-932409; 978-1-934239; 978-1-934800; 978-1-935162; 978-1-936152; 978-1-60972; 978-1-949240; 978-1-68459; 978-1-63862; 979-8-89235)* 501 Grant St., Suite 1075, Pittsburgh, PA 15219 USA Tel 412-690-2442 Toll Free: 888-851-7094
Web site: http://carnegielearning.com.
Carnelian Moon Publishing *See* **Carnelian Moon Publishing, Inc.**
Carnelian Moon Publishing, Inc., *(978-1-7376060)* 15919 Robin Hill Loop, Clermont, FL 34714 USA Tel 352-631-3378
E-mail: debbie@carnelianmoonpublishing.com
Web site: carnelianmoonpublishing.com.
Carney Educational Services, *(978-1-930288)* 1150 Foothill Blvd., Ste B, La Canada, CA 91011 USA Toll Free: 888-511-7737
E-mail: michellecarroll67@gmail.com
Web site: http://www.thebrightmind.com
Dist(s): **Sunbelt Pubns., Inc.**
Carney, Sean Creative LLC *See* **Bull & Brain Creative**
Carnifex Pr., *(978-0-9759727; 978-0-9789583)* P.O. Box 1686, Ormond Beach, FL 32175 USA Tel 386-677-2980
E-mail: carnifexpress@hotmail.com
Web site: http://www.carnifexpress.net.
Carnivore Games, *(978-0-9749150; 978-1-7339749)* Orders Addr.: P.O. Box 846, Londonderry, NH 03053-0846 USA; Edit Addr.: 12 Emerald Dr., Derry, NH 03038 USA
E-mail: brad@carnivoregames.com
Web site: http://www.carnivoregames.com/.
Carol J. Pierre, LLC, *(978-0-578-19829-3)* 2045 Mt. Zion Rd., Suite 366, Morrow, GA 30260 USA Tel 678-615-5965; *Imprints:* Pierre Publishing (PierrePub)
E-mail: millonesinc@yahoo.com; moneymindbook@gmail.com
Web site: www.moneymindbooks.com.
Carol Kalhagen-Tamanaha, *(978-0-9799493)* 36020 Big Trout Rd., Hebo, OR 97122 USA
E-mail: beartotem@earthlink.net
Web site: http://www.CarolKalhagenWildlifeart.com.
Carol Stream Animal Hospital, *(978-1-7367495)* 982 Lockwood Ln 0, BATAVIA, IL 60510 USA Tel 4077709222
E-mail: mondrian79@msn.com
Dist(s): **Ingram Content Group.**
Carole "Lisa Lynn" Gilbert, *(978-0-692-98458-1; 978-0-692-11031-7; 978-0-692-19521-5; 978-0-692-19793-6; 978-1-7329447; 978-1-7346873; 979-8-9861158)* 1708 Quail Valley Rd., Iowa Park, TX 76367 USA Tel 940-592-1136; Fax: 940-592-1136
E-mail: mamagilbert@aol.com
Web site: carolelgilbert.com.
Carolina Academic Pr., *(978-0-89089; 978-1-59460; 978-1-61163; 978-1-5310)* 700 Kent St., Durham, NC 27701 USA (SAN 210-7848) Tel 919-489-7486; Fax: 919-493-5668
E-mail: tim@cap-press.com; css@cap-press.com
Dist(s): **Follett School Solutions.**
Carolina Biological Supply Co., *(978-0-89278; 978-1-4350)* 2700 York Rd., Burlington, NC 27215-3398 USA (SAN 249-2784) Tel 336-584-0381; Fax: 910-584-3399; Toll Free Fax: 800-222-7112; Toll Free: 800-334-5551
E-mail: carolina@carolina.com
Web site: http://www.carolina.com
Dist(s): **Follett School Solutions.**
Carolina Canines for Service Inc., *(978-0-9800070)* P.O. Box 12643, Wilmington, NC 28405-1823 USA Tel 910-362-8181; Fax: 910-362-8184; Toll Free: 866-910-3647
Web site: http://www.carolinacanines.org.
Carolina Children, *(978-0-9794580)* P.O. Box 862, Mauldin, SC 29662 USA
Web site: http://carolinachildren.net.
†Carolina Wren Pr., *(978-0-89587; 978-0-910244; 978-0-932112; 978-1-949467; 978-1-958888)* 811 9th St. Suite 120-137, Durham, NC 27705 USA (SAN 213-0327) Tel 919-682-0555; *Imprints:* Blair (MYID_W_BLAIR)
E-mail: ops@blairpubl.com
Dist(s): **Consortium Bk. Sales & Distribution**
Follett School Solutions
MyiLibrary; *CIP.*
Carolrhoda Bks. *Imprint of* **Lerner Publishing Group**
Carolrhoda Lab™ *Imprint of* **Lerner Publishing Group**
Carolyn & Kristina's Bookshelf, *(978-0-615-18357-2)* 550 Brittany Ct., North Huntingdon, PA 15642 USA
E-mail: prin66@aol.com; cnkbkshelf@aim.com
Dist(s): **Lulu Pr., Inc.**
Carousel Pubns., Inc., *(978-0-9759382)* P.O. Box 225, Springfield, NJ 07081 USA
Web site: http://www.net2infinity/aplaceinthesky.
Carp Cove Pr., *(978-0-9703752)* Orders Addr.: 9099 Oneida River Pk. Dr., Clay, NY 13041 USA Tel 315-652-4964
E-mail: carpcovepress@holisticanimal.com; Colleen@holisticanimal.com
Web site: http://www.holisticanimal.com/.
Carp Hse. Pr., *(978-0-9860663; 978-0-9860663-0-6)* 4403-B Catlin Cir., Carp interim, CA 93013 USA Tel 805-684-0691
E-mail: Gold2@cox.com.
Carpe Diem Pubs., *(978-0-615-35949-6; 978-0-9836691; 978-1-949215)* 17401 Betty Blvd., Canyon, TX 79015 USA Tel 806.433.6321
E-mail: carpediempublishers@gmail.com; craig.keel@gmail.com
Web site: CarpediemPublishers.com.
Carpe Noctem Publishing LLC, *(978-0-9965756; 978-1-950032)* P.O. Box 7949, Little Rock, AR 72217 USA Tel 501-993-2080
E-mail: authorjencrane@gmail.com
Web site: www.JenCraneBooks.com.
Carpe Viam Productions, LLC, *(978-0-9892949)* Orders Addr.: 3217 E. Shea Blvd. No. 305, Phoenix, AZ 85028 USA (SAN 920-8356) Tel 602-762-1473
E-mail: dwight@theLittleRedRacingCar.com
Web site: www.theLittleRedRacingCar.com.
Carpenter Bks., *(978-1-7347798)* 10014 fairway Vista Dr., Rowlett, TX 75089 USA Tel 385-489-4362
E-mail: jesscarpenterwrites@gmail.com
Web site: jesscarpenterwrites.com.
Carpenter's Son Publishing, *(978-0-9832846; 978-0-9835571; 978-0-9839876; 978-0-9849771; 978-0-9849772; 978-0-9851085; 978-0-9883043; 978-0-9883962; 978-0-9885931; 978-0-9889403; 978-0-9893722; 978-1-940262; 978-1-942557; 978-1-942587; 978-1-945507; 978-1-946889; 978-1-948484; 978-1-949572; 978-1-950892; 978-1-7340850; 978-1-952025; 978-1-954437; 978-1-956370) 307 Verde Meadow Dr., Franklin, TN 37067 USA Tel 615-472-1128*
E-mail: larry@christianbookservices.com
Dist(s): **Ingram Publisher Services**
Iron Stream Media
MyiLibrary
Send The Light Distribution LLC
Smashwords.
Carpentino, Michela, *(978-1-63843)* 13820 NE Airport Way Suite No. K322898, PORTLAND, OR 97251 USA Tel 3271428280
E-mail: michelacarpentino@libero.it
Dist(s): **Ingram Content Group.**
Carr Insight, *(978-1-7332637)* P.O. Box 10315, Fayetteville, AR 72703 USA Tel 479-283-3381
E-mail: carrie12001@gmail.com.
Carradice Collection, *(978-0-9985385; 978-0-578-41138-5; 978-0-578-53389-6; 978-0-578-60087-1)* 3925 Ivy St. Apt. 1 Front, East Chicago, IN 46312 USA Tel 219-718-6894; 3925 Ivy St. Apt. 1front, East Chicago, IN 46312
E-mail: ihadadream44@gmail.com; mikey_talbot@hotmail.com
Web site: http://carradicecollection.com.
Carriage Barn Bks., *(978-0-692-30787-8)* P.O. Box 247, Leeds, MA 01053 USA Tel 413-586-0283
Dist(s): **CreateSpace Independent Publishing Platform.**
Carriage House Publishing *See* **American Carriage Hse. Publishing**
Carrier, Therese, *(978-0-9797648)* 2020 Fieldstone Pkwy., Suite 900 PMB 121, Franklin, TN 37069 USA
Web site: http://hwbdproductions.com.
Carrington Bks., *(978-0-9787143; 978-0-9820003; 978-0-9819656)* P.O. Box 451399, Los Angeles, CA 90045 USA Tel 310-628-5557; 12975 Agustin Pl., No. A-109, Playa Vista, CA 90094
Web site: http://www.StudentSafetyTips.com.
Carrion, Whitney, *(978-1-7363277)* 5941 Harrell St., Fort Polk, LA 71459 USA Tel 224-489-8608
E-mail: mdubfitness5@gmail.com
Web site: whitneycarrion.com.
Carroll Pr., *(978-0-9986187)* 1510 Grand Ave, Seattle, WA 98122 USA Tel 206-328-5218
E-mail: mccormick.mj@comcast.net
Web site: susanmccormickbooks.com.

Carroll, Sherry, *(978-0-9752994)* P.O. Box 34603, Washington, DC 20774 USA
E-mail: carrollcom01@aol.com.

Carruthers, Rory, *(978-0-9861036; 978-1-949696)* 1730 N Laurelwood Loop, Canby, OR 97013 USA Tel 949-525-7384
E-mail: rory.carruthers@gmail.com.

Carson, Tracy, *(978-0-9767077)* 1998 66th St., SE, Bismarck, ND 58504-3835 USA
Web site: http://www.grandmaisnowabutterfly.com.

Carson-Dellosa Publishing Company, Incorporated *See* **Carson-Dellosa Publishing, LLC**

Carson-Dellosa Publishing, LLC, *(978-0-88724; 978-1-57156; 978-1-57332; 978-1-59441; 978-1-60022; 978-1-60418; 978-1-936022; 978-1-936023; 978-1-936024; 978-0-9823625; 978-0-9823626; 978-0-9823627; 978-0-692-00200-1; 978-1-60996; 978-1-62057; 978-1-62223; 978-1-62399; 978-1-62442; 978-1-62648; 978-1-4838) Orders Addr.: P.O. Box 35665, Greensboro, NC 27425 USA Tel 336-632-0084; Fax: 336-808-3249; Toll Free: 800-321-0943; Imprints:* DJ Inkers (DJInk); HighReach Learning, Incorporated (HghRchLrn); Brighter Child (BrighterChild); Spectrum (Spectrum Dell); Frank Schaffer Publications (FS Pubns); Instructional Fair (InstFair)
Web site: http://www.carsondellosa.com
Dist(s): **Follett School Solutions.**

Carsume, *(978-0-9883927)* 16509 Old Forest Rd., Hacienda Heights, CA 91745 USA Tel 626-968-2192
E-mail: sumeta@verizon.net.

Carter, Brittaney, *(978-1-7373426)* 277 S Brookhurst St APT No. C312, Anaheim, CA 92804 USA Tel 714-824-0681
E-mail: Brittaney@merchantmama.com.

Carter, Deborah, *(978-0-692-56254-3; 978-0-578-86679-6)* 380 Clocks Blvd., Massapequa, NY 11758 USA Tel 516-557-9562
E-mail: jobmagic@aol.com.

Carter, Pocahontas, *(978-1-7371099)* 10505 Birdie Ln, Upper Marlboro, MD 20774 USA Tel 202-440-5561
E-mail: carterpocahontas@gmail.com.

CarterPr. LLC, *(978-1-950596)* 725 River Rd., Suite 32-174, Edgewater, NJ 07020 USA Tel 866-233-7307
E-mail: zac@carterpress.com
Web site: www.carterpress.com.

Cartoon Connections Pr., *(978-0-9657136)* P.O. Box 10889, White Bear Lake, MN 55110 USA (SAN 299-352X) Tel 651-429-1244; 651-429-7660; 24145 435Th Ave., Aitkin, MN 56431
E-mail: CartoonC@aol.com
Web site: http://www.cartooningbasics.com; http://www.cartoonconnections.com
Dist(s): **Follett School Solutions**
F&W Media, Inc.

Cartoonmario.com, *(978-0-9766755)* 5084 S. 65th St., Greenfield, WI 53220-4504 USA Tel 414-541-9221 (phone/fax)
E-mail: duiliomario@gmail.com; marioduilio@gmail.com; marioduilio@yahoo.com
Web site: http://www.mariomacari.com.

Cartoons & Caricatures *See* **Drawing From History**

Cartwheel Bks. *Imprint of* **Scholastic, Inc.**

Cartwright Publishing, *(978-0-9861613; 978-1-7321736)* P.O. Box 145, Corte Madera, CA 94925 USA Tel 415-354-2388
E-mail: mark@datagroup.com.

Caruso, Kevin M. *See* **Aerospace 1 Pubns.**

Carver, Dennis, *(978-0-578-69367-5)* 4440 Rawleigh Dr, Fort Worth, TX 76126 USA Tel 817-995-6517
E-mail: 4u2BBandme@gmail.com.

Caryn Solutions, LLC, *(978-0-9791046)* Orders Addr.: P.O. Box 635, Naples, FL 34106 USA (SAN 852-4726) Tel 239-404-5820
E-mail: caryn@carynsolutions.com
Web site: http://www.carynsolutions.com.

CaryPress *See* **CaryPr. International Bks.**

CaryPr. International Bks., *(978-0-615-86265-1; 978-1-63103)* 8263 NC HWY 86 N, Providence, NC 27315 USA Tel 3363880248
Web site: http://www.write-a-book.org/; http://memoirtherapist.com/; www.CaryPress.com; ghostwriters-for-hire.com; saleattraction.com
Dist(s): **CreateSpace Independent Publishing Platform.**

Casa Bautista de Publicaciones, *(978-0-311)* Div. of Southern Baptist Convention, Orders Addr.: P.O. Box 4255, El Paso, TX 79914 USA (SAN 220-0139) Tel 915-566-9656; Fax: 915-562-6502; Toll Free: 800-755-5958; *Imprints:* Editorial Mundo Hispano (Edit Mundo)
E-mail: epena@casabautista.org
Web site: http://www.casabautista.org
Dist(s): **Smashwords.**

Casa Creacion *Imprint of* **Charisma Media**

Casa de Estudios de Literatura y Talleres Artisticos Amaquemecan A.C. (MEX) *(978-968-6465) Dist. by* **Lectorum Pubns.**

Casa de Periodistas Editorial, *(978-0-9743102)* Orders Addr.: P.O. Box 9021787, San Juan, PR 00902-1787 USA; Edit Addr.: Calle de la Luna, Esq. Calle de San José, San Juan, PR 00902-1787 USA
E-mail: multiser@coqui.net
Web site: http://www.asppro.org.

Casa de Snapdragon LLC, *(978-0-9793075; 978-0-9840530; 978-0-9845681; 978-1-937240)* Orders Addr.: 12901 Bryce Ave., NE, Albuquerque, NM 87112 USA Tel 505-508-5513
E-mail: sales@casadesnapdragon.com; managingeditor@casadesnapdragon.com
Web site: http://www.casadesnapdragon.com
Dist(s): **Smashwords.**

Casa Nazarena de Publicacions, *(978-1-56344)* 6401 The Paseo, Kansas City, MO 64131 USA Tel 816-333-7000; Fax: 816-333-1748; Toll Free: 800-462-8711
E-mail: donnie@nph.com
Dist(s): **The Foundry Publishing.**

Casa Promesa *Imprint of* **Barbour Publishing, Inc.**

Casalina, *(978-1-7366617)* 2040 Torreon, Los Alamos, NM 87544 USA Tel 505-709-7528
E-mail: casalina@los-alamos.net.

Cascade Design Publishing *See* **Cascade, Inc.**

Cascade, Inc., *(978-0-9726173)* 1085 Commonwealth Ave., PMB 253, Boston, MA 02215 USA Tel 617-558-1038; *Imprints:* Philograph (Philograph)
E-mail: info@philograph.com
Web site: http://www.philograph.com.

Cascade Pass, Inc., *(978-1-880599; 978-0-615-39461-9; 978-1-935999)* Orders Addr.: 4223 Glencoe Ave., Suite C-105, Marina del Rey, CA 90292 USA Tel 310-305-0210; Fax: 310-305-7850; Toll Free: 888-837-0704
E-mail: jlc@cascadepass.com
Web site: http://www.cascadepass.com
Dist(s): **Follett School Solutions.**

Cascade Pr., *(978-0-692-83243-1)* 3411 Greenacres Rd, Mesa, WA 99343 USA Tel 509-430-3390
E-mail: lovewillfindu2@gmail.com
Dist(s): **Independent Pub.**

Cascade Publishing Incorporated *See* **Compass Productions Inc.**

Cascade Writing, *(978-0-9767519)* 1808 Lake Dr., Camano Island, WA 98282 USA Tel 360-387-8023
E-mail: dennisc@whidbey.net.

Cascadia Publishing Hse., LLC, *(978-0-9665021; 978-1-931038; 978-1-68027)* Orders Addr.: 126 Klingerman Rd., Telford, PA 18969 USA Tel 215-723-9125; Fax: 215-721-2312
E-mail: editor@cascadiapublishinghouse; mking@cascadiapublishinghouse.com; contact@cascadiapublishinghouse.com
Web site: http://www.pandorapressus.com; http://www.cascadiapublishinghouse.com
Dist(s): **Follett School Solutions**
Herald Pr.

Cascarano, John *See* **Lock & Mane**

Case, Darrell, *(978-0-615-60186-1; 978-0-692-78774-8; 978-0-692-88205-4)* 4118 W Co Rd 975 N, Farmersburg, IN 47850 USA Tel 812-394-2219 (phone/fax)
Web site: darrellcase.com
Dist(s): **CreateSpace Independent Publishing Platform.**

Casemate Academic, *(978-0-9774094; 978-1-935488)* Orders Addr.: P.O. Box 511, Oakville, CT 06779 USA (SAN 630-9461) Tel 860-945-9329; Fax: 860-945-9468; Toll Free: 800-791-9354; Edit Addr.: 20 Main St., Oakville, CT 06779 USA
E-mail: queries@dbbconline.com
Web site: http://www.oxbowbooks.com
Dist(s): **Casemate Pubs. & Bk. Distributors, LLC.**

Casemate Pubs. & Bk. Distributors, LLC, *(978-0-9711709; 978-1-932033; 978-1-935149; 978-1-61200; 978-1-952715; 978-1-63624; 978-1-955041; 979-8-88857)* Orders Addr.: 1950 Lawrence Rd., Havertown, PA 19083 USA; 22883 Quicksilver Dr., Herndon, VA 20166 (SAN 631-9386) Tel 703-661-1500; Edit Addr.: 180 Varick St. Suite 816, New York, NY 10014 USA
E-mail: casemate@casematepublishing.com
Web site: http://www.casematepublishing.com
Dist(s): **JSTOR**
MyiLibrary
Open Road Integrated Media, Inc.
ebrary, Inc.

Casey Joy Bks., *(978-0-692-96067-7)* 4053 Rivertown Ln, Wyoming, MI 49418 USA Tel 616-293-9908
E-mail: caseyjoybergman@att.net
Dist(s): **Independent Pub.**

Casey N Morris, PhD, *(978-1-7370481)* 448 Olivadi way, Sacramento, CA 95834 USA Tel 510-459-0185
E-mail: cmorristtu@gmail.com
Web site: ballingonward.org.

Caseys World Bks., *(978-0-9765872)* Orders Addr.: 1998 Skyline Dr., Saintughton, WI 53589 USA Tel 608-335-0401 Please call with any questions. Leave a voice message if no answer.
E-mail: kate@caseysworld.net
Web site: http://www.caseysworld.net.

Cash Cow Publishing, *(978-0-578-79414-3)* 9202 St. Clair Dr. NE, Atlanta, GA 30329 USA Tel 601-212-4877
E-mail: brianjonesglobel@gmail.com.

Casion Books *See* **Slangman Publishing**

Casion Pr., *(978-0-9728144)* 315 Richards Ave., Portsmouth, NH 03801-5239 USA Tel 603-431-6823
E-mail: jbf@fergus.com
Web site: http://www.jbf.fergus.com.

Caso, George R., *(978-0-9719290)* 2445 Babylon Tpke., Merrick, NY 11566 USA Tel 516-379-9397.

Caspar's Cottage, *(978-1-7343632; 978-1-7361387)* 21 Bloody Brook Rd, Amherst, NH 03031 USA Tel 603-554-8225
E-mail: casparscottage@gmail.com
Web site: www.casparscottage.com.

Cassandra Armstrong *See* **Storm Moon Pr., LLC**

Cassava Republic Pr. (GBR) *(978-1-911115) Dist. by* **Consort Bk Sales.**

Casscom Media, *(978-1-930034; 978-1-936081; 978-1-62758)* 6000 Industrial Dr., Greenville, TX 75402 USA Tel 903-455-2555; Fax: 903-455-4448; Toll Free: 800-974-1555
E-mail: sue@casscommedia.com; kathy@casscomedia.com
Web site: http://www.casscommedia.com
Dist(s): **Destiny Image Pubs.**
Follett School Solutions.

Cassette & Video Learning Systems *See* **Watch & Learn, Inc.**

Cassette Communications, Incorporated *See* **Casscom Media**

Cassidy Clarke, *(978-0-578-83874-8; 978-1-957993)* 3342 Herrington Dr., Holly, MI 48442 USA Tel 248-802-2072
E-mail: cassidyewriter@gmail.com.

Cast, Inc., *(978-1-930583; 978-0-9898674; 978-1-943085)* 40 Harvard Mill Sq. Ste. 3, Wakefield, MA 01880-3233 USA Toll Free: 888-858-9994
E-mail: publishing@cast.org
Web site: http://www.cast.org; www.castpublishing.org
Dist(s): **Independent Pubs. Group.**

Castadream LLC, *(978-0-692-47520-1)* 69 Shaker CT, GUILFORD, CT 06437 USA Tel 203-361-6300.

Castaneda, Kay *See* **Bk.places Publishing**

Castellated Pr., *(978-0-9746416)* 21325 NE 130th Ave., Fort McCoy, FL 32134 USA
E-mail: shzamek@gmail.com
Web site: http://www.castellatedpress.com.

Casterman, Editions (FRA) *(978-2-203; 978-2-542) Dist. by* **Distribks Inc.**

Castillo, Ediciones, S. A. de C. V. (MEX) *(978-968-6635; 978-968-7415; 978-970-20) Dist. by* **Macmillan.**

Castillo, Ediciones, S. A. de C. V. (MEX) *(978-968-6635; 978-968-7415; 978-970-20) Dist. by* **Mariuccia Iaconi Bk Imports.**

Castillo, Ediciones, S. A. de C. V. (MEX) *(978-968-6635; 978-968-7415; 978-970-20) Dist. by* **Lectorum Pubns.**

Castle Builder Pr. *Imprint of* **Blue Cubicle Pr., LLC**

Castle Creative, *(978-0-692-99043-8; 978-0-692-99044-5)* P.O. Box 391, Mount Hood Parkdale, OR 97041 USA Tel 541-490-2324
E-mail: teamc2g2@gmail.com
Dist(s): **Ingram Content Group.**

Castle Keep Pr. *Imprint of* **Rock, James A. & Co. Pubs.**

Castle Pacific Publishing, *(978-0-9653869; 978-0-9749305; 978-0-9774168)* P.O. Box 77089, Seattle, WA 98177 USA Tel 206-839-0984; Toll Free: 888-756-2665 (888-756-BOOK)
Web site: http://www.castlepacific.com.

Castle Pr., *(978-0-9669263; 978-0-9835012)* 1222 N. Fair Oaks Ave., Pasadena, CA 91103 USA Fax: 626-789-7385
E-mail: george@castlepress.com.

Castle Rock Creative, Inc., *(978-0-9820544; 978-1-939445; 978-1-943754; 978-0-9982107; 978-1-7372401)* 2318 Verona Ct., Champaign, IL 61822 USA (SAN 857-1023) Tel 847-328-2561 (phone/fax)
Web site: http://www.daveneta.com; http://www.Trailblazerbooks.com; http://www.riskinggrace.com.

Castlebay, Inc., *(978-0-9748145)* P.O. Box 168, Round Pond, ME 04564-0168 USA Tel 207-529-5438
E-mail: castlebay@castlebay.net.

Castleberry Farms Pr., *(978-1-891907)* Orders Addr.: P.O. Box 337, Poplar, WI 54864 USA Tel 715-364-8404
E-mail: cbfarmpr@centurytel.net
Web site: http://www.castleberryfarmspress.com; http://www.cbfarmpr.com.

Castlebridge Bks. *Imprint of* **Big Tent Bks.**

Castlebrook Bks., *(978-0-9641697; 978-0-9798242; 978-0-615-99230-3; 978-0-692-53831-9; 978-0-692-61641-3; 979-8-9853201)* Orders Addr.: 1761 Melrose Dr., Bartlesville, OK 74006 USA
E-mail: castlebrookbooks@aol.com
Web site: http://www.youdrawitbooks.com; http://www.castlebrookbooks.com
Dist(s): **CreateSpace Independent Publishing Platform**
Follett School Solutions.

Castlebrook Publications *See* **Castlebrook Bks.**

Castleconal Pr., *(978-0-9677348)* 1517 National Ave., Madison, WI 53716 USA Tel 608-222-6051; Fax: 608-221-5264
E-mail: dfleming@madison.k12.wi.us.

Castlegate Pr., *(978-0-9743588)* 457 Terraces Ct., Mesquite, NV 89027 USA Tel 303-550-3360; Fax: 702-346-2058.

Castleton, Julia J, *(978-0-578-06109-2)* P.O. Box 880371, Pukalani, HI 96788 USA.

Castro, Shirley, *(978-0-9790307; 978-0-578-62659-8)* 9917 Stockholm Pl., Bakersfield, CA 93306 USA Tel 661-331-9546
Web site: http://www.pelicanfamily.com.

Cat Marcs Publishing, *(978-0-9843899; 978-1-943786)* P.O. Box 54, Silverdale, WA 98383 USA Tel 360-271-4448
E-mail: crysmm307@aol.com; info@catmarcs.com
Web site: http://crystalmarcos.com/; http://catmarcs.com/.

Catalpa Pr., *(978-0-9745665; 978-0-9763810; 978-0-615-56579-8)* P.O. Box 27303, Oakland, CA 94602-0303 USA (SAN 256-4068)
E-mail: jack@jackschroder.com; staff@catalpapress.com
Web site: http://www.jackschroder.com; http://www.malpracticebooks.com.

Catalyst Book Press *See* **Catalyst Pr. LLC**

Catalyst Game Labs *Imprint of* **InMediaRes Productions**

Catalyst Pr. LLC, *(978-0-9802081; 978-1-946395; 978-1-946498; 978-1-7335474; 979-8-9854552; 978-1-960803)* 701 La Chapa Unit B, El Paso, TX 79912 USA (SAN 855-4803); *Imprints:* Story Press Africa (MYID_O_STORY P)
E-mail: jlpowers@evaporites.com; jlpowers@catalystbookpress.com
Web site: http://www.catalystpress.org
Dist(s): **Consortium Bk. Sales & Distribution.**

Catamount Publishing LLC, *(978-0-9752922)* P.O. Box 30015, Denver, CO 80218 USA Tel 303-839-1687 Do not confuse with Catamount Publishing LLC in Allenstown, NH.

Catapulta Pr., *(978-0-9762986)* 2242 Hemingway Dr., Suite H, Fort Myers, FL 33912 USA
Dist(s): **Hachette Bk. Group**
Independent Pubs. Group.

Catawba Publishing Co., *(978-1-59712)* 5945 Orr Rd. Ste. F, Charlotte, NC 28213-7314 USA
E-mail: info@catawbapublishing.com
Web site: http://www.catawbapublishing.com.

catBOX Entertainment, Inc., *(978-0-9706062)* Orders Addr.: P.O. Box 1077, Oklahoma City, OK 73101 USA Tel 405-232-1400; Edit Addr.: P.O. Box 1077, Oklahoma Cit OK 73101 USA
E-mail: alohapublishing@aol.com
Web site: http://www.catdetectives.com; http://www.catboxentertainment.com.

Catch 22 Publishing, *(978-0-9759691)* 1228 Tennyson Ln., Naperville, IL 60540 USA
E-mail: kthomaschicago@gmail.com
Web site: http://www.livinglifesociety.com.

Catch 22 Publishing Incorporated *See* **Catch 22 Publishing**

Catch the Spirit of Appalachia *Imprint of* **Ammons Communications, Ltd.**

Catch-A-Winner Publishing, *(978-0-9845630; 978-0-9985254; 978-1-7340800; 978-1-7344586; 978-1-7347381; 978-1-7360767; 978-1-7360786)* P.O. Box 160125, San Antonio, TX 78280 USA Tel 210-387-8189
E-mail: jamestaylor22@live.com.

Catechesis of the Good Shepherd *Imprint of* **Liturgy Training Pubns.**

Caterpillar & Gypsy Moth Pr. *Imprint of* **Reynoso, Michelle**

Cates, Jr., Richard L, *(978-0-692-93813-3)* 5992 Cty. Rd T, Spring Green, WI 53588 USA Tel 608-588-2836; Fax: 608-588-2836
E-mail: richardlcates@gmail.com.

Cathal Entertainment *See* **Cathalson LLC.**

Cathal Entertainment *Imprint of* **Cathalson LLC.**

Cathalson LLC., *(978-0-9822656; 978-0-615-77486-2; 978-0-615-77543-2; 979-8-9860586)* 11381 SW 17th Ct., Miramar, FL 33025 USA Tel 305-206-3699; *Imprints:* Cathal Entertainment (MYID_S_CATHAL)
E-mail: phil.mccalli@gmail.com
Web site: cathalson.com
Dist(s): **CreateSpace Independent Publishing Platform**
INscribe Digital.

Cathedral of the Holy Spirit, *(978-0-917595)* Div. of Chapel Hill Harvester Church, 4650 Flat Shoals Rd., Decatur, GA 30034 USA (SAN 657-1484) Tel 404-243-5020; Fax: 404-243-5927; Toll Free: 800-241-4702.

Cathedrall Pr./Encycloware, *(978-0-9626554)* 2703 Townes Dr., Greenville, NC 27858 USA Tel 252-341-8906
E-mail: encycloware@suddenlink.net
Web site: http://www.KabalyonKey.com.

Catherine Fenquist, *(978-0-692-19381-5; 978-0-692-19382-2; 978-0-578-67052-2; 979-8-218-24575-7)* 7413 10th Hole Dr., Windsor, CA 95492 USA Tel 707-483-9957
E-mail: Catherine.Fenquist@gmail.com
Dist(s): **Ingram Content Group.**

Cathier Pr., *(978-0-9720445)* 156 Gates Rd., Lizella, GA 31052 USA.

Catholic Answers, Inc., *(978-1-888992; 978-1-933919; 978-1-938983; 978-1-941663; 978-1-68357)* 2020 Gillespie Way, El Cajon, CA 92020-0908 USA Tel 619-387-7200; Fax: 619-387-0042; Toll Free: 888-291-8000 (orders)
E-mail: mobrien@catholic.com
Web site: http://www.catholic.com.

Catholic Authors Pr., *(978-0-9776168; 978-0-9789432)* 203 Fairfield Ave., Hartford, CT 06114 USA
E-mail: books@catholicauthors.org
Web site: http://www.catholicauthors.org.

Catholic Bk. Publishing Corp., *(978-0-89942; 978-0-9623410; 978-1-878718; 978-1-933066; 978-1-937913; 978-1-941243; 978-1-947070; 978-1-948843; 978-1-948844; 978-1-953152; 978-1-958237)* 77 West End Rd., Totowa, NJ 07512-1405 USA (SAN 204-3432) Tel 973-890-2400; Fax: 973-890-2410; Toll Free: 800-892-6657; *Imprints:* Resurrection Press (Resurrection Pr)
E-mail: resurpress@aol.com
Web site: http://www.catholicbkpub.com
Dist(s): **ACTA Pubns.**
Moshy Brothers, Inc.
Spring Arbor Distributors, Inc.

Catholic Heritage Curricula *See* **Little Way Pr.**

Catholic Heritage Curricula, *(978-0-9788376; 978-0-9824585; 978-0-9836832; 978-0-9851642; 978-0-9858343; 978-0-9883797; 978-0-9913264; 978-1-946207)*
Web site: https://www.chcweb.com.

Catholic World Mission, *(978-0-9747571; 978-0-9765180; 978-1-933643)* 33 Rossotto Dr., Hamden, CT 06514 USA Tel 203-848-3323; Fax: 203-407-4823
E-mail: george.sirois@catholicworldmission.org
Web site: http://www.catholicworldmission.org.

Catronaut Bks., *(978-0-9893522)* 203 Beaver Ct. No. 11, Colorado Springs, CO 80905 USA Tel 719-575-9355
E-mail: thelastlaunch@hotmail.com.

Cats Corner Publishing, *(978-1-7334195; 978-1-7340097; 978-1-7343502; 978-1-953147)* 615 Lakeridge St, Kingsport, TN 37663 USA Tel 423-366-1234
E-mail: claysprolesbooks@gmail.com
Web site: http://claysproles.com/.

Cats Ink, *(978-0-9763441)* P.O. Box 387, Chagrin Falls, OH 44022 USA Tel 440-247-6486
Web site: http://www.lillieandrose.com.

CatsCurious Pr., *(978-0-9790889)* 5312 Dillon Cir., Haltom City, TX 76137 USA (SAN 852-4084) Tel 210-326-8239; Toll Free Fax: 866-372-2490
E-mail: sonyamshannon@charter.net
Web site: http://www.catscratchbooks.com; http://www.catscuriouspress.com
Dist(s): **Follett School Solutions.**

Catskill Ctr. for Conservation & Development, Inc., *(978-0-9616712)* General Delivery, Arkville, NY 12406 USA (SAN 660-9953) Tel 914-586-2611; Fax: 914-586-3044; Rte. 28, Arkville, NY 12406 (SAN 660-9961)
E-mail: cccd@catskill.net
Web site: http://catshillcenter.org.

atslip Arts, LLC, (*978-0-9729414*) 668 Cook St., Suite 200, Denver, CO 80206 USA Tel 303-322-9483; Fax: 303-758-6388
E-mail: books@catsliparts.com
Web site: http://www.catsliparts.com.

atSpring Living, (*978-0-578-58844-5; 978-0-578-61667-4*) P.O. Box 43, Cat Spring, TX 78933 USA Tel 512-677-4907
E-mail: abianne@catspringyaupon.com.

atSpring Yaupon *See* **CatSpring Living**

atterfly Pr., (*978-0-9741074*) 122 Eagle Ridge Rd., Lake Orion, MI 48360-2612 USA Tel 248-789-2227; Fax: 248-393-2535
E-mail: frejen111@aol.com
Web site: http://www.catterflypress.com.

attLeLogos Brand Management Systems, (*978-0-9745612*) 2522 Lombard St., Suite 300, Philadelphia, PA 19146-1025 USA Fax: 215-827-5578
E-mail: info@cattlelogos.com
Web site: http://www.cattlelogos.com.

Catto Creations, LLC, (*978-0-9702633; 978-1-938078*) 3125 Crusade Ln., Green Bay, WI 54313 USA Tel 920-494-4237; 920 494 4237
E-mail: cattocreations@gmail.com
Web site: http://www.cattocreations.com.

Catton Communications, (*978-0-615-76872-4; 978-0-578-55240-8; 978-0-578-63310-7*) 301 Farmbrook Pass, Canton, GA 30115 USA Tel 918-853-4682
Web site: http://www.cattoncommunications.com
Dist(s): **CreateSpace Independent Publishing Platform.**

Caution Bks., (*978-0-9754148*) P.O. Box 2235, Newport Beach, CA 92659 USA
Web site: http://www.cautionbooks.com.

Cave Hollow Pr., (*978-0-9713497; 978-1-7342678*) 304 Grover St., Warrensburg, MO 64093-2439 USA
E-mail: rmkinder@sprintmail.com
Web site: http://www.cavehollowpress.com.

Caveat Press, Incorporated *See* **White Cloud Pr.**

Cavendish Square *See* **Cavendish Square Publishing LLC**

Cavendish Square *Imprint of* **Cavendish Square Publishing LLC**

Cavendish Square Publishing LLC, (*978-0-7614; 978-1-60870; 978-1-62712; 978-1-5026*) 303 Pk. Ave. S. Suite 1247, New York, NY 10010 USA (SAN 760-9639) Tel 646-205-7426; *Imprints:* Cavendish Square (CavendishSq)
E-mail: hollyc@rosenpub.com; csq_cs@csqpub.com
Web site: http://www.cavendishsq.com
Dist(s): **Follett School Solutions**
MyiLibrary
Rosen Publishing Group, Inc., The.

Cavizzana Press *See* **21st Century Pubs.**

†**Caxton Pr.,** (*978-0-87004*) Div. of Caxton Printers. Ltd., 312 Main St., Caldwell, ID 83605-3299 USA (SAN 201-9698) Tel 208-459-7421; Fax: 208-459-7450; Toll Free: 800-657-6465
E-mail: publish@caxtonprinters.com; sgipson@caxtonpress.com
Web site: http://www.caxtonpress.com
Dist(s): **MyiLibrary**
Univ. of Nebraska Pr.; *CIP.*

Caxton Printers, Limited *See* **Caxton Pr.**

Caxton, Wm Ltd., (*978-0-940473*) P.O. Box 220, Ellison Bay, WI 54210-0220 USA (SAN 135-1303) Tel 920-854-2955.

CB Publishing & Design *Imprint of* **UBUS Communications Systems**

CBAY Bks., 4501 Forbes Blvd., Lanham, MD 20706 USA
Dist(s): **Follett School Solutions**
Independent Pubs. Group.

CBE READERS, 11306 SAGECREEK DR, HOUSTON, TX 77089 USA Tel 832-775-3721.

CBH Bks. *Imprint of* **Cambridge BrickHouse, Inc.**

CBJ Entertainment, (*978-0-9997551*) 7457 Easterly Ln., Memphis, TN 38125 USA Tel 901-690-1956
E-mail: cbjentertainment1@yahoo.com.

CBM Publishing, (*978-0-9743988*) P.O. Box 6938, Lincoln, NE 68506 USA
E-mail: mvbettenhausen@alltel.net.

CC Conglomerate LLC, (*978-0-9998853*) 1430 Seagirt Blvd., Far Rockaway, NY 11691 USA Tel 917-663-0125
E-mail: cynthia@cynthiacordero.com
Web site: cynthiacordero.com.

CCA & B, LLC, (*978-0-9769907; 978-0-9843651; 978-0-9887032; 978-0-9970920; 978-0-9988109; 978-0-9600665; 978-1-7336905; 978-1-957345*) Orders Addr.: 3350 Riverwood Pkwy. Suite 300, Atlanta, GA 30339 USA Fax: 678-990-1182; Toll Free: 877-919-4105
E-mail: sales@elfontheshelf.com; christa@elfontheshelf.com
Web site: http://elfontheshelf.com; http://www.ccaandb.com; http://alightinthenight.com.

CCC of America, (*978-1-56814*) P.O. Box 166349, Irving, TX 75016-6349 USA (SAN 298-7546) Toll Free: 800-935-2222
E-mail: customerservice@cccofamerica.com
Web site: http://www.cccofamerica.com
Dist(s): **Liguori Pubns.**

CCH Services, Inc., (*978-0-9768383*) 8862 Earhart Ave., Los Angeles, CA 90045 USA Tel 562-895-0682
Web site: http://www.realworldrecovery.com.

CCP Publishing & Entertainment, (*978-0-9677385; 978-0-9800655; 978-0-9801265*) 9602 Glenwood Rd., No. 362, Brooklyn, NY 11236 USA
E-mail: brillionaireone@gmail.com
Web site: www.ccppublishing.com; http://www.thecccowanshow.com; http://www.cccowan.com.

CCR Pr., (*978-1-7340503; 978-1-7363529*) 9501 Argyle Dr., Austin, TX 78749 USA Tel 512-784-8492
E-mail: caseychapmanrossphotography@gmail.com
Web site: www.caseychapmanrossphotography.com.

CCRiddles, (*978-0-9785118; 978-0-9819833; 978-1-941747*) 878 Laramie Ct., Newbury Park, CA 91320 USA Tel 805-338-4170; Fax: 805-498-2901
E-mail: ccriddles@gmail.com
Web site: http://www.ccriddles.com.

CCS Pubs., (*978-0-9755819; 978-0-9790679; 978-0-9843110; 978-1-935789; 978-1-950069*) 23890 Brittlebush Cir., Moreno Valley, CA 92557 USA Tel 951-242-1706 (phone/fax); Toll Free: 1-888-344-2355; *Imprints:* CCS Publishing (CCSPubng)
E-mail: joelcomiskey@msn.com
Web site: http://www.joelcomiskeygroup.com.

CCS Publishing *Imprint of* **CCS Pubs.**

CD Publishing, (*978-0-9859042*) 38041 Manzanita St., Newark, CA 94560 USA Tel 510-709-7459
E-mail: caseydevargas@yahoo.com.

CDS Books *See* **Vanguard Pr.**

CE Bilingual Bks. LLC, (*978-0-9801305*) P.O. Box 31848, Philadelphia, PA 19104-1848 USA (SAN 855-2819) Fax: 215-352-0409; 28 Eight St., Hicksville, NY 11801
E-mail: cebilingualbooks@gmail.com
Web site: http://www.cebilingualbooks.com
Dist(s): **Follett School Solutions.**

Ce Code Efficiency, Inc., (*978-0-9769931*) Orders Addr.: P.O. Box 1184, State College, PA 16804-1184 USA; Edit Addr.: 120 E. Beaver Ave., #208, State College, PA 16801 USA
E-mail: rlp188@psu.edu
Web site: http://www.personal.psu.edu/rlp188.

Cebrano Publishing, (*978-0-9761366*) P.O. Box 27236, Barrigada, GU 96921 USA
E-mail: billyb1937@yahoo.com.

Cedar Bay Pr., L.L.C., (*978-1-57555*) P.O. Box 230084, Portland, OR 97281-0084 USA (SAN 298-6361)
E-mail: cedarbay@hotmail.com.

Cedar Creek Publishing, (*978-0-9790205; 978-0-9842449; 978-0-9839192; 978-0-9891465; 978-1-942882*) 1604 Monticello Ave, Unit D, Charlottesville, VA 22902 USA (SAN 857-1368) Tel 434-996-9089
E-mail: cedarcreekbooks@aol.com
Web site: http://www.cedarcreekauthors.com
Dist(s): **BCH Fulfillment & Distribution.**

Cedar Creek Publishing Service, (*978-0-9659419*) P.O. Box 115, Bremo Bluff, VA 23022 USA Tel 434-842-6203 Do not confuse with companies with same or similar names in Hayward, CA, Anderson, IN, Indianapolis, IN
E-mail: cedarcreekbooks@aol.com.

Cedar Crest Bks., (*978-0-910291*) 17 Lookout Ave., Natick, MA 01760 USA (SAN 241-2837) Tel 508-653-8839
E-mail: davidrottenberg@yahoo.com; publisher@cedarcrestbooks.com
Web site: http://www.cedarcrestbooks.com
Dist(s): **Follett School Solutions.**

Cedar Fort, Inc. *Imprint of* **Cedar Fort, Inc./CFI Distribution**

Cedar Fort, Inc./CFI Distribution, (*978-0-88290; 978-0-934126; 978-1-55517; 978-1-59955; 978-1-4621*) 2373 West 700 South, Springville, UT 84663 USA (SAN 170-2858) Tel 801-489-4084; Fax: 801-489-1097; Toll Free: 800-759-2665; *Imprints:* Bonneville Books (Bonneville Bks); Horizon Publishers (HorPubs); Cedar Fort, Incorporated (Cedar Fort); Sweetwater Books (Sweetwater Bks)
E-mail: skybook@cedarfort.com
Web site: http://www.cedarfort.com
Dist(s): **Casemate Pubs. & Bk. Distributors, LLC**
Children's Plus, Inc.
Follett School Solutions
Todd Communications.

Cedar Grove Books *See* **Cedar Grove Publishing**

Cedar Grove Publishing, (*978-0-9740212; 978-0-9835077; 978-1-941958; 978-1-7368501; 979-8-9866872; 979-8-9880527*) 3205 Elmhurst St., Rowlett, TX 75088 USA (SAN 255-3732) Tel 415-364-8292
E-mail: rperry@cedargrovebooks.com
Web site: http://www.cedargrovebooks.com
Dist(s): **Independent Pubs. Group**
Small Pr. United.

Cedar Hse. Pubs., (*978-0-9676289*) Orders Addr.: P.O. Box 399, Monroe, VA 24574 USA Tel 434-929-8002 (phone/fax); Fax: 434-929-1059; Edit Addr.: 407 Eastview Dr., Madison Heights, VA 24572 USA
E-mail: info@cedarhousepublishers.com
Web site: http://www.cedarhousepublishers.com
Dist(s): **Send The Light Distribution LLC.**

Cedar Kroft Studios, (*978-1-7323936*) 3365 Springplace Rd., Lewisburg, TN 37091 USA Tel 931-637-8518
E-mail: wishuwell4ever@yahoo.com.

Cedar Lake Pubns., (*978-1-61104*) Orders Addr.: P.O. Box 7, Cedar Lake, MI 48812 USA Tel 989-244-0030; Edit Addr.: 4769 Feather Trail, Cedar Lake, MI 48812 USA Tel 989-244-0030
E-mail: carijhaus@gmail.com
Web site: http://www.readaclassic.com.

Cedar Loft Productions *See* **Cedar Loft Publishing**

Cedar Loft Publishing, (*978-0-615-95768-5; 978-0-692-22011-5; 978-0-9907449; 978-0-692-31333-6; 978-0-692-43060-6; 978-0-692-44612-6; 978-0-692-54041-1; 978-0-692-62473-9; 978-0-692-65781-2; 978-0-692-66121-5; 978-0-692-68130-5; 978-0-692-70082-2; 978-0-692-73427-8; 978-0-9979156) P.O. Box 1125, Petersburg, WV 26847 USA Tel 304-470-0189*
E-mail: jennymckinney23@gmail.com
Web site: http://clpublishing.net
Dist(s): **CreateSpace Independent Publishing Platform.**

Cedar Shamrock Publishing, (*978-0-9760680*) P.O. Box 70775, Madison, WI 53707 USA
Web site: http://www.wyattwalker.com
Dist(s): **Partners Bk. Distributing, Inc.**

Cedar Tree Bks., (*978-0-9657328; 978-1-892142*) P.O. Box 4256, Wilmington, DE 19807-0256 USA
E-mail: books@ctpress.com
Web site: http://www.cedartreebooks.com.

Cedar Tree Publishing, (*978-0-9658075*) 201 Matilda St NE Ste. B, Grand Rapids, MI 49503-1593 USA Do not confuse with Cedar Tree Publishing, Cedaredge, CO
E-mail: georan@tapshoe,com
Web site: http://www.cedartreepublishing.com; www.johnnietuitel.com
Dist(s): **Austin & Company, Inc.**

Cedar Valley Publishing, (*978-0-615-12024-9*) P.O. Box 621, Jesup, IA 50648 USA Do not confuse with Cedar Valley Publishing in Cascade, WI.

Cedar Valley Publishing, (*978-1-933476*) N6854 Cedar Valley Rd., Fredonia, WI 53021 USA Tel 920-994-9906 Do not confuse with Cedar Valley Publishing in Cascade, WI, Jesup, IA
E-mail: stacey@cedarvalleypublishing.com
Web site: http://www.cedarvalleypublishing.com
Dist(s): **Follett School Solutions.**

Cedartip Co., The, (*978-0-9771844*) Orders Addr.: P.O. Box 231, Manhattan, KS 66505-0231 USA; Edit Addr.: 3004 Pawnee Cir., Manhattan, KS 66502-1973 USA
E-mail: orders@cedartip.com
Web site: http://www.cedartip.com.

Ceej Dwyer, (*978-0-578-93636-9; 978-0-578-93637-6*) 10201 W. 18th Ct., KENNEWICK, WA 99338 USA Tel 617-416-8014
E-mail: ceej.dwyer@gmail.com.

Celebration Media, (*978-0-692-18742-5*) 4600 E. Moody Blvd. 3P, Bunnell, FL 32110 USA Tel 386-517-4523
E-mail: smckenney66@gmail.com
Dist(s): **Ingram Content Group.**

Celebration Pr. *Imprint of* **Savvas Learning Co.**

Celebration Pr., Orders Addr.: 135 South Mount Zion Rd. P.O. Box 2500, Lebanon, IN 46052 USA Toll Free Fax: 800-393-3156; Toll Free: 800-526-9907; *Imprints:* Good Year Books (GYB) Do not confuse with Celebration Press in Onalaska WI, Denver CO
Web site: http://www.aw-bc.com; http://www.pearsonlearning.com/rightsPerm.rtf.

Celeste Ediciones, S.A. (ESP) (*978-84-8211; 978-84-87553*) *Dist. by* **Lectorum Pubns.**

Celestial Arts *Imprint of* **Ten Speed Pr.**

Celestine Pr., (*978-0-9749382; 978-0-578-08538-8*) 25 Ashland St., Rochester, NY 14620 USA (SAN 255-9927)
E-mail: hellerest@earthlink.net
Web site: http://www.celestinepress.com
Dist(s): **Lulu Pr., Inc.**

Cellar Door Publishing, (*978-0-9766831*) 3439 NE Sandy Blvd, Suite 309, Portland, OR 97232 USA
Web site: http://www.cellardoorpublishing.com.

Celltrition, (*978-0-9746378*) 13472 Vidalia Rd., Pass Christian, MS 39571 USA Tel 228-586-2455.

Cellular Publishing, (*978-1-886358*) Div. of Lakeshore Business Services, P.O. Box 119, Sedona, AZ 86339-0119 USA Tel 520-300-7711; Fax: 413-825-8356.

Celo Valley Bks., (*978-0-923687*) 160 Ohle Rd., Burnsville, NC 28714 USA (SAN 251-7973) Tel 828-675-5918
E-mail: diatoday@msn.com.

Celstumo Publishing, (*978-0-9761041*) A Subs. of Celebration Studios of Missouri, Orders Addr.: P.O. Box 201, Glencoe, MO 63038 USA Tel 636-458-1819 (phone/fax)
E-mail: celstumo@celstumo.com
Web site: http://www.celstumo.com.

Celtic Art Store, (*978-0-9969919*) P.O. Box 2997, Crestline, CA 92325-2997 USA Tel 909-338-9353
E-mail: celticartstore@gmail.com
Web site: www.CelticArtStore.net.

Celtic Cat Publishing, (*978-0-9658950; 978-0-9819238; 978-0-9847836; 978-0-9891380; 978-0-9905945; 978-1-947020*) Orders Addr.: 5111 Green Valley Dr, Knoxville, TN 37914 USA Tel 865-541-7130; Edit Addr.: 5111 Green Valley Dr, Knoxville, TN 37901 USA Tel 865-248-3133
E-mail: info@celticcatpublishing.com
Web site: http://www.celticcatpublishing.com.

Celtic Cross Communications, (*978-0-9740981; 978-0-9887271; 979-8-9869454*) P.O. Box 408, Oshtemo, MI 49077 USA Tel 269-207-0397
Web site: http://www.celticcrosscommunications.com
Dist(s): **Send The Light Distribution LLC.**

Celtic Hearts Pr., (*978-1-949575*) 2026 Society Dr, Holiday, FL 34691 USA Tel 727-686-0998
E-mail: cassidyoconnorauthor@gmail.com
Web site: www.cassidykoconnor.com
Dist(s): **Independent Pubs. Group.**

Celtic Song Pr., (*978-1-7377005*) 43 Stoneham Dr., ROCHESTER, NY 14625 USA Tel 585-313-3749
E-mail: celticsongpress@gmail.com.

Celtic Sunrise, (*978-0-9840893*) P.O. Box 174, New Ringgold, PA 17960 USA (SAN 858-3900) Fax: 570-943-2102
Web site: http://www.celticsunrise.com.

CEM Ventures, Ltd., (*978-0-9760072*) P.O. Box 1713, Harwich, MA 02645 USA Tel 508-896-4988; Fax: 508-896-2586; Toll Free: 866-246 — 7800; 112 Griffith's Pond Rd., Brewster, MA 02631
E-mail: cemventures@yahoo.com
Web site: http://www.jaysonthebluejay.com.

Cemetery Dance Pubns., (*978-1-881475; 978-1-58767*) Orders Addr.: 132-B Industry Ln., Unit 7, Forest Hills, MD 21050 USA Tel 410-588-5901; Fax: 410-588-5904
E-mail: cdancepub@aol.com; info@cemeterydance.com
Web site: http://www.cemeterydance.com.

†**Cengage Gale,** (*978-0-13; 978-0-7876; 978-0-8103; 978-0-936474; 978-1-57302; 978-1-878623; 978-1-59413; 978-1-59414; 978-1-59415; 978-1-4144; 978-1-4205; 978-1-59722; 978-1-4328; 978-1-5358*) Subs. of Cengage Learning, Orders Addr.: P.O. Box 9187, Farmington Hills, MI 48333-9187 USA Toll Free Fax: 800 414 5043; Toll Free: 800 877 4253; Edit Addr.: 27500 Drake Rd., Farmington Hills, MI 48331 USA (SAN 213-4373) Tel 248-699-8495 Toll Free: 800-877-4253; a/o Wheeler Publishing, 295 Kennedy Memorial Dr., Waterville, ME 04901 Toll Free: 800 223 1244; *Imprints:* UXL (UXL); Macmillan Reference USA (Macmillan Ref); Charles Scribner's Sons (C Scribners Sons); Kidhaven (Kidhaven); Blackbirch Press, Incorporated (Blackbirch Pr); Lucent Books (Lucent Books); Greenhaven Press, Incorporated (Greenhaven Pr); Five Star (Five Star ME); Wheeler Publishing, Incorporated (Wheel); Five Star Trade (Five Star Trade); Greenhaven Publishing (GreenHav); Kennebec Large Print (Kennebec Lrg); Walker Large Print (Walker Large Pt)
E-mail: gale.salesassistance@thomson.com
Web site: http://www.gale.com
Dist(s): **Follett School Solutions**
Send The Light Distribution LLC
Smashwords
Thorndike Pr.; *CIP.*

†**Cengage Heinle,** (*978-0-8384; 978-0-88377; 978-0-912066; 978-1-4130*) Div. of Cengage Learning, Orders Addr.: 10650 Toebben Dr., Independence, KY 41051 USA Toll Free Fax: 800 487 8488
E-mail: reply@heinle.com
Web site: http://www.heinle.com
Dist(s): **CENGAGE Learning**; *CIP.*

Cengage Learning (GBR) (*978-0-15; 978-1-86152; 978-1-84480; 978-1-4080; 978-1-4737*) *Dist. by* **CENGAGE Learn.**

Cengage Learning *Imprint of* **CENGAGE Learning**

CENGAGE Learning, Orders Addr.: 10650 Toebben Dr., Independence, KY 41051 USA (SAN 200-2213) Tel 859-525-6620; Fax: 859-525-0978; Toll Free Fax: 800-487-8488; Toll Free: 800-354-9706; *Imprints:* Cengage Learning (CengLearning); National Geographic Learning (Nat Geo Learn)
Web site: http://www.cengage.com/
Dist(s): **Amazon Digital Services Inc.**
Delmar Cengage Learning
Follett School Solutions
Johns Hopkins Univ. Pr.
OptumInsight, Inc.

Cengage Learning Australia (AUS) (*978-0-17; 978-0-646-20862-6; 978-0-646-20863-3; 978-0-646-22565-4; 978-0-646-22598-2; 978-0-646-24330-6; 978-0-646-26855-2; 978-0-646-26850-7; 978-0-646-26853-8; 978-0-646-26854-5; 978-0-646-47716-9*) *Dist. by* **Cheng Tsui.**

CENGAGE Learning Custom Publishing, (*978-0-87393; 978-0-931920; 978-0-7593; 978-1-4266; 978-0-357; 978-1-4390; 978-1-111; 978-1-133; 978-1-285; 978-1-305; 978-1-337; 979-8-9852423; 979-8-214*) 5191 Natrop Blvd., Mason, OH 45240 USA Toll Free: 800-543-0487
E-mail: debbie.stowell@cengage.com
Web site: http://www.thomsoncustom.com
Dist(s): **CENGAGE Learning**
Follett School Solutions.

†**Cengage South-Western,** (*978-0-03; 978-0-324; 978-0-538*) Div. of Cengage Learning, 5191 Natorp Blvd., Mason, OH 45040 USA (SAN 202-7518) Tel 513 229 1000; Toll Free Fax: 800-437-8488; Toll Free: 800-354-9706 (orders only); 800-543-0487
Web site: http://www.thomsonedu.com/
Dist(s): **CENGAGE Learning**
International Thomson Computer Pr.; *CIP.*

Cenozoic Pr., (*978-0-615-38180-0; 978-0-615-52278-4*) 354 Via La Canada No. 7, Orange, CA 92869 USA Tel 714-928-6648
E-mail: arajic@gmail.com.

Ctr. for Appalachian Trail Studies, (*978-0-9636342; 978-0-9707916*) Orders Addr.: 17 S. Meadow Dr., Sudbury, MA 01776 USA Tel 781-752-6100 (phone/fax)
E-mail: orders@trailplace.com
Web site: http://trailplace.com/orders.html.

Center for Applications of Psychological Type, Incorporated *See* **Myers & Briggs Foundation, Inc.**

Center for Applied Psychology, Incorporated *See* **Childswork/Childsplay**

Ctr. for Basque Studies, (*978-1-877802; 978-1-935709; 978-1-949805*) 1664 N. Virginia St., MS 2322, Reno, NV 89557-2322 USA Tel 775-784-4854; Fax: 775-784-1355
E-mail: basque@unr.edu; cbspress@unr.edu
Web site: http://basquebooks.myshopify.com/
Dist(s): **University of Nevada Pr.**

Ctr. for Creative Leadership, (*978-0-912879; 978-0-9638301; 978-1-882197; 978-1-932973; 978-1-60491; 978-1-64761*) Affil. of Smith Richardson Foundation, Orders Addr.: 1 Leadership Pl., Greensboro, NC 27410 USA Tel 336-286-4095 (Client Services); Fax: 336-288-3999; Edit Addr.: 1 Leadership Pl., Greensboro, NC 27410 USA Tel 336-286-4437
E-mail: lombardinok@ccl.org
Web site: http://www.ccl.org
Dist(s): **MyiLibrary**
Wiley, John & Sons, Inc.
ebrary, Inc.

Ctr. For Cultural Leadership, (*978-0-9745948*) P.O. Box 70, La Grange, CA 95239 USA
Web site: http://www.christianculture.com.

Center for Economic Research & Social Change *See* **Haymarket Bks.**

Ctr. for Educational Policy Research, (*978-0-9729538*) 720 E. 13th Ave., Suite 201, Eugene, OR 97401 USA Tel 541-346-6153; Fax: 541-346-6154; Toll Free: 877-766-2279
E-mail: Terri_Heath@s4s.org
Web site: http://www.s4s.org.

Center for Labor Research and Education, Univ. of California, Los Angeles, (*978-0-89215; 978-0-615-12275-5; 978-0-9836289*) Orders Addr.: 675 S. Pk. View St., Los Angeles, CA 90057 USA Tel 213-780-4155 x205
E-mail: jamonroe@ucla.edu
Web site: http://www.labor.ucla.edu.

Center for Learning, The, (*978-1-56077*) Orders Addr.: 590 E. Western Reserve Rd. Unit 10-h, Youngstown, OH 44514 USA Tel 800-767-9090; Toll Free Fax: 888-767-8080; Toll Free: 800-767-9090 (ordering); Edit

Addr.: 29313 Clemens Rd. Ste. 2E, Westlake, OH 44145-1052 USA (SAN 248-2029)
E-mail: ahollis@centerforlearning.org
Web site: http://www.centerforlearning.org.

Center for Loss & Life Transition *See* **Companion Pr.**

Center for Safe & Responsible Internet Use *See* **Embrace Civility LLC**

Center for Self-Actualization, Incorporated, The, *(978-0-9758799; 978-0-9788389; 978-0-9823847; 978-0-615-38102-2; 978-0-9846266; 978-0-9851608)* P.O. Box 98466, Atlanta, GA 30359-2166 USA Tel 770-623-4133; Fax: 770-623-3853
E-mail: centerforself@yahoo.com
Web site: http://www.selfactualized.org.

†**Ctr. for Strategic & International Studies,** *(978-0-89206; 978-0-615-19961-0)* 1800 K St., NW, Washington, DC 20006 USA (SAN 281-4021) Tel 202-887-0200; Fax: 202-775-3199; 4501 Forbes Blvd., Lanhan, MD 20706
E-mail: books@csis.org
Web site: http://www.csis.org; http://www.csisbookstore.org
Dist(s): **Books International, Inc.**
Follett School Solutions
MyiLibrary
Rowman & Littlefield Publishers, Inc.
Rowman & Littlefield Unlimited Model; *CIP.*

Ctr. for the Affirmation of Responsible Education, *(978-0-9740071)* 496 Gold Ct., San Andreas, CA 95249 USA Tel 209-754-9218
E-mail: jnorton2@earthlink.net.

Center for the Collaborative Classroom, *(978-1-57621; 978-1-885603; 978-1-59892; 978-1-61003; 978-1-68246; 978-1-64940)* 1001 Marina Village Pkwy Suite 110, ALAMEDA, CA 94501 USA Tel 510-533-0213; Fax: 510-464-3670; Toll Free: 800-666-7270
E-mail: pubs@devstu.org; brandon_holroyd@devstu.org; bholroyd@collaborativeclassroom.org
Web site: http://www.devstu.org; http://www.collaborativeclassroom.org
Dist(s): **Booksource, The.**

Ctr. for Victims of Torture, The, *(978-0-9759789)* 717 E. River Rd., Minneapolis, MN 55455 USA Tel 612-436-4800.

Ctr. for Western Studies, *(978-0-931170)* Div. of Augustana University, Orders Addr.: Augustana Univ. 2001 S. Summit Ave., Sioux Falls, SD 57197 USA (SAN 211-4844) Tel 605-274-4007; Fax: 605-274-4999
E-mail: harry.thompson@augie.edu; cws@augie.edu
Web site: http://augie.edu/cws
Dist(s): **Dakota West Bks.**

Center For Youth Issues, Incorporated *See* **National Ctr. For Youth Issues**

Ctr. of SW Studies, Fort Lewis College, *(978-0-9727664)* 1000 Rim Dr., Durango, CO 81301 USA
E-mail: gulliford_a@fortlewis.edu
Web site: http://www.swcenter.fortlewis.edu.

Ctr. Stage Puppets, *(978-0-9795087)* P.O. Box 8279, Bend, OR 97708 USA Tel 541-420-7943
E-mail: info@centerstagepuppets.com
Web site: http://www.centerstagepuppets.com.

Center Street *Imprint of* **Center Street**

Center Street, 1290 6th Ave., New York, NY 10104 USA; *Imprints:* Center Street (CtrSt)
E-mail: CenterStreet@hbgusa.com
Web site: https://www.centerstreet.com/
Dist(s): **Blackstone Audio, Inc.**
Hachette Bk. Group.

Centering Corp., *(978-1-56123)* 6406 Maple St, Omaha, NE 68104-0600 USA (SAN 298-1815) Tel 402-553-1200; Fax: 402-553-0507
E-mail: j1200@aol.com
Web site: http://www.centering.org
Dist(s): **Follett School Solutions.**

CenterLine Media, *(978-0-9754212; 978-0-9814896)* 115 Greenwood Ave., Ambler, PA 19002-5709 USA Tel 215-646-4591; Fax: 215-933-6819
E-mail: info@centerlinemedia.com
Web site: http://www.centerlinemedia.com.

Centerpunch Pr., *(978-0-9724882)* P.O. Box 43151, Cincinnati, OH 45243 USA Tel 513-561-3392 (phone/fax)
E-mail: info@centerpunchpress.com
Web site: http://www.centerpunchpress.com.

Ctrs. for Spiritual Living, *(978-0-911336; 978-0-917849; 978-0-9727184; 978-1-956198)* Div. of United Church of Religious Science, Orders Addr.: 573 Park Point Dr., Golden, CO 80401-7042 USA (SAN 203-2570) Tel 720-279-1643; 720-496-1370; Fax: 303-526-0913; *Imprints:* Science of Mind Publishing (MYID_Z_SCIENCE)
E-mail: kjohnson@csl.org
Web site: http://www.scienceofmind.com; http://www.spirituallivingpress.com
Dist(s): **DeVorss & Co.**
Red Wheel/Weiser.

Centerstream Publishing, *(978-0-931759; 978-1-57424)* Orders Addr.: P.O. Box 17878, Anaheim Hills, CA 92817 USA (SAN 683-8022) Tel 714-779-9390 (phone/fax)
E-mail: centerstrm@aol.com
Web site: http://www.pma-online.org
Dist(s): **Booklines Hawaii, Ltd.**
Leonard, Hal Corp.
MyiLibrary.

Centipede Dragon A Benevolent Creature *See* **AY Chen Illustration & Design**

Centiramo Publishing, *(978-0-692-98500-7; 978-0-692-14219-6; 978-1-7327815; 978-1-7347256; 978-1-958406)* 11 Minker Pl, Belleville, NJ 07109-1732 USA Tel 201-674-0274; Fax: 201-674-0274
E-mail: pierceram@gmail.com
Web site: www.centiramopublishing.com; www.gilbertluisrcentinaiii.com
Dist(s): **CreateSpace Independent Publishing Platform.**

Central Ave. Pr, *(978-0-9715344; 978-0-9798452)* 8400 Menaul Blvd. NE, Suite A No. 211, Albuquerque, NM 87112 USA
E-mail: oelfkej@aol.com
Web site: http://www.centralavepress.com
Dist(s): **Quality Bks., Inc.**

Central Avenue Publishing (CAN) *(978-1-926760; 978-0-9812737; 978-1-77168) Dist. by* **IPG Chicago.**

Central Coast Bks./Pr., *(978-0-9658776; 978-1-930401)* Orders Addr.: P.O. Box 3654, San Luis Obispo, CA 93403 USA (SAN 631-1547) Tel 805-534-0307 (phone/fax); Edit Addr.: 831 a Via Esteban, Samn Luis, Obispo, CA 94301 USA (SAN 631-1539)
E-mail: ccbooks@surfari.net.

Central Coast Press *See* **Central Coast Bks./Pr.**

Central Conference of American Rabbis/CCAR Pr., *(978-0-88123; 978-0-916694)* 355 Lexington Ave., 18th Flr., New York, NY 10017-6603 USA (SAN 204-3262) Tel 212-972-3636; Fax: 212-692-0819; Toll Free: 800-935-2227; *Imprints:* Reform Judaism Publishing (RfrmJudaism)
E-mail: ccarpress@ccarnet.org; info@ccarnet.org
Web site: http://ccarpress.org.

Central Orb Publishing, *(978-0-9818818)* P.O. Box 830, Orem, UT 84059-0830 USA
E-mail: Thesoulalliance@Hotmail.com
Web site: http://www.createspace.com/3347335; http://www.lulu.com/thesoulalliance; http://www.createspace.com/3351702.

Central Park Media Corp., *(978-1-56219; 978-1-57800; 978-1-887692; 978-1-58664)* 250 W. 57th St. Ste. 1723, New York, NY 10107-1708 USA (SAN 631-3191) Toll Free: 800-833-7456; *Imprints:* CPM Manga (CPM Manga); CPM Comics (CPM Comics); Manga 18 (Manga Eighteen); CPM Manhwa (CPM Manhwa)
E-mail: info@teamcpm.com
Web site: http://www.centralparkmedia.com/; http://www.cpmpress.com/
Dist(s): **Hobbies Hawaii Distributors.**

Central Recovery Pr., *(978-0-9799869; 978-0-9818482; 978-1-936290; 978-1-937612; 978-1-942094; 978-1-949481)* 3321 N. Buffalo Dr. Suite 275, Las Vegas, NV 89129 USA (SAN 854-9532) Tel 702-868-5830; Fax: 702-868-5831
E-mail: phughes@centralrecovery.com; vkilleen@centralrecovery.com
Web site: http://www.centralrecoverypress.com
Dist(s): **Consortium Bk. Sales & Distribution**
Elsevier
Follett School Solutions
Health Communications, Inc.
MyiLibrary.

Centro Bks., LLC, *(978-1-933572)* 3636 Fieldston Rd. Apt. 6P, Bronx, NY 10463-2041 USA (SAN 256-7229)
Web site: http://www.centrobooks.com.

Centro de Informacion y Desarrollo de la Comunicacion y la Literatura (MEX) *(978-968-494) Dist. by* **Continental Bk.**

Centro de Informacion y Desarrollo de la Comunicacion y la Literatura (MEX) *(978-968-494) Dist. by* **AIMS Intl.**

Centro de Informacion y Desarrollo de la Comunicacion y la Literatura (MEX) *(978-968-494) Dist. by* **Mariuccia Iaconi Bk Imports.**

Centro de Informacion y Desarrollo de la Comunicacion y la Literatura (MEX) *(978-968-494) Dist. by* **Lectorum Pubns.**

Centurion Bks., *(978-0-692-37166-4; 978-0-692-86932-1; 978-0-692-90093-2; 978-1-957004)* 8001 Magnolia Ridge Ct, Louisville, KY 40291 USA Tel 502-494-2890
Web site: http://jessicaminyard.com
Dist(s): **CreateSpace Independent Publishing Platform.**

Centurion Pr., *(978-0-9800805)* 740 Breeze Hill Rd., #171, Vista, CA 92081 USA Fax: 760-631-3607
E-mail: fedthought@gmail.com
Web site: http://www.centurionpress.com.

Cepia LLC., *(978-0-9777241)* 121 Hunter Ave., Suite 103, Saint Louis, MO 63124 USA Tel 314-725-4900; Fax: 314-725-4919
E-mail: support@cepiallc.com
Web site: http://www.cepiallc.com.

Ceravolo Maret, Anita, *(978-0-692-92214-9; 978-0-692-93666-5)* 202 Broad St., Bloomfield, NJ 07003 USA Tel 973-747-7697
E-mail: ceravolo_maret@live.com
Dist(s): **CreateSpace Independent Publishing Platform.**

Cerebellum Corp., *(978-1-58198; 978-1-886156; 978-1-59626; 978-1-61867)* 145 Corte Madera Town Ctr, Ste 406, rte Madera, CA 94925 USA (SAN 299-240X) Tel 415-541-9901; Fax: 805-426-8136; Toll Free: 800-238-9669
E-mail: customerservice@cerebellum.com; cerebell@mindspring.com; admin@cerebellum.com
Web site: www.cerebellum.com; http://www.standarddeviants.com
Dist(s): **Follett School Solutions.**

Cerebral Press International, *(978-0-916309)* HC-71 Box 121-1, Thornfield, MO 65762 USA (SAN 295-9461) Tel 417-679-4748
E-mail: lagunapress@braintypes.com
Web site: http://www.braintypes.com.

Ceres Pr., *(978-0-9606138; 978-1-886101)* P.O. Box 87, Woodstock, NY 12498 USA (SAN 217-0949) Tel 845-679-5573; Toll Free: 888-804-8848 Do not confuse with Ceres Pr., Stamford, CT
E-mail: cem620@aol.com
Web site: http://www.heathyhighways.com
Dist(s): **Integral Yoga Pubns.**
New Leaf Distributing Co., Inc.
Nutri-Bks. Corp.
Partners Bk. Distributing, Inc.

Ceres Software, Incorporated *See* **Inspiration Software, Inc.**

Cernunnos (FRA) *(978-2-37495) Dist. by* **HachBkGrp.**

Certified Firearms Instructors, LLC, *(978-0-9741480)* P.O. Box 131254, Saint Paul, MN 55113-1254 USA Tel 952-935-2414; Fax: 952-935-4122
E-mail: jolson@gw.hamline.edu
Web site: http://www.aacfi.com.

Cervena Barva Pr., *(978-0-615-17167-8; 978-0-615-20097-2; 978-0-615-25796-9; 978-0-615-25797-6; 978-0-615-25983-3; 978-0-615-26369-4; 978-0-578-00416-7; 978-0-692-00181-3; 978-0-578-02262-8; 978-0-578-02491-2; 978-0-578-04084-4; 978-0-692-00642-9; 978-0-578-04207-7; 978-0-9844732; 978-0-9831041; 978-0-578-08091-8; 978-0-9883713; 978-0-9910091; 978-0-692-28317-2; 978-0-692-30231-6; 978-0-692-33628-1; 978-0-9861111; 978-0-9966894; 978-0-9981027; 978-0-9984253; 978-0-692-08026-9; 978-0-692-13790-1; 978-1-950063) P.O. Box 440357, West Somerville, MA 02144-3222 USA Tel 617-764-2229*
E-mail: editor@cervenabarvapress.com
Web site: http://www.cervenabarvapress.com
Dist(s): **Instant Pub.**
SPD-Small Pr. Distribution.

CET *Imprint of* **Greater Cincinnati TV Educational Foundation**

C E V Multimedia, Ltd., *(978-1-57078; 978-1-59535; 978-1-60333; 978-1-61459; 979-8-88864)* Orders Addr.: P.O. Box 65265, Lubbock, TX 79464 USA Tel 806-745-8820; Fax: 806-745-5300; Toll Free Fax: 800-243-6398; Toll Free: 800-922-9965; Edit Addr.: 1020 SE Loop 289, Lubbock, TX 79404 USA
E-mail: cev@cevmultimedia.com
Web site: http://www.cevmultimedia.com
Dist(s): **Follett School Solutions.**

CFM, *(978-0-9728620; 978-0-9769071; 978-0-9908661)* 112 Greene St., New York City, NY 10012 USA Tel 212-966-3864; Fax: 212-226-1041
E-mail: info@cfmgallery.com
Web site: http://www.cfmgallery.com.

CG Star, L.L.C. *See* **C-It Entertainment Group, LLC**

C.G.S. Pr., *(978-0-9660726)* P.O. Box 1394, Mountainside, NJ 07092 USA Tel 908-233-8293 (phone/fax)
E-mail: Gwynnic2000@aol.com.

Chacmool Pr., *(978-0-9789391)* 849 W. University Pkwy., Baltimore, MD 21210 USA
E-mail: publisher@chacmoolpress.com
Web site: http://www.chacmoolpress.com.

Chafie Pr., LLC, *(978-0-9833190; 978-0-9903532)* 7557 Rambler Rd. Suite 626, Dallas, TX 75231 USA Tel 214-628-8600
E-mail: trish.jones@chafiehds.com
Web site: http://www.chafiepress.com
Dist(s): **Follett School Solutions**
Pathway Bk. Service.

Chagrin River Publishing Co., *(978-1-929821; 978-0-615-32246-9)* Orders Addr.: P.O. Box 173, Chagrin Falls, OH 44022 USA Tel 440-893-9250; Edit Addr.: 21 E. Summit St., Chagrin Falls, OH 44022 USA
Dist(s): **Follett School Solutions.**

Chai Yo Maui Pr., *(978-0-615-31840-0; 978-0-9855804)* P.O. Box 331, Kihei, HI 96753 USA.

Chaklet Coffee Bks *Imprint of* **Candalyse Publishing**

Chalice Pr., *(978-0-8272)* Div. of Christian Board of Pubn., Orders Addr.: c/o Christian Board of Publication, P.O. Box 933119, Atlanta, GA 31193-3119 USA Tel 800-366-3383; Fax: 770-280-4039; Toll Free: 800-366-3383; Edit Addr.: 483 E Lockwood Ave., Suite 100, Saint Louis, MO 63119 USA Tel 314-231-8500; Fax: 314-231-8524
E-mail: customerservice@chalicepress.com; cpbiz@chalicepress.com
Web site: http://www.chalicepress.com; http://www.lucasparkbooks.com
Dist(s): **Baker & Taylor Publisher Services (BTPS)**
Follett School Solutions
MyiLibrary
Spring Arbor Distributors, Inc.
ebrary, Inc.

Chamberlain Hart Enterprises, Inc., *(978-0-9749756)* P.O. Box 1600, Fairfield, IA 52556 USA Tel 641-469-3717; Fax: 641-469-6647
E-mail: che@iowatelecom.net
Web site: http://www.chamberlainhart.com.

Chambers Kingfisher Graham Publishers, Incorporated *See* **Larousse Kingfisher Chambers, Inc.**

Chambers, Ta'mara, *(978-0-692-11886-3)* 8503 Bridgeway Dr., Fort Wayne, IN 46816 USA Tel 260-210-2642
E-mail: amaralove721@gmail.com.

Chameleon Designs, *(978-0-9701573)* P.O. Box 61855, North Charleston, SC 29419 USA Tel 843-761-7426
E-mail: yeleth@aol.com.

Chamike Pubs., *(978-1-884876)* 9000 Doris Dr., Fort Washington, MD 20744 USA Tel 301-248-4034.

†**Champagne Book Group,** *(978-0-9737261; 978-0-9737627; 978-1-897261; 978-1-926681; 978-1-897445; 978-1-77155; 978-1-926996; 978-1-927454; 978-1-947128; 978-1-957228; 978-1-959036)* 2373 NE Evergreen Ave., Albany, OR 97321 USA Tel 503-961-4918
E-mail: publisher@champagnebooks.com
Web site: http://www.champagnebooks.com
Dist(s): **Smashwords**; *CIP.*

Champagne Books *See* **Champagne Book Group**

CHAMPEAU, BRANDY *See* **Exploring ExPr.ion LLC**

Champion Athlete Publishing Company *See* **National Assn. of Speed & Explosion**

Championship Chess, *(978-0-9729456; 978-0-9772489)* Div. of Teachable Tech, Inc., Orders Addr.: 3565 Evans Rd., Atlanta, GA 30340 USA Toll Free: 888-328-7373
E-mail: dj@championshipchess.net
Web site: http://www.championshipchess.net.

Champlain Avenue Bks., Inc., *(978-0-9855008; 978-0-9896347; 978-0-9908256; 978-1-943063)* 2360 Corporate Cir. Suite 400, Henderson, NV 89074-7722 USA Tel 760-684-5861
E-mail: champlainavenuebooks@hotmail.com
Web site: champlainavenuebooks@hotmail.com
Dist(s): **Smashwords.**

CHAN, ANGELA *See* **Nonsuch Media Pte. Ltd.**

Chan, David, *(978-0-9754302)* 12511 Fox Trace Ln., Houston, TX 77066-4029 USA Tel 281-580-7042
E-mail: david@chancomputerhelp.com.

Chandiramani, Riya, *(978-0-692-05362-1; 978-0-692-05363-8)* 4047 Irving St., Philadelphia, PA 19104 USA Tel (+852) 68089894
E-mail: riya.chandiramani@gmail.com
Dist(s): **Ingram Content Group.**

Chandler Hse. Pr., *(978-0-9636277; 978-1-886284)* P.O. Box 20126, Worcester, MA 01602 USA Fax: 508-753-7419
E-mail: chandlerhousepress@yahoo.com
Web site: http://www.chandlerhousebooks.com
Dist(s): **Follett School Solutions.**

Chandler Publishing, *(978-1-7326823)* 49 Ctr. Ct., Roslyn Heights, NY 11577 USA Tel 310-909-3571
E-mail: whitney@sleepeezkidz.com.

Chandler/White Publishing Co., *(978-1-877804)* 517 W. Midvale Ave., Philadelphia, PA 19144-4617 USA
Dist(s): **Alliance Hse., Inc.**

Chaney, Denise Ann, *(978-0-692-10888-8; 978-0-692-12992-0; 978-0-692-19846-9)* 166 Arrowhead Dr., PAGOSA SPRINGS, CO 81147 USA Tel 719-588-9202
E-mail: neisly@hotmail.com
Dist(s): **Ingram Content Group.**

Change Is Strange, Inc., *(978-0-9755902)* 3630 21st St., Boulder, CO 80304-1608 USA
E-mail: info@changeisstrange.com
Web site: http://www.changeisstrange.com
Dist(s): **Follett School Solutions.**

Changemakers Pr., *(978-1-7346186)* P.O. Box 1400, Rockville, MD 20849 USA
E-mail: carrie@mission.partners
Web site: changemakerspress.com; missionforward.us.

Changing Lives Changing The World, Incorporated *See* **Changing Lives Publishing**

Changing Lives Pr., *(978-0-9850248; 978-0-9882476; 978-0-9894529; 978-0-9904396; 978-0-9909424)* 91-18 159th Ave., Howard Beach, NY 11414 USA Tel 347-304-0625
E-mail: anminerva727@gmail.com; aminerva727@aol.com
Web site: http://www.changinglivespress.com
Dist(s): **BookBaby**
Follett School Solutions
Independent Pubs. Group
Midpoint Trade Bks., Inc.
ebrary, Inc.

Changing Lives Publishing, *(978-0-9653700; 978-0-9774513; 978-0-9798553)* Div. of Changing Lives Changing The World, Inc., P.O. Box 132, Sharpes, FL 32959 USA Tel 321-637-1128; Toll Free: 866-578-1900
E-mail: print2publish@gmail.com
Web site: http://www.print2publish.com.

Changing World Publishing, *(978-0-9829274; 979-8-9889506)* 3214 6A Ave S., Lethbridge , AB T1J1H4 CAN Tel 403-331-9146
E-mail: kindlingkindness1@gmail.com
Web site: www/kindiscoolkids.com.

Changing-Times.net, *(978-0-9741930)* Orders Addr.: P.O. Box 39651, Phoenix, AZ 85069-9651 USA
Web site: http://www.changing-times.net.

Channel Publishing, Ltd., *(978-0-945501; 978-1-933053; 978-1-946729)* 4750 Longley Ln., Suite 209, Reno, NV 89502 USA (SAN 247-1256) Tel 775-825-0880; Fax: 775-825-5633; Toll Free: 800-248-2882
E-mail: info@channelpublishing.com
Web site: http://www.channelpublishing.com.

Chanticlair Publishing, *(978-0-692-22416-8; 978-0-692-80319-6; 978-0-692-07326-1; 978-0-578-51383-6; 978-0-578-51928-9)* P.O. Box 74672, San Clemente, CA 92673 USA Tel 949-378-0287
E-mail: Auntielynny@gmail.com.

Chantilly Books, *(978-0-9841960)* Div. of Boone Amie Publishing, Orders Addr.: 14240-A Sullyfield Cir., Chantilly, VA 20151 USA (SAN 858-6853) Fax: 703-830-7100
E-mail: sue@a-childs-book.com
Web site: http://www.a-childs-book.com.

Chapel Hill Press, Inc., *(978-1-880849; 978-1-59715)* 11312 US 15-501 N Ste 107-223, Chapel Hill, NC 27517 USA Tel 919-929-8389
E-mail: edwina.woodbury@chapelhillpress.com
Web site: http://www.chapelhillpress.com
Dist(s): **Blair**
Follett School Solutions
Univ. of North Carolina Pr.

Chapel Song Publishing *See* **Wild Willow Pr.**

Chapin Hse. Bks. *Imprint of* **Florida Historical Society**

Chapman, Chris & Eric P. Hvolboll, *(978-0-9765061)* 2741 Cuerta Rd., Santa Barbara, CA 93105 USA Fax: 805-882-9897.

Chapman Pr., LLC, *(978-0-9725420)* 949 S. Josephine St., Denver, CO 80209 USA
E-mail: taylor@babsonfarms.com; taylor@babsonfarms.com
Web site: http://www.chapmanpress.com.

Chapter & Verse Pr., *(978-0-9724549)* 7350 Detrick Jordan Pike, Springfield, OH 45502-9660 USA Tel 937-964-0294
E-mail: nashvila@bright.net.

Chapter Bks. *Imprint of* **Spotlight**

Chapterhouse Comics (CAN) *(978-0-9947386; 978-0-9950098; 978-1-988247) Dist. by* **D C D.**

Chara Pr., *(978-0-9862513; 978-1-944705)* 74 Brandywine Rd., Fords, NJ 08863-1320 USA Tel 732-225-5046
E-mail: jamiebee.banta@gmail.com.

Character Arts, *(978-0-9772259)* 37 Pond Rd., Bldg. 2, Wilton, CT 06897 USA Tel 203-834-0323.

Character Assassin Bks., *(978-1-7363459)* 6520 S Shore Dr, Altoona, WI 54720 USA Tel 608-314-5497
E-mail: starr@starrzdavies.com.
Character Development Group, Inc., *(978-0-9653163; 978-1-892056)* Div. of Character Development Group, Inc., Orders Addr.: P.O. Box 35136, Greensboro, NC 27425-5136 USA Tel 336-668-9373; Fax: 336-668-9375; Edit Addr.: 8646 W. Market St. Suite 102, Greensboro, NC 27409 USA
E-mail: info@charactereducation.com
Web site: http://www.charactereducation.com
Dist(s): **Follett School Solutions.**
Character Development Publishing *See* **Character Development Group, Inc,**
Character Kids Publishing *See* **LJM Communications**
Character-in-Action *Imprint of* **Quiet Impact, Inc.**
Characters of Faith Publishing, LLCLLC, *(978-1-7366719)* 134 Roseheart, San Antonio, TX 78259 USA Tel 210-455-3737
E-mail: mkwyrick@cs.com
Web site: charactersoffaithpublishing.com.
Charbonneau, Bradley, *(978-1-7322434)* 15129 Killion St., Sherman Oaks, CA 91411 USA Tel 415-558-8400
E-mail: ingram@likomaisland.com
Dist(s): **Ingram Content Group.**
Charde vera *See* **Charde Vera**
Charde Vera, *(978-1-7374173; 979-8-9885294)*
E-mail: chardemontes@yahoo.com; info@chardevera.com
Web site: chardevera.com.
CharFaye Publishing, Incorporated *See* **FayeHouse. Pr. International**
Charisma Hse. *Imprint of* **Charisma Media**
Charisma Kids *Imprint of* **Charisma Media**
Charisma Media, *(978-0-88419; 978-0-930525; 978-1-59185; 978-1-59979; 978-1-61638; 978-1-62136; 978-1-62998; 978-1-62999; 978-1-63641)* Div. of Creation House Pr., 600 Rinehart Rd., Lake Mary, FL 32746 USA (SAN 677-5640) Tel 407-333-0600; Fax: 407-333-7100; Toll Free: 800-283-8494; *Imprints:* Charisma House (Charisma Hse); Casa Creacion (Casa Cre); Creation House (CreatHse); Siloam Press (Siloam Pr); Charisma Kids (Charisma Kids); Frontline (Frontline FLA); Realms (Realms)
Web site: http://www.charismamedia.com/
Dist(s): **Dake Publishing**
Follett School Solutions
INscribe Digital
Independent Pubs. Group
Lulu Pr., Inc.
Pura Vida Bks., Inc.
SPD-Small Pr. Distribution
Send The Light Distribution LLC.
Charlene Adler, *(978-0-692-94597-1; 978-0-9994165)* 510 E. Washington, DELAVAN, WI 53115 USA Tel 816-813-1708
E-mail: mmmuffin4@gmail.com
Dist(s): **Ingram Content Group.**
Charles River Media, *(978-1-886801; 978-1-58450)* Orders Addr.: P.O. Box 960, Herndon, VA 20172 USA (SAN 254-1564) Fax: 703-996-1010; Toll Free: 800-382-8505; Edit Addr.: 25 Thomson Pl., Boston, MA 02210-1202 USA
E-mail: info@charlesriver.com
Web site: http://www.charlesriver.com
Dist(s): **CENGAGE Learning**
Delmar Cengage Learning
ebrary, Inc.
Charles River Pr., *(978-0-9754913; 978-0-9791304; 978-0-9793844; 978-0-9820946; 978-1-936185; 978-1-940676)* 37 Evergreen Rd., Norton, MA 02766 USA Fax: 508-297-3628; P.O. Box 1122, Mansfield, MA 02048 (SAN 256-2251); *Imprints:* Gap Tooth Publishing (Gap Tooth Pubng) Do not confuse with Charles River Pr. in Alexandria, VA
E-mail: jwomack@charlesriverpress.com; customerservice@charlesriverpress.com
Web site: http://www.charlesriverpress.com.
Charles Scribner's Sons *Imprint of* **Cengage Gale**
Charlesbridge Moves *Imprint of* **Charlesbridge Publishing, Inc.**
Charlesbridge Publishing, Inc., *(978-0-88106; 978-0-935508; 978-1-57091; 978-1-58089; 978-1-879085; 978-1-60734; 978-0-9822939; 978-0-9823064; 978-1-936140; 978-1-63289; 978-1-64537)* Orders Addr.: c/o Penguin Random House, 400 Hahn Rd., Westminster, MD 21157 USA Toll Free Fax: 800-669-1536; Toll Free: 800-733-3000; Edit Addr.: 85 Main St., Watertown, MA 02472 USA (SAN 240-5474) Tel 617-926-0329; Fax: 617-926-5720; Toll Free Fax: 800-926-5775; Toll Free: 800-225-3214; *Imprints:* Mackinac Island Press, Incorporated (Mackinac); Imagine Publishing (ImaginePub); Charlesbridge Teen (CharlesbridgeT); Charlesbridge Moves (CBridge Moves)
E-mail: orders@charlesbridge.com
Web site: http://www.charlesbridge.com
Dist(s): **Children's Plus, Inc.**
Continental Bk. Co., Inc.
Follett School Solutions
Lectorum Pubns., Inc.
MyiLibrary
Penguin Random Hse. Distribution
Penguin Random Hse. LLC
Random Hse., Inc.
Charlesbridge Teen *Imprint of* **Charlesbridge Publishing, Inc.**
Charles-Collins, Kelly *See* **Lady Lawyer Media**
Charlie & Albert, *(978-0-9801329)* 2920 Applewood Ct., Suite 192, Atlanta, GA 30345-1401 USA Tel 770-938-8863.
Charlie Co., *(978-0-578-42731-7)* 1561 East Ave., Rochester, NY 14610 USA Tel 585-303-6121
E-mail: johns@exhibitsandmore.com.
Charlie's Gift, *(978-0-9786795)* 920 York Rd., Suite 350, Hinsdale, IL 60521 USA Tel 630-399-8164.
Charlie's Port, *(978-0-692-90898-3; 978-0-9997510; 978-0-692-03537-5)* 224 Rose Cottage Dr., Woodstock, GA 30189 USA Tel 678-800-8787
E-mail: mc@charliesport.org
Web site: www.charliesport.org.
Charming Pubns., *(978-0-9773531)* Orders Addr.: P.O. Box 90792, Austin, TX 78709-0792 USA Tel 512-288-4803
E-mail: minia.lopez@gmail.com
Web site: http://www.happychildrenbooks.com.
Charming Scoundrel Publishing, *(978-0-692-62829-4; 978-1-7349552)* 2728 N 26th St, Tacoma, WA 98407 USA Tel 253-341-5047
Dist(s): **CreateSpace Independent Publishing Platform.**
Chartwell *Imprint of* **Book Sales, Inc.**
Charwood Pubns., *(978-0-615-58076-0; 978-0-615-66672-3; 978-0-9910347; 978-0-692-79990-1; 978-0-692-80308-0; 978-0-9986914)* Orders Addr.: P.O. Box 14881, Long Beach, CA 90853 USA Tel 562-810-7176
E-mail: charlesfilius@gmail.com
Web site: www.charlesfilius.com; www.charwoodpublications.com.
Chaser Media LLC, *(978-0-9747447)* P.O. Box 99, Dorset, VT 05251 USA
Web site: http://www.chasermedia.com.
Chateau Thierry Pr., *(978-0-935046)* Div. of Joan Thiry Enterprises, Ltd., 2100 W. Estes, Chicago, IL 60645 USA (SAN 281-4056) Tel 773-262-2234; Fax: 773-262-2235
E-mail: percival6390@sbcglobal.net.
Chatelain, Linda, *(978-1-938669)* Orders Addr.: 4106 S. Middlepark Ln., West Valley City, UT 84119 USA Tel 801-654-7793
E-mail: lchat1950@hotmail.com.
Chatoyant, *(978-0-9661452)* P.O. Box 832, Aptos, CA 95001 USA (SAN 253-9454) Tel 831-662-2723
E-mail: books@chatoyant.com
Web site: http://www.chatoyant.com.
Chatting Timmy, 845 16Th St unit 28, San Diego, CA 92101 USA Tel 678-862-2178
E-mail: iracanada@bellsouth.net
Dist(s): **Ingram Content Group.**
Chaucer Pr. *Imprint of* **Altschuler, Richard & Assocs., Inc.**
Chauncey Park Pr., *(978-0-9667808)* Div. of Charles Chauncey Wells, Inc., 735 N. Grove Ave., Oak Park, IL 60302-1551 USA Tel 708-524-0695; Fax: 708-524-0742
E-mail: chauncey@wells1.com
Web site: http://www.wells1.com.
CHB Media, *(978-0-9822819; 978-0-9851507; 978-0-9886315; 978-0-9911189; 978-0-9863842; 979-8-9852374; 979-8-9873184)* Div. of Christian Heartbeat, Inc., 3039 Needle Palm Dr., Edgewater, FL 32141 USA Tel 386-690-9295
E-mail: christianheartbeat@gmail.com
Web site: http://www.chbmediaonline.com.
Cheatham Publishing, *(978-1-7354989)* 3425 S. 176th St., Seatac, WA 98188 USA Tel 206-519-1720
E-mail: hello@jeffcheatham2.com
Web site: www.jeffcheatham2.com.
Checker Bk. Publishing Group, *(978-0-9710249; 978-0-9741664; 978-0-9753808; 978-1-933160; 978-1-61799)* 217 Byers Rd., Miamisburg, OH 45342 USA
Web site: http://www.checkerbpg.com
Dist(s): **Brodart Co.**
Haven Distributors
Tales of Wonder.com.
Checkerboard Library *Imprint of* **ABDO Publishing Co.**
†Checkerboard Pr., Inc., *(978-1-56288)* 1560 Revere Rd., Yardley, PA 19067-4351 USA; *CIP.*
Checkmark Bks. *Imprint of* **Infobase Holdings, Inc.**
Cheerful Cherub, *(978-0-9753417)* Orders Addr.: 10071 S. Maples Ln., Highlands Ranch, CO 80129 USA Tel 303-471-8472; Edit Addr.: 10071 S. Maples Ln., Highlands Ranch, CO 80129 USA
E-mail: coloradodonna@q.com
Web site: http://www.cheerfulcherub.com.
Cheesy Bread Publishing, *(978-1-7323816)* 510 Wallace, Chicago Heights, IL 60411 USA Tel 708-491-6382
E-mail: art.pressley@yahoo.com.
CheeTrann Creations LLC, *(978-0-9834761; 978-1-7320332)* 203 Airport Dr. Unit A5, Sitka, AK 99835 USA Tel 907-738-4303
E-mail: Tom@SKRandolph.com
Web site: www.skrandolph.com.
Chelsea Clubhse. *Imprint of* **Infobase Holdings, Inc.**
Chelsea Green Publishing, *(978-0-930031; 978-1-890132; 978-1-931498; 978-1-933392; 978-1-60358; 978-1-64502)* 85 N. Main St., Suite 120, White River Junction, VT 05001 USA
E-mail: info@chelseagreen.com
Web site: http://www.chelseagreen.com
Dist(s): **Follett School Solutions**
Independent Pubs. Group.
Chelsea lagrange, *(978-0-692-15625-4; 978-0-692-17382-4; 978-0-578-40438-7)* 9078 Blackhawk trl., Lucerne Valley, CA 92356 USA Tel 760-646-2660
E-mail: Chelsealagrange@gmail.com
Dist(s): **Ingram Content Group.**
Chelsea Media *See* **Chelsea Multimedia**
Chelsea Multimedia, *(978-0-9822348)* P.O. Box 4668 19830, New York, NY 10163-4668 USA Tel 203-853-0540; *Imprints:* Chelsea Press (Chelsea Press)
Web site: http://www.chelseapress.com
Dist(s): **CreateSpace Independent Publishing Platform.**
Chelsea Pr. *Imprint of* **Chelsea Multimedia**
Chelsea Publishing Co., Inc. *Imprint of* **American Mathematical Society**
Chelsea The Golden Retriever, *(978-1-951690)* 7215 Eby Dr., Merriam, KS 66204 USA Tel 913-221-9180
E-mail: dantheman4christ@yahoo.com.
Chemical Heritage Foundation, *(978-0-941901)* 315 Chestnut St., Philadelphia, PA 19106-2702 USA (SAN 666-0193) Tel 215-925-2222; Fax: 215-925-1954; Toll Free: 888-224-6006
E-mail: booksales@chemheritage.org
Web site: http://www.chemheritage.org.
Chen, Stephen, *(978-0-692-14249-3)* 5106 E. Palo Brea Ln., Cave Creek, AZ 85331 USA Tel 602-284-6501
E-mail: schendesigns@gmail.com
Dist(s): **Ingram Content Group.**
Cheng & Tsui Co., *(978-0-88727; 978-0-917056; 978-1-62291)* 25 W. St., Boston, MA 02111-1213 USA (SAN 169-3387)
E-mail: service@cheng-tsui.com
Web site: http://www.cheng-tsui.com
Dist(s): **Chinasprout, Inc.**
Follett School Solutions.
Cheng Chung Bk. Co., Ltd. (TWN) *(978-957-09) Dist. by* **Cheng Tsui.**
Cheniere Pr., *(978-0-9725146; 978-0-9786260)* 151 La Jolla Dr., Santa Barbara, CA 93109 USA
E-mail: webmaster@cheniere.org.
Cherakota Books *See* **Cherakota Publishing**
Cherakota Publishing, *(978-0-9795678)* P.O. Box 171, Sandstone, MN 55072 USA
E-mail: joashlyank@gmail.com
Web site: http://www.cherakotapublishing.com.
Cherish the Children *See* **Chris A. Zeigler Dendy Consulting LLC**
Cheriton Children's Bks. (GBR) *(978-1-914383; 978-1-915153) Dist. by* **Lerner Pub.**
Cherokee Bks., *(978-0-9640458; 978-1-930052)* Orders Addr.: 24 Meadow Ridge Pkwy. Dover, De 19904, Dover, DE 19904-5800 USA Tel 302-734-8782; Fax: 302-734-3198 Do not confuse with Cherokee Bks., Ponca City, OK
E-mail: milthanna@aol.com
Web site: http://www.cherokeebooks.com
Dist(s): **Washington Bk. Distributors.**
Cherokee Publishing Company *See* **Cherokee Bks.**
Cherokee Rose Publishing, LLC, *(978-0-9968902; 978-0-9994622)* 2367 Barrett Cottage Pl., Marietta, GA 30066 USA Tel 678-403-2272
E-mail: margeryphelps@msn.com
Web site: www.margeryphelps.com; www.findingmargaret.com; www.cherokeerosepublishing.com.
Cherry Blossom Press *Imprint of* **Cherry Lake Publishing**
Cherry Lake Publishing, *(978-1-60279; 978-1-61080; 978-1-62431; 978-1-62753; 978-1-63137; 978-1-63188; 978-1-63362; 978-1-63470; 978-1-63471; 978-1-63472; 978-1-5341; 978-1-6689)* 1215 Overidgeview Ct., Ann Arbor, MI 48103 USA Tel 248-705-2045; 1750 Northway Dr., Suite 101, North Mankato, MN 56003 (SAN 858-9275) Tel 866-918-3956; Toll Free Fax: 866-489-6490; *Imprints:* Blackbirch Press, Incorporated (Blackbirch Pr); 45th Parallel Press (45 Parallel); Cherry Blossom Press (Cherry Bloss Pr); Torch Graphic Press (TrchGraphicPr)
E-mail: customerservice@cherrylakepublishing.com; benmondloch@me.com; lois.hume@sleepingbearpress.com
Web site: http://cherrylakepublishing.com; www.sleepingbearpress.com
Dist(s): **Follett School Solutions**
MyiLibrary.
Cherry Lane Books *See* **Cherry Lane Music Co.**
†Cherry Lane Music Co., *(978-0-89524; 978-1-57560; 978-1-60378)* 6 E. 32nd St., 11th Flr., New York, NY 10016 USA (SAN 219-0788) Tel 212-561-3000; Fax: 212-251-0822
E-mail: print@cherrylane.com
Web site: http://www.cherrylane.com
Dist(s): **Leonard, Hal Corp.**
MyiLibrary
National Bk. Network; *CIP.*
Cherry Publishing, *(978-0-615-90433-7; 978-0-9864490)* P.O. Box 40, Maury, NC 28554 USA Tel 252-747-8491
Dist(s): **CreateSpace Independent Publishing Platform.**
Cherry Street Pr., *(978-0-9764921)* 139A N. 22nd St., Philadelphia, PA 19103 USA Fax: 215-568-4329
Dist(s): **Follett School Solutions.**
Cherry, Tasha *See* **Pop Academy of Music**
Cherry Tree Bks., *(978-0-9666832; 978-0-9774665)* 433 Perkins Rd., Weybridge, VT 05753 USA Tel 802-545-2474
E-mail: idahw@pshift.com; lmwash@together.net
Web site: http://www.cherrytreebooks.net.
Cherry Tree Lane Publishing, *(978-0-9771858)* 125 Cobblestone Ct., Berea, OH 44017-1079 USA
E-mail: sharesom@wowway.com.
Cherry Tree Pr. LLC, *(978-0-9772771)* Orders Addr.: 525 W. 14th St., #185, Traverse City, MI 49684-4968 USA Tel 231-421-1012; Edit Addr.: 526 W. 14th St., No. 185, Traverse City, MI 49684-4968 USA Do not confuse with Cherry Tree Press in Palo Alto, CA
E-mail: info@cherrytreepress.com
Web site: http://www.CherryTreePress.com; http://www.AmlaColorToo.com
Dist(s): **Partners Bk. Distributing, Inc.**
Cherrymoon Media, *(978-0-9982190)* 3785 Lady Di Ln, Lexington, KY 40517 USA Tel 606-483-1806
E-mail: info@cherrymoonmedia.com
Web site: www.cherrymoonmedia.com.
Cherrytree Bks. (GBR) *(978-0-7451; 978-0-7540; 978-1-84234) Dist. by* **IPG Chicago.**
Cherrytree Pubns., Inc., *(978-0-9677757)* 881 Ocean Dr., No. 18B, Biscayne, FL 33149 USA Tel 305-361-1828.
Chesed Avraham Temple, *(978-0-9801799)* Orders Addr.: P.O. Box 35456, Los Angeles, CA 90035 USA (SAN 855-4137) Tel 310-654-0303
E-mail: meissany@ca.rr.com
Web site: http://www.EbrahimNeissany.com.
Cheshire House Bks., *(978-0-9675073)* P.O. Box 2484, New York, NY 10021 USA Tel 212-861-5404 (phone/fax)
E-mail: Chershirehouse@webtv.net
Web site: http://www.samthecat.com
Dist(s): **Brodart Co.**
Follet Higher Education Grp
Follett School Solutions.
Chess Detective Pr., *(978-0-9761962)* 1 Red Fox Ln., Englewood, CO 80111 USA Tel 303-770-6696 (phone/fax)
Web site: http://www.coloradomasterchess.com
Dist(s): **Follett School Solutions.**
Chess Library, The, *(978-0-9661889)* 12615 SW 297th Way, Vashon, WA 98070 USA
E-mail: pkmccready@netscape.net; admin@thechesslibrary.com
Web site: http://www.thechesslibrary.com.
Chessmore Publishing *See* **Eusebian Publishing**
Chester Comix, LLC, *(978-0-9729616; 978-1-933122; 978-0-692-95704-2; 978-1-7323612)* P.O. Box 5653, Williamsburg, VA 23188 USA
E-mail: chestercomix@yahoo.com
Web site: http://www.chestercomix.com
Dist(s): **Follett School Solutions.**
Chester Music (GBR) *(978-0-7119) Dist. by* **H Leonard.**
Chester Music *Imprint of* **Music Sales Corp.**
Cheval International, *(978-0-9640610; 978-1-885351)* P.O. Box 706, Black Hawk, SD 57718-0706 USA
E-mail: cheval@rapidnet.com
Web site: http://www.chevalinternational.com
Dist(s): **Barnes & Noble Bks.-Imports.**
Cheveux Roux LLC *See* **Gray & Gold Publishing**
Chi Chi Rodriguez Books *See* **Caribbean Experience Con Amor, LLC, A**
Chiang Mai Bks., *(978-0-578-19214-7)* 1006 Marley Manor Dr. Apt 103, Salisbury, MD 21804 USA.
Chiappini, Lydia , *(978-0-9669355)* 60 Gaisler Rd., Blairstown, NJ 07825 USA Tel 908-362-5604
E-mail: lydiachiappini@yahoo.com.
Chiaramonti, Gregory, *(978-0-615-13848-0)* 825 Cherry St., Trenton, NJ 08638-3322 USA
E-mail: gcmonti@yahoo.com
Web site: http://www.probie-thespaceprobe.com
Dist(s): **Lulu Pr., Inc.**
Chicago Children's Museum, *(978-0-9759580)* Navy Pier, 700 E. Grand Ave., Chicago, IL 60611 USA Tel 312-527-1000; Fax: 312-527-9082
Web site: http://www.chichildrensmuseum.org
Dist(s): **Follett School Solutions**
Independent Pubs. Group
ebrary, Inc.
Chicago Distribution Ctr., Orders Addr.: 11030 S. Langley Ave., Chicago, IL 60628 USA (SAN 630-6047) Tel 773-702-7000 (International); Fax: 773-702-7212 (International); Toll Free Fax: 800-621-8476 (USA/Canada); Toll Free: 800-621-2736 (USA/Canada); 800-621-8471 (credit & collections)
E-mail: custserv@press.uchicago.edu; orders@press.uchicago.edu
Web site: http://www.press.uchicago.edu; http://www.press.uchicago.edu/presswide/cdc/.
Chicago Review Pr., *(978-1-941530; 978-1-945053; 978-1-951954)* 814 N. Franklin St., Chicago, IL 60610 USA Tel 312-337-0747; *Imprints:* Interlude Press (InterludePr)
E-mail: lex@interludepress.com; annie@interludepress.com
Web site: http://interludepress.com; http://duetbooks.com
Dist(s): **Independent Pubs. Group.**
†Chicago Review Pr., Inc., *(978-0-89733; 978-0-912777; 978-0-913705; 978-0-914090; 978-0-914091; 978-0-915864; 978-1-55652; 978-1-56976; 978-1-61373; 978-1-61374; 978-1-64160; 979-8-89068)* 814 N. Franklin St., Chicago, IL 60610 USA (SAN 213-5744) Tel 312-337-0747; Toll Free: 800-888-4741 (orders only); *Imprints:* Hill, Lawrence Books (Lawrence Hill); Zephyr Press (ZephPr); Academy Chicago Publishers, Limited (AcadChicagoPubs)
E-mail: frontdesk@chicagoreviewpress.com; orders@ipgbook.com
Web site: http://www.ipgbook.com; http://www.chicagoreviewpress.com
Dist(s): **AK Pr. Distribution**
Children's Plus, Inc.
Cobblestone Publishing Co.
Ebsco Publishing
Follett School Solutions
Gryphon Hse., Inc.
Independent Pubs. Group
Lulu Pr., Inc.
MyiLibrary
Open Road Integrated Media, Inc.
SAGE Pubns., Inc.
ebrary, Inc.; *CIP.*
Chicago Spectrum Pr., *(978-1-58374; 978-1-886094)* Div. of Evanston Publishing Inc., Orders Addr.: 6611 Foxcroft Rd., Prospect, KY 40059 USA Tel 502-899-1919; Toll Free: 800-594-5190; 888-266-5780 (888-BOOKS-80)
E-mail: dorothykavka@twc.com
Web site: http://www.fineartbykavka.com.
Chicago Unzipped, *(978-0-9771699; 978-0-9817538)* 633 Clark St., No. 2-634, Evanston, IL 60208 USA (SAN 856-4558) Tel 847-491-8757
Web site: http://www.chicagounzipped.com.
Chick Light Publishing, *(978-0-9769198)* 845 Monticello Ct., Cape Coral, FL 33904 USA Tel 239-945-1939 (phone/fax)
E-mail: vince@chicklight.com
Web site: http://chicklight.com.
Chick Pubns., Inc., *(978-0-937958; 978-0-7589)* P.O. Box 3500, Ontario, CA 91761-1019 USA (SAN 211-7770) Tel 909-987-0771; Fax: 909-941-8128; Toll Free: 800-932-3050
E-mail: orderdesk@chick.com
Web site: http://www.chick.com.

Chickadee Words *Imprint of* **Chickadee Words, LLC**

Chickadee Words, LLC, *(978-0-9981291; 978-0-9998315; 978-1-7357338)* 5220 N. Randolph Rd, Kansas City, MO 64119 USA Tel 816-807-7025; *Imprints:* Chickadee Words (MYID_S_CHICKAD)
E-mail: kathy@chickadeewords.com
Web site: chickadeewords.com
Dist(s): **BookBaby**
Independently Published
Ingram Bk. Co.

Chickaloon Village Publishing, *(978-0-9767217)* Orders Addr.: P.O. Box 1105, Chickaloon, AK 99674 USA Tel 907-745-0707; Fax: 907-745-0709
E-mail: cvadmin@chickaloon.org
Web site: http://www.chickaloon.org.

Chicken Hse., The *Imprint of* **Scholastic, Inc.**

Chicken Socks *Imprint of* **Klutz**

Chicken Soup for the Soul Publishing, LLC, *(978-1-935096; 978-1-61159)* 132 E. Putnam Ave., Cos Cob, CT 06807 USA; 180 Varick St. Suite 816, New York, NY 10014; *Imprints:* CSS Backlist (CSSBacklist)
E-mail: evergreenstables@hotmail.com
Dist(s): **Follett School Solutions**
Leonard, Hal Corp.
MyiLibrary
Open Road Integrated Media, Inc.
Simon & Schuster
Simon & Schuster, Inc.

chickenscratchPr., *(978-1-7348204; 978-1-7353338)* 14128 Valerio St., Van Nuys, CA 91405 USA Tel 818-426-3939
E-mail: brettha@mac.com
Web site: chickenscratchpress.com.

Chickering-Moller Project, *(978-0-9860799)* 414 W. 16th Street, Traverse City, MI 49684 USA.

Chicory Pr., *(978-0-9785886; 978-0-578-94795-2)* 49 Maple Ave., Morgantown, WV 26501 USA Tel 304-292-1115
E-mail: efaulkes@mail.wvu.edu.

Chien, Paris *See* **La Librairie Parisienne**

Chihuly Workshop, Inc., *(978-0-9608382; 978-1-57684)* Orders Addr.: P.O. Box 70856, Seattle, WA 98127 USA (SAN 240-3579) Tel 206-297-1304; Fax: 206-297-6207; Toll Free: 800-574-7272 (trade orders) Do not confuse with Portland Pr., Inc., Chapel Hill, NC
E-mail: jacobb@portlandpress.net
Web site: http://www.chihuly.com;
http://www.portlandpress.net;
http://www.chihulyworkshop.com
Dist(s): **Follett School Solutions.**

ChikChat(r) Ink, *(978-0-9766634)* P.O. Box 3302, Brentwood, TN 37024-3302 USA Tel 615-731-7422.

Child Advocates, Inc., *(978-0-9754953)* 2401 Portsmouth, Suite 210, Houston, TX 77098 USA Tel 713-529-1396; Fax: 713-529-1390
Web site: http://www.childadvocates.org
Dist(s): **Follett School Solutions.**

Child & Family Pr. *Imprint of* **Child Welfare League of America, Inc.**

Child Life Bks., LLC, *(978-0-9771143; 978-0-9791687)* 22303 Charlotte Dr., Torrance, CA 90505-2118 USA
E-mail: liana@mannersicare.com.

Child Like Faith Children's Bks. LLC, *(978-1-7328586; 978-1-7331584; 978-1-7348268; 978-1-7355149; 978-1-7360718; 978-1-7367544; 978-1-7376779; 979-8-9852530; 979-8-9864500)* 2012 Wages Way, Jacksonville, FL 32218 USA Tel 904-207-5044
E-mail: lsg19596@gmail.com;
kim@abcbookpublishers.com; clfcbs@gmail.com
Web site: https://childlikefaithchildrensbooks.com/;
https://www.amazon.com/Larry-S-Glover/e/B08FYG8XN R/ref=dp_byline_cont_pop_ebooks_1;
https://www.facebook.com/ChildlikeFaithChildrensBooks/.

Child Scope Productions, *(978-0-9678778)* Div. of Moschea Promotions, 5016 N. Lydell Ave., White Fish Bay, WI 53217 USA Tel 414-332-1897; Fax: 414-332-1609
E-mail: mosch@execpc.com.

Child Sensitive Communication, LLC, *(978-0-9743197; 978-1-933803; 978-0-9979174; 978-0-9986292; 979-8-9870550)* P.O. Box 150806, Nashville, TN 37215-0806 USA; *Imprints:* Karyn Henley Resources (Krayn Henley)
Web site: http://www.karynhenley.com;
http://throatofthenight.com
Dist(s): **Brown Bks.**

†**Child Welfare League of America, Inc.,** *(978-0-87868; 978-1-58760)* Orders Addr.: P.O. Box 932831, Atlanta, GA 31193-2831 USA Tel 770-280-4164; Toll Free: 800-407-6273; Edit Addr.: 2345 Crystal Dr., Suite 250, Arlington, VA 22202 USA (SAN 201-9876) Tel 703-412-2400; Fax: 703-412-2401 (orders only); PBD 420 Eagleview Blvd., Exton, PA 19341 (SAN 851-2558) Tel 202-638-2952; Fax: 202-638-4004; *Imprints:* C W L A Press (CWLA Pr); Child & Family Press (Child-Family Pr)
E-mail: order@cwla.org
Web site: http://www.cwla.org/pubs
Dist(s): **Lectorum Pubns., Inc.**; *CIP.*

Child1st Pubns., LLC, *(978-0-9844972; 978-0-9829873; 978-1-936981; 978-1-947484)* Orders Addr.: PO Box 150226, Grand Rapids, MI 49515 USA
Web site: http://www.child1st.com
Dist(s): **Follett School Solutions.**

Childcraft Education Corp., *(978-1-890275; 978-1-58669)* Div. of School Speciality, 2920 Old Tree Dr., Lancaster, PA 17603 USA Tel 717-397-4027; Fax: 717-397-7436; Toll Free: 800-631-5652
E-mail: kmyers@childcrafteducation.com
Web site: http://www.childcrafteducation.com/.

Childhood Anxiety Network *See* **Selective Mutism Anxiety Research & Treatment Ctr.**

Children *Imprint of* **Star Light Pr.**

Children 911 Resources, *(978-0-692-06493-1; 978-1-7327292)* 6639 Buttonwood Ave., Oak Park, CA 91377 USA Tel 818-422-1088
E-mail: children911resources@gmail.com
Dist(s): **CreateSpace Independent Publishing Platform.**

Children Concept Publishing, *(978-0-9745219)* Orders Addr.: P.O. Box 1179, Highland, MI 48357 USA; Edit Addr.: 1651 S. Milford Rd., Highland, MI 48357 USA.

Children Learning Awareness, Safety & Self-Defense, *(978-0-9768273)* Orders Addr.: 16815 Gault St., Lake Balboa, CA 91406 USA Tel 818-990-9909 (phone/fax); *Imprints:* CLASS Publications (CLASS Pubns)
E-mail: janet@classeducation.org;
janet@classpublications.com
Web site: http://www.classeducation.org;
http://www.classpublications.com
Dist(s): **Class Pubns., Inc.**

Children Left Behind, *(978-0-9829203)* P.O. Box 129, Berryville, AR 72616 USA Tel 870-654-3207
E-mail: LKHudd@yahoo.com
Web site: http://childrenleftbehind.org.

Children of Color/The Indra Collection, *(978-0-9746779)* P.O. Box 992, Great Falls, VA 22066 USA
Web site: http://www.childrenofcolor.com.

Children's Author, *(978-0-692-96975-5; 978-0-692-13151-0)* 12425 Hastings Rd, Midwest City, OK 73130 USA Tel 405-816-4011
E-mail: roxiemcbride@sbcglobal.net
Web site: roxiemcbride.com.

Children's Better Health Institute, *(978-1-885453)* Div. of Benjamin Franklin Literary & Medical Society, Inc., 1100 Waterway Blvd., Indianapolis, IN 46202 USA Tel 317-636-8881; Fax: 317-684-8094; Toll Free: 800-558-2376.

Childrens Bible Society, *(978-0-9777446)* Orders Addr.: P.O. Box 96, Hemet, CA 92546 USA Tel 951-652-9456; Edit Addr.: 1123 W. Acacia Ave., Hemet, CA 92543 USA
E-mail: kristy@actstracts.com
Web site: http://www.childrensbiblesociety.org/.

Children's Book Press *Imprint of* **Lee & Low Bks., Inc.**

Children's Bk. Publishing, *(978-0-692-18457-8; 978-0-692-18724-1; 978-0-692-04436-0)* 1523 Moore St., Huntingdon, PA 16652 USA Tel 814-644-9883
E-mail: JandCbooks18@gmail.com
Dist(s): **Ingram Content Group.**

Children's Bookshoppe Stop, The, *(978-0-9728393)* 7719 James Monroe Way, Gloucester, VA 23061 USA Tel 804-601-0707 (phone/fax)
E-mail: jacquelinesbooksforkids@yahoo.com
Web site: http://www.surfcbs.com.

Children's Classic Book Pubs., *(978-0-9794753)* Orders Addr.: 103 Josh Ln., Poolville, TX 76487 USA (SAN 853-5280)
E-mail: orders@snerfycat.com;
misterfish@snerfycat.com; ccbp@snerfycat.com
Web site: www.SnerfyCat.com.

Children's Creative Writing Institute, The, *(978-0-692-24484-5; 978-0-692-24485-2; 978-0-692-24486-9; 978-0-692-24487-6; 978-0-692-24488-3; 978-0-692-24489-0)* 17610 Weddington St., Encino, CA 91316 USA Tel 8185158712
Web site: www.ccwi.net
Dist(s): **CreateSpace Independent Publishing Platform.**

Children's Express Foundation, Inc., *(978-0-9621641)* 1331 H St, NW, Suite 900, Washington, DC 20005 USA (SAN 251-6993) Tel 202-737-7377; Fax: 202-737-0193
E-mail: s1@dc.ce.org
Web site: http://www.ce.org.

Children's Insight *Imprint of* **Insight Services, Inc**

Children's Kindness Network, *(978-0-9662268; 978-0-9745184)* Orders Addr.: 1323 Barkleigh Ln., Franklin, TN 37064 USA Tel 970-453-0410; Fax: 970-453-7375; Toll Free: 800-699-4541
E-mail: ted@moozie.com
Dist(s): **Bibliotech, Inc.**

Children's Legacy, *(978-0-9629365)* Orders Addr.: P.O. Box 300305, Denver, CO 80203 USA; Edit Addr.: 2553 Dexter St., Denver, CO 80207 USA Tel 303-830-7595.

Children's Literacy Pubns., *(978-0-9710432)* P.O. Box 5581, Sun City Center, FL 33571 USA Toll Free Fax: 1-866-350-4502; Toll Free: 1-800-585-1893
E-mail: janet@makereadingfirst.com
Web site: http://www.makereadingfirst.com.

Children's Plus, Inc., 1387 Dutch American, Beecher, IL 60401 USA Tel 708-946-4100; Fax: 709-946-4199
E-mail: danw@childrensplusinc.com
Web site: http://www.childrensplusinc.com
Dist(s): **Stevens, Gareth Publishing LLLP.**

Children's Poetic Pr., *(978-0-692-64574-1; 978-0-692-80728-6; 978-0-578-63313-8; 978-0-578-65781-3; 978-0-578-71497-4; 978-0-578-93508-9; 979-8-218-00470-5)* 415 S. Lombard Ave. Apt No. 305, Oak Park, IL 60302 USA Tel 708-548-7191
Dist(s): **CreateSpace Independent Publishing Platform.**

Children's Pr. *Imprint of* **Scholastic Library Publishing**

Children's Psychological Health Ctr., Inc., The, *(978-0-9790846)* 2105 Divisadero St., San Francisco, CA 94115 USA Tel 415-292-7119; Fax: 415-749-2802
E-mail: gil.kliman@cphc-sf.org
Web site: http://www.cphc-sf.org.

Children's Publishing, *(978-0-9725803; 978-0-9789347)* Orders Addr.: 101 Crepe Myrtle Ln., Georgetown, TX 78633-4724 USA (SAN 254-9328) Toll Free: 877-864-7364
E-mail: carlson@childrenspublishing.com
Web site: http://www.childrenspublishing.com
Dist(s): **Quality Bks., Inc.**
Speech Bin, Inc., The.

Children's Success Unlimited LLC, *(978-0-9829613; 978-1-7363801)* 160 Greentree Dr., Suite 101, Dover, DE 19904 USA Tel 917-208-7785
E-mail: bolbrys@ion-partners.com
Dist(s): **Emerald Bk. Co.**
Greenleaf Book Group.

Children's Village Foundation, Inc., *(978-0-9740481)* 1350 W. Hanley Ave., Coeur d'Alene, ID 83815 USA Tel 208-667-1189; Fax: 208-664-5735
E-mail: tinka@thechildrensvillage.org
Web site: http://www.thechildrensvillage.org.

ChildrenzBks., *(978-0-9748989)* P.O. Box 1431, Tucson, AZ 85702-1431 USA; *Imprints:* Bases Loaded Books (Bases Loaded Bks)
E-mail: sales@childrenzbooks.com
Web site: http://www.childrenzbooks.com.

Child's Play International Ltd. (GBR) *(978-0-85953; 978-1-904550; 978-1-84643; 978-1-78628) Dist. by* **Children Plus.**

Childswork/Childsplay, *(978-1-882732; 978-1-58815; 978-1-931704)* Div. of The Guidance Channel, Orders Addr.: P.O. Box 760, Plainview, NY 11803-0760 USA Tel 516-349-5520; Fax: 516-349-5521; Toll Free Fax: 800-262-1886; Toll Free: 800-962-1141; 45 Executive Dr. Ste. 201, Plainview, NY 11803-1738
E-mail: karens@at-risk.com; info@childswork.com
Web site: http://www.childswork.com.

Chiliric Pubns., *(978-0-9755253)* 1423 6th St., Eureka, CA 95501 USA Tel 707-443-4046
Web site:
http://www.geocities.com/harleysgreatadventures/;
http://www.Geocities.com/harleys_great_adventures.

Chimera Pubns. (GBR) *(978-1-901388; 978-1-903931) Dist. by* **PerseuPGW.**

Chimeric Pr., *(978-0-9847122)* 5299 Rau Rd., West Branch, MI 48661 USA Tel 989-343-9953
E-mail: info@chimericpress.com
Web site: www.chimericpress.com.

Chin & A Pr., *(978-0-9746341)* 2809 79th Ave., Brooklyn Park, MN 55444 USA Tel 763-549-8821
E-mail: jlodien@earthlink.net;
ChinAndAPress@earthlink.net
Web site: http://www.allbeethere.com.

Chin Music Pr., *(978-0-9741995; 978-0-9844576; 978-0-9850416; 978-0-9887693; 978-1-63405)* 2621 24th Ave. W., Seattle, WA 98199 USA Tel 206-380-1947 (phone/fax)
E-mail: bruce@chinmusicpress.com
Web site: http://www.chinmusicpress.com
Dist(s): **Consortium Bk. Sales & Distribution**
Follett School Solutions
MyiLibrary.

China Blue Publishing, *(978-0-9828936)* 202 Calvert Dr. No. 274, Cupertino, CA 95014 USA Tel 408-623-7569
E-mail: chinabluepublishing@gmail.com
Web site: http://chinabluepublishing.com
Dist(s): **Ingram Content Group.**

†**China Books & Periodicals, Inc.,** *(978-0-8351)* 360 Swift Ave., Suite 48, South San Francisco, CA 94080 USA (SAN 145-0557) Tel 650-872-7718; 650-872-7076; Fax: 650-872-7808
E-mail: chris@chinabooks.com
Web site: http://www.chinabooks.com
Dist(s): **Follett School Solutions**
SPD-Small Pr. Distribution; *CIP.*

China Language University Pr. (CHN) *(978-7-88703) Dist. by* **China Bks.**

Chinasoft (AUS) *(978-1-876739; 978-0-646-06656-1; 978-0-646-06657-8; 978-0-646-06658-5; 978-0-646-22330-8; 978-0-646-13326-3; 978-0-646-13327-0; 978-0-646-13328-7; 978-0-646-22328-5; 978-0-646-22329-2; 978-0-646-25096-0; 978-0-646-25097-7) Dist. by* **Cheng Tsui.**

Chinasprout, Inc., *(978-0-9707332; 978-0-9747302; 978-0-9820227; 978-1-945947)* 110 W. 32nd St., Flr. 6, New York, NY 10001-3205 USA Toll Free: 800-644-2611
E-mail: info@chinasprout.com
Web site: http://www.chinasprout.com
Dist(s): **China Books & Periodicals, Inc.**
Follett School Solutions.

Chipman, Marilyn, *(978-0-9745857)* P.O. Box 441233, Aurora, CO 80044-1233 USA
E-mail: chipman@mscd.edu
Web site: http://www.marilynchipman.com.

Chipotle Publishing, LLC, *(978-0-9823918; 978-0-9965218)* 631 N. Stephanie St., Suite 282, Henderson, NV 89014 USA Tel 702-565-0746
E-mail: megan@chipotlepublishing.com
Web site: www.chipotlepublishing.com.

Chippewa Valley Museum, *(978-0-9636191; 978-1-7334036)* Orders Addr.: P.O. Box 1204, Eau Claire, WI 54702 USA Tel 715-834-7871; Fax: 715-834-6624; Edit Addr.: Carson Park Dr., Eau Claire, WI 54702 USA
E-mail: info@cvmuseum.com
Web site: http://www.cvmuseum.com
Dist(s): **Chicago Distribution Ctr.**
Univ. of Wisconsin Pr.

Chiron Pubns., *(978-0-933029; 978-1-888602; 978-1-63051; 978-1-68503)* 932 Hendersonville Rd.; STE 104, Asheville, NC 28803 USA (SAN 689-1659) Tel 828-333-5245; Fax: 828-333-4787; Toll Free: 800-397-8109
E-mail: stevebuser@gmail.com
Web site: http://www.chironpublications.com.

ChironBooks *Imprint of* **Coleman/Perrin**

Chloe Arts and Publishing *See* **Chloe Arts & Publishing,LLC**

Chloe Arts & Publishing,LLC, *(978-0-9824909; 978-0-9885726; 978-0-692-59319-6; 978-0-692-66543-5; 978-0-9991829; 978-1-7358122; 979-8-218-28174-8; 979-8-9891993)* 3549 3rd Ave. S., Minneapolis, MN 55408 USA Tel 612-643-0342
E-mail: New Email chloenterprises@live.com
Web site: www.chloeartsandpublishing.com
Dist(s): **Ingram Content Group.**

Chock-Lit Pubns., *(978-0-9742344)* 26 Douvaine Ct., The Woodlands, TX 77382 USA
E-mail: publisher@chocklitpublications.com
Web site: http://www.chocklitpublications.com.

Chocolate Bits &Things *See* **Skinulicious Services**

Chocolate Sauce, *(978-0-9740268; 978-0-9911314)* 211 E. 60th street, sweet C3, New York, NY 10022 USA
Web site: http://www.chocolatesaucebooks.com
Dist(s): **SPI Bks.**

Choi, Sophia, *(978-0-692-41049-3; 978-0-692-07768-9)* 122 Golden Vale Dr., Riverside, CA 92506 USA Tel 951-756-8883.

Choice PH, *(978-0-9841910; 978-0-9887595; 978-0-9991517)* 412 Olive Ave., Suite 305, Huntington Beach, CA 92648 USA (SAN 858-6829)
E-mail: choiceph@aol.com
Dist(s): **eBookIt.com.**

Choice Point Editions, *(978-0-9778774)* 7883 N. Pershing AVE., Stockton, CA 95207 USA Tel 209-952-7108; Fax: 209-951-3216
E-mail: choicepointeditions@inreach.com
Web site: http://www.choicepointeditions.com.

Choice Publishing House *See* **Choice PH**

ChoiceMaker Pty. Ltd., The (AUS) *(978-0-9805673; 978-1-921790; 978-1-925186; 978-1-925233; 978-1-925234; 978-1-925235; 978-1-925246; 978-1-925247; 978-1-925248; 978-1-925249; 978-1-925250; 978-1-925251; 978-1-925252) Dist. by* **Lerner Pub.**

Choices For Tomorrow, *(978-0-9748689)* 43H Meadow Pond Dr., Leominster, MA 01453 USA
E-mail: moniquehoude@yahoo.com.

Choices International, *(978-0-9768530)* Orders Addr.: P.O. Box 408, Berries Springs, MI 49103 USA Tel 269-471-9718 (phone/fax); Edit Addr.: P.O. Box 408, Berrien Sprgs, MI 49103-0408 USA
E-mail: pennyturner@sbcglobal.net;
yourchoices@choicesinternational.info.

Choices Program, Brown Univ., *(978-1-891306; 978-1-60123)* Choices Program-brown Univ. Box 1948, Providence, RI 02912 USA Tel 401-863-3155; Fax: 401-863-1247
E-mail: choices@brown.edu
Web site: http://www.choices.edu.

Choices Program, Watson Institute, Brown University *See* **Choices Program, Brown Univ.**

Cholita Prints & Pub. Co., *(978-0-9742956; 978-0-692-16734-2)* Orders Addr.: P.O. Box 8018, Sante Fe, NM 87504 USA; Edit Addr.: 655 W. San Francisco St., Sante Fe, NM 87501 USA
E-mail: cholitaprints@comcast.net
Dist(s): **Follett School Solutions.**

Choltus, Rebekah L., *(978-0-692-27186-5)* 3260 SW Evergreen Ter, Portland, OR 97205 USA Tel 503-475-1458
E-mail: choltus@msn.com.

Chong, Lisa, *(978-0-9997557)* 208 8th St., Huntington Beach, CA 92648 USA Tel 714-323-0924
E-mail: LisaKLChong@gmail.com.

Choo Choo Clan, *(978-0-9788670)* 1616 Brockton Ave., Apt. 104, Los Angeles, CA 90025 USA Tel 626-715-3342
E-mail: joey0724@hotmail.com
Web site: http://www.choochooclan.com.

Choose Joy Enterprise *See* **Choose Joy Publishing**

Choose Joy Publishing, *(978-0-692-14977-5; 978-0-578-38810-6; 979-8-9860508)* 4533 Ravenwood Pl, Union city, GA 30291 USA Tel 404-786-1846
E-mail: Miriammuhammad1908@yahoo.com.

Chooseco LLC, *(978-0-9745356; 978-1-933390; 978-1-937133; 978-1-954232)* Orders Addr.: P.O. Box 46, Waitsfield, VT 05673 USA (SAN 852-1131); Edit Addr.: 193 Home Farm Way Suite 3, Waitsfield, VT 05673 USA (SAN 852-1158) Tel 802-214-3300
E-mail: cfrascella@chooseco.com;
webmail@chooseco.com
Web site: http://www.cyoa.com;
http://www.chooseco.com
Dist(s): **Children's Plus, Inc.**
Follett School Solutions.

Choosing The Best Publishing, *(978-0-9724890; 978-0-9819748; 978-0-9819759; 978-0-9974442; 978-1-7334174; 979-8-9886313)* 2625 Cumberland Pkwy., Suite 200, Atlanta, GA 30339 USA Tel 770-803-3100; Fax: 770-803-3110; Toll Free: 800-774-2378
E-mail: bcook@ctbpublishing.com;
book@ctbpublishing.com
Web site: http://www.choosingthebest.org.

Choristers Guild, *(978-1-929187)* 2834 W. Kingsley Rd., Garland, TX 75041-2498 USA (SAN 689-9188) Tel 972-271-1521; Fax: 972-840-3113
E-mail: choristers@choristersguild.org
Web site: http://www.choristersguild.org
Dist(s): **Faith Alive Christian Resources**
Lorenz Corp., The.

Chosen Bks., *(978-0-8007)* Div. of Baker Publishing Group, Orders Addr.: P.O. Box 6287, Grand Rapids, MI 49516-6287 USA Toll Free Fax: 800-398-3111 (orders only); Toll Free: 800-877-2665 (orders only); Edit Addr.: 6030 E. Fulton, Ada, MI 49301 USA Tel 616-676-9185; Fax: 616-676-9573
Web site: http://www.bakerpublishinggroup.com
Dist(s): **Baker Publishing Group**
Faith Alive Christian Resources.

Chosen Word Publishing, *(978-0-9707536; 978-0-9748056; 978-0-9754779)* P.O. Box 481886, Charlotte, NC 28269 USA Tel 704-527-2177; Fax: 704-527-1677
E-mail: jeannette@chosenwordpublishing.com
Web site: http://www.chosenwordpublishing.com.

ChosenButterfly Publishing, *(978-0-9831637; 978-0-9915202; 978-1-945377)*
Web site: http://www.cb-publishing.com
Dist(s): **Smashwords.**

Chou Chou Pr., *(978-0-9606140; 978-0-9716605; 978-0-9789152)* 4 Whimbrel Ct., Okatie, SC 29909 USA (SAN 220-2379) Tel 631-744-5784
E-mail: chouchou@hargray.com; info@bilingualkids.com
Web site: http://www.bilingualkids.com
Dist(s): **Follett School Solutions.**

houette Publishing (CAN) *(978-2-9815807; 978-2-924786; 978-2-89802) Dist. by* **PerseuPGW.**

howder Bay Bks., *(978-0-9795364)* P.O. Box 5542, Lake Worth, FL 33466-5542 USA (SAN 853-7119)
Web site: http://www.chowderbaybooks.com.

HPublishing, Incorporated *See* **Triumphant Living Enterprises, Inc.**

hris A. Zeigler Dendy Consulting LLC, *(978-0-9679911)* P.O. Box 189, Cedar Bluff, AL 35959 USA Fax: 256-779-5203
E-mail: chrisdendy@mindspring.com
Web site: http://www.chrisdendy.com
Dist(s): **Follett School Solutions.**

hris Six Group, The, *(978-0-9899182)* P.O. Box 1829, New York, NY 10159-1829 USA Tel 718-514-0452
E-mail: thechrissixgroup@msn.com.

hrist Inspired, Inc., *(978-1-4183)* 2263 Dicey Rd., Weatherford, TX 76085-3619 USA
Web site: http://www.christinspired.com.

hristen Marie Watson *See* **Shaky Alien Pubns.**

Christian Aid Ministries, *(978-1-885270)* Orders Addr.: P.O. Box 360, Berlin, OH 44610 USA Tel 330-893-2428; Fax: 330-893-2305; Edit Addr.: 4464 S.R. 39 E., Berlin, OH 44610 USA Tel 216-893-2428.

Christian Bible Studies, *(978-0-9763357)* P.O. Box 11155, Lansing, MI 48911 USA Tel 517-272-9076
E-mail: verseyawilliams@sbcglobal.net
Web site: http://www.christianstudies7.com.

Christian Courier Publications *See* **Fortify Your Faith Foundation**

Christian Cowgirl *See* **Sonrise Stable Bks.**

Christian Education Resources, *(978-1-933479)* P.O. Box 320099, Cocoa Beach, FL 32932 USA.

Christian Educational Services, Inc., *(978-0-9628971; 978-0-9786683)* 180 Robert Curry Dr., Martinsville, IN 46151-8076 USA Toll Free: 888-255-6189
Web site: http://www.STFonline.org.

Christian Faith Publishing, *(978-1-68197; 978-1-63525; 978-1-63575; 978-1-64028; 978-1-64079; 978-1-64114; 978-1-64140; 978-1-64191; 978-1-64258; 978-1-64299; 978-1-64349; 978-1-64416; 978-1-64458; 978-1-64492; 978-1-64515; 978-1-64569; 978-1-0980; 978-1-63844; 978-1-63874; 978-1-63903; 978-1-63961; 978-1-68517; 978-1-68570; 979-8-88540; 979-8-88616; 979-8-88685; 979-8-88751; 979-8-88832; 979-8-88943; 979-8-89043; 979-8-89130) 296 Chestnut St., Meadville, PA 16335 USA Tel 646-503-4906; 832 Park Ave., Meadville, PA 16335 Tel 814-253-6442; Toll Free: 866-554-0919*
E-mail: dustin@christianfaithpublishing.com
Web site: www.christianfaithpublishing.com; ChristianFaithPublishing.com.

Christian Focus Pubns. (GBR) *(978-0-906731; 978-1-85792; 978-1-871676; 978-1-84550; 978-1-78191; 978-1-5271) Dist. by* **STL Dist.**

Christian Focus Pubns. (GBR) *(978-0-906731; 978-1-85792; 978-1-871676; 978-1-84550; 978-1-78191; 978-1-5271) Dist. by* **BTPS.**

Christian, Harvey Pubs. Inc., *(978-1-932774)* 3107 Hwy. 321, Hampton, TN 37658 USA Tel 423-768-2297
E-mail: books@harveycp.com
Web site: http://www.harveycp.com.

Christian Heartbeat Incorporated *See* **CHB Media**

Christian Liberty Pr., *(978-1-930092; 978-1-930367; 978-1-932971; 978-1-935796; 978-1-62982)* Div. of Church of Christian Liberty, 502 W. Euclid Ave., Arlington Heights, IL 60004 USA
E-mail: e.shewan@christianlibertypress.com; linak@christianlibertypress.com; larsj@christianlibertypress.com
Web site: http://www.christianlibertypress.com.

Christian Life Bks., *(978-0-9646289; 978-1-931393)* Subs. of River Revival Ministries, Inc., Orders Addr.: P.O. Box 36355, Pensacola, FL 32516-6355 USA Tel 850-457-7057; Fax: 850-458-9339
E-mail: mail@drlarrymartin.org
Web site: http://www.rmi.org.

Christian Life Workshops *See* **Noble Publishing Assocs.**

Christian Light Pubns., Inc., *(978-0-87813; 978-1-63737)* 1066 Chicago Ave., Harrisonburg, VA 22802 USA (SAN 206-7315) Tel 540-434-0768; Fax: 540-433-8896
E-mail: andrew.crider@christianlight.org
Web site: christianlight.org.

Christian Literature Crusade, Incorporated *See* **CLC Pubns.**

Christian Living Books, Inc. *Imprint of* **Pneuma Life Publishing, Inc.**

Christian Logic, *(978-0-9745315; 978-1-7330826)* PO Box 1381, Durango, CO 81302 USA Tel 563-505-5258
E-mail: hansbluedorn@pm.me
Web site: http://www.fallacydetective.com.

Christian Novel Studies, *(978-0-9707712)* 5208 E. Lake Rd., Saginaw, MN 55779 USA Tel 218-729-9733; Fax: 509-271-8614
E-mail: cnsroe@aol.com; chsroe@aol.com
Web site: http://www.christiannovelstudies.homestead.com.

Christian Publishing Corp., *(978-0-9770320)* 19530 E. Dickenson Pl., Aurora, CO 80013 USA Tel 303-752-0845
E-mail: carterpattillo@aol.com.

Christian Science Publishing Society, The *See* **Eddy, The Writings of Mary Baker**

Christian Services Publishing, *(978-1-879854)* Div. of Christian Services Network, 1975 Janich Ranch Ct., El Cajon, CA 92019 USA Tel 619-334-0706; Fax: 619-579-0685; Toll Free: 800-484-6184 Do not confuse with Christian Services, Damascus, MD
E-mail: tim@csnbooks.com
Web site: http://csnbooks.com.

Christian Visionary Communications, *(978-0-9746867)* P.O. Box 63, Sharon Center, OH 44274-0063 USA
E-mail: lorshir3@verizon.net
Web site: http://www.christianary.org.

Christian Visual Arts of California, *(978-0-9766584)* 64969 Pine St., Hume, CA 93628-9619 USA Tel 559-335-2797; Fax: 559-335-2107
E-mail: dajohnson@spiralcomm.net.

Christian Voice Publishing, A, *(978-0-9776747; 978-0-9786580; 978-1-934327)* 2031 W. Superior St. Ste. 1, Duluth, MN 55806-2036 USA.

Christiangela Productions, *(978-0-9720773)* 3340 SE. Federal Hwy., #310, Saintarf, FL 34997 USA.

Christianstar.Me *See* **Fomenky Publishing**

Christine S White, *(978-0-9998133)* 315 W. st N., Ahoskie, NC 27910 USA Tel 252-287-8896
E-mail: destinedtosoar63@yahoo.com
Web site: www.soaringhigh.net.

Christine, Yates, *(978-0-9741210)* 13165 Oak Farm Dr., Woodbridge, VA 22192 USA
Web site: http://www.freekidcrafts.com.

Christine's Closet, *(978-0-9713405)* 10300 Grand Oak Dr., Austin, TX 78750 USA Tel 512-918-9255; Fax: 512-873-9818; Toll Free: 800-591-1165
E-mail: chrissy@chrissy.com
Web site: http://www.chrissy.com.

Christopher Arnold Hill, *(978-0-692-19611-3)* 117 6253 Lankershim Blvd., N. Hollywood, CA 91606 USA Tel 323-632-2510
E-mail: chriswisegamgee@yahoo.com
Dist(s): **Ingram Content Group.**

Christopher Davis, Jr., *(978-0-578-43937-2; 978-0-578-45747-5)* CMR 415, APO, AE 09114 USA Tel 803-350-0503
E-mail: bookingchristopher@gmail.com
Dist(s): **Ingram Content Group.**

Christopher Winkle Products *See* **First Stage Concepts**

Chronicle Bks. *Imprint of* **Chronicle Bks. LLC**

†Chronicle Bks. LLC, *(978-0-8118; 978-0-87701; 978-0-938491; 978-1-4521; 978-1-7972)* Div. of The McEvoy Group, Orders Addr.: 680 Second St., San Francisco, CA 94107 USA (SAN 202-165X) Tel 415-537-4200; Fax: 415-537-4460; Toll Free Fax: 800-286-9471; Toll Free: 800-759-0190 (orders only); Edit Addr.: 3 Center Plaza, Boston, MA 2108 USA; *Imprints:* SeaStar Books (SeaStar Chronic); Chronicle Books (ChronBks)
E-mail: order.desk@hbgusa.com; customer.service@hbgusa.com
Web site: http://www.chroniclebooks.com
Dist(s): **Children's Plus, Inc.**
Diamond Bk. Distributors
Follett School Solutions
Leonard, Hal Corp.
Hachette Bk. Group
Ingram Publisher Services
Music Sales Corp.
Open Road Integrated Media, Inc.; *CIP.*

Chronicle Guidance Pubns., Inc., *(978-0-912578; 978-1-55631)* Orders Addr.: 66 Aurora St., Moravia, NY 13118-3569 USA Tel 315-497-0330; 315-497-3359; Toll Free: 800-622-7284
E-mail: CustomerService@ChronicleGuidance.com
Web site: http://www.chronicleguidance.com
Dist(s): **Follett School Solutions.**

Chronicles *See* **Life Chronicles Publishing**

Chronister, Rachel, *(978-1-7379851)* 10101 E. 91st Cir. N., Owasso, OK 74055 USA Tel 918-996-0746
E-mail: rachel.chronister@owassops.org
Web site: Rachel Chronister.

Chronos Press *See* **WingSpan Publishing**

Chrysalis *Imprint of* **Balm and Blade Publishing**

Chrysalis Education, *(978-1-929298; 978-1-930643; 978-1-931983; 978-1-932333; 978-1-59389)* Div. of The Creative Company, 1980 Lookout Dr., North Mankato, MN 56003 USA Tel 507-388-6273; Fax: 507-388-2746; Toll Free: 800-445-6209
E-mail: schlichted@aol.com; info@thecreativecompany.us
Dist(s): **Creative Co., The.**

Chrysalis Pr., *(978-0-9795933)* Orders Addr.: P.O. Box 13129, Newport Beach, CA 92658 USA (SAN 853-8514)
E-mail: amber@chrysalispress.com
Web site: http://www.Chrysalispress.com
Dist(s): **Follett School Solutions.**

Chrysanthalix Pr., *(978-0-615-72788-2; 978-0-9972029)* 516 S Shore Pines Rd, Post Falls, ID 83854 USA Tel 408-607-1377
Dist(s): **CreateSpace Independent Publishing Platform.**

Chubasco Publishing Company *See* **Perelandra Publishing Co.**

Chucklebks. Publishing, *(978-0-9702730)* 27 Brown St., Andover, MA 01810 USA Tel 978-749-0674
E-mail: jeff@chucklebooks.com
Web site: http://www.chucklebooks.com; http://www.incredibleassemblies.com
Dist(s): **Partners Bk. Distributing, Inc.**

Chun, Anthony, *(978-0-9994539)* 855 1/2 N. Alexandria Ave., Los Angeles, CA 90029 USA Tel 323-383-2034
E-mail: anthonychun72@gmail.com.

Chung, Jo Anne *See* **Vision Unlimited Pr.**

Church at Cane Creek *See* **No Greater Joy Ministries, Inc.**

Church Hymnal Corporation *See* **Church Publishing, Inc.**

Church Publishing, Inc., *(978-0-89869; 978-1-59627; 978-1-59628; 978-1-64065; 978-1-954184)* Orders Addr.: 19 E. 34th St., New York, NY 10016 USA (SAN 857-0140) Tel 212-592-1800; Fax: 212-779-3392; Toll Free: 800-242-1918; Edit Addr.: 19 East 34th st, New York, NY 10016 USA; *Imprints:* Morehouse Publishing (MoreHse Pubng); Living the Good News (LTGN)
E-mail: rmasteller@cpg.org; churchpublishingorders@pbd.com; lort@cpg.org; lsimonello@cpg.org
Web site: http://www.churchpublishing.org
Dist(s): **Abingdon Pr.**
Ingram Publisher Services
Macmillan
MyiLibrary
Open Road Integrated Media, Inc.
Two Rivers Distribution.

Church Without Walls Publications, USA *See* **Masha, Segun Inc.**

ChurchToast, *(978-1-7379864; 979-8-9882688)* 2426 Island Club Way, Orlando, FL 32822 USA Tel 484-547-4883
E-mail: churchtoast@quezart.com
Web site: churchtoast.com.

CHUTE,, PHILLIP B. EA, *(978-0-692-06056-8; 978-1-7328855)* 45506 BAYBERRY PL, TEMECULA, CA 92592 USA Tel 951-302-2285; Fax: 951-719-1853
E-mail: phillipchute1@verizon.net
Web site: temeculataxservice.net; www.silverthreadoflife.com; wwww.phillipbchute.com.

Chuttani, Kabir, *(978-0-9749364)* 8 Nameloc Rd., Plymouth, MA 02360-1418 USA.

CI Publishing Group, *(978-0-692-08310-9; 978-0-692-08313-0; 978-0-578-51677-6)* 3113 Ruhl Ave Apt 11B, Columbus, OH 43209 USA Tel 614-209-4393
E-mail: cipubgroup@gmail.com
Dist(s): **Ingram Content Group.**

Ciardella, James, *(978-1-7332363)* 4816 Rocklin Dr, Union City, CA 94587 USA Tel 510-305-3351
E-mail: jciardella@hotmail.com.

Cicada Bks. (GBR) *(978-0-9562053; 978-1-908714) Dist. by* **Consort Bk Sales.**

CicadaSun, *(978-0-9779808)* P.O. Box 90834, Austin, TX 78709-0834 USA
E-mail: service@cicadasun.com
Web site: http://www.cicadasun.com.

CIFC Pr., *(978-0-615-18435-7)* 65 Bayard St., New York, NY 10013 USA
E-mail: christinaseid@chinatownicecreamfactory.com
Web site: http://www.chinatownicecreamfactory.com
Dist(s): **Lulu Pr., Inc.**

Cideb (ITA) *(978-88-7754; 978-88-530) Dist. by* **Distribks Inc.**

Cider Mill Pr. Bk. Pubs., LLC, *(978-1-933662; 978-1-60433; 978-1-941868; 978-1-64643; 978-1-64785)* PO Box 454 12 Spring St., Kennebunkport, ME 04046 USA (SAN 257-1927) Tel 207-967-8232; Fax: 207-967-8233; *Imprints:* Applesauce Press (Applesauce Pr)
E-mail: johnwhalen@cidermillpress.com
Web site: http://www.cidermillpress.com
Dist(s): **Children's Plus, Inc.**
HarperCollins Christian Publishing
HarperCollins Pubs.
Nelson, Thomas Inc.
Simon & Schuster
Simon & Schuster, Inc.
Sterling Publishing Co., Inc.

Cidermill Bks., *(978-0-9748483)* P.O. Box 32250, San Jose, CA 95152-2250 USA
E-mail: info@cidermillbooks.com
Web site: http://www.cidermillbooks.com.

CiDuMos, *(978-0-692-77143-3; 978-0-692-77666-7; 978-0-692-80223-6; 978-0-692-80597-8; 978-0-692-05074-3; 978-0-692-05076-7; 978-0-578-90491-7; 978-1-7373833)* 405 Woodway Ln., Longview, TX 75605 USA Tel 903-240-6959
Web site: www.cimowrites.com
Dist(s): **CreateSpace Independent Publishing Platform.**

Ciletti Publishing Group, Inc., The, *(978-0-917665; 978-0-9768655)* 2421 Redwood Ct., Longmont, CO 80503 USA Tel 720-494-1473; Fax: 720-494-1471
E-mail: barbaraj@odysseybooks.net
Dist(s): **Follett School Solutions.**

CILLYart4U, *(978-0-9985955)* 236 E. Fairmont DR, Tempe, AZ 85282 USA Tel 480-543-9352
Web site: www.cillyart4u.wix.com/cillyart4u
Dist(s): **CreateSpace Independent Publishing Platform.**

Cinco Puntos Press *Imprint of* **Lee & Low Bks., Inc.**

Cinealta Pr., *(978-0-9821065)* 2060 W. Mulberry Dr., Chandler, AZ 85286-6771 USA
Web site: http://www.cinealtapress.com.

CineBook (GBR) *(978-1-905460; 978-1-84918) Dist. by* **Natl Bk Netwk.**

Cinnamon Bay Entertainment Group, *(978-0-9727116)* 1300 W. Menlo Ave No. 113, Hemet, CA 92543 USA
E-mail: rsdan4043@yahoo.com.

Cinnamon Ridge Publishing, *(978-0-9800762)* 7121 W. Craig Rd., Suite 113, No. 284, Las Vegas, NV 89129 USA.

Circelli, Kristina, *(978-0-9763728; 978-0-615-40270-3; 979-8-218-10047-6)* 9655 Crotty Ave., Hastings, FL 32145 USA Tel 386-290-7294
E-mail: kristinacircelli@gmail.com
Web site: www.kristinacircelli.com.

Circle Journey, Ltd., *(978-0-9741104)* 22 East Gay St., Suite 801, Columbus, OH 43215 USA Fax: 614-564-7795; Toll Free: 877-247-2534
E-mail: connections@circlejourney.com
Web site: http://www.circlejourney.com.

Circle of Courage Pubns., 104 N. Main St., Lennox, SD 57039 USA
E-mail: bookstore@reclaiming.com
Web site: http://www.reclaiming.com
Dist(s): **Lulu Pr., Inc.**

Circle of Friends *Imprint of* **Booksville, U.S.A.**

Circle Pr., *(978-0-9651601; 978-0-9743661; 978-1-933271)* Div. of Circle Media, Inc., Orders Addr.: 33 Rossotto Dr., Hamden, CT 06514 USA Tel 203-230-3805; Fax: 203-230-3838; Toll Free: 888-881-0729; Edit Addr.: 432 Washington Ave., North Haven, CT 06473 USA Do not confuse with companies with the same name in Huntington Beach, CA, New York, NY, Itasca, IL
E-mail: victor@catholicformation.com.

Circle Studios, *(978-0-9768022)* 200 Medicine Way, Eureka Springs, AR 72632 USA Tel 479-253-5826
Dist(s): **Follett School Solutions.**

Circle7531, *(978-1-7355504)* 3451 Via Montebello No. 192-317, Carlsbad, CA 92009 USA Tel 760-271-4574
E-mail: mariafeliciakelley@gmail.com
Web site: Circle7531.com.

Circles Legacy Publishing, LLC, *(978-0-692-94613-8; 978-0-692-95206-1; 978-0-692-95797-4; 978-0-692-95798-1; 978-0-692-95799-8; 978-0-692-95990-9; 978-0-692-96184-1; 978-0-692-05662-2; 978-0-692-09424-2; 978-0-578-42821-5; 978-0-578-50152-9; 978-0-578-55604-8; 978-0-578-61652-0; 978-0-578-66442-2; 978-0-578-70287-2; 978-0-578-74888-7; 978-0-578-28852-9; 978-0-578-29847-4; 979-8-218-11397-1) 84 Liberty Lakes Dr, Valparaiso, IN 46385 USA Tel 281-682-7327*
E-mail: jjoslin3@att.net
Dist(s): **CreateSpace Independent Publishing Platform.**

CircleSquare Projections, *(978-0-578-40667-1; 978-0-578-42399-9; 978-0-578-64385-4; 978-0-578-65233-7; 978-0-578-68406-2; 978-0-578-86429-7; 978-0-578-86701-4; 978-1-7369559; 979-8-218-21036-6)* 9867 haddon ave, pacoima, CA 91331 USA Tel 323-626-1152
E-mail: student7business@gmail.com.

Circling Rivers, *(978-1-939530)* Orders Addr.: P.O. Box 8291, Richmond, VA 23226 USA Tel 804-272-4625; *Imprints:* Gertrude M Books (MYID_M)
Web site: http://www.circlingrivers.com.

Circumpolar Pr., *(978-1-878051)* Subs. of Wizard Works, P.O. Box 1125, Homer, AK 99603 USA Tel 907-235-8757 (phone/fax); Toll Free: 877-210-2665
E-mail: wizard@xyz.net
Web site: http://www.xyz.net/~wizard.

Ciro's Bks., *(978-0-9676643; 978-1-934499)* 4152 Meridian St. PMB 116, Bellingham, WA 98226 USA
Web site: http://www.wrwilkerson.net
Dist(s): **BCH Fulfillment & Distribution Smashwords.**

Cirrus Publishing, LLC, *(978-0-9755678)* Orders Addr.: P.O. Box 291724, Davie, FL 33329-1724 USA Fax: 954-965-2643
E-mail: cirruspublish@aol.com
Web site: http://www.yessy.com/wildimages.

C-It Entertainment Group, LLC, *(978-0-9718151)* 230 S. Hamilton Dr. Unit 204, Beverly Hills, CA 90211 USA Tel 213-925-1535; Fax: 213-291-1473
E-mail: dennischristen@hotmail.com
Web site: http://www.booksnflicks.com.

Citified Pubns., *(978-0-9832174)* 1310 Valley Lake Dr., Schaumburg, IL 60195 USA Tel 708-308-2854
E-mail: djsbchl@gmail.com.

Citizen Pr, *(978-0-9779100)* P.O. Box 1369, Glendale, CA 91209-1369 USA Tel 310-497-7419; Fax: 818-450-0518
E-mail: citizen@citizenpress.net
Web site: http://www.citizenpress.net.

Citizens Publishing, *(978-0-9755597)* 17636 W. Neuberry Ridge Dr., Lockport, IL 60441 USA
Web site: http://www.citizenspublishing.com.

Citizens Rising, *(978-0-9997645; 978-0-578-38766-6)* P.O. Box 1118, Tryon, NC 28782 USA Tel 707-845-5499
E-mail: dhoffman@internews.org.

Citron Concassee, *(978-0-692-91920-0; 978-0-9995927; 979-8-9856546)* 210 Hirschbeck Heights, ABERDEEN, WA 98520 USA Tel 360-637-8559; *Imprints:* Lumen Anime (LumenAnime)
E-mail: vadams@comp-dyn.com
Web site: http://www.citronconcasse.com/
Dist(s): **Ingram Content Group.**

Citrus Roots - Preserving Citrus Heritage Foundation, *(978-0-9669508)* Orders Addr.: P.O. Box 4038, BALBOA, CA 92661 USA Tel 949-673-7877
Web site: http://www.citrusroots.com.

City Castles Publishing, *(978-0-615-22213-4; 978-0-615-26743-2; 978-0-615-56258-2)* 12160 E. Iowa Dr., Aurora, CO 80012 USA
Web site: http://www.citycastles.com.

City Creek Pr., Inc., *(978-1-883841)* P.O. Box 8415, Minneapolis, MN 55408-0415 USA
E-mail: orders@citycreek.com
Web site: http://www.citycreek.com
Dist(s): **Follett School Solutions.**

City Girl Gone Country, *(978-0-9904469)* 1983 Hwy. NN Box 344, Hermann, MO 65041 USA Tel 573-486-3091
E-mail: djweingarth@ktis.net.

†City Lights Bks., *(978-0-87286)* 261 Columbus Ave., San Francisco, CA 94133 USA (SAN 202-1684) Tel 415-362-1901; Fax: 415-362-4921
E-mail: staff@citylights.com
Web site: http://www.citylights.com
Dist(s): **Consortium Bk. Sales & Distribution**
MyiLibrary
SPD-Small Pr. Distribution; *CIP.*

City Lights Pr. *Imprint of* **Wolfpack Publishing**

City Monsters Bks. (CAN) *(978-2-924734) Dist. by* **PerseuPGW.**

City of Elmhurst, *(978-0-9708003)* 209 N. York St., Elmhurst, IL 60126 USA Tel 630-530-3000; Fax: 630-530-3014
E-mail: nancy.wilson@elmhurst.org
Web site: http://www.elmhurst.org.

City of God, St. Joseph's Hill of Hope, *(978-1-892957)* Orders Addr.: P.O. Box 1055, Brea, CA 92822 USA Tel 714-528-6962; Fax: 714-528-0707; Edit Addr.: 7351 Carbon Canyon Rd., Brea, CA 92823 USA
E-mail: mail@themiracleofstjoseph.org
Web site: http://www.themiralceofstjoseph.org.

City of Manassas Department of Social Services, *(978-0-9747385)* 9324 West St. Ste. 201, Manassas, VA 20110-5198 USA.

City of Oaks Publishing *See* **Meder, Julia**

City on a Hill, Inc., *(978-0-9779521)* 4085 Hancock Bridge Pkwy., Suite 111-269, North Fort Myers, FL 33903 USA Tel 614-488-6953
E-mail: info@cityonahillinc.org
Web site: http://www.cityonahillinc.org.

City Point Bks., *(978-0-615-27021-0)* P.O. Box 221, Yulee, FL 32041 USA
Dist(s): **Simon & Schuster, Inc.**

City Salvage Records, *(978-0-9713865)* 195 St. Marks Ave., No. 4, Brooklyn, NY 11238 USA Tel 718-857-6822
E-mail: andy@citysalvagerecords.com
Web site: http://citysalvagerecords.com.

CityLit Pr., *(978-1-936328)* c/o CityLit Project, 120 S. Curley St., Baltimore, MD 21224-2235 USA Tel 410-274-5691
E-mail: info@citylitproject.org
Web site: http://www.citylitprojet.org.

CityWeb Corp., *(978-0-9719803)* P.O. Box 702216, Tulsa, OK 74170-2216 USA Tel 918-369-0544
E-mail: citywebcorporation@acken.com
Web site: http://www.citywebbooks.com.

Civitas Consulting Group, *(978-1-7358233)* 1027 Grace Meade, Ashland City, TN 37015 USA Tel 646-296-5257
E-mail: info@nathalienelsonparker.com
Web site: www.nathalienelsonparker.com.

Civitas:Institute for the Study of Civil Society (GBR) *(978-1-903386) Dist. by* **Coronet Bks.**

CJ Publishing Co., *(978-0-9655777)* Div. of McPhaul, Inc, 1370 electric ave apt 404, lincoln park, MI 48146 USA
E-mail: johnmcphaul@live.com.

CJK Publishing, *(978-0-9889100; 978-1-7353967)* 120 N. Denver St., Dallas, TX 75203 USA Tel 469-223-6244
E-mail: info@cjkpublishing.com
Web site: www.cjkpublishing.com.

CJR, *(978-0-9796411; 978-1-941607; 978-1-943764)* 8079 Barcarole Ct., Springfield, VA 22153-2945 USA Tel 571-481-5396
E-mail: books.kiteb@gmail.com
Web site: http://www.go2melik.org/NewBridgesTextbooks.lsp.

CJT Publishing, *(978-0-692-83362-9)* 500 Veterans Memorial Pkwy., East Providence, RI 02914 USA Tel 843-469-4417
E-mail: cjtalbert@pga.com.

CK Books *See* **CK Books Publishing**

CK Bks., *(978-0-9797580)* 395A S. Hwy. 65, No. 324, Lincoln, CA 95648 USA.

CK Books Publishing, *(978-0-9800529; 978-0-9832984; 978-0-9881993; 978-0-9892152; 978-1-949085)* P.O. Box 214, New Glarus, WI 53574 USA Tel 608-220-1885
Web site: http://ckbookspublishing.com
Dist(s): **Follett School Solutions.**

CKE Pubns., *(978-0-935133; 978-1-932327)* Div. of Carolyn Kyle Enterprises, Orders Addr.: P.O. Box 12869, Olympia, WA 98508-2869 USA (SAN 695-197X) Toll Free: 800-428-7402; Edit Addr.: P.O. Box 12869, Olympia, WA 98508-2869 USA
E-mail: ckepubs@aol.com
Web site: http://www.ckepublications.com.

CKK Educational, LLC., *(978-0-9743499; 978-0-9963087)* 17 W. 8th St., Ocean City, NJ 08226-3430 USA Tel 609-398-1949; Toll Free: 866-543-5463
Web site: http://www.tannersmanners.com.

CKNY Paw Productions, *(978-0-692-92176-0)* 1280 Fifth Ave. Unit 15E, New York, NY 10029 USA Tel 212-810-6105
E-mail: hanakodesignstudio@gmail.com.

cky *See* **Congregation Kehilas Yaakov (CKY)**

CL Bowers Academy LLC, The *See* **High Self-Esteem Group**

CLADACH Publishing, *(978-0-9670386; 978-0-9759619; 978-0-9818929; 978-0-9891014; 978-1-945099)* P.O. Box 336144, Greeley, CO 80633 USA Tel 970-371-9530
E-mail: office@cladach.com
Web site: http://https://cladach.com.

Claim Stake Productions *See* **Claim Stake Publishing, LLC**

Claim Stake Publishing, LLC, *(978-1-936284)* P.O. Box 1586, Aspen, CO 81612 USA
E-mail: pfioravante@tmwent.com
Web site: http://www.travelswithgannonandwyatt.com.

Clair, Aspen, *(978-0-578-20089-7; 978-0-578-20118-4)* 1022 N Anthony Ave, Anthony, KS 67003 USA.

Claire Luana, *(978-0-9977018; 978-1-948947)* 11923 NE Sumner St STE 681096, Portland, OR 97220 USA
E-mail: claire.luana.author@gmail.com
Web site: http://www.liveedgepublishing.com; http://www.claireluana.com.

Claire Pubns. (GBR) *(978-1-871098; 978-1-904572) Dist. by* **Parkwest Pubns.**

Clairmont Pr., Inc., *(978-0-9623319; 978-1-56733)* Orders Addr.: P.O. Box 11743, Montgomery, AL 36111 USA Tel 334-874-8638; Edit Addr.: Rte. 2, Box 191, Selma, AL 36701 USA.

Clandestine Pr., The, *(978-0-9766261)* 314 Taylor Pl., Ithaca, NY 14850-3135 USA Tel 607-273-8036
E-mail: dohertyprint@juno.com.

Clapper Publishing Co., *(978-0-930184)* Div. of Clapper Publishing Co., Inc., 2400 E. Devon, Suite 375, Des Plaines, IL 60018 USA (SAN 210-7104) Tel 847-635-5800; Fax: 847-635-6311.

Clara Denise West, *(978-1-892313)* 122 Beaconsfield Dr, Meridianville, AL 35759 USA Fax: 205-721-1269.

Clara Publishing, *(978-0-9706347; 978-0-692-45828-0; 978-1-7342900)* Orders Addr.: 680 Napa Ct., Claremont, CA 91711-1553 USA (SAN 254-7236)
E-mail: clarapub@ca.rr.com
Web site: http://www.magicunion.com.

Clare Mary Johnson, *(978-0-578-75701-8; 978-0-578-75760-5; 978-0-578-75761-2; 978-0-578-79729-8)* 1544 Alta Vista Dr 0, Vista, CA 92084 USA Tel 7602243649
E-mail: clare333@hotmail.com
Dist(s): **Ingram Content Group.**

Clarence-Henry Bks., *(978-0-615-19572-8; 978-0-578-05235-9; 978-0-615-42297-8; 978-0-9882909)* 4135 Teton Pl., Alexandria, VA 22312 USA.

Claretian Pubns., *(978-0-89570)* 205 W. Monroe St., 9th Flr., Chicago, IL 60606 USA (SAN 207-5598) Tel 312-236-7782
E-mail: schneiderc@claretians.org.

Clarion Bks. *Imprint of* **HarperCollins Pubs.**

Clarion Bks. *Imprint of* **Little Brown & Co.**

Clarionton Press *See* **Twelve Star Pr.**

Clarissa C. Foster, *(978-0-578-46127-4)* 62 Old Agua Fria Rd. W., Santa Fe, NM 87508 USA Tel 505-470-7019
E-mail: clarissa.caldwell@gmail.com
Dist(s): **Ingram Content Group.**

Clark Bks., *(978-0-9741677; 978-0-615-11591-7; 978-0-615-11769-0)* 599 Shapleigh Corner Rd., Shapleigh, ME 04076 USA (SAN 630-2017) Tel 207-636-1769 Do not confuse with Clark Books in Baton Rouge, LA
E-mail: clarkbooks@metrocast.net
Web site: http://www.clarkbooksmaine.com.

Clark, I. E. Publications *See* **Family Plays**

Clark, N. Laurie *See* **Clark Pubs.**

Clark Productions Ltd. Inc., *(978-0-9777289)* P.O. Box 583, Little Rock, AR 72203 USA Tel 501-280-9424
E-mail: ouida-clark56@yahoo.com.

Clark Pubs., *(978-0-9641197)* 133 Chestnut St., Amherst, MA 01002 USA Tel 413-549-0575; 941-255-0431
E-mail: ellusmith@aol.com
Dist(s): **Brodart Co.**
North Country Bks., Inc.
Quality Bks., Inc.

Clark Publishing, Inc., *(978-1-883589; 978-0-9822201; 978-0-9825057; 978-0-9827453; 978-0-9832639)* Orders Addr.: P.O. Box 34102, Lexington, KY 40588 USA Toll Free: 800-944-3995; Edit Addr.: 250 E. Short St., Lexington, KY 40507 USA Toll Free: 859-944-3995 Do not confuse with companies with same or similar names in Tacoma, WA, Topeka, KS, Annapolis, MD
E-mail: bclark@theclarkgroupinfo.com
Web site: http://www.theclarkgroupinfo.com; http://www.kyalmanac.com; http://www.clarkpublishing.com; http://www.clarklegacies.com
Dist(s): **Follett School Solutions.**

Clarkson Potter *Imprint of* **Crown Publishing Group, The**

Clarkson Potter *Imprint of* **Potter/Ten Speed/Harmony/Rodale**

CLASS LLC, *(978-0-9911124; 978-1-955095)* P.O. Box PO Box 2884, PAWLEYS ISLAND, SC 29585 USA Tel 843-235-9600
E-mail: linda@classatpawleys.com
Web site: www.classatpawleys.com.

CLASS Publications *Imprint of* **Children Learning Awareness, Safety & Self-Defense**

Classic Bks. Library *Imprint of* **The Editorium, LLC**

Classic Bks., *(978-1-58201; 978-0-7426)* Orders Addr.: P.O. Box 130, Murrieta, CA 92564-0130 USA Tel 951-767-1803; Fax: 951-767-0133
Dist(s): **Reprint Services Corp.**

Classic Bookwrights *Imprint of* **Lindaloo Enterprises**

Classic Comic Store, Ltd. (GBR) *(978-1-906814; 978-1-910619; 978-1-911238) Dist. by* **Casemate Pubs.**

Classic Textbooks, *(978-1-4047)* Div of Classic Books, Orders Addr.: P.O. Box 130, Murrieta, CA 92564-0130 USA
E-mail: newbookorders@gmail.com.

Classical Academic Pr., *(978-1-60051)* 3920 Market St., Camp Hill, PA 17011-4202 USA
Web site: http://www.classicalacademicpress.com.

Classical Comics (GBR) *(978-1-906332; 978-1-907127) Dist. by* **PerseuPGW.**

Classical Conversations, Inc., *(978-0-9727197; 978-0-9798333; 978-0-692-00116-5; 978-0-9829845; 978-0-9851701; 978-0-9884965; 978-0-9904720; 978-0-9965660; 978-0-9972442; 978-0-9984373; 978-0-9995748; 978-0-9996995; 978-0-9996996; 978-1-7329639; 978-1-7329640; 978-1-951571)* Orders Addr.: 255 Air Tool Dr., Southern Pines, NC 28387 USA (SAN 854-5065) Tel 910-687-0288
E-mail: bortins@yahoo.com; cwidman@classicalconversations.com; spederson@classicalconversations.com; sswigart@classicalconversations.com
Web site: http://www.classicalconversations.com; www.ccinternationalonline.com.

Classical Home Education *See* **Pandia Pr.**

Classical Learning Universe, LLC, *(978-0-9721733; 978-0-9763376; 978-0-9793021)* 305 W. Broadway, Suite 184, New York, NY 10013 USA Tel 718-357-2431; Fax: 718-357-2432; Toll Free: 888-684-5922
E-mail: lindsay@classicallearning.com
Web site: http://www.classicallearning.com.

Classical Magic, Inc., *(978-0-9675997; 978-0-9794947)* P.O. Box 1809, Banner Elk, NC 28604 USA Tel 828-898-7764 (phone/fax); 828-898-9571
E-mail: comapers@skybest.com
Web site: http://www.classicalmagic.net
Dist(s): **Book Clearing Hse.**

Classics International Entertainment, Inc., *(978-1-57209)* 324 Main Ave., Suite 183, Norwalk, CT 06851 USA Tel 203-849-8977; Fax: 203-847-5746.

Classroom Complete Pr. *Imprint of* **Rainbow Horizons Publishing, Inc.**

Classroom Library Company *See* **Classroom Library Co.**

Classroom Library Co., *(978-1-56137; 978-1-58130; 978-1-60878; 978-1-4569; 978-1-5020)* Div. of Conn Education Inc., Orders Addr.: 3901 Union Blvd., Suite 157, Saint Louis, MO 63115 USA (SAN 991-0573) Tel 888-318-2665; Fax: 877-716-7272; 3901 Union Blvd, suite 159, St Louis, MO 63115 (SAN 991-0581) Tel 888-318-2665; Fax: 877-716-7272; *Imprints:* Novel Units, Inc. (NvlUnitsI)
E-mail: ben@classroomlibrary.com
Web site: http://www.classroomlibrarycompany.com.

Clavis (ROM) *(978-973-97411) Dist. by* **PerseuPGW.**

Clavis Publishing, *(978-1-60537)* 814 N. Franklin St., Chicago, IL 60610 USA; 250 West 57Th St. 15Th Flr., New York, NY 10016
E-mail: info@clavis.be
Web site: http://www.clavis.be
Dist(s): **Follett School Solutions**
Legato Pubs. Group
Publishers Group West (PGW).

Claw *Imprint of* **ABDO Publishing Co.**

Clawfoot Publishing, *(978-0-9747881)* 1236 S. Pekin Rd., Woodland, WA 98674 USA Tel 360-901-9932; Fax: 360-225-1311
E-mail: bobsbooks@zerfing.com
Web site: http://www.zerfing.com/bobsbooks.

Claxton, Sarah, *(978-0-692-10369-2; 978-0-692-16261-3)* 27 W. Durham St., Philadelphia, PA 19119 USA Tel 240-938-1562
E-mail: sarah.adler.claxton@gmail.com
Dist(s): **Ingram Content Group.**

Clay Jars Publishing, *(978-0-9843369)* 2232 Ralph Ave., 1st Flr., Brooklyn, NY 11234-5610 USA (SAN 859-1156) Tel 718-502-7935
E-mail: clayjarspublishing@gmail.com; justgottawrite@aol.com
Web site: http://www.clayjarspublishing.com.

Claybar Publishing, *(978-0-9787918)* 4007 Greenbriar Dr., Suite E, Stafford, TX 77477-3923 USA (SAN 851-5778) Tel 281-491-4009; Fax: 281-491-4024; Toll Free: 888-491-9533
E-mail: cbarclay@qdlinc.com
Web site: http://www.qdlinc.com.

Claybrook, Matthew, *(978-0-692-95999-2; 978-0-692-96001-1; 978-0-578-90524-2; 978-0-578-90525-9; 978-0-578-39205-9; 978-0-578-39206-6; 978-0-578-39234-9; 979-8-218-12967-5; 979-8-218-22547-6)* 8453 Southwestern Blvd. apt 5146, DALLAS, TX 75206 USA Tel 405-657-6107
E-mail: sanguinecross1@gmail.com
Dist(s): **Ingram Content Group.**

Clayro Corp., *(978-0-9709523)* P.O. Box 270605, Oklahoma City, OK 73137-0605 USA Tel 405-373-2347; Fax: 405-373-0923
E-mail: waderoddy@yahoo.com
Web site: http://tcpublishers.com.

Clayton, Mike, *(978-0-9772622)* 639 Howard Rd., West Point, NY 10996-1510 USA
Web site: http://www.session6wrestling.com.

CLC Pubns., *(978-0-87508; 978-1-936143; 978-1-61958)* Div. of CLC Ministries International, Orders Addr.: P.O. Box 1449, Fort Washington, PA 19034-8449 USA Tel 215-542-1242; Fax: 215-542-7580; Toll Free: 800-659-1240; 701 Pennsylvania Ave., Fort Washington, PA 19034 (SAN 169-7358) Tel 215-542-1242; Fax: 215-542-7580; Toll Free: 800-659-1240
E-mail: orders@clcpublications.com; church@clcpublications.com; dfessenden@clcpublications.com
Web site: http://www.clcusa.org; http://www.clcpublications.com
Dist(s): **Anchor Distributors**
Appalachian Bible Co.
Calvary Chapel Publishing
Spring Arbor Distributors, Inc.

CLC Publishing, *(978-0-692-91090-0; 978-0-578-44393-5; 978-1-7363318)* 12520 SW 13th St, Yukon, OK 73099 USA Tel 360-674-4370
E-mail: shannon@clcforauthors.com
Web site: www.clcforauthors.com.

Clean Teen Publishing, *(978-0-9894701; 978-1-940534; 978-1-63422)* 1107, Kettlewood Dr., Justin, TX 76247 USA Tel 469-583-8737
E-mail: submissions@cleanteenpublishing.com
Web site: http://www.cleanteenpublishing.com; www.crimsontreepublishing.com; www.changingtidespublishing.com
Dist(s): **Independent Pubs. Group**
Ingram Content Group
Midpoint Trade Bks., Inc.

Clear Braces L.L.C., *(978-0-9790682)* 1530 Palisade Ave., Fort Lee, NJ 07024 USA Tel 201-947-6453
E-mail: drjfortlee@aol.com
Web site: http://www.pediatric-dentistry.com.

Clear Creek Pubs., *(978-0-9653543; 978-0-9975839)* Orders Addr.: 115 Clear Creek Ct., Fayetteville, GA 30215 USA Tel 770-461-9460
E-mail: patcruzan@aol.com.

Clear Fork Publishing *See* **Clear Fork Publishing**

Clear Fork Publishing, *(978-0-9899568; 978-0-9974370; 978-1-946101; 978-1-950169)* 102 S. Swenson, Stamford, TX 79553 USA Tel 325-773-5550; *Imprints:* Spork (Spork)
E-mail: callie@clearfork.media
Web site: clearforkpublishing.com.

Clear Horizon, *(978-0-9773569; 978-1-936187)* 605 Silverthorn Rd., Gulf Breeze, FL 32561 USA Tel 850-934-0819; Fax: 850-934-9981
E-mail: info@maxpress.com; ginac@maxpress.com
Web site: http://www.maxpress.com.

Clear Light Pubs., *(978-0-940666; 978-1-57416)* 823 Don Diego, Santa Fe, NM 87501 USA (SAN 219-7758) Tel 505-989-9590; Fax: 505-989-9519; Toll Free: 800-253-2747; 823 Don Diego, Sante Fe, CA 87501 Do not confuse with Clear Light Pub., Seattle, WA
E-mail: service@clearlightbooks.com; janet@clearlightbooks.com
Web site: http://www.clearlightbooks.com
Dist(s): **Follett School Solutions.**

Clear Water Pr., *(978-0-9742972; 978-0-9828995; 979-8-9854922)* 1909 S. Stagecoach Dr., Olathe, KS 66062 USA Do not confuse with Clear Water Press in Reno, NV
E-mail: editor@clearwaterpress.com
Web site: http://www.clearwaterpress.com
Dist(s): **Send The Light Distribution LLC.**

Clear Wind Publishing, *(978-0-578-42570-2; 978-0-578-42571-9; 978-0-578-48868-4; 978-0-578-51065-1; 978-0-578-59180-3; 978-0-578-77212-7; 978-0-578-77215-8; 979-8-218-09076-0; 979-8-218-10333-0; 979-8-218-12001-6; 979-8-218-12980-4; 979-8-218-15203-1; 979-8-218-15463-9)* 4300 Elmgree Dr., Roanoke, TX 76262 USA Tel 817-333-7060
E-mail: aaronwronko@gmail.com
Dist(s): **Ingram Content Group.**

Clearbridge Publishing, *(978-1-929194)* Div. of Science of Strategy Institute, Orders Addr.: Science Of Strategy Institute 2829 Linkview Dr., Las Vegas, NV 89134 USA (SAN 857-8524) Tel 702-721-9631; *Imprints:* Art of War Plus Books (Art War Plus)
E-mail: gagliardi.gary@gmail.com
Web site: http://www.scienceofstrategy.org.

Clearwater Publishing *See* **Clearwater Publishing, LLC**

Clearwater Publishing, LLC, *(978-0-9769465)* 1101 Waterfall Ln., Lakeland, FL 33803 USA.

ClearWaters Publishing, *(978-0-9841439)* 7539 Parkview Dr., Columbia, SC 29223 USA Tel 803-404-8893
E-mail: clearwatersllc@yahoo.com; thomashuntersjr@yahoo.com
Web site: http://www.tjhunteronline.com.

Cleis Pr. *Imprint of* **Start Publishing LLC**

Clem Publishing, *(978-0-9772225)* P.O. Box 246, Danvers, IL 61732 USA Tel 309-530-0710; 116 W. North St., Danvers, IL 61732
E-mail: josephclem@hotmail.com.

Clements, J. S. Corporation *See* **Clements, Jehan**

Clements, Jehan, *(978-0-9622500)* Orders Addr.: P.O. Box 543, Tarrytown, NY 10591 USA Tel 914-293-7884
E-mail: storyteller1@optonline.net
Web site: http://www.flipoverpicturebooks.com.

Clemons, Bethany, *(978-0-578-67029-4; 978-0-578-91474-9)* 5058 BARRON Pk. DR, SAN JOSE, CA 95136-2903 USA Tel 408-972-1107
E-mail: starlover940@gmail.com.

Clemson University Digital Press *See* **Clemson Univ. Pr.**

Clemson Univ. Pr., *(978-0-9741516; 978-0-9771263; 978-0-9796066; 978-0-9842598; 978-0-9835339; 978-0-9890826; 978-0-9908958; 978-1-942954; 978-1-78694; 978-1-949979; 978-1-63804)* c/o Ctr. for Electronic & Digital Publishing, 611 Strode Tower, Clemson Univ., Clemson, SC 29634-0522 USA
E-mail: amero@clemson.edu
Web site: https://www.clemson.edu/centers-institutes/press/
Dist(s): **Oxford Univ. Pr., Inc.**

Clendenin Fine Art Concepts, *(978-0-9897662)* 8160 Manitoba St., No. 104, Playa del Rey, CA 90293 USA Tel 310-821-3941; Fax: 310-821-2282
E-mail: aclendenin@verizon.net
Web site: www.clendeninfineart.com.

Cleo and Olive, *(978-0-692-75647-8)* 44 Buckelew Bridge Rd., ANNISTON, AL 36207 USA Tel 256-239-3135.

Clerisy Pr. *Imprint of* **AdventureKEEN**

Cleveland Clinic Pr., *(978-1-59624)* c/o Lawrence D. Chilnick, 9500 Euclid Ave., NA32, Cleveland, OH 44195 USA Tel 216-444-1158; Fax: 216-444-9385
E-mail: chilnil@ccf.org
Web site: http://www.clevelandclinicpress.org.

†Cleveland Museum of Art, *(978-0-910386; 978-0-940717; 978-1-935294)* 11150 East Blvd., Cleveland, OH 44106-1797 USA (SAN 278-4572) Tel 216-421-7340; Fax: 216-421-9409; Toll Free: 1-877-262-4748
E-mail: bbradley@clevelnadart.org
Web site: http://www.clevelandart.org
Dist(s): **Art Media Resources, Inc.**
Chicago Distribution Ctr.
D.A.P./Distributed Art Pubs.
Hopkins Fulfillment Services
Hudson Hills Pr. LLC
Indiana Univ. Pr.
Ohio Univ. Pr.
Univ. of Washington Pr.; *CIP.*

Cleveland Stock Images, *(978-0-9617637; 978-0-692-86770-9; 978-1-7338131)* 7124 Baker Ln., Chagrin Falls, OH 44023 USA (SAN 664-8533) Tel 216-548-4484; Fax: 216-249-5828
E-mail: jsjidc@aol.com.

Clever Factory, The, *(978-1-59277; 978-1-64038)* 545 Mainstream Dr., Suite 406, Nashville, TN 37228 USA.

Clever Girl Publishing, *(978-0-692-95655-7; 978-0-692-14357-5; 978-0-692-14362-9; 978-0-692-14619-4; 978-0-578-67317-2; 978-0-578-91970-6)* 33 A St., Bonne Terre, MO 63628 USA Tel 573-631-9284
E-mail: missyannlang@gmail.com.

Clever Media Group, *(978-1-948418; 978-1-949998; 978-1-951100; 978-1-954738; 978-1-956560; 979-8-88887)* 90 State St., Albany, NY 12207 USA Tel 541-255-3815
E-mail: n.vorobyeva@clever-publishing.com
Dist(s): **Hachette Bk. Group**
Quarto Publishing Group USA.

CleverKits,LLC, *(978-0-9778771)* 12 Brinckerhoff Ave, Stamford, CT 06905-3201 USA Fax: 267-821-7523
E-mail: cleverkits@yahoo.com
Web site: http://www.cleverkits.com.

Cleverly Changing Pr., *(978-1-7350498; 978-1-960690)* 7103 Sequoia Terr., Beltsville, MD 20705 USA Tel 410-429-7043
E-mail: cleverlychanging@gmail.com
Web site: CleverlyChanging.com.

CleverlyChanging *See* **Cleverly Changing Pr.**

CLF Publishing, *(978-0-9857372; 978-0-9884237; 978-0-9892358; 978-0-9899408; 978-0-9960815; 978-0-9961971; 978-1-945102)* 10063 Maple Ave., Hesperia, CA 92345 USA Tel 760-669-8149
E-mail: DRCWE@YAHOO.COM
Dist(s): **Lulu Pr., Inc.**

Cliff Road Bks., *(978-1-60261)* 3437 Cliff Rd., Birmingham, AL 35222 USA (SAN 857-409X)
E-mail: holly@cliffroadbooks.com.

iffhanger Bks., *(978-0-615-49921-5; 978-0-615-78254-6)* 2756 Vista Bluff Blvd., Lewisville, TX 75067 USA Tel 972-743-0736
E-mail: khosey@gmail.com; kevin@cliffhangerbooks.com
Web site: http://www.cliffhangerbooks.com
Dist(s): **CreateSpace Independent Publishing Platform.**

lifton Carriage House Pr., *(978-0-9825713)* 12 S. Sixth St., No. 1250, Minneapolis, MN 55402 USA Fax: 612-746-8811
E-mail: wreynolds@briobooks.com
Web site: http://www.briobooks.com.

limb Your Moutain Publishing, *(978-1-7338162)* P.O. Box 245, Sequim, WA 98382 USA Tel 907-942-7563
E-mail: akfishwoman@hotmail.com.

limbing Angel Publishing, *(978-0-9965721; 978-1-956218)* P.O. Box 32381, Knoxville, TN 37930 USA Tel 818-530-3541
E-mail: lisasoland@aol.com.

Clinch, David *See* **Clinch Media**

Clinch Media, *(978-0-9800835)* 1339 Mill Glen Dr., Atlanta, GA 30338 USA (SAN 855-1588) Tel 770-730-1721
E-mail: clinch@bellsouth.net
Web site: http://www.theleprechauntrap.com.

Clocktower Bks., *(978-0-7433)*
E-mail: mohlercullen@gmail.com
Web site: http://www.clocktowerbooks.com; http://www.johntcullen.com
Dist(s): **CreateSpace Independent Publishing Platform**
Smashwords.

Clocktower Fiction *See* **Clocktower Bks.**

Clocktower Hill Research & Publishing Group, LLC, *(978-0-9832130)* 23 Oakfield Dr., Rome, GA 30161 USA Tel 706-936-0254; Fax: 973-201-1755; *Imprints:* Lucas Violet (LucasViolet)
E-mail: davidehrier@clocktowerhill.com
Web site: http://www.clocktowerhill.com.

ClockTower Pubns., *(978-0-9704280)* 203 Skyland Dr., Dept. I, Staunton, VA 24401-2358 USA Tel 540-885-6614
E-mail: trgww@ntelos.net.

Clockwise Pr. (CAN) *(978-0-9939351; 978-1-988347) Dist. by* **Firefly Bks Limited.**

CLOJ Publishing, *(978-0-9767711)* 544 Rialto Ave., Venice, CA 90291-4248 USA (SAN 256-5129) Tel 310-399-6126
E-mail: publisher@clojpublishing.com
Web site: http://www.clojpublishing.com.

Cloonfad Pr., *(978-0-9744744; 978-0-9769404; 978-0-9797772)* Orders Addr.: P.O. Box 106, Cassville, NJ 08527 USA Tel 732-833-9800 (phone/fax)
E-mail: cloonfad@optonline.net
Web site: http://www.cloonfadpress.com
Dist(s): **Gatewood Pr.**

Cloquet River Pr., *(978-0-9720050; 978-0-9792175; 978-1-7324434)* 5353 Knudsen Rd, Duluth, MN 55803 USA Tel 218-721-3213; Fax: 218-725-5074
E-mail: cloquetriverpress@yahoo.com
Web site: http://www.cloquetriverpress.com
Dist(s): **Partners Bk. Distributing, Inc.**

Closer Looks Bks., *(978-0-9763593)* 864 Horns Corners Rd., Cedarburg, WI 53012 USA
E-mail: sggk@wi.rr.com
Web site: http://home.wi.rr.com/acloserlookbooks.

Cloud 9 Ranch, *(978-0-9767690)* 231 Jung Blvd., E, Naples, FL 34120 USA Tel 239-353-6877; Fax: 239-353-7579
E-mail: nsfcloud9@aol.com
Web site: http://www.cloud9ranch.info.

Cloud Chinese *See* **Cloud Learning**

Cloud, Kat Creations, *(978-0-692-88310-5; 978-0-692-88311-2)* 903 E Constitution Dr., Chandler, AZ 85225 USA Tel 480-748-0826
Dist(s): **Ingram Content Group.**

Cloud Lake Publications *See* **Cloud Lake Publishing**

Cloud Lake Publishing, *(978-0-9787054)* 1440 Beaumont Avenue, Ste 2-198, Beaumont, CA 92223 USA Tel 707-239-4060
E-mail: mlarchibald@mac.com
Web site: http://www.winecountrywriter.com.

Cloud Learning, *(978-1-7327063; 978-1-954729)* 237 Locust Rd, Wilmette, IL 60091 USA Tel 847-917-0036
E-mail: chuminghuang@hotmail.com; myeasyshows@gmail.com
Web site: www.mycloudchinese.com.

Cloud Mountain Publishing *See* **Easter Island Foundation**

Cloudbreak Media Inc., *(978-0-692-12942-5)* 4817 Katherine Ave, Sherman Oaks, CA 91423 USA Tel 323-243-2909
E-mail: chrys@chryscoulter.com
Dist(s): **Ingram Content Group.**

Cloudland.net Publishing, *(978-1-882906)* Orders Addr.: HC 33, Box 50-A, Pettigrew, AR 72752-9501 USA Tel 870-861-5536; Fax: 870-861-5736; Toll Free: 800-838-4453
E-mail: tim@timernst.com
Web site: http://www.TimErnst.com
Dist(s): **Chicago Distribution Ctr.**
Univ. of Arkansas Pr.

Cloudless Sky, *(978-0-9978443)* P.O. Box 32992, Santa Fe, NM 87594 USA Tel 505-670-3177
E-mail: derekfs@yahoo.com.

Cloudmaker Entertainment, *(978-0-9743989)* 7654 195th Ave. Ct. E., Bonney Lake, WA 98390 USA Tel 253-862-1490 (phone/fax)
E-mail: trox@cloudmakerentertainment.com
Web site: http://www.cloudmakerentertainment.com.

Cloudstone, *(978-1-879846)* 10 Patchin Pl., New York, NY 10011 USA Tel 212-929-6871.

Cloudwalker Publications *See* **Working Title Publishing**

Clouser, Lisa M., *(978-0-692-53171-6; 978-0-692-63828-6; 978-0-9977202)* 11 Countryside Ct., Camp Hill, PA 17011 USA Tel 717-737-3334
Dist(s): **CreateSpace Independent Publishing Platform.**

Clover Pr., *(978-1-951038; 978-1-951757)* Orders Addr.: 8820 Kenamar Dr. Suite No. 501, San Diego, CA 92121 USA; Edit Addr.: 8820 Kenamar Dr. Suite 501, San Diego, CA 92121 USA Tel 858-342-3215
E-mail: robbie@cloverpress.us
Web site: CloverPress.us
Dist(s): **Diamond Comic Distributors, Inc.**

Clovercroft Publishing, 307 Verde Meadow Dr., Franklin, TN 37067 USA Tel 615-472-1128
E-mail: larry@christianbookservices.com
Dist(s): **Iron Stream Media**
Two Rivers Distribution.

Club Pro Products, *(978-0-9725721)* 153 Raquet Club Dr., Rancho Mirage, CA 92270 USA
E-mail: info@robstanger.com
Web site: http://www.robstanger.com.

Club4Girls *Imprint of* **Club4Girls Publishing Co.**

Club4Girls Publishing Co., *(978-0-9712297)* 4017 Dutch Harbor Ct., Raleigh, NC 27606-8604 USA Tel 919-387-9939; *Imprints:* Club4Girls (ClubFourGirls)
E-mail: bob@sas.com.

ClueSearchPuzzles.com, *(978-0-9753879)* 7645 N. Union Blvd. #175, Colorado Springs, CO 80920-3863 USA Tel 719-659-9034
E-mail: books@cluesearchpuzzles.com
Web site: http://www.cluesearchpuzzles.com.

Cluster Storm Publishing, *(978-1-56998)* Orders Addr.: 507 E. 3750 N., Provo, UT 84604 USA Tel 801-623-9101
E-mail: cjmartell@gmail.com.

Clydesdale Pr., LLC, *(978-0-9729606)* P.O. Box 2375, Kesington, MD 20891 USA
Dist(s): **Simon & Schuster, Inc.**

CMB Publishing Co., *(978-0-9722969)* 24 Appleton St., Suite 1, Boston, MA 02116 USA Tel 617-306-5581; Fax: 617-451-0168
E-mail: info@cmbpublishing.com
Web site: http://www.cmbpublishing.com/.

CMC Publishing, *(978-0-9787336)* 1 Heritage Pl., Nesconset, NY 11767 USA
E-mail: colleenssite@yahoo.com.

CMD UnLtd., LLC, *(978-0-9742796)* 316 Karl Linn Dr. No. 221, North Chesterfield , VA 23225 USA Tel 804-380-4683 Do not confuse with Blessings Unlimited in Bloomington, MN
Web site: http://www.blessingsunlimited.info.

CMK Pubs. LLC, *(978-0-9743159)* .

CMS Enterprises, *(978-0-9768170)* Orders Addr.: P.O. Box 8039, Van Nuys, CA 91409 USA (SAN 256-5226); Edit Addr.: 6429 Whitman Ave., Van Nuys, CA 91406 USA
E-mail: cms55@hotmail.com.

CNJ Bks. & Publishing LLC, *(978-1-7361360)* 4517 Willow Pond Ct E, West Palm Beach, FL 33417 USA Tel 561-714-9006
E-mail: cnjbooks0316@gmail.com
Web site: www.cnjbooksandpublishing.com.

CNL Publishing, *(978-0-9766921)* 105 Wedgewood Dr., Fairfield, AL 35064 USA Tel 205-835-5444; Fax: 205-923-3218.

CNPIECSB, 332 W Cermak Rd., Apt. 2D, Chicago, IL 60616 USA.

CNT Robotics LLC, *(978-0-9993918)*
E-mail: roboteer@comcast.net
Web site: www.cntrobotics.com.

Coach Enterprises, *(978-0-9636706)* 616 Munntown Rd., Finleyville, PA 15332 USA Tel 724-348-4843; Fax: 724-348-5549.

Coach Hse. Bks. (CAN) *(978-1-55245; 978-1-77056) Dist. by* **Consort Bk Sales.**

coach speak & serve, *(978-0-9987829; 978-0-9990044)* 1219 N Classen blvd, oklahoma city, OK 73106 USA Tel 405-246-0077; Fax: 405-246-0077
E-mail: support@coachspeakserve.com
Web site: coachspeakserve.com.

Coachwhip Pubns., *(978-1-930585; 978-1-61646)* 1505 English Brook Dr., Landisville, PA 17538 USA
E-mail: chadarment@verizon.net
Web site: http://www.coachwhipbooks.com.

Coal City Stories, *(978-0-9849028)* 2011 Oak Pk. Ln., Decatur, GA 30032 USA Tel 678-896-9493 (Tel/Fax)
E-mail: emilie.bush@gmail.com; machineseat@hotmail.com
Web site: CoalCitySteam.com.

Coal Hole Productions, *(978-0-9709630)* 207 Hemlock Ln., Bloomsburg, PA 17815 USA Tel 570-784-4561
E-mail: ceo@coalhole.com
Web site: http://www.coalhole.com
Dist(s): **Partners Bk. Distributing, Inc.**

Coal Under Pr.ure, LLC, *(978-0-9763400; 978-0-9913704; 978-1-7326303; 979-8-218-22527-8)* Div. of Coal Under Pressure, LLC, Orders Addr.: 109 Ambersweet Way No. 280, Davenport, FL 33897 USA
E-mail: coalunderpressurepubs@gmail.com
Web site: http://www.coalunderpressure.com.

Coal Under Pressure Publications *See* **Coal Under Pr.ure, LLC**

Coalesce Bookstore *See* **Coalesce Pr.**

Coalesce Pr., *(978-0-9895234)* 845 Main St., Morro Bay, CA 93442 USA Tel 805-772-2880
E-mail: coalescebookstore@gmail.com.

Coast View Publishing, *(978-0-9849732)* 638 Camino De Los Mares Suite H130-157, San Clemente, CA 92673 USA Tel 949-388-7996
E-mail: coastviewpublishing@yahoo.com.

Coastal Carolina Pr., *(978-1-928556)* Orders Addr.: P.O. Box 9111, Chapel Hill, NC 27515-9111 USA
E-mail: books@coastalcarolinapress.org
Web site: http://www.coastalcarolinapress.org
Dist(s): **Blair**
Parnassus Bk. Distributors.

Coastal Publishing Carolina, Inc., *(978-0-9705727; 978-1-931650)* 504 Amberjack Way, Summerville, SC 29485 USA Tel 843-821-6168; Fax: 843-851-6949
E-mail: coastalpublishing@earthlink.net
Web site: http://coastalpublishing.net/.

Coastal Publishing, LLC, *(978-0-9755573)* No. 226, 1133 Bal Harbor Blvd., Suite 1139, Punta Gorda, FL 33950-6574 USA Tel 941-505-5547.

Cobalt Pr., *(978-0-9747805)* P.O. Box 5393, Hauppauge, NY 11788 USA Do not confuse with Cobalt Pr. in Minneapolis, MN
Web site: http://www.geocities.com/corrinedzwi/index.html.

Cobblestone Pr., *(978-0-9649021)* 12356 CULTURED STONE DR, FISHERS, IN 46037 USA Tel 317-253-7476; Fax: 317-475-9578; Toll Free: 800-420-6655 Do not confuse with companies with the same or similar name in Midland, MI, Huntsville, AL
Dist(s): **Publishers Group West (PGW).**

Cobblestone Publishing Co., *(978-0-382; 978-0-942389; 978-0-9607638)* Div. of Cricket Magazine Group, 30 Grove St., Suite C, Peterborough, NH 03458 USA (SAN 237-9937) Tel 603-924-7209; Fax: 603-924-7380; Toll Free: 800-821-0115; P.O. Box 487, Effingham, IL 62401
E-mail: custsvc@cobblestone.mv.com
Web site: http://www.cobblestonepub.com
Dist(s): **Americana Publishing, Inc.**
Follett School Solutions.

Cobblesworth Studio, *(978-0-692-91147-1)* Orders Addr.: 1261 Bistre St, Longmont, CO 80501 USA Tel 720-467-3119; Edit Addr.: 1261 Bistre St, Longmont, CO 80501 USA Tel 720-467-3119
E-mail: cobblesworth@gmail.com; travisrueckert88@gmail.com
Web site: https://www.facebook.com/Cobblesworth
Dist(s): **Independent Pub.**

Cobbs Creations, *(978-0-692-75070-4; 978-0-692-96368-5; 978-0-692-98749-0; 978-0-692-14642-2; 978-0-692-14643-9; 978-0-692-17740-2; 978-0-578-84472-5; 979-8-218-08442-4; 979-8-218-29223-2)* 1861 Holly Point Rd., PROSPERITY, SC 29127 USA Tel 803-924-1947.

Cobbs Creek Publishing, *(978-1-7342219; 978-1-7361533)* 5523 DELANCEY ST, Philadelphia, PA 19143 USA Tel 215-758-7889
E-mail: msmelange123@gmail.com.

Coburn Birge Publishing, *(978-0-9839000)* 2339 Forest Hill-Irene Rd., Germantown, TN 38139 USA Tel 901-248-9134.

Cochise County Juvenile Detention Ctr., *(978-0-9771011)* P.O. Box 208, Bisbee, AZ 85603 USA Fax: 520-432-7136
Web site: http://www.co.cochise.az.us/schools.

Cochran, Russ Co., The, *(978-0-939947; 978-0-9816923)* P.O. Box 469, West Plains, MO 65775 USA (SAN 663-8236) Fax: 417-256-6666
E-mail: russcochran333@gmail.com
Web site: http://www.russcochran.com.

Cochrane Farms, *(978-0-9992841)* 13220 Lowell unit c, Broomfield, CO 80020 USA Tel 720-244-3148
E-mail: cottagesimplicity@gmail.com.

Cockburn Publishing *See* **GoFindHome**

Cockey, EJ & Company *See* **The Painted Word, Ltd.**

Cockney Kid Publishing, *(978-0-9903710)* 986 Woodstock Ln., Ventura, CA 93001 USA Tel 805-258-6325
E-mail: davisivor@yahoo.com
Web site: ivordavisbeatles.com.

Coconut Info, *(978-1-929317)* Orders Addr.: P.O. Box 75460, Honolulu, HI 96836 USA Tel 808-947-6543; Fax: 808-923-6544
E-mail: sales@coconutinfo.com; info@coconutinfo.com
Web site: http://www.coconutinfo.com
Dist(s): **Booklines Hawaii, Ltd.**

Coconut Pr., LLC, *(978-0-9702168; 978-0-9778913; 978-0-578-44083-5)* Div. of Puerto Rico Postcard Co., Inc, Orders Addr.: P.O. Box 309540, Saint Thomas, VI 00803 USA Tel 787-248-3774; Fax: 787-253-8449; Edit Addr.: P.O. Box 79710, Carolina, PR 00984 USA Do not confuse with companies with same or similar names in Coral Gables, FL, Missouri City, TX
E-mail: Angelaspenceley1@msn.com
Dist(s): **Puerto Rico Postcard.**

Coda Grove Publishing, *(978-0-9889113)* P.O. Box 275, Fairfax, VT 05454 USA Tel 802-849-2777
E-mail: codagrovepub@gmail.com.

Cody Roach Enterprises, *(978-1-7322370)* 5 W Winter Pk. St., Orlando, FL 32804 USA Tel 407-579-6453
E-mail: codyroachenterprizes@gmail.com.

Cody's Guide, *(978-0-9755305)* 3855 Humbug Creek Rd., Applegate, OR 97530 USA
Web site: http://www.codysguide.com.

Coe, Kathleen, 6102 Auburndale Dr., Greensboro, NC 27410 USA Tel 336-580-4205
E-mail: kathleenmcoe@aol.com.

Coffee Hse. Ink, *(978-0-9663176)* 32370 SE Judd Rd., Eagle Creek, OR 97022 USA Tel 503-637-3277; Fax: 503-423-7980
E-mail: donmillili@aol.com
Web site: http://www.coffeehouseink.com.

Coffee Hse. Pr., *(978-0-918273; 978-1-56689)* 79 13th Ave NE Ste. 110, Minneapolis, MN 55413-1073 USA (SAN 206-3883); 387 Pk. Ave. S., New York, NY 10016
Web site: http://www.coffeehousepress.org
Dist(s): **BookMobile**
Children's Plus, Inc.
Consortium Bk. Sales & Distribution
Follett School Solutions
MyiLibrary
Open Road Integrated Media, Inc.
SPD-Small Pr. Distribution.

Coffee Seed Bks., *(978-1-943718)* 17611 Redhawk Dr, Arlington, WA 98223 USA Tel 360-631-2422
E-mail: coffeeseedbooks@gmail.com
Web site: www.coffeeseedbooks.com.

Coffragants (CAN) *(978-2-921997; 978-2-89517; 978-2-89558) Dist. by* **Penton Overseas.**

Coghlan Group, The *See* **Phoenix International, Inc.**

Cogi Garden Bks., *(978-0-692-83770-2; 978-0-692-85083-1)* 811 Lyon St NE, Grand Rapids, MI 49503 USA Tel 301-367-2830
E-mail: dirmeyer@gmail.com
Dist(s): **CreateSpace Independent Publishing Platform.**

Cognella, Inc., *(978-0-9763162; 978-1-934269; 978-1-935551; 978-1-60927; 978-1-62131; 978-1-62661; 978-1-63189; 978-1-63487; 978-1-5165; 978-1-7935; 979-8-8233)* 320 South Cedros Ave., Suite 400, Solana Beach, CA 92075 USA (SAN 990-1701) Tel 858-800-2675 Toll Free: 800-200-3908
E-mail: accounting@universityreaders.com; ap@cognella.com; accounting@cognella.com
Web site: http://www.universityreaders.com; http://www.cognella.com
Dist(s): **Independent Pubs. Group.**

Cognisaya, *(978-0-615-60544-9; 978-0-9852568; 978-0-9980759)* 3104 SE Misty Ct, Port Orchard, WA 98367 USA Tel 360-602-1913
Web site: cognisaya.com
Dist(s): **CreateSpace Independent Publishing Platform.**

Cohen, Deanna Moreau, 1626a Garden St., Santa Barbara, CA 93101-1110 USA
E-mail: liftveil2@cs.com.

Cohen, Sonia *See* **Gigi Enterprises**

Cohn, Tricia, *(978-0-9743847)* 16158 Highgate Dr., Riverside, CA 92503-8718 USA Tel 714-272-6972
E-mail: triciacohn@beobi.com
Web site: http://www.beobi.com.

Coho Press *See* **Dot Dot Bks.**

Cokesbury *Imprint of* **Abingdon Pr.**

Cola, Arthur, *(978-0-9789423)* 425 Robins Run, Papa Adventures, Burlington, WI 53105 USA
E-mail: arthurcola@yahoo.com
Dist(s): **Partners Bk. Distributing, Inc.**

Colbert Hse., LLC, The, *(978-1-887399)* Orders Addr.: P.O. Box 786, Mustang, OK 73064-0786 USA Tel 405-204-0043
E-mail: customerservice@colberthouse.com
Web site: http://www.colberthouse.com.

Colbert House, The *See* **Colbert Hse., LLC, The**

Colby Studio, *(978-0-9978198)* P.O. Box 681, Castine, ME 04421 USA Tel 207-322-0432
E-mail: kasey@eternav.com
Web site: ivystories.com.

Cold River Pubns., *(978-0-9712867; 978-0-692-52577-7)* P.O. Box 606, Long Lake, NY 12847-0606 USA Tel 518-624-3581
E-mail: criver@telenet.net; criver@telenent.net
Web site: http://www.coldriverwoodworks.com
Dist(s): **Smashwords.**

Cole, Mark, *(978-0-615-86154-8; 978-0-615-92911-8; 978-0-692-02398-3; 978-0-692-23967-4; 978-0-692-25816-3)* 112 Ash Ridge Pl., Pearl, MS 39208 USA Tel 601-540-5125
E-mail: wnxaz@hotmail.com
Dist(s): **CreateSpace Independent Publishing Platform.**

Cole Publishing, *(978-0-9678779; 978-0-9773973; 978-0-9787317)* 13428 Maxella Ave., Suite 701, Marina Del Rey, CA 90292 USA (SAN 256-856X) Fax: 310-209-2448
E-mail: candace@candacecole.com; ccpprod@aol.com
Web site: http://candacecole.com/.

Cole, Reginald, *(978-0-692-81245-7)* 1705 Inverness Ave., Dundalk, MD 21222 USA Tel 301-502-2964
E-mail: reggie.cole@outlook.com.

Cole-Dai, Phyllis, *(978-0-615-24350-4)* 712 6th St., Brookings, SD 57006 USA Tel 605-692-7001
E-mail: phyllis@phylliscoledai.com; coledai@brookings.net
Web site: http://www.phylliscoledai.com.

Coleman, CJ, *(978-0-9773651)* 2191 Craig Springs Rd., Sturgis, MS 39769 USA Tel 662-312-4383
E-mail: cillycreations@hotmail.com
Web site: http://www.cillycreations.com.

Coleman, Kandis, *(978-0-578-44859-6; 979-8-9855967)* 2323 Bloomfield Dr., Kannapolis, NC 28081 USA Tel 704-907-7675
E-mail: sweat49@gmail.com.

Coleman, Monte C, *(978-0-578-64783-8)* 20121 Runnymede St., Winnetka, CA 91306 USA Tel 818-209-8585
E-mail: whiskerwagglytail@gmail.com.

Coleman Ranch Pr., *(978-0-9677069)* Orders Addr.: P.O. Box 1496, Sacramento, CA 95812 USA Tel 916-393-9032; Toll Free Fax: 888-532-4190; Toll Free: 877-765-3225
E-mail: colemanranch@comcast.net
Web site: http://www.CRPRESS.com.

Coleman, Wim *See* **Coleman/Perrin**

Coleman/Perrin, *(978-1-935178)* 405 Walnut St., Chapel Hill, NC 27517 USA Tel 919-338-8119; *Imprints:* ChironBooks (ChironBooks)
E-mail: wim-pat@gmail.com; info@chironbooks.com
Web site: http://www.playsonideas.com; http://www.chironbooks.com; http://www.madeirapress.com
Dist(s): **BookBaby**
Pathway Bk. Service.

Colibri Children's Adventures *See* **Leaning Rock Pr.**

Colihue (ARG) *(978-950-581) Dist. by* **AIMS Intl.**

Collado, Karin *See* **DELICATE STAYS LLC**

Collective Bk. Studio, The, *(978-1-951412; 978-1-68555)* 4517 Pk. Blvd, Oakland, CA 94602 USA Tel 510-384-8019
E-mail: angela@thecollectivebook.studio
Web site: https://thecollectivebook.studio
Dist(s): **Simon & Schuster, Inc.**

Collector Bks., *(978-0-89145; 978-1-57432; 978-1-60460)* Div. of Schroeder Publishing Co., Inc., Orders Addr.: P.O. Box 3009, Paducah, KY 42003 USA (SAN 157-5368) Tel 270-898-6211; 270-898-7903; Fax: 270-898-8890; 270-898-1173; Toll Free: 800-626-5420 (orders only); Edit Addr.: 5801 Kentucky Dam Rd., Paducah, KY 42003 USA (SAN 200-7479); *Imprints:* American Quilter's Society (Am Quilters Soc)
E-mail: Info@collectorbooks.com; info@AQSquilt.com
Web site: http://www.collectorbooks.com; http://www.americanquilter.com/.

Collectors Pr., Inc., (*978-0-9635202; 978-1-888054; 978-1-933112*) Orders Addr.: P.O. Box 230986, Portland, OR 97281 USA Tel 503-684-3030; Fax: 503-684-3777; Toll Free: 800-423-1848; Edit Addr.: P.O. Box 230986, Portland, OR 97281-0986 USA
E-mail: lperry@collectorspress.com; rperry@collectorspress.com
Web site: http://www.collectorspress.com
Dist(s): **Universe Publishing**
Worldwide Media Service, Inc.

College & Career Pr., LLC, (*978-0-9745251; 978-0-9829210*) P.O. Box 300484, Chicago, IL 60630 USA Tel 773-718-0366; Fax: 777-777-7777; P.O. Box 300484, Chicago, IL 60630
E-mail: andymorkes@gmail.com
Web site: http://www.ccpnewsletters.com; https://natureinchicago.wordpress.com/
Dist(s): **Brodart Co.**
Follett School Solutions.

College Assistance & Scholarship Help, Incorporated *See* **College Assistance, Inc.**

College Assistance, Inc., (*978-0-9760251*) Orders Addr.: 7235 Promenade Dr. Apt. J401, Boca Raton, FL 33433-6982 USA Toll Free: 866-346-7890
E-mail: librodereecy@aol.com; thecollegebook@aol.com
Web site: http://www.librodelauniversidad.com; http://www.thecollegebook.com; http://www.reecysbook.com.

College Hse. Enterprises, LLC, (*978-0-9655911; 978-0-9700675; 978-0-9723567; 978-0-9762413; 978-0-9792581; 978-1-935673*) 5713 Glen Cove Dr., Knoxville, TN 37919-8611 USA (SAN 253-5831) Tel 865-558-6111 (phone/fax)
Web site: http://www.collegehousebooks.com.

College of DuPage Pr., (*978-1-932514*) Orders Addr.: 425 Fawell Blvd., Glen Ellyn, IL 60137 USA Fax: 630-942-3333; Toll Free: 800-290-4474
E-mail: software@cod.edu
Web site: http://www.dupagepress.com.

College Planning Network, (*978-1-380344*) 914 E. Jefferson, Campion Tower, Seattle, WA 98122 USA Tel 206-323-0624; Fax: 206-323-0623
E-mail: seaspn@collegeplan.org
Web site: http://www.collegeplan.org.

College Prowler, Inc., (*978-1-932215; 978-1-59658; 978-1-4274*) 5001 Baum Blvd. Ste. 750, Pittsburgh, PA 15213-1856 USA Toll Free Fax: 800-772-4972; Toll Free: 800-290-2682; *Imprints:* Off The Record (Off The Rcd)
E-mail: joey@collegeprowler.com; luke@collegeprowler.com
Web site: http://www.collegeprowler.com.

Collegiate Kids Bks., LLC, (*978-0-9836211; 978-0-692-01848-4; 978-0-9886542*) 3956 2nd St. Dr. NW, Hickory, NC 28601 USA Tel 828-773-5398
E-mail: bryan@collegiatekidsbooks.com
Web site: http://www.collegiatekidsbooks.com.

Collins *Imprint of* **HarperCollins Pubs.**

Collins Christian Co., The, (*978-0-692-66059-1*) 1043 Myrtle Ln, Cocoa, FL 32922 USA Tel 321-208-1538
E-mail: zlcinc2015@gmail.com.

Collins Couch, (*978-1-7365767; 979-8-9862064*) 3725 Renaissance Cir., ATLANTA, GA 30349 USA Tel 404-574-9810
E-mail: rhgordon36@yahoo.com
Web site: www.collinscouch.com.

Collins Reference *Imprint of* **HarperCollins Pubs.**

Collins, Robert, (*978-0-9766426*) 865 Helke Rd., Vandalia, OH 45377 USA; *Imprints:* Peregrine Communications (Peregrine Comm)
E-mail: adagio@gemair.com
Web site: http://www.ufoconspiracy.com/.

Colonel Davenport Historical Foundation, (*978-0-9755934*) P.O. Box 4703, Rock Island, IL 61204 USA
Web site: http://www.davenporthouse.org.

†Colonial Williamsburg Foundation, (*978-0-87935; 978-0-910412*) P.O. Box 3532, Williamsburg, VA 23187-3532 USA (SAN 128-4630) Fax: 757-565-8999 (orders only); Toll Free: 800-446-9240 (orders only)
Web site: http://www.colonialwilliamsburg.com
Dist(s): **Antique Collectors' Club**
National Bk. Network
University of Virginia Pr.; *CIP.*

Color & Learn, (*978-0-9795190*) P.O. Box 1592, Saint Augustine, FL 32085-1592 USA (SAN 853-6023)
Web site: http://www.colorandlearn.com.

Color & Light Editions, (*978-0-9671527; 978-0-9835239*) 371 Drakes View Dr., Inverness, CA 94937 USA Tel 415-663-1616
E-mail: kathleenpgoodwin@gmail.com
Web site: http://BlairGoodwin.com
Dist(s): **Partners Bk. Distributing, Inc.**

Color Loco *See* **Color Loco, LLC**

Color Loco, LLC, (*978-0-9770652; 978-0-9788778*) 213 Woodland Dr., Downingtown, PA 19335-9335 USA
Web site: http://www.ColorLoco.com.

Colorado Associated University Press *See* **Univ. Pr. of Colorado**

Colorfield Creative, LLC, (*978-1-948227*) 2324 NW 113th St, Oklahoma City, OK 73120 USA Tel 405-249-4254
E-mail: colorfieldcreative@gmail.com.

Colorful Bks. Pr., (*978-0-9746152*) 935 Ottawa Ave., Ypsilanti, MI 48198 USA.

Colorful Crayons For Kids Publishing, LLC *See* **Jeb Cool Kids Entertainment, Inc**

ColoringCrumbs LLC, (*978-1-63965*) 16192 Coastal Hwy., Lewes, DE 19958 USA Tel 160-126-6628
E-mail: steffenmeisel@outlook.com
Web site: coloringcrumbs.com.

Colors Of Me LLC, The, (*978-1-7330624*) 3710 Pelican Lake Dr., Richmond, TX 77406 USA Tel 832-495-3345
E-mail: STEPHANIEOGUCHI82@GMAIL.COM
Web site: www.thecolorsofme.com.

Colossus Bks. *Imprint of* **Amber Bks.**

Colourpoint Bks. (GBR) (*978-1-898392; 978-1-904242; 978-1-906578; 978-1-78073*) *Dist. by* **Casemate Pubs.**

Columba Pr. (IRL) (*978-0-948183; 978-1-85607; 978-1-78218*) *Dist. by* **Dufour.**

†Columbia Univ. Pr., (*978-0-231*) Orders Addr.: 61 W. 62nd St., New York, NY 10023-7015 USA (SAN 212-2480) Toll Free Fax: 800-944-1844; Toll Free: 800-944-8648 x 6240 (orders); Edit Addr.: 61 W. 62nd St., New York, NY 10023 USA (SAN 212-2472) Tel 212-459-0600; Fax: 212-459-3678; 387 Pk. Ave., S., New York, NY 10016
E-mail: cupbooks@columbia.edu
Web site: http://www.columbia.edu/cu/cup
Dist(s): **Cambridge Univ. Pr.**
Casemate Academic
CreateSpace Independent Publishing Platform
De Gruyter, Inc.
Ebsco Publishing
Follett School Solutions
Cengage Gale
ISD
JSTOR
MyiLibrary
Open Road Integrated Media, Inc.
Ingram Academic
Wiley, John & Sons, Inc.
ebrary, Inc.; *CIP.*

Columbine Pr., (*978-0-9651272; 978-0-9768570; 978-0-9965407*) Orders Addr.: P.O. Box 1950, Cripple Creek, CO 80813 USA Tel 719-689-2141; Edit Addr.: 340 Colorado Ave., Cripple Creek, CO 80813 USA Do not confuse with companies with the same name in Bainbridge Island, WA, East Hampton, NY
E-mail: pkmacv@earthlink.net.

Columbine Publishing Group, LLC, (*978-0-615-47989-7; 978-1-945422; 978-1-64914*) P.O. Box 416, Angel Fire, NM 87710 USA Tel 480-639-3700; *Imprints:* Secret Staircase Books, an imprint of Columbine Publishing Group, LLC (MYID_O_SECRET)
Dist(s): **CreateSpace Independent Publishing Platform**
Dummy Record Do Not USE!!!!.

Columbus Pr., (*978-0-9891737; 978-1-63337*) 47 N. 4th St. Suite 204, Zanesville, OH 43701-3416 USA Tel 614-441-9777; *Imprints:* Proving Press (Proving Pr); Boyle & Dalton (Boyle n Dalton)
E-mail: info@columbuspressbooks.com
Web site: www.ColumbusPressBooks.com
Dist(s): **BookBaby.**

Columbus Zoo & Aquarium, The, (*978-0-9841554*) 4850 W. Powell Rd., P.O. Box 400, Powell, OH 43065 USA (SAN 858-589X) Tel 614-645-3400; Fax: 614-645-3465
E-mail: fran.baby@columbuszoo.org
Web site: http://www.columbuszoo.org.

Column Hall Concepts, LLC, (*978-0-9786584*) 217 - 82nd St., Brooklyn, NY 11209 USA Tel 718-836-1072
Web site: http://www.heydadthebook.com
Dist(s): **Follett School Solutions.**

Combel Editorial, S.A. (ESP) (*978-84-7864; 978-84-9825*) *Dist. by* **IPG Chicago.**

Combs, David, (*978-1-7350034*) 625 Hillside Dr., Wilmington, NC 28412 USA Tel 910-262-3809
E-mail: davidcombsauthor@gmail.com.

Combs-Hulme Publishing, (*978-0-9769854*) 1720 Eldridge Ave. W., Saint Paul, MN 55113 USA Tel 651-631-2173 Do not confuse with Combs Publishing in Winston-Salem, NC
E-mail: lvhulme@aol.com.

Come Alive with Candace, (*978-1-7365314*) 47298 908th Rd, Naper, NE 68755 USA Tel 605-633-1738
E-mail: comealivewithcandace@gmail.com
Web site: comealivewithcandace.com.

Come & Get It Publishing, (*978-0-9653042; 978-0-9753883; 978-0-692-64839-1*) Orders Addr.: P.O. Box 1562, Madison, VA 22727 USA Tel 540-829-0516 Toll Free: 800-825-9008; Edit Addr.: 214 E. Spencer St., No. 1, Culpeper, VA 22701 USA
E-mail: comeandgetproducts@gmail.com
Dist(s): **Publishers Group West (PGW).**

Come As A Child, (*978-1-7338134*) 135 Joinda, Vass, NC 28394 USA Tel 910-691-4001
E-mail: debigatlyn@gmail.com.

Come Sing With Us, (*978-1-7360205*) 1268 Blue Parrot Ct, Gilroy, CA 95020 USA Tel 408-714-8416
E-mail: mayuri.amarnath@gmail.com.

Comfort Tales, LLC, (*978-0-9741586*) Orders Addr.: 47 Watsons Way, Medford, NJ 08055 USA (SAN 255-464X) Tel 856-988-0884; Fax: 856-988-8499
E-mail: comforttales@aol.com.

Comic Library International, (*978-1-929515*) 2049 Alfred St., Pittsburgh, PA 15212-1426 USA; *Imprints:* Solovisions (Solovisions)
E-mail: gbstudios@comcast.net
Web site: http://www.geocities.com/SoHo/Cafe/9669/clipage.html
Dist(s): **Diamond Comic Distributors, Inc.**

ComicMix, (*978-1-939888; 978-1-958482*) 71 Hauxhurst Ave., Weehawken, NJ 07086 USA Tel 551-265-9059
E-mail: glenn@comicmix.com
Web site: http://www.comicmix.com
Dist(s): **Diamond Comic Distributors, Inc.**

Comics Lit *Imprint of* **NBM Publishing Co.**

Comics Workshop, (*978-0-9824153; 978-1-7343869*) 93 Bennett Rd., Henniker, NH 03242 USA
Web site: http://www.marekbennett.com.

ComicsOne Corp./Dr. Masters, (*978-1-58899*) P.O. Box 14232, Fremont, CA 94539-1532 USA
Dist(s): **Diamond Comic Distributors, Inc.**
Diamond Bk. Distributors
L P C Group.

ComiXstand *Imprint of* **Zoolook**

Command Performance Language Institute, (*978-0-929724*) 25 Hopkins Ct., Berkeley, CA 94706 USA (SAN 250-1694) Tel 510-524-1191; Fax: 510-527-9880
E-mail: consee@aol.com
Web site: http://www.hometown.aol.com/commandperform1/myhomepage/business.html
Dist(s): **Alta English Publishers**
Applause Learning Resources
Athelstan Pubns.
Betty Segal, Inc.
BookLink
Calliope Bks.
Carlex
Continental Bk. Co., Inc.
Delta Systems Company, Inc.
Educational Showcase
Edumate-Educational Materials, Inc.
European Bk. Co., Inc.
Follett School Solutions
Gessler Publishing Co., Inc.
International Bk. Ctr., Inc.
Midwest European Pubns.
Miller Educational Materials
Multi-Cultural Bks. & Videos, Inc.
Sky Oaks Productions, Inc.
SpeakWare
Teacher's Discovery
Tempo Bookstore
2Learn-English
World of Reading, Ltd.

Command Publishing, LLC, (*978-0-9778356*) 43311 Joy Rd. Suite 201, Canton, MI 48187-2075 USA (SAN 850-2706).

Commercial Communications Incorporated *See* **Great Lakes Design**

Commission on Culture and Tourism, (*978-0-9759389*) 1 Constitution Plz., Hartford, CT 06103-1803 USA
E-mail: kazkozlowski@snet.net.

Committed 2 Win, LLC, (*978-0-578-22353-7*) P.O. Box 22087, Waco, TX 76702 USA Tel 888-926-6648
E-mail: darryl@committed2win.com
Web site: http://darryl.mykajabi.com/.

Committee for Children, (*978-0-9741388*) 568 First Ave. S., Suite 600, Seattle, WA 98104-2804 USA Toll Free: 800-634-4449
Web site: http://www.cfchildren.org.

Common Courtesy, (*978-0-9746148*) 709 Uwharrie St., Asheboro, NC 27203 USA Tel 336-629-5274
E-mail: jjdortch@earthlink.net.

Common Deer Pr. (CAN) (*978-0-9950729; 978-1-988761*) *Dist. by* **Natl Bk Netwk.**

Commonwealth Books, LLC *See* **Commonwealth Books of Virginia, LLC**

Commonwealth Books of Virginia, LLC, (*978-0-9825922; 978-0-9854863; 978-0-9904018; 978-0-9909592; 978-0-9961368; 978-1-943642*) 30 Village Ct., Boothbay Harbor, ME 04538 USA Tel 703-307-7715; 30 Village Ct., Boothbay Harbor, ME 04538 Tel 703-307-7715
E-mail: jct@commonwealthbooks.org; info@commonwealthbooks.org
Web site: http://www.commonwealthbooks.org; http://www.commonwealthbooks.org; www.thomasjeffersonenlightenment.org; www.bayardtberndt.org; www.jamesthompsonauthor.org
Dist(s): **MyiLibrary**
Small Pr. United
ebrary, Inc.

Commonwealth Bks.,Black Widow,
Dist(s): **National Bk. Network.**

Commonwealth Editions *Imprint of* **Applewood Bks.**

Communicate! *See* **Rethinking Schls., Ltd.**

Communication Service Corporation *See* **Gryphon Hse., Inc.**

Community Bks. (CAN) (*978-0-9694180; 978-0-9698407; 978-1-896496*) *Dist. by* **Col U Pr.**

Community Voice Media, LLC, (*978-0-9776613; 978-0-9885741*) P.O. Box 564, Round Hill, VA 20142-5640 USA Tel 540-751-2214; Fax: 540-751-2215
E-mail: bobbicarducci@communityvoicemedia.com
Web site: http://www.communityvoicemedia.com.

Community Works!, (*978-0-9742213*) 13313 Country Way Cir., Fredericksburg, VA 22404 USA
E-mail: arayu1@comcast.net; carol@carolynnfitzpatrick.com
Web site: http://www.carolynnfitzpatrick.com
Dist(s): **New Leaf Distributing Co., Inc.**

Companhia das Letras (BRA) (*978-85-7164; 978-85-85095; 978-85-85466; 978-85-359; 978-65-5921*) *Dist. by* **Distribks Inc.**

Companhia Melhoramentos de Sao Paulo Industrias de Papel (BRA) (*978-85-06*) *Dist. by* **Lectorum Pubns.**

Companion Pr., (*978-1-879651; 978-1-61722*) Div. of Ctr. for Loss & Life Transition, 3735 Broken Bow Rd., Fort Collins, CO 80526 USA Tel 970-226-6050; Fax: 970-226-6051; Toll Free Fax: 800-922-6051 (orders only) Do not confuse with companies with the same name in Santa Barbara, CA, Aliso Viejo, CA
E-mail: wolfelt@centerforloss.com
Web site: http://www.centerforloss.com
Dist(s): **Ebsco Publishing**
Independent Pubs. Group
MyiLibrary
ebrary, Inc.

CompanionHouse Bks. *Imprint of* **Fox Chapel Publishing Co., Inc.**

Company's Coming Publishing, Ltd. (CAN) (*978-0-9690695; 978-0-9693322; 978-1-895455; 978-1-896891; 978-1-897069; 978-1-897477; 978-1-927126; 978-1-77207*) *Dist. by* **Lone Pine.**

Compass *Imprint of* **Raphel Marketing, Inc.**

Compass Books *See* **Lake Street Pubs.**

Compass Flower Pr. *Imprint of* **AKA:yoLa**

Compass Point Bks. *Imprint of* **Capstone**

Compass Pr., (*978-0-9847863; 978-0-9851804; 978-1-939469*) 28437 Hwy 395, Lakeview, OR 97630 USA Tel 541-947-4080 Do not confuse with Compass Press in Eugene, OR
Web site: http://cpdesignandcompasspress.blogspot.com
Dist(s): **CreateSpace Independent Publishing Platform**
Dummy Record Do Not USE!!!!.

Compass Productions Inc., (*978-1-63264*) 9316 Lakeview Ave SW Ste B-1, Lakewood, WA 98499 USA Tel 206-430-6021; *Imprints:* Bookbarn Publishing (MYID_Z_BKBARN)
E-mail: mark@cascade-publishing.com
Dist(s): **Atlas Bks.**
Baker & Taylor Publisher Services (BTPS).

Compassio Veraque *See* **Compassio Veraque LLC**

Compassio Veraque LLC, (*978-1-7352463; 979-8-9866773*) 4710 Shady Ct., Evansville, IN 47712 USA Tel 812-760-0315
E-mail: toddschimmell@gmail.com.

Compassion Outreach Ministry *See* **Stott, Darrel Ministry**

Compassion Pets Publishing, (*978-0-615-13428-4; 978-0-615-30968-2*) 34672 Hardtack Ln., Shingletown, CA 96088 USA (SAN 858-5954) Tel 530-474-1038
E-mail: compassionpet.pub@frontiernet.net
Web site: http://www.compassionpets.com.

Compendium, Inc., Publishing & Communications, (*978-0-9640178; 978-1-888387; 978-1-932319; 978-1-935414; 978-1-938298; 978-1-943200; 978-1-946873; 978-1-970147; 978-1-957891*) Orders Addr.: P.O. Box 5308, Lynnwood, WA 98046-5308 USA (SAN 253-7109) Tel 425-673-2238; Fax: 425-673-6949; Toll Free: 800-914-3327; 2815 E.lake Ave E. Suite 200, Seattle, WA 98102 (SAN 992-4507); Edit Addr.: 600 N. 36th St. Ste. 400, Seattle, WA 98103-8699 USA
E-mail: kobi@compendiuminc.com; connie@compendiuminc.com; carolanne@compendiuminc.com
Web site: http://www.compendiuminc.com; http://www.live-inspired.com
Dist(s): **APG Sales & Distribution Services.**

Competitor Creeds *See* **Moon Chaser Publishing**

Complete in Christ Ministries, Inc., (*978-0-9795007*) P.O. Box 42027, Baton Rouge, LA 70835 USA
E-mail: completeinchrist@cox.net
Web site: http://www.cicmblog.com.

Comprecom, (*978-0-9772809*) 411 Hess Ave., Golden, CO 80401 USA.

Comprehensive Health Education Foundation, (*978-0-935529; 978-1-57021*) 159 S. Jackson St. Ste. 510, Seattle, WA 98104-4416 USA (SAN 696-3668) Toll Free: 800-323-2433
E-mail: chefstaff@chef.org
Web site: http://www.chef.org/.

Compsych Systems, Inc., Pubns. Div., (*978-0-929948*) Div. of Compsych Systems, Inc., P.O. Box 1568, Pacific Palisades, CA 90272 USA (SAN 250-8281) Tel 310-454-6426 (phone/fax)
Web site: http://www.jeanettegriver.com
Dist(s): **Follett School Solutions.**

Compton, Tyler, (*978-0-9893845*) 1627 N. Laurel Ave. No. 5, Los Angeles, CA 90046 USA Tel 323-350-2120
E-mail: ts_compton@yahoo.com.

Computer Age Education *See* **Learning Net, The**

Computer Athlete Media, (*978-0-9820447*) P.O. Box 687, Princeton Junction, NJ 08550 USA
E-mail: support@computerathlete.net
Web site: http://www.computerathlete.net.

Computer Classics (R), (*978-0-9721216; 978-0-9748870; 978-0-9836019; 978-0-9899265*) 5036 Suter Dr., Nashville, TN 37211-5155 USA
E-mail: computerclassics@mindspring.com
Web site: http://www.computer-classics.com.

ComQwest, LLC, (*978-0-9753454*) 1350 E. Flamingo Rd., Suite No. 265, Las Vegas, NV 89119 USA
Web site: http://www.comqwest.com.

Comstock Publishing Assocs. *Imprint of* **Cornell Univ. Pr.**

ComteQ Publishing, (*978-0-9674074; 978-0-9766889; 978-0-9793771; 978-1-935232; 978-1-941501*) Div. of ComteQ Communications, LLC, Orders Addr.: 7806 Marshall Ave., Margate, NJ 08402 USA Tel 609-487-9000
E-mail: publisher@comteqpublishing.com
Web site: http://www.comteqpublishing.com
Dist(s): **BookBaby.**

Comunicadora Koine, Inc., (*978-0-9794682; 978-0-9834966*) Orders Addr.: P.O. Box RR3 Box 3801, San Juan, PR 00926 USA Tel 787-642-2053; Fax: 787-753-7077; Edit Addr.: 1118 Calle Padres Capuchinos, Rio Piedras, PR 00925 USA
E-mail: comunicadorakoine@gmail.com
Web site: http://www.comunicadorakoine.com.

Comyn Publishing, (*978-1-7342301*) 15417 Linden Ave N, Shoreline, WA 98133 USA Tel 206-579-3374
E-mail: barb@live.com.

Conari Press *Imprint of* **Mango Media**

ConArtistE Pubng., (*978-0-9755386*) 6084 Churn Creek Rd., Redding, CA 96002 USA Tel 530-209-4338
E-mail: conartiste@msn.com
Web site: www.conartiste.com.

Concentric Publishing Co., (*978-1-7335950*) 4518 Rocky River Rd, Charlotte, NC 28215 USA Tel 704-701-4191
E-mail: jglad7@me.com.

Concepcion, Jorge, (*978-0-9761779*) 9125 SW 56th Ter., Miami, FL 33173-1605 USA
E-mail: jconcepcion1@msn.com.

Concept Media Group, LLC, The, (*978-0-9864191*) 1408 N. Riverfront Blvd., No. 134, Dallas, TX 75207 USA Tel 214-854-2150
E-mail: sherilyn@theconceptmediagroup.com
Web site: www.TheConceptMediaGroup.com.

Concepts *See* **Developmental Vision Concepts**

Concepts 'N' Publishing, (*978-1-879940*) Orders Addr.: P.O. Box 10413, College Station, TX 77842 USA
Web site: http://www.ethaemm.homestead.com.

oncepts Redefined, *(978-0-692-83922-5; 978-0-692-83939-3; 978-0-9986630; 978-1-7330938; 979-8-9886350)* 11739 Mango cross ct., Seffner, FL 33584 USA Tel 813-598-9481
E-mail: creynolds70@verizon.net; creynolds70@verizon.net; creynolds70@verizon.net
Web site: www.jaycethebee.com
Dist(s): **CreateSpace Independent Publishing Platform.**

oncerned Christians, *(978-0-9768352)* P.O. Box 18, Mesa, AZ 85211 USA Tel 480-833-2537; Fax: 480-833-4116
E-mail: jim@concernedchristians.org
Web site: http://www.concernedchristians.org.

oncerned Communications, *(978-0-936785; 978-1-58938)* Orders Addr.: P.O. Box 1000, Siloam Springs, AR 72761-1000 USA (SAN 699-8623) Tel 501-594-9000; Fax: 501-549-4002; Toll Free: 800-447-4332; Edit Addr.: 200 S Washington St, Siloam Springs, AR 72761 USA (SAN 699-8631)
E-mail: lustwrt@areasonfor.com
Web site: http://www.areasonfor.com
Dist(s): **Project Patch.**

Conciliar Press *See* **Ancient Faith Publishing**

Concinnity Initiatives, *(978-0-9842146; 978-0-615-49009-0; 978-0-615-53946-1)* 2733 Meade St., Denver, CO 80211-4076 USA
E-mail: kevin.mccaffrey@firstpersonpublishing.com; jeffrey.fugate@navy.mil
Web site: http://www.firstpersonpublishing.com.

Concord Theatricals, *(978-0-573)* 235 Pk. Ave. S., 5th Fl., New York, NY 10003 USA; *Imprints:* French, Samuel , Inc. (SamFrnchUSA); French, Samuel , Ltd. (SamFrnchUK)
Web site: www.concord.com; www.concordtheatricals.com.

Concordia Publishing Hse., *(978-0-570; 978-0-7586)* Subs. of Lutheran Church Missouri Synod, 3558 S. Jefferson Ave., Saint Louis, MO 63118-3968 USA (SAN 202-1781) Tel 314-268-1000; Fax: 314-268-1360; Toll Free Fax: 800-490-9889 (orders only); Toll Free: 800-325-3040 (orders only); 800-325-0191
E-mail: cphorder@cph.org
Web site: http://www.cph.org.

Concordis Publishing, *(978-0-578-41781-3; 978-0-578-86307-8; 978-0-578-86794-6; 978-0-578-87263-6; 978-0-578-88362-5; 978-0-578-90021-6; 978-0-578-96411-9; 978-0-578-96860-5; 978-0-578-31171-5; 978-0-578-31172-2; 979-8-218-17843-7; 979-8-218-17845-1; 979-8-218-21931-4) 28160 McBean Pkwy. Unit 25201, VALENCIA, CA 91354 USA Tel 310-650-0213*
E-mail: concordispublishing@gmail.com
Dist(s): **Ingram Content Group.**

Concourse Pr., *(978-0-911323)* Subs. of East-West Fine Arts Corp., Orders Addr.: 14 Ridgeview Rd., Newtown Sq, PA 19073-3002 USA (SAN 269-249X); Edit Addr.: P.O. Box 8265, Philadelphia, PA 19101 USA
E-mail: site.concoursepress@gmail.com
Web site: http://www.ConcoursePress.com
Dist(s): **Brodart Co.**

Concrete Jungle Pr., *(978-0-9749048; 978-1-945610)* 47-04 168th St., Flushing, NY 11358 USA
E-mail: dw@dwaynedworsky.com
Web site: http://www.dwaynedworsky.com; www.alphacentauriandbeyond.com.

Condor Designs, *(978-0-692-80859-7; 978-0-692-80933-4)* P.O. Box 155, FISH CAMP, CA 93623 USA Tel 559-341-8854
E-mail: mscondor@gmail.com; mscondor@gmail.com.

Condor Publishing, Inc., *(978-1-931079)* Orders Addr.: P.O. Box 39, Lincoln, MI 48742-0039 USA Tel 517-736-7426; Fax: 517-724-7054; Edit Addr.: 125 N. Barlow, Lincoln, MI 48742-0039 USA Do not confuse with companies with same or similar names in Ashland, MA, Thousand Oaks, CA
E-mail: condorpub@juno.com.

Conerly, Lawrence, *(978-0-9765669)* 85 Mt. Canaan Rd., Tylertown, MS 39667 USA
E-mail: augsept@bellsouth.net.

Conexion Educativa, *(978-0-9702021)* 900 Alameda St., Villa Granada, San Juan, PR 00923 USA Tel 787-766-4448; Fax: 787-250-8709
E-mail: conexion@coqui.net
Web site: http://home.coqui.net/conexion.

Conflict Games, LLC, *(978-0-9824507; 978-1-7331144)* Orders Addr.: 15 Green Hill Ct., Nanuet, NY 10954 USA Tel 845-689-9014
E-mail: mscott@conflictroleplaying.com
Web site: http://www.conflictbooks.com/.

Cong Bais Tziporah, *(978-0-9728849; 978-0-9767166; 978-1-934098)* 3 Harrison Ave., Spring Valley, NY 10977 USA.

Congregation Agudat Achim, *(978-0-9770172)* 2117 Union St., Schenectady, NY 12309 USA
Web site: http://www.divinekosher.com.

Congregation Kehilas Yaakov (CKY), *(978-0-9770352; 978-0-9847019)* 2 Omni Ct., Lakewood, NJ 08701 USA Tel 732-942-8374.

Congress At Your Fingertips, *(978-1-879617; 978-0-9969346; 978-0-9994368; 978-1-7340022; 979-8-9854054)* Div. of Capitol Advantage, LLC, Orders Addr.: P.O. Box 309, Newington, VA 22122 USA Tel 703-550-9500; Fax: 703-550-0406; Toll Free: 877-827-3321
Web site: http://congressatyourfingertips.com.

Congressional Publishing, Inc., *(978-0-9762916)* P.O. Box 1318, Leesburg, VA 20177 USA Tel 703-777-6737; Fax: 703-777-6272
E-mail: congressionalpub@verizon.net
Web site: http://www.congressionalpublishing.com.

Coniston Designs (AUS) *(978-0-86435) Dist. by* **IPG Chicago.**

Conley, Connie, *(978-0-9800898)* 4555 SW Willow St., Seattle, WA 98136 USA (SAN 855-1731)
E-mail: puppyluck@comcast.net.

Connealy, Joel, *(978-0-692-16637-6)* 2015 W 81st Terr., Leawood, KS 66206-1204 USA Tel 913-515-1536
E-mail: joel5knealy@gmail.com
Dist(s): **CreateSpace Independent Publishing Platform.**

Connect With Your Kid Bks., *(978-0-9746094)* 106 Central Park Sq., No.150, Los Alamos, NV 87544 USA Toll Free: 888-388-5437
E-mail: DrSillyScience@comcast.net
Web site: http://www.DrSillyScience.com.

Connected 2 The Father Publishing *See* **Urban Advocacy**

Connecticut Pr., The, *(978-0-9825468; 978-0-9977907; 979-8-218-00089-9; 979-8-218-06335-1)* 36 Wildlife Ct., Cheshire, CT 06410 USA Tel 203-257-6020
E-mail: pjmalia@connecticutpress.com; celestemalia@connecticutpress.com
Web site: http://www.connecticutpress.com
Dist(s): **Ingram Bk. Co.**
Ingram Content Group.

Connection, *(978-0-9743687)* 601 Daniel Ct., Nashville, TN 37221-6512 USA.

Connelly Pr., The, *(978-0-9797415; 978-1-7341309)* 243 Abrahams Ln., Villanova, PA 19085 USA Tel 610-316-1997
Dist(s): **eBookit.com.**

Connexions Unlimited, *(978-1-929785)* 1021 Silver Lake Blvd., Frankfort, KY 40601 USA Tel 502-695-5181.

Connor Lonning, Kealy, *(978-1-7359945)* 45 Boyden Pkwy., Maplewood, NJ 07040 USA Tel 563-380-8834
E-mail: kealyconnor0716@gmail.com
Web site: www.kealyconnorlonning.com.

Connors, E. W. Publishing Co., *(978-0-9635587)* P.O. Box 691, Buffalo, NY 14205-0691 USA Tel 716-851-1343.

Conquistador Pubns., *(978-0-9978732)* 36 Alcira Ct., St. Augustine, FL 32086 USA Tel 904-834-4160
E-mail: kathleen.caulfield@yahoo.com.

Conscience Studio, *(978-0-9828492; 978-1-7356337)* 90 W. Univ. St., Alfred, NY 14802-1134 USA (SAN 859-9203) Tel 607-587-9111
E-mail: ConscienceStudio@gmail.com
Web site: http://www.consciencestudio.com.

Conscious Culture Publishing, *(978-1-7322051; 978-1-7364666; 979-8-9888245)* 450 Leland Ave., San Francisco, CA 94134 USA Tel 415-902-0557
E-mail: marion@artnomad.com
Web site: https://www.consciousculturepublishing.com/.

Conscious Living Pubns., *(978-1-890580)*
E-mail: info@leonardjacobson.com
Dist(s): **New Leaf Distributing Co., Inc.**

Conscious Pubs., *(978-1-7338234)* 3233 Sharp Rd., Glenwood, MD 21738 USA Tel 760-331-4029
E-mail: tsarchitecture@msn.com.

Consciousness-Based Education Association, *(978-0-9727877)* 1100 Univ. Manor Dr., B-24, Fairfield, IA 52556 USA Tel 641-472-1663; Fax: 641-472-3116; Toll Free: 888-472-1677
E-mail: info@cbeprograms.org
Web site: http://www.cbeprograms.org.

Consejo Estatal Electoral (MEX) *(978-970-58) Dist. by* **Santillana.**

Consilient Pubns., *(978-0-9746242)* 8176 S. Centaur Dr., Evergreen, CO 80439 USA Tel 303-679-1538
E-mail: stephanie@cost-benefit-jr.com
Web site: http://www.cost-benefit-jr.com.

Consortium Bk. Sales & Distribution, Div. of Ingram Content Group, Orders Addr.: 1094 Flex Dr., Jackson, TN 38301-5070 USA; Edit Addr.: 34 13th Ave NE, Suite 100, Minneapolis, MN 55413-1007 USA (SAN 200-6049) Toll Free: 800-283-3572 (orders)
E-mail: info@cbsd.com
Web site: http://www.cbsd.com/
Dist(s): **Follett School Solutions.**

Consortium Publishing Co., *(978-0-9644681; 978-0-9707173; 978-0-9748830; 978-1-7320567)* Div. of Creative Ideas, Inc., Orders Addr.: P.O. Box 998, Jacksonville, IL 62651 USA; Edit Addr.: P.O. Box 1535, Jacksonville, IL 62651-1535 USA Tel 217-243-7628 (phone/fax); Toll Free: 800-419-8698; 888-456-7235; 4 Sunnydale Ave., Jacksonville, IL 62650
E-mail: consortm@aol.com
Web site: http://www.creativeideas.com.

Consortium, The *See* **Consortium Publishing Co.**

Constellate Children's Books (VGB) *Dist. by* **AmplifyPubGrp.**

Constitutional Rights Foundation *Imprint of* **Constitutional Rights Foundation**

Constitutional Rights Foundation, *(978-1-886253)* 601 S. Kingsley Dr., Los Angeles, CA 90005 USA (SAN 225-6401) Tel 213-487-5590; Fax: 213-386-0459; Toll Free: 800-488-4273; *Imprints:* Constitutional Rights Foundation (MYID_C_CONSTIT) Do not confuse with Constitutional Rights Foundation Chicago in Chicago, IL
E-mail: crf@crf.usa
Web site: http://www.crf-usa.org.

Constructing Modern Knowledge Pr., *(978-0-9891511; 978-0-9975543; 978-0-9994776; 978-1-955604)* 21825 Barbara St., Torrance, CA 90503 USA Tel 310-874-8236
E-mail: gary@stager.org; sylvia@cmkpress.com
Web site: cmkpress.com.

Consultant's Unlimited *See* **Schwarz Pauper Pr.**

Consumer Pr., The, *(978-0-9717119)* 6 Berkley Rd., Glenville, NY 12302 USA (SAN 254-5446)
E-mail: richesq@mindspring.com
Web site: http://www.theconsumerpress.com.

†Consumer Reports Bks., *(978-0-89043)* Div. of Consumers Union of U. S., Inc., 101 Truman Ave., Yonkers, NY 10703 USA (SAN 224-1048) Tel 914-378-2000; Fax: 914-378-2925; Toll Free: 800-500-9760 (book dept.)
Web site: http://www.consumerreports.org/; *CIP.*

Consumers Union of U. S., Inc., *(978-0-89043; 978-0-9755388; 978-1-933524)* Orders Addr.: 540 Barnum Ave., Bridgeport, CT 06608 USA (SAN 661-9800); Edit Addr.: 101 Truman Ave., Yonkers, NY 10703 USA (SAN 269-3518) Tel 914-378-2000; Fax: 914-378-2925
Web site: http://ConsumersReports.org
Dist(s): **Ingram Publisher Services**
Macmillan.

Contemplation Corner Pr., *(978-0-9707979; 978-0-9758748)* 1229 Randy Rd., Ashland City, TN 37015 USA Tel 615-746-8220; Fax: 615-746-3697
E-mail: ccpress1@bellsouth.net
Web site: http://www.contemplationcornerpress.com.

Contemporary Fiction *Imprint of* **Noel, Jaren**

Continental Bk. Co., Inc., *(978-0-9626800)* Eastern Div., 80-00 Cooper Ave., Bldg. No. 29, Glendale, NY 11385 USA (SAN 169-5436) Tel 718-326-0560; Fax: 718-326-4276; Toll Free: 800-364-0350; Western Div., 625 E. 70th Ave., No. 5, Denver, CO 80229 (SAN 630-2882) Tel 303-289-1761; Fax: 303-289-1764
E-mail: hola@continentalbook.com; esl@continentalbook.com; bonjour@continentalbook.com; tag@continentalbook.com
Web site: http://www.continentalbook.com
Dist(s): **Follett School Solutions.**

Continental Enterprises Group, Inc. (CEG), Orders Addr.: 108 Red Row St., Easley, SC 29640-2820 USA (SAN 631-0915)
E-mail: ContactUs@centerprisesgrp.com.

Continental Pr., Inc., *(978-0-8454; 978-1-5240)* Orders Addr.: 520 E. Bainbridge St., Elizabethtown, PA 17022 USA (SAN 202-182X) Tel 717-367-1836; Fax: 717-367-5660; Toll Free: 800-233-0759; *Imprints:* Seedling Publications (Seedlg Pubns)
E-mail: educationsales@continentalpress.com
Web site: http://www.continentalpress.com.

Continental Sales, Inc.,; *Imprints:* New in Chess (New Chess); New In Chess,Csi (NEW IN CHESS,C)
Dist(s): **National Bk. Network.**

Continental Shelf Publishing, *(978-0-9822583; 978-0-9831483)* 4602 Sussex Pl., Savannah, GA 31405 USA Tel 912-355-7054 (phone/fax)
E-mail: editor@CSPbooks.com; sales@CSPbooks.com
Web site: http://www.CSPBooks.com
Dist(s): **Follett School Solutions.**

Continuum *Imprint of* **Bloomsbury Academic & Professional**

Contmedia Inc,

Contreras, Chantal, *(978-1-7343441)* 20836 MARGARET ST, CARSON, CA 90745 USA Tel 310-694-6487
E-mail: MRS.CHANTALCONTRERAS@GMAIL.COM.

Conundrum Pr. (CAN) *(978-0-9685161; 978-0-9680364; 978-0-9689496; 978-1-894994; 978-1-77262) Dist. by* **Consort Bk Sales.**

Convergent Bks. *Imprint of* **Crown Publishing Group, The**

CONVERPAGE, *(978-0-9728155; 978-0-9815720; 978-0-9820733; 978-0-9825854; 978-0-9835784; 978-0-9851721; 978-0-9858282; 978-0-615-84393-3; 978-0-9910923)* 23 Acorn St., Scituate, MA 02066-3324 USA
E-mail: pmccallum@comcast.net
Web site: www.converpage.com.

Conversations for Action and Listening Pubn., *(978-0-692-43550-2; 978-0-9977110)* 95 Westminster Dr., Oakland , CA 94618 USA Tel 5102203334
Dist(s): **CreateSpace Independent Publishing Platform.**

Conviction 2 Change, *(978-0-692-72172-8; 978-0-692-10823-9; 978-0-692-14012-3; 978-1-7327121)* P.O. Box 990, New York, NY 10037 USA Tel 917-607-0570
Web site: www.conviction2change.com
Dist(s): **CreateSpace Independent Publishing Platform.**

Conway, Kathleen R., *(978-0-9897763; 978-0-9973737)* 2 Nauset Rd., Sagamore Beach, MA 02562 USA Tel 508-415-1295
E-mail: capecodscribe@yahoo.com
Web site: http://www.capecodscribe.com; https://wickedwhalepublishing.wordpress.com
Dist(s): **BookBaby**
Cape Cod Scribe.

Cook, Cheryl *See* **Heavenly C. Publishing**

Cook Communication, *(978-0-9726996)* Orders Addr.: 6086 Dunes Dr., Sanford, NC 27332 USA Tel 312-859-8090; 919-498-6421; Fax: 866-652-8493
E-mail: cookcomm@gte.net; cookcomm@ameritech.net
Web site: http://www.author-me.com; http://www.reservebooks.com.

Cook, David, *(978-0-9741629)* P.O. Box 657, Albemarle, NC 28001 USA Do not confuse with companies with the same name in Chapel Hill, NC, Boerne, TX
E-mail: info@dac-and.com
Web site: http://www.dac-and.com.

Cook, David C., *(978-0-7814; 978-0-88207; 978-0-89191; 978-0-89693; 978-0-912692; 978-1-55513; 978-1-56476; 978-1-4347)* 4050 Lee Vance View, Colorado Springs, CO 80918 USA (SAN 206-0981) Tel 719-536-0100; Fax: 719-536-3244; Toll Free: 800-708-5550; 800-323-7543 (Customer Service)
E-mail: wendi.lord@davidccook.com
Web site: http://www.davidccook.com
Dist(s): **Follett School Solutions.**

Cook, David C. Publishing Company *See* **Cook, David C.**

Cook, Jahde, *(978-0-9991510)* 973 E. Well Springs Rd., Midvale, UT 84047 USA Tel 801-628-9226
E-mail: jahdeofelia@gmail.com
Web site: www.jahdethewriter.com.

Cook, Ken Co., *(978-0-9652491)* 2855 S Calhoun Rd, New Berlin, WI 53151 USA Tel 414-466-6060; Fax: 414-466-0840
E-mail: nics@kencook.com
Web site: http://www.kencook.com.

Cookbook Resources, LLC, *(978-0-9677932; 978-1-931294; 978-1-59769)* 541 Doubletree Dr., Highland Village, TX 75077 USA (SAN 253-5262) Tel 972-317-0245; Fax: 972-317-6404; Toll Free: 866-229-2665
E-mail: lauren@cookbookresources.com
Web site: http://www.cookbookresourses.com
Dist(s): **Bk. Marketing Plus.**

Cookie Bear Pr., Inc., *(978-0-9701155)* Orders Addr.: P.O. Box 5074, Buffalo Grove, IL 60089 USA (SAN 253-6579) Tel 847-955-0001; 847-478-9202; Fax: 847-955-0002; Edit Addr.: 205 Thompson Blvd., Buffalo Grove, IL 60089 USA
E-mail: info@cookiebearpress.com
Web site: http://www.cookiebearpress.com
Dist(s): **Distributors, The.**

Cookie Jar, *(978-1-933799; 978-1-60095)* Cookie Jar Entertainment, Inc., P.O. Box 35665, Greensboro, NC 27425 USA Fax: 336-808-3249; Toll Free: 800-321-0903; *Imprints:* Doodlebops (Doodiebops)
Web site: http://www.cinar.com/EN/
Dist(s): **Carson-Dellosa Publishing, LLC.**

Cookie O'Gorman, *(978-0-9978174; 978-1-960547)* 105 Carver Ct., Warner Robins, GA 31088 USA Tel 478-218-0166
E-mail: aireeahna@cox.net.

Cool Kids Create, *(978-0-9797297)* 48 Beach 217 St., Breezy Point, NY 11697 USA
Web site: http://www.coolkidscreate.com
Dist(s): **BCH Fulfillment & Distribution.**

Cool, Kim @ Historic Venice Pr., *(978-0-9721655)* 312 Shore Rd., Venice, FL 34285 USA
Web site: http://www.historicvenicepress.com
Dist(s): **American Wholesale Bk. Co.**
Bk. Warehouse
Southern Bk. Service.

Cool Springs Pr. *Imprint of* **Quarto Publishing Group USA**

Cool Things Pr., *(978-0-615-20795-7; 978-0-615-20796-4; 978-0-615-78176-1; 978-0-692-45762-7)* P.O. Box 3852, Concord, NH 03302-3952 USA Tel 6037157852
Dist(s): **CreateSpace Independent Publishing Platform**
Lulu Pr., Inc.

Coolbular Inc, *(978-0-578-15459-6; 978-0-9980946)* PO Box 1764, Evergreen, CO 80439 USA
E-mail: author.adir.rondack@gmail.com
Web site: http://to-kill-a-predator.com/.

Coolidge Corner Pr., *(978-1-7338376)* 28 Oak Sq. Ave., Boston, MA 02135 USA Tel 857-264-0674
E-mail: editor@coolidge-corner-press.com.

Coolmath.com, Inc., *(978-0-9791628)* P.O. Box 4386, Costa Mesa, CA 92628-4386 USA
Web site: http://Coolmath.com.

Cools, Sarah A, *(978-1-7365417)* 951 W Powell Blvd, Gresham, OR 97030 USA Tel 503-828-1136
E-mail: thelightchaserstudio@gmail.com.

CoolSpeak Publishing Co., *(978-0-615-75939-5; 978-0-615-76596-9; 978-0-615-83196-1; 978-0-615-96867-4; 978-0-692-23542-3; 978-0-692-42448-3; 978-0-692-48950-5; 978-0-692-52130-4; 978-0-692-52792-4; 978-0-692-72682-2; 978-0-692-76203-5; 978-0-692-77684-1; 978-0-692-87782-1; 978-0-692-05795-7; 978-0-692-18688-6; 978-0-578-52470-2; 978-0-578-61637-7; 978-0-578-73290-9; 978-0-578-36930-3; 979-8-218-17620-4) 148 Stone Hill Dr., Pottstown, PA 19464 USA Tel 888-300-1880; Fax: 888-300-1880*
E-mail: info@coolspeak.net
Dist(s): **CreateSpace Independent Publishing Platform.**

Coon, Kathy, *(978-0-9741300)* P.O. Box 14267, Baton Rouge, LA 70898 USA
Web site: http://www.dogintelligencetest.com.

Cooper, Gene, *(978-0-615-85312-3)* 6 Peter Cooper Rd. Apt. 3C, New York, NY 10010 USA Tel 212-228-5083
E-mail: cooper.gene82@gmail.com.

Cooper Publishing, *(978-1-59655)* Orders Addr.: P.O. Box 1974, Englewood, FL 34295 USA Tel 941-587-0396
E-mail: cooper.publishing@yahoo.com.

Cooper, Robbi, *(978-0-9749643)* 9 Scott Crescent, Austin, TX 78703 USA
Web site: http://www.everythingfromthegarden.com.

Cooper Square Publishing Llc,
Dist(s): **National Bk. Network**
Rowman & Littlefield Publishers, Inc.

Cooperative Kids, *(978-0-9821121)* P.O. Box 432, Enfield, CT 06083-0432 USA (SAN 857-2917) Tel 860-265-2272
E-mail: info@cooperativekids.com
Web site: http://www.cooperativekids.com.

Cooperfly Books *See* **Cooperfly Creative Arts, Inc.**

Cooperfly Creative Arts, Inc., *(978-0-9669504; 978-0-9970476)* 3184 Plainfield NE PMB 248, Grand Rapids, MI 49525 USA Tel 616-364-5870
E-mail: kevin@tomatocollection.com
Web site: http://www.tomatocollection.com
Dist(s): **Indig, Stanley M. Specialty Pubn.**

Cooper's Pack, *(978-0-9794882)* Div. of Cooper's Pack Publishing, Orders Addr.: 1900 W. Nickerson St., Suite 116-130, Seattle, WA 98119 USA (SAN 853-5825) Tel 206-235-1886 Toll Free: 877-278-3278
E-mail: brandon@cooperspack.com
Web site: http://www.CoopersPack.com.

Copano Bay Pr., *(978-0-9767799; 978-0-9822467; 978-0-9829828; 978-0-9847372; 978-0-9884357; 978-1-941324)* Orders Addr.: P.O. Box 1992, Fulton, TX 78358-1992 USA Tel 361-776-1836; P.O. Box 1992, Fulton, TX 78358
E-mail: orders@booksontexas.com
Web site: http://www.booksontexas.com.

Cope, Jakki, *(978-1-7364311)* 20 Highlander Dr., Scotch Plains, NJ 07076 USA Tel 908-400-5638
E-mail: Jakki03@yahoo.com.

Copeland, Kenneth Pubns., *(978-0-88114; 978-0-938458; 978-1-57562; 978-1-60463)* Subs. of Eagle Mountain International Church, Kenneth Copeland Ministries, Fort

Publisher Name Index

Worth, TX 76192 USA Tel 817-252-2700; Toll Free: 800-600-7395
E-mail: mjohnson@kcm.org
Web site: http://www.kcm.org.contact.html
Dist(s): **Anchor Distributors**
Appalachian Bible Co.
Central South Christian Distribution
Harrison House Pubs.
New Day Christian Distributors Gifts, Inc.
Spring Arbor Distributors, Inc.

Copernicus Pr., *(978-0-9741638)* 933 Dwyer Ave., Saint Louis, MO 63122 USA Tel 314-822-8597 Do not confuse with Copernicus Pr. in Atlanta, GA
E-mail: nikolom@slu.edu
Web site: http://www.Copernicuspress.com
Dist(s): **Unique Bks., Inc.**

Copley Custom Textbooks, *(978-0-87411; 978-1-58152; 978-1-58390)* Div. of XanEdu Publishing Inc., 530 Great Rd., Acton, MA 01720 USA (SAN 687-4959) Tel 978-263-9090; Fax: 978-263-9190; Toll Free: 800-562-2147; *Imprints:* Copley Publishing Group (Copley Pub Grp)
E-mail: textbook@copleypublishing.com; publish@copleycustom.com
Web site: http://www.xanedu.com.

Copley Publishing Group *See* **Copley Custom Textbooks**

Copley Publishing Group *Imprint of* **Copley Custom Textbooks**

Coppenrath, F. Verlag KG (DEU) *(978-3-88547; 978-3-920192; 978-3-8157) Dist. by* **Distribks Inc.**

Copper Moon Press *See* **TangleTown Media Inc.**

Copyright Office *Imprint of* **United States Government Printing Office**

Coram Deo Pr., *(978-0-9769054)* One Nelson Pkwy., 2400 FM 407, Highland Village, TX 75077 USA Tel 972-318-5222; Fax: 972-692-5140
E-mail: press@coramdeoacademy.org
Web site: http://www.coramdeopress.com.

Corbett Features, *(978-0-9762294)* Div. of Corbett Features, 100 Cummings Ctr. Suite 432-a, Beverly, MA 01915 USA Tel 978-232-1124; Fax: 978-232-1124; *Imprints:* Griffin Comics (Griffin Comics)
E-mail: cdesign.ma.ultranet@rcn.com
Web site: http://www.corbettfeatures.com.

Corbus Systems, *(978-0-9742347)* 20368 Forestwood, Southfield, MI 48706 USA Tel 248-356-9427
E-mail: info@corbus-systems.com
Web site: http://www.corbus-systems.com.

Corby Books, *(978-0-9776458; 978-0-9819605; 978-0-9827846; 978-0-9833586; 978-0-9859377; 978-0-9890731; 978-0-9912451; 978-0-9961362; 978-1-7321150; 978-1-7352702)* 51760 Whitestable Ln, South Bend, IN 46637 USA
E-mail: prestonward1@aol.com; jimtach@aol.com.

Corcoran, Nenia, *(978-0-578-89384-6; 978-0-578-89385-3; 979-8-9850375)* 238 Canaan St 0, CANAAN, NH 03741 USA Tel 9788085536
E-mail: neniacorcoran@gmail.com
Dist(s): **Ingram Content Group.**

CORD Communications, *(978-1-55502; 978-1-57837)* Subs. of Ctr. for Occupational Research & Development, Orders Addr.: P.O. Box 21206, Waco, TX 76702-1206 USA Tel 254-776-1822; Fax: 254-776-3906; Toll Free: 800-231-3015; Edit Addr.: 324 Kelly Dr., Waco, TX 76710 USA
E-mail: webmaster@cord.org
Web site: http://www.cord.org/index.cfm.

Cordon Pubns., *(978-0-9822083; 978-0-9826984; 978-0-615-39009-3; 978-0-9829049; 978-0-9834908; 978-0-9839858; 978-1-937912)* 5161 Great Lakes Dr. So., Evansville, IN 47715 USA (SAN 857-5460) Tel 812-303-9070
E-mail: coraseaman@hotmail.com
Web site: http://www.Cordon Publications.com.

Cordoves, Barbara & Gladys M., *(978-0-9637252)* 2800 SW 106th Ave., Miami, FL 33165-2748 USA.

Core Knowledge Foundation, *(978-1-890517; 978-1-933486; 978-1-68380; 979-8-88970)* Orders Addr.: 801 E. High St., Charlottesville, VA 22902 USA Tel 434-977-7550; Fax: 434-977-0021; Toll Free: 800-238-3233
E-mail: mjones@coreknowledge.org; coreknow@coreknowledge.org
Web site: http://www.coreknowledge.org.

Core Library *Imprint of* **ABDO Publishing Co.**

Core Publishing & Consulting, Inc., *(978-1-933079)* 13016 Bee St., Suite 208, Dallas, TX 75234 USA (SAN 256-1514) Tel 214-926-4742; Fax: 972-243-5854
E-mail: stan.peterson@sbcglobal.net
Web site: www.core-publishing.com.

Corelink Solution, The, *(978-0-578-40812-5; 978-0-578-44515-1; 978-1-7336346)* 2207 Concord Pike, Wilmington, DE 19803 USA Tel 610-505-6043
E-mail: jamesrosseau@thecorelinksolution.com
Web site: www.thecorelinksolution.com.

Corey, Richard, *(978-0-9966310)* 1611 Burlington Blvd, North Platte, NE 69101 USA Tel 308-534-5612
E-mail: mrbeepa@allophone.com.

CoreyJF Publishing, *(978-0-9895101)* 12299 Greenleaf Ave., Potomac, MD 20854 USA Tel 301-564-3058
E-mail: corey@coreyjf.com
Web site: www.coreyjf.com; www.egrettheelephant.com.

Corgi Tales Publishing, *(978-0-615-26492-9)* 57715 Hwy. 58, McKittrick, CA 93251 USA
Dist(s): **Lulu Pr., Inc.**

Corimbo, Editorial S.L. (ESP) *(978-84-8470; 978-84-95150) Dist. by* **Distribks Inc.**

Corimbo, Editorial S.L. (ESP) *(978-84-8470; 978-84-95150) Dist. by* **Mariuccia Iaconi Bk Imports.**

Corimbo, Editorial S.L. (ESP) *(978-84-8470; 978-84-95150) Dist. by* **Lectorum Pubns.**

Cork Hill Pr., *(978-1-59408)* P.O. Box 117, Carmel, IN 46082-0117 USA
Web site: http://www.corkhillpress.com
Dist(s): **CreateSpace Independent Publishing Platform.**

Corman Productions, *(978-0-9655749)* 6729 Dume Dr., Malibu, CA 90265 USA Tel 310-457-7524; Fax: 310-457-5941
E-mail: Dikkybird@aol.com.

Cormier, Shawn *See* **Pine View Pr.**

Cormorant Bks. Inc. (CAN) *(978-0-920953; 978-1-896951; 978-1-897151; 978-1-77086) Dist. by* **Orca Bk Pub.**

Corn Crib Publishing, *(978-0-9907688; 978-1-7353663)* 18988 Point Lookout Rd., Lexington Park, MD 20653 USA Tel 301-862-3421
E-mail: Christina@CornCribStudio.com
Web site: corncribstudio.com.

Corn, Richard LLC, *(978-0-9985849)* 8 Colonial Ct., New Canaan, CT 06840 USA Tel 203-561-0865
E-mail: mathtutorct@yahoo.com.

Corn Tassel Pr., *(978-0-9752597)* 9655 Corn Tassel Ct., Columbia, MD 21046 USA Fax: 301-776-6538.

Cornell, A.J. Pubns., *(978-0-9727439; 978-0-9850501)* 18-74 Corporal Kennedy St., Bayside, NY 11360 USA Tel 718-423-4082.

Cornell Lab Publishing Group, The *Imprint of* **WunderMill, Inc.**

Cornell Maritime Pr./Tidewater Pubs. *Imprint of* **Schiffer Publishing, Ltd.**

†Cornell Univ. Pr., *(978-0-8014; 978-0-87546; 978-1-5017)* Orders Addr.: P.O. Box 6525, Ithaca, NY 14851 USA (SAN 281-5680) Tel 607-277-2211; Toll Free Fax: 800-688-2877; Toll Free: 800-666-2211; Edit Addr.: Sage House, 512 E. State St., Ithaca, NY 14851 USA (SAN 202-1862) Tel 607-277-2338; *Imprints:* Comstock Publishing Associates (Comstock Pub); Northern Illinois University Press (NorthIUPr)
E-mail: cupressinfo@cornell.edu; orders@nbninternational.com; cupress-sales@cornell.edu
Web site: http://www.cornellpress.cornell.edu
Dist(s): **CUP Services**
Casemate Academic
De Gruyter, Inc.
Follett School Solutions
Hachette Bk. Group
JSTOR
Longleaf Services
MyiLibrary
Oxford Univ. Pr., Inc.
ebrary, Inc.; *CIP.*

Corner Publishing Group, *(978-0-692-92074-9; 978-0-692-92076-3; 978-0-9993730)* PO Box 1518, Dawsonville, GA 30534 USA Tel 770-815-9494
E-mail: corey.parson@cornerpublishinggroup.com
Web site: cornerpublishinggroup.com.

Corner To Learn Ltd. (GBR) *(978-0-9545353; 978-1-905434; 978-1-908702) Dist. by* **Parkwest Pubns.**

Cornerstone Bk. Publishers *Imprint of* **Cornerstone Bk. Pubs.**

Cornerstone Bk. Pubs., *(978-1-887560; 978-1-934935; 978-1-61342)* 7041 Canal Blvd. No. 107, New Orleans, LA 70124 USA; *Imprints:* Cornerstone Book Publishers (Cstone Bk Pubs)
E-mail: 1cornerstonebooks@gmail.com
Web site: http://www.cornerstonepublishers.com.

Cornerstone Enterprises, *(978-0-9778015)* 6787 W. Tropicana Ave., Suite No. 246, Las Vegas, NV 89103 USA (SAN 850-2757) Toll Free: 800-635-3122
E-mail: admin@cornerstoneserve.com
Web site: http://www.cornerstoneserve.com.

Cornerstone Family Ministries/Lamplighter Publishing, *(978-1-58474)* Orders Addr.: P.O. Box 777, Waverly, PA 18471 USA Tel 717-585-1314; Fax: 717-587-4246; Toll Free: 888-246-7735; Edit Addr.: Waverly Community Ctr., Main St., S. Wing, 2nd Flr., Waverly, PA 18471 USA
E-mail: cfm@epix.net
Web site: http://www.agospel.com
Dist(s): **Follett School Solutions.**

Cornerstone Pr., *(978-0-918476)* 1825 Bender Ln., Arnold, MO 63010-0388 USA (SAN 210-0584) Tel 636-296-9662 Do not confuse with companies with the same name in Edison, NJ, Kents Hill, ME, Pearland, TX, Stevens Point, WI
E-mail: anthsum@sbcglobal.net.

Cornerstone Pr., *(978-0-9658488; 978-0-9774802; 978-0-9846739; 978-1-7333086; 978-1-7377390; 979-8-9861447; 979-8-9896663; 978-1-960329)* c/o Univ. of Wisconsin, Dept. of English, 325 Collins Classroom Center, Univ. of Wisconsin-Stevens Point 1801 Fourth Ave, Stevens Point, WI 54481-3897 USA Tel 715-346-4532; Fax: 715-346-2849 Do not confuse with companies with the same name in Kents Hill, ME, Arnold, MO
E-mail: ross.tangedal@uwsp.edu.

Cornerstone Pr. Chicago, *(978-0-940895)* 939 W. Wilson, Chicago, IL 60640 USA (SAN 664-7200) Tel 773-561-2450; 773-989-4920; Fax: 773-989-2076; Toll Free: 888-407-7377
E-mail: cspress@jpusa.org
Web site: http://www.cornerstonepress.com.

Cornerstone Publishing, Inc., *(978-1-882185)* P.O. Box 23015, Evansville, IN 47724 USA (SAN 298-735X) Tel 812-422-6187 Do not confuse with companies with the same name in Decatur, GA, Altamonte Springs, FL, Wichita, KS
E-mail: cornerstonepublishinghouse@gmail.com
Web site: http://www.cornerstonepublishinghouse.com
Dist(s): **Book Clearing Hse.**
Ingram Content Group.

Cornerstonia, *(978-0-9828588)* 9457 Venezia Plantation Dr., Orlando, FL 32829 USA Tel 407-222-4287
E-mail: author@cornerstonia.com
Web site: http://www.cornerstonia.com.

CornerWind Media, L.L.C., *(978-0-9741072)* Orders Addr.: 2635 Whitehall Ct., Rock Hill, SC 29732 USA Tel 803-329-7140; Fax: 803-329-7145
Web site: http://www.twiggyleaf.com; http://www.cornerwind.com.

Corning Museum of Glass, *(978-0-87290)* One Museum Way, Corning, NY 14830 USA (SAN 202-1897) Fax: 607-974-7365; Toll Free: 800-732-6845
E-mail: cmg@cmog.org; pr@cmog.org
Web site: http://www.cmog.org
Dist(s): **Associated Univ. Presses**
Casemate Academic
Hudson Hills Pr. LLC
National Bk. Network.

Cornsilk Pr., *(978-0-9989337; 978-1-7364525)* 5020 Dory Way, Fair Oaks, CA 95628 USA Tel 916-342-2390
E-mail: ssnavarro22@gmail.com.

Corolishine Bks., *(978-0-692-05498-7; 978-0-692-08080-1)* P.O. Box 394, Forest Knolls, CA 94933 USA Tel 415-419-9390
E-mail: marlenemar1@yahoo.com
Web site: www.marlenesusan.com.

Corona Pr., *(978-1-891619)* 4535 Palmer Ct., Niwot, CO 80503 USA Tel 303-247-1455; Fax: 303-417-0355; Toll Free: 888-648-3877 Do not confuse with Corona Pr., Brooklandville, MD
E-mail: coronapress@aol.com.

Coronet Bks., *(978-0-89563)* 33 Ashley Dr., Schwenksville, PA 19473 USA (SAN 210-6043) Tel 484-919-6486; Fax: 215-717-4655 Do not confuse with Coronet Bks. & Pubns., Eagle Point, OR
E-mail: ronsmolin@earthlink.net; order@coronetbooks.com
Web site: http://www.coronetbooks.com
Dist(s): **ISD**
MyiLibrary.

Coronet, The Multimedia Co., *(978-0-388; 978-0-912034)* Div. of The Phoenix Learning Group, 2349 Chaffee Dr., Saint Louis, MO 63146 USA (SAN 212-3967).

Corpus Communications *See* **Caritas Communications**

Corraini (ITA) *(978-88-86250; 978-88-87942; 978-88-7570) Dist. by* **Dist Art Pubs.**

Corredora Independent Publishing, *(978-0-9995768)* Attn: Kristen Nugent, Esq. 5565 Glenridge Connector NE, Suite 850, Atlanta, GA 30342 USA Tel 203-606-1287
E-mail: kristennugent20@gmail.com.

Corroluna Pr., *(978-0-9986661)* 904 Queenstown Rd., Lancaster, VA 22503 USA Tel 804-387-3653; Fax: 804-387-3653
E-mail: mjbeswickart@gmail.com
Web site: maryjobeswick.com.

Corrugated Sky, LLC *See* **Erendi Publishing**

Cortright Fellowship Pr., *(978-0-9706684)* P.O. Box 434, Allegan, MI 49010 USA
E-mail: ekklesia@accn.org
Web site: http://www.redbay.com/ekklesia.

Corunda, Ediciones, S.A. de C.V. (MEX) *(978-968-6044; 978-968-7444) Dist. by* **AIMS Intl.**

Corwin Pr., *(978-0-7619; 978-0-8039; 978-1-57517; 978-1-879179; 978-1-4129; 978-1-0718; 978-1-5443-1945-2; 978-1-0718-3887-7)* Affil. of Sage Pubns., Inc., 2455 Teller Rd., Thousand Oaks, CA 91320-2218 USA Tel 805-499-9734; 805-499-9774 (customer service); Fax: 805-499-0871; 805-499-5323
E-mail: info@sagepub.com
Web site: http://www.corwinpress.com
Dist(s): **Follett School Solutions**
MyiLibrary
SAGE Pubns., Inc.
ebrary, Inc.

Corwin Press, Incorporated *See* **Corwin Pr.**

Coscia, Alexandra, *(978-1-7335291)* 138 Thornbury Rd. E., Scarsdale, NY 10583 USA Tel 248-835-6617
E-mail: alexandratracey@gmail.com.

Cosimo Classics *Imprint of* **Cosimo, Inc.**

Cosimo, Inc., *(978-1-59605; 978-1-60206; 978-1-60520; 978-1-61640; 978-1-944529; 978-1-945934; 978-1-64679; 979-8-89135)* 733 3rd Ave. 16th Flr., NEW YORK, NY 10017 USA Tel 212-989-3616; Fax: 212-989-3662; *Imprints:* Cosimo Classics (CosClassics)
E-mail: adake@cosimobooks.com; info@cosimobooks.com
Web site: http://www.cosimobooks.com
Dist(s): **Follett School Solutions**
INscribe Digital
Independent Pubs. Group.

COSMIC EDITIONS , LLC, *(978-0-9967223)* P.O. Box 348491, Miami, FL 33234 USA Tel 305-951-6571
E-mail: cosmiceditions@gmail.com
Web site: WWW.COSMICEDITIONS.COM.

Cosmic Gargoyle Creative Solutions, *(978-0-9835843)* 3883 Turtle Creek Blvd. No. 1202, Dallas, TX 75219 USA Tel 214-679-4725; *Imprints:* Lonely Swan Books (Lonely Swan)
E-mail: cosmicgargoyle@gmail.com
Dist(s): **Smashwords.**

Cosmic Media Group, The *See* **COSMIC EDITIONS , LLC**

Cosmic Teapot, *(978-0-9899360; 978-0-9953316-9-3)* 62 W. 106th St. Apt. 2A, New York City, NY 10025 USA Tel 917-659-1600
E-mail: chris@theatheistbook.com.

COSMIC VORTEX, *(978-0-9719580)* Div. of TETRA XII Inc., Orders Addr.: P.O. Box 322, Paia, HI 96779 USA
E-mail: atlantis@archaeologist.com; aloha@mauivortex.com
Web site: http://www.atlantistoday.com; http://atlantis-motherland.com.

Cosmographia Pubns., *(978-0-615-60710-8)* 6 1/2 W. 3rd St., Spencer, IA 51301 USA Tel 712-580-3271
E-mail: hnewgard@gmail.com.

Cosmos Books *See* **Prime**

Cosmos Publishing, *(978-0-9660449; 978-1-932455)* 262 River Vale Rd., River Vale, NJ 07675 USA (SAN 631-0486) Tel 201-664-3494; Fax: 201-664-3402 Do not confuse with companies with the same in Bellevue, WA, Saint Louis, MO
E-mail: info@greeceinprint.com
Web site: http://www.greeceinprint.com.

Cosmos Publishing Company, Incorporated *See* **Cosmos Publishing**

Costa, Adriane Photography, *(978-1-7323726)* 54 Mustang Ct., DANVILLE, CA 94526 USA Tel 925-768-5001
E-mail: adriane.e.costa@gmail.com
Dist(s): **Ingram Content Group.**

Costello, Katelyn, *(978-0-578-40352-6)* 1260 Lehigh Sta. Rd Apt. 705, Henrietta, NY 14467 USA Tel 585-397-4347
E-mail: scripturient101@gmail.com
Dist(s): **Ingram Content Group.**

Costley, Jennifer, *(978-0-692-18888-0)* 607 S. Main St., Pendleton, OR 97801 USA Tel 541-248-0672
E-mail: author@mflorson.com
Dist(s): **Ingram Content Group.**

Costume & Fashion Pr. *Imprint of* **Quite Specific Media Group, Ltd.**

Cosulich, Charlotte, *(978-0-692-18860-6; 979-8-218-20019-0)* 306 E. Ranch Rd., Sacramento, CA 95825 USA Tel 916-485-3915
E-mail: charlotte11@comcast.net.

Cote Literary Group, The, *(978-1-929175)* 483 Old Carolina Ct., Mount Pleasant, SC 29464 USA (SAN 850-4881) Tel 843-881-6080; Fax: 843-278-8456
E-mail: editor@corinthianbooks.com; dickcote@earthlink.net
Web site: http://www.corinthianbooks.com
Dist(s): **Brodart Co.**
Follett School Solutions
Quality Bks., Inc.
eBookit.com.

Coteau Bks. (CAN) *(978-0-919926; 978-1-55050; 978-0-9780316) Dist. by* **Orca Bk Pub.**

Cotler, Joanna Books *Imprint of* **HarperCollins Pubs.**

Cotsen Occasional Pr., *(978-0-9666084; 978-0-9745168; 978-0-9971510)* Div. of Cotsen Family Foundation, 12100 Wilshire Blvd. Suite 905, Los Angeles, CA 90025 USA Tel 310-826-9113
E-mail: jolie@cotsenfamilyoffice.com
Web site: http://www.hesdegraaf.com/hes/.

Cottage Door Pr., *(978-1-68052; 978-1-64638; 979-8-89019)* 5005 Newport Dr. Suite 300, Rolling Meadows, IL 60008 USA (SAN 990-1051) Tel 224-228-6000; *Imprints:* Parragon Books (Parragon Bks)
E-mail: kfinnamore@cottagedoorpress.com; contactus@cottagedoorpress.com; kshully@cottagedoorpress.com; mgrajewski@cottagedoorpress.com
Web site: http://www.cottagedoorpress.com.

cottage in the woods Pr., *(978-0-9971552)* 3917 Lyman Rd, oakland, CA 94602 USA Tel 510-316-7182
E-mail: yosgurl@yahoo.com.

Cotton Candy Pr. *Imprint of* **Unveiled Media, LLC**

Cotton, Karen O., *(978-0-692-25813-2; 978-0-692-27344-9; 978-0-692-85154-8; 978-0-692-04453-7; 978-0-578-40033-4)* 5006 Foxen Ct., Cheyenne, WY 82001 USA Tel 307-214-0277
E-mail: cotton.karen@gmail.com
Web site: karencotton.net.

Cottonwood Graphics, Incorporated *See* **Cottonwood Publishing, Inc.**

Cottonwood Pr., Inc., *(978-1-877673; 978-1-936162)* 109-B Cameron Dr., Fort Collins, CO 80525 USA Tel 970-204-0715; Fax: 970-204-0761; Toll Free: 800-864-4297 Do not confuse with companies with same name in Novato, CA, Lawrence, KS, Wilsonville, OR
E-mail: cottonwood@cottonwoodpress.com
Web site: http://www.cottonwoodpress.com
Dist(s): **ebrary, Inc.**

CottonWood Publishing Co., *(978-0-9766804)* 840 W. Washington St., Ann Arbor, MI 48103 USA Do not confuse with Cottonwood Publishing Company in Saint George, UT Helena MT.

Cottonwood Publishing, Inc., *(978-0-9626999; 978-1-886370)* 296 Willowbrook Dr., Helena, MT 59602-7764 USA Toll Free: 800-937-6343 Do not confuse with Cottonwood Publishing in Saint George, UT Ann Arbor MI
E-mail: oldmt@mt.net
Web site: http://www.oldmontana.com
Dist(s): **CreateSpace Independent Publishing Platform**
Mountain Pr. Publishing Co., Inc.

Coulee Region Pubns., Inc., *(978-0-9650629)* 307 Twin Oak Dr., Altoona, WI 54720-1383 USA.

Counce, Paula, *(978-0-9762776)* 1628 Bob O Link Dr., Venice, FL 34293 USA
Web site: http://www.ajourneyremembered.com.

†Council for Agricultural Science & Technology (CAST), *(978-1-887383)* 4420 W. Lincoln Way, Ames, IA 50014-3347 USA (SAN 225-7416) Tel 515-292-2125; Fax: 515-292-4512; Toll Free Fax: 800-375-2278; Toll Free: 800-762-4232
E-mail: cast@cast-science.org
Web site: http://www.cast-science.org; *CIP.*

Council for Indian Education, *(978-0-89992)* Orders Addr.: 1240 Burlington Ave., Billings, MT 59102-4224 USA Tel 406-248-3465; Fax: 406-248-1297
E-mail: cie@cie-mt.org
Web site: http://www.cie-mt.org
Dist(s): **Follett School Solutions.**

Council Oak Bks., *(978-0-933031; 978-1-57178)* Orders Addr.: 2822 Van Ness Ave., San Francisco, CA 94109 USA (SAN 689-5522) Tel 415-931-7700; Fax: 415-931-9911; Toll Free: 800-247-8850 (orders only)
E-mail: order@counciloakbooks.com; publicity@counciloakbooks.com
Web site: http://www.counciloakbooks.com
Dist(s): **Independent Pubs. Group**
New Leaf Distributing Co., Inc.
Univ. of Oklahoma Pr.

Count On Learning, *(978-0-9771472)* 1406 Arlington Ave., Baton Rouge, LA 70808 USA
E-mail: admin@countonlearning.com
Web site: http://www.countonlearning.com.

Counterbalance Bks., *(978-0-9774906; 978-0-9799592; 978-0-9989923)* P.O. Box 876, Duvall, WA 98019-0876 USA
E-mail: admin@counterbalancebooks.com; publisher@counterbalancebooks.com
Web site: http://www.counterbalancebooks.com.

CounterCulture Ministries *See* **Edifi Publishing LLC**

Counterpath Pr., *(978-1-933996)* P.O. Box 18351, Denver, CO 80218 USA
E-mail: tr@counterpathpress.org
Web site: http://www.counterpathpress.org
Dist(s): **SPD-Small Pr. Distribution.**

Counterpoint LLC *See* **Counterpoint Pr.**

Counterpoint Pr., *(978-1-58243; 978-1-887178; 978-1-59376; 978-1-61902; 978-1-944869; 978-1-64009; 978-1-949017)* 2560 Ninth St., Suite 318, Berkeley, CA 94710-2205 USA Fax: 510-704-0268; *Imprints:* Soft Skull Press (Soft)
E-mail: info@counterpointpress.com
Web site: http://www.counterpointpress.com
Dist(s): **Lulu Pr., Inc.**
MyiLibrary
Open Road Integrated Media, Inc.
Penguin Random Hse. Distribution
Penguin Random Hse. LLC
Publishers Group West (PGW)
Perseus Bks. Group.

Counting Pup Pr., *(978-0-9969452; 978-0-9986572; 978-1-948246)* 3616 Harden Blvd, No. 315, Lakeland, FL 33803 USA Tel 863-255-5438
E-mail: countingpup@gmail.com
Web site: countingpup.com.

Countinghouse Pr., Inc., *(978-0-9664732; 978-0-9786191; 978-0-9911102)* 6632 Telegraph Rd., Suite 311, Bloomfield Hills, MI 48301 USA Tel 248-642-7191; Fax: 248-642-7192
E-mail: lcharla@comcast.net
Web site: http://www.countinghousepress.com.

Country Bookshop, The, *(978-0-9991317)* 140 NW Broad St., Southern Pines, NC 28387 USA Tel 910-692-3211
E-mail: kimberlyddaniels@gmail.com.

Country Boy Publishing Co., *(978-0-9795574)* Orders Addr.: 300 Collier Dr., Winter Haven, FL 33884 USA
E-mail: dgreenl2@tampabay.rr.com
Web site: http://www.countryboypublishing.com.

Country Bumpkin Pubns. USA, *(978-0-9677936)* 212 California Ave., Watertown, NY 13601 USA Tel 315-782-0941
E-mail: bsteve3@twcny.rr.com.

Country Fresh Farms, *(978-0-578-78185-3; 978-0-578-87961-1)* 23851 Cty. Rd. 61, Elbert, CO 80106 USA Tel 720-318-2763
E-mail: msmith@countryfreshfarmsllc.com
Web site: wwwcountryfreshfarmsllc.com.

Country Girl Publishing, *(978-0-615-26902-3)* 5537 Shallowriver Rd., Clinton, MD 20735 USA.

Country Kid Publishing LLC, *(978-0-9754624; 978-0-9963649)* 951 Canyon Tr Ct., Yorkville, IL 60560 USA
E-mail: michaelwaguespack@gmail.com
Web site: http://www.countrykidpublishing.com
Dist(s): **Angler's Bk. Supply**
Follett School Solutions.

Country Messenger Pr. Publishing Group, LLC, *(978-0-9619407; 978-0-9801554; 978-1-937162)* 27657 Hwy. 97, Okanogan, WA 98840 USA (SAN 244-5638) Tel 253-216-6364
E-mail: kfreel@cmppg.org; edna@cmppg.org
Web site: http://www.cmppg.com.

Country Side Pr., The, *(978-0-9746360)* Orders Addr.: 49850 Miller Rd., North Powder, OR 97867 USA Tel 541-856-3239
E-mail: debbys@rconnects.com
Web site: http://www.thecountrysidepress.com.

Courage Publishing, *(978-0-692-05388-1; 978-0-692-16578-2)* 813 12th Ave W., West Fargo, ND 58078 USA Tel 701-200-8480
E-mail: sarahzaun@hotmail.com.

Courage to Change *See* **CTC Publishing**

Courageous Heart Pr., *(978-0-9832514; 978-0-9969984; 978-1-950714)* 127 RAINBOW Dr. No. 2756, Livingston, TX 77399 USA Tel 979-417-2482
E-mail: erin@erin-casey.com
Web site: http://gypsyheartpress.com; http://courageousheartpress.com; http://mywritersconnection.com/.

Couronne et Croix, *(978-0-578-94563-7; 978-0-578-96710-3; 978-0-578-96806-3; 978-0-578-31082-4; 978-0-578-35003-5)* 7959 Tulane St., Taylor, MI 48180 USA Tel 313-463-8561
E-mail: brianadobson2@gmail.com.

Couronne et Cronix *See* **Couronne et Croix**

Course Technology, *(978-0-534; 978-0-619; 978-0-7600; 978-0-7895; 978-0-87709; 978-0-87835; 978-0-89426; 978-0-928763; 978-1-56527; 978-1-878748; 978-1-4188; 978-1-59863; 978-1-4239; 978-1-60334)* Div. of Cengage Learning, Orders Addr.: 20 Channel Ctr St., Boston, MA 02210-3402 USA Toll Free Fax: 800-881-8922
E-mail: Esales@thomsonlearning.com; stacy.hiquet@thomson.com; cheryl.mondillo@thomson.com
Web site: http://www.course.com/
Dist(s): **Alfred Publishing Co., Inc.**
CENGAGE Learning
Delmar Cengage Learning
Ebsco Publishing
Leonard, Hal Corp.
ebrary, Inc.

Courtyard Publishing, LLC, *(978-0-9795260)* Div. of Alchemical Courtyard, LLC, 1688 Meridian Ave., 10th Flr., Miami Beach, FL 33139 USA Tel 305-695-9380
E-mail: info@courtyardpublishing.com
Web site: http://www.courtyardpublishing.com.

Covenant Bks., *(978-0-615-42722-5; 978-0-692-58739-3)* 4200 Kensington High St., Naples, FL 34105 USA Tel 239-643-0887 Do not confuse with Covenant Books in Fort Wayne, IN
E-mail: robertpetterson@msn.com
Dist(s): **CreateSpace Independent Publishing Platform.**

†Covenant Communications, *(978-0-9649122)* 1009 Jones St., Old Hickory, TN 37138 USA Tel 615-847-2066; Fax: 615-860-3601; Toll Free: 800-979-3882 Do nt oconfuse with Covenant Communications in Old Hickory, TN
Dist(s): **Quality Bks., Inc.**; *CIP.*

Covenant Communications, Inc., *(978-1-55503; 978-1-57734; 978-1-59156; 978-1-59811; 978-1-60861; 978-1-62108; 978-1-68047; 978-1-5244)* Orders Addr.: 920 E State Rd Ste F, American Fork, UT 84003-0416 USA (SAN 169-8540) Tel 801-756-9966; 801-756-1041; Fax: 801-756-1049; Toll Free: 800-662-9545; Edit Addr.: 920 E. State Rd., Suite F, American Fork, UT 84003 USA Toll Free: 800-662-9545 Do not confuse with Covenant Communications in American Fork, UT
E-mail: verls@covenant-lds.com
Web site: http://www.covenant-lds.com
Dist(s): **Follett School Solutions.**

Covenant Support Network *See* **The 101 Group, Inc.**

Coventry Pool & Garden Houses *See* **Manor Hse. Publishing Co., Inc.**

Covercraft *Imprint of* **Perfection Learning Corp.**

Covered Bridge Bks., *(978-0-9722027)* 336 Covered Bridge Rd., Cherry Hill, NJ 08034-2949 USA.

Covered Bridge Children's Books *See* **Covered Bridge Bks.**

Covered Wagon Publishing LLC, *(978-0-9723259)* P.O. Box 473038, Aurora, CO 80047 USA (SAN 254-7813) Tel 303-751-0992; Fax: 303-632-6794
E-mail: CoveredWagon@comcast.net
Web site: http://www.RockyMountainMysteries.com.

Covert & Sergiacomi Publishing, *(978-0-578-41850-6)* 10 Saint Augustine Dr., Charleston, SC 29407 USA Tel 843-670-6645
E-mail: covertj1986@gmail.com
Dist(s): **CreateSpace Independent Publishing Platform.**

Covfefe Pr., *(978-0-692-11693-7; 978-0-578-92259-1)* 1300 Pk. W. Blvd. Unit 123, Mount Pleasant, SC 29466 USA Tel 843-830-8831
E-mail: susan@susansloate.com
Web site: susansloate.com
Dist(s): **CreateSpace Independent Publishing Platform.**

Cow Heard Records, *(978-0-9763012)* 3622 Altura Ave., La Crescenta, CA 91214 USA
Web site: http://www.thesunflowers.com.

Cowan, Pricilla J., *(978-0-9822542; 978-0-9841194; 978-0-9840083; 978-0-9891159; 978-0-9896988)* 11594 SW 135th Ave., Tigard, OR 97223 USA
Web site: http://www.storiesbypj.com.

Cowboy Collector Pubns., *(978-0-9628078)* Orders Addr.: P.O. Box 7486, Long Beach, CA 90807 USA Tel 714-840-3942; Edit Addr.: 4677 Rio Ave., Long Beach, CA 90805 USA Tel 213-428-6972
Dist(s): **Hervey's Booklink & Cookbook Warehouse.**

Cowboy Magazine, *(978-0-9765969)* Orders Addr.: P.O. Box 126, La Veta, CO 81055 USA Tel 719-742-5250; Fax: 719-742-3034; Edit Addr.: 124 N. Main St., La Veta, CO 81055 USA
E-mail: workincowboy@amigo.net
Web site: http://www.cowboymagazine.com.

COWCATCHER Pubns., *(978-0-9821521; 978-0-9960533; 978-0-9975172; 979-8-9855785)* 68 S. Port Royal Dr., Hilton Head Island, SC 29928 USA Tel 843-816-7883
Web site: http://www.do-the-write-thing.com.

Cowcatcher Pubns. *See* **COWCATCHER Pubns.**

Cowgirl Peg Bks. *Imprint of* **Cowgirl Peg Enterprises**

Cowgirl Peg Enterprises, *(978-0-9721057; 978-0-615-59075-2; 978-0-692-95998-5; 979-8-9860717)* Orders Addr.: P.O. Box 178, Harper, TX 78631 USA; *Imprints:* Cowgirl Peg Books (Cowgirl Peg Books)
E-mail: cowgirlpeg2@gmail.com
Web site: http://www.cowgirlpeg.com
Dist(s): **Follett School Solutions.**

Cowpokes Cartoon Bks., *(978-0-917207)* P.O. Box 290868, Kerrville, TX 78029-0868 USA (SAN 656-089X) Tel 830-257-7446 (phone/fax); Toll Free: 800-257-7441 (phone/fax)
E-mail: cartoons@cowpokes.com
Web site: http://www.cowpokes.com.

Cox & Castelluccio, 7637 Lauppe Ln., Citrus Heights, CA 95621 USA Tel 530-605-9272
E-mail: amyreneecox@gmail.com
Dist(s): **Ingram Content Group.**

Cox, Audrey Phillips, *(978-0-692-11181-9; 978-0-692-11183-3; 978-1-7324065)* P.O. Box 348 1616 Cadillac Ave, DAUPHIN ISLAND, AL 36528 USA Tel 251-391-6557; *Imprints:* APCWriter & Publisher (APCWriter Pub)
E-mail: apcoxmail@gmail.com; bookinfo@apcwriterpublisher.com; audrey@apcwriterpublisher.com
Web site: http://www.apc-writer-blogger.com; http://www.apc-writer-publisher.com; http://www.audreyphillipscox.com
Dist(s): **Ingram Content Group.**

Cox, Donald, *(978-0-692-07527-2; 978-0-692-13808-3; 978-0-692-16885-1)* 945 San Ildefonso Rd., TRLR 53, Los Alamos, NM 87544 USA Tel 505-426-5410
E-mail: 3times10tothe8th@live.com
Dist(s): **Ingram Content Group.**

Cox, Gene, *(978-0-9669672)* 2309 Limerick Dr., Tallahassee, FL 32308 USA Tel 850-893-1789
E-mail: gccox@mail.istal.com.

Cox, Julie, *(978-0-9742118)* P.O. Box 77966, Fort Worth, TX 76177 USA
E-mail: info@facereadingacademy.com
Web site: http://www.facereadingacademy.com.

Cox, Mark Design *See* **Sympathetic Pr.**

Coyote Canyon Pr., *(978-0-9796607; 978-0-9821298; 978-0-9890080; 978-1-7321903; 979-8-9877655)* 693 Black Hills Dr., Claremont, CA 91711-2928 USA Toll Free Fax: 800-319-4707
E-mail: tom@coyotecanyonpress.com
Web site: http://www.coyotecanyonpress.com.

Coyote Cowboy Co., *(978-0-939343)* Orders Addr.: P.O. Box 2190, Benson, AZ 85602 USA (SAN 663-0820) Tel 520-586-1077; Toll Free: 800-654-2550; Edit Addr.: 1251 S. Red Chile Rd., Benson, AZ 85602 USA
E-mail: cindylou@baxterblack.com
Web site: http://www.baxterblack.com
Dist(s): **Follett School Solutions.**

Coyote Moon Publishing *See* **Cowgirl Peg Enterprises**

CoZi Publishing LLC, *(978-0-9749151)* P.O. Box 211, Rutland, VT 05702-0211 USA
E-mail: publish@cozi.com
Web site: http://www.cozi.com.

Cozy Den Pr. *Imprint of* **Marriwell Publishing**

Cozy Graphics Corp., *(978-1-932002; 978-1-59343)* 61-20 G.C.P., Apt. B1204, Forest Hills, NY 11375 USA Tel 718-592-9782 (phone/fax); *Imprints:* Cozy Publishing House (Cozy Pub Hse)
E-mail: publisher@cozygraphics.com
Web site: http://www.cozygraphics.com.

Cozy Publishing Hse. *Imprint of* **Cozy Graphics Corp.**

CP Production Studios Publishing Co., P.O. Box 64551, Phoenix, AZ 85082 USA Tel 630-788-7839
E-mail: cpprostudios3@gmail.com
Dist(s): **CreateSpace Independent Publishing Platform.**

CPCC Pr., *(978-1-59494)* P.O. Box 35009, Charlotte, NC 28235-5009 USA Tel 704-330-6789
E-mail: cpccpress@cpcc.edu; melissa.wilson@cpcc.edu; amy.rogers@cpcc.edu; emma.reynolds@cpcc.edu
Web site: http://www.cpccservicescorp.com; http://https://cpccpress.com/.

CPM Comics *Imprint of* **Central Park Media Corp.**

CPM Manga *Imprint of* **Central Park Media Corp.**

CPM Manhwa *Imprint of* **Central Park Media Corp.**

CPR Pubng, *(978-0-9778597)* 740 13th St., Fennimore, WI 53809 USA.

CQ Pr. Library Reference *Imprint of* **CQ Pr.**

†CQ Pr., *(978-0-7401; 978-0-87187; 978-0-9625531; 978-1-56692; 978-1-56802; 978-1-933116; 978-1-60426; 978-0-9823537; 978-1-60871; 978-1-0718-1685-1)* Div. of SAGE Pubns., Inc., Orders Addr.: a/o Order Dept., 2300 N. St. NW, Suite 800, Washington, DC 20037 USA (SAN 256-470X) Toll Free: 866-427-7737 (customer service - orders); *Imprints:* C Q Press Library Reference (CQ Pr Lib Ref)
E-mail: customerservice@cqpress.com
Web site: http://www.cqpress.com
Dist(s): **Cengage Gale**
MyiLibrary
SAGE Pubns., Inc.
Sage US Textbks.
ebrary, Inc.; *CIP.*

CR Publishing, *(978-0-9982115)* 947 W. 5950 S., Spanish Fork, UT 84660 USA Tel 801-376-5982; Fax: 801-376-5982
E-mail: christina.utah@gmail.com.

Crabtree Publishing Co. (CAN) *(978-0-7787; 978-0-86505; 978-1-4271; 978-1-0396) Dist. by* **Children Plus.**

Cracker the Crab LLC, *(978-0-9725560)* P.O. Box 80475, Simpsonville, SC 29680-0475 USA Do not confuse with Two Bear Publishing Company in Alpine, CA
E-mail: jillkcogdill@twobearproducts.com; jcogdill@crackerthecrab.com; jkcogdill@msn.com
Web site: http://www.crackerthecrab.com.

Crafterina, *(978-0-9886652; 978-0-9886653; 978-0-692-58583-2; 978-0-692-93016-8; 979-8-9868612)* 505 N. Pinehurst Ave., Salisbury, MD 21801 USA Tel 443-235-1436
E-mail: VanessaEstelleSalgado@gmail.com.

CraftGenie *See* **Pr.Ville**

Craig, Frankye, *(978-0-9794904)* 1735 Caughlin Creek Rd., Reno, NV 89519 USA Tel 775-747-1138; Fax: 775-747-1138
E-mail: FrankyeEBD@aol.com.

Craig Jones *See* **B. Craig Jones**

Crain, Suzanne, *(978-0-9763254)* 10423 Brickey Rd., Red Bud, IL 62278-3519 USA
E-mail: slcrain@hcis.net.

Cram101 Inc., *(978-1-4288; 978-1-61654; 978-1-61698; 978-1-61744; 978-1-61461; 978-1-61490; 978-1-61812; 978-1-61830; 978-1-61905; 978-1-61906; 978-1-4672; 978-1-4784; 978-1-4902; 978-1-4970; 978-1-5388)* 1320 Flynn Rd Unit C, Camarillo, CA 93012 USA (SAN 851-2175)
E-mail: www.palitt.com
Web site: http://www.cram101.com.

Cranberry Quill Publishing Co., *(978-0-9741406; 978-0-9884899; 978-0-9914246; 978-0-9965986)* P.O. Box 26227, Fayetteville, NC 28301-4901 USA Tel 910-257-5109
E-mail: writearlybooks@gmail.com
Web site: http://www.cranberryquill.com.

Crane Bks., *(978-0-9647924)* Div. of Math in Motion, 668 Stony Hill Rd., No. 233, Yardley, PA 19067 USA Tel 215-321-5556; Fax: 215-310-9412
E-mail: info@mathinmotion.com
Web site: http://www.mathinmotion.com.

†Crane Hill Pubs., *(978-0-9621455; 978-1-57587; 978-1-881548)* 3608 Clairmont Ave., Birmingham, AL 35222-3508 USA Tel 205-714-3007; Fax: 205-714-3008
E-mail: cranemail@cranehill.com
Web site: http://www.cranehill.com; *CIP.*

Crane Institute of America, Inc., *(978-0-9744279; 978-0-9855502; 978-1-946269)* 3880 Saint Johns Pkwy., Sanford, FL 32771 USA Tel 407-322-6800; Fax: 407-330-0660; Toll Free: 800-832-2726
E-mail: annc@craneinstitute.com; info@craneinstitute.com
Web site: http://www.craneinstitute.com.

Crane, Kristy, *(978-0-578-45309-5)* 306 S. 7th St., Montpelier, ID 83254 USA Tel 208-847-0150
E-mail: kristyscrane@yahoo.com
Dist(s): **Ingram Content Group.**

Crane Publishing, *(978-0-9753608)* 308 Trinity Rd., Venice, FL 34293 USA Do not confuse with companies with the same name in Paramus, New Jersey.
E-mail: jborza@cranepublishing.net
Web site: http://www.cranepublishing.net.

Cranky Pants Publishing, LLC, *(978-0-9759627)* 2 Upland Rd., W., Arlington, MA 02474 USA
E-mail: ssanzo@yahoo.com.

Crary Pubns., *(978-0-9743438; 978-0-9980887)* 5233 Painted Pebble St., North Las Vegas, NV 89081 USA
E-mail: tabrown@crarypublications.com
Web site: http://www.CraryPublications.com
Dist(s): **Ingram Content Group.**

Craven Street Bks. *Imprint of* **Linden Publishing Co., Inc.**

Crawford, Dana, *(978-0-9742362)* 921 N. Chaparral, Suite 208, Corpus Christi, TX 78401-0208 USA
E-mail: wt.loss@ccinternet.net
Web site: http://www.naturalweight.net.

Crawford, Quinton Douglass, *(978-0-615-14879-3)* 225 Santa Ana Ct., Fairfield, CA 94533 USA
Web site: http://www.knowledgefortomorrow.com
Dist(s): **Lulu Pr., Inc.**

Crayens *See* **Coolidge Corner Pr.**

Crazy 8 Pr., *(978-0-615-56701-3; 978-0-615-75884-8; 978-0-692-20450-4; 978-0-9969275)* 8 Davis Rd., Port Washington, NY 11050 USA Tel 516-883-8079
Dist(s): **CreateSpace Independent Publishing Platform.**

Crazy A, *(978-0-578-45787-1)* 514 Country Club Dr., Stockbridge, GA 30281 USA Tel 770-507-4538
E-mail: thecrazyablogger@gmail.com
Dist(s): **Independent Pub.**

Crazy Dream Publishing, LLC *See* **Waltham Publishing, LLC**

Crazy Man Press, LLC, *(978-0-9743553)* 33 University Sq., Suite 254, Madison, WI 53715-1042 USA Tel 608-215-0532
E-mail: info@crazymanpress.com
Web site: http://www.crazymanpress.com.

Crazy Pet Pr., The, *(978-0-9744749)* 655 N. Azusa Ave., No. 104, Azusa, CA 91708 USA Tel 831-438-2730; Fax: 831-438-2764; Toll Free: 877-860-2100
E-mail: kpbooks@calcentral.com
Web site: http://www.crazydog.com; http://www.crazypetpress.com; http://www.kidoodlepetpress.com.

Crazy Red Head Publishing, *(978-0-692-71498-0; 978-0-692-76622-4; 978-0-692-76623-1; 978-0-9992968)* 3900 Walnut Lake rd, West Bloomfield, MI 48323 USA Tel 248-227-5508
Dist(s): **Independent Pub.**

†CRC Pr. LLC, *(978-0-8493; 978-0-87762; 978-0-87819; 978-0-935184; 978-1-56676; 978-1-57491; 978-1-58488; 978-1-58716; 978-1-4200; 978-1-4398; 978-1-4665; 978-1-4822; 978-1-4987; 978-1-351)* Subs. of Taylor & Francis, Inc., Orders Addr.: 6000 Broken Sound Pkwy., NW, Ste. 300, Boca Raton, FL 33487 USA Tel 800-272-7737 Toll Free Fax: 800-374-3401; Edit Addr.: 270 Madison Ave., New York, NY 10016 USA; *Imprints:* A K Peters/CRC Press (AKPetersCRCPr); Routledge (RoutldgCRC)
E-mail: orders@crcpress.com; Theresa.Gutierrez@taylorandfrancis.com
Web site: http://www.crcpress.com; http://www.taylorandfrancis.com
Dist(s): **Ebsco Publishing**
Follett School Solutions
MyiLibrary
Oxford Univ. Pr., Inc.
Rittenhouse Bk. Distributors
Taylor & Francis Group
Thieme Medical Pubs., Inc.
ebrary, Inc.; *CIP.*

CRE Lease Talk, Incorporated, *(978-0-9820726)* Orders Addr.: P.O. Box 341594, Memphis, TN 38134-1084 USA Tel 901-399-0967
E-mail: valencia.mackie@comcast.net; valencia@creleasetalk.com
Web site: http://www.CRELeaseTalk.com.

Create and Blossom, LLC *See* **Create & Blossom Publishing**

Create & Blossom Publishing, *(978-0-615-76536-5; 978-0-9890039; 978-0-615-83176-3; 978-0-9910489; 978-0-9915412; 978-0-9903486; 978-0-9906662; 978-0-9909652; 978-0-9860866; 978-0-9969105; 978-0-9972921; 978-1-945304; 978-0-692-07007-9; 978-0-692-15731-2; 978-0-692-19174-3;-0-578-98674-6)*
E-mail: createandblossomllc@gmail.com
Web site: www.createandblossomstudios.com.

Create! Bks. *Imprint of* **Bearport Publishing Co., Inc.**

Create Loving Kindness, *(978-0-9977115)* 1313 N. Ritchie Ct., Chicago, IL 60610 USA Tel 310-220-7733
E-mail: debsmazor@gmail.com.

Create Noise Publishing, *(978-0-9961346; 978-1-945109)* 1233 W. 74th St., Los Angeles, CA 90044 USA Tel 323-365-9239
E-mail: drealashon@gmail.com; createnoise1@gmail.com
Web site: www.createnoise.org.

CreateBk.org, *(978-0-692-52480-0; 978-0-9992620; 978-1-7335545; 978-1-953351)* 703 E Main St, Vermillion, SD 57069 USA Tel 605-215-8447
E-mail: patrick@createbook.org
Web site: www.createbook.org
Dist(s): **CreateSpace Independent Publishing Platform.**

Created For You, *(978-0-615-17773-1; 978-0-615-17775-5; 978-0-9819968)* Orders Addr.: P.O. Box 4448, Horseshoe Bay, TX 78657 USA; Edit Addr.: 305 Sunspot, Horseshoe Bay, TX 78657-4448 USA Tel 830-596-2726
Dist(s): **Publishers Services.**

CreateSpace Independent Publishing Platform, *(978-1-58898; 978-1-5423; 978-1-59109; 978-1-59456; 978-1-59457; 978-1-4196; 978-1-4348; 978-1-4382; 978-1-4392; 978-1-4404; 978-1-4414; 978-1-4421; 978-1-61550; 978-1-4486; 978-1-4495; 978-1-4499; 978-1-4505; 978-1-4515; 978-1-4528; 978-1-4536; 978-1-4537; 978-1-4538; 978-1-4563; 978-1-4564; 978-1-4565; 978-1-61789; 978-1-4609; 978-1-4610; 978-1-4611; 978-1-61396; 978-1-61397; 978-1-4635; 978-1-4636; 978-1-4637; 978-1-4662; 978-1-4663; 978-1-4664; 978-1-61914; 978-1-61915; 978-1-61916; 978) Orders Addr.: 4900 LaCross Rd., North Charleston, SC 29406 USA (SAN 255-2132) Tel 843-225-4700 (Ask for ordering department); Fax: 843-577-7506; Toll Free: 866-308-6235; 4900 LaCross Rd., North Charleston, SC 29406; Imprints:* Great UNpublished (Great UNpublished)
E-mail: info@createspace.com
Web site: http://www.createspace.com
Dist(s): **Amazon Digital Services Inc.**
Independently Published.

Creating Worlds with Words, LLC, *(978-1-7320589)* 7972 Crescent Moon Pl., Anchorage, AK 99507 USA Tel 907-354-7413
E-mail: k.t.munson1@gmail.com
Dist(s): **Ingram Content Group.**

Creation By Design, *(978-0-9828077; 978-1-936532)* 95 Bennett Rd., Teaneck, NJ 07666 USA Tel 914-714-3300
E-mail: CrtnByDsgn@aol.com
Dist(s): **Send The Light Distribution LLC.**

Creation Hse. *Imprint of* **Charisma Media**

Creation Instruction Publishing, *(978-1-928765)* Orders Addr.: P.O. Box 304, Plentywood, MT 59254 USA Tel 406-895-2689; Edit Addr.: 1770 S. Overland, Juniata, NE 68955 USA
E-mail: creation1@juno.com
Web site: http://www.creationinstruction.org/.

Creation Nation Animation, *(978-1-7342452)* 2907 Shelter Island Dr. Suite 219, San Diego, CA 92106 USA Tel 619-642-0477
E-mail: info@creationnation.com
Web site: creationnationanimation.com.

Creation Resource Foundation, *(978-0-9672713)* P.O. Box 570, El Dorado, CA 95667 USA Tel 530-626-4447; Fax: 530-626-5215; Toll Free: 800-497-1454
E-mail: info@creationresource.org
Web site: http://www.awesomeworks.com; http://www.creationresource.org/
Dist(s): **Send The Light Distribution LLC.**

Creative 3, LLC, *(978-1-933815)* 2236 E Spring Hill Rd., Springfield, MO 65804 USA Tel 417-882-2145; Fax: 417-882-2145; Toll Free Fax: 800-866-1360; Toll Free: 800-866-1360; *Imprints:* Quirkles, The (The Quirkles)
E-mail: info@quirkles.com; thequirkles@aol.com
Web site: http://www.quirkles.com.

Creative Attic, Inc., The, *(978-0-9653955)* P.O. Box 187, Canterbury, NH 03224 USA Tel 603-783-9103; Fax: 603-783-0118; Toll Free: 888-566-6539
E-mail: the5kids@aol.com.

Creative Avenues Media, *(978-1-7327161)* 3736 SW 10th, 4, Portland, OR 97239 USA Tel 503-754-5831
E-mail: natepjensen@gmail.com
Web site: http://portlandchildrensbookillustrator.com/.

Creative Bk. Pubs., *(978-0-9754818; 978-0-9763093; 978-0-9765467; 978-0-9779662; 978-0-9795460)* 1912 Falcon Dr., Ridgefield, WA 98642 USA
Web site: http://www.creativebookpublishers.com.

Creative Chapps, *(978-1-947997)* 25 River Rock Way, Franklinton, NC 27525 USA Tel 919-400-9935
E-mail: sixchapps@gmail.com.

Creative Communication, *(978-1-60050)* Orders Addr.: P.O. Box 303, Smithfield, UT 84335 USA Tel 435-713-4411; Fax: 435-713-4422; Edit Addr.: 1488 . 200 W., Logan, UT 84341 USA Do not confuse with companies with the same or similar name in Forest Grove, OR, Seattle, WA, Trabuco Canyon, CA, Nixa, MO, Chelan, WA, La Mesa, CA, Kalamazoo, MI
E-mail: drtom@poeticpower.com
Web site: http://www.poeticpower.com
Dist(s): **Independent Pubs. Group.**

Creative Communications for the Parish, *(978-0-9629585; 978-1-889387; 978-1-68279)* 1564 Fencorp Ct., Fenton, MO 63026 USA Tel 636-305-9777; Fax: 636-305-9339; Toll Free Fax: 800-448-6557; Toll Free: 800-325-9414
Web site: http://www.creativecommunications.com.

Creative Co., The, *(978-0-87191; 978-0-88682; 978-0-89812; 978-1-56660; 978-1-56846; 978-1-58341; 978-1-60818; 978-1-62832; 978-1-68277; 978-1-64000; 978-1-64026; 979-8-88989)* 2140 Howard Drive West, North Mankato, MN 56003 USA Tel 507-388-6273; Fax: 507-388-4797; Toll Free: 800-445-6209; *Imprints:* Creative Editions (Creative Eds); Creative Education (Creat Educ); Creative Paperbacks (Creative Paperbks) Do not confuse with The Creative Co., Lawrenceburg, IN
E-mail: info@thecreativecompany.us; rglaser@thecreativecompany.us
Web site: http://www.thecreativecompany.us
Dist(s): **Abraham Assocs. Inc.**
Children's Plus, Inc.
Hachette Bk. Group
RiverStream Publishing.

Creative Continuum, Inc., *(978-0-9713804; 978-1-932252; 978-1-62192)* 2910 E. La Palma Ave. Ste. C, Anaheim, CA 92806-2618 USA
E-mail: info@creativecontinuum.com
Web site: http://www.creativecontinuum.com.

Creative Conversations, *(978-0-9768235)* 11767 W. Coal Mine Dr., Littleton, CO 80127 USA Tel 303-437-8533.

Creative Cranium Concept, The, *(978-0-9741009)* Orders Addr.: 2560 Reed Ave, Marshalltown, IA 50158 USA Tel 303-875-8742; Edit Addr.: 2560 Reed Ave, Marshalltown, IA 50158 USA Tel 303-875-8742
E-mail: Rhonda@RhondaSpellman.com
Web site: http://www.rhondaspellman.com; http://AutismWithRhonda.com.

Creative Creature Publishing, *(978-0-9964983; 978-1-7353083)* 53 Chadwick Ln., Westcliffe, CO 81252 USA Tel 719-285-5650
E-mail: creativecreaturepublishing@gmail.com
Web site: http://www.creativecreaturepublishing.com/.

Creative Curriculum Initiatives *See* **Curriculum Concepts International**

Creative Dreaming Ltd., *(978-0-615-14010-0; 978-0-615-14725-3; 978-0-615-15431-2; 978-0-615-15487-9; 978-0-615-15521-0; 978-0-615-16439-7; 978-0-615-17664-2; 978-0-615-18006-9; 978-0-615-18260-5; 978-0-615-18340-4; 978-0-615-18424-1; 978-0-615-18654-2; 978-0-615-18886-7; 978-0-615-23631-5)* 6433 Topanga Canyon Blvd., No. 120, Woodland Hills, CA 91303 USA
Dist(s): **Lulu Pr., Inc.**

Creative Editions *Imprint of* **Creative Co., The**

Creative Education *Imprint of* **Creative Co., The**

Creative Education & Publishing, *(978-0-9824964; 978-0-9825969; 978-0-9835315; 978-0-9859066; 978-0-9903851)* 3339 Ardley Ct., Falls Church, VA 22041 USA Tel 703-856-7005
E-mail: alameddine_kaddoura@yahoo.com; info@creativeeducationandpublishing.com
Web site: http://www.creativeeducationandpublishing.com.

Creative Educational Video *See* **C E V Multimedia, Ltd.**

Creative Energy, LLC, *(978-0-9821062; 978-0-9829825; 978-1-945372)* 20322 Sequoia Trace, Spring, TX 77379 USA (SAN 857-2771)
E-mail: drkmcleod@yahoo.com.

Creative Enterprises, *(978-1-880675)* 1040 Harvard Blvd., Dayton, OH 45406-5047 USA (SAN 253-5491) Tel 937-278-7159; Toll Free: 888-266-5777 Do not confuse with companies with the same or similar name in Mattapoisett, MA, Cordova, TN, Brooklyn, NY, Kittery, ME, Montgomery Village, MD
E-mail: allen45406@aol.com
Web site: http://creative-enterprises.org.

Creative Home & Family Endeavors, *(978-0-9747306)* 1555 Main St., Suite A-3-287, Windsor, CO 80550 USA Tel 970-221-0737
E-mail: endeavors4@aol.com.

Creative Homeowner *Imprint of* **Fox Chapel Publishing Co., Inc.**

†Creative Homeowner, *(978-0-932944; 978-1-58011; 978-1-880029)* Div. of Courier Corporation, 24 Park Way, Upper Saddle River, NJ 07458-9960 USA (SAN 213-6627) Tel 201-934-7100; Fax: 201-934-8971; Toll Free: 800-631-7795
E-mail: info@creativehomeowner.com
Web site: http://www.creativehomeowner.com
Dist(s): **Dover Pubns., Inc.**
Follett School Solutions
Independent Pubs. Group
MyiLibrary; *CIP.*

Creative House Press *See* **Bourgeois Media & Consulting**

Creative Hse. Kids Pr. *Imprint of* **Bourgeois Media & Consulting**

Creative Image Pubs., *(978-0-9742667)* 102 E. Main, Georgetown, KY 40324 USA
E-mail: Kathy@creativeimagepublishers.com
Web site: http://www.creativeimagepublishers.com.

Creative Impact, *(978-0-9862655)* 111 10th St., Des Moines, IA 50309 USA Tel 515-707-8860
E-mail: ardisglace@gmail.com.

Creative James Media, *(978-1-7332621; 978-1-7353926; 978-1-956183)* 9150 Ft. Smallwood Rd., Pasadena, MD 21122 USA Tel 301-262-2511
E-mail: jeanlowd@gmail.com.

Creative Learning Books *See* **Aradiance Publishing**

Creative Learning Consultants, Incorporated *See* **Pieces of Learning**

Creative Learning Exchange, *(978-0-9753169; 978-0-9960128; 978-1-7379574)* 27 Central St., Acton, MA 01720-3522 USA (SAN 850-8836) Tel 978-287-0070; Fax: 978-287-0080
E-mail: stuntzln@clexchange.org
Web site: http://www.clexchange.org.

Creative Life Publishing, *(978-0-9779072)* 210 Indian Oak Dr., No. 1163, Waleska, GA 30183 USA Tel 770-720-1975
E-mail: affiliate@caroleoconnell.com
Web site: http://www.caroleoconnell.com.

Creative Marketing Concepts, Inc., *(978-0-9761408)* 2775 Jade St., Mora, MN 55051 USA Tel 320-679-4105; Fax: 320-679-3349; Toll Free: 800-605-4280 Do not confuse with companies with the same name in Saint Louis, MO, Los Angeles, CA
E-mail: cmc@creativemk.com
Web site: http://www.creativemk.com.

Creative Media Partners, LLC, *(978-1-115; 978-1-4264; 978-1-4346; 978-1-4375; 978-0-554; 978-0-559; 978-0-526; 978-0-341; 978-0-469; 978-0-699; 978-1-103; 978-1-110; 978-1-113; 978-1-116; 978-1-117; 978-1-140; 978-1-141; 978-1-142; 978-1-143; 978-1-144; 978-1-145; 978-1-146; 978-1-147; 978-1-148; 978-1-149; 978-1-170; 978-1-171; 978-1-172; 978-1-173; 978-1-174; 978-1-175; 978-1-176; 978-1-177; 978-1-178; 978-1-179; 978-1-240; 978-1-241; 978-1-242; 978-1-243; 978-1-244; 978-1-245; 978-1-246; 978-1-247; 978-1-248; 978-1-2) P.O. Box 21206, Charleston, SC 29413 USA Tel 843-696-0416; Fax: 843-853-9251; 33 Cannon St., Charleston, SC 29403 Tel 843-408-2303; Imprints:* BiblioLife (Bibliolife); Nabu Press (Nabu Pr); Gale ECCO, Print Editions (GECCO); British Library, Historical Print Editions (BritLibrary); Wentworth Press (Wentworth Pr); Gale, Study Guides (GaleStudy) 11/15/05 Owner also owns Indigo, Inc. of Charleston, SC but the two companies are not connected. LT
E-mail: jason@creativmedia.io; info@bibliolife.com; info@bibliolabs.com
Web site: support.creativemedia.io; http://www.bibliobazaar.com; www.bibliolabs.com
Dist(s): **MyiLibrary.**

Creative Media Publishing, *(978-0-9826435; 978-0-9835393; 978-1-938438; 978-1-950298)* 10606 La Alba Dr, Whittier, CA 90603-2460 USA Tel 714-542-1212
E-mail: info@creativemedia.net
Web site: http://www.CreativeMedia.net
Dist(s): **Lulu Pr., Inc.**

Creative Medicine: Healing Through Words, LLC, *(978-0-9965324; 978-0-9986011; 978-978-099-000-8; 978-978-099-001-5; 978-978-099-002-2; 978-978-099-003-9; 978-978-099-004-6; 978-978-099-005-3; 978-978-099-006-0; 978-978-099-007-7; 978-978-099-008-4; 978-978-099-653-6)* P.O. Box 2749, Tappahannock, VA 22560 USA Tel 804-833-4171
E-mail: Ronnie@creative-medicine.com
Web site: www.creative-medicine.com.

Creative Mind Energy, *(978-1-939424; 978-1-63849)* 259 W Front St. Ste. 1, Missoula, MT 59802 USA; *Imprints:* Vault Comics (Vault Comics); Wonderbound (MYID_A_WONDERB)
E-mail: damian@vaultcomics.com; publisher@vaultcomics.com
Web site: www.vaultcomics.com
Dist(s): **Diamond Comic Distributors, Inc.**
Diamond Bk. Distributors
Simon & Schuster, Inc.

Creative Minds Pubns., *(978-0-9769737; 978-0-578-58785-1; 978-0-578-65146-0; 978-0-578-88326-7; 979-8-218-06282-8; 979-8-218-18411-7; 979-8-218-18412-4)* Orders Addr.: 2325 Crowncrest Dr., Richmond, VA 23233 USA Tel 804-740-6010; Fax: 804-798-1531
E-mail: kcstarke@aol.com
Dist(s): **Follett School Solutions.**

Creative Ministry Solutions, *(978-1-58302)* P.O. Box 472258, Aurora, CO 80011 USA
E-mail: kj@creativemin.com
Web site: www.creativemin.com.

Creative Nutrition & Wellness, *(978-0-615-12437-7)* P.O. Box 7000-233, Redondo Beach, CA 90277 USA Fax: 310-792-0428
Web site: http://www.creativenutrition.com.

Creative Paperbacks *Imprint of* **Creative Co., The**

Creative Properties LLC, *(978-0-929292; 978-1-934749; 978-1-61315)* Div. of KLMK Communications, Inc., 313 S. 11th St. Suite A, Garland, TX 75040 USA; 313 S. 11th St., Garland, TX 75040
E-mail: louismoore@yahoo.com
Dist(s): **Ingram Content Group**
Spring Arbor Distributors, Inc.

Creative Publishing, *(978-0-9744833)* 2221 Justin Rd., No. 119-123, Flower Mound, TX 75028 USA Tel 281-251-1751 (phone/fax) Do not confuse with companies with the same or similar name in Roseboro, NC, Greenville, SC, Lawrenceville, GA, Shrevport, LA, College Station, TX, Tustin, CA
E-mail: support@creativekidsonthemove.com
Web site: http://www.creativekidsonthemove.com.

Creative Publishing Consultants, *(978-0-9824730)* 19 Hilltopper Ct., Blythewood, SC 29016-8745 USA.

Creative Publishing International *Imprint of* **Quarto Publishing Group USA**

Creative Publishing International *Imprint of* **Quarto Publishing Group USA**

Creative Pursuits Publishing, *(978-1-7367765)* 4436 Highland Ave., San Diego, CA 92115 USA Tel 619-283-1578
E-mail: barbaraellen5@cox.net.

Creative Quill Publishing, Inc., *(978-0-9709906)* Orders Addr.: P.O. Box 4028, Salem, OR 97302 USA; Edit Addr.: 460 Myers S., Salem, OR 97302 USA Tel 503-363-2843
E-mail: mavist@aol.com; Creativequill@aol.com
Web site: http://www.creativequill.us.

Creative Sharp Presentations, Incorporated *See* **SHARP Literacy, Inc.**

Creative Sources, *(978-0-9759613)* 105 N. Harvest Crest Ct., Highland, IL 62249 USA
E-mail: lynnette@kidsdoread.com
Web site: http://www.KidsDoRead.com.

Creative Styles *See* **JFW, Ltd.**

Creative Success Works, *(978-0-9759551)* 752 E. Lake Lndg., Marietta, GA 30062-3876 USA
E-mail: creativesuccess@comcast.net
Web site: http://www.creativesuccessworks.com.

Creative Teaching Assocs., *(978-1-878669; 978-1-930818; 978-1-931474; 978-1-932918)* Orders Addr.: P.O. Box 7766, Fresno, CA 93747 USA (SAN 297-6803) Tel 559-294-2141 Toll Free: 800-767-4282 (800-767-4CTA); Edit Addr.: P.O. Box 7766, Fresno, CA 93747-7766 USA
Web site: http://www.mastercta.com
Dist(s): **Follett School Solutions.**

Creative Teaching Pr., Inc., *(978-0-88160; 978-0-916119; 978-1-57471; 978-1-59198; 978-1-60689; 978-1-61601; 978-1-62186; 978-1-63445; 978-1-68310; 978-1-64474)* Orders Addr.: P.O. Box 2723, Huntington Beach, CA 92647-0723 USA Tel 714-895-5047; Fax: 714-895-6547 Toll Free Fax: 800-444-4287; Edit Addr.: 6262 Katella Ave., Cypress, CA 90630 USA (SAN 294-9180) Tel 714-895-5047; Toll Free Fax: 800-229-9929; Toll Free: 800-444-4287; *Imprints:* Learning Works, The (The Lrning Works)
E-mail: toni.gardner@creativeteaching.com; webmaster@creativeteaching.com; we.listen@creativeteaching.com; emond.ling@creativeteaching.com; denise.clarke@creativeteaching.com
Web site: http://www.creativeteaching.com; http://www.thelearningworks.com; http://www.learntoreadkidsclub.com
Dist(s): **Follett School Solutions**
Pacific Learning, Inc.

Creative Texts Publishers *See* **Creative Texts Pubs., LLC**

Creative Texts Pubs., LLC, *(978-0-692-32201-7; 978-0-692-32220-8; 978-0-692-42754-5; 978-0-692-42766-8; 978-0-692-42772-9; 978-0-692-42777-4; 978-0-692-42846-7; 978-0-692-42868-9; 978-0-692-42875-7; 978-0-692-42882-5; 978-0-692-42919-8; 978-0-692-42927-3; 978-0-692-42986-0; 978-0-692-43308-9; 978-0-692-43311-9; 978-0-692-43323-2; 978-0-692-43324-9; 978-0-692-43331-7; 978-0-692-43340-9; 978-0-692-43346-1; 978-0-692-43349-2; 978-0-692-43353-9; 978-0-692-43362-1; 978-0-692-43390-4; 978-0-692-43395-9; 978-0-692-43412-3;) P.O. Box 50, Barto, PA 19504 USA Tel 610-945-7586*
E-mail: info@creativetexts.com
Web site: http://www.creativetexts.com; www.ColdWest.com
Dist(s): **Ingram Bk. Co.**
Ingram Content Group.

Creative Thinkers, Incorporated *See* **Let's Think-kids Foundation, Inc.**

Creative Unity Productions, *(978-0-9822796; 978-1-949402)* 1550 Harrison Dr., Greenwood, IN 46143 USA (SAN 857-748X)
E-mail: CreativeUnityPublishing@gmail.com; CreationsByDonna@gmail.com.

Creative Well, The, *(978-0-9700108)* P.O. Box 2121, Ashtabula, OH 44005 USA Tel 440-964-0338.

Creative with Words Pubns., *(978-0-936945)* P.O. Box 223226, Carmel, CA 93922 USA (SAN 658-6961) Fax: 408-655-8627
E-mail: cwwpub@usa.net.

Creative Works, *(978-0-9727499)* 3747 Redwood Cir., Palo Alto, CA 94306 USA Tel 650-493-3747.

Creative Writing & Publishing Co., *(978-1-887636)* P.O. Box 511848, Milwaukee, WI 53203-0311 USA
E-mail: Cbritt1@wi.rr.com.

Creative Writing Pr., Inc., *(978-0-9708382)* 1830 Stephenson Hwy., Troy, MI 48083-2173 USA Toll Free: 800-760-6397
E-mail: rodgers@mich.com
Web site: http://thepoetrylady.com.

Creative Year 2014, The *See* **Frog Prince Pr.**

Creatively Hue, *(978-1-7339845)*
E-mail: senditomireya@yahoo.com
Web site: creativelyhue.com.

Creatively Unleashed, *(978-1-7346503)* 25 Evergreen Rd., Norristown, PA 19403 USA Tel 610-504-1146
E-mail: lakeyaguy@yahoo.com.

CreativeMedia, Incorporated *See* **Creative Media Publishing**

Creativity Pr., *(978-1-934396; 978-0-9952290-2-0)* P.O. Box 1313, Anacortes, WA 98221 USA Do not confuse with Creativity Press in Cleveland, OH
E-mail: anne@Anneolwin.com
Web site: http://www.creativitypress.com.

Creatopia Productions - Lamy, New Mexico, *(978-0-9637467; 978-0-9854527)* 719 1/2 No. B, Lamy, NM 87540-9682 USA Tel 505-204-3892
E-mail: wrayl@hotmail.com
Web site: http://www.members.tripod.com/~lyne4lyne/
Dist(s): **Adventures Unlimited Pr.**
Barnes & Noble Bks.-Imports
CreateSpace Independent Publishing Platform.

Crecelius Haus Publishing, *(978-1-7322492; 978-1-7370597)* 31 Sir William Dr., Bedford, IN 47421 USA Tel 812-508-1249
E-mail: author_loriroberts@yahoo.com.

Credible Math, LLC., *(978-0-9903831)* 20 Baltimore Ave, Piscataway, NJ 08854 USA Tel 732-356-3329
E-mail: deboraharey@aol.com.

Credo Hse. Pubs., *(978-0-9787620; 978-1-935391; 978-1-62586)* 2200 Boyd Ct NE, Grand Rapids, MI 49525-6714 USA
E-mail: connect@credocommunications.net
Web site: http://www.credohousepublishers.com.

Credo Italia, *(978-0-9768375)* Orders Addr.: 350 Bay St., Suite 100-124, San Francisco, CA 94123 USA
E-mail: info@ClintAdams.com
Web site: http://www.ClintAdams.com.

Creed, Julie, *(978-0-9728181)* 17 Los Abitos, Rancho Santa Margarita, CA 92688 USA
E-mail: julie@qabranding.com
Web site: http://www.qabranding.com.

Creed Publishing, *(978-1-7357809)* 3106 Raven's Crest Dr., Plainsboro, NJ 08536 USA Tel 609-731-9613
E-mail: aus2503@yahoo.com.

Creek Sound Bks., *(978-0-9743840)* 120 Misty Way, Cosby, TN 37722 USA Tel 606-523-5324
E-mail: rapowell7@msn.com.

reekside Publishing, (*978-0-692-69750-4; 978-1-951763*) 2310 Homestead Rd. Suite C1-155, Los Altos, CA 94024-7302 USA Tel 408-730-1511
E-mail: hansonreading@gmail.com
Web site: www.hansonreading.com.

reekside Publishing, (*978-0-9972349*) 14 Mill St., Morris, NY 13808 USA Tel 607-263-5531
E-mail: LesDiehl60@aol.com
Web site: www.lesleyadiehl.com.

reepy Little Productions, (*978-0-9704159*) 3726 W. Augusta Ave., Phoenix, AZ 85051 USA Tel 602-625-6596; Fax: 602-242-3046
E-mail: christy@atgproductions.com; madamem@creepylittlestories.com
Web site: http://www.creepylittlestories.com
Dist(s): **PSI (Publisher Services, Inc.).**

reevy, Anne *See* **ABC Bks.**

reflo Dollar Ministries Pubns., (*978-1-931172; 978-1-59089*) Orders Addr.: P.O. Box 490124, College Park, GA 30349 USA Tel 770-210-5700; Fax: 770-210-5701; Edit Addr.: 2500 Burdett Rd., College Park, GA 30349 USA
E-mail: mfleming@worldchangers.org; mocarter@worldchangers.org; dfidler@worldchangers.org; tdavis@worldchangers.org
Web site: http://www.creflodollarministries.org
Dist(s): **Independent Pubs. Group**
Send The Light Distribution LLC.

CreoXimius Publishing Company, (*978-0-9776617*) 3314 Granger Rd., Medina, OH 44256 USA
Web site: http://www.debrae.com.

Crescent Moon Pr., (*978-0-9816011; 978-0-9818484; 978-0-9823065; 978-0-9841805; 978-0-9828200; 978-0-9846394; 978-1-937254; 978-1-939173; 978-0-9906274; 978-0-9908827; 978-0-9862871*) 1385 Hwy. 35, Box 269, Middletown, NJ 07748 USA
E-mail: publisher@crescentmoonpress.com
Web site: http://www.crescentmoonpress.com.

Crescent Moon Publishing (GBR) (*978-1-86171; 978-1-871846*) *Dist. by* **indiCo.**

CREST Pubns., (*978-0-9725546; 978-0-9912995*) P.O. Box 481022, Charlotte, NC 28269 USA Do not confuse with Crest Publications, Richardson, TX
Web site: http://www.crestpub.com.

Crested Tern Publishing, (*978-0-578-19682-4*) 2251 Winged Foot Ct., Oxnard, CA 93036 USA.

Creston Bks., (*978-1-939547; 978-1-954354*) 965 Creston Rd., Berkeley, CA 94708 USA Tel 510-928-1765
E-mail: solsetimo@yahoo.com
Dist(s): **Lerner Publishing Group**
Publishers Group West (PGW)
Two Rivers Distribution.

Crews, Nina Studio, (*978-0-692-43447-5; 978-0-578-67097-3*) 653 Carroll St., Brooklyn, NY 11215 USA Tel 718-636-5774
E-mail: letters@ninacrews.com
Web site: www.ninacrews.com.

Crews Pubns., LLC, (*978-0-9795236*) 7483 Garnet Dr., Jonesboro, GA 30236 USA Tel 770-617-9688
E-mail: crewspublications@yahoo.com
Web site: http://www.gscrews.com.

Cribsheet Publishing *See* **Blue Shoe Publishing**

Cricket Bks., (*978-0-8126*) Div. of Carus Publishing Co., 70 E. Lake St. Ste. 300, Chicago, IL 60601-5945 USA Tel 312-701-1720
Web site: http://www.cricketmag.com/home.asp
Dist(s): **Cobblestone Publishing Co.**
Ebsco Publishing
Follett School Solutions.

Cricket Cottage Publishing, LLC, (*978-0-9991224*) 6799 Calistoga Cir., Port Orange, FL 32128 USA Tel 323-207-6213
E-mail: m.owenmurray@gmail.com
Web site: thecricketpublishing.com.

Cricket Productions, Incorporated *See* **Scrumps Entertainment, Inc.**

Cricket Rohman, (*978-0-9896971; 978-0-9975270; 978-0-9994819; 978-1-7355672; 979-8-9868894; 979-8-9888822*) 7618 E. Callisto Cir. No. 123, Tucson, AZ 85715 USA Tel 520-490-7430
E-mail: cricket@cricketrohman.com
Web site: www.cricketrohman.com.

Cricket XPress of Minnesota, (*978-0-9822534*) 504 Bluebird Ct., Sartell, MN 56377 USA Tel 320-267-8978
E-mail: CricketXPressMN@charter.net.

Crickhollow Bks. *Imprint of* **Great Lakes Literary, LLC**

Cridge Mumbly LLC *See* **Cridge Mumbly Publishing**

Cridge Mumbly Publishing, (*978-1-7326245*) 19172 Laurenrae St., Riverside, CA 92508 USA Tel 909-512-2658
E-mail: peirce@yahoo.com
Web site: peirce-clayton.squarespace.com.

CrimethInc. Workers' Collective, (*978-0-9709101; 978-0-9989822*) P.O. Box 13998, Salem, OR 97309 USA Tel 928-222-9129
E-mail: pfm@me.com
Web site: http://www.crimethinc.com
Dist(s): **AK Pr. Distribution.**

Crimson Cloak Publishing, (*978-0-692-30069-5; 978-0-692-31345-9; 978-0-692-32698-5; 978-0-692-33222-1; 978-0-692-36488-8; 978-1-68160*) P.O. Box 36, Pilot Knob, MO 63663 USA Tel 573-639-7591
E-mail: carly@crimsoncloakpublishing; rhianna_al_mere@yahoo.com; carly7698@gmail.com
Web site: www.crimsoncloakpublishing.com
Dist(s): **Ingram Publisher Services.**

Crimson Oak Publishing LLC, (*978-0-9822725; 978-0-9829505*) P.O. Box 1389, Pullman, WA 99163 USA
E-mail: info@crimsonoakpublishing.com
Web site: http://www.crimsonoakpublishing.com
Dist(s): **Smashwords.**

Crimson Pulse Media, (*978-0-615-67903-7; 978-0-615-70396-1; 978-0-615-86304-7; 978-0-692-49583-4; 978-0-692-50626-4; 978-0-692-53074-0; 978-0-692-53165-5; 978-0-692-71751-6; 978-1-946692*) 10108 Antler Creek Dr, Falcon, CO 80831 USA Tel 3093704920
E-mail: thequestfortruthbooks@gmail.com; brock83@gmail.com
Web site: crimsonpulsemedia.com; brockeastman.com
Dist(s): **Independently Published**
Ingram Content Group.

Crippen & Landru Pubs., (*978-1-885941; 978-1-932009; 978-1-936363*) Orders Addr.: P.O. Box 9315, Norfolk, VA 23505-9315 USA Tel 757-622-6656 (phone/fax); Toll Free: 877-622-6656 (phone/fax); Edit Addr.: 627 New Hampshire Ave., Norfolk, VA 23508 USA Tel 757-622-6656 (phone/fax)
E-mail: info@crippenlandru.com
Web site: http://www.crippenlandru.com
Dist(s): **Follett School Solutions.**

Criqueville Pr., (*978-0-9705404*) Orders Addr.: P.O. Box 1227, Princeton, NJ 08542-1227 USA Tel 908-359-7834; Edit Addr.: 2 Dogwood Ln., Princeton, NJ 08542-1227 USA (SAN 255-982X)
E-mail: criquevillepress@hotmail.com.

Crises Research Pr., (*978-0-86627*) 301 W. 45th St., New York, NY 10036 USA (SAN 238-9274).

Crispin Bks. *Imprint of* **Great Lakes Literary, LLC**

Crispus Medical Pr., (*978-0-9640389*) 7923 Leschi Rd., SW, Lakewood, WA 98498 USA Toll Free: 877-464-6469.

Crist, Rachel, (*978-0-578-56390-9*) 2612 W. Laredo St., Broken Arrow, OK 74012 USA Tel 918-944-8333
E-mail: raechull315@gmail.com
Web site: www.rachelcrist.com
Dist(s): **Ingram Content Group.**

Cristal Publishing Co., (*978-0-9779124*) P.O. Box 14-4828, Coral Gables, FL 33114-4828 USA
E-mail: cristal228@bellsouth.net
Dist(s): **Ediciones Universal**
Follett School Solutions.

Critical Path Publishing, (*978-0-9740605*) P.O. Box 1073, Clayton, CA 94517-9073 USA Do not confuse with Critical Path Publishing Company in Denville, NJ
E-mail: cpp@silcon.com
Dist(s): **BPC.**

Critical Thinking Co., The, (*978-0-89455; 978-0-910974; 978-1-60144; 978-1-64420*) Orders Addr.: 1991 Sherman Ave Ste 200, North Bend, OR 97459 USA (SAN 207-0510) Tel 800-458-4849 Toll Free: 800-458-4849
E-mail: GaleO@criticalthinking.com; AbbeyH@criticalthinking.com; service@criticalthinking.com
Web site: http://www.criticalthinking.com
Dist(s): **Follett School Solutions.**

Critical Thinking Company, The *See* **Critical Thinking Co., The**

Crittendon, Kiana, (*978-1-7349857*) 6715 Glyndon Ln., Richmond, VA 23225 USA Tel 804-888-4057
E-mail: mskianarae@yahoo.com.

Critter Camp Inc., (*978-0-9772825*) 1190 Scenic Ave., Lummi Island, WA 98262 USA Tel 360-758-4269 (phone/fax)
E-mail: midiana@clearwire.net.

Critter Pubns., (*978-1-928972*) P.O. Box 413, Leicester, MA 01524-0413 USA
E-mail: del@critterp.com
Web site: http://www.critterp.com.

Critter Publishing, (*978-0-9754615*) Orders Addr.: P.O. Box 585, Readfield, ME 04355 USA Tel 207-685-5527 (phone/fax); Edit Addr.: 70 Walker Rd., Readfield, ME 04355 USA
E-mail: soniccomics@gwi.net
Web site: http://www.sonicpublishing.com.

CritterKin., (*978-0-9960657*) 107 Killam Ct., Cary, NC 27513 USA Tel 919-535-8472
E-mail: JenaBall@CritterKin.com
Web site: www.critterkin.com
Dist(s): **Lulu Pr., Inc.**

Critters Up Close *Imprint of* **National Wildlife Federation**

Crittersinc, (*978-0-9745997*) 19611 Longview Terr., Salinas, CA 93908 USA
Web site: http://www.crittersinc.com.

CRLE Publishing, (*978-0-9972129*) P.O. Box 70437, Odessa, TX 79769 USA Tel 432-553-5867
E-mail: robyn.mitchell1@yahoo.com
Web site: https://www.facebook.com/robynmitchellauthor.

CRM Enterprises, (*978-0-615-13155-9; 978-0-615-13278-5; 978-0-615-33279-6; 978-0-615-96051-7; 978-0-692-80739-2; 978-0-692-19775-2*) 411 Coram Avenue, Shelton, CT 06484 USA.

Croce, Pat & Co., (*978-0-9897533*) P.O. Box 520A, Villanova, PA 19085 USA Tel 610-520-1890; Fax: 610-525-5279
E-mail: sbarbacane@piratesoul.com.

Crocodile Bks. *Imprint of* **Interlink Publishing Group, Inc.**

Crocodiles Not Waterlilies Entertainment, (*978-0-9798297*) 58 Maiden Ln., Fifth Flr., San Francisco, CA 94108 USA (SAN 854-4921) Fax: 801-892-2230
E-mail: jodeen@crocpond.com.

Crofton Creek Pr., (*978-0-9700917; 978-0-9767268*) 2303 Gregg Rd., SW, South Boardman, MI 49680 USA Tel 231-369-2325; Fax: 231-369-4382; Toll Free: 877-255-3117
E-mail: publisher@croftoncreek.com
Web site: http://www.croftoncreek.com
Dist(s): **Partners Bk. Distributing, Inc.**
Wayne State Univ. Pr.

Cromulent Pr., (*978-1-7326840*) 145 Flowering Grove Ln., Mooresville, NC 28115 USA Tel 703-554-7530
E-mail: indiegantz@gmail.com
Dist(s): **CreateSpace Independent Publishing Platform.**

Cronier, Brett, (*978-0-692-15190-7; 978-0-692-15191-4; 978-0-578-42221-3; 978-0-578-42222-0; 979-8-218-15341-0*) 3604 Kelliebrook Ln., Moss Point, MS 39562 USA Tel 228-218-7086
E-mail: brettgcronier@gmail.com
Dist(s): **Ingram Content Group.**

Cronies, (*978-1-929566*) Div. of Reproductive Images, 22738 Roscoe Blvd., No. 225, Canoga Park, CA 91304-3350 USA Tel 818-773-4888; Fax: 818-773-8808; Toll Free: 800-232-8099
E-mail: SethJ@CRONIES.com.

Cronus College, (*978-0-9760045; 978-0-9779897*) Div. of e-Pluribus Unum Publishing Co., P.O. Box 941, Lafayette, CA 94549 USA; *Imprints:* Reluctant Reader Books (ReluctRead)
Web site: http://www.cronuscollege.com.

Crooked Creek Publishing, LLC, (*978-0-9786084*) Orders Addr.: P.O. Box 901 Fourth St., Suite 50, Hudson, WI 54016 USA Tel 715-781-2047; Edit Addr.: 901 Fourth St., Suite 50, Hudson, WI 54016 USA
E-mail: crookedcreekpublishing@gmail.com
Dist(s): **Stevens International.**

Crooked Lane Bks., (*978-1-62953*) Div. of Bookspan, 2 Park Ave., 10th Flr., New York, NY 10016 USA Tel 212-596-2806; Fax: 646-214-0637
E-mail: inquiries@crookedlanebooks.com
Web site: http://www.crookedlanebooks.com/
Dist(s): **Legato Pubs. Group**
Penguin Random Hse. Distribution
Penguin Random Hse. LLC
Publishers Group West (PGW).

Crooked River Pr., (*978-0-9778586*) P.O. Box 21, Cuyahoga Falls, OH 44221 USA Tel 330-701-3375; *Imprints:* Blue Jay Books (Blue Jay Bks)
E-mail: Books@CrookedRiverPress.com
Web site: http://www.CrookedRiverPress.com.

Crooked Tail Pr., (*978-1-946380*) 2302 115th AVE SE, Lake Stevens, WA 98258 USA Tel 425-350-2625
E-mail: joy@thecontentvixen.com
Web site: crookedtailpress.com.

Crooked Tree Stories, (*978-0-692-15525-7*) 6240 Copper Valley Ct. NE, ADA, MI 49301 USA Tel 616-648-5410
E-mail: mbepperly@comcast.net
Dist(s): **Ingram Content Group.**

Crosam Pr., (*978-0-9774822; 978-0-9790337; 978-0-9798351; 978-0-9818903*) Orders Addr.: 681 Beverly Dr., Lake Wales, FL 33853 USA Tel 863-676-5737; Fax: 863-676-2285; Toll Free: 877-676-2285
E-mail: winksampson22@aol.com
Web site: http://www.feathersandfur.com; http://www.crosampress.com.

Crosby Advanced Medical Systems Inc., (*978-0-9846293*) 13556 Dornoch Dr., Ste. 1, Orlando, FL 32828 USA Tel 407-823-9502.

Cross & Crown Publishing, (*978-0-9785523; 978-0-9817728; 978-0-9886778*) 342 Meadow Green Dr., Ringgold, GA 30736 USA Tel 706-937-3798
E-mail: eddunlop@juno.com
Web site: http://www.dunlopministries.com
Dist(s): **Follett School Solutions.**

Cross Dove Publishing, LLC, (*978-0-9656513; 978-1-7335856*) 1704 Esplanade, Front, Redondo Beach, CA 90277-8710 USA Tel 310-375-8400; Fax: 310-373-5912; 27 West 20Th St., New York, NY 10011
Web site: http://www.marysson.com; http://www.crossdove.com
Dist(s): **Follett School Solutions**
MyiLibrary.

Cross, Gregory *See* **Gregory Cross Publishing**

Cross, Michael John, (*978-1-7331414*) 36 Island Pond Rd., Atkinson, NH 03811 USA Tel 603-362-3612
E-mail: lotharcross@hotmail.com.

Cross Pointe Printing, (*978-0-9742154*) 14417 N. 42nd St., Phoenix, AZ 85032-5437 USA
E-mail: dan@crosspointeprinting.com.

Cross Product Pubns., (*978-0-9793087; 978-0-9826837*) 3222 Cascade Hills Dr., NW, Cleveland, TN 37312 USA.

Cross Pubns., (*978-0-9771926; 978-0-9850996; 978-1-7349330*) Orders Addr.: 502 E. Liberty Ave., Stillwater, OK 74075 USA Tel 405-564-5641 Do not confuse with Cross Publications in Safford, AZ, Savannah, GA
Web site: www.lulu.com/greenpheon7
Dist(s): **Lulu Pr., Inc.**

Cross Reference Imprints, (*978-0-9725139*) 3607 Hycliffe Ave., Louisville, KY 40207 USA Tel 502-897-2719
E-mail: Pneuma@eclipsetel.com.

Cross Time *Imprint of* **Crossquarter Publishing Group**

Cross Training Publishing, (*978-1-887002; 978-1-929478; 978-0-9821652; 978-0-9845750; 978-1-938254; 978-0-578-22976-8; 978-1-952222*) P.O. Box 1874, Keary, NE 68848 USA (SAN 298-7406) Tel 308-293-3891; Fax: 308-338-2058; Toll Free: 800-430-8588; 16329 Josphine St., Omaha, NE 68136 Tel 308-293-3891
E-mail: gordon@crosstrainingpublishing.com; gthiessen@mac.com
Web site: http://www.crosstrainingpublishing.com
Dist(s): **Follett School Solutions.**

CrossBearers Publishing, (*978-0-9716365*) Div. of Reconciliation Ministries, Inc., Orders Addr.: 3101 Troost Ave., Kansas City, MO 64109 USA Tel 816-931-4751; Fax: 816-931-0142; P.O. Box 45642, Kansas City, MO 64171 Tel 816-449-2825; Fax: 816-449-5231; *Imprints:* St. Nicholas Press (St Nich Pr)
E-mail: frpaisius@hotmail.com; stnicholaspress@gmail.com
Web site: http://www.stmaryofegypt.net/.

CrossGeneration Comics, Inc., (*978-1-931484; 978-1-59314*) 9030 Lake Chase Island Way, Tampa, FL 33626-1942 USA
E-mail: jbreitbeil@crossgen.com
Web site: http://www.crossgen.com
Dist(s): **Diamond Comic Distributors, Inc.**

Crosshill Creek Pubns., LLC, (*978-1-7341602*) P.O. Box 216, Wicomico Church, VA 22579 USA Tel 804-436-8615
E-mail: gailkenna@gmail.com.

Crossing Guard Bks. *Imprint of* **Crossing Guard Bks., LLC**

Crossing Guard Bks., LLC, (*978-0-9770141*) Orders Addr.: P.O. Box 1792, Loveland, CO 80538 USA Tel 970-672-8078; *Imprints:* Crossing Guard Books (CrossGrdBks)
E-mail: Sarah@CrossingGuardBooks.com
Web site: http://www.CrossingGuardBooks.com

Crossing the T Publishing Co., (*978-1-7331295*) 137 Turtle Cove Ct., Ponte Vedra Beach, FL 32082 USA Tel 904-536-9815
E-mail: jaterry1@att.net
Web site: JuliaTerry@crossingthetpublishingcompany.com.

Crossing Trails Pubns., (*978-0-9726095*) 4804 Kentwood Ln., Woodbridge, VA 22193 USA Tel 703-590-4449; Fax: 703-878-2119
E-mail: whnesbitt@compuserve.com
Web site: http://www.crossingtrails.com.

Cross-Lengua Productions *See* **KALEXT Productions, LLC**

Cross-Over, (*978-0-9749455; 978-0-9882835; 978-0-9987894*) 190 Vista Linda Ave., Durango, CO 81303 USA Tel 970-385-1809 (phone/fax); Toll Free: 866-385-1809
E-mail: info@homeschoolhowtos.com
Web site: http://fastphonics.weebly.com/; http://homeschoolhowtos.com/.

Crossover Comics *See* **Gavila Publishing**

Crossquarter Publishing Group, (*978-1-890109*) Div. of Earth Healers Inc., Orders Addr.: P.O. Box 23749, Santa Fe, NM 87502 USA Tel 505-690-3923 (phone); Fax: 214-975-9715 (fax); Edit Addr.: P.O. Box 23749, Santa Fe, NM 87502-3749 USA; *Imprints:* Cross Time (Crosstime)
E-mail: info@crossquarter.com
Web site: http://www.crossquarter.com
Dist(s): **Follett School Solutions**
New Leaf Distributing Co., Inc.

Crossroad Pr., (*978-0-9834348; 978-1-937530; 978-1-941408; 978-1-946025; 978-1-948929; 978-1-949914; 978-1-950565; 978-1-951510; 978-1-952979; 978-1-63789*) 141 Brayden Dr., HERTFORD, NC 27944 USA Tel 252-340-3952; *Imprints:* Wonderstruck Books (Wonderstruck); Mystique Press (Mystique Pr); Otherside Press (MYID_S_OTHERSI)
E-mail: publisher@crossroadpress.com
Web site: http://store.crossroadpress.com
Dist(s): **Follett School Solutions.**

†Crossroad Publishing Co., The, (*978-0-8245*)
E-mail: production@crossroadpublishing.com; publisher@crossroadpublishing.com
Web site: http://www.crossroadpublishing.com
Dist(s): **Independent Pubs. Group;** *CIP.*

CrossStaff Publishing, (*978-0-9743876; 978-0-9800755*) P.O. Box 288, Broken Arrow, OK 74013 USA Tel 918-369-9293; Fax: 413-723-4384; Toll Free: 866-862-2278
E-mail: info@crossstaff.com
Web site: http://www.crossstaff.com.

Crosswalk Bks., (*978-0-9746269*) P.O. Box 176, American Fork, UT 84003 USA (SAN 255-7657)
Web site: http://www.crosswalkbooks.com.

†Crossway, (*978-0-89107; 978-1-58134; 978-1-4335; 978-1-68216*) Div. of Good News Pubs., 1300 Crescent St., Wheaton, IL 60187 USA (SAN 211-7991) Tel 708-682-4300; Fax: 630-682-4785; Toll Free: 800-323-3890 (sales only); *Imprints:* Crossway Bibles (Crossway Bibles)
E-mail: permissions@gnpcb.org; service@crossway.org; info@crossway.org
Web site: http://www.crossway.org
Dist(s): **Follett School Solutions**
L I M Productions, LLC
Vision Video; *CIP.*

Crossway Bibles *Imprint of* **Crossway**

Crossway Books *See* **Crossway**

Crossways International, (*978-1-891245*) 7930 Computer Ave., S., Minneapolis, MN 55435-5415 USA Tel 952-832-5454; Fax: 952-832-5553; Toll Free: 800-257-7308
E-mail: info@crossways.org
Web site: http://www.crossways.org.

Crosswinds Bks., (*978-0-9726573*) P.O. Box 143, Keller, TX 76244 USA
E-mail: jroach35@earthlink.net.

Crosswinds Pr., Inc., (*978-0-9825559; 978-0-9838155*) 126 Crosswinds Dr., Groton, CT 06340 USA
Web site: http://www.crosswindspress.com.

Crouch, Valeria *See* **Zig the Pig**

Crouse, Donna J., (*978-0-9765339*) P.O. Box 250, Jersey, VA 22481 USA Tel 540-775-7787; Fax: 540-775-1682
E-mail: df_crouse@msn.com.

Crow & Pitcher Pr., (*978-0-9987214; 979-8-9862721*) P.O. Box 1294, Shingle Springs, CA 95682-1294 USA Tel 530-672-0143
E-mail: angelicarjackson@yahoo.com
Web site: https://www.crowandpitcherpress.com/.

Crow Dog Pr., (*978-0-9727656*) 541 Hunter Ave., Modesto, CA 95350 USA
E-mail: jackrandom@earthlink.net
Web site: http://www.jackrandom.com.

Crow, R.L. Pubns., (*978-0-9722958; 978-0-9971780; 978-1-7356296*) P.O. Box 262, Penn Valley, CA 95946 USA
E-mail: wsgainer@comcast.net
Dist(s): **SPD-Small Pr. Distribution.**

Crowder, Jack L., (*978-0-9616589*) Orders Addr.: P.O. Box 250, Bernalillo, NM 87004 USA (SAN 659-8064) Tel 505-867-5812 (phone/fax); Edit Addr.: 500 Beehive Ln., Bernalillo, NM 87004 USA (SAN 659-8072)
E-mail: crowdercon@aol.com.

Crowe, L.J. *See* **ibukku, LLC**

Publisher Name Index

Crowell, Peter T. Pubns., *(978-0-9740290)* 102 Wilson Rd., Phoenixville, PA 19460 USA E-mail: petercrowell@gmail.com Web site: http://www.petertcrowell.com; callmescythe.com *Dist(s):* **Partners Bk. Distributing, Inc.**

Crown *Imprint of* **Crown Publishing Group, The**

Crown Atlantic Publishing, *(978-0-9883375; 978-1-7326123)* 2000 Mariposa Vista Ln. No. 104, St. Augustine, FL 32084 USA Tel 407-925-3053 E-mail: philipucf23@yahoo.com

Crown Books For Young Readers *Imprint of* **Random Hse. Children's Bks.**

Crown Hse. Publishing LLC, *(978-1-899836; 978-1-904424; 978-1-84590; 978-0-9823573; 978-1-935810; 978-1-78135; 978-1-78583)* Orders Addr.: P.O. Box 2223, Williston, VT 05495 USA Fax: 802-864-7626; Toll Free: 877-925-1213; Edit Addr.: Crown Bldg., Bancyfelin, Carmarthen, Dyfed SA33 5ND GBR Tel 01267 211345; 01267 211880; Fax: 01267 211882; 81 Brook Hills Dr., White Plains, NY 10605 Tel 914-946-3517; Toll Free: 866-272-8497; *Imprints:* Independent Thinking Press (IndThinking) E-mail: books@crownhouse.co.uk; info@CHPUS.com Web site: http://www.crownhouse.co.uk/; http://www.CHPUS.com; http://www.crownhousepublishing.com *Dist(s):* **MyiLibrary.**

Crown Media Publishing *See* **Crown Media Publishing**

Crown Media Publishing, *(978-0-692-60979-8; 978-0-692-61041-1; 978-0-692-61106-7; 978-0-692-61190-6; 978-0-692-63234-5; 978-0-692-63291-8; 978-0-692-63333-5; 978-0-9990279)* P.O. Box 4838, Omaha, NE 68104 USA Tel 4025782578 *Dist(s):* **CreateSpace Independent Publishing Platform.**

Crown of Life Ministries, Inc., *(978-0-9997429)* 256 3rd St., Niagara Falls, NY 14303-1231 USA Tel 905-228-0277 E-mail: crownoflifemin@yahoo.com Web site: www.wayoftheeagle.org.

Crown Peak Publishing, *(978-0-9645663)* Orders Addr.: P.O. Box 317, New Castle, CO 81647 USA Tel 970-618-1748 E-mail: ann@annsphotos.com; ann@annramseydesign.com; ann@annlouiseramsey.com Web site: http://www.annramseydesign.com; http://www.annlouiseramsey.com; http://www.annramseyphotography.com

†**Crown Publishing Group, The**, Div. of Random Hse., Inc., Orders Addr.: 400 Hahn Rd., Westminster, MD 21157 USA Tel 410-848-1900; Toll Free Fax: 800-659-2436; Toll Free: 800-733-3000; 800-726-0600; Edit Addr.: 1745 Broadway, New York, NY 10019 USA (SAN 200-2639) Tel 212-751-2600; Toll Free Fax: 800-659-2436; *Imprints:* Clarkson Potter (Clarkson Potter); NAL (NewAmLib); Multnomah (Mltnmah); Potter Style (Potter Style); WaterBrook (WaterBrook); Crown (Crow); Broadway Books (BwayBks); Convergent Books (Convergent Bk); Multnomah (Multnom Bks) E-mail: customerservice@randomhouse.com; crownpublicity@randomhouse.com Web site: http://www.randomhouse.com/ *Dist(s):* **Children's Plus, Inc. Follett School Solutions MyiLibrary Penguin Random Hse. Distribution Penguin Random Hse. LLC Random Hse., Inc.**; *CIP.*

Crowne Pointe *See* **White Phoenix**

Crowned Warrior Publishing *Imprint of* **Walters, Steve Ministries**

Crownover Enterprises, LLC, *(978-0-9785425)* 1194 Berkeley Rd., Avondale Estates, GA 30002 USA E-mail: amy@mybenefitauctioneer.com; dean@mybenefitauctioneer.com Web site: https://mybenefitauctioneer.com/.

CrowsNest Publishing, *(978-0-9710225)* 11513 Crows Nest Rd., Clarksville, MD 21029-1601 USA Tel 410-531-3110 E-mail: hannon@erols.com.

Crowther, Debra, *(978-0-9741295)* P.O. Box 1870, Three Rivers, TX 78071 USA Tel 361-786-4703; Fax: 361-786-2579 Web site: http://www.jackthewestie.com.

Cruce de Caminos, *(978-0-9885392)* 10 Akron St., Suite 100, Cambridge, MA 02138-1281 USA Tel 617-384-9499 E-mail: crucedecaminos.org@gmail.com.

Crucifiction Games, *(978-0-9778263)* P.O. Box 654, Selah, WA 98942 USA Tel 509-697-7393; 509-952-6270 E-mail: cweedin@crucifictiongames.com Web site: http://www.crucifictiongames.com *Dist(s):* **Ingram Content Group.**

Crumb Elbow Publishing, *(978-0-89904)* P.O. Box 294, Rhododendron, OR 97049 USA (SAN 679-128X) Tel 503-622-4798.

CrumbGobbler Pr. *Imprint of* **Downtown Wetmore Pr.**

Crumly, Billie, *(978-0-9760577)* P.O. Box 281, Geraldine, AL 35974 USA.

Crumm, David Media, LLC, *(978-1-934879; 978-1-939880; 978-1-942011)* 42015 Ford Rd., Suite 234, Canton, MI 48187 USA (SAN 855-3637) Tel 734-786-3813 E-mail: admin@DavidCrummMedia.com Web site: http://www.ReadTheSpirit.com.

Crunchpeep Media, *(978-0-9749469)* a/o Steven Merahn, 1700 Market St., 6th Flr., Philadelphia, PA 19103 USA Tel 215-832-0181 E-mail: smerahn@crunchpeep.com.

Crush Publishing (CZE) *(978-80-907532; 978-80-908121) Dist. by* **IPG Chicago.**

Crush Publishing, *(978-0-9798869; 978-0-9853434; 978-0-9910756; 978-0-9995994; 978-1-950935; 978-1-956407)* P.O. Box 6088, Gardnerville, NV 89460 USA Do not confuse with Crush Publishing in Brooklyn, NY E-mail: veronica@veronicablade.com Web site: http://www.crushpublishing.com.

Crushing Hearts and Black Butterfly Publishing, *(978-0-615-60362-9; 978-0-615-60460-2; 978-0-615-60592-0; 978-0-615-60593-7; 978-0-615-60597-5; 978-0-615-61380-2; 978-0-615-61435-9; 978-0-615-62403-7; 978-0-615-63475-3; 978-0-615-66682-2; 978-0-615-66683-9; 978-0-615-66684-6; 978-0-615-66760-7; 978-0-615-67525-1; 978-0-615-68166-5; 978-0-615-68247-1; 978-0-615-69025-4; 978-0-615-70249-0; 978-0-615-70607-8; 978-0-615-70608-5; 978-0-615-70656-6; 978-0-615-71144-7; 978-0-615-72063-0; 978-0-615-72064-7; 978-0-615-72065-4; 978-0-615-72906-0;) 710 Saratoga Cir., Algonquin, IL 60102 USA Tel 224-234-9677* Web site: www.crushingheartsandblackbutterfly.com *Dist(s):* **CreateSpace Independent Publishing Platform.**

CrutchfieldPublishing.com, *(978-1-7378687)* 125 West South St. No. 1952, Indianapolis, IN 46206 USA Tel 317-620-3659 E-mail: jamarandashleyc@gmail.com.

Crying Cougar Pr., *(978-0-615-31150-0; 978-0-615-33106-5; 978-0-615-34888-9; 978-0-615-40439-4; 978-0-615-53634-7; 978-0-9859802; 978-1-7339646)* 3559 Ruffin Rd. Suite 155, San Diego, CA 92123 USA *Dist(s):* **Smashwords.**

Crypto Editions *Imprint of* **Hancock Hse. Pubs.**

Crysalis Publishing, Inc., *(978-0-9745190)* 10 Main St., Suite 4A, PMB 227, Woodbridge, NJ 07095 USA Web site: http://www.chrysalispublishinc.com.

crysta luna studios, *(978-0-615-43657-9; 978-0-9887006)* 14995 SW Onyx Ct., Beaverton, OR 97007 USA Tel 503-933-1817 E-mail: smirlsmirl@gmail.com.

Crystal Ball Publishing, LLC., *(978-1-932277)* 107 Skiff Ave., Frankfort, NY 13340 USA E-mail: Nerbo@msn.com; Sales@CrystalBallPublishing.com; Insight@CrystalBallPublishing.com Web site: http://www.crystalballpublishing.com; http://www.gypsykids.com.

Crystal Bks. *Imprint of* **Words In The Works, LLC**

Crystal Clarity Pubs., *(978-0-916124; 978-1-56589; 978-1-878265)* 1123 Goodrich Blvd, Commerce, CA 90022 USA (SAN 201-1778) Toll Free: 800-424-1055 E-mail: michele@crystalclarity.com; dharmadevi@crystalclarity.com Web site: http://www.crystalclarity.com *Dist(s):* **Instructional Video Koen Pacific Ingram Content Group MyiLibrary National Bk. Network New Leaf Distributing Co., Inc. Nutri-Bks. Corp. Princeton Bk. Co. Pubs. ebrary, Inc.**

Crystal Journeys Publishing, *(978-1-880737)* 130 Cochise Dr., Sedona, AZ 86351-7927 USA Tel 520-284-5730 *Dist(s):* **Light Technology Publishing, LLC.**

Crystal Mosaic Bks., *(978-0-9836303; 978-0-9911061; 978-0-9981136; 978-1-7322046)* PO Box 1276, Hillsboro, OR 97123 USA E-mail: raymond@macalino.com.

Crystal Pr., *(978-0-9632123; 978-0-9670886; 978-0-9746109)* 1750 Orr Ave., Simi Valley, CA 93065 USA Tel 805-527-4369; Fax: 805-582-3949 Do not confuse with Crystal Pr. in Houston, TX E-mail: crystalpress@aol.com Web site: http://www.Crystalpress.org.

Crystal Productions, *(978-0-924509; 978-1-56290)* Orders Addr.: 1812 Johns Dr., Glenview, IL 60025 USA (SAN 920-8224); Edit Addr.: 1812 Johns Dr., Glenview, IL 60025 USA (SAN 653-2489) Tel 847-657-8144; Fax: 847-657-8149; Toll Free Fax: 800-657-8149; Toll Free: 800-255-8629 E-mail: custserv@crystalproductions.com Web site: http://www.crystalproductions.com *Dist(s):* **Baker & Taylor Fulfillment, Inc. Follett School Solutions.**

Crystal Springs Bks. *Imprint of* **Staff Development for Educators**

CS Media Resources, *(978-0-9764992)* Orders Addr.: 12 W. Willow Grove Ave. Suite 121, Philadelphia, PA 19118-3952 USA Toll Free: 877-866-8309 E-mail: csmr@csmediaresources.com Web site: http://www.csmediaresources.com.

Csb Innovations, *(978-0-692-71580-2; 978-0-9996271; 978-1-7335178; 978-1-952330)* 1918 bentwood dr, floresville, TX 78114 USA Tel 210-305-1105 E-mail: csbinnovationssa@gmail.com Web site: www.csbinnovations.com.

CSE Publishing, *(978-0-9743567)* 706 Radcliffe Ave., Lynn Haven, FL 32444-3039 USA (SAN 255-5581) Fax: 850-271-9874; Toll Free: 866-262-8776 E-mail: tchardy@bellsouth.net.

CSI Publishing *See* **Decere Publishing**

CSIR Publishing, *(978-1-7368569)* 5300 S EASTERN AVE, LAS VEGAS, NV 89121 USA Tel 702-496-1134 E-mail: ileanaauthor@gmail.com.

CSIRO Publishing (AUS) *(978-1-922173; 978-1-4863) Dist. by* **Stylus Pub VA.**

CSS Backlist *Imprint of* **Chicken Soup for the Soul Publishing, LLC**

CSS Publishing, *(978-0-9721679)* 108A Gallegos Ln., Tularosa, NM 88352 USA (SAN 254-6477) Fax: 505-585-4908 Do not confuse with C S S Publishing Company in Lima, OH E-mail: rblanks@netmdc.com; csspublishing@hotmail.com.

CT Bookshelf, *(978-0-9837301; 978-0-9972140; 978-0-9974963; 978-1-7376790)* 309 4th St. SE No. 5, Washington, DC 20003 USA Tel 202-546-7126 E-mail: author.travis@gmail.com Web site: www.travisbooks.com.

CTaylorGo, *(978-0-578-40657-2; 978-0-578-50796-5)* 885 Briarcliff Rd. NE. #29, Atlanta, GA 30306 USA Tel 404-374-8449 E-mail: courtney.cnt@gmail.com.

CTC Publishing, *(978-0-9747789; 978-1-934073)* 10431 Lawyers Rd., Vienna, VA 22181-2822 USA (SAN 851-7908) Toll Free: 800-942-0962 E-mail: pitts@ndmc.com Web site: http://www.couragetochange.com/ *Dist(s):* **Follett School Solutions.**

CTK Publishing *See* **Southampton Publishing**

CTO Bks., *(978-0-9724411)* Div. of CTO Publishing LLC, Orders Addr.: P.O. Box 825, Kokomo, IN 46903 USA E-mail: ctobooks@gmail.com Web site: http://www.ctobooks.com *Dist(s):* **MyiLibrary ebrary, Inc.**

Ctr. for Curatorial Studies *Imprint of* **Bard College Pubns. Office**

Ctrl+Alt+Del Prodns., *(978-0-9764678)* P.O. Box 206392, New Haven, CT 06520 USA Tel 508-274-5804 E-mail: absath@ctrlaltdel-online.com Web site: http://www.ctrlaltdel-online.com.

Cub Bks. *Imprint of* **Global Business Information Strategies, Inc.**

Cubbie Blue Publishing, *(978-0-9706341; 978-1-932824)* 546 Flanders Dr., Saint Louis, MO 63122-1618 USA; *Imprints:* Ravencrest (Ravencrest) E-mail: rahandler@earthlink.net Web site: ravencrestpublishing.com *Dist(s):* **BookBaby.**

Cubby Hole Tales, *(978-0-9754591)* 524 Moores Mill Rd., Pelzer, SC 29669 USA Tel 864-947-6426 E-mail: telvajo@bellsouth.net Web site: http://www.talesfromtwocousins.com.

Cube Marketing, *(978-0-9893091)* 51 9th Ave., Newark, NJ 07107 USA Tel 973-482-4101 E-mail: deidre.knight@gmail.com.

Cube17, Inc., *(978-0-9821425; 978-1-945196)* 4364 Bonita Rd. - No. 241, Bonita, CA 91902 USA Tel 619-852-6942 E-mail: Jorge@JorgeOlson.com Web site: http://www.jorgeolson.com.

Cuccia, Louis, *(978-0-9727415)* 603 Winthrop, Smyrna, TN 37167 USA Tel 615-355-6821; Fax: 615-355-0171 E-mail: Lcuccia@aol.com.

Cuddehe Services *See* **Found Link**

Cudworth, Melissa, *(978-0-692-14317-9; 978-0-578-53124-3)* 34529 SE Linden Loop, Snoqualmie, WA 98065 USA Tel 206-300-9957 E-mail: melissa.cudworth@gmail.com *Dist(s):* **CreateSpace Independent Publishing Platform.**

Cuento de Luz SL (ESP) *(978-84-937814; 978-84-15241; 978-84-938240; 978-84-15503; 978-84-15619; 978-84-15784; 978-84-16078; 978-84-16147) Dist. by* **PerseuPGW.**

Culican, J.A. *See* **Dragon Realm Pr.**

Cully, Amanda, *(978-0-9971120)* 5303 e village rd, Long beach, CA 90808 USA Tel 562-494-6179 E-mail: Blebow75@aol.com.

Culpepper, Felix International, Inc., *(978-0-9740435)* Orders Addr.: P.O. Box 70, Jefferson City, TN 37760-0070 USA (SAN 255-2752) Tel 865-475-4993; Fax: 914-470-1091; Edit Addr.: 2476 Tarr Rd., Talbott, TN 37877 USA E-mail: gfac@cshore.com; peteculpepper@helpkidswhohavecancer.org; pete@felixculpepper.com Web site: http://www.bigboxhead.com; http://www.felixculpepper.com *Dist(s):* **American Wholesale Bk. Co.**

Cult Classics Pub., *(978-0-692-54687-1; 978-0-9981068)* 1613 A Black Duck Terr., Carrollton, TX 75010 USA Tel 214-731-8767 Web site: www.Cultclassicspublisher.com *Dist(s):* **CreateSpace Independent Publishing Platform.**

Cultural Connections, *(978-0-9636629; 978-1-57371)* 23499 Shakeridge Rd., Volcano, CA 95689 USA Toll Free: 888-234-5412 E-mail: culture123@volcano.net.

Culturatti Ink, *(978-0-9712383; 978-0-692-42185-7; 978-0-692-42186-4; 978-0-692-92033-6; 978-0-692-06343-9; 978-0-692-10351-7; 978-0-578-40944-3)* 9465 Counselors Row Suite 200, Indianapolis, IN, IN 46240 USA E-mail: erika@culturattikids.net Web site: http://www.culturattiink.com.

Culture Connection, The *See* **Culturatti Ink**

Culture Hse., *(978-0-9676080; 978-0-9819484)* Orders Addr.: P.O. Box 293, Newton, IA 50208 USA Tel 641-792-0920; Edit Addr.: 3830 Harbor Ave., Newton, IA 50208-9040 USA E-mail: museum@pcpartner.net Web site: http://www.mike-chapman.com.

Culture of Life, Inc., *(978-0-9761457)* 1054 Windy Knoll Rd., West Chester, PA 19382-7433 USA.

CultureGrams World Edition *Imprint of* **ProQuest LLC**

Culturelink Pr., *(978-0-9759276)* Web site: http://www.culturelinkpress.com; www.dianeasitimbay.com.

Cumberland Hse. *Imprint of* **Sourcebooks, Inc.**

Cummings Pr., *(978-0-9767063)* 1939 Mt. Vernon Pl., Dunwoody, GA 30338-4417 USA Tel 770-512-8115 (phone/fax).

Cummins Associates International *See* **CAI Publishing**

Cummins, Judi, *(978-0-9760377)* Orders Addr.: P.O. Box 10 Chosen Spot Apartments, Canandaigua, NY 14424 USA E-mail: jcummins1@rochester.rr.com.

Cumquat Publishing Company *See* **Floppinfish Publishing Co., Ltd.**

Cumuli, *(978-0-9709730)* Div. of Cumuli, Inc., P.O. Box 1174, Port Orchard, WA 98366 USA Tel 360-871-9493 (phone/fax) E-mail: fletcher@cumuli.com; susan@cumuli.com Web site: http://www.cumuli.com; http://www.cumulipress.com.

Cune *See* **Cune Pr., LLC**

Cune Pr. Classics *Imprint of* **Rare Bird Bks.**

Cune Pr., LLC, *(978-1-885942; 978-1-61457; 978-1-951082)* Div. of Scott Davis Co., P.O. Box 31024, Seattle, WA 98103 USA (SAN 298-3648) Tel 206-930-1659; Fax: 206-774-0592 E-mail: therese.nasr@cunepress.com; scott.davis@cunepress.com Web site: http://www.cunepress.com; www.cunepress.info; www.cunepress.org; http://www.cunepress.net *Dist(s):* **Publishers Group West (PGW) Smashwords.**

Cunnyngham, Marissa, *(978-1-7374273)* 5016 Briargrove St., Liberty, TX 77575 USA Tel 936-402-4425 E-mail: marissacunnyngham@gmail.com Web site: Marissacunnyngham.com.

Cuppa Tea Productions, Inc., *(978-0-9992405)* 1313 Maltman Ave, Los Angeles, CA 90026 USA Tel 310-803-0594 E-mail: 1devonkelly@gmail.com.

†**Curbstone Pr.**, *(978-0-915306; 978-1-880684; 978-1-931896)* P.O. Box 45, Willimantic, CT 06226-0045 USA (SAN 209-4282) E-mail: info@curbstone.org Web site: http://www.curbstone.org *Dist(s):* **Chicago Distribution Ctr. Lectorum Pubns., Inc. SPD-Small Pr. Distribution**; *CIP.*

Curcumin Bks. *Imprint of* **Davlaw Press**

Cure Media Group, *(978-0-9997666; 978-0-578-88520-9; 978-0-578-92129-7; 978-0-578-96943-5; 978-0-578-35787-4; 978-0-578-39924-9; 979-8-218-18118-5)* 2 Clarke Dr, Cranbury, NJ 08512 USA Tel 609-529-9622; Fax: 609-529-9622 E-mail: nglasser@mdmag.com.

CureBound Publishing *See* **Freiling Publishing**

Curio Creative *Imprint of* **Wasteland Pr.**

Curiosity Quills Pr., *(978-1-62007; 978-1-948099)* Orders Addr.: P.O. Box 2160, Reston, VA 20195 USA (SAN 920-9700) Tel 800-998-2509 E-mail: editor@curiosityquills.com Web site: http://curiosityquills.com

Curiosmith, *(978-0-9817505; 978-1-935626; 978-1-941281; 978-1-946145)* P.O. Box 390293, Minneapolis, MN 55439-0293 USA (SAN 856-4450) E-mail: shopkeeper@curiosmith.com Web site: http://www.curiosmith.com.

Curious Cat Bks. *Imprint of* **Legacy Bound**

Curious Kids Guides, *(978-0-9789140)* 2561 Bunker Hill, Ann Arbor, MI 48105-3432 USA Tel 734-665-0533 E-mail: eisbruchs@aol.com Web site: http://www.CuriousKidsGuides.com *Dist(s):* **Partners Bk. Distributing, Inc.**

CuriousDots, *(978-0-9893751)* 81 Prospect St., Acton, MA 01720 USA Tel 978-263-1713; Fax: 978-263-1713 E-mail: curiousdots@gmail.com.

Curiouser Hse. Publishing, *(978-0-9843093; 978-1-954319)* 7 Walnut St, South Hadley, MA 01075 USA Tel 720-938-7826 E-mail: curiouserhouse@gmail.com Web site: https://curiouser.house.

Curiously Created Bks., *(978-1-959959)* 35-15 80 St., Jackson Heights, NY 11372 USA Tel 347-633-3669 E-mail: kristinalucia@cccokl.com.

Curly & Confident Publishing, *(978-1-7345572)* 860 Johnson Ferry Rd. Ste 140-370, Atlanta, GA 30342 USA Tel 770-405-9292 E-mail: support@beautifulcurlyme.com; info@beautifulcurlyme.com.

Curly Girl Cafe, *(978-0-578-73577-1; 978-0-578-77699-6; 978-0-578-77773-3)* 183 Hillcrest Dr. 0, AUSTELL, GA 30168 USA Tel 4045503057 E-mail: CurlyGirlCafe2020@gmail.com. *Dist(s):* **Ingram Content Group.**

Currach Pr. (IRL) *(978-1-85607) Dist. by* **Casemate Pubs.**

Currach Pr. (IRL) *(978-1-85607) Dist. by* **Dufour.**

Curran, M.J., *(978-0-9768984)* 640 Gooseberry Dr., No. 1207, Longmont, CO 80503 USA Tel 720-206-9099 E-mail: mjcurran@hotmail.com.

Curran Pr. and Editorial Consulting, LLC, *(978-1-970002)* 20 Smith Rd., Rockport, MA 01966 USA E-mail: damaris@curraneditorial.com Web site: curranpress.curraneditorial.com.

Currency Pr. (AUS) *(978-0-86819; 978-0-9596937; 978-1-921428; 978-1-921429; 978-1-925004; 978-1-925005; 978-1-925210; 978-1-925359; 978-1-76062) Dist. by* **Antipodes Bks.**

Current Clinical Strategies Publishing, *(978-0-9626030; 978-1-881528; 978-1-929622; 978-1-934323)* P.O. Box 1753, Blue Jay, CA 92317 USA (SAN 298-4490) Tel 949-348-8404; Fax: 949-348-8405; Toll Free Fax: 800-965-9420; Toll Free: 800-331-8227 E-mail: info@ccspublishing.com Web site: http://www.ccspublishing.com/ccs *Dist(s):* **Majors, J. A. Co. Matthews Medical Bk. Co. Rittenhouse Bk. Distributors.**

Current Publishing Corp., *(978-1-878663)* 30151 Tomas St., Rancho Santa Margarita, CA 92688 USA Toll Free: 800-729-7234.

Curriculum Associates, Incorporated *See* **Curriculum Assocs., LLC**

Curriculum Assocs., LLC, *(978-0-7609; 978-0-89187; 978-1-55915; 978-1-4957; 978-1-7280; 978-1-6630)* Orders Addr.: P.O. Box 2001, North Billerica, MA 01862-0901 USA (SAN 659-6304) Toll Free: 800-225-0248; Edit Addr.: 153 Rangeway Rd., North

Billerica, MA 01862 USA Tel 978-667-8000; Toll Free Fax: 800-366-1158; Toll Free: 800-225-0248
E-mail: info@curriculumassociates.com; info@cainc.com; aclark@cainc.com
Web site: http://www.curriculumassociates.com.

Curriculum Concepts International, *(978-0-9786500; 978-1-60409)* 118 E. 28th Street., Suite 401, New York, NY 10016 USA Tel 212-242-7827; Fax: 212-242-3523
Web site: www.cciny.net.

Curriculum Publishing, Presbyterian Church (U. S. A.), *(978-1-57153)* 100 Witherspoon St., Louisville, KY 40202-1396 USA Tel 502-569-5090; Fax: 502-569-8329; Toll Free: 800-524-2612; *Imprints:* Witherspoon Press (Witherspoon Pr)
Web site: http://www.pcusa.org/pcusa/currpub; http://www.bridgeresources.org
Dist(s): **Westminster John Knox Pr.**

Currie & Smith Publishing *See* **T.Y.M. Publishing**

Currier Davis Publishing *See* **GRAND Media, LLC**

Currituck Booksmiths, *(978-0-9965845)* 1959 Peace Haven Rd No. 246, Winston Salem, NC 27106 USA Tel 888-833-0360
E-mail: cfh1@prospectivepress.com
Web site: prospectivepress.com.

Curry Brothers Publishing Group, *(978-0-9798364; 978-0-9818956)* 608 Sandy Spring Trail, Madison, TN 37115 USA
E-mail: cbmpg@yahoo.com
Web site: http://currybrotherspublishing.com.

Cursack Bks., *(978-1-933439)* 31 Hubbard Rd., Dover, NH 03820 USA
E-mail: info@cursackbooks.com
Web site: http://www.cursackbooks.com
Dist(s): **Ediciones Universal.**

Curtis Aikens, Inc. *See* **Currituck Booksmiths**

Curtis Elliott Designs, Ltd., *(978-0-9742438)* 5250 Franklin St., Unit C-1, Hilliard, OH 43026 USA Tel 614-771-7978
E-mail: info@creativecoloringbooks.com
Web site: http://www.creativecoloringbooks.com.

Curtis Publishing Company *See* **Cedar Creek Publishing Service**

Custom Museum Publishing LLC *See* **Maine Authors Publishing**

Customer Centered Consulting Group, Inc., *(978-0-9762493)* 5729 Lebanon Dr., Suite 144-222, Frisco, TX 75034 USA Tel 469-633-9833; Fax: 469-633-9843
E-mail: dreed@cccginc.com
Web site: http://www.cccginc.com.

Custureri, Mary *See* **Taylor and Seale Publishing**

Cute & Cuddly Productions, Inc., *(978-0-9761318)* 4401 Shallowford Rd., Suite 162-161, Roswell, GA 30075 USA Tel 678-478-6071 (phone/fax)
E-mail: cuteandcuddlyproductions@msn.com
Web site: http://www.bigbillandbuddies.com.

Cutelli, Nick, *(978-0-692-11508-4)* 918 N. Havenhurst Dr. Unit 109, WEST HOLLYWOOD, CA 90046 USA Tel 312-613-4969
E-mail: ncutelli@gmail.com
Dist(s): **Ingram Content Group.**

Cutie Series Co., The, *(978-0-9987568)* 11035 Lavender Hill Dr., Las Vegas, NV 89135 USA Tel 516-459-7966
E-mail: feliciadijohn@gmail.com.

CVD Publishing, *(978-0-9743520)* 1254 Grizzly Flat Ct., Auburn, CA 95603 USA Tel 530-885-4988
E-mail: grizlyflat@jps.net
Web site: http://www.CVDbooks.com.

CVTrahan Publishing, *(978-0-692-74059-0; 978-0-692-78996-4; 978-0-692-80854-2; 978-0-692-89332-6; 978-0-692-90547-0; 978-1-7369473; 979-8-9852517)* 245 Lake Dr, Tioga, TX 76271 USA Tel 940-393-0769; *Imprints:* CVTrahan Publishing, LLC (CVTrahan).

CVTrahan Publishing, LLC *Imprint of* **CVTrahan Publishing**

CWG Pr., *(978-0-9788186; 978-0-9906714)* 1517 NE. 5th Ter Apt 1, Fort Lauderdale, FL 33304 USA Tel 954-524-5953
E-mail: editor@cwgpress.com
Web site: http://www.cwgpress.com.

CWLA Pr. *Imprint of* **Child Welfare League of America, Inc.**

CWS Studios, Inc., *(978-0-9785827; 978-0-615-92291-1)* 5414 W. Barry Ave., Chicago, IL 60641 USA
Web site: http://www.cws-studios.com.

Cyber Education, *(978-0-9980728)* 6377 Marquis Ct., Oak Park, CA 91377 USA Tel 818-414-5674
E-mail: lori@lorigetz.com.

Cyber Haus, *(978-1-931373)* 159 Delaware Ave., #145, Delmar, NY 12054 USA Tel 518-478-9798
E-mail: cyhaus@msn.com
Web site: http://www.revolutionaryday.com/; http://www.cyhaus.com/.

Cyber Publishing Co., *(978-0-9637419; 978-0-9747870)* 421 Ave. De Teresa, Grants Pass, OR 97526 USA (SAN 255-691X) Tel 541-474-1077; Fax: 541-474-2829
E-mail: intrchild@aol.com.

Cyber Tiger Pr., *(978-0-615-18259-9)* Planetarium Station, New York, NY 10024 USA
E-mail: bill@billweberstudios.com
Dist(s): **Lulu Pr., Inc.**

Cyberlab Publishing, *(978-0-9746501)* P.O. Box 618, Dimondale, MI 48821-0618 USA Tel 517-974-8068; Fax: 517-887-9029
E-mail: ministerjd@yahoo.com
Web site: http://www.cyberlabpublishing.com.

Cyberosia Publishing, *(978-0-9709474; 978-0-9742713)* 3864 Shelley Dr., Mobile, AL 36693-3933 USA
E-mail: scottobrown@gmail.com
Dist(s): **Diamond Distributors, Inc.**

Cyberwizard Productions, *(978-0-9795788; 978-0-9815669; 978-0-9821352; 978-1-936021)* 1403 Iron Springs Rd. No. 36, Prescott, AZ 86305 USA; *Imprints:* Banana Oil Books (Banana Oil)
Web site: http://cyberwizardproductions.com; http://www.cyberwizardproductions.com/Chaco_Canyon_Books/; http://wildplainspress.webs.com; http://www.cyberwizardproductions.com/Altered_Dimensions_Press; http://www.cyberwizardproductions.com/Banana_Oil_Books/; http://www.cyberwizardproductions.com/Diminuendo_Poetry/; http://firesidemysteries.webs.com; http://www.cyberwizardproductions.com/Toy_Box_Books/
Dist(s): **Send The Light Distribution LLC**

Cyclops Pr., *(978-0-9740269)* 1342 Van Buren Ave., Saint Paul, MN 55104-1926 USA.

Cyclotour Guide Bks., *(978-1-889602)* Orders Addr.: P.O. Box 10585, Rochester, NY 14610-0585 USA; Edit Addr.: 160 Harvard St., Rochester, NY 14607 USA
E-mail: cyclotour@cyclotour.com; cyclotour@frontiernet.net
Web site: http://www.cyclotour.com.

Cygnet Publishing Group, Inc./Coolreading.com (CAN) *(978-1-55305) Dist. by* **Orca Bk Pub.**

Cymbal Technique 101, *(978-0-9762593)* 440 Ross Rd., Fort Walton Beach, FL 32547 USA
E-mail: edward_capps@cymbaltechnique101.com
Web site: http://www.cymbaltechnique101.com.

Cynthia Eden *See* **Hocus Pocus Publishing, Inc.**

Cynthia Harvest Moon Intuitive Psychic Medium *See* **Cynthia Wildes**

Cynthia Wildes, *(978-0-692-96767-6; 979-8-218-17323-4)* 47732 Cty. 27, Becida, MN 56678 USA Tel 218-854-7265
E-mail: 4darling58@live.com.

Cypress Bay Publishing, *(978-0-9746747)* 910 W. Harney Ln., Lodi, CA 95242 USA (SAN 255-6928) Tel 209-365-6114
E-mail: nclaus@clearwire.net.

Cypress Communications, *(978-0-9636412; 978-0-9896043)* 35 E. Rosemont Ave., Alexandria, VA 22301 USA Tel 703-548-0532 (phone/fax) Do not confuse with companies with similar names in Leawood, KS, Saint Paul, MN, Cypress, TX
E-mail: jcclifford@earthlink.net
Web site: http://www.lighthousehistory.info/; http://www.CivilWarDrummerBoy.com
Dist(s): **Partners Bk. Distributing, Inc.**

Cypress Knees Publishing, *(978-0-9745863; 978-0-9763757)* Div. of Top Brass Outdoors, Orders Addr.: P.O. Box 209, Starkville, MS 39760 USA Tel 662-323-1559; Fax: 662-323-7466; Edit Addr.: 312 Industrial Pk., Rd., Starkville, MS 39759 USA
E-mail: eric@topbrasstackle.com
Web site: http://www.topbrasstackle.com; http://www.outdooryouthadventures.com.

Cypress Knoll Prs., *(978-0-578-19357-1; 978-0-692-92433-4; 978-0-692-08720-6; 978-0-578-41513-0; 978-1-7335913)* 4070 CR 3070, Cookville, TX 75558 USA.

CyPress Pubns., *(978-0-9672585; 978-0-9776958; 978-1-935083)* P.O. Box 2636, Tallahassee, FL 32316-2636 USA Fax: 850-254-7112
E-mail: lraymond@nettally.com
Web site: http://cypresspublications.com
Dist(s): **Smashwords.**

Cypress Publishing *See* **Cypress Communications**

Cypress River Publishing, *(978-0-692-90901-0; 978-0-692-91278-2; 978-0-692-98702-5)* 1402 Vino Blanc Ct., SOUTHLAKE, TX 76092 USA Tel 817-903-2064
E-mail: agellert@yahoo.com
Dist(s): **Ingram Content Group.**

Cyr Design Publishing, *(978-0-9774543)* P.O. Box 1662, Nashua, NH 03061-1662 USA
Web site: http://cyrdesign.com.

Cyrano Bks., *(978-0-615-55618-5; 978-0-9892699)* 3348 kaunaoa St., Honolulu, HI 96815 USA Tel 808-381-5205
E-mail: cindykm@hawaii.rr.com
Web site: www.cyranobooks.com.

Cyrano Bks., *(978-0-9990993; 978-0-692-08214-0; 978-1-7322739; 978-0-578-61568-4; 978-1-7358942)* 918 12th avenue, 1000, honolulu, HI 96816 USA Tel 808-492-4553; Fax: 808-492-4553
E-mail: cmackey11@icloud.com
Web site: www.cyranobooks.com.

CZ Mentoring, LLC, *(978-1-7347556)* 113319 TRAVELERS WAY Cir., HOUSTON, TX 77065 USA Tel 512-924-1659
E-mail: drceciczuniga@gmail.com
Web site: http://drceciczuniga@gmail.com.

Czarnecki, Janina, *(978-0-9888517)* 426 Clifton Blvd., Clifton, NJ 07013 USA Tel 973-249-1164
E-mail: janina.czarnecki@gmail.com
Dist(s): **Ingram Content Group.**

Czech, Cassandra, *(978-1-7330636)* N26 W26691 Prospect Ave, Pewaukee, WI 53072 USA Tel 262-443-7547
E-mail: heckc3@gmail.com.

Czech Revival Publishing *Imprint of* **Distinct Pr.**

Czechoslovak Genealogical Society International, *(978-0-9651932)* Orders Addr.: P.O. Box 16225, Saint Paul, MN 55116-0225 USA Tel 763-595-7799; Edit Addr.: 8582 Timberwood Rd., Woodbury, MN 55125-7620 USA Tel 651-739-7543
E-mail: cgsi@comcast.net
Web site: http://www.cgsi.org.

D. A. Graham *See* **Graham, D. A.**

D. A. W. Enterprise, *(978-0-9628081)* 1314 Bainbridge St., Philadelphia, PA 19147 USA Tel 215-424-2016.

D & S Marketing Systems, Inc., *(978-1-878621; 978-0-9787199; 978-1-934780)* 1205 38th St., Brooklyn, NY 11218-3705 USA Tel 718-633-8383; Fax: 718-633-8385; Toll Free: 800-633-8383
E-mail: dsmarketing@aol.com; info@dsmarketing.com
Web site: http://www.dsmarketing.com.

D B W, Incorporated *See* **Just Like Me, Inc.**

DDDD Pubns., *(978-0-9635341; 978-1-885519)* 3407 Brown Rd., Saint Louis, MO 63114-4329 USA (SAN 631-2675).

D H Publishing LLC, *(978-0-9800263)* 515 E. Carefree Hwy., No. 652, Phoenix, AZ 85085-8839 USA
E-mail: deserthillspublishing@hotmail.com.

D K Publishing, Incorporated *See* **Dorling Kindersley Publishing, Inc.**

D. W. Cope Pr., *(978-0-9770121)* 6310 Hegerman St., Philadelphia, PA 19135 USA
E-mail: wakageryucope@gmail.com
Web site: http://www.ryucope.com.

D. W. Ink *See* **Clara Denise West**

D. W. Publishing, *(978-0-9741774)* 226 McFarland St., Grand Blanc, MI 48439 USA Tel 810-695-8985
E-mail: dan@dwpublishing.com
Web site: http://www.dwpublishing.com.

Da Capo Lifelong *Imprint of* **Hachette Bks.**

Da Capo Pr. Inc. *Imprint of* **Hachette Bks.**

Da Wong Bks., *(978-0-9744360; 978-0-615-73234-3)* 4070 Cactus Rd., Shingle Springs, CA 95682 USA Tel 530-676-6060 (phone/fax)
E-mail: eslhotel@yahoo.com.

DAAB Media Gmbh (DEU) *(978-3-942597) Dist. by* **InnovativeLog.**

Dabel Brothers Production LLC. *See* **Dabel Brothers Publishing LLC**

Dabel Brothers Publishing LLC, *(978-0-9764011; 978-0-9779333; 978-0-9973065; 978-0-692-87763-0; 978-0-9996163)* 6070 Autumn View Trail, Acworth, GA 30101 USA
E-mail: ldabel@dabelbrothers.com
Web site: http://www.dabelbrothers.com/
Dist(s): **Diamond Comic Distributors, Inc.**
Diamond Bk. Distributors.

Dabrishus, Mara, *(978-0-9961872)* 16 Pepper Creek Dr., Pepper Pike, OH 44124 USA Tel 412-818-2116
E-mail: mdabris@gmail.com
Web site: www.maradabrishus.com.

DAC Educational Pubns., *(978-1-930731)* 4325 Carlton Pl., Yorba Linda, CA 92886 USA
E-mail: DACpublis@aol.com.

DaChosen Publishing, *(978-0-9762627; 978-1-951047)* 1931 BRIAN WAY, GA 30033, DECATUR, GA 30033 USA Tel 404-926-6563
E-mail: dachosenorg@gmail.com
Web site: http://www.dachosen.org; www.ratesandroyalty.com.

Dad Wings It Bks., *(978-1-7372061)* 8215 Windy Harbor Way, West Chester, OH 45069 USA Tel 513-218-7205
E-mail: dadwingsit@gmail.com
Web site: www.dadwingsit.com.

Daddy Bean Bks., *(978-0-9842929)* 42 W. 38th St., Suite 1001, New York, NY 10018 USA Tel 212-840-2326
E-mail: Pwalsh@walshfamilymedia.com
Web site: http://www.walshfamilymedia.com.

Daddy's Heroes, Inc., *(978-0-9792111)* 4799 Baxter St., Santa Barbara, CA 93110 USA
E-mail: karun@daddysheroes.com
Web site: http://www.daddysheroes.com.

Dadielte Production, *(978-0-9799273; 978-0-9981419)* Orders Addr.: 12910 Fontainebleau Dr., Moreno Valley, CA 92556-1266 USA (SAN 854-7645)
E-mail: gema118@hotmail.com.

Daedalian Press *See* **Biabe Publishing**

Dahle, Mark Portfolios, *(978-0-615-68498-7; 978-0-615-68502-1; 978-0-615-68515-1; 978-0-615-68518-2; 978-0-615-68718-6; 978-0-615-68727-8; 978-0-615-68729-2; 978-0-615-68732-2; 978-0-615-68733-9; 978-0-615-68735-3; 978-0-615-75042-2; 978-0-615-75046-0; 978-0-615-75047-7; 978-0-615-75049-1; 978-0-615-75053-8; 978-0-615-75054-5; 978-0-615-93016-9; 978-0-615-93750-2; 978-0-615-98110-9; 978-0-615-98111-6; 978-0-692-02252-8; 978-0-692-21589-0; 978-0-692-37061-2; 978-0-692-39866-1; 978-0-692-42329-5; 978-0-692-42332-5) 1645 Emerald St., 2U, San Diego, CA 92109 USA Tel 858-581-1645*
E-mail: MarkDahle@aol.com
Dist(s): **CreateSpace Independent Publishing Platform.**

Dahomey Publishing Co., *(978-0-9723570)* Orders Addr.: 50 Hall Rd., Winchendon, MA 01475 USA (SAN 255-4542) Tel 978-297-1820; Fax: 978-297-2519
Web site: http://www.DahomeyPublishing.com.

Dailey International Pubs., *(978-0-9666251)* 500 Laurel Oaks Ln., Alpharetta, GA 30004-4508 USA
E-mail: franklyn@daileyint.com
Web site: http://www.daileyint.com.

Dailor, Dylan, *(978-0-692-14740-5)* 42 Kittling Ridge Ln., Rochester, NY 14612 USA Tel 585-353-2582
E-mail: DDailor11@gmail.com.

Daimon Verlag (CHE) *(978-3-85630) Dist. by* **BTPS.**

Daisy Mae Bk. Publishing, *(978-0-9998154)* 8024 Michener Ave., Philadelphia, PA 19150 USA Tel 215-601-0106
E-mail: jordylive@yahoo.com.

Daisy Mae Bks., *(978-0-692-04361-5; 978-0-692-04423-0; 978-0-578-46281-3)* 8255 N. Denny Rd., Bloomington, IN 47404 USA Tel 812-327-8493
E-mail: sbaker8493@yahoo.com
Dist(s): **Ingram Content Group.**

Daisy Patch Pr., *(978-1-7362082)* 6249 Williamsburg Blvd, Arlington, VA 22207 USA Tel 703-863-0901
E-mail: liz.j.harr@gmail.com
Web site: daisypatchpress.com.

Daisy Publishing, *(978-0-9740641)* P.O. Box 681171, Franklin, TN 37068 USA Do not confuse with Daisy Publishing in Massapequa Park, NY, Altoona, PA.

Dakitab, Inc., *(978-0-9791059)* Orders Addr.: 2906 W. Grand Blvd., Detroit, MI 48202 USA (SAN 852-4408) Fax: 248-360-6148
E-mail: aid@awaytoread.com
Web site: http://www.awaytoread.com.

Dakota Assocs., Inc., *(978-0-615-14589-1; 978-0-615-18375-6)* P.O. Box 321, W. Bloomfield, NY 14585 USA
Web site: http://www.dakotaassociates.com
Dist(s): **Lulu Pr., Inc.**

Dakota Bks., *(978-0-9632861)* Orders Addr.: 2801 Daubenbiss, No. 1, Soquel, CA 95073 USA (SAN 630-9445) Tel 831-477-7174
E-mail: llogan@cruzio.com.

Dakota Legends, *(978-0-692-65514-6)* 510 S Extension Rd Apt 1044, Mesa, AZ 85210 USA Tel 480-202-7714
Web site: www.timpanogoslegend.com
Dist(s): **CreateSpace Independent Publishing Platform.**

Dakota Rose, *(978-0-9727056)* 23725 260th Ave., Okaton, SD 57562 USA Tel 605-669-2529
E-mail: dakotarose746@goldenwest.net.

Dakota Skies Photography *See* **Johnny Sundby Photography**

Dale Seymour Publications *Imprint of* **Savvas Learning Co.**

Dale, Shelley *See* **Norman Bks.**

Daley, Robert, *(978-0-9800839)* P.O. Box 5518, Keaau, HI 96749-5518 USA Tel 808-982-6688; Fax: 808-982-7824
E-mail: thedaleys@bythebookministries.org.

Dallas, Krissi *See* **Thunderfly Productions**

Dally, James W. Associates *See* **College Hse. Enterprises, LLC**

Dalton Publishing (GBR) *(978-0-9541886) Dist. by* **Midpt Trade.**

Dalton, Steven, *(978-0-692-14600-2; 978-0-692-14601-9)* 12164 S. 3410 W., Riverton, UT 84065 USA Tel 801-403-4144
E-mail: captainteancum@hotmail.com
Dist(s): **Ingram Content Group.**

Dalton, William, *(978-0-9764395)* 1338 N. Laurel Ave., West Hollywood, CA 90046 USA Tel 310-800-0811
E-mail: urban_mystic@yahoo.com.

Damamli Publishing Co., *(978-0-9753584)* 25A Crescent Dr., No.171, Pleasant Hill, CA 94523-3501 USA (SAN 256-100X) Fax: 923-674-9461
E-mail: tookie@tookie.com; president@damamli.com
Web site: http://www.damamli.com.

Damiano Sara, Janeen, *(978-0-9786404)* 108 W. Village Dr., Saint Augustine, FL 32095 USA
Web site: http://www.whereslily.com.

Damnation Bks., *(978-1-61572; 978-1-62929)* P.O. Box 3931, Santa Rosa, CA 95402-9998 USA
Web site: http://www.damnationbooks.com; http://www.eternalpress.biz.

Damon Strom, *(978-0-578-94717-4; 978-0-578-34098-2; 978-0-578-29596-1)* 6559 116TH PL NE, KIRKLAND, WA 98033 USA Tel 425-445-3972
E-mail: damonstrom@hotmail.com.

Dan Dan Fantasy, *(978-0-9834315)* 18483 Five Points, Redford, MI 48240 USA Tel 734-776-5478
E-mail: paintballman@sbcglobal.net.

Dan, Rebekah, *(978-0-692-94753-1)* 1150 Loma Vista Way, Vista, CA 92084 USA Tel 760-298-9404
E-mail: singtonations@gmail.com
Dist(s): **Ingram Content Group.**

Dana Jay, *(978-1-7365493)* 2894 Grand Concourse apt 2i, Bronx, NY 10458 USA Tel 929-416-8871
E-mail: Danajackson27@gmail.com
Web site: DanaJaybooks.com.

Dana Wilkerson *See* **Dana Wilkerson, LLC**

Dana Wilkerson, LLC, *(978-1-948148)* 239 N Broadway, Edmond, OK 73034 USA Tel 970-231-3999
E-mail: wilkerson.dana@gmail.com
Web site: danawilkerson.com.

Dance & Movement Pr. *Imprint of* **Rosen Publishing Group, Inc., The**

Dance Horizons *Imprint of* **Princeton Bk. Co. Pubs.**

Dancer's Publishing, *(978-0-9749848)* 2103 Harrison NW, Suite 2-336, Olympia, WA 98502 USA.

Dances With Horses, Inc., *(978-0-9763489)* P.O. Box 819, Rexburg, ID 83440 USA Tel 800-871-7635; Fax: 208-356-7817; Toll Free: 800-871-7635
E-mail: frankbell@horsewhisperer.com
Web site: http://www.horsewhisperer.com.

Dancing Crows Pr., *(978-0-9704420; 978-1-951543)* 306 Huntington Dr., Temple, GA 30179 USA
E-mail: Dancingcrowspress@gmail.com.

Dancing Crows Unlimited *See* **Dancing Crows Pr.**

Dancing Dakini Pr., *(978-0-9836333)* 77 Morning Sun Dr., Sedona, AZ 86336 USA Tel 505-466-1887
E-mail: editor@dancingdakinipress.com
Web site: www.dancingdakinipress.com.

Dancing Force, The, *(978-0-9726119)* 2249 Reeves Creek Rd., Suite B, Selma, OR 97538 USA (SAN 255-156X) Tel 541-597-2093 (phone/fax)
E-mail: dancingforce@ureach.com
Dist(s): **DeVorss & Co.**

Dancing Horse Pr., *(978-0-9766168; 978-0-9966617; 978-1-7330204; 978-1-7373618)* 7013 S. Telluride St., Centennial, CO 80016-1524 USA
E-mail: mjevansbtm@gmail.com
Web site: www.dancinghorsepress.com.

Dancing Journey Pr., *(978-0-9847662)* 434 Ulman Rd., Thetford Center, VT 05075 USA Tel 802-785-4717
E-mail: Ginger.Wallis@valley.net.

Dancing Magic Heart Bk., *(978-0-9790041)* Div. of Douglas/Steinman Productions, 1841 Broadway, Suite 1103, New York, NY 10023 USA Tel 212-765-9848; Fax: 212-765-9848
E-mail: faithdouglas@earthlink.net
Web site: http://www.douglas-steinman.com
Dist(s): **New Leaf Resources.**

Dancing Mommy Pr., *(978-0-9971084)* 242 St. Paul Dr., Alamo, CA 94507 USA Tel 925-876-4546
E-mail: jeryl@ronjer.com.

Dancing Moon Pr., *(978-1-892076; 978-1-937493; 978-1-945587)* 61535 S Hwy 97 Ste. 5 No. 623, Bend, OR 97702 USA Tel 541-574-7708 (work)
E-mail: kim@dancingmoonpress.com
Web site: http://www.dancingmoonpress.com
Dist(s): **Partners/West Book Distributors.**

Dancing Spirit Publishing, LLC, *(978-0-9997064)* P.O. Box 102, Forked River, NJ 08731 USA Tel 732-403-7146
E-mail: s4mmy415@gmail.com
Web site: DancingSpiritPublishing.com.

Publisher Name Index

For full information on wholesalers and distributors, refer to the Wholesaler and Distributor Name Index

Dancing With Bear Publishing, *(978-0-9988339; 978-1-7325905; 978-1-7342841)* P.O. Box 281, San Marcos, TX 78667 USA Tel 512-665-6188 Do not confuse with Dancing With Bear Publishing in Antlers, OK
E-mail: debbieroppolo@gmail.com
Web site: dwbpublishing.com.

Dancing Words Pr., Inc., *(978-0-9716346)* Orders Addr.: P.O. Box 1575, Severna Park, MD 21146 USA; Edit Addr.: 12 Sonneborn Ln., Severna Park, MD 21146 USA Tel 410-647-1441 (phone/fax)
E-mail: dwpinc@aol.com
Web site: http://www.dancingwordspress.com
Dist(s): **Quality Bks., Inc.**

D&C Publishing, *(978-0-692-77041-2; 978-0-692-78854-7; 978-0-692-19084-5)* 2062 S. Taylor, cleveland heights, OH 44118 USA Tel 216-321-1101
E-mail: ladoshaw@yahoo.com
Web site: www.lwrightbooks.com.

Dandelion Publishing, *(978-0-9793930)* 6234 Eliza Ln., North Las Vegas, NV 89031 USA (SAN 853-330X)
E-mail: sand.d@cox.net
Web site: http://DandelionPublishing.com.

D&L Bks. LLC, *(978-1-7357418; 978-1-7379131)* 34 Long Hill Rd., Long Valley, NJ 07853 USA Tel 908-879-2497
E-mail: dferri1123@gmail.com
Web site: dlbooks.org.

Dandy Lion Pubns., *(978-0-931724; 978-1-883055)* P.O. Box 190, Sn Luis Obisp, CA 93406-0190 USA (SAN 211-5565) Toll Free: 800-776-8032
E-mail: dandy@dandylionbooks.com
Web site: http://www.dandylionbooks.com.

Dangberg, Grace Foundation, Incorporated *See* **Sage Hill Pubs., LLC**

Daniel, Onicka J, *(978-0-692-90518-0; 978-0-692-95713-4; 978-0-692-08712-1; 978-0-578-40429-5)* 562 Candle Ln. No. 101, Newport News, VA 23608 USA Tel 757-358-3677
E-mail: theholidayboys@outlook.com
Web site: www.theholidayboy.com.

Danielle Lacy *See* **My Three Roses**

Danielle Marietta, *(978-1-7357218; 978-1-962140)* 42084 Mansfield Pk. Ct, Chantilly, VA 20152 USA Tel 253-921-1227
E-mail: daniellemariettabook@gmail.com.

Daniel's Hse. Publishing, *(978-0-9637200; 978-0-692-01895-8; 978-0-9915033; 978-0-692-66397-4; 978-0-692-84229-4; 978-0-9988590; 978-1-7365110; 979-8-9885283)* P.O. Box 623, Huntington, IN 46750 USA Tel 260-388-1942; Fax: 260-356-7594.

Dankworth Publishing, *(978-0-9855676; 978-0-9987888)* 309 Reamer Pl., Oberlin, OH 44074 USA Tel 612-309-5126
E-mail: mindybrueggemann@yahoo.com.

DanMar Publishing, *(978-0-9749407)* 112 E. Pennsylvania Blvd., Feasterville, PA 19053 USA Tel 215-364-1112; Fax: 215-364-3231
E-mail: drlavanga@aol.com
Web site: http://www.drlavanga.com.

Danny & Ester's Fortunate Adventures, *(978-0-9833667)* 1979 Willow Ave., Worthington, MN 56187 USA Tel 507-376-5889
E-mail: mccuen@mchsi.com
Dist(s): **Adventure Pubns.**

Dante's Publishing *See* **Solomon's Bks.**

Dantone, Desni, *(978-0-9895090)* 114 Alderwood Dr., Greensburg, PA 15601 USA Tel 724-261-0096
Dist(s): **CreateSpace Independent Publishing Platform.**

Danza Pubns., *(978-0-9774552)* P.O. Box 252053, West Bloomfield, MI 48325 USA Toll Free: 800-457-2157
Web site: http://www.elaineserling.com.

D.A.P./Distributed Art Pubs., *(978-1-881616; 978-1-891024; 978-1-933045; 978-1-935202; 978-1-938922; 978-1-942884; 978-1-63681)* Orders Addr.: 75 Broad St., Suite 630, New York, NY 10004 USA (SAN 630-6446) Tel 212-627-1999; Fax: 212-627-9484; Toll Free Fax: 800-478-3128; Toll Free: 800-338-2665
E-mail: dap@dapinc.com
Web site: http://www.artbook.com/.

DAPHNE JAMES HUFF, *(978-0-578-47414-4; 978-0-578-60170-0; 978-0-578-61387-1; 978-0-578-62784-7; 979-8-9877259)* 257 High St., Acton, MA 01720 USA Tel 240-390-7921
E-mail: daphnejameshuff@gmail.com
Dist(s): **Ingram Content Group.**

Dar Asadeeq Publishing & Distribution, Inc., *(978-0-615-52712-3; 978-0-9853772)* 646 Oaklawn Ave., Chula Vista, CA 91910 USA Tel 619-761-5329
E-mail: alsadeeq.usa@gmail.com
Web site: www.daralsadeeq.com.

Dara Publishing LLC, *(978-0-9975059; 978-0-692-98947-0; 978-1-7321362)* 1649 Nostrand Ave., Brooklyn, NY 11226 USA Tel 347-962-8363
E-mail: denifa@yahoo.com.

Darby Creek *Imprint of* **Lerner Publishing Group**

Darci, *(978-1-7341819)* 5666 Middleboro Rd., Morrow, OH 45152 USA Tel 937-763-6592
E-mail: darci989@yahoo.com.

Dare To Be King Project, *(978-0-615-59706-5; 978-0-615-91386-5; 978-0-692-34347-4; 978-0-692-69126-7; 978-0-692-73435-3; 978-0-692-78432-7; 978-0-692-91727-5; 978-0-692-11044-7; 978-0-578-47744-2; 978-0-578-84273-8; 978-0-578-30221-8; 979-8-218-05870-8)*
E-mail: dmiller3941@gmail.com
Web site: www.daretobeking.net.

Dare to Dream Scholarship, Incorporated *See* **Cole Publishing**

Dare Wright Media, *(978-0-615-75722-3; 978-0-615-76436-8; 978-0-615-77738-2; 978-0-615-77739-9; 978-0-615-77740-5; 978-0-615-82784-1; 978-0-615-82786-5; 978-0-615-82788-9; 978-0-615-83495-5; 978-0-615-97776-8; 978-0-9965827; 978-1-7334312)* 136 Cedar Ln., Santa Barbara, CA 93108 USA Tel 8058848488
Web site: www.darewright.com
Dist(s): **CreateSpace Independent Publishing Platform.**

Dargaud Publishing Co. (FRA) *(978-0-917201; 978-2-205) Dist. by* **Distribks Inc.**

Daring, Doe, *(978-0-9853543)* 601 N. Elm St., Comanche, TX 84105 USA Tel 469-688-6888
E-mail: doedaring@gmail.com.

Dark Circle Comics *Imprint of* **Archie Comic Pubns., Inc.**

Dark Cloud Bks., *(978-0-9978296; 978-0-692-91121-1; 978-0-578-49281-0; 978-0-578-49284-1)* 2808 Bent Leaf Dr., Valrico, FL 33594 USA Tel 813-601-2965
E-mail: stevealtier@outlook.com
Web site: www.stevealtier.com.

Dark Continents Publishing, *(978-0-9831603; 978-0-9836245; 978-0-9848931; 978-0-615-68082-8; 978-0-615-69182-4; 978-0-615-71013-6; 978-0-615-71015-0; 978-0-615-71017-4; 978-0-615-71018-1; 978-0-615-71019-8; 978-0-615-71840-8; 978-0-615-83145-9; 978-0-615-84491-6; 978-0-615-88140-9; 978-0-615-91582-1; 978-0-615-96489-8; 978-0-615-97495-8; 978-0-692-24951-2) P.O. Box 276, Tiskilwa, IL 61368 USA Tel 815-646-4748*
E-mail: DMYoungquist@darkcontinents.com
Web site: www.darkcontinents.com
Dist(s): **CreateSpace Independent Publishing Platform.**

Dark Forest Pr., *(978-0-9764226)* 1310 N. Oak St., Apt. 408, Arlington, VA 22209 USA Tel 202-368-4341; P.O. Box 9133, Arlington, VA 22210 (SAN 256-4475) Tel 202-368-4341 Do not confuse with Dark Forest Press in Denver, CO.

Dark Horse Books *Imprint of* **Dark Horse Comics**

Dark Horse Comics, *(978-1-56971; 978-1-878574; 978-1-59307; 978-1-59582; 978-1-59617; 978-1-61655; 978-1-61659; 978-1-62115; 978-1-63008; 978-1-5067)* 10956 SE Main St., Milwaukie, OR 97222 USA Tel 503-652-8815; Fax: 503-654-9440; *Imprints:* Dark Horse Books (Dark Horse Bks)
E-mail: dhcomics@darkhorse.com
Web site: http://www.darkhorse.com
Dist(s): **Children's Plus, Inc.**
Diamond Comic Distributors, Inc.
Diamond Bk. Distributors
Penguin Random Hse. Distribution
Penguin Random Hse. LLC
Random Hse., Inc.

Dark Ink Media, *(978-0-9984868)* 45977 Houghton Creek Rd., Baker City, OR 97814 USA Tel 541-403-1291
E-mail: kristenwares@protonmail.com.

Dark Mantle Publishing, *(978-0-692-97450-6)* 1301 n dunbarton oaks ln, Liberty Lake, WA 99019 USA Tel 253-905-9563
E-mail: empirial995@gmail.com.

A Dark Matter Pubn., *(978-0-578-22252-3)* 63 E. 9th St., Apt. 7R, New York, NY 10003-6302 USA Tel 972 0506899049
E-mail: adarkmatterpublication@gmail.com.

Dark Oak Pr., *(978-0-9660744; 978-0-9788777; 978-0-9823745; 978-1-937035; 978-1-941754; 978-1-949817)* Div. of Kerlak Enterprises, Inc., 1779 Kirby Pkwy., Suite 1-373, Memphis, TN 38138 USA (SAN 857-9776)
E-mail: agilbreath@kerlakpublishing.com; service@kerlakpublishing.com; agilbreath@darkoakpress.com
Web site: http://www.darkoakpress.com; http://www.darkoakpress.com.

Dark Overlord Media *See* **Empty Set Entertainment**

Dark Passages *Imprint of* **Whorl Bks.**

Dark Skull Studios, *(978-0-9797080)* 17711 Barker Bluff Ln., Cypress, TX 77433 USA (SAN 854-1922) Tel 832-220-6734
E-mail: richardleon@darkskullstudios.com
Web site: http://www.darkskullstudios.com.

Dark Star Publishing, *(978-0-9897435; 978-0-9984263; 978-0-9986260)* P.O. Box 667, Richmond, MI 48062 USA Tel 810-858-1135
E-mail: dayne87@comcast.net
Web site: www.bloodandshadows.net.

Dark Titan, *(978-0-692-48858-4; 978-0-692-49239-0; 978-0-9998204; 978-0-578-46697-2; 978-0-578-56306-0; 978-1-7343300; 978-1-7353154; 978-1-7359429; 978-1-7363782; 978-1-7366984; 978-1-7369944; 978-1-7376143; 979-8-9851109; 979-8-9856344; 978-0-578-29643-2; 979-8-9866393; 979-8-218-09730-1; 979-8-9875065; 979-8-9886918) 5776 Goodland Trace, Alexandria, LA 71301 USA Tel 318-955-7815*
E-mail: trobinsonii@hotmail.com.

Darker Intentions Pr., *(978-0-9769612; 978-0-9827597)* P.O. Box 569, Freehold Twp., NJ 07728-0569 USA Tel 732-299-6212
E-mail: jzdakota@hotmail.com.

Darkerwood Publishing Group, *(978-0-9669788; 978-0-9788975; 978-1-938839)* P.O. Box 2011, Arvada, CO 80001 USA
E-mail: swordarkeereon@gmail.com; ofs.admin@gmail.com; darkerwoodpublishing@gmail.com
Web site: http://www.demonolatry.org/dbpub.htm.

Darlene L. Eason, *(978-0-578-74641-8)* 18 Crownbrook Dr., Waterbury, CT 06704 USA Tel 203-525-2499
E-mail: Our1stprotest@gmail.com.

Darlene Williams, *(978-0-578-83720-8; 978-0-578-98577-0; 979-8-218-22643-5)* 3211 W. Lexington Apt. 1C, Chicago, IL 60624 USA Tel 773-963-3368
E-mail: williamsdarlene70@gmail.com
Web site: 1ihaveavoice.com.

Darling & Co. *Imprint of* **Laughing Elephant**

Darling Pr. LLC, *(978-0-9765761)* Orders Addr.: 19740 SW 49th Ave., Tualatin, OR 97062 USA
Web site: http://www.darlingpress.com
Dist(s): **Bottman Design, Inc.**

Darlyng & Co. Publisher *See* **Darlyng & Co. Publishing**

Darlyng & Co. Publishing, *(978-1-7337778)* 1585 Yanceyville St., No. 14292, Greensboro, NC 27405 USA Tel 929-376-8584
E-mail: info@darlyngandco.com
Web site: www.darlyngandco.com.

Darnell Publishing, *(978-0-9755616)* P.O. Box 341825, Tampa, FL 33694 USA
Web site: http://www.abrink.com.

Darren Scott Engelkemier, *(978-0-692-04110-9)* 1225 Hillview Dr., Menlo Park, CA 94025 USA Tel 650-776-5427
E-mail: darrene@stanfordalumni.org
Dist(s): **Ingram Content Group.**

Dar-Salam.org, *(978-1-948117)* P.O. Box 55573, Houston, TX 77255 USA Tel 713-364-4649
E-mail: hope99@gmail.com.

Dart Publishing, *(978-0-692-80432-2; 978-0-692-84334-5; 978-0-578-54227-0; 978-0-578-56167-7)* 1198 Spruance St., San Jose, CA 95128 USA Tel 408-280-7611
E-mail: juliedart@comcast.ney.

DASANBOOKS, *(978-0-9819542; 978-0-9828016; 978-0-9839594)* 120 Sylvan Ave., Englewood Cliffs, NJ 07632 USA
Dist(s): **Midpoint Trade Bks., Inc.**

Dash & Doodles Productions, *(978-0-615-22279-0; 978-0-578-08121-2)* 4810 Kellywood Dr., Glen Allen, VA 23060 USA Tel 804-527-1033
E-mail: dashanddoodles@aol.com
Web site: http://www.askdash.com
Dist(s): **Lulu Pr., Inc.**

Data Trace Legal Publishers, Incorporated *See* **Data Trace Publishing, Co.**

Data Trace Publishing, Co., *(978-0-9637468; 978-1-57400)* Orders Addr.: P.O. Box 1239, Brooklandville, MD 21022 USA Tel 410-494-4994; Fax: 410-494-0515; Toll Free: 800-342-0454; Edit Addr.: 110 West Rd., Suite 227, Towson, MD 21204 USA
E-mail: info@datatrace.com
Web site: http://www.datatrace.com/legal.

Databooks *See* **Chandler Hse. Pr.**

Daughter Culture Pubns., *(978-0-935281)* P.O. Box 127924, San Diego, CA 92112 USA (SAN 695-7447) Tel 619-432-5491.

Daughters Arise, LLC, *(978-0-9744178)* 2648 E. Workman Ave., Suite 314, West Covina, CA 91791 USA Tel 770-808-1199; Fax: 770-216-1626
E-mail: fhenley@daughtersarise.com
Web site: http://www.daughtersarise.com.

Daughtrey Publishing Hse., *(978-0-578-46710-8)* 5024 3/4 Hayter Ave., Lakewood, CA 90712 USA Tel 562-333-5353
E-mail: sdaughtrey@icloud.com.

DaValle, Grace, *(978-0-578-78405-2)* 3006 Lunada Ln., Alamo, CA 94507 USA Tel 925-967-5481
E-mail: gracedavalle@icloud.com.

Dave Horning LLC *See* **Field of Play Pr.**

Daven, Christian Publishing, *(978-0-578-00257-6)* 6504 Mendius Ave., NE, Albuquerque, NM 87109 USA Tel 505-315-2984
Dist(s): **Lulu Pr., Inc.**

Davenport, May Pubs., *(978-0-943864; 978-0-9603118; 978-0-9794140)* 26313 Purissima Rd., Los Altos Hills, CA 94022-4539 USA (SAN 212-467X) Tel 650-947-1325; Fax: 650-947-1373
E-mail: mdbooks@earthlink.net
Dist(s): **Todd Communications.**

Davenport, Sheena, *(978-0-9747625)* 3535 Riverview Approach, Ellenwood, GA 30294 USA Tel 404-241-3106
E-mail: szdavenport@yahoo.com.

Davey, Daisy & Pete - The Things We Can Dream, *(978-0-578-40850-7; 978-0-578-46097-0)* 5 Novilla, Laguna, CA 92677 USA Tel 951-907-0762
E-mail: tehunter9@yahoo.com
Dist(s): **CreateSpace Independent Publishing Platform.**

David & Charles Pubs. (GBR) *(978-0-7153; 978-1-4463) Dist. by* **TwoRivers.**

David Bradley LLC, *(978-1-7366084)* 200 Hoover Ave, LAS VEGAS, NV 89101 USA Tel 224-392-9245
E-mail: davidbschnitzer@gmail.com.

David, Elizabeth A., *(978-0-9740170)* P.O. Box 766, Fairhaven, MA 02719-0700 USA Tel 508-979-5593
E-mail: yasny@comcast.net
Web site: http://www.zorena.com.

David Fickling Bks. *Imprint of* **Random Hse. Children's Bks.**

†David, Jonathan Pubs., Inc., *(978-0-8246)* 68-22 Eliot Ave., Middle Village, NY 11379 USA (SAN 169-5274) Tel 718-456-8611; Fax: 718-894-2818
E-mail: jondavpub@aol.com
Web site: http://www.jdbooks.com; *CIP.*

David L Lantz, *(978-1-7376114)* 7802 Cannonade Dr., Indianapolis, IN 46217 USA Tel 317-670-8060
E-mail: dlantz@wisejargon.com
Web site: www.wisejargon.com.

†Davidson, Harlan Inc., *(978-0-88295)* 773 Glenn Ave., Wheeling, IL 60090-6000 USA (SAN 201-2375) Tel 847-541-9720; Fax: 847-541-9830
E-mail: harlandavidson@harlandavidson.com
Web site: http://www.harlandavidson.com; *CIP.*

Davies, Sean, *(978-0-692-96866-6)* 514 Americas Way 8806, Box Elder, SD 57719 USA Tel 314-409-0306
E-mail: incrediblemicrobiome@gmail.com.

Davies, Tammy, *(978-0-578-54098-6; 978-0-578-62554-6)* 2213 7th St S, La Crosse, WI 54601 USA Tel 608-314-5497
E-mail: Mordelic@gmail.com
Dist(s): **Ingram Content Group.**

Davis, A. S. Media Group, *(978-0-9666352; 978-0-9729150; 978-0-9759022; 978-0-9766013; 978-0-9776245; 978-0-9787719; 978-1-934724)* Orders Addr.: P.O. Box 590780, San Francisco, CA 94159 USA
E-mail: info@greenlinepub.com
Web site: http://www.greenlinepub.com.

Davis Bks. LLC, *(978-0-9770142)* Orders Addr.: P.O. Box 6291, Cincinnati, OH 45206 USA Tel 513-687-1943
E-mail: georgedisselkamp@yahoo.com
Web site: http://www.davisbooks.cjb.net
Dist(s): **Docustar.**

Davis, Brittney, *(978-0-578-47171-6; 978-0-578-47172-3)* 5143 Derby Forest Dr. N., Jacksonville, FL 32258 USA Tel 904-844-3998
E-mail: brittney3583@yahoo.com
Dist(s): **Ingram Content Group.**

†Davis, F. A. Co., *(978-0-8036; 978-1-7196)* Orders Addr.: 1915 Arch St., Philadelphia, PA 19103 USA; Edit Addr.: 1915 Arch St., Philadelphia, PA 19103 USA (SAN 295-3250) Tel 215-440-3001; Fax: 215-440-3016; Toll Free: 800-323-3555
E-mail: orders@fadavis.com
Web site: http://www.fadavis.com
Dist(s): **Ebsco Publishing**
Majors, J. A. Co.
Majors Scientific Bks., Inc.
Matthews Medical Bk. Co.
MyiLibrary
Oxford Univ. Pr., Inc.
Rittenhouse Bk. Distributors
ebrary, Inc.; *CIP.*

Davis, Gregory B., *(978-0-578-21354-5)* 8 Aintree Walk, Sewell, NJ 08080 USA Tel 856-904-5097
E-mail: gregbdavis@comcast.net.

Davis II, Robert B, *(978-0-9978464)* 6 Greenwood Pl., Menlo Park, CA 94025 USA Tel 650-815-5274
E-mail: robertbdavis93@gmail.com
Web site: jnanayogaphilosophy.com.

Davis, James (Jim), *(978-0-9760960)* 1700 W. Washington St. Apt. A507, Springfield, IL 62702-6447 USA.

Davis, Kevin, *(978-1-7330948)* P.O. Box 544, hindman, KY 41822 USA Tel 606-785-3104
E-mail: kevindavispac@yahoo.com.

Davis, Kristalin, *(978-0-578-59675-4)* P.O. Box P.O. Box 84, Howe, OK 74940 USA Tel 760-898-9764
E-mail: kristalin.davis@yahoo.com.

Davis, nathaniel *See* **Davis, Nathaniel**

Davis, Nathaniel, *(978-0-9997822; 979-8-9876168)* 1627 McDonald St., Houston, TX 77007 USA Tel 281-755-7779
E-mail: peanutbutterandjam2017@gmail.com.

Davis, Paul *See* **Royal Hse. Publishing**

Davis Pubns., Inc., *(978-0-87192; 978-1-61528; 978-1-64164; 979-8-88695)* 30 Beach St., WESTBOROUGH, MA 01581 USA (SAN 201-3002) Tel 508-754-7201; Fax: 508-791-0779; Toll Free: 800-533-2847
E-mail: esperber@davisart.com
Web site: http://www.davisart.com
Dist(s): **Sterling Publishing Co., Inc.**

Davis, Tamela *See* **JacKris Publishing**

Davis, Wayne *See* **LoGiudice Publishing**

Davlaw Press, *(978-0-9776917)* Orders Addr.: P.O. Box 4317, Harrisburg, PA 17111 USA (SAN 257-9863) Tel 717-441-5451; Fax: 717-441-4925; *Imprints:* Curcumin Books (Curcumin Bks)
E-mail: larry@davlawpress.com
Web site: http://www.davlawpress.com.

†Davus Publishing, *(978-0-915317)* 7-190 Argyle St, Simcoe, ON N3Y 0C1 CAN Tel 519-909-2927
E-mail: davus@kwic.com; davuspub@gmail.com
Web site: https://www.davuspublishing.com
Dist(s): **Coutts Information Services;** *CIP.*

DAW *Imprint of* **DAW**

DAW, 375 Hudson St., 3rd Flr., New York, NY 10014 USA; *Imprints:* DAW (DAW)
Dist(s): **Penguin Random Hse. Distribution**
Penguin Random Hse. LLC.

Dawasoft, *(978-0-9764218)* 150-35 119th Rd., Jamaica, NY 11434 USA Tel 347-954-6479
E-mail: dawasoft@yahoo.com.

Dawkins, Latoya, *(978-1-7363021)* 535 Penn Ave. 0, LANCASTER, PA 17602 USA Tel 8189380328
E-mail: capricetoy@gmail.com.

Dawn Chorus Pr. *Imprint of* **Perennis, Sophia**

Dawn of a New Day Pubns., The *Imprint of* **Konkori International**

Dawn of Day Childrens Publishing Co., Inc., *(978-0-9666857)* 73 Ireland Pl., PMB 201, Amityville, NY 11757 USA (SAN 253-0198) Tel 631-225-5513; Fax: 631-225-5431; Toll Free: 800-575-7040
E-mail: information@dawnofday.com
Web site: http://www.dawnofday.com.

Dawn Publications *See* **Take Heart Pubns.**

Dawn Pubns. *Imprint of* **Sourcebooks, Inc.**

DawQuin LLC, *(978-0-9842787)* P.O. Box 1800, Troy, MI 48099 USA (SAN 858-9461) Tel 248-765-7276
E-mail: publisher@dawquin.com
Web site: www.dawquin.com.

Day By Day Recovery Resources, *(978-0-9674915; 978-1-934569)* 35582 Shooting Star Ln. 35582 Shooting Star Ln., Potomic, MT 59823 USA Tel 887-447-1683
E-mail: business@pocketsponsor.com
Web site: http://www.day-by-day.org; http://www.PocketSponsor.com
Dist(s): **Mentor Bks.**

Day By Day Recovery Resources, LLC *See* **Day By Day Recovery Resources**

Day I Hit a Home Run Enterprise, The, *(978-0-9831950)* 7389 Brookville Rd., Oxford, OH 45056 USA Tel 513-290-2189
E-mail: mullenmike122@yahoo.com
Web site: www.thedayihitahomerun.com.

Day to Day Bks. *Imprint of* **Day to Day Enterprises**

Day to Day Enterprises, *(978-1-890905)* Orders Addr.: 8396 Maryland Rd., Lake Shore, MD 21122-4655 USA (SAN

299-7118) Tel 443-817-2129; *Imprints:* Eco Fiction Books (Eco Fiction Bks); Day to Day Books (Day2Day)
E-mail: books@daytodayenterprises.com
Web site: http://www.daytodayenterprises.com; http://www.totallystories.com
Dist(s): **Book Clearing Hse.**

Day3 Productions, Inc., *(978-0-9777361)* 215 Tower Rd, McKenzie, TN 38201 USA (SAN 850-0770) Tel 731-352-6081
E-mail: jeff@day3productions.com
Web site: http://www.day3productions.com.

Daybreak Pr., *(978-0-578-05238-0; 978-0-578-09509-7)* 314 W. 92nd St., 2F, New York, NY 10025 USA; 2307 Broadway, New York, NY 10024
E-mail: lesliefourton2gmail.com.

Daydreamers Pr. *Imprint of* **Penn, Carlotta**

Daylight Bks., *(978-0-9632177; 978-0-9840220)* 671 W. 193rd St. #4j New York, New York, NY 10040 USA Tel 646-265-3294
E-mail: smartin34@earthlink.net
Dist(s): **ebrary, Inc.**

Daylight Pubs., *(978-0-9764103; 978-0-9792755)* 8255 S Wright Pl., Broken Arrow, OK 74014 USA Tel 918-357-1266
E-mail: kathy@daylightpublishers.com
Web site: http://www.daylightpublishers.com.

DayOne Pubns. (GBR) *(978-0-902548; 978-1-903087; 978-1-84625) Dist. by* **STL Dist.**

Days of Glory Publishing, *(978-0-9770206)* 28 Branden Way, Tolland, CT 06084 USA.

DaySpring Cards, *(978-1-58061; 978-1-884009; 978-1-59449; 978-1-60116; 978-1-60817; 978-1-61494; 978-1-63116; 978-1-68408; 978-1-64454; 978-1-64870; 979-8-88602; 979-8-88603)* P.O. Box 1010, Siloam Springs, AR 72761 USA (SAN 298-6302) Tel 479-524-9301; Fax: 479-524-9477; Toll Free: 800-944-8000
E-mail: jkaufman@dayspring.com; laurak@dayspring.com; calis@dayspring.com; dang@dayspring.com
Web site: http://www.dayspring.com
Dist(s): **TNT Media Group, Inc.**

Daystar Press *See* **TopNotch Pr.**

Dayton International Peace Museum *See* **Peace Power Pr.**

Dayton Publishing, *(978-0-9893290; 978-0-9970032; 978-1-7325265; 978-1-7351716)* 608 Barbara Ave., Solana Beach, CA 92075 USA Tel 858-775-3629
E-mail: linneadayt@aol.com.

Dazsling Inc., *(978-0-9749170)* P.O. Box 236, Allston, MA 02134 USA
Web site: http://www.rootfriends.com.

DC Comics, *(978-0-930289; 978-1-56389; 978-1-4012; 978-1-7995)* Div. of Warner Bros.- A Time Warner Entertainment Co., 1700 Broadway, New York, NY 10019 USA Tel 212-636-5400; Fax: 212-636-5979; *Imprints:* Vertigo (Vertigo); Paradox (Paradox); A B C (A B C); Wildstorm (Wildstorm); DC Kids (DCKids); DC Zoom (DC Zoom); DC Ink (DC Ink)
E-mail: booksales@dccomics.com
Web site: http://www.dccomics.com
Dist(s): **Children's Plus, Inc.**
Eastern News Distributors
MyiLibrary
Penguin Random Hse. Distribution
Penguin Random Hse. LLC
Random Hse., Inc.

DC Ink *Imprint of* **DC Comics**

DC Kids *Imprint of* **DC Comics**

DC Zoom *Imprint of* **DC Comics**

DCT Ranch Pr., *(978-0-692-11765-1; 978-1-7339997; 978-1-7340051)* 417 Hidden Ranch Ln., Floresville, TX 78114 USA Tel 512-626-6212
E-mail: mistyandjay@gmail.com
Dist(s): **CreateSpace Independent Publishing Platform.**

DCTS Publishing, *(978-0-9653904)* Div. of Hamilton Ministry, P.O. Box 40216, Santa Barbara, CA 93140 USA Tel 805-570-3168; Toll Free: 800-965-8150
E-mail: dennis@dctspub.com
Web site: http://www.dctspub.com.

de Blegny, Nick Publishing, *(978-0-615-82516-8; 978-0-615-92205-8; 978-0-615-95925-2; 978-0-692-32582-7; 978-0-692-32583-4; 978-0-692-61843-1; 978-0-692-67559-5; 978-0-692-14919-5; 978-1-7332647; 978-1-7373869)* 63 Mount Vernon Street, Apt 9, Boston, MA 02108 USA Tel 12019843148
Dist(s): **CreateSpace Independent Publishing Platform.**

De Boer, Cynthia L. Author/Speaker, *(978-1-7321384)* P.O. Box 50014, Henderson, NV 89016 USA Tel 702-293-0612
E-mail: c.deboerauthorspeaker@gmail.com
Web site: www.CynthiaL.DeBoer.com.

de Contreras, Lantz *See* **Angelic Prince Publishing, The**

de Fosseway, Marquis (GBR) *(978-0-9561561) Dist. by* **LuluCom.**

De Graff, Missy *See* **Stone Phoenix Pr.**

de Gruyter, Walter GmbH (DEU) *(978-0-346; 978-0-8176; 978-0-89925; 978-0-938198; 978-3-11; 978-3-486; 978-3-597; 978-3-598; 978-3-7940; 978-3-907820; 978-90-279; 978-3-89949; 978-3-0346; 978-3-0356; 978-3-922251; 978-83-958150) Dist. by* **IngramPubServ.**

De La Flor (ARG) *(978-950-515) Dist. by* **LD Bks Inc.**

De La Luz Pubns., *(978-0-9748326)* 121 W. Hickory St., Denton, TX 76201 USA Tel 940-367-1651; Fax: 940-323-0488
E-mail: ccarrasco1@chater.net

DE LA O LLC, *(978-0-578-41239-9)* 85 John St. 5C, New York, NY 10038 USA Tel 773-600-3799
E-mail: SD.DELAO@GMAIL.COM
Dist(s): **Independent Pub.**

De Loach, George P., *(978-0-9768362)* 475 W. Fallen Leaf Cir., Wasilla, AK 99654 USA Tel 907-376-2680
E-mail: gdeloach@juno.com.

De Portola Pr., *(978-0-692-47363-4; 978-0-692-18673-2; 979-8-218-10888-5)* 33780 Linda Rosea Rd., Temecula, CA 92592 USA Tel 951-551-5338
Dist(s): **CreateSpace Independent Publishing Platform.**

Dead Fossil Entertainment, *(978-0-578-56868-3; 978-0-578-59357-9)* 4020 E Altadena Ave, Phoenix, AZ 85028 USA Tel 480-266-3808
E-mail: deadfossil@carldang.com
Web site: https://carldang.com.

Deaf Missions, *(978-1-59799)* Orders Addr.: 21199 Greenview Rd., Council Bluffs, IA 51503-4190 USA
E-mail: joseph@deafmissions.com
Web site: http://www.deafmissions.com.

Deal, Darlene, *(978-0-9747299)* P.O. Box 521, North Hollywood, CA 91603-0521 USA Tel 818-752-7065 (phone/fax).

Deane, Jennifer Inc., *(978-0-9825112)* 1061 5th Ave. N., Naples, FL 34102 USA
E-mail: Jenniferdeane@earthlink.net; Jennifer@JenniferDeane.com
Web site: http://www.Jenniferdeane.com; http://www.SiennaBooks.com; http://www.musemediapublishing.com.

DeAngelis, Anthony, *(978-0-9754853)* 101 Cypress Ave., San Bruno, CA 94066-5420 USA
E-mail: a.deangelis@worldnet.att.net.

DeAnna Lynn Books *See* **SOAR Pr.**

Dean's Bks., Inc., *(978-0-9728607)* 1426 S. Kansas Ave., Topeka, KS 66612 USA Tel 785-357-4708
E-mail: contact@oilcanbook.com
Web site: http://www.oilcanbook.com.

Dear You, *(978-1-7321177)* 134-27 166th Pl. No. 10c, Jamaica, NY 11434 USA Tel 646-601-3802
E-mail: Nasheemad@gmail.com.

Dearborn Publishing, *(978-1-891685)* Div. of The Mae Group LLC,
E-mail: johngraham@att.net.

Dearborn Real Estate Education *Imprint of* **Kaplan Publishing**

Dearborn Trade, A Kaplan Professional Company *See* **Kaplan Publishing**

Deats, Dorie, *(978-1-7326064)* 3617 General Taylor St., New Orleans, LA 70125 USA Tel 607-342-8754
E-mail: dorie.deats@gmail.com.

Deb on Air Bks., *(978-0-9727615)* Orders Addr.: P.O. Box 580055, Elk Grove, CA 95758 USA Tel 916-684-3551.

Debate, Editorial (ESP) *(978-84-7444; 978-84-8306) Dist. by* **AIMS Intl.**

Debi, Kennedy *See* **nJoy Bks.**

Deborah Remington Charitable Trust for the Visual Arts, *(978-0-692-75785-7)* 325 E. 79th St., New York, NY 10075 USA Tel 212-535-7050
E-mail: mmbart1@gmail.com
Web site: deborahremington.com
Dist(s): **D.A.P./Distributed Art Pubs.**

Debra L. Wood, *(978-0-578-43189-5; 978-0-578-64475-2)* 381 Colebrook Rd., Gansevoort, NY 12831 USA Tel 518-695-2055
E-mail: jibbitsohio@aol.com, tsart@live.com
Dist(s): **Ingram Content Group.**

DeCa Communications, LLC, *(978-0-9762262)* 300 Williamsburg Dr., Mandeville, LA 70471 USA
Web site: http://www.decacom.info.

Decent Hill, *(978-1-936085)* Div. of Decent Hill Pubs., LLC, Orders Addr.: 6100 Oak Tree Blvd., Ste 200, Independence, OH 44131 USA (SAN 858-2483) Tel 216-236-3315 Personal Cell Phone; Toll Free: 866-688-5325 (phone/fax)
E-mail: Support@DecentHill.com
Web site: http://www.DecentHill.com.

Decent Hill Publishers *See* **Decent Hill**

Decere Publishing, *(978-0-9717013; 978-0-9816572)* 5590 Bunky Way, Atlanta, GA 30338 USA Tel 404-474-2830; Fax: 770-399-5883 Do not confuse with CSI Publishing in Monterey Park, CA
E-mail: mark@decere.com
Web site: http://www.decere.com.

Decesare, Jason, *(978-0-578-50578-7; 978-0-578-50579-4)* 174 Water St., Warren, RI 02885 USA Tel 401-473-6231
E-mail: j.dece1010@gmail.com.

Deck Prism Pubns., *(978-0-9979305)* 471 S. U.S. Hwy. 231, Jasper, IN 47546 USA Tel 812-470-3971
E-mail: deckprism15@gmail.com
Web site: deckprismpublications.com.

deCordova Sculpture Park and Museum *Imprint of* **Yale Univ. Pr.**

Dedalus Bks. Ltd. (GBR) *(978-0-946626; 978-1-873982; 978-1-903517; 978-1-904556; 978-1-907650; 978-1-909232; 978-1-910213; 978-1-912868) Dist. by* **SCB Distributo.**

Dedoni, *(978-1-953118)* 3618 Tamal Ct, Las Vegas, NV 89103 USA Tel 702-413-3747
E-mail: dianasegev@gmail.com
Web site: dedonibooks.com.

Dedoni Books *See* **Dedoni**

Dedushkiny Skazki, *(978-0-692-17234-6; 978-0-692-17238-4)* 5677 Nesbitt Ln., JACKSONVILLE, FL 32277 USA Tel 904-434-0062
E-mail: z.arbatskiy@gmail.com
Dist(s): **Ingram Content Group.**

Dee, *(978-1-7357804)* 7231 Australian St., Navarre, FL 32566 USA Tel 850-826-3705
E-mail: dee4716@gmail.com.

Deep Dish Design, *(978-0-9755033)* 15012 Cherry Ln., Burnsville, MN 55306 USA
E-mail: jb@deepdishdesign.com
Web site: http://www.deepdishdesign.com.

Deep Read Pr., *(978-1-954989)* P.O. Box 412, Lafayette, TN 37083 USA Tel 615-670-1725
E-mail: deepreadpress@gmail.com.

Deep River Bks., *(978-0-9712311; 978-0-9747190; 978-1-933204; 978-1-935265; 978-1-937756; 978-1-940269; 978-1-63269)* 1610 W. Williamson Ave., Sisters, OR 97759 USA Tel 541-549-1139
E-mail: bill@deepriverbooks.com
Web site: http://www.deepriverbooks.com/
Dist(s): **Baker & Taylor Publisher Services (BTPS)**
Send The Light Distribution LLC.

Deep Roots Pubns., *(978-0-9671713; 978-0-9819528)* Orders Addr.: P.O. Box 114, Saratoga, NY 12866 USA Tel 518-583-8920; Fax: 518-584-3919; Edit Addr.: 229 Lake Ave., Saratoga, NY 12866 USA
E-mail: drpalmer2002@yahoo.com
Web site: http://www.deeprootspublications.com
Dist(s): **North Country Bks., Inc.**

Deep Sea Publishing, *(978-0-9834276; 978-1-939535)* 1109 Devon St., Herndon, VA 2010 USA (SAN 860-164X) Tel 571-455-2027
E-mail: erhughes@deepseapublishing.com
Web site: www.deepseapublishing.com
Dist(s): **Lulu Pr., Inc.**

Deep Vellum Publishing, *(978-0-916583; 978-1-56478; 978-0-9892759; 978-1-62897; 978-1-941920; 978-1-943150; 978-0-9985184; 978-1-64605)* 3000 Commerce St., Dallas, TX 75226 USA Tel 512-771-6469
E-mail: deepvellum@gmail.com
Web site: http://deepvellum.org
Dist(s): **Consortium Bk. Sales & Distribution**
MyiLibrary
Publishers Group West (PGW).

Deep Waters Pr., *(978-0-9748171)* Suite 100, 77 Court St., Laconia, NH 03246 USA (SAN 255-8777) Tel 603-520-1214; P.O. Box 452, Meredith, NH 03253 Tel 603-524-2585
E-mail: halcyon@yahoo.com; deepwaterspress@yahoo.com
Web site: http://www.DeepWaterspress.com.

Deeper Revelation Bks., *(978-0-942507; 978-1-949297)* P.O. Box 4260, Cleveland, TN 37320 USA (SAN 667-3619) Tel 423-478-2843; 423-614-7399; Fax: 423-479-2980
E-mail: pastormikeshreve@gmail.com; vicki@deeperrevelationbooks.org; mikeshreve@shreveministries.org
Web site: http://www.deeperrevelationbooks.org; http://www.shreveministries.org
Dist(s): **Anchor Distributors**
Whitaker Hse.

Deeper Roots Pubns. & Media, *(978-1-930547)* Orders Addr.: 13 W. Lakeshore Dr., Cherokee Village, AR 72529 USA
E-mail: deeperroots@aol.com
Web site: http://www.DeeperRoots.com.

Deeper Waters, *(978-0-615-36602-9; 978-0-615-43255-7; 978-0-615-58840-7)* 11520 Grandview Rd., Kansas City,, MO 64137 USA Tel 816-765-9900
E-mail: blake.cadwell@gmail.com.

Deepercalling Media, Inc., *(978-0-9726135; 978-1-59601)* 1200 Mt. Diablo Blvd., Suite 108, Walnut Creek, CA 94596 USA (SAN 254-9360) Fax: 925-939-4010
E-mail: info@deepercalling.com
Web site: http://www.deepercalling.com
Dist(s): **Whitaker Hse.**

Deer Creek Publishing, *(978-0-9651452)* Orders Addr.: P.O. Box 2594, Nevada City, CA 95959 USA Fax: 530-478-1759 Do not confuse with Deer Creek Publishing, Provo, UT.

Deer Horn Pr., *(978-1-7334556)* 4239 Church St., Skokie, IL 60076 USA Tel 773-336-2338; *Imprints:* Little Big Deer (MYID_S_LITTL)
E-mail: tevi@tevster.com; me@tevih.com
Web site: tevih.com.

Deer Oaks, Inc., *(978-0-9764700)* P.O. Box 429, Barrington, IL 60011-0429 USA.

Deerbrook Editions, *(978-0-9712488; 978-0-9828100; 978-0-9904287; 978-0-9975051; 978-0-9991062; 978-0-9600293; 978-1-7343884; 978-1-7368477; 979-8-9865052)* P.O. Box 542, Cumberland, ME 04021-0542 USA Tel 207-233-0158
E-mail: jewilh@gmail.com
Web site: http://www.deerbrookeditions.com; http://deerbrookeditions.wordpress.com
Dist(s): **SPD-Small Pr. Distribution.**

DefConOne Publishing, *(978-0-615-90595-2; 978-0-692-27021-9; 978-0-692-39732-9; 978-0-692-46014-6; 978-0-692-51470-2; 978-0-692-53013-9; 978-0-692-54329-0; 978-0-692-59172-7; 978-0-692-62764-8; 978-0-692-65123-0; 978-0-692-72847-5; 978-0-9977936; 978-1-948280)* 12550 Greenwood Ave N, No. 202, Seattle, WA 98133 USA Tel 206-902-8249
E-mail: bolthy@bolthy.com
Web site: www.defconone.com
Dist(s): **CreateSpace Independent Publishing Platform.**

Defense Acquisition University *Imprint of* **United States Government Printing Office**

Defense Dept. *Imprint of* **United States Government Printing Office**

Defense Research LLC, *(978-0-9749873)* 211 Kirkland Ave. Apt. 216, Kirkland, WA 98033-6578 USA
E-mail: sales@defenseresearch.org
Web site: http://www.defenseresearch.org.

Defiance In Print, *(978-0-9771641)* Orders Addr.: 9412 S Belfort Cr, Tamarac, FL 33321 USA (SAN 256-9663) Tel 561-235-1828
E-mail: miller2554@gmail.com.

Defiant Pr. *Imprint of* **Passkey Online Educational Services**

Defined Mind, Inc., *(978-0-9763767)* 580 Broadway, Suite 912, New York, NY 10012 USA Tel 212-925-5138 (Hours: M-F 9:30 am-5:30 pm)
E-mail: info@defmind.com
Web site: http://www.defmind.com.

DeForest Pr., *(978-0-9649922; 978-1-930374; 978-0-615-99631-8)* Orders Addr.: P.O. Box 383, Rogers, MN 55374 USA Tel 763-428-2997; Fax: 877-747-3123; Toll Free: 877-747-3123; Edit Addr.: P.O. Box 383, Rogers, MN 55374 USA
E-mail: shane@deforestpress.com
Web site: http://www.deforestpress.com.

DeFranco Entertainment, *(978-1-929845)* P.O. Box 1425, Thousand Oaks, CA 91358-1425 USA Fax: 805-376-2953
E-mail: tdefranco@vcnet.com.

Degenhardt, Scott, *(978-0-9765671)* P.O. Box 11182, Murfreesboro, TN 37129 USA Tel 615-890-9484
E-mail: anything@thedegshop.com
Web site: http://www.thedegshop.com.

DeGraaf Publishing, *(978-0-9678385)* 903 W. Morse St., Plant City, FL 33563 USA Tel 813-752-2348; 813-967-7489 (Cell phone)
E-mail: robdegraaf@verizon.net
Web site: http://www.degraafpublishing.com.

Degree Network, LLC *See* **Marilux Pr.**

Dehghanpisheh, Corine, *(978-0-9851930; 978-0-692-41280-0; 978-0-9978985)* P.O. Box 30302, New York, NY 10011 USA Tel 646-580-8655
E-mail: cmardi2@gmail.com.

DeimosWeb Publishing, *(978-1-950485)* 2727 David Lee Dr., Parkersburg, WV 26101 USA Tel 606-371-7706
E-mail: deimosweb@gmail.com
Web site: www.leonarddhilleyii.com.

Dejohn Enterprises, *(978-0-9754526)* 1121 Elm St., Peekskill, NY 10566 USA
E-mail: dejohnenterprise@aol.com
Web site: http://www.theretumofsf.com.

DeJulien Publishing, *(978-0-9722253; 978-0-9822537; 978-0-9977658; 978-0-9997765; 978-1-7344412)* P.O. Box 210686, San Francisco, CA 94121-0686 USA
E-mail: kissfaq@outlook.com
Web site: http://www.kissfaq.com/
Dist(s): **CreateSpace Independent Publishing Platform.**

Deka Pr., *(978-0-9645045)* P.O. Box 812, Christmas Valley, OR 97641 USA Tel 541-576-3900; Fax: 541-576-3909
E-mail: katym@teleport.com.

DEKpress *See* **Parent Positive Pr.**

DeKruyff, Ruth, *(978-0-9797549)* Orders Addr.: P.O. Box 380604, San Antonio, TX 78268 USA; Edit Addr.: 5911 Forest Rim, San Antonio, TX 78240 USA.

Del Alma Pubns., LLC, *(978-0-9822422; 978-1-7364182)* 1713 Delmar, Zapata, TX 78076 USA Tel 956-278-0760
E-mail: delalmapublications@gmail.com
Web site: www.delalmapublications.com.

Del Gatto, Maria, *(978-0-9747509)* 2227 South 3rd St., Philadelphia, PA 19148 USA Tel 215-271-7165
Web site: http://www.shapettes.com.

Del George, Dana, *(978-0-578-00730-4)* 1025 1/2 Magnolia St., South Pasadena, CA 91030 USA
Dist(s): **Lulu Pr., Inc.**

Del Rey *Imprint of* **Random House Publishing Group**

Del Rey *Imprint of* **Random Hse. Worlds**

Del Sol Pubns., *(978-0-9722936)* P.O. Box 1112, Ventura, CA 93002 USA Do not confuse with Del Sol Publications in Two River, WI
E-mail: info@delsolpublications.com
Web site: http://www.delsolpublications.com.

Del Sol Publishing, *(978-1-58186)* 29257 Bassett Rd., Westlake, OH 44145 USA (SAN 299-4178) Tel 440-892-5524; Fax: 440-892-5546; Toll Free: 888-335-7651
E-mail: delsolbooks@telocity.com
Dist(s): **Lectorum Pubns., Inc.**

Del Valle Productions, Inc., *(978-1-7343099)* 4775 Collins Ave., Miami Beach, FL 33140 USA Tel 516-729-8200
E-mail: elainedelvalle@gmail.com
Web site: www.delvalleproductions.com.

Delabarre Publishing, *(978-0-9829247; 978-0-9836125; 978-1-61941)* P.O. Box 714, Conway, MA 01341 USA Tel 413-475-0087
E-mail: jeff@jeffrutherford.com.

Delacorte Bks. for Young Readers *Imprint of* **Random Hse. Children's Bks.**

Delacorte Bks. for Young Readers *Imprint of* **Random House Publishing Group**

Delacorte Pr. *Imprint of* **Random Hse. Children's Bks.**

Delacorte Pr *Imprint of* **Random Hse. Children's Bks.**

Delacorte Pr. *Imprint of* **Random House Publishing Group**

Delacorte Pr *Imprint of* **Random House Publishing Group**

Delaney Green, *(978-0-9982633)* 1928 Ohm Ave., Eau Claire, WI 54701 USA Tel 715-839-7411
E-mail: fitzfool74@gmail.com
Web site: http://www.delaneygreenwriter.com/.

Delatorre, Maria *See* **Father's Hse. Publishing**

DeLaVega, T., *(978-0-9754328)* Orders Addr.: P.O. Box 760, Hanapepe, HI 96716 USA Tel 808-335-2704; Fax: 808-335-5469; Edit Addr.: 3691 Uwao St., Hanapepe, HI 96716 USA
E-mail: tim.delavega@verizon.net
Web site: http://www.napaliphoto.com.

†Delaware &Lehigh National Heritage Corridor, Inc., *(978-0-930973)* Orders Addr.: 2750 Hugh Moore Pk. Rd., Easton, PA 18042 USA; Edit Addr.: 2750 Hugh Moore Pk. Rd., Easton, PA 18042-7743 USA (SAN 678-8831) Tel 610-923-3548; *Imprints:* Canal History & Technology Press (Canal Hist Tech)
E-mail: archives@delawareandlehigh.org; finance@delawareandlehigh.org
Web site: http://www.canals.org; http://www.delawareandlehigh.org; *CIP.*

DeLawrence, Troy, *(978-0-692-79971-0; 978-0-692-80354-7)* 1905 Somersby Ln., VIRGINIA BEACH, VA 23456 USA Tel 757-343-9681.

Deletrea *See* **Deletrea**

Deletrea, *(978-0-9972904; 978-1-7351219)* 1650 Coral Way Suite 502, Miami, FL 33145 USA Tel 954-562-7784
E-mail: casandra@deletrea.net
Web site: www.deletrea.net
Dist(s): **Legato Pubs. Group**
Publishers Group West (PGW).

Publisher Name Index

DELICATE STAYS LLC, *(978-1-7377598)* 8742 Elmhurst Ave. Apt 6C 0, ELMHURST, NY 11373 USA Tel 3474889944
E-mail: karincollado@gmail.com
Dist(s): **Ingram Content Group.**

Delirious Scribbles Ink *See* **Delirious Scribbles Ink Inc**

Delirious Scribbles Ink Inc, *(978-1-944357; 978-1-962063)* 4519 Woodruff Rd Unit 4 No. 108, Columbus, GA 31904 USA Tel 762-212-9396
E-mail: ink@deliriousscribbles.com; publisher@deliriousscribblesink.com
Web site: www.deliriousscribbles.com
Dist(s): **CreateSpace Independent Publishing Platform**
Ingram Content Group.

Delittle Storyteller Co., *(978-1-892633)* Orders Addr.: 1562 Pinehurst Dr., Casselberry, FL 32707 USA Tel 407-699-7769
E-mail: delittlestoryteller@yahoo.com
Web site: http://www.delittlestoryteller.com.

Dell Books for Young Readers *Imprint of* **Random Hse. Children's Bks.**

Dell, Jacob J., *(978-0-9744544)* 6518 Chasethorn Dr., San Antonio, TX 78249-4825 USA
E-mail: books@jacobjdell.com
Web site: http://www.jacobjdell.com/books.

Dellas, Melanie, *(978-0-9830163)* 4405 Pescadero Ave., San Diego, CA 92107 USA Tel 858-442-7916
E-mail: mdellas@hotmail.com
Web site: http://www.Mythological-Creatures.com.

Dellinger, Hampton, *(978-0-615-24971-1)* 4306 Peachway Dr., Durham, NC 27705 USA
Dist(s): **Lulu Pr., Inc.**

Dellwin Publishing Co., Inc., *(978-0-9765267)* P.O. Box 23391, Brooklyn, NY 11202-3391 USA
E-mail: dellwin5@aol.com
Web site: http://www.therockmastersystem.com.

†Delmar Cengage Learning, *(978-0-314; 978-0-7668; 978-0-7693; 978-0-8273; 978-0-87350; 978-0-916032; 978-0-944132; 978-0-9653629; 978-1-56253; 978-1-56593; 978-1-56930; 978-1-4018; 978-1-4180; 978-1-4283; 978-1-4354; 978-1-7319)* Div. of Cengage Learning, Orders Addr.: c/o Thomson Learning Order Fulfillment, P.O. Box 6904, Florence, KY 41022 USA Toll Free Fax: 800 487 8488; Toll Free: 800 347 7707; c/o Thomson Delmar Learning Clinical Health Care Series, P.O. Box 3419, Scranton, PA 18505-0419 Fax: 570-347-9072; Toll Free: 888-427-5800; Edit Addr.: P.O. Box 15015, Albany, NY 12212-5015 USA (SAN 206-7544) Tel 518-348-2300; Fax: 518-373-6345; Toll Free: 800-998-7498; 5 Maxwell Dr., Clifton Park, NY 12065- (SAN 658-0440) Tel 518-348-2300; Fax: 518-881-1256; Toll Free: 800-998-7498
E-mail: matthew.grover@thomson.com; clinicalmanuals@thomson.com
Web site: http://www.delmarlearning.com; http://www.clinicalmanuals.com/
Dist(s): **CENGAGE Learning**
Follett School Solutions
Gryphon Hse., Inc.
OptumInsight, Inc.
Pearson Education
Rittenhouse Bk. Distributors
ebrary, Inc.; *CIP.*

Delor Francis Pr., *(978-0-9838947)* 873 Atwells Ave., Providence, RI 02909 USA Tel 401-421-1222
E-mail: publisher@delorfrancis.com
Web site: www.delorfrancis.com.

DeLorme, *(978-0-89933)* P.O. Box 298, Yarmouth, ME 04096 USA (SAN 220-1208) Tel 207-846-7000; Fax: 207-846-7051; Toll Free Fax: 800-575-2244 (orders); Toll Free: 800-335-6763 (orders only)
E-mail: reseller@delorme.com
Web site: http://www.delorme.com
Dist(s): **Benchmark LLC**
Hammond World Atlas Corp.
Langenscheidt Publishing Group
Many Feathers Bks. & Maps
Rand McNally.

DeLorme Mapping Company *See* **DeLorme**

Delphi Bks., *(978-0-9663397; 978-0-9765185; 978-0-9846015; 978-1-7320512)* Orders Addr.: P.O. Box 6435, Lee's Summit, MO 64064 USA Toll Free: 800-431-1579 (orders)
E-mail: DelphiBks@yahoo.com
Web site: http://www.DelphiBooks.us; http://www.FranBaker.com
Dist(s): **Brodart Co.**
Emery-Pratt Co.
Midwest Library Service.

Delphinium Bks., Inc., *(978-1-883285; 978-1-953002)* 1038 Rock Rimmon Rd., Stamford, CT 06903 USA Tel 917-301-7496 Do not confuse with Delphinium Pr. in Wellfleet, MA
E-mail: joseph@delphiniumbooks.com
Dist(s): **HarperCollins Pubs.**
Ingram Publisher Services
MyiLibrary.

Delta Education, Incorporated *See* **Delta Education, LLC**

Delta Education, LLC, *(978-0-87504; 978-1-58356; 978-1-59242; 978-1-59821; 978-1-60395; 978-1-60902; 978-1-62571; 978-1-64011; 978-1-68535)* 80 Northwest Blvd., Nashua, NH 03063 USA (SAN 630-1711) Toll Free: 800-442-5444
E-mail: ngosselin@delta-edu.com
Web site: http://www.delta-education.com.

Delta Gamma Ctr., *(978-0-9748523)* 1750 S. Big Bend Blvd., Saint Louis, MO 63117-2402 USA Toll Free: 800-341-4310
E-mail: info@dgckids.org
Web site: http://www.dgckids.org.

Delta Stream Media, *(978-0-9776939; 978-1-945899)* Div. of Natural Math, 309 Silvercliff, Cary, NC 27513 USA (SAN 257-9987) Tel 919-388-1721
E-mail: maria@naturalmath.com
Web site: http://www.naturalmath.com
Dist(s): **American Mathematical Society**
Natural Math.

Delta Systems Company, Inc., *(978-0-937354; 978-1-887744; 978-1-932748; 978-1-934960; 978-1-936299; 978-1-936402; 978-1-62167)* Orders Addr.: 1400 Miller Pkwy., McHenry, IL 60050-7030 USA (SAN 220-0457) Tel 815-363-3582; Fax: 815-363-2948; Toll Free Fax: 800-909-9901; Toll Free: 800-323-8270; *Imprints:* Raven Tree Press (Raven Tree Pr)
E-mail: d.patchin@DeltaPublishing.com; L.Bruell@DeltaPublishing.com; j.patchin@deltapublishing.com
Web site: http://www.deltapublishing.com; http://www.raventreepress.com
Dist(s): **Follett Media Distribution**
National Bk. Network.

DeLuca, Robert John *See* **Alliance Publishing & Media, LLC**

DeMaio, Carlo A., *(978-1-7322583; 978-1-950219)* 2726 NE 6th Ln, Wilton Manors, FL 06824-6112 USA Tel 203-395-6760
E-mail: Carlo.DeMaio@Gmail.com.

DeMara-Kirby & Assocs., LLC., *(978-1-947442)* P.O. Box 720335, Mcallen, TX 78504 USA Tel 956-802-0004
E-mail: christinademara@aol.com.

DEMDACO, *(978-1-932139)* Div. of DD Traders, Inc., 5000 W. 134th St., Leawood, KS 66209-7806 USA Toll Free: 888-336-3226
Web site: http://www.demdaco.com.

Demeter Books *See* **Lake Street Pr.**

Demolle,, Chantel K. Inc., *(978-0-692-48641-2; 978-0-578-81385-1)* 608 N. Kingsley Dr., Atlanta, GA 30122 USA Tel 310-927-8879
E-mail: ckdemolle@gmail.com
Web site: www.chanteldemolle.com.

DeMosi *See* **DeMosi Publishing**

DeMosi Publishing, *(978-0-9708523)* Orders Addr.: P.O. Box 60606, Chicago, IL 60660 USA
E-mail: demosipublishing@email.com.

Den Publishing Co., *(978-0-9742195)* P.O. Box 93336, Albuquerque, NM 87199-3336 USA Fax: 505-822-8035.

DeNicest Concepts, *(978-0-9763973)* P.O. Box 1831, Buffalo, NY 14240 USA.

Denim Design Lab LLC, *(978-0-9773012)* P.O. Box 5853, San Clemente, CA 92674-9998 USA Tel 949-366-3307; Fax: 949-366-3304
E-mail: denimdesignlab@aol.com
Web site: http://www.denimdesignlab.com.

Denise K. Cook, *(978-0-578-97665-5)* 14207 Heidi Oaks Ln, Humble, TX 77396 USA Tel 713-829-1950
E-mail: dcook143@outlook.com.

Denise T. Lucas, *(978-1-7365122)* 2531 3rd St. NE, Washington, DC 20002 USA Tel 202-489-3422
E-mail: denisetlucas@gmail.com.

Denison, T. S. & Co., Inc., *(978-0-513)* Orders Addr.: P.O. Box 1650, Grand Rapids, MI 49501-5431 USA (SAN 201-3142) Tel 616-802-3000; Fax: 616-802-3009; Toll Free Fax: 800-543-2690; Toll Free: 800-253-5469
Dist(s): **Lectorum Pubns., Inc.**

Denlinger, Dennis, *(978-0-9742567)* Orders Addr.: 46 Purdy St., Harrison, NY 95821 USA; Edit Addr.: P.O. Box 60431, Sacramento, CA 95860-0431 USA Tel 916-488-9643 Phone/fax); Toll Free: 800-431-1579 fulfilment
E-mail: dennis@footarch.com
Web site: http://www.footarch.com
Dist(s): **Book Clearing Hse.**

Denney Literary Services, *(978-0-9654698; 978-0-9707469)* 2907 Noah St., Chattanooga, TN 37406-1928 USA Tel 423-622-0419; *Imprints:* DLS Books (DLS Bks)
E-mail: denney2907@earthlink.net.

Dennis West, *(978-0-9978774)* 8212 Sleeping Bear Dr NW, Albuquerque, NM 87120 USA Tel 214-505-0179
E-mail: cwickwire@att.net.

Dennison, Donna, *(978-0-9760484)* 121 Tuxedo, San Antonio, TX 78209-3712 USA.

Densmore-Reid Pubns., *(978-0-9700827)* 67 S. 24th St., Richmond, IN 47374 USA Tel 765-939-2984 (phone/fax)
E-mail: ddgreens@netscape.net
Web site: http://www.densmorereid.com/.

Denson Landrieux, Karolyn, *(978-1-7359278; 978-1-7377837)* 134 Parkhurst St., Pittsburgh, PA 15212 USA Tel 412-956-3255
E-mail: karolynd88@gmail.com
Web site: MaxineandBeanie.com.

Dental Wellness Institute, *(978-0-9815630)* 321 S. Main St., No. 503, Sebastopol, CA 95472 USA (SAN 855-8795) Tel 707-829-7220; Toll Free: 800-335-7755
E-mail: dentwell@pacbell.net
Web site: http://www.dentalwellness4u.com
Dist(s): **Cardinal Pubs. Group.**

Denver Broncos, *(978-0-9759579)* INVESCO Field at Mile High, 1701 Bryant St., Suite 900, Denver, CO 80204 USA
Web site: http://www.denverbroncos.com.

Denwit Publishing, *(978-0-9960973; 979-8-88753)* 822 Cotton Grove Rd., Jackson, TN 38305 USA Tel 731-616-5099
E-mail: gcdenwiddie@gmail.com
Web site: gcdenwiddie.com.

DEO Consulting, Inc., *(978-0-9728793)* 16334 Boardwalk Terr., Orland Hills, IL 60477 USA
E-mail: dale@mbd2.com
Web site: http://www.mbd2.com.

DePalma, Vanessa, *(978-0-9728135)* 49 Tropez Point, Rochester, NY 14626 USA Tel 585-723-9699
E-mail: vdepalma@frontiernet.net.

Dept. of Chamorro Affairs, *(978-1-883488)* P.O. Box 2950, Hagatna, GU 96932 USA Tel 671-477-6447
E-mail: lbaguon@yahoo.com
Web site: http://www.dca.guam.gov.

Depot Bks., *(978-0-9717611)* Orders Addr.: 87 Throckmorton Ave., Mill Valley, CA 94941 USA; Edit Addr.: 8 Madrona St., Mill Valley, CA 94941 USA.

Dept. of the Army *Imprint of* **United States Government Printing Office**

Derby Press *See* **MacLaren-Cochrane Publishing**

Dercum Audio, *(978-1-55656)* 1501 County Hospital Rd., Nashville, TN 37218 USA (SAN 658-7607) Tel 615-254-2408
E-mail: DawsonC@locc.com
Web site: http://www.bookcase.com/Dercum
Dist(s): **APG Sales & Distribution Services.**

Dercum Press/Dercum Audio *See* **Dercum Audio**

Derke, Connie, *(978-0-9747063)* 6418 W. 13100 S., Herriman, UT 84065 USA Tel 801-254-8711
E-mail: derke1904@msn.com.

Derrick, Paul, *(978-0-9744875)* Orders Addr.: 918 N. 30th St., Waco, TX 76707-2502 USA Tel 254-753-6920 (phone/fax)
E-mail: pjderrick@aol.com
Web site: http://stargazerpaul.com.

Derry Lane Publishing, *(978-0-692-82325-5; 978-0-692-83659-0)* 1225 Derry Ln., WEST CHESTER, PA 19380 USA Tel 314-800-7731
E-mail: priyaponnapula@gmail.com; priyaponnapula@gmail.com.

Derrydale Pr., The, *(978-1-56416; 978-1-58667)* Div. of Rowman & Littlefield Publishing Group, Orders Addr.: 15200 NBN Way, Blue Ridge Summit, PA 17214 USA Tel 717-794-3800 (Sales, Customer Service, MIS, Royalties, Inventory Mgmt., Dist., Credit & Collections); Fax: 717-794-3803 (Customer Service &/or orders only); 717-794-3857 (Sales & MIS); 717-794-3856 (Royalties, Inventory Mgmt., & Dist.); Toll Free Fax: 800-338-4550 (Customer Service &/or orders); Toll Free: 800-462-6420 (Customer Service &/or orders); Edit Addr.: 4501 Forbes Blvd., Lanham, MD 20706 USA Tel 301-459-3366; Fax: 301-459-5748
E-mail: sdriver@derrydalepress.com
Web site: http://www.derrydalepress.com
Dist(s): **MyiLibrary**
National Bk. Network
Rowman & Littlefield Publishers, Inc.
Rowman & Littlefield Unlimited Model
ebrary, Inc.

Dershowitz, Adena, *(978-0-692-05378-2)* 2540 Shore Blvd. 1st Flr., ASTORIA, NY 11102 USA Tel 570-575-8433
E-mail: adenardershowitz@gmail.com
Dist(s): **Ingram Content Group.**

Desdemona's Dreams LLC, *(978-0-9968874)* 4229 N. Derbigny, New Orleans, LA 70117 USA Tel 818-645-7390
E-mail: zachmohr77@gmail.com
Web site: https://desdemonasdreams.com/.

†Deseret Bk. Co., *(978-0-87579; 978-0-87747; 978-1-57345; 978-1-59038; 978-1-60641; 978-1-60907; 978-1-60908; 978-1-62972; 978-1-62973; 978-1-64933; 978-1-63993)* Div. of Deseret Management Corp., P.O. Box 30178, Salt Lake City, UT 84130 USA (SAN 150-763X) Tel 801-517-3165 (Wholesale Dept.); 801-534-1515; Fax: 801-517-3338; Toll Free: 800-453-3876; *Imprints:* Bookcraft, Incorporated (Bkcraft Inc); Shadow Mountain (ShadMtn)
E-mail: wholesale@deseretbook.com; dbwhsale@deseretbook.com
Web site: http://www.deseretbook.com; http://www.shadowmountain.com
Dist(s): **Blackstone Audio, Inc.**
Children's Plus, Inc.
Shadow Mountain Publishing; *CIP.*

Desert Badger Pr., *(978-0-9767555)* 4147 E. Megan Dr., Tucson, AZ 85712 USA
Web site: http://www.elderlawtucson.com.

Desert Bear Publishing, *(978-0-9765389)* P.O. Box 72313, Phoenix, AZ 85050 USA Tel 480-538-0842; Fax: 602-926-2429.

Desert Hills Publishing *See* **D H Publishing LLC**

Desert Palm Pr., *(978-1-942976; 978-1-948327; 978-1-954213)* 1961 Main St. Suite 220, Watsonville, CA 95076 USA Tel 831-234-9556
E-mail: rleefitz@gmail.com
Web site: www.desertpalmpress.com.

Desert Sage Pr., *(978-0-615-72020-3; 978-0-9897133; 978-1-7373135)* P.O. Box 357, Eagle, ID 83616 USA Tel 208-860-2464; Fax: 208-938-1554
Web site: www.desertsagepress.com
Dist(s): **CreateSpace Independent Publishing Platform.**

Desert Song Productions, *(978-0-9743402)* P.O. Box 35052, Tucson, AZ 85740 USA
E-mail: brian@brianjharris.com
Web site: http://www.brianjharris.com.

Desert Well Network, LLC *See* **Kamal**

Desert West Pubn., *(978-0-9833522)* P.O. Box 1, Logan, UT 84323 USA Tel 435-512-0112
E-mail: hunterkendall@hotmail.com.

Desert West Publishing, *(978-0-578-03542-0)* P.O. Box 35, Fairview, UT 84629 USA
Dist(s): **Lulu Pr., Inc.**

DesertStar Communications, LLC, *(978-0-9769815)* Orders Addr.: P.O. Box 243988, Boynton Beach, FL 33424-3988 USA
Web site: http://www.desertstarcommunications.com.

Desiana Pubns., *(978-0-578-58588-8; 978-0-578-91659-0; 978-1-7377635)* 1510 N Forest St., Bellingham, WA 98225 USA Tel 360-389-1081
E-mail: desiana3@outlook.com
Web site: none.

Desideramus Publishing, *(978-0-9975883)* 802 Peachwood Bend Dr., Houston, TX 77077 USA Tel 281-597-8867
E-mail: Barbarabdenson@gmail.com
Web site: Desideramus.com.

Design Media Publishing Ltd. (HKG) *(978-988-19738-4-9; 978-988-12967) Dist. by* **BTPS.**

Design Originals *Imprint of* **Fox Chapel Publishing Co., Inc**

Design Pr. Bks. *Imprint of* **Savannah College of Art & Design Exhibitions**

Design Studio Pr., *(978-0-9726676; 978-1-933492; 978-1-62465)* Orders Addr.: 3653 Primavera Ave., Los Angeles, CA 90065 USA
Web site: http://www.designstudiopress.com
Dist(s): **Consortium Bk. Sales & Distribution**
Diamond Bk. Distributors
Ingram Publisher Services.

Design to Spec LLC, *(978-0-9744281)* 14 Twist Hill Rd, Newtown, CT 06470 USA
E-mail: designtospec@gmail.com
Web site: http://www.bishamhill.com.

Design Vault, LLC *See* **Design Vault Pr., LLC**

Design Vault Pr., LLC, *(978-0-9768974; 978-0-615-93708-3; 978-0-692-68465-8; 978-1-7351818)* 11813 E 105th St N, Owasso, OK 74055 USA Tel 918.625.1483
E-mail: daniel@designvaultpress.com
Web site: www.designvaultpress.com
Dist(s): **CreateSpace Independent Publishing Platform.**

DesignAbility, *(978-0-9786425)* P.O. Box 9988, Salt Lake City, UT 84109 USA
Web site: http://www.design-ability.com.

Designed World Learning, LLC, *(978-0-9763351)* Suite 105-124, 1933 Hwy. 35, Wall, NJ 07719 USA
Web site: http://www.designedworldlearning.com.

Designer Discipline, *(978-0-692-09750-2; 978-0-692-15182-2; 978-0-692-16568-3)* 3521 Marcey Creek Rd., Laurel, MD 20724 USA Tel 646-246-4063
E-mail: shawnadoyle@outlook.com
Dist(s): **Ingram Content Group.**

Designs For Progress, Inc., *(978-0-9793902)* 24601 Milfay Rd., No. 5, Depew, OK 74028 USA
E-mail: dmccalment@aol.com.

Desktop Prepress Services, *(978-0-615-15679-8; 978-0-615-15817-4; 978-0-615-19039-6; 978-0-615-19643-5; 978-0-615-19723-4; 978-0-615-25624-5; 978-0-578-00424-0; 978-0-578-01448-7; 978-0-578-02385-4; 978-0-578-02469-1; 978-0-578-03167-5; 978-0-578-04693-8; 978-0-578-08235-6; 978-0-578-15292-9) 808 S. New Bethel Blvd., Ada, OK 74820 USA*
Web site: http://www.desktopprepress.com
Dist(s): **Lulu Pr., Inc.**

Deste Foundation (GRC) *Dist. by* **Dist Art Pubs.**

Destination Pubs. *Imprint of* **Pulte, Therese Marie**

Destination Wonder Pr., *(978-1-949752)* P.O. Box 505, Laguna Beach, CA 92652 USA Tel 760-989-2226
E-mail: requests@destinationwonderpress.com
Web site: www.destinationwonderpress.com.

Destined For Greatness Publisher *See* **Empowering People Pub.**

Destinee Media, *(978-0-9759082; 978-0-9832768; 978-1-938367; 978-0-578-47597-4)*
Web site: http://www.destineemedia.com.

Destiny Alignment Publishing, *(978-0-9839779)* 23046 E. Ottawa Dr. No. 106, Aurora, CO 80016 USA Tel 303-888-4509
E-mail: cindy@cindys-studio.net.

Destiny Bks. *Imprint of* **Inner Traditions International, Ltd.**

Destiny Hse. Publishing, *(978-1-936867)* P.O. Box 19774, Detroit, MI 48219 USA Tel 888-890-9455
E-mail: destinyhousepublishing1@yahoo.com.

Destiny Image Europe (ITA) *(978-88-900588; 978-88-89127; 978-88-96727) Dist. by* **STL Dist.**

Destiny Image Pubs., *(978-0-7684; 978-0-914903; 978-1-56043; 978-0-9716036)* 167 Walnut Bottom Rd., Shippensburg, PA 17257 USA (SAN 253-4339) Tel 717-532-3040; Fax: 717-532-9291; Toll Free: 800-722-6774
E-mail: dnj@destinyimage.com; jinori@norimediagroup.com
Web site: http://www.destinyimage.com
Dist(s): **Anchor Distributors**
Appalachian Bible Co.
Nori Media Group
Send The Light Distribution LLC
Spring Arbor Distributors, Inc.

Detail Press *See* **Blue Tree LLC**

Determined Productions, Inc., *(978-0-915696)* P.O. Box 2150, San Francisco, CA 94126-2150 USA (SAN 212-7385) Tel 415-433-0660; Fax: 415-421-0929.

Detroit International Pr., *(978-0-9766622)* 900 Wilshire Dr. Ste. 202, Troy, MI 48084-1600 USA
E-mail: vince@detroitip.com.

Dettling Moreno, Elizabeth, *(978-0-692-18190-4)* 1811 FM. 1299 Rd., Wharton, TX 77488 USA Tel 979-282-9626
E-mail: praise77488@sbcglobal.net
Dist(s): **Ingram Content Group.**

Dettman Design Services, *(978-0-615-38527-3)* 718 Logan Ave., Elgin, IL 60120 USA Tel 847-888-2178
E-mail: t.dettman@sbcglobal.net.

Deutscher Taschenbuch Verlag GmbH & Co KG (DEU) *(978-3-423) Dist. by* **Distribks Inc.**

Deux *Imprint of* **Aurora Publishing, Inc.**

DeuxRay Productions, *(978-0-615-52915-8)* 2401 Capitan Ave., San Diego, CA 92104 USA Tel 619-987-5505; Fax: 619-291-4404
E-mail: deuxray@cox.net
Web site: www.inmyownbackyard.org.

Devadoss, Donna, *(978-1-7338464)* 3855 Creek Rd., Andover, OH 44003 USA Tel 440-858-2185
E-mail: donnadvds@yahoo.com.

DeVane, Thomas G., *(978-0-9705788)* 46 Marmon Ct., Springfield, MA 01129-1335 USA
E-mail: poettlove@aol.com.

Developmental Studies Center *See* **Center for the Collaborative Classroom**

Developmental Vision Concepts, *(978-0-9635507; 978-0-9747810)* Orders Addr.: P.O. Box 400, Tehachapi,

CA 93581 USA Tel 661-822-3106; Edit Addr.: 316 S. Green, Tehachapi, CA 93581 USA
E-mail: stoebner@lightspeed.net.

evenny, Jenny, *(978-0-692-78650-5)* 257 Gold St. Apt. 1002, Brooklyn, NY 10009 USA Tel 917-232-7377
E-mail: jennydevenny@gmail.com.

evere Publishng, Inc., *(978-0-9787988)* P.O. Box 970965, Orem, UT 84097-0965 USA (SAN 851-6456) Tel 801-434-7558 (phone/fax)
E-mail: boblamx@gmail.com
Web site: http://winningorlosing.com.

evil's Due Comics, *(978-1-932796; 978-1-934692; 978-1-7332250; 978-1-7370505; 978-1-957078)* 1658 N Milwaukee Ave 100-5850, Chicago, IL 60647 USA
E-mail: d.davis@devilsdue.net; Kit@devilsdue.net
Web site: http://www.devilsdue.net
Dist(s): **Diamond Comic Distributors, Inc.**
Diamond Bk. Distributors
Publishers Group West (PGW)
Simon & Schuster, Inc.

Devil's Due Digital, Incorporated - A Checker Digital Company *See* **Checker Bk. Publishing Group**

Devil's Due Publishing, Incorporated *See* **Devil's Due Comics**

†Devin-Adair Pubs., Inc., *(978-0-8159)* P.O. Box A, Old Greenwich, CT 06870 USA (SAN 112-062X) Tel 203-531-7755; Fax: 718-359-8568; *CIP.*

DeVincentis, Anna, *(978-0-692-86032-8; 978-0-692-87091-4)* 5200 N Ocean Blvd, Lauderdale by the Sea, FL 33308 USA Tel 954-907-3923
E-mail: annadevincentis@gmail.com
Dist(s): **CreateSpace Independent Publishing Platform.**

Devlin, Jacob, *(978-1-7324984; 978-1-7342803)* 2801 N Park Ave., No. 3, Tucson, AZ 85719 USA Tel 520-647-4572
E-mail: authorjakedevlin@gmail.com
Dist(s): **Ingram Content Group.**

Devon & Keonna Scott, *(978-1-7367653)* 1065 Westmoreland Ln., Lawrenceville, GA 30043 USA Tel 614-599-8572
E-mail: keonna.scott1@gmail.com
Web site: thescottstories.com.

Devonfield, *(978-0-692-34077-6; 978-1-7329612; 979-8-9855399)* 16921 Via de Santa Fe P.O. Box 5005 No. 178, Rancho Santa Fe, CA 92067 USA Tel 858-436-6667; *Imprints:* Britfield (MYID_X_BRITFIE)
E-mail: crsdevonfield@gmail.com
Web site: www.Devonfieldllc.com.

Devonshire Bks., *(978-0-615-33660-2)* 918 W. Browning St., Appleton, WI 54914 USA Tel 920-954-5733
E-mail: flwrgirl3@hotmail.com.

Devora Publishing *Imprint of* **Simcha Media Group**

DeVore & Sons, Incorporated *See* **Fireside Catholic Bibles**

DeVorss & Co., *(978-0-87516; 979-8-88774)* Orders Addr.: P.O. Box 1389, Camarillo, CA 93011-1389 USA (SAN 168-9886) Tel 805-322-9010; Fax: 805-322-9011; Toll Free: 800-843-5743; Edit Addr.: 1100 Flynn Rd., No. 104, Camarillo, CA 93012 USA; *Imprints:* Devorss Publications (Devorss Pubns)
E-mail: service@devorss.com
Web site: http://www.devorss.com
Dist(s): **Health and Growth Assocs.**
New Leaf Distributing Co., Inc.
Publishers Group West (PGW).

Devorss Pubns. *Imprint of* **DeVorss & Co.**

Devotional Publications *See* **GoodLife Publishing**

Dew Bear Enterprises, Inc., *(978-1-942261)* 1289 N Fordham Blvd PMB 413, Chapel Hill, NC 27514 USA Tel 919-382-0068
E-mail: dewbear@mindspring.com
Web site: dewbear.com.

DeWard Publishing Co., Ltd., *(978-0-9798893; 978-0-9819703; 978-1-936341; 978-1-947929)* P.O. Box 6259, Chillicothe, OH 45601 USA Toll Free: 800-300-9778
E-mail: nathan_ward@hotmail.com
Web site: http://www.dewardpublishing.com.

Dewberry Pr., *(978-0-9854076; 978-0-9910340)* P.O. Box 604, Pflugerville, TX 78660 USA Tel 512-522-0596
E-mail: dewberrypress@yahoo.com
Web site: http://www.dewberrypress.com
Dist(s): **Ingram Content Group.**

Dewey Pubns., Inc., *(978-0-9615053; 978-1-878810; 978-1-932612; 978-1-934651; 978-1-941825; 978-1-956013)* 1840 Wilson Blvd Suite 203, Arlington, VA 22201 USA (SAN 694-1451) Tel 703-524-1355
E-mail: deweypublications@gmail.com
Web site: http://www.deweypub.com.

Dewey's Good News Balloons *See* **Glen Enterprises**

DewPuffBaby, *(978-0-578-93353-5; 978-0-578-95639-8; 979-8-9850667)* P.O. Box PO Box 7016, Hudson, FL 34674 USA Tel 813-577-9774
E-mail: osandre1193@gmail.com.

Dey Street Bks. *Imprint of* **HarperCollins Pubs.**

Dezaim Productions and Management, LLC, *(978-0-9770111)* 1385 Chancellor Cir., Bensalem, PA 19020 USA.

Deziner Media International, *(978-0-9743971; 978-0-615-23060-3; 978-0-615-28400-2; 978-0-9819912)* P.O. Box 239, Marrero, LA 70073 USA Tel 504-292-9101; 1472 Ames Blvd., Marrero, LA 70072
E-mail: dezinermedia@aol.com
Web site: http://www.writeabc123.com.

DFC Pubs., *(978-0-9793987)* 31 W. Smith St., Amityville, NY 11701 USA (SAN 853-3695)
E-mail: contactus@urbanclubbooks.com
Web site: http://www.urbanclubbooks.com.

DG Bks. Publishing *Imprint of* **Digital Golden Solutions LLC**

dg ink, *(978-0-9772577)* Orders Addr.: P.O. Box 1182, Daly City, CA 94017-1182 USA Tel 650-994-2662; Fax: 650-991-3050; *Imprints:* Ascribed (Ascribed)
E-mail: dg@dg-ink.net; info@dg-ink.net
Web site: http://www.dg-ink.net
Dist(s): **Follett School Solutions.**

DG Self-Publishing *See* **Social-Emotional Learning Bks.**

DGriffith Publishing, *(978-1-7337270)* 4217 Braidwood Dr, Fort Collins, CO 80524 USA Tel 970-566-0058
E-mail: djofc51@gmail.com
Web site: Munchkintales.com.

DH Strategies, *(978-0-9864080; 978-1-7347427)* 317 N. Fourth St., Festus, MO 63028 USA Tel 978-989-5433
E-mail: sdewitthall@gmail.com
Web site: www.ipromotebooks.com.

†Dharma Publishing, *(978-0-89800; 978-0-913546)* Orders Addr.: 35788 Hauser Bridge Rd., Cazadero, CA 95421 USA (SAN 201-2723) Tel 707-847-3717; Fax: 707-847-3380; Toll Free: 800-873-4276
E-mail: contact@dharmapublishing.com; hughj@mangalamresearch.org; order@dharmapublishing.com
Web site: http://www.kumnyeyoga.com; http://www.centerforskillfulmeans.com; http://www.enjoysitting.com; http://www.mangalamresearch.org; http://www.dharmapublishing.com/
Dist(s): **National Bk. Network**
Wisdom Pubns.; *CIP.*

Dhami, Laisha, *(978-0-578-40064-8)* 5265 Winflow Way, Suwanee, GA 30024-5333 USA Tel 404-539-0773
E-mail: laishadhami@gmail.com.

DHUNAMI, *(978-0-615-21482-5; 978-0-615-32994-9; 978-1-7356332)*
E-mail: paulji@dhunami.guru
Web site: https://www.dhunami.guru.

Di Angelo Pubns., *(978-0-9850853; 978-1-942549; 978-1-955690; 978-1-962603)* 4265 San Felipe No. 1100, Houston, TX 77027 USA Tel 713-960-6636
E-mail: sales@diangelopublications.com; info@diangelopublications.com
Web site: www.diangelopublications.com.

Di Bella, Brenda, *(978-0-615-38253-1)* 6643 Haskell Ave. No. 205, Van Nuys, CA 91406 USA Tel 818-235-3040
E-mail: comiab@yahoo.com
Web site: http://www.imuptobigthings.com.

Di Capua, Michael *Imprint of* **Scholastic, Inc.**

di Capua, Michael Bks. *Imprint of* **Hyperion Bks. for Children**

Di Maggio, Richard *See* **Consumer Pr., The**

Diakonia Publishing, *(978-0-9676528; 978-0-9725609; 978-0-9747278; 978-0-9772483; 978-0-9800877)* P.O. Box 9512, Greensboro, NC 27429-0512 USA Tel 336-707-2610
E-mail: diakoniapublishing@hotmail.com
Web site: http://www.ephesians412.com.

Dial *Imprint of* **Penguin Publishing Group**

Dial Bks *Imprint of* **Penguin Young Readers Group**

Dialogue Systems, Incorporated *See* **Metropolitan Teaching & Learning Co.**

Dialogues in Self Discovery LLC, *(978-1-934450)* P.O. Box 43161, Montclair, NJ 07043 USA (SAN 853-2745) Tel 973-714-2800; Fax: 973-746-2853
E-mail: discoveroption@aol.com.

Dials-Corujo, Shaneen, *(978-1-7351725)* 37 Winding Creek Ln., Columbia, SC 29229 USA Tel 803-378-2910
E-mail: shaneencorujo14@gmail.com.

DIAMOND & HALO PUBLISHING, LLC, *(978-1-955181)* 2043 Hewitt Ave, Cincinnati, OH 45207 USA Tel 513-968-0583
E-mail: montresor2@live.com
Web site: jcornelius.com.

Diamond Bk. Distributors, *(978-1-64031)* Div. of Diamond Comic Distributors, Inc., Orders Addr.: 1966 Greenspring Dr., Suite 300, Timonium, MD 21093 USA (SAN 110-9502) Tel 410-560-7100; Fax: 410-560-2583; Toll Free: 800-452-6642; *Imprints:* William M. Gaines Agent, INC. (WILLIAM M. GAI)
E-mail: books@diamondbookdistributors.com
Web site: http://www.diamondcomics.com; http://www.diamondbookdistributors.com/
Dist(s): **Elsevier**
MyiLibrary
SCB Distributors
SPD-Small Pr. Distribution.

Diamond Book Distributors Inc. *See* **Diamond Comic Distributors, Inc.**

Diamond Clear Vision *Imprint of* **Illumination Arts LLC**

Diamond Comic Distributors, Inc., *(978-1-59396; 978-1-60584)* 1966 Greenspring Dr., Suite 300, Timonium, MD 21093 USA Tel 410-560-7100; Fax: 410-560-2583; Toll Free: 800-452-6642
E-mail: books@diamondbookdistributors.com
Web site: http://www.diamondbookdistributors.com/
Dist(s): **Diamond Bk. Distributors.**

Diamond Creek Publishing, *(978-0-9713811)* P.O. Box 2068, Flagstaff, AZ 86003-2068 USA
Web site: http://www.apathways.com.

Diamond Event Planning, Inc., *(978-0-9766901)* 50-44 193rd St., Fresh Meadows, NY 11365 USA Tel 718-357-6144; Fax: 718-357-6685
E-mail: bridepro@aol.com
Web site: http://www.awedwitharedhead.com.

Diamond Farm Bk. Pubs., Div. of Yesteryear Toys & Books, Inc., Orders Addr.: P.O. Box 537, Alexandria Bay, NY 13607 USA (SAN 674-9054) Tel 613-475-1771; Fax: 613-475-3748; Toll Free Fax: 800-305-5138 (Order Line); Toll Free: 800-481-1353 (Order Line)
E-mail: info@diamondfarm.com
Web site: http://www.diamondfarm.com.

Diamond Fly Publishing, Inc., *(978-0-9817938)* 5224 Kings Mills Rd. Suite 264, Mason, OH 45040-2319 USA (SAN 856-566X)
Web site: http://www.diamondflypublishing.com.

Diamond Media Pr., *(978-1-7333011; 978-1-951302; 978-1-954368)* 217 Fieldstone Dr., Fraziers Bottom, WV 25082 USA Tel 888-322-7392
E-mail: authorsline@diamondmediapress.com
Web site: https://diamondmediapress.com/.

Diamond Select Toys & Collectibles, *(978-1-931724)* Div. of Diamond Comics Distributors, 1966 Greenspring Dr., Suite 300, Timonium, MD 21093 USA Tel 410-560-7100; Fax: 410-560-7589; Toll Free: 800-452-6642
E-mail: wjason@diamondcomics.com
Web site: http://www.diamondselecttoys.com
Dist(s): **Diamond Comic Distributors, Inc.**
Diamond Bk. Distributors
Simon & Schuster, Inc.

Diamond Spine Publishing, *(978-0-9765119; 978-0-9906238)* 42 Lake Ave., Ext., Suite 188, Danbury, CT 06811 USA Fax: 203-775-3311
E-mail: steeling@sinfulnyms.com.

Diamond Springs Pr., *(978-0-9729940)* 8085 Diamond Springs Dr., Helena, MT 59602 USA Tel 406-458-9220
E-mail: sagewood@qwest.net.

Diamond Star Pr., *(978-0-9774335; 978-1-7324591)* P.O. Box 490817, Los Angeles, CA 90049-0817 USA (SAN 257-6457)
E-mail: info@diamondstarpress.com.

Diamond Triple C Ranch, *(978-0-9790652)* 801 Floral Vale Blvd., Yardley, PA 19067 USA (SAN 852-324X) Tel 215-497-3188; Fax: 215-497-3190
Web site: http://www.diamondtriplecranch.com.

DIANE Publishing Co., *(978-0-7881; 978-0-941375; 978-1-56806; 978-0-7567; 978-1-4223; 978-1-4289; 978-1-4379; 978-1-4578)* Orders Addr.: P.O. Box 617, Darby, PA 19023-0617 USA (SAN 667-1217) Tel 610-461-6200; Fax: 610-461-6130; Toll Free: 800-782-3833; Edit Addr.: 330 Pusey Ave., No. 3 rear, Collingdale, PA 19023 USA Tel 610-461-6200; Fax: 610-461-6130; Toll Free: 800-782-3833
E-mail: cfisher@dianepublishing.net
Web site: http://www.dianepublishing.net.

Diarmuid Inc., *(978-1-59347)* Orders Addr.: P.O. Box 357580, Gainesville, FL 32635 USA Toll Free: 877-475-3277; Edit Addr.: 2630 N.W. 41st St., Suite D-1, Gainesville, FL 32606 USA
E-mail: kuc49@aol.com; dalia@greatleaps.com
Web site: http://www.greatleaps.com.

DiaShah Pr., LLC, *(978-0-9761207)* Orders Addr.: P.O. Box 43804, Nottingham, MD 21236 USA
E-mail: diashahpress@yahoo.com
Web site: http://www.debrasawyer.com; http://www.diashahpress.com.

DIASOT Pubns., *(978-0-9844649)* P.O. Box 705, Pittsburg, KS 66762 USA (SAN 859-4759)
E-mail: DIASOTPublications@gmail.com.

Diaspora Vibes Publishing, LLC *See* **Autherine Publishing**

Diaz, Bethany, *(978-0-692-76474-9; 978-0-692-76476-3; 978-0-692-79593-4; 978-0-692-79666-5; 978-0-578-67940-2)* 895 Riverside Dr Apt E157, WENATCHEE, WA 98801 USA Tel 253-820-3953.

Diaz, Olga L, *(978-1-948918)* 2017 Rowe Ave NE, Grand Rapids, MI 40505 USA Tel 616-307-8555; *Imprints:* LectoCultura (MYID_S_LECTOCU)
E-mail: lectocultura2018@gmail.com.

Dibble Institute for Marriage Education, The, *(978-0-9652427; 978-0-9761349; 978-0-9828395; 978-1-940815)* Orders Addr.: P.O. Box 7881, Berkeley, CA 94707-0881 USA Tel 510-528-7975 (Main Office); Fax: 972-226-2824 (Customer Service Fax); Toll Free: 800-695-7975 (Customer Service); Edit Addr.: 728 Coventry Rd., Kensington, CA 94707 USA
E-mail: relationshipskills@DibbleInstitute.org
Web site: http://www.buildingrelationshipskills.org; http://www.DibbleInstitute.org.

Dickens Ghost Publishing, *(978-0-9996219)* 912 Scott St., Beaufort, SC 29902 USA Tel 843-812-3589
E-mail: kimpoovey@gmail.com.

Dickerman, David, *(978-0-692-76993-5; 978-0-692-76994-2)* 317 Hale St., PENNINGTON, NJ 08534 USA Tel 347-834-7819.

Dickherber, Andrea, *(978-1-7344794)* 2002 Dawn St., Lomita, CA 90717-1148 USA Tel 573-253-0730
E-mail: andrea.dickherber.writes@gmail.com.

Dickow, Gregory Ministries, *(978-1-932833)* Orders Addr.: P.O. Box 7000, Chicago, IL 60680 USA Tel 847-645-9100; Fax: 847-842-9200; Edit Addr.: 2500 Beverly Rd., Hoffman Estates, IL 60192 USA
E-mail: gdmpartnerrelations@changinglives.org
Web site: http://www.changinglives.org.

Dickson Keanaghan, LLC, *(978-0-9749146; 978-1-933230)* 265 Jerusalem Ave., Hicksville, Long Island,, NY 11801-4931 USA Tel 516-578-5874 cell phone; Fax: 516-433-5734 office fax
E-mail: jckunzjr@dicksonkeanaghan.com
Web site: DicksonKeanaghan.com
Dist(s): **Ingram Content Group.**

Dickson-Keanaghan Publishing Group, LLC *See* **Dickson Keanaghan, LLC**

Dictionary Project, Inc., The, *(978-0-9745292; 978-0-9771777; 978-1-934669)* P.O. Box 566, Sullivan's Island, SC 29482 USA (SAN 255-5999)
E-mail: wordpower2@aol.com.

Didax Educational Resources, Inc., *(978-1-58324; 978-1-885111)* 395 Main St., Rowley, MA 01969 USA Tel 978-948-2340 (ext. 350); Fax: 978-948-2813; Toll Free: 800-458-0024
Web site: http://www.didax.com.

Didgeridoo Pr., *(978-0-692-85735-9; 978-0-578-78688-9; 978-0-578-98237-3; 978-0-578-98238-0; 978-0-578-28580-1; 979-8-218-06506-5; 979-8-218-21518-7; 979-8-218-27394-1)*
Dist(s): **CreateSpace Independent Publishing Platform.**

Diedre, *(978-0-578-30820-3)* 1410 Cabot Lakes Dr, League City, TX 77573 USA Tel 832-561-1564
E-mail: diedreosundwa@icloud.com.

Dietrich, Melanie, *(978-1-7362512)* 6201 Windrush Hollow, Baton Rouge, LA 70808 USA Tel 225-937-9558
E-mail: chardietrich@cox.net.

Diettribe Enterprises *See* **Steve Diet Goedde**

Dietz Pr., *(978-0-87517; 978-0-692-55454-8; 978-0-692-55455-5)* Orders Addr.: 930 Winfield Rd., Petersburg, VA 23803-4748 USA Tel 804-733-0123; Fax: 804-733-3514; Toll Free: 800-391-6833
E-mail: wsmith@owenprinting.com; customerservice@dietzpress.com
Web site: http://www.dietzpress.com
Dist(s): **American Wholesale Bk. Co.**
Barnes&Noble.com
Emery-Pratt Co.
Follett School Solutions.

Different Friends, *(978-1-892750)* Orders Addr.: P.O. Box 40208, Cincinnati, OH 45240 USA Tel 513-825-1514; Edit Addr.: 703 Yorkhaven Rd., Cincinnati, OH 45246 USA.

Different Mousetrap Pr. LLC, *(978-0-615-65392-1; 978-0-9890696)* 1100 19th Avenue, No. 108 Unit J, Fargo, ND 58102-2269 USA
E-mail: poisonivygulch@aol.com; maxwestart@gmail.com
Web site: http://maxwestart.deviantart.com; http://sunnyvillestories.com; http://www.poisonivygulch.com.

Different Worlds Pubns., *(978-0-9753999)* 1600 Portola Dr., San Francisco, CA 94127-1402 USA (SAN 256-0577)
E-mail: info@diffworlds.com
Web site: http://www.diffworlds.com.

DiFrancesco, Joe, *(978-0-9712682)* 35 Meadow Creek Ln., Glenmoore, PA 19343-2017 USA
E-mail: josephdifran@comcast.net.

Digging Clams n Oregon, *(978-0-9767508)* P.O. Box 746, Newport, OR 97365 USA (SAN 850-9700) Tel 541-265-5847
E-mail: williamlackner001@msn.com.

Digibots Corp., *(978-0-9755725)* Orders Addr.: P.O. Box 6803, Katy, TX 77491 USA Tel 281-599-1095; Fax: 281-599-0391; Toll Free: 877-375-8794; Edit Addr.: 3710 Havenmoor Pl., Katy, TX 77449 USA
E-mail: drew3710@msn.com
Web site: http://www.digibots.us.

Digireads.com *See* **Digireads.com Publishing**

Digireads.com Publishing, *(978-0-9753222; 978-1-59625; 978-1-59674; 978-1-4209)* 3921 Harvard Rd., Lawrence, KS 66049 USA
E-mail: digireads@yahoo.com
Web site: http://www.digireads.com
Dist(s): **Ingram Content Group**
Neeland Media, LLC.

Digital Antiquaria, Inc., *(978-1-58057)* Orders Addr.: 988 Ye Greate St., Greenwich, NJ 08323 USA
E-mail: info@DigitalAntiquaria.com; cutler@DigitalAntiquaria.com
Web site: http://digitalantiquaria.com
Dist(s): **PayLoadz.**

Digital Golden Solutions LLC, *(978-1-948040; 978-1-950280; 978-1-64916)* 11807 Westheimer Rd. Suite 550 PMB 846, HOUSTON, TX 77077 USA Tel 281-305-9245; *Imprints:* DG Books Publishing (MYID_Y_DG BKS)
E-mail: digitalgoldensolutions@gmail.com
Dist(s): **Ingram Content Group.**

Digital Kidz Publishing Hse., *(978-1-7327314)* 5010 Aberdeen Pkwy., Amarillo, TX 79119 USA Tel 806-316-6067
E-mail: kyla@kylahashmi.com.

Digital Manga Distribution *See* **Digital Manga Publishing**

Digital Manga Publishing, *(978-1-56970)* Div. of Digital Manga, Inc., 1487 W. 178th St. Ste. 300, Gardena, CA 90248-3253 USA (SAN 111-817X) Toll Free: 866-897-7300
E-mail: contact@emanga.com
Web site: http://www.dmpbooks.com/
Dist(s): **Diamond Comic Distributors, Inc.**
Diamond Bk. Distributors
Random Hse., Inc.

Digital Quest Inc., *(978-1-934873; 978-1-947262)* 525 Thomastown Ln., Ridgeland, MS 39157 USA Tel 601-856-2237; Fax: 601-856-2576
Web site: http://www.digitalquest.com.

Digital Scanning, Inc., *(978-1-58218)* 344 Gannett Rd., Scituate, MA 02066 USA (SAN 299-8734) Tel 781-545-2100
E-mail: info@digitalscanning.com
Web site: http://www.digitalscanning.com
Dist(s): **Ingram Content Group**
TextStream
ebrary, Inc.

Digital Tech Frontier, LLC., *(978-0-9830127; 978-0-9905354; 978-0-692-51963-9)* Orders Addr.: 2610 E. Mohawk Ln. No. 120, Phoenix, AZ 85050 USA Tel 480-290-2195
E-mail: rsiddell@popartoys.com.

Digital Vista, Inc., *(978-0-9817625; 978-0-9976807; 978-0-9983375; 978-1-950052)* 24 Amity Pl., Massapequa, NY 11758 USA (SAN 856-4825); *Imprints:* DV Books (MYID_W_DV BKS)
E-mail: info@digitalvista.net.

digital@batesjackson llc *See* **Bates Jackson Engraving Co., Inc.**

DigitalKu, *(978-0-9763168)* 7913 N. Highview Dr., Milwaukee, WI 53223 USA
Web site: http://www.digitalku.com/.

Digi-Tall Media, *(978-0-9785728; 978-0-9793944; 978-0-9802093; 978-0-9840655; 978-0-9828950; 978-0-9837334; 978-0-9850007; 978-0-9894024; 978-0-9913654; 978-0-9863958; 978-0-9972356; 978-0-9982406; 978-0-9989286; 978-1-7332411)* 6205 Oregon Ct., Plano, TX 75023 USA Tel 972-352-0324 Digi Tall Media Distributor
E-mail: editorshepherd@gmail.com
Web site: https://www.instagram.com/digi.tall.media.ig/; https://twitter.com/DigiTallMedia1; https://www.facebook.com/groups/207015945987971/; https://www.facebook.com/Digi.Tall.Media.books/; http://www.digi-tall-media.com; http://www.story-e-books.com.

Publisher Name Index

Digitex-U Pubns., (*978-0-615-15579-1*) 6655 Malyem Ave., Philadelphia, PA 19151 USA Tel 215-738-4678
E-mail: raincloud1@gmail.com
Web site: http://www.myspace.com/raincoud1
Dist(s): **Lulu Pr., Inc.**

DiGuiseppi, Joseph, (*978-0-9768348*) Orders Addr.: 4 Richmond Rd., Newtown, CT 06470-1214 USA
E-mail: joedigspi@hotmail.com
Web site: http://www.joedigspi.com.

Dillies, Lyn, (*978-0-615-66530-6; 978-0-615-67484-1*) 15 Laurel Ln., Westport, MA 02790 USA Tel 508-636-2484
E-mail: lyn@magicoflyn.com.

Dilligaf Publishing, (*978-0-9639070; 978-0-9701020; 978-1-931207*) Orders Addr.: 98 Main St., Ellsworth, ME 04605 USA Tel 207-667-5351
E-mail: studio3marty@acadia.net; vze277g4@verizon.net.

Dillon, Elena, (*978-0-9886353; 978-0-9908804*) 15035 Live Oak Springs, Canyon Country, CA 91387 USA Tel 661-406-2369
E-mail: info@elenadillon.com.

Dilly Green Bean Games, (*978-0-9744698; 978-0-9801898*) 33 Hillview Rd., Gorham, ME 04038 USA
E-mail: dillygreenbeangames@dillygreenbeangames.com; jay@indirpg.com; jay@dillygreenbeangames.com
Web site: http://www.dillygreenbeangames.com.

Dimensions, (*978-0-9882694*) 1595 Parliament Ct., Fairfield, OH 45014 USA Tel 513-829-4196; Fax: 513-829-4545
E-mail: hw2000@zoomtown.com
Web site: http://www.henryhwilliamson.com.

Dimensions in Media, Inc., (*978-0-9762273*) 24191 N. Forest Dr., Lake Zurich, IL 60047 USA Tel 847-726-2093
E-mail: debbie@dimensionsinmedia.com
Web site: http://www.be-still.com.

Dingles & Co., (*978-1-891997; 978-1-59646*) P.O. Box 508, Sea Girt, NJ 08750 USA
E-mail: dinglesco@aol.com
Dist(s): **Central Programs**
Gumdrop Bks.

Dingobi Publishing, (*978-0-9772819*) P.O. Box 4533, Rock Island, IL 61204-4533 USA.

Dings Bks., (*978-0-9748890*) 411 Schoolhouse Ln., Shippensburg, PA 17257 USA
E-mail: dingscenter@yahoo.com.

Dino Entertainment AG (DEU) (*978-3-89748; 978-3-932268*) *Dist. by* **Distribks Inc.**

Dinosaur Fund, (*978-0-9748618*) 711 E. St. SE, No. 104, Washington, DC 20003-2879 USA Tel 202-547-3326
E-mail: dinosaurfund@juno.com; shill@laser-image.com
Web site: http://www.dinosaurfund.org.

Dinoship, Inc., (*978-0-9728585; 978-1-933384*) 105 W. 73rd St., No. 1B, New York, NY 10023 USA Tel 212-721-5056; Fax: 212-595-0247; 299 Broadway, No. 1016, New York, NY 10007
E-mail: bob@dinoship.com
Web site: http://www.dinoship.com.

DinRo, (*978-0-9744412*) 7545 Gladstone Dr., No. 205, Naperville, IL 60565 USA Fax: 630-305-3695.

Diogenes Verlag AG (CHE) (*978-3-257*) *Dist. by* **Intl Bk Import.**

Diogenes Verlag AG (CHE) (*978-3-257*) *Dist. by* **Distribks Inc.**

Diomo Square Bks., (*978-0-9765948*) 4911 SW 43rd Ave., Portland, OR 97206-5011 USA
E-mail: diomo@earthlink.net.

Dion's Pubn., (*978-0-9795739; 978-0-9836893*) 3002 Royston Rd., Charlotte, NC 28208 USA Tel 574-307-2496
E-mail: tokereke@gmail.com.

Diotima Pr., (*978-0-9642128*) P.O. Box 608, Stroudsburg, PA 18360 USA Fax: 717-421-7776; Toll Free: 888-269-7266 (orders)
E-mail: amyangel@noln.com
Web site: http://www.bookzone.com/bookzone/10000829.html
Dist(s): **New Leaf Distributing Co., Inc.**
Quality Bks., Inc.

Diplodocus Pr., (*978-0-9771346; 978-0-9800149; 978-0-9860533; 978-1-940999*) 6828 Laurel Canyon Blvd., No. 203, North Hollywood, CA 91605 USA
E-mail: order@diplodocuspress.com
Web site: http://www.diplodocuspress.com.

DIPS publishing Inc, (*978-1-946818*) 4229 e 124, Cleveland, OH 44105 USA Tel 216-801-7886
E-mail: Davidawright73@gmail.com.

DIR 19 Publishing, (*978-1-7346165*) 8127 W. Capitol Dr., Milwaukee, WI 53222 USA Tel 414-553-7837
E-mail: dreamsintorealityllc@gmail.com.

Dire Wolf Bks., (*978-1-943934*) 3300 N. Main St. Suite D 153, Anderson, SC 29621 USA Tel 843-269-5167
E-mail: bpatterson@direwolfbooks.com
Web site: www.direwolfbooks.com.

Direct Access Publishing, (*978-0-9796473*) 1402 Auburn Wy No. No. 232, Auburn, WA 98002 USA (SAN 853-9952) Tel 206-725-3001; Toll Free: 877-725-3009
E-mail: directt_access@yahoo.com.

Direct World Publishing, (*978-0-9787591; 978-0-9987832; 978-1-948562*) Orders Addr.: 15507 S. Normandie Ave No. 316, Gardena, CA 90247 USA Tel 949-302-7738; Edit Addr.: 15507 S. Normandie Ave No. 316, Gardena, CA 90247 USA Tel 949-302-7738
E-mail: jennifer@jenniferyu.com; yu@directworldapp.com; yu@directworldpublishing.com
Web site: www.JenniferYu.com; www.directworldpublishing.com.

Directions in Education, Training & Consultation, (*978-0-9664681*) Orders Addr.: P.O. Box 2478, Gig Harbor, WA 98335 USA Tel 253-858-7261; Edit Addr.: 4720 Birchtree Ln., NW, Gig Harbor, WA 98335 USA
E-mail: lbaker@HarborNet.com
Web site: http://www.pebblesinthepond.com.

DirkDesigns, LLC, (*978-0-9790923*) P.O. Box 3754, West Lafayette, IN 47996 USA.

Dirks Publishing *See* **Dirks Publishing, LLC**

Dirks Publishing, LLC, (*978-0-9823145*) P.O. Box 348, Rantoul, IL 61866-0348 USA Fax: 206-339-8510
E-mail: julie@dirkspublishing.com
Web site: http://www.dirkspublishing.com.

Disciple One Publishing, (*978-0-9791883*) Div. of Disciple Group Production, 10153 1/2 Riverside Dr., No. 467, Toluca Lake, CA 91602 USA Tel 323-654-8579
E-mail: baronjay@yourlittleblackbook.net
Web site: http://www.yourlittleblackbook.net
Dist(s): **Lushena Bks.**

Disciple Publishing Co., (*978-0-615-23763-3*) P.O. Box 554, Beaufort, SC 29901 USA Tel 843-379-9955; Fax: 843-379-9956; Toll Free: 866-245-8182
E-mail: dpc@hargray.com
Web site: http://www.dpchope.com.

Discipleship Pubns. International, (*978-1-57782; 978-1-884553*) 300 5th Ave. Ste. 5, Waltham, MA 02451-8749 USA Toll Free: 888-374-2665
E-mail: spjones@icoc.org; dpibooks@icoc.org
Web site: http://www.dpibooks.org
Dist(s): **ebrary, Inc.**

Discipleship Resources *Imprint of* **Upper Room Bks.**

Discover Writing Company *See* **Discover Writing Pr.**

Discover Writing Pr., (*978-0-9656574; 978-1-931492*) Orders Addr.: P.O. Box 264, Shoreham, VT 05770 USA Tel 802-897-7022; Fax: 802-897-2084; Toll Free: 800-613-8055
E-mail: registrar@discoverwriting.com; ann@discoverwriting.com; administrator@discoverwriting.com; barry@discoverwriting.com
Web site: http://www.discoverwriting.com.

Discover Your Northwest, (*978-0-914019*) 164 S. Jackson St., Seattle, WA 98104 USA (SAN 286-8504) Tel 206-220-4140; Fax: 206-479-4170
E-mail: nwia-publications@nwpubliclands.org
Web site: http://www.nwpubliclands.com
Dist(s): **Hopkins Fulfillment Services**
Partners/West Book Distributors
Univ. of Washington Pr.

Discoveries Publishing llc, (*978-0-9998318; 978-1-7377805*) 100 silver beach Ave. No. 124, daytona beach, FL 32115 USA Tel 860-214-8066
E-mail: acernst24@gmail.com.

DiscoverNet, (*978-0-9728053; 978-0-9742787; 978-0-9746943; 978-1-932813*) 1105 Walnut St. #f-160-25, Cary, NC 27511 USA Tel 919-301-0109; Fax: 919-557-2261
E-mail: lharte@discovernet.com
Web site: http://www.althosbooks.com.

DiscoverRoo *Imprint of* **Pop!**

Discovery Communications *See* **Discovery Education**

Discovery Education, (*978-1-56331; 978-1-58738; 978-1-59527; 978-1-60288; 978-1-60711; 978-0-9824299; 978-1-61629; 978-1-61708; 978-1-61828; 978-1-68220*) One Discovery Pl., Silver Spring, MD 20910 USA Tel 240-662-2000; Toll Free: 888-892-3484
E-mail: megan.faller@discovery.com; sara_fisher@discovery.com
Web site: http://www.discoveryeducation.com
Dist(s): **Explorations**
Follett School Solutions
Insight Guides
Langenscheidt Publishing Group.

Discovery Enterprises, Limited *See* **History Compass, LLC**

Discovery Hse. Pubs., (*978-0-929239; 978-1-57293; 978-1-62707; 978-1-64070*) Div. of R B C Ministries, Orders Addr.: P.O. Box 3566, Grand Rapids, MI 49501 USA (SAN 248-8949) Tel 616-942-9218; Fax: 616-957-5741; Toll Free: 800-653-8333; Edit Addr.: 3000 Kraft Ave., SE, Grand Rapids, MI 49512 USA (SAN 248-8957) Tel 616-942-6770; Fax: 616-974-2224
E-mail: melissa.wade@odb.org; lisa.luckenbaugh@odb.org; carol.waltman@odb.org
Web site: http://www.dhp.org
Dist(s): **CLC Pubns.**

Discovery Pr. Pubns., Inc., (*978-0-9645159*) 400 E. 3rd Ave., No. 901, Denver, CO 80203 USA (SAN 298-5691) Tel 303-355-9689; Fax: 303-733-3474
E-mail: discoverypresspub@comcast.net
Web site: http://www.discoverypresspub.com
Dist(s): **Brodart Co.**
Quality Bks., Inc.

Discovery Pubns. (GBR) (*978-0-9538222; 978-0-9550458*) *Dist. by* **Irish Bks Media.**

Disenos del Arte, Inc., (*978-0-9820784*) P.O. Box 11441, San Juan, PR 00910 USA Tel 787-722-1060; Fax: 787-728-3092
E-mail: dasant@delartepr.com
Web site: http://www.delartepr.com.

Disinformation Co. Ltd., The, (*978-0-9713942; 978-0-9729529; 978-1-932857; 978-1-934708; 978-1-939517*) 220 E. 23rd St., Suite 500, New York, NY 10010 USA
E-mail: books@disinfo.com
Dist(s): **Follett School Solutions**
Red Wheel/Weiser
ebrary, Inc.

Dismondy, Maria Inc., (*978-0-615-47393-2; 978-0-615-51620-2; 978-0-9848558; 978-0-9976085; 978-1-7328418; 978-1-7330359; 978-1-7353451; 979-8-9850233; 979-8-9858051*) Orders Addr.: 5449 Sylvia, Dearborn, MI 48124 USA Tel 248-302-1800; *Imprints:* Cardinal Rule Press (CardinalRule)
E-mail: mariadismondy@mac.com
Web site: http://www.cardinalrulepress.com
Dist(s): **Baker & Taylor Publisher Services (BTPS)**
Independent Pubs. Group
Partners Bk. Distributing, Inc.

Disney Editions *Imprint of* **Disney Pr.**

Disney Lucasfilm Press *Imprint of* **Disney Publishing Worldwide**

†**Disney Pr.**, (*978-0-7868; 978-1-56282; 978-1-4231*) Div. of Disney Bk. Publishing, Inc., A Walt Disney Co., 44 S. Broadway. Flr. 16, White Plains, NY 10601-4411 USA Toll Free: 800-759-0190; *Imprints:* Disney Editions (Disney Ed); Riordan, Rick (RRiordan)
Web site: http://www.disney.com/disneybooks/index.html
Dist(s): **Blackstone Audio, Inc.**
Children's Plus, Inc.
Hachette Bk. Group
Libros Sin Fronteras
Little Brown & Co.
Perfection Learning Corp.; *CIP.*

Disney Press Books *Imprint of* **Disney Publishing Worldwide**

Disney Publishing Worldwide, (*978-1-892309; 978-1-931580; 978-1-4231; 978-1-4847; 978-1-368; 978-1-368-01377-2*) Subs. of Walt Disney Productions, 44 S. Broadway, 10th Flr., White Plains, NY 10601 USA Tel 914-288-4316; 1101 Flower St., Glendale, CA 91201; *Imprints:* Jump at the Sun (Jump at the Sun); National Geographic Children's Books (NGCB); National Geographic (NatlGeo); Riordan, Rick (RRiordan); Under the Stars (UndertheStars); Disney Press Books (Disney Pr Bks); Disney-Hyperion (Disney-Hyperion); Hyperion Books for Children (Hype Bks Children); National Geographic Kids (Nat Geo Kids Disney); Rick Riordan Presents (Rick Riordan); Marvel Press (Marvel Pr); Disney Lucasfilm Press (Lucasfilm Pr); Melissa de la Cruz Studio (MelissaCruz); National Geographic Books (Nat Geo Bks); NatGeo Under the Stars (NatGeo Stars)
Web site: http://www.disney.go.com; http://www.hyperionbooksforchildren.com; books.disney.com
Dist(s): **Blackstone Audio, Inc.**
Children's Plus, Inc.
Follett School Solutions
Penguin Random Hse. LLC.

Disney-Hyperion *Imprint of* **Disney Publishing Worldwide**

Disneyland/Vista Records & Tapes *See* **Walt Disney Records**

Disposition Sketch Bks. *Imprint of* **MacBride, E. J. Pubn., Inc.**

Disruptive Publishing, (*978-1-59654; 978-1-60872; 978-1-62657*) 735 Ivy League Ln., Rockville, MD 20850 USA
E-mail: service.blackmask@gmail.com
Web site: http://www.dispub.com
Dist(s): **Diamond Bk. Distributors.**

Dissected Lives (Auto Biographies) *Imprint of* **Speedy Publishing LLC**

DISTANZ Verlag GmbH (DEU) (*978-3-942405; 978-3-95476*) *Dist. by* **BTPS.**

DiStasi Advisors, LLC, (*978-0-692-49826-2; 978-1-7327067; 978-0-578-33245-1*) 5029 Bristol CT, Loveland, OH 45140 USA Tel (513) 477-7624
Dist(s): **CreateSpace Independent Publishing Platform.**

Distinct Pr., (*978-0-9916089; 978-1-943103*) 6822 22nd Ave. N., St. Petersburg, FL 33710-3918 USA Tel 727-238-7884; *Imprints:* Czech Revival Publishing (MYID_E_CZECH R)
E-mail: theageofattraction@gmail.com; waldorfinspired@yahoo.com
Web site: www.DistinctPress.com; http://czechrevival.com/
Dist(s): **Ingram Content Group.**

Distractions Ink, (*978-0-9713389; 978-0-9821921; 978-0-9827826; 978-0-9835250; 978-0-9838074; 978-0-9852740; 978-0-9852807; 978-0-9884276; 978-0-9889582; 978-0-9913878; 978-0-9861307; 978-0-9970959; 978-0-9980595; 978-0-9990831; 978-0-9996274; 978-1-7330336; 978-1-7377309) Orders Addr.: P.O. Box 15971, Rio Rancho, NM 87144 USA Tel 719-495-1562*
E-mail: marcialmcclure@cs.com
Web site: http://www.marcialynnmcclure.com.

Distribooks, Inc., Div. of MED, Inc., 8124 N. Ridgeway, Skokie, IL 60076 USA (SAN 630-9763) Tel 847-676-1596; Fax: 847-676-1195
E-mail: info@distribooks.com.

Distribuidora Norma, Inc., (*978-1-881700; 978-1-935164*) Div. of Carvajal International, Orders Addr.: P.O. Box 195040, San Juan, PR 00919-5040 USA Tel 787-788-5050; Fax: 787-788-7161; Edit Addr.: Carretera 869 Km 1.5 Barrio Palmas Royal Industrial, Catano, PR 00962 USA
Web site: http://www.norma.com.

Distribuidora Plaza Mayor, 1500 Ave. Ponce de Leon Local 2 El Cinco, San Juan, PR 1 USA.

éditeur, Annika Parance (CAN) (*978-2-923830*) *Dist. by* **Firefly Bks Limited.**

Éditions Chouette (CAN) (*978-2-89450; 978-2-921198; 978-2-89718; 978-2-924734; 978-2-9800909*) *Dist. by* **Distribks Inc.**

Éditions Tourbillon (FRA) (*978-2-84801; 979-10-276*) *Dist. by* **HachBkGrp.**

Ditto Enterprises *See* **Ditto Enterprises**

Ditto Enterprises, (*978-0-9967559; 978-1-7373381*) 138 Biltmore Loop, Montgomery, TX 77316 USA Tel 713-824-3105
E-mail: denfield97@aol.com.

Diverse Medium *See* **Diverse Mediumz**

Diverse Mediumz, (*978-1-7320989*) 15814 Pryor Dr, Missouri city, TX 77489 USA Tel 832-203-9133
E-mail: tiana31510@gmail.com.

Diverse Skills Ctr., (*978-0-692-74605-9; 978-0-692-81700-1; 978-0-578-21625-6*) P.O. Box 290963, Tampa, FL 33687 USA Tel 813-802-4083
E-mail: support@diverseskillscenter.com; cjohns43@yahoo.com
Web site: www.diverseskillscenter.com
Dist(s): **CreateSpace Independent Publishing Platform.**

Diversified A+ Pubns., (*978-0-9773526*) P.O. Box 13, Winchendon, MA 01475 USA
E-mail: Dpipub@aol.com
Web site: http://www.dpublications.com.

Diversified Publishing, 1745 Broadway, New York, NY 1001[illegible] USA; *Imprints:* Random House Large Print (RH LargeP)
Dist(s): **Penguin Random Hse. Distribution**
Penguin Random Hse. LLC
Random Hse., Inc.

Diversion Bks. *Imprint of* **Diversion Publishing Corp.**

Diversion Books *See* **Diversion Publishing Corp.**

Diversion Pr., (*978-1-935290*) P.O. Box 30277, Clarksville, T[illegible] 37040 USA (SAN 857-0264)
E-mail: diversionpress@yahoo.com
Web site: http://www.diversionpress.com.

Diversion Publishing Corp., (*978-0-9845151; 978-0-9829050; 978-0-9833371; 978-0-9838395; 978-0-9839885; 978-1-938120; 978-1-62681; 978-1-68230; 978-1-63576*) 443 Park Aveue S., Ste. 1008, New York, NY 10016 USA (SAN 990-6304) Tel 212-675-5556; 212-961-6390; *Imprints:* Diversion Books (DiversionBks)
E-mail: info@diversionbooks.com; charles@efit.com
Web site: http://www.diversionbooks.com
Dist(s): **Children's Plus, Inc.**
Ingram Publisher Services
MyiLibrary
Open Road Integrated Media, Inc.
Smashwords
Two Rivers Distribution.

Diversity Foundation, The, (*978-0-9797193*) 505 W., 10200 S., South Jordan, UT 84095 USA Tel 801-553-4556; Fax: 801-553-4600; Toll Free: 888-216-2122
Web site: http://www.thediversityfoundation.org
Dist(s): **Partners Pubs. Group, Inc.**

Diversity Ink Publishing, (*978-0-9767258*) P.O. Box 2414, Santa Maria, CA 93457 USA.

Diversity Matters Pr., (*978-0-578-06591-5; 978-0-9839020*) 5555 DTC Pkwy., Suite C3200, Greenwood Village, CO 80111 USA.

Dividion Group, LLC, The, (*978-0-9769366*) Orders Addr.: P.O. Box 2678, North Canton, OH 44720 USA
E-mail: tumekash22@aol.com; bigheds@bigheds.com
Web site: http://www.bigheds.com.

Divine House Ministries *See* **Kingdom Sound Pubs.**

Divine Inspiration Publishing, LLC, (*978-0-9820490*) P.O. Box 210414, Auburn Hills, MI 48326 USA (SAN 857-1090) Fax: 248-927-0357
E-mail: stevecogswell@comcast.net; scogswell@divineinspirationpublishing.com
Web site: http://www.divineinsirationpublishing.com.

Divine Intertwine Publishing, (*978-0-9754489*) P.O. Box 4088, Ocean City, MD 21843 USA.

Divine Mercy Pr., (*978-0-9755471*) 3216 Mission Ave. Apt. 138, Oceanside, CA 92058-1348 USA
E-mail: divinemercy@hypersurf.com.

Divine Ministry of North Florida, Inc., (*978-0-9773356*) P.O. Box 5668, Gainesville, FL 32627-5668 USA (SAN 257-3652)
E-mail: ade0201@yahoo.com
Web site: http://www.divineministry.net.

Divine Physiology International Ministries, (*978-0-9983379*) P.O. Box 159175, Nashville, TN 37215 USA Tel 615-509-5557
E-mail: bnainc@aol.com.

Divine Providence Pr., (*978-0-692-08222-5; 978-1-7351665*) 4616 Loughborough Ave. No. 2E, Saint Louis, MO 63116 USA Tel 314-599-3627; Fax: 314-577-6301
E-mail: jasonkoltuniak@yahoo.com; joshuahren@gmail.com; wisebloodbooks@gmail.com; mauriceprater@hotmail.com
Web site: www.wisebloodbooks.com; www.divineprovidencepress.com.

Divine Works Publishing LLC, (*978-0-9894680; 978-0-9996047; 978-1-949105*) 1128 Royal Palm Beach Blvd Suite 289, Royal Palm Beach, FL 33411 USA Tel 561-990-2665
E-mail: info@divineworkspublishing.com; sbjohn0827@gmail.com
Web site: www.divineworkspublishing.com.

Divot & Swish Publishing, (*978-1-7351700*) P.O. Box 5358, Norman, OK 73070 USA Tel 405-658-3313
E-mail: sbethbrown3@gmail.com.

Dixie W Publishing Corp., (*978-0-9843720; 978-1-68372*) P.O. Box 241901, Montgomery, AL 36124 USA Tel 334-233-7856
E-mail: peter@dixiewpublishing.com
Web site: http://www.dixiewpublishing.com.

Dixon, Emma, (*978-0-692-95138-5*) 475 S Perkins Rd No. 708, Memphis, TN 38117 USA Tel 385-209-6542
E-mail: cristina_wilson@yahoo.com.

Dixon, Nell, (*978-0-9864033*) 820 S. MacArthur Blvd., Coppell, TX 75019 USA Tel 972-510-5574
E-mail: nelldixonministries@hotmail.com.

DJ Blues Publishing, (*978-0-9743985*) 403 Dula Cir., Duncanville, TX 75116 USA
E-mail: hipdjblues@earthlink.net
Web site: http://www.djblues.com.

DJ Inkers *Imprint of* **Carson-Dellosa Publishing, LLC**

DK *Imprint of* **Dorling Kindersley Publishing, Inc.**

DK *Imprint of* **DK Games**

DK, c/o DK Publishing, 1745 Broadway, New York, NY 10019 USA; *Imprints:* Phonic Books (PhBksDKL)
Dist(s): **Penguin Random Hse. LLC.**

DK Children *Imprint of* **Dorling Kindersley Publishing, Inc.**

DK Games, 1745 Broadway, New York, NY 10019 USA; *Imprints:* DK (DK)
Dist(s): **Penguin Random Hse. Distribution**
Penguin Random Hse. LLC.

Dksmo-Press, Izdatel'skaja firma (RUS) (*978-5-04*) *Dist. by* **Distribks Inc.**

DL Grant, LLC, (*978-0-9853713; 978-0-9882084; 978-0-9889947; 978-0-9914542; 978-1-942017; 978-1-958353*)
E-mail: dgauthor@gmail.com.

. Publishing *See* **7Seven Spark Publishing**
.G, LLC *See* **DL Grant, LLC**
ife - For Your Diabetes Life, *(978-0-9777463)* Div. of LifeMed Media, 101 Franklin St., Westport, CT 06880-0688 USA (SAN 850-1254) Tel 203-454-6985; Fax: 203-454-6986
E-mail: info@dlife.com
Web site: http://www.dlife.com.
LS Bks. *Imprint of* **Denney Literary Services**
M Creative, *(978-0-9798445)* 1438 Pine Valley Loop, Fayetteville, NC 28305 USA
Web site: http://www.hamstersam.com; http://davemcdonald.com/.
m Productions, *(978-0-615-14860-1; 978-0-615-15990-4)* 10596 N. Washington Blvd., Indianapolis, IN 46280 USA
Web site: http://dmprod.blogspot.com/
Dist(s): **Lulu Pr., Inc.**
M Publishing, *(978-0-9963006)* 14410 Dracaena Ct., Houston, TX 77070 USA Tel 281-235-4213
E-mail: dean@cdeanmills.com; diann@diannmills.com
Web site: dmpublishing.co; diannmills.com.
DMH Pr., Inc., *(978-0-9746153)* 10 Beachside Dr., No. 302, Vero Beach, FL 32963 USA (SAN 256-0127) Fax: 631-325-1340
Web site: http://www.dollyadventures.com.
DMT Publishing, *(978-0-9726189; 978-0-9749144; 978-0-9785553; 978-0-9800813; 978-0-9824259; 978-1-935821)* 900 N. 400 W. , Bldg. 12, North Salt Lake, UT 84054 USA
Web site: http://www.dmtpublishing.com.
DNA Pr., *(978-0-9664027; 978-0-9748765; 978-1-933255)* P.O. Box 572, Eagleville, PA 19408-0572 USA (SAN 256-5005) Fax: 501-694-5495
E-mail: editors@dnapress.com
Web site: http://www.dnapress.com.
DNA2Market, *(978-0-9992689)* 6800 W. McGlochlin St., Boise, ID 83709 USA Tel 208-870-1911
E-mail: beckydembowski@gmail.com.
do be you, *(978-0-9794262)* 229 Vincent Ave. N., Minneapolis, MN 55405 USA
E-mail: info@i-get-around.com
Web site: http://www.i-get-around.com.
Do Good Pr., *(978-0-9974263)* 9950 Scripps Lake Blvd. No. 104, San Diego, CA 92131 USA Tel 858-800-5080
E-mail: info@dogoodpress.com
Web site: www.dogoodpress.com.
Do Life Right, Inc., *(978-0-9824829; 978-1-937848)* P.O. Box 61, Sahuarita, AZ 85629 USA
E-mail: lisa@wrightontimebooks.com
Web site: http://www.doliferight.com
Dist(s): **CreateSpace Independent Publishing Platform.**
Do The Write Thing Foundation of DC, *(978-1-930357; 978-0-692-86055-7; 978-1-7350773)* 56 T. St. , NW, Washington, DC 20001-1009 USA Tel 202-758-0397; Fax: 202-758-0397
E-mail: chillshil@netscape.net; dothewritething1@gmail.com
Web site: www.dothewritethingdc.com.
Do Well Studio, *(978-0-692-86200-1)* 68 Tupper Rd. No. 7, Sandwich, MA 02563 USA Tel 617-966-4636
E-mail: donna@dowellstudio.com
Web site: dowellstudio.com.
DOAN, DEIRDRA *See* **Tapestry Productions**
Dobie Book Publishing *See* **Mowery, Julia**
Dobral LLC, *(978-0-9971125)* 200 Schermerhorn St., Brooklyn, NY 11201 USA Tel 347-227-8455
E-mail: giftedonesprod@yahoo.com.
Dobson, Kathy, *(978-0-9982820)* 7 Chestnut St., Rhinebeck, NY 12572 USA Tel 617-276-7050
E-mail: kldobson@gmail.com.
Doc Publishing, *(978-0-615-46526-5; 978-0-615-58218-4; 978-0-9967370; 978-1-7358559)* 1149 Brookshire Dr., New Castle, PA 16101 USA Tel 724-658-2189
E-mail: juliannmangino@yahoo.com
Web site: www.docpublishing.org
Dist(s): **Lulu Pr., Inc.**
Doc Roe Publishing, *(978-0-692-06979-0; 978-0-692-16579-9; 978-0-578-48545-4; 978-0-578-48546-1; 978-0-578-60412-1; 979-8-9874897)* 1641 Creek Wood Dr., Midlothian, TX 76065 USA Tel 214-450-3939
E-mail: docroegrandson@gmail.com.
Dockery, Robert, *(978-0-692-12903-6; 978-0-692-12907-4; 978-0-578-66709-6; 978-0-578-66712-6)* 64 INNESS Dr., TARPON SPRINGS, FL 34689 USA Tel 727-938-6029
E-mail: rdock@knology.net
Dist(s): **Ingram Content Group.**
Dockter, Toni, *(978-0-9712201)* P.O. Box 1532, Soquel, CA 95073-1532 USA
E-mail: tonette101@aol.com
Web site: http://percyveerance.com.
Doctor Dolittle's Library *Imprint of* **PhotoGraphics Publishing**
DocUmeant Publishing, *(978-0-9788831; 978-0-9825608; 978-0-9826005; 978-0-9832122; 978-1-937801; 978-0-692-30306-1; 978-1-950075; 978-1-957832)* Orders Addr.: 1730 Rainbow Dr., Clearwater, FL 33755 USA Tel 727-565-2130; Fax: 727-446-2217; Edit Addr.: 244 5th Avenue, Suite G-200, New York, NY 10001 USA; *Imprints:* DP Kids Press (DP Kids Pr)
E-mail: ceo@calomarllc.com; publisher@documeantpublishing.com
Web site: http://www.DocUmeantPublishing.com
Dist(s): **CreateSpace Independent Publishing Platform**
Draft2Digital
Findaway Voices
Ingram Content Group
Lulu Pr., Inc.
Dodi Pr., *(978-0-9767273; 978-0-9851067)* Orders Addr.: 5829 Campbellton Rd., SW Ste 104-224, Atlanta, GA 30331 USA (SAN 860-3200)
E-mail: cherilnc@cherilnclarke.com; monica.r.bey@gmail.com; cheril@phenomenalwriting.com
Web site: http://www.myfamilyproducts.com; http://www.dodipress.com; https://www.cherilnclarke.com.
Dog Ear Publishing, LLC, *(978-0-9762173; 978-0-9766603; 978-1-59858; 978-1-60844; 978-1-4575)* 4010 W. 86th St., Suite H, Indianapolis, IN 46268 USA Tel 317-228-3656; Fax: 317-489-3506; Toll Free: 866-823-9613
E-mail: rayr@dogearpublishing.net
Web site: http://www.dogearpublishing.net
Dist(s): **Ingram Publisher Services**
Ingram Content Group
Lulu Pr., Inc.
Smashwords.
Dog Hair Pr., *(978-1-7324914)* 7706 Marine Rd. 129, North Bergen, NJ 07047 USA Tel 201-295-9992
E-mail: cntp@optonline.net.
DOG ON A LOG Bks. *Imprint of* **Jojoba Pr.**
Dog Soldier Pr., *(978-0-9718658; 978-1-7362743; 978-1-7371362; 979-8-9874524; 979-8-9877380; 979-8-218-25072-0)* P.O. Box 1782, Ranchos de Taos, NM 87557-1782 USA (SAN 254-4733) Tel 575-770-1040
E-mail: dogsoldier@newmexico.com
Web site: http://www.dogsoldierpress.com.
Dog-Eared Pubns., *(978-0-941042)* Orders Addr.: P.O. Box 620863, Middleton, WI 53562-0863 USA (SAN 281-6059) Tel 608-831-1410 (phone/fax); Toll Free: 888-364-3277; Edit Addr.: 4642 Toepfer Rd., Middleton, WI 53562 USA
E-mail: field@dog-eared.com
Web site: http://www.dog-eared.com
Dist(s): **Common Ground Distributors, Inc.**
Paradise Cay Pubns.
Partners/West Book Distributors.
Doggerel Daze, *(978-0-9722820)* 10144 Riedel Pl., Cupertino, CA 95014 USA.
Doggy Diva Show, Inc., The, *(978-0-692-15017-7; 978-0-578-67286-1; 978-0-578-95951-1)* 1800 2nd St. Suite 750, SARASOTA, FL 34236 USA Tel 941-447-4441
E-mail: doggydivashow@aol.com
Dist(s): **Ingram Content Group.**
DogHouse Pr., *(978-0-9761497)* 150 Chestnut St., Park Forest, IL 60466 USA Toll Free: 877-413-8997
E-mail: kimberly@rjsystems.us
Web site: http://www.doghousepress.com.
Doghouse Publishing, Incorporated *See* **Mess Hall Writers**
Dogs Doing Jobs, LLC, *(978-0-9992365)* 224 SHANNON CT, INWOOD, WV 25428 USA Tel 703-980-1442
E-mail: alwssales@gmail.com.
Dogs in Hats Children's Publishing Co., *(978-1-59445)* P.O. Box 182, Grand Haven, MI 49417 USA Tel 616-844-2220; Fax: 616-844-2922
E-mail: customerservice@dogsinhats.com
Web site: http://www.dogsinhats.com
Dist(s): **Follett School Solutions.**
Dogs4dogs, *(978-0-9771265)* P.O. Box 675432, Rancho Santa Fe, CA 92067-5432 USA
Web site: http://www.dogs4dogs.com.
Dogtown Artworks, *(978-0-9777126)* 201 Southland DR N, Tuscola, IL 61953 USA Tel 217-722-9125
E-mail: pringle.photography@gmail.com; pearl.barker@gmail.com
Web site: http://www.dogtownartworks.com.
Dogwalk Pr., *(978-0-9766846)* Div. of Dan Gersten & Assocs., LLC, 29636 Quail Run Dr., Agoura Hills, CA 91301 USA Tel 818-735-0280; Fax: 818-991-1838
Web site: http://www.askcurtisthedog.com.
Dogwise *See* **Dogwise Publishing**
Dogwise Publishing, *(978-1-929242; 978-1-61781)* Orders Addr.: 403 S. Mission, Wentachee, WA 98801 USA (SAN 631-1415) Tel 509-663-9115; Fax: 509-662-7233; Toll Free: 800-776-2665
E-mail: mail@dogwise.com; charlenew@dogwise.com; nate.woodward@dogwise.com
Web site: http://www.dogwise.com.
Dohate Pr., *(978-0-9767003)* Orders Addr.: 1809 Brookhaven Dr., Austin, TX 78704 USA Tel 512-442-0576
E-mail: donbutlerbooks@earthlink.net.
Doherty, Tom Assocs., LLC, *(978-0-312; 978-0-7653; 978-0-8125)* Div. of Holtzbrinck Publishers, Orders Addr.: 16365 James Madison Hwy., Gordonsville, VA 22942-8501 USA Toll Free Fax: 800-672-2054; Toll Free: 888-330-8477; Edit Addr.: 175 Fifth Ave., New York, NY 10010 USA Tel 212-674-5151; Fax: 540-672-7540 (customer service); *Imprints:* Forge Books (Forge Bks); Orb Books (Orb Bks); Tor Books (Tor Books); Starscape (Starscape); Tor Fantasy (Tor Fan); Tor Science Fiction (TorSciFic); Tor Teen (Tor Teen); Tor.com (Torcom); Tor Romance (Tor Romance)
E-mail: inquiries@tor.com
Web site: http://www.tor.com/
Dist(s): **Cambridge Univ. Pr.**
Children's Plus, Inc.
CreateSpace Independent Publishing Platform
Libros Sin Fronteras
Macmillan
MyiLibrary
Perfection Learning Corp.
Westminster John Knox Pr.
Doing Good Ministries, *(978-0-9667054)* 217 Bayview Way, Chula Vista, CA 91910 USA Tel 619-476-7230
E-mail: moehlenpah@aol.com
Web site: http://www.doinggood.org.
Dokument forlag, Fotograf Malcolm Jacobsson (SWE) *(978-91-973981; 978-91-85639) Dist. by* **SCB Distributo.**
Dolan, Katie Lange, *(978-1-7339586)* 60 Beach, Little Compton, RI 02837 USA Tel 914-216-1715
E-mail: katie@katiedolan.net
Web site: katielangedolan.com.
Doley Pubns., *(978-0-9985699)* 4934 Garden Grove Rd., Grand Prairie, TX 75052 USA Tel 972-606-6755
E-mail: stacy.antonino@gmail.com.
Dollison Road Bks., *(978-0-9855540)* 247 E. 4700 N., Provo, UT 84604 USA Tel 417-883-0601
E-mail: JeanStringam@gmail.com
Web site: jeanstringam.com; DollisonRoadBooks.com.
Dollworks, *(978-0-9760064; 978-1-60304)* 6693 Lake Shore Dr., Newport, MI 48166-9716 USA; P.O. Box 66075, Newport, MI 48166
E-mail: nanciejack@aol.com.
Dolly Dimple Ink Children's Bks., *(978-0-9773506)* 5484 Atlantic View, Saint Augustine, FL 32080 USA Tel 904-460-0997
E-mail: effiemaeshearin@aol.com
Web site: http://www.dollydimpleink.com.
Dolphin Media *See* **Blue Brush Media**
Dolphin Publishing, *(978-1-878400)* P.O. Box 16656, West Palm Beach, FL 33416-6656 USA Tel 561-585-8901; Toll Free: 800-547-7867 Do not confuse with companies with the same name in Richardson, TX, Mattawan, MI
E-mail: nicotinefree@bellsouth.net
Web site: http://www.davidcjones.com.
Dolphin Star, *(978-0-9827408; 978-1-7379124)* 12808 Valentano Ave., Bakersfield, CA 93312 USA Tel 661-333-8391
E-mail: dolphinstar@lorenjohnpresley.com
Web site: www.lorenjohnpresley.com.
Dolphins Publishing, *(978-0-9892565)* 1931 SW 17th Pl., Cape Coral, FL 33991 USA
E-mail: coach4u13@yahoo.com.
Domestic Policy Association *See* **National Issues Forums Institute**
Dominick Pictures, *(978-0-9726092)* P.O. Box 1925, New York, NY 10013 USA.
Dominie Elementary *Imprint of* **Savvas Learning Co.**
Dominie Pr., Inc., *(978-0-7685; 978-1-56270)* Div. of Pearson Learning, 145 S. Mount Zion Rd., Lebanon, IN 46052-8186 USA (SAN 630-947X) Toll Free: 800-232-4570
E-mail: info@dominie.com
Web site: http://www.dominie.com.
Dominik, Karen, *(978-0-578-70159-2)* 23211 Foxberry Ln., Bonita Springs, FL 34135 USA Tel 239-287-5756
E-mail: dominikkad@aol.com.
Dominion Publishing, *(978-0-692-87247-5; 978-0-578-45589-1; 978-0-578-58139-2; 978-0-578-71806-4)* P.O. Box 130, Sodus, MI 49126 USA Tel 770-862-5890
E-mail: cornellburtonjr@gmail.com; cornellburtonjr@gmail.com; cornellburtonjr@gmail.com
Web site: www.DominionRevival.com
Dist(s): **CreateSpace Independent Publishing Platform.**
DOMINIONHOUSE Publishing & Design, *(978-0-9755234; 978-0-9815463; 978-0-9828366; 978-0-9839869; 978-0-9888718; 978-0-9905031; 978-0-9971980; 978-1-7323126; 978-1-7353091; 978-1-7367927; 979-8-9865071)* Orders Addr.: P.O. Box 681938, Orlando, FL 32868 USA Tel 407-703-4800 (phone/fax)
Web site: http://www.mydominionhouse.com.
Don Cohen-The Mathman, *(978-0-9621674; 978-0-9779493)* Orders Addr.: 809 Stratford Dr., Champaign, IL 61821-4140 USA (SAN 251-866X) Tel 217-356-4555; Fax: 217-356-4593; Toll Free: 800-356-4559
E-mail: mathman@shout.net
Web site: http://www.shout.net/~mathman
Dist(s): **Rainbow Re-Source Ctr.**
Don Paul Publishing, LLC, *(978-0-9655792; 978-0-9816477; 978-1-941818)* P.O. Box 17062, Portland, OR 97217 USA Tel 503-764-9100
E-mail: jenna7jennifer@gmail.com; jennifer@donpaulpublishing.com
Web site: http://www.donpaulpublishing.com.
Don Quixote Publishing Co. Inc., *(978-0-9749196; 978-0-578-06784-1)* 905 Brickell Bay Dr., Unit 230, Miami, FL 33131 USA (SAN 255-884X) Tel 305-379-6151; Fax: 305-379-5156
E-mail: panza1209@aol.com; camote@manuelmartinezdreamer.com
Web site: http://www.manuelmartinezdreamer.com.
Don Rand's Classy Collectibles, *(978-0-9773775)* 26585 Fawn., Lake Forest, CA 92630-6728 USA.
DONALDSON, STEPHEN /THE BIG RED BUS Co., *(978-1-7379747)* 232 N CRESCENT Dr 203, BEVERLY HILLS, CA 90210 USA Tel 323-590-7529
E-mail: SMDMCR@YAHOO.COM.
DoNascimento.com/Books *See* **Briggs & Schuster**
Donegal Publishing Co., *(978-0-9788128)* Orders Addr.: 1850 Industrial St., #307, Los Angeles, CA 90021 USA (SAN 851-6782) Tel 310-598-6340; Fax: 310-349-3441; Toll Free: 866-964-4919
E-mail: editor@donegalpublishing.com; richie-d@comcast.net; donegalpublishing@mac.com
Web site: http://www.donegalpublishing.com; http://www.jerryland.net.
Dong, Jianming, *(978-0-692-80729-3)* 3181 Louis Rd., PALO ALTO, CA 94303 USA Tel 408-685-1089
E-mail: dongjianming@gmail.com; dongjianming@gmail.com.
Donkey Duck Enterprises, LLC, *(978-0-578-19757-9; 978-0-578-19906-1)* 1315 Deneb Ct., Walnut Creek, CA 94597 USA.
Donkey Penguin, *(978-1-7329164)* 310 S Delaware Ave. Apt. D, Tampa, FL 33606 USA Tel 813-505-4009
E-mail: denisehaunstetter@yahoo.com
Web site: www.donkeypenguin.com.
Donkey Publishing, *(978-0-9887454)* 16582 Hutchison Rd., Odessa, FL 33556 USA Tel 813-781-7143
E-mail: TOM@BRAYFIELDS.COM.
Donkey Quest Books *See* **Donkey's Quest Pr.**
Donkey's Quest Pr., *(978-0-9961139)* 40 Sherwood Rd., Medford, MA 02155 USA
E-mail: ccbaha1@gmail.com
Web site: http://donkeysquestpress.com.
Donnellan, Martha *See* **Pine Cone Pr.**
Donning Co. Pubs., *(978-0-89865; 978-0-915442; 978-1-57864; 978-1-68184)* Subs. of Walsworth Publishing Co., Inc., 184 Business Park Dr. Suite 206, Virginia Bch, VA 23462 USA (SAN 211-6316) Toll Free: 800-296-8572
E-mail: dcpr3@pilot.infi.net
Web site: http://www.donning.com
Dist(s): **Chicago Distribution Ctr.**
Schiffer Publishing, Ltd.
Donor Sibling Registry, *(978-0-692-10693-8; 978-0-692-12226-6; 978-0-692-14016-1; 978-0-578-63337-4; 978-0-578-63338-1)* P.O. Box 1571, Nederland, CO 80466 USA Tel 303-258-0902
E-mail: wendy@donorsiblingregistry.com
Dist(s): **Ingram Content Group.**
Donovan, Kevin M. *See* **Billy the Bear & His Friends, Inc.**
Dont "Diss" Abilities, *(978-1-7323298)* 726 S Nebraska St., Unit 95, Chandler, AZ 85225 USA Tel 480-688-8346
E-mail: nsharvick@cox.net.
Don't Eat Any Bugs Prodns., *(978-0-9728177; 978-0-9802314; 978-0-9887329; 978-1-7326165)* P.O. Box 291, Tehachapi, CA 93581 USA
E-mail: Ray@rayfriesen.com
Web site: http://www.donteatanybugs.com
Dist(s): **National Bk. Network.**
Don't Look Publishing, *(978-0-9728234)* P.O. Box 486, Moose Lake, MN 55767 USA.
Don't Run With Knives Publications *See* **Academic Solutions, Inc.**
Don't Stop Publishing, *(978-0-9992753; 978-1-947884)* 5940 S Rainbow Blvd Ste 400 No. 55447, Las Vegas, NV 89118 USA Tel 702-329-9980
E-mail: jwagner@qtpublish.com.
Don't Sweat It, Inc., *(978-0-9888712; 978-0-692-63804-0; 978-0-692-63805-7)* 547 N. Las Palmas Ave., Los Angeles, CA 90004 USA Tel 310-435-7713
E-mail: ivana@princessivana.com
Web site: http://www.dontsweatitmedia.com.
Dontstickdontstuff, *(978-0-9888861)* 5426 E. Via Los Caballos, Paradise Valley, AZ 85253 USA Tel 480-600-4690
E-mail: dontstickdontstuff@gmail.com
Dist(s): **BookBaby**
New Shelves Distribution.
Doob, Jeanne Reinhardt, *(978-0-578-44964-7; 978-0-578-97431-6)* 728 Stewart Way, Brentwood, CA 94513 USA Tel 925-240-9757
E-mail: jnpdoob@sbcglobal.net.
Doodle and Peck Publishing, *(978-0-692-26513-0; 978-0-692-45586-9; 978-0-692-45589-0; 978-0-9966205; 978-0-9972351; 978-0-9983271; 978-0-9989302; 978-0-9992497; 978-1-7323637; 978-1-7327713; 978-1-7337170; 978-1-7333462; 978-1-7346072; 978-1-7358306; 979-8-9853351; 979-8-9866380) 413 Cedarburg Ct., Yukon, OK 73099 USA Tel 405-354-7422*
E-mail: iluvrocksmj@yahoo.com
Web site: www.doodleandpeck.com
Dist(s): **Brodart Co.**
Ingram Content Group.
Doodle Publishing, *(978-0-9719518)* 2219 Tam-O-Shanter Ct., Carmel, IN 46032 USA Tel 317-538-6995
E-mail: adam10spro@aol.com.
Doodlebops *Imprint of* **Cookie Jar**
DoodleCake *Imprint of* **Irresistible Pr., LLC**
Dooley Bks., Ltd, *(978-0-9786605)* 53 W. Jackson No. 1240, CHICAGO, IL 60604 USA
Web site: http://www.Dooleybooks.com.
Doolittle Edutainment Corp., *(978-0-9793144)* 2445 Fifth Ave., Suite 440, San Diego, CA 92101 USA (SAN 853-0912)
Web site: http://www.doolittleedutainment.com.
Doorlight Pubns., *(978-0-9778372; 978-0-9838653; 978-0-9982233)* 4 Central Ave., South Hadley, MA 01075 USA.
Doorposts, *(978-1-891206)* 5905 SW Lookingglass Dr., Gaston, OR 97119-9241 USA Tel 503-357-4749; Fax: 503-357-4909 Do not confuse with Doorposts, Lansdale, PA
E-mail: orders@doorposts.com
Web site: http://www.doorposts.com.
Dora, Liza *See* **Liza Dora Bks.**
Dorcas Pubns., LLC, *(978-0-9769829)* 890 Woodland Ave., Corydon, IN 47112 USA Tel 812-738-4361; Fax: 812-738-2259
E-mail: wfwilson@aol.com
Web site: http://www.dorcaspublications.com.
Dorcas Publishing, *(978-0-9762375)* Div. of Heavenly Patchwork Charity Bks., Orders Addr.: 12101 N. MacArthur, Suite 137, Oklahoma City, OK 73162-1800 USA Tel 405-751-3885 (phone/fax)
E-mail: buckboardquilts@cox.net
Web site: http://www.heavenlypatchwork.com.
Dorchester Publishing Co., Inc., *(978-0-505; 978-0-8439; 978-1-4285)* Orders Addr.: 200 Madison Ave., Suite 2000, New York, NY 10016 USA (SAN 264-0090); P.O. Box 6640, Wayne, PA 19087 Toll Free: 800-481-9191
Dist(s): **MyiLibrary.**
Dorhauer, Amanda, *(978-1-7327442)* 109 Delta Dr., Oakwood, IL 61858 USA Tel 314-337-2599
E-mail: greendayltd@yahoo.com.
Dork Storm Pr., *(978-1-930964; 978-1-933288)* P.O. Box 45063, Madison, WI 53744 USA Fax: 608-225-1352
Web site: http://www.dorkstorm.com
Dist(s): **PSI (Publisher Services, Inc.).**
†Dorling Kindersley Publishing, Inc., *(978-0-7894; 978-1-56458; 978-1-879431; 978-0-7566; 978-1-4654)* Div. of Penguin Publishing Group, 375 Hudson St., 2nd Flr., New York, NY 10014 USA (SAN 253-0791) Tel 212-213-4800; Fax: 212-213-5240; Toll Free:

877-342-5357 (orders only); *Imprints:* Alpha (AlphaUSA); DK (DKUSA); DK Children (DKChildren)
E-mail: Annemarie.Cancienne@dk.com; customer.service@dk.com
Web site: http://www.dk.com
Dist(s): **Children's Plus, Inc.**
Continental Bk. Co., Inc.
Ebsco Publishing
Follett School Solutions
Cengage Gale
Penguin Random Hse. Distribution
Penguin Random Hse. LLC
Penguin Publishing Group
Hale, Robert & Co., Inc.
Sunburst Communications, Inc.; *CIP.*

Dormouse Productions, Inc., *(978-1-889300)* 25 NE 99th St., Miami, FL 33138-2338 USA Tel 305-379-4990; Fax: 305-379-7990
E-mail: dmouse@juno.com.

Dorn Enterprises *See* **Susy Dorn Productions, LLC**

Dorob International Ltd., *(978-0-9910985; 979-8-218-23453-9)* 1402 Pointe Gate Dr., Livingston, NJ 07039 USA Tel 973-995-9249
E-mail: rdg@genesysassociates.com.

Dorothy Payne & Virginia Letourneau, *(978-0-9747823)* 300 E. 33rd St., Apt. 7C, New York, NY 10016 USA
Web site: http://www.cityislandclamdigger.com.

Dorothy-Frances Bks., *(978-0-9911099; 978-0-692-27734-8; 978-0-9997911; 978-1-7338878; 978-1-7334865; 978-1-7355366; 978-1-957254)* 6469 NW 80th Terr, Parkland, FL 33067 USA Tel 954-742-7777
E-mail: drhdel@gmail.com
Dist(s): **CreateSpace Independent Publishing Platform.**

Dorrance Publishing Co., Inc., *(978-0-8059; 978-1-4349; 978-1-4809; 978-1-64426; 978-1-64530; 978-1-64610; 978-1-64702; 978-1-64804; 978-1-64913; 978-1-64957; 978-1-63661; 978-1-63764; 978-1-63867; 978-1-63937; 978-1-68537; 979-8-88527; 979-8-88604; 979-8-88683; 979-8-88729;-8-88812; 979-8-88925; 979-8-89027; 979-8-89127; 979-8-89211) 701 Smithfield St. Third Flr., Pittsburgh, PA 15222 USA (SAN 201-3363) Tel 412-288-4543; Fax: 412-288-1786; Toll Free: 800-788-7654; 800-695-7599; Imprints:* RoseDog Books (RoseDog Bks)
E-mail: rpiotrowski@dorrancepublishing.com; dorrordr@dorrancepublishing.com
Web site: http://www.dorrancepublishing.com; www.dorrancebookstore.com.

Dorry Pr., *(978-0-615-67780-4; 978-0-615-75213-6; 978-0-615-76920-2; 978-0-615-76921-9; 978-0-692-20424-5; 978-0-692-22048-1; 978-0-692-45609-5; 978-0-9983796; 978-1-951386)* P.O. Box 16537, Chesapeake, VA 23322 USA Tel 757-277-9739; 1041 Baydon Ln., Chesapeake, VA 23322
E-mail: sherryajones@yahoo.com
Dist(s): **CreateSpace Independent Publishing Platform.**

†**Dorset Hse. Publishing**, *(978-0-932633)* 3143 Broadway Suite 2b, New York, NY 10027 USA (SAN 687-794X) Tel 212-620-4053; Fax: 212-727-1044; Toll Free: 800-342-6657
E-mail: info@dorsethouse.com; littlewest@dorsethouse.com
Web site: http://www.dorsethouse.com; http://www.littlewestpress.com; *CIP.*

Dory Pr., *(978-0-9633240)* 13396 Wakefield Rd., Sedley, VA 23878 USA Tel 757-220-9206.

Doses of Reality, Inc., *(978-0-9754024)* 634 Ceape Ave, Oshkosh, WI 54901 USA Tel 920-573-9884
E-mail: dosesofreality@yahoo.com.

Dot Dot Bks., *(978-0-9670750)* 420 16th St., Bellingham, WA 98225 USA Tel 360-220-1686
E-mail: dana.rozier@gmail.com
Dist(s): **Small Pr. United.**

Dot EDU (Educational & Textbooks) *Imprint of* **Speedy Publishing LLC**

Dothan Publishing *See* **Moriah Ministries**

Dottir Pr., *(978-1-948340)* 33 Fifth Ave., New York, NY 10003 USA Tel 917-753-8091
E-mail: jb@dottirpress.com
Web site: dottirpress.com
Dist(s): **Consortium Bk. Sales & Distribution.**

Double B Pubns., *(978-0-929526)* 4123 N. Longview, Phoenix, AZ 85014 USA (SAN 249-6615) Tel 602-996-7129; Fax: 602-996-6928
E-mail: bfischerppg@aol.com.

Double Bridge Publishing, 9812 Mahogany Dr., Gaithersburg, MD 20878 USA Tel 240-551-4234
E-mail: editor@doublebridgepublishing.com
Web site: www.doublebridgepublishing.com.

Double Dagger Pr., *(978-0-9729293)* 256 Ridge Ave., Gettysburg, PA 17325-2404 USA (SAN 255-7517) Tel 717-334-5392
E-mail: mplank@doubledaggerpress.com
Web site: http://www.doubledaggerpress.com.

Double Edge Pr., *(978-0-9774452; 978-0-9819514; 978-1-938002)* Orders Addr.: 72 Ellview Rd., Scenery Hill, PA 15360 USA (SAN 257-5019) Tel 724-518-6737; *Imprints:* Hummingbird World Media (HummbirdWrld)
E-mail: cuttingedge@atlanticbb.net
Web site: http://www.doubleedgepress.com
Dist(s): **ebrary, Inc.**

DOUBLE R Bks. *Imprint of* **Rodrigue & Sons Co./Double R Books Publishing**

Double R Publishing, LLC, *(978-0-9713381; 978-0-9718696; 978-0-9770534)* 7301 W. Flagler St., Miami, FL 33144 USA Tel 305-262-4240; Fax: 305-262-4115; Toll Free: 877-262-4240
E-mail: abcsbook@abcsbook.com
Web site: http://www.abcsbook.com
Dist(s): **ABC'S Bk. Supply, Inc.**

Double Roads *See* **Karenzo Media**

Doubleday Bks. for Young Readers *Imprint of* **Random Hse. Children's Bks.**

Doubleday Canada, Ltd. (CAN) *(978-0-385; 978-0-7704)* *Dist. by* **Random.**

Doubleday Canada, Ltd. (CAN) *(978-0-385; 978-0-7704)* *Dist. by* **Peng Rand Hse.**

Doubleday Publishing *See* **Knopf Doubleday Publishing Group**

Doubleday Religious Publishing Group, The, Div. of Random Hse., Inc., Orders Addr.: 400 Hahn Rd., Westminster, MD 21157 USA Tel 410-848-1900; Toll Free: 800-726-0600 (customer service); 800-733-3000; Edit Addr.: 12265 Oracle Blvd., Suite 200, Colorado Springs, CO 80921 USA (SAN 299-4682) Tel 719-590-4999; Fax: 719-590-8977; Toll Free Fax: 800-294-5686; Toll Free: 800-603-7051; *Imprints:* Multnomah (Mltnmah) Do not confuse with WaterBrook Pr., Great Falls, VA
Web site: http://www.randomhouse.com/waterbrook
Dist(s): **Anchor Distributors**
Children's Plus, Inc.
MyiLibrary
Penguin Random Hse. Distribution
Penguin Random Hse. LLC
Random Hse., Inc.

DOUBLE-R BKS. *Imprint of* **Rodrigue & Sons Co./Double R Books Publishing**

DoubleStar, LLC, *(978-0-9742558)* 9672 Litzsinger Rd., Saint Louis, MO 63124-1494 USA
E-mail: doublestarllc@sbcglobal.net
Web site: http://www.cogno.com.

Dougherty, Elizabeth *See* **School Street Bks.**

Douglas and McIntyre (2013) Ltd. (CAN) *(978-0-88894; 978-1-55365; 978-1-926812; 978-1-77100; 978-1-77162)* *Dist. by* **PerseuPGW.**

Douglas, Bettye Forum, Inc., The, *(978-0-9703183)* 6608 N. Western Ave., No. 327, Oklahoma City, OK 73116 USA Tel 405-528-1773; Fax: 405-842-7541; Toll Free: 800-354-0680
E-mail: bettye_douglas@excite.com
Web site: http://www.bettyedouglas.com.

Doulos Christou Pr., *(978-0-9744796; 978-1-934406)* 57 N. Ruial St. Englewood Christian Church, Indianapolis, IN 46201-3330 USA
E-mail: douloschristoupress@yahoo.com
Web site: http://www.douloschristou.com.

Doumlele, Carol, *(978-0-9992578)* 1500 Jamaica Ct., Marco Island, FL 34145 USA Tel 239-777-0492
E-mail: doumleca@embarqmail.com.

Dove Books and Audio *Imprint of* **Phoenix Bks., Inc.**

Dove Hollow Bks., *(978-0-9969383)* P.O. Box 665, Denton, TX 76202 USA Tel 817-233-8546
E-mail: sarahmactavishtx@gmail.com.

Dove Publishing, Inc., *(978-0-9766578)* P.O. Box 310326, Atlanta, GA 31131 USA Do not confuse with companies with the same or similar name in Houston, TX, Decatur, GA, Forest heights, MD, Lake Konkonkma, NY
Web site: http://www.dovepub.com.

†**Dover Pubns., Inc.**, *(978-0-486; 978-1-60660)* Div. of Courier Corporation, 31 E. Second St., Mineola, NY 11501 USA (SAN 201-338X) Tel 516-294-7000; Fax: 516-873-1401 (orders only); Toll Free: 800-223-3130 (orders only); *Imprints:* bxia Press (bxiaPr)
E-mail: rights@doverpublications.com
Web site: http://www.doverdirect.com; http://www.doverpublications.com
Dist(s): **Continental Bk. Co., Inc.**
Firebrand Technologies
INscribe Digital
Independent Pubs. Group
MyiLibrary
Beeler, Thomas T. Pub.; *CIP.*

DoveTail Hse., Inc., *(978-0-9706244; 978-0-9772935; 978-0-9800099; 978-0-9862832; 978-1-943181)* P.O. Box 501995, San Diego, CA 92150 USA Tel 858-581-5954; Fax: 858-668-1771
E-mail: dovepub@san.rr.com.

Dovetail Publishing, *(978-0-9651284)* P.O. Box 19945, Kalamazoo, MI 49019 USA Tel 616-342-2900; Fax: 616-342-1012; Toll Free: 800-222-0070
E-mail: dovetail@mich.com
Web site: http://www.mich.com/~dovetail
Dist(s): **Quality Bks., Inc.**

Down East Bks., *(978-0-89272; 978-0-924357)* Div. of Rowman & Littlefield Publishing Group, Inc., P.O. Box 679, Camden, ME 04843 USA (SAN 208-6301) Tel 207-594-9544; Fax: 207-594-0147; Toll Free: 800-766-1670 Wholesale orders; 800-685-7962 Retail orders
E-mail: pblanchard@downeast.com; tbregy@downeast.com
Web site: http://www.countrysportpress.com; http://www.downeastbooks.com
Dist(s): **Blackstone Audio, Inc.**
Follett School Solutions
MyiLibrary
National Bk. Network
Rowman & Littlefield Publishers, Inc.
Rowman & Littlefield Unlimited Model
TNT Media Group, Inc.
ebrary, Inc.

Down The Road Publishing, *(978-0-9754427)* 172 White Oak Dr., Batesville, IN 47006 USA (SAN 256-2227)
E-mail: timt@downtheroad.org
Web site: http://www.downtheroad.org.

Down The Shore Publishing, *(978-0-945582; 978-0-9615208; 978-1-59322)* Orders Addr.: P.O. Box 100, West Creek, NJ 08092 USA Tel 609-812-5076; Fax: 609-812-5098; Edit Addr.: P.O. Box 100, West Creek, NJ 08092 USA (SAN 661-082X)
E-mail: downshore@gmail.com
Web site: http://www.down-the-shore.com
Dist(s): **Partners Bk. Distributing, Inc.**
Sourcebooks, Inc.

Down The Shore Publishing Corporation *See* **Down The Shore Publishing**

Down-To-Earth-Bks., *(978-1-878115)* P.O. Box 488, Ashfield, MA 01330 USA Tel 413-628-0227
E-mail: maryskole@aol.com
Web site: http://www.spinningglobe.net.

Downtown Bookworks, *(978-1-935703; 978-1-941367; 978-1-950587)* 285 W. Broadway, Suite 600, New York, NY 10013 USA Tel 646-613-0707
Dist(s): **Children's Plus, Inc.**
Diamond Comic Distributors, Inc.
Simon & Schuster, Inc.

Downtown Revitalization Consultants, *(978-0-9855316)* 2380 Alamo Ave., Chico, CA 95926 USA Tel 530-345-0900; Fax: 530-345-0900
E-mail: campkilbrn@aol.com.

Downtown Wetmore Pr., *(978-0-9795302)* Orders Addr.: 13451 Wetmore Rd., San Antonio, TX 78247 USA (SAN 853-7070) Tel 210-490-7222; Fax: 210-490-8222; Toll Free Fax: 877-490-8222; Toll Free: 877-490-7222; *Imprints:* CrumbGobbler Press (CrumbGobbler)
E-mail: downtownwetmore@earthlink.net; info@crumbgobbler.com
Web site: http://www.downtownwetmore.com.

Doxy, Pascale, *(978-0-578-24929-2; 978-0-578-25778-5; 978-0-578-25779-2; 978-0-578-27797-4; 978-0-578-27798-1)* 3517 Rindle Ct., Charlotte, NC 28269 USA.

Doyle Arts, *(978-0-9853216)* 2621 Blake Rd., Wadsworth, OH 44281 USA Tel 330-466-0238
E-mail: DoyleArts@gmail.com
Web site: http://www.DoyleArts.com.

DP Group LLC, The *See* **DP Group LLC, The**

DP Group LLC, The, *(978-0-9978230; 978-1-949513)* 150 Wrenn Drive, No. 584, cary, NC 27512 USA Tel 919-452-6966
E-mail: divpriti@gmail.com.

DP Kids Pr. *Imprint of* **DocUmeant Publishing**

DPK, Inc., *(978-0-9971308)* 1225 N. 160 W., Orem, UT 84057 USA Tel 801-669-3094
E-mail: dpowersking@gmail.com
Web site: www.davidpowersking.com.

Dr. Donna L Sauer, *(978-0-578-33381-6; 978-0-578-28608-2; 979-8-218-08554-4; 979-8-218-12926-2)* 643 Leonard Rd, Onalaska, WA 98570 USA Tel 360-978-5130
E-mail: De.dlsauer@gmail.com
Web site: www.drdonnaac.com.

Dr. Emily Woolcock, *(978-1-7359319)* 20203 Goshen Rd., Gaithersburg, MD 20879 USA Tel 240-241-7100
E-mail: Nationalorthopaedics@GMAIL.COM
Web site: www.dremilywoolcock.com.

Dr. Gazebo Publishing *See* **Snow In Sarasota Publishing**

Dr. Ingrid Wright, *(978-0-9992143)* 5505 W. Buckskin Trail, Phoenix, AZ 85083-4302 USA Tel 951-440-7063
E-mail: ingridwright07@yahoo.com
Web site: IngridWrightFineArt.com.

Dr. Jay, LLC, *(978-0-9860063)* P.O. Box 422, Green Farms, CT 06838 USA
E-mail: yroehler@bookpublishing.com.

Dr. Joyce STARR Publishing *See* **STARR Publishing**

Dr Ma Publishing, *(978-0-9995813)* 119 N. Fairfax Ave., No. 188, Los Angeles, CA 90036 USA Tel 469-250-0884
E-mail: edna@drednabrands.com
Web site: drEdnabrands.com.

Dr. Mark Stuart Berlin *See* **Berlin, Stuart**

Dr. Mary's Bks., *(978-0-9765453)* 180 90th Ave. SE, Kensal, ND 58455 USA Tel 701-435-2388
E-mail: dwayneerickson@agristar.net
Web site: http://www.shopnd.com.

Dr Monica Y Jackson Education & Design Services, *(978-0-9728674)* 11762 De Palma Rd., Suite 1-C No. 548, Corona, CA 92883 USA.

Dr Monica Y Jackson Educational Services *See* **Dr Monica Y Jackson Education & Design Services**

Dr Palmer Writes, *(978-0-578-97619-8; 978-0-578-97622-8; 978-0-578-97641-9; 979-8-218-01900-6)* 209 E 12th St 0, RICHMOND, VA 23224 USA Tel 8044379735
E-mail: info@audreyhinds.com
Dist(s): **Ingram Content Group.**

Dr. Patricia Garfield's Ctr. for Creative Dreami, *(978-0-692-79633-7; 978-0-692-79635-1; 978-0-578-77503-6)* 130 Rancho Dr., TIBURON, CA 94920 USA Tel 415-383-7770.

Dr. Publishing, 2 Kenen Ct., Burlingame, CA 94010 USA Tel 916-548-2113
E-mail: Drbcool29@aol.com.

Draft2Digital, *(978-1-4977; 978-1-4989; 978-1-5014; 978-1-5022; 978-1-5070; 978-1-5130; 978-1-5163; 978-1-5199; 978-1-5242; 978-1-5337; 978-1-5365; 978-1-5401; 978-1-386; 978-1-393; 978-0-578-64452-3; 978-0-578-78856-2; 978-0-578-79287-3; 979-8-201; 979-8-215; 979-8-223) 9400 N. Broadway Ext. Ste. 410, Oklahoma City, OK 73114 USA Tel 866-336-5099; Toll Free Fax: 866-358-6413*
E-mail: support@draft2digital.com
Web site: www.draft2digital.com
Dist(s): **Independent Pubs. Group.**

Drag City, *(978-0-9656183; 978-0-9820480; 978-1-937112)* 2921 N. Cicero Ave., Chicago, IL 60641 USA Tel 312-455-1015; Fax: 312-455-1057
E-mail: sales@dragcity.com
Web site: http://www.dragcity.com; http://www.soccerclubclub.com
Dist(s): **Independent Pubs. Group**
SPD-Small Pr. Distribution.

Dragon Gate Media, *(978-1-7324359; 979-8-9853734; 979-8-9888163)* 307 Lexington Cir., Newport Beach, CA 92660 USA Tel 949-723-1088
E-mail: carolj10@aol.com.

Dragon Hill Publishing (CAN) *(978-1-896124)* *Dist. by* **Lone Pine.**

Dragon Hoard Pr. *Imprint of* **IYF Publishing**

Dragon Pup Pr., *(978-0-578-45522-8)* 7360 Stoney Pointe, Liberty Township, OH 45044 USA Tel 513-265-3160
E-mail: kftbooks@outlook.com
Web site: katherinethomasart.com.

Dragon Realm Pr., *(978-0-692-73198-7; 978-0-692-98866-4; 978-0-692-09895-0; 978-0-692-15184-6; 978-1-949621)* 14 HOPPYS LN, CAPE MAY COURT HOUSE, NJ 08210-2364 USA Tel 856-332-5306
E-mail: jaculican@gmail.com
Web site: www.dragonrealmpress.com; www.jaculican.com; www.avasilvers.com.

Dragon Scale Publishing, *(978-1-943183)* 8466 N Stonebridge LN, Eagle Mountain, UT 84005 USA Tel 801-471-0502
E-mail: Dragonscalebooks@outlook.com
Web site: www.Dragonscalepublishing.com.

Dragon Tree Bks., *(978-0-9884024; 978-0-9916200; 978-0-9862641; 978-0-9963081; 978-0-9974513; 978-0-9977478; 978-0-9995488; 978-1-7326613; 978-1-7337577; 978-1-7343332; 978-1-7348915; 978-1-7361578; 979-8-9857936; 979-8-9872440)* 1620 SW 5th Ave., Pompano Beach, FL 33060 USA Tel 954-788-4775
E-mail: editors@editingforauthors.com
Web site: http://editingforauthors.com.

Dragon Wings Publishing, *(978-0-9748951)* Orders Addr.: Kaybee Images Marketing Order Division PO Box 659, Dallas, OR 97338 USA.

Dragonbrush Arts, *(978-0-9960374; 979-8-9889155)* 34242 Vauxhill Dr. Apt. No. 7, Paw Paw, MI 49079 USA Tel 269-254-0663
E-mail: dan.monroe.art@gmail.com
Web site: dragonbrushart.com.

Dragoneagle Pr., *(978-0-9787465)* Orders Addr.: P.O. Box Box 30856, Bethesda, MD 20824 USA Tel 732-861-0449; Fax: 301-897-2786
E-mail: info@dragoneagle.com
Web site: http://www.dragoneagle.com.

DragonEye Publishing, *(978-0-9767832; 978-1-61500)* Orders Addr.: c/o ISOTUT Publisher, 753 Linden Place, Apt A, Elmira, NY 14901 USA (SAN 857-7110) Tel 607-333-5256 For questions about ordering
E-mail: Michael.Kiser@DragonEyePublishers.com
Web site: https://www.DragonEyePublishers.com.

Dragonfly Bks. *Imprint of* **Random Hse. Children's Bks.**

Dragonfly Entertainment, *(978-0-9745213)* 97 Chartwell Ct., Rochester, NY 14618-5376 USA; *Imprints:* Dragonfly Flipz (Dragonfly Flipz)
E-mail: dfly@earthlink.net
Web site: http://www.dragonflyent.net.

Dragonfly Farms: The Great Adventure, *(978-0-578-40926-9)* 1803 E. Hickory Hill Rd., Argyle, TX 76226 USA Tel 817-881-3383
E-mail: jennjennortiz@yahoo.com
Dist(s): **CreateSpace Independent Publishing Platform.**

Dragonfly Flipz *Imprint of* **Dragonfly Entertainment**

Dragonfly Ministries, *(978-0-9788289)* 295 Noble Cir., Vernon Hills, IL 60061-2927 USA
E-mail: info@dragonflyministries.com
Web site: http://www.dragonflyministries.com.

Dragonfly Publishing, Inc., *(978-0-9710473; 978-0-9755888; 978-0-9765786; 978-0-9778651; 978-0-9787421; 978-0-9794660; 978-0-9797574; 978-0-9801376; 978-0-9817049; 978-0-9819080; 978-0-9840980; 978-1-936381; 978-1-941278; 978-1-949187)* 2440 Twin Ridge Dr., Edmond, OK 73034-1943 USA Do not confuse with companies with the same or similar name in Mount Enterprise, TX , Whethersfield, CT , San Antonio, TX ,
Web site: http://www.dragonflypubs.com
Dist(s): **Smashwords.**

Dragonflyer Pr., *(978-0-944933)* Div. of American Water Gardens, Inc., 2460 N. Euclid Ave., Upland, CA 91784-1184 USA (SAN 245-7660) Toll Free: 800-558-0676
E-mail: info@dragonflyerpress.com; cuber@uberadv.com
Web site: http://www.vnwg.com; http://www.dragonflyerpress.com
Dist(s): **Midpoint Trade Bks., Inc.**

Dragongate Publishing, *(978-0-9765178; 978-0-578-67655-5; 978-1-7354042)* 44-119 Bayview Haven Pl., Kaneohe, HI 96744 USA Tel 808-534-0452; 1519 Nuuanu Ave., No.18, Honolulu, HI 96817-3739 (SAN 256-4939) Tel 808-234-5508
E-mail: dragongate@hawaii.rr.com.

Dragonhawk Publishing, *(978-1-888767)* Div. of Life Magic Enterprises, Inc., P.O. Box 1316, Jackson, TN 38302 USA Tel 901-987-3334; Fax: 901-987-2484
Dist(s): **Austin & Company, Inc.**
New Leaf Distributing Co., Inc.

Dragonon, Inc., *(978-0-9763398)* 9378 Mason Montgomery Rd., Suite 108, Mason, OH 45040 USA (SAN 256-3398) Tel 513-227-9224
E-mail: dmeyer@dragonon.com.

Dragon's Roost Pr., *(978-0-615-97909-0; 978-0-9988878; 978-1-7351233; 978-1-956824)* 2470 Hunter Rd, Brighton, MI 48114 USA Tel 1 (248) 259-9680
E-mail: editor@thedragonsroost.net
Web site: http://thedragonsroost.biz
Dist(s): **CreateSpace Independent Publishing Platform.**

Dragonscale Pr., *(978-0-9994291)* 613 Gray Head Ln., Knightdale, NC 27545 USA Tel 919-266-6292
E-mail: landsman.nic1129@gmail.com.

Dragonseed Pr., *(978-0-9678115)* Orders Addr.: 19020 Brookfield Dr., Chagrin Falls, OH 44023 USA
E-mail: dragonseedpress@aol.com
Web site: http://www.m-c-ryan.com.

ragonsoul Bks., *(978-0-692-51453-5; 978-0-692-51841-0; 978-0-692-19827-8)* P.O. Box 885, Mechanicsburg, PA 17055 USA Tel 717-648-7012
E-mail: natalie@nataliedamschroder.com
Web site: www.nataliedamschroder.com
Dist(s): **CreateSpace Independent Publishing Platform.**

ragonwick Ink, *(978-0-9987985; 978-0-578-56859-1)* 140 Hensley Rd., Chesnee, SC 29323 USA Tel 864-461-2768
E-mail: lpspms@chesnet.net.

ragonWing Bks., *(978-0-9761444)* 9107 Brunners Run Ct., Columbia, MD 21045 USA Tel 301-509-5451
E-mail: liz@dragonwingbooks.com
Web site: http://www.dragonwingbooks.com.

rake, Edwin, *(978-0-9743405)* R.R. 5, Box 5417, Saylorsburg, PA 18353 USA Tel 570-992-2914
E-mail: edrakee@enter.net.

rake Feltham Publishing, *(978-0-578-10548-2)* 22113 Palos Verdes Blvd., Torrance, CA 90503 USA
Dist(s): **Outskirts Pr., Inc.**

Drake Univ., Anderson Gallery, *(978-0-9749296)* 25th St. & Carpenter Ave., Des Moines, IA 50311 USA Tel 515-271-1994; Fax: 515-271-2558
E-mail: cira.pascual-marquina@drake.edu
Web site: http://www.drake.edu/andersongallery.

Drake Valley Pr., *(978-0-9728186; 978-0-9785632; 978-1-935970)* P.O. Box 979, Clinton, MS 39060 USA Toll Free: 866-442-4990 (fax on demand & phone/fax)
Web site: http://www.drakevalleypress.com
Dist(s): **Palari Publishing LLP.**

Drama Publishers *See* **Quite Specific Media Group, Ltd.**

Drama Tree Pr., *(978-0-9741670; 978-0-9821852; 978-0-9985676)* 150 Iota Ct., Madison, WI 53706 USA
E-mail: dramatree@mail.com
Web site: http://www.dramatree.com.

Dramaline Pubns., *(978-0-940669; 978-0-9611792)* 36851 Palm View Rd., Rancho Mirage, CA 92270-2417 USA (SAN 285-239X) Tel 760-770-6076; Fax: 760-770-4507
E-mail: drama.line@verizon.net
Web site: http://www.dramaline.com
Dist(s): **Distributors, The.**

DramaQueen, L.L.C., *(978-0-9766045; 978-1-933809; 978-1-60331)* Orders Addr.: P.O. Box 2626, Stafford, TX 77497 USA Fax: 281-498-4723; Toll Free: 800-883-1518 (ext. 2)
E-mail: orders@onedramaqueen.com; info@onedramaqueen.com
Web site: http://www.onedramaqueen.com
Dist(s): **AAA Anime Distribution.**

Dramatic Ellipsis, *(978-0-9984397)* P.O. Box 980882, Houston, TX 77098 USA Tel 281-773-2648; *Imprints*: Drivel & Drool (MYID_F_DRIVEL)
E-mail: enparekh@dramaticellipsis.com
Web site: driveIanddrool.com.

Dramatic Improvements Publishing, *(978-0-9768251)* 226 Perrine Ave., Auburn, NY 13021-1715 USA
E-mail: twoods@dramaimp.com
Web site: http://www.dramaimp.com.

Dramatic Pen Press, LLC, The *See* **Dramatic Pen Pr., LLC, The**

Dramatic Publishing Co., *(978-0-87129; 978-1-58342; 978-1-61959)* Orders Addr.: 311 Washington St., Woodstock, IL 60098 USA (SAN 201-5676) Tel 815-338-7170; Fax: 815-338-8981; Toll Free Fax: 800-334-5302; Toll Free: 800-448-7469
E-mail: kjusten@dpcplays.com
Web site: http://www.dramaticpublishing.com.

Dramatists Play Service, Inc., *(978-0-8222)* 440 Park Ave., S., New York, NY 10016 USA (SAN 207-5717) Tel 212-683-8960; Fax: 212-213-1539
E-mail: postmaster@dramatists.com
Web site: http://www.dramatists.com.

Drane, John Wanzer, *(978-0-578-10633-5)* 5 Derry Dr., Horse Shoe, NC 28742 USA.

Draper Publishing, *(978-0-9913342)* 1701 Willow Oak Ln., Dalton, GA 30721 USA Tel 706-260-5496
E-mail: duraniemaria39@yahoo.com
Web site: mariarochelle.com.

Draw Three Lines Publishing, *(978-0-9749418; 978-0-9826202)* P.O. Box 1522, Hillsboro, OR 97123 USA Tel 503-648-9905
E-mail: hastings@draw3lines.com
Web site: http://www.draw3lines.com.

Drawing From History, *(978-0-692-05234-1; 978-0-578-53831-0)* 215 W. Prospect St., Angola, IN 46703 USA Tel 260-665-1988
E-mail: drawingsmiles@yahoo.com
Web site: www.drawingsmiles.com.

Drawn & Quarterly Pubns. (CAN) *(978-0-9696701; 978-1-896597; 978-1-894937; 978-1-897299; 978-1-77046)* *Dist. by* **Macmillan.**

DrDryland.Com, LLC, *(978-0-9766490)* P.O. Box 1281, Ashland, OR 97520 USA
Web site: http://www.DrDryland.Com.

Dream A World *Imprint of* **BrassHeart Music**

Dream Bee Pubns., *(978-0-9661572)* 3325 C 1/2 Rd., Palisade, CO 81526 USA Tel 970-434-7501
E-mail: bee@dreambee.com
Web site: http://www.dreambee.com
Dist(s): **Bks. West**
Partners/West Book Distributors.

Dream Big Publishing, *(978-0-692-63592-6)* 2625 Pk. Avenue, Unit 10-H, Bridgeport, CT 06604 USA Tel 207-317-6099
E-mail: tasha@socialmedia22.com
Web site: www.achievebigger.com.

Dream Big Toy Co., *(978-1-940731)* 249 Merton Ave., Alen Ellyn, IL 60137 USA Tel 877-351-1031
E-mail: jnorgaard@dreambigtoycompany.com
Dist(s): **MyiLibrary.**

Dream Creek Pr., *(978-0-9771515)* 401 Taylor St., Ashland, OR 97520 USA
E-mail: bethart@mind.net
Web site: http://www.bbcreativecards.com.

Dream Dance Pubns., *(978-0-9769192; 978-0-692-96655-6)* 375 Kirkland Ave, Kirkland, WA 98033 USA Tel 425-246-7829
E-mail: briggs870@msn.com.

Dream Factory Bks., *(978-0-9701195)* Orders Addr.: P.O. Box 874, Enumclaw, WA 98022 USA (SAN 253-2611) Tel 360-663-0508; Fax: 360-825-7952; Toll Free Fax: 877-377-7030; Edit Addr.: 58402 114th St., E., Enumclaw, WA 98022-7305 USA
E-mail: sensel@earthlink.net
Web site: http://dreamfactorybooks.com.

Dream Faith Productions, LLC, *(978-0-578-49736-5)* 1303 Emerson Ave. SE, Cairo, GA 39828 USA Tel 404-808-8175
E-mail: tdreamfaith@gmail.com.

Dream, Feral LLC, *(978-0-9835970; 978-1-63820)*
Web site: www.feraldream.com.

Dream Fetchers, *(978-0-578-22846-4; 978-0-578-27068-5)* 8192 Sandcove Cir., 106, Huntington Beach, CA 92646 USA.

Dream House Pr., *(978-0-9671555)* 2714 Ophelia Ct., San Jose, CA 95122 USA Tel 408-274-4574; Fax: 408-274-0786; Toll Free: 877-274-4574
E-mail: mr_art@prodigy.net; dreamhousepress@yahoo.com
Dist(s): **Brodart Co.**
Midwest Library Service
Milligan News Co., Inc.
Partners/West Book Distributors
Yankee Bk. Peddler, Inc.

Dream Image Pr., LLC, *(978-0-9744812)* P.O. Box 454, Northbrook, IL 60065-0454 USA Tel 847-480-8998
E-mail: drashley@dreamimagepress.com
Dist(s): **Follett School Solutions.**

Dream In Magic Publishing, *(978-0-692-87384-7; 978-0-692-10805-5; 978-0-578-51771-1; 978-0-578-60493-0; 978-1-7352093)* 311 Main St, Panhandle, TX 79068 USA Tel 806-681-3723
E-mail: ddc6505@sbcglobal.net; ddc6505@sbcglobal.net; ddc6505@sbcglobal.net
Dist(s): **CreateSpace Independent Publishing Platform.**

Dream Journey Kids Publishing, *(978-1-7350721)* 201 E. 5TH St. STE 1200, Sheridan, WY 82801 USA Tel 917-983-9397
E-mail: dreamtowerllc@gmail.com
Web site: www.dreamjourneykidspublishing.com.

Dream Mastery, *(978-1-7330327)* 30 Ehrbar Ave., Mount Veron, NY 10552 USA Tel 914-619-8867
E-mail: dors7@msn.com.

Dream On Pubns., *(978-0-9761151)* Orders Addr.: P.O. Box 190265, Fort Lauderdale, FL 33319 USA (SAN 256-2057)
E-mail: books@dreamonpublications.com.

Dream Publications, I, Incorporated *See* **BOOKGEMSFORKIDS**

Dream Ridge Pr., *(978-0-9792084)* P.O. Box 625, Aurelia, IA 51005 USA Tel 712-660-8409
E-mail: rainbowfarm2006@yahoo.com; tpeiffer67@yahoo.com
Web site: http://www.lulu.com/trishacp; http://www.rainbowfarmbooks.com; http://www.authorsden.com/trishacp
Dist(s): **Lulu Pr., Inc.**

Dream Scape Publishing, LLC, *(978-0-9795519; 978-0-615-13650-9)* 805 Dunwood Ct., Chesapeake, VA 23322 USA Tel 757-717-2734
E-mail: dreamscape2@cox.net.

Dream Secret Inc., The, *(978-0-615-18103-5)* P.O. Box 2012, Sandy, UT 84091 USA Tel 801-518-7770
E-mail: lscread@yahoo.com.

Dream Ship Publishing Co., *(978-0-9729155)* 1512 River Rock Trace, Woodstock, GA 30188 USA
E-mail: info@dreamshipbooks.com.

Dream Star Productions, *(978-0-9772027)* Orbisson Sq. 4306 S. Peoria Ave., Ste 705, Tulsa, OK 74105-3922 USA Tel 918-630-7580; Fax: 918-749-1717
Web site: http://www.kbaustin.com.

Dream Weaver Ministries, Inc., *(978-0-9800259)* Pmb#123 1631 Rock Springs Rd., Apopka, FL 32712-2229 USA (SAN 855-0239) Toll Free: 888-397-7772.

Dream Workshop Publishing Co., LLC, The, *(978-0-9786940)* Orders Addr.: 4421 Bachelor Creek Rd., Asheboro, NC 27205 USA (SAN 851-3635) Tel 336-879-8108
E-mail: info@dreamworkshoppub.com; publisher@dreamworkshoppub.com
Web site: http://www.dreamworkshoppub.com; http://www.spenceraliens.com.

Dream Yard Pr., *(978-0-615-72969-5)* 1085 Washington Ave., Bronx, NY 10456 USA Tel 718-588-8007; Fax: 718-588-8310
E-mail: neilwald@aol.com
Web site: dreamyard.com; neilwaldman.com.

Dream&Achieve Bks., *(978-0-9859298)* 2609 W. 84th Pl., Merrillville, IN 46410 USA Tel 219-218-5145
Web site: www.weenzcat.com.

Dreambridge, *(978-0-692-10136-0; 978-0-692-10397-5; 979-8-9876843)* 927 Bellview Ave. No. 1, Ashland, OR 97520 USA Tel 541-482-8954
E-mail: angel@thedreambridge.com
Dist(s): **Ingram Content Group.**

Dreamcatcher Bks., *(978-0-9848484)* 892 Jensen Ln., Windsor, CA 95492 USA Tel 707-292-0272 Do not confuse with Dreamcatcher Books in Las Vegas, NM
E-mail: alvarezgang@yahoo.com
Web site: http://www.jenniferlynnalvarez.com/.

Dream-Catcher Pubns., *(978-0-9752878)* 22265 Petersburg, Eastpointe, MI 48021 USA.

DreamDog Pr., *(978-0-9666199)* 2308 Mount Vernon Ave., Alexandria, VA 22301-1328 USA
E-mail: rainey@dreamdog.com
Web site: http://www.dreamdog.com.

DreamerLand, *(978-0-9763250)* Orders Addr.: 1018 3rd St., Hermosa Beach, CA 90254 USA Tel 310-406-9371
E-mail: christo@dreamerland.com; info@dreamerland.com
Web site: http://www.Dreamerland.com
Dist(s): **Diamond Bk. Distributors.**

DreamHse. Publishing Inc.,

Dreaming Big Pubns., *(978-0-692-67563-2; 978-0-692-70106-5; 978-0-692-74058-3; 978-1-947381)* 102 First E. St, Sumrall, MS 39482 USA Tel 601-394-8813
Dist(s): **CreateSpace Independent Publishing Platform.**

Dreaming World Bks., *(978-0-615-96020-3; 978-0-615-99045-3; 978-0-692-22696-4; 978-0-692-23006-0; 978-0-692-26821-6; 978-0-692-28839-9; 978-0-692-56077-8; 978-0-692-61841-7; 978-1-948662)* 2409 35th Ave, Rock Island, IL 61201 USA Tel 309-721-2298
Dist(s): **CreateSpace Independent Publishing Platform.**

DreamLand Mediaworks LLC, *(978-0-9884657)* 3712 Lake Catherine Dr., Harvey, LA 70058 USA Tel 504-756-5589; Fax: 504-366-2606
E-mail: Jacqueline_Buffinet@yahoo.com.

Dreams 2 Wings LLC, *(978-0-9797781)* 100 N. 72nd Ave., Wausau, WI 54401 USA Tel 715-842-1133; Fax: 715-842-1155
E-mail: fred@lanepatents.com.

Dreams Due Media Group, Inc., *(978-0-9789202)* P.O. Box 1018, Firestone, CO 80520 USA Tel 303-241-3155 Toll Free: 877-462-1710
Web site: http://www.dreamsdue.com.

Dreams of Dragons, *(978-0-578-12149-9; 978-0-615-97831-4)* P.O. Box 312, Malden, MO 63863 USA Tel 573-576-7435
E-mail: drwilliamembry@yahoo.com
Web site: http://www.drakoandrawr.com.

Dreamscape, LLC *See* **Dreamscape Media, LLC**

Dreamscape Media, LLC, *(978-0-9745563; 978-0-9747118; 978-0-9760996; 978-0-9761981; 978-0-9771510; 978-0-9772338; 978-0-9774680; 978-0-9776262; 978-0-9777098; 978-1-933938; 978-1-61120; 978-1-62406; 978-1-62923; 978-1-63379; 978-1-68141; 978-1-68262; 978-1-5200; 978-1-9749; 978-1-6905; 978-1-6620; 978-1-6665; 978-1-6666) Orders Addr.: 1417 Timberwolf Dr., Holland, OH 43538 USA Tel 419-867-6965*
E-mail: kruiz@dreamscapeab.com; molah@dreamscapeab.com
Web site: http://www.dreamscapeab.com
Dist(s): **Findaway World, LLC**
Follett School Solutions
Publishers Group West (PGW)
Recorded Bks., Inc.

Dreamscape Publishing, *(978-0-615-51244-0; 978-0-615-55971-1; 978-0-615-69293-7; 978-0-692-53650-6; 978-0-692-57366-2; 978-0-9972394; 978-0-578-78607-0; 978-0-578-98855-9; 978-0-578-98856-6; 978-0-578-98858-0; 978-0-578-98859-7; 978-0-578-98860-3; 978-0-578-36395-0; 979-8-218-03879-3; 979-8-218-07503-3; 979-8-218-12208-9; 979-8-218-22132-4; 979-8-218-22133-1; 979-8-218-22134-8; 979-8-218-22135-5; 979-8-218-22136-2) 5696 NW 39th Ave., Boca Raton, FL 33496 USA Tel 410-218-7233 Do not confuse with DreamScape Publishing in San Francisco, CA*
E-mail: michelle@madow.com
Web site: www.michellemadow.com
Dist(s): **CreateSpace Independent Publishing Platform.**

Dreamschooner Pr., *(978-0-9899128)* 15 Beacon St., Natick, MA 01760 USA Tel 773-368-4386
E-mail: rfelty@gmail.com
Web site: dreamschoonerpress.com.

Dreamspinner Pr., *(978-0-9795048; 978-0-9801018; 978-0-9815084; 978-0-9817372; 978-1-935192; 978-1-61581; 978-1-61372; 978-1-62380; 978-1-62798; 978-1-63216; 978-1-63476; 978-1-63477; 978-1-63533; 978-1-64080; 978-1-64108; 978-1-64405)*; *Imprints*: Harmony Ink Press (HarmonyInk); DSP Publications (DSPPubns)
E-mail: contact@dreamspinnerpress.com
Web site: http://www.dreamspinnerpress.com
Dist(s): **INscribe Digital**
Independent Pubs. Group.

Dreamstreet Studios, Inc. (A Div. of DSMV Industries, Inc.), *(978-0-9892295)* 1800 Grand Ave., Nashville, TN 37212 USA Tel 615-321-9029
E-mail: songmerch@aol.com.

Dreamtime Publishing, *(978-0-9741726)* P.O. Box 834, Tahlequah, OK 74465 USA Tel 918-456-8639.

DREAMTITLE PUBLISHING LLC, *(978-0-615-74249-6; 978-0-615-78551-6; 978-0-692-41154-4; 978-0-692-55532-3; 978-0-692-14674-3; 978-0-578-33555-1; 979-8-218-18700-2)* 1321 S. CLOVERDALE AVE, LOS ANGELES, CA 90019 USA Tel 323-528-7495
E-mail: Bettykbynum@gmail.com
Web site: www.theimagirlcollection.com
Dist(s): **Independent Pubs. Group**
Midpoint Trade Bks., Inc.

Dreamtower Kids Publishing *See* **Dream Journey Kids Publishing**

Dreamwand, *(978-0-615-32313-8; 978-0-9913715)* 715 N. Croft Ave., Los Angeles, CA 90069-5303 USA Tel 323-424-4095
E-mail: dreamwandbooks@yahoo.com; theafflictedgirls@dreamwand.net
Web site: http://www.theafflictedgirls.com.

DreamWorks Animation Pr., *(978-1-941341; 978-1-943452)* 1000 Flower St., Glendale, CA 91201 USA Tel 818-695-3997
E-mail: samantha.suchland@dreamworks.com.

Dreighton Pubns., *(978-0-9981870)* 2645 Kingston rd, Leonard, MI 48367 USA Tel 810-429-0734
E-mail: Jpelkey@residentialhomehealth.com.

Dreistadt, Jessica R., *(978-0-578-02239-0)* 1700 Sullivan Trail, No. 311, Easton, PA 18040 USA
Dist(s): **Lulu Pr., Inc.**

Drenttel, William Editions *See* **Winterhouse Editions**

Dressler, Avi, *(978-0-9744309)* 35 Old Brick Rd., East Hills, NY 11577-1816 USA.

Dressler, Craig, *(978-0-9778247)* 5341 NE Webster Ct., Portland, OR 97218 USA Tel 503-281-4214.

Drew Squared Publishing, *(978-0-578-21799-4)* 12232 Oakmont Cir., Knoxville, TN 37934 USA.

Dries, John D., *(978-0-615-62480-8; 978-0-578-98961-7; 978-0-578-32039-7)* 7251 W. N. Ave., Wauwatosa, WI 53213 USA Tel 414-453-9866; Fax: 414-453-6612
Dist(s): **CreateSpace Independent Publishing Platform.**

Driftwood Pr., *(978-0-9638803)* Orders Addr.: P.O. Box 284, Yachats, OR 97498 USA; Edit Addr.: 62 Gender Dr., Yachats, OR 97498 USA Tel 541-547-3484
E-mail: njguni@clubinernet.fr.

Drinian Pr., LLC, *(978-0-9785165; 978-0-9820609; 978-0-9833069; 978-1-941929)* Orders Addr.: P.O. Box 63, Huron, OH 44839 USA
E-mail: drinianpress@frontier.com
Web site: http://drinianpress.com; http://smithwrite.net.

Drinking Gourd Pr., *(978-0-578-13425-3; 978-0-578-13426-0)* 414 Jefferson Ave., Apt. 1, Brooklyn, NY 11221 USA.

Drivel & Drool *Imprint of* **Dramatic Ellipsis**

Driving Vision, Inc., *(978-0-9766329)* 2117 S. Ventura Dr., Tempe, AZ 85282 USA
Web site: http://www.drivingvision.com.

DrMaster Pubns. Inc., *(978-1-59796)* 48531 Warm Springs Blvd., Suite 408, Fremont, CA 94539 USA Tel 510-687-1388 (phone/fax)
Web site: http://www.drmasterpublications.com
Dist(s): **Diamond Comic Distributors, Inc.**
Diamond Bk. Distributors.

Droemersche Verlagsanstalt Th. Knaur Nachf. - GmbH & Co. (DEU) *(978-3-426) Dist. by* **Distribks Inc.**

Drollery Pr., *(978-0-940920)* 1524 Benton St., Alameda, CA 94501-2420 USA (SAN 223-1808) Tel 510-521-4087.

Dronen, Christina, *(978-0-9997520)* 10705 Northgate St, Culver City, CA 90230 USA Tel 310-710-7614
E-mail: c3stina@gmail.com
Web site: christinadronen.com.

Droogle Inc., *(978-0-578-19933-7; 978-0-692-19024-1; 978-0-578-43477-3; 978-0-578-49174-5; 978-1-7332045)* 3513 Oates Dr., Raleigh, NC 27604 USA
Web site: www.droogledots.com.

DRS Publishing LLC, *(978-0-9852089)* 505 N. Link Rd., Johns Creek, GA 30022 USA Tel 770-475-1772
E-mail: drspubl363@aol.com; drspubl363@aol.com; drspubl@mindspring.com.

DRT Pr., *(978-1-933084)* Orders Addr.: P.O. Box 427, Pittsboro, NC 27312 USA Tel 919-360-7073; Fax: 866-562-5040; Edit Addr.: 395 Bill Thomas Rd., Moncure, NC 27559 USA
E-mail: editorial@drtpress.com
Web site: http://www.drtpress.com
Dist(s): **BWI**
Bk. Hse., The
Brodart Co.
Follett School Solutions
Quality Bks., Inc.

Drucker, Samantha Diener, *(978-0-692-92225-5)* 6070 Oak Bluff Way, Lake Worth, FL 33467 USA Tel 561-568-6430
E-mail: diener.samantha@gmail.com
Dist(s): **CreateSpace Independent Publishing Platform.**

Drummond Publishing Group, The, *(978-0-9755080; 978-1-59763)* 4 Collins Ave., Plymouth, MA 02360-4809 USA Do not confuse with Rec#s 786442, 791375, 1194043
E-mail: f_allen@drummondpub.com
Web site: http://www.drummondpub.com.

Drumstick Media, *(978-0-9764791)* Div. of Old Goats, Inc., 5805 Hwy. 93 S., Whitefish, MT 59937 USA Tel 406-862-8938; Fax: 406-862-8936; Toll Free: 800-404-8279
E-mail: robert@drumstickmedia.com; james@drumstickmedia.com
Web site: http://www.baxterowengraham.com; http://www.drumstickmedia.com.

Drunk Duck Comics, *(978-0-9748960)* P.O. Box 869, Pittston, PA 18640 USA
E-mail: rubbermallet@verizon.net; arrkelaan@hotmail.com
Web site: http://www.drunkduck.com.

Dry Climate Press *See* **Dry Climate Studios**

Dry Climate Studios, *(978-0-9856429; 978-0-9906858; 978-0-9908195; 978-1-942402)* 5119 NE 42nd St., Seattle, WA 98105 USA Tel 206-877-2093
Web site: www.dryclimatestudios.com
Dist(s): **Baker & Taylor Publisher Services (BTPS)**
Publishers Group West (PGW).

Dry Creek Mill, *(978-1-7369208)* 843 S Breezy Way, Post Falls, ID 83854 USA Tel 503-207-5635
E-mail: skhofhiens@yahoo.com
Web site: krhofhiens.com.

Dry, Paul Bks., Inc., *(978-0-9664913; 978-0-9679675; 978-1-58988)* 1616 Walnut St. Ste. 808, Philadelphia, PA 19103-5308 USA
E-mail: pdb@pauldrybooks.com
Web site: http://www.pauldrybooks.com
Dist(s): **Consortium Bk. Sales & Distribution.**

Dryad Pr., *(978-0-931848; 978-1-928755)* P.O. Box 11233, Takoma Park, MD 20913 USA (SAN 206-197X) Tel 301-891-3729
E-mail: dryadpress@yahoo.com
Web site: http://www.dryadpress.com
Dist(s): **SPD-Small Pr. Distribution.**

Publisher Name Index

Dryden Publishing, *(978-0-9644370; 978-1-929204)* P.O. Box 482, Dryden, WA 98821-0432 USA
E-mail: dryden@csiconnect.com.

Dryland, David *See* **DrDryland.Com, LLC**

DSA Publishing & Design, Inc., *(978-0-9774451; 978-0-9818229; 978-0-9848057)* 6900 Edgewater Dr., Mckinney, TX 75070 USA
Web site: http://www.dsapubs.com
Dist(s): **Chicago Distribution Ctr.**

DSP Pubns. *Imprint of* **Dreamspinner Pr.**

DTA Bks., *(978-0-578-09856-2)* 37 Evergreen Ave., Nutley, NJ 07110 USA
E-mail: dta@msn.com.

DTaylor Bks., *(978-0-615-36081-2)* 415 Armour Dr., Apt. 12204, Atlanta, GA 30324 USA Tel 404-838-9678.

DTC Press *See* **Sweetbeet Bks.**

DTJ, LLC, *(978-0-9765731)* P.O. Box 635, Sequim, WA 98382 USA.

D-Tower Pubns., *(978-0-9770386)* 8028 Pine St., Ethel, LA 70730-3853 USA Tel 225-335-0802
E-mail: swbloopers@yahoo.com.

Dube, Tory, *(978-0-9886193)* 3168 41st St. No. 1f, Astoria, NY 11103 USA Tel 603-781-1440
E-mail: torydube@gmail.com
Web site: www.lovelythankyou.com.

Dubois, Ricardo S., *(978-0-615-15411-4; 978-0-615-15412-1; 978-0-615-15413-8; 978-0-615-16958-3; 978-0-615-17232-3; 978-0-615-18220-9; 978-0-615-19724-1)* 16015 Creekround Dr., Praireville, LA 70769 USA Tel 225-802-6001
E-mail: craftycajun@yahoo.com
Dist(s): **Lulu Pr., Inc.**

Duckett, Brenda, *(978-0-615-17289-7)* 27 Millswood Dr., Clarkville, TN 37042 USA Tel 931-906-8649
E-mail: bduckett1@bellsouth.net
Dist(s): **Lulu Pr., Inc.**

Duckpond Publishing, Inc., *(978-0-9720350)* 130 Hillside Ln., Roswell, GA 30076 USA Tel 770-649-9947; Fax: 770-594-8058
E-mail: theducks@duckpondpublishing.com
Web site: http://www.duckpondpublishing.com.

Dudek, Ilene, *(978-0-692-89507-8; 978-0-692-94660-2; 978-0-692-04481-0; 978-0-578-40624-4; 978-0-578-53171-7; 978-0-578-70642-9)* 36 Rhoda Ave., Nutley, NJ 07110 USA Tel 201-390-4381
E-mail: Ilene_Catania@Yahoo.com
Web site: www.littleantstories.com.

Dudek, Mike, *(978-0-9740380; 978-0-9968182)* 505 Duwell St., Johnston, PA 15906 USA Tel 814-536-1500; Fax: 814-536-8952
E-mail: mike@dudekins.com; jetset15906@yahoo.com
Web site: www.rascaljokes.com.

Dudley, Joshua Patrick, *(978-0-615-16396-3; 978-0-615-18871-3)* 4 Heritage Village Dr., Unit 102, Nashua, NH 03062 USA Tel 603-459-9687
E-mail: admin@joshuapatrickdudley.com; lostinozbook@yahoo.com
Web site: http://www.ostinozbook.com; http://www.lostinozbook.com
Dist(s): **Lulu Pr., Inc.**

DUENDE Bks., *(978-0-9777973; 978-0-615-14984-4; 978-0-615-15099-4)* Div. of DeCo Communications, 13900 Fiji Way, Apt. 306, Marina del Rey, CA 90292 USA Tel 310-486-0983
E-mail: denizr@verizon.net
Web site: http://www.duendebooks.blogspot.com
Dist(s): **Lulu Pr., Inc.**

Duffy, Rose Creations, *(978-1-7339434)* 641 Saratoga St. S., St. Paul, MN 55116 USA Tel 651-434-7269
E-mail: One_Rosebud@msn.com
Web site: www.RoseDuffyCreations.com.

†Dufour Editions, Inc., *(978-0-8023)* Orders Addr.: P.O. Box 7, Chester Springs, PA 19425-0007 USA (SAN 201-341X) Tel 610-458-5005; Fax: 610-458-7103; Toll Free: 800-869-5677
E-mail: info@dufoureditions.com
Web site: http://www.dufoureditions.com
Dist(s): **Casemate Pubs. & Bk. Distributors, LLC**; *CIP.*

Dugan, Renee, *(978-0-692-19913-6; 978-0-578-43407-0; 978-1-7339255; 978-1-958927)* P.O. Box 1265, Martinsville, IN 46151 USA Tel 765-346-1927
E-mail: renee.s.dugan@gmail.com.

Duke & Oscar, *(978-0-692-04831-3)* 1521 Boyd Pointe Way, Vienna, VA 22182 USA Tel 408-223-5177
E-mail: czeffy@gmail.com.

Duke Publishing & Software Corp., *(978-0-9745406)* P.O. Box 3429, Los Altos, CA 94024 USA Tel 408-245-3853; Fax: 408-245-9289
E-mail: info@aboutthekids.org
Web site: http://www.aboutthekids.org.

†Duke Univ. Pr., *(978-0-8223; 978-1-4780)* P.O. Box 90660, Durham, NC 27708-0660 USA (SAN 201-3436) Tel 919-687-3600; Fax: 919-688-4574; 905 W. Main S., Ste.18B, Durham, NC 27701 Tel 919-687-3600; Fax: 919-688-4574; Toll Free: 888-651-0122
E-mail: orders@dukepress.edu; subscriptions@dukepress.edu; hlw@dukeupress.edu
Web site: http://www.dukeupress.edu
Dist(s): **JSTOR**
MyiLibrary
ebrary, Inc.; *CIP.*

Dukes World, Inc., *(978-0-9664506)* P.O. Box 85, Yonkers, NY 10704 USA Tel 917-403-7661
E-mail: dukesworldinc@aol.com
Web site: http://www.chillstreetgang.com.

Dulany, Joseph P., *(978-0-9708830)* 6200 Oregon Ave NW Apt. 236, Washington, DC 20015-1529 USA
E-mail: josephdulany@msn.com
Web site: http://www.onceasoldier.com.

Duling Designs, *(978-0-9743445)* P.O. Box 1996, Marco Island, FL 34146-1996 USA
E-mail: jsduling87@aol.com.

†Dumbarton Oaks, *(978-0-88402)* Orders Addr.: c/o Hopkins Fulfillment Services, P.O. Box 50370, Baltimore, MD 21211-4370 USA (SAN 665-6870) Tel 410-516-6965; Fax: 410-516-6998; Toll Free: 800-537-5487; Edit Addr.: 1703 32nd St., NW, Washington, DC 20007 USA (SAN 293-2547) Tel 202-777-0092; Fax: 202-298-8407
E-mail: doaksbooks@doaks.org
Web site: http://www.doaks.org/publications.html
Dist(s): **Harvard Univ. Pr.**; *CIP.*

Dume Publishing *See* **Corman Productions**

Dumplinz Bk. Publishing, *(978-0-615-80362-3; 978-0-9964684)* 2305 Holland Ave. Apt. 1-G, Bronx, NY 10467 USA Tel 718-944-2414
E-mail: isreba1949@optonline.net.

Dunamis Development, *(978-0-9767066)* 3972-J Barranca Pkwy., Suite 115, Irvine, CA 92606 USA Tel 949-263-0063.

Dunbar, Camesha, *(978-1-7371588)* 925E 229th, Bronx, NY 10466 USA Tel 917-615-9815
E-mail: cameshadunbar@yahoo.com.

Dundurn Pr. (CAN) *(978-0-88762; 978-0-88882; 978-0-88924; 978-0-919028; 978-0-919670; 978-0-9690454; 978-1-55002; 978-1-55488; 978-1-4597; 978-1-77070) Dist. by* **PerseuPGW.**

Dundurn Pr. (CAN) *(978-0-88762; 978-0-88882; 978-0-88924; 978-0-919028; 978-0-919670; 978-0-9690454; 978-1-55002; 978-1-55488; 978-1-4597; 978-1-77070) Dist. by* **IngramPubServ.**

Dungeon Mapper, LLC, *(978-0-9903366; 978-1-944592)* P.O. Box 8074, Chandler, AZ 85246 USA Tel 480-369-2918
E-mail: bluemoonskingdom@yahoo.com
Web site: dungeonmapper.com.

Dunlop, Edward *See* **Cross & Crown Publishing**

Dunn, Hunter, *(978-0-9761732)* 410 Old Spring Rd., Danville, VA 24540-5206 USA.

Dunn, Michael *See* **Big Secret, The**

Dunn, Stephen Daingerfield, *(978-0-9985428; 978-0-578-76039-1)* 8828 McCraw Dr., Dallas, TX 75209 USA Tel 214-676-5461
E-mail: dunn7rite@sbcglobal.net.

Dunne, Thomas Bks. *Imprint of* **St. Martin's Pr.**

Dunnigan, Stefanie and Tina Traina, *(978-0-9962796)* 155 Evergreen Rd., Ramsey, NJ 07446 USA Tel 201-452-4190
E-mail: savvyscribbiers@gmail.com
Web site: www.traveltailsbooks.com.

Dunrobin Publishing, *(978-0-9832363; 978-0-9884613; 978-0-9984000; 978-1-949718)* 221 Pleasant Grove Ave, Ballwin, MO 63011-3319 USA Tel 314-913-0674
E-mail: info@dunrobin.us
Web site: www.dunrobin.us
Dist(s): **Lulu Pr., Inc.**

Dunton Publishing, *(978-0-615-55848-6; 978-0-615-56429-6; 978-0-615-76368-2; 978-0-615-76615-7; 978-0-692-48457-9; 978-0-692-48492-0; 978-0-692-54319-1; 978-0-692-73280-9; 978-0-692-06924-0; 978-0-578-40647-3; 978-0-578-78536-3)* P.O. Box 4, New York, NY 10023 USA Tel 212-799-7402
Web site: duntonpublishing.com
Dist(s): **CreateSpace Independent Publishing Platform.**

Duo Pr. LLC, *(978-0-9796213; 978-0-9825295; 978-0-9838121; 978-1-938093; 978-1-946064; 978-1-947458; 978-1-950500; 978-1-955834)* 265 Stanmore Rd., Baltimore, MD 21212 USA
E-mail: info@duopressbooks.com
Web site: http://www.duopressbooks.com
Dist(s): **MyiLibrary**
ebrary, Inc.

Duplicates Printing, *(978-0-9749953)* Orders Addr.: P.O. Box 2398, Pawleys Island, SC 29585 USA Tel 843-237-3998; Edit Addr.: 14329 Ocean Hwy. Unit 115, Pawleys Isl, SC 29585-4816 USA
E-mail: slingshot@sc.rr.com.

Dupuis North Publishing, *(978-0-9749199)* 76 N. Church St., Clayton, GA 30525 USA Tel 828-524-9520; Fax: 828-349-1945.

Duracell & the National Ctr. for Missing & Exploited Children (NCMEC), *(978-0-9795307)* 415 Nadison Ave., New York, NY 10018 USA Tel 212-613-4904.

duran, oscar, *(978-0-615-72225-2; 978-0-9886109)* 6204 sw 18th St, Miramar, FL 33023 USA Tel 954-986-4082; Fax: 954-986-4082
Dist(s): **CreateSpace Independent Publishing Platform.**

Durban House Press, Incorporated *See* **Fireside Pr., Inc.**

Durland Alternatives Library, *(978-0-9740184)* 127 Anabel Taylor Hall, Ithaca, NY 14853-1001 USA Tel 607-255-6486; Fax: 607-255-9985
E-mail: alt-lib@cornell.edu
Web site: http://www.alternativeslibrary.org.

Durst, Sanford J., *(978-0-915262; 978-0-942666; 978-1-886720)* 106 Woodcleft Ave., Freeport, NY 11520 USA (SAN 211-6987) Tel 516-867-3333; Fax: 516-867-3397
E-mail: sjdbooks@verizon.net.

Dust Bunny Games LLC, *(978-0-9747833)* Orders Addr.: 3744 Mistflower Ln., Naperville, IL 60564-5921 USA Tel 630-244-0335; Fax: 630-922-6995; Edit Addr.: 3744 Mistflower Ln., Naperville, IL 60564-5921 USA
E-mail: info@dustbunnygames.com
Web site: http://www.dustbunnygames.com.

DuSum Publishing, LLC, *(978-0-9911276; 978-0-9997044; 978-1-7329780; 978-1-960031)* 549 5th St. NW, Hickory, NC 28601 USA Tel 828-328-5955
E-mail: rdonepudi1969@gmail.com.

Duthaluru, Vidhya, *(978-0-9797657)* 247 Levinberg Ln., Wayne, NJ 07470 USA.

Dutton *Imprint of* **Penguin Publishing Group**

Dutton Books for Young Readers *Imprint of* **Penguin Young Readers Group**

Dutton Caliber *Imprint of* **Penguin Publishing Group**

Dutton Juvenile *Imprint of* **Penguin Publishing Group**

Dutton, Mary, *(978-0-692-90204-2)* 1408 Adams St., PORT TOWNSEND, WA 98368 USA Tel 360-344-2498
E-mail: mhdcashew@juno.com
Dist(s): **Ingram Content Group.**

Duval Publishing, *(978-0-9745637)* Orders Addr.: P.O. Box 4255, Key West, FL 33041 USA Toll Free: 800-355-8562; Edit Addr.: 3717 Eagle Ave., Key West, FL 33040 USA
Web site: http://www.southerncoastaldesigns.com.

DV Bks. *Imprint of* **Digital Vista, Inc.**

DVTVFilm, *(978-0-9678094)* 3 Temi Rd., Framingham, MA 01701 USA
E-mail: todd@dvtvfilm.com; info@themonkeykingsdaughter.com; todd@themonkeykingsdaughter.com
Web site: http://www.dvtvfilm.com; http://www.themonkeykingsdaughter.com.

Dwemhar Realms *See* **Dwemhar Realms**

Dwemhar Realms, *(978-1-7363707)* 4 Helen Ct, Long Branch, NJ 07755 USA Tel 409-502-7878
E-mail: authorjtwilliams@gmail.com
Web site: www.authorjtwilliams.com.

Dwight Buckner *See* **T&J Pubs.**

Dwitt Publishing, *(978-0-9741352)* 9249 17th St SE, Saint Cloud, MN 56304-9709 USA
E-mail: dickawit@aol.com
Web site: http://www.dwittpublishing.com.

DWJJR, *(978-1-7372005)* 18305 Sierra Wind Cove, Elgin, TX 78621 USA Tel 512-775-2139
E-mail: davidwjohns21@yahoo.com.

DWP, *(978-0-692-17974-1; 978-0-578-40120-1; 978-0-578-48090-9; 978-1-7330092)* 5070 SW 141st Ave., Beaverton, OR 97005 USA Tel 503-807-2012
E-mail: polanddw@comcast.net.

Dyeing Arts, *(978-0-9817244; 978-1-7357139)* 231 Mcallister Ave., Kentfield, CA 94904-1631 USA
E-mail: joytroyer@aol.com
Web site: http://www.DyeingArts.com.

Dyer, Rose *See* **Funnel Time Bks.**

Dykema Engineering, Incorporated *See* **Dykema Publishing Co.**

Dykema, Marjorie *See* **One Coin Publishing, LLC**

Dykema Publishing Co., *(978-0-9660705; 978-0-9701538)* Div. of Dykema Engineering, Inc., 3264 W. Normandy Ave., Roseburg, OR 97470 USA Tel 541-957-0259; Fax: 541-677-7146
E-mail: odykema@mcsi.net
Web site: http://www.oregonwriters.com.

Dykes, William R. III, *(978-0-9740987)* 317 Luchase Rd., Linden, VA 22642 USA.

Dykes, Woodrow, *(978-0-615-99769-8; 978-0-692-02493-5; 978-1-7350876)* 28 Bones Pl., Lexington, VA 24450 USA Tel 540-570-2570
E-mail: eafeinauer@gmail.com.

Dylanna Publishing, Inc., *(978-1-942268; 978-1-947243; 978-1-949651; 978-1-64790)* 423 S CREEK DR, OSPREY, FL 34229 USA
E-mail: juliegrady@comcast.net
Web site: www.creativecoloring.co.

Dynagraphix *Imprint of* **Elliott, Jane**

Dynamic Forces, Incorporated *See* **Dynamic Forces, Inc.**

Dynamic Forces, Inc., *(978-0-9749638; 978-1-933305; 978-1-60690; 978-1-5241)* 113 Gaither Dr., Ste. 205 Suite B, Mt. Laurel, NJ 08054 USA; *Imprints:* Dynamite Entertainment (Dyna Enter)
E-mail: marketing@dynamite.com
Web site: http://www.dynamicforces.com; http://www.dynamite.com
Dist(s): **Diamond Comic Distributors, Inc.**
Diamond Bk. Distributors.

Dynamic Publishing Co., Inc., *(978-0-9656808)* Orders Addr.: P.O. Box 120, Calumet City, IL 60409 USA Tel 708-868-0512; Fax: 708-868-0549; Toll Free: 800-884-1840 Do not confuse with Dynamic Publishing, Sugar Land, TX
E-mail: dpc123@ymail.com
Web site: http://www.DynamicPublishingCompany.com.

Dynamiq Press LLC *See* **Rustik Haws LLC**

Dynamite Entertainment *Imprint of* **Dynamic Forces, Inc.**

DynaStudy, Inc., *(978-0-9776270; 978-0-9777909; 978-1-933854; 978-1-935005)* 1401 Broadway St. Suite 100, Marble Falls, TX 78654 USA
E-mail: info@dynastudy.com
Web site: http://dynanotes.com.

Dynasty Publishing, Inc., *(978-0-9790444; 978-0-9793490)* P.O. Box 11997, Kansas City, MO 64138-0997 USA Do not confuse with Dynasty Publishing in Honolulu, HI
E-mail: info@dynastypublishinginc.com
Web site: http://www.dynastypublishinginc.com.

DysCovered Publishing *Imprint of* **Lawson, Tracy**

Dyson, Sarah, *(978-1-7334845; 978-1-962183)* P.O. Box 17253, Jonesboro, AR 72403 USA Tel 870-351-1015
E-mail: Sarah.mdyson@outlook.com.

DZ Publishing, LLC, *(978-0-9753660; 978-0-9889975)* 7360 Lincoln Dr., #2, Scottsdale, AZ 85258 USA Tel 949-922-7042
E-mail: szipp22@gmail.com
Web site: http://www.mycollegesuccess.com.

E & D Bks., Ltd., *(978-0-9794413)* P.O. Box 211, Ruby, NY 12475 USA (SAN 853-4314)
E-mail: info@buddyboobysbirthmark.com
Web site: http://www.buddyboobysbirthmark.com
Dist(s): **Beekman Bks., Inc.**

E & E Publishing, *(978-0-9719898; 978-0-9748933; 978-0-9791606; 978-0-9831499)* P.O. Box 3346, Omaha, NE 68103 USA Tel 402-578-2563 Do not confuse with E & E Publishing, Junction City, OR
E-mail: EveHeidiWrites@gmail.com.

E & H Publishing Co., Inc., *(978-0-9717295)* P.O. Box 4, Burkeville, VA 23922 USA
E-mail: greanes@earthlink.net.

EBP Latin America Group, Inc., *(978-1-56409)* 175 E. Delaware Pl. Apt. 8806, Chicago, IL 60611-7753 USA.

E B S C O Industries, Inc., *(978-0-913956; 978-1-888751)* Orders Addr.: P.O. Box 1943, Birmingham, AL 35201-1943 USA (SAN 201-3584) Tel 205-991-6600; Fax: 205-995-1636; Toll Free: 800-826-3024; Edit Addr.: 5724 Hwy. 280 E., Birmingham, AL 35242 USA
Web site: http://www.ebsco.com.

E C Jackson, *(978-0-9961812; 978-1-7329592)* P.O. Box 701886, Tulsa, OK 74170 USA Tel 918-493-5004
E-mail: christieok8@cox.net.

ECO Herpetological Pub. & Dist., *(978-0-9713197; 978-0-9767334; 978-0-9788979; 978-0-9832789; 978-0-9852936; 978-1-938850)* 4 Rattlesnake Canyon Rd., Rodeo, NM 88056 USA Tel 575-557-5757; Fax: 575-557-7575
E-mail: ecoorders@hotmail.com
Web site: http://www.reptileshirts.com
Dist(s): **BookBaby**
Serpent's Tale Natural History Bk. Distributors, Inc.
T-Rex Products.

EECI, Inc., *(978-0-9649379; 978-0-9722686; 978-1-933193)* 8055 W. Manchester Ave., 1st Flr., Playa Del Rey, CA 90293 USA
E-mail: rwoo@eecinternational.com.

E. F. S. Online Publishing, *(978-0-9701344)* Div. of E. F. S. Enterprises, Inc., 2844 Eighth Ave., Suite 6-E, New York, NY 10039 USA Tel 212-283-8899; Fax: 212-283-6280
E-mail: efsenterprises@hotmail.com
Web site: http://www.efs-enterprises.com.

E Innovative Ideas, *(978-0-9799540)* 800 SE 4th St., Suite 501, Fort Lauderdale, FL 33301 USA Tel 954-527-1070
E-mail: einnovate@aol.com.

E. J. Publishing, *(978-0-9764444; 978-0-9770303)* 4529 Hillcrest Rd., Birmingham, AL 35224-2818 USA Toll Free Fax: 866-864-6087; Toll Free: 866-864-6085
E-mail: elysia@ejpub.com
Web site: http://www.ejpub.com
Dist(s): **Baker & Taylor International**
CreateSpace Independent Publishing Platform.

EKS Publishing Co., *(978-0-939144)* 322 Castro St., Oakland, CA 94607-3028 USA (SAN 216-1281) Tel 510-251-9100; Fax: 510-251-9102; Toll Free: 877-743-2739
E-mail: orders@EKSpublishing.com
Web site: http://www.ekspublishing.com.

E M C Publishing *See* **EMC/Paradigm Publishing**

EMG Networks, *(978-1-56843)* Div. of Educational Management Group, 1 Lake St., No. 3B-47, Upper Saddle River, NJ 07458-1813 USA Tel 602-970-3250; Fax: 602-970-3460; Toll Free: 800-842-6791.

E M McIntyre, *(978-0-9988993)* 2125 S. 108th St., Omaha, NE 68144 USA Tel 402-393-3971; *Imprints:* Little Hound Publishing (MYD_M_LITTLE)
E-mail: redkingtrilogy@gmail.com.

E M Pubns., *(978-0-9749739; 978-0-9794331; 978-0-9893569; 978-0-9905099; 978-0-9997469)* Orders Addr.: P.O. Box 780900, Wichita, KS 67278-0900 USA
Web site: http://www.enloeministries.org.

ERIC Clearinghouse on Rural Education & Small Schls., *(978-1-880785)* Div. of Appalachia Educational Laboratory, Inc., Orders Addr.: P.O. Box 1348, Charleston, WV 25325-1348 USA Tel 304-347-0437; Fax: 304-347-0467; Toll Free: 800-624-9120; Edit Addr.: 1031 Quarrier St., Suite 610, Charleston, WV 25301 USA
E-mail: ericrc@ael.org
Web site: http://www.ael.org/eric.

ESP, Inc., *(978-0-8209)* Orders Addr.: P.O. Box 839, Tampa, FL 33601-0839 USA; Edit Addr.: 1212 N. 39th St., Suite 444, Tampa, FL 33605-5890 USA (SAN 241-497X) Do not confuse with E S P Inc., Woodlands, TX
E-mail: epublish@tampalay.rr.com
Web site: http://www.espbooks.com.

†ETC Pubns., *(978-0-88280)* 700 E. Vereda del Sur, Palm Springs, CA 92262 USA (SAN 124-8766) Tel 760-325-5352; Fax: 760-325-8841; Toll Free: 800-382-7869
E-mail: etcbooks@earthlink.net; *CIP.*

E T Nedder *Imprint of* **Paulist Pr.**

E3 Concepts LLC, *(978-0-9797375)* 3311 Mulberry Dr., Bloomington, IN 47401 USA Tel 812-360-7488; Fax: 888-876-5152
E-mail: chris.berry@linkedblocks.com
Web site: http://www.linkedblocks.com.

E3 Resources, *(978-1-933383)* 317 Main St., Suite 207, Franklin, TN 37064 USA (SAN 631-9076) Toll Free: 888-354-9411
Web site: http://www.e3resources.org.

Eager Minds Pr. *Imprint of* **Warehousing & Fulfillment Specialists, LLC (WFS, LLC)**

Eagle Bay Pr., *(978-0-692-39305-5; 978-0-692-42563-3; 978-0-692-54282-8; 978-0-692-73103-1; 978-0-692-73657-9; 978-0-692-83068-0; 978-0-578-84781-8; 978-0-578-32974-1; 979-8-218-04670-5; 979-8-218-23169-9)* P.O. Box 1391, Cannon Beach, OR 97110 USA Tel 425-239-5501
Dist(s): **CreateSpace Independent Publishing Platform.**

Eagle Bk. Bindery, *(978-0-9772304; 978-1-934333)* 2704 Camelot Ave., NW, Cedar Rapids, IA 52405 USA Tel 319-265-8210
E-mail: sales@eaglebookbindery.com
Web site: http://www.eaglebookbindery.com.

Eagle Creek Pubns., LLC, *(978-0-9769093)* P.O. Box 781166, Indianapolis, IN 46278 USA (SAN 257-3490) Tel 317-870-9902; Fax: 317-870-9904; Toll Free: 866-870-9903 Do not Confuse with Eagle Creek Publications in Prior Lake, MN
E-mail: ben@eaglecreekpubs.com
Web site: http://www.eaglecreekpubs.com.

Eagle Editions, Ltd., *(978-0-914144; 978-0-9660706; 978-0-9721060; 978-0-9761034; 978-0-9794035)* Orders Addr.: P.O. Box 580, Hamilton, MT 59840 USA Tel 406-363-5415; Fax: 406-375-9270; Toll Free: 800-255-1830; Edit Addr.: 752 Bobcat Ln., Hamilton, MT 59840 USA
E-mail: eagle@eagle-editions.com
Web site: http://www.eagle-editions.com
Dist(s): **Hachette Bk. Group**
MBI Distribution Services/Quayside Distribution.

agle Eye Consultancy (UK) Ltd, *(978-0-9996283)* 4 Regency Mews Tadcaster Rd., York, YO241LL GBR Tel 798-180-7467
E-mail: thejontyolivier@gmail.com
Web site: jontyolivier.com.

agle Eye Consultancy US, Inc. *See* **Eagle Eye Consultancy (UK) Ltd**

agle Publishing *See* **Majestic Eagle Publishing**

agle River Type & Graphics *See* **Northbooks**

agle Trail Pr., *(978-0-9851876; 978-0-9892807; 978-0-9974267)* P.O. Box 3671, Parker, CO 80134 USA Tel 720-295-2208
E-mail: info@EagleTrailPress.com.

agle Tree Pr., *(978-0-9792499)* Div. of M. Kay Howell, P.O. Box 1060, Rainier, OR 97048-1060 USA (SAN 852-8950)
Web site: http://fairyempire.biz.

Eaglebrook Press *See* **Oldcastle Publishing**

Eaglehouse, Carolyn, *(978-0-9773263)* 521 E. Uwchian Ave., Chester Springs, PA 19425 USA
Web site: http://www.chesterspringscreamery.com.

Eaglemont Pr., *(978-0-9662257; 978-0-9748411; 978-1-60040)* 13228 NE 20th St. Ste. 300, Bellevue, WA 98005-2049 USA (SAN 254-2102) Toll Free: 877-590-9744
E-mail: info@eaglemontpress.com
Web site: http://www.eaglemontpress.com.

Eaglemoss Publications Ltd (GBR) *(978-0-947837; 978-1-85167; 978-1-85629; 978-1-85875) Dist. by* **Peng Rand Hse.**

Eagle's Wings Educational Materials, *(978-1-931292)* P.O. Box 502, Duncan, OK 73534 USA Tel 580-252-1555 (phone/fax)
E-mail: info@EaglesWingsEd.com
Web site: http://www.EaglesWingsEd.com.

Eaglesquest Publishing, *(978-0-9745860)* LTN Enterprises, 11852 Shady Acres Ct., Riverton, UT 84065 USA
E-mail: lestertn@earthlink.net
Web site: http://www.thepaddedgirdle.com; http://www.findingyour new normal.com.

Eakin Pr. *Imprint of* **Eakin Pr.**

†Eakin Pr., *(978-0-89015; 978-1-57168; 978-0-9789150; 978-1-934645; 978-1-935632)* Div. of Sunbelt Media, P.O. Box 90159, Austin, TX 78709-0159 USA (SAN 207-3633) Tel 254-235-6161; Fax: 254-235-6230; Toll Free: 800-880-8642; *Imprints:* Eakin Press (Eakin Pr); Nortex Press (Nortex Pr)
E-mail: sales@eakinpress.com; kris@eakinpress.com
Web site: http://www.eakinpress.com
Dist(s): **Children's Plus, Inc.**
Follett School Solutions
Hervey's Booklink & Cookbook Warehouse
Twentieth Century Christian Bks.
Wolverine Distributing, Inc.; *CIP.*

Eardley Pubns., *(978-0-937630)* Div. of Elizabeth Claire, Inc., Orders Addr.: 2100 Mccomas Way Suite 607, Virginia Beach, VA 23456 USA (SAN 215-6377) Tel 757-430-4308; Fax: 757-430-4309; Toll Free: 888-296-1090
E-mail: eceardley@aol.com
Web site: http://www.elizabethclaire.com
Dist(s): **BookLink, Inc.**
Delta Systems Company, Inc.

Early Encyclopedias *Imprint of* **ABDO Publishing Co.**

Early Foundations Pubs., *(978-0-9670728; 978-0-9742131; 978-1-936215)* Orders Addr.: 8794 W. S. Ave., Schoolcraft, MI 49087 USA Tel 269-372-4517
E-mail: orders@efpublishers.org
Web site: http://www.efpublishers.org.

Early Learning Assessment 2000, *(978-0-9667830; 978-0-9746447)* P.O. Box 21003, Roanoke, VA 24018 USA
E-mail: eanaatwork@aol.com.

Early Learning Foundation, LLC, *(978-0-9755415)* 5184 Milroy, Brighton, MI 48116 USA
E-mail: bob@earlylearningfoundation.com
Web site: http://www.earlylearningfoundation.com
Dist(s): **Independent Pubs. Group**
Midpoint Trade Bks., Inc.

Early Lighr Pr., LLC, *(978-0-9799179)* P.O. Box 317, Boyds, MD 20841-0317 USA
E-mail: lee@earlylightpress.com
Web site: http://www.earlylightpress.com
Dist(s): **MyiLibrary.**

Early Morning Cocktail, *(978-0-578-55416-7; 978-0-578-55561-4; 978-0-578-66771-3; 978-0-578-72207-8; 978-1-7376022)* 16 Sandra Rd., Voorhees, NJ 08043 USA Tel 856-952-4375
E-mail: mskgarvin@yahoo.com.

Early Rise Pubns., *(978-0-9741082)* Orders Addr.: 350 S. Cty. Rd., Suite 102-134, Palm Beach, FL 33480 USA Tel 877-419-3648 (phone/fax)
E-mail: info@earlyrisepublications.com
Web site: http://www.earlyrisepublications.com
Dist(s): **CreateSpace Independent Publishing Platform.**

EARN, LLC, *(978-1-7361129)* 405 Powers Ferry Rd., Cary, NC 27519 USA Tel 804-402-9422
E-mail: Teo@artisteam.com
Web site: artisteam.com.

Earth Arts NW, *(978-0-9792207)* P.O. Box 25183, Portland, OR 97298-0183 USA
E-mail: tribal@spiritone.com
Web site: http://www.earthandspirit.org.

Earth Aware Editions *Imprint of* **Mandala Publishing**

Earth Aware Editions *Imprint of* **Insight Editions**

Earth Star Pubns., *(978-0-944851)* P.O. Box 117, Pagosa Springs, CO 81147-1800 USA (SAN 244-9315) Tel 970-731-0694; Fax: 970-731-0694 call first
E-mail: starbeacon@gmail.com
Web site: http://earthstar.tripod.com.

Earthatone Enterprises, *(978-0-578-03024-1; 978-0-9914892)* 244 5th Ave., No.2643, New York, NY 10016 USA Tel 212-252-6859; Fax: 208-977-3697
E-mail: earthatone@aol.com
Web site: http://www.earthatone.com.

EarthBound Bks., *(978-0-9771818)* P.O. Box 549, North Egremont, MA 01252 USA (SAN 256-9183) Tel 413-528-9042
E-mail: info@earthboundbooks.com
Web site: www.earthboundbooks.com.

Earthdancer Bks. *Imprint of* **Inner Traditions International, Ltd.**

Earthen Vessel Production, Inc., *(978-1-887400)* 3620 Greenwood Dr., Kelseyville, CA 95451 USA Tel 707-279-9621; Fax: 707-279-8769
E-mail: books@earthen.com; request@earthen.com
Web site: http://www.earthen.com.

Earthlight *See* **Light24**

Earthling Pr. *Imprint of* **Awe-Struck Publishing**

Earthshaker Bks., *(978-0-9790357)* 400 Melville Ave., Saint Louis, MO 63130 USA (SAN 852-2545) Tel 314-862-8177
E-mail: albonnie@mindspring.com
Dist(s): **MyiLibrary**
ebrary, Inc.

EarthTime Pubns., *(978-0-9663286)* Orders Addr.: 5662 Calle Real, #169, Santa Barbara, CA 93117 USA (SAN 299-5727) Tel 805-898-2263; Fax: 805-898-9460
E-mail: donna@seemamoon.com
Web site: http://www.seemamoon.com.

Earthwalk Pr., *(978-0-915749)* 5432 La Jolla Hermosa Ave., La Jolla, CA 92037-7613 USA (SAN 293-9258)
Dist(s): **Booklines Hawaii, Ltd.**
Langenscheidt Publishing Group.

EarthWardProject, *(978-0-9984596)* 20 E. Main St., Haverhill, MA 01830 USA Tel 978-807-1805
E-mail: runawaydandelion@gmail.com.

Earthways *See* **Earthways Guided Canoe Trips and School of Wilderness Living**

Earthways Guided Canoe Trips and School of Wilderness Living, *(978-0-9761714)* 159 Earthways Rd., Canaan, ME 04924 USA Tel 207-426-8138
E-mail: info@earthways.net
Web site: http://www.earthways.net.

Ear Twiggles Productions, Inc., *(978-0-9762573)* 14610 Luna Media, San Diego, CA 92127 USA Tel 858-756-8644; Fax: 858-756-8235
E-mail: contactus@eartwiggles.com
Web site: http://www.eartwiggles.com.

Eas'l Pubns., *(978-1-57377)* Div. of The Idea Shop, Inc., Orders Addr.: P.O. Box 22088, Saint Louis, MO 63126 USA Tel 314-892-9222; Fax: 314-892-9607; Edit Addr.: 11150 Lindbergh Business Ct., Suite 107, Saint Louis, MO 63123 USA
E-mail: easlpub@l1.net
Web site: http://www.easlpublications.com.

East End Hospice, Inc., *(978-0-9754932)* Orders Addr.: P.O. Box 1048, Westhampton Beach, NY 11978 USA Tel 631-288-8400; Fax: 631-288-8492; Edit Addr.: 481 Westhampton River Head Rd., Westhampton Beach, NY 11978 USA
E-mail: info@eeh.org
Web site: http://www.eeh.org.

East River Pr., *(978-0-9791283)* 455 FDR Dr., No. B1205, New York, NY 10002-5915 USA Do not confuse with companies with the same or similar name in Largo, MD, NEw YOrk, NY, Chester, NY.

East Stream Group, LLC, *(978-0-9910342; 978-1-7369507)* 46 Bonnie Brae Dr., Weaverville, NC 28787 USA Tel 828-775-4812
E-mail: robin@eaststreamgroup.com; stefan@eaststreamgroup.com.

East West Discovery Pr., *(978-0-9669437; 978-0-9701654; 978-0-9799339; 978-0-9821675; 978-0-9832278; 978-0-9856237; 978-0-9913454; 978-0-9973947; 978-1-949567)* P.O. Box 3585, Manhattan Beach, CA 90266 USA Tel 310-545-3730; Fax: 310-545-3731
E-mail: info@eastwestdiscovery.com; icy@eastwestdiscovery.com
Web site: http://www.eastwestdiscovery.com
Dist(s): **Follett School Solutions**
Independent Pubs. Group.

East West Hse, *(978-0-9778403)* 899 S. Plymouth Ct. Apt 2106, Chicago, IL 60605 USA.

Easter Island Foundation, *(978-1-880636)* Orders Addr.: P.O. Box 6774, Los Osos, CA 93412-6774 USA Tel 805-528-8558; Fax: 805-534-9301
E-mail: eif@att.net
Web site: http://www.islandheritage.org.

Easter, Robert C. Sr., *(978-1-885257)* 4212 Lost Ridge Dr., Austin, TX 78731 USA Tel 512-346-1692; Fax: 512-349-0802; Toll Free: 800-848-5593
Dist(s): **Quality Bks., Inc.**

Eastern Digital Resources, *(978-0-9815953)* P.O. Box 1451, Clearwater, SC 29822 USA Tel 803-439-2938
E-mail: jrigdon@researchonline.net; sales@researchonline.net
Web site: http://www.researchonline.net.

†Eastern National, *(978-0-915992; 978-1-888213; 978-1-59091)* 470 Maryland Dr., Suite 1, Fort Washington, PA 19034 USA (SAN 630-4044)
E-mail: jasons@easternnational.org
Web site: http://www.easternnational.org; *CIP.*

Eastern National Park & Monument Association *See* **Eastern National**

Eastern Slope Publisher, *(978-0-9746996; 978-0-9839956; 978-1-7368043)* Orders Addr.: 2636 Edgerock Rd., Reno, NV 89519 USA; Edit Addr.: 2636 Edgerock Road., Reno, NV 89519 USA
E-mail: pdcafferata@sbcglobal.net.

Eastland Studios *See* **Eastwind Studios**

Eastlight Pr., *(978-0-9743121)* 1976 Savanna, Fairfield, IA 52556 USA
E-mail: gadef@mac.com.

Easton Studio Pr., LLC, *(978-0-9743806; 978-0-9798248; 978-1-935212; 978-1-63226)* P.O. Box 3131, Westport, CT 06880-3131 USA; *Imprints:* Prospecta Press (ProspectaPr)
Web site: http://www.eastonsp.com/live/
Dist(s): **MyiLibrary**
Two Rivers Distribution
ebrary, Inc.

Eastpoint Enterprises, *(978-0-9996386)* 2228 Nelson Ave Apt. B, Redondo Beach, CA 90278 USA Tel 323-423-8359
E-mail: efadw@msn.com
Web site: glenshoffmanbooks.com.

Eastwaterfront Pr., *(978-0-9769771)* P.O. Box 220-554, Brooklyn, NY 11222 USA
E-mail: pdolack@gis.net.

Eastwind Studios, *(978-0-9755635; 978-0-615-36383-7; 978-0-615-36384-4; 978-0-615-36385-1)* P.O. Box 750, San Bernardino, CA 92402 USA Tel 909-725-7337
E-mail: lindaadams35@yahoo.com; philyeh@mac.com
Web site: http://www.ideaship.com; http://www.wingedtiger.com
Dist(s): **Booklines Hawaii, Ltd.**

Eastword Publications Development, Incorporated *See* **Lincoln Library Pr., Inc., The**

Easy Reach Corp., *(978-0-615-50973-0; 978-0-615-59362-3; 978-0-9883620)* HC 76 Box 121, Daisy, OK 74540 USA Tel 918-569-4803
E-mail: npyle@kiamichiwb.org.

Eat Words Publishing, *(978-0-9892840)* 49 Greene St., Catskill, NY 12414 USA Tel 518-291-6048
E-mail: info@foodtruck411book.com
Web site: eatwordspublishing.com.

Eat Your Peas Publishing, *(978-0-9743210)* 330 Conestoga Rd., Wayne, PA 19087 USA Tel 610-995-0495; Fax: 610-995-0496
E-mail: lisa@richeyassociates.com
Web site: http://www.mannerstogo.com.

EB Benjamin, LLC, *(978-0-615-38727-7; 978-0-615-43887-0)* 413 Mosby Dr, Leesburg, VA 20175 USA Tel 219-669-8474
E-mail: solalife@gmail.com
Dist(s): **CreateSpace Independent Publishing Platform.**

Ebed Pr., *(978-0-9741927; 978-1-933484; 978-0-9774825; 978-1-934050)* 3103 Villa Ave., Bronx, NY 11468-1356 USA Tel 718-788-2484; Fax: 718-788-7760; Toll Free: 800-224-7808
E-mail: info@ebedpress.com
Web site: http://www.ebedpress.com.

Ebeling, Vicki, *(978-0-9779768; 978-0-9981925)* 1250 6th St., Hermosa beach, CA 90254 USA Tel 310-530-0770
E-mail: books@pieravenuepublishing.com
Web site: http://www.educatingamerica.us
Dist(s): **Baker & Taylor Publisher Services (BTPS).**

Ebenezer A.M.E. Church, *(978-0-9748834)* 7707 Allentown Rd., Fort Washington, MD 20744 USA Tel 301-248-8833; Fax: 301-248-6894
Web site: http://www.ebenezerame.org.

Ebks. On The Net *Imprint of* **Write Words, Inc.**

EBL Coaching, *(978-0-9772110; 978-0-9778391)* 167 E. 82nd St., Suite 1A, New York, NY 10023 USA Tel 646-342-9380; Fax: 212-937-2305
E-mail: elevy@eblcoaching.com
Web site: http://www.eblcoaching.com.

Ebon Research Systems *See* **Ebon Research Systems Publishing, LLC**

Ebon Research Systems Publishing, LLC, *(978-0-915960; 978-0-9648313)* 812 Sweetwater Club Blvd., Longwood, FL 32779 USA (SAN 254-6698) Tel 407-786-9200; Fax: 407-682-2384
E-mail: femillionaire@embarqmail.com
Web site: http://www.daretobebooks.com; http://www.ebonresearchsystems.com.

Ebony D. James, *(978-0-578-80634-1; 978-1-7364039)* 1507 Merlin Ave, MEMPHIS, TN 38106 USA Tel 901-569-2684
E-mail: eworles@yahoo.com.

Ebony Pearl's World Bks. & Publishing, *(978-0-9988715)* 194 Ormond St. SW, Atlanta, GA 30315 USA Tel 404-396-5833; Fax: 404-396-5833
E-mail: alishajohnsonedu@gmail.com.

EbonyEnergy Publishing, Incorporated *See* **GEM Bk. Club**

EBk. Writing Hub, *(978-1-955595)* 2282 Oak St., Old Forge, NY 13420 USA Tel 315-369-5754
E-mail: bryan.scott2266@outlook.com.

eBookit.com, *(978-1-4566)* Div. of Archieboy Holdings, LLC, 365 Boston Post Rd., No. 311, Sudbury, MA 01776 USA
Web site: http://www.ebookit.com.

eBooks2go *See* **eBooks2go Inc**

eBooks2go Inc, *(978-1-61813; 978-1-5457)* 1111 N. Plaza Dr., Ste. 300, Schaumburg, IL 60173 USA Tel 847-598-1150
E-mail: ram@ebooks2go.net
Web site: www.gantecpublishing.com; http://www.ebooks2go.com/.

E-Booksgen, *(978-1-893767)* 40 Sandy Pond South, East Wakefield, NH 03830 USA Tel 603-522-9951
E-mail: e-booksgen@e-booksgen.com
Web site: http://www.e-booksgen.com; http://www.e-booksgen.com/E-WW2DOC.html.

eBooksOnDisk.com, *(978-0-9719101; 978-1-932157)* Orders Addr.: P.O. Box 30432, Gulf Breeze, FL 32503 USA Tel 850-261-1981
E-mail: thomas@ebooksondisk.com
Web site: http://www.ebooksondisk.com; http://www.confederatemilitaryhistory.com
Dist(s): **CreateSpace Independent Publishing Platform**
Ingram Content Group.

ebooksonthe.net *See* **Dilligaf Publishing**

ebooksonthe.net *See* **Write Words, Inc.**

eBookstand Books *See* **Bookstand Publishing**

E-BookTime LLC, *(978-0-9717625; 978-1-932701; 978-1-59824; 978-1-60862)* 6598 Pumpkin Rd., Montgomery, AL 36108 USA Toll Free: 877-613-2665
E-mail: publishing@e-booktime.com
Web site: http://www.e-booktime.com.

Ebright, David, *(978-1-7322277)* 152 Moses Creek Blvd, St Augustine, FL 32086 USA Tel 904-466-4173
E-mail: jaxpop8@hotmail.com.

Ebury Publishing (GBR) *(978-0-09; 978-0-426; 978-0-7126; 978-0-7535; 978-0-85223; 978-0-86369; 978-1-85227; 978-0-907080; 978-0-903446; 978-1-905042; 978-1-904978; 978-1-84670; 978-1-905264; 978-1-4735; 978-1-5291; 978-0-427) Dist. by* **IPG Chicago.**

EC Pr. Bks., *(978-0-9983615; 978-1-7330224)* 6456 Dwane Ave, San Diego, CA 92120 USA Tel 760-791-3033
E-mail: elizabethchennamchetty@gmail.com
Web site: elizabethchennamchetty.com.

EC Publishing LLC, *(978-1-970160; 978-1-953821)* 416 Marion Oaks Pass, Ocala, FL 34473 USA Tel 918-938-2068; 352-667-9279
E-mail: ecpublishingllc@outlook.com
Web site: ecpublishing.com
Dist(s): **Ingram Content Group.**

Ecco *Imprint of* **HarperCollins Pubs.**

ecEmedia, a Div. of The EC Corp., *(978-0-9822242; 978-1-948623)* 10511 Hardin Valley Rd, Knoxville, TN 37932 USA Tel 865-789-8324; Fax: 865-789-8324
E-mail: orlinob@gmail.com
Web site: ecEmedia.net.

ECF Bks., *(978-0-9747452)* P.O. Box 77023, Corona, CA 92877 USA
E-mail: rjonesdmin@protonmail.com
Web site: http://www.ecfbooks.com.

Echelon Press Publishing, *(978-1-59080)* Orders Addr.: 9055 Thamesmeade Rd. Apt. G, Laurel, MD 20723-5807 USA; *Imprints:* Quake (Quake)
E-mail: admin@echelonpress.com; echelonpress@gmail.com
Web site: http://www.echelonpress.com; http://quakeme.com
Dist(s): **Brodart Co.**
Ingram Content Group
Partners Bk. Distributing, Inc.
Smashwords.

Echo Point Books and Media, LLC. *See* **Echo Point Bks. & Media, LLC.**

Echo Point Bks. & Media, LLC., *(978-0-9638784; 978-0-615-56118-9; 978-1-62654; 978-1-63561; 978-1-64837)* Orders Addr.: 22 Browne Court, No. 100, Brattleboro, VT 05301 USA
E-mail: editorial@echopointbooks.com; fred@epbm.mygbiz.com
Web site: www.echopointbooks.com
Dist(s): **Open Road Integrated Media, Inc.**
Rodale Institute Bookstore.

Echo Valley Pr, *(978-0-9860734)* P.O. Box 449, Glen Arbor, MI 49636 USA.

Echoes Joint Venture, *(978-0-9759995)* Intensive English Program, UD, 1845 E. Northgate Dr., Irving, TX 75062 USA.

ECity Publishing *Imprint of* **ECity Publishing**

E-City Publishing, *(978-0-615-16430-4)* 150 Rustic Ridge Rd., Fredericksburg, VA 22405 USA
Dist(s): **Publishers Services.**

ECity Publishing, *(978-0-9716006; 978-0-9830425; 978-1-7341046)* Orders Addr.: P.O. Box 5033, Everglades City, FL 34139 USA Tel 239-695-2905; 102 E. Broadway, Everglades City, FL 34139; *Imprints:* ECity Publishing (ECity Pubng)
E-mail: ecitypublishing@earthlink.net
Web site: http://www.ecity-publishing.com.

Eckankar, *(978-1-57043)* Orders Addr.: P.O. Box 27300, Minneapolis, MN 55427 USA (SAN 253-7192) Fax: 952-380-2295; Toll Free: 800-568-3463
E-mail: eckbooks@eckankar.org
Web site: http://www.eckankar.org
Dist(s): **BookMobile.**

Eckerd College Leadership Development Institute, *(978-0-9764173)* 4200 54th Ave. S., St. Petersburg, FL 33711 USA Tel 727-864-8213; Fax: 727-864-7575; Toll Free: 800-753-0444
E-mail: ldi@eckerd.edu
Web site: http://www.eckerd.edu/ldi.

Eckl, Joseph J., *(978-0-9746686)* 346 Country Brook Ln., Harvard, IL 60033-7807 USA
E-mail: ecklindpil@aol.com.

Ecky Thump Bks., Inc., *(978-0-9815883)* 1411 N. California St., Burbank, CA 91505-1902 USA
Web site: http://www.achristmasbox.com
Dist(s): **Partners Pubs. Group, Inc.**

ECLAT Bks., *(978-0-9625706)* Div. of R. K. Interstellar Industries, Inc., 3172 N. Rainbow Blvd., Suite 315, Las Vegas, NV 89108 USA Tel 702-255-7919.

Eclectic Dragon Pr., *(978-0-9746016)* P.O. Box 91, Laie, HI 96762-1294 USA.

Eclectry Bks., *(978-0-9834906)* 107 Bugg Hill Rd, Monroe, CT 06468 USA
E-mail: the.eclectry@gmail.com.

Eclectus Publishing, *(978-1-7362581)* 3 RANDOM RD, ENGLEWOOD, CO 80113 USA Tel 720-236-2413
E-mail: robert123linnane@gmail.com.

Eclipse Pr. *Imprint of* **Blood-Horse, Inc., The**

Eclipse Solutions (UK) Ltd. (GBR) *(978-0-9556910) Dist. by* **LuluCom.**

Eco Fiction Bks. *Imprint of* **Day to Day Enterprises**

Eco Images, *(978-0-938423)* Orders Addr.: P.O. Box 61413, Virginia Beach, VA 23466-1413 USA (SAN 661-230X); Edit Addr.: 4132 Blackwater Rd., Virginia Beach, VA 23457 USA (SAN 661-2318) Tel 757-421-3929
E-mail: wildfood@cox.net
Web site: http://www.ecoimages-us.com.

Eco-Busters, *(978-1-885091)* 1198 Old Castleberry Rd, Brewton, AL 36426 USA.

Publisher Name Index

Eco-Justice Pr., LLC, *(978-0-9660370; 978-0-9891296; 978-1-945432)* P.O. Box 5409, Eugene, OR 97405 USA; *Imprints:* Aurora Books (AuroraBks)
E-mail: info@ecojusticepress.com; orders@ecojusticepress.com
Web site: ecojusticepress.com.

Ecology Comics, *(978-0-9643421)* 465 B. Kawailoa Rd., Kailua, HI 96734 USA Tel 808-261-1018; Fax: 808-531-3177.

Econ for Kids, *(978-0-578-83477-1; 978-1-954945)* P.O. Box 72, alviso, CA 95002 USA Tel 650-353-7525
E-mail: kellyweb@gmail.com.

EcoSeekers, The, *(978-0-9798800)* P.O. Box 637, Nyack, NY 10960 USA (SAN 854-6339)
E-mail: info@theecoseekers.com
Web site: http://www.theecoseekers.com
Dist(s): **Midpoint Trade Bks., Inc.**

Eco-thumb Publishing Co., *(978-0-9778536)* 1212 S. Naper Blvd., Suite 119-337, Naperville, IL 60540 USA (SAN 850-4113) Tel 630-853-9758
Web site: http://www.ecothumb.com; http://www.sendmethesoap.com.

ECS Learning Systems, Inc., *(978-0-944459; 978-1-57022; 978-1-58232; 978-1-60539)* P.O. Box 440, Bulverde, TX 78163 USA (SAN 243-6167) Toll Free Fax: 877-688-3226; Toll Free: 800-688-3224
Web site: http://www.ecslearningsystems.com.

Ecstatic Exchange, The, *(978-0-615-13570-0; 978-0-615-13599-1; 978-0-615-14273-9; 978-0-615-14505-1; 978-0-615-15116-8; 978-0-615-16308-6; 978-0-615-18394-7; 978-0-615-18412-8; 978-0-615-20490-1; 978-0-615-22182-3; 978-0-615-23628-5; 978-0-578-00773-1; 978-0-578-01004-5; 978-0-578-01084-7; 978-0-578-01690-0; 978-0-578-02569-8; 978-0-578-02765-4; 978-0-578-04677-8; 978-0-578-04905-2; 978-0-578-06116-0; 978-0-578-07145-9; 978-0-578-07482-5; 978-0-578-07608-9; 978-0-578-08293-6; 978-0-578-08512-8; 978-0-578-08891-4;) 6470 Morris Pk. Rd., Philadelphia, PA 19151 USA Tel 215-477-8927*
E-mail: abdalhayy@danielmoorepoetry.com; medinatenour@gmail.com
Web site: http://www.danielmoorepoetry.com; www.ecstaticxchange.com
Dist(s): **Lulu Pr., Inc.**

Ectopic Publishing, *(978-0-9759695)* 3638 Lovejoy Ct. NE, Olympia, WA 98506 USA
E-mail: bryanrandall@ectopicpublishing.com
Web site: http://www.ectopicpublishing.com.

ECW Pr. (CAN) *(978-0-920763; 978-0-920802; 978-1-55022; 978-1-77041; 978-1-55490; 978-1-77090; 978-1-77305) Dist. by* **BTPS.**

Ed. Acespanish S.A.C.- Lima, Peru, *(978-0-9762361)* 4806 Alta Loma Dr., Austin, TX 78749 USA Tel 512-784-6333
Web site: http://www.acespanish.com.

E.D. Insight Bks., *(978-0-9761552)* P.O. Box 514, Beverly Hills, CA 90213-0514 USA
E-mail: brady@edinsight.com
Web site: http://www.edinsight.com.

Ed Musica, *(978-1-932637)* 1219 La Casa Dr., San Marcos, CA 92078 USA
E-mail: alfredo@edmusica.com
Web site: www.edmusica.com.

Edamex, Editores Asociados Mexicanos, S. A. de C. V. (MEX) *(978-968-409; 978-970-561) Dist. by* **Giron Bks.**

EDC Publishing, *(978-0-7460; 978-0-86020; 978-0-88110; 978-1-58086; 978-0-7945; 978-1-60130)* Orders Addr.: P.O. Box 470663, Tulsa, OK 74147-0663 USA (SAN 658-0505); Edit Addr.: 10302 E. 55th Pl., Tulsa, OK 74146-6515 USA (SAN 107-5322) Tel 918-622-4522; Fax: 918-665-7919; Toll Free Fax: 800-747-4509; Toll Free: 800-475-4522; *Imprints:* Usborne (UsborneU)
E-mail: edc@edcpub.com
Web site: http://www.edcpub.com
Dist(s): **Children's Plus, Inc.**
Continental Bk. Co., Inc.
Lectorum Pubns., Inc.
Libros Sin Fronteras.

EDCO Publishing, Inc., *(978-0-9712692; 978-0-9749412; 978-0-9798088)* 2648 Lapeer Rd., Auburn Hills, MI 48326 USA (SAN 254-4261) Fax: 248-475-9122; Toll Free: 888-510-3326
E-mail: lynette@edcopublishing.com; martha@edcopublishing.com
Web site: http://www.edcopublishing.com
Dist(s): **Partners Bk. Distributing, Inc.**

EDCON Publishing Group, *(978-0-8481; 978-1-56872)* 30 Montauk Blvd., Oakdale, NY 11769 USA Tel 631-567-7227; Fax: 631-567-8745; Toll Free Fax: 888-518-1564; Toll Free: 888-553-3266
E-mail: dale@edconpublishing.com
Web site: http://www.edconpublishing.com
Dist(s): **Findaway World, LLC**
Follett School Solutions.

Eddie Crabtree Ministries, *(978-0-9765830)* Orders Addr.: P.O. Box 846, Salem, VA 24153 USA Tel 540-562-1500; Fax: 540-562-2695; Edit Addr.: 1928 Loch Haven Dr., Roanoke, VA 24019 USA
E-mail: eddiecrabtreeministries@valleywordministries.org.

Eddy, Eric, *(978-0-578-60866-2; 979-8-218-26753-7)* 82 Covington Dr, Buffalo, NY 14220 USA Tel 716-604-2777
E-mail: eric.eddy59@yahoo.com.

Eddy, The Writings of Mary Baker, *(978-0-87510; 978-0-87952)* Orders Addr.: 210 Massachusetts Ave P03-25, Boston, MA 02115 USA (SAN 203-6541) Tel 617-450-2517
E-mail: gilibertos@csps.com
Web site: http://www.spirituality.com.

Edebé (ESP) *(978-84-236; 978-84-683; 978-84-300-1909-0) Dist. by* **Ediciones.**

Edebé (ESP) *(978-84-236; 978-84-683; 978-84-300-1909-0) Dist. by* **Lectorum Pubns.**

Edelsa Grupo Didascalia, S.A. (ESP) *(978-84-389; 978-84-7711; 978-84-85786) Dist. by* **Distribks Inc.**

Edelsa Grupo Didascalia, S.A. (ESP) *(978-84-389; 978-84-7711; 978-84-85786) Dist. by* **Continental Bk.**

Edelson, Madelyn, *(978-0-9770131)* 69 Bay Ave., H, Huntington, NY 11743 USA
E-mail: mbedelson@optonline.net
Web site: http://www.beechwindpress.com.

Eden Entertainment Ltd., Inc., *(978-0-9672819; 978-0-9835380)* 1277 1st St. Suite 1, Key West, FL 33040 USA Tel 305-294-7928
E-mail: MarcusVarner@Hotmail.com; DanielJReynen@Hotmail.com
Web site: http://www.truesecretof.com; http://www.dietisdead.com; http://www.webefit.com.

Eden Studios, Inc., *(978-1-891153; 978-1-933105)* 6 Dogwood Ln., Londonville, NY 12211 USA Tel 518-331-2063; Fax: 425-962-2593
E-mail: edenprod@aol.com
Web site: http://www.edenstudios.net
Dist(s): **PSI (Publisher Services, Inc.).**

EdenTree Publishing, *(978-0-692-78131-9; 978-0-9982113)* P.O. Box 1174, PORTSMOUTH, OH 45662 USA Tel 740-285-3954
E-mail: frwarnock@yahoo.com.

Edes Publishing Co., *(978-0-9788010; 978-1-943472)* 1224 E. Hadley, Las Cruces, NM 88001 USA (SAN 851-6561)
E-mail: publisher@edes.net
Web site: http://www.edes.net.

Edgar Road Publishing, *(978-0-615-20414-7)* 938 Tuxedo Blvd., Webster Groves, MO 63119 USA Tel 314-541-9235; Fax: 314-961-9044
E-mail: edgarroadpublishing@gmail.com
Dist(s): **Not So Plain Jane Publishing.**

Edge, Inc., *(978-0-692-70443-1; 978-0-9996501)* 6141 Arbutus Dr., Pensacola, FL 32504 USA Tel 850-516-7251; Fax: 850-516-7251
E-mail: deborah-edge@cox.net
Web site: www.edgetherapyseminars.

Edgecliff Pr. LLC., *(978-0-9798659; 978-0-9819271; 978-0-9844622; 978-0-9839486)* Mid-century Modern Bldg. 9066 Long Ln., Cincinnati, OH 45231 USA (SAN 854-6150) Tel 513-348-9120 Hours 9 to 5 EST
E-mail: Info@edgecliffpress.com
Web site: http://www.edgecliffpress.com; http://www.edgecliffkids.com.

EDGEucation Publishing, *(978-1-932689)* Orders Addr.: P.O. Box 852013, Yukon, OK 73085-2013 USA; Edit Addr.: 1441 NW 47th St., Oklahoma City, OK 73085-2013 USA
E-mail: edgeucation@sbcglobal.net.

Edgewise Publishing, *(978-1-7363007)* 4008 Grayson Dr, Obetz, OH 43207 USA Tel 419-549-0726
E-mail: Deedge1@gmail.com.

Edgewood Publishing, LLC, *(978-0-9792645)* P.O. Box 153, Adell, WI 53001 USA Tel 920-994-2483.

EDGSMITH Publishing,LLC, *(978-1-7328750)* 5933 One Penny Dr, Fairfax Station, VA 22039 USA Tel 703-323-6863
E-mail: authoredgsmith@gmail.com.

Ediciones Alas, Inc., *(978-0-9753799)* Orders Addr.: P.O. Box 327495, Fort Lauderdale, FL 33332 USA; Edit Addr.: 6061 SW 195th Ave., Pembroke Pines, FL 33332 USA
E-mail: mm@miilymolo.com
Web site: http://www.miilymolo.com.

Ediciones Alfaguara (ESP) *(978-84-204) Dist. by* **Lectorum Pubns.**

Ediciones Alfaguara (ESP) *(978-84-204) Dist. by* **Santillana.**

Ediciones B (ESP) *(978-84-406; 978-84-7735; 978-84-666; 978-84-9872; 978-84-15420) Dist. by* **Peng Rand Hse.**

Ediciones B Mexico (MEX) *(978-84-406; 978-84-7735; 978-607-480) Dist. by* **Peng Rand Hse.**

Ediciones Cocoli, *(978-0-9650197; 978-0-9994064)* P.O. Box 9023072, San Juan, PR 00902 USA Tel 787-354-8264
E-mail: sofiasaezmatos@gmail.com.

Ediciones Cátedra (ESP) *(978-84-376) Dist. by* **Continental Bk.**

Ediciones de la Torre (ESP) *(978-84-7960; 978-84-85277; 978-84-85866; 978-84-86587) Dist. by* **AIMS Intl.**

Ediciones de la Torre (ESP) *(978-84-7960; 978-84-85277; 978-84-85866; 978-84-86587) Dist. by* **Libros Fronteras.**

Ediciones del Bronce (ESP) *(978-84-8453; 978-84-89854) Dist. by* **Planeta.**

Ediciones del Laberinto (ESP) *(978-84-8483; 978-84-87482) Dist. by* **Ediciones.**

Ediciones Destino (ESP) *(978-84-233; 978-84-9710) Dist. by* **Continental Bk.**

Ediciones Destino (ESP) *(978-84-233; 978-84-9710) Dist. by* **AIMS Intl.**

Ediciones Destino (ESP) *(978-84-233; 978-84-9710) Dist. by* **Lectorum Pubns.**

Ediciones Destino (ESP) *(978-84-233; 978-84-9710) Dist. by* **Planeta.**

Ediciones DiQueSi (ESP) *Dist. by* **Lectorum Pubns.**

Ediciones El Pozo, *(978-0-9821364; 978-0-9884286; 978-0-9861812; 978-0-9986971)* 37 Fairview St., Apt. 4, Oneonta, NY 13820 USA (SAN 857-3581) Tel 607-353-9277
E-mail: gustavoa1234@hotmail.com
Web site: http://www.employees.oneonta.edu/arangog/.

Ediciones El Salvaje Refinado *See* **Refined Savage Editions / Ediciones El Salvaje Refinado, The**

Ediciones Eleos, *(978-0-9650058; 978-1-881741; 978-1-961322)* 164 calle Pitirre Urb. Los Montes, Dorado, PR 00646-9408 USA; *Imprints:* FJ Multimedia LLC (MYID_N_FJ MULT)
E-mail: fjortiz@edicioneseleos.com
Web site: http://www.edicioneseleos.com
Dist(s): **Lushena Bks.**

Ediciones Eleos, Incorporated *See* **Ediciones Eleos**

Ediciones Kiwi S.L. (ESP) *(978-84-941348) Dist. by* **Lectorum Pubns.**

Ediciones La Fragatina (ESP) *(978-84-16226) Dist. by* **IPG Chicago.**

Ediciones la Gota de Agua, *(978-0-9771987; 978-0-9819303; 978-0-9964627; 978-1-7337513)* 1937 Pemberton St., Philadelphia, PA 19146-1825 USA Tel 215-546-9421
E-mail: info@edicioneslagotadeagua.com
Web site: http://edicioneslagotadeagua.com
Dist(s): **Ediciones Universal**
GOBI Library Solutionis from EBSCO.

Ediciones Lea S.A. (ARG) *(978-987-1257; 978-987-21776; 978-987-22032; 978-987-22079; 978-987-634; 978-987-718) Dist. by* **IPG Chicago.**

Ediciones Lerner *Imprint of* **Lerner Publishing Group**

Ediciones Nuevo Espacio *See* **Ediciones Nuevo Espacio-AcademicPressENE**

Ediciones Nuevo Espacio-AcademicPressENE, *(978-1-930879)* Orders Addr.: 39 Redfern Rd., Eatontown, NJ 07724 USA
E-mail: AcademicPressENE@gmail.com
Web site: http://www.editorialene.com; http://www.editorial-ene.com
Dist(s): **Book Wholesalers, Inc.**
Brodart Co.

Ediciones Obelisco (ESP) *(978-84-7720; 978-84-86000; 978-84-9777; 978-84-940745; 978-84-941549; 978-84-16117) Dist. by* **Spanish.**

Ediciones Oniro S.A. (ESP) *(978-84-89920; 978-84-922523; 978-84-9754; 978-84-95456) Dist. by* **Bilingual Pubns.**

Ediciones Oniro S.A. (ESP) *(978-84-89920; 978-84-922523; 978-84-9754; 978-84-95456) Dist. by* **Lectorum Pubns.**

Ediciones Santillana, Inc., *(978-1-57581; 978-1-60484; 978-1-61875)* Div. of Santillana-S. A. (SP), P.O. Box 195462, San Juan, PR 00919-5462 USA Tel 787-781-9800; Fax: 787-782-6149; Toll Free: 800-981-9822
E-mail: molivero@santillanapr.net; areynoso@santillanapr.net; cvazquez@santillanapr.net
Web site: http://www.gruposantillana.com
Dist(s): **Santillana USA Publishing Co., Inc.**

Ediciones Situm, Incorporated *See* **Biblio Services, Inc.**

Ediciones SM, *(978-1-933279; 978-1-934801; 978-1-935556; 978-1-936534; 978-1-939075; 978-1-940343; 978-1-63014; 978-1-64486; 979-8-89076)* Barrio Palmas, 776 Calle 7 Suite 2, Catano, PR 00962-6335 USA Tel 787-625-9800; Fax: 787-625-9799
Web site: http://www.ediciones-smpr.com
Dist(s): **Children's Plus, Inc.**

Ediciones Universal, *(978-0-89729; 978-1-59388)* Orders Addr.: P.O. Box 450353, Miami, FL 33245-0353 USA (SAN 658-0548); Edit Addr.: 3090 SW Eighth St., Miami, FL 33135 USA (SAN 207-2203) Tel 305-642-3355; Fax: 305-642-7978
E-mail: marta@ediciones.com; ediciones@ediciones.com
Web site: http://www.ediciones.com
Dist(s): **Lectorum Pubns., Inc.**

Ediciones Urano de México (MEX) *(978-607-95139; 978-607-7835; 978-607-9344) Dist. by* **Spanish.**

Ediciones Urano S. A. (ESP) *(978-84-7953; 978-84-95618; 978-84-95752; 978-84-86344; 978-84-95787; 978-84-96711; 978-84-96886; 978-84-92916; 978-84-9944) Dist. by* **Spanish.**

Ediciones y Distribuciones Codice, S.A. (ESP) *(978-84-357) Dist. by* **Continental Bk.**

Edifi Publishing LLC, *(978-0-692-02937-4; 978-0-692-09127-2; 978-0-578-44203-7; 978-1-7339305; 979-8-9883419)* 3446 Winder Hwy. No. M195, Flowery Branch, GA 30542 USA Tel 706-631-8672
E-mail: info@edifipublishing.com
Web site: http://www.edifipublishing.com
Dist(s): **Ingram Bk. Co.**

Edifytainment Bks., *(978-0-9753427)* 213 Regent Cir., Inglewood, CA 90301 USA Tel 310-677-9744
E-mail: edifytainmentbooks@prodigy.net
Web site: http://www.bobettejamison-harrison.com/edifytainmentbooks.html.

Edilupa Ediciones, S.L. (ESP) *(978-84-932571; 978-84-932843; 978-84-96252; 978-84-96609) Dist. by* **Lectorum Pubns.**

Edimat Libros, S. A. (ESP) *(978-84-8403; 978-84-923200; 978-84-95002; 978-84-9764; 978-84-9794) Dist. by* **Lectorum Pubns.**

eDimples, Inc., *(978-0-9787759)* 9249 S. Broadway, 200-161, Highlands Ranch, CO 80129 USA Tel 303-284-1331 (phone/fax)
E-mail: greg@edimples.com
Web site: http://www.edimples.com.

Edinboro Bk. Arts Collective, *(978-0-9747001)* Orders Addr.: P.O. Box 77, Edinboro, PA 16412 USA; Edit Addr.: 103 Tarbell Ln., Edinboro, PA 16412 USA
E-mail: winterberger@edinboro.edu.

Edinborough Pr., *(978-1-889020)* P.O. Box 13790, Roseville, MN 55113-2293 USA (SAN 299-2825) Tel 651-415-1034; Toll Free Fax: 800-566-6145; Toll Free: 888-251-6336 (Orders Only)
E-mail: books@edinborough.com
Web site: http://www.edinborough.com
Dist(s): **ebrary, Inc.**

Edinburgh Univ. Pr. (GBR) *(978-0-7486; 978-0-85224; 978-1-4744) Dist. by* **TwoRivers.**

Edinumen, Editorial (ESP) *(978-84-89756; 978-84-85789; 978-84-95986; 978-84-9848) Dist. by* **Cambridge U Pr.**

Edinumen, Editorial (ESP) *(978-84-89756; 978-84-85789; 978-84-95986; 978-84-9848) Dist. by* **IngramPubServ.**

Edit et Cetera *See* **Edit et Cetera Ltd.**

Edit et Cetera Ltd., *(978-0-9746122; 978-0-9769989; 978-0-9832270)* P.O. Box 551, Canon City, CO 81215 USA
E-mail: familybookhouse@aol.com
Web site: http://www.familybookhouse.com.

EDITER'S Publishing Hse., *(978-0-9706814; 978-0-9743743)* 654 Schafer Pl., Escondido, CA 92025 USA Tel 619-339-7030; Fax: 760-294-2685
E-mail: books@editers.com
Web site: http://www.editers.com.

EDITER'S Publishing Hse. (MEX) *(978-968-6966; 978-968-5432) Dist. by* **EDITERS Pub Hse.**

Editex, Editorial S.A. (ESP) *(978-84-7131) Dist. by* **Lectorum Pubns.**

Editing Mee, *(978-1-7348905; 978-1-953109)* 3985 S 900 E Apt 116 0, Salt Lake City, UT 84124 USA Tel 8016744934
E-mail: esuggs92@gmail.com
Dist(s): **Ingram Content Group.**

Editing Partners, *(978-0-578-53665-1; 978-0-578-53715-3; 978-1-7377160)* Grand Central Sta., New York, NY 10163 USA Tel 347-549-1148
E-mail: morfolk@editingpartners.com
Dist(s): **Ingram Content Group.**

Edition Axel Menges GmbH (DEU) *(978-3-930698; 978-3-932565; 978-3-936681) Dist. by* **Natl Bk Netwk.**

Edition Chimaira (DEU) *(978-3-930612; 978-3-89973) Dist. by* **Serpents Tale.**

Edition Q, Inc., *(978-0-86715; 978-1-883695)* 551 N. Kimberly Dr., Carol Stream, IL 60188-1881 USA Tel 630-682-3223; Fax: 630-682-3907; Toll Free: 800-421-0387
E-mail: quintpub@aol.com; service@quintbook.com
Web site: http://www.quintpub.com.

Editions de la Montagne Verte, Inc. (CAN) *(978-0-9737681; 978-1-897277) Dist. by* **Lone Pine.**

Editions de la Paix (CAN) *(978-2-921255; 978-2-922565; 978-2-9800785; 978-2-89599) Dist. by* **World of Reading.**

Editions du Petit Music (FRA) *(978-2-84607) Dist. by* **Distribks Inc.**

Editions du Seuil (FRA) *(978-2-02) Dist. by* **Distribks Inc.**

Editions Fleurus (FRA) *(978-2-215; 978-2-250; 978-2-7289) Dist. by* **Distribks Inc.**

Editions Milan (FRA) *(978-2-7459; 978-2-84113; 978-2-86726; 978-2-408) Dist. by* **Distribks Inc.**

Editora Campamocha, *(978-1-934802)* 1609 Chicago Av., McAllen, TX 78501 USA.

Editores Mexicanos Unidos (MEX) *(978-968-15) Dist. by* **Ediciones.**

Editorial Alma (ESP) *(978-84-15701; 978-84-15618) Dist. by* **IPG Chicago.**

Editorial Anagrama S.A. (ESP) *(978-84-339) Dist. by* **Spanish.**

Editorial Betania *See* **Grupo Nelson**

Editorial Brief (ESP) *(978-84-931888) Dist. by* **IPG Chicago.**

Editorial Buenas Letras *Imprint of* **Rosen Publishing Group, Inc., The**

Editorial Busqueda, *(978-0-9744408; 978-0-9760652; 978-0-9798461; 978-0-9843607)* Calle Pinero, No. 113, San Juan, PR 00925-3612 USA.

Editorial Campana, *(978-0-9725611; 978-1-934370; 978-1-962756)* 109 Echo Hill Rd., Saugerties, NY 12477 USA (SAN 854-2791) Tel 845-559-4757 (phone/fax); *Imprints:* Campanita Books (Campanita Bks)
E-mail: kidcaribooks@gmail.com
Web site: http://www.editorialcampana.com
Dist(s): **Downtown Bk. Ctr., Inc.**

Editorial Cultural, Inc., *(978-1-56758; 978-84-399)* Orders Addr.: P.O. Box 21056, San Juan, PR 00928 USA; Edit Addr.: Calle Robles, No. 51, San Juan, PR 00928 USA
E-mail: angiev@editorialculturalpr.com; alamo48@gmail.com
Web site: http://www.editorialculturalpr.com.

Editorial de Nuevo Extremo S.A. (ARG) *(978-950-9681; 978-987-1068; 978-987-1427; 978-987-609) Dist. by* **IPG Chicago.**

Editorial Diana, S.A. (MEX) *(978-968-13) Dist. by* **Continental Bk.**

Editorial Diana, S.A. (MEX) *(978-968-13) Dist. by* **Lectorum Pubns.**

Editorial Diana, S.A. (MEX) *(978-968-13) Dist. by* **Giron Bks.**

Editorial Edaf, S.L. (ESP) *(978-84-7640; 978-84-7166; 978-84-414) Dist. by* **Spanish.**

Editorial EKEKA (ARG) *Dist. by* **IPG Chicago.**

Editorial El Antillano, Inc., *(978-0-9755661; 978-0-9793026; 978-1-7326361)* 104 Jefferson St., Suite 5-B, Santurce, PR 00911 USA Tel 787-982-4060
E-mail: olga_otero@mspr.net
Web site: http://www.elantillano.com.

Editorial el Pirata (ESP) *(978-84-946115; 978-84-18664) Dist. by* **IPG Chicago.**

Editorial Everest, S.A (ESP) *(978-84-441) Dist. by* **Lectorum Pubns.**

Editorial Flamboyant (ESP) *Dist. by* **Lectorum Pubns.**

Editorial Guipil *Imprint of* **Editorial Guipil**

Editorial Guipil, *(978-0-9992367; 978-1-7335328; 978-1-7332447; 978-1-953689)* 500 W. 5th St. Suite 400, Winston Salem, NC 27101 USA Tel 305-790-6338; *Imprints:* Editorial Guipil (MYID_I_ED.IAL)
E-mail: rebecasegebre@gmail.com
Web site: http://guipilpress.com/; http://editorialguipil.com/.

Editorial Hidra (ESP) *Dist. by* **Lectorum Pubns.**

Editorial Homagno, *(978-0-9727467)* Div. of Homagno Group, Inc., P.O. Box 960227, Miami, FL 33296 USA
Web site: http://www.homagno.com.

Editorial Humanitas, *(978-0-9650104)* Orders Addr.: 2006 23rd Ave., E., Seattle, WA 98112-2936 USA Tel 206-616-9394
E-mail: oberle@mindspring.com
Web site: http://www.mindspring.com/~oberle/PRbirds.htm
Dist(s): **Representaciones Borinquenas, Inc.**

Editorial Imagen, *(978-1-64081; 978-1-64521)* 364 E Main St. Suite 1003, Middletown, DE 19709 USA; *Imprints:* Educando Kids (MYID_M_EDUCAND); Inspira (MYID_Y_INSPIRB).

Editorial John Louis von Neumann, Inc., *(978-0-9748297; 978-0-9779982)* Urb. Villa Fontana, 3NS-15 Via Lourdes, Carolina, PR 00983-4650 USA Tel 787-630-6330; Fax: 787-257-4979
E-mail: josejuandiaz@gmail.com
Web site: http://josejuandiaz.com
Dist(s): **Representaciones Borinquenas, Inc.**

Editorial Leetra (MEX) *Dist. by* **Lectorum Pubns.**

ditorial Libre Albedrío (ESP) *(978-84-947462; 978-84-944172; 978-84-942313) Dist. by* **Lectorum Pubns.**

ditorial Libros en Red, *(978-1-59754; 978-1-62915)* 5018 57th Ave., Apt. B8, Bladensburg, MD 20710 USA
E-mail: administracion@librosenred.com
Web site: http://www.librosenred.com
Dist(s): **Ediciones Universal.**

ditorial Libsa, S.A. (ESP) *(978-84-7630; 978-84-662) Dist. by* **Continental Bk.**

ditorial Libsa, S.A. (ESP) *(978-84-7630; 978-84-662) Dist. by* **Lectorum Pubns.**

ditorial Lucero *See* **Carnaval Editorial**

ditorial Lumen (ESP) *(978-84-264) Dist. by* **Distribks Inc.**

ditorial Lumen (ESP) *(978-84-264) Dist. by* **Lectorum Pubns.**

ditorial Miglo Inc., *(978-0-9671705)* 1560 Grand Concourse, Apt. 504, Bronx, NY 10457 USA
E-mail: jcmalone01@aol.com
Web site: http://www.edimiglo.com.

ditorial Mundo Hispano *Imprint of* **Casa Bautista de Publicaciones**

Editorial Oceano de Mexico (MEX) *(978-607-400; 978-607-557; 978-607-527) Dist. by* **IPG Chicago.**

Editorial Panamericana, Inc., *(978-1-881744; 978-1-934139; 978-1-61725)* Orders Addr.: Urb. Puerto Nuevo 1336 F.d. Roosevelt Ave., San Juan, PR 00920 USA Tel 787-277-7988; Fax: 787-277-7240; Edit Addr.: P.O. Box 25189, San Juan, PR 00928-5189 USA Tel 787-277-7988; Fax: 787-277-7240
E-mail: info@editorialpanamericana.com; cbaez@editorialpanamericana.com
Web site: http://www.editorialpanamericana.com.

Editorial Pax (MEX) *(978-968-860; 978-968-461) Dist. by* **IPG Chicago.**

Editorial Planeta, S. A. (ESP) *(978-84-08; 978-84-320; 978-84-395; 978-84-8460; 978-970-37) Dist. by* **Lectorum Pubns.**

Editorial Planeta, S. A. (ESP) *(978-84-08; 978-84-320; 978-84-395; 978-84-8460; 978-970-37) Dist. by* **TwoRivers.**

Editorial Plaza Mayor, Inc., *(978-1-56328)* Avenida Ponce De Leon 1527, Barrio El Cinco, Rio Piedras, PR 00926 USA Tel 787-764-0455; Fax: 787-764-0465
E-mail: patrigut@prtc.net
Dist(s): **Continental Bk. Co., Inc.**
Ediciones Universal
Cengage Gale
Lectorum Pubns., Inc.
Libros Sin Fronteras.

Editorial Porrua (MEX) *(978-968-432; 978-968-452; 978-970-07) Dist. by* **Continental Bk.**

Editorial Portavoz *Imprint of* **Kregel Pubns.**

Editorial Resources, Inc., *(978-0-9745923)* 4510 Seneca St., Pasadena, TX 77504-3568 USA
E-mail: anng@editorial-resources.com
Web site: http://www.editorial-resources.com.

Editorial Sendas Antiguas, LLC, *(978-1-932789)* 1730 Leffingwell Ave., Grand Rapids, MI 49525-4532 USA Tel 616-365-9073 (phone/fax); 616-365-0699; Fax: 616-365-1990
E-mail: info@sendasantiguas.com; sales@sendasantiguas.com; greendykbill@aol.com
Web site: http://www.sendasantiguas.com
Dist(s): **Send The Light Distribution LLC.**

Editorial Sudamericana S.A. (ARG) *(978-950-07; 978-950-37) Dist. by* **Distribks Inc.**

Editorial Sudamericana S.A. (ARG) *(978-950-07; 978-950-37) Dist. by* **Lectorum Pubns.**

Editorial Unilit, *(978-0-7899; 978-0-945792; 978-1-56063)* Div. of Spanish Hse., Inc., 1360 NW 88th Ave., Miami, FL 33172-3093 USA (SAN 247-5979) Tel 305-592-6136; Fax: 305-592-0087; Toll Free: 800-767-7726
E-mail: sales1@unidial.com
Web site: http://www.editorialunilit.com/
Dist(s): **Bethany Hse. Pubs.**
Lectorum Pubns., Inc.
Pura Vida Bks., Inc.

Editorial Vida Abundante, *(978-0-9765828)* P.O. Box 1073, Fajardo, PR 00738 USA Tel 787-860-3555
Web site: http://www.vidaabundante.org.

Editorial Voluntad S.A. (COL) *(978-958-02) Dist. by* **Continental Bk.**

Editorial Voluntad S.A. (COL) *(978-958-02) Dist. by* **Distr Norma.**

Editorium, The *See* **The Editorium, LLC**

Edivision Compania Editorial, S.A. de C.V. (MEX) *(978-968-890) Dist. by* **Continental Bk.**

Edizioni PIEMME spa (ITA) *(978-88-384; 978-88-566; 978-88-585) Dist. by* **Distribks Inc.**

Edmonds, Doug, *(978-1-7355273)* 3795 Private Rd. 304, Semmes, AL 36575 USA Tel 251-689-4784
E-mail: Edmonds2000.de@gmail.com.

Edmondson, Dayne *See* **Dark Star Publishing**

Edmund, Neo, *(978-0-9883808)* 15135 Ryon Ave., Bellflower, CA 90706 USA Tel 562-324-3860
E-mail: neo@neoedmund.com.

EDR, *(978-0-9794615)* P.O. Box 22, Waterport, NY 14571 USA
E-mail: sakina@edrsinc.com
Web site: http://www.edrsinc.com; http://www.omariworld.com.

EdTechLens, *(978-0-9912337)* 1834 Lenox Rd., SCHENECTADY, NY 12308 USA Tel 518-393-9460
E-mail: ellen@ellensenisi.com
Web site: https://www.edtechlens.com
Dist(s): **Follett School Solutions.**

Edu Designs, *(978-0-9795017; 978-1-7348434)* Orders Addr.: PO Box 660518 Apt B, Arcadia, CA 91066 USA Tel 626-940-4768; Edit Addr.: P.O. Box 660518, Arcadia, CA 91066 USA Tel 626-940-4768
E-mail: edudesigns.org@gmail.com
Web site: http://www.edudesigns.org.

Educa Vision Inc., *(978-1-881839; 978-1-58432; 978-1-62632; 978-1-64382; 978-0-578-24509-6)* 7550 NW 47th Ave., Coconut Creek, FL 33073 USA (SAN 760-873X) Tel 954-968-7433; Fax: 954-970-0330; 2725 NW 19th St., Pompano Beach, FL 33069
E-mail: educa@aol.com
Web site: http://www.educavision.com; http://www.educabrazil.org; http://www.caribbeanstudiespress.com; http://www.educalanguage.com; https://www.educavision.org
Dist(s): **Follett School Solutions.**

Educando Kids *Imprint of* **Editorial Imagen**

Educare Pr., *(978-0-944638)* P.O. Box 17222, Seattle, WA 98107 USA Tel 206-782-4797; Fax: 206-782-4802 Do not confuse with EduCare, Colorado Springs, CO
E-mail: educarepress@hotmail.com
Web site: http://www.educarepress.com.

Education 4 All Now LLC *See* **Garwell Publishing LLC**

Education and More, Inc., *(978-0-9755809)* 1760 Clayton Cir., Cumming, GA 30040-7860 USA Tel 678-455-7667
E-mail: education@educationandmore.com
Web site: http://www.educationandmore.com.

Education Ctr., Inc., *(978-1-56234)* Orders Addr.: P.O. Box 9753, Greensboro, NC 27429 USA Tel 336-854-0309; Fax: 336-547-1590; Toll Free: 800-334-0298; Edit Addr.: 3515 W. Market St., Greensboro, NC 27403 USA (SAN 256-6311) Fax: 336-851-8218; 4224 Tudor Ln. Ste. 101, Greensboro, NC 27410-8145 (SAN 256-632X); *Imprints:* Mailbox Books, The (The Mailbox Bks)
E-mail: jmartin@theeducationcenter.com; mjones@themailbox.com
Web site: http://theeducationcenter.com; http://www.themailbox.com
Dist(s): **Sharpe, M.E. Inc.**

Education Matters Co., *(978-0-9768307; 978-0-692-36454-3; 978-0-9963863)* 1112 S. Holly Dr., Sioux Falls, SD 57105 USA Tel 605-334-8149; Fax: 605-334-2479
E-mail: compasscse@sio.midco.net.

Education Services Australia Ltd. (AUS) *(978-1-86366; 978-0-9758070; 978-1-74200; 978-0-646-19608-4; 978-0-646-24402-0; 978-0-646-24701-4; 978-0-646-25530-9; 978-0-646-21423-8) Dist. by* **Cheng Tsui.**

Education That, LLC, *(978-0-692-73656-2; 978-0-692-77912-5; 978-0-9984254)* 5850 Waterloo Rd. Suite 140, Columbia, MD 21045 USA Tel 443-324-7388; 5850 Waterloo Rd. Suite 140, Columbia, MD 21045
E-mail: mbooker@educationthat.com
Web site: www.educationthat.com.

Educational Activities, Inc., *(978-0-7925; 978-0-89525; 978-0-914296; 978-1-55737)* Orders Addr.: P.O. Box 87, Baldwin, NY 11510 USA; Edit Addr.: 1947 Grand Ave., Baldwin, NY 11510 USA (SAN 207-4400) Tel 516-223-4666; Fax: 516-623-9282; Toll Free: 800-797-3223
E-mail: learn@edact.com
Web site: http://www.edact.com
Dist(s): **Follett School Solutions.**

Educational Adventures *See* **Mighty Kids Media**

Educational Adventures Publishing, *(978-0-9864134)* 12840 Normandy Ln., Los Altos Hills, CA 94022 USA Tel 650-948-5742
E-mail: easyandhealthycooking@yahoo.com.

Educational Consulting by Design, LLC, *(978-0-692-59277-9)* 216 Anderson Rd, Glenoma, WA 98336 USA Tel 360-280-8841
E-mail: jcollierllc@gmail.com.

Educational Development Corporation *See* **EDC Publishing**

Educational Dynamics, LLC *See* **Educational Dynamics, LLC**

Educational Dynamics, LLC, *(978-0-9987753; 978-1-7369903)* 19400 Stubblefield Ln., Edmonad, OK 73012 USA Tel 405-341-4411
E-mail: dcastlerich@gmail.com
Web site: http://wwdonnacastlerichardson.com.

Educational Expertise, LLC, *(978-0-9713450)* 427 E. Belvedere Ave., Baltimore, MD 21212 USA
Web site: http://www.educationalexpertise.com.

Educational Impressions, *(978-0-910857; 978-1-56644)* Orders Addr.: P.O. Box 77, Hawthorne, NJ 07507 USA (SAN 274-4899) Tel 973-423-4666; Fax: 973-423-5569; Toll Free: 800-451-7450; Edit Addr.: 210 Sixth Ave., Hawthorne, NJ 07507 USA
E-mail: awpeller@word.net.att.net
Web site: http://www.awpeller.com
Dist(s): **Continental Bk. Co., Inc.**

Educational Media Corp., *(978-0-932796; 978-1-930572)* Orders Addr.: 1443 Old York Rd., Warminster, PA 18974 USA Fax: 215-956-9041; Toll Free: 800-448-2197; Edit Addr.: 4256 Central Ave. NE, Minneapolis, MN 55421-2920 USA (SAN 212-4203) Tel 763-781-0088; Fax: 763-781-7753; Toll Free: 800-966-3382
E-mail: emedia@educationalmedia.com
Web site: http://www.educationalmedia.com.

Educational Publishing Concepts, Inc., *(978-1-892354)* P.O. Box 665, Wheaton, IL 60189 USA Tel 630-653-5336; Fax: 630-653-5368 Do not confuse with Educational Publishing Concepts, Inc., Walla Walla, WA
E-mail: Jerryw@newkidsmedia.com
Web site: http://www.newkidsmedia.com.

Educational Publishing LLC, *(978-1-60436)* Orders Addr.: 51 Saw Mill Pond Rd., Edison, NJ 08817-6025 USA Toll Free: 800-554-2296; Edit Addr.: 10 W. 33rd St. Rm. 910, New York, NY 10001-3306 USA (SAN 854-2422)
Web site: http://www.earlystartchild.com.

Educational Research & Applications, LLC, *(978-0-9762724)* P.O. Box 1242, Danville, CA 94526 USA.

Educational Resources, Inc., *(978-1-931574)* 1691 Highland Pkwy., Saint Paul, MN 55116 USA Tel 651-592-3688; Fax: 651-690-2188 Do not confuse with companies with same name in Shawnee Mission, KS, Columbia, SC, Elgin, IL
E-mail: Edres1691@aol.com
Web site: http://www.eduresources.org.

Educational Solutions, Inc., *(978-0-87825)* 99 University Pl., 6th Flr., New York, NY 10003-4555 USA (SAN 205-6186) Tel 212-674-2988 Do not confuse with Educational Solutions, Stafford, TX.

Educational Testing Service, *(978-0-88685)* P.O. Box 6108, Princeton, NJ 08541-6108 USA (SAN 238-034X) Tel 609-771-7243; Fax: 609-771-7385 Do not confuse with Educational Testing Service in Washington, DC
E-mail: lsavadge@ets.org; j.womack@ets.org; cbrodsky@ets.org
Web site: http://www.ets.org.

Educational Tools, Inc., *(978-0-9766802; 978-0-9774310; 978-1-933797)* 3500 Beachwood Ct., Suite 102, Jacksonville, FL 32224 USA Fax: 904-998-1941; Toll Free: 800-586-9940
E-mail: rpettus@educationaltools.org
Web site: http://www.educationaltools.org.

Educational Video Resources *See* **Summit Interactive**

Educators for the Environment *See* **Energy Education Group**

Educators Publishing Service, Inc., *(978-0-8388; 978-1-4293)* P.O. Box 9031, Cambridge, MA 02139-9031 USA (SAN 201-8225) Toll Free: 800-435-7728; 625 Mount Auburn St., Cambridge, MA 02138
E-mail: epsbooks@epsbooks.com
Web site: http://www.epsbooks.com.

Educ-Easy Bks., *(978-0-9664217; 978-0-9912724; 978-0-9864034; 978-0-9963893; 978-0-9968972; 978-1-7324211; 978-1-7371990)* POB 6366, Greenville, SC 29606 USA Tel 910-798-5042
E-mail: gisela.hausmann@yahoo.com.

EDUKIT, L.L.C., *(978-0-9765917)* P.O. Box 821, Suffern, NY 10901 USA
E-mail: edukitco@aol.com
Web site: http://www.edukit.biz.

EduMatch, *(978-0-692-99178-7; 978-0-692-04640-1; 978-0-692-06333-0; 978-1-7322487; 978-1-970133; 978-1-953852; 978-1-959347)* P.O. Box 150324, Alexandria, VA 22192 USA Tel 703-398-0533; 415-862-8240
E-mail: sarah@edumatch.org; edumatchbooks@edumatchers.org
Web site: www.edumatch.org; www.edumatchpublishing.com
Dist(s): **CreateSpace Independent Publishing Platform.**

Edupress, Inc., *(978-1-56472)* P.O. Box 800, Fort Atkinson, WI 53538-0800 USA Toll Free: 800-835-7978 Do not confuse with EduPress, Pittsburgh, PA
E-mail: info@edupressinc.com
Web site: http://www.edupressinc.com.

Edu-Steps, Inc., *(978-0-9771101; 978-0-9863690)* Orders Addr.: 4644 N. 22nd St. Suite 1161, Phoenix, AZ 85016-4699 USA Tel 480-570-3888; Fax: 602-795-6837
E-mail: patdoran@edu-steps.com
Web site: http://www.edu-steps.com.

Edutech Learning Resource Ctr., *(978-0-9768208)* 1361 NE 158 St., North Miami Beach, FL 33162 USA Tel 305-947-6393
E-mail: edutech_learning@yahoo.com.

Edutunes, *(978-1-930979)* 2067 Rurline Dr., Saint Louis, MO 63146 USA Tel 808-728-8863
E-mail: missjenny@edutunes.com
Web site: http://www.edutunes.com.

Edward, Isaac Adams, *(978-0-692-80001-0)* 2527 S. Meridian St., Puyallup, WA 98373 USA Tel 206-886-5453
E-mail: menatiiworld@hotmail.com.

Edward J. Flora, *(978-1-7327414)* 370 Pk. St., Hackensack, NJ 07601 USA Tel 917-974-7173
E-mail: edwardjflora@gmail.com.

Edwards, Idella, *(978-0-615-56814-0; 978-0-615-65355-6; 978-0-9896802; 978-0-9986662; 978-1-7327963; 978-1-7364506; 979-8-9862014)* 602 Lake Harbor Dr., Marion, IL 62959 USA Tel 618-997-5237
E-mail: idellapearl@frontier.com.

Edwards, Michael, *(978-0-9720952)* 310 N. Front St., Suite No. 4, Box 248, Wilmington, NC 28401 USA
E-mail: neversanever@hotmail.com.

Edwards, R. G. Publishing, *(978-0-615-13336-2; 978-0-615-16739-8; 978-0-615-17785-4)* P.O. Box 978, Goodlettsville, TN 37070 USA
Dist(s): **Lulu Pr., Inc.**

Edwards, R.G. Publlishing *See* **Edwards, R. G. Publishing**

Edwards, Ryan, *(978-1-7377368)* 1826 Lampost, San Antonio, TX 78213 USA Tel 210-608-3462
E-mail: ryanedwards.crypto@gmail.com.

Edwards, Tyler, *(978-0-578-89608-3; 978-1-7377226)* 5808 Oakbury Ct, Myrtle Beach, SC 29579 USA Tel 9046157910
E-mail: tedwardsccc@gmail.com
Dist(s): **Ingram Content Group.**

ee publishing & productions, inc., *(978-0-9753843; 978-0-9798466)* P.O. Box 7006, Fairfax Station, VA 22039 USA Tel 703-256-1721 (phone/fax)
E-mail: info@eeppinc.com; lsaker@eepinc.com
Web site: http://www.eeppinc.com.

eeBoo Corp., *(978-1-59461; 978-1-68227)* 170 West 74th St., Ste. 102, New York, NY 10023 USA (SAN 860-4371) Fax: 212-678-1922
E-mail: christine@eeboo.com
Web site: http://www.eeboo.com.

Eelman's Pr., *(978-0-9747053; 979-8-218-06293-4)* Orders Addr.: P.O. Box Box 359, South Orleans, MA 02662 USA Tel 607-277-0612; Edit Addr.: Davis Rd., South Orleans, MA 02662 USA.

Eepie Pr., *(978-0-9755606)* 1412 Greenbrier Pkwy., Suite 145-B, Norfolk, VA 23320 USA Tel 757-424-5868; Fax: 757-424-5845
E-mail: info@eepiepress.com
Web site: http://www.eepiepress.com
Dist(s): **Print & Ship.**

Eerdmans Bks For Young Readers *Imprint of* **Eerdmans, William B. Publishing Co.**

†Eerdmans, William B. Publishing Co., *(978-0-8028; 978-1-4674)* 2140 Oak Industrial Dr NE, Grand Rapids, MI 49505 USA (SAN 220-0058) Tel 616-459-4591; Fax: 616-459-6540; Toll Free: 800-253-7521 (orders); *Imprints:* Eerdmans Books For Young Readers (Eerdmans Bks)
E-mail: info@eerdmans.com; customerservice@eerdmans.com
Web site: http://www.eerdmans.com
Dist(s): **Children's Plus, Inc.**
Faith Alive Christian Resources
Forward Movement Pubns.
INscribe Digital
Independent Pubs. Group
Ingram Content Group
Send The Light Distribution LLC; *CIP.*

Eernisse, Rachel, *(978-0-692-97874-0)* 2320 W Windmill Ave, NAMPA, ID 83651 USA Tel 408-796-9963
E-mail: racheleernisse@gmail.com
Dist(s): **Ingram Content Group.**

Eeyagi Tales, *(978-1-7327679)* 225 Skyridge Dr, Atlanta, GA 30350 USA Tel 678-320-0386; Toll Free: 678-320-0386
Web site: www.eeyagitales.com
Dist(s): **CreateSpace Independent Publishing Platform.**

EFFE Bks., *(978-0-9773583)* P.O. Box 3448, Winter Park, FL 32790-23448 USA (SAN 257-3784) Tel 407-645-2326
E-mail: tfunaro@summittech.us
Web site: http://www.effebooks.com
Dist(s): **Midpoint Trade Bks., Inc.**

Effective Literacy Methods, *(978-0-9706094)* 57 Knollwood Dr., Rochester, NY 14618-3512 USA
E-mail: info@newphonics.com; rkb@newphonics.com
Web site: http://www.newphonics.com.

Efforts Unified, *(978-0-9763523)* 244 Fifth Ave., No. N259, New York, NY 10001 USA.

EG Bks., *(978-0-615-54589-9; 978-0-615-55920-9)* 360 Oak St., Oakfield, WI 53065 USA Tel 920-583-3329
E-mail: e.garner3@gmail.com.

Egap Gifa Bks. *Imprint of* **Leafcollecting.com Publishing Co.**

Egbert, Bill, *(978-0-9979779)* 3507 N Cole Rd No. 101, Boise, ID 83704-0770 USA
E-mail: begbert2@yahoo.com.

Egg Hill Pubns., *(978-0-9652351; 978-0-692-56474-5; 978-0-692-16533-1; 978-0-692-16534-8)* Orders Addr.: 113 Cottontail Ln., Centre Hall, PA 16828-8508 USA Tel 814-360-4401
E-mail: jandhfra2@yahoo.com
Dist(s): **Partners Bk. Distributing, Inc.**

Egger Publishing, Inc., *(978-1-886050; 978-1-934262)* P.O. Box 12248, Scottsdale, AZ 85267 USA Tel 480-596-5100; Fax: 480-951-2276; Toll Free: 888-937-7355
E-mail: regger@sittonspelling.com
Web site: http://www.sittonspelling.com
Dist(s): **Northwest Textbook Depository.**

Egia, LLC *See* **Spring Song Pr., LLC**

EGM Pr., *(978-0-692-13687-4)* 2600 Somerset Dr., Nashville, TN 37217 USA Tel 615-917-4473
E-mail: karuis@comcast.net.

Ehly, Bridgette, *(978-1-7328733)* 3005 Darby Creek Dr., Crestwood, KY 40014 USA Tel 502-905-7376
E-mail: bridgettejacobs@gmail.com
Web site: excellentfiction.com.

Eifrig Publishing, *(978-0-9795518; 978-1-936172; 978-1-63233)* P.O. Box 66, Lemont, PA 16851-0066 USA (SAN 858-6462)
E-mail: contact@eifrigpublishing.com
Web site: http://www.eifrigpublishing.com
Dist(s): **BookBaby**
Follett School Solutions.

Eileen Reno Maurer, *(978-0-692-16262-0; 978-0-578-40857-6; 978-0-578-42376-0; 978-0-578-42377-7)* 2241 Baxter Canyon Rd., VISTA, CA 92081 USA Tel 760-420-5938
E-mail: eileenmaurer@yahoo.com
Dist(s): **Ingram Content Group.**

Eileen/Morris *See* **Shnoozles, LLC**

Einstein Underground Pr., *(978-0-692-96717-1; 978-0-692-04667-8; 978-0-578-61292-8; 978-1-7344016)* 5225 Evanswood Ln, Edina, MN 55436 USA Tel 612-220-2140; Fax: 612-220-2140
E-mail: amyminge71@gmail.com
Web site: precociouspublishing.com.

Eisenberg Energy, *(978-1-7322969; 979-8-9888042)* 1607 Jefferson Ave., Louisville, CO 80027 USA Tel 303-579-8381
E-mail: gregg@eisenbergenergy.com
Web site: www.curvedspacecomedy.com.

EJMP, *(978-0-615-77563-0)* 2421 SW Candletree Dr Apt 6, Topeka, KS 66614 USA Tel 785-338-0625
Dist(s): **CreateSpace Independent Publishing Platform.**

EJR Language Service Pty. Ltd. (AUS) *(978-0-9805885; 978-0-9945625; 978-0-6480782; 978-0-6485800; 978-0-6455154) Dist. by* **LightSource CS.**

EK Success Ltd., *(978-1-930232)* P.O. Box 1141, Clifton, NJ 07014-1141 USA Tel 973-458-0092; Fax: 973-594-0545; Toll Free: 800-524-1349
E-mail: success@eksuccess.com
Web site: http://www.eksuccess.com.

EKADOO Publishing Group, *(978-0-9747387)* Orders Addr.: P.O. Box 2286, North Redondo Beach, CA 90278 USA Toll Free: 877-252-3404; Edit Addr.: 123 West First St., Suite 675, Casper, WY 82601 USA
E-mail: info@ekadoo.com
Web site: http://www.ekadoo.com.

Ekaré,
Dist(s): **Lectorum Pubns., Inc.**

Ekaré Europa S.L. (ESP) *(978-84-933060; 978-84-934863; 978-84-936504; 978-84-937212; 978-84-937767; 978-84-936843; 978-84-938429; 978-84-939138; 978-84-939912; 978-84-940256; 978-84-941247; 978-84-941716; 978-84-942081; 978-84-943038; 978-84-944050; 978-84-944291; 978-84-946699; 978-84-947431) Dist. by* **Lectorum Pubns.**

Publisher Name Index

Ekare, Ediciones (VEN) *(978-980-257; 978-84-8351; 978-84-937212; 978-84-937767)* Dist. by **Mariuccia Iaconi Bk Imports.**

Ekare, Ediciones (VEN) *(978-980-257; 978-84-8351; 978-84-937212; 978-84-937767)* Dist. by **Lectorum Pubns.**

Eklektika Pr., Inc., *(978-0-9651672; 978-0-9765465; 978-0-9823250)* Orders Addr.: P.O. Box 157, Chelsea, MI 48118 USA Tel 734-730-5161; Edit Addr.: 6401 Conway Rd., Chelsea, MI 48118 USA
Web site: http://www.theseniorsguide.com; http://www.meandmycaregivers.com
Dist(s): **Alliance Bk. Co.**
Distributors, The.

EKR Pubns., *(978-0-9791348)* 257 N. Calderwood St., #356, Alcoa, TN 37701-2111 USA (SAN 852-5293) Tel 727-517-2767 (publisher contact); Toll Free Fax: 866-790-0417 (orders/publisher); Toll Free: 800-266-5564 (orders/AtlasBooks)
Web site: http://www.willigetsahistorylesson.com; http://www.ekrpublications.com.

Ekwike Books & Publishing *See* **Orange County Publishing**

El Aleph Editores, S.A. (ESP) *(978-84-7669; 978-84-85501)* Dist. by **Ediciones.**

El Assali, Amira, *(978-0-9777650)* 23842 Alicia Pkwy Apt. 248, Mission Viejo, CA 92691 USA Tel 714-478-2114
E-mail: amiraalassaly@hotmail.com.

El Brown Training Solutions, *(978-0-9909512)* 2987 District Ave, Fairfax, VA 22031 USA Tel 571-422-3636
E-mail: elbrown@kinderjam.com
Web site: www.elbrowntrainings.com.

El Cid Editor Incorporated, *(978-0-9669968; 978-1-4135; 978-1-4492; 978-1-5129)* Div. of E-Libro Corp., 17555 Atlantic Blvd. # 4, Sunny Isl Bch, FL 33160-2996 USA; 16699 Collins Ave., No. 1003, Miami, FL 33160 Tel 305-466-0155
E-mail: editor@e-libro.com
Web site: http://www.e-libro.net; http://www.e-libro.com
Dist(s): **MyiLibrary**
ProQuest LLC
ebrary, Inc.

El Gato de Hojalata (ARG) *(978-987-668; 978-987-705; 978-987-751)* Dist. by **Peng Rand Hse.**

El Globo de Antonia (COL) Dist. by **Lectorum Pubns.**

El Hogar y La Moda, S.A. (ESP) *(978-84-7183)* Dist. by **AIMS Intl.**

El Jefe, *(978-0-9742840)* P.O. Box 7871, Pueblo West, CO 81007 USA
E-mail: rearch145@aol.com.

El Publications *See* **Jesus Estanislado**

El Zarape Pr., *(978-0-9789954; 978-0-692-69574-6; 978-0-692-72032-5; 978-1-7328106)* 1413 Jay Ave., McAllen, TX 78504-3327 USA (SAN 852-1514)
E-mail: elzarapepress@gmail.com
Dist(s): **CreateSpace Independent Publishing Platform.**

Eland' Ra, *(978-0-9862361)* 27 Ellsworth Rd., West Hartford, CT 06107 USA Tel 860-543-3302
E-mail: elandra4444@gmail.com
Web site: www.ElandraArts.com.

elci Productions LLC, *(978-0-578-45186-2; 978-0-578-45190-9; 978-0-578-71903-0; 978-0-578-71904-7; 978-0-578-85200-3)* 5610 Southern Hills Dr., North Richland Hills, TX 76180 USA Tel 817-605-1134
E-mail: roosta2000@hotmail.com.

Elder Star Pr., *(978-0-578-41282-5; 978-0-578-49060-1; 978-0-578-58687-8)* 3617 Homeway Dr., Los Angeles, CA 90008 USA Tel 614-266-7482
E-mail: johndbuell3@gmail.com
Dist(s): **Independent Pub.**

Elderberry Press, Inc., *(978-0-9658407; 978-1-930859; 978-1-932762; 978-1-934956)* 1393 Old Homestead Rd., Oakland, OR 97462 USA (SAN 254-6604) Tel 541-459-6043 Do not confuse with Elderberry Pr., Encinitas, CA
E-mail: editor@elderberrypress.com
Web site: http://www.elderberrypress.com
Dist(s): **Smashwords.**

Eldergivers, *(978-0-9742262)* 1755 Clay St., San Francisco, CA 94109 USA
E-mail: info@eldergivers.org
Web site: http://www.eldergivers.org.

Eldorado Ink, *(978-1-932904; 978-1-61900)* P.O. Box 100097, Pittsburgh, PA 15233-4842 USA Tel 412-688-0444; Fax: 412-688-8545; Toll Free: 800-783-6767
E-mail: info@eldoradoink.com
Web site: http://www.eldoradoink.com.

Elea Pr., *(978-0-615-34357-0; 978-0-615-67531-2; 978-0-615-75642-4; 978-0-692-21410-7)* 7922 Sequoia Dr., Roanoke, VA 24019 USA
Web site: http://www.nursiesbook.com; http://www.nightweaning.com
Dist(s): **Ingram Content Group.**

eLectio Publishing, *(978-0-615-77551-7; 978-0-615-79001-5; 978-0-615-79469-3; 978-0-615-79864-6; 978-0-615-80543-6; 978-0-615-81846-7; 978-0-615-82555-7; 978-0-615-82645-5; 978-0-615-83096-4; 978-0-615-83772-7; 978-0-615-83878-6; 978-0-615-84548-7; 978-0-615-85867-8; 978-0-615-87769-3; 978-0-615-88179-9; 978-0-615-88473-8; 978-0-615-90365-1; 978-0-615-90866-3; 978-0-615-91122-9; 978-0-615-91680-4; 978-0-615-92441-0; 978-0-615-93116-6; 978-0-615-93337-5; 978-0-615-93550-8; 978-0-615-93822-6; 978-0-615-94869-0;) 1361 Bristol Ln., Aubrey, TX 76227 USA Tel 2149988361*
Web site: http://www.eLectioPublishing.com
Dist(s): **CreateSpace Independent Publishing Platform.**

Electret Scientific Co., *(978-0-917406)* P.O. Box 4132, Star City, WV 26504 USA (SAN 206-4715) Tel 304-594-1639 (phone/fax)
E-mail: U1a00439@wvnet.edu.

Electric Moon Publishing, *(978-1-943027)* P.O. Box 466, Stromsburg, NE 68666 USA Tel 402-366-2033
E-mail: laree.lindburg@gmail.com
Web site: www.emoonpublishing.com
Dist(s): **Whitaker Hse.**

Electric Quill Press *See* **Shine-A-Light Pr.**

Electric Theatre Radio Hour, *(978-0-9848486; 978-0-578-89476-8; 978-0-578-91134-2; 978-0-578-92783-1; 978-0-578-34760-8; 978-0-578-34761-5; 979-8-218-07246-9)* 2200 Market St. Suite 735, Galveston, TX 77550 USA Tel 409-750-8915
E-mail: brendadonaloio@sbcglobal.net.

Eleftheria Publishing, *(978-0-9826040)* 6041 N. Fifth Pl., Phoenix, AZ 85012 USA Tel 602-214-5695
E-mail: michael@michaelenewton.com
Web site: http://www.eleftheriapublishing.com
Dist(s): **Ingram Content Group.**

Elemental Pubs., *(978-0-9765403)* 4404 Whistling Way, Raleigh, NC 27616 USA Tel 919-217-2092.

Elemental Publishing LLC *See* **Elemental Science Inc.**

Elemental Science Inc., *(978-1-935614; 978-1-953490)* 1800 Kraft DR Suite 207, Blacksburg, VA 24060 USA
E-mail: info@elementalscience.com
Web site: http://www.elementalscience.com.

Elementary Publishing, *(978-1-7351417)* 13030 175th DR SE, Snohomish, WA 98290 USA Tel 206-354-9932
E-mail: leonard@leonardwlambert.com
Web site: www.leonardwlambert.com.

Elena Marcus Negoita, *(978-0-615-57545-2)* 2240 Blake St. No. 315, Berkeley, CA 94704 USA
Web site: www.doghappiness.net
Dist(s): **CreateSpace Independent Publishing Platform.**

ElephantSide Pr., *(978-0-9716873)* 33 Bedford St., Suite 10, Lexington, MA 02420 USA (SAN 255-4062).

Eleuthera Press *See* **Windsong Publishing Co.**

Elevé Arts Publishing *See* **Eleve Publishing**

Elevator Group, The, *(978-0-9786854; 978-0-9820384; 978-0-9819719; 978-0-9824945; 978-0-9825282)* P.O. Box 207, Paoli, PA 19301 USA (SAN 851-3104) Tel 610-296-4966; Fax: 610-644-4436; P.O. Box 207, Paoli, PA 19301 Tel 610-296-4966; Fax: 610-644-4436
E-mail: TheElevatorGroup@comcast.net
Web site: http://www.TheElevatorGroup.com; http://www.TEGFaith.com
Dist(s): **MyiLibrary**
ebrary, Inc.

Eleve Publishing, *(978-0-9827304)* 3001 S. Jay St., Denver, CO 80227 USA Tel 720-560-2448
E-mail: larryelwood@gmail.com.

Eleviv Publishing Group, *(978-0-615-61316-1; 978-0-9886289; 978-0-615-89408-9; 978-0-615-98912-9; 978-0-615-99808-4; 978-0-615-99962-3; 978-0-692-22473-1; 978-0-692-30857-8; 978-0-692-35753-8; 978-0-692-35754-5; 978-0-692-40653-3; 978-0-692-42663-0; 978-0-692-42723-1; 978-0-692-45815-0; 978-0-692-45827-3; 978-0-692-56068-6; 978-0-692-57879-7; 978-0-692-59882-5; 978-0-692-65038-7; 978-0-692-66118-5; 978-0-692-72894-9; 978-0-692-06694-2; 978-0-692-08511-0; 978-0-692-13413-9; 978-0-578-44137-5; 978-0-578-44138-2; 978-)*
Web site: www.elevivpublishing.com
Dist(s): **CreateSpace Independent Publishing Platform.**

Elf Garb, *(978-0-615-64129-4; 978-0-9881822)* 96 Idlewell Bld, Weymouth, MA 02188 USA Tel 781-331-7949
E-mail: kelley@elfgarb.com
Web site: www.elfgarb.com.

ELF Productions, *(978-1-7361404)* 207 Mattawoman Way, Accokeek, MD 20607 USA Tel 240-595-7306
E-mail: serviceiamwear@yahoo.com.

Elfa Bks., *(978-0-578-10974-9; 978-0-578-10978-7; 978-0-578-11908-3; 978-0-578-12216-8; 978-0-578-12227-4; 978-0-578-12965-5; 978-0-578-12975-4; 978-0-578-13661-5; 978-0-578-13735-3)* 14967 Merlot Dr., Sterling Heights, MI 48312 USA Tel 586-634-4321
E-mail: elfabooks@yahoo.com
Web site: http://www.elfabooks.com.

Elfen Media, *(978-0-9992311)* P.O. Box 66103, Austin, TX 78766 USA Tel 512-333-4600
E-mail: c.bair@christopherbair.com
Web site: http://www.elfenmedia.com/.

Elgar, Edward Publishing, Inc., *(978-1-84064; 978-1-85278; 978-1-85898; 978-1-84376; 978-1-84542; 978-1-84720)* Orders Addr.: P.O. Box 960, Herndon, VA 20172-0960 USA Tel 800-390-3149; Fax: 802-864-7626; Edit Addr.: 9 Dewey Ct., Northampton, MA 01060-3815 USA (SAN 299-4615)
E-mail: elgarinfo@e-elgar.com; kwight@e-elgar.com; asturner@e-elgar.com
Web site: http://www.e-elgar.com
Dist(s): **Books International, Inc.**
MyiLibrary.

Elgea Publishing, *(978-0-9972884)* 11960 Tivoli Pk. Row, San Diego, CA 92128 USA Tel 858-649-6311
E-mail: chornermd108@aol.com
Web site: www.drchristinehorner.com.

Elias Pubns., LLC, *(978-0-9726247)* P.O. Box 49704, Sarasota, FL 34230 USA Tel 941-556-5656; Fax: 720-920-7262
E-mail: eliaspublications@hotmail.com
Web site: http://www.eliaspublications.com.

Eliassen Creative, *(978-1-937160; 978-0-9892097)* 10328 Horseback Ridge Ave., las Vegas, NV 89144 USA Tel 702-328-2637
E-mail: sunshinenelson@hotmail.com.

eLiberty Pr., *(978-0-9755608)* 2250 N. University Pkwy. No. 4888, Provo, UT 84604 USA Tel 801-427-6630; Fax: 801-373-5999
E-mail: info@elibertypress.com; sales@elibertypress.com
Web site: http://www.elibertypress.com
Dist(s): **Alibris**
Powells.com.

Elim Publishing, *(978-0-9713711; 978-1-59919)* Div. of Elim Gospel Church, 1679 Dalton Rd., Lima, NY 14485 USA Tel 716-624-5560; Fax: 716-624-9677
E-mail: randy@elimpublishing.com
Web site: http://www.elimpublishing.com
Dist(s): **Ingram Content Group.**

Elissian Publishing Co., *(978-0-615-47664-3)* 9715 FM 620 N No. 11203, Austin, TX 78726 USA Tel 512-913-5553; Fax: 512-436-9796
E-mail: demiolesen@hotmail.com.

Elite Online Publishing, *(978-0-692-89706-5)* 9225 Wickford Dr, Houston, TX 77024 USA Tel 713-545-6268; Fax: 713-545-6268
E-mail: melecj@yahoo.com
Web site: www.eliteonlinepublishing.com.

Eliza Todd Designs/A Peace of Werk, *(978-1-7361918)* 1329 Calamus Ln., Grayslake, IL 60030 USA Tel 847-682-4218
E-mail: eliza@elizatodd.com
Web site: www.apeaceofwerk.com.

Elizabeth Dettling Moreno *See* **Dettling Moreno, Elizabeth**

ELIZABETH DETTLING MORENO *See* **Opportune Independent Publishing Co.**

Elizabooks, *(978-0-9762839)* 5515 Catfish Ct., Waunakee, WI 53597 USA Tel 608-849-1984; Fax: 608-849-1985; Toll Free: 888-603-1984
E-mail: liz@elizabookspublishing.com
Web site: http://www.elizabooks.com.

Elk Lake Publishing, Inc., *(978-0-9793543; 978-0-9913727; 978-0-9903062; 978-0-692-32584-1; 978-1-942513; 978-1-944430; 978-1-946638; 978-1-948888; 978-1-950051; 978-1-951080; 978-1-951970; 978-1-64949; 979-8-89134)* 35 Dogwood Dr, Plymouth, MA 02360 USA (SAN 853-2001) Tel 508-746-1734
Web site: http://elklakepublishing.com.

Elk River Pr., *(978-0-9710389)* 1125 Central Ave., Charleston, WV 25302 USA Tel 304-342-1848; Fax: 304-343-0594 Do not confuse with companies with the same or similar name in Altamont, KS, Athens, AL.
E-mail: wvbooks@verizon.net
Web site: http://www.wvbookco.com
Dist(s): **West Virginia Book Co., The.**

Elkarez Publishing Co., *(978-0-9819100)* 327 Sheldon Ave., Staten Island, NY 10312 USA Tel 718-966-5205
E-mail: info@elkarezpublishing.com
Web site: http://www.elkarezpublishing.com.

Eller Books *See* **Brethren Pr.**

Ellie Claire *Imprint of* **Worthy Publishing**

Elliott, Ann T, *(978-0-692-18507-0)* 601 E. Micheltorena St Unit 105, Santa Barbara, CA 93103 USA Tel 707-694-1914
E-mail: annelliottart@gmail.com
Dist(s): **Ingram Content Group.**

Elliott, Jane, *(978-0-9741254)* 707 Country Club Rd., Schofield, WI 54476 USA; *Imprints:* Dynagraphix (Dynagraphix).

Ellipsis Pr., *(978-0-9637536; 978-1-940400)* 3555 78th St., #41, New York, NY 11372 USA Tel 718-840-9373 Do not confuse with Ellipsis Pr. in Campbell, CA
E-mail: info@ellipsispress.com
Web site: http://www.ellipsispress.com
Dist(s): **SPD-Small Pr. Distribution.**

Ellis Pr., The, *(978-0-933180; 978-0-944024)* Div. of Spoon River Poetry Pr., P.O. Box 6, Granite Falls, MN 56241 USA (SAN 214-008X) Tel 507-537-6463 Do not confuse with Ellis Pr., in Charlottesville, VA
E-mail: pichaske@southwest.msus.edu
Web site: http://www.southwest.msus.edu/faculty/pichaske/plains.htm.

Ellison, Penny, *(978-0-9771121)* Orders Addr.: P.O. Box 510082, Miami, FL 33151 USA Tel 786-222-1443; Edit Addr.: 4877 Registry Ln NW, Kennesaw, GA 30152-2891 USA.

Ellosir Pubns., *(978-0-615-91210-3; 978-0-578-41034-0)* 32 Grove St., Salinas, CA 93901 USA Tel 831-262-9274
Web site: www.antoinetheant.com
Dist(s): **CreateSpace Independent Publishing Platform.**

Elm Grove Publishing, *(978-1-943492; 978-1-958407)* 351 Sharon Dr., San Antonio, TX 78216 USA Tel 210-683-9716
E-mail: diane@elmgrovepublishing.com
Web site: www.elmgrovepublishing.com.

Elm Hill, Div. of HarperCollins Christian Publishing, 836 S. Western Dr., Bloomington, IN 47403 USA Tel 317-552-0111; Toll Free: 888-880-4403
Web site: https://elmhillbooks.com
Dist(s): **HarperCollins Christian Publishing**
Nelson, Thomas Inc.

Elma Colletes & Sons, *(978-0-9719337)* 5895 Gardens Reach Cove, Memphis, TN 38120-2523 USA Fax: 901-747-0040
E-mail: mschnap1@midsouth.rr.com.

Elmdale Park Books *See* **Tabron Publishing**

Elnoir Jane Publishing, *(978-0-578-45111-4)* 6200 E. Sam Houston Pkwy. N. No. 8202, Houston, TX 77049 USA Tel 832-874-8897
E-mail: lashandramhall@gmail.com
Dist(s): **Ingram Content Group.**

ELOHAI International Publishing & Media, *(978-0-9984756; 978-0-9992023; 978-1-7324971; 978-1-7348778; 978-1-953535)* PO Box 64402, Virginia Beach, VA 23467 USA
E-mail: connect@banddbrand.com; hello@elohaiintl.com
Web site: BandDBrand.com; www.ElohaiIntl.com.

Elohim Bks., *(978-0-9768831)* Orders Addr.: P.O. Box 1027, Howell, MI 48844 USA.

Eloquence Pr., *(978-0-9753300; 978-0-9824954; 978-0-9913283; 978-0-692-89832-1)* Orders Addr.: 51689 Via Bendita, La Quinta, CA 92253 USA (SAN 255-9676) Tel 760-698-8482
E-mail: jeadon@cox.net; jeadon2@gmail.com
Web site: http://www.eadonbooks.com; http://www.theamericandramaseries.com; http://.

Eloquent Bks. *Imprint of* **Strategic Book Publishing & Rights Agency (SBPRA)**

Eloquent Rascals, *(978-0-9907094; 978-0-9989949)* 30 Lorden Ln., Weare, NH 03281 USA Tel 845-787-3832
E-mail: eloquentrascals@gmail.com
Web site: www.EloquentRascals.com.

Elora Media, LLC, *(978-0-9786813)* PMB 112, 1201 Yelm Ave., Yelm, WA 98597-9859 USA Tel 360-894-6369
E-mail: betsy@eloramedia.com.

Elora Pr., *(978-0-9786813)* Div. of Elora Media, LLC, PMB 112, 1201 Yelm Ave., Yelm, WA 98597-9859 USA (SAN 851-3228) Toll Free: 888-440-8972
E-mail: betsy@eloramedia.com
Web site: http://www.eloramedia.com.

Elotos Pr., LLC, *(978-0-9821737)* 1220 N. Market St., Suite 808, Wilmington, DE 19808 USA
E-mail: info@elotos.com
Web site: http://www.ELOTOS.com.

ELP Bks., *(978-0-9841650)* P.O. Box 1506, Gardena, CA 90249 USA (SAN 858-6098) Tel 213-928-6724
E-mail: emma_p@sbcglobal.net
Web site: http://www.elpbooks.net.

Elsevier - Health Sciences Div., *(978-0-323; 978-0-443; 978-0-444; 978-0-7020; 978-0-7216; 978-0-7234; 978-0-7236; 978-0-7506; 978-0-8016; 978-0-8151; 978-0-920513; 978-0-932883; 978-1-55664; 978-1-56053; 978-1-898507; 978-1-932141; 978-1-4160; 978-1-4377; 978-1-4557)* Subs. of Elsevier Science, Orders Addr.: a/o Customer Service, 3251 Riverport Ln., Maryland Heights, MO 63043 USA Tel 314-453-7010; Fax: 314-447-8030; Toll Free Fax: 800-535-9935; Toll Free: 800-545-2522; 800-460-3110 (Customers Outside US); 1799 Highway 50, Linn, MO 65051 (SAN 200-2280); Edit Addr.: 1600 John F. Kennedy Blvd., Suite 1800, Philadelphia, PA 19103-2899 USA Tel 215-239-3900; Fax: 215-239-3990; Toll Free: 800-523-4069; *Imprints:* Mosby (MosElsHlth); Mosby Limited (Mosby Ltd)
E-mail: usbkinfo@elsevier.com
Web site: http://www.elsevier.com; http://www.us.elsevierhealth.com/
Dist(s): **Elsevier**
MyiLibrary
TNT Media Group, Inc.
ebrary, Inc.

Elsevier Science - Health Sciences Division *See* **Elsevier - Health Sciences Div.**

Elsewhere Editions *Imprint of* **Steerforth Pr.**

Elsie Publishing Co., *(978-1-7327573)* 2950 Van Ness St. NW Apt 319, Washington, DC 20008 USA Tel 202-670-3282
E-mail: elsie1guerrero@gmail.com
Web site: www.elsieguerrero.com.

Eltsar Pr., *(978-0-9769275; 978-0-9833990; 978-0-9850892)* 40453 Cherokee Oaks Dr., Three Rivers, CA 93271-9617 USA Tel 559-561-3270
Dist(s): **Lulu Pr., Inc.**

Elucidate Publishing, *(978-0-615-18146-2; 978-0-615-18228-5; 978-0-9825299; 978-0-9887120; 978-1-948370)* P.O. Box 1262, Hermitage, PA 16148 USA Do not confuse with Elucidate Publishing in Salt Lake City, UT
Web site: http://www.ellamkaye.com; http://www.lkhunsaker.com; http://www.elucidations.us
Dist(s): **Lulu Pr., Inc.**
Smashwords.

Elv Enterprises, *(978-0-9829669)* P.O. Box 2225, La Jolla, CA 92038 USA Tel 858-336-6499
E-mail: rainierpage@ymail.com.

Elva Resa Publishing, LLC, *(978-0-9657483; 978-1-934617; 979-8-88752)* 8362 Tamarack Village, Suite 119-106, Saint Paul, MN 55125 USA Tel 651-357-8770 orders & general info; *Imprints:* Alma Little (Alma Little)
E-mail: orders@elvaresa.com
Web site: http://www.elvaresa.com
Dist(s): **Follett School Solutions**
Independent Pubs. Group.

ELW Pubns., *(978-0-9766233)* 1831 Secretary's Rd., Scottsville, VA 24590 USA Tel 434-295-1678; *Imprints:* His Grace is Sufficient (HGIS)
E-mail: bridgeministry@aol.com.

Elysian Editions *Imprint of* **Princeton Bk. Co. Pubs.**

Elysian Hills, *(978-0-9635589)* Orders Addr.: P.O. Box 40693, Albuquerque, NM 87196 USA Tel 505-897-2734; Fax: 505-897-4614; Edit Addr.: 919 Western Meadows, Albuquerque, NM 87114 USA
E-mail: EdDziczek@aol.com.

Elyssia Bks., *(978-0-692-90256-1; 978-0-578-49336-7; 978-1-954732)* 12228 28th Pl W, Everett, WA 98204 USA Tel 858-722-4339
E-mail: annaholmeswritesbooks@gmail.com; elyssiabooks@gmail.com
Web site: elyssiabooks.com
Dist(s): **CreateSpace Independent Publishing Platform.**

Elytra & Antenna, *(978-0-9719129; 978-0-9802401)* 4663 Ruby Ln., BRUNSWICK, OH 44212-1159 USA Tel 330-273-1918
E-mail: mantidsassassins@yahoo.com; mantidsassassins@yahoo.com
Web site: http://www.elytraandantenna.com.

ELZ Publishing, *(978-0-9772717)* 33 Sheridan Rd., Wellesley, MA 02481 USA Tel 781-237-7417; Fax: 781-237-7429
E-mail: elzahniser@mindspring.com
Web site: http://elzpublishing.com.

M Greenberg Pr., Inc., *(978-0-9634561; 978-0-615-40288-8)* 1245 Sixteenth St., Suite 210, Santa Monica, CA 90402 USA Tel 310-454-0502 (phone/fax)
E-mail: elainergordonphd@gmail.com
Web site: http://elainegordon.com.

maculate Publishing, *(978-1-931855)* P.O. Box 1804, Woodbridge, VA 22195-1074 USA (SAN 254-2005)
E-mail: emaculatepublishing@yahoo.com; info@emaculatepublishing.com
Web site: http://www.emaculatepublishing.com.

MaginationFlow, Incorporated *See* **CuriousDots**

man Publishing, *(978-0-9841275; 978-1-935948)* P.O. Box 404, Fishers, IN 46038 USA
Web site: http://www.EmanPublishing.com.

marketing Of Michigan, LLC, *(978-0-615-38985-1; 978-0-615-88247-5)* Orders Addr.: 11127 Kings Ct., Sterling Heights, MI 48312 USA Tel 586-838-0099; Fax: 586-275-2295
Web site: http://www.readwithmax.com; http://www.emarketingofmichigan.com.

Ember *Imprint of* **Random Hse. Children's Bks.**

Ember *See* **Elyssia Bks.**

Embolden Bks., *(978-1-7322526)* P.O. Box 1228, Cairo, NY 12413 USA Tel 518-819-1662
E-mail: childofmuses@gmail.com.

Embrace Civility LLC, *(978-0-9724236; 979-8-9878023)* P.O. Box 628, Veneta, OR 97487 USA Tel 541-344-9125
E-mail: info@embracecivility.org
Web site: http://embracecivility.org.

Embrace Communications, *(978-0-9668878)* 6887 Red Mountain Rd., Livermore, CO 80536 USA Tel 970-416-9076; Fax: 970-407-0083
E-mail: suengayReynolds@aol.com
Dist(s): **Spring Arbor Distributors, Inc.**

Embracing Life, *(978-0-9985540)* 709 Phar Lap Ln., Bahama, NC 27503 USA Tel 919-308-8889
E-mail: lfovercash@gmail.com.

EMC Publishing, *(978-0-9884707; 978-0-692-36034-7)* 11718 S.E. Federal Hwy. #245, Hobe Sound, FL 33455 USA Tel 504-669-9099.

†EMC/Paradigm Publishing, *(978-0-7638; 978-0-8219; 978-0-88436; 978-0-912022; 978-1-56118; 978-1-5338)* Div. of EMC Corp., 875 Montreal Way, Saint Paul, MN 55102 USA (SAN 201-3800) Toll Free Fax: 800-328-4564; Toll Free: 800-328-1452
E-mail: publish@emcp.com; educate@emcp.com
Web site: http://www.emcp.com.
Dist(s): **Continental Bk. Co., Inc.**; *CIP*.

Emecé Editores S.A. (ARG) *(978-950-04; 978-950-519) Dist. by* **Lectorum Pubns.**

Emecé Editores S.A. (ARG) *(978-950-04; 978-950-519) Dist. by* **Planeta.**

Emece Editores (ESP) *(978-84-95908) Dist. by* **Ediciones.**

Emece Editores (ESP) *(978-84-95908) Dist. by* **Lectorum Pubns.**

EMedia Corp., *(978-1-891155)* 664 NE Northlake Way, Seattle, WA 98105-6428 USA Toll Free: 888-363-3424
E-mail: custserv@emediamusic.com
Web site: http://www.emediamusic.com.

Emerald *Imprint of* **Emerald Bk. Co.**

Emerald Bk. Co., *(978-1-934572; 978-1-937110)* Div. of Greenleaf Bk. Group, 4425 Mo Pac Expy., Suite 600, Austin, TX 78735 USA; *Imprints*: Emerald (Emerald USA)
Dist(s): **Greenleaf Book Group MyiLibrary.**

Emerald Bks., *(978-1-883002; 978-1-932096; 978-1-62486)* Orders Addr.: P.O. Box 635, Lynnwood, WA 98046 USA (SAN 298-7538) Tel 425-771-1153; Fax: 425-775-2383; Toll Free: 800-922-2143; Edit Addr.: 7825 230th St. SW, Edmonds, WA 98026 USA Do not confuse with Emerald Bks. in Westfield, NJ
E-mail: wlwalsh@seanet.com
Web site: http://www.ywampublishing.com
Dist(s): **YWAM Publishing.**

Emerald City Publishing, *(978-0-9675082)* Do not confuse with A Class Act, Sierra Madre, CA
E-mail: eagle3.fox1@gmail.com.

Emerald Funding Corp, *(978-0-692-52542-5; 978-0-692-80620-3; 978-0-692-12589-2)* 7029 Caviro Ln., BOYNTON BEACH, FL 33437 USA Tel 954-961-3352.

Emerald Hse. Group, Inc., *(978-1-889893; 978-1-932307; 978-1-935507; 978-1-62020; 978-1-64960)* 411 Univ. Ridge, Suite B14, Greenville, SC 29601 USA Tel 864-235-2434; Fax: 864-235-2491; Toll Free: 800-209-8570; *Imprints*: Ambassador-Emerald, International (Ambassador-Emerald); Ambassador International (Ambassador Intl)
E-mail: info@emeraldhouse.com
Web site: http://www.emeraldhouse.com; www.ambassador-international.com
Dist(s): **Christian Bk. Distributors Follett School Solutions Spring Arbor Distributors, Inc.**

Emerald Light Pr., *(978-0-9990977)* 20229 Darlington Dr., Montgomery Village, MD 20886 USA Tel 301-651-9881
E-mail: kate@katekennelly.com
Web site: http://www.katekennelly.com.

Emerald Prairie Pr., *(978-1-7337424; 978-1-957938)* 700 R St., No. 80164, Lincoln, NE 68501 USA Tel 402-440-5237
E-mail: kelly@kellybrakenhoff.com.

Emerald Shamrock Pr. LLC, *(978-0-9841880)* 1031 Parkland Rd., Lake Orion, MI 48360 USA (SAN 858-6675) Tel 248-393-6082
E-mail: bridget.mary@comcast.net
Web site: http://www.onechildoneplanet.com.

Emerald Star Pr., *(978-0-615-29908-2; 978-0-615-36644-9; 978-0-615-39280-6; 978-0-9831993)* P.O. Box 2621, Atlanta, GA 30331 USA.

Emerson & Tilman, *(978-0-9827835; 978-1-947151; 978-1-957272)* 129 17th St., Suite 55, Washougal, WA 98671 USA Tel 360-835-3543
E-mail: Blythe@1blythe.com.

EmersonInk, *(978-1-7323603)* 46 Grandview Ave., White Plains, NY 10605 USA Tel 917-273-5353
E-mail: salwaemerson@gmail.com
Dist(s): **CreateSpace Independent Publishing Platform.**

EMG Asylum, LLC, *(978-0-578-18234-6; 978-0-578-22450-3)* 9940 Richmond Ave., Apt. 2017, Houston, TX 77042 USA; 17230 Lilac Vale Ct., Houston, TX 77084 Tel 757-892-4798.

EMI CMG Distribution,
E-mail: distribution@emicmg.com
Web site: http://www.emicmgdistribution.com.

Emidra Publishing, *(978-0-9723569)* P.O. Box 770, Fair Oaks, CA 95628 USA (SAN 255-0369) Tel 916-961-2540 (phone/fax); 10416 Fair Oaks Blvd., Fair Oaks, CA 95628
E-mail: emidra@msn.com
Web site: http://www.emidrapublishing.com.

Emilia, Cara Pr., *(978-1-7329722)* 414 23rd St., Sacramento, CA 95816 USA Tel 805-503-5716
E-mail: caraemiliadesigns@gmail.com
Web site: www.caraemilia.com.

EMK Pr., *(978-0-9726244; 978-1-942571)* Div. of EMK Group, LLC, 16 Mt. Bethel Rd., No. 219, Warren, NJ 07059 USA (SAN 255-0318) Tel 732-469-7544; Fax: 732-469-7861
E-mail: carriekitze@emkpress.com
Web site: http://www.emkpress.com
Dist(s): **Quality Bks., Inc.**

Emma Lindberg, *(978-0-9997307)* 3406 Stagecoach Rd, Durham, NC 27713 USA Tel 919-808-6019
E-mail: Emilyi@eliglobal.com.

EMMA Pubns., *(978-0-9800074)* P.O. Box 654, Northville, MI 48168 USA (SAN 854-977X)
E-mail: info@emmapublications.com
Web site: http://www.emmapublications.com
Dist(s): **Partners Bk. Distributing, Inc.**

Emma, Sasha, *(978-1-7335173)* 5208 Drystack Ln., Glen Allen, VA 23059 USA Tel 804-938-5574
E-mail: timo.selvaraj@gmail.com.

Emmanuel Bks. LLC, *(978-1-7331211)* 34509 Globe School Ave., Edwards, MO 65326 USA Tel 573-692-6928
E-mail: rrspencer7171@gmail.com.

Emma's Pantry, *(978-0-9648437)* 0373 Sopris Creek Rd., #7, Basalt, CO 81621 USA Tel 970-927-4661
E-mail: eewalling@yahoo.com
Web site: http://www.pages.prodigy.com/legends/.

Emmaus Road, International, *(978-1-880185)* 7150 Tanner Ct., San Diego, CA 92111 USA Tel 619-292-7020
E-mail: emmaus_road@eri.com
Web site: http://www.eri.org.

Emmaus Road Publishing, *(978-0-9663223; 978-1-931018; 978-1-937155; 978-1-940329; 978-1-941447; 978-1-63446; 978-1-945125; 978-1-947792; 978-1-949013; 978-1-64585)* 1468 Parkview Cir., Steubenville, OH 43952 USA Tel 740-264-9535; Fax: 740-283-4011; Toll Free: 800-398-5470
E-mail: cerickson@emmausroad.org
Web site: http://www.emmausroad.org.

Emnes Systems, *(978-0-9661636)* 7212 Antares Dr., Suite 100, Gaithersburg, MD 20879 USA Tel 240-683-8502
E-mail: ecfchang@msn.com
Web site: http://www.emnes.com.

Emotional Content, LLC, *(978-0-9817543)* 1445 S. Carmelina Ave., Los Angeles, CA 90025 USA
E-mail: info@biographicnovel.com; eiji@wadirum.com; latinsamurai@gmail.com
Web site: http://www.biographicnovel.com; http://www.emotionalcontent.net.

Empak Publishing Co., *(978-0-922162; 978-0-9616156)* Subs. of Empak Enterprises, Inc., P.O. Box 8596, Chicago, IL 60680-8596 USA (SAN 699-9182) Tel 312-642-3434; Fax: 312-642-9657; Toll Free: 800-477-4554
E-mail: empak@email.msn.com
Web site: http://www.empakpub.com.

Empire Bks., *(978-1-933901; 978-1-949753)* P.O. Box 491788, Los Angeles, CA 90049 USA (SAN 850-4490) Tel 310-433-6732 Do not confuse with Empire Books in New York, NY
Web site: www.martialartsdigital.com; http://www.empirebooks.com.

Empire Holdings *Imprint of* **Kodel Group, LLC, The**

Empire Holdins - Literary Division for Young Readers *Imprint of* **Kodel Group, LLC, The**

Empire Publishing, *(978-0-9766246)* 1117 Desert Ln., Suite 1362, Las Vegas, NV 89102 USA Fax: 413-714-5213.

Empire Publishing Service, *(978-1-58690)* P.O. Box 1344, Studio City, CA 91614-0344 USA (SAN 630-5687) Tel 818-784-8918
E-mail: empirepubsvc@att.net.

Empire Studies Pr., *(978-0-9991435; 978-1-952520)* 5001 College St. SE, Lacey, WA 98503 USA Tel 360-539-7441
E-mail: tdurwood@gmail.com
Web site: www.empirestudies.com.

Empower Pr., *(978-0-9673093; 978-0-9823344)* Div. of Terry Tripp Ministries, Orders Addr.: P.O. Box 899, Gallatin, TN 37066 USA Tel 615-491-3007; Edit Addr.: 2105 Cages Bend Rd., Gallatin, TN 37066 USA
E-mail: klimley@aol.com
Web site: http://empowerpress.com.

Empowered Entertainment, *(978-0-9767076)* 5853 Liberty Creek Dr. N., Indianapolis, IN 46254 USA
E-mail: andrew@chameleonchronicles.com
Web site: http://www.chameleonchronicles.com.

Empowered Faith International *See* **Enlightened Living Ministries International**

Empowered Flower Girl, *(978-0-9978800)* 4921 Crooks, M-11, Royal Oak, MI 48073 USA Tel 313-492-3879
E-mail: rkamaria@gmail.com
Web site: www.empoweredflowergirl.com.

Empowering People Pub., *(978-0-9762639; 978-0-578-16865-4)* Orders Addr.: P.O. Box 329, Rex, GA 30273 USA Tel 850-328-1698
E-mail: Drtina2@gmail.com; altrellpipkin@yahoo.com
Web site: http://www.tinapipkin.com; http://www.empoweringpeopleinc.com; http://www.altrellpipkin.com.

Emprise Publishing *See* **Emprise Publishing & Media**

Emprise Publishing & Media, *(978-0-9717581; 978-0-9725121)* 3643 South Ave., Springfield, MO 65807 USA
E-mail: martyb@powermarkcomics.com.

Empty Harbor Productions, LLC, *(978-0-9790699)* 4 Sarah Lynn Ln., Suite 127, Conroe, TX 77303 USA Toll Free: 866-419-2921
E-mail: emptyharbor@msn.com
Web site: http://www.sticman.net.

Empty Set Entertainment, *(978-0-615-28744-7; 978-0-615-36542-8; 978-0-9831963; 978-1-939366)* Orders Addr.: PO Box 122710, San Diego, CA 92112-2710 USA (SAN 920-7694)
Dist(s): **Baker & Taylor Publisher Services (BTPS) BookBaby.**

Empty Sky *Imprint of* **Zeromayo Studios, LLP**

Empyrion Publishing, *(978-0-692-21367-4; 978-0-692-22501-1; 978-0-692-23065-7; 978-0-692-25133-1; 978-0-692-26300-6; 978-0-692-29670-7; 978-0-692-32818-7; 978-0-692-34586-3; 978-0-692-35427-8; 978-0-692-35803-0; 978-0-692-37463-4; 978-0-692-39027-6; 978-0-692-39961-3; 978-0-692-50806-0; 978-0-692-53646-9; 978-0-692-56921-4; 978-0-692-57186-6; 978-0-692-57448-5; 978-0-692-58459-0; 978-0-692-59421-6; 978-0-692-60449-6; 978-0-692-61946-9; 978-0-692-62947-5; 978-0-692-71074-6; 978-0-692-71963-3; 978-0-9981013) PO Box 140914, Broken Arrow, OK 74014 USA Tel 9184512676 Do not confuse with Empyrion Publishing in Winter Garden, FL*
E-mail: rickmanis@hotmail.com
Dist(s): **CreateSpace Independent Publishing Platform.**

Emu Editions, *(978-0-692-46644-5)* 543 Virginia Ave, Harrisonburg, VA 22802 USA Tel 5405744414
Dist(s): **CreateSpace Independent Publishing Platform.**

En Prose Publications *See* **EnProse Bks.**

En Route Bks. & Media, *(978-0-9988940; 978-0-9991143; 978-0-9994704; 978-0-9996670; 978-0-9998814; 978-1-7324148; 978-1-7325949; 978-1-950108; 978-1-952464; 978-1-956715; 979-8-88870)* 5705 Rhodes Ave., Saint Louis, MO 63109 USA Tel 314-706-1009; Fax: 314-706-1009
E-mail: smahfood@holyapostles.edu
Web site: http://www.enroutebooksandmedia.com.

Enchanted Children Castle Pubns., *(978-1-7377209)* 9711 Risen Star Dr, Upper Marlboro, MD 20772 USA Tel 301-877-5921
E-mail: rae_0217@hotmail.com.

Enchanted Forest Publishing, *(978-0-9910700)* P.O. Box 453, Volcano, HI 96785-0453 USA Tel 808-333-8052
E-mail: enchantedforestpublishing@gmail.com.

Enchanted Lion Bks., LLC, *(978-1-59270)* 201 Richards St. Ste. 4, Brooklyn, NY 11231-1537 USA; *Imprints*: Unruly (UnrulyEL)
E-mail: zoeclaud@earthlink.com; enchantedlionbooks@yahoo.com
Dist(s): **Abrams, Inc. Consortium Bk. Sales & Distribution Farrar, Straus & Giroux Hachette Bk. Group.**

Enchanted Pages Publishing LLC, *(978-0-9843361; 978-1-941739)* P.O. Box 88876, Carol Stream, IL 60188 USA Tel 630-432-0915
E-mail: enchantedpagespublishing@gmail.com
Web site: ourenchantedpages.com.

Enchanted Self Pr., *(978-0-9798952)* 603 S. Edgemere Dr., West Allenhurst, NJ 07711 USA.

Enchantment Pr., *(978-0-9832074)* 14 Valle Escondido, Placitas, NM 87043 USA Tel 505-350-0227
E-mail: lisa.goldman@comcast.net.

Encore Performance Publishing, *(978-1-57514)* Orders Addr.: P.O. Box 692, Orem, UT 84059 USA Tel 801-785-9343; Fax: 801-785-9394
E-mail: encoreplay@aol.com
Web site: http://www.encoreplay.com.

Encore Pubns., *(978-0-9798718)* P.O. Box 117, Stoughton, WI 53589 USA Tel 608-877-9692; Fax: 608-877-9693
E-mail: masonfinancial@charter.net; bonita.mason@peachbandana.com
Web site: http://PeachBandana.com.

Encyclopaedia Britannica, Inc., *(978-0-7826; 978-0-8347; 978-0-85229; 978-0-87827; 978-1-59339; 978-1-60835; 978-1-61535; 978-0-9823819; 978-0-9823820; 978-0-9823821; 978-0-9823822; 978-0-9823823; 978-0-9823824; 978-1-62513; 978-1-68382)* 325 N. La Salle St., Chicago, IL 60654 USA (SAN 204-1464) Toll Free Fax: 800-344-9624 (fax orders); Toll Free: 800-323-1229; 800-621-3900 (orders); 2nd Flr., Unity Wharf Mill St., London, SE1 2BH Tel 020 7500 7800; Fax: 020 7500 7878
E-mail: enquiries@britannica.co.uk; contact@eb.com
Web site: http://www.eb.com; http://www.britannica.co.uk
Dist(s): **Continental Bk. Co., Inc. Ebsco Publishing Follett School Solutions MyiLibrary Pearson Education Pearson Technology Group ebrary, Inc.**

End Game Pr., *(978-1-63797)* P.O. Box 206, Nesbit, MS 38651 USA Tel 901-231-4688
E-mail: victoria@endgamepress.com
Web site: www.endgamepress.com
Dist(s): **Iron Stream Media.**

Endeavor Press *See* **Endeavor Publishing**

Endeavor Pr., *(978-0-9728656)* P.O. Box 4307, Chicago, IL 60680 USA Tel 312-420-6675 Do not confuse with Endeavor Press in Gilbert, AZ
E-mail: rogerrange@endeavorpress.net
Web site: http://www.endeavorpress.com.

Endeavor Publishing, *(978-0-9743843)* 4204 E. Marshall Ave., Gilbert, AZ 85297 USA Tel 480-632-1306 (phone/fax) Do not confuse with Endeavor Press in Annapolis, MD
E-mail: endeavorpublishing@yahoo.com
Web site: http://www.dowkump.com.

Endeavor Publishing Group, *(978-0-9827432)* 10945 State Bridge Rd. Suite 401-193, Atlanta, GA 30022 USA Tel 888-829-8825; Fax: 888-829-8830
E-mail: dscriven@enrichyourfamily.org
Web site: http://www.enrichyourfamily.org
Dist(s): **Outskirts Pr., Inc.**

Endicott & Hugh Bks., *(978-0-9823167; 978-0-9837115; 978-0-9894291; 978-0-9993646)* P.O. Box 13305, Burton, WA 98013 USA
E-mail: info@endicottandhughbooks.com
Web site: http://www.endicottandhughbooks.com
Dist(s): **Partners/West Book Distributors.**

Endoldeation, LLC. *See* **Power of the Pen, LLC.**

Endurance Pr., *(978-0-9856746; 978-0-9960146; 978-0-9964975; 978-0-9988756; 978-1-7335503; 978-1-7363842)* 577 N. Cardigan Ave., Star, ID 83669 USA Tel 208-794-5647
E-mail: robert@endurancepress.com
Web site: www.endurancepress.com.

Energetic Press, LLC *See* **Four Dolphins Pr., LLC**

Energion Pubns., *(978-1-893729; 978-1-938434; 978-1-63199)* P.O. Box 841, Gonzalez, FL 32560 USA Tel 850-525-3916
E-mail: pubs@energion.com
Web site: http://www.energion.com; https://energiondirect.com.

Energy Education Group, *(978-0-9744765)* Div. of The California Study, Inc., Orders Addr.: 664 Hilary Dr., Tiburon, CA 94920 USA Tel 415-435-4574; Fax: 415-435-7737
E-mail: energyforkeeps@aol.com
Web site: http://www.energyforkeeps.org
Dist(s): **PixyJack Pr., Inc.**

Enfini Innovations, *(978-0-692-17507-1; 978-0-692-17598-9; 978-0-578-63638-2; 978-0-578-63639-9; 978-0-578-67559-6)* 1541 Jonathan Ave., Cincinnati, OH 45207 USA Tel 513-238-1484
E-mail: ztm82@yahoo.com
Dist(s): **Ingram Content Group.**

Engage-N-Learn *See* **Zishka Publishing**

Enger, Norman, *(978-0-9905168)* 8817 Twin Creek Ct., Potomac, MD 20854 USA Tel 301-983-5520
E-mail: Norman.Enger@verizon.net.

EngGoGIC, LLC, *(978-0-9882142)* P.O. Box 364, PLAINSBORO, NJ 08536 USA Tel 609-716-6165
E-mail: contact@enggogic.com
Dist(s): **BookBaby.**

Engine Hse. Bks., *(978-0-615-19130-0; 978-0-615-19495-0; 978-0-615-20663-9; 978-0-615-21565-5; 978-0-578-00775-5; 978-0-578-01960-4; 978-1-936211)* 330 WCR 16 1/2, Longmont, CO 80504 USA
Web site: http://www.enginehousebooks.com
Dist(s): **Lulu Pr., Inc. Smashwords.**

Engineering is Elementary, *(978-0-918866; 978-0-9774084; 978-1-933758; 978-1-936789; 978-1-940314; 978-1-7348782; 978-1-952749; 978-1-63619)* 1 Science Pk., Boston, MA 02114 USA (SAN 210-4687) Tel 617-589-0230
E-mail: mhiggins@mos.org
Web site: www.mos.org/eie.

Enginuity, LLC, *(978-1-929645)* Orders Addr.: P.O. Box 20607, San Jose, CA 95160 USA Tel 408-268-9740; Toll Free Fax: 888-268-9740; Toll Free: 888-618-4263; Edit Addr.: 3629 Bryant St., Palo Alto, CA 94306-4209 USA
E-mail: sales@enginuity.com; support@enginuity.com
Web site: http://www.enginuity.com.

England-McCarthy, Judy, *(978-1-7335816)* 217 Buchanan St., Linden, NJ 07036 USA Tel 908-357-0622
E-mail: jemjtt10@gmail.com.

Englefield & Arnold, Incorporated *See* **Englefield & Assocs., Inc.**

Englefield & Assocs., Inc., *(978-1-884183; 978-1-59230)* Div. of Show What You Know Publishing, Orders Addr.: P.O. Box 341348, Columbus, OH 43234-1348 USA Tel 614-764-1211; Fax: 614-764-1311; Toll Free: 877-727-7464 (877-PASSING); Edit Addr.: 6344 Nicholas Dr., Columbus, OH 43235 USA
E-mail: eapub@eapublishing.com; marketing@eapublishing.com
Web site: http://www.showwhatyouknowpublishing.com/.

Engler, Sherry E, *(978-1-7321786)* 195 S Engler Ln., PAYSON, AZ 85541 USA Tel 928-595-4088
E-mail: sherryengler@gmail.com
Web site: sherryengler.com.

English Garden Talk Pr., *(978-0-9763572; 978-0-9779257; 978-0-9858431; 978-0-9915290; 978-0-9971342; 978-0-9995535; 978-1-7342095; 979-8-9875592)* 536 W. Hoptree Ct., Louisville, CO 80027 USA
E-mail: sanddollar5643@aol.com
Dist(s): **Lulu Pr., Inc.**

English SchoolHouse, The, *(978-0-9960016; 978-0-9976860; 978-0-9992108; 978-1-955130)* 3100 June St., Killeen, TX 76543 USA Tel 254-690-6551
E-mail: tamara_nicole@hotmail.com
Web site: www.theenglishschoolhouse.com.

Publisher Name Index

Enhancing Health, Inc., *(978-0-9744479)* P.O. Box 1882, Duluth, GA 30096 USA
E-mail: info@thefitgolfer.com.

ENHEART Publishing, *(978-0-9654899; 978-0-9838882)* Orders Addr.: P.O. Box 620086, Charlotte, NC 28262 USA Tel 980-272-1410 (phone/fax)
E-mail: info@enheartpublishing.com
Web site: http://www.enheartpublishing.com
Dist(s): **BookBaby**
Parnassus Bk. Distributors.

Enigma Productions *See* **Enigmaw Studios**

Enigmaw Studios, *(978-0-9794321)* 923 W. Stephen Ave, clawson, MI 48017 USA
Web site: http://www.enigmaw.com.

Enisen Publishing, *(978-0-9702908; 978-0-9763070)* 2118 Wilshire Blvd., # 351, Santa Monica, CA 90403-5784 USA (SAN 253-3308) Tel 310-989-4069; Fax: 310-576-7278 Do not confuse with companies with the same name in Clermont, FL, Hollywood, CA, Otis Orchards, WA
E-mail: publishing@enisen.com
Web site: http://www.enisen.com.

Enlighten Learning, *(978-0-9755865)* 269 S. Beverly Dr., No. 139, Beverly Hills, CA 90212 USA Tel 310-358-2995.

Enlighten Pubns., *(978-0-9706226)* Orders Addr.: P.O. Box 525, Vauxhall, NJ 07088 USA Toll Free: 866-862-8626
E-mail: books@enlightenpublications.com
Web site: http://www.authorsden.com/jackiehardrick; www.enlightenpublications.com.

Enlightened Bks., *(978-0-9769541; 978-0-692-02980-0)* Orders Addr.: P.O. Box 7423, NewPort Beach, CA 92658 USA Tel 949-644-1376; Edit Addr.: 1 Belcourt Dr., Newport Beach, CA 92660 USA
E-mail: enlightenedbooks13@gmail.com
Web site: http://www.enlightenedbooks.com.

Enlightened Learners Publishing, *(978-0-692-86351-0; 978-0-692-86392-3; 978-0-692-87855-2)* 1935 Sabra Dr, Tallahassee, FL 32303 USA Tel 631-949-6886
E-mail: quashierf@yahoo.com.

Enlightened Living Ministries International, *(978-0-9768416)* P.O. Box 156, Marietta, GA 30061 USA Tel 770-218-6215
E-mail: doctorbell@ecclive.org
Web site: http://www.empoweredfaith.org; https://www.enlightenedliving.info.

Ennis, Scott, *(978-0-692-71256-6; 978-0-692-82285-2; 978-1-7343125)* 3751 Sommers St., Jacksonville, FL 32205 USA Tel 904-673-5994
Dist(s): **CreateSpace Independent Publishing Platform.**

EnProse Bks., *(978-0-9989163; 978-1-948166)* 5557 Baltimore Ave. Suite 500-2082, Hyattsville, MD 20781 USA
E-mail: drnicoleajones@gmail.com
Web site: enprosebooks.org.

Enricharamics, Inc., *(978-1-889654)* 8416-905 O'Connor Ct., Richmond, VA 23228 USA Tel 804-747-5826.

Ensign Peak *Imprint of* **Shadow Mountain Publishing**

Enslow Elementary *Imprint of* **Enslow Publishing, LLC**

Enslow Publishers, Incorporated *See* **Enslow Publishing, LLC**

Enslow Publishing *Imprint of* **Enslow Publishing, LLC**

†Enslow Publishing, LLC, *(978-0-7660; 978-0-89490; 978-1-59845; 978-1-4644; 978-1-4645; 978-1-4646; 978-1-62285; 978-1-62293; 978-1-62324; 978-1-62400; 978-1-9785)* Orders Addr.: P.O. Box 398, Berkeley Heights, NJ 07922-0398 USA (SAN 213-7518) Tel 908-771-9400; Fax: 908-771-0925; Toll Free: 800-398-2504; Edit Addr.: 40 Industrial Rd., Berkeley Heights, NJ 07922-0398 USA; 101 W. 23rd St., Ste, 240, New York, NY 10011 Toll Free Fax: 877-980-4454; Toll Free: 800-398-2504; *Imprints:* MyReportLinks.com Books (MyRptLnks); Enslow Elementary (Enslow Elmntry); Enslow Publishing (EnslowPubng); West 44 Books (MYID_T_WEST 44)
E-mail: ginas@enslow.com; customerservice@enslow.com; hollyc@rosenpub.com
Web site: http://www.enslow.com; http://www.chasingroses.com; http://www.jasminehealth.com; http://www.enslowclassroom.com; http://www.myreportlinks.com; www.speedingstar.com; www.bluewaveclassroom.com; www.scarletvoyage.com
Dist(s): **Follett School Solutions**
MyiLibrary
Rosen Publishing Group, Inc., The; *CIP.*

Entangled Publishing, LLC, *(978-1-937044; 978-1-62061; 978-1-62266; 978-1-63375; 978-1-943113; 978-1-943114; 978-1-943336; 978-1-943892; 978-1-68281; 978-1-5451; 978-1-64063; 978-1-64937)* 10940 S Parker Rd Suite 327, Parker, CO 80134 USA Fax: 970-797-9107; *Imprints:* Entangled Teen (EntangledTeen)
E-mail: publisher@entangledpublishing.com
Web site: http://www.entangledpublishing.com
Dist(s): **Children's Plus, Inc.**
Ingram Content Group
Macmillan
MyiLibrary
Westminster John Knox Pr.

Entangled Teen *Imprint of* **Entangled Publishing, LLC**

Entegrity Choice Publishing, *(978-0-692-28050-8; 978-0-9909397; 978-0-9974859; 978-0-692-90991-1; 978-0-9991780; 978-1-7325767; 978-1-7330301; 978-1-7351739; 979-8-9850792)* .

Entelechy Education, LLC, *(978-0-9887813)* 10810 Symphony Way, Columbia, MD 21044 USA Tel 410-730-5570
E-mail: Gary@EntelechyEd.com
Web site: www.EntelechyEd.com.

Enterprise Incorporated *See* **TLK Pubns.**

Enterprise Leaf Pr., *(978-0-692-05867-1; 978-0-692-17333-6; 978-0-578-52061-2)* 792 Columbus Ave. APT. 4S, New York, NY 10025 USA Tel 917-623-4686
E-mail: sarayaharon1@gmail.com
Dist(s): **Ingram Content Group.**

Enterprize Publishing Co., Inc., *(978-1-893490)* 1036 Parkway Blvd., Brookings, SD 57006 USA Tel 605-692-7778; Fax: 605-997-3194
E-mail: cfcecil@home.com.

Entertainment Ministry, The, *(978-0-9707798; 978-0-9717316; 978-0-9728003; 978-0-9765142; 978-0-9791259; 978-0-9817549; 978-0-9827891)* 5584 Mountain Rd., Antioch, TN 37013-2311 USA Toll Free: 800-999-0101
Web site: http://www.entmin.com
Dist(s): **Send The Light Distribution LLC.**

Entertainment Pubns., Inc., *(978-1-880248; 978-1-58553; 978-1-59878; 978-1-60967; 978-1-949012; 978-1-950493)* 1401 Crooks Rd. Suite 150, Troy, MI 48084 USA Tel 248-404-1000
E-mail: NationalRetail@entertainment.com
Web site: http://www.entertainment.com
Dist(s): **Waldenbooks, Inc.**

Entertainment Publications Operating Company, Incorporated *See* **Entertainment Pubns., Inc.**

Enthusi Adams, Inc., *(978-0-9670245)* 2792 W. Pekin Rd., Spring Boro, OH 45066 USA Tel 937-743-6381; Fax: 513-743-3292
E-mail: enthusiadams@earthlink.net
Web site: http://www.enthusiadams.com.

Entomological Society of America, *(978-0-938522; 978-0-9776209; 978-0-9966674)* 3 Pk. Pl., Suite 307, Annapolis, MD 21401-3722 USA (SAN 200-9307) Tel 301-731-4535
E-mail: pubs@entsoc.org
Web site: http://www.entsoc.org.

Entropy's Espresso, *(978-0-615-64648-0; 978-0-692-36413-0; 978-0-692-93063-2)*
Dist(s): **CreateSpace Independent Publishing Platform.**

Entry Way Publishing *See* **Digi-Tall Media**

EniCare Consulting, Inc., *(978-0-9710925)* Orders Addr.: 2809 Blairmont Dr., Midland, MI 48642 USA Tel 989-839-9177
E-mail: bstrawter@chartermi.net
Web site: http://www.envicareinc.com.

Environmental Protection Agency *Imprint of* **United States Government Printing Office**

Environmental Systems Research Institute *See* **ESRI, Inc.**

Environments, Inc., *(978-1-59794)* P.O. Box 1348, Beaufort, SC 29901-1348 USA Tel 843-846-8155; Fax: 843-846-2999; Toll Free Fax: 800-343-2987; Toll Free: 800-342-4453
E-mail: environments@eichild.com
Web site: http://www.eichild.com.

Envisage Publishing, *(978-0-9729042)* Orders Addr.: P.O. Box 557, Queens Village, NY 11428 USA; Edit Addr.: 89-52 208th St., Queens Village, NY 11427 USA
E-mail: drndavoren@hotmail.com
Web site: http://www.envisagepublishing.com
Dist(s): **Lulu Pr., Inc.**

Envision Berlin, e.V., *(978-1-940105)* Orders Addr.: Parkstraße 11, Berlin, 13086 DEU; Edit Addr.: Parkstraße 11, Berlin, 13086 DEU
E-mail: jones@viscereality.us; stephen@thepracticalinterculturalist.com; jennie@excegent.com
Web site: http://www.excegent.com; http://www.iamintercultural.com; http://www.thepracticalinterculturalist.com; http://www.viscereality.us
Dist(s): **Ingram Bk. Co.**
Smashwords.

Envision Editions, Limited *See* **Envision Editions Ltd.**

Envision Editions Ltd., *(978-0-9762814)* Orders Addr.: P.O. Box 442, Gaylord, MI 49734 USA; Edit Addr.: 2020 Brink Trail, Gaylord, MI 49735 USA.

Envision EMI, Inc., *(978-0-9745760)* 1919 Gallows Rd. Ste. 700, Vienna, VA 22182-4007 USA.

EoH Publishing *See* **WE, LLC**

E-O-L Publishing Corp., *(978-0-9753705)* P.O. Box 110 Keely Circle, New Smyrna Beach, FL 32168 USA
E-mail: jvoss2@cfl.rr.com
Web site: http://www.eolpublishing.com.

Eos *Imprint of* **HarperCollins Pubs.**

EPEI Press *See* **EPEI Pr.**

EPEI Pr., *(978-0-9729065)* Orders Addr.: 1450 S. New Wilke Rd., Suite 102, Arlington Heights, IL 60005 USA Tel 847-670-6992; Fax: 847-670-7466; Toll Free: 877-670-7444; Edit Addr.: 1749 Golf Rd., No. 204, Mount Prospect, IL 60056 USA
E-mail: sara@getprepared.org
Web site: http://www.getprepared.org.

Ependymoma Research Foundation, *(978-0-578-55473-0; 978-1-7356809)* 1337 Massachusetts Ave No. 219, Arlington, MA 02476 USA Tel 718-538-6755
E-mail: sbfine@gmail.com
Web site: ependymomaresearchfoundation.org.

Ephemeron Pr., *(978-0-912290)* 1510 Perdido Ct., Melbourne, FL 32940 USA Tel 321-752-0167
E-mail: johnknapp2@gmail.com
Web site: http://www.ephemeronpress.com.

EPI Bks., *(978-0-9726075; 978-0-9796536; 978-0-9843655; 978-0-9826006)* 2364 Roll Dr., San Diego, CA 92154 USA Fax: 619-869-8501; *Imprints:* EPI Kid Books (EPI Kid Bks)
Web site: http://www.EPIBooks.com
Dist(s): **Anderson Merchandisers.**

EPI Kid Bks. *Imprint of* **EPI Bks.**

Epic Bks. *Imprint of* **Bellwether Media**

Epic Escape *Imprint of* **EPIC Pr.**

Epic Pr. *Imprint of* **ABDO Publishing Co.**

Epic Pr., *(978-0-9801061; 978-1-941185)*
E-mail: sglittle@grandecom.net
Web site: http://www.epic-press.com
Dist(s): **Ingram Content Group.**

EPIC Pr., *(978-1-68076)* Div. of ADBO Publishing Group, 8000 W. 78th St., Suite 310, Edna, MN 55439 USA Toll Free Fax: 800-862-3480; Toll Free: 800-800-1312; *Imprints:* Epic Escape (EpicEscape)
Web site: https://abdopublishing.com/
Dist(s): **ABDO Publishing Co.**

EPIC Publishing Co., *(978-0-9674025; 978-0-9763870; 978-0-9995925)* 1405 Ten Palms Ct., Las Vegas, NV 89117-1404 USA (SAN 253-2840) Do not confuse with companies with the same or similar name in Erie, PA, Canon City, CO, Greeley, CO
E-mail: rxl@epicpublishing.com
Web site: http://www.epicpublishing.com.

Epicality Bks., *(978-0-9838594; 978-1-954585)*
E-mail: matthewjamesbeier@gmail.com.

Epicality Books, LLC *See* **Epicality Bks.**

Epicenter Literary Software, *(978-0-9760222; 978-1-938609)* 6514 Seventh St., NW, Washington, DC 20012-2622 USA Tel 202-829-2427; 202-277-2649
E-mail: carolivia@carolivia.org; carolivia@gmail.com
Web site: http://www.carolivia.org; http://www.carolivia.com.

Epicenter Pr., Inc., *(978-0-945397; 978-0-9708493; 978-0-9724944; 978-0-9745014; 978-0-9790470; 978-1-60381; 978-0-9800825; 978-1-935347; 978-1-941890)* Orders Addr.: 6524 NE 181st St., No. 2, Kenmore, WA 98028 USA (SAN 246-9405) Do not confuse with companies with similar names in Kanehoe, HI, Long Beach, CA, Oakland, CA
E-mail: info@epicenterpress.com; phil@epicenterpress.com; aubrey@epicenterpress.com
Web site: http://www.epicenterpress.com
Dist(s): **Open Road Integrated Media, Inc.**
Smashwords.

Epigraph Bks., *(978-0-9726357; 978-0-9749359; 978-0-9766843; 978-0-9789427; 978-0-9798828; 978-0-9823246; 978-0-9824530; 978-0-9825255; 978-0-9826441; 978-0-9830517; 978-0-9833589; 978-1-936940; 978-1-939681; 978-1-944037; 978-1-948626; 978-1-948796; 978-1-951937; 978-1-954744; 978-1-960090) a/o Monkfish Book Publishing Company, 22 E. Market St., Ste. 304, Rhinebeck, NY 12572 USA*
Web site: http://www.epigrahps.com
Dist(s): **MyiLibrary**
SPD-Small Pr. Distribution.

Epiphany Movement, *(978-1-7340892)* 28 Nobels Rd., Monticello, MS 39654 USA Tel 601-455-1331
E-mail: tdnelson2@mc.edu
Web site: epiphanymovement.com.

Episode.Media, *(978-0-9986610)* 5060 S. Hillcrest Ln., Veradale, WA 99037 USA Tel 509-435-7401
E-mail: dandaines.episode@gmail.com
Web site: www.dandaines.com; www.Episode.media.

Epistelogic, *(978-0-9748319)* 47 White Pl., Bloomington, IL 61701-1859 USA Tel 309-826-4808
Web site: http://www.epistelogic.com; http://www.scholarpress.com
Dist(s): **Savant Bk. Distribution Co.**

e-Pluribus Unum Publishing Company *See* **Cronus College**

Epoca, Editorial, S.A. de C.V. (MEX) *(978-968-6769; 978-970-627) Dist. by* **Giron Bks.**

EPOCH Studios, LLC, *(978-0-9970208; 978-0-9975570)* 2645 Rosalyn Ln. SE, Smyrna, GA 30080 USA Tel 773-896-6276
E-mail: dxbrooks@aol.com; jbrooks@worldsofepoch.com
Web site: http://www.worldsofepoch.com.

Eppy's Creations, *(978-0-615-16983-5)* P.O. Box 1103, Swansboro, NC 28584 USA
Dist(s): **Lulu Pr., Inc.**

eProduction Services *See* **Kepler Pr.**

EPS Digital, *(978-0-9772315)* P.O. Box 5185, De Pere, WI 54115-5185 USA.

ePub Bud, *(978-1-61061; 978-1-61979; 978-1-62154; 978-1-62314; 978-1-62590; 978-1-62776; 978-1-62840)* 427 California Ave., Santa Monica, CA 90403 USA Tel 310-980-4668
E-mail: josh@epubbud.com
Web site: http://www.epubbud.com
Dist(s): **BookBaby**
INscribe Digital
Lulu Pr., Inc.

ePublishing Works!, *(978-1-61417; 978-1-947833; 978-1-64457)* 644 Shrewsbury Commons Ave, No. 249, Shrewsbury, PA 17349 USA Tel 866-846-5123; Fax: 866-846-5123; *Imprints:* Rise UP Publications (MYID_B_RISE UP)
E-mail: epublishingworks@ebookprep.com
Web site: www.epublishingworks.com
Dist(s): **INscribe Digital**
Independent Pubs. Group.

EQUALS *Imprint of* **Univ. of California, Berkeley, Lawrence Hall of Science**

Equidata Publishing, *(978-0-9714185)* Orders Addr.: P.O. Box 8116, Surprise, AZ 85374 USA Tel 623-476-7503; Edit Addr.: 13781 W. Crocus Dr. Surprise, Az 85379, Surprise, AZ 85379 USA
E-mail: jobrien6@cox.net
Web site: http://www.equidatapublishing.com.

Equimax USA, Inc., *(978-0-9668082)* HC65 Box 271, Alpine, TX 79830 USA Tel 432-371-2610; Fax: 432-371-2612; Toll Free: 800-759-9494
E-mail: employment@equimax.com
Web site: http://www.equimax.com.

Equine Graphics Publishing Group, *(978-1-887932; 978-0-9855309; 978-0-9962336; 978-1-7379710)* 30 Wiemes Ct, Waterford, CT 06385 USA Tel 860-383-9527; *Imprints:* SmallHorse Press (SmallHorse Pr)
E-mail: editor@newconcordpress.com; toniweeone@smallhorse.com; equinegraphicspubs@gmail.com
Web site: http://www.smallhorse.com; http://www.newconcordpress.com; http://www.equinegraphicspublishing.com; http://www.tonileland.com
Dist(s): **Smashwords.**

Equitel Publishing Co., *(978-0-9789131)* 53 Mount Ida Rd., Suite.2, Dorchester, MA 02122-1735 USA
Web site: http://www.equitelpublishing.com.

ER Landron, *(978-1-7324581)* urb las haciendas, 15031 calle camino largo, canovanas, PR 00729 USA Tel 787-312-7474
E-mail: erlandron@gmail.com
Web site: erlandron.com.

Erazo, Carlos, *(978-0-9759757; 978-0-9796253)* P.O. Box 2111, Bayamon, PR 00960-2111 USA
E-mail: erazo2001@prtc.net
Web site: http://www.erazolabor.com
Dist(s): **Representaciones Borinquenas, Inc.**

Erendi Publishing, *(978-0-9982605; 978-1-950903)* 84 Big Oak Rd., Warsaw, VA 22572 USA
E-mail: admin@erendi.com
Web site: http://www.erendi.com.

Erickson Pr., *(978-1-60217)* Orders Addr.: P.O. Box 33, Yankton, SD 57078 USA (SAN 852-0402); Edit Addr.: 329 Broadway, Yankton, SD 57078 USA
Web site: http://www.ericksonpress.com.

Erickson, Rakel L., *(978-0-9744422)* P.O. Box 86, Fertile, MN 56540-0086 USA
E-mail: thomas_robinson@und.nodak.edu.

Erickson, Tim, *(978-1-59492)* 8801 Fremont Ave S., Minneapolis, MN 55420-2642 USA
E-mail: terickson21@mn.rr.com
Web site: http://www.deathswhisper.com.

Erie Harbor Productions, *(978-0-9717828)* Orders Addr.: 223 W. Cornell Ave., Suite B, Pontiac, MI 48340 USA
E-mail: harbormaster@erieharbor.com
Web site: http://www.erieharbor.com.

ErieKIDS, Inc., *(978-0-9779822)* 4544 W. Ridge Rd., Suite One, Erie, PA 16506 USA (SAN 850-668X) Tel 814-835-3430
Web site: http://www.eriekids.com.

Eriginal Bks. LLC, *(978-0-9829213; 978-1-61370)* 13868 SW 151 Ct., Miami, FL 33196 USA Tel 305-763-2706; 10854 SW 88 St Suite 220, Miami, FL 33176
E-mail: marlene.moleon@gmail.com.

Erin Go Bragh Publishing, *(978-0-9882745; 978-1-941345; 978-1-956581)* 1885 FM 2673 No. 3, Canyon Lake, TX 78133 USA Tel 830-515-8187; Fax: 866-652-5165
E-mail: kjs@hamiltontroll.com; kjs@kathleensbooks.com; kathleen@eringobraghpublishing.com
Web site: www.HamiltonTroll.com; www.ErinGoBraghPublishing.com; www.KathleensBooks.com.

Erin Kelly Roberts Flores, *(978-0-692-18743-2; 978-0-692-18744-9)* 35280 Prestwick Ct., Round Hill, VA 20141 USA Tel 949-533-3218
E-mail: kellywahine@gmail.com
Dist(s): **Ingram Content Group.**

Eringer Travel Guides *See* **Writer's Cramp, Inc.**

Erinsillart, *(978-0-9779155)* 739 31 ave, san francisco, CA 94121 USA Tel 415-816-0766
E-mail: erin@erinsillart.com
Web site: http://www.erinsillart.com.

Ernest Michael Olivarez Publishing LLC, *(978-1-7328080)* 1011 Wembley Rd., Arlington, TX 76014 USA Tel 817-525-5187
E-mail: emolivarez@yahoo.com
Web site: josethereindeer.com.

ERPublishing, LLC, *(978-0-9766568)* P.O. Box 152, Old Greenwich, CT 06870 USA
Web site: http://www.erpublishing.com.

ERTLL Pubs., *(978-0-9909929; 978-1-7342708)* 7216 Lotus Ave. No. 7, San Gabriel, CA 91775 USA Tel 626-258-9946
E-mail: RANDYERTLL@YAHOO.COM
Web site: www.randyjuradoertll.com.

Ervin, Imogene *See* **Finer Moments**

Ervin, Lavette, *(978-1-7344278)* 9105 Barton Creek Dr., Rowlett, TX 75089 USA Tel 469-831-0642
E-mail: bfbookadventure01@gmail.com.

Ervin, Randy, *(978-0-578-05732-3; 978-0-578-09147-1; 978-0-578-16686-5; 978-0-578-18433-3; 978-0-578-75824-4)* 1113 Stinson Ave., Mattoon, IL 61938 USA
E-mail: randyjervin@icloud.com
Dist(s): **Independent Pub.**

Ervin, Robert E., *(978-0-9746189)* 552 Keystone Station Rd., Jackson, OH 45640 USA Tel 740-286-2693; Fax: 740-286-0756
E-mail: multicominc@adelphia.net
Web site: http://johnhuntmorgan.com.

Erwin, Amy Leaf *See* **Leaf Publishing, LLC**

Eryn Lace, *(978-0-615-38779-6)* 223 Pacific St. Unit B, Santa Monica, CA 90405 USA Tel 323-620-7434
E-mail: jwkobernick@hotmail.com.

Escape Hatch Bks., *(978-0-9976397)* 27 Main St., Jaffrey, NH 03452 USA Tel 603-721-1230
E-mail: ehb@escapehatchbooks.com
Web site: www.escapehatchbooks.com.

Escher, Ursula, *(978-0-9718609)* Bookmasters (high Mountain Pub) 30 Amberwood Pkwy. P.o. Box 388, Ashland, OH 44805 USA Tel 818-645-8621
E-mail: uescher@hotmail.com.

Eschia Bks. (CAN) *(978-0-9810942; 978-1-926696) Dist. by* **Lone Pine.**

Escritora, *(978-0-578-46574-6; 978-0-578-63419-7; 978-0-578-76663-8; 978-0-578-87444-9)* 1402 William Penn Ln., Wilmington, DE 19803 USA Tel 302-354-2800
E-mail: aida.wasersteinauthor@gmail.com.

Escuela de Musica *See* **Ed Musica**

slinger Hse. Publishing, *(978-0-9763033)* 17762 Neff Ranch Rd., Yorba Linda, CA 92886-9013 USA E-mail: gilberstadt@earthlink.net.

smaili, Inc., *(978-0-9656185)* P.O. Box 421382, Dallas, TX 75342 USA Tel 214-521-9600; Fax: 214-526-9617.

SOL Publishing, *(978-0-9793761)* 10305 Colony View Dr., Fairfax, VA 22032 USA (SAN 853-2796) Tel 703-250-7097 E-mail: ESOLPublishing@aol.com; mcpuginrodas@aol.com Web site: http://www.Createspace.com/3382900 *Dist(s):* **CreateSpace Independent Publishing Platform Reading Matters, Inc.**

spasa Calpe, S.A. (ESP) *(978-84-239; 978-84-339; 978-84-8326; 978-84-670) Dist. by* **Distribks Inc.**

Espasa Calpe, S.A. (ESP) *(978-84-239; 978-84-339; 978-84-8326; 978-84-670) Dist. by* **Continental Bk.**

Espasa Calpe, S.A. (ESP) *(978-84-239; 978-84-339; 978-84-8326; 978-84-670) Dist. by* **Ediciones.**

Espasa Calpe, S.A. (ESP) *(978-84-239; 978-84-339; 978-84-8326; 978-84-670) Dist. by* **Libros Fronteras.**

Espasa Calpe, S.A. (ESP) *(978-84-239; 978-84-339; 978-84-8326; 978-84-670) Dist. by* **Lectorum Pubns.**

Espasa Calpe, S.A. (ESP) *(978-84-239; 978-84-339; 978-84-8326; 978-84-670) Dist. by* **Planeta.**

eSpec Bks., *(978-1-942990; 978-1-949691; 978-1-956463)* Orders Addr.: P.O. Box 242, Pennsville, NJ 08070 USA; Edit Addr.: P.O. Box 242, Pennsville, NJ 08070 USA Tel 856-669-7395; *Imprints:* Paper Phoenix Press (MYID_U_PAPER) E-mail: especbooks@aol.com Web site: www.especbooks.com.

Esperanza Pr., *(978-0-692-30570-6)* 12089 N. 75th St., Longmont, CO 80503 USA Tel 303-772-9868 *Dist(s):* **CreateSpace Independent Publishing Platform.**

Espial Design, *(978-0-692-60881-4; 978-0-692-79727-3; 978-1-7321435)* 16020 SE 42nd Pl., Bellevue, WA 98006 USA Tel 425-615-5609 E-mail: slk_macia@hotmail.com Web site: www.espialdesign.com *Dist(s):* **CreateSpace Independent Publishing Platform.**

Esquire Publishing, Inc., *(978-0-9745045; 978-0-9816554; 979-8-9856998)* 5900 Harper Rd., Suite 107, Solon, OH 44139 USA (SAN 856-146X) Tel 440-318-4234; Fax: 440-528-0157 E-mail: esq@pollock-law.com; esq@esquiresongs.com Web site: http://www.monsterbooks.net *Dist(s):* **Partners Pubs. Group, Inc.**

ESRI, Inc., *(978-1-879102; 978-1-58948)* 380 New York St., Redlands, CA 92373-8100 USA Fax: 909-307-3082; Toll Free: 800-447-9778; *Imprints:* ESRI Press (ESRI Pr) E-mail: esripress@esri.com Web site: http://www.esri.com/esripress *Dist(s):* **Cengage Gale Independent Pubs. Group Ingram Publisher Services MyiLibrary Trans-Atlantic Pubns., Inc.**

ESRI Pr. *Imprint of* **ESRI, Inc.**

Essential Library *Imprint of* **ABDO Publishing Co.**

Essentially Strong, *(978-1-7339972)* 6898 190th Ave SE, Becker, MN 55308 USA Tel 763-439-5508 E-mail: JackieKartakYL@gmail.com.

Estreno Plays, *(978-0-9631212; 978-1-888463)* 18 Van Hise Dr., Perrineville, NJ 08535 USA Tel 609-443-4787; Fax: 212-346-1435 E-mail: iridelens@aol.com; sberardini@aol.com Web site: http://www.rci.rutgers.edu/~estrplay/webpage.html.

ETA hand2mind *See* **hand2mind**

Etcetera Pr. LLC, *(978-0-9785160; 978-0-9826781; 978-1-936824)* 221 Edgewood Dr., Richland, WA 99352 USA (SAN 850-864X) E-mail: great_copy@hotmail.com Web site: http://etcpress.net *Dist(s):* **CreateSpace Independent Publishing Platform Independently Published Ingram Content Group.**

Etched In Stone Pubns., *(978-0-9898907)* 756 S. Orange Ave., Newark, NJ 07106 USA Tel 973-703-8850 E-mail: rodneyjwls@aol.com.

Eternal Foundations Curriculum, *(978-1-932505)* P.O. Box 1213, Atascadero, CA 93423 USA Tel 805-466-1910 E-mail: tsgaddis@tcsn.net.

Eternal Studios, *(978-1-887814)* 15235 Rainhollow, Houston, TX 77070 USA Tel 713-370-8384 *Dist(s):* **Diamond Comic Distributors, Inc.**

Eternity Pr., *(978-0-9758989)* 2828 Brannon Ave., Saint Louis, MO 63139-1438 USA Toll Free: 800-886-7587; 1 Brounger Rd., Constantia, 7806 Tel 447521578414 Web site: http://www.cenveo.com *Dist(s):* **Smashwords.**

Ethan Ellenberg Literary Agency, *(978-1-68068; 978-0-692-03770-6)* 155 Suffolk St., # 2R, New York, NY 10002 USA Tel 212-431-4554.

Ethics Trading (GBR) *(978-0-9556887) Dist. by* **LuluCom.**

Ethos Of Commerce Pubs., Ltd., *(978-0-9741412)* 3535 E. Coast Hwy. No. 216, Corona del Mar, CA 92625 USA Tel 949-862-5826 E-mail: ethosofcommerce@yahoo.com Web site: http://www.geocities.com/EthosOfCommerce.

Etiquette, Etc., LLC *See* **CKK Educational, LLC.**

ETN, Inc., *(978-0-9759629; 978-0-9855450)* 3540 W. Sahara Ave., No. 25, Las Vegas, NV 89102 USA E-mail: eworth@etnbooks.com.

Etopia Pr., *(978-1-936751; 978-1-937976; 978-1-939194; 978-1-940223; 978-1-941692; 978-1-944138; 978-1-947135; 978-1-949719)* 117 Bellevue Ave. Ste. 202B, Newport, RI 02840 USA Tel 401-846-0010 E-mail: apmelton@gmail.com Web site: www.etopia-press.net.

eTreasures Publishing, *(978-0-9740537)* Orders Addr.: P.O. Box 71813, Newnan, GA 30271 USA Tel 770-683-8032; Edit Addr.: 4442 Lafayette St., Marianna, FL 32446 USA Tel 850-209-0329 E-mail: publisher@etreasurespublishing.com Web site: http://www.etreasurespublishing.com *Dist(s):* **Smashwords.**

Etruscan Pr., *(978-0-9718228; 978-0-9745995; 978-0-9797450; 978-0-9819687; 978-0-9832944; 978-0-9839346; 978-0-9886922; 978-0-9897532; 978-0-9903221; 978-0-9977455; 978-0-9987508; 978-0-9997534; 978-1-7336741; 978-1-7364946; 979-8-9858824; 979-8-9881985)* 84 West South St., Wilkes-Barre, PA 18766 USA Tel 570-408-4546; Fax: 570-408-3333 E-mail: bill@etruscanpress.org Web site: http://www.etruscanpress.org *Dist(s):* **Consortium Bk. Sales & Distribution MyiLibrary SPD-Small Pr. Distribution.**

ETS Publishing, *(978-0-9816642)* Orders Addr.: 9341 Clovercroft Rd., Franklin, TN 37067 USA (SAN 856-1583) E-mail: info@etspublishinghouse.com Web site: http://www.thisbespromise.com; http://www.etspublishing.com.

Ettelloc Publishing, *(978-0-615-78622-3; 978-0-615-83429-0; 978-0-9898304)* 734 Franklin Avenue, Suite 235, Garden City, NY 11530 USA Tel 5169244411 *Dist(s):* **CreateSpace Independent Publishing Platform.**

Ettrick Bks., *(978-0-9963451)* P.O. Box 340488, New York, NY 11234 USA Tel 602-743-7426 E-mail: ettrickbooks2015@gmail.com.

Eudon Publishing, *(978-0-9765423)* P.O. Box 9, Goddard, KS 67052 USA Tel 316-210-4649; Fax: 316-233-1075 E-mail: gsmith@EudonPublishing.com Web site: http://www.EudonPublishing.com *Dist(s):* **BWI Brodart Co. Follett School Solutions.**

eugenus(r) STUDIOS *See* **eugenus STUDIOS, LLC**

eugenus STUDIOS, *(978-0-578-09572-1)* 445 Lakeview Rd., Craryville, NY 12521 USA E-mail: victor@eugenus.com Web site: http://www.captaincrossbones.com; http://www.eugenus.com.

eugenus STUDIOS, LLC, *(978-0-9885030; 978-0-9989154; 978-0-692-05160-3; 978-1-7330671; 979-8-218-95259-4)* P.O. Box 213, Valatie, NY 12184 USA Tel 518-610-8270; Fax: 518-610-8270; 170 Cortland Dr., Valatie, NY 12184 E-mail: victor@eugenus.com Web site: www.eugenusSTUDIOS.com.

Eupanapue-Auntella's Rooster Pubns., *(978-0-615-32789-1)* P.O. Box 5803, Denver, CO 80217-5803 USA Tel 720-272-5570; *Imprints:* RoosterBugglePue Books (RoosBugglePue) E-mail: Eupanapue_AuntellasRoosterPub@q.com Web site: http://www.roosterbugglepue.com.

Euphema Press, *(978-0-9779600)* P.O. Box 2314, Bowie, MD 20718 USA Web site: http://www.euphema.com.

Eureka Productions, *(978-0-9712464; 978-0-9746648; 978-0-9787919; 978-0-9825630; 978-0-9963888)* 8778 Oak Grove Rd., Mount Horeb, WI 53572 USA Web site: http://www.graphicclassics.com *Dist(s):* **Diamond Comic Distributors, Inc. Diamond Bk. Distributors.**

Europa Editions, Inc., *(978-1-933372; 978-1-60945; 978-0-9968778; 979-8-88966)* Div. of Edizioni E/O (Rome, Italy), 27 Union Sq. W. Suite 302, New York, NY 10003 USA; Italian Office, Via Gabriela Camozzi 1, Roma, 00195 E-mail: diego@europaeditions.com; editor@europaeditions.com Web site: http://www.europaeditions.com/ *Dist(s):* **MyiLibrary Open Road Integrated Media, Inc. Penguin Publishing Group Publishers Group West (PGW) Random Hse., Inc.**

European Language Institute (ITA) *(978-88-8148; 978-88-85148; 978-88-536) Dist. by* **Distribks Inc.**

Eusebian Publishing, *(978-1-947805)* 5348 Vegas Drive, Suite 1670, Las Vegas, NV 89108 USA Tel 916-291-9903 E-mail: Eusebianpublishing@gmail.com Web site: https://www.eusebian.com/.

EV Publishing Corp., *(978-0-9727787)* 1628 E. Southern Ave., Suite 9, PMB 237, Tempe, AZ 85282 USA Fax: 480-966-8627 E-mail: info@evpub.com Web site: http://www.evpub.com.

Eva Publishing, LLC, *(978-0-9786799)* 345 W. Broadway, Shelbyville, IN 46176 USA (SAN 851-321X) Tel 317-398-0271 (phone/fax) E-mail: jmesser@lightbound.com.

EvaHarleyChiphe, *(978-0-692-10905-2)* P.O. Box 524, Clio, SC 29525 USA Tel 843-862-8524 E-mail: echiphe@gmail.com Web site: www.evaharleychiphe.com.

EvangeCube International *See* **E3 Resources**

Evangel Author Services, *(978-1-933858; 978-0-9823957)* Div. of Brethren in Christ Media Ministries, 2000 Evangel Way, P.O. Box 189, Nappanee, IN 46550 USA Tel 574-773-3164; Fax: 574-773-5934; Toll Free: 800-253-9315 E-mail: info@evangelpublishing.com; sales@evangelpublishing.com Web site: http://www.evangelpress.com; http://www.evangelpublishing.com.

Evangel Press *See* **Evangel Publishing Hse.**

Evangel Publishing Hse., *(978-0-916035; 978-1-928915; 978-1-934233; 978-0-692-00906-2)* Div. of Brethren in Christ Media Ministries, Orders Addr.: P.O. Box 189, Nappanee, IN 46550 USA (SAN 211-7940) Tel 574-773-3164; Fax: 574-773-5934; Toll Free: 800-253-9315 (order); Edit Addr.: 2000 Evangel Way, Nappanee, IN 46550 USA Fax: 574-773-5934; Toll Free: 800-253-9315 E-mail: sales@evangelpublishing.com Web site: http://www.evangelpublishing.com *Dist(s):* **Anchor Distributors Partners Bk. Distributing, Inc. Spring Arbor Distributors, Inc.**

evangeline, *(978-0-692-04736-1; 978-1-7320290)* 5437 Upland way, Philadelphia, PA 19131 USA Tel 610-803-6539 E-mail: ink4inc@gmail.com.

Evangelista, Susan, *(978-0-9769602)* 1261 W. Fulton Ave., Grand Rapids, MI 49504 USA Web site: http://micart.net.

Evan-Moor Educational Pubs., *(978-1-55799; 978-1-59673; 978-1-4409; 978-1-60792; 978-1-60793; 978-1-935353; 978-1-60823; 978-1-60963; 978-1-61365; 978-1-61366; 978-1-61367; 978-1-61368; 978-1-62938; 978-1-64514)* Sub. of Evan-Moor Corporation, 18 Lower Ragsdale Dr., Monterey, CA 93940 USA (SAN 242-5394) Tel 800-976-1915; 831-649-5901; Fax: 831-649-6256; Toll Free Fax: 800-777-4332; Toll Free: 800-777-4362 E-mail: customerservice@evan-moor.com; sterling@evan-moor.com Web site: http://www.evan-moor.com *Dist(s):* **Follett School Solutions Spring Arbor Distributors, Inc.**

Evans Brothers, Ltd. (GBR) *(978-0-237) Dist. by* **IPG Chicago.**

Evans Brothers, Ltd. (GBR) *(978-0-237) Dist. by* **Children Plus.**

†Evans, M. & Co., Inc., *(978-0-87131; 978-1-59077)* 216 E. 49th St., New York, NY 10017 USA (SAN 203-4050) Tel 212-688-2810 E-mail: editorial@mevans.com *Dist(s):* **MyiLibrary National Bk. Network Rowman & Littlefield Publishers, Inc. Rowman & Littlefield Unlimited Model ebrary, Inc.**; *CIP.*

Evans, Margi *See* **Dancing Horse Pr.**

Evans, Robert, *(978-0-9766468; 978-0-9884466)* 1065 Saint Helena Way, Sebastopol, CA 95472 USA E-mail: rgevans@sonic.net.

Even Me Imprinting *See* **Even Me Publishing**

Even Me Publishing, *(978-1-7332436)* 876 Solimar Way, Mary Esther, FL 32569 USA Tel 804-366-4301 E-mail: tena.veney@gmail.com.

Evening Star Enterprise, Inc., *(978-0-9790210; 978-0-9841611)* Orders Addr.: P.O. Box 254, Wilmore, KY 40390-1072 USA (SAN 852-2111) Tel 859-421-0243; Edit Addr.: 408 Kinlaw Dr., Wilmore, KY 40390-1072 USA E-mail: Rgray@Eveningstarenterprise.com Web site: http://www.eveningstarenterprise.com/Home.html.

Evening Sun Pr., *(978-0-9726781)* 8332 Melrose Ave., West Hollywood, CA 90069 USA Tel 310-657-9092 E-mail: lc@pictureentertainment.com.

Evenson, Laurel, *(978-0-9666834)* 675 Moon Lake Dr., Cambridge, MN 55008 USA Tel 612-689-4093.

Event-Based Science Institute, Inc., *(978-0-9747576)* 6609 Paxton Rd., Rockville, MD 20852-3659 USA Web site: http://www.eventbasedscience.com.

Ever Wonder Bks., *(978-0-692-37551-8; 978-0-9966505)* 1620 Rose Walk Dr, Hoover, AL 35244 USA Tel 205-739-8558 *Dist(s):* **CreateSpace Independent Publishing Platform.**

EverAfterPr., *(978-0-578-40973-3; 978-0-578-40974-0)* 3085 Blackthorn Rd., Riverwoods, IL 60015 USA Tel 224-500-2752 E-mail: kanemcloughlin@outlook.com *Dist(s):* **Ingram Content Group.**

Everbind *Imprint of* **Marco Bk. Co.**

Everbind/Marco Book Company *See* **Marco Bk. Co.**

Eveready Letter & Advertising Inc., *(978-0-9758714; 978-0-9777623; 978-0-9814694; 978-0-9820757; 978-0-9826118; 978-0-9837256; 978-0-9858365; 978-0-9897161; 978-0-9963917; 978-0-9981522)* 7105 Peach Court Suite 110, Brentwood, TN 37027 USA Web site: http://eveready-usa.com.

Everest Bks., *(978-0-9754146)* 16026 N. 54th St., Scottsdale, AZ 85254 USA Tel 602-684-5644; Fax: 602-595-7152 E-mail: grahamhfoster@msn.com Web site: http://www.pacificseminars.com.

Everest Editora (ESP) *(978-84-241; 978-972-750) Dist. by* **Continental Bk.**

Everest Editora (ESP) *(978-84-241; 978-972-750) Dist. by* **Lectorum Pubns.**

Everett Pr. *Imprint of* **State Standards Publishing, LLC**

Everette Publishing (EP), LLC, *(978-0-9672539)* 106 Tillerson Dr., Newport News, VA 23602 USA Tel 757-344-9092; 757-877-6943; Fax: 757-988-0909 E-mail: EverettePublish@cox.net Web site: http://www.Webunlimted.com.

Everfield Pr., *(978-1-946785)* 19005 SW 13th AVE, NEWBERRY, FL 32669 USA Tel 352-514-8701 E-mail: karenwhiteporter@gmail.com Web site: Everfieldpress.com.

Evergreen Farm, *(978-1-956233)* P.O. Box 77, Lincoln, VA 20160 USA Tel 800-717-4838 E-mail: nancy@evergreenfarmpublishing.com Web site: evergreenfarmpublishing.com.

Evergreen Pr. *Imprint of* **Genesis Communications, Inc.**

Evergreen Press *See* **Genesis Communications, Inc.**

Evergreen Pr. LLC, *(978-0-9995825)* P.O. Box 22071, Tampa, FL 33622 USA Tel 813-240-1942 E-mail: evergreenpressllc@gmail.com Web site: evergreenpressllc.com.

Evergreen Pr. of Brainerd, LLC, *(978-0-9661599; 978-0-9755252; 978-0-9819766)* P.O. Box 465, Brainerd, MN 56401 USA Tel 218-851-4843; 201 W. Laurel St., Brainerd, MN 56401 E-mail: tenlee@evergreenpress.net Web site: http://www.evergreenpress.net.

Evergreen Publishing, *(978-0-9973726)* 12 Evergreen Ln., Marlton, NJ 08053 USA Tel 856-296-6311 E-mail: chris.depietro13@gmail.com.

EverIncrease LLC *See* **CrutchfieldPublishing.com**

Everlasting Publishing, *(978-0-9778083; 978-0-9824844; 978-0-9852739; 978-0-9983858; 978-1-7348047; 979-8-9886777)* P.O. Box 1061, Yakima, WA 98907 USA (SAN 850-2919) Tel 509-225-9829; P.O. Box 1061, Yakima, WA 98907 USA Tel 509-225-9829 E-mail: dpride42@gmail.com Web site: http://everlastingpublishing.org.

Everwas Publishing, *(978-0-9777735)* 200 Broken Arrow Way S., Sedona, AZ 86351-8743 USA Tel 928-284-0457; Fax: 928-284-9225 E-mail: kroyce88@esedona.net.

Everybody Run Music, *(978-0-578-04648-8)* 186-A W. Lemon Ave., Monrovia, CA 91016 USA E-mail: eshouse@hotmail.com.

Everyday Learning Corp., *(978-0-9630009; 978-1-57039; 978-1-877817)* 2 Prudential Plaza, Suite 1200, Chicago, IL 60601 USA Tel 312-233-7820; Fax: 312-540-5848; Toll Free: 800-382-7670 Web site: http://www.everydaylearning.com.

Everyday Mathtools Publishing Company *See* **Everyday Learning Corp.**

Everydaysanctuary Pubns., *(978-0-9761900)* 12514 Maria Cir., Broomfield, CO 80020-5324 USA Web site: http://www.everydaysanctuary.net.

Everyman Chess (GBR) *(978-1-85744; 978-1-78194) Dist. by* **Natl Bk Netwk.**

Everyman's Library *Imprint of* **Knopf Doubleday Publishing Group**

Everything *Imprint of* **Adams Media Corp.**

Everything Journals, *(978-0-9980714)* 4544 Cielo Ln., Las Vegas, NV 89130 USA Tel 702-458-2201 E-mail: mignard2201@gmail.com.

Everything Journals/Novels, *(978-0-9989428; 978-1-7379017; 979-8-9870530)* 10389 Whispy Willow Way, Las Vegas, NV 89135 USA Tel 702-339-4226 E-mail: annkimbrough123@gmail.com.

Everything Novels *See* **Everything Journals/Novels**

Everything Possible Bks., *(978-0-578-42575-7)* 22 Saint Stanislaus, Florissant, MO 63031 USA Tel 314-600-5036 E-mail: tlupo@sbcglobal.net *Dist(s):* **Independent Pub.**

Evey, *(978-1-7336844)* 62 N. Sabra Ave., Oak Park, CA 91377 USA Tel 310-696-9148 E-mail: evey@eveyclothing.com Web site: www.EveyClothing.com.

Evil Hat Productions LLC, *(978-0-9771534; 978-1-61317)* Orders Addr.: 1905 Blackbriar St, Silver Spring, MD 20903 USA Tel 240-EHP-BLUE (240-347-2583) E-mail: feedback@evilhat.com Web site: http://www.evilhat.com/ *Dist(s):* **Diamond Comic Distributors, Inc. Diamond Bk. Distributors.**

Evil Twin Pubns., *(978-0-9712972; 978-0-9763355)* P.O. Box 2, Livingston Manor, NY 12758 USA Tel 917-971-2450 E-mail: info@eviltwinpublications.com Web site: http://www.eviltwinpublications.com *Dist(s):* **AK Pr. Distribution D.A.P./Distributed Art Pubs.**

eVision, LLC, *(978-0-9768579)* Orders Addr.: 334 Sixth Ave. S., Birmingham, AL 35205 USA Tel 205-283-7690; Fax: 205-252-3090 Web site: http://www.eVisionLLC.net *Dist(s):* **Parnassus Bk. Distributors.**

Evolved Publishing, *(978-0-615-60885-3; 978-0-615-61939-2; 978-1-62253; 979-8-89025)* Orders Addr.: 4985 N 125th St, Butler, WI 53007 USA E-mail: Admin@EvolvedPub.com Web site: http://www.evolvedpub.com/press/ *Dist(s):* **CreateSpace Independent Publishing Platform Draft2Digital Ingram Content Group Smashwords.**

Evolved Self Publishing, *(978-0-9779470)* 723 Springtown Rd., Tillson, NY 12486 USA Tel 845-658-8270; Fax: 845-658-3718 E-mail: publisher@evolvedself.com Web site: http://www.evolvedself.com *Dist(s):* **Smashwords.**

Evolved Teacher Pr. *Imprint of* **499**

EvoraBooks, LLC, *(978-0-9725071)* P.O. Box 397, Canton, CT 06019 USA E-mail: evorabooks@snet.net Web site: http://www.booksbyevora.com.

EW Trading Inc., *(978-0-9985234; 978-1-7355654; 978-1-955013)* 17510 S Broadway St. No. B, Gardena, CA 90248 USA Tel 310-515-9896; Fax: 310-515-9897 E-mail: sales@ewpackaging.com Web site: ewpackaging.com.

Ewers Family Partnership, *(978-0-9987475)* 404 Ridge Rd., Boulder City, NV 89005 USA Tel 702-294-7718; Fax: 702-294-7718 E-mail: lifelake@embarqmail.com.

Ewuramma, *(978-0-9849805)* 1850 Lafayette Ave. Apt. 3A, Bronx, NY 10473 USA Tel 646-220-6432 E-mail: adomkwa1@gmail.com.

Exact Change, *(978-1-878972)* 5 Brewster St., Cambridge, MA 02138 USA Tel 617-492-1934 E-mail: dk@exactchange.com; ny@exactchange.com Web site: http://www.exactchange.com *Dist(s):* **D.A.P./Distributed Art Pubs.**

Exaltation Pr., *(978-1-950067)* 4592 N. Camrose Ct., Wyoming, MI 49519 USA Tel 616-916-8860 E-mail: orthodoxlinguist@gmail.com Web site: www.exaltationpress.com.

Exambusters *Imprint of* **Ace Academics, Inc.**

Examined Solutions PTE. Ltd., *(978-1-68374)* 9450 SW Gemini Dr., No. 21372, Beaverton, OR 97008 USA (SAN 990-1426) Tel 888-248-4521
E-mail: admin@speedypublishing.com; examinedsolutions@gmail.com.

ExamWise *Imprint of* **Total Recall Learning, Inc.**

Excalibur Bks., *(978-1-7330921)* 2635 Second Ave., No. 828, San Diego, CA 92103 USA Tel 619-892-7004
E-mail: simon.grey.yokai@gmail.com.

Exceed, LLC, *(978-0-9771722)* 715 E. 100 N., Lindon, UT 84042 USA (SAN 256-8519) Tel 801-785-7931
E-mail: kcooper@exceed.bz
Web site: http://www.exceed.bz.

Exceeding Abundance Bks., *(978-1-7360316)* 105 Kit Ct., New Bern, NC 28562 USA Tel 252-675-3216
E-mail: teishaglover@teishaglover.com.

Exegent Communication *See* **Envision Berlin, e.V.**

Excel Book Press *See* **Printsbury**

Excel Heritage Group, Inc., *(978-0-692-88807-0)* 2007 Remington Oaks Cir, CARY, NC 27519 USA Tel 678-549-6517
Dist(s): **Ingram Content Group.**

Excellence Enterprises, *(978-0-9627735)* 3040 Aspen Ln., Palmdale, CA 93550-7985 USA Tel 661-267-2220; Fax: 661-267-2946
E-mail: lavonne.taylor@sbcglobal.net
Web site: http://vonnieshealthspot.com.

Excellence Student Incentives, *(978-0-9789612)* 18942 Muirland, Detroit, MI 48221 USA (SAN 852-1107) Tel 313-646-6079; Fax: 313-449-0396
E-mail: beatthemeap@yahoo.com
Web site: http://www.beatthemeap.com.

Excellent Bks., *(978-0-9628014; 978-1-880780)*
E-mail: books@excellentbooks.com
Web site: http://www.excellentbooks.com.

Excite Kids Pr. *Imprint of* **Publishing Services @ Thomson-Shore**

Executive Books *See* **Tremendous Life Bks.**

Executive Performances, Incorporated *See* **Nicholas Rizzo**

Executive Performances Publishing *Imprint of* **Nicholas Rizzo**

Exegetica / Grace Acres Press *See* **Exegetica Publishing**

Exegetica Publishing, *(978-1-60265)* 205 S 8th St No. 310, Fort Dodge, IA 50501 USA (SAN 852-5978) Tel 816-269-8505
E-mail: ccone@agathonedu.com; cat.cone@exegeticapublishing.com
Web site: https://www.graceacrespress.org; https://www.exegeticapublishing.com.

Exeter Pr., *(978-0-9700612; 978-0-9797407)* Orders Addr.: 223 Commonwealth Ave., Boston, MA 02116 USA Tel 617-267-7720; Fax: 617-262-6948; Edit Addr.: 223 Commonwealth Ave., Boston, MA 02116 USA (SAN 854-2554)
E-mail: davidburke@commonwealthfilms.com
Web site: http://www.exeterpress.com.

Exhibit A *Imprint of* **TR Bks.**

Exhibit A Pr., *(978-0-9633954; 978-0-9815519)* 4657 Cajon Way, San Diego, CA 92115 USA Tel 619-286-6350; Fax: 619-286-1591
E-mail: mail@exhibitapress.com
Web site: http://www.exhibitapress.com
Dist(s): **Baker & Taylor Publisher Services (BTPS)**
Independent Pubs. Group
MyiLibrary.

Exisle Publishing Pty Ltd. (AUS) *(978-1-921497; 978-1-921966; 978-1-925335; 978-0-646-95875-0; 978-1-925820; 978-1-922539; 978-1-923011) Dist. by* **TwoRivers.**

Exit 81 Publishing LLC, *(978-1-7324761)* 1530 Davis St. Apt. D, Conway, AR 72032 USA Tel 817-305-6025
E-mail: authorjgabrielle@gmail.com.

Exit Studio, *(978-0-9640868; 978-0-9831891)* 1466 N. Quinn St., Arlington, VA 22209 USA Tel 571-432-8724
E-mail: efontanez@exitstudio.com
Web site: http://www.exitstudio.com
Dist(s): **Follett School Solutions.**

Exley, Helen Giftbooks (GBR) *(978-0-905521; 978-1-85015; 978-1-86187; 978-1-905130; 978-1-84634; 978-1-78485) Dist. by* **Natl Bk Netwk.**

Exodus 35:31 Artistry LLC, *(978-0-9989256; 978-1-7369680)* 49 S. Syracuse St., Denver, CO 80230 USA
E-mail: kimbaltz@hotmail.com; kimbaltz@hotmail.com; kimbaltz@hotmail.com; exoduskb@gmail.com
Dist(s): **CreateSpace Independent Publishing Platform.**

ExpandingBooks.com, *(978-0-9721764; 978-1-934443)* 200 W. 34th, Suite 953, Anchorage, AK 99503 USA Tel 907-278-9800; Fax: 877-552-7200
E-mail: cherylkirk@gmail.com; expandingbooks@gmail.com
Web site: http://www.expandingpress.com; http://www.expandingbooks
Dist(s): **Taku Graphics.**

Expansive Pr., *(978-1-7370573)* 1476 Mulberry Dr., Grass Valley, CA 95945 USA Tel 530-277-4311
E-mail: reonne.haslett@gmail.com.

Expansive West LLC, *(978-1-953356)* 13900 CR 455 Unit 107-138, Clermont, FL 34711 USA Tel 330-474-9610
E-mail: admin@dietstandards.com.

Experiment LLC, The, *(978-0-9620471; 978-1-891011; 978-1-61519)* 220 E. 23rd St. Suite 600, New York, NY 10010 USA (SAN 857-961X)
E-mail: info@theexperimentpublishing.com
Web site: http://www.theexperimentpublishing.com
Dist(s): **Blackstone Audio, Inc.**
Hachette Bk. Group
Open Road Integrated Media, Inc.
Timber Pr., Inc.
Workman Publishing Co., Inc.

Expert Systems for Teachers *Imprint of* **Teaching Point, Inc.**

Explorations Early Learning, *(978-0-615-15718-4; 978-0-615-15719-1)* 1524 Summit St., Sioux City, IA 51103 USA Tel 712-202-1627
E-mail: jeffajohnson@cableone.net
Web site: http://www.explorationsearlylearning.com
Dist(s): **Lulu Pr., Inc.**

Explorer Media *Imprint of* **Simon & Barklee, Inc./ExplorerMedia**

Explorer's Bible Study, *(978-1-889015; 978-0-9787993; 978-1-935424)* 2652 Hwy. 46 S., Dickson, TN 37055 USA Tel 615-446-7316; Fax: 615-446-7951; Toll Free: 800-657-2874; P.O. Box 425, Dickson, TN 37056 Toll Free: 800-657-2874
Web site: http://www.explorerbiblestudy.org.

Exploring California Insects *Imprint of* **Insect Sciences Museum of California**

Exploring ExPr.ion LLC, *(978-0-692-10412-5; 978-1-7324823; 978-1-954057)* 122 Lakewood Dr, Kingsland, GA 31548 USA Tel 405-795-4824
E-mail: exploringexpression@gmail.com.

Express Bks. *Imprint of* **Bellwether Media**

Expressions Woven, *(978-0-9668179)* P.O. Box 1004, Waterford, CT 06385 USA Tel 860-442-1332; Fax: 860-447-9916
E-mail: dreaminthelight@alum.rpi.edu
Web site: http://www.poetryin.com
Dist(s): **Ingram Content Group.**

Expressive Design Group, Inc., *(978-0-9845278; 978-1-936676)* 49 Garfield St., Holyoke, MA 01040 USA (SAN 859-6654) Tel 413-315-6296; Fax: 413-315-6271; Toll Free: 800-848-6685
E-mail: richard.marks@theedg.net
Web site: http://www.theedg.net.

Expressive Ink, *(978-0-9759362)* Orders Addr.: P.O. Box 74, Foreston, MN 56330 USA; Edit Addr.: 305 Pheasant Ln., Foreston, MN 56330-5540 USA Tel 320-294-4022
E-mail: express@bctelco.net
Web site: http://www.natknows.com.

Exquisite Thoughts, Incorporated *See* **CCP Publishing & Entertainment**

Extejt, Gabriele *See* **McGab Publishing**

Extended Blessings, *(978-0-9984267)* 3807 Stonecreek Cir SW, Conyers, GA 30094 USA Tel 404-934-8352; Fax: 404-934-8352
E-mail: msdonita76@gmail.com.

Extra Point Pubs., *(978-0-9801749; 978-0-9840847; 978-0-9846377; 978-0-9882595; 978-0-9904882; 978-0-9973309)* Orders Addr.: P.O. Box 871, Perry, GA 31069 USA; Edit Addr.: 315 Hampton Ct., Perry, GA 31069 USA (SAN 855-4129) Tel 478-224-3267; Fax: 478-218-0306
Web site: http://www.die-hardfans.com.

Extreme Explorers LLC, *(978-0-9996666)* 14113 Deep Lake Dr, Orlando, FL 32826 USA Tel 859-433-6585
E-mail: MrsHasford@gmail.com.

Eye Bks. (GBR) *(978-1-903070; 978-1-908646; 978-1-78563) Dist. by* **IPG Chicago.**

Eye Contact Media, *(978-0-9729187)* 1344 Disc Dr., No. 105, Sparks, NV 89436 USA
Web site: http://www.eyecontactmedia.com.

Eye of Newt, The, *(978-0-9762565)* 5203 Cedar Springs Rd, Dallas, TX 75235-8537 USA Tel 214-520-1739
Web site: http://www.theyeofnewt.com
Dist(s): **Consortium Bk. Sales & Distribution.**

Eyres, John, *(978-0-9769762)* 12713 Willowyck Dr., Saint Louis, MO 63146 USA.

E-z Clothin' *Imprint of* **Prince Zone Publishing**

EZ Comics, *(978-0-9795887)* 5925 Almeda Road, Unit 12018, HOUSTON, TX 77004 USA
E-mail: vshah.ezcomics@gmail.com; vshah@ezcomics.com
Web site: http://ezcomics.com.

EZ Muzik Publishing, *(978-0-615-24181-4; 978-0-9822805; 978-0-692-01686-2)* P.O. Box 50826, Santa barbara, CA 93108 USA Tel 805-886-0799
E-mail: patrikpiano@aol.com.

Ezra's Earth Publishing, *(978-0-9727855)* P.O. Box 3036, South Pasadena, CA 91031 USA (SAN 255-0555)
E-mail: information@ezrasearth.com
Web site: http://www.ezrasearth.com
Dist(s): **Quality Bks., Inc.**

Ezra's Engine Publishing *See* **Ezra's Earth Publishing**

F & S Music KS Publishing Co., *(978-0-9745630; 978-0-9765787)* Orders Addr.: P.O. Box 11805, Jackson, MS 39283 USA; Edit Addr.: 1902 Queens Road Ave., Jackson, MS 39213 USA
E-mail: lanniespann@yahoo.com
Web site: lanniespannmcbride.com.

FC&A Publishing, *(978-0-915099; 978-1-890957; 978-1-932470; 978-1-935574)* 103 Clover Green, Peachtree City, GA 30269-1695 USA (SAN 289-7946) Tel 770-487-6307; Fax: 770-631-4357; Toll Free: 800-537-1275
E-mail: charlotte_carpenter@fca.com; anne_kaufmann@fca.com
Web site: http://www.fca.com.

F E A Publishing *See* **FEA Ministries**

F Publishing *See* **William & William Publishing**

FA LLC, *(978-0-692-74187-0; 978-0-692-79747-1)* 7582 Cresthill Dr., Longmont, CO 80504 USA Tel 303-859-0121; Toll Free: 303-859-0121
Dist(s): **CreateSpace Independent Publishing Platform.**

Fabbri Editori - RCS Libri (ITA) *(978-88-450; 978-88-451; 978-88-452; 978-88-454) Dist. by* **Distribks Inc.**

Faber & Faber Children's Bks. *Imprint of* **Faber & Faber, Inc.**

†Faber & Faber, Inc., *(978-0-571)* Affil. of Farrar, Straus & Giroux, LLC, Orders Addr.: c/o Van Holtzbrinck Publishing Services, 16365 James Madison Hwy., Gordonsville, VA 22942 USA Fax: 540-572-7540; Toll Free: 888-330-8477; Edit Addr.: 19 Union Sq., W, New York, NY 10003-3304 USA (SAN 218-7256) Tel 212-741-6900; Fax: 212-633-9385; *Imprints:* Faber & Faber Children's Books (F&FChildrens)
E-mail: sales@fsgbooks.com
Web site: http://www.fsgbooks.com
Dist(s): **Children's Plus, Inc.**
Continental Bk. Co., Inc.
ISD
Macmillan
MyiLibrary
Penguin Random Hse. Distribution
Penguin Random Hse. LLC
Publishers Group West (PGW); *CIP.*

Faber & Faber, Ltd. (GBR) *(978-0-571; 978-1-78335) Dist. by* **Alfred Pub.**

Faber, David *See* **Faber Pr.**

Faber Music, Ltd. (GBR) *(978-0-571) Dist. by* **Alfred Pub.**

Faber Piano Adventures(r), *(978-1-61677)* 3042 Creek Dr., Ann Arbor, MI 48108 USA Tel 734-975-1995; Fax: 734-332-7823
Dist(s): **Leonard, Hal Corp.**

Faber Pr., *(978-0-9768763)* Orders Addr.: 5638 Lake Murray Blvd., No.206, La Mesa, CA 91942 USA (SAN 256-8071) Tel 619-517-2662; Fax: 619-255-2354
E-mail: annavennis@yahoo.com
Web site: http://www.becauseofromek.com.

Fabled Films LLC, *(978-1-944020)* 200 Park Ave. S., New York, NY 10003 USA Tel 212-220-5804; *Imprints:* Fabled Films Press LLC (Fabled Film)
E-mail: StaceyAshton@fabledfilms.com
Web site: www.fabledfilms.com
Dist(s): **Children's Plus, Inc.**
Consortium Bk. Sales & Distribution
Simon & Schuster, Inc.

Fabled Films Pr. LLC *Imprint of* **Fabled Films LLC**

Fablefy LLC, *(978-0-578-18496-8)* 2515 Plaza Dr., Woodbridge, NJ 07095 USA.

FableVision Pr., *(978-1-891405)* 308 Congress St. # 6, Boston, MA 02210-1027 USA Toll Free: 888-240-3734
E-mail: info@fablevision.com; shoppe@fablevision.com
Web site: http://www.fablevision.com; http://www.fablevision.com/shoppe.

Fabula, *(978-0-9915194; 978-0-9915195)* P.O. Box 2709, Redmond, WA 98073 USA Tel 314-495-6939
E-mail: kkennedy0929@gmail.com.

Fabulicity Lifestyle Creations, *(978-1-7324186)* 429 Main Rd, Maryville, TN 37804 USA Tel 865-679-7948
E-mail: rheimerman@bellsouth.net.

Faccia Brutta, *(978-1-7348413)* 5418 Contera ct, Las Vegas, NV 89120 USA Tel 702-490-1602
E-mail: vickiannbush@gmail.com
Web site: www.vickiannbush.com.

Face 2 Face Games Publishing, *(978-0-9728197; 978-0-9761156)* 36 The Arcade, 65 Weybosset St., Providence, RI 02903 USA Tel 401-351-0362 (phone/fax)
E-mail: lwhalen@face2facegames.com
Web site: http://www.face2facegames.com
Dist(s): **PSI (Publisher Services, Inc.).**

Face of Stone Publishing Co., *(978-0-615-96329-7; 978-0-9960868)* P.O. Box 3462, Columbus, OH 43210 USA Tel 937-654-1748; 937-931-1894
E-mail: tmyadze@yahoo.com.

Facing History & Ourselves, *(978-0-9798440; 978-0-9819543; 978-0-615-47708-4; 978-0-9837870; 978-1-940457; 979-8-218-25924-2)* 16 Hurd Rd., Brookline, MA 02445-6919 USA Tel 617-232-1595
E-mail: catherine_okeefe@facing.org
Web site: http://www.facinghistory.org
Dist(s): **Independent Pubs. Group**
Midpoint Trade Bks., Inc.

Factors Pr., *(978-0-9700582)* Orders Addr.: 14718 Ellison Ave., Omaha, NE 68116-4336 USA
E-mail: Info@FactorsPress.com.

Facts On File *Imprint of* **Infobase Holdings, Inc.**

Faden, Ellen, *(978-0-9821231)* 145 Plaza Dr., Suite 207-224, Vallejo, CA 94590 USA (SAN 857-3166) Tel 415-342-1552
E-mail: efaden1@gmail.com
Web site: http://www.kabbalah-dating.com.

FaeriesINC LLC *See* **Fairy At Work Publishing**

Fagiolina Pr., *(978-0-9986527)* 4605 8th Street, NW, Washington, DC 20011 USA Tel 202-819-4646
E-mail: ninahalper@gmail.com
Web site: www.fagiolinapress.com.

Fahnestock Pr., *(978-0-9747981)* 310 Dennytown Rd., Putman Valley, NY 10579-1423 USA (SAN 255-8564) Tel 212-894-1219
E-mail: weigman676@aol.com.

Faie Miss, *(978-0-9851482)* 513 Memorial Blvd PMB No. 161, Springfield, TN 37172-2905 USA Tel 240-353-8437
E-mail: jen@microparse.com
Web site: www.faiemiss.com
Dist(s): **CreateSpace Independent Publishing Platform**
Ingram Content Group.

Fair, Barbara A., *(978-0-9621174)* Orders Addr.: P.O. Box 241155, Detroit, MI 48224 USA (SAN 250-7447); Edit Addr.: P.O. Box 26101, Fraser, MI 48026-6101 USA (SAN 250-7455).

Fair Havens Pubns., *(978-0-9664803)* P.O. Box 1238, Gainsville, TX 76241 USA Tel 940-668-6044; Fax: 940-668-6984; Toll Free: 800-771-4861
E-mail: fairhavens@fairhavenspub.com
Web site: http://www.fairhavenspub.com; http://www.ageofgrace.com
Dist(s): **Anchor Distributors**
Spring Arbor Distributors, Inc.

Fair Page Media LLC, *(978-0-9989098)* 626 W. Springfield Rd., Springfield, PA 19064-1626 USA Tel 484-432-1486
E-mail: joelmanon.jm@gmail.com
Dist(s): **Ingram Content Group.**

Fair Winds Pr. *Imprint of* **Quarto Publishing Group USA**

Fairchild Bks. *Imprint of* **Bloomsbury Academic & Professional**

Fairchild Bks., *(978-0-87005; 978-1-56367; 978-1-60901)* Div. of Bloomsbury Publishing, c/o Sandra Washington, 750 Third Ave., 8th Floor, New York, NY 10017 USA (SAN 201-470X) Tel 212-630-3875; Fax: 212-630-3868; Toll Free: 800-932-4724
Web site: http://www.fairchildbooks.com
Dist(s): **Bloomsbury Publishing USA**
MyiLibrary.

Fairfax Lectern, Inc., The, *(978-0-9701756)* 4280-Redwood Hwy., No. 11, San Rafael, CA 94903 USA Tel 415-479-1128; Fax: 415-479-9024
E-mail: scalised@aol.com
Web site: http://www.fairfax-lectern.com; http://www.professordave.com
Dist(s): .

Fairfield Language Technologies *See* **Rosetta Stone Ltd.**

Fairhaven Bk. Pubs., *(978-1-929649)* P.O. Box 105, Lucerne Valley, CA 92356 USA Tel 760-248-1086
E-mail: fairhaven-books@outlook.com
Web site: http://www.worldpeace2.com; http://www.themotivationsolution.net; http://www.forebrain.org;;
Dist(s): **Quality Bks., Inc.**

Fairland Bks., *(978-0-9818154)* P.O. Box 63, West Friendship, MD 21794 USA
Web site: http://fairlandbooks.com
Dist(s): **Emerald Bk. Co.**

†Fairmont Pr., Inc., *(978-0-88173; 978-0-915586)* 700 Indian Trail, Lilburn, GA 30047 USA (SAN 207-5946) Tel 770-925-9388; Fax: 770-381-9865
Web site: http://www.fairmontpress.com
Dist(s): **Assn. of Energy Engineers**
CRC Pr. LLC
Ebsco Publishing
Lulu Pr., Inc.
Taylor & Francis Group; *CIP.*

Fairway Pr. *Imprint of* **CSS Publishing Co.**

Fairwood Pr., *(978-0-9668184; 978-0-9746573; 978-1-933846; 978-0-9789078; 978-0-9820730; 978-1-958880)* 21528 104th St. Ct. E., Bonney Lake, WA 98391 USA Tel 253-269-2640; *Imprints:* Media Man! Productions (MeidaMan)
E-mail: patrick@fairwoodpress.com
Web site: http://www.fairwoodpress.com.

Fairy At Work Publishing, *(978-1-7332917)* 54 Music Sq. E, Suite 320, Nashville, TN 37203 USA Tel 615-944-0311
E-mail: hellofairy@fairyclub.love
Web site: www.fairyclub.love.

Fairy Dust Wildflowers, *(978-1-7372800)* 28443 Mountain View Pl., Menifee, CA 92587 USA Tel 951-837-3339
E-mail: fairydustwildflowers@gmail.com.

†Faith Alive Christian Resources, *(978-0-930265; 978-0-933140; 978-1-56212; 978-1-59255; 978-1-62025)* 2850 Kalamazoo Ave., SE, Grand Rapids, MI 49560 USA (SAN 212-727X) Tel 616-224-0784; Fax: 616-224-0834; Toll Free Fax: 888-642-8606; Toll Free: 800-333-8300; P.O. Box 5070, Burlington, ON L7R 3Y8 Toll Free Fax: 888-642-8606; Toll Free: 800-333-8300
E-mail: sales@faithaliveresources.org
Web site: http://www.faithaliveresources.org
Dist(s): **Lulu Pr., Inc.**; *CIP.*

Faith & Action Team, *(978-1-931984; 978-1-60382)* 637 Meadowview Ln, Chestnutridge, MO 65630 USA
E-mail: elizabeth@faithandactionseries.org; Office@FaithAndActionSeries.org
Web site: http://www.faithandactionseries.org; http://www.seriefeyaccion.org
Dist(s): **MyiLibrary.**

Faith & Action/RD *See* **Faith & Action Team**

Faith & Life Pr., *(978-0-87303)* Orders Addr.: P.O. Box 347, Newton, KS 67114-0347 USA (SAN 658-0637) Tel 316-283-5100; Fax: 316-283-0454; Toll Free: 800-245-7894 (orders only); Edit Addr.: 718 Main St., Newton, KS 67114-0347 USA (SAN 201-4726)
E-mail: flp@gcmc.org
Web site: http://www.2southwind.net/~gcmc/flp.html
Dist(s): **Herald Pr.**
Spring Arbor Distributors, Inc.

Faith Baptist Church Publications *See* **FBC Pubns. & Printing**

Faith Bks. & MORE, *(978-0-9820197; 978-0-9841729; 978-0-9842378; 978-0-9845779; 978-0-9846507; 978-0-9852729; 978-0-9860159; 978-0-9860247; 978-1-939761)* 3255 Lawrenceville-Suwanee Rd., Suite P250, Suwanee, GA 30024 USA (SAN 857-0337) Tel 678-232-6156; Fax: 888-479-4540
E-mail: publishing@faithbooksandmore.com
Web site: http://www.faithbooksandmore.com; http://www.facebook.com/corpconnoisseur; http://www.facebook.com/faithbooksandmorepublishing.

Faith Communications *Imprint of* **Health Communications, Inc.**

Faith Pubns., *(978-0-9743167; 979-8-9874006)* 5301 Edgewood Rd., College Park, MD 20740 USA Tel 301-982-2061 Do not confuse with companies with the same name in Milton, FL, Haviland, KS
E-mail: samira@darussalaam.org.

Faith, Substance & Evidence, *(978-0-692-99106-0; 978-0-692-18628-2; 978-0-692-18794-4; 978-0-692-18796-8; 978-0-692-18800-2; 978-0-578-36102-4; 979-8-218-04384-1; 979-8-218-04390-2; 979-8-218-28088-8)* 24706 Timberlake Dr., Greenwood, MO 64034 USA Tel 816-394-8816
E-mail: eacroteau@gmail.com
Dist(s): **Ingram Content Group.**

Faith that Sticks *Imprint of* **Tyndale Hse. Pubs.**

Faithful Friends Publishing, *(978-1-7369459)* 6121 E Caballo Dr, Paradise Valley, AZ 85253 USA Tel 480-577-6619
E-mail: cfinefrock@gmail.com
Web site: CynthiaAnne.com.

Faithful Life Pubs., *(978-0-9749836; 978-0-9821408; 978-0-9824931; 978-0-9845208; 978-0-9829105; 978-0-9832039; 978-1-937129; 978-1-63073)* Div. of With Integrity Ministries, 3335 Galaxy Way, North Fort

Myers, FL 33903-1419 USA Tel 239-652-0135; Toll Free: 800-699-2623
E-mail: editor@FLPublishers.com
Web site: http://www.faithfullife.com; http://www.FLPublishers.com.

aithful Publishing, *(978-0-9759941; 978-0-9779889; 978-1-940911)* P.O. Box 345, Buford, GA 30515-0345 USA Tel 770-932-7335; Fax: 678-482-4446; *Imprints:* Pixelated Publishing (Pixel Pubng)
E-mail: faithfulpublishing@yahoo.com; alwzapri@bellsouth.net
Web site: http://www.eighttwelvepublishing.com.

aithlife Corp., *(978-1-57799; 978-1-68359)* 1313 Commercial St., Bellingham, WA 98225-4307 USA (SAN 853-9731) Tel 360-527-1700; Fax: 360-527-1707; Toll Free: 800-875-6467; *Imprints:* Lexham Press (LexhamPr)
E-mail: editor@lexhampress.com; jesse.myers@faithlife.com; fanny.gonzalez@faithlife.com
Web site: http://www.lexhampress.com
Dist(s): **Anchor Distributors**
Baker & Taylor Publisher Services (BTPS)
Whitaker Hse.

FAITHTOGO, *(978-0-9765898)* P.O. Box 17273, San Antonio, TX 78217 USA
E-mail: faithtogo@msn.com
Web site: http://www.faithtogo.com.

Faithwords *Imprint of* **FaithWords**

FaithWords, *(978-0-446; 978-1-5460)* 10 Cadillac Dr., Suite 220, Brentwood, TN 37027 USA Tel 615-221-0962; Toll Free: 800-423-1247; *Imprints:* Faithwords (Faithwrds); Jelly Telly Press (Jelly Telly Pr)
E-mail: fwpublicity@hbgusa.com
Dist(s): **Blackstone Audio, Inc.**
Hachette Bk. Group
MyiLibrary.

Falcon Guides *Imprint of* **Globe Pequot Pr., The**

Falcon Pr. International, *(978-1-884459; 978-1-7362188)* 2150 Almaden Rd., No. 141, San Jose, CA 95125 USA Tel 408-677-4875
E-mail: getty@gettyambau.com.

Falcon Publishing LTD, *(978-0-9746959)* P.O. Box 6099, Kingwood, TX 77325 USA
E-mail: gwen@falconpublishing.com
Web site: http://www.falconpublishing.com.

Falcor Bks., *(978-0-9723530)* P.O. Box 1055, Yorktown, VA 23692-1055 USA Tel 757-872-6649; Toll Free: 866-872-6649
E-mail: info@falcorbooks.com
Web site: http://www.falcorbooks.com.

†Falk Art Reference, *(978-0-932087)* Div. of artprice.com, Orders Addr.: P.O. Box 833, Madison, CT 06443 USA (SAN 686-5240) Tel 203-245-2246; Fax: 203-245-5116; Toll Free: 800-278-4274; Edit Addr.: 61 Beekman Pl., Madison, CT 06443-2400 USA Do not confuse with companies with the same name in Tacoma, WA
E-mail: info@falkart.com
Web site: http://www.falkart.com; http://www.artprice.com; *CIP.*

Fall Rose Bks., *(978-0-9742185)* 7 Riverwoods Dr. Apt D211, Exeter, NH 03833 USA Tel 207-439-2878
Web site: http://www.fallrosebooks.com.

Fallick, Barbara, *(978-0-692-31163-9; 978-0-9997020; 978-1-7379593)* 1650 Gold St., Eureka, UT 84628 USA Tel 801-746-9052; 801-746-9064; *Imprints:* Gold Street Publishers (Gold Street Pubs)
E-mail: goldstreetpublishers@gmail.com.

Falls Media *See* **Seven Footer Pr.**

False Buddha LLC, *(978-0-692-42228-1; 978-0-692-63933-7; 978-0-692-68590-7; 978-0-692-85521-8; 978-0-692-94805-7; 978-0-578-40243-7; 978-0-578-50508-4; 978-0-578-66785-0; 978-0-578-89261-0; 979-8-218-03374-3; 979-8-218-22161-4)* 1314 E Las Olas Blvd #232, Ft Lauderdale, FL 33301 USA Tel 954-798-3461
Dist(s): **CreateSpace Independent Publishing Platform.**

FAM Publications *See* **iFAM Publishing, LLC**

Fame's Eternal Bks., LLC, *(978-0-9753721; 978-1-7364346)* 3424 Dempsey Ave. SW, Waverly, MN 55390-5040 USA Tel 512-468-8873
E-mail: tammy.mate@isd742.org; tammymate81@gmail.com
Web site: http://www.fameseternalbooks.com.

Familius LLC, *(978-1-938301; 978-1-939629; 978-1-942672; 978-1-942934; 978-1-944822; 978-1-945547; 978-1-64170)* 1254 Commerce Way, Sanger, CA 93657 USA (SAN 990-1515) Tel 801-552-7298; 559-876-2170
E-mail: christopher@familius.com
Web site: www.familius.com
Dist(s): **Abrams, Inc.**
Children's Plus, Inc.
Hachette Bk. Group
MyiLibrary
Open Road Integrated Media, Inc.
Workman Publishing Co., Inc.

Family & Child Development Ctr., *(978-1-7367818)* 500 argylls crest, Alpharetta, GA 30022 USA Tel 404-433-7363
E-mail: lucinda.grapenthin@gmail.com
Web site: familypsychologynorthatlanta.com.

Family Bks., *(978-0-9728460)* Orders Addr.: P.O. Box 730, Petaluma, CA 94953-0730 USA Do not confuse with companies with the same name in Glendale, CA, Dana Point, CA
E-mail: familybooks2003@yahoo.com.

Family Bks. at Home, *(978-0-9753127; 978-1-933200)* 375 Hudson St., 2nd Flr., New York, NY 10014-3657 USA.

Family Christian Ctr., *(978-0-9760416)*
E-mail: FamilyChristianCenter@hotmail.com
Web site: www.FamilyChristianCenterMinistries.com.

Family Enterprises, *(978-0-9773858)* 2678 Challis Creek Rd., Box 981, Challis, ID 83226-0981 USA Do not confuse with Family Enterprises in Milwaukee, WI.

Family Guidance & Outreach Ctr. of Lubbock, *(978-0-9767215)* 5 Briercroft Office Pk., Lubbock, TX 79412-3007 USA Tel 806-747-5577; Fax: 806-747-5119
E-mail: wedwards23@cox.net.

Family Harvest Church, *(978-1-889723)* 18500 92nd Ave., Tinley Park, IL 60477 USA (SAN 801-4817) Tel 708-614-6000; Fax: 708-614-8288; Toll Free: 800-622-0017
E-mail: winner@winninginlife.org
Web site: http://www.winninginlife.org
Dist(s): **Smashwords.**

Family Learning Assn., Inc., *(978-0-9719874)* 3925 Hagan St. Ste. 103, Bloomington, IN 47401-8649 USA
Web site: http://www.kidscanlearn.com.

Family Legacy Ministries, *(978-0-9797879)* Orders Addr.: P.O. Box 811, Rocky Point, NC 28457 USA Tel 910-675-1825
E-mail: publishing@familylegacyministries.org
Web site: http://www.familylegacyministries.org.

Family Life Productions, *(978-1-883761)* 2460 Hobbit Ln., Fallbrook, CA 92028-3679 USA (SAN 239-1090) Tel 760-728-6437; Fax: 760-728-5309; Toll Free: 800-886-2767.

Family Nutrition Ctr. P.C., *(978-0-9770756)* 98 Harding Rd., Glen Rock, NJ 07452-1317 USA
E-mail: everyday7foods@earthlink.net.

Family Of Man Pr., The *Imprint of* **Hutchison, G.F. Pr.**

Family Plays, *(978-0-87602; 978-0-88680)* Div. of Dramatic Publishing, Orders Addr.: 311 Washington St., Woodstock, IL 60098-3308 USA (SAN 282-7433) Tel 815-338-7170
E-mail: msergel@dpcplays.com
Web site: http://www.familyplays.com; http://www.dramaticpublishing.com.

Family Rocks, The, *(978-0-9747466)* 256 S. Robertson Blvd., Beverly Hills, CA 90211-2898 USA Tel 310-358-5106; Fax: 310-734-1594
E-mail: sales@coupon-directory.com
Web site: http://www.coupon-directory.com.

Family Value Publishing, *(978-0-9645180)* R.R. 2, Box 110A, Nevis, MN 56467 USA Tel 218-732-1349.

Family Value Series, *(978-0-9894443)* 257 Blazer Ave, Eugene, OR 97404 USA Tel 541-345-5110
E-mail: rasorprogram@aol.com
Dist(s): **Lulu Pr., Inc.**

FamilyLife, *(978-1-57229; 978-1-60200)* Div. of Campus Crusade for Christ, 5800 Ranch Dr., Little Rock, AR 72223 USA Tel 501-223-8663; Fax: 501-224-2529; Toll Free: 800-404-5052
Web site: http://www.familylife.com.

Familyman Ministries, *(978-0-9821941; 978-1-937639)* 611 S. Main St., Milford, IN 46542 USA Tel 574-658-4376
Web site: http://www.familymanweb.com.

Family:Story:Legacy Pr., *(978-0-615-99214-3; 978-0-692-31896-6; 978-0-578-53318-6; 978-0-578-53320-9; 978-1-7358065)* 4935 Bright Heights Dr., Hernando, MS 38632 USA Tel 9018579610
Web site: http://linesinthegravel.com/
Dist(s): **CreateSpace Independent Publishing Platform.**

Fan, Mary, *(978-1-7321986)* 20 2nd St., Jersey City, NJ 07302 USA Tel 609-240-9808
E-mail: astralcolt@gmail.com
Dist(s): **Ingram Content Group.**

Fanatic4Feelings, *(978-1-7373178)* 2515 W Central Pk. Ave, Davenport, IA 52804 USA Tel 563-349-9595; Fax: 563-265-5875
E-mail: kim@butterflybeginningscounseling.com
Web site: www.butterflybeginningscounseling.com.

FancyCrazy Publishing *See* **TOAT Venture LLC**

FancyCrazy Publishing *Imprint of* **TOAT Venture LLC**

Fandemonium Bks. *Imprint of* **Fandemonium Ltd.**

Fandemonium Ltd., *(978-0-9547343; 978-1-905586; 978-1-80070)* Orders Addr.: 3 Browns Rd., Surbiton, KT58SP GBR; Edit Addr.: P.O. Box 2178, Decatur, GA 30031 USA; *Imprints:* Fandemonium Books (FndmnmBks)
E-mail: fandemonium@blueyonder.co.uk
Web site: http://www.stargatenovels.com.

Fanning, Neli, *(978-0-692-19555-0)* 5654 W. Cornelia Ave., Chicago, IL 60634 USA Tel 347-307-2326
E-mail: nelilalanne@gmail.com
Dist(s): **Ingram Content Group.**

Fantagraphics Bks., *(978-0-930193; 978-1-56097; 978-1-60699; 978-1-68396)* 7563 Lake City Way, NE, Seattle, WA 98115 USA (SAN 251-5571) Tel 206-524-1967; Fax: 206-524-2104; Toll Free: 800-657-1100
E-mail: diva@eroscomix.com; fbicomix@fantagraphics.com
Web site: http://www.fantagraphics.com; http://eroscomix.com
Dist(s): **Diamond Comic Distributors, Inc.**
Diamond Bk. Distributors
Norton, W. W. & Co., Inc.

Fantasías Puertorriqueñas, *(978-0-9785676)* calle Mendez Vigo No. 275, Dorado, PR 00646 USA Tel 787-796-6154
E-mail: drelfrenros@prtc.net.

Fantasy Flight Games *See* **Asmodee North America, Inc.**

Fantasy Island Pr., *(978-0-9766628)* 320 W. 7th St., Beach Heaven, NJ 08008 USA Tel 609-492-4000; Fax: 609-492-3512
E-mail: webmaster@fantasyislandpark.com
Web site: http://www.fantasyislandpark.com.

Fantasy Prone Comics, *(978-0-9762842; 978-0-615-32076-2; 978-0-615-36782-8; 978-0-615-39550-0)* 3625 Fredonia Dr., Suite 2, Hollywood, CA 90068 USA (SAN 631-8606) Tel 310-270-6612
E-mail: blakeleibel1@hotmail.com
Web site: http://www.fantasyprone.com
Dist(s): **Diamond Bk. Distributors.**

Fantoons, LLC, *(978-0-9964185; 978-1-970047)* 15344 Weddington St., Sherman Oaks, CA 91411 USA Tel 818-422-3324; 10067 Riverside Dr., Toluca Lake, CA 91602 Tel 818-210-0383
E-mail: david@fantoons.tv; david@nosecode.tv
Web site: www.fantoons.com; www.fantoons.tv
Dist(s): **Simon & Schuster, Inc.**

Far Moons Pr., *(978-1-7331709)* 125 W. Virginia, No. 116, Gunnison, 81230 SUN Tel 520-490-5613
E-mail: easandrose@farmoons.com.

Far Out Pr., *(978-0-9915285; 978-1-7333589)* 2915 California St., San Francisco, CA 94115 USA Tel 415-746-0430
E-mail: citizenwriter2010@gmail.com
Web site: http://faroutpress.com/.

Farah, Barbara, *(978-0-9769346)* P.O. Box 350, Center Harbor, NH 03226 USA Tel 603-253-7142
E-mail: bbfarah@yahoo.com.

Faraway Publishing, *(978-0-9710130; 979-8-9881761)* Orders Addr.: 125 SPRING VIEW Dr., Black Mountain, NC 28711-0329 USA (SAN 254-2870) Tel 828-482-2346
E-mail: farawaypublishing@gmail.com
Web site: ranshaffner@gmail.com; https://www.ranshaffner.com.

FarBeyond Publishing LLC, *(978-1-936872)* 8185 SW Birchwood Rd., Portland, OR 97225 USA (SAN 920-5276) Tel 503-683-3013
E-mail: publish@farbeyond.com
Web site: http://farbeyond.com
Dist(s): **CreateSpace Independent Publishing Platform**
Quality Bks., Inc.

Farcountry Pr., *(978-0-938314; 978-1-56037; 978-1-59152)* Orders Addr.: P.O. Box 5630, Helena, MT 59604 USA (SAN 220-0732) Tel 406-422-1263; Fax: 406-443-5480; Toll Free: 800-821-3874; 2750 Broadwater, Helena, MT 59602; *Imprints:* Sweetgrass Books (SweetgrassBks)
E-mail: books@farcountrypress.com
Web site: http://www.farcountrypress.com
Dist(s): **INscribe Digital**
Partners Bk. Distributing, Inc.
TNT Media Group, Inc.

Farmer Valley Publishing, *(978-1-7328384)* 779 Cty. Rd., Jackson, MO 63755 USA Tel 573-833-6509
E-mail: rechenberg@yahoo.com
Web site: www.marykoeberlrechenbergwriter.com.

Farmer's Daughter Pr., *(978-0-615-66088-2; 978-0-692-37657-7; 978-0-9979274)* P.O. Box 772, Hebron, CT 06248 USA Tel 860-384-3049
Dist(s): **CreateSpace Independent Publishing Platform.**

Farnsworth, Michelle *See* **Mainspring Foundations Publishing**

Farrand Avenue Faith Publishing, *(978-0-9887841)* 301 Lakeside Dr., Walkerton, IN 46574 USA Tel 219-369-9302
E-mail: wordgirl_mary.allen@yahoo.com.

Farrar, Straus & Giroux *Imprint of* **Farrar, Straus & Giroux**

†Farrar, Straus & Giroux, *(978-0-374; 978-0-571)* Div. of Holtzbrinck Publishers, Orders Addr.: c/o Holtzbrinck Publishers, 16365 James Madison Hwy., Gordonsville, VA 22942 USA Toll Free Fax: 800-672-2054; Toll Free: 888-330-8477; Edit Addr.: 18 W. 18th St., New York, NY 10011-4607 USA (SAN 206-782X); *Imprints:* Farrar, Straus & Giroux (FarStraGir); Hill & Wang (Hill-Wang); Farrar, Straus & Giroux (BYR) (FSGBYR)
E-mail: sales@fsgee.com; fsg.editorial@fsgee.com
Web site: http://www.fsgbooks.com/
Dist(s): **Children's Plus, Inc.**
Continental Bk. Co., Inc.
Lectorum Pubns., Inc.
Macmillan
MyiLibrary
Perfection Learning Corp.
SPD-Small Pr. Distribution
Westminster John Knox Pr.; *CIP.*

Farrar, Straus & Giroux (BYR) *Imprint of* **Farrar, Straus & Giroux**

Farrell Writes, LLC, *(978-0-692-70163-8; 978-0-9991278)* 5859 Landau Dr., Southaven, MS 38671 USA Tel 901-606-5407
E-mail: farrellwrites@gmail.com
Web site: http://farrellwrites.com
Dist(s): **CreateSpace Independent Publishing Platform.**

Farshore (GBR) *(978-0-416; 978-0-603; 978-0-7497; 978-0-7498; 978-1-4052; 978-0-7555; 978-1-78031) Dist. by* **Trafalgar.**

Farshore (GBR) *(978-0-416; 978-0-603; 978-0-7497; 978-0-7498; 978-1-4052; 978-0-7555; 978-1-78031) Dist. by* **IPG Chicago.**

Farshore (GBR) *(978-0-416; 978-0-603; 978-0-7497; 978-0-7498; 978-1-4052; 978-0-7555; 978-1-78031) Dist. by* **HarperCollins Pubs.**

Farshore (GBR) *(978-0-416; 978-0-603; 978-0-7497; 978-0-7498; 978-1-4052; 978-0-7555; 978-1-78031) Dist. by* **Children Plus.**

F.A.S.T. Learning LLC, *(978-1-59792)* 3447 S Birch St, Denver, CO 80222 USA Tel 720-537-7599
E-mail: becky@crsuccesslearning.com
Web site: http://www.fastlearningllc.com.

FASTLANE LLC, *(978-0-9966017; 978-1-64193; 978-1-0717)* PO Box 85073, Richmond, VA 23285 USA; *Imprints:* Bold Illustrations (BoldIllustration).

FastPencil, Inc., *(978-1-60746; 978-1-61933; 978-1-63364; 978-1-4999; 978-1-68133)* 1608 W. Campbell Ave. Suite 239, Campbell, CA 95008 USA Tel 408-540-7571; Fax: 408-540-7572; *Imprints:* Premiere (PremierPenc)
E-mail: operations@fastpencil.com; author_services@fastpencil.com
Web site: http://www.fastpencil.com.

FastPublishing.com *See* **ExpandingBooks.com**

Fasttrack Teaching Materials, *(978-1-893742)* 6215 Lavell Court, Springfield, VA 22152 USA Tel 703-644-4612
E-mail: davburns@fasttrackteaching.com.

Fated Hearts Publishing, *(978-0-9997834; 978-0-578-44491-8)* 25 Country Lake Dr., Oak Ridge, NJ 07438 USA Tel 201-693-1580
E-mail: jpg2msmc@gmail.com
Web site: http://www.jpgrider.com/.

Father & Son Publishing, *(978-0-942407; 978-1-935802)* 4909 N. Monroe St., Tallahassee, FL 32303 USA (SAN 667-0229) Tel 850-562-3927; 850-562-0907; Fax: 850-562-0916; Toll Free: 800-741-2712 (orders only)
E-mail: lance@fatherson.com; jean@fatherson.com
Web site: http://www.fatherson.com
Dist(s): **Dot Gibson Distribution.**

Father's Hse. Publishing, *(978-0-9785308)* Orders Addr.: P.O. Box 161597, Miami, FL 33116 USA Fax: 305-235-0352
E-mail: mariadelatorre9@bellsouth.net.

Father's Pr., LLC, *(978-0-9779407; 978-0-9795394; 978-0-9824982; 978-0-9825321; 978-0-9833739)* 2424 SE 6th. St., Lee's Summit, MO 64063 USA Tel 816-600-6288 (phone/fax)
E-mail: fatherspress@yahoo.com
Web site: http://www.fatherspress.com.

Fathom Publishing Co., *(978-0-9607358; 978-1-888215; 978-1-954896)* Orders Addr.: P.O. Box 200448, Anchorage, AK 99520-0448 USA (SAN 239-7684) Tel 907-272-3305 (phone/fax)
E-mail: Connie@fathompublishing.com
Web site: http://https://www.teachmutualfunds.com; http://https://www.arcticterm.fathompublishing.com; http://https://www.tamarfrankel.com; http://https://www.fathompublishing.com; http://https://www.OpenMeetingLaws.com; http://https://arcticgroundsquirrel.fathompublishing.com.

Fatigato, Donna, *(978-1-7339415; 978-1-7378329)* 1353 Rolling Oaks Dr., Carol Stream, IL 60188 USA Tel 630-234-3402
E-mail: donna@q2fit.com.

Fauna Nirvana LLC, *(978-0-9982242)* 21015 Sylvanwood Ave., Lakewood, CA 90715 USA Tel 626-278-9845
E-mail: steverbarrett7@gmail.com
Web site: www.averyandmasa.com.

Faux Paw Media Group, *(978-0-9777340; 978-0-9779539; 978-0-9825387; 978-1-935824)* 718 Cliff Dr., Laguna Beach, CA 92651 USA (SAN 850-637X)
Web site: http://www.fauxpawproductions.com.

FAVA Pr., *(978-0-9801396)* 1401 Sherman St., Geneva, OH 44041 USA (SAN 855-3173).

Favata, Cody, *(978-1-7371070; 978-1-7377289)* 21 Holly Ln., Londonderry, NH 03053 USA Tel 603-340-0974
E-mail: codyfavata@gmail.com.

Favonian Books *See* **Arts and Minds Studio Inc.**

Favorable Impressions, *(978-0-7808; 978-0-9674698; 978-1-931360)* Div. of Elm Park Pr., Orders Addr.: P.O. Box 69018, Pleasant Ridge, MI 48069 USA Tel 248-544-2421 (phone/fax); Toll Free: 866-246-2341; Edit Addr.: 9 Elm Park Blvd., Pleasant Ridge, MI 48069 USA
E-mail: danoptt@tir.com; danoepp@tir.com.

Favored Publishing, Inc., *(978-0-9791374)* P.O. Box 734, Jackson, MS 39205-0734 USA Tel 601-316-2193
E-mail: jriley_collins@yahoo.com.

Favorite Uncle Bks., LLC, *(978-0-9711665)* 23228 Lawrence, Dearborn, MI 48128 USA Tel 313-406-2040
E-mail: john@johntocco.com.

Favorite World Pr. LLC, *(978-1-948751)* 33 W 84th St., Fourth Flr., New York, NY 10024 USA Tel 646-722-7082
E-mail: lfrench@favoriteworldpress.com.

Favortwou Publishing, *(978-0-9774107; 978-0-9799006; 978-0-615-12362-2; 978-0-9823883)* 6339 Harbin Woods Dr., Morrow, GA 30260-1835 USA
E-mail: favortwou@hotmail.com
Web site: http://www.favortwov.net.

Fawkes Pr., LLC, *(978-1-945419; 978-1-957529)* 724 Timberoaks Dr., Azle, TX 76020 USA Tel 817-919-0638
E-mail: jodi_thompson@yahoo.com
Web site: www.fawkespress.com.

Faye Bks., *(978-0-615-16371-0; 978-0-615-16610-0; 978-0-615-16737-4; 978-0-578-02146-1)* 305 Halls Ln., Shepherdsville, KY 40165 USA; P.O. Box 387, Shepherdsville, KY 40165
Web site: http://www.fayebooks.zoomshare.com
Dist(s): **Lulu Pr., Inc.**

FayeHouse. Pr. International, *(978-0-9655222)* 1568 St. Margaret's Rd., Annapolis, MD 21401 USA Tel 443-822-9144; Fax: 410-349-9413 (Call before faxing)
E-mail: Charletfaye@aol.com.

Fayette Pr., *(978-0-615-95121-8; 978-0-692-37661-4; 978-0-692-62969-7; 978-0-9982078; 978-1-953419)* 1106 Main St. No. 1471, Bastrop, TX 78602 USA Tel 512-998-9781
E-mail: jamie@jamiesfoley.com
Web site: http://www.jamiesfoley.com; http://www.fayettepress.com
Dist(s): **CreateSpace Independent Publishing Platform.**

FayRe Pr., *(978-0-9771301)* 513 Mount Evans Rd., Golden, CO 80401 USA (SAN 257-9340) Tel 303-526-7726 (phone/fax)
E-mail: theblueumbrella@earthlink.net.

FBC Pubns. & Printing, *(978-1-933594; 978-1-60208)* 3794 Oleander Ave., Fort Pierce, FL 34982 USA Tel 772-461-6460; Fax: 772-461-6474
E-mail: printing@fbcpublications.com
Web site: http://www.fbcpublications.com.

FBS Publishing Co., *(978-0-615-18629-0; 978-0-615-18633-7; 978-0-615-21316-3)* 5520 Grandview Ln., Doylestown, PA 18902 USA Tel 877-853-2267
Dist(s): **Publishers Services.**

FCA Pr., *(978-0-9717540; 978-1-932076; 978-1-933322; 978-1-934180; 978-1-936223; 978-1-955324)* 101 Clarke St., Syracuse, NY 13210 USA Toll Free: 800-871-6809
E-mail: fullcastaudio@gmail.com
Web site: http://www.fullcastaudio.com
Dist(s): **Brilliance Publishing, Inc.**

Publisher Name Index

F.C.E. Publishing, *(978-0-615-46463-3; 978-0-692-63419-6; 978-0-692-83736-8; 978-0-692-94214-7; 978-0-692-97980-8)* 1020 Amber Falls Ln., North Las Vegas, NV 89081 USA Tel 702-900-8434; Fax: 702-459-7805
E-mail: jazzwlv@gmail.com.

FDI Publishing, *(978-1-7367004; 978-1-955758)* 2930 Domingo Ave No. 1139, Berkeley, CA 94705 USA Tel 650-762-9060
E-mail: tarak.lyn@gmail.com; tara@firstdesignerin.com; office@fdi.pub
Web site: firstdesignerin.com; kellytilis.com; fdi.pub.

FDI Publishing LLC *See* **FDI Publishing**

FEA Ministries, *(978-0-9618730; 978-0-9749168; 978-1-933716)* Orders Addr.: P.O. Box 1065, Hobe Sound, FL 33475 USA (SAN 668-6877) Tel 772-546-8426; Fax: 772-546-9379; Edit Addr.: 11305 SE Gomez Ave., Hobe Sound, FL 33455 USA
E-mail: orders@gospelpublishingmission.org
Web site: http://www.gospelpublishingmission.org.

Fear2love Pr., *(978-1-937861)* P.O. Box 1824, Point Roberts, WA 98281 USA Tel 814-409-8083
E-mail: lisa@fear2love.com.

FEARON *Imprint of* **Savvas Learning Co.**

Feather Insight Pr., *(978-0-9982769)* 6710 94th St. Ct NW, Gig Harbor, WA 98332-8455 USA Tel 906-361-1047
E-mail: alexandrafolz@gmail.com.

Feather River Publishing, *(978-0-615-16630-8)* 28 S. Garfield Ave., North Platte, NE 69101 USA Tel 308-532-4025
Dist(s): **Publishers Services.**

Feather Rock Bks., Inc., *(978-1-934066)* Orders Addr.: 4245 Chippewa Ln., Maple Plain, MN 55359 USA; Edit Addr.: P.O. Box 99, Maple Plain, MN 55359 USA (SAN 851-1829) Tel 952-473-9091
E-mail: jadams@featherrockbooks.com
Web site: http://www.featherrockbooks.com.

Feather Star Pr., *(978-1-7327242)* P.O. Box 295, Springfield, NH 03284 USA Tel 603-867-1908
E-mail: featherstarpress@gmail.com.

Featherproof Bks., *(978-0-9771992; 978-0-9825808; 978-0-9831863)* 2108 W. North Ave. No. 2N, Chicago, IL 60647 USA
E-mail: mail@featherproof.com
Web site: http://www.featherproof.com
Dist(s): **MyiLibrary**
Publishers Group West (PGW).

Federal Emergency Management Agency *Imprint of* **United States Government Printing Office**

Federal Street Pr., *(978-1-892859; 978-1-59695)* Div. of Merriam Webster, Inc., P.O. Box 281, Springfield, MA 01102 USA (SAN 859-4678) Fax: 413-731-5979; 47 Federal St., Springfield, MA 01105
E-mail: info@federalstreetpress.com; lbrodeur@m-w.com
Web site: http://www.federalstreetpress.com.

Federation Pr. (AUS) *(978-1-86287; 978-1-876067; 978-0-646-17924-7; 978-1-76002) Dist. by* **Gaunt.**

Feed My Sheep, *(978-0-9768958; 979-8-218-15447-9)* P.O. Box 16438, Rural Hall, NC 27045 USA Do not confuse with Feed My Sheep in Brunswick, GA, Detroit, MI.

Feed My Sheep Bks., *(978-0-9769152)* P.O. Box 05340, Detroit, MI 48205 USA Do not confuse with companies with the same name in Rural Hall, NC, Brunswick, GA.

Feeding Minds Pr., *(978-1-948898; 978-1-957306)* 600 Maryland Ave SW, Washington, DC 20024 USA Tel 202-406-3737
E-mail: juliad@fb.org
Web site: www.feedingmindspress.com
Dist(s): **Baker & Taylor Publisher Services (BTPS)**
Independent Pubs. Group
Small Pr. United.

Feeley, Lisa & Craig *See* **CMK Pubs. LLC**

Fegley, Elizabeth *See* **Healing Hands Pr.**

Fehlauer, Michael, *(978-0-578-31336-8; 979-8-9873067)* 7401 Thundersee Dr, Corpus Christi, TX 78413 USA Tel 361-244-6502
E-mail: fehlauer6502@gmail.com; solsen@newlifecorpus.com
Web site: newlifecorpus.com.

Feil, *(978-0-9741588)* 15 Fox Meadow Ln., Merrimack, NH 03054 USA
Web site: http://www.theservingart.com/creativewriting.

Fein, Bruce, *(978-0-9745049)* 5400 Lochmor Ave., Las Vegas, NV 89130 USA
Web site: http://www.oxymoronbooks.com.

Feiner, Bob, *(978-0-9989148)* 6605 Dogwood Creek Dr., Austin, TX 78746 USA Tel 512-289-4737; Fax: 512-289-4737
E-mail: bobfeiner@yahoo.com.

Feisty Scholar Pubns., *(978-1-913619)* 571 Charminster Rd., Bournemouth, BH8 9RG GBR
E-mail: cherjones@hotmail.co.uk.

Feiwel & Friends *Imprint of* **Feiwel & Friends**

Feiwel & Friends, *(978-0-312)* 175 Fifth Ave., New York, NY 10010 USA Tel 646-307-5151; *Imprints:* Feiwel & Friends (Feiwel)
Web site: http://www.holtzbrinckus.com
Dist(s): **Children's Plus, Inc.**
Macmillan
Perfection Learning Corp.
Westminster John Knox Pr.

Feldheim, Philipp Incorporated *See* **Feldheim Pubs.**

†Feldheim Pubs., *(978-0-87306; 978-1-58330; 978-1-59826; 978-1-68025)* 208 Airport Executive Park., Nanuet, NY 10954-5262 USA (SAN 106-6307) Toll Free: 800-237-7149
E-mail: sales@feldheim.com; eli3@feldheim.com
Web site: http://www.feldheim.com
Dist(s): **David, Jonathan Pubs., Inc.**
Libros Sin Fronteras; *CIP.*

Feldick, Les Ministries, *(978-1-885344)* 30706 W. Lona Valley Rd., Kinta, OK 74552 USA Tel 918-768-3218; Fax: 918-768-3219; Toll Free: 800-369-7856
Web site: http://www.lesfeldick.org.

Feldman, Enrique C, *(978-0-9974877)* 4927 N. Sabino Gulch Ct., Tucson, AZ 85750 USA Tel 520-861-3001
E-mail: enriquehankfeldman@gmail.com
Web site: www.globallearning.foundation.

Felix Comics, Inc., *(978-0-615-12660-9)* 123 Rt. 23 S., Hamburg, NJ 07419 USA Toll Free: 800-343-3549 (800-34-FELIX)
Web site: http://www.felixthecat.com.

Fell Pr., The, *(978-0-9759430)* 8926 N. Greenwood, No. 289, Niles, IL 60714 USA
Web site: http://www.thefellpress.com
Dist(s): **SCB Distributors.**

Fellowship Pr., *(978-0-914390; 978-1-943388)* 5820 Overbrook Ave., Philadelphia, PA 19131 USA (SAN 201-6117) Tel 215-879-8929; Fax: 215-879-6307; Toll Free: 888-786-1786
E-mail: info@bmf.org
Web site: http://www.bmf.org
Dist(s): **Ilmhouse Inc.**
New Leaf Distributing Co., Inc.
Omega Pubns., Inc.

Felony & Mayhem, LLC, *(978-1-933397; 978-1-934609; 978-1-937384; 978-1-63194)* 220 W. 98th St., #9e, New York, NY 10025 USA Tel 212-731-2440; Fax: 212-656-1227
E-mail: jo@felonyandmayhem.com
Web site: http://www.felonyandmayhem.com
Dist(s): **MyiLibrary**
Open Road Integrated Media, Inc.
Publishers Group West (PGW).

Felsen Ink, *(978-1-62272)* 1599 NW 101st St., Clive, IA 50325 USA Tel 515-226-9372
E-mail: holly.welch@gmail.com
Web site: www.felsenink.com.

†Feminist Pr. at The City Univ. of New York, *(978-0-912670; 978-0-935312; 978-1-55861; 978-1-936932; 978-1-952177)* 365 Fifth Ave., New York, NY 10016 USA (SAN 213-6813) Tel 212-817-7915; Fax: 212-817-2988
E-mail: jisu@feministpress.org; info@feministpress.org
Web site: http://www.feministpress.org
Dist(s): **Consortium Bk. Sales & Distribution**
Continental Bk. Co., Inc.
CreateSpace Independent Publishing Platform
MyiLibrary
Open Road Integrated Media, Inc.
SPD-Small Pr. Distribution
Women Ink; *CIP.*

Fence Bks. *Imprint of* **Fence Magazine, Inc.**

Fence Magazine, Inc., *(978-0-9663324; 978-0-9713189; 978-0-9740909; 978-0-9771064; 978-1-934200; 978-0-9864373; 978-1-944380; 979-8-218-12409-0)* Div. of Fence Bks., New Library 320 Univ. At Albany 1400 Washington Ave., Albany, NY 12222 USA Tel 518-591-8162 (phone/fax); *Imprints:* Fence Books (Fence Bks)
E-mail: fence@albany.edu
Web site: http://www.fencemag.com; http://www.fencebooks.com
Dist(s): **DeBoer, Bernhard Inc.**
Consortium Bk. Sales & Distribution
SPD-Small Pr. Distribution
Univ. Pr. of New England.

Fencepost Communications Inc., *(978-0-9776487)* Orders Addr.: P.O. Box Fencepost Communications, Inc., P O Box 398, Hinsdale, IL 60522-0398 USA Tel 630-850-9755; Toll Free: 888-648-0008; Edit Addr.: 49 1/2 S. Washington St., Hinsdale, IL 60521 USA.

Feng Liu Productions, *(978-0-9727089)* P.O. Box 248, Mill Valley, CA 94942 USA
Dist(s): **Independent Pubs. Group.**

Fenman, Inc., *(978-1-928534)* Div. of Fenman, Ltd. UK , 116 Beech St., Belmont, MA 02478 USA Tel 617-484-0399; Fax: 617-484-2761; Toll Free: 800-599-9876
E-mail: info@fenman.com
Web site: http://www.fenman.com.

Fennell Adventures, *(978-0-692-94917-7; 978-0-692-95485-0; 978-0-692-04902-0; 978-0-692-08736-7; 978-1-7324796; 978-1-7338306)* 8064 S. fulton Pkwy., fairburn, GA 30213 USA Tel 302-565-9474
E-mail: jennayefennell@yahoo.com.

Fennell, Claire, *(978-0-578-41397-6)* 4070 Virginia Way, Lake Oswego, OR 97035 USA Tel 412-952-4873
E-mail: clairemadelinefennell@gmail.com
Dist(s): **CreateSpace Independent Publishing Platform.**

Fen's Rim, *(978-0-9713603)* Orders Addr.: P.O. Box 885, Elk Rapids, MI 49629 USA Tel 231-264-6800; Edit Addr.: 104 Dexter St., Elk Rapids, MI 49629 USA
E-mail: mail@fensrim.com
Web site: http://www.fensrim.com.

Fenton Publishing Company *See* **Octopus Publishing Co.**

Fenwyn Pr., *(978-0-913062)* Orders Addr.: P.O. Box 245, Rapid City, SD 57709 USA Tel 605-343-6070; Fax: 605-348-2108; Toll Free: 800-821-6343; Edit Addr.: 3635 Homestead St., Rapid City, SD 57703 USA.

Feral Hse., *(978-0-922915; 978-1-932595; 978-1-936239; 978-1-62731)* 1240 W. Sims Way, No. 124, Port Townsend, WA 98368 USA (SAN 251-5423) Tel 323-666-3311; Fax: 323-297-4331
E-mail: info@feralhouse.com
Web site: http://www.feralhouse.com
Dist(s): **Consortium Bk. Sales & Distribution**
MyiLibrary
ebrary, Inc.

Feral Pr., Inc., *(978-0-9649349; 978-1-930094)* 304 Strawberry Field Rd., Flat Rock, NC 28731 USA Tel 828-694-0438; Fax: 828-694-0438; *Imprints:* Rivet Books (Rivet Bks)
E-mail: gchet@feralpressinc.com
Web site: http://www.feralpressinc.com.

Fergus & Lady Publishing, *(978-0-9786975)* 2310 Del Mar Rd., No. 10, Montrose, CA 91020 USA.

Ferguson, Linda, *(978-0-9755288)* 383 Alewine Dr., Boaz, AL 35957-5034 USA
E-mail: lkinspire@yahoo.com
Web site: http://www.l-n-kinspirationalbooks.com/.

Ferguson Publishing, *(978-0-692-34213-8)* 4801 Kona Kove Way, Yorba Linda, CA 92886 USA Tel 714-345-9727
Dist(s): **CreateSpace Independent Publishing Platform.**

Ferguson Publishing Company *Imprint of* **Infobase Holdings, Inc.**

Ferguson, Suzanie Pamela, *(978-0-9658745)* 4609 Maplewood Dr., Suffolk, VA 23435 USA Tel 757-483-5721
E-mail: lferg72184@aol.com.

Fern Creek Pr., *(978-0-9625737; 978-1-893651)* P.O. Box 1322, Clayton, GA 30525 USA Tel 706-782-5379; Fax: 706-782-5379
E-mail: brian@ferncreekpress.com
Web site: http://rabun.net/boyd.

Fern Creek Publishing *See* **Fern Creek Pr.**

Fern Rock Falls Pr., *(978-0-9762409)* 22105 Fisk Rd., Noti, OR 97461-9718 USA Tel 541-935-3920
E-mail: dandq@rio.com.

Fernandez, Mary Lynne, *(978-0-9840031)* 300 Ctr. Drive, Suite G 181, Superior, CO 80027 USA Tel 303-246-6825
E-mail: marylynne@marylynnefernandez.com.

Fernandez USA Publishing, 203 Argonne Ave., Suite B, PMB 151, Long Beach, CA 90803-1777 USA Tel 562-901-2370; Fax: 562-901-2372; Toll Free: 800-814-8080
Web site: http://www.fernandezusa.com
Dist(s): **Continental Bk. Co., Inc.**

Ferne Pr. *Imprint of* **Nelson Publishing & Marketing**

Fernhouse Pr., *(978-0-9759363)* P.O. Box 73, Woodstock, VT 05067 USA
Web site: http://www.fernhouse.com.

Fernhurst Bks. (GBR) *(978-0-906754; 978-1-898660; 978-1-904475; 978-1-909911) Dist. by* **Casemate Pubs.**

Fernweh Bks., *(978-0-692-46359-8; 978-0-578-70639-9; 978-0-578-76426-9)*
Dist(s): **CreateSpace Independent Publishing Platform.**

Fernwood & Hedges Bks., *(978-0-615-72092-0; 978-0-9890698; 978-0-615-80386-9; 978-0-615-81583-1)* 7612 Fountain Ave., West Hollywood, CA 90046 USA Tel 213-910-2887
Dist(s): **CreateSpace Independent Publishing Platform.**

Fernwood Publishing Co., Ltd. (CAN) *(978-1-55266; 978-1-895686; 978-1-77363) Dist. by* **Col U Pr.**

Ferree, Rebecca Ann, *(978-0-692-07066-6)* 3207 N. 31st St, TACOMA, WA 98407 USA Tel 253-752-9060
E-mail: ferreet@asme.org
Dist(s): **Ingram Content Group.**

Ferrell Art Enterprises, *(978-0-9666142)* 112 E. Main St., Elizabeth City, NC 27909 USA Tel 919-338-3579.

Ferrell, Karen, *(978-1-7327341; 978-1-958494)* PO Box 141, Justin, TX 76247 USA Tel 817-233-0542
E-mail: karenferrell141@yahoo.com.

ferrocement.com, *(978-0-9748016)* P.O. Box 31 S. St., Bernardston, MA 01337-0133 USA Fax: 413-648-9098
E-mail: garrett@ferrocement.com.

Fertig, Howard Incorporated *See* **Fertig, Howard Publisher**

†Fertig, Howard Publisher, *(978-0-86527)* Orders Addr.: 80 E. 11th St., New York, NY 10003 USA (SAN 201-4777) Tel 212-982-7922; Fax: 212-982-1099
E-mail: orders@hfertigbooks.com
Web site: http://www.hfertigbooks.com; *CIP.*

Fetch Pr. Publishing, *(978-1-7357990)* 533 Ellynn Dr, Cary, NC 27513 USA Tel 919-618-2053
E-mail: tailsofdogswhohelp@gmail.com
Web site: dogswhohelp.com.

Fetch! Publishing, *(978-0-9746324)* 27881 La Paz Rd., Suite G-124, Laguna Niguel, CA 92677 USA Fax: 877-426-3809; Toll Free Fax: 877-426-3809; Toll Free: 877-899-9454
Web site: http://fetchpublishing.com.

Fetiform Teratoma Productions, *(978-0-692-07054-3; 978-0-692-12868-8; 978-0-578-57993-1)* 19053 Nordhoff St. 304, northridge, CA 91324 USA Tel 818-626-0392
E-mail: haitisworst@hotmail.com
Dist(s): **Independent Pub.**

Fey, Sid Designs, Inc., *(978-0-9753530)* Box 184, 335 E. Geneva Rd., Carol Stream, IL 60188 USA Tel 630-668-6607; Fax: 630-668-6282
E-mail: zpdduda@earthlink.net
Web site: http://www.thebeinggame.com.

Fichter, Brittany, *(978-1-949710)* 302 SEARIGHT DR., FORT BRAGG, NC 28307 USA Tel 702-513-2147
E-mail: BRITTANYFICHTERFICTION@GMAIL.COM
Web site: BrittanyFichterFiction.com.

Fickling, David Bks. (GBR) *(978-0-910200; 978-1-910989; 978-1-78845) Dist. by* **Peng Rand Hse.**

Fiction Focus *See* **Story Direction**

Fiction Hse. Pr., *(978-0-692-28905-1; 978-0-692-29870-1; 978-0-692-30039-8; 978-0-692-31178-3; 978-0-692-35913-6; 978-0-692-36240-2; 978-1-947964; 978-1-64720)*
E-mail: fortunapublications@gmail.com
Web site: www.fortunapublications.com
Dist(s): **CreateSpace Independent Publishing Platform.**

Fiction Publishing, Inc., *(978-0-9796752; 978-0-9814956; 978-0-9819727; 978-0-9825086; 978-0-9826168; 978-0-9827442; 978-0-9830007; 978-0-9837803)* 5626 Travelers Way, Fort Pierce, FL 34982 USA Tel 772-489-5811
E-mail: fictionpub@bellsouth.net
Web site: http://www.fictionpublishinginc.com.

Fiction Works, The, *(978-1-58124)* Orders Addr.: 3328 SW Cascade Ave., Corvallis, OR 97333 USA Tel 541-730-2044; Fax: 541-738-2648
E-mail: fictionworks@me.com
Web site: http://www.fictionworks.com
Dist(s): **Brodart Co.**
Untreed Reads Publishing, LLC.

FictionSpin, *(978-0-9724007; 978-0-9817897)* P.O. Box 885, Pacific Palisades, CA 90272 USA (SAN 255-0431) Tel 310-456-0677
E-mail: ASCBooks@aol.com; FictionSpin@aol.com
Web site: http://ASCBooks@aol.com; http://www.fictionspin.com.

Fiddlehead Pr., *(978-0-615-88594-0; 978-0-615-90572-3; 978-0-692-02414-0; 978-1-68013)* 2129 Bethel St. NE, Olympia, WA 98506 USA Tel 360-357-7800
Dist(s): **CreateSpace Independent Publishing Platform.**

Fiddlesticks Press *See* **Periwinkle Pr.**

Fideli Publishing, Inc., *(978-1-60414; 978-1-948638; 978-1-955622; 978-1-962402)*
E-mail: info@fidelipublishing.com
Web site: http://www.fidelipublishing.com
Dist(s): **BookBaby**
Greenleaf Book Group
MyiLibrary
Smashwords.

Fidelity Heart Publishing, *(978-0-9748522)* Orders Addr.: P.O. Box 1758, Houston, TX 77251 USA; Edit Addr.: 3923 Teal Run Pl., Ct, Fresno, TX 77545-7049 USA
E-mail: slmccraw@fidelityheart.com
Web site: http://www.fidelityheart.com.

Field Mouse Productions, *(978-0-9647586; 978-0-9888021)* Div. of Associated Design Services, Inc., Orders Addr.: P.O. Box 392, Grand Island, NE 68802 USA Tel 308-380-3315; 308-380-3215; Edit Addr.: 454 8th Ave., Palmer, NE 68864 USA
E-mail: skidi@aol.com; rtstron@aol.com; JeanLukesh@aol.com
Web site: http://www.fieldmousebooks.com; http://www.fieldmouseproductions.com
Dist(s): **Ingram Content Group.**

Field of Play Pr., *(978-1-7369592)* P.O. Box PO Box 1555, Hilliard, OH 43026 USA Tel 614-206-7057
E-mail: dave@davehorning.com
Web site: www.davehorning.com.

Field Stone Pubs., *(978-0-9645272)* 331 Fields Hill Rd., Conway, MA 01341 USA Tel 413-369-4091
E-mail: author@johnrdixonbooks.com
Web site: http://www.JohnRDixonBooks.com.

Fielder Group, *(978-0-9639986; 978-0-9789058)* Orders Addr.: P.O. Box 510, Benton, KY 42025 USA Tel 888-255-9248; Fax: 270-362-7130; Toll Free: 888-255-9248
E-mail: barbara@thefieldergroupusa.com
Web site: http://www.thefieldergroupusa.com.

Fielder, John Publishing, *(978-0-9832769; 978-0-9860004; 978-0-9914990; 978-0-9985080; 978-1-7344429; 979-8-218-12246-1)* P.O. Box 26890, Silverthorne, CO 80497 USA Tel 303-907-2179
E-mail: john@johnfielder.com.

Fieldhouse LLC, *(978-0-9768353)* P.O. Box 541, Lawrence, KS 66044 USA
Dist(s): **Independent Pubs. Group**
Midpoint Trade Bks., Inc.

Fielding-Lowe, Thea *See* **T. Fielding-Lowe Co.**

Fields Communications & Publishing *See* **Fields Publishing, Inc.**

Fields of Gold Publishing, Inc., *(978-0-9746296; 978-0-9848034; 978-1-940894)* P.O. Box 128438, Nashville, TN 37212-3304 USA Tel 615-335-2014; 615-567-3371; *Imprints:* Fog Ink (FogInk)
E-mail: tnefitzger@comcast.net; amy@fogink.com
Web site: http://www.fogink.com
Dist(s): **Brodart Co.**
Ingram Content Group.

Fields Publishing, Inc., *(978-1-57843)* 8120 Sawyer Brown Rd. Ste. 108, Nashville, TN 37221-1410 USA
E-mail: Fieldsco@mindspring.com
Web site: http://www.fieldspublishing.com.

Fieldstone Hill Pr., *(978-0-9767762)* 321 Old Saluda Dam Rd., Easley, SC 29640 USA
Web site: http://www.fieldstone-hill.net.

Fierce Girl Publishing Hse., *(978-0-9993880)* 4160 gunnison ct, Estero, FL 33928 USA Tel 952-356-9607
E-mail: georginakane@hotmail.com.

Fierce Publishing, *(978-0-9980154)* 501 Fletcher Ave., Indianapolis, IN 46203 USA.

Fierce Publishing, *(978-0-9837678)* 976 Dolores St., No. 1, San Francisco, CA 94110 USA Tel 415-642-3656
E-mail: therobrosen@yahoo.com
Web site: www.fiercegaybooks.com.

Fiery Studios, *(978-0-9743110)* P.O. Box 51595, Kalamazoo, MI 49005-1595 USA
Web site: http://www.vogelein.com
Dist(s): **Diamond Comic Distributors, Inc.**
Diamond Bk. Distributors.

Fifth Avenue Pr. *Imprint of* **Ann Arbor District Library**

Fifth Ave Pr., *(978-0-9755390)* 413 Salt Pond Rd., Bethany Beach, DE 19930 USA Tel 302-537-9633; Fax: 302-537-0210; Toll Free: 800-862-6443 Do not confuse with Fifth Avenue Press in Fargo, ND and New York, NY.
E-mail: bethanybil@aol.com
Web site: http://www.e-studio8.com/fifthstreetpress.

Fifth Crown Pr., *(978-0-9908713; 978-0-692-99307-1; 978-0-578-51460-4; 978-0-578-81001-0; 978-0-578-87248-3)* PO Box 5506, Somerset, NJ 08875 USA Tel 732-649-3604
E-mail: books@kamrynadams.com
Web site: www.kamrynadams.com/books.

Fifth Hse. Pubs. (CAN) *(978-0-920079; 978-1-895618; 978-1-894004; 978-1-894856; 978-1-897252; 978-1-927083) Dist. by* **Firefly Bks Limited.**

Fifth Paw Press *See* **Jocko Publishing**

fth Pillar Bks., *(978-1-950972)* La Jolla, San Diego, CA 92037 USA Tel 858-926-5828
E-mail: info@fifthpillarbooks.com
Web site: www.fifthpillarbooks.com.

fth Ribb Publishing, *(978-0-9848104; 978-1-7367898)* 7827 Olive Blvd, UNIVERSITY CITY, MO 63130 USA (SAN 991-0786) Tel 314-349-1122
E-mail: pamela.blair@eyeseeme.com.

g & The Vine, LLC, The, *(978-0-9841087; 978-0-615-49661-0; 978-0-615-62717-5; 978-0-9883370; 978-0-692-48233-9; 978-0-578-60456-5; 979-8-218-06435-8; 979-8-218-06436-5)* Orders Addr.: 753 Winthrop St., Mount Pleasant, SC 29464-2946 USA Fax: 843-881-8425; Toll Free Fax: 843-881-8425
E-mail: figandvine@mail.com; wadamacofarms@mail.com
Web site: http://thefigandthevinemedia.com.

g Factor Media LLC *Imprint of* **Fig Factor Media Publishing**

g Factor Media Publishing, *(978-0-615-36808-5; 978-0-9971605; 978-0-9990012; 978-1-7324916; 978-1-7330635; 978-1-7342369; 978-1-7345680; 978-1-952779; 978-1-957058; 978-1-959989; 978-1-961600)* 843 Hathaway Ct., North Aurora, IL 60542 USA Tel 630-441-6057; Fax: 630-786-6116; *Imprints:* Fig Factor Media LLC (Fig Factor)
E-mail: jackie@jjrmarketing.com.

Fighting Dreamers Productions, *(978-1-952117)* 13820 NE Airport Way Suite No. 162809, Portland, OR 97230 USA Tel 778-798-7341
E-mail: FightingDreamersProductions0@gmail.com.

Fighting Words Publishing, *(978-0-9755279; 978-1-959166)* P.O. Box 7, Highwood, IL 60040 USA Tel 847-266-1965; Fax: 847-266-0840
E-mail: magmem@aol.com; mk@robertmkatzmanwriter.com
Web site: http://www.fightingwordsbook.com; http://www.robertmkatzmanwriter.com.

Figueroa Pr., *(978-0-9727625; 978-1-932800)* 840 Childs Way, Suite 401-E, Los Angeles, CA 90089-2540 USA Tel 213-743-4801; Fax: 213-743-4808
Web site: http://www.figueroapress.com.

Figure 8 Pr., *(978-0-9630376)* Orders Addr.: P.O. Box 248, Rolling Ground, WI 54631 USA
E-mail: figure8press@gmail.com
Web site: http://figure8press.com.

Figures In Motion, *(978-0-9818566; 978-1-944481)* 6055 E. Hemmi Ln., Bellingham, WA 98226 USA (SAN 856-7336) Tel 360-966-3500; 510-482-8500
E-mail: cathy@figuresinmotion.com; info@figuresinmotion.com
Web site: http://www.figuresinmotion.com.

Filaretos, William, *(978-0-9724520)* 220 W. Canton St. # 3, Boston, MA 02116-5814 USA
E-mail: william_filaretos@thepotionoftime.com
Web site: http://www.ThePotionofTime.com.

Filion, Rita-Anneliese, *(978-0-9749142)* 26 Elizabeth Ln., Saratoga Springs, NY 12866-2804 USA
E-mail: sirdino@noblebones.com
Web site: http://www.noblebones.com.

Filippucci-Kotz, Renee, *(978-0-578-40718-0)* 6908 Clear Sailing Ln., Raleigh, NC 27615 USA Tel 919-706-5283
E-mail: booksbyrenee@att.net
Dist(s): **Ingram Content Group.**

Filiquarian Publishing, LLC, *(978-0-9770505; 978-1-59986)* Orders Addr.: 110 W. Grant St. Unit 2c, Minneapolis, MN 55403 USA Tel 612-207-2335; *Imprints:* FQ Classics (FQ Classics).

Fillet Of Horn Publishing, *(978-0-9753077)* 35000 Muskrat Rd., Barnesville, OH 43713 USA Tel 740-758-5050; Fax: 740-758-5114
Web site: http://www.filletofhorn.com
Dist(s): **ebrary, Inc.**

Film Black Friday, LLC., The, *(978-0-692-08334-5)* 1450 stokes ave, ATLANTA, GA 30310 USA Tel 404-642-5903
E-mail: thefilmblackfriday@gmail.com
Dist(s): **Ingram Content Group.**

Film Ideas, Inc., *(978-1-57557; 978-1-60572)* 308 N. Wolf Rd., Wheeling, IL 60090 USA Tel 847-419-0255; Fax: 847-419-8933; Toll Free: 800-475-3456
E-mail: info@filmideas.com
Web site: http://www.filmideas.com
Dist(s): **Follett School Solutions.**

Filsinger & Co., Ltd., *(978-0-916754)* 288 W. 12th St., New York, NY 10014 USA (SAN 208-3574) Tel 212-243-7421.

Filter Press, LLC *See* **Filter Pr., LLC**

Filter Pr., LLC, *(978-0-86541; 978-0-910584)* 400 Shy Cir., Westcliffe, CO 81252 USA (SAN 201-484X) Tel 719-481-2420 (phone/fax)
E-mail: info@filterpressbooks.com; julie@filterpressbooks.com
Web site: http://www.filterpressbooks.com.

Financial Safari Pr., *(978-0-9777993)* 1135 Kildaire Farm Rd., Suite 200, Cary, NC 27512 USA Tel 919-657-4201
E-mail: capitaltax@gmail.com.

Finch & Pine Design, *(978-1-7348078)* 10164 E. Pinewood Dr., PARKER, CO 80138 USA Tel 425-478-1921
E-mail: ellie.mclaughlin@gmail.com
Web site: www.finchandpinedesign.com.

Finch Bks. Co., *(978-0-9661457)* Orders Addr.: P.O. Box 545, Tularosa, NM 88352 USA; Edit Addr.: 1418 Apple Ave., Tularosa, NM 88352 USA Tel 505-585-8037; Fax: 505-585-8039
Dist(s): **MBI Distribution Services/Quayside Distribution.**

Find Your Way Publishing, Inc., *(978-0-9824692; 978-0-9849322; 978-1-945290)* P.O. Box 667, Norway, ME 04268 USA
E-mail: melissa@findyourwaypublishing.com
Web site: http://www.findyourwaypublishing.com.

Findaway World, LLC, *(978-1-59895; 978-1-60252; 978-1-60514; 978-1-60640; 978-1-60775; 978-1-60812; 978-1-60847; 978-1-61545; 978-1-61574; 978-1-61587; 978-1-61637; 978-1-61657; 978-1-61707; 978-1-4676; 978-1-5094; 978-1-9871; 978-1-0942; 978-1-6622; 978-1-6649; 978-1-6670; 978-1-6696; 979-8-8226; 979-8-3689; 979-8-8686; 979-8-8687) 31999 Aurora Rd., Solon, OH 44139 USA (SAN 853-8778) Tel 440-893-0808 x108; 4 World Trade Ctr., Fl. 62, New York, NY 10007*
Web site: http://www.findaway.com
Dist(s): **Follett School Solutions**
MyiLibrary.

Findhorn Press *Imprint of* **Inner Traditions International, Ltd.**

Finding Forward Bks., *(978-0-578-92372-7; 978-1-7373157; 979-8-9890657)* P.O. Box PO Box 8182, Long Beach, CA 90808 USA Tel 310-908-7921
E-mail: russthompson95@gmail.com
Web site: www.findingforwardbooks.com
Dist(s): **Ingram Content Group.**

Finding the Cause, LLC, 39738 Calle Azucar, Murrieta, CA 92562 USA Tel 760-724-8104
E-mail: Dr.king@findingthecause.com
Web site: www.FindingTheCause.com.

Finding the JEMS, *(978-1-7323622)*
E-mail: findingthejems@gmail.com.

Fine Art Editions *Imprint of* **North American International**

Fine Eye Media, *(978-1-7357862)* 3449 Country Haven Cir., Thousand Oaks, CA 91362 USA Tel 805-432-6515
E-mail: Rita@FineEyeMedia.com.

Fine Feather Pr. Ltd. (GBR) *(978-1-908489) Dist. by* **IPG Chicago.**

Fine, Melanie, *(978-1-7375009)* 1480 S. Wooster St. No. 1 0, LOS ANGELES, CA 90035 USA Tel 7608080918
E-mail: cantormel@gmail.com
Dist(s): **Ingram Content Group.**

Fine Print Publishing Company *See* **GO Publishing Co.**

Fine Skylark Media, *(978-0-9908146; 978-1-957691)* P.O. Box 1505, Lake Forest, CA 92609-1505 USA Tel 949-378-6691
E-mail: deanna@deannacameron.com
Web site: www.fineskylarkmedia.com.

Fineo Editorial, S.L. (ESP) *(978-84-16470) Dist. by* **IPG Chicago.**

Finer Moments, *(978-0-9771549)* P.O. Box 22102, Robbinsdale, MN 55422 USA Tel 612-302-7830
E-mail: finermoments@earthlink.net
Web site: http://www.finermoments.net.

Finest Bks., *(978-1-935679)* 959 W. Jericho Tpke., Smithtown, NY 11787 USA Tel 615-479-0877; Fax: 631-864-1565
E-mail: michaelsheahan@msn.com
Web site: http://www.finestbks.com.

Fingerprint Books *See* **Gloria List**

Finial Publishing, *(978-1-933791)* P.O. Box 346, Mercer Island, WA 98040 USA
Web site: http://www.finialpublishing.com.

Finkelstein, Ruth, *(978-0-9628157)* 27 Saddle River Rd., Airmont, NY 10952-3034 USA.

Finlay Prints, Inc., *(978-0-9766998)* Orders Addr.: 74 Fifth Ave., 6D, New York, NY 10011 USA Tel 212-463-7173
E-mail: finlayprints@earthlink.net.

Finn & Remy, LLC, *(978-1-7322788)* 5834 Richmond Ave, DALLAS, TX 75206 USA Tel 214-538-5342
E-mail: artbyjanedu@gmail.com
Web site: www.finnandremy.com.

Finnegan, Jeanette Gray Jr., *(978-0-578-46566-1)* 46044 Cape Point Way, Buxton, NC 27920 USA Tel 252-305-7077
E-mail: Tedtorok@gmail.com
Web site: Thelighthousekids.com.

Finneran, Lisa, *(978-0-9777744)* 9709 River Rd., Newport News, VA 23601-2360 USA
E-mail: arkangels@cox.net.

Finney Co., Inc., *(978-0-89317; 978-0-912486; 978-0-933855; 978-0-9617767; 978-0-9639705; 978-1-880654; 978-1-893272)* Orders Addr.: 8075 215th St. W., Lakeville, MN 55044 USA (SAN 206-412X) Tel 952-469-6699; Fax: 952-469-1968; Toll Free Fax: 800-330-6232; Toll Free: 800-846-7027; *Imprints:* Windward Publishing (Windward Publng); Lone Oak Press, Limited (LoneOak)
E-mail: feedback@finneyco.com
Web site: http://www.finneyco.com; http://www.ecopress.com; http://www.pogopress.com; http://www.astragalpress.com
Dist(s): **Book Wholesalers, Inc.**
Brodart Co.
Follett School Solutions
National Bk. Network
Rowman & Littlefield Publishers, Inc.
Rowman & Littlefield Unlimited Model
Southern Bk. Service.

Fire Engineering Bks. & Videos, *(978-0-87814; 978-1-59370; 978-0-9795633)* Orders Addr.: P.O. Box 21288, Tulsa, OK 74121 USA (SAN 282-1567) Tel 918-831-9421; Fax: 918-832-9319; Toll Free Fax: 877-218-1348; Toll Free: 800-752-9764; Edit Addr.: 10050 E 52nd St, Tulsa, OK 74146 USA (SAN 282-1559) Tel 918-931-9421; Fax: 918-831-9555; 918-832-9319; Toll Free Fax: 877-218-1348; Toll Free: 800-752-9764 (orders only)
E-mail: sales@pennwell.com; bookmarketing@pennwell.com; DentalBookSales@pennwell.com; EnergyBookSales@pennwell.com; FireBookSales@pennwell.com
Web site: http://www.pennwellbooks.com; http://www.fireengineeringbooks.com
Dist(s): **Independent Pubs. Group**
Ingram Publisher Services
Majors, J. A. Co.

Fire Flies Entertainment, LLC, *(978-0-9787302)* 1077 North Ave., Suite 114, Elizabeth, NJ 07208 USA Tel 212-561-1654; Fax: 908-351-1888
Dist(s): **INscribe Digital.**

Fire Island Pr., *(978-0-9986438)* 4337 La Cresta Ave, Oakland, CA 94602 USA Tel 510-289-0591
E-mail: gregseff@gmail.com.

Fire Mountain Pr., *(978-1-929374)* Orders Addr.: P.O. Box 3851, Hillsboro, OR 97123 USA Tel 503-846-9057 (phone/fax); 503-219-5643 (phone/fax)
Web site: http://www.firemountainpress.com.

Fire Pit Creek Publishing, *(978-0-9845362)* 31208 E. Heidelberger Rd., Buckner, MO 64016 USA.

Fire Quill Publishing, *(978-0-9969748; 978-0-9984714; 978-1-947649)* 2686 Baughman Ave, Columbus, OH 43211 USA Tel 480-819-5205
E-mail: erichbester@hotmail.com.

Firebird *Imprint of* **Penguin Young Readers Group**

Firebird Creative, *(978-1-63023)* 12042 SE Sunnyside Rd No. 385, Clackamas, OR 97015 USA
E-mail: mark@resurrectionhouse.com; mark@firebirdcreative.net
Web site: http://firebirdcreative.net; http://www.51325books.com; http://www.underlandpress.com; http://www.resurrectionhouse.com
Dist(s): **MyiLibrary**
Publishers Group West (PGW).

Firebrand Publishing, *(978-0-9801310)* 33398 Twin Hills Way, Temecula, CA 92592 USA (SAN 855-286X).

Firebreak Publishing Co., *(978-0-9761448)* Orders Addr.: P.O. Box 995, Pacific Palisades, CA 90272-0995 USA Tel 310-454-3105
E-mail: r.brodie@verizon.net
Web site: http://www.firebreakpublishing.com.

Firebug Fairy Tales, *(978-0-615-58954-1; 978-0-615-58955-8)* P.O. Box 680396, Charlotte, NC 28216 USA Tel 704-398-9923
E-mail: ejkisinger@yahoo.com.

Firefall *See* **Firefall Editions**

Firefall Editions, *(978-0-915090; 978-1-939434)* Div. of Firefallmedia, 4905 Tunlaw St., Alexandria, VA 22312 USA Tel 510-549-2461; *Imprints:* California Street (Calif St)
E-mail: firefallmedia@att.net; literary@att.net
Web site: http://www.firefallmedia.com; http://www.firefallfilms.com; http://www.blotbooks.com; http://www.lostshoerecords.com; http://www.sim-book.com; http://www.lovinglicks.com; http://www.blue-loves.com; http://www.metech.us; http://www.shift-alt-delete.com; http://www.spacespa.net; http://www.1across.com; http://mz.firefallmedia.com; http://www.scifun.us
Dist(s): **Audible.com**
Brodart Co.
Follett School Solutions.

Firefly Bks., Ltd., *(978-0-920668; 978-1-55209; 978-1-895565; 978-1-896284; 978-1-55297; 978-1-55407)* Orders Addr.: c/o Frontier Distributing, 1000 Young St., Suite 160, Tonawanda, NY 14150 USA (SAN 630-611X) Tel 203-222-9700; Toll Free Fax: 800-565-6034; Toll Free: 800-387-5085; Edit Addr.: 8514 Long Canyon Dr., Austin, TX 78730-2813 USA
E-mail: service@fireflybooks.com
Web site: http://www.fireflybooks.com/
Dist(s): **Children's Plus, Inc.**
Lectorum Pubns., Inc.

Firefly Games, *(978-0-9747671)* 7525 Garden Gate Dr., Citrus Hts, CA 95621-1909 USA
E-mail: patrick@firefly-games.com
Web site: http://www.firefly-games.com.

FireFly Lights, *(978-0-9856863)* 1403 Delano St. No. 7, Houston, TX 77003 USA Tel 281-536-3915
E-mail: lacycameywrites@gmail.com.

Firefly Press *See* **Pretty Cool Bks.**

FireFly Publishings & Entertainment *See* **FireFly Publishings & Entertainment LLC**

FireFly Publishings & Entertainment LLC, *(978-0-9774126; 978-0-9846428)* Orders Addr.: P.O. Box 1346, Snellville, GA 30078 USA; Edit Addr.: 845 Common Oak Pl., Lawrenceville, GA 30045 USA (SAN 257-6597)
E-mail: fireflypublishingent@yahoo.com; dorced58@yahoo.com
Web site: http://www.fireflypublishingent.com
Dist(s): **Follett School Solutions.**

Fireglass Publishing, *(978-0-9857523)* 2593 NE Kevos Pond Dr., Poulsbo, WA 98370 USA
E-mail: fiction@slwhyte.com.

FireHydrant Creative Studios, Inc., *(978-0-9826066; 978-1-937176)* 52 Huntleigh Woods, Saint Louis, MO 63132 USA Tel 314-822-0833
E-mail: administrator@FireHydrantCS.com
Web site: http://www.FireHydrantCS.com.

FireLace *See* **FireLace Editions**

FireLace Editions, *(978-1-7331138)* 2405 Kirkwood Ln. N., Plymouth, MN 55441 USA Tel 612-599-2616
E-mail: evetseor@gmail.com.

Firelight Press, Inc., *(978-0-9786555; 978-1-934517)* 550 Larchmont Dr., Cincinnati, OH 45215 USA (SAN 851-2353); P.O. Box 15758, Cincinnati, OH 45215 Tel 513-646-6803; Fax: 513-821-2830 Do not confuse with companies with the same name in Independence, MO, Solvang, CA
E-mail: books@firelightpress.com
Web site: http://firelightpress.com.

Firelight Publishing, Inc., *(978-0-9707206)* Orders Addr.: P.O. Box 444, Sublimity, OR 97385-0444 USA Toll Free: 866-347-3544; Edit Addr.: 226 Division St., SW, Sublimity, OR 97385-9637 USA Tel 503-767-0444; Fax: 503-769-8980; Toll Free: 866-347-3544
E-mail: info@firelightpublishing.com; editor@firelightpublishing.com; webmaster@firelightpublishing.com; orders@firelightpublishing.com
Web site: http://www.firelightpublishing.com
Dist(s): **Partners/West Book Distributors.**

Firenze Pr., *(978-0-9711236)* Orders Addr.: P.O. Box 6892, Wyomissing, PA 19610-0892 USA (SAN 254-315X); Edit Addr.: 612 Museum Rd., Reading, PA 19610-0892 USA Tel 610-374-7048 Do not confuse with Leonardo Pr., Camden, ME
E-mail: hailejohnjr@msn.com; HaileJohnJr@msn.com; InkPenCJH@msn.com
Web site: http://caroljhaile.com.

Fireproof Ministries, *(978-0-9741849)* P.O. Box 150169, Grand Rapids, MI 49515 USA
E-mail: info@fireproofministries.com
Web site: http://www.fireproofministries.com.

Fireship Pr., *(978-1-934757; 978-1-935585; 978-1-61179; 978-1-7320305; 978-1-7353545; 978-1-7366203)* P.O. Box 68412, Tucson, AZ 85737 USA Tel 520-360-6228
E-mail: tmg@en.com
Web site: http://www.FireshipPress.com.

Fireside Catholic Bibles, *(978-1-55665)* Div. of Fireside Catholic Bibles, Orders Addr.: P.O. Box 780189, Wichita, KS 67278-0189 USA Tel 316-267-3211; Fax: 316-267-1850; Toll Free: 888-676-2040; Edit Addr.: 9020 E. 35th St., N., Wichita, KS 67226 USA (SAN 854-0780)
E-mail: info@firesidebibles.com; llear@devore.cc
Web site: http://www.firesidebibles.com
Dist(s): **Spring Arbor Distributors, Inc.**

Fireside Critters, *(978-0-9753248)* Orders Addr.: P.O. Box 283, Vermilion, OH 44089 USA; Edit Addr.: P.O. Box 283, Vermillion, OH 44089 USA
E-mail: FiresideCritters@AOL.com.

Fireside Pr., Inc., *(978-1-930754; 978-0-9779863; 978-0-9800067; 978-0-9818486; 978-1-935451; 978-0-9825292; 978-1-935764)* 10000 N. Central Exp, Suite 400, Dallas, TX 75231 USA
E-mail: info@durbanhouse.com; john7@durbanhouse.com
Web site: http://www.durbanhouse.com
Dist(s): **BookMasters**
MyiLibrary
National Bk. Network
ebrary, Inc.

Firesidenook, *(978-0-9887214)* 10072 Forestedge Ln, Miamisburg, OH 45342 USA Tel 937-776-0019
E-mail: strangedad1@yahoo.com.

Firestorm Editions, *(978-0-9855541)* 14314 Rockdale Rd., Clear Spring, MD 21722 USA Tel 815-642-0700
E-mail: cashives@gmail.com.

Firewater Media Group, *(978-0-9812439; 978-1-7365612)* P.O. Box P.O. Box 782375, ORLANDO, FL 32878 USA Tel 407-488-3171
E-mail: spersad728@aol.com; info@firewatermediagroup.com
Web site: https://www.firewatermediagroup.com
Dist(s): **Independent Pubs. Group.**

Fireweed Pr., *(978-1-878660)* Orders Addr.: P.O. Box 482, Madison, WI 53701-0482 USA; Edit Addr.: 638 Gately Terr., Madison, WI 53711 USA Tel 608-233-0300 Do not confuse with companies with same name in Falls Church, VA, Fairbanks, AK, Evergreen, CO Seattle, WA
E-mail: tmccormi@wisc.edu.

Fireweed Pr., *(978-0-9772528)* Orders Addr.: P.O. Box 31037, Seattle, WA 98103 USA; Edit Addr.: 1807 N. 36th St., Seattle, WA 98103 USA Do not confuse with Fireweed Press in Falls Church, VA Fairbanks, AK, Madison, WI, Evergreen, CO AJ
E-mail: fireweedpress@comcast.net.

First Assist Pubns., *(978-0-9724865)* P.O. Box 608, Woodland Hills, CA 91365 USA Fax: 818-346-8988
E-mail: e21sherr@aol.com.

First Associates Publishing, *(978-0-9618835)* P.O. Box 1281, Richmond, VA 23218-1281 USA (SAN 242-6289) Tel 804-254-0662; Fax: 804-524-5138; Toll Free: 877-247-8343
E-mail: earl@fapbooks.com.

First Avenue Editions *Imprint of* **Lerner Publishing Group**

First Biographies *Imprint of* **Reynolds, Morgan Inc.**

First Bks., *(978-0-912301; 978-0-9823476; 978-1-61007; 978-1-937090)* 6750 SW Franklin St., Suite A, Portland, OR 97223 USA (SAN 297-9063) Tel 503-968-6777; Fax: 503-968-6779
E-mail: customerservice@firstbooks.com
Web site: http://www.firstbooks.com
Dist(s): **Bookazine Co., Inc.**
Partners Bk. Distributing, Inc.

First Century Publishing, *(978-1-885273)* Div. of First Century Church Ministries, P.O. Box 130, Delmar, NY 12054 USA Tel 518-439-3544; Fax: 518-439-0105; Toll Free: 800-570-6060
E-mail: dnbubar1@nycap.rr.com; 1century@nycap.rr.com
Web site: http://www.firstcenturypublishing.com
Dist(s): **Send The Light Distribution LLC.**

First Choice Entertainment *See* **Papilion Pr.**

First Christmas Project, *(978-0-9769828)* 333 Brooks Bend, Brownsburg, IN 46112 USA
Web site: http://www.firstchristmaspresent.com
Dist(s): **Send The Light Distribution LLC.**

First Class Fitness Systems, Inc., *(978-0-9747008)* 23901 Civic Ctr. Way, Suite 342, Malibu, CA 90265 USA Tel 310-456-3043
E-mail: Mario@myfitfamily.com
Web site: http://myfitfamily.com.

First Cup Pr., *(978-1-7336820; 979-8-9876125)* P.O. Box 422, Marlborough, NH 03455 USA Tel 603-876-4430
E-mail: angie@angiefrazier.com.

First Edition Design eBook Publishing *See* **First Edition Design Publishing**

First Edition Design Publishing, *(978-0-9837342; 978-1-937520; 978-1-62287; 978-1-5069)* 5202 Old Ashwood Dr., Sarasota, FL 34233 USA (SAN 860-2719) Tel 941-921-2607; Fax: 617-249-1694; P.O. Box 20217, Sarasota, FL 34276 Tel 941-921-2607; Fax: 941-866-7510
E-mail: dgordon@firsteditiondesign.com
Web site: http://www.firsteditiondesignpublishing.com.

First Flight Bks., *(978-0-9763675; 978-0-9836035; 978-0-9860666; 978-0-9974973)* Div. of The Copy

Workshop, 2144 N. Hudson, RB, Chicago, IL 60614 USA Tel 773-871-1179; Fax: 773-281-4643
E-mail: firstflightbooks@aol.com
Web site: http://www.firstflightbooks.com.

First Lady Pr., *(978-0-9995630; 978-1-7324308; 978-1-7338897; 978-1-7331134)* 5224 Jackpine Rd., Bemidji, MN 56601 USA Tel 218-766-0753
E-mail: schlichtingbarb@gmail.com.

First Light Publishing, *(978-0-9754411; 978-0-692-51651-5; 978-0-692-51652-2)* 14402 Twickenham Pl., Chesterfield, VA 23832 USA Do not confuse with First Light Publishing in Chagrin Falls, OH
E-mail: briantherock@cs.com
Dist(s): **Parklane Publishing.**

First Mom's Club, The, *(978-0-9704876; 978-0-9728180; 978-0-9764557; 978-1-935822)* 367 Eric Way, Grants Pass, OR 97526-8820 USA
E-mail: dianne@thefirstmomsclub.com
Web site: http://www.thefirstmomsclub.com
Dist(s): **Alliance Bk. Co.**

First Person Publishing *See* **Concinnity Initiatives**

First Second Bks. *Imprint of* **Roaring Brook Pr.**

First Stage Concepts, *(978-0-9667719; 978-1-931430)* Orders Addr.: P.O. Box 3390, Redondo Beach, CA 90277-1390 USA Tel 310-371-6834; Fax: 310-370-3392; Edit Addr.: 5410 W. 190th St., No. 98, Torrance, CA 90503-1045 USA
E-mail: quickstartguitar@msn.com
Web site: http://www.QuickStartGuitar.com.

First Steps *Imprint of* **Child's World, Inc, The**

First Steps Pr., *(978-0-9659944)* Orders Addr.: P.O. Box 380122, Clinton Township, MI 48038-0060 USA Tel 810-463-5670; Edit Addr.: 38453 Gail, Clinton Township, MI 48036 USA.

First Steps Publishing, *(978-0-9833164; 978-1-937333; 978-0-9837225; 978-0-9852431; 978-1-938985; 978-1-944072; 978-1-945146)* 105 Westwind St., Gleneden Beach, OR 97388 USA Tel 541-961-7641; *Imprints*: West Wind Press (MYID_Q_WEST WI); White Parrot Press (MYID_H_WHITE P); Soul Fire Press (SoulFire)
E-mail: sfparrott@firststepspublishing.com
Web site: https://www.ChristopherMatthewsPub.com/; https://www.FiresidePress.com/; https://www.FirstStepsPublishing.com.

First Time Pr., *(978-1-7366172)* 3928 Pattentown RD, OOLTEWAH (HAMILTON county), TN 37363 USA Tel 423-715-4694
E-mail: director@sctreehouse.com
Web site: http://firsttimepress.sctreehouse.com/.

First Word Publishing, The, *(978-0-9708590)* 305 Lind Ave., SW, No. 9, Renton, WA 98055 USA Tel 425-254-8575
E-mail: dejonfw@ayhoo.com.

Firsthand *Imprint of* **Heinemann**

First-Sight Publishing, *(978-0-9770363)* 9636 Nevada Ave., Chatsworth, CA 91311 USA Tel 818-207-6334
E-mail: sabrinawright1961@yahoo.com.

Fiscal Pink, LIC, *(978-0-9974001)* 13502 Arrowwood Ln., Bowie, MD 20715 USA Tel 301-875-9020
E-mail: sharon@fiscalpink.com
Web site: www.fiscalpink.com.

Fischer, Carl LLC, *(978-0-8258)* Orders Addr.: 588 N. Gulph Rd. Ste. B, Kng Of Prussa, PA 19406-2831 USA Toll Free: 800-762-2328; Edit Addr.: 65 Bleeker St., New York, NY 10012-2420 USA (SAN 107-4245) Tel 212-772-0900; Fax: 212-477-6996; Toll Free: 800-762-2328
E-mail: cf-info@carlfischer.com
Web site: http://www.carlfischer.com
Dist(s): **Follett School Solutions**
Leonard, Hal Corp.

Fish Creek Productions, LLC, *(978-0-9973651)* P.O. Box 131401, Spring, TX 77393 USA Tel 832-341-2372
E-mail: contact@fishcreekproductions.com.

Fish Decoy.com, Ltd., *(978-0-9748721; 978-0-9759386)* Orders Addr.: P.O. Box 321, Cross River, NY 10518 USA (SAN 256-1093) Tel 914-533-5181; Edit Addr.: 71 Conant Valley Rd., Pound Ridge, NY 10576 USA; 218 Honey Hallow Rd., Pound Ridge, NY 10576
Web site: http://www.fishdecoystore.com
Dist(s): **Antique Collectors' Club.**

Fish Head Pubns., LLC, *(978-1-934627)* 5013 W. Buckskin Tr., Glendale, AZ 85310 USA
Web site: http://www.fishheadpublications.com.

Fish Tales Publishing, *(978-0-9795860)* Orders Addr.: 65 Glen Rd., PMB 128, Garner, NC 27529 USA (SAN 853-8344) Tel 919-320-7428
E-mail: Books@fishtales.org
Web site: http://www.fishtales.org.

Fishbowl International, Inc., *(978-0-9745188; 978-0-9765619)* Orders Addr.: P.O. Box 362, Roxie, MS 39661 USA Tel 601-384-0219; Fax: 601-384-1667
E-mail: fishbowlinternational@yahoo.com
Web site: http://www.fishbowlinternational.com.

Fishcake Publishing, Incorporated *See* **Benicia Literary Arts**

Fisher Amelie, *(978-0-615-48662-8; 978-0-615-58205-4; 978-0-9888125; 978-0-9978769)* 905 Dee Ln., Bedford, TX 76022 USA Tel 817-657-0252
E-mail: mediastem@hotmail.com.

Fisher & Hale Publishing, *(978-0-9742037)* Div. of Horizon Bks., Orders Addr.: 6525 Gunpark Dr. 370, #250, Boulder, CO 80301 USA; Edit Addr.: 18841 E. Cornell Ave., Aurora, CO 80013 USA
E-mail: slmclean@hotmail.com
Web site: http://www.fisherhale.com.

Fisher Enterprises, *(978-0-9767265)* P.O. Box 1342, Eagle, ID 83616 USA Tel 208-939-6650; Fax: 208-939-7480 Do not confuse with Fisher Enterprises, Inc. in Edmonds, WA
E-mail: ggfisher@earthlink.net.

Fisher Hill, *(978-1-878253)* 5267 Warner Ave., No. 166, Huntington Beach, CA 92649 USA (SAN 254-1289) Tel 714-377-9353; Fax: 714-377-9495; Toll Free: 800-214-8110
E-mail: fisher.k@mac.com
Web site: http://www.Fisher-Hill.com
Dist(s): **Delta Systems Company, Inc.**

Fisher, John Wilfred, *(978-0-9771093)* 25216 Arrow Highline Rd., Juliaetta, ID 83535 USA Tel 208-843-7159
E-mail: jwfisher@starband.net.

Fisher King Enterprises, *(978-0-9776076; 978-0-9810344; 978-1-926715; 978-1-77169)* 30 N Gould St Suite 10570, Sheridan, WY 82801 USA (SAN 257-7410) Tel 307-222-9575; 831-238-7799; Fax: 831-621-4667; *Imprints*: il piccolo editions (Il piccolo)
E-mail: orders@fisherkingpress.com; fisherkingpress@gmail.com
Web site: http://www.fisherkingpress.com
Dist(s): **Fisher King Bks.**

Fisher King Press *See* **Fisher King Enterprises**

Fisher Wilcoxon *See* **Fisher Hill**

Fisher-Paner Publishing, *(978-0-615-19778-4; 978-0-615-23931-6)* 1919 Sorrento Pl., Richmond, VA 23238 USA
Dist(s): **Lulu Pr., Inc.**

Fishers Media *See* **Hendrickson, Thomas L**

Fishman, Greg *See* **Fishman, Greg Jazz Studios**

Fishman, Greg Jazz Studios, *(978-0-9766153; 978-0-9843492; 978-0-9914078)* 824 Custer Ave., Evanston, IL 60202 USA
E-mail: greg1111@aol.com
Web site: http://www.gregfishmanjazzstudios.com.

Fishnet Pubns./Ministries, *(978-0-9667517)* 8440 Fairwind Ct., Indianapolis, IN 46256 USA
E-mail: canddjohnson@comcast.net.

Fisticuff Publishing, 2529 Whetstone ln, Myrtle Beach, SC 29579 USA Tel 607-759-5075
Dist(s): **CreateSpace Independent Publishing Platform.**

Fit Kids, *(978-0-9709301)* 175 W. 200 S., Suite 2012, Salt Lake City, UT 84101-1459 USA Tel 801-521-0109; Fax: 801-521-8360; Toll Free: 888-234-8543
E-mail: brucebellco@earthlink.net
Web site: http://www.fitkids.org.

Fit Kids Publishing, *(978-0-9895095)* P.O. Box 4149, Auburn, CA 95604 USA Tel 650-339-2727
E-mail: katherine@fitkidspublishing.com
Web site: http://www.fitkidspublishing.com
Dist(s): **Partners Pubs. Group, Inc.**

Fitch, Michele Marko, *(978-0-615-14996-7)* 2103 Wilkerson St., South Boston, MA 24592 USA
E-mail: familyfitch@myembarg.com
Dist(s): **Lulu Pr., Inc.**

Fitness Information Technology, Inc., *(978-0-9627926; 978-1-885693; 978-1-935412; 978-1-940067)* Orders Addr.: P.O. Box 6116, Morgantown, WV 26506 USA; Edit Addr.: 375 Birch St., Morgantown, WV 26506-6116 USA Tel 304-293-6888; Fax: 304-293-6658; Toll Free: 800-477-4348
E-mail: ICPE@mail.wvu.edu; matthew.brann@mail.wvu.edu
Web site: http://www.fitinfotech.com
Dist(s): **Cardinal Pubs. Group**
National Bk. Network
Unifacmanu International Trading Co., Inc.
ebrary, Inc.

Fitzerald, Seeking String, *(978-0-692-09906-3)* 29431 US HWY 160, South Fork, CO 81154 USA Tel 719-480-1858
E-mail: dplucinskihotel@yahoo.com
Dist(s): **CreateSpace Independent Publishing Platform.**

Fitzgerald Bks., *(978-1-887238; 978-1-59054; 978-1-4242)* Div. of Central Programs, Inc., Orders Addr.: P.O. Box 505, Bethany, MO 64424 USA Tel 660-425-7777; Fax: 660-425-3929; Toll Free: 800-821-7199; Edit Addr.: 802 N. 41st St., Bethany, MO 64424 USA
E-mail: wecare@gumdropbooks.com
Web site: http://www.gumdropbooks.com
Dist(s): **Gumdrop Bks.**

Fitzgerald, Caryn, *(978-0-615-17982-7; 978-0-615-21500-6)* P.O. Box 1343, Mansfield, TX 76063 USA
Web site: http://www.samifitzgerald.com
Dist(s): **Lulu Pr., Inc.**

Fitzhenry & Whiteside, Ltd. (CAN) *(978-0-88902; 978-1-55005; 978-1-55041; 978-1-55455)* *Dist. by* **Firefly Bks Limited.**

Fitzhenry & Whiteside, Ltd. (CAN) *(978-0-88902; 978-1-55005; 978-1-55041; 978-1-55455)* *Dist. by* **Children Plus.**

Fitzroy Bks. *Imprint of* **Regal Hse. Publishing, LLC**

Five Degrees of Frannie, *(978-0-9679115)* P.O. Box 178, North Greece, NY 14515 USA Tel 716-467-9136
E-mail: ohfrannie@aol.com.

Five Oaks Pr., *(978-0-9779325)* P.O. Box 251, Lake Lure, NC 28746-0251 USA
E-mail: davidklett@bellsouth.net
Web site: http://www.lakelurechronicles.com.

Five O'clock Dog, *(978-0-9767887)* Orchid # 1170, Corona del Mar, CA 92625 USA Tel 949-422-5909
Web site: http://www.fiveodog.com.

Five Ponds Pr., *(978-0-9727156; 978-0-9824133; 978-0-9824583; 978-1-935813; 978-1-958361)* 30 Hidden Spring Dr., Weston, CT 06883-1144 USA
E-mail: lou@fivepondspress.com
Web site: http://www.fivepondspress.com.

Five Star *Imprint of* **Cengage Gale**

Five Star Christian Pubns., *(978-0-9740142; 978-0-9777291)* 312 SE 24th Ave., Cape Coral, FL 33990 USA Tel 239-574-1000
E-mail: info@5scp.com
Web site: http://www.gulfcoastbaptistchurch.com; www.fivestarchristianministries.com.

Five Star Pr., *(978-0-9673102)* Orders Addr.: P.O. Box 8454, Richmond, VA 23226 USA Tel 804-282-6069; Edit Addr.: 1910 Byrd Ave., Suite 12, Richmond, VA 23230 USA.

Five Star Publications, Incorporated *See* **Story Monsters LLC**

Five Star Trade *Imprint of* **Cengage Gale**

Five Valleys Publishing (GBR) *(978-0-9566042)* *Dist. by* **LightSource CS.**

Five Vines Pr., *(978-1-7327710)* 530 E. Patriot Blvd. Unit 104, RENO, NV 89511 USA Tel 775-338-4300
E-mail: wav66@yahoo.com
Web site: TheGospelofSantaClaus.com.

FizzBang Science, *(978-0-9718480)* 807 Murlay Dr., Plain City, OH 43064 USA Tel 614-873-8860 (phone/fax)
E-mail: blrohrig@worldnet.att.net
Web site: http://www.fizzbangscience.com.

FJ Multimedia LLC *Imprint of* **Ediciones Eleos**

Flaghouse, Inc., *(978-0-9713648; 978-1-932032)* 601 Rte. 46 W., Hasbrouck Heights, NJ 07604-3116 USA (SAN 631-3086) Tel 201-288-7600; Fax: 201-288-7887; Toll Free Fax: 800-793-7900
Web site: http://www.flaghouse.com.

Flagship Church Resources *Imprint of* **Group Publishing, Inc.**

Flamburis, Georgia, *(978-0-615-47908-8)* 5 Griggs Pl., Allston, MA 02134 USA Tel 617-783-9425
E-mail: gf_mae@yahoo.com.

Flame Tree Publishing (GBR) *(978-1-874634; 978-1-903817; 978-1-904041; 978-1-84451; 978-1-84786; 978-1-78361; 978-1-83964; 978-1-78758)* *Dist. by* **Atlas Bks USA.**

Flaming Pen Pr., *(978-0-615-27115-6; 978-0-615-28423-1; 978-0-615-34476-8; 978-0-615-36650-0; 978-0-615-41089-0; 978-0-615-93500-3; 978-1-950677)* 114 Kingsdale Ct, Simpsonville, SC 29680 USA
Web site: www.flamingpenpress.com
Dist(s): **CreateSpace Independent Publishing Platform.**

Flamingo Bks., *(978-0-9678981)* 17033 Newport Club Dr., Boca Raton, FL 33496 USA (SAN 253-1631) Tel 561-989-0920; Fax: 561-989-9064
E-mail: semotum@aol.com
Dist(s): **Penguin Random Hse. Distribution**
Penguin Random Hse. LLC.

Flamingo Rampant! (CAN) *(978-0-9879763; 978-1-7750840; 978-1-9991562)* *Dist. by* **Orca Bk Pub.**

Flammarion et Cie (FRA) *(978-2-08)* *Dist. by* **Distribks Inc.**

Flammer, Josephine, *(978-0-615-16197-6; 978-0-615-25550-7)* P.O. Box 225, Adirondack, NY 128008 USA
E-mail: joannflammer@aol.com
Web site: http://joannflammer.com
Dist(s): **Lulu Pr., Inc.**

Flash & Fancy Bks., *(978-0-692-04518-3)* 835 Front St. No. C, Georgetown, SC 29440 USA Tel 757-705-6745
E-mail: flashandfancy@gmail.com
Dist(s): **Ingram Content Group.**

Flash Blasters, Incorporated *See* **Ace Academics, Inc.**

Flashlight Pr., *(978-0-9729225; 978-0-9799746; 978-1-936261; 978-1-947277; 978-1-962269)* 527 Empire Blvd., Brooklyn, NY 11225-3121 USA
E-mail: ed.assist@flashlightpress.com
Web site: http://www.flashlightpress.com
Dist(s): **Independent Pubs. Group**
MyiLibrary
ebrary, Inc.

FlashPaws Productions, *(978-0-9674929)* 7714 Rolling Fork Ln., Houston, TX 77040-3432 USA Tel 713-896-8484 (phone/fax)
E-mail: info@flashpaws.com
Web site: http://www.flashpaws.com
Dist(s): **Greenleaf Book Group.**

Flat Hammock Pr., *(978-0-9718303; 978-0-9758699; 978-0-9773725; 978-0-9795949; 978-0-9818960)* 5 Church St., Mystic, CT 06355 USA Tel 860-572-2722; Fax: 860-572-2755
E-mail: info@flathammockpress.com
Web site: http://www.flathammockpress.com.

Flat Kids *Imprint of* **Smart Smiles Co., The**

Flat Pond Publishing, *(978-0-9979179)* 32 Flat Pond Cir., Mashpee, MA 02649 USA Tel 860-214-2121
E-mail: foxgroupct@yahoo.com.

Flat Sole Studio *Imprint of* **Skywater Publishing Co.**

Flathouse, Kara, *(978-1-7362501)* 4918 Oxbow Cir. E. 0, Fulshear, TX 77441 USA Tel 806 683 3029
E-mail: kflathouse@att.net
Dist(s): **Ingram Content Group.**

Flatiron Bks., *(978-1-250-08290-9)* Div. of Macmillan, 175 Fifth Ave., New York, NY 10010 USA Tel 646-307-5151
Web site: www.flatironbooks.com
Dist(s): **Children's Plus, Inc.**
Macmillan
Westminster John Knox Pr.

Flaxenfluff Pr., LLC, *(978-0-9743890)* P.O. Box 2287, Broken Arrow, OK 74013 USA
Web site: http://www.flaxenfluff.com.

Fleischhacker, Daniel, *(978-0-578-49196-7; 978-0-578-51290-7)* 1911 Grand Ave., Kalamazoo, MI 49006 USA Tel 269-381-4191
E-mail: drdanf@gmail.com
Dist(s): **CreateSpace Independent Publishing Platform.**

Fleming, G. Faye *See* **Faye Bks.**

Fleming, Randall, *(978-0-9841616)* P.O. Box 252, Point Reyes Station, CA 94956 USA.

Fletcher, C J Publishing LLC, *(978-0-9755255)* Orders Addr.: P.O. Box 784, Independence, KS 67301 USA (SAN 256-1050) Tel 620-331-5182; Fax: 620-331-5183; Toll Free: 800-814-8513; Edit Addr.: 212- 214 E. Myrtle, Independence, KS 67301 USA
E-mail: cjdcpa@cableone.net.

Fletcher, Kerstin, *(978-0-9891660)* 3529 San Sonita Pl., Santa Rosa, CA 95403 USA Tel 707-523-2174
E-mail: rb1993@sbcglobal.net.

Fletcher, Robert *See* **Iron Mountain Pr.**

Fleur Art Productions, *(978-0-9741277)* 32 N. Goodwin Ave., Elmsford, NY 10523 USA Fax: 914-206-3558; Toll Free: 866-353-8727; *Imprints*: Fleur Publishing (Fleur Pubng)
E-mail: agents@fleur.ws
Web site: http://www.fleur.ws
Dist(s): **E-Pros DG.**

Fleur De Lis Publishing, LLC, *(978-0-9821956)* P.O. Box 2521, South Portland, ME 04116-252121 USA
E-mail: cmunson667@aol.com.

Fleur Publishing *Imprint of* **Fleur Art Productions**

Fleuve Noir (FRA) *(978-2-265)* *Dist. by* **Distribks Inc.**

Flickerfawn *Imprint of* **Barton Bks.**

Flight Time LLC, *(978-0-9858024; 978-0-9943153-4-2)* 1218 Deer Chase Dr., Cincinnati, OH 45240 USA Tel 513-702-3126
E-mail: lalakems@aol.com.

FlightBks., *(978-0-9834147; 978-1-954280)* Orders Addr.: 5505 N Ocean Blvd No. 11-208 11-208, OCEAN RIDGE FL 33435 USA
E-mail: bocatherapy@gmail.com.

FlightBooks Entertainment *See* **FlightBks.**

Flinders Pr., *(978-0-9843955)* P.O. Box 3975, Burbank, CA 91508-3975 USA (SAN 859-2829) Tel 818-714-0455
E-mail: flinderspress@gmail.com
Web site: http://www.flinderspress.com.

Flinn Scientific, Inc., *(978-1-877991; 978-1-933709; 978-1-63709)* Orders Addr.: P.O. Box 219, Batavia, IL 60510 USA (SAN 630-1800) Fax: 866-452-1436; Toll Free: 800-452-1261; Edit Addr.: 770 N. Raddant Rd., Batavia, IL 60510 USA
E-mail: flinn@flinnsci.com.

Flip n Flop Learning, LLC, *(978-0-9801772; 978-0-9853372; 978-1-7334384; 978-1-7353114; 979-8-9868233)* 6752 Castenson Rd., Bryan, TX 77808 USA
E-mail: senoragose@verizon.net
Web site: http://www.flipfloplearning.com.

Flip Publishing, *(978-0-9769342)* P.O. Box 1072, Hawthorne, CA 90251 USA
E-mail: flippublishing@yahoo.com
Web site: www.flippublishing.net.

Flip The Script Bks., *(978-0-692-87184-3; 978-0-692-16870-7; 978-1-951256)* 1708-C August Street, No. 335, Greenville, SC 29605 USA Tel 864-484-6629
E-mail: liagem@liagem.com; flipthescriptbooks@gmail.com
Web site: liagem.com.

Flipp Sports, *(978-0-9744443)* 960 Turnpike St., Canton, MA 02021 USA Tel 781-821-8788; Fax: 781-821-4088
E-mail: jmarnikovic@flippsports.com
Web site: http://www.flippsports.com.

Flippin' Bks. LLC, *(978-0-9742500)* 25450 Williams Ridge, Warrenton, MO 63383 USA Tel 636-456-6224
E-mail: thw@flippinbooks.com
Web site: http://www.flippinbooks.com.

Floating Castles Media Inc. (CAN) *(978-1-988736)* *Dist. by* **IPG Chicago.**

Floating World Editions, *(978-1-891640; 978-1-953225)* 26 Jack Corner Rd., Warren, CT 06777 USA Tel 860-868-0890
E-mail: rayworks@charter.net; rfurse@floatingworldeditions.com
Web site: http://www.floatingworldeditions.com
Dist(s): **Antique Collectors' Club**
National Bk. Network.

FloBound Poems Publications, *(978-0-9705819)* Orders Addr.: P.O. Box 3101, Fredericksburg, VA 22402-3101 USA
E-mail: floboundpoems@aol.com; morningpoemsflog@aol.com
Web site: http://www.floboundpoems.com.

Flood Crest Pr., *(978-1-934130)* 604 E. Spring St., New Albany, IN 47150 USA Tel 812-944-5116; Fax: 812-944-5277
E-mail: ops@destinationsbooksellers.com
Web site: http://www.destinationsbooksellers.com.

Flood, Tim, *(978-0-9797159)* 1349 E. Ellis Dr., Tucson, AZ 85719 USA
Web site: http://www.dreamsofaballinflight.com.

Floodgate Publishing, *(978-0-9761355)* P.O. Box 1475, Castle Rock, WA 98611 USA.

Floppinfish Publishing Co., Ltd., *(978-0-9629124; 978-0-615-70203-2; 978-0-692-34807-9; 978-0-692-87027-3; 978-0-578-52462-7; 978-0-578-84437-4; 979-8-218-14464-7)* P.O. Box 4932, Saint Louis, MO 63108 USA Tel 314-567-8697
E-mail: wm4932@yahoo.com
Web site: http://www.JoeKeylon.com; http://www.pixofpeople.com
Dist(s): **Big River Distribution**
Partners Bk. Distributing, Inc.

Floppy Cat Co., *(978-0-9823818)* 2315 Devon Ave., Tea, SD 57064 USA
E-mail: jenn@greenleafbookgroup.com.

Flora Delaterre Productions, *(978-0-9792302)* P.O. Box 8474, Missoula, MT 59807 USA Tel 406-728-2977
Web site: http://www.floradelaterre.com.

Florencia Gimenez-Levit, *(978-0-692-18100-3)* 7227 Desert Jewel, El Paso, TX 79912 USA Tel 915-401-2536
E-mail: ceflovipa@msn.com.

Flores, Angie, *(978-0-9979738)* 1414 Dalmatia Dr., San Pedro, CA 90732 USA Tel 310-408-3764
E-mail: crafty125@hotmail.com; angiefloresbooks@gmail.com
Web site: https://www.Angiefloresbooks@gmail.com.

Flores, Travis *See* **Inclusive Global Inc.**

Floricanto Pr., *(978-0-915745; 978-0-9796457; 978-1-951088)* Div. of Inter American Development, 7177 Walnut Canyon Rd., Moorpark, CA 93021-1110 USA (SAN 293-9169) Tel 415-793-2662; Fax: 805-517-2991
E-mail: info@floricantopress.com; rcabello@floricantopress.com
Web site: http://www.floricantopress.com.

Florida Div. of Historical Resources, *(978-0-9642289; 978-1-889030)* Div. of Florida Dept. of State, c/o Bureau of Historic Preservation, 500 S. Bronough St., Tallahassee, FL 32399-0250 USA Tel 850-487-2333; Fax: 850-922-0496; Toll Free: 800-847-7278
Web site: http://www.flheritage.com.

Florida Historical Society, *(978-1-886104; 978-0-9771079; 978-0-9817337; 978-1-949810)* 435 Brevard Ave.,

Cocoa, FL 32922 USA Tel 321-690-1971; *Imprints:* Chapin House Books (Chapin Hse)
E-mail: FHSPress@myfloridahistory.org; chris.brotemarkle@myfloridahistory.org
Web site: www.floridabooks.net; www.myfloridahistory.org.

lorida Kids Pr., Inc., *(978-0-9792304; 978-0-9863325)* 11802 Magnolia Falls Dr., Jacksonville, FL 32258-2587 USA
Web site: http://www.janewoodbooks.com
Dist(s): **Ingram Content Group.**

lorida Science Source, Inc., *(978-0-944961)* Orders Addr.: P.O. Box 8217, Longboat Key, FL 34228-8217 USA (SAN 245-6974); Edit Addr.: 28 Eagle Ridge Rd., Sapphire, NC 28774-9681 USA (SAN 245-6982)
E-mail: fssource@aol.com
Web site: http://www.ultimacitrus.com/fssource.

loris Bks. (GBR) *(978-0-86315; 978-0-903540; 978-1-78250) Dist. by* **SteinerBook I.**

Floris Bks. (GBR) *(978-0-86315; 978-0-903540; 978-1-78250) Dist. by* **Gryphon Hse.**

Floris Bks. (GBR) *(978-0-86315; 978-0-903540; 978-1-78250) Dist. by* **Consort Bk Sales.**

Flourish Publishing Hse., *(978-0-9851659)* P.O. Box 1661, Frisco, CO 80443 USA Tel 405-760-1118
E-mail: garystallings@yahoo.com.

Flow Press *See* **Sleepy Cat Pr.**

Flower Press *See* **Flowerfield Enterprises**

Flower Publishing, *(978-0-9852608)* 1003 Deer Creek Church Rd., Forest Hill, MD 21050 USA Tel 443-528-3033
E-mail: gfdbuilders@yahoo.com.

Flower Sprouts, *(978-0-615-21179-4; 978-0-615-21180-0; 978-0-615-21683-6)* P.O. Box 1843, Morro Bay, CA 93443 USA Tel 805-772-5808 (phone/fax); 245 Morro Bay Blvd., Morro Bay, CA 1111
Web site: http://www.seawindgallery.com
Dist(s): **Lulu Pr., Inc.**

Flowerfield Enterprises, *(978-0-942256)* 10332 Shaver Rd., Kalamazoo, MI 49024-6744 USA (SAN 217-7358) Tel 269-327-0108; Fax: 269-327-7009
E-mail: nancy@wormwoman.com
Web site: http://www.wormwoman.com.

Flowerpot Pr., *(978-1-68461)* Div. of MitSo Media Inc., 142 Second Ave., N., Franklin, TN 37064 USA Tel 615-479-0695
E-mail: infor@flowerpotpress.com; anne@flowerpotpress.com
Web site: http://www.flowerpotpress.com
Dist(s): **Baker & Taylor Publisher Services (BTPS).**

Fluckiger, Jay D. *See* **Harmony Hse. Publishing Co.**

Fluckiger, Kory, *(978-0-615-15654-5)* 3640 Gramercy Ave., Ogden, UT 84403 USA Tel 801-791-3461
E-mail: kory@koryfluckiger.com
Web site: http://www.koryfluckiger.com
Dist(s): **Lulu Pr., Inc.**

Fluency Fast Language Classes, Inc., *(978-0-9824687)* Orders Addr.: P.O. Box 165, Manitou Springs, CO 80829 USA Tel 719-633-6000; Toll Free: 866-999-3583; Edit Addr.: 707 Manitou Blvd., Colorado Springs, CO 80904 USA
E-mail: karen@fluencyfast.com
Web site: http://www.fluencyfast.com.

Fluency Matters, *(978-0-9777911; 978-1-934958; 978-1-935575; 978-1-940408; 978-1-945956; 978-1-64498)* TPRS Publishing, Inc., P.O. Box 13409, Chandler, AZ 85248 USA Fax: 480-963-3463; Toll Free: 800-877-4738
E-mail: jlevasseur@waysidepublishing.com; mgorden@waysidepublishing.com
Web site: http://www.tprstorytelling.com.

Flugul Pubng, *(978-0-9779390)* P.O. Box 6090, Cincinnati, OH 45206 USA
E-mail: VLI@flugulpublishing.com
Web site: http://www.Flugulpublishing.com
Dist(s): **Lulu Pr., Inc.**

Fluharty, Linda Cunningham, *(978-0-9759097)* 833 Camforth Dr., Baton Rouge, LA 70810 USA
E-mail: LCFlu@aol.com
Web site: http://www.lindapages.com.

Flurry Group, *(978-1-7333843)* P.O. Box 2015, Winnfield, LA 71483 USA Tel 318-302-0089
E-mail: melissa@theflurrygroup.com.

Flutter-By Productions, *(978-0-9714734)* 1415 Panther Ln. # 214, Naples, FL 34109-7874 USA
Web site: http://www.flutter-byproductions.com
Dist(s): **APG Sales & Distribution Services.**

Flux *Imprint of* **Llewellyn Pubns.**

Flux *Imprint of* **North Star Editions**

Fly High Media, LLC., *(978-0-9600527)* P.O. Box 3983, Akron, OH 44314 USA Tel 866-320-0861
E-mail: sherry@totaloffice.cc
Web site: www.sherrycarnahan.com.

Flyaway Bks. *Imprint of* **Westminster John Knox Pr.**

FlyHigh Media, LLC. *See* **Fly High Media, LLC.**

Flying Cloud Bks., *(978-0-615-13477-2)* 123 Moore Rd., Sudbury, MA 01776 USA
E-mail: mail@paulgreenspan.com
Web site: http://www.paulgreenspan.com
Dist(s): **Lulu Pr., Inc.**

Flying Corgi Media, Inc., *(978-0-9839460)* P.O. Box 422, Chelmsford, MA 01824 USA Tel 978-250-9161
E-mail: corgimail@flyingcorgimedia.com
Web site: flyingcorgimedia.com.

Flying Eagle Pubns., *(978-0-9766268; 978-1-7327688; 978-1-960210)* 139 Brown., Tecumseh, MI 49286 USA
E-mail: dflyingeagle@flyingeaglepublications.com
Web site: http://www.flyingeaglepublications.com/.

Flying Eye Bks. (GBR) *(978-1-909263; 978-1-911171; 978-1-912497) Dist. by* **Peng Rand Hse.**

Flying Frog Pubs.,
Dist(s): **Ideals Pubns.**

Flying Frog Publishing, *(978-0-9666647)* 567 Westcove Dr., Wasilla, AK 99654-7161 USA Tel 907-373-6994 (phone/fax); Toll Free: 888-673-6994 Do not confuse with Flying Frog Publishing, Reisterstown, MD
E-mail: jobshih@corecom.net
Web site: http://www.galaxymall.com/children/alaskariddles
Dist(s): **Todd Communications**
Wizard Works.

Flying Frog Publishing, Inc., *(978-1-57755; 978-1-884628; 978-1-934967; 978-1-60745; 978-1-63560)* 2219 York Rd., Suite 300, Lutherville, MD 21093 USA Tel 443-901-2100; Fax: 443-901-2104
Web site: http://www.flyingfrogpub.com
Dist(s): **Gibbs Smith, Publisher**
Ideals Pubns.

Flying Kea Pr., *(978-0-9897004)* P.O. Box 1293, Cortaro, AZ 85652 USA
E-mail: info@flyingkeapress.com
Web site: www.flyingkeapress.com

Flying Owl Pubns, *(978-0-9820769)* 2268 Brighton, Holland, MI 49424 USA Tel 616-399-3857
E-mail: denuyl@chartermi.net.

Flying Pig Publishing, *(978-0-9746110)* P.O. Box 304, Harvard, MA 01451 USA
E-mail: douglee41@yahoo.com
Web site: http://deelee.net.

Flying Point Pr., *(978-0-9904604)* The Pilot House, Boston, MA 02110 USA Tel 617-734-7560
E-mail: peggy@flyingpointpress.com.

Flying Rhino Productions, Incorporated *See* **Flying Rhinoceros, Inc.**

Flying Rhinoceros, Inc., *(978-1-883772; 978-1-59168; 978-0-9822773)* 1440 NW Overton St., Portland, OR 97209 USA (SAN 857-7501) Tel 503-552-8777; Fax: 503-445-8375; Toll Free: 800-537-4466
E-mail: flyingrhino@flyingrhino.com; melson@flyingrhino.com
Web site: http://www.flyingrhino.com.

Flying Scroll Publishing, LLC, *(978-0-9742432; 978-0-9848099)* P.O. Box 246, Fort Atkinson, WI 53538 USA Tel 920-723-3454
E-mail: info@flyingscrollpublishing.com
Web site: http://www.flyingscrollpublishing.com.

Flying Solo Pr., LLC, *(978-1-940137)* 1116 Cherokee St, Denver, CO 80204 USA Tel 303-733-3751
E-mail: paulaertker@gmail.com
Web site: www.crimetravelers.com.

Flying Squirrel Press *See* **Heritage Heart Farm**

Flying Thru Life Pubns., *(978-0-692-43750-6; 978-0-692-78797-7; 978-1-7324937; 979-8-9874457)* P.O. Box 3351, San Diego, CA 92163 USA Tel 619-368-9410
Web site: www.flyingthrulife.com
Dist(s): **CreateSpace Independent Publishing Platform.**

Flying Turtle Publishing, *(978-0-615-31741-0; 978-0-9851492; 978-0-9911378; 978-0-9907104; 978-0-9989979)* 7216 Birch Ave., Hammond, IN 46324 USA
Web site: http://flyingturtlepublishing.com
Dist(s): **Smashwords.**

Flying Wren Studio, *(978-0-9980141)* 508 Liberty St., Petosky, MI 49770 USA.

Flyleaf Publishing, *(978-0-9658246; 978-1-929262; 978-1-60541)* Orders Addr.: P.O. Box 287, Lyme, NH 03768-0185 USA Tel 800-449-7006; Fax: 888-619-6419; P.O. Box 287, Lyme, NH 03768-0287 Toll Free: 800-449-7006; *Imprints:* Books To Remember (Bks To Remember)
E-mail: laura@flyleafpublishing.com
Web site: http://www.flyleafpublishing.com.

Flywheel Publishing Co., *(978-1-930826)* Orders Addr.: 1375 Sunnyhills Rd., Oakland, CA 94610 USA (SAN 253-2441) Tel 510-407-7577; Fax: 510-373-6060
E-mail: admin@flywheel.us
Web site: http://www.flywheel.us.

FM Rocks Kids, LLC *See* **Playdate Kids Publishing**

FMA Publishing, *(978-0-9774411)* 1920 Pacific Ave. No. 16152, Long Beach, CA 90806 USA (SAN 257-4977) Tel 310-438-3483; Fax: 310-438-3486
E-mail: info@fmapublishing.com
Web site: http://www.fmapublishing.com.

FMG, *(978-0-578-95348-9)* 6396 Walden Pond Ct, LAS VEGAS, NV 89148 USA Tel 725-710-3943
E-mail: thinkfocus1@gmail.com.

Fo Guang Shan International Translation Ctr., *(978-1-943211)* 3456 Glenmark Dr., Hacienda Heights, CA 91745 USA Tel 626-330-8361
E-mail: fgsitc@gmail.com
Web site: fgsitc.org.

Focus *Imprint of* **Hackett Publishing Co., Inc.**

Focus Group, Inc., *(978-0-9766968)* 2201 SW 152nd St. Ste. 3, Burien, WA 98166-2080 USA
E-mail: pubs@focusgroupseattle.com.

†Focus on the Family Publishing, *(978-0-929608; 978-1-56179; 978-1-58997; 978-1-60482; 978-1-62405; 978-1-62471; 978-1-68332; 978-1-68424; 978-1-68428; 978-1-64607; 979-8-88799)* 8605 Explorer Dr., Colorado Springs, CO 80920 USA (SAN 250-0949) Fax: 719-531-3356; Toll Free: 800-232-6459
E-mail: robert.huntrods@fotf.org; permissions@fotf.org
Web site: http://www.focusonthefamily.com
Dist(s): **Follett School Solutions**
Gospel Light Pubns.
Nelson, Tommy
Tyndale Hse. Pubs.
Zondervan; *CIP.*

Focus Publishing, *(978-1-885904; 978-1-936141)* Orders Addr.: P.O. Box 665, Bemidji, MN 56619 USA Tel 218-759-9816 Toll Free: 800-913-6287; Edit Addr.: 502 Third St., NW, Bemidji, MN 56601 USA
E-mail: jan@focuspublishing.com
Web site: http://focuspublishing.com
Dist(s): **Spring Arbor Distributors, Inc.**

Focus Readers *Imprint of* **North Star Editions**

Fog City Pr., *(978-1-875137; 978-1-887451; 978-1-892374; 978-1-929156; 978-1-74089)* Subs. of Weldon Owen, Inc., 2215-R Market St., No. 123, San Francisco, CA 94114 USA Tel 415-626-9636
E-mail: gilblock@sirius.com
Dist(s): **INscribe Digital**
Ingram Publisher Services.

Fog Ink *Imprint of* **Fields of Gold Publishing, Inc.**

Foglight Pr., *(978-0-9755848)* Orders Addr.: P.O. Box 160322, Sacramento, CA 95816 USA
E-mail: info@foglightpress.com
Web site: http://www.foglightpress.com
Dist(s): **Bookazine Co., Inc.**

folder leaf *Imprint of* **Story Time Stories That Rhyme**

Foley, Mark, *(978-0-615-19609-1)* 4 3rd Ave., Annville, PA 17003 USA
Dist(s): **Lulu Pr., Inc.**

Folk Prophet Bks., *(978-0-578-00160-9)* 140 S. 200 E., Lindon, UT 84042 USA
E-mail: books@folkprophet.com
Dist(s): **Lulu Pr., Inc.**

Folklore Publishing (CAN) *(978-1-894864; 978-1-897206; 978-1-926677) Dist. by* **Lone Pine.**

Follett Library Resources *See* **Follett School Solutions**

Follett School Solutions, *(978-0-329; 978-0-88153; 978-0-924917; 978-1-4898; 978-1-5160; 978-1-5181; 978-1-5379; 978-1-5444; 978-1-5490; 978-1-7254; 978-1-7137; 978-1-6868; 979-8-3687)* Div. of the Follett Corp., Orders Addr.: a/o McHenry Warehouse, 1340 Ridgeview Dr., McHenry, IL 60050 USA (SAN 169-1902) Toll Free: 888-511-5114; a/o Patti Hall: R & R Bindery Services, 499 Rachel Rd., Girard, IL 62640 (SAN 155-8412) Tel 815-759-1700; *Imprints:* Follettbound (Follettbnd)
Web site: http://www.follett.com
Dist(s): **Baker & Taylor Bks.**

Follettbound *Imprint of* **Follett School Solutions**

Follmer Group, The, *(978-0-925065; 978-1-933478; 978-1-935871; 978-1-943137)* 5758 S. Blackstone Ave., Chicago, IL 60637 USA Tel 773-643-1902; Fax: 773-643-1903
E-mail: david@thedavidfollmergroup.com
Web site: http://www.thedavidfollmergroup.com.

Folsom Fallies Pr., *(978-0-9760790)* Orders Addr.: P.O. Box 348, Folsom, NM 88419 USA Tel 505-278-2520
E-mail: kristene@folsomfallies.com
Web site: http://www.folsomfallies.com.

Fomenky Publishing, *(978-0-615-97545-0; 978-0-9988929; 979-8-9888585)* 3333 164TH ST SW Apt No. 1613, LYNNWOOD, WA 98087 USA Tel 925-367-5478
E-mail: Berthina@CNATOMD.COM; Kellen@Colemanprfirm.com
Web site: www.FOMENKYPUBLISHING.COM; Colemanprfirm.com; WWW.CHRISTIANSTAR.ME.

Fond du Lac Head Start, *(978-0-615-69899-1)* 1720 Big Lake Rd., Cloquet, MN 55720 USA Tel 218-878-8130; Fax: 218-878-8115
E-mail: barbaraforcier@fdlrez.com
Web site: fdlrez.com.

Fondo de Cultura Económcia,
Dist(s): **Fondo de Cultura Economica USA.**

Fondo de Cultura Economica USA, 2293 Verus St., San Diego, CA 92154 USA (SAN 860-1380) Tel 619-429-0455; Fax: 619-651-9684; Toll Free: 800-532-3872
E-mail: orders@fceusa.com; drazo@fceusa.com; fondosales@fceusa.com
Web site: http://www.fceusa.com
Dist(s): **Giron Bks.**
Latin American Book Source, Inc.
Lectorum Pubns., Inc.

Fondo Editorial Grania, Fundacion Hogares Juveniles Campesinos (COL) *(978-958-8233; 978-958-9321) Dist. by* **Chelsea Green Pub.**

Fons Vitae *See* **Fons Vitae of Kentucky, Inc.**

Fons Vitae of Kentucky, Inc., *(978-1-887752; 978-1-941610)* 49 Mockingbird Valley Dr., Louisville, KY 40207-1366 USA Tel 502-897-3641
E-mail: fonsvitaeky@aol.com
Web site: http://www.fonsvitae.com
Dist(s): **Independent Pubs. Group.**

Fontanka (GBR) *(978-0-9543095; 978-1-906257) Dist. by* **Natl Bk Netwk.**

Food Allergy & Anaphylaxis Network, *(978-1-882541)* 11781 Lee Jackson Hwy. Suite 160, Fairfax, VA 22033 USA Tel 703-691-3179; Fax: 703-691-2713; Toll Free: 800-929-4040
E-mail: faan@foodallergy.org
Web site: http://www.foodallergy.org.

Food Allergy Network *See* **Food Allergy & Anaphylaxis Network**

Food & Agriculture Organization of the United Nations (ITA) *(978-92-5) Dist. by* **Rowman.**

Food Enhancement Enterprises, *(978-0-9747247)* Orders Addr.: P.O. Box 60581, Sacramento, CA 95680 USA; Edit Addr.: 2148 Bluebird Ln., Sacramento, CA 95821 USA
E-mail: hsdell@lanset.com
Web site: http://www.pizzareconsidered.com.

Food Marketing Consultants, Inc., *(978-0-9763307; 978-1-59949)* 2805 N. Commerce Pkwy., Miramar, FL 33025 USA Tel 954-322-2668 Toll Free: 877-493-2633
Web site: http://www.colorallabout.com.

Food Network Kitchens *Imprint of* **Meredith Bks.**

Food Safety & Inspection Service *Imprint of* **United States Government Printing Office**

FoodPlay Productions, *(978-0-9642858)* 1 Sunset Ave., Hatfield, MA 01038 USA Tel 413-247-5400; Fax: 413-247-5405; Toll Free: 800-366-3752 (Orders)
E-mail: store@foodplay.com
Web site: http://www.foodplay.com
Dist(s): **Partners Pubs. Group, Inc.**

Foolosophy Media, *(978-0-9779928)* 1528 Primrose Ln., Panama City, FL 32404 USA (SAN 850-8186) Tel 850-871-2304; 850-899-1972; Fax: 850-871-2304
E-mail: wisemullet@gmail.com.

Foothill-Hydroponics, *(978-0-9669557)* 10705 Burbank Blvd., N., North Hollywood, CA 91601 USA Tel 818-760-0688; Fax: 818-760-0025
E-mail: mohsen@foothillhydroponics.com
Web site: http://www.foothill-hydroponic.com.

Footpath Pr. LLC, *(978-0-9821686; 978-0-615-56745-7; 978-0-615-56749-5; 978-0-692-24094-6)* 408 8 1/2 Ave. NW Apt. E204, Rochester, MN 55901 USA
E-mail: footpathpress@yahoo.com
Dist(s): **CreateSpace Independent Publishing Platform.**

Footprints Pr., *(978-0-9679813)* 71 Hudson St., New York, NY 10013 USA Tel 212-267-9300; Fax: 212-267-9400.

For Children With Love Pubns., *(978-0-578-00980-3; 978-0-9831221; 978-0-9994002; 978-0-578-74995-2)* 23 Robkins rd, Avon, CT 06001 USA Tel 860-940-9878; 23 Robkins rd, Avon , CT 06001
E-mail: Cathy.forchildren@gmail.com
Web site: http://www.forchildrenwithlove.com.

For Dummies *Imprint of* **Wiley, John & Sons, Inc.**

For Him Pr., *(978-0-9858899)* P.O. Box 2207, Morristown, TN 37816 USA Tel 423-307-8137
E-mail: claudia-scribe@live.com
Web site: claudia-clues.com.

For Kids' Sake Publising, Inc., *(978-1-7337502)* P.O. Box 61084, Corpus Christi, TX 78466 USA Tel 361-215-8340
E-mail: debra.hatch@forkissakepublishing.com.

For Little Folks, *(978-0-9771236)* P.O. Box 571, Dresden, OH 43821 USA.

For Such A Time As This Ministries, *(978-0-9725890)* 510 Swank Rd., Hollsopple, PA 15935-8116 USA Tel 814-479-7710; Fax: 814-479-4874; Toll Free: 877-378-4374
E-mail: jpstobaugh@aol.com
Web site: http://www.forsuchatimeasthis.com.

For The Love of Dog Bks., *(978-0-9761124)* 635 NE Buffalo, Portland, OR 97211 USA Tel 503-286-5351
E-mail: stelljes@aol.com
Web site: http://www.silvertonbobbie.com
Dist(s): **Far West Bk. Service**
Partners/West Book Distributors.

Forbes Custom Publishing, *(978-0-8281)* Div. of Forbes, Inc., 60 Fifth Ave., New York, NY 10011 USA (SAN 206-9032) Tel 212-620-2200; Fax: 212-367-4862; Toll Free: 800-242-8786
E-mail: customerservice@forbes.net
Dist(s): **Institute for Healthcare Advancement.**

Forbes Literary Ltd. Inc., *(978-0-9776284)* P.O. Box 494, Grover, MO 63040-1621 USA Tel 314-753-6142; Fax: 636-405-1963
E-mail: forbeslit@sbcgobal.net
Web site: http://www.forbesliterary.com.

Force of Nature LLC, *(978-0-692-87979-5; 978-0-692-94113-3; 978-0-692-04818-4; 978-0-692-08542-4)* 12289 Jamboree Dr, Eastvale, CA 91752 USA
E-mail: info@4orceofnature.com.

Ford, Angela J. *See* **Angela J. Ford, LLC**

Fore Angels Pr., *(978-0-9658920; 978-0-9799947)* 267 Woodbury Rd., Huntington, NY 11743 USA Tel 631-385-0336
E-mail: annaarts@verizon.net.

Foreign Policy Assn., *(978-0-87124)* 551 Fifth Ave. Suite 3000, New York, NY 10176 USA (SAN 212-9426) Tel 212-481-8100; Fax: 212-481-9275; Toll Free: 800-628-5754; 800-477-5836 (orders)
Web site: http://www.fpa.org.

Forelle Graphics, *(978-0-9770918)* 1015 Atlantic Blvd., Suite 89, Atlantic Beach, FL 32233 USA
E-mail: forelle-graphics@yahoo.com.

Forest Hill Publishing, LLC, *(978-0-9759251; 978-0-9771113)* 13200 Forest Hill Ave., East Cleveland, OH 44112 USA Tel 216-761-8316 (phone/fax); Fax: 253-799-8316; *Imprints:* PlayGround (PlayGrnd OH); SpringTree (SpringTree); FortuneChild (FortuneChild) Do not confuse with Forest Hill Publishing in Downers Grove, IL
E-mail: email@foresthillpublishing.com
Web site: http://www.foresthillpublishing.com.

Forest Hse. Publishing Co., Inc., *(978-1-56674; 978-1-878363)* P.O. Box 738, Lake Forest, IL 60045 USA Tel 847-295-8287; Fax: 847-295-8201; Toll Free: 800-394-7323.

Forest Lane Bks., *(978-0-9996735)* P.O. Box 371006, San Diego, CA 92137 USA Tel 619-269-5433
E-mail: ruthmacpete@gmail.com.

Forest Service *Imprint of* **United States Government Printing Office**

Forest Woods Media Productions *Imprint of* **Bunny & The Crocodile Pr., The**

Foresta, David Samuel, *(978-0-578-42370-8)* 3277 Bighorn Cir., Corona, CA 92881 USA Tel 951-549-0789
E-mail: dforesta@arbonne.com.

Forever *Imprint of* **Grand Central Publishing**

Forge Bks. *Imprint of* **Doherty, Tom Assocs., LLC**

Forgotten Bks., *(978-1-60506; 978-1-60620; 978-1-60680; 978-1-4400; 978-1-4510)* 8345 NW 66th St., Miami, FL 33166 USA (SAN 854-9354)
E-mail: director@forgottenbooks.org
Web site: http://www.forgottenbooks.org/
Dist(s): **CreateSpace Independent Publishing Platform.**

Fork in the Road Pubs., *(978-0-9740825)* 1883 145th Pl. SE, Bellevue, WA 98007-6019 USA Tel 425-644-4285
Web site: http://www.raincitycookingschool.com.

Forks Pr., *(978-0-9816641)* 4-02 Summit Ave., Fair Lawn, NJ 07410 USA (SAN 856-1575) Tel 201-310-3297; 646-208-2161
E-mail: info@forkspress.com
Web site: http://www.forkspress.com.

Form 2 Fashion, *(978-1-7370215)* 509 S Chickasaw Trail No. 187 0, ORLANDO, FL 32825 USA Tel 407-710-5565
E-mail: info@form2fashion.com
Dist(s): **Ingram Content Group.**

Formac Publishing Co., Ltd. (CAN) *(978-0-88780; 978-0-921921; 978-1-55277; 978-1-4595)* *Dist. by* **Casemate Pubs.**

Formac Publishing Co., Ltd. (CAN) *(978-0-88780; 978-0-921921; 978-1-55277; 978-1-4595)* *Dist. by* **Lerner Pub.**

Forrestall Consulting, *(978-0-578-54273-7)* 3325 Paloma St, Pasadena, CA 91107 USA Tel 225-413-2405
E-mail: shanna.forrestall@gmail.com
Web site: www.forrestallconsulting.com.

Forsberg, Michael Photography, *(978-0-9754964)* 100 N. 8th St., Suite 150, Lincoln, NE 68508-1369 USA Toll Free: 888-812-3790 Do not confuse with Platte Publishing Company in Denver, CO
E-mail: patty@michaelforsberg.com
Web site: http://www.michaelforsberg.com
Dist(s): **Univ. of Nebraska Pr.**

fortheARTofit Publishing, *(978-0-9897577)* 917 Esplanade Ave. No. 1, New Orleans, LA 70116 USA Tel 347-365-0622
E-mail: books@thecasquettegirls.com
Web site: www.thecasquettegirls.com.

Fortify Your Faith Foundation, *(978-0-9678044; 978-1-932723)* P.O. Box 11746, Jackson, TN 38308 USA Tel 731-256-7280
E-mail: david@christiancourier.com
Web site: http://www.christiancourier.com.

Fortitude Graphic Design & Printing *See* **Fortitude Graphic Design & Printing**

Fortitude Graphic Design & Printing, *(978-0-9741611; 978-0-578-06241-9; 978-0-9863173; 978-0-9977136; 978-0-692-88090-6; 978-0-9991334; 978-1-7328399; 978-1-7353600; 978-1-7370202; 979-8-9868698)* 841 Gibson St., Kalamazoo, MI 49001-2540 USA
E-mail: seasonpub@gmail.com
Web site: www.comvoicesonline.com; www.seasonpressinc.com.

Fortner, Ray, *(978-0-9726365)* Orders Addr.: 3501 Baisden Rd., Pensacola, FL 32503-3458 USA.

Fortress Pr. *Imprint of* **1517 Media**

Fortuna Publications *See* **Fiction Hse. Pr.**

FortuneChild *Imprint of* **Forest Hill Publishing, LLC**

Forward Comix, *(978-0-9886114; 978-0-9904747; 978-1-7344969)* 467 Bay Ridge Pkwy., Brooklyn, NY 11209 USA Tel 718-921-8789
E-mail: jerome@forwardcomix.com
Web site: forwardcomix.com.

Forward Communications *See* **NetNia Publishing Co.**

Forward Movement Pubns., *(978-0-88028)* 300 West Fourth St., Cincinnati, OH 45202 USA (SAN 208-3841) Tel 513-721-6659; Fax: 513-721-0729; Toll Free: 800-543-1813 (orders only)
E-mail: Orders@forwarddaybyday.com
Web site: http://www.forwardmovement.org.

Forword, *(978-0-9623937)* 16526 W. 78th St., Suite 335, Eden Prairie, MN 55346 USA Tel 612-944-7761; Fax: 612-944-8674.

Foster Branch Publishing, 20 Poplar St., No. 2, Jersey City, NJ 07307 USA
E-mail: dolphinupatree@hotmail.com.

Foster, Dennis, *(978-0-9771956)* P.O. Box 363, Millwood, VA 22646 USA.

Foster, Hicks & Assocs., *(978-0-9790709)* Orders Addr.: 4053 Harlan St., loft 201, Emeryville, CA 94608-9460 USA Tel 510-540-1241
E-mail: info@fosterhicks.com.

Foster, Walter Publishing, Incorporated *See* **Quarto Publishing Group USA**

Foston Adolescent Workshop, Inc., *(978-0-9641709; 978-1-930362)* P.O. Box 726, Clarksville, TN 37041 USA Tel 931-906-4623; Fax: 931-645-3500; Toll Free: 800-418-0374
E-mail: mrfoston@aol.com
Web site: http://www.drfoston.com.

Fotopia Pr., *(978-0-9970996)* 9501 S. King Dr., Chicago, IL 60628 USA Tel 773-318-9485
E-mail: adamfotos@rocketmail.com
Web site: adamfotos.com.

Fouch, Robert L., *(978-0-9907913)* 26 Ivy Pl., Valley Stream, NY 11581 USA Tel 516-569-0125
E-mail: robfouch@aol.com
Web site: robertlfouch.com.

Foulsham, W. Co., Ltd. (GBR) *(978-0-572)* *Dist. by* **APG.**

Found Image Pr., *(978-0-9674866; 978-0-9755211; 978-1-933344; 978-1-60150; 978-1-68081; 978-1-64811; 978-1-6695; 979-8-3854)* Orders Addr.: P.O. Box 16116, San Diego, CA 92176-6116 USA Fax: 619-282-4562; Toll Free: 800-927-3722; Edit Addr.: 5155 Santa Fe St.,Suite J, San Diego, CA 92109 USA
E-mail: info@foundimage.com
Web site: http://www.foundimage.com.

Found Link, *(978-0-615-43601-2; 978-0-9836659)* 13125 Ladybank Ln., Herndon, VA 20171 USA Tel 703-966-2175
E-mail: jlcuddehe@verizon.net
Web site: www.CuddeheServices.com.

Foundation For Cosmetic Surgery, The, *(978-0-9799438)* 400 Newport Center Dr. Ste. 800, Newport Beach, CA 92660-7607 USA
E-mail: bryan@griffinpublishing.com; ffps2007@yahoo.com
Web site: http://www.beautybybrennan.com.

Foundation, Pr. The, *(978-0-9765987)* Do not confuse with companies with the same name in New York, NY, Anaheim, CA
Web site: http://www.thefoundationpress.com.

Foundation Pr., *(978-0-9767272)* 13832 Gimbert Ln., Santa Ana, CA 92705-2849 USA Do not confuse with companies with the same name in New York, NY, Westport, CT.

Foundations for Learning, LLC, *(978-0-9726479; 978-1-933546)* 246 W. Manson Hwy., PMB 144, Chelan, WA 98816 USA Toll Free: 800-553-5950
E-mail: info@gophonics.com
Web site: http://www.gophonics.com.

Foundations in Brass *See* **Cymbal Technique 101**

Foundation, Inc., *(978-0-9797125; 978-0-9859251)* 701 E. Gate Dr. Suite 300, Mt. Laurel, NJ 08054 USA Tel 856-533-1600; Fax: 856-533-1601; Toll Free: 888-977-5437
E-mail: rmclaughlin@foundationsinc.org
Web site: http://www.foundationsinc.org.

Founders Hse. Publishing LLC, *(978-0-9843764; 978-0-692-34395-1; 978-0-692-38422-0; 978-0-692-38427-5; 978-0-692-38945-4; 978-0-692-39110-5; 978-0-692-43655-4; 978-0-692-45654-5; 978-0-692-45897-6; 978-0-692-48863-8; 978-0-692-55429-6; 978-0-692-57197-2; 978-0-692-67911-1; 978-0-692-73490-2; 978-1-945810) 420 Commercial St., Danville, IL 61832 USA*
E-mail: sckilgore@foundershousepublishing.com
Web site: https://www.foundershousepublishing.com; https://www.foundershousebooks.com; https://www.mythicmag.com
Dist(s): **CreateSpace Independent Publishing Platform.**

Fountain Blue Publishing, *(978-0-615-81358-5; 978-1-62868)* P.O. Box 657, Squaw Valley, CA 93675 USA Tel 213-986-6835
E-mail: fountainbluepublishing@gmail.com
Web site: www.fountainbluepublishing.com.

Fountain Publishing, *(978-0-9659164; 978-0-9748423; 978-0-9822172; 978-1-936665)* Orders Addr.: P.O. Box 80011, Rochester, MI 48308 USA (SAN 253-8571) Tel 248-651-2934; Toll Free: 877-736-8598; Edit Addr.: 375 Olivewood Ct., Rochester, MI 48306 USA Tel 810-651-1153 Do not confuse with Fountain Publishing in Pittsburgh, PA
E-mail: ftnpublish@aol.com; jk@fountainpublishing.com
Web site: http://www.fountainpublishing.com.

Fountain Square Publishing, *(978-0-9724421)* 786 Old Ludlow, Cincinnati, OH 45220 USA.

Fountainbleau Media, *(978-1-952863)* 2465 W 175th St., Homewood, IL 60430 USA Tel 305-434-0738
E-mail: msanders@fountainbleaumedia.com.

Fountains of Financial Services, LLC, *(978-0-9719706)* 626 S. Ninth St., Las Vegas, NV 89101 USA Tel 702-382-9833; Fax: 702-382-0375
E-mail: pgfox711@aol.com.

Four Blocks, Div. of Carson-Dellosa Publishing Company, Inc., Orders Addr.: P.O. Box 35665, Greensboro, NC 27425 USA Tel 336-632-0084; Fax: 336-808-3249; Toll Free: 800-321-0943
Dist(s): **Carson-Dellosa Publishing, LLC.**

Four Corners Magazine LLC, *(978-0-578-46178-6; 978-0-578-47860-9)* P.O. Box 2252, Flagstaff, AZ 86003 USA Tel 928-300-4452
E-mail: sedonamag@gmail.com.

Four Corners Publishing Co., Inc., *(978-1-893577)* 45 W. Tenth St., New York, NY 10011 USA Tel 212-673-5226; Fax: 516-771-1243
E-mail: RLutnick@aol.com.

Four Dolphins Pr. *Imprint of* **Four Dolphins Pr., LLC**

Four Dolphins Pr., *(978-0-9745746)* Orders Addr.: P.O. Box 93601, Los Angeles, CA 90093 USA (SAN 255-626X) Tel 323-304-2053; Edit Addr.: 2700 N. Cahuenga Blvd., E., Suite 1403, Los Angeles, CA 90068-2139 USA.

Four Dolphins Pr., LLC, *(978-0-9799315)* P.O. Box 833, Scott Depot, WV 25560 USA Tel 304-757-8125; *Imprints:* Four Dolphins Press (Four Dolphin)
Web site: http://www.SadMadGladBooks.com.

Four Dolphins Press/Smart Communications, Incorporated *See* **Four Dolphins Pr.**

Four Elephants Pr., *(978-1-940051; 978-0-9998324)* 11828 La Grange Ave., Los Angeles, CA 90025 USA Tel 310-477-4564
E-mail: annaka.harris@gmail.com
Dist(s): **MyiLibrary**
Publishers Group West (PGW).

Four Foot Pr. LLC, *(978-0-9820817)* 12647 Galveston Ct., Suite 114, Manassas, VA 20112 USA
E-mail: dcgenesis@hotmail.com; fourfootpress@yahoo.com
Web site: http://fourfootpress.com.

Four Menards, The, *(978-0-9887969; 978-0-9891734; 978-0-9903872; 978-0-9904521)* P.O. Box 17265, Asheville, NC 28816 USA Tel 828-335-0284; Fax: 828-484-9873
E-mail: thefourmenards@gmail.com
Web site: N/A.

Four Oaks Publishing *Imprint of* **Santacroce, John**

Four Panel Pr., *(978-0-9674102; 978-0-9971090)* P.O. Box 50032, Eugene, OR 97405 USA Tel 541-343-6436; Fax: 541-684-0787
E-mail: tedlay@comcast.net
Web site: http://www.stonesoupcartoons.com.

Four Phoenixes Publishing, *(978-0-9976205)* 6407 N. Post Oak Rd., Peoria, IL 61603 USA Tel 309-256-6406
E-mail: joechianakas@gmail.com.

Four Pine Farms *See* **Four Pines Farms**

Four Pines Farms, *(978-0-9860701)* 683 Feldhauser Rd, Frederic, MI 49733 USA
E-mail: yroehler@bookpublishing.com.

Four Seasons Bks., Inc., *(978-0-9666858; 978-1-893595)* P.O. Box 395, Ben Wheeler, TX 75754 USA Tel 903-963-1442; Fax: 903-963-1525; Toll Free: 800-852-7484
E-mail: hcmarlow@yahoo.com; editor@fourseasonsbookstore.com
Web site: http://www.herbmarlow.com; http://www.fourseasonsbookstore.com.

Four Seasons Pubs., *(978-0-9656811; 978-1-891929; 978-1-932097)* Orders Addr.: P.O. Box 51, Titusville, FL 32781 USA Tel 321-632-2932; Fax: 321-632-2935; Edit Addr.: 4350 N. U.S. Hwy. 1, Cocoa, FL 32927 USA
E-mail: fseasons@bellsouth.net
Dist(s): **Follett School Solutions.**

Four Seasons Publishing, *(978-0-578-05005-8)* 105 Ansley Pl., Harlem, GA 30814 USA
E-mail: tedhoodjr@arkansas.net
Web site: http://www.thecardinalnest.com.

Four Sonkist Angels, *(978-0-9753117)* 4985 Wiltshire Ln., Suwanee, GA 30024 USA
E-mail: Michelle@FourSonkistAngels.com
Web site: http://www.FourSonkistAngels.com.

Four Star Publishing, *(978-0-9815894)* P.O. Box 871784, Canton, MI 48187 USA
E-mail: fourstarpublishing@comcast.net.

Four Winds Pubns., *(978-1-929113)* 551 Cordova Rd., Suite 112, Santa Fe, NM 87501 USA.

FourFront Media & Music, *(978-0-9743420)* Orders Addr.: 1245 S. 128th St., Seattle, WA 98168 USA Tel 206-282-6116
E-mail: chris@chrisknab.net
Web site: http://www.fourfrontmusic.com.

Foursquare Media, ICFG, *(978-0-9635581; 978-0-9802392)* 1910 W. Sunset Blvd., Suite 200, Los Angeles, CA 90026 USA Tel 213-989-4493; Fax: 213-413-3824
E-mail: rwulfestieg@foursquare.org
Web site: http://www.foursquare.org.

Fourth Generation Pubs., *(978-0-9706186)* PMB 146,14625 Baltimore Ave., Laurel, MD 20707-4902 USA (SAN 253-5513) Tel 301-497-9948.

Fox Chapel Publishing Co., Inc., *(978-0-932944; 978-1-56523; 978-1-57421; 978-1-58011; 978-1-880029; 978-1-896980; 978-1-85974; 978-1-903366; 978-0-9777004; 978-1-905523; 978-1-60765; 978-1-906853; 978-1-4971; 978-1-4972; 978-1-5048; 978-1-908397; 978-1-910456; 978-1-64124; 978-1-64178; 978-1-63741; 978-1-63981; 979-8-89094) Orders Addr.: 1970 Broad St., East Petersburg, PA 17520 USA (SAN 920-8887) Tel 717-560-4703; Fax: 717-560-4702; Toll Free Fax: 888-369-2885; Toll Free: 800-457-9112 (orders); Edit Addr.: 903 Square St., Mount Joy, PA 17552 USA Fax: 888-369-2885; Toll Free: 1-800-457-9112; Imprints:* Design Originals (Design Orig); Creative Homeowner (CreativeHome); CompanionHouse Books (CompanionBks); Quiet Fox Designs (QuietFox)
E-mail: sales@carvingworld.com; alan@foxchapelpublishing.com; Younger@foxchapelpublishing.com; sales@foxchapelpublishing.com
Web site: http://www.foxchapelpublishing.com/; http://www.scrollsawer.com/; http://www.carvingworld.com; http://www.foxchapelpublishing.com; www.d-originals.com
Dist(s): **Children's Plus, Inc.**
Open Road Integrated Media, Inc.

Fox Cottage Pr., *(978-1-7330772)* 23 Ryerson Rd., New Hampton, NY 10958 USA Tel 516-502-8099
E-mail: Fox_cottage@icloud.com.

Fox, Kenneth *See* **Flat Pond Publishing**

Fox Pointe Publishing LLP, *(978-0-692-78291-0; 978-0-692-79187-5; 978-0-692-04582-4; 978-1-7337717; 978-1-7345885; 978-1-952567; 978-1-955743)* P.O. Box 623, Austin, MN 55912 USA Tel 507-993-8929; Fax: 507-512-1373
E-mail: KIERSTEN@FOXPOINTEPUBLISHING.COM; CHELSEA@FOXPOINTEPUBLISHING.COM
Web site: FOXPOINTEPUBLISHING.COM; www.teacup-press.com.

Fox Print Bks., *(978-0-9729587)* 200 Seashore Ave., Peaks Island, ME 04108 USA Tel 207-899-0781
E-mail: eleanor.morse@gmail.com.

Fox Ridge Pubns., *(978-0-9856215; 978-0-9904281; 978-0-9967683)* 10490 Fox Ridge Dr., Hillsboro, WI 54634 USA Tel 715-630-2433
E-mail: lisalickel@gmail.com.

Fox Run Pr., LLC, *(978-0-9819607; 978-0-9825930)* 7840 Bullet Rd., Peyton, CO 80831 USA
Web site: http://www.FoxRunPress.com; http://www.ShadowFoxBook.com.

Fox Song Bks., *(978-0-9744989; 978-0-9837310)* 6185 Ferguson Rd., Port Alberni, BC V9Y 8L4 CAN
E-mail: fox@foxsongbooks.com; orders@foxsongbooks.com; foxsongbooks@gmail.com
Web site: http://foxsongbooks.com; www.faithrichardson.info
Dist(s): **Ingram Content Group.**

Fox Valley Habitat for Humanity, *(978-0-9914127)* 1300 S. Broadway, Montgomery, IL 60538 USA Tel 630-859-3333
E-mail: R.Kelso@foxvalleyhabitat.org
Web site: www.foxvalleyhabitat.org.

FoxAcre Pr., *(978-0-9671783; 978-0-9709711; 978-0-9818487; 978-1-936771)* 401 Ethan Allen Ave., Takoma Park, MD 20912 USA Fax: 301-560-2482
E-mail: info@foxacre.com
Web site: http://www.foxacre.com
Dist(s): **Smashwords.**

Foxcroft, Jennifer, *(978-0-9909895)* P.O. Box 2541, Littleton, CO 80161 USA
E-mail: jenfoxy@me.com
Web site: jenniferfoxcroft.com.

FoxRock, Inc., *(978-0-9643740; 978-0-9714705)* 61 Fourth Ave., No. 4, New York, NY 10003 USA Tel 212-505-6880; Fax: 212-673-1039
E-mail: evergreen@nyc.rr.com
Web site: http://www.evergreenreview.com.

Fox's Den Publishing, *(978-0-9816107)* P.O. Box 6156, Sevierville, TN 37864-6156 USA
E-mail: foxsdenpublishing@hotmail.com.

FoxTales Pr., *(978-1-942023; 978-1-956495)* P.O. Box 658, Cave Creek, AZ 85327 USA Tel 503-689-0100
E-mail: info@foxtalespress.com
Web site: http://danihoots.com.

FPI Publishing, *(978-0-9768215)* P.O. Box 247, Havre de Grace, MD 21078 USA Tel 410-459-9087
E-mail: gyleen@colourfulstitches.com
Web site: http://www.colourfulstitches.com.

FQ Classics *Imprint of* **Filiquarian Publishing, LLC**

FR Publishing *Imprint of* **Razavi, Firouzeh Bks.**

Fragile X Assn. of Georgia, *(978-0-9727865)* 3161 W. Somerset Ct., Marietta, GA 30067-5045 USA Tel 770-988-9275; Fax: 770-988-8255; Rood End Hse., 6 Stortford Rd., Great Dunmow, CM6 1DA Tel 01371 875100
E-mail: info@fragilex.k-web.co.uk; frax@bellsouth.net
Web site: www.fragilex.org.uk; http://www.myextraspecialbrother.com.

Fragmenta Editorial (ESP) *(978-84-92416)* *Dist. by* **IPG Chicago.**

Fragnito, Julie, *(978-1-7370866)* 24 Hidden Pond Ln., Trumbull, CT 06611 USA Tel 516-640-7767
E-mail: taleoftwostories@gmail.com.

Fragrance Ministries, *(978-0-9745260)* 2900 Government Way, No. 161, Coeur d'Alene, ID 83815 USA
E-mail: fragranceministries@yahoo.com
Web site: http://www.fragranceministries.com.

Frances, Celia, *(978-0-692-13655-3)* 424 Parker Ave, DEAL PARK, NJ 07723 USA Tel 732-829-1288
E-mail: celia.ezon@gmail.com
Dist(s): **Ingram Content Group.**

Frances Lincoln Childrens Bks. (GBR) *(978-1-84507; 978-1-84780; 978-1-78603)* *Dist. by* **HachBkGrp.**

Frances More International Teaching Systems, *(978-0-9768234)* Div. of Gray Squirrel, Inc., P.O. Box 26659, Collegeville, PA 19426 USA Tel 610-724-6331
E-mail: sales@graysquirrel.org; francesmore.hangingrock@xtra.co.nz
Web site: http://www.qwertyqik.com; http://www.fingerithmatic.com.

Francesca Studios, *(978-0-9741060)* 26 Dole Hill Rd., Holden, ME 04429 USA.

Francis & Lee Publishing, *(978-1-7371124; 979-8-9869948)* P.O. Box P.O. Box 6536, Waldorf, MD 20603 USA Tel 301-651-7041
E-mail: destiny.w.phillip@gmail.com.

Francis, Jennifer, *(978-0-692-87978-8; 978-0-692-91422-9)* 343 Gold St, 903, Brooklyn, NY 11201 USA Tel 718-930-9813
E-mail: JenHappy2Day@gmail.com.

Franciscan Media, *(978-0-86716; 978-0-912228; 978-1-61636; 978-1-63253; 978-1-63254)* Subs. of Franciscan Friars (St. John Baptist Province), 28 W. Liberty St., Cincinnati, OH 45202 USA (SAN 204-6237) Tel 513-241-5615; Fax: 513-241-1197; Toll Free: 800-488-0488
E-mail: caroleD11@AmericanCatholic.org
Web site: http://www.AmericanCatholic.org
Dist(s): **Firebrand Technologies**
Forward Movement Pubns.
SPD-Small Pr. Distribution
Spring Arbor Distributors, Inc.
St. Anthony Messenger Press.

Franckowiak, Jon, *(978-0-9715415)* 4981 Shallow Ridge Rd., NE., Kennesaw, GA 30144 USA
E-mail: psukeljon@aol.com
Dist(s): **Partners Bk. Distributing, Inc.**

Franco, Nick Art, *(978-0-615-24474-7; 978-0-578-03402-7)* 5757 W. Euglie Ave., No. 2050, Glendale, AZ 85304 USA
E-mail: nickfrancoart@yahoo.com
Web site: http://www.nickfrancoart.com
Dist(s): **Lulu Pr., Inc.**

Frank, Lauren, *(978-1-7353461)* 2030 Redwood Crest, Vista, CA 92081 USA Tel 916-759-7171
E-mail: lbeck27.lb@gmail.com.

Frank Schaffer Pubns. *Imprint of* **Carson-Dellosa Publishing, LLC**

Frankel, David, *(978-0-692-83220-2)* 221 Walton St., WEST HEMPSTEAD, NY 11552 USA Tel 718-404-8914
E-mail: jeffwcrawford5+LVP0003251@gmail.com; jeffwcrawford5+LVP0003251@gmail.com.

Frankie Dove Publishing, *(978-0-9786487; 978-0-9987731)* P.O. Box 3875, Federal Way, WA 98063-3875 USA (SAN 851-2051)
E-mail: georgepettingell@frankiedovepublishing.com.

Franklin, J.E., *(978-0-9746669)* P.O. Box 517, New York, NY 10031 USA Tel 212-283-8666
E-mail: je413@aol.com
Web site: http://www.geocities.com/haveplaywilltravel/playseries.html.

Franklin, Lauren, *(978-0-9972386)* 24827 whitewater, Murrieta, CA 92563 USA Tel 619-384-3914
E-mail: laurenfranklin23@yahoo.com
Web site: Babblingbeth.com.

Franklin Mason Pr., *(978-0-9679227; 978-0-9760469; 978-0-9857218; 978-0-9977250; 978-1-7376768)* Orders Addr.: P.O. Box 3808, Trenton, NJ 08629 USA (SAN 253-1828) Tel 609-291-5030; Fax: 609-291-7807; 415 Route 68, Columbus, NJ 08022
E-mail: lwill0517@aol.com
Web site: http://www.franklinmasonpress.com; http://www.nickyfifth.com
Dist(s): **BMI Educational Services.**

Franklin Publishing, *(978-0-9708129)* 1917 Warrington Rd., SW, Roanoke, VA 24015-3037 USA Tel 540-982-1654 (phone/fax on demand) Do not confuse with Franklin Publishing, Tempe, AZ, Chandler, AZ
E-mail: ampaw@aol.com.

Franklin Scribes, *(978-0-615-68198-6; 978-0-9886433; 978-1-941516)* 301 Apache Ledge, Cibolo, TX 78108 USA Tel 210-363-3843
E-mail: franklinscribeswrites@gmail.com
Web site: www.franklinscribes.com
Dist(s): **CreateSpace Independent Publishing Platform**
Independently Published
Ingram Bk. Co.

Franklin, Stephanie Michelle *See* **Heavenly Realm Publishing**

Fransson, Wade *See* **Something Or Other Publishing**

Frayed Pages Publishing *See* **Frayed Pages Publishing**

ayed Pages Publishing, (*978-0-9753397*) P.O. Box 705, Pickens, SC 29671 USA
E-mail: cjr@watkinsandwatkins.com
Dist(s): **Continental Enterprises Group, Inc. (CEG).**

azee, Patti *See* **LynxGazer Publishing**

razier, Angie *See* **First Cup Pr.**

razier, Jeffrey R. *See* **Egg Hill Pubns.**

razier, Jeremy A., (*978-0-692-78756-4*) 208 Mairead Dr., DOTHAN, AL 36301 USA Tel 803-586-5040.

red Pinsocket Productions, (*978-0-9907941*) 5070 Betlo Ct., San Jose, CA 95130 USA Tel 408-252-7383
E-mail: musicnews@PeterApel.com.

rederic, Marc *See* **World of Whimsy Productions, LLC**

rederic Thomas USA, Inc., (*978-1-945546*) 5621 Strand Blvd, Naples, FL 34110 USA Tel 239-593-8000
E-mail: jbelyea@fredericthomasusa.com
Web site: http://fredericthomasusa.com/.

redonia Bks., (*978-1-58963; 978-1-4101*) 4440 NW 73rd Ave., PTY 362, Miami, FL 33166-6437 USA Tel 407-650-2537 (phone/fax)
E-mail: bip@fredoniabooks.com
Web site: http://www.fredoniabooks.com.

Fredrickson, Anne, (*978-0-615-20146-7*) 6905 290th St. W., Northfield, MN 55057 USA
Dist(s): **Aardvark Global Publishing.**

Free Bird Pr., (*978-1-7365636; 978-1-958764*) 1870 Fairway Pk. Unit A, ESCONDIDO, CA 92026 USA Tel 503-858-2864
E-mail: bethanyjvotaw@gmail.com.

Free Focus Publishing, (*978-0-9826747*) P.O. Box 716, Blaine, WA 98231 USA Tel 310-562-8165 (phone/fax).

Free People Publishing, (*978-0-9838131; 978-0-9991163; 978-1-959341*) 10 Parker Cir., Salem, NH 03079 USA Tel 603-898-6124
E-mail: jzygmont@jeffreyzygmont.com
Web site: https://www.jeffreyzygmont.com; https://www.freepeepub.com
Dist(s): **Free People Books.**

Free Pr. *Imprint of* **Free Pr.**

†Free Pr., (*978-0-02; 978-0-669; 978-0-671; 978-0-684; 978-0-7432*) Orders Addr.: 100 Front St., Riverside, NJ 08075 USA; Edit Addr.: 1230 Ave. of the Americas, New York, NY 10020 USA; *Imprints:* Free Press (Free Imp)
Dist(s): **CreateSpace Independent Publishing Platform**
Simon & Schuster
Simon & Schuster, Inc.; *CIP.*

Free Pr. Pubs., (*978-0-943751*) Orders Addr.: P.O. Box 4717, Monroe, LA 71211 USA (SAN 242-6242) Tel 318-388-1310; Fax: 318-388-2911
E-mail: RooseveltWright@prodigy.net
Web site: http://www.sermonideas.com.

F.R.E.E. Publishing House, (*978-0-86639; 978-0-9762472*) Div. of Friends of Refugees of Eastern Europe, 1383 President St., Brooklyn, NY 11213 USA Tel 718-467-0860 ext 118; Fax: 718-467-2146
E-mail: publications@russianjewry.org
Web site: http://www.JRBooks.org.

Free Spirit Artworks, LLC, (*978-0-9996760*) 1125 Lamar Ave, Altamonte Springs, FL 32714 USA Tel 732-778-0351
E-mail: jessica333@yahoo.com.

†Free Spirit Publishing Inc., (*978-0-915793; 978-1-57542; 978-1-63198; 979-8-88554*) 6325 Sandburg Rd., Ste. 100, Warehouse Docks 42/43, Golden Valley, MN 55427-3674 USA (SAN 293-9584) Tel 612-338-2068; Fax: 612-337-5050; Toll Free: 800-735-7323
E-mail: help4kids@freespirit.com
Web site: http://www.freespirit.com
Dist(s): **Brodart Co.**
Children's Plus, Inc.
Follett School Solutions
Independent Pubs. Group
MyiLibrary
Teacher Created Materials, Inc.; *CIP.*

Free Spirit Publishing, Incorporated *See* **Free Spirit Publishing Inc.**

Free Your Mind Publishing, (*978-0-9760056*) P.O. Box 70, Boston, MA 02131 USA Fax: 202-889-5056; 2724 Knox Terrace, SE, Washington, DC 20020 (SAN 256-1883) Do nopt confuse with Free Your Mind Publishing in Indianapolis, IN
E-mail: omekongo@omekongo.com
Web site: http://www.freeyourmindpublishing.com
Dist(s): **Smashwords.**

FreeBird Foundation of Evergreen, CO, The, (*978-1-7347701; 978-1-7361014*) 2357 Columbine Ln., Evergreen, CO 80439 USA Tel 303-910-0770
E-mail: freebirdevergreen@gmail.com.

Freedom Archives, The, (*978-0-9727422; 978-0-9790789*) 522 Valencia St., San Francisco, CA 94110 USA Tel 415-863-9977
E-mail: info@freedomarchives.org
Web site: http://www.freedomarchives.org
Dist(s): **AK Pr. Distribution**
Consortium Bk. Sales & Distribution
SPD-Small Pr. Distribution.

Freedom in Christ Ministries, (*978-0-9969725; 978-1-7366641*) 9051 Executive Pk. Dr, KNOXVILLE, TN 37932 USA Tel 865-342-4006
E-mail: jshafer@ficm.org
Web site: freedominchrist.com.

Freedom International Bks. LLC, (*978-0-692-10650-1; 978-0-578-62101-2; 978-0-578-74437-7; 978-1-7365260*) 12825 lake vista dr, Gibsonton, FL 33534 USA Tel 727-698-6275
E-mail: ashley@thekeeperofmyheart.com
Web site: Www.thekeeperofmyheart.com.

Freedom International Publishing LLC *See* **Freedom International Bks. LLC**

Freedom of Speech Publishing, Inc., (*978-1-938634*) 4552 W 138 Terr, Leawood, KS 66224 USA Tel 815-290-9605
E-mail: admin@freedomofspeechpublishing.com
Web site: www.freedomofspeechpublishing.com.

Freedom Pr., (*978-0-9989145; 978-1-7354215*) 4131 Biedsoe Ave, Los Angeles, CA 90066 USA Tel 310-390-9937
E-mail: jjiefu2002@icloud.com
Web site: www.jeffjacobsonworld.com.

Freedom Pr., (*978-0-9664326*) P.O. Box 2228, Wrightwood, CA 92397-2228 USA Tel 505-573-0737 Do not confuse with companies with the same name in Allentown, PA, Scottsdale, AZ, Pawcatuck, CT, Southaven, MS, Liberty Lake, WA, Saint Louis, MO, Nutley, NJ
E-mail: freedompress@hotmail.com
Web site: http://freedompress.4t.com
Dist(s): **Bristlecone Publishing Co.**
New Leaf Distributing Co., Inc.

Freedom Reading Foundation, Incorporated *See* **Edu-Steps, Inc.**

Freedom Three Publishing, (*978-0-9714254; 978-0-578-36815-3; 979-8-218-00580-1; 979-8-218-17310-4*) 310 N. Indian Hill Blvd., #442, Claremont, CA 91711 USA Tel 909-447-5320
E-mail: info@freedomthree.com
Web site: http://www.freedomthree.com; http://www.joelharper.net; http://www.allthewaytotheocean.com
Dist(s): **Leonard, Hal Corp.**

Freedom Voices Pubns., (*978-0-915117; 978-0-9625153*) Div. of Tenderloin Reflection & Education Ctr., P.O. Box 423115, San Francisco, CA 94142 USA
E-mail: jess@freedomvoices.org; spottywest@freedomvoices.org; art@arthazelwood.com
Web site: http://www.freedomvoices.org
Dist(s): **AK Pr. Distribution**
Ingram Content Group
SPD-Small Pr. Distribution.

Freedom's Hammer, (*978-0-9884780; 978-1-7359236*) 11 Country Squire Ct., Greenville, SC 29615 USA Tel 864-386-1146
E-mail: cfors10917@aol.com.

Freefox Publishing, (*978-0-9801527*) Orders Addr.: 32 Doncaster Cir., Lynnfield, MA 01940 USA
Web site: http://www.freefoxpublishing.com.

Freelance Fridge, LLC, (*978-0-578-42245-9; 978-0-578-60157-1; 978-1-7364141*) 3806 E. Santa Fe Ln., Gilbert, AZ 85297 USA Tel 480-688-5289
E-mail: jameskoenig1@yahoo.com
Dist(s): **Ingram Content Group.**

FreeStar Pr., (*978-0-9661315*) P.O. Box 54552, Cincinnati, OH 45254-0552 USA Tel 513-734-0102
E-mail: Freestarpr@aol.com.

Freet Publishing, (*978-0-9676717*) Orders Addr.: P.O. Box 219, Willow Hill, PA 17271-0219 USA Tel 717-349-7873 (phone/fax); Edit Addr.: 18028 Pigeon Hill Rd., Willow Hill, PA 17271-0219 USA
E-mail: freepbl@pa.net.

Freeverse Enterprises Inc., (*978-0-9743789*) 1200 E. River Rd. C-35, Tucson, AZ 85718 USA.

Freeze Time Media, (*978-0-9858103; 978-0-9913550; 978-0-9966883; 978-1-946702*) 7133 Depew Ct., Arvada, CO 80003 USA Tel 303-885-8736
E-mail: difreeze@gmail.com
Web site: www.difreeze.com.

Freiling Publishing, (*978-0-692-08071-9; 978-0-692-09075-6; 978-0-692-10203-9; 978-1-950948; 978-1-956267; 979-8-9874834; 979-8-9881634; 979-8-9888007*) 10375 Welhams Ln, Marshall, VA 20115 USA Tel 703-347-4400
E-mail: tom@freiling.agency
Web site: www.FreilingPublishing.com
Dist(s): **Whitaker Hse.**

Fremantle Pr. (AUS) (*978-1-86368; 978-0-909144; 978-0-949206; 978-1-920731; 978-1-921064; 978-1-921361; 978-1-921696; 978-1-921888; 978-0-646-39543-2; 978-0-646-50123-9; 978-1-925160; 978-1-925161; 978-1-925162; 978-1-925163; 978-1-925164; 978-1-925591; 978-1-925815; 978-1-925816; 978-1-76099; 978-1-922089*) *Dist. by* **IPG Chicago.**

French & European Pubns., Inc., (*978-0-320; 978-0-7859; 978-0-8288; 978-1-5479*) 425 E. 58th St., Suite 27D, New York, NY 10022-2379 USA (SAN 206-8109) Fax: 212-265-1094
E-mail: livresny@gmail.com; frenchbookstore@aol.com
Web site: http://www.frencheuropean.com.

French, Samuel , Inc. *Imprint of* **Concord Theatricals**

French, Samuel , Ltd. *Imprint of* **Concord Theatricals**

French Workshop, The *See* **Aaron Levy Pubns., LLC**

FREOMM Publishing, (*978-0-9659891*) 77635 Malone Cir., Palm Desert, CA 92211 USA Tel 760-772-6628
E-mail: odyssey@odysseyofthesoul.org
Web site: http://www.odysseyofthesoul.org
Dist(s): **New Leaf Publishing Group.**

Fresh Ink Group, (*978-1-936442; 978-1-947867; 978-1-947893; 978-1-958922*) 23 Lake Breeze Dr., Guntersville, AL 35976 USA Tel 256-606-6204
E-mail: info@freshinkgroup.com
Web site: freshinkgroup.com.

Freshwater Pr., (*978-1-893555; 979-8-9863020; 979-8-9868502; 978-1-960150; 979-8-218-12972-9*) 400 Corporate Dr. Suite 200, Stafford, VA 22554 USA Tel 757-239-0535
E-mail: freshwaterpress9@gmail.com.

Freundship Pr., LLC, (*978-0-9822204; 978-0-9839957*) P.O. Box 9171, Boise, ID 83707 USA Tel 208-407-7457
E-mail: info@freundshippress.com
Web site: http://www.freundshippress.com.

Frey Hse. Publishing LLC, (*978-1-7329423*) 130 Corridor Rd. No. 116, Ponte Vedra Beach, FL 32004 USA Tel 904-373-5906
E-mail: Freyhousepub@gmail.com.

Frias, Marilyn, (*978-0-692-83460-2*) 100 Meadowood Dr, ASPEN, CO 81611 USA Tel 970-618-5050
E-mail: jeffwcrawford5+LVP0003264@gmail.com; jeffwcrawford5+LVP0003264@gmail.com.

Frick Art & Historical Ctr.,The, (*978-0-9703425; 978-0-615-57373-1; 978-0-615-57374-8*) 7227 Reynolds St., Pittsburgh, PA 15208 USA Tel 412-371-0600; Fax: 412-241-5393
E-mail: tsmart@frickart.org; info@frickart.org
Web site: http://www.frickart.org.

Fried, Scott *See* **TALKAIDS, Inc.**

Frieda B., (*978-0-9843862*) 55 Long Hill Dr., Somers, CT 06071 USA (SAN 859-2640)
Web site: http://www.friedab.com.

Friedman, Michael Publishing Group, Inc., (*978-0-9627134; 978-1-56799; 978-1-58663; 978-1-4114*) Div. of Barnes & Noble, Inc., 122 Fifth Ave., Fifth Flr., New York, NY 10011 USA (SAN 248-9732) Tel 212-685-6610; Fax: 212-633-3327
E-mail: rlamarche@bn.com
Web site: http://www.metrobooks.com
Dist(s): **MyiLibrary**
Sterling Publishing Co., Inc.
Texas A&M Univ. Pr.

Friedman, Yuda, (*978-0-9677313*) 11 Quickway Rd. Unit 103, Monroe, NY 10950-8804 USA.

Friedrich, Paul, (*978-0-9793676*) 323 W. Martin St., SPC 70, Raleigh, NC 27601 USA
Web site: http://onionheadmonster.com.

Friend Family Ministries, (*978-0-9767524*) 1601 Hamilton Richmond Rd., Hamilton, OH 45013 USA.

Friendly Isles Pr., (*978-0-9678979*) Orders Addr.: 8503 Sun Harbor Dr., Bakersfield, CA 93312 USA Tel 661-587-0645
E-mail: ofalisiate@yahoo.com.

Friendly Planet, (*978-0-9742469*) 101 Third St., Cambridge, MA 02141 USA; *Imprints:* Big Books for Little People (Big Bks)
E-mail: mike@friendlyplanet.org
Web site: http://www.friendlyplanet.org.

Friendly Planet Club, (*978-0-692-17569-9*) 3301 Michelson Dr., Apt. No. 1521, Irvine, CA 92612 USA Tel 949-573-3517
E-mail: yaya1582@gmail.com
Web site: https://www.friendlyplanet.club/.

Friends of Hildene, Inc., (*978-0-9754917; 978-0-692-31124-0*) 1005 Hildene Rd., PO Box 377, Manchester, VT 05254 USA Tel 802-362-1788; Fax: 802-362-1564
Web site: http://www.hildene.org.

Friends of Lulu, (*978-0-9740960*) P.O. Box 1114, New York, NY 10013-0866 USA
E-mail: info@friends-lulu.org
Web site: http://www.friends-lulu.org/.

Friends Of The Goshen Grange, The, (*978-0-9771473*) P.O. Box 1016, Goshen, NH 03752-1016 USA.

Friends of Vail Foundation *See* **Proverbial Girl Publishing**

†Friends United Pr., (*978-0-913408; 978-0-944350; 978-1-956149*) 101 Quaker Hill Dr., Richmond, IN 47374 USA (SAN 201-5803) Tel 765-962-7573; Fax: 765-966-1293; Toll Free: 800-537-8839
E-mail: friendspress@fum.org
Web site: http://www.fum.org
Dist(s): **Independent Pubs. Group**; *CIP.*

Frog Bks. *Imprint of* **North Atlantic Bks.**

Frog Children's Bks. *Imprint of* **North Atlantic Bks.**

Frog Legs Ink *Imprint of* **Gauthier Pubns. Inc.**

Frog Light Pr., (*978-0-578-93923-0*) 47 Washington St., Marblehead, MA 01945 USA Tel 347-224-6408
E-mail: rebeccamkwait@gmail.com.

Frog Ltd. *Imprint of* **North Atlantic Bks.**

Frog Pond Enterprises, (*978-0-615-12821-4; 978-0-9915037*) 2821 Sheffield Ct., Trophy Club, TX 76262 USA Tel 862-502-4827
E-mail: joyclassalive2@gmail.com
Web site: www.joyclassalive.com; http://www.joyforchurches.com.

Frog Prince Bks., (*978-1-7325410; 978-1-7348242*) 442 E. Shore Trl, Sparta, NJ 07871 USA Tel 973-670-8324
E-mail: frogprincebooks@gmail.com
Web site: www.frogprincebooks.net.

Frog Prince Pr., (*978-0-615-91119-9; 978-0-9908323*) 480 N Walnut St, Boise, ID 83712 USA Tel 5129647997
Web site: elisabethsharpmcketta.com
Dist(s): **CreateSpace Independent Publishing Platform.**

Frog Street Pr., (*978-1-60128; 978-1-63237; 978-1-63636*) 800 Industrial Blvd Suite 100, Grapevine, TX 76051 USA (SAN 851-0806) Tel 800-884-3764; Fax: 800-759-3828; Toll Free Fax: 800-759-3828; Toll Free: 800-884-3764
E-mail: bhunt@frogstreet.com; mtyndall@frogstreet.com
Web site: http://www.frogstreet.com.

F.R.O.G. the Rock Pubns., (*978-0-9727142*) 3524 Parkview Dr., Marietta, GA 30062 USA Tel 770-587-4902; Fax: 770-993-0394
E-mail: frogtherock@aol.com.

Froglogic Concepts LLC *See* **Leadline Publishing**

From Inside the Heart *See* **WaterWords**

From My Shelf Bks. & Gifts, (*978-0-692-59255-7; 978-0-692-64770-7; 978-0-692-72287-9; 978-0-692-72460-6; 978-0-692-76063-5; 978-0-692-76325-4; 978-0-692-79938-3; 978-0-692-80112-3*) 7 E. Ave, Suite 101, Wellsboro, PA 16901 USA Tel 570-724-5793
E-mail: from_my_shelf@yahoo.com.

From the Asylum Bks. & Pr., (*978-0-9715860*) P.O. Box 1516, Dickinson, TX 77539 USA
Web site: http://www.fromtheasylum.com.

From Your Doctor To You, LLC, (*978-0-692-78615-4; 978-0-9984610*) 8340 Merion Dr., Duluth, GA 30097 USA Tel 404-427-6239
E-mail: fatuforna@hotmail.com.

From Your Heart to Paper Publishing, (*978-0-692-16341-2; 978-0-578-86512-6; 978-0-578-86517-1; 978-0-578-98138-3; 979-8-9861668*) 5232 Judy Lynn Ave., Memphis, TN 38118 USA Tel 901-846-9894
E-mail: tammie@tammieterrellmompreneurs.com
Dist(s): **CreateSpace Independent Publishing Platform.**

Front Page Publishing, LLC, (*978-1-951705*) 5198 Arlington Ave., Suite 335, Riverside, CA 92504 USA Tel 951-809-8833
E-mail: delanolaw319@gmail.com; mary@FirstBookAcademy.com
Web site: www.FrontPagePublishing.com.

Front Porch Publishing, (*978-0-9998139*) 1086 Seefried Ln., Blackfoot, ID 83221 USA Tel 208-694-3484
E-mail: coniet7@hotmail.com.

Front Street *Imprint of* **Astra Publishing Hse.**

Front Street *Imprint of* **Highlights Pr., c/o Highlights for Children, Inc.**

Front Street/Cricket Books *See* **Cricket Bks.**

Fronte, Kathy, (*978-0-9727725*) 5604 Greenwood Cir., Naples, FL 34112 USA.

Frontier Books *See* **Frontier Pr.**

Frontier Image Pr., (*978-0-9634309; 978-1-888571*) Orders Addr.: P.O. Box 3055, Silver City, NM 88061 USA Tel 505-534-4032; Fax: 505-590-1301
E-mail: frontr@cybermcs.com.

Frontier Pr., (*978-0-9768465*) 180 E. Ocean Blvd., Fl 4, Long Beach, CA 90802-9080 USA Tel 562-491-8331; Fax: 562-491-8791
E-mail: new_frontier@usw.salvationarmy.org.

Frontiera, Deborah *See* **Jade Enterprises**

Frontline *Imprint of* **Charisma Media**

Frontline Communications *See* **YWAM Publishing**

Frontline Pr., (*978-0-930201*) Orders Addr.: P.O. Box 764499, Dallas, TX 75376-4499 USA Tel 972-572-8336; Fax: 972-572-8335 Do not confuse with companies with the same or similar name in Washington, DC, Taylors, SC, Charlston, SC
E-mail: info@youthdirect.org
Web site: http://www.youthdirect.org.

Frost, C. A., (*978-0-9847236*) 8113 Cloverglen Ln., Fort Worth, TX 76123 USA Tel 817-994-2420
E-mail: theewordnerd@yahoo.com.

Frost, Heather, (*978-1-7348919; 978-1-959122*) 245 S 1280 W, Logan, UT 84321 USA Tel 435-230-3341
E-mail: heatherfrostauthor@gmail.com
Web site: www.HeatherFrost.com.

Frost Hollow Pubs., LLC, (*978-0-9658523; 978-0-9720922; 978-0-9794273; 978-0-9829636; 978-0-9890965; 978-0-9989136*) 411 Barlow Cemetery Rd., Woodstock, CT 06281 USA Tel 860-974-2081; Fax: 860-974-0813; Toll Free: 877-974-2081
E-mail: frosthollow@mindspring.com
Web site: http://www.frosthollowpub.com.

Frugal Bear Communications, (*978-0-9678694*) P.O. Box 5154, Inglewood, CA 90310 USA; *Imprints:* FrugalBear.com (FrugalBear)
E-mail: regresa@hotmail.com; frugalbear@email.com
Web site: http://www.frugalbear.com.

FrugalBear.com *Imprint of* **Frugal Bear Communications**

Fruit Springs, LLC, (*978-1-970016*) 17330 W Ctr. Rd., Omaha, NE 68130 USA Tel 402-884-5995
E-mail: fruitsprings@conciergemarketing.com.

Fruitbearer Kids *Imprint of* **Fruitbearer Publishing, LLC**

Fruitbearer Publishing, LLC, (*978-1-886068; 978-1-938796; 978-1-955008*) Orders Addr.: P.O. Box 777, Georgetown, DE 19947 USA (SAN 920-380X) Tel 302-856-6649; Fax: 302-856-7742; Edit Addr.: 107 Elizabeth St., Georgetown, DE 19947 USA; *Imprints:* Fruitbearer Kids (Fruitbear Kid)
E-mail: cfa@candyabbott.com; info@fruitbearer.com
Web site: http://www.fruitbearer.com
Dist(s): **BookBaby**
Independently Published
Ingram Content Group
Smashwords.

Fruitful Tree Publishing, (*978-0-9986677; 978-1-7341845*) 509 Aspen Glade Ct., Lexington, SC 29072 USA.

Fruition Online Publishing, (*978-0-9712079*) Div. of Cherokee Ventures, 120 St. Albans Dr., #469, Raleigh, NC 27609 USA Tel 919-743-2500; Fax: 919-743-2501
E-mail: customersupport@fruitiononline.com
Web site: http://www.fruitiononline.com.

Fry, Debbie, (*978-0-9759647*) 301 N. Gleason Ave., Fowler, CA 93625-2162 USA.

F/S *Imprint of* **Worthy Publishing**

FT Richards Publishing, (*978-0-9746561*) 41 Tailwinds Ln., North East, MD 21901 USA
Web site: http://www.fairwindsstables.com.

Ft. Valley Geology Study Ctr. *Imprint of* **InterPress**

FTD, (*978-0-9747637*) 3113 Woodcreek Dr., Downers Grove, IL 60515 USA Toll Free: 800-383-6659.

FTL Pubns., (*978-0-9653575; 978-0-9825232; 978-1-936881*) Orders Addr.: P.O. Box 1363, Minnetonka, MN 55345-0363 USA Tel 952-938-4275; Edit Addr.: 5137 Clear Springs Dr., Minnetonka, MN 55345-4312 USA
E-mail: mail@ftlpublications.com
Web site: http://www.FTLPublications.com
Dist(s): **Diamond Comic Distributors, Inc.**
Smashwords.

Fuchs, Monique, (*978-1-7335624*) 118 Franklin St., No. 3, Brookline, MA 02445 USA Tel 617-738-1739
E-mail: monique_fuchs@yahoo.com.

Fuel Media Group, Incorporated *See* **Amplify Church Group, Inc.**

Fuentes, Krista, (978-1-7370121) 1814 Nantz Ln 0, CONROE, TX 77304 USA Tel 713-289-9771
E-mail: Krista.kay.fuentes@gmail.com
Dist(s): **Ingram Content Group.**

Fuess, Rachel, (*978-0-692-85142-5; 978-0-692-85250-7*) 21203 Pk. Villa, KATY, TX 77450 USA Tel 281-638-2261
E-mail: jeffwcrawford5+LVP0003378@gmail.com; jeffwcrawford5+LVP0003378@gmail.com.

†Fulcrum Publishing, (*978-0-912347; 978-1-55591; 978-1-56373; 978-1-936218; 978-1-938486; 978-1-68275*) Orders Addr.: 4690 Table Mountain Dr.

Publisher Name Index

Suite 100, Golden, CO 80403 USA (SAN 200-2825) Toll Free Fax: 800-726-7112; Toll Free: 800-992-2908
E-mail: info@fulcrumbooks.com
Web site: http://www.fulcrumbooks.com
Dist(s): **Abraham Assocs. Inc.**
Alibris
Copyright Clearance Ctr., Inc.
Independent Pubs. Group
MyiLibrary
ebrary, Inc.; *CIP*.

Fulfill Publishing, *(978-0-9969449)* 3871 S. 850 W., Riverdale, UT 84405 USA Tel 801-695-1673
E-mail: brownjo76@comcast.net.

Full Cast Audio *See* **FCA Pr.**

Full Circle Media, Inc. *Imprint of* **Atma Global Knowledge Media, Inc.**

Full Circle Pr. *Imprint of* **WillowTree Pr., L.L.C.**

Full City Press *See* **Lychgate Pr.**

Full Court Pr., *(978-0-9709477; 978-0-578-01482-1; 978-0-578-02337-3; 978-0-578-02841-5; 978-0-578-03345-7; 978-0-578-05544-2; 978-0-578-05545-9; 978-0-9846113; 978-0-9833711; 978-0-9837411; 978-0-9849536; 978-1-938812; 978-1-946989; 978-1-953728)* 601 Palisade Ave., Englewood Cliffs, NJ 07632 USA Fax: 201-567-7202
Web site: http://writingcenternj.com
Dist(s): **Follett School Solutions.**

Full Cycle Pubns., *(978-0-615-43266-3; 978-0-615-50132-1; 978-0-615-68186-3; 978-0-615-78628-5; 978-0-615-81244-1; 978-0-9905819; 978-0-9966422; 978-1-7325961)* 5837 S. 157 W., Salt Lake City, UT 84107 USA (SAN 860-0953) Tel 213-804-4891
E-mail: nabila@earthlink.net
Dist(s): **BookBaby.**

Full Effect Gospel Ministries, Inc., *(978-0-9679516; 978-0-615-76085-8; 978-0-692-29621-9; 978-1-7338592)* 900 New Lots Ave, Brooklyn, NY 11208 USA Tel 7189270476
Web site: www.effect900.com
Dist(s): **CreateSpace Independent Publishing Platform.**

Full Gospel Family Pubns., *(978-0-9745599)* 419 E. Taft Ave., Appleton, WI 54915-2079 USA Tel 920-734-6693
E-mail: character@characterbuildingforfamilies.com; pilgrims@juno.com
Web site: http://www.characterbuildingforfamilies.com.

Full House Productions, *(978-0-615-27092-0; 978-0-9832564)* 2466 Center Point Rd., Fredericksburg, TX 78624 USA.

Full Moon Creations, Incorporated *See* **LeLeu, Lisa Studios! Inc.**

Full Moon Press *See* **King's Way Pr.**

Full Moon Publishing, LLC, *(978-0-615-81984-6; 978-0-615-84647-7; 978-0-615-89471-3; 978-0-615-89533-8; 978-0-615-99886-2; 978-0-692-20136-7; 978-0-692-02366-2; 978-0-692-02367-9; 978-0-692-20350-7; 978-0-692-22127-3; 978-0-692-40867-4; 978-0-692-43932-6; 978-0-692-47046-6; 978-0-692-53018-4; 978-0-692-58018-9; 978-0-692-58662-4; 978-0-692-58663-1; 978-0-692-60312-3; 978-0-692-63908-5; 978-0-692-65568-9; 978-0-692-66138-3; 978-0-692-68604-1; 978-0-692-68605-8; 978-0-692-74504-5; 978-1-946232) 110 Evergreen St., Glade Spring, VA 24340 USA Tel 276-451-0331*
E-mail: rondacaudill@yahoo.com
Dist(s): **CreateSpace Independent Publishing Platform.**

Full Moon Publishing LLC, *(978-0-9666021; 978-0-9785402; 978-0-9820352; 978-0-9846357; 978-0-9888683; 978-0-9976707)* Orders Addr.: 433 Mystic Point Dr., Bluffton, SC 29909 USA Tel 219-688-3093 Do not confuse with Full Moon Publishing, Norton, MA
E-mail: fullmoonpub@sc.rr.com
Web site: http://www.fullmoonpub.com
Dist(s): **Smashwords.**

Full Quart Pr. *Imprint of* **Holly Hall Pubns., Inc.**

Full Satchel Pr. (CAN) *(978-0-9731960) Dist. by* **MYID_F_GATEWOO.**

Full Tilt Pr. (NZL) *(978-0-473-24742-3) Dist. by* **Lerner Pub.**

Fullerton Bks., Inc., *(978-0-9652918)* Orders Addr.: P.O. Box 1, Waveland, MS 39576 USA Tel 972-412-3131; 228-457-5323; Fax: 509-278-0766
E-mail: info@vincevance.com
Web site: http://www.vincevance.com.

FullofPep Pubns., *(978-0-9760684)* P.O. Box 367, Columbia, SC 29202 USA
E-mail: fullofpeppublications@yahoo.com.

Fulton Bks., *(978-1-63338; 978-1-64654; 978-1-64952; 978-1-63710; 978-1-63860; 978-1-63985; 979-8-88505; 979-8-88731; 979-8-88982; 979-8-89221)* Orders Addr.: 296 Chestnut St, Meadville, PA 16335 USA; Edit Addr.: 296 Chestnut St., Meadville, PA 16335 USA Tel 877-210-0816
E-mail: dusty@fultonbooks.com
Web site: fultonbooks.com.

Fulton, David Pubs. (GBR) *(978-1-85346; 978-1-84312) Dist. by* **Taylor and Fran.**

Fultus *See* **Fultus Corp.**

Fultus Corp., *(978-0-9744339; 978-1-59682)* P.O. Box 50095, Palo Alto, CA 94303 USA Fax: 650-745-0873; *Imprints*: Fultus Publishing (Ful Pubng)
E-mail: production@fultus.com
Web site: http://www.fultus.com; http://elibrary.fultus.com; http://store.fultus.com; http://writers.fultus.com
Dist(s): **Ingram Content Group.**

Fultus Publishing *Imprint of* **Fultus Corp.**

Fun 4 Kids Publishing *Imprint of* **Stray Dog Pr., LLC**

Fun Bks., *(978-0-615-58137-8; 978-0-692-52380-3; 978-0-692-52382-7; 978-0-692-52394-0; 978-0-692-52400-8; 978-0-692-91324-6; 978-1-7329438)* 22 Kowall Pl., Lynbrook, NY 11563 USA Tel 516-754-6287 Do not confuse with Fun Books in Tulsa, OK
Dist(s): **BookBaby**
CreateSpace Independent Publishing Platform.

Fun Family Publishing, *(978-1-7331631)* 9033 SW Burnham St., Portland, OR 97223 USA Tel 503-449-4631
E-mail: kameronkh@yahoo.com
Web site: lamikeandotis.com.

Fun Fitness Publishing, *(978-0-9762483; 978-0-615-35686-0)* 16 Paulsboro Rd., Woolwich, NJ 08055 USA Tel 609-410-3717 (phone/fax); Fax: 609-257-4079
E-mail: jeyre2@comcast.net; funfitness@comcast.net
Web site: http://www.janeeyre-art.com; http://www.funfitnesstraining.weebly.com.

Fun Places Publishing, *(978-0-9646737; 978-0-9833832)* 6124 Capetown St., Lakewood, CA 90713 USA Tel 562-867-5223
E-mail: orders@funplaces.com
Web site: http://www.funplaces.com
Dist(s): **American West Bks.**
Sunbelt Pubns., Inc.

Fun Publishing Co., *(978-0-938293)* 2121 Alpine Pl., No. 402, Cincinnati, OH 45206 USA (SAN 661-1761) Tel 513-533-3636; Fax: 513-421-7269 Do not confuse with companies with the same or similar names in Scottsdale, AZ, Fort Lauderdale, FL, Indianapolis, IN
E-mail: funpublish@aol.com
Web site: http://www.funpublishing.com.

Fun Time Flowers *See* **Flower Sprouts**

Fun to Read Bks. with Royally Good Morals *Imprint of* **MKADesigns**

Funcastle Pubns., *(978-0-9645771)* Orders Addr.: P.O. Box 51217, Riverside, CA 92517 USA Tel 951-653-5200; Fax: 951-653-4300; Edit Addr.: 20833 Millbrook St., Riverside, CA 92508 USA
Dist(s): **Independent Pubs. Group.**

Functional Fitness, LLC, *(978-0-9815551; 978-0-9995034)* 102 Twin Oaks Way, Kemah, TX 77565 USA Tel 281-704-8804
E-mail: functionalfitness@peoplepc.com; patbrill@peoplepc.com
Web site: http://www.functionalfitnessllc.org.

Fundacion Intermon (ESP) *(978-84-604; 978-84-8452; 978-84-89970; 978-84-921977) Dist. by* **Mariuccia Iaconi Bk Imports.**

Fundacion Intermon (ESP) *(978-84-604; 978-84-8452; 978-84-89970; 978-84-921977) Dist. by* **Lectorum Pubns.**

Fundamental Christian Endeavors, *(978-1-931787)* 49191 Cherokee Rd., Newberry Springs, CA 92365 USA Tel 760-257-3503; Fax: 760-652-4808
Web site: http://www.ironwood.org.

Fundamental Wesleyan Pubs., *(978-0-9629383; 978-0-9761003; 978-0-9914251; 978-1-7327926)* 2120 Culverson Ave., Evansville, IN 47714 USA Tel 812-476-2996
E-mail: victorpau@aol.com
Web site: http://www.fwponline.cc.

FUNdamentals/Leap In Faith, *(978-0-9834645)* P.O. Box 491, Abingdon, MD 21009 USA Tel 443-484-2512
E-mail: Fundamentals123@aol.com
Web site: Fundamentals123.com
Dist(s): **Partners Pubs. Group, Inc.**

Fundcraft Publishing, *(978-1-931413; 978-1-935397)* Orders Addr.: P.O. Box 340, Collerville, TN 38027 USA Tel 901-853-7070; Fax: 901-853-6196; Edit Addr.: 410 Hwy. 72 W., Collierville, TN 38017 USA Tel 901-853-7070
E-mail: info@fundcraft.com
Web site: http://www.fundcraft.com.

FungChung, Nikko M, *(978-0-9981497)* 505 Benton Drive, Apt. 4312, Allen, TX 75013 USA Tel 347-724-0000; Fax: 347-724-0000
E-mail: nikko.fungchung@gmail.com
Web site: http://www.awabookseries.com.

Funk, Sherree *See* **Serving One Lord Resources**

Funnel Cloud 9, Inc., *(978-0-9767297)* 545 Tom Treece Rd., Morristown, TN 37814 USA
Web site: http://www.fc9.net.

Funnel Time Bks., *(978-0-9600123)* 2475 S Huckleberry CT, Heber City, UT 84032 USA.

Funny Bone Bks., *(978-0-9771836; 978-0-9790240; 978-0-9799121; 978-0-9822288; 978-0-9841507)* 3435 Golden Ave., No. 302, Apt. 302, Cincinnati, OH 45226 USA
E-mail: dpendery@newforms.com
Web site: http://www.bookmasters.com/funnybones.

FunnyGuy.Comedy, *(978-0-9747398)* 123 N. Kings Rd., Los Angeles, CA 90048 USA
E-mail: dave@funnyguy.com
Web site: http://www.funnyguy.com.

FunStitch Studio *Imprint of* **C & T Publishing**

Fur, George, *(978-0-9752985)* 165 Laurel Ave., Menlo Park, CA 94025 USA
E-mail: yfur@msn.com.

Fura Bks., *(978-1-890224)* P.O. Box 90751, Nashville, TN 37209-0751 USA
E-mail: furabooks@comcast.net
Web site: http://www.powerofhorses.com.

Furry Purry Pr., *(978-0-692-64005-0; 978-0-692-98224-2; 978-0-578-43122-2)* 514 Duck Puddle Rd., Waldoboro, ME 04572 USA Tel 207-563-7127
E-mail: tx22@tidewater.net.

Fury Publishing & Distributing, *(978-0-9747049)* 325 Washington Ave. No. 214, Kent, WA 98032 USA Tel 253-520-3111
E-mail: furypublishing@msn.com
Web site: http://www.fury2000.com.

Fushimi, Tatsuya, *(978-1-7376809)* 13232 Beach St. 0, CERRITOS, CA 90703 USA Tel 562-746-9876
E-mail: tatsufushimi@gmail.com
Dist(s): **Ingram Content Group.**

Fusible, LLC, *(978-1-7367011)* 5501 Merchants View Sq. Suite 180, Haymarket, VA 20169 USA Tel 703-963-5488
E-mail: admin@fusible.com
Web site: fusible.com.

Fusion Bks. *Imprint of* **Bearport Publishing Co., Inc.**

Futech Educational Products, Inc., *(978-0-9627001; 978-1-889192)* 2999 N. 44th St., Suite 225, Phoenix, AZ 85018-7248 USA Tel 602-808-8765; Fax: 602-278-5667; Toll Free: 800-597-6278.

Future Bookworms LLC, 30 N. Gould St., Ste 4000, Sheridan, WY 82801 USA Tel 707-702-3069; Fax: 707-312-8175
E-mail: admin@futurebookworms.com
Web site: http://futurebookworms.com.

Future Comics, *(978-0-9744225)* 220 W. Brandon Blvd., Brandon, FL 33511 USA Tel 813-655-1900; Fax: 813-662-3250; Toll Free: 877-226-6427
E-mail: info@futurecomicsonline.com
Web site: http://www.futurecomicsonline.com.

Future Education, Incorporated *See* **Future Horizons, Inc.**

Future Horizons, Inc., *(978-1-885477; 978-1-932565; 978-1-935274; 978-1-935567; 978-0-9860673; 978-1-941765; 978-1-949177; 978-1-957984)* 721 W. Abram St., Arlington, TX 76013 USA Tel 817-277-0727; Fax: 817-277-2270; Toll Free: 800-489-0727
E-mail: kelly@fhautism.com
Web site: http://www.FHautism.com
Dist(s): **BookBaby**
Follett School Solutions
Ingram Publisher Services
MyiLibrary.

Fuze Publishing, LLC, *(978-0-9841412; 978-0-9849908; 978-0-9897306; 978-0-9965553; 978-0-9974956; 978-0-9998089)* 2305-C Ashland Street, No. 312, Ashland, OR 97520 USA.

FuzionPrint, *(978-0-9844611; 978-0-9909039; 978-0-9974938; 978-1-946195; 978-1-955541; 978-0-578-35085-1; 978-0-578-35087-5)* Orders Addr.: 1250 E 115th St, Burnsville, MN 55337 USA Tel 612-781-2815; Fax: 612-294-3068; Edit Addr.: c/o Brian C. Aubitz, 9948 Portland Ave. S., Bloomington, MN 55420 USA
E-mail: info@fuzionprint.com
Web site: http://www.fuzionprint.com.

FWB Pubns., *(978-0-9829070; 978-0-9847974; 978-0-9887437; 978-0-615-85868-5; 978-1-940609; 978-0-615-87554-5; 978-0-615-87589-7; 978-0-615-89973-2; 978-0-615-91387-2; 978-0-615-94095-3; 978-0-692-21431-2; 978-0-692-30634-5; 978-0-692-30835-6; 978-0-692-34282-4) 1006 Rayme Dr., COLUMBUS, OH 43207-8738 USA Tel 573-330-7728*
E-mail: alton.loveless@prodigy.net
Dist(s): **CreateSpace Independent Publishing Platform.**

FWOMP Publishing, *(978-0-9760096)* 935 Lighthouse Ave. No. 21, Pacific Grove, CA 93950 USA
Web site: http://www.fwomp.com
Dist(s): **Sunbelt Pubns., Inc.**

FX Digital Photo, *(978-0-9769009)* 9 Maison Way, Toms River, NJ 08757-6413 USA
Web site: http://www.fxdigitalphoto.com.

Fyhrie, Stephanie, *(978-0-9989821; 978-0-9989821-0-6)* 13316 E 7th Ave, Spokane Valley, WA 99216 USA Tel 509-499-1445
E-mail: tc@taylorchristianmarketing.com.

FyreSyde Publishing, *(978-0-692-11286-1)* 620 Bluebonnet Ln., Pilot Point, TX 76258 USA Tel 817-773-0635
E-mail: bramsayauthor@gmail.com
Dist(s): **Ingram Content Group.**

G & K Publishing, *(978-0-615-15770-2)* P.O. Box 445, Johnstown, OH 43031 USA
E-mail: eking@byroncarmichael.com
Web site: http://www.byroncarmichael.com; http://GandKPublishing.com.

G & R Publishing, *(978-1-56383)* 509 Industrial St., Waverly, IA 50677 USA Toll Free Fax: 800-866-7496; Toll Free: 800-887-4445
E-mail: gifts@cqbookstore.com
Web site: http://www.cqbookstore.com
Dist(s): **CQ Products.**

G Arts LLC, *(978-0-9721152; 978-0-9765851; 978-0-9777531; 978-0-9793384; 978-0-9801557; 978-0-9822669; 978-0-9823412; 978-0-9823799; 978-0-9832702; 978-0-9851696; 978-0-9881745; 978-0-9891704; 978-0-9913419; 978-0-9903808; 978-0-9905320; 978-0-9862500; 978-0-9962930; 978-1-943876; 978-0-692-84666-7; 978-0-9987474; 978-0-9992430) 322 W. 57th St. No. 19T, New York, NY 10019 USA Tel 212-362-9119; Fax: 646-607-4433; a/o Barcodes/ISBNs, 54 W. 40 St., New York, NY 10018*
E-mail: accounting@glitteratiincorporated.com; ccounting@glitteratieditions.com
Web site: http://www.glitteratiincorporated.com
Dist(s): **National Bk. Network**
Two Rivers Distribution.

G. B. Enterprises *See* **Kent Communications, Ltd.**

G C B Publishing *See* **Holly Hall Pubns., Inc.**

G E Bacques, *(978-0-578-74060-7)* 5250 denny ave No. 202, north hollywood, CA 91601 USA Tel 985-317-9124
E-mail: gbacques@gmail.com
Web site: gebacques.com.

G F W C of South Dakota/Daughters of Dakota *See* **Sky Carrier Pr.**

G. G. Brown, *(978-0-692-78431-0)* P.O. Box 221161, Hollywood, FL 33004 USA Tel 954-638-2858
E-mail: ggbrown@yahoo.com.

G I A Pubns., Inc., *(978-0-941050; 978-1-57999; 978-1-62277)* 7404 S. Mason Ave., Chicago, IL 60638 USA (SAN 205-3217) Tel 708-496-3800; Fax: 708-496-3828; Toll Free: 800-442-1358
E-mail: custserv@giamusic.com
Web site: http://www.giamusic.com
Dist(s): **Faith Alive Christian Resources**
Independent Pubs. Group
MyiLibrary.

G J & B Publishing, *(978-0-9635006)* 22442 University Ave., N., Cedar, MN 55011 USA Tel 612-434-0786.

G. Lamar Wilkie, *(978-0-9971141; 978-1-959245)* 784 Toliver Lake Rd., Manchester, TN 37355 USA Tel 931-952-3736
E-mail: wilkie_family@hotmail.com.

G Pa Rhymes, *(978-1-7348031)* 4 Pierre Vernier Dr, Mashpee, MA 02649 USA Tel 617-640-4438
E-mail: gwakstein@gmail.com.

G Publishing *See* **G Publishing LLC**

G Publishing LLC, *(978-0-9727582; 978-0-9773267; 978-0-9776780; 978-0-9788536; 978-0-9790691; 978-0-9796978; 978-0-9801297; 978-0-9814650; 978-0-9820002; 978-0-9823533; 978-0-9843426; 978-0-9834307; 978-0-9849360; 978-0-9883374; 978-0-9862379; 978-0-9971579; 978-0-9985990; 978-0-9998578; 978-1-7340865; 978-1-7355579; 978-1-7357302; 978-1-7366387; 979-8-9858131; 979-8-9865807; 979-8-9876534) P.O. Box 7169 Highway 72 W Suite A P. O. Box 114, Madison, AL 35758 USA Tel 313-575-0096 Do not confuse with G Publishing in Sebastopol, CA*
E-mail: jhun@gpublishingsuccess.com; juliahunter2020@att.net
Web site: http://www.gpublishingsuccess.com.

G R M Assocs., *(978-0-933813; 978-0-929093)* 290 W. End Ave., 16A, New York, NY 11111 USA Tel 212-874-5964; Fax: 212-874-6425; *Imprints*: Taylor Productions (Taylor Prods)
Dist(s): **Independent Pubs. Group.**

G R Publishing, *(978-0-9668530)* 460 Brookside Way, Felton, CA 95018 USA
E-mail: pub@grandmarose.com
Web site: http://www.grandmarose.com.

G R T Pubns., *(978-0-9678420; 978-0-9716906)* P.O. Box 1845, Provo, UT 84603 USA Tel 801-374-2587 (phone/fax)
E-mail: grtpublications@juno.com
Web site: http://www.rogerpminert.

G Schirmer, Inc. *Imprint of* **Leonard, Hal Corp.**

G. Scott Huggins, *(978-1-7355244)* 4210 Danbury Ln, Mt Pleasant, WI 53403 USA Tel 262-800-3317
E-mail: g.scott.huggins@gmail.com
Web site: gscotthuggins.com.

G T Labs, *(978-0-9660106; 978-0-9788037)* P.O. Box 8145, Ann Arbor, MI 48107 USA Tel 734-994-0474; Fax: 734-764-4487
E-mail: info@gt-labs.com
Web site: http://www.gt-labs.com
Dist(s): **Diamond Comic Distributors, Inc.**
Diamond Bk. Distributors.

G340 Publishing, *(978-0-9843837)* 7115 N. Division St. Suite B #132, Spokane, WA 99207-2242 USA (SAN 859-2462) Tel 509-850-0340
E-mail: service @g340.com; grealy@gmail.com
Web site: http://g340.com.

G7s Design and Business Solutions *See* **Olsen, Erik**

Gabriel Pr., *(978-0-9721888)* 255 Calle San Sebastian, San Juan, PR 00901 USA Do not confuse with companies with the same name in Phoenix, AZ, Ventura, CA, Fort Lauderdale, FL, Saratoga, CA, Sacramento, CA, San Juan, PR, Littleton, CO
E-mail: paolanogueras@gmail.com
Web site: http://www.paolanogueras.net
Dist(s): **Lectorum Pubns., Inc.**

Gabriel Resources, Orders Addr.: P.O. Box 1047, Waynesboro, GA 30830 USA Tel 706-554-1594; Fax: 706-554-7444; Toll Free: 800-732-6657 (8MORE-BOOKS); Edit Addr.: 129 Mobilization Dr., Waynesboro, GA 30830 USA.

Gabriele Capelli Editore Sagl (CHE) *(978-88-87469) Dist. by* **SPD-Small Pr Dist.**

Gabrielle, Ava, *(978-0-578-42242-8)* P.O. Box 177, Exmore, VA 23350 USA Tel 757-442-4195
E-mail: avagabrielle@esprittv.com.

Gaff Pr., *(978-0-9619629)* Orders Addr.: P.O. Box 1024, Astoria, OR 97103 USA (SAN 245-8403); Edit Addr.: P.O. Box 1024, Astoria, OR 97103-1024 USA (SAN 245-8411)
E-mail: gaffpres@pacifier.com
Web site: http://www.gaffpress.com.

Gaffney, Linda, *(978-0-9787501)* Orders Addr.: PMB 2682 2103 Harrison Ave., NW, Olympia, WA 98502 USA Tel 360-584-8566
Web site: http://www.HomeplacePress.com.

Gagnier Enterprises, *(978-0-9993302; 978-0-9995944)* 1514 Canterbury Ln., Fernandina Beach, FL 32034 USA Tel 904-261-3601
E-mail: frankandsue@gagnierenterprises.com.

Gago, Noel, *(978-0-692-44889-2; 978-0-692-72531-3; 978-0-692-72538-2; 978-0-692-09490-7; 978-0-578-45548-8)* 14261 nw 22nd st, PEMBROKE PINES, FL 33028 USA Tel 7182165431.

Gail's Guides, *(978-1-881005)* Orders Addr.: 134 West Canyonview Dr., Longview, WA 98632 USA
E-mail: guides@oz.net; info@gailsguides.com
Web site: http://www.gailsguides.com
Dist(s): **Anderson News - Tacoma**
Aramark
American News Company
Partners/West Book Distributors.

Gain Literacy Skills / Lynette Gain Williams, *(978-0-9779063)* 10659 Rookwood Dr., San Diego, CA 92131-1619 USA (SAN 850-5608)
E-mail: gainliteracy@sbcglobal.net.

Gaines, Alan, *(978-0-692-06251-7)* 8214 S. 3rd Ave., Inglewood, CA 90305 USA Tel 219-406-8028
E-mail: gainesalan22@gmail.com
Dist(s): **Ingram Content Group.**

Gakken Plus Co., Ltd. (JPN) *(978-4-05) Dist. by* **S and S Inc.**

alactic Bookforge, *(978-0-9990324)* 11752 leibacher ave, Norwalk, CA 90650 USA Tel 562-760-4392
E-mail: Aceeducator123@gmail.com.

alactic Bks., *(978-0-9769400)* 9827 Endora Ct., Owings Mills, MD 21117 USA
Web site: http://www.galacticbooks.usafreespace.com.

alactic Pr., *(978-1-7329452)* 1154 E.223rd St. 2nd Fl., Bronx, NY 10466 USA Tel 646-341-3880
E-mail: bfaust646@aol.com.

alahad Publishing, *(978-0-918483)* 6035 Vantage Ave., Suite 100, North Hollywood, CA 91606-4637 USA (SAN 657-680X) Tel 818-761-5198; Fax: 818-766-8645; Toll Free: 888-349-4878
Web site: http://www.GalahadPublishing.com.

alaxia Publishing Group, LLC, *(978-0-9741657)* P.O. Box 61054, Phoenix, AZ 85082-1054 USA Tel 480-279-0836; Fax: 480-279-0863
E-mail: info@galaxiapg.com; LatonyaJordanSmith@yahoo.com
Web site: http://www.galaxiapg.com.

Galaxias Productions, *(978-0-9835631; 978-0-9850529)* 200 W. 90th St. No. 9B, New York, NY 10024 USA Tel 212-712-1540
E-mail: alwooten411@yahoo.com
Web site: www.arthurwooten.com
Dist(s): **Smashwords.**

Galaxy Bks., *(978-0-9671358; 978-0-9935428-2-4)* 244 Madison Ave., PMB 231, New York, NY 10016-2817 USA Fax: 212-428-6747; Toll Free: 877-425-2992
E-mail: Galaxybooks@yahoo.com.

Galaxy Pr., LLC, *(978-1-59212; 978-1-61986)* Orders Addr.: 7051 Hollywood Blvd., Suite 200, Hollywood, CA 90028 USA (SAN 254-6906) Tel 323-466-7815; Fax: 323-466-7817; Edit Addr.: 6121 Malburg Way, vernon, CA 90058 USA
E-mail: jwills@galaxypress.com; kcatalano@galaxypress.com; jgoodwin@galaxypress.com; sarahc@galaxypress.com
Web site: http://www.galaxypress.com/; http://www.battlefieldearth.com; http://www.writersofthefuture.com; http://www.goldenagestories.com
Dist(s): **Follett School Solutions**
Gumdrop Bks.

Galbraith, Sondra R. , *(978-0-578-17085-5)* 10291 Loridan Lane, Sandy, UT 84092 USA.

Gale ECCO, Print Editions *Imprint of* **Creative Media Partners, LLC**

Gale, Study Guides *Imprint of* **Creative Media Partners, LLC**

Galen Pr., Ltd., *(978-1-883620)* Orders Addr.: P.O. Box 64400, Tucson, AZ 85728-4400 USA (SAN 254-1823) Tel 520-577-8363; Fax: 520-529-6459; Toll Free: 800-442-5369 (orders only) Do not confuse with Galen Pr. in Madison, NJ
E-mail: ml@galenpress.com; sales@galenpress.com
Web site: http://www.galenpress.com
Dist(s): **Majors, J. A. Co.**
Matthews Medical Bk. Co.
Rittenhouse Bk. Distributors.

Gali Girls, Inc., *(978-0-9773673)* 48 Cranford Pl., Teaneck, NJ 07666 USA Tel 201-862-1989
Web site: http://www.galigirls.com.

Galileo Pr., *(978-0-913123; 978-0-9817519)* 3222 Rocking Horse, Aiken, SC 29801 USA (SAN 240-6543) Do not confuse with companies with the same or similar name in Edmonds, WA, Brooklyn, NY
E-mail: jawendell@aol.com
Dist(s): **Pathway Bk. Service**
SPD-Small Pr. Distribution.

Galison, *(978-0-7353; 978-0-929648; 978-0-939456; 978-1-56155)* Div. of The McEvoy Group, 28 W. 44th St., Suite 1411-12, New York, NY 10036 USA Tel 212-354-8840; Fax: 212-944-8682; Toll Free: 800-322-6663; *Imprints:* Mudpuppy (Mudpuppy)
E-mail: sales@galison.com
Web site: http://www.galison.com
Dist(s): **Hachette Bk. Group**
McEvoy Group, The.

Gall, Frank, *(978-0-692-18621-3)* 9622 Poynes Dr, Houston, TX 77065 USA Tel 832-567-4892
E-mail: frankcgall@gmail.com.

Gallagher, Carole M., *(978-0-9702197)* 431 S. Main St., Williamstown, NJ 08094 USA Tel 856-875-1575; Fax: 856-875-1998.

Gallagher, Jessica, *(978-1-7367101)* 5453 Burnet Rd Apt 605 0, AUSTIN, TX 78756 USA Tel 919-931-7200
E-mail: jessicaigallagher@yahoo.com
Dist(s): **Ingram Content Group.**

Gallant Gold Media *See* **Gallant Gold Media LLC**

Gallant Gold Media LLC, *(978-0-9653035; 978-1-890570; 978-1-58584)* P.O. Box 10404, Burke, VA 22009 USA Tel 310-926-4100 (phone/fax) Do not confuse with Huckleberry Pr., Gig Harbor, WA
E-mail: gallantgoldmedia@gmail.com; noreenwise@gallantgoldmedia.com
Web site: https://www.gallantgold.com.

Gallant Hse. Publishing, *(978-0-9660373)* 1329 Hwy. 395n, Ste 10 Pmb 114, Gardnerville, NV 89410 USA Toll Free: 877-577-2244
E-mail: gallanthouse@hotmail.com.

Gallant Pr., *(978-0-9990879; 978-1-952553)* 18228 Hastings Way, Porter, CA 91326 USA Tel 323-363-2743
E-mail: production@gallantpress.com
Web site: www.gallantpress.com.

†Gallaudet Univ. Pr., *(978-0-913580; 978-0-930323; 978-1-56368; 978-1-944838; 978-1-954622)* 800 Florida Ave., NE, Washington, DC 20002-3695 USA (SAN 205-261X) Tel 202-651-5488; Fax: 202-651-5489; Toll Free Fax: 800-621-8476; Toll Free: 888-630-9347 (TTY)
E-mail: valencia.simmons@gallaudet.edu
Web site: http://gupress.gallaudet.edu
Dist(s): **Chicago Distribution Ctr.**
Ebsco Publishing
Follett School Solutions
JSTOR; *CIP.*

Gallery Bks. *Imprint of* **Gallery Bks.**

Gallery Bks., 1230 Ave. of the Americas, New York, NY 10020 USA; *Imprints:* Gallery Books (Gallery Imp)
Dist(s): **Children's Plus, Inc.**
Simon & Schuster, Inc.

Galletti, Barbara, *(978-0-9748737)* 2509 Lawnside Rd., Timonium, MD 21093-2605 USA Tel 410-252-6568
E-mail: gallettinotes@hotmail.com.

Gallimard, Editions (FRA) *(978-2-07) Dist. by* **Distribks Inc.**

Gallopade International, *(978-0-635; 978-0-7933; 978-0-935326; 978-1-55609)* Orders Addr.: 6000 Shakerag Hl. # 314, Peachtree Cty, GA 30269-6523 USA (SAN 213-8441) Toll Free Fax: 800-871-2979; Toll Free: 800-536-2438; *Imprints:* Marsh, Carole Family CD-Rom (C Marsh); Marsh, Carole Books (C Mrsh Bks); Marsh, Carole Mysteries (CarolMarshMyst)
E-mail: michael@gallopade.com
Web site: http://www.gallopade.com
Dist(s): **Children's Plus, Inc.**
Follett School Solutions.

Gallopade: Publishing Group *See* **Gallopade International**

Gallup, Ben, *(978-1-7339661)* 1025 NE 72nd St, Seattle, WA 98115 USA Tel 440-339-0219
E-mail: benjaminjgallup@gmail.com
Web site: beboldebewyse.com.

Gallup Pr., *(978-1-59562)* 1251 Avenue of the Americas, 23rd Fl., New York, NY 10020 USA Tel 212-899-4709; Fax: 212-899-4899; Toll Free: 877-242-5587
Web site: http://www.gallup.com
Dist(s): **MyiLibrary**
Simon & Schuster
Simon & Schuster, Inc.

GALT, DANIEL Bks., LLC, *(978-0-9992257)* 650 Univ. Cir., Athens, GA 30605 USA Tel 706-351-3180; Fax: 706-351-3180
E-mail: danielgaltbooks@gmail.com
Web site: https://danielgaltbooks.wordpress.com/.

Galway Pr., *(978-0-9963482)* 51999 hwy 19, stratford, OK 74872 USA Tel 580-759-9698
E-mail: kissb4ugo@gmail.com.

Gambit Pubns., Ltd. (GBR) *(978-1-901983; 978-1-904600; 978-1-906454; 978-1-910093) Dist. by* **TwoRivers.**

Game Changer Ga LLC, *(978-0-692-91915-6; 978-0-692-91979-8; 978-0-692-99638-6)* 3708 tamer Ln., LILBURN, GA 30047 USA Tel 678-789-7485
E-mail: renniecurran@me.com
Dist(s): **Ingram Content Group.**

Game Day Press *See* **Timberwood Pr.**

Game Designers' Workshop, *(978-0-943580; 978-1-55878)* 1418 N. Clinton Blvd., Bloomington, IL 61701 USA (SAN 240-656X) Tel 309-531-4076
E-mail: farfuture@gmail.com
Dist(s): **PSI (Publisher Services, Inc.).**

Game Time Bks., *(978-1-7331651)* 24578 Energy Hwy., New Martinsville, WV 26155 USA Tel 304-771-0659
E-mail: briancroasmun@gmail.com
Web site: briancroasmun.com.

Gamemakers of Pittsburgh, *(978-0-9771001; 978-0-578-13668-4; 978-0-578-46356-8)* 14040 NE 8th St., Suite 233, Bellevue, WA 98007 USA (SAN 256-7660).

Games Workshop, Ltd. (GBR) *(978-1-84154; 978-1-869893; 978-1-872372; 978-1-907964; 978-1-78253) Dist. by* **S and S Inc.**

Gametasia, *(978-0-692-32164-5; 978-0-9862942; 978-0-692-97852-8; 978-0-578-44579-3)* 14252 Morning Glory Rd., Tustin, CA 92680 USA Tel 714-838-9408
E-mail: pamela@freedomwithinfoundation.org.

Gam-Jam Publishing Company *See* **Pendleton Publishing, Inc.**

Gamlin, Stephen, *(978-0-9767993)* P.O. Box 5, Goffstown, NH 03045 USA Tel 603-560-3360; Fax: 603-774-8698; Toll Free: 877-560-3360
E-mail: Steve@InspiredBySteve.com
Web site: http://www.InspiredBySteve.com.

Gamoke, John, *(978-0-9771290)* 6645 Humboldt Ave. S., Richfield, MN 55423 USA; *Imprints:* JoZanephine Originals (MYID_Z_JOZANEP).

GanDale Associates Houston *See* **Holocaust Museum Houston**

Ganeshan, Rajeshwari Iyer, *(978-0-692-14768-9)* 2289 Pinnacle Ct., Erie, PA 16506 USA Tel 262-309-8749
E-mail: ragasspace@gmail.com
Dist(s): **Ingram Content Group.**

Gannon, Ryan, *(978-0-9991760)* 2626 King ST., Denver, CO 80211 USA Tel 720-475-6738
E-mail: ryanwritergannon@gmail.com
Dist(s): **CreateSpace Independent Publishing Platform.**

Gant, Linda G. Gifted Creations *See* **Readers Are Leaders**

Gantt Smith Publishing Hse., *(978-0-9847885)* 875 Victor Ave. Apt., 235, Inglewood, CA 90302 USA Tel 310-673-5114
E-mail: migs13@sbcglobal.net.

Gaon Bks., *(978-0-9820657; 978-0-9825439; 978-1-935604)* Div. of Gaon Institute for Tolerance Studies, P.O. Box 23924, Santa Fe, NM 87502-3924 USA Tel 505-920-7771
E-mail: gaonbooks@gmail.com
Web site: http://www.gaonbooks.com.

Gap Tooth Publishing *Imprint of* **Charles River Pr.**

Garamella, Priscilla, *(978-0-692-99433-7)* 19 Squire Ct., Brookfield, CT 06804 USA Tel 203-313-0819
E-mail: pgaramella@gmail.com.

Garbage Factory, The, *(978-0-692-58125-4; 978-0-9975227)* 188 Lyndon Ave., Athens, GA 30601 USA Tel 706-248-8626
E-mail: johnnypence@gmail.com
Web site: garbagefactory.com.

Garcia, Cezanne, *(978-0-9728041)* 30405 Cupeno Ln., Temecula, CA 92592-2540 USA Tel 951-506-6407 (phone\fax)
E-mail: stgarcia@fda.net.

Garcia, Jeffrey, *(978-0-9840942)* 3000 Avenida Ciruela, Carlsbad, CA 92009 USA Tel 760-822-0222.

Garden Fleetfoot Pr., *(978-0-9762544)* Orders Addr.: P.O. Box 1188, Okemos, MI 48805 USA
E-mail: info@gardenfleetfoot.com
Web site: http://gardenfleetfoot.com
Dist(s): **Partners Pubs. Group, Inc.**

Garden Gallery, *(978-0-9996323)* 247 Lawrence Rd. 216, Black Rock, AR 72415 USA Tel 870-878-1801
E-mail: jdsclark55@yahoo.com.

Garden Publishing Co., The, *(978-0-9833377; 978-0-9966453; 978-1-7333459; 978-1-7355464; 979-8-9867620; 979-8-9868163; 979-8-9890762)* 10403 US Hwy. 87N, Sterling City, TX 76951 USA (SAN 860-1984) Tel 325-650-3381; Fax: 325-378-4020
E-mail: uranch02@gmail.com.

Garden, Randa, *(978-0-615-12322-6)* 3503 Portia Pl., Norfolk, NE 68701 USA Tel 402-371-0544
E-mail: jrgarden@cableone.net
Web site: www.pennythepenguin.com.

Gardner, Colin, *(978-0-9720348; 978-0-615-11851-2)* 1677 S. 75 E., Bountiful, UT 84010-5218 USA Tel 801-296-2109 (phone/fax)
E-mail: colingardner@juno.com.

Gardner, Dianne Lynn, *(978-0-692-47613-0; 978-0-692-89976-2; 978-0-692-90949-2; 978-0-692-91279-9; 978-0-692-92044-2; 978-0-692-92048-0; 978-0-692-92874-5; 978-0-692-97612-8; 978-0-692-98797-1; 978-0-692-98798-8; 978-0-692-05912-8; 978-0-692-05913-5; 978-0-692-05979-1; 978-0-692-15188-4; 978-0-578-45959-2; 978-0-578-88934-4) 9385 Olalla Valley Rd. SE, Port Orchard, WA 98367 USA Tel 253-851-0339*
Web site: http://gardnersart.com
Dist(s): **CreateSpace Independent Publishing Platform.**

Gardner Media LLC, *(978-0-9822550; 978-1-935481; 978-1-935719; 978-1-936979; 978-1-939647; 978-1-941609)* 75 S. Orange Ave., No.215, South Orange, NJ 07079 USA Tel 973-761-4555; Fax: 973-761-1555
E-mail: cplay@earthlink.net
Web site: http://www.gardnermediallc.com.

Gardner Pubns., *(978-0-9659163)* 235 E. Main St., No. 119, Hendersonville, TN 37075 USA Tel 615-824-5100; Fax: 615-824-3400; Toll Free: 800-297-8179
E-mail: harveyjgardner@bbsco.com
Web site: http://www.bbsco.com.

Gareth Stevens Hi-Lo Must Reads *Imprint of* **Stevens, Gareth Publishing LLLP**

Gareth Stevens Learning Library *Imprint of* **Stevens, Gareth Publishing LLLP**

Gareth Stevens Secondary Library *Imprint of* **Stevens, Gareth Publishing LLLP**

Garfein, Stanley, *(978-0-9787422)* 1110 Lasswade Dr., Tallahassee, FL 32312-2845 USA Tel 850-385-1538; Fax: 850-531-0276
E-mail: StaGarfein@aol.com.

Garfield, M., *(978-0-615-96149-1; 978-0-9964930)* 609 Mills St., Lafayette, CO 80026 USA Tel 303-604-6540; *Imprints:* Pennaeth Publishing (Pennaeth Pub)
E-mail: m.garfield@comcast.net.

Garing, Bernard, *(978-0-9765809)* 6304 Caleigh Dr., Charlestown, IN 47111-7713 USA.

Garland City Bks. of Watertown, *(978-0-9890509)* P.O. Box 604, Black River, NY 13612 USA Tel 315-783-0728
E-mail: rothensu@yahoo.com.

Garland, Daniel, *(978-0-9768414)* 6247 Cascade Hwy., NE, Silverton, OR 97381 USA
E-mail: danielggarland@msn.com.

Garland E. Stafford III, *(978-0-578-41744-8; 978-1-7373123)* 875 Cashen Dr., Fernandina Beach, FL 32034 USA Tel 904-556-3015
E-mail: treystafford51@gmail.com
Dist(s): **Independent Pub.**

Garlic Pr., *(978-0-931993; 978-1-930820)* Orders Addr.: 899 S. College Mall, Suite 381, Bloomington, IN 47401 USA (SAN 686-1105) Tel 800-789-0554; Toll Free Fax: 800-789-5576 Do not confuse with companies with the same name in Kirkwood, MO, New London, NH, Abingdon MD, Lenox MA, Kansas City, MO
E-mail: garlic.press@att.net
Web site: http://www.garlicpress.com.

Garr, Sherry B., *(978-0-9759866)* 3456 S. Mulberry Dr., Saint George, UT 84790 USA
Web site: http://www.gumfounded.com.

Garrelts, Christopher *See* **Squarey Head, Inc.**

Garrett, Debbie Behan, *(978-0-615-24202-6; 978-0-615-42184-1)* P.O. Box 210571, Dallas, TX 75211-0571 USA Tel 214-337-5928; Fax: 214-337-8127
E-mail: blackdolls@sbcglobal.net
Web site: http://blackdollcollecting.com.

Garrigues Hse. Pubs., *(978-0-9620844; 978-1-931014)* 2746 Stein Ln., Lewisburg, PA 17837 USA (SAN 249-969X) Tel 570-204-2906; 2746 Stein Ln., Lewisburg, PA 17837 (SAN 249-9703)
E-mail: jim@garrigueshouse.com
Web site: http://www.garrigueshouse.com.

Garry & Donna, LLC, *(978-0-9815617)* P.O. Box 30021, Las Vegas, NV 89173 USA.

Garteiz, John, *(978-0-578-40228-4; 978-1-7337634)* 7316 Steilacoom Blvd. SW, Lakewood, WA 98499 USA Tel 253-970-7095
E-mail: jgarteizalaska@gmail.com.

Garwell Publishing LLC, *(978-1-7355502; 978-1-961424)* 610 Meacham Rd. Suite 1003, Elk Grove Village, IL 60007 USA Tel 404-536-3344
E-mail: tfplatinum@gmail.com
Web site: garwellpublishing.com.

Gasior, Julie, *(978-0-615-18824-9; 978-0-615-18884-3)* 6404 Shadow Oaks Ct., Monmouth Jct, NJ 08852-2297 USA
E-mail: juliespotions@gmail.com
Web site: http://juliespotions.com
Dist(s): **Lulu Pr., Inc.**

Gask Castle Pr., *(978-0-9843717)* 1725 Stamont Trail, Knoxville, TN 37909 USA Tel 865-310-8947
E-mail: phillip@gaskcastlepress.com.

Gaslight Pubns., *(978-0-934468)* P.O. Box 1344, Studio City, CA 91614-0344 USA Tel 818-784-8918
Dist(s): **Empire Publishing Service**
Players Pr., Inc.

GASLight Publishing, *(978-0-9754796; 978-1-933869)* P.O. Box 1025, Leander, TX 78646 USA Tel 512-528-1727; Fax: 512-259-8671
E-mail: ken@gaslightpublishing.com; kenschaefer@totalaccess.net
Web site: http://www.gslightpublishing.com
Dist(s): **Smashwords.**

Gatbonton, Beverly Mabanglo, *(978-1-7322791)* 1083 Independence Blvd, Virginia Beach, VA 23455 USA Tel 757-270-0443
E-mail: bevmmg@gmail.com.

Gatekeeper Pr. *Imprint of* **Gatekeeper Pr.**

Gatekeeper Pr. *Imprint of* **Magic Works Publishing & Production**

Gatekeeper Pr., *(978-0-9724102; 978-1-932549; 978-1-936910; 978-1-61984; 978-1-64237; 978-1-6629)* 7853 Gunn Hwy Suite 209, Tampa, FL 33626 USA Toll Free: 888-234-6896; *Imprints:* Gatekeeper Press (GatekeeperPr); BlogIntoBook.com (BlogIntoBook); Quintessential Press (MYID_L_QUINTES); Breezy Way Publishing (Breezy Way P)
Web site: http://www.priceworldpublishing.com; http://www.GatekeeperPress.com
Dist(s): **Cardinal Pubs. Group**
INscribe Digital
Independent Pubs. Group
MyiLibrary.

GateKeepers International, Incorporated, *(978-0-9745483)* 15245 Jessie Dr., Colorado Springs, CO 80921 USA
E-mail: Femritegki@gmail.com
Web site: http://www.gatekeepersintl.org.

GateKeepers Ministries International, *(978-0-9754535; 978-0-578-21738-3)* 3600 Earl Ave., Pennsauken, NJ 08110 USA Tel 856-406-6101 Toll Free: 866-910-2810
E-mail: gatekeepersmintl@aol.com
Web site: http://www.gkmi.org.

Gateway Hse. Publishing, *(978-0-9995258)* 38 N Gateway, Toms River, NJ 08753 USA Tel 732-239-6752
E-mail: info@gatewayhousepublishing.com
Web site: gatewayhousepublishing.com.

Gateway Learning Corporation *See* **HOP, LLC**

Gateways Bks. & Tapes, *(978-0-89556)* Div. of I.D.H.H.B., Inc., P.O. Box 370, Nevada City, CA 95959 USA (SAN 211-3635) Tel 530-477-8101; Fax: 530-272-0184; Toll Free: 800-869-0658
E-mail: orders@gatewaysbooksandtapes.com; info@gatewaysbooksandtapes.com
Web site: http://www.gatewaysbooksandtapes.com
Dist(s): **Independent Pubs. Group**
MyiLibrary
ebrary, Inc.

Gatewood Pr., *(978-0-9710427)* P.O. Box 356, Johnson City, TX 78636 USA Tel 832-723-7313 Do not confuse with Wilson & Associates, Gig Harbor, WA
E-mail: alvincoog@me.com.

Gathering Place Pubs., Inc., *(978-0-9754622; 978-0-615-38236-4; 978-0-9828311)* P.O. Box 341, Kaysville, UT 84037-8403 USA (SAN 256-0658) Fax: 801-451-6008
E-mail: sales@stonesquest.com
Web site: http://www.rebuildshattereddreams.com; http://www.stonesquest.com.

Gatorbytes *Imprint of* **Univ. Pr. of Florida**

†Gaunt, Inc., *(978-0-912004; 978-1-56169; 978-1-60449)* 3011 Gulf Dr., Holmes Beach, FL 34217-2199 USA (SAN 202-9413) Tel 941-778-5211; Fax: 941-778-5252
E-mail: info@gaunt.com; sales@gaunt.com
Web site: http://www.gaunt.com; *CIP.*

Gaunt, William W. & Sons, Incorporated *See* **Gaunt, Inc.**

Gauntlet, Inc., *(978-0-9629659; 978-1-887368; 978-1-934267)* 5307 Arroyo St., Colorado Springs, CO 80922 USA Tel 719-591-5566; Fax: 719-591-6676
E-mail: gauntlet66@aol.com; info@gauntletpress.com
Web site: http://www.gauntletpress.com
Dist(s): **Independent Pubs. Group.**

Gauthier Pubns. Inc., *(978-0-9820812; 978-0-9833593; 978-0-615-71779-1; 978-1-942314)* P.O. Box 806241, Saint Clair Shores, MI 48080 USA (SAN 857-2119) Tel 313-458-7141; Fax: 586-279-1515; *Imprints:* Frog Legs Ink (Frog Legs Ink); Hungry Goat Press (Hungry Goat)
E-mail: info@gauthierpublications.com
Web site: http://www.FrogLegsInk.com; http://www.EATaBOOK.com
Dist(s): **BWI**
Brodart Co.
CreateSpace Independent Publishing Platform
Diamond Bk. Distributors
Follett School Solutions
OverDrive, Inc.

Gavila Publishing, *(978-0-9748466)* 20-23 43 St., Astoria, NY 11105 USA
Web site: http://www.gavila.com.

Gavin, Fred Enterprises, *(978-0-935668)* 96 Byron St., East Boston, MA 02128 USA (SAN 221-1629).

Gaviota Ediciones (ESP) *(978-84-392) Dist. by* **Lectorum Pubns.**

Gavlak, L.J. Publishing, *(978-0-9740357)* Orders Addr.: P.O. Box 72, Kylertown, PA 16847 USA Tel 814-345-6391; Edit Addr.: Rollingston Rd., Kylertown, PA 16847 USA
E-mail: largav@juno.com.

Gazarik, Rebecca, *(978-0-9802258)* 637 Pine Run Rd., Apollo, PA 15613-9313 USA
Web site: http://www.rebeccagazarik.com/.

Gazelle Pr. *Imprint of* **Genesis Communications, Inc.**

Gazing In Publishing, *(978-0-9839318)* P.O. Box 197, Columbia, SC 29147 USA Tel 803-743-8810
E-mail: winmilawe@gmail.com.

Gazoobi Tales, *(978-0-9679364)* P.O. Box 19614, Seattle, WA 98109-6614 USA
E-mail: info@gazoobitales.com
Web site: http://www.gazoobitales.com.

GB Pr., *(978-0-578-02613-8; 978-0-615-35332-6; 978-0-9828241)* P.O. Box 27224, Boise, ID 83716 USA Tel 208-863-9045
E-mail: ken.mcconnell@gmail.com
Web site: http://gb-press.com
Dist(s): **Lulu Pr., Inc.**

GB4K Inc, *(978-0-9989161)* 1885 Silverstone Dr, Lawrenceville, GA 30045 USA Tel 404-987-9096
E-mail: tjay3@gb4kinc.com.

GDG Publishing, *(978-0-9787549; 978-0-9796625; 978-0-9797952; 978-0-9855335)* Orders Addr.: 2063 Continental Dr. NE, Atlanta, GA 30345 USA (SAN 851-5182) Tel 404-248-0012; Fax: 404-248-1487 Do not confuse with GDG Publishing in Oxnard, CA
E-mail: glennondesign@comcast.net
Web site: http://www.gdgpublishing.com.

GDI Enterprises, *(978-0-692-65587-0; 978-0-692-65590-0; 978-0-692-79315-2; 978-0-692-79317-6; 978-0-578-75456-7; 978-0-578-75464-2; 978-0-578-88837-8; 978-0-578-88848-4; 978-0-578-89442-3; 978-0-578-89443-0; 978-0-578-89577-2; 978-0-578-89578-9; 978-1-7377087)* 411 N Akard St 414, Dallas, TX 75201 USA
E-mail: gdiepublishing@gmail.com
Web site: gdipublishing.com.

GDL Multimedia, LLC, *(978-1-60245)* 2513 179th Ave E., Lake Tapps, WA 98391-6453 USA
E-mail: greg@gdlmultimedia.com
Web site: http://www.gdlmultimedia.com
Dist(s): **KSG Distributing.**

GDM Consulting Services LLC, *(978-0-9763738)* 5 Alluvium Lakes Dr., Voorhees, NJ 08043 USA
Web site: http://www.gdmcs.com.

G.E. Books *See* **Vision Bks. LLC**

Gean Penny Bks., *(978-0-9841638; 978-0-615-59994-6; 978-0-615-60073-4; 978-0-615-63110-3; 978-0-615-63275-9; 978-0-615-63868-3; 978-0-615-68175-7; 978-0-615-71997-9; 978-0-9963778; 978-1-952726)* Div. of Createspace, 870 W Somers LN, Axtell, TX 76624 USA Tel 254-715-9419
E-mail: info@geanpenny.com; author@pgshriver.com
Web site: https://www.geanpenny.com; https://www.thestinkerbooks.com; https://www.runtandarnold.com; https://www.thegiftedonestrilogy.com; https://www.pgshriver.com; https://www.zoomein.com
Dist(s): **CreateSpace Independent Publishing Platform**
Ingram Content Group.

Gecko Pr. (NZL) *(978-0-9582598; 978-0-9582787; 978-0-9582720; 978-1-877467; 978-1-877579; 978-1-927271; 978-1-77657) Dist. by* **Lerner Pub.**

Geckostufs, Incorporated *See* **Words & Pictures Publishing, Inc.**

Geekdazzle, *(978-0-692-80608-1)* 9 Ashford Pl., Albertson, NY 11507 USA Tel 516-294-3335
E-mail: dvtuozzo@gmail.com
Web site: geekdazzle.com.

Geers, Amanda, *(978-1-7365154)* 1720 E. Beaver Lake Dr. SouthE., Sammamish, WA 98075 USA Tel 425-213-4413
E-mail: taytaysnevets@gmail.com
Web site: www.amandageers.com.

Geez Pr., *(978-0-9816574)* P.O. Box 711, Elmore, OH 43416-0711 USA
Web site: http://home.woh.rr.com/geezpress.

Gefen Bks., *(978-0-86343)* 11 Edison Pl., Springfield, NJ 07081 USA (SAN 856-8065)
E-mail: gefenny@gefenpublishing.com
Web site: http://www.gefenpublishing.com.

Gefen Publishing Hse., Ltd (ISR) *(978-965-229; 978-965-7023) Dist. by* **Strauss Cnslts.**

Gefen Publishing Hse., Ltd (ISR) *(978-965-229; 978-965-7023) Dist. by* **Gefen Bks.**

Geist, Sabrina, *(978-0-692-69506-7; 978-0-692-93941-3)* 5628 Cofeen, Sheridan, WY 82801 USA Tel 307-259-6419
E-mail: glannie@msn.com.

Gelos Pubns., *(978-0-9964157; 978-0-9972657; 978-1-7345226)* 332 S. Michigan Ave., Chicago, IL 60604 USA Tel 631-979-5990
E-mail: iansadler64@gmail.com
Dist(s): **Independent Pubs. Group**
Midpoint Trade Bks., Inc.

GEM Bk. Club, *(978-0-9722795; 978-0-9755092; 978-1-59825)* Div. of Highest Good Pubns., Orders Addr.: P.O. Box 43476, Chicago, IL 60643 USA (SAN 255-3953) Tel 773-445-4946; Fax: 773-233-5178; Toll Free: 877-447-1266; *Imprints:* Highest Good Publications (Highest Good Pubns)
E-mail: cherylwash@icloud.com; info@ebonyenergypublishing.com; cherylwash@yahoo.com
Web site: http://www.cherylwash.com; www.globalexecutivemedia.com; www.gembookclub.com; http://www.ebonyenergy.com; http://gemliteraryfoundation.org; http://ebonyenergybooks.com; http://ebonyenergykids.com; http://www.ebonyenergypublishing.com; http://highestgoodpublications.com; http://pocketbooksforyoursoul.com
Dist(s): **Biblio Distribution**
ebrary, Inc.

Gem Bk. Pubs., *(978-0-9633723; 978-1-887651)* Div. of Fred Ward Productions, Inc., Orders Addr.: 2575 Barrymore Dr., Malibu, CA 90265-2955 USA Tel 310-456-9949; Fax: 310-456-9799
E-mail: fred@fredwardgems.com; charlotte@fredwardgems.com
Web site: http://www.fredwardgems.com/.

Gem Printing, *(978-0-9743429)* Orders Addr.: 600 Reisterstown Rd., Suite 200G, Baltimore, MD 21208 USA Tel 410-764-1617; Fax: 410-764-7471; *Imprints:* American Poets Society (Amer Poets)
E-mail: poetryamericaorders@yahoo.com
Web site: http://www.poetryamerica.com.

Gem Pubns., *(978-0-9742354)* 3520 McNally Ave., Altadena, CA 91001 USA
E-mail: gregmiddleton@earthlink.net
Web site: http://www.gempublications.com.

Gemini Bk. Pubns., *(978-0-615-99427-7; 978-0-9978433)* 12458 Mount Bora Dr., Boynton Beach, FL 33473 USA Tel 561-810-5843
E-mail: writerron65@gmail.com
Dist(s): **CreateSpace Independent Publishing Platform.**

GEMS *Imprint of* **Univ. of California, Berkeley, Lawrence Hall of Science**

Gems International Incorporated *See* **Gems International, LLC**

Gems International, LLC, *(978-0-9728626)* 119 Fern St., Darby, PA 19023 USA
E-mail: polishmeprofessional@gmail.com
Web site: www.rayfieldsrules.com.

Gemstone Literary, *(978-0-9801692)* 27943 Seco Canyon Rd., No. 212, Los Angeles, CA 91350 USA
Web site: http://www.GemTal.com.

Gemstone Publishing, Inc., *(978-0-911903; 978-1-888472; 978-1-60360)* Div. of Diamond Comic Distributors, Inc., 1966 Greenspring Dr., Suite 405, Timonium, MD 21093 USA Tel 410-427-9432; Fax: 410-252-4582 Do not confuse with companies with same or similar names in Thornville, OH, Lebanon, OR, Lauderdale Lakes, FL, Sugarland, TX
Web site: http://www.gemstonepub.com
Dist(s): **Diamond Comic Distributors, Inc.**
Diamond Bk. Distributors
SPD-Small Pr. Distribution.

Gen Manga Entertainment, Inc., *(978-0-9836134; 978-0-9850644; 978-1-939012)* 250 Pk. Ave., Suite 7002, New York, NY 10177 USA Tel 646-535-0090
E-mail: editor@genmanga.com
Web site: www.genmanga.com
Dist(s): **Diamond Comic Distributors, Inc.**
Diamond Bk. Distributors.

GenBeam LLC, *(978-1-7325080; 978-1-950491)* 912 Candlewood Dr., El Dorado Hills, CA 95762 USA Tel 916-296-3202; *Imprints:* Tinker Toddlers (MYID_A_TINKER)
E-mail: kaur.handeep@gmail.com.

Gene Caven, *(978-0-578-09100-6; 978-0-9987416)* 61 Hidden Hill Rd, Tryon, NC 28782 USA Tel 828-817-9160.

Gene Keys Publishing, *(978-0-578-03855-1)* P.O. Box 216, Aptos, CA 95001 USA.

Genealogical Publishing Company, Incorporated *See* **Genealogical.com**

†Genealogical.com, *(978-0-8063)* 3600 Clipper Mill Rd. Suite 260, Baltimore, MD 21211-1953 USA (SAN 206-8370) Toll Free: 800-296-6687 (orders & customer service); 3600 Clipper Mill Rd. Suite 260, Baltimore, MD 21211 (SAN 920-8755) Tel 410-837-8271; Fax: 410-752-8492
E-mail: hoffman@genealogical.com
Web site: http://www.Genealogical.com; *CIP.*

General Board of Global Ministries, The United Methodist Church, *(978-1-890569; 978-1-933663)* 475 Riverside Dr. Rm. 1473, New York, NY 10115 USA Tel 212-870-3731; Fax: 212-870-3654; *Imprints:* WD/GBGM Books (WD GBGM)
E-mail: cscott@gbgm-umc.org; KDonato@gbgm-umc.org
Web site: http://www.gbgm-umc.org
Dist(s): **Cokesbury**
Mission Resource Ctr.

General Bks. LLC, *(978-1-234; 978-1-77045; 978-1-150; 978-1-151; 978-1-152; 978-1-153; 978-1-154; 978-1-155; 978-1-156; 978-1-157; 978-1-158; 978-1-159; 978-1-230; 978-1-231; 978-1-232; 978-1-233; 978-1-235; 978-1-236; 978-1-238; 978-1-239; 978-1-130)* Orders Addr.: Box 29000, NAS485, Miami, FL 33102 USA
E-mail: support@general-books.net
Web site: www.general-books.net

Generations of Virtue, *(978-0-9766143; 978-0-9848960)* P.O. Box 62253, Colorado Springs, CO 80920 USA
E-mail: genofvirtue@aol.com
Web site: http://www.generationsofvirtue.org.

Generosity Philosophy, *(978-0-9961703)* 9848 Bobcat St., Aumsville, OR 97325 USA Tel 503-507-7069
E-mail: kim.trumbo@gmail.com.

Genesis Bk. Writing, *(978-1-7379528; 979-8-9859765; 978-1-958207)* M01, Al Zarooni Building, Rigga Street, Deira, Dubai, Westchester, IL 60154 USA Tel 888-638-7617
E-mail: info@genesisbookwriting.com
Web site: https://www.genesisbookwriting.com/.

Genesis Communications, Inc., *(978-0-9637311; 978-1-58169)* P.O. Box 191540, Mobile, AL 36619 USA Tel 251-861-2525; Fax: 251-287-2222; Toll Free: 800-367-8203; *Imprints:* Evergreen Press (Evergrn Pr AL); Gazelle Press (Gazelle Pr); Axiom Press (Axiom Press)
E-mail: Jeff@evergreen777.com
Web site: http://www.evergreenpress.com
Dist(s): **BookBaby**
Spring Arbor Distributors, Inc.

Genesis Iconic, *(978-1-7328022)* P.O. Box 10130, College Station, TX 77842 USA Tel 979-219-3061
E-mail: pjf1010@gmail.com.

Genet Pr. LLC, *(978-0-9846663; 978-1-955310)* 9907 Cranapple Ct., Springdale, MD 20774 USA Tel 301-636-6353
E-mail: mayimona_ngwala@hotmail.com
Web site: www.genetpress.com.

Genius In A Bottle Technology Corp, *(978-0-9768429)* Orders Addr.: 910 NW 42nd St., Miami, FL 33127-2755 USA
E-mail: geniusinfo@geniusinabottle.net
Web site: http://www.geniusinabottle.net; http://www.cafepress.com/forevergirl; http://www.cafepress.com/geniusbooks; http://www.cafepress.com/gumo; http://www.cafepress.com/gkid; http://www.cafepress.com/cleversunburst; http://www.cafepress.com/tou; http://www.cafepress.com/foreverman; http://www.cafepress.com/forever4; http://www.cafepress.com/whateverr; http://www.cafepress.com/robospace; http://www.cafepress.com/battlegirlgear; http://www.cafepress.com/geniusinabottle; http://www.ca

Gennesaret Pr., *(978-0-9845541; 978-0-9997343)* 202 Persimmon Pl., Apex, NC 27523 USA (SAN 859-7278) Tel 919-633-0929
E-mail: joel@joelschnoor.com
Web site: http://www.auntruthgrammar.com.

Gentle Giraffe Pr., *(978-0-9747921; 978-0-9777394; 978-0-9801746)* 7405 Barra Dr., Bethesda, MD 20817 USA Tel 202-423-4205; Fax: 334-460-0724; Toll Free: 888-424-4723
E-mail: info@gentlegiraffe.com
Web site: http://www.gentlegiraffe.com.

Gentle Thoughts for Hard Spots, *(978-0-9988274)* 401 RIVER ROCK Rd., CHALLIS, ID 83226 USA Tel 298-833-4681
E-mail: karenw@custertel.net.

Gently Spoken Communications, *(978-0-9711794; 978-0-9746491; 978-0-9776096; 978-0-615-11369-2; 978-0-615-11845-1; 978-0-692-55642-9)* P.O. Box 365, St. Francis, MN 55070 USA Tel 763-506-9933; Fax: 763-506-9934; Toll Free: 877-224-7886
E-mail: info@gentlyspoken.com
Web site: http://www.gentlyspoken.com.

Genuine Prints, LLC, *(978-0-615-23040-5)* P.O. Box 328, Carpentersville, IL 60110 USA Fax: 847-844-9073; Toll Free: 888-853-0001
E-mail: info@nicoandlola.com
Web site: http://www.nicoandlola.com.

Genuine Six Publishing, *(978-0-9981086)* P.O. Box 843, Morrow, GA 30260 USA Tel 404-835-7422
E-mail: angela@angelaodom.com
Web site: angelaodom.com.

Geographic Tongue, LLC, *(978-0-9841685)* P.O. Box 31461, Tucson, AZ 85751-1461 USA
Web site: http://www.GeographicTongueEditions.com.

Geography Matters, Inc., *(978-0-9702403; 978-1-931397; 978-1-62863)* P.O. Box 92, Nancy, KY 42544 USA Tel 606-636-4678; Fax: 606-636-4697; Toll Free: 800-426-4650
E-mail: geomatters@geomatters.com
Web site: http://www.geomatters.com.

George, H. Publishing, *(978-0-9728183)* Orders Addr.: 14513 Bayes Ave., Lakewood, OH 44107 USA Tel 216-319-4575
E-mail: ninthohio@sbcglobal.net.

George, Richardson , *(978-0-578-18582-8; 978-0-578-19335-9; 978-0-578-20500-7; 978-0-578-20892-3; 978-0-578-21273-9; 978-0-578-24134-0; 978-0-578-24416-7)* 4411 NW 74th Avenue, Miami, FL 33166 USA; 1670 NW 94th Ave. Jet Box, JT - 1379214, Doral, FL 33172
Web site: http://georgesplacett.com/_.

George, Tricia Artist, *(978-1-7338865)* 5 Caballo Sendero, Placitas, NM 87043 USA Tel 415-577-5595
E-mail: tricia.george11@gmail.com
Web site: www.fineartforkidz.com.

Geoscience Information Services, *(978-0-9777100)* Orders Addr.: P.O. Box 911, West Falmouth, MA 02574-0911 USA Tel 508-540-6490
E-mail: geoinfo@comcast.net.

Gequalsa, *(978-0-9792518)* 2710 Walnut St., Orlando, FL 32806 USA.

Gerardian Inkspot & Paint Society, *(978-0-9786675)* St. Gerard's Church, 240 W. Robb Ave., Lima, OH 45801 USA.

Gerber, Brandy Fine Art, *(978-1-7325942)* 8494 Ida Ctr. Rd, Ida, MI 48140 USA Tel 734-755-4039
E-mail: brandygerber@hotmail.com
Web site: www.brandygerber.com.

Gerber, Judie *See* **Seachild**

Gere Publishing, *(978-0-9743995; 978-0-9981987)* 113 Leonard Rd., Shutesbury, MA 01072-9783 USA (SAN 257-4594) Tel 413-259-1741
E-mail: claudia@claudiagereco.com
Web site: http://www.gerepublishing.com.

Gerhardt, Paul L., *(978-0-615-13556-4; 978-0-615-16208-9; 978-0-615-16270-6; 978-0-615-23707-7; 978-0-615-23721-3)* P.O. Box 111141, Tacoma, WA 98411 USA
Web site: http://www.paulgerhardt.com
Dist(s): **Lulu Pr., Inc.**

Geringer, Laura Book *Imprint of* **HarperCollins Pubs.**

Gernand, Linda, *(978-0-9755025)* 523 Oyster Creek Dr., Richwood, TX 77531 USA.

Geronimo Media, Incorporated *See* **Night Raven Publishing**

Gerson Group, The, *(978-0-578-58402-7; 978-0-578-95576-6)* 127 Tullamore Trail, Tyrone, GA 30290 USA Tel 770-827-7977
E-mail: gersongroup45@gmail.com.

Gersten, Dan & Associates LLC *See* **Dogwalk Pr.**

Gerstenblatt, Judith Furedi *See* **Lucky & Me Productions, Inc.**

Gerstorff, Katherine, *(978-0-692-16431-0)* 700 Race St., Jonesboro, IN 46938 USA Tel 765-603-8457
E-mail: gerstorff@gmail.com
Dist(s): **Ingram Content Group.**

gertrude m Bks. *Imprint of* **Circling Rivers**

Gestalt Pubns., *(978-0-9764065)* 3828 Clinton Ave. S., Minneapolis, MN 55409-1314 USA Tel 612-822-4419.

Gestalt Publishing Pty, Ltd. (AUS) *(978-0-9775628; 978-0-9807823; 978-1-922023; 978-1-922335) Dist. by* **C D.**

Get Happy Tips, LLC, *(978-0-9860272)* 515 SW 18th Ave. No. 19, Fort Lauderdale, FL 33312 USA Tel 786-314-8199
E-mail: gethappytips@gmail.com
Web site: http://www.gethappytips.com.

Get Healthy With Dr Cooper / Cooper Internal Medicine, *(978-0-9973379; 978-1-7373042)* 801 E Nolana Ave., Ste 12, McAllen, TX 78504 USA Tel 956-686-8802; Fax: 956-696-8802
E-mail: dondoc91@aol.com
Web site: gethealthywithdrcooper.tv.

Get It Factory, The, *(978-0-578-44095-8; 978-0-578-44596-0; 978-1-7337019; 978-1-7333079; 978-1-953011)* 1021 25th Ave SW, Great Falls, MT 59404 USA Tel 406-217-8644
E-mail: ryanacra@sugarbeetfalls.com
Web site: www.thegetitfactory.com.

Get Kids Golfing, *(978-0-692-92660-4)* 3669 Fanwood Ave, LONG BEACH, CA 90808 USA Tel 562-552-4681
E-mail: info@getkidsgolfing.com
Dist(s): **Ingram Content Group.**

Get Life Right Foundation, The *See* **Life Force Bks.**

Get Published, *(978-1-4501; 978-1-4525)* 1663 Liberty Dr., Bloomington, IN 47403 USA Tel 812-650-0913; Fax: 812-339-6554; Toll Free: 877-217-3420 Do not confuse with Get Published in Valparaiso, IN
E-mail: customersupport@dellartepress.com
Dist(s): **Author Solutions, LLC**
CreateSpace Independent Publishing Platform.

Get the Word Out, Inc, *(978-1-7337970)* 39293 Plymouth Rd., Livonia, MI 48150 USA Tel 734-521-6579
E-mail: letsgwo@gmail.com.

Gettier Group LLC, *(978-0-9860882; 978-0-9971906; 978-0-9994595; 978-1-7358925)* 43150 Broadlands Ctr. Plaza Box 152-218, Broadlands, VA 20148-3800 USA Tel 703-307-7091
E-mail: denisetimpko@verizon.net
Web site: www.gettiergroup.net.

Getting There, *(978-0-9707274)* P.O. Box 1412, Asheville, NC 28802-1412 USA Tel 828-645-5908
E-mail: bmayers@charter.net
Web site: http://www.paddlingasheville.com
Dist(s): **Common Ground Distributors, Inc.**

Getty, J. Paul Trust Publications *See* **Getty Pubns.**

†Getty Pubns., *(978-0-89236; 978-0-941103; 978-1-60606; 978-1-947440; 979-8-88712)* Orders Addr.: P.O. Box 49659, Los Angeles, CA 90049-0659 USA Tel 310-440-7333; Fax: 818-779-0051; Edit Addr.: 1200 Getty Ctr. Dr., Suite 500, Los Angeles, CA 90049-1682 USA (SAN 208-2276) Tel 310-440-7365; Fax: 310-440-7758; Toll Free: 800-223-3431; *Imprints:* J. Paul Getty Museum (J P Getty)
E-mail: pubsinfo@getty.edu; pubsinfo@getting.edu; mwinter@getty.edu
Web site: http://www.getty.edu/publications
Dist(s): **Abrams, Inc.**
Casemate Academic
Chicago Distribution Ctr.
Hachette Bk. Group
JSTOR
Lectorum Pubns., Inc.
Libros Sin Fronteras
Oxford Univ. Pr., Inc.; *CIP.*

Gewanda J. Parker, *(978-1-7353840)* 1556 6th St., West Palm Beach, FL 33401 USA Tel 863-585-9729
E-mail: gcjpboss@gmail.com.

GFC Pr., *(978-0-9792132; 978-0-9840789; 978-0-9839256)* P.O. Box 294, Inglewood, CA 90306 USA (SAN 858-2297) Do not confuse with companies with the same or similar name in Odenton, MD, Cove, OR, Livingston, TX, Dallas, TX, Dunlap, TN, Hume, CA
E-mail: rjdriver5@gmail.com.

GGMI Incorporated *See* **God's Glory Media**

Ghim, John Yun, *(978-0-9656864)* 1139 Queen Anne Pl. Apt. 106, Los Angeles, CA 90019-7105 USA
E-mail: coolghim@yahoo.com.

GHL Publishing LLC, *(978-0-9726419)* P.O. Box 26462, Collegeville, PA 19426 USA (SAN 254-9875) Tel 610-831-1442; Fax: 610-831-1443
E-mail: c.lagunilla@att.net
Web site: http://www.GHLPublishing.com.

Gholson, C. D., *(978-0-9725974)* 2341 W. Pierce, Harrison, MI 48625 USA Tel 898-539-5312
E-mail: goatlocker@msn.com.

Ghost Hse. Bks. *Imprint of* **Lone Pine Publishing USA**

Ghost Hunter Productions, *(978-0-9717234; 978-1-934307)* P.O. Box 1199, Helena, MT 59624 USA
E-mail: info@ibw-books.com
Web site: http://www.ibw-books.com.

G-Host Publishing, *(978-0-9649088)* Orders Addr.: 8701 Lava Pl., West Hills, CA 91304-2126 USA Tel 818-340-6676 (phone/fax)
E-mail: robanne@ix.netcom.com.

Ghost Writing Venture *See* **Publishing Xpert**

Ghostwriters *See* **Self Pub.**

Giant in the Playground, *(978-0-9766580; 978-0-9854139)* 2417 Welsh Rd., Suite 21 No. 328, Philadelphia, PA 19114 USA
E-mail: rich@giantitp.com
Web site: http://www.giantitp.com
Dist(s): **Diamond Comic Distributors, Inc.**
Diamond Bk. Distributors.

Giant in the Playground Games *See* **Giant in the Playground**

Giant Robot Bks., *(978-0-9749492)* P.O. Box 641639, Los Angeles, CA 90064 USA Tel 310-479-7311
E-mail: books@giantrobot.com
Web site: http://www.giantrobot.com
Dist(s): **Trucatriche.**

ibbons-Fitts Ink, *(978-1-941387)* 14 Hillcrest, Tuscaloosa, AL 35401 USA Tel 205-752-5934
E-mail: billfittsauthor@att.net
Web site: billfittsauthor.com.

ibbs, Andrea, 615 Kentucky Dr., Rochester Hills, MI 48307 USA Tel 248-495-9881
E-mail: andrealynngibbs@gmail.com.

ibbs Publishing, *(978-0-9969509)* 8 Evergreen Terr., Ballston Lake, NY 12019 USA Tel 518-877-0759
E-mail: gibbs.pubco@gmail.com.

Gibbs Smith, Publisher, *(978-0-87905; 978-0-941711; 978-1-58685; 978-1-4236)* Orders Addr.: P.O. Box 667, Layton, UT 84041 USA (SAN 201-9906) Tel 801-544-9800; Fax: 801-544-5582; Toll Free Fax: 800-213-3023 (orders); Toll Free: 800-748-5439 (orders); 800-835-4993 (Customer Service order only); Edit Addr.: 1877 E. Gentile St., Layton, UT 84040 USA Tel 801-544-9800; Fax: 801-544-8853; *Imprints:* Anorak Press (Anorak Pr); 7 Cats Press (7 Cats)
E-mail: info@gibbs-smith.com; tradeorders@gibbs-smith.com
Web site: http://www.gibbs-smith.com
Dist(s): **Children's Plus, Inc.**
Firebrand Technologies
Open Road Integrated Media, Inc.
Publishers Group West (PGW)
Publishers Group International, Inc.; *CIP.*

Gibson Bks. *Imprint of* **Glory Days Group Publishing**

Gibson, C. R. Co., *(978-0-7667; 978-0-8378; 978-0-937970)* 401 BNA Dr., Bldg 200, Suite 600, Nashville, TN 37217 USA Toll Free: 800-243-6004 (ext. 2895)
E-mail: customerservice@crgibson.com
Web site: http://www.andersonpress.com.

Gibson, Cita, *(978-0-9727964)* P.O. Box 411236, Melbourne, FL 32941 USA Tel 316-210-6422; Fax: 321-757-7385
E-mail: maloon57@aol.com
Web site: http://www.citagibson.com.

Gibson Tech Ed, Incorporated *See* **GSS Tech Ed**

Gichigami Pr., *(978-0-9906846)* 34145 Pacific Coast Hwy. No. 343, Dana Point, CA 92629 USA Tel 313-310-9115
E-mail: mb@letschatbooks.com
Web site: www.letschataboutbooks.com.

Giddy Up, LLC, *(978-1-932125; 978-1-59524)* 3630 Plaza Dr., Ann Arbor, MI 48108 USA (SAN 255-6847)
E-mail: stiehl@giddyup.com
Web site: http://www.giddyup.com.

Giesy, Mitchell, *(978-0-9993723)* 242 Vine Cliff Dr., Harvest, AL 35749 USA Tel 256-348-8906
E-mail: mitchgiesy@gmail.com.

Gift Gardens *See* **Gift Gardens Pr.**

Gift Gardens Pr., *(978-0-692-09535-5; 978-1-7329293)* 5133 Waterman Blvd., Saint Louis, MO 63108 USA Tel 314-249-8500
E-mail: arthur.culbert@gmail.com
Web site: giftgardens.org.

Gifted Education Pr., *(978-0-910609)* Orders Addr.: P.O. Box 1586, Manassas, VA 20108 USA; Edit Addr.: 10201 Yuma Ct., Manassas, VA 20109 USA (SAN 694-132X) Tel 703-369-5017; Toll Free: 800-484-1406 (code 6857)
E-mail: mfisher345@home.com
Web site: http://GIFTEDEDPRESS.COM.

Gifted Genie Publishing, *(978-0-9897187)* 149 Forestbrook Dr., Madison, AL 35757 USA Tel 256-527-2692; Fax: 866-819-4954
E-mail: giftedgenie1@hotmail.com.

Gifted Kids Bks., *(978-0-692-08230-0)* 207 Hillside Ave., New Hyde Park, NY 11040 USA Tel 718-673-0310
E-mail: mahvashfm@gmail.com.

Gifted Town, *(978-1-7343641)* 4276 Casa Buena Way, No. 167, Oceanside, CA 92057 USA Tel 858-616-7355; Fax: 760-433-5603
E-mail: n.zaborov@icloud.com
Web site: Giftedtown.com.

Gifted UnLtd., LLC, *(978-1-7337758; 978-1-953360)* 12340 U.S. Hwy 42 No. 453, Goshen, KY 40026 USA Tel 502-715-6306
E-mail: giftedunlimitedllc@gmail.com
Web site: http://www.giftedunlimitedllc.com/
Dist(s): **SCB Distributors.**

Gigarjian, Ani & Linda Avedikian, *(978-0-9717799)* 169 S. Main St., Sherborn, MA 01770 USA
E-mail: gigarjian@comcast.net
Web site: http://www.armeniankids.com.

Giggle & Go, *(978-0-9997090)* 450 Wood Duck Ct., Lincoln, CA 95959 USA Tel 530-263-4708
E-mail: joytahoe4@gmail.com
Web site: stubbsworld.net.

Giggletins *Imprint of* **Le Bk. Moderne, LLC**

Giggling Gorilla Productions, LLC, *(978-0-9770700)* 3444 Laredo Ln., Escondido, CA 92025-7807 USA
E-mail: zoomanmike@earthlink.net
Web site: http://www.gigglinggorillaproductions.com.

GiGi Bks., *(978-0-9740847)* 17480 Old Waterford Rd., Leesburg, VA 20176 USA Tel 703-669-9781; Fax: 703-669-9782
E-mail: ganderson@gigiaudiobooks.com
Web site: http://www.gigiaudiobooks.com.

Gigi Costa, *(978-0-692-11572-5)* 3191 Coral Way, Coral Gables, FL 33145 USA Tel 305-978-3266
E-mail: gc@costalawmiami.com.

Gigi Enterprises, *(978-0-615-12926-6)* P.O. Box 133, Irvington, NY 10533-0133 USA Fax: 914-591-9249
E-mail: sonia0904@aol.com.

Gil Harp Bks., *(978-1-7335441; 978-1-956990)* 569 Cty. Line Rd., Wayne, PA 19087 USA Tel 917-971-3337
E-mail: javiergaray@gmail.com.

GIL Pubns., *(978-0-9626035; 978-0-9802185; 978-0-615-75814-5)* P.O. Box 80275, Brooklyn, NY 11208 USA Fax: 718-386-6434
E-mail: kumasi@gilpublications.com
Web site: http://www.gilpublications.com
Dist(s): **A & B Distributors & Pubs. Group**
Bk. Hse., Inc., The.

Gilbert, Drexel Enterprises, Inc., *(978-0-9818464)* Orders Addr.: P.O. Box 364, Daphne, AL 36526 USA
E-mail: drexelgilbert@drexelgilbert.com
Web site: http://www.drexelgilbert.com.

Gilbert Square Bks., *(978-0-9745308)* 2115 Plymouth SE, Grand Rapids, MI 49506 USA Tel 616-245-1050
E-mail: kvidro2003@yahoo.com
Web site: http://www.squarepears.com.

Gilboy Publishing, *(978-0-9774696)* 3521 River Narrows Rd., Hilliard, OH 43026-7833 USA.

Gilchrist & Guy Publishing, *(978-0-9747990)* 2112 Colina Vista Way, Costa Mesa, CA 92627 USA
E-mail: rguy2112@comcast.net.

Gilded Dog Enterprises LLC, *(978-0-9793483)* 106 High Point Dr., Churchville, PA 18966 USA (SAN 853-1943) Tel 215-322-5592; Fax: 215-396-6832
Web site: http://gildeddog.com.

Gilder Lehrman Institute of American History, The, *(978-0-9663843; 978-1-932821; 978-0-9970330; 978-1-953611)* Orders Addr.: 49 W. 45th St., 6th Flr., New York, NY 10036 USA Tel 646-366-9666; Fax: 646-366-9669
E-mail: ahlstrom@gilderlehrman.org
Web site: http://www.gilderlehrman.org.

Gile, John Communications *See* **JGC/United Publishing Corps**

Giles, D. Ltd. (GBR) *(978-1-904832; 978-1-907804; 978-1-911282; 978-1-913875) Dist. by* **Consort Bk Sales.**

Giles, W. Marie *See* **Giles, Willie M.**

Giles, Willie M., *(978-0-9728944)* Orders Addr.: 3555 Nighthawk Ln., Pensacola, FL 32506 USA
Web site: http://www.wix.com/booksbywmariegiles
Dist(s): **CreateSpace Independent Publishing Platform.**

Gilgit Pr., LLC, *(978-0-9746283)* P.O. Box 4881, Richmond, VA 23220 USA
Web site: http://www.gilgitpress.com.

Gill Bks. (IRL) *Dist. by* **Casemate Pubs.**

Gill, Jim Music, *(978-0-9679038; 978-0-9815721)* Subs. of Jim Gill, Inc., Orders Addr.: P.O. Box 2263, Oak Park, IL 60303 USA Tel 708-763-9864; Fax: 708-763-9888; Edit Addr.: 835 N. Kenilworth Ave., Oak Park, IL 60303-9888 USA
E-mail: jimgill@jimgill.com
Web site: http://www.jimgill.com.

Gillespie, Lauren, *(978-0-692-19996-1)* 1311 N Main St, Naperville, IL 60563 USA Tel 480-840-5137
E-mail: orafrying@hotmail.com.

Gillette, Frances A., *(978-0-9636066)* P.O. Box 351, Yacolt, WA 98675 USA
E-mail: copia@copia.com; ward@infinitecolor.com; lithoinusa@centurytel.net
Web site: http://www.copia.com
Dist(s): **Adventure Pubns.**
Publishers Group West (PGW).

Gillgren, John, *(978-0-9798530)* 20716 Rainsboro Dr., Ashburn, VA 20147 USA (SAN 854-5502) Tel 703-724-1150.

Gilliam, T. & Associates, LLC, *(978-0-9762703)* 1696 Georgetown Rd., Unit B, Hudson, OH 44236 USA Tel 330-342-5940; Fax: 330-463-5730; Toll Free: 877-316-5097
E-mail: tgilliam@healthybodyweight.com
Web site: http://www.healthybodyweight.com.

Gilliam-Wilson, Tia, *(978-0-9986073)* P.O. Box 352, Gibsonville, NC 27249 USA Tel 336-267-6998
E-mail: tiagilliamwilson@gmail.com; tiagilliamwilson@gmail.com; tiagilliamwilson@gmail.com
Dist(s): **CreateSpace Independent Publishing Platform.**

Gilligan, Will, *(978-1-7364396)* 13 Madison Ave, Flemington, NJ 08822 USA Tel 908-547-7586
E-mail: willgilliganohmy@gmail.com
Web site: gilligraphic.com.

Gillingham, Elizabeth, *(978-0-692-95423-2)* 3775 Martin Dr., Boulder, CO 80305 USA Tel 7203885153
E-mail: elizabethgillingham@gmail.com
Dist(s): **Ingram Content Group.**

Gillis-Smith, *(978-1-7331652)* 12555 Cherry Grove St., Moorpark, CA 93021 USA Tel 805-558-0561
E-mail: greg@gillis-smith.com
Web site: Gillis-SmithAuthor.com.

Gilpatrick, Gil, *(978-0-9650507)* Orders Addr.: P.O. Box 461, Skowhegan, ME 04976 USA Tel 207-453-6959; Edit Addr.: 369 Middle Rd., Fairfield, ME 04937 USA
E-mail: gil@gilgilpatrick.com
Web site: http://www.gilgilpatrick.com.

Gimme Gimme Toys & Games, Inc., *(978-0-9762524)* 1418 N. Clinton Blvd., Bloomington, IL 61701 USA
Web site: http://www.gimmegimme.ca
Dist(s): **PSI (Publisher Services, Inc.).**

Gin & Tonic Pr. *Imprint of* **Robertson, Colin**

Gina, *(978-1-7344789)* 3101 Ave. I, Apt. 1N, Brooklyn, NY 11210 USA Tel 347-752-0243
E-mail: gina.paul@live.com.

Gina Art Books *See* **Pipton Pr.**

Gina's Ink, *(978-0-9740454)* P.O. Box 11650, Denver, CO 80211 USA
Web site: http://www.cassandrasangel.com.

Ginebra, Fidel, *(978-0-615-15410-7)* Urb. La Plata, M-19 Calle Rubi, Cayey, PR 00736 USA
E-mail: fbloodguard@gmail.com
Dist(s): **Lulu Pr., Inc.**

Ginger Nielson - Children's Bk. Illustration, *(978-0-615-92252-2; 978-0-9913093; 978-0-692-78023-7; 978-0-578-41662-5; 978-0-578-44108-5; 978-0-578-50225-0; 978-0-578-51323-2; 978-0-578-53427-5; 978-0-578-74028-7; 978-0-578-77783-2; 978-0-578-96648-9; 978-0-578-96762-2; 978-0-578-96915-2; 978-0-578-96997-8; 978-0-578-30293-5; 979-8-9858879)* 278 Sand Hill Rd., Peterborough, NH 03458 USA Tel 603-924-3775; *Imprints:* HallaVision Publishing (MYID_X_HALLAVI)
E-mail: gingernielson@gmail.com.

Ginger Pr., The, *(978-0-9785151)* P.O. Box 45753, Omaha, NE 68145-0753 USA
Dist(s): **Greenleaf Book Group**
Independent Pubs. Group.

Gingerbread Hse., *(978-0-940112)* 602 Montauk Hwy., Westhampton Beach, NY 11978 USA (SAN 217-0760) Tel 631-288-5119; Fax: 631-288-5179 Do not confuse with Gingerbread House, The, Savannah GA
Web site: http://www.gingerbreadbooks.com
Dist(s): **Independent Pubs. Group.**

gingerdakin. llc, *(978-0-692-11848-1; 978-0-578-56712-9)* 1312 Village Way S, Blacksburg, VA 24060 USA Tel 540-951-8440
E-mail: gingerdakin@yahoo.com
Web site: gingerdakin.com.

Gingko Pr., Inc., *(978-1-58423; 978-1-934471)* Orders Addr.: 1321 Fifth St., Berkeley, CA 94710 USA (SAN 860-4436) Tel 510-898-1195; Fax: 510-898-1196 Do not confuse with Gingko Pr. in New York, NY
E-mail: account@gingkopress.com
Web site: http://www.gingkopress.com
Dist(s): **MyiLibrary**
Publishers Group West (PGW)
Two Rivers Distribution.

Ginter, Judy, *(978-0-692-16194-4)* 11291 E. Wesley Ave., Aurora, CO 80014 USA Tel 303-695-8608
E-mail: jgginter@msn.com
Dist(s): **Ingram Content Group.**

GIP House *See* **Summit Hse. Pubs.**

Girasol Collectables Inc., *(978-0-9797639; 978-0-9820890; 978-0-9820891; 978-0-9854755)* P.O. Box 5289, Mansfield, OH 44901-5289 USA
Web site: http://www.girasolcollectables.com.

Girl Friday Bks., *(978-1-7348802; 978-1-7363243; 978-1-7363579; 978-1-954854; 978-1-959411)* 318 W Galer St, Ste. 101, Seattle, WA 98119 USA Tel 206-524-4257; *Imprints:* Bird Upstairs (MYID_I_BIRD UP)
E-mail: indie@girlfridayproductions.com
Web site: www.girlfridayproductions.com
Dist(s): **Ingram Publisher Services**
Two Rivers Distribution.

Girl Friday Productions *See* **Girl Friday Bks.**

Girl Named Pants, Inc., A, *(978-0-9755959)* 8954 Stonebriar Dr., Clarence Ctr., NY 14032-9373 USA
Web site: http://www.agirlnamedpants.com.

Girl Pr., Inc., *(978-0-9659754)* P.O. Box 480389, Los Angeles, CA 90048-1389 USA
E-mail: gp@girlpress.com
Web site: http://www.girlpress.com.

Girl Scouts of the USA, *(978-0-88441)* 420 Fifth Ave., New York, NY 10018 USA (SAN 203-4611) Tel 212-852-8000; Fax: 212-852-6511
E-mail: bnelson@girlscouts.org
Web site: http://www.girlscouts.org/.

Girl Twirl Comics, *(978-0-9742450; 978-0-9766707; 978-0-9794207)* Orders Addr.: P.O. Box 88, Sebastopol, CA 95473 USA Tel 707-546-7121 Do not confuse with Jane's World in Seattle, WA
Web site: http://www.janecomics.com
Dist(s): **Diamond Comic Distributors, Inc.**
Diamond Bk. Distributors.

Girl-Confident Brand, *(978-0-578-21743-7; 978-1-7337697)* 3719 Ave. D Brooklyn, Brooklyn, NY 11203 USA Tel 917-331-9614
E-mail: erikasped@gmail.com
Dist(s): **Independent Pub.**

Girls Explore *Imprint of* **Girls Explore LLC**

Girls Explore LLC, *(978-0-9749456)* Orders Addr.: P.O. Box 54, Basking Ridge, NJ 07920 USA (SAN 256-2677) Fax: 908-842-9166; *Imprints:* Girls Explore (GilExplore)
Web site: http://www.girls-explore.com
Dist(s): **Brodart Co.**

Girls In Da Game Publishing, *(978-0-9674454)* Orders Addr.: 5916 Las Virgenes Rd. No. 596, Calabasas, CA 91302 USA
E-mail: corneliagailgroundup@gmail.com
Web site: http://www.facebookthenewlook.com
Dist(s): **Ingram Content Group.**

GIRLS KNOW HOW *Imprint of* **NouSoma Communications, Inc.**

Girls of Faith, *(978-0-9764304)* P.O. Box 535, Rogersville, MO 65742 USA
E-mail: orders@girlsoffaith.com
Web site: http://www.girlsoffaith.com.

Girls-Connect *See* **Bizzy Girls Publishing**

Girn-Dolce, Nora, *(978-0-9974642)* 8502 139th Ave NE, Redmond, WA 98052 USA Tel 425-502-2223
E-mail: gironnora@hotmail.com.

Giro Pr., *(978-1-878857)* Orders Addr.: P.O. Box 203, Croton-on-Hudson, NY 10520 USA Tel 914-271-8924; Fax: 914-271-6552; Edit Addr.: 44 Morningside Dr., Croton-on-Hudson, NY 10520 USA
E-mail: info@giropress.com
Web site: http://www.giropress.com.

Giron Bks., *(978-0-9741393; 978-0-9915442)* 2141 W. 21st St., Chicago, IL 60608-2608 USA Tel 773-847-3000; Fax: 773-847-9197; Toll Free: 800-405-4276
E-mail: juanmanuel@gironbooks.com; carolina@gironbooks.com
Web site: http://www.gironbooks.com.

Gish Creative, *(978-0-9728507; 978-0-615-74202-1)* 1940-A Fountainview, PMB 116, Houston, TX 77057 USA Tel 713-532-1173 (phone/fax)
Web site: http://www.gishcreative.com; http://www.thesummerbook.com.

Giunti Gruppo Editoriale (ITA) *(978-88-09; 978-88-507; 978-88-440) Dist. by* **Distribks Inc.**

Giusti-Gambini, J.M. Publishing, LLC, *(978-0-615-36873-3; 978-0-9829496)* 7259 Creeks Bend Ct., West Bloomfield, MI 48322 USA Tel 248-855-0869
E-mail: jogambini@comcast.net
Web site: http://www.poetino.com; http://www.jmgiusti-gambinipublishing.com.

Gival Pr., LLC, *(978-1-928589; 978-1-940724)* P.O. Box PO Box 3812, Arlington, VA 22203 USA (SAN 852-9787) Tel 703-351-0079 (phone)
E-mail: givalpress@yahoo.com
Web site: http://www.givalpress.com; http://www.givalpressstore.com
Dist(s): **CreateSpace Independent Publishing Platform**
Ediciones Universal
Follett School Solutions.

Givens, Diane C., *(978-1-7328014)* 8253 Seven Oaks Dr., Jonesboro, GA 30236 USA Tel 678-914-9355
E-mail: dianegivens3@gmail.com.

Givens, Florence Rosie *See* **FloBound Poems Publications**

Givinity Pr., *(978-0-9728654; 978-1-943803)* 3374 Maplewood Ct., Fargo, ND 58104-6224 USA (SAN 255-1527) Tel 701-235-4241; Fax: 701-280-2016; Toll Free: 866-221-5860
E-mail: ellen@givinity.com
Web site: http://www.givinity.com
Dist(s): **Brodart Co.**
Follett School Solutions.

GiWU Publishing, *(978-1-7335752)* 134 S. Mason, Chicago, IL 60644 USA Tel 773-688-5128
E-mail: Info@Giwupublishing.com
Web site: www.Giwupublishing.com.

Gizicki-Lipson, Coryn *See* **In the Sky Publishing**

Gizmo Enterprises, Inc, *(978-0-9759638; 978-1-7322455)*
E-mail: Perrytheinventor+bowker@gmail.com; perry@colorcutter.com
Web site: http://www.colorcutter.com; http://www.gizmoLine.com.

Gizmo Enterprises, Incorporated *See* **Gizmo Enterprises, Inc**

Gizmo Pr., *(978-0-9749911)* 6990 Poco Bueno Cir., Sparks, NV 89436 USA Tel 775-626-4533; Fax: 775-425-5290
E-mail: mjarcher@aol.com; greg.nielsen@charter.net.

GL Design, *(978-0-9745882; 978-1-933983)* 1047 Cherryvale Rd., Boulder, CO 80303 USA
E-mail: distrib@gldesignpub.com
Web site: http://www.gldesignpub.com
Dist(s): **Ingram Content Group.**

G.L. Sturdivant Pubs., *(978-1-7337133)* 9752 Charolais Dr., Tuscaloosa, AL 35405 USA Tel 205-586-2641
E-mail: gwarnekia.l.sturdivant@gmail.com.

Gladstone Publishing, *(978-1-928681)* Orders Addr.: 27 Sunny Bend, Newark, DE 19702 USA (SAN 254-8410) Tel 302-533-6831 Do not confuse with Gladstone Publishing, Prescott, AZ
E-mail: admin@yourinnerconfidence.com
Web site: http://www.yourinnerconfidence.com/smart-sojourner; http://www.yourinnerconfidence.com/smart-sojourner
Dist(s): **BookBaby.**

Glas Daggre Publishing, 61 collins St., ATTLEBORO, MA 02703 USA Tel 585-978-1057
E-mail: srstjean@gmail.com
Dist(s): **Ingram Content Group.**

Glass, Michael B. & Assocs., Inc., *(978-0-940429)* 735 Calebs Path/Glaro Bldg., Hauppauge, NY 11788 USA (SAN 664-3574).

Glass Onion Publishing, *(978-0-9986381; 978-1-947678)* 6237 Presidential Ct., No. 140, Fort Myers, FL 33919 USA Tel 239-910-1355; *Imprints:* Happy Dolphin Press (MYID_U_HAPPY D)
E-mail: editor@happydolphinpress.com
Web site: www.PubSmithPress.com; www.GlassOnionPublishing.com; www.HappyDolphinPress.com.

†Glastonbury Pr., *(978-0-944963)* Orders Addr.: 454 Las Gallinas Ave., No. 108, San Rafael, CA 94903 USA Tel 415-492-2140; 415-686-4150 Do not confuse with Glastonbury Pr., Whittier, CA
E-mail: starstone@comcast.net; misty@glastonburypress.com
Web site: http://www.glastonburypress.com
Dist(s): **CreateSpace Independent Publishing Platform**; *CIP.*

Glavin, Kevin, *(978-0-9825466)* 23 Vassar Aisle, Irvine, CA 92612 USA
E-mail: admin@kevinglavinpublishing.com
Web site: http://www.rockstarsrainbow.com; http://www.kevinglavinpublishing.com.

Gleasner, Bill & Diana Inc., *(978-0-9651185)* 7994 Holly Ct., Denver, NC 28037 USA Tel 704-483-9301; Fax: 704-483-6309
E-mail: dgleasner@aol.com
Dist(s): **Booklines Hawaii, Ltd.**

Glen Enterprises, *(978-1-880215)* 1202 Wildwood Dr., Deer Park, TX 77536 USA Tel 281-479-2759
E-mail: purdys@flash.net.

Glenbridge Publishing, Ltd., *(978-0-944435)* 19923 E. Long Ave., Centennial, CO 80016 USA (SAN 243-5403) Tel 720-870-8381; Fax: 720-230-1209; Toll Free: 800-986-4135 (orders only)
E-mail: glenbridge@qwestoffice.net
Web site: http://www.glenbridgepublishing.com.

Glencannon Pr., *(978-0-9637586; 978-1-889901)* Orders Addr.: P.O. Box 1428, El Cerrito, CA 94530 USA; *Imprints:* Palo Alto Books (Palo Alto)
E-mail: merships@yahoo.com
Web site: http://www.glencannon.com.

†Glencoe/McGraw-Hill, *(978-0-02; 978-0-07)* Div. of The McGraw-Hill Education Group, 8787 Orion Pl.,

Publisher Name Index

Columbus, OH 43240-4027 USA Toll Free: 800-334-7344
E-mail: customer.service@mcgraw-hill.com
Web site: http://www.glencoe.com
Dist(s): **Follett School Solutions**
Libros Sin Fronteras
McGraw-Hill Cos., The; *CIP.*

Glenhaven Pr., *(978-0-9637265; 978-0-9741279)* 24871 Pylos Way, Mission Viejo, CA 92691 USA Tel 949-770-1486
E-mail: glenhavn@thevision.net; jacki@hydrasystems.com
Dist(s): **J & J Bk. Sales.**

Glenmere Pr., *(978-0-9852948; 978-0-9903139)* Orders Addr.: 26 Kings Ridge Rd., Warwick, NY 10990 USA
E-mail: lois@glenmerepress.com; lois@wingedbooks.com
Web site: http://www.glenmerepress.com; http://www.wingedbooks.com
Dist(s): **CreateSpace Independent Publishing Platform**
INscribe Digital
Independent Pubs. Group
Ingram Content Group.

Glenn, Lauren, *(978-0-9772459)* 2436 Oakdale St., Tallahassee, FL 32308 USA.

Glenn, Peter Pubns., *(978-0-87314)* 824 E. Atlantic Ave. Ste. 7, Delray Beach, FL 33483-5300 USA (SAN 201-9930)
E-mail: gjames@pgdirect.com
Web site: http://www.pgdirect.com.

Glenn Young Bks., *(978-1-55783)* 253 W. 72nd St., New York, NY 10023 USA Tel 212-595-2082
Dist(s): **Leonard, Hal Corp.**
National Bk. Network.

Glenneyre Pr. LLC, *(978-0-9768040; 978-1-934602)* 20555 Devonshire St., Box 203, Chatsworth, CA 91311-9133 USA
E-mail: myn@wordsushi.com
Web site: http://www.glenneyrepress.com.

Glens Falls Printing LLC, *(978-1-933575)* 51 Hudson Ave., Glens Falls, NY 12801 USA (SAN 256-7148) Tel 518-793-0555; Fax: 518-793-8624; Toll Free: 866-793-0555
E-mail: bob@gfprinting.com
Web site: http://www.gfprinting.com; http://www.spiritoftheadirondacksbook.com; http://www.commonmanbooks.com.

Glitter Creek, Inc., *(978-0-9744520)* 2919 Westridge Ave., Cincinnati, OH 45238 USA Toll Free: 888-982-7335
Web site: http://www.glittercreek.com.

Glitterati Incorporated *See* **G Arts LLC**

GLM Publishing, *(978-0-578-14076-6; 978-0-9863604; 978-0-9973325)* 2165 NW 30th Rd., Boca Raton, FL 33431 USA.

Global Academic Publishing, *(978-0-9633277; 978-1-883058; 978-1-58684)* Global Academic Publishing, Binghamton Univ., Binghamton, NY 13902-6000 USA Tel 607-777-4495; 607-777-2745 (contact Barnes & Noble for orders); Fax: 607-777-6132
E-mail: gporders@binghamton.edu
Web site: http://www.academicpublishing.binghamton.edu
Dist(s): **Hesteria Records & Publishing Co.**
State Univ. of New York Pr.

Global Age Publishing/Global Academy Pr., *(978-1-887176)* 16057 Tampa Palms Blvd., W., No. 219, Tampa, FL 33647 USA Tel 813-991-4982; Fax: 813-973-8166.

Global Alliances, *(978-0-9759126)* 82-09 166th St., Hillcrest, NY 11432 USA.

Global Authors Pubns., *(978-0-9728513; 978-0-9742161; 978-0-9766449; 978-0-9779680; 978-0-9798087; 978-0-9821223; 978-0-9845926; 978-0-9846536; 978-0-9861109; 979-8-9874547)* P.O. Box 954, Green Cove Springs, FL 32043 USA; 730 Donnelly St., Eustis, FL 32726 Tel 904-425-1608
E-mail: gapbook@yahoo.com
Web site: http://www.globalauthorspublications.com.

Global Awareness Publishing Co., *(978-1-885888)* 1102 Hickory St., Madison, WI 53715-1726 USA.

Global Business Info USA *See* **Global Pro Info USA**

Global Business Information Strategies, Inc., *(978-1-60231)* Orders Addr.: P.O. Box 610135, Newton, MA 02461 USA (SAN 852-1980) Tel 617-795-0519; Fax: 617-795-0211; Edit Addr.: 965 Walnut St., Suite 100, Newton, MA 02461 USA; *Imprints:* Cub Books (Cub Bks)
E-mail: publishing@gbisi.com
Web site: http://gbisi.com.

Global Commitment Publishing, *(978-1-884931)* Div. of Alpert & Assocs., 3544 Winfield Ln., NW, Washington, DC 20007 USA Tel 202-338-4975; Fax: 202-835-0668; 5505 Connecticut Ave., Washington, DC 20015.

Global Communications *See* **Inner Light - Global Communications**

Global Community Communications Publishing, *(978-0-9647357; 978-0-9822423; 978-1-937919)* P.O. Box 1613, Tubac, AZ 85646-1613 USA Tel 520-603-9932
E-mail: info@GlobalCommunityCommunicationsPublishing.org
Web site: http://www.GlobalCommunityCommunicationsPublishing.org.

Global Content Ventures, *(978-0-9799901)* P.O. Box 6370, Lancaster, PA 17607 USA.

Global counseling & coaching services , inc *See* **Global Training Coaching & Consulting services , inc**

Global Education Advance, *(978-0-9796019; 978-0-9801674; 978-1-935434; 978-1-950839)* 345 Barton Rd. at Lone Mountain, Dayton, TN 37321-7635 USA Tel 423-775-2949
E-mail: GlobalEdAdvance@aol.com
Web site: http://www.globaledadvance.org.

Global Education Resources, LLC, *(978-1-934046)* 37 Station Rd., Madison, NJ 07940 USA (SAN 851-1012) Tel 973-410-0840; Fax: 973-410-1603
E-mail: myoshida@globaledresources.com
Web site: http://www.globaledresources.com.

Global Footprints *See* **Tiny Global Footprints**

Global Goddess Pr., *(978-0-692-71437-9)* 20212 Village 20, Camarillo, CA 93012 USA Tel 805-504-5050
E-mail: endangeredabcs@yahoo.com.

Global Institute for Maximizing Potential, Incorporated, *(978-0-9772020; 978-0-9825776; 978-0-9830337)* 92 Mt. Zion Way, Ocean Grove, NJ 07756 USA Tel 732-776-7360
E-mail: richert@globalinst.com
Web site: http://www.globalinst.com.

Global Learning, Inc., *(978-1-59867)* 1001 SE Water Ave., Suite 310, Portland, OR 97214 USA Toll Free: 888-548-2787 Do not confuse with Global Learning Inc. in Brielle, NJ
Web site: http://www.litart.com.

Global Partnership, LLC, *(978-0-9644706)* Orders Addr.: P.O. Box 894, Murray, KY 42071 USA (SAN 255-4186) Tel 562-884-0062; Edit Addr.: 100 N. 6th St., Murray, KY 42071 USA
E-mail: steveneschmitt@cs.com; erin@wakeuplive.com
Web site: http://www.businessolympians.com
Dist(s): **Seven Locks Pr.**

Global Pr., *(978-0-9792151)* 2083 Ridge Point Dr., Los Angeles, CA 90049 USA Tel 310-476-8336.

Global Pro Info USA, *(978-0-7397; 978-0-9646241; 978-1-57751; 978-1-4330; 978-1-4387; 978-1-5145)* 6301 Stevenson Ave Suite 1317, Alexandria, VA 22304 USA Tel 703-370-8082; Fax: 703-370-8082; 6301 Stevenson Ave., # 1317, Alexandria, VA 22304 Tel 202-656-2103; Fax: 202-546-3275 Do not confuse with International Business Pubn., Inc. in Cincinnati, OH
E-mail: ibpusa3@gmail.com
Web site: http://www.ibpus.com
Dist(s): **Lulu Pr., Inc.**

Global Publications (S S I P S) *See* **Global Academic Publishing**

Global Publishing, *(978-0-911649)* 51 Bell Rock Plaza, Suite A, PMB 511, Sedona, AZ 86351 USA (SAN 299-3627) Tel 928-284-5544; Fax: 928-284-5545 Do not confuse with companies with the same or similar name in Meiminghan, MI, Costa Mesa, CA, Las Angeles, CA, Florence, MA, Memphis, TN, Sauk Rapids, MN, Fort Lauderdale, FL, Fort Worth, TX, Salt Lake City, UT
E-mail: minorwood@earthlink.net
Web site: http://www.wealthysoul.com
Dist(s): **New Leaf Distributing Co., Inc.**

Global Summit House *See* **Regency Pubs., The**

Global Training Coaching & Consulting services , inc, *(978-0-9905718; 978-1-7328275; 979-8-9864291)*
E-mail: Drstem14@gmail.com
Web site: www.drstemspeaks.com; www.amazon.com; Www.drstemmie.com; www.bouncebackconference.com; www.bouncebackbooks.com; www.womenselfcaresuccess.com.

Global Truth Publishing, *(978-0-9740465)* Orders Addr.: 1001 Bridgeway, Suite 474, Sausalito, CA 94965 USA Tel 415-331-1102; Fax: 415-331-2265
E-mail: sales@globaltruthpublishing.com
Web site: http://www.globaltruthpublishing.com.

Global Village Kids, LLC, *(978-0-9760472)* 4111 Calavo Dr., La Mesa, CA 91941-7051 USA Tel 619-303-0929; Fax: 925-888-8471
E-mail: seth.burns@globalvillagekids.com
Web site: http://www.globalvillagekids.com
Dist(s): **AV Cafe, Inc., The**
BWI
Iaconi, Mariuccia Bk. Imports
Wayland Audio-Visual.

GlobalVision Travel Resources, Inc., *(978-0-9800147)* 4831 Las Virgenes Rd., No. 115, Calabasas, CA 91302-1911 USA
E-mail: LCohen@getglobalvision.com
Web site: http://getglobalvision.com.

GLOBE *Imprint of* **Savvas Learning Co.**

Globe Fearon Educational Publishing, *(978-0-13; 978-0-8224; 978-0-8359; 978-0-87065; 978-0-88102; 978-0-912925; 978-0-915510; 978-1-55555; 978-1-55675)* Div. of Pearson Education Corporate Communications, Orders Addr.: 4350 Equity Dr., P.O. Box 2649, Columbus, OH 43216-2649 USA Toll Free Fax: 800-393-3156; Toll Free: 800-848-9500; 800-321-3106 (customer service); Edit Addr.: One Lake St., Upper Saddle River, NJ 07458 USA
Web site: http://www.pearsonschool.com
Dist(s): **Cambridge Bk. Co.**
Follett School Solutions
IFSTA.

†**Globe Pequot Pr., The,** *(978-0-7627; 978-0-87106; 978-0-88742; 978-0-914788; 978-0-933469; 978-0-934802; 978-0-941130; 978-1-56440; 978-1-57034; 978-1-57392; 978-1-58574; 978-1-59228; 978-1-59921; 978-1-4779; 978-1-4930)* Orders Addr.: P.O. Box 480, Guilford, CT 06437-0480 USA (SAN 201-9892) Tel 888-249-7586; Toll Free Fax: 800-820-2329 (in Connecticut); Toll Free: 800-243-0495 (24 hours); 800-336-8334; Edit Addr.: 246 Goose Ln., Guilford, CT 06437 USA Tel 203-458-4500; Fax: 203-458-4600; Toll Free Fax: 800-336-8334; *Imprints:* Lyons Press (Lyons); Falcon Guides (Fal-Guides); TwoDot (Two-D)
E-mail: info@globepequot.com
Web site: http://www.globepequot.com
Dist(s): **Blackstone Audio, Inc.**
Chelsea Green Publishing
MyiLibrary
National Bk. Network
Rowman & Littlefield Publishers, Inc.
Rowman & Littlefield Unlimited Model; *CIP.*

Globe Pubs., *(978-0-9623653; 978-1-882614)* 724 Fair Meadows Dr., Saginaw, TX 76179-1017 USA.

Globe Publishing, *(978-0-9765168)* Orders Addr.: P.O. Box 3040, Pensacola, FL 32516-3040 USA Tel 850-453-3453; Fax: 850-456-6001; Edit Addr.: 8590 Hwy 98 W., Pensacola, FL 32506 USA Do not confuse with Globe Publishing in Salt Lake City, UT
Web site: http://www.gme.org.

Globo, Editora SA (BRA) *(978-85-217; 978-85-250) Dist. by* **Distribks Inc.**

Globo Libros, *(978-0-9706953)* Orders Addr.: P.O. Box 4025, Sunnyside, NY 11104 USA; Edit Addr.: 402 E. 64th St. Apt. 6C, New York, NY 10021-7826 USA
E-mail: dstockwell@globolibros.com
Web site: http://www.globolibros.com.

Glolar Multimedia Productions, *(978-0-9707746)* P.O. Box 721452, San Diego, CA 92172-1452 USA
E-mail: info@Glolar.com; info@glolar.com
Web site: http://www.glolar.com.

Gloria List, *(978-0-9709861)* 83439 Greenbrier Dr, Indio, CA 92203 USA (SAN 253-7923) Tel 760-574-6616 (phone/fax)
E-mail: glorialist64@gmail.com.

Glory Be Collectibles, *(978-0-9795127; 978-0-578-06528-1; 978-0-578-07491-7)* 2169 Green Canyon Rd., Fallbrook, CA 92028 USA (SAN 853-6627) Tel 760-723-5222; Fax: 760-723-4433
E-mail: sales@glorybe.com
Web site: http://www.glorybe.com.

Glory Bound Books Las Vegas *See* **Glorybound Publishing**

Glory Days Group Publishing, *(978-0-9755145)* P.O. Box 1869, Glen Burnie, MD 21060-1869 USA Tel 410-766-0005 (phone/fax); *Imprints:* Gibson Books (Gibson Bks)
E-mail: drgibson123@yahoo.com
Web site: http://www.glorydayspublishing2day4u.com.

Glorybound Publishing, *(978-0-9766718; 978-0-9779654; 978-0-9802481; 978-1-60789)* 349 S. 6th St., Camp Verde, AZ 86322 USA (SAN 256-4564) Do not confuse with Glory Bound Books in Marlette, MI
E-mail: sherihauser@yahoo.com; gloryboundpublishing@yahoo.com
Web site: http://www.gloryboundpublishing.com.

Glover Publishing and Community Outsourcing, *(978-0-692-81946-3; 978-0-9986222)* 16306 Thornridge Dr., Grand Blanc, MI 48501 USA Tel 810-423-5118
E-mail: gg.writer.glove@gmail.com; gg.writer.glove@gmail.com; gg.writer.glove@gmail.com
Web site: www.GloverPCO.com
Dist(s): **CreateSpace Independent Publishing Platform.**

Glow Word Bks., *(978-0-9859834; 978-1-942514)* P.O. Box 705, Willernie, MN 55090 USA Tel 720-443-3320
E-mail: glowwordbooks@gmail.com
Web site: http://www.glowwordbooks.com
Dist(s): **CreateSpace Independent Publishing Platform**
Ingram Content Group.

Glowacki, Helen, *(978-0-9847211; 978-0-9890214; 978-0-9893807; 978-0-9913916)* 2319 Saratoga Bay Dr., West Palm Beach, FL 33409 USA Tel 561-845-8493
E-mail: wally_helen@yahoo.com
Web site: www.helenglowacki.com.

Gluten & Gluten Free Cooking in Perfect Har, *(978-0-578-41702-8; 978-0-578-60429-9; 978-0-578-39890-7)* 60 Weeden Ave., Rumford, RI 02916 USA Tel 401-263-8068
E-mail: contente6@verizon.net
Dist(s): **Ingram Content Group.**

Glynworks Publishing, *(978-0-9795912)* 2630 International Dr. #929b, Ypsilanti, MI 48197 USA
Web site: http://www.glynworkspublishing.com
Dist(s): **Ingram Content Group.**

GMC Distribution (GBR) *(978-0-946819; 978-1-86108; 978-1-78494) Dist. by* **IngramPubServ.**

GMEC Publishing, *(978-0-9794302)* P.O. Box 4470, Lake Tahoe, NV 89449-4470 USA Tel 704-992-2272; Fax: 704-992-2271
E-mail: MrsButtar@aol.com; StoriesThatTeach@aol.com
Web site: http://www.DebbieButtar.com; http://www.ChildrensStoriesThatTeach.com.

GMI Bks., *(978-0-9841809)* 7250 Franklin Ave., No.1407, Hollywood, CA 90046 USA
E-mail: richard@thegirlfromatlantis.com; doubleosix@aol.com
Web site: http://www.thegirlfromatlantis.com.

GMKelso, *(978-1-7331092)* 20620 Youpon Ln, PORTER, TX 77365 USA Tel 281-755-7330
E-mail: pegasusfury333@yahoo.com
Dist(s): **Ingram Content Group.**

Gnatcatcher Children'S Bks., *(978-0-9778005)* 1451 E. Armando Dr., Long Beach, CA 90807 USA Tel 562-427-1200
E-mail: maryhoch@excite.com.

Gnosophia Pubs., *(978-0-9773391)* 3800 New Hampshire Ave. NW Apt 507, Washington, DC 20011-7932 USA (SAN 257-3210) Tel 202-709-7580; Toll Free Fax: 866-525-0247
E-mail: admin@wisdomforthesoul.org; info@wisdomforthesoul.org; admin@gnosophia.com
Web site: http://www.wisdomforthesoul.org; http://www.gnosophia.com.

Go Ask Anyone, Inc., *(978-0-9742866)* 38 Irwin St., No.3, Winthrop, MA 02152 USA
Web site: http://www.goaskanyone.com.

Go Daddy Productions, Inc., *(978-0-9753938)* 2010 Ripley Point Ct., Odenton, MD 21113 USA Tel 443-226-4747
E-mail: mejagan@yahoo.com
Web site: http://www.go-daddyproductions.com.

Go Flag Football, *(978-0-9772203)* 1978 Shiloh Valley Trail, Kennesaw, GA 30144 USA
Web site: http://www.goflagfootball.com.

Go Jolly Bks., *(978-0-9822824; 978-1-942937)* P.O. Box 2203, Port Angeles, WA 98362 USA
Web site: http://www.gojollybooks.com.

GO Publishing Co., *(978-0-9640713; 978-1-892951; 978-0-9998032; 978-0-578-73897-0)* Orders Addr.: 338 Wekiva Cove Rd., Longwood, FL 32779 USA Tel 407-463-5464
E-mail: wmg@fprint.net.

Go Team, LLC, *(978-0-9797040)* 1427 Heatherwood Rd., Columbia, SC 29205 USA (SAN 854-1566)
E-mail: deliacorrigan@mindspring.com
Web site: http://www.goteambooks.com.

Goal Line Group LLC, *(978-1-7335651)* 4547 Placepointe Dr., Mason, OH 45040 USA Tel 513-972-8023
E-mail: depolen1@gmail.com.

Goal Pubns., *(978-0-9979125; 978-1-949768)* 14 Asylum St, Norwich, CT 06374 USA Tel 860-546-8377
E-mail: professionaljunk@anthroaquatic.com
Web site: www.goalpublications.com.

Goal Standard Publishing, *(978-1-953941)* 900 Commonwealth Pl. Suite 200-1017, Norfolk, VA 23464 USA Tel 833-491-1200
E-mail: betty.hernandez@lsd44.navy.mil
Web site: goalstandardpublishing.com.

Goat Song Publishing, *(978-0-692-90923-2; 978-0-692-92333-7; 978-0-692-98176-4; 978-0-692-06808-3; 979-8-218-02668-4)* 7619 Hwy. 70 S PO Box 218482, NASHVILLE, TN 37221 USA Tel 703-407-4654
E-mail: goatsongpub@gmail.com
Dist(s): **CreateSpace Independent Publishing Platform**
Ingram Content Group.

Goatee Graphics, *(978-0-9657257)* P.O. Box 591840, San Francisco, CA 94159-1840 USA (SAN 256-8985) Tel 415-272-6117
E-mail: goatee848@yahoo.com
Web site: http://www.undertherimbook.com.

Goblin Bks., *(978-1-7340585)* 9153 Broken Oak Pl., Burke, VA 22015-3566 USA Tel 703-451-7470
E-mail: TomCrepeau3@aol.com
Web site: TomCrepeau.com.

Goblin Fern Pr. *Imprint of* **HenschelHAUS Publishing, Inc.**

Goddess Enterprises *See* **Goodness Experience, The**

†**Godine, David R. Pub.,** *(978-0-87923; 978-1-56792; 978-1-57423)* Orders Addr.: P.O. Box 450, Jaffrey, NH 03452 USA Tel 603-532-4100; Fax: 603-532-5940; Toll Free Fax: 800-226-0934; Toll Free: 800-344-4771; Edit Addr.: Fifteen Court Sq., Suite 320, Boston, MA 02108 USA (SAN 213-4381) Tel 617-451-9600; Fax: 617-350-0250; *Imprints:* Non Pareil Books (Non Pareil Bk)
E-mail: info@godine.com; order@godine.com
Web site: http://www.godine.com
Dist(s): **Baker & Taylor International**
INscribe Digital
Independent Pubs. Group
MyiLibrary
Open Road Integrated Media, Inc.
Two Rivers Distribution
eBookit.com; *CIP.*

Godinez-Hammermaster Design, *(978-0-9773205)* Orders Addr.: 411 Garonne St., Oxnard, CA 93036 USA; Edit Addr.: 122 Eugenia Dr., Ventura, CA 93003 USA (SAN 257-7127)
E-mail: artposter3@gmail.com.

Godiva Girl Records & Publishing, Incorporated *See* **Girls In Da Game Publishing**

God's Bible School & College *See* **Revivalist Pr., The**

God's Glory Media, *(978-0-9772647; 978-1-7327861)* Div. of God's Glory Ministries International Inc., P.O. Box 1430, Dacula, GA 30019 USA (SAN 257-1528)
E-mail: office@godsglory.org
Web site: http://www.GodsGlory.org.

God's Greatest Gift, LLC, *(978-0-9796477)* Orders Addr.: P.O. Box 185, Manchester, MI 48158-8513 USA (SAN 853-9855) Tel 734-320-5111; Edit Addr.: 520 City Rd., Manchester, MI 48158-8513 USA Fax: 734-428-0084
E-mail: godsgreatestgift@comcast.net
Web site: http://www.godsgreatestgift.net
Dist(s): **Partners Pubs. Group, Inc.**

God's World Publications *See* **God's World Pubns. Inc.**

God's World Pubns. Inc., *(978-1-882440; 978-0-9844605; 978-0-9855957)* 12 All Souls Crescent, Asheville, NC 28803 USA (SAN 254-1696) Tel 828-253-8063; Fax: 828-253-1556
E-mail: edufeedback@gwpub.com; pub@gwnews.com
Web site: http://www.learnwithworld.com/writewithworld/.

Godspeed Pr., *(978-0-9798250)* 430 Davis Dr., Suite 270, Morrisville, NC 27560 USA Tel 404-457-4097
E-mail: deanthewriter@gmail.com.

Goff Bks. *Imprint of* **ORO Editions**

GoFindHome, *(978-1-887461)* 3919A Iberville St., New Orleans, LA 70119 USA.

GoGo Pr., *(978-0-9769028)* Orders Addr.: 6007 Hickory Valley Rd., Nashville, TN 37205 USA (SAN 257-1412) Tel 615-356-6571; Fax: 615-356-9609
E-mail: info@gogopress.com; paul@pbuff.com
Web site: http://www.gogopress.com.

Goin' Native, Inc., *(978-0-9891323; 978-0-692-83288-2)* P.O. Box 617153, Orlando, FL 32861 USA Tel 407-897-3522; Fax: 407-896-4614
E-mail: info@goinnative.com.

Goins, Marva, *(978-1-7322838)* 940 Drake Ave., Roselle, NJ 07203 USA Tel 908-245-2535
E-mail: Njtriumph46@aol.com.

GoKnow, Incorporated *See* **GoKnow Learning**

GoKnow Learning, *(978-0-9762083; 978-0-9767504; 978-0-9786499)* 2084 S. State St., Ann Arbor, MI 48104-4608 USA Toll Free: 877-482-3439
Web site: http://www.goknow.com.

Gokul Workshops LLC, *(978-1-7359606)* 300 Pk. Ave., NEW YORK, NY 10022 USA Tel 917-770-8408
E-mail: bal.das@gokulworld.com.

Golaboff, Laura J., *(978-0-9996184)* 4797 Westfield Dr., Hampstead, MD 21074 USA Tel 410-374-3435
E-mail: jlgolab@verizon.net.

Golan, Hanna, *(978-0-9779723)* 17340 Hamlin St., Lake Balboa, CA 91406 USA (SAN 850-7732) Tel 818-342-4969
E-mail: hannagolan2000@yahoo.com
Web site: http://blessthechildren.com.

GO-LA-NV Pr., *(978-0-9741828)* P.O. Box 1897, Huntsville, TX 77342-1897 USA Tel 936-291-2906
E-mail: rhvann@sbcglobal.net.

Gold 5 Publishing, *(978-0-9904017)* 5599 Sherwood Ct., Newburgh, IN 47630 USA Tel 334-614-6103
E-mail: gold5publishing@gmail.com.

Gold Angel Press *See* **ONLY1EARTH, LLC**

Gold Boy Music & Pubn., *(978-0-9761992)* 108 Highland Tr., Chapel Hill, NC 27516 USA (SAN 256-2499) Tel 919-500-3023
E-mail: rob@musicgoldboy.com
Web site: thechristmasauntie.com; http://www.musicgoldboy.com
Dist(s): **BCH Fulfillment & Distribution.**

Gold Boy Music & Publishing *See* **Gold Boy Music & Pubn.**

Gold Charm Publishing, LLC, *(978-0-9744855)* Orders Addr.: P.O. Box 161, Nottingham, NH 03290 USA Tel 603-942-7925 (phone/fax); Edit Addr.: 82 Priest Rd., Nottingham, NH 03290 USA.

Gold Design, LLC *See* **Toy Rocket Studios, LLC**

Gold Leaf Pr., *(978-1-886769)* Orders Addr.: 2229 Alter Rd., Detroit, MI 48215 USA Tel 313-331-3571; 262-342-0018 Oleand Publications; Fax: 313-308-3063; 262-342-0018 Oleand Publications; Toll Free: 800-838-8854 Do not confuse with companies with the same name in Seattle, WA, Starke FL
E-mail: rebecca@goldleafpress.com; wings@oleand.com
Web site: http://www.goldleafpress.com; http://www.oleand.com
Dist(s): **Oleand Pubns.**

Gold Street Pr., *(978-1-934533)* 814 Montgomery St., San Francisco, CA 94133 USA Tel 415-291-0100; Fax: 415-291-8841
E-mail: michelle@weldonowen.com
Web site: http://www.weldonowen.com; http://www.goldstreetpress.com.

Gold Street Pubs. *Imprint of* **Fallick, Barbara**

Gold Sun Publishing, *(978-0-9886549; 978-0-578-53091-8; 978-0-578-55939-1; 978-0-578-69936-3; 978-1-7354679)* 1325 Wolf St., Philadelphia, PA 19148 USA Tel 610-241-0256
E-mail: Roncostello@mail.com.

Goldberg, Alena, *(978-1-7353624)* P.O. Box 421, Cannon Beach, OR 97110 USA Tel 480-234-4177
E-mail: alenagoldberg@hotmail.com.

Golden Alley Pr., *(978-0-9895265; 978-0-9984429; 978-1-7320276; 978-1-7333055; 978-1-7373410)* 37 S. 6th St., Emmaus, PA 18049 USA Tel 610-966-4440
E-mail: nsayre@goldenalleypress.com
Web site: http://www.goldenalleypress.com.

Golden Anchor Pr., *(978-1-886864)* 625 Elrod Rd., Bowling Green, KY 42104 USA Tel 270-780-9334
E-mail: smithdale2@aol.com; goldnanchr@aol.com
Web site: http://www.Everykidawinner.com
Dist(s): **Partners/West Book Distributors**
Quality Bks., Inc.
Unique Bks., Inc.

Golden Bks. *Imprint of* **Random Hse. Children's Bks.**

Golden Bks. *Imprint of* **Random Hse., Inc.**

Golden Bks. Adult Publishing Group *Imprint of* **St. Martin's Pr.**

Golden, Brian *See* **PastWays Inc.**

Golden Crown Publishing, LLC, *(978-1-7342322; 978-1-957283)* 445 Pk. St, Deerfield, MI 49238 USA Tel 419-350-1796
E-mail: sarah@sarah-sutton.com
Web site: www.sarah-sutton.com.

Golden Door Pr., *(978-0-692-96859-8)* 82 ellen st, Riverhead, NY 11901 USA Tel 631-727-6728
E-mail: bmasonrast@aol.com.

Golden Dragon Pr., LLC, *(978-0-9894603)* 8501 E. Alameda Ave. Unit 1116, Denver, CO 80230 USA Tel 720-971-3018
E-mail: sacredjoy09@yahoo.com.

Golden Eagle Publishing Hse., Inc., *(978-0-9744205; 978-0-9753533; 978-0-9759122; 978-0-9769364)* 9201 Wilshire Blvd., Suite 205, Beverly Hills, CA 90210 USA Tel 310-273-9176; Fax: 310-273-0954
E-mail: info@goldeneaglepublishing.com
Web site: http://www.goldeneaglepublishing.com
Dist(s): **Greenleaf Book Group.**

Golden Gate National Parks Conservancy, *(978-0-9625206; 978-1-883869; 978-1-932519)* 201 Fort Mason, 3rd Flr., San Francisco, CA 94123 USA Tel 415-561-3000; Fax: 415-561-3033
Web site: http://www.parksconservancy.org/
Dist(s): **Yosemite Conservancy.**

Golden Gate Publishing, *(978-0-9856631; 979-8-9874697)* P.O. Box 27478, San Francisco, CA 94127 USA Tel 415-753-2930
E-mail: GoldenGatePublishing@gmail.com
Web site: GoldenGatePublish.com.

Golden Gryphon Pr., *(978-0-9655901; 978-1-930846)* 3002 Perkins Rd., Urbana, IL 61802 USA (SAN 299-1829) Tel 217-384-4205 (phone/fax); Fax: 217-352-9748
E-mail: Gryphon@goldengryphon.com
Web site: http://www.goldengryphon.com
Dist(s): **MyiLibrary**
ebrary, Inc.

Golden Harvest Publishing Co., *(978-0-9747904)* 4849 Valley Rd., Rosedale, VA 24280 USA Tel 276-880-9862; Fax: 276-880-1146
E-mail: adda@mounet.com.

Golden Imprint Pubns., *(978-0-9989194)* P.O. Box 20333, Rancho Santa Fe, CA 92067 USA Tel 858-754-7987
E-mail: darcyneils@yahoo.com
Web site: www.goldenimprintpublications.com.

Golden Inspirational *Imprint of* **Random Hse. Children's Bks.**

Golden Kingdom Pr., *(978-0-9883280)* P.O. Box 1104, Deland, FL 32721 USA Tel 386-490-1556
E-mail: gkingdommusic@yahoo.com.

GOLDEN LIBERTY, *(978-0-578-59944-1)* 7521 Carpenter St., Port Richey, FL 34668 USA Tel 727-831-8301
E-mail: gloriateschofficial@gmail.com.

Golden Light Factory, *(978-1-7327645)* 4006 Darling Hill Rd, East Burke, VT 05832 USA Tel 802-626-5152
E-mail: hope@goldenlightfactory.com
Web site: www.goldenlightfactory.com.

Golden Mastermind Seminars, Inc., *(978-0-9740924; 978-1-934919; 978-0-692-03130-8; 978-0-578-20058-3)* Orders Addr.: 6507 Pacific Ave., Suite 329, Stockton, CA 95207 USA (SAN 255-2639) Fax: 209-467-3260; Toll Free: 800-595-6632
E-mail: Jeff@goldenmastermind.com; Carolyn@goldenmastermind.com
Web site: http://www.goldenmastermind.com.

Golden Meteorite Pr. (CAN) *(978-1-895385; 978-1-894573; 978-0-929024; 978-1-897480; 978-1-77369) Dist. by* **LuluCom.**

Golden Monkey Publishing, LLC, *(978-0-9719632)* 24 Meadowood Ln., Old Saybrook, CT 06475 USA (SAN 254-5322)
Web site: http://www.goldenmonkeypublishing.com.

Golden Moon Design, *(978-0-692-93327-5)* 3815 N. Kedzie Ave. Unit 3S, Chicago, IL 60618 USA Tel 773-817-5386
E-mail: hemanshoe@gmail.com
Dist(s): **Ingram Content Group.**

Golden Oak Publishers *See* **Golden Oak Pubs. L.P.**

Golden Oak Pubs. L.P., *(978-1-929248; 978-1-936346)* Orders Addr.: P.O. Box 136967, Fort Worth, TX 76163 USA Tel 800-479-3545; Toll Free Fax: 800-479-3545
E-mail: MattS@goldenoakpublishers.com
Web site: http://www.HaroldBullock.com.

Golden Peach Publishing, *(978-1-930655)* 1223 Wilshire Blvd., #1510, Santa Monica, CA 90403 USA Tel 310-623-0835; 310-272-6809
E-mail: marketing@goldenpeachbooks.com; info@goldenpeachbooks.com; goldenpeachbooks@gmail.com
Web site: http://goldenpeachbooks.com.

Golden Perils Pr., *(978-0-615-15007-9; 978-0-615-19452-3; 978-0-578-00320-7; 978-0-578-00360-3; 978-0-578-00361-0)* 2 McKee Dr., Old Orchard Beach, ME 04064 USA Tel 207-934-3074
E-mail: goldenperils@aol.com
Web site: http://www.howardhopkins.com
Dist(s): **Lulu Pr., Inc.**

Golden Poppy Pubns., *(978-0-9890572; 978-1-945329)* 14313 Valley Vista Blvd., Sherman Oaks, CA 91423 USA Tel 818-501-8423
E-mail: dnehamen@gmail.com.

Golden Rain Tree Pr., *(978-0-9744107)* Div. of Leland Foerster Photography, 307 Fowles St., Oceanside, CA 92054 USA Tel 760-433-2554 (phone/fax)
E-mail: lelandfoerster@sbcglobal.net
Web site: http://www.lelandfoerster.com
Dist(s): **Sunbelt Pubns., Inc.**

Golden Seed Books LLC *See* **Coffee Seed Bks.**

Golden Triangle Bike, *(978-0-692-71596-3)* 600 First Ave, Pittsburgh, PA 15219 USA Tel 412-600-0675
E-mail: gapguide@bikepittsburgh.com
Web site: goldentrianglebike.com.

Golden Valley Pr., *(978-0-9718053)* 24905 Mica Ridge Rd., Custer, SD 57730 USA
E-mail: horsted@dakotaphoto.com
Web site: http://www.goldenvalleypress.com.

Golden Voice Enterprises, *(978-0-9643301)* 8503 Summerdale Rd., No. 371, San Diego, CA 92126 USA.

Golden West Publishers *Imprint of* **American Traveler Pr.**

Golden Wings Enterprises, *(978-0-9700103; 978-0-9749241; 978-0-9794340)* P.O. Box 468, Orem, UT 84059-0468 USA
E-mail: BJ@bjrowley.com
Web site: http://www.bjrowley.com.

Golden/Disney *Imprint of* **Random Hse. Children's Bks.**

Goldenrod Pr., *(978-0-9748333)* Orders Addr.: P.O. Box 71, Algona, IA 50511 USA Tel 515-295-7090; Edit Addr.: 2509 S. State St., Algona, IA 50511-7296 USA
E-mail: slotjm@yahoo.com.

Goldest Karat Publishing, *(978-1-939509)* 1700 Northside Dr NW Suite A-7, PMB 513, Atlanta, GA 30318 USA Tel 404-465-4120
E-mail: cswainbates@gmail.com; crystal@goldestkarat.com.

Goldhirsh, Julia, *(978-0-578-55290-3; 978-0-578-56704-4; 978-1-7351697)* 4739 NW 30th St., Coconut Creek, FL 33063 USA Tel 954-812-9644
E-mail: bluemoonroze@gmail.com.

Goldie McCoppertop Publishing, *(978-0-692-05348-5; 978-0-692-12354-6)* 2082 SE Bristol St No. 215, Newport Beach, CA 92660 USA Tel 949-636-5964
E-mail: goldiemccoppertop@gmail.com
Dist(s): **CreateSpace Independent Publishing Platform.**

GoldInk Pubs. LLC, *(978-1-956913)* 530-B HARKLE Rd. STE 100, SANTA FE, NM 87505 USA Tel 505-416-3028
E-mail: moiz.hassan123@yahoo.com
Web site: www.goldinkbooks.com.

Goldleaf Games, LLC, *(978-0-9748757)* P.O. Box 804, Lawrence, KS 66044 USA
E-mail: gary@goldleafgames.com
Web site: http://www.goldleafgames.com.

Goldman Agency, *(978-1-958066)* ¿244 Fifth Avenue, Suite H246, New York, NY 10001 USA Tel 718-285-8189
E-mail: kenjiedeguzman1990@gmail.com
Web site: www.goldmanagency.com.

Goldman Hse. Publishing, *(978-0-9815627; 978-0-9892935; 978-0-9864361; 978-0-9997331)* P.O. Box 6029-117, Artesia, CA 90702 USA
E-mail: goldmanhousepublishing@gmail.com.

Goldmann, Wilhelm Verlag GmbH (DEU) *(978-3-442) Dist. by* **Distribks Inc.**

Goldminds Publishing *Imprint of* **Amphorae Publishing Group**

Goldner, Harriet LLC, *(978-0-9779676)* P.O. Box 480003, Delray Beach, FL 33448 USA
E-mail: hgoldnerbooks@bellsouth.net
Web site: http://www.JewishFamilyFun.com.

Goldsberry, Booty, *(978-0-9792875)* 10 Windsor Pl., Poland, ME 04274 USA Tel 207-998-5710
E-mail: elattanzi@bookmasters.com.

GOLDSUN, LLC, *(978-0-578-96578-9)* 955 E LOBSTER TRAP LN St. Address 2, TEMPE, AZ 85283 USA Tel 480-532-4137
E-mail: tzisis@gmail.com.

GoldTouch Pr., *(978-1-7337013; 978-1-7337014; 978-1-7332264; 978-1-7332265; 978-1-7333366; 978-1-7333367; 978-1-7334028; 978-1-7334396; 978-1-951461; 978-1-952155; 978-1-953791; 978-1-954673; 978-1-955347; 978-1-955955; 978-1-956803; 978-1-957575; 978-1-959143) 420 Lexington Ave., Suite 300, New York, NY 10170 USA Tel 917-108-1114*
E-mail: arianna.parker@goldtouchpress.com
Web site: goldtouchpress.com.

Goldwrite Publishing, *(978-0-9767933; 978-0-615-13858-9; 978-1-7333188)* 11414 Vinea Ln., Hampton, GA 30228 USA Tel 678 510-6941
E-mail: asheagold@yahoo.com
Dist(s): **BookBaby**
Lulu Pr., Inc.

Golf Machine, Ltd.!, *(978-0-9829466)* 8381 S UPHAM WAY No. 103, Littleton, CO 80128 USA Tel 720-799-6816
E-mail: four_4aces@centurylink.net
Web site: http://warriorwong.com.

Golfing Bee, LLC, *(978-0-692-78420-4; 978-0-9983495)* 8815 First Bloom Rd., Charlotte, NC 28277 USA Tel 503-507-2712
E-mail: golfingbee45@gmail.com.

Golgotha Pr., *(978-1-61042; 978-1-62107; 978-1-62917)* 200 N. Ventura, Anaheim, CA 92801 USA Tel 714-404-7182
E-mail: Roboscott@gmail.com.

Golightly Publishing, *(978-0-9617721; 978-0-9966544; 978-1-7339277)* P.O. Box 181533, Dallas, TX 75218-1533 USA (SAN 665-1259) Tel 214-415-6156
E-mail: golightlyinfo@aol.com; david@sellbox.com.

Golly Gee-pers, *(978-0-9964175)* 923 Mountain View Dr., Lafayette, CA 94549 USA Tel 925-324-4418
E-mail: gollygee_pers@yahoo.com
Web site: http://www.gollygee-pers.com.

Golob, Julie, *(978-0-9996456)* 105 S. Jefferson St.,, Kearney, MO 64060 USA Tel 406-230-0824
E-mail: jgoloski@gmail.com
Web site: juliegolob.com.

Gom Foxtail *Imprint of* **Gom Publishing, LLC**

Gom Publishing, LLC, *(978-0-9729197; 978-1-932966)* P.O. Box 211110, Columbus, OH 43221 USA (SAN 255-3988) Tel 614-876-7097; Toll Free Fax: 866-422-8292; Toll Free: 866-466-2608; *Imprints:* Gom Foxtail (Gom Foxtail)
E-mail: sfox@gompublishing.com
Web site: http://www.gompublishing.com.

Gomer Pr. (GBR) *(978-0-85088; 978-0-86383; 978-1-85902; 978-1-84323; 978-1-84851) Dist. by* **Casemate Pubs.**

Gomez Expeditions, *(978-1-7321369; 978-1-7333160; 979-8-9857369; 979-8-9865374)* P.O. Box 246, Nash, TX 75569 USA Tel 910-286-8576
E-mail: sil.gomez@yahoo.com.

Goncalves, John, *(978-0-692-09746-5; 978-0-692-09747-2)* 406 12th Ave. SE, MINNEAPOLIS, MN 55414 USA Tel 401-257-9015
E-mail: john_goncalves@alumni.brown.edu
Dist(s): **Ingram Content Group.**

Gondolin Institute, *(978-1-945658)* 1331 Red Cedar Cir., Fort Collins, CO 80524 USA Tel 970-493-4840
E-mail: gondolinpress@hotmail.com
Web site: www.gondolinpress.com.

Gonsalves, Theresa Joyce, *(978-0-9762347; 978-1-62193)* 2725 Grafton Ct., LAS VEGAS, NV 89117 USA
E-mail: tjgmanage@gmail.com
Web site: http://www.theresagonsalves.com
Dist(s): **BCH Fulfillment & Distribution.**

Gonzalez, David J. Ministries, *(978-0-9741561)* P.O. Box 847, Lake Delton, WI 53940 USA Tel 608-254-5150
E-mail: dgm@mountainfaith.org
Web site: http://www.mountainfaith.org.

Good & True Media, *(978-1-7370796; 978-1-955492; 979-8-9874622)* 1520 S. York Rd, Gastonia, NC 28052 USA (SAN 992-1311) Tel 704-865-1256
E-mail: Goodandtruemedia@gmail.com
Web site: Www.goodandtruemedia.com
Dist(s): **Baker & Taylor Publisher Services (BTPS)**
Baker & Taylor Bks.
Saint Benedict Pr.

Good Beginnings Publishing, LLC, *(978-0-692-84463-2)* 5625 Platte Dr., Ellenwood, GA 30294 USA Tel 404-759-9002
E-mail: aleroa12@hotmail.com.

Good Bks. *Imprint of* **Skyhorse Publishing Co., Inc.**

Good Books *See* **Promise Pr.**

Good Catch Publishing, *(978-0-9772383; 978-0-9785152; 978-0-9792475; 978-1-934635; 978-1-938478; 978-1-68085)* Orders Addr.: P.O. Box 6551, Aloha, OR 97007 USA (SAN 257-0289) Tel 503-475-2005; Fax: 503-356-9685; Toll Free: 877-967-3224; Edit Addr.: 4074 NW 169th Ave., Beaverton, OR 97006 USA Fax: 503-356-9685; Toll Free: 877-967-3224
E-mail: nathanlindley@goodcatchpublishing.com; admingcp@gmail.com
Web site: http://www.goodcatchpublishing.com; http://www.testimonybooks.com.

Good Faith Media, *(978-1-938514; 978-1-63528)* P.O. Box PO Box 721972, Norman, OK 73070 USA Tel 478-719-1033
Web site: www.goodfaithmedia.org.

Good Fun Bks., *(978-0-9995591)* 6716 Gleason Ave. NW, Albuquerque, NM 87120-4409 USA Tel 505-321-8142
E-mail: csteiner5@msn.com
Web site: goodfunbooks.com.

Good Harbor Pr., *(978-0-9799638; 978-0-615-32057-1)* 80 Walsh St., Medford, MA 02155 USA Tel 781-396-1733.

Good Karma Publications *See* **Innerworld Pubns.**

Good MEWD Publishing, *(978-0-578-32261-2; 978-0-578-33095-2; 978-0-578-28599-3)* 465 Green Bay Rd., Highland Park, IL 60035 USA Tel 513-226-6247
E-mail: maggieduplace@yahoo.com.

Good MEWDS Publishing *See* **Good MEWD Publishing**

Good News Connections, *(978-0-9728900)* Orders Addr.: P.O. Box 66573, Austin, TX 78766 USA Toll Free: 888-899-3207 Do not confuse with The Good News Connections, Inc. in Orlando, FL
E-mail: stayton@xc.org
Web site: http://www.GoodNewsConnections.com.

Good News Fellowship Ministries, *(978-0-9629559; 978-1-888081; 978-1-7344999)* Div. of Funtasy Pubns., 220 Sleepy Creek Rd., Macon, GA 31210-5720 USA Tel 478-757-8071; Fax: 478-757-0136; Toll Free: 800-300-9630
E-mail: goodnews@reynoldscable.net
Web site: http://www.goodnews.netministries.org; http://kathiewaltersministry.com
Dist(s): **Anchor Distributors.**

Good News Productions, International, *(978-1-59305)* Orders Addr.: P.O. Box 222, Joplin, MO 64802-0222 USA Tel 417-782-0060; Fax: 417-782-3999; Edit Addr.: 2111 N. Main, Joplin, MO 64802-0222 USA
E-mail: gnpi@gnpi.org
Web site: http://www.gnpi.org.

Good Newz Dudez, *(978-0-9765568)* 4906 Hopespring Dr., Orlando, FL 32829 USA Tel 407-970-3828.

Good Night Bks., *(978-0-9777979; 978-1-60219)* 36 Route 6A, Sandwich, MA 02563 USA
E-mail: adam@goodnightourworld.com
Web site: http://goodnightbooks.com
Dist(s): **Islander Group**
MyiLibrary
Penguin Random Hse. Distribution
Penguin Random Hse. LLC
Random Hse., Inc.
ebrary, Inc.

Good Reading Bks., *(978-1-888042; 978-0-578-17942-1)* Div. of Southern Printing, Imaging & Typography, Inc., 153 Shady Oaks Dr., Lafayette, LA 70506 USA.

Good River Print & Media, *(978-1-956742)* 250 E. 5th St. 15th Flr., Cincinnati, OH 45202 USA Tel 614-321-8079
E-mail: info@goodriverprintandmedia.com.

Good Roots Publishing, *(978-0-9745187)* Orders Addr.: P.O. Box 3493, Homer, AK 99603-3493 USA Tel 907-235-5283; Edit Addr.: 62315 Fireweed Ave., Homer, AK 99603-3493 USA
Dist(s): **Wizard Works.**

Good Sound Publishing, *(978-0-9821563; 978-1-935743)* 295 Olive Ave., Palo Alto, CA 94306 USA Fax: 650-227-2320; Toll Free: 888-686-2669
E-mail: info@goodsoundpublishing.com
Web site: http://www.goodsoundpublishing.com.

Good Stories Publishing, *(978-0-9777135; 978-1-7370092)* 8120 N. Lehigh Ave. Suite 100, Morton Grove, IL 60053 USA (SAN 853-0688) Tel 773-405-3748
E-mail: marlenefbyrne@gmail.com
Web site: https://www.marlenebyrne.com; http://www.projectplaybooks.com; http://www.musichaslegs.com; http://www.goodstoriespublishing.com.

Good Stories Publishing LLC *See* **Good Stories Publishing**

Good Success Publishing, *(978-0-9837895; 978-0-9978332; 978-1-7355882)* P.O. Box 134, Oxon Hill, MD 20750 USA Tel 301-467-8885
E-mail: info@drcelesteowens.com
Web site: www.drcelesteowens.com
Dist(s): **BookBaby.**

Good Thoughts Publishing *See* **Cardinal Pr.**

Good Times at Home LLC, *(978-0-9840338)* 1933 Hwy. 35 Suite 105-335, Belmar, NJ 07719 USA Tel 732-803-1902
E-mail: vinnie@vinniecurto.com.

Good Turn Publishing, *(978-0-9794393)* 1 Bancroft Rd., Wellesley, MA 02481 USA
Web site: http://www.goodturnpublishing.com.

Good Witch of Salem LLC, *(978-1-7352318; 979-8-9879927)* 36 BEACH AVE, SWAMPSCOTT, MA 01907 USA Tel 978-500-0383
E-mail: goodwitchofsalem@gmail.com
Web site: www.goodwitchofsalem.com.

Good Works Pr., *(978-0-9634472; 978-1-888572)* 4121 Whitfield Ave., Fort Worth, TX 76109 USA Tel 817-927-8808.

Good Works Publishing Hse., *(978-0-9744733)* P.O. Box 52217, Houston, TX 77052-2217 USA Tel 832-267-7366; 346-234-3031
E-mail: wonderlandhudson@yahoo.com.

Good Year Bks. *Imprint of* **Celebration Pr.**

Good Year Bks., *(978-1-59647)* P.O. Box 91858, Tucson, AZ 85752-1858 USA (SAN 854-4050) Toll Free Fax: 888-511-1501; Toll Free: 888-511-1530
E-mail: publisher@goodyearbooks.com; sales@goodyearbooks.com; marketing@goodyearbooks.com; orders@goodyearbooks.com
Web site: http://www.goodyearbooks.com.

Goodall, Barry, *(978-0-9763932)* 218 Tucker Sta. Rd, Louisville, KY 40243 USA Tel 502-817-8530
E-mail: bgoodal1@jefferson.k12.ky.us.

Goode, Ty *See* **Tytam Publishing**

Goodheart-Willcox Pub., *(978-0-87006; 978-1-56637; 978-1-59070; 978-1-60525; 978-1-61960; 978-1-63126; 978-1-68311; 978-1-63563; 978-1-64564; 978-1-64925; 978-1-63776; 978-1-68584; 979-8-88817; 979-8-88999; 979-8-89118)* Orders Addr.: 18604 West Creek Dr., Tinley Park, IL 60477-6243 USA (SAN 203-4387) Tel

708-687-5000; Fax: 708-687-5068; Toll Free Fax: 888-409-3900; Toll Free: 800-323-0440
E-mail: custserv@g-w.com; jff@g-w.com
Web site: http://www.g-w.com.

GoodLife Publishing, *(978-1-934345)* Div. of NF Publishing, P.O. Box 1622, Mt Carmel, TN 36745 USA Tel 423-299-3034; Fax: 800-807-9203; Toll Free Fax: 800-807-9203
E-mail: stacey.kohan@theremoteservice.com
Web site: http://www.southwestpublications.net.

goodluck, marquita Publishing, *(978-0-692-19580-2; 978-0-692-19942-8; 978-0-578-59017-2)* 14111 Arbor Forest Dr., Rockville, MD 20850 USA Tel 240-383-7687
E-mail: marquita.goodluck@gmail.com
Dist(s): **Ingram Content Group.**

Goodman, Kathleen, *(978-1-7336080)* 2328 10th Ave E, Seattle, WA 98102 USA Tel 615-708-4238
E-mail: mkgoodman11@gmail.com.

goodman, peggy, *(978-0-9990606)* 212 windsor ave, glasgow, KY 42141 USA Tel 270-651-6366
E-mail: cag3@glasgow-ky.com.

Goodmedia Communications, LLC, *(978-0-615-60107-6; 978-0-9883237; 978-0-9911148; 978-1-7327046; 979-8-9852429)* 25 Highland Pk. Village, No. 100-810, Dallas, TX 75205 USA Tel 214-240-4503
E-mail: info@goodmediapress.com
Web site: www.GoodMediaPress.com.

Goodness Experience, The, *(978-0-9653077; 978-0-692-27102-5; 978-0-692-03668-6)* 2101 Palm Canyon Ct., Las Vegas, NV 89117-1941 USA.

Goodreads Pr., *(978-1-63292)* 454 W. 44, New York, NY 10036 USA Tel 212-713-1633
E-mail: susan@schulmanagency.com.

Goodtimes Software *See* **GT Interactive Software**

Goodwin, Brian, *(978-0-615-16104-4)* 53-823 Kamehameha Hwy., Hauula, HI 96717-9658 USA
Dist(s): **Lulu Pr., Inc.**

Goodwin, Evelyn, *(978-0-615-16145-7; 978-0-615-16344-4)* 2345 Ala Wai Blvd. Apt. 917, Honolulu, HI 96815-5017 USA
Dist(s): **Lulu Pr., Inc.**

goodworksebooks.com, *(978-0-9773192)* 3084 CR 310, Brazoria, TX 77422 USA
Web site: http://goodworksebooks.com.

GoodyGoody Bks., *(978-0-9702546; 978-0-9995920)* P.O. Box 1073, Sun City, AZ 85372-1073 USA
E-mail: charlie-the-cat@cox.net
Web site: http://www.charliethecat.com.

Goodykoontz, Jared, *(978-0-692-04422-3; 978-0-578-45862-5; 978-0-578-54505-9)* 10520 Shields Rd., Ostrander, OH 43061 USA Tel 614-315-5258
E-mail: Jaredgoodykoontz@gmail.com
Dist(s): **Ingram Content Group.**

Goofy Guru Publishing, *(978-0-9726130)* 405 Kiowa Pl., Boulder, CO 80303 USA.

Google, *(978-1-201; 978-1-227; 978-1-122; 978-1-180; 978-1-181; 978-1-182; 978-1-183; 978-1-184; 978-1-185; 978-1-186; 978-1-187; 978-1-188; 978-1-189; 978-1-190; 978-1-191; 978-1-192; 978-1-193; 978-1-194; 978-1-195; 978-1-196; 978-1-197; 978-1-198; 978-1-199; 978-1-200; 978-1-202; 978-1-203; 978-1-204; 978-1-205; 978-1-206; 978-1-207; 978-1-208; 978-1-209; 978-1-210; 978-1-211; 978-1-212; 978-1-213; 978-1-214; 978-1-215; 978-1-216; 978-1-217; 978-1-218; 978-1-219; 978-1-220; 978-1-221; 978-1-123;) 1600 Amphitheatre Pkwy., Mountain View, CA 94043 USA; 440 Broadway, 21st Flr., New York, NY 10018.*

Goon Dog Publishing, *(978-0-9791612)* 309 W. 14th, Suite 32, New York, NY 10014-0014 USA (SAN 852-6206) Tel 212-645-2096
E-mail: monk@ispwest.com
Web site: http://owenopolis.com.

Goops Unlimited, *(978-0-9712368; 978-0-9834865)* P.O. Box 1809, Battle Ground, WA 98604-1809 USA Tel 360-687-1891; Fax: 360-687-2097; Toll Free: 800-861-1891
E-mail: barbara@thegoops.com
Web site: http://www.thegoops.com.

Goose Creek Pubs., Inc., *(978-1-59633)* 4227 Vermont Ave., Louisville, KY 40211 USA Tel 502-714-9985
E-mail: wanda@goosecreekpublishers.com
Web site: http://www.goosecreekpublishers.com.

Goose River Pr., *(978-1-930648; 978-1-59713)* 3400 Friendship Rd., Waldoboro, ME 04572 USA Tel 207-832-6665
E-mail: gooseriverpress@gmail.com
Web site: http://www.gooseriverpress.com
Dist(s): **Ingram Content Group.**

Gooseberry Patch *Imprint of* **Rowman & Littlefield Publishers, Inc.**

Goosebottom Bks. LLC, *(978-0-9845098; 978-0-9834256; 978-1-937463)* P.O. Box 150764, San Rafael, CA 94915 USA (SAN 859-8029)
E-mail: info@goosebottombooks.com; mamagoose@goosebottombooks.com
Web site: http://www.goosebottombooks.com
Dist(s): **Publishers Group West (PGW).**

GoPublish *Imprint of* **Visual Adjectives**

GORDON, JESSICA *See* **Mountain Bell Pr.**

Gordon Rocket, *(978-1-941037)* P.O. Box 120023, Chula, CA 91912 USA Tel 619-272-8235
E-mail: mxreynoso@gmail.com
Web site: gordonrocket.com.

Gordon, Scott, *(978-0-9963574)* 30 Serenity Ln., Laguna Niguel, CA 92677 USA Tel 949-280-2799
E-mail: repioneer32@gmail.com.

Goretti Publishing, *(978-0-9778451)* Orders Addr.: 1150 N. Loop 1604 W., Ste. 108-410, San Antonio, TX 78248 USA (SAN 850-3176) Tel 210-274-2769; Fax: 210-493-6080 attn: 410
E-mail: publishedworks@aol.com
Web site: http://www.thetexasmermaid.com
Dist(s): **Bk. Marketing Plus.**

Gorgias Pr., LLC, *(978-0-9713097; 978-0-9715986; 978-1-931956; 978-1-59333; 978-1-60724; 978-1-61719; 978-1-61143; 978-1-4632)* 954 River Rd., Piscataway, NJ 08854-5504 USA (SAN 853-0629)
E-mail: info@gorgiaspress.com; sales@gorgiaspress.com
Web site: http://www.gorgiaspress.com
Dist(s): **De Gruyter, Inc.**
ebrary, Inc.

Gormer, Jennifer Hobson, *(978-0-692-96829-1)* P.O. Box 382623, DUNCANVILLE, TX 75138 USA Tel 972-302-0082
E-mail: hobson.jennifer@gmail.com
Dist(s): **Ingram Content Group.**

Gormley Publishing, *(978-0-9794500; 978-0-9827503; 978-0-692-61920-9)* Orders Addr.: 1520 Courtney Dr., Washington Court House, OH 43160-8920 USA
Web site: http://www.gormleypublishing.com.

Gorp Group Pr., The, *(978-0-9724249)* 7450 OLIVETAS Ave. No. 386, LA JOLLA, CA 92037 USA Tel 858-412-4424; 208-720-7980; Toll Free: 888-729-4677
E-mail: gorp2@earthlink.net
Web site: http://www.thegorp.com.

†Gospel Advocate Co., *(978-0-89225)* Orders Addr.: 1006 Elm Hill Pike, Nashville, TN 37210 USA (SAN 205-2792) Tel 615-254-8781; Fax: 615-254-7411; Toll Free: 800-251-8446; Edit Addr.: 1006 Elm Hill Pike, Nashville, TN 37210 USA (SAN 662-0213)
E-mail: jodie.duke@gospeladvocate.com
Web site: http://www.gospeladvocate.com; *CIP.*

Gospel Advocate Company, Incorporated *See* **Gospel Advocate Co.**

Gospel Grown, *(978-1-7336615)* 974 Breckenridge Ln. No. 295, Louisville, KY 40207-4619 USA Tel 502-514-9513
E-mail: contact@gospelgrown.org
Web site: www.gospelgrown.org.

Gospel Light *Imprint of* **Gospel Light Pubns.**

Gospel Light Pubns., *(978-0-8307)* Orders Addr.: 1957 Eastman Ave., Ventura, CA 93003 USA (SAN 299-0873) Tel 805-644-9721; Fax: 805-289-0200; Toll Free: 800-446-7735 (orders only); *Imprints:* Gospel Light (Gospel Light); Regal Books (Regal Bks) Do not confuse with companies with similar names in Brooklyn, NY, Delight, AR
E-mail: info@gospellight.com; kyleloffelmacher@gospellight.com
Web site: http://www.gospellight.com
Dist(s): **Christian Bk. Distributors**
Cook, David C.
Faith Alive Christian Resources.

Gospel Missionary Union, *(978-0-9617490; 978-1-890940)* 10000 N. Oak Trafficway, Kansas City, MO 64155 USA (SAN 664-1830) Tel 816-734-8500; Fax: 816-734-4601
E-mail: info@gmu.org
Web site: http://www.gmu.org.

†Gospel Publishing Hse., *(978-0-88243; 978-1-60731)* Div. of General Council of the Assemblies of God, 1445 N. Boonville Ave., Springfield, MO 65802-1894 USA (SAN 206-8826) Tel 417-862-2781; Fax: 417-862-5881; Toll Free Fax: 800-328-0294; Toll Free: 800-641-4310 (orders only)
E-mail: webmaster@gph.com
Web site: http://www.gospelpublishing.com
Dist(s): **Appalachian Bible Co.**
Baker & Taylor Publisher Services (BTPS)
Ingram Publisher Services
Lulu Pr., Inc.
MyiLibrary
Spring Arbor Distributors, Inc.; *CIP.*

Gospel Puzzles *See* **Cluster Storm Publishing**

Goss, Nicholas, *(978-1-7321815)* 100 Hiram Ct, Spring Hill, TN 37174 USA Tel 615-596-6923
E-mail: nickthegoss@gmail.com.

Gossamer Bks., *(978-0-9729016)* 444 Eastwood Dr., Petaluma, CA 94954 USA (SAN 255-2671) Tel 707-765-1992; Fax: 707-765-6507 Do not confuse with Gossamer Books LLC in Belmont, CA
E-mail: dcr530@cs.com.

Gossamer Bks., LLC, *(978-0-9742502)* P.O. Box 455, Belmont, CA 94002 USA Fax: 650-257-4058 Do not confuse with Gossamer Books in Petaluma, CA
E-mail: info@gossamerbooks.com
Web site: http://www.gossamerbooks.com.

Gossamer Wings Pr., *(978-1-7321544)* 23 Telfair Dr., Beaufort, SC 29907 USA Tel 859-644-7077
E-mail: rjchamberlain71@gmail.com
Web site: www.rchamberlainart.com.

Gosselin, Matthew S., *(978-0-692-07476-3; 978-0-692-07483-1; 978-0-692-09304-7; 978-0-692-09305-4; 978-0-578-67389-9)* 872 Cropoked Branch Dr., CLERMONT, FL 34711 USA Tel 407-504-8253
E-mail: mattgosselin@gmail.com
Web site: http://www.MattGosselin.com
Dist(s): **Ingram Content Group.**

Gotham *Imprint of* **Penguin Publishing Group**

Gothenburg Bks., *(978-1-7327275; 978-1-7338677; 978-1-7333061)* 1797 Channing Ave, PALO ALTO, CA 94303 USA Tel 650-561-4101
E-mail: jillianbeckerwriter@gmail.com.

Gothic Image Pubns. (GBR) *(978-0-906362) Dist. by* **SCB Distributo.**

Gottabeareason *See* **Rhodes, Candice Sumner**

Gottlieb, Rachel E, *(978-0-692-60407-6)* 62 Old Orchard Ln., Scarsdale, NY 10583 USA Tel 917-494-7236
E-mail: raycraz1@gmail.com.

Goulart-Johnston, Michelle, *(978-0-9980932)* 1375 E Grand Ave. No. 318, Arroyo Grande, CA 93420 USA Tel 805-539-9214
E-mail: michgoulart@gmail.com.

Goulasche Pr., *(978-0-9771466)* 1352 Ithilien, Excelsior, MN 55331 USA.

Gourley, Deb Nelson *See* **Astri My Astri Publishing**

Govinda Yoga Play, *(978-0-692-16098-5; 978-1-7326062)* 10 Faye Cir., Marblehead, MA 01945 USA Tel 781-639-3543
E-mail: ajgiven@comcast.net
Dist(s): **Ingram Content Group.**

Gozo Bks. *Imprint of* **Premio Publishing & Gozo Bks., LLC**

Gozo Books, LLC *See* **Premio Publishing & Gozo Bks., LLC**

G.P. Hoffman Publishing, *(978-0-9798230)* 2224 Heather Ln., Lincoln, NE 68512 USA.

G.P. Putnam's Sons *Imprint of* **Penguin Publishing Group**

G.P. Putnam's Sons Books for Young Readers *Imprint of* **Penguin Young Readers Group**

Grace & Mercy Publishing, *(978-0-9672049; 978-0-9764763)* Orders Addr.: P.O. Box 11531, Fort Wayne, IN 46857 USA; Edit Addr.: 7408 Mill Run, Suite B, Fort Wayne, IN 46819 USA.

Grace Contrino Abrams Peace Education Foundation *See* **Peace Education Foundation**

Grace Hse. Pr., *(978-0-9995368; 978-1-7332888)* P.O. Box PO Box 1699, Maple Grove, MN 55113 USA
E-mail: bethanyatazadeh@yahoo.com
Web site: www.bethanyatazadeh.com.

Grace Hse. Publishing, *(978-0-9633633)* Div. of R. Allan McCauley Law Office, 6237 N. 15th St., Phoenix, AZ 85014 USA Tel 602-265-9151 Do not confuse with Grace House Publishing in Mahomet, IL.

Grace Publishing, *(978-0-9769985)* P.O. Box 17980, Seattle, WA 98123 USA (SAN 256-6257) Tel 206-818-9769 Do not confuse with companies with the same name in Farmington Hills, MI, Broken Arrow, OK, Waldorf, MD, Richmond, VA, Elma, NY, Woodinville, WA & New Prague, MN
E-mail: vonukk@comcast.net
Web site: http://www.rcberg.com.

Grace to Grow Pubns., *(978-0-9709488; 978-0-9745499; 978-0-9764247; 978-0-9778936; 978-0-9800594; 978-0-9819603; 978-1-62289)* Orders Addr.: 507 State St., Hammond, IN 46320 USA Tel 219-932-0711
E-mail: carol.hunter@pulseprint.org; abby.amoros@pulseprint.org
Web site: https://gracetogrowpublications.com; http://www.pulseprint.org.

Grace Walk Ministries *See* **Grace Walk Resources, LLC**

Grace Walk Resources, LLC, *(978-0-9664736)* Orders Addr.: P.O. Box 6537, Douglasville, GA 30135 USA Tel 800-472-2311; Toll Free: 800-472-2311
E-mail: info@gracewalk.org
Web site: http://www.gracewalk.org.

Graceffa, Leilani, *(978-1-7335558; 978-1-7350952; 978-0-578-76251-7)* 167 Brooklyn Way, Pooler, GA 31322 USA Tel 912-508-6700
E-mail: Japanesemagnolia@icloud.com.

Gracefully Global Group LLC, *(978-0-9834760; 978-0-9973090; 979-8-9856862)* 22568 Mission Blvd No. 427, Hayward, CA 94541 USA Tel 510-967-3339; Fax: 5109273044
E-mail: grace@gracefullyglobal.com; thewonderlady@gmail.com
Web site: http://www.latinnovating.com/; http://www.captainmama.com/; http://www.gracefullyglobal.com/
Dist(s): **Ingram Content Group.**

Gracelight Pr. LLC, *(978-1-952832; 978-1-64984)* 3550 CAMPUS ST, PITTSBURGH, PA 15212-2266 USA Tel 512-237-7349
E-mail: Jeffkid@126.com.

GraceNotes Pr. *Imprint of* **New Shelves Bks.**

GraceWorks Interactive, *(978-0-9760548; 978-1-935915)* P.O. Box 2613, Corvallis, OR 97339-2613 USA Toll Free: 877-785-3496 (phone/fax)
E-mail: tim@graceworksinteractive.com
Web site: http://www.graceworksinteractive.com.

Grady Bunch Bks., LLC, *(978-0-9990075)* 7887 N. 16th St. 204, Phoenix, AZ 85020 USA Tel 602-475-1718
E-mail: joannegrady@gmail.com.

Graffeg Limited (GBR) *(978-0-9544334; 978-1-905582; 978-1-909823) Dist. by* **IPG Chicago.**

grafixCORP, *(978-0-9778374)* Orders Addr.: P.O. Box 1441, Mount Vernon, WA 98273-9827 USA
Web site: http://www.grafixCORP.com.

Grafton and Scratch Pubs. (CAN) *(978-0-9879023; 978-0-9881216; 978-1-927979; 978-1-926495) Dist. by* **BTPS.**

Graham Bay, Jeanette, *(978-0-9771210)* 770 Victor Rd., Macedon, NY 14502 USA.

Graham Cracker Kids, *(978-0-9716475; 978-0-615-11409-5)* 1661 Hunt Rd., El Cajon, CA 92019 USA Tel 619-258-7571; Fax: 619-258-5412
E-mail: grmcrkrkds@aol.com
Web site: http://www.grahamcrackerkids.com.

Graham, D. A., *(978-1-7328819; 978-1-7362483; 979-8-9859164)* 1101 Deer Valley Ln., Arlington, TX 76001 USA Tel 817-846-2853
E-mail: gramedia54@yahoo.com.

Graham, Inna, 13825 Robinson Ct., Oklahoma City, OK 73170 USA Tel 405-602-4984
E-mail: Inna.shch@gmail.com
Dist(s): **Ingram Content Group.**

Graham, Rita, *(978-0-578-13165-8)*.

Grain Valley Press *See* **Grain Valley Publishing**

Grain Valley Publishing, *(978-1-7323047)* 1818 W. 18th St. No. 291, Wichita, KS 67203 USA Tel 316-734-7196
E-mail: grainvalleypress@gmail.com
Web site: www.GrantOverstake.com.

Grampa Jones's Publishing Co., *(978-0-9748266; 978-0-615-11169-8; 978-0-9893868)* P.O. Box 93, Heron, MT 59844-0093 USA (SAN 214-4700)
Web site: http://www.become-a-millionaire.com.

Gran Gran Series, *(978-0-9840237)* 8549 Hartham Pk. Ave., Raleigh, NC 27616 USA Tel 919-295-4750
E-mail: mhopkins25@nc.rr.com.

Grand Bks., Inc., *(978-0-930809)* P.O. Box 212, Crystal, MI 48818 USA (SAN 677-6361) Tel 517-875-4674; 517-235-4427
E-mail: jwrites@yahoo.com.

Grand Canyon Association *See* **Grand Canyon Conservancy**

Grand Canyon Conservancy, *(978-0-938216; 978-1-934656)* Orders Addr.: P.O. Box 399, Grand Canyon, AZ 86023-0399 USA (SAN 215-7675) Tel 928-638-7141; 928-863-3893; Fax: 928-638-2494; Toll Free: 800-858-2808
E-mail: aorrison@grandcanyon.org; cspivey@grandcanyon.org
Web site: http://www.grandcanyon.org.

Grand Canyon Orphan, *(978-0-9764260)* P.O. Box 438, Mina, NV 89422 USA
E-mail: info@grandcanyonorphan.com
Web site: http://www.grandcanyonorphan.com.

†Grand Central Publishing, *(978-0-445; 978-0-446; 978-0-7595; 978-1-4555; 978-1-5387; 978-1-5460)* Orders Addr.: c/o Little Brown & Co., 3 Center Plaza, Boston, MA 02108-2084 USA Toll Free Fax: 800-286-9471; Toll Free: 800-759-0190; Edit Addr.: 237 Park Ave., New York, NY 10017 USA (SAN 281-8892) Fax: 800-331-1664; Toll Free Fax: 800-759-0190; 1290 Avenue of the Americas, New York, NY 10104; *Imprints:* Mysterious Press (MysteriousPr); Vision (VisionC); Business Plus (Busn Plus); Forever (Forever); Sixth Avenue Books (SixthAveBks); Aspect (Aspect); Walk Worthy Press (WalkWorthy)
E-mail: renee.supriano@twbg.com; customer.service@hbgusa.com
Web site: http://www.hbgusa.com
Dist(s): **Blackstone Audio, Inc.**
Children's Plus, Inc.
Findaway World, LLC
Follett School Solutions
Hachette Bk. Group
Lectorum Pubns., Inc.
Libros Sin Fronteras
Little Brown & Co.
MyiLibrary
Norton, W. W. & Co., Inc.
Open Road Integrated Media, Inc.
Perelandra, Ltd.
Beeler, Thomas T. Pub.
TextStream
Thorndike Pr.
iPublish.com; *CIP.*

Grand County Historical Assn., *(978-1-7322461)* P.O. Box 165, Hot Sulphur Springs, CO 80451 USA Tel 970-725-3939
E-mail: shanna@grandcountyhistory.org
Web site: grandcountyhistory.org.

Grand Daisy Pr., *(978-0-9848608; 978-0-9962843)* 625 Stetson Rd., Elkins Park, PA 19027-2524 USA Tel 215-380-6710
E-mail: karenptoz@gmail.com
Web site: www.granddaisypress.com; www.karentoz.com.

Grand Hank Productions, Inc., *(978-0-9767236)* P.O. Box 23488, Philadelphia, PA 19143 USA Tel 215-724-5260
Web site: http://www.grandhank.com.

Grand Kidz, The *Imprint of* **Vertical Connect Pr.**

Grand Marais Publishing, *(978-0-615-34796-7)* 1441 Huntington Dr., No. 234, South Pasadena, CA 91030 USA Tel 626-441-1154
E-mail: grandmaraispublishing@gmail.com.

GRAND Media, LLC, *(978-0-930507; 978-0-615-51541-0)* 4791 Baywood Point Dr. S., Gulfport, FL 33711 USA (SAN 670-963X) Tel 727-327-9039; Fax: 727-323-9587
E-mail: jonmicocci@att.net
Web site: http://www.deathfromchildabuse.com.

Grand Productions, *(978-0-9795386)* 1914 Karly Ct., Panama City, FL 32405 USA (SAN 853-7194).

Grand Teton Assn., *(978-0-931895; 978-1-940093)* P.O. Box 170, Moose, WY 83012 USA (SAN 686-0303) Tel 307-739-3606; Fax: 307-739-3423
E-mail: grte_assoc@partner.nps.gov
Web site: http://www.grandtetonpark.org.

Grand Teton Natural History Association *See* **Grand Teton Assn.**

Grand Valley State Univ., *(978-0-9709811)* 1 Campus Dr., 107 Lake Superior Hall, Allendale, MI 49401 USA Tel 616-895-3488
E-mail: royer@river.it.gvsu.edu
Dist(s): **Michigan State Univ. Pr.**

Grandfeather Pr., *(978-0-9832355)* 1221 S. 7th St., Renton, WA 98057 USA Tel 425-902-1852
E-mail: publishing@grandfeather.com
Web site: www.grandfeather.com
Dist(s): **Ingram Content Group.**

Grandin Bk. Co., *(978-0-910523)* P.O. Box 2206, Provo, UT 84603-2206 USA (SAN 260-1931) Tel 801-225-2020; Fax: 801-222-0176; Toll Free: 800-292-2003.

Grandkidsandme, Inc., *(978-0-9741710)* 1764 Hampshire Ave., Saint Paul, MN 55116 USA (SAN 255-3902) Tel 651-695-1988; Fax: 651-699-5966
E-mail: don@grandkidsandme.com
Web site: http://www.grandkidsandme.com.

Grandma Chubby's Bks., *(978-0-9728535)* P.O. Box 902308, Sandy, UT 84090-2308 USA Tel 801-571-6617; Fax: 801-571-2285
E-mail: lsashby@juno.com
Dist(s): **Granite Publishing & Distribution.**

"Grandma's Hope Notes", *(978-0-9677477)* P.O. Box 868, Anchor Point, AK 99556 USA Tel 907-235-0502 (phone/fax).

Grandoc Publishing, *(978-0-9761739)* 3923 Hidden Way NE, Rochester, MN 55906-5590 USA Tel 507-287-9121
E-mail: grandoc@mac.com; drjohngraner@mac.com.

Grandpa Gardener Publishing Co., *(978-1-935427)* 745 W Calle Las Tunas, Sahuarita, AZ 85629-8712 USA
Web site: http://www.grandpagardener.com.

Grandreams Bks., Inc., *(978-1-59340)* Div. of Robert Frederick, 360 Hurst St., Linden, NJ 07036 USA (SAN 254-9832) Fax: 908-523-0373
E-mail: ssullivan@grandreamsbooks.com.

Granite Publishing & Distribution, *(978-1-890558; 978-1-930980; 978-1-932280; 978-1-59936)* 868 N. 1430 W., Orem, UT 84057 USA (SAN 631-0605) Tel 801-229-9023; Fax: 801-229-1924; Toll Free:

800-574-5779 Do not confuse with companies with same or similar names in Madison, WI, Columbus, NC
E-mail: granite@granitepublishing.biz; gregg@granitepublishing.biz
Web site: http://granitepublishing.biz.

ranite Publishing, LLC, *(978-0-926524; 978-0-9632310; 978-1-893183)* P.O. Box 1429, Columbus, NC 28722 USA Tel 828-894-3088; Fax: 828-894-8454; Toll Free: 800-366-0264; *Imprints:* Wild Flower Press (Wild Flower Pr) Do not confuse with companies with same or similar names in Madison, WI, Orem, UT, Siloam Springs, AR
E-mail: brian@5thworld.com
Web site: http://www.5thworld.com
Dist(s): **New Leaf Distributing Co., Inc.**
Smashwords.

iranity Studios, *(978-1-949520)* 10 Park Terr. E., New York, NY 10034 USA Tel 646-221-2714
Dist(s): **Two Rivers Distribution.**

irannie Annie Family Story Celebration, The, *(978-0-9677685; 978-0-9793296; 978-0-9969394)* P.O. Box 11343, Saint Louis, MO 63105 USA Tel 314-550-6396; Fax: 636-527-2822
E-mail: familystories@thegrannieannie.org
Web site: http://www.TheGrannieAnnie.org.

iranny's Pub Co., *(978-0-9749950)* P.O. Box 1701, Granbury, TX 76048 USA Tel 817-605-9004; Fax: 817-605-1180
E-mail: granny@loralie.com
Web site: http://www.loralie.com.

Grano Salas, *(978-0-692-61295-8; 978-0-692-61296-5; 978-0-692-65013-4; 978-0-692-66349-3; 978-0-692-66825-2; 978-1-7333784)* P.O. Box 4255, Arcata, CA 95518 USA Tel 707-223-5986
E-mail: anthonytovell@gmail.com
Dist(s): **CreateSpace Independent Publishing Platform.**

Grant, Irma, *(978-0-9996033)* 848 Sylvaner Dr., Pleasanton, CA 94566 USA Tel 919-460-5301
E-mail: irmawgrant@gmail.com
Web site: www.irmagrant.com.

Grant, Melinda Gail *See* **Keebie Pr.**

Grant, Tahlonna *See* **BeanSprout Bks.**

Grape Elephant MarketPr., *(978-0-9760646)* 13025 Ct. Pl., Burnsville, MN 55337 USA Tel 612-281-2566
E-mail: jill@grapeelephant.com
Web site: http://www.grapeelephant.com.

Graph Publishing, *(978-1-7359608)* 510 Ave. I, Lawn, TX 79530 USA Tel 325-583-2784
E-mail: deana_carmack@yahoo.com.

Graphic Arts Bks. *Imprint of* **West Margin Pr.**

Graphic Arts Books *See* **West Margin Pr.**

Graphic Expressions *See* **Graphics North**

Graphic Novels *Imprint of* **Spotlight**

Graphic Planet *Imprint of* **ABDO Publishing Co.**

Graphic Planet - Fiction *Imprint of* **Magic Wagon**

Graphic Universe™ *Imprint of* **Lerner Publishing Group**

Graphically Speaking, Inc., *(978-0-9729975)* 15509 Lloyd St., Omaha, NE 68144 USA Tel 402-330-1144; Fax: 402-334-3311
E-mail: fontstudios@cox.net
Web site: http://www.fontstudios.com.

Graphics North, *(978-0-9643452; 978-0-615-29759-0; 978-0-9829503)* P.O. Box 218, Jay, NY 12941 USA Tel 518-946-7741
E-mail: graphicsnorth@yahoo.com
Web site: graphicsnorth.com.

Graphics North, *(978-0-692-79724-2)* 42 Mela Ln., Rancho Palos Verdes, CA 90275 USA Tel 310-780-0643
E-mail: brengreen@gmail.com.

Graphic-Sha (JPN) *(978-4-7661) Dist. by* **Diamond Book Dists.**

Graphic-Sha (JPN) *(978-4-7661) Dist. by* **D C D.**

Graphic International, Inc., *(978-0-916189)* 8780 19th St., No. 199, Alto Loma, CA 91701 USA (SAN 294-9342) Tel 909-987-1921; Fax: 435-514-5975
E-mail: lmartres@phototripusa.com
Web site: http://www.phototripusa.com
Dist(s): **Bks. West**
Canyonlands Pubns.
Mountain n' Air Bks.

Graphis, U.S., Inc., *(978-1-888001; 978-1-931241; 978-1-932026; 978-1-954632)* Orders Addr.: c/o ABDI, Inc., Buncher Commerce Pk. Ave. A, Bldg. 16, Leetsdale, PA 15056-1304 USA Tel 412-741-3679; Fax: 412-741-0934; Toll Free: 800-209-4234 (for Canada & USA); Edit Addr.: 389 5th Ave., Suite No. 1105, New York, NY 10016 USA Tel 212-532-9387 (ext. 226)
Web site: http://www.graphis.com
Dist(s): **Consortium Bk. Sales & Distribution**
Innovative Logistics
National Bk. Network
Watson-Guptill Pubns., Inc.

Graphite Pr., *(978-0-9755810; 978-1-938313)* 2025 Lexington Parkway, Niskayuna, NY 12309-4205 USA (SAN 256-0712) Tel 518-303-6006
E-mail: publish@graphitepress.com
Web site: http://graphitepress.com.

Graphix *Imprint of* **Scholastic, Inc.**

Graphix Network, *(978-0-9740673; 978-0-9752832; 978-0-9762301; 978-0-9777043)* Orders Addr.: P.O. Box 2745, Evans, GA 30809 USA Tel 706-210-1000; Fax: 706-210-1111; Edit Addr.: 4104 Colben Blvd., Suite C, Evans, GA 30809 USA Tel 706-210-1000; Fax: 706-210-1111
E-mail: graphixnetwork@hotmail.com; sales@graphixnetwork.com
Web site: http://www.graphixnetwork.com.

Grappling Arts Pubns., LLC, *(978-0-9721097)* 1282 Watson Ave., Costa Mesa, CA 92626 USA
E-mail: info@grapplingarts.net
Web site: http://www.grapplingarts.net
Dist(s): **Baker & Taylor Publisher Services (BTPS)**
Cardinal Pubs. Group.

Grass Root Enterprises, *(978-1-886075)* 16315 Forest Way Dr., Houston, TX 77090-4716 USA Tel 281-444-4103; Fax: 281-444-5804.

Grassdale Publishers, Incorporated *See* **Saxon Pubs., Inc.**

Grasshopper Dream Productions, *(978-0-615-12337-0; 978-0-615-12724-8; 978-0-615-35616-7)* Orders Addr.: P.O. Box 1831, Saint Petersburg, FL 33731-1831 USA Tel 813-382-4230; Edit Addr.: 121 E. Davis Blvd., No. 104, Tampa, FL 33731 USA
E-mail: kokopelli911@hotmail.com
Web site: http://www.kokopelli-butterfly.com.

Grassleaf Publishing, *(978-0-9990716; 978-1-7334913; 979-8-9862391)* 533 Derby Downs, Lebanon, TN 37087-8607 USA Tel 615-477-5743
E-mail: grassleafbooks@gmail.com.

Grassroots Educational Service *See* **Right On Programs, Inc.**

Grassroots Publishing Group, *(978-0-9794805; 978-0-9975677)* 9404 Southwick Dr., Bakersfield, CA 93312 USA (SAN 853-5493) Tel 661-368-2624; Fax: 661-368-2624; 4560 Woodlands Village Dr., Orlando, FL 32835
E-mail: nesta@sbcglobal.net.

Grateful Abundance Publishing, *(978-0-692-06796-3)* 51 Day Ave., Newark, OH 43055 USA Tel 740-334-9438
E-mail: dayleandtom@gmail.com
Dist(s): **Ingram Content Group.**

Grateful Day Pr., *(978-0-9882804)* 24 Dewey Mt Rd., Saranac Lake, NY 12983 USA Tel 518-891-2278; Fax: 518-891-1645
E-mail: gratefuldaypress@gmail.com.

Grateful Steps, *(978-0-9789548; 978-1-935130; 978-0-9962490; 978-1-945714)* 1091 Hendersonville Rd., Asheville, NC 28801 USA (SAN 856-471X) Tel 828-277-0998; Fax: 828-277-8027
Web site: http://www.gratefulsteps.com.

Gratia et Veritas Press *See* **Papillon Publishing**

Gratitude Works, *(978-0-578-13447-5)* 6255 Whitsett Ave, North Hollywood, CA 91606 USA.

Grau, Ryon, *(978-0-9772559)* 6824 Falstone Dr., Frederick, MD 21702 USA
E-mail: ryon@landmarkletters.com
Web site: http://www.spankledelia.com.

Gravino, Nicholas, *(978-0-615-24099-2; 978-0-578-27738-7)* 8935 Oldham Way, West Palm Bch, FL 33412-1110 USA; 831 SW Pebble Ln., Palm City, FL 34990
E-mail: nicholasgravino@att.net
Web site: http://www.apilotsmemoirsfromthegroundup.com.

Gravitas Pubns., Inc., *(978-0-9749149; 978-0-9765097; 978-0-9799459; 978-0-9817731; 978-0-9823163; 978-1-936114; 978-1-941181; 978-1-950415; 978-1-953542)* PO Box 90338, Albuquerque, NM 87199 USA Tel 505-266-2761; Fax: 505-266-2762; Toll Free: 888-466-2761; *Imprints:* Real Science-4-Kids (RealSci)
E-mail: office@gravitaspublications.com
Web site: http://www.gravitaspublications.com.

Gravley, Debbie Bybee, *(978-0-9771793)* Orders Addr.: P.O. Box 268, Gaston, OR 97119 USA; Edit Addr.: 12320 S.W. Springhill Rd., Gaston, OR 97119 USA.

Graw, Victoria, *(978-0-9787901)* P.O. Box 458, Orange, MA 01364 USA (SAN 851-6138)
E-mail: Vgraw@aol.com.

Gray and Company, Publishers *See* **Gray & Co., Pubs.**

Gray & Co., Pubs., *(978-0-9631738; 978-1-886228; 978-1-59851; 978-1-938441)* Orders Addr.: 1588 E 40th St Ste 1B, Cleveland, OH 44103 USA Tel 216-431-2665; Edit Addr.: 1588 E 40th St Ste 1B, Cleveland, OH 44103 USA Tel 216-431-2665
E-mail: sales@grayco.com
Web site: http://www.grayco.com.

Gray & Gold Publishing, *(978-1-945888; 978-1-64001; 978-1-64520; 978-1-7008)* 14546 Brook Hollow Blvd Num 349, San Antonio, TX 78232 USA
E-mail: sean@papeteriebleu.com.

Gray, Erin, *(978-1-7363366)* 6417 Rte. 380, Sinclairville, NY 14782-9653 USA Tel 716-708-8819
E-mail: eegray804@gmail.com.

Gray Jay Bks., *(978-0-9754539)*
E-mail: Contact@GrayJaybooks.com
Web site: http://www.grayjaybooks.com.

Gray, John, *(978-0-578-43434-6)* 1128 Springfield Valley Rd., Morrisville, NC 27560 USA Tel 318-401-5033; *Imprints:* Misguided Ink (MYID_L_MISGUID)
E-mail: johndonatron@gmail.com.

Gray, Jolie, *(978-1-7340647)* P.O. Box 273, Gonzales, TX 78629 USA Tel 830-857-1731
E-mail: jolie.gray@gmail.com
Dist(s): **Ingram Content Group.**

Gray Publishing, *(978-1-7327006)* 549 Hancock St., Brooklyn, NY 11233 USA Tel 201-320-7396
E-mail: babawesleygray1943@gmail.com.

Gray, Susan *See* **Two's Company**

Graye Castle Pr., *(978-0-692-10934-2; 978-0-692-11865-8)* 202 Brookfield Ave, Chattanooga, TN 37411 USA Tel 423-760-8662
E-mail: kendra@kendrayoung.com.

Grayer Publishing, *(978-0-9785536)* P.O. Box 788, Flossmoor, IL 60422 USA
E-mail: ac@grayerpublishing.com
Web site: http://www.grayerpublishing.com.

Graymalkin Media, *(978-1-935169; 978-1-63168; 978-1-63507)* Orders Addr.: 1413 Greenfield Ave., Suite 103, Los Angeles, CA 90025 USA Tel 310-231-8202 (phone/fax)
Web site: http://www.graymalkin.com
Dist(s): **Follett School Solutions**
Midwest Tape
Open Road Integrated Media, Inc.

Grayson, Kate, *(978-0-9774357)* 2307 58th Ave. E., Bradenton, FL 34203 USA (SAN 257-5000)
E-mail: kgrayson1@aol.com.

Graziano, Claudia *See* **Meerkat's Adventures Bks.**

GRC Bks., *(978-0-578-06866-4; 978-0-578-08611-8; 978-0-578-12011-9)* 704 Robinson Rd., Sebastopol, CA 95472 USA Tel 707-829-9191
E-mail: martyr@sonic.net
Dist(s): **Lulu Pr., Inc.**

Great AD-Ventures, *(978-0-9665053)* P.O. Box 8011, Boise, ID 83707 USA Fax: 208-336-5797; Toll Free: 800-390-5687
E-mail: theplace@lesbois.com; book@freeread.com
Web site: http://www.freeread.com/.

Great Adventures Publishing, *(978-0-9747972)* 465 Hill St., Laguna Beach, CA 92651 USA Tel 949-494-5797
E-mail: paigeturner5@hotmail.com.

Great American Pr., The, *(978-0-9777996; 978-0-9798776; 978-0-9814627)* 551 League City Pkwy., League City, TX 77573 USA (SAN 850-2773) Tel 281-557-4300 (phone/fax)
Web site: http://www.thegreatamericanpress.com.

Great American Pubs., *(978-0-9779053; 978-1-934817)* 171 Lone Pine Church Rd., Lena, MS 39094 USA Tel 601-854-5954; Fax: 601-854-5958
E-mail: info@gapublishers.com; ssimmons@gapublishers.com; tmonk@gapublishers.com
Web site: http://www.greatamericanpublishers.com
Dist(s): **Appalachian Bk. Distributors**
Bk. Marketing Plus
Bks. West
Dot Gibson Distribution
Forest Sales & Distributing Co.
Rumpf, Raymond & Son
Southwest Cookbook Distributors.

Great Authors Online, *(978-0-9773869)* 16440 Monterey St., Lake Elsinore, CA 92530 USA Tel 951-674-3246; Fax: 951-245-3608
E-mail: rodgerolsen@yahoo.com
Web site: http://greatauthorsonline.com.

Great Big Comics *See* **Great Big Comics, Big Tex Films**

Great Big Comics, Big Tex Films, *(978-0-9746784; 978-0-9844728; 978-0-615-49875-1)* Div. of The Big Tex Movin' Picture Company, LLC, 31 E. Bonneymead Cir., The Woodlands, TX 77381 USA
E-mail: bh@wondervista.com; avast@shebuccaneer.com
Web site: http://www.wondervista.com; http://www.greatbigcomics.com
Dist(s): **Diamond Distributors, Inc.**

Great Bks. Foundation, *(978-0-945159; 978-1-880323; 978-1-933147; 978-1-939014; 978-1-951782; 978-1-959042)* 35 E. Wacker Dr. Ste. 400, Chicago, IL 60601-2105 USA (SAN 205-3292) Toll Free: 800-222-5870
E-mail: hurleyp@greatbooks.org
Web site: http://www.greatbooks.org.

Great Bks. Publishing Co., *(978-1-7353487; 978-1-7359497)* 5111 Blackwell Rd, Memphis, TN 38134 USA Tel 901-922-5311
E-mail: chamberskacy@gmail.com
Web site: https://chamberskacy.wixsite.com/website-1.

Great Character Development Workbook, The, *(978-0-9728417)* P.O. Box 1852, Kingston, WA 98346 USA
Web site: http://www.thegreatcharacterdevelopmentworkbook.com.

Great Dog Literary LLC, *(978-0-692-94683-1; 978-0-9993912; 978-1-7331337; 978-1-951388)* P.O. Box 456, Craryville, NY 12521 USA Tel 917-207-8703
E-mail: liz@greatdogliterary.com
Dist(s): **Ingram Content Group.**

Great Expectations Bk. Co., *(978-1-883934)* P.O. Box 2067, Eugene, OR 07402 USA Tel 541-343-2647; Fax: 541-343-0568
E-mail: fred@pinehillgraphics.com.

Great I-AM Publishing Co., The, *(978-0-9762788)* Orders Addr.: P.O. Box 30412, Wilmington, DE 19805 USA Tel 302-888-2477; Fax: 302-416-5085; Edit Addr.: 25 Roselane Rosegate, New Castle, DE 19720 USA
E-mail: watkinstyree2@aol.com.

Great Ideas for Teaching, Inc., *(978-1-886143)* Orders Addr.: P.O. Box 444, Wrightsville Beach, NC 28480-0444 USA Tel 910-256-4494; Fax: 910-256-4493; Toll Free Fax: 800-839-8498; Toll Free: 800-839-8339; Edit Addr.: 6800 Wrightsville Ave., No. 16, Wilmington, NC 28403 USA
E-mail: gift@wilmington.net
Web site: http://www.gift-inc.com.

Great Ideas Pr., Ltd., *(978-1-884949)* 4130 166th Pl. SW, Lynnwood, WA 98037 USA Tel 425-774-6611
E-mail: JamesRobert@jamesrobertdeal.com
Web site: http://www.whattoserveagoddess.com.

Great Kids Helping Great Kids, Incorporated *See* **America's Great Stories**

Great Lakes Design, *(978-0-9761274)* P.O. Box 511534, Milwaukee, WI 53203 USA
Web site: http://www.vikingadventure.net.

Great Lakes Literary, LLC, *(978-1-883953; 978-1-933987)* 3147 S. Pennsylvania Ave., Milwaukee, WI 53207 USA; *Imprints:* Crickhollow Books (Crickhollow); Crispin Books (CrispinBks); Blue Horse Books (BlueHorse)
E-mail: info@CrickhollowBooks.com
Web site: http://www.CrickhollowBooks.com; http://www.CrispinBooks.com
Dist(s): **BookBaby**
BookMobile
Itasca Bks.

Great Lakes Literary, LLCorp. *See* **Great Lakes Literary, LLC**

Great Lakes Press, Inc., *(978-0-9614760; 978-1-881018; 978-1-939085)* Orders Addr.: P.O. Box 374, Cottleville, MO 63338 USA Fax: 636-273-6086
E-mail: service@glpbooks.com
Web site: http://www.glpbooks.com; http://www.greatlakespress.com.

Great Liberty Pub., *(978-1-950772; 978-1-956677)* 5445 Province Pl., Alexandria, LA 71303 USA Tel 305-768-6767
E-mail: stevojionu@gmail.com.

Great Mastiff Corp., *(978-0-9759166)* 9945 E. Whitebirch Rd., Port wing, WI 54865 USA Tel 715-774-3247
E-mail: greatmastiff@hotmail.com
Web site: http://www.greatmastiff.com.

Great Nation Publishing, *(978-0-578-05549-7; 978-0-578-06529-8; 978-0-615-44374-4; 978-0-615-60214-1; 978-0-9891056)* Orders Addr.: 3828 Salem Rd., No. 56, Covington, GA 30016 USA
E-mail: brian@authorbrianthompson.com
Web site: http://www.authorbrianthompson.com
Dist(s): **Smashwords.**

Great Ocean Publishers *See* **Great River Bks.**

Great Persuader Publishing, The, *(978-0-9712581)*
E-mail: greatpersuader@hotmail.com; Info@Poetryisalive.com.

Great Plains Pr., *(978-0-9632459; 978-0-9861616)* 1103 Canyon Rd., Santa Fe, NM 87501 USA
E-mail: dirk@rainbowplace.com
Web site: http://www.greatplainspress.com/.

Great Plains Pubns. (CAN) *(978-0-9697804; 978-1-894283; 978-1-926531; 978-1-927855; 978-1-77337) Dist. by* **IPG Chicago.**

Great Reads Bks., *(978-0-9718694)* P.O. Box 270801, Houston, TX 77277 USA (SAN 254-5462)
E-mail: greatreadsbooks@earthlink.net
Web site: http://www.greatreadsbooks.com.

†Great River Bks., *(978-0-915556)* 161 M St., Salt Lake City, UT 84103 USA (SAN 207-527X) Tel 801-532-4833
E-mail: info@greatriverbooks.com
Web site: http://www.greatriverbooks.com
Dist(s): **Crown Hse. Publishing LLC**
Independent Pubs. Group
Midpoint Trade Bks., Inc.; *CIP.*

Great Smoky Mountains Assn., *(978-0-937207; 978-1-7370351)* 115 Park Headquarters Rd., Gatlinburg, TN 37738 USA (SAN 658-7267) Tel 865-436-7318; Fax: 865-436-6884
E-mail: aaron@gsmassoc.org
Web site: http://www.smokiesinformation.org
Dist(s): **Publishers Group West (PGW).**

Great Smoky Mountains Natural History Association *See* **Great Smoky Mountains Assn.**

Great Source Education Group, Inc., *(978-0-669; 978-0-9638133; 978-1-57185)* Subs. of Houghton Mifflin Harcourt Supplemental Pubs., 181 Ballardvale St., Wilmington, MA 01887 USA Tel 978-661-1500; Fax: 978-661-1331; Toll Free Fax: 800-289-3994; Toll Free: 800-289-4490
Web site: http://www.greatsource.com
Dist(s): **Houghton Mifflin Harcourt Publishing Co.**

Great Success, LLC, *(978-0-9882039; 978-1-63498-451-5)* P.O. Box 1245, Bluffton, SC 29910 USA Tel 678-472-4740
E-mail: rgmincey@gmail.com.

Great Texas Line Pr., *(978-1-892588)* Orders Addr.: P.O. Box 11105, Fort Worth, TX 76110 USA Tel 817-922-8929; Fax: 817-926-0420
E-mail: greattexas@hotmail.com
Web site: http://www.greattexasline.com
Dist(s): **Baker & Taylor Bks.**

Great UNpublished *Imprint of* **CreateSpace Independent Publishing Platform**

Great Valley Bks. *Imprint of* **Heyday**

Great West Publishing, *(978-0-9796199; 978-0-9974553)* Orders Addr.: P.O. Box 31631, Tucson, AZ 85751-1631 USA (SAN 853-9146); *Imprints:* Sentry Books (Sentry Bks)
Web site: http://www.sentrybooks.com.

Great White Bird Publishing, *(978-0-9792474)* Orders Addr.: P.O. Box 667, Hiram, GA 30141-0667 USA Tel 770-947-6817; *Imprints:* GWB (GWB)
E-mail: davidthackston@bellsouth.net
Web site: http://www.myspace.com/thackston.

Greater Cincinnati TV Educational Foundation, *(978-0-9744419)* 1223 Central Pkwy., Cincinnati, OH 45214-2812 USA Tel 513-381-4033; Fax: 513-381-7520; *Imprints:* CET (Cet)
E-mail: edtech@wcet.pbs.org
Web site: http://www.wcet.org.

Greater Reality Pubns., *(978-0-9802111; 978-1-7374106; 978-1-7374107)* 23 Payne Pl., Normal, IL 61761 USA (SAN 855-5028) Tel 309-452-2831; Fax: 309-452-9357; Toll Free: 800-827-3770
E-mail: rchogan@greaterreality.com
Web site: http://greaterreality.com.

Greater Truth Pubs., *(978-0-9653078; 978-1-937151)* P.O. Box 4332, Lafayette, IN 47903 USA Do not confuse with Griffin Publishing, Glendale, CA
E-mail: gtp@ao-soft.com
Web site: http://www.ao-soft.com/gtpub/.

Greatest Books Pub., *(978-1-937775; 978-1-62236; 978-81-8423-059-8)* 2764 N. Green Valley Pkwy., Henderson, NV 89014 USA Tel 951-760-8499
E-mail: lbbooks1234@gmail.com.

Greatful Geek Publishing, *(978-0-578-22716-0; 978-0-578-22717-7)* 2301 E. Rock Creek Rd., Norman, OK 73071 USA.

GreatWineFinds.com *See* **GWF Publishing & Henry's Helpers**

Grecia Saavedra Pinto, *(978-0-692-08728-2; 978-1-7332602; 979-8-9867239)* 32551 Via Los Santos, San Juan Capistrano, CA 92675 USA Tel 949-226-1163
E-mail: gpscastro@gmail.com
Dist(s): **CreateSpace Independent Publishing Platform.**

GreeHee Publishing, *(978-0-9779590)* Orders Addr.: 125 Susan St., Myrtle Creek, OR 97457-9741 USA Tel 541-863-6631
E-mail: astrologyandmore@gmail.com
Web site: http://www.greehee.com; http://www.talesoftamoor.com
Dist(s): **Quality Bks., Inc. Smashwords.**

Green & Purple Publishing *See* **Green & Purple Publishing**

Green & Purple Publishing, *(978-1-7321212; 978-1-950190)* 44864 Linalou Ranch Rd, Temecula, CA 92592 USA Tel 909-938-9932
E-mail: pambowen909@gmail.com
Web site: pamellabowen.com; greenandpurplepublishing.com.

Green Apple Lessons, Inc., *(978-0-692-98638-7; 978-0-692-12278-5; 978-0-578-50526-8)* 24110 Venetian Dr., Richmond, TX 77406 USA Tel 832-612-1224
E-mail: julieannesavage@protonmail.com
Dist(s): **Ingram Content Group.**

Green Beanie Bks., *(978-1-937499)* P.O. Box 7405, Bonney Lake, WA 98391 USA Tel 253-862-4711
E-mail: carla@greenbeaniebooks.com
Web site: greenbeaniebooks.com
Dist(s): **American West Bks.**

Green Buffalo Pr., *(978-0-9905489)* 4313 Chase Ave., Los Angeles, CA 02139 USA Tel 323-533-1459
E-mail: marco.pavia@gmail.com.

Green Butterfly Pr., *(978-0-9817556; 978-0-9823722; 978-1-7362735; 979-8-9850203; 978-1-958625)* 21027 N. Desert Sands Dr., Sun City West, AZ 85375 USA (SAN 856-4639).

Green, C. K. *See* **Kingston Publishing Co.**

Green Card Voices, *(978-0-692-51151-0; 978-0-692-57281-8; 978-0-9974960; 978-1-949523; 978-1-7327906)* 2611 1st Ave S, Minneapolis, MN 55408 USA Tel 612-889-7635
E-mail: greencardvoices@gmail.com
Web site: http://www.greencardvoices.com/
Dist(s): **Consortium Bk. Sales & Distribution CreateSpace Independent Publishing Platform.**

Green Consulting, LLC, *(978-0-615-54194-5; 978-0-692-31813-3; 978-0-9982225; 979-8-9889341)* 2750 Piney Wood Dr., Atlanta, GA 30344 USA Tel 404-290-9857
E-mail: paulapalmergreen@gmail.com
Web site: www.paulapalmergreen.com.

Green Cows Bks. *Imprint of* **K Yee**

†**Green Dragon Bks.,** *(978-0-89334; 978-1-62386)* 2875 S. Ocean Blvd. Ste 200, Palm Beach, FL 33480 USA (SAN 658-0882) Toll Free Fax: 888-874-8844; Toll Free: 800-874-8844; *Imprints:* Humanics Learning (Humanics Lrng) Do not confuse with Humanics ErgoSystems, Inc., Reseda, CA
E-mail: info@greendragonbooks.com
Web site: http://www.greendragonbooks.com; http://www.humanicslearning.com; http://www.humanicsdealer.com
Dist(s): **Borders, Inc. Midpoint Trade Bks., Inc. New Leaf Distributing Co., Inc. Two Rivers Distribution**; *CIP.*

Green E-Bks., *(978-1-938848; 978-0-9990528; 978-0-9994577; 978-1-7329882)* 6145 N. Tapestry Way, Boise, ID 83714 USA Tel 208-608-8325; Fax: 208-441-6024
E-mail: jason@greene-books.com.

Green Egg Media, Incorporated *See* **Three Sixteen Publishing**

Green Ghost Press *See* **Waide Aaron Riddle**

Green Goat Bks., *(978-0-615-15585-2)* P.O. Box 11256, Bainbridge Island, WA 98110 USA Tel 206-842-3412; Fax: 206-842-0570; Toll Free: 866-776-4543
E-mail: contact@greengoatbooks.com
Web site: http://www.greengoatbooks.com
Dist(s): **Greenleaf Book Group.**

Green Hill Publishers *See* **Jameson Bks., Inc.**

Green Igric Pr., *(978-0-9776170)* P.O. Box 82454, Columbus, OH 43202 USA Tel 614-267-9426.

Green Irene, *(978-0-9742280)* P.O. Box 5, Huron, OH 44839 USA
E-mail: chager@buckeye-express.com
Web site: http://www.redandgreenchoices.com.

Green Key Books *See* **Practical Christianity Foundation**

Green Kids Club, Inc., *(978-0-9836602; 978-1-939871)* 1425 Higham St., Idaho Falls, ID 83402 USA Tel 208-528-8718
E-mail: peggy_hinman@yahoo.com.

Green Lady Pr., The *Imprint of* **RealityIsBooks.com, Inc.**

Green Leaf Publishing *See* **BookWise Publishing**

Green Light Books and Publishing, LLC *See* **Greenlight Bks. & Publishing, LLC**

Green Mansion Pr. LLC, *(978-0-9714612; 978-0-9746457)* 501 E. 79th St., Suite 16A, New York, NY 10021-0773 USA (SAN 254-2684) Tel 212-396-2667; Fax: 212-937-4685
E-mail: info@greenmansionpress.com
Web site: http://www.greenmansionpress.com.

Green Mansions, Inc., *(978-0-9728156)* P.O. Box 100, Redmond, OR 97756 USA
E-mail: lewhollander@yahoo.com
Web site: http://www.andchocolateshallleadus.com.

Green, Mary, *(978-0-9764639)* 737 Buffalo Valley Rd., Cookeville, TN 38501-3862 USA
E-mail: greenmajt@frontiernet.net
Web site: http://www.bigfootlady.net.

Green Meeple Bks., *(978-1-7357708)* 3206 146th St 0, URBANDALE, IA 50323 USA Tel 5159891221
E-mail: danallbaugh@gmail.com.

Green Nest LLC, *(978-0-9772392)* 18662 Macarthur Blvd. Suite 200, Irvine, CA 92612 USA Fax: 949-387-3806
Web site: http://www.greennest.com
Dist(s): **Pathway Bk. Service.**

Green Owl, Inc., *(978-0-9727273)* 23834 SE 248th St., Maple Valley, WA 98038 USA (SAN 255-0679)
E-mail: owl@greenowl.org
Web site: http://www.greenowl.org.

Green Pastures Pr., *(978-0-9627643; 978-1-884377)* HC 67, Box 91-A, Mifflin, PA 17058 USA Tel 717-436-9115.

Green Pastures Publishing, Inc., *(978-0-9664276; 978-0-9720580)* Orders Addr.: P.O. Box 804, Windsor, CO 80550 USA Tel 970-686-7242
Dist(s): **Independent Pubs. Group.**

Green Ronin Publishing, *(978-0-9701048; 978-0-9714380; 978-0-9723599; 978-0-9726756; 978-1-932442; 978-1-934547; 978-1-949160)* Orders Addr.: 3815 S. Othello St. Ste 100 #311, Seattle, WA 98118 USA; Edit Addr.: 6731 29th Ave., S, Seattle, WA 98108 USA
E-mail: pramas@greenronin.com; nicole@greenronin.com
Web site: http://www.greenronin.com
Dist(s): **Diamond Comic Distributors, Inc. Diamond Bk. Distributors.**

Green Rose Publishing LLC, *(978-1-7352558)* 4600 NW 24th Ave, Boca Raton, FL 33431 USA Tel 561-414-4576
E-mail: justinesrosen@gmail.com.

Green Sheet Inc., The, *(978-0-9670947)* P.O. Box 6008, Petaluma, CA 94955-6008 USA Fax: 707-586-1738; Toll Free: 800-757-4441
E-mail: gmsht@aol.com
Web site: http://www.greensheet.com.

Green Tiger Pr. *Imprint of* **Laughing Elephant**

Green, Tim, *(978-0-578-51360-7; 978-0-578-51388-1; 978-0-578-51389-8; 978-0-578-51390-4)* 9127 Cresta Dr., Los Angeles, CA 90035 USA Tel 310-365-4865
E-mail: tmrtim@gmail.com
Dist(s): **Ingram Content Group.**

Green Writers Pr., *(978-0-9893104; 978-0-9899838; 978-0-9960872; 978-0-9909733; 978-0-9961357; 978-0-9962676; 978-0-9968973; 978-0-9974528; 978-0-9982604; 978-0-9987012; 978-0-9990766; 978-0-9994995; 978-1-7320815; 978-1-7322662; 978-1-7327434; 978-1-7328540; 978-1-7336534; 978-1-950584; 979-8-9865324; 979-8-9870707; 979-8-9876631; 979-8-9883820; 979-8-9891784) 34 Miller Rd., Brattleboro, VT 05301 USA Tel 802-380-1121*
E-mail: dcdesignteamvt@gmail.com
Web site: www.greenwriterspress.com
Dist(s): **Independent Pubs. Group Midpoint Trade Bks., Inc.**

Greenamyer, Robert S., *(978-0-692-07937-9; 978-0-578-76729-1)* P.O. Box 3480, IDYLLWILD, CA 92549 USA Tel 858-382-4638
E-mail: bgreenamyer@gmail.com
Dist(s): **Ingram Content Group.**

Greenbank, Amy Hernandez, *(978-0-578-47827-2)* 3709 Willow Brook Dr., Jefferson City, MO 65109 USA Tel 217-617-1950
E-mail: a.greenbank82@gmail.com
Web site: Type1Diabitsies.com.

Greenberg, Carmel *See* **Kicks and Giggles Today**

Greenberg, Melanie Hope, *(978-0-692-11664-7; 978-0-578-55212-5; 978-0-578-61903-3)* 168 Hicks St., Brooklyn, NY 11201 USA Tel 718-522-7026
E-mail: melhopegreenberg@aol.com
Web site: http://melaniehopegreenberg.blogspot.com.

Greenberg, Scott *See* **Jump Start Performance Programs**

Greenberry Publishing, LLC *See* **Authors Pr.**

Greenblatt, Kim, *(978-0-9777282; 978-1-60622)* 6600 Melba Ave., West Hills, CA 91307 USA (SAN 850-0649).

Greenbrier/Scentex *See* **Bright of America**

Greenbush Pr., *(978-0-9766720; 978-0-9836460; 978-0-615-95792-0; 978-0-9600297)* Orders Addr.: 21518 Karpathos Ln., Spring, TX 77388-3262 USA (SAN 256-5048) Tel 832-469-1033 Office
E-mail: frank@depressionproofchurch.com; frank@frankbecker.com; frank@greenbushpress.com
Web site: http://www.frankbecker.com.

Greene & Sandell, *(978-0-9834681)* 45 Church St. Apt. 1, Boston, MA 02116 USA Tel 617-426-7278
E-mail: greenesandell@gmail.com.

Greene, A.S. & Co., *(978-0-9761723)* 1828 Kings Hwy., Lincoln Park, MI 48146 USA Fax: 313-388-0447
E-mail: anitac21@yahoo.com.

Greene Bark Pr., Inc., *(978-1-880851)* P.O. Box 1108, Bridgeport, CT 06601-1108 USA Tel 203-372-4861; Fax: 203-371-5856
E-mail: Greenebark@aol.com
Web site: http://www.greenebarkpress.com.

Greene, Brenda H. *See* **Three Willows Pr.**

Greene, Marjorie A., *(978-0-9741764)* 124 Caughman Park Dr., Columbia, SC 29209 USA Tel 803-783-5430; Fax: 803-783-5430
E-mail: remaininme@msn.com.

Greenfield Enterprises, Ltd. (HKG) *(978-962-563) Dist. by* **Cheng Tsui.**

†**Greenfield Review Literary Ctr., Inc.,** *(978-0-87886; 978-0-912678)* 2 Middle Grove Rd., P.O. Box 308, Greenfield Center, NY 12833 USA (SAN 203-4506) Tel 518-583-1440; Fax: 518-583-9741; *Imprints:* Greenfield Review Press (Greenfld Rev Pr)
Web site: http://www.nativeauthors.com
Dist(s): **SPD-Small Pr. Distribution**; *CIP.*

Greenfield Review Pr. *Imprint of* **Greenfield Review Literary Ctr., Inc.**

Greenhaven Pr., Inc. *Imprint of* **Cengage Gale**

Greenhaven Publishing *Imprint of* **Cengage Gale**

Greenhaven Publishing *Imprint of* **Greenhaven Publishing LLC**

Greenhaven Publishing LLC, *(978-1-5345)* 353 3rd Ave., Suite 255, New York, NY 10010 USA (SAN 990-171X) Tel 212-420-1205; Fax: 212-614-7385; Toll Free Fax: 844-317-7405; Toll Free: 844-317-7404; *Imprints:* KidHaven Publishing (KidHaven Publ); Lucent Press (Lucent Pr); Greenhaven Publishing (GreenHav)
E-mail: gh_custserv@greenhaven.com; hollyc@rosenpub.com
Dist(s): **Rosen Publishing Group, Inc., The.**

Greenhill Bks. (GBR) *(978-0-947898; 978-1-85367; 978-1-78438) Dist. by* **Casemate Pubs.**

Greenhill Bks. (GBR) *(978-0-947898; 978-1-85367; 978-1-78438) Dist. by* **HachBkGrp.**

Greenleaf Book Group, *(978-0-9665319; 978-1-929774; 978-0-9790842; 978-1-60832; 978-1-61486; 978-1-62634; 979-8-88645)* Orders Addr.: 4005-B Banister Ln., Austin, TX 78704 USA Tel 512-891-6100; Fax: 512-891-6150; Toll Free: 800-932-5420; Edit Addr.: P.O. Box 91869, Austin, TX 78709 USA; *Imprints:* Greenleaf Book Group Press (GBGP)
E-mail: tanya@greenleafbookgroup.com
Web site: http://www.greenleafbookgroup.com
Dist(s): **CreateSpace Independent Publishing Platform D.A.P./Distributed Art Pubs.**

Greenleaf Book Group Pr. *Imprint of* **Greenleaf Book Group**

Greenleaf Pr., *(978-1-882514)* 1570 Old Laguardo Rd E., Lebanon, TN 37087-8958 USA (SAN 297-8555) Toll Free Fax: 866-725-0785 Do not confuse with Greenleaf Pr., Breckenridge, CO
E-mail: info@greenleafpress.com
Web site: http://www.greenleafpress.com.

Greenleaf Publishing, Inc., *(978-0-578-42560-3; 978-0-578-70790-7; 978-0-578-29230-4)* 5531 W. 93rd St., Bloomington, MN 55437-1941 USA Tel 952-856-2505
E-mail: davegreenleaf@comcast.net
Web site: http://www.greenleafpub.com.

Greenlees Publishing, *(978-1-951098)* 7848 Bavaria Rd., Victoria, MN 55386 USA Tel 323-477-5703
E-mail: lisaumhoefer@gmail.com.

Greenlight Bks. & Publishing, LLC, *(978-0-9755110)* P.O. Box 1965, ORLANDO, FL 32802-1965 USA
E-mail: juan_chisholm@yahoo.com; juan.chisholm@gmail.com
Web site: http://www.greenlightbooks.org.

Greenline Publications *See* **Davis, A. S. Media Group**

GreenPoint Computer Services *See* **GIL Pubns.**

Greenroom Bks., *(978-0-9712163)* 12 N. Juniper St., Hampton, VA 23669-2416 USA (SAN 254-2501) Tel 757-726-2651 (phone/fax)
E-mail: brad@greenroombooks.com; publisher@greenroombooks.com
Web site: http://www.greenroombooks.com
Dist(s): **Brodart Co.**

Greens' Pubns., *(978-0-9975003)* 409 Misty Ridge Way, Woodstock, GA 30189 USA Tel 678-403-1892
E-mail: darrylgreenpubs@gmail.com
Web site: www.greenspublications.com.

Greensboro Historical Museum, Inc., *(978-0-9747456)* 130 Summit Ave., Greensboro, NC 27401-3016 USA Tel 336-373-2043; Fax: 336-373-2204
Web site: http://www.greensborohistory.org.

Greentown Glass Co., *(978-0-9723958)* Orders Addr.: P.O. Box 771, Westfield, IN 46074-0771 USA Tel 765-455-0595; Edit Addr.: 3703 Robin Dr., Kokomo, IN 46902 USA
Web site: http://www.greentownglasscompany.com.

Greenville Family Partnership, *(978-0-9759699)* P.O. Box 10203, Greenville, SC 29603-0203 USA Tel 864-467-4099; Fax: 864-467-4102
Web site: http://www.redribbonworks.org.

Greenwillow Bks. *Imprint of* **HarperCollins Pubs.**

Greenwoman Publishing, LLC, *(978-0-9897056; 978-0-9905385)*
E-mail: maefayne@msn.com
Web site: http://www.greenwomanmagazine.com.

Greenwood *Imprint of* **ABC-CLIO, LLC**

Greenwood *Imprint of* **Bloomsbury Publishing USA**

Greenwood Hill Pr., *(978-0-9797868; 978-0-9836382; 978-0-9846912; 978-0-9881748; 978-0-9915961; 978-0-9989643)* W 7048 Savannah Ln., Delavan, WI 53115 USA; *Imprints:* OddInt Media (OddIntMedia)
E-mail: mjohnson@fullpo.com.

Greenwood, Lisa K., *(978-0-692-08066-5)* 5960 Munger Rd., Dayton, OH 45459 USA Tel 937-609-0891
E-mail: tgreenwood@greentreegroup.com.

Greenwood, Lori Ministries, Inc., *(978-0-9747956)* Orders Addr.: 17622 32nd Pl W., Lynnwood, WA 98037-7714 USA (SAN 255-8297)
E-mail: lgministries@cs.com
Web site: http://www.thevisionlink.com.

Greenwood Street Publishing. GSP, *(978-0-9745553)* 1539 W. Townley Ave., Phoenix, AZ 85021 USA Tel 602-997-4444; Fax: 602-997-5959 Do not confuse with Greenwood Publishing in Wixom, MI
E-mail: julie@gg-az.com; info@greenwoodstreet.com
Web site: http://www.greenwoodstreet.com.

Greever, Millie, *(978-0-692-92784-7; 978-0-692-92786-1; 978-1-7326789)* 8782 N Spring Garden Ln., MOUNT VERNON, IL 62864 USA Tel 618-731-1963
E-mail: millie@teamgreever.com
Dist(s): **Ingram Content Group.**

Gregory, Charles, *(978-0-9745432)* 17697 Palmer St., Melvindale, MI 48122 USA (SAN 255-7991) Tel 313-389-2836
E-mail: charles_gregory@ameritech.net
Web site: http://www.charles_gregory/index.html
Dist(s): **Lulu Pr., Inc.**

Gregory, Charles Matthew, *(978-0-9766442)* 5101 Boarshead Rd. No. 102, Minnetonka, MN 55345 USA Tel 612-845-7134
Web site: www.mikascomic.com.

Gregory Cross Publishing, *(978-0-578-24525-6; 978-0-578-25774-7; 979-8-9869465)* 17888 W 78th Dr., Arvada, CO 80007 USA Tel 720-979-4734
E-mail: gcross@suncompany.net.

Gregory, Marissa, *(978-0-578-89612-0)* 106 Derosa Dr, Hampton, VA 23666 USA Tel 757-927-4663
E-mail: spoiledheartsllc@gmail.com.

Gregory Oliver Publishing *See* **Good River Print & Media**

Grenevitch, Betsy Coffman, *(978-0-9747113)* 1450 Hewatt Rd., Lilburn, GA 30047 USA Tel 678-344-6100 (phone/fax)
E-mail: blindangel@joimail.com.

Grenwood Publishing *See* **Greenwood Street Publishing. GSP**

Gresham, Joel, *(978-0-9708446; 978-0-578-78507-3)* 2201 Morgan Pl., Atlanta, GA 30324 USA Tel 404-512-0445
E-mail: undercolorjg@yahoo.com.

Grettler, Kelly, *(978-0-692-80151-2; 978-0-692-07558-6; 978-0-578-57187-4)* .

Grey Gate Media, LLC *See* **Raven's Wing Bks.**

Grey Gecko Pr., *(978-0-9836185; 978-0-9854400; 978-1-938821; 978-1-945760)* 565 S Mason Rd Ste 154, Katy, TX 77450 USA Tel 713-489-5731
E-mail: jason@greygeckopress.com
Web site: http://www.greygeckopress.com
Dist(s): **Ingram Content Group.**

†**Grey Hse. Publishing,** *(978-0-939300; 978-1-891482; 978-1-930956; 978-1-59237; 978-1-61925; 978-1-68217; 978-1-64265; 978-1-63700; 979-8-89179)* 4919 Rte. 22 PO Box 56, Amenia, NY 12501 USA Tel 518-789-8700; Fax: 518-789-0556; Toll Free: 800-562-2139; 4919 Rte. 22 PO Box 56, Amenia, NY 12501 Tel 518-789-8700; Fax: 518-789-0556; Toll Free: 800-562-2139; *Imprints:* Universal Reference Publications (Universal Ref Pubns)
E-mail: books@greyhouse.com
Web site: http://www.greyhouse.com
Dist(s): **Ebsco Publishing Cengage Gale MyiLibrary ebrary, Inc.**; *CIP.*

GreyCore Pr., *(978-0-9671851; 978-0-9742074)* 3833 Hilton Ave NE, Albuquerque, NM 87110-1059 USA
E-mail: joan123@frontiernet.net.

Greyhound Bks., *(978-0-9724136; 978-1-59677)* 2000 Stock Creek Rd., Knoxville, TN 37920 USA Tel 865-405-3002
E-mail: cynmob@aol.com; editor@bushidopress.com
Web site: http://www.dogbooks.org.

Greyson Media Associates, *(978-1-68399)* 122 W Main St No. 49394, Cookeville, TN 38506 USA
Web site: ChristopherGreyson.com; www.greysonmediaassociates.com.

Greystone Books Ltd. (CAN) *(978-1-55365; 978-1-77100; 978-1-77164; 978-1-77840) Dist. by* **PerseuPGW.**

Grid Pr. *Imprint of* **L & R Publishing, LLC**

Grief Watch, *(978-0-9615197; 978-0-9724241; 978-0-9916312; 978-0-692-37070-4)* Div. of Metanoia Peace Community United Methodist Church, 2116 NE 18th Ave., Portland, OR 97212 USA (SAN 694-2911) Tel 503-284-7426; Fax: 503-282-8985
E-mail: webmaster@griefwatch.com
Web site: http://www.griefwatch.com
Dist(s): **ACTA Pubns. CreateSpace Independent Publishing Platform.**

GRIFFIN *See* **Griffin**

Griffin, *(978-0-312-60750-0)* 915 Electric Ave., Venice, CA 90291 USA.

Griffin Comics *Imprint of* **Corbett Features**

Griffin, Curtis Monroe, *(978-0-9749583)* 3250 Oneal Cir., Boulder, CO 80301-1424 USA.

Griffin Group Publishing LLC, *(978-0-692-01920-7)* 3419 Westminister Suite 320, Dallas, TX 75205 USA.

Griffin Publishing *See* **Greater Truth Pubs.**

Griffin Publishing Group, *(978-1-58000; 978-1-882180)* P.O. Box 28627, Santa Ana, CA 92799-8627 USA Toll Free: 800-472-9741 Do not confuse with Griffin Publishing, Ogden, UT
E-mail: griffinbooks@earthlink.net; mvonarx@griffinpublishing.com
Web site: http://www.griffinpublishing.com
Dist(s): **BHB Fulfillment Sundaykool Bulletins.**

Griffin, Sandi Zambarano, *(978-1-883838)* 10840 Kimberfyld Ln., Port Saint Lucie, FL 34986 USA Tel 561-461-6830
Dist(s): **Bookazine Co., Inc.**

Griffis, Teri Errico, *(978-0-692-88542-0)* 1935 Treebark Dr., Charleston, SC 29414 USA Tel 203-450-7051; Fax: 203-450-7051
E-mail: teresaerrico05@yahoo.com.

Griffith, John *See* **Rosetta Stone Communications**

Griffith, John LLC, *(978-0-692-89931-1; 978-0-692-92090-9; 978-1-7343449)* 6913 Shoreview Dr, McKinney, TX 75070 USA Tel 972-841-5897
E-mail: johngriffithllc@gmail.com.

Griffith, Tara, *(978-0-692-83481-7)* 1330 Worley Ave NW, CANTON, OH 44703 USA Tel 330-617-3594
E-mail: jeffwcrawford5+LVP0003269@gmail.com; jeffwcrawford5+LVP0003269@gmail.com.

Griggs, Amelia, *(978-1-7330666; 978-1-7372096)* 2125 Robin Dr., Warrington, PA 18976 USA Tel 215-343-3681
E-mail: adgriggs1@yahoo.com
Web site: www.amazon.com/author/ameliagriggs.

Griggs Music Co., *(978-0-9753385)* 228 Pope Bend Rd., Cedar Creek, TX 78612 USA Tel 512-303-2744
Web site: http://www.griggsmusic.net.

Grigsby, Cynthia, *(978-0-9786840)* 4304 Hillyer St., Fairfax, VA 22032-1418 USA
E-mail: cgrigsby6@yahoo.com.

Griha, *(978-0-9748503)* 23 Iron Bark Ln., Aliso Viejo, CA 92656 USA
Web site: http://www.griha.com.

Grijalbo, Editorial (MEX) *(978-968-419; 978-970-05) Dist. by* **Continental Bk.**

Grijalbo, Editorial (MEX) *(978-968-419; 978-970-05) Dist. by* **AIMS Intl.**

Grijalbo Mondadori, S.A.-Junior (ESP) *(978-84-253; 978-84-397; 978-84-7419; 978-84-478; 978-84-7423) Dist. by* **Continental Bk.**

Grijalbo Mondadori, S.A.-Montena (ESP) *(978-84-7515; 978-84-85297; 978-84-8441) Dist. by* **Lectorum Pubns.**

Grijalbo-Dargaud, S.A. Editores (ESP) *(978-84-7510) Dist. by* **Distribks Inc.**

Grimes, Richard, (978-0-9770594) 111 Lankford Dr., Georgetown, KY 40324 USA.

Gripper Products, (978-0-916176; 978-1-954519) 787 N. 24th St., Philadelphia, PA 19130-2540 USA (SAN 206-3816) Tel 215-765-9362
E-mail: reluctantspy@gmail.com
Web site: http://www.lookunderrocks.com
Dist(s): **CreateSpace Independent Publishing Platform**
Ingram Content Group
Smashwords.

Grivante Pr., (978-1-62676; 979-8-218-15711-1) P.O. Box 1392, Sagle, ID 83860 USA Tel 208-660-7294; *Imprints:* Melanin Origins, LLC (MYID_G_MELANIN)
E-mail: grivante@gmail.com
Web site: www.grivantepress.com.

Grizlegirl Productions *See* **Bookateer Publishing**

Grizzly Adams Productions, Inc., (978-0-9667985; 978-1-929296; 978-1-931602; 978-1-933424; 978-1-934646) Orders Addr.: P.O. Box 298, Baker City, OR 97814 USA; Edit Addr.: 2850 Myrtle St., Baker City, OR 97814 USA
Dist(s): **Send The Light Distribution LLC.**

Grizzly Bks Publishing, (978-0-9747951; 978-0-9749634) Orders Addr.: PMB Box 136, Dahlonega, GA 30533 USA Tel 706-864-2349 (phone/fax); Edit Addr.: 240 Wal-Mart Way, Dahlonega, GA 30533 USA
E-mail: ancient12@linkamerica.net
Web site: http://www.grizzlybookz.com.

Grizzly Ridge Publishing, (978-0-9793963) P.O. Box 268, West Glacier, MT 59936 USA
Web site: http://www.grizzlyridgepublishing.com.

Grolier *Imprint of* **Scholastic Library Publishing**

Grolier Online *Imprint of* **Scholastic Library Publishing**

Grolier Publishing *See* **Scholastic Library Publishing**

Grolier Publishing, (978-0-516; 978-0-531) 90 Old Sherman Tpke., Danbury, CT 06816E USA Tel 203-797-3500; Fax: 203-797-3657
E-mail: agraham@grolier.com
Web site: www.scholasticlibrary.com.

Grosinger, Crain Publishing, (978-0-9720054) Orders Addr.: P.O. Box 55, Mandan, ND 58554 USA Tel 701-202-1293; Edit Addr.: 210 Collins Ave., Mandan, ND 58554 USA
Web site: http://www.johnsbook.net; http://www.crainbooks.com
Dist(s): **Partners Bk. Distributing, Inc.**

Gross, H. H., (978-0-9754699) P.O. Box 122606, San Diego, CA 92112 USA
E-mail: hhgross@lycos.com
Web site: http://www.hhgross.net.

Gross, Roxanna, (978-0-615-16398-7) 3 S. Cedarwood Ct., Alexandria, KY 41001 USA
E-mail: roxie@zoomtown.com
Dist(s): **Lulu Pr., Inc.**

Grosset & Dunlap *Imprint of* **Penguin Publishing Group**

Grosset & Dunlap *Imprint of* **Penguin Young Readers Group**

Grosset & Dunlap *Imprint of* **Penguin Young Readers Group**

Grossman, Dina *See* **Tzipora Pubns., Inc.**

Groundbreaking Pr., (978-0-9718562; 978-0-9745624; 978-0-9765821; 978-0-9773535; 978-0-9777795; 978-0-9793542; 978-0-9831030; 978-0-9850651; 978-1-7339001; 979-8-9874176) 2050 Ruby Lane #1, Fairfield, IA 52556 USA Tel 512-339-4000; Fax: 512-458-1648
E-mail: bradfregger@gmail.com
Web site: http://www.groundbreaking.com.

GroundSwell Bks. *Imprint of* **BPC**

Groundwood Bks. (CAN) (978-0-88899; 978-1-55498; 978-1-77306) *Dist. by* **PerseuPGW.**

Group Books *See* **Group Publishing, Inc.**

†Group Publishing, Inc., (978-0-7644; 978-0-931529; 978-0-936664; 978-1-55945; 978-1-4707) Orders Addr.: 1515 Cascade Ave., Loveland, CO 80538-8681 USA (SAN 214-4689) Tel 970-669-3836; Fax: 970-679-4373; Toll Free: 800-635-0404; 800-447-1070 (consumer orders only); 800-541-5200 (trade orders only); *Imprints:* Flagship Church Resources (Flagship Church)
E-mail: sjohnson@group.com
Web site: http://www.group.com
Dist(s): **Appalachian Bible Co.**
Faith Alive Christian Resources
Spring Arbor Distributors, Inc.
Twentieth Century Christian Bks.; *CIP.*

Grove Creek Publishing, LLC, (978-1-933963) 1159 N. 950 E., Pleasant Grove, UT 84062 USA Tel 801-471-5652
E-mail: noonws@yahoo.com
Web site: http://www.grovecreekpublishing.com.

Grove Educational Technologies, (978-0-936735) 6435 Yamhill St., SE, Portland, OR 97215-2027 USA (SAN 699-9840); 27 Hy Pl., Lake Grove, NY 11755 (SAN 699-9859)
E-mail: geta@juno.com.

†Grove/Atlantic, Inc., (978-0-8021; 978-0-87113; 978-1-55584; 978-1-61185) 841 Broadway, 4th Flr., New York, NY 10003-4793 USA (SAN 201-4890) Tel 212-614-7850; Fax: 212-614-7886; Toll Free: 800-521-0178; *Imprints:* Black Cat (BlackCat)
Web site: http://www.groveatlantic.com/
Dist(s): **MyiLibrary**
Open Road Integrated Media, Inc.
Publishers Group West (PGW)
Two Rivers Distribution; *CIP.*

Grow Good Publishing, (978-1-7364208) 41 S. Shell Rd., DeBary, FL 32713 USA Tel 407-748-4463
E-mail: juliebishopcassetta@gmail.com
Web site: juliecassetta.com.

Grow Grit Pr., (978-1-7338627; 978-1-951056; 978-1-953399; 978-1-63731) 4400 S. Coltrane Rd, Edmond, OK 73013 USA (SAN 992-0145) Tel 405-971-4888
E-mail: marynhin@gmail.com.

Growing & Learning Pr., (978-0-9795773) 228 Woodward Ave, Buffalo, NY 14214 USA (SAN 853-8093).

Growing Art Pr., (978-1-934367) 419 NW 16th St., Corvallis, OR 97330 USA (SAN 852-9612)
E-mail: stickmaker@comcast.net.

Growing Communities for Peace, (978-0-9646676) P.O. Box 248, Scandia, MN 55073 USA Tel 651-257-2478; Fax: 651-257-2095
Web site: http://www.peacemaker.org.

Growing Field *Imprint of* **Growing Field Bks.**

Growing Field Bks., (978-0-9770391; 978-0-9857057; 978-0-9891881) 514 Elm St., Windsor, CO 80550 USA (SAN 851-7193); *Imprints:* Growing Field (Growing Field) Do not confuse with companies with the same or similar name in Lawrence, KSThomaston, CT, Los Angeles, CA, Huntsville, AL, New YOrk, NY, Glen Head, NY
E-mail: Mhoog@growingfield.com
Web site: http://www.Growingfield.com
Dist(s): **Brodart Co.**
Follett School Solutions
Hertzberg-New Method Inc.

Growing Little Readers, (978-0-9777150) 1105 Kyle Ct., Chesapeake, VA 23322 USA
Web site: http://growinglittlereaders.com.

Growing Senses Pubns., (978-0-9973189) 5842 Cranbrook Trail, Traverse City, MI 49685 USA Tel 231-881-4138
E-mail: growingsensespublications@gmail.com.

Growing with the Saints, Inc., (978-0-9798889) 2812 Longwood Ct., Fort Wayne, IN 46845 USA Tel 260-489-8493
E-mail: melissa@growingwiththesaints.com
Web site: http://www.growingwiththesaints.com.

Growing Years *Imprint of* **Port Town Publishing**

Growsies, (978-0-9980949) 10905 Tree Cactus Loop, Land O Lakes, FL 34638 USA Tel 727-641-7944
E-mail: growsiestories@gmail.com
Web site: www.growsiestories.wordpress.com.

Growth Affirming Co., (978-0-9913804) 2760 150th Ave., Clear Lake, MN 55319-9561 USA Tel 763-856-8646
E-mail: growthaffirm@izoom.net
Web site: Growthaffirm.com.

Growth Publishing, (978-1-893505) Div. of Growth Central LLC, Orders Addr.: 6545 N. Via Divina, Tucson, AZ 85750-0971 USA Tel 520-299-2550; Fax: 520-577-6998
E-mail: growthcentral@gmail.com
Web site: http://www.growthcentral.com/.

Growth-Ink, (978-0-9799636) 4025 State St., No. 9, Santa Barbara, CA 93110 USA (SAN 854-9303)
E-mail: Growthink1@aol.com.

Gruber Enterprises, (978-0-9770413) 21521 Finlan, Saint Clair Shores, MI 48080 USA
Web site: http://www.thelegendofthebrog.com.

Grubish, Donald, (978-0-9771179) 1326 Goodwin Ave N., Saint Paul, MN 55128-6164 USA.

Grubnedor Pr., (978-0-9795407; 978-0-9989368; 978-0-578-58511-6; 978-0-578-58512-3; 978-0-578-63474-6) 8121 Allison Pl., Arvada, CO 80005 USA (SAN 853-7186)
E-mail: dmrodenburg@comcast.net
Web site: grubnedorpress.com.

Grupo Anaya, S.A. (ESP) (978-84-207; 978-84-667; 978-84-678; 978-84-698) *Dist. by* **Distribks Inc.**

Grupo Anaya, S.A. (ESP) (978-84-207; 978-84-667; 978-84-678; 978-84-698) *Dist. by* **Continental Bk.**

Grupo Anaya, S.A. (ESP) (978-84-207; 978-84-667; 978-84-678; 978-84-698) *Dist. by* **AIMS Intl.**

Grupo Anaya, S.A. (ESP) (978-84-207; 978-84-667; 978-84-678; 978-84-698) *Dist. by* **Lectorum Pubns.**

Grupo Nelson, (978-0-8499; 978-0-88113; 978-0-89922; 978-1-60255) Div. of Thomas Nelson, Inc., 501 Nelson Pl., Nashville, TN 37217 USA (SAN 240-6349) Tel 615-889-9000; Fax: 615-883-9376; Toll Free: 800-251-4000
Web site: http://www.editorialcaribe.com
Dist(s): **Ediciones Universal**
HarperCollins Christian Publishing
Libros Sin Fronteras
Luciano Bks.
Nelson, Thomas Inc.
Pan De Vida Distributors
Peniel Productions
Twentieth Century Christian Bks.
Zondervan.

Gryphon House Inc *Imprint of* **Gryphon Hse., Inc.**

Gryphon Hse., Inc., (978-0-87659; 978-0-917505; 978-1-58904; 978-1-63650) Orders Addr.: 6848 Leon's Way, Lewisville, NC 27023 USA (SAN 169-3190) Tel 800-638-0928; Fax: 800-638-7576; Toll Free: 800-638-0928; *Imprints:* Robins Lane Press (Robins Ln Pr); School Age Notes (School-Age); Gryphon House Inc (GHI)
E-mail: info@ghbooks.com
Web site: http://www.gryphonhouse.com
Dist(s): **CENGAGE Learning**
Children's Plus, Inc.
Firebrand Technologies
INscribe Digital
MyiLibrary
ebrary, Inc.

Gryphon Pr., The, (978-0-940719) 6808 Margarets Ln., Edina, MN 55439 USA Tel 952-941-5993; Fax: 952-941-6593
E-mail: eb6@earthlink.net
Dist(s): **Consortium Bk. Sales & Distribution.**

G.S. Enterprises of America Inc., (978-0-9763141) P.O. Box 776, Frankfort, KY 40602-0776 USA Tel 502-227-8226; Fax: 502-227-8223
E-mail: lstafford173@gmail.com
Web site: http://www.bedtimeboomer.com.

GS Publishers *See* **GSVQ Publishing**

GSD Publishing, (978-0-9724658) 5589 Nix Rd., Fayetteville, NC 28314 USA Tel 910-864-5033.

GSP Players, LLC, (978-0-9792640) 8033 Sunset Blvd., No. 1024, Los Angeles, CA 90046 USA.

G-Square Publishing, (978-0-692-10481-1) 888c 8th Ave. suite 424, New York, NY 10019 USA Tel 917-681-2810
E-mail: G-Square-pub@optimum.net
Web site: G-Square.org.

GSR Communications, (978-0-9717507) 6090 SW Elm Ave., Beaverton, OR 97005 USA
E-mail: gsr@teleport.com.

GSS Tech Ed, (978-0-9712340; 978-0-9895576) 31500 Grape St. Bldg. 3-364, Lake Elsinore, CA 92532 USA Tel 951-471-4932; Fax: 951-471-4981; Toll Free Fax: 866-367-6180; Toll Free: 800-422-1100
Web site: http://www.GSSTechEd.com
Dist(s): **All Electronics Corp.**
Pitsco Education.

GSVQ Publishing, (978-1-933156) 1350 E. Flamingo Rd., Suite 50, Las Vegas, NV 89119-5263 USA Tel 866-347-9244; *Imprints:* VisionQuest Kids (VisionQuest Kids); Visikid Books (Visikid Bks)
E-mail: contactus@gsvisionquest.com
Web site: http://www.gsvisionquest.com; http://www.visikidbooks.com.

GT Bks. LLC, (978-0-9765845) 19 Housman Ct., Maplewood, NJ 07040-3006 USA
Web site: http://www.gtbooks.net.

GT Interactive Software, (978-1-56893; 978-1-58869) 417 Fifth Ave., New York, NY 10016 USA Tel 212-726-4243; Fax: 212-726-4204
E-mail: efierro@gtinteractive.com
Web site: http://gtinteractive.com.

GTA Bks., (978-1-7336245; 979-8-9876115) 1017 Ledgewood Trail, Lyndhurst, OH 44124 USA Tel 440-523-8538
E-mail: alex.shaland@gmail.com
Web site: globaltravelauthors.com.

Guadeloupe, Emmanuel & Augustine 'Gus' Logie *See* **Plain Vision Publishing**

Guangdong New Era Publishing Hse. (CHN) (978-7-5405; 978-7-5583) *Dist. by* **Chinasprout.**

Guardian Angel Publishing, (978-0-9763990) 415 Meadow View Dr., Lavon, TX 75166-1245 USA Do not confuse with companies with the same or similar name in Carby, OR, Saint Louis, MO
E-mail: admin@tommytellbooks.com
Web site: http://www.tommytellbooks.com.

Guardian Angel Publishing, Inc., (978-1-933090; 978-1-935137; 978-1-61633; 978-1-951545) 12430 Tesson Ferry Rd., No. 186, Saint Louis, MO 63128 USA (SAN 858-7833) Do not confuse with companies with same name in Canby, OR and Hubbard, OR., The Colony, TX
E-mail: publisher@guardianangelpublishing.com
Web site: http://www.guardianangelpublishing.com.

Guardian of Truth Foundation *See* **Truth Publications, Inc.**

Guardian Publishing, (978-0-615-69862-5; 978-0-9892163; 978-0-9892385; 978-0-9909008; 978-0-9965569; 978-1-7340643) 8044 Montgomery Rd. Suite 440, Cincinnati, OH 45213 USA Tel 800-554-7233; Fax: 866-913-4911
E-mail: jmiller@ojmgroup.com
Web site: www.guardpub.com.

Guardians of Order (CAN) (978-0-9682431; 978-1-894525) *Dist. by* **PSI Ga.**

Guardsman Press *See* **Moondance Publishing**

Guemann, Steven, (978-0-9909120) 13870 Idaho Maryland Rd., Nevada City, CA 95959 USA Tel 530-274-9245
E-mail: sguemann@sbcglobal.net.

Guernica Editions, Inc. (CAN) (978-0-919349; 978-0-920717; 978-1-55071; 978-2-89135; 978-1-77183) *Dist. by* **IPG Chicago.**

Guerra, Justin A., (978-0-692-87963-4; 978-0-692-98756-8; 979-8-218-05563-9) 14685 Eagle River Rd, EASTVALE, CA 92880 USA Tel 760-912-3560
E-mail: jeffwcrawford5+LVP0003671@gmail.com; jeffwcrawford5+LVP0003671@gmail.com.

Guest Cottage, Incorporated, The, 8821 Hwy 47, Woodruff, WI 54568 USA Tel 715-358-5195; Fax: 715-358-9456
E-mail: amherst@networth.net
Web site: www.amherstpress.com
Dist(s): **Chicago Distribution Ctr.**

Guevara, Alexis S., (978-0-9765663) 1625 Palo Alto St., No. 208, Los Angeles, CA 90026 USA
E-mail: sa_guevara@msn.com
Web site: http://www.selectaUSA.com; http://www.alexisguevara.com.

Guia, Elizabeth, (978-0-9764280) 15060 SW 104 St. #1613, Miami, FL 33196 USA
E-mail: eguiam@live.com.

Guide to South Florida Off-Road Bicycling *See* **DeGraaf Publishing**

Guideline Pubns. Co., (978-1-882951) Div. of Marketing Support Services, Orders Addr.: P.O. Box 801094, Atlanta, GA 30101 USA Fax: 770-424-0778; Toll Free: 800-552-1076
E-mail: sales@guidelinepub.com
Web site: http://www.guidelinepub.com.

Guiding Horizons, (978-0-9749763) 2201 Heritage Crest Dr., Valrico, FL 33594-5120 USA
Web site: http://www.guidinghorizons.com.

Guidry Assocs., Inc., (978-0-9724667) P.O. Box 2280, Winchester, VA 22604 USA Tel 540-545-8800; *Imprints:* Who's Who In Sports (Who's Who In Sp)
E-mail: info@whoswhoinsports.com
Web site: http://www.whoswhoinsports.com.

Guiffre Bk. Publishing, (978-0-9830172) Orders Addr.: P.O. Box 202, Inlet, NY 13360 USA; Edit Addr.: 298 Salt Meadow Cove, Kiawah Island, SC 29455 USA Tel 843-714-7040; 315-357-3422; 843-789-3269
E-mail: misspatrish@gmail.com; wguiffre@frontiernet.net.

Guild of Limners, The *Imprint of* **Interset Pr.**

Guilford Pr., The *Imprint of* **Guilford Pubns.**

Guilford Pubns., (978-0-89862; 978-1-57230; 978-1-59385; 978-1-60623; 978-1-60918; 978-1-4625) Orders Addr.: 370 Seventh Avenue, Suite 1200, New York, NY 10001-1020 USA (SAN 212-9442) Tel 212-431-9800; Fax: 212-966-6708; Toll Free: 800-365-7006; *Imprints:* Guilford Press, The (GuilfordPr)
E-mail: info@guilford.com
Web site: http://www.guilford.com
Dist(s): **Ebsco Publishing**
MyiLibrary
Rittenhouse Bk. Distributors
Taylor & Francis Group
ebrary, Inc.

Guilin City Publishing, (978-0-9818622) P.O. Box 9621, Pittsburgh, PA 15226 USA
E-mail: info@guilincitypublishing.com
Web site: http://www.guilincitypublishing.com.

Guilty Mom Pr., (978-0-9708415) 172 Dolphin Cir., Marina, CA 93933 USA Tel 831-384-8459
E-mail: plumtckrd@aol.com
Dist(s): **One Small Voice Foundation.**

Guipil Press *See* **Editorial Guipil**

GuitarVoyager Inc., (978-0-9785992) 3616 Calvend Ln., Kensington, MD 20895 USA Tel 240-486-3849; Fax: 301-949-1647
E-mail: guitarvoyager@gmail.com
Web site: http://www.guitarvoyager.com.

Gullah Girl Publishing, (978-0-9967540)
E-mail: bftafwife1@yahoo.com.

Gulley Institute of Creative Learning, Inc., (978-1-928561) Orders Addr.: P.O. Box 652, Meridian, MS 39302 USA Tel 601-483-0963; Fax: 601-483-0962; Edit Addr.: P.O. Box 1266, Inglewood, CA 90308-1266 USA
E-mail: Gulstem7@aol.com.

Gulley, Wayne, (978-0-9843505; 978-0-9886117; 978-0-9981252) P.O. Box 8807, Spring Valley Lake (Victorville), CA 92395 USA
E-mail: wagpublishing@me.com
Web site: www.michelangelotangelo.com.

Gulliver Bks. *Imprint of* **Harcourt Children's Bks.**

GULP Pr., (978-1-7323810) W3685 Jostad Rd, Mindoro, WI 54644 USA Tel 608-338-9992
E-mail: beth.mattson@gmail.com
Web site: bethmattson.com.

Gultepe, Evin, (978-1-7345359) 2815 Autumn Estates 0, SAN JOSE, CA 95135 USA Tel 8572774901
E-mail: evingultepe@gmail.com
Dist(s): **Ingram Content Group.**

Gumbo Multimedia Entertainment, (978-0-9762838; 978-0-9832329) P.O. Box 371641, Miami, FL 32821 USA
E-mail: srodriguez@lushenabks.com; Jeff@JeffRivera.com
Web site: http://www.JeffRivera.com; http://www.GumboWriters.com
Dist(s): **NetSource Distribution**
Smashwords.

Gumdrop Pr., (978-0-692-50194-8; 978-0-692-54667-3; 978-0-692-54669-7; 978-0-692-54843-1; 978-0-692-56291-8; 978-0-692-56420-2; 978-0-692-56869-9; 978-0-692-57148-4; 978-0-692-57399-0; 978-0-692-57563-5; 978-0-692-57788-2; 978-0-692-57967-1; 978-0-692-57996-1; 978-0-692-58001-1; 978-0-692-58022-6; 978-0-692-58025-7; 978-0-692-58067-7; 978-0-692-58070-7; 978-0-692-58071-4; 978-0-692-58081-3; 978-0-692-58117-9; 978-0-692-58122-3; 978-0-692-58128-5; 978-0-692-58169-8; 978-0-692-58187-2; 978-0-692-58194-0) 12220 Maycheck Ln, Bowie, MD 20715 USA; *Imprints:* Big Blue World Books (Big Blue W)
Web site: http://www.gumdroppress.com
Dist(s): **CreateSpace Independent Publishing Platform.**

GumShoe Press, (978-0-9777538) Orders Addr.: 411 Chartley Pk. Rd., Reisterstown, MD 21136 USA (SAN 850-1769) Tel 410-971-8229
E-mail: tjmysteryauthor@aol.com
Web site: http://www.authorsden.com/tjperkins.

Gunderson, Cindy *See* **Button Pr.**

Gunderson, Lisa M., (978-0-692-96692-1; 978-0-692-96768-3; 978-0-692-12699-8) 6423 W 94th St, Oak Lawn, IL 60453 USA Tel 708-945-7968; *Imprints:* Tea Time Socials, LLC (Tea Time S)
E-mail: lmgmarketingchicago@gmail.com
Web site: www.teatimesocials.com.

Gunnar Swager Foundation, (978-0-578-58721-9) 5915 N Normandie St., Spokane, WA 99205 USA Tel 509-939-2518
E-mail: cot16@live.com
Web site: www.gunnarswagerfoundation.com.

Gunter, Nathan *See* **TGJS Publishing**

Guppy Publishing LLC, (978-0-9788553) PMB 221, 6749 S. Westnedge, Suite K, Portage, MI 49002 USA Fax: 269-327-3168
E-mail: dkennis@charter.net
Web site: http://www.guppypublishing.com.

Gupton, Gary Neil, (978-0-692-95396-9; 978-0-692-97766-8; 978-0-692-14874-7) 1109 Hampton Pines Ct., LELAND, NC 28451 USA Tel 9103710033
E-mail: g.guppy63@gmail.com
Dist(s): **Ingram Content Group.**

Gurevich, Leonid, (978-0-9753458) 4 Remington Ln., Plymouth, MA 02360-1424 USA
E-mail: lgurev3007@aol.com.

Guru Graphics, (978-0-9729759) 500 Creekside Ct., Golden, CO 80403-1903 USA Tel 303-278-0177
E-mail: levropes@attbi.com.

Gurze Bks *Imprint of* **Turner Publishing Co.**

Gustav's Library, (978-0-9758914) 1011 E. High St., Davenport, IA 52803 USA Tel 563-323-2283
E-mail: gustav@gustavslibrary.com
Web site: http://www.gustavslibrary.com.

Gutenberg Publishers *See* **Albatross Pubs.**

Guzman, Maria del C., (978-0-9855639) 39 Arenas St., Aguirre, PR 00794 USA Tel 787-853-2542
E-mail: mguzman_aguirre@yahoo.com.

GW Publishing (GBR) *(978-0-9535397; 978-0-9546701; 978-0-9551564; 978-0-9554145; 978-0-9561211; 978-0-9570844) Dist. by* **MYID_F_GATEWOO.**

Gwarmekia, *(978-0-615-61445-8; 978-0-692-52428-2; 978-0-692-17810-2; 978-0-692-18855-2)* 924 9th Ave., Pleasant Grove, AL 35127 USA Tel 256-682-6834
E-mail: gwarmekia.germany@gmail.com.

GWB *Imprint of* **Great White Bird Publishing**

Gwenwst Bks., *(978-0-9914423)* P.O. Box 457, Willernie, MN 55090 USA Tel 651-280-7232
E-mail: John.digley@gmail.com
Web site: Pending.

GWF Publishing & Henry's Helpers, *(978-0-9768442)*
E-mail: henryshelpers@yahoo.com
Web site: http://www.henryshelpers.com.

GWOG, *(978-0-692-08311-6; 978-1-7344104)* 318 Plaza Del Sol Pk., Houston, TX 77020 USA Tel 832-233-9494
E-mail: elliotgarcia01@gmail.com.

GWW Publishing Co. *See* **Relentless Publishing Hse.**

GYATRi Media, *(978-0-9988778)* 269 S Western Ave No. 212, Los Angeles, CA 90004 USA Tel 310-426-8899
E-mail: strangeway.ji@gmail.com.

Gye Nyame Hse., *(978-1-886098)* Orders Addr.: P.O. Box 42248, Philadelphia, PA 19101 USA (SAN 299-0415) Tel 215 229 1751; Edit Addr.: 6810 Old York Rd., Philadelphia, PA 19126 USA Tel 215-548-2175
E-mail: gyenyamehouse@aol.com.

Gye Nyame Press *See* **Love II Learn Bks.**

Gypsy Heart Press *See* **Courageous Heart Pr.**

Gypsy Hill Publishing,

Gypsy Pubns., *(978-0-9842375; 978-1-938768; 978-1-955640)* 325 Green Oak Dr., Troy, OH 45373-4396 USA
E-mail: fishermh@juno.com; meg.fisher@yahoo.com
Web site: http://www.gypsypublications.com.

Gypsy Shadow Publishing Co., *(978-0-9844521; 978-0-9834027; 978-1-61950)* 222 Llano St., Lockhart, TX 78644 USA Tel 512-428-8816
E-mail: cholley@gypsyshadow.com
Web site: http://www.gypsyshadow.com
Dist(s): **Smashwords.**

Gyrfalcon Pr., *(978-1-7344251)* 5744 N 71st St, Longmont, CO 80503-8623 USA Tel 720-470-9454
E-mail: shannon@sovndal.com.

Gyromagnetic Pr., *(978-0-9764790; 978-1-7334070)* 228 Smith Cross Rd., Cooperstown, NY 13326 USA
E-mail: coinmagic1@aol.com
Web site: http://www.geocities.com/larrybarnowsky/.

H & R Magic Bks., *(978-0-9727938; 978-0-578-27064-7)* 14606 Wisteria Hollow Ln., Houston, TX 77062 USA Tel 281-540-7229; 281-549-2007
Web site: http://www.magicbookshop.com; www.hrmagicbooks.com.

H Bar Pr., *(978-0-9794104; 978-0-9893092; 978-1-7324594; 979-8-9861522)* 29 Village St., East Wallingford, VT 05742 USA (SAN 853-3644) Tel 802-259-6072
E-mail: kwford@verizon.net; hbar.press@verizon.net; puttyhead@aol.com
Dist(s): **Smashwords.**

H E C Software, Inc., *(978-0-928424; 978-1-62382)* 60 N. Cutler Dr., No. 101, North Salt Lake, UT 84054 USA (SAN 669-6201) Tel 801-295-7054; Fax: 801-295-7088; Toll Free: 800-333-0054
E-mail: info@readinghorizons.com
Web site: http://www.readinghorizons.com.

H H Krsna Balaram Swami, *(978-0-9631403)* Orders Addr.: P.O. Box 27127, Baltimore, MD 21230 USA; Edit Addr.: 1613 Webster St., Baltimore, MD 21230 USA Tel 301-752-7531.

H M Bricker, *(978-0-615-42163-6; 978-0-9838738)* Orders Addr.: 2279 Grass Lake Rd., Lindenhurst, IL 60046 USA
E-mail: santanobeard@comcast.net; birdman1211@comcast.net
Web site: http://www.grandpabrickerbooks.com.

H M S Pubns., Inc., *(978-1-888732)* P.O. Box 524, Niantic, CT 06357 USA Tel 860-739-3187; Toll Free: 888-739-3187
E-mail: hmspublications@earthlink.net
Dist(s): **Follett School Solutions**
Quality Bks., Inc.
ebrary, Inc.

H. O. M. E. (Holding Onto Memorable Experiences) *See* **Do The Write Thing Foundation of DC**

H R M Software *See* **Human Relations Media**

HSA Pubns., *(978-0-910621; 978-1-931166)* 4 W. 43rd St., New York, NY 10036 USA (SAN 270-6490) Tel 212-997-0050; Fax: 212-768-7149.

Haag Environmental Press *See* **Haag Pr.**

Haag Pr., *(978-0-9665497; 978-0-9710260; 978-0-9797511)* Div. of Haag Environmental Co., Inc., Orders Addr.: 315 E. Market St., Sandusky, OH 44870 USA (SAN 852-6583) Tel 419-621-9329; Fax: 419-621-8669
E-mail: haagpress@aol.com; help@haagpress.com
Web site: http://www.haagpress.com.

Haan Graphic Publishing Services, Limited *See* **Southfarm Pr.**

Haas, Melissa *See* **Sophisticated Unicorn**

Habakkuk Publishing, *(978-0-9798082; 978-0-9827769; 978-0-692-62872-0; 978-0-578-21055-1)* P.O. Box 871601, Canton, MI 48187 USA; 9376 Westwind Dr., Livonia, MI 48150
Web site: http://www.dudleyministries.com.

Haber-Schaim & Associates *See* **Science Curriculum, Inc.**

Habit House *See* **Roedway Pr.**

Hachai Publications, Incorporated *See* **Hachai Publishing**

Hachai Publishing, *(978-0-922613; 978-1-929628; 978-1-945560; 979-8-88806)* 527 Empire Blvd., Brooklyn, NY 11225 USA (SAN 251-3749) Tel 718-633-0100; Fax: 718-633-0103
E-mail: info@hachai.com
Web site: http://www.hachai.com
Dist(s): **Kerem Publishing.**

Hachette Antoine, *(978-0-692-94283-3; 978-0-578-78619-3)* 525 W 28th St, New York, NY 10001 USA Tel 917-993-0758
E-mail: chaker@chakerkhazaal.com
Web site: http://www.hachette.com/en/maison/hachette-antoine.

Hachette Audio, *(978-1-57042; 978-1-58621; 978-1-59483; 978-1-60024; 978-1-60788; 978-1-5491; 978-1-6686)* Div. of Hachette Book Group, 1290 Ave. of the Americas, New York, NY 10104 USA Tel 212-364-1100; Fax: 212-364-1923; Toll Free: 800-759-0190
E-mail: audiobooks.publicity@hbgusa.com
Web site: http://www.hachettebookgroupusa.com/publishing_hachette-audio.aspx
Dist(s): **Blackstone Audio, Inc.**
Findaway World, LLC
Follett School Solutions
Grand Central Publishing
Hachette Bk. Group
Libros Sin Fronteras
Landmark Audiobooks.

Hachette AudioBooks *See* **Hachette Audio**

Hachette Australia (AUS) *(978-0-340; 978-0-450; 978-0-7336; 978-0-7267; 978-0-7316-4988-4; 978-0-646-26970-2; 978-0-646-26972-6; 978-0-646-42250-3) Dist. by* **HachBkGrp.**

Hachette Bks. *Imprint of* **Hachette Bks.**

Hachette Bk. Group, *(978-0-446; 978-1-60286; 978-1-60941; 978-1-61113; 978-1-61969; 978-1-4789; 978-1-64732; 978-1-63883; 979-8-88585; 979-8-88969)* Div. of Hachette Group Livre, Orders Addr.: 3 Center Plaza, Boston, MA 02108 USA (SAN 852-5463) Tel 617-263-1828; Toll Free Fax: 800-286-9471; Toll Free: 800-759-0190; Edit Addr.: P.O. Box 2146, Johannesburg, 2196 ZAF Tel 2711 783-7565; Fax: 2711 883-6866
Web site: http://www.hachettebookgroup.com
Dist(s): **Blackstone Audio, Inc.**
Findaway World, LLC
Follett School Solutions
MyiLibrary
Open Road Integrated Media, Inc.
Perfection Learning Corp.
Time Inc. Bks.

Hachette Bks., *(978-0-201; 978-0-306; 978-0-7382; 978-0-938289; 978-0-946771; 978-0-9627613; 978-1-55561; 978-1-58097; 978-1-873376; 978-1-882810; 978-1-885119)* Div. of Hachette Book Group, Orders Addr.: 3 Center Plaza, Boston, MA 02108-2084 USA Tel 617-227-0730; Toll Free Fax: 800-286-9471; Toll Free: 800-759-0730; Edit Addr.: 237 Park Ave., New York, NY 10017 USA Tel 212-364-0600; Fax: 212-364-0952; *Imprints:* Hachette Books (HachetteBks); Black Dog & Leventhal Publishers, Inc. (BlackDog Lev); Da Capo Lifelong (DaCapoLF); Da Capo Press, Incorporated (DaCapoPRI)
Dist(s): **Blackstone Audio, Inc.**
Children's Plus, Inc.
Hachette Bk. Group
MyiLibrary
Open Road Integrated Media, Inc.

Hachette Children's Group (GBR) *(978-0-7502; 978-1-85881; 978-1-84255; 978-1-4440; 978-1-4449) Dist. by* **HachBkGrp.**

Hachette Children's Group (GBR) *(978-0-7502; 978-1-85881; 978-1-84255; 978-1-4440; 978-1-4449) Dist. by* **IPG Chicago.**

Hachette Groupe Livre (FRA) *(978-2-01) Dist. by* **Distribks Inc.**

Hachette New Zealand (NZL) *(978-0-340; 978-1-86958; 978-0-908676; 978-1-86971; 978-1-877426) Dist. by* **HachBkGrp.**

†Hackett Publishing Co., Inc., *(978-0-87220; 978-0-915144; 978-0-915145; 978-0-941051; 978-1-58510; 978-1-60384; 978-1-62466; 978-1-64792; 978-1-64793)* Orders Addr.: P.O. Box 44937, Indianapolis, IN 46244-0937 USA (SAN 201-6044) Tel 317-635-9250; Fax: 317-635-9292; Toll Free Fax: 800-783-9213; *Imprints:* Focus (FocusUSA)
E-mail: customer@hackettpublishing.com; lizw@hackettpublishing.com
Web site: http://www.hackettpublishing.com
Dist(s): **ebrary, Inc.**; *CIP.*

Hadassah's Crown LLC *See* **Hadassah's Crown Publishing, LLC**

Hadassah's Crown Publishing, LLC, *(978-0-9981230; 978-0-692-98525-0; 978-0-9980269; 978-1-950894; 978-1-960779)* 634 NE Main St., No. 1263, Simpsonville, SC 29681 USA Tel 864-708-1214
E-mail: soncunnlev@gmail.com
Web site: http://HadassahsCrownPublishing.com.

Hadrosaur Pr., *(978-1-885093; 979-8-9851120)* P.O. Box 2194, Mesilla Park, NM 88047-2194 USA Tel 575-639-3411; *Imprints:* LBF/Hadrosaur (LBF Hadrs)
E-mail: hadrosaur@zianet.com
Web site: http://www.hadrosaur.com.

Hafabanana Press *See* **KB Bks. & More**

Hagan, Theda *See* **Hagan, Theda Bks.**

Hagan, Theda Bks., *(978-0-9678032; 978-0-9827155)* 47 Comer Dr., Madisonville, KY 42431 USA Tel 270-821-6968
E-mail: thedahagan@yahoo.com
Web site: http://www.heavenlyharborbooks.com/default.htm.

Hager, Robert, *(978-0-9727676)* 101 Crawford, Suite 2C, Houston, TX 77002 USA
Web site: http://www.saurcana.com/pages/about_author.html.

Hagnos Editora (BRA) *Dist. by* **Whitaker Hse.**

Hahn, Beverly, *(978-0-9722494)* Orders Addr.: P.O. Box 66, Hilmak, CA 95324 USA; Edit Addr.: 9613 Ailanthus Ave., Delhi, CA 95315 USA (SAN 254-7376).

Hairball Pr., *(978-0-9646781)* 2318 2nd Ave., Suite 591, Seattle, WA 98121 USA Tel 206-932-8173.

Hairston Enterprises, LLC, *(978-0-9762958)* 582 Bristol Ln., Birmingham, AL 35226 USA Tel 205-369-4022
E-mail: kchairston@yahoo.com
Web site: http://www.forgottenrules.com; http://www.forgottenrules.org; http://www.theforgottenrules.com; http://www.theforgottenrules.org.

Hairston, Rodney, *(978-0-9760689)* 75 Fern Oak Cir. Apt. 201, Stafford, VA 22554-8459 USA
E-mail: rhairston@jbmanagement.com.

Haislip, Allen, *(978-0-9767640)* Orders Addr.: 32 Marquette Dr., Florissant, MO 63031-3839 USA.

Haiti World, *(978-0-9793039)* P.O. Box 5663, Vernon Hills, IL 60061 USA Tel 847-514-9967
E-mail: haitiworld@yahoo.com.

Halbur Publishing, *(978-0-9603520)* 142 Angela Dr., Santa Rosa, CA 95403-1702 USA (SAN 212-9469)
E-mail: dhalbur@sonic.net.

Halcyon Pr., *(978-0-941970)* 18-05 215 St., Flushing, NY 11360 USA (SAN 238-244X) Tel 212-631-9640 Do not confuse with companies with same or similar name in Hendersonville, NC, Dallas, TX, Houston, TX.

Halcyon Pr., Ltd., *(978-0-9706054; 978-1-931823; 978-0-9830676)* P.O. Box 260, Pearland, TX 77588-0260 USA (SAN 253-9934) Toll Free: 866-774-5786 Do not confuse with companies with same or similar name in Hendersonville, NC, Flushing, NY, Dallas, TX
E-mail: david.raley@gmail.com
Web site: http://www.halcyonpress.com
Dist(s): **Bk. Marketing Plus.**

Haldane Mason, Ltd. (GBR) *(978-1-902463; 978-1-905339; 978-1-909720) Dist. by* **Trans-Atl Phila.**

Hale Kuamo'o Hawaiian Language Ctr. at UHH, *(978-0-9665331; 978-1-930339; 978-0-9741580)* Div. of Ka Haka 'Ula o Ke'elikolani/College of Hawaiian Language at UH Hilo, 200 W. Kawili St., Hilo, HI 96720-4091 USA Tel 808-974-7339; Fax: 808-974-7686
E-mail: contact@ahapunanaleo.org
Web site: http://www.olelo.hawaii.edu; http://www.ahapunanaleo.org.

Hale Publishing, *(978-0-9636219; 978-0-9729583; 978-0-9772268; 978-0-9815257; 978-0-9823379; 978-0-9845039; 978-0-9833075; 978-0-9847746; 978-0-9858893; 978-1-939847)* 1712 N. Forest St., Amarillo, TX 79106 USA Tel 806-376-9900 Toll Free: 800-378-1317
E-mail: books@ibreastfeeding.com; alicia.ingram@halepublishing.com
Web site: http://www.ibreastfeeding.com.

Haley's, *(978-0-9626308; 978-1-884540; 978-0-9897667; 978-0-9916102; 978-0-9967730; 978-0-9982735; 978-1-948380; 978-1-956055)* Orders Addr.: 488 S. Main St., Athol, MA 01331 USA Tel 978-249-9400 (phone/fax); Toll Free: 800-215-8805 (phone/fax); Edit Addr.: 488 S. Main St., Athol, MA 01331 USA
E-mail: haley.antique@verizon.net
Dist(s): **Follett School Solutions.**

Half Nelson Enterprises, *(978-1-947934; 978-0-578-92189-1)* 306 Greenup St., Covington, KY 41011 USA Tel 513-607-1206
E-mail: richardhunt07@gmail.com.

Half-Pint Kids, Inc., *(978-1-59256)* Orders Addr.: 646 Crabapple Ln., Ellwood City, PA 16117 USA Tel 724-809-8023
Web site: http://halfpintkids.com.

Hall & Humphries Publishing Hse., *(978-0-9758521)* Orders Addr.: P.O. Box 371021, Decatur, GA 30037-1021 USA; Edit Addr.: 2652 Rainbow Pkwy., Decatur, GA 30034 USA Tel 404-625-4486.

Hall, Annalisa, *(978-0-615-22113-7)* 14271 Anabelle Dr., Poway, CA 92064 USA
Dist(s): **Lulu Pr., Inc.**

Hall, Dana, *(978-0-578-40551-3)* 10 Whaton Oaks Ct., Greensboro, NC 27409 USA Tel 336-501-4334
E-mail: danahallgso@gmail.com
Dist(s): **Ingram Content Group.**

Hall, Joan, *(978-0-692-00148-6)* 1209 Jolliff Rd., Chesapeake, VA 23321 USA Tel 757-620-8871.

Hall, Kenneth, *(978-0-615-19649-7)* 1857 Morris Ave., Lincoln Park, MI 48146-1328 USA
E-mail: kenhall321@yahoo.com
Dist(s): **Lulu Pr., Inc.**

Hall, Monique P. Productions, *(978-0-9772634)* 167 Wyatt Earp Loop, Nolanville, TX 76559 USA (SAN 851-6391) Tel 254-462-2990
E-mail: nickiepop777@gmail.com; moniquephallproductions@gmail.com
Web site: http://nickiepopart.com.

Hall, Nancy Inc., *(978-1-884270)* 7 W. 18th St., 6th Flr., New York, NY 10011 USA Tel 212-674-3408; Fax: 212-353-1521
E-mail: Nhallinc@aol.com.

Hall Press *See* **Hallcienda**

Hall, Stephen & Denise, *(978-0-9753305)* 1237 Prairie Dell Rd., Union, MO 63084-4310 USA
E-mail: wordsofahunter@cs.com.

Hall, Wesley F., *(978-0-9717055; 978-0-692-25358-8; 978-0-692-60207-2)* Orders Addr.: P.O. Box 11904, Omaha, NE 68111 USA; Edit Addr.: 10309 Huntington Ave., Omaha, NE 68122 USA
E-mail: whall8882@aol.com.

HallaVision Publishing *Imprint of* **Ginger Nielson - Children's Bk. Illustration**

Hallcienda, *(978-0-932218; 978-0-578-54705-3)* Orders Addr.: P.O. Box 9066, San Bernardino, CA 92427 USA (SAN 211-7061) Tel 909-887-3466; P.O. Box 9066, San Bernardino, CA 92427 USA (SAN 665-7060) Tel 909-887-3466.

Hallelujah Acres Publishing, *(978-0-929619)* P.O. Box 2388, Shelby, NC 28151 USA (SAN 249-7891) Tel 704-481-1700; Fax: 704-481-0345
E-mail: chet@hacres.com
Web site: http://www.hacres.com
Dist(s): **Send The Light Distribution LLC.**

Haller Company, The, *(978-0-9743961)* Orders Addr.: P.O. Box 207, Burlingame, CA 94010 USA Tel 650-348-3900 Fax: 650-558-9012; Edit Addr.: 1325 Howard Ave., Burlingame, CA 94010 USA
Web site: http://www.hallercompany.com.

Hallinan, Claire E., *(978-1-7330356)* 973 NW Calypso Cir, Silverdale, WA 98383-8004 USA Tel 253-221-5742
E-mail: claire.e.hallinan@gmail.com
Web site: https://claireehallinan.wordpress.com/.

Hallmark Card, Inc., *(978-0-87529; 978-1-59530; 978-1-63059)* 2501 McGee, Kansas City, MO 64141-6580 USA (SAN 202-2672) Tel 816-274-5111
Dist(s): **Univ. of New Mexico Pr.**

Hallmark Emporium, *(978-0-9665055)* 9201 Russell Ave., S., Bloomington, MN 55431 USA Tel 612-884-2601; Fax: 612-703-0218
E-mail: dead541@aol.com
Web site: http://members.aol.com/dead 541/index.html.

HallowStyle, LLC, *(978-0-9853082)* 20 Robert Dr., Hyde Park, NY 12538 USA Tel 914-489-9529
E-mail: donnadavies@hallowstyle.com
Web site: www.hallowstyle.com.

Halo Publishing International, *(978-0-9718350; 978-0-9797429; 978-1-935268; 978-1-61244; 978-1-78280; 978-1-63765)* 5549 Canal Rd., Cleveland, OH 44125 USA
Web site: http://www.halopublishing.com.

Hambrick, Brandy , *(978-0-578-18543-9; 978-0-578-21029-2)* 888 Rockdale Ave, Cincinnati, OH 45229 USA.

Hameray Publishing Group, Inc., *(978-1-60559; 978-1-62817; 978-1-64039; 978-1-64387; 978-1-64941; 978-1-68581; 979-8-89073)* 11545 Sorrento Valley Rd., Suite 310, San Diego, CA 92121 USA Tel 858-369-5200; Fax: 858-369-5201; Toll Free Fax: 858-369-5209; Toll Free: 866-918-6173
E-mail: christine@hameraypublishing.com
Web site: http://www.hameraypublishing.com.

Hamilton Bks., *(978-0-7618)* Div. of Rowman & Littlefield Publishing Group, Orders Addr.: 15200 NBN Way, Blue Ridge Summit, PA 17214 USA Tel 717-794-3800 (Sales, Customer Service, MIS, Royalties, Inventory Mgmt., Dist., Credit & Collections); Fax: 717-794-3803 (Customer Service &/or orders only); 717-794-3857 (Sales & MIS); 717-794-3856 Royalties, Inventory Mgmt. & Dist.); Toll Free Fax: 800-338-4550 (Customer Service &/ or orders); Toll Free: 800-462-6420 (Customer Service &/ or orders); Edit Addr.: 4501 Forbes Blvd., Suite 200, Lanham, MD 20706 USA Tel 301-459-3366; Fax: 301-459-5748 Short Discount, please contact rlpgsales@rowman.com
Web site: http://www.rlpgbooks.com
Dist(s): **Follett School Solutions**
MyiLibrary
National Bk. Network
Rowman & Littlefield Publishers, Inc.
Rowman & Littlefield Unlimited Model
ebrary, Inc.

Hamilton Ministries *See* **DCTS Publishing**

Hamilton, Sharon, *(978-0-9857599; 978-0-9963748; 978-0-9963749; 978-0-9969954; 978-0-9969955; 978-1-945020; 978-1-955084)* P.O. Box 5287, Santa Rosa, CA 95402 USA Tel 707-545-9228; Fax: 707-545-7572
E-mail: sharonhamilton2001@gmail.com
Web site: http://www.authorsharonhamilton.com/.

Hamilton Stone Editions, *(978-0-9654043; 978-0-9714873; 978-0-9801786; 978-0-9836668; 978-0-9903767; 978-1-7365001)* P.O. Box 43, Maplewood, NJ 07040 USA; *Imprints:* Irene Weinberger Books (IWeinberger)
E-mail: meredithsuewillis@gmail.com; hstone@hamiltonstone.org
Web site: http://www.hamiltonstone.org
Dist(s): **Smashwords.**

Hamline Univ. Pr., *(978-0-9633686; 978-0-9723721; 978-1-934458)* 1536 Hewitt Ave., MS-C1916, Saint Paul, MN 55104-2490 USA
E-mail: bhansonhegg01@hamline.edu
Web site: http://www.hamline.edu.

Hammad, Salma *See* **Lucent Interpretations, LLC**

Hammersmark Books *See* **Kluis Publishing, LLC**

Hammond, Incorporated *See* **Hammond World Atlas Corp.**

Hammond, Roger, *(978-0-9763822)* 4915 Avon Ln., Sarasota, FL 34238 USA
Web site: http://www.pelithepelican.com.

†Hammond World Atlas Corp., *(978-0-7230; 978-0-8437)* Subs. of Langenscheidt Pubs., Inc., 193 Morris Ave., Springfield, NJ 07081-1211 USA (SAN 202-2702)
E-mail: rstrung@americanmap.com
Web site: http://www.Hammondmap.com
Dist(s): **Langenscheidt Publishing Group**; *CIP.*

Hamner, Shannon, *(978-1-7350764)* 267 Tumbleweed Trail, Denison, TX 75021 USA Tel 903-227-7486
E-mail: shannonhamner@yahoo.com.

Hampton Roads Publishing Co., Inc., *(978-0-9624375; 978-1-57174; 978-1-878901)* Orders Addr.: P.O. Box 8107, Charlottesvle, VA 22906-8107 USA (SAN 299-8874) Toll Free Fax: 800-766-9042; Toll Free: 800-766-8009
E-mail: hrpc@hrpub.com
Web site: http://www.hamptonroadspub.com
Dist(s): **Hay Hse., Inc.**
Red Wheel/Weiser.

Hampton-Brown Books *See* **National Geographic School Publishing, Inc.**

Hamster Huey Pr., *(978-0-9749090)* 7627 84th Ave., Ct., NW, Gig Harbor, WA 98335-6237 USA Tel 253-851-7839; Fax: 253-853-3493
E-mail: phs@oz.net
Web site: http://www.hamsterhueypress.com.

amster Pr., *(978-0-9645669; 978-0-9724630)* Orders Addr.: P.O. Box 27471, Seattle, WA 98125 USA Fax: 206-363-2878
E-mail: hamstrpres@aol.com
Web site: http://www.billschelly.com
Dist(s): **Diamond Comic Distributors, Inc. FM International Syco Distribution.**

anako Studio *See* **CKNY Paw Productions**

Hancock Hse. Pubs., *(978-0-88839; 978-0-919654; 978-1-55205)* No. 104- 4550 Birch Bay-Lynden Rd, Blaine, WA 98230-9436 USA (SAN 665-7079) Tel 604-538-1114; Fax: 604-538-2262; Toll Free Fax: 800-983-2262; Toll Free: 800-938-1114; 19313 Zero Ave., Surrey, BC V3S 9R9 (SAN 115-3730); *Imprints:* Crypto Editions (MYID_W_CRYPTO)
E-mail: sales@hancockhouse.com
Web site: http://www.hancockhouse.com; *CIP.*

Hand Print Pr., *(978-0-9679846; 978-0-615-74893-1; 978-0-9914762)* Orders Addr.: 928 N 9TH ST 928 N 9TH ST, PHILOMATH, OR 97370-9714 USA Tel 541-740-7243; Edit Addr.: 928 N 9TH ST 928 N 9TH ST, PHILOMATH, OR 97370-9714 USA
E-mail: kiko@handprintpress.com
Web site: http://www.handprintpress.com
Dist(s): **Chelsea Green Publishing CreateSpace Independent Publishing Platform.**

†hand2mind, *(978-0-7406; 978-0-914040; 978-0-923832; 978-0-938587; 978-1-57162; 978-1-57452; 978-1-63406)* 500 Greenview Ct., Vernon Hills, IL 60061 USA (SAN 285-7553) Tel 847-816-5050; Fax: 847-816-5066; Toll Free: 800-445-5985; *Imprints:* Hands-On Standards (Hands-OnStand)
E-mail: info@hand2mind.com
Web site: http://www.hand2mind.com; *CIP.*

Handersen Publishing, *(978-1-941429; 978-1-947854; 978-1-64703)* PO Box 21843, Lincoln, NE 68542 USA
E-mail: editors@handersenpublishing.com; stinkwavesmagazine@hotmail.com
Web site: http://handersenpublishing.com/; www.stinkwavesmagazine.com.

H&H Publishing, *(978-0-9975411)* 2403 Craig Rd Se, Olympia, WA 98501 USA Tel 360-918-6976
E-mail: puzzlebabe2002@yahoo.com.

Handle Your Business Girl Publishing, *(978-1-886853)* 1006 Deerfield trace, Mebane, NC 27302 USA (SAN 298-5101) Tel 919-244-6321 Do not confuse with Joshua Publishing, Aurora, CO, Lenexa, KS
E-mail: info@handleyourbusinessgirl.com
Web site: www.paiceducationgroup.org; www.handleyourbusinessgirl.com.

H&M Systems Software, Inc., *(978-1-885936)* 600 E. Crescent Ave., Suite 203, U Saddle Riv, NJ 07458-1846 USA Toll Free: 800-327-3713; *Imprints:* StudioLine Photo (StudioLine)
E-mail: Info@HM-Software.com
Web site: http://www.Gameware.com; http://www.HM-Software.com; http://www.StudioLine.biz
Dist(s): **Victory Multimedia.**

Handprint Bks., *(978-1-929766; 978-1-59354)* 413 Sixth Ave., Brooklyn, NY 11215-3310 USA
E-mail: publisher@handprintbooks.com
Web site: http://www.handprintbooks.com
Dist(s): **Chronicle Bks. LLC Hachette Bk. Group Learning Connection, The Penton Overseas, Inc. Random Hse., Inc.**

Hands to the Plow, Inc., *(978-1-930914)* P.O. Box 567, Webster, WI 54893 USA Tel 715-349-7185
E-mail: tomkelby@handstotheplow.org
Web site: http://www.handstotheplow.org.

Handsome Prince Publishing, *(978-0-9910536; 978-0-9908048; 978-0-9961115)* 2712 Occidental Dr., Sacramento, CA 95826 USA Tel 916-801-5376
E-mail: jam43210@gmail.com
Web site: HandsomePrincePublishing.com.

Hands-On Standards *Imprint of* **hand2mind**

Handstand Kids, *(978-0-9792107; 978-0-9847476)* 23346 Pk. Colombo, Calabasas, CA 91302 USA (SAN 852-7822) Tel 818-917-7200
E-mail: yvette@handstandkids.com
Web site: http://www.handstandkids.com.

Hand-Stitched Publishing, *(978-0-9988637)* 814 La Porte Dr., La Canada, CA 91011 USA Tel 213-590-8058
E-mail: seth34larsen@yahoo.com.

H&W Publishing Inc., *(978-0-9800934)* P.O. Box 53515, Cincinnati, OH 45253 USA Tel 513-687-3968; Fax: 513-761-4221
E-mail: kwatkins1@fuse.net
Web site: http://www.handwpublishing.com.

Handwriting Without Tears, *(978-1-891627; 978-1-934825; 978-1-939814; 978-1-948729; 978-1-950578; 978-1-952970; 978-1-954728; 978-1-955350; 978-1-956794; 979-8-88566)* Div. of No Tears Learning Inc., 8001 MacArthur Blvd., Cabin John, MD 20818-1607 USA Tel 301-263-2700; Fax: 301-263-2707; Toll Free: 888-983-8409
Web site: http://www.hwtears.com; http://www.getsetforschool.com.

Hanes, Gussie, *(978-1-7345773)* 9885 Monte Alto, No. 1, Helotes, TX 78023 USA Tel 210-793-8432
E-mail: gussie.westpoint@yahoo.com.

Hanford Mead Pubs., Inc., *(978-0-9643158; 978-1-59275)* P.O. Box 8051, Santa Cruz, CA 95061 USA (SAN 253-9195) Tel 831-459-6855; Fax: 831-426-4474
E-mail: info@hanfordmead.com
Web site: http://www.hanfordmead.com; http://www.soulcollage.com; http://www.ethicsofcaring.com
Dist(s): **New Leaf Distributing Co., Inc.**

†Hanging Loose Pr., *(978-0-914610; 978-1-882413; 978-1-931236; 978-1-934909)* 231 Wyckoff St., Brooklyn, NY 11217 USA (SAN 206-4960) Fax: 212-243-7499
E-mail: print225@aol.com
Web site: http://www.hangingloosepress.com
Dist(s): **Partners/West Book Distributors SPD-Small Pr. Distribution**; *CIP.*

Hank of America Consulting LLC, *(978-0-692-09239-2; 978-0-692-09241-5; 978-0-692-10267-1; 978-0-692-15867-8; 978-0-692-15869-2; 978-0-578-53482-4)* 11 Riverside DR APT 6kw, NEW YORK, NY 10023 USA Tel 917-686-1979
E-mail: henry.linn@gmail.com
Dist(s): **Ingram Content Group.**

Hanke, Cheryl, *(978-1-7331912)* 6349 Bright Plume, Columbia, MD 21044-3749 USA Tel 314-223-7515; *Imprints:* Screwy Ideas (MYID_M_SCREWY)
E-mail: chaindrivr@yahoo.com
Web site: www.screwyidea.com.

Hanks, Scott, *(978-0-9794157; 978-0-9799518; 978-0-9815083)* 1781 E. 800th Rd., Lawrence, KS 66049 USA (SAN 853-4098) Tel 785-887-2203; Fax: 785-887-2204
E-mail: mt@heritagebaptistchurch.cc
Web site: http://www.heritagebaptistchurch.cc.

Hanna Concern Publishing *See* **Ariella Publishing**

Hanna, Nicholas, *(978-0-615-14369-9)* 3439 NE Sandy Blvd., No. 304, Portland, OR 97232 USA
Dist(s): **Lulu Pr., Inc.**

Hannacroix Creek Bks., Inc., *(978-1-889262; 978-1-938998)* 1127 High Ridge Rd., No. 110, Stamford, CT 06905-1203 USA (SAN 299-9560) Tel 203-968-8098; Fax: 203-968-0193
E-mail: Hannacroix@aol.com
Web site: http://www.hannacroixcreekbooks.com
Dist(s): **Brodart Co. CreateSpace Independent Publishing Platform Emery-Pratt Co. Follett School Solutions Midwest Library Service Quality Bks., Inc. TextStream Unique Bks., Inc.**

Hannel Educational Consulting, *(978-0-9764776)* 1131 W. Palm Ln., Phoenix, AZ 85007-1536 USA Tel 602-524-7647; Fax: 602-253-2693
Web site: http://www.hannel.com.

Hannibal Books *See* **Creative Properties LLC**

Hannover Hse. *Imprint of* **Truman Pr., Inc.**

Hans, Judy E., *(978-0-578-24006-0)* 619 Seeport Dr., Allen, TX 75013 USA.

Hansen, Charles Educational Music & Bks., Inc., *(978-0-8494)* 1820 West Ave., Miami Beach, FL 33139 USA (SAN 205-0609) Tel 305-532-5461; Fax: 305-672-8729
E-mail: khansen507@aol.com
Web site: http://www.hansenpublications.com/
Dist(s): **Hansen Hse.**

Hansen, Diane, *(978-0-9761988)* P.O. Box 1051, Redondo Beach, CA 90278 USA Tel 310-379-8006
Web site: http://thosearemyprivateparts.com.

Hansen, Marc Stuff!, *(978-0-9794643)* P.O. Box 621, Greenville, MI 48838 USA
E-mail: marchansenstuff@gmail.com
Web site: http://www.marchansenstuff.com.

Hanson, Tracie, *(978-0-9799185)* Orders Addr.: 94 Pletcher Dr., Yorkville, IL 60560 USA Tel 815-440-5681
E-mail: tracie777@sbcglobal.net
Web site: http://www.newworldbaby.net.

Happy About, *(978-0-9633302; 978-1-60005; 978-1-60773)* 21265 Stevens Creek Blvd., Suite 205, Cupertino, CA 95014 USA Tel 408-257-3000
E-mail: info@happyabout.info
Web site: http://www.happyabout.info
Dist(s): **Ebsco Publishing MyiLibrary OverDrive, Inc.**

Happy Apple Bks., *(978-0-9890903)* 852 Riven Oak Dr., Murrells Inlet, SC 29576 USA Tel 843-458-8740
E-mail: wickedisbetter@yahoo.com; mattellerin@yahoo.com
Web site: http://www.happyapplebooks.com.

Happy Bks. Pr., *(978-0-9787826)* 29877 Westhaven Dr., Agoura, CA 91301 USA Tel 818-879-1268
E-mail: ghuyette@charter.net; happybookspress@vrillustration.com
Web site: http://www.vrillustration.com.

Happy Cat Bks. (GBR) *(978-1-899248; 978-1-903285; 978-1-905117) Dist. by* **Star Brght Bks.**

Happy Day *Imprint of* **Tyndale Hse. Pubs.**

Happy Dolphin Pr. *Imprint of* **Glass Onion Publishing**

Happy Dolphin Press *See* **Glass Onion Publishing**

Happy Hamster Press, The *See* **Imagination Workshop, The**

Happy Heart Kids Publishing, *(978-0-9763143)* Orders Addr.: 2912 Beane Rd., Lenoir, NC 28645-8653 USA (SAN 256-3029) Tel 828-302-9500; 828-754-4126 (phone/fax); Fax: 828-758-8409
E-mail: mshelen@charter.net
Web site: http://www.happyheartkids.com.

Happy Hearts Family, The, *(978-0-615-34485-0; 978-0-9899470)* 2044 Loggia, Newport Beach, CA 92660 USA Tel 949-701-8296
E-mail: marianal@cox.net
Web site: http://thehappyheartsfamily.com.

Happy Holliday Bks., *(978-0-692-54584-3; 978-0-692-95833-9; 978-0-692-08125-9; 978-0-578-50486-5)* P.O. Box 324, Glendale, CA 91209 USA Tel 818-568-4492
E-mail: thefoodainttheproblem@gmail.com.

Happy Horse Publishing, Ltd., *(978-0-9727849)* Orders Addr.: P.O. Box 15767, Chevy Chase, MD 20825 USA Tel 301-589-8888; Edit Addr.: 5910 Connecticut Ave., Chevy Chase, MD 70875 USA
E-mail: eashe@happyhorse.us
Web site: http://www.happyhorsekids.com.

HAPPY HOUSE PR., *(978-0-615-87080-9; 978-0-615-88154-6)* 1301 Birdsall St., Old Hickory, TN 37138 USA Tel 6155547064 Do not confuse with Happy House Press in Tillamook, OR
Web site: www.happyhousepress.com
Dist(s): **CreateSpace Independent Publishing Platform.**

Happy Kamperz, *(978-0-578-22287-5; 978-0-578-22288-2)* 13180 Garrett Hwy., Suite F PMB 78, Oakland, MD 21550 USA
Dist(s): **Outskirts Pr., Inc.**

Happy Kappy Karacters, *(978-0-615-45522-8; 978-0-615-65651-9)* 20 Secora Rd., Suite 312, Monsey, NY 10952 USA
E-mail: georgegisser@aol.com; marshall@nydesign.com
Web site: www.nydesign.com; www.kappythekangaroo.com.

Happy Place Bks. LLC, *(978-0-9904893)* P.O. Box 291, Massillon, OH 44648 USA Tel 330-830-9223
E-mail: happyplacebooks@cs.com.

Happy Publishing LLC *See* **Happy Publishing LLC**

Happy Publishing LLC, *(978-0-615-73531-3; 978-0-9895554; 978-0-9896332; 978-0-9961712; 978-0-9983708; 978-0-9996603; 979-8-9851442; 978-1-957142)* 7052 Santa Teresa Blvd No. 72, San Jose, CA 95139 USA Tel 408-416-7090; 408-478-0763
E-mail: happypublishing@gmail.com.

Happy Viking Crafts, *(978-0-9740175)* Orders Addr.: P.O. Box 35, Mahomet, IL 61853 USA; Edit Addr.: 1001 Sunrise Cir., Mahomet, IL 61853-3536 USA Tel 217-586-2497.

Happy Women Publishing Co., *(978-0-9745627)* 11487 57th St E., Parrish, FL 34219-5818 USA
E-mail: hwp@toerrific.com
Web site: http://toerrific.com
Dist(s): **Continental Enterprises Group, Inc. (CEG).**

Happy Woods Pr., *(978-0-9894691)* 400 Davey Glen Rd. No. 4323, Belmont, CA 94002 USA Tel 650-802-8369
E-mail: meechie2@sbcglobal.net.

HappyFeet Bks., *(978-0-9992492; 978-1-7329617)* 146 Essex St., Deep River, CT 06417 USA Tel 860-328-1106
E-mail: don@happyfeetbooks.com
Web site: www.happyfeetbooks.com.

Happyland Media, *(978-0-9726418)* Orders Addr.: P.O. Box 20398, Castro Valley, CA 94546 USA; Edit Addr.: 20283 Santa Marie Ave., Castro Valley, CA 94546 USA
E-mail: info@happylandmedia.com
Web site: http://www.happylandmedia.com.

Harambee Pr., *(978-0-9769846)* P.O. Box 353, Macatawa, MI 49434 USA
Web site: http://www.harambeepress.com.

Harbin, Etta, *(978-0-578-78893-7)* 3316 Onyx, Miramar, FL 33025 USA Tel 954-410-7175
E-mail: msih@aol.com.

Harbinger Pr., *(978-0-9674736; 978-0-9723998)* 2711 Buford Rd. PMB 383, Richmond, VA 23235-2423 USA (SAN 299-9994) Do not confuse with companies with the same or similar names in Woodland Hills, CA, Corte Madera, CA
E-mail: keith@harbpress.com
Web site: http://www.harbpress.com.

Harbor Hse., *(978-1-891799)* 629 Stevens Xing., Augusta, GA 30907-9566 USA; *Imprints:* Bat Wing Press (Bat Wing Pr)
E-mail: peggycheney@harborhousebooks.com; harborhouse@harborhousebooks.com
Web site: http://www.harborhousebooks.com.

Harbor Hse. Pubs., Inc., *(978-0-937360)* 221 Water St., Boyne City, MI 49712 USA (SAN 200-5751) Tel 616-582-2814; Fax: 616-582-3392; Toll Free: 800-491-1760
E-mail: harbor@harborhouse.com
Web site: http://www.harborhouse.com.

Harbor Island Bks., *(978-0-9741787)* 1214 W. Boston Post Rd., No. 245, Mamaroneck, NY 10543 USA (SAN 255-9137) Tel 914-420-9782; Fax: 914-835-7897
E-mail: publisher@lyingawake.net; hfurbush@earthlink.net
Web site: http://www.lyingawake.net/
Dist(s): **Partners/West Book Distributors.**

Harborseal Publishing Co., *(978-0-9652963; 978-0-9787308)* Orders Addr.: P.O. Box 126, Seal Cove, ME 04674-0126 USA Tel 207-244-7753; Edit Addr.: Rte. 102, Captain's Quarters Rd., Seal Cove, ME 04674 USA
Dist(s): **Magazines, Inc.**

HarborTown Histories, *(978-0-9710984)* 6 Harbor Way, Santa Barbara, CA 93109 USA
E-mail: baker@sbcc.net.

Harbour Arts, LLC, *(978-0-9778196)* 1790 Philippe Pkwy., Safety Harbor, FL 34695 USA
Web site: http://www.harbourarts.com.

Harbour Bks. *Imprint of* **Mariner Publishing**

Harbourside Pr., *(978-0-9740552)* 7892 Sailboat Key Blvd., Suite 506, South Pasadena, FL 33707 USA Tel 727-543-5855
E-mail: harbours@harboursidepress.com
Web site: http://www.harboursidepress.com
Dist(s): **Greenleaf Book Group.**

Harcourt Achieve *See* **Houghton Mifflin Harcourt Supplemental Pubs.**

Harcourt Brace & Company *See* **Harcourt Trade Pubs.**

Harcourt Brace School Publishers *See* **Harcourt Schl. Pubs.**

Harcourt Briggs, *(978-0-692-91301-7; 978-0-692-96875-8)* 2020 Penn Ave., NW Suite 343, WASHINGTON, DC 20006 USA Tel 202-841-4682
E-mail: funmi@ffjohn.com
Dist(s): **Ingram Content Group.**

Harcourt Children's Bks *Imprint of* **Harcourt Children's Bks.**

Harcourt Children's Bks., *(978-0-15)* Div. of Houghton Mifflin Harcourt Trade & Reference Pubs., Orders Addr.: 6277 Sea Harbor Dr., Orlando, FL 32887 USA Toll Free Fax: 800-235-0256; Toll Free: 800-543-1918; 465 S. Lincoln Dr., Troy, MO 63379 Toll Free Fax: 800-235-0266; Toll Free: 800-543-1918; Edit Addr.: 15 E. 26th St., 15th Flr., New York, NY 10010 USA Tel 212-592-1000; Fax: 212-592-1011; 525 B St., Suite 1900, San Diego, CA 92101 Tel 619-231-6616; *Imprints:* Gulliver Books (Gulliver Bks); Red Wagon Books (Red Wagon Bks); Harcourt Children's Books (HCB)
E-mail: Andrew.porter@harcourt.com
Web site: http://www.HarcourtBooks.com
Dist(s): **Children's Plus, Inc. Houghton Mifflin Harcourt Publishing Co. Harcourt Trade Pubs.**

Harcourt Schl. Pubs., *(978-0-15)* Div. of Houghton Mifflin Harcouty School Publishers, 9205 Southpark Ctr. Loop, Orlando, FL 32819 USA (SAN 299-4585) Tel 407-345-2000; Fax: 407-352-3445; Toll Free Fax: 800-874-6418 (orders); Toll Free: 800-225-5425 (orders)
E-mail: hbspcs@harcourt.com
Web site: http://www.harcourtschool.com/
Dist(s): **Houghton Mifflin Harcourt Trade & Reference Pubs. Lectorum Pubns., Inc.**

†Harcourt Trade Pubs., *(978-0-15)* Div. of Houghton Mifflin Harcourt Trade & Reference Pubs., Orders Addr.: 6277 Sea Harbor Dr., Orlando, FL 32887 USA (SAN 200-285X) Tel 619-699-6707; Toll Free Fax: 800-235-0256; Toll Free: 800-543-1918 (trade orders, inquiries, claims); Edit Addr.: 15 E. 26th St., New York, NY 10010 USA Tel 212-592-1000; Fax: 212-592-1011; 525 B St., Suite 1900, San Diego, CA 92101-4495 (SAN 200-2736) Tel 619-231-6616; *Imprints:* Silver Whistle (Silver Whistle)
E-mail: andrewporter@harcourt.com
Web site: http://www.HarcourtBooks.com
Dist(s): **MyiLibrary**; *CIP.*

hard girl bk. club, *(978-0-9748712)* 4143 S. Adelle, Mesa, AZ 85212 USA Tel 480-241-1351; Fax: 480-354-4727; Toll Free: 800-307-5261
E-mail: tkempton@cox.net
Web site: http://hardgirlbookclub.com.

Hard Made Books *See* **HM Bks.**

Hard Shell Word Factory, *(978-1-58200; 978-0-7599)* Orders Addr.: 6470a Glenway Ave. #109, Cincinnati, OH 45211 USA (SAN 631-4899) Toll Free Fax: 888-460-4752; Toll Free: 888-232-0808; Edit Addr.: 6470a Glenway Ave. #109, Cincinnati, OH 45211 USA Toll Free: 888-232-0808
E-mail: books@hardshell.com; books@mundania.com
Web site: http://www.hardshell.com
Dist(s): **CreateSpace Independent Publishing Platform American News Company.**

Hardeman, *(978-0-692-91025-2; 978-0-692-94242-0)* 2662 River Eagle Ct, Sherwood, AR 72120 USA Tel 501-256-6359
E-mail: Royhardeman@delivering2morrowsfuture.com.

Harder, Polly *See* **R. H. Publishing**

Hardgrove, Jaime, *(978-1-7334509)* 4912 Woodfield Ct, Nashotah, WI 53058 USA Tel 920-266-3687
E-mail: hardjl@yahoo.com.

Hardie Grant Bks. (AUS) *(978-1-86498; 978-1-876719; 978-1-74064; 978-1-74066; 978-1-74270; 978-1-74273; 978-0-9807835; 978-0-646-49937-6; 978-1-74358; 978-1-74379; 978-1-76143; 978-1-76144; 978-1-76145; 978-0-9944772) Dist. by* **HachBkGrp.**

Hardie Grant Children?s Publishing (AUS) *(978-1-920878; 978-1-921098; 978-1-921288; 978-1-921417; 978-1-921502; 978-1-921564; 978-1-921690; 978-1-921759; 978-1-921848; 978-1-74297; 978-1-76121; 978-1-76050; 978-1-76012) Dist. by* **IPG Chicago.**

Hardin Publishing, LLC, *(978-0-9742704)* 1380 W. Paces Ferry Rd., Suite 180, Atlanta, GA 30327 USA Tel 404-504-6619; Fax: 404-264-3583 Do not confuse with Hardin Publishing Company in Avera, GA
E-mail: proper@piedmont-atl.com; yntema@hardinpublishing.net
Web site: http://www.hardinpublishing.net.

Harding Hse. Publishing Sebice Inc., *(978-1-933630; 978-1-937211; 978-1-62524)* 220 Front St., Vestal, NY 13850-1514 USA; *Imprints:* Anamchara Books (Anamchara Bks); Village Earth Press (Village Earth); Candlewood Press (Candlewood Pr.)
E-mail: info@anamcharabooks.com
Web site: http://www.hardinghousepages.com; http://www.villageearthpress.com; http://www.anamcharabooks.com
Dist(s): **Follett School Solutions Smashwords.**

Hardnett Publishing, *(978-0-9789310; 978-0-692-21182-3)* 2114 Keithshire Ct., Conyers, GA 30013 USA
E-mail: info@hardnettpublishing.com
Web site: http://www.hardnettpublishing.com.

Hardtke Publishing Co., *(978-0-9718166)* 2217 Second Ave. E., No. 1, Hibbing, MN 55746-1966 USA (SAN 254-4601) Tel 218-262-6510
Web site: http://www.libertyandlove.com/.

Hardway Pr, *(978-0-9717148; 978-0-9840221; 978-0-9974422; 978-0-692-94359-5; 978-0-578-60308-7)* 2547 La Cara Ave., Las Vegas, NV 89121 USA Tel 702-373-2609
Web site: http://www.brianrouff.com.

Hardy Ink LLC, *(978-1-7329442)* 3605 Woodcliff Dr., Kalamazoo, MI 49008 USA Tel 269-544-2225
E-mail: hardyinklc@gmail.com
Web site: www.hardyink.com.

Hardy, John M. Publishing Company *See* **Texas Bk. Pubs. Assn.**

Hargrave Pr., *(978-0-9744885; 978-0-9817195)* P.O. Box 524, Nantucket, MA 02554 USA (SAN 856-3519)
E-mail: sales@hargravepress.com
Web site: http://www.hargravepress.com
Dist(s): **BookMasters.**

Hargrove Grey Publishing *Imprint of* **Phebe Phillips, Inc.**

Publisher Name Index

Hargrove, Linda Leigh, *(978-0-9909412)* E-mail: linda.l.hargrove@gmail.com.

Hargroves, Ann *See* **Hargroves Publishing Co.**

Hargroves Publishing Co., *(978-0-9742277)* P.O. Box 985, Virginia Beach, VA 23451-0985 USA Web site: http://www.annhhargroves.com.

HarHan, LLC, *(978-0-578-82037-8)* 999 Cleveland Ct., Warrington, PA 18976 USA Tel 267-566-0397 E-mail: MEFREEDM@GMAIL.COM Web site: www.pizzatreebook.com.

Harlan Publishing Company *See* **Diakonia Publishing**

Harlan Rose Publishing, *(978-0-9853466)* 920 Fall Creek, Grapevine, TX 76051 USA Tel 469-951-8499 E-mail: Flyingunicorn99@yahoo.com.

Harlem Pr., LLC., *(978-0-692-97471-1; 978-0-578-73961-8)* 7 William St., Montclair, NJ 07042 USA Tel 973-619-3266; Fax: 973-619-3266 E-mail: coryajones@me.com Web site: HarlemPressLLC.com.

Harlequin Enterprises ULC (CAN) *(978-0-373; 978-1-55166; 978-1-58314; 978-1-55254; 978-0-7783; 978-1-55373; 978-1-4268; 978-1-4592; 978-1-4603; 978-84-687-2370-9; 978-0-919622; 978-1-335; 978-1-4880; 978-1-4882)* *Dist. by* **HarperCollins Pubs.**

Harlin Jacque Pubns., *(978-0-940938)* Orders Addr.: P.O. Box 336, Garden City, NY 11530 USA (SAN 281-7667) Tel 516-489-0120; Fax: 516-292-9120; Edit Addr.: 89 Surrey Ln., Hempstead, NY 11550-3521 USA (SAN 281-7659) Tel 516-489-8564; *Imprints:* Pen & Rose Press (Pen&Rose Pr) E-mail: harlinjacquepub@aol.com Web site: http://www.lindamichellebaron.com.

Harmon, Amanda, *(978-0-578-99158-0)* 3205 Ginny Lake dr., middleburg, FL 32068 USA Tel 904-501-9378 E-mail: amandaharmon1011@gmail.com.

Harmon Creek Pr., *(978-0-9820852)* 1763 Diamond Head Dr., Tiki Island, TX 77554 USA E-mail: lnicholson@bookpublishing.com.

Harmony Enterprises, *(978-0-9647247)* 512 14th St., Modesto, CA 95354 USA Tel 209-571-2725; Fax: 209-571-2520 E-mail: rrvgleser@skysailproductions.com.

Harmony Healing Hse., *(978-0-9787179; 978-0-9854037)* 530 Miramonte Ave., Lakeport, CA 95453 USA (SAN 851-3570).

Harmony Hse. Art Studio, *(978-0-9700127)* 12852 Harmony Pkwy., Westminster, CO 80034 USA Tel 720-289-7926 (phone/fax) E-mail: Vkrudwig@aol.com Web site: http://www.members.aol.com/vkrudwig *Dist(s):* **Bks. West.**

Harmony Hse. Publishing Co., *(978-0-9725289)* P.O. Box 858, Rexburg, ID 83440 USA Tel 208-359-1595 (phone/fax) E-mail: jaydef@cableone.net Web site: http://www.debtfreestepbystep.com.

Harmony Hse. *Imprint of* **Twin Flame Productions**

Harmony Ink Pr. *Imprint of* **Dreamspinner Pr.**

Harmony Pubns., LLC, *(978-0-9787586)* 100 W. Sta. Sq. Dr. Suite 230, Pittsburgh, PA 15219 USA (SAN 851-5468) Tel 412-670-3901; Fax: 724-934-4275 E-mail: harmonypublications@hotmail.com Web site: http://www.colormyworld.info/.

Harmony Spirit Publishing Co., Inc., *(978-0-9762392)* 148 Westgate Dr., Saint Peters, MO 63376 USA E-mail: lynowak@mail.win.org.

Harn Museum of Art, *(978-0-9629384; 978-0-9762552; 978-0-9833085; 978-1-7343235)* Div. of University of Florida, Orders Addr.: P.O. Box 112700, Gainesville, FL 32611-2700 USA; Edit Addr.: 3259 Hull Rd., Gainesville, FL 32608 USA Tel 352-294-7067 (x2116); Fax: 352-392-3892 E-mail: twroath@harn.ufl.edu Web site: http://www.harn.ufl.edu *Dist(s):* **Univ. Pr. of Florida.**

Harold, Elsie L., *(978-0-9764644)* 1701 Eleni Ct., Virginia Bch, VA 23453-2886 USA E-mail: turtlelsie@aol.com.

Harper *Imprint of* **HarperCollins Pubs.**

Harper Design *Imprint of* **HarperCollins Pubs.**

Harper Entertainment *Imprint of* **HarperCollins Pubs.**

Harper Girl Pr., *(978-0-692-85347-4; 978-0-692-92746-5; 978-0-692-07731-3)* 4210 Wilshire Ave., Baltimore, MD 21206 USA E-mail: michelle@iheartgratitude.com Web site: www.harpergirlpress.com.

Harper Horizon *Imprint of* **HarperCollins Focus**

Harper, Janice N, *(978-0-692-88338-9)* 3657 Evans Mill Rd., Lithonia, GA 30038 USA Tel 706-593-4023 E-mail: jnh2005@netzero.net.

Harper, Joel D. *See* **Freedom Three Publishing**

Harper Kids Hse., *(978-0-9747218)* 10061 Riverside Dr., Suite 438, Toluca Lake, CA 91602 USA Tel 818-955-5301; *Imprints:* Young Women Programming (YWProgram) E-mail: hannah@hannahsway.com Web site: http://www.hannasway.com *Dist(s):* **HarperCollins Pubs.**

Harper Large Print *Imprint of* **HarperCollins Pubs.**

Harper Paperbacks *Imprint of* **HarperCollins Pubs.**

Harper Perennial *Imprint of* **HarperCollins Pubs.**

Harper Perennial Modern Classics *Imprint of* **HarperCollins Pubs.**

Harper Trophy *Imprint of* **HarperCollins Pubs.**

Harper, Vicky *See* **Little Bookstore Who Could, The**

Harper Voyager *Imprint of* **HarperCollins Pubs.**

HarperAlley *Imprint of* **HarperCollins Pubs.**

Harper-Arrington Publishing, *(978-0-9764161)* 18701 Grand River Ave., 105, Detroit, MI 48223 USA Tel 313-283-4494; Fax: 248-281-0373; Toll Free: 888-435-9234 E-mail: info@harperarringtonmedia.com Web site: http://www.hapub.com/.

HarperChildren's Audio *Imprint of* **HarperCollins Pubs.**

HarperChristian Resources, *Dist(s):* **Zondervan.**

HarperCollins *Imprint of* **HarperCollins Pubs.**

HarperCollins *Imprint of* **HarperCollins Pubs.**

HarperCollins Canada, Ltd. (CAN) *(978-0-00; 978-0-06; 978-0-690; 978-1-84887; 978-1-4434)* *Dist. by* **HarperCollins Pubs.**

HarperCollins Español, 501 Nelson Pl., Nashville, TN 37214 USA E-mail: hce@harpercollins.com *Dist(s):* **Children's Plus, Inc. HarperCollins Pubs.**

HarperCollins Focus, *(978-0-7852)* P.O. Box 141000, Nashville, TN 37214 USA Tel 615-902-1928; *Imprints:* Harper Horizon (HCHorizon) *Dist(s):* **Brilliance Publishing, Inc. Children's Plus, Inc. HarperCollins Christian Publishing Nelson, Thomas Inc. Open Road Integrated Media, Inc.**

†**HarperCollins Pubs.,** *(978-0-00; 978-0-06; 978-0-380; 978-0-688; 978-0-690; 978-0-694; 978-0-87795; 978-1-55710)* Div. of News Corp., Orders Addr.: 1000 Keystone Industrial Pk., Scranton, PA 18512-4621 USA (SAN 215-3742) Tel 570-941-1500; Toll Free Fax: 800-822-4090; Toll Free: 800-242-7737 (orders only); Edit Addr.: 10 E. 53rd St., New York, NY 10022-5299 USA (SAN 200-2086) Tel 212-207-7000; *Imprints:* Julie Andrews Collection (Julie Andrews); Harper Trophy (HarperTrophy); HarperFestival (HarperFestival); Cotler, Joanna Books (JoCotler); Geringer, Laura Book (LauraGeringer); Greenwillow Books (GreenwillowBks); HarperCollins (HarperCollCh); HarperChildren's Audio (HarperChildAud); Tegen, Katherine Books (KTegenBooks); Morrow, William & Company (WmMorrow); Avon Books (AvonBooks); Eos (Eos Harper); Harper Entertainment (HarperEntert); HarperCollins (HarperCollinsT); Harper Perennial (HarperPerenl); Harper Paperbacks (HarperPaper); Harper Perennial Modern Classics (HarperPMC); Harper Large Print (HarperLargePr); Amistad (AmistadHarper); Rayo (Rayo Harper); Ecco (Ecco Harper); ReganBooks (ReganBooks); Collins (Collins); Morrow, William Cookbooks (MorrowCookbks); Harper Design (HDesign); HarperTeen (HarperTeen); HarperOne (HarperOne); Heartdrum (Heartdrum); Quill Tree Books (QuillTreeBks); Versify (VersifyHC); William Morrow Paperbacks (WILLIAM MORROW); Balzer & Bray (Balzer & Bray); Walden Pond Press (Walden Pond); Avon Impulse (AVON IMPULSE); Newmarket for It Books (NewmarketforItBks); Harper Voyager (HarperVoyager); Dey Street Books (DeyStBks); Collins Reference (Collins Reference); HarperVia (HarperVia); Harper (Harper IMP); HarperAlley (HarperAlley); Clarion Books (ClarionBksHC); Harvest (HarvestHC); Mariner Books (MarinerBksHC) Web site: http://www.harpercollins.com; http://www.harpercollinschildrens.com *Dist(s):* **Blackstone Audio, Inc. Casemate Academic Chicago Distribution Ctr. Children's Plus, Inc. Ebsco Publishing Findaway World, LLC Follett School Solutions F&W Media, Inc. HarperCollins Christian Publishing Lectorum Pubns., Inc. MyiLibrary Open Road Integrated Media, Inc. Outskirts Pr., Inc. Two Rivers Distribution Zondervan**; *CIP.*

HarperCollins Pubs. Australia (AUS) *(978-0-207; 978-0-7322; 978-0-85835; 978-1-86256; 978-1-86371; 978-1-86378; 978-1-876288; 978-0-7304; 978-1-74050; 978-1-921504; 978-1-4607; 978-1-74309; 978-0-7316-3320-3; 978-0-646-10869-8; 978-0-646-39434-3; 978-1-922033)* *Dist. by* **HarperCollins Pubs.**

HarperCollins Pubs. Ltd. (GBR) *(978-0-00; 978-0-01; 978-0-06; 978-0-246; 978-0-261; 978-0-586; 978-0-85152; 978-0-411; 978-1-55468)* *Dist. by* **Trafalgar.**

HarperCollins Pubs. Ltd. (GBR) *(978-0-00; 978-0-01; 978-0-06; 978-0-246; 978-0-261; 978-0-586; 978-0-85152; 978-0-411; 978-1-55468)* *Dist. by* **IPG Chicago.**

HarperCollins Pubs. Ltd. (GBR) *(978-0-00; 978-0-01; 978-0-06; 978-0-246; 978-0-261; 978-0-586; 978-0-85152; 978-0-411; 978-1-55468)* *Dist. by* **HarperCollins Pubs.**

HarperFestival *Imprint of* **HarperCollins Pubs.**

HarperOne *Imprint of* **HarperCollins Pubs.**

HarperTeen *Imprint of* **HarperCollins Pubs.**

HarperVia *Imprint of* **HarperCollins Pubs.**

Harpeth Ridge Pr., *(978-0-9974449)* 304 Harpeth Ridge Dr., Nashville, TN 37221 USA Tel 615-352-1672 E-mail: judithwolfmandell@gmail.com.

Harptoons Publishing, *(978-0-615-35469-9; 978-0-615-41337-2; 978-0-615-45321-7; 978-0-615-59572-6; 978-0-615-68599-1; 978-0-9960197; 978-0-9995290)* 1081 State Rt. 28 Suite B No. 168, Milford, OH 45150 USA (SAN 859-6921) Tel 614-315-9427 E-mail: steve@studioharpster.com Web site: www.harptoons.com.

Harrassowitz Verlag (DEU) *(978-3-447)* *Dist. by* **ISD USA.**

Harren Communications, LLC *See* **OH Industries**

Harrill, R Enterprises, *(978-0-9883082)* 2311 Holly Ln., Shelby, NC 28150 USA Tel 704-692-7052 E-mail: rharrill50@aol.com.

Harrington Artwerkes Booksellers, *(978-0-9778042)* P.O. Box 10648, Burke, VA 22009-0648 USA E-mail: sjph@cox.net Web site: http://www.amazingartbros.com.

Harrington, Katherine, *(978-1-7362665)* 520 Palomas Dr NE 0, ALBUQUERQUE, NM 87108 USA Tel 505 265-0410 E-mail: kjharrington23@gmail.com.

Harrington Park Pr. *Imprint of* **Haworth Pr., Inc., The**

Harriot Publishing, *(978-0-578-17487-7; 978-0-578-19268-0; 978-0-578-19269-7; 978-0-692-05564-9)* 1504 Filmore Rd, Fort Washington, MD 20744 USA.

Harris, Candice *See* **Harris, K Publishing, Inc.**

Harris Communications, Inc., *(978-0-9727520)* 15155 Technology Dr., Eden Prairie, MN 55344-2277 USA (SAN 255-0512) Tel 952-906-1180; Fax: 952-906-1099; Toll Free: 800-825-6758 E-mail: mail@harriscomm.com Web site: http://www.harriscomm.com.

Harris, H. E. & Company *See* **Whitman Publishing LLC**

Harris, Janea D., *(978-1-7334092)* 199 Ivy Ln., Highland Park, IL 60035 USA Tel 404-788-0312 E-mail: Janeadh8@gmail.com Web site: Supherbooks.com.

Harris, Jennifer, *(978-0-9989251)* 1821 Barker Rd., Thompsons Station, TN 37179 USA Tel 615-299-6268 E-mail: jeffandjenniferharris@gmail.com.

Harris, Jessica, *(978-0-692-84752-7)* P.O. Box 2044, MONTGOMERY VILLAGE, MD 20886 USA Tel 240-449-4458 E-mail: jeffwcrawford5+LVP0003345@gmail.com; jeffwcrawford5+LVP0003345@gmail.com.

Harris, K Publishing, Inc., *(978-0-9770331)* P.O. Box 3091, Brandon, FL 33509-3091 USA Web site: http://www.khpinc.com.

Harris, K.L. *See* **Make-believe Pr. LLC**

Harris, Monica *See* **Keep Empowering Yourself Successfully**

Harris, Noah, *(978-0-578-42504-7; 978-0-578-46408-4)* 9 Rosebay Ct., Hattiesburg, MS 39402 USA Tel 601-325-0982 E-mail: noahharris0131@gmail.com *Dist(s):* **Independent Pub.**

Harris, Patrick Monroe, *(978-0-578-48290-3; 978-0-578-50990-7)* 530 E. Patriot Blvd. #248L, RENO, NV 89511 USA Tel 775-671-0219 E-mail: jeffwcrawford5+LVP0003340@gmail.com; jeffwcrawford5+LVP0003340@gmail.com.

Harris, Pleshette Communications Inc. Publishing, *(978-0-9754380)* P.O. Box 491282, Lawrenceville, GA 30049 USA Tel 678-910-6128; Fax: 770-237-9358 E-mail: contact@phc1.org Web site: http://phc1.org.

Harris, Polly, *(978-0-9749375)* 6041 E Akron St., Mesa, AZ 85205 USA Tel 480-654-1213 E-mail: pollyharris@sbcglobal.net.

Harris Publishing, Inc., *(978-1-7340950)* 360 B St., Idaho Falls, ID 83402 USA Tel 208-542-2221 E-mail: janet@harrispublishing.com.

Harris, Samuel, *(978-0-9759253)* 21660 Boschome Dr., Kildeer, IL 60047-8616 USA E-mail: sf864@aol.com; eharris864@aol.com *Dist(s):* **Partners Bk. Distributing, Inc.**

Harris, Thea Publishing, *(978-0-9909170)* P.O. Box 7576, Port St Lucie, FL 34985 USA Tel 772-475-6800 Web site: www.theaharris.com *Dist(s):* **CreateSpace Independent Publishing Platform.**

Harrison and James, *(978-0-692-54055-8; 978-0-692-77913-2; 978-0-692-81389-8)* 11300 S Fairfield Ave, Chicago, IL 60655 USA Tel 773-238-9978 *Dist(s):* **CreateSpace Independent Publishing Platform.**

Harrison, Bobby, *(978-0-9771752)* 444 Shooting Star Tr., Gurley, AL 35748 USA Tel 256-776-2003; Fax: 256-776-2003 E-mail: bnharri@aol.com; ivorybillwp@aol.com Web site: http://www.bobbyharrison.com *Dist(s):* **Impact Photographics.**

Harrison, Gloria M., *(978-1-949185)* P.O. Box PO Box, Dover, DE 19903 USA Tel 302-736-3706 E-mail: hallelu@verizon.net.

Harrison House, Incorporated *See* **Harrison House Pubs.**

†**Harrison House Pubs.,** *(978-0-89274; 978-1-57794; 978-1-60683; 978-1-68031; 978-1-6675; 979-8-218-01386-8)* Orders Addr.: P.O. Box 310, SHIPPENSBURG, PA 17257 USA (SAN 208-676X) Tel 717-532-3040; Toll Free Fax: 800-830-5688; Toll Free: 800-888-4126; Edit Addr.: 167 Walnut Bottom Rd., Shippensburg, PA 17257 USA Tel 717-532-3040; 717-532-9291; Toll Free Fax: 800-830-5688; 800-722-6774; Toll Free: 800-888-4126 E-mail: smckee@norimediagroup.com; jinori@norimediagroup.com Web site: http://www.harrisonhouse.com *Dist(s):* **Anchor Distributors Appalachian Bible Co. Destiny Image Pubs. Distributors, The Nori Media Group Spring Arbor Distributors, Inc.**; *CIP.*

Harry & Stephanie Bks., *(978-0-9760875)* P.O. Box 172, Bronxville, NY 10708 USA Tel 914-961-6601 E-mail: harryandstephanie@yahoo.com Web site: http://www.harryandstephanie.com.

Harseal Publications *See* **Harborseal Publishing Co.**

Hart, Chris Bks. *Imprint of* **Sixth&Spring Bks.**

hart Hse. publishing's, *(978-0-692-68612-6; 978-0-692-88008-1; 978-0-692-92066-4; 978-0-692-96780-5; 978-0-692-14929-4)* 406 E. Walton, Warrenton, MO 63383 USA Tel 636-359-3073 E-mail: cshart45@gmail.com Web site: harthousepublishings.com *Dist(s):* **CreateSpace Independent Publishing Platform.**

Hart Street Pubs., *(978-0-9793637)* 12157 Antibes St., Jacksonville, FL 32224 USA.

Hart-Burn Pr., *(978-0-9740318)* P.O. Box 99, Newton Junction, NH 03859-0099 USA E-mail: stevehart7@yahoo.com Web site: http://www.facebook.com/stevehart7 *Dist(s):* **Smashwords.**

Hartland Pubns., *(978-0-923309; 978-1-60564)* Div. of Hartland Institute of Health & Education, P.O. Box 1, Rapidan, VA 22733 USA (SAN 252-0834) Tel 540-672-3566; Fax: 540-672-3568; Toll Free: 800-774-3566 E-mail: jcarmouche@hartland.edu Web site: http://www.hartlandpublications.com; http://www.hartlandbooks.com.

Hartlyn Kids Media, LLC, *(978-0-615-48984-1; 978-0-615-50182-6; 978-0-615-50503-9; 978-0-615-54948-4)* 45 Cowles St., Hartford, CT 06114 USA Tel 866-962-9993 E-mail: info@hartlynkids.com Web site: http://www.hartlynkids.com.

Hartsuyker, Alice, *(978-0-9770441)* 1258 Fordham Dr. Apt. 204, Glendale Hts, IL 60139-4869 USA E-mail: info@insidedharma.org; info@alicememoir.com Web site: http://www.insidedharma.org; http://www.alicememoir.com.

Hart-Whitlow Pubs., *(978-0-9637951)* 1845 Brandywine Dr., Lenoir City, TN 37772 USA Tel 865-986-8553 E-mail: dickins@utk.edu.

Hartwood Publishing Group, LLC, The, *(978-1-62916)* 12372 W Woodland Ave., Avondale, AZ 85323 USA Tel 347-427-8966 E-mail: georgia@hartwoodpublishing.com Web site: www.hartwoodpublishing.com *Dist(s):* **INscribe Digital Independent Pubs. Group.**

Harvard Business Review Pr., *(978-0-87584; 978-1-57851; 978-1-59139; 978-1-4221; 978-1-62527; 978-1-63369; 978-1-64782)* 60 Harvard Way, Boston, MA 02163 USA (SAN 202-277X) Tel 617-783-7400; 617 495 6181; Fax: 617-783-7492; Toll Free: 888-500-1016 6-19-01 faxed 2nd prefix app, charge, KC E-mail: corpcustserv@hbsp.harvard.edu Web site: http://www.hbsp.harvard.edu; http://www.harvardbusinessonline.com *Dist(s):* **Ingram Publisher Services McGraw-Hill Professional Publishing MyiLibrary Two Rivers Distribution.**

Harvard Business School Press *See* **Harvard Business Review Pr.**

Harvard Education Publishing Group (HEPG), *(978-0-916690; 978-1-891792; 978-1-934742; 978-1-61250; 978-1-68253)* Orders Addr.: c/o Pssc, Harvard Education Press 46 Development Rd., Fitchburg, MA 01420 USA Fax: 978-348-1233 (book order); Toll Free: 888-437-1437 Book Order Line; Edit Addr.: 8 Story St., First Flr., Cambridge, MA 02138 USA (SAN 913-9753) Tel 617-495-3432 editorial office phone; Fax: 617-496-3584 (orders); *Imprints:* Harvard Educational Review Reprint Series (Harv Ed Review) E-mail: laura_clos@harvard.edu; sumita_mukherji@gse.harvard.edu; christina_deyoung@gse.harvard.edu Web site: hepg.org.

Harvard Educational Review Reprint Series *Imprint of* **Harvard Education Publishing Group (HEPG)**

Harvard Perspectives in American Sports *Imprint of* **Harvard Perspectives Pr.**

Harvard Perspectives Pr., *(978-0-9715778)* P.O. Box 400827, Cambridge, MA 02140-0009 USA; *Imprints:* Harvard Perspectives in American Sports (Harvard Pers Amer Sp) E-mail: harvardperspecpr@aol.com; indieKindle@gmail.com Web site: http://indieKindle.blogspot.com.

†**Harvard Univ. Pr.,** *(978-0-674; 978-0-916724; 978-0-935617; 978-0-674-26878-4)* Orders Addr.: c/o Triliteral LLC, 100 Maple Ridge Dr., Cumberland, RI 02864 USA Tel 401-531-2800; Fax: 401-531-2801; Toll Free Fax: 800-406-9145; Toll Free: 800-405-1619; 800-448-2242; Edit Addr.: 79 Garden St., Cambridge, MA 02138 USA (SAN 200-2043) Tel 617-495-2600; Fax: 617-495-5898; *Imprints:* Belknap Press (Belknap) E-mail: contact_hup@harvard.edu Web site: http://www.hup.harvard.edu *Dist(s):* **Blackstone Audio, Inc. Casemate Academic De Gruyter, Inc. Ebsco Publishing JSTOR Open Road Integrated Media, Inc. Wiley, John & Sons, Inc. ebrary, Inc.**; *CIP.*

Harvest *Imprint of* **HarperCollins Pubs.**

Harvest Hse. Pubs., *(978-0-7369; 978-0-89081; 978-1-56507)* 990 Owen Loop, N., Eugene, OR 97402-9173 USA (SAN 207-4745) Tel 541-302-0729; Fax: 541-302-0731; Toll Free: 888-501-6991; *Imprints:* Harvest Kids (Harvest Kids) E-mail: pat.mathis@harvesthousepublishers.com; onix@harvesthousepublishers.com Web site: http://www.harvesthousepublishers.com *Dist(s):* **Faith Alive Christian Resources INscribe Digital Independent Pubs. Group Lulu Pr., Inc. MyiLibrary Twentieth Century Christian Bks.**

Harvest Kids *Imprint of* **Harvest Hse. Pubs.**

Harvest Moon Bks. *Imprint of* **Tully, Jennifer Cahill**

Harvest Pubns., *(978-0-9654272)* 1928 Oxbow Rd., Minneapolis, KS 67467 USA Tel 913-392-2750 Do not confuse with companies with same name in Berkeley,

CA, Arlington Heights, IL, Fort Worth, TX, Jacksonville, TX
E-mail: Adharvest@juno.com
Web site: http://www.pma-online.org/list/7345.html.

arvest Sun Pr., LLC, *(978-0-9743668)* Orders Addr.: P.O. Box 826, Fairacres, NM 88033 USA Tel 479-283-4000; Fax: 505-526-6930; Edit Addr.: 4109 Broken Arrow Cv., Springdale, AR 72764-7503 USA
E-mail: info@harvestsunpress.com
Web site: http://www.harvestsunpress.com.

arvey, Alan, *(978-0-9766354)* P.O. Box 235, Chapel Hill, NC 27514 USA; *Imprints:* Big H Books (Big H Bks)
Web site: http://www.lomeharvey.com.

arwell, William, *(978-0-9728274)* HC 63 Box 1, Hanna, UT 84031 USA.

ashmi, Kyla *See* **Digital Kidz Publishing Hse.**

askell & Judy Rosenthal, *(978-0-9966802)* 2215 Briar Branch Dr., Houston, TX 77042 USA Tel 713-785-4278
E-mail: brosenthal@fb.com.

askell, Rachael A., *(978-0-615-21356-9; 978-0-615-25625-2)* 6177 Sun Blvd., No. 404, Staint Petersburg, FL 33715 USA Tel 727-698-2543; Fax: 727-865-6507
E-mail: hangingwithib@yahoo.com
Dist(s): **Lulu Pr., Inc.**

Hassan, Marian, *(978-0-9766616)* 430 Mendota Rd. W., Suite 219, West Saint Paul, MN 55118 USA
E-mail: mhassan1@yahoo.com.

Hasse, Brenda, *(978-0-9906312; 978-1-7347786; 979-8-9864383)* P.O. Box 124, Fenton, MI 48430 USA Tel 810-955-6121
E-mail: bmh730@aol.com.

Hat Trick Publishing, *(978-0-9860405)* 8169 Outer Dr., S., Traverse City, MI 49685 USA.

Hatch Ideas, Inc., *(978-0-9792558)* P.O. Box 14, Pine Plains, NY 12567 USA.

HATCHBACK Publishing, *(978-0-9778155; 978-0-9817338; 978-0-9891934; 978-0-9906594; 978-0-9988295; 978-1-948708)* P.O. Box 494, Genesee, MI 48437 USA Tel 810-394-8612
E-mail: cynthia@hatchbackpublishing.com
Web site: http://www.cynthialhatcher.com.

Hatchling Pr., *(978-0-692-21870-9)* 4603 Long Beach Blvd, Brant Beach, NJ 08008 USA Tel 6097138130; Toll Free: 6097138130
Dist(s): **CreateSpace Independent Publishing Platform.**

Hatchlings LLC, *(978-1-7333837)* 7 Birchbend, Cleveland, SC 29635 USA Tel 864-243-7795
E-mail: beachrob@mac.com.

Hatherleigh Co., Ltd., The, *(978-1-57826; 978-1-886330; 978-1-961293)* Orders Addr.: 62545 State Hwy. 10 62545 State Hwy. 10, Hobart, NY 13788 USA Tel 800-528-2550; Edit Addr.: 5-22 46th Ave., Suite 200, Long Island City, NY 11101-5215 USA (SAN 298-878X) Tel 212-832-1584; Fax: 212-832-1502; Toll Free Fax: 800-621-8892; Toll Free: 800-367-2550; *Imprints:* Hatherleigh Press (Hath Pr)
E-mail: info@hatherleigh.com
Web site: http://www.hatherleigh.com; http://www.getfitnow.com; https://hatherleighcommunity.com/; http://www.hatherleighpress.com
Dist(s): **MyiLibrary**
Penguin Random Hse. Distribution
Penguin Random Hse. LLC
Random Hse., Inc.

Hatherleigh Pr. *Imprint of* **Hatherleigh Co., Ltd., The**

Hathi Chiti Bks. for Kids, *(978-0-615-37071-2; 978-0-615-37072-9; 978-0-9829362)* 203 Rivington St. Suite 2L, New York, NY 10002 USA Tel 212-920-1844
Web site: http://www.hathichiti.com
Dist(s): **National Bk. Network.**

Hatje Cantz Verlag GmbH & Co KG (DEU) *(978-3-7757)*
Dist. by **Dist Art Pubs.**

Hatpin Press *See* **MusiKinesis**

Hatton, Robert, *(978-0-692-79740-2)* 12010 Teeside Dr., Fredericksburg, VA 22407 USA Tel 804-310-8246
E-mail: roberthattonsr@gmail.com.

Hausen, Julie, *(978-0-692-98786-5)* P.O. Box 12153, Beaumont, TX 77726-2153 USA Tel 409-767-0300
E-mail: hausen.julie@gmail.com.

Have Hope Publishing, *(978-0-9762044)* Orders Addr.: P.O. Box 20892, Baltimore, MD 21209 USA Tel 410-367-6179 (phone/fax); Edit Addr.: 5033 Yellowwood Ave., Baltimore, MD 21209 USA
E-mail: teachertalk@jhu.edu.

Haven Bks., *(978-0-9659480; 978-1-58436)* 10153 1/2 Riverside Dr., Suite 629, North Hollywood, CA 91602 USA Tel 818-503-2518; Fax: 818-508-0299
E-mail: Havenbks@aol.com; reya@havenbooks.net; info@havenbooks.net
Web site: http://www.havenbooks.net
Dist(s): **National Bk. Network**
ebrary, Inc.

Haven Harbor, *(978-0-9729863)* P.O. Box 2197, Huntington Beach, CA 92647-0197 USA
Web site: http://www.havenharbor.com.

HavenBound Publishing, *(978-0-9761733)* Orders Addr.: 1076 Pinnacle Dr., Waynesville, NC 28786 USA; Edit Addr.: 1305 Old Balsam Rd., Waynesville, NC 28786 USA; *Imprints:* HBHavenBound Publishing (HBHavenBnd)
E-mail: joseph@introductiontojesus.com; carolyn@havenbound.net; havenbound@havenbound.net.

Haver, Nancy, *(978-0-9795696)* 19 Moorland St., Amherst, MA 01002 USA Tel 413-549-1337
E-mail: nhaver@crocker.com.

Havet Pr., *(978-0-9882798; 978-0-9864148; 978-0-9983132; 978-1-7346789)* 9519 130th Ave. NE, Kirkland, WA 98033 USA Tel 425-736-7303
E-mail: kortemary@comcast.net.

Hawaii Fine Art Studio, *(978-0-615-21549-5)* 1028 Tirol Ln., Lake Arrowhead, CA 92352 USA.

Hawaii Fishing News, *(978-0-944462; 978-0-9884939)* 6650 Hawaii Kai Dr., No. 201, Honolulu, HI 96825 USA (SAN 243-6612) Tel 808-395-4499; Fax: 808-396-3474
E-mail: fishnews@pixi.com
Web site: http://www.hawaiifishingnews.com/hfn
Dist(s): **Booklines Hawaii, Ltd.**

HAWAII Way Publishing *See* **Hawaii Way Publishing**

Hawaii Way Publishing, *(978-1-945384)* 4118 W. Harold Ct., Visalia, CA 93291 USA Tel 559-972-4168
E-mail: hawaiiwaypublishing@gmail.com
Web site: http://www.hawaiiwaypublishing.com.

Hawaiian Service, Inc., *(978-0-930492)* 94-527 Puahi St., Waipahu, HI 96797-4208 USA (SAN 205-0463) Tel 808-676-5026; Fax: 808-676-5156
Dist(s): **Booklines Hawaii, Ltd.**

Hawaya, Inc., *(978-0-9644149)* Orders Addr.: 11434 LA GRANGE Dr., FRISCO, TX 75035 USA Tel 972-400-9900
E-mail: niveksullivan@gmail.com
Dist(s): **Booklines Hawaii, Ltd.**

Hawes & Jenkins Publishing, Inc, *(978-1-63784)* 16427 N. Scottsdale Road., Scottsdale, AZ 85254 USA Tel 888-430-7450
E-mail: stephen@hawesjenkins.com
Web site: hawesjenkins.com.

Hawk Meadow Pr., *(978-0-9908903)* P.O. Box 178, Pine Mountain Valley, GA 31823 USA Tel 706-628-5676
E-mail: hawkmeadowpress@gmail.com.

Hawk Mountaintop Publishing, *(978-0-9672162)* P.O. Box 88, Piercy, CA 95587 USA Tel 707-247-3409
E-mail: hawk@saber.net.

Hawk Planners, *(978-0-9759702; 978-0-9776843)* 916 Silver Spur Rd. Suite 203, Rolling Hills Estates, CA 90274 USA Toll Free: 888-442-9575
E-mail: matthawkphd@msn.com
Web site: http://www.hawkplanners.com; http://www.satorsports.com
Dist(s): **Cardinal Pubs. Group.**

HAWK Publishing Group, *(978-0-9673131; 978-1-930709)* 7107 S. Yale, No. 345, Tulsa, OK 74136 USA (SAN 299-9293) Tel 918-492-3677; Fax: 918-492-2120
E-mail: wb@hawkpub.com
Web site: http://www.hawkpub.com
Dist(s): **Baker & Taylor Publisher Services (BTPS).**

Hawkeye Enterprises, *(978-0-9743061)* P.O. Box 252, Seal Rock, OR 97376-0252 USA Tel 541-563-4577
E-mail: hawkeye@oregonfast.net.

Hawks, Lyn, *(978-0-9888837)* 310 Ferguson Rd., Chapel Hill, NC 27516 USA Tel 919-929-5344
E-mail: lynhawks@gmail.com
Web site: www.lynhawks.com.

Haworth, Margaret, *(978-0-9740313)* 1625 W. May St. Apt. 3, Wichita, KS 67213-3578 USA.

†Haworth Pr., Inc., The, *(978-0-7890; 978-0-86656; 978-0-917724; 978-1-56022; 978-1-56023; 978-1-56024)* Div. of Taylor & Francis Group, 325 Chestnut St., Philadelphia, PA 19106-2614 USA (SAN 211-0156) Toll Free Fax: 800-895-0582; Toll Free: 800-429-6784; *Imprints:* Harrington Park Press (Harrington Park)
E-mail: orders@haworthpress.com; getinfo@haworthpress.com; barnold@haworthpress.com; docdelivery@haworthpress.com; tbronstein@haworthpress.com
Web site: http://www.haworthpress.com
Dist(s): **Barnes & Noble, Inc.**
Bookazine Co., Inc.
Borders, Inc.
Columbia Univ. Pr.
Distributors, The
Matthews Medical Bk. Co.
New Leaf Distributing Co., Inc.
Quality Bks., Inc.
Rittenhouse Bk. Distributors
SPD-Small Pr. Distribution
Unique Bks., Inc.
Waldenbooks, Inc.; *CIP.*

Hawthorn Pr. (GBR) *(978-0-9507062; 978-1-869890; 978-1-903458; 978-1-907359; 978-1-912480) Dist. by* **IPG Chicago.**

Hawthorne Bks. & Literary Arts, Inc., *(978-0-9716915; 978-0-9766311; 978-0-9790188; 978-0-9833049; 978-0-9834775; 978-0-9838504; 978-0-9860007; 978-0-9893604; 978-0-9904370; 978-0-9970683; 978-0-9988257; 979-8-218-19422-2)* 3636 NE 45th Ave., Portland, OR 97213 USA
E-mail: rhughes@hawthornebooks.com
Web site: Http://hawthornebooks.com
Dist(s): **Publishers Group West (PGW).**

†Hay Hse., Inc., *(978-0-937611; 978-0-945923; 978-1-56170; 978-1-891751; 978-1-58825; 978-1-4019)* Orders Addr.: P.O. Box 5100, Carlsbad, CA 92018-5100 USA (SAN 630-477X) Tel 760-431-7695 ext 112; Fax: 760-431-6948; Toll Free Fax: 800-650-5115 (orders only); Toll Free: 800-654-5126 (orders only); 2776 Loker Ave. W, Carlsbad, CA 92010 (SAN 257-3024) Tel 800-654-5126; Fax: 800-650-5115; *Imprints:* Hay House Lifestyles (Hay Hse Lifestyles)
E-mail: kjohnson@hayhouse.com; pcrowe@hayhouse.com
Web site: http://www.hayhouse.com
Dist(s): **Follett School Solutions**
Lectorum Pubns., Inc.
Penguin Random Hse. Distribution
Penguin Random Hse. LLC; *CIP.*

Hay Hse. Lifestyles *Imprint of* **Hay Hse., Inc.**

Haydenburri Lane, *(978-0-9758785; 978-0-9801849; 978-0-9822149)* 6114 LaSalle Ave., No. 285, Oakland, CA 94611-2802 USA Toll Free: 888-425-2636
Web site: http://www.haydenburrilane.com.

Hayes, Bob (CAN) *(978-0-9867376) Dist. by* **Firefly Bks Limited.**

Hayles, Nanette E., *(978-0-9986666)* 6631 NE 159th St., Vancouver, WA 98686 USA Tel 360-977-5597
E-mail: nehayles@gmail.com.

Haylie's House Of Books *See* **none**

HayMarBks., LLC, *(978-0-9848736)* 1719 Plantation Oaks Dr., Jacksonville, FL 32223 USA Tel 904-655-0801
E-mail: dianeharperbooks@gmail.com
Web site: www.haymarbooks.com.

Haymarket Bks., *(978-1-931859; 978-1-60846; 978-1-64259)* 800 W. Buena Ave, Chicago, IL 60618 USA Tel 773-583-7884
E-mail: info@haymarketbooks.org
Web site: http://www.haymarketbooks.org
Dist(s): **Consortium Bk. Sales & Distribution**
MyiLibrary
Open Road Integrated Media, Inc.
ebrary, Inc.

Haynes Manuals, Inc., *(978-0-8019; 978-1-56392; 978-1-85010; 978-1-85960; 978-1-62092)* Subdivision of J H Haynes, 859 Lawrence Dr., Newbury Park, CA 91320 USA (SAN 200-9838) Tel 805-498-6703; Fax: 805-498-2867; Toll Free: 800-442-9637; 1299 Bridgestone Pkwy., LaVergne, TN 37086 Fax: 615-793-5325; Toll Free: 800-242-4637
Web site: http://www.haynes.com/
Dist(s): **Delmar Cengage Learning**
Hachette Bk. Group
MBI Distribution Services/Quayside Distribution
Quarto Publishing Group USA.

Haynes Media Group, *(978-1-952648)* 108-14 72nd Ave. 2nd Flr., Queens, NY 11375 USA Tel 844-828-0428; Fax: 844-828-0428
E-mail: aliceclark@haynesmediagroup.com
Web site: www.haynesmediagroup.com.

Haynes Publications, Incorporated *See* **Haynes Manuals, Inc.**

Haynes Publishing Group P.L.C. (GBR) *(978-0-85696; 978-0-900550; 978-1-56392; 978-1-85010; 978-1-85260; 978-1-85960; 978-1-84425; 978-0-85733; 978-1-78521) Dist. by* **HachBkGrp.**

Haynes,Chilton,

Hayse, Emily, *(978-0-692-10514-6; 978-1-7332428)* 1939 Pero Lake Rd., Lapeer, MI 48446 USA Tel 810-510-0122
E-mail: blessedhopeem@aol.com.

HazardousWeather Preparedness Institute, *(978-0-9742794)* 5203 N. Oaks Dr., Greensboro, NC 27455-1229 USA
E-mail: rjackson@weatherpreparedness.com
Web site: http://www.weatherpreparedness.com.

Hazel Street Productions, *(978-0-9786988)* P.O. Box 5936, Sherman Oaks, CA 91413-5936 USA
Web site: http://www.hazelst.com.

†Hazelden, *(978-0-89486; 978-0-89638; 978-0-935908; 978-0-942421; 978-1-56246; 978-1-56838; 978-1-59285; 978-1-61649; 978-1-63634)* 15251 Pleasant Valley Rd., P.o. Box 176, Center City, MN 55012-0176 USA (SAN 209-4010) Fax: 651-213-4044; Toll Free: 800-328-9000; P.O. Box 176, RW4, Center City, MN 55012 Tel 651-213-4000; Toll Free: 800-328-9000
E-mail: bosterbauer@hazelden.org
Web site: http://www.hazelden.org
Dist(s): **BookMobile**
Follett School Solutions
Health Communications, Inc.
MyiLibrary
Simon & Schuster, Inc.
ebrary, Inc.; *CIP.*

Hazelden Publishing & Educational Services *See* **Hazelden**

Hazlett, Sandra , *(978-0-578-18864-5)* 843 North 1500 Rd., Lawrence, KS 66049 USA.

Hazy Dell Pr., *(978-0-9965787; 978-1-948931)* 1129 SE Market St, Portland, OR 97206 USA
E-mail: info@hazydellpress.com
Web site: www.hazydellpress.com
Dist(s): **Consortium Bk. Sales & Distribution.**

HB Publishing *See* **Nadine Lalich**

HBHavenBound Publishing *Imprint of* **HavenBound Publishing**

H.B.P., Inc., *(978-0-9753285; 978-0-9789617; 978-0-9853898; 978-0-9971299; 978-0-692-19636-6; 979-8-9865351)* 952 Frederick St., Hagerstown, MD 21740 USA
E-mail: jdaniels@hbp.com
Web site: http://www.hbp.com.

HCI Teens *Imprint of* **Health Communications, Inc.**

Head of Zeus (GBR) *(978-1-908800; 978-1-78185; 978-1-78408; 978-1-78669; 978-1-78497; 978-1-78854; 978-1-80024; 978-1-83893; 978-1-80110; 978-1-78954) Dist. by* **IPG Chicago.**

Head On Dialogue Publishing, *(978-0-9770550)* Orders Addr.: P.O. Box 11400, Oakland, CA 94611 USA; Edit Addr.: 509 El Dorado No. 309, Piedmont, CA 94611 USA Tel 510-677-3267
E-mail: headondialogue@yahoo.com.

Head Pr. Publishing, *(978-0-9758924; 978-0-9832837)* 3804 Pk. Bend Dr., Flower Mound, TX 75022 USA Tel 817-410-9490
E-mail: headpresspublish@aol.com
Web site: http://www.headpress.info
Dist(s): **Send The Light Distribution LLC.**

Headcanon Pr., *(978-0-9984533; 978-1-955343)*
E-mail: contact@shawnacanon.com
Web site: shawnacanon.com.

Headline Bks., Inc., *(978-0-929915; 978-0-938467; 978-1-882658; 978-1-946664; 978-1-951556; 978-1-958914)* Orders Addr.: P.O. Box 52, Terra Alta, WV 26764 USA (SAN 250-8559) Tel 304-789-3001; Toll Free: 800-570-5951; *Imprints:* Publisher Page (Pub Page); Headline Kids (HeadlineKids)
E-mail: cathy@headlinebooks.com
Web site: http://www.headlinebooks.com
Dist(s): **American Wholesale Bk. Co.**
American West Bks.
Brodart Co.
Coutts Information Services
Follett School Solutions
Midwest Library Service
News Group, The.

Headline Kids *Imprint of* **Headline Bks., Inc.**

Headline Publishing Group (GBR) *(978-0-7472; 978-0-7553; 978-1-4722) Dist. by* **Trafalgar.**

Headline Publishing Group (GBR) *(978-0-7472; 978-0-7553; 978-1-4722) Dist. by* **HachBkGrp.**

Headrick, Gordon, *(978-0-9771385)* M. F. W. High School 1775 W. Lowell Ave., Tracy, CA 95376 USA.

Heads First (1st), *(978-0-9761969)* 4207 Magnolia Ln., Sugar Land, TX 77478 USA Tel 281-844-3719
E-mail: heads1st@aol.com
Web site: http://www.headsfirst.com.

Healing Arts Pr. *Imprint of* **Inner Traditions International, Ltd.**

Healing Flood Bks., Inc., *(978-0-9746497)* Orders Addr.: 3108 N. Longmore St., Chandler, AZ 85224 USA
E-mail: freebook@healingflood.com; prb@healingflood.com; sales@hospitalbooks.net; jerry@hospitalbooks.net; marketing@healingflood.com
Web site: http://www.healingflood.com; http://www.hospitalbooks.net.

Healing for People Pr., *(978-0-578-79057-2; 978-0-578-80718-8)* 1408 4th St., San Rafael, CA 94901 USA Tel 415-380-8600
E-mail: Tiffany@HealingforPeople.com
Web site: www.HealingforPeople.com.

Healing Hands Pr., *(978-0-9747686)* Div. of Holistic Home Health Care, 1329 N. Wembley Cir., Port Orange, FL 32128 USA Tel 386-322-4888
Web site: http://www.love-heals.com.

Healing Heart's Publishing Co., *(978-0-692-18461-5)* 10955 Quail Cove Ct., Nampa, ID 83687 USA Tel 208-914-4628
E-mail: heatherorchard88@gmail.com
Dist(s): **CreateSpace Independent Publishing Platform.**

Healing Hounds Publishing LLC, *(978-1-7347787)* 4807 Lancaster Pike, Wilmington, DE 19807 USA Tel 304-692-9099; Fax: 304-285-7388
E-mail: Paul.Rsn@gmail.com.

Healing Society, Inc., *(978-0-9720282; 978-1-932843)* Orders Addr.: P.O. Box 4503, Sedona, AZ 86340-9978 USA; Edit Addr.: 6560 Hwy. 179, Suite 114, Sedona, AZ 86351 USA Toll Free: 877-504-1106
E-mail: dcrenshaw@hspub.com; moh@hspub.com
Web site: http://www.healingsociety.com; http://www.bodynbrain.com
Dist(s): **New Leaf Distributing Co., Inc.**

Healing Tree Arts, *(978-0-9779643)* P.O. Box 3398, Laguna Hills, CA 92654 USA (SAN 850-7775)
E-mail: healingtreearts@yahoo.com
Web site: http://www.healingtreearts.com.

healologie, 2467 Adelaide, Abbotsford, CA 11111 USA Tel 778-552-5117
E-mail: jassal.lakhbir@gmail.com.

Health & Beauty Ctr., LLC, *(978-0-9747253)* P.O. Box 363, Oregon City, OR 97045 USA Toll Free: 888-648-7771
E-mail: support@healthnbeauty.com; support@perfect-prescription.com
Web site: http://www.healthnbeauty.com; http://www.perfect-prescription.com.

Health & Human Services Dept. *Imprint of* **United States Government Printing Office**

†Health Communications, Inc., *(978-0-932194; 978-1-55874; 978-0-7573; 978-0-9910732)* Orders Addr.: 3201 SW 15th St., Deerfield Beach, FL 33442-8190 USA (SAN 212-100X) Tel 954-360-0909; Fax: 954-360-0034; Toll Free: 800-441-5569; *Imprints:* HCI Teens (HCi Teens); Faith Communications (Faith Comns) Do not confuse with Health Communications, Inc., Edison, NJ
E-mail: terip@hcibooks.com; lorig@hcibooks.com
Web site: http://www.hcibooks.com
Dist(s): **Bookazine Co., Inc.**
Children's Plus, Inc.
Islander Group
Partners/West Book Distributors
Simon & Schuster, Inc.
Southern Bk. Service
Western Pubns. Service; *CIP.*

Health New England, *(978-0-9777159)* One Monarch Pl., Springfield, MA 01144-1500 USA (SAN 850-0436) Tel 413-787-4000; Toll Free: 800-842-4464
Web site: http://www.hne.com; http://www.hnestore.com; http://www.hnewhizkidz.com.

Health Press *See* **Health Press NA Incorporated**

Health Press NA Incorporated, *(978-0-929173)* P.O. Box 37470, Albuquerque, NM 87176 USA (SAN 248-5036) Tel 505-888-1394; Fax: 505-212-0612
E-mail: goodbooks@healthpress.com
Web site: http://www.healthpress.com.

Health Success Media, LLC, *(978-0-9820121)* P.O. Box 21092, Bradenton, FL 34204 USA (SAN 857-0043)
E-mail: elana.devorah@gmail.com; Elana@ConquerProstateCancer.com
Web site: http://www.ConquerProstateCancer.com.

Health UnLtd. *See* **Books to UPLIFT**

Healthful Living Bks. *Imprint of* **Unique Executive Pubs.**

HealthMark Multimedia, *(978-0-9717399)* 1828 L St., NW, Suite 250, Washington, DC 20036 USA
E-mail: hm@healthmarkmultimedia.com; amcfarren@healthmarkmultimedia.com
Web site: http://www.HealthMarkMultimedia.com.

Healthnets, *(978-0-615-20972-2)* 2921 Emmorton Rd., Abingdon, MD 21009 USA Tel 410-515-7858
E-mail: milleniumdiet@gmail.com
Web site: http://www.Milleniumdiet.com/.

Healthoot, Inc., *(978-0-9968393)* P.O. Box 2782, Running Springs, CA 92382 USA Tel 909-261-5205
E-mail: jaimestiansen@gmail.com.

HealthSprings, LLC, *(978-0-9718120; 978-0-9740697; 978-0-9748263)* 1759 Grandstand, San Antonio, TX 78238 USA Tel 210-521-7650; Fax: 210-521-7141
E-mail: sabra@zoeyzones.com
Web site: http://www.zoeyzones.com.

Publisher Name Index

HealthTeacher, *(978-0-9785578; 978-0-9817969)* 5200 Maryland Way Ste. 100, Brentwood, TN 37027-5072 USA Toll Free: 800-514-1362 E-mail: tod@relegent.com Web site: http://www.healthteacher.com.

Healthy Life Press *See* **Healthy Life Pr., LLC**

Healthy Life Pr., Inc., *(978-0-9727328)* Orders Addr.: 1574 Gulf Rd., PMB 72, Point Roberts, WA 98281-9602 USA; Edit Addr.: 2667 Stellar Ct., Coquitlam, BC V3E 1H1 CAN Tel 604-682-5838; Fax: 604-468-1217 E-mail: rszefler@shaw.ca; info@starthealthylife.com Web site: http://www.starthealthylife.com.

Healthy Life Pr., LLC, *(978-0-9821466; 978-0-9825800; 978-1-939267; 978-0-578-59920-5; 978-1-7342916)* Orders Addr.: 3004 Shelby Street, Apt 316, Bristol, TN 37620 USA Toll Free: 877-331-2766 Web site: http://www.healthylifepress.com *Dist(s):* **CreateSpace Independent Publishing Platform Outskirts Pr., Inc. Send The Light Distribution LLC.**

Hear My Heart Publishing, *(978-0-9862331; 978-1-945620)* 313 E. Oak St., Skiatook, OK 74070 USA Tel 918-510-1483 E-mail: hearmyheart02@yahoo.com Web site: hearmyheart.net.

Heard Publishing, *(978-1-7357556)* 2908 Wilsonia Way, Virginia Beach, VA 23453 USA Tel 757-309-6848 E-mail: bgowns4more@gmail.com.

Heard Word Publishing, LLC, *(978-0-9801060)* 3051 W. 105th Ave. No. 350253, Westminster, CO 80031 USA E-mail: hispublishingllc@yahoo.com; Beatrice@TheGetOverItGal.com Web site: www.TheGetOverItGal.com.

Hearst Book Group *See* **Hearst Magazine Media**

Hearst Communications, Inc., *(978-0-87851; 978-1-58816)* 250 W. 55th St., New York, NY 10019-5288 USA E-mail: jdeval@hearst.com Web site: http://www.hearst.com *Dist(s):* **Hearst Bks. Sterling Publishing Co., Inc.**

Hearst Magazine Media, *(978-1-950785; 978-1-958395)* Orders Addr.: 300 W. 57th St., New York, NY 10019 USA Tel 212-649-2000 E-mail: andy.nelson63@gmail.com *Dist(s):* **Penguin Random Hse. Distribution Penguin Random Hse. LLC.**

Heart 4 Clowning Pr., A, *(978-0-9799093)* 905 Hwy 321 NW., No. 215, Hickory, NC 28601 USA Tel 828-326-0662 E-mail: aheart4clowning@gmail.com Web site: http://www.AHeart4Clowning.com.

Heart & Harp LLC, *(978-0-9742174)* Orders Addr.: P.O. Box 818, Walled Lake, MI 48390-0818 USA Tel 313-938-9847 E-mail: HeartandHarp@comcast.net Web site: http://www.heartandharp.net.

Heart Arbor Bks., *(978-1-891452)* Orders Addr.: P.O. Box 542, Grand River, OH 44045 USA (SAN 299-6073) Tel 440-257-0722; Toll Free: 877-977-4422.

Heart Bound Pr., *(978-0-615-25721-1; 978-0-578-73329-6)* Orders Addr.: 2141 Via Pacheco, Palos Verdes, CA 90274 USA Tel 310-375-3716; Fax: 310-373-2702 E-mail: heartboundpublishing@yahoo.com.

Heart Communications, *(978-0-9694176; 978-0-9747516)* P.O. Box 710791, Oak Hill, VA 20171 USA (SAN 116-404X) Tel 641-715-3900 (ext. 20889) E-mail: info@heartcommunications.com Web site: http://www.HeartCommunications.com.

Heart Flame Publishing, *(978-0-9726618)* P.O. Box 790038, Virgin, UT 84779-0038 USA (SAN 853-2532) Fax: 435-635-2613 Web site: http://www.heartflamepublishing.com.

Heart Of Dixie Publishing *See* **Bluewater Pubns.**

Heart Path Publishing, *(978-0-9712305)* P.O. Box 44, Keene, TX 76059 USA Tel 817-681-3877 Do not confuse with Heart Path Publishing, Atlanta, GA Web site: http://www.guidemagazine.org.

Heart Seed Pr., *(978-0-615-37628-3; 978-0-9831945; 978-0-578-72051-7; 978-0-578-72052-4; 979-8-218-05414-4)* 3710 Little Walnut Rd. Spc3, Silver City, NM 88061 USA Tel 575-956-5891 E-mail: acircleisdrawn@gmail.com Web site: http://acircleisdrawn.org.

Heart to Heart Publishing, Inc., *(978-0-9742806; 978-0-9802486; 978-1-937008)* Orders Addr.: P.O. Box PO Box 50644, Bowling Green, KY 42102 USA Tel 270-526-5589; Edit Addr.: P.O. Box PO Box 50644, Bowling Green, KY 42102 USA Tel 270-526-5589 E-mail: elizabeth@hearttoheartpublishinginc.com Web site: http://www.lindajhawkins.com; http://www.hearttoheartpublishinginc.com *Dist(s):* **BookBaby.**

Heart2Heart Publishing, *(978-0-578-61465-6; 978-1-7348781)* 103 Ctr. St W No. 1688, Eatonville, WA 98328 USA Tel 253-439-0130 E-mail: DrGMagee@outlook.com Web site: HarmonyRidgeCenter.com.

Heart-centered Productions, *(978-0-692-15583-7; 978-0-692-15585-1; 978-0-578-34855-1; 979-8-218-10687-4; 979-8-218-10688-1)* 282 N 300 E Unit D, American Fork, UT 84003 USA Tel 801-602-2699 E-mail: scotty_amour@yahoo.com *Dist(s):* **Ingram Content Group.**

Heartdrum *Imprint of* **HarperCollins Pubs.**

Heartfelt Bks., *(978-0-9763933)* 149 Thunderbird Trail, Carol Stream, IL 60188-1982 USA.

HeartFelt Stories LLC, *(978-0-9773113)* 5767 Kempton Run Ct., Columbus, OH 43235 USA (SAN 850-3036) E-mail: heartfeltstories@hotmail.com Web site: http://www.heartfeltstoriesllc.com *Dist(s):* **Blu Sky Media Group.**

Heartful Loving Pr., *(978-0-9723639)* Div. of Illui International, 1450 Orange Grove Ave., Santa Barbara, CA 93105 USA Tel 805-687-7442; Fax: 805-687-3042 E-mail: howard@heartfullovingpress.com Web site: http://www.heartfullovingpress.com; http://www.howtobeafamily.com; http://www.firstloveremembrances.com; http://www.howtobethebestlover.com *Dist(s):* **Partners Bk. Distributing, Inc.**

Hearth & Garden Productions, *(978-0-692-59584-8; 978-0-692-91632-2; 978-0-692-04302-8; 978-0-578-98345-5; 978-0-578-98520-6)*.

Hearthstone Rose, *(978-0-9836682)* 1156 Valleyview Dr., Lawrence, PA 15055 USA Tel 724-746-0662 E-mail: conniedonaldson@comcast.net.

Heartland Foundation, Inc., *(978-0-943177)* Orders Addr.: P.O. Box 887, Ames, IA 50010 USA Toll Free: 866-385-2027; Edit Addr.: 413 Northwestern Ave., Ames, IA 50010 USA (SAN 668-3010) Tel 515-232-1054 E-mail: lssn@att.net Web site: http://mcmillenbooks.com *Dist(s):* **McMillen Bk. Distributors.**

Heartlight Girls, *(978-0-9787689)* P.O. Box 370546, Denver, CO 80237 USA Tel 303-690-5603 E-mail: debra@heartlightgirls.com; debragano@aol.com Web site: http://www.heartlightgirls.com.

Heartohopia Pr., *(978-0-9725184)* 2007 NE 59 Pl., Suite 105, Fort Lauderdale, FL 33308 USA Web site: http://www.heartohopia.com.

HeartQuake Publishing *See* **Hunt Thompson Media**

Heartrock Pr., *(978-0-9817668)* P.O. Box 135, Langley, WA 98260 USA Tel 360-321-5603 Web site: http://NWDragons.com.

Heart's Path LLC *See* **Breadcrumbs LLC**

Heartsome Press *See* **Heartsome Publishing**

Heartsome Publishing, *(978-0-9726408)* 220 Norfolk St., Walpole, MA 2081 USA Tel 508-553-3858; Fax: 508-668-1998 Web site: http://www.nolobsterplease.com/.

Heartsome Publishing, *(978-0-9726408)* 220 Norfolk St., Walpole, MA 02081 USA Tel 508-553-3858; Fax: 508-668-1998 E-mail: rrhearts@comcast.net Web site: http://www.nolobsterplease.com/.

Heartstring Productions, LLC, *(978-0-578-53540-1; 978-0-578-81173-4; 978-1-7362294; 979-8-9853393)* 1702 Trey Terr., Huntsville, AL 35802 USA Tel 256-683-8045 E-mail: authormarciaashford@gmail.com *Dist(s):* **Ingram Content Group.**

Heartstring Productions, LLD *See* **Heartstring Productions, LLC**

Heartstrings Publishing, *(978-0-9760733)* Orders Addr.: P.O. Box 8255, Fernando Beach, FL 32035 USA; Edit Addr.: Marchette Burette Market, Amelia Island Plantation, Fernandina Beach, FL 32034 USA E-mail: mledlen@aol.com.

Heart-to-Heart Pubns., *(978-0-9744565)* 18237 N. 51st Pl., Scottsdale, AZ 85254 USA Tel 602-485-0793 E-mail: cpruett1@cox.net.

Heat *Imprint of* **Penguin Publishing Group**

Heath, Jonathan Publishing, *(978-0-9715837)* 10 Willowstream Dr., Vernon, CT 06066 USA Tel 860-875-8373 E-mail: lenpam@snet.net.

Heath Publishing *See* **Lockwood House Publishing**

Heather & Highlands Publishing, *(978-1-58478)* Div. of Heather & Highlands Publishing, Orders Addr.: 2384 Tokay Ct., Paradise, CA 95969 USA (SAN 254-0932) Tel 530-876-8986; Fax: 530-876-8989; Toll Free: 888-999-2358; *Imprints:* Highland Children's Press (Highind Child) E-mail: pawprintsorders@pawprintspress.com; pawprints@pawprintspress.com; tew@tewatsononline.com; heatherandhighlands@heatherandhighlandspublishing.com Web site: http://www.pawprintspress.com; http://www.tewatsononline.com; http://heatherandhighlandspublishing.com *Dist(s):* **Book Wholesalers, Inc. Brodart Co.**

Heather E. Robyn, *(978-1-7345050; 979-8-9857501)* 1049 Coleman Rd Apt 4101, San Jose, CA 95123 USA Tel 619-952-0290 E-mail: wutsupdoc24@gmail.com Web site: heatherrobyn.com.

Heather Kelly, Author *See* **Pocket Moon Pr.**

Heavenly C. Publishing, *(978-0-9746361)* P.O. Box 335, West Chester, OH 45071 USA Web site: http://www.heavenlyCPublishing.com.

Heavenly Realm Publishing, *(978-0-9714874; 978-0-9825589; 978-0-9828802; 978-0-9833418; 978-0-9835202; 978-0-9839969; 978-1-937911; 978-1-944383)* Orders Addr.: P.O. Box 682532, Houston, TX 77268 USA Tel 866-216-0696; Toll Free: 877-599-3237 E-mail: heavenlyrealm@heavenlyrealmpublishing.com Web site: http://www.heavenlyrealmpublishing.com *Dist(s):* **Ingram Content Group.**

HeavensDew Publishing *See* **DewPuffBaby**

Heavy Metal Magazine, *(978-1-882931; 978-1-932413; 978-1-935351)* Div. of Metal Mammoth, Inc., 100 H. Village Ave., Suite IV, Rockville Centre, NY 11570-4801 USA Tel 516-594-2130; Fax: 516-594-2133 E-mail: heavymetal1@rcn.com Web site: http://metaltv.com *Dist(s):* **Diamond Comic Distributors, Inc. TNT Media Group, Inc.**

Hebler, Dave, *(978-0-9765392)* 5891 S. Military Trail, 5A-PMB, Lake Worth, FL 33463-6920 USA Tel 561-642-6696 E-mail: daveahebler@aol.com Web site: http://www.protectingwomen.com.

Hebler, Michael, *(978-0-615-39525-8; 978-0-9833884; 978-0-692-67408-6; 978-0-692-70134-8)* 1344 Kingswood Ct., Fort Myers, FL 33919 USA Tel 562-857-1524; *Imprints:* Night After Night Publications, Incorporated (NightAfterNight) E-mail: michaelhebler@gmail.com Web site: http://www.michaelhebler.com *Dist(s):* **CreateSpace Independent Publishing Platform.**

Hecker, Mark Daniel, *(978-0-692-91079-5)* 1606 Isherwood St. NE No. 2, WASHINGTON, DC 20003 USA Tel 215-205-9902 E-mail: mhecker616@gmail.com *Dist(s):* **Ingram Content Group.**

Hedgebury (AUS) *(978-0-9873437) Dist. by* **NewShelves.**

Hedgehog Hill Pr., *(978-0-615-90068-1; 978-0-692-53693-3; 978-0-692-53695-7; 978-0-692-53696-4; 978-0-692-53804-3; 978-0-692-56005-1; 978-0-692-68211-1; 978-0-692-68510-5; 978-0-692-69829-7; 978-0-692-72830-7; 978-0-692-72835-2; 978-0-692-78517-1; 978-0-692-79765-5; 978-0-692-91674-2; 978-0-692-91758-9; 978-0-692-06689-8)* 7 Urban Dr., Anderson, IN 46011 USA Tel 765-639-5930 *Dist(s):* **CreateSpace Independent Publishing Platform.**

Hedgepeth, Thaabit, *(978-0-578-42865-9)* 502 Everette Ave, Clayton, NC 27520 USA Tel 919-825-7358 E-mail: thaabithedgepeth@gmail.com.

Hedger, Ralph, *(978-0-9753880)* 208 Chaucer Rd., Charlottesville, VA 22901-2215 USA E-mail: rehedger@aol.com.

Heerema, Dina, *(978-0-692-23844-8)* 401 Riverview Dr., Totowa, NJ 07512 USA Tel 973-200-0560 E-mail: dina23n@hotmail.com.

Heersink, Roland, *(978-0-9770473)* 18303 Starboard Dr., Houston, TX 77058-4362 USA Web site: http://www.fairytunes.com.

Heflin & Thrall Language Pubns., Inc., *(978-0-9723341)* 2109 Stanford, Jacksonville, TX 75766 USA Toll Free: 888-313-3310 E-mail: jheflin@language-publications.com.

Hegemony Pr., *(978-0-9754114)* 5205 Pacific Ave., Tacoma, WA 98405 USA Tel 253-671-2665; Fax: 253-475-2665; Toll Free: 888-671-2665.

Heiderer, Conrad, *(978-0-9746699)* P.O. Box 405, Glen Arbor, MI 49636 USA Tel 231-334-6680 Toll Free: 888-877-0994 E-mail: cehj1200@hotmail.com Web site: http://www.twigma.com.

Heifer Project International, *(978-0-9755996; 978-0-9798439; 978-0-9819788)* Orders Addr.: 1 World Ave., Little Rock, AR 72203-8058 USA Tel 800-422-1311; Fax: 501-907-2802 E-mail: info@heifer.org Web site: http://www.heifer.org.

Heights Series, The, *(978-0-692-16632-1)* 511 Andrews Dr., Hampton, GA 30228 USA Tel 305-586-2495 E-mail: denarriuspennell206@outlook.com *Dist(s):* **Ingram Content Group.**

Heinemann *Imprint of* **Capstone**

†**Heinemann,** *(978-0-325; 978-0-434; 978-0-435; 978-1-59469)* Orders Addr.: P.O. Box 6926, Portsmouth, NH 03802 USA Toll Free: 800-225-5800; Edit Addr.: 361 Hanover St., Portsmouth, NH 03801 USA (SAN 210-5829) Tel 603-431-7894; Fax: 603-431-7840; *Imprints:* Firsthand (Firsthnd) E-mail: info@heinemann.com Web site: http://www.heinemann.com *Dist(s):* **ABC-CLIO, LLC Capstone Follett School Solutions Leonard, Hal Corp. Pearson Education Trans-Atlantic Pubns., Inc.**; *CIP.*

Heinemann Educational Books, Incorporated *See* **Heinemann**

.Heinemann-Raintree *See* **Heinemann-Raintree**

Heinemann-Raintree, *(978-0-431; 978-1-57572; 978-1-58810; 978-1-4034; 978-1-4109; 978-1-4329; 978-1-4846)* Div. of Capstone, Orders Addr.: 1710 Roe Crest Dr., North Mankato, MN 56003 USA; Halley Court Freepost PO Box 1125, Oxford, OX2 8YY *Dist(s):* **Capstone Follett School Solutions Lectorum Pubns., Inc.**

Heinle & Heinle Publishers, Inc. *See* **Cengage Heinle**

Heinrich Publishing LLC, *(978-0-578-43837-5; 978-0-578-57110-2)* 1140 N. 27th Ave., Bozeman, MT 59718 USA Tel 605-645-8436 E-mail: savinglikeasloth@gmail.com *Dist(s):* **Ingram Content Group.**

Heinrich, Tyson Chui, *(978-0-615-23894-4; 978-0-578-00492-1; 978-0-578-01337-4; 978-0-578-01343-5; 978-0-9962209)* Web site: http://www.tysonchulheinrich.com.

Heins Pubns., *(978-0-9671762; 978-0-9748680)* 2016 Leonard Ct., Eau Claire, WI 54703 USA Toll Free: 800-554-3467 E-mail: revheins@wwt.net.

Heinz, Derek *See* **Heinz, Derek**

Heinz, Derek, *(978-0-578-19115-7; 978-0-692-98514-4)* 1124 NE Lilac St. 107, Issaquah, WA 98029 USA.

Helden, Rachel, *(978-0-578-87633-7; 978-0-578-96295-5; 978-0-578-96296-2)* 10557 Litz Ave., St. Ann, MO 63074 USA Tel 618-401-4719 E-mail: hello@rachelhelden.com Web site: www.rachelhelden.com.

Helen Bolton Ministries *See* **Bolton Publishing LLC**

Helen Darling *See* **My Darling-Tots Pubns.**

Heliand Publishing Corp., *(978-0-9770712)* P.O. Box 477, Pleasant Grove, UT 84062 USA E-mail: submissions@heliandpublishing.com Web site: http://www.heliandpublishing.com.

Heliograph, Inc., *(978-0-9668926; 978-1-930658)* 26 Porter St., Somerville, MA 02143-2215 USA E-mail: info@heliograph.com Web site: http://www.heliograph.com.

Heliotrope Bks., LLC, *(978-0-9816198; 978-0-9832940; 978-0-9904012; 978-1-942762; 978-1-956474)* 125 E. 4th St., New York, NY 10003 USA Tel 212-477-1783 E-mail: publishers@heliotropebooks.com; nonirose@earthlink.net Web site: http://www.heliotropebooks.com.

Helkenn, Brady, *(978-1-7340909)* 815 Tennessee St, San Francisco, CA 94107 USA Tel 415-637-0541 E-mail: bhelkenn@gmail.com.

Helle Brisson, *(978-0-9884387; 979-8-9856438)* 6443 Amethyst Way, Carlsbad, CA 92011 USA Tel 760-809-7753 E-mail: hellebrisson@yahoo.com Web site: www.hellebrisson.com.

Hellgate Pr. *Imprint of* **L & R Publishing, LLC**

Helm Literary Publishing *See* **Helm Publishing**

Helm Publishing, *(978-0-9723011; 978-0-9760919; 978-0-9769193; 978-0-9778205; 978-0-9792328; 978-0-9801780; 978-0-9820605; 978-0-9841397; 978-0-9830109; 978-0-9850488)* Orders Addr.: 861 37th Ave. N Apt D, St. Petersburg, FL 33704 USA (SAN 254-7562) Tel 815-621-3336; Edit Addr.: 861 27th Ave. N Apt D, St. Petersburg, FL 33704 USA Tel 727-623-5014 E-mail: dianne@publishersdrive.com Web site: http://www.publishersdrive.com.

Helms, Jo Publishing, *(978-0-9745319)* 824 S. Schaefer St., Appleton, WI 54915 USA E-mail: cheesedawg@earthlink.net; ilovegrizz@earthlink.net Web site: http://www.grizz.20megsfree.com.

Helmshines, *(978-0-9969893)* 11203 Ranch Rd. 2222 Unit 2005, AUSTIN, TX 78730 USA Tel 770-630-3620 E-mail: Melissa.Hines.Helms@gmail.com.

HELORO Publishing Group, *(978-0-9785435; 978-0-615-15932-4; 978-0-615-15933-1; 978-0-615-16034-4)* 860 Appletree Ct., Northbrook, IL 60062-3402 USA (SAN 850-9549) Tel 847-207-1087 mobile phone Do not confuse with companies with the same or similar name in Minneapolis, MN, Great Neck, NY Web site: http://www.HELORO.com *Dist(s):* **Lulu Pr., Inc.**

H.E.L.P. for Self-Education, *(978-0-9766991)* 960 Perth Rd., Troutman, NC 28166 USA Tel 704-528-5866; Fax: 704-585-9397 E-mail: swedship@bellsouth.net Web site: http://www.home.bellsouth.net/p/pwp-helpeducate.

Helping Hands Children's Bks., *(978-0-9762274)* 421 26th St., Marion, IA 52302 USA Tel 319-373-4169 E-mail: mary@mysak.com.

Helping Hands Therapeutic Services, *(978-0-9855978)* P.O. Box 1452, Columbus, GA 31902 USA Tel 770-310-0510 E-mail: mirrorbuzz99@gmail.com.

Helpingwords, *(978-0-615-16066-5; 978-0-615-23505-9; 978-0-578-03620-5; 978-0-578-05059-1; 978-0-578-06008-8; 978-0-9828529; 978-0-9977922; 979-8-9852242)* 66 Prospect St., Manchester, NH 03104 USA Tel 603-668-1975 E-mail: kathy@kathybrodsky.com Web site: http://www.kathybrodsky.com *Dist(s):* **Enfield Publishing & Distribution Co., Inc.**

Helps4Teachers, *(978-0-9778548)* 145 Gardenside Ct., Fallbrook, CA 92028 USA (SAN 850-4180) Tel 760-723-0504 E-mail: rstur@roadrunner.com Web site: http://www.helps4teachers.com.

Helvetiq, RedCut Sarl (CHE) *(978-2-940481; 978-3-907293) Dist. by* **Consort Bk Sales.**

Hemed Books, Incorporated *See* **Lambda Pubs., Inc.**

Henderson Publishing, *(978-1-891029)* Orders Addr.: 811 Eva's Walk, Pounding Mill, VA 24637 USA Tel 276-964-2291.

Hendley, Jeff *See* **L'Edge Pr.**

Hendricks, J. L., *(978-0-9974915; 978-1-952634)* 1649 Ironwood PL Unit B, Corona, CA 92879 USA Tel 951-314-6464 E-mail: jlhendricksauthor@gmail.com.

Hendrickson Academic *Imprint of* **Hendrickson Pubs. Marketing, LLC**

Hendrickson Publishers, Incorporated *See* **Hendrickson Pubs. Marketing, LLC**

†**Hendrickson Pubs. Marketing, LLC,** *(978-0-913573; 978-0-917006; 978-0-943575; 978-1-56563; 978-1-59856; 978-1-61970; 978-1-68307)* Orders Addr.: P.O. Box 3473, Peabody, MA 01961-3473 USA (SAN 285-2772) Fax: 978-531-8146; Toll Free: 800-358-3111; Edit Addr.: 140 Summit St., Peabody, MA 01960 USA (SAN 663-6594) Fax: 978-573-8414; *Imprints:* Hendrickson Academic (HendrAcad) Do not confuse with Hendrickson Group, Sandy Hook, CT E-mail: editorial@hendrickson.com Web site: http://www.hendrickson.com *Dist(s):* **Tyndale Hse. Pubs.**; *CIP.*

Hendrickson, Thomas L, *(978-0-9817011)* 19910 W. Monroe St., Buckeye, AZ 85326 USA Web site: http://www.fishersmedia.com.

Henisz, Jerzy E., *(978-0-615-13851-0)* Orders Addr.: P.O. Box 1089, Sharon, CT 06069 USA; Edit Addr.: 33 Hospital Hill Rd., Sharon, CT 06069 USA *Dist(s):* **Lulu Pr., Inc.**

Henrique, Afonso J., *(978-0-692-08329-1; 978-0-692-14855-6)* 400 S 5th St, Elizabeth, NJ 07206 USA Tel 619-997-1353 E-mail: ajhenrique7@gmail.com *Dist(s):* **Ingram Content Group.**

Henry, Ian Pubns. (GBR) *(978-0-86025) Dist. by* **Empire Pub Srvs.**

Henry, Ian Pubns. (GBR) *(978-0-86025) Dist. by* **Players Pr.**

enry, Nelson K. Jr, *(978-0-578-43221-2)* 215 Hidden Springs Dr., Durham, NC 27703 USA Tel 919-824-0370
E-mail: nkhjr05@gmail.com.

enry, Olga, *(978-0-578-76278-4; 978-0-578-83326-2)* 5734 Corbett St, Los Angeles, CA 90016 USA Tel 562-506-5885
E-mail: henry.olga@gmail.com.

enry, Patti, *(978-0-9817155)* 9114 Tepee Trail, Houston, TX 77064 USA (SAN 856-3268) Tel 281-894-4131
E-mail: patti@patti-henry.com
Web site: http://www.patti-henry.com.

enry Quill Pr., *(978-1-883960)* 7340 Lake Dr., Fremont, MI 49412-9146 USA Tel 231-924-3026; Fax: 231-928-2802.

enschelHAUS Publishing, Inc., *(978-0-9647663; 978-0-9722099; 978-1-59598)* 7401 W. Georgia Ave., Milwaukee, WI 53220 USA Tel 608-576-9747; *Imprints:* Goblin Fern Press (Goblin Fern)
E-mail: kira2255@gmail.com
Web site: http://www.goblinfernpress.com; http://www.mavenmarkbooks.com; http://www.henschelHAUSbooks.com; http://www.threetowerspress.com
Dist(s): **Ingram Content Group**
Smashwords.

Hensley, Michael, *(978-0-9747389)* P.O. Box 2952, Ranchos de Taos, NM 87557 USA
Web site: http://www.michaelmhensley.com.

Henson, Annadee, *(978-0-578-55466-2)* 5250 Colodny Dr., No. 25, Agoura, CA 91301 USA Tel 818-445-0975
E-mail: HENSONANNADEE@GMAIL.COM.

Henzel, Richard, *(978-0-9747237; 978-0-9826688; 978-0-9846715)* 1106 N. Taylor, Oak Park, IL 60302 USA Tel 312-296-8396
E-mail: richard@richardhenzel.com
Web site: http://www.richardhenzel.com; http://www.richardhenzel.com/marktwain
Dist(s): **Audible.com**
Midwest Tape.

Her Version of Eventz LLC *See* **HVOE Media**

†Herald Pr., *(978-0-8361; 978-1-5138)* Div. of MennoMedia, Inc., Orders Addr.: 1251 Virginia Ave., Harrisonburg, VA 22802 USA (SAN 202-2915) Tel 1-316-283-0454; Toll Free: 1-800-245-7894; 800-631-6535 (Canada only) Do not confuse with Herald Pr., Charlotte, NC
E-mail: info@mennomedia.org
Web site: http://www.mennomedia.org
Dist(s): **Ebsco Publishing**
Faith Alive Christian Resources
Firebrand Technologies
Send The Light Distribution LLC
Spring Arbor Distributors, Inc.; *CIP.*

†Herald Publishing Hse., *(978-0-8309)* Orders Addr.: P.O. Box 390, Independence, MO 64051-0390 USA Tel 816-521-3015; Fax: 816-521-3066 (customer services); Toll Free: 800-767-8181; Edit Addr.: 1001W. Walnut St., Independence, MO 64051-0390 USA (SAN 111-7556) Tel 816-257-0200
E-mail: sales@HeraldHouse.org
Web site: http://www.heraldhouse.org; *CIP.*

Heraver, Jamie Renee, *(978-0-692-15830-2; 978-0-578-57078-5; 978-0-578-79437-2; 978-0-578-79440-2)* P.O. Box 16, Huntington Beach, CA 92648 USA Tel 714-916-2422
E-mail: jheraver@yahoo.com
Dist(s): **CreateSpace Independent Publishing Platform.**

Herdman, Susan E., *(978-0-578-01491-3)* 4639 Sunset Ridge, Santa Fe, NM 87507 USA
E-mail: susan@susanheerdman.com
Web site: http://americanadolescents.com
Dist(s): **Lulu Pr., Inc.**

Here with an ear publishing, *(978-0-9995675)* 1080 roundelay rd e, Reynoldsburg, OH 43068 USA Tel 614-591-2687
E-mail: daviddwriter@gmail.com.

Heredia, Denise, *(978-0-692-10461-3)* 11819 Central Ave. Apt 213, CHINO, CA 91710 USA Tel 626-905-2517
E-mail: niecyntab@yahoo.com
Dist(s): **Ingram Content Group.**

Heritage Bks., *(978-0-7884; 978-0-917890; 978-0-940907; 978-1-55613; 978-1-888265; 978-1-58549; 978-1-68034)* 5810 Ruatan St, Berwyn Heights, MD 20740 USA (SAN 209-3367) Tel 800-876-6103; Fax: 800-876-6103; Toll Free: 800-876-6103
E-mail: Info@HeritageBooks.com
Web site: http://www.HeritageBooks.com; http://www.WillowBendBooks.com
Dist(s): **CreateSpace Independent Publishing Platform.**

Heritage Heart Farm, *(978-0-9706348)* Orders Addr.: 21387 Rd. 128, Oakwood, OH 45873 USA Tel 419-594-2258
E-mail: heritageheartfarm@roadrunner.com; kohart@tds.net
Web site: http://www.heritageheartfarm.com.

Heritage Hse. (CAN) *(978-0-919214; 978-1-895811; 978-1-894384; 978-0-9690546; 978-1-894974; 978-1-926613; 978-1-926936; 978-1-927051; 978-1-927527; 978-1-77203) Dist. by* **Orca Bk Pub.**

Heritage Music Pr., *(978-0-89328)* Div. of The Lorenz Corp., Orders Addr.: 501 E. Third St., Dayton, OH 45401-0802 USA Tel 937-228-6118; Toll Free: 800-444-1144
E-mail: order@lorenz.com
Web site: http://www.lorenz.com.

Heritage National Publishing, *(978-0-9983202)* 412 S. White St. No. 129, Athens, TN 37303 USA Tel 423-920-0776
E-mail: mountmaaziah@aol.com.

Heritage Pr. Pubns., LLC, *(978-1-937660; 978-1-945464)* 10231 Shallow Creek Dr., Collinsville, MS 39325 USA Tel 601-737-2086; Fax: 888-340-3668
E-mail: hannemoon@heritagepresspublications.com
Web site: heritagepresspublications.com.

Heritage Publishing, *(978-0-9672363)* 23507 E. State Rte. P, Pleasant Hill, MO 64080 USA Tel 816-540-4768; 913-338-3893 Do not confuse with Heritage Publishing with the same or similar names in Dallas, TX, Enumclaw, WA, Chicago, IL, Beverly Hills, CA, Loveland, CO, Valley Center, KS, Peabody, MA, Whitesboro, TX, Pleasant Hill, MO, Springdale, AR, Charlotte, NC, Thomasville, GA, North Little Rock, AR, Baton Rouge, LA, Stockton, CA, carthage, MO
E-mail: peggytucker@juno.com.

Heritage Publishing, *(978-0-692-39278-2; 978-0-692-57340-2; 978-0-692-62722-8; 978-0-9974318; 978-0-692-72236-7; 978-0-692-81935-7; 978-0-9987766)* 1261 Andrew Donelson, Hermitage, TN 37076 USA Tel 615-440-6228
E-mail: jsteph1135@gmail.com.

Heritage Publishing Co., *(978-0-9787462)* 4393 Mission Inn Ave., Riverside, CA 92501 USA (SAN 851-5247) Tel 951-788-7878; Fax: 951-788-1206
E-mail: rich1rodriguez@sbcglobal.net; isabel@isabelelias.com
Web site: http://IsabelElias.com.

Heritage Youth, Inc., *(978-0-9740753)* 6245 Esplanade Ave., Baton Rouge, LA 70806-6144 USA.

Hermes Hse. Pr., *(978-0-9912614)* 1197 Village Cove NE, Atlanta, GA 30319 USA Tel 404-844-3049
E-mail: juleshermes@hermeshousepress.com
Web site: www.hermeshousepress.com.

Hermes Pr., *(978-0-9710311; 978-1-932563; 978-1-61345)* 2100 Wilmington Rd., New Castle, PA 16105-1931 USA Tel 724-652-0511; Fax: 724-652-5597 Do not confuse with companies with same or similar names in Brooks, ME, Vista, CA, Ferndale, MI
Web site: http://www.hermespress.com
Dist(s): **Diamond Comic Distributors, Inc.**
Diamond Bk. Distributors.

Hermes Pubs., Inc., *(978-0-9766543)* P.O. Box 186, Roselle Park, NJ 07207 USA (SAN 256-453X) Toll Free: 888-557-5527
E-mail: dollarnet@aol.com.

Hermit Chum Publishing, *(978-0-9760317)* 6901 S. McClateck, No. 245, Tempe, AZ 89283 USA.

Hermit's Grove, The, *(978-0-9655687; 978-0-9863639)* 16501 County 13, Houston, MN 55943 USA Tel 507-896-3339
E-mail: paul@thehermitsgrove.org
Web site: http://www.thehermitsgrove.org
Dist(s): **New Leaf Distributing Co., Inc.**

Hern, Nick Bks., Ltd. (GBR) *(978-1-85459; 978-1-84842; 978-1-78001; 978-1-78460; 978-1-78850; 978-1-83904) Dist. by* **Consort Bk Sales.**

Hernandez, Theresa, *(978-0-9908688; 978-0-9969393)* 13880 Royal Dornoch Sq., San Diego, CA 92128 USA Tel 858-449-7490
E-mail: theresahernandez1@gmail.com
Web site: http://thhernandez.com.

Hero Builder Comics, *(978-0-615-31157-9)* 1713 Golden Ct., Bellingham, WA 98226 USA.

Hero Dog Pubns., *(978-0-9743659)* 14 Eastview Ave., Pleasantville, NY 10570 USA (SAN 255-545X) Tel 914-525-6483
E-mail: herodogpubl@msn.com
Web site: www.herodogpublications.com
Dist(s): **BCH Fulfillment & Distribution.**

Herobrine Publishing, *(978-0-615-94047-2; 978-0-692-36105-4; 978-0-692-36106-1; 978-0-692-36369-0; 978-0-692-36679-0; 978-0-692-36690-5; 978-0-9864441; 978-1-943330; 978-1-7326265; 978-1-960507)* 18340 Yorba Linda Blvd Suite 107-119, Yorba Linda, CA 92886 USA Tel 7147439845; *Imprints:* Zack Zombie Publishing (MYID_C_ZACK ZO)
E-mail: info@herobrinepublishing.com; info@zackzombiepublishing.com
Web site: http://sapientbizsolutions.com
Dist(s): **CreateSpace Independent Publishing Platform.**

Heroes & Leaders, *(978-0-9801408)* 616 Kaufman St., Forney, TX 75126 USA (SAN 855-3165)
Web site: http://www.zertelo.com.

Heroic Publishing, Inc., *(978-0-929729)* 6433 California Ave., Long Beach, CA 90805 USA (SAN 250-0582) Tel 562-428-4124 (phone/fax)
E-mail: heroicpub@aol.com
Web site: http://www.heroicpub.com
Dist(s): **Diamond Comic Distributors, Inc.**

Herow Pr. *Imprint of* **Krantz, Heather**

Herrington Teddy Bears, *(978-0-9722343)* 8945 Research Dr., Irvine, CA 92618-4237 USA Toll Free: 866-482-2327
E-mail: chris@herringtonco.com
Web site: http://www.herringtonteddybears.com.

Herrod, Ron L. Evangelism Ministries Association (R.H.E.M.A), *(978-0-9763789)* P.O. Box 6447, Sevierville, TN 37864 USA
E-mail: emily@ronherrod.org; ron@ronherrod.org
Web site: http://ronherrod.org.

Herron, Linda *See* **Big Little Pr.**

Hers LA, LLC, *(978-1-7346766)* 1411 35th Ave N, St Petersburg, FL 33704 USA Tel 727-243-7286
E-mail: lesbest2@gmail.com
Web site: Meetlg.com.

hersh, patrice, *(978-0-692-76668-2; 978-0-692-84974-3)* 1865 jacob st, cortlandt manor, NY 10567 USA Tel 914-737-6095
E-mail: pattihersh@aol.com.

Hershberger, Ivan & Fannie, *(978-0-9725806)* 8219 CR 192, Holmesville, OH 44633 USA.

Hershenson, Bruce, *(978-1-887893)* Orders Addr.: P.O. Box 874, West Plains, MO 65775 USA Tel 417-256-9616; Fax: 417-257-6948
E-mail: mail@emovieposter.com
Web site: http://www.emovieposter.com
Dist(s): **Austin & Company, Inc.**
Partners Pubs. Group, Inc.

Heryin Publishing Corp., *(978-0-9762056; 978-0-9787550; 978-0-9845523)* 1033 E. Main St., No. 202, Alhambra, CA 91801 USA Tel 626-289-2238; Fax: 626-289-3865
E-mail: info@heryin.com.

Herzog, Joyce, *(978-1-887225)* 900 Airport Rd., #21, Chattanooga, TN 37421 USA Tel 423-553-6387
E-mail: joyceoffice@aol.com
Web site: http://JoyceHerzog.com; http://JoyceHerzog.info; http://ScaredyCatReadingSystem.com.

Hesperia Publishing, *(978-0-578-33680-0; 978-0-578-37146-7; 978-0-578-37557-1; 979-8-218-03632-4; 979-8-9880142)* 4207 SE Woodstock Blvd No. 294, Portland, OR 97206-6267 USA Tel 2066077810
E-mail: andrew@hesperiapublishing.com
Dist(s): **Ingram Content Group.**

Hesperus Pr. (GBR) *(978-1-84391; 978-1-78094) Dist. by* **IPG Chicago.**

Hess, Alana, *(978-0-578-29621-0; 979-8-218-05420-5)* 1116 w 77th St s dr 0, INDIANAPOLIS, IN 46260 USA Tel 3172922015
E-mail: Alanarhess@gmail.com
Dist(s): **Ingram Content Group.**

Hess, Retha, *(978-1-7349599)* 3601 S Taylor Ave, Milwaukee, WI 53207 USA Tel 262-899-9797
E-mail: islandcoco@ymail.com.

Hester Publishing, *(978-0-9789388)* 219 Blackberry Cir., Colchester, VT 05446 USA
E-mail: sales@hesterpublishing.com
Web site: http://hesterpublishing.com.

Hetherington Hall, *(978-0-9839963)* 888 Logan St. Suite 9A, Denver, CO 80203 USA Tel 720-883-4848
E-mail: lisa@hetheringtonhall.com
Web site: www.hetheringtonhall.com.

Hetman Publishing (GBR) *(978-0-9561592) Dist. by* **LuluCom.**

Hewell Publishing, *(978-1-56870)* 2722 N. Josey Ln. Suite 100, Carrollton, TX 75007 USA
E-mail: sally.hewell@alphagraphics.com
Web site: http://www.hewellpublishing.com.

Hewett, Katherine J.E., *(978-0-578-03065-4; 978-0-578-09202-7)* 625 Gregory Dr. Apt. 85, Crp Christi, TX 78412-3061 USA
E-mail: kathewett@aol.com
Dist(s): **Lulu Pr., Inc.**

Hewitt Research Foundation, Inc., *(978-0-913717; 978-1-57896)* P.O. Box 28010, Spokane, WA 99228-8010 USA (SAN 286-1852) Tel 360-835-8708; Fax: 360-835-8697; Toll Free: 800-348-1750; 8117 N. Division St. Ste D, Spokane, WA 99208
E-mail: orders@hewittlearning.org
Web site: http://hewittlearning.org.

Hewitt Research, Incorporated *See* **Hewitt Research Foundation, Inc.**

Hewlett Packard, *(978-1-131; 978-1-132)* 1501 Page Mill Rd., Palo Alto, CA 94304 USA
Web site: http://www.hp.com.

Hexagon Blue, *(978-0-9729958)* P.O. Box 1790, Issaquah, WA 98027-0073 USA (SAN 255-3406)
E-mail: maryjesse@gmail.com
Web site: http://www.hexagonblue.com
Dist(s): **Ingram Bk. Co.**
Quality Bks., Inc.

Hey Carter!, *(978-1-7339159; 978-1-7379655; 979-8-9883765)* 3185 Ameno Rd., Concord, CA 94519-2220 USA Tel 510-909-7034
E-mail: tsbookher@gmail.com.

Hey U.G.L.Y., Inc., *(978-0-9759004; 978-0-692-15994-1)* 8057 N. 300 E., Rolling Prairie, IN 46371 USA
Web site: http://www.heyugly.org.

Heyday, *(978-0-930588; 978-0-9666691; 978-1-890771; 978-1-59714)* Orders Addr.: P.O. Box 9145, Berkeley, CA 94709 USA (SAN 207-2351) Tel 510-549-3564; Fax: 510-549-1889; 1633 University Ave., Berkeley, CA 94703-1424; *Imprints:* Great Valley Books (Grt Valley Bks)
E-mail: orders@heydaybooks.com; david@heydaybooks.com; christopher@heydaybooks.com
Web site: http://www.heydaybooks.com
Dist(s): **Open Road Integrated Media, Inc.**
Publishers Group West (PGW).

Heyday Books *See* **Heyday**

Heyer Publishing, *(978-1-7338784)* 8505 Oak Way, Arvada, CO 80005 USA Tel 303-808-2230
E-mail: claudiaswest@yahoo.com
Web site: GrammyGiggles.com.

Heyokah Publishing Co., *(978-0-9656124; 978-1-930910)* 7244 Lattigo Dr., Nampa, ID 83687 USA Tel 208-465-5809
E-mail: hiheyokah@aol.com
Dist(s): **New Leaf Distributing Co., Inc.**

Heywood, Joseph, *(978-0-692-82719-2; 978-0-692-82723-9)*

Hez-N-Tales, *(978-0-9745349)* 11037 Hopewell Rd., Boaz, KY 42027 USA
Web site: http://www.feedinghislambs.org.

HF Group, LLC., The, *(978-0-615-33762-3)* 1010 N. Sycamore St., North Manchester, IN 46962 USA Tel 260-982-2107
E-mail: sfultz@thehfgroup.com
Dist(s): **Lectorum Pubns., Inc.**

HH Castle-Mac Publishing, *(978-0-615-21892-2; 978-0-9826684)* 2833 Joppa Ave. S., Suite 2510, St. Louis Park, MN 55416 USA.

Hi Jinx *Imprint of* **Black Rabbit Bks.**

Hi Jinx Pr., *(978-1-57650)* P.O. Box 1814, Davis, CA 95617-1814 USA Tel 530-759-8514; Fax: 530-759-8639.

Hi Willow Research & Publishing, *(978-0-931510; 978-1-933170)* Orders Addr.: P.O. Box 720400, San Jose, CA 95172-0400 USA (SAN 211-3945) Toll Free: 800-873-3043
E-mail: sales@lmcsource.com
Web site: http://www.lmcsource.com
Dist(s): **Follett School Solutions**
L M C Source.

Hibbets, Becky, *(978-1-7346098)* 20323 Fieldstone Crossing Dr., Goshen, IN 46528 USA Tel 574-333-5815
E-mail: HibbetsBecky@gmail.com.

Hibiscus Publishing, *(978-0-9792963; 978-0-9842831)* 1499 Gormican Ln., Naples, FL 34110 USA Fax: 239-514-0238
E-mail: hibiscus311@comcast.net
Web site: http://www.hibiscuspublishing.com.

Hiccup Cottage Pubns., *(978-0-9718724)* 316 10th St., NE, Charlottesville, VA 22902 USA Tel 434-980-5347
E-mail: hiccupcottage@yahoo.com.

Hickle Pickle Publishing, *(978-1-881958)* 4450 Allison Dr., Michigan Center, MI 49254 USA Tel 517-764-1117
E-mail: hicklepickle@modempool.com
Web site: www.hicklepickle.com.

Hickory Bark Productions, *(978-0-9748047)* 3355 N. Five Mile Rd., Suite 332, Boise, ID 83713 USA Tel 208-322-7239.

Hickory Grove Pr., *(978-0-9679915; 978-0-9854725)* Orders Addr.: 3151 Treeco Ln., Bellevue, IA 52031 USA Tel 563-583-4767 (phone/fax) Do not confuse with Hickory Grove Pr., Canton, OH
E-mail: challengemath@aol.com
Web site: http://www.challengemath.com.

Hickory Tales Publishing, *(978-0-9709104; 978-0-9787555)* Orders Addr.: 841 Newberry St., Bowling Green, KY 42103 USA Tel 270-791-3242
E-mail: jadonel@aol.com
Web site: http://www.hickorytales.com.

Hickory Tree Publishing, *(978-0-9893157; 978-0-9985754; 978-1-7334091)* Orders Addr.: 728 S Shore Dr, Holland, MI 49423 USA
E-mail: finley.ra@gmail.com
Web site: http://www.rafinleybooks.com
Dist(s): **eBookit.com.**

Hicks, Christina Creative, *(978-0-692-84858-6; 978-0-9988146)* 21955 N. Douglas Ave, Edmond, OK 73012 USA Tel 405-615-9524
E-mail: christinahickscreative@gmail.com.

Hidden Bower Pr., *(978-0-578-50818-4; 978-1-7377895)* 210 Main St. No. 1021, Farmington, CT 06032 USA Tel 860-897-0828
E-mail: katie@katiejgallagher.com
Dist(s): **Ingram Content Group.**

Hidden Cache Media, *(978-0-692-57398-3; 978-0-9981078)* 7 Cedar Rd., Wallingford, PA 19086 USA Tel 610-800-9437
Web site: joykiefler.com
Dist(s): **CreateSpace Independent Publishing Platform.**

Hidden Curriculum Education, *(978-0-9755103)* Orders Addr.: P.O. Box 222041, Hollywood, FL 33022 USA Tel 954-457-8098; Fax: 954-457-3331
Web site: http://www.collegefaqbook.com.

Hidden Forest Pubs., *(978-0-9755117)* 269 Co. Hwy. 250, Guin, AL 35563-2700 USA.

Hidden Helm Pr., *(978-1-949604)* 42 Aldwick Rise, Fairport, NY 14450 USA Tel 585-269-8692
E-mail: elicelata@gmail.com.

Hidden Manna Pubns., *(978-0-9891683; 978-0-9915261; 978-0-9864066; 978-1-7347503)* 53 Solar Rd., Oldtown, ID 83822 USA Tel 208-412-3087
E-mail: artnbooks@gmail.com
Web site: www.gentleshepherd.com.

Hidden Oasis Publishing, *(978-0-9884636)* P.O. Box 80, Kimberton, PA 19442 USA Tel 610-935-2711
E-mail: pcbaxter@verizon.net.

Hidden Path Pubn., Inc., *(978-0-9711534)* 304 Briarwood Rd., Statesville, NC 28677 USA Tel 704-878-0716; 704-224-4832
E-mail: dkellysteele@aol.com.

Hidden Pictures, *(978-0-9678159; 978-0-9843088)* Orders Addr.: P.O. Box 63, Tipp City, OH 45371-9103 USA (SAN 253-6862) Tel 937-667-6288; Fax: 937-669-4178
E-mail: liz@hiddenpictures.com
Web site: http://www.hiddenpicturepuzzle.com.

Hidden Talent Pr., *(978-0-9776114)* Orders Addr.: P.O. Box 9052, Missoula, MT 59807 USA
Web site: http://www.iysofwar.com.

Hidden Valley Farm Pub., *(978-0-615-17173-9)* P.O. Box 172, Perry, NY 14530 USA
E-mail: theotherherald@yahoo.com
Web site: http://www.tfrice.etsy.com
Dist(s): **Lulu Pr., Inc.**

Hidden Wolf Bks., *(978-0-9911045; 978-0-9968922; 978-0-9994345; 979-8-9869781)* 155 W. Genung St., St. Augustine, FL 32086 USA Tel 904-797-5964
E-mail: nsinatsch@hotmail.com.

HiddenSpring *Imprint of* **Paulist Pr.**

Hide & Seek Ministries, *(978-0-9994901; 978-1-7359547)* P.O. Box 1835, Springfield, MO 65801 USA Tel 417-522-3597
E-mail: contact@hsm4kids.com
Web site: http://www.hideandseekministries.com.

Hide-a-Way Publishing, *(978-0-9988999)* 1405 Westview Ln., Northlake, TX 76226 USA Tel 469-418-3296
E-mail: hideawaypublishingcompany@gmail.com
Web site: www.hideawaypublishing.com.

Hieble, Helen, *(978-0-615-77684-2; 978-0-692-79708-2)* 685 Knox Rd., Wayne, PA 19087 USA Tel 610-688-4961; Fax: 610-688-0869
Dist(s): **CreateSpace Independent Publishing Platform.**

Hierophant Publishing Services *See* **Hieropub LLC**

Hierophantasm, *(978-0-9837905)* 190 W. Fifth Ave. P. O. Box 792, Clifton, IL 60927 USA Tel 815-694-0010
E-mail: awinkel@gmail.com
Web site: hierophantasm.com.

Hieropub LLC, *(978-0-9727940)* P.O. Box 895, Pottstown, PA 19464 USA Tel 610-705-0282
E-mail: patholl@hieropub.com; pholl@comcast.net
Web site: http://www.hieropub.com; http://www.hatheadbooks.com
Dist(s): **Quality Bks., Inc.**

Publisher Name Index

Higgins, Christine, (*978-0-9975649*) 571 Woodbine Ave., Towson, MD 21204 USA Tel 410-825-6404
E-mail: chriswrite73@comcast.net.

Higgins Publishing, (*978-0-9815202; 978-1-941580*) P.O. Box 1463, Cedar Hill, TX 75106 USA Tel 800-364-9734
E-mail: contact@higginspublishing.com
Web site: http://www.higginspublishing.com.

Higginson Bk. Co., (*978-0-7404; 978-0-8328*) 148 Washington St., Salem, MA 01970 USA (SAN 247-9400) Tel 978-745-7170; Fax: 978-745-8025
E-mail: higginsn@cove.com
Web site: http://higginsonbooks.com.

— High Art Forms, LLC, (*978-0-9962188; 978-0-9992019*) P.O. Box 49194, Cookeville, TN 38506 USA Tel 844-370-1730; Fax: 931-537-2218
E-mail: highartforms@frontier.com
Web site: www.highartforms.com.

High Bar Bks., (*978-1-950361*) 3515 Glover Rd, Easton, PA 18040 USA Tel 307-752-7935
E-mail: highbarbooks@gmx.com.

High Country Conservation Advocates, (*978-0-692-90486-2*) PO Box 1066 716 Elk Ave., CRESTED BUTTE, CO 81224 USA Tel 970-349-7104
E-mail: office@hccacb.org
Dist(s): **Ingram Content Group.**

High Desert Libris, (*978-1-7334361*) 8808 New Hampton NE, Albuquerque, NM 87111 USA Tel 505-299-4916
E-mail: rjmcreativearts@gmail.com
Web site: rjmirabal.wordpress.com.

High Desert Productions, (*978-0-9652920*) Orders Addr.: P.O. Box 5506, Bisbee, AZ 85603 USA Tel 520-432-5288; Edit Addr.: 511 Mance St., Bisbee, AZ 85603 USA
Dist(s): **Rio Nuevo Pubs.**

High Flying Pr., (*978-1-7366422*) 1424 Cove Dr, Bowling Green, KY 42101 USA Tel 270-438-3832
E-mail: bobbiefalin@gmail.com
Web site: http://Bobbiefalin.com.

High Ground Productions, Incorporated *See* **High Ground Pubns.**

High Ground Pubns., (*978-0-9720153*) 80 Supai Dr., Sedona, AZ 86351 USA (SAN 254-5748) Tel 360-945-2485
E-mail: Karen@amatteroftime.org
Web site: http://www.amatteroftime.org.

High Hill Pr., (*978-1-60653*) 2731 Cumberland Landing, Saint Charles, MO 63303 USA (SAN 856-2806) Tel 636-928-2212
E-mail: HighHillPress@aol.com
Web site: http://www.highhillpress.com.

High Hopes Publishing, (*978-0-9708417; 978-0-9905129*) Subs. of Communication Arts Multimedia, Inc., 1618 Williams Dr., Suite No. 5, Georgetown, TX 78628 USA Tel 512-868-0548 (phone/fax); Toll Free: 888-742-0074
E-mail: mail@commartsmultimedia.com
Web site: http://www.highhopespublishing.com.

High Interest Publishing (HIP) (CAN) (*978-0-9731237; 978-1-897039; 978-1-926847*) *Dist. by* **Children Plus.**

High Mountain Publishing *See* **Escher, Ursula**

High Noon Bks., (*978-0-87879; 978-1-57128*) Div. of Academic Therapy Publications, Inc., 20 Leveroni Ct., Novato, CA 94949-5746 USA Tel 415-883-3314; Toll Free: 800-422-7249
E-mail: customerservice@academictheapy.com
Web site: http://www.highnoonbooks.com.

High Self-Esteem Group, (*978-1-953453*) P.O. Box 462, Barberton, OH 44203 USA Tel 216-438-0875
E-mail: cynthiabowersmartin@yahoo.com.

High Standards Publishing, Incorporated *See* **True Exposures Publishing, Inc.**

High Star Pr., (*978-0-9981808*) 217 Teaberry Ln., South Abington Township, PA 18411 USA Tel 570-479-6491
E-mail: cindynoonan49@gmail.com
Web site: cindynoonan.com.

High Tide Pubns., (*978-0-9884637; 978-0-615-72863-6; 978-0-692-34939-7; 978-0-692-37913-4; 978-0-692-38423-7; 978-0-692-45585-2; 978-0-692-45595-1; 978-0-692-50369-0; 978-0-692-54851-6; 978-0-692-56405-9; 978-0-692-57700-4; 978-0-692-57708-0; 978-0-692-57961-9; 978-0-692-50854-8; 978-0-692-62932-1; 978-0-692-67079-8; 978-0-692-70597-1; 978-0-692-74482-6; 978-1-945990) Orders Addr.: 1000 Bland Point Rd, Deltaville, VA 23043 USA Tel 804-776-8478*
E-mail: hightidepublications@yahoo.com
Web site: redmarblepublishing.com; hightidepublications.com
Dist(s): **CreateSpace Independent Publishing Platform.**

Higher Age Pr., (*978-0-9979034*) 5222 Univ. Ave NE, No. 304A, Seattle, WA 98105 USA Tel 425-891-9129
E-mail: hansenjake@hotmail.com
Web site: jakehansennovels.com.

Higher Balance Institute, (*978-0-9759080; 978-1-939410*) 515 NW Saltzman Rd., No.726, Portland, OR 97229 USA Tel 503-646-4000; Toll Free: 800-935-4007
E-mail: publishing@higherbalance.com
Web site: http://www.higherbalance.com.

Higher Ground Pr., (*978-0-9766062; 978-0-9838321*) Orders Addr.: P.O. Box PO 1381, Allen, TX 75013 USA Tel 214-680-9779
E-mail: info@highergroundpress.com
Web site: http://www.highergroundpress.com
Dist(s): **Brigham Distribution.**

Higher Power Publishing *See* **NITALUSA PUBLISHING@DISTRIBUTION**

Higher Priority Publishing *See* **Arlington & Ameilia**

HigherLife Development *See* **HigherLife Development Services, Inc.**

HigherLife Development Services, Inc., (*978-0-9793227; 978-1-935245; 978-1-939183; 978-0-9907578; 978-0-9978018; 978-0-9989773; 978-0-9994156; 978-0-9998197; 978-1-7325026; 978-1-7326377; 978-1-7328859; 978-1-7337273; 978-1-7332289; 978-1-951492; 978-1-954533; 979-8-9859212; 978-1-958211) P.O. Box 623307, Oviedo, FL 32762 USA; 83 Geneva Dr., Oviedo, FL 32762*
Web site: http://www.higherlifeservices.com
Dist(s): **Independent Pubs. Group**
Midpoint Trade Bks., Inc.
MyiLibrary
Strauss Consultants
ebrary, Inc.

Highest Good Pubns. *Imprint of* **GEM Bk. Club**

Highflying Press *See* **High Flying Pr.**

Highland Children's Pr. *Imprint of* **Heather & Highlands Publishing**

Highland Press *See* **Highland Pr. Publishing**

Highland Pr., (*978-0-9630273*) Div. of The Alabama Booksmith, 5512 Crestwood Blvd., Birmingham, AL 35212-4131 USA (SAN 297-8628) Do not confuse with companies with the same name in Boerne, TX, Wilsonville, OR, Tonasket, WA, Bryson City, NC, San Rafael, CA, High Springs, FL
E-mail: booksmith@mindspring.com.

Highland Pr., (*978-0-910722*) 10108 Johns Rd., Boerne, TX 78006 USA (SAN 204-0522) Do not confuse with companies of the same name or similar in Birmingham, AL, Wilsonville, OR, Tonasket, WA, Bryson City, NC, San Rafael, CA, High Springs, FL.

Highland Pr. Publishing, (*978-0-9746249; 978-0-9787139; 978-0-9800356; 978-0-9815573; 978-0-9818550; 978-0-9823615; 978-0-9842499; 978-0-9833960; 978-0-9846541; 978-0-9850690; 978-0-9895262; 978-0-9916439; 978-1-942606*) Orders Addr.: P.O. Box 2292, High Springs, FL 32655 USA (SAN 851-4275); *Imprints:* Pandora (Pandora) Do not confuse with companies with the same or similar name in Sacramento, CA, Birmingham, AL, Wilsonville, ORBoerne, TX, San Rafael, CA, Bryson City, NC, Tonasket, WA
E-mail: The.Highland.Press@gmail.com; Mickeytl@aol.com
Web site: http://www.highlandpress.org.

Highlight Publishing, (*978-0-9741734*) P.O. Box 27, Little Falls, MN 56345 USA Tel 320-630-1463; Toll Free: 866-336-6681
E-mail: books@highlightpublishing.com
Web site: http://www.highlightpublishing.com.

Highlights *Imprint of* **Highlights Pr., c/o Highlights for Children, Inc.**

Highlights for Children, (*978-0-87534*) Orders Addr.: P.O. Box 269, Columbus, OH 43216-0269 USA (SAN 281-7810) Tel 614-486-0631; Fax: 614-876-8564; Toll Free: 800-255-9517; Edit Addr.: 803 Church St., Honesdale, PA 18431 USA (SAN 281-7802) Tel 570-253-1080; Fax: 570-253-1179
E-mail: eds@highlights.com
Web site: http://www.highlights.com
Dist(s): **Blackstone Audio, Inc.**
Hachette Bk. Group
INscribe Digital
Ingram Publisher Services
Highlights Pr., c/o Highlights for Children, Inc.
Penguin Random Hse. Distribution
Penguin Random Hse. LLC.

Highlights of Chicago Pr., (*978-0-9710487; 978-0-9907771*) 4325 N. Central Park Ave., Chicago, IL 60618 USA Tel 773-509-0008 (phone/fax)
E-mail: bturner@highlightsofchicago.com
Web site: http://www.highlightsofchicago.com.

Highlights Pr., c/o Highlights for Children, Inc., (*978-1-56397; 978-1-878093; 978-1-886910; 978-1-59078; 978-1-932425; 978-1-62091; 978-1-62979; 978-0-9961172; 978-0-9961173; 978-1-943283; 978-1-68238; 978-1-68329; 978-1-68437; 978-1-64472; 978-1-7922; 978-1-63962*) Div. of Highlights For Children, Inc., 815 Church St., Honesdale, PA 18431 USA (SAN 852-3177) Tel 570-251-4513; 570-251-4592; *Imprints:* Wordsong (Wordsong); Calkins Creek (Calkins Creek); Front Street (FrtSt); Lemniscaat (Lemnisca); Highlights (Highlights)
Dist(s): **Children's Plus, Inc.**
Follett School Solutions
INscribe Digital
Ingram Publisher Services
Lectorum Pubns., Inc.
Penguin Random Hse. Distribution
Penguin Random Hse. LLC
Perfection Learning Corp.
Ingram Academic
Two Rivers Distribution.

High-Lonesome Bks., (*978-0-944383*) Orders Addr.: P.O. Box 878, Silver City, NM 88062 USA (SAN 243-3079) Tel 505-388-3763; Fax: 505-388-5705; Toll Free: 800-380-7323 (orders only)
E-mail: Cherie@High-LonesomeBooks.com
Web site: http://www.high-lonesomebooks.com.

High-Pitched Hum Inc., (*978-0-9759818; 978-0-9777290; 978-0-9787995; 978-0-9792780; 978-1-934666; 978-0-9885818; 978-0-9914847*) 321 15th St., N., Jacksonville Beach, FL 32250 USA
E-mail: breynolds@jettyman.com
Web site: http://www.highpitchedhum.net.

HighPoint Publishing, Inc., (*978-1-933190*) Orders Addr.: 3975 E. Highway 290., Dripping Spgs, TX 78620-4287 USA (SAN 256-2952)
E-mail: kenc@highpointpublishing.com; milena@highpointpublishing.com
Web site: http://www.HighPointPublishing.com.

HighReach Learning, Incorporated *Imprint of* **Carson-Dellosa Publishing, LLC**

†High/Scope Pr., (*978-0-929816; 978-0-931114; 978-1-57379*) Div. of High/Scope Educational Research Foundation, 600 N. River St., Ypsilanti, MI 48198-2898 USA (SAN 211-9617) Tel 734-485-2000; Fax: 734-485-0704; Toll Free Fax: 800-442-4329 (orders); Toll Free: 800-407-7377 (orders only)
E-mail: info@highscope.org
Web site: http://www.highscope.org
Dist(s): **CENGAGE Learning**
Delmar Cengage Learning
Follett School Solutions; *CIP.*

Highsmith Inc., (*978-0-913853; 978-0-917846; 978-1-57950; 978-1-932146; 978-1-59847; 978-1-60213*) P.O. Box 5210, Janesville, WI 53547-5210 USA (SAN 159-8740) Toll Free: 800-448-4887; 401 S. Wright Rd., Janesville, WI 53547 (SAN 858-9674) Toll Free Fax: 800-835-2329; Toll Free: 800-554-4661; *Imprints:* Upstart Books (Upstart Bks)
Web site: http://www.highsmith.com
Dist(s): **Mackin Bk. Co.**

Highsmith Press, LLC *See* **Highsmith Inc.**

Hightree Publishing, (*978-1-7339049; 979-8-9885670*) 10990 Wilshire Blvd., 8th Flr., Los Angeles, CA 90024 USA Tel 516-644-7087
E-mail: lea@hightreepublishing.com; roda@hightreepublishing.com.

Highview Creative, (*978-0-9978518*) 1433 Highview Ave, Eagan, MN 55121 USA Tel 651-303-5202
E-mail: larossin@comcast.net.

Hignites, Tom Miracle Studio, (*978-1-934017*) Orders Addr.: 1977 Mayfield Rd., Richfield, WI 53076-5307 USA (SAN 850-9611) Tel 262-628-5577; Fax: 262-628-5580; Edit Addr.: 3070 Hwy. 145, Richfield, WI 53076-5307 USA
E-mail: jbrown@miracle-homes.com
Web site: http://tomhignitesmiraclestudios.com.

Hilarity Waters Pr., (*978-0-615-49668-9*) 1117 SW 126th St., Oklahoma City, OK 73170 USA Tel 405-990-9891
E-mail: andrews.africabound@gmail.com
Web site: www.hilaritywaterspress.com.

Hildebrand, Betty, (*978-0-9753729*) 116 Rosetta Ct., Springdale, OH 45246 USA
E-mail: deona@bethart.com
Web site: http://www.bethart.com.

Hildebrandt, Sara, (*978-0-578-45179-4; 978-0-578-45201-2*) 14321 NE30th St. Unit AA, Vancouver, WA 98682-8257 USA Tel 360-975-9173
E-mail: sara.hildebrandt@outlook.com
Dist(s): **Ingram Content Group.**

Hill & Wang *Imprint of* **Farrar, Straus & Giroux**

Hill, Brian, (*978-0-692-15774-9; 978-0-578-99407-9*) 736 W. Millard Canyon Rd., Altadena, CA 91001 USA Tel 626-241-8424
E-mail: brian220@pacbell.net
Dist(s): **Ingram Content Group.**

Hill, Lawrence Bks. *Imprint of* **Chicago Review Pr., Inc.**

Hill, Molly, (*978-0-615-54126-6; 978-0-578-46346-9*) 505 26th St., Battle Mountain, NV 89820 USA Tel 775-635-9125.

Hill, Monica *See* **Penway Publishing LLC**

Hill, Napoleon Foundation, (*978-1-880369*) Friends of Napoleon Hill, 19458 S. La Grange Rd., Mokena, IL 60448 USA Tel 847-998-0408; Fax: 847-998-6890; Toll Free Fax: 800-957-9124; Toll Free: 800-957-9114
E-mail: 70543.3377@compuserve.com
Web site: http://www.naphill.org.

Hill Publishing *See* **SunHill Pubs.**

Hill Song Pr., (*978-0-9745159; 978-0-692-29132-0; 978-0-692-41911-3; 978-0-692-68393-4; 978-0-692-82104-6; 978-0-692-88303-7; 978-0-692-11598-5; 978-0-578-65257-3; 979-8-218-96213-5*) Orders Addr.: P.O. Box 486, Lawrence, KS 66044 USA Tel 785-330-3779; Toll Free: 800-266-5564; Edit Addr.: 3807 Hunters Hill Dr., Lawrence, KS 66049 USA
E-mail: tom.mach@yahoo.com
Web site: http://www.hillsongpress.com; https://www.tom-mach.com/
Dist(s): **CreateSpace Independent Publishing Platform.**

Hill, Stephanie & Clarissa, (*978-0-9785539*) P.O. Box 13212, Baltimore, MD 21203-3212 USA (SAN 850-9816) Tel 443-838-9426
E-mail: sachedesignsinc@yahoo.com
Web site: http://www.sachedesigns.com.

Hill Street Pr., LLC, (*978-1-892514; 978-1-58818*) P.O. Box 49468, Athens, GA 30604-9468 USA Toll Free: 800-295-0365
E-mail: info@hillstreetpress.com
Web site: http://www.hillstreetpress.com
Dist(s): **Gibbs Smith, Publisher**
Beeler, Thomas T. Pub.

Hillegass, Anette, (*978-0-692-80034-8; 978-0-692-81058-3; 978-0-692-07155-7*).

Hilliard Pr., (*978-0-9912792; 978-0-9966962; 978-0-9990090; 978-1-7342711; 979-8-9869169*) 204 Dandridge Dr., Franklin, TN 37067 USA Tel 931-446-0047
E-mail: jessasexton@gmail.com.

Hillrow Editions, (*978-0-9897958*) 150 Spreading Oak Dr., Scotts Valley, CA 95066 USA Tel 831-439-9888
E-mail: chriz9@yahoo.com.

Hillside Education, (*978-0-9766386; 978-0-9798469; 978-0-9831800; 978-0-9885106; 978-0-9906720; 978-0-9969986; 978-0-9976647; 978-0-9991706; 978-1-7331383; 978-1-955402*) 475 Bidwell Hill Rd., Lake Ariel, PA 18436 USA (SAN 257-4446)
E-mail: info@hillsideeducation.com; sales@hillsideeducation.com
Web site: http://www.hillsideeducation.com.

Hillside Press *See* **Hillside Pr.**

Hillside Pr., (*978-0-9627530; 979-8-9878244*) Affil. of Ridgetop Pr., Do not confuse with companies with the same name in Los Angeles, CA, Carversville, PA, Vista, CA, Collegeville, PA, Wolcott, CT
E-mail: jhaighak@gmail.com
Web site: waiting4thestorm.com; www.hillsidepressalaska.com
Dist(s): **American News Company**
Partners/West Book Distributors
Todd Communications.

Hillside Pr., (*978-0-9815895*) P.O. Box 241, Midway, FL 32343 USA
E-mail: ljhill@hillsidepress.net
Web site: http://www.hillsidepress.net
Dist(s): **Two Rivers Distribution.**

Hilm Publishing Co., (*978-1-7356123*) 9545 Oak Leaf Way, Granite Bay, CA 95746 USA Tel 510-919-5014
E-mail: shanalondon@ymail.com
Web site: www.hilmpublishing.com.

Hilton Publishing *See* **Hilton Publishing Co.**

Hilton Publishing Co., (*978-0-9654553; 978-0-9675258; 978-0-9716067; 978-0-9743144; 978-0-9764443; 978-0-9773160; 978-0-9777779; 978-0-9800649; 978-0-9815381; 978-0-9841447; 978-0-9847566; 978-0-9904283; 978-0-9983282*) Orders Addr.: 1630 45th Ave. Ste. 103, Munster, IN 46321-3959 USA Toll Free: 866-455-1070
E-mail: info@hiltonpub.com
Web site: http://www.hiltonpub.com
Dist(s): **SCB Distributors.**

Himari Publishing, (*978-0-9981543*)
E-mail: himaripublishing@gmail.com.

Himminbjorg Publishing, Inc., (*978-0-9749416*) P.O. Box 6493, Napa, CA 94581 USA Tel 707-251-9526 (phone/fax)
E-mail: himminbjorg@aol.com
Web site: http://www.wyrdsway.com.

HINDS FEET PUBLISHING, (*978-0-9988206*) 3022 W I-44 Service Rd., No. 57043, Oklahoma City, OK 73112 USA Tel 405-412-6218; Fax: 405-285-5590
E-mail: hindsfeetpublishing@gmail.com
Web site: www.hindsfeetpublishing.com.

Hines, Jerry, (*978-0-615-17723-6*) 2660 Suzanne Cir., White Bear Lake, MN 55110 USA
E-mail: jerryhines@comcast.net
Dist(s): **Lulu Pr., Inc.**

Hinman, Bobbie E. Incorporated *See* **Best Fairy Bks.**

Hinman Publishing, (*978-0-9723525*) 2943 Breakwater Way, Longmont, CO 80503 USA
E-mail: jshinman@earthlink.net.

Hinson, Rebecca Publishing, (*978-1-938360; 978-1-942765; 978-1-947623*) Orders Addr.: 818 N. Palmway, Lake Worth, FL 33460 USA Tel 561-267-5756
E-mail: rebeccahinson@bellsouth.net
Dist(s): **Follett School Solutions.**

Hinterland Sky Pr., (*978-0-9818880*) 37 W. Black Oak Dr., Asheville, NC 28804-1809 USA
E-mail: frances.ruiz@gmail.com
Web site: http://www.hinterlandsky.com.

HinterWelt Enterprises, LLC, (*978-0-9740096*) 7504 W. Hickory Creek Dr., Frankfort, IL 60423-9094 USA
E-mail: winna@hinterwelt.com
Web site: http://www.hinterwelt.com.

Hip Hop Schl. Hse., (*978-0-9768674*) 8618 S. Constance, Chicago, IL 60617 USA Tel 793-218-4204.

Hip Me Publishing, (*978-1-7337395*) 1560 Adams St., Denver, CO 80206 USA Tel 720-232-6514
E-mail: taraemrick@hotmail.com
Web site: www.whyyoubelong.com.

Hippo Park *Imprint of* **Astra Publishing Hse.**

Hippocratic Pr., The, (*978-0-9753516*) 281A Fairhaven Hill Rd., Concord, MA 01742 USA Tel 978-369-0739
E-mail: ccowanmd@hippocraticpress.com
Web site: http://www.hippocraticpress.com.

†Hippocrene Bks., Inc., (*978-0-7818; 978-0-87052; 978-0-88254*) 171 Madison Ave., New York, NY 10016-1002 USA (SAN 213-2060) Tel 718-454-2366 (sales); 212-685-4371 (editorial); Fax: 718-454-1391 (sales/order inquiry); 212-779-9338 (editorial)
E-mail: hippocre@ix.netcom.com
Web site: http://www.hippocrenebooks.com
Dist(s): **Continental Bk. Co., Inc.**
Ingram Publisher Services
Two Rivers Distribution; *CIP.*

Hired Pen, Inc., The *See* **Acacia Publishing, Inc.**

His Feast Publishing, (*978-0-9677722*) Div. of Feast of Tabernacles Ministries, 2720 Mallow Pl., Loveland, CO 80537 USA
E-mail: Hisfeasts@gmail.com; 4Donnamae@gmail.com.

His Glory Creations *See* **His Glory Creations Publishing, LLC**

His Glory Creations Publishing, LLC, (*978-0-692-70633-6; 978-1-7327227; 978-1-950861*) P.O. Box 941, Wendell, NC 27591 USA Tel 919-618-0262
E-mail: hisglorycreations@att.net
Web site: www.felicialucas.com.

His Glory Publishing, LLC, (*978-0-9651007; 978-1-7379092*) P.O. Box 44595, Fort Washington, MD 20749 USA Tel 301-292-3636; P.O. Box P.O. Box 44595, Fort Washington, MD 20749
E-mail: xnate333@gmail.com
Web site: http://www.tanalakepublishing.com
Dist(s): **Evanston Publishing, Inc.**

His Grace Is Sufficient *Imprint of* **ELW Pubns.**

His Hands, Inc., (*978-0-9720881*) Orders Addr.: P.O. Box 7063, Oak Ridge, TN 37831 USA Tel 865-482-9562; Edit Addr.: 82 E. Tennesse Ave., Apt. 117, Oak Ridge, TN 37830 USA (SAN 255-2930) Tel 865-482-9562
E-mail: hishandstn@netzero.com
Web site: http://www.hishands.org.

His Kids Publishing, Inc., (*978-0-9720417*) Orders Addr.: P.O. Box 72172, Marietta, GA 30007 USA Tel 770-998-3240; Fax: 770-998-4943; Edit Addr.: 1544 Sandpoint Dr., Roswell, GA 30075 USA
E-mail: management@intrag-publishing.com
Web site: http://www.intrag-publishing.com.

His Pen Publishing, LLC, (*978-0-9798020; 978-1-944643*)
E-mail: authorlacricia@ymail.com; publisher@hispenpublishing.com; author@lacriciaangelle.com
Web site: http://www.lacriciaangelle.com; www.hispenpublishing.com
Dist(s): **Smashwords.**

s Pencil Publishing, *(978-1-7364021)* 2301 W White Ave No. 1218, McKinney, TX 75071 USA Tel 405-760-0668
E-mail: rayshondafarria@hotmail.com
Web site: www.hispencilpublishing.com.

.I.S. Publishing LLC *See* **Heard Word Publishing, LLC**

is Sonshine, Inc., *(978-0-9758880)* 13214 Barwick Rd., Del Ray Beach, FL 33445 USA.

is Story, *(978-0-9766951)* 1409 Coolhurst, Sherwood, AR 72120 USA
Web site: http://www.hisstory.org.

is Work Christian Publishing, *(978-0-9778328; 978-0-9798290; 978-0-9799189; 978-0-615-43443-8; 978-0-9854469)* Div. of His Work Christian Ministries, Orders Addr.: P.O. Box 563, Ward Cove, AK 99928 USA Tel 206-274-8474; Fax: 614-388-0664
E-mail: hiswork@hisworkpub.com; editor@hisworkpub.com
Web site: http://www.hisworkpub.com
Dist(s): **Ingram Content Group.**

Hispanic Institute of Social Issues, *(978-0-9771167; 978-0-9797814; 978-1-936885)* P.O. Box 50553, Mesa, AZ 85208-0028 USA (SAN 992-6607); *Imprints:* Many Seasons Press (MYID_V_MANY SE)
Web site: http://www.hisi.org; manyseasonspress.com; multimediapublishingproject.com.

Histart Books *See* **Histart Pr.**

Histart Pr., *(978-0-9915597)* 385 EISENHOWER DR, LOUISVILLE, CO 80027 USA Tel 786-354-3631
E-mail: maritillo@gmail.com
Web site: https://histartpress.com/.

Historic Mint Co., The, *(978-0-9753767)* 36 Sandwedge Dr., Henderson, NV 89074-1714 USA Toll Free: 877-264-6266
Web site: http://www.historicmint.com.

Historic Philadelphia, Inc., *(978-0-9855319)* 150 S. Independence Mall, W. Suite 550, Philadelphia, PA 19106 USA Tel 215-629-5801
E-mail: debiflora@about-books.com; msdariaf@gmail.com
Web site: http://www.historicphiladelphia.org.

Historic Pr.-South, *(978-0-9645990)* Orders Addr.: P.O. Box 407, Gatlinburg, TN 37738 USA Tel 423-436-4163; Toll Free: 800-279-2603; Edit Addr.: 367 Buckhorn Rd., Gatlinburg, TN 37738 USA.

Historic Tours of America, Inc., *(978-0-9752698)* 201 Front St., Suite 224, Key West, FL 33040 USA Tel 305-292-8920; Fax: 305-295-4999
E-mail: psmith@historictours.com
Web site: http://www.historictours.com.

Historical Pages Company *See* **Birch Island**

Historical Publishing Network *See* **Ledge Media**

Historical Society of Western Pennsylvania, *(978-0-936340)* 1212 Smallman St., Pittsburgh, PA 15222-4208 USA (SAN 214-0276)
E-mail: babutko@heinzhistorycenter.org
Web site: http://www.einzhistorycenter.org.

History Compass, LLC, *(978-1-57960; 978-1-878668; 978-1-932663)* 25 Leslie Rd., Auburndale, MA 02466 USA (SAN 297-2611) Tel 617-332-2202; Fax: 617-332-2210
E-mail: info@historycompass.com; lisa@historycompass.com
Web site: http://www.historycompass.com.
Dist(s): **Follett School Solutions**
Ingram Publisher Services
Social Studies Schl. Service.

History Factory, *(978-1-882771)* 14140 Parke Long Ct., Suite G, Chantilly, VA 20151 USA Tel 703-631-0500; Fax: 703-631-1124
E-mail: info@historyfactory.com; editorial@historyfactory.com
Web site: https://www.historyfactory.com/.

History Gal's Publishing, *(978-0-578-10958-9)* 8344 W. Smith Rd, Medina, OH 44256 USA.

History Hse Pubs., *(978-0-9679158)* 10624 Tuppence Ct., Rockville, MD 20850 USA Do not confuse with History House Press, Rocky Mount, VA.

History Jukebox, LLC, *(978-0-9791118)* P.O. Box 467, Marshall, MI 49068 USA Tel 269-781-8357; Fax: 269-781-8760; Toll Free: 866-977-7664
E-mail: info@historyjukebox.org
Web site: http://www.historyjukebox.org.

History Pr. Ltd.,The (GBR) *(978-0-7509; 978-0-7524; 978-0-86299; 978-0-904387; 978-1-84165; 978-1-84015)* *Dist. by* **IPG Chicago.**

History Pr., The *Imprint of* **Arcadia Publishing**

Hit Products, *(978-0-9836437)* 6004 Carol St., San Diego, CA 92115 USA Tel 619-286-3661
E-mail: victor2b4@aol.com.

HI-Tech Software, *(978-1-928618; 978-1-936735)* 10 Little Tarn Ct., Hamburg, NJ 07419-1262 USA
E-mail: harry@htsoftware.com
Web site: http://www.htsoftware.com.

Hither Creek Pr., *(978-0-9700555)* 14 Holman St., Laconia, NH 03246-3016 USA Do not confuse with Hither Creek Press in Nantucket, MA
E-mail: hithercreekpress@aol.com.

Hi-Time Pflaum *See* **Pflaum Publishing Group**

HITN, *(978-1-64094)* 63 flushing Ave. bldg. 292 Ste. 211, Brooklyn, NY 11205 USA Tel 646-731-3520; Fax: 212-966-5725
E-mail: mpedroza@hitn.org
Web site: www.hitn.org
Dist(s): **Simon & Schuster, Inc.**

Hive Collective, *(978-0-9884774)* 30 Shelburne Rd., Merrimack, NH 03054 USA Tel 603-423-1071
E-mail: stan@findtheaxis.com
Web site: http://hiveauthors.wordpress.com.

H.J VandeRiet, *(978-0-578-87949-9)* 7313 Trousdale Pl, Stockton, CA 95207 USA Tel 209-774-6312
E-mail: heather.j.vanderiet@icloud.com
Dist(s): **Independent Pub.**

HK Comics Ltd. (HKG) *(978-962-85278; 978-988-98437; 978-988-97972)* *Dist. by* **Diamond Book Dists.**

HM Bks., *(978-0-9796476; 978-0-9820126)* Div. of HM Entertainment Inc.,
E-mail: meja_mwangi@yahoo.com; mejamwangi@yahoo.com
Web site: http://www.mejamwangi.com; http://www.skylineafrica.com.

HMH Books For Young Readers *Imprint of* **Houghton Mifflin Harcourt Publishing Co.**

HMSI, Inc., *(978-0-615-29442-1; 978-0-9842662; 978-0-9826945; 978-0-9851996)* 50768 Van Buren Dr., Plymouth, MI 48170 USA
Web site: http://www.PublishHMSI.com.

HNB Publishing, *(978-0-9664286; 978-0-9728061; 978-0-9828874)* Orders Addr.: 250 W. 78th St., No. 3FF, New York, NY 10024 USA Tel 212-873-5382; 347-260-1376
E-mail: sales@hnbpub.com
Web site: http://www.hnbpub.com.

Hoaki Bks. SL (ESP) *(978-84-936408; 978-84-92810; 978-84-935438; 978-84-935881; 978-84-936508; 978-84-15967; 978-84-17084; 978-84-17656; 978-84-17412; 978-84-16851; 978-84-16504)* *Dist. by* **Consort Bk Sales.**

Hoard, W.D. & Sons Co., *(978-0-932147; 978-0-9960753)* P.O. Box 801, Fort Atkinson, WI 53538-0801 USA (SAN 686-4341) Tel 920-563-5551; Fax: 920-563-7298; *Imprints:* Hoard's Dairyman (Hoards Dairyman)
Web site: http://www.hoards.com.

Hoard's Dairyman *Imprint of* **Hoard, W.D. & Sons Co.**

Hobar Pubns., *(978-0-89317; 978-0-913163; 978-0-933855; 978-0-9616847; 978-1-55797)* Div. of Finney Co., Orders Addr.: 8075 215th St. W., Lakeville, MN 55044 USA (SAN 283-1120) Tel 952-469-6699; Fax: 952-469-1968; Toll Free Fax: 800-330-6232; Toll Free: 800-846-7027
E-mail: feedback@finneyco.com
Web site: http://www.finney-hobar.com
Dist(s): **Book Wholesalers, Inc.**
Brodart Co.
Follett School Solutions
Midpoint Trade Bks., Inc.
National Bk. Network
Rowman & Littlefield Publishers, Inc.
Southern Bk. Service.

Hobbes End Publishing, LLC, *(978-0-9763510; 978-0-9859110)* Div. of Hobbes End Entertainment, P.O. Box 193, Aubrey, TX 76227 USA
Web site: http://www.hobbesendpublishing.com
Dist(s): **Smashwords.**

Hobblebush Bks., *(978-0-9636413; 978-0-9760896; 978-0-9801672; 978-0-9845921; 978-1-939449)* PO Box 1285, Concord, NH 03302 USA
E-mail: info@hobblebush.com; kirsty@hobblebush.com
Web site: www.hobblebush.com
Dist(s): **Distributors, The**
SPD-Small Pr. Distribution.

Hobbs, Brenda F., *(978-0-9772970)* 14303 Greenview Rd., Detroit, MI 48223 USA
E-mail: bhobbs101@aol.com.

Hobbs, Constance (GBR) *(978-0-9556783)* *Dist. by* **LuluCom.**

Hobby Horse Publishing, LLC, *(978-0-615-89154-5)* P.O. Box 22, Peterborough, NH 03458 USA Tel 555-555-5555
E-mail: info@hobbyhorsepublishing.com
Web site: www.HobbyHorsePublishing.com.

Hobby Hse. Publishing Group, *(978-0-9727179)* Orders Addr.: 48 Hickory Hill Rd., Box 1527, Jackson, NJ 08527 USA
Web site: http://www.hobbyhousepublishinggroup.com.

Hobley, Linda Dean, *(978-0-692-17201-8)* 2504 Troost Ave., Kansas City, MO 64108 USA Tel 816-284-9504
E-mail: rosemarybaby18@gmail.com.

Hobnob Pr., *(978-0-9663241)* 2 W. Northfield Rd., Livingston, NJ 07039-3789 USA
Dist(s): **Diamond Comic Distributors, Inc.**

Hobson, Shoshanah, *(978-0-578-74505-3)* 15 Oakland Pl., Brooklyn, NY 11226 USA Tel 646-287-5486
E-mail: alizahsstory@gmail.com
Web site: alizahsstory.com.

Hochman, Steven, *(978-0-9887975)* 5 Wendover Ct., Mount Laurel, NJ 08054 USA Tel 856-778-1282
E-mail: hoc@me.com.

Hocks Out Press, *(978-0-578-14723-9; 978-0-578-15306-3; 978-0-9964421)* .

Hocus Pocus Publishing, Inc., *(978-0-9855544; 978-0-9910276; 978-1-942840; 978-1-952824; 978-1-960633)* PO Box 2960, Daphne, AL 36526 USA Tel 251-454-3244
E-mail: nicholasroussos@gmail.com; cynthia@cynthiaeden.com; info@hocuspocuspublishing.com
Web site: https://hocuspocuspublishing.com; https://cynthiaeden.com.

Hodder & Stoughton (GBR) *(978-0-245; 978-0-340; 978-0-550; 978-0-7131; 978-0-7195; 978-1-85998; 978-1-84032; 978-1-84456; 978-1-84854; 978-1-4447; 978-1-4736)* *Dist. by* **Trafalgar.**

Hodder & Stoughton (GBR) *(978-0-245; 978-0-340; 978-0-550; 978-0-7131; 978-0-7195; 978-1-85998; 978-1-84032; 978-1-84456; 978-1-84854; 978-1-4447; 978-1-4736)* *Dist. by* **HachBkGrp.**

Hodder & Stoughton Canada (CAN) *(978-0-340; 978-0-7131)* *Dist. by* **HachBkGrp.**

Hodder Education Group (GBR) *(978-0-340; 978-0-412; 978-0-450; 978-0-7122; 978-0-7131; 978-0-7506; 978-0-85264; 978-0-947054; 978-0-86003; 978-1-874958; 978-1-902984; 978-1-4441; 978-1-905735; 978-1-4718)* *Dist. by* **Trans-Atl Phila.**

Hodder Education Group (GBR) *(978-0-340; 978-0-412; 978-0-450; 978-0-7122; 978-0-7131; 978-0-7506; 978-0-85264; 978-0-947054; 978-0-86003; 978-1-874958; 978-1-902984; 978-1-4441; 978-1-905735; 978-1-4718)* *Dist. by* **IngramPubServ.**

Hoffman, Mark *See* **Hramiec Hoffman Publishing**

HOFFMAN, MELINDA, *(978-0-578-49295-7; 978-0-578-49750-1; 978-0-578-58928-2; 978-0-578-58963-3; 978-0-578-84604-0)* 100 Brookbend Rd., Mauldin, SC 29662 USA Tel 864-320-0973
E-mail: hoffmanmelinda@bellsouth.net
Dist(s): **Ingram Content Group.**

Hoffmann, Catherine, *(978-0-9753106)* 349 Martin Ln., Bloomingdale, IL 60108-1326 USA
E-mail: publisher@writehappy.com
Web site: http://www.writehappy.com.

Hoffmann Partnership *See* **Hoffmann, Catherine**

Hoffmaster, Casey Camille, *(978-0-692-13484-9)* 1225 Catherine Ct., CARBONDALE, CO 81623 USA Tel 561-252-1610
E-mail: casey.c.hoffmaster@gmail.com
Dist(s): **Ingram Content Group.**

Hogan Publishing LLC, *(978-0-9779504)* 2708 E. Edison, Tucson, AZ 85716 USA
E-mail: benjamin@madseadog.com
Web site: http://www.madseadog.com.

Hogrefe & Huber Publishers *See* **Hogrefe Publishing**

†Hogrefe Publishing, *(978-0-88937; 978-1-61676; 978-1-61334)* Subs. of Hogrefe Publishing GmbH, Orders Addr.: a/o Customer Service Dept., 30 Amberwood Pkwy., Ashland, OH 44805 USA Fax: 419-281-6883; Toll Free: 800-228-3749; Edit Addr.: 361 Newbury St. 5th Flr., Boston, MA 02115 USA (SAN 293-2792) Tel 857-880-2002
E-mail: customerservice@hogrefe.com; publishing@hogrefe.com
Web site: http://www.hogrefe.com/
Dist(s): **Baker & Taylor Publisher Services (BTPS)**
Coutts Information Services
Majors Scientific Bks., Inc.
Matthews Medical Bk. Co.
Metapress
Rittenhouse Bk. Distributors; *CIP.*

Hohm Pr., *(978-0-934252; 978-1-890772; 978-1-935387)* Div. of Hohm, Inc., P.O. Box 2501, Prescott, AZ 86302 USA (SAN 221-0924) Tel 520-778-9189; Fax: 520-717-1779; Toll Free: 800-381-2700 (orders only)
E-mail: staff@hohmpress.com; pinedr@goodnet.com; hpproduction@cableone.net
Web site: http://www.hohmpress.com
Dist(s): **SCB Distributors.**

Holbrook Studios, *(978-0-9762440)* Orders Addr.: P.O. Box 3064, Beverly Hills, CA 90212 USA; Edit Addr.: 754 E. S. Temple, Salt Lake city, UT 84102 USA.

Hole's Greenhouses & Gardens, Ltd. (CAN) *(978-0-9682791; 978-1-894728)* *Dist. by* **Lone Pine.**

Holes In My Socks Publishing, *(978-0-9771891; 978-0-578-41680-9)* P.O. Box 266, Paola, KS 66071 USA Tel 913-557-4508
E-mail: stephgun2@aol.com; christydreiling@att.net.

†Holiday Hse., Inc., *(978-0-8234)* Orders Addr.: 425 Madison Ave., New York, NY 10017 USA (SAN 202-3008) Tel 212-688-0085; Fax: 212-688-0395; *Imprints:* Margaret Ferguson Books (M Ferguson Bks); Neal Porter Books (Neal Porter)
E-mail: holiday@holidayhouse.com
Web site: http://www.holidayhouse.com
Dist(s): **Children's Plus, Inc.**
MyiLibrary
Open Road Integrated Media, Inc.
Penguin Random Hse. Distribution
Penguin Random Hse. LLC
Random Hse., Inc.; *CIP.*

Holiness.com, *(978-0-9743831)* 1271 Washington Ave., PMB 165, San Leandro, CA 94577 USA Tel 510-384-8082
E-mail: suppliers@holiness.com
Web site: http://www.holiness.com.

Holism Publishing, *(978-0-9818297)* Orders Addr.: P.O. Box 3385, Palm Beach, FL 33480-1585 USA Tel 561-533-7704 (phone/fax)
E-mail: curecare@bellsouth.net; info@holismpublishing.com
Web site: http://www.HolismPublishing.com; http://www.HolismMovement.com
Dist(s): **New Leaf Distributing Co., Inc.**

Holland Brown, *(978-0-9797006; 978-0-9897544)* 2509 Portland Ave The Anchor Bldg., Louisville, KY 40202-1008 USA
E-mail: stephanie@thegreenbuilding.com
Web site: http://www.hollandbrownbooks.com.

Holland, Gretchen, *(978-0-9768340)* 4437 Craig Dr., Fort Collins, CO 80526 USA Tel 970-282-1338.

Hollandays Publishing Corp., *(978-0-9708224; 978-0-9728844; 978-0-9753239; 978-0-9769459; 978-0-9799003)* 8459 N. Main St. Ste. 118, Dayton, OH 45415-1324 USA Toll Free: 800-792-3537
E-mail: zhensler@hollandays.net
Web site: http://www.hollandays.net
Dist(s): **Partners Bk. Distributing, Inc.**

Hollar, Cheryl Public Relations, *(978-0-9763826)* Orders Addr.: 218 S. Cheatham St., Franklinton, NC 27525 USA Tel 919-494-2150
E-mail: cherylhollar@yahoo.com; billythebunnybooks@yahoo.com.

Hollenbach, David A, *(978-0-578-41371-6)* 342 Merchant Ave., Marion, OH 43302 USA Tel 740-361-2168
E-mail: daveh8000@gmail.com
Dist(s): **Ingram Content Group.**

Holley, Wendy, *(978-1-7359093)* 122 S Van Ness Ave, Los Angeles, CA 90004 USA Tel 323-380-5029
E-mail: holleywend@yahoo.com.

Hollingale Bks. LLC, *(978-0-9907895)* 55 N. Merchant St. No. 1481, American Fork, UT 84003 USA Tel 801-855-6448
E-mail: paige@hollingale.com
Web site: www.hollingale.com.

Hollingsworth, Kenneth, *(978-0-9771572)* 2215 Janet Ct., Cedar Hill, TX 75104-1021 USA (SAN 256-8926)
Web site: http://www.hollingsworthtexas.com/plantingtheseeds.

Hollow Mountain Publishing LLC, *(978-0-9981676; 978-1-954173)* 2266 Possum Hollow Dr, Camdenton, MO 65020 USA Tel 573-207-0699
E-mail: diannakilpack@outlook.com.

Holloway, Greg, *(978-0-9908100)* 107 Ashburne Glen Ln, Ovilla, TX 75154 USA Tel 214-325-8357
E-mail: info@48hrbooks.com
Web site: hollowaygreg.com.

Holly Hall Pubns., Inc., *(978-0-9645396; 978-1-888306)* P.O. Box 254, Elkton, MD 21922-0254 USA Tel 410-392-2300; Fax: 410-620-9877; Toll Free: 800-211-0719; *Imprints:* Full Quart Press (Full Quart Pr)
Dist(s): **Spring Arbor Distributors, Inc.**

Holly Hill Pr., *(978-0-578-01217-9; 978-0-578-03837-7; 978-0-578-03971-8; 978-0-578-08282-0; 978-0-692-03326-5; 978-0-578-40816-3; 978-0-578-41542-0)* 3 Earl Rd., Box 36, East Sandwich, MA 02537 USA; 135 Corn Shop Ln., Farmington, ME 04938
E-mail: jbeanpalmer@yahoo.com
Dist(s): **Independent Pub.**

Holly Schindler, LLC / InToto Books *See* **InToto Bks.**

HollyBear Pr., *(978-0-9651067)* Orders Addr.: P.O. Box 4257, Prescott, AZ 86302-4257 USA Tel 928-776-4689; Edit Addr.: 910 Stevens Dr., Prescott, AZ 86305 USA
E-mail: monamc2@msn.com.

Hollygrove Publishing, Inc., *(978-0-9777939; 978-0-9840904)* 4100 W. Eldorado Pkwy., Suite 100-182, McKinney, TX 75070 USA (SAN 850-170X) Tel 972-837-6191
E-mail: bsmith@hollygrovepublishing.com
Web site: http://www.hollygrovepublishing.com.

Hollym International Corp., *(978-0-930878; 978-1-56591)* Orders Addr.: 2647 Gateway Rd. No. 105-223, Carlsbad, CA 92009 USA (SAN 992-3551) Tel 760-814-9880; Edit Addr.: 2647 Gateway Rd. No. 105-223, Carlbad, CA 92009 USA (SAN 211-0172) Tel 760-814-9880 Do not confuse with Hollym Corporation Pubs., New York, NY
E-mail: gracepresa@gmail.com; contact@hollym.com
Web site: http://www.hollym.com.

Hollywood Jesus Books *See* **Methow Pr.**

Hollywood Operating System, *(978-1-893899)* 3108 W. Magnolia Blvd., Burbank, CA 91505-3045 USA
E-mail: hollywoodos@aol.com
Web site: http://www.HollywoodOS.com.

HollywoodComics.com, LLC, *(978-0-9740711; 978-1-932983; 978-1-934543; 978-1-935558; 978-1-61227; 978-1-64932)* 18321 Ventura Blvd. Suite 915 Attn: Greg M. Seigel, Tarzana, CA 91356 USA (SAN 255-366X) Tel 818-385-0284; *Imprints:* Black Coat Press (Black Coat Pr)
E-mail: info@hollywoodcomics.com; info@riviereblanche.com; jean-marc@hollywoodcomics.com; info@blackcoatpress.com
Web site: http://www.hexagoncomics.com; http://www.blackcoatpress.com; http://www.riviereblanche.com.

Holmade Publishing, *(978-0-578-20055-2; 978-0-578-20056-9)* 22431 Philiprimm St., Woodland Hills, CA 91367 USA Tel 818-887-4123
E-mail: michaelrholm@yahoo.com.

Holman Bible Pubs. *Imprint of* **B&H Publishing Group**

Holman, Doris Anne, *(978-0-9667192; 978-0-9758630)* 5 Oak Ledge Rd., Harpswell, ME 04079 USA.

Holmes Bookshop *Imprint of* **Belle Lumiere True News**

Holmes Investments & Holdings LLC, *(978-0-9962102; 978-0-9992369)* P.O. Box 1021, Lakewood, CA 90714 USA Tel 562-472-8202
E-mail: quentinholmes@hotmail.com
Web site: www.quentinholmes.com
Dist(s): **Ingram Content Group.**

Holmes, Jinai Michele, *(978-0-9969282)*
E-mail: jinai_holmes@yahoo.com.

Holmgard Pr. (GBR) *(978-1-5262-0211-6)* *Dist. by* **IPG Chicago.**

Holocaust Museum Houston, *(978-0-9659781; 978-0-9773988)* 5401 Caroline St., Houston, TX 77004-6804 USA Tel 713-942-8000; Fax: 713-942-7953
E-mail: info@hmh.org
Web site: http://www.hmh.org
Dist(s): **Hervey's Booklink & Cookbook Warehouse.**

Holocaust Survivors' Memoirs Project, *(978-0-9760739; 978-0-9814686)* c/o World Jewish Congress, 633 Third Ave., Flr. 21, New York, NY 10017 USA Fax: 212-318-6176
E-mail: survivorsmemoirs@aol.com.

Holofcener, Mark, *(978-0-9718626)* 7323 Island Cir., Boulder, CO 80301-3905 USA
E-mail: mark@evansadventure.com
Web site: http://www.evansadventure.com.

Holography Sells, *(978-0-9741087)* 1305 Kirks Ln., Dresher, PA 19025 USA (SAN 255-3627)
E-mail: sales@snookybook.com
Web site: http://www.snookybook.com.

Holon Publishing, *(978-0-615-59702-7; 978-0-9853027; 978-0-9915282; 978-0-9966685; 978-1-955342)* Orders Addr.: 1311 Vine St., Cincinnati, OH 45202 USA; Edit Addr.: 1311 Vine St. Ste. Lotus, Cincinnati, OH 45202 USA Tel 812-269-6390; 812-325-6194
E-mail: Jeremy@holon.co; jeremygotwals@gmail.com
Web site: http://www.Holon.co; http://www.holonpublishing.com.

Holst Bks., *(978-0-9794133; 978-0-615-14014-8; 978-1-955781)* Div. of TV Acres.com, 510 Lexington Ave. 510 Lexington Ave. No Address Provided, Thomasville, NC 27360 USA Tel 336-803-0406
Web site: http://www.holstbooks.com
Dist(s): **CreateSpace Independent Publishing Platform**
Lulu Pr., Inc.

Holt Enterprise, LLC, *(978-0-9740016)* Orders Addr.: P.O. Box 414, Riverside, NJ 08075 USA (SAN 255-2760) Tel 856-764-7043; Fax: 856-764-0851; Toll Free:

Publisher Name Index

888-944-4658; Edit Addr.: 147 N. Fairview St., Riverside, NJ 08075 USA
E-mail: HoltEnterprise@comcast.net; holt109@comcast.net
Dist(s): **Quality Bks., Inc.**

Holt, Henry & Co. *Imprint of* **Holt, Henry & Co.**

Holt, Henry & Co. Bks. For Young Readers *Imprint of* **Holt, Henry & Co.**

†**Holt, Henry & Co.**, *(978-0-03; 978-0-8050)* Div. of Holtzbrinck Publishers, Orders Addr.: 16365 James Madison Hwy., Gordonsville, VA 22942-8501 USA Toll Free Fax: 800-672-2054; Toll Free: 888-330-8477; Edit Addr.: 115 W. 18th St., 5th Flr., New York, NY 10011 USA (SAN 200-6472) Tel 212-886-9200; Fax: 540-672-7540 (customer service); *Imprints*: Metropolitan Books (Metropol Bks); Times Books (Times Bks); Holt, Henry & Company (HenHolt); Holt, Henry & Company Books For Young Readers (HH Bks Yng Read); Holt Paperback (Holt Paperbck)
E-mail: info@hholt.com
Web site: http://www.henryholt.com
Dist(s): **Blackstone Audio, Inc.**
Children's Plus, Inc.
Giron Bks.
Lectorum Pubns., Inc.
Macmillan
Perfection Learning Corp.
Westminster John Knox Pr.
Weston Woods Studios, Inc.; *CIP.*

Holt International, *(978-1-7329647; 979-8-9873556)* 250 Country Club Rd, Eugene, OR 97401 USA Tel 541-687-2202
E-mail: celestes@holtinternational.org
Web site: www.holtinternational.org.

Holt, Max Media., *(978-0-9966104; 978-1-944537)* 303 Casacabel Pl, Mt Juliet, TN 37122 USA Tel 731-819-4241
E-mail: sandymaxholt@yahoo.com
Web site: www.maxholtmedia.com.

Holt McDougal, *(978-0-395; 978-0-8123; 978-0-86609; 978-0-88343; 978-0-618)* Subs. of Houghton Mifflin Harcourt Publishing Co., Orders Addr.: 1900 S. Batavia Ave., Geneva, IL 60134 USA Toll Free: 888-872-8380; Edit Addr.: P.O. Box 1667, Evanston, IL 60204 USA (SAN 202-2532) Toll Free: 800-323-5435; 800-462-6595 (customer service); 909 Davis St., Evanston, IL 60201 Tel 847-869-2300; Fax: 847-869-0841
Web site: http://www.mcdougallittell.com.

Holt Paperback *Imprint of* **Holt, Henry & Co.**

Holt Smith, Ltd., *(978-0-9886493; 978-0-692-31193-6; 978-0-692-31279-7; 978-0-692-55473-9; 978-0-692-57280-1; 978-0-692-57286-3; 978-0-692-58679-2; 978-0-692-68801-4; 978-0-692-70258-1; 978-0-692-70856-9; 978-0-692-72171-1; 978-0-9977938; 978-1-946777; 978-1-959572) 101 W. 23rd Apt. 2Q, New York, NY 10011 USA Tel 917-553-3143*
E-mail: support@holtsmith.com
Dist(s): **CreateSpace Independent Publishing Platform.**

Holt, Tammy, *(978-1-7362177)* 3502 FLATWATER Pl., LAUREL, MD 20724 USA Tel 202-320-1114
E-mail: TAMMYHOLT@GMAIL.COM
Web site: superpowersactivate.org.

Holtz Creative Enterprises, *(978-0-9817247; 978-0-9837617)* 3103 Terry Ln., Eau Claire, WI 54703 USA Tel 715-835-2705
E-mail: holtzenterprises@sbcglobal.net.

Holtzbrinck Publishers *See* **Macmillan**

Holy Child Pubns., *(978-0-615-27752-3; 978-0-615-33948-1; 978-0-615-37502-1; 978-0-615-45181-7; 978-0-615-58648-9; 978-0-615-69219-7; 978-0-615-81249-6; 978-0-692-47633-8; 978-0-692-80495-7; 978-0-692-11629-6; 978-0-578-55615-4; 978-0-578-55616-1; 978-0-578-80955-7) P.O. Box 954, Fairburn, GA 30213 USA*
Web site: http://www.holychildpublications.com.

HOLY COW Bk. Pubs., *(978-0-9773407; 978-0-615-83382-8; 978-1-953232)* 3321 Hugo Ln., Timmonsville, SC 29161 USA Tel 843-229-4641
E-mail: ralphy_jmm@yahoo.com; ollyaga@gmail.com.

Holy Heroes LLC, *(978-0-9801121; 978-1-936330; 978-1-959418)* 728 Hanna Woods, Cramerton, NC 28032 USA (SAN 855-2401)
E-mail: kandkdavison@bellsouth.net; kennethldavison@gmail.com
Web site: http://www.holyheroes.com.

Holy Macro! Bks. *Imprint of* **Tickling Keys, Inc.**

Holy Sparks, *(978-1-937472)* 602 N. Orange Dr., Los Angeles, CA 90036 USA Tel 323-934-6653
E-mail: bowker@askbubbe.com.

Holy Trinity Monastery, *(978-0-88465; 978-1-942699)* P.O. Box 36, Jordanville, NY 13361-0036 USA (SAN 207-3501) Tel 315-858-0940; Fax: 315-858-0505
Dist(s): **Independent Pubs. Group.**

Holzwarth Pubns. (DEU) *(978-3-935567; 978-3-00) Dist. by* **Dist Art Pubs.**

Hom, Jonathan, *(978-0-9974103)* 132 Cityhomes Ln., Foster City, CA 94404 USA Tel 650-477-5315
E-mail: w00tw00tjon@gmail.com.

Homa & Sekey Bks., *(978-0-9665421; 978-1-931907; 978-1-62246)* 3rd Floor, North Tower Mack-Cali Center III 140 East Ridgewood Ave, Paramus, NJ 07652 USA Tel 800-870-HOMA (4662) (Orders only); 201-261-8810; Fax: 201-261-8890
E-mail: info@homabooks.com
Web site: http://www.homabooks.com
Dist(s): **Independent Pubs. Group.**

Homagno Group, Incorporated *See* **Editorial Homagno**

Homawoo, Richard, *(978-0-9983274)* 22432 Bright Sky Dr., Clarksburg, MD 20871 USA Tel 703-303-4183
E-mail: info@gritcrafters.com
Web site: www.gritcrafters.com

Home, *(978-1-7376581)* 135 Mill Creek Dr., CANTON, GA 30115 USA Tel 404-435-9710
E-mail: ChristopherJude1@protonmail.com
Web site: www.adandeliongirl.com.

Home Box Office, Inc., *(978-0-910765; 978-0-9828167)* 1100 Sixth Ave., New York, NY 10036 USA (SAN 260-2032) Tel 212-512-1000.

Home Discipleship Pr., *(978-0-9753133; 978-0-9785678)* 6645 W. Steger Rd., Monee, IL 60449 USA Tel 708-235-1901; Fax: 708-235-1904
E-mail: leaders@homediscipleship.orf
Web site: http://www.homedisciplesshippress.org.

Home For Words, *(978-0-9993323)* 192 Broken Ridge Trl, West End, NC 27376 USA Tel 910-603-5405
E-mail: beckyschrodt@yahoo.com
Web site: www.homeforwordspress.com.

Home Planet Bks., *(978-0-9743712; 978-0-9887978)* 2300 8th St., Olivenhain, CA 92024-6565 USA Tel 760-634-4947
E-mail: sales@homeplanetbooks.com.

Home Planet Bks., *(978-0-692-18826-2; 978-0-578-62406-8; 978-0-578-30384-0)* 2043 New Hampshire St., Lawrence, KS 66046 USA Tel 785-979-2961
E-mail: randi.hacker1@gmail.com.

Home Schl. in the Woods, *(978-0-9720265; 978-0-9815523; 978-0-9842041; 978-0-9913678; 978-1-957525)* 3997 Roosevelt Hwy., Holley, NY 14470 USA Tel 585-672-5882
E-mail: eduardoopak@yahoo.com
Web site: http://www.homeschoolinthewoods.com.

Homecooked Entertainment *See* **Sungrazer Publishing**

Homegrown Pubns.,LLC, *(978-0-9799635)* P.O. Box 173, Red Wing, MN 55066 USA
Web site: http://www.homegrownpublications.com.

Homelight Pr., *(978-0-9749936)* P.O. Box 1901, Huntersville, NC 28070-1901 USA Toll Free: 877-438-6657
E-mail: homeligh@bellsouth.net.

Homer Historical Society, *(978-0-9770022)* 107 N. Main St., Homer, IL 61849 USA Tel 217-896-2549.

Homes for the Homeless Institute, Inc., *(978-0-9641784; 978-0-9724425; 978-0-9825533)* 50 Cooper Sq. Flr. 4, New York, NY 10003-7144 USA; *Imprints*: White Tiger Press (Wht Tiger Pr)
E-mail: info@icphusa.org
Web site: www.icphusa.org; www.whitetigerpress.org.

HomeScholar Bks., *(978-0-9754934)* 2311 Harrison Rd., Nashville, NC 27856 USA Tel 252-459-9279; *Imprints*: Literary Lessons (LitLessons)
Web site: http://www.homescholarbooks.com.

Homeschool Journey, *(978-0-9762918; 978-0-9825006)* 4625 Devon, Lisle, IL 60532 USA Tel 630-277-6200
E-mail: homeschooljourney@gmail.com
Web site: http://www.homeschooljourney.com.

Homestead Publishing, *(978-0-943972)* 4388 17th St., San Francisco, CA 94114 USA (SAN 241-029X) Tel 415-621-5039
E-mail: info@homesteadpublishing.net
Web site: http://homesteadpublishing.net; http://www.homesteadpublishing.net.

Hometown World *Imprint of* **Sourcebooks, Inc.**

Honey Bee, *(978-0-692-86152-3; 978-1-7363045)* 20247 Damman, Harper Woods, MI 48225 USA Tel 313-627-3568
E-mail: shirleybarden204@yahoo.com
Web site: www.myhoneybee.com.

Honey Girl Bks., *(978-0-9984432)* 1725 41st Ave SW, Seattle, WA 98116 USA Tel 574-400-9362
E-mail: juliawsea@gmail.com
Web site: honeygirlbooks.com/.

Honey Ink Publishing LLC, *(978-1-7361861)* 2517 Paintbrush Dr, Palmdale, CA 93551 USA Tel 510-681-3087
E-mail: m.harrison@honeyinkbooks.com
Web site: www.honeyinkbooks.com.

Honey Locust Pr. *Imprint of* **Wolfmont, LLC**

Honey Pot Publishing House *See* **Westside Storybks.**

Honeybee in the Garden, LLC, *(978-0-9857996; 978-1-7323630)* 11619 Greenlane Dr., Potomac, MD 20854 USA Tel 301-765-6248
E-mail: dband@dbandart.com
Web site: www.dbandart.com.

Honeycomb Adventures Pr., LLC, *(978-0-9820886; 978-0-9836808)* P.O. Box 1215, Hemingway, SC 29554 USA Tel 843-558-0133
E-mail: queenbjan@sc rr.com
Web site: http://honeycombadventures.com
Dist(s): **Ingram Content Group.**

Honeycomb Inc., *(978-0-9793799)* 1017 Avon, Flint, MI 48503 USA (SAN 853-3024) Tel 810-397-8025; Fax: 810-234-1794
E-mail: tandtvison@aol.com
Web site: http://www.101waysyoucansave.com.

HoneyKeep Ministries, *(978-0-9989332)* 45 Ruspin Ave., Buffalo, NY 14215 USA Tel 716-235-4575
E-mail: honeykeepministries1cejb@gmail.com
Web site: www.honeykeepministries.org.

Honeysuckle Acres, *(978-0-9963033)* 146 Rockfish Run Rd., Scottsville, VA 24590 USA Tel 434-566-6675
E-mail: kayepearse@gmail.com.

Honor Bound Bks., *(978-0-615-91638-5; 978-0-692-02434-8; 978-0-692-21785-6; 978-0-692-28323-3; 978-0-692-48896-6; 978-0-692-64187-3; 978-0-692-64346-4; 978-0-9977785; 978-1-951587)* 422 W Meadow Creek Way, Middleton, ID 83644 USA Tel 208-800-1355 Do not confuse with Honor Bound Books in Sacramento, CA
Web site: www.honorboundbooks.com
Dist(s): **CreateSpace Independent Publishing Platform.**

Honorable Pr., *(978-0-9719727)* 2432 Wilshire Ct., Decatur, GA 30035 USA.

HonorNet, *(978-0-9753036; 978-0-9788726; 978-0-9820590; 978-1-938021)* P.O. Box 910, Sapulpa, OK 74067 USA
E-mail: mail@honornet.net
Web site: http://honornet.net
Dist(s): **Destiny Image Pubs.**
Whitaker Hse.

Hood, Alan C. & Co., Inc., *(978-0-911469)* P.O. Box 775, Chambersburg, PA 17201 USA (SAN 270-8221) Tel 717-267-0867; Fax: 717-267-0572; Toll Free Fax: 888-844-9433; 4501 Forbes Blvd., Lanham, MD 20706
E-mail: hoodbooks@pa.net
Web site: http://www.hoodbooks.com
Dist(s): **Follett School Solutions.**

Hood, Ted *See* **Four Seasons Publishing**

Hooker, Lou, *(978-0-9755106)* 6900 Chamberlain, Fremont, MI 49412 USA Tel 231-924-3555
E-mail: lvhook@ncats.net.

Hoopoe Bks. *Imprint of* **I S H K**

Hooser, Jack M Van, *(978-0-692-06208-1; 978-0-692-06224-1)* 2809 Meadow Rose Dr., Nashville, TN 37206 USA Tel 615-308-0822
E-mail: jogarrett35@gmail.com
Dist(s): **Ingram Content Group.**

Hoot N' Cackle Pr., *(978-0-9659381)* 1928 S. Mayfair, Springfield, MO 65804 USA Tel 417-887-0837; Fax: 417-886-3994
E-mail: ripe@usipp.net
Web site: http://www.mowrites4kids.drury.edu/authors/lipe/.

Hoots, Dani *See* **FoxTales Pr.**

Hoover, Linda, *(978-0-9981806)* 3050 Craig Rd, Springfield, OH 45502 USA Tel 397-631-1566
E-mail: lhoover2@Hotmail.com.

HOP, LLC, *(978-1-887942; 978-1-931020; 978-1-933863; 978-1-60143; 978-1-60242; 978-1-60498; 978-1-60499)* Educate, Inc., 1407 Fleet St. Flr. 1, Baltimore, MD 21231-2859 USA
Web site: http://www.hookedonphonics.com
Dist(s): **Simon & Schuster, Inc.**

Hope Belle LLC, *(978-0-692-16751-9; 978-0-692-16752-6)* 247 W. 145th St. Apt. 1D, NEW YORK, NY 10039 USA Tel 646-489-9409
E-mail: hopebelle1@gmail.com
Dist(s): **Ingram Content Group.**

Hope Chest Legacy, Inc., *(978-1-59565)* P.O. Box 1398, Littlerock, CA 93543 USA Toll Free: 888-554-7292
E-mail: hopechestlegacy@aol.com
Web site: http://hopechestlegacy.com.

Hope Farm Pr. & Bookshop, *(978-0-910746)* 15 Jane St., Saugerties, NY 12477-1511 USA (SAN 204-0697) Toll Free: 800-883-5778 (orders)
E-mail: hopefarm@hopefarm.com
Web site: http://www.hopefarm.com; http://www.hopefarmbooks.com
Dist(s): **North Country Bks., Inc.**

Hope for Families, Inc., *(978-0-9676489; 978-1-954567)* P.O. Box 238, Hatfield, PA 19440 USA Tel 215-280-5369
E-mail: hopeforfamilies@verizon.net; loristauffer@verizon.net
Web site: Hffbooks.com.

Hope Harvest Ministries *See* **Hope Harvest Publishing**

Hope Harvest Publishing, *(978-0-9716523; 978-0-9763695; 978-0-9771318; 978-0-9779898)* Div. of H&H Bindery & Distribution Centre, P.O. Box 8353, Kentwood, MI 49518 USA Tel 616-307-3080; Fax: 616-458-8991
E-mail: hopeharvest@comcast.net
Web site: http://www.hopeharvest.com; http://www.blessly.com
Dist(s): **Anchor Distributors**
Anderson Merchandisers
H & H Distribution
Spirit Filled Pr., Inc.
Spring Arbor Distributors, Inc.

Hope International Printshop, *(978-0-9748096)* Orders Addr.: P.O. Box 1182, Hobe Sound, FL 33475 USA; Edit Addr.: 8436 SE Bayberry Terr., Hobe Sound, FL 33475 USA.

Hope of Vision Publishing, *(978-0-9753795; 978-0-9818253; 978-0-9831371; 978-0-9837082; 978-0-9852746; 978-0-9884773; 978-0-9912483; 978-1-942871; 978-1-955107)* 43 Yale St., Bridgeport, CT 06605 USA (SAN 856-6410) Tel 203-338-1301; Fax: 203-413-1593
Web site: http://www.hopeofvisionpublishing.com.

Hope Pr., *(978-1-878267)* Orders Addr.: P.O. Box 188, Duarte, CA 91009-0188 USA (SAN 200-3244) Tel 626-303-0644; Fax: 626-358-3520; Toll Free: 800-321-4039; Edit Addr.: 1110 Mill Run, Monvaia, CA 91016 USA Tel 626-303-0644 Do not confuse with Hope Pr., Pittsville, WI
E-mail: hopepress@earthink.net; dcomings@earthlink.net
Web site: http://www.hopepress.com; http://www.didmancreategod.com.

Hope Publishing Hse., *(978-0-932727; 978-7-5379; 978-1-932717)* Affil. of Southern California Ecumenical Council, P.O. Box 60008, Pasadena, CA 91116 USA (SAN 688-4849) Tel 626-792-6123; Fax: 626-792-2121; Toll Free: 800-326-2671 (orders only)
E-mail: hopepub@sbcglobal.net
Web site: http://hope-pub.com
Dist(s): **Chinasprout, Inc.**
Send The Light Distribution LLC.

Hope Rekindled Pr. *See* **Risen Heart Pr.**

Hope Through Healing Pubns., *(978-0-9743626)* P.O. Box 310, Yelm, WA 98597 USA
E-mail: jennifer@correctthetext.com
Web site: http://www.CorrectTheText.com.

Hopecopious Productions, *(978-0-9982922)* 1720 SW 346th Pl, Federal Way, WA 98023 USA Tel 253-927-9279; Fax: 253-927-9279
E-mail: Connect@Hopecopious.com
Web site: Hopecopious.com.

Hopefully You'll Get to See, *(978-0-692-09913-1; 978-1-7373220)* 900 Palisade Ave, Apt. 16N, Fort Lee, NJ 07024 USA Tel 973-214-5608
E-mail: elkins.dani@gmail.com
Dist(s): **CreateSpace Independent Publishing Platform.**

Hopewell Pubns., LLC, *(978-0-9726906; 978-1-933435)* P.O. Box 11, Titusville, NJ 08560-0011 USA Tel 609-818-1049; Fax: 609-964-1718 Do not confuse with companies with the same or similar name in Longmont, CO, Austin, TX, Springdale, AZ
E-mail: publisher@hopepubs.com
Web site: http://www.hopepubs.com
Dist(s): **Univ. Pr. of New England.**

Hopkins, KC, *(978-0-615-23929-3)* 409 Orchid Trail, Franklin, TN 37174 USA Tel 615-618-4997
E-mail: kchopkins1276@yahoo.com
Dist(s): **Lulu Pr., Inc.**

Hopkins Publishing, *(978-0-9839326; 978-1-62080)* 201 Faircrest Dr. No. 3687, Cleburne, TX 76033 USA Tel 210-595-9313; *Imprints*: Azimuth Media (Azimuth Me)
E-mail: leah@hopkinspublishing.com; justin@hopkinspublishing.com
Web site: http://www.facebook.com/churchofchristbooks; http://hopkinspublishing.com/; http://twitter.com/#!/cofcbooks; https://www.smashwords.com/profile/view/hopkinspublishing
Dist(s): **Ingram Content Group**
Send The Light Distribution LLC.

Hoppenbrouwers, Toke *See* **Monte Nido Pr.**

Hopping Mad Pr., *(978-0-692-98113-9; 978-0-692-98114-6)* 219 East N. D St., Gas City, IN 46933 USA Tel 765-667-4822
E-mail: Ardbrowncda@Live.com.

HOPS Pr., LLC, *(978-1-892784)* Orders Addr.: 12 Quartz St., Pony, MT 59747-0697 USA Tel 406-685-3222
E-mail: orders@hollowtop.com
Web site: http://www.hopspress.com
Dist(s): **Chelsea Green Publishing**
Lone Pine Publishing USA
Mountain Pr. Publishing Co., Inc.

Horan Publishing, *(978-0-9769980)* P.O. Box 740485, Orange City, FL 32774-0485 USA
E-mail: horanpublishing@wmconnect.com.

Horizon Bks., *(978-0-9787987)* Orders Addr.: 768 Hardtimes Rd., Farmville, VA 23901 USA (SAN 851-6243) Tel 434-390-7732 (phone/fax)
E-mail: eicherjs@kinex.net
Web site: http://www.readingwithhorizon.com.

Horizon Line Pr., *(978-0-9749426)* 77 N. River Dr., Roseburg, OR 97470 USA
E-mail: dj@knights-of-avalon.com
Web site: http://www.knights-of-avalon.net/.

Horizon Pubs. & Distributors, Inc., *(978-0-88290)* Orders Addr.: P.O. Box 490, Bountiful, UT 84011-0490 USA.

Horizon Pubs. *Imprint of* **Cedar Fort, Inc./CFI Distribution**

Horizons *Imprint of* **Alpha Omega Pubns., Inc.**

Horizons Literary Management LLC *See* **Better Bound Hse.**

Horowitz Creative Media, Incorporated *See* **ArtMar Productions**

Horse & Dragon Publishing, *(978-0-9759488)* 241 Coast Hill Dr., Suite A, Indian Harbour Beach, FL 32937 USA Tel 321-821-2220; Fax: 321-821-2226; Toll Free: 877-374-6815
E-mail: bob@robertclark.us
Web site: http://www.robertclark.us.

Horse Creek Pubns., *(978-0-9722217)* 945 Mockingbird Ln., Norman, OK 73071-4802 USA
E-mail: sue.schrems@horsecreekpublications.com
Web site: http://www.horsecreekpublications.com.

Horseyolo, *(978-0-9966602)* 20 Minuteman Dr., Bluffton, SC 29910 USA Tel 843-368-2115
E-mail: mikoszshowhorses@gmail.com
Web site: horseyolo.com.

Horton, David *See* **Negro Publishing, LLC**

Horvath, Janet, *(978-0-9713735)* 122 Virginia St., Saint Paul, MN 55102 USA (SAN 255-5441) Tel 612-870-4200; Fax: 612-454-2554
E-mail: jhorvathcello@hotmail.com
Web site: http://www.playinglesshurt.com.

Ho's, Jane Children Bks., *(978-0-9619126)* 700 Kipling Ct., El Sobrante, CA 94803 USA (SAN 243-4954) Tel 510-222-2621.

Hosannah Pubns., *(978-0-9786031)* 507 W. Manheim St., Bldg.18 , Apt.D, Philadelphia, PA 19144-4859 USA Tel 215-991-6154; Fax: 215-991-0609
E-mail: fourhosannah@verizon.net.

Hoskins, Jenny, *(978-1-7324318)* 104 E. Fairview Ave. No. 282 Meridian, Meridian, ID 83642 USA Tel 208-996-2692
E-mail: jennyhoskins0213@gmail.com
Web site: jennyhoskins.com.

Hospice & Community Care Pubns., *(978-0-9774691)* Orders Addr.: P.O. Box 993, Rock Hill, SC 29731 USA (SAN 257-6309) Tel 803-329-4663; Fax: 803-329-5935; Toll Free: 800-895-2273; Edit Addr.: P.O. Box 993, Rock Hill, SC 29731-6993 USA
Web site: http://www.hospicecommunitycare.org.

Hospice of Saint John, The, *(978-0-9742849)* 1320 Everett Ct., Lakewood, CO 80215 USA.

Hot Chocolate Pr., *(978-0-9910626; 978-0-9961710; 978-0-692-95409-6; 978-0-692-11452-0; 978-1-7333341; 978-1-7373905)* 338 Zeppelin Way, Fort Collins, CO 80524 USA Tel 970-556-0908
E-mail: kerrie.flanagan@gmail.com
Dist(s): **BookBaby.**

Hot Key Bks. (GBR) *(978-1-4714) Dist. by* **IPG Chicago.**

Hot off the Pr., *(978-0-933491; 978-0-9605904; 978-1-56231; 978-1-59776)* 1250 NW 3rd Ave., Canby, OR 97013 USA (SAN 216-3977) Toll Free: 800-227-9595
E-mail: info@hotp.com
Web site: http://www.craftpizazz.com.

Hot Page Pr. *Imprint of* **Potter Assocs.**

otComb Pr., (978-0-9787940) 6230 Wilshire Blvd., Suite 805, Los Angeles, CA 90048-5104 USA
E-mail: info@hotcombpress.com
Web site: http://hotcombpress.com.
otDiggetyDog Pr., (978-0-9741417; 978-0-9844645) P.O. Box 747, Shepherdsville, KY 40165 USA Tel 502-376-5966; Fax: 208-474-1227
E-mail: leighanne@thewoodybooks.com
Web site: http://www.thewoodybooks.com.
Houghton Mifflin Bks. for Children *Imprint of* **Houghton Mifflin Harcourt Trade & Reference Pubs.**
Houghton Mifflin Company *See* **Houghton Mifflin Harcourt Publishing Co.**
Houghton Mifflin Company (School Division) *See* **Houghton Mifflin Harcourt School Pubs.**
Houghton Mifflin Company Trade & Reference Division *See* **Houghton Mifflin Harcourt Trade & Reference Pubs.**
Houghton Mifflin Harcourt Learning Technology, (978-0-7630; 978-1-930106) Div. of Houghton Mifflin Harcourt Publishing Co., 100 Pine St. Ste. 1900, San Francisco, CA 94111-5205 USA Toll Free: 800-223-6925; 125 Cambridgepark Dr., Cambridge, MA 02140-2329
E-mail: info@riverdeep.net; international@riverdeep.net
Web site: http://www.riverdeep.com
Dist(s): **Follett School Solutions**
Open Road Integrated Media, Inc.
†**Houghton Mifflin Harcourt Publishing Co.,** (978-0-395; 978-0-87466; 978-0-9631591; 978-1-57630; 978-1-881527; 978-0-618; 978-0-544; 978-0-547; 978-1-328; 978-0-358; 979-8-202) Orders Addr.: 9205 Southpark Ctr. Loop, Orlando, FL 32819 USA Toll Free: 800-225-3362; Edit Addr.: 222 Berkeley St., Boston, MA 02116 USA (SAN 215-3793) Tel 617-351-5000; 125 High St., Boston, MA 02110; *Imprints:* HMH Books For Young Readers (HMH Bks FYR)
Web site: http://www.hmco.com
Dist(s): **Blackstone Audio, Inc.**
CENGAGE Learning
Cheng & Tsui Co.
Children's Plus, Inc.
Continental Bk. Co., Inc.
hand2mind
Ebsco Publishing
Firebrand Technologies
Follett School Solutions
Houghton Mifflin Harcourt Trade & Reference Pubs.
Houghton Mifflin Harcourt Supplemental Pubs.
Larousse Kingfisher Chambers, Inc.
Lectorum Pubns., Inc.
MyiLibrary
Open Road Integrated Media, Inc.
Perelandra, Ltd.
TextStream
ebrary, Inc.; *CIP.*
Houghton Mifflin Harcourt School Pubs., (978-0-395; 978-0-669) Orders Addr.: 1900 Batavia Ave., Geneva, IL 60134-3399 USA Toll Free Fax: 800-733-2098; Toll Free: 800-733-2828; 1175 N. Stemmons Fwy., Lewisville, TX 75067-2516 Toll Free: 800-733-2828; Edit Addr.: 222 Berkeley St., Boston, MA 02116 USA Tel 617-351-5000; Fax: 617-227-5409
E-mail: eduwebmaster@hmco.com
Web site: http://www.eduplace.com
Dist(s): **Follett School Solutions.**
Houghton Mifflin Harcourt Supplemental Pubs., (978-1-60032; 978-1-60277) 10801 N. Mopac Expressway, Bldg. 3, Austin, TX 78759 USA
Web site: www.harcourtachieve.com.
Houghton Mifflin Harcourt Trade & Reference Pubs., (978-0-395; 978-0-89919; 978-0-618) Orders Addr.: 9205 Southpark Ctr. Loop, Orlando, FL 32819 USA Tel 978-661-1300; Toll Free: 800-225-3362; Edit Addr.: 222 Berkeley St., Boston, MA 02116 USA (SAN 200-2388) Tel 617-351-5000; Fax: 617-227-5409; 215 Park Ave S., 12th Flr., New York, NY 10003-1621; *Imprints:* Sandpiper (Sandpiper); Houghton Mifflin Books for Children (HMBC)
E-mail: trade_sub_rights@hmco.com
Web site: http://www.hmco.com/; http://www.houghtonmifflinbooks.com
Dist(s): **Blackstone Audio, Inc.**
CENGAGE Learning
Children's Plus, Inc.
CreateSpace Independent Publishing Platform
Ebsco Publishing
Follett School Solutions
Houghton Mifflin Harcourt Publishing Co.
Harcourt Trade Pubs.
HarperCollins Pubs.
Lectorum Pubns., Inc.
MyiLibrary
Open Road Integrated Media, Inc.
Ho'ulu Hou Project: Stories Told by Us *Imprint of* **Na Kamalei Koolauloa Early Education Program**
Hound Dog Pr., The, (978-0-578-42526-9) 6710 River Springs Ct. NW, Atlanta, GA 30328 USA Tel 404-256-0078
E-mail: jimewing21@hotmail.com.
HourGlass Publishing, (978-0-9860205; 978-1-946223) 2095 Hwy. 211 NW Suite 2F-152, Braselton, GA 30517 USA Tel 678-439-9229; Fax: 866-855-1971
E-mail: info@hourglasspublishing.com
Web site: www.HourGlassPublishing.com.
House, David, (978-0-9777086) 1488 Madelyn Ave SE, Salem, OR 97306-3552 USA
Web site: http://www.space-worthy.com.
House of Anansi Pr. (CAN) (978-0-88784; 978-1-77089; 978-1-4870) *Dist. by* **PerseuPGW.**
House of David *See* **Key of David Publishing**
Hse. of Mistofer Christopher, (978-1-7321266) 114-10 202 St., Saint Albans, NY 11412 USA Tel 347-415-6485
E-mail: mistoferchristopher@gmail.com
Web site: Www.mistoferchristopher@gmail.com.
House of Prayer Ministries, Inc., (978-1-882825) 2428 Florian Ct., Decatur, IL 62526 USA Tel 217-428-7077 (phone/fax)
E-mail: vikischerer@comcast.net
Web site: www.houseofprayerministries.com.
House of the Guilded Scribe, (978-0-615-28905-2; 978-0-615-55608-6; 978-0-9914351) P.O. Box 432, Mount Pocono, PA 18344 USA
E-mail: sales@prissyandmissy.com; theguildedscribe@gmail.com; theguildedscribe@yahoo.com; theadventuresofprissyandmissy@yahoo.com
Web site: http://www.wonderfulwondersart.com; http://www.prissyandmissy.com; http://www.prissyandmissy.com.
House of The Lord Fellowship, (978-0-9673530) Orders Addr.: P.O. Box 235, Lock Haven, PA 17745 USA Tel 570-748-6455; Fax: 570-748-6858; Edit Addr.: 201 W. Main St., Lock Haven, PA 17745 USA
E-mail: ssnyder@houseofthelordfellowship.org
Web site: http://www.houseofthelordfellowship.org.
House of Usher *See* **Abysso Bks.**
House Upon A Hill Bks., (978-0-9795826) Orders Addr.: P.O. Box 140322, Broken Arrow, OK 74014 USA; Edit Addr.: 19546 E. 42nd St. S., Broken Arrow, OK 74014 USA.
Houston Enterprises, (978-0-9712861; 978-0-9907800; 978-0-9862339; 978-0-9862349) Orders Addr.: 6320 Rucker Rd. Suite E, Indianapolis, IN 46220 USA Tel 317-726-1901; Fax: 317-726-1902; Toll Free: 888-826-8082
E-mail: info@scotthouston.com
Web site: http://www.scotthouston.com.
Houston, Skyler, (978-0-578-55574-4; 978-0-578-64219-2; 978-0-578-92382-6) 951 Ledge Hill Cove, Lawrenceville, GA 30045 USA Tel 706-207-0177
E-mail: skye_tenese@yahoo.com
Dist(s): **Ingram Content Group.**
Houston Zoo, Inc., (978-0-9762385) 1513 N. MAcGregor, Houston, TX 77030 USA Tel 713-533-6500; Fax: 713-533-6755
E-mail: gwarfield@houstonzoo.org
Web site: http://www.houstonzoo.org.
Houstons Pr., (978-0-578-42900-7; 978-0-578-44878-7; 978-1-7334575) 3035 Stone Mountain St, Lithonia, GA 30058 USA Tel 678-235-4183
E-mail: houstonspressllc@gmil.com.
Houts & Home Pubns. LLC, (978-0-9855084; 979-8-218-06016-9) 26162 Ridge Dr., Maryville, MO 64468 USA Tel 660-562-3122
E-mail: sase@cebridge.net
Web site: www.houtsandhome.com.
How 2 Creative Services, (978-0-9893405; 978-1-7360370) 3220 18th St. S. Suite 8C, Fargo, ND 58104 USA Tel 701-866-4661
E-mail: mark@how2cs.com
Web site: www.how2cs.com.
"How Do You Know", (978-0-9675574) Orders Addr.: P.O. Box 831172, Stone Mountain, GA 30083 USA
E-mail: pjgastonbooks@yahoo.com.
How Great Thou ART Pubns., (978-0-9700405; 978-0-9717874; 978-0-9859000) Orders Addr.: P.O. Box 48, Mcfarlan, NC 28102-0048 USA Tel 704-851-3117; Fax: 704-851-3111; Toll Free: 800-982-3729; Edit Addr.: 357 McFarlin Rd, Morven, NC 28119 USA
E-mail: matthew@howgreatthouart.com
Web site: http://www.howgreatthouart.com/.
How to Make & Keep Friends, LLC, (978-0-692-53121-1; 978-0-9972808) 1 Industrial Way, Tyngsboro, MA 01879 USA Tel 978-392-9865; *Imprints:* Social Success Central, LLC (MYID_B_SOCIAL)
Web site: www.howtomakeandkeepfriends.com
Dist(s): **CreateSpace Independent Publishing Platform.**
Howard Bks. *Imprint of* **Howard Bks.**
Howard, Bob, (978-1-945754) 1304 Buckthorn Cir., Summerville, SC 29483 USA Tel 803-603-3783; *Imprints:* Sunrise Books, LLC (Sunrise Bks LLC)
E-mail: MacBHoward@aol.com
Web site: realbobhoward.com.
Howard Bks., Div. of SIMON & SCHUSTER, 1230 Ave. of the Americas, New York, NY 10020 USA; *Imprints:* Howard Books (Howard Imp)
Dist(s): **Simon & Schuster, Inc.**
Howard, Emma Bks., (978-1-886551) P.O. Box 385, New York, NY 10024-0385 USA Tel 212-996-2590 (phone/fax)
E-mail: emmahowardbooks@verizon.net
Web site: http://www.EellGrassGirls.com.
Howard, Marissa, (978-0-9985935) 104 Hampton Loop Unit 1, Minot AFB, ND 58704 USA Tel 719-439-5500
E-mail: marissahowardbooks@gmail.com.
Howard Printing, Inc., (978-0-9793790) 14 Noahs Ln., Brattleboro, VT 05301 USA Tel 802-254-3550; Fax: 802-257-1453
E-mail: info@howardprintinginc.com
Web site: http://www.howardprintinginc.com.
Howard Ray White, (978-0-9746875; 978-0-9837192; 979-8-9877990) Orders Addr.: 6012 Lancelot Dr., Charlotte, NC 28270 USA Tel 704-242-0022 Howard's cell phone
E-mail: howardraywhite@gmail.com
Web site: http://www.southernhistorians.org; http://www.amazon.com; http://www.howardraywhite.com.
Howard-Hirsch *See* **Howard-Hirsch Publishing**
Howard-Hirsch Publishing, (978-0-9802307) P.O. Box 786, Green, OH 44720 USA (SAN 855-5524)
Web site: http://www.Howardhirschpublishing.com.
Howe, Tina Field, (978-0-9768585) P.O. Box 581, Waverly, NY 14892 USA (SAN 256-8276) Tel 607-329-2458
Web site: http://www.tinafieldhowe.com.
Howell Bk. Hse. *Imprint of* **Wiley, John & Sons, Inc.**
Howell Canyon Pr., (978-1-931210) 1475 N Bundy Dr., Los Angeles, CA 90049 USA (SAN 255-3015) Toll Free: 888-252-0411 (Orders)
E-mail: info@HowellCanyonPress.com
Web site: http://www.AddisonTheDog.com; http://www.howellcanyonpress.com/; http://www.drdeanhowell.com/; http://www.TrishaHowell.com
Dist(s): **Ingram Publisher Services.**
Howell, M Kay *See* **Eagle Tree Pr.**
Howell, Mallory, (978-1-7324216) 128 Tom Pate Rd., Johnson City, TN 37604 USA Tel 423-647-3259
E-mail: malli02@yahoo.com.
Howell, Steven, (978-0-615-15346-9; 978-0-615-19997-9) 697 Superior Ln., Clarksville, TN 37043 USA Tel 931-358-6022
E-mail: mmrshowell2@yahoo.com
Dist(s): **Lulu Pr., Inc.**
Howie, C.J. Co., (978-1-885275) 1695 Quigley Rd., Columbus, OH 43227-3433 USA Tel 614-237-5474.
Howig, Tiffany, (978-0-692-07670-5; 978-0-692-07671-2; 978-0-578-47228-7) 213 Manhattan Blvd., SUNNYVALE, TX 75182 USA Tel 972-655-6916
E-mail: tiffany.howig@gmail.com
Dist(s): **Ingram Content Group.**
HP Bks. *Imprint of* **Penguin Publishing Group**
HPN Publishing, (978-0-9768451) 22902 Sonriente Trail, Trabuco Canyon, CA 92679 USA.
HR Dowling, (978-0-692-83760-3; 978-0-578-40147-8) 5006 51st Ave SW, Seattle, WA 98136 USA Tel 206-747-2055
E-mail: hrdowling@hotmail.com.
H.R. Wallace Publishing, (978-0-692-31112-7; 978-0-692-31125-7; 978-0-692-31138-7; 978-0-692-31621-4; 978-0-692-31624-5; 978-0-692-31627-6; 978-0-692-31634-4; 978-0-692-31635-1; 978-0-692-31637-5; 978-0-692-31639-9; 978-0-692-31644-3; 978-0-692-31646-7; 978-0-692-31648-1; 978-0-692-31649-8; 978-0-692-31651-1; 978-0-692-31660-3; 978-0-692-31667-2; 978-0-692-31668-9; 978-0-692-32363-2; 978-0-692-32368-7; 978-0-692-32370-0; 978-0-692-32374-8; 978-0-692-32377-9; 978-0-692-32378-6; 978-0-692-32501-8; 978-0-692-32502-5;) 909 Mayfield Rd., Sharpsville, PA 16150 USA
Dist(s): **CreateSpace Independent Publishing Platform.**
Hramiec Hoffman Publishing, (978-0-9746901) 6911 M-119 Hwy., Harbor Springs, MI 49740 USA Tel 231-526-1011
Dist(s): **Partners Bk. Distributing, Inc.**
Hub City Pr., (978-0-9638731; 978-1-891885; 978-1-938235; 979-8-88574) Orders Addr.: 186 West Main St., Spartanburg, SC 29306 USA Tel 864-577-9349; Fax: 864-577-0188
E-mail: bteter@bellsouth.net
Web site: http://www.hubcity.org
Dist(s): **Blair**
Publishers Group West (PGW).
Hub City Writers Project *See* **Hub City Pr.**
Hubbard Scientific, Inc., (978-0-8331) Orders Addr.: P.O. Box 760, Chippewa Falls, WI 54729-1468 USA (SAN 202-3121) Tel 715-723-4427; Fax: 715-723-8021; Toll Free: 800-323-8368; Edit Addr.: P.O. Box 760, Chippewa Fls, WI 54729-0760 USA
Web site: http://www.hubbardscientific.com.
Hubbell, Gerald, (978-0-9762042) 4127 Roanoke Rd., Kansas City, MO 64111 USA Tel 816-531-4427
Web site: http://www.malverack.com.
Huckleberry Hill Adventure LLC, (978-0-692-89191-9; 978-0-578-46430-5) 4055 El Bosque Dr., Pebble Beach, CA 93953 USA Tel 831-233-0937
E-mail: huckleberryhilladventure@gmail.com
Web site: huckleberryhilladventure.com.
Hudson, Bidenia, (978-0-692-91356-7; 978-0-578-40023-5) 701 HARVEST GROVE Ln. SE, CONYERS, GA 30013 USA Tel 678-806-5439
E-mail: BHudsonMinistry@gmail.com
Dist(s): **Ingram Content Group.**
Hudson Bks., (978-0-9749860; 978-0-9762502; 978-0-9764459; 978-0-9767789; 978-0-9786296; 978-0-9822553) 244 Madison Ave., No. 254, New York, NY 10016 USA Fax: 718-225-5556; Toll Free: 877-822-2500
Web site: http://www.thefloatingallery.com.
Hudson Hills Press, Incorporated *See* **Hudson Hills Pr. LLC**
†**Hudson Hills Pr. LLC,** (978-0-933920; 978-0-9646042; 978-1-55595) Orders Addr.: P.O. Box 205, Manchester, VT 05254 USA; Edit Addr.: 74-2 Union St., Manchester, VT 05254 USA (SAN 213-0815) Tel 802-362-6450; Fax: 802-362-6459
E-mail: artbooks@hudsonhills.com
Web site: http://www.hudsonhills.com/
Dist(s): **Art Institute of Chicago**
National Bk. Network; *CIP.*
Hudson House Publishing & Productions *See* **Whorl Bks.**
Hudson, Jessie, (978-0-9778922) 14814 Forward Pass, San Antonio, TX 78248 USA
Web site: http://www.OLLIEANDFRIENDS.com.
Hudson, Mary C., (978-0-9627745; 978-0-9722937) 1125 Karen Way, Mountainview, CA 94040 USA Tel 650-948-1270.
Hudson Publishing Group, The *See* **Just Us Bks., Inc.**
Hudson, Russ, (978-0-692-96385-2) 1080 Pinnacle Rd, LIBERTY, ME 04949 USA Tel 802-738-0775
E-mail: russ@cannabizconsultant.com
Dist(s): **Ingram Content Group.**
Hudson-Greenwood, Amonyca, (978-0-578-91748-1) 5720 N. Belt, West Belleville, IL 62207 USA Tel 618-671-0656
E-mail: amonycahudson@yahoo.com.
Hufnagel Software, (978-0-9743881) P.O. Box 747, Clarion, PA 16214-0747 USA Tel 814-226-5600; Fax: 814-226-5551
Web site: http://www.hufsoft.com/books.
Hughes, Betty Barber *See* **Puwaii International, LLC**
Hughes, Millicent, (978-0-692-19146-0; 978-0-578-60746-7) 46 Sydnor St., Hamilton, VA 20158 USA Tel 703-474-1516
E-mail: millicent_hughes@yahoo.com.
Huginn & Muninn, (978-1-937571) 1240 W. Sims Way No. 93, Port Townsend, WA 98368 USA Tel 206-202-0998
E-mail: 2ravens@gmx.com; wyrddesign@unseen.is; huginnandmuninn@gmx.com; heathenmama@gmx.com; carrie@carrieoverton.com; carrie@huginnandmuninn.net
Web site: huginnandmuninn.net.
Hugo House Publishers, Ltd., (978-1-936449; 978-1-948261; 979-8-9888097) 3361 W. Monmouth Ave., Englewood, CO 80110-6336 USA Tel 303-762-1469; Fax: 303-993-5639
E-mail: Patricia@HugoHousePublishers.com.
Hugs Bks. *Imprint of* **Indie Artist Pr.**
Huia Pubs. (NZL) (978-0-908975; 978-1-877266; 978-1-877241; 978-1-877283; 978-1-86969; 978-0-9582517; 978-1-77550-255-5; 978-1-77550-297-5; 978-1-77550-244-9; 978-1-77550-295-1; 978-1-77550-238-8; 978-1-77550-294-4; 978-1-77550-239-5; 978-1-77550-257-9; 978-1-77550-241-8; 978-1-77550-243-2; 978-1-77550-252-4; 978-1-77550-296-8; 978-1-77550-250-0; 978-1-77550-242-5; 978-1-77550-247-0; 978-1-77550-253-1; 978-1-77550-240-1; 978-1-77550-245-6; 978-1-77550-254-8; 978-1-77550-248-7; 978-1-77550-256-2; 978-1-77550) *Dist. by* **UH Pr.**
Hula Moon Pr., (978-0-9794649) P.O. Box 11173, Honolulu, HI 96828 USA Tel 808-947-6470
Dist(s): **BookBaby.**
Hulliberger, Elaine, (978-0-615-31129-6) 1703 Stamping Ground Rd., Georgetown, KY 40324-9130 USA.
Hulme Publishing, (978-0-9991262) 9 Mountain Laurel Dr., Greenwich, CT 06831 USA Tel 203-622-5131
E-mail: dhulme@optonline.net.
Human Consciousness Consortium, (978-1-7324336; 978-1-956129) 3450 Roxboro Road, NE 4111, ATLANTA, GA 30326 USA Tel 833-300-9990
E-mail: snicholas007@gmail.com
Web site: http://SusanNicholas.org.
Human Factor LLC, (978-0-9816472) P.O. Box 3742, Washington, DC 20027 USA (SAN 856-1109)
E-mail: info@humanfactor.net
Web site: http://www.humanfactor.net.
†**Human Kinetics,** (978-0-7360; 978-0-87322; 978-0-88011; 978-0-918438; 978-0-931250; 978-1-4504; 978-1-4925; 978-1-7182) Orders Addr.: P.O. Box 5076, Champaign, IL 61825-5076 USA (SAN 211-7088) Tel 217-351-5076; Toll Free: 800-747-4457; Edit Addr.: 1607 N. Market St., Champaign, IL 61820 USA (SAN 658-0866) Tel 217-351-5076; Fax: 217-351-1549; Toll Free: 800-747-4457
E-mail: humank@hkusa.com; info@hkusa.com
Web site: http://www.humankinetics.com; http://www.hkusa.com
Dist(s): **Follett School Solutions**
MyiLibrary
ebrary, Inc.; *CIP.*
Human Kinetics Publishers *See* **Human Kinetics**
Human Relations Media, (978-1-55548; 978-1-62706) 41 Kensico Dr., Mount Kisco, NY 10549 USA (SAN 287-4873) Tel 914-244-0486; Fax: 914-244-0485; Toll Free: 800-431-2050
Web site: http://www.hrmvideo.com.
Human Values 4 Kids Foundation, The, (978-0-9798986; 978-1-7331428) Orders Addr.: 11498 Pyrites Way, Gold River, CA 95670-6226 USA; Edit Addr.: 11498 Pyrites Way, Gold River, CA 95670-6226 USA
E-mail: vvnambiar@sbcglobal.net
Web site: https://www.hv4k.org/; http://www.thehumanvalues4kidsfoundation.org.
Humana *Imprint of* **Springer New York**
Humane Society Pr. *Imprint of* **National Assn. for Humane & Environmental Education**
Humanics Learning *Imprint of* **Green Dragon Bks.**
Humanics Publishing Group *See* **Green Dragon Bks.**
Humanist Pr. *Imprint of* **American Humanist Assn.**
Humanness Project Pr., The, (978-0-9891086) 63 Beacon Cir., Cranston, RI 02910 USA Tel 401-467-9240
E-mail: colbyahopkins@gmail.com.
Humanoids, Inc., (978-0-9672401; 978-1-930652; 978-1-59465; 978-1-64337) Orders Addr.: 8033 Sunset Blvd. #628, Los Angeles, CA 90046 USA Tel 323-522-5466; Fax: 323-892-2848; *Imprints:* BiG (BiGHuman)
E-mail: alex.donoghue@humanoids.com
Web site: http://www.humanoids.com/
Dist(s): **Diamond Comic Distributors, Inc.**
DKE Toys
Ingram Publisher Services
Simon & Schuster, Inc.
Humble Heart Publishing, (978-0-9712922) 267 Crane Orchard Rd., Brewster, WA 98812 USA
Web site: humblehearpublishing.com.
Humming Meadow Ranch, (978-0-9766431) 47265 Twin Pines Rd., Banning, CA 92220-9656 USA Tel 951-849-1803; Fax: 951-849-9091
E-mail: elaine@hummingmeadowranch.com
Web site: http://www.hummingmeadowranch.com.
Hummingbird, (978-0-615-93231-6; 978-0-692-45597-5; 978-0-578-75086-6) 2081 murdock rd, marietta, GA 30062 USA Tel 4155395777
Dist(s): **CreateSpace Independent Publishing Platform.**
Hummingbird Jewel Pr., (978-0-9981700) 137 So. Reeves Dr., No. 405, Beverly Hills, CA 90212 USA Tel 310-278-3189
E-mail: rjslewis@aol.com.
Hummingbird Mountain Pr., (978-0-9746792) P.O. Box 127, Midpines, CA 95345-0127 USA
Web site: http://www.sierratel.com/hummingbirdmountain.

Publisher Name Index

Hummingbird World Media *Imprint of* **Double Edge Pr.**

Humor & Communication, *(978-0-9677844; 978-0-9820466)* 709 Doe Trail, Edmond, OK 73012 USA
E-mail: hduncan2@cox.net
Web site: http://www.hallduncan.com.

Humphrey, Daniel, *(978-1-7336598)* 7508 Red Oak Ct., Lincoln, NE 68516 USA Tel 402-489-6705
E-mail: dmhumphrey31@yahoo.com.

Humphreys, Kevin, *(978-0-9745727)* P.O. Box 10731, Spokane, WA 99220 USA; 1312 N. Brook Terrace St., Spokane, WA 99224-5678.

Hundred Ways LLC, A, *(978-0-9789544)* 18034 Ventura Blvd., No. 491, Encino, CA 91316 USA Tel 818-708-0558
E-mail: admin@ahundredways.com
Web site: http://www.whenwordsdream.com.

Hungry Bear Publishing, *(978-0-9754007; 978-0-9857607)* Orders Addr.: 40 McClelland St., Saranac Lake, NY 12983 USA Tel 518-891-5559
Web site: http://www.hungrybearpublishing.com
Dist(s): **North Country Bks., Inc.**

Hungry Goat Pr. *Imprint of* **Gauthier Pubns. Inc.**

Hungry Tiger Pr., *(978-0-9644988; 978-1-929527)* 5995 Dandridge Ln., Suite 121, San Diego, CA 92115-6575 USA
E-mail: books@hungrytigerpress.com
Web site: http://www.hungrytigerpress.com.

Hungry Tomato (r) *Imprint of* **Lerner Publishing Group**

Hungry Tomato Ltd. (GBR) *(978-1-910684; 978-1-912108; 978-1-913077; 978-1-913440; 978-1-914087) Dist. by* **BTPS.**

Hunt, J. L. Publishing, *(978-0-9769401)* Orders Addr.: 27881 La Paz Rd., Suite G-124, Laguna Niguel, CA 92677 USA Tel 949-751-7511; Fax: 949-363-8559
E-mail: james@chewnomore.com.

Hunt, J.L. Publishing *See* **Hunt, J. L. Publishing**

Hunt, John Publishing Ltd. (GBR) *(978-1-85608; 978-1-903019; 978-1-84298; 978-1-903816; 978-1-905047; 978-1-84694; 978-1-78099; 978-1-78904) Dist. by* **Natl Bk Netwk.**

Hunt, John Publishing Ltd. (GBR) *(978-1-85608; 978-1-903019; 978-1-84298; 978-1-903816; 978-1-905047; 978-1-84694; 978-1-78099; 978-1-78904) Dist. by* **STL Dist.**

Hunt Thompson Media, *(978-0-9630377)*
E-mail: cjhunt@huntthompsonmedia.com; cjhunt3@gmail.com
Web site: http://www.PerfectHumanDiet.com; http://www.HuntThompsonMedia.com.

Hunter Hse. *Imprint of* **Turner Publishing Co.**

Hunter, J. H. Publishing, *(978-0-9718274)* 8100 Schmuck Rd., Evansville, IN 47712 USA Tel 812-985-5013.

Hunter, Julius K. *See* **J.K.H. Enterprises**

Hunter, Karen Media, *(978-0-9820221; 978-0-9845060)* P.O. Box 632, South Orange, NJ 07079 USA (SAN 857-0167)
Web site: http://www.karenhuntermedia.com; http://www.karenhuntermedia.com; www.readourbooks.com.

Hunter Pubns., *(978-0-9654185)* P.O. Box 433, Vallejo, CA 94589 USA Tel 707-645-8714; Fax: 707-644-7880.

Hunter Publishing, Inc., *(978-1-55650; 978-1-58843)* Orders Addr.: 222 Clematis St., West Palm Beach, FL 33401 USA Do not confuse with Hunter Publishing, Inc., Hobe Sound, FL
E-mail: comments@hunterpublishing.com
Web site: http://www.hunterpublishing.com
Dist(s): **Ebsco Publishing**
Cengage Gale
MyiLibrary
ebrary, Inc.

Hunter, Torrance, *(978-0-692-94807-1)* 1210 Concord Pl, MISSOURI CITY, TX 77459 USA Tel 713-435-9734
E-mail: torrancehunter1@gmail.com
Dist(s): **Independent Pub.**

HuntForMo Creations, *(978-0-9740182)* 3718 Brentford Rd., Randallstown, MD 21133 USA Toll Free: 800-327-9779
E-mail: monique@huntformo.com
Web site: http://www.huntformo.com.

Huntington Library Pr., *(978-0-87328)* Div. of Huntington Library, Art Collections & Botanical Gardens, 1151 Oxford Rd., San Marino, CA 91108 USA (SAN 202-313X) Tel 626-405-2172; Fax: 626-585-0794
E-mail: booksales@huntington.org
Web site: http://www.Huntington.org/HEHPubs.html
Dist(s): **Angel City Pr.**
California Princeton Fulfillment Services
D.A.P./Distributed Art Pubs.
Gibbs Smith, Publisher.

Huntington Library Publications *See* **Huntington Library Pr.**

Huntington Ludlow Media Group, *(978-0-9789057)* 5320 Maverick Dr., Grand Prairie, TX 75052-2617 USA (SAN 851-9080)
Web site: http://www.huntingtonludlow.com.

Huntley, Shannon, *(978-0-578-55297-2)* 1003 Creech Rd, Garner, NC 27529 USA Tel 919-637-6905
E-mail: brainbunts@gmail.com.

Huntly Hse., *(978-0-9885349; 978-0-615-73405-7)* 1965 Murcer Ln., Elgin, IL 60123 USA Tel 847-312-5904
E-mail: cfurtick@huntlyhouse.com
Web site: www.huntlyhouse.com.

Hunton, Carroll & Wenonah, *(978-0-9758873)* P.O. Box 1048, Albuquerque, NM 87103-1048 USA
E-mail: alan@excelstaff.com.

Huqua Pr., *(978-0-615-43791-0; 978-0-9838120; 978-0-9906966; 978-0-692-41659-3; 978-0-692-17579-8; 978-0-578-41353-2; 978-0-578-52073-5; 978-0-578-55090-9; 978-1-7353844; 979-8-218-11731-3)* 8730 Sunset Blvd., Los Angeles, CA 90069 USA Tel 818-981-5262
E-mail: judy@magpyemedia.com
Dist(s): **MyiLibrary**
Open Road Integrated Media, Inc.

Huron River Pr., *(978-1-932399)*
E-mail: info@huronriverpress.com
Web site: http://www.huronriverpress.com
Dist(s): **Partners Bk. Distributing, Inc.**

Hurst, Carol Consultants, *(978-0-9748509)* 41 Colony Dr., Westfield, MA 01085 USA Tel 413-562-3412
E-mail: carol@carolhurst.com
Web site: http://www.carolhurst.com
Dist(s): **Follett School Solutions.**

Huseby, Kirby, *(978-0-9778494)* P.O. Box 8034, Kentwood, MI 49518 USA
E-mail: staytoond@aol.com.

Husk, Braxton, *(978-0-578-18412-8)* 30 Bitterwoord Circle, The Woodlands, TX 77381 USA.

Huskies Pub *Imprint of* **MacLaren-Cochrane Publishing**

Husky Trail Pr. LLC, *(978-0-9722918; 978-1-935258)* Orders Addr.: P.O. Box 705, East Lyme, CT 06333-0705 USA Tel 860-739-7644; Fax: 860-739-3702
Web site: http://www.huskytrailpress.com.

Huss Publishing *See* **Huss, Sally Inc.**

Huss, Sally Inc., *(978-0-9822625; 978-0-692-31737-2; 978-0-692-33084-5; 978-0-692-33945-9; 978-0-692-34415-6; 978-0-692-34837-6; 978-0-692-35119-2; 978-0-692-35180-2; 978-0-692-35238-0; 978-0-692-35546-6; 978-0-692-36087-3; 978-0-692-36353-9; 978-0-692-36513-7; 978-0-692-36666-0; 978-0-692-38150-2; 978-0-692-38247-9; 978-0-692-38875-4; 978-0-692-39364-2; 978-0-692-39483-0; 978-0-692-39581-3; 978-0-692-39598-1; 978-0-692-39683-4; 978-0-692-39848-7; 978-0-692-40015-9; 978-0-692-40262-7; 978-0-692-40587-1; 978-) Orders Addr.: 10 El Sereno Dr., Colorado Springs, CO 80906 USA*
Dist(s): **CreateSpace Independent Publishing Platform.**

Hussl, Gloria, *(978-0-9791468)* 5818 Trinity Rd., Needville, TX 77461 USA Tel 832-595-5678
E-mail: gloriasunrisefarms@yahoo.com.

Hutchings, John Pubs., *(978-1-935014)* 621 Dogleg Ln., Bartlett, IL 60103 USA Tel 630-736-6088; *Imprints:* Lessons From The Vine (LFTV)
E-mail: kaththompson@att.net.

Hutchings, Vicki, *(978-0-578-72760-8)* 1945 S. 800 W., Mapleton, UT 84664 USA Tel 801-489-5994
E-mail: vickihutchings@gmail.com.

Hutchison, G.F. Pr., *(978-1-885631; 978-0-9796279)* 319 S. Block, Suite 17, Fayetteville, AR 72701-6484 USA Tel 479-587-1726; *Imprints:* Family Of Man Press, The (Family Of Man Pr)
E-mail: drwriterguy@netscape.net
Web site: http://www.thehappinessplace.com.

Hutman Productions, *(978-0-9702386; 978-0-9833573; 978-0-9854486; 978-1-7320830; 978-1-7352875)* P.O. Box 268, Linthicum, MD 21090 USA Tel 410-789-0930
E-mail: cbladey@verizon.net
Web site: http://www./cbladey.com/hutmanA.html.

Hutt, Sarah, *(978-0-9743417)* 1140 Washington St., No. 7, Boston, MA 02118 USA Tel 617-482-4722
Web site: http://www.mymotherslegacy.com.

Hutton Electronic Publishing, *(978-0-9742894; 978-0-9785171; 978-0-9888775)* 160 N. Compo Rd., Westport, CT 06880 USA
E-mail: huttonbooks@hotmail.com
Web site: http://www.huttonelectronicpublishing.com.

Huu, Andre, *(978-0-578-40283-3)* 4911 Harvest Chase Ln., Sugar Land, TX 77479 USA Tel 832-418-8860
E-mail: andrePT228@aol.com
Web site: www.golfroundofyourlife.com.

Huzon Fyrst Pr., *(978-0-9970483)* 19805 Shearwater Point Dr., Cornelius, NC 28031 USA Tel 704-892-8899
E-mail: wolfeskin@hotmail.com
Web site: www.149waystowipeyourass.com.

HVOE Media, *(978-1-954829)* 964 S 4th St., Philadelphia, PA 19147 USA Tel 267-255-8888
E-mail: whoisnikihurtz@gmail.com.

Hybrid Age Pr., *(978-1-7323192)* 34 Dodd St, Montclair, NJ 07042 USA Tel 862-220-1634
E-mail: tanejaarchitecture@gmail.com; info@hybridagepress,com
Web site: hybridagepress.com.

Hydra Productions Online LLC, *(978-1-951178)* 2500 E Pk. Blvd, Plano, TX 75074 USA Tel 214-298-3132
E-mail: hydraproductions2018@gmail.com.

Hydra Pubns., *(978-0-615-43242-7; 978-0-615-49378-7; 978-0-615-49820-1; 978-0-615-49950-5; 978-0-615-50445-2; 978-0-615-56017-5; 978-0-615-56345-9; 978-0-615-56584-2; 978-0-615-59650-1; 978-0-615-59651-8; 978-0-615-59822-2; 978-0-615-60737-5; 978-0-615-63328-2; 978-0-615-63783-9; 978-0-615-63858-4; 978-0-615-63863-8; 978-0-615-63882-9; 978-0-615-65016-6; 978-0-615-67766-8; 978-0-615-67970-9; 978-0-615-67972-3; 978-0-615-67974-7; 978-0-615-68018-7; 978-0-615-68422-2; 978-0-615-68969-2; 978-0-615-69010-0;) 337 Clifty Dr., Madison, IN 47250 USA Tel 812-574-4113*
Web site: http://www.hydrapublications.com
Dist(s): **CreateSpace Independent Publishing Platform**
Dummy Record Do Not USE!!!!.

Hydra Publishing *See* **Hylas Publishing**

Hydrangea Pr., *(978-0-9768418)* 22 Plumer Rd., Epping, NH 03042 USA Tel 603-679-9544
E-mail: mswegles@comcast.net
Web site: http://www.plumercrest.com.

Hylas Publishing, *(978-1-59258)* 129 Main St., Irvington, NY 10533 USA Fax: 914-591-3220
E-mail: hydrapublishing@mac.com
Dist(s): **St. Martin's Pr.**

Hyles Publications *See* **Grace to Grow Pubns.**

Hylton, Scott, *(978-0-615-97172-8)* 32215 Big Oak LN, Castaic, CA 91384 USA Tel 661-702-9972
E-mail: oneworldpeacenow@yahoo.com.

Hyperion Books for Children *Imprint of* **Disney Publishing Worldwide**

†**Hyperion Bks. for Children,** *(978-0-7868; 978-1-56282)* Div. of Disney Bk. Publishing, Inc., A Walt Disney Co., Orders Addr.: 3 Center Plaza, Boston, MA 02108 USA Toll Free: 800-759-0190; Edit Addr.: 114 Fifth Ave., New York, NY 10011 USA Tel 212-633-4400; Fax: 212-633-4833; *Imprints:* Jump at the Sun (Jump at the Sun); Volo (Volo); di Capua, Michael Books (diCapua Bks)
Web site: http://www.disney.com; http://www.hyperionbooksforchildren.com
Dist(s): **Children's Plus, Inc.**
Disney Publishing Worldwide
Hachette Bk. Group
Little Brown & Co.; *CIP.*

†**Hyperion Paperbacks for Children,** *(978-0-7868; 978-1-56282)* Div. of Disney Bk. Publishing, Inc., A Walt Disney Co., 114 Fifth Ave., New York, NY 10011 USA Tel 212-633-4400; Fax: 212-633-4833
Web site: http://www.disney.com
Dist(s): **Hachette Bk. Group**
Little Brown & Co.; *CIP.*

†**Hyperion Pr.,** *(978-0-7868; 978-1-56282; 978-1-4013)* Div. of Disney Bk. Publishing, Inc., A Walt Disney Co., Orders Addr.: c/o HarperCollins Publishers, 1000 Keystone Industrial Park, Scranton, PA 18512-4621 USA Toll Free: 800-242-7737; Edit Addr.: 114 Fifth Ave., New York, NY 110011 USA Tel 917-661-2000
Web site: http://www.hyperionbooks.com
Dist(s): **Blackstone Audio, Inc.**
Children's Plus, Inc.
Follett School Solutions
Hachette Bk. Group
MyiLibrary; *CIP.*

hyperwerks *See* **Hyperwerks Entertainment**

Hyperwerks Entertainment, *(978-0-9770213)* 1830 Stoner Ave. Apt. 6, Los Angeles, CA 90025-7319 USA
Web site: http://www.hyperwerks.com.

HyphenatedPr., *(978-0-615-75998-2)* 6737 Roosevelt Dr, Sylvania, OH 43560 USA Tel 419-340-4654
E-mail: chadmichaelsimon@gmail.com.

i ZGOOL Media, *(978-0-9885898)* 100 Andover Pk. W Suite 150-237, Tukwila, WA 98188 USA Tel 206-851-1065
E-mail: fredbc11@gmail.com.

I AM Children Bks., *(978-1-7362195)* 9 Horseshoe, Oak Ridge, NJ 07438 USA Tel 201-264-5542
E-mail: Janine@iamchildrenbooks.com
Web site: iamchildrenbooks.com.

I AM Foundation, The, *(978-0-9645224; 978-0-9831780; 978-0-615-70944-4)* 7825 Fay Ave., Suite 200, La Jolla, CA 92037 USA Tel 619-297-7010
E-mail: iam@iamfoundation.org
Web site: http://www.iamfoundation.org
Dist(s): **CreateSpace Independent Publishing Platform**
DeVorss & Co.
New Leaf Distributing Co., Inc.

I Am My Life Publishing, LLC, *(978-0-9973805)* 611 Pennsylvania Ave., SE No. 120, Washington, DC 20003 USA Tel 720-252-9578; *Imprints:* Kaleidoscope Books (KaleidoscopebKS)
E-mail: rachelfosterstuart@gmail.com.

I AM Publishing, *(978-0-9905276)* 2370 Hwy 89A No. 11, Sedona, AZ 86336 USA Tel 805-729-0515
E-mail: danielposney@gmail.com
Web site: www.OneWhiteStone.com.

I Am Your Playground LLC, *(978-0-9769580)* P.O. Box 301, Fanwood, NJ 07023-0301 USA Fax: 908-301-0777; Toll Free: 888-759-4736 (888-PLY-GRND)
E-mail: john@iamyourplayground.com
Web site: http://www.iamyourplayground.com.

I & L Publishing, *(978-0-9661244; 978-1-930002)* 174 Oak Dr. Pkwy., Oroville, CA 95966 USA Tel 530-589-5048; Fax: 530-589-3551; Toll Free: 888-443-4722
E-mail: iolamoore@juno.com
Dist(s): **Morris Publishing.**

i. b. d., Ltd., *(978-0-88431)* 24 Hudson St., Kinderhook, NY 12106 USA (SAN 630-7779) Tel 518-758-1755; Fax: 518-758-6702
E-mail: lankhof@ibdltd.com
Web site: http://www.ibdltd.com.

IBE, Inc., *(978-0-916547; 978-0-9785848)* Div. of Inspiration Bks. East, Inc., Orders Addr.: P.O. Box 352, Jemison, AL 35085 USA (SAN 295-4672) Tel 205-646-2941; Edit Addr.: 170 Cty. Rd. 749, Jemison, AL 35085 USA
E-mail: communications@inbookseast.org
Web site: http://www.inbookseast.org.

I. B. Hoofinit Co., *(978-1-928890)* Orders Addr.: 94 Rte. 130, Forestdale, MA 02644 USA
E-mail: ibhoofinit@yahoo.com
Web site: http://ibhoofinit.com.

I. B. Tauris & Co., Ltd. (GBR) *(978-0-302; 978-0-85667; 978-1-85043; 978-1-86064; 978-1-84511; 978-1-84885; 978-1-78076; 978-0-85772; 978-0-85771; 978-1-78672; 978-1-78673; 978-1-78831; 978-0-7556; 978-0-85773; 978-1-78453; 978-1-78130) Dist. by* **Macmillan.**

I C A, *(978-0-9747506)* P.O. Box 910, Wayne, MI 48184-9998 USA Fax: 734-595-1869
E-mail: codemanray@aol.com
Web site: http://www.thefemalecode.com.

I C Legacy LLC, *(978-1-7320698)* 18 First Ave, Westbury, NY 11590 USA Tel 646-883-5393
E-mail: creations@iclegacy.com
Web site: www.iclegacy.com.

I Can Do All Things Productions, *(978-0-9745787)* 8 Loveland St., Madison, NJ 07940 USA Tel 973-377-5970; Fax: 973-377-5970
E-mail: seucony@optonline.net
Web site: http://www.perfectpraisebooks.com.

I E E E * Standards *See* **IEEE**

I F D Publishing, *(978-0-9671912; 978-0-9887767; 978-0-9965536; 978-0-9988466; 978-0-9996656; 978-1-7342978; 979-8-9852827)* P.O. Box 40776, Eugene, OR 97404 USA Tel 541-461-3272; Fax: 541-461-3686
E-mail: contact@ifdpublishing.com
Web site: http://www.ifdpublishing.com.

I F V, Inc., *(978-1-931861)* 1045 Coddington Rd., Ithaca, NY 14850 USA
E-mail: ifv@lightlink.com
Web site: http://www.classicalfencing.com.

I Follow the Leader, LLC, *(978-1-7321045)* 2001 Windcliff Dr Marietta, GA 30067 USA Tel 404-324-6310
E-mail: thegreenfamilybooks@gmail.com
Web site: thegreenfamilybooks.com.

I Global, *(978-0-692-29250-1; 978-0-692-32768-5; 978-0-692-32769-2; 978-0-692-32770-8; 978-0-692-32771-5; 978-0-692-32772-2; 978-0-692-32774-6; 978-0-692-32775-3)* 400 Shelton St. Greensboro, NC 27405 USA Tel 3105703425.

I Have A Voice Enterprises, *(978-0-9746192)* P.O. Box 83, Peshtigo, WI 54157 USA
Web site: http://www.thehidersstory.com.

I Play Math Games *See* **IPMG Publishing**

I S H K, *(978-0-86304; 978-0-900860; 978-1-883536; 978-1-933779; 978-1-942698; 978-1-944493; 978-1-946270; 978-1-948013; 978-1-949358; 978-1-953292; 978-1-958289; 978-1-959393; 978-1-960884)* Div. of Institute for the Study of Human Knowledge, Ishk-hoopoe-malor 548 Market St. No. 39187, San Francisco, CA 91404-5401 USA (SAN 226-4536) Tel 408-445-9639; Ishk-hoopoe-malor 548 Market St. No. 39187, San Francisco, CA 91404-5401 Tel 408-445-9639; *Imprints:* Malor Books (Malor Bks); Hoopoe Books (Hoopoe Books)
E-mail: ishkadmin@ishk.net
Web site: http://www.ishk.net; http://www.hoopoebooks.com; http://www.malorbooks.com.

I S M Teaching Systems, Inc., *(978-1-56775)* 14132 Desert Willow, El Paso, TX 79938 USA Tel 915-856-6365; Fax: 915-856-6367; Toll Free: 800-453-4476
E-mail: Email4ism@aol.com
Web site: http://www16.inetba.com/ismteachingsystemsinc.

I S R P Press *See* **Sound Reading Solutions**

I Save A Tree, *(978-0-9714299; 978-0-9744670; 978-0-9745659; 978-1-61015)* Orders Addr.: P.O. Box 3006, Arcadia, FL 34265 USA
Web site: http://www.garrettbooks.com; http://www.isaveatree.com.

I See Puppy, LLP, *(978-0-9774277)* Orders Addr.: 107 Richard Mine Rd., Dover, NJ 07801 USA (SAN 257-554X) Tel 973-361-8637; Fax: 973-361-8035
E-mail: info@iseepuppy.com
Web site: http://www.iseepuppy.com.

I WANNA BEE DESIGNS, *(978-0-9986664)* 2117 Markland Dr., Chesapeake, VA 23325 USA Tel 757-424-1357
E-mail: maadukes@yahoo.com.

i wantz Publishing, *(978-0-9727998)* P.O. Box 9305, Grand Rapids, MI 49509-0305 USA
E-mail: elizabeth@iwantz.com
Web site: http://www.iwantz.com.

i-5 Publishing LLC, *(978-0-87714; 978-0-944875; 978-0-9629525; 978-1-882770; 978-1-889540; 978-1-931993; 978-1-59378; 978-0-9745407; 978-1-933342; 978-1-933958; 978-1-935484; 978-1-937049; 978-1-62008; 978-1-62187)* 10 Bridge St., Bldg. C, Metuchen, NJ 08840 USA Tel 949-855-8822 (ext. 1003); Fax: 732-960-3107
Dist(s): **MyiLibrary.**

IAC Publishing, *(978-0-9748383)* 3432 Denny St., No. 3, Pittsburgh, PA 15201 USA Toll Free: 877-592-0237
Web site: http://www.irishamericancatholic.com.

Iaconi, Mariuccia Bk. Imports, *(978-0-9628720)* P.O. Box 77023, San Francisco, CA 94107-0023 USA (SAN 161-1364) Toll Free: 800-955-9577
E-mail: mibibook@ixnetcom.com
Web site: http://www.mibibook.com
Dist(s): **Lectorum Pubns., Inc.**

IAHunt, *(978-0-9986851)* 7102 Capitol View Dr., McLean, VA 22101 USA Tel 703-893-0809
E-mail: iah2nd@aol.com.

IamCoach.com Publishing, *(978-0-9754761)* P.O. Box 60088, King of Prussia, PA 19406 USA
E-mail: publishing@iamcoach.com
Web site: http://www.IamCoach.com/chess/publishing/
Dist(s): **SCB Distributors.**

IAMPress, *(978-0-9768782; 978-0-9794839)* 3053 Dumbarton Rd., Memphis, TN 38128 USA Tel 901-358-2226; Fax: 901-358-8102
E-mail: renford@iam-cor.org
Web site: http://www.iam-cor.org
Dist(s): **Lulu Pr., Inc.**

IAMSA Creations, LLC *See* **Unlimited Possibilities Publishing, LLC**

IbbiLane Pr., *(978-0-692-23847-9; 978-0-692-45419-0; 978-0-692-56380-9; 978-0-692-64185-9; 978-0-692-67314-0; 978-0-692-68980-6; 978-0-692-69439-8; 978-0-692-73498-8; 978-0-692-74914-2; 978-0-692-76249-3; 978-0-692-77268-3; 978-0-692-78145-6; 978-0-692-80913-6; 978-0-692-81980-7; 978-0-692-82333-0; 978-0-692-83308-7; 978-0-692-83863-1; 978-0-692-87396-0; 978-0-692-92279-8; 978-0-692-97660-9; 978-0-692-04470-4; 978-0-692-07227-1; 978-0-692-11264-9; 978-0-692-19171-2; 978-0-578-45573-0; 978-0-578-62139-5;) 9233 E Carolyn Fraser Ln, Pearce, AZ 85625 USA Tel 5205071027*
E-mail: fitzgeraldtoo@yahoo.com
Dist(s): **CreateSpace Independent Publishing Platform.**

IBE, *(978-1-7336854)* 3908 Webster St, Brentwood, MD 20722 USA Tel 954-498-6573
E-mail: royalblackbook@gmail.com.

erian Press *See* **7 Robots, Inc.**

ex Pubs., Inc., *(978-0-936347; 978-1-58814)* Orders Addr.: P.O. Box 30087, Bethesda, MD 20824 USA (SAN 696-866X) Tel 301-718-8188; Fax: 301-907-8707; Toll Free: 888-718-8188
E-mail: info@ibexpub.com
Web site: http://www.ibexpublishers.com.

J Custom Publishing, *(978-0-9745673; 978-0-9776675; 978-0-9798830; 978-1-934922; 978-1-939550; 978-1-950143)* 41 E. Washington St., Suite 200, Indianapolis, IN 46204 USA.

3J Media Custom Publishing *See* **IBJ Custom Publishing**

Bks., Inc.,
Dist(s): **National Bk. Network.**

books, Inc., *(978-0-671; 978-0-7434; 978-1-58824; 978-1-59176; 978-1-59687; 978-1-59687-543-2)* 100 Jericho Quadrangle. Ste. 300, Jericho, NY 11753-2702 USA; *Imprints:* Milk & Cookies (Milk-Cookie); ipicturebooks (Ipicbks)
Web site: http://www.ibooksinc.com.

books, Incorporated/ipictures.com *See* **ibooks, Inc.**

bukku, LLC, *(978-0-9896324; 978-0-9862586; 978-0-9965541; 978-1-944278; 978-1-946035; 978-1-64086; 978-1-68574)* 3723 Haven Ave. Suite 109, Menlo Park, CA 94025 USA Tel 650-204-1962
E-mail: luiscrowe@gmail.com; ljcrowe@ibukku.com
Web site: https://ibukku.com.

I C Creative, Inc., *(978-0-9742714)* 2300 Michigan Ct., Suite B, Arlington, TX 76016 USA Tel 817-459-8079; Fax: 817-460-0430
E-mail: joi@stayintouchmail.com
Web site: http://www.stayintouchmail.com.

ICAN Press *See* **Black Forest Pr.**

ICanPublish, *(978-0-9711480)* Div. of Heckman Bindery, Inc., P.O. Box 89, North Manchester, IN 46962 USA (SAN 253-9500) Tel 260-982-2107; Fax: 260-982-1130; Toll Free: 800-334-3628
E-mail: dave_mcintyre@heckmanbindery.com.

Ice Age Park and Trail Foundation, Inc., *(978-0-9627079)* 2453 Atwood Ave. STOP 4, Madison, WI 53704-5682 USA
E-mail: iat@iceagetrail.org
Web site: http://www.iceagetrail.org.

Ice Cube Pr., LLC, *(978-1-888160; 978-1-948509)* 205 N. Front St., North Liberty, IA 52317 USA (SAN 298-9085) Tel 319-626-2055; 319-594-6022
E-mail: steve@icecubepress.com
Web site: http://www.icecubepress.com
Dist(s): **Quality Bks., Inc.**

Ice Mountain Publishing, *(978-0-9748814)* P.O. Box 1418, Salida, CO 81201 USA
E-mail: nathanward@amigo.net.

Ice Wine Productions, Inc. *See* **Ice Wine Productions, Inc.**

Ice Wine Productions, Inc., *(978-0-9981666; 979-8-9863836)* 4415 N Bayview Rd., Southold, NY 11971 USA Tel 631-765-8287; *Imprints:* An Ice Wine book. (MYID_W_AN ICE)
E-mail: writegw@gmail.com
Web site: www.geoffreywellsfiction.com.

Icecat Bks., *(978-0-9764308; 978-0-9768670)* 1243 Old Canyon Dr., Hacienda Heights, CA 91745 USA Tel 626-333-2430
E-mail: contact@icecatbooks.com
Web site: http://www.icecatbooks.com.

Ichabod Ink, *(978-0-9766641)* 418 Lake George Cir., West Chester, PA 19382 USA.

iCharacter.org, *(978-1-62387; 978-1-63474)* Orders Addr.: 6-9 Trinity St., Dublin, 2 IRL; *Imprints:* Kidible (Kidible)
E-mail: info@icharacter.org
Web site: www.icharacter.org.

Icilcle Falls Publishing Co., *(978-0-9749360)* Orders Addr.: HC 31, Box 5118A, Wasilla, AK 99654 USA; Edit Addr.: Hc31 B0x 5118a, Wasilla, AK 99654 USA
Web site: www.alaskanstoires.com
Dist(s): **American News Company.**

Icon Bks., Ltd. (GBR) *(978-1-874166; 978-1-84046; 978-1-906850; 978-1-84831; 978-1-78578)* *Dist. by* **PerseuPGW.**

Icon Group International, Inc., *(978-0-7576; 978-0-7418; 978-0-597; 978-0-497; 978-0-546; 978-1-114)* Div. of Icon Group, Ltd., P.O. Box 27740, Las Vegas, NV 89126-7440 USA (SAN 299-8122) Tel 858-635-9410; Fax: 858-635-9414
E-mail: ula@icongroupbooks.com; meta@icongroupbooks.com; orders@icongroupbooks.com
Web site: http://www.icongrouponline.com
Dist(s): **CreateSpace Independent Publishing Platform**
Ebsco Publishing
MyiLibrary.

Icon Language Systems, Inc. *See* **Ampersand, Inc.**

ICONS Foundation, The *See* **ICONS Foundation, The**

iCreate Publishing, *(978-0-578-42588-7)* 2650 FM 407 E. Ste 145/150, Bartonville, TX 76226 USA Tel 505-330-9076
E-mail: admin@peopleprosper.com
Dist(s): **Independent Pub.**

ICS Pr., *(978-1-890825)* Div. of International Community of Submitters/Masjid Tucson (I C S), Orders Addr.: P.O. Box 43476, Tucson, AZ 85733-3476 USA Tel 520-323-7636; Edit Addr.: 5010 E. Bellevue St., Tucson, AZ 85716 USA
Web site: www.masjidtucson.org.

ICT Intuition, *(978-1-7359830)* 1804 Sycamore Ridge, Kearney, MO 64060 USA Tel 920-216-6379
E-mail: nruzicka@ictintuition.com.

Idaho State Journal, *(978-0-9749865; 978-0-615-47497-7)* Orders Addr.: P.O. Box 431, Pocatello, ID 83204 USA; Edit Addr.: P.O. Box 431, Pocatello, ID 83204-0431 USA
Web site: http://www.journalnet.com.

Idea & Design Works, LLC, *(978-0-9712282; 978-0-9719775; 978-1-932382; 978-1-933239; 978-1-60010; 978-1-61377; 978-1-62302; 978-1-63140; 978-1-68405; 978-1-68406; 978-1-64936; 979-8-88724)* 2765 Truxtun Rd., San Diego, CA 92106 USA (SAN 255-1926) Tel 858-270-1315; Fax: 858-270-1308; 5080 Santa Fe St., San Diego, CA 92109-1609; *Imprints:* Worthwhile Books (Worthwhile Bks)
E-mail: tara@idwpublishing.com
Web site: http://www.idwpublishing.com/
Dist(s): **Chicago Distribution Ctr.**
Children's Plus, Inc.
Diamond Comic Distributors, Inc.
Diamond Bk. Distributors
L P C Group
MyiLibrary
Open Road Integrated Media, Inc.
Penguin Random Hse. Distribution
Penguin Random Hse. LLC
Random Hse., Inc.

Idea Group Incorporated *See* **IGI Global**

Idea, Inc., *(978-0-9701566)* 403 5th Pl NW, Austin, MN 55912-3051 USA Toll Free: 800-828-1231 (phone/fax)
E-mail: Idea_inc@smig.net
Web site: http://www.ccjournal.com.

Idea Magic Bks., *(978-1-932062)* 373 E Shaw Ave, Fresno, CA 97310 USA Tel 503-729-3167
E-mail: Tressa.Bundren@gmail.com
Web site: https://SapnaConsulting.com; http://LifeWorkandLove.com.

Idea Magic Media *See* **Idea Magic Bks.**

Idea Network LA Inc., *(978-0-9773301)* 201 S. Santa Fe Ave. No. 105, Los Angeles, CA 90012 USA Tel 213-613-1252; Fax: 213-613-1440.

IdeaList Enterprises, Inc., *(978-0-9758794)* P.O. Box 1967, Evanston, IL 60204 USA.

Ideals Pubns. *Imprint of* **Worthy Publishing**

IdeaStormPress, *(978-0-9820686; 978-1-945313)* 296 Hanbury Dr., Lake Zurich, IL 60047 USA
Web site: http://www.ideastormpress.com.

Ideate Prairie, *(978-0-9762564)* P.O. Box 65, Genoa, IL 60135 USA Tel 815-986-6577; *Imprints:* American Dog (Am Dog)
E-mail: cpierce@ideate-prairie.com
Web site: http://www.americandogtales.com; http://www.ideate-prairie.com.

Identity Pr., *(978-0-9753482)* P.O. Box 46224, Cincinnati, OH 45246-0224 USA Tel 513-313-5907 Do not confuse with companies with the same or similar name in Fountain Valley, CA, Cambridge, MA
E-mail: discovteenesteem@aol.com.

Ideopage Pr. Solutions, *(978-1-948928; 978-1-949735; 978-1-951394)* 295 Madison Ave, New York City, NY 10017 USA Tel 646-512-9981
E-mail: kirkabellacanete@gmail.com.

Idle Time Pr., *(978-1-7329258; 978-1-7372629)* Orders Addr.: 4616 Pin Oak Ln., Bellaire, TX 77401-2504 USA; Edit Addr.: 4616 Pin Oak Ln., Bellaire, TX 77401-2504 USA Tel 250-423-2186
E-mail: cynthia@idletimepress.com
Web site: www.idletimepress.com.

Idle Winter Pr., *(978-0-615-75103-0; 978-0-615-75329-4; 978-0-615-75375-1; 978-0-615-75790-2; 978-0-615-89153-8; 978-0-692-36927-2; 978-0-692-37191-6; 978-0-692-37441-2; 978-0-692-37871-7; 978-0-692-37934-9; 978-0-692-37993-6; 978-0-692-38122-9; 978-0-692-38502-9; 978-0-692-41873-4; 978-0-692-41874-1; 978-0-692-45244-8; 978-0-692-55074-8; 978-0-692-68244-9; 978-1-945687) 4525 SE 61st Ave., Portland, OR 97206 USA Tel 503-772-1214*
E-mail: books@idlewinter.com
Web site: http://IdleWinter.com
Dist(s): **CreateSpace Independent Publishing Platform.**

Idlehour Entertainment, *(978-0-9778063)* P.O. Box 12048, Glendale, AZ 85318 USA (SAN 850-3001) Tel 623-780-1434; Fax: 623-780-1438
Web site: http://www.idlehourentertainment.com.

Idyllworks, LLC, *(978-0-9794647)* 2904 Rippling Brook Ln., Dickinson, TX 77539-6199 USA
Web site: http://www.JamboNation.com.

†IEEE, *(978-0-7803; 978-0-87942; 978-1-55937; 978-0-7381; 978-1-4244; 978-1-61284; 978-1-4577; 978-1-4673; 978-1-62195; 978-1-4799; 978-1-5044; 978-1-5090; 978-1-5386; 978-1-7281; 978-1-6654; 978-1-958504; 979-8-3503; 979-8-8557; 978-1-962716)* Orders Addr.: P.O. Box 1331, Piscataway, NJ 08855-1331 USA (SAN 250-6130) Tel 732-981-0060; Fax: 732-981-0027; Toll Free: 800-701-4333; Edit Addr.: 445 Hoes Ln., Piscataway, NJ 08855-1331 USA Tel 732-981-0060; 732-981-5300; 732-562-3828; 800-678-4333; 732-562-3966; Fax: 732-981-1769; 732-562-1746; 732-562-1971
E-mail: confpubs@ieee.org; customer-service@ieee.org
Web site: http://www.ieee.org
Dist(s): **Curran Assocs., Inc.**
MyiLibrary
Oxford Univ. Pr., Inc.
Wiley, John & Sons, Inc.; *CIP.*

IEM Publishing, *(978-1-7362240)* 811 N 15th St., Philadelphia, PA 19130 USA Tel 215-605-0111
E-mail: J_C_Avery2@hotmail.com.

IEP - Intelligence Bk. Div., *(978-0-9729659)* P.O. Box 583, Hopkinton, MA 01748 USA Tel 508-308-3376
E-mail: intellepublishing@yahoo.com.

IEP Resources *Imprint of* **Attainment Co., Inc.**

iFAM Publishing, LLC, *(978-0-9861924)* 3035 SE Maricamp Rd. Ste 104-222, Ocala, FL 34471 USA
E-mail: ifam.publishing@gmail.com.

IFLY Bks., *(978-0-9758888)* P.O. Box 894134, Temecula, CA 92589 USA.

I.Form Ink, Publishing, *(978-0-9763274)* Div. of Insu-Form, Inc., 41921 Beacon Hill, Suite A, Palm Desert, CA 92211 USA Tel 760-779-0657; Fax: 760-779-5143
E-mail: john@hackergroup.org.

IFWG Publishing (AUS) *(978-0-646-56641-2; 978-0-646-59588-7; 978-0-9923020; 978-0-9923654; 978-1-925148; 978-0-9945229; 978-1-925496; 978-1-925759; 978-1-925956; 978-1-922556; 978-1-922856)* *Dist. by* **IPG Chicago.**

IFWG Publishing Inc., *(978-0-9843298; 978-0-615-50936-5; 978-0-615-51846-6; 978-0-615-52105-3; 978-0-615-55249-1; 978-0-615-55424-2; 978-0-615-55642-0; 978-0-615-56093-9; 978-0-615-56121-9)* 302 Horseshoe Ln., Rockaway Beach, MO 65740 USA (SAN 859-0842) Toll Free: 800-337-3038
E-mail: ifwg-publishing@live.com; r.a.knowlton@ifwgpublishing.com
Web site: http://ifwgpublishing.weebly.com/index.html
Dist(s): **CreateSpace Independent Publishing Platform.**

Ig Publishing *See* **Ig Publishing, Inc.**

Ig Publishing, Inc., *(978-0-9703125; 978-0-9752517; 978-0-9771972; 978-0-9788431; 978-0-9815040; 978-1-935439; 978-1-939601; 978-1-63246)* 260 ACADEMY St., South Orange, NJ 07079 USA (SAN 254-0444)
Web site: http://www.igpub.com
Dist(s): **Children's Plus, Inc.**
Consortium Bk. Sales & Distribution
Publishers Group West (PGW)
SPD-Small Pr. Distribution
ebrary, Inc.

IGC Japan Ltd., *(978-0-578-42441-5)* 279 E. 52nd St., San Bernardino, CA 92404 USA Tel 909-883-0299
E-mail: lance@igcjapan.com
Dist(s): **Independent Pub.**

IGI Global, *(978-1-878289; 978-1-930708; 978-1-931777; 978-1-59140; 978-1-59904; 978-1-60566; 978-1-61520; 978-1-61692; 978-1-60960; 978-1-61350; 978-1-4666; 978-1-5225; 978-1-68318; 978-1-7998; 978-1-6684; 979-8-3693)* 701 E. Chocolate Ave., Hershey, PA 17033-1240 USA (SAN 858-4265) Tel 717-533-8845 (ext. 100) 717-533-7115; Toll Free: 866-342-6657; *Imprints:* Information Science Publishing (Info Scie Pub)
E-mail: econtent@igi-global.com; cust@igi-global.com; it-accounts@igi-global.com
Web site: https://www.igi-global.com
Dist(s): **Ebsco Publishing**
Cengage Gale
ebrary, Inc.

IGI Pr., *(978-0-9709443; 978-0-9777121; 978-0-9799963; 978-0-9820870; 978-0-9825503; 978-0-9829273)* 241 First Ave. N., Minneapolis, MN 55401 USA (SAN 854-1876) Tel 612-338-8973 Toll Free: 888-805-8973
E-mail: igi@igipublishing.com
Web site: http://www.igipublishing.com.

IGlobal Educational Services, *(978-0-9882271; 978-1-944346)* 1000 Heritage Ctr. Cir., Round Rock, TX 78664 USA Tel 800-427-8422
E-mail: iglobal.educational@gmail.com.

Igloo Bks. (GBR) *(978-1-84561; 978-1-84817; 978-1-84852; 978-0-85734; 978-0-85780; 978-1-78197; 978-1-78343; 978-1-78440; 978-1-78557; 978-1-78670; 978-1-78810)* *Dist. by* **S and S Inc.**

IGMI Publishing, *(978-0-9655933)* Div. of PrissyH, P.O. Box 1735, Las Vegas, NM 87745-9602 USA Tel 505-425-9292
E-mail: favplagget@aol.com.

Ignatius Pr., *(978-0-89870; 978-1-58617; 978-1-62164; 978-1-68149; 978-1-64229)* Orders Addr.: P.O. Box 1339, Fort Collins, CO 80522-1339 USA (SAN 855-3556) Tel 970-221-3920; Fax: 970-221-3964; Toll Free Fax: 800-278-3566; Toll Free: 877-320-9276 (bookstore orders); 800-651-1531 (credit card orders, no minimum, individual orders); 1915 Astor Rd. Sycamore, Sycamore, IL 60178 (SAN 991-4595); Edit Addr.: 1348 10th Ave., San Francisco, CA 94122 USA (SAN 214-3887) Toll Free: 800-651-1531
E-mail: info@ignatius.com
Web site: http://www.ignatius.com
Dist(s): **Follett School Solutions**
Independent Pubs. Group
Midpoint Trade Bks., Inc.
Spring Arbor Distributors, Inc.

Ignite! Learning, *(978-0-9791935; 978-0-9798418; 978-1-934763; 978-1-937822)* 2905 San Gabriel Suite 212, Austin, TX 78705 USA Tel 512-697-7000; Fax: 512-697-7001; Toll Free: 866-464-4648
E-mail: support@ignitelearning.com; jbohls@ignitelearning.com
Web site: http://www.ignitelearning.com.

Ignite Reality, *(978-0-9776771; 978-0-9816258)* P.O. Box 1804, Burlingame, CA 94011-1804 USA (SAN 856-0781)
E-mail: drjenniferleigh@gmail.com
Web site: http://www.drjenniferaustinleigh.com.

Ignition Pr. *Imprint of* **Publishing Services @ Thomson-Shore**

igou, asia, *(978-0-692-67491-8; 978-0-692-75292-0)* 317 Riblett Ln., Wilmington, DE 19808 USA Tel 302-332-7564.

IGR Limited *See* **EKADOO Publishing Group**

Iguana Adventures Publishing *See* **Publish To Go Pubns.**

I.H.S. Pubs., *(978-0-9847656; 979-8-9851141)* 3920 S. Old Hwy. 94 Suite 33, St. Charles, MO 63304 USA Tel 636-447-6000.

II, Paul Duane Rhodeman, *(978-0-578-44805-3)* 2445 Wedgwood Dr. W., Florissant, MO 63033 USA Tel 314-225-8922
E-mail: pdrhodemanii@gmail.com
Dist(s): **Ingram Content Group.**

IIEI Pr., *(978-0-9773098; 978-0-9797244; 978-0-615-52608-9)* 11225 N. 28th Dr., Suite B-201, Phoenix, AZ 85029 USA Tel 602-648-5750; Fax: 602-648-5755; Toll Free: 800-474-8013
E-mail: info@expandglobal.com
Web site: http://www.expandglobal.com/iiei-press/.

IIG Pub, *(978-1-64615; 978-1-6904)* 12759 NE Whitaker Way, Portland, OR 97230 USA Tel 971-247-4552; 13820 NE Airport Way, Portland, OR 97251.

Ijiwola Pr., Gregory *Imprint of* **Summit Hse. Pubs.**

IJN Publishing, Inc., *(978-1-933894)* 724 NE. 4th St. #9, Hallandale, FL 33009 USA (SAN 850-4474) Fax: 954-457-2277; P.O. Box 630577, Miami, FL 33163
E-mail: gerald@ijnpublishing.com
Web site: http://www.whatliesbeneaththebed.com; http://www.ijnpublishing.com.

IJustWantToSleep, Inc., *(978-0-9744357)* 18 Timothy Ln., Candler, NC 28715 USA
E-mail: store@ijustwanttosleep.com; author@ijustwanttosleep.com
Web site: http://www.ijustwanttosleep.com.

IKIDS *Imprint of* **Innovative Kids**

il piccolo editions *Imprint of* **Fisher King Enterprises**

ILCP, *(978-0-9967007)* 15323 Weddingto st No. 302, Sherman Oaks, CA 91411 USA Tel 818-445-5383
E-mail: mollajani@yahoo.com.

Ile Orunmila Communications, *(978-0-9644247; 978-0-9714949; 978-0-9825100)* Orders Addr.: P.O. Box 2326, San Bernardino, CA 92405 USA Tel 909-475-5851; Fax: 909-475-5850; Toll Free: 888-678-6645; Edit Addr.: 515 W. 21st St., San Bernardino, CA 92405 USA
E-mail: fsorunmila@aol.com
Web site: http://www.IleOrunmila.com
Dist(s): **Original Pubns.**

iLearn.vip, *(978-0-9668718)*
E-mail: dawn@dawnmartin.com
Web site: http://www.dawnmartin.com
Dist(s): **Distributors, The.**

Illui International *See* **Heartful Loving Pr.**

Illumify Media Group, *(978-0-9987896; 978-1-947360; 978-1-949021; 978-1-955043; 978-1-959099; 979-8-218-09919-0)* 6561 S. Simms Way, Littleton, CO 80127 USA Tel 303-523-4813
E-mail: mklassen@illumifymedia.com
Web site: www.illumifymedia.com
Dist(s): **Independent Pubs. Group**
Midpoint Trade Bks., Inc.

Illumina Publishing, *(978-0-9718600; 978-0-9818092)* P.O. Box 2643, Friday Harbor, WA 98250-2643 USA Tel 360-378-6047
E-mail: illumina@rockisland.com
Web site: http://www.illuminapublishing.com; http://www.illuminabookdesign.com.

Illuminate YA *Imprint of* **LPC**

Illumination Arts *See* **Inspire Every Child dba Illumination Arts**

Illumination Arts LLC, *(978-0-9829225; 978-0-9846874)* 6788 Lakeview Dr, FRAZIER PARK, CA 93225 USA Tel 617-472-1443; 661-289-5007; *Imprints:* Diamond Clear Vision (DiamondClear)
E-mail: thpjr52@aol.com
Web site: http://www.illuminationarts.us; http://www.diamondclearvision.com.

Illumination Arts Publishing Co., Inc., *(978-0-935699; 978-0-9701907; 978-0-9740190)* Orders Addr.: P.O. Box 1865, Bellevue, WA 98009 USA (SAN 696-2599) Tel 425-644-7185; Fax: 425-644-9274; Toll Free: 888-210-8216; Edit Addr.: 808 6th St S. Ste. 200, Kirkland, WA 98033-6768 USA
E-mail: liteinfo@illumin.com
Web site: http://www.illumin.com
Dist(s): **DeVorss & Co.**
Follett School Solutions
Koen Pacific
New Leaf Distributing Co., Inc.
Partners/West Book Distributors
Quality Bks., Inc.

Illumination Pubns., *(978-0-9789511)* 2802 Floore Ct., Louisville, KY 40299-1610 USA (SAN 852-0313) Tel 502-491-5664 Do not confuse with Illumination Publications in West Toluca lake, CA.

Illumination Studios, *(978-0-9741381)* 5924 Woodoak Dr., Dallas, TX 75249 USA
E-mail: contact@illuminationstudios.com
Web site: http://www.illuminationstudios.com.

Illusion Factory, The, *(978-0-9747331; 978-1-932949)* 21800 Burbank Blvd., Suite 225, Woodland Hills, CA 91367 USA (SAN 255-7096) Tel 818-598-8400; Fax: 818-598-8494
E-mail: ewong@illusionfactory.com
Web site: http://www.illusionfactory.com.

Illusionary Magic LLC, *(978-0-9834201)* 104 Donato Cir., Scotch Plains, NJ 07076 USA Tel 877-322-2723; Fax: 908-322-0421
E-mail: info@bradross.com
Web site: http://www.BradRoss.com.

Illustrate to Educate, *(978-0-9892732)* 2313 Quincy St. Apt. No. 2, Durham, NC 27703 USA Tel 919-908-1254
E-mail: everettar@hotmail.com.

Illustrated Bks. *Imprint of* **Jorge Pinto Bks.**

ILMHOUSE LLC, *(978-0-9726607)* P.O. Box 535, Unionville, PA 19375-0535 USA
Web site: http://www.thetruemarriage.com.

ILT Publishing, *(978-0-9774409)* Div. of Integrated Learning Technology, Inc., 1410 Steeplechase Rd., Downingtown, PA 19335 USA (SAN 257-4950) Tel 484-883-7107 (phone/fax)
E-mail: info@iltpublishing.com; rebejames@smartmail.com; presetco@iltpublishing.com
Web site: http://www.iltpublishing.com; http://www.tommilance.com; http://rebejames.com.

I.M. Enterprises, *(978-0-9777882)* P.O. Box 111, Rochester, MA 02770 USA (SAN 850-1645); *Imprints:* Light Works Publishing (Light Works)
E-mail: imenterprises@hotmail.com
Web site: http://www.imenterprises.org.

IM Pr., *(978-0-9654651; 978-0-9716911; 978-0-615-43634-0; 978-0-9857952)* Orders Addr.: P.O. Box 5346, Takoma Park, MD 20913-5346 USA Tel 301-587-1202; Edit Addr.: 7214 Cedar Ave., Takoma Park, MD 20912 USA Do not confuse with companies with the same name in Cincinnati, OH, Fairfax Station, VA
E-mail: efaine@yahoo.com
Web site: http://www.takoma.com/ned/home.htm
Dist(s): **Book Clearing Hse.**

Publisher Name Index

Imaajinn This, (978-0-9767342) P.O. Box 294, West Haven, CT 06516 USA (SAN 256-484X) Tel 203-710-4906 Web site: http://www.robleyblake.com.

Image Cascade Publishing, (978-0-9639607; 978-1-930009; 978-1-59511) 420 Lexington Ave., Suite 300, New York, NY 10170 USA (SAN 253-2972) Tel 212-297-6240; Toll Free: 800-691-7779
E-mail: jc@imagecascade.com
Web site: http://www.imagecascade.com
Dist(s): **Baker & Taylor Publisher Services (BTPS)**
Baker & Taylor Bks.

Image Comics, (978-1-58240; 978-1-887279; 978-1-60706; 978-1-63215; 978-1-5343) 2001 Center St., Berkeley, CA 94704 USA
E-mail: info@imagecomics.com
Web site: http://www.imagecomics.com/
Dist(s): **Children's Plus, Inc.**
Diamond Comic Distributors, Inc.
Diamond Bk. Distributors
L P C Group
Simon & Schuster, Inc.
Trucatriche.

Image Express Inc., (978-0-9664634; 978-0-615-50572-5) P.O. Box 66536, Austin, TX 78766 USA Tel 512-401-4900; Toll Free: 888-794-4300
Web site: http://greatday.com
Dist(s): **CreateSpace Independent Publishing Platform.**

Image Formation, (978-0-9763440) 23233 N. Pima, No. 113-102, Scottsdale, AZ 85255 USA
E-mail: lance@themummymountainstory.com
Web site: http://www.themummymountainstory.com.

Image Pr., Inc., (978-1-891548) Orders Addr.: P.O. Box 2407, Edmond, OK 73083-2407 USA Tel 405-844-6007; Fax: 405-348-5577; Edit Addr.: 247 N. Broadway, Suite 101, Edmond, OK 73034 USA.

Image Publishing, Ltd., (978-0-911897) Subs. of Roger Miller Photo, Ltd., 1411 Hollins St., Baltimore, MD 21223 USA (SAN 264-6781) Tel 410-566-1222; 410-233-1234; Fax: 410-233-1241 Do not confuse with companies with the same or similar names in Encino, CA, Wilton, CT
E-mail: rmpl.ipl@verizon.net
Web site: http://www.rogermillerphoto.com.

IMAGECRAFTERS, (978-0-9773478) Orders Addr.: 1644 Masters Ct., Naperville, IL 60563 USA (SAN 257-3709) Tel 630-355-1449
E-mail: imgcft@mc.net.

Imagery Pr., (978-0-9754287) P.O. Box 337, Carpinteria, CA 93014-0337 USA
E-mail: books@imagerypress.com.

Images & Pages, (978-0-9788332) P.O. Box 118120, Carrollton, TX 75007 USA
E-mail: deguzman@imagesandpages.com
Web site: http://imagesandpages.com.

Images Company *See* **Images SI Inc.**

Images For Presentation, (978-0-9749531) 176 Second St., Saint James, NY 11780 USA Tel 631-361-7908
E-mail: imagesforpres@aol.com.

Images Pr., (978-1-891577) 27920 Roble Alto St., Los Altos Hills, CA 94022 USA (SAN 299-4844) Tel 650-948-9251; 650-948-8251; Fax: 650-941-6114 Do not confuse with companies with the same name in San Leandro, CA, New York, NY
E-mail: bugsmom2@aol.com
Web site: http://www.images-press.com
Dist(s): **Quality Bks., Inc.**

Images SI Inc., (978-0-9677017; 978-1-62385) 109 Woods of Arden Rd., Staten Island, NY 10312 USA
E-mail: john.iovine@gmail.com; sales@imagesco.com; john.iovine@imagesco.com; melissa@imagesco.com
Web site: http://www.imagesco.com.

Images Unlimited Publishing, (978-0-930643) 124 N. Grand Ave., Maryville, MO 64468 USA (SAN 242-0163) Tel 660-582-4279; *Imprints:* Snaptail Press (Snaptail Pr)
E-mail: images@cebridge.net; info@imagesunlimitedpub.com; Lee@imagesunlimitedpub.com
Web site: http://www.imagesunlimitedpub.com; http://www.snaptail.com; http://www.snaptailpress.com; http://www.imagesunlimitedpublishing.com; http://www.cookingandkids.com/blog; http://www.healthykidseatingtips.com; http://www.caringmomshealthykids.com
Dist(s): **Brodart Co.**
Follett School Solutions.

ImaginAISHAn Media LLC, (978-0-692-94911-5; 978-0-692-12037-8; 978-0-692-12044-6; 978-0-692-14985-0; 978-0-578-51561-8; 978-0-578-92080-1; 978-0-578-34008-1) 2038 Prentiss Dr., Downers Grove, IL 60532 USA
E-mail: tempestt.williams@yahoo.com
Web site: imaginaishan.net
Dist(s): **Ingram Content Group.**

Imaginarium Pr., (978-0-615-45112-1; 978-0-9978066; 978-1-7334752) 254 W. 98th St. Apt.1E, New York, NY 10025 USA Tel 410-963-1854
E-mail: josephrbecker@gmail.com.

Imaginary Lines, Incorporated *See* **Sally Ride Science**

Imagination Arts Pubns., (978-0-9746119) P.O. Box 103, Mahwah, NJ 07430 USA Tel 201-529-5105; Fax: 201-529-5105
E-mail: imaginationarts@optonline.net
Web site: http://www.iapbooks.com.

Imagination Bk. Works, (978-0-692-88301-3; 978-0-692-07550-0; 978-0-692-14913-3; 978-0-578-68300-3; 978-0-578-79381-8) 10N164 Chapman Rd, hampshire, IL 60140 USA Tel 630-337-9019
Dist(s): **CreateSpace Independent Publishing Platform.**

Imagination Publishing-Orlando, (978-0-9817123; 978-0-615-38566-2) P.O. Box 802, Loughman, FL 33858 USA (SAN 856-3152)
E-mail: paul@HubbleRevealsCreation.com
Web site: http://www.TheSecretDoorway.com; http://www.HubbleRevealsCreation.com/
Dist(s): **BookBaby.**

Imagination Stage, Inc., (978-0-9723729) 4908 Auburn Ave., Bethesda, MD 20814 USA Tel 301-961-6060; Fax: 301-718-9526
E-mail: lagogliati@aol.com
Web site: http://www.imaginationstage.org.

Imagination Station Pr., (978-0-9742575) 4560 N. 25th Rd., Arlington, VA 22207-4147 USA Tel 703-528-5828
E-mail: epyatt1@comcast.net.

Imagination UnLtd., (978-0-692-24980-2) P.O. Box 270, Raymond, NH 03077 USA Tel 603-793-8447
E-mail: iunlimitedllc@gmail.com.

Imagination Workshop, The, (978-0-9744437) 4150 Abbott Ave., N., Minneapolis, MN 55422 USA
E-mail: imaginationworkshop@yahoo.com.

Imaginative Publishing, Ltd., (978-0-9743335; 978-0-9767948) P.O. Box 150008, Fort Worth, TX 76108 USA Tel 817-246-6436 (phone/fax); Toll Free: 877-246-6436 (phone/fax)
E-mail: publisher@imaginativepublishing.com
Web site: http://www.imaginativepublishing.com.

Imaginator Pr., (978-0-9745603; 978-1-936917) 6400 Baltimore National Pike Suite 170A-194, Baltimore, MD 21228-3915 USA
E-mail: sruth@ImaginatorPress.com
Web site: http://www.ImaginatorPress.com
Dist(s): **Beagle Bay Bks.**
Ingram Content Group.

Imagine & Wonder, (978-1-953652; 978-1-63761) 28 Sycamore Ln., Irvington, NY 10533 USA Tel 646-644-0403
E-mail: steven@imagineandwonder.com; john.shableski@imagineandwonder.com; dr.simonmills@ignitioncapital.com
Web site: www.imagineandwonder.com
Dist(s): **APG Sales & Distribution Services**
Independent Pubs. Group.

Imagine Books *See* **Imagine! Studios**

Imagine Creatively *Imprint of* **BaBk.y**

Imagine Publishing *Imprint of* **Charlesbridge Publishing, Inc.**

Imagine Publishing, (978-0-9758899) 7620 Dogleg Rd., Dayton, OH 45414 USA Fax: 937-890-7949
E-mail: skyblu40@earthlink.net.

Imagine! Studios, (978-0-9761317; 978-0-9764353; 978-0-9767913; 978-1-937944) PO Box 1362, Sarasota, FL 34230 USA Tel 941-999-1278
E-mail: contact@artsimage.com
Web site: http://www.artsimagine.com
Dist(s): **BookBaby.**

Imagine That Design, (978-0-578-77344-5; 979-8-218-14062-5) 299 E. 10th St No. 3, New York, NY 10009 USA Tel 212-228-2128
E-mail: itdnyc@icloud.com.

Imagine That Enterprises, (978-0-9723067) P.O. Box 29315, Saint Louis, MO 63126 USA
E-mail: underthedove@hotmail.com
Web site: http://www.underthedove.com.

Imagine the Possibilities, LLC *See* **Imaging Possibilities**

Imagineland, Ltd., (978-0-9765038) P.O. Box 10134, College Station, TX 77842-0134 USA
Web site: http://www.imagineland.com
Dist(s): **Smashwords.**

IMAGINEX, LLC, (978-0-9753620) P.O. Box 1375, Frisco, TX 75034 USA; *Imprints:* Bible Game (BibleGame)
Web site: http://www.imnex.net.

Imagining Possibilities, (978-0-9747426) P.O. Box 266, Gwynedd Valley, PA 19437-0266 USA.

ImaginOn Bks., (978-1-954405) 4401 Barclay Downs Dr, Suite 518, CHARLOTTE, NC 28209-4606 USA Tel 704-796-1997
E-mail: imaginonbooks@gmail.com.

Imago, (978-0-9765179) 14220 Duckett Rd., Brandywine, MD 20613-9343 USA Tel 856-812-0400; Toll Free Fax: 866-268-9003; Toll Free: 866-413-6864.

Imago Pr., (978-0-9725303; 978-0-9799341; 978-1-935437; 978-0-9981791) 3710 E. Edison St., Tucson, AZ 85716-2912 USA; *Imprints:* As Sabr Publications (AsSabr)
Web site: http://www.imagobooks.com; http://www.oasisjournal.org.

ImaJinn Bks. *Imprint of* **BelleBks., Inc.**

Imani Productions, (978-0-615-14325-5) 2261 Bernwood Dr., Erie, PA 16510 USA Tel 814-897-0502
E-mail: umemesababu@aol.com
Web site: http://www.imaniproductions.org.

Imani-MCHS, (978-0-9729586) 3445 W. 66th Pl., Chicago, IL 60629 USA Tel 773-925-6473
E-mail: imanimchs@aol.com.

I-Mar, (978-0-9741052) 5150 Rancho Rd., Huntingtn Bch, CA 92647-2074 USA
Web site: http://www.i-mar.net.

ImaRa Publishing, (978-0-9843111) Orders Addr.: 3002 230th Ln., SE, Sammamish, WA 98075 USA
E-mail: vrpearce@msn.com
Web site: http://www.imarapublishing.com.

ImBost Inc., (978-0-9848626) 158 E. 100 St. Ste 6R, New York, NY 10029 USA Tel 917-482-5178
E-mail: taekwontales@gmail.com.

Imbrifex Bks., (978-0-9972369; 978-1-945501; 978-1-955307) 8275 S. Eastern Ave., Las Vegas, NV 89123 USA Tel 702-320-4866
E-mail: mark@imbrifex.com
Dist(s): **Legato Pubs. Group**
Publishers Group West (PGW).

Imdalind Pr., (978-0-9884837; 978-0-9914313; 978-0-9964632; 978-1-949725) 6980 S. Boulder Dr., Cottonwood Heights, UT 84121 USA Tel 385-229-7434
E-mail: me@rebeccaethington.com.

Immediex Publishing, (978-1-932968) 540 Evelyn Pl., Beverly Hills, CA 90210 USA Tel 310-273-1585
E-mail: rodney@immediex.com
Web site: www.immediex.com
Dist(s): **Smashwords.**

Immedium, (978-1-59702) P.O. Box 31846, San Francisco, CA 94131 USA
Web site: http://www.immedium.com
Dist(s): **Consortium Bk. Sales & Distribution**
MyiLibrary.

Immortal Works LLC, (978-0-692-78113-5; 978-0-692-83650-7; 978-0-692-88092-0; 978-0-9990205; 978-1-7324674; 978-1-7339085; 978-1-7343866; 978-1-7349046; 978-1-953491) 1505 Glenrose Dr., SALT LAKE CITY, UT 84104 USA Tel 801-651-4024.

Immortality Pr., (978-0-9795753) 1005 Winthrope Chase Dr., Alpharetta, GA 30004 USA
E-mail: publisher@immortalitypress.com; order@immortalitypress.com
Web site: http://www.immortalitypress.com.

IMMPACT Communications *See* **Humble Heart Publishing**

Imogen Rose, (978-0-615-34507-9; 978-0-615-37681-3; 978-0-9828002; 978-0-9850797; 978-0-9856766; 978-1-940015) 18 Westwinds Dr., Princeton Junction, NJ 08550 USA
E-mail: portalchronicles@hotmail.com
Dist(s): **Lulu Pr., Inc.**
Smashwords.

IMPACT Books *Imprint of* **Penguin Publishing Group**

Impact Pubns., (978-0-942710; 978-1-57023) Div. of Development Concepts, Inc., 7820 Sudley Rd Ste 100, Manassas, VA 20109 USA (SAN 240-1142) Tel 703-361-7300; Fax: 703-335-9486 Do not confuse with companies with the same name in Evanston, IL, Mandeville, LA, Southfield, MI
E-mail: krannich@impactpublications.com
Web site: http://www.impactpublications.com
Dist(s): **Follett School Solutions**
MyiLibrary
National Bk. Network
ebrary, Inc.

Impact Publications, Incorporated *See* **Specialty Pr., Inc.**

Impact Pubs. *Imprint of* **New Harbinger Pubns.**

Imparted Joy LLC, (978-1-7370347; 979-8-9892382) 2715 Pinewood Ct, Clearwater, FL 33761 USA Tel 727-709-0474
E-mail: jilliande412@gmail.com
Web site: impartedjoy.com.

Impetus Pr., (978-0-9776693) P.O. Box 10025, Iowa City, IA 52240-0001 USA Tel 319-321-6282 Do not confuse with Impetus Press in Atlanta, GA
E-mail: jennifer@impetuspress.com
Web site: http://www.impetuspress.com
Dist(s): **SPD-Small Pr. Distribution.**

Important Publishing, 12759 NE Whitaker Way R993, Portland, OR 97230 USA Tel 971-247-4552
E-mail: tommy@sleekpublishers.com
Dist(s): **Ingram Content Group.**

Impossible Dreams Publishing Co., (978-0-9786422; 978-1-7364565) 4123 Rancho Grande Pl., NW., Albuquerque, NM 87120 USA (SAN 851-139X)
E-mail: Quixote1818@aol.com
Web site: http://www.impossibledreamspub.com
Dist(s): **Baker & Taylor Publisher Services (BTPS).**

Impower Group, The, (978-1-7336419; 979-8-9887656)
E-mail: mranthonybrice@gmail.com.

Impressions By Veronica, (978-0-692-80171-0) .

Impressions Ink, (978-1-882626) 3918 Peachtree Ln., Memphis, TN 38135-9115 USA Tel 901-388-5382; Fax: 901-385-0256; Toll Free: 800-388-5382.

Imprexions Publishing Co., (978-0-9742922) 4398 Dunkeld Rd., Reno, NV 89519 USA
E-mail: listinsky@hotmail.com.

Imprint (IND) (978-81-902436) *Dist. by* **Macmillan.**

ImPrint, (978-0-9850454) 30-84 14th St. Apt. 6, Astoria, NY 11102 USA Tel 347-392-1280
E-mail: charlesm.fraser@hammerandcyclemessengerservice.com.

Imprint.li, (978-0-9894891; 978-0-9897418) 11015 122nd Ave. Kp N., Gig Harbor, WA 98329 USA Tel 253-853-4199
E-mail: carolyn@imprint.li
Web site: www.imprint.li.

Imprints, (978-1-883986) Div. of Spectrum Bks., Orders Addr.: P.O. Box 4365, Thousand Oaks, CA 91359 USA Tel 808-707-3336; Fax: 808-707-4446; Edit Addr.: 32151 Sailview Ln., Westlake Village, CA 91359 USA
Dist(s): **Continental Bk. Co., Inc.**

Impulse Surf, (978-0-9744247) Orders Addr.: 1106 Second St., PMB 823, Encinitas, CA 92024 USA Tel 760-431-6883; Fax: 760-436-7158; Edit Addr.: 7200 Ponto Dr., Carlsbad, CA 92009 USA
E-mail: franklinlives@yahoo.com
Web site: http://www.impulsesurf.com.

Impulsum Pr., (978-1-7367481) 25 Calverton Rd, SAINT LOUIS, MO 63135 USA Tel 314-276-5397
E-mail: jennaterese@paperbacksoftware.com
Web site: jennaterese.com.

In Ardua Tendit Pr., (978-0-9749673) 464 Leton Dr., Columbia, SC 29210 USA Tel 803-608-0804
E-mail: mail@jessmaccallum.com
Web site: http://www.jessmaccallum.com
Dist(s): **BookBaby.**

In Audio *Imprint of* **Sound Room Pubs., Inc.**

In Between Bks., (978-0-935430; 978-0-9802007) P.O. Box 790, Sausalito, CA 94966 USA (SAN 213-6236) Tel 415-383-8447; Fax: 415-381-1938; 415-381-3513
E-mail: inbetweenbooks@atthebutterflytree.com; karla@inbetweenbooks.com; juno@inbetweenbooks.com
Web site: http://www.atthebutterflytree.com.

In Cahoots, (978-0-9745990) 105 Los Padres Way, Unit 6, Buellton, CA 93427 USA Do not confuse with In Cahoots in Marietta, GA
Dist(s): **SPD-Small Pr. Distribution.**

In Cider Pr., (978-0-9721716) P.O. Box 228, Barton, VT 0582 USA Tel 802-754-8889.

In Easy Steps Ltd. (GBR) (978-1-84078) *Dist. by* **PerseuPGW.**

In Heels Publishing, (978-0-578-15732-0; 978-0-692-80485-8; 978-0-9989264) 17412 Ventura Blvd, No. 441, Encino, CA 91316 USA.

In Motion Books Incorporated *See* **Dakitab, Inc.**

In Our Words Inc., (978-1-938040) 6104 City Pl., Edgewater, NJ 07020 USA Tel 201-280-7399
E-mail: ahn.jaesuk@gmail.com.

In Search Of The Universal Truth (ISOTUT) *See* **DragonEye Publishing**

In the Desert, (978-0-9744005) 7990 E. Snyder Rd., No. 5106, Tucson, AZ 85750-9009 USA
Web site: http://www.inthedesert.biz.

In the Hands of a Child, (978-1-60308) Eclectically Me Niki, 3271 Kerlikowske Rd., Coloma, MI 49038-8913 USA
E-mail: sales@handsofachild.com
Web site: http://www.Handsofachild.com; http://www.eclecticallymeniki.com.

In The Hse. Publishing Co., (978-0-9760441) 1122 N. 84th St., Seattle, WA 98103 USA
E-mail: projectfile@hotmail.com
Web site: http://www.projectgirl.com.

In The Lead Publishing *See* **Lone Cypress Pubs.**

In the Sky Publishing, (978-0-9740438) Orders Addr.: 26300 Ford Rd., No. 407, Dearborn Heights, MI 48127 USA Tel 313-792-0694
E-mail: cmlipson@wideopenwest.com
Web site: http://www.intheskypublishing.com.

In the Spirit of Healing, (978-1-7367755) 6 Oakwood St., East Greenbush, NY 12061 USA Tel 518-527-3043
E-mail: inthespiritofhealing820@gmail.com
Web site: inthespiritofhealing.net.

In the Think of Things *See* **Rainbow Resource Ctr., Inc.**

In the Think of Things *Imprint of* **Rainbow Resource Ctr., Inc.**

In This Together Media, (978-0-9858956; 978-0-9898166) 5 Evergreen Ln., Larchmont, NY 10538 USA Tel 914-833-1189
E-mail: calbertine@gmail.com
Web site: www.inthistogethermedia.com
Dist(s): **INscribe Digital.**

In Time Pubns. Inc., (978-0-9762857) P.O. Box 190537, Fort Lauderdale, FL 33319 USA
Web site: http://www.intimepublications.com.

In Your Heart Lives a Rainbow, (978-0-9857824) 25 Strauss Ave., Selden, NY 11784 USA Tel 516-483-1899
E-mail: kare4you2@yahoo.com.

In Your Own Words, (978-0-578-55767-0) 100 Bridgeton Dr., Bluffton, SC 29910 USA Tel 912-777-8643
E-mail: deedeehassan5@gmail.com.

Inane Blabbering Bks. (GBR) (978-0-9559798) *Dist. by* **LuluCom.**

Inanna Pubns. & Education, Inc. (CAN) (978-0-9681290; 978-0-9736709; 978-0-9782233; 978-0-9808822; 978-1-926708; 978-1-77133) *Dist. by* **SPD-Small Pr Dist.**

Incentive Pubns., Inc., (978-0-86530; 978-0-913916; 978-1-62950) 233 N. Michigan Ave., Suite 2000, Chicago, IL 60601 USA (SAN 203-8005) Toll Free: 800-421-2830
E-mail: info@incentivepublications.com
Web site: http://www.incentivepublications.com
Dist(s): **MyiLibrary**
ebrary, Inc.

Inch By Inch Pubns., LLC, (978-0-9670941) P.O. Box 15, Okemos, MI 48805 USA Tel 716-688-1515; Fax: 716-636-4058; Toll Free: 877-462-4967
E-mail: chofner@aol.com
Web site: http://www.inchbyinchbooks.com
Dist(s): **Partners Pubs. Group, Inc.**

Inclement Pr., (978-0-9819736; 978-0-9886669) P.O. Box 120, Sidney, IA 51652 USA.

INCLUDAS Publishing, (978-0-9861927; 978-1-949983) PO Box 893566, Temecula, CA 92589 USA Tel 818-350-3652
E-mail: inquiries@includas.com
Web site: includas.com.

Inclusive Books LLC, (978-0-9778143) 3027 New Natchez Trace, Nashville, TN 37215 USA Tel 615-383-1065
E-mail: estelle@estellecondra.com
Web site: http://www.inclusivebooks.com.

Inclusive Global Inc., (978-0-9759077) P.O. Box 143, Newport, OH 45768 USA Tel 740-516-1143 (phone/fax)
E-mail: sparkeythespider@aol.com
Web site: http://www.inclusive.global; http://www.sparkeythespider.com; http://www.travisflores.org.

Incorgnito Publishing Pr. *Imprint of* **Incorgnito Publishing Pr. LLC**

Incorgnito Publishing Press *See* **Incorgnito Publishing Pr. LLC**

Incorgnito Publishing Pr. LLC, (978-0-9861953; 978-0-9969111; 978-1-944589) 1651 Devonshire Ln, Sarasota, FL 34236-7512 USA Tel 888-859-0792; *Imprints:* Incorgnito Publishing Press (MYID_H_INCORGN)
E-mail: mconant@incorgnitobooks.com.

Incorporated Trustees of the Gospel Worker Society, The, (978-0-9617506; 978-1-59843; 978-1-934981; 978-1-935338; 978-1-936272; 978-1-936897; 978-1-936898; 978-1-64495) Div. of Union Gospel Pr., 19695 COMMERCE PKWY, Cleveland, OH 44130 USA (SAN 664-2845) Tel 800-638-9988
Web site: http://www.uniongospelpress.com.

Incredible Kid, LLC, (978-0-9755836) 7095 Hollywood Blvd., Suite 461, Hollywood, CA 90028 USA.

Publisher Name Index

da, Michelle, (*978-0-692-79108-0; 978-0-578-46397-1*) 5 Atherton St., Roxbury, MA 02119 USA Tel 617-599-8730
E-mail: lnda.2006@yahoo.com.

dependence Books *See* **America Star Bks.**

dependent Media Institute *See* **AlterNet Bks.**

dependent Pub., (*978-1-4243; 978-1-59975; 978-1-60402; 978-1-60461; 978-1-60530; 978-1-60585; 978-1-60643; 978-1-60702; 978-1-60725; 978-1-60743; 978-1-61539; 978-1-61584; 978-1-61623; 978-1-61658; 978-1-4507; 978-1-4675; 978-1-4951; 978-0-9927847; 978-1-5323;-1-7923; 978-0-578-33228-4; 978-0-578-33515-5; 978-0-578-33612-1; 978-0-578-35450-7; 979-8-3507; 979-8-218-21167-7; 979-8-218-21168-4; 979-8-218-28747-4; 979-8-218-28748-1*) *Div. of Bar Code Graphics, 875 N. Michigan Ave., Suite 2650, Chicago, IL 60615 USA Fax: 312-595-0725; Toll Free: 800-662-0701; 65 E. Wacker Pl., 18th Flr., Chicago, IL 60601 Tel 312-595-0600; Toll Free: 800-662-0703 Do not confuse with Independent Publishers in Bountiful, UT*
E-mail: pubserv@barcode-us.com
Web site: http://www.publisherservices-us.com; http://www.isbn-us.com
Dist(s): **Consortium Bk. Sales & Distribution**
D.A.P./Distributed Art Pubs.
Ebsco Publishing
Epicenter Pr., Inc.
Follett School Solutions
Greenleaf Book Group
Leonard, Hal Corp.
Hay Hse., Inc.
Independent Pubs. Group
Ingram Publisher Services
Lulu Pr., Inc.
Midpoint Trade Bks., Inc.
Outskirts Pr., Inc.
SCB Distributors
SPD-Small Pr. Distribution
Smashwords
TNT Media Group, Inc.
Univ. of Arkansas Pr.
eBookit.com
ebrary, Inc.

Independent Pub., (*978-1-62951; 978-1-63041; 978-1-63102; 978-1-63415; 978-1-943438; 978-1-943579; 978-1-943730; 978-1-943932; 978-1-944169; 978-1-944170; 978-1-944171; 978-1-944541; 978-1-944819; 978-1-944820; 978-1-945239; 978-1-945563; 978-1-63535; 978-1-947099*) *427 California Ave Unit 1, Santa Monica, CA 90403 USA Tel 310-980-4668 Do not confuse with Independent Publisher in Chicago, IL, Pasadena, CA*
E-mail: ahoohooahoo@yahoo.com
Dist(s): **Lulu Pr., Inc.**

Independent Publisher Services, (*978-1-4243; 978-0-692-73622-7*) Orders Addr.: 444 N. Michigan Ave., #3500, Chicago, IL 60611 USA Toll Free: 800-662-0701
E-mail: sales@barcode-us.com
Dist(s): **Follett School Solutions**
Islander Group
Miller Trade Bk. Marketing.

Independent Pubs. Group, (*978-1-4956*) 814 N. Franklin, Chicago, IL 60610 USA Tel 773-722-5527; 312-337-0747; Fax: 312-337-5985
Web site: http://www.ipgbook.com.

Independent Pubs. Group, (*978-1-4956; 979-8-3688*) Subs. of Chicago Review Pr., 814 N. Franklin, Chicago, IL 60610 USA (SAN 201-2936) Tel 312-337-0747; Fax: 312-337-5985; Toll Free: 800-888-4741
E-mail: frontdesk@ipgbook.com
Web site: http://www.ipgbook.com; http://www.trafalgarsquarepublishing.com
Dist(s): **Children's Plus, Inc.**

Independent Publishing *See* **New Pubns.**

Independent Spirit Publishing, (*978-0-9666919; 978-0-578-09203-4; 978-0-615-86951-3; 978-0-615-93315-3; 978-0-615-95976-4*) 15994 325th St., Goodhue, MN 55027 USA
Web site: http://www.nataliebuskethomas.com
Dist(s): **Lulu Pr., Inc.**

Independent Thinking Press *Imprint of* **Crown Hse. Publishing LLC**

INDI, LLC, (*978-0-9789247; 978-1-935636*) 15508 W. Bell Rd. Suite 101-315, Surprise, AZ 85374-3436 USA Tel 623-556-2751; Fax: 602-524-7550; *Imprints:* INDI Best (INDIBest)
E-mail: jerry@writersreaders.com
Web site: http://www.writersreaders.com
Dist(s): **BookBaby**
Smashwords.

INDI Publishing Group *See* **INDI, LLC**

Indian Hill Gallery of Fine Photography, (*978-0-9669079*) 671 River Rd., Wells, VT 05774 USA Tel 802-325-2274; Fax: 802-325-2276
E-mail: info@stephenschaub.com
Web site: http://www.indianhillgallery.com
Dist(s): **RAM Pubns. & Distribution.**

Indian Territory Publishing, (*978-0-9727068*) P.O. Box 43, Bennington, OK 74723-0043 USA
E-mail: wes@wesparker-itp.com; wes.parker@us.army.mil
Web site: http://www.wesparker-itp.com.

†Indiana Historical Society, (*978-0-87195*) 450 W. Ohio St., Indianapolis, IN 46202-3269 USA (SAN 201-5234) Tel 317-233-9557; 317-232-1882; Fax: 317-233-0857; Toll Free: 800-447-1830
E-mail: rvaught@indianahistory.org; cbennett@indianahistory.org
Web site: http://www.indianahistory.org
Dist(s): **Distributors, The**
Indiana Univ. Pr.; *CIP.*

†Indiana Univ. Pr., (*978-0-253; 978-0-86196*) 601 N. Morton St., Bloomington, IN 47404-3797 USA (SAN 202-5647) Fax: 812-855-7931; Toll Free: 800-842-6796
E-mail: iuporder@indiana.edu
Web site: http://www.iupress.indiana.edu
Dist(s): **Blackstone Audio, Inc.**
Ebsco Publishing
Cengage Gale
JSTOR
Johns Hopkins Univ. Pr.
Ingram Content Group
MyiLibrary
Open Road Integrated Media, Inc.
Transaction Pubs.
Two Rivers Distribution
ebrary, Inc.; *CIP.*

., Orders Addr.: 528 E. Lorain St., Oberlin, OH 44074-1298 USA (SAN 134-2118) Tel 440-775-7777; Toll Free Fax: 800-344-5059; Toll Free: 800-321-3883 (orders only); 800-458-9303 (backorder status only); 800-334-9882 (support programs/technical support); Whitlow Campus Store-indiCo 1 1550 Clarke Dr., DUBUQUE, IA 52001-3198 (SAN 990-560X)
E-mail: service@goindico.com; orders@goindico.com
Web site: http://www.nacscorp.com.

INDICOMM, (*978-0-578-43404-9; 978-1-7358536*) P.O. Box 714, Grayson, GA 30017 USA Tel 216-393-7973
E-mail: info.indicomm@gmail.com
Dist(s): **CreateSpace Independent Publishing Platform.**

Indie Artist Pr., (*978-1-62522*) Orders Addr.: 90 W 100 N No. 6, Price, UT 84501 USA; *Imprints:* Hugs Books (Hugs Bks)
Web site: http://www.indieartistpress.com
Dist(s): **Suite 3 Productions.**

Indie Owl Pr., (*978-0-692-73714-9; 978-0-692-80949-5; 978-0-9990126; 978-1-949193*) 4700 Millenial Blvd Ste 175 No. 90776, Orlando, FL 32839 USA Tel 386-212-2835
E-mail: nightowlfreelance@gmail.com
Web site: http://IndieOwlPress.com; http://NightOwlFreelance.com.

Indie Publishing Group, (*978-0-692-43389-8; 978-1-988656*) 242 W dilcrest, Florence, KY 41042 USA Tel (859)3718242
Web site: JacobCartlidge.com
Dist(s): **CreateSpace Independent Publishing Platform.**

IndieArtz, Inc., (*978-0-9753252*) 1650 Margaret St., Suite 302-131, Jacksonville, FL 32204-3869 USA
Web site: http://www.indieartz.com.

Indigo Custom Publishing *See* **Sphinx Publishing**

Indigo House Publishing, LLC *See* **Leia Stone, LLC**

Indigo Impressions, (*978-0-9788339*) Orders Addr.: P.O. Box 501, Speonk, NY 11972-0501 USA
E-mail: meghanspd@yahoo.com
Dist(s): **BookBaby.**

Indigo, LLC, (*978-0-9758995*) 7486 North Shore Rd., Norfolk, VA 23505 USA Tel 757-622-3319
E-mail: lee@indigoart.net
Web site: http://www.indigoart.net
Dist(s): **Norfolk SPCA.**

Indigo Pubns., (*978-0-9646680*) Orders Addr.: 68-1030 Mauna Lani Point Dr., Kamuela, HI 96743 USA (SAN 298-9921) Tel 808-345-2001; 808-345-0805
E-mail: mei@malinowski.com; judy@malinowski.com
Web site: http://www.snorkelguides.com.

Indigo Sea Pr., LLC, (*978-1-935171; 978-1-938101; 978-1-63066*) 931-B S. Main St., Box 145, Kernersville, NC 27284 USA
E-mail: willhodam@yahoo.com; indigoseapress@gmail.com
Web site: http://secondwindpublishing.com/; http://indigoseapress.com
Dist(s): **Smashwords.**

Indigo Skye, (*978-0-9994924*) 1517 Mackenzie St., WASHINGTON, IL 61571 USA Tel 309-472-0565
E-mail: Indigo.Skye@comcast.net.

Individualized Education Systems/Poppy Lane Publishing, (*978-0-938911*) Orders Addr.: P.O. Box 5136, Fresno, CA 93755 USA (SAN 661-8405) Tel 559-299-4639; Edit Addr.: 134 Poppy Ln., Clovis, CA 93612 USA (SAN 661-8413)
E-mail: Bette1234@aol.com
Web site: http://www.poppylane.com
Dist(s): **American West Bks.**

IndoEuropeanPublishing.com, (*978-1-60444*) 4215 Vineland Ave., No. 17, Studio City, CA 91602 USA
E-mail: Alfredagha@gmail.com
Web site: http://IndoEuropeanPublishing.com.

Indomita Press, (*978-0-578-20983-8*) 17 Colby Ct., Sacramento, CA 95825 USA Tel 646-477-7810
E-mail: pjoshualaskey@hotmail.com
Web site: indomitapress.com.

Indulgence Pr., (*978-0-9742191*) 250 N. 3rd Ave. #224, Minneapolis, MN 55401 USA Tel 612-379-4743
Web site: http://www.indulgencepress.com.

Industrial Gingerbread, (*978-0-9860691*) 61-33 ALDERTON ST, REGO PARK, NY 11374 USA Tel 718-478-8537
E-mail: richard.a.west@jpmchase.com.

Indy Pub, (*978-1-0878; 978-1-0879; 978-1-0880; 978-1-0881; 978-1-0882; 978-0-578-64405-9; 978-0-578-64518-6; 978-0-578-64713-5; 978-0-578-66570-2; 978-0-578-67285-4; 978-0-578-70875-1; 978-0-578-70940-6; 978-0-578-72593-2; 978-0-578-75332-4; 978-0-578-75333-1; 978-0-578-75336-2; 978-0-578-75734-6; 978-0-578-76746-8; 978-0-578-77291-2; 978-0-578-78480-9; 978-0-578-78943-9; 978-0-578-79216-3; 978-0-578-80947-2; 978-0-578-81096-6; 978-0-578-82083-5; 978-0-578-84621-7; 978-0-578-85240-9; 978-0-578-86115-*) *Ingram Content Group, One Ingram Blvd., LaVergne, TN 37086 USA.*

IndyPublish.com, (*978-1-58827; 978-1-4043; 978-1-4142; 978-1-4219; 978-1-4280; 978-1-4353; 978-1-4378; 978-1-4491*) 170 Gore St. Suite 405, Cambridge, MA 02141 USA
E-mail: info@indypublish.com
Dist(s): **Ingram Content Group**
TextStream.

InExTra LLC, (*978-1-946972*) 929 Lehigh Cir., Naperville, IL 60565 USA Tel 773-340-9259
E-mail: walz@inextra.biz.

Infant Learning Co., The, (*978-0-9657510; 978-1-931026*) 5009 Isle Royal Ct., Oceanside, CA 92057 USA Tel 760-630-6204; Fax: 760-630-3894; Toll Free: 888-463-2681
E-mail: brendan@infantlearning.com; lisa@infantlearning.com; sharon@infantlearning.com
Web site: http://www.infantlearning.com; http://www.yourbabycanlearn.com
Dist(s): **Penton Overseas, Inc.**

Infini Pr., LLC, (*978-1-932457*) Orders Addr.: P.O. Box 9096, Cincinnati, OH 45209-9096 USA Toll Free: 800-765-5885; Edit Addr.: 1120 Ave. of the Americas, Fourth Flr., New York, NY 10036 USA; *Imprints:* Asia for Kids (Asia for Kids)
E-mail: info@infinipress.com
Web site: http://www.infinipress.com
Dist(s): **Follett School Solutions**
Master Communications, Inc.

Infinite Adventure, (*978-0-9790720*) 6043 S. Danielson Way, Chandler, AZ 85249 USA
E-mail: amb0457@cox.net
Web site: http://www.members.cox.net/valuevolga.

Infinite Light Publishing, (*978-0-9884537; 978-0-9970467; 978-1-947925; 978-1-957256*) 5142 Hollister Ave. No. 115, Santa Barbara, CA 93111 USA Tel 805-350-3239
E-mail: ayn@infinitelightpublishing.com; info@infinitelightpublishing.com; aynsgold@yahoo.com
Web site: www.ayncatessullivan.com; www.astoryofbecoming.net; www.infinitelightpublishing.com
Dist(s): **BCH Fulfillment & Distribution**
New Leaf Distributing Co., Inc.

Infinite Love Publishing, (*978-0-9794827*) 15127 NE 24th St., No. 341, Redmond, WA 98052 USA (SAN 853-5264) Toll Free: 888-733-7105
E-mail: sales@jackiechristie.com; dotti@dotdesign.net
Web site: http://www.jackiechristie.com.

Infinite Visions Forum, (*978-0-9770405*) Orders Addr.: P.O. Box 938, La Verne, CA 91750 USA Tel 909-593-7332 (phone/fax); Edit Addr.: 4095 Fruit St., SP 938, La Verne, CA 91750 USA
E-mail: ivforum@aol.com.

Infinity Bks. USA, (*978-1-7374425*) 405 S. 8th St., Council Bluffs, IA 51501 USA Tel 712-325-9292
E-mail: infinitybooksusa@gmail.com.

Infinity Flower Publishing, LLC *Imprint of* **Barrera, Elizabeth Paige**

Infinity Oak Bks., (*978-0-9885066*) Orders Addr.: P.O. Box 195964, Dallas, TX 75219 USA Tel 972-803-4744
E-mail: jillksayre@me.com.

Infinity One Publishing, (*978-0-9772888*) P.O. Box 725394, Atlanta, GA 31139 USA Tel 678-760-6664; Fax: 617-507-8352
E-mail: thesleepysteve@yahoo.com.

Infinity Plus Publishing, (*978-1-7333739; 978-1-7378202*) P.O. Box 92308, Lakeland, FL 33804 USA Tel 813-358-8104
E-mail: info@letsgodreaming.com
Web site: www.letsgodreaming.com.

Infinity Publishing *See* **Macro Publishing Group**

Infinity Publishing, (*978-0-9665678; 978-1-892896; 978-0-7414; 978-1-4958*) Div. of Buy Books On The Web.Com, 1094 New Dehaven St., Suite 100, West Conshohocken, PA 19428 USA Tel 610-941-9999; Fax: 610-941-9959; Toll Free: 877-289-2665
E-mail: info@infinitypublishing.com
Web site: http://www.buybooksontheweb.com; http://www.infinitypublishing.com/
Dist(s): **Smashwords.**

Infinity Publishing, (*978-0-9640184*) 8525 Evergreen Ln., Darien, IL 60561 USA Tel 708-985-2300; Fax: 708-985-2339 Do not confuse with companies with same name in Seattle WA, Lansing IL, West Palm Beach, FL.

Infinity Publishing Co., (*978-0-9799487*) 11111 N. Scottsdale Rd., Suite 205, Scottsdale, AZ 85260 USA Tel 480-703-0606
E-mail: pchambers8@cox.net
Web site: http://www.infinitypublishingcompany.com.

Infinity Studios LLC, (*978-1-59697*) 2601 Hilltop Dr. Apt. 815, San Pablo, CA 94806-5797 USA Do not confuse with companies with the same or similar name in Austin, TX
E-mail: info@infinitystudios.com
Web site: http://www.infinitystudios.com
Dist(s): **Diamond Comic Distributors, Inc.**
Diamond Bk. Distributors.

Influence, (*978-1-936699; 978-1-937830; 978-1-938309; 978-1-62912*) 1445 N. Boonville Ave., Springfield, MO 65802 USA Tel 417-831-8000; Fax: 417-862-5881
E-mail: apargo@ag.org; SUPPORT@INFLUENCERESOURCES.COM; tbledsoe@ag.org
Web site: http://store.influenceresources.com/
Dist(s): **Baker & Taylor Publisher Services (BTPS)**
Lulu Pr., Inc.
MyiLibrary
ebrary, Inc.

Infobase Holdings, Inc., (*978-0-7808; 978-0-7910; 978-0-8160; 978-0-87196; 978-1-55888; 978-1-60825; 978-1-61616; 978-1-61733; 978-1-62102; 978-1-62290; 978-1-68272; 978-1-63521; 978-1-64023; 978-1-64198; 978-1-64347; 978-1-64481; 978-1-64623; 978-1-64693; 978-1-64867;-1-63722; 978-1-68566; 979-8-88678; 979-8-88725; 979-8-89206*) *132 West 31st St., 17th Flr., New York, NY 10001 USA Tel 1-800-322-8755; Imprints:* Facts On File (MYID_P_FACTS O); Bloom's Literary Criticism (BlmLtIBH); Chelsea Clubhouse (ChelsChIBH); Ferguson Publishing Company (FergPCIBH); Checkmark Books (ChckmrkIBH)
E-mail: info@infobase.com; CustServ@infobase.com
Web site: https://www.infobase.com; https://infobasepublishing.com/,
Dist(s): **Facts On File, Inc.**
Cengage Gale
Omnigraphics, Inc.

Infobase Learning *See* **Infobase Holdings, Inc.**

Infobus, Inc., (*978-0-9771184*) 19 Yellow Brook Rd., Holmdel, NJ 07733-1967 USA Tel 732-332-0232.

InfoHi Publishing, (*978-0-9678605; 978-0-9717849*) P.O. Box 1688, Fremont, CA 94538 USA Tel 831-685-1063
E-mail: linda@infohi.com
Web site: http://www.infohi.com
Dist(s): **Booklines Hawaii, Ltd.**

INFORMA INC, (*978-0-692-90984-3; 978-1-948346; 978-1-948817; 978-1-949338; 978-1-950024; 978-1-950771; 978-1-951306; 978-1-951822; 978-1-952309; 978-1-952852; 978-1-956073; 978-1-957039*) 30 Wall St 8th Flr., New York City , NY 10005 USA Tel 866-257-9368; 607 Deemer PL Suite 424, New Castle, DE 19720 Tel 866-256-1278
E-mail: vanessa.jones@bookartpress.us.

Information Age Publishing, Inc., (*978-1-930608; 978-1-931576; 978-1-59311; 978-1-60752; 978-1-61735; 978-1-62396; 978-1-68123; 978-1-64113; 978-1-64802; 979-8-88730*) P.O. Box 79049, Charlotte, NC 28271 USA (SAN 925-9228) Tel 704-752-9125; Fax: 704-752-9113 Do not confuse with Information Age Publishing in Exeter, NH
E-mail: iap@infoagepub.com; info@infoagepub.com
Web site: http://www.infoagepub.com
Dist(s): **Ambassador Bks. & Media**
Midwest Library Service
Blackwell
ebrary, Inc.

Information Science Publishing *Imprint of* **IGI Global**

Infusionmedia Publishing, (*978-0-9704852; 978-0-9718677; 978-0-9796586; 978-0-9843101*) 140 N. 8th St., Suite 205, Lincoln, NE 68508-1358 USA (SAN 253-9136) Tel 402-477-2065 (phone/fax)
E-mail: info@infusionmediapublishing.com
Web site: http://www.infusionmediapublishing.com
Dist(s): **Smashwords.**

Ingenuity 31 Inc., (*978-0-578-05331-8*) 109 N. Church St., Waynesboro, PA 17268 USA
E-mail: ingenuity31@yahoo.com.

Ingle, Rosalie, (*978-0-578-09876-0*) P.O. Box 8636, St. Joseph, MO 64508 USA.

Ingleside Pr., (*978-1-929883*) P.O. Box 30029, Baltimore, MD 21215 USA
E-mail: inglesidepress@yahoo.com
Web site: http://inkwell62.wixsite.com/inglesidepress.

InGrace Pubns., (*978-0-9679145; 978-0-9719262; 978-0-9858764; 978-1-7338976; 979-8-9860253*) 24126 N. Quentin Rd., Lake Zurich, IL 60047 USA Tel 847-438-4494 ext 1071; Fax: 847-438-4232; Toll Free: 800-784-7223
E-mail: contact@ingrace.us
Web site: http://ingrace.us.

Ingram Bk. Co., (*978-1-61522; 978-1-60894*) Subs. of Ingram Industries, Inc., Orders Addr.: 1 Ingram Blvd., P.O. Box 3006, La Vergne, TN 37086-1986 USA (SAN 169-7978) Tel 615-213-5000; Fax: 615-213-3976 (Electronic Orders); Toll Free Fax: 800-285-3296 (fax inquiry US & Canada); 800-876-0186 (orders); 877-663-5367 (Canadian orders); Toll Free: 800-937-8000 (orders only); 800-937-8200 (customer service US & Canada); 800-289-0687 (Canadian orders only customer service); 800-234-6737 (electronic orders US & Canada)) Do not confuse with Ingram Pr., Sacramento, CA
E-mail: flashback@ingrambook.com; customerservice@ingrambook.com; ics-sales@ingrambook.com
Web site: http://www.ingrambook.com.

Ingram Content Group, Orders Addr.: 1246 Heil Quaker Blvd., LaVergne, TN 37086 USA (SAN 179-6976) Tel 615-213-4595; Fax: 615-213-4426; 860 Nestle Way - LSI Lightning Source, Breingsville, PA 18031 (SAN 920-4288)
E-mail: edi@ingramcontent.com.

Ingram Publisher Services, Orders Addr.: Customer Services, Box 512 1 Ingram Blvd., LaVergne, TN 37086 USA Toll Free Fax: 800-838-1149; Edit Addr.: 1 Ingram Blvd., LaVergne, TN 37086 USA (SAN 631-8630) Tel 615-793-5000; Fax: 615-213-5811
E-mail: customer.service@ingrampublisherservices.com; Publisher@ingrampublisherservices.com; Retailer@ingrampublisherservices.com
Web site: http://www.ingrampublisherservices.com.

Ingram, Sean Inc., (*978-0-9749049; 978-0-615-11910-6*) 176 Lane Rd., Stantonsburg, NC 27883 USA Tel 919-517-7326; Fax: 919-870-7227
E-mail: sean@seaningram.com
Web site: http://www.seaningram.com.

Ingram Spark, (*978-0-9965609; 978-1-7350397*) P.O. Box 93, Maplecrest, NY 12454 USA Tel 518-275-7754
E-mail: josiemoonpelham@gmail.com.

Ingram's Nutrition Consultations, (*978-0-9769379*) 43889 Bayview Ave. Apt. 40107, Clinton Twp, MI 48038-7073 USA; 7701 Corporate Dr., No.212, Houston, TX 77036 (SAN 850-5179) Tel 281-513-4596; Fax: 713-771-2177
E-mail: admin@ingramsnutritionconsultations.com
Web site: http://www.ingram's nutrition.com.

IngramSpark *See* **Indy Pub**

IngramSpark, (*978-0-578-90124-4; 978-0-578-90125-1*) 5130 Saint Michael Ave, Belle Isle, FL 32812-1139 USA Tel 407-443-2805
E-mail: shanmcd77@hotmail.com.

Ingramspark, (*978-0-578-53031-4; 978-0-578-61343-7*) 918 N Harrison, Sherman, TX 75090 USA Tel 903-209-9332
E-mail: Japhetangono78@yahoo.com.

Ingramspark, *(978-0-578-35393-7)* 209 Reigate dr, El Paso, TX 79928 USA Tel 504-609-9499
E-mail: edorsey222@gmail.com.

INgrooves *See* **INscribe Digital**

Inhabit Education Bks. Inc. (CAN) *(978-0-9938975; 978-0-9940216; 978-1-77266; 978-1-987876; 978-1-987958; 978-0-2287; 978-1-77450) Dist. by* **Consort Bk Sales.**

Inhabit Media Inc. (CAN) *(978-0-9782186; 978-1-926569; 978-1-927095; 978-1-77227) Dist. by* **Consort Bk Sales.**

Inheritance Pr., Inc., *(978-0-9638066; 978-0-9749501)* Orders Addr.: P.O. Box 580, Trenton, NC 28585-0580 USA; Edit Addr.: 388 Henderson Ln., Trenton, NC 28585 USA.

Inherst, Marie, *(978-0-9749785)* 52670 TH 180, Beallsville, OH 43716-9226 USA.

Ink & Feathers Comics, *(978-0-9664974)* Div. of Ink & Feathers Calligraphy, Orders Addr.: 202 E. Grove St., Streator, IL 61364 USA Tel 815-672-1171
E-mail: nerwonduh@hotmail.com
Web site: http://www.ifcomics.com.

Ink & Quill Pubs. *Imprint of* **Mystic Pubs., Inc.**

Ink & Scribe, *(978-0-9679817; 978-1-931947)* Div. of Wise River Companies, Inc., 3101 Kintzley Ct. Unit J, Laporte, CO 80535-9393 USA Toll Free: 888-616-7720
E-mail: books@northfortynews.com
Web site: http://www.inkandscribe.com.

Ink Monster, *(978-0-9894050; 978-0-9960864; 978-0-9906352; 978-1-943858; 978-1-955974)*
E-mail: info@inkmonster.net
Dist(s): **INscribe Digital**
Independent Pubs. Group.

Ink queens publishing, *(978-1-7359312; 979-8-218-24771-3)* 211 Ft. Edward dr, ARLINGTON, TX 76002 USA Tel 682-559-7878
E-mail: d_preyor@yahoo.com.

Ink Well, *(978-0-9767578)* P.O. Box 786, Winlock, WA 98596 USA; *Imprints:* Ink Well Publishing (I W P) Do not confuse with Ink Well in Hermosa Beach, CA.

Ink Well Publishing *Imprint of* **Ink Well**

Inkberry Pr., *(978-0-9742148)* 15521 Shell Point Blvd., Fort Myers, FL 33908 USA Tel 239-466-2757
E-mail: wallykain@comcast.net.

Inkberry Pr., *(978-0-9838293)* 4110 S. Highland Dr. Suite 340, Salt Lake City, UT 84124 USA Tel 801-949-1083
E-mail: editorial@leatherwoodpress.com.

Inkblot Bks., *(978-1-932461)* Orders Addr.: 1285 Stratford Ave STE-G No. 115, Dixon, CA 95620 USA; Edit Addr.: 415 Mast Ct, Dixon, CA 95620 USA
E-mail: kathompson@gmail.com
Web site: http://www.inkblotbooks.com
Dist(s): **Smashwords.**

Inkchanted Publishing LLC, *(978-0-578-43819-1)* P.O. Box 572, Princeton, LA 71067 USA Tel 318-518-0800
E-mail: inkchantedpublishing@gmail.com.

InkDrops Publishing, *(978-1-7337947)* 73 N. State Rd., Upper Darby, PA 19082 USA Tel 267-574-1545; *Imprints:* Brown Brainy Brilliant Books (MYID_R_BROWN)
E-mail: inkdropspublications@gmail.com.

Inkling Bks., *(978-1-58742)* 584 Homewood Dr., Auburn, AL 36830 USA Tel 334-369-9613
E-mail: editor@inklingbooks.com
Web site: http://www.inklingbooks.com/
Dist(s): **CreateSpace Independent Publishing Platform**
Smashwords.

Inklings Publishing, *(978-0-9910211; 978-1-944428)* 7222 Granvia Dr., Houston, TX 77083 USA Tel 281-736-7168
E-mail: fbrady.03@comcast.net
Web site: http://inklingspublishing.com.

Inknbeans Pr., *(978-0-615-62429-7; 978-0-615-62896-7; 978-0-615-63408-1; 978-0-615-64400-4; 978-0-615-68085-9; 978-0-615-71952-8; 978-0-615-72837-7; 978-0-615-73222-0; 978-0-9886670; 978-0-615-73861-1; 978-0-615-74204-5; 978-0-615-74488-9; 978-0-615-74719-4; 978-0-615-74944-0; 978-0-615-74958-7; 978-0-615-74961-7; 978-0-615-75145-0; 978-0-615-75791-9; 978-0-615-75854-1; 978-0-615-76442-9; 978-0-615-76749-9; 978-0-615-77178-6; 978-0-615-77534-0; 978-0-615-78970-5; 978-0-615-80657-0; 978-0-615-81135-2; 978-) 25060 Hancock Ave. Bldg 103 Suite 458, Murrieta, CA 92560 USA Tel 951-471-8184*
Web site: inknbeans.com
Dist(s): **CreateSpace Independent Publishing Platform**
Steuben Pr.

Inkshares, *(978-1-941758; 978-1-942645; 978-1-947848; 978-1-950301)* 415 Jackson St Suite B, San Francisco, CA 94111 USA Tel 919-418-0835
E-mail: thad@inkshares.com
Web site: http://www.inkshares.com
Dist(s): **Publishers Group West (PGW)**
Two Rivers Distribution.

Inkspil Publishing, *(978-0-9833877; 978-0-615-79874-5)* 1676 W. Bryn Mawr, Chicago, IL 60660 USA Tel 708-824-8465
E-mail: inkspillbooks@gmail.com
Web site: www.inkspillbooks.com
Dist(s): **CreateSpace Independent Publishing Platform.**

Inkspill Publishing House *See* **Inkspil Publishing**

Inkstone Literary, *(978-1-958169; 978-1-960362; 978-1-961119)* 14412 Lemongrass Ln., Pflugerville, TX 78660 USA Tel 310-734-8854
E-mail: ajames.finance@gmail.com
Web site: https://inkstoneliterary.com.

Inkwell Books LLC, *(978-0-9658158; 978-0-9718155; 978-0-9728118; 978-0-9749701; 978-0-9766340; 978-0-9786202; 978-0-9814648; 978-0-9829589; 978-0-9833247; 978-0-9848019; 978-0-9852501; 978-0-9883568; 978-1-939625; 978-0-9861743; 978-0-578-50033-1; 978-0-578-66486-6; 978-0-578-70836-2; 978-0-578-84662-0; 978-1-7366445; 979-8-9880779) Orders Addr.: 10632 N. Scottsdale Rd. Unit 695, Scottsdale, AZ 85254 USA Tel 480-315-3781*
E-mail: info@inkwellbooksllc.com
Web site: http://inkwellbooksllc.com/.

Inkwell Productions, LLC *See* **Inkwell Books LLC**

InMediaRes Productions, *(978-0-9792047; 978-1-934857; 978-1-936876; 978-1-941582; 978-1-942487; 978-1-947335; 978-1-63861; 979-8-9853598; 979-8-9853599; 979-8-98872; 979-8-88918)* 303 91st Ave., PMB 202 E502, Lake Stevens, WA 98258 USA Fax: 425-948-1301; *Imprints:* Catalyst Game Labs (Catalyst Game)
Web site: http://www.imrpro.com; http://www.catalystgamelabs.com
Dist(s): **PSI (Publisher Services, Inc.).**

Innate Foundation Publishing, *(978-0-9745866)* 276 Cherry St., Blaine, WA 98230 USA Tel 360-441-9156
E-mail: rca@robertclydeaffolter.com
Web site: http://www.innatefoundation.com.

Inner Circle Publishing, *(978-0-9770682)* 1407 Crane St., Schenectady, NY 12303 USA Tel 518-377-0548.

Inner City Publications *See* **Citified Pubns.**

Inner Light - Global Communications, *(978-0-938294; 978-1-892062; 978-1-60611)* Orders Addr.: P.O. Box 753, New Brunswick, NJ 08903 USA (SAN 662-0191) Tel 646-331-6777; Edit Addr.: 1231 Hamilton St., Somerset, NJ 08873 USA
E-mail: mrufo@hotmail.com
Dist(s): **Distributors, The**
Distributors International
New Leaf Distributing Co., Inc.
Quality Bks., Inc.
Red Wheel/Weiser
Unique Bks., Inc.

Inner Peace Pr., *(978-1-7351738; 978-1-958150)* 3360 SOUTHGATE CT, Eau Claire, WI 54701, Eau Claire, WI 54701 USA Tel 715-379-1823
E-mail: heatherafelty@gmail.com; heather@innerpeacepress.com
Web site: https://innerpeacepress.com.

Inner Quality Publishing, *(978-0-9988319)* 13258 Spruce Run Dr., North Royalton, OH 44133 USA Tel 440-877-9390; *Imprints:* Nana Says (NanaSays)
E-mail: lauren@centerforinnerquality.com.

Inner Reaches Pr., *(978-0-9821782)* 13420 Query Mill Rd., North Potomac, MD 20878 USA (SAN 857-460X)
Web site: http://www.innerreaches.com.

†Inner Traditions International, Ltd., *(978-0-89281; 978-0-905249; 978-1-899171; 978-0-906191; 978-0-9504268; 978-1-84409; 978-1-59477; 978-1-62055; 978-1-64411; 979-8-88850)* Orders Addr.: P.O. Box 388, Rochester, VT 05767-0388 USA Tel 802-767-3174; Fax: 802-767-3726; Toll Free Fax: 800-246-8648; Edit Addr.: One Park St., Rochester, VT 05767 USA (SAN 208-6948) Tel 802-767-3174; Fax: 802-767-3726; *Imprints:* Destiny Books (Destiny Bks); Healing Arts Press (Heal Arts VT); Bindu Books (Bindu Bks); Findhorn Press (FindhornPr); Earthdancer Books (EarthdancerBks)
E-mail: customerservice@innertraditions.com; info@innertraditions.com
Web site: http://www.innertraditions.com
Dist(s): **Beekman Bks., Inc.**
Book Wholesalers, Inc.
Bookazine Co., Inc.
Brodart Co.
Independent Pub.
Integral Yoga Pubns.
Library Sales of N.J.
Lotus Pr.
MyiLibrary
New Leaf Distributing Co., Inc.
Nutri-Bks. Corp.
Partners/West Book Distributors
Quality Bks., Inc.
Simon & Schuster
Simon & Schuster, Inc.
Unique Bks., Inc.; *CIP.*

Inner Wisdom Pubns., *(978-0-9656741; 978-0-9774921)* 22850 Summit Rd., Los Gatos, CA 95033 USA (SAN 299-2450) Tel 408-353-2050; Fax: 408-353-4663; Toll Free: 888-468-4335
E-mail: 15minutemiracle@verizon.net
Web site: http://www.15MinuteMiracle.com.

InnerChamp Bks., *(978-0-9663949)* P.O. Box 11362, Santa Rosa, CA 95406 USA Tel 707-571-8023; Fax: 707-546-3764
E-mail: inrchamp@aol.com
Web site: http://www.innerchamp.com.

Innerchild Publishing, Inc., *(978-0-9768078)* Orders Addr.: P.O. Box 142317, Fayetteville, GA 30214-2317 USA.

Innerchoice Publishing, *(978-0-9625486; 978-1-56499)* 24426 S. Main, Carson, CA 90745 USA Tel 310-816-3085; Fax: 310-816-3092
Dist(s): **Jalmar Pr.**

InnerCircle Publishing, *(978-1-882918; 978-0-9723191; 978-0-9755214; 978-0-9762924)* 522 Sadie St. Apt. 2, Laurens, IA 50554-1553 USA
Web site: http://www.innercirclepublishing.com; http://www.rev-press.com.

InnerPrize Group, LLC, *(978-1-947485)* 411 SE Delaware Ave. Unit 204, ANKENY, IA 50021 USA Tel 312-399-0886; *Imprints:* Mine Rich In Gems (MYID_B_MINE RI)
E-mail: innerprizeceo@gmail.com; innerprizecfo@gmail.com; innerprizecco@gmail.com; lilishang9@gmail.com
Web site: www.innerprizegroup.com; www.auntielili.com; www.minerichingems.com.

InnerRESOURCES Pubns., *(978-0-9728389)* 109 E. 73rd St., New York, NY 10021 USA
E-mail: jeff@jefflandau.com; jefflandau@innerresources.org
Web site: http://jeffs.smugmug.com/; http://www.jefflandau.com; http://www.innerresources.org; http://www.flickr.com/photos/8ideas/
Dist(s): **Ingram Content Group.**

innertuber, *(978-0-9742742)* 2124 NE 7th St., Gainesville, FL 32609 USA.

Innerworld Pubns., *(978-1-881717; 978-1-939983)* P.O. Box 1613, San German, PR 00683 USA Tel 787-264-3587 (phone/fax)
E-mail: devashish@coqui.net
Web site: http://www.innerworldpublications.com.

Innov8 Studios, *(978-0-9754544)* 16 Cedarwood Dr., Ballston Lake, NY 12019 USA
E-mail: innov8studios@nycap.rr.com.

Innovation Game, The, *(978-0-9643819)* 8509 Irvington Ave., Bethesda, MD 20817 USA Tel 301-530-4299.

Innovation Pr., The, *(978-1-943147; 978-1-959244)* 7511 Greenwood Ave N, Seattle, WA 98103 USA Tel 360-870-9988
E-mail: acitro@theinnovationpress.com
Web site: http://www.theinnovationpress.com
Dist(s): **Baker & Taylor Publisher Services (BTPS)**
Blackstone Audio, Inc.
Legato Pubs. Group.

Innovative Christian Pubns. *Imprint of* **Baker Trittin Pr.**

Innovative Eggz LLC, *(978-1-945644; 978-1-64032)* 7208 W Angela Dr, Glendale, AZ 85308 USA Tel 517-817-8093; *Imprints:* Puppet Theater Books (MYID_H_PUPPET) .

Innovative Kids, *(978-1-58476; 978-1-60169)* Div. of Innovative USA, Inc., 18 Ann St., Norwalk, CT 06854-2258 USA Tel 203-838-6400; Fax: 203-855-5582; *Imprints:* IKIDS (IKIDS)
E-mail: info@innovativekids.com
Web site: http://www.innovativekids.com
Dist(s): **Hachette Bk. Group.**

Innovative Language, LLC, *(978-0-9765236)* P.O. Box 1593, Eugene, OR 97440-1593 USA.

Innovative Logistics, Orders Addr.: 575 Prospect St., Lakewood, NJ 08701 USA (SAN 760-6532) Tel 732-534-7001; 732-363-5679; Fax: 732-363-0338
E-mail: innlogorders@innlog.net
Web site: http://www.innlog.net.

Innovo Pr. *Imprint of* **Innovo Publishing, LLC**

Innovo Publishing, LLC, *(978-0-9815403; 978-1-936076; 978-1-61314; 979-8-88928)* 159 College St., Collierville, TN 38017 USA Fax: 901-221-4055; Toll Free: 888-546-2111; *Imprints:* Innovo Press (Innovo Pr)
E-mail: info@innovopublishing.com
Web site: http://www.innovopublishing.com; christianpublishingportal.com.

Inprint Bks., *(978-0-9814510; 978-0-9973316)* 1223 Wilshire Blvd., Suite 1413, Santa Monica, CA 90403 USA (SAN 855-5923).

INscribe Digital, *(978-1-61750; 978-1-62517)* Div. of Independent Publishers Group, 55 Francisco St. Suite 710, San Francisco, CA 94105 USA; *Imprints:* Brown Girls Publishing (BrownGirls)
E-mail: digitalpublishing@ingrooves.com
Web site: http://www.INscribeDigital.com
Dist(s): **Independent Pubs. Group**
Lulu Pr., Inc.

Insect Lore, *(978-1-891541)* Orders Addr.: P.O. Box 1535, Shafter, CA 93263 USA Tel 661-746-6047; Fax: 661-746-0334; Toll Free: 800-548-3284; Edit Addr.: 132 S. Beech St., Shafter, CA 93263 USA
E-mail: john@insectlore.com
Web site: http://www.insectlore.com.

Insect Sciences Museum of California, *(978-0-9764454)* 3644 Calafia Ave., Oakland, CA 94605 USA; *Imprints:* Exploring California Insects (Ex CA In)
E-mail: insectnet@aol.com
Web site: http://www.bugpeople.org.

Inside Out Publishing *See* **Building Authors Publishing**

Insight Editions, *(978-1-933784; 978-1-60887; 978-0-615-39977-5; 978-0-615-50360-8; 978-0-615-50366-0; 978-1-68298; 978-1-68383; 978-1-64722; 979-8-88663)* 800 A St., San Rafael, CA 94901 USA; P.O. Box 3088, San Rafael, CA 94912 Tel 415-526-1370; Fax: 866-509-0515 eFax; *Imprints:* Earth Aware Editions (EarthAware)
Dist(s): **Children's Plus, Inc.**
Hachette Bk. Group
Open Road Integrated Media, Inc.
Simon & Schuster, Inc.

Insight Publishing Group, *(978-1-930027; 978-1-932503; 978-1-960452)* Div. of Insight International, Inc., 8801 S. Yale, Suite 410, Tulsa, OK 74137 USA Tel 918-493-1718; Fax: 918-493-2219; Toll Free: 800-924-8264 Do not confuse with companies with similar names in Parker, CO, Yreka,CA, Jacksonville, FL, Woodbridge, VA, Salt Lake City, UT
E-mail: info@freshword.com
Web site: http://www.freshword.com
Dist(s): **Smashwords.**

Insight Services, Inc, *(978-0-9786034)* 1020 Hummingbird Ct., Springfield, TN 37172-5563 USA (SAN 851-092X); *Imprints:* Children's Insight (Children's Insight)
E-mail: childrensinsight@learnlivebetter.com
Web site: http://www.learnlivebetter.com.

Insight Studios, LLC *See* **Bugeye Bks.**

Insight Technical Education, *(978-0-9722058; 978-0-9755280)* 13410 NE 92nd St., Vancouver, WA 98682 USA Tel 360-852-6152
E-mail: webinfo@sixbranches.com
Web site: http://www.insightteched.com.

Insights Productions - Innovating Education, *(978-0-9753827)* P.O. Box 1323, Fall City, WA 98024 USA Tel 206-391-5993; Fax: 425-222-7549
E-mail: alandelaossa@centurytel.net.

Inspira *Imprint of* **Editorial Imagen**

Inspirasian Pr. LLC, *(978-0-9743882)* P.O. Box 460256, San Francisco, CA 94146-0256 USA Tel 415-282-7925; Fax: 415-282-6427
Web site: http://www.inspirasian.com.

Inspiration Pr. Inc., *(978-0-9798395)* 8598 N. W. St., Coral Springs, FL 33071 USA
Dist(s): **TNT Media Group, Inc.**

Inspiration Software, Inc., *(978-0-928539; 978-1-932463; 978-1-933238; 978-1-934425)* 9400 SW Beaverton Hillsdale Hwy., No. 300, Beaverton, OR 97005 USA (SAN 670-8234) Toll Free: 800-877-4292
E-mail: jbrooks@inspiration.com
Web site: http://www.inspiration.com
Dist(s): **Follett School Solutions.**

Inspirational Hse. of America, *(978-0-9768598)* 93 Jay Ln., Gasburg, VA 23857 USA.

Inspirations by Grace LaJoy, *(978-0-9747583; 978-0-9814607; 978-0-615-34652-6; 978-0-9829404; 978-0-9987117; 978-0-692-89959-5; 978-0-692-89977-9; 978-1-7341868)* P.O. Box 181, Raymore, MO 64083 USA
Web site: http://www.gracelajoy.com.

Inspire Bks., *(978-1-950685; 978-1-961065)* 1860 Burlington Dr., York, SC 29745 USA Tel 330-416-4916
E-mail: beth@inspire-books.com
Web site: www.inspire-books.com.

Inspire Every Child dba Illumination Arts, *(978-0-615-50779-8; 978-0-9855417)* 808 6th St. S., Ste 200, Kirkland, WA 98033 USA Tel 425-968-5097; Fax: 425-968-5634
E-mail: jthompson@illumin.com
Web site: www.illumin.com.

Inspire Media, LLC *See* **Motivision Media**

Inspire Press, Inc., *(978-0-9741800)* P.O. Box 33241, Los Gatos, CA 95030 USA Tel 408-395-2003; Fax: 408-904-4662
E-mail: sharper@inspirepress.com
Web site: http://www.inspirepress.com.

Inspire Pubns., *(978-0-9725292)* 13229 Middle Canyon Rd., Carmel Valley, CA 93924 USA (SAN 255-1225) Tel 831-917-6059; Fax: 831-659-8460
E-mail: larryhayes@mynamestartswith.com; lhayes@mynamestartswith.com
Web site: http://www.mynamestartswith.com.

Inspire U., LLC, *(978-0-9792361)* 30520 Rancho California Rd., Suite 107-64, Temecula, CA 92591 USA (SAN 852-8535).

Inspired By Family, *(978-0-9787074)* 1332 Westmore Ct., Stevens Point, WI 54481 USA
Web site: http://www.inspiredbyfamily.com.

Inspired by the Beach Co., *(978-0-9790415)* Orders Addr.: P.O. Box 174, Simpsonville, MD 21150-0174 USA
E-mail: mjareaux@ureach.com
Web site: http://www.26thingstoteach.com.

Inspired By the Beach Publishing *See* **Inspired by the Beach Co.**

InspirEd Educators, *(978-1-933558; 978-1-938275)* 350 Waverly Hall Cir., Roswell, GA 30075 USA Tel 770-649-7571; Fax: 770-642-7568; Toll Free: 866-WE-INSPIRE (866-934-6774)
E-mail: sharon@inspirededucators.com; lainey@inspirededucators.com
Web site: http://www.inspirededucators.com.

Inspired Idea, *(978-1-931203)* 4105 Buckthorn Ct., Flower Mound, TX 75028 USA
E-mail: Eve@pharaohsofthebible.com; Eve@Engelbrite.com
Web site: https://inspiredideapress.com; http://www.kneelingmedia.org.

Inspired Imaginations, LLC, *(978-0-9903752; 978-1-945200)* 1405 S. Bascom Ave., San Jose, CA 95128 USA Tel 408-835-5911
E-mail: todd@maxrhymes.com
Dist(s): **Follett School Solutions.**

Inspired Potentials, *(978-0-9974966)* 7617 Jewel Lake, Anchorage, AK 99502 USA Tel 907-349-2653
E-mail: courtneystrum@gmail.com
Web site: www.inspiredpotentials.com.

Inspired Studios Inc. *See* **Inspired Studios Inc.**

Inspired Studios Inc., *(978-0-7396; 978-0-88149; 978-1-57713; 978-1-943758; 978-1-64183)* 9920 Royal Cardigan Way, West Palm Beach, FL 33411 USA (SAN 287-7589) Tel 561-509-6119; Fax: 561-333-9143; 12862 Whitehorn Way, Boynton Beach, FL 33473
E-mail: DKasen@Inspired-Studios.com; dkasen@inspired-studios.com
Web site: http://www.peterpan.com; www.inspired-Studios.com
Dist(s): **Follett School Solutions**
INscribe Digital
Independent Pubs. Group
Midwest Tape.

InspiredByVanessa, *(978-0-692-68689-8; 978-0-9994246; 978-0-578-58187-3; 978-1-7351788; 978-1-7363669; 978-1-957522)* 21777 Peterson Ave., Sauk Village, IL 60411 USA Tel 312-843-0877
Web site: www.InspiredByVanessa.com
Dist(s): **CreateSpace Independent Publishing Platform.**

InspireGrowth Enterprises, LLC, *(978-0-578-55405-1; 978-0-578-55407-5; 978-1-7340080)* 108 Jefferson St., Highland Mills, NY 10930 USA Tel 646-246-0911
E-mail: stevepiriano@yahoo.com
Dist(s): **Ingram Content Group.**

Inspiring Honey Publishing, *(978-0-578-41328-0; 978-0-578-77769-6; 978-0-578-77770-2; 979-8-218-03401-6; 979-8-218-08971-9; 979-8-218-23186-6; 979-8-218-23187-3)* 201 Pkwy. Dr., Livingston, AL 35470 USA Tel 205-499-3791
E-mail: honeybookseries@gmail.com
Dist(s): **Ingram Content Group.**

Inspiring Jreams Publishing *See* **Sade Harvison**

Inspiring Voices *Imprint of* **Author Solutions, LLC**

Instant Help Books *Imprint of* **New Harbinger Pubns.**

stant Pub., *(978-1-59196; 978-1-59872; 978-1-60458; 978-1-61422)* Orders Addr.: P.O. Box 985, Collierville, TN 38027 USA Tel 901-853-7070; Fax: 901-853-6196; Toll Free: 800-259-2592; Edit Addr.: 410 Hwy, 72 W., Collierville, TN 38017 USA
Web site: http://www.instantpublisher.com
Dist(s): **BookBaby**
Lulu Pr., Inc.
Smashwords.

stantpublisher.com *See* **Instant Pub.**

stitute For Behavior Change Incorporated The, *(978-0-9770503)* 9900 W. Sample Rd., Suite 300, Coral Springs, FL 33065 USA Tel 954-755-6639; Fax: 954-755-4100
E-mail: rhall3318@acn.net
Web site: http://www.afterthestormchildrensbook.com.

stitute for Conscious Change, The, *(978-0-9743443)* Div. of BioPlan Associates, Inc., Orders Addr.: 8987 E. Tanque Verde Rd. Ste. 309, Tucson, AZ 85749-9399 USA
E-mail: info@ConsciousChange.org
Web site: http://www.ConsciousChange.org.

Institute for Creation Research, *(978-0-932766; 978-1-935587; 978-1-946246; 978-1-957850)* 1806 Royal Ln., Dallas, TX 75229 USA Tel 214-615-8300.

Institute for Disabilities Research & Training, Inc., *(978-0-9667589; 978-0-9752933; 978-0-9760818; 978-0-9789373)* 11323 Amherst Ave., Wheaton, MD 20902 USA Tel 301-942-4326; Fax: 301-942-4439
E-mail: sales@idrt.com
Web site: http://www.idrt.com.

Institute for Economic Democracy Pr., Inc., *(978-0-9624423; 978-0-9753555; 978-1-933567)* 13851 N. 103rd Ave., Sun City, AZ 85351-4520 USA Tel 623-583-2518; Toll Free: 888-533-1020 (credit card orders)
E-mail: cc@ccus.info; ied@ied.info
Web site: http://www.ied.info.

Institute for Food & Development Policy/Food First Bks., *(978-0-935028; 978-0-9970989)* 398 60th St., Oakland, CA 94618-1212 USA (SAN 213-327X) Tel 510-654-4400; Fax: 510-654-4551
E-mail: marthak@foodfirst.org
Web site: http://www.foodfirst.org
Dist(s): **Ingram Publisher Services**
L P C Group.

Institute For Outdoor Awareness, Inc, *(978-0-9835176; 978-0-9915227)* 41 Linden Ave., Rutledge, PA 19070 USA Tel 610-544-8335
E-mail: phil@bartowassoc.com
Web site: phil@bartowassoc.com.

Institute for Preventative Sports Med., *(978-0-9745655)* P.O. Box 7032, Ann Arbor, MI 48107 USA Tel 734-434-3390; Fax: 734-572-4503
E-mail: admin@ipsm.org
Web site: http://www.ipsm.org.

Institute in Basic Life Principles, *(978-0-916888)* P.O. Box 1, Oak Brook, IL 60522-3001 USA (SAN 208-6972) Tel 630-323-9800
Web site: http://www.iblp.org; http://www.store.iblp.org; http://www.iblp.org.mx.

Institute in Basic Youth Conflicts *See* **Institute in Basic Life Principles**

Institute of Cybernetics Research, Inc., *(978-1-893375; 978-1-58578)* Orders Addr.: 15 W. 139th St. Apt. 10G, New York, NY 10037-1516 USA
E-mail: icri@usa.net; journal_of_amateur_computing-subscribe@yahoogroups.com
Web site: http://groups.yahoo.com/groups/journal_of_amateur_computing/join
Dist(s): **American Heritage Magazine**
Analog Magazine
Theme Stream, Inc.
Wiley, John & Sons, Inc.

Institute of Physics Publishing, *(978-0-7503; 978-0-85274; 978-0-85498)* The Public Ledte Bldg., Suite 1035 150 S. Independence Mall, W., Philadelphia, PA 19106 USA (SAN 298-2315) Tel 215-627-0880; Fax: 215-627-0879; Toll Free: 800-632-0880; Dirac House Temple Back, Bristol, BS1 6BE Tel 44 (0) 117 929 7481; Fax: 44 (0) 117 930 1186
E-mail: book.enquiries@iop.org
Web site: http://bookmark.iop.org
Dist(s): **CRC Pr. LLC**
National Bk. Network.

Instream Flow Council, *(978-0-9716743)* c/o Wyoming Game & Fish, 5400 Bishop Blvd., Cheyenne, WY 82002 USA Tel 307-777-4600; Fax: 307-777-4611
E-mail: tannea@state.wy.us.

Instructional Fair *Imprint of* **Carson-Dellosa Publishing, LLC**

Instructional Resources Co., *(978-1-879478)* P.O. Box 111704, Anchorage, AK 99511-1704 USA Tel 907-345-6689 (phone/fax)
E-mail: susan@susancanthony.com
Web site: http://www.susancanthony.com.

Instrument Society of America *See* **ISA**

Insu-Form, Incorporated *See* **I.Form Ink, Publishing**

Insundry Productions Bks., *(978-1-7368013; 978-1-962056)* 890 Bollen Cir., GARDNERVILLE, NV 89460 USA Tel 775-392-1367
E-mail: NICKCOOK1@EARTHLINK.NET.

Intaglio, Inc., *(978-0-9748034)* P.O. Box 211296, Montgomery, AL 36109 USA Tel 706-593-2749; Fax: 334-260-9373
E-mail: sperez@intaglioinc.com
Web site: http://www.intaglioinc.com.

Intaglio Pr., *(978-0-944091)* Orders Addr.: P.O. Box 9952, College Station, TX 77842 USA (SAN 242-7133) Tel 409-696-7800; Toll Free: 800-768-5565; Edit Addr.: 8709 Bent Tree, College Station, TX 77845 USA (SAN 242-7141)
E-mail: HDETHL9414@aol.com.

†**Integral Yoga Pubns.,** *(978-0-932040; 978-1-938477)* Satchidananda Ashram-Yogaville, 108 Yogaville Way, Buckingham, VA 23921 USA (SAN 285-0338) Tel 434-969-3121 ex 102; Fax: 434-969-1303; Toll Free: 800-262-1008 (orders)
Web site: http://www.yogaville.org
Dist(s): **Baker & Taylor Publisher Services (BTPS)**
MyiLibrary
New Leaf Distributing Co., Inc.
ebrary, Inc.; *CIP.*

integrated health publishing, *(978-0-615-72324-2; 978-0-9981472; 978-0-578-46893-8)* 9305 fraser Ln., Chesterland, OH 44026 USA Tel 2164692160
E-mail: drlori27@gmail.com
Web site: doctorlori.net
Dist(s): **CreateSpace Independent Publishing Platform.**

Integrity Consulting Enterprise, LLC, *(978-0-9964038)* P.O. Box 651, Menomonee Falls, WI 53052 USA Tel 262-292-9533; 875 N. Michigan Avenue, Suite 3100 John Hancock Ctr., Chicago, IL 60611; *Imprints*: Riley Press (Riley P)
E-mail: candegail@gmail.com; carolyn@lifetc.org
Web site: www.megalife.life; www.rileypress.com; www.integritycce.com; www.carolynganderson.com.

Intellect, Character, & Creativity Institute *See* **Arbor Center for Teaching**

Intelligence e-Publishing Company *See* **IEP - Intelligence Bk. Div.**

Intelligent Concepts, Inc., *(978-0-9740612)* 1889 N. Airport Dr., Lehi, UT 84043 USA Tel 801-766-0262
E-mail: joe@intelcon.biz
Web site: http://www.intelcon.biz.

Intelligent Design Pr., Ltd., *(978-0-9993322)* 1150 First Ave., STE 511, King of Prussia, PA 19406 USA Tel 732-757-7989
E-mail: steph.krell@gmail.com.

Intellipop, LLC, *(978-0-9743805)* 2701 Troy Center Dr., Suite 275, Troy, MI 48084 USA Tel 248-269-6091; Fax: 248-269-6092
E-mail: info@intellipop.com
Web site: http://www.intellipop.com.

Intense Media, LLC, *(978-0-615-31401-3; 978-0-9854709)* 3324 E. Carla Vista Dr., Gilbert, AZ 85295 USA
Dist(s): **CreateSpace Independent Publishing Platform**
Ingram Content Group.

Interaction Point Games, LLC, *(978-1-936326)* 4544 Chowen Ave. N., Robbinsdale, MN 55422 USA
E-mail: brent@interactionpoint.com; info@interactionpoint.com
Web site: http://www.interactionpoint.com.

Interaction Pubs., Inc., *(978-1-57336)* Orders Addr.: P.O. Box 900, Fort Atkinson, WI 53538 USA; Edit Addr.: W5527 State Rd. 106, Fort Atkinson, WI 53538-0800 USA (SAN 631-2950) Tel 920-563-9571; Fax: 920-563-7395; Toll Free: 800-359-0961
E-mail: sales@interact-simulations.com; interact@highsmith.com
Web site: http://www.interact-simulations.com/; http://www.teachinteract.com.

Interactive Eye, L.L.C. *Imprint of* **Interactive Knowledge, Inc.**

Interactive Knowledge, Inc., *(978-0-9759464)* 142 High St., No. 618, Portland, ME 04101 USA Tel 207-775-2278; Fax: 413-778-6861; *Imprints*: Interactive Eye, L.L.C. (InterEye) Do not confuse with Interactive Knowledge, Inc., Charlotte, NC
E-mail: support@iknow.net
Web site: http://www.iknow.net.

Interactive Media Publishing, *(978-0-9744391; 978-1-934332)* Orders Addr.: P.O. Box 1407, Phoenix, OR 97535-1407 USA (SAN 256-095X) Tel 541-535-5552; Fax: 888-900-1598; *Imprints*: Once Upon A Time in a Classroom (OnceUponTime)
E-mail: orders@i-mediapub.com; linda@i-mediapub.com
Web site: http://www.interactivemediapub.com; http://www.edfortech.com; http://www.exploringrobotics.com
Dist(s): **New Leaf Distributing Co., Inc.**

Interactive Pubns. Pty, Ltd. (AUS) *(978-1-876819; 978-1-921479; 978-1-921869; 978-0-646-32685-6; 978-0-646-32746-4; 978-1-922332; 978-1-922830; 978-1-922120; 978-1-925231) Dist. by* **LightSource CS.**

Interactive Pubns. Pty, Ltd. (AUS) *(978-1-876819; 978-1-921479; 978-1-921869; 978-0-646-32685-6; 978-0-646-32746-4; 978-1-922120; 978-1-925231; 978-1-922332; 978-1-922830) Dist. by* **CreateSpace.**

Interactive Stories, *(978-0-692-23199-9; 978-0-692-36847-3; 978-0-692-37008-7; 978-1-945906)* 2001 Kingston Rd, Farmington, UT 84025 USA Tel 801-867-7493
Web site: http://minecraft-interactive.com
Dist(s): **CreateSpace Independent Publishing Platform.**

Intercultural Communication Services, Inc., *(978-0-9741881; 978-0-9773359)* 2580 SW 76th Ave., Portland, OR 97225-3305 USA Fax: 503-292-6817
E-mail: jolinda@jolindaosborne.com
Web site: http://www.jolindaosborne.com.

Interdimensional Pr., *(978-0-9827753; 978-0-9911970)* 480 Lakeview Dr. Suite 107, Brentwood, CA 94513 USA Tel 925-513-1596 (phone/fax)
E-mail: pmcculley@comcast.net
Dist(s): **Ingram Content Group.**

Interface Publishing *See* **IGI Pr.**

Interior Dept. *Imprint of* **United States Government Printing Office**

Interlink Bks. *Imprint of* **Interlink Publishing Group, Inc.**

Interlink Publishing Group, Inc., *(978-0-940793; 978-1-56656; 978-1-62371)* 46 Crosby St., Northampton, MA 01060-1804 USA (SAN 664-8908) Tel 413-582-7054; Fax: 413-582-6731; Toll Free: 800-238-5465; *Imprints*: Crocodile Books (Crocodile Bks); Interlink Books (Interlink Bks)
E-mail: info@interlinkbooks.com; editor@interlinkbooks.com
Web site: http://www.interlinkbooks.com
Dist(s): **MyiLibrary**
Publishers Group West (PGW)
Simon & Schuster, Inc.

Interlink Resources International *See* **CJR**

Interlude Pr. *Imprint of* **Chicago Review Pr.**

Intermedia Publishing Group, *(978-0-9820458; 978-0-9819682; 978-1-935529; 978-1-935906; 978-1-937654; 978-0-615-56309-1)* Orders Addr.: P.O. Box 2825, Peoria, AZ 85380 USA Tel 623-337-8710; Fax: 623-867-9469
E-mail: halton@intermediapr.com; ldavis@intermediapr.com
Web site: http://www.intermediapub.com.

Intermedio Editores S.A. (COL) *(978-958-637) Dist. by* **Random.**

International Alliance Pro-Publishing, LLC, *(978-1-60942)* 7260 W. Azure Dr. 140-744, Las Vegas, NV 89130 USA Tel 206-339-9080
E-mail: therebox@yahoo.com
Web site: http://www.iappublishing.net.

International Arts & Artists, *(978-0-9662859; 978-0-9767102; 978-0-9883497; 978-0-9973099; 978-1-7377492)* 9 Hillyer Ct., NW, Washington, DC 20008 USA Fax: 202-333-0758
E-mail: design@artsandartists.org; designstudio@artsandartists.org
Web site: http://www.artsandartists.org
Dist(s): **Tuttle Publishing**
Univ. of Washington Pr.

†**International Bk. Ctr., Inc.,** *(978-0-86685; 978-0-917062)* 2007 Laurel Dr., P.O. Box 295, Troy, MI 48099 USA (SAN 169-4014) Tel 248-879-7920; 586-254-7230; Fax: 586-254-7230
E-mail: ibc@ibcbooks.com
Web site: http://www.ibcbooks.com; *CIP.*

International Bk. Import Service, Inc., Orders Addr.: 161 Main St., P.O. Box 8188, Lynchburg, TN 37352-8188 USA (SAN 630-5679) Tel 931-759-7400; Fax: 931-759-7555; Toll Free: 800-277-4247
E-mail: IBIS@IBIService.com
Web site: http://www.IBIService.com.

International Children's Books *See* **Calabrese, Christine**

International Church of the Foursquare Gospel *See* **Foursquare Media, ICFG**

International Comics & Entertainment L.L.C., *(978-1-929090; 978-1-932575)* 1005 Mahone St., Fredericksburg, VA 22401 USA Tel 540-899-9186; Fax: 540-899-9196
E-mail: kblue@ic-ent.com
Web site: http://www.ic-ent.com
Dist(s): **Diamond Comic Distributors, Inc.**

International Council for Computers in Education *See* **International Society for Technology in Education**

International Council for Gender Studies, *(978-1-929656)* Orders Addr.: P.O. Box 702, Waxahachie, TX 75168 USA Fax: 972-937-9930; Toll Free: 800-317-6958
E-mail: rivilian@yahoo.com; icgsinfo@yahoo.com
Web site: http://www.fiveaspects.com; www.5aspects.org.

International Debate Education Assn., *(978-0-9702130; 978-0-9720541; 978-1-932716; 978-1-61770)* 224 W. 57th St., New York, NY 10019 USA Tel 212-547-6932; Fax: 646-557-2416; 105 E. 22nd St. Suite 915, New York, NY 10010 Tel 212-300-6076 x9
E-mail: martin.greenwald@opensocietyfoundations.org
Web site: http://www.idebate.org
Dist(s): **Books International, Inc.**

International Development Ctr., *(978-0-9774483; 978-0-9799873)* P.O. Box 25163, Arlington, VA 22202 USA Tel 703-766-0643
E-mail: mi.productions@yahoo.com; ouatiss@yahoo.com.

International Educational Improvement Ctr. Pr., *(978-1-884169)* Orders Addr.: c/o Dr. Archie W. Earl, Sr., Mathematics Dept. School of Science & Technology Norfork State University, Norfolk, VA 23504 USA Tel 757-823-9564
E-mail: awearl@nsu.edu
Web site: http://www.webspawner.com/users/ieicpress/index.html.

International Graphic Group, *(978-0-9821692)* 838 Reedy St., Cincinnati, OH 45202 USA Tel 513-321-7884; Fax: 513-621-1619
E-mail: sales@iggbooks.com.

International Institute for Ecological Agriculture, *(978-0-9790437)* 309 Cedar St. No.127, Santa Cruz, CA 95060 USA (SAN 852-2847) Tel 831-471-9164; Toll Free: 888-737-6228
E-mail: ourstore@permaculture.com
Web site: http://www.permaculture.com.

International Language Centre, 1753 Connecticut Ave., NW, Washington, DC 20009 USA (SAN 209-1615) Tel 202-332-2894; Fax: 202-462-6657
E-mail: richard@newsinform.com; zisa@newsinform.com
Web site: http://www.newsinform.com.

International Learning Systems, Incorporated *See* **International Language Centre**

International Linguistics Corp., *(978-0-939990; 978-1-887371; 978-0-9814540)* 12220 Blue Ridge Blvd., Suite G, Grandview, MO 64030 USA (SAN 220-2573)
E-mail: jennifer@learnables.com
Web site: http://www.learnables.com.

International Literary Properties, *(978-1-953380)* 630 Ninth Ave., New York, NY 10036 USA Tel 914-907-3017
E-mail: subscriptions@ilpliterary.com
Web site: https://www.internationalliteraryproperties.com/.

International Localization Network, *(978-1-935018; 978-1-945423)* 109 Sunset Ct. No. 2., Hamburg, NY 14075 USA Tel 913-773-8323
E-mail: randy2905@gmail.com
Web site: www.ilncenter.com.

International Marine/Ragged Mountain Pr. *Imprint of* **McGraw-Hill Professional Publishing**

†**International Monetary Fund,** *(978-0-939934; 978-1-55775; 978-1-58906; 978-1-61635; 978-1-4518; 978-1-4519; 978-1-4527; 978-1-4552; 978-1-4623; 978-1-4639; 978-1-4755; 978-1-4843; 978-1-4983; 978-1-5135; 979-8-4002)* c/o Publications Department, 700 19th St., NW, Washington, DC 20431 USA (SAN 203-8188) Tel 202-623-7899; P.O. Box 92780, Washington, DC 20090
E-mail: tdelrosario@imf.org; salavi@imf.org; jbeardow@imf.org
Web site: http://www.imf.org; http://.www.cibrary.imf.org
Dist(s): **Bernan Assocs.**
MyiLibrary
Rowman & Littlefield Publishers, Inc.
ebrary, Inc.; *CIP.*

International Pacific Halibut Commission, *(978-0-9776931)* P.O. Box 95009, Seattle, WA 98145-2009 USA Tel 206-634-1838
E-mail: lauri@iphc.washington.edu
Web site: http://www.iphc.washington.edu.

International Scientific Ctr., *(978-0-9630594)* 2655 E. 21st St., Brooklyn, NY 11235 USA Tel 718-368-2918.

International Society for Technology in Education, *(978-0-924667; 978-1-56484; 979-8-88837)* 175 W. Broadway., Suite 300, Eugene, OR 97401-3003 USA (SAN 296-7693) Toll Free: 800-336-5191
E-mail: iste@iste.org
Web site: http://www.iste.org
Dist(s): **Follett School Solutions**
Cengage Gale
Ingram Publisher Services
Two Rivers Distribution.

International Society of Sephardic Leadership Council *See* **ISLC**

International Specialized Book Services *See* **ISBS Publisher Services**

International Step by Step Assn., *(978-1-931854; 978-1-60195)* 400 W. 59th St., New York, NY 10019 USA
E-mail: info@issa.nl
Web site: http://www.issa.nl.

International Training, Incorporated *See* **ITI Holdings, Inc.**

International Univ. Line, *(978-0-9636817; 978-0-9720774; 979-8-9890695)* P.O. Box 2525, La Jolla, CA 92038 USA Tel 858-457-0595; Fax: 858-581-9073
E-mail: info@iul-press.com.

International Vaquero Productions, *(978-0-9761103)* 730 W. 8th St., Claremont, CA 91711 USA
E-mail: ivp1@me.com
Web site: http://www.kurtbeardsley.com.

International Wizard of Oz Club, The, *(978-1-930764)* P.O. Box 26249, San Francisco, CA 94126-6249 USA Fax: 510-642-7589 Do not confuse with International Wizard of OZ Club, Appleton, WI
E-mail: phanff@library.berkeley.edu
Web site: http://ozclub.org.

Interpact Press *See* **Schwartau, Winn LLC**

Interplay Productions, *(978-1-57629)* 16815 Von Karman Ave., Irvine, CA 92606-4920 USA Tel 714-553-6655; Fax: 714-252-2820.

InterPress, *(978-0-9744173)* 14056 Fort Valley Rd., Fort Valley, VA 22652 USA; *Imprints*: Fort Valley Geology Study Center (Ft Valley)
E-mail: wjmelson@shentel.net
Web site: http://interpressusa.com.

Interpreting Time's Past, LLC, *(978-0-692-31046-5; 978-0-9964304; 978-1-7328333)* 450 Old Richmond Rd. S, Crab Orchard, KY 40419 USA Tel 770-364-6512
E-mail: connie@cmhuddleston.com
Web site: www.cmhuddleston.com.

InterRelations Collaborative, Inc., *(978-0-9761753)* P.O. Box 6280, Hamden, CT 06517-3503 USA.

Interset Pr., *(978-1-57433)* Orders Addr.: 35 Burns Hill Rd., Wilton, NH 03086 USA Tel 603-654-2949; *Imprints*: Guild of Limners, The (Guild Limners)
E-mail: artistafloat@earthlink.net; woad@earthlink.net
Dist(s): **Lulu Pr., Inc.**

Interstellar Publishing Co., *(978-0-9645957; 978-1-889599)* Orders Addr.: P.O. Box 7306, Beverly Hills, CA 90212 USA (SAN 298-5829) Tel 310-247-8154 (orders); Fax: 310-247-0622
E-mail: Interstlr@aol.com
Web site: http://www.interstellarpublishing.com.

Interstellar Trading & Publishing Company *See* **Interstellar Publishing Co.**

†**InterVarsity Pr.,** *(978-0-8308; 978-0-87784; 978-1-5140)* Div. of InterVarsity Christian Fellowship of the USA, Orders Addr.: P.O. Box 1400, Downers Grove, IL 60515 USA (SAN 202-7089) Tel 630-734-4000; Fax: 630-734-4200; Toll Free: 800-843-7225 (other depts.); 800-843-9487 (orders); 800-843-1019 (customer service); 800-873-0143 (electronic ordering); *Imprints*: IVP Books (IVP Bks); IVP Kids (IVPkids)
E-mail: email@ivpress.com
Web site: http://www.ivpress.com
Dist(s): **INscribe Digital**
Independent Pubs. Group
Midpoint Trade Bks., Inc.
christianaudio
ebrary, Inc.; *CIP.*

Intervisual/Piggy Toes *Imprint of* **Bendon, Inc.**

InterWeave Corp., *(978-0-9771936; 978-0-9841041)* Orders Addr.: 5364 Ehrlich Rd. No. 248, Tampa, FL 33624 USA Tel 813-933-4431; Fax: 813-933-4311
E-mail: kimberly@wheredoyoufindgod.com; kking@wheredoyoufindgod.com
Web site: http://www.wheredoyoufindgod.com.

IntoPrint Publishing LLC, *(978-1-62352; 978-0-578-44926-5)* 4322 Harding Pike, SUite 417, Nashville, TN 37205 USA Tel 615-210-8593
E-mail: jpcampbell3@mac.com; jonathanperry@comcast.net.

InToto Bks., *(978-0-9961667; 978-0-9968616; 978-1-950514)* 1125 E. Westchester Dr., Springfield, MO 65810 USA Tel 417-887-4782
E-mail: hollyschindler@sbcglobal.net
Web site: hollyschindler.com.

Intralife Systems Publishing, *(978-0-9703102)* P.O. Box 1555, Layton, UT 84041 USA Tel 801-544-2470; Fax: 801-544-2518
E-mail: admin@frogbuster.com
Web site: http://www.frogbuster.com.

Intrepid Films, LLC, *(978-1-929931)* Orders Addr.: P.O. Box 566, Boulder, CO 80306-0566 USA Tel 303-443-2426; Fax: 303-541-9737; Toll Free: 800-279-0802
E-mail: sportinc@msn.com; marya@intrepidfilms.com
Web site: http://www.intrepidfilms.com.

Intrepid Ink, LLC, *(978-0-9843857; 978-1-935774; 978-1-937022; 978-1-943403)* Orders Addr.: P.O. Box 302, McFarland, WI 53558 USA Tel 608-318-3636; *Imprints:* Resurrected Press (ResurrectedPr)
E-mail: publisher@intrepidink.com; irene@intrepidink.com
Web site: http://www.intrepidink.com.

Intrigue Publishing, *(978-0-9762181; 978-0-9794788; 978-0-9893696; 978-1-940758; 978-1-7337793; 979-8-9885333)* 10200 Twisted Stalk Ct., Upper Marlboro, MD 20772 USA
E-mail: dbcamacho@hotmail.com
Web site: http://www.intriguepublishing.com
Dist(s): **Independent Pubs. Group.**

Intuitive Arts Pr., *(978-0-9741334)* 15 E. Northwest Hwy., Suite 15 B, Palatine, IL 60067 USA
E-mail: katychance@juno.com
Web site: http://www.peakperformanceliving.info.

Investigaciones LLEJ *See* **KCL Publishing & Tutoring**

Investing for Kids *Imprint of* **LINX Corp.**

Invisible College Pr., LLC, The, *(978-1-931468)* Orders Addr.: P.O. Box 209, Woodbridge, VA 22194 USA Tel 703-590-4005; Edit Addr.: 1206 N. Danville St., Arlington, VA 22201 USA; 3703 Del Mar Dr., Woodbridge, VA 22193
E-mail: manager@invispress.com
Web site: http://www.invispress.com/.

Invision Pubns., *(978-0-9767337)* 1136 Sherman Ave., Suite C4, Bronx, NY 10456 USA Tel 718-538-6102
E-mail: puzzles@puzzlesforus.com
Web site: http://www.puzzlesforus.com.

Invoke A Blessing Inc., *(978-0-9831902)* P.O. Box 163772, Fort Worth, TX 76161-3772 USA
E-mail: yuritereshchenko@hotmail.com; Yuritereshchenko@hotmail.com.

Invoke A Blessing Ministry *See* **Invoke A Blessing Inc.**

Inward Core, Inc., *(978-0-9796546)* Orders Addr.: P.O. Box 792, Roswell, GA 30077 USA (SAN 854-0284)
E-mail: nancialeath@inwardcore.com; passionnancia@gmail.com
Web site: http://www.inwardcorebooks.com.

Inward Reflections, Inc., *(978-0-9746783)* P.O. Box 1747, Brockton, MA 02303-1747 USA
E-mail: inwardreflections@homestead.com.

Inyati Press, *(978-0-9777440)* P.O. Box 453, fulton, CA 95439 USA
E-mail: milton@webbellis.org
Web site: http://www.webbellis.org.

I.Om.Be Pr., *(978-1-882161)* Orders Addr.: P.O. Box 1387, New York, NY 10159 USA
Web site: http://about.me/josefinaBaezAyombeT.

IONA Pubs., *(978-1-948056)* 413 Mosby Dr, Leesburg, VA 20175 USA Tel 219-669-8474
E-mail: ben@ionapublishers.com.

IOS Pr., Inc., *(978-90-407; 978-90-5199; 978-90-6275; 978-0-9673355; 978-1-58603; 978-90-298; 978-1-60750; 978-1-61499; 978-1-64368)* 4502 Rachael Manor Dr., Fairfax, VA 22032 USA Tel 703-323-5600; Fax: 703-323-3668; Nieuwe Hemweg 6B, Amsterdam, 1013 BG (SAN 858-995X) Tel 31 (0)20 688 33 55; Fax: 31 (0)20 687 00 19
E-mail: iosbooks@iospress.com; orders@iospress.com
Web site: http://www.iospress.com
Dist(s): **Ebsco Publishing**
Metapress
MyiLibrary
ebrary, Inc.

Iowa Greyhound Association *See* **McKinnon, Robert Scott**

Ipaatti, *(978-0-9984282)* 12500 Flatwood circel, Fairfax, VA 22033 USA Tel 703-901-7904
E-mail: kumar.sivalingam@ipaatti.com
Web site: www.ipaatti.com.

IPG Publishing, *(978-1-957317)* 814 N Franklin St, Chicago, IL 60610 USA Tel 312-337-0747
E-mail: rwilliams@ipgbook.com
Web site: www.ipgbook.com
Dist(s): **Independent Pubs. Group.**

ipicturebooks *Imprint of* **ibooks, Inc.**

iPlayMusic, Inc., *(978-0-9760487; 978-0-9797683)* P.O. Box 391775, Mountain View, CA 94039 USA Tel 650-969-3387; Fax: 650-969-3680; Toll Free: 866-594-3344
E-mail: quincy@iplaymusic.com
Web site: http://www.iplaymusic.com
Dist(s): **Leonard, Hal Corp.**
Music Sales Corp.

IPMG Publishing, *(978-1-934218)* 18362 Erin Bay, Eden Prairie, MN 55347 USA (SAN 852-2057)
E-mail: webmaster@iplaymathgames.com
Web site: http://www.iplaymathgames.com.

Ippolito, Eva Marie, *(978-0-9705350; 978-0-615-11326-5)* 10316 W. Oakmont Dr., Sun City, AZ 85351-3528 USA.

iPulpFiction.com, *(978-0-9828090; 978-0-692-37516-7; 978-0-692-37518-1; 978-0-692-37526-6; 978-0-692-38410-7; 978-0-692-38411-4; 978-0-692-38412-1; 978-0-692-38413-8; 978-0-692-38414-5; 978-0-692-38428-2; 978-0-692-38690-3; 978-0-692-41603-7; 978-0-692-45613-2; 978-0-692-45695-8; 978-0-692-46161-7; 978-0-692-46508-0; 978-0-692-48539-2; 978-0-692-66826-9; 978-0-692-95944-2; 978-0-692-96162-9; 978-0-692-96166-7; 978-0-692-97715-6)* 1630 W. Gail Dr., Chandler, AZ 85224 USA Tel 480-773-8958
E-mail: publisher@ipulpfiction.com
Web site: http://www.iPulpFiction.com
Dist(s): **CreateSpace Independent Publishing Platform.**

Iran Books *See* **Ibex Pubs., Inc.**

Irene, Jan Pubns., *(978-0-9653428)* Orders Addr.: P.O. Box 934, Sonora, CA 95370 USA Tel 209-532-2470; Fax: 209-532-0277; Edit Addr.: 19575 Roselyn Ln., Sonora, CA 95370 USA
E-mail: janirene@mlode.com.

Irene Press *See* **Quindaro Pr.**

Irene Weinberger Bks. *Imprint of* **Hamilton Stone Editions**

Iris Pallas-Luke E-Writings/E-Literature, *(978-0-9765637)* 12472 Lake Underhill Rd., Suite 267, Orlando, FL 32828 USA
E-mail: irispallasluke@msn.com; noir@noirpallasluke.com
Web site: http://www.irispallas-luke.com; http://www.barbarapallas-luke.com; http://www.vernninapallas-luke.com; http://www.noirpallas-luke.com.

Iris Pr. *Imprint of* **Iris Publishing Group, Inc., The**

Iris Publishing Group, Inc., The, *(978-0-916078; 978-1-60454)* 969 Oak Ridge Turnpike, No. 328, Oak Ridge, TN 37830-8832 USA Tel 865-483-0837; Fax: 865-481-3793; Toll Free: 800-881-2119; *Imprints:* Iris Press (Iris)
E-mail: rcumming@irisbooks.com
Web site: htt://irisbooks.com.

Irish Academic Pr. (IRL) *(978-0-7165) Dist. by* **IPG Chicago.**

Irish American Bk. Co., Subs. of Roberts Rinehart Pubs., Inc., P.O. Box 666, Niwot, CO 80544-0666 USA Tel 303-652-2710; Fax: 303-652-2689; Toll Free: 800-452-7115
E-mail: irishbooks@aol.com
Web site: http://www.irishvillage.com.

Irish Bks. & Media, Inc., *(978-0-937702)* Orders Addr.: 2904 41st Ave S., Minneapolis, MN 55406-1814 USA (SAN 111-8870) Toll Free: 800-229-3505 Do not confuse with Irish Bks. in New York, NY
E-mail: Irishbook@aol.com
Web site: http://www.irishbook.com.

Irish Genealogical Foundation, *(978-0-940134)* Div. of O'Laughlin Pr., P.O. Box 7575, Kansas City, MO 64116 USA (SAN 218-4834) Tel 816-454-2410
E-mail: mike@Irishroots.com
Web site: http://www.IrishRoots.com
Dist(s): **Irish Bks. & Media, Inc.**

Iron Arm International, *(978-0-9746989)* 1 Reid St., Amsterdam, NY 12010-3424 USA Tel 518-842-9299
E-mail: Ironarm1@aol.com
Web site: http://www.uechiryu-karate.com
Dist(s): **Tuttle Publishing.**

Iron Circus Comics, *(978-0-9708731; 978-0-9794080; 978-0-9890207; 978-1-945820; 978-1-63899)* Orders Addr.: 329 W 18th St Suite 604, Chicago, IL 60616 USA
Web site: http://www.ironcircus.com
Dist(s): **Consortium Bk. Sales & Distribution**
Diamond Comic Distributors, Inc.

Iron Fire Publishng Co., *(978-0-9817791)* 3702 Manhattan Ave., Suite 101, Fort Collins, CO 80526 USA (SAN 856-5465)
E-mail: mike@iron-fire.com
Web site: http://www.destinationstationseries.com.

Iron Mountain Pr., *(978-0-9722961)* Orders Addr.: P.O. Box 7, New Milford, NY 10959 USA (SAN 256-0097)
E-mail: info@ironmountainpress.com
Web site: http://www.ironmountainpress.com.

Iron Stream Media, *(978-1-56309; 978-1-59669)* 100 Missionary Ridge, Birmingham, AL 35242 USA Toll Free Fax: 888-811-9934; *Imprints:* New Hope Publishers (NewHopePub)
Dist(s): **Baker & Taylor Publisher Services (BTPS).**

Ironbound Pr., *(978-0-9763857)* P.O. Box 250, Winter Harbor, ME 04693-0250 USA Tel 207-963-2355; Fax: 320-323-2434 Do not confuse with Ironbound Pr. in Scotch Plains, NJ
E-mail: sales@ironboundpress.com
Web site: http://www.ironboundpress.com.

Ironcreek Pr., *(978-0-9766017)* 147 S. Randolph Ave., Asheboro, NC 27203 USA Tel 336-521-9105
E-mail: crottymartha@yahoo.com.

Ironcroft Publishing, *(978-0-9771688)* 11093 Alberta Dr., Brighton, MI 48114 USA
Web site: http://www.ironcroft.com
Dist(s): **BookBaby**
Partners Bk. Distributing, Inc.

Irongate Pr., *(978-0-9754746)* Orders Addr.: 1237 W. Seascape Dr., Gilbert, AZ 85233 USA Tel 480-813-2056
E-mail: jpascoe@irongatepress.com; j3pascoe@gmail.com
Web site: http://www.irongatepress.com
Dist(s): **Canyonlands Pubns.**
Forest Sales & Distributing Co.
Rio Nuevo Pubs.

Ironhorse Publishing Co., *(978-0-9747039)* 308 B W. Market St., Gratz, PA 17030 USA Fax: 717-365-7399 do not confuse with Ironhorse Publishing in Hayden Lake, ID
E-mail: pennvalleyprint@epix.net.

IRONSTREAM Pr., *(978-0-9794563; 978-0-578-86314-6; 978-0-578-90420-7)* 392 Cty. Rd. Cty. Rd., Sheffield, MA 10576 USA Tel 914-450-3517
Web site: IRONSTREAM PRESS; IRONSTREAM PRESS; IRONSTREAM PRESS
Dist(s): **Ingram Publisher Services.**

Irresistible Pr., LLC, *(978-1-946047)* 150 Ogilvie Dr., John Day, OR 97845 USA Tel 541-575-4387; *Imprints:* DoodleCake (DoodleCake)
E-mail: ccnrs@craigemcmillan.com
Web site: www.irresistiblepress.com
Dist(s): **Ingram Content Group.**

I.R.Vasquez, *(978-1-7354762)* 11125 SW 3rd St, Miami, FL 33174 USA Tel 786-413-5871
E-mail: ishmaelvasquez@outlook.com.

†Irvington Pubs., *(978-0-512; 978-0-8290; 978-0-8422; 978-0-89197)* Orders Addr.: P.O. Box 286, New York, NY 10276-0286 USA Fax: 212-861-0998; Toll Free Fax: 800-455-5520; Toll Free: 800-472-6037
Dist(s): **Addicus Bks.**
MyiLibrary; *CIP.*

Irwin, Christine, *(978-0-615-15008-6; 978-0-578-00787-8)* 4N 265 Avard Rd., West Chicago, IL 60185 USA
Dist(s): **Lulu Pr., Inc.**

Irwin, Esther L., *(978-0-9778462)* 3531 Grove Dr., Cheyenne, WY 82001 USA Tel 307-632-2060
E-mail: Elivroman@bresnan.net.

Irwin, Wesley, *(978-0-692-08872-2; 978-0-692-19774-5; 978-0-578-51975-3; 978-0-578-70070-0; 978-0-578-80266-4; 978-0-578-33541-4)* 12354 Sandpoint Way NE, Seattle, WA 98125 USA Tel 206-665-0360
E-mail: wesleydirwin@gmail.com
Dist(s): **Ingram Content Group.**

is for Animal, A, *(978-0-578-74937-2; 978-0-578-74938-9)* 5015 Addison Cir., Addison, TX 75001 USA Tel 413-883-3754
E-mail: hspires@texaswillslawyer.com.

†ISA, *(978-0-87664; 978-1-55617; 978-0-9791330; 978-0-9792343; 978-1-934394; 978-1-936007; 978-1-937560; 978-1-939660; 978-1-941546; 978-1-945541; 978-1-64331)* 67 Alexander Dr., Research Triangle Park, NC 27709 USA (SAN 202-7054) Tel 919-549-8411; Fax: 919-549-8288
E-mail: info@isa.org; ebell@isa.org; lelrod@isa.org
Web site: http://www.isa.org
Dist(s): **INscribe Digital**; *CIP.*

Isaac Publishing *See* **Ajoyin Publishing, Inc.**

Isaac Publishing, *(978-0-9787141; 978-0-9825218; 978-0-9853109; 978-0-9885930; 978-0-9892905; 978-0-9916145; 978-0-9967245; 978-0-9977033; 978-1-7321952; 978-1-952450)* 80 Abbeyville Rd., Lancaster, PA 17603 USA Tel 703-288-1681
E-mail: usa@barnabasaid.org
Web site: https://isaac-publishing.com/
Dist(s): **BookBaby**
Independent Pubs. Group
Midpoint Trade Bks., Inc.
Send The Light Distribution LLC.

Isaacs, John, *(978-0-9779606)* 643 N. Main St., Lawrenceburg, KY 40342 USA (SAN 850-6191) Tel 502-418-1521
E-mail: jisaacs@kheaa.com.

Isabella Media Inc, *(978-0-9994459; 978-1-7330416; 978-1-7357256; 979-8-9862460)* 270 Bellevue Ave, Newport, RI 02840 USA Tel 401-354-2445
E-mail: steveg@isabellamedia.com
Web site: www.isabellabooks.com; www.isabellamedia.com.

Isabella Products, Inc., *(978-1-936503; 978-1-62334; 978-1-63083; 978-1-68186)* 23 Bradford St. 2nd Flr., Concord, MA 01742 USA Tel 978-287-0007; Fax: 309-405-1865; *Imprints:* StarWalk Kids Media (StarWalkKids)
E-mail: liz.nealon@isabellaproducts.com; support@fablelearning.com; gabrielle.howard@fablelearning.com
Web site: http://www.fablelearning.com; http://www.isabellaproducts.com
Dist(s): **INscribe Digital**
Independent Pubs. Group
StarWalk Kids.

ISBS Publisher Services, 920 NE 58th Ave., Suite 300, Portland, OR 97213-3786 USA (SAN 169-7129) Tel 503-287-3093; Fax: 503-280-8832; Toll Free: 800-944-6190
E-mail: info@isbs.com
Web site: http://www.isbs.com
Dist(s): **ebrary, Inc.**

iScribe Pubns. LLC, *(978-0-9883126)* 1006 Westbriar Dr., Henrico, VA 23238 USA Tel 804-441-3400; Fax: 804-741-7741
E-mail: info@iscribepublications.com.

ISD, 70 Enterprise Dr., Suite 2, Bristol, CT 06010 USA Tel 860-584-6546; Fax: 860-540-1001
E-mail: orders@isdistribution.com
Web site: https://www.isdistribution.com/.

Isha Enterprises, Inc., *(978-0-936981)* P.O. Box 25970, Scottsdale, AZ 85255 USA (SAN 658-7895) Tel 480-502-9454; Fax: 480-991-5635; Toll Free: 800-641-6015
E-mail: info@easygrammar.com
Web site: http://www.easygrammar.com.

Ishi Pr. International, *(978-0-923891; 978-1-63711)* Div. of The Ishi Pr. (Japan), 1664 Davidson Ave Apt 1B, Bronx, NY 94903-1327 USA (SAN 249-0749) Tel 917-507-7226
E-mail: samhsloan@gmail.com
Web site: http://www.anusha.com/ordering.html.

ISIS Large Print Bks. (GBR) *(978-0-7531; 978-1-85089; 978-1-85695) Dist. by* **Transaction Pubs.**

Isis Publishing Hse., Inc., *(978-0-9662281)* 4620 Kings Hwy., Brooklyn, NY 11234 USA
E-mail: isispublishingco@aol.com.

Iskierka, Kristine, *(978-0-692-13533-4; 978-0-692-13534-1; 978-0-692-15852-4; 978-0-692-17114-1)* 16515 Yakima St. N.W., Andover, MN 55304 USA Tel 763-355-7680
E-mail: krisiskierka@gmail.com
Dist(s): **Ingram Content Group.**

Islamic Bk. Service, 1209 Cleburne, Hoston, TX 77004 USA (SAN 169-2453) Tel 713-528-1440; Fax: 713-528-1085.

Islamic Ctr. of Sacramento, The, *(978-0-9769245)* Div. of Sacramento Computers, c/o Sacramento Computers, 2022 4th St. #2, Sacramento, CA 95818 USA
E-mail: shamdani@mindspring.com
Web site: http://www.hineaf.net.

Islamic Foundation, Ltd. (GBR) *(978-0-9503954; 978-0-86037) Dist. by* **Consort Bk Sales.**

Islamic Supreme Council of America, *(978-1-930409; 978-1-938058)* Orders Addr.: 17195 Silver Pkwy. #401 Fenton, MI 48430, Fenton, MI 48430 USA Tel 810-593-1222; Fax: 810-815-0518; Toll Free: 800-278-6624; Edit Addr.: 17195 Silver Pkwy. #401 Fenton Michigan 48430, Fenton, MI 48430 USA
E-mail: staff@islamicsupremecouncil.org; aliyah@sunnah.org
Web site: http://www.islamicsupremecouncil.org; http://www.worde.org.

Island Books *See* **Island Bks.**

Island Bks., *(978-0-9843998; 978-0-9983759; 978-0-9994378; 978-0-9998479; 978-1-7356324; 979-8-9883619)*
E-mail: ericwiberg@sbcglobal.net
Web site: http://www.ericwiberg.com
Dist(s): **SPD-Small Pr. Distribution.**

Island Friends LLC, *(978-0-9729987)* 11 Promontory Ct., Hilton Head Island, SC 29928 USA
E-mail: benjo@adelphia.net
Web site: http://www.islandfriends.net
Dist(s): **Sandlapper Publishing Co., Inc.**

Island Heritage Publishing, *(978-0-89610; 978-0-931548; 978-1-59700)* Div. of The Madden Corp., 94-411 Koaki St., Waipahu, HI 96797 USA (SAN 211-1403) Tel 808-564-8800; Fax: 808-564-8888; Toll Free: 800-468-2800
E-mail: ihorders@welcometotheislands.com
Web site: http://www.welcometotheislands.com
Dist(s): **Independent Pubs. Group**
Madden Corp., The
Midpoint Trade Bks., Inc.
Univ. of Hawaii Pr.

Island In The Sky Publishing Co., *(978-0-9760328)* 60 Meadow Lakes, East Windsor, NJ 08520 USA
Web site: http://www.MemoriesOfWWII.com.

Island Ink, *(978-0-9657849)* Orders Addr.: P.O. Box 1818, Indiantown, FL 34956 USA Tel 561-597-3778; Fax: 561-597-4691.

Island Institute, *(978-0-942719; 978-0-9835613)* 386 Main St., Box 648, Rockland, ME 04841-3345 USA (SAN 667-7274) Tel 207-594-9209; Fax: 207-594-9314
E-mail: inquiry@islandinstitute.org; publications@islandinstitute.org
Web site: http://www.islandinstitute.org
Dist(s): **Magazines, Inc.**

Island Media Publishing, LLC, *(978-0-9829908)* 120 N. 15th St., Fernandina Beach, FL 32034 USA Tel 904-556-3002
E-mail: islandmediapublishing@gmail.com.

Island Moon Pr., *(978-0-9755605)* P.O. Box 956, Oaks, PA 19456-0956 USA Tel 610-935-2378; Toll Free: 877-252-8262
E-mail: islandquest@msn.com
Web site: http://www.IslandMoonPress.com.

Island Nation Pr., LLC, *(978-0-9657437; 978-1-892738)* Orders Addr.: 144 Rowayton Woods Dr., Norwalk, CT 06854 USA Tel 203-852-0028; Fax: 203-852-0528; Toll Free: 888-356-1450 [Direct Order Line]
E-mail: cvaleallen@earthlink.net
Web site: http://www.charlottevaleallen.com.

Island Paradise Publishing, *(978-0-9705889; 978-0-9855153)* Orders Addr.: P.O. Box 163, Haleiwa, HI 96712 USA Tel 808-638-9640; Edit Addr.: 59-465 KeWaena Rd., Haleiwa, HI 96712 USA
E-mail: CooperKool@Hawaii.rr.com
Dist(s): **Booklines Hawaii, Ltd.**

Islandport Pr., Inc., *(978-0-9671662; 978-0-9763231; 978-1-934031; 978-1-939017; 978-1-944762; 978-1-952143)* Orders Addr.: P.O. Box 10, Yarmouth, ME 04096 USA Tel 207-846-3344; Fax: 207-846-3955; Edit Addr.: 267 US Rte. 1, Suite B, Yarmouth, ME 04096 USA
E-mail: deanlunt@islandportpress.com; piper@islandportpress.com
Web site: http://www.islandportpress.com
Dist(s): **Baker & Taylor Publisher Services (BTPS)**
Follett School Solutions
INscribe Digital
Independent Pubs. Group
MyiLibrary
ebrary, Inc.

Islandrdjodib, *(978-1-7374014)* 1141 sw 87th ave, Pembroke Pines, FL 33025 USA Tel 954-665-9766
E-mail: Jodibrd@gmail.com.

IslandWood, *(978-0-9821633)* Orders Addr.: 4450 Blakely Ave. NE, Bainbridge Island, WA 98110 USA Tel 206-855-4300; Fax: 206-855-4301
Web site: http://www.IslandWood.org.

ISLC, *(978-0-9763226)* c/o Alfassa, 15 W. 16th St., 6th Flr., New York, NY 10011 USA Tel 917-207-4344
E-mail: shelomo@alfassa.com.

Isle of Dogs Publishing, Co., *(978-0-9741321)* 4008 - 83rd Ave. SE, Snohomish, WA 98290 USA
E-mail: connieraestrain@msn.com; ConnieRaeStrain@IsleofDogsPublishing.com
Web site: http://www.isleofdogspublishing.com.

Isles of the Sea Pubs., *(978-0-9728126)* Orders Addr.: P.O. Box 51352, Provo, UT 84605-1352 USA Tel 801-427-5209; Edit Addr.: 2052 S. California Ave., No. 12, Provo, UT 84044 USA
E-mail: drrlesa@hotmail.com.

Islewest Publishing, *(978-0-9641919; 978-1-888461)* Div. of Carlisle Communications, Ltd., 4242 Chavenelle Dr., Dubuque, IA 52002-2650 USA (SAN 299-5018)
E-mail: mjgraham@carcomm.com
Web site: http://www.islewest.com
Dist(s): **Independent Pubs. Group.**

Israel Book Shop *See* **Israel Bookshop Pubns.**

Israel Bookshop Pubns., *(978-0-9670705; 978-1-931681; 978-1-60091; 979-8-88673)* 501 Prospect St., No. 97, Lakewood, NJ 08701 USA Tel 732-901-3009; Fax: 732-901-4012; Toll Free: 888-536-7427
E-mail: sales@israelbookshoppublications.com
Web site: http://www.israelbookshoppublications.com.

rael, Tabitha Bks., *(978-0-578-64715-9; 978-1-7347778)* 9585 Downs Ct., Jonesboro, GA 30238 USA Tel 470-778-1421
E-mail: PTWITCHER9@GMAIL.COM.

S, *(978-1-934942)* 2 Shaker Rd. Ste. D103, Shirley, MA 01464-2535 USA (SAN 855-6164)
E-mail: print@issexpress.com
Web site: http://www.imagesoftware.com.

storia Hse., *(978-0-9816538)* Orders Addr.: P.O. Box 6342, Vernon Hills, IL 60061 USA (SAN 856-1370)
E-mail: info@istoriahouse.com
Web site: http://www.istoriahouse.com.

talica Pr., *(978-0-934977; 978-1-59910)* 99 Wall St. Suite 650, New York, NY 10005 USA (SAN 695-1805) Tel 917-371-0563
E-mail: inquiries@italicapress.com
Web site: http://www.italicapress.com
Dist(s): **JSTOR.**

tasca Bks., *(978-0-9767054)* Orders Addr.: 5120 Cedar Lake Rd. S., Minneapolis, MN 55416 USA (SAN 855-3823) Tel 952-345-4488; Fax: 952-920-0541; Toll Free: 800-901-3480
E-mail: mjung@itascabooks.com
Web site: http://www.itascabooks.com
Dist(s): **BookMobile.**

iTeenBooks Inc., *(978-0-9798997; 978-0-9852925)* P.O. Box 171, Middletown, NJ 07748-0171 USA.

Ithaca Pr. *Imprint of* **Authors & Artists Publishers of New York, Inc.**

iThink Bks., *(978-0-9766797)* P.O. Box 50, Saratoga Springs, NY 12866 USA Tel 518-782-0723 (phone/fax)
E-mail: mwayne2@mac.com
Web site: http://www.ithinkbooks.com
Dist(s): **Book Clearing Hse.**

Ithuriel's Spear, *(978-0-9749502; 978-0-9793390; 978-0-9835791; 978-1-943209)* 939 Eddy St., Apt. 102, San Francisco, CA 94109 USA Tel 415-440-3204
plainfeather@gmail.com
E-mail: plainfeather@gmail.com
Web site: http://www.ithuriel.com
Dist(s): **BookMobile**
SPD-Small Pr. Distribution.

ITI Holdings, Inc., *(978-1-931451; 978-1-61011)* 1321 SE Decker Ave, Stuart, FL 34994 USA Tel 207-729-4201; Fax: 207-729-4453; Toll Free: 888-778-9073
E-mail: flemming.elleboe@tdisdi.com; brian.carney@tdisdi.com; worldhq@tdisdi.com
Web site: http://www.tdisdi.com.

Itiya Publishing, Inc., *(978-0-9770312)* 217 Ave. Unvi. Interanericana PMB 161, San German, PR 00683 USA
E-mail: gpita@itiyainc.com
Web site: http://www.itiyainc.com.

ITRON Publishing, *(978-0-9786863)* 6510 LBJ Freeway, Suite 200, Dallas, TX 75240 USA (SAN 851-2817) Tel 972-934-2811; Fax: 972-934-1705.

It's A Habit! Co., The, *(978-0-9713664)* 2238 Harwood St., Los Angeles, CA 90031-1238 USA Tel 323-254-7772
Web site: http://www.itsahabit.com.

It's a Lifestyle Fitness, *(978-0-9890227)* 1 Evergreen Pl., Morristown, NJ 07960 USA (SAN 920-783X) Tel 973-267-2121
E-mail: gregorycrawford@ymail.com.

It's About Time, Herff Jones Education Division *See* **It's About Time, Herff Jones Education Div.**

It's About Time, Herff Jones Education Div., *(978-1-891629; 978-1-58591; 978-1-60720; 978-1-68231)* Orders Addr.: 333 N. Bedford Rd. # 110, Mt. Kisco, NY 10549 USA Tel 914-273-2233; Fax: 914-273-2227; Toll Free: 888-698-8463 Do not confuse with companies with the same name in Los Gatos, CA, Santa Monica, CA
E-mail: generalinfo@herffjones.com
Web site: http://www.its-about-time.com.

It's Good 2B Good LLC,
Dist(s): **Baker & Taylor Publisher Services (BTPS).**

It's Me Briana, LLC, *(978-0-9793904; 978-0-9838492)* P.O. Box 12386, Atlanta, GA 30355 USA
Web site: http://www.brianasneighborhood.com.

It's My Hair! Magazine, *(978-0-692-74966-1; 978-0-692-77197-6; 978-0-692-83141-0; 978-0-692-88297-9; 978-0-692-93394-7)* P.O. Box 18593, ATLANTA, GA 31126 USA Tel 470-755-2061.

ITSMEEE Industries, *(978-0-9677231)* 13918 E. Mississippi Ave., No 213, Aurora, CO 80012 USA Tel 303-229-7584
E-mail: itsmeeeindustries@outlook.com.

Itsy Bitsy Muslims *See* **Itsy Bitsy Muslims**

Itsy Bitsy Muslims *Imprint of* **Itsy Bitsy Muslims**

Itsy Bitsy Muslims, *(978-1-7321600); Imprints:* Itsy Bitsy Muslims (MYID_B_ITSY BI)
E-mail: alielsayed.92@gmail.com; Elsayed.neda@gmail.com
Web site: https://www.itsybitsymuslims.com/.

Itty Bitty Bks., *(978-0-9760691)* 1682 NW 785 Rd., Bates City, MO 64011 USA Tel 816-697-3617 (phone/fax)
E-mail: waynedyer@gmail.com.

Itty Bitty Kitty *Imprint of* **Singing Moon Pr.**

Itty Bitty Witch Works, *(978-0-9768573)* P.O. Box 532, Kernville, CA 93238 USA Tel 760-376-3973 (phone/fax)
E-mail: ittybittywitch@sierranet.us
Web site: http://ittybittywitch.com.

iUniverse, Inc. *Imprint of* **iUniverse, Inc.**

iUniverse, Inc., *(978-0-9665514; 978-1-58348; 978-0-9668591; 978-1-893652; 978-0-595; 978-0-9795279; 978-1-60528; 978-1-4401; 978-1-936236; 978-1-4502; 978-1-4620; 978-1-4697; 978-1-4759; 978-1-4917; 978-1-5320; 978-1-6632)* Orders Addr.: 1663 Liberty Dr., Suite 300, Bloomington, IN 47403 USA (SAN 254-9425) Toll Free: 800-288-4677; *Imprints:* Writers Club Press (Writers Club Pr); Writer's Showcase Press (Writers Showcase); Backinprint.com (Backinprint); ASJA Press (ASJA Pr); Authors Choice Press (Authors Choice Pr); Mystery Writers of America Presents (Myst Write Amer); Mystery & Suspense Press (Mystery & Suspense); Weekly Reader Teacher's Press (Weekly Rd Tch); Writers Advantage Press (Writers Adv Pr); iUniverse, Inc. (iUni Inc); iUniverse Star (iUniverse Star)
Web site: http://www.iUniverse.com; http://iuniverse.com; www.balboapress.com
Dist(s): **Author Solutions, LLC**
Baker & Taylor Publisher Services (BTPS)
CreateSpace Independent Publishing Platform
Smashwords
Zondervan.

iUniverse Star *Imprint of* **iUniverse, Inc.**

iUniverse.com, Incorporated *See* **iUniverse, Inc.**

Ivanov, Dimitar, *(978-1-7354603)* 20243 Mohegan Dr. 0, ASHBURN, VA 20147 USA Tel +12026843474
E-mail: dcivanov85@gmail.com
Dist(s): **Ingram Content Group.**

Iverson, Theodore, *(978-0-9747378)* P.O. Box 3671, Grand Canyon, AZ 86023-3671 USA.

Ivey Leaf Publishing, *(978-0-9981801)* 8508 Jean Parrish Ct. NE, Albuquerque, NM 87122 USA Tel 505-400-1785
Dist(s): **CreateSpace Independent Publishing Platform.**

Ivoryton Pr., *(978-0-9814663)* P.O. Box 485, Ivoryton, CT 06442 USA Tel 860-581-8133
E-mail: Ivoryton.Press@gmail.com.

IVP Bks. *Imprint of* **InterVarsity Pr.**

IVP Kids *Imprint of* **InterVarsity Pr.**

IVS Pr., *(978-0-9981871; 978-1-959829)* 1515 NW 7th Pl., Gainesville, FL 32603-1208 USA Tel 570-814-2150
E-mail: ivspublishing@gmail.com.

IVS Publishing *See* **IVS Pr.**

Ivy Advising LLC, *(978-0-9771568)* 50 Livingston St., Brooklyn, NY 11201 USA (SAN 256-8934).

Ivy Fund, The, *(978-0-9754003)* 33 Irving St., Waltham, MA 02451-0758 USA
E-mail: courtney@ivysplace.org
Web site: http://ivysplace.org.

Ivy Group, The (GBR) *Dist. by* **HachBkGrp.**

Ivy Hill Bunch, LLC, *(978-0-9743619)* P.O. Box 1053, La Quinta, CA 92253 USA Tel 760-771-0834; Fax: 760-771-1910; Toll Free: 866-892-5795
E-mail: lynn@ivyhillbunch.com
Web site: http://www.saddyandgladdy.com.

Ivy House Publishing Group *Imprint of* **Pentland Pr., Inc.**

IvyStone Pr., *(978-0-9755771)* P.O. Box 50, Emmalena, KY 41740 USA
E-mail: hodson@tgtel.com
Web site: http://www.mountainrainbow.com.

iwishyouicecreamandcake, *(978-0-9792019)* 3871 W. Millers Bridge Rd., Tallahassee, FL 32312 USA Fax: 850-893-9616
E-mail: carolhmoore@yahoo.com
Web site: http://iwishyouicecreamandcake.com.

Ixia Pr. *Imprint of* **Dover Pubns., Inc.**

Iyengar, Malathi, *(978-0-9753912)* 14748 Morrison St., Sherman Oaks, CA 91403 USA
E-mail: msiyengar@yahoo.com
Web site: http://www.rangoli.org.

IYF Publishing, *(978-0-692-69861-7; 978-0-9998780; 978-1-7345152; 978-1-7378129)* 501 S Jackson St, Beverly Hills, FL 34465 USA Tel 239-272-8613; *Imprints:* Dragon Hoard Press (MYID_Y_DRAGON)
Web site: www.SandyLenderInk.com
Dist(s): **CreateSpace Independent Publishing Platform.**

iynx publishing (GBR) *(978-0-9535413; 978-0-9540583) Dist. by* **Dufour.**

IZA Publishing Co., *(978-0-9674241)* 253 Pvt. Rd. 2410, Uvalde County, TX 78801 USA Tel 361-946-3132; Fax: 361-946-2000
E-mail: smith-ma@swhell.net.

IZS, Inc., *(978-0-9764684)* 34 E. Franklin St., Bellbrook, OH 45305-1746 USA Tel 937-848-8896
E-mail: pantherbay@aol.com
Web site: http://www.pantherbay.com.

IzzyBella Bks., *(978-0-578-49304-6; 978-0-578-56938-3; 978-0-578-63492-0)* 8828 Meridian Pl. NE B 102, Lake Stevens, WA 98258 USA Tel 360-784-9390
E-mail: abbi.mckee@yahoo.com.

J A G Pubns., *(978-0-943327)* 11288 Ventura Blvd., No. 301, Studio City, CA 91604 USA (SAN 668-4157) Tel 818-505-9002 (phone/fax) Do not confuse with Jag Publications in Los Angeles, CA
E-mail: info@jagpublications-esl.com
Web site: http://www.jagpublications-esl.com.

J A Interests, Inc., *(978-0-9769648)* P.O. Box 1472, Versailles, KY 40383 USA.

J A S Pr., Inc., *(978-0-9666920; 978-0-9773316)* Orders Addr.: P.O. Box 1925, Bolingbrook, IL 60440 USA Tel 630-226-1635; Edit Addr.: 155 Ashcroft Dr., Bolingbrook, IL 60490 USA Tel 630-226-1635
E-mail: jaspress@mindspring.com.

J & J Publishing Co., *(978-0-9759831)* Box 305, 9728 US Hwy. 277, Elgin, OK 73538 USA Do not confuse with companies with same or similar name in Los Angeles, CA, Buffalo, NY, Englewood, CO, Darien, IL, Frankfurt, IL MD
E-mail: djw73@aol.com.

J & J Publishing Co., *(978-0-9705008; 978-0-615-73754-6; 978-0-9961018)* P.O. Box 291205, Columbia, SC 29229 USA Tel 803-968-5196
E-mail: jjpublisher@yahoo.com
Web site: http://www.jandjpublishingonline.com.

J & K Publishing, *(978-0-9790487)* 5221 Collins St., Suite 101, Panama City, FL 32404 USA
E-mail: jnbowen@netscape.com.

J&M Publishing, *(978-0-9646590)* 2417 Valley View Rd., Narvon, PA 17555 USA Tel 610-286-5489 Do not confuse with companies with the same name in Lebanon, TN, Fayetteville, NC, Phoenix, AZ.

J. B. Bks., LLC, *(978-1-7366421)* 5501 Blue Heron Dr, Greensboro, NC 27455-0821 USA Tel 336-209-7179
E-mail: Jbbrownbooks@aol.com.

J B Communications, Inc., *(978-1-55987)* 101 W. 55th St., No. 2D, New York, NY 10019-5346 USA Tel 212-246-0900; *Imprints:* Sunny Books (Sunny Bks).

J. B. J. Enterprises *See* **Morgan, E. A.**

J. Caro & Associates *See* **Cowboy Collector Pubns.**

J. David Lubinger, *(978-1-7368466)* 11509 Chautauqua Trail, Brecksville, OH 44141 USA Tel 440-655-5961
E-mail: jdavidlubinger@hotmail.com.

J J Publishing, *(978-0-9604610)* 1312 Arthur St., Hollywood, FL 33019 USA (SAN 220-0090) Tel 954-929-3559 (phone/fax).

J. K. Eckert & Co., Inc., *(978-0-9835675; 978-0-9913571; 978-0-9915252; 978-0-692-27860-4)* 513 Dona Dr., Nokomis, FL 34275 USA Tel 941-882-8760; *Imprints:* Susanna Lagoon Books (SusLagoonBks)
E-mail: tech@jkeckert.com.

J L Publishing Co., *(978-0-9740774)* 2901 Ranch Rd, Apt. 511, Paragould, AR 72450 USA.

J M D's Business Services, *(978-0-9712641)* 67 Darling St., Southington, CT 06489 USA
E-mail: jmdsbussrv@liquidchariot.com
Web site: http://www.jmdsbusinessservices.com; http://www.liquidchariot.com.

J. M. Jensen, *(978-0-578-42147-6; 978-0-578-42167-4)* 9606 Fox Den Dr., Littleton, CO 80125 USA Tel 970-372-6263
E-mail: jmjensenart@yahoo.com
Dist(s): **Ingram Content Group.**

J M Pubns., *(978-0-9638007)* Orders Addr.: P.O. Box 753427, Memphis, TN 38115 USA; Edit Addr.: 3830 Scottsdale Ave., Memphis, TN 38115 USA (SAN 255-0598) Tel 901-368-3414; Fax: 901-566-1978; Toll Free: 888-321-4747
E-mail: jmpub1@midsouth.rr.com
Web site: http://www.jmpublications.com.

J. Paul Getty Museum *Imprint of* **Getty Pubns.**

J. R. Johnson, *(978-0-578-39328-5)* PO Box 56, Santa Barbara, CA 93102 USA Tel 213-249-3941
E-mail: apgsba@gmail.com.

J. Taylor Publishing, *(978-0-9834058; 978-1-937744)* 5448 Apex Peakway No. 198, Apex, NC 27502 USA Tel 919-249-7318
E-mail: production@jtaylorpublishing.com
Web site: http://www.jtaylorpublishing.com.

J2B Publishing LLC, *(978-0-9911994; 978-1-941927; 978-1-948747; 978-1-954682)* 4251 Columbia Pk. Rd., Pomfret, MD 20675 USA Tel 202-557-8097
E-mail: GladToDoIt@gmail.com
Web site: www.GladToDoIt.net; www.J2BLLC.com.

J3Russell, LLC., *(978-1-7350437)* 575 NE 162nd St., Miami, FL 33162 USA Tel 786-838-7403
E-mail: j3russell@yahoo.com
Web site: http://www.j3russellbooks.wordpress.com
Dist(s): **Ingram Content Group.**

J.A. Pr., *(978-0-578-60055-0; 978-0-578-38844-1; 978-0-578-38845-8)* 947 Devine St., ALLIANCE, OH 44601 USA Tel 812-361-3055
E-mail: jon@jonathonallen.com
Web site: Jacpress.com.

JA Pubns., Ltd., *(978-0-9746093; 978-0-9794124)* Orders Addr.: P.O. Box 7275, Loveland, CO 80537 USA Tel 970-776-8395; Fax: 970-692-2492
E-mail: julieaydlott@gmail.com; info@japublicationsltd.com
Web site: http://www.startabookkeepingbusiness.com/; http://www.thevitalicsystem.com
Dist(s): **Emery-Pratt Co.**
Midwest Library Service.

Jabberwocky Literary Agency, Inc., *(978-1-936535; 978-1-62567)* Orders Addr.: P.O. Box 4558, Sunnyside, NY 11104 USA Tel 718-392-5985; Edit Addr.: 41-16 47th Ave., No. 2D, Sunnyside, NY 11104 USA Tel 718-392-5985
E-mail: jessie@awfulagent.com
Web site: www.awfulagent.com
Dist(s): **INscribe Digital**
Independent Pubs. Group
Open Road Integrated Media, Inc.

Jacera Publishing, *(978-1-943992)* 14918 EL TESORO DR, HOUSTON, TX 77083 USA Tel 281-772-2549
E-mail: jen.m.gabler@gmail.com.

Jack Hook Publishing, *(978-0-9837863)* 1288 Columbus Ave., No. 279, San Francisco, CA 94133 USA Tel 310-889-4728
E-mail: susan.saville@jackhook.com
Web site: www.jackhook.com.

Jack, Penney, *(978-1-7323308)* 2666 E. 73rd St., Chicago, IL 60649 USA Tel 773-580-8012
E-mail: Sunsum1234@aol.com.

Jack Walker Pr., *(978-1-945378)* 945 Bay View Cir., Mukwonago, WI 53149 USA Tel 262-955-6675
E-mail: amyloujenkins@gmail.com
Web site: www.JackWalkerPress.com.

Jackal Moon Pr. *Imprint of* **P. Anastasia**

Jackie Jordan, *(978-0-578-32911-6; 978-0-578-32912-3)* 4102 Curled Dock Ln., Odenton, MD 21113 USA Tel 404-295-3519
E-mail: jackiejl68@gmail.com.

JacKris Publishing, *(978-0-9772923; 978-0-9821196; 978-0-9826608; 978-0-9836089)*
E-mail: sales@growingwithgrammar.com; tonydee64@sbcglobal.net
Web site: http://www.jackrispublishing.com; http://www.growingwithgrammar.com.

Jack's Bookshelf, Inc., *(978-1-928907)* 224 Woodland Dr., Vista, CA 92083 USA.

Jackson, Amber, *(978-0-692-84096-2; 978-0-578-60073-4)* 5390 Amber Cove Way, FLOWERY BRANCH, GA 30542 USA Tel 404-694-4387
E-mail: jeffwcrawford5+LVP0003324@gmail.com; jeffwcrawford5+LVP0003324@gmail.com.

Jackson Joy LLC, *(978-0-692-84728-2; 978-0-692-84760-2; 978-0-692-07026-4; 978-0-578-91290-5; 978-0-578-91292-9)* P.O. Box 922, GRAYSON, GA 30017 USA Tel 770-375-0635
E-mail: jeffwcrawford5+LVP0003332@gmail.com; jeffwcrawford5+LVP0003332@gmail.com.

Jackson, Kristen M., *(978-0-615-13580-9)* 1604 N. 7th St. Apt. 26, Longview, TX 75601-4014 USA
Dist(s): **Lulu Pr., Inc.**

Jackson, Linda *See* **Jackson Publishing**

Jackson, Lucas L. *See* **RBHC LLC.**

Jackson Publishing, *(978-0-9716442)* 7661 Forstoria Cove, Southaven, MS 38672 USA Tel 901-413-5748 Do not confuse with companies with the same name in Jackson, MS; Clarkston, MI
E-mail: jackson35015@bellsouth.net.

Jackson, Robert, *(978-0-9761420)* 12807 Prospect Knolls Dr., Bowie, MD 20720 USA
E-mail: trebor_jackson@yahoo.com
Web site: http://www.amazingliberteens.com.

Jacobob Pr., LLC, *(978-0-9705827; 978-0-9772817; 978-0-9820960; 978-0-9838072; 978-0-9852887; 978-0-9857477; 978-0-9860361; 978-0-9911151; 978-0-9914066; 978-0-9916416; 978-0-692-53701-5; 978-0-692-55660-3)* 11035 Ridge Forest Ct., Saint Louis, MO 63126-3429 USA (SAN 257-1862) Tel 314-843-4829
E-mail: jacobobsw@sbcglobal.net
Web site: http://jacobobpress.com
Dist(s): **Follett School Solutions**
Jacobob Pr. Distributing
Unique Bks., Inc.

Jacobs, Karen, *(978-0-9850440; 978-0-9982119; 978-1-7363194)* 40 Indian Carry Rd., Moultonborough, NH 03254 USA Tel 617-838-1872
E-mail: kjacobs@bu.edu.

Jacqueline Bell *See* **Body by Bella, LLC**

Jacqueline Beverly Hills, *(978-0-9664783)* 650 The Village. Unit 215, Redondo Beach, CA 90277-2734 USA
E-mail: jacquih3@yahoo.com
Web site: http://jbhbooks.com.

Jacquelyn Morris-Hundal, *(978-1-7368110)* PO Box 366 0, ANDOVER, NH 03216 USA Tel 6037315257
E-mail: Morrisj1@findlay.edu
Dist(s): **Ingram Content Group.**

Jacques, Ednar, *(978-1-7372387)* 635 12th Ave NE Apt 3, St Petersburg, FL 33701 USA Tel 863-510-9975
E-mail: Jacquesednar@gmail.com
Web site: storiesfromej.com.

Jacquet-Acea, Russell, *(978-0-9771919)* 3645 Whitman Ave. N., Seattle, WA 98103 USA Tel 206-547-7026; Fax: 810-454-1721
E-mail: rjacquet2@msn.com
Web site: http://rjacquet.tripod.com.

JACS Publishing, *(978-1-7361535)* 831 Madison St., Brooklyn, NY 11221 USA Tel 718-715-8247
E-mail: asoto831@gmail.com.

JADA Pr., *(978-0-9747501; 978-0-9761110; 978-0-9764115; 978-0-9771343; 978-0-9788724; 978-0-9800629; 978-0-9843558; 978-0-9848365; 978-0-9907961)* 4375 Confederate Point Rd. #6-H, Jacksonville, FL 32210 USA Tel 904-226-8876 (leave a message)
Web site: http://www.jadapress.com.

JadaStar *See* **Star Publish LLC**

Jade Enterprises, *(978-0-9753410)* 26106 Franklin, Calumet, MI 49913 USA Tel 713-416-0109
Web site: http://www.authorsden.com/deborahkfrontiera.

Jade Publishing, *(978-0-9985390; 978-1-949299)* 700 Ciro St., Donna, TX 78537 USA Tel 956-570-1023
E-mail: rossylima@jadepublishing.org
Web site: www.jadepublishing.org.

Jade Ram Publishing, *(978-1-877721)* 3003 Wendy's Way, No. 9, Anchorage, AK 99517-1466 USA Tel 907-248-0979; Fax: 907-272-8432
E-mail: jaderam@alaska.net
Dist(s): **Publication Consultants**
Todd Communications
Wizard Works.

Jade Tree Bks., *(978-0-9888610)* P.O. Box 2132, Cherry Hill, NJ 08034 USA Tel 215-913-3456
E-mail: pangj@comcast.net.

Jadenaila Publishing, *(978-0-615-12544-2)* 7340 S. Union Creek Way 5G, Salt Lake City, UT 84047 USA Tel 801-916-1037
E-mail: kidsbooksbynaila@hotmail.com
Web site: http://www.kidsbooksbynaila.com.

Jades Publishing, *(978-0-9743352)* Orders Addr.: P.O. Box 485, Fayette, OH 43521 USA Tel 419-237-3128; Edit Addr.: 24022-T, Fayette, OH 43521 USA
E-mail: amadsj@bright.net; amadsj@bright.nett.

Jaffe Book Solutions, Div. of Booksource, 1230 Macklind Ave, Saint Louis, MO 63110-1432 USA
Dist(s): **Booksource, The.**

Jaffee, Diane, *(978-0-692-19766-0; 978-1-7350254)* 7799 Wills Run Ln, Blacklick, OH 43004 USA Tel 614-933-0608
E-mail: Jaffwoman@gmail.com.

Jaffrey, Kamal, *(978-0-9753673)* 400 Technology Sq., Cambridge, MA 02139 USA.

Jahs Publishing Group, *(978-0-9701144; 978-0-9747550; 978-0-615-49893-5; 978-0-615-50005-8)* 6304 Somerset Rd., Riverdale, MD 20737 USA Tel 301-326-6468
Web site: http://www.jahspublishing.com
Dist(s): **CreateSpace Independent Publishing Platform.**

Jair Collections LLC, *(978-1-7367664)* 617 Orlando Ave, Normal, IL 61761 USA Tel 312-804-8624
E-mail: jasmineshegog721@gmail.com
Web site: www.jaircollections.com.

JaJa's Publishing, *(978-0-578-63866-9; 978-1-7357335)* 3033 Hughes Ln. 0, HAYES, VA 23072 USA Tel 8048153358
E-mail: fromdeesdesk@gmail.com
Dist(s): **Ingram Content Group.**

Jajou, Rafee, *(978-0-692-19219-1)* 7341 Cornell Ave., La Mesa, CA 91942 USA Tel 619-204-6291
E-mail: rjajou@gmail.com
Dist(s): **Ingram Content Group.**

Publisher Name Index

Jakal LLC, *(978-0-9745734; 978-1-941662)* Div. of Viridian City Media, E-mail: adastra@perasperapress.com; jakkoke@koke.org Web site: http://www.perasperapress.com/ *Dist(s):* **Brodart Co. Partners/West Book Distributors.**

Jakkar Enterprises, *(978-0-692-15099-3; 978-0-692-15949-1; 978-0-692-17649-8; 978-0-578-43447-6; 978-0-578-51473-4; 978-0-578-54902-6; 978-0-578-55096-1; 978-0-578-69512-9; 978-0-578-69513-6)* 777 W. Germantown Pike Apt. 926, Plymouth Meeting, PA 19462 USA Tel 215-300-2904 E-mail: lenny1908@yahoo.com Web site: www.leonardandersonjr.com.

Jakki Joy Publishing, *(978-0-692-69630-9; 978-1-7339436)* 7010 Alpine Way, Yakima, WA 98908 USA Tel 509-930-4611 *Dist(s):* **CreateSpace Independent Publishing Platform.**

Jakobi Publishing, LLC, *(978-0-9972358)* 5820 Perry Rd., Elkton, FL 32033 USA Tel 904-377-3915 E-mail: heather.hamel@hotmail.om Web site: heatherhamel.com.

Jalali, Yassaman *See* **Saman Publishing**

Jalmar Pr., *(978-0-915190; 978-0-935266; 978-1-880396; 978-1-931061)* Subs. of B. L. Winch & Assocs., P.O. Box 370, Fawnskin, CA 92333-0370 USA (SAN 113-3640) Toll Free: 800-662-9662 (orders) E-mail: jalmarpress@att.net Web site: http://jalmarpress.com *Dist(s):* **Winch, B. L. & Assocs. Brodart Co.**

JA-M Pubs., LLC, *(978-0-9728975)* Orders Addr.: 23 May St., Battle Creek, MI 49037 USA Tel 269-363-2955 Primary business telephone; 4149 N. Castle Ridge Dr. #296, Grand Rapids, MI 49508 Do not confuse with companies with the same or similar name in Mount Pleasant, SC, Comstock Park, MI E-mail: joycex4@msn.com Web site: http://ja-mpublishers.weebly.com.

Jama Kids, *(978-0-9772711)* 612 N. St., Beaufort, SC 29902 USA Tel 843-522-1577 E-mail: janspringle@earthlink.net.

Jamaldinian, Yousef, *(978-0-9766657)* 5207 Olley Ln., Burke, VA 22015 USA Tel 571-212-9471 E-mail: joedinian@yahoo.com.

JaMarque Publishing *See* **JK Pr.**

Jambor Publishing (CAN) *(978-0-9732928; 978-1-989055) Dist. by* **IPG Chicago.**

James A. Parker, *(978-1-7366534)* 150 Moeller St., Binghamton, NY 13904 USA Tel 607-242-2746 E-mail: parker19995james@gmail.com Web site: https://www.parkerajames.com/.

James, JoAnn, *(978-0-9764406)* P.O. Box 11459, Eugene, OR 97440 USA E-mail: joann_james@comcast.net.

James Lorimer & Co. Ltd., Pubs. (CAN) *(978-0-88862; 978-1-55028; 978-1-55277; 978-1-4594) Dist. by* **Casemate Pubs.**

James Lorimer & Co. Ltd., Pubs. (CAN) *(978-0-88862; 978-1-55028; 978-1-55277; 978-1-4594) Dist. by* **Lerner Pub.**

James Lorimer & Co. Ltd., Pubs. (CAN) *(978-0-88862; 978-1-55028; 978-1-55277; 978-1-4594) Dist. by* **Children Plus.**

James Matthew Thompson, *(978-0-692-17501-9)* 762 Coriander Rd., Blythewood, SC 29016 USA Tel 803-466-4006 E-mail: jamathompson@gmail.com *Dist(s):* **Ingram Content Group.**

James parker *See* **James A. Parker**

James, Roger, *(978-0-692-58272-5; 978-0-578-88259-8; 978-0-578-89880-3; 978-0-578-90565-5; 978-0-578-90594-5; 978-0-578-93546-1; 978-0-578-94686-3)* 6603 Oliver St., Riverdale, MD 20737 USA Tel 301-922-4539 E-mail: rjam1974@gmail.com Web site: www.jamesstudio.com.

James Stevenson Pub., *(978-1-885852)* 1500 Oliver Rd., Suite K-109, Fairfield, CA 94533 USA Tel 707-469-0237; Fax: 206-350-2954 E-mail: ceo@jspub.com Web site: http://www.jspub.com *Dist(s):* **Marangio, Charles F. Distribution.**

†Jameson Bks., Inc., *(978-0-89803; 978-0-915463; 978-0-916054)* 722 Columbus St., P.O. Box 738, Ottawa, IL 61350 USA (SAN 281-7578) Tel 815-434-7905; Fax: 815-434-7907; Toll Free: 800-426-1357 E-mail: jamesonbooks@yahoo.com *Dist(s):* **Midpoint Trade Bks., Inc.**; *CIP.*

Jamestown, *(978-0-07; 978-0-8092; 978-0-8442; 978-0-89061; 978-0-913327; 978-0-941263; 978-1-56943)* Div. of Glencoe/McGraw-Hill, Orders Addr.: P.O. Box 543, Blacklick, OH 43004-0543 USA Fax: 614-860-1877; Toll Free: 800-334-7344; Edit Addr.: P.O. Box 508, Columbus, OH 43216 USA Toll Free: 800-872-7323 Web site: http://www.jamestowneducation.com *Dist(s):* **Libros Sin Fronteras McGraw-Hill Cos., The.**

Jamie Jai, *(979-8-9888716)* 687 Valley View Way, Travis AFB, CA 94535 USA Tel 214-498-0406 E-mail: Jamiejaifitness@gmail.com *Dist(s):* **Ingram Content Group.**

Jamilian Bks., *(978-0-578-87645-0; 978-1-7379224)* 1608 6th St, Harlan, IA 51537 USA Tel 712-308-0804 E-mail: jjh00@aol.com.

Jamiram Publishing, *(978-0-9790434)* 1760 Harbeck Rd., Grants Pass, OR 97527 USA Web site: http://jamiram.com.

Jamisonk.com, *(978-0-692-08517-2; 978-0-692-08518-9; 978-0-692-08985-9; 978-0-578-55500-3; 978-0-578-62136-4; 978-0-578-98616-6; 978-0-578-98635-7)* Tiny Ranch 5 Paso Mediano, Carmel Valley, CA 93924 USA Tel 831-236-2036 E-mail: jamisonk@mac.com *Dist(s):* **Ingram Content Group.**

JamSum Limited, *(978-0-9770754)* 621 S. Main St., Bellefontaine, OH 43311-1725 USA Toll Free: 866-857-2061 E-mail: publish@jamsum.com Web site: http://www.jamsum.com.

Jan & San *See* **Jerome, Janice**

Janaway Publishing, Inc., *(978-0-9703211; 978-0-9741957; 978-1-59641)* 2412 Nicklaus Dr., Santa Maria, CA 93455 USA Tel 805-925-1038; Fax: 805-925-5228 E-mail: jim@janawaygenealogy.com Web site: http://www.janawaygenealogy.com.

Jan-Carol Publishing, INC., *(978-0-9767793; 978-0-9801504; 978-0-9822337; 978-0-9841870; 978-0-9843192; 978-0-9845470; 978-0-9846398; 978-0-9834885; 978-0-9848050; 978-0-9850272; 978-1-939289; 978-1-945619; 978-1-950895; 978-1-954978; 978-1-962561)* Orders Addr.: PO Box 701, Johnson City, TN 37605 USA Tel 423-926-9983; *Imprints:* Little Creek Books (LittleCreek) Web site: www.voicemagazineforwomen.com; www.jancarolpublishing.com.

Jandie Jams Music LLC, *(978-0-9796150)* 1036 Katy Ln., Longmont, CO 80504 USA (SAN 853-8999) E-mail: jandiejams@comcast.net Web site: http://www.kidcleveronline.com.

J&M Pubs, *(978-0-9726492)* Orders Addr.: P.O. Box 648, Florence, SC 29501 USA Fax: 410-981-5456; Toll Free: 800-989-1170 E-mail: jmpublishers@comcast.net Web site: http://www.jmpublishers.net.

Jane & Street Pubs. Ltd., *(978-0-9745077)* 302-A W. 12th St., No. 197, New York, NY 10014 USA Web site: http://www.janeandstreet.com.

Janelle Pubns., Inc., *(978-0-9626739; 978-1-890265)* Orders Addr.: P.O. Box 811, De Kalb, IL 60115-0811 USA Tel 815-756-2300; Fax: 815-756-4799; Toll Free: 800-888-8834; Edit Addr.: 1189 Twombley Rd., De Kalb, IL 60115 USA E-mail: info@janellepublications.com Web site: http://www.janellepublications.com.

Jane's World *See* **Girl Twirl Comics**

Janik Pr., *(978-0-9883938)* P.O. Box 12034, Fort Wayne, IN 46862 USA Tel 260-804-8044 E-mail: nikbenedict@yahoo.com.

Janis, Tim Ensemble, Inc., *(978-0-9773335)* P.O. Box 315, Kennebunk, ME 04043 USA (SAN 257-280X) Tel 207-985-3463.

Jank Publishing LLC *See* **Bks. for the Culture LLC**

Janneck Bks., *(978-1-7322236; 978-1-7329687; 978-1-950434)* 100 N. Prospect St, Crescent City, FL 32112 USA Tel 904-874-2608 E-mail: turtlemay@gmail.com.

Janosky, Brandon, *(978-0-692-83634-7)* 905 Evans Ave, Kirkwood, MO 63122 USA Tel 314-315-7006 E-mail: brandon@daddytries.com Web site: www.daddytries.com.

Jan's Bks., *(978-0-9797139)* Orders Addr.: 1780 Phillips, Berkley, MI 48072 USA Tel 248-545-5160.

Jan's Looks & Books *See* **Jan's Bks.**

Jan¿s Lulu Books *See* **Jans Lulu Bks.**

Jans Lulu Bks., *(978-1-7369608)* 3652 Bay Ave, Chico, CA 95973 USA Tel 530-521-4885 E-mail: jan@janicecondon.com; janmaxcon@gmail.com Web site: Janmaxcon.com.

Jansen, Marilyn, *(978-0-9761070)* P.O. Box 278, Makawao, HI 96768 USA Tel 808-572-0699 phone/fax E-mail: jamarilyn2008@aol.com Web site: http://amaryllisofhawaii.com *Dist(s):* **Booklines Hawaii, Ltd.**

Jansen, Michael, *(978-0-578-41166-8; 978-0-578-41168-2; 978-0-578-49333-6; 978-0-578-49334-3)* 5942 N. Michigan St., Portland, OR 97217 USA Tel 503-826-3547 E-mail: mikedjansen@gmail.com *Dist(s):* **Ingram Content Group.**

January Joyce Author, *(978-0-578-86212-5; 978-0-578-86213-2; 978-0-578-89349-5; 978-0-578-92839-5; 979-8-218-06737-3)* 3009 Cornell St. 0, Bakersfield, CA 93305 USA Tel 6615652917 E-mail: tamibeaulieu93263@aol.com *Dist(s):* **Ingram Content Group.**

Janze Pubns., *(978-0-9629142; 978-0-9794955)* 930 Bargo St, London, KY 40741-2713 USA E-mail: janzepub@windstream.net.

Japan Pubns. (U.S.A.), Inc., *(978-0-87040; 978-1-57863)* Subs. of Japan Pubns., Inc. (Tokyo, Japan), 160 Spruce Knob Rd., Middletown Springs, VT 05757-4432 USA (SAN 680-0513) Tel 802-235-2814 *Dist(s):* **Diamond Comic Distributors, Inc. Diamond Bk. Distributors Oxford Univ. Pr., Inc.**

Japanime Co., Ltd. (JPN) *(978-4-921205) Dist. by* **Diamond Book Dists.**

Japanime Co., Ltd. (JPN) *(978-4-921205) Dist. by* **D C D.**

Jappa Pubns., *(978-0-9720694)* 1808 N. 79th St., Kansas City, KS 66112 USA Tel 913-205-2361 E-mail: Ongi.entertainment@gmx.com Web site: http://www.pandaoki.com.

Jappamation Studios *See* **Jappa Pubns.**

Jarndyce & Jarndyce Pr., *(978-0-9721916; 978-0-9772720; 978-0-9817269; 978-0-9836173; 978-0-9894271; 978-0-9910077; 978-0-9864238; 978-0-9995747; 978-1-7327493; 978-1-7349967; 978-1-7355873; 978-1-7365991; 978-1-7378038; 979-8-9870255)* Div. of PSA Consulting, Inc., 305 Snow Shoe Dr., Southgate, KY 41071 USA (SAN 860-2433) Tel 513-382-4315; 513-304-3633; Fax: 855-361-8591 Web site: http://www.cincybooks.com *Dist(s):* **BookBaby.**

Jarrel, Ashley Creations Inc, *(978-0-578-56421-0)* 6831 Hwy. 53 W., Dawsonville, GA 30534 USA Tel 678-776-2620 E-mail: Ashleybrandtjarrel@gmail.com.

Jarrett Publishing Co., *(978-0-9624723; 978-1-882422; 978-0-9795493; 978-1-935022)* P.O. Box 1460, Ronkonkoma, NY 11779-0426 USA Toll Free: 800-859-7679 E-mail: info@jarrettpub.com Web site: http://www.jarrettpub.com.

Jarvis Printing *See* **Mitchell, Damien Pardow**

Jasmine Pr., *(978-0-930069)* 2224 Ogden Ave., Bensalem, PA 19020 USA (SAN 669-9650) Tel 215-244-0525.

Jasnans Publishing Co., *(978-0-9761759)* P.O. Box 873633, Wasilla, AK 99687-3633 USA E-mail: hallaifa@mtaonline.net Web site: http://www.jasnanspublishing.com.

Jason & Nordic Pubs., *(978-0-944727)* P.O. Box 441, Hollidaysburg, PA 16648 USA (SAN 244-9374) Tel 814-696-2920; Fax: 814-696-4250; *Imprints:* Turtle Books (Turtle Books) E-mail: turtlbks@jasonandnordic.com Web site: http://www.jasonandnordic.com.

Jason Foundation for Education *See* **JASON Project, The**

Jason Jacques Gallery Pr. The, *(978-0-9788371; 978-0-615-55775-5; 978-0-578-41302-0)* 29 E. 73rd St., No. 1, New York, NY 10021-3501 USA (SAN 851-7568) Tel 212-535-7500; Fax: 212-535-5757 E-mail: jason@jasonjacques.com Web site: http://www.jasonjacques.com.

Jason, Michael, *(978-1-953732)* 3064 Zappia Dr., Florence, KY 41042 USA Tel 859-283-5674 E-mail: 550197436@qq.com.

JASON Project, The, *(978-0-9763809; 978-0-9787574; 978-1-935211; 978-1-945126)* Orders Addr.: 44983 Knoll Sq. Suite 150, Ashburn, VA 20147 USA Tel 703-822-7238; Fax: 703-673-1060; Toll Free: 888-527-6600 E-mail: info@jason.org Web site: http://www.jason.org.

Jasper State Brand, Inc., *(978-0-9820228; 978-0-9833366)* 311 N. Robertson Blvd., Suite 363, Beverly Hills, CA 90211 USA (SAN 857-0213) Tel 310-801-7737 E-mail: judith@jasperstate.com.

Jauregui, Julian, *(978-0-578-43568-8)* 4214 Lotus Ave., Sacramento, CA 95823 USA Tel 661-563-4453 E-mail: Julianjauregui77@yahoo.com *Dist(s):* **Ingram Content Group.**

javariBook, *(978-0-9679161)* P.O. Box 230551, New York, NY 10023 USA E-mail: javaribook@javari.com Web site: http://www.javaribook.com; http://www.globalwidetrade.com.

Jawbone Publishing Corp., *(978-0-9702959; 978-1-59094)* P.O. Box PO Box 3741, Costa Mesa, CA 92626 USA (SAN 253-5335); *Imprints:* Top Shelf (Top); Jawbreakers for Kids (Jawbreakers) E-mail: tara@taraballman.com Web site: http://www.jawbonepublishing.com.

Jawbreakers for Kids *Imprint of* **Jawbone Publishing Corp.**

JaxPublishing.net, *(978-0-9798316)* 11727 Invierno Dr., San Diego, CA 92124-2883 USA Tel 619-757-7016; Fax: 858-277-6418 E-mail: atom@atomart.net Web site: http://www.atomart.net.

Jay Media Publishing *See* **JayMedia Publishing**

Jay Mikael Publishing, *(978-0-9841181)* P.O. Box 3, Omaha, NE 68101-0003 USA.

Jay, Ronald Publishing, *(978-0-9744383)* 301 33rd St., Fort Madison, IA 52627 USA (SAN 255-769X) Tel 319-372-4781 E-mail: racrooks@lisco.com.

Jay Street Pubs., *(978-0-9639999; 978-1-889534)* Div. of G-Communications, P.O. Box 230944, New York, NY 10023-0016 USA E-mail: jaystpub@i-2000.com.

Jay Wertz & Associates, LLC *See* **Monroe Pubns.**

JayJo Bks., LLC, *(978-0-9639449; 978-1-891383)* Orders Addr.: P.O. Box 760, Plainview, NY 11803-0760 USA (SAN 178-5435) Tel 516-349-5520; Fax: 800-262-1886; Toll Free: 800-999-6884; Edit Addr.: 45 Executive Dr. Ste. 201, Plainview, NY 11803-1738 USA E-mail: jayjobook@guidancechannel.com Web site: http://www.jayjo.com *Dist(s):* **Follett School Solutions Quality Bks., Inc. Unique Bks., Inc.**

Jaylil Publishing Co., *(978-0-9748165)* Orders Addr.: P.O. Box 656551, Flushing, NY 11365 USA E-mail: jaylilpublishing@aol.com Web site: http://www.jaylilpublishing.com *Dist(s):* **Culture Plus Bk. Distributors Seaburn Bks.**

JayMedia Publishing, *(978-0-9849290; 978-1-7334432; 978-1-7358701; 978-1-957443)* 9429 Nicklaus Ln., Laurel, MD 20708 USA Tel 301-613-3478 E-mail: jaymediapublishing2018@gmail.com Web site: www.jaymediagroup.net.

JayZ Pubns., *(978-0-578-18666-5; 978-0-578-21162-6)* 48 S. New York Rd., B-7, Smithville, NJ 08205 USA.

Jazwares Distribution, Inc., *(978-0-9724983; 978-0-9765714; 978-1-933752)* 555 Sawgrass Corporate Pkwy., Sunrise, FL 33325-6211 USA E-mail: julio@jazwares.com Web site: http://www.projectkitsforkids.com.

Jazz Path Publishing, *(978-0-9760977)* P.O. Box 381810, Cambridge, MA 02238 USA Web site: http://www.jazzpath.com.

Jazzy Kitty Greetings Marketing & Publishing Company *See* **Jazzy Kitty Pubns.**

Jazzy Kitty Pubns., *(978-0-9768540; 978-0-9843255; 978-0-9830548; 978-0-9851453; 978-0-9892656; 978-0-9916648; 978-0-9970848; 978-0-9988433; 978-0-692-10602-0; 978-1-7324523; 978-1-7349014; 978-1-7357874; 978-1-954425)* E-mail: anelda@jazzykittypublications.com; jazzykittygreetingpublishing@gmail.com Web site: http://www.jazzykittypublications.com.

JB Bks. LLC, *(978-0-578-33589-6; 978-0-578-33590-2; 978-0-578-34797-4)* 301 S 1200 E Unit 34 0, SAINT GEORGE, UT 84790 USA Tel 435-676-3605 E-mail: jbrockguthrie@gmail.com *Dist(s):* **Ingram Content Group.**

JB Information Station, *(978-0-934334)* P.O. Box 19333, Saint Louis, MO 63125 USA (SAN 213-4128) Tel 314-638-3404; 3888 Via Miralesta Dr., Saint Louis, MO 63125 E-mail: empoweredparenting@earthlink.net Web site: http://www.JoanBramsch.com.

JBall Publishing, *(978-0-9764179)* 393 W. 300 N., Smithfield, UT 84335 USA Tel 435-563-9437 Web site: http://pumpkinglow.com.

JBiRD iNK, Ltd., *(978-0-9715253; 978-0-9850732)* 109 Knutson Dr., Madison, WI 53704 USA Tel 608-554-0803 E-mail: info@jbirdink.com Web site: http://www.jbirdink.com.

JBT Publishing, *(978-0-9792059)* Orders Addr.: 1485 Christina Ln., Lake Forest, IL 60045 USA (SAN 852-7644) Tel 781-760-2357; Fax: 419-735-0603 E-mail: jtedesco@gis.net.

JC Burdine, P.O. Box 3017, SOUTHAMPTON, NY 11968 USA Tel 646-352-1413 E-mail: jcburdine1@aol.com *Dist(s):* **Ingram Content Group.**

JCCJ Pr., *(978-0-9770207)* 81 River Rd., Norfolk, MA 02056 USA Tel 508-528-4767.

JCTT, LLC, *(978-0-9766926; 978-1-7338960)* 412 Capote Peak Dr., Georgetown, TX 78633 USA E-mail: linleyw@msn.com Web site: http://www.mathemagicians.info.

JD & RB Enterprise Inc. *See* **JD PUBLISHING**

JD Entertainment, *(978-0-9772240)* 1731 Cherry Rd., Memphis, TN 38117 USA E-mail: directorrsp@yahoo.com Web site: http://www.jkdenny.com *Dist(s):* **Partners Bk. Distributing, Inc.**

J.D. Hines, *(978-0-578-42047-9; 978-0-578-47336-9; 978-0-578-47341-3; 978-0-578-49357-2; 978-0-578-57818-7; 978-0-578-58350-1; 978-0-578-58532-1; 978-0-578-58824-7; 978-0-578-60020-8; 978-0-578-60124-3; 978-0-578-72920-6; 978-0-578-72922-0; 978-1-7357396; 978-0-578-81146-8; 978-0-578-34166-8; 978-0-578-35313-5) 2380 Central Ave., Riverside, CA 92506 USA Tel 951-784-7024* E-mail: jdwriter@rocketmail.com *Dist(s):* **Ingram Content Group.**

J.D. Publishing *See* **Onion Publishing**

JD PUBLISHING, *(978-0-9991838)* P.O. Box 1774, Bunnell, FL 32110 USA Tel 386-263-2325; Fax: 386-263-2325 E-mail: jorjao@msn.com Web site: www.jorjao2013.com.

JD Publishing, *(978-0-9793972)* Div. of Redpsych Production, P.O. Box 696, Fairfax, CA 94978 USA (SAN 853-3431) Tel 773-793-7622 E-mail: redpsychproductions@yahoo.com Web site: http://www.redpsych.com; http://www.monkeyandtheengineer.com.

JDonniniLLC, *(978-0-578-50831-3; 978-0-578-57484-4; 978-1-7346606)* 55 Layton Rd., Pilesgrove, NJ 08098 USA Tel 609-364-4599 E-mail: jdonninibooks@gmail.com Web site: JDonninibooks.com.

J.E. Reed, *(978-0-578-49409-8; 978-0-578-57279-6; 978-0-578-77646-0; 979-8-9873410)* 4310 Long Acres Dr., Apt. C, Cincinnati, OH 45245 USA Tel 513-767-6083 E-mail: J.E.reedauthor@gmail.com *Dist(s):* **Ingram Content Group.**

JE Solinski, *(978-0-9989096)* 80 Danbury Dr., Redding, CA 96003 USA Tel 530-339-6268 E-mail: jody@jesolinski.com Web site: jesolinski.com.

Jean Voice Dart, *(978-1-7339327)* 347 Carmel Ave. Spc 54, Marina, CA 93933 USA Tel 831-272-2752 E-mail: jeanvoicedart@gmail.com *Dist(s):* **Ingram Content Group.**

JeanneArleneGale, *(978-1-7322986)* 1304 Williams St., Eureka, CA 95501 USA Tel 707-445-9835 E-mail: jeannegale8@gmail.com.

Jeb Cool Kids Entertainment, Inc, *(978-0-9744123; 978-0-9859430)* 8208 Norton Ave., Unit 2, Los Angeles, CA 90046 USA E-mail: jebcoolkids@gmail.com Web site: http://www.jebcoolkids.com *Dist(s):* **BookBaby.**

JEBWizard Publishing, *(978-1-7335264; 978-1-7343553; 978-1-7362146; 978-1-7368288; 979-8-9850177; 979-8-9877174)* 37 Pk. Forest Rd, Cranston, RI 02802 USA Tel 401-533-3988 E-mail: Joe.Broadmeadow@JEBWizardpublishing.com Web site: www.jebwizardpublishing.com *Dist(s):* **AudioBks. Unleashed.**

JEC Publishing Company *See* **Recipe Pubs.**

Jeffers Pr., *(978-0-9745776; 978-0-9777618)* 2700 Neilson Way, Suite 1428, Santa Monica, CA 90405 USA Tel 310-450-4008; Toll Free: 877-450-4008 E-mail: mark@jefferspress.com Web site: http://www.jefferspress.com *Dist(s):* **National Bk. Network.**

Jefferson Pr., *(978-0-9718974; 978-0-9778086; 978-0-9800164; 978-0-615-27680-9)* P.O. Box 115, Lookout Mountain, TN 37350 USA E-mail: dmagee@jeffersonpress.com; info@jeffersonpress.com Web site: http://www.jeffersonpress.com.

Jefferson, Thomas University Press *See* **Truman State Univ. Pr.**

ffrey Sterling, (978-0-692-17587-3) 5808 Woodrow Wilson Blvd. NE, St. Petersburg, FL 33703 USA Tel 727-798-5850
E-mail: Scottsterling81@gmail.com
Dist(s): Ingram Content Group.
effries Bks., (978-1-7358658; 978-1-957079) 9734 S MILLARD AVE, EVERGREEN PARK, IL 60805 USA Tel 678-386-6906
E-mail: zackgeoffroy@gmail.com
Web site: https://www.zjeffries.com.
elly Telly Pr. Imprint of FaithWords
ellyroll Productions See Osborne Enterprises Publishing
ellysquid Books See Jellysquid Bks. LLC
ellysquid Bks. LLC, (978-0-578-68183-2; 978-0-578-97158-2; 979-8-9887273) 721 W Boston St. 0, BROKEN ARROW, OK 74012 USA Tel 9186880154
E-mail: hannahtindle324@gmail.com
Dist(s): Ingram Content Group.
IEM Bks., Inc., (978-0-9754317) 10466 E. Sheena Dr., Scottsdale, AZ 85255-1742 USA
E-mail: rmahoney@jem-books.com
Web site: http://www.jem-books.com.
Jen Jen W. Cherieperrault, (978-0-9984684) 40 Musket Dr., shirley, NY 11967 USA Tel 347-319-2747; Fax: 631-399-2919
E-mail: netnich@gmail.com.
Jenis Group, LLC, (978-1-942674) 975 Alvin St., San Diego, CA 92114-1838 USA Tel 619-955-9284
E-mail: aynixon@yahoo.com.
Jenkins, Keisha See World Is Mine Publishing LLC
Jenkins, Tranise, (978-0-692-84008-5; 978-0-578-71922-1; 978-0-578-74895-5; 978-0-578-74896-2; 978-0-578-75303-4; 978-0-578-75356-0) 5684 Whinstone Way, CHAMBERSBURG, PA 17202 USA Tel 717-263-0425
E-mail: jeffwcrawford5+LVP0003313@gmail.com; jeffwcrawford5+LVP0003313@gmail.com.
Jenkins-Simmons, Glenda, (978-0-9758586) 692 Mulberry Dr., Biloxi, MS 39532 USA Tel 228-388-7540
E-mail: res55472@cs.com.
Jennie's Music Room Bks., (978-0-9842392; 978-0-578-33214-7; 979-8-218-20287-3) 4241 Filmore St., Chincoteague Island, VA 23336 USA (SAN 858-8236)
Web site: http://www.ginasfamilystore.com; http://www.jmrbooks.com
Dist(s): Smashwords.
Jennifer Hartinger, (978-0-9964588) Div of BYS Books, 315 12Th St No. B, Seal Beach, CA 90740 USA
E-mail: jchartinger@hotmail.com
Web site: http://www.jenniferhartinger.com.
Jennifer Lynne Kennard, (978-0-692-34412-5; 978-0-692-56862-0; 978-0-578-43066-9; 978-0-578-48077-0; 978-0-578-97678-5) 1135 Belvidere Dr., Nashville, TN 37204-3915 USA Tel 615-424-4529
E-mail: jenniferlynnkennard@gmail.com.
Jennifer Lynn-Gates Jackson, (978-1-7368164) 2626 E PACIFIC CT, BREA, CA 92821 USA Tel 626-260-1212
E-mail: gatez1@yahoo.com.
Jennings, J. Publishing Company See Jennings Publishing
Jennings Publishing, (978-0-9700038) 5012 Kahn St., Carmichael, CA 95608 USA Tel 916-863-1638; Fax: 916-863-5807
E-mail: jane@jenningspub.com
Web site: http://www.jenningspub.com
Dist(s): Omnibus Pr.
Jenpet Publishing, (978-0-9726794) P.O. Box 2542, Alameda, CA 94501 USA Tel 510-521-3582
E-mail: jj@jenpet.com
Web site: http://www.jenpet.com.
JenPrint Pubns., LLC, (978-0-9653791) 12195 Hwy. 92 Suite 114-162, Woodstock, GA 30188 USA
E-mail: margarette@jenprint.com
Web site: http://www.jenprint.com
Dist(s): Book Clearing Hse.
Follett School Solutions
Quality Bks., Inc.
Jensen, Lissa, (978-0-9666973) 958 Summer Holly Ln., Encinitas, CA 92024 USA Tel 760-944-6345.
JENSEN, TRAVIS, (978-0-9754439) 600 N. Central Ave. #533, Glendale, CA 91203 USA
E-mail: TRAVIS@TRAVISJENSENPHOTO.COM
Web site: http://WWW.TRAVISJENSENPHOTO.COM.
Jensonbooks, (978-0-9794415) P.O. Box 416, Greenfield, MA 01302-0416 USA (SAN 853-4322).
Jentmedia, (978-0-578-03676-2) P.O. Box 1304, Lonbard, IL 60148 USA
Dist(s): Lulu Pr., Inc.
Jeremy's Things, (978-0-9747878) 410 Fifth Ave., 2nd Flr., Brooklyn, NY 11215 USA Tel 718-788-3987
E-mail: jeremy@jeremybullis.com
Web site: http://www.jeremybullis.com.
Jeriel Works, (978-0-9994364) 2855 Poirier Rd., Blanchard, ID 83804 USA Tel 208-437-0719
E-mail: jessicapaintsjesus@hotmail.com.
Jeriger Pr., (978-1-59810) P.O. Box 1249, Stafford, TX 77477-1249 USA Tel 888-447-5495 (phone/fax)
E-mail: info@jeriger.com
Web site: http://www.jeriger.com.
Jerome, Janice, (978-0-9729741) 273 Roy Huie Rd., Riverdale, GA 30274 USA
E-mail: feedback@providerhouse.com
Web site: http://www.providerhouse.com.
Jersey Classic Publishing, (978-0-9765261) 75 Locust Ave., Wallington, NJ 07057 USA.
Jerusalem Pubns., (978-0-9707572; 978-0-9743911; 978-0-9761862; 978-0-9773885; 978-0-9792230; 978-0-9815567; 978-0-9844921; 978-0-9888958; 978-0-9863253; 978-0-9987055) 4917 Ravenswood Dr., Apt. 513, San Antonio, TX 78232 USA Tel 732-901-3009; Fax: 732-901-4012
E-mail: rapaport@netvision.net.il
Web site: http://www.israelbookshop.com/; http://www.feldheim.com/
Dist(s): Feldheim Pubs.
Israel Bookshop Pubns.
Jessa Lynn Pease Garrett, (978-0-578-43550-3; 978-0-578-43888-7; 978-0-578-70803-4; 978-0-578-70804-1) 1432 Shades Crest Rd., Hoover, AL 35226 USA Tel 678-794-6356
E-mail: Jessalynnpease@gmail.com
Dist(s): Ingram Content Group.
Jessian Pr., (978-0-692-70523-0) 21 Saddlerock Dr., Poughkeepsie, NY 12603 USA Tel 917-833-4580
Dist(s): CreateSpace Independent Publishing Platform.
Jessica D. Stovall, (978-0-578-33304-5) 1281 Brockett Rd, Clarkston, GA 30021 USA Tel 404-543-0149
E-mail: JSTOVALL93@GMAIL.COM.
Jessica Nelson, (978-0-692-95114-9; 978-0-692-95115-6; 978-0-692-95394-5; 978-0-692-95397-6; 978-0-692-95403-4) 2318 n 450 w, Harrisville, UT 84414 USA Tel 801-505-1323
E-mail: jeffwcrawford5+LVP0003523@gmail.com; jeffwcrawford5+LVP0003523@gmail.com.
Jessie Street Pr., (978-0-9888080) P.O. Box 3013, Sausalito, CA 94966 USA Tel 415-806-4083
E-mail: btcolor@yahoo.com
Web site: www.jessiestreetpress.com.
JESSPress See JESSPress/Susie Yakowicz
JESSPress/Susie Yakowicz, (978-0-9652546) 4231 Wexford Way, Eagan, MN 55122 USA Tel 651-681-9537
E-mail: syakowicz@comcast.net
Web site: http://www.jesspress.com; susieyakowicz.com/blog.
Jester Bks., (978-0-9723382) 39 E. 12th St., 506, New York, NY 10003 USA Tel 212-529-9209 Do not confuse with companies with the same or similar names in Woodland Hills, CA, Orinda, CA
E-mail: davidmkorn@earthlink.net.
Jesus Estanislado, (978-0-9776291) P.O. Box 6373, Lakewood, CA 90714 USA
E-mail: jesscortez01@gmail.com.
Jet City Comics Imprint of Amazon Publishing
JETM Publishing & Distribution See I Am Your Playground LLC
Jetpack Publishing, (978-0-9898533) 3 Maybrook Dr., Glenville, NY 12302 USA Tel 518-929-1895
E-mail: ethancrownberry@nycap.rr.com.
Jetty Hse. Imprint of Randall, Peter E. Pub.
Jetway Geographer, LLC, (978-0-9711640) Orders Addr.: 431 S. Cooke, Helena, MT 59601 USA Tel 406-586-6879
E-mail: jgeographer@bresnan.net
Web site: http://www.jetwaygeographer.com.
Jew-El Pr. Co., (978-0-9767618) 40022 Milkmaid Ln., Murrieta, CA 92562 USA Tel 951-600-7054 (phone/fax)
E-mail: jew-el-press@verizon.net
Web site: http://www.jew-el-press.com.
Jewel Publishing, (978-0-9744944) P.O. Box 38, Chino Hills, CA 91709 USA Fax: 909-606-1092 Do not confuse with companies with the same or similar name in Baltimore, MD, Denver, CO, Detroit, MI, Cincinnati, OH
E-mail: cmckee7721@aol.com.
Jewel Publishing LLC, (978-0-9629715; 978-1-936499) Orders Addr.: 6815 W. Floyd Ave., Denver, CO 80227 USA Tel 303-980-1957 Do not confuse with companies with similar names in Cincinnati, OH, New York, NY, Baltimore, MD, Detroit, MI, Chino Hills, CA
E-mail: sandy7lardinois@gmail.com; sandy@jewelpublishing.com
Web site: http://jewelpublishing.com.
Jewell Histories, (978-0-9678413) 143 Breckenridge St., Gettysburg, PA 17325 USA Tel 717-420-5344
E-mail: jewellhistories@superpa.net.
Jewell, Vickie, (978-0-692-99078-0) 1702 S. 7th ave. No. 17, Marshalltown, IA 50158 USA Tel 641-750-8041
E-mail: vtjewell@outlook.com.
Jewelvision Publishing LLC., (978-0-9992781) 4045 S. Buffalo Dr., Las Vegas, NV 89147 USA Tel 702-614-6931
E-mail: Jewelvision@cox.net.
Jewish Community Federation of Rochester, NY, Inc., (978-0-9710686) 441 East Ave., Rochester, NY 14607 USA Tel 585-461-0490; Fax: 585-461-0912
E-mail: bappelbaum@jewishrochester.org
Web site: http://www.jewishrochester.org
Dist(s): Wayne State Univ. Pr.
Jewish Educational Media, (978-1-931607; 978-1-932349; 978-0-9890522) 784 Eastern Pkwy., Suite 403, Brooklyn, NY 11213 USA Tel 718-774-6000; Fax: 718-774-3402
E-mail: eli@jemedia.org
Web site: http://www.jemedia.org
Dist(s): Kehot Pubn. Society.
Jewish Girls Unite, (978-0-9841624; 978-0-578-40595-7; 978-0-578-44571-7; 978-0-578-53297-4; 978-0-578-55652-9; 978-0-578-68652-3; 978-0-578-70328-2; 979-8-218-07771-6; 979-8-218-10574-7; 979-8-218-22939-9; 979-8-218-25105-5; 979-8-218-28877-8) P.O. Box 215, Sharon, MA 02067-0215 USA (SAN 858-5938) Toll Free: 888-492-5324
E-mail: leahmcaras@gmail.com
Web site: http://www.yaldah.com.
Jewish Learning Group, The, (978-1-891293) 6 Tokay Ln., Monsey, NY 10952-1701 USA Toll Free: 888-565-3276
E-mail: info@jewishlearninggroup.com
Web site: http://www.jewishlearninggroup.com
Dist(s): Independent Pubs. Group.
Jewish Lights Publishing Imprint of LongHill Partners, Inc.
†Jewish Pubn. Society, (978-0-8276) Orders Addr.: 22883 Quicksilver Dr., Dulles, VA 20166 USA (SAN 253-9446) Tel 703-661-1165; 703-661-1529; Fax: 703-661-1501; Toll Free: 800-355-1165; Edit Addr.: 2100 Arch St., 2nd Flr., Philadelphia, PA 19103-1399 USA Tel 215-832-0600
E-mail: marketing@jewishpub.org
Web site: http://www.jewishpub.org
Dist(s): Ebsco Publishing
MyiLibrary
Univ. of Nebraska Pr.; CIP.
Jezowski, Savannah, (978-0-578-98355-4) 500 23 Mile Rd, Homer, MI 49245 USA Tel 231-206-8217
E-mail: dragonwriter84@gmail.com
Dist(s): Ingram Content Group.
JFA Productions, (978-0-9723024) 806 Homestead Ave., Maybrook, NY 12543 USA Tel 845-427-5008
E-mail: carrdero@warwick.net.
Jfalcock, (978-0-9890111; 979-8-9854174) 4262 Althea Way, Palm Beach Gardens, FL 33410 USA Tel 561-252-3350
E-mail: jfalcock@gmail.com.
JFAR Bks., (978-0-615-45886-1) Orders Addr.: P.O. Box 331621, West Hartford, CT 06133 USA Tel 617-388-2489
E-mail: J_Farquharson@yahoo.com
Web site: www.PlaytimetoBedtime.com.
JFK Online Studios, LLC, (978-0-9742249) 293 2nd Ave., West Haven, CT 06516-5127 USA
Web site: http://www.jfkonlinestudios.com.
JFW, Ltd., (978-0-9710071) 400 N. Church St., Unit 602, Charlotte, NC 28202 USA Tel 704-277-8378 (phone/fax)
E-mail: create2000@earthlink.net; jfwbird@earthlink.com.
JG Pr. Imprint of World Pubns. Group, Inc.
JGC/United Publishing Corps, (978-0-910941) 1717 Harlem Blvd., Rockford, IL 61103 USA (SAN 270-5109) Tel 815-968-6601
E-mail: mailbox@jgcunited.com
Web site: http://www.jgcunited.com.
J.G.R. Enterprises, (978-0-9758746) 100 Oak St., Patchogue, NY 11772 USA Tel 631-790-0932
E-mail: joannros12@aol.com.
JGracia Publishing, (978-0-9837403) 2998 Valley View Cir., Powder Springs, GA 30127 USA Tel 678-668-6286
E-mail: jgraciaenterprises@gmail.com
Dist(s): Lulu Pr., Inc.
JHAMS Media Legacy, (978-0-578-55169-2; 978-0-578-34413-3; 979-8-9860217) 4375 Cascade Rd., Apt. Q225, Atlanta, GA 30331 USA Tel 678-361-9968
E-mail: msakinah7@gmail.com
Web site: sensoryxplosionboutique.com.
JHAMS Media Legacy/JHAMS Forever See JHAMS Media Legacy
Jib & Jigger, Inc., (978-0-692-17283-4) 826 E. Pk. Ave., Port Townsend, WA 98368 USA Tel 800-979-1930
E-mail: josh@smallcraftadvisor.com
Dist(s): Ingram Content Group.
Jill Knapp-Zitron See Sunflower Pr.
jilljohnsonyoung.com, (978-0-692-97586-2; 978-0-9997886; 978-1-7359323) 2549 Flanders Rd., Riverside, CA 92506 USA Tel 951-990-9186
E-mail: jilljohnsonyoung@gmail.com; admin@jilljohnsonyoung.com
Web site: www.jilljohnsonyoung.com
Dist(s): CreateSpace Independent Publishing Platform
Ingram Content Group.
Jim C. Hines, (978-1-7352662) 1923 Pageant Way, Holt, MI 48842 USA Tel 517-889-2143
E-mail: jchines42@hotmail.com
Web site: https://www.jimchines.com.
JIMAPCO, Inc., (978-1-56914) Orders Addr.: P.O. Box 1137, Clifton Park, NY 12065 USA Fax: 518-899-5093; Toll Free: 800-627-7123; Edit Addr.: 2095 Rte. 9, Round Lake, NY 12151 USA Tel 518-899-5091
E-mail: cfisk@jimapco.com
Dist(s): Benchmark LLC
Langenscheidt Publishing Group
Rand McNally.
Jimmy Patterson Imprint of Little Brown & Co.
Jimmyland Corp., (978-0-9760140; 978-0-9792672; 978-0-9820618; 978-0-9837021) Jimmyland Corp., Orders Addr.: 2804 E. Crosley Dr., Suite H, West Palm Beach, FL 33415 USA Tel 561-602-1400
E-mail: jimmydrobinson@comcast.net
Web site: http://www.jimmydrobinson.com
Dist(s): BookBaby.
Jimsam Incorporated See Jimsam Inc. Publishing
Jimsam Inc. Publishing, (978-0-9790768; 978-0-9816914; 978-0-9820587; 978-0-9841074; 978-0-615-57183-6; 978-0-615-66583-2; 978-0-615-67879-5) P.O. Box 3363, Riverview, FL 33569 USA Tel 813-748-9523
E-mail: contact@jimsaminc.com; ms1free@aol.com
Web site: http://www.jimsam-inc.com.
Jinks, Elizabeth Schneider, (978-0-9666312) 7624 W. Mauna Loa Ln., Peoria, AZ 85381-4388 USA Tel 602-486-5362
E-mail: ee_jinks@qwest.net.
JINKS Studio Art & Publishing, (978-0-9749672) Orders Addr.: 9421 Woodlief Rd., Wake Forest, NC 27587-8993 USA
E-mail: jinksstudio@comcast.net
Web site: http://www.jinksstudio.com.
Jiovanie, (978-0-578-10152-1) 503 La Costa, Leander, TX 78641 USA.
JIST Life Imprint of JIST Publishing
†JIST Publishing, (978-0-942784; 978-1-56370; 978-1-57112; 978-1-59357; 978-1-63332) Div. of EMC Publishing, 875 Montreal Way, Saint Paul, MN 55102 USA (SAN 240-2351) Tel 651-290-2800 Toll Free Fax: 800-547-8329; Imprints: KIDSRIGHTS (Kidsrts); JIST Works (JIST Works); JIST Life (JIST Lfe)
E-mail: info@jist.com
Web site: http://www.jist.com
Dist(s): Cardinal Pubs. Group
Ebsco Publishing
Follett School Solutions
Linx Educational Publishing, Inc.
MyiLibrary
O'Reilly Media, Inc.; CIP.
JIST Works Imprint of JIST Publishing
JIST Works, Incorporated See JIST Publishing
Jitterbug Bks., (978-0-9763031; 978-0-615-49452-4) 25 Whale Rock Rd., Jamestown, RI 02835 USA Tel 401-423-2823
E-mail: jitterbugbooks@cox.net.
J.J. Pips Publishing, (978-0-9982343) 2461 Santa Monica Blvd., Suite 519, Santa Monica, CA 90404 USA Tel 310-710-5345
E-mail: jj@jjpips.com
Web site: http://www.jjpips.com.
JJR Marketing Consultants LLC See Fig Factor Media Publishing
JK Pr., (978-0-9667853; 978-0-9667853-1-9; 978-1-7329347; 978-1-7359233; 978-1-7378969) 2054 SW 25th ST, Redmond, OR 97756 USA
E-mail: james5of7@yahoo.com.
J.K.H. Enterprises, (978-0-9761422) MSC 5033, Busch Student Center 20 N. Grand Blvd., Saint Louis, MO 63103 USA
E-mail: juliushunter@slu.edu
Web site: http://juliushunter.tripod.com.
JL De Castro, (978-1-7324219) P.O. Box 25, Hummels Wharf, PA 17831-0025 USA Tel 570-374-8294
E-mail: jldecastrolivros@yahoo.com
Web site: janetldecastro.com.
JL Thomas Pub., (978-0-9786537) 1287 Hadaway Trl., Lawrenceville, GA 30043-4670 USA
E-mail: jlthomas@jlthomas-author.com
Web site: http://jlthomas-author.com.
JLM CD-ROM Publishing Co., (978-0-9749905) 150 Idora Ave., San Francisco, CA 94127-1016 USA (SAN 255-9552)
Web site: http://www.jlmcd-rompublishing.com.
JM Publishing, (978-0-578-14249-4; 978-0-9907424) 64 Elm St, Georgetown, MA 01833 USA.
J.M. Roman See Jose M. Roman
JM Studio, (978-1-7321442) 48 E. 1050 N., Chesterton, IN 46304 USA Tel 219-926-8937
E-mail: mullindesign@gmail.com.
JM2 Publishing Co., (978-0-9767210) 6316 Monte Cresta, Richmond, CA 94806 USA Fax: 510-237-4305
E-mail: jeanmock@comcast.net.
JMC Printing, (978-0-9638586) Div. of JMC Marketing, Orders Addr.: 6730 W. 84th Cir. Suite 88, Arvada, CO 80003 USA Tel 303-564-1606 mobile
E-mail: jmcpublishing@aol.com.
JMG Studio, (978-0-9771117) Div. of John-Marc Grob Studios, 6 Southwind Dr., Flanders, NJ 07836 USA (SAN 256-8691) Tel 973-347-5399
E-mail: johnmarc@jmgstudio.net
Web site: http://www.jmgstudio.net.
JMK Music Publishing, (978-0-9743218) 22 Maple Ln., Northborough, MA 01532 USA
Web site: http://www.jmkmusicpub.com.
JMN, (978-1-7356679) 540 Vine St., Oceanside, CA 92054 USA Tel 619-251-6437
E-mail: Jared.nelson07@gmail.com.
Jmpendleton, (978-1-7364435) 18927 Cir. of the Oaks, Newhall, CA 91321 USA Tel 805-416-3954
E-mail: teachincolors@gmail.com
Web site: Jmpendleton.com.
J.N. Courtney Pubns., (978-0-9967059) 51 Hilltop Dr., Penfield, NY 14526 USA Tel 585-313-1995
E-mail: jeancourt59@gmail.com.
JNB Pr., (978-0-615-38122-0; 978-0-692-79347-3; 978-0-9993017) 40 Glen St., Melrose, MA 02176 USA Tel 617-957-2076; Fax: 617-957-2076
E-mail: janice@janicecooks.com
Web site: https://janicecooks.com/.
J-Novel Club, (978-1-7183) 22542 Alabado, San Antonio, TX 78261 USA Tel 210-900-7853
E-mail: contact@j-novel.club
Web site: http://www.j-novel.club
Dist(s): Consortium Bk. Sales & Distribution
Ingram Publisher Services.
JoAnn Vergona Krapp & Gene Zaner, (978-0-9722576) 94 Sunset Ave., Farmingdale, NY 11735 USA
E-mail: jkrapp1940@aol.com.
Joanna Nabholz, (978-0-692-95912-1) 330 170th Pl. SE, Bothell, WA 98012 USA Tel 408-859-7879; Fax: 408-859-7879
E-mail: wlodawer@gmail.com.
Joanne Faye Pr., (978-0-9747375) c/o Goblin Fern Pr., Inc., 852 Hemlock Dr., Verona, WI 53593 USA Tel 608-835-5523; Fax: 608-442-0212
E-mail: jritland@mac.com
Web site: http://www.loveybooks.com.
Joanne Frances Pr., (978-0-9777640) Orders Addr.: 210 Piney Hill Rd., Oakland, MI 48363-1449 USA Toll Free: 800-960-2347
Web site: http://www.JoanneFrancesPress.com.
JoAnne/Horatio Books See Gumbo Multimedia Entertainment
JoanRuddimanEdD, (978-1-7363061) 75 Lakeview Drve, Allentown, NJ 08501 USA Tel 609-529-6701
E-mail: joan.ruddiman@gmail.com
Web site: JoanRuddimanEdD.
JoBen Books, LLC See Unveiled Media, LLC
Jocko Publishing, (978-0-9816188; 979-8-9871452) 4247 Eagle Rock Blvd Unit 502, Los Angeles, CA 90065 USA Tel 718-288-6141
E-mail: jbozak@jockopublishing.com; jonbozak@gmail.com
Web site: http://www.jockopublishing.com; www.warriorkid.com
Dist(s): Ebsco Publishing.
Jodan Collections, (978-0-9747181) Orders Addr.: 2716 N. Univ. Rd., Spokane, WA 99206 USA Tel 509-927-1882; Edit Addr.: 6405 S. Dishman Mica Rd., Spokane, WA 99206 USA
E-mail: joanne@inlandbindery.com
Web site: http://www.inlandbindery.com.

Publisher Name Index

Jodaviste Publishing, *(978-0-9789016)* P.O. Box 473444, Charlotte, NC 28247 USA (SAN 851-920X)
E-mail: jodavistepublishing@earthlink.net
Web site: www.margosmagictrunk.com.

Joe Girl Ink, *(978-0-9766080)* 111S. Morgan, No. 502, Chicago, IL 60607 USA.

Joe Joe Dawson, *(978-0-692-70463-9; 978-0-692-87713-5; 978-0-692-97245-8; 978-0-692-05949-4; 978-0-692-18205-5; 978-0-692-18206-2; 978-0-692-19908-4; 978-0-578-40269-7; 978-0-578-42130-8; 978-0-578-42415-6; 978-0-578-43891-7; 978-0-578-44456-7; 978-0-578-51625-7; 978-0-578-52644-7; 978-0-578-62380-1; 978-0-578-69190-9; 978-0-578-69191-6; 978-0-578-69193-0).*

Joel-Taiwo, Olubusola, *(978-0-578-41500-0)* 5415 N. Sheridan Rd. Apt. 2807, Chicago, IL 60640 USA Tel 312-890-5198
E-mail: author4kidss@gmail.com
Dist(s): **Ingram Content Group.**

Joewolf Pubs., *(978-0-9671344)* Orders Addr.: P.O. Box 80127, Conyer, GA 30013 USA Tel 770-922-6655; Fax: 770-388-0521
E-mail: joewolf@bellsouth.net.

Joey Bks. *Imprint of* **Acclaim Pr., Inc.**

Joey Publishing, *(978-0-9799444)* 300 Atlantic St., Suite 500, Stamford, CT 06902 USA Fax: 203-363-7825
E-mail: jeanne@joeypublishing.com.

Johannesen Printing & Publishing, *(978-1-881084)* Orders Addr.: P.O. Box 24, Whitethorn, CA 95589 USA Tel 707-986-7465; Fax: 707-986-1656
E-mail: books@johannesen.com
Web site: http://www.johannesen.com.

Johansson, J.R. *See* **Midnight Media**

John, *(978-0-9886232)*
E-mail: altj1a@gmail.com.

John John Bks., *(978-0-9980527)* 6704 Nashville Ave., Lubbock, TX 79413 USA Tel 806-789-3269; Fax: 806-698-6855
E-mail: johnjohnbooks@yahoo.com.

John M. Jimerson, *(978-0-578-44197-9)* 5900 Timber Creek Ln. No. 1315, Raleigh, NC 27612 USA Tel 919-561-1950
E-mail: john@johnjimerson.com
Dist(s): **Ingram Content Group.**

John R. Mitchell, *(978-0-692-16571-3)* 694 Maple Leaf Ln., LA PORTE, IN 46350 USA Tel 219-362-3038
E-mail: jmitchell694@comcast.net
Dist(s): **Ingram Content Group.**

Johnny Magory Business (IRL) *(978-0-9935792; 978-1-8382152) Dist. by* **Casemate Pubs.**

Johnny Sundby Photography, *(978-0-9747152)* 4780 Easy St., Rapid City, SD 57702 USA Tel 605-343-5646
E-mail: dsp@rap.midco.net
Web site: http://www.johnnysundby.com.

Johnnycopywriter, *(978-0-692-93913-0)* 825 Bayshore Dr Apt 505, Pensacola, FL 32507 USA Tel 850-723-6923; Fax: 850-723-6923
E-mail: johngllgskns@gmail.com
Web site: johncwaite.com.

†**Johns Hopkins Univ. Pr.,** *(978-0-8018; 978-1-4214)* Div. of Johns Hopkins Univ., Orders Addr.: P.O. Box 50370, Baltimore, MD 21211-4370 USA; Edit Addr.: 2715 N. Charles St., Baltimore, MD 21218-4319 USA (SAN 202-7348) Fax: 410-516-4189; Toll Free: 800-537-5487
E-mail: webmaster@press.jhu.edu
Web site: http://muse.jhu.edu/; http://www.press.jhu.edu/books/
Dist(s): **Casemate Academic**
Ebsco Publishing
Hopkins Fulfillment Services
Open Road Integrated Media, Inc.
Wiley, John & Sons, Inc.
ebrary, Inc.; *CIP.*

Johnson, Anthony, *(978-0-9773760)* P.O. Box 731, Burbank, CA 91503-0731 USA (SAN 257-4187) Fax: 818-558-6771
E-mail: leedobug@hotmail.com.

Johnson Bks. *Imprint of* **Bower Hse.**

Johnson, Bonnie, *(978-0-9769756)* Orders Addr.: 6 Son Ct., Valley Center, KS 67147-2659 USA.

Johnson, Colleen, *(978-0-9785002)* 2500 63rd St NW, Minot, ND 58703 USA Tel 701-839-5768
E-mail: gchristi@minot.com
Web site: http://icecreamforbreakfastbook.com.

Dr. Dionna Hancock Johnson International Corp., *(978-0-9913988)* 2328 Spice Pecan Way, Palmdale, CA 93551 USA Tel 858-869-7368
E-mail: energeticlifecoaching@gmail.com.

Johnson, Earl Photography, *(978-0-9649645; 978-0-9779024)* Orders Addr.: P.O. Box 870165, Stone Mountain, GA 30087 USA Tel 678-476-3950; Fax: 678-476-3951
E-mail: books@earljohnsontruckbooks.com
Web site: http://earljohnsontruckbooks.com.

Johnson, Gary, *(978-0-9791794)* 938 E. Lois Ln., Phoenix, AZ 85020-1189 USA (SAN 852-6931) Tel 602-944-7517 (phone/fax); Toll Free: 888-665-2762
E-mail: gjohnson@molarman.com
Web site: http://www.molarman.com.

Johnson, James *See* **Strategies Publishing Co.**

Johnson, Jenna Elizabeth, *(978-0-9976442)* 729 Calle Bendita, Arroyo Grande, CA 93420 USA Tel 805-478-0244
E-mail: authorjejohnson@gmail.com
Web site: www.jennaelizabethjohnson.com.

Johnson, Paula, *(978-1-7363704)* 13 Hausmann Ct., Maplewood, NJ 07040 USA Tel 973-204-8046
E-mail: pyjohn136@hotmail.com.

Johnson Publishing, *(978-0-692-12227-3; 978-1-7343662)* 1105 Urban Dr., Desoto, TX 75115 USA Tel 214-938-6621
E-mail: Booksonly03@yahoo.com.

Johnson, Renee B., *(978-0-578-46891-4; 978-1-7340409)* 2900 Gilbert Ln, Alton, IL 62002-5504 USA Tel 618-465-0764
E-mail: Rbj2040@aol.com.

Johnson, Suzanne, *(978-0-9968220; 978-1-7325921)* 814 Chickasaw Ave., Auburn, AL 36830 USA Tel 504-301-6414
E-mail: suzannej3523@gmail.com
Web site: http://www.suzannejohnsonauthor.com.

Johnson Tribe Publishing, *(978-0-9896733; 978-0-692-30715-1; 978-0-9977522; 978-0-692-14788-7; 978-0-578-43285-4; 978-1-7337844; 978-1-7352637; 978-1-7363274; 978-0-578-89270-2; 978-1-7374632; 979-8-9857140; 979-8-218-23902-2; 979-8-9892527)* 1484 Uncle Ben Dr., Powder Springs, GA 30127 USA Tel 770-815-6477
E-mail: johnsontribepublishing@gmail.com
Web site: dradairspeaks.net; johnsontribepublishing.com.

Johnson, Verlena, *(978-0-578-41470-6)* 18445 Collins St., No. 210, Tarzana, CA 91356 USA Tel 562-277-4661
E-mail: Verlenaj2004@yahoo.com
Dist(s): **Ingram Content Group.**

Johnson-Young,, Jill LCSW *See* **jilljohnsonyoung.com**

Johnston, Ann, *(978-0-9656776)* Orders Addr.: P.O. Box 388, Ashland, OH 44805 USA Toll Free: 800-247-6553 (ordering & shipping information); Edit Addr.: P.O. Box 944, Lake Oswego, OR 97034 USA (SAN 852-9043) Tel 503-635-6791; Fax: 503-675-0366
E-mail: order@bookmaster.com
Web site: http://www.annjohnston.net
Dist(s): **CreateSpace Independent Publishing Platform.**

Johnston, Ann, *(978-0-9796010)* 2409 Crest St., Alexandria, VA 22302 USA Tel 703-629-2175
E-mail: growhealthy@gmail.com.

Johnston, Lissa, *(978-0-9973068)* 721 Wildwood Rd., Leesville, SC 29070 USA Tel 803-487-9385
E-mail: lissajohnston@gmail.com.

Johnston-Brown, Anne Publishing Co. *See* **Retriever Pr.**

Joint Committee on Printing *Imprint of* **United States Government Printing Office**

Joint Committee on Taxation *Imprint of* **United States Government Printing Office**

Joint Heir Multimedia, *(978-0-9796148)* P.O. Box 108, Edgewater, NJ 07020 USA
Web site: http://www.jointheirmultimedia.net.

Joint Publishing Co. (HKG) *(978-962-04) Dist. by* **China Bks.**

Joint Publishing Co. (HKG) *(978-962-04) Dist. by* **Chinasprout.**

Jojoba Pr., *(978-1-949471; 978-1-64831)* P.O. Box 1281, Tucson, AZ 85702 USA; *Imprints:* DOG ON A LOG Books (MYID_T_DOG ON)
E-mail: jojobapress@gmail.com
Web site: www.dogonalogbooks.com.

Jokar Productions, LLC *See* **Save Our Seas, Ltd.**

Jolley Chronicles, *(978-1-7331821; 978-1-7373296; 978-1-958734)* 606 20 Rd, Grand Junction, CO 81507 USA Tel 970-361-1520
E-mail: tylerhjolley@gmail.com
Web site: http://www.jolleychronicles.com.

Jolly Fish Pr. *Imprint of* **North Star Editions**

Jolly Geranium, Inc., *(978-0-9644524)* 2953 E. Pawnee Dr., Sierra Vista, AZ 85635-8511 USA Tel 520-321-4747.

Jolly Journey Publishing, *(978-0-615-28357-9; 978-0-615-31956-8; 978-0-9980791)* 1321 Bantry Dr, Smyrna, TN 37167 USA.

Jolly Learning, Ltd. (GBR) *(978-1-870946; 978-1-903619; 978-1-84414) Dist. by* **Am Intl Dist.**

Jollyrhymes, *(978-1-7336364; 978-1-952717)* 1586 Johnson St., North Bend, OR 97459 USA Tel 541-252-1397
E-mail: jollyllama23@gmail.com
Web site: www.jollyrhymes.com.

Jolt, *(978-0-9831498)* Orders Addr.: P.O. Box 201013, Montgomery, AL 36120 USA Tel 256-390-3722
E-mail: information@jolt-books.com
Web site: http://www.jolt-books.com.

Jonathan, *(978-0-9910704)* P.O. Box 113, Bayville, NJ 08721 USA Tel 609-290-3728
E-mail: jonathan@jonathan-mcelroy.com.

†**Jones & Bartlett Learning, LLC,** *(978-0-7637; 978-0-86720; 978-1-4496; 978-1-284)* 5 Wall St., Burlington, MA 01803 USA (SAN 285-0893) Toll Free: 800-832-0034
Web site: http://www.jblearning.com
Dist(s): **Ebsco Publishing**
Rittenhouse Bk. Distributors
ebrary, Inc.; *CIP.*

Jones & Bartlett Publishers, Incorporated *See* **Jones & Bartlett Learning, LLC**

Jones, Augustine R., *(978-0-9743223)* 4213 N. Knoll Ridge Rd. Apt. B2, Peoria, IL 61614-7439 USA.

Jones, Bob University Press *See* **BJU Pr.**

Jones Bks., *(978-0-9721217; 978-0-9763539; 978-0-9790475)* 3 Loon Ln., Madison, WI 53717-1854 USA
E-mail: info@jonesbooks.com
Web site: http://www.jonesbooks.com.

jones, coral, *(978-1-7375240)* 10708 Wild Oak dr 0, FT WORTH, TX 76140 USA Tel 4194678978
E-mail: coraljonessu@yahoo.com
Dist(s): **Ingram Content Group.**

Jones, Janice, *(978-1-7371874)* 43 FRANK ST, VALLEY STREAM, NY 11580 USA Tel 917-688-5305
E-mail: janicebnichols@gmail.com.

Jones, Jim Enterprises LLC, *(978-1-7350356)* 32256 Woodfield Dr., Avon Lake, OH 44012 USA Tel 419-297-5552
E-mail: jimjone@aol.com
Web site: www.JimBasketballJones.com.

Jones, John Paul, *(978-0-9858362)* 879 W. 23rd st., San Pedro, CA 90731 USA Tel 310-880-2076; Fax: 310-514-9111
Dist(s): **CreateSpace Independent Publishing Platform.**

Jones, Kaylie Books *Imprint of* **Akashic Bks.**

Jones, Kirk, *(978-0-9759688)* P.O. Box 74702, Richmond, VA 23236 USA
E-mail: kirkjonesillustrations@juno.com.

Jones, Linda, *(978-0-9776450)* 2700 Woodland Park Dr. Apt. 705, Houston, TX 77082-6605 USA
E-mail: amiasthefirst@aol.com.

Jones, Madelyn, *(978-1-7354851)* 16816 SW 137TH AVE, APT 1204, MIAMI, FL 33177 USA Tel 334-477-2406
E-mail: majones536@gmail.com.

Jones, Maria F. *See* **Doodle and Peck Publishing**

Jones, Oyindamola, *(978-0-578-90657-7; 978-0-578-92439-7; 978-0-578-95151-5)*
E-mail: missjones_567@yahoo.com.

Jones Publishing LLC, *(978-0-9836783)* P.O. Box 15156, Lansing, MI 48910 USA Tel 517-505-9797
E-mail: jlpwordpress@gmail.com.

Jones, Randell, *(978-1-7345623)* 4937 Castlewood Dr., Lilburn, GA 30047 USA Tel 404-569-0714
E-mail: randellj68@gmail.com.

Jones, Stephanie, *(978-0-578-33079-2)* 2090 108th Ave, Farmington, IA 52626 USA Tel 563-886-7229
E-mail: d_414@aol.com.

Jones, Van, *(978-0-578-71012-9)* 3249 Woodhollow Cir, ABILENE, TX 79606 USA Tel 325-692-6464
E-mail: jonesvm52@yahoo.com.

Jones, Vivian Ann, *(978-0-692-91819-7)* 574 Dandelion Loop, Kyle, TX 78640 USA Tel 512-743-8174
E-mail: padellatemp4@yahoo.com.

JonesHarvest Publishing, *(978-0-9794455; 978-1-60388)* 5400 E. State Rd. 45, Bloomington, IN 47408 USA Tel 812-323-2330; Fax: 812-323-2339; Toll Free: 877-400-0075
E-mail: jonesharvest@sbcglobal.net
Web site: http://www.jonesharvest.com.

Jonquil Books *See* **Miglior Pr.**

Jon'taar Graphxs, *(978-0-9764385)* 75 Lantern Chase Dr., Delaware, OH 43015 USA Tel 740-972-6321
E-mail: msuplicki@jontaar.com; information@mirthburdz.com
Web site: http://www.jontaar.com; http://www.mirthburdz.com.

Jordan Elise Durbin, *(978-0-692-18001-3; 978-0-578-77551-7)* 399 E. Ave., Tallmadge, OH 44278 USA Tel 330-491-6831
E-mail: Jordandurbin79@gmail.com
Dist(s): **Ingram Content Group.**

Jordan Music Productions, Inc., *(978-1-895523; 978-1-894262; 978-1-55386)* M.P.O. Box 490, Niagara Falls, NY 14302-0490 USA
E-mail: sjordan@sara-jordan.com
Web site: http://www.sara-jordan.com; http://www.SongsThatTeach.com; http://www.edu-mart.com
Dist(s): **Follett Media Distribution**
iLeon.

Jordan Publishing Hse., *(978-1-890875)* Orders Addr.: P.O. Box 671, Columbia, CA 95310 USA Fax: 209-532-5503; Edit Addr.: 22620 Parrotts Ferry Rd., Columbia, CA 95310 USA Do not confuse with companies with the same name in Las Vegas, NV, Nappanee, IN, Reston, VA, Phoenix, AZ, Prescott, AZ
E-mail: gpview@erli.net.

Jordan, Sara Publishing, *(978-1-895523; 978-1-894262; 978-1-55386)* Div. of Jordan Music Productions, Inc., Orders Addr.: M.P.O. Box 490, Niagara Falls, NY 14302-0490 USA (SAN 118-959X) Tel 416-760-7664; Fax: 416-762-2770; Toll Free Fax: 800-229-3855; Toll Free: 800-567-7733
E-mail: sjordan@sara-jordan.com
Web site: http://www.edu-mart.com; http://www.sara-jordan.com; http://www.songsthatteach.com
Dist(s): **Follett School Solutions.**

Jordan Valley Heritage Hse., *(978-0-939810)* P.O. Box 99, Stayton, OR 97383-0099 USA (SAN 216-7425) Tel 503-769-4236
E-mail: jvhh5@wvi.com.

Jorge Pinto Bks., *(978-0-9742615; 978-0-9774724; 978-0-9790766; 978-0-9795576; 978-0-9801147; 978-1-934978; 978-1-7364215)* 6216 Vorlich Ln., Bethesda, MD 20816 USA (SAN 853-7526); *Imprints:* Illustrated Books (Illus Bks)
Web site: http://www.pintobooks.com; jpintobooks.com
Dist(s): **D.A.P./Distributed Art Pubs.**

Jorlan Publishing *See* **Jorlan Publishing, Inc.**

Jorlan Publishing, Inc., *(978-0-9710696; 978-1-933830)* P.O. Box 2882, Cedar City, UT 84721-2882 USA
Web site: http://www.jorlanpublishing.com.

Jose M. Roman, *(978-0-692-60566-0; 978-1-7324943)* 200 Thunderbird Hill Rd., Sebring, FL 33872 USA Tel 863-414-1621
E-mail: jmr508@yahoo.com
Dist(s): **CreateSpace Independent Publishing Platform.**

Joseph, Dr. Angela Banner, *(978-1-943945)* 37-29 104th Street, Apt. 3D, Corona, NY 11368 USA Tel 347-669-0151
Dist(s): **CreateSpace Independent Publishing Platform.**

Joseph Henry Pr. *Imprint of* **National Academies Pr.**

Joseph Pubns., *(978-0-9773243)* P.O. Box 401, Killington, VT 05751 USA Tel 917-502-7328
Web site: http://www.josephpublications.com.

Joseph's Coat Publishing *See* **Breezy Reads**

Joseph's Heartprint, *(978-0-9787035)* 728 Creek Rd., Carlisle, PA 17013 USA Tel 717-258-8796; Fax: 717-243-4254
E-mail: george@catholicartworks.com
Web site: http://www.catholicartworks.com.

Joseph's Labor, *(978-0-9729800)* P.O. Box 176265, Covington, KY 41017-6265 USA Tel 859-578-8112
E-mail: JosephsLabor@aol.com.

Joshua Pr., Inc. (CAN) *(978-1-894400) Dist. by* **Gabriel Res.**

Joshua Publishing *See* **Handle Your Business Girl Publishing**

Joshua Tree Publishing, *(978-0-9710954; 978-0-9768677; 978-0-9778311; 978-0-9823703; 978-0-9845904; 978-0-9829803; 978-0-9886577; 978-1-941049; 978-1-956823)* 3 Golf Ctr. No. 201, Hoffman Estates, IL 60169 USA Tel 312-893-7525; 3 Golf Ctr. No. 201, Hoffman Estates, IL 60169 Tel 312-893-7525 Do not confuse with companies with the same or similar names in Mentor, OH, Lake San Marcos, CA
E-mail: info@joshuatreepublishing.com
Web site: https://joshuatreepublishing.com; https://centaurbooks.com; https://chiralhouse.com.

Jossey-Bass *Imprint of* **Wiley, John & Sons, Inc.**

Jostens Bks., *(978-0-9759530; 978-0-9788398)* 116 Independence Dr., Indian Trail, NC 28079-9452 USA Toll Free: 800-458-0319
E-mail: sherry.clontz@jostens.com
Web site: http://www.jostens.com.

Jotopia Productions, LLC, *(978-1-7366082)* 5198 Lupine Ln., Acworth, GA 30102 USA Tel 678-956-9716
E-mail: jo@livinginjotopia.com.

Jots & Tittles Publishing, *(978-0-9894379)* 310 W. 39th St., Vancouver, WA 98660 USA Tel 360-566-2781
E-mail: ghost@writingasaghost.com.

Joubert, Christopher, *(978-0-692-19093-7; 978-0-692-19094-4)* 5420 Downs Rd., Beaumont, TX 77705-6900 USA Tel 409-673-9073
E-mail: cjoubert11@aol.com
Dist(s): **Ingram Content Group.**

Journal Joy, LLC, *(978-1-7361688; 978-1-957751)* P.O. Box 2500 Dallas Highway St 202 #259, Marietta, GA 30064 USA Tel 404-227-1169
E-mail: Amiyra@thatmommyjoy.com
Web site: WWW.THEJOURNALJOY.COM.

Journals Unlimited, Inc., *(978-1-892033; 978-0-9818414; 978-0-9842578; 978-0-9832414; 978-0-9859025; 978-0-9907307; 978-0-9973031; 978-0-9995079; 978-1-7345331)* P.O. Box 1882, Bay City, MI 48706 USA Tel 989-686-3377; Fax: 989-686-3380; Toll Free Fax: 800-897-8529; Toll Free: 800-897-8528
E-mail: orders@journalsunlimited.com
Web site: http://www.journalsunlimited.com.

Journalstone, *(978-0-9828119; 978-1-936564; 978-1-940161; 978-1-942712; 978-1-945373; 978-1-947654; 978-1-950305; 978-1-68510)* 3205 Sassafras Trl, Carbondale, IL 62901 USA Tel 415-235-6734
E-mail: christophercpayne@journalstone.com
Web site: http://journalstone.com.

Journey 2 Free Publishing *See* **Journey 2 Free Publishing**

Journey 2 Free Publishing, *(978-1-954553)* 52 Arrowbrook Rd, Windsor, CT 06095 USA Tel 860-219-9024
E-mail: journey2free2013@gmail.com
Web site: journey2free.com.

Journey Pubns., LLC, *(978-0-9728716; 978-0-9748087; 978-0-9772078; 978-0-9798171; 978-1-7378994)* Orders Addr.: P.O. Box 2442, Warminster, PA 18974-2442 USA (SAN 255-1675) Do not confuse with companies with the same or similar names in Woodstock, NY, Savannah, GA, Avon Park, FL, Metairie, LA, Lacey, WA
E-mail: journeypubs@aol.com
Web site: http://www.journeypublications.com.

Journey Stone Creations, LLC, *(978-0-9758709; 978-1-59958)* 3533 Danbury Rd., Fairfield, OH 45014 USA Fax: 513-860-0176; *Imprints:* A.W.A. Gang (AWA Gang)
E-mail: pat@journeystonecreations.com
Web site: http://www.journeystonecreations.com; http://www.myezbookclub.com; http://www.jscbooks.com.

JourneyForth *Imprint of* **BJU Pr.**

Journeys Press *See* **Whirlwind Publishing Group**

JourneytimeBks., *(978-0-615-43624-1; 978-0-692-43867-1)* 407 8TH Ave., TROY, NY 12182 USA Tel 518-237-8622
E-mail: mgraber@journeytimebooks.com.

Journique Publishing Group, Inc., *(978-0-9795586)* P.O. Box 524, Knightdale, NC 27545 USA Fax: 407-796-6394
E-mail: pjordan@journique.com
Web site: http://www.journique.com
Dist(s): **Ingram Content Group.**

Joy of my Youth Pubns., The, *(978-0-9774345)* P.O. Box 128702, Cincinnati, OH 45212 USA Tel 513-531-2709
E-mail: thejoyofmyyouth@netzero.net
Web site: http://www.thejoyofmyyouth.com.

Joy on Your Shoulders TM, *(978-0-9840353; 978-1-7364587)* 104 Parkview Dr., Brevard, NC 28712 USA Tel 440-476-0960
E-mail: joy@joyonyourshoulders.com
Web site: https://www.joyonyourshoulders.com.

J.O.Y. Pubns., *(978-0-9762975)* 186 Gatewood Ave., Rochester, NY 14624-1737 USA Do not confuse with companies with the same or similar name in Santa Maria, CA Gardena, CA, Pittsboro, NC, Woburn, MA
E-mail: rainbowvillagecc@yahoo.com; rainbowvillage@homewithGod.net
Web site: www.our.homewithGod.com/rainbowvillage/.

J.O.Y. Publishing, *(978-0-9755454)* Orders Addr.: P.O. Box 540912, Merritt Island, FL 32954-0912 USA; *Imprints:* Laughing Zebra - Books for Children (Laugh Zebra)
E-mail: jdelgado@laughing-zebra-children-books.com
Web site: http://zooprisepartyfiestazoorpresa.blogspot.com; http://www.laughing-zebra-children-books.com.

Joy Revolution *Imprint of* **Random Hse. Children's Bks.**

Joya Cultural Enterprises Inc., *(978-0-9904135)* 4644 W. Gandy Blvd. 4 - 102, Tampa, FL 33611 USA Tel 813-388-8385
E-mail: info@joya-inc.com.

Joyce Miriam Friedman, *(978-0-578-41520-8; 978-0-578-48355-9)* 50 Dorset Rd., Waban, MA 02468-1406 USA Tel 617-645-3186
E-mail: joycefriedman625@gmail.com
Dist(s): **Ingram Content Group.**

JoyceHerzog.com, Incorporated *See* **Herzog, Joyce**

yful Breath Pr., *(978-1-7357836)* 30159 Southampton Bridge Rd., SALISBURY, MD 21804 USA Tel 860-916-9755
E-mail: maxelwrites@gmail.com
Web site: www.meaghanaxel.com.

yful by Design, *(978-0-9976590; 978-1-7340288)* 4025 Forsythe Way, Tallahassee, FL 32309 USA Tel 850-570-0415
E-mail: sarajoym@yahoo.com
Web site: www.saramarchessault.com.

oyful Learning Publications, LLC, *(978-0-9836580)* 3148 Plainfield Ave NE suite 153, Grand Rapids, ME 49525-3285 USA Tel 207-693-5257
E-mail: sandyjane05@yahoo.com.

oyful Learning Publishing *See* **Joyful Learning Publications, LLC**

Joyful Noise, *(978-0-9772109)* 312 Stonewall Rd., Concord, VA 24538 USA (SAN 257-0149)
E-mail: j.b.designs@att.net.

Joyful Pubs., *(978-0-9992868)* 941 Fry Rd, Greenwood, IN 46142 USA Tel 317-888-3333
E-mail: kiwidenis@gmail.com.

Joyride Bks., *(978-1-937791)* 9200 Alpine Rd., La Honda, CA 94020 USA Tel 650-747-0796 (phone/fax); *Imprints:* Kid Fuse (Kid Fuse)
E-mail: laurie@fuseliterary.com; joyridebooks@gmail.com; gordon@fuseliterary.com
Web site: http://fuseliterary.com/shortfuse; http://joyridebooks.com.

JoyRox, LLC, *(978-0-9754972)* 11585 Hooker St., Westminster, CO 80031-7121 USA
E-mail: info@joy-rox.com
Web site: http://www.joy-rox.com.

JoySoul Corp., *(978-0-9727786)* Orders Addr.: 1214 Rose St., Lisbon, ND 58054-0071 USA
E-mail: jscontact@joysoul.com
Web site: http://www.joysoul.com.

JoyWrites, *(978-1-7322831)* 10430 Morado Cir. No. 1820, Austin, TX 78759 USA Tel 512-796-6974
E-mail: joy@joywrites.com.

JoZanephine Originals *Imprint of* **Gamoke, John**

Jozef Syndicate, *(978-0-615-95569-8; 978-0-692-21665-1; 978-0-692-52958-4; 978-1-944155)* P.O. Box 318013, Baton Rouge, LA 70831 USA Tel 225-926-5693
E-mail: books@jozefpa.com
Web site: www.jozefsyndicate.com
Dist(s): **CreateSpace Independent Publishing Platform.**

JPA Assocs., *(978-0-9727125)* 11026 Maple Rd., Lafayette, CO 80026 USA Tel 303-665-6764.

JR Comics (KOR) *(978-89-94208; 978-89-92836; 978-89-98341) Dist. by* **Lerner Pub.**

Jr Imagination, *(978-0-9837404; 978-0-9893189)* 17310 Trosa St., Granada Hills, CA 91344 USA Tel 818-366-4194; Fax: 818-366-2134
E-mail: marty@jrimagination.com
Web site: https://www.jrimagination.com; https://www.samatart.com; https://www.doublemgraphics.com; https://www.marjoriesamat.com.

J.R. Molt, *(978-0-578-78358-1; 978-0-578-78361-1; 978-1-7370585)* 1816 W 51st St. Pl. 0, KEARNEY, NE 68845 USA Tel 3086279302
E-mail: rockingchairsandbookshelves@gmail.com.

JRayDesigns *See* **Smorgasbord Pubns.**

JRP Ringier Kunstverlag AG (CHE) *(978-2-940271; 978-3-905701; 978-3-905770; 978-3-03764; 978-3-905829) Dist. by* **Dist Art Pubs.**

JRSK Bks., *(978-0-9837709; 978-0-9850733)* 1120 Ellison Pk. Cir., Denton, TX 76205 USA Tel 940-383-0426
E-mail: jrskipling@yahoo.com
Web site: www.jrodneyshort.com.

JRV Bks., LLC, *(978-1-7340315; 978-1-953346)* 1805 W. 7600 S. No. D302, West Jordan, UT 84084 USA Tel 307-679-8964
E-mail: jrvaineo@gmail.com
Dist(s): **Ingram Content Group.**

JRV Publishing, *(978-0-9771250)* P.O. Box 82, West Simsbury, CT 06092 USA
E-mail: jverney1@jrvpublishing.com.

J.R.V.P., *(978-0-578-65610-6; 978-0-578-81314-1; 978-1-7371572)* 1306 Delaware Blvd, Madison, WI 53704 USA Tel 608-333-2684
E-mail: jasonrvanpelt@gmail.com.

JSP Bks., *(978-0-9728519)* 6886 Hickory Lake Cove, Memphis, TN 38119 USA Tel 901-757-0694
E-mail: contact@jspbooks.com
Web site: http://www.jspbooks.com.

JT Taylor Consulting *See* **JT Taylor LLC**

JT Taylor LLC, *(978-0-578-34798-1; 978-0-578-34955-8)* 1455 NE 2nd Ct., Boca Raton, FL 33432 USA Tel 561-762-7712
E-mail: jonathantaylor8429@gmail.com.

JU Pr., *(978-0-578-52674-4)* 1709 S. State Rte. 560, Urbana, OH 43078 USA Tel 937-869-3882
E-mail: Jessie.k.uthoff@gmail.com.

Juba Bks. *Imprint of* **NetNia Publishing Co.**

Jubilee LLC, 1712 Pioneer Ave. Suite 2019, Cheyenne, WY 82001 USA Tel 307-222-4729
E-mail: ccformemail@gmail.com
Web site: http://www.LeepCalendar.com.

Judah Bks., Inc., *(978-0-9767469)* 3535 W. Tierra Buena Ln., Apt. No. A273, Phoenix, AZ 85053 USA.

Judaica Pr., Inc., The, *(978-0-910818; 978-1-880582; 978-1-932443; 978-1-60763)* 123 Ditmas Ave., Brooklyn, NY 11218 USA (SAN 204-9856) Tel 718-972-6200; Fax: 718-972-6204; Toll Free: 800-972-6201; *Imprints:* Shayach Comics (Shayach Comics)
E-mail: info@judaicapress.com
Web site: http://www.judaicapress.com.

Judd, Robert, *(978-0-692-05202-0)* P.O. Box 186, Forest City, NC 28043 USA Tel 828-245-3950; Fax: 828-245-3950
E-mail: robertjudd7067@att.net.

JuDe Publishing, *(978-0-9712585)* Orders Addr.: P.O. Box 264 s lacienega blvd #1283, beverly hills, CA 90211 USA Tel 310-600-9729
E-mail: judepublishing@yahoo.com
Dist(s): **Bookazine Co., Inc.**

Judie, Sharon Y. *See* **Golden Quill LLC, The**

Judith VT Wilson, *(978-0-692-07753-5; 978-0-692-14615-6)* 191 Delhi Ct, Smyrna, DE 19977 USA Tel 302-653-6862
E-mail: jwilson191@comcast.net
Web site: www.growingsmartercenter.com.

†Judson Pr., *(978-0-8170)* Div. of American Baptist Churches, U.S.A., Orders Addr.: 1075 First Ave., King of Prussia, PA 19406 USA (SAN 201-0348) Fax: 610-768-2107; Toll Free: 800-458-3766
E-mail: gale.tull@abhms.org
Web site: http://www.judsonpress.com
Dist(s): **Anchor Distributors**
Spring Arbor Distributors, Inc.; *CIP.*

Juice & Berries(r), The *Imprint of* **Asiana Media**

Jujapa Pr., *(978-0-9650233; 978-1-7321976; 978-1-952493)* PO Box 269, Hansville, WA 98340 USA.

Juju Press *See* **Huqua Pr.**

Julenda Enterprises, *(978-0-9747994)* 219 E. El Valle, Green Valley, AZ 85614-2903 USA Tel 520-393-0071
E-mail: judylgarcia@aol.com
Web site: http://www.judylenore.com.

Julia Inserro, *(978-1-947891)*
E-mail: jhmiles2@gmail.com.

Julian's Legacy, *(978-0-615-22488-6; 978-0-578-48848-6; 978-1-7361667)* 65 Futch Rd., Allenhurst, 31313 SUN
Web site: tamaratheauthor.com.

Julie Andrews Collection *Imprint of* **HarperCollins Pubs.**

Julie Causton, phD, *(978-0-578-44374-4)* 7704 Berkshire Pkwy., Manlius, NY 13104 USA Tel 315-692-2026
E-mail: julie@inclusiveschooling.com
Dist(s): **Ingram Content Group.**

Julie Christiansen, *(978-0-578-61891-3)* 10900 SE Seminole Terr., Jupiter, FL 33469 USA Tel 561-234-0353
E-mail: ruthiemayc@gmail.com.

Julien, Shevon *See* **SNJ Enterprises**

Juliette's Adventures, 85 Sturbridge Ln., Grand Island, NY 14072 USA Tel 716-773-3694
E-mail: dawn_cardin@yahoo.com
Dist(s): **Ingram Content Group.**

Julio C. Malone *See* **Editorial Migio Inc.**

Julson, D. K., *(978-0-9746564; 978-0-615-11699-0)* 28704 County Hwy B., Richland Ctr, WI 53581-6721 USA.

July Publishing Inc. *See* **Social Motion Publishing**

July-Eight Publishing *See* **Three Socks Publishing**

Jumbo Minds, Inc., *(978-1-944049)* P.O. Box 1153, Fairport, NY 14450 USA Tel 585-747-4242
E-mail: admin@JumboMinds.com
Web site: JumboMinds.com.

Jump at the Sun *Imprint of* **Disney Publishing Worldwide**

Jump at the Sun *Imprint of* **Hyperion Bks. for Children**

Jump! Inc. *See* **Jump! Inc.**

Jump! Inc., *(978-1-62031; 978-1-62496; 978-1-64128; 978-1-64527; 978-1-63690; 979-8-88524; 979-8-88996; 979-8-89213)* 5357 Penn Ave. S., Minneapolis, MN 55419 USA (SAN 920-8143) Tel 888-960-1346; *Imprints:* Bullfrog Books (BullfrogBks); Pogo (Pogo)
Web site: http://www.jumplibrary.com
Dist(s): **Follett School Solutions Independent Pubs. Group.**

Jump Pr., *(978-0-9754902; 978-0-9980733)* 717 Atlantic Ave. No. 5D, Boston, MA 02111 USA
E-mail: emily@emilysper.com
Web site: http://blueirisdesign.com
Dist(s): **Children's Plus, Inc.**

Jump Start Performance Programs, *(978-1-893962)* P.O. Box 3448, Van Nuys, CA 91407 USA Toll Free Fax: 800-990-9667; Toll Free: 800-450-0432
E-mail: scott@scottgreenberg.com
Web site: http://www.scottgreenberg.com.

Jumping Cow Pr., *(978-0-9801433; 978-0-9980010; 978-1-7356962; 979-8-9885395)* P.O. Box 2732, Briarcliff Manor, NY 10510 USA (SAN 855-305X) Tel 914-373-9816
E-mail: jumpingcowpress@gmail.com
Web site: http://www.JumpingCowPress.com
Dist(s): **Brown Books Publishing Group.**

Jumping Jack Pr., *(978-0-9795441; 978-1-60580; 978-1-62348)* Div. of Up With Paper, LLC, 6049 Hi-Tek Ct., Mason, OH 45040 USA Tel 513-759-7473; Fax: 513-336-3119
E-mail: info@upwithpaper.com; georgew@upwithpaper.com
Web site: http://www.jumpingjackpress.com
Dist(s): **Ingram Publisher Services.**

June & Lucy, *(978-1-64608; 979-8-88561)* 627 Stoneway Dr, San Antonio, TX 78258 USA Tel 210-569-9083
E-mail: bowker@junelucy.com.

June & The Wolves Publishing, *(978-0-615-74511-4; 978-0-615-89550-5; 978-0-692-36512-0)* 148 E St. RD 177, FEASTERVILLE, PA 19053 USA Tel 480-999-1877
Dist(s): **CreateSpace Independent Publishing Platform.**

June Bks., LLC, *(978-0-9835558)* 408 W. Lotta St. Suite No. 1, Sioux Falls, SD 57105 USA Tel 512-630-3380
E-mail: trevor@junebooks.com; hello@junebooks.com
Web site: http://www.junebooks.com.

Junebug Bks. *Imprint of* **NewSouth, Inc.**

JuneOne Publishing Hub, *(978-0-9763082)* 27762 Antonio Pkwy., L1-404, Ladera Ranch, CA 92694 USA Tel 949-364-6179; Fax: 757-299-4407; *Imprints:* A JuneOne Production (A JuneOne Prod)
E-mail: info@juneonehub.com
Web site: http://www.juneonehub.com.

Jung, Loretta, *(978-0-9724174)* 1738 Fifth Ave., NE, Jamestown, ND 58401 USA Tel 701-952-4741
E-mail: jung.loretta@gmail.com
Web site: http://www.bowkerbios.com.

Junge, Michael, *(978-0-692-75722-2; 978-0-692-75723-9; 978-0-692-77029-0)* 10 Algerwood, Ladera Ranch, CA 92694 USA Tel 949-887-6085.

Jungle Communications, Incorporation *See* **Allergic Child Publishing Group**

JUNGLE Gym, The, *(978-0-578-42236-7)* 8566 N. Oswego Ave., Portland, OR 97203 USA Tel 312-802-2323
E-mail: antonfrederickcobb@gmail.com
Dist(s): **Ingram Content Group.**

Jungle Hse. Pubns., *(978-0-9769332)* Orders Addr.: 736 Cardium St., Sanibel, FL 33957-6704 USA Tel 239-395-4518
E-mail: junglehousepub@yahoo.com
Web site: http://junglehousepublications.com.

Jungle Jeep Press *See* **Jungle Wagon Pr.**

Jungle Tales, *(978-0-615-70807-2)* 229 edgecomb Ave Apt No. 3, New York, NY 10030 USA Tel 714-856-1768
E-mail: Jeff Zorrilla@gmail.com.

Jungle Wagon Pr., *(978-0-9834092; 978-0-9904271)* 5116 Didier Ave., Rockford, IL 61101 USA (SAN 920-6426) Tel 815-988-9048
E-mail: junglewagonpress@gmail.com
Web site: http://www.junglewagonpress.com.

Jungler *See* **Yunka Publishing**

Junior History Pr., *(978-0-9744556)* Orders Addr.: P.O. Box 157, Summerville, SC 29484-0157 USA Tel 843-873-8117; Edit Addr.: 1311 Jahnz Ave., Summerville, SC 29485 USA
E-mail: gteaster@juniorhistory.com
Web site: http://www.juniorhistory.com.

Junior League of Central Westchester, *(978-0-615-16563-9)* 1039 Post Rd., Scarsdale, NY 10583 USA Tel 914-723-6139; Fax: 914-723-6016
E-mail: jlcw@verizon.net
Web site: http://www.jlcentralwestchester.org.

Junior League of Grand Rapids Michigan, Inc., *(978-0-9611316; 978-0-9634927)* 25 Sheldon Blvd., Suite 124, Grand Rapids, MI 49503 USA (SAN 282-9452) Tel 616-451-0452; Fax: 616-451-1936
E-mail: juniorleague@iserv.net
Web site: http://www.juniorleagegr.com.

Junior League of Omaha, *(978-0-9609146)* 608 N. 108th Ct., Omaha, NE 68154-1762 USA (SAN 241-5348) Tel 402-330-0197.

Junior League of Tyler, Inc., The, *(978-0-9607122)* 1919 S. Donnybrook, Tyler, TX 75701 USA (SAN 238-9975) Tel 903-593-8141; Fax: 903-595-1362.

Juniper Berry Pr., *(978-0-9760076)* 6609 Cornelia Dr., Edina, MN 55435 USA Tel 952-285-4447
E-mail: gjudso@aol.com
Web site: http://www.juniperberrypress.com.

Juniper Grove, *(978-1-60355)* 2129 E. Stearns, Fayetteville, AR 72703 USA (SAN 853-5078)
E-mail: JuniperGrove@gmail.com
Web site: http://www.junipergrove.com
Dist(s): **CreateSpace Independent Publishing Platform.**

Juniper Publishing (CAN) *(978-1-988002) Dist. by* **S and S Inc.**

Juping Horse Pr., *(978-0-615-55671-0; 978-0-615-75585-4)* 845 N. 27th St., Philadelphia, PA 19130 USA Tel 215-978-0844
E-mail: karin@jumpinghorsepress.com
Web site: http://www.jumpinghorsepress.com.

Jupiter Coins *See* **Adventure in Discovery**

Jupiter Kids (Childrens & Kids Fiction) *Imprint of* **Speedy Publishing LLC**

juputer2 bks., *(978-0-9779404)* 309 Claymille Pl., Nashville, TN 37207 USA
Web site: http://www.juputer2books.com.

Juris Prudence LLC, *(978-1-946456)* 5115 8th St. NW, Washington, DC 20011 USA Tel 804-937-4598
Dist(s): **CreateSpace Independent Publishing Platform.**

Just Be, LLC *See* **Just Be Publishing**

Just Be Publishing, *(978-1-7357166)* 294 Griswold St, Glastonbury, CT 06033 USA Tel 860-978-8121
E-mail: liz.kametz@gmail.com
Web site: justbethejourney.com.

Just Be Publishing, Inc., *(978-0-9668219)* 746 E. Rosemore Ct., Salt Lake City, UT 84107 USA (SAN 299-7479) Tel 801-265-3435 (phone/fax)
E-mail: bl_ehrler@att.net
Web site: http://www.justbepublishing.com.

Just Chill Pubns., *(978-0-9726548)* P.O. Box 5990, Chicago, IL 60680 USA
E-mail: chill1960@comcast.net; contact@justchill.org; contact@communityaccessresources.org
Web site: http://www.justchill.org; http://www.communityaccessresources.org.

Just Enjoyable Memorable Story Bks., *(978-0-9724472)* 8258 Balsam Way, Arvada, CO 80005 USA
E-mail: jemsbooks@hotmail.com.

Just For Kids Pr., LLC, *(978-1-934650; 978-1-935498; 978-1-935747; 978-1-936918; 978-1-937962)* 360 Hurst St., Linden, NJ 07036 USA
E-mail: ssullivan@justforkidspress.com.

Just Fun Bks. & Things, *(978-0-692-87442-4; 978-0-9990471)* 4991 Manor Ridge Ln., San Diego, CA 92130 USA Tel 858-461-1935
E-mail: barbgay95@gmail.com.

Just Imagine Bks. & Services, LLC, *(978-0-9986934; 978-0-9989696)* 102 Washington Ave, Point Richmond, CA 94801 USA Tel 510-422-5304
E-mail: tamarashiloh@gmail.com
Web site: tamarashiloh.com.

Just Jessica, L.L.C., *(978-0-692-92654-3; 978-0-578-63561-3; 978-0-578-63563-7; 978-0-578-36506-0)* 529 Brooklyn Tpke., Hampton, CT 06247 USA Tel 203-218-7864
E-mail: Fred.wills@att.net
Web site: Just Jessica.org.

Just Like Me, Inc., *(978-1-928889)* 525 Tailgate Terr., Landover, MD 20785 USA
E-mail: jlm1922@gmail.com
Web site: http://www.justlikemeworld.com
Dist(s): **Ingram Bk. Co.**

Just Me Productions, *(978-0-9821118)* 4255 Us 1 S., Suite 18-212, Saint Augustine, FL 32086 USA Tel 904-797-7242
Web site: http://www.justmeproductions.com.

Just Think Bks. *Imprint of* **Canary Connect Pubns.**

Just Us Bks., Inc., *(978-0-940975; 978-1-933491)* 395 Pleasant Valley Way Suite B, West Orange, NJ 07052 USA (SAN 664-7413) Tel 973-672-7701; *Imprints:* Sankofa Books (Sankofa Bks)
E-mail: justusbook@aol.com
Web site: http://www.justusbooks.com.

Just Us Bks., Inc., *(978-1-60349)* 395 Pleasant Valley Way Suite B, West Orange, NJ 07052 USA Tel 973-672-7701; Fax: 973-677-7570; *Imprints:* Marimba Books (MarimbaBks)
E-mail: justusbook@aol.com
Dist(s): **Just Us Bks., Inc.**

Just Write Bks., *(978-0-9722839; 978-0-9766533; 978-0-9777614; 978-0-9788628; 978-1-934949; 978-1-944386)* Just Write Communications, 13 Williams Dr., Topsham, ME 04086 USA (SAN 855-5109) Tel 207-837-0558
E-mail: jstwrite@jstwrite.com
Web site: http://www.jstwrite.com.

Just Write Pubns., *(978-0-578-31556-0; 978-0-578-31930-8; 978-0-578-33458-5; 978-0-578-34465-2; 978-0-578-35455-2; 978-0-578-35456-9; 978-0-578-36393-6; 978-0-578-37952-4; 979-8-9859369; 979-8-9878870)* 4509 Parkgate Dr. 0, MATTHEWS, NC 28105 USA Tel 7042214405
E-mail: boywithantsinhispants@gmail.com
Dist(s): **Ingram Content Group.**

Justice Brothers Publishing *See* **Justice, Israel**

Justice, Israel, *(978-0-9997969)* 2429 Arborwood Dr, Valrico, FL 33596 USA Tel 813-956-7605
E-mail: israeljustice04@gmail.com.

Justice Link Publishing, *(978-0-692-00612-2)* P.O. Box 3144, Glendale, CA 91221 USA.

Justice, Mable, *(978-1-7333171)* PSC 78 Box 3824, APO, MD 96326 USA Tel 757-966-6026
E-mail: mjust410@yahoo.com.

Justice Tales Pr., *(978-0-578-75627-1; 978-0-578-76977-6; 978-0-578-91821-1)* 946 Sousa Dr., Walnut Creek, CA 94597 USA Tel 925-935-6621
E-mail: llewzanne@gmail.com.

Justine A. P. Louis *See* **VivLiv Bks.**

Justkym, *(978-0-692-90715-3)* 1907 Rambling Ln., Brandon, FL 33510 USA Tel 813-317-1004
E-mail: justkym@gmail.com.

JustTheBox, LLC, *(978-0-692-92371-9)* 600 Excel Cir, SE, Brownsboro, AL 35741 USA Tel 256-457-5355
E-mail: rdunford21@gmail.com
Dist(s): **Independent Pub.**

Juvenescent Research Corp., *(978-0-9600148; 978-1-884996)* 807 Riverside Dr., Apt. 1F, New York, NY 10032 USA (SAN 206-7250) Tel 212-795-3749
Dist(s): **Barnes & Noble, Inc.**

Juventud, Editorial (ESP) *(978-84-261) Dist. by* **Distribks Inc.**

Juventud, Editorial (ESP) *(978-84-261) Dist. by* **Continental Bk.**

Juventud, Editorial (ESP) *(978-84-261) Dist. by* **AIMS Intl.**

Juventud, Editorial (ESP) *(978-84-261) Dist. by* **Lectorum Pubns.**

JVED Publishing, *(978-0-9768833)* 13570 Grove Dr. No. 361, Maple Grove, MN 55311 USA
Web site: http://www.jvedpublishing.org.

JVGray, *(978-0-9982387)* 71 Snowden Ave, Ossining, NY 10562 USA Tel 914-713-4104
E-mail: jvgray01@gmail.com
Web site: jvgray.com.

JWall Publishing, *(978-0-9760518)* 287 Jones Rd., Statham, GA 30666 USA Tel 770-725-7465.

JWD Publishing, *(978-0-9816437; 978-0-9843365; 978-0-9846315; 978-1-941574)* 217 New Trails Ln, Lafayette, LA 70508 USA Tel 912-687-5546
E-mail: jwpublishing@gmail.com
Web site: http://www.revolutionarydisciples.com; www.jaribooks.com.

JY *Imprint of* **Yen Pr. LLC**

J.Y. Johnson-Garcia, *(978-1-7339560)* 1178 Broadway, Third Floor, No. 1076, New York, NY 10001 USA Tel 201-898-0115
E-mail: busyjenn@gmail.com
Web site: jyjohnsongarcia.com.

JYZ Books, LLC *See* **JYZ Bks., LLC**

K and K Publishing, *(978-0-9828886)* P.O. Box 20517, Carson City, NV 89721 USA Tel 775-885-7986
E-mail: okmarge@charter.net; marge@kankpublishing.com
Web site: http://kankpublishing.com.

K Jacks Publishing, *(978-0-9978108)* 20 Deerfield Dr., Franklin, NJ 07416 USA Tel 973-827-0684
E-mail: kristenjaccodine@hotmail.com.

K T Graphics, *(978-0-9755259)* 5300 Standing Rock Pl., Las Vegas, NV 89130 USA Tel 702-808-3773
Web site: http://www.ktgraphicsolutions.com.

K Yee, *(978-0-9992730; 978-1-955188)* 3126 Allen Way, Santa Clara, CA 95051 USA Tel 650-714-1005; *Imprints:* Green Cows Books (MYID_H_GREEN)
E-mail: greencows2@gmail.com
Web site: www.greencowsbooks.com.

K12, *(978-1-931728; 978-1-60153)* 2300 Corporate Park Dr., Herndon, VA 20171 USA Tel 703-483-7000; Fax: 703-483-7330
Web site: http://www.k12.com.

K-Twelve MicroMedia Publishing, Inc., *(978-0-943646; 978-1-56419)* 16 McKee Dr., Mahwah, NJ 07430 USA (SAN 286-990X) Tel 201-529-4500; Fax: 201-529-5282; Toll Free: 800-292-1997
E-mail: sales@k12mmp.com
Web site: http://www.k12mmp.com.

K4K Bks. LLC, *(978-1-935368)* 21 N 13th St, Niles, MI 49120 USA
E-mail: editorial_staff@K4KBooks.com
Web site: http://www.K4KBooks.com.

KA Productions, LLC, *(978-1-888018)* Orders Addr.: P.O. Box 21, Alexandria, VA 22313-0021 USA Tel 703-371-4325 (phone/fax); *Imprints:* Word of Mouth Books (Word of Mouth Bks)
E-mail: stephanie@bookinaday.com
Web site: http://www.kwamealexander.com
Dist(s): **SPD-Small Pr. Distribution.**

Kabet Pr. (GBR) *(978-0-948662) Dist. by* **Empire Pub Srvs.**

KAC Publishing *See* **Fifth Crown Pr.**

Kachejian, Malinda, *(978-1-7342941)* 130 Juniper Ave., Smithtown, NY 11787 USA Tel 631-335-4708
E-mail: Malindakachejian@gmail.com.

Kacy C. Chambers *See* **Great Bks. Publishing Co.**

Kade, Carly Creative, *(978-0-9968879; 978-1-7334763)* 4137 N. 42nd St., Phoenix, AZ 85018 USA Tel 201-927-5135
E-mail: carly.kade@yahoo.com
Web site: www.carlykadecreative.com.

Kadima Pr., *(978-0-9723229)* 410 Pine St. No., 802 C, Abilene, TX 79601-5163 USA Fax: 501-636-7425
E-mail: KadimaPress@juno.com
Web site: http://www.kadimapress.com; http://www.AuntLaya.com
Dist(s): **Bks. West.**

Kaeden Bks. *Imprint of* **Kaeden Corp.**

Kaeden Corp., *(978-1-57874; 978-1-879835; 978-1-61181; 978-1-63584; 978-1-64132)* Orders Addr.: P.O. Box 16190, Rocky River, OH 44116 USA Tel 440-617-1400; Fax: 440-617-1403; Toll Free: 800-890-7323; *Imprints:* Kaeden Books (Kaeden)
E-mail: info@kaeden.com; gurmston@kaeden.com; customerservice@kaeden.com
Web site: http://www.kaeden.com
Dist(s): **Follett School Solutions.**

Kagan Cooperative Learning *See* **Kagan Publishing**

Kagan Publishing, *(978-1-879097; 978-1-933445)* Div. of Resources for Teachers, Orders Addr.: P.O. Box 72008, San Clemente, CA 92673 USA Tel 949-545-6300; Fax: 949-545-6301; Toll Free: 800-933-2667
E-mail: carol@kaganonline.com; parker@kaganonline.com; Hannah@KaganOnline.com
Web site: http://www.kaganonline.com.

Kagelmacher, Leonard W. *See* **Buffalo Arts Publishing**

Kahl, Helen Barry, *(978-0-692-13055-1; 978-0-692-19734-9)* 907 Governor Bridge Rd., Davidsonville, MD 21035 USA Tel 202-528-7569
E-mail: helenbarry@msn.com
Dist(s): **CreateSpace Independent Publishing Platform.**

kahla, bob, *(978-1-882820; 978-0-692-75067-4)* P.O. Box 134, Stowell, TX 77661 USA Tel 409-201-4614
E-mail: poss1108@msn.com.

Kahley, Glenn, *(978-0-9788914)* 1575 England Dr., Columbus, OH 43240 USA
E-mail: kahley.1@osu.edu; glennkahley@gmail.com.

Kai Adventures, *(978-0-692-63587-2)* 10700 Brunswick Rd., Apt. 107, Bloomington, MN 55438 USA Tel 612-987-5945
E-mail: juneoliver2@aol.com; joliver@isd271.org.

Kaimanu Prodns., Ltd., *(978-0-9764474)* 135-A Kaimanu Pl., Kihei, HI 96753 USA Tel 808-268-9092; Fax: 808-442-0013
E-mail: customerservice@kaimanu.net
Web site: http://www.kaimanu.net
Dist(s): **Booklines Hawaii, Ltd.**

Kaio Publications, Inc. *See* **Kaio Pubns., Inc.**

Kaio Pubns., Inc., *(978-0-9960430; 978-1-7326661; 978-1-952955; 978-1-7359815; 979-8-218-01089-8; 979-8-218-12848-7)* P.O. Box 118, Spring Hill, TN 37174 USA Tel 615-828-4363
E-mail: joe@kaiopublications.org
Web site: www.kaiopublications.org.

Kairos Publishing, *(978-0-9665831; 978-0-9818864; 978-0-615-92130-3; 978-0-692-55816-1; 978-0-692-67177-1; 979-8-218-26647-9; 979-8-218-27171-8)* Orders Addr.: P.O. Box 450, Clarence, NY 14031 USA Tel 716-759-1058; Edit Addr.: 10501 Main St., Clarence, NY 14031 USA Do not confuse with Kairos Publishing in Llano de San Juan, NM
E-mail: office@eagleswings.org
Web site: http://www.eagleswings.org
Dist(s): **Destiny Image Pubs.**
Send The Light Distribution LLC.

KAK, *(978-0-615-40229-1)* 776 Highland Hills Dr., Howard, OH 43028 USA Tel 740-294-3202
E-mail: saucie776@yahoo.com.

Kalandraka Ediciones Andalucía, S.L. (ESP) *(978-84-96388; 978-84-933755; 978-84-933759; 978-84-933780) Dist. by* **Lectorum Pubns.**

Kalandraka Editora, S.L. (ESP) *(978-84-8464; 978-84-923553; 978-84-95123) Dist. by* **Mariuccia Iaconi Bk Imports.**

Kalandraka Editora, S.L. (ESP) *(978-84-8464; 978-84-923553; 978-84-95123) Dist. by* **Lectorum Pubns.**

Kalawantis Computer Services, Incorporated *See* **Kalawantis Publishing Services, Inc**

Kalawantis Publishing Services, Inc, *(978-0-9665909)* Orders Addr.: P.O. Box 25004, Charlotte, NC 28227 USA Tel 704-754-1108
E-mail: publisher@kalawantis.com
Web site: http://www.kalawantis.com.

Kalcom Publishing, *(978-0-9797530)* 84-01 Lefferts Blvd., Kew Gardens, NY 11415 USA Tel 718-805-5555
E-mail: yek@kalcom.com.

Kaleidoscope Bks. *Imprint of* **I Am My Life Publishing, LLC**

Kales Pr., *(978-0-9670076; 978-0-9798456; 978-1-7333958; 978-1-7378327; 979-8-9859558)* 7031 Columbine, Carlsbad, CA 92011 USA
E-mail: books@kalespress.com
Web site: http://www.kalespress.com
Dist(s): **Norton, W. W. & Co., Inc.**
Penguin Random Hse. Distribution
Penguin Random Hse. LLC.

Kaleta Publishing, LLC, *(978-0-615-39881-5; 978-0-9830222)* 161 Trail E., Pataskala, OH 43062 USA Tel 614-352-3583
E-mail: mindyjkaleta@gmail.com
Dist(s): **MyiLibrary.**

KALEXT Productions, LLC, *(978-0-9617451; 978-0-9748792)* 12795 75th Lane N., West Palm Beach, FL 33412 USA (SAN 664-0613) Tel 561-310-4338; Fax: 561-790-6294 Call 561-310-4338 first
E-mail: xela319@comcast.net
Web site: http://www.bilingualgames.com; http://www.biznizgames.com.

Kalindi Pr., *(978-1-935826; 978-0-9838455)* 2508 Shadow Valley Ranch Rd., Prescott, AZ 86305 USA Tel 928-636-3759
E-mail: balazuccarello@gmail.com
Web site: http://www.kalindipress.com
Dist(s): **SCB Distributors.**

Kaliyan Publishing, *(978-0-9762065)* P.O. Box 473, Stephens City, VA 22655-9998 USA.

†Kalmbach Media Co., *(978-0-8238; 978-0-87116; 978-0-89024; 978-0-89778; 978-0-913135; 978-0-933168; 978-1-62700; 978-1-961200)* Orders Addr.: P.O. Box 1612, Waukesha, WI 53186 USA (SAN 201-0399) Tel 262-796-8776 Toll Free: 800-533-6644 (customer sales); 800-446-5489 (customer service); 800-558-1544 (trade sales); Edit Addr.: 21027 Crossroads Cir., Waukesha, WI 53186 USA Tel 262-796-8776
E-mail: mlundin@kalmbach.com
Web site: http://www.kalmbach.com
Dist(s): **Publishers Group West (PGW)**
Watson-Guptill Pubns., Inc.; *CIP.*

Kalmbach Publishing Company, Books Division *See* **Kalmbach Media Co.**

Kalmia Publishing, *(978-0-9676620)* Orders Addr.: 826 Amiford Dr., San Diego, CA 92107 USA Tel 619-222-7074 (phone/fax)
E-mail: pixieh@mymailstation.com; folsom@islc.net
Web site: http://www.islc.net/~folsom/language.

Kaloustian, Varak, *(978-0-9987773; 978-1-7338185)* 13903 Otsego St., Sherman Oaks, CA 91423 USA Tel 818-383-0621; *Imprints:* TLOV Publishing (MYID_H_TLOV PU)
E-mail: info@thelegendofv.com
Web site: thelegendofv.com.

KAM Publishing, *(978-0-9795474)* Orders Addr.: 1716 Worley St., Durant, OK 74701-2468 USA
E-mail: sharonm@llibs.com
Web site: http://www.llibs.com
Dist(s): **Library Integrated Solutions & Assocs.**

Kamahoi Pr. *Imprint of* **Bishop Museum Pr.**

Kamal, *(978-1-59236)* P.O. Box 1026 Florin Rd, #303, Sacramento, CA 95831 USA
E-mail: admin04@desertwellnetwork.com
Web site: http://www.DesertWellNetwork.com
Dist(s): **Ingram Content Group.**

Kamara, Feremusu, *(978-0-692-19390-7)* 1224 Waugh Chapel Rd, Gambrills, MD 21054 USA Tel 202-378-8185
E-mail: musukamara@hotmail.com.

Kamaron Institute Pr., Div. of Kamaron Institute for Rapid Business Results, 104 Strawflower Path, Peachtree City, GA 30269 USA
E-mail: info@kamaron.org; kamaroninstitute@earthlink.net
Web site: http://www.kamaron.org.

†Kamehameha Publishing, *(978-0-87336)* 567 S. King St., Suite 118, Honolulu, HI 96813 USA Tel 808-534-8205; Fax: 808-541-5305
E-mail: publishing@ksbe.edu
Web site: http://www.kamehamehapublishing.org
Dist(s): **Bess Pr., Inc.**
Booklines Hawaii, Ltd.
Follett School Solutions
Native Bks.; *CIP.*

Kamehameha Schools Press *See* **Kamehameha Publishing**

Kana'i Records, *(978-0-9754567)* 95-1168 Makaikai St. Apt. 113, Mililani, HI 96789-4392 USA
E-mail: bhelemano@aol.com
Dist(s): **Booklines Hawaii, Ltd.**

K&B Products, *(978-0-9646181; 978-0-9740841; 978-0-9772372; 978-1-935122)* P.O. Box 548, Yellville, AR 72687 USA Toll Free Fax: 888-871-5856; Toll Free: 800-700-5096
E-mail: brmp@aol.com
Web site: http://www.thecompletepet.com; http://www.whitehallpublishing.com
Dist(s): **Western International, Inc.**

Kandon Publishing *See* **Kandon UnLtd., Inc.**

Kandon UnLtd., Inc., *(978-0-9829277; 978-0-9912905; 978-1-970163; 978-1-7359571; 978-1-7359572)* 6977 Navajo Rd. No. 105, San Diego, CA 92119 USA
Web site: http://kandonunlimited.com/.

Kane, Gillian, *(978-0-692-14579-1)* 3305 Gina Lynne Ct., Murrysville, PA 15668 USA Tel 724-325-9047
E-mail: 15kaneg@comcast.net
Dist(s): **Ingram Content Group.**

Kane, Kimberly Brougham, *(978-0-615-17610-9; 978-0-578-04556-6)* 1406 Campfire Rd., Lake Charles, LA 70611 USA
Web site: http://www.mommysheart.com
Dist(s): **Lulu Pr., Inc.**

†Kane Miller, *(978-0-916291; 978-1-929132; 978-1-933605; 978-1-935279; 978-1-61067; 978-1-68464)* Div. of EDC Publishing, Orders Addr.: P.O. Box 470663, Tulsa, OK 74146 USA (SAN 295-8945) Tel 800-475-4522; 918-622-4522; Fax: 800-743-5660; Edit Addr.: P.O. Box 8515, La Jolla, CA 92038 USA Tel 858-456-0540
E-mail: info@kanemiller.com
Web site: http://www.kanemiller.com; http://www.edcpub.com
Dist(s): **Children's Plus, Inc.**
EDC Publishing; *CIP.*

Kane Press *Imprint of* **Astra Publishing Hse.**

Kane/Miller#Book Publishers, Incorporated *See* **Kane Miller**

Kanlearn, Inc., *(978-0-9772077)* 8950 W. Olympic Blvd., No. 128, Beverly Hills, CA 90211 USA Tel 310-430-6806
E-mail: mattie3rd@yahoo.com
Web site: www.thekanlearnfoundation.com.

Kansas Alumni Assoc., *(978-0-9742918)* 1266 Oread Ave., Lawrence, KS 66044 USA
Web site: http://www.kualumni.org.

Kansas City Guidebooks, *(978-0-9763873)* P.O. Box 14082, Parkville, MO 64152 USA
Web site: http://www.kckidsguide.com.

Kanto Productions, LLC, *(978-1-929956)* P.O. Box 630435, Simi Valley, CA 93063 USA Tel 805-584-9639; Fax: 310-507-0142; Toll Free: 800-335-2686
E-mail: info@atophill.com
Web site: http://www.atophill.com.

KAOS PR., *(978-0-692-68535-8; 978-0-692-68536-5; 978-0-9975836; 978-0-578-58895-7; 978-1-954111; 978-0-578-36232-8; 978-0-578-36446-9)* 1904 CEDAR LANE, NASHVILLE, TN 37212 USA Tel 615-383-8964
Dist(s): **Independent Pub.**

Kaplan, Hadas, *(978-0-578-21404-7; 978-0-578-46844-0; 978-0-578-47442-7; 978-0-578-74856-0)* 8131 Havitshire Way Apt. 101, Centerville, OH 45458 USA.

†Kaplan Publishing, *(978-0-7931; 978-0-88462; 978-0-913864; 978-0-936894; 978-0-942103; 978-1-57410; 978-1-60714; 978-1-60978; 978-1-61865; 978-1-62523; 978-1-5062)* 395 Hudson St., New York, NY 10014 USA (SAN 211-2280); 395 Hudson St., New City, NY 10014; *Imprints:* Dearborn Real Estate Education (Dearbrn Real Est Ed); Kaplan Test Prep (Kaplan Test Prep); Barron's Educational Series, Incorporated (BarronsEd)
E-mail: deb.darrock@kaplan.com; shayna.webb@kaplan.com; alexander.noya@kaplan.com
Web site: http://www.kaplanpublishing.com; http://www.kaplanprofessional.com
Dist(s): **BookBaby**
Cranbury International
Dearborn Financial Publishing, Inc.
JAGCO & Associates Inc.
LibreDigital
MBI Distribution Services/Quayside Distribution
Simon & Schuster
Simon & Schuster, Inc.; *CIP.*

Kaplan Test Prep *Imprint of* **Kaplan Publishing**

Kapp Bks. LLC, *(978-1-60346; 978-1-64035)* Orders Addr.: 204-Mohan Complex , H block Market Phase 1, New Delhi, 110052 IND; Edit Addr.: 3602 Rocky Meadow Ct., Fairfax, VA 22033 USA Fax: 703-621-7162
E-mail: pravin@kappbooks.com; sundeep@macawbooks.com
Web site: http://www.kappbooks.com; http://www.macawbooks.com/.

Karadjian, Kayl, *(978-0-692-79862-1; 978-0-9989635)* 14324 Lake Price Dr., ORLANDO, FL 32826 USA Tel 954-551-8169.

Kar-Ben Publishing *Imprint of* **Lerner Publishing Group**

Kardec, Allan Educational Society, *(978-0-9649907)* 5020 N. Eighth St., Philadelphia, PA 19120 USA Tel 215-329-4010 (phone/fax)
E-mail: akesbooks@cox.net
Web site: http://www.allan-kardec.org.

Kardooni, Azadeh Afsar, *(978-0-692-14501-2)* 9 Gemstar Ln., LAS VEGAS, NV 89135 USA Tel 949-500-3949
E-mail: azyafsar@gmail.com
Dist(s): **Ingram Content Group.**

Karen Pokras Toz *See* **Grand Daisy Pr.**

Karenzo Media, *(978-0-9798164; 978-0-9899318)* 451 Tequesta Dr, Tequesta, FL 33469 USA Tel 772-882-8582
E-mail: karenzomedia@gmail.com; khsilvestri@live.com
Web site: http://www.karenyvonnehamilton.com; http://www.publishersmarketplace.com/members/kazsilvestri/; http://www.writingyourlifetales.com.

karilogue, *(978-0-9994504)* 2211 urbana pike, Ijamsville, MD 21754 USA Tel 301-401-9951
E-mail: kariann.marti@gmail.com
Web site: www.karilogue.com.

Karina Library Pr., *(978-0-9824491; 978-1-937902)* P.O. Box 35, Ojai, CA 93024-9302 USA Tel 805-500-4535
E-mail: michael@karinalibrary.com; sails@karinalibrary.com
Web site: http://www.karinalibrary.com.

Karleen Tauszik *See* **Tip Top Bks.**

Karlin, Malcolm, *(978-0-692-16851-6; 978-0-692-16854-7; 978-0-692-17566-8; 978-0-692-19405-8; 978-0-692-19413-3)* 1065 Pk. Ave., New York, NY 10128 USA Tel 212-779-3375
E-mail: mkarlin@karlinpimsler.com
Dist(s): **Ingram Content Group.**

Karma Kollection LLC, *(978-0-9896966; 978-0-692-33207-8; 978-0-692-33208-5)* 549 W. Eugenie St., Chicago, IL 60614 USA Tel 312-952-0776
E-mail: roopaweber@gmail.com
Web site: www.messypenny.com.

Karma Valley Music, *(978-0-9746011)* 505 Lovins Ln., Somerset, KY 42503 USA Tel 606-274-5194
E-mail: flo@floydlovins.com.

Karmen Dalyte Presents, *(978-1-7353630)* 4729 ALLUVIAL CIR, Alvin, TX 77511 USA Tel 832-882-4505
E-mail: demi_fowler@yahoo.com
Web site: Karmen Dalyte Presents.

Karnak Co., *(978-0-9630951)* Orders Addr.: P.O. Box 497-158, Chicago, IL 60649-7158 USA Tel 773-684-5298; Edit Addr.: 1616 E. 50th Pl., No. 5-C, Chicago, IL 60615 USA
E-mail: t.greer57@yahoo.com.

Karosa Publishing, *(978-0-9706312)* 4636 Almond Ln., Boulder, CO 80301 USA Tel 303-484-8856 Do not confuse with companies with same or similar name in Lower Burnell, PA, Paradise Valley, AZ, Sheffield, PA, hailey, ID
E-mail: karpub@comcast.net
Web site: http://www.spadesbook.com.

Karsonkina, Tatiana, *(978-0-9779672)* P.O. Box 191, Brooklyn, NY 11223 USA.

Karten, Ryan, *(978-0-9987424)* 1020 N Vista St., West Hollywood, CA 90046 USA Tel 323-810-5841; Fax: 323-810-5841
E-mail: ryankarten@gmail.com
Web site: ryankarten.com.

Karuna Press *See* **Utopia Pr.**

Karyn Henley Resources *Imprint of* **Child Sensitive Communication, LLC**

Kaseberg, W. G. Publishing, *(978-0-9761138)* 49 Red Bud Ln., Glen Carbon, IL 62034 USA Tel 618-288-5269; Fax: 618-288-0712
E-mail: wgkasebergpub@empowering.com.

Kashvi'sArtwork, *(978-0-692-04749-1; 978-0-692-05070-5)* 6605 W, 126th Terr., Overland Park, KS 66209 USA Tel 913-660-0945
E-mail: kashvi.silswal@gmail.com
Dist(s): **Ingram Content Group.**

Kasian Publishing, *(978-1-943207; 978-1-951871)* 15582 Eastbrook Ln., Apple Valley, MN 55124 USA Tel 612-414-9173
E-mail: kristin@kristinvanrisseghem.com
Web site: www.kristinvanrisseghem.com.

Kasson Publishing, *(978-0-9729435)* 201 E. St., Elmo Rd., Austin, TX 78745-1217 USA Tel 512-447-1988 (phone/fax)
E-mail: publishing@kassonscastings.com
Web site: http://www.kassonscastings.com.

Kat Tales Publishing *See* **EMC Publishing**

Kat Tales Publishing, *(978-0-9744330)* 2515 Clarkson St., Denver, CO 80205 USA Tel 303-394-6380
E-mail: alluptojah@aol.com.

KATastroPHE, *(978-0-9769698)* 6389 Florio St., Oakland, CA 94618 USA Tel 510-601-9631
E-mail: info@katastrophemusic.com
Web site: http://www.katastrophemusic.com.

Kate DeL, *(978-1-7352597)* 6730 Sturbridge Pl, Poland, OH 44514 USA Tel 330-501-8888
E-mail: contact@katedel.com
Web site: www.katedel.com.

Katheryn Maddox Haddad *Imprint of* **Northern Lights Publishing Hse.**

Kathleen Bertoldie, *(978-1-7349933)* 1808 N. Patriot Dr., Ozark, MO 65721 USA Tel 417-224-3263
E-mail: thebertoldies@yahoo.com.

Kathryn Marie, *(978-1-7348323)* 55 Spencer St, Lynn, MA 01905 USA Tel 774-230-4074
E-mail: kathryn.marie.maiden@gmail.com
Web site: https://www.authorkathrynmarie.com/.

Kathryn Sommer *See* **KMS Productions**

Kathy Dawson Books *Imprint of* **Penguin Young Readers Group**

Kathy Wall, *(978-0-9971001)* 101 Sierra Point Rd., Brisbane, CA 94005 USA Tel 415-608-4168
E-mail: kwallprudential@aol.com.

Kathy's Pen, *(978-0-9777034)* 24 Ridgewood Pkwy, Newport News, VA 23608 USA Tel 757-872-6258
E-mail: regmcc@cox.net
Web site: http://www.kathyspen.com.

Kati Bee & Friends Publishing, *(978-0-9793760)* 8304 Limonite Ave. Suite D-3, Riverside, CA 92509 USA (SAN 853-2818) Tel 951-685-7256; Fax: 951-332-0436
E-mail: ContactKati@katibeeandfriends.com
Web site: http://www.katibeeandfriends.com.

Katie Cook, *(978-0-9883554)* 1201 Kenwood Dr., Nashville, TN 37216 USA Tel 615-430-8128
E-mail: cookontv@comcast.net.

Katie Gigliotti, *(978-1-7374300)* 1920 Birch Dr., Culpeper, VA 22701 USA Tel 540-812-5380
E-mail: Katie@katiegigliotti.com
Web site: KatieGigliotti.com.

Katieleimkuehler.com, *(978-0-615-82843-5; 978-0-578-38126-8; 978-0-578-38129-9)* 101 N. Wacker, Chicago, IL 60606 USA Tel 440-935-5023
E-mail: katieleimkuehler@gmail.com
Web site: www.shytowngirls.com.

Katrina A. Weston, *(978-0-578-74579-4; 978-0-578-90891-5)* 1631 Westchester Blvd., Westchester, IL 60154 USA Tel 773-742-6360
E-mail: katrinaweston24@gmail.com.

Katrina Denise, *(978-0-692-77541-7; 978-0-692-84082-5; 978-1-7343535)* 26 Pickersgill Sq., Owings Mills, MD 21117 USA Tel 443-416-5177
Dist(s): **CreateSpace Independent Publishing Platform.**

Katrina'sWORKS, *(978-0-692-21505-0; 978-0-692-24403-6; 978-0-692-29174-0; 978-0-692-29925-8; 978-0-692-38043-7; 978-0-692-48068-7; 978-0-692-58983-0; 978-0-9982189)*
E-mail: caiytee@yahoo.com
Dist(s): **CreateSpace Independent Publishing Platform.**

Kat's Kids Kreation, A, *(978-0-9749516)* 413 Fairlawn Ave., Saint Louis, MO 63119-2614 USA Fax: 314-963-0494
E-mail: katbuck123@aol.com.

Kat's Socks, *(978-1-7322448; 978-1-7340750; 978-1-7351053; 979-8-9873927)* P.O. Box 3081, Bismarck, ND 58502 USA Tel 701-527-7322
E-mail: kats@katssocks.com
Web site: www.katssocks.com.

Katsoris, Nicholas C. *See* **NK Pubns.**

attan, Peter I., *(978-0-615-15334-6; 978-0-615-18718-1; 978-0-578-03642-7)* 147-29 182nd St. Box AMM 2232, Springfield Gardens, NY 11413 USA Tel 718-553-8740
E-mail: info@kindergardensudoku.com; info@petrabooks.com
Web site: http://www.kindergardensudoku.com
Dist(s): **Lulu Pr., Inc.**

aty Warren, *(978-0-9995221)* 8747 Phinney Ave N, No. 6, Seattle, WA 98103 USA Tel 206-291-2021
E-mail: kathlyn_warren@yahoo.com; tulipandpiggy@gmail.com.

atydid Pubns., *(978-1-879945)* Orders Addr.: P.O. Box 526, Point Lookout, MO 65726 USA; Edit Addr.: Acacia Club Rd., Hollister, MO 65672 USA Tel 417-335-8134
E-mail: mgcameron@aol.com; kay@camerons-crag.com
Web site: http://www.katydid-publications.com.

atydid Publishing LLC, *(978-0-9724272)* 5845 Eldorado, San Joaquin, CA 93660 USA Tel 559-693-4565 Do not confuse with Latydid Publishing in Mincie, IN.

Katzman, Lori, *(978-1-7335992)* 24 Claremont Dr., Short Hills, NJ 07078 USA Tel 732-809-7499
E-mail: lakatzman@me.com.

Kaufman, A. Shandle, *(978-1-7333098)* 540 Cardinal Ln., Bellville, TX 77418 USA Tel 979-877-8120
E-mail: akaufman@academicplanet.com.

Kaukini Ranch Pr., *(978-0-9643674)* P.O. Box 2462, Wailuku, HI 96793 USA Tel 808-244-3371; Fax: 808-395-0738.

Kav Books, Incorporated *See* **Royal Fireworks Publishing Co.**

Kawabata, Thomas *See* **Purring Pr.**

Kawainui Pr., *(978-0-943357)* P.O. Box 163, Captain Cook, HI 96704 USA (SAN 668-6427) Tel 808-328-9126 (phone/fax)
E-mail: herbkane@kona.net
Web site: http://www.hitrade.com
Dist(s): **Booklines Hawaii, Ltd.**

Kay, James Publishing, *(978-0-9728288; 978-0-9850113; 978-1-943245)* Orders Addr.: P.O. Box 470733, Tulsa, OK 74147-0733 USA
E-mail: alongtheway89@sbcglobal.net
Web site: www.jameskaypublishing.com.

Kay, Janet Consulting, *(978-0-9768786)* 115 Brighton Pk., Battle Creek, MI 49015 USA.

Kay Kay Publishing, LLC, *(978-0-9987769)* 19 Clyde Road, Suite 202, Somerset, NJ 08873 USA Tel 732-873-6464; Fax: 732-873-6480
E-mail: khebbon@yahoo.com
Web site: www.kaykaypublishing.com.

Kay Press, *(978-0-9860831)* 4908 Bennington Drive, Schwenksville, PA 19473 USA.

Kay Productions LLC, *(978-0-9707201)* Orders Addr.: 1115 W. Lincoln Ave., Suite 107, Yakima, WA 98902 USA Tel 509-853-0860; Fax: 509-853-0861; Toll Free: 800-619-4345; Edit Addr.: 732 Summitview Ave., Suite 628, Yakima, WA 98902 USA Do not confuse with Kay Productions, San Rafael, CA
E-mail: marketing@kayproductions.com
Web site: http://www.kayproductions.com.

Kay, Sjoukje, *(978-0-9789698)* 4500 Broadway Suite 6i, New York, NY 10040 USA
E-mail: pdolan@fairpoint.net
Web site: http://www.thedonutyogi.com.

Kaya 20 LLC, *(978-1-948633)* 1039 Constitution Way, Cumming, GA 30040-1295 USA Tel 404-618-8988; *Imprints*: Kitab Press (Kitab Pr)
E-mail: kaya20llc@gmail.com.

Kaya Production *See* **Muae Publishing, Inc.**

KayStar Publishing, *(978-0-9749886)* P.O. Box 571, Saddle River, NJ 07458 USA Fax: 201-825-3912.

Kazi Pubns., Inc., *(978-0-933511; 978-0-935782; 978-1-56744; 978-1-871031; 978-1-930637)* 3023 W. Belmont Ave., Chicago, IL 60618 USA (SAN 162-3397) Tel 773-267-7001; Fax: 773-267-7002
E-mail: info@kazi.org
Web site: http://www.kazi.org.

KaZoom Kids Bks., Inc., *(978-1-885242; 978-1-7354504)* 4850 S. Lake Park, Unit 1801, Chicago, IL 60615 USA.

KB Bks. & More, *(978-0-9761128; 978-1-934486)* Orders Addr.: P.O. Box 56, Channing, TX 79018 USA Tel 806-235-2665; Fax: 866-282-1658; 715 Sante Fe, Channing, TX 79018 Fax: 866-282-1658
E-mail: kbbooks@windstream.net
Dist(s): **Follett School Solutions.**

KB Publishing, *(978-0-9768129)* 11 Running Fox Rd., Columbia, SC 29223 USA.

KBA, LLC, *(978-1-880931)* P.O. Box 3673, Carbondale, IL 62902 USA Tel 618-549-2893
E-mail: thriving@colorado.net
Web site: http://www.benziger.org.

KBK Publishing LLC, *(978-1-7358841; 978-1-956860)* 350 schoen st, Atlanta, GA 30315 USA Tel 404-863-7444
E-mail: yalandasweney@gmail.com; hello@kbkpublish.com
Web site: www.kbkpublish.com.

KBR Mutti's Pubns., *(978-0-9762664)* P.O. Box 907431, Santa Barbara, CA 93190 USA
E-mail: kbrmutts@cox.net
Web site: http://www.matthewsbox.com.

K.C. Fox Publishing, *(978-0-9767078)* Div. of The Kerr Co., P.O. Box 5446, Takoma Park, MD 20913 USA Tel 301-434-9191
E-mail: publisher@kcfoxpublishing.com
Web site: http://www.poutorpurpose.com; http://www.kcfoxpublishing.com.

KC13 Corp., *(978-1-945918)* 5440 Strand No. 203, Hawthorne, CA 90250 USA Tel 909-576-7002
E-mail: kccorp13@gmail.com.

KCI Sports *See* **KCI Sports Publishing**

KCI Sports Publishing, *(978-0-9758769; 978-0-9798729; 978-0-9843882; 978-0-9831985; 978-0-9837337; 978-0-9885458; 978-1-940056; 978-1-957005)* 3340 Whiting Ave., Suite 5, Stevens Point, WI 54481 USA Fax: 715-344-2668; Toll Free: 800-697-3756
Web site: http://www.kcisports.com
Dist(s): **Partners Bk. Distributing, Inc.**

KCL Publishing & Tutoring, *(978-0-692-05332-4; 978-0-692-18636-7; 978-0-578-46591-3; 978-0-578-50656-2; 978-1-7334681)* 683 SE Juniper Ave., Dallas, OR 97338 USA Tel 503-910-4445
E-mail: kathy.martin123@gmail.com
Dist(s): **CreateSpace Independent Publishing Platform.**

K.Co.Kids, LLC, *(978-0-9801423)* 6804 Peter's Path, Colleyville, TX 76034 USA (SAN 855-3092) Tel 817-886-8402
E-mail: kristine@kcokids.com
Web site: http://www.kcokids.com; http://www.katieandthemagicumbrella.com
Dist(s): **Midpoint Trade Bks., Inc.**

KDC Enterprises *See* **KDC Enterprises LLC**

KDC Enterprises LLC, *(978-0-692-13866-3; 979-8-9853206)* 12523 S Union Ave., Chicago, IL 60628 USA Tel 773-552-2463; 773-552-2463
E-mail: contactkdcenterprises@gmail.com
Web site: www.deirdrelcunningham.com.

Kean, Marcia, *(978-0-578-60062-8)* 48 Churchill St, Newtonville, MA 02460 USA Tel 617-413-1295
E-mail: marciakean@gmail.com.

Keane, Sharon L, *(978-1-7352954)* 4003 W. Bay Ave., Tampa, FL 33616 USA Tel 813-310-6557
E-mail: sk5102w@verizon.net.

Kearia, *(978-0-578-50561-9)* 2493 W. 85th Ln., Merrillville, IN 46410 USA Tel 219-276-7416
E-mail: keariaShontell1@yahoo.com.

Keaster, Diane W. *See* **ZC Horses Series of Children's Bks.**

Keebie Pr. *Imprint of* **Keebie Pr.**

Keebie Pr., *(978-0-692-91210-2; 978-0-692-91211-9; 978-0-692-92913-1; 978-0-692-98591-5; 978-0-692-98592-2; 978-0-692-98832-9; 978-0-578-42135-3; 978-0-578-42137-7; 978-0-578-42333-3; 978-0-578-54500-4; 978-1-7358875)* 327 N. Brooke Dr., CANTON, GA 30115 USA Tel 925-768-2102; *Imprints*: Keebie Press (Keebie Press)
E-mail: mgailgrant@gmail.com
Web site: MGailGrant.com
Dist(s): **Ingram Content Group.**

Keen Communications *See* **AdventureKEEN**

Keen Vision Publishing, LLC *See* **Keen Vision Publishing, LLC**

Keen Vision Publishing, LLC, *(978-0-692-59693-7; 978-0-692-63481-3; 978-0-692-64894-0; 978-0-692-64975-6; 978-0-692-65811-6; 978-0-692-66053-9; 978-0-692-67212-9; 978-0-692-69096-3; 978-0-692-70406-6; 978-0-692-71010-4; 978-0-692-71312-9; 978-0-692-72314-2; 978-0-692-74401-7; 978-0-692-74789-6; 978-0-692-75265-4; 978-0-692-75657-7; 978-0-692-75939-4; 978-0-692-77086-3; 978-0-692-77378-9; 978-0-9982523; 978-0-9987200; 978-0-9990740; 978-0-9992657; 978-1-948270; 978-1-955316) 620 D Julia St., Huntsville, AL 35816 USA Tel 2563485610*
E-mail: keenvisionediting@gmail.com
Web site: www.keen-vision.com
Dist(s): **CreateSpace Independent Publishing Platform.**

Keenan Tyler Paine, *(978-0-9740907)* 1715 Brae Burn Rd., Altadena, CA 91001 USA (SAN 255-3414)
E-mail: pmgoddard@earthlink.net.

Keene Publishing, *(978-0-9724853; 978-0-9766805; 978-0-9792371; 978-0-9815972)* P.O. Box 54, Warwick, NY 10990-0054 USA (SAN 254-8631) Tel 845-987-7750; Fax: 845-987-7845; *Imprints*: Moo Press (Moo)
E-mail: dtinney@KeeneBooks.com; info@KeeneBooks.com; mbrowne@KeeneBoooks.com
Web site: http://www.KeeneBooks.com.

Keen's Martial Arts Academy, *(978-0-9702958; 978-1-60243)* Orders Addr.: P.O. Box 144, Tannersville, PA 18372-0144 USA (SAN 852-3002)
E-mail: LOHON6@msn.com
Web site: http://www.kmaa.info.

Keenspot Entertainment, *(978-0-9722350; 978-1-932775)* Orders Addr.: P.O. Box 110, Cresbard, SD 57435 USA Tel 605-324-3332; Toll Free: 888- 533-6776
E-mail: TeriCrosby@gmail.com
Web site: http://www.keenspot.com
Dist(s): **Simon & Schuster, Inc.**

Keep Bks., *(978-1-893986)* Div. of The Ohio State Univ., 1100 Kinnear Rd., Columbus, OH 43212 USA Tel 800-678-6484; Fax: 614-688-3452; Toll Free: 800-678-6484
E-mail: keepbooks@osu.edu
Web site: https://keepbooks.osu.edu/.

Keep Coming Back *See* **Puddledancer Pr.**

Keep Empowering Yourself Successfully, *(978-0-9762009)* 5630 S. Division, Grand Rapids, MI 49548 USA Tel 616-261-3000; Fax: 616-261-3355
E-mail: monicaharris@grar.com
Web site: http://www.successfulkeys.com.

Keep Hope Alive, *(978-1-887831)* P.O. Box 270041, West Allis, WI 53227 USA Tel 414-545-6539; Fax: 414-329-0653
E-mail: khope@access4less.net
Web site: http://www.keephopealive.org
Dist(s): **New Leaf Distributing Co., Inc.**

Keep Me Company Publishing Co., *(978-0-9718632)* 214 Blue Ridge Rd., Plymouth Meeting, PA 19462 USA Tel 610-828-2641.

Keepers of Wisdom and Peace Bks., *(978-0-9844079)* P.O. Box 1314, Woodstock, NY 12498 USA (SAN 859-3159) Tel 845-679-9258
E-mail: KeepersofWisdomandPeace@gmail.com
Web site: http://KeepersofWisdomandPeace.com
Dist(s): **Ingram Publisher Services.**

Keepin' Up Wit *See* **Keepin' Up Wit Pr.**

Keepin' Up Wit Pr., *(978-0-578-61884-5; 978-0-578-62544-7; 978-1-7350797; 978-1-953567)* 2200 Greywing St., WOODBRIDGE, VA 22191 USA Tel 571-237-9749
E-mail: RACHELLEJONESSMITH@GMAIL.COM
Web site: rjonessmith.online.

Keepsake Productions *Imprint of* **Keepsake Productions**

Keepsake Productions, *(978-0-615-63929-1; 978-0-9882979)* 2485 W. Mericrest Way, Queen Creek, AZ 85142-6066 USA Tel 480-659-9682; *Imprints*: Keepsake Productions (KeepsakeProdns)
Dist(s): **CreateSpace Independent Publishing Platform.**

Keepworthy Creations LLC, *(978-0-9833155)* P.O. Box 3529, Peoria, IL 61612 USA
E-mail: bob@keepworthy.com
Web site: www.keepworthy.com.

Kegel, Gina M, *(978-1-7339512)* 6562 Rennrick Cir, Huntington Beach, CA 92647 USA Tel 562-234-4488
E-mail: Ginaiswrite@yahoo.com
Web site: Ginakegel.com.

Kehas, Alethea, *(978-0-692-92157-9; 978-0-692-12357-7; 978-0-578-40031-0)* 26 Jonathan Ln, Bow, NH 03304 USA Tel 603-233-1846
E-mail: aekehas@gmail.com
Dist(s): **Independent Pub.**

Kehot Pubn. Society, *(978-0-8266)* Div. of Merkos L'Inyonei Chinuch, Orders Addr.: 291 Kingston Ave., Brooklyn, NY 11213 USA Tel 718-778-0226; Fax: 718-778-4148; Toll Free: 877-463-7567 (877-4MERKOS); Edit Addr.: 770 Eastern Pkwy., Brooklyn, NY 11213 USA (SAN 220-7060) Tel 718-604-2785
E-mail: orders@kehotonline.com; info@kehot.com
Web site: http://www.kehotonline.com
Dist(s): **Follet Higher Education Grp**
Follett School Solutions.

Keira Pr., *(978-0-9824506)* P.O. Box 815, Joliet, IL 60434 USA Tel 815-726-4200
Web site: http://www.keirapress.com.

Keith Pubns., LLC, *(978-1-936372; 978-1-62882)* Orders Addr.: 1526 W. Sea Haze Dr., Gilbert, AZ 85233 USA
E-mail: KeithPublications@cox.net; mary@keithpublications.com
Web site: http://www.keithpublications.com.

Keiva DA, *(978-1-7335596)* 131 E. Central Ave., Maywood, NJ 07607 USA Tel 201-888-6060
E-mail: keivada@gmail.com.

Keller, Ed, *(978-1-7347439)* 2014 9th Ave., Morgantown, WV 26508-8401 USA Tel 304-296-8587
E-mail: ekeller.westpoint@gmail.com
Web site: https://www.clarestomatobook.com/.

Kelley, James *See* **Lypton Publishing**

Kelley, L. A., *(978-1-7321537)* 513 Pheasant Ct., Pensacola, FL 32514 USA Tel 850-477-0067
E-mail: l.a.kelley.author@gmail.com.

Kelley, Mark, *(978-1-880865; 978-0-9744053)* Orders Addr.: P.O. Box 32077, Juneau, AK 99803 USA Tel 907-586-1993; Fax: 907-586-1201; Edit Addr.: PO Box 32077, Juneau, AK 99803 USA
E-mail: photos@markkelley.com
Web site: http://www.markkelley.com.

KelleyGreenworks Publishing, *(978-0-9791029)* Orders Addr.: 607 Woodsman Way, Crownsville, MD 21032 USA
Web site: http://www.readysetgo-organic.com.

Kellie Ann Briseno, *(978-0-578-57205-5; 978-0-578-60915-7; 978-0-578-77522-7)* 6100 York River Dr., Arlington, TX 76018 USA Tel 817-807-3870
E-mail: kellie.briseno@gmail.com.

Kelly Bear Pr., Inc., *(978-0-9621054)* 20493 Pine Vista, Bend, OR 97702 USA (SAN 250-5746) Fax: 541-330-6846; Toll Free: 800-431-1934 (orders only)
E-mail: kellybear@bendcable.com
Web site: http://www.kellybear.com
Dist(s): **Sunburst Visual Media.**

Kelly Cochran Publishing, *(978-0-578-42665-5)* 2261 N Beachwood Dr. K-114, Los Angeles, CA 90068 USA Tel 205-265-0102
E-mail: caremoresharemore@gmail.com
Dist(s): **Independent Pub.**

Kelly, D Scott, *(978-0-9755442)* 208 W. Lincoln, Charlevoix, MI 49720 USA Tel 231-547-1144; Fax: 231-547-4970
E-mail: info@basesteencenter.org
Web site: http://www.basesteencenter.org.

Kelly, Elaine A., *(978-0-578-06873-2)* 5 Appletree Ln., Newtown Square, PA 19073 USA
E-mail: eakgck@hotmail.com.

Kelly, Jason Pr., *(978-0-9664387)* 15 Ken Pratt Blvd. Suite 200, Longmont, CO 80501 USA Tel 303-772-7209
E-mail: jason@jasonkelly.com
Web site: http://www.JasonKelly.com
Dist(s): **BookBaby.**

Kelly, Katherine, *(978-0-9773481)* 4203 Cty. Rd., 3100, Lubbock, TX 79403-7869 USA
E-mail: kellytomkat@sptc.net
Web site: www.informationsleuth.wordpress.com.

Kelly, Kimberly, *(978-0-9747363)* 9801 E. Homestead Rd., Poplar, WI 54864 USA
E-mail: kimkellykimkelly@yahoo.com
Dist(s): **Partners Bk. Distributing, Inc.**

Kelly Lee Culbreth, *(978-0-578-43267-0; 978-0-578-49777-8; 978-0-578-56447-0; 978-0-578-32630-6)* 641 Creek Oak Dr., Murfreesboro, TN 37128 USA Tel 615-480-7747
E-mail: studio627@gmail.com
Dist(s): **Ingram Content Group.**

Kelly, Tiffany, *(978-0-692-83022-2; 978-0-578-71835-4)* 9001 Bramblewood Way, Elk Grove, CA 95758 USA Tel 916-877-0378; Fax: 916-877-0378
E-mail: TiffanyKelly616@yahoo.com.

Kelsey Enterprises Publishing *See* **Cheval International**

†Kelsey Street Pr., *(978-0-932716)* 2824 Kelsey St., Berkeley, CA 94705-2302 USA (SAN 212-6729)
E-mail: kelseyst@sirius.com
Web site: http://www.kelseyst.com
Dist(s): **BookMobile**
SPD-Small Pr. Distribution; *CIP.*

Kelton, Inc., *(978-0-692-86206-3)* 200 2nd Ave SE, Sleepy Eye, MN 56085 USA Tel 715-533-5880
E-mail: jediblender1986@gmail.com.

Kempston, Megan, *(978-0-9975660)* 19275 Hidden Springs Ln., Boulder Creek, CA 95006 USA Tel 520-904-0546
E-mail: megankempston@gmail.com.

Kemtec Educational Corp., *(978-1-877960)* 4780 Interstate Dr., Cincinnati, OH 45246-1112 USA Toll Free: 877-536-8321
E-mail: prekem@kemtecscience.com
Web site: http://www.kemtecscience.com.

Ken Bangs Writing, *(978-1-7331194; 979-8-9868611)* 606 Courtney Ln., McKinney, TX 75071 USA Tel 214-842-4817
E-mail: kenbangs1@gmail.com
Web site: https://author.amazon.com/home.

Ken Floro III, *(978-0-615-52118-3; 978-0-9847117; 978-0-9892839)* 4745 Goethe, St. Louis, MO 63116 USA Tel 314-541-4021
E-mail: kenfloro3@sbcglobal.net.

Ken Pr., *(978-1-928771)* 4001 N. Paseo de los Rancheros, Tucson, AZ 85745 USA (SAN 299-9714) Tel 520-743-3200; Fax: 520-743-3210
E-mail: office@kenpress.com
Web site: http://www.kenpress.com
Dist(s): **Distributors, The.**

Kenamar, Inc., *(978-0-9753207)* P.O. Box 689, West Dundee, IL 60110-0689 USA
E-mail: kenamarpublish@aol.com.

Kendahl Hse. Pr. *Imprint of* **Youngs, Bettie Bks.**

Kendall Hunt Publishing Co., *(978-0-7872; 978-0-8403; 978-0-7575; 978-1-4652; 978-1-5249; 978-1-7924; 979-8-7657; 979-8-3851)* Orders Addr.: P.O. Box 1840, Dubuque, IA 52004-1840 USA; Edit Addr.: 4050 Westmark Dr., Dubuque, IA 52002 USA (SAN 203-9184) Tel 563-589-1000; Fax: 563-589-1046; Toll Free Fax: 800-772-9165; Toll Free: 800-228-0810
E-mail: orders@kendallhunt.com; kkelly@kendallhunt.com
Web site: http://www.kendallhunt.com
Dist(s): **Smashwords.**

Kendar Publishing Company *See* **Kendar Publishing, Inc.**

Kendar Publishing, Inc., *(978-1-889506)* 310 5th St., Suite 101, Racine, WI 53403 USA Tel 262-632-4070; Fax: 262-632-7089; Toll Free: 866-632-7040.

Kenealy, Kevin Patrick, *(978-0-692-15485-4; 978-0-692-15487-8; 978-0-692-15576-9; 978-0-692-15577-6; 979-8-9852098)* 14307 Wooded Path Ln., Orland Park, IL 60462 USA Tel 708-299-2486
E-mail: kevin.kenealy@gmail.com
Dist(s): **Ingram Content Group.**

Kennebec Large Print *Imprint of* **Cengage Gale**

Kennedy Christian Publishing, *(978-0-9743136)* P.O. Box 5385, Texarkana, TX 75505-5385 USA
E-mail: knndytgr@aol.com.

Kennedy Enterprises, LLC, *(978-0-9836230)* 600 Baver St., Clarksburg, WV 26301 USA Tel 304-685-1239
E-mail: kennedykonnection@yahoo.com
Dist(s): **Lulu Pr., Inc.**

Kenneth B. White, *(978-0-9979291; 978-0-692-04983-9; 978-1-7340222; 978-1-7354384)* 1108 Wellesley Ave., Modesto, CA 95350 USA Tel 209-567-0600.

Kenneth R. Luchterhand *See* **Luchterhand, Kenneth R.**

Kensington Bks. *Imprint of* **Kensington Publishing Corp.**

Kensington Publishing Corp., *(978-0-7860; 978-0-8065; 978-0-8184; 978-0-8217; 978-1-55817; 978-1-57566; 978-0-7582; 978-1-4201; 978-1-59983; 978-1-60183; 978-0-9817144; 978-0-9818905; 978-0-9824170; 978-0-9841132; 978-1-61650; 978-1-61773; 978-1-4967; 978-1-5161; 978-1-63573; 978-1-64566) 119 W. 40th St., New York, NY 10018 USA Tel 212-407-1500; Fax: 212-935-0699; Toll Free: 800-221-2647; 499 North Canon Dr., Beverly Hills, CA 90210 Tel 310-887-7082; Imprints:* Kensington Books (Knsington); K-Teen (K-TEEN); K-Teen/Dafina (K-TEEN/DAFINA); Urban Renaissance (Urban Renais)
E-mail: jmclean@kensingtonbooks.com; melley@kensingtonbooks.com
Web site: http://www.kensingtonbooks.com
Dist(s): **Blackstone Audio, Inc.**
Children's Plus, Inc.
Ebsco Publishing
Hachette Bk. Group
Independent Pubs. Group
MyiLibrary
Open Road Integrated Media, Inc.
Penguin Random Hse. Distribution
Penguin Random Hse. LLC
Penguin Publishing Group
Random Hse., Inc.
Worldwide Media Service, Inc.

Kent Communications, Ltd., *(978-0-9627106; 978-1-888206; 978-0-9830963)* Orders Addr.: 25 Poplar Plain Rd., Westport, CT 06880 USA Tel 203-454-9646; *Imprints*: Kent Press (Kent Pr)
E-mail: mhoule@gbiplaw.com
Dist(s): **Independent Pubs. Group**
MyiLibrary
National Bk. Network
Small Pr. United.

Kent Fine Art *See* **Kent Gallery**

Kent Gallery, *(978-1-878607)* P.O. Box 684, New York, NY 10012-0013 USA
E-mail: info@kentfineart.net
Web site: http://www.kentfineart.net.

Kent, Madigan, *(978-1-7358926)* 105 Michaels Way, Chapel Hill, NC 27516 USA Tel 312-758-1295
E-mail: madigankent@gmail.com
Web site: www.madigankent.com.

Kent Pr. *Imprint of* **Kent Communications, Ltd.**

†Kent State Univ. Pr., *(978-0-87338; 978-1-60635; 978-1-61277; 978-1-63101)* Orders Addr.: c/o BookMasters, Inc., 30 Amberwood Pkwy., Ashland, OH 44805 USA Tel 419-281-1802; Fax: 419-281-6883; Toll Free: 800-247-6553; Edit Addr.: 1118 Univ. Library Bldg.

1125 Risman Dr., Kent, OH 44242-0001 USA (SAN 201-0437) Tel 330-672-7913; Fax: 330-672-3104; *Imprints:* Black Squirrel Books (Blck Squir)
E-mail: scash@kent.edu
Web site: http://www.kentstateuniversitypress.com
Dist(s): **Baker & Taylor Publisher Services (BTPS)**
Follett School Solutions
MyiLibrary
Partners Bk. Distributing, Inc.
ebrary, Inc.; *CIP.*

Kentauron, *(978-1-64673)* 11923 NE Sumner St, Portland, OR 97220 USA Tel 408-695-3872
E-mail: kentauron@kentauron.com.

Keogh, Anne, *(978-1-938993)* 132 S. Battery St., Charleston, SC 29401 USA Tel 843-722-7350
E-mail: akeogh98@hotmail.com
Web site: www.annetoddbooks.com.

Keokee Bks. *Imprint of* **Keokee Co. Publishing, Inc.**

Keokee Co. Publishing, Inc., *(978-1-879628)* Orders Addr.: P.O. Box 722, Sandpoint, ID 83864 USA Tel 208-263-3573; Fax: 208-263-4045; Toll Free: 800-880-3573; Edit Addr.: 405 Church St., Sandpoint, ID 83864-1346 USA; *Imprints:* Keokee Books (Keokee Bks)
E-mail: books@keokee.com; officemanager@keokee.com
Web site: http://www.keokee.com; http://www.keokeebooks.com.

Kepler Pr., *(978-0-9713770)* Orders Addr.: P.O. Box 400326, Cambridge, MA 02140 USA (SAN 255-6014) Tel 617-413-7204
E-mail: ealex@keplerpress.com
Web site: http://www.keplerpress.com
Dist(s): **Ingram Content Group.**

Keriouspyeseries LLC, *(978-0-615-45033-9; 978-0-615-55447-1; 978-0-9899654; 978-0-692-88383-9; 978-1-7324965)* 12437 N. Portland Ave., Mequon, WI 53092 USA Tel 262-243-1299
E-mail: keriouspyeseries@att.net.

Kerlak Enterprises, Inc. *See* **Dark Oak Pr.**

Kerpluggo Bks. LLC, *(978-0-9762429)* 1015 W. Webster Ave., Suite 3, Chicago, IL 60614 USA Tel 773-665-8075
E-mail: mbwillian2@yahoo.com.

Kerr, Alex, *(978-0-9753076)* 145 Lincoln Rd. Apt. 2L, Brooklyn, NY 11225-4017 USA
E-mail: alexkerr@earthlink.net.

Kerr, Charles H. Publishing Co., *(978-0-88286; 978-1-7326067; 978-1-7378971)* Orders Addr.: 8901 S. Exchange Ave., Chicago, IL 60617 USA (SAN 207-7043) Tel 773-465-7774 (orders); 847-328-2132 (orders); Fax: 773-472-7857 (orders)
E-mail: charles.h.kerr.pub@gmail.com; arcane@ripco.com
Web site: http://www.charleshkerr.net
Dist(s): **AK Pr. Distribution**
SPD-Small Pr. Distribution.

Kerr Company, The *See* **K.C. Fox Publishing**

Kerr, Justin & Shelley, *(978-0-9716408)* 10735 Atascadero Ave., Atascadero, CA 93422-5723 USA
Web site: http://www.kirra-rincon.com.

Kes & Kyd Publishing, *(978-1-960925)* 97 S Mann Cir, Camp Verde, AZ 86322 USA Tel 602-323-7002
E-mail: navarreedward@gmail.com.

Kessinger Publishing Company *See* **Kessinger Publishing, LLC**

Kessinger Publishing, LLC, *(978-0-7661; 978-0-922802; 978-1-56459; 978-1-4179; 978-1-4191; 978-1-4192; 978-1-4253; 978-1-4254; 978-1-4286; 978-1-4304; 978-1-4325; 978-1-4326; 978-0-548; 978-1-4365; 978-1-4366; 978-1-4367; 978-1-4368; 978-1-4369; 978-1-4370; 978-1-4371; 978-1-4372; 978-1-4373; 978-1-4374; 978-1-104; 978-1-120; 978-1-160; 978-1-161; 978-1-162; 978-1-163; 978-1-164; 978-1-165; 978-1-166; 978-1-167; 978-1-168; 978-1-169) Orders Addr.: P.O. Box 1404, Whitefish, MT 59937 USA (SAN 251-4621) Fax: 406-897-7825*
E-mail: kpreply55@runbox.com
Web site: http://www.kessinger.net
Dist(s): **Ingram Content Group.**

Kesterson & Associates *See* **Big Valley Publishing**

Kestrel Pubns., *(978-0-9628472; 978-0-9881925)* 1811 Stonewood Dr., Dayton, OH 45432-4002 USA Tel 937-426-5110; Fax: 937-320-1832; Toll Free: 800-314-4678 (orders only)
E-mail: invisiblei@aol.com.

Keszler, E., *(978-0-615-19548-3; 978-0-615-36360-8)* 6779 Sienna Club Pl., Lauderhill, FL 33319 USA
E-mail: uniqueart613@gmail.com.

Ketabe Gooya Publishing LLC, *(978-1-933429)* Orders Addr.: 6400 Canoga Ave., Suite 355, Woodland Hills, CA 91367 USA Tel 818-346-8338; Toll Free: 800-515-0069
E-mail: nasser@farrokh.us
Web site: http://www.ketabegooya.com.

Ketman Publishing *See* **Wooster Bk. Co., The**

Kevin W W Blackley Bks., LLC, *(978-0-9960839; 978-1-950039)* 280 E. Treehaven Rd, BUFFALO, NY 14215 USA Tel 716-316-6336
E-mail: kevin.blackley@gmail.com.

kevindkone, *(978-0-9997562)* 10116 lonesome pine Dr., knoxville, TN 37932 USA Tel 801-380-1142
E-mail: kevindkone@gmail.com.

Kew Publishing (GBR) *(978-0-947643; 978-1-900347; 978-0-85521; 978-1-84246) Dist. by* **Chicago Distribution Ctr.**

Key Answer Products, Inc., *(978-0-9642823)* 108 S. Third St., Suite 4, Bloomingdale, IL 60108 USA (SAN 255-805X) Tel 630-893-4007; Fax: 630-893-4030; Toll Free: 800-539-1233
E-mail: dcowhey@ci-inc.com
Web site: http://www.ci-inc/what/what.htm.

Key of David Publishing, *(978-1-886987)* Subs. of House of David, Orders Addr.: PO Box 947, Palatka, FL 32178 USA Tel 800-829-8777 (phone/fax); Toll Free: 800-829-8777 Do not confuse with Key of David Publishing, Poughquag, NY
E-mail: info@redeemedisrael.com
Web site: http://www.keyofdavidpublishing.com.

Key Publishers, Incorporated *See* **City Creek Pr., Inc.**

Key, Veverly & Prinzwono, *(978-0-615-13786-5)* 5081 Cates Ave., Saint Louis, MO 63108 USA
Dist(s): **Lulu Pr., Inc.**

Keyboarding First, LLC, *(978-0-9768426)* 6919 Prairie Dr., Middleton, WI 53562-5356 USA Tel 608-836-4404 (phone/fax); Fax: 608-836-4405
E-mail: psm.janet@tds.net.

KEYGARD, *(978-0-9767086)* Orders Addr.: 7887 Broadway, Suite 506, San Antonio, TX 78209 USA Tel 210-829-5074; Fax: 210-829-5132
E-mail: bhkeyser@aol.com.

Keyhole Pr., *(978-0-9821512; 978-0-615-59031-8; 978-0-615-61927-9; 978-0-692-83815-0)* Div. of Dzanc Bks.,
E-mail: info@keyholepress.com
Web site: http://www.keyholepress.com
Dist(s): **Consortium Bk. Sales & Distribution**
CreateSpace Independent Publishing Platform
MyiLibrary
Smashwords.

Keylon, Robi, *(978-0-578-92961-3)* 5815 Aster Rd., Knoxville, TN 37918 USA Tel 865-382-1253
E-mail: ratstudioart@gmail.com
Web site: https://www.lulu.com/.

Keysquake Music, *(978-0-9760837)* 42 Blackfoot Ct., Guilford, CT 06437 USA
E-mail: bgillie48@yahoo.com
Web site: http://www.briangillie.com.

Keystone College Pr., *(978-0-9623862; 978-1-879205; 978-1-64042)* One College Green, La Plume, PA 18440-0200 USA Tel 570-945-5141 x 3007; *Imprints:* Swingin' Bridge Books (SwinginBridge)
E-mail: raymond.hammond@keystone.edu; nightshadepress@keystone.edu; kcpress@keystone.edu
Web site: http://www.keystone.edu.

Keytochange Publishing, Inc., *(978-0-9729798)* 7484 University Ave. Ste. T, La Mesa, CA 91941-6030 USA
E-mail: sjones@keytochange.com
Web site: http://www.keytochange.com.

Keywords Press *Imprint of* **Atria Bks.**

Khalexandra Bks., *(978-1-949558)* 500 Westover Dr. No. 13880, Sanford, NC 27330 USA Tel 937-421-6511
E-mail: khalexandra80@gmail.com
Web site: www.khalexandra.com.

Khalfani, Natasha, *(978-0-692-38558-6)* 4500 Governor Pratt Ct., Upper Marlboro, MD 20772 USA Tel 301-580-3786
E-mail: khalfani.law@gmail.com.

Khanna, Rachel, *(978-0-9779568)* 163 John St., Greenwich, CT 06831 USA (SAN 850-7260)
Web site: http://www.liveeatcookhealthy.com.

Khesed Foundation, *(978-0-9785077)* Orders Addr.: 633 S. Plymouth Ct, Chicago, IL 60605-6060 USA Tel 615-792-1449; Edit Addr.: 1030 Trouble Ct., No. 1005, Ashland City, TN 37015-6060 USA (SAN 850-7236)
E-mail: hankbo@juno.com.

Khunum Productions, Inc., *(978-0-9797010)* Khunum Productions, Inc. 149 Bainbridge St., Suite 3, Brooklyn, NY 11233 USA Tel 718-924-8779
E-mail: Khunumproductions@gmail.com; Nehprii@msn.com
Web site: http://www.NehpriiAmenii.com.

Kia Harris, LLC (Publishing Co.), *(978-1-7342186; 978-1-953237)* 295 Princeton Highstown Rd 11-314, West Windsor, NJ 08550-3123 USA Tel 732-658-2018
E-mail: info@khpublishers.com
Web site: www.khpublishers.com.

Kiazpora LLC, *(978-0-9966362; 978-1-946057; 978-1-960768)* P.O. Box 2184, Union City, CA 94587 USA Tel 408-230-0340
E-mail: info@kiazpora.com.

Kick The Ball, *(978-0-9790396; 978-1-934372; 978-1-61320)* Orders Addr.: 8595 Columbus Pike Suite 197, Lewis Center, OH 43035 USA
E-mail: pfwilson@triviagamebooks.com; tprippey@triviagamebooks.com
Web site: http://www.triviagamebooks.com; http://www.bythenumberbook.com
Dist(s): **Partners Bk. Distributing, Inc.**

Kickapoo Farms *See* **Genuine Prints, LLC**

Kicks and Giggles Today, *(978-0-615-20924-1; 978-0-615-54874-6)* P.O. Box 1023, Ross, CA 94957 USA
Web site: http://www.kicksandgigglestoday.com.

Kicky Cane Pr., *(978-1-7342789)* 221 W. Illinois St., Bellingham, WA 98225 USA Tel 206-992-9259
E-mail: courtneyshannonstrand@gmail.com
Web site: courtneyshannonstrand.com.

Kid by Kid, Incorporated, *(978-0-9745496)* 54249 Myrica Dr., Macomb, MI 48042 USA Tel 586-781-2345 (phone/fax)
E-mail: kidbykid@comcast.net
Web site: http://www.crystalkids.net.

Kid Fuse *Imprint of* **Joyride Bks.**

Kid Niche Christian Bks., *(978-0-9852712; 978-0-9904626; 978-0-9994837)* 9958 Edgewood Ave, Traverse City, MI 49686-5845 USA.

Kid Niche Publishing *See* **Kid Niche Christian Bks.**

Kid Prep, Inc., *(978-1-58312)* 6942 FM 1960 E-132, Humble, TX 77346 USA Tel 281-852-5261; Fax: 281-852-4901; *Imprints:* Little Chameleon Books (Little Chameleon)
E-mail: customerservice@kidprep.com
Web site: http://www.kidprep.com.

KiD Sounds, *(978-0-9767650)* P.O. Box 13888, Las Vegas, NV 89112-1888 USA
Web site: http://www.kid-sounds.com.

kid2kid publishing, *(978-0-615-48783-0; 978-0-692-58147-6)* 2577 Cove Point Pl., Virginia Beach, VA 23455 USA Tel 757-375-5020
E-mail: kfk1313@yahoo.com
Dist(s): **CreateSpace Independent Publishing Platform.**

KidBiz 3000 *See* **Achieve3000**

KidBookInk Publishing, LLC, *(978-0-9776772)* Orders Addr.: 25809 Nichols Rd., Columbia Station, OH 44028 USA (SAN 257-9103) Tel 440-725-7587; Fax: 440-236-5356; Toll Free: 888-978-1669
E-mail: dbvanhorn@yahoo.com
Web site: http://www.kidbookink.com; http://www.storyboard4kidz.com.

Kidder, Clark, *(978-0-615-15313-1; 978-0-692-58895-6; 978-0-692-82942-4; 978-1-7364884)* 1620 Sienna Crossing, Janesville, WI 53546 USA
Web site: http://www.clarkkidder.com.

Kidderature Publishing, *(978-0-9729703)* P.O. Box 612, Hammondsport, NY 14840 USA Tel 607-292-3026
E-mail: bobhicks@citlink.net
Web site: http://www.kidderature.com.

Kiddy Chronicles Publishing (CAN) *(978-0-9699203; 978-0-9733994) Dist. by* **Firefly Bks Limited.**

Kid-E Bks. *Imprint of* **Word Productions**

Kidhaven *Imprint of* **Cengage Gale**

KidHaven Publishing *Imprint of* **Greenhaven Publishing LLC**

Kidible *Imprint of* **iCharacter.org**

Kidpub Pr., *(978-0-9840807; 978-1-936184; 978-1-61018)* P.O. Box 724, North Attleboro, MA 02761 USA (SAN 858-365X) Tel 401-466-4176; Toll Free: 800-252-5224 (orders/editorial)
E-mail: pd@kidpub.com; orders@kidpub.com
Web site: http://bookstore.kidpub.com; http://www.kidpub.com.

Kidrich Corp., *(978-0-9761051)* 347 5th Ave., Suite 610, New York, NY 10016 USA Tel 718-767-5135; Toll Free: 800-231-7385
Web site: http://www.kidrich.com.

Kids 4 Ever, *(978-0-9764433)* P.O. Box 1784, Holland, MI 49422 USA Tel 616-566-1231
E-mail: kids4ever@charter.net
Web site: http://www.kids4everbooks.com.

Kids Activity Publishing, *(978-1-946525; 978-1-954392; 978-1-956397)*
E-mail: activitypublishingkids@gmail.com.

Kids Ahead Bks. *Imprint of* **WND Bks, Inc.**

Kids At Heart Publishing & Books *See* **Kids At Heart Publishing, LLC**

Kids At Heart Publishing, LLC, *(978-0-615-36340-0; 978-0-9828109; 978-0-9836641; 978-0-9855202; 978-0-9886360; 978-0-9899472; 978-0-9905734; 978-0-9964962; 978-0-9969574; 978-1-946171; 978-1-956628)* P.O. Box 492, Milton, IN 47357 USA Tel 765-478-5873
Dist(s): **Davis/Books Distribution.**

Kids At Our House, Inc., The, *(978-0-9705773; 978-1-942390)* Orders Addr.: 47 Stoneham Pl., Metuchen, NJ 08840 USA Tel 732-548-1779
E-mail: info@dannyandkim.com
Web site: www.dannyandkim.com
Dist(s): **Follett School Solutions**
Indig, Stanley M. Specialty Pubn.

Kids Bk. Pr., *(978-0-692-23217-0; 978-0-692-37117-6; 978-0-692-37484-9; 978-0-692-46037-5; 978-0-692-51635-5; 978-0-692-51675-1; 978-0-692-54962-9; 978-0-692-56562-9; 978-0-692-58944-1; 978-0-692-59953-2; 978-0-692-61637-6; 978-0-692-62920-8; 978-0-692-71803-2; 978-0-692-73023-2) 1352 E. Sunshine, Springfield, MO 65804 USA Tel 417-881-6537*
E-mail: sharon@paperback-press.com
Dist(s): **CreateSpace Independent Publishing Platform.**

Kids Books Rule! *See* **Anthropology Major Publishing**

Kids Camping Bks., *(978-1-951633)* 6960 Kirkridge Ct., Shelby Township, MI 48316 USA Tel 703-597-1511
E-mail: teamsponsler@gmail.com
Web site: www.kidscampingbooks.com.

Kids Can *Imprint of* **Proactive Publishing**

Kids Can Pr., Ltd. (CAN) *(978-0-919964; 978-0-921103; 978-1-55074; 978-1-55337; 978-1-894786; 978-1-55453; 978-1-77138) Dist. by* **HachBkGrp.**

Kids Can Pr., Ltd. (CAN) *(978-0-919964; 978-0-921103; 978-1-55074; 978-1-55337; 978-1-894786; 978-1-55453; 978-1-77138) Dist. by* **Children Plus.**

Kids Children & Teens World 2000 & Beyond, *(978-0-9747543)* Orders Addr.: P.O. Box 385, Brandywine, MD 20613 USA Fax: 301-372-9979; Edit Addr.: 8300 Belding Ct., Brandywine, MD 20613 USA
E-mail: djospeh301@aol.com.

Kids Core *Imprint of* **ABDO Publishing Co.**

Kid's Creative Classics *Imprint of* **BrassHeart Music**

Kids, Critters & Country Publishing, *(978-0-9755200)* P.O. Box 866874, Plano, TX 75086-6874 USA
E-mail: jlarsen@chasewest.com
Web site: http://www.kidscrittersandcountry.com.

Kids Donate, Inc., *(978-0-9754131)* 221 Chesley Ln., Chapel Hill, NC 27514 USA Tel 919-967-0882.

Kids For Health, Inc., *(978-0-9759517; 978-1-933847)* P.O. Box 326, Springdale, AR 72763 USA Tel 479-756-9551; Fax: 479-756-0949.

Kids Go Europe, Inc., *(978-0-9772699)* P.O. Box 4014, Menlo Park, CA 94026 USA Tel 650-743-7404
E-mail: info@kidsgoeurope.com
Web site: http://www.kidsgoeurope.com.

Kids in Ministry International, *(978-0-9767647; 978-0-9815940)* P.O. Box 549, Mandan, ND 58554-0549 USA
Web site: http://www.kidsinministry.com.

Kids Life Pr., *(978-0-9755348; 978-0-9903172)* P.O. Box 3484, Pismo Beach, CA 93448-3484 USA Fax: 805-888-2838; Toll Free: 800-262-8973; 109 Hermosa Drive, Pismo Beach, CA 93449 Tel 805-773-4422
E-mail: tuzee@charter.net.

Kids Rehab Spa, *(978-0-692-92453-2)* 1220 Heritage Lakes Dr., Mableton, GA 30126 USA Tel 404-317-4894
E-mail: Kimgreene563@gmail.com.

Kid's Shelf, *(978-0-9729339)* 19600 Baker Rd., Gambier, OH 43022 USA Tel 740-247-2427.

Kids Think Big LLC, *(978-0-9797362)* P.O. Box 11013, Greenwich, CT 06831 USA (SAN 854-2597)
E-mail: info@kidsthinkbig.com
Web site: http://www.kidsthinkbig.com
Dist(s): **Distributors, The**
Follett School Solutions.

Kids Write On, LLC, *(978-0-615-23574-5)* Orders Addr.: P.O. Box 700924, Dallas, TX 75370 USA Tel 972-862-7257; Fax: 972-862-0194; Toll Free: 877-596-7257
Web site: http://www.thestaplercaper.com.

Kids1st Bks. *Imprint of* **BC Publishing**

Kidsafety of America, *(978-1-884413)* 6288 Susana St., Chino, CA 91710 USA
E-mail: peter@kidsafetystore.com
Web site: http://www.kidsafetystore.com
Dist(s): **Follett School Solutions.**

Kidsbooks, Incorporated *See* **Kidsbooks, LLC**

Kidsbooks, LLC, *(978-0-942025; 978-1-56156; 978-1-58865; 978-1-62885; 978-1-63854)* 5307 Ballard Ave NW, Seattle, WA 98107 USA (SAN 666-3729)
E-mail: jolesek@kidsbookspublishing.com
Web site: http://www.kidsbookspublishing.com
Dist(s): **Independent Pubs. Group.**

KidsCanPublish.Org, *(978-0-692-76150-2; 978-0-692-77349-9; 978-0-692-78442-6; 978-0-692-84092-4; 978-0-692-07621-7)* 1020 Brookview Ct., Morgan Hill, CA 95037 USA Tel 408-607-0986
E-mail: kidscanpublish@gmail.com
Web site: www.KidsCanPublish.Org.

Kidscope, Inc., *(978-0-9647798)* 2045 Peachtree Rd NE Ste. 150, Atlanta, GA 30309-1405 USA.

KidsDiscuss.com, *(978-0-9749244)* PCS, Orders Addr.: P.O. Box 6102, Edmonds, WA 98026 USA
E-mail: JeanTracy@KidsDiscuss.com
Web site: http://www.KidsDiscuss.com.

KidsGive, LLC, *(978-0-9792912; 978-0-9845910)* 5757 W. Century Blvd., Suite 800, Box 8, Los Angeles, CA 90045 USA (SAN 853-0297) Tel 310-665-9777; Fax: 310-665-9494
E-mail: lmuniz@kidsgive.com
Web site: http://www.kidsgive.com.

Kidskills America *Imprint of* **Kidskills International**

Kidskills International, *(978-0-9710641)* Div. of Creekside Creations, 1031 Cahoon Rd., Westlake, OH 44145-1232 USA Tel 440-835-5071 (phone/fax); *Imprints:* Kidskills America (Kidskills Amer)
E-mail: kidskills@wowway.com; diane@kidskills.com
Web site: http://www.kidskills.com.

KIDSRIGHTS *Imprint of* **JIST Publishing**

Kidsrights, 10100 Park Cedar Dr., Charlotte, NC 28210 USA (SAN 299-2809) Tel 704-541-0100; Fax: 704-541-0113; Toll Free: 888-970-5437 Do not confuse with Kidsrights, Mount Dora, FL.

Kidstalk, LLC, *(978-0-9776144)* P.O. Box 520, Sherman, TX 75091 USA (SAN 257-7992) Tel 903-436-0858; Fax: 903-893-1614
E-mail: kidstalk@cableone.net
Web site: http://www.kidstalkmag.com.

Kidstory Pr., *(978-0-9772231)* P.O. Box 75, Brighton, MI 48116-0075 USA Tel 517-204-9030
E-mail: kidstorypress@comcast.net
Web site: http://www.kidstorypress.home.comcast.net.

KidsWorld Bks. (CAN) *(978-0-9938401; 978-1-988183; 978-0-9940069) Dist. by* **Lone Pine.**

Kidware Software, LLC, *(978-1-937161; 978-1-937161-25-5; 978-1-951077)* P.O. Box 701, Maple Valley, WA 98038 USA Tel 425-413-1185
E-mail: phil@kidwaresoftware.com; phil@biblebytebooks.com
Web site: http://www.kidwaresoftware.com; http://www.biblebytebooks.com; http://www.computerscienceforkids.com.

Kidwick Bks., *(978-0-9703809)* 363 S. Saltair Ave., First Fl., Los Angelas, CA 90049 USA Tel 310-471-2472; Fax: 310-861-8111
E-mail: mail@kidwick.com
Web site: http://www.kidwick.com
Dist(s): **National Bk. Network.**

Kidz & Katz Publishing Co., *(978-1-883371)* 752 Brandon Pl., Wheeling, IL 60090 USA Fax: 708-860-0513.

Kidz By Dezign Pr., Inc., *(978-0-9771030)* 1881 Kingston Way, Lawrenceville, GA 30044 USA (SAN 256-7121) Tel 770-962-2181; Fax: 678-615-2247; Toll Free: 800-719-5439
E-mail: info@slumbergirls.com
Web site: http://www.slumbergirls.com.

Kidz Entertainment, Inc., *(978-0-9795049; 978-0-9891954)* P.O. Box 0301, Baldwin, NY 11510 USA Fax: 516-223-6546
E-mail: dcorrado@optonline.net
Web site: http://www.chanteusemusic.com.

Kidz Krave Inc., *(978-0-9764144)* P.O. Box 88350, Houston, TX 77288 USA
Web site: http://www.prettypainful.com.

Kidzpoetz Publishing, *(978-0-9760220)* P.O. Box 621, New City, NY 10956 USA Tel 845-536-5505; Fax: 845-323-4272
E-mail: robertkurkela@kidzpoetz.com
Web site: http://www.kidzpoetz.com
Dist(s): **Quality Bks., Inc.**

Kidzup Productions, *(978-1-894281; 978-1-894677)* 555 VT Rte. 78, Suite 146, Box 717, Swanton, VT 05488 USA Toll Free: 888-321-5437 (888-321-KIDS)
E-mail: info@kidzup.com
Web site: http://www.kidzup.com
Dist(s): **Penton Overseas, Inc.**

eliszewski, Shelia, *(978-0-615-25575-0; 978-0-578-00002-2)* 2192 Willow Springs Dr., Stevens Point, WI 54481 USA
E-mail: shellabrt@yahoo.com
Dist(s): **Lulu Pr., Inc.**

ies Publishing Co., *(978-0-9767437)* Orders Addr.: P.O. Box 923572, Sylmar, CA 91392-3572 USA Tel 818-367-8416
E-mail: kies@kies.org
Web site: http://www.kies.org.

iki Hse. Pr., *(978-1-7365263)* 7s910 Camp Dean, Big rock, IL 60511 USA Tel 630-450-1652
E-mail: bmenzel122@aol.com.

ila Springs Pr., *(978-0-9716481; 978-1-7338479)* Div. of Kila Springs Group, 4231 Oak Meadow Rd., Placerville, CA 95667 USA Tel 530-621-2297; Fax: 206-202-1309
E-mail: press@kilasprings.net
Web site: http://kilasprings.net/KSPress.html.

Kilbride, Harry, *(978-0-578-14015-5; 978-0-578-14016-2)*.

Killer Sports Publishing, *(978-1-933135)* Orders Addr.: P.O. Box 862, Berea, OH 44017 USA Tel 440-239-1854; Edit Addr.: 201 S. Rocky River Rd., Berea, OH 44017 USA
Web site: http://www.killersports.com.

Killingbeck, Dale, *(978-0-9762758)* 18300 Tustin Rd., Tustin, MI 49677 USA Tel 231-829-3084.

Kilsby, Raymond *See* **RK Enterprises, Inc.**

Kim Is Thirsty Again, *(978-0-9725827)* 1256 Cranwood Square N., Columbus, OH 43229-1341 USA Tel 614-975-3989
E-mail: kfreeman2038@sbcglobal.net
Web site: http://www.kimisthirstyagain.com.

Kim Lucretia Writes, *(978-0-615-72408-9; 978-0-692-02264-1; 978-0-692-02265-8; 978-0-692-37020-9; 978-0-692-37121-3; 978-0-692-11369-1; 978-0-578-86862-2)* 4290 Weston Dr., Lilburn, GA 30047 USA Tel 404-207-9181
E-mail: edwardskim5@aol.com
Web site: kimlucretia.com.

Kim Pearson, *(978-1-881849)* 16442 SE 42nd Pl., Issaquah, WA 98027 USA Tel 425-865-0409 (phone/fax)
E-mail: info@primary-sources.com
Web site: http://www.primary-sources.com/
Dist(s): **Smashwords.**

Kimball, Robert, *(978-1-7345064)* 7 Wessale Ln., Patagonia, AZ 85624 USA Tel 520-394-2481
E-mail: robertkimball326@gmail.com.

Kimber Stories, *(978-0-9767773)* Orders Addr.: P.O. Box 143, Woodlake, CA 93286 USA; Edit Addr.: 37811 Millwood Dr., Woodlake, CA 93286 USA
E-mail: kimberstories@yahoo.com.

KimberCourt Pr., *(978-0-9891822)* 3001 W. 10th St. Unit 219, Panama City, FL 32401 USA Tel 850-668-0514
E-mail: info@bootshensel.com
Web site: www.bootshensel.com.

Kimberlite Publishing Co., *(978-0-9632675)* 44091 Olive Ave., Hemet, CA 92544-2609 USA Tel 951-927-7726 Do not confuse with Kimberlite Publishing, Ventura, CA
E-mail: frumpypapa@yahoo.com.

Kimberly Freeman *See* **Kim Is Thirsty Again**

Kimberly M. Nesmith *See* **Ms. Education Publishing, LLC**

Kimberly Pr., LLC, *(978-0-9668611)* 100 Westport Ave., Norwalk, CT 06851 USA (SAN 251-2483) Tel 203-750-6101; Fax: 203-846-3472.

Kimble, George J., *(978-0-9767024)* 4941 Hickory Woods E., Antioch, TN 37013 USA
Web site: http://www.theroadpoet.com.

Kimm Irwin, *(978-1-7359158)* 13600 NE 228th Ct, Brush Prairie, WA 98606 USA Tel 541-571-5312
E-mail: kimmsirwin@gmail.com.

Kin Pr., *(978-0-9989293; 979-8-9880365)*
E-mail: affinitystudio@yahoo.com
Web site: www.kinpress.org.

Kincy, Karen, *(978-1-7379251)* 749 Haverhill Dr, Sunnyvale, CA 94087 USA Tel 425-246-1215
E-mail: KarenLKincy@gmail.com
Web site: www.karenkincy.com.

Kind Critter Junction, *(978-0-9752842)* P.O. Box 30249, Indianapolis, IN 46220 USA Toll Free: 888-366-3525
E-mail: info@kindcritterjunction.com
Web site: http://www.kindcritterjunction.com.

Kind Eye Publishing, *(978-0-9992262)* P.O. Box 511, MASON, OH 45040 USA Tel 202-270-8470
E-mail: avanti@kindeyepublishing.com
Web site: www.kindeyepublishing.com.

Kind Word Publishing, *(978-1-7358815)* po box 143, Woodstock, VT 05091 USA Tel 802-291-4272
E-mail: jooliveryeager@gmail.com.

Kind World Publishing & Consulting, LLC, *(978-1-63894)* 4789 LONDON LN, EAGAN, MN 55122 USA Tel 952-457-7749
E-mail: pstockland@kindworldpublishing.com
Web site: www.kindworldpublishing.com
Dist(s): **Publishers Group West (PGW).**

Kinder Shpiel USA, Inc., *(978-1-937637; 978-1-68091)* 199 Lee Ave. PMB 148, Brooklyn, NY 11211 USA Tel 718-305-7540
Web site: WWW.Kindershpiel.com.

KinderBach L.L.C., *(978-0-9773005)* P.O. Box 336, Hudson, IA 50643 USA (SAN 257-2397) Toll Free: 866-988-9814
E-mail: info@kinderbach.com
Web site: http://www.kinderbach.com.

Kinderhaus Publishing Co., *(978-0-578-05104-8)* 2970 Edgewick Dr., Glendale, CA 91206 USA
E-mail: bettyfritz@kinderhauspublishing.com.

Kindermusik International, *(978-0-945613; 978-1-931127; 978-1-58987; 978-1-948952)* Orders Addr.: 2606 Phoenix Dr., Greensboro, NC 27406 USA (SAN 247-3747) Tel 336-273-3363; Fax: 336-273-2023; Toll Free: 800-628-5687; Edit Addr.: 6204 Corporate Park Dr., Browns Summit, NC 27214 USA (SAN 247-3755)
E-mail: info@kindermusik.com; dkells@kindermusik.com
Web site: http://www.kindermusik.com.

Kindle Health + Fox Song Books *See* **Fox Song Bks.**

Kindness Kids, *(978-0-578-94381-7; 978-0-578-94382-4)* 370 S. Peralta Hills Dr., Anaheim, CA 92807 USA Tel 646-724-4102
E-mail: m.mahoney@eevijones.com.

Kindness Learning Co. LLC, The, *(978-0-9967943; 979-8-9880557)* 300 E 54th St Apt 34BC, New York, NY 10022 USA Tel 914-752-8378
E-mail: carazelas@gmail.com.

Kindness Queen's Empire, The, *(978-0-9889060)* 7850 Wildwood Rd., Jacksonville, FL 32211-6046 USA Tel 904-723-0116
E-mail: dbsmith10@comcast.net.

Kindred Press *See* **Kindred Productions**

Kindred Productions, *(978-0-921788; 978-0-919797)* Orders Addr.: 315 S. Lincoln St., Hillsboro, KS 67063 USA Tel 316-947-3151; Fax: 316-947-3266; Toll Free: 800-545-7322
E-mail: kindred@mbconf.ca
Web site: http://www.mbconf.org/kindred.htm
Dist(s): **Spring Arbor Distributors, Inc.**

Kindred Trade LLC, *(978-0-692-08598-1)* 2809 W Bluefield Ave., Phoenix, AZ 85053 USA Tel 602-315-0259
E-mail: sales@kindredtrade.com
Web site: www.thedesertmermaid.com.

Kinfolk Research Pr., *(978-0-9712564)* P.O. Box 6303, Plymouth, MI 48170 USA Tel 734-454-1883
E-mail: KinfolkPress@aol.com
Web site: http://cheekfamilychronicles.homestead.com/CheekFamilyChronicles.html.

King & Castle Publishing LLC *See* **King & Castle Publishing LLC**

King & Castle Publishing LLC, *(978-1-949778)* 2134 W Ditch Creek Dr, Meridian, ID 83646 USA Tel 623-455-6426
E-mail: kelvan@yahoo.com.

King, Cawanna, *(978-1-7353856)* 5703 Gloria Dr., Suitland, MD 20746 USA Tel 202-557-8601
E-mail: kingcawanna@gmail.com.

King Joe Educational Enterprises, Inc., *(978-0-9728596; 978-0-9773902)* Orders Addr.: P.O. Box 86, Los Alamitos, CA 90720 USA Tel 562-430-8600; Fax: 562-598-5940; Toll Free: 866-818-5464 (866-818-KING); Edit Addr.: 3112 Inverness Dr., Los Alamitos, CA 90720 USA
E-mail: lindarodgers@kingjoe.com
Web site: http://www.kingjoe.com.

King, Joel, *(978-0-9787820)* 547 McLean Ave., Hopkinsville, KY 42240 USA
E-mail: joelk3@bellsouth.net.

King, Julia, *(978-0-615-34585-7; 978-0-615-37032-3; 978-0-9839827)* 13565 Watsonville Rd., Morgan Hill, CA 95037 USA Tel 408-591-6465
E-mail: wyethia3@yahoo.com.

King, Laurence Publishing (GBR) *(978-1-85669; 978-1-898113; 978-1-78067; 978-1-78627) Dist. by* **HachBkGrp.**

King, Marcy, *(978-0-9850752)* 4107 Sunset Ave., Chester, VA 23831 USA Tel 804-683-0517
E-mail: marcy.king@yahoo.com.

King Production, A, *(978-0-9755811; 978-0-9843325; 978-0-9860045; 978-0-9913890; 978-1-942217; 979-8-9861059; 978-1-958834)* P.O. Box 912, Collierville, TN 38017 USA Tel 917-279-1363; Fax: 201-624-7225
E-mail: joyking1993@yahoo.com
Web site: www.joydejaking.com
Dist(s): **Children's Plus, Inc.**

King, Rose, *(978-1-7340008; 978-1-7362060)* 23063 Plumbrooke Dr., Southfield, MI 48075 USA Tel 248-796-9510
E-mail: susanne.collyer@gmail.com.

King St Bks./Stabler-Leadbeater Apothecary Museum, *(978-0-9763945)* 410 S Fairfax St., Alexandria, VA 22314 USA Fax: 703-456-7890
Web site: http://apothecarymuseum.org.

King, Terri Ann *See* **Paulus Publishing**

Kingdom Builders Pubn., *(978-0-578-12048-5; 978-0-578-13238-9; 978-0-578-13304-1; 978-0-578-13488-8; 978-0-578-13932-6; 978-0-578-13991-3; 978-0-578-14385-9; 978-0-578-14627-0; 978-0-578-14843-4; 978-0-578-14903-5; 978-0-578-14909-7; 978-0-578-15487-9; 978-0-692-38109-0; 978-0-692-38120-5; 978-0-692-38123-6; 978-0-692-39146-4; 978-0-692-40038-8; 978-0-578-15969-0; 978-0-692-41566-5; 978-0-692-45673-6; 978-0-692-45674-3; 978-0-692-45975-1; 978-0-692-50699-8; 978-0-692-52648-4; 978-0-692-53342-0; 978-0-692-53343-7;) 1641 Omarest Dr., Columbia, SC 29210 USA*
Web site: www.kingdombuilderspublications.com
Dist(s): **CreateSpace Independent Publishing Platform.**

Kingdom Come Pr., *(978-0-9749423)* 15122 N. Berwick Ln., Upper Marlboro, MD 20774 USA (SAN 255-8874) Tel 202-607-0496
E-mail: info@bookwormbooks.biz
Web site: http://www.bookwormbooks.biz.

Kingdom Door Publishing LLC, *(978-0-9974913)* P.O. Box 2144, Amarillo, TX 79105 USA Tel 806-676-5087
E-mail: wholehearted8@yahoo.com
Web site: kingdomdoor.org.

Kingdom Kaught Publishing LLC, *(978-0-9824550; 978-0-9964040; 978-0-9982100; 978-1-947741)* 1350 Blair Dr., Odenton, MD 21113 USA (SAN 858-2033)
E-mail: kingdompublishingllc@gmail.com
Web site: http://www.kingdompublishingllc.com.

Kingdom Publishers *See* **Cathedral of the Holy Spirit**

Kingdom Publishing Co., *(978-0-9765636)* 17100 Halsted St., Harvey, IL 60426-6131 USA.

Kingdom Publishing Group, Inc., *(978-0-9745324; 978-0-9772964; 978-0-9792074; 978-0-9796130; 978-0-9801564; 978-0-9817706; 978-0-9821411; 978-0-9824084; 978-0-9825104; 978-0-9825849; 978-0-9826370; 978-0-9827484; 978-0-9829775; 978-0-9831452; 978-0-9833651; 978-0-9835721; 978-0-9839090; 978-0-9848940; 978-0-9852679; 978-0-9854693; 978-0-9896581; 978-0-9862492; 978-0-9962629; 978-0-9971518) P.O. Box 3273, Henrico, VA 23228-9705 USA*
Web site: http://www.kingdompublishing.org.

Kingdom Sound Pubs., *(978-0-9662666; 978-0-9856206)* Orders Addr.: P.O. Box 371917, Decatur, GA 30037 USA Tel 404-384-3795; Edit Addr.: 3622 Summit Trace, Suite 400, Decatur, GA 30034 USA
E-mail: kvjackson@yahoo.com.

Kingdom Talk Publishing, Incorporated *See* **Rapha Publishing**

Kingfisher *Imprint of* **Roaring Brook Pr.**

Kingfisher Bks., *(978-0-9662218)* Orders Addr.: P.O. Box 4628, Helena, MT 59604 USA Tel 406-442-2168; Toll Free: 800-879-4576; Edit Addr.: 2480 Broadway, No. 18D, Helena, MT 59601 USA
Dist(s): **Houghton Mifflin Harcourt Trade & Reference Pubs.**
Partners/West Book Distributors.

Kingfisher Publications, plc (GBR) *(978-0-7523; 978-0-7534; 978-1-85697; 978-0-86272) Dist. by* **Children Plus.**

KingMaker Bks. LLC, *(978-0-9744870)* 13315 E. Cindy St., Chandler, AZ 85225 USA
E-mail: mbogumill@juno.com.

King's Kids Trading Cards, Inc., *(978-0-9703880)* P.O. Box 923271, Sylmar, CA 91392-3271 USA Fax: 818-364-2443; Toll Free: 800-910-2690
E-mail: visioninprint@brandx.net
Web site: http://www.kingskidscards.com.

King'S Land Pr. Inc,

King's Treasure Box Ministries, The, *(978-0-9910841)* 7735 Castle Combe Ct., Cumming, GA 30040 USA Tel 678-455-3710
E-mail: roy.nancyj@gmail.com
Web site: www.kingstreasurebox.org.

King's Way Pr., *(978-0-9814748; 978-0-615-22720-7; 978-0-615-29920-4; 978-0-692-67787-2; 978-0-692-70065-5; 978-0-692-70141-6; 978-0-692-70487-5; 978-0-692-71717-2; 978-0-9988367)* 3721 New Macland Rd. Suite 200-141, Powder Springs, GA 30127 USA (SAN 855-6539) Tel 404-642-5113
E-mail: publisher@kings-way-press.com
Web site: https://stolenjesus.com/; http://www.kwp-books.com
Dist(s): **CreateSpace Independent Publishing Platform.**

Kingston Pr. (CAN) *(978-1-894997) Dist. by* **SCB Distributo.**

Kingston Publishing Co., *(978-0-9969540; 978-1-949050; 978-1-970068; 978-1-64533)* 1521 NW 31st St., Lawton, OK 73505 USA
E-mail: crystal@kingstonpublishing.com
Web site: http://www.kingstonpublishing.com.

Kingsway Pubns. (GBR) *(978-0-85476; 978-0-86065; 978-0-902088; 978-1-84291) Dist. by* **STL Dist.**

KiniArt Publishing, *(978-0-578-06335-5)* 658 SE Jerome St., Oak Harbor, WA 98277 USA
E-mail: publishing@kiniart.com
Dist(s): **Lulu Pr., Inc.**

KINJIN Global, *(978-0-9759152)* 4960 SW 32nd Ave., Dania Beach, FL 33312 USA Tel 347-826-6272
E-mail: i@dangoldman.net
Web site: http://dangoldman.net; http://redlightproperties.com.

Kinkachoo Pr., The, *(978-0-9729285)*
Web site: http://www.zhibit.org/bolan.

Kinkajou Pr. *Imprint of* **Artemesia Publishing, LLC**

Kinsey, Michael, *(978-0-578-67223-6; 978-0-578-67227-4)* 53 W. 8th St. 4RE, New York, NY 10011 USA Tel 6504715670
E-mail: michael.charles.kinsey@gmail.com
Dist(s): **Ingram Content Group.**

KinYori Bks. LLC, *(978-1-7340945)* 46036 Michigan Ave., Canton, MI 48188 USA Tel 248-321-2239
E-mail: KinyelFriday@gmail.com.

KinYori Books,LLC *See* **KinYori Bks. LLC**

Kip Kids of New York, *(978-0-9789384)* 85 Christopher St., Suite No. 5B, New York, NY 10014 USA
E-mail: KipKids@aol.com
Web site: http://www.KipKids.com.

Kirin Rise Studios, LLC, *(978-1-946003)* 120 e. anita ave, mount prospect, IL 60056 USA Tel 847-800-9679
E-mail: info@kirinrise.com
Web site: kirinrise.com.

Kirk Hse. Pubs., *(978-1-886513; 978-1-932688; 978-1-933794; 978-1-942304; 978-1-952976; 978-1-959681)* Orders Addr.: P.O. Box 390759, Minneapolis, MN 55439 USA Tel 952-835-1828; Fax: 952-952-2613; Toll Free: 888-696-1828; Edit Addr.: PO Box 390759, Minneapolis, MN 55439 USA
E-mail: publisher@kirkhouse.com; publisher@lutheranupress.org; publisher@quill-house.com
Web site: http://www.kirkhouse.com; http://www.lutheranupress.org; http://www.quill-house.com.

Kirkham, Sharon Birlson, *(978-0-9767100)* 1530 Michigan Ave., La Porte, IN 46350 USA
Dist(s): **INscribe Digital.**

KIRKLAND, JUSTIN B., *(978-0-615-81456-8)* 906 BENDLETON TRACE, ALPHARETTA, GA 30004 USA Tel 404-434-8035
E-mail: KIRKLANDJUSTIN@YMAIL.COM.

KishKnows Publishing, *(978-0-9700561; 978-1-7325756; 978-0-578-84171-7; 978-0-578-84173-1; 979-8-218-08842-2)* 3831 Janis Dr., Richton Park, IL 60471 USA Tel 708-212-4469.

Kiss A Me Productions, Inc., *(978-1-890343)* 90 Garfield Ave., Sayville, NY 11782 USA Tel 516-589-4886; Fax: 516-218-8927; Toll Free: 888-547-7263.

Kissell, Nicole, *(978-0-578-89176-7; 978-1-7371859)* 329 WashingtonAve 0, PHOENIXVILLE, PA 19460 USA Tel 6105637009
E-mail: nickikissell@gmail.com
Dist(s): **Ingram Content Group.**

KISSFAQ.COM Publishing *See* **DeJulien Publishing**

KitaabWorld.Com, LLC, *(978-0-9995476)* P.O. Box 268, MENLO PARK, CA 94025 USA Tel 650-421-3409
E-mail: gauri@kitaabworld.com
Dist(s): **Ingram Content Group.**

Kitab Pr. *Imprint of* **Kaya 20 LLC**

Kitanie Bks., *(978-0-9821262; 978-0-9841195; 978-1-935734)* P.O. Box 97, Saratoga Springs, NY 12866 USA (SAN 857-3263)
Web site: http://www.kitanie.com.

Kitanie Coloring Books *See* **Kitanie Bks.**

Kitchen Ink Publishing, *(978-1-943016)* 114 John St., New York, NY 10038 USA Tel 617-312-9026
E-mail: dottarr@kitcheninkpublishing.com
Web site: www.kitcheninkpublishing.com
Dist(s): **Hachette Bk. Group**
Independent Pubs. Group.

Kitchen Table Bks., *(978-1-7335882)* 9110 Renato St., San Diego, CA 92129 USA Tel 619-742-4280
E-mail: mmcdevitt@pacbell.net.

Kitchen Table Pubs., *(978-0-9707685)* Orders Addr.: 136 Cook-McDonald Rd., Collins, MS 39428 USA Tel 601-765-8329; Edit Addr.: 802 S. Cherry St., Collins, MS 39428 USA Tel 601-765-8329
E-mail: knight3230@bellsouth.net.

Kitchens, E. J., *(978-0-9993509; 978-1-958167)* P.O. Box 1985, Tuscaloosa, AL 35403 USA Tel 205-542-6689
E-mail: elizabeth.j.kitchens@gmail.com
Web site: www.elizabethjanekitchens.com.

Kite Tales Publishing, *(978-1-935332)* 9122 N Tennyson Dr, Milwaukee, WI 53217 USA Tel 414-803-9259
E-mail: cbohlen@wi.rr.com
Web site: http://kitetalespublishing.com.

Kitsune Bks., *(978-0-9792700; 978-0-9819495; 978-0-9827409; 978-0-9840058; 978-0-9840059)* P.O. Box 1154, Crawfordville, FL 32326-1154 USA (SAN 852-9760) Tel 850-926-3464
E-mail: anne@kitsunebooks.com; contact@kitsunebooks.com
Web site: http://www.kitsunebooks.com
Dist(s): **Bella Distribution**
Smashwords.

Kitsune Inc., *(978-0-692-53331-4; 978-0-9978028; 978-0-9989942; 978-1-951904)* 10610 S. 48th St. 2090, Phoenix, AZ 85044 USA Tel 480-235-8151
Web site: http://varnellbrandon.wix.com/brandon-author
Dist(s): **CreateSpace Independent Publishing Platform.**

Kittyco Pr., *(978-1-937922)* 6D Auburn Ct., Alexandria, VA 22305 USA Tel 703-684-3699
E-mail: kittyerussell@comcast.net.

Kiva Publishing, Inc., *(978-1-885772)* 21731 E. Buckskin Dr., Walnut, CA 91789 USA Tel 909-595-6833; Fax: 909-860-5424; Toll Free: 800-634-5482
E-mail: kivapub@aol.com
Web site: http://www.kivapub.com
Dist(s): **Canyonlands Pubns.**
New Leaf Distributing Co., Inc.
Quality Bks., Inc.
Rio Nuevo Pubs.

Kivel, Lee, *(978-0-9774999)* 6010 E. Paseo Santa Teresa, Tucson, AZ 85750 USA Tel 520-529-2802
E-mail: ghostriver@gainusa.com.

KiwE Publishing, Ltd., *(978-1-931195; 978-1-933973)* 2980 Glacier St., Anchorage, AK 99508 USA Tel 907-333-5493
E-mail: kiwe@kiwepublishing.com
Web site: http://www.kiwepublishing.com.

Kiwi Media Group, Inc., *(978-0-9743319)* P.O. Box 493, Hopkinton, MA 01748 USA Tel 508-435-4986; Fax: 508-435-0378.

Kiwi Publishing *See* **Kiwi Media Group, Inc.**

Kiykioglu, Tamer, *(978-0-578-49227-8)* 13350 SW Lancewood St, Beaverton, OR 97008 USA Tel 503-330-0196
E-mail: Tamerk007@gmail.com.

KJ Pubns., *(978-0-9792383)* 7069 Middlebury Dr., Boynton Beach, FL 33436 USA
E-mail: contactus@kidshyperspace.com
Web site: http://www.thenutrigang.com.

Kjasen, *(978-0-692-68195-4; 978-0-692-69120-5; 978-0-692-70341-0; 978-0-692-71040-1; 978-0-692-71147-7; 978-0-692-71188-0; 978-0-692-71192-7; 978-0-692-71675-5; 978-0-692-72916-8; 978-0-9977821; 978-1-7328521; 978-1-956106)* 2215 Rippling Rill St, San Antonio, TX 78232 USA Tel 210-788-0452; Toll Free: 210-788-0452
Dist(s): **CreateSpace Independent Publishing Platform.**

Kjellberg & Sons, Incorporated *See* **Kjellberg, Inc.**

Kjellberg, Inc., *(978-0-912868)* 805 W. Liberty Dr., Wheaton, IL 60187-4844 USA (SAN 201-5102) Tel 630-653-2244; Fax: 630-653-6233; *Imprints:* Kjellberg Publishers (Kjellberg Pubs)
E-mail: wsc@kjellbergprinting.com
Web site: http://kjellbergprinting.com.

Kjellberg Pubs. *Imprint of* **Kjellberg, Inc.**

KK, *(978-1-940689)* 149 Amapola Ave, Pacifica, CA 94044 USA Tel 650-284-3303
E-mail: kk@kk.org
Web site: http://www.kk.org.

Kladnik, Mary, *(978-1-7345516)* P.O. Box 592, Los Alamos, CA 93440 USA Tel 805-453-3234; Fax: 805-344-4663
E-mail: Mkauthor@verizonl.net
Web site: Www.maggiestories.com.

Klapheke, Alisha, *(978-0-9987379; 978-0-9998314; 978-1-7361833; 979-8-9852764; 979-8-9871228; 979-8-9888358)* 3975 New Hwy. 96 W, Franklin, TN 37064 USA Tel 615-440-3717
E-mail: alisha@alishaklapheke.com.

Klare & Taylor Publishing Company *See* **Klare Taylor Pubs.**

Klare Taylor Pubs., *(978-0-9764403)* P.O. Box 637, Ashland, OR 97520 USA
Web site: http://www.klaretaylorpublishers.com; http://www.pacificwestcom.com/klare; http://www.pacificwestcom.com/amazon; http://www.pacificwestcom.com/shipsofchildren; http://www.pacificwestcom.com/richardpoem.

KLC Publishing, *(978-0-9995734)* P.O. Box 10162, Dothan, AL 36303 USA Tel 334-405-4519
E-mail: info@tianapatrice.com
Dist(s): **CreateSpace Independent Publishing Platform.**

K.L.Corgliano, *(978-0-615-56735-8)* 926 Holly hills Ct., Keller, TX 76248 USA Tel 817-914-2344
E-mail: corgliano@verizon.net.

Klein, Sharon, *(978-0-578-81659-3)* 6233 N. Camino Miraval, Tucson, AZ 85718 USA Tel 520-299-0344
E-mail: Sfklein@aol.com.

Klemm, Rebecca Charitable Foundation *See* **NumbersAlive! Pr.**

Klett Lerntraining bei PONS (DEU) *(978-3-12) Dist. by* **Intl Bk Import.**

Klett Lerntraining bei PONS (DEU) *(978-3-12) Dist. by* **Continental Bk.**

Klink, Hannah Designs, *(978-1-7373245)* 9102 N 134th E Ave, Owasso, OK 74055 USA Tel 805-264-5945
E-mail: hklink17@gmail.com.

Klobe, Anne-Marie *See* **Walking The Way**

Kloria Publishing LLC, *(978-1-933737)* Orders Addr.: 401 E. 8th St. Suite 214-568, Sioux Falls, SD 57103 USA
E-mail: orders@kloria.com
Web site: https://www.kloria.com/
Dist(s): **Concordia Publishing Hse.**

KLS LifeChange Ministries *Imprint of* **Skinner, Kerry L.**

KLT & Assocs., *(978-0-9799119)* 11829 E. Parkview Ln., Scottsdale, AZ 85255 USA Tel 480-342-9638.

Kluge, Matt, *(978-0-578-51574-8; 978-0-578-80427-9)* 7012 Hadrian Dr, Joliet, IL 60431 USA Tel 630-740-8832
E-mail: mattsbooks33@gmail.com.

Kluis Publishing, LLC, *(978-0-9776878; 978-0-9830382)* Orders Addr.: 901 Twelve Oaks Ctr. Dr. Suite 907, Wayzata, MN 55391 USA Tel 952-767-5504; Toll Free: 888-345-2855
E-mail: info@kluispublishing.com; kt@alkluis.com
Web site: http://www.alkluis.com.

Klutz, *(978-0-932592; 978-1-57054; 978-1-878257; 978-1-59174)* Div. of Scholastic, Inc., 450 Lambert St., Palo Alto, CA 94306 USA (SAN 212-7539) Tel 650-857-0888; Fax: 650-857-9110; Toll Free: 800-737-4123; *Imprints:* Chicken Socks (Chick Socks); Klutz Certified (Klutz Cert)
E-mail: thefolks@klutz.com
Web site: http://www.klutz.com
Dist(s): **Scholastic, Inc.**

Klutz Certified *Imprint of* **Klutz**

Klutz Latino (MEX) *Dist. by* **IPG Chicago.**

KMB Creative, *(978-0-692-19239-9; 978-0-578-40991-7)* 1409 Tuscany Way, Boyton Beach, FL 33435 USA Tel 561-449-7071
E-mail: too2koi@gmail.com
Web site: www.kellymbcreative.com.

KMR Scripts, *(978-1-932240)* P.O. Box 189, Webster City, IA 50595 USA
Web site: http://www.kmrscripts.com.

KMS Productions, *(978-0-9719665)* P.O. Box 162, Garnett, KS 66032 USA (SAN 254-5527)
Web site: https://booklocker.com/11653.

KnackPacks, Inc., *(978-0-9726619)* P.O. Box 3716, Oak Park, IL 60303-3716 USA Tel 708-358-1760
E-mail: comments@knackpacks.com
Web site: http://www.knackpacks.com.

KnausWorks, *(978-0-9758742)* 4160-87 Jade St., Capitola, CA 95010 USA
E-mail: ltrsfmspace@aol.com.

Knee Patch Publishing, *(978-1-7323319)* 1643 Coastal Rd, Brooksville, ME 04617 USA Tel 808-866-8046
E-mail: abrambarrett@gmail.com.

Knee-High Adventures, *(978-0-615-16825-8)* 13450 Oak Hollow, Cypress, TX 77429 USA
Web site: http://www.davidsdonkeytales.com
Dist(s): **Lulu Pr., Inc.**

Knight Publishing, *(978-0-9740535)* P.O. Box 7452, Fremont, CA 94537-7452 USA Tel 209-743-7390; Fax: 510-818-1166
E-mail: knightpublishing@sbcglobal.net; childrenbooks@sbcglobal.net.

Knight Watch Publishing, *(978-0-9974351)* 8663 Oak Dr, Rancho Cucamonga, CA 91730 USA Tel 626-824-1099
E-mail: contact@knightwatchpublishing.com
Web site: www.knightwatchpublishing.com.

Knighted Phoenix Publishing, *(978-1-7330574; 978-1-958797)*
E-mail: charity-mae@outlook.com
Web site: charity-mae@outlook.com.

Knights of Soul Publishing *See* **DHUNAMI**

KNK Books *See* **California Is Me**

KnockKnock LLC, *(978-1-60106; 978-1-68349)* 11111 Jefferson Blvd No. 5167, Culver City, CA 90231 USA Tel 310-396-4132; Fax: 310-396-4385; Toll Free: 800-656-5662
E-mail: kk1@knockknockstuff.com; gil.vizconde@whosthere.com; ops@whosthere.com
Web site: http://www.knockknockstuff.com.

†Knoll, Allen A. Pubs., *(978-0-9627297; 978-1-888310)* 200 W. Victoria St., Santa Barbara, CA 93101 USA (SAN 299-0539) Tel 805-564-3377 (orders); Fax: 805-966-6657 (orders); Toll Free: 800-777-7623 (orders)
E-mail: accounts@knollpublishers.com
Web site: http://www.knollpublishers.com
Dist(s): **Brodart Co.**
Follett School Solutions; *CIP.*

Knopf *Imprint of* **Knopf Doubleday Publishing Group**

†Knopf, Alfred A. Inc., *(978-0-394)* Div. of The Knopf Publishing Group, Orders Addr.: 400 Hahn Rd., Westminster, MD 21157 USA Tel 410-848-1900; Toll Free: 800-726-0600 (orders); Edit Addr.: 1745 Broadway, New York, NY 10019 USA (SAN 202-5825) Tel 212-782-9000; Toll Free: 800-726-0600
E-mail: customerservice@randomhouse.com
Web site: http://www.randomhouse.com/knopf
Dist(s): **Libros Sin Fronteras**
MyiLibrary
Penguin Random Hse. Distribution
Penguin Random Hse. LLC
Random Hse., Inc.; *CIP.*

Knopf Bks. for Young Readers *Imprint of* **Random Hse. Children's Bks.**

†Knopf Doubleday Publishing Group, *(978-0-307; 978-0-385-17470-1)* Div. of Doubleday Broadway Publishing Group, Orders Addr.: 400 Hahn Rd., Westminster, MD 21157 USA (SAN 281-6083) Tel 410-848-1900; Toll Free: 800-726-0600; Edit Addr.: 1745 Broadway, New York, NY 10019 USA (SAN 201-0089) Tel 212-782-9000; 212-572-4961 Bulk orders; Toll Free Fax: 800-659-2436 Orders only; Toll Free: 800-669-1536 Electronic orders; 800-726-0600 Customer service; *Imprints:* Knopf (KnoG); Everyman's Library (Everymns Lib); Pantheon (Pantheon); Schocken (Schocken); Vintage (Vin Bks); Anchor (AncKPG)
E-mail: ddaypub@randomhouse.com
Web site: http://www.doubleday.com
Dist(s): **Children's Plus, Inc.**
Follett School Solutions
MyiLibrary
Penguin Random Hse. Distribution
Penguin Random Hse. LLC
Random Hse., Inc.
Sourcebooks, Inc.; *CIP.*

Knosis, LLC *See* **SkyMark Corp.**

Knot Garden Pr., *(978-0-9655018)* 7712 Eagle Creek Dr., Dayton, OH 45459 USA Tel 937-433-2592 (phone/fax)
E-mail: marthaboice@aol.com.

Knott, Joan, *(978-0-9779895)* 132 W. High St., Jackson, MI 49203 USA.

Know Me Pubn. LLC, *(978-0-9790934)* Orders Addr.: 1679 Valdosta Cir., Pontiac, MI 48340 USA Tel 248-212-0204
E-mail: knowmepub@yahoo.com
Web site: http://www.cwren.bravehost.com.

Know Wonder Publishing, LLC, *(978-0-615-18112-7)* 12832 71st Ave., Kirkland, WA 98034 USA
Dist(s): **Publishers Services.**

Knowing Pr., The, *(978-0-936927)* Orders Addr.: 400 Sycamore, McAllen, TX 78501 USA (SAN 658-361X) Tel 956-686-4033
E-mail: janseale@rgv.rr.com.

Knowledge Bks. & Software (AUS) *(978-1-875219; 978-1-920696; 978-1-920824; 978-1-74162; 978-1-921016; 978-1-925398; 978-1-925714; 978-1-922370; 978-1-922516; 978-1-76127) Dist. by* **Lerner Pub.**

Knowledge Box Central, *(978-1-61625; 978-1-62472)* 403 N. Jodie St., Shreveport, LA 71007 USA Tel 318-207-2454
Web site: http://www.knowledgeboxcentral.com.

Knowledge College Planning, *(978-0-9761218)* P.O. Box 321, Stockbridge, GA 30281 USA Tel 770-331-0739
Web site: http://www.kcplan.com.

Knowledge Kids Enterprises, Incorporated *See* **LeapFrog Enterprises, Inc.**

Knowledge Power Communications *See* **KP Publishing Co.**

Knowledge Quest, *(978-1-932786)* P.O. Box 474, Boring, OR 97009-0474 USA Tel 503-663-1210; Fax: 503-663-0670 Do not confuse with Knowledge Quest, Dieterich, IL
E-mail: orders@knowledgequestmaps.com; terri@knowledgequestmaps.com
Web site: http://www.knowledgequestmaps.com.

Knowledge Wand, LLC, *(978-0-9766680)* 100 Kennewyck Cir., Slingerlands, NY 12159 USA Tel 518-456-3110; Fax: 518-456-6990; Toll Free: 800-376-5669
E-mail: djahnel@gmail.com
Web site: http://www.knowledgewand.com.

KnowledgeGain, *(978-0-9779844)* 1607 Crescent Ridge Rd NW, ROCHESTER, MN 55901 USA (SAN 850-802X) Tel 507-398-2384
E-mail: Chris@KnowledgeGain.com
Web site: http://www.KnowledgeGain.com.

KnowledgeGain Inc. *See* **KnowledgeGain**

Knowtivate, LLC, *(978-0-9787021)* Orders Addr.: 116 Milton St., Lake Mills, WI 53551-5355 USA Tel 920-478-3936; Edit Addr.: N7894 Cty. Rd., O, Waterloo, WI 53594-5355 USA
Web site: http://www.knowtivate.com.

Knox, John Press *See* **Westminster John Knox Pr.**

KO Kids Bks., *(978-0-9723946)* 16 Baytree Rd., San Rafael, CA 94903-3801 USA
Web site: http://www.kokidsbooks.com
Dist(s): **Publishers Group West (PGW).**

Koala Jo Publishing, *(978-0-9764698)* Orders Addr.: 352 N. El Camino Real, San Mateo, CA 94401 USA
Web site: http://www.koalajo.com.

KOBZ, *(978-0-9772222)* 2230 Rockingham Dr., Maryville, TN 37803 USA Tel 865-980-7755.

Koch, Chris, *(978-0-9764338)* 3344 Louisville Rd., Harrodsburg, KY 40330-9190 USA.

Kochevar, Steven, *(978-0-9763546)* 7 Beth Lee Dr., Grafton, MA 01519-1139 USA.

†Kodansha America, Inc., *(978-0-87011; 978-1-56836; 978-1-935429; 978-1-61262; 978-1-63236; 978-1-64651; 979-8-88877)* 451 Park Ave S. Flr. 7, New York, NY 10016-7390 USA (SAN 201-0526) Toll Free: 800-451-7556; *Imprints:* Vertical (Vrtical); Vertical (Vertical)
E-mail: t-sumi@kodansha-usa.com
Web site: www.kodansha.us
Dist(s): **Oxford Univ. Pr., Inc.**
Penguin Random Hse. Distribution
Penguin Random Hse. LLC
Random Hse., Inc.; *CIP.*

Kodansha International (JPN) *(978-4-7700) Dist. by* **Cheng Tsui.**

Kodansha International (JPN) *(978-4-7700) Dist. by* **Kodansha.**

Kodansha USA Publishing *See* **Kodansha America, Inc.**

Kodel Group, LLC, The, *(978-0-9844784; 978-0-9850142; 978-1-62485)* Orders Addr.: P.O. Box 38, Grants Pass, OR 97528-0003 USA (SAN 859-4961) Tel 541-471-1234; Edit Addr.: 132 NW 6th St., Grants Pass, OR 97528 USA; *Imprints:* Empire Holdings (Empire Holds); Empire Holdins - Literary Division for Young Readers (EH LDYR)
E-mail: info@kodelgroup.com
Web site: stevietenderheart.com; kodelempire.com.

Kodzo Bks., *(978-1-943960; 979-8-88577)* 1125 Hilltop Dr., Rock Springs, WY 82901 USA Tel 801-414-2550
E-mail: lkodzo@live.com.

Koehler Bks., *(978-0-9835013; 978-0-9840316; 978-1-938467; 978-1-940192; 978-1-63393; 978-1-64663; 979-8-88824)* 210 60th St., Virginia Beach, VA 23451 USA Tel 757-289-6006
E-mail: john@koehlerbooks.com
Web site: http://www.koehlerbooks.com/.

Koehntopp, James, *(978-0-578-61820-3)* 715 Harrison Ct., West Bend, WI 53090 USA Tel 715-379-5013
E-mail: shazam791@yahoo.com.

Koenisha Pubns., *(978-0-9700458; 978-0-9718758; 978-0-9741685; 978-0-9759621; 978-0-9800098; 978-1-7351485)* 3196-53rd St., Hamilton, MI 49419 USA
E-mail: shar@sewingmachinemuseum.com
Web site: http://www.sewingmachinemuseum.com; http://www.hearingaidbrigade.com.

Kofford, Greg Books, Inc., *(978-1-58958)* P.O. Box 1362, Draper, UT 84020 USA (SAN 253-5882) Tel 801-572-7417; Fax: 801-576-0583
E-mail: gregk@koffordbooks.com
Web site: http://www.gregkofford.com.

Kogan Page, Ltd. (GBR) *(978-0-7494; 978-0-85038; 978-1-85091; 978-1-78966; 978-1-78757; 978-1-78967; 978-1-3986) Dist. by* **IngramPubServ.**

Kogan, Sheila, *(979-8-218-15955-9)* 8 Highland Blvd., Kensington, CA 94707 USA Tel 510-527-9741
E-mail: sheilakogan@hotmail.com
Dist(s): **Ingram Content Group.**

Kohls, Jacqueline B, *(978-1-7340428)* 20073 Rd. S, Fort Jennings, OH 45844 USA Tel 567-242-8335
E-mail: jackiekohls@gmail.com.

Koho Pono, LLC, *(978-0-9845424; 978-1-938282; 978-1-941379)* 15024 SE Pinegrove Loop, Clackamas, OR 97015-7629 USA (SAN 859-6956) Tel 503-723-7392
E-mail: burrs@kohopono.com
Web site: http://kohopono.com.

Kokila *Imprint of* **Penguin Young Readers Group**

Kokopelli Pr., *(978-0-9759270)* 9611 Paseo del Rey NE, Albuquerque, NM 87111-1649 USA Do not confuse with companies with the same name in Las Cruces, NM, Sedona, AZ.

Kolaj, Paul, *(978-0-578-42916-8)* 245 Main St., White Plains, NY 10601 USA Tel 914-413-6100
E-mail: pk@famousfamiglia.com
Dist(s): **Ingram Content Group.**

Koldarana Pubns., *(978-1-884993)* Orders Addr.: P.O. Box 973, Dover, AR 72837 USA; Edit Addr.: 958 SR 164 E., Dover, AR 72837 USA
E-mail: ctn47496@yahoo.com.

Kollath-Stensaas Pubs., *(978-0-9673793; 978-0-9792006; 978-1-936571)* 394 Lake Ave., S., Suite 406, Duluth, MN 55802 USA Tel 218-341-3350
E-mail: sparkystensaas@hotmail.com
Web site: http://www.kollathstensaas.com
Dist(s): **Adventure Pubns.**
Publishers Group West (PGW).

Kolluri, Alina M., *(978-0-9787319)* 10124 Queens Park Dr., Tampa, FL 33647-3179 USA
E-mail: alinakolluri@yahoo.com.

Komikwerks, LLC, *(978-0-9742803; 978-0-9778809; 978-1-933925)* 1 Ruth St., Worcester, MA 01602 USA; *Imprints:* Actionopolis (Actionopolis); Agent of Danger (AgentofDanger)
E-mail: patrick@komikwerks.com; shannon@komikwerks.com; kristendenton@gmail.com
Web site: http://www.komikwerks.com; http://www.actionopolis.com.

Kommon Cents, Inc., *(978-0-9745982)* Orders Addr.: P.O. Box 313274, Jamaica, NY 11431-3274 USA Tel 917-541-8568; Toll Free: 877-566-2368
E-mail: info@kommoncents.com
Web site: http://www.kommoncents.com.

Kommon Cents Publishing Company *See* **Kommon Cents, Inc.**

Konaa Publishing *See* **Smallbag Bks.**

Konecky & Konecky *Imprint of* **Konecky, William S. Assocs., Inc.**

Konecky, William S. Assocs., Inc., *(978-0-914427; 978-1-56852)* 72 Ayers Point Rd., Old Saybrook, CT 06475-4301 USA (SAN 663-2432) Tel 860-388-0878; Fax: 860-388-0273; *Imprints:* Konecky & Konecky (Konecky & Konecky)
E-mail: seankon@comcast.net.

Konkori International, *(978-0-9647012)* P.O. Box 102441, Denver, CO 80250 USA Tel 303-744-6318; Fax: 303-296-9113; *Imprints:* Dawn of a New Day Publications, The (Dawn of a New Day)
E-mail: dabdulai@yahoo.com
Dist(s): **Emery-Pratt Co.**

Konopka, Ann Marie, *(978-0-615-18598-9)* 20 Palmer Rd., Kendall Pk., NJ 08824 USA Tel 732-821-5415
E-mail: annmkonopka@yahoo.com
Dist(s): **Lulu Pr., Inc.**

Konstellation Pr., *(978-0-9987482; 978-0-9991989; 978-1-7346421; 979-8-9868432)* 4367 Narragansett Ave., San Diego, CA 92107 USA Tel 619-517-5017
E-mail: corneliafeye@gmail.com.

Kontis, Alethea, *(978-1-942541)* PO Box 512, Mims, FL 32754 USA
E-mail: akontis@gmail.com
Web site: http://www.aletheakontis.com.

Koobville, *(978-1-7334786)* 4934 Cartagena Dr., Toledo, OH 43623 USA Tel 440-465-9976
E-mail: kristinwinovich@gmail.com.

Kookalook Publishing, *(978-0-9706323)* 53 Garden Pl., Brooklyn, NY 11201-4501 USA
E-mail: kookypubs@hotmail.com.

Kopecky, Jessica Design, LLC, *(978-1-7369641)* 845 Everest Dr., Rothschild, WI 54474 USA Tel 715-340-7781
E-mail: design@jessicakopecky.com
Web site: www.jessicakopecky.com.

Korab, Kat *See* **Purple Unicorn Pr.**

Korean Culture Research, Inc., *(978-0-9762990)* 38 W. 32nd St., Suite 1112, New York, NY 10001 USA Tel 212-563-5763; Fax: 212-563-6707
E-mail: leekle@sprynet.com
Web site: http://www.learnkoreannow.com.

Kores, Michelle, *(978-0-692-78763-2; 978-0-692-78765-6)* 633 Montrose Ave., Delano, MN 55328 USA Tel 701-446-7048.

Korin, Steve, *(978-0-578-92115-0; 978-0-578-92117-4; 978-0-578-94459-3; 978-0-578-94542-2; 978-0-578-98641-8; 979-8-9859658)* 1151 brighton beach ave apt 5L 0, BROOKLYN, NY 11235 USA Tel 3472444850
E-mail: Slavakorin75@gmail.com.

Koroknay, Thomas, *(978-0-9749705)* 3718 Lindsey Rd., Lexington, KY 44904 USA Tel 419-884-0222.

Kortus, Author Rob, *(978-0-578-55119-7; 978-0-578-55319-1; 978-0-578-59172-8; 978-0-578-82249-5; 978-0-578-82460-4)* 10016 Casa Nuestra Dr., Charlotte, NC 28214 USA Tel 828-545-0445
E-mail: whendogpalsfly@gmail.com
Web site: www.whendogpalsfly.com.

Kory Industries, *(978-0-578-40186-7; 978-0-578-42596-2; 978-0-578-50961-7; 978-0-578-68647-9; 978-0-578-68648-6; 978-0-578-93124-1; 978-0-578-93125-8)* 17617 SE 293rd PL, KENT, WA 98042 USA Tel 425-941-9352
E-mail: flyacecat@hotmail.com
Dist(s): **Ingram Content Group.**

Kotowicz, Anetta *See* **ArtsKindred**

Kotzig Publishing, Inc., *(978-0-9715411; 978-0-9767163)* 1109 NW 16th St., Delray Beach, FL 33444 USA
E-mail: susan@kotzigpublishing.com
Web site: http://www.kotzigpublishing.com
Dist(s): **Independent Pubs. Group.**

Kountz Marketing Group *See* **Texas Pride Publishing**

Kovels Antiques, Inc., *(978-0-9646683; 978-0-9970825)* 22000 Shaker Blvd., Shaker Heights, OH 44122 USA Tel 216-752-2252; Fax: 216-752-3115; Toll Free: 800-303-1996
E-mail: kkovel@kovels.com
Web site: www.kovels.com.

Kowalewski, Billie, *(978-0-692-04643-2; 978-0-578-48323-8; 979-8-218-23852-0)* P.O. Box 106, MOODUS, CT 06469 USA Tel 860-861-5115
E-mail: billie@enlightenedbook.net
Dist(s): **Ingram Content Group.**

KP Bks., *(978-0-9748549)* 354 Sequoia Ct., Antioch, IL 60002-2600 USA
E-mail: pudaitem@sbcglobal.net; bluehorizon1@sbcglobal.net; marylpk625@me.com.

KP Publishing Co., *(978-0-9818790; 978-0-9854107; 978-0-9888644; 978-0-9907199; 978-0-9967162; 978-0-9976622; 978-0-9981701; 978-0-9993455; 978-1-7322665; 978-1-950936; 979-8-9857184; 979-8-9869907; 978-1-960001)* 24307 Magic Mountain Pkwy, No. 386, Valencia, CA 91355 USA (SAN 856-8189) Tel 661-513-0308
E-mail: willa@kp-pub.com
Web site: http://www.kp-pub.com.

KPPages, *(978-1-7374325)* 7010 Kayleigh Ct., Sugar Land, TX 77479 USA Tel 501-291-1064
E-mail: kploundy@gmail.com
Web site: www.kppages.com.

KPT Publishing, LLC, *(978-1-944833)* 2600 E. 26th St., Minneapolis, MN 55406 USA Tel 612-721-5017; Fax: 612-721-7968
E-mail: david.koechel@kpadesign.com
Web site: KPTpublishing.com
Dist(s): **Penguin Random Hse. Distribution**
Penguin Random Hse. LLC.

Kraal, Luisette, *(978-0-578-57401-1; 978-1-7370056; 978-1-7379647; 978-1-960509)* 2650 W. Albion Ave. Unit 2, Chicago, IL 60645 USA Tel 210-322-5728
E-mail: saved.serve@gmail.com
Dist(s): **Ingram Content Group.**

Kraemer, Jean, *(978-0-9897694)* 28627 Essex St., Roseville, MI 48066 USA Tel 586-777-0113
E-mail: jeangirlk60@att.net.

Krafft, Steve, *(978-1-7374687)* 3043 E. Dry Creek Rd., Phoenix, AZ 85048 USA Tel 602-300-2302
E-mail: stevekrafft7@gmail.com.

Kramer, H.J. Inc., *(978-0-915811; 978-1-932073)* P.O. Box 1082, Tiburon, CA 94920 USA (SAN 294-0833) Fax: 415-435-5364; Toll Free: 800-972-6657
E-mail: hjkramer@jps.net
Web site: http://www.newworldlibrary.com
Dist(s): **New Leaf Distributing Co., Inc.**
New World Library
Publishers Group West (PGW).

Kramer, Julie, *(978-0-578-89964-0)* P.O. Box 809, Ansonia, OH 45303 USA Tel 937-423-2432
E-mail: kramerjulie84@yahoo.com.

Kramer, Sarah, *(978-0-692-99173-2)* 3909 W 124th St., Leawood, KS 66209 USA Tel 417-214-6721
E-mail: sarahfarrellkramer@gmail.com
Dist(s): **Ingram Content Group.**

rane, Garet, *(978-0-692-15119-8; 978-0-692-15216-4)* 466 Gregory Lane, 604, Acworth, GA 30102 USA Tel 321-317-2978
E-mail: garetekrane@yahoo.com
Web site: Garetkrane.com.

ranichfeld, Andrew, *(978-0-692-51647-8; 978-0-692-51648-5; 978-0-692-51649-2; 978-0-692-52541-8; 978-0-692-61529-4; 978-0-692-84206-5)* 3425 Kingsbridge Ave. Apt. 606, BRONX, NY 10463 USA Tel 914-227-0645.

rantz, Heather, *(978-0-9987037; 978-1-952881)* 2967 NW Starview Dr, Bend, OR 97703 USA Tel 541-948-5641; *Imprints:* Herow Press (HerowPr)
E-mail: zwillinga@bendbroadband.com.

rash Publishing *See* **Place Mark Bks.**

rassa, Arlene, *(978-0-578-45100-8; 978-0-578-45105-3)* 14520 Fincher Rd., Ball Ground, GA 30107 USA Tel 678-848-8041
E-mail: arlenekrassa@gmail.com
Dist(s): **Ingram Content Group.**

Kraszewski, Terry, *(978-0-9821989)* 2162 Avenida De La Playa, La Jolla, CA 92037 USA (SAN 857-5223) Tel 858-456-9283; Fax: 858-456-9551
E-mail: ricswave@cox.net
Web site: http://www.surfangelbook.com.

Krause, Claudia, *(978-0-9655689)* P.O. Box 7083, Capistrano Beach, CA 92624 USA Tel 714-492-7778.

Kravec & Kravec & Associates *See* **Bellaboozle Books, Inc.**

Krazy Duck Productions, *(978-0-9776739; 978-0-9961622)* Orders Addr.: P.O. Box 105, Danville, KY 40423 USA Tel 606-787-2571; Fax: 606-787-8207; Edit Addr.: 2227 Wood Creek Rd., Liberty, KY 42539 USA
E-mail: KrazyduckProductions@msn.com
Web site: http://www.krazyduck.com.

KRBY Creations, LLC, *(978-0-9745715)* 2 Leeds Ct., Brick, NJ 08724-4011 USA
E-mail: krbyenterprises@comcast.net
Web site: http://www.krbycreations.com.

Kre8u, LLC., *(978-0-578-84888-4)* 738 TORRINGTON PL 0, DAYTON, OH 45406 USA Tel 2168320690
E-mail: cmjames31@gmail.com
Dist(s): **Ingram Content Group.**

Kreations *See* **Worn Pants**

Kreativ Kaos, *(978-0-9790572)* P.O. Box 27955, Anaheim Hills, CA 92809 USA (SAN 852-310X)
E-mail: admin@kreativkaos.com
Web site: http://www.kreativkaos.com.

Kreative Character Kreations, Inc., *(978-0-9641381)* 9 Endicott Dr., Huntington, NY 11743 USA Tel 516-673-8230; Fax: 516-346-6620.

Kreative X-Pressions Pubns., *(978-0-9798536; 978-0-9800552)* Orders Addr.: 87 Kennedy Dr., Colchester, CT 06415-1315 USA (SAN 854-5561) Tel 860-537-2673
E-mail: novelwriter@comcast.net
Web site: http://www.kreativexpressionsonline.com.

KreativeMindz Prodns. LLC, P.O. Box 2413, New York, NY 10108 USA Tel 212-222-3069
E-mail: KLB@kreativemindzproductions.com
Web site: http://www.kreativemindzproductions.com.

Kreder, Mary Ellen DeLuca, *(978-0-615-92430-4; 978-0-9913232)* 364 Quaker St., Wallkill, NY 12589 USA Tel 845-853-2803
E-mail: MaryEd4466@verizon.net.

†Kregel Pubns., *(978-0-8254)* Div. of Kregel, Inc., Orders Addr.: P.O. Box 2607, Grand Rapids, MI 49501-2607 USA (SAN 206-9792) Tel 616-451-4775; Fax: 616-451-9330; Toll Free: 800-733-2607; Edit Addr.: 733 Wealthy St., SE., Grand Rapids, MI 49503-5553 USA (SAN 298-9115); *Imprints:* Editorial Portavoz (Edit Portavoz)
E-mail: kregelbooks@kregel.com; acquisitions@kregel.com
Web site: http://www.kregel.com
Dist(s): **Faith Alive Christian Resources**
INscribe Digital
Send The Light Distribution LLC
Spring Arbor Distributors, Inc.; *CIP.*

Kreizel Enterprises, Inc., *(978-0-9729232)* P.O. Box 224, Monsey, NY 10952 USA; 26 Charles Ln., Spring Valley, NY 10977-3330
E-mail: info@kreizelplating.com; books@kreizelplating.com.

Kremer Pubns, Inc., *(978-0-9707591; 978-0-9745631; 978-0-9817272)* 12615 W. Custer Ave., Butler, WI 53007 USA Toll Free: 800-669-0887
E-mail: info@kremerpublications.com
Web site: http://www.kremerpublications.com.

Krevat, Shaina, *(978-1-7325013)* P.O. Box 2565, Kirkland, WA 98083 USA
E-mail: shainakrevat@gmail.com
Web site: shainakrevat.com.

Krickett Enterprises, *(978-1-7333567)* 18013 Duncan St., Encino, CA 91316 USA Tel 818-384-1697
E-mail: krickett@drumtolearn.com
Dist(s): **Ingram Content Group.**

Krickle Forest Adventures, *(978-0-9855997)* 4081 Jeri Rd., Interlochen, MI 49643 USA Tel 231-753-6025
E-mail: customerservice@krickleforest.com
Web site: http://www.krickleforest.com.

Kringle Enterprises Company *See* **North Pole Pr.**

Kris, *(978-0-9984291)* 660 King Street, Apt 302, San Francisco, CA 94107 USA Tel 617-763-6129
E-mail: krishanthirondonfuentes@gmail.com.

Krisaran Publishing Co., *(978-0-9773146)* 850 NC 55 E., Mount Olive, NC 28365 USA (SAN 257-3983)
E-mail: bjackson@esn.net; brenda@krisaran.com
Web site: http://www.krisaran.com.

Krishnan, Laura, *(978-0-692-78397-9)* 13560 NE 54th PL, BELLEVUE, WA 98005 USA Tel 832-687-3560.

Kristy High, *(978-0-578-91514-2; 979-8-218-16409-6; 979-8-218-17513-9)* 7831 New England Ct., West Chester, OH 45069 USA Tel 336-455-2567
E-mail: khigh81@gmail.com.

KRO Publishing *See* **Preschool Prep Co.**

Kronos Publishing, *(978-0-615-44390-4; 978-0-9833951)* 297 Billerica Rd., Chelmsford, MA 01730 USA Tel 978-947-3042
E-mail: Indrani.Ghosal@kronos.com
Web site: kronos.com
Dist(s): **INscribe Digital.**

Krown Up, *(978-1-7369083)* 3195 BRIDGEPOINT DR, NASHVILLE, TN 37207 USA Tel 504-237-4811
E-mail: talldelly@yahoo.com.

Kruger, Wolfgang Verlag, GmbH (DEU) *(978-3-8105) Dist. by* **Intl Bk Import.**

Kruger, Wolfgang Verlag, GmbH (DEU) *(978-3-8105) Dist. by* **Distribks Inc.**

Krullstone Publishing, LLC, *(978-0-9833237; 978-0-9882170; 978-0-9889578; 978-1-941851)* 114 Oakwood Ave., FAIRHOPE, AL 36532 USA (SAN 860-1240) Tel 251-270-7173
E-mail: charlotte@krullstone.com
Web site: www.krullstone.com
Dist(s): **Krullstone Distributing, LLC**
Smashwords.

Krystal Lee Enterprises (KLE Publishing), *(978-0-9971378; 978-1-945066)* 1264 Mill Crest Walk NW, Conyers, GA 30012 USA Tel 404-667-2051
E-mail: krystalleeenterprises@gmail.com
Web site: www.klepub.com.

K's Kids Publishing, *(978-0-9797208)* 12706 SW 94 Ct., Miami, FL 33176 USA (SAN 854-1892) Tel 305-969-5570
E-mail: ks_kids@bellsouth.net.

†Ktav Publishing Hse., Inc., *(978-0-87068; 978-0-88125; 978-1-60280; 978-965-524)* Orders Addr.: 930 Newark Ave. 4th Flr., Jersey City, NJ 07306 USA (SAN 201-0038) Tel 201-963-9524; Fax: 201-963-0102; Toll Free Fax: 800-626-7517 (orders)
E-mail: orders@ktav.com; editor@ktav.com; questions@ktav.com
Web site: http://www.ktav.com
Dist(s): **Academic Studies Pr.**
ISD
eBookit.com; *CIP.*

K-Teen *Imprint of* **Kensington Publishing Corp.**

K-Teen/Dafina *Imprint of* **Kensington Publishing Corp.**

ktf-writers-studio, *(978-0-615-41134-7; 978-0-615-44161-0; 978-3-9523908; 978-0-578-10595-6; 978-0-9913395; 978-0-9969890; 978-0-9986927)* 5712 Ashley Sq. S., Memphis, TN 38120 USA Tel 901-683-4210; 478 W. Racquet Club Pl., Memphis, TN 38117
E-mail: frigonormfr@aol.com; ktf-writers-studio@hotmail.com
Web site: www.ktf-writers-studio.ch.

KTH Investment Group, *(978-0-692-85894-3; 978-0-692-08213-3; 978-0-692-09811-0; 978-0-692-09812-7; 978-0-578-42213-8; 978-0-578-42215-2)* 592 N Peppercorn Ln., Rossville, GA 30741 USA Tel 423-463-2720
E-mail: jeffwcrawford5+LVP0003448@gmail.com; jeffwcrawford5+LVP0003448@gmail.com.

Ku, Elizabeth, *(978-0-692-11406-3)* 9 Keyes St, Florham Park, NJ 07932 USA Tel 845-505-4116
E-mail: ebperley@gmail.com.

Kube Publishing Ltd. (GBR) *(978-1-84774) Dist. by* **Consort Bk Sales.**

Kudu, *(978-0-9849294; 978-1-938624; 978-1-943294; 978-1-950718; 978-1-954089; 978-1-957369; 978-1-959095; 978-1-960678; 978-1-962401)* 225 W Seminole Blvd No. 105, Sanford, FL 32771 USA Tel 407-900-5838
E-mail: cara.fm@gmail.com; sarahp@fourriversmedia.com
Dist(s): **Independent Pubs. Group**
Send The Light Distribution LLC
Whitaker Hse.

Kudzu King Productions, *(978-0-9961370)* 864 Heiferhorn Trace, Columbus, GA 31904 USA Tel 706-315-9117
E-mail: stephen.scott@mchsi.com
Web site: www.thekudzuking.com.

KuhnWorks Publishing, *(978-1-7365722)* 830 S 9th St, Terre Haute, IN 47807 USA Tel 217-808-2008
E-mail: kuhnworkspublishing@gmail.com
Web site: www.kuhnworks.com.

Kulupi Pr., *(978-0-9661867; 978-0-9817653)* 5082 Warm Springs Rd., Glen Ellen, CA 95442 USA Tel 707-996-1149
E-mail: kulupi@vom.com
Web site: http://www.kulupi.com
Dist(s): **Partners Bk. Distributing, Inc.**

Kumar, Sheila, *(978-0-578-58218-4)* 7247 Clamshell Ln., Naples, FL 34114 USA Tel 202-999-0585
E-mail: sheilakumar123@gmail.com.

Kumon Publishing North America, Inc., *(978-1-933241; 978-4-7743; 978-1-934968; 978-1-935800; 978-1-941082; 978-0-692-47466-2; 978-0-692-57875-9; 978-0-692-59884-9; 978-0-692-67737-7; 978-0-692-69890-7; 978-0-692-74109-2; 978-0-692-76435-0; 978-0-692-76436-7; 978-0-692-76437-4; 978-0-692-76438-1; 978-0-692-76658-3; 978-0-692-76659-0; 978-0-692-76660-6; 978-0-692-76661-3; 978-0-692-76662-0; 978-0-692-86678-8; 978-0-692-86679-5; 978-0-9989219; 978-0-9998787; 978-1-7331689; 978-1-953845)* 55 Challenger Rd. Suite 300, Ridgefield Park, NJ 07660 USA Tel 201-836-2105; Fax: 201-836-1559; Toll Free: 800-657-7970; 4-10-18 Takanawa Minato-Ku, 13th Flr. Chiyoda-ku, Tokyo, 108-8617 Tel 0081 0332343485; Fax: 0081 0332344018
E-mail: books@kumon.com
Web site: http://www.kumonbooks.com
Dist(s): **Bookazine Co., Inc.**
Independent Pubs. Group
Ingram Publisher Services
Sterling Publishing Co., Inc.

Kumon U.S.A., Inc., *(978-0-9702092)* 300 Frank W. Burr Blvd., Teaneck, NJ 07666 USA
E-mail: falcbooks@home.com.

Kumquat Kids Productions, LLC, *(978-0-692-06661-4; 978-1-7334138)* 14590 NE Brazee Ct. Portland, OR 97230 USA Tel 360-281-9512
E-mail: rjmockford@gmail.com
Web site: https://kumquatkids.com/.

Kunce, Craig LLC *See* **Windhill Bks. LLC**

Kung, Jeannie M., *(978-0-578-18737-2)* 815 S. Songbird Cir., Anaheim Hills, CA 92808 USA Tel 714-809-5634
E-mail: jeanniekung@sbcglobal.net.

Kunz, Dan, *(978-1-7340777)* 533 NE 3rd. Ave., Fort Lauderdale, FL 33301 USA Tel 954-234-5095
E-mail: Dankunz54@gmail.com.

Kunz, Matt, *(978-0-9976298)* 730 Sable Pointe Rd, Milton, GA 30004 USA Tel 404-386-0354
E-mail: mkunz59@hotmail.com.

Kuperman, Marina, *(978-0-9801109)* 8 Forge Rd., Hewitt, NJ 07421 USA Tel 973-728-0835
E-mail: marinakuperman@yahoo.com
Web site: http://turtlefeetsurfersbeat.com.

Kupu Kupu Pr., *(978-0-9883448)* 1710 Franklin No. 300, Oakland, CA 94612 USA Tel 510-452-1912
E-mail: inno@designaction.org
Web site: http://aisforactivist.com.

Kurdyla, E L Publishing LLC, *(978-1-61751)* Orders Addr.: P.O. Box 958, Bowie, MD 20718-0958 USA Tel 301-805-2191; Fax: 301-805-2192; Edit Addr.: P.O. Box 958, Bowie, MD 20718-0958 USA Tel 301-805-2191; Fax: 301-805-2192; *Imprints:* 4th Division Press (FourthDiv)
E-mail: publisher@kurdylapublishing.com
Web site: http://www.kurdylapublishing.com.

KURIKURI INC, *(978-0-578-96285-6; 978-1-7378805)* 1230 20th Pl., Hermosa Beach, CA 90254 USA Tel 925-256-6703
E-mail: admin@howietales.com
Web site: howietales.com.

Kurjan, Sally, *(978-0-692-13852-6; 978-0-692-19276-4; 978-0-578-44656-1; 978-0-578-52747-5; 978-0-578-70592-7; 979-8-218-17970-0; 979-8-218-28600-2)* 1703 Warner Ct., Mineral Ridge, OH 44440 USA Tel 330-519-5319
E-mail: sally3510@hotmail.com
Web site: www.bernietheoneeyedpuppy.com.

Kurtz Art Studio Inc, *(978-0-9982674)* 64 Austin Storey Cir., Newnan, GA 30263 USA Tel 404-435-3647
E-mail: kurtzartwork@gmail.com
Web site: johnkurtzart.com.

Kurz, Ron, *(978-0-939829)* P.O. Box 95551, Las Vegas, NV 89193 USA (SAN 663-8333) Tel 702-837-6395 (phone/fax); 3060 Sunrise Heights Dr., Henderson, NV 89052 (SAN 663-8341) Tel 702-870-5968
E-mail: ronkurz@earthlink.net
Web site: http://www.ronkurz.com.

Kush Univ. Pr., *(978-1-893731)* Orders Addr.: 8247 S. Oglesby Ave., Chicago, IL 60617 USA Tel 773-598-5707; *Imprints:* Mandolin House (MandolinHse)
E-mail: esmith334@kushuniversitypress.net
Web site: http://kushuniversitypress.net/opencart/; http://kushuniversitypress.net/KU_press.html.

Kutie Kari Bks., Inc., *(978-1-884149)* 4189 Ethan Dr., Eagan, MN 55123 USA Tel 651-450-7427
E-mail: gharbo@garyharbo.com
Web site: http://www.garyharbo.com.

Kvale Good Natured Games LLC, *(978-0-9793583)* 771 Parkview Ave., Saint Paul, MN 55117-4045 USA Tel 651-204-6781; Fax: 651-204-6966
E-mail: admin@kvalegames.com
Web site: http://www.kvalegames.com.

Kvalvasser, Leonid, *(978-0-9753110)* 1124 Blake Ct. # 1A, Brooklyn, NY 11235-5219 USA.

Kwazy Kitty Publishing Co., *(978-0-9770012)* Orders Addr.: P.O. Box 178, Monkton, MD 21111-0178 USA.

KWE Publishing LLC, *(978-0-9974025; 978-0-9993620; 978-0-9997254; 978-1-7321034; 978-1-7326273; 978-1-950306; 978-1-956092)* 5015 Takach Rd., Prince George, VA 23875 USA Tel 804-536-1972
E-mail: Kimkokomo804@gmail.com
Dist(s): **Morgan James Publishing.**

Kwist, Karla, *(978-0-9795046)* 2420 Golden Arrow, Las Vegas, NV 89120 USA Tel 702-768-8406
E-mail: karlakk@aol.com
Web site: http://www.karlakwist.com.

Kyburg Publishing, *(978-1-7337650)* 1307 W. Hawk Ct., Nampa, ID 83651 USA Tel 208-697-3478
E-mail: authorbenjaminvogt@gmail.com.

Kymberli Mulford, Inc., *(978-1-7323504; 978-1-7329444)* 869 E Schaumburg Rd., PMB 218, Schaumburg, IL 60169 USA Tel 847-627-0984
E-mail: onionskin1@gmail.com
Web site: www.kymberlimulford.com.

Kyoodoz, *(978-0-9771172)* Orders Addr.: P.O. Box 5431, Beaverton, OR 97006-0431 USA
E-mail: customerservice@kyoodoz.com; sales@kyoodoz.com
Web site: http://www.kyoodoz.com.

Kyra, *(978-0-578-34428-7; 979-8-218-00963-2; 979-8-9865016)* 7618 altacrest pl, Charlotte, NC 28217 USA Tel 980-939-4394
E-mail: kyracathcart900@gmail.com.

L A 411 Publishing Company *See* **Reed Business Information**

L. A. Eng Bks., *(978-0-9748598)* 231 W. Hillcrest Blvd., Inglewood, CA 90301 USA
E-mail: luis_arevalo@lennox.k12.ca.us.

L. A. Media, LLC *See* **Mardi Gras Publishing, LLC**

L And J Bks. LLC, *(978-0-692-65385-2; 978-0-9977470)* 15 Ann St., West Harrison, NY 10604 USA Tel 914-837-0199
Web site: www.landjbooks.com
Dist(s): **CreateSpace Independent Publishing Platform.**

L & L Enterprises, *(978-0-9760046)* 6960 W. Peoria Ave. LOT 132, Peoria, AZ 85345-6038 USA
Web site: https://www.latinandlanguage.com.

L & R Publishing, LLC, *(978-1-55571; 978-1-954163)* Subs. of Publishing Services, Inc., P.O. Box 3531, Ashland, OR 97520 USA (SAN 218-9240) Tel 541-973-5154; *Imprints:* Hellgate Press (Hellgate Pr); Grid Press (Grid Pr); Paloma Books (PalomaBks)
E-mail: sales@hellgatepress.com
Web site: http://www.hellgatepress.com; www.palomabooks.com
Dist(s): **Independent Pubs. Group**
Midpoint Trade Bks., Inc.
MyiLibrary
ebrary, Inc.

L. C. D., *(978-0-941414)* 663 Calle Miramar, Redondo Beach, CA 90277 USA (SAN 239-0035) Tel 310-375-6336
E-mail: lenduncan@earthlink.net
Web site: http://www.phonicsplus.com.

LED Publishing, *(978-1-885674)* Div. of Logical Expression In Design, 1730 M St. NW, Suite 407, Washington, DC 20036 USA Tel 703-558-0100; Fax: 703-558-4970.

L G Productions *See* **L G Publishing**

L G Publishing, *(978-0-9768486)* Orders Addr.: 281 Fielding, Ferndale, MI 48220 USA
E-mail: admin@lgproductions.info
Web site: http://www.lgproductions.info.

L L Teach, *(978-0-9676545; 978-1-931104)* 709 Country Club Rd., Bridgewater, NJ 08807-1601 USA Tel 908-575-8830; Fax: 908-704-1730; Toll Free: 800-575-7670
E-mail: ann4480@aol.com; llteach5757670@aol.com
Web site: http://www.LLteach.com.

LMA Publishing, *(978-1-892426)* Div. of Lifestyle Management Assocs., 111 Grove St., Apt. 1, West Roxbury, MA 02132 USA Tel 617-325-6752 (phone/fax)
E-mail: pentzj@ix.netcom.com
Web site: http://www.lifestylemanagement.com.

L P D Enterprises *See* **LPD Pr.**

L W S Bks., *(978-0-9704361)* 227 Bayshore Dr., Hendersonville, TN 37075 USA Tel 615-826-3871; Fax: 615-826-3883; Toll Free: 800-643-4718
E-mail: clazzy@mindspring.com
Web site: http://www.janethan.com; http://www.imsonofman.com.

L W S Publishers *See* **L W S Bks.**

La Caille Nous Publishing Co., *(978-0-9647635; 978-0-9718191)* 328 Flatbush Ave, Suite 240, Brooklyn, NY 11238 USA Tel 212-726-1293; Fax: 212-591-6465
E-mail: gcadet@lcnpub.com.

La Di La Dah, *(978-0-9816629)* 5508 Vantage Point Rd., Columbia, MD 21044-2631 USA
E-mail: r.higgins@xs4all.net
Dist(s): **Lulu Pr., Inc.**

La Frontera Publishing, *(978-0-9785634; 978-0-9857551; 978-0-9974757)* 1712 Pioneer Ave., Suite 181, Cheyenne, WY 82001 USA (SAN 851-0180) Tel 307-778-4752 general office number
E-mail: company@lafronterapublishing.com
Web site: http://www.lafronterapublishing.com
Dist(s): **Univ. of New Mexico Pr.**

La Galera, S.A. Editorial (ESP) *(978-84-246; 978-84-7515; 978-84-85297) Dist. by* **AIMS Intl.**

La Galera, S.A. Editorial (ESP) *(978-84-246; 978-84-7515; 978-84-85297) Dist. by* **Lectorum Pubns.**

La Librairie Parisienne, *(978-0-615-54542-4; 978-0-9886058; 978-0-578-32208-7)* 17844 Porto Marina Way, Pacific Palisades, CA 90272 USA Tel 424-268-4898; 310-343-1941
E-mail: JACKIEMANCUSO@GMAIL.COM; steve@lalibrairieparisienne.com
Web site: http://www.jackiemancuso.com/la-librairie-parisienne
Dist(s): **Independent Pubs. Group.**

La Luz Comics, *(978-0-9755193)* 1516 10th Ave. S., No. 6, Minneapolis, MN 55404-1795 USA
E-mail: sam@samhiti.com
Web site: http://www.samhiti.com.

La Mancha Publishing Group, *(978-1-890701)* 14534 Victory Blvd., Van Nuys, CA 91411 USA Tel 818-994-8195.

La Montagne Secrete (CAN) *(978-2-923163) Dist. by* **IPG Chicago.**

La Oferta Publishing Co., *(978-0-9665876; 978-0-9791624)* 1376 N. Fourth St., San Jose, CA 95112 USA Tel 408-436-7850; Fax: 408-436-7861; Toll Free: 800-336-7850
E-mail: sales@laoferta.com; mary@laoferta.com
Web site: http://www.laoferta.com
Dist(s): **Bilingual Pubns. Co., The**
Lectorum Pubns., Inc.
Libros Sin Fronteras
SPD-Small Pr. Distribution.

la Orilla Farm, *(978-0-9986447; 978-0-9986447-0-7)* 2401 Black Mesa Loop SW, Albuquerque, NM 87105 USA Tel 505-877-2877
E-mail: skreed47@gmail.com.

La Puerta Pubns., *(978-0-692-99026-1; 978-0-692-99855-7; 978-1-948563)* 4510 Catalina Pkwy., McFarland, WI 53558 USA Tel 608-772-3894
E-mail: lapuertapublications@gmail.com
Dist(s): **CreateSpace Independent Publishing Platform.**

LA Ruocco, *(978-0-9743454; 978-1-941593)* Orders Addr.: 31 Lake St., Brooklyn, NY 11223 USA
E-mail: laruocco@cs.com.

Laasya Design, *(978-0-9774147)* 400 N. Catalina St., Burbank, CA 91505 USA
E-mail: info@laasyadesign.com
Web site: http://www.laasyadesign.com.

Lab-Aids, Inc., *(978-1-887725; 978-1-933298; 978-1-60301; 978-1-63093; 979-8-89101)* 17 Colt Ct., Ronkonkoma, NY 11779 USA Tel 631-737-1133; Fax: 631-737-1286; Toll Free Fax: 800-381-8003
E-mail: lab-aids@lab.aids.com.

Labarco, *(978-0-9762439)* P.O. Box 1734, Alief, TX 77411 USA
Web site: http://www.cushcity.com; http://www.Amazon.com.

LaBassiere, Glenda, *(978-0-578-96761-5)* 1277 E 87th St, BROOKLYN, NY 11236 USA Tel 646-623-7314
E-mail: deiyabas@yahoo.com.
L'Abeille Publishing Incorporated *See* **Orndee Omnimedia, Inc.**
Labor, Editorial S. A. (ESP) *(978-84-335) Dist. by* **Continental Bk.**
Labosh Publishing, *(978-0-9744341)* P.O. Box 588, East Petersburg, PA 17520-0588 USA Tel 717-898-3813 (phone/fax)
E-mail: laboshpublishing@msn.com
Web site: http://laboshpublishing.com.
Lab-Volt Systems, Inc., *(978-0-86657; 978-1-60533)* Orders Addr.: P.O. Box 686, Farmingdale, NJ 07727 USA (SAN 238-7050) Tel 732-938-2000 Toll Free: 800-522-8658
E-mail: us@labvolt.com; lvanbrug@labvolt.com
Web site: http://www.labvolt.com.
Lacey Productions, *(978-0-9771076)* 611 Druid Rd., Suite 705, Clearwater, FL 33767 USA
E-mail: sherry@laceyproductions.com
Web site: http://www.laceyproductions.com.
Lacey Publishing Co., *(978-0-9709249)* 29 Bounty Rd W., Benbrook, TX 76132-1003 USA Tel 817-738-3185 (phone/fax)
E-mail: jamesb50@charter.net
Web site: http://www.marfalightsresearch.com
Dist(s): **MyiLibrary**
ebrary, Inc.
LaChrisAnd Productions, *(978-0-9765063)* P.O. Box 969, Desert Hot Springs, CA 92240 USA Tel 760-309-2263
Web site: http://www.lachrisandproductions.com.
Lackner, William *See* **Digging Clams n Oregon**
Lacson, Zsarina Lorna L *See* **Zee Lacson**
Ladd, David Pr., *(978-0-9774563)* 56 Coolidge Ave., South Portland, ME 04106 USA Tel 207-767-2836
E-mail: davidladdpress@yahoo.com.
Ladd-Reese Group, LLC, The, *(978-0-9980271)* 5069 Parkside Cir., Hoover, AL 35244 USA Tel 205-533-5392
E-mail: theladdreesegroup@gmail.com.
LaDow Publishing, *(978-0-9723623)* 308 Reynolds Ln., West Chester, PA 19380-3300 USA Tel 219-689-4565; Fax: 610-918-9571
E-mail: wmladow@aol.com
Web site: http://www.wmladow.com.
Lady Hawk Pr., *(978-0-9829082)* 3831 Abbey Ct., Newbury Park, CA 91320 USA Tel 310-460-8744
Web site: ladyhawkpress.com
Dist(s): **ebrary, Inc.**
Lady Illyria Pr., *(978-0-9765572)* 30 Lamprey Ln., Lee, NH 03824 USA Tel 603-659-3826
E-mail: patricia.emison@unh.edu.
Lady Knight Enterprises Publishing, *(978-0-615-44985-2; 978-0-615-67175-8; 978-0-615-79318-4; 978-0-692-16488-4; 978-0-692-17728-0; 978-0-9980263; 978-1-7358663; 979-8-9858272)* 3628 Satellite Blvd. #956265, Duluth, GA 30095 USA Tel 678 667-2311; 3628 Satellite Blvd., Duluth, GA 30095 Tel 678-667-2311
E-mail: ladyrhondaknight@gmail.com
Web site: http://rhondaknight.com
Dist(s): **CreateSpace Independent Publishing Platform**
Dummy Record Do Not USE!!!!.
Lady Lawyer Media, *(978-1-7354880)* 7242 Branchtree Dr., Orlando, FL 32835 USA Tel 770-476-9865
E-mail: kelly@kellycharlescollins.com
Web site: www.kellycharlescollins.com.
Ladybug Writings, *(978-1-7322968)* P.O. Box 310786, New Braunfels, TX 78131 USA Tel 432-853-6409
E-mail: authorkwendt@gmail.com
Web site: www.kwendt.online.
Lael Marketing, LLC *See* **Lael Publishing, LLC**
Lael Publishing, LLC, *(978-0-9916515)* 3925 Philpark Dr., Winston Salem, NC 27106 USA Tel 336-745-1501
E-mail: angela.laelmarketing@gmail.com.
Laffin Minor Pr., *(978-0-9770516)* P.O. Box 273, Alma, CO 80420 USA Tel 970-409-8857; Fax: 207-967-5492
E-mail: lydia@laffinminorpress.com
Web site: http://www.laffinminorpress.com.
Lagesse Stevens *Imprint of* **Martell Publishing Co**
Lagida-Ostling, Dorota, *(978-1-7353312)* 1320 S Hardy Dr. - 205, Tempe, AZ 85281 USA Tel 480-416-6925
E-mail: dlagidaostling@gmail.com.
LaGrange Publishing Co., Inc., *(978-1-881499)* Orders Addr.: P.O. Box 148, LaGrange, IN 46761-0148 USA Tel 219-463-2166; Fax: 219-463-2734; Toll Free: 800-552-2404; Edit Addr.: Junction 100S, State Rd. 9, LaGrange, IN 46761 USA
E-mail: lagpubco@Kuntrynet.com.
Laguna Press/BTI *See* **Cerebral Press International**
Lainez, Stephanie, *(978-0-9820358)* P.O. Box 1471, La Mirada, CA 90637-1471 USA (SAN 857-068X)
E-mail: storyhousebooks@yahoo.com.
Lake 7 Creative, LLC, *(978-0-9774122; 978-0-9821187; 978-0-9883662; 978-1-940647; 978-1-960084)* 530 Pk. St S, Mora, MN 55051 USA (SAN 257-5167)
E-mail: ryan@lake7creative.com
Web site: http://www.lake7creative.com
Dist(s): **Adventure Pubns.**
Publishers Group West (PGW).
Lake Isle Pr., Inc., *(978-0-9627403; 978-1-891105)* 16 W. 32nd St., Suite 10B, New York, NY 10001 USA Tel 212-273-0796; Fax: 212-273-0198; Toll Free: 800-462-6420 (Orders only)
E-mail: lakeisle@earthlink.net; hiroko@lakeislepress.com
Web site: http://www.lakeislepress.com
Dist(s): **National Bk. Network.**
Lake Limericks, *(978-0-9761711)* P.O. Box 478, Lake Waccamaw, NC 28450 USA Tel 910-646-4998; Fax: 910-371-1133
E-mail: aldrich@weblnk.net.
Lake 'n Moor, Ltd., *(978-1-936748)* Orders Addr.: 5448 Apex Peakway No. 315, Apex, NC 27502 USA Tel 919-815-9769; Edit Addr.: 5448 Apex Peakway No. 315, Apex, NC 27502 USA Tel 919-815-9769
E-mail: info@lakenmoor.com.
Lake Ridge Pr., *(978-0-9790401; 978-1-61876)* 233 Coastal Ave., Stafford, VA 22554 USA Do not confuse with companies with a similar name in Lincoln, NE, Lambertville, NJ, Springfield, MO
E-mail: makleen81@gmail.com
Dist(s): **Follett School Solutions.**
Lake Street Pr., *(978-1-936181)* 4918 N Oakley Ave., Chicago, IL 60625 USA
Web site: http://www.lakestreetpress.com
Dist(s): **Ingram Content Group**
Partners Pubs. Group, Inc.
Quality Bks., Inc.
Lake Street Pubs., *(978-1-58417)* Orders Addr.: 4537 Chowen Ave S., Minneapolis, MN 55410-1364 USA
E-mail: compass@sd.cybernex.net.
Lake Superior Port Cities, Incorporated *See* **Lake Superior Publishing LLC**
Lake Superior Publishing LLC, *(978-0-942235; 978-1-938229)* Orders Addr.: P.O. Box 16417, Duluth, MN 55816-0417 USA Tel 218-722-5002; Fax: 218-722-4096; Toll Free: 888-244-5253; Edit Addr.: 310 E. Superior St. #125, Duluth, MN 55802-3134 USA (SAN 666-9980)
E-mail: edit@lakesuperior.com
Web site: http://www.lakesuperior.com.
Lakefront Research LLC, *(978-0-9764665)* P.O. Box 667, East Hampstead, NH 03826-0667 USA.
Lakeshore Curriculum Materials Company *See* **Lakeshore Learning Materials**
Lakeshore Learning Materials, *(978-1-929255; 978-1-58970; 978-1-59746; 978-1-60666)* Orders Addr.: 2695 E. Dominguez St., Carson, CA 90895 USA (SAN 630-0251) Toll Free: 800-421-5354; Edit Addr.: 2695 E. Dominguez St., Carson, CA 90895 USA Tel 310-537-8600; Fax: 310-632-8314
E-mail: ubeckham@lakeshorelearning.com
Web site: http://www.lakeshorelearning.com.
Lakeside Medical Publishing LLC, *(978-1-7353957)* 14174 Moffett Dr., Fenton, MI 48430 USA Tel 810-208-0360; Fax: 810-720-1790
E-mail: monahardaskiran@gmail.com
Web site: hardasobgyn.com.
Lakeside Pr., *(978-1-879653; 978-0-9978959)* Do not confuse with companies with the same name in Anacortes, WA, Tamarac, FL
E-mail: larry.martin@roadrunner.com.
Lakeside Publishing MI, *(978-0-9907446; 978-1-7360457)* 6175 Kinyon Dr., Brighton, MI 48116 USA Tel 810-599-0481
E-mail: carol.trembath3@gmail.com.
Lakeview Pr., *(978-0-9749677)* c/o Jan Devereux, 255 Lakeview Ave., Cambridge, MA 02138 USA Do not confuse with Lake View Press in New Orleans, LA, Mooresville, NC, Lake Oswego, OR.
Lakin, Laqwacia, *(978-0-9891103)* 3290 Osterley Way, Cumming, GA 30041 USA Tel 678-237-8495
E-mail: llakin.consulting@gmail.com.
Lakota Language Consortium, Inc., *(978-0-9761082; 978-0-9821107; 978-0-9834363; 978-1-941461)* 2620 N Walnut St. Suite 1280, Bloomington, IN 47404 USA Tel 812-961-0140; Fax: 812-961-0141; Toll Free: 888-525-6828
E-mail: orders@lakhota.org; sales@lakhota.org
Web site: http://www.lakhota.org; http://www.languagepress.com; http://www.llcbookstore.com.
Lala Dunn, *(978-1-7365473)* 631 Vaughan Dr, Hampton, GA 30228 USA Tel 213-245-0748
E-mail: ceojaminc@gmail.com
Web site: Www.Maryslittlegoat.com.
Lamar, Mel Ministries *See* **Lamar, Melvin Productions**
Lamar, Melvin Productions, *(978-0-9716068)* 900 Downtowner Blvd., Apt. 89, Mobile, AL 36609-5409 USA
E-mail: melvinelamar@att.net; melvinlamar31@gmail.com.
LaMarca, Tiffany Productions, *(978-1-7365283)* 138 E 700 S, Beryl, UT 84714 USA Tel 775-750-4762
E-mail: iownfakeplants@hotmail.com.
Lamb, Laura, *(978-1-7375344)* 5069 Summer Dr SE, Acworth, GA 30102 USA Tel 770-401-6051
E-mail: lstar63155@bellsouth.net.
Lamb, Wendy Bks. *Imprint of* **Random Hse. Children's Bks.**
Lambda Pubs., Inc., *(978-0-915361; 978-1-55774)* 3709 13th Ave., Brooklyn, NY 11218-3622 USA (SAN 291-0640) Tel 718-972-5449; Fax: 718-972-6307
E-mail: judaica@email.msn.com.
Lambert Bk. Hse., Inc., *(978-0-89315)* 4139 Parkway Dr., Florence, AL 35630-6347 USA (SAN 180-5169) Tel 256-764-4098; 256-764-4090; Fax: 256-766-9200; Toll Free: 800-551-8511
E-mail: Info@lambertbookhouse.com
Web site: http://www.lambertbookhouse.com.
LaMothe, Karin, *(978-0-9728763)* P.O. Box 672, Belleville, MI 48112-0672 USA
Web site: http://www.angelslullaby.com.
Lamp Post Inc., *(978-0-9708587; 978-1-933428; 978-1-60039)* 29348 Ariel St., Murrieta, CA 92563 USA
E-mail: burner@lamppostpubs.com
Web site: http://www.lamppostpubs.com
Dist(s): **Diamond Comic Distributors, Inc.**
Diamond Bk. Distributors.
Lamp Post Publishing, Inc., *(978-1-892135)* 1741 Tallman Hollow Rd., Montoursville, PA 17754 USA (SAN 253-4681) Tel 570-435-2804; Fax: 570-435-2803; Toll Free: 800-326-9273
E-mail: lamppostp@aol.com
Web site: http://www.lamppostpublishing.com; http://www.beyondthegloesmur.com; http://www.heartstringsbio.com.
Lamplight Pubns., *(978-0-615-23329-1; 978-0-9819815)* 11123W US Hwy 60, Olive Hill, KY 41164 USA
E-mail: joan2728@windstream.net.
Lampo Licensing, LLC *See* **Ramsey Pr.**
Lampstand Pr., Ltd., *(978-1-935301)* Orders Addr.: P.O. Box 5798, Derwood, MD 20855 USA Tel 301-963-0808; Fax: 301-963-1868; Toll Free: 800-705-7487; Edit Addr.: 8073 Snouffer School Rd., Derwood, MD 20855 USA
Web site: http://www.lampstandpress.com.
Amur Bks., *(978-0-9776563; 978-0-9847118; 978-0-9855601; 978-0-9894940; 978-0-9914901; 978-0-9908299; 978-0-9963966; 978-1-7377229)* P.O. Box 102697, Denver, CO 80250 USA Tel 303-777-4155
E-mail: amurbooks@msn.com
Web site: http://www.childrenare.com.
LaMuth Publishing Company *See* **Fairhaven Bk. Pubs.**
Lamweg Publishing, *(978-0-9801146)* 176 W. 100 S., Kouts, IN 46347 USA Tel 219-766-2174.
Lancaster, Paula, *(978-1-7322513)* 4809 Briercrest Ct., Bowie, MD 20720 USA Tel 301-262-2366
E-mail: paula@paulalancaster.com.
Lance Schaubert, *(978-1-949547)* 887 5th Ave Apt 11, BROOKLYN, NY 11232 USA Tel 618-335-1193
E-mail: lanceschaubert@gmail.com
Dist(s): **Ingram Content Group.**
Landauer Corporation *See* **Landauer Publishing, LLC**
Landauer Publishing, LLC, *(978-0-9646870; 978-1-890621; 978-0-9770166; 978-0-9793711; 978-0-9800688; 978-0-9818040; 978-0-9825586; 978-1-935726; 978-1-947163)* 3100 100th St., Urbandale, IA 50322 USA (SAN 915-2334) Tel 515-287-2144; Fax: 515 276 5102; Toll Free: 800-557-2144; 3100 100th St., Urbandale, IA 50322 (SAN 915-2334) Tel 515-287-2144; Fax: 515 276 5102; Toll Free: 800-557-2144
E-mail: info@landauercorp.com; jeramy@landauercorp.com; acounting@landauercorp.com
Web site: http://www.landauerpub.com
Dist(s): **American Wholesale Bk. Co.**
Baker & Taylor Bks.
Bookazine Co., Inc.
Brodart Co.
Fox Chapel Publishing Co., Inc.
Landfall Co., The, *(978-0-9747445)* 18640 Mack Ave., P.O. Box 36551, Grosse Pointe Farms, MI 48236 USA Fax: 313-886-6250
E-mail: mhslandfall@landfallcompany.com.
Landmark Editions, Incorporated *See* **landmark Hse., Ltd.**
landmark Hse., Ltd., *(978-0-933849; 978-0-9822874)* 1949 Foxridge Dr., Kansas City, KS 66106 USA
Web site: http://www.landmarkhouse.com.
Landmark Publishing Inc., *(978-0-9726738)* P.O. Box 46403, Minneapolis, MN 55446 USA (SAN 254-9689) Tel 763-694-8907; Fax: 763-694-8909
E-mail: info@brainerdbound.com
Web site: http://www.brainerdbound.com.
Landrum, Warren, *(978-0-9787355; 978-1-7333195)* 1334 E. Chandler Blvd., Suite 5-D67, Phoenix, AZ 85048 USA
E-mail: warrenglandrum@hotmail.com.
Landstrider Pr., *(978-0-9969936)* 2944 NE Sawdust Hill Rd, Poulsbo, WA 98370 USA Tel 206-498-7944
E-mail: bors.vesterby@gmail.com.
Lane, Sondra Corp., *(978-0-9743874)* 2436 N. Federal Hwy., No. 300, Lighthouse Point, FL 33064 USA
Web site: http://www.hallelujahkids.com.
Lane, Veronica Bks., *(978-0-9637597; 978-0-9762743; 978-0-9826513; 978-0-9910083; 978-0-9992573; 978-1-7341800; 978-1-7351910; 978-1-7359974; 978-1-7364567; 979-8-9868809; 979-8-9876036; 979-8-9890770)* 11420 US-1 Suite 124, N. Palm Beach, FL 33408 USA (SAN 298-1157) Tel 310-621-2144 (phone/fax)
E-mail: etan@veronicalanebooks.com
Web site: http://www.veronicalanebooks.com
Dist(s): **Bored Feet Pr.**
DeVorss & Co.
Follett School Solutions
INscribe Digital
Independent Pubs. Group
Integral Yoga Pubns.
New Leaf Distributing Co., Inc.
Lang Graphics, Ltd., *(978-0-933617; 978-1-55962; 978-1-57832; 978-0-7412)* Div. of Perfect Timing, Inc., Orders Addr.: P.O. Box 1605, Waukesha, WI 53188 USA; Edit Addr.: 514 Wells St., Delafield, WI 53018 USA (SAN 692-4689) Tel 414-646-3399; Fax: 414-646-2224; Toll Free: 800-262-2611
E-mail: support@shop.lang.com
Web site: http://www.lang.com
Dist(s): **TNT Media Group, Inc.**
Lang Verhaal Co., *(978-0-578-41140-8; 978-0-578-41707-3; 978-1-7339503; 979-8-9857781)* 3902 N Kenneth Ave Flr. 2, Chicago, IL 60641 USA Tel 630-777-1056
E-mail: jaynesnoelle@gmail.com
Dist(s): **Ingram Content Group.**
Langberg, Daniel, *(978-0-578-82325-6; 978-0-578-36084-3)* 5743 PIGNUT MOUNTAIN DR, WARRENTON, VA 20187 USA Tel 571-426-3278
E-mail: dlangberg@hotmail.com.
Langenscheidt Publishing Group, *(978-0-88729; 978-1-58573)* Subs. of Langenscheidt KG, Orders Addr.: 15 Tyger River Dr., Duncan, SC 29334 USA Fax: 888-773-7979; Toll Free: 800-432-6277; Edit Addr.: 36-36 33rd St., Long Island City, NY 11106 USA
Web site: http://www.americanmap.com; http://www.langenscheidt.com
Dist(s): **Bilingual Pubns. Co., The.**
Lange-Patton, Lorraine, *(978-0-9752874)* P.O. Box 96811, Las Vegas, NV 89193-6811 USA.
Langille, Cody, *(978-0-692-87818-7; 978-0-692-87819-4)* 1808 S 2095 W, Woods Cross, UT 84087 USA Tel 801-358-8934
E-mail: jeffwcrawford5+LVP0003669@gmail.com; jeffwcrawford5+LVP0003669@gmail.com.
Langley, Jan *See* **Captain & Harry LLC, The**
Langley, Rachel, *(978-0-578-43763-7; 978-0-578-44664-6; 978-0-578-66803-1; 978-0-578-66804-8; 978-0-578-80100-1)* 1557 Inland Ave., Charleston, SC 29412 USA Tel 706-399-7896
E-mail: rlangley13@gmail.com
Dist(s): **Ingram Content Group.**
Langley Research & Consulting, *(978-0-578-91600-2; 978-0-578-91604-0; 978-0-578-91778-8; 978-1-7375704)* 1422 Swan Creek Pl., LOUISVILLE, KY 40299 USA Tel 5024728612
E-mail: langleyresearch@outlook.com
Dist(s): **Ingram Content Group.**
LangMarc Publishing, *(978-1-880292)* Orders Addr.: P.O. Box 90488, Austin, TX 78709 USA (SAN 297-519X) Tel 512-394-0989; Fax: 512-394-0829; Toll Free: 800-864-1648 (orders only); Edit Addr.: 7500 Shadowridge Run, No. 28, Austin, TX 78749 USA
E-mail: langmarc@booksails.com
Web site: http://www.langmarc.com.
Langson, Bridgett Bell, *(978-0-9994376)* 2330 Thornridge Rd, Charlotte, NC 28226 USA Tel 704-582-0982; *Imprints:* Tale Wag Press (Tale Wag Pr)
E-mail: bblangson@aol.com.
Langston Publishing, *(978-1-7343273; 978-1-7344325; 978-0-578-76411-5)* 135 arlington ave, Jersey City, NJ 07305 USA Tel 317-645-8045
E-mail: brooklynnmlangston@gmail.com.
Language 911, Inc., *(978-1-933451)* 12924 Calais Cir., Palm Beach Gardens, FL 33410 USA.
Language Adventure Pubns., *(978-0-9671053; 978-0-9976698)* 2311 E. Stadium Blvd., Suite 105 N, Ann Arbor, MI 48104 USA Tel 734-763-8378; Fax: 734-769-8409
E-mail: andrearojo@aol.com.
Language Quest Corp., *(978-0-9744691)* 1 Tartan Lakes, Westmont, IL 60559 USA.
Language Research Educational Series, *(978-0-9609446)* 4309 20th St., NE, Washington, DC 20018 USA (SAN 260-0927) Tel 202-636-9306
E-mail: lresduke@gmail.com.
Language Resource Manual for Schools *Imprint of* **Language Treasures**
Language Transformer Bks. *Imprint of* **Velichko, Vera**
Language Treasures, *(978-0-9765293)* 2141 SE 113th Ave., Portland, OR 97216 USA; *Imprints:* Language Resource Manual for Schools (L R M S)
E-mail: vrisk@comcast.net
Web site: http://www.languagetreasures.com.
Language Workshop for Children, The, *(978-0-9754205; 978-0-9755659; 978-0-9759664; 978-0-9819458)* 888 Lexington Ave., 2nd Flr., New York, NY 10065 USA (SAN 256-0704)
E-mail: info@professortoto.com
Web site: http://www.professortoto.com
Dist(s): **China Books & Periodicals, Inc.**
Lanico Media Hse., *(978-0-9886772; 978-0-9862057; 978-0-9967799; 978-0-9986520; 979-8-88792)* 3305 Lake Desiard Dr., Monroe, LA 71201 USA Tel 318-805-6589
E-mail: lacresha.hayes@gmail.com
Web site: www.lanicomediahouse.com.
Lanier Pr. *Imprint of* **BookLogix**
LANIUS Software *See* **PassionQuest Technologies, LLC**
Lanoue, Michelle, *(978-0-692-10170-4; 978-0-692-11265-6)* 81 Cummings Rd., Athol, MA 01331 USA Tel 978-868-5825
E-mail: lanoue72@yahoo.com
Dist(s): **Ingram Content Group.**
Lanphier Pr., *(978-0-9762151; 978-0-9786039; 978-1-934570)* Div. of Corporate Chaplains of America, 1300 Corporate Chaplain Dr., Wake Forest, NC 27587-6596 USA
E-mail: dwhite@chaplain.org
Dist(s): **Send The Light Distribution LLC.**
Lantana Publishing (GBR) *(978-0-9932253; 978-1-911373) Dist. by* **Lerner Pub.**
Lantern Books *See* **Lantern Publishing & Media**
Lantern Publishing & Media, *(978-1-930051; 978-1-59056)* Div. of Booklight, Inc., 128 2nd Pl., Brooklyn, NY 11231-4102 USA
E-mail: martin.lanternpm.org
Web site: https://lanternpm.org/
Dist(s): **Red Wheel/Weiser**
Smashwords
SteinerBooks, Inc.
Lantia *See* **Lantia LLC**
Lantia LLC, *(978-1-62934; 978-1-63503; 978-1-5243)* 1321 Upland Dr., No. 1320, Houston, TX 77043 USA
Web site: http://www.lantia.com
Dist(s): **Lulu Pr., Inc.**
Lapid, Yosef, *(978-0-9973899; 978-0-9993361; 978-1-949091)* 928 Raleigh Rd., Las Cruces, NM 88005 USA Tel 575-524-3201
E-mail: ioji158@gmail.com.
LAPOP (Latin American Public Opinion Project), *(978-0-9777042; 978-0-9792178; 978-0-9817299; 978-0-9821456; 978-0-9846260; 978-0-9846303; 978-1-939186)* 230 Appleton Pl, PMB 505 PSCI Dept at Vanderbily Univ., Nashville, TN 37203 USA
E-mail: liz.zechmeister@vanderbilt.edu
Web site: http://vanderbilt.edu/lapop.
LaPorte, Margaret, *(978-0-578-87100-4)* 18411 Carrington Ct., Hazel Crest, IL 60419 USA Tel 708-799-3554
E-mail: laporte26@sbcglobal.net.
Laposata, Michael, *(978-1-7327750)* 1006 Palm Cove Ct., Galveston, TX 77554 USA Tel 617-717-8546
E-mail: Mikelaposata@yahoo.com.
Laramie, Charles, *(978-0-9769536)* 11 W. St., Fair Haven, VT 05743 USA Tel 802-265-3538
E-mail: chucklaramie@adelphia.net.
†Laredo Publishing Co., Inc., *(978-1-56492)* 465 Westview Ave., Englewood, NJ 07631 USA Tel 201-408-4048; Fax: 201-408-5011
E-mail: info@laredopublishing.com
Web site: http://www.laredopublishing.com; *CIP.*
Large Print Bk. Co., The, *(978-1-59688)* P.O. Box 970, Sanbornville, NH 03872-0970 USA Tel 603-569-4215
Web site: largeprintbookco.com.
Large Print Pr. *Imprint of* **Thorndike Pr.**
Lark Bks., *(978-0-937274; 978-1-57990; 978-1-887374; 978-1-60059; 978-1-4547)* Div. of Sterling Publishing Co.,

Inc., 67 Broadway St., Asheville, NC 28801-2919 USA (SAN 219-9947)
E-mail: info@larkbooks.com
Web site: http://www.larkbooks.com
Dist(s): **Hearst Bks.**
Open Road Integrated Media, Inc.
Sterling Publishing Co., Inc.

Larksdale, *(978-0-89896)* P.O. Box 801222, Houston, TX 77280 USA (SAN 220-0643) Tel 713-461-7200; Fax: 713-467-4770 (purchase orders); Toll Free: 877-461-7200; *CIP.*

Larksong Productions *See* **Larksong Productions, Earthsong, Inc.**

Larksong Productions, Earthsong, Inc., *(978-0-9744878)* Div. of Earthsong, Inc., 1663 N. Circle Dr., Tempe, AZ 85281 USA Tel 480-599-4830
E-mail: mail@meadowlarkmusic.com; lynn@lynntrombetta.com; trombetta.wordsmith@gmail.com
Web site: http://www.meadowlarkmusic.com; http://choosinggreatness.com/; http://www.lynntrombetta.com.

Larousse, Ediciones, S. A. de C. V. (MEX) *(978-968-6042; 978-968-6147; 978-968-6347; 978-970-607; 978-970-22) Dist. by* **Continental Bk.**

Larousse, Ediciones, S. A. de C. V. (MEX) *(978-968-6042; 978-968-6147; 978-968-6347; 978-970-607; 978-970-22) Dist. by* **IPG Chicago.**

Larousse, Ediciones, S. A. de C. V. (MEX) *(978-968-6042; 978-968-6147; 978-968-6347; 978-970-607; 978-970-22) Dist. by* **HM.**

Larousse, Ediciones, S. A. de C. V. (MEX) *(978-968-6042; 978-968-6147; 978-968-6347; 978-970-607; 978-970-22) Dist. by* **Giron Bks.**

Larousse, Editions (FRA) *(978-2-03) Dist. by* **IPG Chicago.**

Larousse, Editions (FRA) *(978-2-03) Dist. by* **HM.**

Larousse Kingfisher Chambers, Inc., *(978-0-7534; 978-1-85697)* 215 Park Ave., S., New York, NY 10003 USA (SAN 297-7540); 181 Ballardvale St., Wilmington, MA 01887
Dist(s): **Macmillan.**

Larry Huch Ministries, *(978-0-9745301)* Orders Addr.: P.O. Box 2197, Mansfield, TX 76063-0039 USA
E-mail: cory@larryhuchministries.com
Web site: http://www.larryhuchministries.com
Dist(s): **Anchor Distributors.**

Larry W. Mitchell, *(978-0-578-98461-2)* 509 Turning Stone, Cibolo, TX 78108 USA Tel 210-218-1782
E-mail: MitchellLW@icloud.com.

Lars Muller Pubs. (CHE) *(978-3-907044; 978-3-906700; 978-3-907078; 978-3-03778) Dist. by* **Dist Art Pubs.**

Larson Learning, Inc., *(978-0-9639121; 978-1-58123; 978-1-887050)* Div. of Larson Texts, Inc., 1762 Norcross Rd., Erie, PA 16510-3838 USA Tel 814-824-6365; Fax: 814-824-6377; Toll Free: 800-530-2355
Web site: http://www.larsonlearning.com.

Larson Pubns., *(978-0-943914; 978-1-936012)* 4936 Rte. 414, Burdett, NY 14818 USA (SAN 241-130X) Tel 607-546-9342; Fax: 607-546-9344; Toll Free: 800-828-2197 Do not confuse with Larson Pubns., Joliet, IL
E-mail: larson@lightlink.com
Web site: http://www.larsonpublications.org
Dist(s): **National Bk. Network**
New Leaf Distributing Co., Inc.
Red Wheel/Weiser
ebrary, Inc.

Larstan Publishing, Inc., *(978-0-9764266; 978-0-9776895; 978-0-9789182)* 209 Canterbury Ct., Blue Bell, PA 19422 USA (SAN 256-3460) Fax: 707-922-7280
E-mail: sgenkin@larstan.net
Web site: http://www.theblackbooks.com.

LaRyssa K. Hodges, *(978-0-578-42133-9; 978-0-578-49315-2)* 5139 W. Headstall Trail, Phoenix, AZ 85083 USA Tel 770-312-2193
E-mail: laryssa68@icloud.com
Dist(s): **Ingram Content Group.**

Laser Productions *See* **Global Publishing**

Lash & Assocs. Publishing/Training, Inc., *(978-1-931117)* Orders Addr.: 100 Boardwalk Dr. Suite 150, Youngsville, NC 27596 USA Tel 919-556-0300 phone; Fax: 919-556-0900 fax
E-mail: keith@lapublishing.com
Web site: http://www.lapublishing.com.

Lashley, Shane, *(978-0-578-80470-5)* 159 E. 93rd St., Brooklyn, NY 11212 USA Tel 646-413-2329
E-mail: mybestfriendbrowny@gmail.com.

lasirenaBks.01@yahoo.com, *(978-0-578-67625-8; 978-1-7352457; 979-8-9853228)* PO Box 856 0, West seneca, NY 14224 USA Tel 3477430818
E-mail: lasirenabooks01@yahoo.com
Dist(s): **Ingram Content Group.**

Last Gasp Eco-Funnies, Incorporated *See* **Last Gasp of San Francisco**

Last Gasp of San Francisco, *(978-0-86719)* Orders Addr.: 777 Florida St., San Francisco, CA 94110 USA (SAN 216-8308); Edit Addr.: 777 Florida St., San Francisco, CA 94110-2025 USA (SAN 170-3242) Tel 415-824-6636; Fax: 415-824-1836; Toll Free: 800-366-5121
E-mail: colin@lastgasp.com
Web site: http://www.lastgasp.com
Dist(s): **SCB Distributors.**

Last Knight Publishing *See* **Last Knight Publishing Co.**

Last Knight Publishing Co., *(978-0-9720442)* P.O. Box 270006, Fort Collins, CO 80527 USA Tel 970-391-6857
Web site: http://www.lastknightpublishing.com
Dist(s): **Bks. West.**

Last Play Publishing, *(978-0-9760181)* 17931 Inverness Ave., Baton Rouge, LA 70810 USA Tel 225-751-6419
E-mail: djones@dow.com.

Lasting Bks. Publishing Co., *(978-0-9767511)* 8433 Briggs Dr., Roseville, CA 95747-5951 USA
E-mail: director@lastingbooks.com
Web site: http://www.lastingbooks.com.

Lata de Sal Editorial S.L. (ESP) *(978-84-940584; 978-84-941136; 978-84-941784; 978-84-942451; 978-84-942867) Dist. by* **Lectorum Pubns.**

Latham, Jon Bks., *(978-1-7322763)* 455 Bliss Ave., Clovis, CA 93611 USA Tel 559-900-7158
E-mail: mnjonman@gmail.com
Web site: www.jonlathambooks.com.

Latinarte *See* **I.Om.Be Pr.**

Latino, Frank Publishing Co., *(978-0-9640474)* 6806 Newport Lake Cir., Boca Raton, FL 33496 USA Tel 561-241-3880; Fax: 561-995-6975; Toll Free: 800-922-8565
E-mail: frank@hollyboy.com
Web site: http://www.hollyboy.com.

Latino Literacy Press *See* **Lectura Bks.**

Latitude 20 *Imprint of* **Univ. of Hawaii Pr.**

Lato, Greg, *(978-0-692-91633-9; 978-0-578-28833-8; 979-8-218-01545-9)* 16 Marian Ave, Narragansett, RI 02882 USA Tel 401-952-1581
E-mail: greglato@gmail.com.

Latricia Edwards Scriven, *(978-1-7363269; 978-1-7373784)* 2162 Golden Eagle Dr. W, Tallahassee, FL 32312 USA Tel 225-603-7278
E-mail: endeavortolearn@yahoo.com.

Lauco Pr., *(978-0-692-32492-9; 978-0-692-48432-6; 978-0-9976422)* 8206 Kittama Dr., Clinton, MD 20735 USA Tel 3018683221; Toll Free: 3018683221
Dist(s): **CreateSpace Independent Publishing Platform.**

Laudati, Joe, *(978-0-615-20324-9; 978-0-578-06902-9)* 425 E. 76th St., No. 9B, New York, NY 10021-2516 USA Tel 212-737-3515
E-mail: joelaudati33@earthlink.net
Web site: http://www.joelaudati.com
Dist(s): **Lulu Pr., Inc.**

Lauerman, Rosalie, *(978-0-692-50783-4; 978-0-692-08224-9)* 1201 Redtail Cir., Woodstock, IL 60098 USA Tel 815-337-3501
E-mail: rosalielauerman@msn.com.

Laugh-A-Lot Bks., *(978-0-615-28469-9)* 25 W. Broadway, Apt. 310, Long Beach, NY 11561 USA
Web site: http://www.laughalotpoetry.com; http://www.laughalotbooks.com.

Laughing Baby Pubns., *(978-0-615-18948-2)* 3662 Big Spring Rd., Lake Almanor, CA 96137 USA Tel 530-596-4397
E-mail: jennifer@babyinspirations.net
Web site: http://www.laughingbabypublications.com.

Laughing Elephant, *(978-0-9621131; 978-1-883211; 978-1-59583; 978-1-5149)* Orders Addr.: 3645 Interlake Ave., N., Seattle, WA 98103 USA Tel 206-447-9229; Fax: 206-447-9189; Toll Free: 800-354-0400 (orders only); Edit Addr.: 4649 Sunnyside Ave., N., Seattle, WA 98103 USA (SAN 250-7722) Tel 206-632-7075; Fax: 206-632-0466; *Imprints*: Darling & Company (Darling & Comp); Green Tiger Press (Gm Tiger Pr)
E-mail: laughingelephant@laughingelephant.com
Web site: http://www.laughingelephant.com
Dist(s): **Ingram Publisher Services**
SCB Distributors.

Laughing Gull Pr., *(978-0-9726699)* P.O. Box 23272, Brooklyn, NY 11202-3272 USA
E-mail: laughinggullpress@earthlink.net.

Laughing Rhino Bks., *(978-0-9859603)* 23830 25th Dr. SE, Bothell, WA 98021 USA Tel 425-420-8144
E-mail: gordon.glessner@gmail.com
Web site: www.laughinrhinobooks.com.

Laughing Zebra - Bks. for Children *Imprint of* **J.O.Y. Publishing**

Laura Booth Swanson, *(978-0-578-84249-3)* 11048 Marine View Pl SW, Seattle, WA 98146 USA Tel 206-920-0422
E-mail: nadira@nadira.com.

Laura Kate Genevish, *(978-1-7358728)* 22201 Northgate Dr., Carrollton, VA 23314 USA Tel 757-541-3731
E-mail: laura.genevish.12@cnu.edu.

Laurel *Imprint of* **Random House Publishing Group**

Laurel & Herbert, Inc., *(978-0-9619155)* P.O. Box 440266, Sugarloaf Shores, FL 33044 USA (SAN 243-4687) Tel 305-745-3506; Fax: 305-745-9070.

Laurel Leaf *Imprint of* **Random Hse. Children's Bks.**

Laurel Press *See* **Laurel & Herbert, Inc.**

Laurel Rose Publishing, *(978-0-692-41643-3; 978-0-692-42391-2; 978-0-692-56797-5; 978-1-944583)* 1930 Holston Rd, Senatobia, MS 38619 USA Tel 6625196505; Toll Free: 6626120703
Web site: www.laurelrosepublishing.com
Dist(s): **CreateSpace Independent Publishing Platform.**

Laurel Valley Graphics, Inc., *(978-0-9717475; 978-0-9853454)* 1511 Monastery Dr., Latrobe, PA 15650 USA Fax: 724-532-1957
E-mail: mike@lvgraphics.net
Web site: http://www.lvgraphics.net.

Lauren Blakely Bks., *(978-0-692-57203-0; 978-1-7325755; 979-8-9872405)* PO Box 22481, Seattle, WA 98122 USA
E-mail: videofishbowl@gmail.com.

Lauren Elizabeth Design, *(978-0-9779594)* 2002 Duboin Rd, New Iberia, LA 70560 USA
E-mail: chad@turnkeybid.com.

Lauren Simone Publishing Company *See* **Lauren Simone Publishing Hse.**

Lauren Simone Publishing Hse., *(978-0-9979520; 978-1-948071)* 41 Henderson Dr., East Hartford, CT 06108 USA Tel 860-478-3897
E-mail: laurensimonepubs@gmail.com; info@laurensimonepubs.com
Web site: http://laurensimonepubs.com/.

Laurob Pr., *(978-0-9787376)* 4204 Anjou Ct., Chico, CA 95973 USA.

Laurus Books *See* **Laurus Co., Inc., The**

Laurus Co., The, Orders Addr.: 524 Guinevere Court, McDonough, GA 30252 USA (SAN 858-608X) Tel 678-814-4047; Fax: 678-272-7255; Toll Free: 800-596-7370
E-mail: thelaurusco@charter.net
Web site: http://www.thelauruscompany.com.

LaVa Pubns., *(978-0-9638838; 978-0-9714261; 978-0-9761449; 978-0-9792400)* Div. of Field O Dreams Farm, Orders Addr.: P.O. Box 9372, Dothan, AL 36303 USA (SAN 255-2027)
E-mail: spharr@centurytel.net.

Lavabrook Publishing Group *See* **Lavabrook Publishing, LLC**

Lavabrook Publishing, LLC, *(978-0-9892064; 978-1-942662)* 675 E. Santa Clara St. No. 1478, Ventura, CA 93001 USA Tel 805-637-4813
E-mail: laurathalassa.author@gmail.com.

Lavender Books *See* **Lavender Bks.**

Lavender Bks., *(978-0-9742739)* 11111 Jefferson Blvd., Culver City, CA 90230 USA
E-mail: lavenderbooks333@sbcglobal.net
Web site: www.dotiq.net.

Lavergne, Teresa *See* **Teresa E Lavergne**

Laverne Story Stanley, *(978-1-7334611)* 152 Lost Forest St., San Antonio, TX 78233 USA Tel 210-632-9856
E-mail: stilstory@gmail.com.

Lavoie, Louis, *(978-0-9791018)* 1300 W. Medicine Lake Dr., No. 211, Plymouth, MN 55441 USA
E-mail: lavoielouis6@hotmail.com.

Law Offices of Harry Glick *See* **Rai Consulting & Publishing**

Lawe Street Bks., *(978-0-9713179)* 1818 S. Lawe St., Appleton, WI 54915 USA Tel 920-739-4577
E-mail: stedjee@aol.com.

Lawells Publishing, *(978-0-934981)* P.O. Box 1338, Royal Oak, MI 48068-1338 USA (SAN 694-602X) Tel 248-543-5297
E-mail: lawells@tm.net
Web site: http://www.lawells.net.

Lawley Enterprises, *(978-1-7336444; 978-1-952209; 978-1-956357; 978-1-958302; 978-1-960137)* 1448 E Lexington Ave, Gilbert, AZ 85234 USA Tel 480-225-5576
E-mail: laralaw76@gmail.com
Web site: Lawleypublishing.com.

LawMux *See* **Billie Holladay Skelley**

LawMux Pr. *Imprint of* **Billie Holladay Skelley**

Lawrence Educational Services, Inc., *(978-1-932959; 978-1-59699)* Orders Addr.: P.O. Box 6256, Bridgewater, NJ 08807 USA Tel 908-575-8830; Fax: 908-704-1730; Toll Free: 800-575-7670; Edit Addr.: 674 Rte. 202-206 N, Suite 4, Bridgewater, NJ 08807 USA
E-mail: llteach5757670@aol.com
Web site: http://www.llteach.com.

Lawrence Publishing, *(978-0-9716039)* Div. of Educational Services & Publications, 2935 E. Rose Ln., Phoenix, AZ 85016 USA Tel 602-912-9553 Do not confuse with companies with the same or similar names in Flower Mound, TX, Van Nuys, CA, Los Angeles, CA, Wichita, KS, Baton Rouge, LA
E-mail: llawre2222@aol.com; walton90@alltel.net.

Lawson, Archie B., *(978-0-9762660)* 1168 Shashas Way, Riverton, UT 84065-4111 USA Tel 801-302-0440
E-mail: archiebl@msn.com.

Lawson, Joseph, *(978-1-7328071)* 7123 Yacht Basin Ave. Apt. 316, Orlando, FL 32835 USA Tel 704-770-8069
E-mail: jblawson@bellsouth.net
Web site: LunchboxLovenotesBook.com.

Lawson, Tracy, *(978-0-9966108; 979-8-9876123)* 405 N. Ballard AVe., Wylie, TX 75098 USA Tel 614-439-6291; *Imprints*: DysCovered Publishing (DysCovered)
E-mail: tracy.s.lawson@gmail.com
Web site: http://counteractbook.com; https://tracylawsonbooks.com.

Laybrinth Road *Imprint of* **Random Hse. Children's Bks.**

Layla M. Gatlin, *(978-1-7371797)* 3215 Gatlin Dr., TRASKWOOD, AR 72167 USA Tel 501-545-9774
E-mail: laylagatlin_author@yahoo.com.

Layla the Ladybug Bk. Publishing, *(978-0-692-59563-3; 978-0-9988693)* P.O. Box 3246, McKinney, TX 75070 USA Tel 817-504-9094
E-mail: lemonscd7@yahoo.com.

Layman Theologian Ministries, *(978-0-692-13099-5; 978-0-692-13100-8; 978-0-692-14894-5; 978-0-692-16646-8; 978-0-692-17632-0; 978-0-578-44392-8; 978-0-578-50562-6)* 597 W. Burrough Rd., BOWDOIN, ME 04287 USA Tel 207-248-1007
E-mail: davidthms600@gmail.com
Dist(s): **Ingram Content Group.**

Layne Morgan Media, Inc., *(978-0-9762904; 978-0-9772007; 978-0-9774803; 978-1-4265)* 2101 W. Chesterfield Blvd. Ste. A102, Springfield, MO 65807-8672 USA
E-mail: kimberlym@laynemorgan.com
Web site: http://www.laynemorgan.com.

Lazarus Tribe Media, LLC, *(978-1-7324486; 978-1-7331747; 978-1-7350284; 978-1-7370450)* 504 Riverside Pkwy. Suite 608, Rome, GA 30161 USA Tel 706-936-2936
E-mail: lazarustribemedia@gmail.com.

Lazy 2 Y Publishing, *(978-1-7322569)* 22801 Jensen Rd, Wall, SD 57790 USA Tel 605-381-4630
E-mail: angelalytle50@gwtc.net.

LBel Bks., *(978-1-7327887)* 460 Calle De La Mesa, Novato, CA 94949 USA Tel 415-261-7811
E-mail: lindbel@gmail.com.

LBF Bks., LLC, *(978-0-9754533; 978-0-9773082)* Orders Addr.: P.O. Box 7989, Pittsburgh, PA 15216 USA; Edit Addr.: 1537 Dormont Ave., Pittsburgh, PA 15216 USA
E-mail: lbf@lbfbooks.com.

LBF/Hadrosaur *Imprint of* **Hadrosaur Pr.**

LC Design Publishing, *(978-0-9975743)* 8504 Firestone No. 230, Downey, CA 90241 USA Tel 562-400-0799; Fax: 562-862-3007
E-mail: lak-leon@hotmail.com
Web site: leoraleon.com.

LCD Publishing *See* **LC Design Publishing**

L'Chaim Pubns., *(978-0-9766946)* 521 Fifth Ave., Suite 1740, New York, NY 10175 USA
E-mail: lchaim@att.biz
Web site: http://lchaimpublications.com/.

LD Bks., Inc., *(978-0-9772669; 978-0-9785897; 978-1-939048; 978-1-940281; 978-1-943387)* 8313 NW 68th St., Miami, FL 33166 USA (SAN 631-8088) Tel 305-406-2292; Fax: 305-406-2293
E-mail: vilmac@ldbooks.com; sales@ldbooks.com
Web site: http://www.sinlimites.net; http://www.ldbooks.com.

LD Coach, LLC, *(978-0-9745938; 978-0-9764112)* 1401 Johnson Ferry Rd., Suite 328-C13, Marietta, GA 30062-5241 USA Toll Free: 888-848-6224
E-mail: bill.allen@ldcoach.com
Web site: http://www.ldcoach.com.

LDawn, *(978-1-7360418)* 4906 Burnt Knob Rd, Murfreesboro, TN 37129 USA Tel 423-430-0905
E-mail: leslieruth88@gmail.com.

LDS & Assocs., *(978-1-883574)* Orders Addr.: 13681 Newport Ave., Suite 8 #831, Tustin, CA 92780 USA Toll Free: 800-331-3610
E-mail: trainers@ldsassoc.com
Web site: http://www.ldsassoc.com.

Le Bk. Moderne, LLC, *(978-0-9768450)* 2849 W. 23rd Ave., Denver, CO 80211 USA Tel 303-523-6401; *Imprints*: Giggletins (Gigglet)
E-mail: michael@lebookmoderne.com
Web site: http://www.lebookmoderne.com.

Le Gendre, Kimaada, *(978-1-7326320; 978-1-7376409)* 115-44 217th St., Queens, NY 11411 USA Tel 917-795-5344
E-mail: naturebellainc@gmail.com.

Le, Jordan, *(978-1-7372706)* 7705 Lyons Ln, Yakima, WA 98903 USA Tel 253-414-2535
E-mail: jordanle15@yahoo.com.

Le Petit Chien, *(978-0-9717019)* 2415 Daybreaker Dr., Park City, UT 84098 USA.

Le Reve Enterprises, LLC *See* **13th & Joan**

Le Robert (FRA) *(978-2-85036; 978-2-84902) Dist. by* **Distribks Inc.**

Le Robert (FRA) *(978-2-85036; 978-2-84902) Dist. by* **Continental Bk.**

Le Rue Publishing, *(978-0-9985437; 978-1-7335960; 978-1-951714)* 320 S. Boston Ave., Ste. 1030, Tulsa, OK 74103 USA Tel 918-216-0180
E-mail: robertsdenton@gmail.com
Web site: www.leruepublishing.com.

Lead Life Pr., LLC, *(978-0-9762408)* The Lead Life Institute, 2111 Deerfield Dr., New Hope, PA 18938 USA Tel 215 794 8516; Fax: 215 794 8532
E-mail: mdec@leadlifeinstitute.com.

Lead U, *(978-0-578-55634-5)* 511 3rd Ave., Asbury Park, NJ 07712 USA Tel 732-998-4027
E-mail: jd.wilson@leaduthere.com
Web site: www.leaduthere.com.

Leaderbrook, *(978-0-9719079)* P.O. Box 864, Amherst, OH 44001-0864 USA Tel 440-985-5844
E-mail: timothy@clevelandceo.com
Web site: http://www.leaderbrook.com.

LeaderMetrix Inc., *(978-1-7325236)* 3321 Caldeira Dr., Livermore, CA 94550 USA Tel 408-832-8111
E-mail: gary@leadermetrix.com
Web site: www.leadermetrix.com.

Leaders Press *See* **Leaders Pr. SRL**

Leaders Pr. SRL, *(978-0-9831547; 978-1-943386; 978-1-63735)* Via Trento e Trieste 49 P.IVA:01493340119, Levanto, 19015 ITA Tel 334-286-7691
E-mail: alina.rutkowska@gmail.com
Dist(s): **Blackstone Audio, Inc.**
Simon & Schuster, Inc.

Leadership Development Group, The, *(978-0-692-21198-4; 978-0-578-44950-0; 978-0-578-76418-4; 978-0-578-80123-0; 978-1-7370815)* 13131 Castle Harbour Dr M5, Naples , FL 34110 USA Tel 651-399-3556
E-mail: dd@theLDG.org
Web site: www.theLDG.org.

Leadership Horizons, LLC, *(978-0-9668868)* 959 Keystone Way, Carmel, IN 46032-2823 USA Tel 317-844-5587; Fax: 317-581-9226; Toll Free: 888-262-2477
E-mail: ron@leadershiphorizons.com.

Leadership Loft, The *See* **Green Owl, Inc.**

LeaderTreks NFP, *(978-1-934577; 978-1-939031)* 25w560 Geneva Rd. #30, Carol Stream, IL 60188 USA Tel 630-668-0936; Fax: 630-668-0980; Toll Free: 800-502-0699
E-mail: danc@leadertreks.com; angie@leadertreks.com
Web site: http://www.leadertreks.com; http://www.leadertreks.org.

Leading Lady Pubns., *(978-0-9776746; 978-0-9798084; 978-0-9802468; 978-0-9818753)* Orders Addr.: P.O. Box 35, Worton, MD 21678 USA Toll Free: 800-597-9428; Edit Addr.: 306 Sunrise Ave., Ridgely, MD 21660 USA
Web site: http://www.publishyourchristianbook.com
Dist(s): **CreateSpace Independent Publishing Platform**
Lushena Bks.

Leadline Publishing, *(978-0-9801464)* Orders Addr.: 2101 NW Corporate Blvd Ste 206, Boca Raton, FL 33431 USA
Web site: http://www.teamfroglogic.com.

Leaf & Thorn Pr., LLC, *(978-1-945040)* 1080 Pebble Brook Dr., Columbus, OH 43240 USA Tel 614-396-6055
E-mail: kathleengroger@gmail.com.

Leaf & Vine Bks, *(978-0-9786087; 978-0-615-18762-4)* 387 Ivy St., San Francisco, CA 94102 USA
E-mail: editor@leafvinebooks.com
Dist(s): **Lulu Pr., Inc.**

Leaf Publishing, LLC, *(978-0-692-19308-2; 978-0-578-44020-0; 978-0-578-49097-7; 978-0-578-51021-7; 978-1-7363809)* 1470 Baracoa Ave., Coral Gables, FL 33146 USA Tel 305-725-8821
E-mail: amy.l.erwin@comcast.net.

Publisher Name Index

Leaf Storm Pr., *(978-0-9914105; 978-0-9970207; 978-1-945652)* P.O. Box 4670, Santa Fe, NM 87502 USA (SAN 920-7406)
E-mail: LeafStormPress@gmail.com
Web site: http://leafstormpress.com
Dist(s): **Legato Pubs. Group**
Publishers Group West (PGW).

Leafcollecting.com Publishing Co., *(978-0-9747654)* 189 N. Jefferson Ave., Bradley, IL 60915-1829 USA Tel 815-932-0850; *Imprints:* Egap Gifa Books (Egap Gifa Bks)
E-mail: Darlene@leafcollecting.com; Thegreatlakes189@yahoo.com
Web site: http://www.leafcollecting.com.

Leafcutter Pr., LLC, *(978-0-9818734; 978-0-9997992)* P.O. Box 102, Southworth, WA 98386 USA (SAN 856-7999) Tel 360-990-5422
E-mail: kevinhwirth@gmail.com.

Leafprint Pr., *(978-1-7341869)* 4212 Markham St., Lyons Falls, NY 13368 USA Tel 315-717-1153
E-mail: lydia.johnson.huntress@gmail.com
Web site: www.lydiajohnsonhuntress.com.

Leafwood Pubs. *Imprint of* **Abilene Christian Univ. Pr.**

Leah St. James Bks., *(978-0-9853123; 978-0-9967663; 978-0-9983730)*
E-mail: jscottprice@gmail.com; leahdprice@gmail.com; thedaveprice@gmail.com
Web site: http://www.leahstjames.com
Dist(s): **BookBaby.**

Leah Venegas, *(978-0-578-40046-4; 978-0-578-41972-5)* 1017 Klondyke Loop, Somers, MT 59932 USA Tel 406-858-0496
E-mail: leah@leahvenegas.com
Dist(s): **Ingram Content Group.**

Lean Pr., *(978-1-932475)* Div. of Hopefuls, Inc., Orders Addr.: P.O. Box 80334, Portland, OR 97280-1334 USA (SAN 255-6286) Tel 503-708-4415; Fax: 503-626-9098
E-mail: sean@leanpress.com; mike@leanpress.com
Web site: http://www.leanpress.com.

Leaning Rock Pr., *(978-0-9994985; 978-0-9998744; 978-1-7328519; 978-1-950323; 978-1-960596)* P.O. Box 44, Gales Ferry, CT 06335 USA Tel 860-464-6454; 860-235-2552
E-mail: leaningrockpress.gmail.com; bobrobinnelson@hotmail.com
Web site: www.colibrichildrensadventures.com; www.colibrichildrenspress.com; www.leaningrockpress.com.

Leap Bks., *(978-1-61603)* P.O. Box 112, Reidsville, NC 27320-0112 USA (SAN 858-5431)
E-mail: leapbks@gmail.com
Web site: http://www.leapbks.com.

Leap Forward Pubns., *(978-0-9743664)* 12108 Scribe Dr., Austin, TX 78759-3133 USA
E-mail: mjanthony@sbcglobal.net.

L.E.A.P. (Learning through an Expanded Arts Program, Inc), *(978-0-9713649)* 441 W. End Ave., Suite 2G, New York, NY 10024 USA Tel 212-769-4160; Fax: 212-724-4479
E-mail: leap@leapnyc.org
Web site: http://www.leapnyc.org.

Leap Year Marketing, *(978-0-692-08633-9; 978-0-692-17389-3; 978-0-578-97349-4; 978-0-578-97350-0; 978-0-578-32151-6; 978-0-578-32152-3)* 18 Towle Pasture Dr., EPSOM, NH 03234 USA Tel 603-344-8843
E-mail: jmrwtpl@gmail.com
Dist(s): **Ingram Content Group.**

LeapFrog Enterprises, Inc., *(978-1-58605; 978-1-932256; 978-1-59319; 978-1-60685)* 6401 Hollis St., Suite 125, Emeryville, CA 94608 USA Tel 510-420-5000; Fax: 510-596-6821; *Imprints:* LeapFrog School House (LeapSchHse)
E-mail: crymer@leapfrog.com; leo_lui@vtech.com; mtellegen@leapfrog.com
Web site: http://www.leapfrog.com.

Leapfrog Pr., *(978-0-9654578; 978-0-9679520; 978-0-9728984; 978-0-9796415; 978-0-9815148; 978-1-935248; 978-1-948585)* Orders Addr.: P.O. Box 2110, Teaticket, MA 02536 USA; Edit Addr.: 59 Tanglewood Dr., Teaticket, MA 02536 USA Do not confuse with Leapfrog Pr., Wyandotte, MI
E-mail: books@leapfrogpress.com
lisa@leapfrogpress.com
Web site: http://www.leapfrogpress.com
Dist(s): **Children's Plus, Inc.**
Consortium Bk. Sales & Distribution
MyiLibrary
SPD-Small Pr. Distribution.

Leapfrog Press, Incorporated, The *See* **Leapfrog Pr.**

LeapFrog Schl. Hse. *Imprint of* **LeapFrog Enterprises, Inc.**

Leaping Antelope Productions, *(978-0-9659222; 978-0-9762059; 979-8-9887370)* Div. of Armadillo Pr., Orders Addr.: 101 Industrial Way Ste. 10, Belmont, CA 94002-8207 USA (SAN 253-7974) Toll Free: 888-909-5327
E-mail: print123@leapingantelope.com
Web site: http://www.leapingantelope.com
Dist(s): **Distributors, The**
Quality Bks., Inc.

Learn & Sign Funtime *See* **Learn & Sign Funtime Bks.**

Learn & Sign Funtime Bks., *(978-0-9753717)* Orders Addr.: 0255 E. Yellowstone Trail, Hamlet, IN 46532 USA Tel 219-775-7080; Fax: 888-308-2606; 0255 E. Yellowstone Trail Hamlet, In 46532, Hamlet, IN 46532
E-mail: learnandsign@aol.com; jujub121@aol.com.

Learn As You Grow, L.L.C., *(978-0-9824652)* P.O. Box 103, Mount Horeb, WI 53572 USA
E-mail: chad.lindley@learnasyougrow.com.

Learn2study, *(978-0-9729557)* 1935 Columbia Pike No. 24, Arlington, VA 22204 USA
Web site: http://www.learn2study.org.

Learning All About Me, LLC, *(978-0-9763961)* Orders Addr.: P.O. Box 161923, Boiling Springs, SC 29316 USA; Edit Addr.: 8 Montford Ave., Boiling Springs, SC 29316 USA.

Learning Challenge, Inc., *(978-1-59203)* 36 Washington St., Wellesley, MA 02481 USA Tel 781-239-9900; Fax: 781-239-3273
Web site: http://www.learningchallenge.com.

Learning Connection, The, *(978-1-56831)* Orders Addr.: 4100 Silver Star Rd. Ste. D, Orlando, FL 32808-4618 USA Toll Free: 800-218-8489
Web site: http://www.tlconnection.com.

Learning Curve Brands, Incorporated *See* **TOMY International, Inc.**

Learning Fasten-Ations, Inc., *(978-0-9673268; 978-0-9729476)* 5014-16th Ave., Suite 195, Brooklyn, NY 11204 USA Tel 718-854-3808; Fax: 718-854-9436; Toll Free: 800-252-8152
Web site: http://www.velcroboards.com.

Learning in Motion, *(978-1-889775)* 113 Cooper St., Santa Cruz, CA 95060-4526 USA Toll Free: 800-560-5670 Do not confuse with Learning in Motion, Mount Laurel, NJ
Web site: http://www.learn.motion.com.

Learning Line Media, The, *(978-0-9831191; 978-0-9971257; 978-1-7363722; 978-1-959457)* 451 A E. Ojai Ave., Ojai, CA 93023 USA Tel 805-218-2443
E-mail: dave@ojaidigital.com; dreeser@davidreeser.com; dvw@thelearninglinemedia.com
Web site: bluejayink.com.

Learning Links Inc., *(978-0-7675; 978-0-88122; 978-0-930448; 978-1-56982)* Orders Addr.: 26 Haypress Road, Cranbury, NJ 08512 USA (SAN 241-3302) Tel 516-437-9071; Fax: 516-437-5392; Toll Free: 800-724-2616
E-mail: info@learninglinks.com
Web site: http://www.learninglinks.com; http://www.novel-ties.com/estore/search/.

Learning Management Systems *See* **Active Learning Corp.**

Learning Net, The, *(978-1-887946)* 567 Catnip Rd., Cullowhee, NC 28723 USA Tel 828-293-2542.

Learning Parent, The, *(978-0-9708770; 978-0-9777685; 978-0-9785859; 978-0-9860433)* 2430 Sunnymeade Rd., Rustburg, VA 24588 USA Tel 434-845-8345; Fax: 434-845-3020
E-mail: learningparent@aol.com
Web site: http://www.thelearningparent.com.

Learning Props, *(978-0-9741549; 978-0-9768706; 978-1-935292)* 2818 N. 68th St., Milwaukee, WI 53210 USA Toll Free: 877-776-7750
E-mail: bev@learningprops.com
Web site: http://www.learningprops.com
Dist(s): **Follett School Solutions.**

Learning Research Associates, Incorporated *See* **National Reading Styles Institute, Inc.**

Learning Resources, Inc., *(978-1-56911)* 380 N. Fairway Dr., Vernon Hills, IL 60061 USA (SAN 630-057X) Tel 847-573-8400; Fax: 847-573-8425
E-mail: info@learningresources.com
Web site: http://www.learningresources.com.

Learning Series Pr., *(978-0-9769701)* P.O. Box 590812, Fort Lauderdale, FL 33359 USA (SAN 256-6060) Tel 954-552-4855
E-mail: mdgeddes@comcast.net
Web site: http://www.learningtodream.com.

Learning to Give, *(978-0-9774155)* 16924 Buchanan St., Grand Haven, MI 49417-8625 USA
Web site: http://www.learningtogive.org.

Learning Together, *(978-1-931840)* 5509b W. Friendly Ave. Ste. 201, Greensboro, NC 27410-4279 USA
E-mail: wtleci@aol.com.

Learning Tools Co., *(978-0-938017)* Orders Addr.: P.O. Box 657, Berkeley Springs, WV 25411 USA (SAN 692-7297) Tel 304-258-1304; Edit Addr.: 714 Rockwell St., Berkeley Springs, WV 25422 USA.

Learning with Millie & Suzie, *(978-1-7352163)* 24570 Stewart St, Pittsburgh, PA 15219 USA Tel 561-449-4923
E-mail: authors@millieandsuzie.com
Web site: millieandsuzie.com.

Learning Wood, LLC, *(978-1-933577)* 3535 W. Peterson Ave., Chicago, IL 60659 USA Tel 773-509-0707; Fax: 773-509-0404.

Learning Works, The *Imprint of* **Creative Teaching Pr., Inc.**

Learning Wrap-Ups, Inc., *(978-0-943343; 978-1-59204)* 1660 West Gordon Ave., No. 4, Layton, UT 84041 USA (SAN 668-3975) Tel 801-497-0050; Fax: 801-497-0063; Toll Free: 800-992-4966
E-mail: info@learningwrapups.com
Web site: http://www.learningwrapups.com.

Learning ZoneXpress *See* **Visualz**

LearningExpress, LLC, *(978-1-57685; 978-1-61103)* 2 Rector St., Flr. 26, New York, NY 10006-3754 USA Tel 646-274-6453; 800-295-9556
E-mail: info@learnatest.com; customerservice@learnatest.com
Web site: http://www.learnatest.com
Dist(s): **MyiLibrary**
National Bk. Network
ebrary, Inc.

LearningSuccess Pr., *(978-0-9772350)* 1147 E. Main St., Ventura, CA 93001 USA (SAN 257-0726) Tel 805-648-1739
Web site: http://www.learningsuccessinstitute.com.

Learnovation, LLC, *(978-0-9705790; 978-0-9796434; 978-0-9969528)* Orders Addr.: P.O. Box 502150, Indianapolis, IN 46250 USA (SAN 255-4577); Edit Addr.: 10831 Thistle Ridge, Fishers, IN 46038 USA Tel 317-577-1190; Fax: 317-598-0816; Toll Free: 888-577-1190
E-mail: anna@learnovation.com; karen@learnovation.com
Web site: http://learnovation.com.

Leather & Leaf Bks., *(978-1-7362197)* 3906 Thomas Ave. N., Minneapolis, MN 55412 USA Tel 612-512-8928
E-mail: tyrelvonanderberg@gmail.com.

Leatherbound Bestsellers, *(978-1-62715)* Orders Addr.: 20325 N. 51st. Ave. Suite 134, Glendale, AZ 85308 USA Tel 602-616-4334
E-mail: leatherboundbestsellers@gmail.com
Web site: www.leatherboundbestsellers.com.

Leatherbound Booksellers *See* **Leatherbound Bestsellers**

Leatherman, Diane *See* **Bounty Project, The**

Leathers Publishing, *(978-0-9646898; 978-1-890622; 978-1-58597)* Div. of Ad Ctr., 4500 College Blvd., Overland Park, KS 66211-1760 USA Tel 913-498-2625; Fax: 913-498-1561; Toll Free: 888-888-7696
E-mail: barbara@leatherspublishing.com
Web site: http://www.leatherspublishing.com.

Leatherwood Press *See* **Walnut Springs Bks.**

Leatherwood Publishing, *(978-0-9741725)* 20395 Cty. 86, Long Prairie, MN 56347 USA Tel 320-732-2879
E-mail: tann0042@umn.edu
Web site: http://www.alexweb.net/whimsy/index.htm.

Leave No Sister Behind Pubns., *(978-0-9787004)* Orders Addr.: 13 Pecan Ln., Long Beach, MS 39560 USA (SAN 851-3759)
E-mail: info@leavenosisterbehind.net
Web site: http://www.leavenosisterbehind.net
Dist(s): **Ingram Content Group.**

LeBlanc, Terry Leonard, *(978-0-9755913)* Orders Addr.: P.O. Box 387, Loyalton, CA 96118 USA; Edit Addr.: 805 Mill St., Loyalton, CA 96118 USA
E-mail: terrythetrashman@cwo.com.

Lectio Ediciones (ESP) *(978-84-96754; 978-84-15088) Dist. by* **IPG Chicago.**

LectoCultura *Imprint of* **Diaz, Olga L**

Lectorum Pubns., Inc., *(978-0-9625162; 978-1-880507; 978-1-930332; 978-1-933032; 978-1-941802; 978-1-63245; 978-1-64684)* Orders Addr.: 10 New Maple Ave. Suite 303, Pine Brook, NJ 07058 USA (SAN 990-0802) Tel 201-559-2232; Edit Addr.: 10 New Maple Ave. Suite 303, Pine Brook, NJ 07058 USA (SAN 860-0597) Tel 201-559-2200; Fax: 201-559-2201; Toll Free Fax: 877-532-8676; Toll Free: 800-345-5946
E-mail: acorrea@lectorum.com; ffebus@lectorum.com; letlarry@verizon.net
Web site: http://www.lectorum.com; http://www.libreríalectorum.com
Dist(s): **Children's Plus, Inc.**
Libros Sin Fronteras
MyiLibrary
Perfection Learning Corp.

Lectorum, S.A. de C.V. (MEX) *(978-968-7748; 978-968-5270; 978-970-732) Dist. by* **LD Bks Inc.**

Lectura Bks., *(978-0-9716580; 978-0-9772852; 978-1-60448)* 1107 Fair Oaks Ave., Suite 225, South Pasadena, CA 91030 USA
E-mail: ktdelmonte@lecturabooks.com; info@lecturabooks.com
Web site: http://www.lecturabooks.com.

Lectura Colaborativa (ARG) *(978-987-45) Dist. by* **IPG Chicago.**

Lederer/Messianic Jewish Publishers & Distributors *See* **Messianic Jewish Pubs.**

Ledford Publishing, *(978-0-9840777; 978-1-951466)* 16117 Hwy 101 S No. 64, BROOKINGS, OR 97415 USA (SAN 858-3587) Tel 541-661-8170
E-mail: dledford11@gmail.com
Web site: http://www.fructosemalabsorptionhelp.com; http://www.brewtourbooks.com/; https://rardledford.homesteadcloud.com/.

Ledge Media, *(978-0-9654999; 978-1-893619; 978-1-935377; 978-1-939300; 978-1-944891; 979-8-89177)* FRE-Enterprises, Orders Addr.: P.O. Box 230054, Encinitas, CA 92023 USA
E-mail: daphne@ledgemedia.net; info@ledgemedia.net; info@hpnbooks.com
Web site: http://www.hpnbooks.com; http://www.ledgemedia.net; http://www.hpncustommedia.net
Dist(s): **Independent Pubs. Group**
Midpoint Trade Bks., Inc.
Partners Bk. Distributing, Inc.

L'Edge Pr., *(978-0-9762014; 978-1-935256)* P.O. Box 1653, Boone, NC 28607 USA
E-mail: jeffhendley@charter.net
Web site: http://www.upsidedownministries.com.

LeDor Publishing, *(978-0-9747382)* 4885 McKnight Rd., No. 350, Pittsburgh, PA 15237 USA Tel 888-624-9094; Fax: 412-421-1628; Toll Free: 888-624-9094
E-mail: drichman@ledorgroup.com
Web site: http://www.ledorgroup.com.

Lee & Low Bks., Inc., *(978-0-89239; 978-0-938317; 978-1-880000; 978-1-885008; 978-1-58430; 978-1-933693; 978-1-60060; 978-1-935955; 978-1-62014; 978-1-941026; 978-1-947627; 978-1-64379)* 95 Madison Ave., New York, NY 10016 USA (SAN 920-7546) Tel 212-779-4400 (General info./Editorial); Fax: 212-683-1894 (orders); Toll Free: 888-320-3190 (ext. 28, orders); *Imprints:* Tu Books (Tu Books); Children's Book Press (ChilBkPr); Shen's Books (ShensBks); Cinco Puntos Press (5PuntosPr)
E-mail: clow@leeandlow.com
Web site: http://www.leeandlow.com
Dist(s): **Children's Plus, Inc.**
Follett School Solutions
Lectorum Pubns., Inc.
Perfection Learning Corp.

Lee, Angela *See* **Your Destiny Productions**

Lee, Anna, *(978-1-7367889)* 26751 Bernwood Rd., Beachwood, OH 44122 USA Tel 216-245-6373
E-mail: avklee1@gmail.com.

Lee,, Bernard N. Jr., *(978-0-692-31304-6; 978-0-9995576)* 2300 Mallory Cir., Conyers, GA 30094 USA Tel 7706486884; Fax: 7706486884
E-mail: bernie@bernardleejr.com
Dist(s): **CreateSpace Independent Publishing Platform.**

Lee Bks., *(978-0-9660653)* Orders Addr.: 514 Jamacha Rd., No. 16J, El Cajon, CA 92019 USA Tel 619-447-8789 Do not confuse with other companies with the same or similar names in San Anselmo, CA, Columbia, SC
E-mail: leebooks@juno.com
Web site: http://www.readatleebooks.com.

Lee, Collin, *(978-0-692-82896-0; 978-0-692-82897-7)*
E-mail: jeffwcrawford5+LVP0003213@gmail.com; jeffwcrawford5+LVP0003213@gmail.com.

Lee, Deborah I, *(978-0-9858839)* 3800 Bexley Sq., Reno, NV 89503 USA Tel 775-848-7797
E-mail: debbaleereno@yahoo.com.

Lee Enterprise Group *See* **Lee's Pr. and Publishing Co.**

Lee, Howard, *(978-0-9766137)* 191 Lorraine Dr., Berkeley Heights, NJ 07922 USA.

Lee Instruments, *(978-0-9704913)* Orders Addr.: P.O. Box 460-999, Leeds, UT 84746 USA; Edit Addr.: 555 E. 900 N., Leeds, UT 84746 USA; 1050 N. Main, Leeds, UT 84746 Tel 435-879-6907
E-mail: leeinst@infowest.com; violguy@infowest.com
Web site: http://kevinleeluthier.com.

Lee, J. & L. Co., *(978-0-934904)* P.O. Box 5575, Lincoln, NE 68505 USA (SAN 213-8557) Tel 402-488-4416; Fax: 402-489-2770; Toll Free: 888-665-0999
E-mail: leebooks@radiks.net
Web site: http://www.leebooksellers.com
Dist(s): **Big River Distribution.**

Lee, James V. *See* **Salado Pr., LLC**

Lee, Keith Russel Publishing *See* **Lee, Keith Russel Publishing Hse.**

Lee, Keith Russel Publishing Hse., *(978-0-9768684)* 6223 Spruce St., Philadelphia, PA 19139 USA
E-mail: krlteaches@gmail.com
Web site: http://www.keithrlee.com.

Lee, Michael, *(978-0-9766830)* 5503 Harvard, Detroit, MI 48224 USA.

Lee, Quentin Daschel, *(978-0-9789007)* 4949 Harris Ave., Las Vegas, NV 89110 USA (SAN 851-867X) Tel 702-463-9692.

Lee, Shelley, *(978-0-9786757)* Orders Addr.: 441 Frazee Ave., Suite A, Bowling Green, OH 43402-1834 USA Tel 419-354-4673
E-mail: bgpc@wcnet.org
Web site: http://BeforeIKnewYou.com.

LeeBurton Publishing *See* **Education Matters Co.**

Leedan Publishing, *(978-1-893802; 978-0-9991828)* 65 S. Orchard Dr., Park Forest, IL 60466 USA Tel 858-999-4329
E-mail: antigone.blackwell@hotmail.com
Web site: www.adsloane.com.

Leelanau Pr., *(978-0-9742068; 978-0-9785465)* 6898 MacFarlane Rd., Glen Arbor, MI 49636 USA
Web site: leelanaupress.com
Dist(s): **Partners Bk. Distributing, Inc.**

Lee's Pr. and Publishing Co., *(978-0-615-78939-2; 978-0-692-62219-3; 978-0-692-63484-4; 978-0-692-69067-3; 978-0-692-69812-9; 978-0-692-72335-7; 978-0-692-74689-9; 978-0-9978623; 978-0-9993103; 978-1-7329441; 979-8-9860989; 979-8-9886270)* P.O. Box 481628, Charlotte, NC 28269 USA Tel 704-903-7710
Dist(s): **CreateSpace Independent Publishing Platform.**

Leeth, Dawna, *(978-0-9799184)* Orders Addr.: 400 W. Bay Dr., Largo, FL 33770 USA Fax: 727-536-6863.

Leeway Pubs., *(978-0-9744929)* Div. of Leeway Artisans, Orders Addr.: P.O. Box 1577, Laurel, MD 20707 USA Tel 301-404-3355
E-mail: info@LeewayArtisans.com
Web site: http://www.LeewayArtisans.com.

Lefall & Co., Inc., *(978-0-9761778)* 2020 Edmondson Ave., Baltimore, MD 21223 USA (SAN 256-2596)
E-mail: lefallandco@aol.com
Web site: http://www.jockobook.com.

Leffler, Susan, *(978-0-9906244)* P.O. Box 4352, Tumwater, WA 98501 USA Tel 360-866-1841
E-mail: whitestarloghome@hotmail.com.

Left - Write Ink, *(978-0-9761301)* 8407 Shadow Oaks, College Station, TX 77845 USA (SAN 256-2383) Tel 979-693-0224
E-mail: lwink2@aol.com.

Left Brain Craft Brain, *(978-0-692-78236-1)* 516 Balra Dr., EL CERRITO, CA 94530 USA Tel 510-909-4971.

Left Field,Angel Gate,

Left Hand Pubs., LLC, *(978-0-9996839; 978-1-949241)* 1417 Sadler Rd. No. 245, Fernandina Beach, FL 32034 USA Tel 980-505-7677
E-mail: editor@lefthandpublishers.com
Web site: http://LeftHandPublishers.com.

Left Hand Publishing Co., *(978-0-9744799)* P.O. Box 253, Moose Lake, MN 55767 USA
E-mail: nemadji@computerpro.com
Web site: http://computerpro.com/~nemadji.

Left Paw Pr., *(978-0-9818360; 978-0-615-17884-4; 978-0-9829132; 978-0-9838044; 978-1-943356)* Orders Addr.: P.O. Box 133, Greens Fork, IN 47345 USA; Edit Addr.: 17 Washington Blvd., Greens Fork, IN 47345 USA
E-mail: lauren@laurenoriginals.com
Web site: http://www.leftpawpress.com
Dist(s): **Lulu Pr., Inc.**

Left Shoe Lost, *(978-0-9986932)* 66 Maple Ave, Maplewood, NJ 07040 USA Tel 310-614-0693
E-mail: daelo@me.com.

Legacies & Memories, *(978-0-9759533; 978-0-9972523; 978-1-7322135; 978-1-7347007; 978-1-7375505)* 5 Willard Dr., No. 644, Saint Augustine, FL 32086 USA
E-mail: info@legaciesandmemories.com
Web site: http://www.legaciesandmemories.com.

Legacy *Imprint of* **WordWright.biz, Inc.**

Legacy Book Publishing, Incorporated *See* **Legacy Family History, Inc.**

Legacy Bound, *(978-0-9677057; 978-0-9766264; 978-0-9794202; 978-0-9801045; 978-0-9819307; 978-0-9835189; 978-0-9883508; 978-0-9904014)* 7701 Commerce Way, Eden Prairie, MN 55344 USA Tel

800-909-9698; *Imprints:* Curious Cat Books (Curious Cat Bks)
E-mail: laura@legacybound.net; brad@legacybound.net
Web site: http://www.legacybound.net
Dist(s): **Baker & Taylor Publisher Services (BTPS)**
Brodart Co.
Eastern National
Follet Higher Education Grp.

Legacy Bound, Inc *See* **Legacy Bound**

Legacy Family History, Inc., *(978-0-9655835; 978-0-9716705; 978-0-9998770)* 5902 Woodshire Ln., Highland, UT 84003 USA Tel 801-763-1686 (phone/fax)
E-mail: tristantolman@comcast.net
Dist(s): **Send The Light Distribution LLC.**

Legacy Group Productions, LLC, *(978-0-9740585)* 3980 Greenmount Rd., Harrisonburg, VA 22802-0504 USA Toll Free: 877-227-6027
E-mail: cheryl@legacymatters.org
Web site: http://www.legacymatters.org.

Legacy Now International, *(978-0-692-46274-4; 978-0-692-77997-2; 978-0-692-91885-2; 978-0-692-10069-1; 978-0-692-11056-0; 978-0-692-11715-6; 978-0-692-15733-6; 978-0-692-18414-1; 978-0-692-19350-1; 978-0-692-19408-9; 978-0-578-52652-2; 978-0-578-52999-8; 978-0-578-53887-7; 978-0-578-56391-6; 978-0-578-61399-4; 978-0-578-62538-6; 978-0-578-65960-2; 978-0-578-68597-7; 978-0-578-72157-6; 978-0-578-88420-2; 978-0-578-89098-2; 978-0-578-90346-0; 978-0-578-92013-9; 978-0-578-92568-4; 978-0-578-31751-9; 978-0-578-33050-1;) 7200 Marlbrook Dr., Charlotte, NC 28212 USA Tel 980-819-1899*
Dist(s): **CreateSpace Independent Publishing Platform.**

Legacy of Negasi, *(978-1-7372458)* 13806 E Rockhill St., Wichita, KS 67230 USA Tel 316-617-6167
E-mail: raisingroyaltybooks@gmail.com
Web site: info@legacyofnegasi.com.

Legacy Planning Partners, LLC, *(978-0-9719177; 978-0-9823220)* 254 Plaza Dr., Suite B, Oviedo, FL 32765 USA Tel 407-977-8080; Fax: 407-977-8078
E-mail: peggy@hoytbryan.com.

Legacy Pr. *Imprint of* **Rainbow Pubs. & Legacy Pr.**

Legacy Pr., *(978-0-9653198; 978-0-9777897)* 11381 Mallard Dr., Rochester, IL 62563 USA Tel 217-498-8159; Fax: 217-498-7178 Do not confuse with companies with the same or similar name in Pensacola, FL, Fort Lauderdale, FL, Columbus, GA, Thinelander, WI, Sacremento, CA, Hollywood, FL, Fairfax, VA, Argle, TX
E-mail: legacypressbooks@aol.com
Web site: http://legacypress.homestead.com.

Legacy Pr. of Florida, inc, *(978-0-9980128; 978-1-947718; 978-1-958923)* 1883 Lee Rd., Winter Park, FL 32789 USA Tel 407-647-3787; Fax: 321-594-7637
E-mail: gabrielvaughn@earthlink.net
Web site: LegacyBookPublishing.com.

Legacy Pubns., *(978-0-933101)* Subs. of Pace Communications, Inc., Orders Addr.: 1301 Carolina St., Greensboro, NC 27401 USA (SAN 860-4495) Tel 800-248-3204; Fax: 336-378-8271 Do not confuse with companies with the same or similar name in Tumon GU, Overland KS, Brentwood TN, Canyon TX, Irving TX, Lilburn GA, Midlothian, VA
E-mail: legacy.publications@paceco.com
Web site: http://www.legacypublications.com.

Legacy Pubs., *(978-1-932957)* 1866 Oak Harbor Dr., Ocean Isle Beach, NC 28469 USA Tel 910-755-6873 Do not confuse with Legacy Publishers in Natural Bridge, VA, Austin, TX
E-mail: mtdixon@atmc.net.

Legacy Pubs., *(978-0-9754685)* 12126 Trotwood Dr., Austin, TX 78753 USA Tel 512-837-5366 Do not confuse with Legacy Publishers in Snellville GA, Natural Bridge VA
E-mail: legacypublishers@austin.rr.com.

Legacy Pubs. International, *(978-1-880809)* P.O. Box 9690, Rcho Santa Fe, CA 92067-4690 USA (SAN 257-0718)
E-mail: Michele@LegacyPublishersInternational.com; dmiller@hccweb.org
Web site: http://www.LegacyPublishersInternational.com
Dist(s): **Destiny Image Pubs.**

Legacy Publishing Services, Inc., *(978-0-9628733; 978-0-9708395; 978-0-9764982; 978-0-9776777; 978-1-934449; 978-1-937952)* 1883 Lee Rd. Ste. B, Winter Park, FL 32789-2108 USA Tel 407-647-3787 Do not confuse with companies with the same or similar name in Ojai, CA, Berkeley, CA, Atlanta, GA, West Chester, OH, Birmingham, AL, Daty, TX, Fort Meyers, Fl, Baton Rouge, LA
E-mail: legacybookpublishing@yahoo.com; legacypublishing@earthlink.net
Web site: http://www.legacybookpublishing.com
Dist(s): **BookBaby.**

Legacy Tree, LLC, *(978-0-9974834)* 19537 Lake Rd., Rocky River, OH 44116 USA Tel 216-509-2828
E-mail: ckozak@scratchoffworks.com
Web site: www.thejesusfamilytree.com
Dist(s): **Ingram Publisher Services**
Spring Arbor Distributors, Inc.

Legacy Voice Productions, *(979-8-9856062; 978-1-960179)* 3015 Button Cir., Loganville, GA 30052 USA Tel 678-462-0238
E-mail: legacyvoiceproductions@gmail.com.

Legaia Bks. USA, *(978-1-946946; 978-1-948738; 978-1-950543; 978-1-951932)* 555 Fayetteville St. Suite 201, Raleigh, NC 27601 USA Tel 704-216-4194
E-mail: michael.luke@legaiabooks.com.

Legend eXpress Publishing, *(978-0-9773648; 978-0-9846324; 978-0-9982261)* 3831 E. Clovis Ave., Mesa, AZ 85206-8520 USA Tel 480-664-1047; Fax: 800-528-0295
E-mail: jo@lxpaz.com
Web site: http://www.lxpaz.com.

Legend Publishing Co., *(978-0-615-22552-4; 978-0-615-22553-1; 978-0-615-22554-8; 978-0-9821687; 978-0-9909373; 978-0-9991813)* Orders Addr.: P.O. Box 429, Garden City, MI 48136 USA Tel 734-595-0663; Edit Addr.: 33807 Calumet Ct., Westland, MI 48186 USA
E-mail: bobwilly81897@Yahoo.com.

Legendary Comics, *(978-1-937278; 978-1-68116)* 2900 W Alameda Ave. 15th Flr., Suite 1500, Burbank, CA 91522 USA
E-mail: bschreck@legendary.com
Web site: www.legendary.com
Dist(s): **Penguin Random Hse. Distribution**
Penguin Random Hse. LLC
Random Hse., Inc.
Simon & Schuster, Inc.

Legenderry.com, *(978-0-9776967)* 6154 Meadowbrook Dr., Morrison, CO 80465 USA Fax: 720-222-0490
Web site: http://www.legenderry.com.

LegendMaker Scriptoria, *(978-0-9759355)* 9400 Wade Blvd. #817, Frisco, TX 75035 USA Tel 413-313-9127
E-mail: scriptoria@legendmaker.com
Web site: http://legendmaker.com.

Legends of Erin, *(978-0-9996189)* 19342 Saylor Terr., Santa Ana, CA 92705 USA Tel 714-333-7225
E-mail: meadowgriffin@yahoo.com
Web site: www.legendsoferin.com.

Legends of the West Publishing Co., *(978-0-9786904)* 174 Santa Rosa Ave., Sausalito, CA 94965-2060 USA (SAN 851-2825) Do not Confuse with Know DeFeet Publishing Company 2 Different companies. LD
E-mail: knowdefeet@aol.com.

Legler, Caroline, *(978-0-9771233)* Orders Addr.: 1930 Bonanza Ct., Winter Park, FL 32792 USA
E-mail: glegler@cfl.rr.com.

Legwork Team Publishing, *(978-0-578-00665-9; 978-0-578-00666-6; 978-0-578-01705-1; 978-0-578-01865-2; 978-0-578-01866-9; 978-0-578-01999-4; 978-0-578-02016-7; 978-0-578-02310-6; 978-0-578-02407-3; 978-0-578-02845-3; 978-0-9841535; 978-0-9843539; 978-0-9827337; 978-1-935905) 4 Peacock Ln., Commack, NY 11725 USA*
Web site: http://www.legworkteam.com
Dist(s): **Follett School Solutions.**

leharperwilliamsdesign group, *(978-0-615-37424-6)* 3819 Wake Forest Rd., Decatur, GA 30034 USA Tel 770-593-4687; Fax: 770-593-5466
E-mail: lhwdesign@me.com
Web site: http://leharperwilliamsdesign.com.

Lehman, Kim *See* **Lucky Stars Publishing, LLC**

Lehman Publishing, *(978-0-9792686)* 15997 Hough, Allenton, MI 48002 USA
E-mail: dlehman@lwarp.net; dana@lehmanpublishing.com
Web site: http://www.lehmanpublishing.com
Dist(s): **Partners Bk. Distributing, Inc.**

Lehmann, Peter Publishing, *(978-0-9788399)* P.O. Box 11284, Eugene, OR 97440-3484 USA Tel 541-345-9106; Fax: 541-345-3737; Toll Free: 877-623-7743
E-mail: info@peter-lehmann-publishing.com
Web site: http://www.peter-lehmann-publishing.com.

Lehotay, Brennan, *(978-1-7364543)* 222 Avondale Ave, Columbus, OH 43223 USA Tel 614-354-6392
E-mail: brennanlehotay@gmail.com.

Lehua, Inc., *(978-0-9647491)* P.o. Box 25548, Honolulu, HI 96825-0548 USA
E-mail: lehua@ohia.com
Web site: http://www.lehuainc.com
Dist(s): **Booklines Hawaii, Ltd.**

Leia Stone, LLC, *(978-0-615-17978-0; 978-0-9820687; 978-1-951578)* 22018 N 33rd Pl., Phoenix, AZ 85050 USA
Web site: http://www.leiastone.com.

Leicester Bay Bks., *(978-0-615-68523-6; 978-0-615-69470-2; 978-0-615-90725-3; 978-0-692-23263-7; 978-0-692-34862-8; 978-0-692-36091-0; 978-0-692-46080-1; 978-0-692-63220-8; 978-0-692-73508-4; 978-0-692-93091-5; 978-0-692-95237-5)* 3877 Leicester Bay, South Jordan, UT 84095 USA Tel 801-282-8159
Web site: www.leicesterbaybooks.com
Dist(s): **CreateSpace Independent Publishing Platform.**

Leigh, A.J., *(978-0-692-50916-6; 978-0-692-81630-7; 978-0-692-88013-5; 978-0-578-55962-4)* 18822 Salt Lake Pl., PORTER RANCH, CA 91326 USA Tel 818-437-0483.

Leigh, Kimbra, *(978-0-9718851)* P.O. Box 20255, Rochester, NY 14602 USA
Web site: http://www.kimbraleigh.com.

Leiser, Savannah, *(978-0-9991614; 979-8-9868624)* 4654 N Kenmore Ave, Chicago, IL 60640 USA Tel 302-593-9779
E-mail: savyleiser@gmail.com
Web site: savyleiser.com.

Leisure Arts, Inc., *(978-0-942237; 978-1-57486; 978-1-60140; 978-1-60900; 978-1-4647)* Orders Addr.: 5701 Ranch Dr., Little Rock, AR 72223 USA (SAN 666-9565) Tel 501-868-8800; Fax: 501-868-1001; Toll Free Fax: 877-710-5603; Toll Free: 800-643-8030 (customer service); 800-526-5111
E-mail: hermine_linz@leisurearts.com
Web site: http://www.leisurearts.com
Dist(s): **Checker Distributors**
Midpoint Trade Bks., Inc.
Notions Marketing.

Leisure Time Pr., *(978-0-9890270)* 27259 Prescott Way, Temecula, CA 92591 USA Tel 951-219-3168
E-mail: j13m@aol.com
Web site: www.leisuretimepress.com.

Lekha Murali *Imprint of* **Lekha Vippu**

Lekha Pubs., LLC, *(978-0-9725901; 978-1-937675; 978-1-951569)* 263 Ridgeview Dr., Tracy, CA 95377 USA Tel 209-666-2068
Web site: http://www.lekhaink.com.

Lekha Vippu, *(978-0-692-13010-0; 978-1-7327053)* 12807 Duck Pond Dr, GERMANTOWN, MD 20874 USA Tel 301-250-5745; *Imprints:* Lekha Murali (Lekha Murali)
E-mail: lekhavippu@gmail.com
Web site: lmexpressions.com
Dist(s): **Ingram Content Group.**

LeLeu, Lisa Puppet Show Bks. *Imprint of* **LeLeu, Lisa Studios! Inc.**

LeLeu, Lisa Studios! Inc., *(978-0-9710537; 978-0-9770299)* 100 Mechanics St., Doylestown, PA 18901 USA Tel 215-345-1233; Fax: 215-348-5378; *Imprints:* LeLeu, Lisa Puppet Show Books (L LeLeu Puppet)
E-mail: lisa.leleu@lisaleleustudios.com; Frederic.Leleu@LisaLeLeuStudios.com
Web site: http://www.LisaLeLeuStudios.com.

Lemniscaat *Imprint of* **Highlights Pr., c/o Highlights for Children, Inc.**

Lemon Grove Pr., *(978-0-9815240)* 1158 26th St. #502, Santa Monica,, CA 90403 USA Tel 310-471-1740; Fax: 310-476-7627
E-mail: info@lemongrovepress.com
Web site: http://www.lemongrovepress.com
Dist(s): **Brodart Co.**
MyiLibrary
ebrary, Inc.

Lemon Pr. LLC, *(978-0-9844183; 978-1-936617)* Orders Addr.: P.O. Box 459, Emerson, GA 30137 USA (SAN 859-3477) Tel 404-791-7742
E-mail: lemonpresspublishing@gmail.com
Web site: http://www.lemonpresspublishing.com
Dist(s): **Smashwords.**

Lemon Shark Pr., *(978-0-9741067)* 1604 Marbella Dr., Vista, CA 92081-5463 USA Tel 760-727-2850 [phone after 9AM PCT]
E-mail: lemonsharkpress@yahoo.com
Web site: http://www.lemonsharkpress.com
Dist(s): **Coutts Information Services**
Eastern Bk. Co.
Yankee Bk. Peddler, Inc.

Lemon Sherbet Pr., *(978-0-9897411)* 87 Guernsey St., Roslindale, MA 02131 USA Tel 781-799-5412
E-mail: lemonsherbetpress@gmail.com.

Lemon Vision Productions, *(978-1-934789)* 27475 Ynez Rd., No. 642, Temecula, CA 92591 USA (SAN 854-9346) Tel 951-526-2942 Toll Free: 866-580-1675
E-mail: info@lemonvision.com
Web site: http://www.lemonvision.com.

Lemonade Bks., *(978-0-9994330)* 7701 Covered Bridge Dr, Austin, TX 78736 USA Tel 949-302-1760; Fax: 949-302-1760
E-mail: ann.orsinger@gmail.com
Web site: www.lemonade-books.com.

Lemondrop Pr., *(978-0-9704718)* 2121 Loudenslager Dr., Thompson's Station, TN 37179 USA.

Lemonflavor Productions, *(978-0-9740169)* 100 Pk. Ave., 18th Flr. (Dept. MSM), New York, NY 10017 USA Tel 212-316-4278; Fax: 212-937-2211
E-mail: info@lemonflavor.com
Web site: http://www.lemonflavor.com.

Lemur Conservation Foundation, *(978-0-9766009; 978-0-9856728; 978-0-615-97588-7)* P.O. Box 249, Myakka City, FL 34251 USA Tel 941-322-8494; Fax: 941-322-9264
Web site: http://www.lemurreserve.org.

Leni Bks., *(978-0-9828173)* 11036 S. Tripp, Oak Lawn, IL 60453 USA Tel 708-712-4021; Fax: 708-398-1546
E-mail: ntalty@me.com
Web site: http://cilie-yack-is-under-attack.com.

LENKK Pr., *(978-0-9988004; 979-8-9855037)* 9612 Albert Dr, Dublin, CA 94568 USA Tel 925-289-0120
E-mail: julie@jkroyce.com
Web site: www.jkroyce.com.

Leo Publishing, *(978-0-9834735; 978-1-941157)* 303 Augusta Cir., Saint Augustine, FL 32086 USA Tel 310-598-8943
E-mail: lp10leo@gmail.com.

Leo Publishing Works, Inc., *(978-0-615-35488-0)* 3 Monroe Pkwy., Suite P455, Lake Oswego, OR 97035 USA Tel 800-675-7564; Fax: 888-362-5891
E-mail: bethany@leopublishingworks.com
Web site: http://www.LeoPublishingWorks.com.

Leonard, Dennis Publications *See* **Legacy Pubs. International**

†**Leonard, Hal Corp.,** *(978-0-634; 978-0-7935; 978-0-87910; 978-0-87930; 978-0-88188; 978-0-931340; 978-0-9607350; 978-1-56516; 978-1-57467; 978-1-4234; 978-1-936098; 978-1-61713; 978-1-61774; 978-1-61780; 978-1-4584; 978-1-4768; 978-1-4803; 978-1-62906; 978-1-4950; 978-1-5400; 978-1-7051; 979-8-3501) Orders Addr.: P.O. Box 13819, Milwaukee, WI 53213-0819 USA Tel 414-774-3630; Fax: 414-774-3259; Toll Free: 800-524-4425; Edit Addr.: 7777 W. Bluemound Rd., Milwaukee, WI 53213 USA (SAN 239-250X) Tel 414-777-3630; Fax: 414-774-4176; Imprints:* G Schirmer, Incorporated (G Schirmer); Limelight Editions (LimelightEd); Amadeus Press (AmadeusPress); Applause Theatre & Cinema (ApplauseTheatr)
E-mail: halinfo@halleonard.com
Web site: http://www.halleonard.com
Dist(s): **Blackstone Audio, Inc.**
Follett School Solutions
Giron Bks.
Hachette Bk. Group
MyiLibrary
National Bk. Network
Penguin Random Hse. Distribution
Penguin Random Hse. LLC
Penguin Publishing Group
Rowman & Littlefield Publishers, Inc.
Rowman & Littlefield Unlimited Model; *CIP.*

Leonard Pr., *(978-0-9769114; 978-1-934223)* P.O. Box 752, Bolivar, MO 65613-0752 USA Tel 417-326-5001
Web site: http://www.leonardpress.com.

Leonardo Press *See* **Firenze Pr.**

Leonardoverse Books *See* **Beyond Bks.**

Leonard's, Stew Holdings, LLC *See* **Kimberly Pr., LLC**

Leonine Pubs. LLC, *(978-0-9843001; 978-0-9836740; 978-0-9859483; 978-0-9887729; 978-0-9860552; 978-1-942190)* P.O. Box 1040, Laveen, AZ 85339 USA Tel 602-237-7487
E-mail: laura@leoninepublishers.com; info@leoninepublishers.com
Web site: http://www.leoninepublishers.com.

Leopard Books LLC *See* **Kids Activity Publishing**

Leprechaun Trappers Assn. Ltd., *(978-0-578-44732-2)* 3192 Ash Meadow Ln., Franklin, OH 45005 USA Tel 513-824-5173
E-mail: BRFiesin@gmail.com
Dist(s): **Ingram Content Group.**

Lerner Digital *Imprint of* **Lerner Publishing Group**

†**Lerner Publishing Group,** *(978-0-7613; 978-0-8225; 978-0-87406; 978-0-87614; 978-0-929371; 978-0-930494; 978-1-57505; 978-1-58013; 978-1-58196; 978-1-4677; 978-1-5124; 978-1-5415; 978-1-7284; 979-8-7656)* Orders Addr.: 241 1ST AVE N, MINNEAPOLIS, MN 55401 USA (SAN 256-0283) Tel 612-332-3344; Fax: 612-204-9208; Edit Addr.: 241 First Ave., N., Minneapolis, MN 55401 USA (SAN 201-0828) Tel 612-332-3344; Fax: 612-215-6230; Toll Free Fax: 800-332-1132; Toll Free: 800-328-4929; *Imprints:* First Avenue Editions (First Ave Edns); Lerner Publications (Lerner Publctns); Kar-Ben Publishing (Kar-Ben); Carolrhoda Lab™ (CarolrhodaLAB); Hungry Tomato (r) (Hungry Tomato); Zest Books (ZstBk); Carolrhoda Books (Carolrho Bks); Ediciones Lerner (EdiciLerner); Millbrook Press (Millbrok Pr); Twenty-First Century Books (TwentFrstCent); Graphic Universe™ (Graphic Univ); Darby Creek (DarbyCreek); Lerner Digital (LernerDigital)
E-mail: info@lernerbooks.com; custserve@lernerbooks.com
Web site: http://www.lernerbooks.com; http://www.karben.com
Dist(s): **Blackstone Audio, Inc.**
Children's Plus, Inc.
Ebsco Publishing
Follett School Solutions
Hachette Bk. Group
Ingram Publisher Services
MyiLibrary
Open Road Integrated Media, Inc.
Perfection Learning Corp.; *CIP.*

Lerner Pubns. *Imprint of* **Lerner Publishing Group**

LERN-LEARN, *(978-0-9763195)* 340 Vallejo Dr., Suite 82, Millbrae, CA 94030 USA.

Lerone Landis, *(978-0-692-33396-9; 978-0-578-54977-4)* 6026 Shady Valley Ct., GARLAND, TX 75043 USA Tel 469-855-9373.

Lerue Pr., LLC, *(978-0-9797460; 978-1-938814)* Orders Addr.: 280 Greg St., #10, Reno, NV 89502 USA Tel 775-849-3814
E-mail: janiceh@lerurpress.com; custserv@leruepress.com; lrp@lrpnv.com
Web site: http://www.leruepress.com; http://www.lrpnv.com
Dist(s): **Ingram Bk. Co.**

Les Lum Publishers *See* **Little Gene Pr.**

Les Penseurs, *(978-0-9764999; 978-0-9820676)* 309 Weatherstone Ln., Marietta, GA 30068 USA Tel 678-575-7052; Fax: 678-560-1580
E-mail: jsands@lespenseurs.com
Web site: http://www.lespenseurs.com.

Lesen Pub., *(978-0-9767200)* 2207 Shermont Pl., Brandon, FL 33511 USA Tel 813-857-6629; Fax: 813-684-7876
E-mail: jem2207@aol.com.

LeShaun, Temara, *(978-0-578-27883-4)* 737 Parkbluff Way, Lewis Center, OH 43035 USA.

LeShelle B. Flagg, *(978-1-7377725)* 12109 Chip Shot Ln, Upper Marlboro, MD 20772 USA Tel 301-237-4285
E-mail: leshelleflagg@gmail.com.

Leslie, Beverly J., *(978-0-9769722)* 1911 Patton Pl., Lithonia, GA 30058 USA Tel 770-987-8769; Fax: 770-987-8018
E-mail: bjleslie1@comcast.net; Beverly@lesliegraphicdesigns.com
Web site: http://LeslieGraphicDesigns.com.

leslie, shaquela, *(978-1-7365502)* 267 Plainville Ave, Unionville, CT 06085 USA Tel 518-888-4521
E-mail: shaquelal@yahoo.com.

Less is More Publishing, LLC, *(978-0-9769618)* 405 N. Woodlawn Ave., Kirkwood, MO 63122 USA
Web site: http://www.aboutheaven.net
Dist(s): **Big River Distribution.**

Less Pr., *(978-0-9657367)* 100 Hannah Niles Way, Braintree, MA 02184-7261 USA Tel 781-848-0555.

Lesson Ladder, *(978-0-9848657; 978-0-9884499; 978-0-9964067)* 21 Orient Ave, Melrose, MA 02176 USA Tel 800-301-4647
E-mail: accounting@xamonline.com
Dist(s): **Ingram Publisher Services.**

Lessons From The Vine *Imprint of* **Hutchings, John Pubs.**

Let Us Learn Together, *(978-0-692-19272-6)* 1802 Hackett Ave, Mountain View, CA 94043 USA Tel 415-412-5051
E-mail: kris@letuslearntogether.com
Web site: www.letuslearntogether.com.

LeTay Publishing, *(978-0-9753434; 978-0-9830731)* Div. of LeTay Corp., Orders Addr.: P.O. Box 170233, Atlanta, GA 30317 USA Tel 404-667-2810; Edit Addr.: P.O. Box 310043, Atlanta, GA 31131 USA
E-mail: booksales@letaypublishing.com; publisher@letaypublishing.com
Web site: http://www.letaypublishing.com; www.prussellmccloud.com
Dist(s): **Ingram Content Group.**

Letendre, Susan, *(978-0-9962152)* 16 Mill Pond Rd., North Kingstown, RI 02852 USA Tel 401-268-9810
E-mail: sevenstorymarket@verizon.net
Dist(s): **Ingram Publisher Services.**

Publisher Name Index

Letitia de Graft-Johnson, *(978-1-7374048; 978-1-956776)* 13405 Saint Charles Blvd, LITTLE ROCK, AR 72211 USA Tel 501-960-2601
E-mail: tishadegraft@hotmail.com.

Letona, Oscar, *(978-0-615-24938-4)* 51 Cedar Pl., Yonkers, NY 10705 USA
E-mail: mrletona@thetrojancurse.com; mrletona@hotmail.com
Web site: http://www.thetrojancurse.com.

Letourneau, *(978-0-692-07912-6)* 49 W. Gill Rd., Gill, MA 01354 USA Tel 413-863-8291
E-mail: dolly.letourneau@yahoo.com.

LETRA 2 EDITORES, *(978-0-9830875; 978-1-7360963)* W8-36 Calle Tirso Molina, San Juan, PR 00926 USA Tel 787-344-3144
E-mail: hiramalbertosanchez@gmail.com
Web site: www.letra2editores.com.

Lets Go Publish, *(978-0-9899957; 978-0-9962454; 978-0-9977667; 978-0-9980848; 978-0-9982683; 978-0-9986282; 978-0-9988111; 978-1-947402; 978-1-951562; 978-0-578-35789-8)* 11 Marjorie Ave., Wilkes Barre, PA 18702 USA Tel 570-829-5926
E-mail: jmac@kellyconsulting.com; bkelly@kellyconsulting.com
Web site: http://letsgopublish.com; http://www.bookhawkers.com
Dist(s): **BookHawkers Internet BookSeller.**

Let's Grow Leaders, *(978-1-7322647; 979-8-9868164)* 8505 Young Rivers Ct., Laurel, MD 20723 USA Tel 303-898-7018
E-mail: david.dye@letsgrowleaders.com
Web site: https://letsgrowleaders.com.

Let's Learn Library of Knowledge Series, *(978-0-9771015)* P.O. Box 9910, Canoga Park, CA 91309-9910 USA (SAN 256-7849)
E-mail: letslearn@letslearnlibrary.net
Web site: http://www.letslearnlibrary.net.

Let's Pretend Childrens Bks., *(978-0-9986480; 978-1-7324256; 979-8-9864368)* 126 Fitchburg Dr, Woodstock, GA 30189 USA Tel 404-644-6888; Fax: 404-644-6888
E-mail: pcsclean@bellsouth.net
Web site: www.amazon.com/author/cindyshirley.

Let's Think-kids Foundation, Inc., *(978-1-58237)* 3925 Blackburn Ln., Burtonsville, MD 20866 USA Toll Free: 800-841-2883
E-mail: thinkkids@aol.com; sftierno@aol.com
Web site: http://www.LTKF.org.

Lettra *See* **Lettra Pr. LLC**

Lettra Pr. LLC, *(978-1-949746; 978-1-64552; 978-1-951559; 978-1-951913; 978-1-953150; 978-1-955363)* 30 N. Gould St. Ste. 4753, Sheridan, WY 82801 USA
E-mail: chrisclay@lettrapress.com
Web site: www.lettrapress.com.

Levanter Publishing, *(978-0-9847237; 978-1-940576)* 910 S. Skylake Dr., Woodland Hills, UT 84653 USA Tel 801-423-8409
E-mail: loislane@digis.net
Dist(s): **Smashwords.**

Level 603 LLC *See* **35th Parallel Concepts LLC**

Level Green Bks., *(978-0-9788771)* 11 Level Green Rd., Brooktondale, NY 14817 USA (SAN 851-8319).

Level Ground Pr., *(978-0-9773461)* 2810 San Paula Ave., Dallas, TX 75228 USA Tel 214-796-2135
Web site: http://www.levelgroundfilms.com.

Levels2Learning, *(978-0-578-34326-6)* 189 Harmon Ave, Cranston, RI 02910 USA Tel 401-516-0080
E-mail: Info@levels2learning.com
Web site: Levels2learning.com.

Levenger Pr., *(978-1-929154)* 420 S. Congress Ave., Delray Beach, FL 33445 USA Tel 561-276-2436; Fax: 561-276-3584
E-mail: mvogel@levenger.com
Web site: http://www.levenger.com.

Leverage Factory, *(978-0-9773000)* 38 Rogerson Dr., Chapel Hill, NC 27517-4037 USA (SAN 257-2710)
E-mail: info@leveragefactory.com
Web site: http://www.beawriter.us; http://www.leveragefactory.com
Dist(s): **Independent Pubs. Group.**

Levi Bass Publishing, *(978-0-9835651)* PO Box 608355, Orlando, FL 32860 USA Tel 407-709-0578; Fax: 407-271-8552
E-mail: carolyndenise@ymail.com
Web site: www.carolyndenise.com.

Levine, Arthur A. Bks. *Imprint of* **Scholastic, Inc.**

Levine, Bette M., *(978-0-9721094)* 4605 Regiment Way, Manlius, NY 13104 USA
E-mail: rampa505@aol.com.

Levine Querido, *(978-1-64614)* 220 E 74th St, New York, NY 10021 USA Tel 201-983-9470
E-mail: nick@levinequerido.com
Web site: www.levinequerido.com
Dist(s): **Children's Plus, Inc.**
Chronicle Bks. LLC
Hachette Bk. Group.

Levinson, Ralph D, *(978-1-7327889)* 10563 Troon Ave., Los Angeles, CA 90064 USA Tel 310-839-1075; Fax: 310-839-1075
E-mail: ralphdlevinson@gmail.com
Web site: ralphlevinson.com.

levitin, sarah, *(978-0-578-43972-3)* 891 33rd Ave., San Francisco, CA 94121 USA Tel 415-305-7808
E-mail: sarah_ll@sbcglobal.net
Dist(s): **Ingram Content Group.**

Levity Pr., *(978-0-615-64986-3; 978-0-615-68151-1; 978-0-615-70890-4; 978-0-615-70893-5; 978-1-939896)* 10170 Palm Glen Dr. No. 46, Santee, CA 92071 USA
Web site: www.englishcorner.me
Dist(s): **CreateSpace Independent Publishing Platform.**

Lewis & Clark Bicentennial Corps of Discovery Arch, *(978-0-9763970)* 1907 NE 75th Ave., Portland, OR 97213 USA Tel 503-201-2494
E-mail: faith.ruffing@bicencorpsarchive.com
Web site: http://www.bicencorpsarchive.com.

Lewis International, Inc., *(978-0-9666771; 978-1-930983)* 2201 NW 102nd Pl., No. 1, Miami, FL 33172 USA Tel 305-436-7984; Fax: 305-436-7985; Toll Free: 800-259-5962.

Lewis, Kathrine, *(978-1-7355790)* 606 S Mulberry St, Statesville, NC 28677 USA Tel 480-710-5706
E-mail: kathrinefuentestewis@gmail.com.

Lewis Lynn Bks., *(978-0-9745544)* 1143 N. Carey Ave., Clovis, CA 93611-7371 USA Fax: 559-322-9038
E-mail: cconn@cwnet.com
Web site: http://www.brainiansector.com.

Lewis-Thornton, Rae, *(978-0-9747983)* 1507 E. 53rd St., Suite 315, Chicago, IL 60615 USA Tel 773-643-4316; Fax: 773-643-4356
E-mail: rae_lewis_thornton@hotmail.com
Web site: http://www.raelewisthornton.org.

Lexham Pr. *Imprint of* **Faithlife Corp.**

Lexicon Marketing Corporation *See* **Lexicon Marketing, LLC**

Lexicon Marketing, LLC, *(978-1-59172)* 6380 Wilshire Blvd. Ste. 1400, Los Angeles, CA 90048-5018 USA
E-mail: Jbelletti@lexiconmarketing.com; icruz@lexiconmarketing.com.

Lexingford Publishing, *(978-0-9844938; 978-0-9859480; 978-0-9863343; 978-0-9963948; 978-0-9981665; 978-0-9986060; 978-1-947373; 978-1-7329576)* 255 redlands st., Playa del Rey, CA 90293 USA (SAN 859-5674) Tel 415-328-5465
E-mail: abell@clarkson.edu.

Lexington Books *See* **Lexington Bks.**

Lexington Bks., *(978-0-7391; 978-1-4985; 978-1-9787; 978-1-7936; 978-1-6669)* Div. of Rowman & Littlefield Publishing Group, Inc., Orders Addr.: 15200 NBN Way, Blue Ridge Summit, PA 17214 USA Tel 717-794-3800 (Sales, Customer Service, MIS, Royalties, Inventory Mgmt., Dist., Credit & Collections); Fax: 717-794-3803 (Customer Service &/or orders only); 717-794-3857 (Sales & MIS); 717-794-3856 (Royalties, Inventory Mgmt., & Dist.); Toll Free Fax: 800-338-4550 (Customer Service &/or orders); Toll Free: 800-462-6420 (Customer Service &/or orders); 67 Mowat Ave., Suite 241, Toronto, ON M6K 3E3 Tel 416-534-1660; Fax: 416-534-3699; Edit Addr.: 4501 Forbes Blvd., Blvd., Ste. 200, Lanham, MD 20706 USA Tel 301-459-3366; Fax: 301-429-5749; Toll Free: 1-800-462-6420 Short Discount, contact rlpgsales@rowman.com
E-mail: custserv@rowman.com; edebusk@rowman.com; lexingtonbooks@rowman.com
Web site: http://www.lexingtonbooks.com; http://www.rlpgbooks.com; http://www.rowman.com
Dist(s): **CreateSpace Independent Publishing Platform**
Ebsco Publishing
Follett School Solutions
MyiLibrary
National Bk. Network
Rowman & Littlefield Publishers, Inc.
Rowman & Littlefield Unlimited Model
Send The Light Distribution LLC
Transaction Pubs.
ebrary, Inc.

Lexington Pubs., *(978-1-933361)* P.O. Box 750018, Arlington Heights, MA 02475 USA
E-mail: lexingtonpublishers@gmail.com.

Leyva, Barbara, *(978-0-9729056)* P.O. Box 3295, Clewiston, FL 33440-3295 USA; *Imprints:* Balticbard Publishing (Balticbard Pub)
E-mail: balticbard@yahoo.com
Web site: http://www.geocities.com/balticbard/index.html.

LFF Consultant, *(978-0-9843472)* 127 Peck Hill 1200 Harford Ave, N.Scituate, RI 02857 USA (SAN 859-1326) Tel 401-688-0217
E-mail: admin@lifestyleinstitute.org
Web site: Lifestyleinstitute.org.

L.G. Publishing, *(978-0-615-16242-3)* P.O. Box 5098, Sarasota, FL 34277 USA Tel 941-312-4725
E-mail: glickmanfamily@aol.com.

LGBTQI Pr. NZ, *(978-1-7348044)* 6616 7th Ave Cir W, Bradenton, FL 34209 USA Tel 617-600-0241
E-mail: jeffreydb32@gmail.com.

LGE Performance Systems, Inc., *(978-0-9778776)* 9757 Lake Nona Rd., Orlando, FL 32827 USA (SAN 850-5055) Tel 407-438-9911; Fax: 407-438-6667.

LGR Productions *See* **LGR Publishing, Inc.**

LGR Publishing, Inc., *(978-0-9657610)* 3219 NW C St., Richmond, IN 47374 USA Tel 765-939-8924 (phone/fax)
E-mail: jwilde@indiana.edu; mcphd@infocom.com
Web site: http://www.angerchillout.com.

Lóguez Ediciones (ESP) *(978-84-85334; 978-84-89804; 978-84-96646) Dist. by* **Lectorum Pubns.**

LH Pubns. & Productions, *(978-0-9749013)* Orders Addr.: P.O. Box 914, Center Harbor, NH 03226 USA
E-mail: mcat_lh@yahoo.com
Web site: http://www.laurahickey.com.

LHC Publishing, *(978-0-615-71668-8; 978-0-615-86013-8; 978-0-615-93103-6; 978-0-692-02397-6; 978-0-692-47441-9; 978-0-692-47443-3; 978-0-9970254; 978-1-7323733; 978-1-952517)*
E-mail: yvijones@hotmail.com
Web site: www.LHCpublishing.com
Dist(s): **CreateSpace Independent Publishing Platform.**

Li, Richard T., *(978-0-9675988)* 4554 Rose Tree Ct., Fort Worth, TX 76137 USA Tel 817-656-5178; Fax: 817-656-4138.

LiArt-Literature & Art, *(978-1-931481)* P.O. Box 245686, Pembroke Pines, FL 33024-5686 USA Tel 954-986-6886 (phone/fax)
E-mail: liartpe@aol.com.

Liber Publishing Hse., *(978-1-950425)* Orders Addr.: Tres de Abril St., Punta Princessa, Labangon, Cebu City, 6000 PHL Tel 315-820-1714; Edit Addr.: Tres de Abril St., Punta Princessa, Labangon, Cebu City, 6000 PHL Tel 315-820-1714
E-mail: bookprojects18@gmail.com
Web site: http://www.liberpublishing.com; www.royalehousepub.com.

Liberation's Publishing, *(978-0-9843827; 978-0-615-76642-3; 978-0-9891348; 978-0-692-02160-6; 978-0-692-02161-3; 978-0-692-02162-0; 978-0-692-02163-7; 978-0-692-02164-4; 978-0-692-27755-3; 978-0-692-36183-2; 978-0-692-37137-4; 978-0-692-37138-1; 978-0-692-39174-7; 978-0-692-39217-1; 978-0-692-42144-4; 978-0-692-42913-6; 978-0-692-53789-3; 978-1-7320846; 978-1-7326934; 978-1-7336754; 978-1-951300; 979-8-218-14808-9; 979-8-218-14986-4; 978-1-960853) Orders Addr.: 183 Cottrell St 183 Cottrell St, West Point, MS 39773 USA Fax: 800-325-8028; Edit Addr.: 183 Cottrell St., West Point, MS 39773 USA (SAN 859-242X) Tel 662-605-0382*
E-mail: nicole@liberationspublishing.com
Web site: http://www.liberationspublishing.com
Dist(s): **CreateSpace Independent Publishing Platform**
Ingram Content Group
Lulu Pr., Inc.

Libertary Company *See* **Booktrope**

Liberty Artists Management, *(978-0-9785427)* Orders Addr.: 31 Liberty St., Catskill, NY 12414-1442 USA
E-mail: admin@libertyartists.com
Web site: http://www.beckyblume.com; http://www.libertyartists.com.

Liberty Communications House *See* **JB Information Station**

Liberty Fund, Inc., *(978-0-86597; 978-0-913966; 978-1-61487)* Orders Addr.: c/o Total Response, Inc., 5804 Churchman By-Pass, Indianapolis, IN 46203 USA; Edit Addr.: 8335 Allison Pointe Trail, No. 300, Indianapolis, IN 46250-1684 USA (SAN 202-6740) Tel 317-842-0880; Fax: 317-579-6060; Toll Free: 800-866-3520; 800-955-8335 (customer service); *Imprints:* Amagi Books (Amagi Bks)
E-mail: webmaster@libertyfund.org
Web site: http://www.libertyfund.org
Dist(s): **Chicago Distribution Ctr.**
Ingram Publisher Services
MyiLibrary
ebrary, Inc.

Liberty Hill Publishing *Imprint of* **Salem Author Services**

Liberty Junkies, *(978-0-578-55856-1; 978-0-578-59388-3; 978-0-578-82886-2)* 626C ADMIRAL Dr. No. 219, Annapolis, MD 21401 USA Tel 202-288-6287
E-mail: Julie@LibertyJunkies.com.

Liberty Manuals Co., *(978-0-9710748; 978-0-9820955; 978-1-940069)* Orders Addr.: P.O. Box 453, Rumson, NJ 07760 USA Tel 732-842-3000; Fax: 732-741-5820.

Liberty Publishing Group, *(978-1-893095; 978-1-946291)* Div. of The Holton Consulting Group, Inc., Orders Addr.: 1405 Autumn Ridge Dr., Durham, NC 27712-2680 USA Tel 919-767-9620; Toll Free Fax: 866-500-7697; Toll Free: 877-819-7489
E-mail: bil@holtonconsulting.com; cher@holtonconsulting.com
Web site: http://www.holtonconsulting.com; http://www.prosperityPublishing.com; http://www.themetaphysicalwebsite.com
Dist(s): **Prosperity Publishing Hse.**
Smashwords.

Liberty Publishing Hse., Inc., *(978-0-914481; 978-1-932686; 978-1-62804)* P.O. Box 1058, New York, NY 10024-0547 USA (SAN 289-6869)
E-mail: info@libertypublishinghouse.com
Web site: https://www.libertypublishinghouse.com.

Liberty St. *Imprint of* **Time Inc. Bks.**

Liberty University Press, *(978-0-9819357; 978-1-935986; 978-0-9976828; 978-1-7326376)* 1971 University Blvd., Lynchburg, VA 24502 USA Tel 434-592-3100
E-mail: libertyuniversitypress@liberty.edu.

Librado Pr., *(978-1-879571)* 11223 Leatherwood Dr., Reston, VA 22091 USA Tel 703-476-0516 Do not confuse with Librad Press in San Francisco, CA.

Librairie du Liban Pubns. (FRA) *Dist. by* **Intl Bk Ctr.**

Librairie Larousse (FRA) *(978-2-03) Dist. by* **Distribks Inc.**

Libraries Unlimited *Imprint of* **ABC-CLIO, LLC**

Libraries Unlimited *Imprint of* **Bloomsbury Publishing USA**

Library Assn. of La Jolla, *(978-0-9744804; 978-0-9828289; 979-8-9869448)* 1008 Wall St., La Jolla, CA 92037-4418 USA Tel 858-454-5872; Fax: 858-454-5835; *Imprints:* Athenaeum Music & Arts Library (Athenaeum Music)
E-mail: Athlibrary@pacbell.net; kpeterson@ljathenaeum.org
Web site: http://www.ljathenaeum.org.

Library Ideas, LLC, *(978-1-936348; 978-1-948381; 978-1-952183; 978-0-692-03681-5; 978-0-692-03682-2; 978-1-954635; 978-1-955675; 979-8-88519)* 333 Maple Ave., Vienna, VA 22182 USA Tel 571-730-4300; 703-938-2592
E-mail: info@libraryideas.com
Web site: http://www.libraryideas.com.

Library of America, The, *(978-0-940450; 978-1-883011; 978-1-931082; 978-1-59853)* Div. of Literary Classics of the U. S., Inc., 14 E. 60th St., New York, NY 10022 USA (SAN 286-9918) Tel 212-308-3360; Fax: 212-750-8352
E-mail: info@loa.org
Web site: http://www.loa.org
Dist(s): **MyiLibrary**
Penguin Random Hse. Distribution
Penguin Random Hse. LLC
Penguin Publishing Group
Random Hse., Inc.

Library Reprints, Inc., *(978-0-7222)* Orders Addr.: P.O. Box 890820, Temecula, CA 92589-0820 USA (SAN 254-0258) Fax: 951-767-1803; 951-767-0133
E-mail: newbookorders@gmail.com
Dist(s): **Amazon Digital Services Inc.**

Library Sales of N.J., *(978-1-888032)* Orders Addr.: P.O. Box 335, Garwood, NJ 07027-0335 USA Tel 908-232-1446; Edit Addr.: 607 S. Chestnut St., Westfield, NJ 07090-1369 USA
E-mail: Librarysalesofnj@aol.com.

Library Tales Publishing, Inc., *(978-0-615-39884-6; 978-0-578-07458-0; 978-0-578-07790-1; 978-0-615-47817-3; 978-0-615-48528-7; 978-0-615-50393-6; 978-0-615-51583-0; 978-0-615-52116-9; 978-0-615-56273-5; 978-0-615-56822-5; 978-0-615-56823-2; 978-0-615-65368-6; 978-0-615-66879-6; 978-0-615-69556-3; 978-0-615-74800-9; 978-0-615-75793-3; 978-0-615-76875-5; 978-0-615-77415-2; 978-0-615-83527-3; 978-0-615-83638-6; 978-0-615-86816-5; 978-0-615-91241-7; 978-0-615-91251-6; 978-0-615-91956-0; 978-0-615-94763-1; 978-0-615-94799-0;) Div. of Library Tales Entertainment Group, 180 Riverside Blvd 40C, New York, NY 10069 USA*
E-mail: Office@Librarytales.com
Web site: http://www.librarytalespublishing.com
Dist(s): **CreateSpace Independent Publishing Platform**
Ingram Content Group.

LIBRI Bks., Division of Seasons & A Muse, Incorporated *See* **LIBRI Pubs.**

LIBRI Pubs., *(978-0-9763952)* P.O. Box 5849, Playa Del Rey, CA 90296-5849 USA Tel 310-827-6495; Fax: 310-827-8166
E-mail: libri@seasonsandamuse.com
Web site: http://www.seasonsandamuse.com.

Libris Draconis Pr., *(978-0-9728124)* PMB 279 1296 E. Gibson Rd., Suite A, Woodland, CA 95776 USA (SAN 255-1179)
Dist(s): **Baker & Taylor Publisher Services (BTPS).**

Libro Studio LLC, *(978-1-63578)* 1012 Pk. Ave. NW., Willmar, MN 56201 USA Tel 320-293-7702; Fax: 320-293-7702
E-mail: LibroStudioLLC@gmail.com.

Libros del Zorro Rojo (ESP) *(978-84-933361; 978-84-933976; 978-84-934032; 978-84-96509; 978-84-92412; 978-84-940336; 978-84-941041; 978-84-941619; 978-84-941645; 978-84-942473; 978-84-942918) Dist. by* **Lectorum Pubns.**

Libros Desafio, *(978-0-939125; 978-1-55883; 978-1-55955)* Subs. of CRC Pubns., 2850 Kalamazoo Ave., SE, Grand Rapids, MI 49560 USA (SAN 248-9775) Tel 616-224-0785; Fax: 616-224-0834; Toll Free: 800-333-8300
E-mail: info@librosdesafio.org
Web site: http://www.librosdesafio.org.

Libros, Encouraging Cultural Literacy, *(978-0-9675413; 978-0-9710860)* Orders Addr.: P.O. Box 453, Long Beach, NY 11561 USA Tel 516-889-6077; Fax: 516-889-6365; Toll Free: 800-260-9915; Edit Addr.: 160 LaFayette Blvd., Long Beach, NY 11561 USA (SAN 253-374X)
E-mail: librospress@msn.com
Web site: http://www.librospress.com.

Libros in Spanish, LLC, 1941 NE 147th Terr., North Miami, FL 33181 USA Tel 786-274-1556; Fax: 305-948-0333
E-mail: admin@librosinspanish.com.

Libros Liguori *Imprint of* **Liguori Pubns.**

Libros Para Ninos *Imprint of* **Libros Para Ninos**

Libros Para Ninos, Div. of Simon & Schuster Children's Publishing, 1230 Ave. of the Americas, New York, NY 10020 USA; *Imprints:* Libros Para Ninos (LibPara)
Dist(s): **Children's Plus, Inc.**
Simon & Schuster
Simon & Schuster, Inc.

Libros Publishing, *(978-0-9837458; 978-0-9851769; 978-0-9906713; 978-0-9987031)* 24040 Camino Del Avion No. A225, Monarch Beach, CA 92629 USA Tel 949-201-9477; Fax: 949-661-9098
E-mail: librospublishing@cox.net
Dist(s): **Baker & Taylor Publisher Services (BTPS)**
Follett School Solutions
ebrary, Inc.

Libros Sin Fronteras, P.O. Box 2085, Olympia, WA 98507 USA Tel 360-357-4332; Fax: 360-357-4964
E-mail: info@librossinfronteras.com
Web site: http://www.librossinfronteras.com.

Libros-Latin American Treasures For Kids *See* **Libros, Encouraging Cultural Literacy**

Librujas, *(978-0-9771566)* 4335 Van Nuys Blvd., Suite 117, Sherman Oaks, CA 91403 USA (SAN 256-887X) Tel 818-905-7221
E-mail: jamie@librujas.com; patricia@librujas.com
Web site: http://www.librujas.com
Dist(s): **Quality Bks., Inc.**

Liburdi, Marlana *See* **Happy Hearts Family, The**

Lickel, Lisa Publishing, also operating as Five Loaves *See* **Fox Ridge Pubns.**

Lieberherr, Ruth, *(978-1-7328877)* 8 Red Coach Ln., Winchester, MA 01890 USA Tel 781-721-2663
E-mail: ruth.lieberherr@gmail.com
Dist(s): **Ingram Content Group.**

Liebling Pr., Inc., *(978-0-9642874)* 2971 Bellmore Ave., Bellmore, NY 11710 USA Tel 516-781-9419; Fax: 516-781-8187; Toll Free: 800-781-9419.

Life Action Inc., *(978-0-940110; 978-0-9667124; 978-1-934718; 978-1-959704)* Orders Addr.: P.O. Box 31, Buchanan, MI 49107 USA Tel 269-697-8600; Fax: 269-695-2974; Toll Free: 800-321-1538; Edit Addr.: 2727 Niles Buchanan Rd., Buchanan, MI 49107 USA (SAN 220-2859)
Web site: http://www.lifeaction.org; http://www.ReviveOurHearts.com.

Life Action Publishing *See* **Life Action Inc.**

fe Arts Bks., LLC, *(978-1-948364)* 1 Piney Creek Ct, Monkton, MD 21111 USA Tel 443-845-4614
E-mail: info@lifeartbooks.com
Web site: www.lifeartsbooks.com.

fe by Design Youth Leadership Resources *See* **Youthleadership.com**

fe Changers International Church *See* **Dickow, Gregory Ministries**

ife Chronicles Publishing, *(978-0-692-64191-0; 978-0-692-77302-4; 978-0-692-84946-0; 978-0-9989114; 978-0-692-98651-6; 978-1-7328944; 978-1-950649; 978-1-958242)* 4414 S 318th St, FEDERAL WAY, WA 98023 USA Tel 253-508-8876
E-mail: sharon.blake@outlook.com
Web site: www.lifechroniclespublishing.com
Dist(s): **CreateSpace Independent Publishing Platform.**

Life force *See* **Therapy Art Theater LLC**

Life Force Bks., *(978-0-9795331; 978-0-9896540; 978-0-9962386; 978-1-7324453)* P.O. Box 302, Bayside, CA 95524 USA; *Imprints:* Zardoz Press (ZardozPr)
E-mail: jjsemple@suddenlink.net; jjsemple@lifeforcebooks.com
Web site: http://www.lifeforcebooks.com; http://www.goldenflowermeditation.com; http://www.commonsensekundalini.com; http://www.kundaliniconsortium.org/
Dist(s): **Smashwords.**

Life is a Story Problem LLC, *(978-1-63270)* 2910 N. Powers No. 326, Colorado Springs, CO 80922 USA Tel 720-940-8153
E-mail: demcadams@demcadams.com
Web site: www.demcadams.com.

Life Letters Publishing, *(978-0-9746022)* P.O. Box 360111, Strongsville, OH 44136 USA
E-mail: lifeletter@aol.com
Web site: http://www.lifeletter.net.

Life Line, Inc., *(978-0-9647089)* P.O. Box 7990, New York, NY 10116-8715 USA Tel 212-947-0661; Fax: 212-947-0681
Do not confuse with Life Lines, Rimrock, AZ
E-mail: lifel@aol.com.

Life Line Publishing, *(978-0-9761604)* P.O. Box 1482, Bridgeport, CT 06601-1482 USA Do not confuse with Life Line Publishing in Franklin, VA.

Life Link Worldwide Pubs., *(978-1-880608)* 175 Raymond Ct., Fayetteville, GA 30214 USA Tel 770-994-1683.

Life of Asil, The, *(978-0-615-31907-0)* 8302 turnberry St., Rowlett, TX 75089 USA.

Life Pubs. International, *(978-0-7361; 978-0-943258; 978-1-890219; 978-0-578-79485-3; 979-8-218-27980-6)* 1625 N. Robberson Ave., Springfield, MO 65803 USA (SAN 213-5817) Tel 417-831-7766; Fax: 417-831-6445; Toll Free: 888-776-2425
E-mail: info@lifepublishers.org
Dist(s): **Charisma Media.**

Life Rich Publishing *Imprint of* **AuthorHouse**

Life Sentence Publishing, Inc., *(978-0-9832016; 978-1-62245; 979-8-88936)* P.O. Box 652, Abbotsford, WI 54405 USA Tel 715-223-3013; *Imprints:* ANEKO Press (ANEKOPr)
E-mail: jeremiah@lspbooks.com
Web site: zeiset.org; http://www.anekopress.com
Dist(s): **Carson-Dellosa Publishing, LLC**
Ingram Content Group
North Star Editions
Send The Light Distribution LLC
Spring Arbor Distributors, Inc.

Life Story Publishing, LLC *See* **Wizard Academies, LLC**

Life Works Pr., *(978-0-9755938)* P.O. Box 2174, Clinton, MD 20735 USA Tel 602-561-1354; Toll Free: 888-786-7526
Web site: http://www.byrongarrett.com.

Lifeforce Enterprises, Inc., *(978-0-9709796)* 250 Pacific Ave., Suite 326, Long Beach, CA 90802 USA Tel 562-366-2617; Toll Free: 866-543-3367
E-mail: ajyager@entertheforce.com
Web site: http://www.entertheforce.com
Dist(s): **Midpoint Trade Bks., Inc.**

Lifelight Bks., *(978-0-9743801)* 2629 262nd Pl SE, Sammamish, WA 98075-7900 USA (SAN 850-8070)
E-mail: lynne@lifelightbooks.com
Web site: http://www.lifelightbooks.com.

LifeLine Studios, Inc., *(978-0-9714753)* 1390 W. Main St., Lancaster, TX 75146 USA Tel 972-275-0468; Fax: 972-275-0469
E-mail: afoutsjr@lifelinestudios.com
Web site: http://www.lifelinestudio.com.

Lifelong Friends Pub., *(978-0-9971221)* po box 483, Mansfield Center, CT 06250 USA Tel 860-428-7691
E-mail: ssptbp@charter.net
Web site: www.lifelongfriends.com.

Lifepac *Imprint of* **Alpha Omega Pubns., Inc.**

Liferays Publishing, *(978-0-9795397)* 5390 Elliott Rd., Powder Springs, GA 30127-3803 USA Tel 770-943-6123
E-mail: liferays@bellsouth.net
Web site: http://liferays02.googlepages.com/home.

LifeReloaded *See* **LifeReloaded Specialty Publishing LLC**

LifeReloaded Specialty Publishing LLC, *(978-0-9776414; 978-1-60800)* 2256 Huber Dr., Manheim, PA 17545 USA; *Imprints:* American Literary Publishing (Amer Literary)
E-mail: Mike@lifereloaded.com
Web site: http://www.LifeReloaded.com.

Life's Journey of Hope Pubns., *(978-0-9747815)* Orders Addr.: P.O. Box 1277, Groton, MA 01450 USA (SAN 255-7789) Tel 978-448-1252; Edit Addr.: 90 Martins Pond Rd., Groton, MA 01450 USA
E-mail: LLeonard@lifesjourneyofhope.com; lifesjourneyofhope@hotmail.com
Web site: http://www.lifesjourneyofhope.com.

Lifeskills Press *See* **Uplift Pr.**

LifeSong Pubs., *(978-0-9718306; 978-0-9799116)* Orders Addr.: P.O. Box 183, Somis, CA 93066-0183 USA Tel 805-504-3916; Toll Free: 866-266-6917
Web site: http://www.lifesongpublishers.com
Dist(s): **Send The Light Distribution LLC.**

Lifestage, Inc., *(978-0-9799905)* 496 Smithtown ByPass, Suite 202, Smithtown, NY 11787 USA (SAN 854-9192) Tel 631-366-4265
E-mail: lifestage_2000@yahoo.com
Web site: http://www.lifestage.org.

LifeStory Publishing, *(978-0-9711004; 978-0-9758988; 978-0-578-41243-6; 978-0-578-58575-8)* 5328 Runnymede Rd., Jackson, MS 39211 USA Tel 601-978-3478
E-mail: joemaxwell@me.com.

LifeTime Media, Inc., *(978-0-9675967; 978-0-9816368; 978-0-9822171; 978-0-9823975)* 352 Seventh Ave., 7th Flr., New York, NY 10001 USA (SAN 856-0978) Tel 212-631-7524; Fax: 212-631-7529
E-mail: sales@lifetimemedia.com; jgrace@lifetimemedia.com
Web site: http://www.lifetimemedia.com.

Lifetime Relationship Center *See* **Intralife Systems Publishing**

Lifetrack Resources, *(978-0-9743826)* 709 Univ. Ave. W., Saint Paul, MN 55104-4804 USA Tel 651-227-8471; Fax: 651-227-0621
E-mail: familiestogether@lifetrackresources.org
Web site: http://www.lifetrackresources.org.

Lifevest *Imprint of* **Lifevest Publishing, Inc.**

Lifevest Publishing, Inc., *(978-0-9724680; 978-1-932338; 978-1-59879)* 4910 E. Dry Creek Rd., Suite 170, Centennial, CO 80122 USA Tel 303-221-1007; Fax: 303-771-1166; Toll Free Fax: 877-843-1007; *Imprints:* Lifevest (Livevst)
E-mail: ric.simmons@lifevestpublishing.com; publisher@lifevestpublishing.com
Web site: http://www.lifevestpublishing.com.

Lifeway Christian Resources, *(978-0-7673; 978-0-633; 978-1-4158; 978-1-4300; 978-1-5359; 978-1-0877; 979-8-3845)* Div. of The Southern Baptist Convention, One Lifeway Plaza, Nashville, TN 37234 USA Tel 615-251-2000; Fax: 615-277-8221 (product info., ordering, order tracking); 615-251-2626 (shipping/transportation); Toll Free Fax: 800-296-4036; Toll Free: 800-458-2772 (product info., ordering); 800-251-3225; 200 Powell Pl., Suite 100, Brentwood, TN 37027 Tel 615-251-2000; 615-251-2657; Toll Free Fax: 800-296-4036; Toll Free: 800-458-2772; *Imprints:* Serendipity House (Serendip Hse)
E-mail: customerservice@lifeway.com; support.lifeway.com
Web site: http://www.lifewaystores.com; http://www.lifeway.com; http://www.bhpublishinggroup.com
Dist(s): **Spring Arbor Distributors, Inc.**

Lifeworks Enterprises, *(978-0-692-04543-5)* 417 S Sterling Rd, Elkins Park, PA 19027 USA Tel 215-635-1266
E-mail: flohannah18@gmail.com.

Liffey Pr., The (IRL) *(978-1-904148; 978-1-905785; 978-1-908308) Dist. by* **Dufour.**

Light 4 You, *(978-1-7349991)* 1150 N Columbus St, Lancaster, OH 43130 USA Tel 740-919-1499
E-mail: nikkijlong@icloud.com.

Light & Life Publishing Co., *(978-0-937032; 978-1-880971; 978-1-933654)* Orders Addr.: 4808 Park Glen Rd., Minneapolis, MN 55416 USA (SAN 213-8565) Tel 952-925-3888; Fax: 888-925-3918; Toll Free Fax: 888-925-3918
E-mail: ivy@light-n-life.com
Web site: http://www.light-n-life.com.

Light Bugs Publishing, *(978-0-9765514)* 1400 Champions Green Dr., Gulf Breeze, FL 32563 USA Tel 850-932-9325
E-mail: allen911@bellsouth.net; russ@lightbugspublishing.com; jan@lightbugspublishing.com
Web site: http://www.lightbugspublishing.com.

Light Energy Bks., *(978-0-9740480)* 731 Mandana Blvd., Oakland, CA 94610 USA Tel 510-268-9999.

Light Horse Publishing, *(978-0-9966754)* 2500 Sawmill Rd., Santa Fe, NM 87505 USA Tel 505-660-4456
E-mail: camkattell@yahoo.com.

Light Internal Publishing, *(978-0-9823732)* Orders Addr.: 6130 E. Fair Ave., Centennial, CO 80111 USA (SAN 857-9822)
E-mail: marnie@lightinternal.com
Web site: http://www.lightinternal.com.

Light Line, *(978-0-9773244)* 353 E. Pittsfield St., Pennsville, NJ 08070 USA (SAN 257-2540) Toll Free: 877-427-8271
E-mail: jlldadf@comcast.net.

Light Messages Publishing, *(978-0-9679937; 978-0-9800756; 978-1-61153)* 5216 Tahoe Dr., Durham, NC 27713 USA (SAN 920-9298) Tel 919-361-5041; Toll Free Fax: 919-797-9368; *Imprints:* Torchflame Books (TorchflameBks)
E-mail: books@lightmessages.com
Web site: http://www.lightmessages.com
Dist(s): **INscribe Digital**
Independent Pubs. Group
New Leaf Distributing Co., Inc.

Light Network, The, *(978-0-9966403; 978-0-9975727; 978-0-9987043; 978-1-7320268; 978-1-7335939; 978-1-7330436; 978-1-7341814; 978-1-7356648; 979-8-9850627; 979-8-9876176)* 151 4th St. W., Ketchum, ID 83340 USA Tel 208-721-3324
E-mail: keidikeating@yahoo.co.uk
Web site: www.thelightnetwork.com.

Light of Logos Pr., *(978-0-615-82703-2; 978-0-9896356)* 15 Fairfield Rd, Wayland, MA 01778 USA
E-mail: yuegang_zhang@yahoo.com.

Light On Pubns., *(978-1-7325066)* 32 Longcourse Ln., Paoli, PA 19301 USA Tel 727-772-3809
E-mail: patriciasmccandless@gmail.com
Web site: savingthemagicofchildhood.com.

Light Pubns., *(978-0-9702642; 978-0-9824707; 978-1-940060)* Orders Addr.: P.O. Box 2462, Providence, RI 02906 USA Tel 401-272-8707; Edit Addr.: 393 Morris Ave., Providence, RI 02906 USA (SAN 852-7407) Tel 401-272-8707
E-mail: info@lightpublications.com
Web site: http://www.lightpublications.com.

Light Sword Publishing, LLC *See* **LSP Digital, LLC**

Light Works Publishing *Imprint of* **I.M. Enterprises**

Light24, *(978-0-9700002)* Orders Addr.: 85-42 160th St., Jamaica Queens, NY 11432 USA Tel 718-526-7021 Do not confuse with companies with the same name in Worthington, OH, Kirkland, WA.

LightBurst Media, *(978-0-692-59600-5; 978-0-692-63807-1; 978-0-692-63810-1; 978-0-692-63813-2; 978-0-692-64039-5; 978-0-692-64283-2; 978-0-692-65893-2; 978-0-692-66096-6; 978-0-692-67320-1; 978-0-692-70346-5; 978-0-692-70858-3; 978-0-692-70961-0; 978-0-692-71084-5; 978-0-692-73769-9; 978-0-9979389) 3226 se gladstone st, portland, OR 97202 USA Tel 347-551-3121*
Web site: www.lightburstmedia.com
Dist(s): **CreateSpace Independent Publishing Platform.**

Lighted Hill, *(978-0-9966539; 978-0-692-50004-0)* 5207 Candlewood Dr., Northport, AL 35473 USA Tel 205-792-9611
E-mail: joshua.horton@sfwbcmail.com
Web site: www.hortonbooks.com
Dist(s): **CreateSpace Independent Publishing Platform.**

Lighted Lamp Pr., *(978-1-888350)* Orders Addr.: P.O. Box 1234, Wheat Ridge, CO 80034 USA; Edit Addr.: 4945 Gray St., Denver, CO 80212 USA (SAN 298-8348)
E-mail: robertjinye@msn.com.

Lighten Press *See* **Lighten Pr., LLC**

Lighten Pr., LLC, *(978-0-9980410)* 2633 N. 22nd St., Mesa, AZ 85213 USA
E-mail: authororasmith@gmail.com
Web site: www.lightenpress.com.

Lighthearted Pr., Inc., *(978-0-9659225)* Orders Addr.: P.O. Box 90125, Portland, OR 97290 USA Tel 503-786-3085; Fax: 503-786-0315; Edit Addr.: 10585 SE Fairway Dr., Happy Valley, OR 97086 USA
E-mail: davis@lightheartedpress.com
Web site: http://www.lightheartedpress.com.

Lighthouse, *(978-0-692-51925-7)* 1300 Wind Leaf Dr., Unit O, Reston, VA 20194 USA Tel 571-246-7198
E-mail: alana.rudkovsky@gmail.com.

Lighthouse Bk. Publishing, *(978-0-9791168)* Orders Addr.: P.O. Box 310534, Houston, TX 77231 USA Toll Free: 800-247-9100
E-mail: book@journeytoseetheking.com
Web site: http://www.journeytoseetheking.com.

Lighthouse Christian Products Co., *(978-0-9712894)* 1050 Remington Rd., Schaumburg, IL 60173-4518 USA
Web site: http://lcpgifts.com.

Lighthouse eBooks *See* **Lighthouse Publishing**

Lighthouse for Leaders, *(978-0-9820576)* P.O. Box 1990, San Benito, TX 78586 USA; *Imprints:* Lighthouse for Leaders, A (LighthseforLea)
Web site: http://www.LighthouseforLeaders.com.

Lighthouse for Leaders, A *Imprint of* **Lighthouse for Leaders**

LightHouse Global Publishing & PR *See* **LightHse. Global Publishing & PR LLC**

LightHse. Global Publishing & PR LLC, *(978-1-950621)* 506 S. Spring St. No. 13308, SMB 4527, Los Angeles, CA 90013 USA
E-mail: agent@lighthouseglobalinc.com
Web site: www.lighthouseglobalinc.com.

Lighthouse Point Pr., *(978-0-9637966; 978-0-9792998)* Div. of Yearick-Millea, Inc., 7412 Lighthouse Point, Pittsburgh, PA 15221 USA Tel 412-242-9382; Fax: 412-242-9382
Web site: http://lighthousepointpress.com.

LightHouse Pr., *(978-0-9703823; 978-0-9724442; 978-0-9747189; 978-0-9762898; 978-0-9791372; 978-0-9823218)* 2053 Williams Valley Dr., Madison, TN 37115-7610 USA Do not confuse with companies with the same or similar names in Culver City, CA, Millersburg, OH, York, ME, Marblehead, MA, Deerfield Beach, FL, La Junta, CO, Rochester, NY, San Mateo, CA.

Lighthouse Pr., Inc., *(978-0-9677347; 978-0-9795392; 979-8-9859383)* 5448 Apex Peakway #230, Apex, NC 27502-3924 USA (SAN 253-0961) Do not confuse with companies with the same or similar names in York, ME, Marblehead, MA, La Junta, CO, Deerfield Beach, FL, San Mateo, CA, Sanford, MI, Minneapolis, MN, Millersburg, OH
E-mail: swagner@lighthouse-press.com
Web site: http://www.lighthouse-press.com
Dist(s): **Independently Published**
Ingram Bk. Co.

Lighthouse Publication *See* **MainSpringBks.**

Lighthouse Publications *See* **I AM Foundation, The**

Lighthouse Publishing *See* **LightHse. Publishing**

LightHse. Publishing, *(978-0-9755438)* 6761 W. Sonnet Dr., Glendale, AZ 85308 USA Tel 602-535-9379; Fax: 858-720-8733; Toll Free: 888-357-7313
E-mail: julieginn@gmail.com.

Lighthouse Publishing, *(978-0-9773766; 978-0-9797863; 978-1-935079; 978-0-9981577; 978-1-64373)* 754 Roxholly Walk, Buford, GA 30518 USA (SAN 257-4330)
E-mail: andyoverett@lighthousechristianpublishing.com
Web site: http://www.lighthouseebooks.com; http://www.lighthousechristianpublishing.com; http://www.loneoakpublishing.com
Dist(s): **CreateSpace Independent Publishing Platform.**

Lighthouse Publishing of the Carolinas *See* **LPC**

LightHse. Pr. *Imprint of* **LightHse. Bks., The**

Lightly Pr., *(978-0-9794452)* 26 Quay Ct., No. 65, sacramento, CA 95831-1540 USA Tel 916-427-7840
E-mail: regdown@hotmail.com.

Lightnin Bug Pr., *(978-0-9824289)* 422 S. Maple, Harrison, AR 72690-5832 USA (SAN 858-1428).

Lightning Bug Flix *See* **Santa Fe Communications, Inc.**

Lightning Bug Learning Corporation *See* **Lightning Bug Learning Pr.**

Lightning Bug Learning Pr., *(978-0-9817826; 978-0-9832098)* Reviewer Relations Dept. 316 Mid Valley Ctr., #130, Carmel, CA 93923 USA (SAN 856-5449) Tel 831-250-1866; Fax: 971-250-2582; Toll Free: 877-695-7312
E-mail: mail@lightningbuglearning.com
Web site: http://www.lightningbuglearning.com; http://www.lightningbuglearningpress.com
Dist(s): **Book Clearing Hse.**

Lightning Creek *See* **Perceval Pr.**

Lightning Fast Bk. Publishing, *(978-0-9916682; 978-0-9965411; 978-0-9974925; 978-0-9994653; 978-1-7348113; 979-8-9852917; 979-8-9882743)* 1812 Hollydale Rd., Fort Washington, MD 20744 USA Tel 240-605-1106
E-mail: matt@matthewchorne.com
Web site: www.lfbookpublishing.com.

Lightning Source, LLC *See* **Ingram Content Group**

LightningBolt Pr., *(978-0-9746398)* 1481 Applegate Dr. Suite 101, Naperville, IL 60565-1225 USA Tel 630-778-7310; Fax: 630-778-7890
E-mail: info@mygreatdebate.net
Web site: http://www.greatdebate.net.

Lightport Bks., *(978-0-9712425; 978-0-578-84351-3; 978-0-578-93066-4; 978-0-578-38634-8)* P.O. Box 7112, Berkeley, CA 94707 USA
E-mail: haconrad@earthlink.net
Web site: http://www.lightportbooks.com.

Lightwatcher Publishing *See* **Illumina Publishing**

Ligonier Ministries, *(978-1-56769; 978-1-64289)* Orders Addr.: P.O. Box 547500, Orlando, FL 32854-7500 USA Tel 407-333-4244; Fax: 407-333-4233; Edit Addr.: 400 Technology Park Dr., Lake Mary, FL 32746 USA
Web site: http://www.ligonier.org
Dist(s): **christianaudio.**

Liguori Pubns., *(978-0-7648; 978-0-89243)* One Liguori Dr., Liguori, MO 63057-9999 USA (SAN 202-6783) Tel 636-464-2500; Fax: 636-464-8449; Toll Free Fax: 800-325-9526; Toll Free: 800-325-9521 (orders); *Imprints:* Libros Liguori (Libros Liguori)
E-mail: liguori@liguori.org
Web site: http://www.liguori.org
Dist(s): **ACTA Pubns.**
Follett School Solutions
MyiLibrary.

LikeMinds Pr., *(978-0-9764724; 978-0-9915853)* Orders Addr.: 3151 Airway Ave. Suite K-205 Suite K-205, Costa Mesa, CA 92626 USA Fax: 714-556-2354
E-mail: shendi@cox.net
Web site: http://www.likemindspress.com.

Lil' Chakras, *(978-0-578-99170-2)* 4695 Camelot Dr., Harbor Springs, MI 49740 USA Tel 949-400-5632
E-mail: robbie@neumann5.com.

Lil' Libros *Imprint of* **Little Libros, LLC**

Lilac Daggers Press *See* **Lilac Daggers Pr. LLC**

Lilac Daggers Pr. LLC, *(978-1-7349004)* 9429 MONTICELLO DR, TWINSBURG, OH 44087 USA Tel 330-620-0440
E-mail: authorsydneyhawthorn@gmail.com
Web site: worldofsydneyhawthorn.com.

Lilac Pr., *(978-0-9662568)* Orders Addr.: P.O. Box 1356, Scottsdale, AZ 85252-1356 USA Fax: 480-368-5551; Edit Addr.: 6268 N. 85th St., Scottsdale, AZ 85250 USA
E-mail: lilacp@cholesterolnodiet.com; lilacp@frontiernet.net
Web site: http://www.cholesterolnodiet.com.

Lilacs in Litearture *See* **Lilacs in Literature**

Lilacs in Literature, *(978-0-692-74509-0; 978-0-692-74510-6; 978-0-9981958; 978-1-7340099)* 3014 Coventry Ct., Cocoa, FL 32926 USA Tel 321-525-9612
E-mail: wandalu64@gmail.com
Web site: www.wandaluthman.wordpress.com.

LiliArte, *(978-0-692-88040-1; 978-0-692-92873-8)* 21 SHENEMAN DR, BELLA VISTA, AR 72715 USA Tel 501-588-1365
E-mail: christyhn@yahoo.com.

Lillenas Publishing Co., *(978-0-8341)* Div. of Nazarene Publishing Hse., P.O. Box 419527, Kansas City, MO 64141 USA (SAN 298-7619) Tel 816-931-1900; Fax: 816-753-4071; Toll Free Fax: 800-849-9827; Toll Free: 800-877-0700 (Orders Only)
E-mail: music@lillenas.com
Web site: http://www.lillenas.com
Dist(s): **The Foundry Publishing**
Leonard, Hal Corp.
Spring Arbor Distributors, Inc.

Lillian Press *See* **Smith & Assocs.**

Lillis, Holly, *(978-0-9762733)* P.O. Box 1082, Aptos, CA 95001-0000 USA.

Lill-Till Pr., *(978-0-9742808)* 15305 Walvern Blvd., Maple Heights, OH 44137 USA.

Lily & Co. Publishing, *(978-1-929265)* Orders Addr.: 15 Willow Rd., Greenville, RI 02828 USA
E-mail: erinesquedesign@mac.com
Web site: http://www.lilycopublishing.com.

Lily The Reindeer, *(978-0-692-87764-7; 978-0-692-15777-0)* 55 Myrtle Pk. Point, Ponte Vedra, FL 32081 USA Tel 516-819-1234; Toll Free: 516-819-1234
E-mail: jackbunkerdavid@aol.com; jackbunkerdavid@aol.com; jackbunkerdavid@aol.com
Web site: https://lilythereindeer.com/
Dist(s): **CreateSpace Independent Publishing Platform.**

Lily Wish Factory, *(978-0-9792472)* 44 W. Main St., Mystic, CT 06355 USA (SAN 852-8861) Tel 860-245-0629
E-mail: shipandshimmer@aol.com
Web site: http://shipandshimmer.com.

LilyBoo Pr., *(978-1-7346422)* 4822 S 133 St, Ste 200, Omaha, NE 68137 USA Tel 402-884-5995
E-mail: lilyboo@conciergemarketing.com.

Lima Bear Pr LLC, The, *(978-1-933872)* 2305 MacDonough Rd., Wilmington, DE 19805 USA
E-mail: lbp.books@yahoo.com
Web site: http://www.limabearpress.com.

Publisher Name Index

Limelight Editions *Imprint of* **Leonard, Hal Corp.**

Limerock Bks., *(978-0-9746589)* 15 Mechanic St., Thomaston, ME 04861 USA Tel 207-354-8191 Do not confuse with Limerock Books, Inc., New Canaan, CT
E-mail: limebks@midcoast.com
Web site: http://www.ChristopherFahy.com
Dist(s): **Brodart Co.**

Limitless Bks., *(978-0-9998865)* 101 Parkhurst Rd, Gansevoot, NY 12831 USA Tel 518-396-8376
E-mail: ian@bicyclebenefits.org
Web site: www.limitlessbooks.us.

Limitless Ink Press, LLC, *(978-1-939672; 978-0-615-93665-9; 978-1-947218)* P.O. Box 8802, Erie, PA 16505 USA Tel 913-271-7804
E-mail: patricemichelle@gmail.com.

Limitless Publishing, LLC, *(978-0-615-68509-0; 978-0-615-76957-8; 978-0-615-78296-6; 978-0-615-78347-5; 978-1-68058; 978-1-64034; 978-1-954194)* 701 N. Kalaheo, Kailua, HI 96734 USA
E-mail: jennifer@limitlesspublishing.com; dixie@limitlesspublishing.com
Web site: http://www.limitlesspublishing.com
Dist(s): **CreateSpace Independent Publishing Platform.**

Lin, Chen, *(978-1-7334156)* 80 Hillcrest Rd., Needham, MA 02492 USA Tel 781-400-1632
E-mail: crystalchenlin@hotmail.com.

Lincoln Bks., *(978-0-9910560)* 406 Diana Ct., Highland Heights, OH 44124 USA Tel 440-813-0274
E-mail: robthomas@hotmail.com
Web site: Rob Thomas.

Lincoln, Emma *See* **Awesome Bk. Publishing**

Lincoln Learning Solutions, *(978-0-9816745; 978-1-935193; 978-1-936318; 978-1-938165; 978-1-943303; 978-1-944075; 978-1-68379)* 294 Massachusetts Ave., Rochester, PA 15074 USA Toll Free: 866-990-6637
Web site: http://www.nndsonline.org; lincolnlearningsolutions.org.

Lincoln Library Pr., Inc., The, *(978-0-912168)* Orders Addr.: 812 Huron Rd., SE, Suite 401, Cleveland, OH 44115-1126 USA (SAN 205-5953) Fax: 216-781-9559 (phone/fax); Toll Free: 800-516-2656
E-mail: tgall@thelincolnlibrary.com
Web site: http://www.thelincolnlibrary.com
Dist(s): **Follett School Solutions INscribe Digital.**

Lincoln Public Schls., *(978-0-9671920)* P.O. Box 82889, Lincoln, NE 68501 USA (SAN 508-9964) Tel 401-436-1628; Fax: 401-436-1638
E-mail: dpeters@lps.org
Web site: http://www.lps.org.

Lincross Publishing, *(978-0-9987566; 978-0-9991896; 978-1-948581; 978-1-7370953)* 4480 - H South Cobb Drive, Suite 391, Smyrna, GA 30080 USA Tel 678-308-9971
E-mail: lincrosspublishing@gmail.com
Web site: www.lincrosspublishing.com.

Linda Cardillo, Author *See* **Bellastoria Pr.**

Linda Hall Library, *(978-0-9763590)* 5109 Cherry St., Kansas City, MO 64110-2498 USA Tel 816-363-4600; Fax: 816-926-8790
E-mail: bradleyb@lindahall.org
Web site: http://www.lindahall.org.

Linda Kaye's Birthdaybakers, Partymakers, *(978-0-9759161)* 195 East 76th St., New York, NY 10021 USA Tel 212-288-7112; Fax: 212-879-6785
E-mail: lindak@partymakers.com
Web site: http://www.partymakers.com.

Linda M. Penn Author, *(978-0-9852488; 978-0-9908807; 978-1-7321454)* 2023 Eagles Landing Dr., Lagrange, KY 40031 USA Tel 502-262-7870
E-mail: lindampenn@gmail.com.

Lindaloo Enterprises, *(978-0-9800923; 978-1-937564)* P.O. Box 90135, Santa Barbara, CA 93190 USA; *Imprints:* Classic Bookwrights (ClassicBook)
E-mail: sales@lindaloo.com
Web site: http://www.lindaloo.com; http://www.tporigami.com
Dist(s): **Ingram Content Group.**

Linden Hill Publishing, *(978-0-9704754; 978-0-9820153)* Subs. of Arcadia Productions, 11923 Somerset Ave., Princess Anne, MD 21853 USA Tel 410-651-0757 (phone/fax)
E-mail: lindenhill2@comcast.net
Web site: http://www.lindenhill.net.

Linden Publishing Co., Inc., *(978-0-941936; 978-1-933502; 978-1-61035)* 2006 S. Mary, Fresno, CA 93721 USA (SAN 238-6089) Tel 559-233-6633 (phone/fax); Toll Free: 800-345-4447 (orders only); *Imprints:* Craven Street Books (Craven St Bks) Do not confuse with Linden Publishing in Avon, NY
E-mail: richard@lindenpub.com
Web site: http://www.lindenpub.com
Dist(s): **CreateSpace Independent Publishing Platform Ingram Publisher Services Quality Bks., Inc. Smashwords.**

Lindisfarne Bks. *Imprint of* **SteinerBooks, Inc.**

Lindsay Pubns., Inc., *(978-0-917914; 978-1-55918)* Orders Addr.: P.O. Box 12, Bradley, IL 60915 USA (SAN 209-9462) Tel 815-935-5353; Fax: 815-935-5477.

Lindsey Publishing, Incorporated *See* **KaZoom Kids Bks., Inc.**

Lindsley, David Studio, *(978-0-9796008)* P.O. Box 431, Springville, UT 84663 USA.

Line By Lion Pubns. *Imprint of* **3 Fates Pr.**

Linear Wave Publishing, *(978-0-9767196)* P.O. Box 177, Liberty, KY 42539-0177 USA Tel 606-787-8189
E-mail: blaine.staat@linearwavepublishing.com
Web site: http://www.linearwavepublishing.com.

Linehan Authors, *(978-1-7336855)* 807 Callant Dr., Little River, SC 29566 USA Tel 860-942-1623
E-mail: judithlinehan@gmail.com; thomas.linehan@yahoo.com
Web site: www.linehanauthors.com.

Lingenfelser, Lynda L., *(978-0-615-13290-7; 978-0-615-14072-8)* 3284 Spruce Creek Glen, Daytona Beach, FL 32198 USA; P.O. Box 290714, Port Orange, FL 32129
Dist(s): **Lulu Pr., Inc.**

Linger Longer Books *See* **Artists' Orchard, LLC, The**

Lingo Pr. LLC, *(978-0-9777419)* 1020 Janet Dr., Lakeland, FL 33805 USA (SAN 850-119X) Tel 863-868-5996 (phone/fax)
E-mail: customerservice@lingopress.com
Web site: http://www.lingopress.com.

Linguatechnics Publishing, *(978-0-9767837)* 2114 Pauline Blvd., Ann Arbor, MI 48103 USA Tel 734-662-0434; Fax: 734-662-0248
E-mail: info@linguatechnics.com
Web site: http://www.linguatechnics.com.

LinguaText, Limited *See* **LinguaText, LLC**

LinguaText, LLC, *(978-0-936388; 978-0-942566; 978-1-58871; 978-1-58977)* Orders Addr.: 103 Walker Way, Newark, DE 19711-6119 USA (SAN 238-0307) Tel 302-453-8695
E-mail: text@linguatextbooks.com; libros@juandelacuesta.com
Web site: http://www.LinguatextLtd.com; http://www.MoliereandCo.com; http://www.LinguaTextBooks.com; http://www.CervantesandCo.com; http://www.EuropeanMasterpieces.com; http://www.JuandelaCuesta.com
Dist(s): **Baker & Taylor Publisher Services (BTPS) Follett School Solutions Yankee Bk. Peddler, Inc.**

Linguistic Artistry, *(978-1-7372648)* 1720 Shadewood Dr., Modesto, CA 95355 USA Tel 209-484-3540
E-mail: danceisbreath@gmail.com.

LinguiSystems, Inc., *(978-0-7606; 978-1-55999)* 3100 Fourth Ave., East Moline, IL 61244-9700 USA Tel 309-755-2300; Fax: 309-755-2377; Toll Free: 800-776-4332; 800-577-4555
E-mail: kmicka@linguisystems.com
Web site: http://www.linguisystems.com.

Linhardt, Mitch, *(978-0-578-13379-9; 978-0-578-17373-3; 978-0-578-18616-0; 978-0-578-18748-8; 978-0-578-78198-3)* 921 Union Pl., Herculaneum, MO 63048 USA Tel 314-223-8689
E-mail: mclinhardt@yahoo.com.

Linive Kreyol Publishing, *(978-0-9720954)* 339 Howell Dr. SE, Suite 3-F, Atlanta, GA 30316 USA.

Link & Rosie Pr., *(978-0-9762434)* Orders Addr.: c/o Goblin Fern Press, Inc., 1118 Sequoia Trail, Madison, WI 53713 USA Tel 608-335-0542; Fax: 608-210-7235
E-mail: ssharron@sbcglobal.net
Web site: http://www.linkandrosie.com.

Linky & Dinky Enterprises, *(978-0-9768588)* P.O. Box 418, Oldsmar, FL 34677 USA
E-mail: uncle-url@linkydinky.com
Web site: http://www.linkydinky.com.

Linmore Publishing, Inc., *(978-0-916591; 978-1-934472)* Orders Addr.: P.O. Box 1545, Palatine, IL 60078 USA (SAN 662-2291) Fax: 612-729-9125; Toll Free: 800-336-3656
E-mail: linmore@linmore.com
Web site: http://www.linmore.com.

LinWood Hse. Publishing, *(978-0-9753098; 978-0-692-98408-6; 978-1-7321891)* 3652 Kissimmee Pk. Rd., Saint Cloud, FL 34772 USA Tel 407-595-6220
E-mail: zippityzem@comcast.net
Dist(s): **CreateSpace Independent Publishing Platform Smashwords.**

Linworth Publishing, Inc. *Imprint of* **ABC-CLIO, LLC**

LINX Corp., *(978-0-9642386; 978-0-9802118; 978-1-936961)* P.O. Box 613, Great Falls, VA 22066 USA Tel 703-216-9314; *Imprints:* Investing for Kids (Investing); VRguy publishing (VRguy)
E-mail: orders@linxcorp.com; steve@linxcorp.com
Web site: http://www.linxcorp.com
Dist(s): **Bookazine Co., Inc.**

Linx Educational Publishing, Inc., *(978-1-891818; 978-0-9797510)* P.O. Box 50009, Jacksonville Beach, FL 32240 USA Tel 904-241-1861; Fax: 904-241-3279; Toll Free Fax: 888-546-9338; Toll Free: 800-717-5469
E-mail: mimi@linxedu.com; info@linxedu.com
Web site: http://www.linxedu.com
Dist(s): **American Assn. for Vocational Instructional Materials Films Media Group Follett School Solutions JIST Publishing S V E & Churchill Media.**

†**Lion Bks.,** *(978-0-87460)* 235 Garth Rd. Apt. D5A, Scarsdale, NY 10583-3994 USA (SAN 241-7529)
Dist(s): **Baker & Taylor Publisher Services (BTPS);** *CIP.*

Lion Crest Leadership *See* **Victoria Tecken**

Lion Forge *Imprint of* **Oni Pr., Inc.**

Lion Hudson PLC (GBR) *(978-0-7459; 978-0-85648; 978-0-85721) Dist. by* **Trafalgar.**

Lion Hudson PLC (GBR) *(978-0-7459; 978-0-85648; 978-0-85721) Dist. by* **IPG Chicago.**

Lion Hudson PLC (GBR) *(978-0-7459; 978-0-85648; 978-0-85721) Dist. by* **Kregel.**

Lion Hudson PLC (GBR) *(978-0-7459; 978-0-85648; 978-0-85721) Dist. by* **BTPS.**

Lion of Judah Publishing, *(978-0-578-39015-4)* 738 No. Superior St., Duluth, MN 55802 USA Tel 218-341-9339; Fax: 218-722-1971
E-mail: bonniejoy55802@gmail.com
Web site: jesuslovesyoubook.com.

Lion Stone Bks., *(978-0-9658486; 978-0-9859618)* Orders Addr.: 4921 Aurora Dr., Kensington, MD 20895 USA Tel 301-949-3204; Fax: 301-949-3860
E-mail: lionstone@juno.com
Dist(s): **Book Wholesalers, Inc. Brodart Co. Follett School Solutions.**

Lionel A. Blanchard, Pub., *(978-0-9972984; 978-1-7335858)* 2580 Dixon Dr., Santa Clara, CA 95051 USA Tel 408-406-8470
E-mail: l.a.blanchard@comcast.net.

Lioness Publishing, *(978-0-9961606)* 2120 W.96th St., Los Angeles, CA 90047 USA Tel 323-477-3530
E-mail: livia.latrice@gmail.com.

Lionheart Foundation, The, *(978-0-9644933; 978-0-9799338; 978-0-578-59124-7; 978-0-578-62058-9; 978-0-578-68961-6; 978-0-578-74284-7; 978-0-578-76336-1; 978-0-578-90894-6; 979-8-218-10647-8)* P.O. Box 194, Boston, MA 02117 USA Tel 781-444-6667; Fax: 781-444-6855
E-mail: judith@lionheart.org
Web site: http://www.lionheart.org.

Lionheart Group Publishing, *(978-0-9845127; 978-1-938505)* Div. of Lionheart Group, LLC, 1501 Main St No. 1023, Canon City, CO 81215 USA
E-mail: admin@lionheartgrouppublishing.com
Web site: www.redenginepress.com; www.lionheartgrouppublishing.com.

Lionheart Pr., *(978-0-9964246)* 3711 Fews Ford Ln., Durham, NC 27712 USA Tel 919-812-6204
E-mail: hejafred@gmail.com
Web site: www.timberhowligan.com.

Lion's Crest Pr., *(978-0-9763798)* 1900 S. Rock Rd., Suite 5205, Wichita, KS 67207 USA Tel 316-305-5813.

Lions Den Publishing, LLC, *(978-0-9786786)* P.O. Box 91254, Washington, DC 20090-1254 USA (SAN 851-2477) Tel 202-256-0508.

Lions Gate Home Entertainment, *(978-0-940245; 978-1-57362; 978-1-58817; 978-1-59435)* 2700 Colorado Ave. Ste. 200, Santa Monica, CA 90404-5502 USA
E-mail: schandani@lgecorp.com
Web site: http://www.trimarkpictures.com
Dist(s): **Follett Media Distribution Follett School Solutions.**

Lion's Historian Pr., *(978-1-7371629; 978-1-956051)* 509 Spruce St, Eagan, MN 55123 USA Tel 320-492-3045
E-mail: rosaak2000@gmail.com
Web site: www.rosemondowens.com; https://www.lionshistorian.net.

Lion's Tale Pr., LLC, *(978-0-9748478)* 4895 Kings Valley Dr., Suite 200, Roswell, GA 30075 USA Tel 770-998-3302; Fax: 770-998-3874
E-mail: ebbenator@mindspring.com.

LionX Publishing, *(978-0-9716085)* 24988 Blue Ravine Rd., #108-113, Folsom, CA 95630 USA (SAN 254-2021) Tel 916-939-9422; Fax: 916-939-9424
E-mail: info@lionxpublishing.com
Web site: http://www.lionxpublishing.com.

LIP Publishing LLC, *(978-0-9771114)* 903 Oakridge Dr, Suite 100, Round Rock, TX 78681 USA
E-mail: thelifeip@yahoo.com
Web site: http://www.thelifeip.com.

†**Lippincott Williams & Wilkins,** *(978-0-316; 978-0-397; 978-0-683; 978-0-7817; 978-0-8067; 978-0-8121; 978-0-88167; 978-0-89004; 978-0-89313; 978-0-89640; 978-0-911216; 978-1-881063; 978-1-60547; 978-1-60831; 978-1-60929; 978-1-4698)* Orders Addr.: P.O. Box 1620, Hagerstown, MD 21741 USA Fax: 301-223-2400; Toll Free: 800-638-3030; Edit Addr.: 530 Walnut St., Philadelphia, PA 19106-3621 USA (SAN 201-0933) Tel 215-521-8300; Fax: 215-521-8902; Toll Free: 800-638-3030; 351 W. Camden St., Baltimore, MD 21201 Tel 410-528-4000; 410-528-4209
E-mail: custserv@lww.com; orders@lww.com
Web site: http://www.lww.com
Dist(s): **Igaku-Shoin Medical Pubs. MyiLibrary;** *CIP.*

Lippincott-Raven Publishers *See* **Lippincott Williams & Wilkins**

Liquid Space Publishing, *(978-0-9710366)* 37 Endicott St., Salem, MA 01970 USA Tel 978-745-5529
E-mail: donniedives@earthlink.net
Web site: http://www.home.earthlink.net/~donniedives.

Lire Bks., *(978-0-9849323; 978-1-939652)* 7 Debaun Pl., Spring Valley, NY 10977 USA Tel 845-659-2018
E-mail: raedanbocs@gmail.com
Web site: lirebooks.com.

Lisa Bushong-Holgate, *(978-0-692-94611-4)* 5216 Univ. Dr., Santa Barbara, CA 93111 USA Tel 510-265-4714
E-mail: lmbushong@yahoo.com.

Lisa Nicole Publishing, *(978-1-7356342; 978-1-7375515; 979-8-9878940)*
E-mail: info@lisanicolealexander.org.

Lisa The Weather Wonder Inc., *(978-0-9740997)* 187 Summer Lake Dr., Marietta, GA 30060 USA
Web site: http://www.lisamozer.com.

Lisboa, David, *(978-0-9752740)* 9060 Palisade Ave., Apt. 307, North Bergan, NJ 07047 USA Tel 201-869-3494.

Lissarette, *(978-0-578-82621-9; 978-1-7366439)* 426 E 120th St., New York, NY 10035 USA Tel 646-600-0069
E-mail: lissarette@gmail.com; lissarette@lissarette.com
Web site: www.lissarette.com.

Listen & Live Audio, Inc., *(978-1-885408; 978-1-931953; 978-1-59316; 979-8-88642)* Orders Addr.: P.O. Box 817, Roseland, NJ 07068 USA Tel 201-558-9000; Fax: 201-558-9800; Toll Free: 800-653-9400; Edit Addr.: 1700 Manhattan Ave., Union City, NJ 07087-5473 USA
E-mail: Alfred@Listenandlive.com
Web site: http://www.listenandlive.com
Dist(s): **Audible.com Ebsco Publishing Findaway World, LLC Follett School Solutions OverDrive, Inc. Smashwords.**

Listening Library *Imprint of* **Random Hse. Audio Publishing Group**

Lister, Tresina, *(978-0-9791171)* 541 S. Staunton Dr., Tucson, AZ 85710 USA Tel 520-751-8630.

Liszka, Jesse, *(978-1-7333597)* 156 Gregory M. Sears Dr., Gilberts, IL 60136 USA Tel 630-890-8936
E-mail: jessejpalmer@yahoo.com
Web site: jesseliszka.com.

Lit Noire Publishing, *(978-0-9719052; 978-0-578-50965-5)* P.O. Box 26183, Brooklyn, NY 11201 USA Tel 212-656-1762
E-mail: duewa@duewaworld.com
Web site: http://www.duewaworld.com
Dist(s): **CreateSpace Independent Publishing Platform Lulu Pr., Inc.**

Lit Torch Publishing, *(978-1-887357)* 4204 Danmire Dr., Richardson, TX 75082 USA Tel 312-239-8633 (phone/fax)
E-mail: littorch@gmail.com
Web site: http://www.littorch.com.

Literacy Resources, Inc., *(978-0-9759575; 978-1-947260; 978-1-960968)* 805 Lake St. No. 293, Oak Park, IL 60301 USA Tel 708-366-5947
E-mail: hello@heggerty.org
Web site: www.heggerty.org.

Literal Publishing Inc., *(978-0-9770287; 978-0-9897957; 978-1-942307)* 5425 Renwick Dr., Houston, TX 77081 USA Tel 713-626-1433.

Literally Speaking Publishing Hse., *(978-1-929642)* 2020 Pennsylvania Ave., NW, No. 406, Washington, DC 20006 USA (SAN 852-8896) Tel 202-491-5774; Fax: 202-403-3535
E-mail: Distribution@LiterallySpeaking.com; bookinfo@literallyspeaking.com
Web site: http://www.literallyspeaking.com.

Literary Architects, LLC, *(978-1-933669)* 1427 W. 86th St., Suite 324, Indianapolis, IN 46260 USA Tel 317-462-6329
E-mail: info@literaryarchitects.com
Web site: http://www.literaryarchitects.com.

Literary Legacies Publishing, *(978-0-692-95440-9; 978-0-692-15422-9; 978-0-692-15965-1; 978-0-578-49765-5; 978-0-578-49766-2; 978-0-578-49767-9)* 1355 James Ct., Morgan Hill, CA 95037 USA Tel 4084107886
E-mail: info@literarylegacies.org
Dist(s): **CreateSpace Independent Publishing Platform.**

Literary Lessons *Imprint of* **HomeScholar Bks.**

Literary Licensing, LLC, *(978-1-258; 978-1-4940; 978-1-4941; 978-1-4978; 978-1-4979; 978-1-4980; 978-1-4981)* P.O. Box 1404, Whitefish, MT 59937 USA Fax: 406-897-7825
E-mail: literarylicensing@runbox.com
Web site: http://www.literarylicensing.com
Dist(s): **ISD.**

Literary Works Specialist, *(978-0-9746687)* P.O. Box 58908, New Orleans, LA 70158-8908 USA
E-mail: rdomio@aol.com
Web site: http://www.lwspublishing.net.

Literate Chigger Pr., Ink, Inc., The, *(978-0-9759042; 978-0-615-56517-0)* 1175 Queen Anne Rd., Teaneck, NJ 07666 USA Tel 201-741-6529
E-mail: emily@hipbo.org.

Literati, *(978-1-7374508; 978-1-958388)* 1021 E. 7th Street, Suite 103, Austin, TX 78702 USA Tel 405-315-6224
E-mail: charles@literati.com
Web site: literati.com.

Literature Dramatization Pr., *(978-0-9644186)* 1089 Sunset Cliffs Blvd., San Diego, CA 92107-4037 USA Tel 619-222-2462
Dist(s): **Educational Bk. Distributors Empire Publishing Service Lectorum Pubns., Inc.**

LITHBTH Educational Services, *(978-0-9744920)* P.O. Box 55495, Hayward, CA 94545-5495 USA
E-mail: teachingkids@mindspring.com
Web site: http://www.home.mindspring.com/~teachingkids.

Litho Tech, LLC, *(978-0-9742791)* 3045 Highland Ave., Grants Pass, OR 97526 USA Tel 541-479-8905; Fax: 541-474-6937
E-mail: gpprint@charterinternet.com; lithotech541@charter.net.

LitJoy Crate, *(978-1-7350633; 978-1-955876)* 1375 S 500 E, American Fork, UT 84003 USA Tel 801-717-0466
E-mail: jenny@litjoycrate.com
Web site: litjoycrate.com.

Litkus Pr., *(978-1-932629)* P.O. Box 34785, Los Angeles, CA 90034 USA Tel 310-391-5629
E-mail: litkuspress@earthlink.net.

Litmocracy Pubns., *(978-0-9798861)* 9175 Middlefield Dr., Riverside, CA 92508 USA (SAN 854-6606)
E-mail: dscotese@litmocracy.com
Web site: http://www.litmocracy.com.

Little A *Imprint of* **Amazon Publishing**

Little Acorn Assocs., Inc., *(978-0-9741579; 978-0-9844010; 978-1-937257; 978-1-946557)*
E-mail: liacorn53@gmail.com.

Little Acorn Associates, Incorporated *See* **Little Acorn Assocs., Inc.**

Little Acorn LLC, *(978-0-9766703; 978-0-9964448)* Orders Addr.: 112 W. Calista Dr., Tahlequah, OK 74464-7446 USA
E-mail: info@littleacornkids.net
Web site: http://www.littleacornkids.net.

Little Adventures *Imprint of* **Amberjack Publishing Co.**

Little Balloon Pr., *(978-0-9843922)* 988 Belmont Terr., No. 2, Sunnyvale, CA 94086 USA (SAN 859-2721)
Web site: http://www.littleballoonpress.com.

Little Band Man Co., LLC, The, *(978-0-615-12596-1)* 1415 Easy St., New Iberia, LA 70560 USA Tel 337-365-4136; Fax: 337-365-4137
E-mail: jady@littlebandman.com
Web site: http://www.littlebandman.com.

For full information on wholesalers and distributors, refer to the Wholesaler and Distributor Name Index

ttle Bay Pr., *(978-0-9745192)* 40 Salmon Beach, Tacoma, WA 98407 USA Tel 253-756-0987
E-mail: kcampbell@littlebaypress.com
Web site: http://www.littlebaypress.com.

ttle Bear Pr., *(978-0-615-57443-1; 978-0-615-90320-0)* 448 Pear Tree Point Rd., Chestertown, MD 21620 USA Tel 301-775-0164; 410-778-6270
Dist(s): **CreateSpace Independent Publishing Platform.**

ittle Bee Books Inc., *(978-1-4998)* Div. of Bonnier Publishing USA, 275 7th Ave 7 FL, New York, NY 10001 USA (SAN 992-0242) Toll Free: 844-321-0237; *Imprints*: Sizzle Press (SizzlePr); BuzzPop (BuzzPop)
E-mail: info@littlebeebooks.com
Web site: http://www.littlebeebooks.com
Dist(s): **Children's Plus, Inc.**
Simon & Schuster, Inc.

.ittle Big Bay LLC, *(978-0-9834330; 978-0-9892822; 978-0-9968071; 978-0-578-29773-6; 979-8-218-06704-5; 979-8-218-16556-7)* 124 E. Bennett St., Mellen, WI 54546 USA Tel 715-919-0179
E-mail: ros@wintemet.com
Web site: www.littlebigbayshop.com
Dist(s): **Ingram Publisher Services**
Ingram Content Group.

Little Big Deer *Imprint of* **Deer Horn Pr.**

Little Big Tomes, 1275 Trail Ridge Dr., Canyon Lake, TX 78133 USA Tel 830-899-6888
E-mail: cottage@gvtc.com.

Little Bigfoot *Imprint of* **Sasquatch Bks.**

Little Bird Bks., *(978-0-615-66291-6; 978-0-9913003; 978-0-578-79622-2; 979-8-218-02482-6)* 585 Mountain View Rd., Santa Cruz, CA 95065 USA
E-mail: masperling@gmail.com.

Little Bird Publishing, *(978-0-9728838)* 285 W. 8th St., Ship Bottom, NJ 08008 USA Tel 609-494-7485; Fax: 609-494-9569
E-mail: gwennhotaling@aol.com
Web site: http://www.gwennhotaling.com.

Little Black Paws Publishing, *(978-0-9992704)* 2803 Sarento Pl. No. 107, Palm Beach Gardens, FL 33410 USA Tel 203-249-9838
E-mail: sandramendelson@yahoo.com.

Little Blue Flower Pr. *Imprint of* **Raven's Wing Bks.**

Little Blue Hse., 1600 Cliff Rd. E, Burnsville, MN 55337 USA; *Imprints*: Little Blue Readers (LBlueRead)
Dist(s): **North Star Editions.**

Little Blue Pr., *(978-0-9725584)* 14403 Little Blue Rd., Kansan City, MO 64136 USA Tel 816-455-1110
E-mail: littlebluepress@softhome.net.

Little Blue Readers *Imprint of* **Little Blue Hse.**

Little Bookroom *Imprint of* **New York Review of Bks., Inc., The**

Little Bookstore Who Could, The, *(978-0-9746997)* 1303 Windsong Way, Augusta, GA 30907 USA Tel 706-868-0075
E-mail: vickyharperselah@yahoo.com; vicky@thelittlebookstorethatcould.com
Web site: http://www.thelittlebookstorethatcould.com.

Little Boots Publishing, *(978-0-9767230)* P.O. Box 3110, Pawtucket, RI 02861 USA Tel 401-475-5852 (phone/fax)
E-mail: Info@littlebootspublishing.com
Web site: http://www.littlebootspublishing.com.

Little Britches Childrens Bks., *(978-0-9798189)* P.O. Box 1188, Willow, AK 99688-1188 USA.

†Little Brown & Co., *(978-0-316; 978-0-8212; 978-0-7595)* Div. of Hachette Bk. Group, Orders Addr.: 3 Center Plaza, Boston, MA 02108-2084 USA (SAN 630-7248) Tel 617-227-0730; Toll Free Fax: 800-286-9471; Toll Free: 800-759-0190; Edit Addr.: 237 Park Ave., New York, NY 10017 USA (SAN 200-2205) Tel 212-364-0600; Fax: 212-364-0952; *Imprints*: Back Bay Books (Back Bay); Ansel Adams (Ansel Adams); Reagan Arthur Books (ReagArthur); Jimmy Patterson (JimmyPat); Springboard Press (Sprngbrd); Clarion Books (ClarionBksHC)
E-mail: customer.service@hbgusa.com
Web site: http://www.hachettebookgroup.com
Dist(s): **Blackstone Audio, Inc.**
Children's Plus, Inc.
Continental Bk. Co., Inc.
Follett School Solutions
Grand Central Publishing
Hachette Bk. Group
Hastings Bks.
Lectorum Pubns., Inc.
MyiLibrary
Open Road Integrated Media, Inc.
Rounder Kids Music Distribution
Beeler, Thomas T. Pub.
TextStream
Thorndike Pr.; *CIP.*

Little, Brown Book Group Ltd. (GBR) *(978-0-09; 978-0-316; 978-0-349; 978-0-351; 978-0-7088; 978-0-7474; 978-0-7499; 978-0-7515; 978-0-8212; 978-0-86188; 978-0-948164; 978-1-85004; 978-1-85487; 978-1-85703; 978-1-85018; 978-1-84119; 978-0-7221; 978-0-86007; 978-0-9536151; 978-1-903608; 978-1-84529; 978-1-84528; 978-1-4087; 978-1-908974; 978-1-84901)* *Dist. by* **HachBkGrp.**

Little, Brown Bks. for Young Readers, *(978-0-316; 978-0-8212; 978-0-7595; 978-0-7596)* Div. of Hachette Bk. Group, 1271 Ave. of the Americas, New York, NY 10020 USA Tel 212-522-8700; Fax: 212-522-2067; Toll Free: 800-343-9204; 3 Center Plaza, Boston, MA 02108-2084 Tel 617-227-0730; Toll Free Fax: 800-286-9471; Toll Free: 800-759-0190; *Imprints*: Tingley, Megan Books (Megan Tingley Bks); Poppy (Poppy)
Dist(s): **Blackstone Audio, Inc.**
Children's Plus, Inc.
Follett School Solutions
Grand Central Publishing
Hachette Bk. Group
Lectorum Pubns., Inc.
Little Brown & Co.
MyiLibrary.

Little Brown Children's Books *See* **Little, Brown Bks. for Young Readers**

Little Bunny Bks., *(978-0-615-46734-4; 978-0-615-58595-6; 978-0-615-66757-7; 978-0-692-48194-3)* P.O. Box 151, Cabin John, MD 20818 USA Tel 978-712-8669
E-mail: littlebunnybooks@gmail.com
Dist(s): **CreateSpace Independent Publishing Platform.**

Little Buzz Bk. Club, *(978-0-9975981; 978-1-947099-46-3)* 2146 Roswell Rd., Marietta, GA 30062 USA Tel 770-744-9390; Fax: 770-744-9390
E-mail: membership@littlebuzzbookclub.com
Web site: www.littlebuzzbookclub.com.

Little CAB Pr., *(978-0-692-76264-6)* 17220 E Desert Ln., GILBERT, AZ 85234 USA Tel 602-791-8410
Dist(s): **Independent Pub.**

Little Cabbagehead Books *See* **Luthie M West**

Little Chameleon Bks. *Imprint of* **Kid Prep, Inc.**

Little Clive Pr., *(978-0-615-58866-7; 978-0-615-69435-1; 978-0-615-79920-9; 978-0-9911479)* 306 N. 19th Ave., Kelso, WA 98626 USA Tel 503-381-3923
E-mail: bendertzu@yahoo.com; joey.wardell@gmail.com
Web site: www.littleclivepress.com.

Little Cottonwood River Bks., *(978-0-9884268)* 2918 71st St., Dundee, MN 56131 USA Tel 507-274-5316
E-mail: paplowp@gmail.com.

Little Crab Productions, *(978-1-7344633)* 415 S. Prospect Ave., Redondo Beach, CA 90277 USA Tel 818-325-6425
E-mail: littlecrabastrology@gmail.com
Web site: www.littlecrabastrology.com.

Little Creek Bks. *Imprint of* **Jan-Carol Publishing, INC.**

Little Creek Press, *(978-0-9828023; 978-0-9849245; 978-0-9896431; 978-0-9899780; 978-0-9899784; 978-1-942586; 978-1-955656)* Div. of Kristin Mitchell Design, LLC, 5341 Sunny Ridge Rd., Mineral Point, WI 53565 USA (SAN 920-2862) Tel 608-987-3370
E-mail: info@littlecreekpress.com
Web site: www.littlecreekpress.com
Dist(s): **Independent Pubs. Group.**

Little Cubans, LLC, *(978-1-934113)* P.O. Box 260944, Pembroke Pines, FL 33026-7944 USA
E-mail: littlecubans@bellsouth.net
Web site: http://www.littlecubans.com.

Little, Cynthia M. *See* **Sleepless Warrior Publishing**

Little Danny's Bks., Inc., *(978-1-7328515; 978-1-7339326; 978-1-7377060)* 16900 Heller Ln., Saint Robert, MO 65584 USA Tel 805-320-8058
E-mail: littledannysbooks@gmail.com.

Little Deer Pr., *(978-1-891360)* P.O. Box 1220, Rainier, WA 98576 USA Tel 360-894-3459
E-mail: mollypiper@hotmail.com
Web site: http://www.focusbloom.com.

Little Devil Bks., *(978-0-9858280; 978-0-9911534)* 5139 Maxon Terr., Sanford, FL 32771 USA Tel 407-443-6494
E-mail: dave@littledevilbooks.com
Web site: www.littledevilbooks.com
Dist(s): **Ingram Content Group**
Smashwords.

Little Dixie Publishing Co., *(978-0-9628099; 978-0-692-55835-5; 979-8-218-08690-9; 979-8-218-25898-6)* Orders Addr.: P.O. Box 215, Wynnewood, OK 73098 USA Tel 405-665-4811 Do not confuse with Rebel Pr., Chino, CA
E-mail: LittleDixie@litnet.net
Web site: www.michaelandrewgrissom.com.

Little Dog Press *See* **Lauren Blakely Bks.**

Little Dog Pubns., *(978-0-9774143)* P.O. Box 8680, Kansas City Missouri, MO 64114-0680 USA (SAN 257-5051)
E-mail: jeffr@littledogpress.net
Web site: http://littledogpress.net.

Little Feet Pr., *(978-0-9990120)* 13913 Boquita Dr., Del Mar, CA 92014 USA Tel 650-714-8004
E-mail: dani.chammas@gmail.com.

Little Feminist, *(978-1-7341824; 979-8-9867049)* 2625 Alcatraz Ave, Berkeley, CA 94705 USA Tel 510-473-7598
E-mail: brittany@littlefeminist.com
Web site: littlefeminist.com
Dist(s): **Baker & Taylor Publisher Services (BTPS).**

Little Fiddle Co., Inc., The, *(978-0-9700489; 978-0-9798643)* 700 Kinderkamack Rd., Oradell, NJ 07649 USA Fax: 201-265-6499; Toll Free: 888-678-5636
E-mail: info@minimaestro.com; jeofficemgr@osen.us
Web site: http://www.minimaestro.com
Dist(s): **Penton Overseas, Inc.**

Little Fisch, *(978-0-578-55307-8; 978-0-578-55406-8; 978-1-7360598)* 16245 Caisson Rd, Kimball, MN 55353 USA Tel 320-293-1582
E-mail: katefischer@littlefisch.com
Dist(s): **Itasca Bks.**
Ingram Content Group.

Little Gene Pr., *(978-0-9792000)*.

Little Genius Bks., *(978-1-953344; 978-1-960107)* 49 W. Mt. Pleasant Ave. No. 1639, Livingston, NJ 07039 USA Tel 407-499-0819
E-mail: sean@bigboxbooks.com; peter@bigboxbooks.com
Dist(s): **Simon & Schuster, Inc.**

Little Germ That Could..Creations, Inc., The, *(978-0-9763233; 978-0-9960186)* 6815 Edgewater Dr., No.108, Coral Gables, FL 33133 USA Tel 305-775-0281
Web site: www.littlegerm.com.

Little Grandma Bks., *(978-0-692-55126-4; 978-0-692-60419-9; 978-0-9997637)* 813 Los Arboles NW, Albuquerque, NM 87107 USA
Dist(s): **CreateSpace Independent Publishing Platform.**

Little Grasshopper Bks. *Imprint of* **Publications International, Ltd.**

Little Guardians, Inc., *(978-0-9660879)* 111 Melody Dr., Metairie, LA 70001 USA Tel 504-837-3328; Fax: 504-835-9993; Toll Free: 800-582-4923.

Little Hands Bk. Co., LLC, *(978-0-9814878)* 32094 Vintage Way, Afton, OK 74331-5600 USA
Web site: http://www.littlehandsbook.com.

Little Hare Bks. (AUS) *(978-1-877003; 978-1-921049; 978-1-921272; 978-1-921541; 978-1-921714; 978-1-921894)* *Dist. by* **IPG Chicago.**

Little Hat Bks., *(978-0-9980763)* 13216 Mira Mar Dr, Sylmar, CA 91342 USA Tel 818-632-2909
E-mail: cloudgirlbook@gmail.com.

Little Hero, *(978-0-9769057)* P.O. Box 771371, Orlando, FL 32877 USA
E-mail: whitlockmatt@hotmail.com
Web site: http://www.littlehero.net.

Little Hill Pubs., *(978-0-9835048)* Orders Addr.: P.O. Box 282, Ashland, MA 01721 USA; Edit Addr.: 18 Pennock Rd., Ashland, MA 01721 USA Tel 508-881-0011
E-mail: contact@littlehillpublishers.com.

Little Hippo Bks., *(978-1-949679; 978-1-950416; 978-1-950951; 978-1-951356; 978-1-952137; 978-1-952592; 978-1-953756; 978-1-955044; 978-1-956818; 978-1-957842; 978-1-958774; 978-1-960009; 978-1-960765; 978-1-962271)* 145 Pinelawn Rd., Melville, NY 11747 USA Tel 631-390-8822
E-mail: kdoherty@usmediapartners.net; jschiavello@usmediapartners.net
Web site: www.littlehippobooks.com.

Little Hound Publishing *Imprint of* **E M McIntyre**

Little Hse. Site Tours LLC, *(978-0-9765951)* 2430 Marlette Rd., Applegate, MI 48401 USA Tel 810-633-9973; Fax: 810-633-9027
E-mail: lhsitetours@email.com
Web site: http://www.lhsitetours.homestead.com.

Little Island (IRL) *(978-1-84840; 978-1-908195; 978-1-910411; 978-1-910031; 978-1-912417)* *Dist. by* **Consort Bk Sales.**

Little Island Press (NZL) *(978-1-877484)* *Dist. by* **UH Pr.**

Little, Jeanna, *(978-0-578-92584-4; 978-0-578-93263-7)* 3017 Island Creek Rd. 0, PIKEVILLE, KY 41501 USA Tel 6064224135
E-mail: jeannalittle@yahoo.com
Dist(s): **Ingram Content Group.**

Little Johnny Bks., *(978-0-692-09259-0; 978-0-692-09706-9; 978-0-578-44093-4; 978-0-578-44118-4)* 720 Williams White Rd, Zebulon, NC 27597 USA Tel 919-426-5527
E-mail: alfordjp88@gmail.com
Dist(s): **CreateSpace Independent Publishing Platform.**

Little Labradoodle Publishing, LLC, *(978-1-7324566; 978-1-7339605; 978-1-7375570)* 245 Manton St., Pawtucket, RI 02861 USA Tel 401-288-9957
E-mail: info@thelittlelabradoodle.com
Web site: www.thelittlelabradoodle.com.

Little Lamb Bks., *(978-0-9986243; 978-1-7323158; 978-1-7332828; 978-1-953456)* P.O. Box 211724, Bedford, TX 76021 USA
E-mail: rachel@littlelambbooks.com
Web site: www.littlelambbooks.com
Dist(s): **Independent Pubs. Group**
Ingram Content Group
Small Pr. United.

Little League Pr., *(978-0-9747883)* P.O. Box 249, Stanleytown, VA 24168 USA
E-mail: hooneybgood@adelphia.net
Dist(s): **Bassett Printing Corp.**

Little Libros, LLC, *(978-0-9861099; 978-1-947971; 978-1-948066; 978-1-962227)* Orders Addr.: 1960 Hawkins Cir., Los Angeles, CA 90001 USA (SAN 990-6312) Tel 323-484-9758; *Imprints*: Lil' Libros (LIL LIBROS)
E-mail: hola@littlelibros.com; info@littlelibros.com
Web site: www.LilLibros.com; www.LittleLibros.com
Dist(s): **Gibbs Smith, Publisher.**

Little Light Pr., *(978-0-9755374)* Orders Addr.: 549 Broadway, Bethpage, NY 11714 USA Tel 516-938-3343 Do not confuse with Little Light Press in Oklahoma City, OK
E-mail: littlelightpress@yahoo.com
Web site: http://www.littlelightpress.biz.

Little Linguists Press, *(978-0-9777085)* P.O. Box 169, Owings Mills, MD 21117 USA.

Little Lion Pr., *(978-0-9796393)* 4911 Cumberland Ave., Chevy Chase, MD 20815 USA Tel 301-980-4344; Fax: 301-656-0086.

Little Lollipop Pr., *(978-0-9996151)* 4125 Glenshire St., Houston, TX 77025 USA Tel 615-779-6594
E-mail: lkjaxn@gmail.com
Web site: www.littlelollipoppress.com.

Little Lost Creations, *(978-0-9965766; 978-1-7352850)* 3650 N. 3650 W, Darlington, ID 83255 USA Tel 208-406-4777
E-mail: brendaskidsbooks@gmail.com
Web site: https://brendaskidsbooks.com.

Little Lyrics Pubns., *(978-1-893429)* 12310 Old Barn Rd., Elbert, CO 80106 USA Tel 719-495-4941
E-mail: littlelyrics@prodigy.com
Web site: http://www.littlelyrics.com.

little m Bks., *(978-0-9830487)* 756 Pompton Ave., Cedar Grove, NJ 07009 USA Tel 201-704-7886
E-mail: wmadsen@me.com.

Little Mai Pr., *(978-1-893237)* 102 River Dr., Lake Hiawatha, NJ 07034 USA Tel 973-331-9648; Fax: 973-331-1856; Toll Free: 800-438-2719
E-mail: lmaipress@aol.com; f1promo@aol.com
Web site: http://www.littlemaipress.com.

Little Melody Pr. *Imprint of* **Brighter Minds Children's Publishing**

Little Mice Press *See* **Econ for Kids**

Little Mole & Honey Bear, *(978-0-578-45849-6; 978-1-7332232)* 3245 Irving Ave. S., Minneapolis, MN 55408 USA Tel 612-825-9060
E-mail: zipes001@umn.edu
Web site: https://jackzipes.com
Dist(s): **Wayne State Univ. Pr.**

Little Moose Pr., *(978-0-9720227; 978-0-9786049; 978-0-9841021; 978-0-9841441; 978-0-9831161; 978-0-9838386; 978-0-9893988)* Orders Addr.: 269 S. Beverly Dr. #1065, Beverly Hills, CA 90212 USA (SAN 254-9778) Tel 310-862-2574; 310-862-2575; Toll Free: 866-234-0626
E-mail: ellen@littlemoosepresspub.com; bookshep@mac.com
Web site: http://www.littlemoosepresspub.com; www.louisegaylordauthor.com; www.pippinpb.com
Dist(s): **Book Clearing Hse.**
Pathway Bks.
Smashwords.

Little Munchkin Bks., *(978-0-9773936)* 2893 Rockefeller Rd., Willoughby Hills, OH 44092-1423 USA (SAN 257-411X) Tel 440-585-4950
E-mail: tara_tabernik@yahoo.com
Web site: http://www.littlemunchkinbooks.com.

Little Noggin LLC, *(978-0-9743760)* 1350 Grand Summit Dr., Suite 288, Reno, NV 89523 USA Tel 916-435-9737; Fax: 530-673-9680
E-mail: info@akidatart.com
Web site: http://www.akidatart.com.

Little Ones *Imprint of* **Port Town Publishing**

Little P Pr. Co., *(978-0-9853430)* 6387 Camp Bowie Blvd Ste B PMB No. 292, Fort Worth, TX 76116 USA Tel 817-501-8229
E-mail: pitch129@aol.com
Web site: ChazzKids.com.

Little Patriot Pr. *Imprint of* **Regnery Publishing**

Little Paws Pr. *Imprint of* **Veillette, Roseanne**

Little Pear Pr., *(978-0-9746911)* P.O. Box 343, Seekonk, MA 02771-1409 USA
Web site: http://www.littlepearpress.com.

Little Pemberley Pr., *(978-0-9763359)* Orders Addr.: 1528 Tulane St., Suite F, Houston, TX 77008-4146 USA Tel 713-862-8542; Fax: 713-862-6399
E-mail: littlepemberleypress@hotmail.com
Web site: http://www.giraffeofmontana.com; http://www.littlepemberleypress.com.

Little People Bks., *(978-0-9764114)* 2 Victor Ave., Worcester, MA 01603 USA Tel 508-963-2004.

Little Petals *Imprint of* **Roses Are READ Productions**

Little Pickle Pr. *Imprint of* **Sourcebooks, Inc.**

Little Pickle Press LLC *See* **March 4th, Inc.**

Little Pigeon Bks., *(978-0-9818976)* 5354 Washington St., Downers Grove, IL 60515 USA Tel 630-541-3700
Dist(s): **ebrary, Inc.**

Little Pink Pr., *(978-0-692-91027-6; 978-1-7329494; 978-1-7355918; 978-1-7372754; 979-8-9870085)* 11 Dallis Pl., Beacon, NY 12508 USA Tel 914-838-0439
E-mail: keryl@kerylpesce.com
Dist(s): **CreateSpace Independent Publishing Platform.**

Little Prince Publishing, *(978-0-615-46053-6; 978-0-615-46977-5; 978-0-615-47049-8; 978-0-9835220; 978-0-615-58516-1; 978-0-615-59301-2; 978-0-615-59908-3; 978-0-615-59909-0; 978-1-939947; 978-0-692-56834-7)* 7942 Indica Ct., North Charleston, SC 29418 USA
E-mail: sybilnelson@hotmail.com
Web site: www.sybilnelson.com; www.littleprincepublishing.com
Dist(s): **CreateSpace Independent Publishing Platform**
Dummy Record Do Not USE!!!!
Smashwords.

Little Red Acorns *Imprint of* **Little Red Tree Publishing LLC**

Little Red Cat Publishing, *(978-0-9726375)* 939A Terra Bella Ave., Mountainview, CA 94043 USA (SAN 254-9549) Tel 650-960-4040; Fax: 650-960-1040
E-mail: email@comprintingco.com; e-mail@comprintingco.com.

Little Red Tree Publishing LLC, *(978-0-9789446; 978-1-935656)* 635 Ocean Ave., New London, 06320 SUN (SAN 852-0143) Tel 860-287-1660; *Imprints*: Little Red Acorns (LR Acorns)
E-mail: mikelinnard@yahoo.co.uk
Web site: http://www.littleredtree.com.

Little Redhaired Girl Publishing, Inc., *(978-0-9729264)* 120 Riverside Blvd., #2e, New York, NY 10069 USA (SAN 857-6041) Fax: 225-410-6739; *Imprints*: Books for Brats (Books for Brats)
E-mail: booksforbrats@aol.com
Web site: http://www.booksforbrats.com.

Little River Bookshelf, *(978-0-9769856)* 2707 Silver Leaf Ct., Grapevine, TX 76051 USA Tel 817-308-2510
E-mail: mark.storer@usa.net.

Little Roni Publishers *See* **Little Roni Pubs. LLC**

Little Roni Pubs. LLC, *(978-0-615-67830-6; 978-0-615-71945-0; 978-0-615-72674-8; 978-0-615-74782-8; 978-0-615-76043-8; 978-0-615-77770-2; 978-0-615-77827-3; 978-0-615-78997-2; 978-0-615-79198-2; 978-0-615-98426-1; 978-0-9960505; 978-0-692-22923-1; 978-0-692-23688-8; 978-0-692-30350-4; 978-0-692-44071-1; 978-0-692-44075-9; 978-0-692-51300-2; 978-0-692-63119-5; 978-0-692-63662-6; 978-0-692-64496-6; 978-0-692-65319-7; 978-0-692-67214-3; 978-0-692-67304-1; 978-0-692-83128-1; 978-0-692-05040-8; 978-0-692-09849-3; 978-) 109 Friendship Cir., Clanton, AL 35045 USA Tel 256-558-1341 Do not confuse with Little Roni Publishers in Byhalia, MS*
Web site: www.littleronipublishers.com
Dist(s): **CreateSpace Independent Publishing Platform.**

Little Santa Bks., Inc., *(978-0-615-17411-2)* P.O. Box 806, Buffalo, NY 14220 USA Tel 716-316-1545
E-mail: sergioroguez@gmail.com
Web site: http://www.littlesantaclaus.com.

Little Scary Mouse, *(978-1-7326042; 979-8-9873926)*
E-mail: littlescarymouse@gmail.com.

Little Scribblers Bks., LLC, *(978-0-9747689)* 2545 NW 55th Pl., Oklahoma City, OK 73112-7101 USA Tel 405-615-8662
E-mail: littlescribblers@cox.net
Web site: http://www.littlescribblers.com.

Publisher Name Index

Little Shepherd *Imprint of* **Scholastic, Inc.**

Little Simon *Imprint of* **Little Simon**

Little Simon, *(978-0-671; 978-0-689; 978-1-4169)* Div. of Simon & Schuster Children's Publishing, 1230 Ave. of the Americas, New York, NY 10020 USA; *Imprints:* Little Simon (LSimon)
Dist(s): **Children's Plus, Inc.**
Simon & Schuster
Simon & Schuster, Inc.

Little Simon Inspirations *Imprint of* **Little Simon Inspirations**

Little Simon Inspirations, Div. of Simon & Schuster Children's Publishing, 1230 Ave. of the Americas, New York, NY 10020 USA; *Imprints:* Little Simon Inspirations (LSimoninsp)
Dist(s): **Simon & Schuster, Inc.**

Little Soundprints *Imprint of* **Soundprints**

Little Sparrow *Imprint of* **Viident Co.**

Little Sprout Publishing Hse., *(978-0-9779194)* Orders Addr.: 520 Berry Way, La Habra, CA 90631 USA; *Imprints:* Psalms for Kidz (Psalms for Kidz)
Web site: http://psalmsforkidz.com.

Little Star, *(978-1-7323915; 978-1-7358872; 979-8-9861299)* 702 Devon Rd., Henrico, VA 23229 USA Tel 804-405-8990
E-mail: joni@littlestarcommunications.com.

Little Steps Bks (AUS) *(978-0-9805750; 978-0-9807237; 978-1-921928-59-8; 978-1-921928-62-8; 978-1-921928-63-5; 978-1-921928-64-2; 978-1-921928-74-1; 978-1-925117; 978-1-925545; 978-0-6482673; 978-0-6482674; 978-1-925839; 978-1-922358; 978-1-922678; 978-1-922833) Dist. by* **IPG Chicago.**

Little Steps Bks (AUS) *(978-0-9805750; 978-0-9807237; 978-1-921928-59-8; 978-1-921928-62-8; 978-1-921928-63-5; 978-1-921928-64-2; 978-1-921928-74-1; 978-1-925117; 978-1-925545; 978-0-6482673; 978-0-6482674; 978-1-925839; 978-1-922358; 978-1-922678; 978-1-922833) Dist. by* **Lerner Pub.**

Little Thoughts For Little Ones Publishing, Inc., *(978-0-9748884; 978-0-9861870)* Orders Addr.: P.O. Box 665, Tavernier, FL 33070 USA
E-mail: vhandelsman@att.net
Web site: http://www.littlethoughtspublishing.com.

Little Tiger Pr., *(978-1-888444; 978-1-58431)* Div. of Futech Interactive Products, 39 S. La Salle St. Ste. 1410, Chicago, IL 60603-1706 USA Toll Free: 800-541-2205 Do not confuse Little Tiger Press in San Francisco, CA
E-mail: jody@futechsales.com
Dist(s): **Futech Educational Products, Inc.**
Lectorum Pubns., Inc.
MyiLibrary.

Little Treasure Bks., *(978-0-9639838; 978-0-9814571)* P.O. Box 362, Bensalem, PA 19020-0362 USA
Web site: http://www.littletreasurebooks.com.

Little Treasure Publications, Incorporated *See* **Little Treasure Bks.**

Little T's Corner *See* **Zadunajsky, Donna M.**

Little Tule Bks., *(978-0-9773133)* P.O. Box 549, Carmel Valley, CA 93924-0549 USA (SAN 257-2311) Tel 831-659-0107; Fax: 831-659-0106
E-mail: bill@littletulebooks.com
Web site: http://www.littletulebooks.com.

Little Vegan Monsters Publishing, *(978-0-9787590)* P.O. Box 9258, New Haven, CT 06533 USA
E-mail: Lourdes@littleveganmonsters.com
Web site: http://www.littleveganmonsters.com.

Little Village Comics Co., *(978-0-9976193)* 4 E Ing St., Kingston, OH 45644 USA Tel 740-703-8755
E-mail: wes@wesdraws.com.

Little Way Pr., *(978-0-9764691)* 18252 Little Fuller Rd., Twain Harte, CA 95383 USA
Web site: http://www.littlewaypress.com
Dist(s): **Catholic Heritage Curricula.**

Little Willow Tree Bks., *(978-0-9743795)* 4900 Dodd St., Lynchburg, VA 24502 USA Do not confuse with Willow Tree Press in Monsey, NY
E-mail: willowtreebooks@yahoo.com.

Little Wooden Bks., *(978-0-929949)* 11001 S. Degray Ln., Spokane, WA 99224 USA (SAN 250-7943) Tel 509-932-4729.

Little Worm Publishing, *(978-0-9911382)* 920 Litchfield Pl., Roswell, GA 30076 USA Tel 706-258-8925
E-mail: hetheringtonlin@gmail.com
Web site: www.littlewormpub.com.

Littleberry Pr. LLC, *(978-0-9841725; 978-0-9837622; 978-0-9860357; 978-1-940750)* 1281 Win Hentschel Blvd., West Lafayette, IN 47906 USA (SAN 858-6233) Tel 765-237-3390; Fax: 765-594-4302; 1281 Win Hentschel Blvd., W. Lafayette, IN 47906 Tel 765-237-3390; Fax: 765-594-4302
E-mail: anita.schafer@schoolhousepartners.net; pubs@schoolhousepartners.net
Web site: http://www.schoolhousepartners.net.

Littletonhouse Publishing, *(978-0-9746849; 979-8-9870015)* Orders Addr.: P.O. Box 2954, Littleton, CO 80161-2954 USA (SAN 256-3371) Tel 303-740-2003; Fax: 303-771-0305
E-mail: info@thesecretcovebook.com; treis@littletonhousepublishing.com
Web site: http://www.thesecretcovebook.com; http://www.virobacter.com.

Liturgical Pr. Bks. *Imprint of* **Liturgical Pr.**

†**Liturgical Pr.,** *(978-0-8146; 978-0-916134; 979-8-4008)* Div. of Order of St. Benedict, Inc., Orders Addr.: a/o St. Johns Abbey, P.O. Box 7500, Collegeville, MN 56321-7500 USA (SAN 202-2494) Tel 320-363-2213; 612 363 2326; Fax: 320-363-3299; Toll Free Fax: 800-445-5899; Toll Free: 800-858-5450; *Imprints:* Liturgical Press Books (Liturg Pr Bks)
E-mail: sales@litpress.org; bwoods@csbsju.edu
Web site: http://www.litpress.org; http://sjbible.org; http://cistercianpublications.com
Dist(s): **BookMobile**
Metapress
MyiLibrary; *CIP.*

Liturgies, PC, *(978-0-578-40675-6; 978-0-578-42606-8; 978-0-578-50885-6; 978-0-578-56276-6; 978-0-578-60052-9; 978-0-578-91781-8)* 3426 Admiralty Ln., Indianapolis, IN 46240 USA Tel 317-402-2139
E-mail: drtim@liturgies.org
Dist(s): **Ingram Content Group.**

Liturgy Training Pubns., *(978-0-929650; 978-0-930467; 978-1-56854; 978-1-61671; 978-1-61833)* Div. of Archdiocese of Chicago, 3949 S. Racine Ave., Chicago, IL 60609-2523 USA (SAN 670-9052) Toll Free Fax: 800-933-7094 (orders); Toll Free: 800-933-1800 (orders); *Imprints:* Catechesis of the Good Shepherd (Catechesis Good Shepherd)
E-mail: lguzman@ltp.org
Web site: http://www.ltp.org.

Litwin, April Lynn, *(978-0-692-18539-1; 978-0-692-18540-7)* 273 Lyceum Ave., Philadelphia, PA 19128 USA Tel 732-616-7576
E-mail: alitwin273@gmail.com
Dist(s): **Ingram Content Group.**

Liu, Katrina *See* **Lychee Pr.**

Live Like Noah Foundation, *(978-1-7325254)* 7033 Quartz Ave, Winnetka, CA 91306 USA Tel 818-339-1216
E-mail: keith.michaelis@hotmail.com
Web site: www.livelikenoah.org.

Live Oak Games, *(978-0-9764394)* P.O. Box 780932, Orlando, FL 32878 USA Toll Free Fax: 800-214-4632 (phone/fax)
E-mail: sales@liveoakgames.com
Web site: http://www.liveoakgames.com.

Live Oak Media, *(978-0-87499; 978-0-941078; 978-1-59112; 978-1-59519; 978-1-4301)* Orders Addr.: P.O. Box 652, Pine Plains, NY 12567-0652 USA (SAN 217-3921) Tel 518-398-1010; Fax: 518-398-1070; Toll Free: 800-788-1121
E-mail: info@liveoakmedia.com
Web site: http://www.liveoakmedia.com
Dist(s): **AudioGO**
Ebsco Publishing
Findaway World, LLC
Follett School Solutions
Greathall Productions, Inc.
Lectorum Pubns., Inc.
Lerner Publishing Group.

Live with Intention Publishing, *(978-1-7350173)* 9560 Cuyamaca St. 104, santee, CA 92071 USA Tel 760-420-8489
E-mail: Dramandamorrismft@gmail.com
Web site: www.coachingwithdramandamorris.com.

†**Liveright Publishing Corp.,** *(978-0-87140; 978-1-63149)* Subs. of W. W. Norton Co., Inc., 500 Fifth Ave., New York, NY 10110 USA (SAN 201-0976) Tel 212-354-5500; Fax: 212-869-0856; Toll Free Fax: 800-458-6515; Toll Free: 800-233-4830
Web site: http://www.wwnorton.com
Dist(s): **Penguin Random Hse. Distribution**
Penguin Random Hse. LLC; *CIP.*

Liverpool Univ. Pr. (GBR) *(978-0-7463; 978-0-85323; 978-1-84631; 978-1-78138; 978-1-78694; 978-1-78962; 978-1-80034; 978-1-80085; 978-1-80207) Dist. by* **OUP.**

Living Bks. Pr., *(978-0-9790876; 978-0-9818093; 978-1-938192)* 5497 S. Gilmore Rd., Mount Pleasant, MI 48858 USA (SAN 852-4114) Toll Free: 888-331-3481
E-mail: lbcinfo@livingbookscurriculum.com
Web site: http://www.livingbookscurriculum.com.

Living Breathing Story Pubns., *(978-0-578-41938-1)* 8039 Genesta Ave., Van Nuys, CA 91406 USA Tel 805-217-9199
E-mail: kellyanott@gmail.com
Dist(s): **Independent Pub.**

Living Dead Pr., *(978-1-935458; 978-1-61199)* 58 Dedham St., Revere, MA 02151 USA
Dist(s): **Smashwords.**

Living History Pr., *(978-0-9664925)* 7426 Elmwood Ave., Middleton, WI 53562 USA Tel 608-836-7426; Fax: 608-836-0176 Do not confuse with Living History Pr., Bellevue, WA
E-mail: pferd@itis.com
Web site: http://www.inwave.com/Milton/MiltonHouse/.

Living in Grace, *(978-0-9659319)* 10051 Siegen Ln., Baton Rouge, LA 70810 USA Tel 504-769-8844; Fax: 504-767-5655; Toll Free: 800-484-2046 ext. 9506
E-mail: QRBC@aol.com.

Living Ink Bks. *Imprint of* **AMG Pubs.**

Living Library Pr., *(978-0-692-74615-8; 978-0-692-81047-7; 978-0-692-83664-4; 978-0-692-87488-2; 978-0-692-97395-0; 978-0-692-07532-6; 978-0-692-09071-8; 978-0-578-42451-4; 978-0-578-48822-6; 978-0-578-50090-4; 978-0-578-58239-9; 978-0-578-94801-0; 979-8-218-22856-9) 318 Meadow Dr., BRISTOL, VA 24201 USA Tel 276-644-9169.*

Living Life Publishing Co., *(978-0-9768773; 978-0-9769166; 978-0-9774499; 978-1-934796)* Div. of Bianca Productions, LLC, 24165 IH-10, W., Suite 217-474, San Antonio, TX 78257 USA (SAN 256-5684) Tel 210-698-6392; Fax: 210-698-1754
E-mail: livinglifepublishing@msn.com
Web site: http://www.livinglifepublishing.com; http://www.biancaproductions.com.

Living Ministry, Inc., *(978-0-9763167)* 800 Prospect Blvd., Pasadena, CA 91103 USA Tel 626-356-9491; Fax: 626-584-0290
Web site: http://www.livingministry.com.

Living My Shadows, LLC, *(978-0-578-65363-1)* 24 Dalton Dr, Newark, DE 19702 USA Tel 302-353-9841
E-mail: livingmyshadows@gmail.com
Web site: http://www.livingmyshadows.org.

Living Parables, Incorporated. *See* **Living Parables of Central Florida, Inc.**

Living Parables of Central Florida, Inc., *(978-0-9834624; 978-0-9890225; 978-1-941733; 978-1-945975; 978-1-945976; 978-1-952369; 978-1-953114; 978-1-955309)* 1136 W. Winged Foot Cir., Winter Springs, FL 32708 USA Tel 407-712-3431
E-mail: cheri@eabookspublishing.com
Web site: http://www.Living-Parables.com; http://www.eabookspublishing.com
Dist(s): **Iron Stream Media.**

Living Room Adventures, *(978-0-578-16641-4; 978-0-692-79945-1; 978-0-692-99751-2)* 9545 S 2500 W, South Jordan, UT 84095 USA Tel 801-414-5790; Fax: 866-226-0309
E-mail: mattsprunt@gmail.co
Dist(s): **CreateSpace Independent Publishing Platform.**

Living Sacrifice Books *See* **VOM Bks.**

Living Stone Arts, *(978-0-9763901)* 3806 Owl Dr., Rolling Meadows, IL 60008 USA
Web site: http://www.livingstonearts.com.

Living Stream Ministry, *(978-0-7363; 978-0-87083; 978-1-57593; 978-1-5360)* 2431 W. La Palma Ave., Anaheim, CA 92801 USA (SAN 253-4266) Tel 714-236-6001; 714-991-4681; Fax: 714-991-4685; Toll Free: 800-549-5164
E-mail: books@lsm.org
Web site: http://www.lsm.org
Dist(s): **Anchor Distributors**
Spring Arbor Distributors, Inc.

Living the Good News *Imprint of* **Church Publishing, Inc.**

Living Tree Pr., *(978-1-7320355; 978-1-7330477)*
E-mail: editor@livingtreepress.com
Web site: livingtreepress.com.

Living Water Pubns., *(978-1-59521)* P.O. Box 4653, Rockford, IL 61110-4653 USA Fax: 815-394-0140 Do not confuse with Living Water Publications in Edwardsville, KS
E-mail: lwministry@aol.com
Web site: http://www.livingwaterpublications.org.

Living Waters Publishing Co., *(978-0-9798154; 978-0-9814532; 978-0-9821153)* P.O. Box 1361, Marion, AR 72364-1361 USA
E-mail: administration@livingwaterspc.com
Web site: http://www.livingwaterspc.com
Dist(s): **Ingram Content Group.**

Livingston Pr., *(978-0-930501; 978-0-942979; 978-1-931982; 978-1-60489)* Div. of Univ. Of West Alabama, Orders Addr.: Sta. 22, One College Dr. Univ. of W. Alabama, Livingston, AL 35470 USA (SAN 851-917X) Tel 205-652-3470 Do not confuse with Livingston Pr., Anaheim, CA
E-mail: jwt@uwa.edu
Web site: https://livingstonpress.uwa.edu
Dist(s): **SPD-Small Pr. Distribution.**

Livingstone Corporation *See* **Barton-Veerman Co.**

Livity Books LLc *See* **Livity Bks. LLC**

Livity Bks. LLC, *(978-1-941632)* 1110 C Parkside Green Dr., Greenacres, FL 33415 USA Tel 561-373-4439
E-mail: lifegatepublishing@yahoo.com.

Livraria Martins Editora (BRA) *(978-85-336) Dist. by* **Distribks Inc.**

Liza Dora Bks., *(978-0-692-43392-8; 978-0-692-43393-5; 978-0-692-53087-0; 978-0-692-59885-6; 978-0-692-88259-7; 978-0-578-47420-5; 978-1-7340576)* 2205 Charlestown, Clarksville, TN 37043 USA Tel 713-534-7538
E-mail: lizabrightdora@gmail.com.

lizbethBks., *(978-1-7377535)* 1217 Rocky Ridge Blvd, Douglasville, GA 30134 USA Tel 470-360-9238
E-mail: liz4god84@gmail.com.

LizStar Bks, *(978-0-9779753)* 2648 Jolly Acres Rd., White Hall, MD 21161 USA Tel 410-557-9388
E-mail: tracy@lizstarbooks.com
Web site: http://www.lizstarbooks.com.

Lizzie Joy Lukens, *(978-0-692-97943-3)* 924 Bedford Ave SW, Canton, OH 44710 USA Tel 330-754-8984; Fax: 330-754-8984
E-mail: creativelizzie@gmail.com.

Lizzy Anne's Adventures, *(978-0-9845887; 978-0-9835168)* P.O. Box 97, Monrovia, MD 21770-0097 USA (SAN 859-8320)
Web site: http://www.lizzyannesadventures.com.

LJK Publishing LLC, *(978-0-9771476)* P.O. Box 993, Springer, NM 87747 USA Tel 505-483-2451 (fax as well - phone to turn on)
E-mail: chieftalkjaw@aol.com.

LJM Communications, *(978-0-578-85094-8)* 760 Kearney St, Denver, CO 80220 USA Tel 917-583-4665
E-mail: lesliejmitchell101@hotmail.com.

LJM Publishing, *(978-0-615-46906-5; 978-0-615-48518-8; 978-0-9897175; 978-0-615-92333-8; 978-0-9861946)* 2597 CR 2101, Palestine, TX 75801 USA Tel 214-956-5656; 817-703-1844
Web site: www.RachelsLittleQuoteBook.org
Dist(s): **CreateSpace Independent Publishing Platform.**

LL Cameron Group, LLC, *(978-0-930249)* 121 Merryhill Drive, Rochester, NY 14625 USA
E-mail: pattiup@rochester.rr.com
Web site: http://www.rochesternyeats.com
Dist(s): **North Country Bks., Inc.**

Llama Press *See* **Birchall Publishing**

LLC, Plum Tuckered Out, *(978-0-578-89225-2; 978-0-578-89226-9; 978-1-7370675)* 5045 W. Baseline Rd. Suite 482, Laveen, AZ 85339 USA Tel 602-300-8952
E-mail: mjreeves1527@gmail.com.

Llegaci Agency *See* **Kristy High**

†**Llewellyn Pubns.,** *(978-0-7387; 978-0-87542; 978-1-56718)* Div. of Llewellyn Worldwide, Ltd., Orders Addr.: 2143 Wooddale Dr., Woodbury, MN 55125-2989 USA Tel 651-291-1970; Fax: 651-291-1908; Toll Free: 800-843-6666; *Imprints:* Flux (FluxUSA)
E-mail: sales@llewellyn.com
Web site: http://www.llewellyn.com; http://www.midnightinkbooks.com
Dist(s): **Children's Plus, Inc.**
Follett School Solutions
Lectorum Pubns., Inc.
Libros Sin Fronteras
Llewellyn Worldwide Ltd.
New Leaf Distributing Co., Inc.
Partners/West Book Distributors
Perrone; *CIP.*

Lloyd Chiasson, *(978-1-7353032)* 312 Windsor Dr., Thibodaux, LA 70301 USA Tel 985-448-1294
E-mail: theranatanlandtales@gmail.com.

Llumina Christian Bks. *Imprint of* **Aeon Publishing Inc.**

Llumina Kids *Imprint of* **Aeon Publishing Inc.**

Llumina Pr. *Imprint of* **Aeon Publishing Inc.**

LM Azpiazu, *(978-0-692-58185-8; 978-0-692-59170-3)* 3519 Woodlawn Dr., HONOLULU, HI 96822 USA Tel 808-988-6158.

LM Digital, *(978-0-9760770)* 4501 Mirador Dr., Pleasanton, CA 94566-7435 USA
E-mail: luke@lm-digital.com
Web site: http://www.lm-digital.com.

LMA Publishing, *(978-0-692-63132-4)* 8635 W Sahara Ave, Las Vegas, NV 89117 USA Tel 310-402-8677
E-mail: mzabner08@gmail.com.

LMBPN Publishing, *(978-1-64202; 978-1-64971; 978-1-68500; 979-8-88541; 979-8-88878)* PMB 196 2540 S. Maryland Pkwy, Las Vegas, NV 89109 USA Tel 239-821-7655
E-mail: steve@lmbpn.com
Web site: www.lmbpn.com.

LML Designs *See* **US Ghost Writing**

LMS Bks., *(978-0-9764185)* 1007 Manor Dr., Ripon, CA 95366 USA Tel 209-599-4685.

LMW Works, *(978-1-889584)* 85 St. Michael Way NE., Hanceville, AL 35077 USA Tel 716-946-1060
E-mail: lynne@lmwworks.com; pviverito@yahoo.com
Web site: http://www.lmwworks.com.

LNG LLC, *(978-0-692-27681-5; 978-0-692-29319-5; 978-0-692-29448-2; 978-0-9908808; 978-0-9863584; 978-1-943255)* 4504 W. Memphis St, Broken Arrow, OK 74012 USA Tel 918-893-3121
E-mail: andresvarela@hotmail.com
Web site: www.roundyandfriends.com.

LOA Quantum Growth LLC, *(978-0-9786158)* 7805 Tylerton Dr., Raleigh, NC 27613-1554 USA Tel 919-368-8041; Fax: 919-571-8769
E-mail: publisher@loaquantumgrowth.com
Web site: http://www.loaquantumgrowth.com.

Lobster Pr. (CAN) *(978-1-894222; 978-1-897073) Dist. by* **Orca Bk Pub.**

Local Color Pr., *(978-0-9716607; 978-0-578-18575-0; 978-0-578-18576-7)* 526 W. 26th St., Studio No. 506, New York, NY 10001 USA Tel 212-242-2660; Fax: 212-242-2661
E-mail: localcolorpress@aol.com
Web site: http://www.localcolorpress.com.

Local History Co., The, *(978-0-9711835; 978-0-9744715; 978-0-9770429)* Orders Addr.: 112 N. Woodland Rd., Pittsburgh, PA 15232 USA (SAN 257-5264); *Imprints:* Towers Maguire Publishing (Towers Mag)
E-mail: Sales@TheLocalHistoryCompany.com; Sales@TowersMaguire.com
Web site: http://www.TheLocalHistoryCompany.com; http://www.TowersMaguire.com.

Lock & Mane, *(978-0-615-20562-5; 978-0-615-30969-9; 978-0-615-62282-8)* 2012 Spring Garden St., No. 3, Philadelphia, PA 19130 USA.

Lockegee Bks., *(978-1-7354440)* 200 Sypherd Dr, Newark, DE 19711-3627 USA Tel 302-824-3976
E-mail: prbrewer@gmail.com.

Locket Designs, LLC, *(978-1-7337457)* 17337 E. Rosita Dr., Fountain Hills, AZ 85268 USA Tel 480-861-6275
E-mail: debnov@cox.net
Web site: www.debinovotny.com.

Lockman, James Consulting, *(978-0-9759988)* P.O. Box 278, Gorham, ME 04038-0278 USA
E-mail: james@jameslockman.com
Web site: http://www.jameslockman.com.

Lockman, Vic, *(978-0-936175)* 233 Rogue River Hwy No. 360, Grants Pass, OR 97527 USA (SAN 697-2063) Fax: 541-472-1083
E-mail: vlockman@budget.net.

Lockwood House Publishing, *(978-0-578-07258-6; 978-0-578-15354-4; 978-0-578-15986-7; 978-0-578-16662-9; 978-0-578-18530-9; 978-0-578-18592-7; 978-0-578-20154-2; 978-1-7321478)* 103 Seaview Ave., Monmouth Beach, NJ 07750 USA.

LOCO Publishing, *(978-1-7365927)* 814 Flatirons Ct, Louisville, CO 80027 USA Tel 303-579-1584
E-mail: hjwhiton@comcast.net
Web site: https://hilarywhiton.com/.

Lodestone Pr., *(978-0-9678922)* 17 Appleby Rd., Suite B-2, Wellesley, MA 02482 USA
E-mail: books@lodestone.nu
Web site: http://www.lodestone.nu.

Loew-Cornell, Inc., *(978-0-9776925; 978-0-9794445)* Div. of Jarden Corporation, 2834 Schoeneck Rd., Macungie, PA 18062-9679 USA
E-mail: joleary@loew-cornell.com
Web site: http://www.loew-cornell.com
Dist(s): **Watson-Guptill Pubns., Inc.**

Loewe Verlag GmbH (DEU) *(978-3-7855; 978-3-8390; 978-3-7320; 978-3-7432) Dist. by* **Distribks Inc.**

LoewenHerz-Creative *See* **LHC Publishing**

OF Publishing, (*978-0-9764441*) Orders Addr.: 7500 Bellerive, Suite 412, Houston, TX 77036 USA Tel 832-251-6867
E-mail: pslam144ym@aol.com; info@lofpublishing.com
Web site: http://www.lofpublishing.com; http://www.mbridges05.com.

og Cabin Bks., (*978-0-9755548; 978-0-9848911; 978-0-9973251; 978-0-692-07651-4; 978-1-7330891*) 6607 Craine Lake Rd., Hamilton, NY 13346 USA Tel 315-750-9157
Web site: http://www.logcabinbooks.us/; http://www.logcabinbooks.com/.

ogan Bks., (*978-0-9728691*) P.O. Box 21451, Columbia Heights, MN 55421 USA
Web site: http://www.loganbooks.com.

ogan, Emily, (*978-1-7332166*) 897 Nanu St., Honolulu, HI 96818 USA Tel 443-995-5285
E-mail: elogan_1@yahoo.com.

ogan Hse., (*978-0-9674123; 978-0-9769935*) Orders Addr.: Rte. 1, Box 154, Winside, NE 68790 USA Tel 402-286-4891; Edit Addr.: Rte. 1 Box 154, Winside, NE 68790 USA
E-mail: jim@loganhousepress.com
Web site: http://www.loganhousepress.com.

Logic of English, Inc, (*978-1-936706; 978-1-942154; 978-1-950632*) 4865 19th St. NW Suite 130, Rochester, MN 55901 USA (SAN 860-0694)
E-mail: jenny.knutson@logicofenglish.com
Web site: http://www.logicofenglish.com/.

LoGiudice Publishing, (*978-1-940803*) 749 Silver Bluff Rd. E62, Aiken, SC 29803 USA Tel 260-499-0777
E-mail: odavis909@yahoo.com.

Logos Productions, Inc., (*978-0-9618891; 978-1-885361*) 6160 Carmen Ave., E., Inver Grove Heights, MN 55076-4422 USA Tel 612-451-9945; Fax: 612-457-4617; Toll Free: 800-328-0200 Do not confuse with Logos Productions, Carmel, CA
E-mail: lpstaff@mn.uswest.net
Web site: http://www.1logos.com.

Logos Research Systems, Incorporated *See* **Faithlife Corp.**

LOGOS System Assocs., (*978-0-9727146; 978-0-9752605; 978-0-9768168*) 1405 Frey Rd., Pittsburgh, PA 15235 USA Tel 412-372-1341; Fax: 412-372-8447; Toll Free: 877-937-2572
E-mail: patjanssen@logos-system.org
Web site: http://www.logos-system.org.

Logos-Rhema Publishing *See* **Triumph Publishing**

LOLchemy, (*978-0-9723769*) P.O. Box 1209, Point Reyes, CA 94956 USA
Web site: http://www.schmoozeletter.com.

Lollipop Media Productions, LP, (*978-0-9815111; 978-0-9824926; 978-0-9909073*) 3600 S. Harbor Blvd. Apt No. 81 Apt. No. 81, Channel Islands Harbor, CA 93035 USA
E-mail: Suzy@keopu.com.

Lollipop Publishing, LLC, (*978-0-9709793; 978-1-931737*) P.O. Box 6354, Chesterfield, MO 63006-6354 USA Tel 314-434-6011; Fax: 314-434-6040; Toll Free: 800-383-7767
E-mail: jbenigas@aol.com
Web site: http://www.lollippoppublishing.com.

Lollipop Publishing, LLC, (*978-0-615-30165-5; 979-8-218-04979-9*) 10710 Moore Cir., Westminster, CO 80021 USA.

Lolliwolliworld Publishing, (*978-0-692-85138-8; 978-0-692-99931-8; 978-0-692-09392-4; 978-0-692-17814-0; 978-0-578-57863-7; 978-0-578-88485-1*) 330 SW 43rd St., Suite K 532, Renton Washington, WA 98057 USA Tel 206-697-1980
E-mail: info@lolliwolliworld.com
Web site: https://www.lolliwolliworld.com/.

Lollypop Bks., (*978-1-7323550*) 25 Burriana, SAN CLEMENTE, CA 92672 USA Tel 949-361-9316
E-mail: ashley@lollypopbooks.com; steve@lollypopbooks.com
Web site: www.lollypopbooks.com
Dist(s): **Ingram Content Group.**

Loma, LLC, (*978-0-9769460*) 6 Bryan Valley Ct., O'Fallon, MO 63366-3465 USA
E-mail: dudleytg@aol.com.

London Publishing, (*978-969-30; 978-0-578-15413-8; 978-0-578-16496-0; 978-0-578-16507-3*) 84 Red Alder Court, Danville, CA 94506 USA
E-mail: jrespanosa@yahoo.com
Web site: http://www.myspiffykids.com
Dist(s): **Outskirts Pr., Inc.**

London Town Pr., (*978-0-9666490; 978-0-9766134; 978-0-9799759*) 2026 Hilldale Dr., La Canada, CA 91011 USA
E-mail: martin@londontownpress.com
Web site: http://www.londontownpress.com
Dist(s): **Publishers Group West (PGW).**

Lone Butte Pr., (*978-0-9666860; 978-0-9893518*) 32 S. Fork Extended, Santa Fe, NM 87508 USA Tel 505-424-3574; Fax: 505-473-1227
E-mail: wilddogbooks@cnsp.com
Dist(s): **Wild Dog Bks.**

Lone Cypress Pubs., (*978-0-9741413*) 3588 Hwy. 138 S.E., No. 193, Stockbridge, GA 30281 USA Tel 404-421-7445
E-mail: graysenwalles@yahoo.com
Web site: http://www.lonecypresspublishers.com.

Lone Dragonfly Bks., (*978-0-9967350*) 5565 Seminary Rd. Apt. 105, Falls Church, MD 22041 USA Tel 443-824-6854
E-mail: geoff@lonedragonflybooks.com
Web site: http://lonedragonflybooks.com.

Lone Oak Pr., Ltd. *Imprint of* **Finney Co., Inc.**

Lone Pine Publishing USA, Orders Addr.: 1808 B St., NW Suite 140, Auburn, WA 98001 USA (SAN 859-0427) Tel 253-394-0400; Fax: 253-394-0405; Toll Free Fax: 800-548-1169; Toll Free: 800-518-3541; *Imprints:* Ghost House Books (Ghost Hse Bks)
E-mail: mikec@lonepinepublishing.com
Web site: http://www.lonepinepublishing.com; http://www.companyscoming.com/; http://overtimebooks.com; http://www.folklorepublishing.com/.

Lone Star Bks., (*978-1-58907*) Orders Addr.: 15200 NBN Way, Blue Ridge Summit, PA 17214 USA Tel 717-794-3800 ((Sales, Customer Service, MIS, Royalties, Inventory Mgmt., Dist., Credit & Collections); Fax: 717-794-3803 (Customer Service &/or orders only); 717-794-3857 (Sales & MIS); 717-794-3856 (Royalties, Inventory Mgmt., & Dist.); Toll Free Fax: 800-338-4550 (Customer Service &/or orders); Toll Free: 800-462-6420 (Customer Service &/or orders); Edit Addr.: 4501 Forbes Blvd., Suite 200, Lanham, MD 20706 USA Toll Free Fax: 301-459-5748; Toll Free: 301-459-3366
Dist(s): **National Bk. Network.**

Lone Star Pubns., (*978-0-9766157*) P.O. Box 810872, Dallas, TX 75381 USA Do not confuse with Lone Star Publication in Dallas, TX
E-mail: info@lonestarpublications.com
Web site: http://www.lonestarpublications.com.

Lone Star Publishing Co., (*978-0-9777274*) 906 SW St., Lucie W. Blvd., Port Saint Lucie, FL 34986 USA Tel 772-486-3214; Fax: 772-785-8496 do not confuse with companies with the same name in Paradise, TX, Amarillo, TX, Bryan, TX.

Lone Wolf Productions *See* **Canis Lupus Productions**

Lonejack Mountain Pr., (*978-0-9729101*) P.O. Box 28424, Bellingham, WA 98228-0424 USA.

Lonely Child Pr., (*978-0-9969401*) 16200 Mitchell Creek Dr., Fort Bragg, CA 95437 USA Tel 707-964-6810
E-mail: grorby@mcn.org
Web site: www.ginnyrorby.org.

Lonely Planet Global Ltd. (IRL) (*978-1-78657; 978-1-78701; 978-1-78868; 978-1-83869*) *Dist. by* **HachBkGrp.**

Lonely Planet Pubns., (*978-1-55992*) Orders Addr.: 124 Linden St., Oakland, CA 94607 USA (SAN 659-6541) Tel 510-893-8555; Fax: 510-893-8572; Toll Free: 800-275-8555 (orders, 9am - 5pm Pacific Time); 230 Franklin Rd., Bldg. 2B, Franklin, TN 37064; Edit Addr.: 315 W 36th St., 10th Flr., New York, NY 10018 USA
E-mail: orders@lonelyplanet.com; lonelyplanet.kids@lonelyplanet.com; customerservice@lonelyplanet.com
Web site: http://www.lonelyplanet.com.

Lonely Swan Bks. *Imprint of* **Cosmic Gargoyle Creative Solutions**

Lonestar Abilene Publishing *Imprint of* **LoneStar Abilene Publishing, LLC**

LoneStar Abilene Publishing, LLC, (*978-0-9749725*) 402 Cedar St., Suite 208, Abilene, TX 79601 USA Tel 325-676-9800; Fax: 325-676-2790; *Imprints:* Lonestar Abilene Publishing (LoneStarAbil)
E-mail: michael@yrbks.com
Web site: http://www.yrbks.com/LoneStar.html.

Long Beach City Schl. District, (*978-0-9677925*) 235 Lido Blvd., Lido Beach, NY 11561 USA Tel 516-897-2104; Fax: 516-897-2107
E-mail: RLF@li.net.

Long Bridge Publishing, (*978-0-9842723; 978-1-938712*) 2875 Benjamin Ave., San Jose, CA 95124 USA
E-mail: info@longbridgepublishing.com; orders@longbridgepublishing.com
Web site: http://www.longbridgepublishing.com
Dist(s): **Ingram Content Group.**

Long Dash Publishing, (*978-1-59899*) 49 Orchard St., Hackensack, NJ 07601-4806 USA
E-mail: longdash@gmail.com
Web site: http://www.longdash.com.

Long, George Children's Books, (*978-0-9844946*) P.O. Box 3672, Irmo, SC 29063 USA Tel 803-781-5528
E-mail: GL@GeorgeLongChildrensBooks.com
Web site: www.GeorgeLongChildrensBooks.com.

Long Life Publishing Co., (*978-0-9725836*) P.O. Box 1564, Escondido, CA 92033 USA.

Long, Nikki *See* **Light 4 You**

Long Riders' Guild Pr., The, (*978-1-59048*) 2201 Coyle Ln., Walla Walla, WA 99362-8873 USA
E-mail: longriders@thelongridersguild.com
Web site: http://www.thelongridersguild.com.

Long Stories LLC, (*978-0-615-15295-0; 978-0-615-18961-1*) N3865 County Rd. H, Lake Geneva, WI 53147 USA
E-mail: chad@lycanjournal.com
Web site: http://www.lycanjournal.com.

Longevity Publishing, LLC, (*978-0-9777323*) Orders Addr.: 10179 E. Pinewood Ave., Englewood, CO 80111 USA Tel 720-489-7243
E-mail: info@longevitypublishing.com
Web site: http://www.longevitypublishing.com
Dist(s): **Partners Bk. Distributing, Inc.**

LongHill Partners, Inc., (*978-0-943763; 978-1-58023; 978-1-879045; 978-1-893361; 978-1-59473; 978-0-9904152*) P.O. Box 237, Woodstock, VT 05091 USA; *Imprints:* Jewish Lights Publishing (JewishLights); Skylight Paths Publishing (SkylightPaths)
E-mail: production@longhillpartners.com
Dist(s): **Two Rivers Distribution.**

Longhorn Creek Pr., (*978-0-9714358; 978-0-9764026; 978-0-615-99574-8*) 3780 County Road 4317., De Kalb, TX 75559-5681 USA
E-mail: editor@longhorncreekpress.com; Ron@longhorncreekpress.com
Web site: http://www.longhorncreekpress.com
Dist(s): **CreateSpace Independent Publishing Platform**
Gatewood Pr.

Longleaf Services, Orders Addr.: P.O. Box 8895, Chapel Hill, NC 27515-8895 USA Tel 800-848-6224; Fax: 800-272-6817; 919-962-2704 (24 hours)
E-mail: customerservice@longleafservices.org; orders@longleafservices.org
Web site: http://www.longleafservices.org/.

Longline Imprints Ltd, (*978-1-7326530*) 11956 KIOWA AVE APT 9, Los Angeles, CA 90049-5908 USA Tel 753-509-3876
E-mail: peterwibaux@theindiaroad.com.

Longman Publishing, (*978-0-02; 978-0-06; 978-0-13; 978-0-201; 978-0-205; 978-0-321; 978-0-582; 978-0-673; 978-0-7248; 978-0-8013; 978-1-57322; 978-0-7339*) 75 Arlington St., Boston, MA 02116 USA Tel 617-848-7500
Web site: http://www.aw-bc.com
Dist(s): **Giron Bks.**
Libros Sin Fronteras
Pearson Education.

†Longman Publishing Group, (*978-0-13; 978-0-201; 978-0-321; 978-0-582; 978-0-8013*) Div. of Addison Wesley Longman, Inc., The Longman Bldg., 10 Bank St., White Plains, NY 10606-1951 USA (SAN 202-6856) Tel 914-993-5000; Fax: 914-997-8115 800-922-0579 (college, bkstores, customer service only)
Web site: http://www.pearsonlongman.com
Dist(s): **Coronet Bks.**
Giron Bks.
MyiLibrary
Pearson Education
Pearson Technology Group
Sourcebooks, Inc.
Trans-Atlantic Pubns., Inc.; *CIP.*

Longoria, Eugene R., (*978-0-9796818*) 2222 W. Central Ave., Coolidge, AZ 85228 USA (SAN 854-1116)
E-mail: ElJunior@ElJunior.com
Web site: http://eljunior.com; http://eugenelongoria.com.

Longs Peak Publishing, Incorporated *See* **Crossing Guard Bks., LLC**

Longseller S.A. (ARG) (*978-987-550; 978-987-9481; 978-987-98516*) *Dist. by* **Bilingual Pubns.**

Longseller S.A. (ARG) (*978-987-550; 978-987-9481; 978-987-98516*) *Dist. by* **Libros Fronteras.**

Longshot Publishing, (*978-0-9834770; 978-1-953076*) 251 Alta Loma Ave., Daly City, CA 94015 USA Tel 650-922-2349 Do not confuse with Longshot Publishing in Bishop, CA
E-mail: marcanthonyjohnson@gmail.com.

LongTale Publishing, LLC, (*978-0-9818054; 978-0-9854705; 978-1-941515*) P.O. Box 266597, Houston, TX 77207-6597 USA Fax: 713-896-9701
Web site: http://www.iggytheiguana.com.

Longwood Publishing, (*978-0-692-51554-9; 978-0-692-73478-0; 978-1-7324181*) 14 Longwood Dr., Kennebunk, ME 04043 USA Tel 207-468-7100
Dist(s): **CreateSpace Independent Publishing Platform.**

LonnaDee Pr., (*978-0-9898594*) 24171 Frontage Rd, Bozeman, MT 59718 USA Tel 972-800-2153
E-mail: chounzet@gmail.com
Web site: www.diamondwilson.com.

Look Again Pr., LLC, (*978-0-9801113*) 2461 Mountain Vista Dr., Birmingham, AL 35243 USA (SAN 855-2266) Tel 205-823-8556
Web site: www.lookagainpress.com
Dist(s): **CreateSpace Independent Publishing Platform.**

Look, Learn & Do Pubns., (*978-1-893327*) 24 Highland Blvd., Kensington, CA 94707 USA Fax: 510-524-7577
E-mail: professor@lldkids.com
Web site: http://www.looklearnanddo.com
Dist(s): **Ten Speed Pr.**

Look-About Bks., (*978-0-9800208*) P.O. Box 1907, Nampa, ID 83653 USA (SAN 854-9869) Tel 208-466-6260
E-mail: lpowersraptor@msn.com
Web site: http://www.look-aboutbooks.com.

Looking Glass Library *Imprint of* **Magic Wagon**

Loon Song Publishing, (*978-0-9965070*) 17198 Crane Dr., Bend, OR 97707 USA Tel 503-267-6339
E-mail: nick@nvasilieff.com
Web site: www.nvasilieff.com.

Loonfeather Pr., (*978-0-926147*) Orders Addr.: P.O. Box 1212, Bemidji, MN 56619 USA
E-mail: books@loonfeatherpress.com
Web site: http://www.loonfeatherpress.com.

Loose Cannon, (*978-0-9851292; 978-1-939812; 978-1-944476*) 444 Sutter St., Petaluma, CA 94954 USA Tel 530-762-7002
E-mail: stevhutch@loose-cannon.com.

Loose Change, (*978-0-944707*) 936 Sixth St., Los Banos, CA 93635 USA (SAN 244-9692) Tel 209-826-3797; Fax: 209-826-1514
E-mail: nco4242@sbcglobal.net.

Loose In The Lab, (*978-0-9660965; 978-1-931801*) 9462 S. 560 W., Sandy, UT 84070 USA Tel 801-568-9596; Fax: 801-568-9586; Toll Free: 888-403-1189
E-mail: mail@looseinthelab.com
Web site: http://www.looseinthelab.com.

Loose Leaves Publishing, (*978-1-62432*) 4218 E. Allison Rd, Tucson, AZ 85712 USA Tel 520-310-7528
E-mail: Talminia@gmail.com.

Lopata, Melanie ~ Author, (*978-0-578-45341-5*) 208 Stimson St, Herkimer, NY 13350 USA Tel 315-940-1555
E-mail: melanie.author@yahoo.com
Web site: http://melanielopata.weebly.com/.

Lopez, Daniela J., (*978-0-692-96618-1; 978-0-692-12471-0; 978-0-578-59508-5; 979-8-9868446*) 826 E. 16th Street, Apt 4B, Brooklyn, NY 11230 USA Tel 718-781-6246
E-mail: tallgirldani@gmail.com
Dist(s): **CreateSpace Independent Publishing Platform.**

Lopez, David, (*978-0-9744097*) 3441 Twinberry Ct., Bonita Springs, FL 34134 USA Tel 239-947-2532 (phone/fax)
E-mail: jazzpop@aol.com
Web site: http://www.maddiesmagicmarkers.com.

Loquacious Publishing Co., (*978-0-9763811*) 2115 Wintermere Pointe Dr., Winter Garden, FL 34787-5439 USA.

Loqueleo *Imprint of* **Santillana USA Publishing Co., Inc.**

Lord & Dooney Pr., (*978-1-7328166*) 145 Town Ctr., Corte Madera, CA 94925 USA Tel 415-235-8557
E-mail: wcafdn@yahoo.com
Web site: margotelainejones.com.

Lore, Czidor LLC, (*978-0-9903799; 978-0-9971227; 978-0-9993829; 978-1-7371147*) 421 San Eduardo Ter., Sunnyvale, CA 94085 USA Tel 408-746-5779
E-mail: czidorlorellc@outlook.com
Dist(s): **Lulu Pr., Inc.**

LORE Mountain Productions, (*978-0-9970294; 978-1-946807*) 20875 Jerusalem Grade, Lower Lake, CA 95457 USA Tel 707-987-8577; *Imprints:* MonkeyBear Publishing (MonkeyBear Pub)
E-mail: info@loremountain.com
Web site: www.gracieandmonkeybear.com; www.loremountain.com.

Lorenc, Micah, (*978-0-692-50795-7*) 9604 Dawn Trl, San Antonio, TX 78254 USA Tel 210-417-8178
E-mail: micahlorenc@gmail.com.

Lorenz Corp., The, (*978-0-7877; 978-0-88335; 978-0-89328; 978-1-55863; 978-1-57310; 978-1-885564; 978-1-4291*) 501 E. Third St., Dayton, OH 45401-0802 USA (SAN 208-7413) Tel 937-228-6118; Fax: 937-223-2042; Toll Free: 800-444-1144
E-mail: service@lorenz.com
Web site: http://www.lorenz.com.

Lorenz Educational Pubs., (*978-1-885564*) Div. of The Lorenz Corp., 501 E. Third St., Dayton, OH 45401-0802 USA Tel 937-228-6118 (phone/fax); Fax: 937-223-2042; Toll Free: 800-444-1144
Web site: http://www.lorenzeducationalpress.com
Dist(s): **Rainbow Horizons Publishing, Inc.**

Lorenz, Theo, (*978-0-9975738*) 1773 Lafond Ave, Saint Paul, MN 55104-1716 USA Tel 651-278-7865
E-mail: tiernsshadow@gmail.com.

Lorian Assn., The, (*978-0-936878*) P.O. Box 1368, Issaquah, WA 98027 USA (SAN 666-6663) Tel 425-427-9071
E-mail: info@lorian.org
Web site: http://www.lorian.org.

Lorian Press *See* **Lorian Assn., The**

Lorito Bks., Inc., (*978-0-9815686; 978-0-9842981; 978-0-9835197; 978-0-9883561; 978-0-9904930; 978-0-9998903*) 10395 W. 74th Pl., Arvada, CO 80005 USA (SAN 855-8876) Fax: 303-425-3277; Toll Free: 800-420-6936
Web site: http://www.loritobooks.com
Dist(s): **Follett School Solutions.**

Lormax Communications, (*978-0-9641239*) P.O. Box 40304, Raleigh, NC 27629 USA Tel 919-878-9108.

Lorraine Atieno Oduor, (*978-1-953350*) 11697 Charter Oak Ct. 202, Reston, VA 20190 USA Tel 202-834-9355
E-mail: Lijera@gmail.com
Dist(s): **Ingram Content Group.**

Los Alamos Historical Society Publications *See* **Bathtub Row Pr.**

Los Andes Publishing Co., (*978-0-9637065; 978-1-57159*) P.O. Box 190, Chino Hills, CA 91709 USA Tel 562-789-1540; Toll Free: 800-532-8872
E-mail: losandes@losandes.com
Web site: http://www.losandes.com
Dist(s): **Lectorum Pubns., Inc.**

Los Espada, (*978-0-692-75653-9; 978-0-692-93404-3; 978-0-692-99059-9; 978-0-692-10489-7; 978-0-578-65894-0; 978-0-578-78599-8; 978-0-578-99465-9*) 111-03 76 Dr., Forest Hills, NY 11375 USA Tel 917-406-4498
E-mail: losespada@yahoo.com
Web site: losepada.com
Dist(s): **CreateSpace Independent Publishing Platform.**

Los Perros Publishing Co., (*978-0-9764685*) 3565 Parches Cove, Union Grove, AL 35175-8422 USA
E-mail: jr@losperros.com; mrgsd@hiwaay.net
Web site: http://www.mrgsd.com.

Losantiville Pr., Inc., (*978-0-9794946; 978-1-7326293*) Orders Addr.: P.O. Box 42604, Cincinnati, OH 45242-6040 USA; Edit Addr.: 7012 Beech Hollow Dr., Cincinnati, OH 45236 USA
E-mail: losantivillepress@fuse.net.

Lost Art Pr. LLC, (*978-0-9850777; 978-0-9906230; 978-0-9978702; 978-1-7322100; 978-1-7333916; 978-1-954697*) 26 Greenbriar Ave., Fort Mitchell, KY 41017 USA Tel 859-445-6075
E-mail: cms@lostartpress.com
Web site: http://www.lostartpress.com.

Lost Candy Bar Pr., LLC, (*978-0-9786794*) P.O. Box 5193, Madison, WI 53705-0193 USA Tel 608-233-5690; Fax: 608-231-2312
Web site: http://www.lostcandybarpress.com.

Lost Classic Bks.,
Dist(s): **National Bk. Network.**

Lost Classics Bk. Co., (*978-0-9652735; 978-1-890623*) Orders Addr.: P.O. Box 1756, Fort Collins, CO 80522 USA Tel 970-493-3793 (Distribution Center); Toll Free Fax: 888-211-2665 (Libraries & Schools); Toll Free: 888-611-2665 (credit card orders only); Edit Addr.: P.O. Box 3429, Lake Wales, FL 33859-3429 USA Tel 863-678-3149; Fax: 863-678-0802
E-mail: mgeditor@lostclassicsbooks.com
Web site: http://lcbcbooks.com; http://www.lcbcbooks.com/homeright.htm
Dist(s): **National Bk. Network.**

Lost Coast Pr., (*978-1-882897; 978-1-935448*) 155 Cypress St., Fort Bragg, CA 95437 USA Tel 707-964-9520; Fax: 707-964-7531; Toll Free: 800-773-7782
E-mail: forms@cypresshouse.com
Web site: http://www.cypresshouse.com
Dist(s): **Continental Bk. Co., Inc.**
Cypress Hse.
New Leaf Distributing Co., Inc.
Partners/West Book Distributors.

Lost Hills Bks., (*978-0-9798535*) P.O. Box 3054, Duluth, MN 55803 USA (SAN 854-5553)
Web site: http://www.losthillsbks.com.

Lost Island Pr., *(978-1-7341745; 979-8-9850102)* 3778 Hoen Ave., Santa Rosa, CA 95405 USA Tel 707-536-5524
E-mail: meliclark19@gmail.com;
melctorrefranca@gmail.com
Web site: lostislandpress.com.

Lost Lake Pr., *(978-0-9906450; 978-0-9981736)* N7130 N. Lost Lake Rd., Randolph, WI 53956 USA Tel 920-326-5554
E-mail: LostLakePress@gmail.com
Web site: http://www.LostLakePress.com.

Lost Language Pr. LLC, *(978-0-9975009)* 1128 Chesterton Dr., Richardson, TX 75080 USA Tel 214-340-9837
E-mail: fbuchly@sbcglobal.net
Web site: buchly.wordpress.com.

Lost Mountain Pr., *(978-0-9982279)* 1667 Broussard Way, Marietta, GA 30066 USA
E-mail: hollymaxx1@gmail.com
Web site: lostmountainpress.com.

Lost Scout Pr., *(978-0-9741310)* P.O. Box 86, Loveland, OH 45140-0086 USA (SAN 255-7193) Fax: 719-457-5952; 1283 Sand Trap Ct., Loveland, OH 45140-6060
E-mail: hq@lostscout.com
Web site: http://www.lostscout.com.

Lotharin Pubns., *(978-1-7377474)* 3210 Wind Song Ct., Melbourne, FL 32934 USA Tel 321-313-2325
E-mail: arthurwrotethis@gmail.com
Web site: https://rapunculusseries.com/.

Lotti, Marc, *(978-1-932341)* P.O. Box 5841, Carefree, AZ 85377-5841 USA
E-mail: mlotti@mandragore.com.

Lotus Art Works Inc., *(978-0-9800637)* 11833 Mississippi Ave., Suite 200, Los Angeles, CA 90025 USA Tel 310-442-3335.

Lotus Blossom Bks., *(978-0-9801414)* 1220 Rosecrans St., No. 325, San Diego, CA 92106 USA (SAN 855-3181) Tel 619-224-7771
E-mail: publisher@lotusblossombooks.com
Web site: http://www.lotusblossombooks.com
Dist(s): **BookBaby.**

Lotus Lights Publications *See* **Lotus Pr.**

Lotus Petal Publishing, *(978-0-9787672; 978-0-9820949)* Div. of Lotus Petal, P.O. Box 1394, Nashville, IN 47448-1394 USA Tel 812-988-1250; Toll Free Fax: 800-867-4851
E-mail: info@lotuspetalpublishing.com
Web site: http://www.lotuspetalpublishing.com.

Lotus Pond Media, *(978-0-9791021)* 176 Broadway, Suite 9C, New York, NY 10038 USA Tel 212-608-3329
E-mail: scgrant@goatkids.net;
scgrant@customerresearchcenter.com
Web site: http://www.goatkids.net;
http://www.highimpactquality.com.

Lotus Pr., *(978-0-910261; 978-0-914955; 978-0-940676; 978-0-940985; 978-0-941524; 978-1-60869)* Div. of Lotus Brands, Inc., P.O. Box 325, Twin Lakes, WI 53181 USA (SAN 239-1120) Tel 262-889-2461; Fax: 262-889-8591; Toll Free: 800-824-6396 Do not confuse with companies with the same or similar name in Lotus, CA, Westerville, OH, Bokeelia, FL, Brattleboro, VT, Detroit, MI, Tobyhanna, PA
E-mail: lotuspress@lotuspress.com
Web site: http://www.lotuspress.com
Dist(s): **National Bk. Network.**

Lotus Publications *See* **Johnson, Earl Photography**

Louck, Cheryl, *(978-0-9744230)* 2708 Avalon Ln., Montgomery, IL 60538 USA Tel 630-853-0653
Web site: http://www.cheryllouck.com.

Loucks Studios Inc. *See* **Loucks Studios Inc.**

Loucks Studios Inc., *(978-0-9725311; 978-1-59819; 978-0-9771365)* Orders Addr.: P.O. Box 9177, Rochester, MN 55903 USA (SAN 256-8969); *Imprints:* Pickled Eggs Press (TM) (P E P); Waiting Room to Heaven (Wait Room Hvn)
E-mail: publisher@bookentree.com;
loucksstudiosinc@gmail.com; lisa@lisalc.com;
lisa@storyantics.com; lcpbooks@gmail.com
Web site: http://bowwowdetectives.com;
http://meowmeowdetectives.com; bookentree.com;
archives.lisalc.com; storyantics.com; Loucksstudios.com;
personalised.storyantics.com
Dist(s): **Ecompass Business Ctr.**

Loughton Bks., *(978-0-9704974)* 101 W. 23rd St., New York, KS 37215 USA Do not confuse with companies with similar names in Newport, RI, San Diego, CA, Mary Esther, FL,
E-mail: mbraden@loghtonbooks.com
Web site: http://www.loughtonbooks.com.

Louisana Museum of Modern Art (DNK) *(978-87-90029; 978-87-91607; 978-87-92877) Dist. by* **Dist Art Pubs.**

Louisiana Ladybug Pr., *(978-0-9753435)* 210 Pinecrest Rd., Arcadia, LA 71001 USA
Web site: http://www.LouisianaPotpourriFromAtoZ.com.

†Louisiana State Univ. Pr., *(978-0-8071)* 3990 W. Lakeshore Dr., Baton Rouge, LA 70808 USA Tel 225-578-6294; Fax: 225-578-6461; Toll Free Fax: 800-272-6817; Toll Free: 800-848-6224
E-mail: lsupress@lsu.edu
Web site: http://lsupress.org/
Dist(s): **Ebsco Publishing**
Longleaf Services
ebrary, Inc.; *CIP.*

Love + Lifestyle Media Group (CAN) *(978-0-9920874; 978-1-77210) Dist. by* **BTPS.**

Love & Blessings *See* **Self-Mastery Pr.**

Love Bug Bks., *(978-0-9787174)* 1117 Ariana Rd., Suite 102, San Marcos, CA 92069-8122 USA Tel 760-798-9415; Fax: 760-798-9415
E-mail: rolwink@cox.net
Web site: http://www.lovebugbooks.com.

Love Cultivating Editions, *(978-0-9744999)* 2665 Reed Rd., Hood River, OR 97031-9609 USA
Web site: http://www.lovecultivatingeditions.com.

Love II Learn Bks., *(978-0-9796679)* 860 Johnson Ferry Rd., Suite 140-345, Atlanta, GA 30342 USA (SAN 854-0535) Tel 404-808-0458
Web site: http://www.booksbykobie.com;
http://www.loveiilearbooks.com
Dist(s): **Baker & Taylor Publisher Services (BTPS).**

Love Ink LLC, *(978-1-940426)* 65257 Solar Rd, Montrose, CO 81403 USA
E-mail: Love_Ink_LLC@outlook.com
Web site: www.love-ink-llc.com.

Love Language Pubns., *(978-0-9749924)* 2111 E. Santa Fe, No. 268, Olathe, KS 66062 USA
E-mail: anne@lovelanguageforbabies.com
Web site: http://www.lovelanguageforbabies.com.

Love of Kids Bks. Publishing, *(978-0-692-91699-5)* 164 Rendition Dr., None, Mcdonough, GA 30253 USA Tel 770-912-1124
E-mail: loveofkidsbookspublishing@gmail.com.

Love, Semone *See* **Victorious Publishing Group**

Love Truth, *(978-0-9977016; 978-8-9868475)* 353 SW Wakonda Beach Rd., Waldport, OR 97394 USA Tel 541-832-1300
E-mail: jeanann_w@yahoo.com
Web site: http://joshua-mom.blogspot.com/.

Love Your Life, *(978-0-9664806; 978-0-9798554; 978-0-9820477)* Orders Addr.: P.O. Box 2, Red Lion, PA 17356 USA (SAN 256-1387) Tel 717-200-2852; Fax: 310-496-0716; Edit Addr.: 755 Conndly Dr., Red Lion, PA 17356 USA Tel 717-200-2852; Fax: 310-496-0716
E-mail: publish@loveyourlife.com
Web site: http://www.loveyourlife.com.

Loveland Pr., LLC, *(978-0-9662696; 978-0-9744851)* P.O. Box 7001, Loveland, CO 80537-0001 USA Tel 970-593-9557 Toll Free: 800-593-9557
E-mail: info@lovelandpress.com
Web site: http://www.lovelandpress.com.

LoveLight Media, *(978-0-9893181)* 216 Regina Dr., Fort Collins, CO 80525 USA Tel 970-218-2592
E-mail: Deidre@lovelightmedia.com
Web site: None yet.

Love-LovePublishing, *(978-0-9852015; 978-0-9973200; 978-1-7334454; 978-1-7377052; 978-1-961823)* P.O. Box 258136, Madison, WI 53725 USA Tel 608-576-2064
E-mail: contact@love-lovepublishing.com
Web site: http://love-lovepublishing.com.

Love's Creative Resources, *(978-1-929548)* Orders Addr.: P.O. Box 44306, Charlotte, NC 28215 USA Tel 704-563-7469
E-mail: ml9734@yahoo.com.

Lovestruck Literary, *(978-0-9833980; 978-0-9856574; 978-0-9960356)* 1643 Rodney Dr. APT 1, Los Angeles, CA 90027 USA
E-mail: afletcher@lovestruckliterary.com
Web site: lovestruckliterary.com
Dist(s): **Smashwords.**

LoveWorld Publishing, *(978-978-51521-6-6)* ., ., CA 1 USA
Web site: http://www.rhapsodyofrealities.org
Dist(s): **Smashwords**
Whitaker Hse.

Lovin Ovens, Inc., *(978-0-9617468)* 57 Chof Trail, Flagstaff, AZ 86001 USA (SAN 664-1180) Tel 928-525-1527
E-mail: GandCFox@msn.com.

Loving Guidance, Inc., *(978-1-889609; 978-1-7350640)* P.O. Box 622407, Oviedo, FL 32762 USA Tel 407-366-0233; 407-977-8862; Fax: 407-366-4293; Toll Free: 800-842-2846; 50 Smith St., Oviedo, FL 32765-9608
E-mail: bryan@lovingguidance.com;
kate@lovingguidance.com;
becky.bailey@consciousdiscipline.com
Web site: http://www.beckybailey.com;
http://www.consciousdiscipline.com
Dist(s): **Gryphon Hse., Inc.**

Loving Healing Pr., Inc., *(978-1-932690; 978-1-61599)* 5145 Pontiac Trail, Ann Arbor, MI 48105-9279 USA (SAN 255-7770) Tel 734-662-6864; Fax: 734-663-6861; Toll Free: 888-761-6268; *Imprints:* Marvelous Spirit Press (MarvelousSpir); Modern Software Press (ModernSoftware)
E-mail: info@lovinghealing.com
Web site: http://www.beyondtrauma.com/;
http://www.TurtleDolphinDreams.com;
http://www.TIRbook.com; http://www.LifeSkillsBook.com;
http://www.VictorianHeritage.com;
http://www.PhysicalLoss.com; http://www.gotparts.org;
http://www.lovinghealing.com/
Dist(s): **New Leaf Distributing Co., Inc.**
Quality Bks., Inc.
ebrary, Inc.

Lovstad, Joel Publishing, *(978-0-9749058)* 701 Henry St., No. 203, Waunakee, WI 53597 USA
E-mail: jlfred@chorus.net
Web site: http://www.joellovstad-books.com.

†Lowell Hse., *(978-0-7373; 978-0-8092; 978-0-929923; 978-1-56565)* 2020 Avenue of the Stars, Suite 300, Los Angeles, CA 90067-4704 USA (SAN 250-863X) Tel 310-552-7555; Fax: 310-552-7573
Dist(s): **Independent Pubs. Group**
McGraw-Hill Trade; *CIP.*

Lowell Hse. Juvenile, *(978-0-7373; 978-0-929923; 978-1-56565)* 2020 Avenue of the Stars, No. 300, Los Angeles, CA 90067 USA Tel 310-552-7555; Fax: 310-552-7573; *Imprints:* Roxbury Park Juvenile (Roxbury Pk Juvenile)
Dist(s): **McGraw-Hill Trade.**

Lowell, Meryl, *(978-0-578-21442-9; 978-1-7342037)* 1221 Ottawa Dr., South Lake Tahoe, CA 96150 USA Tel 352-427-8525
E-mail: meryllowell@yahoo.com
Web site: www.merylbestlowell.com.

Lowell Milken Ctr. for Unsung Heroes, *(978-0-9988266)* 1 S. Main, Fort Scott, KS 66701 USA Tel 620-223-1312
E-mail: lmcwerling@gmail.com
Web site: lowellmilkencenter.org.

†Lowell Pr., The, Gallion Communications, *(978-0-913504; 978-0-932845)* Orders Addr.: P.O. Box 411877, Kansas City, MO 64141-1877 USA (SAN 207-0774) Tel 816-753-4545; Fax: 816-753-4057; Toll Free: 800-736-7660 Do not confuse with Lowell Pr. in Eugene, OR
E-mail: plowell@accessus.net;
sales@thelowellpress.com
Web site: http://www.thelowellpress.com; *CIP.*

Lowell, Shelley, *(978-0-9765344)* Orders Addr.: c/o Montage Gallery, 925 South Charles St., Baltimore, MD 21230 USA.

Lower Kuskokwim Schl. District, *(978-1-58084)* Orders Addr.: P.O. Box 305, Bethel, AK 99559 USA Tel 907-543-4928; Fax: 907-543-4935
E-mail: catalog@fc.lksd-do.org
Web site: http://www.lksd.org/catalog.

Lower Lane Publishing LLC, *(978-0-9797790)* 2105 Carehill Rd., Vienna, VA 22181 USA.

Lowney, Amanda *See* **Amanda Lowney Bks. LLC**

Lowrance, Carrie, *(978-0-9995069; 978-1-960783)* Orders Addr.: 755 Saint Andrews Dr. Apt 22-104, Murfreesboro, TN 37128 USA Tel 309-444-0209; Edit Addr.: 1900 Highview Rd. Apt. C8, East Peoria, IL 61611 USA Tel 309-444-0209
E-mail: Carrie.Lowrance@yahoo.com
Web site: www.carrielowrance.com.

Loyola Grupo de Comunicacion (ESP) *Dist. by* **Lectorum Pubns.**

†Loyola Pr., *(978-0-8294)* 8770 W. Bryn Mawr Av. Suite 1125, Chicago, IL 60631 USA (SAN 211-6537) Fax: 773-281-0555; Toll Free: 800-621-1008; *Imprints:* 4U2B Books & Media (4U2BBnM)
E-mail: customerservice@loyolapress.com
Web site: http://www.loyolapress.com
Dist(s): **ISD**
Spring Arbor Distributors, Inc.; *CIP.*

LP Publishing, *(978-0-578-00530-0; 978-0-578-01791-4; 978-0-615-56110-3; 978-0-9859790)* 2941 S. Comett Dr., Ridgefield, WA 98642 USA
Dist(s): **Lulu Pr., Inc.**

L.Patrick Publishing, *(978-0-9774418)* 2710 W. 76th St., Inglewood, CA 90305 USA.

LPC, *(978-0-9822065; 978-0-9833196; 978-0-9847655; 978-1-938499; 978-0-615-89890-2; 978-1-941103; 978-1-946016; 978-1-64526)* Div. of Christian Devotions Ministries, Orders Addr.: 2333 Barton Oaks Dr., Raleigh, NC 27614 USA; *Imprints:* Brimstone Fiction (BrimstoneFict); Illuminate YA (Illuminate YA)
E-mail: lighthousepublishingcarolinas@gmail.com
Web site: http://LPCBooks.com
Dist(s): **CreateSpace Independent Publishing Platform**
Iron Stream Media
Spring Arbor Distributors, Inc.

LPD Pr., *(978-0-9641542; 978-1-890689; 978-1-936744; 978-1-943681)* 925 Salamanca, NW, Los Ranchos, NM 87107-5647 USA Tel 505-269-8324; *Imprints:* Rio Grande Books (Rio Grande Bks)
E-mail: LPDPress@q.com
Web site: http://www.nmsantos.com
Dist(s): **Smashwords.**

LRS, *(978-1-58118)* 14214 S. Figueroa St., Los Angeles, CA 90061-1034 USA Tel 310-354-2610; Fax: 310-354-2601; Toll Free: 800-255-5002
E-mail: lrsprint@aol.com
Web site: http://www.lrs-largeprint.com
Dist(s): **Beeler, Thomas T. Pub.**

LS Co., 17901 NW 48 CT, Miami Gardens, FL 33055 USA Tel 239-234-4377.

Ls Dream, *(978-0-578-81664-7)* 722 Richbrook Dr, Claremont, CA 91711 USA Tel 626-833-3294
E-mail: dwyer77l@gmail.com.

LSF, *(978-1-7359942)* 36722 Paulita, San Benito, TX 78586 USA Tel 956-241-9711
E-mail: Santos.vallejo3121@gmail.com
Web site: www.LSFmotivation.com.

LSG Pubns., *(978-1-933532)* 29165 Clover Ln., Big Pine Key, FL 33043-6046 USA
E-mail: lisagaljanic@optonline.net
Web site: http://www.lsgpublications.com.

LSP *Imprint of* **LSP Digital, LLC**

LSP Digital, LLC, *(978-0-9792030; 978-0-9800733; 978-0-9817654)* P.O. Box 851556, Westland, MI 48185 USA Tel 734-355-3733; Fax: 734-261-0155; *Imprints:* LSP (LSP USA)
E-mail: admin@lspdigital.com
Web site: http://www.lspdigital.com.

LSW Strategies, LLC, *(978-1-7322440; 978-1-959250)* 1941 So. 42nd St. Suite 502, Omaha, NE 68105 USA Tel 402-740-6034
E-mail: twobeepublishing@gmail.com
Web site: http://ww.twobeepublishing.com.

LTI Publishing, *(978-0-9743048)* Div. of Let's Talk Interactive, Inc., P.O. Box 371, Huntersville, NC 28070 USA
E-mail: art@LTIPublishing.net
Web site: http://www.letstalkinterctive.com;
http://www.FathersTouch.com;
http://www.SexualAbuse.ws;
http://www.ChildHoodItShouldNotHurt.com;
http://www.ChildHoodShouldNotHurt.com;
http://www.AgainstSexualAbuse.org;
http://www.LetsTalkCounseling.com.

LTL Media LLC, *(978-0-9785744)* P.O. Box 12766, Tempe, AZ 85284 USA
Web site: http://www.mylittlethinkers.com.

LtoJ Pr., *(978-1-7330110; 978-1-956457; 978-1-956680)* 11445 E. Via Linda, Scottsdale, AZ 85259 USA Tel 480-221-7603
E-mail: lee@ltoj.net
Web site: ltoj.net.

Lu, Melissa Productions, *(978-0-9726832)* 5356 Rose Ridge Ln., Colorado Springs, CO 80917 USA Fax: 719-594-6993
E-mail: patsy@melissalu.com
Web site: http://www.melissalu.com.

Lua Publishing, *(978-0-9746304)* P.O. Box 3250, Fairfield, C 94533 USA Tel 707-426-9480
E-mail: info@luapublishing.com
Web site: http://www.luapublishing.com
Dist(s): **New Leaf Distributing Co., Inc.**

Luath Pr. Ltd. (GBR) *(978-0-946487; 978-1-84282; 978-1-905222; 978-1-906307; 978-1-906817; 978-1-908373; 978-1-910021) Dist. by* **Midpt Trade.**

Lubbers, Theresa *See* **Mr. Emmett Publishing**

Lucas Co., *(978-0-9715916)* P.O. Box 9245, Moscow, ID 83843 USA
Web site: http://www.lucasco.com.

Lucas Enterprises, *(978-0-9770611)* P.O. Box 9201, Chico, CA 95927 USA
E-mail: lucasent1@earthlink.net.

Lucas, Mattie, *(978-0-9762456)* P.O. Box 47070, Windsor Mills, MD 21244 USA Fax: 410-944-2597
E-mail: bishop@digc.org.

Lucas Violet *Imprint of* **Clocktower Hill Research & Publishing Group, LLC**

Lucasleo, *(978-1-7340134)* 511 N. 14th St., Nashville, TN 37206 USA
Dist(s): **CreateSpace Independent Publishing Platform.**

†Luce, Robert B. Pubs., *(978-0-88331)* Owned by Renaisance Book Services Corp., 2490 Black Rock Tpke., Fairfield, CT 06432 USA Tel 203-372-0300; Fax: 203-374-4766; Toll Free: 800-786-5427
E-mail: info@aslanpublishing.com
Web site: http://www.aslanpublishing.com
Dist(s): **APG Sales & Distribution Services**; *CIP.*

Lucent Bks. *Imprint of* **Cengage Gale**

Lucent Interpretations, LLC, *(978-0-9787849; 978-1-935146)* P.O. Box 3931, Lisle, IL 60532-8831 USA (SAN 856-6364)
E-mail: salmahammad@hotmail.com.

Lucent Pr. *Imprint of* **Greenhaven Publishing LLC**

Luchterhand, Kenneth R., *(978-0-692-17183-7; 978-0-578-68619-6; 978-0-578-68846-6; 978-0-578-68847-3; 978-1-7365891)* N3309 Cty. Rd. N., Melrose, WI 54642 USA Tel 608-488-2102
E-mail: thomsincharge@yahoo.com
Dist(s): **CreateSpace Independent Publishing Platform.**

Lucia Pubs., *(978-0-9762297)* Orders Addr.: P.O. Box 3, Churubusco, IN 46723-0003 USA Tel 260-693-0852; Fax: 260-693-0082; Edit Addr.: 209C S. Main St., Churubusco, IN 46723 USA
E-mail: diannegg@peoplepc.com; giannakeff@iquest.net
Web site: http://www.luciapublishers.com.

Lucky & Me Productions, Inc., *(978-0-9721256; 978-0-615-71754-8)* Orders Addr.: 410 East 74th St., 6H, New York, NY 10021-3918 USA (SAN 255-0873) Tel 212-288-7203; Fax: 401-783-7815 call before faxing/not always on
E-mail: writermyst@aol.com
Web site: http://www.dearjohnlennon.com
Dist(s): **CreateSpace Independent Publishing Platform.**

Lucky Bear Pubns., *(978-0-9729938)* 1144 Langwood Dr., Gallatin, TN 37066 USA Tel 615-452-3242 (phone/fax)
E-mail: perryluckybear@comcast.net
Web site: http://www.myluckybear.com.

Lucky Duck Designs, *(978-0-9790632)* P.O. Box 2192, Petaluma, CA 94953-2192 USA
E-mail: stuart@lucky-duck.com
Web site: http://www.lucky-duck.com.

Lucky Jenny Publishing, *(978-0-9847982; 978-0-615-69429-0; 978-0-615-87941-3; 978-0-615-88036-5; 978-0-615-88053-2; 978-0-615-92528-8; 978-0-615-93423-5; 978-0-615-97849-9; 978-0-692-26564-2; 978-0-692-33703-5; 978-0-692-34748-5; 978-0-692-35226-7; 978-0-692-35675-3; 978-0-692-44777-2; 978-0-692-46799-2; 978-0-692-48929-1; 978-0-692-61369-6; 978-0-692-66141-3; 978-1-7323301) P.O. Box 331, Plymouth, CA 95669 USA Tel 209-256-2465*
E-mail: publisher@luckyjenny.com
Web site: www.luckyjenny.com
Dist(s): **CreateSpace Independent Publishing Platform**
Ingram Content Group.

Lucky Publications *See* **Covered Wagon Publishing LLC**

Lucky Red Pr., LLC, *(978-0-9790690)* 10061 Riverside Dr., Suite 812, Toluca Lake, CA 91602 USA Tel 818-795-2388; Fax: 818-566-4995
E-mail: Susan@frankiespals.com
Web site: http://www.frankiespals.com.

Lucky Stars Publishing, LLC, *(978-0-9895637; 978-0-692-56883-5; 978-0-692-56890-3; 978-0-692-56891-0; 978-0-692-56895-8; 978-0-692-56900-9; 978-1-944759)* 6303 Riverfront Dr., Royersford, PA 19468 USA Tel 215-892-4161
E-mail: kimvlehman@gmail.com
Dist(s): **CreateSpace Independent Publishing Platform.**

Lucky 3 Ranch, Inc., *(978-1-928624)* 2457 S. County Rd. 19, Loveland, CO 80537-9044 USA Tel 970-663-0066; Fax: 970-663-0676; Toll Free: 800-816-7566
E-mail: meredith@luckythreeranch.com
Web site: http://www.luckythreeranch.com/
Dist(s): **MediaTech Productions.**

LuckySports, *(978-0-935938)* 39844 Somerset Ave., Palm Desert, CA 92211 USA (SAN 213-7453) Tel 760-861-2174 (cell)
E-mail: chuck@LuckySports.net
Web site: http://www.bogiegolf.com;
http://www.sportcartoonbooks.com;
http://www.LuckySports.net.

Lucy Rose Publishing LLC, *(978-0-9789386; 978-0-9821936)* P.O. Box 3034, Fort Polk, LA 71459 USA
E-mail: admin@lucyrosepublishing.com
Web site: http://www.lucyrosepublishing.com.

Ludwig Creative, Inc., *(978-0-578-55326-9; 978-0-578-63568-2)* P.O. Box 25505, Portland, OR 97298-0505 USA Tel 503-329-9873; Fax: 503-297-7773
E-mail: trudy@trudyludwig.com
Web site: trudyludwig.com.

Ludwig, Michael, *(978-0-692-14696-5; 978-0-692-14699-6)* 20 W. St., West Hatfield, MA 01088 USA Tel 774-200-7707
E-mail: mike.luddy@yahoo.com
Dist(s): **Ingram Content Group.**

Lueck Studios, *(978-0-9774547)* 8353 11th Ave. NW, Seattle, WA 98117 USA (SAN 257-6023)
E-mail: jenny@lueckstudios.com
Web site: http://www.chicabee.com
Dist(s): **Baker & Taylor Publisher Services (BTPS).**

Luisalchemy *See* **Alchemy Hero Publishing**

Luke & Lori Bks., *(978-0-9747792)* Orders Addr.: 5908 90th St., Lubbock, TX 79424 USA Tel 806-783-9941; Fax: 806-783-3099
E-mail: Melissa@lukeandlori.com
Web site: http://www.LukeAndLori.com.

Lukeman Literary Management, Ltd., *(978-0-9829537; 978-0-9839778; 978-0-9849753; 978-1-939416; 978-1-63291; 978-1-64029; 978-1-0943; 978-0-578-36268-7)* 157 Bedford Ave., Brooklyn, NY 11211 USA Tel 718-599-8988; Fax: 775-264-2189
E-mail: noah@lukeman.com.

Lulilite Productions, *(978-0-9759631)* P.O. Box 20847, Sedona, AZ 86341-0847 USA Tel 928-284-5442 (phone/fax)
E-mail: ariamagi@npgcable.com
Web site: http://www.lulilites.com.

Lulu Enterprises Inc. *See* **Lulu Pr., Inc.**

Lulu Pr., Inc., *(978-1-4116; 978-1-84728; 978-1-4303; 978-1-4357; 978-1-60552; 978-0-557; 978-1-4583; 978-1-257; 978-1-105; 978-1-300; 978-1-4834; 978-1-304; 978-1-312; 978-1-326; 978-1-329; 978-1-365; 978-1-5342; 978-0-359; 978-0-578-42336-4; 978-1-68470; 978-1-68471; 978-1-68474; 978-1-716; 978-0-578-73052-3; 978-0-578-89171-2; 978-0-692-03785-0) 26-28 Hammersmith Grove, London, W6 7BA GBR; 700 Park Offices Dr#250, Research Traingle Park, NC 27709; Imprints:* Red Button Press (MYID_Y_RED BUT)
E-mail: rbraynin@lulu.com; dllamas@lulu.com
Dist(s): **Amazon Digital Services Inc.**
Booklines Hawaii, Ltd.
Copyright Clearance Ctr., Inc.
CreateSpace Independent Publishing Platform
Ingram Content Group
Smashwords
Valjean Pr.

Lulu.com (GBR) *(978-1-84753; 978-1-4092; 978-1-4461; 978-1-4457; 978-1-4452; 978-1-84799; 978-1-4476; 978-1-4466; 978-1-4467; 978-1-4475; 978-1-4477; 978-1-4478; 978-1-4709; 978-1-4710; 978-1-291; 978-1-4717; 978-1-4716; 978-1-326; 978-1-387; 978-1-7947; 978-1-7948; 978-0-244; 978-1-6780; 978-1-6781; 978-1-6671; 978-1-008) Dist. by* **LuluCom.**

Luma Studio, *(978-1-7352647; 978-1-954137)* 4601 S. Atlantic ave 606, Ponce Inlet, FL 32127 USA Tel 407-462-8828
E-mail: Lu.matuonto@gmail.com
Web site: https://www.luciamatuonto.com/.

Lumadix Pr., *(978-0-9981647)* 1615 Buck St, West Linn, OR 97068 USA Tel 503-707-1438
E-mail: rio4kovlak@gmail.com
Web site: www.riokoviak.com.

Lumberloft Pr., *(978-0-9993743; 978-1-7345497)* 2551 Wellesley Ave., Los Angeles, CA 90064 USA Tel 603-494-4604
E-mail: mavitabile@gmail.com.

Lumen (ARG) *(978-950-724; 978-950-9017; 978-987-00) Dist. by* **Lectorum Pubns.**

Lumen Anime *Imprint of* **Citron Concassee**

LUMEN-US Pubns., *(978-0-9703611; 978-0-9787788; 978-0-9794862; 978-0-9815359; 978-0-9819935; 978-1-936405)* 234 Main St., Park Forest, IL 60466-2098 USA Toll Free: 866-219-9637
E-mail: Lumenuspubl@aol.com
Web site: http://www.lumen-us.com
Dist(s): **BookBaby.**

Lumina Pr. LLC, *(978-0-9708442)* P.O. Box 1106, Wrightsville Beach, NC 28480-1106 USA Do not confuse with Lumina Press in Springfield, MO
E-mail: david@luminapress.com.

Luminade Publishing, *(978-1-7347835)* 172 Erion Ln., Woodland, WA 98674 USA Tel 503-726-9333
E-mail: matthew.smith@kla.com.

Luminare Pr., LLC, *(978-1-937303; 978-1-944733; 978-1-64388; 979-8-88679)* 467 W. 17th Ave., Eugene, OR 97401 USA Tel 541-554-7574
E-mail: pmarshall17@comcast.net.

Luminary Media Group *Imprint of* **Pine Orchard, Inc.**

Luminate 7 Publishing, *(978-0-9765496)* 676 A 9th Ave., No. 142, New York, NY 10036 USA Tel 917-647-6740; Fax: 212-957-9191
E-mail: luminate7@aol.com.

Luminate Pr., *(978-0-578-56624-5; 978-0-578-99991-3)* 8840 Hood Mountain Way, Santa Rosa, CA 95409 USA Tel 310-980-2444
E-mail: kristenj@kemediagroup.net.

Luminations Media Group, Inc., *(978-0-9821199; 978-1-61222)* P.O. Box 538, Monterey Park, CA 91754 USA Tel 626-571-0115
E-mail: office@luminationsmedia.com
Web site: http://www.LuminationsMedia.com.

Luminis Bks., Inc., *(978-1-935462; 978-1-941311)* 13245 Blacktern Way, Carmel, IN 46033 USA (SAN 857-8125) Tel 317-250-9539
E-mail: publisher@luminisbooks.com
Web site: http://www.luminisbooks.com
Dist(s): **MyiLibrary**
ebrary, Inc.

Luminosity Media Group LLC, *(978-0-9969639; 978-0-9982907; 978-0-578-74140-6; 978-0-578-34241-2; 979-8-218-06890-5)* 12100 Archeleta Blvd. Unit 315, Austin, TX 78739 USA Tel 248-701-1995
E-mail: SafetyTrilogy@Yahoo.com.

Luminous Libros, *(978-1-7358182)* 921 SW 87 Terr., Pembroke Pines, FL 33025 USA Tel 954-559-9916
E-mail: llrodrig1@aol.com
Web site: booksoftherealm.com.

Lumpkin, Carol *See* **Peace Rug Company, Inc., The**

Luna Publishing, *(978-0-9791785)* Orders Addr.: 5815 82nd St., No. 145, PMB 137, Lubbock, TX 79424 USA Tel 806-687-3479; Fax: 806-687-3401 Do not confuse with Luna PUblishing Company in Los Angeles, CA
E-mail: ccrmgr2@nts-online.net
Web site: http://www.lunapublish.com.

Luna, Rachel Nickerson *See* **Howard, Emma Bks.**

Luna Rising *Imprint of* **Northland Publishing**

Lunada Pr., LLC, *(978-0-937176)* 2510 W. 237th, Suite 100, Torrence, CA 90505 USA Tel 435-632-8349
E-mail: jeannemaree@charter.net
Dist(s): **Ingram Content Group.**

Lunar Donut Pr., *(978-0-9725638)* P.O. Box 692625, Orlando, FL 32869 USA Tel 407-298-7779; Fax: 407-298-7779
E-mail: caricatureconnection@cfl.rr.com
Web site: http://www.caricatureconnection.com.

Lunasea Studios, *(978-0-9799290)* 9450 Mira Mesa Blvd., Suite B-107, San Diego, CA 92126 USA
Web site: http://www.lunasea-studios.com/.

Lunatic Pr., *(978-0-9772590)* P.O. Box 4571, West Hills, CA 91308 USA
Web site: http://www.lunaticpress.com.

Lunchbox Lessons, *(978-1-60507)* 970 E. Broadway, Suite 406, Jackson, WY 83001 USA (SAN 854-9540) Tel 307-462-4173
E-mail: info@lunchboxlessons.com
Web site: http://www.lunchboxlessons.com.

Lunchbox Stories Inc., *(978-0-9798059)* 20425 NW Quail Hollow Dr., Portland, OR 97229 USA
Web site: http://www.lunchboxstories.com.

Lundy, Dylan, *(978-0-578-19800-2)* 2955 Talon Court, Virginia Beach, VA 23453 USA.

Luse, Sandra I., *(978-0-615-22394-0)* P.O. Box 431, Wilber, NE 68465 USA Tel 402-821-2641.

Lushena Bks., *(978-1-930097; 978-1-63182; 978-1-63923; 979-8-89096)* 607 Country Club Dr., Unit E, Bensenville, IL 60106 USA (SAN 630-5105) Tel 630-238-8708; Fax: 630-238-8824
E-mail: Lushenabks@yahoo.com
Web site: http://www.lushenabks.com/.

Luther T. Collins *See* **Legacy Voice Productions**

Lutherworth Pr., The (GBR) *(978-0-7188) Dist. by* **ISD USA.**

Luthie M West, *(978-0-9986548; 978-1-7322514)* 3979 N. Clarey St., Eugene, OR 97402 USA Tel 541-915-1664
E-mail: Arpeer@gmail.com.

Lutz, William G., *(978-0-615-15622-4; 978-0-615-18287-2; 978-0-615-21273-9)* 10248 Ramm Rd., Whitehouse, OH 43571 USA
Dist(s): **Lulu Pr., Inc.**

Luv U Bks., *(978-0-9715322)* P.O. Box 42037, Cincinnati, OH 45242-0037 USA
E-mail: luvubooks@fuse.net
Web site: http://www.luvubooks.com.

Luvlife Publishing, *(978-0-9764316)* Orders Addr.: 69 Shore Dr., Old Lyme, CT 06371 USA Tel 860-434-0723
E-mail: mistilove@earthlink.net
Web site: http://www.snakesofnewengland.com.

LuvLuv *Imprint of* **Aurora Publishing, Inc.**

Luz Pubns., *(978-0-9673300)* 1110 Laguna St., Santa Barbara, CA 93101 USA Tel 805-636-6530
E-mail: TWSpeaks@yahoo.com.

L.W. Communications, *(978-0-9723378)* 16815 Victory Blvd. #226, Van Nuys, CA 91406-5550 USA Tel 818-787-9550 (phone, fax - call first)
E-mail: lancecoach@aol.com
Web site: http://www.lancecoach.com.

Lycan Valley Press *See* **Lycan Valley Press Pubns.**

Lycan Valley Press Pubns., *(978-0-9987489; 978-1-64562)* 1625 E. 72nd St, STE 700 PMB 132, Tacoma, WA 98404 USA Tel 425-270-7097
E-mail: writer.mj.sydney@gmail.com
Web site: www.TheCrowsInMyAttic.com; www.LycanValley.com.

Lyceum Books, Incorporated *See* **Follmer Group, The**

Lychee Pr. *Imprint of* **Lychee Pr.**

Lychee Pr., *(978-1-7339671; 978-1-953281; 979-8-89111)* 57 Arbor St., San Francisco, CA 94131 USA Tel 415-265-8888; *Imprints:* Lychee press (MYID_G_LYCHEE)
E-mail: katrinaliu@gmail.com.

Lychgate Pr., *(978-0-615-65502-4; 978-0-9882887; 978-0-9976116)* 529 N.W. 31st St., Corvallis, OR 97330 USA Tel 541-752-5211
Web site: editor@fullcitypress.com
Dist(s): **CreateSpace Independent Publishing Platform.**

Lynch Legacy, *(978-1-7361183)* 7152 Saddle Creek Cir., Sarasota, FL 34241 USA Tel 941-921-1043
E-mail: LynchLegacy224@gmail.com
Web site: iftodayyouhearhisvoice.com.

Lynch, Marietta & Patricia Perry, *(978-0-9610962)* 240 Atlantic Rd., Gloucester, MA 01930 USA (SAN 265-2722) Tel 508-283-6322.

Lynda Fern Bks., *(978-0-9961982)* 12918 Oakland Hills Ct., Jacksonville, FL 32225 USA Tel 904-565-8495
E-mail: lyndafernbooks@gmail.com.

Lynn Schulman George, *(978-0-578-34807-0)* 11204 SW 53rd Ave., PORTLAND, OR 97219 USA Tel 503-308-0105
E-mail: lynnstergeorge@yahoo.com.

Lynn Tyner Mitchum & James Rogers, *(978-0-9745191)* P.O. Box 5799, Sevierville, TN 37864 USA
Web site: http://jamesrogersonline.com.

Lynne Ellen, Inc., *(978-0-9748889)* 670 N. Stiles Dr., Charleston, SC 29412 USA Tel 843-817-2530
E-mail: lynne@metoomommy.com.

Lynn's Bookshelf, *(978-0-9618608)* Orders Addr.: P.O. Box 2224, Boise, ID 83701 USA (SAN 667-1314) Tel 208-331-1987 (phone/fax); Edit Addr.: 3423 Scenic Dr., Boise, ID 83703 USA
E-mail: decker.barbara@ymail.com; lynnsbooks@cableone.net.

†Lynx Hse. Pr., *(978-0-89924)* 420 W. 24th Ave., Spokane, WA 99203-1922 USA (SAN 250-3344) Tel 309-624-4594; Fax: 309-623-4238
E-mail: cnhowell@mail.ewu.edu
Dist(s): **SPD-Small Pr. Distribution**
Univ. of Washington Pr.; *CIP.*

LynxGazer Publishing *Imprint of* **LynxGazer Publishing**

LynxGazer Publishing, *(978-0-9984806)* 1313 Westwood Hills Rd., St. Louis Park, MN 55426 USA Tel 952-545-2767; *Imprints:* LynxGazer Publishing (MYID_D_LYNXGAZ)
E-mail: pfrazee@pattifrazee.com.

Lyon, Ernest Media Productions, *(978-0-9741328; 978-0-9991661)* P.O. Box 26101, San Francisco, CA 94126-6101 USA (SAN 255-7460) Tel 415-387-5569 (phone/fax)
E-mail: davidlyon@mindspring.com.

Lyons Pr. *Imprint of* **Globe Pequot Pr., The**

Lypton Publishing, *(978-0-9752780)* 35409 S. Fairbank Point, Drummond Island, MI 49726 USA (SAN 256-0143).

Lyrical Cat Publishing, *(978-0-9969094)* P.O. Box 1072, Millbrae, CA 94030 USA Tel 650-697-1023
E-mail: bros225@gmail.com.

Lyrical Learning, *(978-0-9646367; 978-0-9741635; 978-0-692-37347-7; 978-0-692-38790-0; 978-0-9964731)* 8008 Cardwell Hill, Corvallis, OR 97330 USA Tel 541-754-3579 (phone/fax); Toll Free: 800-761-0906
Web site: http://www.lyricallearning.com.

Lyrical Plight Publishing, *(978-0-692-98448-2; 979-8-218-21349-7)* 2212 Jefferson Ave, Berkeley , CA 94703 USA Tel 510-491-5509
E-mail: fsali324@gmail.com.

Lyrical Plight Publishinh *See* **Lyrical Plight Publishing**

Lyrically Korrect Publishing *See* **Bk. Her Publishing**

M & B Publishing, *(978-0-9758580)* 930 Edgecliffs Dr., Langley, WA 98260 USA
E-mail: wistful@whidbey.com.

M & D Publishing, Inc., *(978-0-9768667)* 2980 SE Fairway W., Stuart, FL 34997 USA Tel 772-286-9781; Fax: 772-286-5169 Do not confuse with M & D Publishing in Phoenix, AZ
E-mail: manddpublishing@bellsouth.net.

M D C T Publishing, *(978-0-9674491; 978-0-692-06540-2; 978-0-692-06544-0; 978-0-578-42274-9; 978-0-578-43146-8; 978-0-578-54083-2; 978-0-578-54088-7; 978-0-578-59982-3)* 31990 SW Village Crest Ln., Wilsonville, OR 97070-8427 USA
E-mail: mdundy@teleport.com
Dist(s): **Partners/West Book Distributors.**

M G L S, Inc., *(978-0-9601682; 978-1-888833)* 700 S. First St., Marshall, MN 56258 USA (SAN 212-2170) Tel 507-532-4311; Fax: 507-532-4313
E-mail: carberry@mgls.com.

M K L Publishing, *(978-0-9746204)* Orders Addr.: P.O. Box 407, Ballston Spa, NY 12020 USA; Edit Addr.: 5019 Fairground Ave., Ballston Spa, NY 12020 USA
E-mail: mklpublishing@aol.com.

MM Co., *(978-1-883473)* 15007 Avon St., Independence, MO 64055 USA Tel 816-246-6365.

M. M. Ray, *(978-1-7376791)* P.O. Box 25381, Memphis, TN 38125 USA Tel 901-624-2575
E-mail: mario06ray@gmail.com.

M Q Pubns., *(978-1-84072; 978-1-897954; 978-1-84601; 978-0-9797400)* 12 The Ivories 6-8 Northampton St., London, N1 2HY GBR Tel 020 7359 2244; Fax: 020 7359 1616; 49 W. 24th St., 8th Flr., New York, NY 10010 Tel 212-223-2320; Fax: 212-675-8026; Toll Free: 800-398-2848
E-mail: mail@mqpublications.com
Web site: http://www.mqpublications.com
Dist(s): **Advanced Global Distribution Services**
Hachette Bk. Group
Mercedes Distribution Ctr., Inc.
Sterling Publishing Co., Inc.
Wybel Marketing Group.

M R L, Inc., *(978-1-892860)* 1445 Cannon St., Louisville, CO 80027-1453 USA Tel 303-666-8164
E-mail: moyazena@aol.com.

M T E, Ltd., *(978-1-888679)* 3095 S. Trenton St., Denver, CO 80231-4164 USA Tel 303-696-0839.

M2M Partners, *(978-0-9768884)* P.O. Box 60923, Phoenix, AZ 85082-0923 USA Toll Free: 800-658-8790
Web site: http://www.mamaroses.com; http://www.printserve.net; http://www.nonnieskitchen.com
Dist(s): **Partners/West Book Distributors.**

MAA Pr. *Imprint of* **American Mathematical Society**

Ma"at American Aborigine Tribal Nation, *(978-1-931671)* Orders Addr.: P.O. Box 10618, Casa Grande, AZ 85130 USA; P.O. Box 10618, Casa Grande, AZ 85130
E-mail: fmpublishing2011@gmail.com; theuniversalmaat@pm.me; mayloemrojo@gmail.com; helpcenterinc@pm.me; aborigine@maatribalnation.org
Web site: http://https://www.theuniversalmaat.org
Dist(s): **Independently Published.**

MAAT Resources, Inc., *(978-0-9624096; 978-1-893447)* 130 East Grand Ave., South San Francisco, CA 94080 USA Tel 650-871-4449; 650-871-4111; Fax: 650-871-4551; *Imprints:* Bilingual Language Materials (Biling Lang)
E-mail: info@blmteachaids.com
Web site: http://www.blmteachaids.com/; http://www.transparentpower.com/.

Mabbul Publishing Co., *(978-0-9762860)* 915 Hunting Horn Way, Evans, GA 30809 USA
Web site: http://www.mabbul.com.

Mabela Publishing, *(978-0-9981307; 978-0-9995544)* 602 1st Ave E, Oskaloosa, IA 52577 USA Tel 641-295-1871; Fax: 641-295-1871
E-mail: karikaydb@gmail.com.

Mabrey, Chris, *(978-0-9979042; 979-8-218-06861-5)* 5410 Nighthawk Dr, Indianapolis, IN 46254 USA Tel 317-513-6413
E-mail: cmabrey@comcast.net.

MAC Productions, *(978-1-878591)* P.O. Box 84, Duvall, WA 98019 USA Tel 425-258-2652; Fax: 425-749-7065
E-mail: macproductions1@verizon.net
Web site: http://www.macsgolfguides.com
Dist(s): **Partners/West Book Distributors.**

MacAdam/Cage Publishing, Inc., *(978-1-878448; 978-0-9673701; 978-1-931561; 978-1-59692)* 155 Sansome St., Suite 550, San Francisco, CA 94104 USA (SAN 299-9730) Tel 415-986-7503; Fax: 415-986-7414
E-mail: david@macadamcage.com
Web site: http://www.macadamcage.com.

Macalester Park Publishing Co., Inc., *(978-0-910924; 978-0-930286; 978-1-886158)* 24558 546th Ave., Austin, MN 55912 USA (SAN 110-8077) Tel 507-396-0135; Toll Free: 800-407-9078
E-mail: macalesterpark@macalesterpark.com
Web site: http://www.macalesterpark.com
Dist(s): **Bookmen, Inc.**
Spring Arbor Distributors, Inc.

Macaronic Pr., *(978-0-9766859; 978-1-59864)* P.O. Box 1542, Sebastopol, CA 95473-1542 USA Tel 707-813-7047; Toll Free: 888-364-8253
E-mail: vivienka@msn.com
Web site: http://www.macaronicpress.com.

Macaulay, David Studio *Imprint of* **Roaring Brook Pr.**

Macauley, Myron Christian, *(978-0-578-05300-4)* 106 Monroe St., No. 2, Brooklyn, NY 11216 USA
E-mail: danae@kgn6.com.

Macaw Books LLC *See* **Kapp Bks. LLC**

MacBeath, Emmaline, *(978-1-7324073)* P.O. Box 55014, Shoreline, WA 98155 USA Tel 541-653-6904
E-mail: emmalinerosebooks@gmail.com
Web site: https://emmalinerosebooks.com.

MacBride, E. J. Pubn., Inc., *(978-1-892511)* 129 W. 147th St., No. 20B, New York, NY 10039 USA; *Imprints:* Disposition Sketch Books (Disposition Sketch).

Macdonald III, Fred G, *(978-1-7340888)* 1131 Bell Creek Rd., Pass Christian, MS 39571 USA Tel 228-255-3141
E-mail: Ststigertraining@aol.com.

MacGill, William V. & Company, *(978-0-9744720)* 1000 N. Lombard Rd., Lombard, IL 60148-1232 USA Tel 800-323-2841; Toll Free Fax: 800-727-3433
E-mail: macgill@macgill.com; nickh@macgill.com
Web site: http://www.macgill.com.

MacGregor Bks., Inc., *(978-0-9833751; 978-0-9962315)* 1371 N. Stevens Blvd., Cleveland, OH 44101 USA Tel 303-349-8957
E-mail: nepal511@yahoo.com.

MacGregor, Doug, *(978-0-9654843; 978-0-9995030)* 1578 Rosada Way, Fort Myers, FL 33901 USA Tel 941-337-3980
E-mail: mactoons@comcast.net.

MacIntyre Purcell Publishing Inc. (CAN) *(978-0-9738063; 978-0-9784784; 978-0-9810941; 978-1-926916; 978-1-927097; 978-1-77276) Dist. by* **BTPS.**

Mack, DeAriesha, *(978-0-578-23705-3; 978-0-578-23891-3; 978-1-7373287)* 5616 Lexington Ave., Apt. 303, Los Angeles, CA 90038 USA
E-mail: astrodeestars@gmail.com
Web site: Astrodeestars.com.

Mack N' Morris Entertainment, *(978-1-950490)* 209 E. Elm St., Bluffton, OH 45817 USA Tel 419-306-7415
E-mail: macknmorris@gmail.com
Dist(s): **Ingram Content Group.**

MacKenzie Press, *(978-1-7334619)* 14835 Sunny Ln., Orland Park, IL 60462 USA Tel 708-269-9130
E-mail: maywoodindustries@sbcglobal.net
Web site: maywoodindustries@sbcglobal.net.

Mackenzie Smiles, LLC, *(978-0-9790347; 978-0-9815761)* P.O. Box 1373, Sausalito, CA 94965 USA Toll Free: 888-800-5978; P.O. Box 1373, Sausalito, CA 94965
Web site: http://www.mackenziesmiles.com.

Mackie, Valencia *See* **CRE Lease Talk, Incorporated**

Mackin, Dan, *(978-0-615-12303-5)* 8395 SE Palm St., Hobe Sound, FL 33455 USA Tel 772-546-3008; Fax: 772-546-5374
E-mail: danmackinartist@aol.com
Web site: http://www.danmackin.com.

Mackinac Island Press, Inc. *Imprint of* **Charlesbridge Publishing, Inc.**

Mackinac Island State Park Commission *See* **Mackinac State Historic Parks**

Mackinac State Historic Parks, *(978-0-911872)* Orders Addr.: P.O. Box 873, Mackinaw City, MI 49701 USA; Edit Addr.: 207 W. Sinclair, Mackinaw City, MI 49701 USA (SAN 202-5981) Tel 231-436-5564; Fax: 231-436-4210.

MackStorm Productions, Inc., *(978-0-9753078)* 1410 Prairie Crossing Dr., West Chicago, IL 60185 USA Tel 630-231-3998
E-mail: marilee@americanslidechart.com.

MacLaren-Cochrane Publishing, *(978-1-64372)* 4020 Stope Dr, Placerville, CA 95667 USA; *Imprints:* Huskies Pub (MYID_X_HUSKIES)
E-mail: Maclarencochranepublishing@gmail.com
Dist(s): **Follett School Solutions.**

MacMenamin Pr., *(978-0-9761414)* P.O. Box 133, Zionsville, PA 18092 USA Tel 610-739-9527
E-mail: sales@macmenaminpress.com
Web site: http://www.macmenaminpress.com.

Macmillan, *(978-0-374; 978-1-4668; 978-1-68274)* Div. of Holtzbrinck Publishing, Orders Addr.: 16365 James Madison Hwy., Gordonsville, VA 22942 USA (SAN 631-5011) Tel 540-672-7600; Fax: 540-672-7664; 540-672-7540 (Customer Service); Toll Free Fax: 800-672-2054 (Order Dept.); Toll Free: 888-330-8477; Edit Addr.: 175 Fifth Ave., 20th Flr., New York, NY 10010

USA Tel 212-674-5151; Fax: 212-677-6487; Toll Free Fax: 800-258-2769; Toll Free: 800-488-5233
E-mail: customerservice@mpsvirginia.com
Web site: http://www.macmillan.com
Dist(s): **Child's World, Inc, The**
Children's Plus, Inc.
Consortium Bk. Sales & Distribution
Follett School Solutions
Cengage Gale
National Bk. Network
ebrary, Inc.

Macmillan Audio, (*978-0-940687; 978-1-55927; 978-1-893564; 978-1-59397; 978-1-59768; 978-1-4272*) Div. of Macmillan, Orders Addr.: 16365 James Madison Hwy., Gordonsville, VA 22942-8501 USA Toll Free Fax: 800-672-2054; Toll Free: 888-330-8477; Edit Addr.: 175 Fifth Ave., Suite 315, New York, NY 10010 USA (SAN 665-1275) Tel 646-307-5000; Fax: 917-534-0980; Toll Free: 800-221-7945
E-mail: audio@hbpub.com
Web site: http://www.macmillanaudio.com
Dist(s): **AudioGO**
Findaway World, LLC
Follett School Solutions
Landmark Audiobooks
MPS
Macmillan.

Macmillan Caribbean (GBR) (*978-0-333; 978-1-4050*) *Dist. by* **Interlink Pub.**

Macmillan Education, Ltd. (GBR) (*978-0-333; 978-1-4050; 978-0-230; 978-1-4472; 978-1-349; 978-1-78632; 978-1-380*) *Dist. by* **Players Pr.**

†Macmillan Publishing Co., Inc., (*978-0-02; 978-0-87605; 978-0-89256*) Orders Addr.: 200 Old Tappan Rd., Old Tappan, NJ 07675 USA (SAN 202-5574)
Dist(s): **MyiLibrary**; *CIP.*

Macmillan Pubs., Ltd. (GBR) (*978-0-330; 978-0-333; 978-1-4050*) *Dist. by* **Trafalgar.**

Macmillan Reference USA *Imprint of* **Cengage Gale**

Macmillan/McGraw-Hill Schl. Div., (*978-0-02*) Div. of The McGraw-Hill Education Group, Orders Addr.: 220 E. Daniel Dale Rd., DeSoto, TX 75115 USA Fax: 972-228-1982; Toll Free: 800-442-9685
Dist(s): **McGraw-Hill Cos., The.**

MacPherson G. International Publishing, Inc., (*978-1-931286*) P.O. Box 1966, Windham, ME 04062 USA Tel 207-893-1252.

Macro Publishing Group, (*978-0-9702699; 978-0-9754130; 978-0-9826829; 978-1-7326225; 978-1-7331782; 978-1-952871*) 1507 E. 53rd Street, No. 858, Chicago, IL 60615 USA Tel 773-263-6512; Toll Free: 888-854-8823 (phone/fax)
E-mail: lissawoodson@aol.com
Dist(s): **INscribe Digital**
Independent Pubs. Group.

Macromedia Education *Imprint of* **Macromedia, Inc.**

Macromedia, Inc., (*978-0-9742273; 978-1-932719*) 600 Townsend St., San Francisco, CA 94103 USA Tel 415-252-2000; Fax: 415-832-5555; Toll Free: 800-457-1774; *Imprints:* Macromedia Education (Macromedia Educ) Do not confuse with Macromedia, Inc. in Lake Placid, NY
Web site: http://www.macromedia.com/education.

Macy, Carolyn, (*978-0-9988838; 978-0-9989127; 978-1-7328604*) 6227 81st Ave. N.E., Norman, OK 73026 USA Tel 405-401-2012
E-mail: cmacy2@aol.com.

Mad Cave Studios *Imprint of* **Mad Cave Studios**

Mad Cave Studios, (*978-1-59707; 978-1-62991; 978-0-9981215; 978-1-5458; 978-1-952303; 978-1-960578*) 8838 SW 129 St., Miami, FL 33176 USA Tel 786-953-4195; *Imprints:* Mad Cave Studios (MYID_Z_MAD CAV); Papercutz (PapercutzMA)
E-mail: cfernandez@madcavestudios.com
Web site: www.madcavestudios.com
Dist(s): **Diamond Comic Distributors, Inc.**
Independent Pubs. Group
Simon & Schuster, Inc.

Mad Creek Bks. *Imprint of* **Ohio State Univ. Pr.**

Mad Dash Co., The, (*978-0-9975965*) 111 Windermere Way, Warwick, RI 02886 USA Tel 401-527-5700
E-mail: lumpybones@gmail.com.

Mad Hatter Publishing, Inc., (*978-0-9994692*) P.O. Box 20973, Ferndale, MI 48220-0973 USA Tel 248-560-7372
E-mail: info@madhatterpublishinginc.com.

Mad Libs *Imprint of* **Penguin Young Readers Group**

Mad Stork Publishing, LLC, (*978-1-7348077; 978-1-7351058; 978-1-954331*) 4932 SW Fairvale Ct, Portland, OR 97221 USA Tel 914-506-2430
E-mail: profstork@gmail.com; nmrosen@gmail.com
Web site: www.profstork.com; www.madstorkpublishing.com; www.professorstork.com.

Mad Yak Pr., (*978-0-9717995*) 8232 Styers Ct., Laurel, MD 20723-2100 USA Tel 301-317-8817
Dist(s): **Diamond Comic Distributors, Inc.**
Diamond Bk. Distributors.

Madala, Amanda, (*979-8-9850239*) 302 S. Stratford Dr., Tucson, AZ 85716 USA Tel 303-570-0305
E-mail: amandamadala6@hotmail.com.

Madame Cat Publishing, (*978-0-9983859*) 6491 Smooth Thorn Ct, Jacksonville, FL 32258 USA Tel 904-955-9967
E-mail: meldow14@gmail.com.

Madame Fifi Pubns., (*978-0-9667418; 978-0-9762900; 978-0-9821707*) P.O. Box 310967, Newington, CT 06131-0967 USA
Web site: http://www.madamefifi3.com.

Madd Mindz Publishing, Inc., (*978-0-9802262*) P.O. Box 20437, Brooklyn, NY 11202-0437 USA Tel 347-661-4030; Fax: 718-425-9919
E-mail: C.Brandon@MaddMindzPublishing.com
Web site: http://www.maddmindzpublishing.com.

Maddness, Inc., (*978-0-9761619*) P.O. Box 76551, Oklahoma City, OK 73147-2551 USA
E-mail: osheashamir@aol.com
Web site: http://www.osheashamir.com.

Mader, Lothar, (*978-0-615-24577-5; 978-0-578-05621-0*) 2130 Professional Dr., Suite 240, Roseville, CA 95661 USA
Dist(s): **Lulu Pr., Inc.**

Madison Ave. & Co., (*978-1-7374869*) 2244 Menlo Ave, Glenside, PA 19038-4740 USA Tel 267-549-3645
E-mail: dawnls32@gmail.com.

Madison Carter Janes *See* **Bjork Print**

Madison, Dr. Ron *See* **Ned's Head Productions**

Maerkle Pr., (*978-0-9721966; 978-0-9819479; 979-8-9852522*) 66 E. Shore Blvd., Timberlake, OH 44095 USA Tel 440-269-8653; Fax: 440-269-8035
Web site: http://www.maerklepress.com.

Maerov, Jeffrey, (*978-0-578-11402-6; 978-0-578-11504-7*) 24 Fecamp, Newport Coast, CA 92657 USA.

Maestro Classics, (*978-1-932684*) Div. of Simon & Simon, LLC, Orders Addr.: 1745 Broadway 17th Fl, New York, NY 10019 USA Tel 212-519-9847
E-mail: bsimon@maestroclassics.com
Web site: http://www.MaestroClassics.com
Dist(s): **CD Baby**
Follett School Solutions.

Maestro Heights, (*978-1-7346937*) 1248 Beecher Ave, Galesburg, IL 61401 USA Tel 309-323-9799
E-mail: gail.masinda@yahoo.com
Web site: gailmasinda.com.

Maestro Learning, (*978-0-9740533*) 24 Chilton St., Cambridge, MA 02138-6802 USA
E-mail: peter@maestrolearning.com
Web site: http://www.maestrolearning.com.

MaestroMedia Pr., (*978-0-9773731*) 408 Pearl St., Richmond, IN 47374 USA Tel 765-962-8380
E-mail: rosecitysp@msn.com.

Maeva, Ediciones, S.A. (ESP) (*978-84-86478; 978-84-95354; 978-84-92695; 978-84-96231; 978-84-96748; 978-84-15120; 978-84-15532; 978-84-15893; 978-84-17108*) *Dist. by* **Lectorum Pubns.**

Mafiq Foundation, Inc., (*978-0-9700372*) P.O. Box 4916, Silver Spring, MD 20914-4916 USA Tel 301-236-0233 (phone/fax)
E-mail: msuc@hotmail.com.

Mage Pubs., Inc., (*978-0-934211; 978-1-933823; 978-1-949445*) PO Box 70881, Chevy Chase, MD 20815 USA (SAN 693-0476)
E-mail: as@mage.com
Web site: http://www.mage.com.

Magee, Burke & Glenna, (*978-0-9748424*) Orders Addr.: P.O. Box 581, Carnation, WA 98014 USA; Edit Addr.: 2015 290th Ave., NE, Carnation, WA 98014 USA
E-mail: rtg@returntogod.com
Web site: http://www.returntogod.com.

Maggid *Imprint of* **Toby Pr. LLC, The**

Maggie Keefe, (*978-0-578-35743-0; 978-0-578-38048-3; 979-8-9864872*) 776 Morrill Rd, Danville, VT 05828 USA Tel 979-500-5592
E-mail: Neomaggie@yahoo.com.

MaggieMooseTracks, (*978-0-9895205*) P.O. Box 764, Nixon, TX 78140 USA Tel 650-280-0248
E-mail: girlfins@aol.com.

Magic Cat (GBR) (*978-1-913520-38-0*) *Dist. by* **Abrams.**

Magic Crystal Pr., (*978-0-9986487*) 727 W. 7th St. Suite 503, Los Angeles, CA 90017 USA Tel 949-278-8005
E-mail: jrc@magiccrystalpress.com
Web site: www.magiccrystalpress.com.

Magic Factory, LLC, The, (*978-1-938155*) Orders Addr.: 3818 Somerset Dr., Durham, NC 27707 USA; Edit Addr.: 3818 Somerset Dr., Durham, NC 27707 USA
E-mail: orders@magicfactory.com; orders@magicfactory.com; info@magicfactory.com; books@magicfactory.com
Web site: http://magicfactory.com; http://signofthesandman.com; http://rangerbaldy.com.

Magic Lamp Pr., (*978-1-56891; 978-1-882629*) Div. of Magic Lamp Productions, 1838 Washington Way, Venice, CA 90291-4704 USA (SAN 256-1670) Tel 310-822-2985; Fax: 310-827-9123; Toll Free: 800-367-9661
E-mail: videopage@earthlink.net
Web site: http://www.magiclamppress.com
Dist(s): **Smashwords.**

Magic Lamp Productions *See* **Magic Lamp Pr.**

Magic Moon Bks., LLC, (*978-0-615-97740-9; 978-0-9983137; 979-8-9876050*) 915 S 2560 E, Spanish Fork, UT 84660 USA Tel 385-495-6393
Web site: http://magicmoonchildrensbooks.com
Dist(s): **CreateSpace Independent Publishing Platform.**

Magic Mountain Pr., (*978-0-9715946; 978-1-7338765*) P.O. Box 1933, Asheville, NC 28802 USA Tel 828-231-0041 Do not confuse with Magic Mountain Press, The in Lafayette, IN
E-mail: karon@ashevillerealtygroup.com
Web site: http://www.the12keys.com.

Magic of African Rhythm (TMOAR), The, (*978-0-9820926*) Orders Addr.: P.O. Box 14724, Raleigh, NC 27620-4724 USA Tel 919-828-1906; Fax: 419-781-8209
E-mail: shabutaso@gmail.com.

Magic Penny Pr., (*978-0-9982777*) 3336 Lone Hill Ln, Encinitas, CA 92024 USA Tel 858-367-8541
E-mail: massiveart@gmail.com.

Magic Penny Reading *See* **Magic Penny Reading**

Magic Penny Reading, (*978-0-9761987; 978-0-9899114*) 8659 Finch Rd., Colden, NY 14033 USA Tel 800-873-0396; Fax: 888-728-0754
E-mail: sandyschneider@magicpennyreading.org
Web site: http://magicpennyreading.org.

Magic Picture Frame Studio, LLC, (*978-0-9749269*) Orders Addr.: P.O. Box 2603, Issaquah, WA 98027 USA Tel 425-222-7562
E-mail: publisher@magicpictureframe.com; mvm@magicpictureframe.com; class@magicpictureframe.com
Web site: http://www.magicpictureframe.com
Dist(s): **Baker & Taylor Publisher Services (BTPS).**

Magic Propaganda Mill, (*978-0-9760117*) Please Send All Correspondence To: Info@mpmill.com, Brooklyn, NY 11238 USA
E-mail: info@mpmill.com
Web site: http://www.magicpropagandamill.com.

Magic Space, (*978-0-615-32034-2; 978-0-9983113*) 14749 Croft St., Dade City, FL 33525 USA Tel 352-521-5653.

Magic Valley Pubs., (*978-0-9716681; 978-0-9774833; 978-0-9785509; 978-0-9800879; 978-0-9821496; 978-0-9845275*) 6390 E. Willow St., Long Beach, CA 90815 USA Tel 562-795-0289; Fax: 562-795-0490 Do not confuse with Magic Valley Publishers in Burly, ID
Web site: http://www.magicvalleypub.com.

Magic Wagon, (*978-1-60270; 978-1-61641*) Div. of ADBO Publishing Group, Orders Addr.: P.O. Box 398166, Minneapolis, MN 55439-8166 USA Fax: 952-831-1632; Toll Free: 800-458-8399; Edit Addr.: 8000 W. 78th St., Suite 310, Edina, MN 55439 USA Toll Free: 800-458-8399; *Imprints:* Looking Glass Library (LookngGlassLib); Graphic Planet - Fiction (Graphic Planet); Short Tales (Short Tales); Calico Chapter Books (CalicoChap Bks); Spellbound (SpellboundUSA)
E-mail: info@abdopublishing.com
Web site: http://www.abdopublishing.com
Dist(s): **ABDO Publishing Co.**
Carson-Dellosa Publishing, LLC
Follett School Solutions
MyiLibrary.

Magic Woman Pubns., (*978-0-9760062*) 1527 Veteran Ave., Suite 7, Los Angeles, CA 90024-5566 USA Tel 310-478-7743; Fax: 310-478-9892
E-mail: artdivin@yahoo.com
Web site: http://www.magicwomanpublications.com.

Magic Wordweaver Pr., (*978-0-9754116; 978-0-615-12456-8*) Orders Addr.: P.O. Box 1315, Conifer, CO 80433 USA (SAN 255-8459) Tel 303-838-7515 (phone/fax); Edit Addr.: 29580 S. Sunset Trail, Conifer, CO 80433 USA
E-mail: premalee108@yahoo.com.

Magic Works Publishing & Production, (*978-0-9799545*) 27 Greenmoor, Irvine, CA 92614 USA Tel 714-309-4824; Fax: 949-651-8895; *Imprints:* Gatekeeper Press (MYID_L_GATEKEEPER PRESA)
E-mail: selina@superachievement.net
Web site: http://SuperAchievement.net.

Magical Beginnings, (*978-0-692-54966-7; 978-0-692-59310-3; 978-0-692-61084-8; 978-0-692-61356-6; 978-0-692-62334-3; 978-0-9973594; 978-0-692-65326-5; 978-0-692-71224-5*) 10940 S. Parker Rd. No. 791, Parker, CO 80134-7440 USA
Web site: www.FairyVillageBooks.com
Dist(s): **CreateSpace Independent Publishing Platform.**

Magical Bk. Works, (*978-1-943196; 978-0-692-42748-4; 978-0-692-44762-8; 978-0-692-57982-4; 978-0-692-61750-2; 978-0-692-66030-0; 978-0-692-68311-8; 978-0-692-71417-1; 978-0-692-71697-7*) 2597 Amethyst Dr., Suite 10, Santa Clara, CA 95051-1154 USA Tel 408-480-0505; Fax: 512-727-0580
E-mail: pennyannecole@gmail.com
Web site: www.magicalbookworks.com
Dist(s): **CreateSpace Independent Publishing Platform.**

Magical Child Bks. *Imprint of* **Shades of White**

Magical Creations, (*978-0-9744879*) P.O. Box 324, Chicago Park, CA 95712 USA Tel 530-477-7429
E-mail: doris_rainville@hotmail.com.

Magical Mischief Maker, (*978-0-9754004*) P.O. Box 1075, Douglasville, GA 30133 USA
Web site: http://www.magicalmischiefmaker.com.

MagicStar Inc., (*978-0-9821387*) 2021 Midwest Rd., Suite 200, Oak Brook, IL 60523 USA (SAN 857-3336) Tel 510-740-4045
E-mail: publisher@magiscstarpub.com
Web site: http://www.magicstarpub.com.

Magination, (*978-1-881597*) 3579 E. Foothill Blvd., No. 330, Pasadena, CA 91107 USA Tel 626-306-1190; Fax: 626-306-1193.

Magination Pr. *Imprint of* **American Psychological Assn.**

Magiscule Publishing Group, L.L.C., (*978-0-9772232*) 12 Armstrong Ave., Suite 3 W., Providence, RI 02903 USA Fax: 401-861-7030
E-mail: Krystalstream@excite.com.

Magliano, Robert, (*978-0-578-62079-4; 978-0-578-96470-6; 978-0-578-96471-3*) 301 Elizabeth St., 2C, New York, NY 10012 USA Tel 914-525-7565
E-mail: Robert.anthony.magliano@gmail.com
Dist(s): **Ingram Content Group.**

Maglione, Concetta A., (*978-0-692-12892-3; 978-0-578-42594-8; 978-0-578-43322-6; 978-0-578-47604-9; 978-0-578-50761-3; 978-0-578-56312-1; 978-0-578-56314-5; 978-0-578-62037-4; 978-0-578-66580-1; 978-0-578-66612-9; 978-0-578-67922-8; 978-0-578-67923-5; 978-0-578-77845-7) 8 Thorngate Ct., Princeton, NJ 08540 USA Tel 609-577-1453*
E-mail: concettascanvas@gmail.com
Web site: concettascanvas.com.

Magna Large Print Bks. (GBR) (*978-0-7505; 978-0-86009; 978-1-84137; 978-1-85057; 978-1-78502*) *Dist. by* **Ulverscroft US.**

Magnatic Music, (*978-0-9719897*) 13806 Delaney Rd., Dale City, VA 22193 USA
E-mail: alstonsongs@aol.com.

Magner Publishing *See* **Magner Publishing & American Binding & Publishing**

Magner Publishing & American Binding & Publishing, (*978-1-929416; 978-1-60080*) P.O. Box 60049, Corpus Christi, TX 78466 USA Tel 361-658-4221; Toll Free: 800-863-3708
E-mail: rmmagner@pyramid3.net
Web site: http://www.americanbindingpublishing.com.

Magness, Robert Pubns., LLC, (*978-0-9774577*) 1412 Kent St., Sturgis, MI 49091-2334 USA Tel 269-651-7473
E-mail: sengam@netzero.com.

Magnetar Venture Group, LLC, (*978-0-692-37543-3; 978-0-9861212*) P.O. Box 540324, Houston, TX 77254 USA Tel 5127632652
Dist(s): **CreateSpace Independent Publishing Platform.**

Magnetic Image, Inc., (*978-0-9678542*) 900 SW 13th St., Boca Raton, FL 33486 USA
E-mail: info@magneticimageinc.com
Web site: http://www.magneticimageinc.com.

Magnetic Pr., (*978-1-942367; 978-1-951719; 978-1-962413*) 5415 N Sheridan Rd Apt 5101, CHICAGO, IL 60640 USA Tel 312-259-7356
E-mail: mike@magnetic-press.com
Web site: www.magnetic-press.com
Dist(s): **Diamond Comic Distributors, Inc.**

Magni Co., The, (*978-1-882330; 978-1-937026*) Orders Addr.: 181 GRAND Ave. Suite 212, SOUTHLAKE, TX 76092 USA Tel 972-540-2050; Fax: 972-540-1057; Edit Addr.: 7106 Wellington Point Rd., McKinney, TX 75072 USA Tel 469-214-4148; Fax: 972-540-1057
E-mail: sales@magnico.com; info@magnico.com
Web site: http://www.magnico.com
Dist(s): **BPC.**

Magnolia, (*978-0-578-53453-4; 978-1-7363928*) 1093 Golden Grove Dr., The Villages, FL 32162 USA Tel 908-601-7037; Fax: 352-268-3291
E-mail: dbraddom@gmail.com.

Magnolia Nook Pubns., (*978-0-692-80164-2; 978-0-692-06306-4*) 145 Delatte Ln., Gheens, LA 70355 USA Tel 985-258-6351
E-mail: magnolianook@yahoo.com
Web site: https://magnolianookpublications.com.

Magpie Children's Bks., (*978-1-7321012*) 158 N 300 E, Provo, UT 84606 USA Tel 623-742-5820
E-mail: morty.joshua@gmail.com
Web site: www.joshualeemortensen.com.

Magpie Press *See* **Magpie Pr., Pine Mountain Club, CA**

Magpie Pr., Pine Mountain Club, CA, Orders Addr.: P.O. Box 6434, Pine Mountain Club, CA 93222-6434 USA Tel 661-242-1265 (phone/fax) Do not confuse with Magpie Pr. in Wallington, NJ
E-mail: MagSmith1265@msn.com
Web site: www.magpiepress.com.

Magrane, Etna International, (*978-0-9741167*) 8 Hill Point Ave., San Francisco, CA 94117 USA Tel 415-681-5157; Fax: 415-681-5820
E-mail: emagrane@aol.com.

Magsimba Pr., (*978-1-932956*) 1821 Bruce Rd., NE, Atlanta, GA 30329-2508 USA Tel 404-633-9153
E-mail: info@magsimba.org
Web site: http://www.magsimba.org; http://www.tagalog1.com/Ordinary/Learn_Filipino.jsp
Dist(s): **Quality Bks., Inc.**

Mahle,, Robin D. Author *See* **Whiskey & Willow Publishing**

Mahogany Bard Pr., (*978-1-7365395*) 2418 Clipper's Sq. 0, HOUSTON, TX 77058 USA Tel 2819170705
E-mail: benjaminhewett@verizon.net
Dist(s): **Ingram Content Group.**

Maia Ocean Printing, (*978-0-692-08522-6*) 2101 E Trant Rd., Kingsville, TX 78363 USA Tel 305-780-9062
E-mail: simplebychoice@gmail.com
Dist(s): **Ingram Content Group.**

Mailbox Bks., The *Imprint of* **Education Ctr., Inc.**

Main Asset Pubns., (*978-0-9667617*) P.O. Box 1153, Teaneck, NJ 07666 USA Tel 201-837-6400; Fax: 201-837-8842
E-mail: mathispublishing@aol.com
Web site: http://www.whyarentumarried.com.

Main Coon Publishing, (*978-0-9983035*) 58 St. George Rd., Wingdale, NY 12594 USA Tel 845-832-6076
E-mail: osusanna@outlook.com.

Main Event Pr., (*978-0-9774129*) 1714 Boxwood Cir., Saint Cloud, MN 56303-0148 USA.

Main Frame Pr., (*978-0-615-49914-7; 978-0-9856790*) 858 Third Ave. No. 320, Chula Vista, CA 91911 USA Tel 619-253-4312
E-mail: gilbert@gilbertklein.com
Web site: www.football101.net.

Main Street Pubns., (*978-0-9745033*) 11810 Dice Rd., Freeland, MI 48623 USA.

Main Street Publishing, Incorporated *See* **Yetto Publishing Co.**

Maine Authors Publishing, (*978-0-9788008; 978-0-9825684; 978-0-9827021; 978-1-936447; 978-1-938883; 978-1-63381*) 12 High St, Thomaston, ME 04861 USA (SAN 851-660X) Tel 207-594-0090
E-mail: info@custommuseumpublishing.com
Web site: www.maineauthorspublishing.com.

Maine Mediator, The, (*978-0-9991718*) 25 Stony Brook Way, Bar Harbor, ME 04609 USA Tel 601-618-6447
E-mail: trishmadell@gmail.com.

Mainspring Foundations Publishing, (*978-1-7368988*) P.O. Box PO Box 186, Riva, MD 21140 USA Tel 202-400-5027
E-mail: mfarnsworth.transformations@gmail.com
Web site: www.mainspringfoundations.com.

MainSpringBks., (*978-1-946854; 978-1-947352; 978-1-64133*) 5901 W Century Blvd. Suite 750, Los Angeles, CA 90045 USA
E-mail: production@mainspringbooks.com
Web site: https://mainspringbooks.com/.

Mainstay, LLC, (*978-0-9798854*) 4134 W. View Pointe Dr., Highland, UT 84003 USA
Web site: http://www.MainstayEducation.com.

Mainstay Publishing, (*978-0-9832901; 978-0-9899479*) Mainstay Publishing P.O. Box 293, Middletown, DE 19709 USA Tel 302-223-6636
E-mail: denise@mainstaypublishing.com.

Mainstream Ctr., Schl. for the Deaf, The, (*978-0-9797287*) 48 Round Hill Rd., Northampton, MA 01060-2124 USA Tel 413-582-1121; Fax: 413-586-6654
E-mail: akot@clarkeschool.org
Web site: http://www.clarkeschool.org.

Mainstream Connections Publishing, (*978-1-60336*) 10103 Queens Cir., Ocean City, MD 21842 USA Tel

410-213-7861 fax or email requests; *Imprints:* Adventures of Everyday Geniuses, The (Adv Evryday)
E-mail: barb.esham@mainstreamconnections.org; lisa.spielman@mainstreamconnections.org
Web site: http://www.mainstreamconnections.org
Dist(s): **Brodart Co.**
Emery-Pratt Co.
Follett School Solutions
Quality Bks., Inc.
Yankee Bk. Peddler, Inc.

lainstreet Systems & Software Inc., *(978-0-9726871)* P.O. Box 577, Harleysville, PA 19438-0577 USA (SAN 255-335X) Toll Free: 800-257-4535
E-mail: epwhelan@netcarrier.com
Web site: http://www.promotecopyrights.com.

laire, Lucy Bedoya, *(978-0-9768436)* Orders Addr.: P.O. Box 2632, Westport, CT 06880 USA Tel 203-454-5204; Fax: 203-454-5204; Edit Addr.: 19 River Oak Rd., Westport, CT 06880 USA
E-mail: twelvetreasures@yahoo.com
Dist(s): **Raimond Graphics Inc.**

Majestic Eagle Publishing, *(978-0-9797495)* Div. of James J. Brown & Assoc., Inc., 6649 Navajo, Lincolnwood, IL 60712 USA Tel 847-679-3447; Fax: 847-679-6191
E-mail: jola1@aol.com.

Majestic Kids *Imprint of* **MP Pubns., Inc.**

Majestic Publishing, LLC, *(978-0-9755314; 978-1-942156)* Orders Addr.: P.O. Box 1560, Lithonia, GA 30058 USA Tel 770-482-9129 Do not confuse with Majestic Publishing, LLC in Santa Barbara, CA
E-mail: majpublish@gmail.com
Web site: http://www.majesticpublishing.net.

Majesty Publishing, *(978-0-9754839)* 12 Paddock Ln., Hampton, VA 23669 USA
E-mail: customerservice@faithfrontier.com
Web site: http://www.faithfrontier.com.

Major, Christina, *(978-0-692-02524-6; 978-0-692-46530-1; 978-1-7374635)*
E-mail: delphina2k@gmail.com
Web site: http://www.horizonscape.com.

Major Masterpieces *See* **Major Masterpieces Ltd.**

Major Masterpieces Ltd., *(978-0-692-52666-8; 978-1-7336564)* 1842 First Ave., Pottsville, PA 17901 USA Tel 570-622-9364
E-mail: nannettebrophymajor@gmail.com
Web site: www.majormasterpieces.com.

Majority Press, Incorporated, The *See* **Majority Pr., The**

Majority Pr., The, *(978-0-912469)* Orders Addr.: 46 Development Rd., Fitchburg, MA 01420 USA (SAN 249-3012) Tel 978-342-9676; Fax: 978-348-1233; Edit Addr.: P.O. Box 538, Dover, MA 02030 USA (SAN 265-2757) Tel 508-744-6097 (phone/fax)
E-mail: tmpress@earthlink.net
Web site: http://www.themajoritypress.com
Dist(s): **A & B Distributors & Pubs. Group**
Lexicon Pubns., Inc.

Majzik, Bill *See* **Mill Creek Metro Publishing**

Makai Concepts, LLC, *(978-0-9744035)* Orders Addr.: 3 King William Ct., Hilton Head Island, SC 29926 USA (SAN 255-6219)
E-mail: betsys@hargray.com.

Makdan Publishing, *(978-0-9819283)* P.O. Box 7560, Bonney Lake, WA 98391 USA Tel 253-720-1059
E-mail: jimlandgraf@hotmail.com.

Make Believe Ideas (GBR) *(978-1-905051; 978-1-84610; 978-1-84879; 978-1-78065; 978-1-78235; 978-1-78393; 978-1-78598)* *Dist. by* **Nelson.**

Make Believe Ideas (GBR) *(978-1-905051; 978-1-84610; 978-1-84879; 978-1-78065; 978-1-78235; 978-1-78393; 978-1-78598)* *Dist. by* **Scholastic Inc.**

MAKE BELIEVE PUBLISHING, *(978-0-692-90006-2; 978-0-9998833; 978-1-7359784)* P.O. Box 1009, BLANCHARD, OK 73010 USA Tel 661-549-2498
E-mail: MakeBelieve63@hotmail.com
Web site: makebelievepublishing.com; www.authordebbiefogle.com
Dist(s): **CreateSpace Independent Publishing Platform.**

Make Me A Story Pr., *(978-1-878847)* 1737 N. 2580 E. Rd., Sheldon, IL 60966 USA Tel 815-429-3501 (phone/fax)
E-mail: info@earthesquirrel.com
Web site: http://www.earthesquirrel.com.

Make Me a World *Imprint of* **Random Hse. Children's Bks.**

Make-A-Wish Middle Tennessee, *(978-0-578-54356-7; 978-0-578-54892-0; 978-0-578-61226-3; 978-0-578-63451-7)* 600 Hill Ave. Suite 201, Nashville, TN 37210 USA Tel 615-221-2200
E-mail: Ltemple@middletennessee.wish.org
Dist(s): **Ingram Content Group.**

Make-believe Pr. LLC, *(978-1-7323686)* P.O. Box P.O. Box 30114, Columbia, MO 65205 USA Tel 310-906-7730
E-mail: masterofmakebelieve@gmail.com
Web site: www.make-believepress.com.

Maker, Azmaira H. *See* **Aspiring Families Press**

Making Ripples Publishing, *(979-8-9852783)* 2500 Fathers Care Dr., Westminster, MD 21157 USA Tel 443-992-2071
E-mail: susanaturfle369@gmail.com
Web site: https://makingripplespublishing.wordpress.com.

Makwa Enewed *Imprint of* **Michigan State Univ. Pr.**

Malachite Quills Publishing *See* **MQuills Publishing**

Malamih Publishing Hse., *(978-0-9820804)* 4311 Jamboree Rd., No. 170, Newport Beach, CA 92660 USA.

Malamute Pr., *(978-0-9722180)* Orders Addr.: P.O. Box W, Aspen, CO 81612 USA; Edit Addr.: P.O. Box W, Aspen, CO 81612-7424 USA
E-mail: info@dodogsvote.com; sales@malamutepress.com
Web site: http://www.malamutepress.com.

Malbrough, Michael, *(978-0-9758883)* 163-167 N. Pk. St., Apt. 5, East Orange, NJ 07019 USA.

Malcolm Down Publishing Ltd. (GBR) *(978-1-910786; 978-1-912863)* *Dist. by* **BTPS.**

Malekowsky, Marie, *(978-1-7361055)* P.O. Box 3145, Montclair, CA 91763 USA Tel 909-786-6751
E-mail: MMalekowsky@gmail.com.

Malene Kai Bell, *(979-8-218-04493-0; 979-8-218-14583-5)* 5603 Foxwood Dr. Apt A., Oak Park, CA 91377 USA Tel 747-755-9670
E-mail: malenebell@gmail.com.

Malenga, Mubita, *(978-0-9991946; 978-0-578-40787-6; 978-1-7345744; 979-8-218-11666-8)* 8641 N. Servite Dr. Unit 205, Milwaukee, WI 53223 USA Tel 414-688-5333
E-mail: mubitam@yahoo.com.

Malibu Bks. for Children, *(978-1-929084)* Div. of Malibu Films, Inc., 48 Broad St., No. 134, Red Bank, NJ 07701 USA Tel 732-933-0446 (phone/fax); Toll Free: 888-629-9947 (phone/fax)
E-mail: malibuinc@aol.com
Web site: http://www.malibubooks.com.

Malik, Sakinah A. *See* **EDR**

Malinda Real Estate Holding LLC, *(978-1-954075)* 446 W HILLSBORO BLVD 0, DEERFIELD BEACH, FL 33441 USA Tel ?+39 351 7983717
E-mail: malindareholding@gmail.com
Dist(s): **Ingram Content Group.**

Malka, Artist Naomi, *(978-1-950411)* 4300 N. Ocean Blvd., Fort Lauderdale, FL 33308 USA Tel 813-308-4451
E-mail: henry@artistnaomimalka.com
Web site: www.artistnaomimalka.com.

Mallon Publishing (AUS) *(978-1-875696)* *Dist. by* **D C D.**

Malone-Ballard Book Publishers, *(978-0-9729484)* 160 S. Third St., Lansing, IA 52151 USA Tel 319-389-7174 (phone/fax)
Web site: http://www.malone-ballard.com
Dist(s): **Partners Bk. Distributing, Inc.**

Malor Bks. *Imprint of* **I S H K**

Malpaso Ediciones SL (ESP) *(978-84-15996; 978-84-16420; 978-84-17081)* *Dist. by* **IPG Chicago.**

Malzone, Carol, *(978-0-578-11108-7; 978-0-578-83952-3)* 1018 Royal Pass Rd., Tampa, FL 33602 USA.

Mama Incense Publishing, *(978-0-9761523)* P.O. Box 4635, Long Beach, CA 90804-9998 USA Tel 310-490-9097
E-mail: mama@mamaincense.com
Web site: http://www.mamaincense.com.

Mama Koku's Storytellin', *(978-0-615-50391-2; 978-0-578-77641-5; 979-8-218-20398-6; 979-8-9885366)* 1769 Mercer Ave., College Park, GA 30337 USA Tel 404-313-2038
E-mail: koku@mamakoku.com.

Mama Specific Productions, *(978-0-9749480)* P.O. Box 110393, Cleveland, OH 44111-0393 USA Tel 440-396-1963; Fax: 801-640-2494; *Imprints:* MSPpress (MSPpr)
E-mail: info@msppress.com; trula@MSPpress.com
Web site: http://www.msppress.com.

Mama's Boyz, Inc., *(978-0-9796132; 978-1-7323184)* 304 Main Ave. #114, Norwalk, CT 06851 USA (SAN 854-1914)
E-mail: jerrycraft@aol.com
Web site: http://www.jerrycraft.net
Dist(s): **Follett School Solutions.**

MaMbabooks.com, *(978-0-9817448; 978-0-9887867; 978-1-948407; 978-1-954251)* Div. of Mamba Books & Publishing, 355 Liberty St., Dendron, VA 23839 USA
E-mail: mambabooks@gmail.com
Web site: http://www.mambabooks.com; http://www.mambabooks.biz.

Mambooks (AUS) *(978-0-9751837)* *Dist. by* **Ingram Bk Co.**

Mammi, Joseph John, *(978-0-9988090)* 669 Dulaney Rd NW, Floyd, VA 24091-3607 USA Tel 540-763-2253
E-mail: jjmammi@lycos.com.

Mammoth, Math, *(978-1-942715; 978-1-954358; 978-1-954379; 978-1-954380)* 915 Lounds St., Inverness, FL 34450 USA Tel 813-728-9831
E-mail: maria_miller@mathmammoth.com
Web site: www.mathmammoth.com.

Mamoo Hse., *(978-1-933014)* 17 W. Browning Rd., Collingswood, NJ 08108 USA Tel 856-858-6616
E-mail: melisma@earthlink.net
Web site: http://www.mamoohouse.com.

MAMP Creations, *(978-0-9772210)* P.O. Box 1316 Landmark Trail South, Hopkins, MN 55343 USA Tel 952-938-9320 (phone/fax); *Imprints:* Phil the Pill & Friends (Phil PillFrnds)
E-mail: APritcha6@gmail.com; mampcreations@gmail.com
Web site: http://https://www.amazon.com/M.-Ann-Machen-Pritchard/e/B002BM9DLM/; http://www.cafepress.com/mampcreations.

Management Services, *(978-0-9747418)* 302 S. 2nd St. Apt. 711, Champaign, IL 61820-4141 USA Do not confuse with Managment Services Incorporated in Atlanta, GA
E-mail: aepelbaum@yahoo.com
Web site: http://moscowtechchicago.com.

Manassas Museum, The, *(978-1-886826)* Orders Addr.: P.O. Box 560, Manassas, VA 20108 USA Tel 703-368-1873; Edit Addr.: 9101 Prince William St., Manassas, VA 201110-5615 USA
Web site: http://www.manassasmuseum.org.

Mance Ian Wright, *(978-0-578-42961-8)* 600 Benton St., Mountain Home, AR 72653 USA Tel 870-580-0166
E-mail: adaniels.wright@gmail.com
Dist(s): **Ingram Content Group.**

Manchester Univ. Pr. (GBR) *(978-0-7190; 978-1-84779; 978-1-5261; 978-1-78499; 978-1-78170)* *Dist. by* **TwoRivers.**

Mandala Publishing, *(978-0-945475; 978-1-886069; 978-1-932771; 978-1-60109)* 3160 Kerner Blvd. Ste. 108, San Rafael, CA 94901-5454 USA Toll Free: 800-688-2218 (orders only); *Imprints:* Earth Aware Editions (Earth Aware)
E-mail: info@mandala.org
Web site: http://www.mandala.org; http://earthawareeditions.com/catalog/
Dist(s): **MyiLibrary**
Simon & Schuster, Inc.

Mandala Publishing Group *See* **Mandala Publishing**

Mandel Vilar Pr., *(978-1-941493; 978-1-942134)* 19 Oxford Ct., Simsbury, CT 06070 USA Tel 860-431-5269; *Imprints:* Moment Books (MYID_G_MOMENT)
E-mail: Robert@americasforconservation.org
Web site: www.mvpublishers.org
Dist(s): **Consortium Bk. Sales & Distribution.**

Mandell, Ted, *(978-0-9749156)* 2232 Pine Creek Ct., South Bend, IN 46628 USA Tel 574-631-6953
E-mail: tmandell@nd.edu.

Mandeville, Terry M., *(978-0-9762475)* 7933 NE 124th St., Kirkland, WA 98034 USA
E-mail: terrymand@aol.com.

M&J Southwest, Inc., *(978-0-9744534)* 4402 E. Desert Willow Rd., Phoenix, AZ 85044 USA Tel 480-940-4046
E-mail: michaelc@gotwords.com
Web site: http://www.gotwords.com.

Mandolin House *See* **Kush Univ. Pr.**

Mandolin Hse. *Imprint of* **Kush Univ. Pr.**

Mandracchia Bks. *Imprint of* **Mandracchia, Charles**

Mandracchia, Charles, *(978-0-9721957)* 7914 Rockaway Beach Blvd. Apt. 6L, Rockaway Beac, NY 11693-2081 USA; *Imprints:* Mandracchia Books (Mandracchia Bks)
E-mail: charlesmandracchia@yahoo.com
Web site: http://www.kungfoogrannys.com; http://www.showtoonz.com.

Mandragora (ITA) *(978-88-7461; 978-88-85957)* *Dist. by* **Natl Bk Netwk.**

Mandy & Andy Bks., Inc., *(978-0-9772757)* 124 Meridian Ave., Poinciana, FL 34759-3241 USA (SAN 257-1765) Tel 407-319-3880; 863-427-4643
E-mail: wadams23@cfl.rr.com
Web site: http://mandyandandybooks.com.

Mandy & Pandy Bks., LLC, *(978-0-9800156; 978-0-9834411)* 2590 Cook Creek Ct., Ann Arbor, MI 48103 USA Tel 734-904-1916
E-mail: tsinkule@heulegordon.com
Dist(s): **China Books & Periodicals, Inc.**

Manga 18 *Imprint of* **Central Park Media Corp.**

Manga Classics Inc., *(978-1-947808)* 2194 Esperanca Ave., Santa Clara, CA 95054 USA Tel 647-400-8366; Fax: 647-400-8366
E-mail: erikko@gmail.com
Web site: www.mangaclassics.com
Dist(s): **Diamond Comic Distributors, Inc.**
Diamond Bk. Distributors.

Manga Punk, *(978-0-9748966)* P.O. Box 966, Meadows of Dan, VA 24120 USA
Web site: http://www.mangapunk.com.

MANGACANDY, LLC, *(978-0-9785891)* 13937 W. 73rd St., Shawnee, KS 66216 USA Tel 913-638-9940
E-mail: nami.bunny@gmail.com
Web site: http://www.mangacandy.com.

Mango (FRA) *(978-2-7404; 978-2-84270; 978-2-910635)* *Dist. by* **Distribks Inc.**

Mango Media, *(978-1-63353; 978-1-64250; 978-1-68481)* 2850 Douglas Rd. Suite 301, Coral Gables, FL 33134 USA (SAN 920-8275) Tel 305-428-2299; *Imprints:* Conari Press (ConariMango)
E-mail: info@mangomedia.us
Web site: www.mangomedia.us
Dist(s): **Ingram Publisher Services**
MyiLibrary
Open Road Integrated Media, Inc.
Publishers Group West (PGW)
Red Wheel/Weiser.

Mango Tree Pr., *(978-0-9708571)* Orders Addr.: P.O. Box 853, Mackinaw City, MI 49701 USA Tel 231-627-7322 (phone/fax); Edit Addr.: 2562 Pinewood Cir., Cheboygan, MI 49721 USA
E-mail: lds@mangotreepress.com; lds@mangotreepress.com
Web site: http://www.mangotreepress.com
Dist(s): **Partners Bk. Distributing, Inc.**

Mangrove Seed Expressions *Imprint of* **Mangrove Seed, Inc.**

Mangrove Seed, Inc., *(978-0-9797158)* Orders Addr.: P.O. Box 2, Sarasota, FL 34230-0002 USA Toll Free: 866-549-1549 to contact publisher; P.O. Box 02, Sarasota, FL 34230; *Imprints:* Mangrove Seed Expressions (Mangve Seed)
E-mail: dan@mangroveseed.org
Web site: http://www.mangroveseed.org; http://www.mangroveseedchronicles.com.

Mangrum, Kaylea J., *(978-0-9883009)* 1521 Carrick Dr., Murfreesboro, TN 37128 USA Tel 615-579-3663
E-mail: donmangrum@yahoo.com; phillipmangrum@mac.com.

Mangrum-Strichart Learning Resources, *(978-0-9745999; 978-0-9797723; 978-0-9978079; 978-1-7336069)* 2634 Glendale Dr., Loveland, CO 80538 USA Tel 970-593-1586; Fax: 970-962-0057; Toll Free: 866-409-0585
E-mail: study@mangrum-strichart.com
Web site: http://www.mangrum-strichart.com.

Manhattan Academia, *(978-0-615-16120-4; 978-0-615-18454-8; 978-0-615-18503-3; 978-1-936581)* 26 Norwood Terr., Millburn, NJ 07041 USA
Web site: http://www.manhattanacademia.com
Dist(s): **Lulu Pr., Inc.**

Manic D Pr., *(978-0-916397; 978-1-933149; 978-1-945665)* Orders Addr.: P.O. Box 410804, San Francisco, CA 94141 USA (SAN 670-6932) Tel 415-648-8288 (phone/fax); Edit Addr.: 250 Banks St., San Francisco, CA 94110 USA
E-mail: info@manicdpress.com
Web site: http://www.manicdpress.com
Dist(s): **Consortium Bk. Sales & Distribution**
Last Gasp of San Francisco
MyiLibrary
SPD-Small Pr. Distribution.

Manifest Pubns., *(978-0-9627896; 978-1-929354)* Orders Addr.: P.O. Box 429, Carpinteria, CA 93014 USA Tel 805-684-4905; Fax: 805-684-3100; Edit Addr.: P.O. Box 429, Carpinteria, CA 93014-0429 USA
E-mail: editor@manifestpub.com; publisher@manifestpub.com
Web site: http://www.manifestpub.com
Dist(s): **Sunbelt Pubns., Inc.**

Manifesting Pages Publishing *See* **MITWA**

Manifold Grace Publishing Hse., *(978-1-937400; 978-1-952926)* 25163 Greenbrooke Dr., Southfield, MI 48033 USA Tel 248-910-5616
E-mail: darlene@mgph.org
Web site: manifoldgracepublishinghouse.com
Dist(s): **BookBaby.**

Maninge Mali, *(978-0-9729698)* 204 Garden Pl., Radnor, PA 19087 USA (SAN 255-4623) Tel 610-254-0846
E-mail: maningemali@aol.com.

Manis, Shirley, *(978-0-9839286)* 2205 Francesco Cr., Capitola, CA 95010 USA Tel 831-462-4126
E-mail: smanis@cruzio.com.

Manitowish River Pr., *(978-0-9656763; 978-0-9998157)* 4245N State Hwy. 47, Mercer, WI 54547 USA (SAN 990-8900) Tel 715-476-2828
E-mail: manitowish@centurytel.net
Web site: www.manitowishriverpress.com
Dist(s): **Adventure Pubns.**

Mankamyer, Laura, *(978-0-9728431)* 343 Stonebrook Dr., Canonsburg, PA 15317-3409 USA.

Mann Publishing Group, *(978-0-9726888; 978-1-932577; 978-1-933673)* 710 Main St., 6th Flr., Rollinsford, NH 03869 USA (SAN 255-5409) Tel 603-601-0325; Fax: 603-601-0334; Toll Free: 877-877-6266; *Imprints:* BookMann Press (BkMann Pr)
E-mail: tmann@mannpublishing.com
Web site: http://www.askopus.com; http://www.rationalpress.com; http://www.agilitypress.com; http://www.incpress.com; http://www.mannpublishing.com.

Mann Publishing Inc. *See* **Mann Publishing Group**

Manners Toy Co., LLC, *(978-0-615-17967-4)* Orders Addr.: 2546 Lochness Rd, Richmond, VA 23235 USA Tel 804-307-5154
E-mail: mmadore@mannerstoycompany.com.

Mannheim Steamroller L.L.C., *(978-0-9656909; 978-0-9754149)* 9130 Mormon Bridge Rd., Omaha, NE 68152 USA Tel 402-457-4341; Fax: 402-457-4332
Web site: http://www.amgram.com; www.mannheimsteamroller.com.

Manning Pubns. Co. LLC, *(978-1-884777; 978-1-930110; 978-1-932394; 978-1-933988; 978-1-935182; 978-1-61729; 978-1-63343; 978-1-63835)* 20 Baldwin Road, Shelter Island, NY 11964 USA Tel 203-626-1510 Editorial
E-mail: bowker@manning.com
Web site: https://www.manning.com
Dist(s): **Ebsco Publishing**
O'Reilly Media, Inc.
ProQuest LLC
Simon & Schuster, Inc.

Manns, Marlo, *(978-0-9976399)* 7631 S. Perry Ave., Chicago, IL 60620 USA
E-mail: myheartknewlove@yahoo.com
Web site: www.myheartknewlove.com.

Manoa Pr., *(978-1-891839)* 2702 Menoa Rd., Honolulu, HI 96822 USA Tel 808-988-4904
Dist(s): **Native Bks.**

Manor Hse. Publishing Co., Inc., *(978-0-9645844; 978-0-9796239; 978-0-9836634; 978-0-9858774)* 880 Louis Dr., Warminster, PA 18974-2819 USA Tel 215-259-1700 Toll Free: 800-768-3222
E-mail: rdean@mgadvertising.com
Web site: http://www.poolspaliving.com.

Mansfield, J. Hse. Publishing Co., *(978-0-9707428)* P.O. Box 191575, Los Angeles, CA 90019 USA Fax: 323-935-6169
E-mail: jlmansfield@usa.net.

Mansion Publishing, Ltd., *(978-0-9675941)* c/o The Maggiore Companies, 60 Mycopia Rd., Winchester, MA 01890 USA Tel 781-729-7210; 781-718-2003; Fax: 781-729-6444
E-mail: mansionpub@aol.com
Web site: http://wdressingthewholeperson.com.

Mantra Lingua (GBR) *(978-1-85269; 978-0-947679; 978-1-84444; 978-1-84611)* *Dist. by* **Chinasprout.**

Manual In Truth, A, *(978-0-9763252)* P.O. Box 541486, Miami, FL 33054 USA
E-mail: customersupport@amanualintruth.com
Web site: http://www.amanualintruth.com.

Manufacturing Application Konsulting Engineering (MAKE)in, *(978-1-62495)* 705 W. Azure Ln., Litchfield PArk, AZ 85340 USA Tel 469-265-8212
E-mail: trythaiketco@gmail.com
Web site: www.trythaiketco.net
Dist(s): **Lulu Pr., Inc.**

Many Kites Pr., *(978-0-9618469; 978-0-9729002)* Orders Addr.: P.O. Box 711, Cass Lake, MN 56633 USA Tel 605-341-4232 (phone/fax); Toll Free: 800-486-8940; Edit Addr.: 6511 160th St. NW, Cass Lake, MN 56633 USA
E-mail: info@manykites.com; jamie@manykites.com
Web site: http://www.manykites.com; http://www.manykites.org
Dist(s): **Smashwords.**

Many Seasons Pr. *Imprint of* **Hispanic Institute of Social Issues**

Many Voice Pr., *(978-0-9795185; 978-0-9833679; 978-1-7336918)* Flathead Valley Community College 777 Grandview Dr., Kalispell, MT 59901 USA (SAN 853-6686) Tel 406-756-3907; Fax: 406-756-3815 Do not confuse with companies with the same name in Long Island City, NY, Cincinnati, OH
E-mail: ljaegermontana@gmail.com; hmbissell@gmail.com
Dist(s): **SPD-Small Pr. Distribution.**

Manzanita Falls Pubs., *(978-0-9763916)* P.O. Box 991920, Redding, CA 96099-1920 USA (SAN 256-3347)
Web site: http://www.manzanitafallspublishers.com.

MAP Creative LLC, *(978-0-9856967)* Orders Addr.: 128 Hamilton Rd, Bloomfield Hills, MI 48301 USA Tel 248-731-7065
E-mail: mattdamman@gmail.com
Web site: www.thesmallsports.com.

Mapin Publishing Pvt. Ltd (IND) *(978-81-85822; 978-81-88204) Dist. by* **Natl Bk Netwk.**

Maple Bend Farms Pr., *(978-0-9740799)* 4804 Laurel Canyon Blvd., Suite 224, Valley Village, CA 91607 USA
E-mail: ocsage@aol.com
Web site: http://www.maplebend.com.

Maple Canyon Co., *(978-0-9669760; 978-0-9787164)* P.O. Box 565, Mapleton, UT 84663 USA Tel 801-489-8948
E-mail: chuckclifton@maplecanyon.com; customerservice@maplecanyon.com
Web site: http://www.maplecanyon.com.

Maple Corners Press *Imprint of* **Attic Studio Publishing Hse.**

Maple Creek Media, *(978-0-9837967; 978-0-9859678; 978-0-9895471; 978-0-9912442; 978-0-9907392; 978-1-942914)* 1194 N. Carroll St., Hampstead, MD 21074 USA Tel 410-259-8295
E-mail: craig.schenning@maplecreekmedia.com
Web site: http://www.maplecreekmedia.com.

maple, Jessie, *(978-0-692-94817-0)* 658 HANSELL ST SE, Atlanta, GA 30312 USA Tel 347-551-0250
E-mail: jessielmaple@aol.com.

Maple Lane Writing & Desktop Publishing, *(978-0-9667527)* 16821 W. County Hill Rd., Hayward, WI 54843 USA Tel 715-634-9600; Fax: 715-634-1871
E-mail: maplein@win.bright.net.

Maple Leaf Ctr., *(978-0-9759850; 978-0-9827210)* 167 N. Main St., Wallingford, VT 05773 USA Tel 802-446-3601; Fax: 802-446-3801
E-mail: mapleleaf@vermontel.net
Web site: http://www.mapleleafcenter.com.

Maple Leaf Publishing *See* **Spreeda Publishing**

Maple Pr., *(978-1-882029; 978-1-938232)* 481 E. San Carlos St, San Jose, CA 95112 USA (SAN 248-1375) Tel 408-297-1000; Fax: 408-297-1057
E-mail: copy@maplepress.net.

Maple Road Publishing, Inc., *(978-0-9844453)* Orders Addr.: P.O. Box 10143, McLean, VA 22102 USA
Web site: http://www.mapleroadpublishing.com.

Maps For Kids Inc., *(978-0-9759433)* 1550 Poly Dr., Billings, MT 59102 USA Tel 406-238-7131; Fax: 406-259-4021; Toll Free: 877-897-7131
E-mail: banjo@floberg.com
Web site: http://www.mapsforkids.com.

Maps.com, *(978-1-930194)* 120 Cremona Dr. Ste. 260, Goleta, CA 93117-5564 USA (SAN 254-4180) Toll Free: 800-929-4627
E-mail: info@maps.com
Web site: http://www.maps.com
Dist(s): **Cram, George F. Co., Inc.**

Marable, Justin, *(978-0-9831104)* 136 SW Kendall Ave., Topeka, KS 66606 USA Tel 785-286-7944
E-mail: justinmarableks@gmail.com.

Maracle, Derek, *(978-0-9991138; 978-1-7321056; 978-1-950594)* 13 Wesley St, Camden, DE 19934 USA Tel 302-697-1243; *Imprints:* Bickering Owls Publishing (BickeringOwls)
E-mail: dcm1977@comcast.net.

Maraj Pr., *(978-1-952912)* 315 Bedford Pl, Moraga, CA 94556 USA Tel 954-695-3415
E-mail: sharada.maraj@gmail.com.

Marak, Michael, *(978-0-9795866)* 6205 Daffan Ln., Austin, TX 78724-1501 USA
E-mail: sue@rezulting.com.

Marandu, Thobias L., *(978-0-9767605)* 2913 Columbiana Rd. Apt. B, Birmingham, AL 35216-3537 USA
E-mail: tlekundayo@yahoo.com.

Marble Hse. Editions, *(978-0-9677047; 978-0-9786745; 978-0-9815345; 978-0-9834030; 978-0-9966224; 978-1-7332299)* 67-66 108th Street, Suite D27, Forest Hills, NY 11375 USA (SAN 253-6536); 67-66 108th Street, Suite D27, Forest Hills, NY 11375 (SAN 253-6536)
E-mail: elizabethuhlig7@gmail.com
Web site: http://www.marble-house-editions.com/.

Marble Mountain Pr., *(978-0-9748552)* PMB 214, 2019 Aero Way, Suite 103, Medford, OR 97504 USA Tel 530-926-2473
E-mail: marblemountain@snowcrest.net
Web site: http://www.rvinnz.com.

Marble Pr., *(978-1-958325)* 2260 Hanover St., Palo Alto, CA 94306 USA Tel 510-219-3515
E-mail: susan.szecsi@gmail.com
Web site: www.marblepress.com
Dist(s): **Baker & Taylor Publisher Services (BTPS).**

Marbury, Tawanda, *(978-0-578-23593-6; 978-0-578-23594-3; 978-1-7367719)* 729 Old Indian Camp Rd., Grovetown, GA 30813 USA Tel 334-524-7253
E-mail: tawandamarbury95@gmail.com.

Marcabru Publishing, *(978-0-615-61495-3)* 108 E. 38th St., New York, NY 10016 USA Tel 917-596-0650
Web site: www.glennberger.net
Dist(s): **CreateSpace Independent Publishing Platform.**

Marcasa Bks., *(978-0-9763015)* Paloma del Lago No. 67, Campolago, Cidra, PR 00739-9361 USA Tel 787-960-3517 (phone/fax)
E-mail: mmartinezpr@gmail.com.

March 4th, Inc., *(978-0-9840806; 978-0-9829938; 978-1-939775)* 3701 Sacramento St. #494, San Francisco, CA 94118 USA (SAN 858-3641) Fax: 415-366-1520; Toll Free: 877-415-4488
E-mail: info@littlepicklepress.com
Web site: http://www.littlepicklepress.com
Dist(s): **MyiLibrary**
Publishers Group West (PGW)
Sourcebooks, Inc.

March Media, Inc., *(978-0-9634824)* 1114 Oman Dr., Brentwood, TN 37027 USA Tel 615-377-1146; Fax: 615-373-1705
E-mail: etta.wilson@comcast.net.

March Street Pr., *(978-0-9624453; 978-1-882983; 978-0-9745909; 978-1-59661)* 3413 Wilshire Dr., Greensboro, NC 27408-2923 USA Fax: 336-282-9754 prefer orders by email (rbixby@earthlink.net)
E-mail: rbixby@earthlink.net
Web site: http://www.marchstreetpress.com
Dist(s): **Bottom Dog Pr.**

Marcia's Menagerie, *(978-0-9777359)* 2960 W. Stuart St., A-203, Fort Collins, CO 80526 USA Tel 970-493-6373
E-mail: tangome27@hotmail.com.

Marcinson Pr., *(978-0-9893732; 978-0-9967207; 978-1-946932)* 11111-70 San Jose Blvd. Suite 136, Jacksonville, FL 32223 USA Tel 352-263-0910
E-mail: editor@marcinsonpress.com.

Marco Bk. Co., *(978-0-9710756; 978-0-9729765)* 60 Industrail Rd., Lodi, NJ 07644 USA Tel 973-458-0485; Fax: 973-458-5289; Toll Free: 800-842-4234; *Imprints:* Everbind (Everbind)
E-mail: everbind5@aol.com
Dist(s): **Bks. & Media, Inc.**

MAR*CO Products, Inc., *(978-1-57543; 978-1-884063)* Orders Addr.: 1443 Old York Rd., Warminster, PA 18974 USA Tel 215-956-0313; Fax: 215-956-9041; Toll Free: 800-448-2197
E-mail: csfunk@marcoproducts.com; marcoproducts@comcast.net
Web site: http://www.store.yahoo.com/marcoproducts; http://www.marcoproducts.com.

Marcoux, Tom Media, LLC, *(978-0-9624660; 978-0-9800511; 978-0-615-78342-0; 978-0-615-78657-5; 978-0-615-80157-5; 978-0-615-80934-2; 978-0-615-81302-8; 978-0-615-83582-2; 978-0-615-91576-0; 978-0-615-92869-2; 978-0-615-97539-9; 978-0-615-99188-7; 978-0-692-21096-3; 978-0-692-22704-6; 978-0-692-22972-9; 978-0-692-23525-6; 978-0-692-33069-2; 978-0-692-35850-4; 978-0-692-38436-7; 978-0-692-45951-5; 978-0-692-52718-4; 978-0-692-56195-9; 978-0-692-60115-0; 978-0-692-60208-9; 978-0-692-63808-8; 978-0-692-64737-0; 978-0-69) 674 Morse Ave. Unit F, Sunnyvale, CA 94085 USA Tel 415-572-6609*
Dist(s): **CreateSpace Independent Publishing Platform.**

Marcovaldo Productions *See* **Green Buffalo Pr.**

Marczak Innovations, *(978-0-692-85726-7; 978-0-692-19627-4; 978-0-578-74872-6)* 38 Oxford Rd, Newport News, VA 23606 USA Tel 757-207-0231
E-mail: chris.marczak.1@gmail.com; info@chrismarczak.com
Dist(s): **CreateSpace Independent Publishing Platform.**

Mardi Gras Publishing, LLC, *(978-0-9787262; 978-0-9789024; 978-0-9789986; 978-0-9790649; 978-0-9791570; 978-1-934329)* 6845 Hwy. 90 E. Suite 255, Daphne, AL 36526 USA
E-mail: contactlamedia@gmail.com
Web site: http://lamediaonline.com.

Mardick Pr., *(978-1-940413)* P.O. Box 10701, Houston, TX 77206 USA Tel 713-254-7285; *Imprints:* Blackbirch Press, Incorporated (Blackbirch Pr)
E-mail: publisher@mardickpress.com.

Marduk Publishing Inc., *(978-1-893138)* Orders Addr.: a/o Marduk Publishing Inc., P.O. Box 480608, Delray Beach, FL 33448 USA (SAN 256-3053) Tel 561-638-6070; 516 695-8077; Toll Free: 888-462-7385 (phone/fax)
E-mail: docbloc@marduk1.com; docbloc@marpub.com; docbloc@hotmail.com
Web site: http://www.marpub.com; http://www.marduk1.com; http://www.all-a.us; http://www.all-ace.com.

Mareldon, *(978-1-7334828)* 2619 Sessions St, Eau Claire, WI 54701 USA Tel 715-379-2583
E-mail: eldon.utilities@gmail.com.

Marn Green Publishing, Inc., *(978-1-934277; 978-1-958069)* 7900 Excelsior Blvd. Suite 105k, Hopkins, MN 55343 USA (SAN 852-4920) Toll Free: 800-287-1512
E-mail: toddsnow@marengreen.com
Web site: http://www.marengreen.com.

Maresca, Wendi, *(978-0-9772897)* 6130 Murifield Dr., Gurnee, IL 60031-5357 USA.

Margaret Ferguson Books *Imprint of* **Holiday Hse., Inc.**

Margaret Quinlin Books *Imprint of* **Peachtree Publishing Co. Inc.**

Margaret Sutton Bks., *(978-1-7355300)* 953 Courtyard Ln. Unit 41, ORLANDO, FL 32825 USA Tel 321-200-5537
E-mail: margaretsuttonbooks@gmail.com
Web site: www.MargaretSuttonBooks.com.

Margaret Weis Productions, Ltd., *(978-1-931567; 978-1-936685)* P.O. Box 1131, Williams Bay, WI 53191 USA Fax: 866-668-5730 Do not confuse with Sovereign Pr. in Rochester, WA
E-mail: margaret@margaretweis.com; christi@margaretweis.com
Web site: http://www.margaretweis.com
Dist(s): **Diamond Comic Distributors, Inc.**
Diamond Bk. Distributors
PSI (Publisher Services, Inc.).

Margolis, Amy Publishing, *(978-0-9776692)* Orders Addr.: 31 Saddle Ln., Old Brookville, NY 11545 USA (SAN 257-9294)
E-mail: Amy@ButterfliesandMagicalWings.com
Web site: http://www.ButterfliesandMagicalWings.com.

Margolis, Marion, *(978-0-9753184)* 1 W. 72nd St., Apt. No. 95, New York, NY 10023 USA Tel 212-595-7555
E-mail: chasmargolis@aol.com
Dist(s): **Xlibris Corp.**

Marhouse, Inc., *(978-0-9752703)* Orders Addr.: a/o Marhouse Inc., P.O. Box 150605, Altamonte Springs, FL 32715 USA Tel 407-499-5307 (phone/fax)
E-mail: marhouse12@yahoo.com
Web site: http://www.adventurefox.com.

Maria, Jillian, *(978-1-7338635)* P.O. Box 958, Mt. Clemens, MI 48046 USA Tel 586-909-9917
E-mail: byjillianmaria@gmail.com
Web site: https://www.byjillianmaria.com/.

Marian Pr., *(978-0-944203; 978-1-932773; 978-1-59614)* Marian Helpers Ctr., Eden Hill, Stockbridge, MA 01263-0004 USA (SAN 243-1548) Tel 413-298-3691; Fax: 413-298-1356; Toll Free: 800-462-7426
E-mail: marianpress@marian.org
Web site: http://www.marian.org
Dist(s): **Send The Light Distribution LLC.**

Marianist Pr., *(978-0-9628309)* Orders Addr.: 1116 Imperial Blvd., Kettering, OH 45419-2434 USA Tel 937-298-8509; Edit Addr.: 233 E. Helena St., Dayton, OH 45404-1003 USA.

Marianne Richmond Studios, Inc. *Imprint of* **Sourcebooks, Inc.**

Marilux Pr., *(978-0-9710281)* 4100 Corporate Sq., Suite 161, Naples, FL 34104 USA Tel 239-398-7018; Fax: 917-591-0387
E-mail: sales@mariluxpress.com
Web site: http://www.MariluxPress.com.

Marimba Bks. *Imprint of* **Just Us Bks., Inc.**

Marinaro, Stacy, *(978-0-615-20684-4; 978-0-615-20807-7; 978-0-615-20883-1; 978-0-615-21988-2; 978-0-578-02365-6)* 420 Matthews St., Bristol, CT 06010 USA
E-mail: stacymarinaro@yahoo.com
Dist(s): **Lulu Pr., Inc.**

Mariner Bks. *Imprint of* **HarperCollins Pubs.**

Mariner Publishing, *(978-0-9768238; 978-0-9776841; 978-0-9800077; 978-0-9820172; 978-0-9841128; 978-0-9833478; 978-0-9835565; 978-0-9849214; 978-0-9909653; 978-0-9975226; 978-0-9992885; 978-0-9997629; 978-1-7339720; 978-1-7341842; 978-1-7349136; 978-1-7378864; 979-8-9863592; 979-8-9867383; 979-8-9892186) Div. of Mariner Media, Inc., 131 W. 21st St., Buena Vista, VA 24416 USA Tel 540-264-0021; Fax: 540-261-1881; Imprints:* Harbour Books (HarbourBks) Do not confuse with Mariner Publishing in Tampa, FL Oklahoma City, OK
E-mail: andy@marinermedia.com
Web site: http://www.marinermedia.com
Dist(s): **Virginia Pubns.**

Mariposa Pr., *(978-0-9666899)* 551 W. Cordova Rd., Santa Fe, NM 87501 USA Tel 505-471-7846; Fax: 505-986-0690 Do not confuse with companies with same or similar names in Gainesville, FL, Chicago, IL, Hurleyville, NY, Boulder, CO, Abilene TX.

Maritime Kids Quest Pr., *(978-0-9761178)* P.O. Box 700, Manteo, NC 27954 USA Tel 252-473-6933
E-mail: maritimekidsquest@earthlink.net.

Maritime Museum Assn. of San Diego, *(978-0-944580)* 1492 N. Harbor Dr., San Diego, CA 92101 USA (SAN 279-5027) Tel 619-234-9153; Fax: 619-234-8345
E-mail: museumstore@sdmaritime.com
Web site: http://www.sdmaritime.com/mains'lhaul
Dist(s): **Sunbelt Pubns., Inc.**

MARK & Assocs. LLC, *(978-0-692-13906-6)* 1622 Country Club Dr., Pittsburgh, PA 15237 USA Tel 412-369-8231
E-mail: reginakmunsch@gmail.com.

Mark Boone, *(978-0-9772515)* 6141 Dixon Dr, Lisle, IL 60532-4151 USA; 6141 Dixon Dr., Lisle, IL 60532-4151
E-mail: maboone1@comcast.net
Dist(s): **National Bk. Network.**

Marked Writers Publishing, *(978-0-692-36079-8; 978-0-692-36179-5; 978-0-692-38117-5; 978-0-692-41586-3; 978-0-692-41587-0; 978-0-692-41588-7; 978-0-692-45389-6; 978-0-692-53897-5; 978-0-692-59419-3; 978-0-692-60911-8; 978-0-692-60912-5; 978-0-692-84543-1; 978-0-692-88868-1; 978-0-692-88869-8; 978-0-692-90722-1; 978-0-692-04653-1; 978-0-692-14283-7; 978-0-578-21503-7; 978-0-578-45854-0; 978-1-7334333; 979-8-9850662) 5809 LAGO VISTA DR, CORPUS CHRISTI, TX 78418 USA Tel 3617286518; 5809 Lago Vista Dr., Corpus Christi, TX 78414*
Dist(s): **CreateSpace Independent Publishing Platform.**

Marker, Margaret Penfield, *(978-0-9716721)* 64 Colonial Dr., Rancho Mirage, CA 92270-1600 USA
E-mail: tmlmarker@aol.com.

Market 1 Group Inc., *(978-0-9748109)* 118 Worthington Business Ctr. 1550 Douglas Ave., Charleston, IL 61920 USA Tel 217-345-8281
E-mail: bmcelwee@consolidated.net
Web site: http://www.familyjourneys.net.

Market Place Publisher *See* **Market Place Publishing**

Market Place Publishing, *(978-1-7326799)* 11442 CALIFORNIA, BRIDGMAN, MI 49106-9362 USA Tel 269-449-1100
E-mail: cherissehavlicek@gmail.com
Web site: http://AuthorCherisse.com/.

Markins Enterprises, *(978-0-937729)* 2039 SE 45th Ave., Portland, OR 97215 USA (SAN 659-3224) Tel 503-235-1036.

Marks, Ginger *See* **DocUmeant Publishing**

Marks, William *See* **MPC Pr. International**

Markwin Pr., *(978-0-9740793)* Orders Addr.: P.O. Box 1143, Silver Springs, NV 89429 USA Tel 775-577-0676; Edit Addr.: 3220 E. 9th St., Silver Springs, NV 89429 USA
E-mail: softgaits@wildblue.com
Web site: www.TheFabulousFloatingHorses.com.

Marlena Brown-Holcomb, *(978-0-578-41006-7; 978-0-578-96552-9)* 905 W. Idylwild Dr., Midwest City, OK 73110 USA Tel 405-414-3711
E-mail: lenabrow38@yahoo.com
Dist(s): **Independent Pub.**

Marley-Goeste, *(978-1-7320306)* 9 Old Timber Ln., Palos Park, IL 60464 USA Tel 708-846-9630
E-mail: marc.mattson@gmail.com.

Marlor Pr., Inc., *(978-0-943400; 978-1-892147)* 4304 Brigadoon Dr., Saint Paul, MN 55126 USA (SAN 240-7140) Tel 651-484-4600; Fax: 651-490-1182; Toll Free: 800-669-4908
E-mail: marlor@minn.net
Dist(s): **Independent Pubs. Group**
MyiLibrary.

MarMooWorks,LLC, *(978-0-9853579; 978-0-9853580; 978-1-7379766)* 318 Beverly Dr., Erie, PA 16505 USA Tel 814-464-6271
E-mail: mamoodey@gmail.com
Web site: jason@conveyorarts.org.

Maroma Bks., *(978-0-9796465)* 5615 Kirby Dr., Suite 820, Houston, TX 77005 USA Toll Free Fax: 800-525-0910; Toll Free: 888-627-6628
E-mail: molly@maromabooks.com
Web site: http://www.maromabooks.com
Dist(s): **Ingram Content Group.**

Marquand Bks., Inc., *(978-0-9706394; 978-0-9744202; 978-0-9778028; 978-0-9815762; 978-0-615-22812-9; 978-0-615-27788-2; 978-0-615-31547-8; 978-0-615-31690-1; 978-0-615-33169-0; 978-0-615-35171-1; 978-0-615-35172-8; 978-0-615-36404-9; 978-0-615-39016-1; 978-0-615-39126-7; 978-0-615-39579-1; 978-0-615-41782-0; 978-0-615-45883-0; 978-0-615-47180-8; 978-0-615-55154-8; 978-0-615-56154-7; 978-0-615-56155-4; 978-0-615-56156-1; 978-0-615-56210-0; 978-0-615-56585-9; 978-0-9849864; 978-0-615-59005-9; 978-0-615-59427-9; 9) 1400 2nd Ave, Seattle, WA 98101 USA Tel 206-624-2030; Fax: 206-624-1821*
E-mail: Adrian@luciamarquand.com
Web site: http://www.luciamarquand.com
Dist(s): **Antique Collectors' Club**
D.A.P./Distributed Art Pubs.
National Bk. Network
Univ. of Oklahoma Pr.
Univ. of Washington Pr.

Marquette Bks., *(978-0-922993; 978-0-9816018; 978-0-9826597; 978-0-9833476; 978-1-7327197)* 16421 N. 31st Ave., Phoenix, AZ 85053 USA (SAN 251-5261) Tel 509-290-9240
E-mail: books@marquettebooks.com
Web site: http://www.marquettebooks.com
Dist(s): **Ambassador Bks. & Media**
Bk. Hse., The
Brodart Co.
Coutts Information Services
Eastern Bk. Co.
Emery-Pratt Co.
Ingram Bk. Co.
Levant USA, Inc.
Midwest Library Service
Blackwell.

Marquette Books, LLC *See* **Marquette Bks.**

Marquise Publishing, *(978-0-9745264)* 11459 Mayfield Rd Suite 338, Cleveland, OH 44106 USA
E-mail: marquisepublishing@gmail.com
Web site: http://www.marquisepublishing.com.

Marrero Illustrations, *(978-1-7347020; 978-0-578-90533-4; 978-0-578-90581-5; 978-0-578-90583-9; 978-0-578-90584-6; 978-0-578-90587-7; 978-0-578-90588-4; 978-0-578-90589-1)* 73 Glover Ave. 3rd Flr., Quincy, MA 02171 USA Tel 617-481-8959
E-mail: mcregal75@gmail.com
Web site: www.marreroillustrations.com.

Marrero, Rafael, *(978-0-9747569)* 2121 Red Rd., Ave., Coral Gables, FL 33155-2232 USA Tel 305-267-0163
E-mail: rafeltomarrero@hotmail.com.

Marriwell Publishing, *(978-0-9742891)* P.O. Box 116, Center Valley, PA 18034 USA; *Imprints:* Cozy Den Press (MYID_B_COZY DE)
Web site: http://www.marriwell.com.

Marro, Jon, *(978-1-7341906)* 6329 La Paloma Ln., Oceanside, CA 92057 USA Tel 410-207-2307
E-mail: jon@jonmarro.com
Dist(s): **Ingram Content Group.**

Mars Hill Ink, *(979-8-9851816; 978-1-957387)* 703 Sta. St, Waynesboro, ND 82001 USA Tel 917-633-4970; Fax: 917-633-4234
E-mail: supportdesk@marshillink.com
Web site: https://www.marshillink.com/.

Mars Media Publishers *See* **Audio Holdings, LLC**

Marsh, Carole Bks. *Imprint of* **Gallopade International**

Marsh, Carole Family CD-Rom *Imprint of* **Gallopade International**

Marsh, Carole Mysteries *Imprint of* **Gallopade International**

Marsh Creek Pr., *(978-0-937750)* Div. of Don Aslett, Inc., Orders Addr.: P.O. Box 700, Pocatello, ID 83204 USA (SAN 216-1028) Tel 208-232-3535; Fax: 208-235-5481; Edit Addr.: 311 S. Fifth Ave., Pocatello, ID 83201 USA
E-mail: Tobih@aol.com
Web site: http://www.aslett.com.

Marsh Media *See* **Witcher Productions**

Marsh, Thomas E. Inc., *(978-0-9633682)* 914 Franklin Ave., Youngstown, OH 44502 USA Tel 216-743-8600; Toll Free: 800-845-7930.

Marshall, Angela, *(978-0-692-98157-3)* 10221 MAIN ST, HANOVERTON, OH 44423 USA Tel 330-853-0889
E-mail: redcow06@gmail.com.

Marshall Cavendish (GBR) *(978-0-7614; 978-0-86307; 978-1-85435; 978-0-9533784; 978-1-902741; 978-0-462; 978-0-85080; 978-1-905992) Dist. by* **Marshall C.**

†Marshall Cavendish Corp., *(978-0-7614; 978-0-85685; 978-0-86307; 978-1-85435; 978-1-60870)* Member of Times Publishing Group, 99 White Plains Rd., Tarrytown,

NY 10591-9001 USA (SAN 238-437X) Tel 914-332-8888; Fax: 914-332-8882; Toll Free: 800-821-9881
E-mail: mce@marshallcavendish.com
Web site: www.MCEducation.us
Dist(s): **BookBaby**
Brilliance Publishing, Inc.
Children's Plus, Inc.
Ebsco Publishing
Follett School Solutions
Fujii Assocs.
Lectorum Pubns., Inc.
MyiLibrary
National Bk. Network; *CIP.*

Marshall Cavendish International (Asia) Private Ltd. (SGP) *(978-981-204; 978-981-232; 978-2-85700; 978-981-261; 978-981-4302; 978-981-4312; 978-981-4328; 978-981-4346; 978-981-4351; 978-981-4361; 978-981-4382; 978-981-4398; 978-981-4408; 978-981-4426; 978-981-4430; 978-981-4433; 978-981-4435; 978-981-4484; 978-981-4516; 978-981-4561; 978-981-4771; 978-981-4828; 978-981-4794) Dist. by* **IPG Chicago.**

Marshall, George Publishing, *(978-0-9729403)* P.O. Box 375, Bedford, VA 24523 USA.

Marshall, John High Schl. Alumni Assn., *(978-0-9759618)* 347 Pineview Cir., Berea, OH 44017 USA
E-mail: jmhalumni@ameritech.com
Web site: http://www.jmhalumni.com.

Marshlands Group LLC, *(978-0-692-98575-5; 978-0-692-98760-5; 978-0-9600605)* PO Box 481624, Charlotte, NC 28269 USA
E-mail: marshlandsgroup@gmail.com
Dist(s): **CreateSpace Independent Publishing Platform**
Ingram Content Group.

Martell Publishing Co, *(978-1-893181; 978-1-930200)* P.O. Box 83554, San Diego, CA 92138-3554 USA Toll Free Fax: 800-805-3329; *Imprints:* Lagesse Stevens (LageseS)
E-mail: martell@martellpublishing.com.

Martella, Liz, *(978-0-615-14941-7; 978-0-615-25506-4)* 393 Lathrop Rd., Lathrop, CA 95330 USA
E-mail: lizmartella@yahoo.com
Web site: http://www.lulu.com/lizmartella
Dist(s): **Lulu Pr., Inc.**

Marten Pr., *(978-1-7324588; 978-1-954335)* 3646 W Keyworth Dr., South Jordan, UT 84095 USA Tel 801-319-6982
E-mail: kaylmoody@gmail.com
Dist(s): **Ingram Content Group.**

Marti Bks., *(978-0-9766006)* Orders Addr.: P.O. Box 603, West Tisbury, MA 02575 USA Tel 508-696-7496 (phone/fax); Edit Addr.: 635 State Rd., West Tisbury, MA 02575 USA
E-mail: fferr2@aol.com
Web site: http://www.martibooks.com.

Martin, Amy, *(978-0-9882051)* 2733 Braden Way, Lexington, KY 40509 USA Tel 859-797-0156
E-mail: amart71@rocketmail.com.

Martin & Brothers, *(978-0-9719842; 978-0-9767500)* Orders Addr.: P.O. Box 122, Abbott, TX 76621 USA Tel 254-235-8588; Edit Addr.: 101 Bordon, Abbott, TX 76621 USA
E-mail: martinbrothers@aol.com.

Martin, Carolyn, *(978-0-9746808)* 1890 N. 36th St., Galesburg, MI 49053-9528 USA Tel 269-665-9963 Do not confuse with Carolyn Martin in Philadelphia, PA
E-mail: carmartin@earthlink.net
Web site: http://www.finefrets.com/metalhorses.

Martin, Danielle, *(978-0-578-41023-4; 978-0-578-28357-9)* 192 S 6th St, Jefferson, OR 97352 USA Tel 541-788-7875
E-mail: daniellemccallister@hotmail.com
Dist(s): **Ingram Content Group.**

Martin, Elizabeth B., *(978-0-578-12912-9; 978-0-578-12913-6; 978-0-9910543; 978-0-9904213)*
E-mail: elizabeth@elizabethbmartin.com
Dist(s): **Lulu Pr., Inc.**

Martin, Erika, *(978-1-7375858)* 7022 Shallowford Rd. Suite 1 Unit No. 633, Chattanooga , TN 37421 USA Tel 931-801-9619
E-mail: emartinteaching@gmail.com.

Martin, Jack & Assocs., *(978-0-9649530)* Orders Addr.: 9422 S. Saginaw, Grand Blanc, MI 48439 USA Tel 810-694-5698; Fax: 810-694-7851
E-mail: jdmart@tir.com
Web site: http://www.Pre-Apprenticetraining.com.

Martin, James Jr., *(978-0-9799465)* P.O. Box 4207, Greenwitch, CT 06831 USA Fax: 516-060-1177
E-mail: JMJ723@optonline.com
Web site: http://williamthegarbagetruck.com.

Martin, Kevin, *(978-0-578-10705-9)* 7450 Globe Rd., Lenoir, NC 28645 USA.

Martin Publishing, *(978-0-9753992)* 1600 S. 30th, Lot 36, Escanaba, MI 49829 USA Do not confuse with companies with the same or similar name in Fort Morgan, CO; Tampico, IL; La Mesa, CA; Perry, OK; Cowpens, SC; Lincoln, ME.

Martin the Marlin, *(978-0-615-59965-6; 978-0-692-52925-6; 978-0-578-46126-7)* 334 Fairview Rd., Westbrook, CT 06498 USA Tel 860-944-9022
Dist(s): **CreateSpace Independent Publishing Platform.**

Martin, Vicki, *(978-1-7336214)* 2636 Dolly Ridge Rd., Birmingham, AL 35243 USA Tel 205-969-1660
E-mail: internist1209@gmail.com.

Martina Franklin Poole, *(978-0-578-42884-0)* P.O. Box 21122, Keizer, OR 97303 USA Tel 541-505-0386
E-mail: martina.f.poole@gmail.com
Dist(s): **Ingram Content Group.**

Martinez, Leroy F., *(978-0-9748002)* 4045 E. 3rd St. Unit 111, Long Beach, CA 90814-2883 USA Tel 562-443-7727
Web site: http://leroymartinez.com.

Martinez, Patty & Logan, *(978-1-7332949)* 176 Broadway, New York, NY 10038 USA Tel 212-665-0252
E-mail: patty@pattyadams.net.

Martinez, Richard A., *(978-1-7329511)* 8961 Jackson St., Weedsport, NY 13166 USA Tel 315-237-8959
E-mail: capt.jack1064@gmail.com.

†Martingale & Co., *(978-0-943574; 978-1-56477; 978-1-60468; 978-1-68356)* Orders Addr.: 19021 120th Ave. NE. Suite 102, Bothell, WA 98011 USA (SAN 665-7923) Tel 425-483-3313; Fax: 425-486-7596; Toll Free: 800-426-3126; *Imprints:* That Patchwork Place (That Patchwrk Pl)
E-mail: ssanta@martingale-pub.com; mburns@martingale-pub.com; info@martingale-pub.com
Web site: http://www.martingale-pub.com
Dist(s): **Bookazine Co., Inc.**; *CIP.*

Martino,, Carmela Arquilla freelance writing *See* **Arquilla Pr.**

Martino Fine Bks., *(978-1-57898; 978-1-888262; 978-1-61427; 978-1-68422)* P.O. Box 913, Eastford, CT 06242 USA Tel 860-974-2277; 118 Westford Rd., Eastford, CT 06242
E-mail: martinofinebooks@hotmail.com
Web site: http://www.martinofinebooks.com.

Martino Publishing *See* **Martino Fine Bks.**

Martin's *See* **Green Pastures Pr.**

Marvel Age *Imprint of* **Spotlight**

Marvel Enterprises, Incorporated *See* **Marvel Worldwide, Inc.**

Marvel Pr. *Imprint of* **Disney Publishing Worldwide**

Marvel Universe *Imprint of* **Marvel Worldwide, Inc.**

Marvel Worldwide, Inc., *(978-0-7851; 978-0-87135; 978-0-939766; 978-0-9604146; 978-1-4695; 978-1-302)* Subs. of The Walt Disney Co, 135 W. 50th St., New York, NY 10020 USA (SAN 216-9088); c/o Marvel Enterprises Japan, Inc., Hill House B, 9-10 Hachiyama-cho Sibuya, Tokyo, 150-0034; *Imprints:* Marvel Universe (Marvel Universe); Outreach/New Reader (Outreach)
E-mail: mail@marvel.com; amorales@marvel.com
Web site: http://www.marvel.com
Dist(s): **Children's Plus, Inc.**
Penguin Random Hse. LLC.

Marvelous Dream, *(978-0-9771016)* Div. of Marvelous World LLC, P.O. Box 252, Bloomfield, NJ 07003-9998 USA (SAN 256-7857).

Marvelous Spirit Pr. *Imprint of* **Loving Healing Pr., Inc.**

Marvis Duo Productions, *(978-1-7345987)* 4447 CR 2546, Quinlan, TX 75474 USA Tel 214-236-5145
E-mail: robyng@lakepointe.org.

MarWel Enterprises, Inc., *(978-0-9759582)* P.O. Box 31227, Washington, DC 20030 USA
E-mail: marwel@earthlink.net.

Marx Group, The, *(978-0-9773962; 978-1-935309)* 2111 Jefferson Davis Hwy. 303N., Arlington, VA 22202 USA Tel 703-418-1956; Fax: 703-418-0224
E-mail: don@themarxgroup.com
Web site: http://www.the marxgroup.com.

Marx, Jeff, *(978-0-9667824; 978-0-9793134)* 3160 N. 35th St., Hollywood, FL 33021-2630 USA (SAN 853-1021)
E-mail: JeffMarx@schoolelection.com
Web site: http://www.schoolelection.com.

Mary B./French, *(978-0-9852821)* 1355 Pine St. # 5, San Francisco, CA 94109 USA Tel 415-931-8691.

Mary Christine Abushar Books *See* **Mary Christine Abushar Bks. LLC**

Mary Christine Abushar Bks. LLC, *(978-0-692-67003-3; 978-0-692-67648-6; 978-0-692-70535-3; 978-0-692-71575-8; 978-0-692-77582-0; 978-0-692-77604-9; 978-1-7332598; 978-1-7332599; 978-1-7355591; 978-1-7368642; 979-8-218-03373-6; 979-8-9872372)* 222 N Rose St. Burbank, CA 91505 USA Tel 818-399-3948
E-mail: makurban@hotmail.com.

Mary Ellen Spencer, *(978-0-578-86621-5)* 3904 Eagle Way, Prospect, KY 40059 USA Tel 502-974-4318
E-mail: maryspe50@gmail.com.

Mary Jane Hayes, *(978-0-9819634; 978-0-578-45139-8; 979-8-9886902)* 3490 Caroline Blvd No. D310, Green Cove Springs, FL 32043 USA
E-mail: maryjanehayes@bellsouth.net; maryjanehayes5@gmail.com
Web site: https://mjhayesauthor.com
Dist(s): **Chicago Distribution Ctr.**

Mary Ryan, *(978-0-578-40941-2; 978-0-578-40963-4; 978-1-7338945; 978-1-961683)* 403 S. Lincoln St. Suite 4 PMB 140, Port Angeles, WA 98362 USA Tel 443-909-6297
E-mail: MaryTruly92@icloud.com
Dist(s): **Ingram Content Group.**

Mary Sunshine Bks., *(978-0-9652337)* 1710 Sunnymede Ave., South Bend, IN 46615 USA Tel 219-233-6064; Fax: 219-631-6767; Toll Free: 800-231-6580.

Maryann, *(978-1-7320725; 979-8-9868458)* P.O. Box 770624, Woodside, NY 11377-0624 USA Tel 646-620-8402
E-mail: SantaMaria1345@yahoo.com.

Maryknoll Fathers & Brothers *See* **Maryknoll Missioners**

Maryknoll Missioners, *(978-0-941395)* P.O. Box 308, Maryknoll, NY 15054-0308 USA (SAN 219-3752) Tel 914-941-7590; Toll Free: 800-227-8523
E-mail: jgoldbeck@maryknoll.org.

†Maryland Ctr. for History & Culture, *(978-0-938420; 978-0-9842135; 978-0-9965944)* 610 Pk. Ave., Baltimore, MD 21201 USA (SAN 203-9788) Tel 410-685-3750; Fax: 410-385-2105
E-mail: mkado@mdhs.org
Web site: http://www.mdhs.org
Dist(s): **Hood, Alan C. & Co., Inc.**
Johns Hopkins Univ. Pr.; *CIP.*

Maryland Historical Society *See* **Maryland Ctr. for History & Culture**

Maryland Secretarial Services, Inc., *(978-0-692-31692-4; 978-0-692-31693-1; 978-0-692-31694-8; 978-0-692-56468-4)* 12105 Whiston Ct, Bowie, MD 20715 USA Tel 3013527927.

Maryleigh Bucher *See* **Bucher, Maryleigh**

Maryruth Bks., Inc., *(978-0-9713518; 978-0-9720295; 978-0-9746475; 978-1-933624; 978-1-62544)* 18660 Ravenna Rd. Bldg. 2, Chagrin Falls, OH 44023 USA Tel 440-834-1105; Toll Free Fax: 800-951-4077
E-mail: admin@maryruthbooks.com
Web site: http://www.maryruthbooks.com.

Marzell, Paul, *(978-0-578-84119-9)* 240 Glenwood Dr., Washington, PA 15301 USA Tel 724-344-2302
E-mail: pmarzell@hotmail.com.

Marzetta Bks., *(978-0-9657033)* P.O. Box 274, Lombard, IL 60148 USA Tel 630-424-1403
E-mail: marzetta@concentric.net.

Masalai Pr., *(978-0-9714127)* 368 Capricorn Ave., Oakland, CA 94611-2058 USA
E-mail: THSlone@yahoo.com
Web site: http://THSlone.tripod.com/masalaipress.html.

Mascot Books *Imprint of* **Amplify Publishing Group**

Mascot Books, Incorporated *See* **Amplify Publishing Group**

Mascot Kids *Imprint of* **Amplify Publishing Group**

Mascots for Kids, *(978-0-9762636)* Div. of Wells Yeager Best Co., Inc., 400 S. 7th St., Lafayette, IN 47901 USA Tel 765-742-7648; Fax: 765-742-1049
E-mail: aklink@nlci.com
Web site: http://www.mascotsforkids.com
Dist(s): **Indiana Univ. Pr.**
Two Rivers Distribution.

Masha, Segun Inc., *(978-0-9755927; 978-1-7336338)* Div. of SEGUN MASHA, INC., 400 Galleria Parkway, Suite 1500, atlanta, GA 30339 USA
E-mail: segunmashainc@gmail.com
Web site: http://www.segunmasha.com; www.marketplacemissions.com.

Mashack Productions *See* **HOLY COW Bk. Pubs.**

MASK, ACE, *(978-0-692-81950-0; 978-0-692-13064-3; 978-0-692-13736-9; 978-0-578-75934-0)* 1988 HEATHER CIRCLE, BREA, CA 92821 USA Tel 714-529-0850
E-mail: acemask@yahoo.com; acemask@yahoo.com.

mason, cathy, *(978-0-692-18311-3; 978-0-692-18340-3; 979-8-218-20488-4)* 7516 Georgia Ridge Rd., Alma, AR 72921 USA Tel 479-997-2774
E-mail: cathy@cathymasonfineart.com
Dist(s): **Ingram Content Group.**

Mason Crest, *(978-1-59084; 978-1-59482; 978-1-4222)* Div. of Highlights Inc., Orders Addr.: 450 Parkway Dr., Suite D, Broomall, PA 19008-0914 USA Tel 610-543-6200; Fax: 610-543-3878; Toll Free: 866-627-2665 (866-MCP-Book)
E-mail: gbaffa@masoncrest.com
Web site: http://www.masoncrest.com
Dist(s): **Follett School Solutions**
Simon & Schuster, Inc.
Smashwords.

Mason Crest Publishers *See* **Mason Crest**

Mason Mill Publishing Hse., *(978-0-9986455)* 4371 Allen Dr, Brownsburg, IN 46112 USA Tel 317-225-3412
E-mail: authorsavannahgoins@gmail.com.

Massachusetts Continuing Legal Education, Inc., *(978-0-944490; 978-1-57589; 978-1-68345)* 10 Winter Pl., Boston, MA 02108 USA (SAN 226-3033) Tel 617-482-2205; Fax: 617-482-9498; Toll Free: 800-966-6253
Web site: http://www.mcle.org.

Massey Publishing, *(978-0-9640883)* P.O. Box 8945, Atlanta, GA 31106-0945 USA Tel 404-406-5034 (phone/fax)
E-mail: galemassey7@aol.com
Dist(s): **New Leaf Distributing Co., Inc.**

Massey University Press (NZL) *(978-0-9941300; 978-0-9941325; 978-0-9941363; 978-0-9941407; 978-0-9941415; 978-0-9941473; 978-0-9951001; 978-0-9951029; 978-0-9951095; 978-0-9951135; 978-0-9951230; 978-0-9951229; 978-0-9951318; 978-0-9951354; 978-0-9951378; 978-0-9951407; 978-0-9951431; 978-0-9951465; 978-1-991016; 978-1-9911511) Dist. by* **IPG Chicago.**

Master Books *Imprint of* **New Leaf Publishing Group**

Master Communications, Inc., *(978-1-888194; 978-1-60480)* 2692 Madison Rd., Suite N1-307 N1-307, Cincinnati, OH 45208 USA (SAN 299-2140) Tel 513-563-3100; Fax: 513-563-3105; Toll Free: 800-765-5885
E-mail: sales@master-comm.com
Web site: http://www.worldculturemedia.com; http://www.master-comm.com
Dist(s): **Follett School Solutions.**

Master Pr., *(978-0-9646543; 978-0-9759049; 978-0-9790296; 978-0-9834326; 978-0-9885057; 978-0-9913121; 978-0-9993750)* 318 SE. 4th Terrace, Cape Coral, FL 33990 USA Tel 239-772-0634 (phone/fax); Fax: 239-772-0634; Toll Free: 800-325-9136
E-mail: neil@ezraproject.org.

Master Publishing, Inc., *(978-0-945053)* 2640 Summit Dr. Suite 307, Glenview, IL 60025 USA (SAN 245-8829) Tel 847-363-2704
E-mail: pete@w5yi.com
Web site: http://www.MasterPublishing.com; http://www.ForrestMims.com; http://www.w5yi.org
Dist(s): **WFiveYI Group, Inc., The.**

Master Strategies Publishing, *(978-0-9766485)* 5806 Chatsworth Ct., Arlington, TX 76018 USA Toll Free: 888-792-5105.

Mastermind Resource Group, *(978-1-7333883)* 1248 Lacey Oak Loop, Round Rock, TX 78681 USA Tel 512-964-1631
E-mail: maverickmoses@gmail.com.

Masterpiece Comics Inc., *(978-0-692-09414-3; 978-0-692-09415-0)* 6320 Dogwood Rd., Baltimore, MD 21207 USA Tel 443-824-3424
E-mail: dmogul63@gmail.com
Dist(s): **Independent Pub.**

Masterpiece Creations Graphics & Publishing, *(978-0-615-23057-3; 978-0-9842171)* 305 Friendship Ln., Suite 100, Gettysburg, PA 17325 USA (SAN 858-7507) Tel 717-337-1829
E-mail: dj@masterpiececreations.biz
Web site: http://www.masterpiececreations.biz.

MasterVision, *(978-1-55919)* 969 Park Ave., New York, NY 10028 USA Tel 212-879-0448
E-mail: stadin1@aol.com
Web site: http://www.mastervision.com/.

Masterwork Bks., *(978-0-9845162)* 14128 Reflection Lakes Dr., Foty Myers, FL 33907 USA (SAN 859-6212)
E-mail: MasterworkBooks@aol.com
Web site: http://www.masterworkbooks.com.

Mastery Education Corporation *See* **Charlesbridge Publishing, Inc.**

Mastery For Strings Pubns., *(978-0-9753919)* 1005 Meriden Ln., Austin, TX 78703 USA Tel 512-474-8196
E-mail: musipro@aol.com.

Mastery Learning Systems, *(978-1-888976)* 532 N. School St., Ukiah, CA 95482 USA Fax: 707-462-9307; Toll Free: 800-433-4181 (phone/fax)
E-mail: mastery@pacific.net
Web site: http://www.masterylearningsystems.com.

Masthof Pr., *(978-1-883294; 978-1-930353; 978-1-932864; 978-1-60126)* 219 Mill Rd., Morgantown, PA 19543-9701 USA Tel 610-286-0258; Fax: 610-286-6860
E-mail: mast@masthof.com
Web site: http://www.masthof.com.

Matchbox Pr., *(978-0-578-80819-2; 978-1-7378871)* 111 S Kenilworth Ave, Mount Prospect, IL 60056 USA Tel 312-415-0783
E-mail: hilary.yelvington@gmail.com.

Matchstick Literary, 3000 Atrium Way, Mt. Laurel, NJ 08054 USA Tel 888-306-8885
E-mail: mgomez@matchliterary.com
Web site: www.matchliterary.com.

Matchu Pichu Press *See* **Matchu Pichu Pr.**

Matchu Pichu Pr., *(978-1-7328684)* 1740 Tristen Dr., Newtown, PA 18940 USA Tel 610-574-4746
E-mail: matthew.elliot.sherman@gmail.com
Web site: http://www.matthew-sherman.com.

Mateboer, Johannes Aart, *(978-0-9759487)* Div. of Captain's Publishing, 6514 Wakehurst Rd., Charlotte, NC 28226 USA Tel 704-540-7617 (phone/fax)
E-mail: hlmateboer@hotmail.com
Web site: http://www.captainspublishing.com
Dist(s): **eBookit.com.**

Math Essentials, *(978-0-9666211; 978-0-9821901; 978-0-9843629; 978-0-9994433; 978-1-7335018; 978-1-7345880; 978-0-578-81771-2; 978-0-578-81772-9; 978-1-7372633; 978-0-578-36861-0; 979-8-9888207)* P.O. Box 1723, Los Gatos, CA 95031 USA (SAN 991-0069) Fax: 408-358-3738; Toll Free: 866-444-6284; 265 Carlton Ct., Los Gatos, CA 95032
E-mail: math.essentials@verizon.net
Web site: http://www.mathessentials.com.

Math in Motion *See* **Crane Bks.**

Math Solutions, *(978-0-941355; 978-1-935099)* Div. of Marilyn Burns Education Assocs., Orders Addr.: 150 Gate 5 Rd., Sausalito, CA 94965 USA (SAN 665-5424) Tel 415-332-4181; Fax: 415-331-1931; Toll Free Fax: 877-942-8837; Toll Free: 800-868-9092
E-mail: info@mathsolutions.com; jcross@mathsolutions.com; jwayland@mathsolutions.com
Web site: http://www.mathsolutions.com
Dist(s): **MyiLibrary**
Scholastic, Inc.

Math Solutions Publications *See* **Math Solutions**

Math Studio, The, *(978-1-929362)* 271 Lafayette St., Salem, MA 01970-5404 USA
E-mail: cdraper@mathstudio.com
Web site: http://www.mathstudio.com.

Math4Minors LLC, *(978-1-7328503; 979-8-9870497)* 321 Rt 59 No. 444, Tallman, NY 10982 USA Tel 845-369-7723
E-mail: info@mathmilemarkers.com
Web site: www.mathmilemarkers.com.

Mathematical Sciences Research Institute, *(978-0-9639903; 978-0-9824800)* 17 Gauss Way, Berkeley, CA 94720-5070 USA Tel 510-642-0143; Fax: 510-642-8609
E-mail: librarian@msri.org
Web site: http://www.msri.org/.

Mathematical Solutions Publishing Company *See* **Twianie Roberts Consulting**

Mathieson Creative Media, *(978-1-940350)* 9140 SW Chelan Pl, Beaverton, OR 97008 USA
E-mail: MathiesonCreativeMedia@outlook.com.

Mathis, Stefan, *(978-0-692-89659-4; 978-0-578-86023-7)* 420 Somerset Dr, AUBURNDALE, FL 33823 USA Tel 863-585-9621
Dist(s): **Ingram Content Group.**

MathisJones Communications, LLC, *(978-0-9799482; 978-0-9840117; 978-0-9850542; 978-0-9853093; 978-0-9889643; 978-0-9964948; 978-1-7321345)* Orders Addr.: P.O. Box 569, Chesterfield, MO 63006-0569 USA (SAN 854-8102) Tel 636-938-1100; Fax: 636-349-1100; Edit Addr.: 1 Putt Ln., Eureka, MO 63025-2828 USA
E-mail: info@mathisjones.com
Web site: monographpublishing.com
Dist(s): **eBookit.com.**

Mathis-Njie, Joan J. *See* **Anointed Pubs.**

MATHSTORY.COM, *(978-0-9702641)* Div. of Rak Productions, P.O. Box 20226, New York, NY 10025-1511 USA Tel 212-864-5462
E-mail: mathstory2000@aol.com
Web site: http://mathstory.com.

MathWord Pr., LLC, *(978-0-9840425; 978-1-939431)* 97 Fennbrook Dr., Hamden, CT 06517 USA Tel 203-288-8114
E-mail: mathwordpress@aol.com
Web site: mwpenn.com.

Matinicus Pr., *(978-0-9765689)* 734 Cleveland Ave., Brackenridge, PA 15014-1501 USA.

Matisse Studios, *(978-0-9630069)* 4572 Via Marina 207, Marina Del Rey, CA 90292 USA
E-mail: LauriAnneMatisse@gmail.com
Web site: www.laurimatisse.com; http://www.matissestudios.com; www.evesmemoirs.com.

MatJo International, *(978-0-9996107)* P.O. Box 232154, Encinitas, CA 92023-2154 USA Tel 310-429-9099
E-mail: happylittlegarbagetruck@gmail.com
Web site: happylittlegarbagetruck.

Matos, Melissa, *(978-1-7364970)* 3119 Willits Rd. 0, PHILADELPHIA, PA 19114 USA Tel 2155282941
E-mail: melissa@momtoast.com
Dist(s): **Ingram Content Group.**

Matter of Africa America Time, *(978-0-9760523)* 2114 Vincent Ave. N., Minneapolis, MN 55411 USA.

Matter of Rhyme, A *See* **Matter of Rhyme, A**

Matthew E Nordin, *(978-0-578-47509-7; 978-0-578-61523-3; 978-1-7355573)* 105 Broad St., Grinnell, IA 50112 USA Tel 402-670-3664
E-mail: matthewenordin@gmail.com
Web site: http://www.scenerychanges.com/
Dist(s): **Ingram Content Group.**

Matthew Upholz, *(978-0-578-42185-8)* 13 Scofield Ct., Bloomington, IL 61704 USA Tel 440-829-1628
E-mail: scottbowlshiner@gmail.com
Dist(s): **Ingram Content Group.**

Matthews, Marion, *(978-1-7379314)* 920 I St., Petaluma, CA 94952 USA Tel 707-853-9381
E-mail: MMATTHEWS_BARBEROSA@YAHOO.COM.

Matting Leah Publishing Co., *(978-0-9761528; 978-0-9905764)* 21 Grand St., WARWICK, NY 10990-0265 USA
Web site: http://www.mattingleahpublishing.com.

Matzah Ball Bks., *(978-0-9753629; 978-1-7367301)* 3469 Redwood Ave., Los Angeles, CA 90066 USA
E-mail: info@matzahballbooks.com
Web site: http://www.matzahballbooks.com.

Mau, C. Publishing Co., *(978-0-9778843)* Orders Addr.: P.O. Box 30084, Edmond, OK 73003-0002 USA
E-mail: cmaupublishing@cox.net.

Maui Arthoughts Co., *(978-0-945045)* P.O. Box 967, Wailuku, HI 96793-0967 USA (SAN 245-8799) Tel 808-244-0156; Toll Free: 800-403-3472
E-mail: books@maui.net
Web site: http://www.booksmaui.com
Dist(s): **Quality Bks., Inc.**

Mauldin Publishing & Literacy House, *(978-0-9786565)*
E-mail: mauldinpublishingliteracyhouse@gmail.com
Web site: http://www.naypree-enterprises.com.

Maupin House Publishing *Imprint of* **Capstone**

Maval Medical Education *See* **Maval Publishing, Inc.**

Maval Publishing, Inc., *(978-1-884083; 978-1-59134)* Div. of Maval Printing Co., 5335 Victoria Cir., Firestone, CO 80504 USA Tel 303-682-9424
E-mail: info@jejerre.com
Web site: http://www.jejerre.com
Dist(s): **Majors Scientific Bks., Inc.**
Matthews Medical Bk. Co.

Maven Of Memory Publishing, *(978-0-9768042; 978-0-9833277; 978-0-9864412)* P.O. Box 398, Hurst, TX 76053-0398 USA Fax: 817-282-0000
Web site: http://www.mavenofmemory.com.

MavenMark Books, LLC *See* **HenschelHAUS Publishing, Inc.**

Maverick Arts Publishing (GBR) *(978-1-84886) Dist. by* **Lerner Pub.**

Maverick Bks. *Imprint of* **Trinity Univ. Pr.**

Maverick Bks., *(978-0-9672355)* P.O. Box 897, Woodstock, NY 12498 USA (SAN 253-9284) Toll Free: 866-478-9266 (phone/fax) Do not confuse with Maverick Books, Perryton, TX
E-mail: maverickbooks@aol.com; hank1@ptsi.net.

Maverick Bks., Inc., *(978-0-916941; 978-0-9608612; 978-1-59188)* Orders Addr.: P.O. Box 549, Perryton, TX 79070 USA (SAN 240-7183) Tel 806-435-7611; Fax: 806-435-2410; Edit Addr.: 14492 N.W. Loop 143, Perryton, TX 78070 USA Do not confuse with Maverick Books, Woodstock, NY
E-mail: hank1@ptsi.net
Web site: http://www.hankthecowdog.com
Dist(s): **Children's Plus, Inc.**
Follett School Solutions
Ingram Publisher Services.

Maverick Press *See* **Maverick Bks.**

Mawco, Inc., *(978-0-9853523)* 22172 Bakers Mill Rd., Dacula, GA 30019 USA Tel 404-202-7615
E-mail: a1missy@aol.com.

Mawi, Inc., *(978-0-9743901)* P.O. Box 471666, Chicago, IL 60647-6525 USA
E-mail: info@mawibooks.com
Web site: http://www.mawibooks.com.

Max & Leo Bks., *(978-1-7358214)* 3229 W. Gloria Switch Rd, Church Point, LA 70525 USA Tel 404-448-1504
E-mail: maxandleobookseries@gmail.com.

Max Osterhagen *See* **Brumby Kids**

Max Publication, Inc., *(978-0-9633577; 978-0-9799882; 978-0-692-76992-8; 978-0-9995882)* Div. of DL Services, Inc., Orders Addr.: 825 Malvern Hill, Alpharetta, GA 30022 USA Tel 770-851-0935; Fax: 770-740-0188
E-mail: info@mrandmrsitaly.com
Web site: www.mrandmrsitaly.com; www.mrandmrsitaly.com.

MAX Publishing, LLC, *(978-1-970097)* 5252 Olde Towne Rd Suite A, Williamsburg, VA 23188 USA
E-mail: tagconsulting123@gmail.com
Web site: www.tijuanagholson.com.

Max West *See* **Different Mousetrap Pr. LLC**

Maxim Pr., *(978-0-9767096)* 6947 Coal Creek Pkwy. SE, No. 137, Newcastle, WA 98059-3159 USA
E-mail: lg@maximpress.com
Web site: http://www.maximpress.com/.

Maximilian Pr. Pubs., *(978-0-9668650; 978-1-930211; 978-0-9827717)* Orders Addr.: P.O. Box 64841, Virginia Beach, VA 23467-4841 USA Tel 757-482-2273; Fax: 757-482-0325; Edit Addr.: 920 S. Battlefield Blvd., No. 100, Chesapeake, VA 23322 USA
E-mail: mp-publishing@inter-source.org
Web site: http://www.maximilianpressbookpublishers.com/.

Maximus Publishing, *(978-0-9792439)* P.O. Box 4455, Whitefish, MT 59937-4455 USA (SAN 852-8829)
E-mail: MaximusPublishing@bresnan.net
Web site: http://www.maximuspublishing.com.

Maxwell, Andre, *(978-0-578-10115-6; 978-0-578-10116-3; 978-0-9881811)* 722 Sawyer St. SE, Olympia, WA 98501 USA Tel 253-509-4022
E-mail: aleighmaxwell@gmail.com
Dist(s): **Follett School Solutions.**

Maxwell, Joseph *See* **LifeStory Publishing**

Maxwell, Mackenzie, *(978-0-692-05134-4; 978-0-692-05135-1)* 7209 Deerfield Dr., Rowlett, TX 75089 USA Tel 2145044598
E-mail: freelance.mackenzie@gmail.com
Dist(s): **Ingram Content Group.**

Maxx Out Pubns., *(978-0-692-51684-3; 978-0-578-49406-7; 978-0-578-52269-2)* 7931 s drexel ave, chicago, IL 60619 USA Tel 773-817-0750
Dist(s): **CreateSpace Independent Publishing Platform.**

May 3rd Bks., Inc., *(978-0-692-72921-2; 978-1-945891)* 201 E. Patrick St. No. 3212, Frederick, MD 21701 USA Tel 202-740-5137
E-mail: info@may3rdbooks.com
Web site: www.may3rdbooks.com.

May, Cynthia D., *(978-0-615-12578-7)* 7720 W. 14 Rd., Mesick, MI 49668-9792 USA.

May December Pubns. LLC, *(978-0-9845372; 978-1-936730; 978-1-940734)* P.O. Box 5132, Beaverton, OR 97006 USA
E-mail: twbrown@maydecemberpublications.com
Web site: http://www.maydecemberpublications.com.

May, L. B. & Assocs., 3517 Neal Dr., Knoxville, TN 37918 USA Tel 865-922-7490; Fax: 865-922-7492
E-mail: lbmay@aol.com.

MAY Publishing, *(978-0-9881804; 978-1-960056)* P.O. Box 1212, Midlothian, VA 23113 USA Tel 804-423-1452
E-mail: maypublishing@yourish.com
Web site: https://merylyourish.com/.

Maya & Me Pubns., *(978-0-692-47111-1; 978-0-9972566)* 12060 Cty. Line Rd Suite J No. 197, Madison, AL 35756 USA Tel 520-241-6559
E-mail: efalva@yahoo.com
Web site: www.maya-and-me.com.

Mayhaven Publishing, Inc., *(978-1-878044; 978-1-932278; 978-1-939695)* P.O. Box PO Box 557, Mahomet, IL 618530557 USA Tel 217-586-4493; *Imprints*: Wild Rose (Wild Rose)
E-mail: mayhavenpublishing@mchsi.com
Web site: http://www.mayhavenpublishing.com
Dist(s): **Brodart Co.**
Deseret Bk. Co.
Distributors, The
Follett School Solutions
Mumford Library Bks., Inc.
Quality Bks., Inc.

Mayhem Bks., *(978-0-9770055)* P.O. Box 313, Bon Secour, AL 36511 USA
E-mail: sweetzer@gulftel.com.

Mayhematic Pr. *Imprint of* **Wheeler, Zachry**

Maylin, Grace, *(978-0-9792384)* 204 S. Roycroft Blvd., Cheektowaga, NY 14225 USA
E-mail: gmds@adelphia.net.

Maynard, Vernal *See* **Maynard, Vernal Hugo**

Maynard, Vernal Hugo, *(978-0-692-91009-2; 978-0-692-05785-8; 978-0-692-05786-5; 978-0-692-05787-2; 978-0-692-07746-7; 978-0-692-17816-4; 978-0-692-17817-1; 978-0-578-48739-7; 978-0-578-48741-0)* 306 Mt. Bethel Rd., Harmony, NC 28634 USA Tel 816-922-9357
E-mail: junecaniel@gmail.com; info@jcaniel.com
Dist(s): **CreateSpace Independent Publishing Platform.**

Maynestream Pr., *(978-0-9715183)* 3189 Cocoplum Cir., Coconut Creek, FL 33063 USA
E-mail: contact@maynestream.com
Web site: http://www.weirdthings.com.

Mayo, Jerry, *(978-0-9985792)* 7524 Via Desierto NE, Albuquerque, NM 87113 USA Tel 505-344-1857
E-mail: Mayo505@gmail.com.

Mayo, Johnny, *(978-0-9765918)* P.O. Box 5484, Columbia, SC 29250 USA Tel 803-767-6756
E-mail: k9heroes@att.net
Web site: http://www.bucksheroes.com.

Mayor of Venice, *(978-0-9998956; 978-1-950698)* 2302 Pacific Ave., Venice, CA 90291 USA Tel 650-740-5018
E-mail: felivesey@gmail.com
Web site: www.ignisla.com
Dist(s): **Ingram Content Group.**

Mayreni *Imprint of* **Mayreni Publishing**

Mayreni Publishing, *(978-0-9653718; 978-1-931834)* Orders Addr.: Vatche Ghazarian 239 Rolling Hill Rd., PORTSMOUTH, RI 02871 USA Tel 831-655-4377; Edit Addr.: Vatche Ghazaraian 239 Rolling Hill Rd., PORTSMOUTH, RI 02871 USA; *Imprints*: Mayreni (Mayreni)
E-mail: mayrenipublishing@comcast.net; vatcheg@gmail.com
Web site: http://https://www.mayreni.net.

Maytag Messerschmitt Media Concern, *(978-0-9768470)* 931 W. 19th St., Santa Ana, CA 92706 USA.

Mazaa, LLC, *(978-0-9849624)* 1555 Botelho Dr., No. 433, Walnut Creek, CA 94596 USA Tel 925-954-7182
E-mail: jofarrell@mazaallc.com.

Maze Creek Studio, *(978-0-9742285)* Orders Addr.: 1495 E. Thirteenth St., Carthage, MO 64836-9507 USA Tel 417-359-8787
E-mail: studio@andythomas.com
Web site: http://www.andythomas.com.

Mazeology, *(978-0-9793043)* 284 W. 12th St., No. 2, New York, NY 10014-6000 USA Tel 212-929-0734
E-mail: mazeology@yahoo.com
Web site: http://www.mazeology.net.

Mazie, Bernard *See* **Pangus Publishing**

Mazo Pubs., *(978-965-90462; 978-965-7344; 978-1-936778; 978-1-946124; 978-1-956381)* P.O. Box 10474, Jacksonville, FL 32247 USA Tel 815-301-3559 (phone/fax)
E-mail: mazopublishers@gmail.com; cm@mazopublishers.com
Web site: http://www.mazopublishers.com
Dist(s): **Smashwords.**

Mazur, Kathy *See* **Spring Ducks Bks., LLC**

Mazzola, Gigi, *(978-0-578-99878-7; 978-0-578-99879-4)* 530 21st St, Beaumont, TX 77706 USA Tel 409-363-3288
E-mail: gigimazzola@hotmail.com.

MB Publishing, LLC, *(978-0-9624166; 978-0-9850814; 978-0-9913646; 978-0-9908430; 978-0-9994463; 979-8-9871401)* 7831 Woodmont Ave., Pmb 312, Bethesda, MD 20814 USA Toll Free: 866-530-4732
Web site: http://www.mbpublishing.com
Dist(s): **BWI**
BookBaby
Quality Bks., Inc.

MBG Creations, *(978-0-578-41008-1)* 9214 Sydney Ln., Brentwood, TN 37027 USA Tel 336-209-1180
E-mail: Katguiliano@gmail.com
Dist(s): **Ingram Content Group.**

MBK Publishing, *(978-1-7378330)* 106 Deleon Rd., Cocoa Beach, FL 32931 USA Tel 321-213-0866
E-mail: zachary.w.ernst@gmail.com.

MBM Pr., *(978-0-578-92302-4)* 2932 Marlatt Ave, Manhattan, KS 66502 USA Tel 503-887-9559
E-mail: jamiebosse@gmail.com
Web site: www.moneybossmom.com.

Mbongiou, Franziska, *(978-0-578-58549-9)* 2609 Amy Dr., Jeffersonville, PA 19403 USA Tel 610-805-5277
E-mail: gmbongiou@yahoo.com.

MBS Onsite llc *See* **This Little Light Productions**

MBT, *(978-0-9768419)* P.O. Box 215, Guilford, CT 06437 USA.

MC Basset, LLC, *(978-0-9774800)* P.O. Box 241, Asbury, NJ 08802 USA Tel 908-537-6410 (phone/fax)
E-mail: mkuderka@mcbasset.com.

M.C. Beynon, *(978-0-578-49900-0; 978-0-578-49907-9; 978-1-7349499)* 4955 Bode Ln., McHenry, IL 60050 USA Tel 773-619-9264
E-mail: merwojo73@yahoo.com
Dist(s): **Ingram Content Group.**

MC Math Comics, *(978-0-9728453)* 720 Sutton Dr., Carlisle, PA 17013 USA Tel 717-243-4470
E-mail: clarkcherry@aol.com
Web site: http://plusman.org.

MC Publishing & Design Group, *(978-0-578-00109-8; 978-0-9966696)* 4207 Forest Ln., Nacogdoches, TX 75965 USA Toll Free: 800-781-4890.

MC Wheeler Enterprises, *(978-0-692-68048-3; 978-0-692-80814-6)* 657 Highland Ave., FALL RIVER, MA 02720 USA Tel 401-835-2718.

MC123 *See* **Taven Hill Studio**

MCA Denver, *(978-0-692-76221-9; 978-0-692-76318-6; 978-0-692-78930-8; 978-0-692-87222-2; 978-0-578-43484-1; 978-0-578-72961-9)* 1485 Delgany St., Denver, CO 80202 USA Tel 720-236-1813
E-mail: zoel@mcadenver.org
Web site: www.mcadenver.org
Dist(s): **D.A.P./Distributed Art Pubs.**

McArdle, Donald, *(978-0-615-14212-8)* 11556 110th Ter., Largo, FL 33778-3716 USA
Web site: http://www.santaandbugsy.com
Dist(s): **Lulu Pr., Inc.**

McBeth, Mary, *(978-0-692-06303-3; 978-0-692-06328-6)* 710 S. Loop St., San Marco, TX 78666 USA Tel 210-393-6883
E-mail: megmcbeth@yahoo.com
Dist(s): **Ingram Content Group.**

McBook Pubs., LLC, *(978-0-9705777)* Orders Addr.: P.O. Box 35513, Tulsa, OK 74005 USA Tel 918-671-6656
E-mail: jdokla@cableone.net.

McBride Collection of Stories LLC, *(978-0-692-81414-7; 978-0-692-82418-4; 978-0-692-84474-8; 978-0-692-85606-2; 978-0-692-03985-4; 978-0-692-03986-1; 978-1-7361082; 978-1-7371528)* 70-02 Parsons Blvd, No. 7c, Fresh Meadows, NY 11365 USA Tel 917-771-4463
E-mail: mcbridestories@gmail.com
Dist(s): **CreateSpace Independent Publishing Platform.**

McBride, Danielle, *(978-0-578-44099-6; 978-0-578-44101-6)* 147-24 230th St., Jamaica, NY 11413 USA Tel 917-771-4463
E-mail: amaritasway@gmail.com
Dist(s): **Ingram Content Group.**

McBride, Heddrick, *(978-0-615-70075-5; 978-0-615-70923-9; 978-0-615-71693-0; 978-0-615-72059-3; 978-0-615-72339-6; 978-0-615-78846-3; 978-0-615-86353-5; 978-0-615-91076-5; 978-0-615-95937-5; 978-0-692-68651-5)* 70-02 parsons blvd. apt 7c, Flushing, NY 11365 USA Tel 917-771-4463
Web site: www.mcbride-collection-of-stories.com
Dist(s): **CreateSpace Independent Publishing Platform.**

McCaid Paul Books, *(978-0-9996145; 978-1-7357299)* P.O. Box 909, DeFuniak Springs, FL 32435 USA Tel 850-305-6343
E-mail: cmccaidpaul@gmail.com.

McCallie, Julia M., *(978-0-9980665)* P.O. Box 7663, MESA, AZ 85216 USA Tel 702-444-5547; Fax: 000-000-0000
E-mail: jmmccallie@yahoo.com.

McCaney Publishing, Inc., *(978-0-692-09204-0)* 12400 Hwy. 157, Florence, AL 35633 USA Tel 256-483-6080
E-mail: maurice_mccaney@yahoo.com.

McCarthy, Maria Skantzaris, *(978-0-9755844)* P.O. Box 1308, Westford, MA 01886 USA
E-mail: msmccarthy@mindspring.com.

McCarthy, Sally Studios, *(978-0-9898968)* 7 Patriot Ln., Whitman, MA 02382 USA Tel 781-771-3394
E-mail: sallyjm@comcast.net.

McCarthy-Contreras, Shannon, *(978-0-692-99294-4)* 2872 W Ribera Pl, Tucson, AZ 85742 USA Tel 520-981-6620
E-mail: smccarthc@gmail.com
Dist(s): **Ingram Content Group.**

McCaw, Matt, *(978-1-7337301)* 614 Kingfisher Creek Dr., Austin, TX 78748 USA Tel 512-350-0634
E-mail: wmmccaw@gmail.com.

McCaw, Pat, *(978-1-7328606)* 27335 205th Ave, Eldridge, IA 52748 USA Tel 563-285-9163
E-mail: patmccawauthor@gmail.com.

McClain Printing Co., *(978-0-87012)* Orders Addr.: P.O. Box 403, Parsons, WV 26287-0403 USA (SAN 203-9478) Tel 304-478-2881; Fax: 304-478-4658; Toll Free: 800-654-7179
E-mail: mcclain@mcclainprinting.com; mmckinnie@mcclainprinting.com
Web site: http://www.McClainPrinting.com.

McClanahan Publishing Hse., Inc., *(978-0-913383; 978-1-934898; 978-0-9829785; 978-0-615-40157-7; 978-0-9836687; 978-0-9847933; 978-0-9895424; 978-0-9897078)* P.O. Box 100, Kuttawa, KY 42055 USA (SAN 285-8371) Tel 270-388-9388; Fax: 270-388-6186; Toll Free: 800-544-6959
E-mail: books@kybooks.com
Web site: http://www.kybooks.com
Dist(s): **Partners Bk. Distributing, Inc.**

McClelland & Stewart (CAN) *(978-0-396; 978-0-7710) Dist. by* **Random.**

McClelland & Stewart (CAN) *(978-0-396; 978-0-7710) Dist. by* **Peng Rand Hse.**

McClendon, Rosheda, *(978-0-578-87705-1)* 1226 Goins Rd., Wrightsville, GA 31096 USA Tel 478-290-7258
E-mail: lookmamaican@gmail.com.

McClenney Publishing *See* **First Associates Publishing**

McClure Publishing Inc., *(978-0-9790450; 978-0-9833697; 978-0-9915335; 978-0-9989223; 978-1-7347595; 979-8-9853967; 979-8-9877802)* Orders Addr.: 5185 Mudville Ln., Waldorf, MD 20602 USA; Edit Addr.: 398 W. Army Trail Rd., Suite 124, Bloomingdale, IL 60108 USA (SAN 852-2782) Tel 800-659-4908; Toll Free: 800-659-4908 (phone/fax)
E-mail: kathymcclurepublishing@outlook.com
Web site: http://www.mcclurepublishing.com.

McConnell, Eric, *(978-0-578-48113-5; 978-0-578-62782-3; 978-0-578-76813-7; 978-0-578-81257-1; 978-0-578-91497-8; 978-0-578-92047-4; 978-0-578-96518-5)* 7409 Blix St., San Diego, CA 91403 USA Tel 818-789-3571; 818-808-8953
E-mail: ericsurf8@sbcglobal.net; youngnoahadventures@gmail.com
Dist(s): **Ingram Content Group.**

McConnell, Gregory Austin, *(978-1-7331602)* 5505 N. 17th St., Ozark, MO 65721 USA Tel 417-988-3830
E-mail: officialtempestpictures@gmail.com.

McCormick, Susan *See* **Carroll Pr.**

McCourtie, Anne, *(978-0-9744448)* 15700 154th Rd., Mayetta, KS 66509 USA.

McCowan, Linda, *(978-0-9814596)* 1739 S. Hwy., 89 A, Kanab, UT 84741 USA.

McCoy, Amy, *(978-0-692-65141-4; 978-1-7330362)* 142 Fairview Terr., South Glastonbury, CT 06073 USA Tel 516-551-9390
Dist(s): **CreateSpace Independent Publishing Platform.**

McCracken, Amie, *(978-0-9981052)* 716 Frederick St, Royal Oak, MI 48067 USA Tel 313-539-9087
E-mail: amie.mccracken@gmail.com.

McCray, Kathy *See* **Kathy's Pen**

McCray-Garrison, Rispba, *(978-0-692-15397-0; 978-0-692-16987-2; 978-0-692-16989-6)* 5009 Isla Canela Ln., League City, TX 77573 USA Tel 409-599-9934
E-mail: rispba.garrison@gmail.com
Dist(s): **CreateSpace Independent Publishing Platform.**

McCullough, Jameka, *(978-0-578-80502-3)* 300 Kirkstall Dr 2720, HOUSTON, TX 77090 USA Tel 972-754-8898
E-mail: Jene8711@gmail.com.

McCuskerHill Productions, *(978-1-7365907)* 146 Indigo St., Mystic, CT 06355 USA Tel 860-803-5053
E-mail: mhmccusker@gmail.com.

McDaniel Group, *(978-1-7332194)* 2274 Salem Rd SE Ste 106 No. 5148, Conyers, GA 30013 USA Tel 678-978-4409
E-mail: mcdanielsyl@gmail.com.

McDaniel Group/Kush Kingdom Publications *See* **McDaniel Group**

McDaniel, Megan Faux *See* **25 Dreams Educational Media**

McDonald & Woodward Publishing Co., The, *(978-0-939923; 978-1-935778)* Orders Addr.: 431-B E. College St., Granville, OH 43023-1319 USA (SAN 663-6977) Tel 740-321-1140; Fax: 740-321-1141; Toll Free: 800-233-8787
E-mail: mwpubco@mwpubco.com
Web site: http://www.mwpubco.com.

McDonald, Marie *See* **Poppy Publishing Hse.**

McDonald Publishing Co., *(978-1-55708; 978-1-934256; 978-1-937664; 978-1-943600)* 567 Hanley Industrial Ct., Saint Louis, MO 63144 USA (SAN 249-5813) Tel 314-781-7400; Toll Free: 800-722-8080
E-mail: janet@mcdonaldpublishing.com.

McDonald, Wendy Goodall MD, *(978-0-9993341)* 4241 S. Martin Luther King, Dr., CHICAGO, IL 60653 USA Tel 312-320-6862; Fax: 312-320-6862
E-mail: wendygmcdonald16@gmail.com
Web site: dreverywoman.com.

McDougal & Assocs., *(978-0-9777053; 978-1-934769; 978-1-940461; 978-1-950398)* 18896 Greenwell Springs Rd., Greenwell Springs, LA 70739 USA
E-mail: hmcdougal@bellsouth.net
Web site: http://www.thepublishedword.com.

McDougal Littell Incorporated *See* **Holt McDougal**

McDougal Publishing Co., *(978-1-58158; 978-1-884369)* Orders Addr.: P.O. Box 3595, Hagerstown, MD

21742-3595 USA (SAN 856-8286) Tel 301-797-6637; Fax: 301-733-2767; Toll Free: 800-962-3684
E-mail: publishing@mcdougal.org
Web site: http://www.mcdougalpublishing.com.

cDowell Health-Science Bks., LLC, *(978-0-9741238)* P.O. Box 81, Lafayette, CO 80026 USA Tel 303-570-7231; Fax: 303-604-0773
E-mail: McDPubCo@mcdowellpublishing.com; McDPubCo@aol.com; healthscience@mcdowellpublishing.com
Web site: http://www.mcdowellpublishing.com.

lcElderry, Margaret K. Bks. *Imprint of* **McElderry, Margaret K. Bks.**

lcElderry, Margaret K. Bks., Div. of Simon & Schuster Children's Publishing, 1230 Ave. of the Americas, New York, NY 10020 USA; *Imprints:* McElderry, Margaret K. Books (MMcElderry)
Dist(s): **Children's Plus, Inc.**
Simon & Schuster, Inc.

McElreath, K.M., *(978-0-9769271)* 10420 Rivertown Rd., Fairburn, GA 30213 USA Tel 770-969-1718; Fax: 770-969-0183
E-mail: tmcelreath@bellsouth.net.

McElroy & Assocs., *(978-0-9673917)* 6651 Avignon Blvd., Falls Church, VA 22043-1724 USA Tel 703-237-5993; Fax: 703-237-5994
E-mail: roland@mcelroyassoc.com
Web site: http://www.mcelroyassoc.com.

McEvoy, N. L., *(978-0-615-95144-7; 978-0-9908933)* 3767 Winding Lake Cir., Orlando, FL 32835 USA Tel 8477369375
Dist(s): **CreateSpace Independent Publishing Platform.**

McEwen, Judith A., *(978-0-9780693)* 22342 Chimayo Bend, San Antonio, TX 78258 USA Tel 210-630-9226; Fax: 210-595-7490
E-mail: chickensonthego@hotmail.com
Web site: http://www.chickensonthego.com.

McFadden, Linnea, *(978-0-9984681)* 1740 Alden Ln., Wyomissing, PA 19610 USA Tel 610-656-9173
E-mail: lbqtmm@gmail.com.

†McFarland & Co., Inc. Pubs., *(978-0-7864; 978-0-89950; 978-1-4766; 979-8-3686)* Orders Addr.: P.O. Box 611, Jefferson, NC 28640 USA (SAN 215-093X) Tel 336-246-4460; Fax: 336-246-5018; 336-246-4403; Toll Free: 800-253-2187 (orders only); Edit Addr.: 960 Hwy., 88 W., Jefferson, NC 28640 USA
E-mail: info@mcfarlandpub.com; vtomlinson@mcfarlandpub.com
Web site: http://www.mcfarlandbooks.com
Dist(s): **Ebsco Publishing**
Follett School Solutions
Metapress
MyiLibrary
ebrary, Inc.; *CIP.*

McFinn Press *See* **Captain McFinn and Friends LLC, McFinn Pr.**

McGab Publishing, *(978-0-9788092)* 12438 Prather Ave., Pt Charlotte, FL 33981-1352 USA
Web site: http://weirdobook.com.

McGarry, Donna *See* **Pollux Ink**

McGee, Tori *See* **Rowboat Pr.**

McGinley, Aaron, *(978-1-7330859)* 27 Willowick Dr., Asheville, NC 28803 USA Tel 828-808-8425
E-mail: aaronmcginley001@gmail.com
Dist(s): **Ingram Content Group.**

McGovern, Matthew /700acres Communications, *(978-0-9749445)* 27 McGovern Dr., Buxton, ME 04093 USA
E-mail: matt@mattmcgovern.com
Web site: http://www.mattmcgovern.com.

McGowan, Linda G. LLC dba LM, *(978-1-7336947)* 27200 Cty. Rd. 313, Lot 19, Buena Vista, CO 81211 USA Tel 719-238-2590
E-mail: ragingravin@gmail.com
Web site: www.unicornandthemaster.com.

mcgraw, cecilia, 65 Fairway Dr., San Rafael, CA 94901 USA Tel 415-246-8721
E-mail: ccmcgraw@aol.com.

McGraw, Jason A., *(978-0-615-13681-3)* 254 Westminster Rd., Rochester, NY 14607 USA Tel 585-771-7777
E-mail: jaymcgraw18@aol.com
Dist(s): **Lulu Pr., Inc.**

†McGraw-Hill Cos., The, *(978-0-07)* 6480 Jimmy Carter Blvd., Norcross, GA 30071-1701 USA (SAN 254-881X) Tel 614-755-5637; Fax: 614-755-5611; Orders Addr.: 860 Taylor Station Rd., Blacklick, OH 43004-0545 USA (SAN 200-254X) Fax: 614-755-5645; Toll Free: 800-722-4726 (orders & customer service); 800-338-3987 (college); 800-525-5003 (subscriptions); 800-352-3566 (books - US/Canada orders); P.O. Box 545, Blacklick, OH 43004-0545 Fax: 614-759-3759; Toll Free: 877-833-5524
E-mail: customer.service@mcgraw-hill.com
Web site: http://www.mcgraw-hill.com; http://www.ebooks.mcgraw-hill.com/
Dist(s): **Cambridge Univ. Pr.**
Children's Plus, Inc.
Ebsco Publishing
Libros Sin Fronteras
McGraw-Hill Osborne
McGraw-Hill Create (TM)
MyiLibrary
Sams Technical Publishing, LLC
ebrary, Inc.; *CIP.*

McGraw-Hill Education (GBR) *(978-0-07) Dist. by* **McGraw.**

McGraw-Hill Education, *(978-1-259; 978-1-260; 978-1-264; 978-1-265; 978-1-266; 979-8-219; 979-8-220; 979-8-221; 979-8-222)* Two Penn Plaza, New York, NY 10121-2298 USA Tel 212-904-2000; a/o The Mcgraw-Hill Companies, 8787 Orion Pl., Columbus, OH 43240 (SAN 256-3908) Tel 614-755-5637; Fax: 614-755-5611
E-mail: customer.service@mcgraw-hill.com
Web site: http://www.mheducation.com/custserv.html; http://www.mcgraw-hill.com
Dist(s): **Brilliance Publishing, Inc.**
McGraw-Hill US Higher Ed ISE
McGraw-Hill US Higher Ed USE
McGraw-Hill Cos., The
McGraw-Hill Professional Publishing
McGraw-Hill Higher Education
MyiLibrary
ebrary, Inc.

McGraw-Hill Higher Education, *(978-0-07; 978-1-121)* Orders Addr.: P.O. Box 545, Blacklick, OH 43004-0545 USA Toll Free: 800-338-3987; Edit Addr.: 1333 Burr Ridge Pkwy., 3rd Flr., Burr Ridge, IL 60527 USA; *Imprints:* McGraw-Hill/Dushkin (Dshkn McG-Hill); McGraw-Hill Science, Engineering & Mathematics (McG-H Sci Eng)
E-mail: customer.service@mcgraw-hill.com
Web site: http://www.mhhe.com
Dist(s): **Follett School Solutions**
McGraw-Hill US Higher Ed USE Legacy
McGraw-Hill US Higher Ed USE
McGraw-Hill Cos., The
McGraw-Hill Education
McGraw-Hill Professional Publishing
MyiLibrary
Oxford Univ. Pr., Inc.
ebrary, Inc.

McGraw-Hill Osborne, *(978-0-07; 978-0-88134; 978-0-931988)* Div. of The McGraw-Hill Professional, 160 Spear St. Flr. 7, San Francisco, CA 94105-1544 USA (SAN 274-3450) Toll Free: 800-227-0900
E-mail: customer.service@mcgraw-hill.com
Web site: http://www.osborne.com
Dist(s): **Ebsco Publishing**
McGraw-Hill Cos., The
MyiLibrary
ebrary, Inc.

McGraw-Hill Professional Book Group *See* **McGraw-Hill Schl. Education Group**

McGraw-Hill Professional Publishing, *(978-0-07)* Div. of McGraw-Hill Higher Education, Orders Addr.: P.O. Box 545, Blacklick, OH 43004-0545 Fax: 614-755-5645; Toll Free: 800-722-4726; Edit Addr.: 2 Penn Plaza, New York, NY 10121-2298 USA Tel 212-904-2000; *Imprints:* International Marine/Ragged Mountain Press (Inter Mar/Rag)
Dist(s): **AMACOM**
American Pharmacists Assn.
Berrett-Koehler Pubs., Inc.
Ebsco Publishing
Entrepreneur Media Inc/Entrepreneur Pr.
Harvard Business Review Pr.
McGraw-Hill Cos., The
McGraw-Hill Medical Publishing Div.
McGraw-Hill Trade
MyiLibrary
ebrary, Inc.

McGraw-Hill Schl. Education Group, *(978-0-07; 978-0-7602; 978-0-8306; 978-0-911314; 978-0-917253; 978-1-55738; 978-1-307)* Div. of The McGraw-Hill Companies, Orders Addr.: P.O. Box 545, Blacklick, OH 43004-0545 USA Fax: 614-755-5645; Toll Free: 800-442-9685 (customer service); 800-722-4726; Edit Addr.: 8787 Orion Pl., Columbus, OH 43240 USA Tel 614-430-4000; Toll Free: 800-344-7344; c/o Grand Rapids Distribution Center, 3195 Wilson NW, Grand Rapids, MI 49544 (SAN 253-6420) Fax: 614-755-5611
E-mail: customer.service@mcgraw-hill.com
Web site: http://www.accessmedbooks.com; http://www.MHEducation.com
Dist(s): **Ebsco Publishing**
McGraw-Hill Cos., The
Urban Land Institute
ebrary, Inc.

McGraw-Hill Science, Engineering & Mathematics *Imprint of* **McGraw-Hill Higher Education**

McGraw-Hill Trade, *(978-0-07; 978-0-658; 978-0-8442)* Div. of McGraw-Hill Professional, Orders Addr.: P.O. Box 545, Blacklick, OH 43004-0545 USA Tel 800-722-4726; Fax: 614-755-5645; Edit Addr.: 2 Penn Plaza, New York, NY 10121 USA Tel 212-904-2000; *Imprints:* Passport Books (Passport Bks)
E-mail: Jeffrey_Krames@mcgraw-hill.com
Web site: http://www.books.mcgraw-hill.com
Dist(s): **Ebsco Publishing**
McGraw-Hill Cos., The
MyiLibrary
ebrary, Inc.

McGraw-Hill/Contemporary, *(978-0-658; 978-0-8092; 978-0-8325; 978-0-8442; 978-0-88499; 978-0-89061; 978-0-913327; 978-0-940279; 978-0-941263; 978-0-9630646; 978-1-56626; 978-1-56943; 978-1-57028)* Div. of McGraw-Hill Higher Education, Orders Addr.: P.O. Box 545, Blacklick, OH 43004-0545 USA Toll Free Fax: 800-998-3103; Toll Free: 800-621-1918; Edit Addr.: 4255 W. Touhy Ave., Lincolnwood, IL 60712 USA (SAN 169-2208) Tel 847-679-5500; Fax: 847-679-2494; Toll Free Fax: 800-998-3103; Toll Free: 800-323-4900; *Imprints:* National Textbook Company (Natl Textbk Co)
E-mail: ntcpub@tribune.com
Web site: http://www.ntc-cb.com
Dist(s): **Continental Bk. Co., Inc.**
Ebsco Publishing
Giron Bks.
Libros Sin Fronteras
McGraw-Hill Cos., The
ebrary, Inc.

McGraw-Hill/Dushkin *Imprint of* **McGraw-Hill Higher Education**

McHay, Micki, *(978-0-9786826)* 8212 Dolphin Bay Ct., Las Vegas, NV 89128 USA (SAN 854-655X).

McIntyre, Connie *See* **Grannie Annie Family Story Celebration, The**

McJimpsey, Erica *See* **RUACH PUBLISHING Co.**

McKatlib Pr., *(978-0-9745440)* P.O. Box 76693, Atlanta, GA 30358-1693 USA
Web site: http://www.bethanyadventures.com.

†McKay, David Co., Inc., *(978-0-679; 978-0-88326; 978-0-89440)* Subs. of Random Hse., Inc., Orders Addr.: 400 Hahn Rd., Westminster, MD 21157 USA Tel 410-848-1900; Toll Free: 800-733-3000 (orders only); Edit Addr.: 201 E. 50th St., MD 4-6, New York, NY 10022 USA (SAN 200-240X) Tel 212-751-2600; Fax: 212-872-8026
Dist(s): **Libros Sin Fronteras**; *CIP.*

McKellen-Caffey, *(978-0-9794191)* 15543 Sprig St., Chino Hills, CA 91709-2853 USA (SAN 853-4144) Tel 909-393-0894
E-mail: mckellencaffey@yahoo.com
Web site: http://chiselhedgehog.com.

McKenna, Mark, *(978-0-9727681)* P.O. Box 633, Florida, NY 10921 USA.

McKenna Publishing Group, *(978-0-9713659; 978-1-932172)* 425 Poa Pl., San Luis Obispo, CA 93405 USA Tel 805-550-1667; Fax: 805-783-2317
E-mail: ric@mckennapubgrp.com
Web site: http://www.mckennapubgrp.com
Dist(s): **Booklines Hawaii, Ltd.**

McKenny, Stephanie L. *See* **J & J Publishing Co.**

McKenzie, Cheryl, *(978-1-7320103)* 21436 Roaring Water Way, Los Gatos, CA 95033 USA Tel 408-335-3442; *Imprints:* C. Lee McKenzie (C Lee Mc)
E-mail: clee38@gmail.com
Dist(s): **Ingram Content Group.**

McKinney, David, *(978-0-692-42801-6; 978-0-692-60111-2; 978-0-692-86325-1; 978-0-692-98324-9)* 7311 E 64 St, Tulsa, OK 74133 USA Tel 918-252-2360 Do not confuse with David McKinney in Phoenix, AZ
E-mail: sardsfamily@cox.net.

McKinnon, Robert Scott, *(978-0-9651943)* 1608 Seventh St., S., Great Falls, MT 59405 USA Tel 406-452-3500
E-mail: maddog526@bresnan.net
Web site: http://home.bresnan.net/~maddog526/.

McKinsey, *(978-1-7334748)* 3360 San Antonio St., Tilques, TX 78411 USA Tel 361-855-3534
E-mail: Mary_Meaney@McKinsey.com.

McKiver, Debbie dba Strong & Healthy Temple, *(978-0-692-18080-8)* 2650 Foxglove Dr SW, MARIETTA, GA 30064 USA Tel 770-850-0603
E-mail: debmac@bellsouth.net
Dist(s): **Ingram Content Group.**

McLellan Bks., *(978-0-9747536)* Orders Addr.: P.O. Box 341, Claymont, DE 19703-0341 USA Tel 302-798-4006; Fax: 302-798-2567
E-mail: richardmclellan@dca.net; richard@mclellanbooks.com
Web site: http://www.mclellanbooks.com.

MCM Prime, Inc., *(978-0-9742351)* 6355 E. Duke Ranch Rd., Pearce, AZ 85625-6113 USA Tel 520-824-4051; Fax: 775-249-9133
E-mail: paulmc@vtc.net
Web site: http://www.mcmprime.pair.com/mcmpindx.htm.

MCM Publishing *Imprint of* **Thompson, Jeniffer**

McManus, Steve, *(978-0-9964485; 978-1-7349083)* 5807 Radford Ave, Valley Village, CA 91607 USA Tel 323-573-0986
E-mail: steve@stevemcmanus.com.

McMillan, Carol, *(978-0-9907106)* 12 Marigold Dr, Bellingham, WA 98229 USA Tel 509-429-0293
E-mail: sylvanease@msn.com.

McMillen Publishing, *(978-0-9635812; 978-1-888223)* Orders Addr.: 304 Main St., Ames, IA 50010 USA (SAN 254-9085) Tel 515-232-0208; Fax: 515-232-0402 (orders); Toll Free: 800-750-6997 (In Iowa); 800-453-3960 (Outside Iowa)
E-mail: denise.sunvold@sigler.com
Web site: http://www.mcmillenbooks.com.

McMurtrey, Martin A., *(978-0-9623961)* 808 Camden, San Antonio, TX 78215 USA Tel 210-223-9680.

McNair Publishing, *(978-0-9976406)* 1751 Mizell Ave., Winter Park, FL 32789 USA Tel 407-644-5662
E-mail: TrudyMcNair@outlook.com
Web site: www.mcnairpublishing.com.

McNatmar Ventures LLC, *(978-0-9787540)* P.O. Box 1324, Clover, SC 29710-7533 USA Tel 803-222-4043
E-mail: rhcisjdm@comporium.net
Web site: http://www.mcnatmar.com.

McNaughton Publishing, *(978-1-64640)* 1776 White Oak Dr., Eugene, OR 97405 USA Tel 800-313-0999
E-mail: info@mcnaughtonpublishing.com.

McNeil & Richards, *(978-0-9825602)* 2715 N. Wisconsin Ave., Peoria, IL 61603 USA.

McNeil Publishing, *(978-1-7340908)* 130 Veracruz Dr., Ponte Vedra Beach, FL 32082 USA Tel 904-742-8487
E-mail: vivianpinner@gmail.com
Web site: vivianpinnertherapy.com.

McNeill, Lance, *(978-0-692-75992-9; 978-0-692-75994-3; 978-0-692-97350-9; 978-0-692-16251-4; 978-0-578-53977-5)* 6200 Honey Dew Ct., AUSTIN, TX 78749 USA Tel 512-964-6040.

McPeake Design, *(978-0-578-14032-2; 978-0-692-92511-9)*.

McPhaul Publisher *See* **CJ Publishing Co.**

McPugh, Kathleen, *(978-0-9742062)* Orders Addr.: P.O. Box 8372, Fresno, CA 93747 USA; Edit Addr.: P.O. Box 2552, Fallbrook, CA 92088-2552 USA
Web site: http://home.att.net/~kathfreeman/book.html; http://home.att.net/~kathfreeman
Dist(s): **Ingram Content Group.**

McQueen Publishing Co., *(978-0-917186)* 1211 S. Osceola Ave., Orlando, FL 32806-2223 USA (SAN 203-9516).

MCrc Industries, LLC *See* **MCrc Industries, LLC — A Publishing Hse.**

MCrc Industries, LLC — A Publishing Hse., *(978-0-692-10760-7; 978-0-692-13581-5; 978-0-692-13718-5; 978-0-692-14425-1; 978-0-692-14426-8; 978-0-692-14442-8; 978-1-7325521; 978-0-578-98118-5)* 8220 Bridgeport Bay Cir., MT Dora, FL 32757 USA Tel 407-245-1254; *Imprints:* ANGI PERRETTI (MYID_G_ANGI PE)
E-mail: angiperretti@outlook.com; angiperretti@gmail.com
Dist(s): **Ingram Content Group.**

McRitchie, Mike, *(978-0-578-03644-1)* 109 Falcon Creek Dr., McKinney, TX 75070 USA Tel 972-540-6800
E-mail: mmcritichie@tx.rr.com
Dist(s): **Lulu Pr., Inc.**

Mcruffy Pr., *(978-1-59269)* P.O. Box 212, Raymore, MO 64083 USA Tel 816-331-2500; Fax: 816-331-3868; Toll Free Fax: 888-967-1300; Toll Free: 888-967-1200
E-mail: brian@mcruffy.com
Web site: http://www.mcruffy.

McSellin Ray II, *(978-0-692-17897-3; 978-0-692-17898-0; 978-1-7363423; 978-0-578-32526-2; 979-8-218-20231-6)* 157 Forest Pl., Stockbridge, GA 30281 USA Tel 404-664-4036
E-mail: mcsellinr@gmail.com
Dist(s): **Ingram Content Group.**

McSweeney's Books *See* **McSweeney's Publishing**

McSweeney's Publishing, *(978-0-9703355; 978-0-9719047; 978-1-932416; 978-1-934781; 978-1-936365; 978-1-938073; 978-1-940450; 978-1-944211)* Orders Addr.: 849 Valencia St., San Francisco, CA 94110-1736 USA (SAN 254-3184)
E-mail: custservice@mcsweeneys.net
Web site: http://www.mcsweeneys.net
Dist(s): **Baker & Taylor Publisher Services (BTPS)**
Children's Plus, Inc.
MyiLibrary
Publishers Group West (PGW).

MCW Publishing, *(978-0-9753773)* 50 Brookdale Ave., Rochester, NY 14621 USA Tel 585-317-5780
E-mail: itm2000@hotmail.com.

McWilliams Mediation Group Ltd., *(978-0-9768663; 978-1-7350243)* P.O. Box 6216, Denver, CO 80206 USA (SAN 257-5442) Tel 303-830-0171
E-mail: joan@peacefinder.com
Web site: http://www.peacefinder.com
Dist(s): **ebrary, Inc.**

McWitty Pr., Inc., *(978-0-9755618; 978-0-9852227; 978-0-9977554)* 1835 NE Miami Gardens Dr. 150, MIAMI, FL 33179 USA Tel 305-466-0652
E-mail: jo@momentumtours.com
Web site: http://www.mcwittypress.com
Dist(s): **MyiLibrary**
Publishers Group West (PGW).

McWong Ink, *(978-0-9820881)* 440 Kent Ave., Apt. PH1B, Brooklyn, NY 11211 USA
Web site: http://www.gordonandlili.com
Dist(s): **Emerald Bk. Co.**
Greenleaf Book Group.

MD Ford, *(978-1-7346389; 978-1-7369555; 979-8-9880059)* 222 W Brown Rd Unit 25, Mesa, AZ 85201 USA Tel 480-415-5353
E-mail: whisperderdarlene@gmail.com; randall.ford@mdford.com
Web site: www.mdford.com.

m.d. hughes, *(978-0-9788541)* 9 Pasadena Rd., Branford, CT 06405 USA
Web site: http://www.cryofthefalcon.com.

Avitable Pub., *(978-0-9769794; 978-0-578-09899-9)* P.O. Box 38, East Meadow, NY 11554 USA Fax: 516-826-6843
E-mail: milliemsrd@aol.com
Web site: http://www.CaloriestheBottomLine.com.

ME Creations, LLC, *(978-1-7377412)* 1213 Morgan Ave, Drexel Hill, PA 19026 USA Tel 610-924-0162
E-mail: ebradley870@gmail.com.

ME Media LLC *See* **Tiger Tales**

Me On the Page, *(978-0-578-42980-9; 978-1-7338064; 978-1-7368399; 979-8-9855827)* 2895 Dandelion Cir., Antioch, CA 94531 USA Tel 925-382-8986
E-mail: Pelang@comcast.net
Dist(s): **Ingram Content Group.**

Mead, Brian Publishing, *(978-0-9717509)* 203 E. Grove Rd., Long Grove, IA 52756 USA (SAN 255-2329)
E-mail: meadpub@juno.com; mattedeye@aol.com.

Mead Lommen Publishing *See* **Calaroga Publishing**

Meadow Road Publishing, *(978-1-7334393)* 360 Bayhead Dr, Melbourne, FL 32940-7705 USA Tel 321-543-7054
E-mail: SillyYaya@SillyYaya.com
Web site: SillyYaya.com.

†Meadowbrook Pr., *(978-0-88166; 978-0-915658)* 5451 Smetana Dr., Minnetonka, MN 55343 USA (SAN 207-3404) Tel 612-930-1100; Fax: 612-930-1940; Toll Free: 800-338-2232
E-mail: mballard@meadowbrookpress.com
Web site: http://www.meadowbrookpress.com
Dist(s): **Hachette Bk. Group**
Simon & Schuster
Simon & Schuster Children's Publishing; *CIP.*

Meadowlark, *(978-0-692-26616-8; 978-0-692-43466-6; 978-0-9966801; 978-0-692-56779-1; 978-1-7322410; 978-1-7342477; 978-1-7362232; 978-1-956578)* Orders Addr.: P.O. Box P.O. Box 333, Emporia, KS 66801 USA; Edit Addr.: 206 Rural St., Emporia, KS 66801 USA Tel 620-794-9320
Web site: www.meadowlark-books.com
Dist(s): **CreateSpace Independent Publishing Platform.**

Meadowview Pubs., *(978-0-9741218)* Orders Addr.: P.O. Box 444, Portland, CT 06480 USA Tel 860-342-2646; Edit Addr.: 221 E. Cotton Hill Rd., Portland, CT 06480 USA
E-mail: marketbase@peoplepc.com.

MeAgain Publishing, *(978-0-9993012; 979-8-218-27682-9)* 3180 Fox Squirrel Dr., Orange Park, FL 32073 USA Tel 904-338-3008
E-mail: beth@meagainpublishing.com
Web site: www.meagainpublishing.com.

Publisher Name Index

Means To An End, (978-0-9995852) 7250 Old Redmond Rd. Apt M147, Redmond, WA 98052-6817 USA Tel 425-861-8042
E-mail: vsches@frontier.com.

MEAR LLC, (978-0-9787628) 636 Twp. Rd., 2724, Loudonville, OH 44842 USA Tel 419-994-3462 (phone/fax)
E-mail: mearllc@gmail.com
Web site: www.twralphabetbook.com.

MEC Publishing, (978-0-9746865) 1923 W. 17th St., Santa Ana, CA 92706 USA (SAN 256-405X)
E-mail: mecpublishing@aol.com
Web site: http://www.mecpublishing.com.

Mechanech Pubns., (978-0-9702861; 978-0-9856497) 4 Kaser Terr., Monsey, NY 10952 USA Tel 914-352-1926.

Mechling Bookbindery, (978-0-9703825; 978-0-9744657; 978-0-9760563; 978-0-9793772; 978-0-9841400; 978-1-938184) Div. of Mechling Associates, Inc., Orders Addr.: 1124 Oneida Valley Rd., Route 38, Chicora, PA 16025-3820 USA Tel 724-287-2120; Fax: 724-285-9231; Toll Free: 800-941-3735
E-mail: sales@mechlingbooks.com
Web site: http://www.mechlingbooks.com.

MECROSS Pubns., (978-0-9995179; 979-8-9875247) P.O. Box 1061, Gorham, ME 04038 USA Tel 732-580-5070
E-mail: rsnyderhalo@gmail.com
Web site: branwensmajor.com.

Medal Bks., (978-0-9764300; 978-0-9785667) Orders Addr.: 11711 Royal Palm Blvd. #1-202, CORAL SPRINGS, FL 33065 USA
E-mail: RonanBlazeBooks@aol.com
Web site: http://.

Medallion Pr., Inc., (978-0-9743639; 978-1-932815; 978-1-933836; 978-1-934755; 978-1-60542; 978-1-942546) Orders Addr.: 4222 Meridian Pkwy. Ste 110, Aurora, IL 60504 USA (SAN 255-5360) Tel 630-513-8316; Fax: 630-513-8362
E-mail: jeanne@medallionmediagroup.com
Web site: http://www.medallionmediagroup.com
Dist(s): **Legato Pubs. Group**
MyiLibrary
Publishers Group West (PGW).

Meder, Julia, (978-0-9967304; 978-1-944260) Kurpfalzstr. 156, Neustadt, 67435 DEU Tel 984-255-5049
E-mail: info@dreamfinder-coaching.com.

Medernach, T.K. *See* **ThunderBolt Pubns.**

Media Alert!, (978-0-9676616) P.O. Box 735, Littleton, CO 80160-0735 USA Toll Free: 800-986-5560 (code 02)
E-mail: CNFsueLS@aol.com.

Media Angels, Inc. *See* **Knowledge Box Central**

Media Angels, Inc., (978-0-9700385; 978-1-931941) Orders Addr.: 15720 S. Pebble Ln., Fort Myers, FL 33912-2341 USA
E-mail: felice@mediaangels.com
Web site: http://www.mediaangels.com
Dist(s): **Send The Light Distribution LLC.**

Media Assocs., (978-0-918501) 221 6th. St., Galt, CA 95632 USA (SAN 657-3207) Tel 916-320-4042; *Imprints*: Archives Pr. (Archives Pr) Do not confuse with Media Assocs., Marina Del Rey, CA
E-mail: lovekillsbook@gmail.com; moyturra@gmail.com.

Media Blasters, Inc., (978-1-890228; 978-1-58655; 978-1-59883) 132 W. 36th St. Rm. 401, New York, NY 10018-8837 USA (SAN 859-5712)
E-mail: info@media-blasters.com
Web site: http://www.media-blasters.com; http://www.kittymedia.com
Dist(s): **Diamond Comic Distributors, Inc.**
Diamond Bk. Distributors
Follett School Solutions.

Media Creations, Incorporated *See* **Aeon Publishing Inc.**

Media For Life, (978-0-9675068) 300 Main St. No. 540, Madison, NJ 07940 USA Fax: 201-490-1801
E-mail: EduFun@aol.com.

Media Hatchery, (978-0-9971276; 978-1-955180) 42 Green Lake Dr., Orchard Park, NY 14127 USA Tel 716-245-1634
E-mail: bill@mediahatchery.com
Web site: https://MediaHatchery.com; https://NostalgicBuffalo.com.

Media Magic New York, (978-0-9744211) 15 W. 39th St., 13th Flr., New York, NY 10018 USA Tel 212-926-5575
E-mail: mediamagicny@aol.com; info@mediamagic-ny.com.

Media Man! Productions *Imprint of* **Fairwood Pr.**

Media Mint Publishing, (978-0-9842778; 978-0-9846897; 978-0-9895364; 978-0-9969446) 2021 Brae Trail, Birmingham, AL 35242-7134 USA Tel 205-408-0363
E-mail: bodatnow@me.com
Web site: http://www.mediamint.net
Dist(s): **Smashwords.**

Media Publishing Group, The, (978-0-692-82027-8) 11 Penn plaza 5th Flr., NEW YORK, NY 10001 USA Tel 718-473-9819
E-mail: Sylfronia.king@mail.com; Sylfronia.king@mail.com.

Media Rodzina (POL) (978-83-7278; 978-83-85594) *Dist. by* **Distribks Inc.**

MediaTek Grafx, (978-0-692-30348-1; 978-0-692-16738-0; 978-0-578-52228-9) POB 62 938 Chestnut Grove S. Rd., Bonnieville, KY 42713 USA Tel 7169695632.

Medical Alternative Pr., (978-0-9660882) 4173 Fieldbrook Rd., West Bloomfield, MI 48323 USA Tel 248-851-3372; Fax: 248-851-0421; Toll Free: 888-647-5616 Do not confuse with Medical Alternative Pr., Colleyville, TX
E-mail: alselko@hotmail.com
Web site: http://www.drbrownstein.com.

Medical Manor Bks., (978-0-934232) Subs. of Manor Hse. Pubns., Inc., 3501 Newberry Rd., Philadelphia, PA 19154 USA (SAN 217-2526) Tel 800-343-8464; Fax: 215-440-9255; Toll Free: 800-343-8464
E-mail: info@diet-step.com; sales@diet-step.com; sales@medicalmanorbooks.com; marketing@diet-step.com; DrWalk@diet-step.com; info@medicalmanorbooks.com
Web site: http://www.medicalmanorbooks.com/; http://www.peace-healingbooks.com; http://www.manorhousepublications.com
Dist(s): **Baker & Taylor Publisher Services (BTPS)**
Distributors, The
Follett School Solutions
Quality Bks., Inc.
Unique Bks., Inc.
ebrary, Inc.

Medici Publishing, Inc., (978-0-9743791; 978-0-9823853) P.O. Box 282, Beulah, CO 81023 USA Tel 719-485-1167
E-mail: marcprat@juno.com
Web site: http://www.medicibooks.org.

Medicine Wheel Education (CAN) (978-0-9938694; 978-1-989122) *Dist. by* **Orca Bk Pub.**

Medicine Wheel Pr., (978-0-9754072) P.O. Box 8254, Edmond, OK 73083-8254 USA Tel 405-204-5479
E-mail: wildcatelder@yahoo.com
Web site: http://www.medicinewheelpress.org
Dist(s): **Publishers Group West (PGW).**

Medicine Woman Inc., The, (978-0-9771906) Orders Addr.: P.O. Box 613, Cascade, ID 83611 USA Tel 208-382-6653; Edit Addr.: 843 S. Main Hwy. 55, Cascade, ID 83611 USA
E-mail: tmw@ctcweb.net
Web site: http://www.themedicinewoman.com.

Medicus Pr., Inc., (978-0-9787727) P.O. Box 284, Leonia, NJ 07605-0284 USA (SAN 851-5905) Tel 201-816-7363; Fax: 201-266-0537
E-mail: medicuspress@yahoo.com.

Medina Publishing, Ltd. (GBR) (978-0-9570233; 978-1-909339; 978-0-9564170; 978-0-9567081) *Dist. by* **Casemate Pubs.**

Medio Media *See* **Medio Media Publishing**

Medio Media Publishing, (978-0-9666941; 978-0-9725627; 978-1-933182) 627 N. 6th Ave., Tucson, AZ 85705-8330 USA Toll Free: 800-324-8305
E-mail: JoeD846136@aol.com; meditate@mediomedia.org
Web site: http://www.mediomedia.org
Dist(s): **Continuum International Publishing Group, Inc.**
Macmillan
National Bk. Network.

Medley, (978-1-890034) 1620 Los Alamos, SW, Albuquerque, NM 87104 USA Tel 505-247-3921; *Imprints*: Medley Publications (Medley Pubns)
E-mail: litchman@unm.edu.

Medley, Cynthia, (978-0-9861178; 978-0-9974021; 978-0-9989748; 978-1-7342690) 805 Brunson St., Prairie du Chien, WI 53821 USA Tel 608-379-1691
E-mail: cmedley49@yahoo.com.

Medley Pubns. *Imprint of* **Medley**

MedPress & Quality Publishers *See* **Quality Pubs.**

Medusa Road Pr., (978-0-9779295) 6 Rte. 75, Norton Hill, NY 12083 USA Tel 518-966-5281
E-mail: MedusaRoadStudio@aol.com
Web site: http://CarolynsWebsite.net.

Medwag Publishing, (978-0-9654963) P.O. Box 36037, Richmond, VA 23235 USA Tel 804-794-8186
E-mail: alrx1@juno.com.

Meehl Foundation Pr., (978-0-9767049) P.O. Box 2089, Brazoria, TX 77422-2089 USA Tel 979-798-7972
E-mail: meehlfou@meehlfoundation.org
Web site: http://www.meehlfoundation.org.

MeeraMasi, Inc., (978-0-9773645; 978-0-9797191) 449 London Pk. Ct., San Jose, CA 95136 USA Tel 408-365-8044; Fax: 408-225-8586
E-mail: info@meeramasi.com; sonali@meeramasi.com
Web site: http://www.meeramasi.com.

Meerkat Pr., (978-0-692-37854-0; 978-0-9966262; 978-1-946154) 200 River Vista Dr. Suite 522, Atlanta, GA 30339 USA Tel 678-439-7675
Web site: www.meerkatpress.com
Dist(s): **CreateSpace Independent Publishing Platform**
Independent Pubs. Group
Midpoint Trade Bks., Inc.

Meerkat's Adventures Bks., (978-0-9778072) 510 Diamond St, Suite A, San Francisco, CA 94114 USA (SAN 850-2862)
Web site: http://www.meerkatsadventures.com.

Meet Bks., LLC, (978-0-615-31579-9; 978-0-615-38973-8) 806 Seale Ave., Palo Alto, CA 94303 USA.

Meet the Author *Imprint of* **Owen, Richard C. Pubs., Inc.**

MeetMinnie, (978-0-9997646) P.O. Box 1628, Columbia, MD 21044 USA Tel 443-808-3201
E-mail: books@meetminnie.com
Web site: www.meetminnie.com.

Mefford, David, (978-0-9762143) 274 W. 700 N., American Fork, UT 84003 USA
E-mail: david@mefford.org.

Meg and Lucy Bks. (GBR) *Dist. by* **IPG Chicago.**

Megami Pr. LLC, (978-0-615-39156-4; 978-0-615-40446-2; 978-0-9853471) P.O. Box 128557, Nashville, TN 37212 USA
E-mail: Megamipress@gmail.com
Web site: http://www.megamipress.com.

Megtree Organics, (978-1-948347) 3914 Clear Creek Ct, Richardson, TX 75082 USA Tel 214-242-9141
E-mail: bijoy@megtree.com.

Megyeri, Graham Bks., (978-0-9711971; 978-0-9791994) 3030 Lyon St., San Francisco, CA 94123 USA Tel 415-567-0462
E-mail: minnmemory@aol.com
Web site: http://www.minnesotamemories.com
Dist(s): **Partners Bk. Distributing, Inc.**

Mehr Iran Publishing Co. *See* **Mehriran Publishing Co.**

Mehriran Publishing Co., (978-0-9633129) 14900 Talking Rock Ct., Suite B, N. Potomac, MD 20878 USA Tel 301-279-6778; Fax: 301-738-2174
E-mail: pirnia@pirnia.com
Web site: http://www.pirnia.com.

MEIER Enterprises Inc., (978-0-9726808) 8697 Gage Blvd., Kennewick, WA 99336 USA Tel 509-735-1589; Fax: 509-783-5075; Toll Free: 800-239-7589
E-mail: sranderson@meierinc.com; info@learningtowrite.com
Web site: http://www.meierinc.com; http://www.learningtowrite.comw.

Meinbach, Anita, (978-0-692-82765-9; 978-0-578-46259-2) 7620 SW 149 St., Miami, FL 33158 USA Tel 305-495-4818
E-mail: ajm2100@att.net; nancysica@aurelioandfriends.com
Web site: www.whatluckbear.com.

Meirovich, Igal, (978-0-9820556; 978-1-60796) 6408 Elray Dr., Apt. E, Baltimore, MD 21209 USA Tel 410-764-6423
E-mail: lightoncds@gmail.com
Dist(s): **BookBaby**
Lulu Pr., Inc.

Meister-Home, Inc., (978-0-9702497) P.O. Box 471250, Charlotte, NC 28247-1250 USA (SAN 256-1794) Tel 704-968-6741; Fax: 704-544-2034; *Imprints*: Meister-Home Press (Meister-Home Pr)
E-mail: ragilmartin@hotmail.com; rgilmartin@meister-home.com
Web site: http://www.meister-home.com.

Meister-Home Pr. *Imprint of* **Meister-Home, Inc.**

Mel Bay Pubns., Inc., (978-0-7866; 978-0-87166; 978-1-56222; 978-1-60974; 978-1-61065; 978-1-61911; 978-1-5134) 16 N Gore Ave Ste 203, Saint Louis, MO 63119-2315 USA (SAN 657-3630) Tel 636-257-3970; Fax: 636-257-5062; Toll Free: 800-863-5229
E-mail: email@melbay.com; sharon@melbay.com
Web site: http://www.melbay.com; www.melbaydealers.com
Dist(s): **Alfred Publishing Co., Inc.**

Mel Ona, (978-0-9716585) Div. of ONA New Body - New Life, Inc., 1203 Kamehame Dr., Honolulu, HI 96825 USA
E-mail: doctormelona@gmail.com
Web site: http://www.doctormelona.com
Dist(s): **Baker & Taylor Publisher Services (BTPS).**

Melanated Magic Bks., (978-1-7361873; 979-8-9856371) 5323 Osage Ave, Philadelphia, PA 19143-1410 USA Tel 267-987-4102
E-mail: staceymat@gmail.com.

Melanie, (978-0-692-64200-9) 208 Stimson St, Herkimer, NY 13350 USA Tel 315-219-1316
E-mail: melanie.lopata@yahoo.com.

Melanie Hooyenga, (978-0-692-72747-8; 978-0-692-72753-9; 978-0-692-72755-3; 978-0-692-04449-0) 15008 Lakeshore Dr., GRAND HAVEN, MI 49417 USA Tel 616-502-6410.

Melanin Grace Publishing, LLC, (978-0-692-87205-5; 978-0-692-87206-2; 978-0-692-97827-6; 978-0-692-97828-3) 7440 Maple Spice Ave, CANAL WINCHESTER, OH 43110 USA Tel 614-946-6475
E-mail: jeffwcrawford5+LVP0003584@gmail.com; jeffwcrawford5+LVP0003584@gmail.com.

Melanin Origins, LLC *Imprint of* **Grivante Pr.**

Melbourne Univ. Publishing (AUS) (978-0-522; 978-0-646-05507-7) *Dist. by* **IPG Chicago.**

Melbournestyle Bks. (AUS) (978-0-9757047; 978-0-9924917; 978-0-6485684; 978-0-6459106) *Dist. by* **IPG Chicago.**

melian, eugenia, (978-1-7325477) 22 saint andrew's Pl., alamo, CA 94507 USA Tel 510-280-4010
E-mail: eugenia@emmanage.net.

Melissa Ahonen LLC, (978-1-7377121) 156 Allen Dr, Lincoln, ND 58504 USA Tel 701-400-0084
E-mail: melissa@melissaahonen.com; melissaahonen@yahoo.com
Web site: www.melissaahonen.com.

Melissa & Doug, LLC, (978-1-950013; 978-1-951733) P.O. Box 590, Westport, CT 06881 USA Tel 203-762-4500
E-mail: NRitchey@melissaanddoug.com.

Melissa Boyd, (978-0-692-18983-2; 978-1-7339390; 978-1-955170) 6745 Plum Point Dr., Aberdeen Proving Ground, MD 21005 USA Tel 215-983-6366
E-mail: melimunro.boyd@yahoo.com.

Melissa de la Cruz Studio *Imprint of* **Disney Publishing Worldwide**

Melissa Productions, Inc., (978-0-9842394; 978-0-9834751; 978-0-9898293) 2003 Arundale Ln., Matthews, NC 28104 USA (SAN 858-8252) Tel 704-246-7304
E-mail: melissa@melissaproductions.com
Web site: http://www.melissaproductions.com.

MelissaCrickard, (978-0-692-22392-5; 978-0-692-25853-8; 978-0-692-91565-3; 978-0-9992059; 978-1-7325856; 978-1-7326808; 978-1-951482) 483 Park Pl., Grand Island, NY 14072 USA Tel 7168648978
Dist(s): **CreateSpace Independent Publishing Platform.**

MELJAMES, Inc., (978-0-9755195; 978-1-933419) 107 Suncreek Dr., Suite 300, Allen, TX 75013 USA
Web site: http://www.meljamesinc.com.

Melland Publishing, LLC, (978-0-9966876; 978-0-9971885; 978-0-9998957) 5515 Hargrove Ave., Caldwell, ID 83607 USA Tel 208-546-1306
E-mail: v19501971@msn.com
Web site: www.maryvine.com.

mellano, jean, (978-0-692-53981-1; 978-0-692-06685-0) 3620 demott ave, wantagh, NY 11793 USA Tel 516-221-5951
E-mail: spinjunkie53@hotmail.com
Web site: www.slippedaway.org.

†Mellen, Edwin Pr., The, (978-0-7734; 978-0-88946; 978-0-935106; 978-0-7799; 978-1-4955) Orders Addr.: P.O. Box 67, Queenston, ON LOS 1L0 CAN; Edit Addr.: P.O. Box 450, Lewiston, NY 14092-0450 USA (SAN 207-110X) Tel 716-754-2266; 716-754-2788; Fax: 716-754-1860
E-mail: sales@mellenpress.com
Web site: http://www.mellenpress.com; *CIP*.

Melquist, Justin, (978-0-578-45882-3) 2504 Fircrest Blvd., Anacortes, WA 98221 USA Tel 360-320-3895
E-mail: justin.melquist@gmail.com
Dist(s): **Ingram Content Group.**

Melton Hill Media, (978-0-9816793; 978-0-9990919) 9119 Solway Ferry Rd., Oak Ridge, TN 37830 USA (SAN 856-2288)
E-mail: wendy@meltonhillmedia.com
Web site: http://www.familyroadmap.org; http://www.meltonhillmedia.com.

Melzee's Production, (978-0-9722738) P.O. Box 394, Hawthorne, CA 90251-0394 USA Tel 310-263-7804
E-mail: melzee3@juno.com.

Me+Mi Publishing, (978-0-9679748; 978-1-931398) 400 Kno St. Ste. B, Wheaton, IL 60187-4557 USA Toll Free: 888-251-1444
E-mail: m3@memima.com
Web site: http://www.memima.com
Dist(s): **Lectorum Pubns., Inc.**
Quality Bks., Inc.

Memoir Bks., (978-0-9793387; 978-1-937748) Div. of Heidelberg Graphics, Orders Addr.: 2 Stansbury Ct., Chico, CA 95928 USA Tel 530-342-6582
Web site: http://www.heidelberggraphics.com.

Memoria Pr., (978-1-930953; 978-1-61538; 978-1-5477) Orders Addr.: 4603 Poplar Level Rd., Louisville, KY 40213-2337 USA Toll Free: 877-862-1097
E-mail: magister@memoriapress.com
Web site: http://www.memoriapress.com
Dist(s): **Chicago Distribution Ctr.**

Memories Publishing, (978-0-9748984; 979-8-9877315) P.O. Box 82516, Austin, TX 78708 USA Tel 512-907-1821
E-mail: mindyred@aol.com.

Memories Publishing, (978-0-615-78560-8; 978-0-615-81047-8; 978-0-9906120; 978-0-692-44500-6; 978-0-9981265; 978-0-9997622; 978-1-7352249) P.O. Box 82516, Austin, TX 78708 USA
E-mail: mindyred@aol.com; mindyfreedauthor25@gmail.com
Web site: mindyfreed.com; www.authorsassistant.com
Dist(s): **CreateSpace Independent Publishing Platform.**

MENDIAS, LJ, (978-0-692-94394-6) 23765 Jayhawk Ave, COLORADO SPRINGS, CO 80928 USA Tel 719-683-7424
E-mail: createillustratedesign@gmail.com
Dist(s): **Ingram Content Group.**

Mendoza, Mireida, (978-1-7376218) 11870 Caminito Ronaldo Unit 139, San Diego, CA 92128 USA Tel 209-606-7924
E-mail: mireidamendozabooks@gmail.com
Web site: mireidamendoza.com.

Mennonite Board of Missions *See* **Mennonite Mission Network**

Mennonite Mission Network, (978-1-877736; 978-1-933845) 500 S. Main St., P.O. Box 370, Elkhart, IN 46515-0370 USA Tel 219-294-7523; Fax: 574-294-8669; Toll Free: 866-866-2872
E-mail: Beyond@MennoniteMission.net
Web site: http://www.mennonitemission.net
Dist(s): **Follett School Solutions**
Herald Pr.

Mennonite Pr. Inc., (978-0-9772745; 978-0-692-03234-3) Orders Addr.: P.O. Box 867, Newton, KS 67114 USA Tel 316-283-4680; Fax: 316-283-2068; Toll Free: 800-536-4686; Edit Addr.: 532 N. Oliver Rd., Newton, KS 67114 USA
E-mail: reliability@mennonitepress.com
Web site: http://www.mennonitepress.com.

Menon, Dr. Sujeeta E., (978-0-578-25859-1) 1729 Nichole Woods Dr., Houston, TX 77047 USA
E-mail: sulizmenon@gmail.com
Web site: bit.ly/imasocialworker.

Mental Health Historic Preservation Society Of Central Illinois, (978-0-9748742) 209 Arnold Ave., East Peoria, IL 61611 USA Tel 309-699-3051
E-mail: aparr12345@aol.com
Dist(s): **Partners Bk. Distributing, Inc.**

Mentoring Minds, LP, (978-0-9763559; 978-0-9767940; 978-1-935123; 978-1-938935; 978-1-62763) P.O. Box 8843, Tyler, TX 75711 USA Fax: 800-838-8186; Toll Free: 800-585-5258
E-mail: gavin@mentoringminds.com
Web site: http://www.mentoring-minds.com.

MentorSource, LLC, (978-0-9773324) P.O. Box 24436, Minneapolis, MN 55424 USA Tel 612-269-8242
E-mail: gianna_bl@msn.com
Web site: http://www.rosyproses.com.

Mentzer Printing Ink, (978-0-9746705; 978-0-9786276; 978-0-9797502; 978-0-9894927) 1054 Virginia Ave., Indianapolis, IN 46203-1754 USA Toll Free: 800-514-6017
E-mail: info@m2print.com
Web site: http://www.m2print.com.

Menucha Pubs. Inc., (978-1-61465; 979-8-88839) 1235 38th St., BROOKLYN, NY 11218 USA (SAN 860-2115) Tel 718-232-0856; Fax: 718-232-0856
E-mail: hirsch@menuchapublishers.com.

Meomya, (978-0-9985664) 144 Cereus Ln., Saint Augustine, FL 32086 USA Tel 904-891-2956
E-mail: katie@meomya.com.

Meraki Co. *See* **Meraki Co.**

Meraki Co., (978-0-578-21845-8) 7386 Long Lake Rd. SE, Port Orchard, WA 98367 USA Tel 210-910-7428
E-mail: juliannefritz14@gmail.com.

†Mercer Univ. Pr., (978-0-86554; 978-0-88146) 1501 Mercer Univ. Dr., Macon, GA 31207 USA (SAN 220-0716) Tel 478-301-2880; Fax: 478-301-2585; Toll Free: 866-895-1472
E-mail: mupressorders@mercer.edu
Web site: http://www.mupress.org; *CIP*.

Mercesart, (978-0-9907894) 65 Dean St., Hicksville, NY 11801 USA Tel 646-269-2080
E-mail: Mercesart@hotmail.com
Web site:
Dist(s): **Lulu Pr., Inc.**

Merchant Bks. *Imprint of* **Rough Draft Printing**

Mercier Pr., Ltd., The (IRL) (978-0-85342; 978-0-900068; 978-0-947962; 978-1-85635; 978-1-86023; 978-1-901737; 978-1-78117) *Dist. by* **Casemate Pubs.**

Mercury Publishing, Inc., *(978-0-9778793)* Orders Addr.: 35 Fieldstone Way, Alpharetta, GA 30005 USA (SAN 850-5020)
E-mail: goga7n@gmail.com
Dist(s): **BCH Fulfillment & Distribution.**

Mercury West Publishing, *(978-1-948577)* 4748 Shands Dr, Mesquite, TX 75150 USA Tel 404-580-2958
E-mail: authorcmhealy@gmail.com

Mercy Grace Publishing, *(978-0-615-70230-8; 978-0-692-93247-6; 978-0-692-96818-5; 978-0-578-49654-2)* 164 Potash, Guilford, VT 05301 USA Tel 617-759-3643
E-mail: belogour@aol.com.

Mercy Place, Inc., *(978-0-9677402; 978-0-9707919)* P.O. Box 134, Shippensburg, PA 17257 USA Tel 717-532-6899; Fax: 717-532-8646; Toll Free: 800-722-6774
E-mail: mpm@reapernet.com
Web site: http://mercyplace.com
Dist(s): **Destiny Image Pubs.**

†Meredith Bks., *(978-0-696; 978-0-89721; 978-0-917102)* Div. of Meredith Corp., Orders Addr.: 1716 Locust St., LN-110, Des Moines, IA 50309-3023 USA (SAN 202-4055) Tel 515-284-2363; 515-284-2126 (sales); Fax: 515-284-3371; Toll Free: 800-678-8091; *Imprints:* Food Network Kitchens (Food Net) Do not confuse with Meredith Pr. in Skaneateles, NY
E-mail: John.OBannon@meredith.com
Web site: http://www.bhgstore.com
Dist(s): **Children's Plus, Inc.**
Follett School Solutions
MyiLibrary
Sterling Publishing Co., Inc.; *CIP.*

Meredith Etc, *(978-0-692-46265-2; 978-0-692-46804-3; 978-0-692-60643-8; 978-0-692-62432-6; 978-0-692-69480-0; 978-0-692-71820-9; 978-0-9993226; 978-1-7341578; 978-1-7378843)*
Web site: https://meredithetc.com/
Dist(s): **CreateSpace Independent Publishing Platform.**

Meredith Group Ltd., The, *(978-0-9765341)* Orders Addr.: 24 N. Bryn Mawr Ave., Box117, Bryn Mawr, PA 19010 USA (SAN 256-4920) Tel 610-642-0199; Edit Addr.: 71 Eden View Rd. # 6, Elizabethtown, PA 17022-3124 USA
E-mail: mmbellamy1@verizon.net
Web site: http://www.goldiesbook.com.

Meridia Pubs. LLC, *(978-0-615-40498-1; 978-0-9832330; 978-0-9904031)* 29439 Sayle Dr., Willoughby Hills, OH 44092 USA Tel 440-944-8047
E-mail: al.ruksenas@gmail.com
Dist(s): **BookBaby**
Smashwords.

Meridian Creative Group *See* **Larson Learning, Inc.**

Meritage Publishing, *(978-0-9769866)* Orders Addr.: 12339 Meritage Ct., Rancho Cucamonga, CA 91739 USA
E-mail: meritagepub@charter.net
Dist(s): **Quality Bks., Inc.**

Meriwether Publishing *Imprint of* **Meriwether Publishing, Ltd.**

Meriwether Publishing, Ltd., *(978-0-916260; 978-1-56608)* Div. of Pioneer Drama Service, Inc., Orders Addr.: P.O. Box 4267, Englewood, CO 80155-4267 USA (SAN 208-4716) Tel 303-779-4035; Fax: 303-779-4315; Edit Addr.: P.O. Box 4267, Englewood, CO 80155 (SAN 990-2856) Tel 303-779-4035; Fax: 303-779-4315; Edit Addr.: 9707 E. Easter Ln. Suite A, Englewood, CO 80112 USA Tel 303-779-4035; *Imprints:* Meriwether Publishing (MeriwetherPub)
E-mail: lori@pioneerdrama.com; books@pioneerdrama.com; wholesale@pioneerdrama.com
Web site: http://https://www.christianpub.com/; http://www.pioneerdrama.com
Dist(s): **Follett School Solutions.**

Merkos L'Inyonei Chinuch, *(978-0-8266)* 291 Kingston Ave., Brooklyn, NY 11213 USA Tel 718-778-0226; Fax: 718-778-4148
E-mail: yonason@kehot.net
Web site: http://www.kehotonline.com.

Merlin, Debbi, *(978-0-9793568)* 12339 Scarcella Ln., Stafford, TX 77477-1609 USA (SAN 853-232X)
E-mail: merlin@merlinmagic.cc
Web site: http://www.merlinmagic.cc.

Merlin Enterprises, *(978-0-9761017)* Orders Addr.: 11881 S. Fortuna Rd., No. 451, Yuma, AZ 85367 USA
E-mail: napuff@gmail.com
Web site: http://cafepress.com/npuff.

Merlot Group, LLC, The, *(978-0-9816123; 978-0-9887117)* P.O. Box 302, Covington, KY 41012-0302 USA Tel 859-743-1003
Web site: http://www.merlotgroup.com
Dist(s): **Lulu Pr., Inc.**

Meroe Publishing, *(978-0-9768306)* P.O. Box 664, Cusseta, GA 31805 USA
E-mail: tonieshort@meroepublishing.com
Web site: http://www.meroepublishing.com.

Merriam-Webster *Imprint of* **Merriam-Webster, Inc.**

Merriam-Webster, Inc., *(978-0-87779; 978-1-68150)* Subs. of Encyclopaedia Britannica, Inc., Orders Addr.: 47 Federal St., Springfield, MA 01102 USA (SAN 202-6244) Tel 413-734-3134; Fax: 413-731-5979; 413-734-2014; Toll Free: 800-828-1880; *Imprints:* Merriam-Webster (Merriam-Webstr); Merriam-Webster Kids (MW-Kids)
E-mail: sales@Merriam-Webster.com; orders@Merriam-Webster.com; jsantoro@Merriam-Webster.com
Web site: http://www.WordCentral.com; http://www.Merriam-Webster.com
Dist(s): **CENGAGE Learning**
Delmar Cengage Learning
Perfection Learning Corp.

Merriam-Webster Kids *Imprint of* **Merriam-Webster, Inc.**

Merrimack Bk. Works, *(978-0-9799090)* 23 Pleasant St., No. 508, Newburyport, MA 01950-2632 USA (SAN 854-7424) Tel 978-417-9277
E-mail: mary@maryleemattison.com
Web site: http://www.maryleemattison.com.

Merrimack Media, *(978-1-939166; 978-1-945756)* 665 Washington St. No. 2507, Boston, MA 02111 USA Tel 508-932-0865
E-mail: jenny@merrimackmedia.com
Web site: http://merrimackmedia.com.

Merritt Publishing *See* **Silver Lake Publishing**

Merriwell, Frank Inc., *(978-0-8373)* Subs. of National Learning Corp., 212 Michael Dr., Syosset, NY 11791 USA (SAN 209-259X) Tel 516-921-8888; Toll Free: 800-645-6337
Dist(s): **Independent Pubs. Group.**

Merry Dissonance Pr., *(978-1-939919)* 3113 Soaring Eagle Ln., Castle Rock, CO 80109 USA Tel 213-448-7701
E-mail: donnamazzitelli@gmail.com
Web site: merrydissonancepress.com.

Merry Lane Pr., *(978-0-9744307)* 18 E. 16th St., 7th Flr., New York, NY 10003 USA Tel 212-633-6505; Fax: 212-242-6077
E-mail: alan@merrylanepress.com
Web site: http://www.merrylanepress.com.

Merry Tales Publishing, *(978-0-9845471)* 209 Bobbitt Rd., Clayton, NC 27520-6557 USA (SAN 859-709X) Tel 919-550-0107.

Merryant Pubs., *(978-1-877599)* P.O. Box 1921, Vashon, WA 98070-1921 USA Toll Free: 800-228-8958
E-mail: jmboule@aol.com.

Merrybooks & More, *(978-0-9615407; 978-1-882607)* 1214 Rugby Rd., Charlottesville, VA 22903 USA (SAN 695-5053) Tel 804-979-3658; Fax: 804-296-8446; Toll Free: 800-959-2665.

MerryHeartInk, *(978-0-9856481)* 17007 SE Tong Rd., Damascus, OR 97089 USA Tel 971-285-1255
E-mail: mainsthome@earthlink.net.

Mesmer, Sandy Bergstrom Designs, *(978-1-7336945)* 1509 Bonair St., Clearwater, FL 33755 USA Tel 727-452-5745
E-mail: sandy@smesmer.com
Web site: https://www.etsy.com/shop/SandyMesmerDesigns.

Mesorah Pubns., Ltd., *(978-0-89906; 978-1-57819; 978-1-4226)* 4401 Second Ave., Brooklyn, NY 11232 USA (SAN 213-1269) Tel 718-921-9000 Toll Free: 800-637-6724; *Imprints:* ArtScroll Series (ArtScroll Series); Shaar Press (Shaar Pr)
E-mail: info@ArtScroll.com
Web site: http://www.artscroll.com.

Mesquite Tress Pr., LLC, *(978-0-9729835)* Orders Addr.: P.O. Box 17513, Louisville, KY 40217 USA; Edit Addr.: 212 W. Ormsby Ave, Louisville, KY 40203 USA
Web site: http://www.onetinytwig.com; http://www.mesquitetreepress.com; http://bluegrassbreeze.com.

Mess Hall Writers, *(978-1-885531)* P.O. Box 1551, Jeffersonville, IN 47130 USA Tel 812-288-9888; Fax: 812-288-9695
E-mail: fooddudes2@aol.com.

Message In a Bottle Translators *See* **Pangloss Publishing**

Messenger Publishing, *(978-1-7320717)* 116 S. Alcott St., Denver, CO 80219 USA Tel 303-221-4409
E-mail: CharolM@aol.com
Web site: www.thenewhumanityauthor.com.

Messiah Publishing - Pearables, *(978-0-9792446)* P.O. Box 272000, Fort Collins, CO 80527 USA (SAN 852-8837) Tel 719-549-0662
Web site: http://www.pearables.com.

Messianic Jewish Pubs., *(978-1-880226; 978-1-936716; 978-1-7339354; 978-1-951833)* Div. of The Lewis & Harriet Lederer Foundation, Inc., 6120 Day Long Ln., Clarksville, MD 21029 USA Tel 410-531-6644; Fax: 410-531-9440; Toll Free: 800-410-7367 (individual orders only)
Web site: http://www.MessianicJewish.net
Dist(s): **Anchor Distributors**
Baker & Taylor Publisher Services (BTPS)
Christian Bk. Distributors
INscribe Digital
Ingram Content Group
Messianic Jewish Resources International
Spring Arbor Distributors, Inc.

Messianic Perspectives, *(978-0-9674319; 978-0-9882120; 978-0-9898240)* Orders Addr.: P.O. Box 345, San Antonio, TX 78292-0345 USA Tel 210-226-0421; Fax: 210-226-2140; Toll Free: 800-926-5397; Edit Addr.: 611 Broadway St., San Antonio, TX 78215 USA
E-mail: info@cjfm.org
Web site: http://www.cjfm.org.

Messimer, Maria S, *(978-0-578-43171-0; 978-0-578-44132-0; 978-0-578-50848-1; 978-0-578-51225-9; 978-0-578-54301-7; 978-0-578-54307-9; 978-0-578-56645-0; 978-0-578-56820-1)* 5375 Main St., Kelseyville, CA 95451 USA Tel 707 245-5445
E-mail: msmessimer@msn.com
Dist(s): **Ingram Content Group.**

Messineo, Joe *See* **Socrates Solutions Incorporated**

Meta Adventures *See* **Meta Adventures Publishing & DIA Publishing**

Meta Adventures Publishing & DIA Publishing, *(978-0-9721202)* Orders Addr.: P.O. Box 1894, Sedona, AZ 86339 USA (SAN 254-6183) Tel 928-204-1560
E-mail: info@dreamsinaction.us; publishing@dreamsinaction.us; orderinfo@dreamsinaction.us
Web site: http://www.dreamsinaction.us; http://www.MrSedona.com
Dist(s): **Dreams in Action Distribution.**

Metacognition Pr., *(978-0-9859707)* 48 Michael Ln., Orinda, CA 94563 USA Tel 925-360-9159
E-mail: Metacognitionblog@yahoo.com.

Metal Lunchbox Publishing, *(978-0-9843437; 978-1-7335118)* 5257 Buckeystown Pike #508, Frederick, MD 21704 USA (SAN 859-1202) Tel 412-916-0211
E-mail: information@metallunchboxpublishing.com; sfvarney@metallunchboxpublishing.com
Web site: http://www.metallunchboxpublishing.com.

Metalmark Pr., *(978-0-9767239)* 7116 New Sharon Church Rd., Rougemont, NC 27572 USA
E-mail: birdcr@concentric.net
Web site: http://www.rlephoto.com.

Metamedix, Incorporated *See* **Science2Discover, Inc.**

Metamorphosis, *(978-0-9774589)* 100 State St S., Kirkland, WA 98033-6667 USA
E-mail: christinemerritt@earthlink.net
Web site: http://www.iahp.com/metamorphosis.

Metaphrog (GBR) *(978-0-9534932; 978-0-9545984) Dist. by* **D C D.**

Metapublishing, *(978-0-9654522)* 500 Center Ave. Apt. 211, Westwood, NJ 07675-1677 USA Do not confuse with Metapublishing, North Miami Beach, FL
Dist(s): **New Leaf Distributing Co., Inc.**

Metchnikoff, Elie Memorial Library, *(978-0-9634067)* 230 Orange St., No. 6, Oakland, CA 94610-4139 USA Tel 510-444-3435; Fax: 510-642-7175
E-mail: bibel@lonemountain-art.com.

Methow Pr., *(978-0-9759577; 978-0-9787554; 978-1-7366537)* P.O. BOX 1213, TWISP, WA 98856 USA Tel 206-241-6149
E-mail: editor@hjbooks.com
Web site: http://www.hjbooks.com.

Metonymy Pr. (CAN) *(978-0-9940471; 978-1-9990588) Dist. by* **SPD-Small Pr Dist.**

Metric Moon Press *See* **Graphite Pr.**

Metrix, *(978-0-692-19417-1)* 13250 W. Lincoln Hwy A502, Dekalb, IL 60115 USA Tel 815-995-7207
E-mail: Cassiemdodd1@gmail.com
Dist(s): **CreateSpace Independent Publishing Platform.**

Metro Bks., *(978-0-9752732)* 1706 W. Jarvis, 1W, Chicago, IL 60626 USA.

Metropolitan Bks. *Imprint of* **Holt, Henry & Co.**

Metropolitan Museum of Art, The, *(978-0-87099; 978-1-58839)* 1000 Fifth Ave., New York, NY 10028 USA (SAN 202-6279) Tel 212-879-5500; Fax: 212-396-5062
Web site: http://www.metmuseum.org
Dist(s): **California Princeton Fulfillment Services**
Casemate Academic
Chicago Distribution Ctr.
Continental Bk. Co., Inc.
ISD
Princeton Univ. Pr.
Yale Univ. Pr.

Metropolitan Teaching & Learning Co., *(978-0-928415; 978-1-58120; 978-1-58830)* 317 Madison Ave., New York, NY 10017 USA Tel 212-475-8826; Fax: 212-475-8311; Toll Free: 800-235-6931
Web site: http://metrotlc.com.

Meyer & Meyer Sport, Ltd. (GBR) *(978-1-84126; 978-1-78255) Dist. by* **Lewis Intl Inc.**

Meyer & Meyer Sport, Ltd. (GBR) *(978-1-84126; 978-1-78255) Dist. by* **Cardinal.**

Meyer Enterprises *See* **Western New York Wares, Inc.**

Meyer, Tjaden, *(978-0-9744536)* Orders Addr.: P.O. Box 230015, Saint Louis, MO 63123 USA Tel 314-352-2253; Edit Addr.: 7045 Parkwood St., Saint Louis, MO 63116 USA
E-mail: klmeyer@worldnet.att.net.

Meza, Marti, *(978-0-615-16571-4)* 1515 W. 7th St., Apt. 4-D, Brooklyn, NY 11204 USA
Dist(s): **Lulu Pr., Inc.**

MF Unlimited, *(978-0-9712278)* P.O. Box 55346, Atlanta, GA 30308 USA
Web site: http://www.mfunews.com
Dist(s): **Ingram Content Group.**

Mfg Application Konsulting Engineering, *(978-0-9762208)* 1071 E. 425 N., Ogden, UT 84404 USA.

M-Graphics *Imprint of* **M-Graphics Publishing**

M-Graphics Publishing, *(978-0-9753075; 978-0-9777003; 978-0-9792808; 978-1-934881; 978-1-940220; 978-1-950319; 978-1-960533)* One Dead Eye Run, Swampscott, MA 01907 USA Tel 781-990-8778 Weekdays 9AM - 4 PM; *Imprints:* M-Graphics (M-Grap)
E-mail: mgraphics.books@gmail.com
Web site: http://www.mgraphics-books.com.

M.H. Gill & Co. U. C. (IRL) *(978-0-7171; 978-0-9516306; 978-1-898256; 978-1-84889; 978-1-903464; 978-1-905172) Dist. by* **Casemate Pubs.**

M.H. Gill & Co. U. C. (IRL) *(978-0-7171; 978-0-9516306; 978-1-898256; 978-1-903464; 978-1-905172; 978-1-84889) Dist. by* **Dufour.**

MHC Ministries, *(978-0-9895422)* 1170 NE 133rd St., North Miami, FL 33161 USA Tel 786-286-5210
E-mail: mmuc31@gmail.com
Web site: www.mhcministries.com.

Mia Sharon, Inc., *(978-0-9759098)* 600 Academy Dr., No. 130, Northbrook, IL 60062 USA Tel 847-826-8196
Web site: http://www.miasharon.com.

†Micah Pubns., *(978-0-916288)* 255 Humphrey St., Marblehead, MA 01945 USA (SAN 209-1577) Tel 781-631-7601; Fax: 781-639-0772; Toll Free: 877-268-9963
E-mail: micah@micahbooks.com
Web site: http://www.micahbooks.com
Dist(s): **David, Jonathan Pubs., Inc.**
BPC; *CIP.*

Miceli, *(978-0-9888654)* P.O. Box 2027, Danvers, MA 01923 USA Tel 978-626-1429
E-mail: mary_miceli@comcast.net.

Miceli, Mary Anne, *(978-0-578-08747-4; 978-0-578-10145-3; 978-0-578-10979-4)* 10 Daniels Rd., Wenham, MA 01984 USA; P.O. Box 2027, Danvers, MA 01923
E-mail: mary_miceli@comcast.net
Web site: bostonnorthshorestoriesandpoems.com.

Micelle Pr., Inc., *(978-0-9608752; 978-1-870228)* Orders Addr.: P.O. Box 1519, Port Washington, NY 11050-0306 USA Tel 516-767-7171; Fax: 516-944-9824
E-mail: micellepress@googlemail.com
Web site: http://www.scholium.com
Dist(s): **Scholium International, Inc.**

MiceWorks, *(978-0-9764719)* 544 13th Ave., W., Kirkland, WA 98033 USA.

Michael Kastre Publishing, LLC *See* **Michael Kastre Publishing, LLC**

Michael Kastre Publishing, LLC, *(978-0-9860675; 978-0-9903754; 978-0-9964726; 978-1-7356527)* 6312 Seven Corners Ctr., Falls Church, VA 22044 USA Tel 703-298-4650
E-mail: michael@michaelkastre.com
Web site: stmichaelspress.com.

Michael Neugebauer Bks. *Imprint of* **North-South Bks., Inc.**

Michael-Christopher Bks., *(978-0-9710398)* Orders Addr.: P.O. Box 75313, Washington, DC 20013-0313 USA Tel 301-927-3179
E-mail: mc@michael-christopher.com
Web site: http://www.michael-christopher.com
Dist(s): **BookBaby.**

MichaelsMind LLC *See* **Right Stuff Kids Bks.**

Michaelson Entertainment, *(978-0-9727702; 978-1-932530; 978-1-60730)* 36 Cabrillo Terr., Aliso Viejo, CA 92656 USA Tel 949-916-0575 phone; Fax: 949-916-0574 fax; *Imprints:* 101 Book (101 Bk); ABC Book (ABCBk)
E-mail: brad@michaelsonentertainment.com
Web site: http://www.michaelsonentertainment.com
Dist(s): **Partners Bk. Distributing, Inc.**

Michalek, Curtis, *(978-0-9786177)* P.O. Box 403, Montezuma, IA 50171 USA Tel 641-623-3368
E-mail: c.a.michalek@hotmail.com
Web site: www.aluris.com.

Michele, Mary, *(978-0-615-25486-9)* 27638 N. 45th Way, Cave Creek, AZ 85331 USA Tel 602-952-8604
E-mail: scriptsrelief@cox.net
Dist(s): **Lulu Pr., Inc.**

Michelle F. Bradley, *(978-1-7372689)* 167 Ramona Ave., STATEN ISLAND, NY 10312 USA Tel 646-957-2201
E-mail: MBradley814@aol.com.

Michelle, Incorporated *See* **Dreamscape Publishing**

Michelle, Patrice *See* **Limitless Ink Press, LLC**

michelle s lazurek-author, *(978-0-692-89435-4; 978-0-692-18987-0; 978-0-578-83857-1; 978-0-578-83858-8)* 3 alliance ave, coudersport, PA 16915 USA Tel 814-274-9298
E-mail: michellelazurek@yahoo.com
Web site: www.michellelazurek.com.

Michelle's A & E (KOR) *(978-89-954869) Dist. by* **APG.**

Michelle's Bks. & More, Ltd. Co., *(978-0-9763080)* 800 Fabric X-Press Way, Dallas, TX 75234 USA Tel 972-625-1444; Fax: 972-406-1321
E-mail: michelle@michellesbooks.com
Web site: http://www.michellesbooks.com.

Michelle's Designs, *(978-0-9789694; 978-0-9817663; 978-0-9842520)* 3702 Sandpoint Ct, Carlsbad, CA 92010 USA Tel 760-720-4335; Fax: 802-609-2629
E-mail: patterns@michelles-designs.com; jen@condormedia.com
Web site: http://www.michelles-designs.com.

Michigan Publishing, *(978-0-9745109; 978-1-4181; 978-1-4255; 978-1-60785; 978-1-64315)* Div. of University of Michigan Library, 1210 Buhr Bldg, 839 Greene St., Ann Arbor, MI 48109 USA (SAN 255-9889)
E-mail: spo.pod@umich.edu; lib.pod@umich.edu
Web site: http://www.lib.umich.edu/michigan-publishing
Dist(s): **Chicago Distribution Ctr.**
Univ. of Chicago Pr. Distribution Clients
Univ. of Michigan Library.

Michigan State Univ., Julian Samora Research Institute, *(978-0-9650557)* 301 Nisbet Bldg., 1407 S. Harrison, East Lansing, MI 48823-586 USA Tel 517-432-1317; Fax: 517-432-2221
E-mail: info@jsri.msu.edu
Web site: http://jsri.msu.edu.

†Michigan State Univ. Pr., *(978-0-87013; 978-0-937191; 978-1-60917; 978-1-61186; 978-1-938065; 978-1-62895; 978-1-62896; 978-1-941258; 978-0-9967252; 978-1-68430; 978-1-947134; 978-1-948314)* Orders Addr.: 1405 S. Harrison Rd. Suite 25, East Lansing, MI 48823-5245 USA (SAN 202-6295) Tel 517-884-6901; Fax: 517-432-2611; Toll Free: 800-621-2736; 800-621-8476; *Imprints:* Makwa Enewed (MakwaEnewed)
E-mail: msupress@msupress.org
Web site: http://www.msupress.org
Dist(s): **Chicago Distribution Ctr.**
JSTOR; *CIP.*

mickego art, *(978-0-692-89076-9; 978-0-692-16315-3; 978-0-578-35321-0; 978-0-578-35912-0)* 12257 Hill Rd., Swartz Creek, MI 48473 USA Tel 989-277-1585
Dist(s): **Ingram Content Group.**

Micro Publishing Media, Inc., *(978-0-9827716; 978-1-936517; 978-1-944068; 978-1-953321)* 29 Pk. St., Stockbridge, MA 01262 USA; *Imprints:* Pop Pop Press (Pop Pop Pr)
E-mail: Deborah@micropublishingmedia.com
Web site: http://www.micropublishingmedia.com
Dist(s): **Cardinal Pubs. Group.**

Microcosm Publishing, *(978-0-9726967; 978-0-9770557; 978-0-9788665; 978-1-934620; 978-1-62106; 978-1-64841)* Orders Addr.: 2752 N. Williams Ave., Portland, OR 97227 USA (SAN 992-5635) Tel 503-799-2698; Toll Free Fax: 888-503-0599
E-mail: joe@microcosmpublishing.com
Web site: http://www.microcosmpublishing.com
Dist(s): **Baker & Taylor Publisher Services (BTPS).**

Microsoft Pr. *Imprint of* **Pearson Education**

†Microsoft Pr., *(978-0-7356; 978-0-914845; 978-0-925550; 978-1-55615; 978-1-57231; 978-1-879021)* Orders Addr.: 3 Center Plaza, Boston, MA 02108-2084 USA Toll Free: 800-677-7377; Edit Addr.: One Microsoft Way, Redmond, WA 98052-6399 USA (SAN 264-9969) Tel 425-882-8080;

Publisher Name Index

206-882-8080; 425-703-0942; Fax: 425-936-7329 Do not confuse with Microsoft Pr., Dunmore, PA
E-mail: msporder@msn.com; duanedr@microsoft.com; chriscai@microsoft.com
Web site: http://www.microsoft.com/mspress/
Dist(s): **Follett School Solutions**
Pearson Education; *CIP.*

Mid Ohio Chiropractic, *(978-0-9989090; 978-1-7346488)* 714 N. Sandusky Aveunue, Upper SAndusky, OH 43351 USA Tel 419-294-0832
E-mail: BettyLok@live.com.

Mid-Atlantic Highlands Publishing *Imprint of* **Publishers Place, Inc.**

Middelhauve Verlags GmbH (DEU) *(978-3-7876)* *Dist. by* **Distribks Inc.**

†Middle Atlantic Pr., *(978-0-912608; 978-0-9705804; 978-0-9754419)* 400 Pond View Dr., Moorestown, NJ 08057 USA Tel 856-273-9062; Fax: 856-273-7526
E-mail: blake@middleatlanticpress.com; info@middleatlanticpress.com
Web site: http://www.middleatlanticpress.com
Dist(s): **Partners Bk. Distributing, Inc.**; *CIP.*

Middle Coast Publishing, *(978-0-934523)* Div. of Merco Global Inc., P.O. Box 535, hills, IA 52235 USA (SAN 693-9031) Tel 319-321-3127
E-mail: timothybanse@yahoo.com; editor@middle-coast-publishing.com
Web site: http://www.marineenginedigest.com; http://www.middle-coast-publishing.com; www.shootersreport.com; www.goldenbeetyoga.com; www.GreatBigTravel.com
Dist(s): **Quality Bks., Inc.**

Middle River Pr., *(978-0-9785656; 978-0-9817036; 978-0-9846071; 978-0-9838203; 978-0-9857295; 978-0-9896724; 978-0-9964086; 978-1-946886)* 1498 NE 30th Ct., Oakland Park, FL 33334-4414 USA Tel 954-630-8192
E-mail: info@middleriverpress.com
Web site: http://www.middleriverpress.com.

Middlebury Hse. Publishing, *(978-0-9792067)* 3225 Middlebury Ln., Charleston, SC 29414 USA
Web site: http://www.rwridley.com; http://www.choytcaldwell.com.

Middleton, Patricia Miniseries, *(978-0-578-63989-5; 978-1-7361260)* 241 Sunderland Way, Stockbrigde, GA 30281 USA Tel 404-395-0443
E-mail: trish01@bellsouth.net
Web site: Patriciamiddletonministries.org.

Middleton Publishing *See* **Unique Coloring**

Midnight Hologram, LLC, *(978-1-938516)* 1180 Beacon Hill Crossing, Alpharetta, GA 30005 USA Tel 678-393-0420
E-mail: yvet77@comcast.net
Web site: www.midnighthologram.com.

Midnight Media, *(978-1-7340089; 979-8-9874737)* 1085 N. 910 E., Orem, UT 84097 USA Tel 801-473-5673
E-mail: jenn@jennjohansson.com.

Midpoint Trade Bks., Inc., *(978-1-940416)* Orders Addr.: 1263 Southwest Blvd., Kansas City, KS 66103 USA (SAN 631-3736) Tel 913-831-2233; Fax: 913-362-7401; Toll Free: 800-742-6139 (consumer orders); Edit Addr.: 27 W. 20th St., No. 1102, New York, NY 10011 USA (SAN 631-1075) Tel 212-727-0190; Fax: 212-727-0195
E-mail: info@midpointtrade.com
Web site: http://www.midpointtrade.com; http://www.midpointtradebooks.com/
Dist(s): **Children's Plus, Inc.**
Ingram Bk. Co.
ebrary, Inc.

MidRun Pr., *(978-0-9664095; 978-0-9824397)* 90 Larch Row, Wenham, MA 01984-1624 USA Tel 978-468-9953 (phone/fax)
E-mail: midrunpress@aol.com
Web site: http://www.midrunpress.com.

Midwest Christian Center *See* **Family Harvest Church**

Midwest Cylinder Management, Inc., *(978-0-9729026)* 1203 Paramount Pkwy., Batavia, IL 60510-1458 USA Tel 630-673-9770; Fax: 630-406-9922
E-mail: prminalt@yahoo.com
Web site: http://www.kidsmenus.com.

Midwest Graphics, Inc., *(978-0-9776893)* 180 N. Wacker Dr., Suite 104, Chicago, IL 60606 USA Tel 312-641-2236; Fax: 312-641-2256
E-mail: mark@mwgchicago.com
Web site: http://www.mwgchicago.com.

Midwest Writng, *(978-0-9778290; 978-0-9818089; 978-0-9834116; 978-0-9906190; 978-1-7334802; 979-8-9865825)* c/o RIPL 401 19th St., Rock Island, IL 61201 USA Tel 309-732-7330
Web site: http://www.mwcqc.org.

Mielcarek, David, *(978-0-9785480)* 3387 Ocean Beach Hwy, Longview, WA 98632 USA
E-mail: thebook@timeforyourmind.com
Web site: http://timeforyourmind.com.

Mighty & Meek, *(978-0-578-59860-4; 978-1-7373981)* 68 Lowry Dr., Wilmington, DE 19805 USA Tel 302-743-7240
E-mail: zebradaze@gmail.com.

Mighty Kids Media, *(978-0-9765953; 978-0-9770455; 978-1-933934; 978-0-9884241)* 4201 Congress St, Suite 451, Charlotte, NC 28209 USA Toll Free Fax: 877-723-3388 Do not confuse with companies with the same name in Dobbs Ferry, NY, Medofrd, OR, Lanett, AL
Web site: http://www.dangerrangers.com.

Mighty Lion Ventures, *(978-0-615-30860-9; 978-0-9831449)* P.O. Box 2950, Cypress, TX 77410 USA.

Mighty Media Junior Readers *Imprint of* **Mighty Media Pr.**

Mighty Media Kids *Imprint of* **Mighty Media Pr.**

Mighty Media Pr., *(978-0-9765201; 978-0-9798249; 978-0-9824584; 978-0-9830219; 978-1-938063)* Div. of Mighty Media, 1201 Currie Ave., Minneapolis, MN 55403 USA Tel 612-455-0252; Fax: 612-338-4817; *Imprints:* Mighty Media Junior Readers (MMJrRead); Mighty Media Kids (MMKids)
E-mail: info@scarlettapress.com; josh@scarlettapress.com
Web site: http://www.mightymediapress.com
Dist(s): **Continental Enterprises Group, Inc. (CEG)**
MyiLibrary
Publishers Group West (PGW).

Mighty Publishing, LLC, *(978-0-9966739)* 701 Niagara St, Denver, CO 80220 USA Tel 303-355-3120
E-mail: kbcinspires@gmail.com.

Miglior Pr., *(978-0-9827614; 978-0-9836484)* P.O. Box 7487, Athens, GA 30604 USA Tel 706-338-0017
E-mail: info@migliorpress.com
Web site: http://migliorpress.com.

Mijade Editions (BEL) *(978-2-87142)* *Dist. by* **Distribks Inc.**

Mikaya Pr., *(978-0-9650493; 978-1-931414)* 12 Bedford St., New York, NY 10014 USA Tel 212-647-1831; Fax: 212-727-0236
E-mail: Waldman@Mikaya.com
Web site: http://www.mikaya.com
Dist(s): **Firefly Bks., Ltd.**

Mikazuki Jujitsu *See* **Mikazuki Publishing Hse.**

Mikazuki Publishing Hse., *(978-0-615-47311-6; 978-0-615-48054-1; 978-0-9835946; 978-1-937981; 978-0-9910285; 978-1-942825)* 530 E. 8th St. Suite 400, Los Angeles, CA 90014 USA
E-mail: kambizmostofizadeh1@gmail.com
Dist(s): **BookBaby**
Ingram Content Group.

Mike the Wolf, *(978-0-692-49135-5; 978-0-692-77057-3; 978-0-578-48583-6)* 1045 e. 3rd St. #5, long beach, CA 90802 USA Tel 562-726-8551
Web site: www.mikethewolf.com
Dist(s): **CreateSpace Independent Publishing Platform.**

Mike-Auri Bks., *(978-0-9747587)* P.O. Box 420966, Del Rio, TX 78842 USA Tel 830-774-2789
E-mail: dfitzgibbon@stx.rr.com
Web site: http://www.texasredhen.com; http://www.mikeauri.com.

Mike-Mike Distribution, *(978-0-9741043)* 1003 N., Fifth St., Champaign, IL 61820 USA Tel 217-352-4215.

Mikenzi's Kardz & Bks. Llc., *(978-0-9792647)* 1115 S. Alhambra Cir., Coral Gables, FL 33146-3711 USA
E-mail: sgbarrow@hotmail.com.

Milano, Jacque & Assocs., *(978-0-9728432)* 700 N. Dobson Rd., No. 15, Chandler, AZ 85224 USA; *Imprints:* Carefree Publishing (Carefree Pubng)
Web site: http://www.carefreepublishing.com.

Mile High Pr., Ltd., *(978-1-885331; 979-8-218-06865-3; 978-1-959737)* Div. of Briles Group, Inc., Orders Addr.: P.O. Box 460880, Aurora, CO 80046 USA Tel 303-627-9179; Fax: 303-627-9184; Toll Free: 800-594-0800; Edit Addr.: 14160 E. Bellewood Dr., Aurora, CO 80015 USA Tel 303-745-4590
E-mail: info@milehighpress.com; milehighpress@aol.com.

Mile Oak Publishing, Inc. (CAN) *(978-1-896819)* *Dist. by* **Austin and Co.**

Miles & Assocs., *(978-0-9778623)* P.O. Box 15566, Phoenix, AZ 85060 USA Tel 386-446-9291
E-mail: drlinda03@aol.com
Web site: http://www.thenewmarriage.com.

Miles Kelly Publishing, Ltd. (GBR) *(978-1-902947; 978-1-84236; 978-1-84810; 978-1-78617; 978-1-78209)* *Dist. by* **Parkwest Pubns.**

Miles, Linda *See* **Miles & Assocs.**

Miles Music, *(978-0-9710446)* Div. of Miles Enterprises, 3060 Larson Rd., Weippe, ID 83553 USA Tel 208-435-4600; Fax: 208-435-1116
E-mail: milesmusic@idamall.com
Web site: http://www.idamall.com.

Milestone Pr., Inc., *(978-0-9631861; 978-1-889596)* Orders Addr.: P.O. Box 158, Almond, NC 28702 USA Tel 828-488-6601 (phone/fax)
E-mail: maryellenhammond@milestonepress.com
Web site: http://www.milestonepress.com
Dist(s): **America's Cycling Pubns.**
Common Ground Distributors, Inc.

Milestones Publishing, *(978-0-9786154)* P.O. Box 1556, Wylie, TX 75098 USA Tel 214-403-9852; Fax: 972-442-1613
E-mail: kaylasadams@hotmail.com
Web site: http://www.kaylaadams.net.

Milet Publishing, *(978-1-84059; 978-1-78508)* P.O. Box 2459, Chicago, IL 60690-2459 USA
E-mail: info@milet.com
Web site: http://www.milet.com; www.milet.co.uk
Dist(s): **Chinasprout, Inc.**
Independent Pubs. Group
Tuttle Publishing.

Milk & Cookies *Imprint of* **ibooks, Inc.**

Milk Mug Publishing, *(978-0-9721882)* 9190 W. Olympic Blvd., Suite 253, Beverly Hills, CA 90212 USA Tel 310-278-1153 (phone/fax)
E-mail: orders@thehoopsterbook.com
Web site: http://www.thehoopsterbook.com
Dist(s): **SCB Distributors.**

Milken Family Foundation, *(978-0-9646425)* 1250 Fourth St., 4th Flr., Santa Monica, CA 90404-1353 USA Tel 310-998-2825; Fax: 310-998-2899
E-mail: jboone@mff.org
Web site: http://www.milkenexchange.org.

Milkman Ink, *(978-1-7332370)* 980 Sandpoint Pond Ln., Henderson, NV 89002 USA Tel 702-600-5393
E-mail: milkman.ink.llc@gmail.com.

Milkweed Editions, *(978-0-915943; 978-1-57131)* 1011 Washington Ave. S., Suite 300, Minneapolis, MN 55415-1246 USA (SAN 294-0671) Tel 612-332-3192; Fax: 612-215-2550; Toll Free: 800-520-6455
E-mail: market@milkweed.org
Web site: http://www.milkweed.org; http://www.worldashome.org
Dist(s): **MyiLibrary**
Open Road Integrated Media, Inc.
Publishers Group West (PGW).

Milky Way Picture Bks. (CAN) *(978-1-990252)* *Dist. by* **Abrams.**

Mill City Press, Inc *Imprint of* **Salem Author Services**

Mill Creek Metro Publishing, *(978-0-9741989)* P.O. Box 90134, Youngstown, OH 44509 USA Tel 330-797-0024
E-mail: ianjcue@ianjcue.com
Web site: http://www.ianjcue.com
Dist(s): **Book Clearing Hse.**

Mill Creek Pr., *(978-0-9897760; 978-0-9916474; 978-1-942236; 978-1-951085)* 2308 Mt Vernon Ave Suite 408, Alexandria, VA 22301 USA Tel 703-638-8395; *Imprints:* At Home With Cristin (MYID_U_AT HOME)
E-mail: cristin@cristinharber.com.

Mill Park Publishing, *(978-0-9728225; 978-0-9883980; 978-0-9975871)* E & M Group, LLC, 6676 N Double Eagle Ln, Meridian, ID 83616 USA Tel 208-890-8122
E-mail: elaine@elaineambrose.com; elaine@millparkpublishing.com
Web site: http://www.Elaineambrose.com; www.millparkpublishing.com
Dist(s): **Lulu Pr., Inc.**

Mill Street Forward, The, *(978-0-9654628)* 15 1/2 Van Houten St., Apt. 117, Paterson, NJ 07505 USA Tel 973-345-9539.

Millbrook Pr. *Imprint of* **Lerner Publishing Group**

millea, john, *(978-0-692-98653-0; 978-0-578-62165-4)* 4661 mira vista dr., Frisco, TX 75034 USA Tel 469-714-5990
E-mail: john.millea@yahoo.com
Dist(s): **Ingram Content Group.**

Millennial Mind Publishing *Imprint of* **American Bk. Publishing Group**

Millennium Marketing & Publishing, *(978-1-886161)* 2455 Glen Hill Dr., Indianapolis, IN 46240-3460 USA Tel 317-815-9828; Fax: 317-815-9829
E-mail: MMPbooks@comcast.net
Web site: http://www.chicksguidetofootball.com
Dist(s): **Cardinal Pubs. Group**
Journey Pubns., LLC
Quality Bks., Inc.

Millennium Workshop Production, *(978-0-9725344)* 11501 Maple Ridge Rd., Reston, VA 20190-3604 USA (SAN 255-1624) Tel 703-925-0610 (phone/fax)
E-mail: victor@millenniumworkshop.com
Web site: http://www.millenniumworkshop.com.

Miller, Ann *See* **Jaylil Publishing Co.**

Miller, Bruce, *(978-0-9765598)* 10011 Bridgeport Way SW., Suite 1500 PMB128, Lakewood, WA 98499 USA Tel 253-227-2292
E-mail: warofpowers@comcast.net.

Miller, Deanna, *(978-0-9725424)* 12215 Fuller St., Silver Spring, MD 20902 USA
E-mail: info@deannamiller.com
Web site: http://www.deannamiller.com.

Miller, Debra Juanita, *(978-0-9706782; 978-0-9776014)* P.O. Box 20593, Chicago, IL 60620 USA
E-mail: monogrambooklets@yahoo.com; djpmspinsstories@yahoo.com.

Miller, D.M., *(978-1-7339768)* 4146 E Mendez St, Long Beach, CA 90815 USA Tel 562-498-9730
E-mail: dglenns@hotmail.com.

Miller, Don G., *(978-0-615-12836-8)* 5051 S. 172nd. St., Omaha, NE 68135 USA.

Miller, Elizabeth, *(978-0-692-10115-5; 978-0-692-10126-1)* 6641 Golf Club Dr., Longmont, CO 80503 USA Tel 303-949-1932
E-mail: liz.w.miller@icloud.com
Dist(s): **Ingram Content Group.**

Miller, J. Cris & Assocs., *(978-0-9725308)* 10555 W. 74th St., Countryside, IL 60525 USA Tel 708-579-1707 (phone/fax)
E-mail: jcmtales@hotmail.com.

Miller, J. Garnet Ltd. (GBR) *(978-0-85343)* *Dist. by* **Empire Pub Srvs.**

Miller, Michael, *(978-0-9723474; 978-0-9743522; 978-0-9825155; 978-0-9839356)* 2418 Hagerman St., Colorado Springs, CO 80904 USA Tel 719-600-9315; Fax: 501-421-1495
E-mail: michael@mail.sabineundmichael.com
Web site: http://www.sabineundmichael.com.

Miller, Peter Mitchell *See* **Silver Print Pr., Inc.**

Miller, Randy, *(978-0-9770530)* 17 N. Rd. No. 282, Alstead, NH 03602 USA Tel 603-835-7889
E-mail: randy.fiddle@gmail.com
Web site: http://www.fiddlecasebooks.com.

Miller, Sharon, *(978-0-9774756)* 4544 Foco Rd., Standish, MI 48658 USA
E-mail: sjmlady@gmail.com.

Miller, Smit Enterprises, *(978-0-9769433)* 112 Misty Creek Dr., Colorado Springs, CO 80132-6032 USA
E-mail: dawn@dawnsmit.com.

MillerWords, *(978-0-615-94052-6; 978-0-692-41237-4; 978-0-692-48617-7; 978-0-692-56102-7; 978-0-692-61478-5; 978-0-692-63441-7; 978-0-692-65983-0; 978-0-692-66359-2; 978-0-692-74074-3; 978-0-692-74075-0; 978-0-692-74141-2; 978-0-9982986; 978-0-9996195; 978-1-7342676; 979-8-9852760) P.O. Box 322, Lansing, KS 66043 USA Tel 352-385-4499*
E-mail: mark@millerwords.com
Web site: www.millerwords.com
Dist(s): **CreateSpace Independent Publishing Platform.**

MillerWrite, Inc., *(978-0-9723948)* 2875-F Northtowne Ln., No. 302, Reno, NV 89512-2062 USA Tel 775-673-2152
E-mail: chrisshelton78@msn.com; jmiller@millerwrite.com
Web site: http://www.millerwrite.com.

Milligan Books *See* **Professional Publishing Hse. LLC**

Million Words Publishing, LLC, *(978-1-891282; 978-0-578-47415-1)* 1946 Mora Ln., Jennings, MO 63136 USA.

Millman, Selena, *(978-0-9793058; 978-0-9794584; 978-0-9795756; 978-0-9798417; 978-0-9798603; 978-0-9802400; 978-0-615-15137-3; 978-0-615-23804-3; 978-0-578-00466-2; 978-0-578-00564-5)* 4984 Ridgebury, Lyndhurst, OH 44124 USA
Web site: http://www.freewebs.com/heal4michael
Dist(s): **Lulu Pr., Inc.**

Millmark Education, *(978-1-4334; 978-1-61618)* Orders Addr.: 7272 Wisconsin Ave, Suite 300, Bethesda, MD 20814-2081 USA (SAN 852-4912) Tel 301-941-1974; Fax: 301-656-0183; Edit Addr.: 7272 Wisconsin Ave. Suite 300, Suite 300, Bethesda, MD 20814-2081 USA
E-mail: rachel.moir@millmarkeducation.com; info@millmarkeducation.com
Web site: http://www.millmarkeducation.com/.

Mills & Morris Publishing Corporation *See* **Bluebonnets, Boots & Bks. Pr.**

Mills, Rebecca, *(978-0-692-98800-8; 978-0-692-98801-5; 978-0-692-14807-5; 978-0-578-77936-2; 978-0-578-31727-4; 978-0-578-31729-8)* 7412 Bevelhymer Rd., New Albany, OH 43054 USA Tel 330-760-2862
E-mail: rmgreenfield1@gmail.com
Dist(s): **Ingram Content Group.**

Milner Crest Publishing, LLC, *(978-0-9820651)* P.O. Box 10754, Portland, OR 97296-0754 USA (SAN 857-1376)
E-mail: danielbruton@gmail.com
Web site: http://www.milnercrestpublishing.com
Dist(s): **BookBaby.**

Milner, Ommi, *(978-0-692-16998-8)* 8180 Vincetta Dr, LA MESA, CA 91942 USA Tel 619-254-0696
E-mail: ommi.milner@hotmail.com.

Milo Educational Bks. & Resources, *(978-1-933668; 978-1-60698)* P.O. Box 41353, Houston, TX 77241-1353 USA Tel 713-466-6456; Fax: 713-896-6456
E-mail: milo_books@yahoo.com
Web site: http://www.miloeducationalbooks.com.

MiLo Ink Bks., *(978-0-615-70687-0; 978-0-9910909; 979-8-9850493)* 10353 Sophia Ave., Granada Hills, CA 91344 USA
E-mail: info@miloinkbooks.com
Web site: https://miloinkbooks.com/
Dist(s): **CreateSpace Independent Publishing Platform.**

Milstein & Hauptman Publishing *See* **Wonderful Publishing**

Miltenberg, Robert Allen, *(978-0-615-63925-3; 978-0-615-66467-5; 978-0-615-77522-7; 978-0-9893031)* 210 LIME KEY Ln., NAPLES, FL 34114 USA Tel 310-994-2407
E-mail: Rmiltenberg@yahoo.com
Web site: www.blurb.com; www.artworq.com.

MiMar Publishing, *(978-0-9754241; 978-0-615-16688-9; 978-0-615-16689-6)* 714 Enchanted Rock Trail, Georgetown, TX 78633 USA
Web site: http://www.bakerstreetbunch.com
Dist(s): **Lulu Pr., Inc.**

Mimaxion, *(978-1-68321)* 40 E. Main St., Newark, DE 19711 USA (SAN 990-0896)
E-mail: cedric.dufay@gmail.com; admin@speedypublishing.com
Web site: http://www.mimaxion.com/.

Mimi Bee Pubns., *(978-0-9745944)* Orders Addr.: P.O. Box 188, Accord, NY 12404 USA
E-mail: mimibee@att.com
Web site: http://mrallergyhead.com.

Mimi's Funhouse, LLC, *(978-0-9841589)* 10611A Crystal Cove Dr., Magnolia, TX 77354 USA
Web site: http://www.mimisfunhouse.com.

Mims Hse., *(978-0-9798621; 978-0-9852134; 978-1-62944)* 1309 S. Broadway, Little Rock, AR 72209 USA
Web site: mimshousebooks.com.

Minardi Photography, *(978-1-878444)* 5501 Harvest Scene Ct., Columbia, MD 21044 USA Tel 410-964-5403; Fax: 410-964-5643.

Minch, John Publishing, *(978-0-9631090; 978-0-9990251)* 27441 Betanzos, Mission Viejo, CA 92692 USA Tel 714-501-4162
E-mail: jmainc@earthlink.net.

Mind - Stretch, *(978-0-9676409)* 3124 Landrum Rd., Columbus, NC 28722 USA Tel 828-863-4235; Fax: 828-863-2584; Toll Free: 888-538-8911
E-mail: marklevin@alltel.net
Web site: http://www.mindstretch.com.

Mind Candy, LLC, *(978-0-9786929)* P.O. Box 2185, Garden City, NY 11531-2185 USA (SAN 851-3392) Tel 516-318-4433
Web site: http://mindcandymedia.com.

Mind Thrive Publishers *See* **MindThrive Pubs.**

Mind Trip Press *See* **Big Ransom Studio**

Mind Trip Productions, *(978-1-7361375)* 224 Kamahao Cir., Wailuku, HI 96793 USA Tel 831-334-0406
E-mail: julia@mindtripproductions.org
Web site: venusandherflytrip.net.

Mindanao Publishing Co., *(978-0-9710841)* 1222 Hazel St., N., Saint Paul, MN 55119-4500 USA Tel 651-274-6602; Fax: 651-771-9772
E-mail: jararick@worldnet.att.net
Web site: http://www.sanpedrocollege.org; http://www.eslseminarschina.org; http://www.eslseminars.org; http://www.ielts4nurses.org.

Mind/Body Workshops, *(978-0-9748548)* 131 S. Euclid, Westfield, NJ 07090 USA Tel 718-273-3682
Web site: http://www.kickoutstress.com.

Mindcastle Bks., Inc., *(978-0-9677204)* Orders Addr.: P.O. Box 3005, Woodinville, WA 98072 USA Tel 425-424-8860; Fax: 425-398-1354
E-mail: vanessa@mindcastle.com
Web site: http://www.mindcastle.com.

MindCatcher Pr., *(978-0-9724113)* 284 Mattison Dr., Concord, MA 01742 USA Tel 978-369-7868
E-mail: marian@mindcatcherpress.com
Web site: http://www.mindcatcherpress.com; http://www.readylady.com.

Mindful Matters LLC, *(978-0-692-05033-0)* P.O. Box 3, Hazlet, NJ 07730 USA Tel 908-358-5249
E-mail: nikki@mindfulmattersliving.com
Web site: www.mindfulmattersliving.com.

Mindful Wonders, LLC, *(978-0-578-67378-3; 978-0-578-68214-3)* 1187 40th Ave NE 0, ST PETERSBURG, FL 33703 USA Tel 4402125110
E-mail: mindfulwonders@gmail.com
Web site: www.mindfulwonders.com
Dist(s): **Ingram Content Group.**

Mindfull Publishing, *(978-0-9669551)* 177 W. Norwalk Rd., Norwalk, CT 06850 USA Tel 203-831-0855
E-mail: mindfullpub@hotmail.com
Web site: http://www.homestead.com/mindfullpublishing/.

Mindfull Publishing Co., *(978-0-9720308)* Orders Addr.: P.O. Box 34, Clairton, PA 15025 USA Toll Free: 888-946-0816; Edit Addr.: 329 Mitchell Ave., Clairton, PA 15025 USA
E-mail: gbberryauthor@yahoo.com.

MindMaze Publishing Co., *(978-0-9747668)* P.O. Box 251278, Woodbury, MN 55125 USA
E-mail: mindmaze@comcast.net.

Mindo Pr., *(978-0-9747971)* P.O. Box 34, Danielsville, PA 18038-9754 USA
E-mail: rshade@fast.net.

MindOH! Foundation, The, *(978-0-9773689)* 2525 Robinhood St., Houston, TX 77005 USA (SAN 257-3741) Tel 713-533-1138 Toll Free: 866-646-3641
Web site: http://www.mindohfoundation.org.

Mind's Eye Publishing, *(978-0-615-84820-4; 978-0-692-86716-7; 978-0-578-62441-9; 978-0-578-71175-1; 978-0-578-71177-5; 978-0-578-71995-5)* 120 Azalea Dr., Mountain View, CA 94041 USA Tel 408-807-0612 Do not confuse with Mind's Eye Publishing in Saint Louis, MO
Dist(s): **CreateSpace Independent Publishing Platform.**

Minds With Motives, *(978-0-578-77889-1)* 3683 W. 132nd St., Cleveland, OH 44111 USA Tel 216-333-6358
E-mail: cwestbrooks77@gmail.com
Web site: www.mindswithmotives.com.

Mindset CS, *(978-0-9989794)* 123 2nd St. Apt 1, Laurel, MD 20707 USA Tel 202-696-0487
E-mail: sudanrr@yahoo.com
Web site: createmindset.com.

Mindsong Math, *(978-0-9758592)* 7757 N. Basin Way, Boise, ID 83714 USA Tel 208-371-7668
E-mail: karlalaland@gmail.com
Web site: http://www.thewhaleslibrary.com.

MindsOrb, Inc., *(978-0-9741877)* P.O. Box 162706, Austin, TX 78716 USA
Web site: http://www.mindsorb.com.

Mindstir Media, *(978-0-9819648; 978-0-9836771; 978-0-9853650; 978-0-9858398; 978-0-9883162; 978-0-9885180; 978-0-9886409; 978-0-9889595; 978-0-9890288; 978-0-9892711; 978-0-9894748; 978-0-9897168; 978-0-9898820; 978-0-9910324; 978-0-9911512; 978-0-9913190; 978-0-9914884; 978-0-9916230; 978-0-9903626; 978-0-9906106; 978-0-9908137; 978-0-9862149; 978-0-9863057; 978-0-9961434; 978-0-9962872; 978-0-9964615; 978-0-9967294; 978-0-9969689; 978-0-9970334; 978-0-9972233; 978-0-9973575; 978-0-9975435; 978-0-9977466; 1931 Woodbury Ave. No. 182, Portsmouth, NH 03801 USA Toll Free: 800-767-0531*
Web site: www.mindstirmedia.com
Dist(s): **Smashwords.**

MindThrive Pubs., *(978-1-7336314)* 15 Azalea Pl., Piscataway, NJ 08854 USA Tel 732-659-4075
E-mail: joireneeapparel@gmail.com; joirenee@mindthrivepublishers.com
Web site: www.findingjoi.us.

MindVista Pr., *(978-1-7347844)* 586 Plymouth Ct., Brentwood, CA 94513 USA Tel 408-564-1101
E-mail: visualartist@yahoo.com
Web site: MindVistaPress.com.

MindWare Holdings, Inc., *(978-0-9648481; 978-1-892069; 978-1-933054; 978-0-9814636; 978-1-936300)* 2100 County Rd. C W., Roseville, MN 55113 USA (SAN 859-9157) Fax: 651-582-0556; Toll Free: 800-999-0398
Web site: http://mindware.com.

Mindwing Concepts, Inc., *(978-0-9761393; 978-0-9769527; 978-0-9791307; 978-0-9792917; 978-0-9793185; 978-0-9816818; 978-0-9996043)* 1 Federal St. Bldg. 103-1, Springfield, MA 01105 USA Toll Free: 888-228-9746
Web site: http://www.mindwingconcepts.com.

MindWorks Pr., *(978-1-886554)* 4019 Westerly Pl., Suite 108, Newport Beach, CA 92660 USA (SAN 850-4873) Tel 949.266.3714; Fax: 949.266.3770; Toll Free: 800-626-2720
E-mail: mindworkspress@aol.com; sposs@amenclinic.com
Web site: http://www.mindworkspress.com
Dist(s): **Lulu Pr., Inc.**

Mine Rich In Gems *Imprint of* **InnerPrize Group, LLC**

Minecraft Interactive *See* **Interactive Stories**

Minedition *Imprint of* **Penguin Young Readers Group**

Minerva Bks., *(978-0-9620125)* Div. of Hulbert Performance Rating, Inc., 316 Commerce St., Alexandria, VA 22314 USA (SAN 247-493X) Tel 703-683-5905 Do not confuse with companies with the same or similar name in Palo Alto, CA, New York, NY, Louisville, KY.

Minerva Bks., Ltd., *(978-0-8056)* 30 W. 26th St., New York, NY 10010 USA (SAN 205-8367) Tel 212-675-0465; Fax: 212-675-0573 Do not confuse with companies with the same or similar name in Alexandria, VA, Palo Alto, CA, Louisville, KY
Dist(s): **Continental Bk. Co., Inc.**
Lectorum Pubns., Inc.

Minetos, Sophia, *(978-1-7355933)* 7429 Chaco Rd. NE, Albuquerque, NM 87109 USA Tel 505-610-4384
E-mail: sminet97@gmail.com.

Mini Enterprises - M.E. *See* **AGB Publishing**

Minikin Pr., *(978-0-9772320)* P.O. Box 528, Barrington, RI 02806-0280 USA (SAN 257-0076) Tel 401-245-7960
E-mail: jill@minikinpress.com
Web site: http://www.minikinpress.com.

Minimal Pr., The, *(978-0-9742516; 978-0-615-25627-6; 978-0-615-25629-0; 978-0-9824665)* 406 Colchester Ave., Burlington, VT 05401 USA
Dist(s): **Lulu Pr., Inc.**

Ministry of Whimsy Press *See* **Wyrm Publishing**

Mink, Connie J *See* **Saturn Music & Entertainment**

Minko, Alyssa, *(978-0-692-09217-0)* 131 Oak Mills Crossing, WEST HENRIETTA, NY 14586 USA Tel 724-575-2210
E-mail: btswu.art@gmail.com
Dist(s): **Ingram Content Group.**

Minna Pr., *(978-0-9829630; 978-1-7324034; 978-1-7353069)* 108 Hamilton Ave., Lehigh Acres, FL 33936 USA Tel 239-308-6139
E-mail: lj1838@gmail.com
Dist(s): **BookBaby.**

Minna Press & Inspire Publications *See* **Minna Pr.**

Minnesota Assn. for Children's Mental Health, *(978-0-9820482)* 165 Western Ave., N., Suite 2, Saint Paul, MN 55102 USA Tel 651-644-7333; Fax: 651-644-7391; Toll Free: 800-528-4511
E-mail: info@macmh.org
Web site: http://www.macmh.org.

Minnesota Department of Economic Security *See* **Minnesota Dept. Employment & Economic Development**

Minnesota Dept. Employment & Economic Development, *(978-0-9670505; 978-0-9845780; 978-0-615-50484-1)* 332 Minnesota St. Ste. E200, Saint Paul, MN 55101-1349 USA Toll Free: 888-234-1114
E-mail: Amy.yerkes@state.mn.us
Web site: http://www.positivelyminnesota.com.

†**Minnesota Historical Society Pr.**, *(978-0-87351; 978-1-68134)* Orders Addr.: 11030 S. Langley Ave., Chicago, IL 60628 USA Toll Free Fax: 800-621-8476; Toll Free: 800-621-2736; Edit Addr.: 345 Kellogg Blvd., W., Saint Paul, MN 55102-1906 USA (SAN 202-6384) Tel 651-297-2221; 651-259-3202; Fax: 651-297-1345; Toll Free: 800-647-7827; *Imprints:* Borealis Book (Borealis Book)
E-mail: greg.britton@mnhs.org
Web site: http://www.mnhs.org/mhspress; mnhspress.org
Dist(s): **BookMobile**
Chicago Distribution Ctr.
Ingram Publisher Services; *CIP.*

Minnesota Humanities Ctr., *(978-0-9629298; 978-1-931016; 978-0-578-03464-5; 978-0-9884539)* 987 E. Ivy Ave., Saint Paul, MN 55106-2046 USA Tel 651-774-0105 Toll Free: 866-268-7293
E-mail: info@minnesotahumanities.org
Web site: http://www.minnesotahumanities.org.

Minnesota Humanities Commission *See* **Minnesota Humanities Ctr.**

Minnesota's Bookstore, *(978-0-9647451; 978-0-9754338)* 660 Olive St., Saint Paul, MN 55155 USA Tel 651-297-3000; Fax: 651-215-5733; Toll Free: 800-657-3757
E-mail: mnbookstore@state.mn.us
Web site: http://www.minnesotasbookstore.com
Dist(s): **Univ. of Texas Pr.**

Minnewaska Pr., *(978-0-9799410)* 1406 S Darling Dr. NW, Alexandria, MN 56308 USA
E-mail: minnewaskapress@yahoo.com
Web site: http://www.debmercier.com.

Minnich, Quinn, *(978-1-7364491)* 216 W Newport Rd, Lititz, PA 17543 USA Tel 717-892-8231
E-mail: chessdragon@gmail.com.

Minnie Troy Pubs., *(978-0-9727480; 978-0-9997346)* Div. of Historically Speaking, 309 Union St., Murfreesboro, NC 27855 USA Tel 252-398-5098
E-mail: lion5098@aol.com.

Minon, S.A. (ESP) *(978-84-355) Dist. by* **Lectorum Pubns.**

Minotaur Bks. *Imprint of* **St. Martin's Pr.**

Minotauro Ediciones (ESP) *(978-84-450) Dist. by* **Distribks Inc.**

Minotauro Ediciones (ESP) *(978-84-450) Dist. by* **Lectorum Pubns.**

Minotauro Ediciones (ESP) *(978-84-450) Dist. by* **Planeta.**

Minton, Art, *(978-0-615-15948-5)* Orders Addr.: P.O. Box 16294, Jackson, MS 39236-6294 USA Tel 601-966-6699; Fax: 206-202-3329; Edit Addr.: 1939 Cherokee Dr., jackson, MS 39211 USA
E-mail: rentjackson@gmail.com
Web site: http://birdingforchildren.com.

Minuteman Press of Green Bay *See* **EPS Digital**

Mira Pr., The, *(978-0-9762947)* P.O. Box 590207, Newton Centre, MA 02459 USA.

Miracle Pr., *(978-0-929889)* 2808 W. Lexington Way, Edmond, OK 73003-4224 USA (SAN 250-975X) Tel 405-359-0369; Fax: 703-883-1861
E-mail: miraclepress@cox.net.

Miraculous Fingerprints Pubs., *(978-1-886134)* 74565 Dillon Rd., MH 15, Desert Hot Springs, CA 92241 USA Tel 760-251-3037.

Miramax Bks., *(978-0-7868; 978-1-4013; 978-1-4464)* Div. of Walt Disney Productions, 11 Beach St., 5th Flr., New York, NY 10013 USA Fax: 212-625-5075
Web site: http://www.miramax.com
Dist(s): **Children's Plus, Inc.**
Disney Publishing Worldwide
Hachette Bk. Group
Hyperion Pr.

MiraQuest, *(978-0-9748329; 978-0-615-26973-3; 978-0-9819958)* Orders Addr.: P.O. Box 29722, Los Angeles, CA 90029-0722 USA
Web site: http://www.islandlili.com
Dist(s): **Ingram Content Group.**

Mirasee, *(978-0-692-97782-8; 978-0-9996500)* 4200 Cabarrus Ct. E., Greensboro, NC 27407 USA Tel 336-404-7165
E-mail: ashlee@mirasee.com
Web site: www.mirasee.com.

Miraux Publishing *See* **Publify Consulting**

Mirhady, Farhad, *(978-0-9760323)* 2055 Beverly Beach Dr NW, Olympia, WA 98502-3427 USA
E-mail: fmirhady@comcast.net
Web site: http://www.poeticliterature.com.

MIROGLYPHICS, *(978-0-9773064; 978-0-9801073)* Orders Addr.: 5734 N. 4th St., Philadelphia, PA 19120 USA (SAN 257-2451) Tel 215-224-2486; *Imprints:* Romoulous (Romoulous)
E-mail: germic2008@gmail.com; mnik1972@aol.com
Web site: http://www.miroglyphics.biz
Dist(s): **Ingram Content Group.**

Mirror Pond Publishing, *(978-0-9777683)* 63090 Casey Pl., Bend, OR 97701 USA Tel 541-385-6927
E-mail: speedyread@hotmail.com.

Mirror Publishing, *(978-0-9796519; 978-0-9800675; 978-0-9815904; 978-0-9817521; 978-0-9821171; 978-0-9822560; 978-1-936046; 978-1-936352; 978-1-61225)* 6434 W. Dixon St., Milwaukee, WI 53214-1750 USA Tel 414-763-1034
E-mail: info@pagesofwonder.com
Web site: http://www.pagesofwonder.com
Dist(s): **Ingram Content Group.**

Mirrorstone *Imprint of* **Wizards of the Coast**

MirthMarks Publishing, *(978-0-9789591)* 675 Deis Dr., STE 123, Fairfield, OH 45014 USA
E-mail: flymaster@coppershoo.com.

Mirubi Group Ltd. Liability Co., *(978-0-9997795)* 1972 Port Seabourne Way, Newport Beach, CA 92660 USA Tel 551-427-2675
E-mail: davesaber@yahoo.com.

Mirviss, Suzanne Artist, *(978-0-692-81043-9; 978-0-578-45222-7; 978-0-578-73341-8; 979-8-218-08764-7)* 463 Wood Hollow Dr., Novato, CA 94945 USA Tel 415-328-6177
E-mail: suzmirviss@comcast.net
Web site: n/a.

Misch Masch *See* **Prime Bks.**

Mischief Productions, *(978-0-9998328)* 15 Vine Ave, Quincy, MA 02169 USA Tel 720-503-6697
E-mail: Cujo2828@gmail.com.

Misfit Mous *See* **Misfit Mouse**

Misfit Mouse, *(978-0-578-11067-7; 978-0-578-12084-3; 978-0-578-15002-4; 978-0-692-42251-9; 978-0-692-48383-1; 978-0-9972406)* 3382 Habersham Rd. NW, Atlanta, GA 30305 USA
Web site: www.misfitmouse.com.

Misguided Ink *Imprint of* **Gray, John**

Miss Lana Pr., *(978-1-7361811)* 4620 Kester Ave. Apt 119, Sherman Oaks, CA 91403 USA Tel 818-253-9044
E-mail: rachaneelumayno@gmail.com
Web site: www.rachanee.net.

Miss Teacher Mom Publishing, *(978-1-7351382)* 4 Wallingford St., Dover, NH 03820 USA Tel 978-569-0783
E-mail: katlynne.mirabal@gmail.com.

MissFoxCreations, *(978-0-692-18325-0; 978-0-578-51496-3; 978-1-7346681)* 323 W4 St., New York, NY 10014 USA Tel 917-586-1850
E-mail: lightfox82@gmail.com
Dist(s): **CreateSpace Independent Publishing Platform.**

Missick Publishing Co., *(978-0-578-88784-5)* 4613 S Langley, Chicago, IL 60653 USA Tel 773-225-6970
E-mail: Nurseraniawrites@gmail.com.

Missing Lid Bk.Hse., *(978-0-9838068)* 13526 Omega Cir., Littleton, CO 80124 USA Tel 303-799-8982
E-mail: tjterbush@yahoo.com.

Missing Piece Pr., *(978-0-9703729; 978-0-9977959; 978-1-7340123; 978-1-7350312; 978-1-7361381; 978-1-957035)* 37042 S. Hollygreen Dr., Tucson, AZ 857398 USA Tel 520-338-2582
E-mail: Questions@MissingPiecePress.com
Web site: http://www.missingpiecepress.com
Dist(s): **Reveal Entertainment, Inc.**

Mission City Pr., Inc., *(978-1-928749; 978-1-934306)* 8122 Datapoint Dr. Ste. 1000, San Antonio, TX 78229-3273 USA Toll Free: 800-840-2641
E-mail: busaffair@missioncitypress.com
Web site: http://www.alifeoffaith.com
Dist(s): **Zondervan.**

Mission Creek Studios, *(978-0-929702)* 1040 Mission Canyon Rd., Santa Barbara, CA 93105-2122 USA (SAN 249-9630) Tel 805-682-6724; Fax: 805-682-6761
E-mail: dave@missioncreek.com
Web site: http://www.missioncreek.com.

Mission Manuscripts, Inc., *(978-0-9768880)* 1000 Jorie Blvd., Suite 206, Oak Brook, IL 60523 USA Tel 630-990-0220; Fax: 630-990-2556
E-mail: kathy.hill@arends-inc.com.

Mission Mill Museum, *(978-0-9753484)* 1313 Mill St., SE, Salem, OR 97301 USA Tel 503-585-7012; Fax: 503-588-9902
E-mail: info@missionmill.org
Web site: http://www.missionmill.org.

Mission Partners *See* **Changemakers Pr.**

Mision Ridge Pr., *(978-0-9763956)* 4660 Eastus Dr., San Jose, CA 95129 USA.

†**Mississippi Museum of Art**, *(978-1-887422)* 380 S. Lamar St., Jackson, MS 39201-4007 USA (SAN 279-6198)
E-mail: rpb@netdoor.com
Web site: http://www.msmuseumart.org
Dist(s): **Pennsylvania State Univ. Pr.**
Univ. Pr. of Mississippi
Univ. of Washington Pr.; *CIP.*

Missouri Botanical Garden Pr., *(978-0-915279; 978-1-930723; 978-1-935641)* Orders Addr.: P.O. Box 299, Saint Louis, MO 63166-0299 USA (SAN 290-0157) Tel 314-577-9547 marketing and publishing questions; Toll Free: 888-271-1930 orders department; Edit Addr.: 4500 Shaw Blvd., Saint Louis, MO 63110 USA
E-mail: mbgpress@mobot.org; press.coordinator@mobot.org; allison.brock@mobot.org
Web site: http://www.mbgpress.org
Dist(s): **Chicago Distribution Ctr.**

Missouri Historical Society Pr., *(978-1-883982; 979-8-9855716)* P.O. Box 775460, Saint Louis, MO 63177 USA Fax: 314-746-4548
E-mail: jstevens@mohistory.org
Web site: http://www.mohistory.org
Dist(s): **Chicago Distribution Ctr.**
SPD-Small Pr. Distribution
Univ. of Missouri Pr.
Univ. of New Mexico Pr.
Wayne State Univ. Pr.

Missy Sheldrake, *(978-1-7345896)* 6818 Chasewood Cir., Centreville, VA 20121 USA Tel 703-203-2420
E-mail: Missy@variable.org
Dist(s): **Ingram Content Group.**

Mister C Music, *(978-0-9755333)* P.O. Box 28, Rochester, PA 15074 USA Toll Free: 877-687-4258
E-mail: misterc437@aol.com
Web site: http://www.mistercmusic.com.

Mistofer Christopher *See* **Hse. of Mistofer Christopher**

MIT Kids Press *Imprint of* **Candlewick Pr.**

†**MIT Pr.**, *(978-0-262; 978-0-89706)* Orders Addr.: c/o Triliteral LLC, 100 Maple Ridge Dr., Cumberland, RI 02864 USA Tel 401-531-2800; Fax: 401-531-2801; Toll Free Fax: 800-406-9145; Toll Free: 800-405-1619; Edit Addr.: One Rogers St., Cambridge, MA 02142-1209 USA (SAN 202-6414) Tel 617-253-5646; Fax: 617-253-6779
E-mail: orders@triliteral.org
Web site: http://mitpress.mit.edu
Dist(s): **Ebsco Publishing**
JSTOR
MyiLibrary
Penguin Random Hse. Distribution
Penguin Random Hse. LLC
TriLiteral, LLC
Wiley, John & Sons, Inc.
ebrary, Inc.; *CIP.*

Mitchell, Carol *See* **CaribbeanReads**

Mitchell, Damien Pardow, *(978-0-615-18469-2)* 13834 Doolittle Dr., San Leandro, CA 94577 USA
Web site: http://jarvisprinting.com
Dist(s): **Publishers Services.**

MITCHELL E. ALBAUGH, *(978-0-578-79989-6)* 1132 VALLEY CREEK RUN, WINTER PARK, FL 32792 USA Tel 407-430-7463
E-mail: malbaugh@winterparklawyers.com.

Mitchell, Karan, *(978-0-9763793)* 79 Baruch Dr., Apt.5E, New York, NY 10002-3659 USA Tel 212-982-7977
E-mail: mtchllkrn@aol.com.

Mitchell Lane Pubs., *(978-1-883845; 978-1-58415; 978-1-61228; 978-1-68020)* 2001 SW 31st Ave, Hallandale, FL 33009 USA (SAN 858-3749) Tel 954-985-9400; Fax: 954-987-2200; Toll Free: 800-814-5484
E-mail: Phil@mitchelllane.com
Web site: http://www.mitchelllane.com
Dist(s): **Cengage Gale.**

Mitchell Lane Publishers, Incorporated *See* **Mitchell Lane Pubs.**

Mitchell, P. S., *(978-0-615-80354-8)* 3682 King St. Unit 16831, Alexandria, VA 22302 USA Tel 571-214-4805
E-mail: psmitchellbook@gmail.com.

Mitchell Publishing, *(978-1-7322689)* 212 Peach Grove Pl., Mauldin, SC 29662 USA Tel 843-860-6742
E-mail: katisha.mitchell@gmail.com.

Mitchell Publishing, Incorporated *See* **Teaching & Learning Co.**

Mitchell Publishing, Inc., *(978-0-938188)* 160 Spear St. Ste. 700, San Francisco, CA 94105-1562 USA (SAN 215-7896) Toll Free: 800-435-2665 Do not confuse with companies with the same or similar names in Spokane, WA, Medina, NY, Medicine Lodge, KS.

MiTeen Press *Imprint of* **Candlewick Pr.**

Mitre's Touch Gallery, The, *(978-0-9764384)* PO Box 139., Imbler, OR 97841 USA Tel 541-910-0155
E-mail: weframe@eoni.com.

Mittal, Chitwan (IND) *(978-81-953886) Dist. by* **IPG Chicago.**

Mitten Pr. *Imprint of* **Ann Arbor Editions LLC**

MITWA, *(978-0-692-90196-0; 978-0-692-96959-5; 978-0-692-97666-1; 978-0-692-08942-2; 978-0-578-61119-8)* 949 OAK CREEK CIR, APT C, DOUGLASVILLE, GA 30134 USA Tel 404-374-5196; Fax: 404-374-5196
E-mail: info@manifestinginc.com.

MixedKids&Co, *(978-1-7368802)* 3085 Knob Dr., Los Angeles, CA 90065 USA Tel 310-406-4324
E-mail: info@mixedkidsco.com
Web site: www.mixedkidsco.com.

Mixta Publishing Co., *(978-0-9675951)* 3179 San Francisco Ave., Long Beach, CA 90806 USA Tel 562-427-4270
E-mail: michael.archuleta@gte.net; michael@mixtapublishing.com
Web site: http://www.mixtapublishing.com; http://www.mixtapublishing.net
Dist(s): **Leonard, Hal Corp.**

Mizzou Media - University BookStores *See* **Mizzou Publishing - The Mizzou Store**

Mizzou Publishing - The Mizzou Store, *(978-1-61600)* Div. of University of Missouri, Mu Student Ctr. 911 E. Rollins St., Columbia, MO 65211 USA Tel 573-882-8567; Fax: 573-884-8050
E-mail: mizzoupublishing@missouri.edu.

MJ Brooks Co. *See* **Picket Press**

MJ Pierson, *(978-0-578-40144-7)* 11578 222 St., Cambra Heights, NY 11411 USA Tel 718-570-4627
E-mail: jcollen85@gmail.com
Dist(s): **CreateSpace Independent Publishing Platform.**

Publisher Name Index

MJA Creative, LLC, *(978-0-9910894; 978-1-7324180)* P.O. Box 3997, Covington, LA 70434 USA Tel 985-789-3423
E-mail: mike@mikeartell.com
Web site: www.mikeartell.com.

MJS Music & Entertainment, LLC, *(978-0-9762917; 978-0-9817451)* 9699 W. Fort Island Trail, Crystal River, FL 34429 USA Tel 352-257-3261; Fax: 352-795-1658 Do not confuse with comapnies with the same or similar name in Boyertown, PA, Searsport, ME
E-mail: msternal@mjspublications.com; wriverroad@aol.com
Web site: http://www.mjspublications.com
Dist(s): **Dumont, Charles Son, Inc.**
Omnibus Pr.
TNT Media Group, Inc.

MJS Music Publications *See* **MJS Music & Entertainment, LLC**

MJS Publishing Group LLC, *(978-0-9764336)* P.O. Box 6582, Evanston, IL 60204-6582 USA Tel 847-869-5901; Fax: 847-745-0219
E-mail: mjspg@ameritech.net
Web site: http://www.mjspub.com.

MK Pubs., *(978-0-9993790; 978-1-7320448; 978-1-7346643)* 3901 Bixler Church RD, Westminster, MD 21158 USA Tel 410-857-6373
E-mail: monakerby@gmail.com.

MK Publishing, *(978-0-9720484; 978-0-9747147; 978-0-9760534; 978-0-9763271; 978-0-9770933; 978-0-9785081)* 25123 22nd Ave. S., Saint Cloud, MN 56301 USA; P.O. Box 945, St Cloud, MN 56302 (SAN 256-4092) Tel 320-252-1023; Fax: 320-252-4574
Web site: http://www.yourbookpublisher.net
Dist(s): **Closet Case Bks.**
J & N Creations, LLC
JMS Distribution
Main Trail Productions
Ozark Bk. Distributors
Perfume River Pubns.
Puzzle Piece Pubns.

MKADesigns, *(978-0-9745839; 978-0-578-74636-4)* 5 American Ave., Huntsville, AL 35824 USA Tel 256-721-0200; *Imprints:* Fun to Read Books with Royally Good Morals (Fun to Read Bk)
E-mail: mike.dozier@mkadesigns.com
Web site: http://www.mkadesigns.com.

MKBks., *(978-1-7371250)* 587 Ft. Washington Ave Apt 9C, New York, NY 10033 USA Tel 917-224-9695
E-mail: marina.royzman@gmail.com
Web site: MKingbooks.yolasite.com.

ML Networks *Imprint of* **Sonis, Gabriela**

ML Publishing, *(978-0-9768347)* Div. of MIHP, 31500 Dequindre Rd., Warren, MI 48092-1057 USA Tel 586-268-6942
E-mail: smclaughlin@mihp.net
Web site: http://mlpublishing.com.

MLM Ranch Publishing, *(978-0-9743098)* P.O. Box 910251, St. George, UT 84791 USA.

MLR Pr., LLC, *(978-0-9793110; 978-1-934531; 978-0-615-13459-8; 978-1-60820; 978-1-944770; 978-1-64122)* 3052 Gaines Waterport Rd., Albion, NY 14411 USA (SAN 853-1013) Tel 585-589-7831
E-mail: mlrpress@gmail.com
Web site: http://www.mlrpress.com
Dist(s): **Lulu Pr., Inc.**

MMB Enterprises, LLC, *(978-0-9747443; 978-0-615-57676-3)* Orders Addr.: P.O. Box 5887, Santa Barbara, CA 93150 USA
E-mail: pabujack@me.com
Web site: http://www.michellemadridbranch.com.

MMC Companies LLC dba Moonglade Press *See* **Moonglade Pr.**

MMG Technology Corp., *(978-0-9754886)* 379 Amherst St., Suite 204, Nashua, NH 03063 USA
Web site: http://www.the-common.com.

MMJ Foundation, *(978-0-9827972)* 4350 Von Karman, 4th Flr., Newport Beach, CA 92660 USA Tel 949-244-5544
E-mail: mjanavs@hotmail.com.

M-m-mauleg Publishing, *(978-0-9790111)* Orders Addr.: P.O. Box 5258, Mangilao, GU 96923 USA; Edit Addr.: 303 University Dr., Mangila, GU 96923-5258 USA
E-mail: millhoff@uog.edu.

MMP *See* **Millennium Marketing & Publishing**

MMR Enlightened Investors, LLC, *(978-0-9821291)* P.O. Box 3326, Mesquite, NV 89024 USA
E-mail: beatnycparkingtickets.com
Web site: http://beatnycparkingtickets.com.

MNMC, *(978-0-9728518; 978-0-9763532)* 17 Old Shelter Rock Rd., Danbury, CT 06810 USA Tel 203-798-6936; Toll Free: 866-210-0004
E-mail: order@muslimplanet.com
Web site: http://www.muslimpublisher.com.

Mo' Bks., *(978-1-7353502)* 1695 Highland Cir., Fairfield, CA 94534 USA Tel 707-718-0707
E-mail: vdhillon123@gmail.com.

Mo MacPhail, *(978-1-7320581)* 95 Hillside Dr., East Longmeadow, MA 01028 USA Tel 413-250-9753
E-mail: momacphail@aol.com.

Mo Peanuts Publishing, *(978-0-9971513)* 1019 Ft. Salonga Rd., Northport, NY 11768 USA Tel 631-682-1768
E-mail: trelfp@gmail.com
Web site: www.TheAlienClub.com.

Moberly, Emily, *(978-1-7357054)* 4880 charles lewis way, san diego, CA 92102 USA Tel 760-688-6251
E-mail: emily.moberly@gmail.com.

Mobius Communications, Ltd., *(978-1-891304; 978-1-928583)* Div. of Publication Services, Inc., 1802 S. Duncan Rd., Champaign, IL 61822-5222 USA Fax: 217-398-3923; Toll Free: 800-662-4875
Web site: http://www.8-mobius.com.

Mocha Enterprises, *(978-0-9707163)* 6322 Chesapeake Cir., Stockton, CA 95219 USA (SAN 253-620X) Tel 209-478-0635 (phone/fax); 209-946-3064
E-mail: mochaenterprises@aol.com
Web site: http://www.welcometotheprofessionalwork.com.

Mockingbird Cottage Pr., *(978-0-692-68327-9; 978-0-9983519)* 1014 Richland Ct, Ashland City, TN Bell USA Tel 615-473-2757
Dist(s): **CreateSpace Independent Publishing Platform.**

Mockingbird Lane Pr., *(978-0-9856906; 978-0-9889542; 978-0-9893105)* 2441 Washington Rd., Maynard, AR 72444 USA Tel 870-647-2137
E-mail: mockingbirdlanepress@gmail.com.

Mockingbird Pr., *(978-0-9981364; 978-1-946774; 978-1-953450; 978-1-68493)* 933 Branch Ct. No. 274, Grovetown, GA 30813 USA Tel 770-778-6475
E-mail: jkraft12@gmail.com.

Mockingbird Publishing, *(978-0-9828528)* Orders Addr.: P.O. Box 442, Fairhope, AL 36533 USA Tel 334-546-0710
E-mail: ashley@mockingbirdpublishing.com
Web site: http://www.mockingbirdpublishing.com.

Modern Curriculum Pr. *Imprint of* **Savvas Learning Co.**

†Modern Curriculum Pr., *(978-0-7652; 978-0-8136; 978-0-87895)* Div. of Pearson Education, Orders Addr.: P.O. Box 2500, Lebanon, IN 46052-3009 USA (SAN 206-6572) Toll Free: 800-526-9907 (Customer Service)
Web site: http://www.pearsonlearning.com
Dist(s): **Follett School Solutions**
Lectorum Pubns., Inc.
Pearson Learning; *CIP.*

Modern Evil Pr., *(978-1-934516)* 913 S 2nd Ave, Phoenix, AZ 85003-2511 USA Tel 602-999-6449
E-mail: teel@modernevil.com
Web site: http://modernevil.com/
Dist(s): **Smashwords.**

Modern Learning Pr., *(978-0-935493; 978-1-56762)* P.O. Box 167, Rosemont, NJ 08556 USA Tel 609-397-2214; Fax: 845-277-3548; Toll Free Fax: 888-558-7350; Toll Free: 800-627-5867
E-mail: Rlow@tasa.com.

Modern Library *Imprint of* **Random House Publishing Group**

Modern Living Media *See* **Pirouz, Raymond**

Modern Publishing, *(978-0-7666; 978-0-87449; 978-1-56144)* Div. of Unisystems, Inc., 155 E. 55th St., New York, NY 10022 USA (SAN 253-2921) Tel 212-826-0850; Fax: 212-759-9096
E-mail: info@modernpublishing.com
Web site: http://www.modernpublishing.com.

Modern Software Pr. *Imprint of* **Loving Healing Pr., Inc.**

Modica, Marianne, *(978-1-7351005)* 1025 EDWIN DR, PHOENIXVILLE, PA 19460-2226 USA Tel 610-917-1495
E-mail: mmodica4@gmail.com
Web site: mariannemodica.com.

MoGho Bks., LLC, *(978-0-9712559; 978-0-615-11888-8)* Box 200, 9801 Hartley Rd., Hallsville, MO 65255 USA Tel 573-696-3537 (phone/fax)
E-mail: moghobks@tranquility.net
Dist(s): **Cowley Distributing, Inc.**
Univ. of Missouri Pr.

Mogul Comics, *(978-0-9657723)* 102 6th Ave. 2nd Flr., WaterVliet, NY 12189 USA.

Moheke Pr., *(978-0-692-77907-1; 978-0-692-19036-4; 978-0-578-60751-1; 978-0-578-32515-6; 978-0-578-29366-0)* 34 Walnut Pl., Huntington, NY 11743 USA Tel 631-385-8708
Dist(s): **CreateSpace Independent Publishing Platform.**

Mohsena Memorial Foundation, Inc., *(978-0-9617273)* P.O. Box 2309, Princeton, NJ 08543 USA (SAN 663-5075) Tel 609-799-6545; Fax: 609-799-7311.

Mohsena Memorial Trust *See* **Mohsena Memorial Foundation, Inc.**

MoJo InkWorks, *(978-0-9820381)* 16 Foxglove Row, Riverhead, NY 11901 USA Tel 516-695-6690
E-mail: maureensullivan@gmail.com
Web site: http://www.maureensullivancommunications.com.

Molino, Editorial (ESP) *(978-84-272) Dist. by* **Distribks Inc.**

Molino, Editorial (ESP) *(978-84-272) Dist. by* **Continental Bk.**

Molino, Editorial (ESP) *(978-84-272) Dist. by* **AIMS Intl.**

Molino, Editorial (ESP) *(978-84-272) Dist. by* **Lectorum Pubns.**

Molino, Editorial (ESP) *(978-84-272) Dist. by* **Santillana.**

Molino RBA,
Dist(s): **Children's Plus, Inc.**
Lectorum Pubns., Inc.

Molly Brave, *(978-1-61245)* 3682 Quiet Pond Ln., Sarasota, FL 34235 USA Tel 941-955-0091
E-mail: mollybrave@gmail.com
Web site: http://www.mollybrave.com.

Molly The Owl Bks., *(978-0-9828638)* 2033 San Elijo Ave. No. 482, Cardiff by the Sea, CA 92007 USA Tel 760-716-6535
E-mail: eric@ericblehm.com
Web site: http://www.mollytheowlbooks.com.

Molo Global Consulting, LLC, *(978-1-7350720; 978-1-955512)* 10777 Lester St., Silver Spring, MD 20902 USA Tel 202-549-0929
E-mail: morganmlimo@gmail.com; consultant@mologlobalconsulting.com
Web site: mologlobalconsulting.com.

Moltiverse, *(978-0-9761844)* Orders Addr.: 76 northampton ave, springfield, MA 01109 USA Tel 413-433-6456; Edit Addr.: 76 northampton ave, springfield, MA 01109 USA
E-mail: pricevanray@gmail.com
Web site: http://pricevanray.com.

Mom of 4, The *See* **Anna Stilianessis**

Moment Bks. *Imprint of* **Mandel Vilar Pr.**

Momentpoint Media, *(978-0-9710448)* 2385 Friesian Rd., York, PA 17406 USA Tel 717-848-4528 (phone/fax) Do not confuse with Moment Point Press Inc. of NH/ME.
E-mail: momentpoint@suscom.net
Web site: http://www.momentpointmedia.com.

MOMENTUM *Imprint of* **Child's World, Inc, The**

Momentum Books, Limited *See* **Momentum Bks., LLC**

Momentum Bks., LLC, *(978-0-9618726; 978-1-879094; 978-1-938018)* Div. of Hour Media, LLC, 117 W. Third St., Royal Oak, MI 48067 USA (SAN 668-7067) Tel 248-691-1800; Fax: 248-691-4531
E-mail: info@momentumbooks.com
Web site: http://www.momentumbooks.com
Dist(s): **Baker & Taylor Publisher Services (BTPS)**
SCB Distributors
TNT Media Group, Inc.

Mometrix Media LLC, *(978-1-60971; 978-1-61072; 978-1-61073; 978-1-61402; 978-1-61403; 978-1-62120; 978-1-62733; 978-1-63094; 978-1-5167)* 3827 Phelan No. 179, Beaumont, TX 77707 USA (SAN 860-0430) Tel 800-673-8175.

MomGeek.com *Imprint of* **Wood Designs, Inc.**

Momma Dot Publishing LLC, *(978-0-9967667)* 11632 18th St SE, Lake Stevens, WA 98258 USA Tel 425-314-9746
E-mail: thenuetzs@gmail.com.

Mommy Has Tattoos, *(978-0-9770232)* P.O. Box 231059, New York, NY 10023-0023 USA
E-mail: info@mommyhastattoos.com
Web site: http://www.mommyhastattoos.com.

Mommy Workshop Bks., *(978-0-9817565)* P.O. Box 265, Doylestown, PA 18901 USA (SAN 856-4655) Tel 215-489-8649; Fax: 480-393-5692
E-mail: kristie@mommyworkshop.com
Web site: http://www.mommyworkshop.com/.

Momotombo Pr., *(978-0-9710465; 978-0-9797446)* Institute for Latino/University of Notre Dame, Notre Dame, IN 46556 USA; Inst. for Latino Studies Univ. of Notre Dame 230 McKenna Hall, Notre Dame, IN 46556
E-mail: faragon@nd.edu
Web site: http://www.momotombopress.com
Dist(s): **SPD-Small Pr. Distribution.**

Mom's Pride Enterprises, *(978-0-9720549)* 16521 N. 69th Dr., Peoria, AZ 85382 USA Tel 623-487-7589; Fax: 623-487-1504
E-mail: mrsb4kids@yahoo.com
Web site: http://www.mrsbstorytime.com.

Monacelli Pr., Inc., *(978-1-58093; 978-1-885254)* 1745 Broadway., New York, NY 10019-4305 USA Tel 212-782-9000
E-mail: info@monaddcellipress.com
Web site: http://www.monacellipress.com
Dist(s): **Hachette Bk. Group**
MyiLibrary
Penguin Random Hse. Distribution
Penguin Random Hse. LLC
Penguin Publishing Group
Random Hse., Inc.

Monarch Baby Publishing, *(978-0-9749499)* Orders Addr.: P.O. Box 22, Salem, VA 24153 USA Tel 504-669-1044
E-mail: monarchbaby@blackbutterflyrecords.com
Web site: http://blackbutterflyrecords.com\monarch_baby_publishing.thml.

Monarch Butterflies *See* **Papillons Monarques**

Monarch Comics, LLC, *(978-1-7358368)* 7700 Fern Hollow Dr., Chesterfield, VA 23832 USA Tel 631-514-1050
E-mail: nbseals@monarchcomics.com
Web site: www.monarchcomics.com.

Monarch Pubs., *(978-0-9774038; 978-0-615-12659-3)* Orders Addr.: 305 Holly Tree Ln., Simpsonville, SC 29681 USA
E-mail: joconnor@uscupstate.edu
Web site: http://www.monarchpublishers.com
Dist(s): **Follett School Solutions**
Parnassus Bk. Distributors
Bryan, R. L.

Monarch Publishing Hse., *(978-0-9797861)* 2573 Lake Cir., Jackson, MS 39211-6630 USA (SAN 859-4627) Tel 601-982-1233.

Monarchs in the Classroom, *(978-0-9800653)* 1980 Folwell Ave., 200 Hodson Hall, Saint Paul, MN 55108 USA Tel 612-624-8706; Fax: 612-625-5299
E-mail: oberh001@umn.edu
Web site: http://www.monarchlab.org.

Monares Collective LLC, *(978-1-7341098)* 1716 67th Ave, Greeley, CO 80634 USA Tel 970-518-0536
E-mail: sarahjmonares@gmail.com
Web site: www.sarahmonares.com.

Mondadori (ITA) *(978-88-04; 978-88-356; 978-88-86372; 978-88-520; 978-88-521) Dist. by* **Distribks Inc.**

Monday Creek Publishing, *(978-0-692-83683-5; 978-0-692-85102-9; 978-0-692-86331-2; 978-0-692-86452-4; 978-0-692-87827-9; 978-0-692-87898-9; 978-0-692-88706-6; 978-0-692-88741-7; 978-0-692-89299-2; 978-0-692-89826-0; 978-0-692-91214-0; 978-0-692-91631-5; 978-0-692-92731-1; 978-0-692-93730-3; 978-0-692-96396-8; 978-0-692-96419-4; 978-0-692-96759-1; 978-0-692-96947-2; 978-0-692-98321-8; 978-0-692-04512-1; 978-0-692-06638-6; 978-0-692-06990-5; 978-0-692-07295-0; 978-0-692-09300-9; 978-0-692-10561-0; 978-0-692-10676-1;) P.O. Box 399, Buchtel, OH 45716 USA Tel 740-590-3987*
E-mail: gmcknight11@gmail.com
Web site: www.mondaycreekpublishing.com
Dist(s): **CreateSpace Independent Publishing Platform.**

Mondial, *(978-1-59569)* 203 W 107th St., No. 6C, New York, NY 10025 USA
E-mail: contact@mondialbooks.com
Web site: http://www.mondialbooks.com
Dist(s): **Smashwords.**

Mondo Fax Publishing, *(978-0-9710095)* 26235 Ravenhill Rd., Suite M, Santa Clarita, CA 91350-4754 USA Tel 661-250-0990; Fax: 661-251-4452
E-mail: argapc@socal.rr.com
Web site: http://mondofax.com.

Mondo Publishing, *(978-1-57255; 978-1-879531; 978-1-58653; 978-1-59034; 978-1-59336; 978-1-60201; 978-1-60715; 978-1-61736; 978-1-62889; 978-1-63060; 978-1-63061; 978-1-68156; 978-1-64064)* Div. of Music Plus, Inc., 980 6th Ave., New York, NY 10018 USA Toll Free: 888-268-3560
E-mail: ckracuna@mondopub.com
Web site: http://www.mondopub.com.

Money Jar LLC, *(978-1-7339874)* P.O. Box 180143, Brooklyn NY 11218 USA Tel 718-801-7769
E-mail: moneyjarllc@gmail.com.

Money Management Books *See* **Prism Hse. Media**

Mongoose on the Loose dba Other Worlds Ink *See* **Other Worlds Ink**

Mongoose Pr., *(978-0-9791482; 978-1-936277)* 1005 Boylston St., Suite 324, Newton Highlands, MA 02461 USA Tel 617-875-6298
E-mail: info@mongoosepress.com
Web site: http://www.MongoosePress.com
Dist(s): **MyiLibrary**
National Bk. Network
ebrary, Inc.

Mongoose Publishing (GBR) *(978-1-903980; 978-1-904577; 978-1-904854; 978-1-905176; 978-1-905476; 978-1-905471; 978-1-905850; 978-1-906103; 978-1-906508; 978-1-907218) Dist. by* **Diamond Book Dists.**

Monique Patrice Hall *See* **Hall, Monique P. Productions**

Monkey Barrel Pr., *(978-0-9802000)* 4738 Andrea Way, Union City, CA 94587 USA
Web site: http://www.monkeybarrelpress.com.

Monkey Brain Factory, *(978-0-692-93725-9)* 245 N Alvarado St No. 305, Los Angeles, CA 90026 USA Tel 213-291-5633
E-mail: brandonifd@gmail.com
Dist(s): **CreateSpace Independent Publishing Platform.**

Monkey Business *See* **Monkeying Around**

Monkey Mantra, *(978-0-692-59340-0; 978-0-9977181; 978-1-7374627; 979-8-9874059)* 2050 Jamison Pl., Santa Clara, CA 95051 USA Tel 408-506-0156
E-mail: deven@monkeymantra.com
Web site: https://www.monkeymantra.com/.

MonkeyBear Publishing *Imprint of* **LORE Mountain Productions**

MonkeyGod Enterprises, *(978-0-9708094; 978-0-9717729; 978-0-9728197)* Div. of Face 2 Face Games Publishing, 36 The Arcade, 65 Weybosset St., Providence, RI 02903 USA Tel 401-351-0362 (phone/fax)
E-mail: fmf@pipeline.com
Web site: http://www.monkeygodenterprses.com.

Monkeying Around, *(978-0-9700437; 978-0-9799753; 978-0-9975907)* P.O. Box 10131, Rochester, NY 14610 USA Tel 585-256-2660; Fax: 585-442-2965
E-mail: info@monkeyingaround.com
Web site: http://www.monkeyingaround.com.

MonkeyMantra *See* **Monkey Mantra**

Monkeyshines Publishers *See* **Allosaurus Pubs.**

Monkeytoes Pr., *(978-0-615-12555-8)* 125 Sycamore Rd., Braintree, MA 02184-7318 USA
E-mail: jvgandkdlarson@comcast.net
Web site: http://www.monkeytoespress.com.

Monnar *See* **Readers Are Leaders U.S.A.**

Monocle Pr., *(978-1-7321189; 978-1-952938)* 11600 Broadway Ext, Oklahoma City, OK 73114 USA Tel 405-507-6447
E-mail: christina@monoclepress.com
Web site: www.monoclepress.com.

Monogram Booklets *See* **Miller, Debra Juanita**

Monolith Graphics, *(978-0-9675756; 978-0-9788857; 978-0-9824899)* Orders Addr.: P.O. Box 360801, Strongsville, OH 44136 USA
E-mail: goth@monolithgraphics.com; nox@noxarcana.com
Web site: http://www.monolithgraphics.com; http://www.noxarcana.com.

Monotheist Productions International *See* **ICS Pr.**

Monroe Educational Media, *(978-0-9721146)* 2965 Taylor Rd., Reynoldsburg, OH 43068 USA Tel 614-866-4289; Fax: 740-927-9131
E-mail: jon@gooddebt.com
Web site: http://www.monroemedia.com.

Monroe, Guy, *(978-0-9742443)* P.O. Box 2325, Newport, OR 97365-0171 USA Toll Free: 877-562-3866
Web site: http://www.pinerystreet.com.

Monroe Media *See* **Monroe Educational Media**

Monroe Pubns., *(978-0-9842127; 978-0-9988893; 978-1-7326315)* 1152 Mae Street, No. 242, Hummelstown, PA 17036 USA Tel 717-497-0881
E-mail: billbreidenstine@gmail.com
Dist(s): **Casemate Pubs. & Bk. Distributors, LLC.**

Monsoon Bks. Pte. Ltd. (SGP) *(978-981-05; 978-981-4358; 978-981-4423; 978-981-4625) Dist. by* **Tuttle Pubng.**

Monsoon Bks. Pte. Ltd. (SGP) *(978-981-05; 978-981-4358; 978-981-4423; 978-981-4625) Dist. by* **Natl Bk Netwk.**

Monster Ivy Publishing, *(978-0-9987426; 978-1-948095)* 104 Candis CT, Springtown, TX 76082 USA Tel 817-805-4418
E-mail: marycgray@icloud.com.

MonsterHaven, *(978-0-615-38690-4)* 385 Camino dos Palos, Thousand Oaks, CA 91360 USA Tel 805-208-8383
E-mail: marmaxdesigns@hotmail.com
Web site: http://www.monsterhaven.com.

Monsters in My Head, LLC, The, *(978-0-9792860; 978-0-9914952; 979-8-9870894)* PO Box 502, New Providence, NJ 07974 USA (SAN 853-0254) Tel 917-881-8326
E-mail: info@worrywoos.com
Web site: http://www.worrywoos.com.

Montag Pr., *(978-0-9822809; 978-1-940233; 978-1-957010)* 1066 47th Ave., Unit #9, Oakland, CA 94601 USA Tel 916-806-8341
E-mail: c.lanfranco@gmail.com
Dist(s): **SPD-Small Pr. Distribution.**

Montana Publishing Group *See* **Loughton Bks.**

Montanha Bks. (GBR) *(978-0-9559856) Dist. by* **LuluCom.**

Montanha Pr., *(978-0-9743380)* 1547 Palos Verdes Mall , Suite 139, Walnut Creek, CA 94597 USA.

Montanye Arts, *(978-0-9779702; 978-1-951801)* P.O. Box 148, Bullville, NY 10915 USA Tel 845-361-2029
E-mail: jmontanye@earthlink.net
Web site: http://www.montanyearts.com.

Monte Nido Pr., *(978-0-9742663)* Rm 9L19, 1240 Mission Rd., Los Angeles., CA 90033 USA Tel 323-226-3406; Fax: 323-226-3440
E-mail: hoppenbrou@earthlink.net
Web site: http://www.toke.hoppenbrouwers.net.

Montemayor Pr., *(978-0-9674477; 978-1-932727)* P.O. Box 526, Millburn, NJ 07041 USA Tel 973-761-1341
E-mail: mail@montemayorpress.com
Web site: http://www.montemayorpress.com.

†Monterey Bay Aquarium, *(978-1-878244)* 886 Cannery Row, Monterey, CA 93940 USA Tel 831-648-4942; 408-648-4800; 831-648-4847; Fax: 831-644-7568; Toll Free: 877-665-2665
E-mail: mmckenzie@mbayaq.org
Web site: http://www.montereybayaquarium.org; *CIP.*

Monterey Bay Sanctuary Foundation, *(978-0-9742810)* 299 Foam St., Monterey, CA 93940 USA
E-mail: info@mbnmsf.org
Web site: http://www.mbnmsf.org
Dist(s): **Sunbelt Pubns., Inc.**

Montessori Advantage, *(978-0-9766453)* Orders Addr.: P.O. Box 272, Wickatunk, NJ 07765 USA Toll Free: 888-946-2114; Edit Addr.: 257 Rt. 79N, Wickatunk, NJ 07765 USA.

Montevallo Historical Pr., *(978-0-9658624; 978-1-956250)* 9052 Old Hickory Ct., Manassas, VA 20110 USA Tel 703-789-2407
E-mail: dean@mhpress.com
Web site: https://www.mhpress.com.

Montevallo Historical Press, Incorporated *See* **Montevallo Historical Pr.**

Montgomery County Historical Society, *(978-0-9720965)* 1000 Carillon Blvd., Dayton, OH 45409-2023 USA Do not confuse with Montgomery County Historical Society in Rockville MD, Fort Johnson NY
Web site: http://www.daytonhistory.org.

Montgomery, Nancy, *(978-1-7374052)* 491 Neptune Ave., Encinitas, CA 92024 USA Tel 808-387-9508
E-mail: nmont491@gmail.com.

Montier Shannon, *(978-1-7332029; 979-8-9857780)* 2295 Trieste Dr., High Ridge, MO 63049 USA Tel 314-609-2480
E-mail: lwhit@msn.com.

Montlake Romance *Imprint of* **Amazon Publishing**

Montoya, Amanda, *(978-0-578-45106-0; 978-0-578-45594-5)* 202 Woodway Dr., Laredo, TX 78041 USA Tel 956-286-8848
E-mail: amandamontoya4@icloud.com
Dist(s): **Ingram Content Group.**

Montville Pr., *(978-0-9706527)* P.O. Box 4304, Greensboro, NC 27410-4304 USA Tel 336-292-8268; Fax: 336-218-0410
E-mail: bas236@aol.com.

Moo Pr. *Imprint of* **Keene Publishing**

Moo Press, Incorporated *See* **Keene Publishing**

†Moody Pubs., *(978-0-8024; 978-1-881273; 978-1-60066)* Div. of Moody Bible Institute, Orders Addr.: 210 W. Chestnut, Chicago, IL 60610 USA; Edit Addr.: 820 N. LaSalle, Chicago, IL 60610 USA (SAN 202-5604) Tel 312-329-2101; Fax: 312-329-2144; Toll Free: 800-678-8812; 215 W. Locust, Chicago, IL 60610 (SAN 297-6404) Tel 312-329-2110; Fax: 312-329-8062; Toll Free: 800-678-8001; *Imprints:* Northfield Publishing (Northfield); WingSpread Publishers (WingSpre Pub)
E-mail: mpcustomerservice@moody.edu
Web site: http://www.moodypublishers.com
Dist(s): **Anchor Distributors**
BJU Pr.
Children's Plus, Inc.
Follett School Solutions
Send The Light Distribution LLC; *CIP.*

Moody Valley, *(978-1-59513)* 475 Church Hollow Rd., Boone, NC 28607 USA Tel 828-963-5331; Fax: 828-963-4101
E-mail: moodyvalley@skybest.com
Web site: http://www.moodyvalley.com
Dist(s): **Partners Bk. Distributing, Inc.**

Moody, William, *(978-0-9762556)* 301 Willard Hall, Univ. of Delaware, Newark, DE 19711 USA Tel 302-831-1658; Fax: 302-831-0591
E-mail: wmoody@udel.edu
Web site: http://www.udel.edu/educ/solveit.htm.

Mookind Pr., *(978-0-9792761)* 1600 S. Eads St., Suite 822N, Arlington, VA 22202 USA Tel 703-920-1884
E-mail: cnadel999@yahoo.com.

Moombaya Bks., *(978-0-9766799)* 2118 Wilshire Blvd., Suite 528, Santa Monica, CA 90403-9040 USA
E-mail: diponzagroup@aol.com.

Moon, Alice *See* **PeachMoon Publishing**

Moon Bear Pr., *(978-0-944164)* P.O. Box 468, Velarde, NM 87582 USA (SAN 242-9144) Tel 505-852-4897
E-mail: orders@moonbearpress.com
Web site: http://www.moonbearpress.com
Dist(s): **New Leaf Distributing Co., Inc.**

Moon Bound Pr. LLC, *(978-0-9967401; 978-1-7362025)* 208 Seamoor Dr, Fredericksburg, TX 78624 USA Tel 830-613-0100
E-mail: stephanie_kay88@yahoo.com
Web site: www.stephanieknееse.com.

Moon Chaser Publishing, *(978-0-9987338)* 220 Mare Pond Pl., Hampstead, NC 28443 USA Tel 714-713-2831
E-mail: ask1rd@aol.com.

Moon Lantern Studios *See* **Pr. Brush**

Moon Leaf Publishing LLC, *(978-0-9997612)* 876 N. Water St, Henderson, NV 89011 USA Tel 702-743-5289
E-mail: moontime@prodigy.net
Dist(s): **Ingram Content Group.**

Moon Mountain Publishing, Inc., *(978-0-9677929; 978-1-931659)* P.O. Box 188, West Rockport, ME 04865 USA Tel 207-236-0958; Fax: 978-719-6290; Toll Free: 800-353-5877
E-mail: hello@moonmountainpub.com
Web site: http://www.moonmountainpub.com.

Moon Over Mountains Publishing (M.O.M.), *(978-1-891665)* Div. of Gallery of Diamonds Jewelers, 1528 Brookhollow Dr. Suite 200, Santa Ana, CA 92705 USA (SAN 299-5492) Tel 714-549-2000; Fax: 714-545-8000; Toll Free: 800-667-4440
E-mail: info@galleryofdiamonds.com
Web site: http://www.whymomdeservesadiamond.com.

Moon Pie Pr., *(978-0-9761744)* 53 Faye Dr., Smithfield, VA 23430 USA Tel 757-356-1690
E-mail: cathyk@visi.net
Web site: http://www.moonpiepress.net.

Moon Trail Bks., *(978-0-9773140)* 24 W. 4th St., Bethlehem, PA 18015-1604 USA (SAN 850-6922) Tel 610-866-6482
E-mail: pnmca21@aol.com.

Moon Travel Handbooks *See* **Avalon Publishing**

Moon Valley Productions, *(978-0-934290)* P.O. Box 1342, Healdsburg, CA 95448 USA (SAN 221-2900) Tel 707-823-9340; 707-523-8525
E-mail: zaksartandsoul@yahoo.com
Web site: http://www.zakzaikine.com.

MoonArtDesign, *(978-1-7339724)* 19 Benjamin St, Manchester, NH 03109 USA Tel 978-424-8240
E-mail: moonart.design@gmail.com
Web site: mimcart.com.

Moonbow Pr., LLc, *(978-0-9789092)* P.O. Box 95, Bethel, OH 45106 USA (SAN 851-9110).

Moondance *Imprint of* **Quarto Publishing Group USA**

Moondance Publishing, *(978-0-9671865; 978-1-931524)* Orders Addr.: P.O. Box 16, Upper Black Eddy, PA 18972 USA Tel 610-442-1951; Fax: 610-982-5331; Edit Addr.: 1525 Oak Ln., Upper Black Eddy, PA 18972 USA (SAN 254-5101) Tel 610-442-1951
E-mail: caravan@moondancepublishing.com
Web site: http://www.moondancepublishing.com.

Moonfire Publishing, *(978-0-9993744; 978-1-954555)* 1207 Dwane St., South St. Paul, MN 55075 USA Tel 612-200-3359
E-mail: scott@moonfire-publishing.com
Web site: http://www.moonfire-publishing.com.

Moonglade Pr., *(978-0-9987639; 978-0-692-90592-0; 979-8-9855042)* P.O. Box 350296, Grand Island, FL 32735 USA Tel 541-728-3579
E-mail: crystal@moongladepress.com
Web site: https://moongladepress.com.

Moonjar, LLC, *(978-0-9724282; 978-0-9764231)* 612 19th Ave., E., Seattle, WA 98112 USA Fax: 206-726-0769; Toll Free: 888-323-0001
E-mail: contact@moonjar.com
Web site: http://www.moonjar.com
Dist(s): **Ten Speed Pr.**

Moonlight Bks., *(978-0-9971833; 978-1-945360; 978-1-7327603; 978-1-950244)* 160 W 77th St, New York, NY 10024 USA Tel 212-799-6416
E-mail: sunnydaysbook@gmail.com
Web site: www.jeanjoachimbooks.com.

Moonlight Mesa Assocs., *(978-0-9774593; 978-0-9827585; 978-1-938628)* P.O. Box 20925, Wickenburg, AZ 85358-2410 USA (SAN 257-6147)
E-mail: orders@moonlightmesaassociates.com
Web site: http://Moonlightmesaassociates.com; http://www.westernswhalesandoceans.com.

Moonlight Publishing, Ltd. (GBR) *(978-0-907144; 978-1-85103) Dist. by* **IPG Chicago.**

MoonRattles, *(978-0-9790920)* P.O. Box 939, Carmel, CA 93921 USA; 70 Dapplegray Rd., Bell Canyon, CA 91307 (SAN 854-2201) Fax: 818-932-9631; Toll Free: 800-961-6073
E-mail: info@moonrattles.com
Web site: http://www.moonrattles.com.

Moons & Stars Publishing For Children, *(978-1-929063)* Div. of Moon Star Unlimited, Inc., P.O. Box 1763, Pasadena, TX 77505 USA Tel 713-473-7120; Fax: 713-473-1105
E-mail: services@dorpexpress.com
Web site: http://www.dorpexpress.com.

moonshadow publishing, *(978-1-7324129)* 19 Brook St., Whitingham, VT 05361 USA Tel 802-368-7536
E-mail: tfooj@yahoo.com.

Moonshell Bks., Inc. *Imprint of* **Shelley Adina**

Moonshine Cove Publishing LLC, *(978-1-937327; 978-1-945181; 978-1-952439)* 150 Willow Pt., Abbeville, SC 29620 USA Tel 864-446-7570
E-mail: publisher@moonshinecovepublishing.com
Web site: http://www.moonshinecovepublishing.com
Dist(s): **Ingram Content Group.**

Moonspinners Enterprise, 2787 N. Cambridge Rd., JEFFERSONVILLE, VT 05464 USA Tel 888-785-4888
E-mail: lesleynase@moonspinnersenterprise.com
Dist(s): **Ingram Content Group.**

MoonStar Pr., *(978-0-9672107)* 4360 E. Main St., Suite 408, Ventura, CA 93003 USA Tel 805-648-7753
E-mail: toutzhag@earthlink.net
Dist(s): **New Leaf Distributing Co., Inc.**

Moonstone, *(978-0-9710129; 978-0-9712937; 978-0-9721668; 978-0-9726443; 978-0-9748501; 978-1-933076; 978-1-936814; 978-1-944017)* Div. of Amazing Fantasy Comic Shop Ltd., 582 Torrence Ave., Calumet City, IL 60409 USA Fax: 708-891-0644
E-mail: afbooks_frankfort@sbcglobal.net
Web site: http://www.moonstonebooks.com
Dist(s): **Diamond Comic Distributors, Inc.**
Diamond Bk. Distributors.

Moonstone Lily Publishing, *(978-0-9992724)* P.O. Box PO Box 90367, San Diego, CA 92169 USA Tel 858-361-5239; Fax: 858-361-5239
E-mail: publisher@moonstonelily.com
Web site: http://moonstonelily.com/.

Moonstone Pr., LLC, *(978-0-9707768; 978-0-9727697; 978-0-9769542; 978-0-9834983)* 4816 Carrington Cir., Sarasota, FL 34243 USA (SAN 852-5625) Tel 301-765-1081; Fax: 301-765-0510
E-mail: mazeprod@erols.com
Web site: http://www.moonstonepress.net
Dist(s): **Independent Pubs. Group**
Lectorum Pubns., Inc.
PSI (Publisher Services, Inc.).

Moonswept Pr., *(978-0-9718629; 978-1-60087)* 20203 Goshen Rd. No. 374, Gaithersburg, MD 20879 USA Tel 240-389-3459
Web site: http://www.moonsweptpress.com.

Moonview Pr., *(978-0-9828987)* 5460 Linda Ln., Santa Rosa, CA 95404 USA Tel 707-578-2269
E-mail: ctmarkee@gmail.com
Web site: http://www.charlesmarkee.comzbandit
Dist(s): **Smashwords.**

Moonwater Products, *(978-0-9769033)* 63 Roycroft Dr., Rochester, NY 14621 USA
E-mail: djed_ra_maat@yahoo.com.

Moore, Ammanuel, *(978-0-9744060)* P.O. Box 3295, Baltimore, MD 21228 USA Tel 410-788-7271
E-mail: info@acmoorebooks.com
Web site: http://www.acmoorebooks.com.

Moore, Evans, *(978-0-9709762)* P.O. Box 30311, Washington, DC 20030 USA Tel 202-889-3648
E-mail: evansmoore@hotmail.com.

Moore, Greg Publishing, *(978-0-9639495)* Orders Addr.: 6202 Wallina Ct., SE, Salem, OR 97309 USA Tel 503-749-1393; Fax: 503-588-7707
E-mail: yoyo@tdn.com.

Moore, Hugh Historical Park & Museums, Incorporated *See* **Delaware &Lehigh National Heritage Corridor, Inc.**

Moore, Hullihen, *(978-0-9785775)* P.O. Box 116, Oldhams, VA 22529 USA (SAN 850-9468).

Moore, Lonnie W. *See* **I & L Publishing**

Moore Publishing, *(978-0-9800791)* 646 Beautiful Run Rd., Madison, VA 22727 USA.

Moore, Sharon, *(978-0-578-03132-3)* 1009 Bay Ridge Ave., No.138, Annapolis, MD 21403 USA Tel 410-757-1474; Toll Free: 877-786-6564
E-mail: sharon@sharon-moore.com.

Moose Egg Productions, *(978-0-578-48781-6)* 1139 Trinity Trl, Saginaw, TX 76131 USA Tel 817-739-1006
E-mail: mooseegg1982@yahoo.com
Web site: www.mooseeggproductions.com.

Moose Hill Bks., Inc., *(978-0-9728627)* P.O. Box 222271, Anchorage, AK 99522 USA (SAN 255-1616)
E-mail: publisher@moosehillbooks.com
Web site: http://www.moosehillbooks.com.

Moose Run Productions, *(978-0-9766315)* 22010 Highview, Clinton Township, MI 48036 USA Tel 586-718-7700
Web site: http://www.moose-run.com.

Moosehead Publishing, *(978-0-615-43399-8; 978-0-692-49597-1; 978-0-692-51854-0; 978-0-692-54977-3; 978-1-9161804-1-3)* 3 Marsh Rd., Tiburon, CA 94920 USA Tel 415-990-5019
Dist(s): **CreateSpace Independent Publishing Platform**
Dummy Record Do Not USE!!!!.

Moppet Bks., *(978-0-9977145; 978-0-9988205; 978-1-7337921)* 10668 SW 41ST AVE, Portland, OR 97219 USA Tel 323-717-3976
E-mail: fredrik@kinderguides.com
Web site: www.kinderguides.com
Dist(s): **SCB Distributors.**

Morals & Values Pr., *(978-0-9754191; 978-0-9842140; 978-0-9898501; 978-1-7355487)* P. O. Box 4785, Los Angeles, CA 90231 USA
E-mail: mischa@mischainspires.com
Web site: http://www.moralsandvaluespress.com; http://www.greatnessnow.org.

Moran, Kristyna, *(978-0-692-79225-4)* 5016 Thorne Dr. #14, LA MESA, CA 91942 USA Tel 619-787-3785.

Morari Specialties Inc., *(978-0-9770618)* 13901 SW 22nd St., Miami, FL 33175-7006 USA
Web site: http://www.moraripecialties.com.

Morcan, Dorina, *(978-0-9763663)* P.O. Box 1564, Malvern, AR 72104 USA Fax: 501-262-4127
E-mail: dmorcan@ix.netcom.com.

More Books Press *See* **SCOJO ENTERTAINMENT**

More, Frances International Teaching Systems *See* **Frances More International Teaching Systems**

More, Francisco J., *(978-0-9747851)* 221 Majorca Ave., No. 207, Coral Gables, FL 33134-4429 USA Tel 305-448-5081.

More Heart Than Talent Publishing, Incorporated *See* **Golden Mastermind Seminars, Inc.**

More Pr., *(978-0-9743394)* Div. of More Consulting Co., 1634 E. 53rd St., Chicago, IL 60615-4389 USA
E-mail: shaharimoore@aol.com.

M.O.R.E. Pubs., *(978-0-9719984; 978-0-9758549; 978-0-9801647; 978-0-9820354; 978-0-9830325; 978-0-692-27449-1; 978-1-945344)* Orders Addr.: P.O. Box 621, Collierville, TN 38027-0621 USA; Edit Addr.: 4466 Elvis Presley Blvd. 1st Memphis Plaza - Suite 103, Memphis, TN 38116 USA (SAN 255-1055)
E-mail: stlouiswpguild@aol.com; MOREPublishersCO@AOL.com
Web site: http://www.MOREPublishers.biz; http://www.TheScaleMagazine.MagCloud.com.

More to Life Publishing, *(978-0-9632564; 978-0-9766971; 978-0-9825746; 978-9949-9251)* 1549 22nd St N, Arlington, VA 22209 USA; Aarekoidu tee 10 Alliku Kula, Saue vald, Harjumaa, 76403 Tel 372 50 81 944
E-mail: kimismore@gmail.com; morepublish@gmail.com
Web site: http://www.askrealjesus.com; http://www.morepublish.com
Dist(s): **SCB Distributors.**

Moredo-Burich, John, *(978-1-7360766; 979-8-9859029)* 3222 K St., Eureka, CA 95503 USA Tel 828-301-6422
E-mail: viralmedicinces@gmail.com.

Morehouse Education Resources, *(978-1-60674)* 1313 Steele St., Suite 400, Denver, CO 80203 USA Tel 303-832-4427; Fax: 202-832-4971; Toll Free: 800-242-1918
Web site: http://www.morehouseeducation.org
Dist(s): **Abingdon Pr.**
Church Publishing, Inc.
Ingram Publisher Services
Open Road Integrated Media, Inc.
Two Rivers Distribution.

Morehouse Publishing *Imprint of* **Church Publishing, Inc.**

moreland story, *(978-0-9993488)* 381 N. Liberty Rd, River Falls, WI 54022 USA Tel 651-308-3084; Fax: 651-308-3084
E-mail: our5thhouse@gmail.com
Web site: www.autismlm.com.

Morelli, Laura, *(978-0-9893671; 978-1-942467; 978-1-942778)* PO Box 30002, Sea Island, GA 31561 USA; *Imprints:* Scriptorium, The (ScriptoriumThe)
E-mail: laura@lauramorelli.com
Web site: www.lauramorelli.com.

Morelmasters LLC, *(978-0-615-12829-0)* Orders Addr.: 6294 Reynolds Ridge Rd., Potosi, WI 53820 USA Tel 608-732-2175; Fax: 608-763-2799
E-mail: morelmasters@tds.net
Web site: http://www.morelmasters.com.

Morewellson, Ltd *See* **Morewellson, Ltd.**

Morewellson, Ltd., *(978-0-9994402; 978-1-950452)* P.O. Box 49726, Colorado Springs, CO 80949-9726 USA Tel 719-460-5425
E-mail: vikki@vikkiwalton.com.

Morgan & Claypool Pubs., *(978-1-59829; 978-1-60845; 978-1-62705; 978-1-970001; 978-1-68173; 978-1-68174; 978-1-947487; 978-1-64327; 978-1-63639)* Orders Addr.: a/o c/o. bLogistics, 82 Winter Sport Ln., Williston, VT 05495 USA (SAN 256-5153) Tel 888-822-9942; Edit Addr.: 1210 5th Ave. Suite 250, San Rafael, CA 94901 USA Tel 415-785-8003; Fax: 415-785-2507
E-mail: info@morganclaypool.com
Web site: http://www.morganclaypool.com
Dist(s): **American International Distribution Corp.**
ebrary, Inc.

Morgan, Briana, *(978-1-7340010)* 208 Cumberland Way SE, Smyrna, GA 30080 USA Tel 407-719-0418
E-mail: brianammorgan@gmail.com.

Morgan, E. A., *(978-0-9631975)* Orders Addr.: P.O. Box 7452, Naples, FL 34101 USA Fax: 941-598-9809
E-mail: rhymetime@mailstation.com.

Morgan, Elizabeth Jane, *(978-0-692-92320-7; 978-0-692-04614-2; 978-0-692-07610-1)* 2245 E. Racquet Club Rd., PALM SPRINGS, CA 92262 USA Tel 760-413-1458
E-mail: ejm92262@gmail.com
Dist(s): **Ingram Content Group.**

Morgan Foundation Pubs.: International Published Innovations, *(978-1-885679)* 8514 La Palomita Rd NE, Albuquerque, NM 87111-4518 USA Tel 505-433-4290; Fax: 815-550-4456
E-mail: morganfoundation@earthlink.net
Web site: http://www.morganfoundationpublishers.com.

Morgan James Publishing, *(978-0-9746133; 978-0-9758570; 978-0-9760901; 978-0-9768491; 978-1-933596; 978-1-60037; 978-0-9815058; 978-0-9817906; 978-0-9820750; 978-0-9823793; 978-0-9846170; 978-0-9828590; 978-0-9833715; 978-0-9835013; 978-1-61448; 978-0-9837125; 978-0-9840316; 978-1-938467; 978-1-63047; 978-1-63195; 978-1-68350; 978-0-9985823; 978-1-64279; 978-1-63698) Div. of Morgan James, LLC, 23rd Flr. 5 Penn Plaza, New York, NY 10001 USA*
E-mail: kim@morganjamespublishing.com
Web site: http://www.morganjamespublishing.com
Dist(s): **Consortium Bk. Sales & Distribution**
Ingram Content Group
Lulu Pr., Inc.
MyiLibrary
Open Road Integrated Media, Inc.
Publishers Group West (PGW)
Two Rivers Distribution.

Morgan Publishing Co., *(978-0-9639940)* Orders Addr.: P.O. Box 28718, San Jose, CA 95159 USA (SAN 298-1432) Fax: 408-637-1674; Edit Addr.: 338 Fifth St., Hollister, CA 95023 USA Tel 408-637-7031.

Morgan Publishing, Incorporated *See* **Augustine Pr.**

Morgan Rice *Imprint of* **Morgan Rice Bks.**

Morgan Rice Bks., Div. of Lukeman Literary Management Ltd., 157 Bedford Ave., Brooklyn, NY 11211 USA Tel 718-599-8988; Fax: 718-264-2189; *Imprints:* Morgan Rice (MYID_X_MORGAN) ; Noah Lukeman (MYID_P_NOAH LU)
Dist(s): **Lukeman Literary Management, Ltd.**
MyiLibrary.

Morgan's Magical Media, *(978-0-692-65214-5; 978-0-578-17921-6; 978-0-692-69248-6; 978-0-692-76332-2; 978-0-578-27716-5)* 2 Foxhall Ct., Silver Spring, MD 20906 USA
Web site: https://morgansmagical.com
Dist(s): **CreateSpace Independent Publishing Platform.**

Moriah Ministries, *(978-0-9728454; 978-0-9774836)* P.O. Box 23823, Chagrin Falls, OH 44023 USA Tel 440-543-9304 (phone/fax)
E-mail: info@davidicdance.com; info@moriahministries.org
Web site: http://www.davidicdance.com; http://www.moriahministries.org.

Morin, Frank *See* **Whipsaw Pr.**

Mormon Comics, *(978-0-9764965)* 435 N. 150 W., Blackfoot, ID 83221 USA Tel 208-785-4558 (phone/fax)
E-mail: info@mormoncomics.com
Web site: http://www.mormoncomics.com.

Mornin' Light Media, *(978-0-9763534)* Orders Addr.: 31203 N. Course View, Franklin, TN 37067 USA; *Imprints:* Mornin'Light Media (MorninLight)
E-mail: shawnsurber@comcast.net; hopebook@bellsouth.net
Web site: http://www.thehopebook.com.

morning circle media, *(978-0-9834702; 978-0-578-65314-3; 978-0-578-71951-1)* 519 Toll Rd., Oreland, PA 19075 USA Tel 215-572-9375
E-mail: cynthiakreilick@aol.com.

†Morning Glory Pr., Inc., *(978-0-930934; 978-1-885356; 978-1-932538; 978-0-9844283)* 6595 San Haroldo Way, Buena Park, CA 90620 USA (SAN 211-2558) 888-327-4362; Toll Free: 888-612-8254 Do not confuse with Morning Glory Press in Nashua, NH
E-mail: jwl@morningglorypress.com; info@morningglorypress.com
Web site: http://www.morningglorypress.com
Dist(s): **MyiLibrary**; *CIP.*

Morning Glory Pubns., *(978-0-9762929)* Orders Addr.: 1104 Blue ridge Dr., Clarkston, MI 48348 USA
E-mail: klinejane@hotmail.com.

Morning Joy Media, *(978-0-9826102; 978-1-937107)* 359 Bridge St., Spring City, PA 19475 USA Tel 610-256-2906
E-mail: debbie@morningjoymedia.com
Web site: http://www.morningjoymedia.com
Dist(s): **BookBaby.**

Morning Star Music Pubs., *(978-0-944529)* 1727 Larkin Williams Rd., Fenton, MO 63026 USA (SAN 243-8496)
E-mail: morningstar@morningstarmusic.com
Web site: http://www.morningstarmusic.com
Dist(s): **BookBaby.**

Morning Sun Bks., Inc., *(978-0-9619058; 978-1-58248; 978-1-878887)* 9 Pheasant Ln., Scotch Plains, NJ 07076 USA (SAN 243-1157) Tel 908-755-5454; Fax: 908-755-5455
E-mail: morningsunbooks@comcast.net
Web site: http://www.morningsunbooks.com
Dist(s): **Walthers, William K. Inc.**

MorningGlory Publishing, *(978-0-9705090)* Orders Addr.: P.O. Box 15523, Plantation, FL 33318-5523 USA Tel 954-370-7205; Fax: 954-370-6817; Edit Addr.: 9951 NW Sixth Ct., Plantation, FL 33324 USA
E-mail: tandtsm@aol.com.

Morningside Publishing, LLC, *(978-1-936210)* 1705 W Riley Rd, Payson, AZ 85541 USA (SAN 858-835X)
Web site: http://www.morningsidepublishing.com
Dist(s): **Smashwords.**

Morningstar Christian Chapel, *(978-0-9715733; 978-0-9729477; 978-0-9842943; 978-1-940198; 978-0-9964131)* 16241 Leffingwell Rd., Whittier, CA 90603 USA Tel 562-943-0297; Fax: 562-943-3608
E-mail: jacobeelen@morningstarcc.org
Web site: http://www.morningstarcc.org.

MorningStar Pubns., Inc., *(978-1-878327; 978-1-929371; 978-1-59933; 978-1-60708)* Div. of MorningStar Fellowship Church, 375 Star Light Dr., Fort Mill, SC 29715 USA Tel 803-802-5544 (phone/fax); Toll Free: 800-542-0278 (orders only) Do not confuse with Morningstar Pubns., Boulder, CO
E-mail: info@morningstarministries.org
Web site: http://www.morningstarministries.org
Dist(s): **Anchor Distributors**
Destiny Image Pubs.
Whitaker Hse.

Morningtide Pr., *(978-0-9790395)* P.O. Box 312, St. Augustine, FL 32085-0312 USA
Web site: http://www.morningtidepress.com
Dist(s): **Quality Bks., Inc.**

Mornin'Light Media *Imprint of* **Mornin' Light Media**

Morris, Nicole, *(978-0-692-89340-1)* 5 Washington Ave, PRINCETON, NJ 08540 USA Tel 908-256-4205
E-mail: lilniki45@gmail.com
Dist(s): **Ingram Content Group.**

Morris Publishing, *(978-0-7392; 978-0-9631249; 978-1-57502; 978-1-885591; 978-0-9863567; 978-0-578-26187-4)* Orders Addr.: P.O. Box 2110, Kearney, NE 68847 USA Fax: 308-237-0263; Toll Free: 800-650-7888 Do not confuse with companies with the same Wesley Chapel, FL, Elkhart, IN
E-mail: publish@morrispublishing.com
Web site: http://www.morrispublishing.com.

Morris, Shanon, *(978-1-7325821)* 272 W. 117th st Apt 2E, NEW YORK, NY 10026 USA Tel 516-972-4513
E-mail: shanonmorris@gmail.com
Web site: www.shanonmorris.com.

Morris, Tami *See* **2B Pr.**

Morrison, Mackenzie, *(978-0-692-04337-0; 978-0-578-54934-7; 978-0-578-67441-4)* 256 S. Norton Ave., Los Angeles, CA 90004 USA Tel 310-600-4737
E-mail: mackenzie.claire.morrison@gmail.com
Dist(s): **Ingram Content Group.**

Morrison Meyer Pr., *(978-1-7323292)* 31 Le Conte, Laguna Niguel, CA 92677 USA Tel 949-395-8364
E-mail: Paulecke@gmail.com.

Morrison-Andrews, Sharalyn, *(978-0-9962889; 978-0-9974305; 978-0-9975343; 978-1-7335614; 979-8-9864768)* 15 Grover Rd, Cape Elizabeth, ME 04107 USA Tel 207-799-3664
E-mail: sharalynlovesanimals@gmail.com
Web site: sharalynlovesanimals.com.

Morrow Circle Publishing, LLC, *(978-0-9989801)* 7333 Woodward Claypool Rd., Morrow, OH 45152 USA Tel 513-310-0280
E-mail: Janet@JanetKassalenAuthor.com
Web site: www.JanetKassalenAuthor.com.

Morrow, William Cookbooks *Imprint of* **HarperCollins Pubs.**

Morrow, William & Co. *Imprint of* **HarperCollins Pubs.**

Morten Moore Publishing, *(978-0-9672576; 978-0-9991108)* Div. of K & M Marketing, 415 E. Mohawk, Flagstaff, AZ 86001 USA Tel 928-380-4982; Fax: 000-000-0000
Dist(s): **Canyonlands Pubns.**

mortensen, charles, *(978-1-7367405)* 723 e. angeleno ave, BURBANK, CA 91501 USA Tel 818-521-0320
E-mail: charles_mortensen@yahoo.com.

Mortensen, Joshua *See* **Magpie Children's Bks.**

Morton Arts Media, *(978-0-9796868)* P.O. Box 233, Cornelius, NC 28031 USA.

Morton Bks., *(978-1-929188)* 47 Stewart Ave., Irvington, NJ 07111 USA Tel 973-374-8327; Fax: 973-374-1125
E-mail: rmo1033555@aol.com
Web site: http://www.mortonbooks.com.

MOS, Inc., *(978-0-9778570)* 5271 E MANN RD, Pekin, IN 47165-8807 USA Tel 812-967-2531; Fax: 812-967-2980; Toll Free: 800-451-3993
E-mail: info@joyfulcatholic.com
Web site: http://www.traditionalcatholicpublishing.com/.

Mosaic Consortium Group, LLC, *(978-0-578-07392-7; 978-0-9852542)* 3 Pascc Ct., Pikesville, MD 21208 USA (SAN 920-2889) Tel 877-733-7308
E-mail: mosaicconsortium1@gmail.com; knight3333@outlook.com
Web site: http://www.onyxgavel.com; www.complexcollective.com.

Mosaic Paradigm Group, LLC *See* **Mosaic Consortium Group, LLC**

Mosaic Pr. (CAN) *(978-0-88962; 978-1-77161) Dist. by* **IPG Chicago.**

Mosaic Publishing *See* **Branded Black Publishing**

Mosby *Imprint of* **Elsevier - Health Sciences Div.**

Mosby Ltd. *Imprint of* **Elsevier - Health Sciences Div.**

Moscow Ballet *Imprint of* **Sports Marketing International, Inc.**

Mosdos Pr., *(978-0-9671009; 978-0-9742160; 978-0-9801670; 978-0-9858078; 978-0-9888286)* Div. of Mosdos Ohr Hatorah, 1508 Warrensville Ctr. Rd., Cleveland, OH 44121 USA Tel 216-291-4158; Fax: 216-291-4169
E-mail: mosdospress@moh1.org; jfactor@moh1.org
Web site: http://www.mosdospress.com.

Moselle Productions, Inc., *(978-0-9701289)* P.O. Box 1304, League City, TX 77574 USA Tel 732-623-9908; Toll Free: 800-598-2519
Web site: http://www.mangoandmarlie.com.

Mosely, Winifred, *(978-0-9769610)* 6600 E. River Rd., Tucson, AZ 85750 USA Tel 520-327-3681
E-mail: njmosely@comcast.net.

Moses, Yvonne, *(978-1-7348957)* 71 Johnson St, Amityville, NY 11701 USA Tel 631-608-8561
E-mail: eviemoses.ym@gmail.com.

Moshire Pr., *(978-0-615-39082-6)* 2355 Carlysle Cove, Lawrenceville, GA 30044 USA Tel 404-784-5987
Web site: http://www.moshirepress.com.

Mosley, Kim, *(978-0-9663215)* 1312 W. 40th St., Austin, TX 78756-3615 USA Tel 512-762-6790
E-mail: mrkimmosley@gmail.com
Web site: http://kimmosley.com/workbook.

Moss, Francis C., *(978-1-7327910)* 7709 Vista Rd., Joshua Tree, CA 92252 USA Tel 818-692-1575
E-mail: fcmoss@gmail.com.

Moss, Marc, *(978-0-578-69598-3; 978-1-7353614; 978-1-7373392)* 704B Ravenel St., Spartanburg, SC 29302 USA Tel 864-921-7813
E-mail: marcmoss77@gmail.com.

Moss, Michael, *(978-0-9763003)* 610 Prestwick Dr., Frankfort, IL 60423 USA Tel 312-437-7827 (312-437-STAR)
Web site: http://www.5starpc.com.

Moss Press Publishing, *(978-0-578-12603-6)* 616 Corporate Way Suite 2-4348, Valley Cottage, NY 10989 USA.

Mosscovered Gumbo Barn, *(978-0-9725853)* 15960 Highland Rd., Baton Rouge, LA 70810 USA
Dist(s): **Greenleaf Book Group.**

Mossy Moot, *(978-0-9977134)* 127 KINGS HWY, HACKETTSTOWN, NJ 07840 USA Tel 908-852-7050
E-mail: Susimage66@gmail.com.

Mostats, Marie C., *(978-0-9742848)* Orders Addr.: P.O. Box 230053, Las Vegas, NV 89123-0001 USA; Edit Addr.: 608 NW 29th St., Wilton Manors, FL 33311-2443 USA.

Mot de Mere Publishing, *(978-0-692-15641-4; 978-0-578-45015-5; 978-0-578-45658-4; 978-0-578-48293-4; 978-0-578-51508-3)* 27506 N. 3979 Dr., Ochelata, OK 74051 USA Tel 918-277-7691
E-mail: scon555@gmail.com.

Mota, Anastasia De La *See* **Seymour Reide**

Mother Bear Pr., *(978-0-692-19773-8; 978-0-692-04346-2)* 1590 Amsterdam Ave. Apt. 22, New York, NY 10031 USA Tel 225-505-2203
E-mail: dcassidy1228@gmail.com
Dist(s): **Ingram Content Group.**

Mother Goose Programs, *(978-0-9753985; 978-0-9841366; 978-1-935784)* P.O. Box 423, Chester, VT 05143-0423 USA
E-mail: debbi@mothergooseprograms.org
Web site: http://www.mothergooseprograms.org
Dist(s): **National Bk. Network.**

Mother Hubbard & Co. LLC *Imprint of* **Mother Hubbard & Co. LLC**

Mother Hubbard & Co. LLC, *(978-0-692-18722-7; 978-0-578-41143-9; 978-1-7330681)* 3375 Centerville Hwy. No. 391385, Snellville, GA 30039 USA Tel 404-740-7835; *Imprints:* Mother Hubbard & Co. LLC (MYID_Z_MOTHER)
E-mail: MotherHubbardCo@gmail.com
Web site: MotherHubbard.us.

Mother Lode Pr. LLC, *(978-0-615-34241-2; 978-0-692-78184-5)* P.O. Box 2526, Bay Saint Louis, MS 39521 USA Tel 571-926-3443
E-mail: jonfaust@helicopterharry.com.

Mother Moose Pr., *(978-0-9724570)* Orders Addr.: 21010 Southbank St., PMB No. 435, Potomac Falls, VA 20165 USA Tel 571-223-6472
E-mail: books@mothermoosepress.com
Web site: http://www.mothermoosepress.com.

Mother Necessity Inc., *(978-0-9796579)* P.O. Box 2135, Bonita Springs, FL 34133 USA
E-mail: cfergus@mothernecessity.com
Web site: http://www.mothernecessity.com.

M.O.T.H.E.R. Publishing Co., Inc., The, *(978-0-9718431)* Orders Addr.: P.O. Box 477, Rock Springs, WY 82902 USA Tel 307-382-5027; Fax: 307-382-6492; Edit Addr.: 616 Elias Ave., Rock Springs, WY 82901 USA
E-mail: motherpublishing@wyoming.com
Web site: http://www.motherpublishing.com.

Motherboard Bks., *(978-0-9749653; 978-0-692-42438-4; 978-0-692-42562-6; 978-0-692-43162-7; 979-8-9866999)*
E-mail: phylliswheeler@phylliswheeler.com
Web site: phylliswheeler.com
Dist(s): **CreateSpace Independent Publishing Platform.**

Motherhood Beyond Bars, *(978-1-7375111)* 1799 Briardiff Rd. Box 15276, Atlanta, GA 30333 USA Tel 678-404-1397
E-mail: info@motherhoodbeyond.org
Web site: www.motherhoodbeyond.org.

Motherhood Printing & Etc., *(978-1-60225)* Orders Addr.: 45973 Rd. 795, Ansley, NE 68814-5126 USA (SAN 852-1212) Tel 308-880-1021; Fax: 308-732-3280
E-mail: mary@motherhoodprinting.com
Web site: http://motherhoodprinting.com.

Motherly Way Enterprises, *(978-0-9671428)* P.O. Box 11, Marylhurst, OR 97036-0011 USA Tel 503-723-2879; Toll Free: 877-666-7929
E-mail: julie@motherlyway.com
Web site: http://www.motherlyway.com.

Mother's Love Publishing, A, *(978-0-9777022)* 4962 Bristol Rock Rd, Florissant, MO 63033 USA (SAN 257-9707)
Dist(s): **Lushena Bks.**

Mothwing Pr. *Imprint of* **Mothwing.com**

Mothwing.com, *(978-0-9724528)* 80 Sheffield Rd., Waltham, MA 02451-2374 USA Tel 781-899-8153; *Imprints:* Mothwing Press (Mothwng Pr)
E-mail: mothwingpress@mothwing.com; andylevesque@rcn.com
Web site: http://www.mothwing.com/mothwingpress.

Motina Bks., *(978-1-945060; 979-8-88784)* 115 Colt St., Van Alstyne, TX 75495 USA Tel 303-668-0440
E-mail: diane@warthog.com.

Motion Fitness LLC, *(978-0-9744568)* P.O. Box 2179, Palatine, IL 60078-2179 USA
E-mail: sales@motionfitness.com
Web site: http://www.motionfitness.com.

Motivision Media, *(978-0-9722332)* 9528 Blossom Valley Rd., El Cajon, CA 92021 USA
E-mail: dehaven@motivisionmedia.com; dehaven1@cox.net
Web site: http://www.motivisionmedia.com; http://www.MyFootballMentor.com.

Motorbooks *Imprint of* **Quarto Publishing Group USA**

†Mott Media, *(978-0-88062; 978-0-915134; 978-0-940319)* 1130 Fenway Cir., Fenton, MI 48430 USA (SAN 207-1460) Tel 810-714-4280; Fax: 810-714-2077 Do not confuse with Mott Media in Stamford, CT
E-mail: sales@mottmedia.com; bill@mottmedia.com
Web site: http://www.mottmedia.com
Dist(s): **Spring Arbor Distributors, Inc.**; *CIP.*

Mottley, William, *(978-0-9769216)* 428 N. Genito Rd., Burkeville, VA 23922 USA Tel 434-767-5594
E-mail: emottley@ceva.net
Web site: http://www.narrowstrip.com.

Motto, Amy, *(978-0-692-14862-4; 978-0-692-14935-5; 978-0-692-14939-3)* 1915 Myrtle Ave, Las Cruces, NM 88001 USA Tel 575-541-8070
E-mail: ray.karen7@gmail.com
Dist(s): **Ingram Content Group.**

Moulton, Shirley *See* **Magic Moon Bks., LLC**

Mount Baldy Pr., Inc., *(978-0-9715863; 979-8-9867744)* P.O. Box 469, Boulder, CO 80306-0469 USA (SAN 254-2625) Tel 415-413-8052; Fax: 303-532-1007
E-mail: simeon@mountbaldy.com
Web site: http://www.mountbaldy.com
Dist(s): **New Leaf Distributing Co., Inc.**
Quality Bks., Inc.

Mount Helicon Pr. *Imprint of* **Rock, James A. & Co. Pubs.**

Mount Olive College Pr., *(978-0-9627087; 978-1-880994; 978-1-59761)* Mount Olive College, Administration Bldg. 634 Henderson St., Mount Olive, NC 28365 USA (SAN 297-7729) Tel 919-658-2502; Toll Free Fax: 800-653-0854.

Mount Orleans Pr. (GBR) *(978-1-912945) Dist. by* **IPG Chicago.**

Mount Rushmore Bookstores, *(978-0-9646798; 978-0-9752617; 978-0-9798823; 978-0-692-63993-1)* Div. of Mount Rushmore National Memorial Society, 13030 Hwy. 244, Keystone, SD 57751 USA Tel 605-341-8883; Fax: 605-341-0433; Toll Free: 800-699-3142
E-mail: debbie_ketel@mtrushmore.org
Web site: http://www.mountrushmoresociety.com
Dist(s): **Partners Distributing.**

Mount Rushmore History Association *See* **Mount Rushmore Bookstores**

†Mount Vernon Ladies' Assn. of the Union, *(978-0-931917)* Orders Addr.: P.O. Box 110, Mount Vernon, VA 22121 USA (SAN 225-3976); Edit Addr.: 3200 Mount Vernon Memorial Hwy., Mount Vernon, VA 22121 USA
E-mail: ajohnson@mountvernon.org
Web site: http://www.mountvernon.org
Dist(s): **University of Virginia Pr.**
Wimmer Cookbooks; *CIP.*

Mountain Air Bks., *(978-0-615-24940-7; 978-0-615-24941-4; 978-0-615-26703-6; 978-0-615-29319-6; 978-0-615-29829-0; 978-0-615-41620-5; 978-0-615-56237-7; 978-0-615-64830-9)* 1045 University Ave. Apt. 2, Rochester, NY 14607-1624 USA
E-mail: scottkny@yahoo.com; mairbooks123@yahoo.com.

Mountain Bell Pr., *(978-0-578-93746-5)* 123 Kit Carson Peak CT 0, NEW CASTLE, CO 81647 USA Tel 3039198976
E-mail: jesturpin@gmail.com
Dist(s): **Ingram Content Group.**

Mountain Bk. Co., P.O. Box 778, Broomfield, CO 80038-0778 USA Tel 303-436-1982; Fax: 917-386-2769
E-mail: wordguise@aol.com
Web site: http://www.mountainbook.org.

Mountain Brook Fire *Imprint of* **Mountain Brook Ink**

Mountain Brook Ink, *(978-0-9960068; 978-1-943959; 978-1-953957)* 26 Moore Rd., White Salmon, WA 98672 USA Tel 509-493-3953; *Imprints:* Mountain Brook Fire (MYID_B_MNTN BR)
E-mail: miraleef@gmail.com
Web site: www.miraleeferrell.com.

Mountain Gap Bks., *(978-0-692-98919-7; 978-1-7323277; 978-1-7329720)* 221 Forestview Dr., Jonesborough, TN 37659-5622 USA Tel 423-773-7225
E-mail: bjmg1049@gmail.com; publisher@mountaingapbooks.com
Web site: mountaingapbooks.com.

Mountain Girl Press *See* **Jan-Carol Publishing, INC.**

Mountain Horse Pr., *(978-0-9995431)* 1859 Tower Rd., St. Johnsbury, VT 05819 USA Tel 802-748-5455
E-mail: robin.kristoff@gmail.com
Web site: mountainhorsepress.com.

Mountain Maid *See* **Light Messages Publishing**

Mountain Memories Bks. *Imprint of* **Quarrier Pr.**

Mountain Ministries, *(978-0-9787761)* 18055 100th St., Lindsay, OK 73052-3308 USA Do not confuse with Mountain Ministries Sitka, Alaska.

Mountain n' Air Bks., *(978-1-879415)* Div. of Mountain n' Air Sports, Inc., Orders Addr.: P.O. Box 12540, La Crescenta, CA 91224 USA (SAN 630-5598) Tel 818-248-9345; Toll Free Fax: 800-303-5578; Toll Free: 800-446-9696; Edit Addr.: 2947-A Hololulu Ave., La Crescenta, CA 91214 USA (SAN 631-4198); *Imprints:* Bearly Cooking (Bearly Cooking)
E-mail: books@mountain-n-air.com
Web site: http://mountain-n-air.com
Dist(s): **CreateSpace Independent Publishing Platform.**

Mountain Path Pr., *(978-0-9653149)* 111 Bank St., Ste 152, Grass Valley, CA 95945 USA Toll Free: 888-224-9997
E-mail: Info@MountainPathPress.com
Web site: http://www.mountainpathpress.com
Dist(s): **Bks. West**
Integral Yoga Pubns.
New Leaf Distributing Co., Inc.
Partners Bk. Distributing, Inc.

Mountain Path Publications *See* **Mountain Path Pr.**

†Mountain Pr. Publishing Co., Inc., *(978-0-87842)* Orders Addr.: P.O. Box 2399, Missoula, MT 59806-2399 USA (SAN 202-8832) Tel 406-728-1900; Fax: 406-728-1635; Toll Free: 800-234-5308; Edit Addr.: 1301 S. Third West, Missoula, MT 59801 USA (SAN 662-0868)
E-mail: jrimel@mtnpress.com; info@mtnpress.com; anne@mtnpress.com
Web site: http://www.mountain-press.com
Dist(s): **Bks. West**
Partners Bk. Distributing, Inc.; *CIP.*

Mountain States Specialties, *(978-0-9726022)* 1671 Valtec Ln., Boulder, CO 80301 USA Tel 303-444-6186 Toll Free: 800-353-2147.

Mountain Stream Publishing, *(978-0-615-89002-9; 978-0-692-22188-4; 978-0-692-26072-2; 978-0-692-28524-4; 978-0-692-33655-7; 978-0-692-33933-6; 978-0-692-35039-3; 978-0-692-37723-9; 978-0-692-52377-3; 978-0-692-76014-7)* 5327 W. HILL Rd., BOISE, ID 83703 USA Tel 2088639839
Dist(s): **CreateSpace Independent Publishing Platform.**

Mountain Thunder Publishing, *(978-0-615-69738-3; 978-0-9887625)* P.O. Box 6264, Snowmass Village, CO 81615 USA Tel 6462836884
Dist(s): **CreateSpace Independent Publishing Platform.**

Mountain Valley Publishing, LLC, *(978-1-59453; 978-1-60002; 978-1-934940)* Orders Addr.: 1420 Maple Ct., Martinsville, IN 46151 USA Tel 765-349-8908; Fax: 765-349-8908
E-mail: bdenton308@comcast.net
Web site: http://www.mountainvalleypublishing.com.

Mountain Voices Pubs., *(978-0-9671908)* Orders Addr.: 2 Junaluska Rd., Andrews, NC 28901 USA Tel 828-321-5553; Fax: 828-321-2446
E-mail: MountainTeller@mountainvoice.com
Web site: http://www.mountainvoice.com.

Mountain World Media LLC, *(978-0-9763309)* Orders Addr.: P.O. Box 687, Telluride, CO 81435 USA Tel 970-729-0289; Edit Addr.: 135 Hillside Ln., Telluride, CO 81435 USA
E-mail: damon@mountainworldmedia.com
Web site: http://www.mountainworldmedia.com
Dist(s): **Alpenbooks Pr. LLC**
Bks. West.

Mountaintop Pr., *(978-0-9711106)* Orders Addr.: P.O. Box 550, Cary, NC 27512-0550 USA Tel 919-567-9550; Fax: 919-567-9694; Edit Addr.: 201-D Foliage Cir., Cary, NC 27511 USA
Dist(s): **Send The Light Distribution LLC.**

MountainView *Imprint of* **Treble Heart Bks.**

Mountan Creek Pubns., *(978-0-615-52752-9; 978-0-615-55170-8; 978-0-9853574)* 80 Post Ave., Rochester, NY 14619 USA Tel 585-966-9669
E-mail: nailahbaniti@gmail.com
Web site: Mountaincreekpublications.com.

Mountcastle Co., *(978-0-913063)* 860 Dolphin Dr., Danville, CA 94526 USA (SAN 285-6689) Tel 925-548-0554
E-mail: support@mntcastle.com
Web site: www.mntcastle.com
Dist(s): **Independent Pubs. Group.**

Mountcastle, Deirdre D. PA, *(978-0-9992073)* 16 Marshview Dr., St Augustine, FL 32080-9182 USA Tel 904-687-5667
E-mail: Dee.Mountcastle.Books@gmail.com.

Mountz Media & Publishing, *(978-0-9840673; 978-0-9891429; 978-1-7347117)* Orders Addr.: P.O. Box 702398, Tulsa, OK 74170 USA; Edit Addr.: 5721 E. 101st Pl., Tulsa, OK 74137 USA
E-mail: mamountz@cox.net.

Mourning Enterprises LLC, *(978-1-7344173)* 4801 Kenmore Ave., Alexandria, VA 22304 USA Tel 203-512-8507
E-mail: mourningknows@gmail.com
Web site: www.mourningknows.com.

ouse! Publishing, *(978-0-9643512)* Orders Addr.: P.O. Box 1674, Honolulu, HI 96806 USA Tel 808-625-7522; Fax: 808-284-5516; Edit Addr.: 419 South St., Suite 133, Honolulu, HI 96813 USA
Dist(s): **Booklines Hawaii, Ltd.**
ouse Works, *(978-0-7364; 978-1-57082)* Div. of Disney Bk. Publishing, Inc., A Walt Disney Co., 114 Fifth Ave., New York, NY 10011 USA (SAN 298-0797) Tel 212-633-4400; Fax: 212-633-4811
Web site: http://www.disneybooks.com
Dist(s): **Random Hse., Inc.**
Mousetime Bks. *Imprint of* **Mousetime Media LLC**
Mousetime Media LLC, *(978-0-9723213)* 7960-B Soquel Dr., No. 297, Aptos, CA 95003 USA; *Imprints:* Mousetime Books (Msetime Bks)
E-mail: books@mousetime.com
Web site: http://www.mousetime.com.
Move Mountains Publishing, *(978-0-9991698)* 2925 Gulf Fwy S Ste. B-248, League City, TX 77573 USA Tel 281-671-7689
E-mail: gobedolive@gmail.com.
Movement Makers International, *(978-0-9766930)* P.O. Box 3940, Broken Arrow, OK 74013-3940 USA
Web site: http://www.j12.com.
Movies for the Ear, LLC, *(978-1-935793)* 8362 Tamarack Village No. 119-327, St. Paul, MN 55125 USA Tel 612-209-3884
E-mail: moviesfortheear@comcast.net
Web site: www.CreepersMysteries.com
Dist(s): **Ingram Content Group.**
Moving Finger Pr., *(978-0-9774214)* 369 Jersey St., San Francisco, CA 94114-3709 USA Tel 415-285-0926; Fax: 415-840-0038
E-mail: editor@movingfingerpress.com
Web site: http://movingfingerpress.com.
Moving Stories, *(978-0-9986877)* P.O. Box 371505, Las Vegas, NV 89137 USA Tel 702-793-8376
E-mail: arlenacohen@gmail.com
Web site: acohenauthor.wordpress.com.
Mowery, Julia, *(978-0-9710529)* 6308 Starfish Ave, North Port, FL 34291 USA
E-mail: storyteller2000@msn.com; storytellerjm@aol.com
Web site: http://dobiebookpublishing.com.
Moznaim Publishing Corp., *(978-0-940118; 978-1-885220)* 4304 12th Ave., Brooklyn, NY 11219 USA (SAN 214-4123) Tel 718-438-7680; Fax: 718-438-1305; Toll Free: 800-364-5118.
MP Pubns., Inc., *(978-0-9823601)* Orders Addr.: P.O. Box 2061, Clifton, NJ 07015-9831 USA Tel 973-471-1787; Toll Free: 877-673-8346; *Imprints:* Majestic Kids (MajesticKids)
E-mail: info@mpministries.org
Web site: http://www.mpministries.org.
MP2ME Enterprise LLC *See* **MP2ME Enterprise LLC**
MP2ME Enterprise LLC, *(978-0-9717947; 978-0-9776679; 978-0-9841360)* 3035 NE Roxy Pl, Bend, OR 97701 USA Tel 425-326-0335
E-mail: mpighin1@comcast.net; marcasmajor@gmail.com
Web site: marcasmajor.com
Dist(s): **Ingram Content Group.**
MPC Pr. International, *(978-0-9628453; 978-0-9715541)* P.O. Box 26142, San Fransisco, CA 94126-6142 USA
E-mail: info@laughingcookiejar.com
Web site: http://www.laughingcookiejar.com.
MPI Publishing, *(978-0-9960179)* 173 Torringford St, Winsted, CT 06098 USA Tel 860-909-1011
E-mail: jldost@aol.com.
MPL Bks., *(978-0-692-09634-5; 978-0-578-41783-7; 978-0-578-62865-3; 978-0-578-69358-3; 978-0-578-69359-0; 978-0-578-69373-6; 978-0-578-69402-3; 978-0-578-69929-5; 978-0-578-89486-7; 979-8-218-02295-2)* 6448 Owl Way, Livermore, CA 94551 USA Tel 617-943-9087
E-mail: manda.pepper@gmail.com
Dist(s): **Ingram Content Group.**
MPR Publishing, *(978-0-9831857)* 3550 N. Daisy Dr., Rialto, CA 92377 USA Tel 323-259-2884
E-mail: sales@mprpublishing.com.
MPublishing *See* **Michigan Publishing**
MQuills Publishing, *(978-0-615-55835-6; 978-0-615-56307-7; 978-0-615-63989-5; 978-1-62375)* 4179 Choteau Cir., Rancho Cordova, CA 95742 USA Tel 916-205-6999; *Imprints:* Calibum Books (Calibum Bks); Paramance (Paramance)
E-mail: mquills@mquills.com
Web site: www.mquills.com
Dist(s): **CreateSpace Independent Publishing Platform**
Ingram Content Group.
Mr. Cal Cumin, *(978-0-9987788)* 9433 Hwy 87, shepherd, MT 59079 USA Tel 406-690-1763; Fax: 406-690-1763
E-mail: cuminster@gmail.com.
Mr Do It All, Inc., *(978-0-9722038)* 2212 S. Chickasaw Trail, No. 220, Orlando, FL 32825 USA Toll Free: 800-425-9206
E-mail: info@planet-heller.com
Web site: http://www.planet-heller.com.
Mr. Emmett Publishing, *(978-0-9759346)* 37 Harleston Pl., Charleston, SC 29401 USA Tel 843-853-5728
E-mail: talubbers@comcast.net.
Mr. Fuzzy Ears LLC, *(978-0-692-14309-4; 978-0-692-18421-9; 978-0-692-18424-0)* 4970 N. Grandview Dr., Peoria Heights, IL 61616 USA Tel 317-753-1028
E-mail: Donna@CarrRoberts.com
Dist(s): **Ingram Content Group.**
Mr Nick Productions, *(978-0-692-35762-0; 978-0-692-60806-7; 978-0-692-65952-6; 978-0-692-85504-1; 978-0-692-85547-8; 978-0-692-10167-4; 978-0-692-10169-8; 978-0-578-47954-5; 978-0-578-47955-2; 978-0-578-50645-6; 978-0-578-54782-4; 978-0-578-58877-3; 978-0-578-63692-4; 978-0-578-68046-0; 978-0-578-68307-2; 978-0-578-69452-8; 978-0-578-69453-5; 978-0-578-69456-6; 978-0-578-69484-9; 978-0-578-69514-3; 978-0-578-69558-7; 978-0-578-69559-4; 978-0-578-70320-6; 978-0-578-74253-3; 978-0-578-78692-6; 978-0-578-86267-5;) 16 Wayto Ln., Ballston Lake, NY 12019 USA Tel 518-598-4194.*
Mr. Theodore Bear, *(978-0-9862968)* 5720 Belaire cir, Granbury, TX 76048 USA Tel 8174080634; Toll Free: 8174080634
Web site: http://mrtheobear.blogspot.com/
Dist(s): **CreateSpace Independent Publishing Platform.**
Mr. V. Consulting Services, *(978-0-692-75108-4; 978-0-692-94960-3; 978-1-7323085)* 938 Buck Way, Sevierville, TN 37876 USA Tel 210-365-1843
E-mail: villareal.mark@yahoo.com
Web site: www.markvillareal.com.
Mr. Wayne Edmiston *See* **WEDmiston Publishing**
Mracek, Ann, *(978-0-9766488)* 22 Morwood Ln., Creve Coeur, MO 63141 USA (SAN 257-0009) Tel 314-432-5713; Fax: 314-569-2202
E-mail: anmracek@springmail.com.
MrDuz.com, *(978-0-9796226)* 1325 W. Sunshine No. 515, Springfield, MO 65807 USA (SAN 853-9332) Tel 417-831-9898; Fax: 417-863-6655 (please include To: MrDuz.com on cover pg.); Toll Free: 866-966-7389
E-mail: patrick@patrickwellman.com; patrick@mrduz.com
Web site: http://www.mrduz.com; http://www.patrickwellman.com.
MrExcel.com Publishing *See* **Tickling Keys, Inc.**
MRG Professional Services, *(978-0-9760310)* 6255 Cherry Ln. Farm Dr., West Chester, OH 45069 USA
E-mail: kgillis85@gmail.com.
MRN Pubns., *(978-0-9630495)* 1417 Noble St., Longwood, FL 32750 USA Tel 407-831-2947 (phone/fax)
E-mail: marjorie@partnersinlearning.com
Web site: http://www.partnersinglelearning.com.
Mroczka Media, *(978-0-9846800; 978-1-938397; 978-0-692-54800-4; 978-0-692-55469-2; 978-0-692-56464-6)* 7202 Barker Cypress Rd. Suite 10302, Cypress, TX 77433 USA; *Imprints:* Pagan Writers Press (PaganWriters)
E-mail: angie@mroczkamedia.com
Web site: http://www.lostenchantressbooks.com
Dist(s): **CreateSpace Independent Publishing Platform.**
Mrs, *(978-1-7329078)* 702 Commercial Ste. 1C, Emporia, KS 66801 USA Tel 620-340-1001
E-mail: debirsik@gmail.com
Web site: dairsik.wordpress.com.
Mrs. Cottontail & Friends, *(978-1-7359680)* 5748 REMINGTON DR, WINSTON-SALEM, NC 27104 USA Tel 336-766-1444
E-mail: christi@mrscottontailandfriends.com
Web site: www.mrscottontailandfriends.com.
Mrs. L's Reading Room, *(978-0-9767278)* Orders Addr.: 110 Wedgefield Dr., Hilton Head Island, SC 29926 USA Tel 843-682-2820 (telephone/fax)
Web site: http://www.readroom.com.
Mrs. Raven's World, *(978-0-578-42837-6; 978-0-578-42839-0)* 2524 Cty. Rt. 60, Elmira, NY 14901 USA Tel 607-873-8011
E-mail: mrsravensworld@gmail.com
Dist(s): **Ingram Content Group.**
Mrs. Weisz Books *See* **Mrs. Weisz Bks.**
Mrs.Pippicocky, LLC., *(978-1-7322364)* 8861 E.Saddleback Dr., Tucson, AZ 85749 USA Tel 609-731-1994
E-mail: wds@pipltd.com
Web site: www.mrspippycocky.com.
Ms. *See* **Brooklyn Girl Bks.**
Ms., *(978-1-7344611)* 301 Frankel Blvd, Merrick, NY 11566 USA Tel 516-238-1414; Fax: 516-378-8122
E-mail: tinablevine@gmail.com
Web site: Read On Books .com.
Ms., *(978-1-7324808)* 12801 N 32nd Ave, Phoenix, AZ 85029 USA Tel 623-826-3715
E-mail: lakotam@cox.net.
Ms. Education Publishing, LLC, *(978-1-7333696)* PO Box 1814, Pawleys Island, SC 29585 USA Tel 843-833-4323
E-mail: kimberlylmeans@gmail.com
Web site: www.kimberlymnesmith.com
Dist(s): **Ingram Content Group.**
msblueheron productions llc, *(978-1-7362675)* 14 Stock Farm Rd., Bluffton, SC 29910 USA Tel 843-540-7814
E-mail: msblueheron@gmail.com.
M.S.C. Bks. *Imprint of* **Mustard Seed Comics**
Msila, Vuyisile, *(978-1-58908)* 1308H Univ. Village, East Lansing, MI 48823 USA Tel 517-355-6135
E-mail: vmsila@hotmail.com.
MSJ Music Publighing, *(978-0-9764521)* P.O. Box 3185, Rancho Santa Fe, CA 92067-3185 USA.
MSP *Imprint of* **Yetto Publishing Co.**
MSPpress *Imprint of* **Mama Specific Productions**
MsRevenda.com, *(978-0-9768538)* P.O. Box 370109, Decatur, GA 30037 USA
Web site: http://www.msrevenda.com.
M.T. Publishing Co., Inc., *(978-1-932439; 978-1-934729; 978-1-938730; 978-1-945306; 978-1-949478; 978-1-957962)* Orders Addr.: P.O. Box 6802, Evansville, IN 47719-6802 USA Toll Free: 888-263-4702; Edit Addr.: 209 NW 8th St., Evansville, IN 47708 USA
Web site: http://www.mtpublishing.com.
MTE Publishing, *(978-0-692-84269-0; 978-0-692-85975-9; 978-0-692-85976-6; 978-0-692-89859-8; 978-0-692-91465-6; 978-0-692-92876-9; 978-0-692-93998-7; 978-0-692-94523-0; 978-0-9994400; 978-0-692-97461-2; 978-1-7335709; 978-1-7375310; 979-8-9858809; 979-8-9862446; 979-8-9874925) 1212 NW 12th Ave. Suite C-4, Gainesville, FL 32615 USA Tel 352-363-4944*
E-mail: kandraalbury@mtepublishing.com; victoria@mtepublishing.com
Web site: www.mtepublishing.com.
mTrellis Publishing, Inc., *(978-0-9663281; 978-1-930650)* Orders Addr.: P.O. Box 280, New York Mills, MN 56567 USA (SAN 299-6669) Fax: 218-385-3708; Toll Free: 800-513-0115
E-mail: trellis2@aol.com; mary@trellispublishing.com
Web site: http://www.trellispublishing.com
Dist(s): **Independent Pubs. Group**
MyiLibrary
Small Pr. United.
MTV Bks. *Imprint of* **MTV Books**
MTV Books, 1230 Ave. of the Americas, New York, NY 10020 USA; *Imprints:* MTV Books (MTV Imp)
Dist(s): **Simon & Schuster, Inc.**
Mu Alpha Theta, National High Schl. Mathematics Club, *(978-0-940790)* 601 Elm Ave., Rm. 423, Norman, OK 73019 USA (SAN 204-0077) Tel 405-325-4489; Fax: 405-325-7184
E-mail: matheta@ou.edu
Web site: http://www.mualphatheta.org.
Muae Publishing, Inc., *(978-1-885030; 978-1-935717)* c/o 3620 S Vermont Ave KAP 462, Los Angeles, CA 90089 USA
E-mail: sunyoung@panix.com; kaya@kaya.com
Web site: http://www.kaya.com
Dist(s): **D.A.P./Distributed Art Pubs.**
SPD-Small Pr. Distribution
Two Rivers Distribution.
Mud Pie Pr., *(978-0-9714941)* 4201 Morrow Ave., Waco, TX 76710 USA Tel 254-716-3193
E-mail: bjelmore@msn.com; belmore1@hot.rr.com
Web site: http://www.mudpiepress.com
Dist(s): **Quality Bks., Inc.**
Mud Puddle, Inc., *(978-1-59412; 978-1-60311)* 54 W. 21st St., Suite 601, New York, NY 10010 USA Tel 212-647-9168.
Mudd, Harvey, *(978-0-9908597)* P.O. Box 1367, Brewster, MA 02631 USA Tel 508-892-8036
E-mail: harveymuddauthor@gmail.com
Dist(s): **Itasca Bks.**
Muddle Puddle Bks. (CAN) *(978-0-9686586) Dist. by* **BTPS.**
Muddy Boots Pr., *(978-1-63076; 978-0-692-44652-2)* 421 Ponderosa Dr, Harker Heights, TX 76548 USA Tel 240-515-1042
Web site: http://www.muddybootspress.com
Dist(s): **CreateSpace Independent Publishing Platform**
National Bk. Network
Rowman & Littlefield Publishers, Inc.
Rowman & Littlefield Unlimited Model.
Mudpuppy *Imprint of* **Galison**
Mudpuppy Pr., *(978-0-7353; 978-0-929648; 978-0-939456; 978-1-56155)* Div. of Galison Bks., 28 W. 44th St., Suite 1411, New York, NY 10036 USA (SAN 216-3888) Tel 212-354-8840
Dist(s): **Hachette Bk. Group.**
Mudturtle Media LLC, *(978-1-948360)* 27475 Westover Way, Valencia, CA 91354 USA Tel 805-402-7626
E-mail: sean@mudturtlemedia.com
Web site: mudturtlemedia.com.
Mueller, Mary L. Bks. LLC, *(978-0-692-90164-9; 978-0-692-90545-6)* 1352 Holmes Landing Dr, FLEMING ISLE, FL 32003 USA Tel 239-823-5240
E-mail: talktomarymueller@gmail.com
Dist(s): **Ingram Content Group.**
Mugdan, Elana, *(978-0-578-82572-4)* 251-31 42nd Ave., Little Neck, NY 11363 USA Tel 917-515-2130
E-mail: shivnath.productions@gmail.com
Web site: www.allentria.com.
Mugen Pr., *(978-1-942920)* 110 Isolda Dr., Pittsburgh, PA 15209 USA Tel 412-401-3264
E-mail: mugenpress@gmail.com
Web site: www.mugenpress.com.
Mugsy and Sugar Pressed, *(978-0-9798886)* 1117 Nobb Hill Dr., West Chester, PA 19380 USA
E-mail: tlaurento@comcast.net.
Muir Design Inc., *(978-0-578-24324-5; 978-0-578-24337-5; 978-0-578-24603-1; 978-0-578-26638-1; 978-0-578-27073-9)* 501 Surf Ave., 23H, Brooklyn, NY 11224 USA Tel 917-628-1431
E-mail: robbi@muir-design.com
Web site: https://www.muir-artworks.com/.
Mukund Pubns., *(978-0-9663831)* 3033 Arbor Bnd., Birmingham, AL 35244-1573 USA
E-mail: pratibhakhare@hotmail.com
Web site: http://www.learnhindi.com.
Mulberry Street Publishing, *(978-1-7330663)* 1 League No. 61653, Irvine, CA 92602 USA Tel 714-658-1671
E-mail: andie@andiemichaels.com
Web site: https://andiemichaels.com/.
Mulholland Teacher Resources *See* **Sonic Sword Productions**
Mullen, Peter, *(978-0-692-77226-3; 978-0-692-77229-4)* 440 Dixon Landing Rd. Apt# I-306, MILPITAS, CA 95035 USA Tel 408-691-6581.
Mullen Pr., *(978-1-7323458; 978-1-954016)* 4600 POWDER MILL RD STE 450, Beltsville, MD 20705 USA Tel 240-351-7269
E-mail: contact.us@mullenpress.com
Web site: www.MullenPress.com.
Mulley, Bradley, *(978-0-9996420)* 133 Steep Mountain Ct., Livermore, CO 80546 USA Tel 970-407-7271
E-mail: bradmulley@gmail.com.
Mullings Media, *(978-0-9767657)* P.O. Box 934, Woodbridge, NJ 07095 USA.
Mullins Pubns. & Apparel, LLC, *(978-0-9760160)* 6600 Plaza Dr., No.2000, New Orleans, LA 70127 USA.
Mulry, Peter J., *(978-0-692-78821-9)* 2401 Bayshore Blvd .No. 1002, Tampa, FL 33629 USA Tel 850-221-1045
E-mail: pete@petemulry.com
Web site: www.peterjmulryfoundation.org.
Multables, Inc., *(978-0-9645004)* 6398 S. Louthan St., Littleton, CO 80120 USA Tel 303-794-0786; Toll Free: 800-320-6857.
Multicultural Pubns., *(978-0-9634932; 978-1-884242)* 936 Slosson St., Akron, OH 44320 USA Tel 330-865-9578; Fax: 330-734-0737; Toll Free: 800-238-0297
E-mail: multiculturalpub@prodigy.net
Web site: http://www.multiculturalpub.net
Dist(s): **Brodart Co.**
Follett School Solutions.
Multi-Language Pubns., *(978-0-9703210; 978-1-931891)* 2500 George Dieter, El Paso, TX 79936 USA Tel 915-857-5852; Fax: 915-857-7644; Toll Free: 800-876-1388
E-mail: paul.hartman@wels.net; jan.gamble@wels.net.
Multi-Language Publications Program *See* **Multi-Language Pubns.**
Multnomah *Imprint of* **Crown Publishing Group, The**
Multnomah *Imprint of* **Doubleday Religious Publishing Group, The**
Multnomah Bks. *Imprint of* **Crown Publishing Group, The**
Mumblefish Bks., *(978-0-9759649)* Orders Addr.: P.O. Box 139, Point Pleasant, PA 18950-0139 USA Tel 215-297-5002; Fax: 215-297-5299
E-mail: info@mumblefishbooks.com
Web site: http://mumblefishbooks.com.
Mumford Institute, *(978-0-615-25457-9; 978-0-692-00349-7)* 330 Shore Dr., Unit C5, Highlands, NJ 07732 USA Tel 732-291-8243.
Munagala, Krithi, *(978-0-692-12315-7; 978-1-7332943)* PO Box 1324, Folsom, CA 95763 USA Tel 916-753-5085
E-mail: kreativekrithi@gmail.com
Web site: www.kreativekrithi.com.
Mundania Pr. *Imprint of* **Mundania Pr.**
Mundania Pr., *(978-0-9723670; 978-1-59426; 978-1-60659)* 6470A Glenway Ave., No. 109, Cincinnati, OH 45211 USA (SAN 255-013X) Tel 513-490-2822; Fax: 513-598-9220; *Imprints:* Mundania Press (MundPr)
E-mail: bob@mundania.com; books@mundania.com
Web site: http://www.mundania.com; http://www.phaze.com
Dist(s): **Ingram Content Group.**
Mungai, Peter, *(978-1-7341043)* 25355 Cypress Ave., Apt. 221, Hayward, CA 94544 USA Tel 510-921-7771
E-mail: unlimitedprose@gmail.com.
Munson, Craig *See* **Fleur De Lis Publishing, LLC**
Murasaki Press *See* **Murasaki Pr.**
Murasaki Pr., *(978-1-7328995; 978-1-7363835)* PO Box 152313, Austin, TX 78715 USA Tel 512-790-3526
E-mail: brittajensen@me.com
Web site: www.britta-jensen.com.
Murdoch Bks. Pty Ltd. (AUS) *(978-0-86411; 978-1-74045; 978-1-921259; 978-1-921208; 978-1-74196; 978-1-74266; 978-0-7316-4258-8; 978-1-74336; 978-1-74325; 978-0-646-32800-3) Dist. by* **HachBkGrp.**
Murdock, Bob E., *(978-0-9754363)* 352 Carly Ln., Rock Hill, SC 29732-7750 USA Tel 803-366-2666 (phone/fax)
E-mail: pbmurdock@comporium.net
Web site: http://www.sermonsforchildren.com.
Murdock Publishing Co., *(978-0-9743359; 978-1-934102)* Orders Addr.: 127 Belk Ct., Clayton, NC 27520 USA Tel 919-934-2393; Fax: 919-938-2394
Web site: http://www.murdockmedia.com.
Murine Pubns., *(978-0-9753093; 978-0-9792665; 978-0-9815971; 978-0-692-00084-7; 978-0-9824994; 978-1-936690; 978-0-615-58775-2; 978-1-940849; 978-1-950330; 978-1-957990)* Div. of Murine Communications, 1804 Miekle Ave, Woodland, CA 95776 USA
Web site: https://www.bigfontbooks.com
Dist(s): **CreateSpace Independent Publishing Platform**
Ingram Content Group
Lulu Pr., Inc.
Murine Publications LLC *See* **Murine Pubns.**
Murphey, Hiromi, *(978-0-9761350)* 4049 Madison Ave. Apt. 102, Culver City, CA 90232-3246 USA
Web site: http://www.nabiland.com.
Murphy, D. L., *(978-1-7329658)* 4470 Long Ln., Franklin, TN 37064 USA Tel 615-714-0030
E-mail: dlrestivo@aol.com
Web site: Kingslandtales.com.
Murphy, Indera *See* **Tolana Publishing**
Murphy, Michael, *(978-0-692-17801-0)* 13436 N. Locust St., Dexter, MO 63841 USA Tel 573-624-7144
E-mail: dunning53@hotmail.com
Dist(s): **CreateSpace Independent Publishing Platform.**
Murphy's Bone Publishing, *(978-0-9748226)* P.O. Box 56835, Sherman Oaks, CA 91413-6835 USA Toll Free: 877-811-2663
E-mail: murphysbone@aol.com
Web site: http://www.murphysbone.com.
Murrah, Emma-Grace, *(978-1-7321239)* 3002 W. Georgia Rd, Piedmont, SC 29673 USA Tel 864-407-8797
E-mail: bemurrah@gmail.com
Web site: sharpenedarrows4christ@gmail.com.
Murray, Aryn D, *(978-0-578-46906-5)* 1840 W. Thomas Rd., Apt. 3, Phoenix, AZ 85015 USA Tel 602-810-0668
E-mail: whatawhoot@gmail.com.
Murray, Cynthia, *(978-0-578-05770-5; 978-0-578-14613-3)* P.O. Box 7564, Charlottesville, VA 22906 USA
E-mail: crm702004@yahoo.com
Web site: http://www.divinewomenofdestiny.com.
Murray, David M., *(978-0-9729807)* Orders Addr.: , Seekonk, MA 02916 USA; Edit Addr.: 30 Wnterberry Ln., Seekink, MA 02771-4816 USA.
Murray, Dax, *(978-0-692-14243-1)* 1705 E. W. Hwy. 117, Silver Spring, MD 20910 USA Tel 202-642-4764
E-mail: dax@dax.codes
Dist(s): **Ingram Content Group.**
Murray, Eleanor, *(978-0-692-93265-0; 979-8-218-25502-2)* 4701 Port Charlotte, Las Vegas, NV 89131 USA Tel 702-982-8946
E-mail: cassie.salde@aol.com
Dist(s): **Ingram Content Group.**

Publisher Name Index

Murray Hill Bks., LLC, *(978-0-9719697; 978-1-935139)* 7 Evergreen Ln., Woodstock, NY 12498 USA (SAN 256-3622) Tel 845-679-6749
E-mail: robinsegal@earthlink.net; info@murrayhillbooks.com
Web site: http://www.murrayhillbooks.com
Dist(s): **Learning Connection, The.**

Murray, Regina Waldron, *(978-0-9636918; 978-0-9664042)* 300 Hollinshead Spring Rd. Apt. AL137, Skillman, NJ 08558-2049 USA
E-mail: reginawmurray@yahoo.com.

Musa Publishing, *(978-1-61937; 978-1-68009)* 4815 Iron Horse Trail, Colorado Springs, CO 80917 USA Tel 719-393-2398
E-mail: kerry@musapublishing.com
Web site: www.musapublishing.com.

Muscatello Publishing, *(978-0-9722774)* P.O. Box 620011, Orlando, FL 32862-0011 USA Tel 407-888-3060; Fax: 407-650-3222; Toll Free: 877-888-3060
E-mail: info@muscatellopublishing.com
Web site: http://www.muscatellopublishing.com.

Muscle Bks. *Imprint of* **AGM Communications**

Muse Media LLC *See* **Deane, Jennifer Inc.**

Muse Media LLC - Halftime Magazine, *(978-1-7359331)* P.O. Box PO Box 428738, Cincinnati, OH 45242 USA Tel 310-594-0050
E-mail: christine@halftimemag.com
Web site: halftimemag.com.

Museum of Fine Arts, Houston, *(978-0-89090)* P.O. Box 6826, Houston, TX 77265-6826 USA (SAN 202-2559) Tel 713-639-7300
Dist(s): **D.A.P./Distributed Art Pubs.**
Texas A&M Univ. Pr.
Two Rivers Distribution
Univ. of Texas Pr.
Yale Univ. Pr.

Museum of Glass, *(978-0-9726649; 978-0-692-46250-8; 978-0-692-78193-7)* 1801 Dock St., Tacoma, WA 98402 USA Toll Free: 866-468-7386 (866-4-MUSEUM)
Web site: http://www.museumofglass.org
Dist(s): **Univ. of Washington Pr.**

Museum of Glass: International Center for Contemporary Art *See* **Museum of Glass**

Museum of Modern Art, *(978-0-87070; 978-1-63345)* 11 W. 53 St., New York, NY 10019-5497 USA (SAN 202-5809) Tel 212-708-9700; Fax: 212-333-1127; Toll Free: 800-447-6662 (orders)
E-mail: MoMA_Publications@moma.org
Web site: http://www.moma.org/publications
Dist(s): **Abrams, Inc.**
D.A.P./Distributed Art Pubs.
Hachette Bk. Group.

Museum of New Mexico Pr., *(978-0-89013)* Div. of New Mexico Department of Cultural Affairs, Orders Addr.: 11030 S. Langley Ave., Chicago, IL 60628 USA (SAN 202-2575) Tel 773-702-7000; 800-621-2736; Fax: 773-702-7212; Toll Free: 800-249-7737; Edit Addr.: P.O. Box 2087, Santa Fe, NM 87504-2087 USA Tel 505-476-1160
E-mail: orders@press.uchicago.edu
Web site: http://www.mnmpress.org
Dist(s): **Chicago Distribution Ctr.**

Museum of Science *See* **Engineering is Elementary**

Museum of Texas Tech Univ., *(978-0-9640188; 978-1-929330)* Div. of Texas Tech Univ., 3301 4th St., Box 43191, Lubbock, TX 79409-3191 USA Tel 806-742-2442; Fax: 806-742-1136
E-mail: museum.texastech@ttu.edu
Web site: http://www.museum.ttu.edu.

Museyon, *(978-0-9822320; 978-0-9846334; 978-1-938450; 978-1-940842)* Orders Addr.: 1177 Ave. Of The Americas, 5th Flr., New York, NY 10036 USA (SAN 857-6033)
E-mail: chiba@museyon.com
Web site: http://www.museyon.com
Dist(s): **Independent Pubs. Group**
MyiLibrary.

Museyon Guides *See* **Museyon**

Mushgush Pr., *(978-0-9795818)* 335 Cantlegate Close, Johns Creek, GA 30022 USA
Web site: http://tidalpress.com.

Mushkins, *(978-0-9987478)* 14 Waldron Pl., Palm Coast, FL 32164 USA Tel 386-569-5684
E-mail: mushmom@bellsouth.net
Web site: www.mushkins.com.

Mushroom Cloud Pr. of Orlando, *(978-0-9679552)* 278 Leslie Ln., Lake Mary, FL 32746 USA Tel 407-328-7311
E-mail: mushroomcloudpress@hotmail.com.

Music Awareness, *(978-0-9753599)* P.O. Box 188, Amherst, MA 01004 USA Tel 413-253-4216; Fax: 413-253-1397
E-mail: pwb@valinet.com
Web site: http://www.musicawareness.com.

Music Bks. & Games, *(978-0-9744427)* P.O. Box 97, McNeil, TX 78651 USA
E-mail: info@musicbooksandgames.com
Web site: http://www.musicbooksandgames.com/.

Music City Bk. Farm, *(978-0-578-56678-6)* 903 Fatherland St., Nashville, TN 37206 USA Tel 828-238-6371
E-mail: jamie.polen@gmail.com.

Music City Publishing, *(978-1-933215)* P.O. Box 41696, Nashville, TN 37204-1696 USA (SAN 256-288X)
E-mail: manager@musiccitypublishing.com
Web site: http://www.musiccitypublishing.com.

Music for Little People, Inc., *(978-1-56628; 978-1-877737)* 390 Lake Benbow Dr., No. C, Garberville, CA 95542 USA Tel 707-923-3991; Fax: 707-923-3241; Toll Free: 800-346-4445
Web site: http://www.musicforlittlepeople.com
Dist(s): **Educational Record Ctr., Inc.**
Follett School Solutions
Goldenrod Music, Inc.
Linden Tree Children's Records & Bks.
Music Design, Inc.
New Leaf Distributing Co., Inc.
Rounder Kids Music Distribution
Western Record Sales.

Music Institute of California, *(978-0-9624062; 978-1-883993)* Orders Addr.: P.O. Box 3535, Vista, CA 92085-3535 USA (SAN 297-5955) Tel 760-891-0226
Dist(s): **BookBaby**
Brodart Co.

Music, Movement & Magination Bks., *(978-0-9818635; 978-1-935572)* 3165 S. Alma School Rd., Suite 29-195, Chandler, AZ 85248 USA (SAN 856-7662) Tel 480-247-3129; Fax: 480-634-7148; Toll Free: 888-637-1313
E-mail: info@MMMKids.com
Web site: http://www.MMMKids.com.

Music Resources International *See* **Kindermusik International**

Music Sales Corp., *(978-0-7119; 978-0-8256; 978-1-84609)* Orders Addr.: 445 Bellvale Rd., P.O. Box 572, Chester, NY 10918 USA (SAN 662-0876) Tel 845-469-2271; Fax: 845-469-7544; Toll Free Fax: 800-345-6842; Toll Free: 800-431-7187; Edit Addr.: 257 Park Ave., S., 20th Flr., New York, NY 10010 USA (SAN 282-0277) Tel 212-254-2100; Fax: 212-254-2103; *Imprints:* Amsco Music (Amsco Music); Chester Music (Chester Music); Ashley (Ashley)
E-mail: info@musicsales.com
Web site: http://www.musicroom.com; http://www.musicsales.com
Dist(s): **Beekman Bks., Inc.**
Dumont, Charles Son, Inc.
Chesbro Music Co.
Leonard, Hal Corp.
Quality Bks., Inc.

Music Together, LLC, *(978-0-615-32865-2; 978-0-9855719; 978-0-9897814)* 66 Witherspoon St., Princeton, NJ 08542 USA Tel 609-945-0354
Web site: http://www.musictogether.com.

Musical Linguist, The, *(978-0-9706829)* Orders Addr.: 14419 Greenwood Ave. N., Suite A, No. 354, Seattle, WA 98133 USA Fax: 509-693-4160; Toll Free: 866-297-2128
E-mail: mlinguist@aol.com
Web site: http://www.musicalspanish.com.

Musical Novels Press *See* **Golden Poppy Pubns.**

Musictech College Pr., *(978-0-9729879)* 19 Exchange St., E., Saint Paul, MN 55101 USA Tel 651-291-0177; Fax: 651-291-0366; Toll Free: 800-594-9500
E-mail: dsmith@musictech.com
Web site: http://www.musictech.com.

MusicWorks, *(978-0-9763194; 978-0-9820900)* Orders Addr.: P.O. Box 1971, Maryland Heights, MO 63043 USA; Edit Addr.: 13233 Amiot Dr., Saint Louis, MO 63146 USA; P.O. Box 1971, Saint Louis, MO 63043 (SAN 857-2291) Tel 314-439-5334 Do not confuse with MusicWorks in Marietta, GA
Web site: http://www.the-music-works.com; http://www.the-music-works.net.

MusiKinesis, *(978-0-9701416)* 3734 Cross Bow Ct., Ellicott City, MD 21042 USA Fax: 410-465-8472
E-mail: monicadale@musikinesis.com
Web site: http://www.musikinesis.com.

Muslim Writers Publishing, *(978-0-9767861; 978-0-9793577; 978-0-9819770; 978-0-9854638)* 1029-B5 Avent Hill., Raleigh, NC 27606 USA Tel 919-817-8656
E-mail: debmcnichol@gmail.com
Web site: http://www.muslimwriterspublishing.com
Dist(s): **Smashwords.**

Mustang BKS, *(978-0-9766270)* P.O. Box 1193, Crooked River Ranch, OR 97760 USA Tel 541-504-9620.

Mustard Hill Pr., *(978-0-9977897)* 492 Pala Way, Sacramento, CA 95819 USA Tel 916-455-2797
E-mail: caron@caronvikre.com.

Mustard Seed Comics, *(978-0-9769819; 978-0-9826975; 978-0-9964631)* 1609 Stoney Grove Church Rd., Warrenton, GA 30828 USA Tel 706-466-1633; *Imprints:* M.S.C. Books (MSCBks)
E-mail: mail@mustardseedcomics.com; benitomsc@yahoo.com
Web site: http://www.mustardseedcomics.com.

Mustard Seed Pr., *(978-0-9797703)* 263 Northampton Rd., Amherst, MA 01002 USA
Web site: http://www.bagelsbuddyandme.com.

Muszynski, James A., *(978-0-9766461)* 1446 Yoder Rd., Manister, MI 49660 USA Tel 231-723-6500 (phone/fax)
E-mail: lsmuszyk@hotmail.com
Web site: http://www.jaminjimbooks.com.

Mutaneers, *(978-1-892619)* 1011 Univ. Village, Salt Lake City, UT 84108 USA Tel 707-616-6893
E-mail: mutaneers@gmail.com
Web site: http://www.mutaneers.com; http://www.crazyuseful.com.

Mutant Prophet Publishing, *(978-0-9864420; 978-0-692-13289-0)* 4933 Rock Haven Dr. SW, Lilburn, GA 30047 USA Tel 678-266-0262
E-mail: violethaze999@yahoo.com.

Mutual Publishing LLC, *(978-0-935180; 978-1-56647; 978-1-939487; 978-0-9971305; 978-1-949307; 978-1-7325030; 978-1-7347824; 978-1-7376774; 979-8-9883393)* 1215 Center St., Suite 210, Honolulu, HI 96816 USA (SAN 222-6359) Tel 808-732-1709; Fax: 808-734-4094
E-mail: info@mutualpublishing.com
Web site: http://www.mutualpublishing.com
Dist(s): **Booklines Hawaii, Ltd.**
Islander Group
Mel Bay Pubns., Inc.

MVCD, Inc., *(978-0-9753617)* 4711 E. Falcon Dr., Suite 251, Mesa, AZ 85215 USA.

MVmedia, *(978-0-9800842; 978-0-9960167; 978-0-9992789; 978-1-7346279; 978-1-7372277; 979-8-9857336)* 145 Ridgewood Dr., Fayetteville, GA 30215 USA.

MVP Kids Media, 7205 E. Southern Ave., #105, Mesa, AZ 85209 USA Tel 480-495-7694
E-mail: info@realMVPkids.com
Web site: http://www.realMVPkids.com
Dist(s): **Baker & Taylor Publisher Services (BTPS).**

MX No Fear, *(978-0-9766918)* 2251 Faraday Ave., Suite A, Carlsbad, CA 92008 USA Toll Free: 866-787-3691
Web site: http://www.mxnofear.com.

My Ancestors, My Heroes *Imprint of* **Parker-Wallace Publishing Co., LLC**

My Bench Productions, *(978-0-9977858)* 5479 Wellesley Dr., Calabasas, CA 91302 USA Tel 818-880-6811
E-mail: lauren@mybenchproductions.com
Dist(s): **Greenleaf Book Group.**

My Campus Adventure, Inc., *(978-1-935159)* Orders Addr.: 7705 Orly Ct., Plano, TX 75025 USA (SAN 856-6690)
E-mail: kim@mycampusadventure.com
Web site: http://www.mycampusadventure.com.

My Children Publishing Inc., *(978-0-9799376)* 17410 Vinwood Ln., Yorba Linda, CA 92886 USA (SAN 854-7890)
Web site: http://www.mychildrenpublishing.com.

My Darling-Tots Pubns., *(978-0-9797674)* 2256 Delbert Rd., Columbus, OH 43211 USA
E-mail: hdarling30@yahoo.com
Web site: http://www.helendarling.com.

My Dream Bk. Pr., *(978-1-7362818)* 1010 Stuyvesant Ave., Irvington, NJ 07111 USA Tel 954-918-0826
E-mail: Dreams_2reality@outlook.com
Web site: Authormarciaharris.com.

My Father's House Publishing Company *See* **KishKnows Publishing**

My Grandma & Me Pubs., *(978-0-9742732)* 1275 E. Parks Rd., Saint Johns, MI 48879 USA
E-mail: info@mygrandmaandme.com; janemarysinke@gmail.com
Web site: http://www.mygrandmaandme.com
Dist(s): **Partners Pubs. Group, Inc.**

My Heart Yours Publishing, *(978-1-932721)* P.O. Box 4975, Wheaton, IL 60187 USA (SAN 255-6774)
E-mail: tanya@myheartyours.com; jeannine@myheartyours.com
Web site: http://www.myheartyours.com.

My Journey Bks., *(978-0-9766295)* P.O. Box 1169, Olney, MD 20830-1169 USA Toll Free: 877-965-2665
E-mail: KGF@billiesworld.com; KGF@myjourneybooks.com
Web site: http://www.billiesworld.com; http://www.myjourneybooks.com.

My Kinda Bks., *(978-0-9830781)* P.O. Box 1910, Beaverton, OR 97075 USA Tel 512-923-4501
E-mail: sharigetzcreative@gmail.com
Web site: www.mykindabooks.com.

My Litte Eagle *See* **My Litte Eagle Pr.**

My Litte Eagle Pr., *(978-1-955117)* 9001 Regent Pkwy., Brooklyn Park, MN 55443 USA Tel 904-861-5034
E-mail: merici_f@hotmail.com.

My Little Jessie Pr., *(978-0-9740743)* Orders Addr.: P.O. Box 529, Bethel, VT 05032 USA (SAN 255-321X) Tel 802-234-9725; Edit Addr.: One Cushing Ave., Bethel, VT 05032 USA
E-mail: jhaywardburnham@aol.com.

My Little One, Incorporated *See* **Mylo Publishing**

My Lyric's Hse., *(978-0-9761446)* 593 Vanderbilt Ave., No. 135, Brooklyn, NY 11238 USA Tel 347-408-7786
E-mail: itsmeisha@yahoo.com.

My Pal Mark, *(978-0-9823750)* 9-15 Essex Pl., Fair Lawn, NJ 07410 USA
E-mail: mypalmark@aol.com
Web site: http://www.mypalmark.com.

My Purple Toes, LLC, *(978-0-9844556; 978-0-9834778)* P.O. Box 826, Mt. Pleasant, SC 29465 USA
E-mail: blair@blairhahnbooks.com
Web site: http://www.blairhahnbooks.com; http://www.mypurpletoes.com
Dist(s): **Emerald Bk. Co.**

My Second Language Publishing, USA, *(978-0-615-23709-1; 978-0-615-24460-0; 978-0-615-26150-8; 978-0-615-26238-3; 978-0-615-26239-0; 978-0-615-26240-6; 978-0-578-00208-8; 978-0-578-00209-5; 978-0-578-02214-7)* 165 River Hills Dr., Clayton, NC 27527 USA
E-mail: publisher@mysecondlanguagepublishingusa.com
Web site: http://www.mysecondlanguagepublishingusa.com
Dist(s): **Lulu Pr., Inc.**

My Special Thoughts, *(978-0-9743019)* P.O. Box 150747, Nashville, TN 37215 USA Fax: 615-297-3138
Web site: http://www.myspecialthoughts.com.

My Story His Glory Publishing, LLC *See* **His Glory Publishing, LLC**

My Student-Athlete, Inc., *(978-0-9767250)* P.O. Box 15, Redan, GA 30074 USA Tel 770-981-3000
Web site: http://www.morethanvictories.com.

My Sunshine Bks., *(978-0-9749561)* 1370 Little Brier Creek Rd., Warrenton, GA 30828 USA Toll Free: 800-765-4663.

My Three Roses, *(978-1-7335753)* 4 Spring Dr., Tabernacle, NJ 08088 USA Tel 609-792-3925
E-mail: Daniellesmason@outlook.com.

My Three Sisters Publishing, *(978-0-615-73283-1; 978-0-615-73697-6; 978-0-615-73769-0; 978-0-615-74341-7; 978-0-615-74542-8; 978-0-615-74664-7; 978-0-615-74890-0; 978-0-615-74922-8; 978-0-615-75048-4; 978-0-615-75245-7; 978-0-615-75261-7; 978-0-615-75276-1; 978-0-615-75367-6; 978-0-615-75421-5; 978-0-615-75460-4; 978-0-615-75518-2; 978-0-615-75534-2; 978-0-615-75556-4; 978-0-615-75716-2; 978-0-615-75752-0; 978-0-615-75770-4; 978-0-615-75825-1; 978-0-615-75897-8; 978-0-615-75904-3; 978-0-615-75910-4; 978-0-615-75938-8;)* 13817 W. Rovey Ave., Litchfield Park, AZ 85340 USA Tel 847-769-9824
E-mail: Jenniseco@aol.com
Dist(s): **CreateSpace Independent Publishing Platform.**

My Three Sons *See* **Life of Asil, The**

My Three Sons Publishing, *(978-1-7367156)* 185 Shenandoah Loop, Troutman, NC 28166 USA Tel 778-878-4367
E-mail: brucealnightly@icloud.com
Web site: mythreesonspublishing.com.

My Time Pubns., *(978-0-9820530; 978-0-9843257; 978-0-9830518)* 2984 Spring Falls Dr., West Carrollton, OH 45449 USA Tel 937-344-4805
E-mail: leila@mytimepublications.com; ljeff25@yahoo.com
Web site: http://www.mytimepublications.com.

MyBoys3 Pr., *(978-0-9893414; 978-0-9861473; 978-1-947881)* P.O. Box 2555, Midlothian, VA 23113 USA
E-mail: steve@myboys3.com
Web site: www.stevensawyerbooks.com; www.myboys3.com.

MyBrothersKeeper, *(978-0-692-97059-1)* 2 28th St. Apt 6H, Newport News, VA 23607 USA Tel 757-277-8504
E-mail: trinitymylove378@gmail.com.

Myers & Briggs Foundation, Inc., *(978-0-935652)* 203 NE. 1st St., Gainesville, FL 32601 USA (SAN 213-9162) Tel 352-375-0160; Fax: 352-378-0503; Toll Free: 800-777-2278
E-mail: purnima@capt.org; research@capt.org
Web site: http://www.capt.org.

Myers, Connie Ellis *See* **Say Out Loud, LLC**

Myers, Jack Ministries, Inc., *(978-0-9720928)* P.O. Box 158, Orland Park, IL 60462-0158 USA
E-mail: jmm.revival@juno.com
Web site: http://www.jackmyersministries.com.

Myers Publishing Co., *(978-0-9745210; 978-0-9745929)* Orders Addr.: 207 Shelley Ct., Roseville, CA 95747 USA Tel 916-987-7668 (phone/fax) Do not confuse with Myers Publishing Company in Tarpon Springs, FL
E-mail: myerspubco@myerspublishing.com
Web site: http://www.myerspublishing.com.

Myers Publishing Co., *(978-0-9729381)* 1426 Vermont Ave., Tarpon Springs, FL 34689-3871 USA Tel 727-938-6855; Fax: 727-934-4562 Do not confuse with Myers Publishing Company in Sacramento, CA
E-mail: kmyers2@tampabay.rr.com.

MyHandiwork, *(978-0-9742555)* 7520 Walker St., Saint Louis Park, MN 55426-4042 USA Fax: 952-935-2840
E-mail: myhandiwork@earthlink.net
Web site: http://www.myhandiwork.com.

MYHRECO, *(978-0-9753704)* 9033 1/2 Hubbard St., Culver City, CA 90232-2508 USA.

Myinnervision, *(978-0-578-34626-7)* 98 Edgars Ln., Hastings-on-Hudson, NY 10706 USA Tel 917-574-3666
E-mail: justin@myinnervision.com.

Mylemarks LLC, *(978-0-9964154)* P.O. Box 1252, Chesapeake, VA 23327 USA Tel 757-620-8539
E-mail: andrew.jatau@mylemarks.com.

Mylestones & Co LLC, *(978-1-7360727)* 1335 Jefferson Rd., Rochester, NY 14692 USA Tel 585-319-7828
E-mail: nicolex.matthews@yahoo.com.

Mylo Publishing, *(978-0-9910341)* 4 Narrow Creek Ct., Trophy Club, TX 76262 USA Tel 682-465-6845
E-mail: znscurry@hotmail.com
Web site: www.mylopublishing.com.

Mymilou Pr., *(978-0-615-93163-0; 978-0-692-79069-4)* 2923 Bighorn Dr., Corona, CA 92881 USA Tel 714-390-6139
E-mail: amarestaing@hotmail.com.

MyPublica *See* **MyPublica Pr.**

MyPublica Pr., *(978-1-7331309)* 8744 SW 206 Ln., Cutler Bay, FL 33189 USA Tel 305-232-5666
E-mail: Caro.Sant22@gmail.com.

Myrddin Publishing Group, *(978-0-9883828; 978-1-939296; 978-1-68063)* 54 Mill Pond Rd., Jackson, NJ 08527 USA Tel 732-822-8920
E-mail: alisondeluca@hotmail.com; cjjasp@gmail.com
Dist(s): **Lulu Pr., Inc.**

MyReportLinks.com Bks. *Imprint of* **Enslow Publishing, LLC**

Myrick, Corinthia *See* **Myrick, Corinthia A.**

Myrick, Corinthia A., *(978-0-9600629)* 1896 Hillsdale Dr., Decatur, GA 30032 USA Tel 770-286-2848
E-mail: corinthia.myrick@yahoo.com
Web site: corinthiamyrick.com.

Myrin Institute, Incorporated *See* **Orion Society, The**

Myrtle Learns, *(978-1-930694)* Orders Addr.: P.O. Box 3645, Rancho Cucamonga, CA 91729 USA Fax: 909-428-2401 (phone/fax); Edit Addr.: 14034 Fort Ross Ct., Fontana, CA 92336 USA Tel 909-428-2401
E-mail: jaajdeem@aol.com
Web site: http://myrtlelearns.com.

MySheri Enterprises, LLC, *(978-0-9766782)* P.O. Box 141111, Detroit, MI 48214 USA.

Myst of the Oracle Corp., *(978-0-9786812)* P.O. Box 133, Piney Creek, NC 28663 USA
E-mail: administrator@mystoftheoracle.com
Web site: http://www.mystoftheoracle.com.

Mysteries by Vincent, LLC, *(978-1-932169)* Orders Addr.: 2707 Mountain Green Trail, Kingwood, TX 77345 USA Tel 281-312-0120; Toll Free: 866-946-3864 1-866-WHODUNIT
E-mail: robert@mysteriesbyvincent.com; cindy@mysteriesbyvincent.com
Web site: http://www.mysteriesbyvincent.com; http://www.buckleyandbogey.com; http://www.whodunitpress.com.

Mysterious Pr. *Imprint of* **Grand Central Publishing**

Mystery & Suspense Pr. *Imprint of* **iUniverse, Inc.**

Mystery Writers of America Presents *Imprint of* **iUniverse, Inc.**

mysterygirl publishing *See* **Mysterygirl Publishing**

Mysterygirl Publishing, *(978-0-692-28118-5; 978-0-692-30501-0; 978-0-692-40686-1;*

978-0-692-40740-0; 978-0-692-90018-5) 15 Fairview Ln., Springfield, IL 62711 USA Tel 217-836-0229
E-mail: mlibrisigle@yahoo.com
Web site: www.marleyparker.com
Dist(s): **CreateSpace Independent Publishing Platform.**

Mystic Arts, LLC, (*978-0-9771700*) P.O. Box 1110, Riverton, UT 84065 USA (SAN 256-8217)
Web site: http://www.reading-with-kids.com.

Mystic Harbor Pr., LLC, (*978-1-933660; 978-0-578-01793-8; 978-1-61899*) Orders Addr.: P.O. Box 1707, Conroe, TX 77305 USA (SAN 257-2680) Tel 281-826-4026 (phone/fax); *Imprints*: Tadpole Press 4 Kids (Tadpole Pr)
E-mail: cmcginnis@smoothsailingpress.com
Web site: http://www.smoothsailingpress.com
Dist(s): **Follet Higher Education Grp**
Ingram Content Group.

Mystic Hippo Media Publishing, (*978-0-9848694*) 5 Bald Hill Ct., Saint Peters, MO 63304 USA Tel 636-922-3593
E-mail: 88fingerslouie@att.net

Mystic Jaguar Publishing, (*978-0-9792294*) 10821 Margate Rd., Suite A, Silver Spring, MD 20901-1615 USA (SAN 852-8365)
E-mail: Mysticjaguar@verizon.net.

Mystic Night Bks. *Imprint of* **Pink Stucco Pr.**

Mystic Pubs., Inc., (*978-0-9727840; 978-1-934051; 978-1-941271; 978-1-948266; 978-0-578-96906-0; 978-0-578-33045-7; 978-1-957374*) 614 Mosswood Dr., Henderson, NV 89002 USA; *Imprints*: Ink & Quill Publishers (Ink&Quill)
E-mail: richard@themackennasaga.com
Web site: http://www.mysticpublishers.com; www.iqpublishing.com; www.newlinkpublishing.com
Dist(s): **ebrary, Inc.**

Mystic Publishing, (*978-0-9747454*) 16613 195th Ave., Mystic, IA 52574-8678 USA Do not confuse with Mystic Publishing in North, VA
E-mail: sharon@freddiethefrog.com; sharon@freddiethefrogbooks.com
Dist(s): **Leonard, Hal Corp.**

Mystic Ridge Bks., (*978-0-9672182; 978-0-9742845*) Div. of Mystic Ridge Productions, Inc., 222 Main St., Sutie 142, Farmington, CT 06032 USA (SAN 853-9898)
E-mail: mysticridge@att.net
Web site: http://www.mysticridgebooks.com; http://www.blackjacktoday.com; http://www.helixeye.com.

Mystic River Ink, (*978-0-9724752*) P.O. Box 441357, Somerville, MA 02144 USA
Web site: http://www.mysticriverink.com.

Mystic Waters Publishing *See* **Winkelstein Studios**

Mystic World Pr., (*978-0-9854289*) 115 San Jose Ave. No. 2, San Francisco, CA 94110 USA Tel 415-373-8533
E-mail: william@mysticworldpress.com.

Mystical Publishing, (*978-0-578-19966-5; 978-1-7379444; 978-0-578-28358-6; 979-8-218-06125-8*) 4200 Maple Leaf Dr., New Orleans, LA 70131 USA Tel 504-579-6534
E-mail: keiffertj@gmail.com.

Mystical Willow Productions, (*978-0-9763205*) P.O. Box 95, Wheaton, IL 60189 USA
E-mail: mysticalwillow@comcast.net.

MysticMountain Pr., (*978-0-9905938*) 483 Apache Rd., Arrey, NM 87930 USA Tel 505-550-5530
E-mail: sheilaofthejungle@yahoo.com.

Mystique International, Ltd., (*978-0-9745333*) 2533 N. Carson St., Suite 593, Carson City, NV 89706-0147 USA
E-mail: metamind@eznet.net.

Mystique Pr. *Imprint of* **Crossroad Pr.**

Myth Breakers *See* **Happy About**

MYTHIKAS, (*978-0-9983011*) 8215 Lake Dr., Doral, FL 33166 USA Tel 786-487-8049; Fax: 786-545-7636
E-mail: infomythikas@gmail.com.

MythSeries, (*978-0-9776472*) P.O. Box 211, Millville, MN 55957 USA (SAN 257-8743) Tel 507-798-2450
E-mail: lisa@mythseries.com
Web site: http://mythseries.com.

Mz. Rosa Notions, (*978-0-9740267*) P.O. Box 114, Turlock, CA 95380 USA
E-mail: ninarule62@aol.com.

NAPSAC Reproductions, (*978-0-934426; 978-1-932747; 978-0-615-45573-0*) Rte. 4, Box 646, Marble Hill, MO 63764 USA (SAN 222-4607) Tel 573-238-4846; Fax: 573-238-2010
E-mail: napsac@clas.net
Dist(s): **Send The Light Distribution LLC.**

N&N Publishing Co., Inc., (*978-0-9606036; 978-0-935487*) 18 Montgomery St., Middletown, NY 10940 USA (SAN 216-4221) Tel 845-342-1677; Fax: 845-342-6910; Toll Free: 800-664-8398; *Imprints*: STAReviews (STAReviews); X-treme Reviews (X-treme Reviews)
E-mail: info@nandnpublishing.com; sales@nandnpublishing.com
Web site: http://www.nandnpublishing.com; http://www.nn4text.com; http://www.starreview.com; http://www.big8review.com.

N Gallerie Pr. LLC, (*978-0-9818347; 978-0-9962748*) Div. of N Gallerie Studios, LLC, Orders Addr.: 1213 Culbreth Dr. Suite 233, Wilmington, NC 28405 USA Tel 910-398-6411
E-mail: sales@ngallerie.com
Web site: http://www.ngallerie.com.

N2Print *Imprint of* **New Age World Publishing**

N8TIVE, (*978-0-9769575*) 620 S. 19th St., Philadelphia, PA 19146 USA
Web site: http://www.n8tve.com.

n/a, (*978-1-7367124*) 9441 Sunrise Lakes Blvd, Sunrise, FL 33322 USA Tel 954-213-5137
E-mail: lfm41301@yahoo.com.

Na Kamalei Koolauloa Early Education Program, (*978-0-9773495; 978-0-9760892; 978-1-935111*) P.O. Box 900, Hauula, HI 96717 USA Tel 808-237-8500; Fax: 808-237-8501; *Imprints*: Ho'ulu Hou Project: Stories Told by Us (Houlu Hou)
E-mail: nkpublishing@nakamalei.org
Web site: http://www.nakamalei.org.

Nabors, Murray W., (*978-0-615-38301-9; 978-0-615-40572-8; 978-0-615-49157-8; 978-0-615-85999-6*) 3051 NE State Rte. W, Saint Joseph, MO 64507 USA Tel 816-244-0354
E-mail: mnabors@missouriwestern.edu.

Nabu Pr. *Imprint of* **Creative Media Partners, LLC**

NACSCORP, Incorporated *See* **.**

NADER, LILLIAN, (*978-1-7323175*) 18421 Lemon Drive, Apt 507, YORBA LINDA, CA 92886 USA Tel 714-693-0951
E-mail: LNADER1910@SBCGLOBAL.NET
Web site: https://lilliannader.com.

Naderi, Fariedeh, (*978-1-7322683; 979-8-9882621*) 4656 Lawson Dr., Decatur,, IL 62526 USA Tel 217-358-6100
E-mail: naderi.farideh@gmail.com.

Nadine Lalich, (*978-0-9711776; 978-0-615-19967-2; 978-1-7374587*)
E-mail: nadinelalich@yahoo.com
Web site: http://hbpublishing.net.

Nadine the Queen of Quarantine, LLC, (*978-0-578-75493-2*) 330 E 57th St, 8, New York, NY 10022 USA Tel 917-364-7478
E-mail: gskortye@yahoo.com.

Nadores Publishing & Research, (*978-0-9797847*) Orders Addr.: P.O. Box 1202, Gilroy, CA 95021-1202 USA
E-mail: regulo-zapata@Verizon.net
Web site: http://www.nadorespublishing.com.

Nags Head Art, Inc., (*978-0-9616344; 978-1-878405*) Orders Addr.: P.O. Box 2149, Manteo, NC 27954 USA (SAN 200-9145) Tel 252-441-7480; Fax: 252-475-9893; Toll Free Fax: 800-246-7014; Toll Free: 800-541-2722; Edit Addr.: 7728 Virginia Dare Trail, Manteo, NC 27954 USA (SAN 658-8107)
E-mail: suzannetate@yahoo.com
Web site: http://www.suzannetate.com
Dist(s): **Florida Classics Library**
Mistco, Inc.

NAHSH M'ISTAH Pub., (*978-0-9665427*) 8614 E. Dahlia Dr., Scottsdale, AZ 85260 USA Tel 480-998-8189
E-mail: nashmista@aol.com.

Nailah, Michele, (*978-0-578-47322-2*) 1 Merrimac Way, Unit G, Tyngsboro, MA 01879 USA Tel 617-504-0369
E-mail: nailahmichele720@gmail.com.

Naim, Deborah, (*978-0-9762828*) 20801 Biscayne Blvd., Suite 403, Aventura, FL 33180 USA
E-mail: dnaim@mercadoecologico.com.

Nakota Publishing, (*978-0-9882442*) 7240 W Shaw Butte, Peoria, AZ 85345 USA Tel 602-750-3662
E-mail: vitreude@cox.net.

NAL *Imprint of* **Crown Publishing Group, The**

NAL *Imprint of* **Penguin Publishing Group**

Nambennett Publishing, (*978-0-9742208*) 11748 Fremont Ave. N., Seattle, WA 98133 USA
E-mail: kelly@nambennett.com
Web site: http://www.nambennett.com.

namelos llc, (*978-1-60898*) 133 Main Ave., South Hampton, NH 03827 USA Tel 828-221-
E-mail: roxburgh@namelos.com
Web site: http://www.namelos.com.

Nana Says *Imprint of* **Inner Quality Publishing**

Nana's Stories, (*978-0-9857362*) 22 St. Nicholas Ave., Worcester, MA 01606 USA Tel 508-560-5888
E-mail: kfinneron@yahoo.com.

Nancy Becklean Tobin *See* **Thalian Bks.**

Nancy Paulsen Bks. *Imprint of* **Penguin Publishing Group**

Nancy Paulsen Books *Imprint of* **Penguin Young Readers Group**

Nancy's Artworks, (*978-0-9748074*) Orders Addr.: 6185 Faxon Ct., Colorado Spgs, CO 80922-1839 USA
E-mail: sales@nancyweb.com
Web site: http://www.multcamp.com; http://www.nancyweb.com; http://www.seanotes.net.

Nanette Pattee Francini, (*978-1-7360695*) 585 Hanley Ave, Los Angeles, CA 90049 USA Tel 760-776-1522
E-mail: nanettefrancini@cochisecap.com.

Nanie C. Memeh, (*978-1-7327876*) 17433 52nd Ave W, Lynnwood, WA 98037 USA Tel 253-202-1225
E-mail: n.m.divis@gmail.com.

NANUQ Publishing, (*978-0-9795400; 978-0-692-97169-7*) 111 Linwood Ave., Williamsville, NY 14221 USA Tel 716-634-4379
E-mail: crait37@yahoo.com.

NAO Pubns., (*978-0-9760838*) 35895 Conroy Rd., Suite 1015, Orlando, FL 32839 USA
E-mail: bbgwyn12@netzero.net; briangwyn@bellsouth.net
Web site: http://www.notanotheroverdraft.com; http://notanotheroverdraft.blogspot.com.

Naphtali Publishing, (*978-0-692-90267-7*) 2221 80th Ave, Unit B, OAKLAND, CA 94605 USA Tel 510-332-2782
E-mail: janrenee418@gmail.com.

NAPNAP, (*978-0-9749769*) 20 Brace Rd., Suite 200, Cherry Hill, NJ 08034-2634 USA Tel 856-857-9700; Fax: 856-857-1600
E-mail: info@napnap.org
Web site: http://www.napnap.org.

Napue & Tucker Publishing, L.L.C. *See* **NT Publishing, L.L.C.**

NA-r *Imprint of* **Capstone**

Narragansett Graphics, (*978-0-615-12390-5*) P.O. Box 1492, Coventry, RI 02816-0029 USA
E-mail: lsousa@narragansettgraphics.com
Web site: http://www.narragansettgraphics.com.

NarraGarden LLC, (*978-0-9907434*)
E-mail: info@narragarden.com; bradley.blankenship@gmail.com
Web site: www.papadadandme.com; www.narragarden.com.

Nash, Patrick, (*978-1-7342771*) 46 Hancock St., Wrentham, MA 02093 USA Tel 508-282-9202
E-mail: pnash5@comcast.net.

Nassau-Street.com, (*978-1-60290*) Nassau Street Media LLC, 3906 Irving St, San Francisco, CA 941222 USA
E-mail: nassaustreetmedia@gmail.com
Web site: http://nassau-street.com.

Nastari, Nadine, (*978-0-9798387*) 8408 Salerno Rd., Fort Pierce, FL 34951-4506 USA Tel 772-475-7787
Web site: http://www.three-leggedcat.com.

NASW Pr. *Imprint of* **National Assn. of Social Workers/NASW Pr.**

Natalie Lee Martin, (*978-1-7363011*) 1339 Weedon Dr., EVANS, GA 30809 USA Tel 228-243-9392
E-mail: leenatal24@yahoo.com
Web site: natalieleemartin.com.

Natavi Guides, (*978-0-9719392; 978-1-932204*) 44 Pine St., West Newton, MA 02465-1425 USA
E-mail: info@nataviguides.com
Web site: http://www.nataviguides.com.

NatGeo Under the Stars *Imprint of* **Disney Publishing Worldwide**

Nathan, Fernand (FRA) (*978-2-09*) *Dist. by* **Distribks Inc.**

Nathaniel Max Rock, (*978-0-9749392; 978-1-59980*) 1418 S. Orange Ave., Monterey Park, CA 91755 USA
Web site: http://rockmath.com.

†**National Academies Pr.,** (*978-0-309*) Orders Addr.: 8700 Spectrum Dr., Landover, MD 20785 USA; Edit Addr.: 500 Fifth St., NW Lockbox 285, Washington, DC 20001 USA (SAN 202-8891) Tel 202-334-3313; Fax: 202-334-2451; Toll Free: 888-624-7654; *Imprints*: Joseph Henry Press (Joseph Henry Pr)
E-mail: zjones@nas.edu
Web site: http://www.nap.edu
Dist(s): **Ebsco Publishing**
MyiLibrary
ebrary, Inc.; *CIP*.

National Academy Press *See* **National Academies Pr.**

†**National Archives & Records Administration,** (*978-0-911333; 978-1-880875*) Orders Addr.: 700 Pennsylvania Ave., NW, Washington, DC 20408 USA (SAN 210-363X) Tel 301-713-6800; Fax: 310-713-6169; Toll Free: 800-234-8861
E-mail: katherine.coram@nara.gov
Web site: http://www.nara.gov
Dist(s): **United States Government Printing Office**; *CIP*.

National Assn. for Humane & Environmental Education, (*978-0-941246*) Div. of Humane Society of the U.S., P.O. Box 362, East Haddam, CT 06423 USA (SAN 285-0680) Tel 860-434-8666; Fax: 860-434-9579; *Imprints*: Humane Society Press (Humane Soc Pr)
E-mail: nahee@nahee.org
Web site: http://www.nahee.org.

National Assn. for Visually Handicapped, (*978-0-89064*) 3201 Balboa St., San Francisco, CA 94121 USA (SAN 202-0971) Tel 415-221-3201; Fax: 415-221-8754; 111 E. 59th St. # 6, New York, NY 10022-1202 (SAN 669-1870)
E-mail: staff@navh.org
Web site: http://www.navh.org.

†**National Assn. of Social Workers/NASW Pr.,** (*978-0-87101*) Orders Addr.: P.O. Box 431, Annapolis Junction, MD 20701 USA Fax: 301-206-7989; Toll Free: 800-227-3590; Edit Addr.: 750 First St., NE, Suite 700, Washington, DC 20002-4241 USA (SAN 202-893X) Tel 202-408-8600; Fax: 202-336-8312; Toll Free: 800-638-8799; *Imprints*: N A S W Press (NASW Pr)
E-mail: press@naswdc.org
Web site: http://www.naswpress.org; *CIP*.

National Assn. of Speed & Explosion, (*978-0-938074*) P.O. Box 1784, Kill Devil Hills, NC 27948 USA (SAN 215-6148) Tel 252-441-1185; Fax: 252-449-4125
E-mail: naseinc@aol.com.

National Bk. Network, Div. of Rowman & Littlefield Pubs., Inc., Orders Addr.: 15200 NBN Way, Blue Ridge Summit, PA 17214 USA (SAN 630-0065) Tel 717-794-3800; Fax: 717-794-3828; Toll Free Fax: 800-338-4550 (Customer Service); Toll Free: 800-462-6420 (Customer Service); a/o Les Petriw, 67 Mowat Ave., Suite 241, Toronto, ON M6P 3K3 Tel 416-534-1660; Fax: 416-534-3699
E-mail: custserv@nbnbooks.com
Web site: http://www.nbnbooks.com.

National Braille Pr., (*978-0-939173*) Orders Addr.: 88 St. Stephen St., Boston, MA 02115 USA (SAN 273-0952) Tel 617-266-6160; Fax: 617-437-0456; Toll Free: 800-548-7323
E-mail: orders@nbp.org
Web site: http://www.nbp.org.

National Ctr. For Youth Issues, (*978-1-931636; 978-1-937870; 978-1-953970*) Orders Addr.: P.O. Box 22185, Chattanooga, TN 37422-2185 USA Tel 423-899-5714; Fax: 423-899-4547; Toll Free: 800-477-8277; Edit Addr.: 6101 Preservation Dr., Chattanooga, TN 37416 USA (SAN 990-1590)
E-mail: info@ncyi.org; mhuff@ncyi.org
Web site: http://www.ncyi.org
Dist(s): **Children's Plus, Inc.**
Follett School Solutions
MAR*CO Products, Inc.
Youthlight, Inc.

National Children's Book Project *See* **Public Square Bks.**

National Conference of State Legislatures, (*978-0-941336; 978-1-55516; 978-1-58024*) 7700 E. First Pl., Denver, CO 80230-7143 USA (SAN 225-1000) Tel 303-364-7700; Fax: 303-364-7800
E-mail: rita.morris@ncsl.org
Web site: http://www.ncsl.org.

†**National Council of Teachers of English,** (*978-0-8141*) 340 N. Neil St. No. 104, Champaign, IL 61820 USA (SAN 202-9049) Tel 217-328-3870 Main Switchboard; Fax: 217-328-0977 Editorial Fax; 217-328-9645 Customer Service Fax; Toll Free: 800-369-6283 Main Switchboard Toll Free Tel; 877-369-6283 Customer Service Toll Free Tel
E-mail: kaustin@ncte.org; orders@ncte.org
Web site: https://ncte.org
Dist(s): **APG Sales & Distribution Services**
Consortium Bk. Sales & Distribution; *CIP*.

†**National Council of Teachers of Mathematics,** (*978-0-87353; 978-1-68054*) 1906 Association Dr., Reston, VA 20191-1502 USA (SAN 202-9057) Tel 703-620-9840; Fax: 703-476-2970; 703-715-9536; Toll Free Fax: 800-220-8483; Toll Free: 800-235-7566 (orders only)
E-mail: info@nctm.org; mdonovan@nctm.org
Web site: http://www.nctm.org; *CIP*.

National Crime Prevention Council, (*978-0-934513; 978-1-929888; 978-1-59686*) 2345 Crystal Dr. Suite 500, Arlington, VA 22202 USA (SAN 693-8574) Tel 202-466-6272; Fax: 202-296-1356; Toll Free: 800-627-2911 (orders only) Do not confuse with The National Crime Prevention Assn., also in Washington, D.C.
E-mail: kirby@ncpc.org; demenno@ncpc.org
Web site: http://www.ncpc.org; http://www.mcgruff.org.

National Dance Education Organization, (*978-1-930798*) 8609 2nd Ave. Ste. 203B, Silver Spring, MD 20910-6359 USA
E-mail: ndeo@erols.com
Web site: http://www.ndeo.org
Dist(s): **Chicago Distribution Ctr.**

National Deacons Association *See* **Tommy Bks. Pubng.**

National Defense University *Imprint of* **United States Government Printing Office**

†**National Education Assn.,** (*978-0-8106*) Orders Addr.: P.O. Box 404846, Atlanta, GA 30384-4846 USA (SAN 203-7262) Tel 202-822-7208; Fax: 202-822-7377; Toll Free: 800-229-4200; Edit Addr.: 1201 16th St., NW. Suite 514, Washington, DC 20036 USA Tel 770-280-4080; Fax: 770-280-4134
E-mail: nea-orders@pbd.com
Web site: http://www.nea.org/books; *CIP*.

National Educational Systems, Inc., (*978-1-893493*) P.O. Box 691450, San Antonio, TX 78269-1450 USA Toll Free: 800-442-2604.

National Film Network LLC, (*978-0-8026*) Orders Addr.: 4501 Forbes Blvd., Lanham, MD 20706 USA (SAN 630-1878) Tel 301-459-8020 ext 2066
E-mail: info@nationalfilmnetwork.com
Web site: http://www.nationalfilmnetwork.com.

National Foundation for Teaching Entrepreneurship, The, (*978-1-890859*) Orders Addr.: 120 Wall St., 29th Flr., New York, NY 10005 USA Tel 212-232-3333; Fax: 212-232-2244; Toll Free: 800-367-6383
E-mail: nfte@nfte.com
Web site: http://www.nfte.com.

National Gallery of Australia (AUS) (*978-0-646-30472-4; 978-0-646-84218-9*) *Dist. by* **U of Wash Pr.**

National Gallery of Victoria (AUS) (*978-1-925432; 978-0-85848*) *Dist. by* **Antique Collect.**

National Gallery of Victoria (AUS) (*978-1-925432; 978-0-85848*) *Dist. by* **Natl Bk Netwk.**

National Gallery Singapore (SGP) (*978-981-09-1091-4; 978-981-09-7349-0; 978-981-09-7352-0; 978-981-09-7353-7; 978-981-09-7384-1; 978-981-09-7385-8; 978-981-09-7498-5; 978-981-09-8433-5; 978-981-09-9561-4; 978-981-11-0189-2; 978-981-11-0190-8; 978-981-11-0608-8; 978-981-11-2236-1; 978-981-11-2373-3; 978-981-11-2374-0; 978-981-11-2375-7; 978-981-14-0606-5; 978-981-14-0607-2; 978-981-14-0652-2; 978-981-14-0664-5; 978-981-14-0720-8; 978-981-14-1043-7; 978-981-14-1147-2; 978-981-14-1960-7; 978-981-14-1961-4; 978-981-14-1962-1;*) *Dist. by* **Pa St U Pr.**

National Geographic *Imprint of* **Disney Publishing Worldwide**

National Geographic *Imprint of* **National Geographic Society**

National Geographic Books *Imprint of* **Disney Publishing Worldwide**

National Geographic Children's Bks. *Imprint of* **Disney Publishing Worldwide**

National Geographic Children's Bks. *Imprint of* **National Geographic Society**

National Geographic Kids *Imprint of* **Disney Publishing Worldwide**

National Geographic Learning *Imprint of* **CENGAGE Learning**

National Geographic School Publishing, Inc., (*978-0-7362; 978-0-917837; 978-1-56334*) Div. of CENGAGE Learning, Orders Addr.: 10650 Toebben Dr., Independence, KY 41051 USA Tel 859-282-5700; Toll Free Fax: 800-487-8488; Toll Free: 800-354-9706; 888-915-3276; Edit Addr.: 1 Lower Ragsdale Dr., Bldg. 1, Suite 200, Monterey, CA 93940 USA
Web site: http://www.hampton-brown.com
Dist(s): **CENGAGE Learning.**

†**National Geographic Society,** (*978-0-7922; 978-0-87044; 978-1-4262; 978-1-4263*) 1145 17th St., NW, Washington, DC 20036 USA (SAN 202-8956) Tel 202-857-7000; Fax: 301-921-1575; Toll Free: 800-647-5463; 800-548-9797 (TTD users only); *Imprints*: National Geographic Children's Books (NGCB); National Geographic (NatiGeo)
E-mail: askngs@nationalgeographic.com
Web site: http://nationalgeographic.com
Dist(s): **Benchmark LLC**
Children's Plus, Inc.
Follett Media Distribution
Follett School Solutions
Hachette Bk. Group
Lectorum Pubns., Inc.
MyiLibrary
Penguin Random Hse. Distribution
Rand McNally
Random Hse., Inc.
Simon & Schuster, Inc.; *CIP*.

National Honor Roll, LLC, (*978-0-9714201; 978-0-9721652; 978-0-9729406; 978-1-932654*) 777 Sunrise Hwy. Ste. 300, Lynbrook, NY 11563-2950 USA Toll Free: 800-416-2185
Web site: http://www.nationalhonorroll.org.

Publisher Name Index

National Horseman Publishing Inc., The, *(978-0-9762854)* 16101 N. 82nd St., Suite 10, Scottsdale, AZ 85260-1830 USA Tel 480-922-5202
Web site: http://www.tnh1865.com.

National Institute on Alcohol Abuse & Alcoholism *Imprint of* **United States Government Printing Office**

National Issues Forums Institute, *(978-0-945639; 978-1-943028; 978-1-946206)* 100 Commons Rd., Dayton, OH 45459 USA (SAN 247-2163) Tel 937-434-7300; Fax: 937-439-9804; Toll Free: 800-221-3657
E-mail: dsacksteder@kettering.org
Web site: http://www.nifi.org
Dist(s): **Atlas Bks.**
Baker & Taylor Publisher Services (BTPS).

National Learning Corp., *(978-0-8293; 978-0-8373; 978-1-7318; 978-1-7993)* 212 Michael Dr., Syosset, NY 11791 USA (SAN 206-8869) Tel 516-921-8888; Fax: 516-921-8743; Toll Free: 800-645-6337
E-mail: sales@passbooks.com
Web site: nlcpassbooks@aim.com
Dist(s): **Independent Pubs. Group.**

National Marfan Foundation, The, *(978-0-918335)* 22 Manhasset Ave., Prt Washingtn, NY 11050-2023 USA (SAN 657-2855) Toll Free: 800-862-7326
E-mail: staff@marfan.org
Web site: http://www.marfan.org.

National Marine Fisheries Service *Imprint of* **United States Government Printing Office**

National Maritime Museum (GBR) *(978-0-905555; 978-0-948065; 978-0-9501764; 978-1-906367; 978-1-8384596) Dist. by* **Casemate Pubs.**

National Network of Digital Schools *See* **Lincoln Learning Solutions**

†National Park Service Div. of Pubns., *(978-0-912627)* Harpers Ferry Ctr., Harpers Ferry, WV 25425 USA (SAN 282-7980) Tel 304-535-6018; Fax: 304-535-6144
Dist(s): **United States Government Printing Office**; *CIP.*

National Reading Styles Institute, Inc., *(978-0-929192; 978-1-883186; 978-1-933533)* Orders Addr.: P.O. Box 737, Syosset, NY 11791 USA (SAN 248-8191) Tel 516-921-5500; Fax: 516-921-5591; Toll Free: 800-331-3117; Edit Addr.: 179 Lafayette Dr., Syosset, NY 11791 USA (SAN 248-8205)
E-mail: readingstyle@nrsi.com
Web site: http://www.literacy.org; http://www.nrsi.com.

National Rehabilitation Services *See* **Northern Speech Services**

National Review, Inc., *(978-0-9627841; 978-0-9758998; 978-0-9847650)* 215 Lexington Ave., 4th Flr., New York, NY 10016 USA (SAN 226-1685) Tel 212-679-7330; Fax: 212-696-0340
E-mail: jfowler@nationalreview.com
Web site: http://www.nationalreview.com
Dist(s): **Chicago Distribution Ctr.**

National Science Resources Center (NSRC) *See* **Smithsonian Science Education Ctr. (SSEC)**

†National Science Teachers Assn., *(978-0-87355; 978-1-933531; 978-1-935155; 978-1-936137; 978-1-936959; 978-1-938946; 978-1-941316; 978-1-68140; 978-1-952109)* 1840 Wilson Blvd., Arlington, VA 22201 USA (SAN 203-7173) 703-243-7177; Toll Free Fax: 888-433-0526 (orders); Toll Free: 800-277-5300 (orders); 800-722-6782
E-mail: pubsales@nsta.org; dyudkin@nsta.org
Web site: http://www.nsta.org/store
Dist(s): **Ebsco Publishing**
Independent Pubs. Group
MyiLibrary
ebrary, Inc.; *CIP.*

National Self-Esteem Resources & Development Ctr., *(978-0-9632276)* 851 Irwin St., Suite 205, San Rafael, CA 94901-3343 USA Tel 415-457-4411; Fax: 415-457-0356.

National Society of Professional Engineers, *(978-0-915409)* 1420 King St., Alexandria, VA 22314-2715 USA (SAN 225-168X) Tel 703-684-2800; Fax: 703-836-4875; Toll Free: 888-285-6773
E-mail: customer.service@nspe.org
Web site: http://www.nspe.org.

National Textbook Co. *Imprint of* **McGraw-Hill/Contemporary**

National Training Network, Inc., *(978-1-57290)* Orders Addr.: P.O. Box 36, Summerfield, NC 27358 USA
E-mail: l.schueren@ntnmath.com
Web site: http://www.ntnmath.com.

National Wildlife Federation, *(978-0-937934; 978-1-888153; 978-1-932396; 978-1-938811; 978-1-946318)* 1260 Audubon Rd., Park Hills, KY 41011-1904 USA (SAN 215-8299) Toll Free: 800-477-5034; *Imprints:* Zoo Books (Zoo Bks); Critters Up Close (Critters Up Close)
E-mail: sales@zoobooks.com
Web site: http://www.zoobooks.com.

National Writers Pr., The, *(978-0-88100)* Div. of National Writers Assn., 17011 Lincoln Ave., No. 421, Parker, CO 80134 USA (SAN 240-320X) Tel 720-851-1944; Fax: 303-841-2607
E-mail: natlwritersassn@hotmail.com
Web site: http://www.nationalwriters.com.

National Writing Institute, *(978-1-888344)* PMB 248, 624 W. University Dr., Denton, TX 76201-1889 USA Tel 940-382-0044; Fax: 940-383-4414; Toll Free Fax: 888-663-7855; Toll Free: 800-688-5375
E-mail: info@writingstrands.com
Web site: http://www.writingstrands.com.

Nations Hope, Inc., The, *(978-0-9761415)* P.O. Box 691446, Orlando, FL 32869-1446 USA
Web site: http://www.nationshope.org.

Native American Pubns., *(978-0-9745867)* Orders Addr.: P.O. Box 9, Dulac, LA 70353-0009 USA Tel 985-223-3857; Edit Addr.: 443 Ashland Dr., Houma, LA 70363-7283 USA
E-mail: ccbilliot@aol.com.

Native Nature *See* **Niche Publishing & Marketing**

Native Sun Pr., *(978-0-9746848)* Orders Addr.: P.O. Box 1139, Summerland, CA 93067 USA (SAN 255-6839) Tel 805-969-2234 (phone/fax); Edit Addr.: 2240 Banner Ave., Summerland, CA 93067 USA.

Native Voices *Imprint of* **BPC**

Natl Bk. Network,
Dist(s): **Perfection Learning Corp.**

NaTroy Publishing Co., *(978-0-9755246)* Orders Addr.: P.O. Box 93442, Cleveland, OH 44101 USA Tel 216-376-4810.

Nattosoup Studio, *(978-1-7355678)* 592 Willowridge Dr., Luling, LA 70070 USA Tel 504-256-5992
E-mail: becca.hillburn@gmail.com
Web site: https://nattosoup.com.

Natural Genius Bks., *(978-0-9765070)* P.O. Box 191088, Sacramento, CA 95819 USA Toll Free: 800-917-9321
E-mail: mjsee3@earthlink.net
Web site: http://www.naturalgeniusbooks.com.

Natural History Museum Pubns. (GBR) *(978-0-565) Dist. by* **IPG Chicago.**

Natural Learning Concepts, Inc., *(978-0-9778866; 978-0-9800300)* 21 Gallatin Dr., Suite B, Dix Hills, NY 11746 USA Tel 631-858-0188 (phone/fax); Toll Free: 800-823-3430
E-mail: sales@nlconcepts.com
Web site: http://www.nlconcepts.com.

Natural Life Energy LLC, *(978-1-7320958)* 13130 SW 16th St., Davie, FL 33325 USA Tel 917-450-4717
E-mail: aqiyl.henry@gmail.com
Web site: http://www.naturallifeenergy.com.

Natural Math *See* **Delta Stream Media**

Naturally You Can Sing, *(978-0-9708397)* 3026 South St., East Troy, WI 53120 USA (SAN 255-4712)
E-mail: mary@flowformsamerica.com
Web site: http://www.naturallyyoucansing.com
Dist(s): **SteinerBooks, Inc.**

Nature Connection, *(978-0-9996944)* 31745 140th St., St. Peter, MN 56082 USA Tel 507-931-4399
E-mail: jbieder@wildblue.net.

Nature, Inc., *(978-0-692-97495-7)* 4195 Cedarcrest Ln., Anacortes, WA 98221 USA Tel 360-969-6170
E-mail: info@natureday.com
Dist(s): **Ingram Content Group.**

Nature Works Press, *(978-0-915965)* Orders Addr.: P.O. Box 469, Talent, OR 97540 USA (SAN 293-9738) Tel 541-535-3189; Toll Free Fax: 866-749-3077
E-mail: irene@natureworkspress.com; natureworks1@gmail.com
Web site: http://www.natureworkspress.com
Dist(s): **Bks. West**
Partners/West Book Distributors.

Naturegraph Pubs., Inc., *(978-0-87961; 978-0-911010)* Box 1047, 3543 Indian Creek Rd., Happy Camp, CA 96039 USA (SAN 202-8999) Tel 530-493-5353; Fax: 530-493-5240; Toll Free: 800-390-5353
E-mail: nature@sisqtel.net
Web site: http://www.naturegraph.com
Dist(s): **American West Bks.**
Gem Guides Bk. Co.
New Leaf Distributing Co., Inc.
Sunbelt Pubns., Inc.

NaturEncyclopedia *Imprint of* **Stemmer Hse. Pubs.**

Naturenurturemade, *(978-1-7360126; 978-1-957416)* 2203 Dunbrook Dr., Chapel Hill, NC 27517 USA Tel 919-428-3586
E-mail: iprofessonelove@gmail.com
Web site: Naturenurturemade.com.

Natures Beauty Publishing, *(978-0-9754701)* P.O. Box 107, Oxford, MI 48371-0107 USA Tel 248-236-9314; Fax: 248-236-9315
E-mail: Ron@Naturesbeautyphotography.com
Web site: http://www.naturesbeautyphotography.com.

Nature's Hopes & Heroes, *(978-0-9822942)* 265 Kings Hwy., Boulder Creek, CA 95006 USA Tel 831-423-8973
E-mail: jimcruz@cruzers.com.

Nature's Pr., *(978-0-9741883)* Orders Addr.: P.O. Box 371, Mercer, WI 54547 USA
Web site: http://www.naturespressbooks.com.

Naumann, Jennifer, *(978-0-9883902)* 2777 420th Ave, Elmore, MN 56027 USA Tel 507-943-3673
E-mail: jen.naumann@yahoo.com.

Nautilus Pr., *(978-0-9916616; 979-8-9885391)* 5080 Via Ricardo, Yorba Linda, CA 92886 USA Tel 714-340-6384 Do not confuse with Nautilus Press in La Jolla, CA
E-mail: n.m.macarthur@aol.com.

†Naval Institute Pr., *(978-0-87021; 978-1-55750; 978-1-59114; 978-1-61251; 978-1-68247; 978-1-68269)* Orders Addr.: 291 Wood Rd, Annapolis, MD 21402-5034 USA (SAN 662-0930) Tel 410-268-6110; Fax: 410-295-1084; Toll Free: 800-233-8764; Edit Addr.: 291 Wood Rd., Beach Hall, Annapolis, MD 21402-5034 USA (SAN 202-9006)
E-mail: tskord@usni.org; books@usni.org
Web site: http://www.usni.org
Dist(s): **Fujii Assocs.**
MyiLibrary
Publishers Group West (PGW); *CIP.*

Navarro, Sandra *See* **Cornsilk Pr.**

NavPress Publishing Group, *(978-0-89109; 978-1-57683; 978-1-60006; 978-1-61521; 978-1-61747; 978-1-61291; 978-1-63146; 978-1-64158)* 3820 N. 30th St., Colorado Springs, CO 80904 USA Fax: 719-260-7223; Toll Free Fax: 800-343-3902; Toll Free: 800-366-7788; *Imprints:* Th1nk Books (Th1nk Bks)
Web site: http://www.navpress.com
Dist(s): **Follett School Solutions**
Tyndale Hse. Pubs.

Nay Seyers *See* **WARTS etc.**

Nay Vogel Photography & Design, *(978-0-692-80195-6; 978-0-692-81723-0)*.

Naydus Pr., *(978-1-7341936)* 8407 Capricorn Dr., Montgomery, OH 45249 USA Tel 510-206-7155
E-mail: jordan.finkin@gmail.com
Dist(s): **ISD.**

Naylor, Christopher, *(978-0-692-12074-3; 978-0-578-40320-5)* 2804 E 9th Ave Apt 23, WINFIELD, KS 67156 USA Tel 316-648-9013
E-mail: cjmnaylor@yahoo.com
Dist(s): **Ingram Content Group.**

Naynay Bks *See* **Naynay Bks.**

Naynay Bks., *(978-0-9769589)* 122 Arbor Rd., NW, Minerva, OH 44657 USA
E-mail: naynaybooks@aol.com
Web site: http://www.naynaybooks.com.

Naypree Enterprises, LLC *See* **Mauldin Publishing & Literacy House**

Nazarene Publishing House *See* **The Foundry Publishing**

NBM Publishing Co., *(978-0-918348; 978-1-56163; 978-1-68112)* Orders Addr.: 40 Exchange Pl., Suite 1308, New York, NY 10005 USA (SAN 210-0835) Tel 212-643-5407; Fax: 212-643-1545; Toll Free: 800-886-1223; Edit Addr.: 160 Broadway, Suite. 700, E. Wing, New York, NY 10038 USA Tel 646-559-4681; Fax: 212-643-1545; Toll Free: 800-886-1223; *Imprints:* Comics Lit (Comics Lit); Amerotica (Amerotica)
E-mail: catalog@nbmpublishing.com
Web site: http://www.nbmpub.com
Dist(s): **Children's Plus, Inc.**
Independent Pubs. Group
MyiLibrary.

N'Deeo Beauty *See* **N'Deeo, LLC**

N'Deeo, LLC, *(978-0-9724203; 978-0-9753811)* Orders Addr.: P.O. Box 460574, Aurora, CO 80046 USA Tel 770-896-6606; P.O. Box 1425, Mableton, GA 30126; Edit Addr.: 20511 E. Union Ave., Aurora, CO 80015 USA
E-mail: cservice@ndeeo.com
Web site: http://www.ndeeo.com.

Ndegwa, Catherine W., *(978-0-9742688)* Orders Addr.: P.O. Box 220411, Saint Louis, MO 63122-0411 USA; Edit Addr.: 119 Oakside Ln., Saint Louis, MO 63122-0411 USA
E-mail: catherine@varietystl.com.

NdueCzon Publishing Group, *(978-0-9755679)* P.O. Box 341825, Tampa, FL 33694 USA Tel 813-269-9351; Fax: 813-968-1941
E-mail: ndueczon@aol.com
Dist(s): **Culture Plus Bk. Distributors.**

Neal, Ann-Marie F, *(978-0-9747734; 978-0-9862096)* 903 Dale St., Edgewater, MD 21037 USA Tel 401-662-2411
E-mail: sunflower683@reagan.com
Web site: http://www.clarencethefrog.com.

Neal Morgan Publishing, *(978-0-9786117)* 51 Arrowgate Dr., Randolph, NJ 07869 USA Tel 973-598-9601; Fax: 973-927-8722
E-mail: Daleb6@aol.com.

Neal Porter Bks *Imprint of* **Holiday Hse., Inc.**

†Neal-Schuman Pubs., Inc., *(978-0-918212; 978-1-55570)* Div. of American Library Assn., 100 William St., Suite 2004, New York, NY 10038 USA (SAN 210-2455) Tel 212-925-8650; Fax: 212-219-8916; Toll Free Fax: 800-584-2414
E-mail: info@neal-schuman.com
Web site: http://www.neal-schuman.com
Dist(s): **Chicago Distribution Ctr.**
ebrary, Inc.; *CIP.*

Nearaway Far Pubns., *(978-0-9969878)* 22330 Victory Blvd., Woodland Hills, CA 91367 USA Tel 805-300-0738
E-mail: thehopefulprince@gmail.com
Web site: thehopefulprince.com.

Nebador Archives, *(978-1-936253)* P.O. Box 592, Kelso, WA 98626 USA
E-mail: jzc23@nebador.com
Web site: http://www.nebador.com.

Nebbadoon Pr., *(978-1-891331)* Div. of Nebbadoon, Inc., Orders Addr.: 371 Hubbard St., Glastonbury, CT 06033 USA Toll Free: 800-500-9086
E-mail: george@4554.com
Web site: http://www.nebbadoonpress.com.

Nebe, Charles, *(978-0-9773091)* Orders Addr.: P.O. Box 631143, Irving, TX 75063-1143 USA
Web site: http://www.boonefiles.com.

Nebraska Wealth.com, *(978-0-9746206)* 1803 Stagecoach Rd., Grand Island, NE 68801 USA
Web site: http://www.nebraskawealth.com.

Necessary Evil Pr., *(978-0-9753635)* P.O. Box 178, Escanaba, MI 49829 USA
E-mail: info@necessaryevilpress.com
Web site: http://www.necessaryevilpress.com.

Nechalec Pr., *(978-0-692-06188-6; 978-0-692-06506-8; 978-0-578-48645-1)* 448 E. Due W. Ave., Madison, TN 37115 USA Tel 615-496-8953
E-mail: jondbwriter@gmail.com
Dist(s): **Ingram Content Group.**

Nectar Pubns., *(978-0-9859986)* P.O. Box 6552, Savannah, GA 31414 USA Tel 912-631-9214
E-mail: contact@nectarpublications.com
Web site: www.nectarpublications.com.

Ned's Head Productions, *(978-1-887206)* 307 State St., Apt. B3, Johnstown, PA 15905 USA (SAN 253-8059) Tel 814-255-6646 (phone/fax)
E-mail: drron@charter.net
Web site: http://nedsheadbooks.com
Dist(s): **APG Sales & Distribution Services.**

Need To Know Publishing, *(978-1-940705)* 11019 N. 73rd St., Scottsdale, AZ 85260 USA Tel 888-377-3158; Fax: 888-377-3158
E-mail: brad@needtoknowpublishing.com
Dist(s): **MyiLibrary**
Publishers Group West (PGW).

Needle Rock Pr., *(978-1-943500)* 341 Flounce Rock Rd., Prospect, OR 97536 USA Tel 541-951-1662
E-mail: sandycathcart@gmail.com
Web site: needlerockpress.com.

Neely, Judy, *(978-1-893968)* 54505 NW Scofield Rd., Buxton, OR 97109 USA Tel 503-324-8222; Fax: 503-324-8252
E-mail: jneely@neelyranch.com
Web site: http://www.neelyranch.com.

Neema's Children Literature Assn., Inc., *(978-0-9740653)* Orders Addr.: P.O. Box 440073, Chicago, IL 60644-1937 USA Tel 773-378-0607; Fax: 773-378-0042; Edit Addr.: 5345 W. Ferdinand St., Chicago, IL 60644-1937 USA Tel 773-575-4639
E-mail: nclapub@gmail.com.

Neena The LAST Brand, *(978-0-692-16362-7; 978-0-578-80585-6; 978-0-578-80586-3; 978-1-7366939)* 1468 Berry Rd., Birmingham, AL 35226 USA Tel 205-306-4032
E-mail: neenathelastbrand@gmail.com.

Nefu Bks. *Imprint of* **Africana Homestead Legacy Pubs., Inc.**

Negro Publishing LLC *Imprint of* **Negro Publishing, LLC**

Negro Publishing, LLC, *(978-0-9763583)* Orders Addr.: P.O. Box 78, Mableton, GA 30126 USA Tel 770-265-0822; Fax: 770-948-2460; *Imprints:* Negro Publishing LLC (Negro Pub)
E-mail: supadave@negropublishing.com; dhhorton_2000@yahoo.com
Web site: http://www.negropublishing.com
Dist(s): **Culture Plus Bk. Distributors.**

NEHA Training LLC, *(978-0-944111)* 720 S. Colorado Blvd. Ste. 1000N, Denver, CO 80246-1926 USA
E-mail: support@nehatraining.com
Web site: http://www.nehatraining.com.

Neighborhood Pubs., *(978-0-9779601)* P.O. Box 8, McDonough, NY 13801 USA
Dist(s): **BCH Fulfillment & Distribution.**

Neighborhood Pubs., *(978-0-615-75249-5)* 3317 Manor Rd., Austin, TX 78723 USA Tel 512-291-2314
E-mail: johnatpbp@yahoo.com.

Nelsbok Publishing, *(978-0-9763072)* 3312 Cedar Ave S., Minneapolis, MN 55407-2335 USA
Web site: http://www.nelsbok.com.

Nelsen, Margie, *(978-0-615-22008-6; 978-0-615-25480-7)* 804 Spruce Pl., Saint Peter, MN 56082 USA
E-mail: margienelsen@mchsi.com
Web site: http://www.snuggiebooks.com.

Nelson, Linda J., *(978-0-692-18458-5; 978-0-578-50119-2)* 47 N. Rd., NEW IPSWICH, NH 03071 USA Tel 603-878-2121
E-mail: linda_nel@msn.com
Dist(s): **Ingram Content Group.**

Nelson, Mikaela, *(978-1-7368287)* 717-R Audubon Lake Dr., Durham, NC 27713 USA Tel 716-997-4054
E-mail: mickeynelson3@gmail.com.

Nelson Multimedia, LLC, *(978-0-9721360)* 1 Airport Rd., Suite 2, Minden, NV 89423 USA.

Nelson Publishing & Marketing, *(978-1-933916; 978-0-9785075; 978-1-938326)* 366 Welch Rd., Northville, MI 48167-1160 USA Tel 248-735-0418; *Imprints:* Ferne Press (Ferne Press)
E-mail: marian@nelsonpublishingandmarketing.com; kris@nelsonpublishingandmarketing.com
Web site: http://nelsonpublishingandmarketing.com
Dist(s): **Children's Plus, Inc.**
Partners Pubs. Group, Inc.

Nelson Publishing, LLC, *(978-0-9794171)* 6710 Laurel Bowie Road, suite 441, Bowie, MD 20718 USA; *Imprints:* Adventures of Hillary, The (AdventuresHillary)
E-mail: nelsonpublishingbooks@gmail.com
Web site: http://www.nelsonpublishingbooks.com.

Nelson, R. E. & Assoc., *(978-0-9749636)* 1535 SW Plass Ave., Topeka, KS 66604 USA Tel 785-235-3041
Web site: http://www.renelson.com.

Nelson, Roy *See* **Nelson, R. E. & Assoc.**

†Nelson, Thomas Inc., *(978-0-529; 978-0-7852; 978-0-8407; 978-0-8499; 978-0-86605; 978-0-88113; 978-0-89840; 978-0-89922; 978-0-918956; 978-0-7180; 978-1-4002; 978-1-4003; 978-1-4016; 978-1-59145; 978-1-4041; 978-1-59554; 978-1-59555; 978-1-4185; 978-1-59951; 978-1-4261; 978-1-60255; 978-1-4845; 978-1-5000; 978-1-5314; 978-1-6623) Div. of HarperCollins Christian Publishing, Orders Addr.: P.O. Box 141000, Nashville, TN 37214-1000 USA (SAN 209-3820) Fax: 615-902-1866; Toll Free: 800-251-4000; Edit Addr.: 501 Nelson Pl., Nashville, TN 37214 USA; Imprints:* Tommy Nelson (Tommy Nel USA)
Web site: http://www.harpercollinschristian.com
Dist(s): **Brilliance Publishing, Inc.**
Children's Plus, Inc.
Christian Bk. Distributors
CreateSpace Independent Publishing Platform
Follett School Solutions
Open Road Integrated Media, Inc.
Twentieth Century Christian Bks.; *CIP.*

Nelson Thornes Ltd. (GBR) *(978-0-17; 978-0-7487; 978-0-85950; 978-1-871402; 978-1-873732; 978-1-4085) Dist. by* **Trans-Atl Phila.**

Nelson Thornes Ltd. (GBR) *(978-0-17; 978-0-7487; 978-0-85950; 978-1-871402; 978-1-873732; 978-1-4085) Dist. by* **OUP.**

Nelson, Tracy C., *(978-0-9990974)* 4011 Overcup Oak Ln., Cary, NC 27519 USA Tel 919-408-9911; Fax: 919-408-9911
E-mail: stephy.costarica@gmail.com.

Nemec LLC, *(978-1-947608)* 3812 Elbert Ave, Alexandria, VA 22305 USA Tel 571-214-4222
E-mail: GaleNemecBooks@gmail.com
Web site: www.GaleNemecBooks.com.

NEMESIS Enterprises, L.P., *(978-0-9713230)* Orders Addr.: 1048 S. Wardsboro Rd., Wardsboro, VT 05355 USA
E-mail: nemesis@myfairpoint.net
Web site: http://www.gophergo.com.

Nemeth, Karen, *(978-0-9899899)* 126 Cambridge Ln., Newtown, PA 18940 USA Tel 215-860-1480
E-mail: karenlela1@gmail.com.

Nemo Publishing, LLC, *(978-0-9817132)* 86 Newbury St., Portland, ME 04101 USA (SAN 856-3381) Tel 207-761-0807; Fax: 207-775-5567
E-mail: tami@maine.rr.com
Web site: http://www.captneli.com
Dist(s): **Diamond Comic Distributors, Inc.**
Diamond Bk. Distributors.

Nemsi Bks., *(978-0-9718164; 978-0-9766400; 978-0-9794855; 978-0-9815313; 978-0-9821427; 978-0-9825011)* Div. of Morphtek.com, Inc., P.O. Box 191, Pierpont, SD 57468-0191 USA Fax: 605-325-3393
E-mail: psiccusa@dailypost.com
Web site: http://www.nemsi-books.net.

Neon Squid *Imprint of* **St. Martin's Pr.**

Neo-Tech Publishing Co., *(978-0-911752)* P.O. Box PO Box 531330, Henderson, NV 89053-1330 USA (SAN 202-3156)
E-mail: rapper@neo-tech.com
Web site: http://www.neo-tech.com; http://www.neo-tech.com/front/cservice.html.

Nerdel Co., The, *(978-0-9823357)* 1000 West McNab Road, Pompano Beach, FL 33069 USA (SAN 858-7205)
Web site: http://www.nerdel.com.

NERO International Holding Co., Inc. *See* **Valenti, Joseph**

NESFA Pr. *Imprint of* **New England Science Fiction Assn., Inc.**

Neshee Pubn., *(978-0-9747017; 978-0-9770907; 978-0-9785794; 978-0-9823053)* P.O. Box 48028, Philadelphia, PA 19144 USA
E-mail: info@nesheepublicaiton.com
Web site: http://www.nesheepublication.com.

Neshui Publishing, Inc., *(978-0-9652528; 978-1-931190)* 6310 Rosebury Ave. #2, Saint Louis, MO 63105 USA
E-mail: info@neshuipress.com
Web site: http://www.neshuipress.com
Dist(s): **Raven West Coast Distribution.**

Nesting Tree Bks. *Imprint of* **Raven Publishing Inc. of Montana**

NetClinger, *(978-0-9760308)* P.O. Box 38144, Houston, TX 77238-8144 USA
Web site: http://www.netclinger.com.

Netcomics, *(978-1-60009)* P.O. Box 16484, Jersey City, NJ 07306 USA
Dist(s): **Diamond Comic Distributors, Inc.**
Diamond Bk. Distributors.

NetLeaves, *(978-0-9798056; 979-8-9825224)* 110 Bay Dr., Bellevue, WA 98008 USA (SAN 854-428X)
Web site: http://www.netleaves.com
Dist(s): **Smashwords.**

NetNia Publishing Co., *(978-1-884163)* 9218 Rockbrook Dr., Dallas, TX 75220 USA; *Imprints*: Juba Books (Juba Bks)
E-mail: jeffery.bradley@outlook.com
Web site: http://www.howtogrowdreadlocks.com; http://www.africanamericanchildrenplays.com
Dist(s): **Ingram Content Group.**

NETroplex Books *See* **Yankee Cowboy**

Netto, J.D. Design Inc., *(978-0-692-18446-2; 978-0-692-18492-9; 978-0-578-55609-3; 978-0-578-56454-8; 978-0-578-75179-5; 978-0-578-77111-3; 978-0-578-36809-2; 979-8-218-09859-9; 979-8-218-11940-9; 979-8-218-18257-1)* 5630 Pacific Blvd. No. 802, Boca Raton, FL 33433 USA Tel 508-740-2103
E-mail: info@jdnetto.com
Dist(s): **Ingram Content Group.**

Network CPU Learning Technologies, *(978-1-932257)* 172 Fifth Ave., Suite 37, Brooklyn, NY 11217-3504 USA (SAN 254-9298)
E-mail: roxceyluv@yahoo.com.

NETWORK Inc., The, *(978-1-878234)* Div. of NETWORK, Inc., 136 Fenno Dr., Rowley, MA 01969-1004 USA Tel 978-948-7764; Fax: 978-948-7836; Toll Free: 800-877-5400
E-mail: info@thenetworkinc.org
Web site: http://www.thenetworkinc.org.

Networking Univ., *(978-0-9885108)* 4900 Brook Ln., Anna, TX 75409 USA Tel 214-592-5196
E-mail: DebraPope@Networking-University.com.

Networlding, *(978-0-9883471; 978-1-944027)* 910 W Madison, No. 905E, IL, IL 60607 USA Tel 312-560-0982; Fax: 312-560-0982; *Imprints*: Purple Butterfly Press (MYID_M_PURPLE)
E-mail: melissa@networlding.com
Web site: www.networlding.com.

Neuburger Publishing, *(978-0-9762419)* Orders Addr.: P.O. Box 3928, Tualatin, OR 97062-3928 USA Tel 503-925-0400; Edit Addr.: 24386 SW Baker Rd., Sherwood, OR 97140 USA
Web site: http://www.takethefearoutofmath.com.

Neumann Pr. *Imprint of* **TAN Bks.**

Neurosculpting Institute, *(978-0-692-80006-5)*
Dist(s): **CreateSpace Independent Publishing Platform.**

Nevaeh Publishing, LLC, *(978-0-9787899; 978-0-9839187)* 3523 Morton's Landing Dr., Ellenwood, GA 30294 USA (SAN 851-6111) Tel 404-216-6111
E-mail: dwanabrams@gmail.com
Web site: http://www.dwanabrams.com
Dist(s): **Smashwords.**

Never Not Knitting, *(978-0-9883249)* P.O. Box 1635, Atascadero, CA 93423 USA Tel 805-270-5648
E-mail: nevernotknitting@gmail.com
Web site: www.nevernotknitting.com
Dist(s): **Independent Pubs. Group.**

Never Quit Productions, Inc., *(978-0-615-26231-4)* 4832 Wind Hill Ct. W., Fort Worth, TX 76179 USA
Dist(s): **Lulu Pr., Inc.**

Never Stop Reading Never Stop Learning, *(978-0-9741750)* 3221 S. Indiana St., Lakewood, CO 80228 USA Tel 303-829-8699
E-mail: neverstopreading@aol.com
Web site: http://www.jdmcdoil.com.

Neverland Publishing Co., LLC, *(978-0-9826971; 978-0-9888290; 978-0-9903148; 978-0-9965595)* 24 NW 102 St., Miami Shores, FL 33150 USA (SAN 990-0187) Tel 786-521-0731
E-mail: editor@neverlandpublishing.com
Web site: http://www.neverlandpublishing.com.

Nevruz, Cori, *(978-0-692-89979-3; 978-0-692-92312-2; 978-0-692-12243-3; 978-0-692-15523-3; 978-0-692-16469-3; 978-0-578-41158-3; 978-0-578-44673-8; 978-0-578-50825-2; 978-0-578-57209-3; 978-0-578-67292-2; 978-0-578-67296-0; 978-0-578-81713-2; 978-0-578-83831-1)* 1121 Military Cutoff, Wilmington, NC 28405 USA Tel 919-610-8532
E-mail: corinevruz@gmail.com.

New Academia Publishing, LLC, *(978-0-9744934; 978-0-9767042; 978-0-9777908; 978-0-9787713; 978-0-9794488; 978-0-9800814; 978-0-9818654; 978-0-9823867; 978-0-9844062; 978-0-9828061; 978-0-615-43269-4; 978-0-9832451; 978-0-9836899; 978-0-9845832; 978-0-9855698; 978-0-9860216; -0-9886376; 978-0-9899169; 978-0-9915047; 978-0-9904471; 978-0-9906939; 978-0-9864353; 978-0-9966484; 978-0-9974962; 978-0-9981477; 978-0-9986433; 978-0-9995572; 978-1-7326988; 978-0-578-50586-2; 978-1-7330408; 978-1-7333980; 978-1-7348659; 978-1-)* 4401-A Connecticut Ave. NW No. 236, Washington, DC 20008 USA; *Imprints*: Vellum Books (Vellum)
Web site: http://www.newacademia.com
Dist(s): **Ingram Content Group**
Open Road Integrated Media, Inc.
eBookit.com.

New Age Beauty Corp, *(978-0-578-50265-6; 978-1-7346298)* 6296 SW 165 Pl., Miami, FL 33193 USA Tel 720-202-1360
E-mail: looleebook@gmail.com
Dist(s): **Ingram Content Group.**

New Age Dimensions, Incorporated *See* **Adrema Pr.**

New Age Lab, *(978-1-7377203)* 1001 N Federal Hwy office 300, Hallandale Beach, FL 33009 USA Tel 561-609-8175
E-mail: Julia.davify@gmail.com; labnewage7@gmail.com.

New Age Literary Agency, *(978-1-955531; 978-1-959071; 978-1-961358)* 9461 Charleville Blvd No. 750, Beverly Hills, CA 90212 USA Tel 424-600-3399
E-mail: info@newageliteraryagency.com
Web site: https://newageliteraryagency.com/.

New Age World Publishing, *(978-1-59405)* 27 Dove Ln., El Sobrante, CA 94803-2827 USA; *Imprints*: N2Print (N2Print)
E-mail: nawpublishing@hotmail.com
Web site: http://www.nawpublishing.com.

New & Living Way Publishing Co., *(978-0-910003)* P.O. Box 830384, Tuskegee, AL 36083-0384 USA (SAN 241-2314) Tel 334-727-5372
E-mail: nlwpc@bellsouth.net; clgpgt@bellsouth.net
Web site: http://www.clgpgt.org/NLW/nlw1.html.

New & Living Way Publishing House *See* **New & Living Way Publishing Co.**

New Art & Vision, LLC, *(978-0-9742322)* 1360 E. 300 N., Layton, UT 84040 USA Tel 801-543-3383
E-mail: bnybo@elmojackson.com
Web site: http://www.elmojackson.com.

New Awareness Network, Inc., *(978-0-9652855; 978-0-9711198; 978-0-9768978; 978-0-9849285; 978-0-9894058; 978-0-9960986; 978-0-9975404; 978-1-7325883)* 86 Dennis St., Manhasset, NY 11030 USA Tel 516-869-9108; 516-365-1547; Fax: 516-365-1624
E-mail: sumari@sethcenter.com
Web site: http://www.sethcenter.com.

New Baby Productions, *(978-0-9818530)* Orders Addr.: 4143 Tanglewood Ct., Bloomfield Township, MI 48301 USA (SAN 856-7298)
E-mail: eric@elementalfources.com
Web site: http://www.ElementalFources.com
Dist(s): **Haven Distributors**
Ingram Content Group.

New Birth Publishing, *(978-0-9755489)* 1900 Preston Rd., No. 267, PMB 264, Plano, TX 75093 USA
Web site: http://www.newbirthpublishing.com.

New Buds Publishing Hse. (CHN) *(978-7-5307) Dist. by* **Chinasprout.**

New Canaan Publishing Co. LLC, *(978-1-889658)* 2384 N. Hwy. 341, Rossville, GA 30741 USA Tel 423-285-8672
E-mail: djm@newcanaanpublishing.com
Web site: http://www.newcanaanpublishing.com
Dist(s): **Send The Light Distribution LLC.**

New Castle Publishing Co., *(978-0-9740195)* 512 Wadsworth Dr., Richmond, VA 23236 USA
E-mail: newcastlepubl@aol.com.

New Century Pr., *(978-1-890035)* Orders Addr.: 1055 Bay Blvd., Suite C, Chula Vista, CA 91911-1628 USA (SAN 859-3760) Tel 619-476-7400; Fax: 619-476-7474; Toll Free: 800-519-2465 (orders) Do not confuse with companies with the same or similar name in Bermuda Dunes CA, New York NY
E-mail: sales@newcenturypress.com
Web site: http://www.newcenturypress.com.

New Century Pr., *(978-0-9748013)* P.O. Box 73381, Richmond, VA 23235-8040 USA Tel 804-897-2824 Do not confuse with companies with the same or similar name in Bermuda Dunes CA, Chula Vista CA, New York NY
E-mail: newcenturypress@aol.com.

New Century Publishing, LLC, *(978-0-9768052; 978-0-9820729; 978-0-9822344; 978-0-9824711; 978-0-9841819; 978-0-9843666; 978-0-9844661)* 1040 E. 86th St., Suite 42A, Indianapolis, IN 46240 USA Tel 317-663-8741; Fax: 317-663-8745
E-mail: dwcaswell@newcentrypublishing.org
Web site: http://www.newcenturypublishing.org.

New City Community Pr., *(978-0-9712996; 978-0-9819560; 978-0-9840429; 978-0-9887635; 978-0-692-83625-5)* 7715 Crittenden St., #222, Philadelphia, PA 191182 USA Tel 315-443-1912 Do not confuse with New City Press in Hyde Park, NY
E-mail: sjparks@syr.edu
Web site: http://www.newcitypress.org
Dist(s): **Chicago Distribution Ctr.**
Longleaf Services
SPD-Small Pr. Distribution.

New City Press *See* **New City Press of the Focolare**

New City Press *See* **New City Community Pr.**

†**New City Press of the Focolare**, *(978-0-911782; 978-1-56548)* 202 Comforter Blvd., Hyde Park, NY 12538 USA (SAN 203-7335) Tel 845-229-0335; Fax: 845-229-0351; Toll Free: 800-462-5980 (orders only)
E-mail: info@newcitypress.com
Web site: http://www.newcitypress.com; *CIP.*

New Classics Pr., *(978-0-9755704)* 2400 Ridgecroft SE, Grand Rapids, MI 49546 USA.

New Concepts Publishing, *(978-1-891020; 978-1-58608; 978-1-60394)* 5202 Humphreys Rd., Lake Park, GA 31636 USA Tel 229-257-0367; Fax: 229-219-1097
E-mail: newconcepts@newconceptspublishing.com; service@newconceptspublishing.com
Web site: http://www.newconceptspublishing.com
Dist(s): **Smashwords.**

New Dawn Pr., Inc., *(978-0-9729607; 978-1-932705)* 244 S. Randall Rd., No. 90, Elgin, IL 60123 USA
E-mail: maildrop@newdawnpress.com
Web site: http://www.newdawnpress.com.

New Dawn Publishing, *(978-0-9721948)* P.O. Box 11151, Portland, ME 04104 USA Tel 207-839-8809 Do not confuse with companies with the same or similar name in Elk Mills, MD, Dexter, NY
Web site: http://www.mynewdawn.com.

New Day Initiative, *(978-1-7377220)* 1025 Winterhawk Dr., St. Augustine, FL 32086 USA Tel 904-599-1927
E-mail: nicolemillerndi@gmail.com.

New Day Pr., *(978-0-913678)* c/o Karamu Hse., 2355 E. 89th St., Cleveland, OH 44106 USA (SAN 279-2664) Tel 216-795-7070 ext 228; Fax: 216-795-7073 Do not confuse with New Day Press in Las Vegas, NV
E-mail: editor@newdaypress.com.

New Day Publishing, Inc., *(978-0-9789056; 978-0-9798247)* 26 Bluff Ridge Ct., Greensboro, NC 27455 USA Tel 336-545-1545; Fax: 336-545-1640; Toll Free: 866-763-2977 Do not confuse with companies with the same or similar name in Winston-Salem, NC, Phoenix, AZ, North Miami, FL
E-mail: ateich@newdaypublishing.net
Web site: http://www.newdaypublishing.net.

†**New Directions Publishing Corp.**, *(978-0-8112)* 80 Eighth Ave., New York, NY 10011 USA (SAN 202-9081) Tel 212-255-0230; Fax: 212-255-0231; Toll Free: 800-233-4830
E-mail: nd@ndbooks.com
Web site: http://www.ndpublishing.com
Dist(s): **Continental Bk. Co., Inc.**
Norton, W. W. & Co., Inc.
Penguin Random Hse. Distribution
Penguin Random Hse. LLC
SPD-Small Pr. Distribution; *CIP.*

New Eden Publishing, *(978-0-9882368; 978-0-692-32667-1; 978-0-9980950)* 50513 W Esch Trail, Maricopa, AZ 85139 USA Tel 480-217-0776
E-mail: anitasmail3@gmail.com
Dist(s): **Lulu Pr., Inc.**

New England Bible Sales, *(978-0-9839522; 978-1-941776)* 262 Quaker Rd., Sidney, ME 04330 USA Tel 207-512-2636
E-mail: jptbooks@gmail.com
Web site: www.NewEnglandBibleSales.com.

New England Science Fiction Assn., Inc., *(978-0-915368; 978-1-886778; 978-1-61037)* P.O. Box 809, Framingham, MA 01701-0809 USA (SAN 223-8187) Tel 508-653-7397; Fax: 617-776-3243; *Imprints*: N E S F A Press (NESFA Pr)
E-mail: bowker@nesfa.org
Web site: http://www.nesfa.org/press/.

New Family Pr., *(978-0-9742008)* 389 Belmont St., Suite 105, Oakland, CA 94610 USA Tel 510-866-3984
E-mail: newfamilypress@yahoo.com
Dist(s): **Book Wholesalers, Inc.**

New Forums Pr., *(978-0-913507; 978-1-58107)* Orders Addr.: P.O. Box 876, Stillwater, OK 74076 USA (SAN 285-8673) Tel 405-372-6158; Fax: 405-377-2237; Toll Free: 800-606-3766; Edit Addr.: 1018 S. Lewis, Stillwater, OK 74074 USA
E-mail: dougdollar@provalue.net; design@newforums.com
Web site: http://www.newforums.com
Dist(s): **BookBaby.**

New Frontier Publishing (AUS) *(978-0-9581463; 978-0-9750907; 978-0-9750896; 978-1-921042; 978-0-9579884; 978-1-921928; 978-1-925059; 978-1-925594; 978-1-922326) Dist. by* **Lerner Pub.**

New Generation Publishing (GBR) *Dist. by* **IPG Chicago.**

New Global Publishing, *(978-0-9762292; 978-0-9770043; 978-0-9785609; 978-0-9791748; 978-0-9830940; 978-0-9896334)* Orders Addr.: 2310 SE. Bordeaux Ct., Port Saint Lucie, FL 34952 USA
Web site: http://www.newglobalpublishing.com.

New Growth Pr., *(978-0-9762308; 978-0-9770807; 978-0-9785567; 978-1-934885; 978-1-935273; 978-1-936768; 978-1-938267; 978-1-939946; 978-1-942572; 978-1-945270; 978-1-948130; 978-1-64507)* Orders Addr.: P.O. Box 4485, Greensboro, NC 27404 USA; Edit Addr.: 1301 Carolina St. Suite 124, Greensboro, NC 27401 USA Tel 336-378-7775; Fax: 336-464-2722
E-mail: aprentzas@newgrowthpress.com; gretchen@newgrowthpress.com
Web site: https://newgrowthpress.com
Dist(s): **Cook, David C.**

New Harbinger Pubns., *(978-0-934986; 978-1-57224; 978-1-879237; 978-1-60882; 978-1-62625; 978-1-68403; 978-1-64848)* Orders Addr.: 5720 Shattuck Ave., Oakland, CA 94609 USA (SAN 205-0587) Tel 510-652-2002; 510-652-0215; Fax: 510-652-5472; Toll Free: 800-652-1613; *Imprints*: Impact Publishers (ImpactPubs); Instant Help Books (Instant Help Bks)
E-mail: customerservice@newharbinger.com; patricia.cram@newharbinger.com
Web site: http://www.newharbinger.com
Dist(s): **MyiLibrary**
ebrary, Inc.

New Holland Pubs., Ltd. (GBR) *(978-1-85368; 978-1-85974; 978-1-84330; 978-1-84636; 978-1-84537; 978-1-84773; 978-1-78009) Dist. by* **Sterling.**

New Holland Pubs. Pty, Ltd. (AUS) *(978-1-86436; 978-1-875580; 978-1-876334; 978-1-877069; 978-1-74110; 978-1-921024; 978-1-921073; 978-1-921072; 978-1-921517; 978-1-921580; 978-1-921655; 978-1-74268; 978-1-921740; 978-1-921836; 978-1-76079; 978-1-74257; 978-0-7316-1991-7; 978-0-646-15496-1; 978-1-74337; 978-1-925546) Dist. by* **Tuttle Pubng.**

New Holland Pubs. Pty, Ltd. (AUS) *(978-1-86436; 978-1-875580; 978-1-876334; 978-1-877069; 978-1-74110; 978-1-921024; 978-1-921073; 978-1-921072; 978-1-921517; 978-1-921580; 978-1-921655; 978-1-74257; 978-1-74268; 978-1-921740; 978-1-921836; 978-0-7316-1991-7; 978-0-646-15496-1; -1-74337; 978-1-925546; 978-1-76079) Dist. by* **IPG Chicago.**

New Holland Pubs. Pty, Ltd. (AUS) *(978-1-86436; 978-1-875580; 978-1-876334; 978-1-877069; 978-1-74110; 978-1-921024; 978-1-921073; 978-1-921072; 978-1-921517; 978-1-921580; 978-1-921655; 978-1-74257; 978-1-74268; 978-1-921740; 978-1-921836; 978-0-7316-1991-7; 978-0-646-15496-1; -1-74337; 978-1-925546; 978-1-76079) Dist. by* **Midpt Trade.**

New Hope *See* **Woman's Missionary Union**

New Hope Pubs. *Imprint of* **Iron Stream Media**

New Horizons Christian Ctr., *(978-0-9728532)* 16 Foxbriar Rd., Hilton Head, SC 29926 USA.

New Horizons Pr., *(978-0-9647933)* Orders Addr.: 26 Nottingham Dr., Cartersville, GA 30121 USA; Edit Addr.: 2815 New South Dr., Marietta, GA 30066 USA Do not confuse with companies with the same name in, Lake Mary, FL, Ferrisburgh, VT, Leesburg, VA, Orlando, FL.

New Idea Publishing, *(978-1-7329952)* 102 Church St., Sardis, MS 38666 USA Tel 662-380-6316
E-mail: writingtoliz@gmail.com
Web site: www.lizbarrettfoster.com.

New in Chess *Imprint of* **Continental Sales, Inc.**

New In Chess,Csi *Imprint of* **Continental Sales, Inc.**

New Internationalist Pubns., Ltd. (GBR) *(978-1-869847; 978-0-9540499; 978-1-904456; 978-1-906523; 978-1-78026; 978-1-912408; 978-0-9955900) Dist. by* **Consort Bk Sales.**

New Island Books (IRL) *(978-1-85186; 978-1-874597; 978-1-902602; 978-1-904301; 978-1-905494) Dist. by* **Casemate Pubs.**

New Issues Poetry & Prose, Western Michigan Univ., *(978-0-932826; 978-1-930974; 978-1-936970)* 1903 West Michigan Ave. Western Michigan University, Kalamazoo, MI 49008 USA (SAN 276-6299) Tel 269-387-8185; Fax: 269-387-2562
E-mail: new-issues@wmich.edu
Web site: http://www.wmich.edu/newissues
Dist(s): **Chicago Distribution Ctr.**
SPD-Small Pr. Distribution
Univ. of Chicago Pr. Distribution Clients.

New Kid Safety, *(978-0-9829371)* 4824 Smallwood Rd. Suite 214, Columbia, SC 29223 USA Tel 803-740-0861; Fax: 803-736-0223
E-mail: info@newkidsafety.com
Web site: http://www.newkidsafety.com.

New Leaf Bks. *Imprint of* **WigWam Publishing Co.**

New Leaf Education, Inc. *See* **New Leaf Educ., Inc.**

New Leaf Educ., Inc., *(978-0-9722452; 978-0-9764217; 978-1-933655)* Orders Addr.: P.O. Box 16230, Baltimore, MD 21210 USA Tel 410-467-7835; Fax: 410-951-0419; Edit Addr.: 2050 Rockrose Ave., Baltimore, MD 21211 USA
E-mail: contactus@newleafeducation.com
Web site: http://www.newleafeducation.com.

New Leaf Media, LLC, *(978-1-970072; 978-1-952027; 978-1-955136)* 410 E. Royal Forrest Blvd., Columbus, OH 43214 USA Tel 951-465-4621
E-mail: info@thenewleafmedia.com; simon.lee@thenewleafmedia.com
Web site: www.thenewleafmedia.com.

New Leaf Pr. *Imprint of* **New Leaf Publishing Group**

New Leaf Press *See* **Park Place Pubns.**

New Leaf Press, Incorporated *See* **New Leaf Publishing Group**

New Leaf Publishing Group, *(978-0-89051; 978-0-89221; 978-1-61458; 978-1-68344)* P.O. Box 726, Green Forest, AR 72638 USA (SAN 207-9518) Tel 870-438-5288; Fax: 870-438-5120 Toll Free: 800-643-9535; 800-999-3777; *Imprints*: New Leaf Press (NLP); Master Books (MasterBks) Do not confuse with companies with the same or similar name in Los Angeles, CAStone Mountain, GA
E-mail: nlp@nlpg.com
Web site: http://www.nlpg.com; http://www.masterbooks.com
Dist(s): **MyiLibrary**
Spring Arbor Distributors, Inc.
ebrary, Inc.

New Learning Publishing, *(978-0-9793576)* 123 Wolcott Ave., Rochester, NY 14606 USA (SAN 853-2273) Tel 585-426-9454
E-mail: callen10@rochester.rr.com.

New Library Press LLC, *(978-0-7950)* Orders Addr.: 3419 Chapman Ave. #133, Orange, CA 92869 USA; Edit Addr.: P.O. Box 130, Murrieta, CA 92564 USA
E-mail: newbookorders@gmail.com.

New Life Clarity Publishing, *(978-0-578-43624-1; 978-0-578-44336-2; 978-0-578-46230-1; 978-0-578-46231-8; 978-0-578-51069-9; 978-0-578-51070-5; 978-0-578-54962-0; 978-0-578-54976-7; 978-0-578-55470-9; 978-0-578-55471-6; 978-0-578-57850-7; 978-0-578-57851-4; 978-0-578-59038-7; 978-0-578-59039-4; 978-0-578-59798-0; 978-0-578-59799-7; 978-0-578-77614-9; 978-0-578-77615-6; 978-0-578-77720-7;*

Publisher Name Index

978-0-578-77722-1; 978-1-7361193; 978-0-578-98699-9; 978-0-578-98700-2) 205 W. 300 S., Brigham City, UT 84302 USA Tel 435-695-4456
E-mail: newlifeclaritypublishing@gmail.com
Dist(s): **Ingram Content Group.**

New Life Publishing Hse., *(978-0-9785573)* Orders Addr.: 2835 Cedar Ln., Vienna, VA 22180 USA (SAN 850-8844) Tel 703-942-8440 (phone/fax)
E-mail: garrygenser@me.com.

New Line Bks., *(978-1-57717; 978-1-880908; 978-1-59764)* 245 Eighth Ave., No. 180, New York, NY 10011-1607 USA Toll Free Fax: 888-719-7723; Toll Free: 888-719-7722
E-mail: info@newlinebooks.com
Web site: http://www.newlinebooks.com.

New Millenium Pr., The, *(978-0-9706728)* 311 E. Seventh St., Tama, IA 52339 USA Tel 515-484-2313 Do not confuse with New Millennium Press in Augusta, GA.

New Millennium Bks., *(978-0-9672333)* c/o Gail Mathabane, 901 SW King St. Suite 1006, Portland, OR 97205 USA Tel 503-758-2628 Do not confuse with New Millennium Bks., Petersburg, VA
E-mail: gem@mathabane.com
Web site: http://www.mathabane.com.

New Monic Bks., *(978-0-9652422; 978-0-9840966)* P.O. Box 511314, Punta Gorda, FL 33951-1314 USA Toll Free: 800-741-1295
E-mail: bburchers@earthlink.net
Web site: www.vocabularycartoons.com.

New Montgomery Pr., *(978-0-692-77662-9; 978-0-578-59072-1; 978-0-578-64136-2; 978-1-7347046)* 2422 Dundee Rd, Louisville, KY 40205 USA Tel 502-767-9312
Web site: http://louisrats.wixsite.com/witchrabbit
Dist(s): **CreateSpace Independent Publishing Platform.**

New Native Pr., *(978-1-883197)* P.O. Box 661, Cullowhee, NC 28723 USA Tel 828-293-9237
E-mail: newnativepress@hotmail.com
Dist(s): **SPD-Small Pr. Distribution.**

New Orleans Stories, *(978-0-9758996)* 7401 Slaughter Ln., PMB 5015, Austin, TX 78739 USA Tel 512-923-5015
E-mail: sean@neworleansstories.com
Web site: http://neworleansstories.com
Dist(s): **Forest Sales & Distributing Co.**

New Page Bks. *Imprint of* **Red Wheel/Weiser**

New Paige Pr., LLC, *(978-0-578-19803-3; 978-0-692-09269-9; 978-0-692-15613-1; 978-0-578-48389-4; 978-0-578-49638-2; 978-0-578-52178-7; 978-0-578-53533-3; 978-0-578-53808-2; 978-0-578-55758-8; 978-0-578-59464-4; 978-1-7345980; 979-8-9859623)* 414 Hackensack Ave suite 1126, Hackensack, NJ 07601 USA Tel 917-887-1993
E-mail: jmiletsky@newpaigepress.com
Dist(s): **Independent Pub.**

New Paradigm Bks., *(978-1-892138)* 22491 Vistawood Way, Boca Raton, FL 33428 USA Tel 561-482-5971; Fax: 561-852-8322; Toll Free: 800-808-5179
E-mail: darbyc@earthlink.net
Web site: http://www.newpara.com
Dist(s): **New Leaf Distributing Co., Inc.**

New Paradigm Pubns., *(978-0-615-35944-1; 978-0-9827673; 978-1-7326610)* 12 Cherokee St., Dover, NH 03820 USA (SAN 860-2255) Tel 603-742-4162
E-mail: jim@mastromedia.com; info@newparadigmpublications.com
Web site: http://www.newparadigmpublications.com.

New Poets Series, Incorporated/Chestnut Hills Press/Stonewall *See* **BrickHouse Bks., Inc.**

New Pr., The, *(978-1-56584; 978-1-59558; 978-1-62097)* 38 Greene St., 4th Flr., New York, NY 10013 USA Tel 212 629 8802; Fax: 212 629 8617; Toll Free Fax: 800 458 6515; Toll Free: 800 233 4830
E-mail: newpress@thenewpress.com
Web site: http://www.thenewpress.com
Dist(s): **China Books & Periodicals, Inc.**
Ingram Publisher Services
MyiLibrary
Open Road Integrated Media, Inc.
Two Rivers Distribution
ebrary, Inc.

New Pubns., *(978-0-692-52964-5; 978-1-944156; 978-0-9933594-1-5)* 5 Bradley Rd., Enfield, NH 03585 USA Tel 603-838-6444
E-mail: darin@theinspiragroup.com
Dist(s): **CreateSpace Independent Publishing Platform.**

New Reformation Pubns., *(978-1-945500; 978-1-945978; 978-1-948969; 978-1-956658; 978-1-962654)* Orders Addr.: 24701 Raymond Way, Spc 225, Lake Forest, CA 92630 USA (SAN 990-638X) Tel 949-748-0616
E-mail: ted@1517.org; steve@1517.org; sam@1517.org
Web site: http://www.1517.org
Dist(s): **1517 Media**
Independent Pubs. Group.

New Seasons *Imprint of* **Publications International, Ltd.**

New Shelves Bks., *(978-1-935355; 978-0-692-73191-8)* Orders Addr.: 20 Office Pkwy. No. 126, Pittsford, NY 13534 USA (SAN 857-3700) Tel 518-261-1300; Fax: 518-633-1211; *Imprints:* GraceNotes Press (GraceNotes Pr)
Web site: http://www.newshelves.com.

New Shelves Distribution, 103 Remsen St., Cohoes, NY 12047 USA Tel 518-391-2300; Fax: 518-391-2365
Web site: http://www.newshelvesdistribution.com.

New Song Publishing Co., *(978-0-942925)* Div. of Al Menconi Ministries, Orders Addr.: P.O. Box 131147, Carlsbad, CA 92013 USA (SAN 667-8475) Tel 760-591-4696; Toll Free: 800-786-8742; Edit Addr.: 1635 S. Rancho Santa Fe Rd., Suite 105, San Marcos, CA 92069 USA (SAN 667-8483)
E-mail: patty@almenconi.com; al@almenconi.com
Web site: http://www.AlMenconi.com.

New Star Bks., Ltd. (CAN) *(978-0-919573; 978-0-919888; 978-0-921586; 978-1-55420) Dist. by* **SPD-Small Pr Dist.**

New Strategist Pr., LLC, *(978-0-9628092; 978-1-885070; 978-1-933588; 978-1-935114; 978-1-935775; 978-1-937737; 978-1-940308)* Orders Addr.: P.O. Box 635, Amityville, NY 11701 USA Tel 631-608-8795; Edit Addr.: 26 Austin Ave., Amityville, NY 11701 USA (SAN 860-4002) Tel 800-848-0842; 631-608-8795; Fax: 631-691-1770
E-mail: accounting@newstrategist.com
Web site: http://www.newstrategist.com
Dist(s): **Cengage Gale**
MyiLibrary.

New Sweden Pr., *(978-0-9702646)* 10509 Schmidt Ln., Manor, TX 78653 USA Fax: 512-278-1251 Do not confuse with New Sweden Pr., South Saint Paul, MN
E-mail: shrout@mail.utexas.edu.

New Tribes Mission, Inc., *(978-1-890040; 978-1-61565; 978-0-9968348)* 1000 E. First St., Sanford, FL 32771-1487 USA Tel 407-323-3430; Fax: 407-330-0376; 407-547-2450; Toll Free: 800-321-5375
E-mail: ntm@ntm.org; doug_lotz@ntm.org
Web site: http://www.ntm.org.

New Village Pr., *(978-0-9766054; 978-0-9815593; 978-1-61332)* Div. of Architects/Designers/Planners for Social Responsibility, 400 Central Pk. W, 12B, New York, NY 10025 USA Tel 510-717-3101
E-mail: hello@newvillagepress.net
Web site: http://www.newvillagepress.net
Dist(s): **Consortium Bk. Sales & Distribution**
Ingram Publisher Services
MyiLibrary
New York Univ. Pr.
Two Rivers Distribution.

New Virginia Pubns., *(978-0-9755030)* 9185 Matthew Dr., Manassas Park, VA 20111 USA (SAN 256-0453) Tel 703-928-8316; Fax: 703-331-0577
E-mail: lab49@att.net.

New Vision Entertainment, LLC, *(978-0-9778310)* Orders Addr.: 30 Estuary Trail, Clearwater, FL 33759 USA
E-mail: jim@newvisionentertainment.us.

New Voices Publishing Co., *(978-1-931642)* Div. of KidsTerrain, Inc., P.O. Box 560, Wilmington, MA 01887 USA (SAN 253-9047) Tel 978-658-2131; Fax: 978-988-8833 Do not confuse with companies with the same or similar names in Sarasota, FL, Flushing, NY
E-mail: egilmartin@kidsterrain.com
Web site: http://www.newvoicespublishing.com; http://www.kidsterrain.com.

New Wave Bks. & CD, *(978-0-9727753; 978-0-9741493)* Orders Addr.: 7850 S. Normandie Ave., Apt. 69, Los Angeles, CA 90044 USA; Edit Addr.: 11050 Bryant St., No. 292, Yucaipa, CA 92399 USA.

New Wave Internet Services Incorporated *See* **Healthy Life Pr., Inc.**

New Wave Pubns., *(978-0-9749674; 978-0-9786660; 978-0-9800452; 979-8-9872669; 979-8-9882644)* 1419 New York Ave., Rm 3A, New York, NY 11210-1221 USA Do not confuse with New Wave Publications in Lincoln, NE.

†New Win Publishing, *(978-0-8329; 978-0-87691)* 9682 Telstar Ave., Suite 110, El Monte, CA 91731 USA (SAN 217-1201) Tel 626-448-4422; *Imprints:* Z Health Books (Z Hlth Bks)
E-mail: info@AcademicLearningCompany.com
Web site: http://www.newwinpublishing.com; *CIP.*

†New World Library, *(978-0-931432; 978-0-945934; 978-1-57731; 978-1-880032; 978-1-60868; 978-1-955831)* 14 Pamaron Way, Novato, CA 94949 USA (SAN 211-8777) Tel 415-884-2100; Fax: 415-884-2199; Toll Free: 800-972-6657 (retail orders only) Do not confuse with New World Library Publishing Co., Los Altos, CA
E-mail: escort@nwlib.com
Web site: http://www.newworldlibrary.com
Dist(s): **Brilliance Publishing, Inc.**
Ebsco Publishing
Islander Group
Landmark Audiobooks
New Leaf Distributing Co., Inc.
Publishers Group West (PGW); *CIP.*

New World Press *See* **New World Pr., Inc.**

New World Pr., Inc., *(978-0-9759730)* 5626 Platte Dr., Ellenwood, GA 30294 USA Tel 770-389-2766
E-mail: casa83@aol.com
Web site: http://www.members.aol.com/casa83/nwp.htm.

New World Publishing, *(978-0-9771939; 978-0-9776818; 978-0-9787112; 978-0-9796815; 978-0-9821528)* 4540 State Rd., Cleveland, OH 44109 USA Tel 216-635-1671 Do not confuse with New World Publishing in Riverdale, GA, Scottsdale, AZ and Auburn, CA
E-mail: rkisner5@sbcglobal.net
Web site: http://www.silverquillpoetry.net.

New World Revelation Pr., *(978-0-9762105)* Orders Addr.: P.O. Box 839, Ellijay, GA 30540 USA Tel 706-635-7720; Fax: 706-635-8170
E-mail: fess1944@etcmail.com; office@awakeandlive.org
Web site: http://www.awakeandlive.org
Dist(s): **Ingram Content Group.**

New Worlds Press *See* **Institute for Economic Democracy Pr., Inc.**

New Year Publishing, *(978-0-9671565; 978-0-9760095; 978-0-9799885; 978-1-935547; 978-1-61431)* 144 Diablo Ranch Ct., Danville, CA 94506 USA Tel 925-348-0481; Fax: 425-984-7256 Do not confuse with New Year Publishing in Oceanside, CA
E-mail: dmorris@newyearpublishing.com
Web site: http://www.newyearpublishing.com
Dist(s): **Distributors, The**
Innovative Logistics.

New York Review of Bks., Inc., The, *(978-0-940322; 978-1-59017; 978-1-68137)* 435 Hudson St., 3rd Flr. Suite 300, New York, NY 10014 USA (SAN 220-3448) Tel 212-757-8070; Fax: 212-333-5374; *Imprints:* NYR Children's Collection (NY Rev Child); NYRB Classics (NYRB Class); NYRB Kids (NYRB Kids); Little Bookroom (LittleBkrm)
E-mail: mail@nybooks.com; nyrb@nybooks.com
Web site: http://www.nyrb.com
Dist(s): **Children's Plus, Inc.**
MyiLibrary
Penguin Random Hse. Distribution
Penguin Random Hse. LLC
Random Hse., Inc.

New York Times Educational Publishing *Imprint of* **Rosen Publishing Group, Inc., The**

†New York Univ. Pr., *(978-0-8147; 978-1-4798)* Div. of New York Univ., Orders Addr.: 838 Broadway, 3rd Flr., New York, NY 10003-4812 USA (SAN 658-1293) Tel 212-998-2575; Fax: 212-995-3833; Toll Free: 800-996-6987 (ordering); *Imprints:* NYU Press (NYUPr)
E-mail: orders@nyupress.org
Web site: http://www.nyupress.org
Dist(s): **CreateSpace Independent Publishing Platform**
Ebsco Publishing
ISD
Ingram Publisher Services
JSTOR
Two Rivers Distribution
ebrary, Inc.; *CIP.*

Newburyport Pr., *(978-1-882266)* Orders Addr.: P.O. Box 389, Newburyport, MA 01950 USA Tel 978-465-5751; Fax: 978-462-2043; Toll Free: 800-491-4700 (in Massachusetts only); Edit Addr.: 477 Commerce Blvd., Oldsmar, FL 34677-2809 USA
E-mail: mail@newburyportpress.com
Dist(s): **D.A.P./Distributed Art Pubs.**

Newburyport Press, Incorporated *See* **Newburyport Pr.**

Newcastle Bks., 11923 NE Sumner St. Ste. 808916, Portland, OR 97220 USA Tel 503-568-1586
E-mail: newcastlebooksofficial@gmail.com.

NeWest Pubs., Ltd. (CAN) *(978-0-920316; 978-0-920897; 978-1-896300; 978-1-897126; 978-1-927063; 978-1-988732; 978-1-926455) Dist. by* **Strauss Cnslts.**

NewLife Publications *See* **Campus Crusade for Christ**

Newman Educational Publishers *See* **Newman Educational Publishing Co.**

Newman Educational Publishing Co., *(978-0-938990)* P.O. Box 461, Glen Ellyn, IL 60138 USA (SAN 239-8273) Tel 630-668-7027
E-mail: bizfootstep@aol.com
Web site: http://www.ugrr.illinois.com.

Newman Springs Publishing, Inc., *(978-1-64096; 978-1-64531; 978-1-64801; 978-1-63692; 978-1-63881; 978-1-68498; 979-8-88763; 979-8-89061)* 320 Broad St., Red Bank, NJ 07701 USA Tel 800-305-0243
E-mail: info@newmansprings.com.

Newmark Learning LLC, *(978-1-60719; 978-1-61269; 978-1-4788)* 145 Huguenot St. 8th Flr., New Rochelle, NY 10801 USA Tel 1-877-279-8388; 1-877-280-0375
E-mail: bhaggerty@benchmarkeducation.com
Dist(s): **Follett School Solutions.**

Newmarket for It Bks. *Imprint of* **HarperCollins Pubs.**

†Newmarket Pr., *(978-0-937858; 978-1-55704)* Div. of Newmarket Publishing & Communications Corp., 18 E. 48th St., New York, NY 10017 USA (SAN 217-2585) Tel 212-832-3575; Fax: 212-832-3629; Toll Free Fax: 800-458-6515 (trade orders); Toll Free: 800-233-4830 (trade orders)
E-mail: mailbox@newmarketpress.com
Web site: http://www.newmarketpress.com
Dist(s): **MyiLibrary**
Worldwide Media Service, Inc.
ebrary, Inc.; *CIP.*

Newport Pr., *(978-0-692-08971-2; 978-0-692-09139-5; 978-0-692-09364-1; 978-0-578-36884-9; 978-0-578-38197-8; 979-8-9876778)* 303 Euer Ct, Folsom, CA 95630 USA Tel 916-890-7083
E-mail: wallace95630@yahoo.com
Dist(s): **CreateSpace Independent Publishing Platform.**

Newport Valley Pr, *(978-0-9778602; 978-1-959410)* P.O. Box 32, Solon, IA 52333-0032 USA Tel 319-351-8854.

NewsChannelChurch *See* **Asiana Media**

NewSound, LLC, 81 Demeritt Pl., Waterbury, VT 05676 USA Tel 802-244-7858; Fax: 802-244-1808; Toll Free: 800-342-0295 (wholesale orders)
E-mail: sales@newsoundmusic.com.

NewSouth Bks. *Imprint of* **NewSouth, Inc.**

NewSouth, Inc., *(978-1-58838; 978-1-60306)* P.O. Box 1588, Montgomery, AL 36102-1588 USA Tel 334-834-3556; Fax: 334-834-3557; Toll Free: 866-639-7688; *Imprints:* NewSouth Books (NewSouth AL); Junebug Books (Junebug Bks)
E-mail: info@newsouthbooks.com
Web site: http://www.newsouthbooks.com
Dist(s): **Blair**
Univ. of Georgia Pr.
ebrary, Inc.

NewSouth Publishing (AUS) *(978-0-86840; 978-0-909465; 978-0-908237; 978-1-921410; 978-1-74223; 978-1-74224; 978-0-646-09872-2; 978-1-76117; 978-0-646-27463-8) Dist. by* **IPG Chicago.**

Newton, J. Britt *See* **Twelve Stones Publishing LLC**

Newtonian Golf & Particle Physics, Inc., *(978-0-9725355)* 107 Bordeaux Ln., Cary, NC 27511 USA Tel 919-469-0180
E-mail: sales@saintmulligan.com
Web site: http://www.stmulligan.com.

New-Wolf Moon Publishing, *(978-0-615-34422-5; 978-0-578-44976-0; 978-0-578-44977-7; 978-0-578-63028-1; 978-0-578-63677-1; 978-0-578-65072-2; 978-0-578-67219-9; 978-0-578-73131-5; 978-0-578-80519-1; 978-0-578-83319-4; 978-0-578-92288-1; 978-0-578-38487-0; 979-8-218-12747-3)* 3035 *Washington Blvd., Cleveland Heights, OH 44118 USA Tel 216-371-1668*
E-mail: clemys@sbcglobal.net.

NExcell Consulting, *(978-0-578-23708-4)* 13 Dora St., Stamford, CT 06902 USA Tel 203-570-9844
E-mail: info@nexcellconsulting.com
Web site: www.nexcellconsulting.com.

Next Century Foundation *See* **Next Century Publishing Co.**

Next Century Publishing *See* **Pilot Communications Group, Inc.**

Next Century Publishing Co., *(978-0-9632937)* Orders Addr.: P.O. Box 3020, Carefree, AZ 85377 USA; Edit Addr.: 8548 Silver Saddle Dr., Carefree, AZ 85377 USA Tel 602-488-9600
Dist(s): **Indiana Univ. Pr.**
Ingram Publisher Services
Midpoint Trade Bks., Inc.
Two Rivers Distribution.

Next Chapter Pr., *(978-0-692-92978-0; 978-0-578-37316-4)* 590 Hallmark Dr., Martinsburg, WV 25403 USA Tel 304-261-3876
E-mail: nextchapterpress@gmail.com
Dist(s): **Ingram Content Group.**

Next Chapter Pr., *(978-0-9816265)* P.O. Box 1937, Boca Grande, FL 33921 USA.

Next Generation Pr., *(978-0-9762706; 978-0-9815595)* P.O. Box 603252, Providence, RI 02906 USA Tel 401-247-7665; Fax: 401-245-6428
E-mail: info@nextgenerationpress.org
Web site: http://www.nextgenerationpress.org.

Next Step Magazine, Inc., The, *(978-0-9752926)* 86 W. Main St., Victor, NY 14564 USA Tel 585-742-1260; Fax: 585-742-1263; Toll Free: 800-771-3117
Web site: http://www.nextstepmagazine.com.

Next Step Pr., *(978-1-892876)* Sub. of New Wisdom, Inc., 1201 Delta Glen Ct., Vienna, VA 22182-1320 USA Tel 703-757-7945; Fax: 703-757-7946
E-mail: Wyattwoodsmall@compuserve.com
Web site: http://www.peoplepatterns.com; http://www.mindcoach.org
Dist(s): **Two Rivers Distribution.**

Next Stop Publishing, *(978-1-942144)* 3225 McLeod Dr. Suite 100, Las Vegas, NV 89121 USA Tel 702-998-2837; Fax: 702-989-4627
E-mail: info@nextstopinc.com
Web site: www.nextstopinc.com.

Nextone Inc., *(978-1-64112; 978-1-952019)* 2681 Spruill Ave., North Charleston, SC 29405 USA; *Imprints:* Palmetto Publishing Group (PalmettoPub); Vertel Publishing (VertelPub)
Dist(s): **Independent Pubs. Group.**

Nextpos Corporation *See* **Aldelo Systems Inc.**

Neyborhood Enterprises, *(978-0-578-19088-4; 978-0-578-19089-1; 978-0-9989848)* 178 Maya Ct., St. Augustine, FL 32086 USA.

NFB Publishing, *(978-0-578-04711-9; 978-0-578-08224-0; 978-0-615-48945-2; 978-0-615-51315-7; 978-0-615-54031-3; 978-0-615-56207-0; 978-0-615-58847-6; 978-0-615-59426-2; 978-0-615-61034-4; 978-0-615-62237-8; 978-0-615-62696-3; 978-0-615-66171-1; 978-0-615-66520-7; 978-0-615-66821-5; 978-0-615-70800-3; 978-0-615-70801-0; 978-0-615-72411-9; 978-0-615-72567-3; 978-0-615-75542-7; 978-0-615-75973-9; 978-0-615-78493-9; 978-0-615-78813-5; 978-0-615-81005-8; 978-0-615-81239-7; 978-0-615-82396-6; 978-0-615-83012-4;)* 119 *Dorchester, Buffalo, NY 14213 USA*
E-mail: mark@nfbpublishing.com
Web site: http://nfbpublishing.com
Dist(s): **CreateSpace Independent Publishing Platform**
Ingram Content Group.

Ngbanda, Cecile, *(978-0-578-83189-3; 978-0-578-86958-2)* 27 Wallingford Ave, Wallingford, PA 19086 USA Tel 267-315-4869
E-mail: cecile.rodrigue@gmail.com.

Nhinjo Press *See* **Grow Grit Pr.**

Ni, Kaiyao, *(978-0-692-89319-7)* 713 churchill rd, chester springs, PA 19425 USA Tel 517-420-7984
E-mail: nikaiyao@gmail.com.

Nia & Ntombi Adventures, *(978-0-578-92130-3; 978-0-578-35604-4; 978-0-578-38780-2)* 12217 Westview Dr., Upper Marlboro, MD 20772 USA Tel 240-381-4602
E-mail: youngnia@yahoo.com
Web site: https://niaandntombi.com/.

Nia Publishing Company, Incorporated *See* **Urban Spirit!**

Nicco Boss, LLC, *(978-0-9891635)* 524 Cala Morlanda St., Las Vegas, NV 89138 USA Tel 702-595-4884
E-mail: niccoboss@yahoo.com.

Niccum, Jewels, *(978-0-578-61998-9)* 83 Deerwood Ct., Hudson, WI 54016 USA Tel 715-338-9275
E-mail: jewels@nccmco.com
Web site: jewelsniccum.com.

Nicewood Imagined, *(978-0-9720334)* 6823 NW 52nd Ln., Gainesville, FL 32653 USA Tel 352-271-3306 (phone/fax)
E-mail: nicewoodimagined@yahoo.com
Web site: http://www.macecora.com.

Niche Content Pr., *(978-0-9989987)* 671 Eastern Ct., Ridgewood, NJ 07450 USA Tel 732-687-4725; Fax: 732-687-4725
E-mail: anthony@engineeredcontent.com.

Niche Publishing & Marketing, *(978-0-9726628; 978-1-7347388)* 3310 Bexley Pk. Rd., Columbus, OH 43213 USA Tel 614-390-5748
E-mail: sairapriest@me.com
Web site: http://www.nichepublishing.us; http://www.zenofhoarding.com.

NicheMarket.com *See* **Passion Profit Co., The/NicheMarket**

Nicho The Tiger LLC, *(978-0-9820801)* 43-31 223 St., Bayside, NY 11361 USA Tel 347-853-2694.

icholas Rizzo, *(978-0-9748220)* ; *Imprints:* Executive Performances Publishing (Exec Perform Pubng)
E-mail: nicholasrizzomd@aol.com.

ichols, Brady, *(978-0-692-78919-3)* 605 Capricorn Ln., Madison, WI 53718 USA Tel 608-335-3775
E-mail: bnichols07@hotmail.com.

ichols, frank, *(978-0-692-47926-1; 978-0-692-48464-7)* 27110 ben howard rd, MONROE, WA 98272 USA Tel 727-320-3158.

ick Of Time Media, Inc., *(978-1-940775)* 8661 NW 16th St., Pembroke Pines, FL 33024 USA Tel 888-540-7593
E-mail: Bsamarel33414@yahoo.com
Web site: http://www.nickoftime.us.

Nick The Cat, LLC, *(978-1-936193)* 26541 Dundee Rd., Huntington Woods, MI 48070 USA Tel 313-570-7996
Dist(s): **Baker & Taylor Publisher Services (BTPS).**

Nickel Pr., *(978-1-57122; 978-1-879424)* Div. of S.R. Jacobs & Assocs., 107 Knob Hill Pk. Dr., Reisterstown, MD 21136 USA Do not confuse with Nickel Press, Inc., Enterprise, AL.

Nicksich, Karen M., *(978-0-692-68768-0; 978-0-578-49282-7; 978-0-578-49577-4; 978-0-578-66845-1; 978-0-578-72532-1)* 1641 Brantingham Rd., Richland, WA 99352 USA Tel 509-737-7637
E-mail: emeraldhalo@earthlink.net.

Nicole Publishing, *(978-0-9648278)* Orders Addr.: P.O. Box 557, South Holland, IL 60473-2129 USA Tel 847-339-2739; Fax: 708-339-7357; Edit Addr.: 16416 S. Prairie Ave., South Holland, IL 60473-2129 USA.

Nicole's Story, *(978-0-578-95488-2; 978-0-578-95522-3)* 1506 E 16th Ave, Cordele, GA 31015 USA Tel 305-834-9050
E-mail: simplinicole@yahoo.com
Web site: www.simplinicoletrahan.com.

Nicolin Fields Publishing, Inc., *(978-0-9637077; 978-1-892066)* 861 Lafayette Rd., Unit 2A, Hampton, NH 03842-1232 USA Toll Free: 800-431-1579 (orders only)
E-mail: nfp@nh.ultranet.com
Web site: http://www.nicolinfields.com
Dist(s): **Alpenbooks Pr. LLC**
Peregrine Outfitters
Quality Bks., Inc.
Univ. Pr. of New England.

Nicoll Creations, *(978-0-9747527)* 5608 Evergreen, Midland, MI 48642 USA Tel 989-839-8293
E-mail: hgnicoll@sbcglobal.net.

Nicolo Whimsey Pr., *(978-1-935550)* 14411 Baden Westwood Rd., Brandywine, MD 20613 USA
Dist(s): **Consortium Bk. Sales & Distribution**
MyiLibrary.

Nicolosi, Gaetano, *(978-0-9763828)* 74 W. Fountain Ave., Delaware, OH 43015-1629 USA
E-mail: ciaogaetano@yahoo.com.

Niedermaier, Andrew, *(978-0-578-74515-2)* 110 Livingston St Apt 9T, Brooklyn, NY 11201 USA Tel 619-808-7060
E-mail: agnieder@gmail.com.

NIEJE Production LLC, *(978-0-692-72812-3; 978-0-692-77187-7; 978-0-578-19895-8; 978-0-578-19899-6; 978-0-692-99480-1)* 1002 Attilio Ct, Harrison City, PA 15636 USA Tel 724-640-8877.

Nielsen, Lester *See* **Eaglesquest Publishing**

Nielsen, Tara L., *(978-0-9973881)* 470-795 Emerson Ct, Susanville, CA 96130 USA Tel 530-250-3737
E-mail: nielsen.tara.l@gmail.com.

Nielsen-Bks., *(978-0-9701670)* 11 Greenway Plaza, No. 2700, Houston, TX 77046 USA Tel 713-963-8740; Fax: 713-572-7728
Web site: http://nielsen-books.com.

Night After Night Pubns., Inc. *Imprint of* **Hebler, Michael**

Night Heron Media, *(978-0-9704729; 978-0-9709987; 978-1-931721; 978-1-933979; 978-1-936474; 978-1-939055; 978-1-942945)* Orders Addr.: 2365 Rice Blvd., Suite 202, Houston, TX 77005 USA Tel 713-533-9300; Fax: 713-528-2432 Do not confuse with Breakaway Bks., Halcottsville, NY
E-mail: info@nightheronmedia.org
Web site: www.nightheronmedia.org
Dist(s): **Follett School Solutions**
Independent Pubs. Group
MyiLibrary
Sterling Publishing Co., Inc.
ebrary, Inc.

Night Howl Productions, *(978-0-9702176)* P.O. Box 1, Clay Center, NE 68933 USA Tel 402-984-2566
E-mail: dirtytricksforchicks@yahoo.com
Dist(s): **AK Pr. Distribution.**

Night Light Pubns., LLC, *(978-0-9740418; 978-0-9743785)* 6101 E. Wethersfield Rd., Scottsdale, AZ 85254 USA Tel 480-948-2607; Fax: 480-948-9921
E-mail: reg@nightlightpublications.com
Web site: http://www.nightlightpublications.com.

Night Raven Publishing, *(978-0-9755984)* 18221 Mandarin Lane. Ste A, Yorba Linda, CA 92886 USA
E-mail: Julie@JulieBelmont.com
Web site: www.JulieBelmont.com.

Night Sky Bks., *(978-1-59014)* Div. of North-South Books, Inc., 11 E. 26th St., 17th Flr., New York, NY 10010 USA Tel 212-706-4545; Fax: 212-706-4546; Toll Free: 800-282-8257 Do not confuse with companies with the same name in Santa Fe, NM
E-mail: nightsky@northsouth.com
Web site: http://www.northsouth.com
Dist(s): **Lectorum Pubns., Inc.**

Night Sky, LLC, *(978-0-9888901)* 4 Buckskin Heights Dr., Danbury, CT 06811 USA Tel 203-826-9690
E-mail: jrivot@yahoo.com.

Nightengale Pr., *(978-0-9743348; 978-0-9761289; 978-1-933449; 978-1-935993; 978-1-945257)* Div. of Nightengale Entertainment LLC, 3743 Brookwood Dr., Cookeville, TN 38501 USA Tel 931-854-1390
E-mail: publisher@nightengalepress.com
Web site: http://www.nightengalepress.com
Dist(s): **Ingram Bk. Co.**

Nightlight Pr., *(978-0-9982992; 978-1-947607)* Orders Addr.: P.O. Box 8345, Miami, FL 33166 USA
E-mail: hpancakeslab@gmail.com.

NIIS Publishing, *(978-0-9745013; 978-0-615-11294-7)* 7349 Milliken, No. 140164, Rancho Cucamonga, CA 91730 USA.

Nile Publishing, *(978-0-9768485)* 213 Hancock St., Brooklyn, NY 11216 USA Tel 718-810-1148 Do not confuse with Nile PUblishing in Cincinnati, OH
E-mail: wale1@hotmail.com.

Nilsson Media, *(978-0-9724771)* Box 1371, Brentwood, TN 37024-1371 USA Tel 615-776-2593; Fax: 615-776-3193; Toll Free: 888-801-5190; *Imprints:* Nilsson, Troy (Troy Nilsson)
E-mail: books@nilssonmedia.org
Web site: http://www.nilssonmedia.com.

Nilsson, Troy *Imprint of* **Nilsson Media**

Nimble Bks. LLC, *(978-0-9754479; 978-0-9765406; 978-0-9777424; 978-0-9788138; 978-0-9799205; 978-1-934840; 978-1-60888)* 2846 S Knightsbridge Cir, Ann Arbor, MI 48105-9288 USA Tel 734-545-5369
E-mail: wfz@nimblebooks.com
Web site: http://www.nimblebooks.com
Dist(s): **Smashwords.**

Nimbus Publishing, Ltd. (CAN) *(978-0-919380; 978-0-920852; 978-0-921054; 978-1-55109; 978-1-77108) Dist. by* **Orca Bk Pub.**

Nimbus Publishing, Ltd. (CAN) *(978-0-919380; 978-0-920852; 978-0-921054; 978-1-55109; 978-1-77108) Dist. by* **BTPS.**

Nine Petal Pr., *(978-0-9984256; 979-8-9871264)* 702 Keywe Pl., Duncanville, TX 75116 USA Tel 214-226-9352
E-mail: unity9@sbcglobal.net
Web site: www.NinePetalPress.com.

NineStar Pr., *(978-1-945952; 978-1-947139; 978-1-947904; 978-1-948608; 978-1-949340; 978-1-949909; 978-1-950412; 978-1-951057; 978-1-951880; 978-1-64890)* P.O. Box 91792, Albuquerque, NM 87199 USA Tel 505-217-4491
E-mail: kat@ninestarpress.com
Web site: www.ninestarpress.com.

Ninety & Nine Records *See* **Blooming Twig Books LLC**

Ninos Aprenden Ingles Corp., *(978-1-934665)* 15476 NW 77 Ct., No. 360, Miami Lakes, FL 33016 USA (SAN 854-249X)
E-mail: ar@childrenlearninglanguages.com
Web site: http://www.ChildrenLearningLanguages.com.

Ninth Planet Pr., *(978-0-615-41386-0; 978-0-615-54486-1; 978-0-615-60901-0; 978-0-692-26010-4; 978-0-692-41572-6; 978-0-9983351)* 402 Buckeye Trail, Austin, TX 78746 USA Tel 512-330-1726; Fax: 512-289-0595; 909 Live Oak Ridge Rd., Austin, TX 78746
E-mail: bmccandless@austin.rr.com.

Nissi Publications *See* **Nissi Publishing, Inc.**

Nissi Publishing, Inc., *(978-0-944372)* 1404 Summer Ridge Ct., Roanoke, TX 76262 USA (SAN 243-4148) Tel 817-337-8681
E-mail: dfreeman@nissipub.com
Web site: http://www.nissipub.com.

Nistraman Consulting, *(978-0-9706387)* P.O. Box 1314, Brookline, MA 02446 USA
E-mail: alex_belenky@lycos.com.

NITALUSA PUBLISHING@DISTRIBUTION, *(978-0-9787631)* 1809 Country CT, Garland, TX 75040 USA Tel 469-569-2684
Web site: http://www.higherpowerpublishing.biz
Dist(s): **Ingram Content Group.**

Nithyananda Univ., *(978-0-9790806; 978-1-934364; 978-1-60607)* 9720 Central Ave., Montclair, CA 91763 USA Tel 909-625-1400
E-mail: galleriaorders@yahoo.com
Web site: http://www.lifeblissfoundation.org.

Nithyananda Yoga & Meditation University *See* **Nithyananda Univ.**

Niyah Net *See* **Niyah Pr.**

Niyah Pr., *(978-0-9822215; 978-1-945873)* 8050 W. Pkwy., Detroit, MI 48239 USA
E-mail: zarinahelamin@gmail.com
Dist(s): **Ingram Content Group.**

NJL College Preparation, *(978-0-9753913)* 880 Willis Ave., Albertson, NY 11507 USA Tel 516-741-3550
E-mail: njlcp@aol.com
Dist(s): **Topical Review Bk Co., Inc.**

NJM *See* **Allen-Ayers Bks.**

nJoy Bks., *(978-0-9769959)* Orders Addr.: 18 S. 2nd St., Madison, WI 53704 USA
E-mail: office@njoybooks.com
Web site: http://www.njoybooks.com.

NK nPrint *See* **nVision Publishing**

NK Pubns., *(978-0-9705100; 978-0-9841610)* P.O. Box 1735, New York, NY 10101-1735 USA
E-mail: nkatsoris@aol.com
Dist(s): **Michigan State Univ. Pr.**

NKB Bks. LLC, *(978-0-9988101; 978-1-7331064)* 1415 23rd St., Canyon, TX 79015 USA Tel 806-655-4046; Fax: 806-655-5558
E-mail: nkbbooksllc@gmail.com; natalie@nataliebright.com
Web site: nataliebright.com.

NLAlex Publishing *See* **Joe Girl Ink**

NLM ENTERPRISES LLC, *(978-1-7372288)* 740 Dragonfly Dr, Myrtle Beach, SC 29579 USA Tel 843-446-8287
E-mail: nikkimerrill.author@gmail.com.

No Agenda Publishing, LLC, *(978-1-7320058)* 7594 Wolftever TRL, Ooltewah, TN 37363 USA Tel 423-619-0917
E-mail: april.royer@icloud.com.

No Doubt Imagination, *(978-0-692-11422-3)* 2055 N. Redding Way, Upland, CA 91784 USA Tel 909-200-8034
E-mail: sargent25@roadrunner.com.

No Dream Too Big LLC, *(978-0-9745717; 978-0-9838415)* Div. of AsAMan Thinketh.net LLC, P.O. Box 1220, Melrose, FL 32666 USA
E-mail: ebooks@asamanthinketh.net
Web site: http://www.asamanthinketh.net
Dist(s): **CreateSpace Independent Publishing Platform.**

No Frills Buffalo *See* **NFB Publishing**

No Greater Joy Ministries, Inc., *(978-1-892112; 978-0-9786372; 978-1-934794; 978-1-935370; 978-1-61644)* 1000 Pearl Rd., Pleasantville, TN 37033 USA (SAN 914-5958) Toll Free: 866-292-9936
E-mail: ngj@nogreaterjoy.org; cjoyner@nogreaterjoy.org
Web site: http://www.nogreaterjoy.org
Dist(s): **Baker & Taylor Publisher Services (BTPS)**
Follett School Solutions
MyiLibrary
Send The Light Distribution LLC
ebrary, Inc.

No Limits Communications, *(978-0-9712842)* P.O. Box 220, Horsham, PA 19044 USA Tel 215-675-9133; Fax: 215-675-9376.

No Limitz Productions, Inc., *(978-0-9766942)* 3257 Primera Ave., Los Angeles, CA 90068 USA Tel 323-876-7149
E-mail: nolimitz@aol.com
Web site: http://www.suzannelopez.com.

No Name, *(978-1-7323493)* 5926 Cove Point Ct, Columbus, OH 43228 USA Tel 614-572-7409
E-mail: salley.ayad@gmail.com.

No Starch Pr., Inc., *(978-1-886411; 978-1-59327; 978-1-7185)* 555 De Haro St., Suite 250, San Francisco, CA 94107 USA Tel 415-863-9900; Fax: 415-863-9950; Toll Free: 800-420-7240; 245 8th St., San Francisco, CA 94103 Tel 415-863-9900; Fax: 415-863-9950; Toll Free Fax: 800-420-7240 Do not confuse with No Starch Pr., in Berkeley, CA
E-mail: bill@nostarch.com; business@nostarch.com
Web site: https://nostarch.com
Dist(s): **Wiley & Sons, Inc., John**
Children's Plus, Inc.
Ebsco Publishing
Follett School Solutions
O'Reilly Media, Inc.
Penguin Random Hse. Distribution
Penguin Random Hse. LLC.

No Voice Left Behind Publishing, *(978-0-9773513)* P.O. Box 1109, Ceres, CA 95307 USA Tel 209-968-3425
E-mail: fernando_pena@sbcglobal.net
Web site: http://www.nvlb.net.

N.O.A.H Bks., *(978-0-615-59068-4; 978-0-9859770; 979-8-9850636)* 1915 Quarterpath Dr., Richmond, TX 77406 USA Tel 832-769-1166; Fax: 713-458-4473; 1915 Quarterpath Dr., Richmond, TX 77406
E-mail: jaiden01@windstream.net; cheryl.hill1914@gmail.com
Web site: http://www.empoweringchildrentoread.blogspot.com/.

Noah Educational Projects *See* **N.O.A.H Bks.**

Noah Lukeman *Imprint of* **Morgan Rice Bks.**

Noble Hero Pr., *(978-0-9768410)* 3754 Salem Walk, No. A1, Northbrook, IL 60062 USA
E-mail: mike@nobleheropress.com
Web site: http://www.nobleheropress.com.

Noble, Holly, *(978-0-578-73048-6)* 1812 Spanish Trail, Plano, TX 75023 USA Tel 450-602-3322
E-mail: holly.h.noble@gmail.com.

Noble, John A. Collection *See* **Noble Maritime Collection, The**

†Noble Maritime Collection, The, *(978-0-9623017)* 1000 Richmond Terr., Staten Island, NY 10301-1114 USA Tel 718-447-6490
E-mail: erinurban@earthlink.net; *CIP.*

Noble Publishing Assocs., *(978-0-923463; 978-1-56857)* 1300 NE 131st Cir., Vancouver, WA 98685 USA (SAN 251-656X) Tel 360-258-3119; Fax: 360-258-3122; Toll Free: 800-225-5259; 1300 NE 131st St., Vancouver, WA 98685-3164
E-mail: noblebooks@noblepublishing.com
Web site: http://www.noblepublishing.com.

Noble Success Publishing, *(978-0-578-21278-4; 978-0-578-44910-4)* 2048 Igou Crossing Dr., Chattanooga, TN 37421 USA Tel 423-508-9642
E-mail: drdb@noblesuccessllc.com
Web site: johncmaxwellgroup.com/davidbanks.

Noble Washitaw Mothers Olmec Muur Trust *See* **Ma"at American Aborigine Tribal Nation**

Nobrow Ltd. (GBR) *(978-1-907704; 978-0-9562135; 978-1-910620) Dist. by* **Peng Rand Hse.**

Nodin Pr., *(978-0-931714; 978-1-932472; 978-1-935666; 978-1-947237)* c/o The Bookmen, Inc., 530 N. Third St., Suite 120, Minneapolis, MN 55401 USA (SAN 204-398X) Tel 612-333-6300; Fax: 612-333-6303
Dist(s): **Adventure Pubns.**
Itasca Bks.
Publishers Group West (PGW).

Noel, Jaren, *(978-0-9993015)* 8941 Miami St, Unit 2, Omaha, NE 68134 USA Tel 308-870-1157; Fax: 308-870-1157; *Imprints:* Contemporary Fiction (MYD_ FICTION)
E-mail: jaren.zimmerman@gmail.com.

Noesis, Inc., *(978-0-9742091)* 10530 Linden Lake Plaza, Manassas, VA 20109 USA Tel 703-369-2924; Fax: 703-392-7978
E-mail: fstilley@noesis-inc.com
Web site: http://www.noesis-inc.com/drydockhistory.

Noesis Publishing, *(978-0-9794328)* Div. of Noesis Communications International, Orders Addr.: 4425 S., Mo Pac Expway Suite 600, Austin, TX 78735 USA Tel 512-891-6100 Greenleaf Book Group; Edit Addr.: 5777 W. Century Blvd., Suite 200, Los Angeles, CA 90045 USA Tel 310-645-5604 Noesis Publishing; 512-891-6100 Greenleaf Book Group; Fax: 310-215-3018 Noesis Publishing
E-mail: diana@cmsbiz.com; candice@greenleafbookgroup.com
Web site: http://noesispublishing.com; http://www.greenleafbookgroup.com; http://www.kandide.com
Dist(s): **Greenleaf Book Group.**

Noguer y Caralt Editores, S. A. (ESP) *(978-84-217; 978-84-279) Dist. by* **Lectorum Pubns.**

Noguera, Ivette Garcia (ESP) *(978-84-87825; 978-84-89825; 978-84-921332; 978-84-938175; 978-84-939339; 978-84-941224; 978-84-942949; 978-84-944379; 978-84-947589) Dist. by* **Lectorum Pubns.**

Noixia's Reading Circle, *(978-0-9749122)* 8002 Avenida Navidad, San Diego, CA 92122 USA Tel 858-550-9519
E-mail: contact@noixia.com
Web site: http://www.noixia.com.

Nolia Crown Prods., *(978-0-9767047)* P.O. Box 150682, Arlington, TX 76015 USA
E-mail: noliacrown@gmail.com
Web site: http://www.noliacrown.com.

Noller, Gail, *(978-0-9744877)* 1416 Oakwood Dr., Anoka, MN 55303 USA Tel 763-427-6897
E-mail: nolle005@tc.umn.edu.

Nomad Pr., *(978-0-9659258; 978-0-9722026; 978-0-9749344; 978-0-9771294; 978-0-9785037; 978-0-9792268; 978-1-934670; 978-1-936313; 978-1-936749; 978-1-61930; 978-1-64741)* Div. of Nomad Communications, Inc., 2456 Christian St., White River Junction, VT 05001 USA Tel 802-649-1995; Fax: 802-649-2667 Do not confuse with Nomad Pr., Clewiston, FL, Fort Collins, CO
E-mail: rachel@nomadcom.com; rachel@nomadpress.net
Web site: http://www.nomadpress.net
Dist(s): **Baker & Taylor Publisher Services (BTPS)**
Children's Plus, Inc.
Ebsco Publishing
Follett School Solutions
Legato Pubs. Group
MyiLibrary
Publishers Group West (PGW)
Perseus Bks. Group.

Non Pareil Bks. *Imprint of* **Godine, David R. Pub.**

Nona Design, *(978-1-7327917; 978-1-951640)* 26828 Maple Valley Hwy., Maple Valley, WA 98038 USA Tel 253-459-2575
E-mail: nona@nona.design.

none *See* **Barbara Browning**

NONE, *(978-1-7365728)* 3338 FRAZIER Rd., KNOXVILLE, TN 37914 USA Tel 865-304-5501
E-mail: sdnichols63@gmail.com.

none, *(978-0-578-50776-7; 978-0-578-51922-7)* 10569 131st, Queens, NY 11419 USA Tel 347-592-6055
E-mail: maharajnathalie@gmail.com.

none, *(978-1-949684)* 1213 Wea Ave., Lafayette, IN 47905-1880 USA Tel 765-532-3535
E-mail: gunzai57@gmail.com
Web site: mellygreywriter/weebly.

Nonetheless Pr., *(978-1-932053)* 20332 W. 98th St., Lenexa, KS 66220-2650 USA Tel 913-254-7266; Fax: 913-393-3245
E-mail: mschutte@nonethelesspress.com
Web site: http://www.nonethelesspress.com; http://www.lookingglasspress.com
Dist(s): **Bookazine Co., Inc.**
Brodart Co.
Greenleaf Book Group
Midwest Library Service.

Non-ISBN Publisher, 630 Central Ave., New Providence, NJ 07974 USA.

Nonsuch Media Pte. Ltd., *(978-1-954145; 979-8-89214)* 68 Circular Road, No. 02-01, Singapore, 049422 SGP
E-mail: ao@nonsuchmedia.com; nec168@gmail.com.

Noodle Holdings LLC, *(978-0-615-41968-8)* Rood Hill Farm 53 Rood Hill Rd., Sandisfield, MA 01255 USA
E-mail: hoover205@gmail.com
Web site: http://www.stevehooverauthor.com.

Noodle Pr., *(978-0-9601022)* Orders Addr.: P.O. Box 42542, Washington, DC 20015 USA; Edit Addr.: P.O. Box 42542, Washington, DC 20015 USA (SAN 208-7871) Tel 202-363-5078; Fax: 202-364-0090
E-mail: Noodleprss@aol.com.

NOOK Press *See* **Barnes & Noble Pr.**

Noonan, Stefanie, *(978-0-9997378)* 25093 Grange Hall Rd., Philomath, OR 97370 USA Tel 541-760-6703
E-mail: stefnoonan@msn.com.

Nooni Publishing, *(978-0-9796832)* 1211 Garden Lake Dr., Riverdale, GA 30296 USA
E-mail: Nooni-pub@hotmail.com.

Noor Foundation-International, *(978-0-9632067; 978-0-9766972; 978-1-942043)* P.O. Box 758, Hockessin, DE 19707 USA (SAN 854-3712) Tel 302-234-8860; Fax: 208-279-5341; Toll Free: 888-937-2665; 249 Peoples Way, Hockessin, DE 19707
E-mail: cyrusomar@hotmail.com; alnoorfoundation@hotmail.com
Web site: http://www.islamusa.org.

Noorart, Inc., *(978-1-933269)* 1356 Exchange Dr., Richardson, TX 75081 USA; 6126 Clear Creek Dr., Garland, TX 75044
E-mail: ammar@noorart.com
Web site: http://www.noorart.com.

Noorart, Incorporated *See* **Noorart, Inc.**

NooVoo Publishing LLC, *(978-0-9767513)* 28257 Thornybrae, Farmington Hills, MI 48331 USA Tel 248-762-4858
E-mail: glennrader@noovoo.com.

Nop, Mony Publishing, *(978-0-9997918)* 1926 Railroad Ave. No. 102, Livermore, CA 94550 USA Tel 925-575-1602
E-mail: mony@monynop.com.

Nora Hse., *(978-0-9752958)* 9122 White Eagle Ct., Raleigh, NC 27617 USA
E-mail: oren2a@yahoo.com.

Norcor Enterprises, (*978-0-9622469*) 6147 N. Sheridan Rd., Chicago, IL 60660 USA Tel 773-743-6792
E-mail: norcorent@juno.com.

Nordic Studies Pr., (*978-0-9772714*) 5226 N. Sawyer, Chicago, IL 60625-4716 USA (SAN 257-1498) Tel 773-610-4283
E-mail: cpeterson@igc.org
Web site: http://www.nordicstudiespress.com.

Nordikgirl, (*978-0-9997737*) 14192 209th St. N., Scandia, MN 55073 USA Tel 651-491-5151; Fax: 651-491-5151
E-mail: ccolonna15@gmail.com
Web site: www.nordikgirl.com.

Nordman, Michael W., (*978-0-9998933*) N8941 Bootz Bluff Rd., Tomahawk, WI 54487 USA Tel 715-966-1082; 4072 Champeau Rd., New Franken, WI 54229 Tel 715-966-1082
E-mail: justmikenord@prodigy.net.

Nordskog Publishing, Inc., (*978-0-9796736; 978-0-9824929; 978-0-9827074; 978-0-9831957; 978-0-9882976; 978-0-9903774; 978-0-9974221; 978-1-946497*) Orders Addr.: 4562 Westinghouse St. Suite E., Ventura, CA 93003 USA; Edit Addr.: 2716 Sailor Ave., Ventura, CA 93001 USA
E-mail: Jerry@NordskogPublishing.com; staff@nordskogpublication.com
Web site: http://www.NordskogPublishing.com.

Norfleet Pr., Inc., (*978-0-9649934*) 1 Gracie Ter. Apt. 4C, New York, NY 10028-7956 USA
Dist(s): **Continental Enterprises Group, Inc. (CEG)**
North Country Bks., Inc.

Norgannan Publishing LLC, (*978-0-692-63209-3; 978-0-692-65539-9; 978-0-692-08818-0; 978-1-7323676*)
Web site: http://www.norgannanpublishing.com
Dist(s): **CreateSpace Independent Publishing Platform.**

Norilana Bks., (*978-1-934169; 978-1-934648; 978-1-60762*) Orders Addr.: P.O. Box 224, Highgate Center, VT 05459-0224 USA (SAN 851-8556); Edit Addr.: 145 Dubois Dr., Highgate Center, VT 05459-0224 USA; *Imprints:* YA Angst (YA Angst)
E-mail: service@norilana.com; vnazarian@gmail.com
Web site: http://www.norilana.com/
Dist(s): **Smashwords.**

NORKY AMERICA, (*978-0-9769209*) Orders Addr.: 4712 Admiralty Way, No. 614, Marina Del Rey, CA 90292 USA Tel 310-985-3039
Web site: http://www.norky.com.

Norma Editorial, S.A. (ESP) (*978-84-7904; 978-84-8431; 978-84-85475; 978-84-86595; 978-84-679*) *Dist. by* **IPG Chicago.**

Norma Editorial, S.A. (ESP) (*978-84-7904; 978-84-8431; 978-84-85475; 978-84-86595; 978-84-679*) *Dist. by* **D C D.**

Norma S.A. (COL) (*978-958-04; 978-958-45*) *Dist. by* **Continental Bk.**

Norma S.A. (COL) (*978-958-04; 978-958-45*) *Dist. by* **AIMS Intl.**

Norma S.A. (COL) (*978-958-04; 978-958-45*) *Dist. by* **Distr Norma.**

Norma S.A. (COL) (*978-958-04; 978-958-45*) *Dist. by* **Lectorum Pubns.**

Normally Unstable, (*978-1-7364248*) 5851 W. 88th St., los angeles, CA 90045 USA Tel 909-835-3786
E-mail: dmalonejr22@gmail.com.

Norman & Globus, Inc., (*978-1-886978*) Orders Addr.: P.O. Box 20533, El Sobrante, CA 94803 USA; Edit Addr.: 4130 Lakeside Dr., San Pablo, CA 94806-1941 USA
E-mail: info@electrowiz.com; drpenny@sciencewiz.com
Web site: http://www.electrowiz.com; http://www.sciencewiz.com.

Norman Bks., (*978-0-9708617*) 900 Euclid St., Suite 302, Santa Monica, CA 90403 USA Tel 310-899-9310; Fax: 503-961-9523
E-mail: normanbooks411@gmail.com
Web site: http://www.normanbooks.com
Dist(s): **Book Wholesalers, Inc.**
Follett School Solutions
Quality Bks., Inc.
Sunbelt Pubns., Inc.

Norman, Tyrone A., (*978-0-692-09248-4*) 4828 Skyway, Fair Oaks, CA 95628 USA Tel 916-257-3461
E-mail: mrsteppingstone@yahoo.com
Dist(s): **CreateSpace Independent Publishing Platform.**

Normandy's Bright Ideas, (*978-0-615-32843-0; 978-0-578-10096-8; 978-0-9859329; 978-0-9979349; 979-8-9855654*) 5704 Dalden Dr., Tampa, FL 33617 USA Tel 813-985-6089.

Norris-Jones, Charmaine *See* **Triddias**

Nortex Pr. *Imprint of* **Eakin Pr.**

North American International, (*978-0-88265*) P.O. Box 251, Penn Laird, VA 22846 USA (SAN 202-9200) Tel 540-435-6454; *Imprints:* Fine Art Editions (Fine Art Edtns)
E-mail: naibooks@yahoo.com; naibooks@gmail.com
Web site: http://erniehippo.ecrater.com; http://finekidsbooks.webs.com; http://kidsbook.zoomshare.com.

North American Mission Board, SBC, (*978-1-59312*) 4200 North Point Pkwy, Alpharetta, GA 30022-4176 USA Tel 770-410-6100; Fax: 770-410-6051; Toll Free: 866-407-6262
E-mail: marketing@namb.net
Web site: http://www.namb.net.

North American Vexillological Assoc. (NAVA), (*978-0-9747728*) 101 Belair Dr., New Milford, CT 06776 USA
E-mail: tmealf@aol.com
Web site: http://www.nava.org.

†North Atlantic Bks., (*978-0-913028; 978-0-938190; 978-0-942941; 978-1-55643; 978-1-883319; 978-1-58394; 978-1-62317; 979-8-88984*) Div. of The Society of the Study of Native Art & Science, Orders Addr.: P.O. Box 12327, Berkeley, CA 94712 USA (SAN 203-1655) Fax: 510-559-8277; Toll Free: 800-337-2665 (orders only); Edit Addr.: 1435 4th St. # A, Berkeley, CA 94710-1335 USA; 2526 Martin Luther King Jr. Way, Berkeley, CA 94704 Tel 510-549-4270; Fax: 510-549-4276; *Imprints:* Frog Limited (Frog Ltd); Frog Books (FrogBks); Frog Children's Books (FrogChld)
E-mail: orders@northatlanticbooks.com
Web site: http://www.northatlanticbooks.com
Dist(s): **China Books & Periodicals, Inc.**
MyiLibrary
Nutri-Bks. Corp.
Penguin Random Hse. Distribution
Penguin Random Hse. LLC
Random Hse., Inc.
SPD-Small Pr. Distribution; *CIP.*

North Bay Bks., (*978-0-9725200; 978-0-9749098*) Orders Addr.: P.O. Box 21234, El Sobrante, CA 94820-1234 USA Tel 510-758-4276; Fax: 510-758-4659; Toll Free: 800-870-3194; Edit Addr.: 3110 Whitecliff Ct., Richmond, CA 94803 USA Do not confuse with companies with the same name in El Sobrante, CA, Richmond, CA
Web site: www.northbaybooks.com.

North Bks., (*978-0-939495; 978-1-58287*) P.O. Box 1277, Wickford, RI 02852 USA (SAN 663-4052) Tel 401-294-3682; Fax: 401-294-9491
E-mail: north@ids.net.

North Bound Bks., (*978-0-9759089*) P.O. Box 63, Norwich, VT 05055 USA.

North Cape Pubns., Inc., (*978-1-882391*) P.O. Box 1027, Tustin, CA 92781 USA Tel 714-832-3621; Fax: 714-832-5302; Toll Free: 800-745-9714
E-mail: ncape@ix.netcom.com
Web site: http://www.northcapepubs.com.

North Carolina 4H, NC State Extension Campus Box 7602, Raleigh, NC 27695 USA
Dist(s): **Univ. of North Carolina Pr.**

North Carolina Division of Archives & History *See* **North Carolina Office of Archives & History**

North Carolina Office of Archives & History, (*978-0-86526*) Orders Addr.: Historical Publications Section 4622 Mail Service Ctr., Raleigh, NC 27699-4622 USA (SAN 203-7246) Tel 919-733-7442 ext. 0; Fax: 919-733-1439
Web site: http://www.ncpublications.com
Dist(s): **Univ. of North Carolina Pr.**

North Carolina State Univ. Humanities Extension Pubns./Program, (*978-1-881507; 978-1-885647*) North Carolina State Univ., Box 8101 026 Winston Hall, Raleigh, NC 27695 USA Tel 919-515-1334; Fax: 919-515-8738
Web site: http://www.ncsu.edu/chass/extension.

North Carolina Symphony Society, Inc., The, (*978-0-9618952*) 4361 Lassiter At North Hills A. Ste. 105, Raleigh, NC 27609-5781 USA (SAN 242-5378).

†North Country Bks., Inc., (*978-0-925168; 978-0-932052; 978-0-9601158; 978-1-59531*) 220 Lafayette Street, Utica, NY 13502 USA (SAN 110-828X) Tel 315-735-4877; Fax: (315) 738-4342
E-mail: ncbooks@verizon.net
Web site: http://www.northcountrybooks.com
Dist(s): **Rowman & Littlefield Publishers, Inc.**
Rowman & Littlefield Unlimited Model; *CIP.*

North Country Pr., (*978-0-945980; 978-1-943424*) P.O. Box 501, Unity, ME 04988 USA (SAN 247-9680) Tel 207-948-2208; Fax: 207-948-9000 Do not confuse with North Country Pr., White Cloud, MI
E-mail: info@northcountrypress.com
Web site: http://www.northcountrypress.com.

North Cover Prs, (*978-0-578-18862-1*) 7 North Cover Rd, Old Saybrook, CT 06475 USA.

North Cover Press *See* **North Cover Prs**

North Dakota Center for Distance Education *See* **State Historical Society of North Dakota**

North Dakota State University, Institute for Regional Studies *See* **North Dakota State Uiv. Pr.**

North Dakota State Univ. Libraries, (*978-0-9629777; 978-1-891193*) Orders Addr.: NDSU Dept 2080, Fargo, ND 58105-6050 USA Tel 701-231-8416; Fax: 701-231-7138; Edit Addr.: 1201 Albrecht Blvd., Fargo, ND 58105 USA
E-mail: michael.miller@ndsu.edu; jeremy.kopp@ndsu.edu
Web site: http://library.ndsu.edu/grhc/.

North Dakota State Uiv. Pr., (*978-0-911042; 978-1-946163*) Div. of North Dakota Institute for Regional Studies, Orders Addr.: 1210 Albrecht Blvd., Fargo, ND 58108-6050 USA (SAN 203-1574) Tel 701-231-6848; Fax: 701-231-1047
E-mail: suzzanne.kelley@ndsu.edu; kelley@kindredhouse.net; ndsu.press@ndsu.edu
Web site: www.ndsupress.org; https://www.facebook.com/NDSUPress/.

North Gap Publishing, (*978-0-9677379*) 636 Golden Hill St., Cheyenne, WY 82009 USA Tel 307-778-8761
E-mail: twalkwyo@hotmail.com.

North Loop Pr. *Imprint of* **Salem Author Services**

North Node LLC, (*978-1-7340857*) 2121 Newcastle Ave., Cardiff by the Sea, CA 92007 USA Tel 760-330-0947
E-mail: cee@ceehunt.com
Web site: www.northnodellc.com.

North Pole Chronicles, (*978-0-9636442*) 7306 Park Ln., Dallas, TX 75225-2462 USA Tel 214-696-1717; Fax: 214-696-5288.

North Pole Pr., (*978-0-9787129; 978-0-9992977; 978-1-7323782; 978-1-7324958; 978-1-7336761*) 432 Ruth Riggs Way, Maryville, TN 37801 USA Tel 865-207-2703
E-mail: tennesseesanta@gmail.com; mary@thenorthpolepress.com; joe@thenorthpolepress.com
Web site: http://thenorthpolepress.com; http://northpolepress.com.

North River Press, Incorporated *See* **North River Pr. Publishing Corp., The**

†North River Pr. Publishing Corp., The, (*978-0-88427*) P.O. Box 567, Great Barrington, MA 01230 USA (SAN 202-1048) Tel 413-528-0034 (phone/fax); Toll Free Fax: 800-266-5329; Toll Free: 800-486-2665
E-mail: agallagher@northriverpress.com
Web site: http://www.northriverpress.com; *CIP.*

North Shore Records, Inc., (*978-0-9746229*) Orders Addr.: P.O. Box 1035, Los Alamos, CA 93440 USA (SAN 257-3733) Tel 800-771-7531
E-mail: info@jacirae.com
Web site: http://www.winningromance.com; http://www.christmaswithlove.com; http://www.theindieguide.com; http://www.winningpoints.net; http://www.jacirae.com; http://www.thequeenofgreen.com; http://www.pennymeals.com.

North Star Editions *Imprint of* **North Star Editions**

North Star Editions, (*978-0-9848801; 978-0-9886491; 978-1-939967; 978-1-63163; 978-1-63517; 978-1-63583; 978-1-64185; 978-1-64493; 978-1-64494; 978-1-64619; 978-1-952455; 978-1-63738; 978-1-63739; 979-8-88998*) Subs. of Big Timber Media, 1600 Cliff Rd. E, Burnsville, MN 55337 USA (SAN 990-2325) Tel 952-446-7222; *Imprints:* Flux (FluxUSA); Focus Readers (FocusRead); Jolly Fish Press (JollyFishPr); North Star Editions (MYID_K_NORTH S); Apex (MYID_O_APEX)
E-mail: info@northstareditions.com
Web site: www.fluxnow.com; www.northstareditions.com; www.focusreaders.com
Dist(s): **Children's Plus, Inc.**
Independent Pub.
Llewellyn Pubns.

North Star Press of Saint Cloud *See* **North Star Pr. of St. Cloud**

†North Star Pr. of St. Cloud, (*978-0-87839; 978-1-68201*) P.O. Box 451, Saint Cloud, MN 56302-0451 USA (SAN 203-7491) Tel 320-558-9062; Toll Free: 888-820-1636; *Imprints:* Polaris Publications (PolarisPubns)
E-mail: info@northstarpress.com
Web site: http://www.northstarpress.com
Dist(s): **Independent Pubs. Group**
Midpoint Trade Bks., Inc.
Partners Bk. Distributing, Inc.; *CIP.*

North Star Way *Imprint of* **Simon & Schuster**

North Street Publishing, (*978-0-9883860*) 40 N. St., Grafton, MA 01519 USA Tel 508-839-5298
E-mail: fwvincent@verizon.net.

Northampton Hse., (*978-1-937997; 978-1-950668*) 7018 Wildflower Ln., Franktown, VA 23354 USA Tel 757-442-3013
E-mail: northamptonhousepress@gmail.com
Web site: www.northampton-house.com.

Northbooks, (*978-0-9653074; 978-0-9720604; 978-0-9789766; 978-0-9815193; 978-0-9830764; 978-0-9888954*) Orders Addr.: P.O. Box 671832, Chugiak, AK 99567 USA Tel 907-696-8973
E-mail: tg@northbooks.com
Web site: http://www.northbooks.com.

Northern Illinois Univ. Pr. *Imprint of* **Cornell Univ. Pr.**

Northern Lights Pr., (*978-0-692-69115-1; 978-0-692-77087-0; 978-0-692-05523-6; 978-0-692-14419-0; 978-1-7337534; 979-8-9852649*) 2403 Dilloway Dr., Midland, MI 48640 USA Tel 989-839-4820
E-mail: jodyhedlund@hotmail.com
Web site: jodyhedlund.com.

Northern Lights Publishing House *See* **Northern Lights Publishing Hse.**

Northern Lights Publishing Hse., (*978-1-948462; 978-1-952261*) 668 W. Jardin Dr., Casa Grande, AZ 85122 USA Tel 520-510-3835; *Imprints:* Katheryn Maddox Haddad (MYID_D_KATHERY)
E-mail: khaddad1940@gmail.com
Web site: https://inspirationsbykatheryn.com.

Northern Publications, Incorporated *See* **Northern Publishing**

Northern Publishing, (*978-0-9639869; 978-0-9741684*) P.O. Box 871803, Wasilla, AK 99687 USA Tel 907-376-6474
E-mail: tony@tonyruss.com
Web site: http://www.tonyruss.com
Dist(s): **American News Company**
Partners Bk. Distributing, Inc.
Partners/West Book Distributors.

Northern Speech Services, (*978-0-9708947; 978-0-9761967; 978-0-9765497; 978-0-9785581; 978-0-9799245; 978-0-9823449; 978-1-935578*) 325 Meecher Rd., Gaylord, MI 49735 USA Toll Free Fax: 888-696-9655; Toll Free: 888-337-3866; P.O. Box 1247, Gaylord, MI 49734
E-mail: tslominski@nss-nrs.com
Web site: http://www.nss-nrs.com
Dist(s): **BookBaby.**

Northern State Univ. Pr., (*978-1-883120*) Div. of NSU Foundation, Orders Addr.: Northern State Univ. 1200 S Jay St, Aberdeen, SD 57401 USA.

Northern Virginia Writing Project, (*978-0-9759524*) GMU, MSN3E4, 4400 University Dr., Fairfax, VA 22030 USA Tel 703-993-1168; Fax: 703-993-1184
E-mail: sbaker@gmu.edu; contact@nvwp.org
Web site: http://www.nvwp.org.

Northfield Publishing *Imprint of* **Moody Pubs.**

Northland Press *See* **Northland Publishing**

†Northland Publishing, (*978-0-87358*) Div. of Rowman & Littlefield Publishing Group, Orders Addr.: P.O. Box 15200 NBN Way, Blue Ridge Summit, PA 17214 USA Tel 301-459-3366; Fax: 301-429-5745; Toll Free Fax: 800-338-4550; Toll Free: 800-462-6420; *Imprints:* Rising Moon Books for Young Readers (Rising Moon Bks); Luna Rising (Luna Rising) Do not confuse with companies with the same or similar name in Memomonie, WI, Cleveland, OH
E-mail: dbreier@nbnbooks.com
Dist(s): **Children's Plus, Inc.**
Fujii Assocs.
Lectorum Pubns., Inc.
Libros Sin Fronteras
Learning Connection, The
National Bk. Network; *CIP.*

Northlight Communications, Inc. *See* **Sign2Me Early Learning / Northlight Communications, Inc.**

Northopolis, (*978-0-615-69125-1; 978-0-9898090*) 1105 Jasmine, Weslaco, TX 78596 USA Tel 956-373-1134
E-mail: rbanda@gmail.com
Web site: www.northopolis.com.

Northshire Pr., (*978-1-60571*) 592 Vt Rte. 153, West Rupert, VT 05776 USA Tel 802-549-4443; *Imprints:* Shires Press (Shires Pr)
E-mail: debbiwraga@gmail.com; writteninstonevt@gmail.com
Web site: http://www.childrensbooksbeloved.com; http://www.writteninstonevt.com.

†North-South Bks., Inc., (*978-0-7358; 978-1-55858; 978-1-58717*) 350 7th Ave. Rm. 1400, New York, NY 10001-5013 USA; *Imprints:* Michael Neugebauer Books (M Neugebauer Bks)
E-mail: mnavarro@northsouth.com
Web site: http://www.northsouth.com
Dist(s): **Children's Plus, Inc.**
Continental Bk. Co., Inc.
Lectorum Pubns., Inc.
Libros Sin Fronteras
Simon & Schuster, Inc.; *CIP.*

Northstar Entertainment Group, LLC, (*978-0-9741544*) 9009 Danwood Manor Ter., Richmond, VA 23227-1269 USA; *Imprints:* Baby Faye Books (Baby Faye)
E-mail: northstarent2003@yahoo.com
Web site: http://www.northstarent.net.

Northstone Publishing, Inc. (CAN) (*978-1-55145; 978-1-896836; 978-1-77064*) *Dist. by* **Westminster John Knox.**

Northwest Interpretive Association *See* **Discover Your Northwest**

Northwestern Publishing Hse., (*978-0-8100*) 2949 N. Mayfair Rd., Suite 200, Milwaukee, WI 53222 USA (SAN 206-7943) Tel 414-454-2100; Fax: 414-454-2170; N16W23379 Stone Ridge Dr., Waukesha, WI 53188
E-mail: kuehlt@nph.wels.net; johnsonr@nph.wels.net; schoenecks@nph.wels.net
Web site: http://www.nph.net.

Northwestern Univ. Pr., (*978-0-8101*) Orders Addr.: c/o Univ. of Chicago Pr. Distribution Ctr., 11030 S. Langley Ave., Chicago, IL 60628 USA Tel 773-568-1550; Fax: 773-660-2235; Toll Free Fax: 800-621-8476; Toll Free: 800-621-2736; Edit Addr.: 629 Noyes St., Evanston, IL 60208-4210 USA (SAN 202-5787) Tel 847-491-5313; 847-491.2046; Fax: 847-491-8150
E-mail: nupress@northwestern.edu
Web site: http://www.nupress.northwestern.edu
Dist(s): **Chicago Distribution Ctr.**
JSTOR
MyiLibrary
Random Hse., Inc.
Univ. of Chicago Pr.
Univ. of Chicago Pr. Distribution Clients
ebrary, Inc.

Northwind Sailing, Inc., (*978-0-9752700*) P.O. Box 973, Grand Marais, MN 55604-0973 USA.

NorthWord Bks. for Young Readers *Imprint of* **T&N Children's Publishing**

Norton, Frances M., (*978-0-9632938*) 1012 N. Wheaton Ave., Wheaton, IL 60187 USA Tel 630-665-0249.

Norton Simon Museum, (*978-0-9726681; 978-0-9891956*) 411 W. Colorado Blvd., Pasadena, CA 91105 USA (SAN 122-4700) Tel 818-449-6840
E-mail: info@nortonsimon.org
Web site: http://www.nortonsimon.org.

†Norton, W. W. & Co., Inc., (*978-0-393; 978-0-88150; 978-0-914378; 978-0-936399; 978-0-942440; 978-1-58157; 978-1-324; 978-1-68268*) Orders Addr.: c/o National Book Company, 800 Keystone Industrial Pk., Scranton, PA 18512 USA (SAN 157-1869) Tel 570-346-2029; Fax: 570-346-1442; Toll Free Fax: 800-458-6515; Toll Free: 800-233-4830; Edit Addr.: 500 Fifth Ave., New York, NY 10110-0017 USA (SAN 202-5795) Tel 212-354-5500; Fax: 212-869-0856; Toll Free: 800-223-2584; *Imprints:* Norton Young Readers (Norton Young)
Web site: http://www.wwnorton.com
Dist(s): **Penguin Random Hse. Distribution**
Simon & Schuster
Taylor & Francis Group
Wiley, John & Sons, Inc.; *CIP.*

Norton Young Readers *Imprint of* **Norton, W. W. & Co., Inc.**

Norvik Pr. (GBR) (*978-1-870041; 978-1-909408*) *Dist. by* **Dufour.**

Norwen Pubns., (*978-0-9852869*) 820 West Shore Dr., Culver, IN 46511 USA.

Norwood Hse. Pr., (*978-1-59953; 978-1-60357; 978-1-68404; 978-1-68450*) Orders Addr.: P.O. Box 316598, Chicago, IL 60631 USA (SAN 257-1552) Tel 773-467-0837; Fax: 773-467-9686; Toll Free Fax: 866-565-2901; Toll Free: 866-565-2900
E-mail: lisa@norwoodhousepress.com
Web site: http://www.norwoodhousepress.com
Dist(s): **Follett School Solutions.**

Nosey Trunk, (*978-0-9911454*) Orders Addr.: 240 Dolores St., No. 216, San Francisco, CA 94103 USA Tel 650-218-2986
E-mail: ranjani_krishnaswamy@hotmail.com.

Nostra Ediciones (MEX) (*978-607-7603*) *Dist. by* **IPG Chicago.**

Nosy Crow *Imprint of* **Candlewick Pr.**

Nosy Crow Inc, (*979-8-88777*) 30 Tower Rd., Lincoln, MA 01773 USA Tel 978-314-2424
E-mail: imogen@nosycrow.com
Web site: www.nosycrow.com
Dist(s): **Hachette Bk. Group.**

Not Available Books *Imprint of* **Not Available Comics**

Not Available Comics, (*978-0-9744767*) Orders Addr.: 2627 Pulaski St., Hamtramck, MI 48212 USA; *Imprints:* Not Available Books (NotAvailBks)
E-mail: feazell038@comcast.net
Web site: http://www.cynicalman.com.

For full information on wholesalers and distributors, refer to the Wholesaler and Distributor Name Index

ot Home Yet Publishing, *(978-0-615-20928-9; 978-0-615-21258-6)* 8 Catamount Ln., Littleton, CO 80127 USA Tel 303-972-0895
E-mail: nothomeyetmin@msn.com.
ot So Plain Jane Publishing, *(978-0-9700741; 978-1-59664)* 4322 Declaration Cir., Belcamp, MD 21017 USA Tel 443-866-9672; Fax: 212-681-8002
E-mail: steph.guzman@icloud.com
Web site: http://www.oliverthectownfish.com.
otable Kids Publishing, *(978-0-9970851; 978-1-7333548)* 10267 Celestine Pl., Parker, CO 80134 USA Tel 303-910-1884
E-mail: info@notablekidspublishing.com
Web site: notablekidspublishing.com
Dist(s): **Independent Pubs. Group**
Midpoint Trade Bks., Inc.
Notgrass Co., *(978-1-933410; 978-1-60999)* 975 Roaring River Rd, Gainesboro, TN 38562 USA Tel 800-211-8793; Fax: 800-891-8335; Toll Free: 800-211-8793
E-mail: books@notgrass.com
Web site: http://www.notgrass.com
Dist(s): **BookBaby.**
Nothing But The Truth, LLC, *(978-0-9883754; 978-0-615-73258-9; 978-0-9904652; 978-0-9963074; 978-0-9968999; 978-0-9972962; 978-1-946706)* 1010 Sir Francis Drake Blvd Suite 102, Kentfield, CA 94904 USA Tel 4157067067
Dist(s): **CreateSpace Independent Publishing Platform**
Publishers Group West (PGW).
Notion Pr., Inc., *(978-0-9975577; 978-1-945400; 978-1-945497; 978-1-945579; 978-1-945621; 978-1-945688; 978-1-945825; 978-1-945926; 978-1-946048; 978-1-946129; 978-1-946204; 978-1-946280; 978-1-946390; 978-1-946436; 978-1-946515; 978-1-946556; 978-1-946641; 978-1-946714; 978-1-946822; 978-1-946869; 978-1-946983; 978-1-947027; 978-1-947137; 978-1-947202; 978-1-947283; 978-1-947349; 978-1-947429; 978-1-947498; 978-1-947586; 978-1-947634; 978-1-947697; 978-1-947752; 978-1-947851; 978-1-947949; 978-1-947988; 978) 800 W. El Camino Real, Suite 180,, Mountain View, CA 94040 USA Tel 984-041-8723*
E-mail: editor@notionpress.com
Web site: www.notionpress.com.
Notto, Kristie, *(978-0-692-64682-3)* 1404 Newcastle Ln., Bartlett, IL 60103 USA Tel 847-244-8450
E-mail: kristie.notto@gmail.com
Web site: http://www.awesomesaucemarketing.net.
NouSoma Communications, Inc., *(978-0-9743604)* 500 Waldron Pk. Dr., Haverford, PA 19041-1932 USA Tel 610-658-5889; *Imprints*: GIRLS KNOW HOW (Girls Know How)
Web site: http://www.nousoma.com; http://girlsknowhow.com/
Dist(s): **Book Wholesalers, Inc.**
Brodart Co.
Nova Blue, Inc., *(978-0-9725584)* 14403 Little Blue Rd., Kansas City, MO 64136 USA Tel 816-737-8895
E-mail: novablueco@aol.com.
Nova Media, Inc., *(978-0-9618567; 978-1-884239)* 1724 N. State St., Big Rapids, MI 49307-9073 USA (SAN 668-0372) Tel 231-796-4637 (phone/fax)
E-mail: trund@netonecom.net
Web site: http://www.novamediainc.com.
Nova Pr., *(978-0-9637371; 978-1-889057; 978-0-692-38359-9; 978-1-944595)* Orders Addr.: 9058 Lloyd Pl., West Hollywood, CA 90069 USA (SAN 858-8317) Tel 310-275-3513; Fax: 310-281-5629; Toll Free: 800-949-6175
E-mail: novapress@aol.com
Web site: http://www.novapress.net
Dist(s): **CreateSpace Independent Publishing Platform**
Ebsco Publishing
Ingram Content Group
ebrary, Inc.
†Nova Science Pubs., Inc., *(978-0-941743; 978-1-56072; 978-1-59033; 978-1-59454; 978-1-60021; 978-1-60456; 978-1-60692; 978-1-60741; 978-1-60876; 978-1-61668; 978-1-61728; 978-1-61761; 978-1-61122; 978-1-61209; 978-1-61324; 978-1-61470; 978-1-62100; 978-1-61942; 978-1-62081; 978-1-62257; 978-1-62417; 978-1-62618; 978-1-62808; 978-1-62948; 978-1-63117; 978-1-63321; 978-1-63463; 978-1-63482; 978-1-63483; 978-1-63484; 978-1-63485; 978-1-53061; 978-1-68507; 979-8-88697; 979-8-89113) 400 Oser Ave., Suite 1600, Hauppauge, NY 11788 USA (SAN 666-0266)*
E-mail: nova.main@novapublishers.com
Web site: http://www.novapublishers.com
Dist(s): **Ebsco Publishing**
ebrary, Inc.; *CIP.*
Novak, Lindy, *(978-0-692-16739-7; 978-1-7331556)* 701 Miner Rd., Orinda, CA 94563 USA Tel 925-258-9432
E-mail: lindy@spottwoode.com.
Novalis, Brigitte *See* **Novalis Pr.**
Novalis Pr., *(978-0-9835035; 978-0-9886559; 978-1-944870)*
E-mail: brigi@brigittenovalis.com
Web site: www.brigittenovalis.com
Dist(s): **Smashwords.**
Novanglus Publishing, LLC, *(978-0-9837186)* Orders Addr.: 15 E. Putnam Avenue, No. 232, Greenwich, CT 06830 USA (SAN 920-4504) Tel 203-885-7476; 15 E. Putnam Ave., #232, Greenwich, CT 06830 Tel 203-885-7476; Fax: 203-724-1867
E-mail: mpeacockphd@gmail.com; michelle@novanglus publishing.com
Web site: http://www.novanglus publishing.com; http://fairandsquarebook.com.
Novarena, *(978-1-7328925)* 18 Central St., Woburn, MA 01801 USA Tel 832-381-4233
E-mail: Info@novarena.com
Web site: Www.novarena.com.
Novel Security, *(978-0-578-42305-0; 978-0-578-42309-8)* 3341 Regent Blvd. Ste. 130-363, Irving, TX 75063 USA Tel 214-536-2422
E-mail: lee@leeparrish.com
Dist(s): **Ingram Content Group.**
Novel Units, Inc. *Imprint of* **Classroom Library Co.**
Novello & Co., Ltd. (GBR) *(978-0-85360) Dist. by* **H Leonard.**
Novello Festival Pr., *(978-0-9708972; 978-0-9760963; 978-0-9815192; 978-0-615-15969-0; 978-0-615-16624-7)* Div. of Public Library of Charlotte & Mecklenburg County, 310 N. Tryon St., Charlotte, NC 28202 USA (SAN 254-3206) Tel 704-416-0706
Dist(s): **Blair.**
Novelstream, LLC *See* **Chicago Review Pr.**
November Media Publishing and Consulting Firm, *(978-0-692-76179-3; 978-0-9981622; 978-0-9990431; 978-0-9998274; 978-1-7326897; 978-1-7337724; 978-0-578-70900-0; 978-1-7354542; 978-0-578-94398-5; 979-8-9852149)* 2212 123rd St., Unit 1, Blue Island, IL 60406 USA Tel 708-515-7114
E-mail: novmedia10@gmail.com
Web site: http://www.novembermediapublishing.com/
Dist(s): **CreateSpace Independent Publishing Platform.**
Novus Via Music Group Inc. (CAN) *(978-1-897379) Dist. by* **H Leonard.**
Now Age Knowledge, *(978-0-9729259)* Orders Addr.: 8315 Lake City Way, NE, Seattle, WA 98115 USA; Edit Addr.: 16626 6th Ave. W. #m301, Lynnwood, WA 98037 USA (SAN 255-2876) Do not confuse with Awaken Publishing in Houston, TX
E-mail: nowageknowledge@gmail.com
Web site: http://nowageknowledge.com.
Now Pubs., *(978-1-933019; 978-1-60198; 978-1-68083; 978-1-63828)* Orders Addr.: 167 Washington St, Norwell, MA 02061 USA Tel 781-871-0245; Edit Addr.: P.O. Box 1024, Hanover, MA 02339 USA Tel 781-871-0245; Fax: 781-871-6172; P.O. Box 179, Delft, 3315BH Tel 31-6-51115274
E-mail: mike.casey@nowpublishers.com; alet.heezemans@nowpublishers.com
Web site: http://www.nowpublishers.com
Dist(s): **Ebsco Publishing**
GOBI Library Solutions from EBSCO
Ingram Content Group
MyiLibrary
ebrary, Inc.
NOW SC Pr., *(978-0-9987391; 978-0-9995845; 978-1-7326611; 978-1-7341809; 978-1-7369388; 979-8-9870349)* 4219 Hartwood Ln., Tampa, FL 33618 USA Tel 253-468-8801
E-mail: liza@nowscpress.com
Web site: www.nowscpress.com.
Nowata Pr. Publishing & Consulting, LLC, *(978-0-615-21595-2; 978-0-692-00130-1; 978-0-692-01778-4; 978-0-615-81419-3; 978-0-9907950)*
E-mail: dellington@nowatapressllc.com
Web site: https://www.nowatapressllc.com/.
Nowata Press Publishing Consultants *See* **Nowata Pr. Publishing & Consulting, LLC**
Nowicki, Sandra Ann, *(978-0-615-70430-2; 978-0-615-85821-0; 978-0-692-36203-7; 978-0-692-80375-2; 978-0-692-18617-6; 978-0-692-18618-3; 978-0-578-82847-3)* 9035 Fox River Rd., Burlington, WI 53105 USA Tel 262-889-4802
E-mail: sannowicki@aol.com
Web site: www.pegasusspetportraits.com.
Nowlin, Roberta J, *(978-0-9862905)* 103 Columbia Way, Montrose, CO 81401 USA Tel 818-792-6189
E-mail: robertajeanmurphy@gmail.com.
Nozithus Bks., *(978-1-7377428)* 1701 sunburst dr, El Cajon, CA 92021 USA Tel 619-226-9895
E-mail: nozithus@gmail.com
Web site: https://nozithus.com.
NPG Newspapers, Inc., *(978-0-9724933)* Orders Addr.: P.O. Box 29, St Joseph, MO 64502-0029 USA Tel 816-271-8500; Fax: 816-271-8631; Toll Free: 800-779-6397; Edit Addr.: 825 Edmond St., St Joseph, MO 64502-0029 USA
E-mail: brucek@npgco.com.
Npustin Pr., *(978-0-9816834; 978-0-9963704)* P.O. Box 683, Arlee, MT 59821-0452 USA
E-mail: npustin@gmail.com
Web site: http://www.npustin.org.
NQSBks., *(978-0-9793168)* 47 Brentview Hills Dr., Nashville, TN 37220 USA Tel 615-832-1125
E-mail: nqsbooks@comcast.net
Web site: http://www.nqsbooks.com.
NRG Pubns., *(978-0-9741647)* 3510 Plum Brook, Missouri City, TX 77459 USA
E-mail: info@nrgpublications.com
Web site: http://www.nrgpublications.com.
NRS Enterprises, *(978-0-615-27983-1)* 2237 NW. Terr. Pines Dr., Bend, OR 97701 USA.
N-Spired Productions, *(978-0-9814774)* P.O. Box 2033, Westfield, NJ 07090 USA Tel 9083720203
Web site: www.NspiredProductions.com
Dist(s): **CreateSpace Independent Publishing Platform**
Lulu Pr., Inc.
NSR Pubns., *(978-0-9761724)* 1482 51st Rd., Douglass, KS 67039 USA Tel 620-986-5472; Toll Free: 866-677-2624
E-mail: gumm@wheatstate.com
Web site: http://www.nsrpublications.com.
NT Publishing, L.L.C., *(978-0-9741864; 978-0-9787123)* P.O. Box 461540, Aurora, CO 80047 USA Tel 303-484-1071; Fax: 303-484-1072
E-mail: questions@ntpublishing.net
Web site: http://www.ntpublishing.net.
NTC/Contemporary Publishing Company *See* **McGraw-Hill/Contemporary**
NUA Multimedia, *(978-0-9777573)* Orders Addr.: 15480 Annapolis Rd., Suite 202, No. 422, Bowie, MD 20715 USA Tel 410-710-2700
E-mail: pr@nuamultimedia.com; orders@nuamultimedia.com
Web site: http://www.soniahayes.com
Dist(s): **Brodart Co.**
Follett School Solutions.
NuAngel, Inc., *(978-0-9626614)* 14717 Friend Rd., Athens, AL 35611 USA Tel 256-729-5000; Fax: 256-729-5111
E-mail: sales@nuangel.com
Web site: www.nuangel.com.
NuBaby, Incorporated *See* **NuAngel, Inc.**
NubeOcho Ediciones (ESP) *(978-84-942360; 978-84-942929; 978-84-17123-11-6) Dist. by* **Consort Bk Sales.**
Nubiangodess Publishing, *(978-0-9744291)* P.O. Box 12224, Columbus, GA 31917-2224 USA
E-mail: ngpublishing@cs.com; admin@nubiangodesspublishing.com
Web site: http://www.nubiangodesspublishing.com.
Nubiano Project, Inc., The, *(978-0-9762837)* P.O. Box 371, Chapel Hill, NC 27514 USA
E-mail: info@thenubianoproject.com.
Nude Son Publishing *See* **Canoed Sun Publishing, LLC**
Nuevo Bks., *(978-1-936745)* 925 Salamanca NW, Los Ranchos, NM 87107 USA Tel 505-344-9382; Fax: 505-345-5129
E-mail: paul@nmsantos.com
Web site: www.NuevoBooks.com.
Nuf-Love Publishing, *(978-0-9636109)* P.O. Box 120976, Clermont, FL 34712 USA
E-mail: ashersbooks@earthlink.net
Web site: http://www.ashersbooks.com.
Nugent, Kristen Independent Publishing *See* **Corredora Independent Publishing**
Nugget Pr., *(978-0-9828259)* 4340 E. Indian School Rd. Suite 21-576, Phoenix, AZ 85018 USA Tel 602-248-7810; Fax: 602-248-0913
E-mail: nanmar@cox.net.
Nui Media & Entertainment, LLC, *(978-0-9817388)* P.O. Box 364, Santa Monica, CA 90406 USA
E-mail: publishing@nui.com.
NUMA LLC, *(978-0-9977196)* P.O. Box 52, Mystic, CT 06355 USA Tel 860-501-3316
E-mail: msoni.author@gmail.com.
Number 6 Publishing LLC, *(978-1-7321116)* 1799 Rampart Dr., Alexandria, VA 22308 USA Tel 703-360-6054
E-mail: sdressing@number6publishing.com.
Number One Fan Pr., *(978-0-615-16416-8; 978-0-615-17221-7; 978-0-615-38550-1; 978-0-615-85320-8)* 34 Robert St., Braintree, MA 02184 USA
Dist(s): **Lulu Pr., Inc.**
Publishers Services.
NumbersAlive! Pr., *(978-0-9853667)* 975 F St., NW., Washington, DC 20004-1454 USA Tel 202-652-1820; Fax: 202-667-5793
E-mail: rebecca@numbersalive.org
Web site: http://www.numbersalive.org.
Nu-Nature, *(978-0-9759008)* 858 Heritage Valley Rd., Norcross, GA 30093 USA Tel 404-376-8917
E-mail: nunatureinfo@aol.com
Web site: http://www.nu-nature.com.
Nunes, H. William, *(978-0-9646934; 978-0-9787994)* 3029 Mark Trail, Glen Carbon, IL 62034 USA Tel 618-288-5185; Fax: 618-205-3053
E-mail: bnunesbook@aol.com
Dist(s): **Big River Distribution**
Partners Bk. Distributing, Inc.
Nur Pubns., *(978-0-9764947)* Orders Addr.: 562 Sawmill River Rd., Millwood, NY 10546 USA
E-mail: s_nadimi@yahoo.com
Web site: http://www.nurpublications.com.
Nuriel, Tal, *(978-0-692-96604-4; 978-0-9997262)* 493 Amsterdam Ave, Apt 2C, New York, NY 10024 USA Tel 646-369-8445
E-mail: tnuriel@gmail.com.
Nursery Bks., *(978-0-9894505)* 30 jannas Ln., Madison, CT 06443 USA Tel 860-308-4303
E-mail: sophie.helenek@gmail.com
Web site: www.nurserybooks.net.
Nurture Wellness now, *(978-0-9998845)* 786 burden lake Rd., Aiken, SC 29803 USA Tel 803-646-1067; Fax: 803-646-1067
E-mail: tania@nurturewellnessnow.com
Web site: nurturewellnessnow.com.
Nurturing Faith, Incorporated *See* **Good Faith Media**
Nurturing Potential, *(978-0-692-96815-4)* 6709 Ave. A, New Orleans, LA 70124 USA Tel 706-201-3927
E-mail: zibbie39@gmail.com.
Nurturing Your Children Pr., *(978-0-9767198)* P.O. Box 5066, Larkspur, CA 94977-5066 USA Tel 415-927-4839 (phone/fax)
E-mail: nurturingpress@aol.com
Web site: http://nurturingyourchildren.com.
Nutrishare Publishing, *(978-0-9764116)* 10519 E. Stockton Blvd., Suite 110, Elk Grove, CA 95624 USA.
Nutrition Network Pubs., Inc., *(978-0-9898633)* 5 Arleigh Rd., Great Neck, NY 11021 USA Tel 516-773-4754
E-mail: daunlester@gmail.com.
Nutshell Publishing *See* **Enisen Publishing**
NuVision Designs, *(978-0-578-19006-8; 978-0-578-19207-9; 978-0-578-19422-6; 978-0-578-19430-1; 978-0-578-19652-7; 978-0-578-19832-3; 978-0-578-20333-1; 978-0-578-20531-1; 978-0-578-21836-6; 978-0-578-21966-0; 978-0-578-22265-3)* P.O. Box 4455, Wilmington, NC 28406 USA; 5027 Lamppost Cir., Wilmington, NC 28403 Tel 240.439.5294
Web site: www.nuvisiondesigns.biz.
NuVision Pubns., LLC, *(978-1-932681; 978-1-59547; 978-1-61536)* 1504 E. 70th St N., Sioux Falls, SD 57104-9429 USA
E-mail: nuvisionpub@gmail.com
Web site: http://www.nuvisionpublications.com
Dist(s): **CreateSpace Independent Publishing Platform**
Ingram Content Group.
Nvision Publishing *Imprint of* **Power Play Media**
nVision Publishing, *(978-0-9766086)* Div. of Written by Nicole Kearney Enterprises, P.O. Box 88731, Indianapolis, IN 46208 USA Tel 317-724-8926
E-mail: nicoleckearney@yahoo.com
Web site: http://www.nicolekearney.com.
N'Writing, *(978-0-9990976)* 14869 Arlington Ave., Allen Park, MI 48101 USA Tel 734-634-1817
E-mail: overstart2002@yahoo.com.
NY Media Works, LLC, *(978-0-9890914)* 112 Franklin St. First Flr., New York, NY 10013 USA (SAN 920-5187) Tel 646-369-5681
E-mail: jgribble@nymediaworks.com
Web site: http://www.nymediaworks.com
Dist(s): **Brodart Co.**
Quality Bks., Inc.
NY Studio Gallery LLC, *(978-0-692-49726-5; 978-0-692-62127-1; 978-0-692-62269-8; 978-0-692-65367-6; 978-0-692-67000-2; 978-0-692-67277-8; 978-0-692-67300-3; 978-0-692-72251-0; 978-0-692-78710-6; 978-0-692-80005-8; 978-0-692-80410-0; 978-0-692-80916-7; 978-0-692-80920-4) 420 N. Ohioville Rd, NEW PALTZ, NY 12561 USA Tel 612-987-1473.*
Nye Products, *(978-0-9746665)* P.O. Box 177, Wexford, PA 15090-0177 USA Tel 724-935-8710
E-mail: nyeproducts@stargate.net
Web site: http://nyeproducts.com; http://www.beverlynye.com/.
Nymeria Publishing, *(978-1-7363027; 979-8-9851572; 979-8-9883332)* 224 Springs Ct., West Columbia, SC 29710 USA Tel 402-999-3495
E-mail: admin@nymeriapublishing.com.
Nypa Distributing, LLC, *(978-0-578-08858-7; 978-0-578-08859-4; 978-0-9997400)* 1733 N. 40 E., Tooele, UT 84074 USA Tel 435-224-4286
E-mail: NypaDistributing@gmail.com.
NYR Children's Collection *Imprint of* **New York Review of Bks., Inc., The**
NYRB Classics *Imprint of* **New York Review of Bks., Inc., The**
NYRB Kids *Imprint of* **New York Review of Bks., Inc., The**
NYU Pr. *Imprint of* **New York Univ. Pr.**
O & H Bks., *(978-0-9960057; 978-1-959703)* 528 Spence Ln Apt 105, Martins Ferry, OH 43935 USA
E-mail: smithgift264@gmail.com
Web site: http://www.oandhbooks.com.
OSS Publishing Co., *(978-0-9660286)* Orders Addr.: P.O. Box 610, White Plains, NY 10603 USA Tel 914-946-6521; Fax: 914-949-5380; Toll Free: 888-677-6521
E-mail: OSSpublishing@att.net
Web site: http://www.osspublishing.com.
Oak Court Pr., *(978-0-9767696)* 34612 Oak Ct., Elizabeth, CO 80107 USA Tel 303-703-6633
E-mail: oakcourtpress@msn.com.
Oak Hill Studios, *(978-0-9848818)* 2150 Farnsworth Dr., O'Fallon, MO 63368 USA Tel 314-560-0041; Fax: 636-978-1135
E-mail: nealwriter1@charter.net
Web site: letterstomillie.com
Dist(s): **BookBaby.**
†Oak Knoll Pr., *(978-0-938768; 978-1-884718; 978-1-58456; 978-1-872116)* 310 Delaware St., New Castle, DE 19720 USA (SAN 216-2776) Tel 302-328-7232; Fax: 302-328-7274; Toll Free: 800-996-2556 Do not confuse with Oak Knoll Press in Hardy, VA
E-mail: oakknoll@oakknoll.com
Web site: http://www.oakknoll.com; *CIP.*
Oak Lake Pr., *(978-0-9744115)* Orders Addr.: 1432 Higuera, San Luis Obispo, CA 93406 USA Tel 916-791-2309; Edit Addr.: P.O. Box 529, Loomis, CA 95650 USA
E-mail: abowler@surewest.net
Web site: http://www.annmartinbowler.net.
Oak Leaf Systems, *(978-0-9659546; 978-0-9848809)* 2710 John Tyler Hwy., Williamsburg, VA 23185 USA Tel 757-208-0200 Landline; 757-634-1441 Mobile
E-mail: carolfeltman@gmail.com
Web site: ATruckNamedTravis.com.
Oak Manor Publishing, Inc., *(978-0-9747361; 978-0-9791757)* 161 Boutwell St., Manchester, NH 03102-2933 USA Tel 603-860-5551
E-mail: customerservice@aokmanorpublishing.com
Web site: http://www.oakmanorpublishing.com.
Oak Ridge Publishing, *(978-0-9814735; 978-0-9843270; 978-0-9851416)* P.O. Box 682, Lady Lake, FL 32158 USA Tel 352-259-7450
E-mail: ldridgley@comcast.net.
Oak Solid Publishers, *(978-1-59999)* 204 Govenors Dr., Forest Park, GA 30297-2183 USA Tel 404-392-5209
Web site: http://www.oaksolidholding.com.
Oak Tree Publishing, *(978-1-892343; 978-1-61009)* Orders Addr.: 1820 W. Lacey Blvd. #220, Hanford, CA 93230 USA; *Imprints*: Acorn (AcornIL) Do not confuse with companies with the same or similar name in Virginia Beach, VA, Seminole, FL
E-mail: oaktreepub@aol.com; Publisher@oaktreebooks.com; info@oaktreebooks.com
Web site: http://www.oaktreebooks.com; http://www.otpblog.blogspot.com.
Oak Valley Publishing, *(978-0-9962753)* 14152 S. Senior Band, Draper, UT 84020 USA Tel 951-249-4577
E-mail: arsenalman@me.com.
Oakana Hse., *(978-0-9762197)* Orders Addr.: P.O. Box 1680, Ramona, CA 92065 USA (SAN 257-5418)
Web site: http://OakanaHouse.com.
Oakdale Pr., *(978-0-9656364)* Orders Addr.: P.O. Box 555, Caulfield, MO 65626 USA Tel 417-284-3512; Fax:

417-284-3623 Do not confuse with companies with the same name in Lincoln., MA, Tallahassee, FL
E-mail: oakdale@webound.com
Web site: http://www.oakdalepress.com.

Oaklawn Marketing, Inc., *(978-0-9764628)* P.O. Box 190615, Dallas, TX 75219 USA Tel 713-542-7642; Fax: 832-550-2079
E-mail: admin@bookofcontext.com.

Oaklea Pr., The, *(978-0-578-46335-3)* 41 Old Mill Rd., Richmond, VA 23226 USA Tel 804-218-2394
E-mail: shmartin@shmartin.com.

OakTara Publishing Group LLC *See* **Nassau-Street.com**

Oakwood Solutions, LLC, *(978-1-893806; 978-1-933093)* 4 Brookwood Ct., Appleton, WI 54914-8618 USA
E-mail: bschmitz@conovercompany.com; sales@conovercompany.com
Web site: http://www.conovercompany.com.

Oasis Audio, *(978-1-55536; 978-1-886463; 978-1-58926; 978-1-59859; 978-1-60814; 978-1-60981; 978-1-61375; 978-1-62188; 978-1-63108; 978-1-64091; 978-1-64555; 978-1-68592; 979-8-88605)* Div. of Domain Communications, 289 S. Main Pl., Carol Stream, IL 60188 USA (SAN 854-3534) Tel 630-668-5300; Fax: 630-668-0158; Toll Free: 800-323-2500 ext. 110
E-mail: info@oasisaudio.com
Web site: http://www.oasisaudio.com
Dist(s): **Blackstone Audio, Inc.**
Follett School Solutions
TNT Media Group, Inc.
Tyndale Hse. Pubs.

Oasis, Producciones Generales de Comunicacion, S.L. (ESP) *(978-84-7871; 978-84-7901; 978-84-85351) Dist. by* **Lectorum Pubns.**

Oasis Pubns., *(978-0-9652736; 978-0-9837859)* 2344 Cambridge Dr., Sarasota, FL 34232 USA Tel 941-371-2223; Fax: 941-342-1228
E-mail: oasis.dianne@juno.com
Web site: http://www.nutrikid2.com
Dist(s): **Nelson's Bks.**
New Leaf Distributing Co., Inc.
Teva Nature.

Oasis Studios Inc, *(978-0-9785605)* Orders Addr.: 7701 Witherspoon Dr., Baltimore, OH 43105 USA Tel 740-862-8620
E-mail: ekayzer@hotmail.com
Web site: http://www.championoasisstudios.com
Dist(s): **Send The Light Distribution LLC.**

OASYS Pr., *(978-0-9863965)* 5916 E. Lake Pkwy. Suite 195, McDonough, GA 30253 USA Tel 678-561-5655; Fax: 877-720-8705
E-mail: alonzo@theoasysgroup.com
Web site: www.HiringMadeEasyasPIE.com; www.TheOASYSGroup.com.

†Oberlin College Pr., *(978-0-932440; 978-0-9973355)* 50 N. Professor St., Oberlin, OH 44074 USA (SAN 212-1883) Tel 440-775-8408; Fax: 440-775-8124
E-mail: oc.press@oberlin.edu
Web site: http://www.oberlin.edu/ocpress
Dist(s): **CUP Services**
Chicago Distribution Ctr.; *CIP.*

Oberon Bks., Ltd. (GBR) *(978-0-948230; 978-1-84002; 978-1-870259; 978-1-84943; 978-1-78319; 978-1-78682) Dist. by* **Macmillan.**

Obert, Christopher Publishing, *(978-0-9749291; 978-0-9821983; 978-1-62502)* Orders Addr.: 20 S. Porter St., Bradford, MA 01835-7646 USA; Edit Addr.: 20 S. Porter St., Bradford, MA 01835 USA
E-mail: Chris@PearTreePublishing.net; Information@PearTreePublishing.net
Web site: http://www.PearTreePublishing.net.

Oblique Angles Pr., *(978-0-9905641; 978-0-9980604; 978-1-7355586; 978-1-955696)* 4475 N. Benton Ct., Bloomington, IN 47408 USA Tel 812-333-1384
E-mail: kawyle@att.net
Web site: http://www.KarenAWyle.net; http://www.KarenAWyle.com.

O'Brien, Gerard, *(978-0-9743850)* 115 Essex St., Indian Orchard, MA 01151-1409 USA Tel 413-543-5939
E-mail: gob@ifriendly.com.

OBrien, Kathryn, *(978-0-692-15101-3)* 12740 N.W. 78th Manor, Parkland, FL 33076 USA Tel 312-285-6189
E-mail: kobauthor@yahoo.com
Dist(s): **Ingram Content Group.**

O'Brien, Lara Publishing, *(978-0-9896752)* 47 Davis st, Vineyard Haven, MA 02568 USA Tel 774-563-0292
E-mail: laraeobrien@yahoo.com.

O'Brien Pr., Ltd., The (IRL) *(978-0-86278; 978-0-86322; 978-0-905140; 978-0-9502046; 978-1-902011; 978-1-84717; 978-1-78849) Dist. by* **Casemate Pubs.**

O'Brien Pr., Ltd., The (IRL) *(978-0-86278; 978-0-86322; 978-0-905140; 978-0-9502046; 978-1-902011; 978-1-84717; 978-1-78849) Dist. by* **Dufour.**

OBrien, Wiley Workspace, *(978-0-615-29492-6; 978-0-615-97038-7)* 125 Washington St., Canandaigua, NY 14424 USA
Web site: http://www.WonderlandBook.com.

Obscurity Books *See* **Home Planet Bks.**

Ocean Aire Productions, Inc, *(978-1-7334684; 978-1-953979)* 111 Ocean Aire Terr. N., Ormond Beach, FL 32176 USA Tel 386-290-3588
E-mail: sarah@oceanaireproductions.com.

Ocean Crest Publishing, LLC, *(978-0-9981322)* P.O. Box 842, Palm Beach, FL 33480 USA Tel 561-629-2528
E-mail: chelow@comcast.net
Web site: www.oceancrestpublishing.com.

Ocean Front Bk. Publishing, Inc., *(978-1-934190)* Orders Addr.: 9101 W. Sahara Ave. Suite 105-130, Las Vegas,, NV 89117 USA (SAN 852-0046) Tel 702-499-0608; 9101 W. Sahara Ave. Suite 105-130, Las Vegas,, NV 89117 (SAN 852-0046) Tel 702-499-0608
E-mail: jhorowitz@oceanfrontbooks.com
Web site: http://www.oceanfrontbooks.com.

Ocean World Photography, *(978-0-9766749)* 6461 Running Brook Rd., Manassas, VA 20112 USA
E-mail: wgregorybrown@comcast.net
Web site: http://www.wgregorybrown.com.

OceanAir Publishing *See* **Mayreni Publishing**

Oceano Grupo Editoria, S.A. (ESP) *(978-84-494; 978-84-7069; 978-84-7505; 978-84-7555; 978-84-7764; 978-84-85317; 978-84-9719) Dist. by* **Gale.**

OceanPubns., *(978-1-7321546)* 12827 SW 133rd ST, MIAMI, FL 33186 USA Tel 727-247-6078
E-mail: oceanpublications@gmail.com
Web site: oceanpublications.us.

Oceanus Bks. *Imprint of* **Warrington Pubns.**

Oceanview Publishing, *(978-1-933515; 978-1-60809)* 61 Paradise Rd., Ipswich, MA 01938 USA Tel 978-356-1897; Fax: 978-356-3526 Do not confuse with Oceanview Publishing, Newport Beach, CA
E-mail: mail@oceanviewpub.com
Web site: http://www.oceanviewpub.com
Dist(s): **Follett School Solutions**
Independent Pubs. Group
Midpoint Trade Bks., Inc.
MyiLibrary
ebrary, Inc.

Ocher Moon Pr., *(978-0-9765303)* 391 Joppa Mountain Rd., Rutledge, TN 37861 USA Tel 865-828-8280
E-mail: jeri@hopalonggreetings.com
Web site: http://www.hopalonggreetings.com.

O'Connor, Cassidy K. *See* **Celtic Hearts Pr.**

OCRS, Incorporated *See* **River Pr.**

Octagon Pr., Ltd., *(978-0-86304; 978-0-900860)* Orders Addr.: P.O. Box 400541, Cambridge, MA 02140 USA; Edit Addr.: 171 Main St. No. 140, Los Altos , CA 94022 USA
Web site: http://www.octagonpress.com
Dist(s): **I S H K.**

Octagon Pr./ISHK Bk. Service *See* **I S H K**

Octane Pr., *(978-0-9821733; 978-0-9829131; 978-1-937747; 978-1-64234)* Orders Addr.: 815A Brazos St No. 658, Austin, TX 78701 USA Tel 512-430-1943; Edit Addr.: 815a Brazos St. No. 653, Austin, TX 78701 USA (SAN 920-9395) Tel 512-334-9441
E-mail: lee@octanepress.com; sales@octanepress.com
Web site: http://octanepress.com
Dist(s): **Bookazine Co., Inc.**
Ingram Content Group.

OctiRam Publishing Co., *(978-0-9830423)* Orders Addr.: P.O. Box 5859, Vancouver, WA 98668 USA Tel 360-464-7670
E-mail: raski@comcast.net.

Octobooks, *(978-0-9843297)* P.O. Box 1554, La Jolla, CA 92038-1554 USA (SAN 859-0834)
E-mail: jack@octoboks.com; millie@millietheoctopus.com
Web site: http://www.millietheoctopus.com.

Octobre Pr., *(978-0-615-69253-1; 978-0-615-84019-2; 978-0-692-34554-2; 978-0-692-61301-6; 978-0-692-82604-1; 978-0-692-98457-4; 978-1-7329768; 979-8-218-11986-7)* 3310 Oak Brook Ln., Vero Beach, FL 32963 USA Tel 772-538-4805
E-mail: virginiabest@me.com
Web site: http://www.pansythepoodle.com
Dist(s): **National Bk. Network.**

Octopoda Pr., *(978-0-9858506; 978-0-9908818)* P.O. Box 8943, Ketchikan, AK 99901 USA Tel 907-225-8212
E-mail: evon@evonzerbetz.com
Web site: octopodapress.com.

Octopus Publishing Co., *(978-0-9824433)* Div. of Octopus Enterprises LLC, 100 S. River Bend, Jackson, GA 30233-3204 USA
E-mail: rogerfen@bellsouth.net; geletaf@bellsouth.net.

Octopus Publishing Group (GBR) *(978-0-600; 978-0-905879; 978-1-84091; 978-1-86007; 978-1-84202; 978-1-84430; 978-1-904705; 978-1-84403; 978-1-84696; 978-1-905814; 978-1-84898; 978-1-908150; 978-1-907579; 978-1-78157; 978-1-78325; 978-1-913183) Dist. by* **HachBkGrp.**

Octopus Publishing Group (GBR) *(978-0-600; 978-0-905879; 978-1-84091; 978-1-86007; 978-1-84202; 978-1-84430; 978-1-904705; 978-1-84403; 978-1-84696; 978-1-905814; 978-1-84898; 978-1-908150; 978-1-907579; 978-1-78157; 978-1-78325; 978-1-913183) Dist. by* **Children Plus.**

Odd Dot *Imprint of* **St. Martin's Pr.**

Odd Duck Ink, Inc., *(978-1-933069)* P.O. Box 533, Norwell, MA 02061-0533 USA
E-mail: jennifer@oddduckink.com
Web site: http://www.oddduckink.com.

OddInt Media *Imprint of* **Greenwood Hill Pr.**

Oddo Publishing, Inc., *(978-0-87783)* Storybook Acres, Box 68, Fayetteville, GA 30214 USA (SAN 282-0757) Tel 770-461-7627.

Odds Bodkin Storytelling Library, The *Imprint of* **Rivertree Productions, Inc.**

Oddvark & Co., *(978-1-7330514)* 1743 Highland Rd., Osprey, FL 34229 USA Tel 941-220-3818
E-mail: ltoddvark2@gmail.com
Web site: oddvarkandcompany.com.

ODE, *(978-0-692-87176-8; 978-0-578-41922-0; 978-0-578-46012-3; 978-0-578-46197-7; 978-0-578-70537-8; 978-0-578-85511-0)* 1708C 4th Ave N, Nashville, TN 37208 USA Tel 818-427-1901
E-mail: cdaymusic@gmail.com
Dist(s): **Independent Pub.**

Oden, Rachel, *(978-0-9729914)* 133 E. Graham Ave., Council Bluffs, IA 51503 USA Tel 712-323-7222 (phone/fax)
E-mail: cbmarketadmin@juno.com.

Odenwald Pr., *(978-0-9623216; 978-1-884363)* 6609 Brooks Dr., Temple, TX 76502 USA Tel 254-773-4884; Fax: 254-773-4884
E-mail: CSho777@aol.com
Dist(s): **SMMA Distributors.**

Odeon Livre, *(978-1-947961; 978-1-64574)* 1111 Old Barn Rd., Buffalo Grove, IL 60089 USA Tel 847-917-9575; Fax: 847-917-9575; *Imprints*: Oui Love Books (MYID_Y_OUI LOV)
E-mail: ethan@odeonlivre.com
Web site: https://odeonlivre.com.

odod bks. *Imprint of* **Uncivilized Bks.**

Odon Livre *See* **Odeon Livre**

Odubayo Thompson, Linda, *(978-1-7322096; 978-1-7348876; 978-1-7363400)* 3-6 Steven Dr., Ossining, NY 10562 USA Tel 914-944-1474
E-mail: linda@ghostbookwritergoldilocks.com
Web site: http://www.ghostbookwritergoldilocks.com.

Odysia Pr., *(978-0-692-98154-2; 978-0-692-99104-6; 978-0-692-99115-2; 978-0-692-99123-7; 978-0-692-99124-4; 978-0-692-04566-4; 978-0-692-19708-0; 978-0-578-42424-8; 978-0-578-42428-6; 978-0-578-42431-6; 978-0-578-44094-1; 978-0-578-44816-9; 978-0-578-82850-3; 978-0-578-83126-8; 979-8-218-13364-1; 979-8-218-15737-1) 705 B SE Melody Ln. No. 320, LEES SUMMIT, MO 64063 USA Tel 816-607-1801*
E-mail: djpedersen@gmail.com
Dist(s): **Ingram Content Group.**

Odyssey Bks. (AUS) *(978-0-9806909; 978-0-9872325; 978-1-922200; 978-1-925652; 978-1-922311) Dist. by* **LightSource CS.**

Oelrich, Josh, *(978-0-692-11120-8)* 300 Koch Dr., Hollister, CA 95023 USA Tel 408-710-0650
E-mail: josh.oelrich@gmail.com
Dist(s): **Ingram Content Group.**

Oembe Publishing, *(978-0-9773520; 979-8-218-13381-8; 979-8-218-16677-9; 979-8-9881667)* 3141 Tiger Run Ct. Suite 102, Carlsbad, CA 92010 USA (SAN 257-3180)
E-mail: elaine@elaineswann.com
Web site: http://www.elaineswann.com; http://https://www.ws-publishing.com/.

OES, *(978-0-692-07456-5)* W6350 Old Lake Ln., Shawano, WI 54166 USA Tel 715-508-0250
E-mail: doug.pebs@gmail.com.

Off The Record *Imprint of* **College Prowler, Inc.**

Officer Byrd Publishing Co., *(978-0-9787322)* 15730 Williams Cir., Lake Mathews, CA 92570 USA (SAN 851-4712) Tel 951-334-6111
E-mail: officerbyrd@aol.com.

OffTheBookshelf.com *See* **Micro Publishing Media, Inc.**

Oglethorpe Pr., Inc., *(978-1-891495)* 326 Bull St., Savannah, GA 31401 USA Tel 912-231-9900; Fax: 912-234-7258
E-mail: sjackel@comcast.net
Dist(s): **Parnassus Bk. Distributors.**

Ogma Pr., *(978-0-9785853)* 4717 Broad Rd., Syracuse, NY 13215 USA Tel 315-491-9339
E-mail: bernie@ogmapress.com
Web site: http://www.ogmapress.com.

Ogonor, Fyne, *(978-1-7321995; 978-1-951460)* 2579 Jenna Ln., Lithia Springs, GA 30122 USA Tel 404-402-7986
E-mail: fcogonor@gmail.com.

Ogorek, Elchanan, *(978-0-692-76640-8)*.

OH Industries, *(978-0-9667359; 978-0-9831032)* Southern Belle Books, P.O. Box 10543, Tallahassee, FL 32302 USA Tel 850-576-2370; *Imprints*: BeanPole Books (BeanPole Bks)
E-mail: publisher@beanpolebooks.com; linda@belladist.com; jess@belladist.com
Web site: http://www.beanpolebooks.com
Dist(s): **Two Rivers Distribution.**

Oh My Stars Publishing, *(978-0-615-20153-5)* 222 3rd St., Suite 4, Lemoyne, PA 17043 USA
Dist(s): **APG Sales & Distribution Services**
Lulu Pr., Inc.

OHC Group LLC, *(978-0-9763213)* P.O. Box 7839, Westlake Village, CA 91359 USA Tel 805-384-4800
Web site: http://www.onlyheartsclub.com.

Ohio Distinctive Publishing, Inc., *(978-0-9647934; 978-1-936772)* 6500 Fiesta Dr., Columbus, OH 43235 USA Tel 614-459-0453; Fax: 614-457-2488
E-mail: tim@ohio-distinctive.com
Web site: http://www.ohio-distinctive.com.

†Ohio State Univ. Pr., *(978-0-8142)* 1070 Carmack Rd., Columbus, OH 43210 USA (SAN 202-8158) Tel 614-292-6930; 773-568-1550 (orders); Fax: 614-292-2065; Toll Free Fax: 800-621-8476 (orders); Toll Free: 800-621-2736 (orders); *Imprints*: Mad Creek Books (MadCreekBks)
E-mail: ohiostatepress@osu.edu
Web site: http://www.ohiostatepress.org
Dist(s): **Chicago Distribution Ctr.**
JSTOR
Partners Bk. Distributing, Inc.
Univ. of Chicago Pr.
Univ. of Chicago Pr. Distribution Clients; *CIP.*

†Ohio Univ. Pr., *(978-0-8214)* Orders Addr.: 11030 S. Langley Ave., Chicago, IL 60628 USA Tel 773-702-7000; Fax: 773-702-7212; Toll Free Fax: 800-621-8476; Toll Free: 800-621-2736; Edit Addr.: 19 Circle Dr. The Ridges, Athens, OH 45701 USA (SAN 282-0773) Tel 740-593-1154; Fax: 740-593-4536; *Imprints*: Swallow Press (Swallow Pr)
Web site: https://www.ohioswallow.com/
Dist(s): **Chicago Distribution Ctr.**
Ebsco Publishing
JSTOR
Trajectory, Inc.
Univ. of Chicago Pr.
ebrary, Inc.; *CIP.*

Ohnick Enterprises, *(978-0-9746222)* Orders Addr.: P.O. Box 969, Meade, KS 67864-0969 USA Tel 620-873-2900; Fax: 620-873-2603; Toll Free: 800-794-2356; Edit Addr.: 102 N. Fowler, Meade, KS 67864-0969 USA
E-mail: nancy@prairiebooks.com
Web site: http://backroomprinting.com.

Oka, Joseph *See* **Joseph's Labor**

Okafor, Gloria, *(978-1-7345830)* 1414 SW 27th Ct, Gresham, OR 97080 USA Tel 971-570-2223
E-mail: ngokafor@msn.com
Web site: Www.okaforbooks.com.

Okasan & Me, *(978-0-9743613)* 829 N. Sixth St., San Jose, CA 95112 USA
Web site: http://www.okasanandme.com.

Okay Enterprises, *(978-0-9675399)* P.O. Box 297, Sebastopol, CA 95473 USA Tel 707-495-4480; Fax: 707-829-3825.

O'Keefe, Cameron, 3 N. Covington Meadows, OLIVETTE, MO 63132 USA Tel 314-406-0069
E-mail: iamcameronkillian@gmail.com
Dist(s): **Ingram Content Group.**

Oki, Blessed, *(978-0-9721336)* 2465 Heaton Dr., Suite A, East Point, GA 30344 USA
E-mail: blessiebeke@yahoo.com.

Oklahoma Energy Resources Board, *(978-0-615-19844-6; 978-0-615-39316-2; 978-0-692-63684-8)* 3555 NW 58th St., Suite 430, Oklahoma City, OK 73112 USA Tel 405-942-5323; Fax: 405-942-3435; Toll Free: 800-664-1301
Web site: http://www.oerb.com.

Oklahoma Heritage Assn., *(978-1-885596; 978-1-938923)* Orders Addr.: 1400 Classen Dr., Oklahoma City, OK 73106 USA Tel 405-235-4458; 405-523-3202; Fax: 405-235-2714; Toll Free: 888-501-2059
E-mail: gmc@oklahomaheritage.com
Web site: http://www.oklahomaheritage.com
Dist(s): **Partners Bk. Distributing, Inc.**

O.K.P LLC, *(978-0-9995168)* 1001 N. Tonopah Dr, Las Vegas, NV 89016 USA Tel 702-480-8603
E-mail: adventuresoflo@gmail.com.

Olabooks International *See* **OlaBks. International**

OlaBks. International, *(978-1-7353671; 978-1-7363889)* 866 Yuma St. SE, Washington, DC 20032 USA Tel 202-341-3504
E-mail: oyekolaadeola@gmail.com
Web site: olabooksinternational.com.

Olahauski Bks., *(978-1-956527)* 207 Andover Ln., Noblesville, IN 46060 USA Tel 248-793-8743
E-mail: olahauski@gmail.com.

Olandar Pr. Ltd., *(978-0-9729502)* Orders Addr.: 2222 Parview Rd., Middleton, WI 53562 USA Tel 608-831-1222; Fax: 608-831-1647
Web site: http://www.leighmccloskey.com.

Ola's Hanalei LTD, *(978-0-9763907)* P.O. Box 488, Hanalei, HI 96714 USA
E-mail: olashanalei@hawaiiantel.net.

Old Bay Publishing, *(978-0-9745854)* 19 Meeting St., Huntsville, AL 35806-5230 USA
E-mail: msikes@hiwaay.net
Dist(s): **Partners Bk. Distributing, Inc.**

Old Bess Publishing Co., *(978-0-9631912; 978-0-9762132)* Orders Addr.: P.O. Box 277, Brunswick, ME 04011 USA Tel 207-725-8575; P.O. Box P.O. Box 277, Brunswick, ME 04011
E-mail: sbutcherr@mcn.net.

Old Coal Publishing, *(978-0-578-54166-2; 978-0-578-65387-7)* 28509 North Pk. Dr., North Olmsted, OH 44070 USA Tel 440-429-6161
E-mail: modernvictorian@yahoo.com.

Old Farm Pr., *(978-0-9788227)* P.O. Box 20894, Oklahoma City, OK 73156-0894 USA (SAN 851-6995) Tel 405-748-7072; Fax: 405-748-7073
E-mail: spi@mbo.net
Web site: http://www.BobbyBrightBooks.com.

Old Farmer's Almanac *Imprint of* **Yankee Publishing, Inc.**

Old Hogan Publishing Co., *(978-0-9638851)* Orders Addr.: P.O. Box 91978, Tucson, AZ 85752 USA Tel 520-579-9321; Fax: 520-579-0502; Toll Free: 800-867-1506; Edit Addr.: 3600 W. Mesa Ridge Trail, Tucson, AZ 85742 USA
E-mail: mgaraway@juno.com
Web site: http://www.oldhogan.com
Dist(s): **Hispanic Bks. Distributors & Pubs., Inc.**
Rio Nuevo Pubs.

Old Hundredth Pr., *(978-0-9793911)* 2885 Gordon Rd., NW, Dover, OH 44622 USA.

O.L.D. Inc., *(978-0-9830470)* 118 N Ross St No. 6, Auburn, AL 36830 USA Tel 334-787-1713
E-mail: cwjones@oldinc.net.

Old Maps, *(978-0-911653; 978-0-9747639)* P.O. Box 54, West Chesterfield, NH 03466 USA (SAN 264-2689)
E-mail: daven@sover.net
Web site: http://www.old-maps.com.

Old Schl. Squirrel, *(978-1-7370641)* 638 N Humphrey Ave, Oak Park, IL 60302 USA Tel 773-213-5370
E-mail: eleyostudio@gmail.com.

Old Scout Pr., *(978-0-692-85277-4; 978-0-692-11902-0; 978-0-578-54238-6)* 4033 Kingsgate Pl., Charlotte, NC 28211 USA Tel 434-996-7318
E-mail: KDSherry@gmail.com; oldscoutpresscharlotte@gmail.com
Web site: katesliteracycorner.weebly.com; oldscoutpresscharlotte.com.

Old Silver Pr., *(978-0-9800975)* 224 Coonamessett Cir., East Falmouth, MA 02536 USA
E-mail: OldSilverPress@yahoo.com.

Old Soldier Publishing, *(978-0-9764167)* Orders Addr.: P.O. Box 1113, Richmond, TX 77469 USA Tel 281-341-0781 (phone/fax); Edit Addr.: 1110 Pioneer Dr., Richmond, TX 77469 USA
Dist(s): **ebrary, Inc.**

Old St. Augustine Pubns., *(978-0-9833684; 978-0-692-38918-8)* P.O. Box 162056, Altamonte Springs, FL 32716 USA Fax: 407-774-8799
E-mail: doug@oldstaugustinepublications.com
Web site: http://www.oldstaugustinepublications.com
Dist(s): **Ingram Content Group.**

Old Stone Pr., *(978-1-938462)* 520 Old Stone Ln., Louisville, KY 40207 USA Tel 502-693-1506
E-mail: john@oldstonepress.com; john@jhclarkandassociates.com
Web site: http://OldStonePress.com
Dist(s): **Baker & Taylor Publisher Services (BTPS).**

Old Time Stories, *(978-0-9792770)* 116 Beasley Rd., Cusseta, GA 31805-3206 USA.

ld Town Publishing, *(978-1-7329703; 978-1-7338129; 978-1-7332138; 979-8-9851650; 978-1-961776)* 5014 College View Ave, Los Angeles, CA 90041 USA Tel 818-415-4616
E-mail: uspnow@aol.com
Web site: www.oldtownpublishing.com.

ld Tree Hse. Publishing, *(978-0-9989775; 978-1-7371646)* 421 King St., Hanover, MA 02339 USA Tel 512-250-8546
E-mail: jillsylvester@adminismith.com.

ld Vine Oublishing Co., *(978-0-9794291)* P.O. Box 6774, Pine Mountain Club, CA 93222-6774 USA.

Old West Company, The *See* **Old West Co., The**

Oldcastle Bks., Ltd. (GBR) *(978-0-948353; 978-1-874061; 978-1-84243; 978-1-84344; 978-1-904915) Dist. by* **IPG Chicago.**

Oldcastle Publishing, *(978-0-932529)* Orders Addr.: P.O. Box 1193, Escondido, CA 92033 USA (SAN 297-9039) Tel 760-489-0336; Fax: 760-747-1198; Edit Addr.: 3415 Laredo Ln., Escondido, CA 92025 USA (SAN 297-9047)
E-mail: abcurtiss@cox.net
Web site: http://www.abcurtiss.com; http://www.depressionisachoice.com
Dist(s): **National Bk. Network.**

Olde Milford Pr., The, *(978-0-9662019; 978-1-7331780; 978-1-7342334)* Orders Addr.: P.O. Box 5342, Milford, CT 06460 USA; Edit Addr.: 108 Clark Hill Rd., Milford, CT 06460 USA
E-mail: oldemilfordpress@msn.com
Web site: http://www.oldemilfordpress.com.

Olde Springfield Shoppe *See* **Masthof Pr.**

Olde Town Publishing, *(978-0-9755906)* 703 W. Main, Jonesborough, TN 37659 USA
Web site: http://www.drisbell.com.

Olde Towne Publishing, *(978-0-9794935)* P.O. Box 98, Old Mission, MI 49673 USA Do noty confuse with Olde Towne Publishing Company in Fredericksburg, VA
Web site: http://www.strolltraversecity.com
Dist(s): **Partners Bk. Distributing, Inc.**

Oldenworld Bks., *(978-0-578-41700-4; 978-0-578-41703-5; 978-1-7339429; 978-1-956623)* 9207 NE 104th St., Vancouver, WA 98662 USA Tel 360-771-3367
E-mail: jd@jackdublin.net
Web site: https://JackDublin.net
Dist(s): **Independent Pub.**

O'Leary, Stephanie, *(978-0-692-16597-3; 978-0-692-17154-7; 978-0-692-04451-3)* 1313 N Lucy Montgomery Way, Olathe, KS 66061 USA Tel 316-841-1322
E-mail: caoghlan@yahoo.com
Dist(s): **Ingram Content Group.**

Oleson, Susan, *(978-0-9779251)* 511 E Iowa St, Monona, IA 52159 USA
E-mail: sammytails@netins.net.

Olive & Ink, *(978-0-578-16978-1; 978-0-692-76874-7; 978-0-692-76882-2)* 21 South Main St., Perry, NY 14530 USA.

Olive Branch & The Frog LLC., The, *(978-1-7377672)* 300 Inwood Dr., Wheeling, IL 60090 USA Tel 847-370-2592
E-mail: klpr99@aol.com.

Olive Branch Bks., *(978-0-9769100)* 1105 Yorkshire St., Port Charlotte, FL 33952 USA Tel 941-627-0493
E-mail: service@arabvoicesspeak.com
Web site: http://www.arabvoicesspeak.com
Dist(s): **Norton, W. W. & Co., Inc.**

Olive Branch Publishing, LLC *See* **OlivesAngels Publishing, LLC**

Olive Grove Pubs., *(978-0-9752508)* 1420 King Rd., Hinckley, OH 44233 USA Tel 330-278-4028
E-mail: RSpirko@Roadrunner.com
Web site: http://www.atlasbooks.com
Dist(s): **American Wholesale Booksellers Assn.**
Baker & Taylor Publisher Services (BTPS)
Book$mart, Inc.
New Leaf Distributing Co., Inc.
ebrary, Inc.

Olive Leaf Pubns., *(978-0-9761583)* 782 San Gabriel Loop, New Braunfels, TX 78132 USA (SAN 256-6206) Tel 830-626-7671
E-mail: sharon3572@att.net; sharon3572@icloud.com
Web site: http://www.oliveleafpublications.com
Dist(s): **Ingram Content Group.**

Olive Pr. Pub., *(978-0-9790873; 978-0-9847111; 978-0-9855241; 978-1-941173)* P.O. Box 163, Copenhagen, NY 13626 USA Tel 315-941-6710.

Olive Pr., The, *(978-0-9769298)* Orders Addr.: P.O. Box 2056, Saintllwater, MN 55082 USA Tel 651-251-3063 Do not confuse with Olive Press i Ann Arbor, MI West Orange, NJ Estes Park, CO
E-mail: olivepressinc@yahoo.com
Web site: http://jumpstartfuture.com.

Olive Tree of Life, *(978-0-9768182)* P.O. Box 344, Tijeras, NM 87059 USA
Web site: http://www.olivetreeoflife.com.

Oliver Pr., Inc., *(978-1-881508; 978-1-934545)* Orders Addr.: 5707 W. 36th St., Minneapolis, MN 55416-2510 USA Tel 952-926-8981; Fax: 952-926-8965; Toll Free: 800-865-4837
E-mail: orders@oliverpress.com
Web site: http://www.oliverpress.com.

Oliver Pr. LLC, *(978-0-692-42047-8; 978-0-692-42048-5; 978-0-692-78667-3; 978-0-692-87956-6)* 1935 Chene Ct. Apt. 1505, Detroit, MI 48207 USA Tel 313-744-8543
E-mail: grimlyjane@yahoo.com
Dist(s): **CreateSpace Independent Publishing Platform**
Ingram Content Group.

Oliver, Sarah (GBR) *(978-0-9559820) Dist. by* **LuluCom.**

Oliver the Brave, *(978-0-692-60184-6; 978-0-692-73809-2; 978-0-578-80566-5; 978-0-578-81802-3; 978-0-578-93756-4; 979-8-218-02473-4)* 2163 Benefit St., Merrick, NY 11566 USA Tel 516-589-2429
E-mail: Oliverthebrave@yahoo.com.

Oliver, Wade, *(978-0-9768030)* P.O. Box 1605, Logan, UT 84322-1605 USA
E-mail: wademan@cache.net
Web site: http://www.dovepage.com.

Oliver-Heber Bks., *(978-0-9884974; 978-0-9898408; 978-1-942820; 978-0-692-38796-2; 978-0-692-45257-8; 978-1-947204; 978-1-64839)* PO Box 216, Suttons Bay, MI 49682 USA Tel 214-734-8333
E-mail: tanya@tanyaannecrosby.com
Web site: http://www.oliver-heberbooks.com
Dist(s): **CreateSpace Independent Publishing Platform**
INscribe Digital
Independent Pubs. Group.

OlivesAngels Publishing, LLC, *(978-0-9793147)* P.O. Box 940725, Plano, TX 75094-0725 USA (SAN 853-0955) Tel 972-977-4881
E-mail: olivesangels@tx.rr.com.

Olivo, Andy, *(978-0-9743376)* 1807 Glengarry St., Carrollton, TX 75006 USA Tel 972-242-0924; Fax: 972-242-1754;
Imprints: Brown Books (Brown BksTX).

OLLY Publishing Co., *(978-0-9720427)* 4335 Lake Michigan Dr., NW Suite H, Grand Rapids, MI 49544 USA (SAN 254-587X) Tel 616-735-0553
E-mail: diane@ollypublishing.com
Web site: http://www.ollypublishing.com.

Olmstead LLC *See* **Olmstead Publishing LLC**

Olmstead Publishing LLC, *(978-0-9667696; 978-1-934194)* Orders Addr.: 2629 Grassmoor Lp, Apopka, FL 32712-5005 USA Tel 954-559-0192 (phone); Fax: 650-479-8273
E-mail: olmsteadpublishing@usa.com
Web site: http://www.olmsteadpublishing.com; http://https://squareup.com/market/olmstead-publishing-llc; http://www.facebook.com/olmsteadpublishing.

Olsen, Erik, *(978-0-578-59023-3; 978-0-578-63149-3)* Barili, Cebu, Barili, TT 06036 USA Tel 995-565-4656
E-mail: girlou.7@gmail.com.

Olsen, Mary Bks., *(978-0-9715374)* P.O. Box 882, Eastsound, WA 98245-0882 USA
E-mail: mary@maryolsenbooks.com.

Olson, Robin, *(978-0-9818695)* P.O. Box 5294, Laytonsville, MD 20882 USA (SAN 856-7719)
E-mail: robin@robinsweb.com
Web site: http://www.robinsweb.com.

Olympiad Publishing, *(978-0-692-79374-9; 978-0-692-12415-4; 978-0-692-15582-0; 978-0-578-40719-7; 978-0-578-43205-2; 978-0-578-47497-7; 978-0-578-48495-2; 978-0-578-49148-6; 978-0-578-51326-3; 978-0-578-65065-4; 978-0-578-65719-6; 978-0-578-76860-1; 978-0-578-79768-7; 978-0-578-33151-5; 979-8-218-10317-0; 979-8-218-21381-7; 979-8-218-24551-1) 7418 Legend Point, San Antonio, TX 78244 USA Tel 210-273-5578*
E-mail: chrispittard@olympiadpublishing.com.

Oma Publishing Co., *(978-0-9747175)* 2217 Eden Rd., Seguin, TX 78155-0179 USA Tel 210-684-3200.

Omaha Bks., *(978-0-9745410; 978-0-9788429; 978-0-9908000)* Div. of Eventive Marketing, 5037 Parker St., Omaha, NE 68104 USA (SAN 857-1295) Tel 402-679-5854
E-mail: kristine.gerber@cox.net; jkgerber@cox.net
Dist(s): **Partners Bk. Distributing, Inc.**

Omaha World-Hearld *See* **Omaha World-Herald**

Omaha World-Herald, *(978-0-615-37076-7; 978-0-615-41175-0; 978-0-615-42369-2; 978-0-615-51155-9; 978-0-615-55822-6; 978-0-615-70853-9; 978-0-615-71539-1; 978-0-615-71549-0; 978-0-615-79394-8; 978-0-615-87516-3; 978-0-615-89513-0; 978-0-615-90983-7; 978-0-692-26499-7; 978-0-692-31051-9; 978-0-692-31055-7; 978-0-692-31859-1; 978-0-692-55512-5; 978-0-692-55518-7; 978-0-692-62399-2; 978-0-692-74658-5; 978-0-692-79875-1; 978-0-692-79878-2; 978-0-692-88708-0; 978-0-692-94259-8; 978-0-692-96277-0; 978-1-7322317; 978-) 1314 Douglas St., Omaha, NE 68102 USA Tel 402-444-1204; Fax: 402-346-7158*
E-mail: rich.warren@owh.com
Web site: http://www.omaha.com.

O'Mara, Michael Bks., Ltd. (GBR) *(978-1-85479; 978-0-946429; 978-0-948397; 978-1-84317; 978-1-903840; 978-1-904613; 978-1-907151; 978-1-78243; 978-1-910552; 978-1-912785; 978-1-78929) Dist. by* **IPG Chicago.**

O'Mara, Michael Bks., Ltd. (GBR) *(978-1-85479; 978-0-946429; 978-0-948397; 978-1-84317; 978-1-903840; 978-1-904613; 978-1-907151; 978-1-78243; 978-1-910552; 978-1-912785; 978-1-78929) Dist. by* **Trans-Atl Phila.**

Omega Hse. Publishing, *(978-0-9672519)* Div. of Spectrum Group, Inc., Orders Addr.: P.O. Box 68, Three Rivers, MI 49093 USA Tel 269-273-7070; Fax: 269-273-7026; Edit Addr.: 58690 US 131, Three Rivers, MI 49093 USA
E-mail: zendra@omega777.com.

Omega Pr., *(978-0-9626087; 978-0-9754923; 978-1-933951)* 5823 N. Mesa, No. 839, El Paso, TX 79912-3340 USA Tel 915-478-1114; 915-219-4210; Toll Free: 888-560-1243 Do not confuse with companies with the same name in Tustin, CA
E-mail: ken@kenhudnall.com
Web site: http://www.omegapress.us; http://www.kenhudnall.com; http://shop.kenhudnall.com.

Omega Prime, LLC, *(978-0-9897588)* 3521 Hartzdale Dr., Camp Hill, PA 17011-7231 USA Tel 717-579-0038
E-mail: SusanRShutt@OmegaPrime.net
Web site: http://www.loveoffizz.com; http://www.fortheloveoffizz.com; http://www.omegaprime.net.

Omega Publishing, *(978-0-9748494)* P.O. Box 53626, Lubbock, TX 79453 USA (SAN 255-8815) Tel 806-748-9880; Fax: 806-748-9870; Toll Free: 877-842-9880 do not confuse with companies iwth the same or similar name in Madisonville, KY, Stockton, GA, Snohomish, WA, Norcross, GA
E-mail: jpartin@omega-pub.com
Web site: http://www.omega-pub.com.

Omega Publishing Hse., *(978-1-886297)* Subs. of B. C. & G. Graphics, Orders Addr.: 2935 Glenwood Ave., Youngstown, OH 44511 USA Tel 330-881-1344; Fax: 330-782-7599
E-mail: omegapublishing@ymail.com; craiga2356@msn.com
Web site: http://omegapublishinghouse.com.

Omen Sky Pubns., *(978-0-9744192)* 3600 Brookewind Way, No. 1201, Lexington, KY 40515 USA Tel 859-543-2026 (phone/fax)
E-mail: omensky@qx.net.

Omni Arts Publishing *Imprint of* **Read Street Publishing, Inc.**

Omni Arts Publishing, Incorporated *See* **Read Street Publishing, Inc.**

Omnibook Co., 1171 Decorah Rd., West Bend, WI 53095-9509 USA (SAN 282-6941) Tel 414-675-2760; Fax: 414-675-2340.

Omnibus Publishing, *(978-0-9740599)* 3402 Beresford Ave., Belmont, CA 94002 USA Tel 650-622-9702; Fax: 650-240-3586
E-mail: yuhogan@omnibuspublishing.com
Web site: http://www.omnibuspublishing.com.

Omnific Publishing, *(978-1-936305; 978-1-62342)* P.O. Box 793871, Dallas, TX 75379 USA Fax: 214-975-4889
E-mail: publisher@omnificpublishing.com
Web site: http://www.omnificpublishing.com
Dist(s): **Simon & Schuster, Inc.**

O'More Publishing, *(978-0-9717444; 978-0-9800285; 978-0-9822618; 978-0-9846244; 978-0-9860150; 978-0-9860244)* 423 S. Margin St., Franklin, TN 37064 USA Fax: 615-790-1662; 615-790-1666
E-mail: mhilliard@omorecollege.edu; jsexton@omorecollege.edu
Web site: http://www.omorepublishing.com.

On Cape Pubns., *(978-0-9653283; 978-0-9719547; 978-0-9758502; 978-0-9785766; 978-0-9913401; 978-1-64907)* Orders Addr.: 87 Barley Neck Rd., Orleans, MA 02638 USA Tel 508-385-2108 Toll Free: 877-662-5839
E-mail: chopi@goodnightbooks.com
Web site: http://www.oncapepublications.com.

On The Ball Publishing, *(978-0-615-21079-7; 978-0-615-25047-2; 978-0-615-45284-5; 978-0-615-45296-8; 978-0-9834341)* 12821 Stratford Dr. Suite 114, Oklahoma City, OK 73120 USA Tel 405-549-1174
E-mail: admin@ontheballpublishing.com
Web site: http://www.ontheballpublishing.com
Dist(s): **Lulu Pr., Inc.**

On The Edge Pubns., *(978-0-9762360)* P.O. Box 690007, Stockton, CA 95269 USA Tel 209-473-8553
E-mail: ontheedgepublications@msn.com
Web site: http://www.ontheedgepublications.com.

On The Fly Publications *See* **Perspicacious Publishing**

On the Reelz Pr., *(978-0-9778048)* 13813 Congress Dr., Suite 610, Rockville, MD 20853 USA Tel 202-288-5562
E-mail: ibefg@hotmail.com
Web site: http://www.onthereelz.com.

On the Spot! Bks., *(978-0-9652998)* 1492 Tipperary St., Boulder, CO 80303 USA Tel 303-666-0550
E-mail: onthespotbooks@msn.com
Web site: www.kerryleemaclean.com
Dist(s): **Bks. West**
New Leaf Distributing Co., Inc.

On Tour Publishing, *(978-0-9767234)* Orders Addr.: 512 Northampton St., 151, 303, Edwardsville, PA 18704 USA
E-mail: otp@ontourpublishing.com.

ON Words Publishing, LLC, *(978-0-9787589)* 8720 Ferguson Ave., Savannah, GA 31406 USA.

ONA Healthy Life, L.L.C. *See* **Mel Ona**

Once Upon A Dance *See* **Once Upon a Dance**

Once Upon a Dance, *(978-1-7359844; 978-1-7363536; 978-1-7365899; 978-1-7368750; 978-1-955555)* 16123 NE 42nd Ct, Redmond, WA 98052 USA Tel 425-883-0836
E-mail: terreld@msn.com; terrel@onceuponadance.org
Web site: www.OnceUponADance.com; www.creativemovementstories.com; www.DanceStories.com; www.OnceUponADance.org.

Once Upon A Page Pr., *(978-1-7346573; 979-8-9852839; 978-1-958369)* 394 Deuce Dr., Wall, NJ 07719 USA Tel 732-977-7825
E-mail: brittanyplumeri12@gmail.com.

Once Upon A Time in a Classroom *Imprint of* **Interactive Media Publishing**

Oncekids, *(978-0-9844207; 978-1-938806)* 119 Maono Pl., Honolulu, HI 96821 USA (SAN 859-3574)
E-mail: oncekids@gmail.com
Dist(s): **Baker & Taylor Publisher Services (BTPS).**

Oncology Nursing Press, Incorporated *See* **Oncology Nursing Society**

Oncology Nursing Society, *(978-1-890504; 978-1-935864; 978-1-63593)* Subs. of Oncology Nursing Society, 125 Enterprise Dr., Pittsburgh, PA 15275-1214 USA (SAN 689-8041) Tel 412-859-6100
E-mail: apetyak@ons.org; rgeffrey@ons.org
Web site: http://www.ons.org.

One Arm Publishing, *(978-0-9746024)* 3344 Via La Selva, Palos Verdes Estates, CA 90274 USA
E-mail: mariana1969@hotmail.com
Web site: http://www.onearmpublishing.com.

One Armed Operation *See* **One Arm Publishing**

One Coin Publishing, LLC, *(978-0-615-31066-4)* 6876 Towhee, Portage, MI 49024 USA.

One Elm Books *Imprint of* **Red Chair Pr.**

One Eyed Pr., *(978-0-9665430; 978-0-615-26684-8)* 272 Rd. 6RT, Cody, WY 82414 USA Tel 307-272-9628; 307-587-6136
E-mail: one_eyed_press@yahoo.com
Web site: http://www.one-eyed-press.com
Dist(s): **Bks. West**
CreateSpace Independent Publishing Platform
Todd Communications.

One Eyed Tiger Publishing, *(978-0-9971588)* 1420 NE Brockman Pl, Seattle, WA 98125 USA Tel 206-228-5954
E-mail: hindmank@gmail.com.

One Faithful Harp Publishing Co., *(978-0-9666701)* 138 N. 2nd St., Catawissa, PA 17820-1210 USA
E-mail: info@onefaithfulharp.com
Web site: http://www.onefaithfulharp.com.

One Foot in the Grave Media, *(978-0-9721327)*
E-mail: andrea@onefootinthegravemedia.com
Web site: onefootinthegravecomics.com.

One Horse Pr., *(978-0-9725650)* 963 Maple Hill Dr., Erie, PA 16509 USA Tel 814-923-4086
E-mail: stephanie@stephaniewincik.com
Web site: http://www.stephaniewincik.com.

One in Me, The, *(978-0-9898437)* 503 Wicklow Pl., Acworth, GA 30102 USA Tel 470-800-2355
E-mail: tgodoy@comcast.net; barard@theoneinme.com; godoy@theoneinme.com
Web site: www.theoneinme.com.

One In The Son Publishing, *(978-0-9973723)* 16745 SE Division St. No. 127, Portland, OR 97236 USA Tel 503-730-4688
E-mail: littleredappletree@hotmail.com
Web site: oneintheson.com.

One iron Pr., *(978-1-7355640)* 2804 Scott Mill Pl., Jacksonville, FL 32223 USA Tel 904-262-8960
E-mail: RLQ@oneironpress.com
Web site: oneironpress.com.

One Little Miracle, *(978-0-9743948)* 1449 Highland Ct., Stillwater, MN 55082 USA Tel 651-439-3250
E-mail: allieschield@hotmail.com
Web site: http://www.onelittlemiracle.com.

One Little Spark, *(978-0-615-53981-2; 978-0-578-12711-8)* 239 W. Lime Ave., Monrovia, CA 91016 USA Tel 818-621-3466; Fax: 626-486-9456
E-mail: vicki@onelilspark.com
Web site: onelilspark.com.

One Little Spark Publishing, *(978-1-7378820)* 24 Valerie Ln., Hamilton, NJ 08690 USA Tel 609-558-2933
E-mail: lindsay.yacovino@gmail.com.

One Love Assn. Bks., *(978-0-9776603)* 306 Trillick Ct., Rolesville, NC 27571 USA (SAN 257-8654)
E-mail: ras@newkemet.com; gerald@newkemet.com
Web site: http://www.newkemet.com/gerald.

One Monkey Bks., *(978-0-9777082; 978-1-940722)* 156 Diamond St., San Francisco, CA 94114-2414 USA (SAN 850-0320).

One Moore Bk., *(978-0-615-66119-3; 978-0-615-66120-9; 978-0-615-66121-6; 978-0-615-66122-3; 978-0-615-66123-0; 978-0-615-66124-7; 978-0-615-66125-4; 978-0-615-70631-3; 978-0-615-72179-8; 978-0-615-73636-5; 978-0-615-73900-7; 978-0-615-73998-4; 978-0-615-73999-1; 978-0-615-74001-0; 978-0-615-74002-7; 978-0-615-74004-1; 978-0-615-74005-8; 978-0-615-80172-8; 978-0-615-97703-4; 978-0-692-49285-7; 978-0-692-77875-3; 978-1-7335161) 80 Broad St. 5th Flr. Suite 503, New York, NY 10004 USA Tel 212-837-7818*
Dist(s): **CreateSpace Independent Publishing Platform.**

One Night Bks. *Imprint of* **WordWright.biz, Inc.**

One Nine Pr., *(978-1-7368509)* 1119 Sassafras Cir., Eldersburg, MD 21784 USA Tel 917-621-6257
E-mail: martine.foreman@gmail.com.

One Odd Duck Bks., *(978-0-578-40036-5; 978-0-578-32846-1)* 122 Alden Ave., Chattanooga, TN 37405 USA Tel 325-668-7808
E-mail: jessalyndalrem@gmail.com
Dist(s): **Ingram Content Group.**

One of a Kind Books, Incorporated *See* **Webster Henrietta Publishing**

One Part Rain, *(978-0-692-79233-9)* 340 E. 4380 N., PROVO, UT 84604 USA Tel 801-420-8087.

One Peace Bks., Inc., *(978-0-9785084; 978-1-935548; 978-1-944937; 978-1-64273)* 43-32 22nd St. #204, Long Island City, NY 11101 USA (SAN 850-7430) Tel 718-482-9100; Fax: 718-482-9101
E-mail: mcguire@onepeacebooks.com
Web site: http://www.onepeacebooks.com
Dist(s): **SCB Distributors.**

One Pink Rose, *(978-0-9722991)* 111921 Rawson Rd., Red Bluff, CA 96080 USA
E-mail: pinkwhirlwind@cablespeed.com; squallsknight@yahoo.com
Web site: http://www.darkfedora.com.

One Rib Pubns., *(978-0-9722625; 978-0-9746191; 978-1-944414; 978-1-959806)* Orders Addr.: 2801 nw 55TH Ct. Bldg. 6W, Ft. Lauderdale, FL 33309 USA Tel 954-603-7285; Edit Addr.: 2801 nw 55TH Ct. Bldg. 6W, Fort Lauderdale, FL 33309 USA Tel 954-815-1538; 2801 nw 55TH Ct. Bldg. 6W, Fort Lauderdale, FL 33309 Tel 954-815-1538.

1 Sleeve Publishing, *(978-0-9729153)* Orders Addr.: P.O. Box 1865, North Mankato, MN 56002-1865 USA; Edit Addr.: 442 Belgrade Ave., No. 13, North Mankato, MN 56003 USA
E-mail: onesleeve@hotmail.com.

One Source Publishing, LLC, *(978-0-9779374)* 63 Gates St, White River Junction, VT 05001 USA Fax: 802-295-5338
E-mail: hphipps@onesourcefg.com.

One Too Tree Publishing, *(978-0-9820781)* 106 Calendar Ct., No. 108, La Grange, IL 60525-2325 USA (SAN 857-1732)
E-mail: publisher@onetootree.com
Web site: http://www.OneTooTree.com.

Publisher Name Index

One True Faith (Religion & Spirituality) *Imprint of* **Speedy Publishing LLC**

One Voice Recordings, *(978-0-9708022)* 16835 Halper St., Encino, CA 91436 USA Tel 818-501-8145 (phone/fax) E-mail: ddavies858@aol.com.

One Way Bks., *(978-0-9800451; 978-1-936459)* Div. of Waht About You?, Inc., 2269 S. Univ. Dr. #330, Fort Lauderdale, FL 33324 USA Tel 954-680-9095 Web site: http://www.OneWayBooks.org *Dist(s):* **MyiLibrary Send The Light Distribution LLC ebrary, Inc.**

One Way Street, Incorporated *See* **Creative Ministry Solutions**

O'Neal, Carolyn, *(978-0-9966878)* 708 Acorn Ln., Charlottesville, VA 22903 USA Tel 434-882-0362 E-mail: carolynoneal@comcast.net Web site: http://authorcarolynoneal.com/.

O'neal Publishing, *(978-0-615-49338-1; 978-0-9851318; 978-0-9972555; 978-0-9984748)* 2594 Pinewood Ln., Layton, UT 84040 USA Tel 8015445045 E-mail: cindymhogan@yahoo.com *Dist(s):* **Brigham Distribution CreateSpace Independent Publishing Platform.**

OneHope *See* **OneHope, Inc.**

OneHope, Inc., *(978-1-890525; 978-1-931940; 978-1-59480; 978-1-63049; 978-1-64653; 979-8-89107)* 600 SW 3rd St., Pompano Beach, FL 33060-6936 USA Toll Free: 800-448-2425 E-mail: andreadragotas@onehope.net *Dist(s):* **Whitaker Hse.**

ONeill, Gene & Assoc., *(978-0-9747797)* 10163 Potter Rd., Des Plaines, IL 60016 USA.

O'Neill, Hugh & Assocs., *(978-0-9675919; 978-0-615-76348-4)* Orders Addr.: P.O. Box 1297, Nevada City, CA 95959 USA Tel 530-265-4196; Edit Addr.: 227 Prospect St., Nevada City, CA 95959 USA E-mail: info@bydb.com Web site: http://www.bydb.com *Dist(s):* **CreateSpace Independent Publishing Platform.**

O'Neill, Jan, *(978-0-9746409)* 5681 Rives Junction Rd., Jackson, MI 49201-9413 USA.

ONeill, Robert L. , *(978-1-7327613)* 437 W. 46th St. No. 4fw, New York, NY 10036 USA Tel 646-431-0956 E-mail: robloneill@aol.com.

O'Neill-Sheehan, Elizabeth, *(978-0-692-69931-7; 978-0-692-76666-8; 978-0-692-76678-1)* 30 Vreeland Ave, East Longmeadow, MA 01028 USA Tel 413-519-5393.

OneLight Publishing, *(978-0-9909270)* E-mail: JOSHGOTTSEGEN@ME.COM Web site: http://www.onelightstudios.com.

OneLight Studios *See* **OneLight Publishing**

OneMoreWord Bks., *(978-1-937533; 978-1-62456)* P.O. Box 165, New Philadelphia, OH 44663 USA Web site: http://HollyLisle.com.

OneShare Educational Pr., *(978-0-9788438)* 3450 Third St. Bldg. 1-D, San Francisco, CA 94124 USA (SAN 851-7487) Tel 415-777-1777; Fax: 415-777-1677; Toll Free: 888-777-6919 Web site: http://www.oneshare.com.

Oneworld Pubns. (GBR) *(978-1-85168; 978-1-78074; 978-1-78607) Dist. by* **S and S Inc.**

Oni Pr., Inc., *(978-0-9667127; 978-1-929998; 978-1-932664; 978-1-934964; 978-1-62010)* 1305 SE Martin Luther King Jr. Blvd., Suite A, Portland, OR 97214 USA Tel 503-233-1377; Fax: 503-233-1477; *Imprints:* Lion Forge (LionFrgl) E-mail: chris@onipress.com Web site: http://www.onipress.com *Dist(s):* **Children's Plus, Inc. Diamond Comic Distributors, Inc. Simon & Schuster, Inc.**

Onion Publishing, *(978-1-7337647)* P.O. Box 54, Pontotoc, MS 38863 USA Tel 662-586-1156 E-mail: starksjessica2013@gmail.com.

Onion River Pr., *(978-0-9657144; 978-0-9976458; 978-1-949066; 978-1-957184)* 21 Essex Way No. 407, Essex Junction, VT 05452 USA (SAN 990-1736) Tel 802-872-7111 (phone/fax) E-mail: michael@phoenixbooks.biz; rachelf@phoenixbooks.biz Web site: http://www.onionriverpress.com; www.phoenixbooks.biz.

ONLY1EARTH, LLC, *(978-0-9763354)* 3146 The Alameda Suite 7, San Jose, CA 95126 USA E-mail: only1earthinc@gmail.com Web site: http://www.theturtlekey.com.

Onondaga Hill Publishing, *(978-0-9794908)* 4586 Bloomsbury Dr., Syracuse, NY 13215 USA Tel 315-420-3025 E-mail: mdunn@imsolv.com; matthew@matthewdunn.net Web site: http://www.matthewdunn.net *Dist(s):* **BookBaby.**

Onstage Publishing, LLC, *(978-0-9700752; 978-0-9753367; 978-0-9790857)* Orders Addr.: 190 Lime Quarry Rd., Suite 106 J, Madison, AL 35758 USA Tel 256-461-0661; Fax: 256-461-0661 E-mail: onstage123@knology.net Web site: http://www.onstagepublishing.com.

ONTRAK, *(978-0-9765502)* P.O. Box 205, Bethel, CT 06801-0153 USA Do not confuse with Ontrak in Yorba Linda, CA E-mail: plumtrees@snet.net.

Onwuemene Publishing Group, *(978-1-948960)* 8311 Brier Creek Pkwy, Raleigh, NC 27617 USA Tel 919-695-3847 E-mail: opubgroup@gmail.com Web site: opubgroup.com.

Onyx Pubns., *(978-0-9702628)* 2002 Tioga Pass Way, Antioch, CA 94531 USA Do not confuse with Onyx Publications, Inglewood, CA E-mail: onyxpub04@aol.com.

ooli & tooli llc, *(978-0-9987126)* 65 crest Dr. N., cresskill, NJ 07626 USA Tel 551-206-5577; Fax: 551-206-5577 E-mail: pollak.ora@gmail.com Web site: ooliandtooli.com.

Ooligan Pr., *(978-1-932010; 978-1-947845)* Div. of Portland State Univ., Dept. of English, Orders Addr.: Dept. of English Portland State Univ. P.O. Box 751, Portland, OR 97207 USA Tel 503-725-9410; Fax: 503-725-3561; Edit Addr.: 630 SW Mill St., 97201, Rm. Nh405, Portland, OR 97201 USA E-mail: ooligan@ooliganpress.pdx.edu; agaterud@pdx.edu Web site: http://www.ooliganpress.pdx.edu; http://www.publishing.pdx.edu *Dist(s):* **Ingram Publisher Services.**

OPA Author Services, *(978-0-911041)* Div. of Optimum Performance Associates, 777 W. Chandler Blvd., No. 1322, Chandler, AZ 85225-2511 USA (SAN 254-9255) Tel 480-275-5270; 480-393-1646 (phone/fax) Web site: http://www.opaauthorservices.com; http://www.opapublishing.com *Dist(s):* **OPA Publishing & Distributing.**

OPA Publishing *See* **OPA Author Services**

Opacity, Inc., *(978-0-615-14266-1)* 7086 SW Iron Horse St., Wilsonville, OR 97070 USA *Dist(s):* **Lulu Pr., Inc.**

Open Arms Publishing, *(978-0-9770841)* 607 Knob Ct., Fayetteville, NC 28303 USA Tel 910-258-3941 E-mail: sallymander66@earthlink.net; thoglenn@yahoo.com Web site: http://www.oaim.net.

Open Bk. Publishing, *(978-0-9719167; 978-0-9740321; 978-1-932621)* Rte. 2, Box 2607, Birch Tree, MO 65438 USA Tel 573-292-3368; Fax: 573-292-8115 Do not confuse with Open Book Publising Company in Huntington beach, CA E-mail: lfann@socket.net; ifann@socket.net Web site: http://www.openbookpublishing.com.

Open Bk. Publishing Co., *(978-0-9753349)* P.O. Box 3602, Huntington Beach, CA 92649 USA Tel 714-264-7284; Fax: 714-846-6782 Do not confuse with Open Book Publishing in Birch Tree, MO E-mail: k.cutt@verizon.net Web site: http://www.openbookpublishingcompany.com.

†Open Court, *(978-0-8126; 978-0-87548; 978-0-89688; 978-0-912050; 978-0-8126-9956-2)* Div. of S R A/McGraw-Hill, 220 E. Daniel Dale Rd., DeSoto, TX 75115 USA Fax: 972-228-1982; Toll Free: 888-772-4543; 800-442-9685 (orders) Web site: https://www.sraonline.com *Dist(s):* **Libros Sin Fronteras Publishers Group West (PGW) SRA/McGraw-Hill**; *CIP.*

Open Court Publishing Co., *(978-0-8126; 978-0-87548; 978-0-89688; 978-0-912050)* Div. of Carus Publishing Co., Orders Addr.: c/o Publishers Group West, 1700 Fourth St., Berkeley, CA 94710 USA Fax: 510-528-3444; Toll Free: 800-788-3123; Edit Addr.: 70 E. Lake St. Ste. 300, Chicago, IL 60601-5945 USA Toll Free: 800-815-2280 E-mail: opencourt@caruspub.com Web site: http://www.opencourtbooks.com *Dist(s):* **Follett School Solutions MyiLibrary Publishers Group West (PGW).**

Open Door Pr., *(978-1-942264)* 42299 Chisolm Trail, Murrieta, CA 92562 USA Tel 951-461-9072 E-mail: khales@me.com Web site: www.opendoor-press.com *Dist(s):* **Greenleaf Book Group.**

Open Door Publishers, Inc., *(978-0-9841721; 978-1-937138)* 2373 Rte. 9, Mechanicville, NY 12118 USA (SAN 858-625X) Tel 518-899-2097 E-mail: adamiszyn@hotmail.com; ladean@opendoorpublishers.com Web site: http://www.ladeanwarner.com; http://opendoorpublishers.com/.

Open Gate Publishing, *(978-0-9717036; 978-1-937195; 978-1-950641)* Div. of Open Gate Sangha, Inc., Orders Addr.: P.O. Box 112107, Campbell, CA 95011-2107 USA; Edit Addr.: 1299 Del Mar Ave., Suite 200, San Jose, CA 95128-3548 USA E-mail: jerilyn@adyashanti.org Web site: http://www.adyashanti.org *Dist(s):* **New Leaf Distributing Co., Inc.**

Open Gate Sangha *See* **Open Gate Publishing**

Open Hand Publishing, LLC, *(978-0-940880)* P.O. Box 20207, Greensboro, NC 27420 USA (SAN 219-6174) Tel 336-292-8585; Fax: 336-292-8588 E-mail: info@openhand.com Web site: http://www.openhand.com.

Open Heaven Pubns., *(978-0-9752622)* P.O. Box 457, Moravian Falls, NC 28654 USA Web site: http://www.garyoates.com.

Open Mind Pr., *(978-0-9755157)* P.O. Box 1338, Garden Grove, CA 92844 USA Tel 714-322-3049 Do not confuse with Open Mind Press in Garner, NC E-mail: openmindpress@albalagh.net Web site: http://www.openmindpress.com.

Open Pages Publishing, *(978-0-9785937)* Orders Addr.: P.O. Box 420788, Houston, TX 77242 USA (SAN 851-0822); Edit Addr.: 3130 Walnut Bend Ln., Unit No. 317, Houston, TX 77042-4778 USA E-mail: goodstory@openpagespublishing.com.

Open Range Publishing, *(978-0-615-70960-8; 978-0-9956877-6-9)* 9415 Wolfe Pl., Highlands Ranch, CO 80129 USA Tel 303-346-8483 *Dist(s):* **CreateSpace Independent Publishing Platform.**

Open Road Integrated Media, Inc., *(978-1-58586; 978-0-7592; 978-1-936317; 978-1-4532; 978-1-61756; 978-0-9832929; 978-1-937624; 978-1-937957; 978-1-938582; 978-0-615-65097-5; 978-1-62467; 978-1-4804; 978-1-4976; 978-1-5040)* 180 Varick St. Suite 816, New York, NY 10014 USA Tel 212-691-0900; Fax: 212-691-0901; 345 Hudson St., Suite 6C, New York, NY 10014 Tel 212-691-0900; Fax: 212-691-0901; *Imprints:* Open Road Media Young Readers (OpenRdMedia); Open Road Media E-riginal (OpenRdMedE-rig) E-mail: acolvin@openroadmedia.com Web site: http://www.openroadmedia.com *Dist(s):* **Children's Plus, Inc. Follett School Solutions Independent Pubs. Group Ingram Publisher Services MyiLibrary.**

Open Road Media E-riginal *Imprint of* **Open Road Integrated Media, Inc.**

Open Road Media Young Readers *Imprint of* **Open Road Integrated Media, Inc.**

Open Spaces Publishing (Rupen), LLC, *(978-0-9768752; 978-0-9846494)* 1411 Timberlake Circle, Richardson, TX 75080 USA E-mail: chistinerhoden@att.net.

Open Suitcase, *(978-0-9985496)* 461 Wildwood Dr., St. Augustine, FL 32086-2903 USA Tel 352-316-2355 E-mail: Myopensuitcase@gmail.com Web site: Myopensuitcase.com.

Open Texture, *(978-0-9742391; 978-1-933900)* 9457 S. Univ. Blvd. #409, Highlands Ranch, CO 80126 USA Toll Free: 866-546-6459 (phone/fax) E-mail: sales@opentexture.com Web site: http://www.opentexture.com.

Open Vision Entertainment Corp., *(978-0-9721825)* 48 Summer St., Stoneham, MA 02180 USA Tel 781-438-7939; Fax: 781-438-8115 Web site: http://www.open-visions.com *Dist(s):* **Fell, Frederick Pubs., Inc.**

Open Water Pr., *(978-1-7324597)* 31 Greenlawn Dr, Fairfield, CT 06825 USA Tel 860-917-7424 E-mail: thectwebbers@optonline.net.

Open Window Publishing, *(978-0-9798505)* P.O. Box 1436, Clarkston, MI 48347-1436 USA (SAN 854-5642).

Openvein, *(978-0-9764033)* 3760 SE Morrison St., Portland, OR 97214-3210 USA Web site: http://www.openvein.com/.

Opocensky, Helene, *(978-1-7348732)* 321 Reeds Landing, Springfield, MA 01109 USA Tel 413-285-8433 E-mail: Hopocensky@outlook.com.

Oppenheim Toy Portfolio, Inc., *(978-0-9664823; 978-0-9721050)* 40 E. Ninth St., Suite 14M, New York, NY 10003 USA (SAN 255-2175) Tel 212-598-0502; Fax: 212-598-9709 E-mail: stephanie@toyportfolio.com Web site: http://www.toyportfolio.com *Dist(s):* **Brodart Co.**

Oppenlander Enterprises LLC, *(978-0-9977800)* 4110 E Morningside Dr., Bloomington, IN 47408 USA Tel 812-391-6310 E-mail: annette.oppenlander@yahoo.com Web site: annetteoppenlander.com.

Opportune Independent Publishing Co., *(978-0-9965694; 978-1-945532; 978-1-970079; 978-1-63616)* 113 Live Oak St, Houston, TX 77003 USA Tel 832-263-1700; 832-792-8269 E-mail: info@opportunepublishing.com Web site: www.opportunepublishing.com.

Opposable Thumb Pr., *(978-0-9786570)* P.O. Box 409107, Chicago, IL 60640 USA E-mail: Dawn@opposablethumbpress.com Web site: http://opposablethumbpress.com.

Options Galore, *(978-0-9801426)* 22890 S. Woodland Rd., Suite 100, Shaker Heights, OH 44122 USA Tel 216-965-8599.

Optiview Publishing, *(978-0-9723066)* 7725 Martin Mill Pike, Knoxville, TN 37920 USA E-mail: mmediajohn@ao.com Web site: http://www.optiviewpubs.com.

OPUS II Bks., *(978-0-9796210)* Orders Addr.: 1216 Purple Sage Loop, Castle Rock, CO 80104 USA (SAN 853-9367) Tel 720-371-1872 E-mail: egualberto@opusiibooks.com Web site: http://www.opusiibooks.com.

Oracle Institute Pr., LLC, The, *(978-0-9773929; 978-1-937465)* Div. of The Oracle Institute, Orders Addr.: 88 Oracle Way, Independence, VA 24348 USA (SAN 257-4780) Tel 276-773-3308 E-mail: Laura@TheOracleInstitute.org Web site: http://www.TheOracleInstitute.org; https://theoracleinstitute.org/bookstore *Dist(s):* **Ingram Content Group New Leaf Distributing Co., Inc.**

Orage Publishing, *(978-0-9740901)* 1460 Wren Ct., Punta Gorda, FL 33950 USA Tel 941-639-6144 E-mail: ntoupsschmitt@comcast.net.

Orange County Historical Society, Inc., *(978-1-932547)* 130 Caroline St., Orange, VA 22960 USA Tel 540-672-5366 (Wednesday afternoon) E-mail: info@orangecohist.org Web site: http://www.orangecohist.org.

Orange County Publishing, *(978-0-9661598; 978-0-9789972; 978-1-7326619)* Orders Addr.: P.O. Box 487, Middletown, NY 10940 USA; Edit Addr.: 4417 Edson Ave., Bronx, NY 10466 USA Tel 917-306-7244 (cell) E-mail: ikebezi@juno.com.

Orange Day Media, *(978-0-615-98797-2; 978-0-9905750)* 4319 S. Ridgewood Ave., Port Orange, FL 32127 USA Tel 386-235-9056 *Dist(s):* **CreateSpace Independent Publishing Platform.**

Orange Frazer Pr., *(978-0-9619637; 978-1-882203; 978-1-933197; 978-1-939710; 978-1-949248)* Orders Addr.: P.O. Box 214, Wilmington, OH 45177 USA (SAN 245-9299) E-mail: ofrazer@erinet.com Web site: http://www.orangefrazer.com *Dist(s):* **Partners Bk. Distributing, Inc.**

Orange Hat Publishing, *(978-1-937165; 978-1-943331; 978-1-948365; 978-1-64538)* 259 S. St. Suite B, Waukesha, WI 53186 USA Tel 414-212-5477; *Imprints:* TEN16 Press (MYID_F_TEN16 P) E-mail: Shannon@orangehatpublishing.com Web site: www.orangehatpublishing.com; www.ten16press.com *Dist(s):* **Blackstone Audio, Inc.**

Orange Hippos! (GBR) *(978-1-85868; 978-1-84222; 978-1-84442; 978-1-84732; 978-1-78097; 978-1-78739; 978-1-911610; 978-1-83861; 978-1-80069) Dist. by* **TwoRivers.**

Orange, Michael Nicholas, *(978-0-9758877)* Orders Addr.: P.O. Box 236, Half Moon Bay, CA 94019 USA; Edit Addr.: 646 Filbert St., Half Moon Bay, CA 94019-2112 USA.

Orange Ocean Pr., *(978-1-885021)* 127 Bennett Ave., Long Beach, CA 90803-2935 USA; *Imprints:* Tangerine Tide (Tang Tide) E-mail: nextmag@aol.com.

Orange Spot Publishing, *(978-0-9785191)* P.O. Box 224, Freeland, WA 98249 USA Web site: http://www.pugetsoundbackyardbirds.com.

OrangeFoot Publishing Co., *(978-0-9760651)* P.O. Box 3694, Pittsburgh, PA 15230-3694 USA E-mail: orangefootpublishing@zoominternet.net; info@orangefootpublishing.com.

Oratia Media (NZL) *(978-1-877514; 978-0-473-17634-1; 978-0-947506; 978-1-990042) Dist. by* **UH Pr.**

Orb Bks. *Imprint of* **Doherty, Tom Assocs., LLC**

Orbis Publications, Incorporated *See* **Bilingual Dictionaries, Inc.**

Orbit, Div. of Hachette Book Group, 237 Park Ave., New York, NY 10017 USA *Dist(s):* **Blackstone Audio, Inc. Hachette Bk. Group MyiLibrary.**

Orca Bk. Pubs. (CAN) *(978-0-920501; 978-1-55143; 978-1-55469; 978-1-4598) Dist. by* **Orca Bk Pub.**

Orca Bk. Pubs. USA, *(978-0-920501; 978-1-55143; 978-1-55469)* Orders Addr.: P.O. Box 468, Custer, WA 98240-0468 USA (SAN 630-9674) Tel 250-380-1229; Fax: 250-380-1892; Toll Free: 800-210-5277 E-mail: orca@orcabook.com Web site: http://www.orcabook.com *Dist(s):* **Children's Plus, Inc.**

Orchard Bks. *Imprint of* **Scholastic, Inc.**

Orchard Bks. *Imprint of* **Scholastic Library Publishing**

Orchard Books *See* **Healing Heart's Publishing Co.**

Orchard House Press *See* **Blue Forge Pr.**

Orchard Pr. *Imprint of* **Point Publishing**

Orchid Isle Publishing Co., *(978-1-887916)* 131 Halai St., Hilo, HI 96720 USA.

Orchid Publishing Co., *(978-0-9740898)* 14906 SW 104 St., Miami, FL 33196 USA.

Orchid Publishing, Inc., *(978-0-9831641; 978-0-9838325)* 333 N. Michigan Ave. Suite 222, Chicago, IL 60601 USA Tel 312-332-7200 E-mail: efimova@russianpointe.com.

Oregon Ctr. for Applied Science, Inc., *(978-1-933898)* 260 E. 11th Ave., Eugene, OR 97401-3291 USA (SAN 850-5284) Toll Free: 888-349-5472 E-mail: orcas@orcasinc.com Web site: http://www.orcasinc.com.

Oregon State Univ. Extension Service, *(978-1-931979; 978-0-578-95066-2; 979-8-9855282)* Extension & Station Communications 422 Kerr Administration, Corvallis, OR 97331 USA Tel 541-737-0807; Fax: 541-737-0817 Web site: http://extension.oregonstate.edu/eesc/.

†Oregon State Univ. Pr., *(978-0-87071; 978-1-962645)* 121 The Valley Library, Corvallis, OR 97331 USA (SAN 202-8328) Tel 541-737-3166; 541-737-4620; Fax: 541-737-3170 E-mail: osu.press@oregonstate.edu Web site: http://osupress.oregonstate.edu/ *Dist(s):* **American Society of Civil Engineers Chicago Distribution Ctr. Partners Bk. Distributing, Inc. University of Arizona Pr. Univ. of Oklahoma Pr. Univ. of Chicago Pr. Distribution Clients**; *CIP.*

O'Reilly & Associates, Incorporated *See* **O'Reilly Media, Inc.**

O'Reilly Media, Inc., *(978-0-937175; 978-1-56592; 978-3-89721; 978-3-930673; 978-4-900900; 978-0-596; 978-4-87311; 978-1-60033; 978-1-4493; 978-1-4919; 978-1-4920; 978-1-4571; 978-1-0981)* Orders Addr.: 1005 Gravenstein Hwy. N., Sebastopol, CA 95472 USA (SAN 658-5973) Fax: 707-829-0104; Toll Free: 800-998-9938; Edit Addr.: 10 Fawcett St. Ste. 4, Cambridge, MA 02138-1175 USA Toll Free: 800-775-7731; 4 Castle St, Farnham, GU9 7HR Tel 01252 71 17 76; Fax: 01252 73 42 11 E-mail: order@oreilly.com; information@oreilly.co.uk; nuts@ora.com; isbn-info@oreilly.com Web site: http://www.oreilly.com; http://www.editions-oreilly.fr; http://oreilly.co.uk; http://oreilly.com.tw; http://www.ora.com; http://www.oreilly.fr/; http://www.oreilly.com.cn/ *Dist(s):* **CreateSpace Independent Publishing Platform Ebsco Publishing Follett School Solutions Ingram Publisher Services MyiLibrary Two Rivers Distribution Wiley, John & Sons, Inc.**

Oren Village, LLC, *(978-0-9777272)* P.O. Box 1111, Worthington, OH 43085 USA Tel 614-937-8513 E-mail: author@alanstjean.com Web site: http://www.alanstjean.com.

Orenda Pr., LLC, *(978-0-9907453; 978-0-9967920)* P.O. Box 1445, Cedar Park, TX 78630 USA Tel 512-961-0531 E-mail: kristen@orendapress.com Web site: Orendapress.com.

resjozef Pubns., (978-1-885566) 167 Canton St., Randolph, MA 02368 USA Tel 781-961-5855; Toll Free: 617-851-0100
E-mail: ojozef@massed.net
Dist(s): **Educa Vision Inc.**
Haitiana Pubns., Inc.

rgan Buddies Inc., (978-0-615-32940-6) 110 Blue Ribbon Dr, North Wales, PA 19454 USA Tel 267-253-8462; Fax: 215-393-8464
E-mail: leedowning8@msn.com
Web site: www.organbuddies.com.

OrganWise Guys Inc., The, (978-0-9648438; 978-1-931212; 978-0-9858048) 450 Satellite Blvd. NE Suite M, Suwanee, GA 30024 USA Tel 770-844-8686; Fax: 770-844-6580; Toll Free: 800-786-1730 Do not confuse with Wellness, Inc., Boston, MA
E-mail: karen@organwiseguys.com
Web site: http://www.organwiseguys.com.

Orion Publishing Group, Ltd. (GBR) *(978-0-304; 978-0-460; 978-0-575; 978-0-7528; 978-1-85797; 978-1-85798; 978-1-85881; 978-1-86047; 978-1-84188; 978-1-84255; 978-1-4091; 978-0-85782; 978-1-4072; 978-1-4719; 978-1-78771-955-2; 978-1-78062; 978-1-905619) Dist. by* **Trafalgar.**

Orion Publishing Group, Ltd. (GBR) *(978-0-304; 978-0-460; 978-0-575; 978-0-7528; 978-1-85797; 978-1-85798; 978-1-85881; 978-1-86047; 978-1-84188; 978-1-84255; 978-1-905619; 978-1-4091; 978-1-78062; 978-0-85782; 978-1-4072; 978-1-4719; 978-1-78771-955-2) Dist. by* **HachBkGrp.**

Orion Society, The, (978-0-913098; 978-0-578-62162-3) Orders Addr.: 187 Main St., Great Barrington, MA 01230-1601 USA (SAN 204-0182) Tel 413-528-4422; Fax: 413-528-0676; Toll Free: 888-909-6568
E-mail: gagne@orionmagazine.org
Web site: http://www.orionmagazine.org.

Orion Wellspring, Inc., (978-0-9794614) 20 Blaine St., Seattle, WA 98109 USA Tel 206-931-4656; Fax: 206-374-2149
E-mail: tom.masters@orionwellspring.com; info@orionwellspring.com
Web site: http://www.orionwellspring.com.

Orion-Cosmos, (978-0-9752725) 3609 Candleknoll Cir., San Antonio, TX 78244 USA
E-mail: customerservice@orion-cosmos.com
Web site: http://www.orion-cosmos.com.

Orison Pubs., (978-0-9763800; 978-0-9827944; 978-1-945169; 978-1-960007) P.O. Box 188, Grantham, PA 17027 USA
E-mail: marsha@orisonpublishers.com
Web site: http://www.discovertheauthor.com; http://www.orisonpublishers.com
Dist(s): **Independently Published**
Ingram Publisher Services
Pennsylvania State Univ. Pr.

Ormond, Jennifer, (978-0-9792010) 77 Pkwy., Quincy, MA 02169 USA
E-mail: jennormond@gmail.com
Web site: http://www.jenniferormond.com.

Orndee Omnimedia, Inc., (978-0-9774260; 978-0-9822229) 36 West 37th St. Penthouse, New York, NY 10018 USA Tel 212-203-0363
E-mail: Publishing@Orndee.com
Web site: http://www.Orndee.com.

ORO Editions, *(978-0-9746800; 978-0-9774672; 978-0-9793801; 978-0-9795395; 978-0-9814628; 978-0-9820607; 978-0-9819857; 978-0-9826226; 978-1-935935; 978-1-941806; 978-1-939621; 978-1-940743; 978-1-943532; 978-1-951541; 978-1-954081; 978-1-957183; 978-1-961856) Orders Addr.: P.O. Box 150338, San Rafael, CA 94915 USA Tel 415-663-0678; Fax: 415-457-3650; Edit Addr.: 31 Commercial Blvd., Suite F, Novato, CA 94945 USA Tel 415-883-3300; Fax: 415-883-3309; Imprints*: Goff Books (GoffBks)
E-mail: gordon@oroeditions.com; christy@oroeditions.com; info@oroeditions.com
Web site: http://www.oroeditions.com
Dist(s): **Actar D**
Consortium Bk. Sales & Distribution
D.A.P./Distributed Art Pubs.
Ingram Publisher Services
Publishers Group West (PGW).

Oron's, (978-1-947095) 30 Chapin Rd, Unit 1201, Pine Brook, NJ 07058-9392 USA Tel 973-740-0095
E-mail: ohagit@gmail.com.

Orpen Pr. (IRL) *(978-1-871305; 978-1-84218; 978-1-909895; 978-1-78605; 978-1-909518) Dist. by* **Dufour.**

Orr Bks., (978-0-9800611; 978-0-9827764; 978-0-9851760) 608 Seitz St., Easton, PA 18042-6544 USA Tel 610-258-5479
E-mail: derek@beachfrontpress.com; peter@beachfrontpress.com
Web site: http://www.orrbooks.net; http://www.beachfrontpress.com.

Ortells, Alfredo Editorial S.L. (ESP) *(978-84-7189) Dist. by* **Continental Bk.**

Ortiz, Enrique Publishing, (978-0-615-25622-1; 978-0-615-25637-5; 978-0-615-26124-9; 978-0-578-00134-0; 978-0-578-00135-7) 1538 Bullbush Way, Oviedo, FL 32765 USA
Dist(s): **Lulu Pr., Inc.**

Osage Bend Publishing Co., (978-0-9626245; 978-1-58389) 213 Belair Dr., Jefferson City, MO 65109 USA Tel 573-635-5580; Toll Free: 888-243-9772
E-mail: OBPC@Socket.net
Dist(s): **Follett School Solutions.**

Osani Studios, (978-1-7327189) 19318 Riverwood Ln., Lake Oswego, OR 97035 USA Tel 503-415-1586
E-mail: osanistudios@gmail.com.

Osanto Univ. Pr. *Imprint of* **Benjamin Franklin Pr.**

Osborne Enterprises Publishing, (978-0-932117) P.O. Box 255, Port Townsend, WA 98368 USA (SAN 242-7567) Tel 360-385-1200; Toll Free: 800-246-3255 (orders only)
E-mail: jpo@olympus.net
Web site: http://www.jerryosborne.com.

Osborne Pr., (978-1-928856) Div. of David M. Osborne, Inc., 16726 Comstock, Livonia, MI 48154 USA Tel 734-464-7002; Fax: 734-464-6837
E-mail: osborne@mich.com
Web site: http://www.mich.com/~osborne.

Osborne, Wanda, (978-1-953895) 4 Canyon Ct., Algonquin, IL USA, IL 60102 USA Tel 847-909-6520
E-mail: lynn095@comcast.net.

Osborne/McGraw-Hill *See* **McGraw-Hill Osborne**

Oscar, Erica, (978-0-9747262) 20424 Packard, Detroit, MI 48234 USA.

O'Shea, Ellen Storyteller, (978-1-7321023) 751 Old Eaglemount Rd., Port Townsend, WA 98368 USA Tel 360-301-1662
E-mail: elleno@peak.org
Web site: Ellenosheastoryteller.com.

Osherbert Bks., LLC, (978-0-9885461) P.O. Box 1591, Gig Harbor, WA 98335 USA Tel 253-651-8997
E-mail: seshell@gmail.com.

Osmosis, LLC, (978-0-9727886; 978-0-9816281) 8 Findlay Ave., Hartsdale, NY 10530-2613 USA Tel 914-328-8898; Fax: 914-328-1124; Toll Free: 866-676-6747
E-mail: osmosis@earthlink.net
Web site: http://www.learningbyosmosis.com; http://www.osmosis.tv.

Osprey *Imprint of* **Bloomsbury Publishing USA**

Osprey Pr., (978-0-9673711) 2107 Ibis Dr., Buffalo, MN 55313 USA Tel 763-682-4558 Do not confuse with companies with the same or similar names in St. Johnsbury, VT, Wiscasset, ME
E-mail: ospreypress@charter.net
Web site: http://www.planetearthhome.com
Dist(s): **Random Hse., Inc.**

Osteogenesis Imperfecta Foundation, (978-0-9642189) 804 W. Diamond Ave., Suite 210, Gaithersburg, MD 20878 USA Tel 301-947-0083; Fax: 301-947-0456; Toll Free: 800-981-2663
E-mail: bonelink@oif.org
Web site: http://www.oif.org.

Osterman, Lisa, (978-1-7353506; 979-8-9857114) 248 Selby Ranch Rd. 1, Sacramento, CA 95864 USA Tel 916-487-2987
E-mail: Lisa@ArribasPress.com
Web site: ArribasPress.com.

Ostermeyer Photography, (978-0-9794228; 978-0-615-74538-1; 978-0-692-02001-2) 1813 Country Brook Ln., Allen, TX 75002 USA Tel 972-542-7065
E-mail: tim@ostermeyer-photography.com
Web site: http://www.ostermeyer-photography.com.

Ostrageous Publishing, (978-0-9785144) P.O. Box 2867, Hot Springs, AK 71914 USA Tel 501-525-4245.

Otago University Pr. (NZL) *(978-0-908569; 978-1-877133; 978-1-877276; 978-1-877372; 978-1-877578; 978-1-988531; 978-1-927322; 978-1-988592) Dist. by* **IPG Chicago.**

Other Road Pr., (978-0-9837329) 31 Beaman Rd., Princeton, MA 01541 USA Tel 508-787-7863
E-mail: otherroadpress@gmail.com
Web site: http://www.otherroadpress.com
Dist(s): **Smashwords.**

Other Worlds Ink, (978-1-7323075; 978-1-955778) P.O. Box 19341, Sacramento, CA 95819 USA Tel 925-788-8896
E-mail: scott@otherworldsink.com
Dist(s): **Ingram Content Group.**

Otherside Pr. *Imprint of* **Crossroad Pr.**

Otis & Randolph Pr., (978-0-9752516) 1229 Bishop's Lodge Rd., Santa Fe, NM 87501 USA.

Otis, Beverly J., (978-0-615-27994-7; 978-0-615-72483-6) 1138 Oakhill St., Seffner, FL 33584 USA
Web site: http://www.beverlyotis.web.officelive.com.

Otis, Dorcas Marie *See* **Zion Publishing**

Otter Falls Publishing, (978-0-692-84835-7; 978-0-692-95401-0; 978-0-692-04557-2; 978-0-578-21284-5; 978-0-578-57496-7; 978-0-578-67954-9) 2085 Bridgewater Blvd S, Cambridge, MN 55008 USA Tel 612-741-9185
E-mail: bbfellerer@yahoo.com.

Otter Run Bks. LLC, (978-0-9760796) 16965 Nicolet Rd., Townsend, WI 54175 USA Tel 715-276-6515 (phone/fax)
E-mail: kathiemarsh@yahoo.com
Web site: http://www.otterrunbooks.com.

Otter Track Pr., (978-0-9848229; 978-0-9998070) Div. of MRose Group, LLC, 103 Turtle Bend, Georgetown, TX 78628 USA Tel 251-752-2416.

Otter-Barry Bks. (GBR) *(978-1-910959; 978-1-913074) Dist. by* **IPG Chicago.**

OTTN Publishing, (978-1-59556) 16 Risler Street, Stockton, NJ 08559 USA Tel 609-397-4005; Fax: 609-397-4007
E-mail: jgallagher@ottnpublishing.com
Web site: http://www.ottnpublishing.com.

Otto PD, (978-0-692-70958-0; 978-0-9981412) 4801 Laguna Blvd #105-310, Elk Grove, CA 95758 USA Tel 408-836-8918; Toll Free: 408-836-8918
Dist(s): **CreateSpace Independent Publishing Platform.**

Ouattara, Issoufou *See* **International Development Ctr.**

Oui Love Bks. *Imprint of* **Odeon Livre**

Our Blueprint-A Recipe for Wellness, (978-0-692-05847-3; 978-0-692-08757-2; 978-0-692-04442-1; 978-0-578-42078-3; 978-0-578-42357-9; 978-0-578-49451-7) 1442 E. Lincoln Ave No. 310, Orange, CA 92865 USA Tel 714-910-5141
E-mail: TONY@ob4w.com; tonyisactive@gmail.com
Web site: www.ob4w.com
Dist(s): **CreateSpace Independent Publishing Platform.**

†**Our Child Pr.**, (978-0-9611872; 978-1-893516) P.O. Box 4379, Philadelphia, PA 19118 USA (SAN 682-272X) Tel 610-308-8988
E-mail: ourchildpress@aol.com
Web site: http://www.ourchildpress.com; *CIP.*

Our Companions, Inc., (978-0-9753257) 84 N. Acoma Blvd., No. 100-33, Lake Havasu City, AZ 86403 USA Tel 928-486-4508.

Our Inspiring Stories Publishing Co., (978-0-9995246) 6983 Seabreeze Dr., Suite 100, Grand Prairie, TX 75054 USA Tel 682-554-1743
E-mail: sandraannwalters@gmail.com
Web site: www.ourispiringstories.com.

Our J.O.Y.C.E. Incorporated *See* **BeMana LLC**

Our Kids Pr., (978-0-9660884; 978-0-9860290) Orders Addr.: P.O. Box 486, Bellingham, WA 98227 USA Tel 360-734-2335; Edit Addr.: 3804 Ridgemont Way, Bellingham, WA 98227 USA
Web site: ourkidspress.com.

Our Lady of Victory Schl., (978-1-931555) 103 E. Tenth Ave., Post Falls, ID 83854 USA Tel 208-773-7265; Fax: 208-773-1951
E-mail: lepanto@olvs.org
Web site: http://www.olvs.org.

Our Little Secret Pr., (978-0-9720978) 140 Timberlink Dr., Grand Island, NY 14072 USA.

Our Story Pubns., (978-0-9765554) P.O. Box 7514, Round Rock, TX 78683 USA Tel 512-663-1471
E-mail: nicoleeutsey@ourstorypublications.com
Web site: http://www.ourstorypublications.com.

Our Sunday Visitor, Publishing Div., (978-0-87973; 978-0-9707756; 978-1-931709; 978-1-59276; 978-1-61278; 978-1-68192; 978-1-63966) 200 Noll Plaza, Huntington, IN 46750 USA (SAN 202-8344) Tel 260-356-8400; Fax: 260-359-9117; 260-356-8472; Toll Free: 800-348-2440
E-mail: osvbooks@osv.com; ntopp@osv.com
Web site: http://www.osv.com
Dist(s): **Baker & Taylor International**
MyiLibrary
Spring Arbor Distributors, Inc.

Our World of Books *See* **Good Night Bks.**

OurRainbow Pr., LLC, (978-0-9752860; 978-1-934214) Orders Addr.: 2600 Penrick Dr., Marietta, GA 30064-1809 USA Tel 770-514-8794; Toll Free: 877-600-7323
E-mail: publisher@ourrainbow.com; ameadows@ourrainbow.com; anthony.meadows@gmail.com; sheila.meadows@gmail.com
Web site: http://www.ourrainbowpress.com; http://orpbooks.com.

Out of the Box, (978-0-9726849) P.O. Box 24234, Minneapolis, MN 55424 USA Tel 612-822-5151; Fax: 612-823-4164
E-mail: info@ootbooks.com
Web site: http://www.ootbooks.com
Dist(s): **Brodart Co.**
Follett School Solutions
Quality Bks., Inc.

Out of the Box Publishing, Inc., (978-0-9664517; 978-0-9708554; 978-0-9716729; 978-1-932359) 609 Bennett Rd., Dodgeville, WI 53533 USA (SAN 760-5269) Toll Free: 800-540-4201 Do not confuse with Out of the Box Publishing, Cincinnati, OH
E-mail: sales@otb-games.com; brad@otb-games.com
Web site: http://www.otb-games.com.

Out There Bks., (978-0-9827906; 978-1-7353204) 1324 Alta Vista Ave., Austin, TX 78704 USA Tel 512-577-7808.

Outcomes Unlimited Pr., Inc., (978-0-925640) P.O. Box 8013, Asheville, NC 28814-8497 USA
E-mail: drdossey@drdossey.com
Web site: http://www.drdossey.com.

Outdoor Originals LLC, (978-0-9762971) 1052 California Ave. W., Saint Paul, MN 55117 USA.

Outdoor Writing & Photography, Limited *See* **Visions Of Nature**

Outer Banks Pr., (978-0-9713890; 978-0-9778924; 978-1-7326805) Div. of OBBC, Inc., P.O. Box 2829, Kitty Hawk, NC 27949 USA (SAN 254-3958) Tel 252-261-0612; Toll Free Fax: 800-215-9648
E-mail: linda@outerbankspress.com
Web site: http://www.outerbankspress.com.

outerBks., (978-0-692-37891-5; 978-0-692-43092-7; 978-0-692-70647-3; 978-0-692-92649-9) 32 jazz way, mt laurel, NJ 08054 USA Tel 856-914-0850
E-mail: rkingsbury32@comcast.net
Web site: http://www.outerbooks.com.

OutFlow Publishing, (978-1-7329995) 929 Main St W., Valdese, NC 28690 USA Tel 828-874-4457
E-mail: allenking@outflowpublishing.com
Web site: www.outflowpublishing.com.

Outland Communications, LLC, (978-0-9714102; 978-1-932820) Orders Addr.: P.O. Box 534, Skaneateles, NY 13152 USA; Edit Addr.: 4022 Mill Rd., Skaneateles, NY 13152-9319 USA
Web site: http://www.outlandbooks.com.

Outlaw Bks., (978-0-9656946) 419 Centre St., Hereford, TX 79045 USA Tel 806-364-2838; Fax: 806-364-5522; Toll Free: 888-583-9408 Do not confuse with Outlaw Books, Bozeman, MT
Dist(s): **Hervey's Booklink & Cookbook Warehouse.**

Outlaw Pubns., (978-1-886709) Orders Addr.: P.O. Box 1424, Red Oak, TX 75154 USA Tel 972-504-6608; Edit Addr.: P.O. Box 3043, Desoto, TX 75115 USA.

Outlet Book Company, Incorporated *See* **Random Hse. Value Publishing**

Outlook Publishing, Inc., (978-0-9711667; 978-0-9817755) Orders Addr.: P.O. Box 278, Laurel, MT 59044 USA Tel 406-628-4412; Fax: 406-628-8260; Edit Addr.: 415 E. Main St., Laurel, MT 59044 USA
E-mail: publisher@laureloutlook.com
Web site: http://www.laureloutlook.com.

Outlook Words & Art, (978-0-692-83201-1; 978-0-692-83667-5; 978-0-9986426; 978-0-9986593; 978-1-7320896) 12057 Open Run Rd., Ellicott City, MD 21042 USA Tel 310-990-5529
E-mail: t.pryce@outlookco.com
Dist(s): **Diamond Comic Distributors, Inc.**
Independent Pubs. Group.

Outreach Publications *See* **DaySpring Cards**

Outreach/New Reader *Imprint of* **Marvel Worldwide, Inc.**

Outrival Publishing, (978-0-9885603) P.O. Box 130345, Houston, TX 77219 USA Tel 832-878-6162; Fax: 713-861-1501
E-mail: kimpedigo@gmail.com.

Outside the Box Publishing, LLC, (978-0-9817398) 326 2nd St. No. 3, Brooklyn, NY 11215 USA Tel 202-905-3442
E-mail: info@otbpublishing.com; dax@daxdevlonross.com; daxdevlonross@gmail.com
Web site: http://www.otbpublishing.com
Dist(s): **Ingram Content Group.**

Outskirts Pr., Inc., (978-0-9725874; 978-1-932672; 978-1-59800; 978-1-4327; 978-0-615-20388-1; 978-1-4787; 978-1-9772) 10940 S. Parker Rd. - 515, Parker, CO 80134 USA (SAN 256-5420)
Web site: http://www.OutskirtsPress.com
Dist(s): **Aardvark Global Publishing**
Smashwords.

Outskirts Press, Incorporation *See* **Outskirts Pr., Inc.**

Ovation Bks., (978-1-933538; 978-0-9790275; 978-0-9814534) 2100 Kramer Ln., Suite 300, Austin, TX 78758 USA Tel 512-478-2028; Fax: 512-478-2117
E-mail: awillis@bookpros.com; sboulden@ovationbooks.net
Web site: http://www.bookpros.com; http://www.ovationbooks.net.

Over The Edge Studios, (978-0-9984716; 978-1-7339086; 978-1-957422) 3942 State Rd. 135 S., Nashville, IN 47448 USA Tel 812-350-4807
E-mail: tc@tcbartlett.com.

Over the Rainbow *Imprint of* **Pearn & Assocs. Inc.**

Over The Rainbow Bks. Publishing, (978-0-9793882) 1810 New Palm Way, No. 410, Boynton Beach, FL 33435 USA Tel 561-704-6581
E-mail: famuffy@aol.com.

Over the Rainbow Productions, (978-0-9661330) 1715 Rosedale, Suite B, Houston, TX 77004 USA Tel 713-523-1276; Fax: 713-526-0571
E-mail: apb3@prodigy.net
Web site: http://www.imneecie.com.

Overcup Pr., (978-0-9834917; 978-1-7326103; 979-8-9856527) 4760 SE 58th Ave., Portland, OR 97206 USA Tel 503-453-0091
E-mail: pat@overcupbooks.com
Web site: www.overcupbooks.com
Dist(s): **Independent Pubs. Group**
SCB Distributors.

Overdue Bks., (978-0-9786850) P.O. Box 259462, Madison, WI 53725 USA Do not confuse with Overdue Books in West Linn, OR
E-mail: theoverduebooks@yahoo.com.

Overhead Pr., LLC, (978-0-9985067) 18 Whitetail Crossing, Lunenburg, MA 01462 USA
E-mail: jaredperrine@hotmail.com.

Overlook Connection Pr., The, (978-0-9633397; 978-1-892950; 978-1-62330) Orders Addr.: P.O. Box 1934, Hiram, GA 30141 USA Tel 678-567-9777; Edit Addr.: 364 Valerie Cir., Hiram, GA 30141 USA
E-mail: overlookcn@aol.com
Web site: http://www.overlookconnection.com; http://www.overlookconnection.com
Dist(s): **Diamond Comic Distributors, Inc.**

Overlook Pr., The *Imprint of* **Abrams, Inc.**

Overman, Ryan, (978-0-578-51968-5) 5626 E. Le Marche Ave, Scottsdale, AZ 85254 USA Tel 623-512-2753
E-mail: ryanoverman21@yahoo.com.

Overmountain Pr., (978-0-932807; 978-0-9644613; 978-1-57072; 978-1-935692) P.O. Box 1261, Johnson City, TN 37605 USA (SAN 687-6641) Tel 423-926-2691; Fax: 423-232-1252; Toll Free: 800-992-2691 (orders only); *Imprints*: Silver Dagger Mysteries (Silver Dagger)
E-mail: beth@overmtn.com
Web site: http://www.silverdaggermysteries.com; http://www.overmountainpress.com
Dist(s): **Partners Pubs. Group, Inc.**

Overstreet, Mae *See* **Overstreet Pub. & Mktg.**

Overstreet Pub. & Mktg., (978-0-9746253) P.O. Box 3808, Yountville, CA 94599 USA
Web site: http://www.bettyoverstreet.com.

Overview Publishing, (978-0-9760685) 1081 Crown River Pkwy., McDonough, GA 30252 USA Tel 678-583-0898
E-mail: cindy@overviewpublishing.com
Web site: http://www.overviewpublishing.com
Dist(s): **Quality Bks., Inc.**

OVI Healthcare, (978-1-7362243) P.O. Box PO Box 250, Somerset, KY 42502 USA Tel 606-219-6701
E-mail: contact@OVIHealthcare.org
Web site: www.OVIHealthcare.org.

Owen, Jessica, 16 Via Tranquila, Rancho Santa Margarita, CA 92688 USA Tel 949-300-6702
E-mail: carolowen@coastalexec.com
Dist(s): **Ingram Content Group.**

Owen, Richard C. Pubs., Inc., (978-0-913461; 978-1-57274; 978-1-878450) P.O. Box 585, Katonah, NY 10536 USA (SAN 285-1814) Tel 914-232-3903; Fax: 914-232-3977; Toll Free: 800-336-5588 (orders); *Imprints*: Meet the Author (Meet Author); Books for Young Learners (Bks Yng Learn); Author at Work (Author at Work)
Web site: http://www.RCOwen.com.

Owens, David A., (978-0-578-05417-9) 4253 October Woods Dr., Antioch, TN 37013 USA.

Owens, Mimi, (978-1-7322175) 213 Penfold Pl, Harahan, LA 70123 USA Tel 504-210-6610
E-mail: mikaseaux@me.com.

Owens, Ralinda, (978-0-9993228) 5633 Tiger Trail, Fort Worth, TX 76126 USA Tel 817-800-5853
E-mail: ralindaowens@att.net.

Owensby, Legertha, *(978-0-9742739)* 6820 Chiffview Dr., No. E, Indianapolis, IN 46214 USA
E-mail: legethac@yahoo.com
Web site: http://earvino.tripod.com.

Owl About Books Publisher, Incorporated *See* **Owl About Bks. Pubs.**

Owl About Bks. Pubs., *(978-1-937752)* 1632 Royalwood Cir., Joshua, TX 76058 USA Tel 682-553-9078; Fax: 817-558-8983
E-mail: owlaboutbooks@gmail.com
Web site: http://www.owlaboutbooks.com
Dist(s): **Ingram Content Group.**

Owl Creek Farm Bks. *Imprint of* **Owl Tree Pr.**

Owl Creek Media Ltd., *(978-1-60404)* 490 Trego Rd., Waverly, OH 45690 USA Tel 740-493-1939; Toll Free: 800-305-0339 Please leave a message
E-mail: james@owlcreekmedia.com
Web site: http://www.owlcreekmedia.com; http://www.localbookproject.com.

Owl Hollow Pr., *(978-1-945654; 978-1-945654-04-6; 978-1-958109)* 224 S. Main St. No. 452, Springville, UT 84663 USA Tel 703-597-4720
E-mail: exec.editor@owlhollowpress.com
Web site: https://owlhollowpress.com/.

Owl Hollow Publishing, *(978-0-9726826)* 13704 Lawrence 2187, Verona, MO 65769 USA Tel 417-498-6964
E-mail: zona@mo-net.com.

Owl of Minerva Press *See* **Minerva Bks.**

Owl Pals, *(978-0-9799196)* 10210 NE. 12th St. Unit C301, Bellevue, WA 98004 USA Tel 206-948-2629
Web site: http://www.owlpals.com.

Owl Room Pr., *(978-0-692-95930-5; 978-0-692-08784-8; 978-0-578-46643-9; 978-0-578-58923-7; 978-0-578-61915-6; 978-1-7351366)* 1630 15th Ave SW, Albany, OR 97321 USA Tel 541-223-3894
E-mail: RocketshipGD@yahoo.com
Dist(s): **CreateSpace Independent Publishing Platform.**

Owl Tree Pr., *(978-1-929424)* P.O. Box 292, Saint Helens, OR 97051 USA Tel 503-397-3667; Fax: 503-397-3684; *Imprints:* Owl Creek Farm Books (Owl Creek Farm Bks)
E-mail: jdnyberg@ados.com
Web site: http://www.owltreepress.com.

Owlkids Bks. Inc. (CAN) *(978-0-919872; 978-0-920775; 978-1-895688; 978-2-920660; 978-1-894379; 978-2-89579; 978-1-77147) Dist. by* **PerseuPGW.**

Own Path Pr., *(978-1-7369807)* 8253 Taunton Pl, Springfield, VA 22152 USA Tel 202-213-4330
E-mail: etainenorris@hotmail.com
Web site: https://www.facebook.com/BlueberryDay.

Oxbow Bks., *(978-0-9771129)* 76 Presidio Dr., Novato, CA 94949 USA
E-mail: dchaller@horizoncable.com.

Oxfam Publishing (GBR) *(978-0-85598; 978-1-78748) Dist. by* **Stylus Pub VA.**

Oxford Museum Pr., *(978-1-930127)* 5790 Stillwell-Beckett Rd., Oxford, OH 45056 USA Tel 513-756-9386; Fax: 513-756-9123; Toll Free: 877-127-1941
E-mail: omp@oxfordmuseumpress.com
Web site: http://www.oxfordmuseumpress.com.

Oxford Univ. Pr. (GBR) *(978-0-19) Dist. by* **OUP.**

Oxford Univ. Pr., Inc., *(978-0-19; 978-0-87893; 978-1-60535)* Orders Addr.: 2001 Evans Rd., Cary, NC 27513 USA (SAN 202-5892) Tel 919-677-0977 (general voice); Fax: 919-677-1303 (customer service); Toll Free: 800-445-9714 (customer service - inquiry); 800-451-7556 (customer service - orders); Edit Addr.: 198 Madison Ave., New York, NY 10016-4314 USA (SAN 202-5884) Tel 212-726-6000 (general voice); Fax: 212-726-6440 (general fax)
E-mail: custserv@oup-usa.org; orders@oup-usa.org
Web site: http://www.oup.com/us
Dist(s): **Chicago Distribution Ctr.**
Children's Plus, Inc.
CreateSpace Independent Publishing Platform
Ebsco Publishing
Follett School Solutions
Cengage Gale
Hancock Hse. Pubs.
Independent Pubs. Group
ISD
MyiLibrary
Oxford University Press USA - OSO
World Bank Pubns.
ebrary, Inc.

Oxfordshire Publishing Co., *(978-0-9745895)* 900 Lincoln Hwy., Box 180, East Mckeesport, PA 15035 USA Tel 412-823-1700
E-mail: blissman@pghmail.com.

Oyebanji, Adam, *(978-0-692-09941-4; 978-0-692-19443-0; 978-0-692-19444-7)* 4769 Wallingford St. 0, Pittsburgh, PA 15213 USA Tel 7736360268; *Imprints:* Andromeda Press (MYID_Q_ANDROME)
E-mail: adam@adam-alexander.net
Web site: adam-alexander.net
Dist(s): **Ingram Content Group.**

OZA.Inc.Co, *(978-1-7330602)* 2980 Brogans Bluff Dr., Colorado Springs, CO 80919 USA Tel 530-314-1766
E-mail: OZA_1@MSN.COM.

Ozark Mountain Publishing, Inc., *(978-0-9632776; 978-1-886940; 978-1-940265; 978-1-950608; 978-1-950639; 978-1-956945)* Orders Addr.: P.O. Box 754, Huntsville, AR 72740 USA Tel 479-738-2348; Fax: 479-738-2448; Toll Free: 800-935-0045 Do not confuse with Ozark Mountain Pubs., Springfield, MO
E-mail: nancy@ozarkmt.com
Web site: http://www.ozarkmt.com
Dist(s): **D.A.P./Distributed Art Pubs.**
Red Wheel/Weiser.

Ozark Publishing, *(978-1-56763; 978-1-59381)* P.O. Box 228, Prairie Grove, AR 72753 USA (SAN 298-4318) Tel 214-649-0188; Fax: 501-846-2853; Toll Free: 800-321-5671
E-mail: srg304@aol.com
Web site: http://www.ozarkpublishing.com
Dist(s): **Central Programs**
Gumdrop Bks.

Ozo Pr., *(978-1-946618)* 8098 Hollygrape Ln., Colorado Springs, CO 80927 USA Tel 719-323-1576
E-mail: stacysjensen@gmail.com
Web site: ozopress.com.

Ozone Publishing, Corp., *(978-0-9773285)* PMB 500, RR-8 Box 1995, Bayamon, PR 00956-9676 USA Tel 787-562-5200; Fax: 787-730-0987
E-mail: info@ozonepublishing.net
Web site: http://www.ozonepublishing.net.

Ozten, *(978-0-9752966)* 347 NW 87th St., Seattle, WA 98117 USA
E-mail: shout@ozten.com
Web site: http://www.ozten.com.

P A Reading Pr., *(978-1-7357314; 979-8-9886818)* 1537 Lincoln Ave, Calumet City, IL 60409 USA Tel 708-646-1981
E-mail: pareadingpress@gmail.com.

P. Anastasia, *(978-0-9862567; 978-0-9974485; 978-1-952425)* ; *Imprints:* Jackal Moon Press (Jackal Moon)
E-mail: wolferene@gmail.com
Web site: www.fatesaflame.com; www.panastasia.com; www.FluorescenceBooks.com; www.DarkDiaryNovel.com.

P & P Publishing LLC, *(978-0-9797020)* 4957 Lakemont Blvd., SE, Suite C-4, No. 316, Bellevue, WA 98006 USA Tel 425-557-0257 Do not confuse with companies with the same or similar name in Frankermuth, MI, Warren, MI, Temple, TX, Wauwatosa, WI.

P & R Publishing, *(978-0-87552; 978-1-59638; 978-1-62995)* Orders Addr.: 1102 Marble Hill Rd., Harmony, Phillipsburg, NJ 08865 USA (SAN 658-1463) Tel 908-454-0505; Fax: 908-859-2390; Toll Free: 800-631-0094 Do not confuse with P & R Publishing Co. in Sioux Center, IA
E-mail: tara@prpbooks.com; jesse@prpbooks.com
Web site: http://www.prpbooks.com
Dist(s): **CLC Pubns.**
Faith Alive Christian Resources.

P C I Education, *(978-1-884074; 978-1-58804; 978-1-61975)* 4560 Lockhill-Selma, Suite 100, San Antonio, TX 78265-4270 USA Tel 210-377-1999; Fax: 210-377-1121; Toll Free Fax: 888-259-8284; Toll Free: 800-594-4263
E-mail: lboulet@pcieducation.com
Web site: http://www.pcieducation.com
Dist(s): **Attainment Co., Inc.**

P C I Educational Publishing *See* **P C I Education**

P.C. Pubns., *(978-0-9709123; 978-0-578-18965-9)* 22 Williams St., Batavia, NY 14020 USA Tel 716-343-2810 (phone/fax); 444 Ellicott St., Batavia, NY 14020
E-mail: patti.chadwick@juno.com
Web site: http://www.historyswomen.com.

P K I Ds, *(978-1-929524)* P.O. Box 5666, Vancouver, WA 98668 USA Tel 360-695-0293; Fax: 360-695-6941; Toll Free: 877-557-5437
E-mail: pkids@pkids.org
Web site: http://www.pkids.org.

PM Bk., *(978-0-9676060)* 2240 Encinitas Blvd., Suite D., Encinitas, CA 92024 USA Tel 760-633-1100; Fax: 858-483-5803
E-mail: jmneill@san.rr.com
Dist(s): **Postal Corner.**

P.O.W. (Pubns. of Worth), *(978-1-877898)* 2561 E. 1980 N., Layton, UT 84040-7928 USA.

PSI & Assocs., *(978-0-938261; 978-1-55993)* 9745 SW 125th Terr., Miami, FL 33176-4941 USA (SAN 659-834X).

P2 Publishing, *(978-0-9856336)* 10455 N. Central Expwy Suite 109-115, Dallas, TX 75231 USA Tel 214-223-0366
E-mail: pickleproductionspc@gmail.com
Web site: www.PiperandPickle.com.

P4K Publishing, *(978-0-9744570)* 5699 Kanan Rd., Suite 373, Agoura Hills, CA 91301 USA Tel 818-991-5764; Fax: 818-879-9646
E-mail: lori@prosperity4kids.com
Web site: http://www.prosperity4kids.com.

Paarmann, Al International, *(978-0-9715963)* 368 El Gaucho Rd., Santa Barbara, CA 93111 USA Tel 805-964-2830 (phone/fax)
E-mail: alpaarmann@aol.com.

Pace Products, Inc., *(978-1-58295; 978-1-880592)* P.O. Box 470970, Lake Monroe, FL 32747-0970 USA Toll Free: 800-541-7670
E-mail: PaceProd@aol.com
Web site: http://www.paceplace.com.

Pacesetters Bible School *See* **Energion Pubns.**

Pach Resources, *(978-1-7379012)* 1066 Pine Meadow ct, Vernon hills, IL 60061 USA Tel 847-814-7025
E-mail: solaiswriting@gmail.com.

Pacific Bks., *(978-1-7373291)* 8911 Vernon RD No. 125, Lake Stevens, WA 98252 USA Tel 425-773-2930
E-mail: info@trianing-academy.org
Web site: www.Pacific-Books.com.

Pacific Bks., *(978-1-885375)* Orders Addr.: P.O. Box 3562, Santa Barbara, CA 93130 USA (SAN 630-2548) Tel 805-687-8340; Fax: 805-687-2514; Edit Addr.: 2573 Treasure Dr., Santa Barbara, CA 93105 USA; *Imprints:* Shore Line Press (Shore Line Pr).

Pacific Dogwood Pr., *(978-0-9896145)* 6400 Claremont Ave., Richmond, CA 94805 USA Tel 510-255-5067
E-mail: karin@manycycles.com
Web site: www.pacificdogwoodpress.com.

Pacific Heritage Bks., *(978-0-9635906; 978-1-928753)* Orders Addr.: P.O. Box 998, Palos Verdes, CA 90274 USA Tel 310-541-8818; Fax: 310-791-9069; Toll Free: 888-810-9891; Edit Addr.: 532 Via del Monte, Palos Verdes Estates, CA 90274 USA
E-mail: amawong@worldnet.att.net
Web site: http://www.pacificheritagebooks.com
Dist(s): **Distributors, The**
Quality Bks., Inc.

Pacific Learning, Inc., *(978-1-59055; 978-1-60457; 978-1-61391; 978-1-59055-000-7; 978-1-958041; 978-1-962364)* Orders Addr.: P.O. Box 2723, Huntington Beach, CA 92647-0723 USA; Edit Addr.: 6262 Katella Ave., Cypress, CA 90630 USA Tel 800-279-0737; Toll Free: 800-279-0737
E-mail: customer.service@pacificlearning.com
Web site: http://www.pacificlearning.com
Dist(s): **Brightpoint Literacy.**

Pacific Moon Pubns., *(978-0-9729524)* Orders Addr.: 2334 Monroe Blvd. Suite 703, Ogden, UT 84401-1727 USA
Dist(s): **Ingram Content Group.**

Pacific Northwest Ballet, *(978-0-9745415)* 301 Mercer St., Seattle, WA 98109 USA Tel 206-441-9411; Fax: 206-441-2440
E-mail: kaolivier@mac.com
Web site: http://www.pnb.org.

Pacific Pr. Pubns., *(978-0-9678122)* 3260 Monument, Ann Arbor, MI 48108 USA Tel 734-975-1877 (phone/fax)
E-mail: hailstormx@aol.com.

†Pacific Pr. Publishing Assn., *(978-0-8163; 978-1-5180)* P.O. Box 5353, Nampa, ID 83653-5353 USA (SAN 202-8409) Tel 208-465-2500; Fax: 208-465-2531; Toll Free: 800-447-7377
E-mail: donlay@pacificpress.com
Web site: http://www.AdventistBookCenter.com; http://www.pacificpress.com; *CIP.*

Pacific Pubs., *(978-0-936521; 978-1-931120)* P.O. Box 480, Bolinas, CA 94924 USA (SAN 697-9335) Tel 415-868-2909; Fax: 415-868-9040
E-mail: tideguy@fastmail.fm
Web site: http://www.tidelog.com.

Pacific Publishing Studio, *(978-0-9823756; 978-0-9824454; 978-1-936136)* 1425 Broadway, No. 435, Seattle, WA 98122 USA.

Pacific Raven Press *See* **Pacific Raven Pr.**

Pacific Raven Pr., *(978-0-9841228; 978-0-9840204; 978-0-9860755)* P.O. Box 195, Wailuku, HI 96793 USA (SAN 931-4946)
E-mail: pacificravenpress@gmail.com
Web site: http://www.pacificravenpress.com.

Pacific Ridge Press, LLC *See* **Parra Grande Pr.**

Pacific View Pr., *(978-1-881896)* 2864 Harrison St., San Francisco, CA 94110 USA Tel 415-285-8538; 510-849-4216; Fax: 415-285-2620; 510-843-5835
E-mail: pvp2@mindspring.com
Web site: http://www.pacificviewpress.com
Dist(s): **Cheng & Tsui Co.**
China Books & Periodicals, Inc.
Chinasprout, Inc.
Publishers Group West (PGW).

Pacifica Island Art, Inc., *(978-0-9727594; 978-0-9758721; 978-1-933735)* Orders Addr.: P.O. Box 120, Haiku, HI 96708 USA Fax: 808-575-2072; Edit Addr.: 810 Haiku Rd., No. 331, Haiku, HI 96708 USA
E-mail: joseph@islandartcards.com
Web site: http://www.islandartcards.com.

Pack, Kristin, *(978-0-9993624)* 938 N Elston Ave, No. 2, Chicago, IL 60642 USA Tel 989-400-8819; Fax: 989-400-8819
E-mail: kristinlynnpack@gmail.com
Web site: www.emmagoestoschool.com.

Packard, Boyle & Jackson *See* **Apollo Pubs.**

Padah Pr., *(978-0-9721269)* Orders Addr.: P.O. Box 231285, Gresham, OR 97281 USA Tel 971-219-1861
E-mail: eileen@padah.net; eileen@eileenscott.com
Web site: http://www.eileenscott.com.

Paddle Wheel Publishing, *(978-0-9657612)* Div. of Arabia Steamboat Museum, 400 Grand Blvd., Kansas City, MO 64106 USA Tel 816-471-1856; Fax: 816-471-1616; Toll Free: 800-471-1856
E-mail: greghawley@comcast.net
Web site: http://www.1856.com.

Paddywhack Lane LLC., *(978-0-9794286; 978-1-936169)* 9849 Bluestar Dr., Parker, CO 80138 USA (SAN 858-6497) Tel 303-841-1163; Fax: 888-840-0169; Toll Free: 800-796-1163
E-mail: bob@paddywhacklane.com
Web site: http://www.paddywhacklane.com.

Padma Light, *(978-1-7353151)* 4822 S 133 St, Ste 200, Omaha, NE 68137 USA Tel 402-884-5995
E-mail: padmalight@conciergemarketing.com.

Padula, Stacy A. *See* **Briley & Baxter Publications**

Padwolf Publishing Inc., *(978-1-890096; 978-1-958310)* 85 Denison Pkwy E No. 313, CORNING, NY 12792-0117 USA
E-mail: padwolf@padwolf.com
Web site: http://www.padwolf.com.

Padwolf Publishing, Incorporated *See* **Padwolf Publishing Inc.**

Pagan Writers Pr. *Imprint of* **Mroczka Media**

Pagan Writers Press *See* **Mroczka Media**

Page A Day Math, *(978-1-947286; 978-1-948949)* 7661 E. Camino Amistoso, Tucson, AZ 85750 USA Tel 520-780-1079
E-mail: janice@pageadaymath.com
Web site: www.pageadaymath.com.

Page Pond Pr., *(978-0-9913977; 978-0-9907600)* 1512 Hilltop Dr., Tallahassee, FL 32303 USA Tel 850-385-7472
E-mail: susan.womble@gmail.com.

Page Publishing *See* **Page Publishing Inc.**

Page Publishing, *(978-0-578-03557-4)* 1010 Winter Hill Dr., No. A, Cookeville, TN 38501 USA.

Page Publishing Inc., *(978-0-9854504; 978-1-62838; 978-1-63417; 978-1-68139; 978-1-68213; 978-1-68289; 978-1-68348; 978-1-68409; 978-1-63568; 978-1-64027; 978-1-64082; 978-1-64138; 978-1-64214; 978-1-64298; 978-1-64334; 978-1-64350; 978-1-64424; 978-1-64462; 978-1-68456; 978-1-64544; 978-1-64584; 978-1-64628; 978-1-64701; 978-1-6624; 979-8-88654; 979-8-88793; 979-8-88960; 979-8-89157)* 101 Tyrellan Ave., Suite 100 New York, NY 10309 USA Toll Free: 866-315-2708; 320 Water St., Conneaut Lake, PA 16316 Toll Free: 866-315-2708
E-mail: accounts@pagepublishing.com
Web site: http://www.pagepublishing.com.

Page Street Publishing Co., *(978-1-62414; 978-1-64567; 979-8-89003)* 31 Forest Ave., Essex, MA 01929 USA Tel 978-768-0168
E-mail: williamkiester@gmail.com
Dist(s): **Macmillan**
Westminster John Knox Pr.

Page Two Bks., Inc. (CAN) *(978-0-9952665; 978-1-989025) Dist. by* **Macmillan.**

PageFree Publishing, Inc., *(978-1-929077; 978-1-930252; 978-1-58961)* P.O. Box 60, Otsego, MI 49078-0060 USA Toll Free: 1-866-GO BOOKS
E-mail: pagefreepublish@aol.com; publisher@pagefreepublishing.com
Web site: http://www.pagefreepublishing.com
Dist(s): **BookBaby**
Ingram Content Group
Midpoint Trade Bks., Inc.
Univ. of Hawaii Pr.

PageMaster Publishing, *(978-0-9797759)* 2884 Britton Rd., B34, Perry, MI 48872 USA (SAN 854-3453)
E-mail: Gwen@pagemasterpublishing.com
Web site: http://www.pagemasterpublishing.com.

Pages of Life, *(978-0-615-24716-8; 978-0-615-48466-2; 978-0-615-48467-9)* Div. of Lavender Belle Enterprises, 6328 Joe Klustch Dr., Fort Washington, MD 20744 USA Tel 202-251-2210
E-mail: LavenderBelle@verizon.net
Web site: http://pagesoflife.wordpress.com.

PageSpring Publishing, *(978-1-939403)* 2671 Bristol Rd., Columbus, OH 43221 USA Tel 614-204-2548
E-mail: rseum@pagespringpublishing.com
Web site: www.pagespringpublishing.com; www.luckymarblebooks.com; www.cupofteabooks.com.

PageTurner: Pr. & Media, *(978-1-948304; 978-1-64376; 978-1-64908; 978-1-63871; 979-8-88622; 979-8-88963; 979-8-89174)* 601 E. Palomar St., Suite C-478, Chula Vista, CA 91911 USA Tel 888-447-9651
E-mail: info@pageturner.us
Web site: www.pageturner.us.

Pageturners Publishing Co., *(978-0-9755102)* Orders Addr.: P.O. Box 6, Jacksonville, FL 32234-0006 USA (SAN 256-1719) Tel 904-266-3393; Fax: 904-266-3394
E-mail: publisher@pageturnerspublishing.com
Web site: http://www.pageturnerspublishing.com.

Pageway Publishing LLC, *(978-0-9831631)* 10053 Diamond Dr., St. Louis, MO 63137 USA Tel 314-740-7446
E-mail: montrice1@msn.com.

Paginas de Espuma (ESP) *(978-84-95642; 978-84-931243; 978-84-8393) Dist. by* **Lectorum Pubns.**

Pagkaihang, Katesalin, 55/1 Moo.10, Chang Keng, 50270 THA
E-mail: Katesalin.pagkaihang@icloud.com.

Paidea Classics, *(978-0-9749900; 978-1-947816)* 304 Robinhood Dr., Irving, TX 75061 USA
Web site: http://paideaclassics.org.

Paige Martin Books *See* **Paige Martin Bks. & Art**

Paige Martin Bks. & Art, *(978-0-578-06864-0; 978-0-578-08272-1; 979-8-218-95152-8)* 11101 Silver Aspen Ct., Hampton, GA 30228 USA
Web site: paigelackeymartin.com
Dist(s): **Smashwords.**

Paige Publishing, *(978-0-9769375)* 5708 Washington St., Downers Grove, IL 60516 USA Do not confuse with companies with the same or similar name in Lexington, OK, Mesa, AZ La Harba, CA San Antonio, TX .

Paige, Sharyn, *(978-0-692-40687-8)* 250 E. 105th St, New York, NY 10029 USA Tel 917-822-7539
E-mail: shaysensuals@gmail.com.

Paige Tate & Co. *Imprint of* **Blue Star Pr.**

Paigerac, Patricia & Allan Choi *See* **Paigerac, Patricia M.**

Paigerac, Patricia M., *(978-0-9801137)* 30110 Crown Valley Pkwy., Suite 103, Laguna Niguel, CA 92677 USA.

Paino, Francine, *(978-0-692-59550-3; 978-0-692-96128-5; 978-1-7326489)* 8020 Journeyville Dr., Austin, TX 78735 USA Tel 512-551-2824
E-mail: franpaino@gmail.com
Web site: francinepaino.com
Dist(s): **CreateSpace Independent Publishing Platform.**

Paint Creek Press, Limited *See* **Archus Pr., LLC**

Paintbox Pr., *(978-0-9669433; 978-0-9777905; 978-1-951574)* 3 Malaga Cove Plaza Suite 206, Palos Verdes, CA 90274 USA Tel 800-920-5075; 800-920-5075; Fax: 800-920-5075
E-mail: ppease@paintboxpress.com
Web site: http://www.paintboxpress.com
Dist(s): **Follett School Solutions.**

Paintbrush Tales Publishing, LLC, *(978-0-9846151)* 20 Webber Ave., Beverly, MA 01915 USA Tel 978-239-9895
E-mail: caustin36@yahoo.com.

Painted Daisies Inc., *(978-0-615-34491-1)* 3433 Hwy. 190 PMB 377, Mandeville, LA 70471 USA Tel 985-674-0398; Fax: 985-674-2965; 978 Bald Cypress Dr., Mandeville, LA 70448
E-mail: kborg95@gmail.com.

Painted Gate Publishing, *(978-0-692-41111-7; 978-0-692-41563-4; 978-0-692-42495-7; 978-0-692-42641-8; 978-0-9963480; 978-0-692-44686-7; 978-0-692-45093-2; 978-0-692-45163-2; 978-1-943871; 978-0-578-41474-4; 978-1-952465)* P.O. Box 681, Spearfish, SD 57783 USA Tel (605) 645-1725
Dist(s): **CreateSpace Independent Publishing Platform.**

Painted Horse Pubns., Inc., *(978-0-9708066; 978-0-9729482)* 45 Wingate St., Haverhill, MA 01835 USA Tel 978-521-1740
E-mail: sully@stopforastory.com.

Painted Leaf Publishing, *(978-0-692-49942-9; 978-0-692-49945-0; 978-0-692-16754-0; 978-0-578-52703-1)* 18870 Painted Leaf Ct., JUPITER, FL 33458 USA Tel 561-972-8690.

Painted Pony, Inc., *(978-0-9759806)* Orders Addr.: P.O. Box 661, Fort Washakie, WY 82514 USA Tel 307-335-7330; Fax: 307-335-7332; Edit Addr.: 47 N. Fork Rd., Fort Washakie, WY 82514 USA Do not confuse with companies with similar name in Atlanta, GA and La Conner, WA.
E-mail: ppi@wrdf.org.

Painted Quill Publishing, *(978-0-9909471)* 230 Parker Oaks Ln., Hudson Oaks, TX 76087 USA
E-mail: paintedquill@gmail.com.

Painted Sky Productions *See* **Emerald City Publishing**

Painted WORD Studios, *(978-0-9721845; 978-0-9771809; 978-0-9845644)* P.O. Box 1606, Crosby, TX 77532-1606 USA Tel 281-456-8810 Toll Free: 866-241-7510
E-mail: paintedwordstudios@gmail.com
Web site: http://www.paintedwordstudios.com.

Painter, Annie & Assocs., *(978-1-928875)* P.O. Box 2135, Sisters, OR 97759 USA Tel 541-549-9539 (phone/fax)
E-mail: monamouse@cox.net.

Painting the Pages Publishing, *(978-0-9843487)* 673 Potomac Station Dr., No. 628, Leesburg, VA 20176 USA (SAN 859-1393)
Web site: http://www.paintingthepages.com.

Painting With Words, *(978-0-9743080)* 10 B State St., Windsor, VT 05089 USA Tel 802-674-5514; Fax: 802-674-9810.

Pair'a Spurs Pr., *(978-0-9749518)* Rt. 2 Box 20, Hollis, OK 73550 USA.

Paisley Publishing, *(978-0-9761710)* 7240 Sagebrush Dr., Parker, CO 80138 USA Fax: 303-841-5229 Do not confuse with Paisley Publishing in Anchorage, AK
E-mail: mlheinze11@aol.com.

Paizo Inc., *(978-0-9770071; 978-0-9776778; 978-1-60125; 978-1-64078)* 7120 185th Ave. NE. Ste 120, Redmond, WA 98052-0577 USA
E-mail: mike.webb@paizo.com
Web site: http://www.paizo.com
Dist(s): **Diamond Comic Distributors, Inc.**
Diamond Bk. Distributors.

Paizo Publishing, LLC *See* **Paizo Inc.**

Pajama Pr. (CAN) *(978-0-9869495; 978-1-927485; 978-1-77278) Dist. by* **PerseuPGW.**

Pajama Pr. (CAN) *(978-0-9869495; 978-1-927485; 978-1-77278) Dist. by* **IngramPubServ.**

Pajarito, Conjeo y Oso *Imprint of* **American Reading Co.**

PAJE Publishing Co., *(978-0-9753200)* 267 Henley Rd., Wynnewood, PA 19096 USA Tel 610-642-1729; Fax: 610-642-9891; Toll Free: 877-561-1377
E-mail: jay.scott@verizon.net
Dist(s): **Quality Bks., Inc.**

Pakkins Presents, *(978-0-9700241)* Orders Addr.: P.O. Box 10503, Salinas, CA 93912 USA Tel 831-422-3442; Edit Addr.: 637 Carmelita Dr., No. 23, Salinas, CA 93901 USA
E-mail: Pakkins-Land@worldnet.att.net
Web site: http://www.pakkinsland.com.

Pal Toys, LLC, *(978-0-9726170; 978-0-9763648; 978-0-9841459)* P.O. Box 2531, Palos Verdes Peninsula, CA 90274 USA Tel 310-938-6125 Toll Free: 877-725-8880; 26 Santa Bella Rd., Rolling Hills Estates, CA 90274
E-mail: info@paltoys.com; marymoepal@cox.net
Web site: http://www.paltoys.com.

Palabra, Ediciones S.A. (ESP) *(978-84-7118; 978-84-8239) Dist. by* **Lectorum Pubns.**

Palace Press International *See* **ORO Editions**

Palace Press International *See* **Insight Editions**

Paladin Timeless *Imprint of* **Twilight Times Bks.**

Palari Publishing LLP, *(978-1-928662)* Orders Addr.: P.O. Box 9288, Richmond, VA 23227-0288 USA Tel 804-355-1035; Toll Free Fax: 866-570-6724 (on demand); Toll Free: 866-570-6724; *Imprints:* Richmondmom.com Publishing (Richmondmom)
E-mail: dave@palaribooks.com
Web site: http://www.palaribooks.com
Dist(s): **Bookazine Co., Inc.**
Smashwords.

Palazzo Editions, Ltd. (GBR) *(978-0-9545103; 978-0-9553046; 978-0-9564448; 978-0-9564942; 978-0-9571483; 978-1-78675) Dist. by* **IPG Chicago.**

Pale Horse Bks., *(978-1-939917)* 108 Maid Marion Pl., Williamsburg, VA 23185 USA Tel 757-220-0146
E-mail: jwconl@wm.edu
Web site: palehorsebooks.com.

Pale Silver Rainplop Pr., *(978-0-9794396; 978-0-615-14670-6)* P.O. Box 1285, Sioux City, IA 51102 USA
Web site: http://www.katieandkimbleblog.com
Dist(s): **Lulu Pr., Inc.**

Palgrave *See* **Palgrave Macmillan**

Palgrave Macmillan *Imprint of* **Palgrave Macmillan**

Palgrave Macmillan, *(978-0-312; 978-0-333; 978-1-4039; 978-0-230; 978-1-4472; 978-1-137; 978-1-349; 978-1-78632)* Orders Addr.: 16365 James Madison Hwy., Gordonsville, VA 22942-8501 USA Toll Free Fax: 800-672-2054; Toll Free: 888-330-8477; Edit Addr.: 175 Fifth Ave., New York, NY 10010 USA Tel 212-982-9300; Fax: 212-777-6359; Toll Free Fax: 800 672-2054 (Customer Service); Toll Free: 800-221-7945; 888-330-8477 (Customer Service); *Imprints:* Palgrave Macmillan (PalgMac); Palgrave Pivot (Palgr Pivot)
E-mail: customerservice@vhpsva.com
Web site: http://www.palgrave.com
Dist(s): **China Books & Periodicals, Inc.**
Ebsco Publishing
Independent Pubs. Group
Libros Sin Fronteras
Macmillan
MyiLibrary
Springer
Trans-Atlantic Pubns., Inc.
ebrary, Inc.

Palgrave Macmillan Ltd. (GBR) *(978-0-312; 978-0-333; 978-1-4039; 978-0-230; 978-1-137) Dist. by* **Macmillan.**

Palgrave Macmillan Ltd. (GBR) *(978-0-312; 978-0-333; 978-1-4039; 978-0-230; 978-1-137) Dist. by* **Spri.**

Palgrave Pivot *Imprint of* **Palgrave Macmillan**

PALH, *(978-0-9719458; 978-1-953716)* P.O. Box 5099, Santa Monica, CA 90409 USA
E-mail: palh@aol.com
Web site: http://www.palhbooks.com.

Palibrio, *(978-1-61764; 978-1-5065)* Div. of Author Solutions, Inc., 1663 Liberty Dr., Bloomington, IN 47403 USA Tel 812-674-9757; Fax: 812-355-1576; Toll Free: 877-407-5847
Web site: http://www.palibrio.com
Dist(s): **Author Solutions, LLC.**

Palladium Bks., Inc., *(978-0-916211; 978-1-57457)* 39074 Webb Ct., Westland, MI 48185-7606 USA (SAN 294-9504)
E-mail: palladiumbooks@palladiumbooks.com
Web site: http://www.PalladiumBooks.com.

Palm, *(978-1-7329843; 979-8-9853077)* 6120 Torrington Dr., Reno, NV 89511 USA Tel 775-848-6096
E-mail: dkinsley0321@hotmail.com.

Palm Canyon Pr., *(978-0-9960794)* 24 Crockett St., Rowayton, CT 06853 USA Tel 203-853-1512
E-mail: pmorrison101@gmail.com; pagemcbrier@gmail.com
Web site: www.abracadabratut.com; www.palmcanyonpress.com; www.pagemcbrier.com.

Palm Pen Press, *(978-0-9666942; 978-1-933678)* Orders Addr.: 7881 Barrancas Ave., Bokeelia, FL 33922 USA (SAN 299-7835) Tel 239-283-3975 Toll Free: 877-725-6782
Web site: http://www.dlhavlin.com.

Palm Publishing LLC, *(978-0-9753548)* 1016 N. Dixie Hwy., West Palm Beach, FL 33401 USA Tel 561-833-6333; Fax: 561-833-0070
Web site: http://www.phfpbc.org.

Palm Tree Pubns., *(978-0-9787128; 978-0-9795480; 978-0-9799879; 978-0-9817054; 978-0-9822237; 978-0-9826954; 978-0-9846311; 978-0-9847653; 978-0-9857942; 978-0-9862033; 979-8-9873538)* Div. of Palm Tree Productions, Orders Addr.: 3401 Chalkstone Cir., Corinth, TX 76208 USA Tel 817-357-5359; Edit Addr.: 3401 Chalkstone Cir., Corinth, TX 76208 USA Tel 817-431-8574; 817-357-5359 Do not confuse with Palm Tree Publications in Baton Rouge, LA
E-mail: wendy@wendykwalters.com
Web site: http://www.wendykwalters.com; http://www.palmtreeproductions.com
Dist(s): **BookBaby.**

Palmer, Barbara A., *(978-0-9728228)* 486 Manitou Beach Rd., Hilton, NY 14468 USA Tel 585-392-3391; Fax: 585-392-1322
E-mail: bpforlkart@aol.com.

Palmer Enterprises *See* **Palmer Pr., The**

Palmer Lake Historical Society, *(978-0-9755989)* 66 Lower Glenway St., Palmer Lake, CO 80133 USA Tel 719-559-0837
E-mail: plhs@palmerdividehistory.org
Web site: www.PalmerDivideHistory.org.

Palmer Pr., The, *(978-0-912479)* P.O. Box 1347, Loomis, CA 95650 USA (SAN 215-1650) Tel 916-652-3225; Fax: 916-652-8665.

Palmer Publications, Incorporated/Amherst Press *See* **Amherst Pr.**

Palmer Publishing, *(978-0-9744410)* 604 4th N.W., Ardmore, OK 73401 USA Tel 580-504-2609 Do not confuse with companies with the same or similar name in Palmer, AK, Ocala, FL
E-mail: charlsie@duracom.net.

Palmer-Pietsch Assocs., *(978-0-935278; 978-1-61847)* 18200 NW Sauvie Island Rd., Portland, OR 97231 USA
E-mail: info@palmerpietsch.com; wisner.palmerpietsch@gmail.com
Web site: http://www.palmerpietsch.com
Dist(s): **Independent Pubs. Group**
MyiLibrary.

Palmetto Publishing, *(978-1-64111; 978-0-578-68178-8; 978-1-64990; 978-1-63837; 978-0-578-89794-3; 978-0-578-91356-8; 978-1-68515; 978-0-578-96009-8; 978-0-578-99015-6; 978-0-578-30165-5; 978-0-578-35615-0; 979-8-88590; 978-0-578-28342-5; 978-0-578-28344-9; 978-1-958284; 979-8-218-00180-3; 979-8-218-03052-0; 979-8-8229; 979-8-218-04286-8; 979-8-218-06790-8; 979-8-218-06843-1; 979-8-218-06844-8; 979-8-218-06847-9; 979-8-218-06863-9; 979-8-218-06866-0; 979-8-218-06902-5; 979-8-218-06907-0; 979-8-218-06908-7; 979-) 2681 Spruill Ave, N. Charleston, SC 29405 USA; 2837 Rivers Ave., N. Charleston, SC 29405 Tel 843-606-1820*
E-mail: info@palmettopublishinggroup.com; info@palmettopublishinggroup.com.

Palmetto Publishing Group *Imprint of* **Nextone Inc.**

Palmetto Publishing Group *See* **Palmetto Publishing**

Palmetto Street Publishing, *(978-0-615-49043-4; 978-0-9848782)* 106 W. Augusta Pl., Greenville, SC 29605 USA Tel 864-242-3906
E-mail: gabbehoward@gmail.com
Web site: n/a.

Palmetto Tree Pr., *(978-0-9742532)* 821 Calhoun St., Columbia, SC 29201 USA (SAN 255-5832) Tel 803-771-9300; Fax: 803-407-0766
E-mail: follybeech@aol.com.

Palmland Publishing *See* **Palm Pen Press**

Palmore, Julie, *(978-0-9722653)* 3203 Harwood, Tyler, TX 75701-7642 USA.

Palo Alto Bks. *Imprint of* **Glencannon Pr.**

Paloma Bks. *Imprint of* **L & R Publishing, LLC**

Palomina Publishing, *(978-0-9763393)* 338 Napa Rd., Sonoma, CA 95476 USA.

Palomino Publishing, *(978-1-892344)* Div. of Programs for the Arts, Inc., 1535 E. Broadway, Tucson, AZ 85719 USA Tel 520-623-4000; Fax: 520-623-9102
E-mail: madaras@worldnet.att.net
Dist(s): **TNT Media Group, Inc.**

Palski, Leona, *(978-0-615-91591-3; 978-0-692-20236-4; 978-0-692-52664-4; 978-0-692-78301-6; 978-0-692-91612-4)* P.O. Box 47, Antes Fort, PA 17720 USA Tel 570-398-2726
E-mail: leonapalski@yahoo.com.

Pamir LLC, *(978-0-9888649)* 460 Jameson Hill Rd., Clinton Corners, NY 12514 USA Tel 845-266-0064
E-mail: natasha_rafi@hotmail.com.

Pampa Publishing, *(978-0-9744675; 978-0-615-11346-3)* Orders Addr.: P.O. Box 3481, Olympia, WA 98509-3481 USA; Edit Addr.: 4613 Shincke Rd. NE, Olympia, WA 98506 USA
E-mail: pampapublishing@comcast.net; ma2ka@home.com.

Pan Asia Pubns. (USA), Inc., *(978-1-57227)* 29564 Union City Blvd., Union City, CA 94587 USA (SAN 173-685X) Tel 510-475-1185; Fax: 510-475-1489; Toll Free: 800-909-8088
E-mail: sales@panap.com; hchan@panap.com; info@panap.com
Web site: http://www.panap.com; http://www.cjkv.com
Dist(s): **China Books & Periodicals, Inc.**
Chinasprout, Inc.
Follett School Solutions
Lectorum Pubns., Inc.

Pan Asian Pubns. (U S A), Inc., *(978-1-57227)* 29564 Union City Blvd., Union City, CA 94587 USA Tel 510-475-1185; Fax: 510-475-1489
E-mail: schiu@panap.com.

Pan Macmillan (GBR) *(978-0-283; 978-0-312; 978-0-330; 978-0-333; 978-0-7522; 978-1-85283; 978-1-4050; 978-1-904633; 978-1-904919; 978-1-905716; 978-1-907360; 978-1-4472; 978-1-909621; 978-1-5098; 978-1-5290) Dist. by* **Trafalgar.**

Pan Macmillan (GBR) *(978-0-283; 978-0-312; 978-0-330; 978-0-333; 978-0-7522; 978-1-85283; 978-1-4050; 978-1-904633; 978-1-904919; 978-1-905716; 978-1-907360; 978-1-4472; 978-1-909621; 978-1-5098; 978-1-5290) Dist. by* **Macmillan.**

Pan Macmillan (GBR) *(978-0-283; 978-0-312; 978-0-330; 978-0-333; 978-0-7522; 978-1-85283; 978-1-4050; 978-1-904633; 978-1-904919; 978-1-905716; 978-1-907360; 978-1-4472; 978-1-909621; 978-1-5098; 978-1-5290) Dist. by* **IPG Chicago.**

Pan Macmillan (GBR) *(978-0-283; 978-0-312; 978-0-330; 978-0-333; 978-0-7522; 978-1-85283; 978-1-4050; 978-1-904633; 978-1-904919; 978-1-905716; 978-1-907360; 978-1-4472; 978-1-909621; 978-1-5098; 978-1-5290) Dist. by* **Trans-Atl Phila.**

Pan Macmillan Australia Pty, Ltd. (AUS) *(978-0-330; 978-0-7251; 978-0-7329; 978-1-4050; 978-1-74198; 978-1-74197; 978-1-74261; 978-1-74262; 978-1-74303; 978-1-74328; 978-1-74329; 978-1-74334; 978-1-74351; 978-1-74353; 978-1-74354; 978-1-76008; 978-1-76009; 978-1-76030; 978-1-925479; 978-1-925480; 978-1-925481; 978-1-925482; 978-1-925483; 978-1-76055; 978-1-76078; 978-1-76098; 978-1-76126; 978-1-76156) Dist. by* **IPG Chicago.**

Panacea Pr., *(978-0-9791309; 978-0-9842147; 978-0-9893645; 978-0-9861012)* P.O. Box 292005, Nashville, TN 37229-2005 USA Tel 615-406-822
E-mail: king2dw@aol.com.

Panacea Publishing, *(978-0-9743432)* Orders Addr.: 5002 Barlow Dr., Round Rock, TX 78681 USA Tel 512-228-1388; Fax: 512-906-1579; Toll Free: 877-723-6110 Do not confuse with Panacea Publishing in North Attleboro MA, South Yarmouth MA
E-mail: sales@panaceabooks.com
Web site: http://www.panaceabooks.com
Dist(s): **Brodart Co.**
Midwest Library Service
Quality Bks., Inc.

Panama Hat Publishing, Ltd., *(978-0-9852202; 978-1-943317)* P.O. Box 343, Green Mountain Falls, CO 80819-0343 USA Tel 970-368-2665
E-mail: admin@panamahatpublishing.com
Web site: http://www.panamahatpublishing.com/.

Pan-American Publishing Co., *(978-0-932906)* P.O. Box 1505, Las Vegas, NM 87701 USA (SAN 212-5366).

Panamericana Editorial (COL) *(978-958-30) Dist. by* **Lectorum Pubns.**

Panda Bear Pr., *(978-0-9724699)* Orders Addr.: 612 Museum Rd., Reading, PA 19611-1427 USA (SAN 255-5328) Tel 610-374-7048; Fax: 610-478-7992
E-mail: HaileJohnJr@msn.com
Web site: http://www.caroljhaile.com
Dist(s): **Firenze Pr.**

PANDA BKS. PR., *(978-0-692-78668-0; 978-0-692-80099-7)* 47 bristol St., thomaston, CT 32968 USA Tel 772-766-6549
E-mail: kramer535@bellsouth.net
Web site: www.musicboxstory.com.

Panda Pubns., *(978-0-9818392; 978-1-7374818)* P.O. Box 595, Wilkes Barre, PA 18703 USA
E-mail: pandapublications@verizon.net; antobianco@msn.com.

Panda Publishing, L.L.C., *(978-0-9740180; 978-1-932724)* Orders Addr.: P.O. Box 670608, Dallas, TX 75367 USA (SAN 255-8165) Toll Free: 800-807-1776; Edit Addr.: 6215 Rex Dr., Dallas, TX 75230 USA; *Imprints:* Bios for Kids (Bios for Kids)
E-mail: info@biosforkids.com.

Pandalily Bks., *(978-0-692-92150-0; 978-0-9995804)* 8505 Laberta Blvd., Savannah, GA 31406 USA Tel 912-704-2301
E-mail: jamie@youhaveawildimagination.com; reservedsav@gmail.com
Web site: youhaveawildimagination.com.

Pandia Pr., *(978-0-9766057; 978-0-9798496; 978-0-9977963; 978-1-7334441)* 18400 SE Hwy.42, Weirsdale, FL 32195 USA
Web site: http://www.PandiaPress.com.

Pandora *Imprint of* **Highland Pr. Publishing**

Pandora Press U. S. *See* **Cascadia Publishing Hse., LLC**

PANGAEA, *(978-0-9630180; 978-1-929165)* Orders Addr.: 226 Wheeler St., S., Saint Paul, MN 55105-1927 USA Tel 651-226-2032
E-mail: info@pangaea.org
Web site: http://www.pangaea.org
Dist(s): **Follett School Solutions.**

Pangaea Publishing *See* **PANGAEA**

Pangea Books *See* **Character Assassin Bks.**

Pangea Software, Inc., *(978-0-9761505)* 12405 John Simpson Ct., Austin, TX 78732-2112 USA Tel 512-266-9991
Web site: http://www.pangeasoft.net.

Pangloss Pr., *(978-0-9668784; 978-0-692-51345-3)* Orders Addr.: P.O. Box 2225, Ballston Spa, NY 12020 USA Tel 518-584-4034 phone/fax; Edit Addr.: 63 Franklin St., Saratoga, NY 12866 USA Do not confuse with Pangloss Pr., Malibu, CA
E-mail: tuckerb@global2000.net.

Pangloss Publishing, *(978-0-9768586; 978-0-615-12424-7)* 3904 Becker Ave., Austin, TX 78751-5209 USA Fax: 512-453-1486
E-mail: candide@grandecom.net.

Pangus Publishing, *(978-0-9769715)* Orders Addr.: 1637 S. Iseminger St., Philadelphia, PA 19148 USA; Edit Addr.: P.O. Box 15763, Philadelphia, PA 19148 USA.

Panigrahy, Sonia, *(978-0-9975956)* 129 W. 89th St., New York, NY 10024 USA Tel 646-648-1898
E-mail: sonia1211@gmail.com.

†Panjandrum Bks., *(978-0-915572)* 6156 Wilkinson Ave., North Hollywood, CA 91606-4518 USA (SAN 282-1257) Tel 818-985-7259
Dist(s): **Coutts Information Services**
New Leaf Distributing Co., Inc.; *CIP.*

Pankratz Creations, *(978-0-9742637)* 355 S. Fairlane Dr., Tooele, UT 84074-2623 USA
E-mail: customerservice@pankratzcreations.com; pankratz@mstar2.net
Web site: http://www.pankratzcreations.com.

Panline U.S.A., Inc., *(978-0-9713507; 978-0-615-23938-5; 978-0-9822010; 978-0-9847127)* 251 Union St., Northvale, NJ 07647 USA (SAN 920-5772) Tel 201-750-8010; Fax: 201-750-8030
E-mail: info@alextoys.com
Web site: http://www.alextoys.com.

Pannonia Pr., *(978-0-9657793)* P.O. Box 1062, Palatine, IL 60078-1062 USA Tel 847-277-0806; Fax: 847-228-6847
E-mail: pannoniapress2000@sbcglobal.net
Web site: http://www.pannoniapress.com.

Pannycake Pubn., *(978-0-9769538)* 1710 Vallejo St., Unit B, Seaside, CA 93955 USA Tel 831-393-1358; Fax: 831-753-6085
E-mail: carmelalayne@yahoo.com.

Panoply Pubns., *(978-0-9818391)* P.O. Box 2329, North Hollywood, CA 91610-0329 USA Tel 818-761-8757
E-mail: panoplypub@aol.com
Web site: http://www.panoplypublications.com.

Panorama Pr., Inc., *(978-0-9768642)* P.O. Box 183, Boulder, CO 80306-0183 USA.

Pantera Pr. (AUS) *(978-0-9807418; 978-0-9870685; 978-1-921997; 978-1-925700; 978-0-6485084; 978-0-6485715; 978-0-6486769; 978-0-6486770; 978-0-6487488; 978-0-6487489; 978-0-6487951; 978-0-6487952; 978-0-6487953; 978-0-6489874; 978-0-6489875; 978-0-6489876; 978-0-6452400; 978-0-6452401; 978-0-6453508; 978-0-6454129; 978-0-6454767; 978-0-6454984; 978-0-6454985; 978-0-6456246; 978-0-6457579; 978-0-6458179; 978-0-6458180; 978-0-6458690; 978-0-6458691; 978-0-6458581; 978-1-925399; 978-0-6456245; 978-0-6457578; 97) Dist. by* **IPG Chicago.**

Pantheon *Imprint of* **Knopf Doubleday Publishing Group**

Panther Creek Pr., *(978-0-9678343; 978-0-9718361; 978-0-9747839; 978-0-9771797)* Orders Addr.: P.O. Box 130233, Spring, TX 77393-0233 USA (SAN 253-8520); Edit Addr.: 104 Plum Tree Ter. Apt. 115, Houston, TX 77077-5375 USA
E-mail: panthercreek3@hotmail.com; guidamj@juno.com
Web site: http://www.panthercreekpress.com.

Pants On Fire Pr., *(978-0-9827271; 978-0-9860373; 978-0-615-88989-4; 978-0-615-89685-4; 978-0-615-89931-2; 978-0-615-91719-1; 978-0-615-96453-9; 978-0-615-98402-5; 978-0-692-02170-5; 978-0-692-02171-2; 978-0-692-20585-3; 978-0-692-20941-7; 978-0-692-21000-0; 978-0-692-21001-7; 978-0-692-21003-1; 978-0-692-30738-0; 978-0-692-35957-0; 978-0-692-44415-3; 978-0-692-44416-0; 978-0-692-57238-2; 978-0-692-69868-6) 2062 Harbor Cove Way, Winter Garden, FL 34787 USA*
E-mail: david@pantsonfirepress.com; editor@pantsonfirepress.com
Web site: http://www.pantsonfirepress.com
Dist(s): **CreateSpace Independent Publishing Platform**
INscribe Digital
Independent Pubs. Group.

Paon Pubns., *(978-0-9711721)* 608 S. Webik Ave, Clawson, MI 48017 USA Tel 248-288-5621.

Papa & Punchanella, *(978-1-7334888)* 5059 Carriage Dr, Lake Park, GA 31602 USA Tel 352-272-8671
E-mail: peterfshorejr@gmail.com.

Papa Koj Bks., *(978-0-9981152)* 21 Washburn Pk., Rochester, NY 14620 USA Tel 330-256-3224
E-mail: cbrownlie@frontiernet.net
Web site: craigbrownlie.com.

Publisher Name Index

Papaloizos Pubns., Inc., *(978-0-932416)* 11720 Auth Ln., Silver Spring, MD 20902-1645 USA (SAN 220-9853) Tel 301-593-0652
E-mail: info@greek123.com
Web site: http://www.greek123.com.

Papas & Nellie Pr., *(978-0-9719925)* 2110 Lakeland Ave., Madison, WI 53704 USA Tel 608-661-0508
E-mail: papasandnellie@tds.net.

Papell, David, *(978-0-615-17531-7; 978-0-615-17931-5; 978-0-615-17932-2)* 5601 Riverdale Ave., Bronx, NY 10471 USA Tel 718-601-3771
E-mail: dpapell@earthlink.net
Web site: http://www.davidpapell.net
Dist(s): **Lulu Pr., Inc.**

Papenberg, Jami, *(978-1-7357248)* 325 S Main, Red Bud, IL 62278 USA Tel 618-201-6259
E-mail: jcpapenberg@gmail.com.

Paper Airplane Publishing, LLC, *(978-1-947677)* 2205 Willow, Liberty, TX 77575 USA Tel 281-734-0330
E-mail: lindastreetely@gmail.com
Web site: http://paperairplanepublishing.com/.

Paper Crane Pr., *(978-0-9650833)* P.O. Box 29292, Bellingham, WA 98228-1292 USA Tel 360-676-0266; Toll Free: 800-356-9315
E-mail: carolrj@nas.com
Dist(s): **Brodart Co.**
New Leaf Distributing Co., Inc.
Unique Bks., Inc.
Upper Access, Inc.

Paper Doll Publishing, *(978-0-9748252)* Orders Addr.: a/o Orders, P.O. Box 72028, Phoenix, AZ 85050 USA (SAN 255-8084)
E-mail: michael@paperdollpublishing.com; books@paperdollpublishing.com
Web site: http://www.paperdollpublishing.com.

Paper Jam Publishing, *(978-1-888345)* Orders Addr.: P.O. Box 435, Eastsound, WA 98245 USA Tel 360-376-3200 (phone/fax); Toll Free: 877-757-2665; Edit Addr.: 531 Fern St., Eastsound, WA 98245 USA
E-mail: paperjam@rockisland.com
Web site: http://www.rockisland.com/~paperjam.

Paper Mermaid, The, *(978-1-7322065)* 57 Main St., ROCKPORT, MA 01966 USA Tel 978-546-3553
E-mail: info@papermermaid.com
Web site: www.papermermaid.com; www.romeaday.com
Dist(s): **Ingram Content Group.**

Paper Phoenix Pr. *Imprint of* **eSpec Bks.**

Paper Posie *See* **Paper Posie Publishing Co., The**

Paper Raven, *(978-1-7363042)* 1202 rustic ridge, Joplin, MO 64804 USA Tel 417-396-3332
E-mail: Drlanceb2003@yahoo.com.

Paper Republic LLC, *(978-1-945295)* 7548 Ravenna Ave NE, Seattle, WA 98115 USA Tel 929-202-6717
E-mail: eric@paper-republic.org
Web site: https://paper-republic.org.

Paper Studio Pr., *(978-0-9790668; 978-0-9795053; 978-1-935223; 978-1-942490)* Orders Addr.: P.O. Box 14, Kingfield, ME 04947 USA Tel 207-265-2500
Web site: http://paperstudiopress.com.

Paper Tiger, Incorporated, The *See* **Paper Tiger, The**

Paper Tiger, The, *(978-1-889439)* Orders Addr.: 722 Upper Cherrytown Rd., Kerhonkson, NY 12446 USA Tel 845-626-5354
E-mail: fredweiss@papertig.com
Web site: http://www.papertig.com.

Paperback Press, LLC *See* **Kids Bk. Pr.**

Paperbacks for Educators, *(978-0-9702376; 978-1-59721)* 426 W. Front St., Washington, MO 63090 USA (SAN 103-3379) Tel 636-239-1999; Fax: 636-239-4515; Toll Free Fax: 800-514-7323; Toll Free: 800-227-2591
E-mail: paperbacks@usmo.com
Web site: http://www.any-book-in-print.com.

Paperchase Solution, *(978-1-63626)* 191 Stephens St., BELLEVILLE, NJ 07109 USA Tel 551-222-0018
E-mail: elliot.carter@paperchasesolution.com
Web site: www.paperchasesolution.com.

Papercutz *Imprint of* **Mad Cave Studios**

Papercutz, *(978-1-59707; 978-1-62991; 978-1-5458)* 160 Broadway, E. Wing Suite 700, New York, NY 10038 USA (SAN 850-9670) Tel 646-559-4681
E-mail: nantier@papercutz.com
Web site: http://www.papercutz.com
Dist(s): **Children's Plus, Inc.**
Diamond Comic Distributors, Inc.
Macmillan
Simon & Schuster, Inc.
Westminster John Knox Pr.

Papergraphics Printing, *(978-0-9773322)* 4 John Tyler St., Suite 1, Merrimack, NH 03054-3054 USA Tel 603-880-1835; Fax: 603-880-1751; Toll Free: 800-499-1835
E-mail: prepress@papergraphics.biz
Web site: http://www.papergraphics.biz.

Paperhat Publishing, *(978-1-7371945)* 1006 N Bend Dr, Austin, TX 78758 USA Tel 832-419-4879
E-mail: morgan.pinales@gmail.com
Web site: www.paperhatpublishing.com.

PaperMaze Media, *(978-0-692-08981-1)* 5418 Gosforth Dr., Katy, TX 77449 USA Tel 8329740639
E-mail: papermazebooks@gmail.com
Dist(s): **Ingram Content Group.**

Papilion Pr., *(978-1-884429)* Orders Addr.: P.O. Box 54502, Phoenix, AZ 85078-4502 USA Tel 602-931-0556
E-mail: firstchoiceent05@msn.com.

Papillon Pr., Inc., *(978-0-9667476)* 23 Seagull Pl., Vero Beach, FL 32960-5212 USA
Dist(s): **New Leaf Distributing Co., Inc.**

Papillon Publishing *Imprint of* **Blue Dolphin Publishing, Inc.**

Papillon Publishing, *(978-0-9651048)* P.O. Box 12044, Dallas, TX 75225 USA Tel 214-722-1297 (phone/fax) Do not confuse with Papillon Publishing in Rochester, MN
E-mail: ford.lawrence@sbcglobal.net.

Papillons Monarques, *(978-1-7345858; 979-8-9883999)* 1105 Summerwood Dr, Clarkston, GA 30021 USA Tel 646-500-4244
E-mail: w.dig@aol.com.

PAPO Brand *Imprint of* **Planet Bronx Productions**

Pa-Pro-Vi Publishing, *(978-0-692-69871-6; 978-1-7352429; 978-1-7363032; 978-1-7374348; 979-8-9857315; 978-1-959667)* 283 Park Ridge Ct., Riverdale, GA 30274 USA Tel 678-608-9948; Toll Free: 678-608-9948
E-mail: paprovipublishing@yahoo.com; laquita@afailure2communicate.com
Web site: www.afailure2communicate.com
Dist(s): **CreateSpace Independent Publishing Platform.**

Papyrus & Pen, *(978-0-9770687)* 2923 Cecil B. Moore Ave., Suite 3, Philadelphia, PA 19121 USA Tel 267-539-7540
E-mail: dmccrary@papyrusandpen.com
Web site: http://www.papyrusandpen.com
Dist(s): **Ingram Content Group.**

Papyrus Publishing, Inc., *(978-0-9675581; 978-0-9882883)* 7409 Edgewood Ave. N., Brooklyn Park, MN 55428 USA Tel 612-481-6417 Do not confuse with Papyrus Publishing in Missouri City, TX
E-mail: PapyrusPublishing@msn.com
Web site: http://www.mahmoudelkati.com; http://www.papyruspublishinginc.com.

Para-Anchors International, *(978-1-878832)* Orders Addr.: P.O. Box 19, Summerland, CA 93067 USA Tel 805-966-4837; Fax: 805-966-0782; Toll Free: 800-350-7070; Edit Addr.: 21 E. Canon Perdido, Suite 303, Santa Barbara, CA 93101 USA
E-mail: victor1pai@netscape.com; victor1cnp@netscape.com
Web site: http://www.jerustar.com
Dist(s): **Quality Bks., Inc.**

†Parable Pr., *(978-0-917250)* P.O. Box 51, Vinalhaven, ME 04863-0051 USA (SAN 208-4449); *CIP.*

Parable Venture Partners, LLC, *(978-0-9728501)* 12946 SW 133 Ct., Suite B, Miami, FL 33186 USA Tel 305-252-0905; Fax: 305-245-9974
E-mail: info@ethansparables.com
Web site: http://www.ethansparables.com.

Parables & Bks., *(978-0-9833188; 978-1-939682)* 24 S. Front St., Bergenfield, NJ 07621 USA Tel 201-338-4953
E-mail: sandy@parablesandbooks.com
Web site: www.parablesandbooks.com.

Parabola Bks., *(978-0-930407)* 656 Broadway, Suite 615, New York, NY 10012-2317 USA (SAN 219-5763) Tel 212-505-6200; Fax: 212-979-7325; Toll Free: 800-560-6984
E-mail: ads-promo@parabola.org; orders@parabola.org; JoeKulin@aol.com; editors@parabola.org
Web site: http://www.parabola.org/; http://www.cinemaofthespirit.org
Dist(s): **Consortium Bk. Sales & Distribution**
New Leaf Distributing Co., Inc.

Parabola Magazine/Society for Study of Myth & Tradition *See* **Parabola Bks.**

Parachute Jump Publishing, *(978-0-9852469; 978-0-9888905; 978-0-9915405; 978-0-9903660)* 50 Brighton 1st Rd. Apt. 16D, Brooklyn, NY 11235 USA Tel 718-593-7717
E-mail: kpaulet@verizon.net
Dist(s): **BookBaby**
Ingram Content Group.

Parachute Press, Incorporated *See* **Parachute Publishing, LLC**

Parachute Publishing, LLC, *(978-0-938753; 978-1-57351)* 156 Fifth Ave., New York, NY 10010 USA (SAN 661-5554) Tel 212-691-1421; Fax: 212-645-8769
E-mail: ppibooks@aol.com.

Paraclete Pr., Inc., *(978-0-941478; 978-1-55725; 978-1-61261; 978-1-64060)* Orders Addr.: P.O. Box 1568, Orleans, MA 02653 USA (SAN 282-1508) Fax: 508-255-5705; Toll Free: 800-451-5006; Edit Addr.: 36 Southern Eagle Cartway, Brewster, MA 02631 USA (SAN 664-6239) Do not confuse with companies with the same or similar names in Indianapolis, IN, Pentwater, MI
E-mail: smercy@paracletepress.com; miao@paracletepress.com
Web site: http://www.paracletepress.com
Dist(s): **BookMasters**
Follett School Solutions
Forward Movement Pubns.
MyiLibrary.

Paradigm Accelerated Curriculum, *(978-1-928629; 978-1-59476)* Div. of Paradigm Alternatives Centers, Inc., Orders Addr.: P.O. Box 200, Dublin, TX 76446-0200 USA Tel 254-445-4272; Fax: 254-445-3947; Edit Addr.: 112 S. Grafton, Dublin, TX 76446-0200 USA
E-mail: learn@pacworks.com
Web site: http://www.pacworks.com.

Paradigm Alternatives Centers, Incorporated *See* **Paradigm Accelerated Curriculum**

Paradigm Publishing, *(978-0-9746013)* Orders Addr.: P.O. Box 872, LaPorte, CO 80535 USA; Edit Addr.: 3106 Kintzley Ct., D, LaPorte, CO 80535 USA Do not confuse with companies with the same or similar name in Oklahoma City OK, San Dimas CA, Chicago IL, McFarland WI, Saint Paul MN, Midvale UT, Pembroke Pines FL, Pocatello ID, Brookline MA, Boulder CO, Laguna Park, TX , Washington, DC
E-mail: sales@paradigmpublish.com
Web site: http://www.paradigmpublish.com.

Paradise Cay Pubns., *(978-0-939837; 978-1-937196)* P.O. Box 29, Arcata, CA 95518-0029 USA (SAN 663-690X) Tel 707-822-9063; Fax: 707-822-9163; Toll Free: 800-736-4509 (orders only)
E-mail: jim@paracay.com
Web site: http://www.paracay.com
Dist(s): **Independent Pubs. Group**
Hale, Robert & Co., Inc.
Univ. of Hawaii Pr.

Paradise Copies, Inc., *(978-0-9836716)* 21 Conz St., Northampton, MA 01060 USA Tel 413-585-0414; Fax: 413-585-0417
E-mail: Carol@paradisecopies.com
Web site: http://paradisecopies.com.

Paradise Pr. & Assocs., LLC, *(978-0-9755970)* P.O. Box 783573, Winter Garden, FL 34778-3573 USA Tel 321-354-5881 (phone/fax)
E-mail: bbeehy@gmail.com
Web site: none.

Paradise Pr., Inc., *(978-1-57657; 978-1-884907; 978-1-4194)* 1776 N. Pine Island Rd. Ste. 218, Plantation, FL 33322-5223 USA Do not confuse with companies with the same or similar names in Crested Butte, CO Corte Madera, CA, Santa Monica, CA, Ridgefield, CA, Chicago, IL, Herdon, VA, Temple Terrace, FL
E-mail: buybooks@paradisepress.us.

Paradise Research Pubns., Inc., *(978-1-885803)* Orders Addr.: P.O. Box 837, Kihei, HI 96753-0837 USA Tel 808-874-4876 (phone/fax)
E-mail: dickb@dickb.com
Web site: http://www.dickb.com/index.html
Dist(s): **Globe Pequot Pr., The**
Good Bk. Publishing Co.

Paradox *Imprint of* **DC Comics**

Paradoxal Pr., *(978-0-9766132)* 28916 NE 34th Ct., Redmond, WA 98053-9114 USA
Web site: http://www.paradoxalpress.com.

Paradoxical Pr., The, *(978-0-9786663)* 48 Cranford Pl., Teaneck, NJ 07666 USA Tel 201-281-8112
E-mail: info@theparadoxicalpress.com
Web site: http://www.theparadoxicalpress.com.

Paraglyph, Inc., *(978-1-932111; 978-1-933097)* 3533 E. Friess Dr., Phoenix, AZ 85032-5318 USA; 3533 E. Friess Dr., Phoenix, AZ 85032-5318; *Imprints:* Paraglyph Press (Paraglyph Pr)
E-mail: ccaldwell@paraglyphpress.com; stevesayre@paraglyphpress.com
Web site: http://www.paraglyphpress.com
Dist(s): **Ingram Publisher Services**
O'Reilly Media, Inc.

Paraglyph Pr. *Imprint of* **Paraglyph, Inc.**

Paragon Agency, Pubs., The *Imprint of* **Paragon Agency, The**

Paragon Agency, The, *(978-1-891030; 978-0-9710012; 978-1-942329)* Orders Addr.: P.O. Box 1281, Orange, CA 92856 USA Tel 714-771-0652; *Imprints:* Paragon Agency, Publishers, The (PAP)
E-mail: Paragon@SpecialBooks.com
Web site: http://www.SpecialBooks.com.

Paragon Expedition Pr., The, *(978-1-952417)* 746 Yearling, Columbus, OH 43213 USA Tel 614-231-4709; Fax: 614-237-0420
E-mail: SusanRW67@gmail.com.

†Paragon Hse. Pubs., *(978-0-88702; 978-0-89226; 978-0-913729; 978-0-943852; 978-1-55778; 978-1-885118; 978-1-61083)* Orders Addr.: 3600 Labore Rd., Suite 1, Saint Paul, MN 55110-4144 USA (SAN 286-1704) Tel 651-644-3087; Fax: 651-644-0997; Toll Free Fax: 800-494-0997; Toll Free: 800-447-3709
E-mail: paragon@paragonhouse.com
Web site: http://www.paragonhouse.com
Dist(s): **Baker & Taylor Publisher Services (BTPS)**; *CIP.*

Paraklesis Pr., *(978-1-947446)* 113 Winn Ct, Waleska, GA 30183 USA Tel 404-695-5517
E-mail: sally@sally-apokedak.com.

Parallax, Inc., *(978-1-928982)* 599 Menlo Dr., No. 100, Rocklin, CA 95765-3708 USA Tel 916-624-8333; Fax: 916-624-8003; Toll Free: 888-512-1024
E-mail: info@parallaxinc.com
Web site: http://www.parallaxinc.com.

Parallax Pr., *(978-0-938077; 978-1-888375; 978-1-935209; 978-0-9846271; 978-1-937006; 978-1-941529; 978-1-946764; 978-1-952692)* Orders Addr.: 2236 B 6th St, Berkeley, CA 94710 USA (SAN 663-4494) Tel 800-863-5290; Fax: 734-487-1890; Toll Free: 800-863-5290; Edit Addr.: 2236 6th St., Berkeley, CA 94710-2219 USA; *Imprints:* Plum Blossom Books (Plum Blossom)
E-mail: orders@parallax.org; hisae@parallax.org; admin@parallax.org; jacob@parallax.org
Web site: http://www.parallax.org
Dist(s): **MyiLibrary**
Penguin Random Hse. Distribution
Penguin Random Hse. LLC
Random Hse., Inc.
SPD-Small Pr. Distribution.

Parallel Vortex, *(978-0-578-20654-7; 978-1-7335610)* 11264 E. Bath Rd, Byron, MI 48418 USA Tel 517-294-5420
E-mail: thechaderway@gmail.com.

Paramance *Imprint of* **MQuills Publishing**

Paraphrase, LLC, *(978-0-9815879; 978-1-953566)* Orders Addr.: P.O. Box 56508, Sherman Oaks, CA 91413 USA (SAN 855-9643) Tel 818-219-4377; Toll Free Fax: 888-863-4377
Web site: http://www.paraphrasellc.com; http://www.espete.com.

Parascension, Inc., *(978-0-9729380; 978-0-615-18212-4)* 222 Oak Grove Rd., Suite 201, Bradfordwoods, PA 15015-1338 USA; *Imprints:* Parascension Press (Parascen)
E-mail: jameshayhurst@zoominternet.net
Web site: http://www.parascension.com; http://www.badcommandments.com; http://www.adventuresofmercurylane.com.

Parascension Pr. *Imprint of* **Parascension, Inc.**

ParaTomb Studios, *(978-0-578-44423-9; 978-1-7336825)* 23441 Via Burriana, Mission Viejo, CA 92691 USA Tel 530-867-7875
E-mail: drew@paratombstudios.com
Web site: paratombstudios.com.

Parchment Global Publishing, *(978-1-950981; 978-1-952302; 978-1-957009; 978-1-959483)* 4152 Barnett St, Philadelphia, PA 19135 USA Tel 323-522-4624
E-mail: mialopez@parchmentglobalpublishing.com
Web site: www.parchmentglobalpublishing.com.

Parence, Tamekia, *(978-1-7366965)* 4930 Rapahoe Trail, Atlanta, GA 30349 USA Tel 912-661-4208
E-mail: parence_tamekia@hotmail.com.

Parent Brigade Company, The, *(978-0-9774998)* 530 New Los Angeles Ave., Suite 115-332, Moorpark, CA 93021 USA Fax: 805-523-0119.

Parent Child Pr., Inc., *(978-0-939195; 978-0-9601016)* Orders Addr.: 11 W 9th St, Santa Rosa, CA 95401 USA (SAN 208-4333) Tel 707-579-3003; Fax: 707-579-1604; Toll Free: 866-727-3682; Edit Addr.: 11 W 9th St, Santa Rosa, CA 95401 USA (SAN 662-7331)
E-mail: smcmath@montessoriservices.com
Web site: http://http://www.montessoriservices.com/parent-child-press.

Parent Perks, Inc., *(978-0-9822150)* 217 Bellevue St., Newton, MA 02458 USA (SAN 857-569X)
E-mail: parentperks@yahoo.com.

Parent Positive Pr., *(978-0-9721502)* 446 Willis Ave., No. 118, Williston Park, NY 11596-0118 USA (SAN 257-4438) Tel 516-997-0051
E-mail: info@parentpositive.com
Web site: http://www.girlsonlyweightloss.com.

Parental Interventional Tools, Inc, *(978-0-9778274)* P.O. Box 547, Southbury, CT 06488 USA Tel 203-264-1054
E-mail: pittools@aol.com
Web site: http://www.drketch.com; www.pit-inc.com.

†Parenting Pr., Inc., *(978-0-943990; 978-0-9602862; 978-1-884734; 978-1-936903)* Orders Addr.: P.O. Box 75267, Seattle, WA 98175 USA (SAN 215-6938) Tel 206-364-2900; Fax: 206-364-0702; Toll Free: 800-992-6657; Edit Addr.: P.O. Box 75267, Seattle, WA 98175 USA (SAN 699-5500)
E-mail: cthreadgill@ParentingPress.com
Web site: http://www.parentingpress.com
Dist(s): **Brodart Co.**
Children's Plus, Inc.
Follett School Solutions
Independent Pubs. Group
Midwest Library Service
MyiLibrary; *CIP.*

Parents Publishing Group *Imprint of* **Big Tent Bks.**

Pares Forma Press *See* **Pares Forma Pr. Will Way Bks., Inc.**

Pares Forma Pr. Will Way Bks., Inc., *(978-1-7327837; 978-1-7332880; 978-1-7370203; 979-8-9883976)* 212 Will Way, Byron, GA 31008 USA Tel 478-972-3448
E-mail: miepmary@gmail.com; MargaretRodeheaverAuthor@gmail.com
Web site: www.margaretrodeheaver.com.

Paris Loves Bks., *(978-0-578-89894-0; 978-1-7370830)* 1001 W. N. Ave Unit D, Villa Park, IL 60181 USA Tel 630-812-9114
E-mail: paris.rodgers@yahoo.com.

Paris Pr., *(978-1-880203)* R.R. 2, Box 218, Paris, MO 65275 USA Tel 816-327-5576 Do not confuse with Paris Pr. in Northampton, MA.

Parish, Alex (GBR) *(978-0-9561613) Dist. by* **LuluCom.**

Parity Pr., *(978-0-9762015)* 1450 W. Horizon Ridge Pkwy, B-304-226, Henderson, NV 89012-4480 USA Tel 702-260-8989; Fax: 702-364-8988; Toll Free: 877-260-8989
E-mail: info@paritypress.biz
Web site: http://www.ShiftingRings.com.

Park Ave Pr., *(978-0-9995526)* 110 Park Ave., Yakima, WA 98902 USA Tel 509-339-5464; *Imprints:* Park Avenue Press (MYID_M_PARK AV)
E-mail: larsen.ideas@gmail.com.

Park Avenue Pr. *Imprint of* **Park Ave Pr.**

Park Bench Pubs., *(978-1-7361601)* 6740 S Depew St, Littleton, CO 80128 USA Tel 720-235-7315
E-mail: adeichtheauthor@gmail.com
Web site: www.amandadeich.com.

Park Hse. Bks., *(978-0-9755097)* 838 N. 6th St., Saint Clair, MI 48079 USA
E-mail: parkhousebooks@yahoo.com; mmerkau@yahoo.com
Web site: http://www.familyunity.us.

Park Place Pubns., *(978-1-877809; 978-1-935530; 978-1-943887; 978-0-578-65279-5; 978-1-953120)* P.O. Box 722, Pacific Grove, CA 93950-0829 USA (SAN 297-5238) Tel 831-649-6640 Do not confuse with Park Place Pubns. in Fort Lauderdale, FL
E-mail: publishingbiz@sbcglobal.net
Web site: http://www.parkplacepublications.com; lifeinpacificgrove.com; http://lifeinpacificgrove.com/; http://keepersofourculture.com/; pacificgrovebooks.com
Dist(s): **CreateSpace Independent Publishing Platform.**

Park Tutor Schl., *(978-0-9612740)* 7200 N. College Ave., Indianapolis, IN 46240 USA (SAN 289-7903) Tel 317-415-2700; Fax: 317-254-2714; Toll Free: 888-782-5861
E-mail: info@parktudor.org
Web site: http://www.parktudor.org.

Parker Girl Publishing, *(978-0-9855074)* 227 Shoreline Dr., Honey Brook, PA 19344 USA Tel 610-496-5070
E-mail: Huganursem@gmail.com.

Parker Hayden Media, *(978-1-941528; 978-1-950349)* 5740 N. Carefree Cir. Suite 120-1, Colorado Springs, CO 80917 USA Tel 205-582-2750
E-mail: admin@parkerhaydenmedia.com.

Parker Hse. Publishing, *(978-0-9895474; 978-0-692-46594-3; 978-0-692-47078-7; 978-0-692-47152-4; 978-0-692-51134-3; 978-0-692-52702-3; 978-0-692-55109-7; 978-0-692-56447-9; 978-0-692-58121-6; 978-0-692-60015-3; 978-0-692-63049-5; 978-0-692-64457-7; 978-0-692-65297-8; 978-0-692-73196-3; 978-0-692-73527-5; 978-0-692-78063-3; 978-0-692-79499-9;*

978-0-692-82457-3; 978-0-692-83776-4; 978-0-692-90853-2; 978-0-692-93111-0; 978-0-692-93808-9; 978-0-692-94055-6; 978-0-692-95112-5; 978-0-692-98617-2; 978-1-7328427; 978-1-73) 474 Great Oaks Blvd, Monticello, FL 32344 USA Tel 850-997-4595
E-mail: docneedles@aol.com
Dist(s): **CreateSpace Independent Publishing Platform.**

Parker, Laurie, *(978-0-9729615; 978-0-9980060)* 111 Dunbrook Dr., Starkville, MS 39759 USA.

Parker Publishing Company *See* **Parker-Wallace Publishing Co., LLC**

Parker Publishing Inc., *(978-1-60043)* 12523 Limonite Ave. #440-438, Mira Loma, CA 91752 USA Fax: 681-685-8036
E-mail: miriam@parker-publishing.com
Web site: http://www.parker-publishing.com
Dist(s): **CreateSpace Independent Publishing Platform.**

Parker-Wallace Publishing Co., LLC, *(978-0-9654700; 978-1-893091)* Orders Addr.: P.O. Box 1111, Stroudsburg, PA 18360 USA; *Imprints:* My Ancestors, My Heroes (My Ancestors)
E-mail: thebusiness2@yahoo.com.

Parkhurst Brook Pubs., *(978-0-9615664)* 303 Perrin Rd., Potsdam, NY 13676 USA (SAN 695-9121) Tel 315-265-9037
E-mail: mhcharle@northnet.org.

Parkhurst Brothers, Inc., Pubs., *(978-1-935166; 978-1-62491)* Orders Addr.: 110 West Main, Marion, MI 49665 USA (SAN 856-7107) Tel 5015153224
E-mail: ted@parkhurstbrothers.com
Web site: www.parkhurstbrothers.com; http://www.parkhurstbrothers.com
Dist(s): **Chicago Distribution Ctr.**
Univ. of Chicago Pr. Distribution Clients.

Parkhurst, R.M., *(978-0-9770323)* Orders Addr.: P.O. Box 1033, Redwood City, CA 94064 USA; Edit Addr.: P.O. Box 1013, Atascadero, CA 93423-1013 USA
E-mail: parkhurst@bigfoot.com.

Parklane Publishing, *(978-1-59384)* Div. of Book Club of America, 100 Marcus Blvd. Ste. 8, Hauppauge, NY 11788-3749 USA
E-mail: lbaumert@bookclubusa.com
Web site: http://www.parklanepublishing.com.

Parks Publishing *Imprint of* **RBC Publishing Co., Inc.**

Parkside Pubns., Inc., *(978-0-9617266; 978-0-9820774)* 601 Union St. Ste. 2600, Seattle, WA 98101 USA (SAN 663-4907) Do not confuse with Parkside Pubns., Inc., Davis, SD
E-mail: info@parksidepublications.com
Web site: http://www.parksidepublications.com
Dist(s): **Partners Bk. Distributing, Inc.**

Parkway Pr., Ltd., *(978-0-9826641; 978-0-9828089)* 330 Smith St., Niles, OH 44446-1735 USA Tel 330-505-8113
E-mail: dlbrown88@yahoo.com
Web site: www.parkwaypress.com.

Parkway Pubs., Inc., *(978-0-9635752; 978-1-887905; 978-1-933251)*
E-mail: parkwaypub@hotmail.com
Web site: http://www.parkwaypublishers.com
Dist(s): **Blair**
Julia Taylor Ebel.

Parkwest Pubns., Inc., *(978-0-88186)* P.O. Box 310251, Miami, FL 33231 USA (SAN 264-6846) Tel 305-256-7880; Fax: 305-256-7816
E-mail: parkwest@parkwestpubs.com; info@parkwestpubs.com
Web site: http://www.parkwestpubs.com
Dist(s): **Independent Pubs. Group.**

Parlance Publishing, *(978-0-9721032)* Orders Addr.: P.O. Box 841, Columbus, MS 39703-0841 USA (SAN 255-0806) Tel 662-327-4064; Fax: 662-327-4504; Edit Addr.: 1099 Southdown Pkwy., Columbus, MS 39701 USA
E-mail: parlancepub@aol.com; mail@abookery.com
Web site: http://www.parlancepublishing.com; http://www.abookery.com.

Parlor Pr., *(978-0-9724772; 978-1-932559; 978-1-60235; 978-1-64317)* Orders Addr.: 3015 Brackenberry Dr., Anderson, SC 29621 USA (SAN 254-8879) Tel 765-409-2649; Fax: 206-600-5076
E-mail: editor@parlorpress.com; sales@parlorpress.com
Web site: http://www.parlorpress.com
Dist(s): **Chicago Distribution Ctr.**
Ebsco Publishing
MBS Textbook Exchange, Inc.
SPD-Small Pr. Distribution
ebrary, Inc.

Parnassus Bk. Service, *(978-1-7327626; 978-1-956087)* P.O. Box 33, Yarmouthport, MA 02675 USA Tel 508-362-6420
E-mail: eben@parnassusbooks.com
Web site: www.parnassusbooks.com.

Parra, Beverly, *(978-0-615-14717-8; 978-0-615-14718-5; 978-0-615-14719-2; 978-0-615-14720-8; 978-0-615-15090-1; 978-0-615-17711-3; 978-0-578-01306-0)* 20412 Tufts Cir., Walnut, CA 91789 USA
E-mail: mrsparra@charter.net
Dist(s): **Lulu Pr., Inc.**

Parra Grande Pr., *(978-0-9815541; 978-0-615-19049-5)* 211 E. Carrillo St., No. 301, Santa Barbara, CA 93101 USA (SAN 855-8671) Tel 805-899-3210; Fax: 805-899-3211
E-mail: jb657@verizon.net.

Parragon Books *Imprint of* **Cottage Door Pr.**

Parragon, Inc., *(978-0-7525; 978-1-85813; 978-1-4054)* Div. of Parragon Publishing, 440 Park Ave. S, 13th Flr., New York, NY 10016 USA (SAN 256-7385) Tel 212-629-9773; Fax: 212-629-9756
Dist(s): **Central Programs.**

Parramon Ediciones S.A. (ESP) *(978-84-342) Dist. by* **Continental Bk.**

Parramon Ediciones S.A. (ESP) *(978-84-342) Dist. by* **Distr Norma.**

Parramon Ediciones S.A. (ESP) *(978-84-342) Dist. by* **Lectorum Pubns.**

Parrish, Fayrene, *(978-0-9826717)* 264 Country Club Dr., Avila Beach, CA 93424 USA Tel 805-500-5481
Dist(s): **CreateSpace Independent Publishing Platform.**

Parrot Pr., *(978-0-615-17122-7)* 6200 Vista Del Mar, Suite 313, Playa del Rey, CA 90293 USA Tel 310-574-0911
E-mail: mira@miramarmango.com
Web site: http://www.parrotstory.com
Dist(s): **Partners Pubs. Group, Inc.**

Parrotlet Pr. LLC, *(978-1-7376599; 978-1-961435)* 15-2714 PAHOA VILLAGE RD, Pahoa, HI 96778 USA Tel 720-295-2406
E-mail: ccordovabooks@gmail.com
Web site: booksbycc.com.

PARSEC Ink, *(978-0-9743231; 978-0-615-15280-6; 978-0-615-23540-0; 978-0-578-03103-3)* P.O. Box 3681, Pittsburgh, PA 15230-3681 USA
E-mail: dianeturnshek@gmail.com; renaissancewomn04@gmail.com
Web site: http://parsecink.com/
Dist(s): **Lulu Pr., Inc.**

PARSEC Publishing *See* **PARSEC Ink**

Parson Place Pr., LLC, *(978-0-9786567; 978-0-9842163; 978-0-9888528)* 10701 Tanner Williams Rd., Mobile, AL 36608-8846 USA (SAN 851-254X); P.O. Box 8277, Mobile, AL 36689-0277 Tel 251-645-9803
E-mail: info@parsonplacepress.com; mlwhite@parsonplacepress.com
Web site: http://www.parsonplacepress.com
Dist(s): **Ingram Content Group**
Spring Arbor Distributors, Inc.

Parsons Porch Bks., *(978-0-9826337; 978-0-9829413; 978-1-936912; 978-0-692-25814-9; 978-0-692-30031-2; 978-0-692-30040-4; 978-0-692-30872-1; 978-0-692-32034-1; 978-0-692-32056-3; 978-0-692-32058-7; 978-0-692-32063-1; 978-0-692-32066-2; 978-0-692-32067-9; 978-0-692-32776-0; 978-0-692-33452-2; 978-0-692-33526-0; 978-0-692-33625-0; 978-0-692-33626-7; 978-0-692-35217-5; 978-0-692-35889-4; 978-0-692-35891-7; 978-0-692-35894-8; 978-0-692-36083-5; 978-0-692-36086-6; 978-0-692-38065-9; 978-0-692-38067-3; 978-0-692-380) 121 Holly Trail NW, Cleveland, TN 37311 USA Tel 423-476-4122*
E-mail: dtullock@parsonsporch.com
Web site: http://www.parsonsporch.com
Dist(s): **CreateSpace Independent Publishing Platform.**

Parsons Technology, *(978-1-57264)* Subs. of The Learning Co., Orders Addr.: P.O. Box 100, Hiawatha, IA 52233-0100 USA (SAN 665-6161) Tel 319-395-9626; Fax: 319-378-0335; Toll Free: 800-833-3241
Dist(s): **Spring Arbor Distributors, Inc.**

Partae Pr., *(978-0-9662608)* 703 Ivinson Ave., Laramie, WY 82070 USA (SAN 254-1688) Tel 307-745-6893
E-mail: press@partae.com
Web site: http://www.partae.com.

Parthenon Pr., *(978-0-9718398)* 4839 Fullmoon Dr., El Sobrante, CA 94803-2139 USA Tel 510-223-6850 Do not confuse with Parthenon Pr., in New York, NY
E-mail: wakingthetiger@yahoo.com
Web site: http://expage.com/tigerspirit
Dist(s): **CreateSpace Independent Publishing Platform.**

Parthian Bks. (GBR) *(978-0-9521558; 978-1-902638; 978-1-905762; 978-1-906998; 978-1-907476; 978-1-912681; 978-1-910409; 978-1-913640) Dist. by* **IPG Chicago.**

PartnerPress.org, *(978-1-944098)*
E-mail: publish@partnerpress.org.

Partners in Development *See* **Partners in Development Foundation**

Partners in Development Foundation, *(978-1-933835)* 2040 Bachelot St., Honolulu, HI 96817 USA Tel 808-595-2752; Fax: 808-595-4932
E-mail: pid@pidfoundation.org
Web site: http://www.pidfoundation.org
Dist(s): **Islander Group.**

Partners in Learning, Incorporated *See* **MRN Pubns.**

Partridge Pub., *(978-1-4828; 978-1-5437)* 1663 Liberty Dr., Bloomington, IN 47403 USA Tel 812-334-5223; Fax: 812-334-5223; Toll Free: 877-655-1722
E-mail: sfurr@authorsolutions.com; jburns@authorsolutions.com
Web site: http://www.partridgepublishing.com.

PartridgeIndia *Imprint of* **Author Solutions, LLC**

Pascha Pr., *(978-0-9964045)* P.O. Box 944, Schererville, IN 46375 USA Tel 844-472-7242
E-mail: mkunch@paschapress.com
Web site: www.paschapress.com.

Pasco Scientific, *(978-1-886998; 978-1-937492)* 10101 Foothills Blvd., Roseville, CA 95678-8905 USA Tel 916-786-3800; Fax: 916-786-8905.

Pascualina Producciones S.A., 150 42nd Ave. E., Seattle, WA 98112 USA Tel 206-940-5412; Fax: 206-621-7956
E-mail: magdelenarossa@aol.com
Dist(s): **Independent Pubs. Group.**

Pasiteles Publishing Co., *(978-0-9785270)* 743 Belmont St., Belmont, MA 02478 USA
Web site: http://www.pasiteles.com.

Passage Point Publishing, *(978-1-7368910; 978-1-7368911)* 9552 E. Silent Hills Pl., Lone Tree, CO 80124 USA Tel 720-253-2412
E-mail: susan.lintonsmith@gmail.com.

Passage Publishing, *(978-0-9715926; 978-0-9724619; 978-0-9814833)* Div. of Art by Marianne, P.O. Box 148304, Nashville, TN 37214 USA Tel 615-828-3657 Do not confuse with Passage Publishing in Seattle, WA
E-mail: upcountrygirl@comcast.net; marsydotes1@live.com; upcountrygirl7@msn.com
Web site: http://www.upcountrycreations.com; http://www.artbymarianne.com.

Passion Profit Co., The/NicheMarket, *(978-0-9629202; 978-0-9745313; 978-0-9835808)* Div. of A Company Called W, P.O. Box 503991, SAIPAN, NP 96950 USA Tel 646-481-4238
E-mail: waltonsaipan@gmail.com
Web site: http://www.passionprofit.com; http://www.fastandgrowyoung.com; http://www.agelessadept.com; http://www.hiphopbiz.com.

Passion Pubns., *(978-0-9729904; 978-1-957101)* 7005 Woodbine Ave, Sacramento, CA 95822 USA Tel 916-280-8445 Do not confuse with Passion Publications in Davie, FL
E-mail: tellthetruthsac@gmail.com; passionbookpub@gmail.com
Web site: tttmi.org; https://passionbookpub.wixsite.com/pbps.

Passionate Purpose, *(978-0-9898579)* 377 Carodon Dr., Ruckersville, VA 22968 USA Tel 850-890-2768
E-mail: wildcatdtt@yahoo.com.

PassionQuest Technologies, LLC, *(978-0-9679338; 978-0-9912611)* P.O. Box 912, Marysville, OH 43040 USA (SAN 254-4326) Tel 707-688-2848; 5055 Business Ctr. Dr. Suite 108, Pmb 110, Fairfield, CA 94534 Tel 707-688-2848; *Imprints:* Wings-on-Disk (Wings Disk)
E-mail: john@earnprofitsfromyourpassion.com
Web site: http://www.OnMyMountain.com.

Passkey Learning Systems Nevada *See* **Passkey Online Educational Services**

Passkey Online Educational Services, *(978-0-9818971; 978-0-9822660; 978-1-935664; 978-1-937361)* 5348 Vegas Dr. 1670, Las Vegas, NV 89108 USA (SAN 856-8782); *Imprints:* Defiant Press (DefiantPr)
E-mail: admin@passkeyonline.com
Web site: https://www.kristianalva.com/; http://www.passkeyonline.com
Dist(s): **CreateSpace Independent Publishing Platform**
Ingram Content Group
Lulu Pr., Inc.

Passport Bks. *Imprint of* **McGraw-Hill Trade**

Pastime Pr., *(978-0-9711632; 978-1-932046)* Div. of CICA Industries, Inc., P.O. Box 741084, Boynton Beach, FL 33474 USA Tel 561-731-3400; Toll Free: 800-370-1174 Do not confuse with Pastime Press in Seattle, WA
E-mail: cicausadotcom@aol.com
Web site: http://www.pastimepress.com.

Pastime Pubns., *(978-0-9760276)* 1370 Trancas St., No. 372, Napa, CA 94558 USA Do not confuse with Pastime Publications in Walnut Creek, CA; Oakhill, VA; Herndon, VA
Web site: http://napavalleypastime.com.

Pastime Pubns., LLC, *(978-0-692-77305-5)* 1303 Waterfront Dr., Virginia Beach, VA 23451 USA Tel 724-961-2922
E-mail: scott@pastimepublicationsllc.com.

Pastorpreneur Ministries, *(978-0-9716489; 978-0-9831958)* Orders Addr.: 6243 Camellia Ct., Rocklin, CA 95765 USA Tel 916-872-5435
E-mail: john@pastorpreneur.com
Web site: http://www.pastorpreneur.com.

PastWays Inc., *(978-0-9671075)* Orders Addr.: P.O. Box 551, Farmington, MI 48332-0551 USA Tel 248-701-8112; Edit Addr.: 33414 Oakland, Suite 2, Farmington Hills, MI 48335-3571 USA
E-mail: bgolden@pastways.info
Web site: http://www.pastways.info.

Patagonia, *(978-0-9790659; 978-0-9801227; 978-1-938340; 978-1-952338)* 259 W. Santa Clara St., Ventura, CA 93001-2717 USA Tel 805-643-8616; Fax: 805-643-2367; Toll Free: 800-638-6464
E-mail: karla_olson@patagonia.com
Web site: http://www.Patagonia.com
Dist(s): **D.A.P./Distributed Art Pubs.**
MyiLibrary
Publishers Group West (PGW).

Patagonia Books *See* **Patagonia**

Patagonia Pr., *(978-1-882695)* P.O. Box 284, Bagdad, FL 32530 USA Tel 904-623-5790 Do not confuse with Patagonia Pr., Inc., Patagonia AZ
E-mail: Patagoniapress@aol.com.

Patchwork Pr., *(978-0-615-88322-9; 978-0-615-91877-8; 978-0-615-93512-6; 978-0-615-98429-2; 978-0-692-20253-1)* 7707 Red Maple Dr., Plainfield, IL 60586 USA Tel 815-416-8236
Dist(s): **CreateSpace Independent Publishing Platform.**

Paternoster Publishing USA *See* **Authentic Media**

Paterson Museum for Italian Girls Press *See* **Mill Street Forward, The**

Path of Peace Inc., The, *(978-0-9766702)* 6610 Dorel St., Suite B, Philadelphia, PA 19142 USA Tel 215-681-6592
E-mail: blessbango@yahoo.com
Web site: http://www.thepathofpeace.net.

Pathlight Bks., *(978-0-9860251; 978-1-7365341)* 20188 Country Rd. 407, Newberry, MI 49868 USA Tel 906-658-3301
E-mail: paulabooks@jamadots.com.

Paths International, Ltd. (GBR) *(978-1-84464) Dist. by* **IPG Chicago.**

Pathway Pr., *(978-0-87148; 978-1-59684; 978-1-64288)* Div. of Church of God Publishing Hse., Orders Addr.: P.O. Box 2250, Cleveland, TN 37320-2250 USA (SAN 665-7567); Edit Addr.: 1080 Montgomery Ave., Cleveland, TN 37311 USA (SAN 202-8727) Tel 423-476-4512; Fax: 423-478-7616; Toll Free: 800-553-8506 (trade only) Do not confuse with Pathway Press, San Rafael, CA
E-mail: stephanie@pathwaypress.org; elaine_mcdavid@pathwaypress.org
Web site: http://www.pathwaypress.org.

Pathways into Science, *(978-0-9779427)* 7417 River Falls Dr., Potomac, MD 20854 USA (SAN 850-5683) Tel 301-365-7593
Web site: http://pathwaysintoscience.com.

Pathwinder, Llc *See* **Pathwinder Publishing**

Pathwinder Publishing, *(978-1-7360999)*
E-mail: pathwinderpublishing@gmail.com.

Patii Jean Ostrander, *(978-1-7333848)* 4621 Camberwell Cir., Clarence, NY 14031 USA Tel 716-912-5302
E-mail: pattijeanostrander.book@gmail.com
Dist(s): **Ingram Content Group.**

Patmos, Inc., *(978-0-9741748)* P.O. Box 124, Maple Hill, KS 66507-0124 USA
Web site: http://www.patmos.us.

Patmos Publishing, *(978-0-9768545)* 4591 Jernigan Rd., Milton, FL 32571-1921 USA Tel 850-994-0908 (phone/fax) Do not confuse with Patmos Publications in Bristol GBR
E-mail: patmosprinting@gmail.com
Web site: http://www.patmospublishing.com.

Patou Bks., LLC, *(978-0-9767756)* 1550 Larimer St., Suite 459, Denver, CO 80202-1602 USA.

Patrenialla Turner, Queen , *(978-0-578-14812-0)* .

PatriceMFoster.com, *(978-0-578-18146-2; 978-0-692-75921-9; 978-0-9981874; 978-1-7332984; 978-1-7345369; 978-1-7345624; 978-1-7346231; 978-1-7348657; 979-8-9865728; 979-8-9869237; 979-8-9873174)* 237 Cobblestone Ln., McDonough, GA 30252 USA
E-mail: patricemfoster@gmail.com
Web site: https://patricemfoster.com/; https://attractgoodlife.com; https://actnowhelpteens.com.

Patricia D. Ensing, *(978-1-7361707)* 1074 S. Green Bay Rd., Lake Forest, IL 60045 USA Tel 847-363-1234
E-mail: butterflymarty9005@gmail.com
Web site: www.wingitpress.com.

Patrick Edward Moyer, *(978-0-578-43754-5)* 16406 E. Garrison Dr., Marina, CA 93933 USA Tel 831-245-8063
E-mail: pem95023@netscape.net
Dist(s): **Ingram Content Group.**

Patrick Henry College Pr., *(978-0-9714458)* 1 Patrick Henry Cir., Purcellville, VA 20132 USA Tel 540-338-1776; Fax: 540-338-8707
E-mail: info@phc.edu
Web site: http://www.phc.edu.

†Patrick's Pr., *(978-0-944322; 978-0-9609412)* Orders Addr.: P.O. Box 5189, Columbus, GA 31906 USA (SAN 274-466X) Tel 706-322-1584; Fax: 706-322-5806; Toll Free: 800-654-1052; Edit Addr.: 2218 Wynnton Rd., Columbus, GA 31906 USA (SAN 243-2773)
E-mail: quizbowl@aol.com
Web site: http://www.patrickspress.com
Dist(s): **Peller, A. W. & Assocs.**; *CIP.*

Patriot Media, Inc., *(978-0-9791642; 978-0-9845777; 978-0-9846638; 978-0-9888930; 978-0-9905724; 978-1-7323764)* Orders Addr.: P.O. Box 5414, Niceville, FL 32578 USA Tel 850-897-4204 (phone/fax)
E-mail: dari.bradleyceo@patriotmediainc.com; dari@patriotmediainc.com
Web site: http://www.patriotmediapublishing.com; http://www.patriotmediainc.com; http://www.patriotmediainternational.com; http://www.silentbattleground.com; http://www.dmulmer.com; http://www.staffmonkeys.com; http://www.paulsherbo.com; http://www.booksbynelson.com; http://www.those67blues.com
Dist(s): **CreateSpace Independent Publishing Platform.**

Patriot Media Publishing *See* **Patriot Media, Inc.**

Patriot Pr., *(978-0-9796000; 978-1-941020)* 1505 Knoxlyn Rd., Gettysburg, PA 17325 USA (SAN 853-8735)
E-mail: patriotpress@live.com
Web site: http://www.patriotpressbooks.com; http://www.jessicajamesbooks.com.

Patriot Publishing, *(978-0-9789936)* Ernest Beath, III, 2216 Horn Point Rd., Cambridge, MD 21613-3379 USA Tel 410-228-5771
E-mail: docprb@bluecrab.org.

Patten Point Marketing Services, Incorporated *See* **Liberty Manuals Co.**

Pattern Pr., *(978-0-9729248; 978-1-935559; 978-1-941961)* Orders Addr.: P.O. Box 2737, Fallbrook, CA 92088 USA; Edit Addr.: 40521 De Luz Rd., Fallbrook, CA 92028 USA
E-mail: patternpress1@gmail.com
Web site: http://www.patternpress.com.

Patterson, Felicia, *(978-0-578-34786-8; 978-0-578-37282-2; 978-1-958189)* 4630 Hwy. 77, chipley, FL 32428 USA Tel 850-629-9424
E-mail: adropfromedensgarden@gmail.com.

Patterson, Stacey Lynn, *(978-0-578-21593-8)* 1030 Strahley Pl., Pittsburgh, PA 15220 USA
Web site: http://shermangc2014.wixsite.com/slpatterson.

Patton, Lashunda, *(978-0-692-27864-2; 978-0-692-09452-5)* 2500 Thomason Cr No. 100, Arlington, TX 76006 USA Tel 817-680-5492
E-mail: lashunda.patton@yahoo.com.

Patty Huston-Holm, *(978-0-692-92156-2; 978-0-692-04996-9; 978-0-692-14271-4; 978-0-578-72034-0; 978-0-578-86224-8; 978-0-578-89208-5)* 9685 Slough Rd., CANAL WINCHESTER, OH 43110 USA Tel 614-837-0164
E-mail: hustonpat@gmail.com
Dist(s): **Ingram Content Group.**

Patty's Blooming Words, *(978-0-615-78050-4; 978-0-9893303)* 693 Springlake Dr., Franklin, TN 37064 USA Tel 615-790-0109
E-mail: pattysbloomers@me.com.

Paul F. Meier, *(978-0-578-72414-0; 978-0-578-72415-7; 978-0-578-73776-8; 978-1-7370400)* 13420 Princeton Ln. 0, EDMOND, OK 73013 USA Tel 19187666120
E-mail: paulfmeier@Yahoo.com
Dist(s): **Ingram Content Group.**

Paul Ferrante, *(978-1-7324857)* 41 A Buckskin Ln., STRATFORD, CT 06614 USA Tel 203-384-1131
E-mail: pnferrante21@optimum.net.

Paul Publishing *See* **Bk. Bunny Publishing**

Paula Deen Ventures *See* **Kitchen Ink Publishing**

†Pauline Bks. & Media, *(978-0-8198)* 50 St. Paul's Ave., Boston, MA 02130-3491 USA (SAN 203-8900) Tel

617-522-8911; Fax: 617-524-8035; Toll Free: 800-876-4463 (orders only)
E-mail: editorial@pauline.org; kcorina@paulinemedia.com
Web site: http://www.PAULINE.org
Dist(s): **MyiLibrary**
O'Reilly Media, Inc.
St Pauls/Alba Hse. Pubs.; *CIP.*

Paulisich, Laura, *(978-0-692-72544-3; 978-0-9981899; 978-0-692-97710-1; 978-0-9997728; 978-0-692-19039-5; 978-0-578-63490-6)* 112 N. St. #3 please leave package without signature, HUDSON, WI 54016 USA Tel 715-808-1897.

†Paulist Pr., *(978-0-8091; 978-1-893757; 978-1-58768; 978-1-61643)* 997 MacArthur Blvd., Mahwah, NJ 07430-2096 USA (SAN 202-5159) Tel 201-825-7300 (ext. 232); Fax: 201-825-8345; Toll Free Fax: 800-836-3161; Toll Free: 800-218-1903; *Imprints:* HiddenSpring (HidSpring); E T Nedder (ETNedder); Ambassador Books (Ambass Bks)
E-mail: info@paulistpress.com
Web site: http://www.paulistpress.com
Dist(s): **Bookazine Co., Inc.**
Spring Arbor Distributors, Inc.; *CIP.*

Paulsen, Marc Productions, Incorporated *See* **Stance Pubns.**

Paulus Publishing, *(978-0-9744863)* 6115 E. Hillview St., Mesa, AZ 85205 USA.

Paved Roads Productions, *(978-0-9795862)* Orders Addr.: P.O. Box 640173, Pike Road, AL 36064 USA.

Pavilion Bks. (GBR) *(978-0-85177; 978-0-86101; 978-0-86283; 978-1-85470; 978-1-85585; 978-1-85753; 978-1-85833; 978-0-947553; 978-1-84138; 978-1-85561; 978-0-904609; 978-1-85028; 978-1-84065; 978-1-85600; 978-1-902616; 978-1-85993; 978-1-84333; 978-1-903954; 978-1-84411; 978-1-86222; 978-1-84340; 978-1-84458; 978-0-86124; 978-1-85841; 978-1-908449; 978-1-909397; 978-1-911670; 978-1-911624; 978-1-910904; 978-1-906388; 978-0-86288) Dist. by* **Trafalgar.**

Pavilion Bks. (GBR) *(978-0-85177; 978-0-86101; 978-0-86283; 978-1-85470; 978-1-85585; 978-1-85753; 978-1-85833; 978-0-947553; 978-1-84138; 978-1-85561; 978-0-904609; 978-1-85028; 978-1-84065; 978-1-85600; 978-1-902616; 978-1-85993; 978-0-86288; 978-1-84333; 978-1-903954; 978-1-84411; 978-1-86222; 978-1-84340; 978-1-84458; 978-0-86124; 978-1-85841; 978-1-906388; 978-1-908449; 978-1-909397; 978-1-911670; 978-1-911624; 978-1-910904) Dist. by* **HarperCollins Pubs.**

Pavilion Bks. (GBR) *(978-0-85177; 978-0-86101; 978-0-86283; 978-1-85470; 978-1-85585; 978-1-85753; 978-1-85833; 978-0-947553; 978-1-84138; 978-1-85561; 978-0-904609; 978-1-85028; 978-1-84065; 978-1-85600; 978-1-902616; 978-1-85993; 978-0-86288; 978-1-84333; 978-1-903954; 978-1-84411; 978-1-86222; 978-1-84340; 978-1-84458; 978-0-86124; 978-1-85841; 978-1-906388; 978-1-908449; 978-1-909397; 978-1-911670; 978-1-911624; 978-1-910904) Dist. by* **Peng Rand Hse.**

Pavilion Pr., Inc., *(978-1-4145)* 1213 Vine St., Philadelphia, PA 19107 USA Tel 215-569-9779; Fax: 215-569-8814
Web site: http://www.pavilionpress.com.

Pavilion Pubs., *(978-0-88432; 978-1-57970)* Div. of Pavilion Publishers, LLC, P.O. Box 1460, Guilford, CT 06437 USA (SAN 213-957X) Tel 518-605-5179; Toll Free: 800-243-1234
E-mail: Antonydaou@gmail.com; Mcgradylaura@gmail.com
Web site: http://www.audioforum.com
Dist(s): **Bolchazy-Carducci Pubs.**

Paw Print Pubns., *(978-0-9785473)* Orders Addr.: 4206 NE Newbury Ct., Lees Summit, MO 64064-1617 USA (SAN 850-9573) Toll Free: 877-267-9482; *Imprints:* Austin & Charlie Adventures (Austin & Charlie Adventures)
E-mail: lparker154@aol.com; pawfacts@aol.com; linda8000@sbcglobal.net
Web site: http://www.austincharlieadventures.com
Dist(s): **Book Clearing Hse.**

Paw Print Publishing, *(978-0-9770898)* Orders Addr.: P.O. Box 48309, Cumberland, NC 28331-8309 USA
Web site: www.k9fluffy.com.

Paw Prints *Imprint of* **Baker & Taylor, CATS**

Paw Prints Press *See* **Heather & Highlands Publishing**

Pawl, Jacqueline, *(978-0-578-44031-6)* 676 Cambridge Way, Bolingbrook, IL 60440 USA Tel 630-345-0370
E-mail: jackiepawl21@aol.com
Dist(s): **Ingram Content Group.**

PawlingPr., *(978-0-692-95226-9)* 24809 Magic Mtn Pkwy, Apt 1733, Valencia, CA 91355 USA Tel 310-730-9060
E-mail: jdmcmah@gmail.com
Web site: www.pawlingpress.com.

Paws and Claws Publishing, LLC, *(978-0-9846724; 978-0-9906067; 978-1-946198)* 1586 Skeet Club Rd. Ste 102-175, High Point, NC 27265 USA Tel 336-297-9783
E-mail: jcappoen@pawsandclawspublishing.com
Web site: http://www.pawsandclawspublishing.com.

Paws In the Sand Publishing, *(978-0-9790057)* Orders Addr.: 4644 Pepper Mill St., Moorpark, CA 93021-9302 USA (SAN 852-193X) Fax: 805-553-9253
Web site: http://pawsinthesand.com.

Paxen Publishing LLC *See* **Paxen Publishing LLC**

Paxen Publishing LLC, *(978-1-934350; 978-1-7326905; 978-1-7337320; 978-1-7345284; 978-1-7345285; 978-1-7345289; 978-1-7346206; 978-1-7351585; 978-1-7351586; 978-1-7356953)* 2194 Hwy. A1A Suite 208, Indian Harbour Beach, FL 32937 USA Tel 321-425-3030; 866-547-1895
Web site: http://www.paxenpublishing.com.

Paycock Pr., *(978-0-931181; 978-0-9602424)* 3819 N. 13th St., Arlington, VA 22201 USA (SAN 212-5420) Tel 703-525-9296 phone/fax
E-mail: gargoyle@gargoylemagazine.com
Web site: http://www.gargoylemagazine.com.

Payne, Christine, *(978-0-9740643)* P.O. Box 951, Mountain Home, AR 72654-0951 USA.

Payne, Elaine, *(978-0-578-85757-2)* P.O. Box PO Box 302, Morrisville, NC 27560 USA Tel 919-884-7484
E-mail: epayneinfo@gmail.com.

Payne, Michael G II, *(978-0-692-14407-7)* 259 Utility Lewisport Rd., Lewisport, KY 42351 USA Tel 270-993-7963
E-mail: mgeoffpayne@gmail.com.

Payne, Yadira V. Publishing, *(978-0-9747350)* 341 Lamplighter Ln., Martinez, GA 30907 USA Tel 706-414-9566
E-mail: yvppublishing@knology.net.

PAZ Publishing, *(978-0-942253)* Div. of PAZ Percussion, Orders Addr.: 2415 Bevington St. NW, North Canton, OH 44709-2221 USA (SAN 666-8100) Tel 330-493-6661 (phone/fax)
E-mail: PAZPublishing@aol.com
Web site: http://www.PAZPublishing.com.

PB&J OmniMedia *Imprint of* **Takahashi & Black**

PBD, Inc., *(978-0-9846038; 978-0-9837260; 978-1-62219)* 1650 Bluegrass Lakes Pkwy., Alpharetta, GA 30004 USA (SAN 126-6039) Tel 770-442-8633; Fax: 770-442-9742
Web site: http://www.pbd.com.

PBL Stories LLC, *(978-0-9792379)* Orders Addr.: P.O. Box 393, Lynn Haven, FL 32444-4272 USA Tel 850-348-0718; Fax: 850-265-9815; Edit Addr.: 1812 S. Hwy. 77, Suite. 115, Lynn Haven, FL 32444-4272 USA
E-mail: booksales@pblstories.com
Web site: http://www.pblstories.com.

PC Treasures, Inc., *(978-1-933796; 978-1-60072)* 1795 N. Lapeer Rd., Oxford, MI 48371-2415 USA (SAN 857-0930)
E-mail: lthomas@pctreasures.com; jbrandt@pctreasures.com; jadams@pctreasures.com
Web site: http://www.pctreasures.com.

PCG Publishing Group *See* **Blue Star Pr.**

PCS Edventures, Inc., *(978-0-9753193; 978-0-9827203)* 345 Bobwhite Ct., Suite 200, Boise, ID 83706 USA Tel 208-343-3110; Fax: 208-343-1321; Toll Free: 800-429-3110
E-mail: rmwright@pcsedu.com; rgrover@pcsedu.com; agranger@pcsedu.com
Web site: http://www.edventures.com.

PD Hse. Holdings, LLC, *(978-0-9815333; 978-0-9984644; 978-1-7370004)* 910 S. Meadow Dr., Sandusky, OH 44870 USA (SAN 855-806X)
E-mail: pjgron@pjgrondin.com
Web site: http://www.pjgrondin.com.

PDG *Imprint of* **Publishers Design Group, Inc.**

†Peabody Essex Museum, *(978-0-87577; 978-0-88389)* Orders Addr.: East India Sq., Salem, MA 01970 USA Tel 978-745-9500 ext 3047; Fax: 978-740-3622; Toll Free: 800-745-4054 ext 3047
E-mail: wholesale@pem.org
Web site: http://www.pem.org
Dist(s): **Antique Collectors' Club**
Ingram Publisher Services
Univ. Pr. of New England
Univ. of Washington Pr.; *CIP.*

†Peabody Museum of Archaeology & Ethnology, Harvard Univ., Pubns. Dept., *(978-0-87365)* Orders Addr.: 11 Divinity Ave., Cambridge, MA 02138 USA (SAN 203-1426) Tel 617-496-9922; 617-495-3938; Fax: 617-495-7535
E-mail: ddickers@fas.harvard.edu
Web site: http://www.peabody.harvard.edu/publications
Dist(s): **Harvard Univ. Pr.**
Univ. Pr. of New England
Univ. of New Mexico Pr.; *CIP.*

Peabody Publishing Co., *(978-0-9963323)* 325 Thames Dr., Colorado Springs, CO 80906 USA Tel 719-237-8014
E-mail: drphineaspeabody@gmail.com.

Peace B Still Ministries Pr., *(978-0-9752665)* 205 Joel Blvd., Suite 107, Lehigh Acres, FL 33972-0202 USA
E-mail: gduncan316@aol.com.

Peace Education Foundation, *(978-1-878227; 978-1-934760; 978-1-953045)* 1900 Biscayne Blvd., Miami, FL 33132-1025 USA Tel 305-576-5075; Fax: 305-576-3106; Toll Free: 800-749-8838
Web site: http://www.peaceeducation.com.

Peace Evolutions, LLC, *(978-0-9753837; 978-0-9912489)* P.O. Box 458, Glen Echo, MD 20812-0458 USA (SAN 256-2146) Fax: 301-263-9280
E-mail: info@peace-evolutions.com; julie@peace-evolutions.com
Web site: http://www.peace-evolutions.com.

Peace Hill Press *See* **Well-Trained Mind Pr.**

Peace Love Karma Publishing, *(978-0-9743540)* 2584 Rim Rock Way, Santa Rosa, CA 95404 USA
E-mail: Carol@peacelovekarma.com; 11lovepoet@gmail.com
Web site: http://www.peacelovekarma.com
Dist(s): **New Leaf Distributing Co., Inc.**

Peace of Mind Inc, *(978-0-692-53539-4; 978-0-9976954; 978-1-7373423)* 5540 Nevada Ave. NW, Washington, DC 20015 USA Tel 202-494-2624; *Imprints:* Peace of Mind Press (P M P)
E-mail: teachpeacedc@gmail.com
Web site: www.teachpeaceofmind.com.

Peace of Mind LLC *See* **Peace of Mind Inc**

Peace of Mind Pr. *Imprint of* **Peace of Mind Inc**

Peace of Sky, *(978-1-7370839)* 4822 S 133 St, Ste 200, Omaha, NE 68137 USA Tel 402-884-5995
E-mail: peaceofsky@conciergemarketing.com.

Peace Power Pr., *(978-0-9824601)* 6044 Waterloo Rd., Dayton, OH 45402-3015 USA (SAN 858-2254) Tel 937-227-3223
Web site: http://daytonpeacemuseum.org.

Peace Rug Company, Inc., The, *(978-0-9763949)* 407 W. Emery St., Dalton, GA 30720 USA Tel 706-272-0200; Fax: 706-226-2296; Toll Free: 888-732-2378
E-mail: info@peacerug.com
Web site: http://www.peacerug.com.

Peaceable Kingdom Pr., *(978-1-56890; 978-1-59395)* 950 Gilman, Suite 200, Berkeley, CA 94710 USA Tel 510-558-2051; Fax: 510-558-2052; Toll Free: 800-444-7778 Do not confuse with Peaceable Kingdom Press in Greenville, VA
E-mail: djaffe@pkpress.com
Web site: http://www.pkpress.com.

Peaceable Productions, *(978-0-9709187)* Orders Addr.: P.O. Box 708, Center Hill, FL 33514 USA (SAN 254-4946) Tel 352-793-7516; Edit Addr.: 6698 SE 57th Rd., Center Hill, FL 33514 USA Tel 352-793-7516; Fax: 775-514-8681
E-mail: yvonne@atlantic.net.

Peaceful Thoughts Pr., *(978-0-9725118)* 598 Straton Chase SE, Marietta, GA 30067 USA
Web site: http://www.peacefulthoughts.net.

PeaceLight Pr., *(978-0-9971661)* 1206 Lineberry St., Ramseur, NC 27316 USA Tel 336-633-9938
E-mail: chip.womick@twc.com.

Peacemakers Press *See* **Positive Spin Pr.**

Peach Blossom Pubns., *(978-0-941367)* 120 E. Beaver Ave. Apt. 212, State College, PA 16801-4991 USA (SAN 665-4800)
E-mail: inezwaterson@prodigy.net
Dist(s): **Quality Bks., Inc.**

Peach Plum Pr., *(978-0-578-04395-1)* 123 Picnic Ave., San Rafael, CA 94901 USA
E-mail: marymitchelldesign@comcast.net.

Peach Tree Pr., *(978-0-9893120; 978-1-62910)* 1321 Upland Dr., Houston, TX 77043 USA Tel 919-502-0151
E-mail: arpl.dropbox@gmail.com.

PeachMoon Publishing, *(978-0-9795831)* 3915 Bonnett Creek Ln., Hoschton, GA 30548-6204 USA (SAN 853-814X)
E-mail: Alice@peachmoonpublishing.com
Web site: http://luckythelizard.com; http://peachmoonpublishing.com.

Peachtree Junior *Imprint of* **Peachtree Publishing Co. Inc.**

Peachtree Publishers *See* **Peachtree Publishing Co. Inc.**

†Peachtree Publishing Co. Inc., *(978-0-931948; 978-0-934601; 978-1-56145; 978-1-68263)* 1700 Chattahoochee Ave., NW, Atlanta, GA 30318-2112 USA (SAN 212-1999) Tel 404-876-8761; Fax: 404-875-2578; Toll Free Fax: 800-875-8909; Toll Free: 800-241-0113; *Imprints:* Peachtree Junior (Peachtree); Margaret Quinlin Books (M Quinlin Books)
E-mail: sales@peachtree-online.com; palermo@peachtree-online.com; McManus@peachtree-online.com
Web site: http://www.peachtree-online.com; www.cheshirecheesecat.com; www.christmasinthetrenches.info; www.14cowsforamerica.com
Dist(s): **Children's Plus, Inc.**
Heinecken & Assoc., Ltd.
Lectorum Pubns., Inc.
MyiLibrary
Open Road Integrated Media, Inc.
Penguin Random Hse. Distribution
Penguin Random Hse. LLC; *CIP.*

Peacock Tree Publishing, *(978-1-9160491)* 52 Parkgrove Dr., Edinburgh, EH4 7QG GBR Tel 07476 303909 Admin
E-mail: madly.chatterjee@gmail.com
Web site: http://www.madlychatterjee.com.

Peak City Publishing, LLC, *(978-1-935711)* 104B N. Salem St., Apex, NC 27502 USA Tel 919-758-9516
Web site: http://www.peakcitypublishing.com.

PEAK League Pr. LLC, *(978-1-7365043)* 9212 Fry Rd. Ste. 105-128, Cypress, TX 77433 USA Tel 281-732-4999; Fax: 832-681-8370
E-mail: info@peakleaguepress.com.

Peak Writing, LLC, *(978-0-9717330; 978-0-9767961)* Orders Addr.: P.O. Box 14196, Savannah, GA 31416 USA Tel 912-398-2987; Toll Free Fax: 888-226-4811; Edit Addr.: 12 Mercer Rd., Savannah, GA 31411 USA Do not confuse with Peak Writing in Frisco, CO
E-mail: info@peakwriting.com
Dist(s): **Quality Bks., Inc.**
Send The Light Distribution LLC
Spring Arbor Distributors, Inc.

Peaks Pr. LLC, *(978-1-938032)* 630 Race St., Denver, CO 80206 USA Tel 720-560-3779
E-mail: info@peakspress.com
Dist(s): **BookBaby.**

Peanut Butter Publishing, *(978-0-89716; 978-1-59849)* 2207 Fairview Ave. E., Houseboat No. 4, Seattle, WA 98102 USA (SAN 212-7881) Tel 206-860-4900 Toll Free: 877-728-8837
E-mail: ewolfpub@aol.com
Web site: http://www.peanutbutterpublishing.com.

Peapod Pr. *Imprint of* **PublishingWorks**

Peapod Publishing, Inc., *(978-0-9729507; 978-0-9894591; 979-8-9850807)* P.O. Box 951599, Lake Mary, FL 32795-1599 USA Tel 407-333-3030
E-mail: info@peapodpublishing.com; diana@peapodpublishing.com
Web site: http://www.adventureswithpawpaw.com; http://www.pawpawspals.org; http://www.peapodpublishing.com; http://www.borntoflybook.com; http://www.born2fly.org
Dist(s): **BookBaby.**

Pearl & Dotty, *(978-0-9772441)* Orders Addr.: P.O. Box 2162, Seattle, WA 98111-2162 USA
E-mail: pearlanddotty@gmail.com; holler@pearlanddotty.com
Web site: http://www.pearlanddotty.com.

Pearl Pr., *(978-0-9674525)* Orders Addr.: P.O. Box 266, Eastport, MI 49627 USA (SAN 299-9870) Tel 231-599-2372 (phone/fax); Edit Addr.: 6027 M-88 Hwy., Eastport, MI 49627 USA Do not confuse with Pearl Pr., Nazareth, PA, Sacramento CA
E-mail: Beebystudio@mailbug.com.

Pearl Pr., *(978-0-9741332)* 3104 O St., No. 175, Sacramento, CA 95816 USA Do not confuse with Pearl Press in Nazareth PA, Eastport MI
E-mail: info@pearlpress.net
Web site: http://www.pearlpress.net
Dist(s): **Quality Bks., Inc.**

Pearl Publishing, LLC, *(978-0-9785264; 978-0-9826175; 978-1-937390)* 2587c Southside Blvd., Melba, ID 83641 USA Tel 888-499-9666
E-mail: info@pearlpublishing.net
Web site: http://wupublishing.com; http://666america.com; http://pearlpublishing.net.

Pearlman, Beth, *(978-0-9767522)* 1773 Diane Rd., Mendota Heights, MN 55118 USA.

Pearls & Ivy Publishing *See* **Monster Ivy Publishing**

Pearlsong Pr., *(978-0-9713247; 978-1-59719)* P.O. Box 58065, Nashville, TN 37205 USA (SAN 255-9188) Tel 615-356-5188
E-mail: contact@pearlsong.com
Web site: http://www.pearlsong.com.

PearlStone Publishing, Inc., *(978-0-9724586; 978-0-9816883; 978-0-9841899; 978-1-936513; 978-1-944348; 978-1-944348-20-5; 978-1-958740)* 514-201 Daniels St., Raleigh, NC 27603 USA
E-mail: publish@pendiumpublishing.com
Web site: http://www.pendiumpublishing.com.

Pearn & Assocs. Inc., *(978-0-9777318; 978-0-9841683; 978-0-9846523; 978-0-9897242; 978-1-7357731)* 1428 S. California Ave., Suite 4, Loveland, CO 80537-7177 USA Tel 970-599-8924; *Imprints:* Over the Rainbow (Over the Rain)
E-mail: victorpearn@ymail.com.

Pearson Custom Publishing *See* **Pearson Learning Solutions**

Pearson Education, *(978-0-13; 978-0-582; 978-0-7686; 978-1-5093)* Orders Addr.: 200 Old Tappan Rd., Old Tappan, NJ 07675 USA (SAN 200-2175) Tel 201-767-5000 (Receptionist); Toll Free Fax: 800-445-6991; Toll Free: 800-428-5331; 800-922-0579; Edit Addr.: One Lake St., Upper Saddle River, NJ 07458 USA Tel 201-236-7000; 201-236-5321; Fax: 201-236-6549; 800 E. 96th St., Suite 300, Indianapolis, IN 46240 Toll Free: 800-571-4580; *Imprints:* Microsoft Press (MicrosoftPress)
E-mail: communications@pearsoned.com
Web site: http://www.pearsoned.com; www.pearson.com
Dist(s): **Gaunt, Inc.**
InterVarsity Pr.
MyiLibrary
Trans-Atlantic Pubns., Inc.

Pearson Education Australia (AUS) *(978-0-7248; 978-0-7342; 978-0-7312; 978-1-86391; 978-1-74140; 978-1-876209; 978-1-74085; 978-1-74103; 978-1-74091; 978-1-74081; 978-1-74206; 978-0-86911; 978-0-7316-1261-1; 978-0-646-30941-5; 978-0-7339; 978-0-85859; 978-0-86462; 978-0-646-24199-9; 978-0-646-31855-4; 978-0-646-32904-8; 978-0-646-32905-5; 978-1-4860; 978-1-74009; 978-1-4425; 978-0-646-29552-7) Dist. by* **Cheng Tsui.**

Pearson Education, Ltd. (GBR) *(978-0-201; 978-0-273; 978-0-321; 978-0-582; 978-0-673; 978-1-4058; 978-1-84479; 978-1-84658; 978-1-84959; 978-1-84878; 978-1-84776; 978-1-4479; 978-1-292; 978-1-78726) Dist. by* **Trans-Atl Phila.**

Pearson Education, Ltd. (GBR) *(978-0-201; 978-0-273; 978-0-321; 978-0-582; 978-0-673; 978-1-4058; 978-1-84479; 978-1-84658; 978-1-84959; 978-1-84878; 978-1-84776; 978-1-4479; 978-1-292; 978-1-78726) Dist. by* **Pearson Educ.**

Pearson ESL, *(978-0-582)* Div. of Pearson International, 75 Arlington St., Boston, MA 02116 USA
Dist(s): **Pearson Education.**

Pearson Learning, *(978-0-7652; 978-1-4284)* Div of Pearson Education, Orders Addr.: P.O. Box 2500, Lebanon, IN 46052 USA Toll Free Fax: 800-393-3156; Toll Free: 800-321-3106; Edit Addr.: 1 Lake St., U Saddle Riv, NJ 07458-1813 USA Toll Free: 800-526-9907 (Customer Service)
E-mail: jeff.hoitsma@pearsonlearning.com
Web site: http://www.pearsonlearning.com
Dist(s): **Follett School Solutions.**

Pearson Learning Solutions, *(978-0-536; 978-0-8087; 978-1-4386; 978-0-555; 978-0-558; 978-1-256; 978-1-269; 978-1-323)* Div. of Simon & Schuster Higher Education Publishing Group, 501 Boylston St., Suite 900, Boston, MA 02116 USA (SAN 214-0225) Tel 617-671-2900; 617-671-2926; 617-671-2000; Fax: 617-671-2994; Toll Free: 800-428-4466 (orders only)
Web site: http://www.pearsoncustom.com; http://www.pearsonlearningsolutions.com
Dist(s): **Pearson Education.**

Pearson School *See* **Savvas Learning Co.**

Pearson, Shelley, *(978-1-7324082)* 16437 SE Stephens St, Portland, OR 97233 USA Tel 503-734-6202
E-mail: shelleypearsonwrites@gmail.com
Web site: shelleypearsonwrites.com.

Peartree (r), *(978-0-935343)* Orders Addr.: P.O. Box 14533, Clearwater, FL 33766 USA Tel 727-531-4973 (phone/fax)7275314973
E-mail: peartreebooks@yahoo.com
Web site: http://www.peartree-books.com
Dist(s): **Brodart Co.**
Follett School Solutions.

Pease, Kathy, *(978-1-7361462)* 4610 Dorchester Ln., Granite Bay, CA 95746 USA Tel 916-812-0749
E-mail: kkp1986@outlook.com.

Pebble *Imprint of* **Capstone**

Pebble Beach Pr., Ltd., *(978-1-883740)* P.O. Box 1171, Pebble Beach, CA 93953-1171 USA Tel 408-372-5559; Fax: 408-375-4525.

Pebbles Pr., *(978-1-7337582)* 130 Malcolm X Blvd, Apt 328, New York, NY 10026 USA Tel 646-541-7127
E-mail: cenydgaleria@mac.com
Web site: www.pebblespress.com.

Pebbleton Pr., *(978-0-9760011)* P.O. Box 1894, Duxbury, MA 02331 USA
E-mail: pebbletonpress@comcast.net
Web site: http://www.pebbletonpress.com.

ebbyville Pr., *(978-1-7357060)* 300 Poplar Ct., Ellettsville, IN 47429 USA Tel 812-345-0169
E-mail: ryanpeek777@yahoo.com
Web site: www.ryanpeek.com.

ecan Tree Publishing, *(978-0-9821114; 978-0-9832078; 978-0-615-67485-8; 978-0-9888969; 978-1-7328311; 978-1-7341058; 978-1-7347430; 978-1-7358295; 978-1-7372621; 979-8-9855014; 979-8-9864215; 979-8-9884334)* Orders Addr.: 2238 Greene St., Hollywood, FL 33020 USA Tel 786-763-1295
E-mail: adminservices@pecantreebooks.com; info@pecantreebooks.com
Web site: http://www.pecantreebooks.com/shop-ptp.html; http://www.pecantreebooks.com
Dist(s): **Ingram Bk. Co.**

ecci Educational Pubs., *(978-0-943220)* 440 Davis Ct., No. 405, San Francisco, CA 94111 USA (SAN 240-558X) Tel 415-391-8579; Fax: 970-493-8781
E-mail: pecci@sirius.com
Web site: http://www.onlinereadingteacher.com.

Pecsi, Louis John, *(978-0-9841162)* 285 Somsert Rd., Deptford, NJ 08096 USA
E-mail: indieflixguy96@aol.com.

PeDante Pr., *(978-0-9790199; 978-1-940844)* 4 White Oak, Danbury, CT 06410 USA Tel 203-350-9288
E-mail: erikagrey@rocketmail.com
Web site: www.erikagrey.com.

Peddlers Group, *(978-0-9802257; 978-0-9829177)* 1127 Parrish Rd., Leesville, SC 29070 USA Tel 803-657-5324; Fax: 803-753-9824
E-mail: peddlersgroup@gmail.com
Web site: http://www.peddlersgroup.com.

Pedia Learning, Inc. *See* **Logic of English, Inc**

Pedigree Bks., Ltd. (GBR) *(978-1-874507; 978-1-904329; 978-1-906450; 978-1-907602; 978-1-908152) Dist. by* **Diamond Book Dists.**

†Pedipress, Inc., *(978-0-914625)* Orders Addr.: 125 Red Gate Ln., Amherst, MA 01002 USA (SAN 287-7570) Tel 413-549-7798 M - Thurs. 8:30 to 4:30 EST; Fax: 413-549-4095; Toll Free: 800-611-6081 M - Thurs. 8:30 to 4:30 EST
E-mail: tplautassistant@gmail.com
Web site: http://www.pedipress.com
Dist(s): **INscribe Digital**; *CIP.*

Peebco Publishing Hse., The, *(978-0-9644758; 978-0-578-55731-1; 978-0-578-55739-7)* P.O. Box 45333, Saint Louis, MO 63145 USA (SAN 298-6760) Tel 636-346-7179
E-mail: info@PeebcoPublishing.com
Web site: http://www.PeebcoPublishing.com.

Peek-A-Boo Publishing, *(978-1-943154)* 500 Montgomery St., Alexandria, VA 22314 USA Tel 703-348-9898; *Imprints:* See-Saw Publishing (See-SawPub)
E-mail: info@peekaboopublishing.com
Web site: peekaboopublishing.com.

PeekaBoo Publishing LLC, *(978-0-578-88450-9; 978-0-578-36682-1)* 1220, Atlanta, GA 30327 USA Tel 404-808-8582
E-mail: meredithpope@ymail.com.

Peel Productions, Inc., *(978-0-939217; 978-1-943158)* 9415 NE Woodridge, Vancouver, WA 98664 USA; *Imprints:* Blackbirch Press, Incorporated (Blackbirch Pr)
E-mail: ddub@drawbooks.com
Web site: http://www.drawbooks.com; http://www.peelbooks.com; http://www.123draw.com; http://www.1-2-3.draw.com
Dist(s): **F&W Media, Inc.**
Pathway Bk. Service
Two Rivers Distribution.

Peeler, Casey, *(978-0-9906984; 978-0-9961521)* 2424 Olan Dr., Shelby, NC 28152 USA Tel 704-472-9384
E-mail: caseypeelerauthor@gmail.com.

Peepal Tree Pr., Ltd. (GBR) *(978-0-948833; 978-1-900715; 978-1-84523) Dist. by* **IPG Chicago.**

Peeper & Friends *Imprint of* **Tree Of Life Publishing**

Peepy Squeeky Publishing, *(978-0-9998736)* 4625 Southport Crossing, Norcross, GA 30092 USA Tel 770-368-1485
E-mail: denslow4625@comcast.net.

Peer Leadership Advisory Network, *(978-0-578-57578-0; 978-1-7343063)* 17130 Downing St., Gaithersburg, MD 20877 USA Tel 240-499-4489
E-mail: daphnebwell@gmail.com.

Peerless Publishing, L.L.C., *(978-0-9666076)* Orders Addr.: P.O. Box 20466, Ferndale, MI 48220 USA Tel 248-542-1930; Fax: 248-542-3895; Edit Addr.: 414 W. Lewiston, Ferndale, MI 48220 USA
E-mail: peerlesspublishing@ameritech.net
Web site: http://www.spannet.org/peerless/index.html.

Pegasus Bks. for Children, *(978-0-9824095; 978-0-615-82835-0)* P.O. Box 681, Flossmoor, IL 60422 USA Tel 708-990-8111; Fax: 708-747-4659
E-mail: stallionbooks@gmail.com
Web site: http://www.stallionbooks.com
Dist(s): **CreateSpace Independent Publishing Platform.**

Pegasus Pubns., *(978-0-9747023)* 1055 E., 16th St., Brooklyn, NY 11230 USA Do not confuse with companies with the same name in Point Reyes Statio, CA, San Antonio, TX.

Pegatha Press *See* **Rosasharn Pr.**

Peggy's Trunk, *(978-0-9706967)* 3809 Juniper Rd., Baltimore, MD 21218-1828 USA Tel 410-366-1785; Fax: 410-467-0641 (to call first)
E-mail: mdpagan@erols.com.

Pegwood Publishing, *(978-0-578-48526-3; 978-1-7331060; 979-8-9879809)* 3419 E 1000 N., Roanoke, IN 46783 USA Tel 260-433-2817
E-mail: peggysuewells@gmail.com
Web site: PeggySueWells.com.

Peiffer, Trisha Cousineau *See* **Dream Ridge Pr.**

Peine, Jan *See* **Ashway Pr.**

Pelagia Pr. *Imprint of* **Calm Unity Pr.**

Pelican Book Group *See* **Pelican Ventures, LLC**

Pelican Lake Pr., *(978-0-9649139)* Div. of Healthy Lifestyle, Inc., Box 250, Ketchum, ID 83340 USA Tel 858-888-2278
E-mail: tomiselin@gmail.com
Web site: http://www.tomiselin.com.

Pelican Press *See* **booksonnet.com**

Pelican Press *See* **Pelican Pr. Pensacola**

Pelican Pr. Pensacola, *(978-0-9771102; 978-0-9911640; 978-1-7342203)* Div. of The Pelican Enterprise, LLC, Orders Addr.: 9121 Carabella St., Pensacola, FL 32514 USA Tel 850-475-8179; 850-206-4608 preferred Do not confuse with companies with the same name in Prather, CA, Santa Barbara, CA, Aptos, CA, Saint Augustine, FL, Belvedere, CA
E-mail: linda.wasserman@att.net
Dist(s): **BookBaby**
CreateSpace Independent Publishing Platform
Lulu Pr., Inc.

Pelican Publishing *Imprint of* **Arcadia Publishing**

Pelican Ventures, LLC, *(978-0-9712522; 978-0-9842968; 978-1-61116; 978-1-5223)* Div.of Pelican Ventures LLC, Orders Addr.: P.O. Box 1738, Aztec, NM 87410 USA; Edit Addr.: 2307 E. Main St., Farmington, NM 87401 USA; *Imprints:* Watershed Books (WatershedBks)
Web site: http://www.harbourlightbooks.com; http://www.whiterosepublishing.com; http://www.pelicanbookgroup.com
Dist(s): **Independent Pubs. Group.**

Pella Road Publishing, *(978-1-7342148; 979-8-9873408)* 26540 SW 2nd St., Martell, NE 68404 USA Tel 402-430-2721
E-mail: Severin2721@gmail.com
Web site: Https://claudiaseverin.wordpress.com.

Peller, A. W. & Associates, Incorporated *See* **Educational Impressions**

Pemberley Publishing, *(978-1-947032)* 621 Hudson St., Eau Claire, WI 54703 USA Tel 715-456-0880
E-mail: pemberleypublishing@aol.com.

Pemblewick Pr., *(978-0-9656557; 978-0-9718507)* Orders Addr.: P.O. Box 321, Lincoln, MA 01773 USA (SAN 254-0886); Edit Addr.: 155 S. Great Rd., Lincoln, MA 01773 USA Tel 781-259-8832 (phone/fax); 617-259-8389; 617 259 8389
E-mail: pemblewick@aol.com
Web site: http://www.pemblewickpress.com.

Pembroke Pubs., Ltd. (CAN) *(978-0-921217; 978-1-55138) Dist. by* **Stenhsa Pubs.**

Pemmican Pubns., Inc. (CAN) *(978-0-919143; 978-0-921827; 978-1-894717) Dist. by* **Firefly Bks Limited.**

Pen + Ink (GBR) *(978-1-911475) Dist. by* **SCB Distributo.**

Pen 2 Pen Publishing, *(978-0-615-80160-5; 978-0-692-28587-9; 978-0-692-51434-4; 978-0-9973704; 978-1-7357666)* 260 Peachtree St. NW Suite 2122, Atlanta, GA 30303 USA Tel 910-465-7914; 404-426-1590
Web site: pen2penpublishing.com
Dist(s): **CreateSpace Independent Publishing Platform**
INscribe Digital.

Pen & Pad Publishing, *(978-0-9769050)* P.o. Box 2995, Orcutt, CA 93457-2995 USA Tel 805-938-1307
E-mail: JBest@BestFamilyAdventures.com
Web site: http://BestFamilyAdventures.com
Dist(s): **Central Coast Bks.**

Pen & Paper Publishing, *(978-0-9703876)* 5450 Saluson Ave., PMB 15, Culver City, CA 90230 USA Fax: 323-933-3851; Toll Free: 800-662-9066 Do not confuse with Pen & Paper Publishing in Horn Lake, MS
E-mail: sixrags@earthlink.net
Web site: http://www.penandpaper.net.

Pen & Publish Incorporated *See* **Pen & Publish, LLC**

Pen & Publish, LLC, *(978-0-9768391; 978-0-9779530; 978-0-9790446; 978-0-9800429; 978-0-9817264; 978-0-9823850; 978-0-9842258; 978-0-9844600; 978-0-9845751; 978-0-9846359; 978-0-9852737; 978-0-9859367; 978-1-941799; 978-1-956897)* Orders Addr.: 4719 Holly Hills Ave, Saint Louis, MO 63116 USA; Edit Addr.: 4719 Holly Hills Ave, Saint Louis, MO 63116 USA Tel 314-827-6567; Toll Free: 866-326-7768
E-mail: info@penandpublish.com; info@brickmantelbooks.com
Web site: http://www.penandpublish.com; http://transformationmediabooks.com; http://openbookspress.com; http://brickmantelbooks.com
Dist(s): **Smashwords.**

Pen & Rose Pr. *Imprint of* **Harlin Jacque Pubns.**

Pen & Sword Bks. Ltd. (GBR) *(978-0-7232; 978-0-85052; 978-1-84415; 978-1-84468; 978-1-84832; 978-1-84884; 978-1-78159; 978-1-78383; 978-1-4738; 978-1-78337; 978-1-78340; 978-1-3990; 978-1-78303; 978-1-78346; 978-1-5267) Dist. by* **Casemate Pubs.**

Pen & Sword Publishing Co., The, *(978-0-9745798)* 522 N. Holly St., Philadelphia, PA 19104 USA
E-mail: nancy@theaalamgroup.com; nk81dove@yahoo.com; melodicg2003@hotmail.com.

Pen It Pubns., *(978-0-692-96536-8; 978-1-948390; 978-1-949609; 978-1-950454; 978-1-951263; 978-1-952011; 978-1-952894; 978-1-954004; 978-1-954868; 978-1-63984)* 5110 W Cty. Rd. 400 N, SCIPIO, IN 47273 USA Tel 812-371-4128
E-mail: penitpublications@yahoo.com
Web site: www.penitpublications.com
Dist(s): **Ingram Content Group**
Open Road Integrated Media, Inc.

Pen It! Publications, LLC *See* **Pen It Pubns.**

Pen Name Publishing, *(978-1-941541)* 54 N. St., Bargersville, IN 46106 USA Tel 317-422-5682
E-mail: dionne@pennamepublishing.com
Web site: www.pennamepublishing.com.

Pen of the Writer, LLC, *(978-0-9786066; 979-8-9865108)* 893 S. Main St. PMB 175, Englewood, OH 45322 USA (SAN 851-1047) Tel 937-307-0760
E-mail: info@penofthewriter.com
Web site: http://www.penofthewriter.com
Dist(s): **Send The Light Distribution LLC**
Smashwords.

Pen of Writer, The, *(978-0-578-42430-9)* 1144 Raccoon Creek Rd., Dallas, GA 30132 USA Tel 404-754-9610
E-mail: thepenofthewriter139@gmail.com
Dist(s): **Ingram Content Group.**

Pen Pearls, *(978-0-9989905; 978-1-7355145; 978-1-7372901; 979-8-9870417; 979-8-9892422)* 13653 Thunderhawk Pl., Victorville, CA 92392 USA Tel 760-617-6039; Fax: 888-464-3229
E-mail: suzanneholbrook@yahoo.com
Web site: www.penpearls.com.

Pen Row Productions, *(978-0-9766695)* 9461 Charleville Blvd., No. 506, Beverly Hills, CA 90212 USA Tel 310-924-9167
E-mail: bwasz1@verizon.net
Web site: http://www.penrowproductions.com.

Pencil Point Pr., Inc., *(978-1-58108; 978-1-881641)* P.O. Box 634, New Hope, PA 18938-0634 USA Toll Free: 800-356-1299
E-mail: penpoint@ix.netcom.com
Web site: http://www.pencilpointpress.com.

Pendant Pr., LLC, *(978-0-9906617)* 130 N. Garland Court, No. 1703, Chicago, IL 60602 USA Tel 615-579-4422
E-mail: carolinelee99@yahoo.com
Web site: http://www.maxzyne.com/.

Pendentive Pubns., *(978-0-9853817)* 405 Serrano Dr., Apt. 9-K, San Francisco, CA 94132 USA Tel 415-586-1806
E-mail: mpowers2004@yahoo.com
Dist(s): **Lulu Pr., Inc.**

Pendleton Publishing, *(978-0-578-47649-0; 978-0-578-52782-6)* 106 N. Pendleton Ave., Pendleton, IN 46064 USA Tel 317-430-9677
E-mail: pendletonpublishing@yahoo.com
Dist(s): **Ingram Content Group.**

Pendleton Publishing, Inc., *(978-0-9654480; 978-0-9711564)* Orders Addr.: P.O. Box 5004, Laurel, MD 20726 USA Tel 301-604-4076; Fax: 301-317-5746; Edit Addr.: 3113 Burning Springs Rd., No.1A, Laurel, MD 20724 USA
E-mail: newauthorsandartists@msn.com; gamjampublishing@yahoo.com.

Pendraig Publishing, *(978-0-9796168; 978-0-9820318; 978-0-9843302; 978-0-9827263; 978-1-936922)* 10625 Mt Gleason Ave., Sunland, CA 91040 USA Tel 818-642-4510
E-mail: Peter.Paddon@pendraigpublishing.com
Web site: http://www.pendraigpublishing.com; http://www.aimidbooks.com
Dist(s): **Ingram Content Group.**

Pendulum Pr., Inc., *(978-0-87232; 978-0-88301)* Academic Bldg., Saw Mill Rd., West Haven, CT 06516 USA (SAN 202-8808) Tel 203-933-2551 Do not confuse with companies with same or similar names in Jacksonville, FL, Palm Coast, FL, Minneapolis, MN.

Penelope Pipp Publishing, *(978-0-9882369)* 38 McCreedy Dr., McHenry, MS 39561 USA Tel 228-254-6711
E-mail: admin@penelopepipp.com
Web site: http://www.penelopepipp.com.

Penfield Bks., *(978-0-941016; 978-0-9603858; 978-1-57216; 978-0-9717025; 978-1-932043)* 215 Brown St., Iowa City, IA 52245 USA Tel 319-337-9998; Fax: 319-351-6846
E-mail: penfield@penfieldbooks.com
Web site: http://www.penfieldpress.com; http://www.penfieldbooks.com
Dist(s): **Partners Bk. Distributing, Inc.**
Penfield Pr.

PenGame Publishing LLC, *(978-0-9771444)* Orders Addr.: P.O. Box 341361, Jamaica, NY 11434 USA (SAN 256-8802)
E-mail: PenGameLLC@aol.com
Web site: http://www.PenGamePublishing.com.

Penguin AudioBooks *Imprint of* **Penguin Publishing Group**

Penguin Bks. *Imprint of* **Penguin Publishing Group**

Penguin Bks. *Imprint of* **Penguin Young Readers Group**

Penguin Bks. India PVT, Ltd (IND) *(978-0-14; 978-0-670) Dist. by* **IPG Chicago.**

Penguin Bks., Ltd. (GBR) *(978-0-14; 978-0-241; 978-0-670; 978-0-7232; 978-1-4059; 978-1-4093) Dist. by* **Diamond Book Dists.**

Penguin Bks., Ltd. (GBR) *(978-0-14; 978-0-241; 978-0-670; 978-0-7232; 978-1-4059; 978-1-4093) Dist. by* **Penguin Grp USA.**

Penguin Bks., Ltd. (GBR) *(978-0-14; 978-0-241; 978-0-670; 978-0-7232; 978-1-4059; 978-1-4093) Dist. by* **IPG Chicago.**

Penguin Bks., Ltd. (GBR) *(978-0-14; 978-0-241; 978-0-670; 978-0-7232; 978-1-4059; 978-1-4093) Dist. by* **D C D.**

Penguin Bks., Ltd. (GBR) *(978-0-14; 978-0-241; 978-0-670; 978-0-7232; 978-1-4059; 978-1-4093) Dist. by* **Peng Rand Hse.**

Penguin Books *Imprint of* **Penguin Publishing Group**

Penguin Books *Imprint of* **Penguin Young Readers Group**

Penguin Canada (CAN) *(978-0-14; 978-0-216; 978-0-451; 978-0-452; 978-0-453; 978-0-670; 978-0-7232; 978-1-55305; 978-0-7723) Dist. by* **Peng Rand Hse.**

Penguin Classics *Imprint of* **Penguin Publishing Group**

Penguin Family Publishing, *(978-0-9637985)* P.O. Box 471, Orland, CA 95963 USA.

Penguin Global *Imprint of* **Penguin Publishing Group**

Penguin Group India (IND) *(978-0-14; 978-0-670) Dist. by* **Penguin Grp USA.**

Penguin Group New Zealand, Ltd. (NZL) *(978-0-14; 978-0-670) Dist. by* **IPG Chicago.**

Penguin Group (USA) Incorporated *See* **Penguin Publishing Group**

Penguin Ireland (IRL) *(978-1-84488) Dist. by* **IPG Chicago.**

Penguin Publishing Group, *(978-0-14; 978-0-399; 978-0-425; 978-0-452; 978-0-525; 978-0-698; 978-0-87477; 978-1-58542; 978-1-933438; 978-1-4295; 978-1-934511; 978-1-4362; 978-1-4406; 978-1-101; 978-1-937007)* Orders Addr.: 405 Murray Hill Pkwy., East Rutherford, NJ 07073-2136 USA (SAN 282-5074) Fax: 201-933-2903 (customer service); Toll Free Fax: 800-227-9604; Toll Free: 800-526-0275 (reseller sales); 800-631-8571 (reseller customer service); 800-788-6262 (individual consumer sales); Edit Addr.: 375 Hudson St., New York, NY 10014 USA Tel 212-366-2000; Fax: 212-366-2666; 405 Murray Hill Pkwy., East Rutherford, NJ 07073 (SAN 852-5455) Tel 201-933-9292; *Imprints:* Ace (Ace Bks); Avery (Avr); Berkley (BerkBks); Dial (Dial); Dutton (Dut); Dutton Juvenile (DuttJuv); Warne (Warne); Putnam Juvenile (PutnaJuv); Gotham (GotBksHard); Grosset & Dunlap (Gross-Dun); HP Books (HPTrade); NAL (NewAmLib); Penguin AudioBooks (PengAudBks); Penguin Classics (PenClassics); Philomel (PhilPG); Plume (PlumPG); Portfolio (PortfolTrade); Price Stern Sloan (PSS); Puffin (PufBks); Penguin Global (PenGlobal); Roc (Roc); Razorbill (Razrbil); Riverhead Books (RivhdHC); Sentinel (Senti); Signet (SigBks); Viking Adult (VikiPG); Prentice Hall Press (PHPP); Heat (Heat); Nancy Paulsen Books (Nancy Paulsen); Viking (MYID_L_VIKING); Penguin Books (PenguinYR); Dutton Caliber (DuttonCaliber); IMPACT Books (IMPACTBks); TarcherPerigee (TarcherPerigee); G.P. Putnam's Sons (GPPutnams); Penguin Books (Penguin Bks)
E-mail: customer.service@us.penguingroup.com
Web site: http://penguingroup.custhelp.com; http://booksellers.penguingroup.com; http://www.penguinputnam.com
Dist(s): **Casemate Pubs. & Bk. Distributors, LLC**
Casemate Academic
Children's Plus, Inc.
Ebsco Publishing
Follett School Solutions
Independent Pubs. Group
Lectorum Pubns., Inc.
MyiLibrary
Penguin Random Hse. Distribution
Pearson Education
Penguin Random Hse. LLC
Perfection Learning Corp.
Viking Penguin
ebrary, Inc.

Penguin Random House Audio Publishing Group, *(978-1-61176)* 375 Hudson St., New York, NY 10014 USA Tel 212-366-2000; Fax: 212-366-2873; *Imprints:* Random House Audio (RHAudio)
Web site: www.penguin.com
Dist(s): **Blackstone Audio, Inc.**
Follett School Solutions
Penguin Random Hse. Distribution
Penguin Random Hse. LLC
Penguin Publishing Group.

Penguin Random Hse. Distribution, *(978-0-593; 978-1-101; 978-1-9848)* 375 Hudson St. 3rd Fl., New York, NY 10014 USA.

Penguin Random House Grupo Editorial (ESP) *(978-84-7888; 978-84-86033; 978-84-8365; 978-9974-899) Dist. by* **Casemate Pubs.**

Penguin Random House Grupo Editorial (ESP) *(978-84-7888; 978-84-86033; 978-84-8365; 978-9974-899) Dist. by* **Peng Rand Hse.**

Penguin Random Hse. Grupo Editorial (USA) LLC, *(978-1-941999; 978-1-945540; 978-1-947783; 978-1-949061; 978-1-64473; 979-8-89098)* 2711 Centerville Rd., Wilmington, DE 19808 USA Tel 305-527-8286; *Imprints:* Aguilar (Aguilar RH)
E-mail: monica.delgado@penguinrandomhouse.com
Web site: http://www.penguinrandomhousegrupoeditorial.com/en/
Dist(s): **Penguin Random Hse. Distribution**
Penguin Random Hse. LLC
Two Rivers Distribution.

Penguin Random House LLC *See* **Penguin Random Hse. Distribution**

Penguin Random Hse. LLC, *(978-0-593; 978-1-101; 978-1-9848; 979-8-217)* Orders Addr.: 400 Hahn Rd., Westminster, MD 21157 USA Toll Free Fax: 800-659-2436; Toll Free: 800-733-3000; Edit Addr.: 375 Hudson St. 3rd Flr., New York, NY 10014 USA Tel 212-366-2424
E-mail: brittany.wienke@us.penguingroup.com
Web site: http://www.PenguinRandomHouse.com.

Penguin Random House SEA Pte. Ltd. (SGP) *(978-981-4867; 978-981-4882; 978-981-4914; 978-981-5017) Dist. by* **IPG Chicago.**

Penguin Random House South Africa (ZAF) *(978-0-86977; 978-0-86978; 978-0-86966; 978-1-86825; 978-1-86872; 978-1-875015; 978-1-86870; 978-1-86809; 978-0-947024; 978-0-9584195; 978-0-9584468; 978-1-77007; 978-1-86823; 978-1-4859) Dist. by* **Casemate Pubs.**

Penguin Random Hse. (GBR) *(978-0-09; 978-0-224; 978-0-7126; 978-1-86046; 978-1-870516; 978-0-85265; 978-1-84413; 978-1-84657; 978-1-84655; 978-1-84853; 978-1-4881; 978-1-78089; 978-1-911215) Dist. by* **Trafalgar.**

Penguin Random Hse. (GBR) *(978-0-09; 978-0-224; 978-0-7126; 978-1-86046; 978-1-870516; 978-0-85265; 978-1-84413; 978-1-84657; 978-1-84655; 978-1-84853; 978-1-4881; 978-1-911215; 978-1-78089) Dist. by* **IPG Chicago.**

Penguin Random Hse. (AUS) *(978-0-14; 978-0-670; 978-0-86914; 978-0-7343; 978-1-920989; 978-1-921382; 978-1-921383; 978-1-921384; 978-1-921518; 978-1-74228; 978-1-74253; 978-1-74348; 978-0-85796; 978-0-85797; 978-1-74377; 978-1-76014; 978-1-76089; 978-1-76104; 978-1-76134; 978-1-76135) Dist. by* **IPG Chicago.**

Penguin Workshop *Imprint of* **Penguin Young Readers Group**

Penguin Young Readers *Imprint of* **Penguin Young Readers Group**

Penguin Young Readers Group, 375 Hudson St., New York, NY 10014 USA; *Imprints:* Grosset & Dunlap (Gross-Dun);

Publisher Name Index

Puffin (PufBks); Rosen Classroom (RosenClassrm); Speak (SpeakPeng); Puffin Books (PuffPeng); Warne (WarneUSA); Dial Books (DialYoung); Viking Books for Young Readers (VikingBksforYR); Dutton Books for Young Readers (Dutt BksYR); Firebird (Firebird); Razorbill (RazorbillUSA); G.P. Putnam's Sons Books for Young Readers (GPPutnam); Grosset & Dunlap (GrosDunl); Kathy Dawson Books (Kathy Daws); Price Stern Sloan (PriceSternSloan); Philomel Books (PhilomelBks); Nancy Paulsen Books (NancyPaul); Penguin Young Readers (Penguin YR); Penguin Books (Penguin Bks); Penguin Books (PenguinYR); Mad Libs (MadLibs); Penguin Young Readers Licenses (PenYngRead); Penguin Workshop (PenguinWrkshop); Kokila (Kokila); Minedition (MiNeEd); Rocky Pond Books (RockyPond)
Dist(s): **Children's Plus, Inc.**
Independent Pubs. Group
Penguin Random Hse. Distribution
Penguin Random Hse. LLC
Penguin Publishing Group.

Penguin Young Readers Licenses *Imprint of* **Penguin Young Readers Group**

Penknife Pr., *(978-0-9741949; 978-1-59997)* 1837 N. Oak Pk. Ave., Chicago, IL 60707 USA Tel 773-733-0830
E-mail: publisher@penknifepress.com
Web site: http://www.penknifepress.com
Dist(s): **Ingram Content Group.**

Pen-L Publishing, *(978-0-9851274; 978-1-940222; 978-1-942428; 978-1-68313)* 12 W. Dickson St., No. 4455, Fayetteville, AR 72702 USA
E-mail: duke@pen-l.com
Web site: Pen-L.com.

Penland, Alexandra Brooke, *(978-0-692-95173-6; 978-0-692-08775-6; 978-0-692-14955-3; 978-0-692-14956-0)* 1513 Olde Hickory Rd. Apt. 3, Coralville, IA 52241 USA Tel 7035097972
E-mail: penlandab@gmail.com
Dist(s): **Ingram Content Group.**

Penlight Pubns., *(978-0-9838685; 978-1-7324955)* 572 Empire Blvd., Brooklyn, NY 11225 USA Tel 718-972-5449
E-mail: urim_pub@netvision.net.il
Web site: www.penlightpublications.com
Dist(s): **Independent Pubs. Group.**

PenLit Publishing, *(978-1-7321263; 978-1-7354329)* 1212 NE 192nd Ave, Portland, OR 97230 USA Tel 503-348-2106
E-mail: nick.buckingham@penlit.com
Web site: www.penlit.com.

Penman Productions, *(978-0-9767978; 978-0-9914804; 978-0-9988968)* P.O. Box 400, Gleneden Beach, OR 97388-0400 USA; *Imprints:* Shalu Children's Series, The (MYID_O_SHALU C)
E-mail: penmanproductions@gmail.com; ronsterbooks@gmail.com
Web site: http://www.penmanproductions.com
Dist(s): **Epicenter Pr., Inc.**
Partners Bk. Distributing, Inc.
Partners/West Book Distributors.

Penman Publications *See* **Voice & Vision Pubns.**

Penman Publishing, Inc., *(978-0-9700486; 978-0-9707646; 978-0-9712808; 978-0-9720775; 978-1-932496; 978-1-7322390)* Div. of Pathway Pr., Orders Addr.: P.O. Box 3933, Cleveland, TN 37320-2250 USA; Edit Addr.: 1705 Overhead Bridge Rd., Cleveland, TN 37312 USA Tel 423-478-7613
Web site: http://www.penmanpublishing.com.

Pen-Mar News Distributors *See* **Americana Souvenirs & Gifts**

Penn, Carlotta, *(978-0-692-96718-8; 978-0-9996613)* 701 Linwood Ave, Columbus, OH 43203 USA Tel 614-599-1170; *Imprints:* Daydreamers Press (DaydreamPr)
E-mail: carlottamichelle@gmail.com
Dist(s): **Ingram Content Group.**

Penn Creek Pr., *(978-1-7370236)* 63 Little Run Rd., Camp Hill, PA 17011 USA Tel 919-604-4537
E-mail: lois.bartholomew@gmail.com
Web site: https://www.loisthompsonbartholomew.com/.

Pennaeth Publishing *Imprint of* **Garfield, M.**

Penned By Fafa, LLC, *(978-0-692-92795-3)* 1709 Walker Ave., Apt. C, Union, NJ 07083 USA Tel 973-651-7838
E-mail: pennedbyfafa@gmail.com
Dist(s): **Ingram Content Group.**

Penner/Lynn Publishing, *(978-0-9763025)* P.O. Box 7393, Naples, FL 34104 USA
E-mail: pennerlynn@msn.com
Web site: http://www.pennerlynn.com.

Pennie Rich Publishing, *(978-0-9820328; 978-0-9824960)* 4755 Cty. Rd. 27, Monte Vista, CO 81144-9314 USA (SAN 857-0884)
E-mail: pennierich@pennierich.com
Web site: http://www.pennierich.com.

†Pennsylvania State Univ. Pr., *(978-0-271; 978-1-64602; 978-1-63779; 978-0-271-09566-0)* Orders Addr.: 820 N. University Dr., USB-1 Suite C, University Park, PA 16802 USA (SAN 213-5760) Tel 814-865-1327; Fax: 814-863-1408; Toll Free Fax: 877-778-2665 (orders only); Toll Free: 800-326-9180 (orders only)
E-mail: http://www.eisenbrauns.org; info@psupress.org; log-ins@press.psu.edu
Web site: http://www.psupress.org
Dist(s): **Diamond Comic Distributors, Inc.**
Ebsco Publishing
ISD
JSTOR
MyiLibrary
ebrary, Inc.; *CIP.*

PennWell Corporation *See* **Fire Engineering Bks. & Videos**

Penny Candy Pr. *Imprint of* **Brighter Minds Children's Publishing**

Penny Farthing LLC *See* **Penny Farthing Publishing**

Penny Farthing Publishing, *(978-1-952527)* 491 N. Bluff St. Suite 106, Saint George, UT 84770 USA Tel 435-669-2220
E-mail: pennyfarthingllc@gmail.com.

Penny Laine Papers, Inc., *(978-1-890703)* 2211 Century Center Blvd. Ste. 110, Irving, TX 75062-4960 USA Toll Free: 800-456-6484; *Imprints:* Bookmates (Bkmates)
E-mail: cardwhiz1@mindspring.com.

Penny Lane Pubns., Inc., *(978-0-911211)* P.O. Box 3005, New York, NY 10012-0009 USA (SAN 274-4961) Tel 212-570-9666.

Penny Pr. *Imprint of* **Penny Pubns., LLC**

Penny Pubns., LLC, *(978-0-944422; 978-1-55956; 978-1-59238)* 6 Prowitt St., Norwalk, CT 06855 USA (SAN 243-6485); *Imprints:* Penny Press (Penny Pr)
E-mail: ltrutnau@pennypublications.net
Web site: http://www.pennydellpuzzles.com; http://www.analogsf.com; http://www.asimovs.com; http://www.themysteryplace.com; http://www.dellhoroscope.com; http://www.thecrosswordsclub.com.

Pennydragon Pr., *(978-0-9988614)* 645 Sumner Way No. 5, Oceanside, CA 92058 USA Tel 310-435-2022
E-mail: zoedragon@yahoo.com
Web site: pennydragon.com.

Penny-Farthing Press, Incorporated *See* **Penny-Farthing Productions, Inc.**

Penny-Farthing Productions, Inc., *(978-0-9673683; 978-0-9719012; 978-0-9842143; 978-0-9991709)* One Sugar Creek Ctr. Blvd., Suite 820, Sugar Land, TX 77478 USA Tel 713-780-0300; Fax: 713-780-4004; Toll Free: 800-926-2669
E-mail: corp@pfproductions.com; edit@pfproductions.com; design@pfproductions.com
Web site: http://www.pfpress.com; http://www.pfproductions.com
Dist(s): **Diamond Comic Distributors, Inc.**

Pennypack Productions, Inc., *(978-0-9704184)* 21 Tree Farm Ct., Glen Arm, MD 21057 USA Tel 410-420-3828; Fax: 410-420-2243
E-mail: ppennypack@comcast.net
Web site: http://www.kinderfun.net.

Penny's Publishing *Imprint of* **Balloon Magic**

Pennywhistler's Pr., *(978-0-9623456; 978-0-9727516)* Orders Addr.: P.O. Box 2473, New York, NY 10108 USA Tel 212-247-3231 (phone/fax); Edit Addr.: 467 W. 46th St., New York, NY 10036 USA
E-mail: info@pennywhistle.com
Web site: http://www.pennywhistle.com
Dist(s): **Book Clearing Hse.**
Mel Bay Pubns., Inc.

Pennywise Pubns., Inc., *(978-0-9702944)* 10550 St. Rd. 84, L98, Davie, FL 33324 USA Tel 954-472-8776 (phone/fax)
E-mail: filmpeny@bellsouth.net.

Penrod/Hiawatha Co., *(978-0-942618; 978-1-893624; 978-1-940691)* 10116 M140, Berrien Center, MI 49102 USA (SAN 238-5546) Tel 269-461-6993; Fax: 269-461-4170; Toll Free: 800-632-2823
Web site: http://www.penrodhiawatha.com
Dist(s): **Partners Bk. Distributing, Inc.**

Pentacle Pr., *(978-0-9604760; 978-0-9763500; 978-0-9825047; 978-1-937313)* Orders Addr.: P.O. Box 9400, Scottsdale, AZ 85252 USA (SAN 255-4860) Tel 480-922-2759; Fax: 480-443-8333; Edit Addr.: 5432 E. Desert Jewel Dr., Paradise Valley, AZ 85253 USA
E-mail: djm543@cox.net
Web site: http://www.missionscalifornia.com; http://www.pentacle-press.com
Dist(s): **Sunbelt Pubns., Inc.**

Pentatonic Pr., *(978-0-9773712)* 1232 Second Ave., San Francisco, CA 94122 USA Tel 415-564-1597; Fax: 415-566-6828
E-mail: Goodkindg@aol.com
Web site: http://www.douggoodkin.com
Dist(s): **Independent Pubs. Group**
Midpoint Trade Bks., Inc.

Pen-Tech Professional, *(978-0-9820962)* P.O. Box 67, Greenville, WI 54942 USA Tel 920-203-0563
Web site: http://www.pentechprofessional.com.

Pentland Pr., Inc., *(978-1-57197)* 5122 Bur Oak Cir., Raleigh, NC 27612 USA (SAN 298-5063) Tel 919-782-0281; Fax: 919-781-9042; Toll Free: 800-948-2786; *Imprints:* Ivy House Publishing Group (Ivy Hse Pubng Grp)
E-mail: janetevans@ivyhousebooks.com
Web site: http://www.ivyhousebooks.com
Dist(s): **Independent Pubs. Group.**

Penton Kids *Imprint of* **Penton Overseas, Inc.**

Penton Overseas, Inc., *(978-0-939001; 978-1-56015; 978-1-59125; 978-1-60379)* 1958 Kellogg Ave., Carlsbad, CA 92008 USA (SAN 631-0826) Tel 760-431-0060; Fax: 760-431-8110; Toll Free: 800-748-5804; *Imprints:* Penton Kids (Penton Kids); Smart Kids (Smrt Kds)
E-mail: kellie@pentonoverseas.com; susan@pentonoverseas.com
Web site: http://www.pentonoverseas.com
Dist(s): **Ideals Pubns.**

Pentucket Publishing, *(978-0-615-78644-5; 978-0-615-96648-9; 978-0-692-35910-5; 978-0-692-39153-2; 978-0-692-39154-9; 978-0-692-59416-2; 978-1-948134)* P.O. Box 482, Andover, MA 01810-0009 USA Tel 978-659-2107
Web site: http://www.pentucketpublishing.com/
Dist(s): **CreateSpace Independent Publishing Platform.**

Penury Pr., *(978-0-9676344)* 8701 Utah Ave S., Bloomington, MN 55438 USA Tel 952-829-1811
E-mail: penurypress@hotmail.com
Web site: http://www.penurypress.com
Dist(s): **Adventure Pubns.**
Adventures Unlimited Pr.
Partners Bk. Distributing, Inc.

Penway Publishing LLC, *(978-0-578-49149-3)* P.O. Box 21117, Louisville, KY 40221 USA Tel 502-450-1203
E-mail: penwaypublishing@gmail.com.

Penworthy Co., LLC, The, *(978-0-87617; 978-1-64310; 978-1-64697; 978-1-68505; 979-8-89033)* 219 N. Milwaukee St., Milwaukee, WI 53202 USA (SAN 630-2300) Fax: 414-287-4602; Toll Free: 800-262-2665
E-mail: info@penworthy.com
Web site: http://www.penworthy.com.

Penzart, *(978-0-9966940)* 9206 White Chimney Ln., Great Falls, VA 22066 USA Tel 571-989-2432.

People, Incorporated *See* **People Ink Pr.**

People Ink Pr., *(978-0-9789476; 978-0-9845983)* 1219 N. Forest Rd., Williamsville, NY 14231 USA Tel 716-634-8132; Fax: 716-817-7558
Web site: http://www.people-inc.org.

People Ink Pr., *(978-0-9858052; 978-0-9893267; 978-0-9862182; 978-0-9977740)* 1219 N. Forest, Williamsville, NY 14223 USA Tel 716-629-3602
E-mail: scrocker@people-inc.org; npalumbo@people-inc.org.

People Skills International, *(978-1-881165)* Orders Addr.: 2910 Baily Ave., San Diego, CA 92105 USA Tel 619-262-9951; Fax: 619-262-0505
E-mail: idagreene@earthlink.net
Web site: http://www.idagreene.com.

People's Literature Publishing Hse. (CHN) *(978-7-02) Dist. by* **China Bks.**

People's Literature Publishing Hse. (CHN) *(978-7-02) Dist. by* **Chinasprout.**

Pep & Olie Publishing, *(978-0-9912023)* 1355 Hilda Ave. No. 6, Glendale, CA 91205 USA Tel 818-552-2642
E-mail: sahin@ersoz.com
Web site: www.pepandolie.com.

Peppermint Bks., *(978-0-9828852)* P.O. Box 16512, Edina, MN 55416 USA (SAN 859-9424) Tel 651-815-8137
E-mail: orders@peppermintbooks.com
Web site: http://www.peppermintbooks.com.

Peppernut Publishing, *(978-0-9796500)* P.O. Box 31126, Omaha, NE 68131-1126 USA Tel 402-556-5591
E-mail: evyboonyawiroj@yahoo.com.

Peppertree Pr., The, *(978-0-9778525; 978-0-9787740; 978-1-934246; 978-0-9814894; 978-0-9817572; 978-0-9818683; 978-0-9820479; 978-0-9821654; 978-0-9822540; 978-0-9823002; 978-1-936051; 978-1-936343; 978-1-61493)* 1269 First St., Suite 7, Sarasota, FL 34236-5518 USA
Web site: http://www.peppertreepublishing.com.

Peppery Pr., *(978-0-9764813)* 504 Springcreek Dr., Longwood, FL 32779 USA Tel 407-786-6113
E-mail: pruben@cfl.rr.com
Web site: http://www.pepperypress.com.

Per Aspera Press *See* **Jakal LLC**

Peralta Publishing, LLC, *(978-0-9798620)* 9908 E. Desert Trail Ln., Gold Canyon, AZ 85218 USA Tel 480-288-4306
E-mail: thomaspreiss@msn.com.

Perceval Pr., *(978-0-9721436; 978-0-9747078; 978-0-9763009; 978-0-9774869; 978-0-9819747; 978-0-9895616; 978-0-9969227; 978-1-7368138)* 1223 Wilshire Blvd. No. F, Santa Monica, CA 90403 USA
E-mail: info@percevelpress.com; michele@percevalpress.com
Web site: http://www.percevalpress.com
Dist(s): **D.A.P./Distributed Art Pubs.**
SPD-Small Pr. Distribution.

Peregrine Communications *Imprint of* **Collins, Robert**

Perelandra Publishing Co., *(978-0-9640858)* Orders Addr.: P.O. Box 697, Cardiff, CA 92007 USA; Edit Addr.: 2387 Montgomery, Cardiff, CA 92007 USA Tel 760-753-4469.

Perennial Dreams Pubns., *(978-0-9764779)* P.O. Box 671, Lehi, UT 84043-0671 USA.

Perennis, Sophia, *(978-0-900588; 978-1-59731)* P.O. Box PO Box 931, Philmont, NY 12565 USA Tel 415-509-6969; *Imprints:* Dawn Chorus Press (DawnChrous)
E-mail: jameswetmore@mac.com
Web site: http://www.sophiaperennis.com
Dist(s): **Ingram Content Group**
SPD-Small Pr. Distribution.

Perennis, Sophia Et Universalis *See* **Perennis, Sophia**

Perfect 4 Preschool, *(978-0-9769239)* 428 N. Nelson St., Arlington, VA 22203 USA (SAN 850-0614) Tel 703-351-5843
E-mail: bjmischel@aol.com
Web site: http://www.perfect4preschool.

Perfect Bound Marketing, *(978-0-9769923; 978-0-9795588; 978-0-9887022; 978-1-939614; 978-1-7339087)* 12558 W. Maya Way, Peoria, AZ 85383 USA Tel 602-996-1766
E-mail: vickie@perfectboundmarketing.press
Web site: www.PerfectBoundMarketing.press
Dist(s): **eBookit.com.**

Perfect Page, The, *(978-0-692-54554-6)* 939 Palm Ave., No. 306, West Hollywood, CA 90069 USA Tel 310-652-8438
E-mail: jamesradford@hotmail.com.

Perfect Pen Publishing, *(978-1-7329230)* 2418 N. Albert St., Lutcher, LA 70071 USA Tel 225-317-2209
E-mail: leron.stewart@yahoo.com.

Perfect Praise Publishing, *(978-0-9679240; 978-0-9915735; 978-1-7359061; 978-1-959574)* 1228 4th Ave E., Williston, ND 58801 USA
E-mail: chuck@chuckblack.com; admin@chuckblack.com
Web site: http://www.chuckblack.com; http://www.kingdomseries.com; http://www.perfect-praise.com.

Perfect Publishing, *(978-0-9895012; 978-0-9915608; 978-1-942688; 978-1-949907; 978-1-64810)* 6030 Marshallee Dr. Suite 711, Elkridge, MD 21075 USA Tel 443-904-4545
E-mail: Natalie@theumbrellasyndicate.com
Web site: https://www.facebook.com/PerfectPublishing.

Perfecting Parenting Pr., *(978-0-9790420)* 3943 Jefferson Ave, Emerald Hills, CA 94062-3437 USA Tel 650-364-4466; Fax: 650-364-2299
Web site: http://www.perfectingparentingpress.com.

Perfection Form Company, The *See* **Perfection Learning Corp.**

Perfection Learning Corp., *(978-0-7807; 978-0-7891; 978-0-8124; 978-0-89598; 978-1-56312; 978-0-7569; 978-1-60686; 978-1-61563; 978-1-61383; 978-1-61384; 978-1-62299; 978-1-62359; 978-1-62765; 978-1-62766; 978-1-62974; 978-1-63419; 978-1-68064; 978-1-68065; 978-1-68240; 978-1-5311; 978-1-6903; 978-1-6636)* 1000 N. 2nd Ave., Logan, IA 51546 USA (SAN 221-0010) Tel 712-644-2831; Fax: 712-644-2392; Toll Free Fax: 800-543-2745; Toll Free: 800-831-4190; Imprints: Covercraft (Covercraft)
E-mail: orders@perfectionlearning.com
Web site: http://www.perfectionlearning.com.

Performance Publishing Group, *(978-0-615-26354-0; 978-0-578-03804-9; 978-0-615-42489-7; 978-0-615-47898-2; 978-0-578-08878-5; 978-0-9839570; 978-0-9847547; 978-0-9915724; 978-0-9906553; 978-0-9861254; 978-0-9965021; 978-0-9975762; 978-1-946629; 978-1-956914; 978-1-961781)* 6841 Virginia Pkwy., Suite 103-124, McKinney, TX 75071 USA.

Performance Strategies, *(978-0-9742333)* 209 Main Ave., Hayti, SD 57241 USA Tel 605-691-2007
E-mail: coleenliebsch@hotmail.com
Web site: www.PublishPS.com.

Pergot Pr., *(978-0-936865)* 19 Prospect Ave., Sausalito, CA 94965 USA (SAN 699-9441) Tel 415-332-0279; Fax: 415-332-5588.

Perigree *Imprint of* **PRI Publishing/Perigree Publishing**

Perinatal Loss *See* **Grief Watch**

Perio Reports, *(978-0-9659236)* Orders Addr.: P.O. Box 30367, Flagstaff, AZ 86003-0367 USA Tel 520-526-2523; Fax: 520-526-0852; Edit Addr.: 1640 N. Spyglass Way, Flagstaff, AZ 86004 USA
Dist(s): **Jenkins Group, Inc.**

Peripatetic Productions, LLC, *(978-0-578-02360-1; 978-0-9842385)* 4145 Joan Ave., Concord, CA 94521-2737 USA Tel 925-798-1311 (phone/fax)
Web site: http://www.peripateticproductions.com
Dist(s): **Lulu Pr., Inc.**

PeriplusEdition *Imprint of* **Tuttle Publishing**

Periscope Film, LLC, *(978-0-9786388; 978-0-9816526; 978-1-935327; 978-1-935700; 978-1-937684; 978-1-940453)* P.O. Box 341474, Los Angeles, CA 90034 USA
E-mail: contact@periscopefilm.com
Web site: http://www.periscopefilm.com.

Periscope Pr., *(978-0-9718546)* 15736 Horton Ln., Overland Park, KS 66223-3491 USA (SAN 254-9700)
Web site: http://www.hearthisorg.com
Dist(s): **Midwest Library Service**
Quality Bks., Inc.

Periscopefilm.com *See* **Periscope Film, LLC**

Periwinkle Pr., *(978-1-7323592)* 706 McGraw Dr., Fort Collins, CO 80526 USA Tel 970-219-9079
E-mail: maripat.borowski@yahoo.com
Dist(s): **Ingram Content Group.**

Periwinkle Studios, *(978-0-9759385)* P.O. Box 5134, Roselle, IL 60172 USA
E-mail: periwinklestudios@comcast.net.

Perkins Crawford, *(978-0-9762935)* 2605 Treyburne Ln., Owens Crossroads, AL 35763 USA Tel 256-536-5391
E-mail: e_vroom@bellsouth.net
Web site: http://www.perkinscrawford.com.

Perkins Miniatures, *(978-0-9759198)* 1708-59th St., Des Moines, IA 50322 USA Tel 515-279-6639
E-mail: gladon@earthlink.net.

Perkins Schl. for the Blind, *(978-0-9657170; 978-0-9743510; 978-0-615-26039-6; 978-0-9822721; 978-0-9881713; 978-0-692-69882-2; 978-0-9991766; 978-0-9992637; 978-1-947954)* a/o Publications Dept., 175 N. Beacon St., Watertown, MA 02472 USA
Web site: http://www.Perkins.org
Dist(s): **eBookit.com.**

Perkins-Stell, Crystal, *(978-0-9740705)* P.O. Box 8044, Edmond, OK 73013-8044 USA Tel 405-216-0224; Fax: 405-216-0224
E-mail: cleva@crystalstell.com
Web site: http://www.crystalstell.com.

Perks, Brad Lightscapes Photo Gallery, *(978-0-9788442)* 4055 Kimberly Pl., Concord, CA 94521-3359 USA
E-mail: bradperks@yahoo.com; bradperks@pcimagenetwork.com
Web site: http://pcimagenetwork.com; http://bradperks.com.

Perky Penguin Prs, *(978-0-578-18046-5; 978-0-578-18047-2)* 1808 E. Oxford Dr., Tempe, AZ 85283 USA.

Perkyideas Publishing, *(978-0-578-47574-5)* 29266 Pilgrim Ct., Valencia, CA 91354 USA Tel 818-967-3402
E-mail: perkinstmb@yahoo.com.

Perlina Pr., *(978-0-9971333; 979-8-9863202)* 20 Udine St., Arlington, MA 02476 USA Tel 781-643-3162
E-mail: irerasin@yahoo.com.

Perlycross Pubs., *(978-0-9741743)* Orders Addr.: a/o Bryce D. Gibby, P.O. Box 9725, Ogden, UT 84409 USA Tel 801-732-8600; Fax: 801-732-8602; Edit Addr.: 2711 Centerville Rd., Suite 120, PMB 5544, Wilmington, DE 19808 USA.

Perman, LeAnn, *(978-0-615-79750-2; 978-0-9892677)* 2295 S. Hiawassee Rd. Suite 208, Orlando, FL 32835 USA Tel 801-243-8463
Dist(s): **BookBaby**
CreateSpace Independent Publishing Platform.

Permanent Productions, Incorporated *See* **Permanent Productions Publishing**

Permanent Productions Publishing, *(978-0-9818204)* Orders Addr.: 904 Silver Spur Rd., No. 510, Rolling Hills Estates, CA 90274 USA (SAN 856-6348) Tel 310-366-4996; Fax: 310-521-9329; Toll Free: 866-698-7376
E-mail: c.jackson@permproductions.com
Web site: http://www.permproductions.com.

Permiso Por Favor Publishing Co., *(978-0-9747272)* 8568 Riverwood Farms, Cordova, TN 38016 USA Tel 901-756-0663
E-mail: permisoporfavor@hotmail.com.

ermuted Press, 1230 Avenue of the Americas, New York, NY 10020 USA
Dist(s): **Simon & Schuster, Inc.**

erpendicular Pr., *(978-0-9740234)* 64 Estabrook Rd., Carlisle, MA 01741-1724 USA
E-mail: info@perpendicularpress.com
Web site: http://www.perpendicularpress.com.

Perpetual Motion Machine Publishing, *(978-0-9887488; 978-0-9860594; 978-1-943720)* 152 Dew Fall Trail, Cibolo, TX 78108 USA Tel 210-573-7796
E-mail: pmmpublishing@gmail.com
Web site: www.perpetualpublishing.com.

Perri, Jessica, *(978-0-692-91830-2)* 600 S Ridgeley, Los Angeles, CA 90036 USA Tel 847-828-4343; *Imprints:* Wild Meadow (WildMeadow)
E-mail: jperri43@gmail.com.

Perri Tales Pubns., *(978-0-9763442)* Orders Addr.: 45 W. 132nd St., Suite 12K, New York City, NY 10037-3123 USA; Edit Addr.: 19601 Kings Hwy., Warrensville Heights, OH 44122 USA
E-mail: perrigaffney@aol.com
Web site: http://www.perritales.com.

Perrin & Kabel Publishing, *(978-0-9725364)* 145 Waverly Dr., Pasadena, CA 91105 USA Tel 626-577-1023; Fax: 626-577-1024
E-mail: perrinkabel@earthlink.net.

Perrin, Leslie, *(978-0-692-11002-7)* 11817 Timbermill Ln, Fredericksburg, VA 22407 USA Tel 540-845-6161
E-mail: lesliekperrin@gmail.com.

Perrine, Jared *See* **Overhead Pr., LLC**

Perry, Brenda, *(978-0-692-18619-0; 979-8-9857814)* 290 Pk. Ave. W. 122, Denver, CO 80205 USA Tel 720-883-6784
E-mail: bjp830@gmail.com
Dist(s): **Ingram Content Group.**

Perry, Brien, *(978-0-9980260)* 13718 Chandler Blvd., Sherman Oaks, CA 91401 USA Tel 310-977-0129
E-mail: brienjtperry@yahoo.com
Web site: brienperry.com.

Perry Enterprises, *(978-0-941518)* 3907 N. Foothill Dr., Provo, UT 84604 USA (SAN 171-0281) Tel 801-226-1002.

Perry Heights Pr., *(978-0-9630181)* P.O. Box 102, Georgetown, CT 06829 USA Tel 203-767-6509; *Imprints:* A Road to Discovery Series Guide (Rd Discovery)
E-mail: contact@perryheightspress.com; contact@cttrips.com
Web site: http://www.cttrips.com.

Perry, Molly A., *(978-0-692-83558-6; 978-1-7359427)* 3689 Silsby Rd., University Heights, OH 44118 USA Tel 216-990-9519
E-mail: mperry4077@gmail.com
Dist(s): **Independent Pub.**

Perry Pubns./Performance Pr., *(978-0-942442)* P.O. Box 5894, Oak Ridge, TN 37830 USA (SAN 238-1877) Tel 865-927-4912; Fax: 423-927-4912 Do not confuse Perry Publications, Silver Spring, Fl., Boerne, TX
E-mail: larryperry@worldnet.att.net.

Perry Publishing, *(978-1-7351506)* 592 Calamint Pt, West Palm Beach, FL 33411 USA Tel 850-566-8481
E-mail: K-Fairclough@hotmail.com.

Perryman Hse. of Design, *(978-1-7320969)* 260 Waterview Terr., Vallejo, CA 94591 USA Tel 707-319-5903
E-mail: gpman@gmail.com.

Pers, *(978-1-932179)* Div. of Pers Corp., 5255 Stevens Creek Blvd., No. 232-5, Santa Clara, CA 95051-6664 USA (SAN 254-7716) Toll Free Fax: 800-505-7377
E-mail: info@pers.com
Web site: http://www.pers.com
Dist(s): **APG Sales & Distribution Services**
Brodart Co.
Emery-Pratt Co.
Quality Bks., Inc.

Pers Publishing *See* **Pers**

†Persea Bks., Inc., *(978-0-89255)* 853 Broadway, Suite 604, New York, NY 10003 USA (SAN 212-8233) Tel 212-260-9256; Fax: 212-260-1902
E-mail: info@perseabooks.com
Web site: http://www.perseabooks.com
Dist(s): **Norton, W. W. & Co., Inc.**
Penguin Random Hse. Distribution
Penguin Random Hse. LLC; *CIP.*

Perseus Bks. Group, *(978-0-7382; 978-0-938289; 978-1-58097; 978-1-882810; 978-1-903985; 978-1-78239)* Div. of Hachette Book Group, Orders Addr.: 2465 Central Ave., Suite 200, Boulder, CO 80301-5728 USA Toll Free: 800-343-4499 (customer service); Edit Addr.: 387 Park Ave., S., 12th Flr., New York, NY 10016-8810 USA Tel 212-340-8100; Fax: 212-340-8105
Web site: http://www.perseusbooksgroup.com.

Perseus Distribution *See* **Two Rivers Distribution**

Perseus-PGW *See* **Publishers Group West (PGW)**

Persnickety Pr. *Imprint of* **WunderMill, Inc.**

Personal, *(978-0-9856724)* P.O. Box 661, Monticello, IL 61856 USA Tel 217-649-1589
E-mail: flygrl78@gmail.com.

Personal Best Motivional Sciences, Inc., *(978-0-9769988)* P.O. Box 562, Social Circle, GA 30025-0562 USA
Web site: http://www.babysimplerecipe.com/.

Personal Freedom Publishing, *(978-0-615-29044-7; 978-0-615-91370-4; 978-0-9973994)* 410 V Pl. SE, Auburn, WA 98002 USA
Web site: viviangale.com; http://www.thepersonalfreedomcenter.com/.

Personal Genesis Publishing, *(978-0-9747395)* 110 Pacific Ave., No. 204, San Francisco, CA 9411 USA Toll Free: 888-337-7776
Web site: http://www.ForgottenFaces.org.

Personal Power Press *See* **Personal Power Pr.**

Personal Power Pr., *(978-0-9616046; 978-0-9772321; 978-0-9821568; 979-8-9867593)* Div. of Institute for Personal Power, 5225 3 Mile Rd, Bay City, MI 48706 USA (SAN 698-0155) Tel 989-239-8628
E-mail: Personalpowerpress@gmail.com
Web site: www.personalpowerpress.com
Dist(s): **Austin & Company, Inc.**
Independent Pubs. Group
Midpoint Trade Bks., Inc.
Partners Pubs. Group, Inc.

Personal Promise Bible, *(978-0-9759578)* 470 Heritage Hills Dr., Richland, WA 99352 USA Tel 509-627-2607; Fax: 775-402-2106; Toll Free: 866-968-7242
Web site: http://www.personalpromisebible.com.

Personal Security, *(978-0-9675357)* 24366 Falcon, Lake Forest, CA 92630 USA Tel 949-461-9552; Fax: 949-472-8018
E-mail: xwordshicklers@hotmail.com.

Personality Wise *See* **Uniquely You Resources**

Personify Creative, LLC, *(978-1-7329172)* 15429 Schuyler Dr., Omaha, NE 68154 USA Tel 402-493-4727
E-mail: gkermc@cox.net.

Personify Pr., *(978-0-9797491)* 1959 Camino a los Cerros, Menlo Park, CA 94025 USA.

Perspective Publishing, Inc., *(978-0-9622036; 978-1-930085)* 2528 Sleepy Hollow Dr., No. A, Glendale, CA 91206 USA Tel 818-502-1270; Fax: 818-502-1272; Toll Free: 800-330-5851 Do not confuse with Perspective Publishing, Memphis, TN
E-mail: books@familyhelp.com
Web site: http://www.familyhelp.com
Dist(s): **Quality Bks., Inc.**

Perspectives Pr., Inc., *(978-0-944934; 978-0-9609504)* P.O. Box 90318, Indianapolis, IN 46290-0318 USA (SAN 262-5059) Tel 317-872-3055
E-mail: patjohnston@perspectivespress.com
Web site: http://www.perspectivespress.com
Dist(s): **Smashwords.**

Perspicacious Publishing, *(978-1-61463)* 1392 Turf Farm Way No. 242, Payson, UT 84651 USA Tel 435-314-9126
E-mail: jaimebuckley@wantedhero.com; jaimebuckley@gmail.com; jaime@jaimebuckley.com
Web site: http://www.ontheflypublications.com; https://wantedhero.com; https://jaimebuckley.com; https://perspicaciouspublishing.com
Dist(s): **Lulu Pr., Inc.**

PES, Inc., *(978-0-9766962)* P.O. Box 5501, Virginia Bch, VA 23471-0501 USA
E-mail: sailingthroughbusiness@cox.net
Web site: http://www.sailingthroughbusiness.com.

Pesavento, James, *(978-1-7377799)* 217 W Crestview Dr, Palm Springs, CA 92264 USA Tel 206-790-3429
E-mail: jamespes@hotmail.com
Web site: TheTrueHistoryofDragonsAndWizards.com.

PESI, *(978-0-941161; 978-1-55957; 978-0-9722147; 978-0-9749711; 978-0-9790217; 978-0-9820398; 978-1-936128; 978-0-9845254; 978-1-937661; 978-1-68373)* P.O. Box 1000, Eau Claire, WI 54702 USA; 3839 White Ave., Eau Claire, WI 54702; *Imprints:* PESI Publishing & Media (PESIPub)
E-mail: dkirby@pesi.com
Web site: http://www.pesi.com
Dist(s): **Baker & Taylor Publisher Services (BTPS)**
BookBaby.

PESI Publishing & Media *Imprint of* **PESI**

Pesout, Christine, *(978-0-615-47220-1)* 14 Dinan Ct., Lake St. Louis, MO 63367 USA Tel 314-443-6319
E-mail: cpesout@hotmail.com.

Pet Pundit Publishing, *(978-0-9853752; 978-1-948444)* P.O. Box 91733, Austin, TX 78209-1733 USA Tel 512-358-4515
E-mail: cathy@petpundit.com
Web site: www.petpunditpublishing.com.

Petalous Publishing, LLC, *(978-0-9777811)* PO Box 1332, Bluffton, SC 29910 USA.

Peter Pauper Pr. Inc., *(978-0-88088; 978-1-59359; 978-1-4413)* 3 International Dr, Suite 310, Rye Brook, NY 10573 USA (SAN 204-9449) Tel 914-681-0144; Fax: 914-681-0389
E-mail: orders@peterpauper.com; customerservice@peterpauper.com
Web site: http://www.peterpauper.com.

PeterCottonBks., *(978-0-692-57072-2)* 2736 Magnolia Woods Dr., Mount Pleasant, SC 29464 USA Tel 843-814-1872
E-mail: petercotto@gmail.com
Web site: www.petercottontales.com.

Peterman, Melvin G. *See* **Insight Technical Education**

Peters & Pardee Pubs., *(978-0-9626279)* Orders Addr.: 1039 NW Hwy. 101, Lincoln City, OR 97367 USA.

Peters, Chelsea, *(978-0-9992786)* 908 Dove Ridge Cir, Nashville, TN 37221 USA Tel 662-816-2554
E-mail: chelspeters7@gmail.com.

Peters, Michelle Lee, *(978-0-692-14933-1; 978-0-692-14936-2)* 2304 S Lakeline Blvd., No. 582, Cedar Park, TX 78613 USA Tel 210-860-8943
E-mail: uxbymichelle@gmail.com
Dist(s): **Ingram Content Group.**

Petersburg Museums, The, *(978-0-9744824)* 15 W. Bank St., Petersburg, VA 23803 USA Tel 804-733-2402 Toll Free: 800-368-3595.

Peterson, Kristi, 127 W. Second St 1E, Monroe, MI 48161 USA Tel 734-731-0482
E-mail: margiekpfudge@gmail.com
Dist(s): **Ingram Content Group.**

Peterson, Mark, *(978-0-692-76713-9; 978-0-692-96981-6; 978-0-692-13912-7; 978-0-692-13913-4; 978-0-692-15178-5)*.

Peterson-Boyce, Linda, *(978-0-9766034)* P.O. Box 2942, North Babylon, NY 11703 USA.

†Peterson's, *(978-0-7689; 978-0-87866; 978-1-56079)* Div. of Nelnet, Orders Addr.: P.O. Box 67005, Lawrenceville, NJ 08648-6105 USA (SAN 200-2167); Edit Addr.: 2000 Lenox Dr., 3rd Flr., Lawrenceville, NJ 08648 USA (SAN 297-5661) Tel 609-896-1800; Fax: 609-896-1811; Toll Free: 800-338-3282 X5660;Customer Service; *Imprints:* Arco (Arco); B.E.S. Publishing (BESPubPete)
E-mail: custsvc@petersons.com
Web site: http://www.petersons.com
Dist(s): **Children's Plus, Inc.**
Cengage Gale
Hachette Bk. Group
Ingram Publisher Services
MyiLibrary
Simon & Schuster
Two Rivers Distribution; *CIP.*

Petey, Rock & Roo Children's Pubns., *(978-0-9789642)* Orders Addr.: 1657 Broadway, New York, NY 10019 USA (SAN 852-0585)
E-mail: tash@timessquarechurch.org
Web site: http://www.timessquarechurch.org.

Petit Chou Chou, LLC, *(978-0-615-54492-2; 978-0-9882306)* P.O. Box 470875, Fort Worth, TX 76147 USA Tel 817-793-2594
E-mail: jdrez@att.net
Web site: http://goodnightcowtown.com.

Petra Publishing *See* **Petra Publishing Co.**

Petra Publishing Co., *(978-0-9712429)* 385 S. Lemon Ave., Suite E314, Walnut, CA 91789 USA Tel 404-452-3374
E-mail: admin@petrapublishingcompany.com
Web site: http://www.petrapublishingcompany.com; http://www.positivemag.com.

Petrine Day Mitchum, *(978-0-692-93173-8; 978-0-692-94429-5)* P.O. Box 1703, SANTA YNEZ, CA 93460 USA Tel 805-698-3488
E-mail: Trineday@comcast.net
Dist(s): **Ingram Content Group.**

Pet's Playground *See* **Singing Moon Pr.**

Pex Publishing Co., *(978-0-933767)* 8625 Boysenberry Dr., Tampa, FL 33635 USA (SAN 692-7645).

P.F.B. Publishing, *(978-0-9741273)* P.O. Box 149, Warren, OH 44482-0149 USA Fax: 330-373-0211
E-mail: pat@southparktitle.com.

Pflaum Publishing Group, *(978-0-89837; 978-0-937997; 978-1-933178; 978-1-935042; 978-1-939105; 978-1-947358)* Div. of Bayard, Inc., 3055 Kettering Blvd., Suite 100, Dayton, OH 45439 USA (SAN 661-2539) Fax: 937-293-1310; Toll Free Fax: 800-370-4450; Toll Free: 800-543-4383; 3055 Kettering Blvd., Suite 100, Dayton, OH 45439 (SAN 661-2539) Fax: 937-293-1310; Toll Free Fax: 800-370-4450; Toll Free: 800-543-4383
E-mail: service@pflaum.com; lcavender@pflaum.com
Web site: http://www.pflaum.com
Dist(s): **ACTA Pubns.**

P.F.P. Pubs., *(978-0-615-18028-1; 978-0-615-18027-4; 978-0-615-18157-8; 978-0-615-18343-5; 978-0-615-18415-9; 978-0-615-18648-1; 978-0-615-18873-7; 978-0-615-19123-2; 978-0-615-19266-6; 978-0-615-19773-9; 978-0-615-22198-4)* 35 Stone Ridge Blvd., Hermitage, PA 16148 USA
E-mail: p.f.p.publishers@gmail.com
Web site: http://www.pfppublishers.com
Dist(s): **Lulu Pr., Inc.**

Pfun-omenal Stories, *(978-0-578-13510-6; 978-0-9906494; 978-0-578-95701-2; 978-0-578-95729-6)* 1105 Denicola Dr., The Villages, FL 32163 USA Tel 631-988-2500
E-mail: pfunomenalstories@gmail.com
Web site: www.PfunomenalStories.com.

PGC Publishing *See* **Hope of Vision Publishing**

PH Publishing, *(978-0-9835863; 978-0-9835863-7-1; 978-1-7320421)* 3446 13th Ave. SW, Naples, FL 34117 USA Tel 239-352-1889
E-mail: pphayton@yahoo.com.

Phaidon Pr., Inc., *(978-0-7148)* 180 Varick St., 14th Flr., New York, NY 10014-4606 USA (SAN 253-3367) Tel 212-652-5400; Fax: 212-652-5410; Toll Free Fax: 800-286-9471 (Orders only); Toll Free: 800-759-0190 (Orders only); 877-742-4366 (Editorial)
E-mail: ussales@phaidon.com
Web site: http://www.phaidon.com
Dist(s): **Children's Plus, Inc.**
Hachette Bk. Group.

Phantom Hill Pr., *(978-1-7328813)* 114 Chocolate Gulch, Ketchum, ID 83340 USA Tel 208-726-4052
E-mail: pattyketchum@gmail.com.

Phantom Pubns., Inc., *(978-0-9625372)* 9451 Page Rd., Wattsburg, PA 16442-2005 USA
Dist(s): **Empire Publishing Service.**

Pharmasoft Publishing *See* **Hale Publishing**

phazelFOZ Co., LLC., The, *(978-0-9819645; 978-0-9834876; 978-0-9859333; 978-0-9960781; 978-0-692-61390-0; 978-0-9974257; 978-0-9988803; 978-1-7328646)* 858 W. Armitage Ave., No. 365, Chicago, IL 60614 USA.

PHD Ink, *(978-0-9897278; 978-1-941104)* P.O. Box 4295, Sarasota, FL 34230 USA Tel 347-661-2073
E-mail: rkclark@aol.com.

Pheasant Tale Productions, *(978-0-9817001)* P.O. Box 73, Skamokawa, WA 98647-0073 USA (SAN 856-2814)
E-mail: rajj@iinet.com; adventureinborneo@gmail.com
Web site: http://https://sites.google.com/site/adventureinborneo/.

Phebe Phillips, Inc., *(978-0-9846454; 978-0-9837820)* P.O. Box 190748, Dallas, TX 75219 USA Tel 214-762-5727; *Imprints:* Hargrove Grey Publishing (Hargrove GP)
E-mail: phebe@phebephillips.com
Web site: http://www.phebephillips.com.

Phelps, Diane *See* **Red Rock Mountain Pr. LLC**

Phelps Publishing, *(978-1-887627)* P.O. Box 22401, Cleveland, OH 44122 USA Tel 216-752-4938; Fax: 216-752-4941
E-mail: earl@phelpspublishing.com; earl@edna-reco.com
Web site: https://www.phelpspublishing.com; https://drawsupercharacters.com/
Dist(s): **Brodart Co.**
Follett School Solutions
Ingram Bk. Co.

Phelps Publishing Company *See* **Phelps Publishing**

Phenomenal One Pr., *(978-0-9841989; 978-0-9850251; 978-0-9969195; 978-1-7329247; 978-1-7379476)* 1463 Akeke Pl., Kailua, HI 96734 USA
E-mail: lprstn@hotmail.com
Web site: http://www.phenomenalonepress.com
Dist(s): **Ingram Content Group**
MyiLibrary.

Phi Sigma Omega, Alpha Kappa Alpha Sorority, Inc., *(978-0-9785269)* P.O. Box 1784, Gonzales, LA 70707-1784 USA Tel 225-936-1665
Web site: http://phisigmaomega2000.org.

Phidal Publishing, Inc./Editions Phidal, Inc. (CAN) *(978-2-89393; 978-2-920129; 978-2-7643) Dist. by* **AIMS Intl.**

Phil the Pill & Friends *Imprint of* **MAMP Creations**

Philadelphia Folklore Project, *(978-0-9644937)* 735 S. 50th St., Philadelphia, PA 19147 USA Tel 215-726-1106; Fax: 215-726-6250
E-mail: pfp@folkloreproject.org
Web site: http://www.folkloreproject.org.

Philadelphia Inquirer, The, *(978-1-58822)* Div. of Philadelphia Newspapers, Inc., 400 N. Broad St., Philadelphia, PA 19101 USA Tel 215-854-2000
Web site: http://www.philly.com.

†Philadelphia Museum of Art, *(978-0-87633)* 2525 Pennsylvania Ave., Philadelphia, PA 19130 USA (SAN 203-0969)
Web site: http://www.philamuseum.org
Dist(s): **Antique Collectors' Club**
Art Media Resources, Inc.
D.A.P./Distributed Art Pubs.
ISD
National Bk. Network
Pennsylvania State Univ. Pr.
Yale Univ. Pr.; *CIP.*

Philio International *See* **Philio Publishing**

Philio Publishing, *(978-0-9622996; 978-0-9964356)* 1138 N. Germantown Pkwy. Suite 101-294, Cordova, TN 38018 USA Tel 901-201-4058
Dist(s): **Lulu Pr., Inc.**

Philip J. Damiani, *(978-0-9980258)* 129 Southridge Dr., Cranberry Twp., PA 16066 USA Tel 412-979-4444
E-mail: pdamiani05@aol.com.

Philip M. Hudson *Imprint of* **BookCrafters**

Philipp, Cathy Publishing, *(978-0-9655848)* P.O. Box 1954, Thousand Oaks, CA 91358-1954 USA Tel 805-498-0611; Fax: 805-498-7331
E-mail: philifam@adelphia.net.

Philippine American Literary House *See* **PALH**

Philippine American Writers & Artists, Inc., *(978-0-9763316; 978-0-9968032; 978-0-9981792)* P.O. Box 31928, San Francisco, CA 94131-0928 USA
E-mail: pawa@pawainc.com
Web site: http://www.pawainc.com.

Philips, Fleur, *(978-0-9889299)* 250 N. College Pk. Dr. No. U33, Upland, CA 91786 USA Tel 909-908-3788
E-mail: fleurphilips@gmail.com
Dist(s): **BookBaby.**

PHILLIPS, JACQUELINE J. LLC., *(978-0-9994550)* 250 Goge Rd., Cliffside Park, NJ 07010 USA Tel 646-526-4781
E-mail: imagecosmetics@yahoo.com
Web site: www.starsbehindthestars.com.

Philograph *Imprint of* **Cascade, Inc.**

Philokalos Pr., *(978-0-9912472)* P.O. Box 3811, McLean, VA 22103 USA Tel 703-586-1353
E-mail: philokalospress@gmail.com
Web site: www.philokalospress.org.

Philomel *Imprint of* **Penguin Publishing Group**

Philomel Bks. *Imprint of* **Penguin Young Readers Group**

Philos Pr., *(978-0-9831075)* 22545 SW Miami Dr., Tualatin, OR 97062 USA Tel 503-885-8877; Fax: 503-885-1847
E-mail: maryandonian@yahoo.com.

†Philosophical Library, Inc., *(978-0-8022)* P.O. Box 1789, New York, NY 10010 USA (SAN 201-999X) Tel 212-886-1873; Fax: 212-873-6070
Dist(s): **Kensington Publishing Corp.**
MyiLibrary
Open Road Integrated Media, Inc.
Open Road Distribution
Rowman & Littlefield Publishers, Inc.; *CIP.*

Philothea Pr., *(978-0-9826867)* P.O. Box 1262, West Chester, OH 45071 USA Tel 513-805-6766.

Phlare, Inc., *(978-0-9741147)* 9565 W. 52nd Ave., Arvada, CO 80002 USA Tel 303-513-1565; Toll Free: 888-731-2398
Web site: http://www.phlare.com.

Phoenix Bks., Inc., *(978-1-59777; 978-1-60747; 978-1-61467; 978-1-7345201; 978-1-7357227; 978-1-955822)* 9465 Wilshire Blvd., Suite 840, Beverly Hills, CA 90212-2609 USA; *Imprints:* Pickwick Press (PickwickPr); Dove Books and Audio (Dove Bks)
Dist(s): **Independent Pubs. Group.**

Phoenix Books, Incorporated *See* **Phoenix Bks., Inc.**

Phoenix Cry Publishing, *(978-0-9995191)* PSC 37 Box 162, APO, AE 09459 USA Tel 405-225-8606
E-mail: jennie.gillham@gmail.com
Web site: www.courageouschiropractor.com.

Phoenix Films & Video, *(978-0-7919)* 2349 Chaffee Dr., Saint Louis, MO 63146 USA (SAN 653-5224) Tel 314-569-0211; Fax: 314-569-2834; Toll Free: 800-221-1274
E-mail: phoenixfilm@worldnet.att.net
Web site: http://www.phoenix-bfa-coronet.com
Dist(s): **Follett School Solutions**
Weston Woods Studios, Inc.

Phoenix Flair Pr., *(978-0-9846124)* 2704 W. Royerton Rd., Muncie, IN 47303 USA (SAN 859-8967).

Phoenix International, Inc., *(978-0-9650485; 978-0-9713470; 978-0-9768007; 978-0-9824295; 978-0-9835615; 978-0-9899356)* 17762 Summer Rain Rd., Fayetteville, AR 72701 USA Tel 479-521-2204 Do not confuse with

companies with the same or similar names in Oxon Hill, MD, Nampa, ID
E-mail: john@phoenixpub.com
Web site: http://www.phoenixbase.com
Dist(s): **Chicago Distribution Ctr.**
Univ. of Arkansas Pr.

Phoenix International Publications, Inc., *(978-0-7853; 978-1-4127; 978-1-60553; 978-1-4508; 978-1-5037; 978-1-64269; 978-1-64996; 979-8-7654; 979-8-3846)* 8501 West Higgins Rd., Suite 300, Chicago, IL 60631 USA (SAN 860-424X); *Imprints:* PIL Kids (PIL Kids); PI Kids (PI Kids); Sequoia Publishing & Media LLC (SequoiaPub); Sunbird Books (SunbirdBKS); Sequoia Kids Media (SequoiaKM)
E-mail: b2b.customerservice@pikidsmedia.com
Web site: www.phoenixintpub.com
Dist(s): **Hachette Bk. Group.**

Phoenix Learning Resources, LLC, *(978-0-7915)* Orders Addr.: P.O. Box 510, Honesdale, PA 18431 USA (SAN 246-148X) Tel 570-251-6871; Fax: 570-253-3227; Toll Free: 800-228-9345
E-mail: rich@phoenixlr.com
Web site: http://www.phoenixlr.com.

Phoenix Publishing, *(978-1-928812)* Orders Addr.: P.O. Box 8231, Missoula, MT 59807 USA Fax: 406-721-6195; Toll Free: 800-549-8371; Edit Addr.: 309 SW Higgins, Missoula, MT 59803 USA Do not confuse with companies with the same or similar names in Redmond, WA, W. Kennebunk, ME, Rocklin, CA, Bloomington, IN, Miami, FL, Fairfield, FL, Tolono, IL, Newark, NJ, Lansing, MI, Alpharetta, GA, Custer, WA, Marina del Ray, CA, Half Moon Bay, CA, New York, NY
E-mail: phoenixi@phoenixpub.com
Web site: http://www.phoenixpub.com.

Phoenix Publishing, *(978-0-615-20417-8)* 308 W. Burnside Ave., Fairland, IN 46126 USA
E-mail: kphoenix_3@sbcglobal.net
Dist(s): **Lulu Pr., Inc.**

Phoenix Rising LLC, *(978-0-9800807)* 11684 Ventura Blvd., Suite 886, Studio City, CA 91604 USA (SAN 855-1464)
E-mail: phoenixrising@earthlink.net.

Phonic Bks. *Imprint of* **DK**

Phonic Monic, *(978-1-943241)* 472 Trident Maple Terr., Fremont, CA 94539 USA Tel 510-573-1646
E-mail: cammieho123@gmail.com
Web site: www.phonicmonic.com.

Phosphene Publishing Co., *(978-0-9796968; 978-0-9851477; 978-0-9986316; 978-1-7369307)* 4019 River Dr., Houston, TX 77017 USA
Web site: phosphenepublishing.com.

PhotoGraphics Publishing, *(978-0-9643844; 978-0-9793813; 978-0-9829730)* 23 Cool Water Ct., Palm Coast, FL 32137 USA Tel 386-246-3672; Fax: 386-445-7365; *Imprints:* Doctor Dolittle's Library (Doctor Dolittle)
E-mail: joycehuber47@hotmail.com
Web site: http://www.photographicspublishing.com.

Photographs Naturally, Inc., *(978-0-9710343)* 57 Laurel Oak, Amelia Island, FL 32034 USA Tel 904-277-4403; Fax: 904-277-0749.

Photographs Naturally, Incorporated *See* **Photographs Naturally, Inc.**

Photography in Pearls LLC, *(978-1-7334206; 979-8-9870280)* 1097 Hawthorn Dr, Pawleys Island, SC 29585 USA Tel 843-543-0054
E-mail: photographyinpearls@gmal.com.

PhotoHutch, *(978-0-9824925)* P.O. Box 482, Alamo, CA 94507 USA
Web site: http://www.bisforbufflehead.com; http://www.photohutch.com.

Photon Pubns., *(978-0-9744128; 978-0-615-11954-0)* 7532 Mason Dells Dr., Dallas, TX 75230-3246 USA
E-mail: j1jagger@aol.com
Dist(s): **Baker & Taylor Publisher Services (BTPS).**

PI Kids *Imprint of* **Phoenix International Publications, Inc.**

Piano Pr, *(978-0-9673325; 978-1-931844; 979-8-88790)* Orders Addr.: P.O. Box 85, Del Mar, CA 92014-0085 USA Tel 619-884-1401; Fax: 858-755-1104; Edit Addr.: 1425 Ocean Ave., No. 17, Del Mar, CA 92014 USA Tel 619-884-1401
E-mail: eaxford@aol.com; pianopress@pianopress.com; lizaxford@pianopress.com
Web site: http://www.pianopress.com
Dist(s): **Book Wholesalers, Inc.**
Coutts Information Services
Blackwell
Wayland Audio-Visual.

Pianomouse Productions, *(978-0-9889068)* Orders Addr.: 8789 Auburn Folsom Rd. Ste. C416, Granite Bay, CA 95746 USA Tel 916-204-8110
E-mail: kathleen@pianomouse.com
Web site: www.pianomouse.com.

Piñata Books *Imprint of* **Arte Publico Pr.**

Picador, *(978-0-312)* Div. of Holtzbrinck Publishers, Orders Addr.: 16365 James Madison Hwy., Gordonsville, VA 22942-8501 USA Fax: 800-672-2054; Toll Free: 888-330-8477; Edit Addr.: 175 Fifth Ave., New York, NY 10010 USA Tel 212-674-5151; Fax: 540-672-7540 (customer service)
Web site: http://www.picadorusa.com
Dist(s): **Libros Sin Fronteras**
Macmillan
Westminster John Knox Pr.

Picaro Press *See* **One Eyed Pr.**

Piccadilly Bks., Ltd., *(978-0-941599; 978-1-936709)* P.O. Box 25203, Colorado Springs, CO 80936 USA (SAN 665-9969) Tel 719-550-9887
E-mail: info@piccadillybooks.com
Web site: http://www.piccadillybooks.com
Dist(s): **MyiLibrary**
New Leaf Distributing Co., Inc.
Nutri-Bks. Corp.

Piccadilly Pr., Ltd. (GBR) *(978-1-85340; 978-0-946826; 978-1-84812; 978-1-4714) Dist. by* **IPG Chicago.**

Piccolo Tales, *(978-0-9881689; 978-1-7360810)* 10640 Riverlake Dr., Knoxville, TN 37922 USA Tel 865-966-0274; Fax: 865-966-0274
E-mail: bc2bls@yahoo.com.

Pick It Publishing, *(978-0-615-26122-5)* P.O. Box 284, Danville, IA 52623 USA
Dist(s): **Lulu Pr., Inc.**

Pick Me Up N Go Publishing Co., *(978-0-615-15832-7)* 10312 S. Prospect Ave., Chicago, IL 60643 USA
E-mail: felice@pickmeupngo.com
Dist(s): **Lulu Pr., Inc.**

Picket Press, *(978-0-9787864)* 767 N. Pine St., Colville, WA 99114 USA Tel 808-347-1311
E-mail: amakihi@startmail.com.

Pickett Fennell Group, The, *(978-0-615-31289-7; 978-0-9833864)* 619 Castlewood Dr., Upper Marlboro, MD 20774 USA
E-mail: pfgpublishing@gmail.com.

Pickett Publishing *See* **Pickett Fennell Group, The**

Pickle Blossom Pr., *(978-0-9965763)* 20225 Haynes St., Winnetka, CA 91306 USA Tel 323-275-8801; Fax: 818-884-1148
E-mail: jule.r.armstrong@gmail.com.

Pickled Eggs Press (TM) *Imprint of* **Loucks Studios Inc.**

Pickled Herring Pr., *(978-0-9778276)* 2380 W. Hill Dr., Madison, WI 53711 USA.

Picklesisters, *(978-0-9767542)* 224 Red Oak Dr E. Apt. F, Sunnyvale, CA 94086-6612 USA
E-mail: editor@picklesisters.com
Web site: http://www.picklesisters.com.

Pickrell, Karen, *(978-0-9993482)* 5717 Balfor Rd., Rocklin, CA 95765 USA Tel 916-435-0256
E-mail: karen_pick@sbcglobal.net
Web site: kareninreallife.com.

Pickup, Terry Lowey *See* **Terry Lowey's Children's Stories, LLC**

Pickwick Pr. *Imprint of* **Phoenix Bks., Inc.**

Picnic Publishing Ltd. (GBR) *(978-0-9556105) Dist. by* **Trans-Atl Phila.**

Pictorial Legends, *(978-0-939031)* Subs. of Event Co., 435 Holland Ave., Los Angeles, CA 90042 USA (SAN 662-8486) Tel 213-254-4416
Dist(s): **Igram Pr.**

Picture Bk. *Imprint of* **Spotlight**

Picture Bk. Learning, Inc., *(978-0-9760725)* P.O. Box 270075, Louisville, CO 80027 USA
E-mail: todd@picturebooklearning.com
Web site: http://www.picturebooklearning.com.

Picture Entertainment *See* **Evening Sun Pr.**

Picture Me Books, Incorporated *See* **Playhouse Publishing**

Picture Window Bks. *Imprint of* **Capstone**

Pie in the Sky Publishing, LLC, *(978-1-893815)* 8031 E. Phillips Cir., Centennial, CO 80112 USA
E-mail: PieintheSkyPublishing@msn.com
Web site: http://www.pieintheskypublishing.com
Dist(s): **Bks. West.**

Pie Plate Publishing Co., *(978-0-9855906; 978-1-941175)* P.O. Box 760151, Lathrup Village, MI 48076 USA Tel 248-508-7749
E-mail: joddo@pieplatepublishing.com
Web site: www.pieplatepub.com.

Pieces of Learning, *(978-0-9623835; 978-1-880505; 978-1-931334; 978-1-934358; 978-1-937113)* Div. of Creative Learning Consultants, Inc., 1990 Market Rd., Marion, IL 62959 USA (SAN 298-461X) Tel 618-964-9426; Fax: 618-964-1897; Toll Free Fax: 800-844-0455; Toll Free: 800-729-5137
E-mail: piecesoflearning@frontier.com; stan@piecesoflearning.com
Web site: http://www.piecesoflearning.com.

Piedra Santa, Editorial (GTM) *(978-84-8377; 978-99922-1; 978-99922-58) Dist. by* **Libros Fronteras.**

PIEEYE Publishing, Inc., *(978-0-9759435)* 116 Consumer Sq., Suite 333, Plattsburgh, NY 12901 USA Tel 514-684-0434; Toll Free: 888-474-3393
E-mail: jocelyne@pieeyepublishing.com; info@pieeyepublishing.com
Web site: http://www.pieeyepublishing.com/.

Piequet, Linda, *(978-1-7379409)* 25 Blystone Ct., Brea, CA 92821 USA Tel 562-697-2211
E-mail: lmpk715@aol.com.

Pier Media, *(978-0-9715980)* Div. of Pier Video, Inc., P.O. Box 190, Gardiner, NY 12525 USA Tel 212-481-0031; Fax: 212-481-0892
E-mail: joe514@aol.com
Web site: http://www.marcusantebi.com.

Pieras Inc. Editorial, *(978-0-9729719)* Div. of Pieras Inc., Y-9 México Ave. and Colorado St. Parkville Extension, Guaynabo, PR 00962-3923 USA (SAN 255-3112) Tel 787-299-4486
E-mail: jorge@elbien.org
Web site: http://www.wakebooks.com
Dist(s): **Ingram Content Group.**

Pieras Incorporated *See* **Pieras Inc. Editorial**

Pierce, Paul, *(978-0-9741819)* 1400 15th St., Columbus, GA 31901 USA
E-mail: prpierce@mindspring.com
Dist(s): **Parnassus Bk. Distributors.**

Pierce Pr., *(978-0-9776396; 978-0-9970975; 978-0-9970681; 978-0-9996592)* P.O. Box 206, Arlington, MA 02746 USA Tel 339-368-5656; Fax: 339-368-5656
E-mail: charlotte@piercepress.com; publisher@piercepress.com
Web site: https://piercepress.com; https://facebook.com/PiercePressBooks; https://peeragogy.org; https://piercepress.com/face-the-book-tv; https://twitter.com/piercepress; https://facebook.com/DanielMcDougalMcDouglasMcFly; https://kidinakilt.com.

Pierre Publishing *Imprint of* **Carol J. Pierre, LLC**

Pig Iron Pr., *(978-0-917530)* Orders Addr.: P.O. Box 237, Youngstown, OH 44501 USA (SAN 209-0937) Tel 330-747-6932; Fax: 330-747-0599; Edit Addr.: 26 N. Phelps, Youngstown, OH 44503 USA (SAN 241-8193)
E-mail: pigironpress@cboss.com.

Pikes Peak Library District, *(978-1-56735)* 5550 N. Union, Colorado Springs, CO 80918 USA Tel 719-531-6333; Fax: 719-389-8161
E-mail: tblevins@ppld.org.

Pikku Publishing (GBR) *(978-0-9928050; 978-1-9996398) Dist. by* **Casemate Pubs.**

Pik-Ware Publishing, *(978-0-9744190)* P.O. Box 110, Crisfield, MD 21817 USA Tel 410-968-3873 (phone/fax)
E-mail: pat@funkyseagull.com
Web site: http://www.pik-ware.com.

PIL Kids *Imprint of* **Publications International, Ltd.**

PIL Kids *Imprint of* **Phoenix International Publications, Inc.**

Pilate, Victoria, *(978-0-9759665)* P.O. Box 75433, Washington, DC 20013 USA.

Pilgrim Press *See* **Kinfolk Research Pr.**

Pilgrim Pr., The/United Church Pr., *(978-0-8298)* Div. of United Church Board for Homeland Ministries, 700 Prospect Ave. E., Cleveland, OH 44115-1100 USA Tel 216-736-3848; Fax: 216-736-2207
E-mail: ucpress@ucc.org; pilgrim@ucc.org; bresnahana@ucc.org
Web site: http://www.ucpress.com; http://www.thepilgrimpress.com
Dist(s): **BookBaby**
Faith Alive Christian Resources
Women Ink.

Pilgrim Voyage Pr., *(978-0-9891166)* 989 Scarlett Pl., Tracy, CA 95376 USA Tel 209-229-1375
E-mail: chase@pilgrimvoyage.com
Web site: www.pilgrimvoyage.com.

Pilinut Pr., Inc., *(978-0-9779576; 978-1-944390)* 41 W. Lee Hwy., Suite 59, #808, Warrenton, VA 20186 USA.

Pill Bug Pr., *(978-0-9761623)* 1868 Bridgeport Ave., Claremont, CA 91711 USA Tel 909-624-9985 (phone/fax).

Pill Hill Pr., *(978-0-9842610; 978-1-61706)* 343 W. 4th St., Chadron, NE 69337 USA
E-mail: pillhillpress@gmail.com
Web site: http://www.pillhillpress.com
Dist(s): **BookBaby.**

Pillar of Enoch Ministry Bks., *(978-0-9759131)* The Pillar of Enoch Ministry, 1708 N. 77th Ave., Elmwood Park, IL 60707-4107 USA
E-mail: helena@pillar-of-enoch.com
Web site: http://www.pillar-of-enoch.com
Dist(s): **Ingram Content Group.**

Pillar Rock Publishing, *(978-0-9764109)* P.O. Box 86571, Portland, OR 97286 USA
Web site: http://www.zoppa.com.

Pillowtalks Publishing, *(978-0-692-82809-0)* 105 Beverly Blvd., Hobart, IN 46342 USA Tel 219-942-1821; Fax: 219-942-1821
E-mail: sherryfinnerty@gmail.com.

Pilot Bks. *Imprint of* **Bellwether Media**

Pilot Communications Group, Inc., *(978-0-9791957; 978-0-9824967; 978-0-9826665; 978-1-936417; 978-1-939268; 978-1-62903)* 317 Appaloosa Trl., Woodway, TX 76712-8816 USA
Dist(s): **Independent Pubs. Group**
Midpoint Trade Bks., Inc.

Pilumeli, Tanya *See* **FAVA Pr.**

Pina Bird Bks. LLC, *(978-1-7347321; 978-1-7370682)* 3 Calder Bridge Dr., Stamford, CT 06903 USA Tel 203-912-5754
E-mail: pinabasone@gmail.com.

Pinata Pubns., *(978-0-934925)* P.O. Box 13252, Oakland, CA 94611 USA (SAN 694-6062) Tel 510-336-0819 (phone/fax)
E-mail: bsalinas@ousd.k12.ca.us
Dist(s): **Lectorum Pubns., Inc.**
Libros Sin Fronteras
Teacher's Discovery.

Pinata Publishing (CAN) *(978-0-9685097; 978-0-9809163) Dist. by* **IPG Chicago.**

Pinchey Hse. Pr., *(978-0-9820342; 979-8-9850281)* 1805 Mummasburg Rd., Gettysburg, PA 17325 USA (SAN 857-0655)
Web site: https://www.pkbutler.com
Dist(s): **Follett School Solutions.**

Pine Cone Pr., *(978-0-9791982; 978-0-692-20517-4)* 2870 Callie Still Rd., Lawrenceville, GA 30045 USA
E-mail: marty@donnellan.com
Web site: http://www.frendibles.com
Dist(s): **CreateSpace Independent Publishing Platform.**

Pine Hill Graphics, *(978-0-9714103; 978-0-9727279; 978-1-933150; 978-0-615-29527-5; 978-0-578-25858-4)* 28441 Briggs Hill Rd., Eugene, OR 97405 USA Fax: 541-343-0568
Web site: https://www.dnb.com/business-directory/company-profiles.pine_hill_graphics.dd9f654ade1dfcb45d
Dist(s): **Leonard, Hal Corp.**

Pine Hill Pr., *(978-1-57579)* Div. of Print Right Printing, 1808 N. K Ave., Sioux Falls, SD 57104 USA Tel 605-362-9200; Fax: 605-362-9222 Do not confuse with Pine Hill Pr., Lafayette, CA8
E-mail: print@pinehillpress.com
Web site: http://www.printrightprinting.com.

Pine Orchard, Inc., *(978-0-9645727; 978-1-930580)* Orders Addr.: 2850 Hwy 95 South. P.O. box 9184, Moscow, ID 83843 USA (SAN 253-4258) Tel 208-882-4838; Fax: 208-882-4845; Toll Free: 877-354-7433; *Imprints:* Ulyssian Publications (Ulyssian Pubns); Luminary Media Group (Luminary Media)
E-mail: orders@pineorchard.com; pineorch@pineorchard.com
Web site: http://www.pineorchard.com
Dist(s): **Brodart Co.**

Pine Orchard Press *See* **Pine Orchard, Inc.**

Pine View Pr., *(978-0-9740151)* Orders Addr.: 42 Central St., Southbridge, MA 01550 USA (SAN 255-3309) Tel 508-764-7415; Fax: 508-765-1963
E-mail: shawnpcormier@aol.com
Web site: http://www.pineviewpress.com
Dist(s): **Partners Bk. Distributing, Inc.**

Pineapple Pr., Inc., *(978-0-910923; 978-1-56164; 978-1-68334)* Div. of The Globe Pequot Press, 4501 Forbes Blvd., Suite 200, Lanham, MD 20706 USA (SAN 285-0850) Tel 301-459-3366; Fax: 301-429-5748 Do not confuse with companies with same or similar names in Saint Johns, MI, Middletown, RI, Northampton, MA, Wimberley, TX
Dist(s): **American Wholesale Bk. Co.**
Children's Plus, Inc.
MyiLibrary
National Bk. Network
Rowman & Littlefield Publishers, Inc.
Rowman & Littlefield Unlimited Model.

Pineapple Publishing and Consulting LLC, *(978-0-9794608; 978-1-938188)* 1046 W. 42nd St., Houston, TX 77018-4314 USA
Web site: http://www.pineapplepublishing.com.

Pinecone Bk. Co., *(978-1-949053)* P.O. Box 65, Evergreen, CO 80437 USA Tel 303-670-3628
E-mail: bethfostered@gmail.com
Web site: BethFosterED.com.

Pinefield Publishing, *(978-0-9746397)* 9801 Fall Creek Rd., Suite 318, Indianapolis, IN 46256 USA Tel 317-258-6211; Fax: 317-576-9154
E-mail: Pinefieldpublishing@comcast.net
Web site: http://www.Pinefieldpublishing.com.

Pines Publishing, *(978-0-9766820)* 9896 Lincoln Rd., Morrison, KY 61270-9498 USA
E-mail: info@pinespublishing.com
Web site: http://www.pinespublishing.com.

Pinetree Pubns., *(978-0-9709408)* 6523 Oregon Chickadee Rd., Weeki Wachee, FL 34613-8353 USA Tel 352-592-5292 (phone/fax)
E-mail: lwnorris@hitter.net; lwnorris@bellsouth.net.

Pink Elephant Pr. The, *(978-0-9772975)* P.O. Box 1153, Jonesboro, GA 30236-1153 USA (SAN 257-2532) Toll Free: 800-583-1439 (phone/fax)
E-mail: info@thepinkelephantpress.com
Web site: http://www.thepinkelephantpress.com.

Pink Granite Pr., *(978-0-9766737)* P.O. Box 231, Thousand Island Park, NY 13692-0231 USA Tel 613-549-6575.

Pink Hyacinth Press *See* **Kelly, Katherine**

Pink Kiss Publishing Co., *(978-0-615-29068-3; 978-0-9828795; 978-0-9835756; 978-0-9847455; 978-0-9851909; 978-0-9858299; 978-0-9885632; 978-0-9895580; 978-0-9904442; 978-0-9962965)* 2316 Greenway Dr., Gautier, MS 39553 USA
E-mail: pinkkisspublishing@pinkkisspublishing.com; glenda099@cableone.net
Web site: http://www.pinkkisspublishing.com.

Pink Lemonade, LLC, *(978-0-9799159)* 297 Sunset Pk. Dr., Prescott, AZ 86303 USA
E-mail: zuzu@cableone.net
Web site: http://www.thecupcakesclub.com.

Pink Pig Pr., *(978-0-9816360)* 980 Broadway, Suite 248, Thornwood, NY 10594 USA Tel 914-747-8188.

Pink Stucco Pr., *(978-0-9717796)* 36 Dexter St., Waltham, MA 02453-5017 USA; *Imprints:* Mystic Night Books (Mystic Night Bks)
E-mail: publishing@pinkstucco.net
Web site: http://www.pinkstucco.net/psp/.

Pink&Brown Publishing, LLP, *(978-0-615-36448-3)* 35 E. Main St. Suite 373, Avon, CT 06001 USA Tel 860-674-0292
E-mail: marycashman@comcast.net
Dist(s): **West.**

Pinkney, Gail, *(978-0-9799320)* 1185 Collier Rd NW Apt. 10E, Atlanta, GA 30318-8218 USA
E-mail: pinkneycorey@yahoo.com
Web site: http://www.dreamteambook.com.

Pinkney Wilcox, JoAnn, *(978-0-9764191)* Orders Addr.: 4044 George Busbee Pkwy. #8304, Kennesaw, GA 30144 USA Tel 678-768-5644
E-mail: joannpwilcox@yahoo.com
Web site: http://www.booksbyjpw.com.

PinkPowerful Bks. *Imprint of* **PinkPowerful LLC**

PinkPowerful LLC, *(978-0-9859171; 978-1-955300)* 1573 E Sahuaro Blossom Pl, Tucson, AZ 85718-7877 USA Tel 650-374-6200; *Imprints:* PinkPowerful Books (PinkPowerfulBks)
Web site: Pinkpowerful.com.

Pinkston, Anastasia, *(978-0-9790515)* 500 Moonraker Dr. Apt. 107, Chesapeake, VA 23320-4051 USA
E-mail: anapinkston@yahoo.com
Web site: http://www.cafepress.com/pinkston.

Pinnacle Press *See* **Mountaintop Pr.**

Pinnacle Press *See* **Capital Communications, Inc.**

Pinnacle Pr., *(978-0-9745542)* 25 Country Estates W., East Durham, NY 12423 USA Tel 518-239-8003 Do not confuse with companies with the same name in Little Rock, AR, Cary, NC, Spokane, WA, Nashville, TN, Franklin, TN, Saint Louis, MO
E-mail: foxykate2001@yahoo.com.

Pinninti Pubns., *(978-0-9703474)* 120 Carter Rd., Princeton, NJ 08540-2111 USA
E-mail: pkrao@dr.com
Web site: http://www.pinnintipublishers.com.

Pinpoint Color *See* **Pinpoint Printing**

Pinpoint Printing, *(978-0-9702324)* 5115 E. Highland Dr., Jonesboro, AR 72401 USA Tel 870-931-6200; Fax: 870-931-5800
E-mail: dkelley@mkbmarketing.com
Web site: http://www.pinpointprinting.com.

Pinter & Martin Ltd. (GBR) *(978-0-9530964; 978-1-905177; 978-1-78066) Dist. by* **Natl Bk Netwk.**

Pinto, Vincent, *(978-0-578-48648-2)* 951 Willow Ln., Sleepy Hollow, IL 60118 USA Tel 224-410-2925
E-mail: predeclined@gmail.com.

ntos, Yoselem G., (*978-0-9800127; 978-1-61196*) 3024 E 30TH AVE APT D101, Spokane, WA 99223 USA Tel 646-634-9490
E-mail: yoselem@hotmail.com.

inup Vintage *See* **Pinup Vintage**

inup Vintage, (*978-0-692-76674-3; 978-0-692-76689-7*) .

inwheel Bks., (*978-0-9832577; 978-0-9854248; 978-1-940741*) Orders Addr.: PO BOX 491470, Key Biscayne, FL 33149 USA Tel 617-794-7976
E-mail: publisher@pinwheelbooks.com
Web site: www.pinwheelbooks.com.

inyon Publishing, (*978-0-9821561; 978-1-936671*) 23847 V66 Trail, Montrose, CO 81403 USA Tel 970-596-8676
E-mail: susanelliott@pinyon-publishing.com
Web site: http://www.pinyon-publishing.com.

Pinz, Shelley Music, (*978-0-9700251*) Orders Addr.: P.O. Box 275, Atlantic Beach, NY 11509 USA Tel 516-371-4437; Fax: 516-371-4437 (*51); Edit Addr.: 2100 Atlantic Blvd., Atlantic Beach, NY 11509 USA.

Pioneer Clubs, (*978-0-9743503; 978-1-934725; 978-0-9853008; 978-0-9885794*) Orders Addr.: P.O. Box 788, Wheaton, IL 60187-0788 USA (SAN 225-4891) Tel 630-293-1600; Fax: 630-293-3053; Toll Free: 800-694-2582; Edit Addr.: 27 W. 130 St. Charles Rd., Carol Stream, IL 60188-1999 USA (SAN 669-2419)
E-mail: info@pioneerclubs.org
Web site: http://www.pioneerclubs.org.

Pioneer Poet Publishing, (*978-0-615-55095-4; 978-0-615-65742-4*) 10651 MacGregor Dr., Pensacola, FL 32514 USA Tel 850-748-8895
E-mail: gincru@gmail.com
Dist(s): **CreateSpace Independent Publishing Platform**
Lulu Pr., Inc.

Pioneer Valley Bks. *Imprint of* **Pioneer Valley Bks.**

Pioneer Valley Bks., (*978-1-58453; 978-1-932570; 978-1-60343; 979-8-88829*) 155A Industrial Drive, Northhampton, MA 01060 USA Fax: 4137278211; *Imprints:* Pioneer Valley Books (PioValley Bks)
E-mail: lauri@pvep.com; gina@pvep.com; nick@pvep.com
Web site: http://www.pioneervalleybooks.com.

Pioneer Valley Educational Press, Incorporated *See* **Pioneer Valley Bks.**

Piper, Aaron, (*978-0-578-21215-9*) 62 Salzburg Blvd., Columbus, IN 47201 USA Tel 567-204-2841
E-mail: aaronjpiper@hotmail.com.

Piper, J.G., (*978-0-9916561*) P.O. Box 14018, Columbus, OH 43214 USA Tel 614-262-7896
E-mail: books@jgpiper.com
Web site: http://jgpiper.com.

†Piper Publishing, Inc., (*978-0-87832*) 2523 Portland Ave., S., Suite 910, Minneapolis, MN 55404 USA (SAN 202-005X) Tel 612-870-8787 Do not confuse with Piper Publishing LLC in Easton, CT; *CIP.*

Piper Punches, (*978-0-9910936; 978-1-7353895*) 30 Citori Ct., Troy, MO 63379 USA Tel 636-346-7028
E-mail: denise_mcgrail@yahoo.com
Web site: www.piperpunches.com.

Piper Verlag GmbH (DEU) (*978-3-492; 978-3-89029; 978-3-8225; 978-3-89521; 978-3-921909*) *Dist. by* **Distribks Inc.**

Pippa's Passion, (*978-0-9988337*) 308 S. Bozeman Ave, Bozeman, MT 59715 USA Tel 406-581-6383
E-mail: edmonia308@yahoo.com.

Pippin & Maxx Arts & Entertain, LLC, (*978-0-9818747*) 533 Choctaw Rd., Jackson, MS 39206-3920 USA (SAN 856-7794) Tel 601-982-9394 (phone/fax)
E-mail: amile@pippinandmaxx.com
Web site: http://www.pippinandmaxx.com.

Pippin Pr., (*978-0-945912*) Orders Addr.: P.O. Box 1347, New York, NY 10028 USA (SAN 247-8366) Tel 212-288-4920; Fax: 732-225-1562; Edit Addr.: 229 E. 85th St., New York, NY 10028 USA.

Pipton Pr., (*978-0-9828203*) Orders Addr.: 1457 Capri Ave., Petaluma, CA 94954 USA; Edit Addr.: 2506 Castello St., Oakland, CA 94602 USA
E-mail: ginaartbooks@gmail.com.

Pirate Island Pr., (*978-0-9799326*) 3750-A Airport Blvd., No. 224, Mobile, AL 36608 USA (SAN 855-0026) Tel 251-650-4147; Fax: 251-928-9841; Toll Free: 877-689-6660
E-mail: pirateisland@bellsouth.net
Web site: http://www.tnrivers.com; http://www.jihadgerm.com.

Pirate Publishing International, (*978-0-9674081*) 6323 St. Andrews Cir., No. 5, Fort Myers, FL 33919-1719 USA Tel 941-939-4845
E-mail: SuperK@juno.com
Dist(s): **ebrary, Inc.**

Pirouette Publishing, (*978-0-9861711; 978-0-578-57132-4*) 2631 Ashleigh Ln., Alpharetta, GA 30004 USA Tel 678-570-0623
E-mail: 1tabathajames@gmail.com.

Pirouz, Raymond, (*978-0-9729815*) Orders Addr.: 2014 Holland Ave. #719, Port Huron, MI 48060 USA (SAN 255-3899)
Web site: http://www.raymondpirouz.com.

Pisteuo Pubns., (*978-0-578-40998-6; 978-0-578-40999-3; 978-0-578-42903-8; 978-0-578-85998-9; 978-0-578-39635-4*) 649 Pecan Ln., Cottonwood Shores, TX 78657 USA Tel 830-220-3408
E-mail: julien@julienjamar.com
Dist(s): **Ingram Content Group.**

P.I.T. Pubns., (*978-0-9760608*) 120 Deweese Dr., Waggaman, LA 70094-2480 USA Tel 504-436-7012.

Pitcher, Jan, (*978-0-9795877*) 208 Tait Ave., Los Gatos, CA 95030 USA
E-mail: janpitcher@verizon.net.

Pitchford, D. L., (*978-0-9987945*) 628 E Morningside, Springfield, MO 65807 USA Tel 417-298-1916; *Imprints:* Straight on till Morningside Prints (Straightontil)
E-mail: dlpitchfordauthor@gmail.com; admin@dlpitchford.com
Web site: dlpitchford.com.

Pitchstone LLC, (*978-0-9728875; 978-0-9844932; 978-0-9852815; 978-1-939578; 978-1-63431*) 848 Sedgefield St., Durham, NC 27705-4251 USA
Web site: http://www.pitchstonepublishing.com
Dist(s): **BookBaby**
Follett School Solutions
Independent Pubs. Group
MyiLibrary
ebrary, Inc.

Pitspopany Pr. *Imprint of* **Simcha Media Group**

Pittsburgh Literary Arts Network LLC, (*978-0-9727319*) P.O. Box 226, Oakmont, PA 15139 USA Tel 412-820-2507; *Imprints:* Blacktypewriter Press (Blacktypewriter Pr)
E-mail: info@blacktypewriter.com
Web site: http://www.blacktypewriter.com.

PitziGil Pr. *Imprint of* **PitziGil Pubns.**

PitziGil Pubns., (*978-0-9846397; 978-0-9914760; 978-0-9970488; 978-0-9985426*) Orders Addr.: P.O. Box 1315, Gaffney, SC 29342-1315 USA (SAN 860-1550) Tel 864-488-7320; *Imprints:* PitziGil Press (PitziGil Pr)
E-mail: pitzigil@yahoo.com; dl@pitzigilpublications.com
Web site: www.pitzigilpublications.com.

Pivot Point Pubns., (*978-1-7335230*) 3 Jersey St., Londonderry, NH 03053 USA Tel 603-770-9288
E-mail: kmcintire5@comcast.net.

Pivotal Force, (*978-0-9740473*) 632 Skyview Rd., Bellville, TX 77418 USA (SAN 256-4319) Tel 979-865-9213
E-mail: pivotalforce@evl.net
Web site: http://www.pivotalforce.com.

Pivotal Publishing, (*978-0-9990332; 978-1-960668*) 246 Churchill St., Northfield, IL 60093 USA
E-mail: chliu0219@gmail.com; cynthealiu2@gmail.com.

Pivotal Publishing Inc. *See* **Pivotal Publishing**

Pixel Coast Publishing, (*978-0-9985159*) P.O. Box 17877, Reno, NV 89511 USA Tel 310-339-1019
E-mail: klasekan@gmail.com.

Pixel Kid Publishing, (*978-0-9990681; 978-1-949216*) 690 S US Hwy. 89, Suite 200, Jackson, WY 83001 USA Tel 307-222-9093; Fax: 307-222-9093
E-mail: info@pixelkidpublishing.com.

Pixel Mouse Hse., (*978-1-939322*) P.O. Box 20241, Huntington Station, NY 11746 USA Tel 631-850-3497
E-mail: info@pixelmousehouse.com
Web site: http://www.pixelmousehousebooks.com.

Pixelated Publishing *Imprint of* **Faithful Publishing**

Pixel+Ink, (*978-1-64595*) 85 Broad St., New York, NY 10004 USA Tel 917-301-5632
E-mail: bbuck@tbridgemedia.com
Dist(s): **Penguin Random Hse. Distribution**
Penguin Random Hse. LLC.

Pixelpics Publishing, (*978-0-9747826*) 4801 Secret Harbor Dr., Jacksonville, FL 32257 USA
Web site: http://www.pixelpics.net.

Pixels Publishing, (*978-0-9728743*) P.O. Box 10, La Fox, IL 60147 USA
E-mail: customerservice@pixelspublishing.com
Web site: http://www.pixelspublishing.com.

Pixie Ears Pr., (*978-1-939157*) 97 Mountain View Rd., Santa Cruz, CA 95065 USA
E-mail: lisa@pixieearspress.com.

Pixie Stuff LLC, (*978-0-9761421; 978-0-9795832; 978-0-9826081; 978-0-9833364; 978-0-9850897; 978-0-9850898; 978-0-9854666; 978-0-9890806; 978-0-9916167; 978-0-9862115; 978-0-9966836; 978-0-9974255; 978-0-9978570; 978-1-7336728*) Orders Addr.: 18 Brighton Way, Saint Louis, MO 63105 USA Tel 314-721-4107; Fax: 314-721-4107
E-mail: jennifer@thumbsupjohnnie.com; jennifer@hiredink.com
Web site: http://www.thumbsupjohnnie.com; www.hiredink.com.

PixyJack Pr., Inc., (*978-0-9658098; 978-0-9773724; 978-1-936555*) Orders Addr.: P.O. Box 149, Masonville, CO 80541 USA Tel 303-810-2850; Toll Free Fax: 888-273-7499
E-mail: info@pixyjackpress.com
Web site: http://www.pixyjackpress.com.

Pizzazz Publishing, (*978-0-9744936*) Orders Addr.: P.O. Box 415, Victoria, MN 55386 USA Tel 952-368-1903; Fax: 952-944-0399
E-mail: psimenson@aol.com
Web site: http://www.pizzazzpublishing.com
Dist(s): **Quality Bks., Inc.**

PJR Assocs., Ltd., (*978-0-9790796*) Orders Addr.: P.O. Box 2482, Alexandria, VA 22301 USA Fax: 703-683-4348; Edit Addr.: 910 Junior St., Alexandria, VA 22301 USA
E-mail: patrichards@pjrassociates.com
Web site: http://www.pjrassociates.com.

PJs Corner *See* **PJs Corner Gift Shoppe**

PJs Corner Gift Shoppe, (*978-0-9745615; 978-1-933158*) Orders Addr.: P.O. Box 1842, Pecos, TX 79772 USA Tel 432-448-4243; Edit Addr.: P.O. Box 1842, Pecos, TX 79772 USA Tel 432-448-4243
E-mail: memories@pjscornergiftshoppe.com
Web site: http://www.pjscornergiftshoppe.com.

PJS Publishing, (*978-0-9743177; 978-0-615-40511-7*) 40344 Redbud Dr., Oakhurst, CA 93644 USA Tel 559-641-5994
E-mail: steve@tycooney.com.

PK Bks. Inc., (*978-0-9827347; 978-0-9846799; 978-0-9891177*) 512 Terrace Rd., Bayport, NY 11705-1528 USA
E-mail: jnewbauer6@hotmail.com
Dist(s): **Ingram Content Group.**

pk potts publishing, (*978-0-615-65613-7; 978-0-578-48767-0*) 2058 Pine Field Ct #622, N. Charleston, SC 29405 USA Tel 843-729-0787
Dist(s): **CreateSpace Independent Publishing Platform.**

Place 33 Presses, (*978-0-9915700*) 10275 Fairfield Ave, Las Vegas, NV 89183 USA Tel 702-717-2137
E-mail: Graphicartist@aol.com
Web site: http://www.place33.org.

†Place In The Woods, The, (*978-0-932991*) 3900 Glenwood Ave., Golden Valley, MN 55422-5302 USA (SAN 689-058X) Tel 763-374-2120; Fax: 952-593-5593
E-mail: placewoods@aol.com; differentbooks@aol.com
Dist(s): **Social Studies Schl. Service;** *CIP.*

Place Mark Bks., (*978-0-9815991; 978-1-941032*) P.o. Box 602, Conneaut, OH 44030 USA (SAN 855-9929).

Place Of Rest Music, (*978-0-9969050*) 2018 Brilliant Dr., Raleigh, NC 27616 USA Tel 919-480-1817
E-mail: swaithe.valles@gmail.com
Web site: www.susanvalles.com.

Placenames Press *See* **Back Channel Pr.**

Plaidswede Publishing, (*978-0-9626832; 978-0-9755216; 978-0-9790784; 978-0-9840650; 978-0-9837400; 978-0-9890176; 978-0-9962182; 978-1-7323648; 978-1-7333556*) P.O. Box 269, Concord, NH 03302-0269 USA Tel 603-226-1020; Toll Free: 800-267-9044
E-mail: gnews@empire.net
Web site: http://www.plaidswede.com.

Plain View Pr., (*978-0-911051; 978-1-891386; 978-0-9819731; 978-1-935514; 978-1-63210*) Orders Addr.: 1101 W 34th Street, STE 404, Austin, TX 78705 USA (SAN 264-3073)
E-mail: pk@plainviewpress.net; support@plainviewpress.net
Web site: http://www.plainviewpress.net; http://www.plainviewpress.com
Dist(s): .

Plain Vision Publishing, (*978-0-9761628; 978-0-9848234; 978-0-9910594; 978-0-9971664; 978-1-947820*) Eb#141 Paria Dr. Aripero Village Rousillac, La Brea, TTO Tel 868-704-6397; 984 Ashford St., Brooklyn, NY 11207 Tel 347-652-0883 Do not confuse with Plain Vision Publishing in Kihei, HI
E-mail: info@pvppress.com; eguadeloupe@pvppressl.com
Web site: http://www.pvppress.com
Dist(s): **Ingram Content Group.**

Plain White Pr., LLC, (*978-0-9760250; 978-0-9777383; 978-0-9815004; 978-0-9815964; 978-1-936005*) Orders Addr.: 17 Chadwick Rd., West Harrison, NY 10604-1802 USA (SAN 850-0886)
E-mail: julie@plainwhitepress.com
Web site: http://www.plainwhitepress.com.

Plan B Bks, (*978-0-9785798*) P.O. Box 300307, University City, MO 63130 USA
E-mail: abby@planbbooks.com
Web site: http://www.planbbooks.com.

Planet Bronx Productions, (*978-0-9765566*) Orders Addr.: 3563 Bainbridge Ave. Apt 6g, Bronx, NY 10467 USA Tel 646-643-4786; *Imprints:* PAPO Brand (PAPO)
E-mail: ivanvelezjr@planetbronx.com; admin@planetbronx.com; ivanvelezjr@gmail.com
Web site: http://www.planetbronx.com.

Planet Gina Media, (*978-0-9991410; 978-0-9991410-0-7*) 813 Hayfield Ct., Doylestown, PA 18901 USA Tel 609-678-6494; Fax: 609-678-6494
E-mail: Jenniep.hamel@gmail.com.

Planeta Mexicana Editorial S. A. de C. V. (MEX) (*978-968-406; 978-970-690*) *Dist. by* **Lectorum Pubns.**

Planeta Publishing *Imprint of* **Planeta Publishing Corp.**

Planeta Publishing Corp., (*978-0-9715256; 978-0-9719950; 978-0-9748724; 978-1-933169; 978-0-9795042*) 999 Ponce De Leon Blvd. Ste. 1045, Coral Gables, FL 33134-3047 USA; *Imprints:* Planeta Publishing (PlanPubng)
E-mail: mnorman@planetapublishing.com
Web site: http://www.planeta.es
Dist(s): **Ediciones Universal**
Ingram Publisher Services
Two Rivers Distribution.

PLANit Brands, LLC, (*978-0-578-49755-6; 978-1-7331188*) P.O. Box 21484, Beaumont, TX 77720 USA
E-mail: donna4430@att.net.

PLANit Lifestyle *See* **PLANit Brands, LLC**

Plankton Pr., (*978-0-9774074*) 5692 Kalanianaole Hwy., Honolulu, HI 96821 USA Tel 808-373-1016; Fax: 808-373-5381
Web site: www.planktonpress.com.

†Planned Parenthood Federation of America, Inc., (*978-0-934586; 978-1-930996; 978-1-935100*) 123 William St. 10th Flr., New York, NY 10038 USA (SAN 205-1281) Tel 212-261-4602
E-mail: julia.scheinbeim@ppfa.org
Web site: https://marketplace.plannedparenthood.org/brochures; *CIP.*

Planning/Communications, (*978-0-9622019; 978-1-884587*) 7215 Oak Ave., River Forest, IL 60305-1935 USA (SAN 253-8717) Tel 708-366-5200; Fax: 708-366-5280; Toll Free: 888-366-5200 (orders only)
E-mail: info@planningcommunications.com; dl@planningcommunications.com
Web site: http://www.jobfindersonline.com; http://www.planningcommunications.com; http://www.dreamitdoit.net.

Plant Kingdom Communications, (*978-0-9834114*) 1503 Gates Ct., Morris Plains, NJ 07950 USA Tel 201-745-5494
E-mail: basia@plantkingdomcommunications.com
Web site: www.PlantKingdomCommunications.com.

Plant the Seed Publishing, (*978-0-9759790*) 4361 Fiesta Ln., Houston, TX 77004 USA Tel 713-747-0026
E-mail: rr4361@aol.com
Web site: http://hometown.aol.com/rr4361/myhomepage/business.

Plantain Pr., Inc., (*978-0-9816262*) P.O. Box 37, Cruz Bay, VI 00831-0037 USA (SAN 856-0838) Tel 340-344-6123
E-mail: info@vitaxhelp.com.

Plata Publishing, (*978-1-61268; 978-1-950138*) 4330 N. Civic Ctr. Plaza Suite 100, Scottsdale, AZ 85251 USA Tel 480-998-6971
E-mail: d.leong@richdad.com
Dist(s): **Ingram Publisher Services**
Smashwords
Two Rivers Distribution.

Plataforma Editorial SL (ESP) (*978-84-15115; 978-84-15577; 978-84-15750; 978-84-15880; 978-84-16096; 978-84-16256; 978-84-935962; 978-84-96981*) *Dist. by* **Lectorum Pubns.**

Platinum Bks., (*978-0-9746503*) P.O. Box 660876, Arcadia, CA 91066-0876 USA (SAN 255-7525) Do not confuse with companies with the same name in Alpharetta, GA, Washington, DC
E-mail: hongdenise@yahoo.com
Web site: http://www.happierkids.com.

Platinum Medallion Children's Bks., (*978-1-929489*) Div. of EDS Design & Animation, 2705 Ridge Rd., Huntingtown, MD 20639 USA Tel 410-535-6992; Fax: 410-535-7643
E-mail: doug@dougweb.com; edsdesign@dsmith.com
Web site: http://www.platinum-medallion.com.

Platinum Paw Pr., (*978-0-9817067; 978-0-692-78049-7; 978-0-9984121; 978-1-7331972*) 104 Vassar St., Inverness, FL 34452 USA (SAN 856-3047)
E-mail: info@platinumpawpress.com
Web site: http://www.platinumpawpress.com.

Platinum Rose Publishing, (*978-0-9742948*) 16619 W. Sierra Hwy., Canyon Country, CA 91351 USA
Web site: http://www.platinumrose.com.

Platte Publishing *See* **Forsberg, Michael Photography**

Platypus Media, L.L.C., (*978-1-930775; 978-1-951995*) Orders Addr.: 725 Eighth St., SE, Washington, DC 20003 USA Tel 202-546-1674; Fax: 202-546-2356; Toll Free: 877-752-8977
E-mail: info@platypusmedia.com
Web site: http://www.platypusmedia.com
Dist(s): **MyiLibrary**
National Bk. Network.

Play Ball Publishing, (*978-0-615-17947-6*) 891 Juliana Cove, Collierville, TN 38017 USA Tel 901-240-1353
E-mail: tmanso9@aol.com.

Play Odyssey Inc., (*978-0-9799441; 978-0-9825931*) 3 Alan Rd., Spring Valley, NY 10977 USA (SAN 854-8463) Tel 520-400-5188; Fax: 310-575-8873
E-mail: mgill@playoi.com
Web site: http://playoi.com; http://worksheetlab.com.

Play Snippets Pr., (*978-1-7335901*) 5581 Gallery Pk. Dr., Ann Arbor, MI 48103 USA Tel 734-929-5881
E-mail: acusleah@gmail.com.

Playdate Kids Publishing, (*978-1-933721*) 1901 Main St., Santa Monica, CA 90405 USA (SAN 257-571X) Toll Free: 800-587-1501
E-mail: info@fmrockskids.com
Web site: http://www.theplaydatekids.com/.

Player Piano Mouse Productions (PPMP), (*978-0-9797794*) 883 S. Iowa St., Suite 105, Dodgeville, WI 53533 USA.

Player Pr., (*978-0-9623966*) 139-22 Caney Ln., Rosedale, NY 11422 USA Tel 718-528-3285 Do not confuse with Player Press LLC in New York, NY.

Players Pr., Inc., (*978-0-88734*) P.O. Box 1132, Studio City, CA 91614-0132 USA (SAN 239-0213) Tel 818-789-4980
E-mail: Playerspress@att.net
Dist(s): **Empire Publishing Service.**

Playful Mind Pr., (*978-1-7378625*) PO Box 21115, Boulder, CO 80308 USA Tel 303-829-5122
E-mail: eklassen@adventuresintotheheart.com
Web site: https://www.adventuresintotheheart.com/.

PlayGround *Imprint of* **Forest Hill Publishing, LLC**

Playground Pr., (*978-0-9790033*) 1951 W. Rochelle Ave., Glendale, WI 53209 USA (SAN 852-1832) Tel 414-352-1590
E-mail: trishwilliams@trishwilliams.net
Web site: http://www.trishwilliams.net.

Playhouse Publishing, (*978-1-57151; 978-1-878338*) 1566 Akron Peninsula Rd., Akron, OH 44313 USA Tel 330-762-6800; Fax: 330-762-2230; Toll Free: 800-762-6775
E-mail: info@playhousepublishing.com
Web site: http://www.nibble-me-books.com; http://www.playhousepublishing.com; http://www.littlelucyandfriends.com.

Playing Pig Pr., (*978-0-9788324*) 922 S. 87th Ave., Omaha, NE 68114 USA (SAN 851-7452) Tel 402-399-0516
E-mail: bettyhan@cox.net
Web site: http://FrecklesandMaya.com.

PlayinTime Productions, Inc., (*978-1-932895; 978-1-59860*) 19525 Valdez Dr., Tarzana, CA 91356-4946 USA Toll Free: 800-310-0087
E-mail: playintime@aol.com
Web site: http://www.playintime.com.

Playmore, Incorporated, Publishers *See* **Waldman Publishing Corp.**

Playor, Editorial, S.A. (ESP) (*978-84-359*) *Dist. by* **Continental Bk.**

PlayPen Publishing, (*978-0-9855865; 978-0-692-42878-8; 978-0-692-42879-5; 978-0-692-42880-1; 978-0-692-42881-8; 978-0-692-42936-5; 978-0-9994380; 978-1-7343610; 978-1-954529*) 1469 Panola Rd., Ellenwood, GA 30294 USA Tel 678-708-5398
E-mail: mzroodyp@aol.com
Web site: http://playpenpublishing.com.

Playroom Pr., (*978-0-9660958*) 1163 Hopper Ave., No. 26, Santa Rosa, CA 95403 USA Tel 707-522-0150
E-mail: rfd5b4@aol.com
Web site: http://www.mansonfamilypicnic.com
Dist(s): **Casemate Pubs. & Bk. Distributors, LLC.**

Playscripts, Inc., (*978-0-9709046; 978-0-9819099; 978-1-62384; 978-1-68069*) 450 Fashion Ave. Ste. 809, New York, NY 10123-0805 USA Toll Free Fax: 866-203-4519
E-mail: info@playscripts.com
Web site: http://www.playscripts.com
Dist(s): **Consortium Bk. Sales & Distribution.**

Playscripts.com *See* **Playscripts, Inc.**

Playwrights Canada Pr. (CAN) *(978-0-88754; 978-0-919834; 978-1-55155)* Dist. by **Consort Bk Sales.**

Plaza & Janes Editories, S.A. (ESP) *(978-84-01)* Dist. by **Distribks Inc.**

Plaza & Janes Editories, S.A. (ESP) *(978-84-01)* Dist. by **Peng Rand Hse.**

Plaza Joven, S.A. (ESP) *(978-84-7655)* Dist. by **Lectorum Pubns.**

Pleasant Company Publications *See* **American Girl Publishing, Inc.**

Pleasant Plains Pr., *(978-0-9790906)* 366 Kingsberry Dr, Suite 100, Annapolis, MD 21409 USA Tel 410-757-1318
E-mail: boaterbrenda@comcast.net
Web site: http://www.pleasantplainspress.com.

Pleasant St. Pr., *(978-0-9792035; 978-1-935025)* P.O. Box 520, Raynham Center, MA 02768 USA (SAN 852-7598) Tel 508-822-3075; Fax: 508-977-2498
E-mail: orders@pleasantstpress.com; info@pleasantstpress.com
Web site: http://www.pleasantstpress.com.

Pleasure Boat Studio *See* **Pleasure Boat Studio: A Literary Pr.**

Pleasure Boat Studio: A Literary Pr., *(978-0-912887; 978-0-9651413; 978-1-929355; 978-1-7364799; 978-1-7370520; 979-8-9871521)* 3710 SW Barton St., Seattle, WA 98126 USA (SAN 299-0075)
E-mail: pleasboat@nyc.rr.com; pleasboatpublishing@gmail.com
Web site: http://www.pleasureboatstudio.com
Dist(s): **Brodart Co.**
Partners/West Book Distributors
SPD-Small Pr. Distribution
Smashwords.

Plebeian Media, *(978-0-692-82854-0; 978-0-9992658)*
E-mail: juliannorthauthor@gmail.com; juliannorthauthor@gmail.com; juliannorthauthor@gmail.com
Web site: www.juliannorth.com
Dist(s): **CreateSpace Independent Publishing Platform.**

Pleiness Publishing, *(978-0-9742472)* 45937 Duke Dr., Chesterfield Township, MI 48051 USA
E-mail: cpbusy@comcast.net.

Plenus Gratia Pubns., *(978-0-9980465; 978-1-7356595)* 7253 Watson Rd No. 2006, Saint Louis, MO 63119-4401 USA
E-mail: plenusgratiatoday@gmail.com
Web site: plenusgratia.com.

PLEO, *(978-0-9660617)* 302 Park Tree Terr Bldg. 1311, Orlando, FL 32825-3474 USA Tel 407-277-3776; 321-297-5531.

pleo leonard productions *See* **PLEO**

Plexus Publishing, Ltd. (GBR) *(978-0-85965)* Dist. by **PerseuPGW.**

Plicata Pr. LLC, *(978-0-9828205; 978-0-9848400; 978-0-9903102; 978-1-7322963)* P.O. Box 32, Gig Harbor, WA 98335 USA Tel 253-851-2444
E-mail: janwalker@centurytel.net; info@plicatapress.com
Web site: http://www.plicatapress.com.

PloohFX Investments, *(978-0-692-15499-1; 978-0-692-15510-3; 978-0-692-19825-4; 978-0-578-40010-5; 978-0-578-40940-5; 978-0-578-75928-9; 978-0-578-75929-6)* 3127 Watsons Bend, Alpharetta, GA 30004 USA Tel 678-749-4063
E-mail: info@zardangs.com
Dist(s): **Ingram Content Group.**

Plouffe, Delci, *(978-0-692-84708-4; 978-0-578-54018-4; 978-0-578-38274-6; 979-8-218-16612-0)* 1102 Clark Ave, Lewistown, MT 59457 USA Tel 406-366-4174
E-mail: jeffwcrawford5+LVP0003374@gmail.com; jeffwcrawford5+LVP0003374@gmail.com.

†**Plough Publishing Hse.,** *(978-0-87486; 978-1-63608)* 151 Bowne Dr., Walden, NY 12586 USA (SAN 202-0092) Tel 845-572-3455; Fax: 845-572-3472; Toll Free: 800-521-8011
E-mail: info@plough.com; mariahine@ccimail.com
Web site: http://www.plough.com
Dist(s): **Ingram Publisher Services**
MyiLibrary
Spring Arbor Distributors, Inc.; *CIP.*

Plowshare Media, *(978-0-9821145; 978-0-9860428; 978-1-7341443)* P.O. Box 278, La Jolla, CA 92038 USA (SAN 857-2933) Tel 858-454-5446
E-mail: tt@plowsharemedia.com
Web site: http://www.plowsharemedia.com.

Pluegl Bks., *(978-0-9760868)* Orders Addr.: P.O. Box 16622, Chapel Hill, NC 27516-6622 USA; Edit Addr.: 114 Waverly Forest Ln., Chapel Hill, NC 27516 USA.

Plum Blossom Bks. *Imprint of* **Parallax Pr.**

Plum Street Pr., *(978-0-692-35865-8)* 550 W. 54th St., New York, NY 10019 USA Tel 310-592-9053
E-mail: laurawilde100@gmail.com
Dist(s): **CreateSpace Independent Publishing Platform.**

Plum Street Press, *(978-1-943169)* Div. of Yes, MAM Creations, P.O. Box 13899, New Orleans, LA 70185-3899 USA Tel 904-307-6411
E-mail: YesMAMCreations@outlook.com.

Plum Tree Pr., *(978-0-9653535; 978-1-892476)* Orders Addr.: 531 Silcott Rd., Clarkston, WA 99403 USA Tel 509-758-2820; 509-332-1520 (Pine Orchard Distributors)
E-mail: bookinfo@pineorchard.com; gpducky@aol.com
Web site: http://www.pineorchard.com/plumtree; http://www.chinchinian.com
Dist(s): **Partners/West Book Distributors**
Pine Orchard, Inc.

Pluma Productions, *(978-1-889848)* Div. of Southern Dominican Province, USA, Orders Addr.: P.O. Box 1138, Los Angeles, CA 90078-1138 USA Tel 213-463-6488; Fax: 213-466-6645; Edit Addr.: 1977 Carmen Ave., Los Angles, CA 90068 USA
E-mail: pluma@eathlink.net.

Plume *Imprint of* **Penguin Publishing Group**

Plumlette Publishing, *(978-0-692-15944-6; 978-0-692-15946-0; 978-0-578-60024-6; 978-0-578-60026-0; 978-0-578-60028-4; 978-0-578-75305-8)* 5501 Abercorn St. Suite D, No. 134, Savannah, GA 31405 USA Tel 206-694-9315
E-mail: natalie.broulette@gmail.com
Dist(s): **Ingram Content Group.**

Pluriverse Publishing, *(978-0-9846119)* 37 Elm St. Sanbornville, Nh 03872, Sanbornville, NH 03872-3709 USA
E-mail: sluckau@comcast.net; information@ePluriverse.com
Web site: http://www.ePluriverse.com.

Plushy Feely Corp, *(978-0-9837668)* 11 San Rafael Ave., San Anselmo, CA 94960 USA Tel 415-454-4600 (Tel/Fax)
E-mail: kerri@kimochis.com
Web site: www.kimochis.com.

Pluteo Pleno, *(978-1-937847)* 803 S. Durbin St., Casper, WY 82601 USA Tel 307-277-9010
E-mail: pete@pluteopleno.com
Web site: http://www.pluteopleno.com.

Pluto Project, *(978-0-9662982)* 601 Van Ness, No. E3801, San Francisco, CA 94102-3200 USA Tel 415-647-5501; Fax: 415-840-0060; Toll Free: 888-227-5886
E-mail: walter@plutoproject.com
Web site: http://www.plutoproject.com
Dist(s): **New Leaf Distributing Co., Inc.**
Quality Bks., Inc.

Pluton Ediciones (ESP) *Dist. by* **Lectorum Pubns.**

Plyler, Clint, *(978-0-692-18569-8; 978-1-7356561)* 1627 Fairwood Forest Dr., Saint Peters, MO 63376 USA Tel 570-604-2014
E-mail: plylermo@gmail.com.

PM, INK, *(978-0-9753852)* 522 aNDERSON aVE., Rockville, MD 20850 USA (SAN 256-0275) Tel 301-424-0638 (phone/fax)
E-mail: pm.ink@verizon.net
Web site: http://www.pmink.net.

PM Moon Pub., LLC, *(978-0-9817777; 978-0-615-15573-9; 978-0-615-15734-4)* 3308 W. 111th St., Cleveland, OH 44111-3642 USA
Dist(s): **Lulu Pr., Inc.**

PM Pr., *(978-1-60486; 978-1-62963; 979-8-88744)* P.O. Box 23912, Oakland, CA 94623 USA
Web site: http://www.pmpress.org
Dist(s): **AK Pr. Distribution**
Ebsco Publishing
Follett School Solutions
Publishers Group West (PGW)
ebrary, Inc.

P.M. Publishing, *(978-0-9798346)* Orders Addr.: P.O. Box 185, Lottsburg, VA 22511 USA (SAN 854-5200); Edit Addr.: 353 Walmsley Rd., Callao, VA 22435 USA
E-mail: pinkie_thecat@yahoo.com.

PMK Press *See* **Dancer's Publishing**

Pneuma Life Publishing, Inc., *(978-1-56229)* Orders Addr.: 12138 Central Ave. #251, Mitchellville, MD 20721 USA (SAN 297-3057); *Imprints:* Christian Living Books, Inc. (Christian Livng)
E-mail: Info@christianlivingbooks.com
Web site: http://www.pneumalife.com; http://christianlivingbooks.com
Dist(s): **Anchor Distributors**
Ingram Content Group
Smashwords
Spring Arbor Distributors, Inc.

Pocamug Pr., *(978-0-9908877; 978-0-9984790; 978-1-7333656)* 5037 Alhambra Rd., Mayslick, KY 41055-9786 USA Tel 702-425-6189
E-mail: michaeid42@aol.com.

POCEE Publishing, *(978-0-9824812)* 1260 Wesley Ave., Pasadena, CA 91104 USA Tel 626-794-8524.

Pocket Books, *(978-1-4165)* 1230 Avenue of the Americas, New York, NY 10020 USA
Dist(s): **Diamond Comic Distributors, Inc.**
Simon & Schuster, Inc.

Pocket Books/Star Trek *Imprint of* **Pocket Bks./Star Trek**

Pocket Bks./Star Trek, 1230 Avenue of the Americas, New York, NY 10020 USA; *Imprints:* Pocket Books/Star Trek (PockBksStar)
Dist(s): **Simon & Schuster, Inc.**

Pocket Moon Pr., *(978-1-952834)* 22 S WOODSIDE AVE, WELLESLEY, MA 02482 USA Tel 508-333-6313
E-mail: hegkelly@gmail.com.

Pocket Pr., Inc., *(978-1-884493; 978-1-61371)* P.O. Box 25124, Portland, OR 97298 USA Toll Free Fax: 877-643-3732; Toll Free: 888-237-2110
E-mail: sales@pocketpressinc.com
Web site: http://www.pocketpressinc.com.

Pocket Pubn., A, *(978-0-9721333)* 6701 Democracy Blvd., Suite 300, Bethesda, MD 20817 USA Tel 301-468-4905 Do not confuse with Pocket Publications in York, PA
E-mail: david_new@msn.com
Web site: http://www.home.talkcity.com/LibertySt/davidwnew.

PockitBook Publishing, Inc., *(978-0-9761716)* P.O. Box 6753, Athens, GA 30604-4120 USA Tel 706-354-8380
E-mail: pockitbook@bellsouth.net
Web site: http://www.pockitbook.com.

Poco Bks., *(978-1-7368626)* 214 Tyne Dr., Franklin, TN 37064 USA Tel 615-294-1412
E-mail: pamnightingale15@gmail.com.

Pocol Pr., *(978-1-929763; 979-8-9852820)* 320 Sutton St., Punxsutawney, PA 20124-1333 USA (SAN 253-6021) Tel 703-870-9611
E-mail: chrisandtom@erols.com
Web site: http://www.pocolpress.com.

Podengo Publishing, *(978-1-941876)* 123 Mohawk Rd., Lyons, CO 80540 USA Tel 970-324-0861
E-mail: marianwynkoop@hotmail.com.

POE Holistic Health, *(978-0-692-19206-1; 978-0-692-19207-8)* 8 Cottonwood Cir., Shrewsbury, MA 01545 USA Tel 508-769-5884
E-mail: kristenleepoe@yahoo.com
Web site: www.poeholistichealth.com.

Poesy Project LLC, *(978-1-7358421)* 3080 N Hozoni Rd, Prescott, AZ 86305 USA Tel 928-910-2907
E-mail: poesyproject@gmail.com
Web site: www.poesyproject.com.

Poet Tree Pubns., *(978-0-9658926)* P.O. Box 571444, Salt Lake City, UT 84157-1444 USA Tel 801-685-9398; Fax: 801-262-2324
Dist(s): **Tree Hse. Distribution.**

Poetic Matrix Pr., *(978-0-9714003; 978-0-9789597; 978-0-9824276; 978-0-9827343; 978-0-9852883; 978-0-9860600; 978-0-9981469; 978-1-7337025)* Orders Addr.: P.O. Box 1051, Lake Isabella, CA 93240 USA Tel 559-673-9402
E-mail: poeticmatrix@icloud.com
Web site: http://www.poeticmatrix.com
Dist(s): **Bored Feet Pr.**
SPD-Small Pr. Distribution.

Poetose Pr., *(978-1-945366; 978-1-64672)* 7 Farrington Ave, Allston, MA 02134 USA Tel 401-935-0696
E-mail: meia_geddes@alumni.brown.edu
Dist(s): **Ingram Bk. Co.**

Poet's Passage Pr., The, *(978-0-9841252; 979-8-9889693)* Calle Cruz 203, Old San Juan, PR 00901 USA (SAN 858-4826) Tel 787-567-9235
E-mail: ducart@yahoo.com
Web site: Poetspassage.com.

Poets Wear Prada, *(978-0-9817678; 978-0-9841844; 978-0-615-60020-8; 978-0-615-60651-4; 978-0-615-65019-7; 978-0-615-76123-7; 978-0-615-81963-1; 978-0-615-83322-4; 978-0-615-84885-3; 978-0-615-86358-0; 978-0-615-87926-0; 978-0-615-88477-6; 978-0-615-91007-9; 978-0-615-97110-0; 978-0-615-98830-6; 978-0-692-22769-5; 978-0-692-28457-5; 978-0-692-30379-5; 978-0-692-45069-7; 978-0-692-67933-3; 978-0-9979811; 978-1-946116) 533 Bloomfield St., 2nd Flr., Hoboken, NJ 07030 USA (SAN 856-5031) Tel 201-253-0561 office; 201-600-9462*
E-mail: roxy533@yahoo.com; publisher@poetswearprada.com; atelierprincipen@gmail.com; fuerstherbert533@gmail.com
Web site: http://thesmokingbook.blogspot.com; http://poetsweaprada.blogspot.com; http://twitter.com/pradapoet; http://pwpbooks.blogspot.com; http://issuu.com/pradapoet/; http://www.facebook.com/pages/Poets-Wear-Prada/4148 3895438; https://rainbowliterary.blogspot.com/; https://www.buzzsprout.com/42914
Dist(s): **CreateSpace Independent Publishing Platform.**

POEZIA.US, *(978-1-7348742)* 2495 Emerald Ln., Lindenhurst, IL 60046 USA Tel 847-915-1601
E-mail: mrakhunov@yahoo.com
Dist(s): **Ingram Content Group.**

Pogo *Imprint of* **Jump! Inc.**

Pohl, Brittiany Publishing, *(978-0-692-10794-2)* P.O. Box 2574, ELIZABETH, CO 80107 USA Tel 303-898-0848
E-mail: brittianylpohl@gmail.com.

Pohl, J. Assocs., *(978-0-939332)* 307 N. Shady Ave., Houston, PA 15342 USA (SAN 220-181X) Tel 724-746-1178
E-mail: judepohl@comcast.net.

Pohrte, Dorey Publishing, Inc., *(978-0-9722296)* 917 Maple Rd., Buffalo, NY 14221 USA Tel 716-631-1256
E-mail: kathysue1@adelphia.net.

Point of Grace Entertainment Group, *(978-0-9706112; 978-0-9727644)* 3575 N. Beltline Rd., Suite 345, Irving, TX 75062 USA Tel 972-331-2538; Fax: 972-331-2569; Toll Free: 877-447-2233
E-mail: pgedist@yahoo.com.

Point of Life, Inc., *(978-0-9668069; 978-0-9819367)* 3032 E. Commercial Blvd., Ft. Lauderdale, FL 33308 USA
E-mail: mikmikl@aol.com
Web site: http://www.pointoflife.com.

Point Publishing, *(978-0-9663560)* Orders Addr.: 960 Sage Crest Dr., Wenatchee, WA 98801 USA Tel 509-670-6250; *Imprints:* Orchard Press (Orchard Press) Do not confuse with Point Publishing, Madison, WI
E-mail: thacken@genext.net
Dist(s): **Lulu Pr., Inc.**

Point To Point Publishing, *(978-0-9714147)* 5108 Brittany Dr., Old Hickory, TN 37138 USA Fax: 615-758-8495.

Poisoned Apple Publishing, *(978-1-7348272; 978-1-955222)* 33 Chesterfield Ct, KINGS MOUNTAIN, NC 28086 USA Tel 803-504-3993
E-mail: poisonedapplepublishing@gmail.com
Web site: www.poisonedapplepublishing.com/.

Poisoned Pen Press *Imprint of* **Sourcebooks, Inc.**

Poitous of Browningtion, Llc, *(978-1-7377523)* 153 hillside dr, Newport, VT 05855 USA Tel 239-872-7333
E-mail: Barifischer@gmail.com.

Pokemon, USA, Inc., *(978-1-933743; 978-1-60438)* 777 108th Ave. NE, Suite 2000, Bellevue, WA 98004 USA
Web site: http://www.pokemon-tcg.com
Dist(s): **Diamond Bk. Distributors**
Simon & Schuster, Inc.

Pokeweed Pr. (CAN) *(978-1-894323)* Dist. by **IngramPubServ.**

Polaire Pubns., *(978-0-9708500; 978-0-9795218; 978-1-936315)* Div. of Polaire Entertainment Group, Inc., 422 Wolf Run Rd., Bartonville, TX 76226 USA (SAN 254-8291)
E-mail: chmeezepal@earthlink.net
Web site: http://www.animalcompanionsandtheirpeople.com
Dist(s): **DeVorss & Co.**

Polan, Shanna, *(978-1-7365801)* 23 Highpoint, Cedar Grove, NJ 07009 USA Tel 732-763-0526
E-mail: shannapolan@gmail.com.

Polar Bear & Company *See* **Solon Ctr. for Research & Publishing**

Polar Bear Buds, *(978-0-578-88688-6)* 251 Smith Un, Brunswick, ME 04011 USA Tel 929-366-2010
E-mail: basmattiedookie@yahoo.com.

Polar Club Publishing, *(978-0-615-22038-3)* 635 Sandy Ridge Dr., Glen Burnie, MD 21061 USA
Dist(s): **Lulu Pr., Inc.**

Polar Surf Enterprises *See* **NORKY AMERICA**

Polaris Bks., *(978-0-9741443)* 11111 W. 8th Ave., Unit A, Lakewood, CO 80215-5516 USA Tel 303-980-0890; Fax: 303-980-0753
E-mail: zubrin@aol.com
Web site: http://www.polarisbooks.net.

Polaris Pubns. *Imprint of* **North Star Pr. of St. Cloud**

Polark, Kelly *See* **Big Smile Pr., LLC**

Polebridge Pr., *(978-0-944344; 978-1-59815)* Orders Addr.: P.O. Box 7268, Santa Rosa, CA 95407 USA Tel 707-523-1323; Fax: 707-523-1350; Toll Free: 877-523-3545
E-mail: accounts@polebridgepress.com
Web site: http://www.polebridgepress.com
Dist(s): **Spring Arbor Distributors, Inc.**

Policy Studies Organization *See* **Westphalia Press**

Polis Bks., *(978-1-940610; 978-1-943818; 978-1-947993; 978-1-951709; 978-1-957957)* 1201 Hudson St. No. 211S, Hoboken, NJ 07030 USA; *Imprints:* Armina Press (ArminaPr); Agora (Agora)
E-mail: jpinter@polisbooks.com
Web site: www.polisbooks.com
Dist(s): **MyiLibrary**
Publishers Group West (PGW).

Polistampa (ITA) *(978-88-8304; 978-88-85977)* Dist. by **CasemateAcad.**

Political Status Education Coordinating Commission *See* **Dept. of Chamorro Affairs**

Polity Pr. (GBR) *(978-0-7456; 978-1-5095)* Dist. by **Wiley US.**

Poliva, Oren, *(978-0-692-93318-3; 978-0-9993687; 978-0-9993688)* 8940 Sage Rd., Oakland, CA 94605 USA Tel 510-292-1790
E-mail: polivaoren@hotmail.com.

Polka Dot Publishing, *(978-0-9709995; 978-0-9791072; 978-1-937032)* Orders Addr.: 3312 Woodview Dr., Lafayette, CA 94549 USA Tel 916-570-3839 our Distributor; Edit Addr.: 9034 Western Skies Dr., Reno, NV 89521 USA Tel 775-852-2690
E-mail: lifeoffred@yahoo.com
Web site: http://www.polkadotpublishing.com
Dist(s): **Z-Twist Bks.**

Poll, Michael Publishing *See* **Cornerstone Bk. Pubs.**

Pollard, Christopher, *(978-1-7359829)* 2421 W Horatio St, Unit 835, Tampa, FL 33609 USA Tel 813-760-8790
E-mail: ChristopherRoyPollard@gmail.com.

Polley Publishing, *(978-1-7320580)* 29 Pond St., Essex, MA 01929 USA Tel 508-641-5535
E-mail: buyersbrokerdiane@gmail.com
Web site: dianepolley.com.

PollieMarieSolutions, *(978-0-578-18749-5)* 2111 E. Blue Lake Dr., Magnolia, TX 77354 USA.

Pollux Ink, *(978-0-9820827; 978-0-615-26320-5; 978-0-9982201)* Div. of Zodiacts, 418 Centre Ave. Nyack, Nyack, NY 10960 USA (SAN 857-2186)
E-mail: mcgarryd6@gmail.com
Web site: http://zodiacts.com
Dist(s): **CreateSpace Independent Publishing Platform**
Lulu Pr., Inc.

PollyCraig, *(978-0-9848613)* 682 Bedford Ct., Woodstock, GA 30188 USA Tel 770-517-7919
E-mail: pollycraig@att.net.

PollyRhythm Productions, *(978-0-9701249)* Orders Addr.: P.O. Box 7707, New York, NY 10150 USA Tel 212 688 3900; Toll Free Fax: 800 701 7981
E-mail: prprd@attglobal.net
Web site: http://www.pollyrhythm.com.

Pollywog Bog Bks. (CAN) *(978-0-9810575)* Dist. by **IngramPubServ.**

Polychrome Publishing Corp., *(978-1-879965)* 4509 N. Francisco, Chicago, IL 60625-3808 USA Tel 773-478-4455; Fax: 773-478-0786
E-mail: polypub@earthlink.net
Web site: http://www.home.earthlink.net/~polypub.

Polyface, Inc., *(978-0-9638109)* 363 Shuey Rd., Swoope, VA 24479 USA Tel 540-885-3590; Fax: 540-885-5888
Dist(s): **Chelsea Green Publishing.**

Polyglot Pr., Inc., *(978-1-931927; 978-1-4115)* 111 Caenarvon Ln., Haverford, PA 19041-1049 USA Do not confuse with Polyglot Press in Fairfax, VA
E-mail: david@polyglotpress.com
Web site: http://www.polyglotpress.com.

Polygon Publishing, *(978-0-9764768)* 73 Sutton Pl. W., Palm Desert, CA 92211 USA (SAN 256-4521) Tel 760-346-0544; Fax: 760-406-9333
E-mail: polygnpublishing@aol.com
Web site: http://www.polygonpublishing.com/.

Polymath Publishing House *See* **Polymath Publishing Hse. LLC**

Polymath Publishing Hse. LLC, *(978-1-953149)* 3400 Cottage Way, Ste G2 No. 11542 Ste G2 No. 11542, Sacramento, CA 95825 USA Tel 970-371-5444
E-mail: polymathpublishinghouse@gmail.com.

Polytope Pr., *(978-0-9670526)* Div. of Tarescent Synductions, Orders Addr.: P.O. Box 1349, Phoenix, AZ 85001 USA Tel 602-271-9922; Fax: 602-230-1991; Edit Addr.: 321 E. Portland, No. 6, Phoenix, AZ 85004 USA
E-mail: polytope@hotmail.com.

Pomegranate Communications, Inc., *(978-0-7649; 978-0-87654; 978-0-917556; 978-1-56640; 978-1-0875)* Orders Addr.: 19018 NE. Portal Way, Portland, OR 97230 USA (SAN 860-2077) Toll Free: 800-227-1428; Edit Addr.: 19018 NE. Portal Way, Portland, OR 97230 USA Tel 503-328-6500; 503-328-6525; Fax: 503-328-9330; Toll Free: 800-227-1428; *Imprints:* POMEGRANATE KIDS (POMEGRANATEKID)
E-mail: info@pomegranate.com
Web site: http://www.pomegranate.com.

OMEGRANATE KIDS *Imprint of* **Pomegranate Communications, Inc.**
omegranate Publishing, *(978-0-9767377)* P.O. Box 43, Carpinteria, CA 93014 USA Do not confuse with Pomegranate Publishing in Loma Linda, CA
Web site: http://www.pomegranatepublishing.com.
omelo Bks., *(978-1-937057)* 4580 Province Line Rd., Princeton, NJ 08540 USA Tel 609-924-4580
E-mail: info@pomelobooks.com
Web site: pomelobooks.com.
Pomeroy, James, *(978-0-578-78275-1)* 3228 N Clifton Ave No. 3N, Chicago, IL 60657 USA Tel 812-459-9705
E-mail: jamescpomeroy@gmail.com.
Ponder Rose-A, The, *(978-0-692-88996-1)* 110 Keel Ct., Grover, NC 28073 USA Tel 704-487-7224
E-mail: roseoday2@yahoo.com.
Pontius, Heather, *(978-1-7362982)* 5024 Southern Star Terr., Columbia, MD 21044 USA Tel 757-338-0392
E-mail: pontiush@gmail.com.
Pontrelli, Jeany, *(978-0-9778456)* 6156 Solstice Dr., Sparks, NV 89436 USA.
PONY *Imprint of* **Stabenfeldt Inc.**
Pony Rock Pr., *(978-0-9759598)* 23484 150th Ave. NE, Thief River Falls, MN 56701 USA.
Poodle Suit Publishing, *(978-0-9728429)* P.O. Box 9844, Phoenix, AZ 85068 USA (SAN 255-1608) Tel 602-943-6766 Toll Free: 800-547-8247
E-mail: lougold@cox.net
Web site: http://www.poodlesuit.com.
Poor Magazine, *(978-0-9742007)* 255 9th St., 3, San Francisco, CA 94103 USA Tel 415-863-6306; Fax: 415-865-1932
E-mail: alex@poormagazine.org
Web site: http://www.poormagazine.org.
PoorHse. Publishing LLC, *(978-0-9896335; 978-1-943468)* 905 Myrtle Ave., Big Bear City, CA 92314 USA (SAN 920-6027) Tel 909-272-0059
E-mail: info@poorhousepublishingllc.com
Web site: poorhousepublishingllc.com
Dist(s): **BookBaby**
Small Pr. United.
Pop!, *(978-1-5321; 978-1-0982-4005-9)* 8000 W. 78th St., Ste. 310, Edina, MN 55439 USA; *Imprints:* Pop! Cody Koala (Pop Cody K); DiscoverRoo (DiscoverRoo)
Web site: https://abdobooks.com/pop-books
Dist(s): **North Star Editions.**
Pop Academy of Music, *(978-0-9887710; 978-0-692-39597-4; 978-0-9961631; 978-1-947029)* 4912 Bendahl valley Terr., Richmond, VA 23237 USA Tel 7576131097
Dist(s): **CreateSpace Independent Publishing Platform.**
Pop! Cody Koala *Imprint of* **Pop!**
Pop Pop Pr. *Imprint of* **Micro Publishing Media, Inc.**
Pop Sandbox, Inc. (CAN) *(978-0-9864884) Dist. by* **Diamond Book Dists.**
Pop the Cork Publishing, *(978-0-9741854)* 1629 McGilvra Blvd., E., Seattle, WA 98112 USA Tel 206-720-9779; Fax: 206-720-9771
E-mail: sallyv@isomedia.com
Dist(s): **Hara Publishing Group.**
Pop The World, *(978-0-9846257)* 462 N. Linden Dr. Ste 430, Beverly Hills, CA 90212 USA Tel 310-274-1462
E-mail: poptheworld@att.net
Web site: www.privilegeofparenting.com.
Pope, Bryson, *(978-0-692-10683-9)* 710 N. 970 E., Springville, UT 84663 USA Tel 801-854-8260
E-mail: brysonrpope@gmail.com
Dist(s): **Ingram Content Group.**
Pope, Justin, *(978-0-615-78484-7; 978-0-578-81351-6; 978-0-578-34039-5; 979-8-218-01576-3; 979-8-218-06854-7)* 4355-301 Birchwood Dr., Wilmington, NC 28405 USA Tel 919-920-5590
E-mail: jwpope25@gmail.com.
Popol Vuh Press *See* **Talisman Pr.**
Popover Pr. LLC, *(978-1-7348163)* 1817 218th PL NE, Sammamish, WA 98074 USA Tel 425-749-0425
E-mail: Allegrolyn@aol.com.
Poppy *Imprint of* **Little, Brown Bks. for Young Readers**
Poppy Blossom Pr., *(978-0-615-24059-6)* 8713 Glenbury Ct., S. Suite 102, Jacksonville, FL 32256 USA
E-mail: hello@poppyblossom.com.
Poppy Publishing Hse., *(978-1-7351193)* 1120 E. 6th St., Unit 9, Des Moines, IA 50316 USA Tel 515-718-5175
E-mail: author@mariebooks.com
Web site: mariebooks.com.
Pops & Hops Publishing *See* **Pops & Hops Publishing**
Pops & Hops Publishing, *(978-1-7342071)* 6081 Bayberry Ave., Manheim, PA 17545 USA Tel 610-751-2355
E-mail: mresh10@gmail.com
Web site: www.mikeresh.com.
Popstheclub.com, Inc., *(978-0-692-29061-3; 978-0-692-43666-0; 978-0-692-43667-7; 978-0-9988382; 978-0-578-47758-9; 978-0-578-47759-6)* 4160 Lyceum Ave., Los Angeles, CA 90066 USA Tel 3107092484.
Popular Bk. Co. (USA) Ltd., *(978-1-942830; 978-1-960500)* 2615 N. Sheffield Ave., Chicago, IL 60614 USA Tel 775-529-0347
E-mail: popularbookcanada@gmail.com
Dist(s): **Firebrand Technologies.**
Popular Truth, Inc., *(978-0-9631547)* P.O. Box 40656, Indianapolis, IN 76260 USA Toll Free: 888-342-8156
E-mail: anyike@netscape.net.
Porfyris, Eleni, *(978-1-7367085)* 228 Campbell Ave., Williston Park, NY 11596 USA Tel 516-304-1897
E-mail: Eporfyris@yahoo.com.
Porpoise Publishing, *(978-1-930328)* Div. of Life On Purpose, Orders Addr.: P.O. Box 834, Flat Rock, NC 28731 USA Tel 828-697-9239; Fax: 828-697-6038; Toll Free: 800-668-0183; Edit Addr.: 1160 W. Blue Ridge Rd., Flat Rock, NC 28731 USA
E-mail: publishing@lifeonpurpose.com
Web site: http://www.lifeonpurpose.com
Dist(s): **BookBaby.**
Porro, Guillermo Fermin III, *(978-0-692-99603-4; 978-0-692-11503-9; 978-0-692-17179-0)* 3307 SE Cty. Rd. 760, Aracdia, FL 34266 USA Tel 786-413-5689
E-mail: dadeshark19@yahoo.com
Dist(s): **Ingram Content Group.**
Port, Cynthia L., *(978-0-9912278)* 2513 E. Poplar Ct., Bloomington, IN 47401 USA Tel 812-322-7897
E-mail: cynthia.l.port@gmail.com.
Port Hole Pubns., *(978-0-9700274; 978-0-9768107; 978-0-9827627; 978-0-9882659; 978-0-9892608; 978-1-943119)* P.O. Box 205, Westlake, OR 97493-0205 USA
E-mail: porthole@digisys.net
Web site: http://www.ellentaylor.com.
Port Ludlow Bks., *(978-0-9729884)* 20 Keefe Ln., Port Ludlow, WA 98365 USA
E-mail: gidyerjr@waypt.com.
Port Town Publishing, *(978-0-9700544; 978-0-9716239; 978-0-9725990; 978-0-9740833; 978-1-59466)* 5832 Lambom Ave., Superior, WI 54880-6231 USA; *Imprints:* Little Ones (Little Ones); Growing Years (Growing Years)
E-mail: porttownpublish@aol.com
Web site: http://www.porttownpublishing.bigstep.com.
Port Washington Public Library, *(978-0-9615059)* 1 Library Dr., Port Washington, NY 11050 USA (SAN 694-163X) Tel 516-883-4400.
Port Yonder Pr., LLC *See* **Port Yonder Pr.**
Port Yonder Pr., *(978-0-9841694; 978-1-935600)* 6332 - 33rd Ave. Dr., Shellsburg, IA 52332 USA (SAN 858-6160)
E-mail: Contact@PortYonderPress.com
Web site: http://PortYonderPress.com.
Portable COO, The *See* **Mathieson Creative Media**
Portable Pr. *Imprint of* **Printers Row Publishing Group**
Portable Press *See* **Akashic Bks.**
Portage & Main Pr. (CAN) *(978-0-919566; 978-0-920541; 978-0-9694264; 978-1-894110; 978-1-895411; 978-1-55379) Dist. by* **Orca Bk Pub.**
Portal Ctr. Pr., *(978-1-936902; 978-0-9834956)* 215 Hwy 101 No. 2 P O Box 2024, Waldport, OR 97394 USA; *Imprints:* SpiritBooks (SpiritBooks)
E-mail: editor@portalcenterpress.com; sales@portalcenterpress.com
Web site: portalcenterpress.com.
Portal Pubns., Ltd., *(978-0-7371; 978-0-931929; 978-1-55809; 978-1-57928; 978-1-4030)* Div. of Devon Publishing Group, 100 Smith Ranch Rd. Flr. 2, San Rafael, CA 94903-5552 USA (SAN 208-9882) Toll Free: 800-255-1849 Do not confuse with Portal Publications Big Indian, NY
E-mail: reception@portalpub.com
Web site: http://www.portalpub.com.
Portals Publishing, *(978-0-692-51890-8; 978-0-692-52862-4; 978-0-9970512; 978-1-946469)* P.O. Box PO Box 973, Eagle Lake, FL 33839 USA Tel 863-640-6709
Web site: http://ShelteringTree.Earth
Dist(s): **CreateSpace Independent Publishing Platform.**
Porter, Inman, *(978-0-9979766)* 32 Leroy St., Apt. 10, New York, NY 10014 USA Tel 478-290-2815
E-mail: inmanporter@gmail.com
Web site: www.inmanporter.com.
Porter, Rosanna *See* **Raisykinder Publishing**
Portfolio *Imprint of* **Penguin Publishing Group**
Portfolio Press *See* **Portfolio Pr. Corp.**
Portfolio Pr. Corp., *(978-0-942620)* Orders Addr.: 130 Wineow St., Suite 3, Cumberland, MD 21502 USA Tel 301-724-2795; Fax: 301-724-2796; Toll Free: 877-737-1200; Edit Addr.: 1107 Broadway, 12th Flr., New York, NY 10010 USA (SAN 238-5554) Tel 212-989-8700; Fax: 212-691-3073
E-mail: portfolio@hereintown.net
Web site: http://www.portfoliopress.com.
Portico Bks., *(978-0-9664867)* Orders Addr.: P.O. Box 6094, Chesterfield, MO 63006 USA Tel 636-527-2822 (phone/fax); Toll Free: 888-641-5353 (phone/fax); Edit Addr.: 1316 Rusticview Dr., Ballwin, MO 63011 USA
E-mail: info@grammarandmore.com
Web site: http://www.grammarandmore.com.
Portland Press, Incorporated *See* **Chihuly Workshop, Inc.**
Portland State University, Ooligan Press *See* **Ooligan Pr.**
Portland Studios, Inc., *(978-0-9797183)* The Point At Pk. Pl. 112 Poinsett Hwy., Greenville, SC 29609 USA (SAN 854-1744) Tel 864-241-0810; Fax: 864-241-0811
E-mail: jpeterson@portlandstudios.com
Web site: http://www.beowulfthebook.com; http://www.portlandstudios.com
Dist(s): **Pioneer Enterprises.**
Portrait Health Publishing, *(978-0-9853555)* Orders Addr.: 175 E Hawthorn Pkwy. Suite 235, Vernon Hills, IL 60061 USA Tel 847-236-0943
E-mail: jeremywarner97@gmail.com
Web site: http://www.portraithealthpublishing.com.
Portunus Publishing Co., *(978-0-9641330; 978-1-886440)* 27875 Berwick Dr., Carmel, CA 93923 USA Tel 831-622-0604; Fax: 310-399-5644
E-mail: service@portunus.net
Dist(s): **Lectorum Pubns., Inc.**
Positive Action For Christ, *(978-1-929784; 978-0-9719491; 978-1-59557)* P.O. Box 700, Whitakers, NC 27891 USA Tel 252-437-7771; Fax: 252-437-3297; Toll Free: 800-688-3008; *Imprints:* ProTeens (ProTeens)
Web site: http://www.positiveaction.org.
Positive Imaging, LLC, *(978-0-615-16787-9; 978-0-615-18693-1; 978-0-9842480; 978-0-9856876; 978-1-944071; 978-1-951776)* 9016 Palace Pwky., Austin, TX 78748 USA (SAN 858-8430) Tel 512-217-4803; 512-282-5717; Fax: 877-288-5496
E-mail: bill@positive-imaging.com; awbenitez@hotmail.com
Web site: http://www.positive-imaging.com; http://www.handyman-business-guide.com/; http://www.woodworking-business.com; http://www.selfpublishingworkbook.com; http://woodworking-biz-solutions.com; http://billbenitez.com; http://self-publish-your-writing.com; http://woodworkingbusinessbook.com; http://selfpublishingworkbook.com; http://woodworking-business-guide.com; http://notesonrelationship.com; http://awilliambenitez.com; http://goodrelationships101.com; http://self-publishing-suppo
Dist(s): **CreateSpace Independent Publishing Platform**
Ingram Bk. Co.
Lulu Pr., Inc.
Smashwords.
Positive Pasta Publishing, LLC, *(978-1-947645)* 8526 Eversham Rd, Henrico, VA 23294 USA Tel 804-385-4150
E-mail: getinspired@positivepasta.com.
Positive Productions, *(978-1-928726)* 934 E. 84th Pl., Suite A, Chicago, IL 60619 USA Tel 773-846-6131; Fax: 773-846-6555; Toll Free: 800-306-3064.
Positive Spin Pr., *(978-0-9773096)* P.O. Box 653, Warren, MI 02885-9998 USA
E-mail: info@positivespinpress.com; lisa@studiocvr.com
Web site: http://www.thehalloweenfairy.com.
Positive Strokes, *(978-0-9673490)* Orders Addr.: P.O. Box 97271, Raleigh, NC 27624 USA
E-mail: pstrokes@aol.com; healheartsbooks@aol.com.
Positively Black Publishing, *(978-0-578-64303-8; 978-0-578-71258-1)* 3478 Paradise Rd., Las Vegas, NV 89169 USA Tel 702-542-2348
E-mail: ned.bry.mas@gmail.com
Web site: educatedthug.com.
Positively for Kids, Inc., *(978-0-9634650; 978-0-9765722; 978-0-9778237; 978-0-9786838)* P.O. Box 3283, Kirkland, WA 98083-3283 USA Toll Free: 800-600-5437
E-mail: customerservice@positivelyforkids.com
Web site: http://www.positivelyforkids.com
Dist(s): **American West Bks.**
Brodart Co.
Mackin Bk. Co.
Positively Rich, *(978-1-7328391)* 245 Maple St, Moscow, PA 18444 USA Tel 570-977-5434
E-mail: rludka7@hotmail.com.
Possum Products, *(978-0-615-12548-0)* 712 Warren Dr., Annapolis, MD 21403 USA Fax: 410-510-1003; 410-263-4473 (call 410-263-1847 first)
E-mail: possumpalette@aol.com.
Possum Trot Productions LLC, *(978-0-9962289)* Orders Addr.: P.O. Box 15341, Kansas City, MO 64106 USA Tel 816-895-2924
E-mail: info@possumtrotproductions.com
Web site: http://possumtrotkc.com.
Post Hill Pr., *(978-1-64293; 978-1-63758; 979-8-88845)* 1604 Westgate Cir. Suite 100, Brentwood, TN 37027 USA Tel 615-261-4646
E-mail: contact@posthillpress.com
Web site: http://www.posthillpress.com
Dist(s): **MyiLibrary**
Simon & Schuster
Simon & Schuster, Inc.
Post Mortem Publications, Inc., *(978-0-615-30090-0; 978-0-9839074; 978-1-941880)* 146 E. Broad St., Groveland, FL 34736 USA.
Post Oak Hill, *(978-0-9636122)* 235 Shady Hill Ln., Double Oak, TX 75067-8270 USA Tel 817-430-1182.
Posture & Breathing, LLC, *(978-0-615-35980-9; 978-0-9894962; 978-0-578-82718-6; 978-0-578-82719-3)* 11 Malke Dr., Ocean Township, NJ 07712 USA Tel 845-802-3949.
Potenial Psychotherapy Counseling & Remedial Service, *(978-0-9759889)* 1525 E. 53rd St., Suite 516, 11-2, Chicago, IL 60615 USA.
Potential Developing Ministries, Inc., *(978-0-9745554)* 455 Grason Hwy., Suite 111 Box 153, Lawrenceville, GA 30045 USA
E-mail: pdm@winning.com.
Potential Unlimited Publishing *See* **Red Letter Publishing & Media Group**
Potocar, Lisa Y., *(978-0-9990488)* 19 Outlet Rd., Ballston Lake, NY 12019 USA Tel 518-225-9695
E-mail: lisapotocar@gmail.com
Web site: lisapotocarauthor.com.
Potoma, Alison Elise, *(978-1-940602)* 6234 Avalon Dr., Wilmington, MA 01887 USA Tel 845-461-1065
E-mail: alisonpotoma@gmail.com
Web site: http://www.alisonpotoma.com.
Potter Assocs., *(978-0-9758672)* 2305 Jacob Dr., Santa Clara, UT 84765 USA Tel 435-986-3886; Fax: 435-986-3887; *Imprints:* Hot Page Press (HotPP)
E-mail: stanpot@sisna.com.
Potter Craft *Imprint of* **Potter/Ten Speed/Harmony/Rodale**
Potter Publishing, *(978-0-9856350)* 100 Cherry Tree Hill Ln., Barton, VT 05822 USA Tel 802-525-3311 Do not confuse with Potter Publishing in Elmsford, NY
E-mail: info@cherryam.com.
Potter Style *Imprint of* **Crown Publishing Group, The**
Potters Publishing LLC, *(978-0-9745810)* Orders Addr.: 2204 Blackjack Oak St., Ocoee, FL 34761 USA Tel 407-877-7444
Web site: http://www.potterspublishing.com.
Potter/Ten Speed/Harmony/Rodale, 1745 Broadway, New York, NY 10019 USA; *Imprints:* Clarkson Potter (Clarkson Potter); Potter Craft (PotterCraft); Ten Speed Press (TenSpeedPr); Watson-Guptill (WatsonG); Rodale Books (Rodale Books)
Dist(s): **MyiLibrary**
Penguin Random Hse. Distribution
Penguin Random Hse. LLC
Random Hse., Inc.
Potter/TenSpeed/Harmony/Rodale *See* **Potter/Ten Speed/Harmony/Rodale**
PottyMD LLC, *(978-0-9762877)* 2216 White Ave., Knoxville, TN 37916 USA Tel 865-525-0000; Fax: 865-525-0262; Toll Free: 877-769-8963
E-mail: support@pottymd.com
Web site: http://www.pottymd.com
Dist(s): **SCB Distributors.**
Poudre Landmarks Foundation, *(978-0-9753849)* 108 N. Meldrum St., Fort Collins, CO 80521 USA Tel 970-221-4220; 970-221-0553
Web site: http://www.poudreiandmarks.com.
Pounce To Success International, Inc., *(978-0-9776074)* 608 1/2 W. Park St., Lamar, CO 81052 USA (SAN 257-7364) Tel 719-201-7470; Toll Free: 800-768-6238.
Pounders Publishing, *(978-0-692-33113-2)* 4545 Barfield Rd, Memphis, TN 38117 USA Tel 901-278-6868
E-mail: pounders@anfa.com.
Pouring the Oil: Poetic Praise Pubns., *(978-0-9760734; 978-0-9841968)* Orders Addr.: P.O. Box 944, Brewster, NY 10509 USA; Edit Addr.: P.O. Box 253, Danbury, CT 06813-0253 USA
E-mail: pouringtheoil@yahoo.com; info@pouringtheoilpublications.com
Web site: http://www.pouringtheoilpublications.com.
POW! Kids Bks., 32 Adams St., Brooklyn, NY 11201 USA Tel 212-604-9074
Web site: http://powkidsbooks.com/
Dist(s): **Simon & Schuster, Inc.**
Powell Hill Pr., *(978-0-9760648)* 8 Packett's Glen, Fairport, NY 14450 USA Tel 585-388-8622
E-mail: scoopwrite@aol.com
Web site: http://www.spiritwolf.info; http://www.powellhillpress.com
Dist(s): **North Country Bks., Inc.**
Powell, Mebane, *(978-0-578-99943-2)* 25 Devoe Rd., Chappaqua, NY 10514 USA Tel 914-486-1907
E-mail: mepo1945@gmail.com.
Power Corner Press.com *See* **Power Corner Pr.com(r)**
Power Corner Pr.com(r), *(978-1-950817)* 2355 Fairview Ave N 330, Roseville , MN 55113 USA Tel 952-374-9438
E-mail: williams_charday@yahoo.com
Web site: Power Corner Press.com; Powercornerpress.com; Ellaandkaykay.org.
Power For Kids, *(978-0-615-64680-0)* 12021 Wilshire Blvd #924, Los Angeles , CA 90025 USA Tel 310 445 3250; Fax: 310 445 3251
Web site: www.powerforkids.com
Dist(s): **CreateSpace Independent Publishing Platform.**
Power In Words Publishing, *(978-0-9759717)* P.O. Box 301, Grant City, MO 64456 USA
E-mail: cjblanchard@solemnword.com
Web site: http://www.solemnword.com.
Power Life Project, *(978-1-7363146)* 4222 Escondito Cir, Sarasota, FL 34238-4520 USA Tel 941-232-3552
E-mail: lacookiestar@gmail.com.
Power of One , LLC, *(978-0-692-81445-1; 978-0-692-96952-6; 978-0-692-18208-6; 978-0-578-57561-2; 978-1-7351969)* 48641 Denton Rd apt 209, Belleville, MI 48111 USA Tel 734-699-6483
E-mail: lajuana_jackson@att.net.
Power of the Pen, LLC., *(978-1-7355823; 978-1-954781)*
E-mail: murray.ayanna@gmail.com.
Power Play Media, *(978-0-9724003; 978-0-9741394; 978-1-934230)* P.O. Box 423, Brandywine, MD 20613 USA Tel 240-375-6908; Fax: 301-579-9913; *Imprints:* Nvision Publishing (NvisPub)
E-mail: tressa428@cs.com
Web site: http://www.nvisionpublishing.com/
Dist(s): **INscribe Digital.**
Power Pr., *(978-0-9748508; 978-0-9825568)* P.O. Box 622, Tyrone, GA 30290 USA Tel 770-486-0758; Fax: 770-486-6687 Do not confuse with Power Press in Torrance CA, Chico CA, Sonoma CA
E-mail: ratto@mindspring.com.
Power Pubns., Inc., *(978-0-9629858; 978-0-9724194; 978-0-615-40283-3; 978-0-615-41417-1)* 185 Randon Terr., Lake Mary, FL 32746 USA (SAN 254-6817) Tel 407-732-4322 (phone/fax) Do not confuse with Power Publications, Inc. in Phoenix, AZ, Mountain City, GA
E-mail: igilbert@cfl.rr.com.
Power Through Faith, *(978-0-9707320)* 1702 Capps St., Durham, NC 27707 USA Tel 919-596-7753.
Power Writings, *(978-0-9641640)* 9019 Wall St., 6F, North Bergen, NJ 07047 USA Fax: 201-869-9179
E-mail: fmelfa02@yahoo.com
Web site: http://www.pharmalanding.com.
Power Your Dreams Publishing LLC, *(978-1-7361268)* 600 BILTMORE WAY, CORAL GABLES, FL 33134 USA Tel 305-505-0699
E-mail: Nolagdq@gmail.com
Web site: PowerYourDreamsPublishing.com.
Powerband, LLC, *(978-0-9746445)* 16199 Kennedy Rd., Los Gatos, CA 95032-9503 USA Fax: 408-402-0617; 16199 Kennedy Rd., Los Gatos, CA 95032-9503
E-mail: clelliott@mac.com
Web site: http://www.powerbandllc.com.
Power-Glide Foreign Language Courses, *(978-1-58204)* 1682 W. 820 N., Provo, UT 84601 USA Tel 801-373-3973; Fax: 801-343-3912; Toll Free: 800-596-0910
E-mail: deloyh@power-glide.com
Web site: http://www.power-glide.com.
powerHouse Bks. *Imprint of* **powerHse. Bks.**
powerHse. Bks., *(978-1-57687; 978-1-64823)* 32 Adams St, Brooklyn, NY 11201 USA (SAN 850-5845); *Imprints:* powerHouse Books (pwerHse Bks); PowerHouse Kids (PowerKids)
E-mail: daniel@powerhousebooks.com
Web site: http://www.powerhousebooks.com; www.powkidsbooks.com; www.archways.us
Dist(s): **MyiLibrary**
Simon & Schuster, Inc.
powerHouse Cultural Entertainment, Incorporated *See* **powerHse. Bks.**
PowerHouse Kids *Imprint of* **powerHse. Bks.**
PowerKids Pr. *Imprint of* **Rosen Publishing Group, Inc., The**
PowerMark Productions, *(978-0-9705669; 978-0-9713412; 978-0-9717876; 978-0-9729135; 978-0-9747026; 978-0-9749339; 978-0-9795833; 978-0-9827990; 978-1-935980)* Div. of Quest Ministries International, 380 E. Hwy. Cc Suite E104, Nixa, MO 65714 USA Tel

Publisher Name Index

417-724-1222; Fax: 417-724-0119; Toll Free: 877-769-2669
E-mail: linda@qminternational.com
Web site: http://www.powermarkcomics.com
Dist(s): **New Day Christian Distributors Gifts, Inc.**

PowerMoves, *(978-0-9748298)* P.O. Box 92907, Washington, DC 20090 USA Tel 301-568-9111
Web site: http://www.powermoves.org.

Powers, Beverly, *(978-0-9982536)* 212 Philadelphia Pike, Wilmington, DE 19809 USA Tel 302-588-4254
E-mail: bevjpowers@gmail.com
Web site: beverlypowers.com.

Powers, Elaine A., *(978-0-9991669)* 8540 N Yellowstone Ave, ORO VALLEY, AZ 85704 USA Tel 520-297-3402
E-mail: lizlady@comcast.net
Dist(s): **Ingram Content Group.**

Powerstart Pr. *Imprint of* **Rosen Publishing Group, Inc., The**

PowWow Publishing, *(978-0-9819789; 978-0-9859577)* P.O. Box 31855, Tucson, AZ 85751 USA
E-mail: brent@powwowinc.com
Web site: http://www.powwowpublishing.com; http://www.katemathis.net.

P.R.A. Enterprises Incorporated *See* **P.R.A. Publishing**

P.R.A. Publishing, *(978-0-9727703; 978-0-9821407; 978-0-9840142; 978-1-941416)* Orders Addr.: P.O. Box 211701, Martinez, GA 30917 USA (SAN 991-5419) Tel 706-855-6173
E-mail: lucindaclark@phoenixrisingarts.com; info@prapublishing.com; ljclark08@gmail.com
Web site: http://www.prapublishing.com; http://www.phoenixrisingarts.com; http://www.phoenixrisingart.wordpress.com
Dist(s): **BookBaby**
Ingram Content Group.

PRAAL ENTERTAINMENT LLC,, *(979-8-9875953; 979-8-218-18782-8)* 675 S. Gulfview Blvd. No. 1004, Cleawater Beach, Florida 33767, Clearwater Beach, FL 33767 USA Tel 440-319-5744
E-mail: bubbasq@icloud.com
Web site: www.bubbab7.com.

Practical Christianity Foundation, *(978-0-9705996; 978-1-932587; 978-1-60098)* 2514 Aloha Pl., Holiday, FL 34691 USA (SAN 254-4377) Tel 727-934-0927; Fax: 727-934-4241; Toll Free: 888-278-3300
E-mail: cseitz@greenkeybooks.com
Web site: http://www.greenkeybooks.com
Dist(s): **Send The Light Distribution LLC.**

Practical Green Pr., *(978-0-9834112)* 407 Del Rio Ct., Allen, TX 75013 USA Tel 214-785-8680
E-mail: office@practicalgreenpress.com
Web site: www.practicalgreenpress.com.

PRACTICAL SOLUTIONS Writing, Editing, Consulting, *(978-0-615-19350-2; 978-0-615-19351-9; 978-0-615-32636-8)* P.O. Box 1484, Wake Forest, NC 27588 USA Tel 919-604-4585; Fax: 901-273-1852
E-mail: Jfaulk28@nc.rr.com
Web site: http://stores.lulu.com/store.php?fAcctID=1906985; http://www.jefferyafaulkerson.com
Dist(s): **Lulu Pr., Inc.**

Praeger *Imprint of* **ABC-CLIO, LLC**

Pragma Design, Inc., *(978-1-7322836; 978-1-958367)* P.O. Box 413, Bertram, TX 78605 USA (SAN 991-1200) Tel 512-277-5424
E-mail: jeffhoo.bowker@pragma-design.com
Web site: www.pragma-design.com; http://pragma.media.

Pragmatic Bookshelf, The *Imprint of* **Pragmatic Programmers, LLC, The**

Pragmatic Programmers, LLC, The, *(978-0-9745140; 978-0-9766940; 978-0-9776166; 978-0-9787392; 978-1-934356; 978-1-937785; 978-1-941222; 978-1-68050; 979-8-88865)* 9650 Strickland Rd., Suite 103, No. 255, Raleigh, NC 27615 USA; 2831 El Dorado Pkwy., No. 103-381, Frisco, TX 75033 Toll Free Fax: 800-699-7764; *Imprints:* Pragmatic Bookshelf, The (Pragmatic Bkshelf)
E-mail: andy@pragprog.com
Web site: http://www.pragmaticprogrammer.com
Dist(s): **Ingram Publisher Services**
O'Reilly Media, Inc.

Prairie Arts, Inc., *(978-0-9725382)* 3100 Birch Bark Ln., Oklahoma City, OK 73120 USA Tel 405-755-5432; 405-728-1350; Fax: 405-728-9813
E-mail: dgordonart@aol.com.

Prairie Heart Publishing, *(978-0-9793668)* 8967 W. Driftwood Dr., Coeur d'Alene, ID 83814 USA Tel 208-777-8079 (phone/fax)
E-mail: aprairieheart@earthlink.net; sdianewood@earthlink.net
Web site: http://www.prairievirtuedolls.com.

Prairie Hills Publishing, *(978-0-9821084)* 1101 4th St. NW, Watertown, SD 57201 USA
Web site: http://www.prairiehillspublishing.com.

Prairie Moon Pubs., *(978-0-9994765)* P.O. Box 779, Nevada, MO 64772 USA Tel 678-777-2584
E-mail: marilyn.kmay@yahoo.com
Web site: www.PrairieMoonPublishers.com.

Prairie Shore Creative, Inc., *(978-0-9740542)* 2500 S. Corbett, Chicago, IL 60608 USA
E-mail: PSCreative@AOL.come
Web site: http://www.Prairieshorecreative.com.

Prairie Winds Publishing, *(978-0-9778240)* 15154 W. 231st St., Spring Hill, KS 66083 USA Tel 913-592-5002
E-mail: cyndi@gertrudemccluck.com
Web site: http://www.gertrudemccluck.com.

Prairieland Pr., *(978-0-9759829; 978-1-944132)* P.O. Box 2404, Fremont, NE 68026-2404 USA Tel 402-721-0241
E-mail: nlsharpwriter@gmail.com
Web site: http://www.prairielandpress.com; http://writesharp.com.

Praising Pages Publishing, *(978-0-578-69214-2)* 20 Highland Ave., Pompton Plains, NJ 07444 USA Tel 973-641-1941
E-mail: praisingpagespublishing@gmail.com.

Prakash Bk. Depot (IND) *(978-81-7234; 978-81-7977; 978-81-85897) Dist. by* **IPG Chicago.**

Pranayama Institute, Inc., The, *(978-0-9724450)* Orders Addr.: P.O. Box 40731, Albuquerque, NM 87196 USA Tel 706-889-5035 (phone/fax); Fax: 505-212-0097
E-mail: ssaranam@pranayama.org; publicity@pranayama.org
Web site: http://www.pranayama.org; http://www.godwithoutreligion.com.

Prancing Pony, The, *(978-0-9763555)* Orders Addr.: 104802 W. Foisy Rd., Prosser, WA 99350 USA
Web site: http://www.herbleonhard.com.

Pransky & Assocs., *(978-0-9988742)* 210 Morris St., La Conner, WA 98257 USA Tel 360-466-5200
E-mail: mail@pranskyandassociates.com
Web site: www.pranskyandassociates.com.

Prasana Pr., *(978-0-9765352; 978-0-9973591; 979-8-218-19251-8)* 105 S. Arnaz Ave., Ojai, CA 93023 USA Tel 805-646-7601 (phone/fax)
E-mail: catherinejones@wayofstory.com
Web site: http://www.wayofstory.com.

Prater, Maurice *See* **Divine Providence Pr.**

Prather, Anastasia, *(978-0-692-09851-6)* 1916 S 2nd St., SPRINGFIELD, IL 62704 USA Tel 217-720-6974
E-mail: dalek0802@gmail.com
Dist(s): **Ingram Content Group.**

Pratt Ctr. The, *(978-0-9772835)* Orders Addr.: Four Main St., Suite 210, Los Altos, CA 94022 USA Tel 650-949-2997; Fax: 650-949-2442
E-mail: prattcenter@covad.net.

Pratt, Deidre, *(978-0-692-32929-0; 978-0-692-17793-8; 978-0-578-54435-9; 978-0-578-72253-5; 978-0-578-28940-3)* 3120 Arbor Oaks Dr., Snellville, GA 30039 USA Tel 404-751-7442
E-mail: myworthministries@gmail.com.

Praxis Pr., Inc., *(978-0-9754305; 978-1-934278)* 1515 Skelton Rd.5-100, Gainesville, GA 30504 USA Tel 770-846-5978
Web site: http://www.praxispress.com.

Prayer Bk. Pr., Inc., *(978-0-87677)* Subs. of Media Judaica, Inc., Orders Addr.: 1363 Fairfield Ave., Bridgeport, CT 06605 USA (SAN 207-0022) Tel 203-384-2284; Edit Addr.: 304 E. 49th St., New York, NY 10017 USA (SAN 282-1788) Tel 212-319-6666.

PRAZZ Pubns., *(978-0-9776356)* Orders Addr.: P.O. Box 636, Upper Marlboro, MD 20773-0636 USA (SAN 257-8212); Edit Addr.: 8419 Thornberry Dr., West Upper Marlboro, MD 20772 USA
E-mail: ycsmallwood@yahoo.com.

Preadtend Publishing, *(978-0-9890174)* 219 Bullfants Blvd., Williamsburg, VA 23188 USA Tel 757-293-8408
E-mail: kendra@pREADtend.com.

Precept, *(978-1-888655; 978-1-934884; 978-1-62119; 978-1-63687)* Orders Addr.: P.O. Box 182218, Chattanooga, TN 37422 USA Tel 423-892-6814; Fax: 423-894-2449; Toll Free: 800-763-8280; Edit Addr.: 7324 Noah Reid Rd., Chattanooga, TN 37421 USA
E-mail: info@precept.org; psimmons@precept.org
Web site: http://www.precept.org.

Precept Ministries *See* **Precept**

Preciado, Evelina, *(978-1-7357306)* 1345 NW 98TH CT (STE2), Miami, FL 33172-2780 USA Tel 703-732-6298
E-mail: evelinapreciado@gmail.com.

Precious Little Bks., *(978-0-9787235)* 9353 SE. Yardarm Terr., Hobe Sound, FL 33455-3214 USA (SAN 851-3813) Tel 561-307-2367; Fax: 772-545-4944
E-mail: clarke@preciouslittlebooks.com
Web site: http://www.preciouslittlebooks.com.

Precious Moments, Inc., *(978-0-9817159; 978-0-9819885; 978-0-9825809)* 2850 W. Golf Rd., Suite 250, Rolling Meadows, IL 60008 USA (SAN 856-3403)
Web site: http://www.preciousmoments.com
Dist(s): **Midpoint Trade Bks., Inc.**

Precioustymes Entertainment, LLC, *(978-0-9729325; 978-0-9776507)* 229 Governors Pl., No. 138, Bear, DE 19701 USA Tel 302-294-6980 (office line); Fax: 302-294-6980
E-mail: PrecioustymesEnt@aol.com
Web site: http://www.precioustymes.com; http://www.platinumteen.org
Dist(s): **A & B Distributors & Pubs. Group**
Afrikan World Bk. Distributor.

Precision Cad/Cam Systems, Inc., *(978-0-9707464)* 9564 Deereco Rd., Luthvie Timon, MD 21093-2119 USA
E-mail: info@cadcam4u.com
Web site: http://www.cadcam4u.com.

Precocious Publishing *See* **Einstein Underground Pr.**

Precocity Pr., *(978-0-9987963; 978-0-692-18056-3; 978-1-7352921; 978-1-7362174; 978-1-7373539; 978-1-7377235; 979-8-9851494; 979-8-9873501; 979-8-9877766; 979-8-9892043)* 612 Santa Clara Ave, Venice, CA 90291 USA Tel 310-392-5382
E-mail: sunnedae@gmail.com.

Preferred Enterprises, *(978-1-885143)* P.O. Box 848, Lakewood, NJ 08701-0848 USA.

Preferred Marketing *See* **American Historical Pr.**

Prefinity Publishing, LLC, *(978-0-9991739)* 226 Corsair Ave., Lauderdale By the Sea, FL 33308 USA Tel 954-647-3554
E-mail: leverard@prefinitypublishing.com
Web site: www.prefinitypublishing.com.

PremaNations Publishing, *(978-1-892176)* Div. of PremaNations, Inc., P.O. Box 321447, Cocoa Beach, FL 32932-1447 USA (SAN 299-5808) Tel 310-417-9195; Fax: 407-784-5372; Toll Free Fax: 877-372-4660; Toll Free: 877-372-4664
E-mail: Paradigm@PremaNations.com
Web site: http://www.PremaNations.com
Dist(s): **New Leaf Distributing Co., Inc.**
Quality Bks., Inc.

Prematurely Yours, *(978-0-9614786)* Orders Addr.: P.O. Box 9141, Chesapeake, VA 23321 USA (SAN 692-9907) Tel 757-483-9879; Fax: 757-484-8267; Toll Free: 800-767-0023
E-mail: kbryant@prematurelyyours.com
Web site: http://www.prematurelyyours.com.

Premier Schl. Agendas, *(978-1-884272; 978-1-59923; 978-1-63080)* 400 Sequoia Dr., Ste. 200, Bellingham, WA 98226 USA Tel 360-734-1153; Fax: 360-734-3014; Toll Free Fax: 800-880-3287; Toll Free: 800-447-2034
E-mail: ruth.richardson@schoolspecialty.com; nancy.fosberg@schoolspecialty.com; arielle.bons@schoolspecialty.com; whitney.ochs@schoolspecialty.com
Web site: http://www.premier.us.

Premiere *Imprint of* **FastPrncil, Inc.**

Preminger, Tanya, *(978-0-692-13441-2; 978-0-578-46358-2; 978-0-578-48039-8; 978-0-578-30808-1; 979-8-218-28145-8; 979-8-218-28146-5)* 8391 Beverly Blvd No. 419 C/O Tomer Grassiany, Los Angeles, CA 90048 USA Tel 054-630-9273
E-mail: tanyapr@gmail.com
Web site: sean-wants-to-be-messi.com.

Premio Publishing & Gozo Bks., LLC, *(978-0-9776065; 978-0-615-43691-3; 978-0-615-44230-3; 978-0-615-44305-8; 978-0-615-49278-0; 978-0-9853988; 978-0-615-68823-7; 978-0-615-68824-4; 978-0-615-69229-6; 978-0-615-85615-5; 978-0-615-85616-2; 978-0-615-85617-9; 978-0-615-87686-3; 978-0-692-22096-2; 978-0-692-22097-9; 978-0-692-22098-6; 978-0-692-22099-3; 978-0-692-40797-4; 978-0-692-42677-7; 978-0-692-43639-4; 978-0-692-64859-9; 978-1-7320696; 978-1-951599) Div. of Premio Publishing, 648 W. Wasatch St., Midvale, UT 84047 USA Tel 801-953-3793; Imprints:* Gozo Books (Gozo Bks)
E-mail: karl@premiobooks.com; karlbx@gmail.com
Web site: https://Premiobooks.com; https://gozobooks.com; https://twitter.com/PremioBooks; https://premiopublishing.com; https://twitter.com/karlbeckstrand; https://karlbeckstrand.com
Dist(s): **Baker & Taylor Publisher Services (BTPS)**
Brodart Co.
CreateSpace Independent Publishing Platform
Follett School Solutions
Ingram Bk. Co.
Smashwords.

Premium Pr. America, *(978-0-9637733; 978-1-887654; 978-1-933725)* Div. of Schnitzer Communications, Inc., Orders Addr.: P.O. Box 159015, Nashville, TN 37215-9015 USA Tel 615-256-8484; Fax: 615-256-8524; Toll Free: 800-891-7323; Edit Addr.: 2606 Eugenia Ave., Suite C, Nashville, TN 37211-2177 USA
E-mail: bbsgcs@aol.com
Web site: http://www.premiumpress.com
Dist(s): **Send The Light Distribution LLC.**

Prentice Hall *Imprint of* **Prentice Hall PTR**

Prentice Hall *Imprint of* **Savvas Learning Co.**

Prentice Hall Bks., *(978-0-13)* Orders Addr.: 200 Old Tappan Rd., Old Tappan, NJ 07675 USA Toll Free Fax: 800-445-6991; 800-835-5327; Toll Free: 800-223-1360; 800-282-0693 (Single-Copy Phone Orders)
Web site: http://www.prenhall.com
Dist(s): **Langenscheidt Publishing Group.**

Prentice Hall General Reference & Travel *See* **Prentice Hall Bks.**

Prentice Hall Pr. *Imprint of* **Penguin Publishing Group**

Prentice Hall Pr., *(978-0-13; 978-0-7352)* Orders Addr.: 200 Old Tappan Rd., Old Tappan, NJ 07675 USA; Edit Addr.: 240 Frisch Ct., Paramus, NJ 07652 USA Tel 201-909-6200; Fax: 201-909-6360; Toll Free: 800-288-4745; 800-223-2336 (customer service); a/o Prentice Hall Direct, P.O. Box 11075, Des Moines, IA 50336 USA Tel 515-284-6719; Toll Free: 800-947-7700
E-mail: pearsoned@eds.com
Web site: http://www.phdirect.com
Dist(s): **Penguin Random Hse. Distribution**
Pearson Education
Penguin Random Hse. LLC
Penguin Publishing Group
ebrary, Inc.

†Prentice Hall PTR, *(978-0-13; 978-0-201; 978-0-672)* Div. of Pearson Technology Group, Orders Addr.: 200 Old Tappan Rd., Old Tappan, NJ 07675 USA Fax: 416-447-2819 (orders - Canada); Toll Free Fax: 800-835-5327 (individual single copy orders - US); 800-445-6991 (government orders); Toll Free: 800-282-0693 (individual single copy orders - US); 800-922-0579 (government orders); 800-567-3800 (orders - Canada); Edit Addr.: 405 Murray Hill Pkwy., E Rutherford, NJ 07073-2136 USA; *Imprints:* Prentice Hall (Prentice Hall)
Web site: http://www.phptr.com/
Dist(s): **Cambridge Bk. Co.**
Continental Bk. Co., Inc.
Ebsco Publishing
IFSTA
MyiLibrary
Pearson Education
Pearson Technology Group
Rittenhouse Bk. Distributors
Trans-Atlantic Pubns., Inc.; *CIP.*

Prentice Hall (Schl. Div.), *(978-0-13)* Div. of Pearson Education, Orders Addr.: P.O. Box 2500, Lebanon, IN 46052-3009 USA Toll Free: 800-848-9500; P.O. Box 2649, Columbus, OH 43216-2649; Edit Addr.: 160 Gould St. (Northeast Region), Needham Heights, MA 02194-2310 USA Tel 617-455-1300; 8445 Freeport Pkwy., Suite 400 (South Central Region), Irving, TX 75063 Tel 214-915-4255
Web site: http://www.phschool.com/
Dist(s): **Pearson Education.**

Prentice-Hall *See* **Prentice Hall PTR**

Prepare For Rain Pr., *(978-0-9889537)*
E-mail: Joel@PrepareForRain.com.

Presbeau Publishing, Inc., *(978-0-9831380; 978-1-7357496)* 43238 London Dr., Parker, CO 80138 USA
E-mail: carmens222@comcast.net
Web site: www.presbeaupublishing.com.

Presbyterian & Reformed Publishing Company *See* **P & R Publishing**

Presbyterian Publishing Corporation *See* **Curriculum Publishing, Presbyterian Church (U. S. A.)**

Preschool Prep Co., *(978-0-9767008; 978-0-9770215; 978-0-9801717; 978-0-9820331; 978-1-935610; 979-8-88721)* P.O. Box 1159, Danville, CA 94526 USA Tel 925-743-1400; Fax: 925-886-4843; Toll Free: 866-451-5600
Web site: http://www.preschoolprepco.com
Dist(s): **Follett School Solutions.**

Presence Publishing, *(978-0-9729676)* Orders Addr.: 25909 Plantation Ave., Denham Springs, LA 70726 USA
E-mail: presencepub@bellsouth.net; sharonelliott@bellsouth.net
Dist(s): **Baker & Taylor Publisher Services (BTPS).**

Preserving Memories, *(978-0-9742576; 978-0-9817835; 979-8-9881476)* 5809 Stonebridge Ln., Waxhaw, NC 28173 USA
Web site: http://www.preservememories.net.

Presidential Publishing, *(978-0-9729095)* Orders Addr.: P.O. Box 221834, Sacramento, CA 95822 USA (SAN 255-1977) Tel 916-447-2460
E-mail: contactus@presidentialcookies.com; contactus@presidentialpublishing.com
Web site: http://www.presidentialcookies.com; http://www.presidentialpublishing.com
Dist(s): **Baker & Taylor Publisher Services (BTPS).**

Presley, Loren John, *(978-0-615-18136-3; 978-0-615-18404-3; 978-0-615-26213-0)* 12808 Valentino Ave., Bakersfield, CA 93312 USA
E-mail: whitecrowpresley@bak.rr.com
Dist(s): **Lulu Pr., Inc.**

Press Americana, *(978-0-9789041; 978-0-9829558; 978-0-9967779; 978-1-7353601)* 7095 Hollywood Blvd, 1240, Hollywood, CA 90028-8903 USA (SAN 851-9013) Tel 747-333-9144
E-mail: editor@americanpopularculture.com
Web site: http://www.americanpopularculture.com.

Pr. & Brand Productions, *(978-0-615-25883-6)* 2515 34th St., No. 6, New York, NY 11103 USA Tel 718-267-8771
Dist(s): **Lulu Pr., Inc.**

Press Box Bks. *Imprint of* **Wheatmark, Inc.**

Pr. Brush, *(978-1-7337601)* 5459 Jasmine Spur, Bulverde, TX 78163 USA Tel 805-698-9311
E-mail: tim@teruo.com
Web site: moonlanternstudios.com.

Press North America, *(978-0-938271)* P.O. Box 105, Gustavus, AK 99826 USA (SAN 659-8285) Tel 907-697-2303 (phone/fax, press start); Fax: 907-697-2760.

Press of the Camp Pope Bookshop *See* **Camp Pope Publishing**

Press Release Group Corp., *(978-0-9764633)* Orders Addr.: P.O. Box 651, New York, NY 10276 USA
E-mail: info@prgroup.info
Web site: http://www.prgroup.info.

Pr. Room Editions LLC, *(978-1-62143; 978-1-63494)* 1686 Cliff Rd. E., Burnsville, MN 55337-1300 USA Tel 952-746-7867; Fax: 952-746-4287
E-mail: btemple@reditorial.com
Dist(s): **Amicus Learning**
North Star Editions
RiverStream Publishing.

Presses Pocket (FRA) *(978-2-266) Dist. by* **Distribks Inc.**

Pr.Ville, *(978-1-63996)* 2650 Tulare St, Fresno, CA, United States, Fresno, CA 93721 USA Tel 074-696-6383
E-mail: madalinaevlad@gmail.com.

Prestel Publishing, *(978-3-7913)* Orders Addr.: c/o VNU, 575 Prospect St., Lakewood, NJ 08701 USA Tel 732-363-5679; Fax: 732-363-0338; Toll Free Fax: 877-227-6564; Toll Free: 888-463-6110; Edit Addr.: 900 Broadway, Suite 603, New York, NY 10003 USA Tel 212-995-2720; Fax: 212-995-2733
E-mail: sales@prestel-usa.com
Web site: http://www.prestel.com; http://www.die-gestalten.de; http://www.scalo.com
Dist(s): **Children's Plus, Inc.**
VNU.

Prestel Verlag GmbH & Co KG. (DEU) *(978-3-7913) Dist. by* **Peng Rand Hse.**

Preston, Matt LLC, *(978-1-7337215)* 15474 Nelsons Walk Ct., North Fort Myers, FL 33917 USA Tel 206-948-0207
E-mail: violet544@outlook.com
Web site: paulshadingerauthor.com.

Preston Publishing, *(978-0-9964464; 978-1-7345879; 978-1-7353855)* 4822 S. 133rd St., Omaha, NE 68137 USA Tel 402-884-5995
E-mail: preston@conciergemarketing.com.

Preston-Speed Pubns., *(978-1-887159; 978-1-931587)* 51 Ridge Rd., Mill Hall, PA 17751 USA Tel 570-726-7844; Fax: 570-726-3547
E-mail: doug@prestonspeed.com
Web site: http://www.prestonspeed.com.

Prestwick Hse., Inc., *(978-1-58049; 978-1-60389; 978-1-60843; 978-1-935464; 978-1-935465; 978-1-935466; 978-1-935467; 978-1-935468; 978-0-9823095; 978-0-9823096; 978-0-9823097; 978-0-692-00136-3; 978-0-692-00137-0; 978-1-62019)* Orders Addr.: P.O. Box 658, Clayton, DE 19938 USA Fax: 302-734-0549; Toll Free: 800-932-4593; Edit Addr.: 58 Artisan Dr., Smyrna, DE 19977 USA (SAN 154-5523) Tel 800-983-4593; Fax: 302-659-2792
E-mail: info@prestwickhouse.com; keith@prestwickhouse.com
Web site: http://www.prestwickhouse.com.

Pretty Cool Bks., *(978-1-7328341)* 3725 Courtois St., Saint Louis, MO 63123-7712 USA Tel 314-631-0320
E-mail: paulkell4842@att.net
Web site: prettycoolbooks.com.

retty Paper Pr., (*978-0-9746315; 978-0-9858814*) 14 Everett St., East Orange, NJ 07017 USA
E-mail: moody4u@verizon.net
Web site: http://www.moodyholiday.com.

retty Please Pr., Inc., (*978-0-9759378*) 105 E. 29th St., 6th Flr., New York, NY 10016 USA.

revail Publishing Group, (*978-1-7343683*) 12227 Glendale Pk., San Antonio, TX 78254 USA Tel 210-778-8077
E-mail: baseemgregg@gmail.com.

Prevention Through Puppetry, Inc., (*978-0-9768827*) 468 Boyle Rd., Port Jefferson Station, NY 11776 USA Tel 631-476-3099; Fax: 631-476-7680
Web site: http://www.sunshinepreventionctr.org.

PrevinPublications *See* **TortoiseBrand Bks.**

PRF Pubs., (*978-0-578-03405-8; 978-0-578-04719-5*) 221 Hopewell Amwell Rd., Hopewell, NJ 08525 USA
E-mail: s.schwinn1@verizon.net
Web site: http://www.henrythelamb.com.

PRH Canada Young Readers (CAN) *Dist. by* **Peng Rand Hse.**

PRI Publishing *See* **PRI Publishing/Perigree Publishing**

PRI Publishing/Perigree Publishing, (*978-0-9703269; 978-0-9835636; 978-0-578-19593-3*) Orders Addr.: 1646 Seascape Cir., Tarpon Springs, FL 34689 USA (SAN 253-3693) Tel 419-869-7901; 245 Philadelphia Blvd., Palm Harbor, FL 34684 Tel 419-869-7901; *Imprints:* Perigree (Perigre) Do not confuse with PRI Publishing, Tampa, FL
E-mail: proreach@aol.com
Web site: http://LowcountryRising.com.

Price, Diane Joan, (*978-0-9789637*) 10508 Courtney Cove, Las Vegas, NV 89144 USA
E-mail: dpcontact@netzero.net.

Price, Mathew Ltd., (*978-1-935021; 978-0-9844366*) 12300 Ford Rd. Ste. 455, Dallas, TX 75234-8136 USA (SAN 856-0471)
Web site: http://www.mathewprice.com.

Price Stern Sloan *Imprint of* **Penguin Publishing Group**

Price Stern Sloan *Imprint of* **Penguin Young Readers Group**

Price World Publishing *See* **Gatekeeper Pr.**

Priceless Ink Publishing Co., Inc., (*978-0-9778937*) Orders Addr.: P.O. Box 218538, Nashville, TN 37221 USA
E-mail: apricelessgiftcom@yahoo.com; audreylprice@yahoo.com
Web site: http://apricelessgift.com.

Priceless Moments Publishing, (*978-1-7340249*) 170 Dreiser Loop, Apt. 21A, Bronx, NY 10475 USA Tel 917-815-6857
E-mail: Pricelessmoments0519@gmail.com.

PricePoint+Publications, (*978-0-9661661; 978-0-9741627; 978-0-9772614; 978-0-9826838; 978-0-9838033*) P.O. Box 26, Alto, NM 88312 USA (SAN 257-067X) Tel 575-973-3277
E-mail: laura@pricepointcreative.com; laurareynoldsdesigner@gmail.com
Web site: http://www.ppcbookpublishing.com; http://www.pricepointcreative.com.

Prickly Pair Bks., (*978-0-578-14536-5; 978-0-578-21252-4; 978-0-578-22392-6; 978-0-578-23157-0*)

Prickly Pear Pr., (*978-0-9764323*) P.O. Box 69, Sahuarita, AZ 85629-0069 USA Tel 520-625-1587; Fax: 520-625-3655 Do not confuse with Prickly Pear Press in San Francisco CA, Cedar Park TX, Scottsdale AZ, Tucson AZ.
E-mail: pricklypearpress@msn.com
Web site: http://pricklypearpress.info.

Prickly Pr., (*978-1-893463*) 11695 Rosehill Rd, Overland Park, KS 66210 USA Tel 913-648-2034 (phone/fax)
E-mail: ikesmith@kc.rr.com
Web site: http://www.readwest.com/flouncesmith.thm.

Priddy Bks. *Imprint of* **St. Martin's Pr.**

Priest, Gerald L., (*978-0-9743871*) 4801 Allen Rd., Allen Park, MI 48101 USA Toll Free: 800-866-0111.

Priest Rapids Pr., (*978-0-615-85681-0; 978-0-615-92080-1; 978-0-9994629*) 16006 Rd. 28 SW, Mattawa, WA 99349 USA Tel 509-840-9846; 2059 Hudson Ave., Richland, WA 99354 Tel 509-840-9846
E-mail: michelle.priestrapidspress@gmail.com
Web site: www.michelleahansen.com
Dist(s): **CreateSpace Independent Publishing Platform.**

Priester, Jennifer, (*978-1-7320765*) 250 Middleton Ct., ORTONVILLE, MI 48462 USA Tel 810-841-0213
E-mail: Jesusjen@hotmail.com
Dist(s): **Ingram Content Group.**

Prima Games *Imprint of* **Random Hse. Information Group**

Primary Concepts, Inc., (*978-1-893791; 978-1-60184*) 1338 Seventh St., Berkeley, CA 94710 USA
E-mail: info@primaryconcepts.com
Web site: http://www.primaryconcepts.com.

Primary Concepts/Concepts to Go *See* **Primary Concepts, Inc.**

Primary Sources *See* **Kim Pearson**

Prime, (*978-0-8095; 978-0-9668968; 978-1-930997; 978-1-894815*) Div. of Wildside Press, P.O. Box 301, Holicong, PA 18928 USA
E-mail: sean@wildsidepress.com
Web site: http://www.primebooks.net
Dist(s): **Diamond Comic Distributors, Inc.**
Diamond Bk. Distributors.

Prime Bks. *Imprint of* **Prime Bks.**

Prime Bks., (*978-1-60701*) 13862 Crosstie Dr., Germantown, MD 20874 USA; *Imprints:* Prime Books (Prime Bks)
Web site: http://www.prime-books.com/
Dist(s): **Diamond Comic Distributors, Inc.**
Diamond Bk. Distributors.

Primedia eLaunch LLC, (*978-1-62209; 978-1-62890; 978-0-615-88236-9; 978-0-615-88337-3; 978-0-615-88403-5; 978-1-63173; 978-1-63315; 978-1-63443; 978-1-942526; 978-1-942573; 978-1-942574; 978-1-942748; 978-1-942749; 978-0-692-36411-6; 978-1-942844; 978-1-942845; 978-1-942846; 978-1-943090; 978-1-943091; 978-1-943092; 978-1-943093; 978-1-943274; 978-1-943275; 978-1-943276; 978-1-943277; 978-1-943278; 978-1-943279; 978-1-943280; 978-1-943281; 978-0-692-42561-9; 978-1-943842; 978-1-943843; 978-1-943844; 978-1-943845*)
E-mail: josh@primediaelaunch.com
Web site: http://www.primediaelaunch.com; https://www.isbnservices.com
Dist(s): **Academic Studies Pr.**
Amazon Digital Services Inc.
BookBaby
Chelsea Green Publishing
CreateSpace Independent Publishing Platform
Lulu Pr., Inc.
Publishers Group West (PGW)
eBookit.com.

Primordia, (*978-0-9759007*) P.O. Box 2455, Santa Barbara, CA 93120 USA (SAN 256-1018).

Primrose Hse. Publishing, (*978-0-9988440*) P.O. Box 724723, Atlanta, GA 31139 USA Tel 678-409-0320; Fax: 678-409-0320
E-mail: thevestigemovie@gmail.com
Web site: www.PrimroseHousePublishing.com.

Primrose Layne Pr., (*978-0-692-85825-7*) 494 Landsdown Cir., ROHNERT PARK, CA 94928 USA Tel 707-664-8110
E-mail: jeffwcrawford5+LVP0003479@gmail.com; jeffwcrawford5+LVP0003479@gmail.com.

Primrose Pr., (*978-0-9673171*) Orders Addr.: P.O. Box 2577, Prescott, AZ 86302 USA (SAN 299-9331) Tel 520-445-4567; Fax: 520-445-0517; Edit Addr.: 815 Bertrand Ave., Prescott, AZ 86303 USA Do not confuse with companies with the same name in Antelope, CA, Alhambra, CA, San Francisco, CA.

Primrose Presses *See* **Scarlet Primrose Pr.**

Prince Motivation, (*978-0-692-88507-9*) 1033 SW 167th ave, Pembroke Pines, FL 33027 USA Tel 954-868-8102
E-mail: 954prince@gmail.com
Web site: http://www.instagram.com/IamPaulMompremier.

Prince Zone Publishing, (*978-0-9785256; 978-1-7353648*) Div. of prince george/warzone comics, records, art etc., 2230 E. 113th St. Apt No. 236, los angeles, CA 90059 USA Tel 424-732-9673 cell phone; Fax: 323-538-7060; *Imprints:* E-z Clothin' (EzCloth)
E-mail: warzonecomicswzc@hotmail.com
Web site: http://www.warzonecomicswzc.com.

Princess Khrystle & Prince Michael, Inc., (*978-0-9772565*) Orders Addr.: P.O. Box 960176, Miami, FL 33296 USA; Edit Addr.: 14631 SW 104 Ct., Miami, FL 33176 USA
E-mail: khrystle19@aol.com
Web site: http://www.princesskhrystle.org.

Princeton Architectural Pr., (*978-0-910413; 978-0-9636372; 978-1-56898; 978-1-878271; 978-1-885232; 978-1-61689; 978-1-7972; 978-1-64896*) Div. of The McEvoy Group, 202 Warren St., Hudson, NY 12534 USA (SAN 260-1176) Tel 518-671-6100
E-mail: sales@papress.com
Web site: https://papress.com/
Dist(s): **Chronicle Bks. LLC**
Hachette Bk. Group
McEvoy Group, The
Metapress
Open Road Integrated Media, Inc.
ebrary, Inc.

Princeton Bk. Co. Pubs., (*978-0-87127; 978-0-916622*) Orders Addr.: P.O. Box 831, Hightstown, NJ 08520-0831 USA (SAN 630-1568) Tel 609-426-0602; Fax: 609-426-1344; Toll Free: 800-220-7149; 614 Rte. 130, Hightstown, NJ 08520 (SAN 244-8076); *Imprints:* Dance Horizons (Dance Horizons); Elysian Editions (Elysian Editions)
E-mail: pbc@dancehorizons.com; elysian@aosi.com
Web site: http://www.dancehorizons.com
Dist(s): **Ebsco Publishing**
Follett School Solutions
Independent Pubs. Group
MyiLibrary.

Princeton Health Pr., (*978-0-933665; 978-0-9835782; 978-1-940175*) 711 Westchester Ave., West Harrison, NY 10604-3504 USA (SAN 692-5391) Toll Free: 800-293-4969
E-mail: ksilloway@nhpamail.com
Web site: http://www.lifeskillstraining.com.

Princeton Review *Imprint of* **Random Hse. Children's Bks.**

†Princeton Univ. Pr., (*978-0-691*) Orders Addr.: California-Princeton Fulfillment Services, 1445 Lower Ferry Rd., Ewing, NJ 08618 USA Tel 800-777-4726; Fax: 800-999-1958; Edit Addr.: 41 William St., Princeton, NJ 08540 USA (SAN 202-0254) Tel 609-258-4900; Fax: 609-258-6305; 3 Market Place, Woodstock, OX20 1SY Tel (0) 1993 814501; Fax: (0) 1993 814504
E-mail: webmaster@pupress.princeton.edu
Web site: http://www.press.princeton.edu
Dist(s): **Casemate Academic**
De Gruyter, Inc.
Ebsco Publishing
Cengage Gale
ISD
JSTOR
MyiLibrary
Ingram Academic
Princeton University Press_mupo
Two Rivers Distribution
Wiley, John & Sons, Inc.
ebrary, Inc.; *CIP.*

Principle Bks. Pubs., (*978-0-9848410; 978-0-9961897; 978-0-9970069; 978-0-9970070; 978-1-7331855*) 14165 Mt. Pleasant Rd., Jacksonville, FL 32225 USA Tel 904-220-2247 (Tel/Fax)
E-mail: Logosman@aol.com
Web site: http://www.HelenJordanDavis.com.

Prindle House *See* **Prindle Hse. Publishing Co.**

Prindle House Publishing Co. *Imprint of* **Prindle Hse. Publishing Co.**

Prindle Hse. Publishing Co., (*978-0-9759527; 978-0-9819372; 978-0-9826846; 978-0-9835320; 978-0-9889080; 978-1-7333874; 979-8-9874545*) Orders Addr.: P.O. Box 18761, Jacksonville, FL 32229 USA Tel 904-710-6529; Fax: 904-751-9338; Toll Free: 866-877-4635; Edit Addr.: 62 W. 27th St., Jacksonville, FL 32206 USA; *Imprints:* Prindle House Publishing Company (PrinHsePubCo)
E-mail: twylaprindle@yahoo.com
Web site: http://www.prindlehouse.com; http://www.twylaprindle.com; www.kashkids.com.

Prinit Pr., (*978-0-932970*) 211 NW Seventh St., Richmond, IN 47374-4051 USA (SAN 212-680X) Tel 765-966-7130; Fax: 765-966-7131; Toll Free: 800-478-4885
Web site: http://www.printpress.com.

Print & Media, Westpoint, (*978-1-7361332; 978-1-956001; 978-1-957582; 978-1-959895*) 135 Sable Heights, SAN ANTONIO, TX 78258 USA Tel 929-624-6101
E-mail: westpointpminfo@gmail.com
Web site: www.westpointprintandmedia.com.

Printers Row Publishing Group, (*978-1-57145; 978-0-7944; 978-1-59223; 978-1-60710; 978-1-62686; 978-1-944991; 978-1-68412; 978-1-948991; 978-1-950146; 978-1-64588*) 9717 Pacific Heights Blvd., San Diego, CA 92121 USA; *Imprints:* Thunder Bay Press (Thunder Bay); Silver Dolphin Books (Silver Dolph); Portable Press (Portable Pr); Canterbury Classics (Canterbury Class); Studio Fun International (StudioFun Intl)
Web site: http://www.printersrowpublishinggroup.com/to-order/
Dist(s): **Children's Plus, Inc.**
Open Road Integrated Media, Inc.
Publishers Group West (PGW)
Readerlink Distribution Services, LLC
Simon & Schuster, Inc.

Printing Systems, (*978-0-9767595; 978-1-59916*) Orders Addr.: 2249 14th St SW, Akron, OH 44314-2007 USA Toll Free: 800-231-0521
E-mail: info@48HrBooks.com
Web site: http://www.48HrBooks.com.

Printmedia Bks., (*978-0-9778591; 978-0-9788447; 978-0-9790999; 978-1-934379*) Div. of The Printmedia Cos. of Southern California, 3355 E. Miraloma Ave., Bldg. 165, Anaheim, CA 92806 USA Tel 714-729-0789; Fax: 714-729-0790
E-mail: peter@printmediabooks.com; books@printmediabooks.com
Web site: http://www.printmediabooks.com.

printONDEMANDpublisher.com, (*978-0-9765725*) 325 W. Belden Ave., Chicago, IL 60614-3817 USA Tel 773-988-8619; Fax: 773-935-9967
E-mail: george@georgevalko.com
Web site: http://www.printondemandpublisher.com.

Prints By Mail, (*978-0-9740173*) 33 Jose I Garica Rd., Belen, NM 87002 USA; 33 Jose I Garcia Rd., Belen, NM 87002
E-mail: books@printsbymail.com
Web site: http://www.printsbymail.com.

Printsbury, (*978-0-9712249; 978-0-9718254; 978-0-9749202; 978-0-9786376; 978-1-7328955; 979-8-9880092*) Printsbury, 611 Lake Bridge Dr., Lake Dallas, TX 75065 USA Tel 214-228-8636
E-mail: hello@printsbury.com
Web site: http://www.printsbury.com.

Prioleau, Jivonne, (*978-0-615-25200-1; 978-0-578-00427-3; 978-0-578-08744-3*) 5701 Rafferty Ave., McClellan, CA 95652 USA
Dist(s): **Lulu Pr., Inc.**

Prioritybooks Pubns., (*978-0-9753634; 978-0-9792823; 978-0-9816483; 978-0-9819913; 978-0-9834860; 978-0-9896502*) 7 Behlmann Estates Ct., Florissant, 63034 USA (SAN 853-0130) Tel 314-741-6789 (phone/fax); 314-306-2972; Fax: 314-475-5613
E-mail: rosbeav03@yahoo.com
Web site: http://www.prioritybooks.com
Dist(s): **Brodart Co.**
Follet Higher Education Grp
Ingram Content Group
Lushena Bks.

Prism Comics, (*978-0-9759164*) 2621 E. Madison, Seattle, WA 98122-4711 USA Fax: 206-770-6137
Web site: http://www.prismcomics.org.

Prism Hse. Media, (*978-0-9748088*) Orders Addr.: 126 Quail Hollow Dr., San Jose, CA 95128 USA Tel 407-461-4999
E-mail: paulpelley@gmail.com
Dist(s): **Review & Herald Publishing Assn.**

Pristine Pubs., Inc., (*978-0-9716633*) 18 Buckthorn Cove, Jackson, TN 38305 USA (SAN 254-2420) Tel 731-660-3333 Toll Free: 866-565-3311
E-mail: Kathy@pristinepublishers.com
Web site: http://www.readysetgofitness.com; http://www.questforasdin.com; http://www.pristinepublishers.com; http://www.gabrielsmagicornament.com.

Pristine Publishing *See* **Wise Writer Publishing**

†Pritchett & Hull Assocs., Inc., (*978-0-939838; 978-1-933638; 978-1-943234*) 3440 Oakcliff Rd., NE, Suite 110, Atlanta, GA 30340 USA (SAN 216-9258) Tel 770-451-0602; Fax: 770-454-7130; Toll Free: 800-241-4925
E-mail: phsales@p-h.com
Web site: http://www.p-h.com/; *CIP.*

Privacy Trust Group, The, (*978-0-9777457*) Div. of JR The Trust Group Inc., Orders Addr.: 240 S. Elizabeth #h1-116, ELizabeth, CO 80107 USA (SAN 850-122X) Tel 303-648-3496; Fax: 303-648-3205; Toll Free: 877-648-0119; 240 S. Elizabeth #h1-116, Elizabeth, CO 80107 Tel 303-648-3496; Fax: 303-648-3205
Web site: http://www.privacytrustgroup.com.

Privateer Pr., Inc., (*978-0-9706970; 978-1-933362; 978-1-939480; 978-1-943693*) 13434 NE 16th St. Ste. 120, Bellevue, WA 98005-2335 USA Do not confuse with Privateer Pr. in New Orleans, LA
E-mail: mw@privateerpress.com
Web site: http://www.privateerpress.com
Dist(s): **Diamond Bk. Distributors**
PSI (Publisher Services, Inc.).

Privatgaeste Verlag, (*978-0-9712545*) c/o Ute Kruedewagen, 3168 Harrison St., No. 106, Oakland, CA 94611 USA
Web site: http://www.privatgaeste.com.

Privileged Communications, LLC, (*978-0-9802302*) 844 25th St., Santa Monica, CA 90403 USA Fax: 310-828-9590
E-mail: lester310@earthlink.net
Web site: http://www.theboywhowouldntsitstill.com.

PRL Publishing, (*978-0-9743957*) 2245 E. Colorado Blvd., No. 104 PMB 243, Pasadena, CA 91107 USA Tel 626-255-1743
E-mail: info@prldesigns.com
Web site: http://www.prlpub.com.

†Pro Lingua Assocs., Inc., (*978-0-86647*) Orders Addr.: 74 Cotton Mill Hill, Suite A315, Brattleboro, VT 05301 USA (SAN 216-0579) Tel 802-257-7779; Fax: 802-257-5117; Toll Free: 800-366-4775
E-mail: info@prolinguaassociates.com; orders@prolinguaassociates.com
Web site: http://www.prolinguaassociates.com; http://www.lexicarry.com
Dist(s): **Independent Pubs. Group**; *CIP.*

Pro-Actif Communications (GBR) (*978-0-9559121; 978-1-908211*) *Dist. by* **IngramPubServ.**

Proactive Publishing, (*978-0-9767324*) 260 Gateway Dr., Suite 21-C, Bel Air, MD 21014 USA Tel 410-893-9016; Fax: 410-893-9380; *Imprints:* Kids Can (Kids Can)
Web site: http://www.proactive-solutions.net.

Probity Publishing, Ltd, (*978-1-7348834*) 541 Hawks Nest Way, Fort Collins, CO 80524 USA Tel 419-438-4962
E-mail: imebourret@yahoo.com
Web site: www.probitypublishing.org.

Process Inc U. S. *See* **Process Transition International, Inc.**

Process Transition International, Inc., (*978-0-9646008*) P.O. Box 1988, Annapolis, MD 21404 USA Tel 301-261-9921; Fax: 410-295-5037
E-mail: spi@processtransition.com
Web site: http://www.processtransition.com.

Proclaim Publishing, (*978-1-885831*) P.O. Box 415, Palmer, TX 75152-0415 USA
E-mail: jo@awake-ministries.org; mreaves872@earthlink.net.

Prodigy Kids Pr., (*978-1-7357829*) 4 Lake View Dr, Coto De Caza, CA 92679 USA Tel 949-322-0390
E-mail: naylamichelle@cox.net
Web site: https://elenasouthworth.com/.

Production 101, Inc., (*978-0-9729706; 978-0-9767765*)
E-mail: julie@smartkids101.com
Web site: http://www.smartkids101.com
Dist(s): **Big Kids Productions, Inc.**

Productivity, Incorporated *See* **Productivity Pr.**

†Productivity Pr., (*978-0-527; 978-0-915299; 978-1-56327*) Orders Addr.: 7625 Empire Dr., Florence, KY 41042-2919 USA (SAN 290-036X) Toll Free Fax: 800-248-4724; Toll Free: 800-634-7064 (orders)
Dist(s): **CRC Pr. LLC**
MyiLibrary
Taylor & Francis Group; *CIP.*

Products & Activities for Christian Education (PACE) LTD, (*978-0-9964043; 978-1-949604*) P.O. Box 1923, Youngstown, OH 44506 USA Tel 919-215-4456
E-mail: linda@abc-jesus.com
Web site: www.abc-jesus.com.

Products With A Purpose, (*978-0-9641134*) 16430 N. 34th Pl., Phoenix, AZ 85032 USA Tel 602-595-1188
E-mail: maryalice@ev1.net.

Profane Existence, (*978-0-9662035*) P.O. Box 8722, Minneapolis, MN 55408-0722 USA
E-mail: blackened@visi.com
Web site: http://www.propaneexistence.com
Dist(s): **AK Pr. Distribution.**

Professional Book Distributors, Incorporated *See* **PBD, Inc.**

Professional Education Systems, Incorporated *See* **PESI**

Professional Publishing Hse. LLC, (*978-1-881524; 978-0-9719749; 978-0-9725941; 978-0-9742811; 978-0-9753504; 978-0-9759654; 978-0-9764690; 978-0-9767678; 978-0-9771082; 978-0-9786032; 978-0-9792016; 978-0-9799308; 978-0-9815783; 978-0-9824292; 978-0-9826704; 978-0-9834444; 978-0-9853259; 978-0-9891960; 978-0-9861557; 978-0-692-79600-9; 978-0-9983089; 978-1-7328982*) *1425 W. Manchester Ave., Suite B, Los Angeles, CA 90047 USA (SAN 852-7563) Tel 323-750-3592; Fax: 323-750-2886*
Web site: http://www.professionalpublishinghouse.com.

Professional Publishing Services *See* **WayaMedia**

Professor Beaver *Imprint of* **Speedy Publishing LLC**

Professor Stork *See* **Mad Stork Publishing, LLC**

Proficient Support, (*978-0-692-42712-5; 978-0-692-52047-5; 978-0-692-64309-9; 978-0-692-78052-7; 978-0-692-86622-1; 978-0-692-17245-2; 978-0-692-19292-4; 978-0-578-41773-8; 978-0-578-47505-9; 978-0-578-58713-4; 979-8-218-03022-3; 979-8-218-18920-4*) 5467 Benttree Way, Antioch, CA 94531 USA Tel 9257279027.

Profile Bks. Ltd. (GBR) (*978-1-86197; 978-0-9536969; 978-0-9535895; 978-0-9541303; 978-1-903942; 978-0-9547913; 978-1-84668; 978-0-9551384; 978-0-9551904; 978-1-84765; 978-0-9556476; 978-1-906994; 978-1-906507; 978-0-9873178; 978-1-78125; 978-1-908990; 978-1-78816*) *Dist. by* **Consort Bk Sales.**

Profile Entertainment, Inc., (*978-0-88013; 978-0-931064; 978-0-934551*) 475 Park Ave., S., 8th Flr., New York, NY 10016 USA (SAN 212-1247) Tel 212-689-2830; Fax: 212-889-7933
E-mail: dee.erwine@starloggroup.com
Dist(s): **Kable Media Services.**

Profit Publishing, (*978-0-9773757*) 39 W. Trace Creek Dr., Spring, TX 77381 USA.

Profitable Publishing *Imprint of* **Thornton Publishing, Inc.**

Publisher Name Index

Profits Publishing, *(978-1-933817)* Orders Addr.: 1300 Boblett St., Unit A-218, Blaine, WA 98230 USA Fax: 604-944-7993; Toll Free: 866-492-6623
E-mail: bwburnham@gmail.com
Web site: http://www.profitspublishing.com
Dist(s): **Ingram Content Group**
Whitewing Pr.

Profound Impact Group, Inc., *(978-0-9760564; 978-0-9887900; 978-1-942151)* Orders Addr.: P.O. Box 506, Alpharetta, GA 30009 USA Tel 303-437-7827
Web site: http://www.profoundgroup.com; http://www.BusterBlank.com; http://www.DomTesta.com; http://www.EricSwan.com
Dist(s): **Bks. West.**

Progeny Pr., *(978-1-58609)* Div of MG Publishers Group LLC, Orders Addr.: P.O. Box 223, Eau Claire, WI 54702-0223 USA Tel 715-838-0171; Fax: 715-836-0176; Toll Free: 877-776-4369; Edit Addr.: 133 S. State St., Box 100, Fall Creek, WI 54742 USA
E-mail: progeny@progenypress.com
Web site: http://www.progenypress.com.

Progreso, Editorial, S. A. (MEX) *(978-970-641; 978-968-436) Dist. by* **Lectorum Pubns.**

Progreso Publishing Group , LLC, *(978-1-930584)* 2733 East Battlefield #283, Springfield, MO 65804 USA Tel 417-234-0084
E-mail: sanderson@progresopublishing.com
Web site: www.progresopublishing.com.

Progressive Language, Inc., *(978-0-9758759; 978-0-9899749)* 5804 Lost Dutchman Ave NE, Albuquerque, NM 87111-5901 USA
Web site: http://www.progressivelangauge.com.

Progressive Rising Phoenix Pr., LLC, *(978-0-615-68352-2; 978-0-615-68666-0; 978-0-615-68667-7; 978-0-615-69091-9; 978-0-615-70515-6; 978-0-615-74990-7; 978-0-9888568; 978-0-615-76159-6; 978-0-615-77265-3; 978-0-615-78287-4; 978-0-615-80027-1; 978-0-615-86717-5; 978-0-615-87169-1; 978-0-615-89836-0; 978-1-940834; 978-1-944277; 978-1-946329; 978-1-950560; 978-1-958640) 100 Goldmine Ct., Aledo, TX 76008 USA Tel 817-757-7143*
E-mail: contact@progressiverisingphoenix.com
Web site: www.progressiverisingphoenix.com.

Project Chaos Entertainment (PrCh Ent.), *(978-1-7326437; 978-1-7359038)* P.O. Box 374, Artesia, CA 90702 USA Tel 714-496-4699
E-mail: prch438@gmail.com.

Project Management Excellence Ctr., Inc., The, *(978-0-9726656; 978-0-9787468)* Div. of Sturgeon Publishing, P.O. Box 30291, Phoenix, AZ 85046-0291 USA Tel 623-321-8068
E-mail: info@perfectscoresoftware.com
Web site: http://www.perfectscoresoftware.com.

Project WET Foundation, *(978-1-888631; 978-0-9857384; 978-0-9903620; 978-0-9907143; 978-1-942416; 978-1-950726)* 1001 W. Oak St. Suite 210, Bozeman, MT 59715 USA Tel 406-585-2236; Fax: 406-522-0394
E-mail: kristen.read@projectwet.org; linda.hveem@projectwet.org; sandra.deyonge@projectwet.org; stephanie.kaleva@projectwet.org
Web site: http://www.projectwet.org

Projector Books Publishing *See* **Gean Penny Bks.**

Projects For Asia, *(978-0-692-98633-2; 978-0-692-98634-9)* 1009 cuervo Ct., Chesapeake, VA 23322 USA Tel 916-554-8570
E-mail: pfasia98@aol.com
Dist(s): **Ingram Content Group.**

Prologo Pubns., *(978-0-9764264)* 4109 N. O Connor Rd., Irving, TX 75062-3748 USA
E-mail: layne@msu.edu; prologo@comcast.net
Web site: http://www.prologopublications.com.

Prom Girl Publishing, Inc., *(978-0-9726917)* 808 Broadway, Penthouse C, New York, NY 10003 USA
Web site: http://www.promgirl.com.

†Prometheus Bks., Pubs., *(978-0-87975; 978-1-57392; 978-1-59102; 978-1-61592; 978-1-61614; 978-1-63388)* Orders Addr.: 59 John Glenn Dr., Amherst, NY 14228-2197 USA (SAN 202-0289) Tel 716-691-0133; Fax: 716-691-0137; Toll Free: 800-421-0351
Web site: http://www.prometheusbooks.com
Dist(s): **Casemate Academic**
MyiLibrary
National Bk. Network
Random Hse., Inc.
Rowman & Littlefield Publishers, Inc.
Simon & Schuster, Inc.; *CIP.*

Promise Pr., *(978-0-578-90580-8)* 10001 Dallas Ave., Silver Spring, MD 20901 USA Tel 970-481-8342
E-mail: davidj@sylvandale.com.

Promocion Editorial Inca S.A., PEISA (PER) *(978-9972-40; 978-9972-721) Dist. by* **Mariuccia Iaconi Bk Imports.**

Promontory Pr. (CAN) *(978-0-9866722; 978-1-927559; 978-1-987857) Dist. by* **IPG Chicago.**

Promotora de prensa internacional S.A (ESP) *(978-84-936408; 978-84-92810; 978-84-935438; 978-84-935881; 978-84-936508; 978-84-15967) Dist. by* **Consort Bk Sales.**

ProNailTech.com, *(978-0-9748796)* P.O. Box 260515, Lakewood, CO 80226 USA Tel 720-935-1761
Web site: http://www.pronailtech.com.

Pronghorn Pr., *(978-0-9714725; 978-1-932636; 978-0-9885533; 978-1-941052)* Orders Addr.: P.O. Box 707, Greybull, WY 82426 USA; Edit Addr.: 335 2nd Ave., N., Greybull, WY 82426 USA
Web site: http://www.pronghornpress.org
Dist(s): **INscribe Digital.**

Pronoun, Inc., *(978-0-9842977; 978-1-936321; 978-0-9846202; 978-1-936792; 978-1-61430; 978-1-62539; 978-1-62921; 978-1-63295; 978-1-63461; 978-1-68105; 978-1-5080; 978-1-5183; 978-1-5312; 978-1-5378; 978-1-64186; 978-1-64203)* Orders Addr.: 229 W. 43rd St. Flr. 8, New York, NY 10036 USA
E-mail: distribution@pronoun.com; alex@pronoun.com
Web site: http://www.pronoun.com.

Prop-Abilities Inc., *(978-0-9827461)* 1502 Fairway Grn, Mamaroneck, NY 10543 USA Tel 914-309-4383.

Propeller Pr., *(978-0-9678577)* P.O. Box 729, Fort Collins, CO 80522 USA (SAN 253-1704) Tel 970-482-8807; Fax: 970-493-1240
E-mail: propress@frii.com
Web site: http://www.propellerpress.com.

Prophecy Pubns., *(978-0-941241)* P.O. Box 7000, Oklahoma City, OK 73153 USA (SAN 665-5319) Tel 405-634-1234; Fax: 405-636-1054; Toll Free: 800-245-5577.

Prophecy, The *Imprint of* **Simon & Son Publishing**

Propos Bks., A, *(978-1-7334683)* 4337 Duval Dr., Jacksonville Beach, FL 32250 USA Tel 904-993-7679
E-mail: jerrychap3@aol.com.

ProPress Bks., Inc., *(978-0-9845197; 978-0-9915627; 978-0-9908641; 978-0-9969945; 978-0-9969946)* 645 Franklin Ave., Massapequa, NY 11758 USA
E-mail: gmpro07@optonline.net
Web site: http://www.ProPressBooks.net.

ProQuest Information and Learning *See* **ProQuest LLC**

ProQuest LLC, *(978-0-14; 978-0-608; 978-0-7837; 978-0-8357; 978-0-88692; 978-0-89093; 978-0-912380; 978-1-55655; 978-0-591; 978-0-9702937; 978-0-599; 978-1-931694; 978-1-59399; 978-0-496; 978-0-542; 978-1-4247; 978-0-9778091; 978-1-60205; 978-1-4345; 978-0-549; 978-1-109; 978-1-124; 978-1-267; 978-1-303; 978-1-321; 978-1-339; 978-1-369; 978-0-355; 978-0-438; 978-1-392; 978-0-578-52671-3; 978-0-578-52672-0; 978-0-578-52673-7; 978-1-7331884; 978-1-7331885; 978-0-578-52675-1; 978-1-0732; 978-1-0739; 978-1-0) 5252 N. Edgewood Dr., Suite 125, Provo, UT 84604 USA Tel 801-765-1737; 789 Eisenhower Pkwy., Ann Arbor, MI 48108 Tel 734-761-4700; Toll Free: 800-521-0600; Imprints:* CultureGrams World Edition (CultureGram Wrld)
E-mail: sales@csa.com
Web site: http://www.culturegrams.com; http://www.proquest.com/
Dist(s): **Cengage Gale.**

Prose & Concepts, *(978-1-7323275; 978-1-952820)* 5 Jeremiahs Ln., Worcester, MA 01602 USA Tel 508-756-5744
E-mail: linhnguyenng@gmail.com
Web site: www.proseandconcepts.com.

ProsePress, *(978-0-9833073; 978-0-9851889; 978-0-9886194; 978-0-9893063; 978-1-941069; 978-1-950768; 978-0-578-79970-4)* 75 Red Maple Dr., Pawleys Island, SC 29585 USA Tel 843-237-9929
E-mail: prose-cons@outlook.com
Web site: prosepress.biz.

Prospect Palo Alto Publishing, *(978-0-9891043)* 435 Tasso Street, Suite 200, Palo Alto, CA 94301 USA Tel 650-327-8800
E-mail: dschnell@prospectventures.com.

Prospect Park Bks. *Imprint of* **Turner Publishing Co.**

Prospecta Pr. *Imprint of* **Easton Studio Pr., LLC**

Prospective Pr., *(978-1-943419; 978-1-63516)* 1959 Peace Haven Rd No. 246, Winston Salem, NC 27106-4850 USA Tel 888-833-0360
E-mail: contact@prospectivepress.com
Web site: prospectivepress.com.

Prosperity & Profits Unlimited, Distribution Services, P.O. Box 416, Denver, CO 80201-0416 USA (SAN 200-4682) Tel 303-575-5676; Fax: 303-575-1187
E-mail: nonstopsuccess@gmail.com
Web site: http://www.breadpudding.net; http://www.contentprovidermedia.com; http://www.gumbomedia.com.

Prospero's Pr., *(978-0-9727315)* P.O. Box 4616, Boulder, CO 80306-4616 USA (SAN 255-0121) Tel 303-817-5622
Web site: http://www.ahouseforamouse.com.

Protar Hse., LLC, *(978-0-9720910)* 829 Ann St., East Lansing, MI 48823 USA Tel 517-974-7993
E-mail: info@protarhouse.com
Dist(s): **Partners Bk. Distributing, Inc.**

Protea Boekhuis (ZAF) *(978-1-86919; 978-1-919825) Dist. by* **Casemate Pubs.**

Protecting Our Diversity (POD), *(978-0-9727714)* P.O. Box 231598, Encinitas, CA 92023-1598 USA Tel 760-944-0852
E-mail: email@kidspod.com
Web site: http://www.kidspod.com.

Protective Hands Communications, *(978-0-9787394; 978-0-9818990; 978-0-9845161; 978-0-615-57240-6; 978-0-615-60403-9; 978-0-615-63600-9; 978-0-9857105; 978-0-9892028; 978-0-692-32229-1; 978-0-692-40426-3; 978-0-692-46613-1; 978-0-9975272; 978-1-7337496; 978-1-7349267; 978-1-7376132; 979-8-9877584) Orders Addr.: 1668 Essex Ln., Riviera Beach, FL 33404 USA Toll Free: 866-457-1203*
E-mail: info@protectivehands.com; steve@protectivehands.com
Web site: http://protectivehands.com.

Protectors of The Wood, *(978-0-692-85933-9; 978-0-692-90065-9; 978-0-692-91472-4; 978-0-692-91475-5; 978-0-578-45016-2; 978-0-578-46955-3)* 1678 8th Ave., BROOKLYN, NY 11215 USA Tel 917-531-3724
E-mail: jeffwcrawford5+LVP0003485@gmail.com; jeffwcrawford5+LVP0003485@gmail.com.

ProTeens *Imprint of* **Positive Action For Christ**

ProTips(TM) Media, *(978-0-9740600)* 810 Adair Pl., Del Rey Oaks, CA 93940 USA
E-mail: tom@rivelli.com
Web site: http://www.protipsmedia.com.

Proton Arts, *(978-0-9752647; 978-0-9905028; 978-1-945857)* 5051 Grand Beech Ct., Haymarket, VA 20169-2586 USA
E-mail: info@protonarts.com
Web site: http://www.protonarts.com.

Proud Peacock Publishing, *(978-0-9859437)* 930 Palm Ave. Apt. 136, West Hollywood, CA 90069 USA Tel 925-520-5528
E-mail: marcelino.rosas@ymail.com.

Proud 2-B Me Publishing!, *(978-0-9655726)* 3653-F Flakes Mill Rd., PMB-F188, Decatur, GA 30034 USA Tel 770-808-2301.

Prous, J. R. S.A. (ESP) *(978-84-499; 978-84-300; 978-84-401; 978-84-86973) Dist. by* **Continental Bk.**

Proverbial Girl Publishing, *(978-0-578-54481-6; 979-8-9870382)* 1720 Venture Farms Rd., Pilot Point, TX 76258 USA Tel 940-367-2567
E-mail: cscranch@gmail.com.

Providence Hse Pubs., *(978-1-57736; 978-1-881576)* 238 Seaboard Ln., Franklin, TN 37067 USA Tel 615-771-2020; Fax: 615-771-2002; Toll Free: 800-321-5692
E-mail: books@providencehouse.com
Web site: http://www.providencehouse.com.

Providence Publishing, *(978-0-9651661; 978-0-9753004; 978-0-9819222; 978-1-60934)* 9500 Tomahawk Trail, Fort Worth, TX 76244 USA; 1317 Ben Hur, Houston, TX 77055 Tel 713-480-7069 Do not confuse with companies with the same or similar name in Salt Lake City, UT, Martinez, CA
E-mail: info@providencepublishing.com; woodtee@aol.com
Web site: http://www.providencepublishing.com
Dist(s): **Gatewood Pr.**

Providence Publishing Corporation *See* **Providence Hse Pubs.**

Provine Pr., *(978-1-889883)* 832 Cerrito St., Albany, CA 94706 USA Tel 510-528-7055
E-mail: jmbartlett@sbcglobal.net.

Proving Pr. *Imprint of* **Columbus Pr.**

Provision Pr., *(978-1-957593)* PO Box 394, Cabin John, MD 20818 USA Tel 773-680-2927
E-mail: jeanette0113@yahoo.com
Web site: www.blackdiamondseries@yahoo.com.

PRPublishing, *(978-0-9712258)* 2830 N. Fifth St., Kalamazoo, MI 49009 USA Tel 616-375-5909; Fax: 616-375-7649
E-mail: freelanceediting@ameritech.net.

PRS Inc., *(978-0-9768441)* PRS Ctr. Suite 200, PO Box 852, Latrobe, PA 15650 USA Tel 724-539-7820; Fax: 724-539-1388; Toll Free: 800-338-3688
E-mail: prsinfo@prsrx.com; alexr@prsrx.com
Web site: http://www.prsrx.com.

Prudden, Suzy, *(978-0-9987597; 978-0-9992211; 978-0-9996519; 978-1-7322946; 978-1-7329566; 978-1-950326; 978-1-959964)* 464 1/2 Kelton Ave, Los Angeles, CA 90025 USA Tel 310-722-6515
E-mail: suzyprudden@gmail.comm
Web site: IttyBittyPublishing.com.

Prufrock Pr., *(978-1-882664; 978-1-59363; 978-1-61821; 978-1-64632)* Orders Addr.: P.O. Box 8813, Waco, TX 76714-8813 USA Tel 254-756-3337; Fax: 254-756-3339; Toll Free Fax: 800-240-0333; Toll Free: 800-998-2208; Edit Addr.: 6898 Woodway Dr., Woodway, TX 76712-6158 USA (SAN 851-9188); 1935 Brookdale Rd, Ste 139, Naperville, IL 60563
E-mail: info@prufrock.com
Web site: http://www.prufrock.com
Dist(s): **Children's Plus, Inc.**
Follett School Solutions
MyiLibrary
Sourcebooks, Inc.

Pruggus Publishing, *(978-0-9844037; 978-0-9900225; 978-1-7325779; 979-8-9876128)* P.O. Box 1655, Taos, NM 87571 USA.

Prytania Pr., *(978-0-9742602; 978-1-7362327)* Orders Addr.: P.O. Box 1892, Gray, LA 70359 USA Tel 225-346-8811
E-mail: ameliastreet@go.com.

Psalms for Kidz *Imprint of* **Little Sprout Publishing Hse.**

Pseudepigrapha Publishing, *(978-1-931608)* Div. of Chi Xi Stigma Publishing Co., LLC, 2113 Elmwood Ln., Pueblo, CO 81005-2724 USA Tel 719-564-3025 Do not confuse with Penny Dreadful Publishers in Jackson, MI
E-mail: hrothbeorht@hotmail.com.

PSI (Publisher Services, Inc.), 3095 Kingston Ct., Norcross, GA 30071-1231 USA Toll Free: 800-755-9653; 877-578-4774.

PSI Research *See* **L & R Publishing, LLC**

Psychedelic Otter Publishing, *(978-1-7321763)* 400 E. 10th St., Leadville, CO 80461 USA Tel 719-293-0148
E-mail: psychedelicotterpublishing@gmail.com
Web site: www.energysmagic.com.

PT Publishing, *(978-0-615-21675-1; 978-0-615-27677-9; 978-0-9839147)* P.O. Box 2668, Oak Bluffs, MA 02557 USA
Dist(s): **Lulu Pr., Inc.**

PTO Pr., *(978-0-9760187)* P.O. Box 5394, Snowmass Village, CO 81615 USA.

P2 Educational Services, Inc., *(978-1-885964)* 4915 S. 146th Cir., Omaha, NE 68137-1402 USA Tel 712-727-3772.

Puarose Publishing, *(978-1-933593)* P.O. Box 1597, Gilroy, CA 95021 USA Tel 408-846-0116
E-mail: admin@puarosepublishing.com
Web site: http://www.puarosepublishing.com.

Public Education Foundation, The, *(978-0-9788980; 978-0-9988332)* 3360 W. Sahara Ave., Suite 160, Las Vegas, NV 89102 USA Tel 702-799-1042; Fax: 702-799-5247
E-mail: dkchristensen@interact.ccsd.net
Web site: http://www.thepef.org.

Public Ink, *(978-0-9772371)* 314 Sandpiper Ct., Novato, CA 94949 USA Fax: 415-883-7669
E-mail: sdunwell@earthlink.net.

Public Square Bks., *(978-1-59497)* 307 Seventh Ave., Suite 1601, New York, NY 10001 USA (SAN 255-8149) Tel 212-604-0415; Fax: 212-604-0390; Toll Free: 800-732-3321
Web site: http://www.publicsquarebooks.com
Dist(s): **Diamond Comic Distributors, Inc.**
Diamond Bk. Distributors.

Public8tion Nation, *(978-0-692-95216-0)* 16331 Willow Bend Ave., Oklahoma City, OK 73165 USA Tel 405-922-6300
E-mail: velazquez0312@yahoo.com.

Publicaciones Citem, S.A. de C.V. (MEX) *(978-970-656; 978-968-6792; 978-968-7668) Dist. by* **Lectorum Pubns.**

Publicaciones Educativas, Inc., *(978-0-9767623; 978-0-9767624; 978-0-9779806)* Orders Addr.: P.O. Box 192337, San Juan, PR 00919-2337 USA Tel 787-250-8252; Fax: 787-274-1671; Edit Addr.: 1117 Ave. Munoz Rivera, San Juan, PR 00925 USA Do not confuse with Publicaciones Educativas, Inc. in Hato Rey, PR, Rio Piedras, PR
E-mail: peduc@coqui.net
Web site: http://www.libreriaeducativapr.com.

Publicaciones Fher, S.A. (ESP) *(978-84-243) Dist. by* **AIMS Intl.**

Publicaciones Papelandia, *(978-0-9759194; 978-0-9765805)* 843 Waukee Pass, San Antonio, TX 78260-1919 USA
E-mail: wjconaway@yahoo.com
Web site: http://www.mexicowalkingtours.com.

Publicaciones Puertorriquenas, Inc., *(978-0-929441; 978-1-881713; 978-1-881720; 978-1-932243; 978-1-933485; 978-1-934630; 978-1-935145; 978-1-935606; 978-1-62537)* Orders Addr.: P.O. Box 195064, San Juan, PR 00919-5064 USA; Edit Addr.: 46 Mayaguez St., San Juan, PR 00917-4915 USA (SAN 249-4272) Tel 787-759-9673; Fax: 787-250-6498
Web site: http://www.publicacionespr.com.

Publicaciones Urbanas, *(978-0-615-41660-1)* Garden Hills PLaza PMB 359, Carr. 19, Guaynabo, PR 00966 USA Tel 787-793-1164 (phone/fax).

Publicaciones y Ediciones Salamandra, S.A. (ESP) *(978-84-9838) Dist. by* **Spanish.**

Publicaciones y Ediciones Salamandra, S.A. (ESP) *(978-84-9838) Dist. by* **Peng Rand Hse.**

PublicAffairs, *(978-1-891620; 978-1-58648; 978-1-61039; 978-1-5417; 978-1-4789-2184-4)* A Member of Perseus Books Group, 1290 Avenue of the Americas, New York, NY 10104 USA Toll Free: 800-759-0190 (and fax)
E-mail: customer.service@hbgusa.com
Web site: http://www.hbgusa.com
Dist(s): **Blackstone Audio, Inc.**
Ebsco Publishing
Follett School Solutions
Hachette Bk. Group
MyiLibrary
ebrary, Inc.

Publication Consultants, *(978-0-9644809; 978-1-888125; 978-1-59433; 978-1-63747)* 8370 Eleusis Dr., Anchorage, AK 99502 USA Tel 907-349-2424; Fax: 907-349-2426; *Imprints:* Publishing Consultants (Pubng Consultants)
E-mail: evan@publicationconsultants.com
Web site: http://www.publicationconsultants.com
Dist(s): **INscribe Digital**
American News Company
Todd Communications
Wizard Works.

Publications International, Ltd., *(978-0-7853; 978-0-88176; 978-1-56173; 978-1-4127; 978-1-60553; 978-1-4508; 978-1-68022; 978-1-64030; 978-1-64558; 978-1-63938)* 8140 Lehigh Ave., Morton Grove, IL 60053-2627 USA (SAN 263-9823) Tel 847-676-3470; Fax: 847-676-3671; Toll Free: 800-745-9299; *Imprints:* New Seasons (New Seasons); PIL Kids (PIL Kids); Little Grasshopper Books (MYID_T_LITTLE GRASSHOPPER BKA)
E-mail: customer_service@pubint.com
Web site: http://www.pilbooks.com
Dist(s): **Penguin Publishing Group**
Send The Light Distribution LLC.

Publications Unltd, *(978-0-9767450)* Orders Addr.: 2706 Cooleemee Dr, Raleigh, NC 27608 USA; Edit Addr.: 2706 Cooleemee Dr, Raleigh, NC 27608 USA Do not confuse with Publications Unlimited in Lake Worth, FL
E-mail: cfmajors@gmail.com
Web site: http://www.publicationsunltd.com.

PublicSpeakKing, *(978-1-7322127)* 5218 Brookside dr, Madison, WI 53718 USA Tel 848-213-7871
E-mail: vnramakrishna@gmail.com
Web site: www.PublicSpeakKing.com.

Publify Consulting, *(978-1-7353705; 978-1-7359627; 978-1-7369513; 978-1-7372768; 979-8-9851566; 979-8-9854412; 979-8-218-06414-3; 979-8-218-14709-9)* 3956 Town Ctr. Blvd, Orlando, FL 32837 USA Tel 321-900-0048
E-mail: mimie@publifyconsulting.com.

Publify Consulting, *(978-0-692-56490-5; 978-0-692-88671-7; 978-0-692-92100-5; 978-0-692-06589-1; 978-1-7338857; 978-1-7343346; 978-1-7347356)* 608 Bohannon Blvd, Orlando , FL 32824 USA Tel 407-308-5948
Dist(s): **CreateSpace Independent Publishing Platform.**

Publish For Christ, Incorporated *See* **Nathaniel Max Rock**

Publish To Go Pubns., *(978-0-9669289; 978-0-9728923; 978-0-9745110)* Orders Addr.: 8812 SW Fishermans Wharf Dr., STUART, FL 34997 USA; Edit Addr.: 8812 SW Fishermans Wharf Dr., STUART, FL 34997 USA Tel 561-350-4770 (phone/fax)
E-mail: marknemcek@comcast.net.

Publish Wholesale, *(978-1-943767; 978-1-970024)* 836 S. Western Dr., Bloomington, IN 47403 USA Tel 812-323-1334
E-mail: isbn@accurance.com
Dist(s): **INscribe Digital.**

PublishAmerica, Inc., *(978-1-893162; 978-1-58851; 978-1-59129; 978-1-59286; 978-1-4137; 978-1-4241; 978-1-60441; 978-1-60474; 978-1-60563; 978-1-60610; 978-1-60672; 978-1-60703; 978-1-60813; 978-1-60836; 978-1-60749; 978-1-61546; 978-1-61582; 978-1-4489;*

978-1-4512-;1-4560; 978-1-4626; 978-1-62709; 978-1-63000; 978-1-63004; 978-1-62772; 978-1-62907; 978-1-63084) Div. of America Hse. Bk. Pubs., Orders Addr.: P.O. Box 151, Frederick, MD 21705 USA Fax: 301-631-9073; Edit Addr.: 230 E Patrick St, Frederick, MD 21701 USA; 230 E. Patrick St., Frederick, MD 21701
E-mail: pratherm@publishamerica.com; support@publishamerica.com; tina@publishamerica.com; retta@publishamerica.com; alice@publishamerica.com
Web site: http://www.publishamerica.com
Dist(s): **America Hse. Bk. Pubs.**

Published by Westview, Inc., *(978-0-9819172; 978-0-9819325; 978-1-935271; 978-1-937763; 978-1-62880; 978-0-692-95380-8; 978-0-692-10895-6)* P.O. Box 210183, Nashville, TN 37082 USA Tel 615-646-6134; Fax: 615-662-0946.

Publisher Media Services *See* **Independent Publisher Services**

Publisher Page *Imprint of* **Headline Bks., Inc.**

Publisher Plus, *(978-1-888537)* Div. of Montana Ole Store, Orders Addr.: 200 Choteau St., Sun River, MT 59483 USA Tel 406-264-5953; Fax: 406-264-5672
E-mail: rebeccahei2000@yahoo.com
Web site: http://www.montanaolestore.com.

Publishers Design Group, Inc., *(978-1-929170)* Orders Addr.: P.O. Box 37, Roseville, CA 95678 USA Tel 916-784-0500; Fax: 916-773-7421; Toll Free: 800-587-6666; Edit Addr.: 1655 Booth Rd., Roseville, CA 95747 USA; *Imprints:* PDG (PDG)
E-mail: books@publishersdesign.com; orders@publishersdesign.com; admin@publishersdesign.com; marketing@publishersdesign.com
Web site: http://www.publishersdesign.com; http://www.tearoomguide.com
Dist(s): **Quality Bks., Inc.**
Send The Light Distribution LLC.

Publishers' Graphics, L.L.C., *(978-0-9663402; 978-1-930847; 978-1-933556; 978-1-934703; 978-1-935590)* 140 Della Ct., Carol Stream, IL 60188 USA (SAN 990-0241) Toll Free: 888-404-3769
Web site: http://www.pubgraphics.com.

Publishers Group West (PGW), Div. of Ingram Content Group, Orders Addr.: 1094 Flex Dr., Jackson, TN 38301-5070 USA (SAN 631-7715) Tel 731-423-1973; Toll Free Fax: 800-351-5073; Toll Free: 800-343-4499; Edit Addr.: 387 Park Avenue South, New York, NY 10016 USA (SAN 631-760X) Tel 212-340-8100; Fax: 212-340-8195
E-mail: info@pgw.com
Web site: http://www.pgw.com/home
Dist(s): **Children's Plus, Inc.**

Publishers Place, Inc., *(978-0-9676051; 978-0-9744785; 978-0-9771978; 978-0-9840757; 978-0-9864267; 978-0-9994072; 978-0-578-96807-0)* Div. of Grace Associates, 821 4th Ave., Suite 201, Huntington, WV 25701 USA Tel 304-697-3236; Fax: 304-697-3399; *Imprints:* Mid-Atlantic Highlands Publishing (Mid Atlantic WV)
E-mail: publishersplace@gmail.com
Web site: http://www.publishersplace.org.

Publishers' Pr., *(978-0-943592)* Orders Addr.: P.O. Box 86421, Portland, OR 97286 USA (SAN 240-7558) Do not confuse with Publishers Pr., Salt Lake City, UT.

Publishers@TreeHouse, The, *(978-0-9708816)* 2658 Patapsco Rd., Finksburg, MD 21048 USA Tel 410-848-9306
E-mail: pix4u@qis.net.

Publishing Assocs., Inc., *(978-0-942683)* Subs. of Financial & Commercial Printing Services, 5020 Montcalm Dr., Atlanta, GA 30331 USA (SAN 667-2183) Tel 404-349-4678; Fax: 404-629-5533
E-mail: fcpublish@aol.com.

Publishing by the Seas *See* **Seven Seas Pr.**

Publishing Consortium, LLC, The, *(978-1-62225)* 435 State Rd. U, Urbana, MO 65767 USA Tel 308-249-4643
E-mail: guy@ny0k.com; guy@guyanthonydemarco.com
Web site: http://www.ThePublishingConsortium.com; http://www.VillainousPress.com.

Publishing Consultants *Imprint of* **Publication Consultants**

Publishing Cooperative, The *Imprint of* **Publishing Factory, The**

Publishing Designs, Inc., *(978-0-929540; 978-1-945127)* Orders Addr.: P.O. Box 3241, Huntsville, AL 35810 USA (SAN 249-6372) Tel 256-533-4301; Fax: 256-533-4302; Edit Addr.: 517 Killingsworth Cove Rd., Gurley, AL 35748 USA (SAN 249-6380) Tel 205-859-9372
E-mail: info@publishingdesigns.com
Dist(s): **Send The Light Distribution LLC**
Twentieth Century Christian Bks.

Publishing Factory, The, *(978-0-9722741)* 1836 Blake St., Suite 200, Denver, CO 80202 USA Tel 303-297-1233; Fax: 303-297-3997; *Imprints:* Publishing Cooperative, The (Publishing Coop)
E-mail: editorinchief@penclay.com.

Publishing Hse. Gelany, *(978-0-9712665; 978-0-9728301; 978-0-9747248; 978-0-9777566; 978-0-9781529; 978-0-9827833)* Orders Addr.: P.O. Box 61472, Staten Island, NY 10306 USA Tel 718-668-1375
E-mail: gelany@juno.com
Web site: http://www.zagorizontom20megsfree.com.

Publishing in Motion, *(978-1-61279)* 2502 Canada bld. No. 1, Glendale, CA 91208 USA Tel 818-547-1554
E-mail: publishinginmotion@yahoo.com
Web site: www.publishinginmotion.com.

Publishing Services @ Thomson-Shore, *(978-0-9841658; 978-1-936672; 978-1-943290; 978-1-7337427; 978-0-578-46731-3; 978-0-578-46732-0)* 7300 W. Joy Rd., Dexter, MI 48130 USA (SAN 991-028X) Tel 734-426-6248; *Imprints:* Excite Kids Press (ExciteKids); Ignition Press (IgnitionPr)
E-mail: jerryf@tshore.com
Web site: http://thomsonshore.com/publishing/
Dist(s): **Seattle Bk. Co.**

Publishing Syndicate LLC,
Dist(s): **MyiLibrary.**

Publishing Xpert, *(978-1-956630)* 201 S Orange Ave No. 1011, Orlando, FL, Orlando, FL 32801 USA Tel 786-605-0003
E-mail: dav.blake401@gmail.com
Web site: https://ghostwritingventure.com/.

PublishingWorks, *(978-0-9744803; 978-1-933002; 978-1-935557)* 151 Epping Rd., Exeter, NH 03833-4522 USA Toll Free: 800-333-9883; 151 Epping Rd., Exeter, NH 03833-4522 (SAN 850-4806) Toll Free: 800-333-9883; *Imprints:* Townsend, J. N. Publishing (JNTown); Peapod Press (PeapodPr) Do not confuse with The Publishing Works in Waldport, OR
E-mail: bookpub@worldpath.net; jeremy@publishingworks.com
Web site: http://www.publishingworks.com
Dist(s): **MyiLibrary.**

PublishNext *See* **Publishing Services @ Thomson-Shore**

Pucker Art Pubns. *Imprint of* **Pucker Gallery**

Pucker Gallery, *(978-0-9635318; 978-1-879985)* 240 Newbury St. 3rd Flr., Boston, MA 02116-2897 USA Tel 617-267-9473; Fax: 617-424-9759; *Imprints:* Pucker Art Publications (Pucker Art)
E-mail: contactus@puckergallery.com; jeanne@puckergallery.com
Web site: http://www.puckergallery.com
Dist(s): **Longleaf Services**
Syracuse Univ. Pr.
Univ. Pr. of New England
Univ. of Washington Pr.

Pucker Safrai Gallery *See* **Pucker Gallery**

Puckett Publishing, Inc., *(978-0-9764938)* P.O. Box 528, Columbia, IL 62236 USA.

Puddinhead LLC, *(978-0-615-24552-2)* 6470 Fogle Ct., Westerville, OH 43082 USA Tel 614-899-6112.

Puddle Jump Pr., Ltd., *(978-0-9726487; 979-8-9868946)*
E-mail: puddlejumppress@gmail.com; betsfeeney@gmail.com
Web site: http://www.puddlejumppress.com; www.betsyfrancofeeney.com
Dist(s): **Follett School Solutions.**

Puddledancer Pr., *(978-0-9647349; 978-1-892005; 978-1-934336; 978-1-960272)* Orders Addr.: 2240 Encinitas Blvd, Encinitas, CA 92024 USA Toll Free: 877-367-2849; Edit Addr.: 3245 Rim Rock Cir., Encinitas, CA 92024 USA
E-mail: email@puddledancer.com; neill@puddledancer.com; meiji@puddledancer.com
Web site: http://www.puddledancer.com; http://www.nonviolentcommunication.com
Dist(s): **Ebsco Publishing**
Independent Pubs. Group
MyiLibrary
ebrary, Inc.

Puddletown Publishing Group, Inc., *(978-1-61413)* 4125 SE 63rd, Portland, OR 97206 USA Tel 503-320-1242
E-mail: lachance@puddletowngroup.com
Web site: puddletowngroup.com
Dist(s): **BookBaby.**

Pueblo Magico Pr., *(978-1-7323960)* 5849 Castana Ave, Lakewood, CA 90712 USA Tel 562-673-2683
E-mail: kgpenaflorLMFT@gmail.com.

Pueblo Mgico Press *See* **Pueblo Magico Pr.**

Puentes, *(978-0-9993479; 978-1-7322780; 978-1-7333464; 978-1-7362438; 978-1-956594)* 4 Ingleside Ave., Norwalk, CT 06850 USA Tel 203-671-3165
E-mail: jadegen9@gmail.com.

Puffin *Imprint of* **Penguin Publishing Group**

Puffin *Imprint of* **Penguin Young Readers Group**

Puffin Books *Imprint of* **Penguin Young Readers Group**

Puget Sound Bks., *(978-0-9715019)* Div. of Angel Fire Pr., Orders Addr.: 14403 N. Silverado Dr., Fountain Hls, AZ 85268-3048 USA Tel 480-304-2948
E-mail: almoeblog@yahoo.com.

Pugh, Val, *(978-0-692-54429-7; 978-0-692-68624-9; 978-0-9982706)* 3536 Del Rio St., Shreveport, LA 71109 USA Tel 318-550-1272
E-mail: valerie@valpughlove.com
Web site: www.valpughlove.com.

Pulp Collector Press *See* **Adventure Hse.**

Pulpit to Page Publishing Co., *(978-0-578-44504-5; 978-0-578-56660-3)* 501 S. Washington St., Warsaw, IN 46580 USA Tel 574-527-6154
E-mail: npoe@pulpittopage.com
Dist(s): **Ingram Content Group.**

Pulte, Therese Marie, *(978-0-9746557)* 1278 Glenneyre St., Suite 39, Laguna Beach, CA 92651 USA; *Imprints:* Destination Publishers (Destin Pubs)
Web site: http://www.destinationpublishers.com.

Pump it up magazine, *(978-0-692-17690-0; 978-0-692-17691-7; 978-0-578-40007-5; 978-0-578-40008-2; 978-0-578-42490-3; 979-8-218-22930-6)* 30821 Russell Ranch Rd., Ste. 140, Westlake Village, CA 91362 USA Tel 877-841-7414
E-mail: anissa@editions-la.com
Dist(s): **Ingram Content Group.**

Pumpkin Hill Productions, *(978-0-9793602)* P.O. Box 165, Hawleyville, CT 06440 USA
E-mail: nmroddas@aol.com.

Pumpkin Patch Publishing, *(978-0-9754823)* 10911 E. Skinner Dr., Scottsdale, AZ 85262 USA.

Pumpkin Ridge Publishing, *(978-0-9754459)* P.O. Box 1668, North Plains, OR 97113-6157 USA (SAN 256-1379) Tel 503-647-5970
E-mail: prpublish@msn.com
Web site: http://www.factoryride.com.

Pumpkin Seed Pr., *(978-0-9700273)* 68335 355th Ave., Humphrey, NE 68642 USA Tel 402-923-1682; Fax: 402-923-9110; Toll Free Fax: 877-923-1682
E-mail: rjnoona@megavision.com; rjnoona@magavision.com
Web site: http://www.usedhomeschoolbooks.com/bgh.htm.

Pumpkin Seeds Pr., *(978-0-615-17159-3)* 24 Uranus Rd., Sewell, NJ 08080 USA
Dist(s): **Lulu Pr., Inc.**

Pumpkins Pansies Bunnies & Bears, *(978-0-9747367)* Orders Addr.: 19 Treevine Ct., The Woodlands, TX 77381 USA Tel 281-785-0755
E-mail: paklppbb@aol.com; tricialowenfield@gmail.com
Web site: http://www.tricialowenfielddesign.com.

Pumpkrin Press *See* **Stone Hollow Pr.**

Punch Press Publications *See* **New Growth Pr.**

Punching Pandas, *(978-0-9998235; 978-0-578-53038-3; 978-0-578-53039-0; 978-0-578-53576-0)* 218 Main St Suite 916, Kirkland, WA 98033 USA Tel 503-475-9824
E-mail: nolen@punchingpandas.com.

Punkin Pr., *(978-1-60149)* 1221 S. Sherbourne Dr., Apt. No. 5, Los Angeles, CA 90035 USA
E-mail: punkinpress@hotmail.com
Web site: http://www.punkinpress.net.

Punta Gorda Pr., *(978-1-929528)* 2760 W. Marion Ave., Punta Gorda, FL 33950 USA
E-mail: joeinnovations@gmail.com
Web site: http://www.puntagordapress.com.

Punto de Lectura *Imprint of* **Santillana USA Publishing Co., Inc.**

Puppet Rescue, *(978-0-9799958)* 711 9th St., No. 2, Santa Monica, CA 90402 USA (SAN 854-9516) Tel 310-656-7738
E-mail: darinvents@adelphia.net
Web site: http://www.puppetrescue.com.

Puppet Theater Bks. *Imprint of* **Innovative Eggz LLC**

Puppetry in Practice, *(978-0-9720183)* 1923 Haring St., Brooklyn, NY 11229-3713 USA
E-mail: tovaa@aol.com
Web site: http://www.puppetryinpractice.com.

Puppy Tale, LLC, *(978-0-9903030)* 555 S. Main St., Providence, RI 02903 USA Tel 508-789-2641
E-mail: lkelley9@msn.com
Web site: livefreelovetuggie.com.

Pups & Purrs Pr., *(978-0-9966612)* 4288 S. Alton St., Greenwood Village, CO 80111 USA Tel 303-547-8138
E-mail: sunny@sunnyweber.com
Web site: www.SunnyWeber.com.

Puptattle Pr., Inc., *(978-0-9786947)* 21813 S. Embassy Ave., Carson, CA 90810 USA
Web site: http://www.puptattle.com.

†Purdue Univ. Pr., *(978-0-911198; 978-1-55753; 978-1-61249; 978-1-62260; 978-1-62261; 978-1-62671)* Orders Addr.: P.O. Box 388, Ashland, OH 44805 USA Toll Free: 800-247-6553; Edit Addr.: 504 W. State St. Stewart Ctr. 190, West Lafayette, IN 47907-2058 USA (SAN 203-4026) Tel 765-494-2038; Fax: 765-496-2442 Do not confuse with Purdue Univ. Pubns., same address
E-mail: pupress@purdue.edu
Web site: http://www.thepress.purdue.edu/
Dist(s): **Baker & Taylor Publisher Services (BTPS)**
Ebsco Publishing
Follett School Solutions
JSTOR
Longleaf Services
MyiLibrary
Trajectory, Inc.; *CIP.*

Pure Faith Ministry *See* **Darlene Williams**

Pure Joy Pubns., *(978-0-9749578)* P.O. Box 482, Wheat Ridge, CO 80034-0482 USA
E-mail: purejoypublicatrions@comcast.net.

Pureheart UnLtd. media, *(978-1-7327547)* 875 Boynton ave, Bronx, NY 10473 USA Tel 646-260-9987
E-mail: Jphunny3@gmail.com.

PureLight Pubns., *(978-0-9787597; 978-0-615-23432-8; 978-0-9825988)* Orders Addr.: P.O. Box 720193, Dallas, TX 75372 USA Tel 214-770-0206 weekdays 9am to 5 pm
E-mail: pl.publications@yahoo.com; seaonducote@aol.com
Web site: http://www.seaonducoteproductions.com; http://www.purelightpublications.org
Dist(s): **Lulu Pr., Inc.**

Pureplay Pr., *(978-0-9714366; 978-0-9765096; 978-1-7352908)* 11353 Missouri Ave., Los Angeles, CA 90025-5553 USA (SAN 852-5404) Tel 310-479-8773; Fax: 310-473-9384
E-mail: editor@pureplaypress.com
Web site: http://www.pureplaypress.com
Dist(s): **Baker & Taylor Publisher Services (BTPS).**

pureplaypress.com *See* **Pureplay Pr.**

Purfect Promises, *(978-0-9759343)* 149 Summerhill Dr., Rockwall, TX 75032 USA Tel 972-771-9528; Fax: 972-772-5403
E-mail: purfectpromises@aol.com.

Purgatory Publishing, Inc., *(978-1-932867)* 904 Colonial Ct., Coatesville, PA 19320 USA; *Imprints:* West End Games (W End Games)
Web site: http://www.westendgames.com
Dist(s): **Century Pr.**
Diamond Distributors, Inc.

Purity Pr. Pubs., *(978-0-9728797)* P.O. Box 2896, Decatur, GA 30031 USA.

Purolove Bks., *(978-1-7364707)* P.O. Box PO Box 25207 PTY 7762, Miami, FL 33102 USA Tel 850-588-1818
E-mail: info@purolove.net
Web site: www.purolove.net/books.html.

Purple Bear Bks., Inc., *(978-1-933327)* 300 Park Ave., Suite 1700, New York, NY 10022 USA.

Purple Brick Road Pr., *(978-0-578-91933-1)* 9208 Raeford Dr., Dallas, TX 75243 USA Tel 469-866-6488
E-mail: a.pouzar.000@gmail.com.

Purple Butterfly Pr. *Imprint of* **Networlding**

Purple Butterfly Pr. *Imprint of* **WritePublishSell**

Purple Cotton Candy Arts, *(978-1-7329897; 978-1-7374406; 978-1-958753)* 5040 Jackson St. No. 86, North Highlands, CA 95660 USA Tel 916-993-8798
E-mail: chrissivilla@gmail.com.

Purple Cow Pr., *(978-0-9820983)* 14688 Denmark Ct., Apple Valley, MN 55124 USA Tel 952-322-1419
E-mail: wdwaibel@aol.com
Web site: http://www.rudyslittleworld.com.

Purple Crayon Studios, *(978-0-9706491)* 0-115 Luce, SW, Grand Rapids, MI 49055 USA Tel 616-822-3186; Toll Free Fax: 877-710-2368
E-mail: beryl@pca3d.com
Web site: http://www.mushtons.com.

Purple Finch Pr., *(978-0-9633740)* P.O. Box 758, Dewitt, NY 13214 USA Tel 315-445-8087 (phone/fax)
E-mail: Nbenson@twcny.rr.com.

Purple Flower Films, *(978-0-692-78410-5)* 1434 Blvd. Lorraine, Atlanta, GA 30311 USA Tel 404-966-2251
E-mail: robinson.dj@gmail.com.

Purple Haze Pr., *(978-0-9773200; 978-1-935183)* Orders Addr.: 2195 Malibu lake Cir., No. 1134, Naples, FL 34119 USA; Edit Addr.: 2430 Vanderbilt Beach Rd., No. 108, PMB 167, Naples, FL 34109 USA
E-mail: v@purpleV.com; p_tomasello@yahoo.com
Web site: http://www.purplehazepress.com
Dist(s): **Baker & Taylor Publisher Services (BTPS)**
ebrary, Inc.

Purple Hse. Pr., *(978-1-930900; 978-1-948959; 979-8-88818)* Orders Addr.: P.O. Box 787, Cynthiana, KY 41031 USA; Edit Addr.: 8100 US Hwy. 62 E., Cynthiana, KY 41031-6796 USA
E-mail: ray@purplehousepress.com
Web site: http://www.purplehousepress.com.

Purple Ink, Inc., *(978-0-9801002; 978-1-939119)* Orders Addr.: P.O. Box 41232, Houston, TX 77241 USA (SAN 855-1987) Tel 713-705-5530; Fax: 713-474-5529
E-mail: onediagage@purpleink.net
Web site: http://www.purpleink.net.

Purple Ink Publishing *See* **Purple Owl Publishing**

Purple Lady Productions, *(978-0-9714506)* P.O. Box 1277, Tiburon, CA 94920-4277 USA Tel 415-435-0720
E-mail: purpleladybythebay@earthlink.net.

Purple Lizard Pr. LLC, *(978-0-9762902)* Orders Addr.: P.O. Box 68883, Tucson, AZ 85737-7076 USA Tel 520-575-6660
E-mail: Julie@PurpleLizardPress.com
Web site: http://www.purplelizardpress.com.

Purple Mountain Pr., Ltd., *(978-0-916346; 978-0-935796; 978-1-930098; 978-0-578-22378-0)* Orders Addr.: P.O. Box 309, Fleischmanns, NY 12430-0309 USA (SAN 222-3716) Tel 845-254-4062; Fax: 845-254-4476; Toll Free: 800-325-2665; Edit Addr.: 1060 Main St., Fleischmanns, NY 12430 USA; 1064 Main St., Fleischmanns, NY 12430 Tel 845-254-4062; Toll Free Fax: 800-325-2665 Do not confuse with Purple Mountain Pr., Carson City, NV
E-mail: purple@catskill.net
Web site: http://www.catskill.net/purple.

Purple Owl Publishing, *(978-1-7326371; 978-1-952800)* 7 Kingman Rd, Newton, MA 02461 USA Tel 617-630-1141
E-mail: dharkins1@verizon.net.

Purple Peaks Pr., *(978-0-9971266)* Orders Addr.: 305 Ocean Meadows, Fairhaven, MA 02719 USA Tel 908-763-6397; Edit Addr.: 305 Ocean Meadows, Fairhaven, MA 02719 USA Tel 908-763-6397
E-mail: mepsteinagain@comcast.net.

Purple Penguin Publishing, *(978-0-9765473)* 3929 Hummingbird Ln., Roanoke, VA 24018 USA Tel 540-400-7220; Toll Free: 800-788-3196
E-mail: tanyapenguin@aol.com
Web site: http://www.underragingskies.tanyaadams.com.

Purple People, Inc., *(978-0-9707793)* P.O. Box 3194, Sedona, AZ 86340-3194 USA Tel 928-204-6400
E-mail: info@purplepeople.com
Web site: http://www.purplepeople.com.

Purple Pig Publishing, *(978-0-9700380; 978-1-8380523)* Orders Addr.: P.O. Box 1083, Bethel, CT 06801 USA Tel 203-797-1857; Edit Addr.: 7 Wixon Rd., Danbury, CT 06811 USA
E-mail: jshaboo@att.net.

Purple Plume Pr., *(978-0-9744923)* 5980 Peach Ave., Manteca, CA 95337 USA Tel 209-825-7602
E-mail: purpleplumepress@cs.com; purpleplumeprss@cs.com.

Purple Sage Publishing, *(978-0-9674639; 978-0-9836690)* P.O. Box 1431, Goldthwaite, TX 76844 USA Tel 830-563-5223
E-mail: karencrumley@hotmail.com
Dist(s): **BookBaby.**

Purple Toad Publishing, Inc., *(978-1-62469)* 204 S. Union St., Kennett Square, PA 19348 USA Tel 610-444-8259
E-mail: cynthia@purpletoadpublishing.com.

Purple Unicorn Pr., *(978-0-692-36341-6; 978-0-692-64540-6)* 1635 35th Ave., Seattle, WA 98122 USA Tel 206-909-8562
E-mail: kat@hopmann.org.

Purpose Publishing LLC, *(978-0-9828379; 978-0-9858266; 978-0-9903010; 978-0-692-29002-6; 978-0-692-34417-0; 978-0-692-36388-1; 978-0-692-37278-4; 978-0-9861063; 978-0-692-37292-0; 978-0-692-40519-2; 978-0-692-40694-6; 978-0-692-41809-3; 978-0-692-42942-6; 978-0-692-44440-5; 978-0-692-48067-0; 978-0-692-48131-8; 978-0-692-52811-2; 978-0-692-55730-3; 978-0-692-55755-6; 978-0-692-57347-1; 978-0-692-68532-7; 978-0-692-70090-7; 978-0-692-70520-9; 978-0-692-70817-0; 978-0-692-71002-9; 978-0-692-71427-0; 978-0-692-72346-) 1503 Main St. No. 168, Grandview, MO 64030 USA Tel 816-401-7527*
E-mail: michelle_gines@yahoo.com
Web site: www.purposepublishing.com
Dist(s): **BookBaby**
CreateSpace Independent Publishing Platform.

Purposeful Pen Publishing, *(978-0-692-04181-9; 978-1-7335789)* 1114 GA Hwy. 96 Suite C-1, No. 353 0, Kathleen, GA 31047 USA Tel 478 213-7892
E-mail: P3@awsindustries-inc.com
Dist(s): **CreateSpace Independent Publishing Platform.**

Purposely Created Publishing Group, *(978-0-615-91309-4; 978-0-615-99099-6; 978-0-692-20774-1;*

Publisher Name Index

978-0-692-23081-7; 978-0-692-29474-1; 978-0-692-29487-1; 978-0-692-29749-0; 978-0-692-32010-5; 978-0-692-34783-6; 978-0-692-35442-1; 978-1-942838; 978-1-945558; 978-1-947054; 978-0-692-92776-2; 978-0-692-92779-3; 978-0-692-92780-9; 978-1-948400; 978-1-949134; 978-0-692-19826-1; 978-1-64484; 978-0-578-87409-8) P.O. Box PO BOX 66546, Baltimore, MD 21239 USA Toll Free: 866-674-3340
E-mail: tie@publishyourgift.com
Web site: www.publishyourgift.com
Dist(s): **CreateSpace Independent Publishing Platform.**

Purpus Publishing, (*978-0-615-65777-6; 978-0-615-75871-8; 978-0-615-76330-9; 978-0-615-93055-8; 978-0-692-22125-9; 978-0-692-26721-9; 978-0-692-35472-8; 978-0-692-78583-6; 978-0-692-94556-8; 978-1-7326402*) 19824 87th Ave. SW, Vashon, WA 98070 USA Tel 206-463-2754
Dist(s): **CreateSpace Independent Publishing Platform.**

Purring Pr., (*978-1-7363577*) 142 Old Piedmont Cir., Chapel Hill, NC 27516 USA Tel 860-235-7376
E-mail: ttkawabata1@gmail.com
Web site: www.keikicomics.com.

PUSH *Imprint of* **Scholastic, Inc.**

Pushkin Children's Bks. *Imprint of* **Steerforth Pr.**

Pushkin Collection *Imprint of* **Steerforth Pr.**

Pushkin Press *Imprint of* **Steerforth Pr.**

Putnam Juvenile *Imprint of* **Penguin Publishing Group**

Putnam Productions, (*978-0-9762728*) P.O. Box 525, Buckner, MO 64016 USA Tel 816-305-6916
E-mail: toby@sagebrushexchange.com
Web site: http://www.prairielabyrinth.com; http://www.chakralabyrinth.com

Putney,, Mary Jo Inc., (*978-1-948880*) P.O. Box 243, Riderwood, MD 21139 USA Tel 410-530-0480; Fax: 410-321-5405
E-mail: mjp624@aol.com
Web site: www.maryjoputney.com.

Putschakap?n Pr., (*978-0-9978943*) 1720 Spruce St., Philadelphia, PA 19103 USA Tel 267-318-7297
E-mail: edmundweisberg@yahoo.com.

Putumayo World Music & Crafts, (*978-1-885265; 978-1-58759*) Div. of Putumayo, Inc., 324 Lafayette St., 7th Flr., New York, NY 10012 USA Tel 212-625-1400; Fax: 212-460-0095; Toll Free: 800-995-9588
E-mail: info@putumayo.com
Web site: http://www.putumayo.com
Dist(s): **Follett School Solutions**
Recorded Bks., Inc.
Rhino Entertainment Co, A Warner Music Group Co.
Rounder Kids Music Distribution.

Puumakaa Pr., (*978-0-9762387*) Orders Addr.: P.O. Box 500, Na'Alehu, HI 96772 USA; Edit Addr.: 94-6448 Mamalahoa Hwy., Na'Alehu, HI 96772 USA
E-mail: elizabeth@fastnethi.com
Web site: http://www.inka-online.com.

Puwaii International, LLC, (*978-0-9787949*) 7326 N. 61 St., Paradise Valley, AZ 85253 USA
E-mail: jerrelvanier@yahoo.com
Web site: http://www.puwaiiadventures.com.

Puzzle Piece Publishing, (*978-1-7355952*) 35 Ohia Lehua Pl, MAKAWAO, HI 96768 USA Tel 808-419-1120
E-mail: jasmine.puzzlepiecepublishing@gmail.com.

Puzzlewright *Imprint of* **Sterling Publishing Co., Inc.**

PW.Co., (*978-0-9745102*) 774 Henry St., Apt. 1E, Brooklyn, NY 11231-3153 USA
E-mail: tregeryefim@aol.com.

PWS Pubs., (*978-0-534; 978-0-87150; 978-0-87872*) 7625 Empire Dr, Florence, KY 41042-2978 USA
Dist(s): **CENGAGE Learning.**

PXL Media, LLC, (*978-0-9749322*) P.O. Box 99, LeClaire, IA 52753-0099 USA
E-mail: pxlmedia@aol.com.

Pyle, Robert Associates *See* **Avocus Publishing, Inc.**

Pyr *Imprint of* **Start Publishing LLC**

Pyramid Dancer Pubns., (*978-0-9659913*) P.O. Box 5263, Colorado Spgs, CO 80931-5263 USA
E-mail: rjb@phoenixbonsai.com
Web site: http://www.phoenixbonsai.com.

Pyramid Educational Products, Inc., (*978-1-928598*) Div of Pyramid Educational Consultants, Incorporated, 13 Garfield Way, Newark, DE 19713-3450 USA
E-mail: dbittner@pyramidproducts.com
Web site: http://www.pyramidproducts.com.

Pyramid Pubs., (*978-0-9851514; 978-0-9982014; 978-1-7351068*) 1314 Grandview Cir., Buffalo, MN 55313 USA Tel 763-390-4853
E-mail: patrickday@pyramidpublishers.com.

Pyramid Publishing, Inc., (*978-1-885920; 978-1-934008*) Orders Addr.: P.O. Box 129, Zenda, WI 53195-0129 USA Tel 414-275-3384; Fax: 414-275-3584; P.O. Box 129, Zenda, WI 53195 Do not confuse with companies with the same name in Utica, NY, Montgomery, AL
E-mail: pyramid2mail@gmail.com.

Pyrola Publishing, (*978-0-9618348*) P.O. Box 80961, Fairbanks, AK 99708 USA (SAN 667-3503) Tel 907-455-6469 (phone/fax)
E-mail: mshields@mosquitonet.com
Web site: http://www.maryshields.com.

Pysher, Brock, (*978-0-692-98452-9; 978-0-692-98453-6*) 138 Harvester Ave., Batavia, NY 14020 USA Tel 585-201-8778
E-mail: TheBrassBadger@gmail.com
Dist(s): **Ingram Content Group.**

Pyxie Moss Press *See* **Fun Fitness Publishing**

Q & A Books *See* **Paradoxical Pr., The**

Q & J Bird Pr., LLC, (*978-0-615-16566-0*) 141 Morey Pl., Greensburg, PA 15601 USA
E-mail: icanbe@qandjbirdpress.com
Web site: http://www.qandjbirdpress.com.

QEB Publishing Inc., (*978-1-59566; 978-1-60992; 978-1-68297*) Div. of QED Publishing, 6 Orchard, Ste. 100, Lake Forest, CA 92630 USA Tel 949-380-7510
Web site: http://www.qed-publishing.co.uk; http://www.quarto.com
Dist(s): **Hachette Bk. Group**
Lerner Publishing Group
Quarto Publishing Group USA
Scholastic Bk. Fairs.

QED Publishing *See* **QEB Publishing Inc.**

Quackenbush, Robert Studios, (*978-0-9612518; 978-0-9712757*) Orders Addr.: 460 E. 79th St., Suite 14E, New York, NY 10021 USA (SAN 656-0458) Tel 212-744-3822; Fax: 212-861-2761
E-mail: rqstudios@aol.com
Web site: http://www.rquackenbush.com.

Quackenworth Publishing, (*978-1-933211*) P.O. Box 4747, Culver City, CA 90230-4747 USA Tel 310-945-5634; Fax: 310-945-5709
E-mail: info@quackenworth.com
Web site: http://www.quackenworth.com.

Quad Cities' Learning, Incorporated *See* **Quad City Pr.**

Quad City Pr., (*978-0-9824448; 978-0-9863898; 978-0-692-52738-2*) 2127 3rd St., Suite B, East Moline, IL 61244-2409 USA (SAN 858-1819)
Web site: http://www.weeklywilson.com
Dist(s): **CreateSpace Independent Publishing Platform.**

QuadMama Pr., (*978-1-944701*) 538 Sinton Ave, Colorado Springs, CO 80906 USA Tel 719-391-8980
E-mail: MyBusinessTweets@outlook.com.

Quadradrillion, LLC - Publishing Division *See* **Transaltar Publishing**

Quagan, Brittany, (*978-0-578-20155-9*) P.O. Box 582, East Granby, CT 06026 USA.

Quagmire Pr., Ltd. (CAN) (*978-0-9783409; 978-1-926695*) *Dist. by* **Lone Pine.**

Quail High Bks., (*978-0-9825443*) 7120 Patriots Colony Dr., Williamsburg, VA 23188 USA.

Quail Ridge Pr., Inc., (*978-0-937552; 978-1-893062; 978-1-934193; 978-1-938879*) Orders Addr.: P.O. Box 123, Brandon, MS 39043 USA (SAN 257-8794) Tel 601-825-2063; Fax: 601-825-3091; Toll Free Fax: 800-864-1082; Toll Free: 800-343-1583
E-mail: lward@quailridge.com
Web site: http://www.quailridge.com
Dist(s): **Booklines Hawaii, Ltd.**
Gibson, Dot Pubns.
Forest Sales & Distributing Co.
Islander Group
Southwest Cookbook Distributors.

Quake *Imprint of* **Echelon Press Publishing**

Quaker Press of Friends General Conference *See* **QuakerPress**

QuakerPress, (*978-0-9620912; 978-1-888305; 978-1-937768*) Div. of Friends General Conference, 1216 Arch St., 2B, Philadelphia, PA 19107 USA (SAN 225-4484) Tel 215-561-1700; Fax: 215-561-0759; Toll Free: 800-966-4556
E-mail: publications@fgcquaker.org; bookstore@fgcquaker.org
Web site: http://www.fgcquaker.org/services/fgc-publications.

Quale Pr. LLC, (*978-0-9656161; 978-0-9700663; 978-0-9744503; 978-0-9792999; 978-1-935835; 978-1-939606*) 2 Hillcrest Rd., Niantic, CT 06357 USA Tel 860-739-9153 (phone/fax); P.O. Box 642, Niantic, CT 06357 Tel 860-739-9153
E-mail: central@quale.com
Web site: http://www.quale.com
Dist(s): **ConsuLogic Consulting Services**
SPD-Small Pr. Distribution.

Quality Nature Displays by Eddie Dunbar *See* **Insect Sciences Museum of California**

Quality of Life Publishing Co., (*978-0-9675532; 978-0-9816219; 978-0-9972612*) 6210 Shirley St., Suite 112, Naples, FL 34109-6258 USA Toll Free: 877-513-0099
Web site: http://www.qolpublishing.com
Dist(s): **Baker & Taylor Publisher Services (BTPS).**

Quality Pr., (*978-0-87389; 978-1-951058; 978-1-952236; 978-1-953079; 978-1-63694*) Div. of American Society for Quality, 600 N. Plankinton Ave., P.O. Box 3005, Milwaukee, WI 53203 USA (SAN 683-5244) Tel 414-272-8575; Fax: 414-270-8810; Toll Free: 800-248-1946
E-mail: books@asq.org; lmcanally@asq.org; ebarse@asq.org
Web site: https://asq.org/quality-press
Dist(s): **American Technical Pubs., Inc.**
Follett School Solutions.

Quality Pubs., (*978-0-9671107*) Orders Addr.: P.O. Box 691546, San Antonio, TX 78269 USA Tel 210-699-9007; Fax: 210-641-6334; Edit Addr.: 11238 Jade Green, San Antonio, TX 78249 USA Toll Free: 888-633-9898
E-mail: aroman@qualitypublishers.com
Web site: http://www.medpress.com.

Quality Publishing Inc., (*978-0-9745741; 978-0-9759309*) 1005 E. Highland Ave., Rome, GA 30161 USA Fax: 706-290-1223; Toll Free: 800-262-4404
E-mail: bbmonday@comcast.net.

Quality Time Publishing *See* **Don't Stop Publishing**

Quantalore *Imprint of* **Spatterlight Pr.**

Quantum Manifestations Publishing, (*978-0-9718099; 978-1-933505*) 1360 University Ave., W. Suite #104-192, Saint Paul, MN 55104 USA Tel 678-227-3162
E-mail: pm@quantumdatingclub.com
Web site: http://www.quantummanfestationspublishing.com.

Quantum One Publishing, (*978-0-9755681*) 1728 Spruce Ln., Linton, IN 47441 USA Tel 812-847-8708; Fax: 812-847-8712
E-mail: jdsapara@iglide.net.

Quarrier Pr., (*978-0-938985; 978-0-9646197; 978-1-891852; 978-1-942294*) 1125 Central Ave., Charleston, WV 25302 USA Tel 304-342-1848; Fax: 304-343-0594; Toll Free: 888-982-7472; *Imprints:* Mountain Memories Books (Mtn Memories Bks)
E-mail: clemmtstate@gmail.com
Web site: http://www.wvbookco.com
Dist(s): **West Virginia Book Co., The.**

Quarry Bks. *Imprint of* **Quarto Publishing Group USA**

Quarry Books *Imprint of* **Quarto Publishing Group USA**

Quarrystone Bond *See* **Club4Girls Publishing Co.**

Quarter Milestones Publishing, (*978-0-9748216*) Orders Addr.: P.O. Box 441, Milligan College, TN 37682-0441 USA Tel 423-542-0159; Fax: 423-542-9532; Edit Addr.: 1682 Powder Branch Rd., Johnson City, TN 37601-6220 USA
E-mail: qmp@preferred.com
Web site: http://www.quartermilestones.com
Dist(s): **Overmountain Pr.**

Quarto Publishing Group UK (GBR) (*978-0-7112; 978-1-85410; 978-0-948149; 978-0-906053; 978-0-946544; 978-0-906459; 978-1-84092; 978-1-85076; 978-1-84543; 978-1-84507; 978-1-84538; 978-1-84513; 978-1-84780; 978-1-78131; 978-1-78493; 978-1-84835; 978-1-78171; 978-1-910277*) *Dist. by* **HachBkGrp.**

Quarto Publishing Group USA, (*978-0-7603; 978-0-86573; 978-0-89738; 978-0-912612; 978-0-929261; 978-0-9640392; 978-1-55832; 978-1-56010; 978-1-888608; 978-1-930604; 978-1-58923; 978-1-59186; 978-1-59233; 978-1-59253; 978-1-60058; 978-1-61673; 978-1-936309; 978-1-61058; 978-1-61059; 978-1-61060; 978-1-937994; 978-1-939581; 978-1-62788; 978-1-63106; 978-1-63159; 978-1-63322; 978-1-942875) Orders Addr.: Retail Order Dept., Quayside Publishing Group 18705 Lake Dr. E., Chanhassen, MN 55317 USA Tel 1-952-936-4700; Fax: 1-952-099-9101; Toll Free: 1-800-328-0590; Edit Addr.: 3 Wrigley Suite A, Irvine, CA 92618-2748 USA (SAN 249-051X) Toll Free: 800-426-0099; Imprints:* Creative Publishing International (Creativ Pub); Quarry Books (QuarryBks); Walter Foster (WalterFoster); Walter Foster Jr (WalterFostJr); Cool Springs Press (CoolSpringsPr); Fair Winds Press (FairWindsPr); Motorbooks (Motorbooks); Zenith Press (ZenithPr); Quarry Books (QuarryBksUSA); Rock Point Gift & Stationery (RockPtGift); Voyageur Press (VoyageurUSA); Creative Publishing International (CreatPubIntl); Rockport Publishers (Rockport); Seagrass Press (Seagrass); Moondance Press (Moondance)
E-mail: rebecca.razo@quartous.com
Web site: https://www.quartoknows.com/division/Quarto-Publishing-Group-USA/
Dist(s): **Arcadia Publishing**
Hachette Bk. Group
Lerner Publishing Group
MyiLibrary
Open Road Integrated Media, Inc.

Quatemion Pr., (*978-0-9672535*) P.O. Box 700564, San Antonio, TX 78270 USA Tel 210-497-1096.

Que, (*978-0-7897; 978-0-88022; 978-1-56529*) Div. of Pearson Technology Group, 201 W. 103rd St., Indianapolis, IN 46290-1094 USA Tel 317-581-3500; Toll Free: 800-428-5331 (orders); 800-858-7674 (customer service) Do not confuse with Que Software, also a division of Macmillan Computer Publishing, same address
E-mail: customerservice@macmillanUSA.com
Web site: http://www.quepublishing.com
Dist(s): **Alpha Bks.**
Ebsco Publishing
MyiLibrary
Pearson Education
Pearson Technology Group
Sams Technical Publishing, LLC.

Quebec Amerique (CAN) (*978-2-89037; 978-2-920948; 978-0-88552; 978-2-7644*) *Dist. by* **Orca Bk Pub.**

Quebla, (*978-0-9772738*) P.O. Box 958073, Duluth, GA 30095 USA Tel 404-906-3993
E-mail: support@quebla.com
Web site: http://www.quebla.com.

Queen Adisa, (*978-0-9979672*) 1621 Nelson Rd, Weaver, AL 36277 USA Tel 205-362-5000
E-mail: adisasalim@gmail.com
Web site: www.queenadisa.com.

Queen Alexandra Foundation for Children (CAN) (*978-0-9880536*) *Dist. by* **Orca Bk Pub.**

Queen Pubns, (*978-0-9778377*) Orders Addr.: P.O. Box 496, Antioch, IL 60002 USA
E-mail: apascascio@comcast.net
Web site: http://www.queenpublications.com.

Queen V Publishing, (*978-0-9817436; 978-0-9825984; 978-0-9962991; 978-1-7358162*) Div. of Pen of the Writer, LLC, 893 S. Main St. PMB 175, Englewood, OH 45322 USA Tel 937-307-0760; Fax: 888-802-1802; Toll Free: 888-802-1802
E-mail: colemanbfp@aol.com
Web site: http://www.queenvpublishing.com; http://www.penofthewriter.com; http://www.passionatepens.com
Dist(s): **Smashwords.**

Queen V Publishing - Ohio *See* **Queen V Publishing**

Queen's Knight, (*978-0-9752810*) 8741 Saline Waterwirks Rd., Saline, MI 48176 USA.

Queens Museum of Art, (*978-0-9604514; 978-1-929641*) New York City Bldg., Flushing Meadows Park, Queens, NY 11368-3398 USA (SAN 280-2147) Tel 718-592-9700; Fax: 718-592-5778
Web site: http://www.queensmuseum.org
Dist(s): **D.A.P./Distributed Art Pubs.**
Univ. Pr. of New England.

Quercus (GBR) (*978-1-905204; 978-1-84724; 978-1-906694; 978-1-84916; 978-0-85705; 978-0-85738; 978-1-84866; 978-1-78087; 978-1-78206; 978-1-78747; 978-1-78648; 978-1-5294; 978-1-78429*) *Dist. by* **HachBkGrp.**

Quercus Pr., (*978-0-9793444*) P.O. Box 46163, Plymouth, MN 55446-0163 USA (SAN 853-1773)
Web site: http://www.windingoak.com.

Quercus Publishing, (*978-0-9827470; 978-0-9864456; 978-1-78429*) 59 Tanglewood Dr., East Falmouth, MA 02536 USA Tel 508-274-2710
E-mail: editor@readmyink.com
Web site: http://www.quercuspublishing.com
Dist(s): **Hachette Bk. Group.**

Quest Bks. *Imprint of* **Theosophical Publishing Hse.**

Questmarc Publishing, (*978-0-9634251; 978-0-9755801; 978-0-9819946; 978-1-939532*) Orders Addr.: P.O. Box 340, Yankton, SD 57078 USA Tel 605-660-0335; Fax: 605-260-6873; Edit Addr.: 811 W. 8th, Yankton, SD 57078 USA Tel 605-660-0335
E-mail: questmarc@mail.com
Web site: http://www.questmarc.com.

Quick Book Publishing *See* **FREOMM Publishing**

Quick, Kelsey, (*978-1-7330724*) 1204 S Oak Ave, Broken Arrow, OK 74012 USA Tel 918-704-4558
E-mail: kelseydquick@gmail.com.

Quick Quest Pubns. LLC, (*978-0-9760372*) Orders Addr.: P.O. Box 9934, Alexandria, VA 22306 USA Toll Free Fax: 800-682-6576; Edit Addr.: P.O. Box 9934, Alexandria, VA 22304 USA Tel 978-726-5713
E-mail: nathanialportis@yahoo.com; mnportis@yahoo.com
Web site: http://www.quickquestpub.com.

Quick Wisdom Publishers *See* **Aylen Publishing**

Quickpresspublishing Incorporated *See* **Quick Quest Pubns. LLC**

Quiet Fox Designs *Imprint of* **Fox Chapel Publishing Co., Inc.**

Quiet Impact, Inc., (*978-0-9713749; 978-0-9754629*) 140 Cherry St., No. 388, Hamilton, MT 59840 USA Tel 406-375-9378; Fax: 406-363-5234; *Imprints:* Character-in-Action (Character-in-Action)
E-mail: elhamilton@quietimpact.com; elhamilton@character-in-action.com
Web site: http://www.character-in-action.com; http://www.quietimpact.com.

Quiet Man, (*978-0-9744251*) 28 W. 44th St., Suite 2105, New York, NY 10036-6600 USA (SAN 255-7150) Tel 212-921-4444; Fax: 212-921-4504
E-mail: dawn@quietman.net
Web site: http://www.quietman.net.

Quiet Man Publishing, (*978-0-9742829*) 27542 Berkshire Hills Pl., Valencia, CA 91354 USA
E-mail: jh1429@yahoo.com
Web site: http://www.Quietmanpublishing.com.

Quiet Owl Bks., (*978-0-615-54891-3; 978-0-615-59366-1; 978-0-615-64284-0; 978-0-615-64677-0; 978-0-615-65835-3; 978-0-9859443; 978-0-615-67800-9; 978-0-9898331*) 85 E. Point Rd., Montrose, PA 18801 USA Tel 323-253-1411; 570-278-6332
E-mail: books@quietowl.com
Web site: http://quietowl.com/
Dist(s): **CreateSpace Independent Publishing Platform**
Dummy Record Do Not USE!!!!.

Quiet Storm Publishing Group, (*978-0-9714296; 978-0-9728819; 978-0-9744084; 978-0-9749608; 978-0-9758571; 978-0-9770070; 978-0-9787528*) Orders Addr.: P.O. Box 1666, Martinsburg, WV 25401 USA; Edit Addr.: 1045 Needmore Rd., Martinsburg, WV 25401 USA
E-mail: quietstormbooks@yahoo.com
Web site: http://www.quietstormpublishing.com.

Quiet Time Pr. *Imprint of* **Quiet Time Publishing**

Quiet Time Publishing *See* **Quiet Time Publishing**

Quiet Time Publishing, (*978-1-884743; 978-0-9755812; 978-0-9825090*) P.O. Box 4 Venice, Ca, Venice, CA 90294 USA Tel 310-452-2922; Fax: 310-399-9206; *Imprints:* Quiet Time Press (QuietTimePr)
E-mail: Quiettimepress@gmail.com; cgreco@earthlink.net
Web site: http://www.quiettimepress.com.

Quiet Vision Publishing, (*978-1-57646; 978-1-891595; 978-1-60545*) Orders Addr.: 12155 Mountain Shadow Rd., Sandy, UT 84092-5812 USA Tel 801-572-4018; Fax: 801-571-8625; Toll Free: 800-442-4018
E-mail: john@quietvision.com; info@quietvision.com
Web site: http://www.quietvision.com.

Quiet Waters Pubns., (*978-0-9663966; 978-1-931475; 978-1-962698*) 1318 N. Nias Ave., Springfield, MO 65802 USA
E-mail: david.trobisch@gmail.com
Web site: http://www.quietwaterspub.com.

Quigley, Karen, (*978-0-9800449*) P.O. Box 535, Blackwood, NJ 08012 USA (SAN 855-076X)
E-mail: loveelwood @comcast.net
Web site: http://www.EveryoneLovesElwood.com.

Quill & Hearth Publishing Hse., (*978-0-9984597*) 8 Hammer Ln., Rustburg, VA 24588 USA Tel 540-535-8952
E-mail: jessiebiggs@ymail.com.

Quill & Parchment Press *See* **Quill Ink & Parchment Pubns.**

Quill Driver Bks., (*978-1-884956; 978-1-61035*) 2006 S. Mary St., Fresno, CA 93721-3311 USA (SAN 298-2196) Toll Free: 800-497-4909
E-mail: info@QuillDriverBooks.com
Web site: http://www.quilldriverbooks.com
Dist(s): **American West Bks.**
Bookazine Co., Inc.
Bookpeople
Heinecken & Assoc., Ltd.
Independent Pubs. Group
Ingram Publisher Services
Libros Sin Fronteras
MyiLibrary
Partners/West Book Distributors
Quality Bks., Inc.
Unique Bks., Inc.

uill Ink & Parchment Pubns., *(978-1-7368702; 979-8-9867467)* 4692 NW 133RD St., Opa Locka, FL 33054 USA Tel 242-558-1512
E-mail: info@quillinkparchment.com
Web site: www.quillinkparchment.com.

uill Space *See* **Access Media Group**

uill Tree Bks. *Imprint of* **HarperCollins Pubs.**

uiller Publishing, Ltd. (GBR) *(978-1-904057; 978-1-84689)*
Dist. by **IPG Chicago.**

uillpen, *(978-0-9673504)* 1520 Waverly Dr., Trenton, MI 48183 USA Tel 734-676-1285; Fax: 734-676-9822
E-mail: bfquillpen@msn.com.

Quillquest Books, *(978-0-940075; 978-0-9769272)* Div. of Quilliquest Publishing Co., Orders Addr.: 388 Knights Run Dr., Heathsville, VA 22473 USA Tel 804-580-8815; 805-724-3869
E-mail: quilquestbooks@msn.com
Web site: http://www.frankmosco.com; http://www.lulu.com/quillquestbooks
Dist(s): **CreateSpace Independent Publishing Platform**
Ingram Content Group
Lulu Pr., Inc.

Quillrunner Publishing LLC, *(978-0-9796330; 978-0-9851157)* 8423 Los Reyes Ct., NW, Albuquerque, NM 87120 USA (SAN 853-9669) Tel 505-890-0723
E-mail: khickman@comcast.net
Web site: http://www.quillrunner.com.

Quilt in a Day, *(978-0-922705; 978-1-891776)* 1955 Diamond St., Unit A, San Marcos, CA 92069 USA (SAN 251-5644) Tel 760-591-0081; Fax: 760-591-4424; Toll Free: 800-777-4852
E-mail: qiad@quilt-in-a-day.com
Web site: http://www.quilt-in-a-day.com
Dist(s): **MyiLibrary**
ebrary, Inc.

Quimby & Sneet Publications *See* **405 Pubns.**

Quindaro Pr., *(978-0-9669258; 978-0-9764434; 978-1-946248)* 3808 Genessee St., Kansas City, MO 64111 USA Tel 913-565-8335
E-mail: quindaropress@gmail.com
Web site: https://www.quindaropress.com
Dist(s): **Pathway Bk. Service.**

Quindim *See* **KINJIN Global**

Quinlan Pr., *(978-0-933341; 978-0-9611268; 978-1-55770)* 1 Devonshire Pl., No. 3108, Boston, MA 02109-3515 USA (SAN 226-4641).

Quinn Entertainment, *(978-0-9773099)* 7535 Austin Harbour Dr., Cumming, GA 30041 USA (SAN 257-2575) Tel 770-356-3847; Fax: 770-886-1475
E-mail: stephaniequinn@bellsouth.net
Web site: http://www.startabusinessteachingkids.com.

Quinn Micheal Publishing, Incorporated *See* **Rhapsody Branding, Inc.**

Quinnova Pr., *(978-0-615-82605-9; 978-0-578-35332-6; 978-0-578-35333-3; 979-8-9856726)*
E-mail: chey@cheyanneyoung.com
Web site: www.cheyanneyoung.com
Dist(s): **CreateSpace Independent Publishing Platform.**

†**Quintessence Publishing Co., Inc.**, *(978-0-86715; 978-0-931386; 978-1-85097; 978-1-883695; 978-1-64724)* 4350 Chandler Dr., Hanover Park, IL 60133-6763 USA (SAN 215-9783)
E-mail: service@quintbook.com
Web site: http://www.quintpub.com
Dist(s): **Publishers Group West (PGW)**; *CIP.*

Quintessential Corp., *(978-0-9715298)* P.O. Box 9224, Mclean, VA 22102 USA Tel 703-734-4900
E-mail: info@qproductsarchery.com
Web site: http://qproductsarchery.com.

Quintessential Pr. *Imprint of* **Gatekeeper Pr.**

Quintessential Productions, *(978-1-7337067)* 808 Concord Rd., Marlborough, MA 01752 USA Tel 774-249-4976
E-mail: kathleenquinton@yahoo.com.

Quintessential Publishing Hse., *(978-1-7365605; 979-8-9877098; 978-1-962442)* 1016 Stoneykirk Rd, Pelham, AL 35124 USA Tel 205-531-1507
E-mail: tellis.deven@gmail.com.

Quirk Bks., *(978-1-931686; 978-1-59474; 978-1-68369)* 215 Church St., Philadelphia, PA 19106 USA Tel 215-627-3581; Fax: 215-627-5220
E-mail: jane@quirkbooks.com
Web site: http://www.quirkbooks.com
Dist(s): **Hachette Bk. Group**
MyiLibrary
Penguin Random Hse. Distribution
Penguin Random Hse. LLC
Random Hse., Inc.

Quirkles, The *Imprint of* **Creative 3, LLC**

Quisqueyana Pr., *(978-0-578-62770-0; 978-1-7354562; 979-8-9855858; 979-8-9879833)* 13625 Antelope Sta., Poway, CA 92064-1355 USA Tel 760-532-8442
E-mail: mariaadukealabi@gmail.com
Web site: www.quisqueyanapress.com.

†**Quite Specific Media Group, Ltd.**, *(978-0-89676)* Orders Addr.: 7373 Pyramid Pl., Hollywood, CA 90046-1312 USA (SAN 213-5752) Tel 323-851-5797; Fax: 323-851-5798; *Imprints:* Costume & Fashion Press (Costume & Fashion Pr)
E-mail: info@quitespecificmedia.com
Web site: http://www.quitespecificmedia.com; *CIP.*

Quitt & Quinn, Pubs., *(978-1-7328489; 978-1-7372600)* 4811 Tullamore Dr., Bloomfoeld Hills, MI 48304 USA Tel 248-594-6376
E-mail: wsthomson@mac.com.

Quixote Pr., *(978-1-57166; 978-1-878488)* 1854 345th Ave., Wever, IA 52658-9597 USA Tel 319-372-7480; Fax: 319-372-7485; Toll Free: 800-571-2665 Do not confuse with Quixote Pr., Houston, TX, Los Angeles, CA
E-mail: heartsnturnmies@hotmail.com
Dist(s): **Bookmen, Inc.**

Qum, *(978-1-7320292)* 2000 Ascot Pkwy, Vallejo, CA 94591 USA Tel 510-325-7548; Fax: 707-731-0493
E-mail: hfeltuscurry@gmail.com.

Quoi Happens LLC, *(978-1-7338375)* 6247 S. Locust St., Centennial, CO 80111 USA Tel 508-733-0542
E-mail: jlowryauthor@gmail.com
Web site: janelowry.com.

Quoir, *(978-0-9765222; 978-0-9827446; 978-1-938480; 978-0-9913345; 978-1-957007)* 11520 Green Ln., Oak Glen, CA 92399 USA Tel 714-403-1922
E-mail: rafael@quoir.com
Web site: www.quoir.com.

QuotationWorld Pubns., *(978-0-9741868)* 3035 Shannon Lakes Dr., N., Tallahassee, FL 32309 USA Tel 850-894-1903 (phone/fax)
E-mail: admin@quotationworld.com
Web site: http://www.quotationworld.com.

Quoth Pubns., *(978-0-692-13221-0; 978-0-692-14800-6; 978-0-578-47684-1; 978-0-578-55089-3; 978-0-578-56760-0; 978-0-578-60105-2; 978-0-578-61180-8)* 4420 Carter Rd. No. 6, Saint Augustine, FL 32086 USA Tel 904-229-7944
E-mail: jkentholloway@gmail.com.

Quotidian, Incorporated *See* **Quotidian Pubs.**

Quotidian Pubs., *(978-0-934391)* Orders Addr.: 377 River Rd., Cushing, ME 04563-9502 USA (SAN 693-8094) Tel 207-354-7091
E-mail: judydownmaine@roadrunner.com.

Quranic Educational Society, *(978-0-9760681)* Orders Addr.: P.O. Box 597969, Chicago, IL 60659 USA; Edit Addr.: 6355 N Claremont Ave., Chicago, IL 60659 USA Tel 773-743-9345
E-mail: qeschicago@sbcglobal.net
Web site: http://www.qesonline.org.

R & D Educational Center *See* **Boarding House Publishing**

R & D Publishing of Lakeland, Florida, *(978-0-9797566)* 5709 LaSerena Ave., Lakeland, FL 33809-4262 USA Tel 863-859-2984.

R & J Publishing, *(978-0-615-15136-6)* 1136 5th Ave. S., Anoka, MN 55303-2726 USA
E-mail: bobhelf.1@juno.com.

R & R Advertising, *(978-0-9765225)* 3409 Executive Ctr. Dr., No. 202, Austin, TX 78731 USA Tel 512-342-0110; Fax: 512-342-0142
E-mail: info@rradinc.com
Web site: http://www.rradinc.com.

R & R Publishing, LLC, *(978-0-9764845; 978-0-615-34449-2; 978-0-9829599; 978-0-9830577)* Div. of GlutenFree Passport, Orders Addr.: 80 Burr Ridge Pkwy. Suite 141, Burr Rudge, IL 60527 USA Tel 312-244-3702; Fax: 312-276-8001 Do not confuse with companies with the same or similar name in Torrance, CA, Brimingham, AL, Shelton, WA, San Antonio, TX, Washington, DC, Baldwin City, KS
E-mail: info@rrpublishing.com; kkoeller@glutenfreepassport.com
Web site: http://www.glutenfreepassport.com.

R & R Reflection Stories LLC, *(978-1-7371762)* 1501 Elderberry Rd, Suffolk, VA 23435 USA Tel 757-228-9859
E-mail: choricialakemyers@gmail.com
Web site: http://rreflectionstories.com.

R & S Bks. (SWE) *(978-91-29) Dist. by* **Macmillan.**

R & S Pubns., *(978-0-615-18520-0; 978-0-615-18814-0)* 6799 Durham Rd., Whitehall, MI 49461 USA
E-mail: beckywlt@charterinternet.com
Web site: http://www.rspublications.com
Dist(s): **Lulu Pr., Inc.**

RBC Publishing Co., Inc., *(978-0-9703178; 978-0-9721547)* Orders Addr.: P.O. Box 1330, Elk Grove, CA 95759 USA Tel 916-685-5578; Fax: 916-685-5958; Edit Addr.: 9107 Voos Ct., Elk Grove, CA 95624 USA; *Imprints:* Parks Publishing (Parks Publ)
E-mail: scituate@citlink.net
Web site: http://www.rbcpublishingco.com.

R.B. Media, Inc., *(978-0-9700021; 978-0-9797932)* 14064 Monterey Estates Dr., Delray Beach, FL 33446-2217 USA Tel 561-498-5922; Fax: 561-498-2369
E-mail: mabudnik@comcast.net
Web site: http://www.rbmediainc.com.

R. C. Bk. Publishing, *(978-0-615-14106-0)* 2309 Sunkist Country Club Rd., Biloxi, MS 39532 USA
E-mail: rc.publishing@yahoo.com
Web site: http://www.rcbookpublishing.com
Dist(s): **Lulu Pr., Inc.**

R. E. Farrellbooks, LLC, *(978-0-9759116; 978-0-9963587)* Orders Addr.: 18212 N. 130th Ave, Sun City West, AZ 85375-5015 USA
E-mail: ref40@msn.com
Web site: http://www.refarrellbooks.com.

REP Pubs., *(978-0-9604876)* Orders Addr.: 733 Turrentine Trail, St. Louis, MO 63141 USA (SAN 239-3786) Tel 314-434-1833
E-mail: Richard@reppublishers.com
Web site: www.reppublishers.com
Dist(s): **Unique Bks., Inc.**

R F T Publishing Company *See* **aha! Process, Inc.**

R.H. Boyd Publishing Corp., *(978-1-58942; 978-1-68167; 979-8-88635)* 6717 Centennial Blvd., Nashville, TN 37209-1049 USA Tel 615-350-8000; Fax: 615-350-9018
E-mail: dgroves@rhboyd.com; lboyd@rhboyd.com; ocloud@rhboyd.com
Web site: http://www.rhboyd.com.

R. H. Publishing, *(978-0-9772460; 978-0-9976907; 978-1-945693; 978-1-960494)* 5021 S. 30th St., Lincoln, NE 68516 USA Tel 214-605-0162
Dist(s): **Ingram Content Group.**

R. Herst Rose, *(978-0-9857934)* 5 Timber Ridge Dr., Simsbury, CT 06070 USA Tel 860-658-4767
E-mail: robin.h.rose@gmail.com.

R J Communications, LLC *See* **Not So Plain Jane Publishing**

R. M. Stone, *(978-1-7369930)* 184 Pine View Loop, Bastrop, TX 78602-9513 USA Tel 678-896-8923
E-mail: asa@carpenter.cx.

R. N. M., Incorporated *See* **Onion River Pr.**

RSVP Pr., *(978-0-930865; 978-1-60209)* 619 Gay Rd., Monroe, NC 28112-8214 USA (SAN 657-6346)
E-mail: writemet@aol.com
Web site: http://www.rsvpbooks.com; http://www.members.aol.com/writernet/rsvp.htm.

R T A Pr., *(978-0-929768)* Div. of Rochester Teachers Assn., 30 N. Union St., Suite 301, Rochester, NY 14607 USA Tel 716-546-2681; Fax: 716-546-4123
E-mail: ddsigns@servtech.com.

RVS Bks., Inc., *(978-0-9634257)* P.O. Box 683, Lebanon, TN 37088-0683 USA (SAN 298-7325) Tel 615-449-6725; Fax: 615-449-6910.

R5 Comics, LLC, *(978-1-7327976; 978-1-954167)* 27103 Kelsey Woods Ct., Cypress, TX 77433 USA Tel 281-795-0728
E-mail: josh@red5comics.com; red5scott@gmail.com
Web site: www.red5comics.com
Dist(s): **Simon & Schuster, Inc.**

Rabbit Ears Pr. & Co., *(978-0-9748922)* Orders Addr.: P.O. Box 1952, Davis, CA 95617 USA Tel 530-220-3289
Web site: http://www.rockythemudhen.com
Dist(s): **Partners Bk. Distributing, Inc.**

Rabbit Pubs., *(978-1-943785)* a/o Mr. Mark A. Poe, 1624 W. Northwest Hwy., Arlington Heights, IL 60004 USA Tel 858-513-7150
E-mail: plewis@smartfamilies.com
Web site: www.smartfamilies.com
Dist(s): **Diamond Comic Distributors, Inc.**
Whitaker Hse.

Rabbit Room Pr., *(978-0-615-32542-2; 978-0-9826214; 978-0-9889632; 978-0-9863818; 978-0-9983112; 978-1-7326910; 978-1-951872)* 940 Davidson Dr., Nashville, TN 37205 USA
Web site: http://www.rabbitroom.com.

Rabbit's Foot Pr. *Imprint of* **Blue Mountain Arts Inc.**

Racehorse Publishing *Imprint of* **Skyhorse Publishing Co., Inc.**

Racemaker Pr. LLC, *(978-0-9766683; 978-1-935240; 978-0-9998754)* 39 Church St., Boston, MA 02116 USA (SAN 256-4513) Tel 617-723-6533
E-mail: admin@racemaker.com
Web site: www.racemaker.com.

Rach, W. Dennis, *(978-0-9792579)* 9965 Portofino Dr., Orlando, FL 32832 USA (SAN 852-9299) Tel 407-625-8528
E-mail: dennis@rachfamily.com.

Rachel Garnet, *(978-0-578-86744-1)* 11605 Longstreet Dr., spotsylvania, VA 22551 USA Tel 540-842-0604
E-mail: info@tickingclocktheatre.com
Web site: rachelgarnet.com.

Racing to Joy Press LLC *See* **Linda M. Penn Author**

Racom Communications, *(978-0-9704515; 978-1-933199)* 150 N. Michigan Ave. Ste. 2800, Chicago, IL 60601 USA (SAN 852-7210)
E-mail: rahagle@aol.com
Dist(s): **Baker & Taylor Publisher Services (BTPS).**

Raconteurs, Inc., *(978-0-9621758)* 1305 W. Wisconsin Ave., No. 114, Oconomowoc, WI 53066-2646 USA (SAN 252-080X) Tel 414-567-4009.

Rada Press, Inc., *(978-0-9604212; 978-1-933011)* Orders Addr.: 1277 Fairmount Ave., Saint Paul, MN 55105-2701 USA Fax: 888-288-6401
E-mail: rm@radapress.com
Web site: http://www.radapress.com.

Radford, Marsha, *(978-0-9785872; 978-0-9903726; 978-1-952205)* 1020 W. Angeleno Ave. No. 1, Burbank, CA 91506 USA Tel 818-940-5704
E-mail: writetomarsha@gmail.com
Web site: http://www.arcanaland.com.

Radiance Pubs., *(978-0-918224)* Div. of S. K. Publications, Orders Addr.: 1042 Maple Ave., Lisle, IL 60532 USA Tel 630-577-7624
E-mail: nlarson@radiancepublishers.com
Web site: http://www.radiancepublishers.com.

Radical Reformation Bks., *(978-0-9818973)* 34 Cindia Ln, Ephrata, PA 17522 USA (SAN 856-8790) Tel 717-738-9099
E-mail: deantaylorfamily@gmail.com; dean@radicalreformation.net
Web site: http://www.radicalreformation.com.

Radical Women, *(978-0-615-62458-7; 978-0-615-73142-1; 978-0-692-58373-9; 978-0-9983308; 978-1-7325363; 978-1-7340398; 979-8-9886485)* P.O. Box 782, Granbury, TX 76048 USA Tel 817-269-9066
E-mail: lisabell@bylisabell.com
Web site: www.bylisabell.com
Dist(s): **CreateSpace Independent Publishing Platform.**

RADIOIONICS RESEARCH, *(978-1-930216)*
E-mail: bruceperreault@roadrunner.com
Web site: http://www.radioionics.com.

Rae, Karyn Publishing, *(978-0-9960922; 978-1-946847)* 13 Colonel Hazzard Rd., Okatie, SC 29909 USA Tel 573-424-0155
E-mail: krp@karynraepublishing.com
Web site: www.karynraepublishing.com.

Raea Gragg Bks., *(978-0-615-97032-5; 978-0-9916269; 978-1-7360124; 979-8-9869023)* 845 Mountain View Dr., Lafayette, CA 94549 USA Tel 510-719-2555
E-mail: karao@overaa.com.

Raedan Bocs *See* **Lire Bks.**

Raemark Pr., *(978-1-7325090)* 346 Rd. 21, Sedan, KS 67361 USA Tel 620-216-0332
E-mail: hjspire@yahoo.com.

Rafka Pr. LLC, *(978-0-9779628; 978-0-9911958)* P.O. Box 8099, Phoenix, AZ 85066 USA
Web site: http://www.rafkapress.com.

Rag Mag *See* **Black Hat Pr.**

Ragan, Jewel, *(978-0-9853809)* 24206 SE 248th St., Maple Valley, WA 98038 USA Tel 425-413-6032
E-mail: jewelragan@gmail.com.

Rageldar Pr., *(978-0-9993390)* 80 Westminster rd, 2, Rochester, NY 14607 USA Tel 585-727-0207; Fax: 585-727-0207
E-mail: Leah.fricano@yahoo.com.

Ragged Sky Pr., *(978-0-9633092; 978-1-933974)* 270 Griggs Dr., Princeton, NJ 08540 USA
E-mail: ellen_foos@pupress.princeton.edu
Web site: http://Raggedsky.com.

Raging Bull Publishing, LLC *See* **Command Publishing, LLC**

Ragtown Pr., *(978-1-7320968)* 21145 Bank Mill Rd., Saratoga, CA 95070-5706 USA Tel 408-823-2476
E-mail: andrew.john.grose@gmail.com.

Rai Consulting & Publishing, *(978-0-9717419)*
Web site: http://www.harryglick.com.

Rai Publishing, *(978-0-9765641)* P.O. Box 918, Grover Beach, CA 93483 USA Tel 805-473-9025
E-mail: donrai@ix.netcom.com.

Raiche, Janet, *(978-1-7353593)* PO Box 208, Dillon Beach, CA 94929 USA Tel 415-308-2714
E-mail: jgraiche@mac.com.

Raider Publishing International, *(978-0-9772054; 978-0-9790799; 978-1-934360; 978-1-935383; 978-1-61667)* 350 5th Ave., 59th Flr., New York, NY 10118 USA Tel 917-267-7912; Toll Free: 800-293-1653
E-mail: johnraider@hotmail.com; jraider@raiderpublishing.com
Web site: http://www.raiderpublishing.com.

Rain Lily Press *See* **River Lily Pr.**

Rain Tree Bks., *(978-0-9764129)* Orders Addr.: P.O. Box 1290, DeQueen, AR 71832 USA; Edit Addr.: 146 Treating Plant Rd., DeQueen, AR 71832 USA Tel 870-582-3565.

Raina Nightingale, *(978-1-952176)* P.O. Box 579, Dunlap, CA 93621 USA Tel 559-907-6037
E-mail: KNIGHTSOFTHEPROMISE@GMAIL.COM.

Rainbow Bks., Inc., *(978-0-935834; 978-1-56825)* P.O. Box 430, Highland City, FL 33846-0430 USA (SAN 213-5515) Tel 863-648-4420; Fax: 863-647-5951 Do not confuse with companies with the same or similar name in Middleburg, VT, Amstgerdam, NY, New York, NY, Sparks, NV
E-mail: RBIbooks@aol.com
Web site: http://www.RainbowBooksInc.com
Dist(s): **BCH Fulfillment & Distribution**
Book Clearing Hse.
Smashwords.

Rainbow Bridge Publishing, *(978-1-887923; 978-1-932210)* Div. of Carson-Dellosa Publishing Co., Inc., Orders Addr.: P.O. Box 571470, Salt Lake City, UT 84157-1470 USA Tel 801-268-8887; Fax: 801-268-2770; Toll Free: 800-598-1441; Edit Addr.: P.O. Box 571470, Salt Lake Cty, UT 84157-1470 USA
E-mail: danell@rbpbooks.com
Web site: http://www.rbpbooks.com
Dist(s): **Carson-Dellosa Publishing, LLC**
Midpoint Trade Bks., Inc.

Rainbow Children Media Group *See* **Mama Koku's Storytellin'**

Rainbow Communications, *(978-0-9725479; 978-0-9728737; 978-0-9888554)* 471 NW Hemlock Ave, Corvallis, OR 97330 USA Tel 541-753-3335
E-mail: varsell4@comcast.net.

†**Rainbow Horizons Publishing, Inc.**, *(978-1-55319)* Orders Addr.: P.O. Box 19729, San Diego, CA 92159 USA Toll Free Fax: 800-663-3608; Toll Free: 800-663-3609; *Imprints:* Classroom Complete Press (Classrm Comp)
E-mail: paul@classroomcompletepress.com
Web site: http://www.ccpinteractive.com; http://www.rainbowhorizons.com; http://www.classroomcompletepress.com
Dist(s): **Follett School Solutions**
OverDrive, Inc.
ebrary, Inc.; *CIP.*

Rainbow Morning Music Alternatives, *(978-0-938663; 978-0-9615696)* 2121 Fairland Rd., Silver Spring, MD 20904 USA (SAN 218-2963) Tel 301-384-9207; Fax: 312-337-5985; Toll Free: 800-881-4741
E-mail: barrylou@ziplink.net
Web site: http://www.barrylou.com
Dist(s): **Baker & Taylor Publisher Services (BTPS)**
MyiLibrary.

Rainbow Pony Publishing, *(978-0-9728871)* 368 S. McCaslin Blvd., PMB No. 226, Louisville, CO 80027 USA.

Rainbow Pony Publising *See* **Rainbow Pony Publishing**

Rainbow Publishers *See* **Rainbow Pubs. & Legacy Pr.**

Rainbow Pubs. & Legacy Pr., *(978-0-937282; 978-1-885358; 978-1-58411)* Orders Addr.: P.O. Box 261129, San Diego, CA 92196 USA (SAN 256-4718) Tel 858-668-3260; Fax: 858-668-3328; Toll Free Fax: 800-331-0297; Toll Free: 800-323-7337; Edit Addr.: P.O. Box 70130, Richmond, VA 23255-0130 USA; *Imprints:* Legacy Press (Lgacy Pr)
E-mail: rainbowed@earthlink.net; drmiley@juno.com
Web site: http://www.rainbowpublishers.com
Dist(s): **Appalachian Bible Co.**
Spring Arbor Distributors, Inc.

Rainbow Reach, *(978-0-9829490)* 2340 Bedfordshire Cir., Reston, VA 20191 USA
E-mail: susan@rainbowreach.com
Web site: www.rainbowreach.com
Dist(s): **Ingram Content Group.**

Rainbow Resource Ctr., Inc., *(978-1-933407; 978-1-942446)* P.O. Box 391, Williamsfield, IL 61489 USA; *Imprints:* In the Think of Things (IntheThink).

Rainbow Star Bks., *(978-0-9802363)* P.O. Box 422, Centereach, NY 11720 USA (SAN 855-5680)
Web site: http://www.rainbowstarbooks.com.

Rainbow Star, Incorporated *See* **Rainbow Star Bks.**

Rainbow Valley Publishing Co., *(978-0-9748558)* 2189 Hwy. 90 W., Sulphur, LA 70663 USA Tel 337-528-1157.

Rainbows Within Reach, *(978-0-9705987; 978-0-578-03944-2; 978-0-578-06631-8)* 5765 Westbourne Ave., Columbus, OH 43213 USA
E-mail: debbie@rainbowswithinreach.com
Web site: http://www.rainbowswithinreach.com
Dist(s): **Follett School Solutions**
TNT Media Group, Inc.

Publisher Name Index

Raincoast Bk. Distribution (CAN) *(978-0-920417; 978-1-55192; 978-1-895714; 978-1-894542) Dist. by* **PerseuPGW.**

Raindrop Bks., *(978-0-9766129)* 423 Hicks St., No. 6-H, Brooklyn, NY 11201 USA Tel 718-855-2918
E-mail: lgliessner@aol.com.

Raindrop Bks., *(978-0-9799677)* 10 Sunderland St., Melville, NY 11747 USA
Web site: http://www.learnalongwithlily.com; http://www.raindropbooks.com
Dist(s): **Big Tent Bks.**

Raining Popcorn Media, *(978-0-9797304)* P.O. Box 91244, San Antonio, TX 78209 USA Tel 210-320-0548; Toll Free: 866-503-3088
E-mail: info@rainingpopcorn.com; lisa@rainingpopcorn.com
Web site: http://www.RainingPopcorn.com.

Rains, Charlotte, *(978-0-692-90412-1; 978-0-692-97125-3; 978-0-578-48057-2; 979-8-218-27028-5)* 405 W. Taylor Ave., COOLIDGE, AZ 85128 USA Tel 520-518-5114
E-mail: bokz4kidz@hotmail.com
Dist(s): **Ingram Content Group.**

Rainstorm Pr., *(978-0-615-47986-6; 978-0-615-49269-8; 978-0-615-53082-6; 978-1-937758; 978-1-4748-9005-2)* P.O. Box 391038, Anza, CA 92539 USA Tel 760-270-8641
E-mail: Lyle@rainstormpress.com
Web site: http://www.RainstormPress.com
Dist(s): **CreateSpace Independent Publishing Platform.**

Raintree *Imprint of* **Capstone**

Raintree Steck-Vaughn Publishers *See* **Steck-Vaughn**

Rainy Day Entertainment, LLC *See* **Apologue Entertainment, LLC**

Rairarubia Bks., *(978-0-9712206)* 1000 San Diego Rd., Santa Barbara, CA 93103 USA Fax: 805-966-4697
E-mail: raira@silcom.com
Web site: http://www.rairarubia.com.

Raising Supaman Project, The *See* **Two Crabs & A Lion LLC**

Raising World Children LLC, *(978-1-7335649; 978-1-956870)* 11604 Kenilworth Pl., Glen Allen, VA 23059 USA Tel 908-338-4650
E-mail: aditi.ws@gmail.com
Web site: https://raisingworldchildren.com/.

Raisykinder Publishing, *(978-0-615-21798-7; 978-0-615-27779-0; 978-0-9825530; 978-0-9907348; 978-0-9978111; 978-0-9992760)* 1713 Golden Ct., Bellingham, WA 98226 USA
E-mail: raisykinderpub@aol.com
Web site: http://www.raisykinderpublishing.com.

Rakha, Marwa *See* **Malamih Publishing Hse.**

Rakowski, Diane, *(978-0-9760194)* 11402 W. Parkhill Dr., Littleton, CO 80127-4716 USA
E-mail: dsjsit@juno.com.

Raku Bks., *(978-0-615-12445-2; 978-0-615-12561-9)* Orders Addr.: P.O. Box 51954, Palo Alto, CA 94303 USA
E-mail: rapimus@yahoo.com.

Raku Publishing, *(978-0-9770662)* 30799 Pinetree Rd., No. 411, Pepper Pike, OH 44124 USA Tel 216-299-0613
Dist(s): **BookBaby.**

Ralston Store Publishing, *(978-0-9822585; 978-1-938322)* P.O. Box 4513, Durango, CO 81302-4513 USA
Web site: http://www.ralstonstorepublishing.com
Dist(s): **Smashwords.**

Ramahi, Yasmin, *(978-1-7323382)* 930 NW 35th St., Corvallis, OR 97330 USA Tel 831-224-6449
E-mail: ThePurplePrincessSeries@gmail.com.

Ramos, Raymond G., *(978-0-9855114)* 11600 Mendel Dr. Apt. 3, Orlando, FL 32826 USA Tel 407-756-5730
E-mail: congabuena@yahoo.com.

Rampant Loon Media LLC, *(978-0-9828974; 978-1-938834; 978-1-958333)* P.O. Box 111, Lake Elmo, MN 55042-0111 USA Tel 651-773-8717.

Ramsey Dean, Inc., *(978-0-9893372)* 1555 N. Dearborn Pkwy. No. 14A, Chicago, IL 60610 USA Tel 312-860-2021
E-mail: ramseydeaninc@gmail.com
Web site: www.ridingonabeamoflight.com.

Ramsey Pr., *(978-0-9635712; 978-0-9718554; 978-0-9720044; 978-0-9726323; 978-0-9753033; 978-0-9769630; 978-0-9774895; 978-0-9777767; 978-0-9785620; 978-0-9786577; 978-1-934629; 978-0-9800873; 978-0-9816839; 978-0-9829862; 978-1-936948; 978-1-937077; 978-1-938400; 978-1-942121; 979-8-88782) 1011 Reams Fleming Blvd, Franklin, TN 37064 USA Tel 615-515-3223; 888-227-3223; Fax: 615-371-5007; Toll Free: 888-227-3223*
E-mail: ken.murray@ramseysolutions.com; preston.cannon@ramseysolutions.com; mandi.snyder@ramseysolutions.com
Web site: http://www.ramseysolutions.com
Dist(s): **Ingram Publisher Services**
Nelson, Thomas Inc.

Ranch Gate Bks., *(978-0-9618660)* 2409 Dormarion, Austin, TX 78703 USA (SAN 668-4033) Tel 512-476-2185.

†**RAND Corp., The,** *(978-0-8330; 978-1-9774)* Orders Addr.: P.O. Box 2138, Santa Monica, CA 90407-2138 USA (SAN 218-9291) Tel 310-393-0411; Fax: 310-393-4818; Toll Free: 877-584-8642; Edit Addr.: 1776 Main St., Santa Monica, CA 90401-3208 USA (SAN 665-763X) Tel 310-393-0411; Fax: 412-802-4981
E-mail: jwarren@rand.org; correspondence@rand.org; randell@rand.org; cs@rand.org
Web site: http://www.rand.org
Dist(s): **CreateSpace Independent Publishing Platform**
Ebsco Publishing
JSTOR
MyiLibrary
National Bk. Network
ebrary, Inc.; *CIP.*

†**Rand McNally,** *(978-0-528)* Orders Addr.: 9855 Woods Dr., Skokie, IL 60077-1074 USA Toll Free Fax: 800-934-3479 (Orders); Toll Free: 800-333-0136 (ext. 4771); 800-678-7263 (Orders); 8770 W Bryn Mawr Ave., Chicago, IL 60631 Tel 800-333-0136; Fax: 847-329-6139
E-mail: Education@randmcnally.com
Web site: http://www.randmcnally.com
Dist(s): **Benchmark LLC**
Bryant Altman Map, Inc.; *CIP.*

Rand Media Co, *(978-0-9818935; 978-0-9824390; 978-0-9841393; 978-0-9844418; 978-0-692-01528-5; 978-0-9852818; 978-0-9988392)* Orders Addr.: 265 Post Rd. W., Westport, CT 06880 USA (SAN 925-4919) Tel 203-226-8727; Fax: 203-221-7677; *Imprints:* Skinny On (tm), The (Skinny on)
E-mail: cmonroy@randmediaco.com
Web site: http://www.theskinnyon.com; http://randmediaco.com/money/money-book-1/; http://randmediaco.com/
Dist(s): **Lulu Pr., Inc.**

RAND Publishing *See* **Rand Media Co**

Randall, Charles Inc., *(978-0-9624736; 978-1-890379)* Orders Addr.: 30 Amberwood Pkwy., Ashland, OH 44805 USA Fax: 419-281-6883; Toll Free: 800-247-6553; Edit Addr.: P.O. Box 1656, Orange, CA 92856 USA (SAN 253-7737)
E-mail: peter@randallonline.com
Web site: http://www.randallonline.com; http://www.charlesrandall.com
Dist(s): **Follett School Solutions**
Independent Pubs. Group
MyiLibrary
ebrary, Inc.

Randall, Cheri, *(978-0-9767213)* P.O. Box 2176, Belton, TX 76513 USA Tel 254-939-8776 (phone/fax)
E-mail: hrandallmail@aol.com
Web site: http://www.harveyrandall.org.

Randall Fraser Publishing *See* **RandallFraser Publishing**

Randall Hse. Pubns., *(978-0-89265; 978-1-61484)* 114 Bush Rd., Nashville, TN 37217 USA (SAN 207-5040) Tel 615-361-1221; Toll Free: 800-877-7030
E-mail: books@randallhouse.com; danny.conn@randallhouse.com
Web site: http://www.randallhouse.com; http://www.d6family.com.

Randall International *See* **Randall, Charles Inc.**

†**Randall, Peter E. Pub.,** *(978-0-914339; 978-1-931807; 978-0-9817898; 978-0-9828236; 978-1-937721; 978-0-692-22144-0; 978-1-942155; 978-0-692-51521-1; 978-0-9971567; 978-0-9600735; 978-1-7331500)* 5 Greenleaf Woods Dr., Unit 102, Portsmouth, NH 03801 USA (SAN 223-0496) Tel 603-431-5667; Fax: 603-431-3566; 60 Main St., Nashua, NH 03060 Toll Free: 844-777-7812; *Imprints:* Jetty House (Jetty Hse)
E-mail: deidre.randall@me.com; lois@loishermann.com; media@perpublisher.com
Web site: http://www.perpublisher.com; www.loishermann.com
Dist(s): **Bondcliff Bks.**
BookBaby
MyiLibrary
Pathway Bk. Service; *CIP.*

Randall, Robert E. *See* **Zander Pubns.**

RandallFraser Publishing, *(978-0-9745143)* 2082 Business Ctr. Dr., Suite 163, Irvine, CA 92612 USA Fax: 949-250-9020; Toll Free: 866-339-3999
E-mail: algreen51@comcast.net
Web site: http://www.Deweydooit.com
Dist(s): **National Bk. Network.**

R&B Trading Co., *(978-0-9718784)* 7619 Belmont Stakes Dr., Midlothian, VA 23112 USA (SAN 254-4741) Tel 804-739-8073; Fax: 775-243-6578
E-mail: dwindsofdestiny@aol.com
Web site: http://www.RnBtradingco.net/home.html.

Randle, Ian Pubs., Inc., *(978-0-9729358; 978-0-9742155; 978-0-9753529)* 25 SE Second Ave., Suite 1105, Miami, FL 33131 USA Tel 305-358-1588; Fax: 305-358-1589
E-mail: info@ianrandlepublishers.com
Web site: http://www.ianrandlepublishers.com
Dist(s): **Indiana Univ. Pr.**

R&N Productions, *(978-0-615-14376-7)* 698 Talbert Ave., Simi Valley, CA 93065 USA
E-mail: norm@kuvina.com
Web site: http://www.troublestreet.com
Dist(s): **Lulu Pr., Inc.**

Randolph, Connie, *(978-0-9994285)* 1153 Strada Cristallo, Henderson, NV 89011 USA Tel 330-610-6023
E-mail: casp2800@gmail.com
Web site: casperjoe.com.

Randolph Publishing, *(978-1-932258)* 4125 Braswell Church Rd., Good Hope, GA 30641-160 USA Do not confuse with companies with the same or similar names in Dunnellon, FL, Dallas, TX, Indianapolis, IN, Princeton, TX
E-mail: randolphpublishing@EarthLink.net
Web site: http://www.RandolphPublishing.com.

Random Ace Ink, *(978-0-9978475)* 18950 N Hills Dr., Brookfield, WI 53045 USA Tel 262-527-9963
E-mail: randomaceink@gmail.com.

Random House *Imprint of* **Random House Publishing Group**

Random House Adult Trade Publishing Group *See* **Random House Publishing Group**

Random House Audio *Imprint of* **Penguin Random House Audio Publishing Group**

Random Hse. Audio Publishing Group, Div. of Random House, Inc., Orders Addr.: 400 Hahn Rd., Westminster, MD 21157 USA (SAN 201-3975) Tel 410-848-1900; Toll Free: 800-726-0600; Edit Addr.: 1745 Broadway, New York, NY 10036 USA Tel 212-782-9000; *Imprints:* Listening Library (Listening Lib)
Web site: http://www.randomhouse.com/audio
Dist(s): **Ebsco Publishing**
Follett School Solutions
Penguin Random Hse. Distribution
Penguin Random Hse. LLC
Random Hse., Inc.

Random Hse. Bks. for Young Readers, *(978-0-375; 978-0-394; 978-0-517; 978-0-679; 978-1-4000)* Orders Addr.: 400 Hahn Rd., Westminster, MD 21157 USA; Edit Addr.: 1540 Broadway, New York, NY 10036 USA
Dist(s): **Children's Plus, Inc.**
MyiLibrary.

Random House Children's Books (GBR) *(978-1-4090; 978-1-4464) Dist. by* **Trafalgar.**

Random House Children's Books (GBR) *(978-1-4090; 978-1-4464) Dist. by* **IPG Chicago.**

Random House Children's Books (GBR) *(978-1-4090; 978-1-4464) Dist. by* **Perfect Learn.**

Random Hse. Children's Bks., *(978-0-7364-4312-8)* Div. of Random Hse., Inc., Orders Addr.: 400 Hahn Rd., Westminster, MD 21157 USA Tel 410-848-1900; Toll Free: 800-726-0600; Edit Addr.: 1745 Broadway, 10th Flr., New York, NY 10019 USA Tel 212-782-8491; 212-782-9000; Fax: 212-782-9577; Toll Free: 800-200-3552; *Imprints:* Delacorte Books for Young Readers (Delacorte Bks); Lamb, Wendy Books (Wendy Lamb); Random House Para Ninos (ParaNinos); Crown Books For Young Readers (CBYR); Dell Books for Young Readers (DBYR); Knopf Books for Young Readers (Knop); RH/Disney (RH Disney); Golden Books (Gold Bks); Random House Books for Young Readers (RHBYR); Doubleday Books for Young Readers (Doubleday Bk Yng); Yearling (Year); Dragonfly Books (Dragonfly Bks); Laurel Leaf (LaurelLeaf); Golden/Disney (Gold Disney); Delacorte Press (DelacortePr); Bluefire (BluefireR); Princeton Review (PrinceReview); Sylvan Learning Publishing (Sylvan Lea); Tricycle Press (Tricycle); Rodale Kids (Rodale Kid); Joy Revolution (Joy Revolution); Schwartz & Wade (Schwartz & Wade); Yearling (Yearling RHCB); Robin Corey Books (Robin Corey); Golden Inspirational (Gold Inspir); Rosen Classroom (RosenClassrm); Delacorte Press (DelacorRHP); Ember (Ember); David Fickling Books (DavidFickling); Underlined (Underlined); Make Me a World (Make Me a Wrld); Bright Matter Books (Bright Matter Bks); Laybrinth Road (Laybrinth Road)
E-mail: pmuller@randomhouse.com; kids@random.com
Web site: http://www.randomhouse.com/kids/
Dist(s): **Children's Plus, Inc.**
Follett School Solutions
Libros Sin Fronteras
MyiLibrary
Penguin Random Hse. Distribution
Penguin Random Hse. LLC
Random Hse., Inc.

Random House, Incorporated *See* **Random Hse., Inc.**

†**Random Hse., Inc.,** *(978-0-307; 978-0-345; 978-0-375; 978-0-385; 978-0-394; 978-0-440; 978-0-449; 978-0-517; 978-0-553; 978-0-593; 978-0-609; 978-0-676; 978-0-679; 978-0-7364; 978-0-7366; 978-0-7615; 978-0-7679; 978-0-7704; 978-0-8041; 978-0-8052; 978-0-8129; 978-0-8230; 978-0-87637; 978-0-87665; 978-0-87788; 978-0-88070; 978-0-913369; 978-0-914629; 978-0-930014; 978-0-945564; 978-1-57082; 978-1-57673; 978-1-57856; 978-1-878867; 978-1-884536; 978-1-885305; 978-1-58836; 978-1-4000; 978-1-59052; 978-1-4159; 978-) Div. of Penguin Random House LLC, Orders Addr.: 400 Hahn Rd., Westminster, MD 21157 USA (SAN 202-5515) Tel 410 848 1900; Toll Free Fax: 800 659 2436; Toll Free: 800 726 0600 (customer service/orders); Edit Addr.: 1745 Broadway, New York, NY 10019 USA (SAN 202-5507) Tel 212 782 9000; Fax: 212 302 7985; Imprints:* Golden Books (Golden Books)
E-mail: customerservice@randomhouse.com
Web site: http://www.randomhouse.com
Dist(s): **Ebsco Publishing**
Follett School Solutions
Giron Bks.
Libros Sin Fronteras
MyiLibrary
Penguin Random Hse. Distribution
Penguin Random Hse. LLC
Perfection Learning Corp.; *CIP.*

Random Hse. Information Group, Div. of Random Hse., Inc., Orders Addr.: 400 Hahn Rd., Westminster, MD 21157 USA Tel 410-848-1900; Toll Free: 800-726-0600; Edit Addr.: 1745 Broadway, New York, NY 10019 USA Tel 212-751-2600; Toll Free: 800-726-0600; *Imprints:* Random House Puzzles & Games (RHPG); Prima Games (PrimGames)
E-mail: customerservice@randomhouse.com
Web site: http://www.randomhouse.com/
Dist(s): **Bilingual Pubns. Co., The**
Children's Plus, Inc.
Ediciones Universal
Libros Sin Fronteras
MyiLibrary
Penguin Random Hse. Distribution
Penguin Random Hse. LLC
Random Hse., Inc.
Simon & Schuster, Inc.

Random House Large Print *Imprint of* **Diversified Publishing**

Random Hse. Large Print, Div. of Random House, Inc., Orders Addr.: 400 Hahn Rd., Westminster, MD 21157 USA Tel 410-848-1900 Toll Free: 800-726-0600 (customer service); Edit Addr.: 1745 Broadway, New York, NY 10019 USA Tel 212-782-9000
E-mail: editor@randomhouse.com; customerservice@randomhouse.com
Web site: http://www.randomhouse.com
Dist(s): **Libros Sin Fronteras**
MyiLibrary
Penguin Random Hse. Distribution
Penguin Random Hse. LLC
Random Hse., Inc.
Thorndike Pr.

Random House Para Ninos *Imprint of* **Random Hse. Children's Bks.**

Random House Publishing Group, *(978-1-4070)* Orders Addr.: 400 Hahn Rd., Westminster, MD 21157 USA (SAN 852-5579) Tel 410-848-1900; 410-386-7560; Toll Free: 800-726-0600; Edit Addr.: 1745 Broadway, New York, NY 10019 USA Tel 212-751-2600; Fax: 212-572-4949; Toll Free: 800-726-0600; *Imprints:* Delacorte Books for Young Readers (Delacorte Bks); Random House Trade Paperbacks (RH Trade Bks); Modern Library (Mod Lib); Villard (Villard Bks); Random House (Random House); Del Rey (Del Rey); Ballantine Books (Ballantine Bks); Bantam (Bant); Delacorte Press (DelacorRHP); Laurel (LaureRH); Delacorte Press (DelacortePr)
E-mail: lstark@randomhouse.com
Dist(s): **Children's Plus, Inc.**
Follett School Solutions
Independent Pubs. Group
Libros Sin Fronteras
MyiLibrary
Penguin Random Hse. Distribution
Penguin Random Hse. LLC
Perfection Learning Corp.
Random Hse., Inc.

Random House Reference & Information Publishing *See* **Random Hse. Information Group**

†**Random Hse. Value Publishing,** Div. of Random House, Inc., Orders Addr.: 400 Hahn Rd., Westminster, MD 21157 USA Tel 410-848-1900 Toll Free: 800-726-0600 (Customer Service); Edit Addr.: 280 Park Ave., 11th Flr., New York, NY 10017 USA Tel 212 572 2400
Web site: http://www.randomhouse.com
Dist(s): **Penguin Random Hse. Distribution**
Penguin Random Hse. LLC
Random Hse., Inc.; *CIP.*

Random Hse. Worlds, *Imprints:* Del Rey (Del Rey)
Dist(s): **Penguin Random Hse. Distribution**
Penguin Random Hse. LLC.

Random Hse. Australia (AUS) *(978-1-86359; 978-0-86824; 978-0-947189; 978-1-86325; 978-0-7338; 978-0-900882; 978-1-74166; 978-1-86471; 978-1-4230; 978-1-74274; 978-1-74275; 978-0-646-19362-5; 978-0-646-31636-9; 978-0-646-32934-5; 978-0-85798; 978-1-925324; 978-0-646-29047-6; 978-1-74051; 978-0-646-08769-6; 978-0-646-23850-0) Dist. by* **IPG Chicago.**

Random Hse. Bks. for Young Readers *Imprint of* **Random Hse. Children's Bks.**

Random Hse. of Canada (CAN) *(978-0-09; 978-0-307; 978-0-375; 978-0-394; 978-0-676; 978-0-679; 978-0-7704; 978-1-4000) Dist. by* **Random.**

Random Hse. of Canada (CAN) *(978-0-09; 978-0-307; 978-0-375; 978-0-394; 978-0-676; 978-0-679; 978-0-7704; 978-1-4000) Dist. by* **Peng Rand Hse.**

Random Hse. Puzzles & Games *Imprint of* **Random Hse. Information Group**

Random Hse. Trade Paperbacks *Imprint of* **Random House Publishing Group**

R&R Blackburn Enterprises, *(978-0-9907603)* P.O. Box 27577, Fresno, CA 93729 USA Tel 559-287-4149
E-mail: rlb737@gmail.com
Web site: www.TwasWithATwist.com.

R&R Endeavors, Inc., *(978-0-9740444)* Orders Addr.: P.O. Box 301, Indianapolis, IN 46217 USA; Edit Addr.: 1350C W. Southport Rd., Indianapolis, IN 46217 USA
E-mail: editor@writerpublishing.com
Web site: http://www.writerpublishing.com.

R&R Graphics, Incorporated *See* **Steuben Pr.**

Randy Jay Richards, *(978-0-578-45210-4)* 1918 S. 19th St., Grand Forks, ND 58201 USA Tel 701-213-2150
E-mail: randyrichards.gop@gmail.com
Dist(s): **Ingram Content Group.**

Rang Jung Yshe Pubns. (HKG) *(978-962-7341) Dist. by* **PerseuPGW.**

Ransom, L. M., *(978-1-7320588)* 1414 S. 102nd Ave., Shelby, MI 49455 USA Tel 231-301-0066
E-mail: lmransom75@gmail.com
Web site: lmransom.com.

Ransom Pr. International, *(978-0-931221; 978-1-64765)* 4918 Roosevelt St., Hollywood, FL 34135 USA (SAN 682-0166) Tel 218-256-1514 (phone/fax); 727-279-7877 Do not confuse with Ransom Pr. Moscow, ID
E-mail: ransompress@outlook.com.

RAPC - Sparkle & Shine Project, *(978-0-9760282)* 116 Jackson St., Sylva, NC 28779 USA Tel 828-586-0661; Fax: 828-586-0663
Web site: http://www.sparkle-shine.com.

RAPHA, Inc., *(978-0-9740081)* Orders Addr.: P.O. Box 1184, Groton, CT 06340 USA Tel 860-938-2599; Edit Addr.: 45 South Rd., Apt. 9A, Groton, CT 06340 USA Tel 860-514-7266
E-mail: joyindamornin@earthlink.net.

Rapha Publishing, *(978-0-9763686)* 431 Beechwood Ave., Carnegie, PA 15106 USA Tel 412-249-0669
E-mail: raphapublishing@yahoo.com
Web site: http://www.raphapublishing.com/.

Raphel Marketing, Inc., *(978-0-9624808; 978-0-9711542; 978-0-9826644; 978-1-938406)* Orders Addr.: 211 North Ave., St Johnsbury, VT 05819-1626 USA Tel 802-751-8802; *Imprints:* Compass (CompassUSA)
E-mail: neil@raphel.com
Web site: http://www.raphel.com; http://www.brigantinemedia.com; http://compasspublishing.org.

Rapids Christian Pr., Inc., *(978-0-915374)* P.O. Box 717, Ferndale, WA 98248-0717 USA (SAN 205-0986) Tel 360-384-1747
E-mail: gundersonwv@aol.com.

Rapier Publishing Co., LLC, *(978-0-9839483; 978-0-9966083; 978-0-9970307; 978-0-9977029; 978-1-946683)* 135 Lakeside Dr., Dothan, AL 36301 USA Tel 256-553-9410; Fax: 334-699-5550
E-mail: petefannie@aol.com.

Rare Bird Bks., *(978-0-9839255; 978-0-9854902; 978-0-9887456; 978-0-9889312; 978-1-940207; 978-1-942600; 978-0-9971486; 978-0-9974407; 978-1-945572; 978-0-9983147; 978-1-947856; 978-1-64428; 978-0-578-95982-5)* 6044 N Figueroa St,

Los Angeles, CA 90042 USA Tel 213-623-1773; *Imprints:* Vireo Book, A (VireoBk); Secular Media Group (MYID_B_SECULAR); Cune Press Classics (MYID_E_CUNE PR)
E-mail: tyson@rarebirdlit.com
Dist(s): **MyiLibrary**
Publishers Group West (PGW)
SPD-Small Pr. Distribution.

Rare Bks. Distributors, *(978-1-57154)* Orders Addr.: P.O. Box 13975, Columbus, OH 43213 USA (SAN 253-7869) Tel 614-651-7508; Fax: 614-258-6745
E-mail: mjabbar@ix.netcom.com
Web site: http://www.thechirstmyth.com.

R.A.R.E. TALES, *(978-0-9760303)* 14120 River Rd., Fort Myers, FL 33905-7436 USA
E-mail: kphchance@comcast.net
Web site: http://www.raretales.net.

Rarecity Pr., *(978-0-9760959)* 17 Yardley Dr., Medford, NJ 08055 USA Tel 201-788-9746
E-mail: jason@rarecity.com.

Rasa Music Co., *(978-0-9766219)* 409 Glenview Rd., Glenview, IL 60025-3262 USA Tel 847-486-0416; Fax: 847-657-9459
E-mail: lleifer@northpark.edu
Web site: http://www.admin.northpark.edu/lleifer/.

Rascal Treehouse Publishing, *(978-0-9759321)* 1523 Morris St. - Suite 330, Lincoln Park, MI 48146 USA
E-mail: lscoffman@lscoffman.com
Web site: http://www.lscoffman.com.

Rasmussen, Author Debbie Ihler, *(978-1-7334645; 979-8-9851721)* 4340 W. 5255 S., Kearns, UT 84118 USA Tel 951-704-3442
E-mail: authordebbieihlerrasmussen@gmail.com
Web site: www.authordebbieihlerrasmussen.com.

Raspberry Bks., *(978-0-9848749)* 4346 Mammoth Ave. No. 4, Sherman Oaks, CA 91423 USA Tel 818-633-9190
E-mail: tammy@tammylaframboise.com.

Ratatat Graphics LLC *See* **Studio Moonfall**

Ratatoskr Pr., *(978-1-946552; 978-1-951439; 978-1-958606)* 11920 TILTON TRL N, ROGERS, MN 55374 USA Tel 763-428-0191; Fax: 763-428-0191
E-mail: KateMacLeod42@gmail.com.

Rattle OK Pubns., *(978-0-9626210; 978-1-883965)* Orders Addr.: P.O. Box 5614, Napa, CA 94581 USA (SAN 297-5475) Tel 707-253-9641; Edit Addr.: 296 Homewood Ave., Napa, CA 94558-5617 USA
Dist(s): **Gryphon Hse., Inc.**

Ratway, Michael, *(978-0-9724696)* 37462 Bonnie St., Ocean View, DE 19970 USA
E-mail: yawtar@earthlink.net
Web site: http://www.earthlink.net/~yawtar.

Rauch, Linda Gallery, *(978-0-692-04341-7; 978-0-578-74232-8; 979-8-218-02863-3)* 246 A Ledoux St., Taos, NM 87571 USA Tel 512-417-0116
E-mail: lrauchartist@yahoo.com
Dist(s): **Ingram Content Group.**

Raven Bks. *Imprint of* **Raven Productions**

Raven House Media, *(978-0-9983624)* 1625 SW 173rd Ter, Beaverton, OR 97003 USA Tel 503-459-8547
E-mail: rmseidler@gmail.com
Web site: rmseidler.com.

Raven Mad Studios, *(978-0-9896269)* 16327 197th Ave. NE, Woodinville, WA 98077 USA Tel 206-310-7246
E-mail: randybriley@comcast.net.

Raven Press *See* **Raven House Media**

Raven Productions, *(978-0-9764091)* 325 E. 2550 N, Suite 117, North Ogden, UT 84414 USA Tel 801-782-0872; *Imprints:* Raven Books (RavenBks) Do not confuse with companies with the same or similar name in Delta Junction, AKEly, MN
E-mail: gshaw@post.harvard.edu
Dist(s): **MyiLibrary.**

Raven Productions, Inc., *(978-0-9914157)* Orders Addr.: P.O. Box 188, Ely, MN 55731 USA Do not confuse with companies with the same or similar name in Delta Junction, AK, North Ogden, UT
E-mail: raven@ravenwords.com.

Raven Publishing *See* **Raven Publishing Inc. of Montana**

Raven Publishing Inc. of Montana, *(978-0-9714161; 978-0-9772525; 978-0-9820893; 978-0-9827377; 978-1-937849)* P.O. Box 2866, Norris, MT 59745 USA (SAN 254-5861) Tel 406-685-3545; Fax: 406-685-3599; Toll Free: 866-685-3545; *Imprints:* Nesting Tree Books (NestingTree) Do not confuse with companies with the same or similar name in Bronx, NY, Pittsfield, MA
E-mail: janet@ravenpublishng.net
Web site: http://www.ravenpublishing.net
Dist(s): **Bks. West**
Distributors, The
Follett School Solutions
Partners/West Book Distributors
Quality Bks., Inc.
Smashwords
Wolverine Distributing, Inc.
Western International, Inc.

Raven Rocks Pr., *(978-0-9615961)* 53650 Belmont Ridge, Beallsville, OH 43716 USA (SAN 696-5679) Tel 740-926-1481 (phone/fax)
E-mail: jmrpress@1st.net.

Raven Tree Pr. *Imprint of* **Delta Systems Company, Inc.**

Raven Wing, *(978-0-9887762; 978-0-9969351; 978-0-9989157; 978-1-7329767; 978-1-7342468; 978-1-954888)* 1837 Talon Rd, Rocklin, CA 95765 USA Tel 916-742-0671
E-mail: susan144@me.com
Web site: www.sbalexander.com.

Ravencrest *Imprint of* **Cubbie Blue Publishing**

Ravenhart Pr., *(978-0-9996106)* 8635 W Sahara Avenue, No. 677, Las Vegas, NV 89117 USA Tel 702-219-5698; Fax: 702-219-5698
E-mail: ravenhartpress@gmail.com
Web site: http://ravenhartpress.com.

Ravenhawk Bks., *(978-1-893660)* Div. of The 6DOF Group, 7739 E. Broadway Blvd. Suite 95, Tucson, AZ 85710 USA Tel 520-886-9885 (phone/fax); Toll Free: 800-520-9885
E-mail: 76673.3165@compuserve.com
Web site: http://www.ravenhawk.org.

RavenMark, *(978-0-9713998; 978-0-615-55902-5)* 27 E. State St., Montpelier, VT 05602-3011 USA Tel 802-223-5507
E-mail: rebecca@ravenmark.com
Dist(s): **Brayshaw, R. C.**

Raven's Wing Bks., *(978-0-9787318; 978-0-9801004; 978-1-61807)* 52 Ridgewood Dr., Yarmouth Port, MA 03303 USA Tel 508-744-7038; *Imprints:* Little Blue Flower Press (Little Blue Flow).

Ravensburger Buchverlag Otto Maier GmbH (DEU) *(978-3-473) Dist. by* **Distribks Inc.**

Ravensdaughter Designs *See* **Celtic Art Store**

Ravenstone Pr., *(978-0-9659712)* Orders Addr.: Ravenstone Press 2056 Berry Roberts Dr., Sun City Center, FL 33573-6130 USA Tel 813-633-5759; Fax: 813-633-5759; Edit Addr.: 2056 Berry Roberts Dr., Sun City Ctr, FL 33573-6130 USA
E-mail: writerjerri@gmail.com
Web site: http://www.ravenstonepress.com.

Ravenwood Publishing, *(978-0-9899275)* 133 Rob Rd., Brooklin, ME 04616 USA Tel 207-359-2451
E-mail: ruthjohnhowell@gmail.com.

Ravenwood Studios, *(978-0-9718604; 978-1-933420)* P.O. Box 197, Diamond Springs, CA 95619 USA
E-mail: ravenwoodstudios@me.com; maureenedgecomb@me.com; todd.ryan@comcast.net
Web site: http://www.maureenedgecomb.com; http://www.ravenwoodstudios.net; http://www.marcyinmanhattan.com.

Ravette Publishing, Ltd. (GBR) *(978-0-948456; 978-1-85304; 978-0-906710; 978-1-84161) Dist. by* **Parkwest Pubns.**

Ravishing Gecko Publishing, *(978-0-9989938)* 2127 Hopkins Pl. Ct, Duluth, GA 30096 USA Tel 470-564-0914
E-mail: naynuk@ravishinggecko.com.

Raw Dog Screaming Pr., *(978-0-9745031; 978-1-933293; 978-1-935738; 978-1-947879)* 2802 Farris Ln., Bowie, MD 20715 USA (SAN 255-7673)
E-mail: books@rawdogscreaming.com
Web site: http://www.rawdogscreaming.com.

Raw Junior, LLC *See* **TOON Books / RAW Junior, LLC**

Rawlings Bks., LLC, *(978-0-9908565; 978-0-9984053; 978-1-7347447)* 2232 Rio Rancho Dr., Virginia Beach, VA 23456 USA Tel 757-773-8769
E-mail: sdill2@yahoo.com.

Ray, *(978-0-9856890)* 551 Atlanta Ave., San Jose, CA 95125 USA Tel 917-647-4899
E-mail: rmfvento@gmail.com.

Ray Greer, Mary Lou, *(978-0-9749161)* P.O. Box 1740, Eagar, AZ 85925 USA Tel 520-850-6209.

Rayden Rose, *(978-1-7349025)* 5641 Lookout Crest. St., Las Vegas, NV 89031 USA Tel 702-561-1734
E-mail: Jared.Rosequist@gmail.com.

Rayenear Publishing, *(978-0-692-97667-8)* 633 F St., Martinez, CA 94553 USA Tel 925-332-9892
E-mail: rayenearpublishing@gmail.com.

Rayna Holloway, *(978-1-7352521)* 2820 Grasslands Dr 714 0, SACRAMENTO, CA 95833 USA Tel 7077711415
E-mail: raynadenise@yahoo.com
Dist(s): **Ingram Content Group.**

Raynear Publishing *See* **Rayenear Publishing**

Raynestorm Bks. *Imprint of* **Silver Rose Publishing**

Rayo *Imprint of* **HarperCollins Pubs.**

Rayve Productions, Inc., *(978-1-877810)* Orders Addr.: P.O. Box 726, Windsor, CA 95492 USA (SAN 248-4250) Tel 707-838-6200; Fax: 707-838-2220; Toll Free: 800-852-4890
E-mail: rayvepro@aol.com
Web site: http://www.rayveproductions.com; http://www.rayvepro.com
Dist(s): **Brodart Co.**
Follett School Solutions
Lippincott Williams & Wilkins
Quality Bks., Inc.
Unique Bks., Inc.

Razavi, Firouzeh Bks., *(978-0-692-08968-2; 978-0-692-11249-6; 978-0-692-15929-3; 978-0-578-42265-7; 978-0-578-42329-6; 978-0-578-80671-6; 978-1-7373557)* 497 S. El Molino No. 211, Pasadena, CA 91101 USA Tel 626-379-7608; *Imprints:* FR Publishing (FR Publish)
E-mail: thefirouzehrazavi@gmail.com
Dist(s): **CreateSpace Independent Publishing Platform.**

Razorbill *Imprint of* **Penguin Publishing Group**

Razorbill *Imprint of* **Penguin Young Readers Group**

RBA Libros, S.A. (ESP) *(978-84-89662; 978-84-7871; 978-84-7901; 978-84-85351; 978-84-9867; 978-84-9006) Dist. by* **Lectorum Pubns.**

RBA Libros, S.A. (ESP) *(978-84-89662; 978-84-7871; 978-84-7901; 978-84-85351; 978-84-9867; 978-84-9006) Dist. by* **Santillana.**

RBHC LLC., *(978-0-692-99523-5; 978-0-578-45901-1)* 111 E. 26th St. Apt. B9, New York, NY 10010 USA Tel 917-209-0960
E-mail: rugbytrader@gmail.com
Dist(s): **CreateSpace Independent Publishing Platform.**

RCL Benziger Publishing, *(978-0-89505; 978-0-913592; 978-1-55924)* A Kendall Hunt Company, Orders Addr.: 8805 Governor's Hill, Suite 400, Cincinnati, OH 45249 USA (SAN 299-0628) Toll Free Fax: 800-688-8356; Toll Free: 877-275-4725
E-mail: customerservice@rclbenziger.com
Web site: http://www.rclweb.com/
Dist(s): **Spring Arbor Distributors, Inc.**

RD Vincent, *(978-0-692-56221-5)* 4000 Essex Ln. Apt 1301, Houston, TX 77027 USA Tel 845-699-6664
E-mail: rayd792002@yahoo.com.

RDM Publishing, *(978-0-9766038)* 605 CR 1040E, Norris City, IL 62869 USA Tel 618-265-3225
E-mail: earthart@midwest.net.

RDR Bks., *(978-0-9636161; 978-1-57143)* 1487 Glen Ave., Muskegon, MI 49441-3101 USA; 960 S. Sherman, Muskegon, MI 49441
E-mail: books@rdrbooks.com
Web site: http://www.rdrbooks.com
Dist(s): **Alpen Bks**
American West Bks.
Book Wholesalers, Inc.
Bookazine Co., Inc.
Brodart Co.
Follett School Solutions
New Leaf Distributing Co., Inc.
Quality Bks., Inc.
Sunbelt Pubns., Inc.
Unique Bks., Inc.
Yankee Bk. Peddler, Inc.

Re, Joseph Del, *(978-0-692-99876-2)* 777 N. Orange Ave., Orlando, FL 32801 USA Tel 407-595-7336
E-mail: babaorlley74@gmail.com
Dist(s): **Ingram Content Group.**

Reaching Beyond, Inc., *(978-0-9741893)* Orders Addr.: P.O. Box 12364, Columbus, GA 31917-2364 USA Tel 706-573-5942; Edit Addr.: P.O. Box 12364, Columbus, GA 31917-2364 USA
E-mail: nccjohnson@hotmail.com
Web site: http://Www.charlotterjohnson.com
Dist(s): **Book Clearing Hse.**

Reaching Higher Pr. LLC, *(978-0-578-84656-9; 978-0-578-84657-6; 978-1-7367539)* 210 Fieldstown Rd Ste 100 No. 449 0, Gardendale, AL 35071 USA Tel 2053357610
E-mail: office@reachinghigherpressllc.com
Web site: www.BreddanBudderman.com; www.BreddanBuddermanBooks.com
Dist(s): **Ingram Content Group**
Outskirts Pr., Inc.

Reachment Publications *See* **Southeast Media**

Read 2 Children, *(978-0-9755839)* P.O. Box 4113, Warren, NJ 07059 USA Tel 732-805-9073
Web site: http://www.read2children.com.

Read All Over Publishing, *(978-0-9728779)* 17705 Ingleside Rd., Cleveland, OH 44119 USA Tel 216-486-8615 ext. 3
E-mail: readallover@sbcglobal.net.

Read More! Run More!, *(978-0-692-82924-0; 978-0-692-92465-5)* 3900 Woodchase Dr Apt152, HOUSTON, TX 77042 USA Tel 443-739-4339
E-mail: jeffwcrawford5+LVP0003230@gmail.com; jeffwcrawford5+LVP0003230@gmail.com.

Read My Ink Editing & Self-Publishing *See* **Quercus Publishing**

Read Publishing, *(978-0-9762868)* Orders Addr.: 3918 Dorcas Dr., Nashville, TN 37215 USA Tel 615-279-9988; Fax: 615-385-2651
E-mail: snea5001@bellsouth.net; jennie0120@aol.com.

Read Street Publishing, Inc., *(978-0-942929)* 133 W. Read St., Baltimore, MD 21201 USA (SAN 667-8505) Tel 410-837-1116; Fax: 410-727-3174; *Imprints:* Omni Arts Publishing (Omni Arts Pubng)
E-mail: editor@omnititles.com; editor@tablespr.com; editor@readstreetpublishing.com
Web site: http://www.omnititles.com; http://www.tablespr.com; http://www.readstreetpublishing.com.

Read Together Bks., *(978-0-9822615)* 1526 208th St, Fl 2, Bayside, NY 11360 USA Tel 917-757-5868
E-mail: mike@readtogetherbooks.com
Web site: http://www.readtogetherbooks.com.

Read Us For Fun Publishing, *(978-0-9820363)* P.O. Box 623, Dover, MA 02030 USA Tel 508-523-9414
E-mail: mking426@msn.com
Web site: http://readusforfun.com.

Read Well Publishing Inc., *(978-0-9630539; 978-0-9703400; 978-1-933873)* Div. of Apodixis, Inc., Orders Addr.: P.O. Box 671053, Dallas, TX 75367 USA Tel 972-241-1366; Fax: 972-241-5345 (call first); Toll Free: 800-522-3341; Edit Addr.: 3975 High Summit Dr., Dallas, TX 75244 USA
E-mail: jillsmithusa@att.net
Web site: http://www.learning-apodixis.com.

read2yourchild LLC, *(978-1-7367605)* P.O. Box 1366, Pottstown, PA 19464 USA Tel 215-791-1277
E-mail: aguerrant@read2yourchild.com
Web site: read2yourchild.com.

ReadaClassic.com *See* **Cedar Lake Pubns.**

Reader Publishing Group, *(978-0-9837873; 978-1-7323345)* 1900 E. Ocean Blvd. No. 1001, Long Beach, CA 90802 USA Tel 562-900-0953
E-mail: cunham@aol.com.

Readerlink Distribution Services, LLC, *(978-0-934429; 978-1-57145; 978-0-7944; 978-1-59223; 978-1-60710; 978-1-62686; 978-1-68412; 978-1-64147; 978-1-64517; 978-1-0785; 978-1-6672; 979-8-3690)* 9717 Pacific Heights Blvd Suite 100, San Diego, CA 92121 USA (SAN 630-8090) Toll Free: 800-284-3580; *Imprints:* Thunder Bay Press (Thunder Bay); Silver Dolphin Books (Silver Dolph)
E-mail: lnordland@readerlink.com
Web site: http://www.silverdolphinbooks.com; http://www.printersrowpublishinggroup.com; http://www.thunderbaybooks.com/; http://www.bathroomreader.com; http://www.readerlink.com
Dist(s): **Publishers Group West (PGW)**
Simon & Schuster, Inc.

Readers Are Leaders, *(978-0-9673625)* 908 Ashland Dr., Mesquite, TX 75149 USA Tel 972-288-5806 (phone/fax)
E-mail: rlgant@airmail.net.

Readers Are Leaders U.S.A., *(978-0-9768035; 978-0-9800397)* 2315 SW 5th Ave., Miami, FL 33129-1939 USA (SAN 855-0557)
Web site: http://www.readersareleadersusa.net; http://monnar.net/.

†Reader's Digest Assn., Inc., The, *(978-0-7621; 978-0-89577; 978-0-86438; 978-1-60652)* One Bedford Rd., Pleasantville, NY 10570 USA (SAN 282-2091) Toll Free: 800-463-8820; 800-334-9599; 800-635-5006
Web site: http://www.readersdigest.com; http://www.rd.com
Dist(s): **Children's Plus, Inc.**
Leonard, Hal Corp.
Penguin Publishing Group
Simon & Schuster, Inc.
Tuttle Publishing; *CIP.*

Reader's Digest Children's Bks. *Imprint of* **Studio Fun International**

Reader's Digest Children's Publishing, Incorporated *See* **Studio Fun International**

Reader's Digest Young Families, Inc. *Imprint of* **Studio Fun International**

READERS to EATERS, *(978-0-9836615; 978-0-9984366; 978-0-9980477; 978-1-7351522)* 1620 Broadway No. 6, San Francisco, CA 94109 USA Tel 206-849-1962
E-mail: philip@readerstoeaters.com
Web site: www.ReadersToEaters.com
Dist(s): **Publishers Group West (PGW).**

Reading Co., The *Imprint of* **Rhoades & Assocs.**

Reading Reading Bks., LLC, *(978-1-933727; 978-1-60892)* P.O. Box 6654, Reading, PA 19610 USA
E-mail: service@rrbooks.com; orangetabbycat2000@yahoo.com
Web site: http://www.rrbooks.com.

Reading Resc., *(978-0-9755561; 978-0-9795648)* 314 Knowles Hill Rd., Alexandria, NH 03222 USA (SAN 853-7771) Tel 603-744-5803 Do not confuse with Reading Resources, Inc. in Worthington, OH
E-mail: laberge001@gmail.com; readingresources@metrocast.net.

Reading Rock Books *See* **Reading Rock, Inc.**

Reading Rock, Inc., *(978-1-929591)* P.O. Box 67, Athens, MI 49011 USA Tel 616-729-9440
Web site: http://www.Readingrockbook.com.

Reading Studio Pr., *(978-0-9767506)* 250 W. 90th St., Suite 12F, New York, NY 10024 USA Tel 212-724-6232
E-mail: readingstudio@aol.com
Web site: http://www.alphieandthealphabets.com.

Reading Tree Pr., *(978-0-615-92763-3; 978-0-692-38179-3)*
Dist(s): **CreateSpace Independent Publishing Platform.**

Reading with Rose, *(978-0-9891006)* 317 S. Elm St. Loft 313, Owosso, MI 48867 USA Tel 989-274-1053
E-mail: rtithof@gmail.com.

Reading's Fun/Books are Fun, Limited *See* **Bks. Are Fun, Ltd.**

Ready Blade *Imprint of* **Blooming Tree Pr.**

Ready Writer Pr., *(978-0-9884614; 978-1-7352867)* 8681 Able St NE, Blaine, MN 55434 USA
E-mail: jessapphire@gmail.com.

Ready Writer Publishing, LLC, *(978-0-9748748)* P.O. Box 18197, Shreveport, LA 71138 USA Tel 318-470-0538
E-mail: satbeau1@bellsouth.net.

ReadZone Bks. (GBR) *(978-1-78322) Dist. by* **IPG Chicago.**

Reagan Arthur Bks. *Imprint of* **Little Brown & Co.**

Reagent Pr. Bks. for Young Readers *Imprint of* **RP Media**

Reagent Pr. Echo *Imprint of* **RP Media**

Reagent Pr. Signature Editions *Imprint of* **RP Media**

Reagent Press *See* **RP Media**

Reaktion Bks., Ltd. (GBR) *(978-0-948462; 978-1-86189; 978-1-78023; 978-1-78914) Dist. by* **Chicago Distribution Ctr.**

Real Bks. 360, *(978-0-692-97002-7; 978-0-692-14235-6)* 4510 Charlotte Ave., Apt. 301, Nashville, TN 37209 USA Tel 615-829-3600
E-mail: freddy.sturman@gmail.com
Dist(s): **CreateSpace Independent Publishing Platform.**

R.E.A.L. Pubns., *(978-0-9724503; 978-0-9748003)* 109 La Costa Dr., Georgetown, KY 40324 USA (SAN 255-867X) Tel 859-539-2463
E-mail: austinandbelinda@gmail.com
Web site: http://www.arealeducation.com.

R.E.A.L. Publishing *See* **R.E.A.L. Pubns.**

Real Reads Ltd. (GBR) *(978-1-906230; 978-1-911091) Dist. by* **Casemate Pubs.**

Real Rhymes LLC, *(978-0-9702216; 979-8-218-26644-8)* 740 Lakeview Dr., Palm Harbor, FL 34683 USA Tel 727-458-4327
E-mail: thoover@therealrhymes.com
Dist(s): **Independent Pub.**

Real Science-4-Kids *Imprint of* **Gravitas Pubns., Inc.**

Real Simple Bks. *Imprint of* **Time Inc. Bks.**

Real World Productions, *(978-1-60855; 978-1-60856)* 131 Ave. B, No. 1B, New York, NY 10009 USA.

Real Writing Press *See* **Real Writing UnLtd.**

Real Writing UnLtd., *(978-0-9742196)* 172 WETLEAU DR, Lowell, OR 97452 USA Tel 541-729-4693
E-mail: areswhy@gmail.com.

Realistically Speaking Publishing Co., *(978-0-9727874)* 10808 Foothill Blvd. No. 160-260, Rancho Cucamonga, CA 91730 USA
E-mail: sherea@vejauan.com
Web site: http://www.vejauan.com.

Reality Living Publishing, Inc., *(978-0-9643021; 978-1-888220)* 8720 E. 55th St., Kansas City, MO 64129 USA Tel 816-358-1515 ext 2062; Fax: 816-358-3439 ext 2062
E-mail: sehle@kcbt.org
Web site: http://www.realityliving.org.

Realtyls Bks. *Imprint of* **RealtylsBooks.com, Inc.**

RealtylsBooks.com, Inc., *(978-0-9791317; 978-0-9817137; 978-0-9843883; 978-0-9847390; 978-0-578-41238-2; 978-1-7334578)* 1327 Winslowe Dr., Unit 304, Palatine, IL 60074 USA Tel 847-305-4657; Toll Free: 866-534-3366; *Imprints:* Realtyls Books (Realtyls Bks); Green Lady Press, The (GreenLady)
E-mail: publish@realtyisbooks.com
Web site: http://www.realtyisbooks.com.

Really Big Coloring Bks., Inc., *(978-0-9727833; 978-0-9729753; 978-0-9763186; 978-1-935266; 978-1-61953)* 224 N. Meramec, Saint Louis, MO 63105

Publisher Name Index

USA Tel 314-725-1452; Fax: 314-725-3553; Toll Free: 800-244-2665 (1-800-Big-Book)
E-mail: wayne@bigcoloringbooks.com; ken@bigcoloringbooks.com; derek@bigcoloringbooks.com
Web site: http://www.bigcoloringbook.com; http://www.spanishcoloringbooks.com; http://www.wholesalecoloringbooks.com; http://www.coloringbook.com; http://www.coloringbookpublishers.com
Dist(s): **MeadWestvaco.**

Realms *Imprint of* **Charisma Media**

RealWord Pubns., *(978-0-9743088)* Orders Addr.: P.O. Box 931461, Norcross, GA 30093-1461 USA Fax: 678-406-9178; Edit Addr.: 6450 Indian Acres Trail, Norcross, GA 30093 USA
E-mail: wrcomm@comcast.net
Web site: http://www.climbeveryobstacle.com.

Reardon, Anne E., *(978-1-7320197; 978-1-7344770)* 10725 S. Ocean Dr. -31, Jensen Beach, FL 34957 USA Tel 772-342-4300
E-mail: Annie2yk@aol.com.

Reasor, Teresa J., *(978-0-615-50243-4; 978-0-9850069; 978-0-9886627; 978-1-940047)* P.O. Box 124, Corbin, KY 40702 USA Tel 606-528-0819
Web site: http://www.teresareasor.com
Dist(s): **CreateSpace Independent Publishing Platform**
Smashwords.

Reaves, Dawn, *(978-1-7367763)* 520 E 39th St, Brooklyn, NY 11203 USA Tel 917-673-0729
E-mail: dawn.r.reaves@gmail.com.

Rebecca E Blair *See* **Blair, Rebecca E**

Rebecca Hse., *(978-0-945522)* 1550 California St., Suite 330, San Francisco, CA 94109 USA (SAN 247-1361) Tel 415-752-1453; Toll Free: 800-321-1912 (orders only)
E-mail: Rebeccahse@aol.com
Dist(s): **New Leaf Distributing Co., Inc.**

Rebecca's Bks., *(978-0-9744346)* P.O. Box 644, Watertown, WI 53094 USA.

Rebel Girls, *(978-1-7331761; 978-1-7333292; 978-1-7342641; 978-1-7348770; 978-1-953424; 979-8-88964)* 520 Broadway, Santa Monica, CA 90401 USA Tel 424-334-0040
E-mail: services@timbuktu.me; services@rebelgirls.com
Web site: www.rebelgirls.com
Dist(s): **Penguin Random Hse. LLC**
Simon & Schuster, Inc.

Rebel Press *See* **Little Dixie Publishing Co.**

Rebel Pr., *(978-1-64339; 978-0-578-50410-0)* 9020-1 N. Capital Of Texas HWY, Suite 180, Austin, TX 78759 USA Tel 512-201-4140
E-mail: morgan@goread.com
Web site: www.rebelpress.com.

Rebel Redd Bks., *(978-0-9984228)* 2807 Doralane, Dodge City, KS 67801 USA Tel 620-682-5070
E-mail: rebelreddbooks@outlook.com.

Rebel Satori Pr., *(978-0-9790838; 978-1-60864)* P.O. Box 363, Hulls Cover, ME 04644 USA Fax: 207-669-4200
E-mail: publisher@rebelsatoripress.com
Web site: http://www.rebelsatori.com; http://www.queermojo.net
Dist(s): **Smashwords.**

Rebellion (GBR) *(978-1-904265; 978-1-906735; 978-1-907519; 978-1-84997; 978-1-907992; 978-1-78108; 978-1-78618) Dist. by* **S and S Inc.**

Rebman, Robin B. *See* **Cane Creek Productions**

Recinos, Sheryl, *(978-1-7328500; 978-1-951542)* 21667 Allison Dr., Santa Clarita, CA 91350 USA Tel 951-259-7113
E-mail: sherylrecinos@gmail.com
Web site: www.sherylrecinosmd.com.

Recipe Pubs., *(978-0-9778057; 978-0-9816282; 978-0-9824801; 978-0-9826424; 978-0-9828531; 978-0-9898137)* Orders Addr.: 610 N. Elmwood Ave, Springfield, MO 65802 USA (SAN 930-8873) Tel 417-619-4939; Toll Free: 800-313-5121
E-mail: jec1963@sbcglobal.net; jec@recipepubs.com
Web site: http://www.recipepubs.com.

Recirculation Art, *(978-0-692-11283-0)* 28 K St. SE, Washington, DC 20003 USA Tel 631-664-2277
E-mail: Recirculationart@gmail.com
Web site: www.recirculationart.com.

Reclam, Philip jun., Verlag GmbH (DEU) *(978-3-15) Dist. by* **Intl Bk Import.**

Record Stockman & Coyote Cowboy *See* **Coyote Cowboy Co.**

Recorded Bks., Inc., *(978-0-7887; 978-1-55690; 978-1-84197; 978-1-4025; 978-1-4193; 978-1-84505; 978-1-4281; 978-1-4361; 978-1-4407; 978-1-4498; 978-1-4561; 978-1-4618; 978-1-4640; 978-1-4703; 978-1-4906; 978-1-5019; 978-1-9800; 978-1-7050; 979-8-88956; 979-8-89059; 979-8-89178) Subs. of W. F. Howes Limited, Orders Addr.: 8400 Corporate Dr., Landover, MD 20785 USA (SAN 920-7414); Edit Addr.: 8400 Corporate Dr., Landover, MD 20785 USA (SAN 111-3984) Fax: 410-535-5499; Toll Free: 800-638-1304*
E-mail: mmitchell@recordedbooks.com
Web site: https://www.rbmediaglobal.com; https://rbmediaglobal.com/recorded-books/
Dist(s): **Blackstone Audio, Inc.**
Brilliance Publishing, Inc.
Ebsco Publishing
Follett School Solutions.

Recorded Books, LLC *See* **Recorded Bks., Inc.**

Recorded Sound Research *See* **Trescott Research**

Rector Pr., Ltd., *(978-0-7605; 978-0-934393; 978-1-57205)* Orders Addr.: The Ledge House 130 Rattlesnake Gutter Rd. Suite 1000, Leverett, MA 01054-9726 USA (SAN 693-8108) Tel 413-367-0303 (International Book Sales); Fax: 413-367-2853
E-mail: info@rectorpress.com; info@runanywhere.com
Web site: http://www.rectorpress.com; http://twitter.com/Lewisxxxusa; http://twitter.com/Rectorpress.

Rector Tales, *(978-0-9969085)* 22154 Barrington Way, Santa Clarita, CA 91350 USA Tel 661-449-9103
E-mail: cuffsbyrector@gmail.com
Web site: RectorTales.com.

Red & Black Pubs., *(978-0-9791813; 978-1-934941; 978-1-61001)* P.O. Box 7542, Saint Petersburg, FL 33734 USA
E-mail: info@redandblackpublishers.com
Web site: http://www.redandblackpublishers.com.

Red Barn Reading Inc., *(978-0-9753059)* P.O. Box 540, Alanson, MI 49706 USA
E-mail: thecathy@tm.net.

Red Brick Learning *Imprint of* **Capstone**

Red Bud Publishing, *(978-0-9759421)* 2425 Lakeshore Ct., Lebanon, IN 46052 USA.

Red Button Pr. *Imprint of* **Lulu Pr., Inc.**

Red CalacArts Publications *Imprint of* **Calaca Pr.**

Red Cardinal Publishing, LLC, *(978-0-9906649)* 91 School St., Chelmsford, MA 01824 USA Tel 617-240-5245
E-mail: patricia_brogdon@hotmail.com
Dist(s): **Lulu Pr., Inc.**

Red Carpet Publishing, *(978-0-9719657; 978-0-9722829)* P.O. Box 309, Noblesville, IN 46061-0309 USA (SAN 255-755X) Tel 317-847-9553; Fax: 317-773-5375
Web site: http://www.redcarpetpublishing.com.

Red Chair Pr., *(978-1-936163; 978-1-937529; 978-1-939656; 978-1-63440; 978-1-947159; 978-1-64371)* P.O. Box 333, South Egremont, MA 01258 USA (SAN 858-6209); *Imprints*: Rocking Chair Kids (Rocking Chair Kids); One Elm Books (One Elm Bks)
E-mail: redchairpress@gmail.com; info@redchairpress.com
Web site: http://www.redchairpress.com; http://www.lernerbooks.com
Dist(s): **Follett School Solutions**
Lerner Publishing Group
MyiLibrary.

RED CLAY / Young Pubs. Global Network, *(978-0-9795370)* P.O. Box 4221, Greenville, MS 38704 USA Tel 662-773-2048
E-mail: YPGNtwk@peoplepc.com
Web site: http://www.ypgn.net.

Red Cove, *(978-0-9861987; 979-8-9874481)* 1056 Franklin Pierce Hwy., Barrington, NH 03825 USA Tel 603-767-3043
E-mail: Peisland@gmail.com.

†Red Crane Bks., Inc., *(978-1-878610)* Orders Addr.: P.O. Box 33590, Santa Fe, NM 87954 USA; Edit Addr.: 2008 Rosina St., Suite C, Santa Fe, NM 87505 USA Tel 505-988-7070; Fax: 505-989-7476; Toll Free: 800-922-3392
E-mail: publish@redcrane.com
Web site: http://www.redcrane.com
Dist(s): **Chicago Distribution Ctr.**
Continental Bk. Co., Inc.
Libros Sin Fronteras; *CIP.*

Red Cygnet Pr., *(978-1-60108)* 2245 Enterprise St. Ste. 110, Escondido, CA 92029-2060 USA
E-mail: info@redcygnet.com
Web site: http://www.redcygnet.com
Dist(s): **Rosen Publishing Group, Inc., The Soundprints.**

Red Deer Pr. (CAN) *(978-0-88995) Dist. by* **Firefly Bks Limited.**

Red Door Pr., *(978-0-9763770)* 1704 Black Oak Ln., Silver Spring, MD 20910 USA Tel 301-588-7599; Fax: 301-838-9771 Do not confuse with Red Door Press in San Francisco, CA
E-mail: trishbaur@comcast.net.

Red Earth Publishing, *(978-0-9779993)* 2041 NW 20th St., Oklahoma City, OK 73106-1609 USA.

Red Earth Publishing, *(978-0-9767748)* Orders Addr.: 104 Candace Dr., Ponca City, OK 74604 USA Tel 580-763-7003
E-mail: deborahjuckes@gmail.com
Web site: http://www.redearthpub.com.

Red Engine Pr., *(978-0-9663276; 978-0-9743758; 978-0-9745652; 978-0-9785158; 978-0-9800064; 978-0-9800332; 978-0-9827923; 978-0-9834930; 978-1-937958; 978-1-943267)* 18942 State Hwy. 13, Suite F107, Branson West, MO 65737 USA Tel 417-230-5555
E-mail: riverroadpress@yahoo.com
Web site: http://www.redenginepress.com.

Red Feather *Imprint of* **Schiffer Publishing, Ltd.**

Red Fox Publishing, *(978-0-692-78504-1; 978-0-692-78506-5; 978-0-578-92907-1; 979-8-218-11994-2)* 19706 N Ramsey Rd, Rathdrum, ID 83858 USA Tel 208-709-7762.

Red Giant Entertainment *Imprint of* **Active Media Publishing, LLC**

Red Giant Publishing, *(978-0-9767661)* P.O. Box 5, San Mateo, CA 94401 USA
E-mail: questions@redgiantpublishing.com
Web site: http://www.redgiantpublishing.com.

Red Hawk Bks., *(978-0-9892851)* 12903 Pt. Richmond Dr., Gig Harbor, WA 98332 USA Tel 253-858-8794; Fax: 253-858-8795
E-mail: torreylystra@gmail.com.

Red Hawk Pr., *(978-0-9971488)*
E-mail: marykincaid2001@yahoo.com.

†Red Hen Pr., *(978-0-931093)* P.O. Box 454, Big Sur, CA 93920 USA (SAN 678-9420) Tel 831-667-2726 (phone/fax) Do not confuse with Red Hen Pr. in Casa Grande, AZ, Granada Hills, CA
E-mail: HopeHen@aol.com
Dist(s): **Book Wholesalers, Inc.**
Brodart Co.
Follett School Solutions; *CIP.*

Red Hen Pr., *(978-1-888996; 978-1-59709; 978-1-939096; 978-0-9890361; 978-1-63628)* P.O. Box 3537, Granada Hills, CA 91394 USA Tel 818-831-0649; Fax: 818-831-6659; *Imprints*: Xeno Books (XenoBooks)
E-mail: editors@redhen.org
Web site: http://www.redhen.org
Dist(s): **Chicago Distribution Ctr.**
Mintright, Inc.
Open Road Integrated Media, Inc.
SPD-Small Pr. Distribution
Two Rivers Distribution
Valentine Publishing Group.

Red Hills Writers Project, *(978-0-9759339)* 1509 Hasosaw Nene, Tallahassee, FL 32301 USA Tel 850-216-2016; Fax: 831-308-3285
E-mail: info@redhillswritersproject.org
Web site: http://www.redhillswritersproject.org.

Red Ink Pr., *(978-0-9788401)* 1914 N. Roan St., Suite 106-223, Johnson City, TN 37601 USA (SAN 851-724X) Tel 423-741-2835
Web site: http://www.redinkpress.com
Dist(s): **Book Hub, Inc.**

Red Jacket Pr., *(978-0-9748895)* 3099 Maqua Pl., Mohegan Lake, NY 10547-1054 USA
E-mail: info@redjacketpress.com
Web site: http://www.redjacketpress.com
Dist(s): **Pathway Bk. Service.**

Red Letter Pr., *(978-0-9661199; 978-0-9794420; 978-0-692-43517-5)* Orders Addr.: 6148 Rutledge Hill, Columbia, SC 29209-1315 USA Tel 843-344-2221 Do not confuse with Red Letter Pr., Seattle, WA
E-mail: redletterpress@gmail.com
Web site: http://redletterpress.googlepages.com
Dist(s): **CreateSpace Independent Publishing Platform.**

Red Letter Publishing & Media Group, *(978-0-9740003)* 3744 N. Odell Ave., Chicago, IL 606034 USA Tel 630-728-6046
E-mail: screenwriter1914@gmail.com.

Red Lotus Reads LLC, *(978-1-7355974)* P.O. Box PO Box 712, Hillside, IL 60162 USA Tel 312-399-7393
E-mail: author.honeythomas@gmail.com.

Red Men Interprises, *(978-0-9744682)* 8 Boton Rd., Lloyd Harbor, NY 11743 USA Tel 516-769-9720
E-mail: jason@drugfreeteen.com
Web site: http://www.drugfreeteen.com.

Red Mitten Bks., LLC, *(978-1-7333034)* 4222 W Bay View Ave, Tampa, FL 33611 USA Tel 813-758-2298
E-mail: barbara.escher@gmail.com
Web site: http://redmittenbooks.com.

Red Mountain Creations, *(978-0-9759858; 978-0-9910804; 978-1-7345037)* P.O. Box 172, High Ridge, MO 63049 USA Tel 636-677-3088; Toll Free: 866-732-4857
E-mail: redmountain@swbell.net
Web site: http://www.byronvonrosenberg.com.

Red Mud Pr., *(978-0-9672996)* Orders Addr.: P.O. Box 1257, Sedona, AZ 86336-4357 USA Tel 520-282-5285; Edit Addr.: 51 Remuda Rd., Sedona, AZ 86336 USA
E-mail: Crawford@sedora.net.

Red Owl Pubns., *(978-0-9754279)* 7857 Sedgewick Dr., Freeland, MI 48623 USA Tel 989-737-4486
E-mail: ckblack@redowlpublications.com
Dist(s): **MyiLibrary.**

Red Penguin Bks., *(978-0-9997460; 978-1-949864; 978-1-952859; 978-1-63777)* 27 Ontario Rd., Bellerose Village, NY 11001 USA Tel 516-448-4993; Fax: 516-740-5899
E-mail: stephanie@redpenguinbooks.com
Web site: http://redpenguinbooks.com.

Blue Pheonix Bks., *(978-0-9726290; 978-1-937781; 978-1-938969)* 809 W. Dike St., Glendora, CA 91740 USA
E-mail: Service@redphoenixbooks.com; cja@redphoenixbooks.com; claudia.alexander@gmail.com
Web site: http://www.redphoenixbooks.com
Dist(s): **Partners Pubs. Group, Inc.**

Red Planet Pictures, *(978-0-9719031)* 1800 S. Robertson Blvd., No. 153, Los Angeles, CA 90035 USA Tel 310-659-8386 (phone/fax)
E-mail: markm@laube.com
Dist(s): **Consortium Bk. Sales & Distribution.**

Red Poppy Pr., *(978-0-9778249)* 30524 Sparrow Hawk Dr., Canyon Lake, CA 92587 USA
E-mail: dharlenemarie@redpoppypress.co
Web site: http://https://www.dharlenemariefahl.com; http://https://www.redpoppypress.com.

Red Pumpkin Pr., *(978-0-9711572; 978-0-9849284)* P.O. Box 40, Rutledge, TN 37861 USA Tel 865-828-3362; Fax: 865-828-4578
E-mail: centar123@aol.com.

Red Raven Publishing, *(978-0-9774482; 978-0-9796720)* 2780 Locker Ave., Carlsbad, CA 92010 USA (SAN 257-5876) Tel 760-602-1260; Fax: 760-602-9284
E-mail: angie@hudsonsd.com.

Red River Pr. *Imprint of* **Red River Pr.**

Red River Pr., *(978-0-910653)* 3900 Roy Rd., Suite 37, Shreveport, LA 71107 USA (SAN 270-1774) Fax: 318-309-1653; *Imprints*: Red River Press (Red River Pr)
E-mail: rrp_asi@Bellsouth.net
Web site: http://www.ArchivalServicesInc.com.

Red Rock Mountain Pr. LLC, *(978-0-615-30253-9; 978-0-615-40473-8; 978-0-615-73121-6; 978-0-578-55760-1; 978-0-578-55761-8; 978-0-578-82959-3; 979-8-218-26529-8)* 7601 E Indian Bend Rd Apt 1064, Scottsdale, AZ 85250 USA.

Red Rock Pr., Inc., *(978-0-9669573; 978-0-9714372; 978-1-933176)* 331 W. 57th. Street, suite 175, New York, NY 10019 USA Tel 212-362-8304; Fax: 212-362-6216; Toll Free: 800-488-8040
E-mail: richard@redrockpress.com
Web site: http://www.redrockpress.com
Dist(s): **MyiLibrary.**

Red Rock Unicorn Bks., *(978-0-578-45942-4)* P.O. Box 251, Bayside, CA 95524 USA Tel 818-726-4426
E-mail: tiffany@redrockunicornbooks.com
Web site: redrockunicornbooks.com.

Red Sage Publishing, *(978-0-9648942; 978-0-9754516; 978-1-60310)* Div. of Red Sage Publishing, Inc., P.O. Box 4844, Seminole, FL 33775 USA (SAN 859-0249) Tel 727-391-3847 (phone/fax)
E-mail: alekendall@aol.com
Web site: http://www.eRedSage.com
Dist(s): **Brodart Co.**
Cowley Distributing, Inc.
OverDrive, Inc.

Red Sky Presents, *(978-1-941015)*
E-mail: redskypresents@gmail.com
Web site: www.redskypresents.com.

Red Sneakers Pr., *(978-1-7331597)* 20 Upper Ladue Rd., St. Louis, MO 63124 USA Tel 314-606-2200; Fax: 314-716-1280
E-mail: ssbrauer@yahoo.com.

Red Summit Pubs., *(978-0-615-76924-0; 978-1-944650)* 346 Pine Springs Dr., Debary, FL 32713 USA Tel 949-246-0980
E-mail: swoffingtonliterary@gmail.com
Web site: sandrawoffington.com; https://warriorsandwatcherssaga.com/
Dist(s): **CreateSpace Independent Publishing Platform.**

Red Tail Publishing, *(978-0-9635757; 978-0-9847756; 978-1-941950)* Orders Addr.: P.O. Box 1477, Anderson, CA 96007 USA Tel 530-365-5863
E-mail: livingston@redtail.com; info@redtail.com
Web site: http://www.redtail.com.

Red Team Ink, *(978-0-9982349; 978-0-9984881; 978-1-7322129)* 9480 W. River Beach Ln., Boise, ID 83714 USA Tel 208-870-8359; Fax: 208-870-8359
E-mail: Redteamink@gmail.com
Web site: www.redteamink.com.

Red Truck LLC, *(978-0-615-73703-4; 978-0-578-51086-6)* 6568 Finch Ct., Fort Collins, CO 80525 USA Tel 970-215-4191
E-mail: jimcampain@comcast.net.

Red Wagon *See* **Magic Wagon**

Red Wagon Bks. *Imprint of* **Harcourt Children's Bks.**

†Red Wheel/Weiser, *(978-0-87728; 978-0-943233; 978-1-56414; 978-1-57324; 978-1-57863; 978-1-59003; 978-1-60163; 978-1-60925; 978-1-61283; 978-1-61852; 978-1-61940; 978-1-938875; 978-1-63265; 978-1-63341; 978-1-942785; 978-1-64297; 978-0-692-19811-7; 978-1-953650;-1-63748) Div. of Weiser Bks., Orders Addr.: 65 Parker St., Suite 7, Newburyport, MA 01950 USA (SAN 255-8610) Tel 978-465-0504; Fax: 978-465-0243; Toll Free Fax: 877-337-3309; Toll Free: 800-423-7087 (orders only); Imprints*: New Page Books (New Page Bks); Career Press (CareerPr)
E-mail: customerservice@redwheelweiser.com
Web site: http://www.redwheelweiser.com
Dist(s): **Abyss Distribution**
D.A.P./Distributed Art Pubs.
Ebsco Publishing
Ingram Publisher Services
New Leaf Distributing Co., Inc.
Open Road Integrated Media, Inc.; *CIP.*

Red Yellow Blue, *(978-0-578-91226-4; 978-0-578-91227-1; 978-1-7374068)* 777 Carson St. 0, MEMPHIS, TN 38111 USA Tel 9012107885
E-mail: d12pray@yahoo.com
Dist(s): **Ingram Content Group.**

Redback Publishing (AUS) *(978-0-9946247; 978-1-925630; 978-1-925860; 978-1-922322; 978-1-76140) Dist. by* **IPG Chicago.**

Redcay Publishing, *(978-0-615-17346-7)* 2953 Grandview Blvd., West LAwn, PA 19609 USA Tel 610-678-5636
E-mail: mwkreitz@msn.com
Web site: http://www.divcothelittlemilktruck.com.

Redding, Marion T. *See* **Redding Stenner, Marion**

Redding Pr., *(978-0-9658879)* Orders Addr.: c/o Mary Mahony, P.O. Box 366, Belmont, MA 02178 USA Fax: 617-489-9476; Toll Free: 800-267-6012; Edit Addr.: P.O. Box 366, Belmont, MA 02178 USA
E-mail: mary@reddingpress.com
Web site: http://www.channel.com/users/msmahony; http://www.reddingpress.com
Dist(s): **Quality Bks., Inc.**

Redding Stenner, Marion, *(978-0-9671701)* Starbourne House, Orders Addr.: 13911 State Rte. 38, Marysville, OH 43040 USA (SAN 254-4024) Tel 740-369-4952
E-mail: marionredding@icloud.com; starbourne53@gmail.com
Web site: http://www.davidredding.net.

Redel, Nicole, *(978-0-9769738)* 2125 David Dr., Florissant, MO 63031-4321 USA Tel 314-839-3242
E-mail: gospelpitbull@sbcglobal.net
Web site: http://www.gospelpitbull.com.

Redemption Pr., *(978-1-63232; 978-1-68314; 978-1-7329625; 978-1-64645; 978-1-951310; 978-1-951350)* 1730 Railroad St., Enumclaw, WA 98022 USA Tel 360-226-3488; Toll Free Fax: 855-498-6595; Toll Free: 888-305-2967; P.O. Box 427, Enumclaw, WA 98022 Tel 360-226-3488; Toll Free: 844-273-3336; *Imprints*: Reliant Publishing (MYID_A_RELIANT)
E-mail: accounting@redemption-press.com
Web site: www.redemption-press.com
Dist(s): **Spring Arbor Distributors, Inc.**

Redhawk Publishing, *(978-0-9641861; 978-0-9769267)* Orders Addr.: 602 Pompa St., Carlsbad, NM 88220 USA Tel 505-885-1748; *Imprints*: RWP Books (RWP Bks)
E-mail: randy@rwpbooks.com
Web site: http://www.rwpbooks.com
Dist(s): **CreateSpace Independent Publishing Platform.**

RedJack *See* **Mutaneers**

Redleaf Pr., *(978-0-934140; 978-1-884834; 978-1-929610; 978-1-933653; 978-1-60554)* Div. of Resources for Child Caring, Inc., 10 Yorkton Ct., Saint Paul, MN 55117-1065

USA (SAN 212-8691) Toll Free Fax: 800-641-0115; Toll Free: 800-423-8309
E-mail: sales@redleafpress.org
Web site: http://www.redleafpress.org
Dist(s): **Capstone**
Consortium Bk. Sales & Distribution
Gryphon Hse., Inc.
Lectorum Pubns., Inc.
MyiLibrary.

Redline Bks., *(978-0-9727440)* 2280 Jones Creek Rd., White Bluff, TN 37187 USA Tel 615-797-3043 (phone/fax)
E-mail: redlinebooks@bardyoung.com; bardyoung@bardyoung.com.

RedMEDIA, *(978-0-9721708)* 41 Schermerhorn St., No. 147, Brooklyn, NY 11201 USA Tel 718-857-6638; Fax: 718-857-6427
E-mail: rmedia3@aol.com
Web site: http://www.tgoodlife.com; http://www.ibrooklyn.com/redmedia.

Redmond, Pamela, *(978-0-9760767)* P.O. Box 169, Topping, VA 23169-0169 USA.

Reece, Kim Taylor Prodns. LLC, *(978-0-9660395; 978-1-59779)* 53-866 Kamehameha Hwy., Hauula, HI 96717 USA Tel 808-293-2000; Fax: 808-293-2136; Toll Free: 800-657-7966
E-mail: info@kimtaylorreece.com
Web site: http://www.kimtaylorreece.com
Dist(s): **Booklines Hawaii, Ltd.**
Islander Group.

Reed Business Information, *(978-0-9614276; 978-1-879930; 978-1-931625; 978-0-9764027; 978-0-9851869)* 5900 Wilshire Blvd. Ste. 3100, Los Angeles, CA 90036-5030 USA (SAN 687-3944) Toll Free: 800-545-2411
E-mail: nlongman@reedbusiness.com; steve.atinsky@reedbusiness.com
Web site: http://www.la411.com
Dist(s): **SCB Distributors.**

Reed, Robert D. Pubs., *(978-1-885003; 978-1-931741; 978-1-934759; 978-1-944297)* P.O. Box 1992, Bandon, OR 97411 USA Tel 541-347-9882; Fax: 541-347-9883
E-mail: 4bobreed@msn.com
Web site: http://www.rdrpublishers.com
Dist(s): **Independent Pubs. Group**
Midpoint Trade Bks., Inc.
Todd Communications.

Reedale Karma Pr., *(978-0-615-67492-6; 978-0-615-90362-0; 978-0-692-88606-9; 978-0-692-09330-6; 978-0-692-13563-1)* 52 Timarron Trail, Rochester, NY 14612 USA Tel 585-368-0383
Dist(s): **CreateSpace Independent Publishing Platform.**

Reedswain, Inc., *(978-0-9651020; 978-1-890946; 978-1-59164)* Orders Addr.: 88 Wells Rd., Spring City, PA 19475-8628 USA Toll Free: 800-331-5191
E-mail: bryan@reedswain.com
Web site: http://www.reedswain.com
Dist(s): **Cardinal Pubs. Group.**

Reedy Pr., *(978-0-9753180; 978-1-933370; 978-1-935806; 978-1-68106)* Orders Addr.: P.O. Box 5131, Saint Louis, MO 63139 USA Toll Free Fax: 866-999-6916 fax
E-mail: jstevens@reedypress.com; dkorte@reedypress.com
Web site: http://www.reedypress.com
Dist(s): **Partners Bk. Distributing, Inc.**

Reel Productions, LLC, *(978-0-9675010; 978-0-9707422)* P.O. Box 1069, Monument, CO 80132 USA Toll Free: 800-964-0439
E-mail: support@reelproductions.net; jolene@explorationfilms.com
Web site: http://www.explorationfilms.com; http://www.reelproductions.net
Dist(s): **Exploration Films**
Send The Light Distribution LLC.

Reeves Bay Press, *(978-0-9860833)* 17 Huntington Lane, Flanders, NY 11901 USA.

Reeves, Emily, *(978-0-9821506)* P.O. Box 15861, Savannah, GA 31416 USA.

Reference Service Pr., *(978-0-918276; 978-1-58841)* 5000 Windplay Dr., Suite 4, El Dorado Hills, CA 95762 USA (SAN 210-2633) Tel 916-939-9620; Fax: 916-939-9626
E-mail: findaid@aol.com; info@rspfunding.com
Web site: http://www.rspfunding.com.

ReferencePoint Pr., Inc., *(978-1-60152; 978-1-68282; 978-1-6782)* P.O. Box 27779, San Diego, CA 92198 USA (SAN 858-6845) Tel 858-618-1314; Fax: 858-618-1730; Toll Free: 888-479-6436; 17150 Via Del Campo. Ste. 205, San Diego, CA 92127-2138; *Imprints:* BrightPoint Press (MYID_J_BRIGHTP)
E-mail: dan@referencepointpress.com; orders@referencepointpress.com; info@referencepointpress.com
Web site: http://www.referencepointdigital.com; http://www.brightpointpress.com; http://www.referencepointpress.com.

Refined Savage Editions / Ediciones El Salvaje Refinado, The, *(978-0-9713175; 978-0-9746855; 978-0-9761940; 978-0-9768868; 978-0-9791011; 978-0-9802008; 978-0-9816968)* 10 Delaware Ave., Charleston, WV 25302-1950 USA
E-mail: esrefinado@aol.com
Web site: http://www.esrefinado.net.

Reflect 14, *(978-1-7355451)* 3281 Logan Dr, Fremont, CA 94536 USA Tel 650-804-6318
E-mail: reflect.fourteen@gmail.com.

Reflection Pr., *(978-0-9671543)* 3430 W. 98th Pl. Unit A, Westminster, CO 80031 USA Tel 303-862-4868 Do not confuse with companies with the same name in Huntsville, AL, Berkeley, CA
E-mail: mbsmith48@gmail.com.

Reflection Pr., *(978-0-9843799; 978-1-945289)* 3452 16th St. No. 102 3452 16th St. No. 102, San Francisco, CA 94114 USA
E-mail: info@reflectionpress.com; manager@reflectionpress.com; hello@genderwheel.com
Web site: https://www.genderwheel.com; https://www.reflectionpress.com.

Reflection Publishing, *(978-0-9797618; 978-1-936629)* P.O. Box 2182, Citrus Heights, CA 95621-2182 USA Fax: 916-726-2768
E-mail: contact@reflectpublishing.com
Web site: http://www.reflectpublishing.com.

Reflection Publishing Company *See* **Imprints**

Reflection Publishing Co., *(978-0-9657561; 978-0-9712142)* 1813 4th St W., Palmetto, FL 34221-4303 USA (SAN 299-2787) Toll Free: 888-677-0101
E-mail: lakepm@msn.com
Web site: http://www.reflectionpublishing.com
Dist(s): **Brodart Co.**
Spring Arbor Distributors, Inc.

Reflections Publishing Hse., *(978-0-9837231; 978-0-9965296)* 925 N. Inglewood Ave No. 10, Inglewood, CA 90302 USA Tel 310-695-9800
E-mail: dabellis@sbcglobal.net
Web site: www.reflectionspublishings.net.

Reflections Publishing, Incorporated *See* **GFC Pr.**

Reform Judaism Publishing *Imprint of* **Central Conference of American Rabbis/CCAR Pr.**

Reformation Herald Publishing Assn., *(978-0-9745295; 978-1-934308)* P.O. Box 7240, Roanoke, VA 24019-0240 USA
Web site: http://www.sdarm.org.

Reformation Heritage Books *See* **Reformation Heritage Bks.**

Reformation Heritage Bks., *(978-1-892777; 978-1-60178; 979-8-88686)* 3070 29th St. SE, Grand Rapids, MI 49512 USA
E-mail: jay.collier@heritagebooks.org
Web site: http://www.heritagebooks.org
Dist(s): **Send The Light Distribution LLC**
christianaudio.

Reformed Church Pr., Reformed Church in America, *(978-0-916466)* 4500 60th St., SE, Grand Rapids, MI 49512-9670 USA Tel 616-698-7071; Fax: 616-698-6606; Toll Free: 800-968-7221 (orders); 475 Riverside Dr., 18th Flr., New York, NY 10115 (SAN 207-4508)
Dist(s): **Faith Alive Christian Resources.**

Reformed Free Publishing Assn., *(978-0-916206; 978-1-936054; 978-1-944555; 978-1-7368154; 978-1-959515; 979-8-9871614)* Orders Addr.: 1894 Georgetown Ctr. Dr., Jenison, MI 49428-7137 USA Tel 616-457-5970
E-mail: mail@rfpa.org
Web site: http://www.rfpa.org.

Refugee Pr., *(978-0-692-43628-8; 978-0-692-88712-7; 978-0-692-95136-1; 978-0-578-48744-1; 978-0-578-48745-8; 978-0-578-60339-1; 978-0-578-92842-5)* 2511 Buck Quarter Farm Rd., Hillsborough, NC 27278 USA Tel 919 625-4502
Dist(s): **CreateSpace Independent Publishing Platform.**

Regal Bks. *Imprint of* **Gospel Light Pubns.**

Regal Enterprises, *(978-0-9727771; 978-0-9729960)* 16310 Garfield Ave., Paramount, CA 90723-4806 USA (SAN 255-2477)
Dist(s): **Timberwolf Pr., Inc.**

Regal Hse. Publishing, LLC, *(978-0-9912612; 978-0-9988398; 978-1-947548; 978-1-64603)* ; *Imprints:* Fitzroy Books (MYID_F_FITZROY)
E-mail: info@regalhousepublishing.com; jaynieroyal@regalhousepublishing.com
Web site: www.pactpress.com; www.fitzroybooks.com; https://regalhousepublishing.com; https://regalhouseinitiative.org/
Dist(s): **Independent Pubs. Group.**

Regan Arts, *(978-0-615-97507-8; 978-1-941393; 978-1-942872; 978-0-692-44842-7; 978-0-692-44843-4; 978-1-68245; 978-0-9973114)* 65 Bleecker St., 8th Flr., New York, NY 10012 USA Tel 646-589-0317
E-mail: kurt@reganarts.com; info@reganarts.com
Web site: http://www.reganarts.com
Dist(s): **Simon & Schuster, Inc.**

ReganBooks *Imprint of* **HarperCollins Pubs.**

Regency Hse., Ltd., *(978-0-9716923)* 6538 Pardee, Taylor, MI 48180-1771 USA Tel 313-291-9242
Dist(s): **Baker & Taylor Publisher Services (BTPS).**

Regenold Publishing, *(978-0-9773085)* P.O. Box 621967, Littleton, CO 80162-1967 USA (SAN 257-2583) Tel 303-797-8881
Web site: http://www.regenoldpublishing.com.

Regent Pr., *(978-0-916147; 978-1-889059; 978-1-58790)* 2747 Regent St., Berkeley, CA 94705-1212 USA (SAN 294-9717) Tel 510-845-1196 Do not confuse with Regent Pr., Oxnard, CA
E-mail: regentpress@mindspring.com
Web site: http://www.regentpress.net
Dist(s): **Ingram Content Group.**

Regina Orthodox Pr., *(978-0-9649141; 978-1-928653)* Orders Addr.: P.O. Box 5288, Salisbury, MA 01952 USA Fax: 978-462-5079; Toll Free: 800-636-2470; Edit Addr.: 6 Second St., Salisbury, MA 01952 USA
E-mail: reginaorthodoxpress@comcast.net
Web site: http://www.reginaorthodoxpress.com
Dist(s): **National Bk. Network.**

Regina Pr., Malhame & Co., *(978-0-88271)* Orders Addr.: P.O. Box 608, Melville, NY 11747-0608 USA (SAN 203-0853) Tel 631-694-8600; Edit Addr.: 10 Hub Dr., Melville, NY 11747 USA
E-mail: customerservice@malhame.com
Web site: http://www.malhame.com/
Dist(s): **Catholic Bk. Publishing Corp.**

Reginetta Pr., LLC, *(978-0-9823714)* P.O. Box 7042, Aurora, IL 60507 USA
Web site: http://www.HookandJill.com; http://www.ReginettaPress.com
Dist(s): **Ingram Bk. Co.**
New Leaf Distributing Co., Inc.

Region 4 Education Service Ctr., *(978-1-932524; 978-1-932797; 978-1-933049; 978-1-933521; 978-1-934950; 978-1-937403; 978-1-945615; 978-1-950577)* 7145 W. Tidwell, Houston, TX 77092-2096 USA Tel 713-462-7708; Fax: 713-744-6514
E-mail: daniesha.debose@esc4.net
Web site: http://www.esc4.net
Dist(s): **Consortium Bk. Sales & Distribution.**

Region IV Education Service Center *See* **Region 4 Education Service Ctr.**

Regional Laboratory for Educational Improvement of the Northeast & Islands *See* **NETWORK Inc., The**

Regnery Kids *Imprint of* **Regnery Publishing**

†Regnery Publishing, *(978-0-89526; 978-1-882926; 978-1-932236; 978-1-59698; 978-1-933859; 978-1-935191; 978-1-61017; 978-1-62157; 978-1-68451)* Div. of Caron Broadcasting, Inc., 122 C Street, N.W., Suite 515, Washington, DC 20001 USA (SAN 210-5578) Tel 202-216-0600; *Imprints:* Little Patriot Press (LittlePatriot); Regnery Kids (REGNERY KIDS)
E-mail: sales@regnery.com; subrights@regnery.com
Web site: http://www.regnery.com
Dist(s): **Continental Bk. Co., Inc.**
MyiLibrary
Simon & Schuster, Inc.
ebrary, Inc.; *CIP.*

Regnery Publishing, Incorporated, An Eagle Publishing Company *See* **Regnery Publishing**

†Regular Baptist Pr., *(978-0-87227; 978-1-59402; 978-1-60776; 978-1-62940; 978-1-64213; 979-8-88973)* Div. of General Assn. of Regular Baptist Churches, 244 S RANDALL RD, ELGIN, IL 60123 USA (SAN 205-2229) Tel 847-843-1600 (foreign orders); 708-843-1600; Fax: 847-843-3757; Toll Free: 800-727-4440 (orders only)
E-mail: rbporders@garbc.org; LOLSON@GARBC.ORG
Web site: http://www.regularbaptistpress.org; *CIP.*

REHammer Pr., *(978-0-692-99749-9; 978-0-578-39862-4; 979-8-218-19334-8)* 6039 Spencer Ave., Bronx, NY 10471 USA Tel 917-678-4977
E-mail: Hammertime217@gmail.com.

Reich, Tina, *(978-1-7343186)* 40 Oleander Ln, Turlock, CA 95380 USA Tel 209-648-2119
E-mail: reichtina320@gmail.com.

Reid For Read Publishing, LLC, *(978-1-7341125)* 6402 Redcliff Dr., Fayetteville, NC 28311 USA Tel 910-257-7227
E-mail: reidforread@gmail.com.

Reid, Hunter, *(978-1-958920; 978-1-961225)* 250 E. 5th St. 15th Flr., Cincinnati, OH 45202 USA Tel 513-202-6559
E-mail: hunterreid127@gmail.com.

Joseph Reidhead & Co. Pubs., *(978-0-9830615; 978-0-9886685; 978-1-940777)* Orders Addr.: 366 Moll Rd., Augusta, MO 63332 USA Tel 314-724-0949
E-mail: reidhead@gmail.com
Web site: http://sotinapublishing.com; http://sentinel.sotinapublishing.com; http://dialectics.sotinapublishing.com; http://jmissouri.com; http://sacredwindspress.com.

Reiki Blessings, *(978-0-9743679)* P.O. Box 2000, Byron, GA 31008-2000 USA (SAN 255-7045) Fax: 801-705-1802
E-mail: reikiblessings@earthlink.net
Web site: http://www.rbpress.com.

Reily Garrett, *(978-0-9989265; 978-1-7339585; 978-1-7363050; 979-8-9867391)* 11400 urieville Ln., Worton, MD 21678 USA Tel 443-480-0639
E-mail: rylankillian@gmail.com
Web site: reilygarrett.com.

Reimann Bks., *(978-0-9820941; 978-0-9838148; 978-0-9852254; 978-1-938743)* Orders Addr.: 305 Parkton Dr, Richlands, NC 28574 USA
E-mail: reimannbooks@gmail.com
Web site: http://www.reimannbooks.com.

Reinhart, Patrick *See* **Curiouser Hse. Publishing**

Reinoso, Marta, *(978-0-9676203)* World Educational Guild, Inc. 1330 E. 223rd., Suite 501, Carson, CA 90745 USA Tel 310-816-1100; Fax: 310-816-1103
E-mail: wegi@earthnet.com.

Reisman, Dave *See* **Jumping Cow Pr.**

Rejoyce Pubns., *(978-0-9661564)* 5205 Aryshire Dr., Dublin, OH 43017 USA Tel 614-766-2771; Fax: 614-766-1731.

Relationship Resources, Inc., *(978-0-9721728)* P.O. Box 63383, Colorado Springs, CO 80962 USA
E-mail: gaylyn@relationshipresources.org
Web site: http://www.relationshipresources.org
Dist(s): **Send The Light Distribution LLC.**

Relde Publishing, *(978-0-9701863)* Subs. of Solutions Training & Development LLC, P.O. Box 21304, Jackson, MS 39289 USA Tel 601-926-4375; Fax: 601-926-4374; Toll Free: 800-489-3439
E-mail: solut2000@aol.com.

Release Repurpose Reorganize LLC, *(978-1-7359684)* 945 Roberts Landing Cove, Sandy Springs, GA 30350 USA Tel 678-537-1160
E-mail: dnqsolutions@gmail.com
Web site: www.releaserepurpose.com.

Relentless Publishing Hse., *(978-0-9991975; 978-1-948829; 978-1-955819)* 136-4 Forum Dr. No. B8, Columbia, SC 29229 USA Tel 803-200-1094
E-mail: info@relentlesspublishing.com
Web site: https://www.relentlesspublishing.com.

Relevant Graces Productions, *(978-0-9822375)* 1044 Cresswood Dr., Richlands, VA 24641 USA.

Relevant Media Group, Inc., *(978-0-9714576; 978-0-9729276; 978-0-9746942; 978-0-9760357; 978-0-9763642; 978-0-9768175; 978-0-9776167; 978-0-9777480)* 1220 Alden Rd., Orlando, FL 32803-2546 USA; 600 Rinehart Rd., Lake Mary, FL 32746
E-mail: nick@relevantmediagroup.com
Web site: http://www.relevantbooks.com/
Dist(s): **Charisma Media.**

Relevant Pages Pr., *(978-0-615-82759-9; 978-0-615-87121-9; 978-0-692-31475-3; 978-0-692-50308-9; 978-0-692-56515-5; 978-0-692-58351-7; 978-0-692-58360-9; 978-0-692-58792-8; 978-0-692-64319-8; 978-0-9982211; 978-1-947303)* 3301 Heathland Way, Mt. Pleasant, SC 29466 USA Tel 843-813-0172
Web site: www.narthexacademyseries.com
Dist(s): **CreateSpace Independent Publishing Platform.**

Relevant Ventures, LLC, *(978-0-9760259)* 4279 Roswell Rd., Suite 102-273, Atlanta, GA 30342-4145 USA (SAN 256-4483) Tel 404-842-1930; Fax: 404-842-1021
E-mail: td3@mac.com; tom@relevantventures.com
Web site: http://www.relevantventures.com.

Reliant Energy, *(978-0-9791383)* 1000 Main St., Houston, TX 77002 USA
E-mail: jmolholt@reliant.com.

Reliant Publishing *Imprint of* **Redemption Pr.**

Religion Res. Institute, *(978-0-9765024; 978-0-578-41422-5; 978-0-578-67382-0)* P.O. Box 7505, Prospect Heights, IL 60070 USA Tel 773-396-0147
E-mail: info@religionresearchinstitute.org
Web site: http://www.religionresearchinstitute.org.

Reluctant Reader Bks. *Imprint of* **Cronus College**

Remarco Publishing, *(978-0-9770762)* P.O. Box 644, Ames, IA 50010 USA (SAN 256-6958) Tel 515-203-0358
Web site: http://www.remarcopublishing.com.

RemarkableMe, *(978-0-9776642)* 3905 W 10260 N, CEDAR HILLS, UT 84062 USA Tel 801-796-6486; Fax: 801-796-6486
E-mail: charless@utahweb.com
Web site: http://www.remarkableme.com.

Remedia Pubns., *(978-1-56175; 978-1-59639; 978-1-61394; 978-1-949581; 978-1-64807)* 15887 N. 76th St., Suite 120, Scottsdale, AZ 85260-1696 USA Tel 602-661-9900; Fax: 602-661-9901; Toll Free: 800-826-4740
E-mail: christina@rempub.com; Becky@rempub.com
Web site: http://www.rempub.com.

Remey, Lisa, *(978-0-9855445)* PSC 2 Box 6496, APO, AE 85718 USA
E-mail: rlremey@aol.com.

Reminders Of Faith, Inc., *(978-0-9748160; 978-0-9763691)* 518 Overhead Dr., Moon Township, PA 15108 USA Fax: 412-264-7857
E-mail: kathyb@remindersoffaith.com
Dist(s): **Send The Light Distribution LLC.**

Remnant Pubns., Inc., *(978-1-883012; 978-1-933291; 978-0-9777445; 978-1-937718; 978-1-62913)* Orders Addr.: 649 E. Chicago Rd., Coldwater, MI 49036-9497 USA Tel 517-279-1304 (ext. 23); Fax: 517-279-1804; Toll Free: 800-423-1319
Web site: http://www.remnantpublications.com.

RemStar Ink, *(978-0-9988791)* 5209 Melvin Ave., Tarzana, CA 91356 USA Tel 818-977-3023
E-mail: remace@yahoo.com.

Renaissance Books *See* **New Millennium Bks.**

Renaissance Learning, Inc., *(978-0-9646404; 978-1-893751; 978-0-9708138; 978-1-931731; 978-1-931819; 978-1-932299; 978-1-59455)* 2911 Peach St., Wisconsin Rapids, WI 54494 USA Tel 715-424-3636; Toll Free: 800-338-4204; P.O. Box 8036, Wisconsin Rapids, WI 54495-8036
E-mail: answers@renlearn.com
Web site: http://www.renlearn.com.

Renaissance Pubns., *(978-1-929473)* Div. of Mission Renaissance, 5744 San Fernando Rd., Glendale, CA 91202-2104 USA Toll Free: 800-430-4278 Do not confuse with Renaissance Publications, Worthington, OH

Renegado Pr., The, *(978-0-9754616)* Orders Addr.: 29 Lynn Way, Indiana, PA 15701 USA Tel 724-388-3958
E-mail: mackelly@renegadopress.com
Web site: http://www.theavatarthenovel.com.

Reney Editions, Inc., *(978-0-9752688)* 35 Sands Brook Dr., New Hemstead, NY 10977 USA Tel 845-548-4029
E-mail: ethan@reney.com
Web site: http://www.reney.com.

Renner Writes, *(978-0-9990586; 978-1-7357351)* 1111 E Le Marche Ave, Phoenix, AZ 85022 USA Tel 602-228-7451
E-mail: barb.renner@gmail.com
Web site: www.rennerwrites.com.

Rennie Road Books *See* **Tuxbury Publishing LLC**

Renovo Partners LLC, *(978-1-935310)* 8220 Jones Rd., Suite 100, Houston, TX 77065-5375 USA (SAN 857-1163) Tel 281-677-9568; Fax: 281-677-9480; Toll Free: 877-773-6686
E-mail: customers@renovopartners.com; barhorw@nationwide.com
Web site: http://www.renovopartners.com.

Repko, Marya *See* **ECity Publishing**

Repressed Publishing LLC, *(978-1-4622; 978-1-5042; 978-1-5222)* P.O. Box 1242, Provo, UT 84603 USA; 223 W. Bulldog Blvd., Number 420, Provo, UT 84604 Tel 385-204-4408
E-mail: orders@repressedpublishing; customerservice@repressedpublishing.com
Web site: http://www.repressedpublishing.com/.

†Reprint Services Corp., *(978-0-7812; 978-0-932051; 978-1-4227)* P.O. Box 130, Murrieta, CA 92564-0130 USA (SAN 686-2640) Fax: 951-699-5065
E-mail: Reprintservices@gmail.com; *CIP.*

Requiem Pr., *(978-0-9758542; 978-0-9788687)* Orders Addr.: 3271 Timrod Rd., Bethune, SC 29009 USA Toll Free: 888-708-7675; P.O. Box 7, Bethune, SC 29009 Tel 843-334-6222; Toll Free: 888-708-7675
E-mail: info@requiempress.com
Web site: http://www.requiempress.com.

Research & Education Assn., *(978-0-7386; 978-0-87891)* Div. of Courier Corporation, Orders Addr.: 61 Ethel Rd.,

Publisher Name Index

W., Piscataway, NJ 08854 USA (SAN 204-6814) Tel 732-819-8880; Fax: 732-819-8808; Toll Free: 800-822-0830
E-mail: jcording@rea.com; info@rea.com
Web site: http://www.rea.com
Dist(s): **Dover Pubns., Inc.**
Firebrand Technologies
INscribe Digital
Independent Pubs. Group
MyiLibrary.

†**Research Centre of Kabbalah,** *(978-0-924457; 978-0-943688; 978-1-57189; 978-1-7334303; 978-1-952895)* 83-84 115th St., Richmond Hill, NY 11418 USA (SAN 210-9484) Tel 718-805-9122; Fax: 718-805-5899; Toll Free: 888-522-2252
Web site: http://www.kabbalah.com/kabbalah/
Dist(s): **MyiLibrary**; *CIP*.

Research Evaluation & Statistics *See* **Image Cascade Publishing**

Research In Time Publications, *(978-0-9764341)* 101 Hotchkiss Grove Rd., No. 4, Branford, CT 06405 USA
E-mail: raradune@comcast.net.

Research In Time Publishers *See* **Research In Time Publications**

Research Institute Pr., The, *(978-0-9752986)* 5000 Enighed Pmb 356, Saint John, VI 00830 USA Tel 340-998-9597
E-mail: asewer@triinformation.com; info@triinformation.com
Web site: www.triinformation.com.

Research Pr., *(978-0-87822)* Orders Addr.: P.O. Box 7886, Champaign, IL 61826-9177 USA (SAN 282-2490) Toll Free: 800-519-2707; Edit Addr.: 2612 N. Mattis Ave., Champaign, IL 61822 USA (SAN 282-2482) Tel 217-352-3273; Fax: 217-352-1221 Do not confuse with Research Pr., Prairie Village, KS
E-mail: products@researchpress.com; permissions@researchpress.com
Web site: http://www.researchpress.com.

Resilience Learning Academy LLC, *(978-1-7335296; 978-1-7335297; 978-1-7335298; 978-1-7335299; 978-1-7335300; 978-1-7335301; 978-1-7335302)* 15329 Chicago Rd., Apt.12, Dolton, IL 60419 USA Tel 708-916-2121
E-mail: bcrump2014@gmail.com.

Resilient Walker, *(978-0-578-44762-9)* P.O. Box 41979, Nashville, TN 37204 USA Tel 615-425-1631
E-mail: resilientwalker@gmail.com
Dist(s): **Ingram Content Group.**

Resolution Pr., *(978-0-9838886; 978-0-9982423-0-9)* 8301 SW 6th Ave., Portland, OR 97219 USA Tel 503-957-5219
E-mail: betsyshand@hotmail.com
Web site: www.survivingnaturaldisastersbook.com
Dist(s): **Baker & Taylor Publisher Services (BTPS).**

Resort Gifts Unlimited, Incorporated *See* **RGU Group, The**

ReSource Guides, Inc., *(978-0-9755370)* 13110 Vista del Mundo, San Antonio, TX 78216-2200 USA Tel 210-493-3974
E-mail: resource@resourceguides.com
Web site: http://www.resourceguides.com.

†**Resource Pubns., Inc.,** *(978-0-89390)* 160 E. Virginia St., No. 290, San Jose, CA 95112-5876 USA (SAN 209-3081) Tel 408-286-8505; Fax: 408-287-8748; Toll Free: 888-273-7782 Do not confuse with Resource Pubns. in Los Angeles, CA
E-mail: info@rpinet.com
Web site: http://www.rpinet.com
Dist(s): **Empire Publishing Service**
Feldheim Pubs.; *CIP*.

Resource Publishing, *(978-0-9706429; 978-0-615-22022-2; 978-0-692-49159-1)* 3736 Brookwood Rd., Birmingham, AL 35223 USA Tel 205-967-3446 Do not confuse company with same or similar name in Greensboro, NC, Baton Rouge, LA, San Francisco, CA
E-mail: hoytwilson1@charter.net.

Resource Pubns.(OR) *Imprint of* **Wipf & Stock Pubs.**

Resources for Children with Special Needs, Inc., *(978-0-9678365; 978-0-9755116)* 116 E. 16th St., 5th Flr., New York, NY 10003 USA
E-mail: dlittwin@resourcesnyc.org
Web site: http://www.resourcesnyc.org.

Resources for Christian Living *See* **RCL Benziger Publishing**

Resources on the Net Publishing, *(978-0-9722803)* 250 32 St., No. 307, Bellingham, WA 98225-0943 USA.

RESPONDER911, Inc., *(978-0-9746186)* 17011 Beach Blvd., Suite No. 900, Huntington Beach, CA 92647 USA Tel 714-375-6693; Fax: 714-375-6694
Web site: http://www.responder911.com.

Restart Enterprises *See* **DGriffith Publishing**

Restless Bks., *(978-0-9899832; 978-1-63206)* 232 3rd St. No. A111, Brooklyn, NY 11215 USA Tel 646-202-9498
E-mail: joshua@restlessbooks.com
Web site: https://restlessbooks.org/
Dist(s): **INscribe Digital**
Publishers Group West (PGW)
Simon & Schuster, Inc.

Restore Order Professional Organizeg *See* **Restore Order Professional Organizing**

Restore Order Professional Organizing, *(978-0-692-18566-7)* 6110 Farmwood Way, Mableton, GA 30126 USA Tel 770-744-5970
E-mail: naeemah.fordgoldson@gmail.com
Web site: www.restoreordernow.com.

Resurrected Pr. *Imprint of* **Intrepid Ink, LLC**

Resurrecting Faith, *(978-0-9729876)* P.O. Box 43217, Minneapolis, MN 55443-0217 USA
E-mail: admin@churchofminneapolis.org; cerise.lewis@comcast.net
Web site: http://www.resurrectingfaith.org; http://www.churchofminneapolis.org.

Resurrection House *See* **Firebird Creative**

Resurrection Pr. *Imprint of* **Catholic Bk. Publishing Corp.**

Resurrection Resources LLC, *(978-0-9653723; 978-0-9710950; 978-0-9792338)* 8362 Tamarack Village, Ste. 119, Woodbury, MN 55125 USA
E-mail: editor@thefathersbooks.com; sales@thefathersbooks.com
Web site: http://www.thefathersbooks.com
Dist(s): **Send The Light Distribution LLC.**

Rethinking Resiliency, LLC, *(978-0-578-53381-0; 978-0-578-62750-2; 978-1-7345026; 979-8-218-17379-1; 979-8-9885597)* 5009 Bobwhite Ln., Richmond, VA 23227 USA Tel 804-709-2777
E-mail: davisal5484@marybaldwin.edu
Web site: www.rethinkingresiliency.com.

Rethinking Schls., Ltd., *(978-0-942961; 978-1-937730; 978-0-9998640)* 6737 W. Washington St Ste 3249, Milwaukee, WI 53214 USA (SAN 667-9633) Tel 414-964-9646; Toll Free: 800-669-4192
E-mail: office@rethinkingschools.org
Web site: http://www.rethinkingschools.org
Dist(s): **Publishers Storage & Shipping.**

Retired Professor, *(978-1-7372178; 979-8-9877782)* 2100 3rd Ave Apt 1201, SEATTLE, WA 98121 USA Tel 916-205-0240
E-mail: artzau@gmail.com.

Retriever Pr., *(978-0-9760718; 978-0-615-55790-8)* 3689 Ridge Line Dr., San Bernardino, CA 92407 USA.

Retro Recess *See* **Crownover Enterprises, LLC**

Return To The Word, *(978-0-9709763)* Div of LIFE Fellowship Family Bible Church, 11500 Sheridan Blvd., Westminster, CO 80020 USA Tel 303-451-5433; Fax: 303-469-1787
E-mail: truthquester@aol.com
Web site: http://www.returntotheworld.org.

Retzlaff Publishing Co., *(978-0-9752525)* 1516 Piedmont Pl., Savannah, TX 76227 USA Tel 817-975-1115
E-mail: DonRetzlaff@gmail.com
Web site: http://RPC.macroenterprisesinc.com.

Retzler, Laura, *(978-0-692-98820-6)* 5302 MacArthur Blvd., Washington, DC 20016 USA Tel 202-286-2179
E-mail: lretzler@yahoo.com
Dist(s): **Ingram Content Group.**

REUTS Pubns., *(978-0-9896499; 978-1-942111)* 13811 NE 65th St, Vancouver, WA 98682 USA Tel 707-362-6326
E-mail: kisa@reuts.com
Web site: http://www.reuts.com.

Revelation Products LLC, *(978-0-9792510)* 11746 Manhattan Ave., Saint Louis, MO 63131-4625 USA Tel 314-984-8180; Fax: 314-984-8194; Toll Free: 888-344-0606
E-mail: info@rpideas.com.

†**Revell,** *(978-0-8007)* Div. of Baker Publishing Group, Orders Addr.: P.O. Box 6287, Grand Rapids, MI 49516-6287 USA Toll Free Fax: 800-398-3111; Toll Free: 800-877-2665; Edit Addr.: 6030 E. Fulton, Ada, MI 49301 USA Tel 616-676-9185; Fax: 616-676-9573
E-mail: sharlow@bakerbooks.com
Web site: http://www.bakerbooks.com
Dist(s): **Baker Publishing Group**; *CIP*.

Revell, Fleming H. Company *See* **Revell**

Reveno, Katherine, *(978-0-692-94881-1)* 1001 mclynn ave ne, Atlanta, GA 30306 USA Tel 503-716-6500
E-mail: kreveno20@grcton.org.

Reverence Design Team Hair Salon, The *See* **D&C Publishing**

Reverence for Life, *(978-1-880757)* P.O. Box 222, Rectortown, VA 20140 USA Tel 540-364-1282; Fax: 540-364-7636
E-mail: sananda@erols.com
Web site: http://www.1spirit.com/sananda.

Reverie Publishing Co., *(978-1-932485)* Orders Addr.: 130 South Wineow St., Suite 3, Cumberland, MD 21502 USA Tel 301-722-2373; Fax: 301-722-2374; Toll Free: 888-721-4999; Edit Addr.: 127 West 96th St., 6-D, New York, NY 10025 USA Tel 212-662-7627
E-mail: info@reveriepublishing.com
Web site: http://www.reveriepublishing.com.

†**Review & Herald Publishing Assn.,** *(978-0-8127; 978-0-8280)* P.O. Box 2150, Hagerstown, MD 21742 USA (SAN 203-3798) Tel 301-393-3000
E-mail: mworden@rhpa.org
Web site: http://www.reviewandherald.com/
Dist(s): **Spring Arbor Distributors, Inc.**; *CIP*.

Revival Pubns. (GBR) *(978-0-9536768) Dist. by* **Consort Bk Sales.**

Revival Waves of Glory, *(978-0-615-94231-5; 978-0-615-94271-1; 978-0-615-94272-8; 978-0-615-94273-5; 978-0-615-94286-5; 978-0-615-94292-6; 978-0-615-94831-7; 978-0-615-95143-0; 978-0-615-95145-4; 978-0-615-96815-5; 978-0-615-96817-9; 978-0-692-20785-7; 978-0-692-21429-9; 978-0-692-21499-2; 978-0-692-21554-8; 978-0-692-21663-7; 978-0-692-22184-6; 978-0-692-22285-0; 978-0-692-22331-4; 978-0-692-22921-7; 978-0-692-23397-9; 978-0-692-24064-9; 978-0-692-26625-0; 978-0-692-27285-5; 978-0-692-27996-0; 978-0-692-32262-8;) P.O. Box 596, Litchfield, IL 62056 USA Tel 217-851-0361*
E-mail: bill.vincent@yahoo.com
Web site: http://www.revivalwavesofgloryministries.com
Dist(s): **BookBaby**
CreateSpace Independent Publishing Platform
Send The Light Distribution LLC.

Revivalist Pr., The, *(978-0-9749186; 978-0-9891979)* Div. of God's Bible School & College, 1810 Young St., Cincinnati, OH 45202 USA
E-mail: president@gbs.edu
Web site: http://www.gbs.edu.

Revolutionary Strategies, *(978-0-9769354; 978-0-9825493; 978-0-9883527; 978-0-9981269; 978-1-949775)* P.O. Box 900, Dripping Springs, TX 78620 USA Tel 512-858-0974
Web site: http://www.rickgreen.com.

Rexroad International, *(978-0-9817742; 978-1-946650)* Div. of Rexroad International, 616 Upham Pl. NW, Vienna, VA 22180 USA; *Imprints*: Rexroad Kids (MYID_G_REXROAD)
E-mail: fred@rexroad.us; fred.rexroad@yahoo.com; riff28@sbcglobal.net
Web site: TannerDent.com; www.fredrexroad.com; WhizTanner.com; http://Rexroad.International
Dist(s): **CreateSpace Independent Publishing Platform**
Ingram Content Group.

Rexroad Kids *Imprint of* **Rexroad International**

Reyes, Jose, *(978-0-9794731)* 422 Sabal Palm Ln., Pearland, TX 77584-7770 USA
E-mail: thelordsfield@sbcglobal.net; riff28@sbcglobal.net.

REYES, MARIA DE LA LUZ, *(978-0-9972790)* 985 SAN PABLO Dr., SAN MARCOS, CA 92078 USA Tel 760-685-3101
E-mail: mdlaluz@icloud.com.

Reynolds & Hearn (GBR) *(978-1-903111; 978-1-905287) Dist. by* **Trafalgar.**

REYNOLDS, CHRIS, *(978-1-7348939)* 2403 NW 49 Ln., BOCA RATON, FL 33431 USA Tel 561-289-2954
E-mail: CHRIS@CREYDG.COM
Web site: authorChrisReynolds.com.

Reynolds, Justin, *(978-0-578-81463-6; 978-0-578-92267-6)* 151-35 84th St Apt 5K, Howard Beach, NY 11414 USA Tel 516-761-1217
E-mail: jcam986@gmail.com.

Reynolds, Morgan Inc., *(978-1-883846; 978-1-931798; 978-1-59935)* 620 S. Elm St., Suite 223, Greensboro, NC 27406 USA (SAN 858-4680) Tel 336-275-1311; Fax: 336-275-1152; Toll Free Fax: 800-535-5725; Toll Free: 800-535-1504; *Imprints*: First Biographies (First Biographies)
E-mail: sales@morganreynolds.com; editorial@morganreynolds.com
Web site: http://www.morganreynolds.com
Dist(s): **Follett School Solutions.**

reynolds, patricia *See* **Reynolds, Patricia**

Reynolds, Patricia, *(978-0-9998348)* 2625 NE Goodwin Rd., Camas, WA 98607 USA Tel 310-922-0926
E-mail: dreamthisone@yahoo.com.

Reynolds, Patrick, *(978-0-692-51354-5; 978-0-578-61405-2)* 134 Boerum St., Brooklyn, NY 11206 USA Tel 339-788-8326
E-mail: patrickjmreynolds@gmail.com.

Reynolds Publishing Co., The, *(978-0-9665128)* Orders Addr.: P.O. Box 13535, Overland Park, KS 66282 USA Tel 913-492-7401 Questions/Communication
E-mail: kmhumbolt9@gmail.com.

Reynolds, Tom K., *(978-0-692-63594-0; 978-0-578-50131-4)* 13535 39th Ave NE, Seattle, WA 98125 USA Tel 206-523-6628
E-mail: tomnoir@seanet.com
Web site: reynoldswrites.net.

Reynoso, Michelle, *(978-0-9997189)* 11 Henry St., Bergenfield, NJ 07621 USA Tel 973-306-8964; *Imprints*: Caterpillar & Gypsy Moth Press (MYID_F_CATERPI)
E-mail: mtr@MichelleReynoso.com
Web site: http://www.michellereynoso.com.

RFH-RLP Real Life Publishing, LLC, *(978-1-7362828)* 688 Glover Rd., River Falls, WI 54022 USA Tel 715-426-0432
E-mail: rf.hartwich@gmail.com
Web site: rf.hartwich@gmail.com.

RFPublishing, *(978-0-9969173)* 244 5th Ave., New York, NY 10001 USA Tel 212-726-1453
E-mail: 007sdropybur007@gmail.com.

RG Mincey Group, LLC, The *See* **Great Success, LLC**

RGC Pr., LLC, *(978-0-9728876; 978-0-9779886)* P.O. Box 2921, Indianapolis, IN 46206-2921 USA (SAN 255-4747) Tel 317-926-0541
E-mail: info@RGCPress.com
Web site: http://www.RGCPress.com.

RGS Resilience LLC, *(978-1-7370619)* 202 Perrine Ave., Piscataway, NJ 08854 USA Tel 201-401-3003
E-mail: oadessese@gmail.com
Web site: www.childresilience.com.

RGU Group, The, *(978-1-891795)* 560 W. Southern Ave., Tempe, AZ 85282 USA (SAN 299-9366) Tel 480-736-9862; Fax: 480-736-9863; Toll Free: 800-266-5265
E-mail: mpagnozzi@theRGUgroup.com
Web site: http://www.thergugroup.com
Dist(s): **Send The Light Distribution LLC.**

RGZ Consulting, *(978-0-615-80196-4)* P.O. Box 153, South Woodstock, VT 05071 USA Tel 802-457-5861
E-mail: zamenhof@alum.mit.edu.

Rhapado Quick Reference, *(978-0-9719588; 978-0-9814940)* 702 S. Fairview St., Riverside, NJ 08075-3950 USA (SAN 855-7020) Tel 856-255-5492
E-mail: dvillari@rhapado.com
Web site: http://www.rhapadopublishing.com.

Rhapsody Branding, Inc., *(978-0-9667232)* Orders Addr.: 14027 N. Miami Ave., Miami, FL 33168 USA Tel 305-681-0489
E-mail: pumba66@yahoo.com; Don@notw8.com; Don@nightofthewitches.com
Web site: http://www.nightofthewitches.com
Dist(s): **Bk. Warehouse**
Distributors, The
Southern Bk. Service.

Rhapsody Productions *See* **Rhapado Quick Reference**

RH/Disney *Imprint of* **Random Hse. Children's Bks.**

Rhea Leto Media Group, *(978-0-9904727; 978-1-947185)* 6854 Orcutt Ave., Long Beach, CA 90805 USA Tel 424-757-8134
E-mail: Rhea@rhealeto.com; cj@phabb5.org
Web site: www.RheaLeto.Com.

Rheiss, *(978-0-692-91113-6)* 141 Hunter Rd., Simpsonville, SC 29681 USA Tel 607-342-4433
E-mail: rsh023@gmail.com
Dist(s): **CreateSpace Independent Publishing Platform.**

Rhemalda Publishing, *(978-0-615-32885-0; 978-0-9827437; 978-1-936850)* P.O. Box 1790, Moses Lake, WA 98837 USA
E-mail: emmaline@rhemalda.com
Web site: http://www.rhemalda.com; http://shop.rhemalda.com/
Dist(s): **MyiLibrary**
Smashwords.

R.Herst Rose *See* **R. Herst Rose**

Rhette Enterprises, Inc., *(978-0-9702319)* 3316 Shorewood Ave., Fort Gratiot, MI 48059 USA Tel 810-385-9416; Fax: 810-385-2304
E-mail: bobjan@futureone.com.

Rhinehart, Joseph, *(978-1-7360854)* 235 Harry S Truman Dr., Largo, MD 20774 USA Tel 240-601-6428
E-mail: josephrhinehart@gmail.com.

Rhino Entertainment Co, A Warner Music Group Co., *(978-0-7379; 978-0-930589; 978-1-56826; 978-0-9797278)* 3400 W. Olive Ave., Burbank, CA 91505 USA (SAN 677-5454) Tel 818-238-6110; Fax: 818-562-9239
E-mail: gladys.sanchez@wmg.com; tracie.bowers@wmg.com
Web site: http://www.rhino.com.

Rhizoo Publishing, *(978-0-9762723)* P.O. Box 1249, Stephenville, TX 76401 USA.

Rhoades & Assocs., *(978-1-930006; 978-0-9841378)* 8070 19th St., No. 326, Alta Loma, CA 91701 USA (SAN 858-5369) Tel 909-297-3436; Fax: 909-657-5446; Toll Free: 888-699-0685; *Imprints*: Reading Company, The (Reading Co)
E-mail: jacquie@readingcompany.us
Web site: http://www.readingcompany.us.

Rhode Island State Council, International Reading Assn., *(978-0-9664455)* 4 Gardner Ave., North Providence, RI 02911 USA.

Rhode, Steve Inc., *(978-0-9742781; 978-1-59840)* 310 Watkins Pond Blvd., Rockville, MD 20850 USA
E-mail: steve@steverhode.com
Web site: http://www.steverhode.com.

Rhodes, Candice Sumner, *(978-0-9895439)* 268 loch stone st, Fort Mill, SC 29715 USA Tel 323-474-9293
E-mail: candicerhodes@yahoo.com.

Rhodes Educational Pubns., *(978-0-9743214)* P.O. Box 501155, Dallas, TX 75250 USA
Web site: http://www.nativeamericanrhymes.com.

Rhodes, Edwin Books LLC *See* **Rhodes, EL. Bks., LLC**

Rhodes, EL. Bks., LLC, *(978-0-615-24550-8; 978-0-578-01988-8; 978-0-578-03719-6; 978-0-692-82552-5)* 7710 Tinkers Creek Dr., Clinton, MD 20735 USA.

Rhombus Publishing Co., *(978-0-936455; 978-0-578-55329-0)* Orders Addr.: P.O. Box 806, Corrales, NM 87048 USA (SAN 698-0287) Tel 505-897-3700; Edit Addr.: 3817 Corrales Rd., Corrales, NM 87048 USA (SAN 698-2425)
E-mail: jaminradford@gmail.com; jradford19@comcast.net
Web site: http://www.ScientificParanormalInvestigation.net; http://www.RhombusBooks.com
Dist(s): **Rio Nuevo Pubs.**
Treasure Chest Bks.

RHS Consulting, *(978-0-9990937)* 104 Pine Lake Dr., Whispering Pines, NC 28327 USA Tel 910-633-1169
E-mail: rhsconsulting@outlook.com.

Rhymeglow LLC, *(978-0-9786912; 978-0-578-15239-4)* Orders Addr.: 14625 Baltimore Ave., #869, Laurel, MD 20707 USA; Edit Addr.: P.O. Box 869, Laurel, MD 20707 USA.

Rhyolite Press LLC *See* **Rhyolite Pr. LLC**

Rhyolite Pr. LLC, *(978-0-9839952; 978-0-9896763; 978-1-943829)* P.O. Box P.O. Box 60144, Colorado Springs, CO 80960 USA Tel 719-359-2848
E-mail: donsphoto@q.com
Web site: www.rhyolitepress.com.

Rhythm & Reasoning Pubns., *(978-1-949301)* 6250 Lyons Rd No. 11, Garland, TX 75043 USA Tel 972-203-1990
E-mail: AlyssaLynnDonovan@tx.rr.com.

Rialp, Ediciones, S.A. (ESP) *(978-84-320; 978-84-321) Dist. by* **Lectorum Pubns.**

Ribbing, John, *(978-0-9987219)* 4866 Charles, Shelby Township, MI 48316 USA Tel 248-310-7551
E-mail: jribbing@yahoo.com.

Ribbonwood Pr., *(978-0-9800291; 978-0-473-38865-2; 979-8-9859903)* P.O. Box 390375, Anza, CA 92539 USA Tel 951-763-2060
E-mail: nancylee202004@yahoo.com.

Ric Design LLC, *(978-0-9758704; 978-0-9859684)* 2245 Stony Hill Rd., Boulder, CO 80305 USA Toll Free: 800-432-7346 (phone/fax)
E-mail: ricdiz13@gmail.com
Dist(s): **Bookazine Co., Inc.**

R.I.C. Publications Asia Co, Inc. (JPN) *(978-4-902216) Dist. by* **CEG.**

R.I.C. Pubns. (AUS) *(978-1-86311; 978-1-74126; 978-1-921750; 978-1-922116; 978-1-925201; 978-1-925431; 978-1-925660; 978-1-925686; 978-1-925698; 978-1-925812; 978-1-925837; 978-1-925926; 978-1-922313; 978-1-922426; 978-1-922526; 978-1-922841; 978-1-922842; 978-1-922843; 978-1-923005) Dist. by* **SCB Distributo.**

Ricciardi, Charles, *(978-0-9996986; 978-1-7363221)* 155 Henry Street, No. 404, New York, NY 10002 USA Tel 646-334-0330
E-mail: charlesricciardi@gmail.com
Web site: torinopictures.com.

Rich Gamble Assocs., *(978-0-692-16775-5; 978-1-7338052; 979-8-9884105)* P.O. Box 163, Los Alamos, CA 93440 USA Tel 805-344-3259
E-mail: rlawsongamble@gmail.com
Web site: rlawsongamble.com.

Rich List *See* **Rich Register, The**

ich Pr., *(978-1-933914)* 4330 N. Civic Center Plaza, #100, Scottsdale, AZ 85251 USA (SAN 850-5209)
E-mail: kathy@richdad.com
Dist(s): **Ingram Publisher Services.**

ich Publishing, *(978-0-9726670)* 4175 W. 5345 S., Salt Lake City, UT 84118 USA Tel 801-965-6200; Fax: 801-965-6199; Toll Free: 800-224-3221 Do not confuse with companies with the same or similar name in Houston, TX, Temecula, CA
E-mail: milton@zeestlouis.com
Web site: http://www.miltonrich.com.

Rich Register, The, *(978-0-9633933; 978-0-9831368)* P.O. Box 29955, Austin, TX 78755 USA Tel 512-477-8871
E-mail: jda@richregister.com
Web site: www.richregister.com.

Richale R. Reed, *(978-1-7349078)* 351 Wagoner Dr. Suite 135, Fayetteville, NC 28303 USA Tel 910-248-9372
E-mail: richale@inpoweryou.com
Web site: inpoweryou.com.

Richard Hall II, *(978-0-692-07897-6)* 130 Berwick Lakes Blvd., POOLER, GA 31322 USA Tel 912-484-9669
E-mail: lavontrichie@aol.com
Dist(s): **Ingram Content Group.**

Richard Vaughn Linville, *(978-0-692-99711-6; 978-0-692-12447-5)* 18489 Fir Ave., Tuolumne, CA 95379 USA Tel 209-918-2534; P.O. Box 1034, Tuolumne, CA 95379
E-mail: Richardvlinville@gmail.com
Dist(s): **Ingram Content Group.**

Richards, Erin, *(978-0-9911264; 978-1-943800)* 1720 Tahoe Cir., Tracy, CA 95376 USA Tel 209-832-3249
E-mail: erinrichards@att.net
Web site: www.erinrichards.com.

Richards, Markita, *(978-0-578-45805-2; 978-0-578-71391-5; 978-0-578-77757-3; 978-0-578-89653-3)* 12085 Jojo Ct., Hampton, GA 30228 USA Tel 678-668-1454
E-mail: lynn0786@gmail.com.

Richards, Michael, *(978-0-692-16268-2; 978-0-692-16269-9; 978-0-578-61478-6)* 3935 Jasmine St., Paris, TX 75462 USA Tel 972-795-5656
E-mail: Mrichards@reagan.com
Dist(s): **Ingram Content Group.**

Richardson, Lilith, *(978-0-578-00920-9; 978-0-578-04792-8; 978-0-578-07481-8)* 360 Dusty Rd., St. Augustine, FL 32095 USA
Dist(s): **Lulu Pr., Inc.**

Richardson Production, Inc., *(978-0-9761222)* Orders Addr.: P.O. Box 543, Marietta, OH 45750 USA Tel 740-373-0861; Edit Addr.: 177 Acme St., Marietta, OH 45750 USA
Web site: http://www.richardsonproductions.tv.

Richardson Publishing Group, LLC, The, 6963 Annie Walk, Lithonia, GA 30038 USA Tel 404-803-5962
E-mail: lakaii.richardson@elavon.com
Dist(s): **Independent Pubs. Group**
Ingram Content Group.

Richardson Publishing, Inc., *(978-0-9637991; 978-1-935683)* 321 Montgomery Rd. No. 162115, Altamonte Springs, FL 32716-2115 USA Tel 407-529-8539
E-mail: usabookcoach@gmail.com; coachrik@aol.com
Web site: http://www.RickFeeney.com; http://www.PublishingSuccessOnline.com.

Richardson, Whitni, *(978-0-9903665)* 61 Harry S Truman Dr. Apt 23, Largo, MD 20774 USA Tel 443-535-2880
E-mail: richardson.whitni@gmail.com.

Richer Life, LLC, *(978-0-9744617; 978-0-9855699; 978-0-9892884; 978-0-9899001; 978-0-9903291; 978-0-9863544; 978-0-9970831; 978-0-9988773; 978-1-7335693; 979-8-9863598)* 5725 S. 21st Pl., Phoenix, AZ 85040 USA Tel 602-708-4268; Fax: 602-772-4910
E-mail: earlcobb@earthlink.net; earlcobb1@gmail.com; earl@richerlifellc.com; charlotte@richerlifellc.com; cobbcare@yahoo.com
Web site: http://www.richerlifellc.com.

Richer Life, LLC (dba RICHER Publications) *See* **Richer Life, LLC**

Richer Resources Pubns., *(978-0-9776269; 978-0-9797571; 978-0-9818162; 978-1-935238; 978-1-63464)* 1926 N. Woodrow St., Arlington, VA 22207-2410 USA (SAN 853-2931) Tel 800-856-3060; Fax: 703-276-0193
E-mail: info@richerresourcespublications.com; publisher@richerresourcespublications.com
Web site: http://www.richerresourcespublications.com.

Riches Publishing Co., *(978-0-9728219)* P.O. Box 02232, Detroit, MI 48202 USA
E-mail: kirich@sbcglobal.net
Web site: http://www.kirich.com.

Richeson, John W., *(978-0-9675315)* P.O. Box 710371, San Diego, CA 92171 USA
E-mail: john@VBAtech.com
Web site: http://vbatech.com.

Richie, Morgan W., *(978-0-692-06695-9)* 6370 Hawaii Kai Dr. No. 39, Honolulu, HI 96825 USA Tel 808-321-7757
E-mail: morganwrichie@gmail.com
Dist(s): **Ingram Content Group.**

Richlee Publishing, *(978-0-9799265)* 2898 Morning Creek Rd., Chula Vista, CA 91914-4311 USA
E-mail: jmacgregor@cadencemarketinggroup.com.

Richlyn Publishing *See* **Richlyn Publishing**

Richlyn Publishing, *(978-0-9722264)* 12045 W Brandt Pl, Littleton, CO 80127-4572 USA Tel 303-263-1241
E-mail: richlyn2@msn.com
Web site: http://www.richlynpublishing.com.

Richmond *Imprint of* **Santillana USA Publishing Co., Inc.**

Richmondmom.com Publishing *Imprint of* **Palari Publishing LLP**

Rick Riordan Presents *Imprint of* **Disney Publishing Worldwide**

Rickshaw Press *See* **Ragged Sky Pr.**

Riddering, Marggie, *(978-0-9765977)* P.O. Box 770, Hormigueros, PR 00660 USA Fax: 787-833-2260.

Riddle Creek Publishing, *(978-0-9725894; 978-0-9835009)* 232 Cty. Rd. 19, Haleyville, AL 35565-7416 USA
E-mail: riddlecreek@centurytel.net
Web site: http://www.riddlecreekpublishing.com.

Rider Franklin Reynolds Publishing *See* **Belisarian Bks.**

Riders Elite Academy, Inc., *(978-0-9741628)* 23120 Garrison Rd., Corcoran, MN 55340-9103 USA Tel 763-498-6565 (phone/fax)
E-mail: books@riderselite.com
Web site: http://www.riderselite.com.

Ridge, Jacqueline, *(978-1-7321403)* 130 Shorewood Dr, Valparaiso, IN 46385 USA Tel 219-213-5432
E-mail: jacquelinemridge@gmail.com.

Ridge Rock Pr., *(978-0-9670177)* Div. of Ridge Rock, Inc., Orders Addr.: P.O. Box 255, Healy, AK 99743 USA (SAN 253-6595) Tel 907-322-8185 (cell); 907-683-7737 (phone/fax); Edit Addr.: Mile 261 Parks Hwy., Box 255, Healy, AK 99743 USA
E-mail: ridgerock@gtemail.net
Dist(s): **Todd Communications.**

Ridge Row Press *See* **Univ. of Scranton Pr.**

Ridgewood Group, The, *(978-0-9716907)* P.O. Box 8011, Manchester, CT 06040 USA (SAN 254-3419) Tel 860-432-4537 (phone/fax); *Imprints*: Ridgewood Publishing (Ridgewd Pub)
E-mail: info@theridgewoodgroup.com
Web site: http://www.hermanthecrab.com.

Ridgewood Pr., *(978-0-9650434)* 2160 Aztec Dr., dyersburg, TN 38024 USA Do not confuse with Ridgewood Pr., Jefferson City, MO
E-mail: bartonsn@mac.com.

Ridgewood Publishing *Imprint of* **Ridgewood Group, The**

Ridgway Park Publishing, *(978-0-9706219; 978-0-692-19391-4)* P.O. Box 2591, La Mesa, CA 91943-2591 USA Tel 619-698-3414; Fax: 619-698-2061
E-mail: pamela@crooks.com; editor@ridgwaypark.com
Web site: http://www.ridgwaypark.com
Dist(s): **Sunbelt Pubns., Inc.**

Ridley Madison, LLC, *(978-1-946284)* 921 Washington St., Hoboken, NJ 07030-5105 USA Tel 201-400-2418
E-mail: mark@ridleymadison.com
Web site: www.ridleymadison.com.

†**Rienner, Lynne Pubs.**, *(978-0-89410; 978-0-931477; 978-0-931816; 978-1-55587; 978-1-56549; 978-1-58826; 978-1-935049; 978-1-62637; 978-1-955055; 978-1-68585; 978-1-962551)* 1800 30th St., Suite 314, Boulder, CO 80301-1026 USA (SAN 683-1869) Tel 303-444-6684; Fax: 303-444-0824
E-mail: cservice@rienner.com; sglover@rienner.com; questions@rienner.com
Web site: http://www.rienner.com; *CIP*.

Rigby Education, *(978-0-7635; 978-0-7578; 978-1-4189)* Div. of Houghton Mifflin Harcourt Supplemental Pubs., Orders Addr.: 6277 Sea Harbor Dr., 5th Flr., Orlando, FL 32887 USA Toll Free Fax: 877-578-2638; Toll Free: 888-363-4266; Edit Addr.: 10801 N. Mopac Expressway, Bldg. 3, Austin, TX 78759 USA Toll Free Fax: 800-699-9459; Toll Free: 800-531-5015
Web site: http://www.harcourtachieve.com
Dist(s): **Follett School Solutions**
Houghton Mifflin Harcourt Supplemental Pubs.

Riggott, Dean Photography, *(978-0-9659875)* 831 10 1/2 St., SW, Rochester, MN 55902 USA Tel 507-285-5076; Fax: 253-540-6093
Web site: http://www.riggottphoto.com
Dist(s): **Partners Bk. Distributing, Inc.**

Riggs, Jon, *(978-0-692-06813-7)* 912 SE Combs Flat Rd., Prineville, OR 97754 USA Tel 360-597-6110
E-mail: j.riggs4@students.clark.edu.

Riggs, Theresia, *(978-0-9746132)* 8910 Dogwood Dr., Tomball, TX 77375 USA Tel 281-351-2329 (phone/fax)
E-mail: Ohringen@aol.com
Web site: http://www.CosmicSisters.com.

Right On Programs, Inc., *(978-0-933426)* 522 E. Broadway, Suite 101, Glendale, CA 91205 USA (SAN 212-5099) Tel 818-240-1683; Fax: 818-240-2858.

Right Side Publishing, *(978-0-692-65951-9; 978-0-9988644; 978-1-955050)* P.O. Box 336, Reynoldsburg, OH 43068 USA Tel 614-626-3800
E-mail: feliciacauley@rightsidepublishing.com
Web site: www.rightsidepublishing.com
Dist(s): **CreateSpace Independent Publishing Platform.**

Right Stuff Kids Bks., *(978-0-9704597; 978-1-932317)* 5600 Claire Rose Ln., Atlanta, GA 30327 USA
E-mail: satiller@bellsouth.net
Web site: http://www.michaelsmind.com.

Right Track Reading LLC, *(978-0-9763290)* P.O. Box 1952, Livingston, MT 59047 USA
E-mail: mmgagen@earthlink.net.

Right-Away, Inc., *(978-0-9709095)* P.O. Box 741993, Riverdale, GA 30274 USA Tel 404-798-7508
E-mail: jakiharris2004@yahoo.com; rightaway1@hotmail.com.

Righteous Readings, *(978-0-9883634)* 2801 W. 83rd St., Chicago, IL 60652 USA Tel 773-744-8162
E-mail: righteousrayray@gmail.com; rsmith@righteousrayray.com
Web site: www.righteousrayray.com.

Righteous Readings LLC *See* **Righteous Readings**

Righter Publishing Co., Inc., *(978-0-9706823; 978-0-9747735; 978-0-9766032; 978-0-9778948; 978-0-9796209; 978-1-934936; 978-1-938527)* Orders Addr.: 410 River Oaks Pkwy., Timberlake, NC 27583 USA Fax: 336-597-8881
E-mail: righterpub@esinc.net
Web site: http://www.righterbooks.com
Dist(s): **CreateSpace Independent Publishing Platform.**

RiJan Publishing, *(978-0-615-79949-0; 978-0-692-20342-2; 978-0-9906179; 978-1-7329739)* 7100 Chase Oaks Blvd Apt 4411, Plano, TX 75025-5938 USA Tel 4694500784
Web site: www.jansikes.com
Dist(s): **CreateSpace Independent Publishing Platform.**

Riker, Dale, *(978-0-9771621)* 6937 W. Country Club Dr. N, Unit 152, Sarasota, FL 34243-3507 USA.

Riley Pr. *Imprint of* **Integrity Consulting Enterprise, LLC**

Riley Pr., *(978-0-9728958)* P.O. Box 202, Eagle, MI 48822 USA Tel 517-626-7027
E-mail: rileypress@yahoo.com
Web site: http://rileypress.hypermart.net.

Rilly Silly Bk. Co., The, *(978-0-9747054)* 11130 W. Heatherbrae Dr., Phoenix, AZ 85037 USA Tel 623-877-6020
Web site: http://www.rillysilly.com.

Rime Quill Publishing Co., *(978-0-9988709; 978-1-7330283)* 150 Central Ave S No. 320, Wayzata, MN 55391 USA Tel 864-504-9293
E-mail: janetascher@gmail.com
Web site: janholmesfrost.com.

Rincon Point, LLC, *(978-0-692-97467-4; 978-0-578-48064-0)* 140 Riverside Blvd, New York City, NY 10069 USA Tel 559-553-5506
E-mail: kkloss12@gmail.com.

Rincon Publishing Co., *(978-0-9660858)* Orders Addr.: 1913 Skyline Dr., Orem, UT 84097 USA Tel 801-377-7657; Fax: 801-356-2733
E-mail: RinconPub@Utahtrails.com
Web site: http://www.utahtrails.com
Dist(s): **Partners/West Book Distributors.**

Rind, Sherry, *(978-0-9674729)* Orders Addr.: 959 Evonshire Ln., Great Falls, VA 22066 USA; Edit Addr.: 8419 NE 144th St., Bothell, WA 98011-5055 USA
E-mail: AIREBIRD@hotmail.com; KCBROOM@erols.com
Web site: http://www.airedaleterriers.org.

Rindle Books Inc *See* **Rindle Bks. Inc.**

Rindle Bks. Inc., *(978-1-942214)* 1200 Westlake Ave. N, Seattle, WA 98109 USA Tel 206-430-6021
E-mail: mark@rindlebooks.com
Web site: www.rindlebooks.com
Dist(s): **Baker & Taylor Publisher Services (BTPS).**

Rinehart, Roberts Pubs., *(978-0-911797; 978-0-943173; 978-1-57098; 978-1-57140; 978-1-879373; 978-1-58979)* Div. of Rowman & Littlefield Pubs., Inc., Orders Addr.: 15200 NBN Way, Blue Ridge Summit, PA 17214 USA Tel 717-794-3800 (Customer Service &/or orders); Fax: 717-794-3803 (Customer Service &/or orders only); 717-794-3857 (Sales & MIS); 717-794-3856 (Royalties, Inventory Mgmt., & Dist.); Toll Free Fax: 800-338-4550 (Customer Service &/or orders); Toll Free: 800-462-6420 (Customer Service &/or orders); Edit Addr.: 4501 Forbes Blvd., Suite 200, Lanham, MD 20706 USA Tel 301-459-3366; Toll Free: 800-462-6420
E-mail: nrothschild@rowman.com
Web site: http://www.robertsrinehart.com
Dist(s): **Ebsco Publishing**
Follett School Solutions
National Bk. Network
Rowman & Littlefield Publishers, Inc.
Rowman & Littlefield Unlimited Model
ebrary, Inc.

Rio Grande Bks. *Imprint of* **LPD Pr.**

Rio Nuevo Pubs., *(978-0-918080; 978-1-887896; 978-0-9700750; 978-1-933855; 978-1-940322)* Orders Addr.: P.O. Box 5250, Tucson, AZ 85703-0250 USA (SAN 209-3251) Tel 520-623-9558; Fax: 520-624-5888; Toll Free Fax: 800-715-5888; Toll Free: 800-969-9558; Edit Addr.: 451 N. Bonita Ave., Tucson, AZ 85745 USA Tel 602-623-9558; *Imprints*: Rio Nuevo Publishers (Rio Nuevo)
E-mail: info@rionuevo.com; info@treasurechestbooks.com; aarond@rionuevo.com
Web site: http://www.treasurechestbooks.com; http://www.rionuevo.com/
Dist(s): **Treasure Chest Bks.**

Rio Nuevo Pubs. *Imprint of* **Rio Nuevo Pubs.**

Rio Wildflower Pubns., *(978-0-9786168)* P.O. Box 246, Almont, CO 81210 USA Tel 970-642-0272
E-mail: wildflowercd@peoplepc.com.

Riordan, Rick *Imprint of* **Disney Publishing Worldwide**

Riordan, Rick *Imprint of* **Disney Pr.**

Rip Squeak, Inc., *(978-0-9672422; 978-0-9747825)* Orders Addr.: c/o Raven Tree Press, 1400 Miller Pkwy., McHenry, IL 60050 USA Tel 815-363-3582; Fax: 815-363-2948; Edit Addr.: 840 Capitolio Way, Suite B, San Luis Obispo, CA 93401-7130 USA Tel 805-594-0184; Fax: 805-543-5782; Toll Free: 800-251-0654; *Imprints*: Rip Squeak Press (Rip Squeak Pr)
E-mail: Beda@RipSqueak.com; dawnj@delta-systems.com
Web site: http://www.RipSqueak.com; http://www.raventreepress.com
Dist(s): **Delta Systems Company, Inc.**

Rip Squeak Pr. *Imprint of* **Rip Squeak, Inc.**

Ripley Entertainment, Inc., *(978-1-893951; 978-1-60991)* Div. of The Jim Pattison Group, 7576 Kingspointe Pkwy., Suite. 188, Orlando, FL 32819-6510 USA (SAN 299-9498)
E-mail: meyer@ripleys.com; dula@ripleys.com
Web site: http://www.ripleys.com
Dist(s): **Children's Plus, Inc.**
Mint Pubs. Group
Simon & Schuster, Inc.

Rippee, Zachariah J., 308 Pershing St, WILLARD, MO 65781 USA Tel 417-207-0948
E-mail: jeffwcrawford5+LVP0003495@gmail.com; jeffwcrawford5+LVP0003495@gmail.com.

Ripple Grove Pr., *(978-0-9913866; 978-0-9990249)* P.O. Box 86740, Portland, OR 97286 USA Tel 774-230-3556
E-mail: amanda@ripplegrovepress.com
Web site: www.ripplegrovepress.com
Dist(s): **Independent Pubs. Group**
Midpoint Trade Bks., Inc.
Small Pr. United.

Riptide Pr., Inc., *(978-0-9723456)* 233 Walnut Creek Dr., Clayton, NC 27520 USA Tel 919-359-2852; Fax: 919-882-9924 Do not confuse with companies with the same or similar name in New York, NY, Fredericksburg, VA
E-mail: info@riptidebooks.com; info@riptidepress.com
Web site: http://www.riptidebooks.com; http://www.riptidepress.com.

Risa Publications, *(978-0-9771404)* 8424-A Santa Monica Blvd., Suite 175, West Hollywood, CA 90069 USA
Web site: http://www.lisahaisha.com.

Rise Up, *(978-0-9896904; 978-1-940473)* 25036 Meadowdale Ln., Veneta, OR 97487 USA Tel 626-629-0195 Do not confuse with Stonebridge Publications in Chesapeake, VA
E-mail: stonebridgepublications@outlook.com.

Rise UP Pubns. *Imprint of* **ePublishing Works!**

Risen Heart Pr., *(978-0-9764497)* 554 Bruns Dr., Rossford, OH 43460 USA Tel 419-666-6269
E-mail: rjbaden@wcnet.org.

Rising Bks., *(978-0-9644456)* P.O. Box 1408, Conyers, GA 30012 USA (SAN 298-5438) Tel 404-378-7464; Fax: 770-761-9865
E-mail: chadfoster@mindspring.com
Web site: www.chadfoster.com.

Rising Glory Productions, *(978-1-7331264; 979-8-9883574)* 452 Squire Dr., Gainesville, FL 32607 USA Tel 813-735-9037
E-mail: India.White.123@gmail.com
Web site: www.india-white.com.

Rising Moon Bks. for Young Readers *Imprint of* **Northland Publishing**

Rising Son International, Ltd., *(978-0-9915370; 978-0-9961358)* 218 Beach Rd., Washington, MA 01223 USA Tel 413-623-6112
E-mail: anniegutherie@risingsonrecords.com
Web site: www.risingsonrecords.com.

Rising Star Publishers *See* **WeWrite LLC**

Rising Star Studios, LLC., *(978-1-936086; 978-1-936770)* 5251 W. 73rd St. Suite C, Edina, MN 55439 USA Tel 952-831-8532; Fax: 952-831-5809
E-mail: mark@risingstarstudios.com; info@risingstarstudios.com; sales@risingstarstudios.com
Web site: http://www.risingstarstudios.com
Dist(s): **Follett School Solutions.**

Rising Sun Publishing, *(978-0-9883642)* 1331 SE 71st Ct, Hillsboro, OR 97123 USA Tel 503-642-2090; Fax: 503-642-2090
E-mail: juanimahiatt@gmail.com.

Rising Sun Publishing, Inc., *(978-1-880463)* P.O. Box 70906, Marietta, GA 30007-0906 USA Tel 770-518-0369; Fax: 770-587-0862; Toll Free: 800-524-2813 Do not confuse with Rising Sun Pubng in Fairfield, OH
E-mail: info@rspublishing.com; sholland@rspublishing.com
Web site: http://www.rspublishing.com.

Rising Tide Pr., *(978-0-913844)* Div. of American-Canadian Pubs., Inc., P.O. Box 6136, Santa Fe, NM 87502-4595 USA (SAN 298-217X) Do not confuse with Rising Tide Pubs., Tucson, AZ.

Rissarae Designs, *(978-0-692-45001-7; 978-0-692-53652-0; 978-1-7322949)* 621 88th Ave. N. Apt. 3, St. Petersburg, FL 33702 USA Tel 6263241249; Toll Free: 6263241249
Web site: www.thefairybabybooks.com
Dist(s): **CreateSpace Independent Publishing Platform**
Ingram Bk. Co.

Rissylyn, *(978-0-9894933)* 2 12th St. Apt. 1012, Hoboken, NJ 07030 USA Tel 917-859-4751
E-mail: info@dreambigacademy.com.

Ritchie, John Ltd. (GBR) *(978-0-946351; 978-1-904064; 978-1-907731; 978-1-909803; 978-1-910513) Dist. by* **BTPS.**

Ritchie Unlimited Pubns., *(978-0-939656)* 1427 Anderson Rd. Suite B, Springfield, OR 97477 USA (SAN 216-6461) Tel 541-741-0794 (phone/fax)
E-mail: ralph-ritchie@comcast.net
Web site: http://www.ritchieunlimitedpublications.com.

Rite Lite Limited, *(978-0-9772560)* 333 Stanley Ave., Brooklyn, NY 11207 USA Tel 718-498-1700; Fax: 718-498-1251; Toll Free: 800-942-0707
E-mail: mail@riteliteltd.com
Web site: http://www.riteliteltd.com.

Rite Quest, *(978-0-9801484; 979-8-9871752)* 1308 Turnberry Ct., Chesapeake, VA 23320-9445 USA.

Ritz, Lee Pubns., *(978-1-940840)* 2934 Ames St., Wheat Ridge, CO 80214 USA Tel 303-330-2477
E-mail: leeritz@leeritzpublications.com
Web site: www.leeritzpublications.com.

Rivendell Bk. Factory, *(978-0-944353)* 217 Country Club Park Crestline Village, PMB321, Mountain Brook, AL 35213 USA Tel (205) 871-5915; Fax: (205) 871-5945
Dist(s): **Cardinal Pubs. Group.**

River Canyon Pr., *(978-0-9815914; 978-0-9827531)* Orders Addr.: P.O. Box 191, Oakland, OR 97462 USA (SAN 855-9651) Tel 541-530-2061
Web site: http://www.rivercanyonpress.com
Dist(s): **CreateSpace Independent Publishing Platform**
River Canyon Distributing.

River City Kids *Imprint of* **River City Publishing**

River City Pr., *(978-0-9706962; 978-0-9764232; 978-0-9776713)* 4301 Emerson Ave. N., Minneapolis, MN 55412 USA Tel 612-521-9633 (phone/fax); Toll Free: 888-234-3559 Do not confuse with River City Pr. in New Orleans, LA
E-mail: bwolf@rivercitypress.net
Web site: http://www.rivercitypress.net.

Publisher Name Index

River City Publishing, *(978-0-913515; 978-0-9622815; 978-1-57966; 978-1-880216; 978-1-881320)* 1719 Mulberry St., Montgomery, AL 36106 USA (SAN 631-4910) Tel 334-265-6753; Fax: 334-265-8880; Toll Free: 877-408-7078; *Imprints:* River City Kids (River City Kids) Do not confuse with companies with the same or similar names in Richland, WA, South Bend, IN
E-mail: sales@rivercitypublishing.com
Web site: http://www.rivercitypublishing.com.

River Grove Bks., *(978-1-938416; 978-1-63299)* 4005 B Banister Ln. Three Pk. Pl., Austin, TX 78704 USA Tel 512-891-6100
E-mail: jgoff@greenleafbookgroup.com
Dist(s): **Greenleaf Book Group.**

River Lake Pr., *(978-0-615-36951-8)* 1799 Ashland Ave., Saint Paul, MN 55104 USA Tel 651-646-2915
E-mail: bethanymasters@riverlakepress.com
Web site: http://www.bethanymasters.com.

River Lily Pr., *(978-0-9725562)* 7595 Heuermann Rd., San Antonio, TX 78256 USA.

River of Life Publishing, *(978-0-9746345)* 3700 Chestnut Lake Ct., Jonesboro, GA 30236-5502 USA Do not confuse with River of Life Publishing in Kremmling, CO.

River Pointe Pubns., *(978-0-9758805; 978-0-9817258; 978-0-9848103)* 612 River Pointe Ct., Milan, MI 48160 USA Tel 734-439-8031
E-mail: riverptpub@sbcglobal.net.

River Pr., *(978-0-9725796; 978-0-9849909)* Div. of OCRS, Inc., Orders Addr.: 52 Tuscan Way Ste 202 # 404, Saint Augustine, FL 32092 USA (SAN 850-5098) Tel 904-563-6277; Fax: 904-940-5178; Edit Addr.: 52 Tuscan Way Ste 202 box 404, St Augustine, FL 32092 USA
E-mail: wrcsacriver@comcast.net
Web site: http://randycribbsauthor.com.

River Rain Creative Arts, *(978-0-9792713)* 1302 E. 30th St., Suite A, Texarkana, AR 71854 USA Tel 870-216-2243 (phone/fax)
E-mail: teaching2win@gmail.com.

River Rain Ministries *See* **River Rain Creative Arts**

River Road Pubns., Inc., *(978-0-938682)* 1433 Fulton St., Grand Haven, MI 49417-1572 USA (SAN 253-8172) Toll Free: 800-373-8762
E-mail: Pandex@prodigy.net
Web site: http://www.riverroadpublications.com.

River Rocks Publishing, LLC, *(978-1-7360059)* 1000 W. Main St., Ridge Spring, SC 29129 USA Tel 803-743-8386
E-mail: selfmanic@gmail.com
Web site: www.ameliagsides.com.

River Sanctuary Publishing, *(978-0-9841140; 978-1-935914; 978-1-952194)* P.O. Box 1561, Felton, CA 95018 USA (SAN 858-4532) Tel 831-335-7283
Web site: http://www.riversanctuarypublishing.com.

River Styx Publishing Co., *(978-0-9788997; 978-1-61704)* 1400 Ash St., Terre Haute, IN 47804 USA; P.O. Box 3246, Terre Haute, IN 47803
E-mail: pessy74@aol.com
Web site: http://fixitprogram.zoomshare.com.

Rivera Engineering, *(978-0-9801695)* 227 Brahan Blvd., San Antonio, TX 78215 USA (SAN 855-3874) Tel 210-771-2662; Fax: 210-226-9027
E-mail: alanegarivera@yahoo.com
Web site: http://www.rivera-engineering.com.

Riverbank Publishing, *(978-0-9753320)* 1917 Winterport Cluster, Reston, VA 20191 USA
Web site: http://www.riverbankpublishing.com.

Riverbend Publishing, *(978-1-931832; 978-1-60639)* Orders Addr.: P.O. Box 5833, Helena, MT 59604 USA Tel 406-449-0200; Fax: 406-449-0330; Toll Free: 866-787-2363; Edit Addr.: 1660 B St., Helena, MT 59601 USA (SAN 254-5020) Do not confuse with companies with the same or similar names in Elizabeth, CO, Marion, KY, Knoxville, TN
Web site: http://www.riverbendpublishing.com
Dist(s): **Bks. West**
High Peak Bks.
National Bk. Network
Partners Bk. Distributing, Inc.
Rowman & Littlefield Unlimited Model
Smashwords
TNT Media Group, Inc.
Wolverine Distributing, Inc.

Rivercity Pr. *Imprint of* **Amereon Ltd.**

RiverCreek Bks., Inc., *(978-0-9745171)* Orders Addr.: P.O. Box 1146, Buies Creek, NC 27506 USA Tel 910-893-8853.

RiverCrest Publishing, *(978-0-9667421; 978-1-930004; 978-1-942091)* Div. of Power of Prophecy, 1708 Patterson Rd., Austin, TX 78733-6507 USA (SAN 920-9972) Tel 512-263-9780; Fax: 512-263-9793; Toll Free: 800-234-9673
E-mail: Prophecy@texemarrs.com
Web site: http://www.texemarrs.com.

Riverdale Bks. *Imprint of* **Riverdale Electronic Bks.**

Riverdale Electronic Books *See* **Riverdale Electronic Bks.**

Riverdale Electronic Bks., *(978-0-9712207; 978-1-932606)* 4420 Bonneville Dr., Cumming, GA 30041 USA Tel 770-891-2710; *Imprints:* Riverdale Books (RiverdBks)
E-mail: jtm@riverdalebooks.com
Web site: http://www.riverdaleebooks.com.

Riverdeep, Incorporated *See* **Houghton Mifflin Harcourt Learning Technology**

RiverEarth, *(978-0-9787722; 979-8-9892637)* P.O. Box 684, Lenoir, NC 28645 USA (SAN 851-5824) Tel 828-750-5983; P.O. Box 684, Lenoir, NC 28645
E-mail: info@riverearth.com
Web site: lostseaexpedition.com; http://riverearth.com.

Riverhead Bks. *Imprint of* **Penguin Publishing Group**

RiverPlace Development Corp., *(978-0-9785538)* Orders Addr.: P.O. Box 6218, Reading, PA 19610-0218 USA
E-mail: info@RiverPlacePA.com
Web site: http://www.RiverPlacePA.com.

RIVERRUN BOOKSTORE INC, *(978-0-9856073; 978-0-9885370; 978-1-939739; 978-1-944393; 978-1-950381; 978-1-958669)* 86 Morning St, Portsmouth, NH 3801 USA Tel 603-431-2100
E-mail: riverrunbookstore@gmail.com.

Rivers, Swannee, *(978-0-9749216; 978-0-578-04160-5)* 1629 Index Ave. Se, Suite No. 400, Renton, WA 98058 USA Fax: 425-277-2950
E-mail: swanneerivers@mindspring.com
Web site: http://www.swanneerivers.com.

Rivershore Bks., *(978-0-615-79091-6; 978-0-615-80212-1; 978-0-615-82977-7; 978-0-615-84337-7; 978-0-615-89413-3; 978-0-615-90629-4; 978-0-615-93301-6; 978-0-615-94046-5; 978-0-615-94307-7; 978-0-615-95626-8; 978-0-615-96614-4; 978-0-615-97239-8; 978-0-615-97851-2; 978-0-615-97975-5; 978-0-692-02353-2; 978-0-692-22526-4; 978-0-692-22528-8; 978-0-692-22625-4; 978-0-692-25882-8; 978-0-692-26386-0; 978-0-692-27118-6; 978-0-692-31180-6; 978-0-692-32102-7; 978-0-692-33564-2; 978-0-692-34741-6; 978-0-692-39052-8;) 8982 Van Buren St. NE, Blaine, MN 55434 USA Tel 7636708677*
Web site: www.rivershorebooks.com
Dist(s): **CreateSpace Independent Publishing Platform.**

Riverside Art Museum, *(978-0-9802207; 978-0-692-41917-5)* 3425 Mission Inn Ave., Riverside, CA 92501-3304 USA
E-mail: mcarlson@riversideartmuseum.org
Dist(s): **D.A.P./Distributed Art Pubs.**

Riverside Park Pr., *(978-0-9864246; 979-8-9883768)* 8811 E Florian Ave, Mesa, AZ 85208 USA Tel 480-201-6048
E-mail: valerieipson@ymail.com
Web site: riversideparkpress.com.

Riverstone Group Publishing, *(978-0-9706117; 978-0-9763092; 978-0-9906166; 978-1-7346235; 979-8-9857349)* 331 Laiken Dr., Jasper, GA 30143 USA; 331 Laiken Dr., Jasper, GA 30143 Tel 404-219-1008
E-mail: ep@rsgroup.us
Web site: http://www.riverstonegroup.com.

RiverStream Publishing, *(978-0-9834972; 978-1-62243)* Orders Addr.: P.O. Box 227, Mankato, MN 56002 USA; Edit Addr.: 2140 Howard Drive West, North Mankato, MN 56003 USA Tel 800-445-6209
E-mail: info@thecreativecompany.us
Web site: https://riverstreampublishing.net
Dist(s): **Creative Co., The.**

Rivertide Publishing, *(978-0-9826252)* 890 Kensington Ave., Astoria, OR 97103 USA Tel 503-440-1002
E-mail: karenleedom@gmail.com.

Rivertree Media, *(978-0-9705018; 978-1-7321457; 978-0-578-39327-8; 979-8-218-00950-2; 979-8-9865456)* 4790 Caughlin Pkwy., Suite 143, Reno, NV 89509 USA
E-mail: glebeck@wingsnv.com
Web site: http://www.wingsnv.com.

Rivertree Productions, Inc., *(978-1-882412)* P.O. Box 410, Bradford, NH 03221 USA Tel 603-938-5120; Fax: 603-938-5616; Toll Free: 800-554-1333; *Imprints:* Odds Bodkin Storytelling Library, The (Odds Bodkin)
E-mail: rivertree@conknet.com
Web site: http://www.oddsbodkin.com
Dist(s): **Penton Overseas, Inc.**

Riverview Foundation, *(978-0-9771639)* Orders Addr.: P.O. Box 310, Topsham, ME 04086 USA (SAN 256-8357) Tel 207-729-7399; Fax: 207-797-5676; Edit Addr.: 610 Augusta Rd., Tomsham, ME 04086 USA
E-mail: office@riverviewfoundation.com
Web site: http://www.riverviewfoundation.com.

Rivet Bks. *Imprint of* **Feral Pr., Inc.**

RIXKIN, *(978-0-9842069)* P.O. Box 11922, Atlanta, GA 30355 USA Tel 888-674-1679; Fax: 888-674-2577
E-mail: info@rixkin.com; pr@rixkin.com; orders@rixkin.com
Web site: http://www.rixkin.com
Dist(s): **Quality Bks., Inc.**

†Rizzoli International Pubns., Inc., *(978-0-8478; 978-0-88363; 978-0-941807; 978-1-932183; 978-1-59962)* Subs. of RCS Rizzoli Editore Corp., 300 Park Ave., S., 3rd Flr., New York, NY 10010 USA (SAN 111-9192) Tel 212-387-3400; Fax: 212-387-3535; *Imprints:* White Star (White Star NY); Rizzoli Universe Promotional Books (RUPB); Skira (Skira); Welcome Books (Welcome)
Web site: http://www.rizzoliusa.com/
Dist(s): **Casemate Academic**
D.A.P./Distributed Art Pubs.
MyiLibrary
Penguin Random Hse. Distribution
Penguin Random Hse. LLC
Random Hse., Inc.; *CIP.*

Rizzoli Universe Promotional Bks. *Imprint of* **Rizzoli International Pubns., Inc.**

RJ Blackstone Ltd, *(978-0-9769949; 979-8-218-02094-1; 979-8-218-25618-0)* Div. of Stuart and Weitz Publishing, 7101 s central ave, los angeles, CA 90001 USA
E-mail: rjblackstone@aol.com
Web site: http://www.stuartweitzpublishing.com.

R.J. Bob Chavez Images, *(978-0-9778110)* 9760 W 76th Pl., Arvada, CO 80005 USA Tel 303-423-6982
E-mail: rjbcimages@aol.com.

RJ Pubns., *(978-0-9769277; 978-0-9786373; 978-0-9817773; 978-0-9819998; 978-1-939284)* 3900 Mountain Way Cove, Snellville, GA 30039 USA (SAN 256-5919); 3900 mountain way cove, Snellville, GA 30039
Web site: http://www.rjpublications.com.

RJA Enterprises, *(978-0-615-76035-3; 978-0-692-31377-0; 978-0-692-35527-5; 978-0-692-55194-3; 978-0-692-58517-7; 978-0-692-68642-3; 978-0-692-75532-7; 978-0-692-79835-5; 978-0-692-12173-3; 978-0-578-40450-9; 978-1-7334754)* 2924 Oakton Ridge Cir., Oakton, VA 22124 USA Tel 703-242-1798
Dist(s): **CreateSpace Independent Publishing Platform.**

RJI Publishing, *(978-1-885184; 979-8-9863591)* Orders Addr.: 9520 Dragonfly Ave., Las Cruces, NM 88012 USA Tel 520-500-7295
E-mail: ronjkramer@gmail.com.

RK Enterprises, Inc., *(978-0-9743775)* 22581 NE State Route 3., Belfair, WA 98528-9303 USA
E-mail: rkilsby@wavecable.com
Web site: http://www.gooshu.com.

R.K. Heckman, *(978-1-7363097)* 204 2nd Ave E, Williston, ND 58801 USA Tel 719-684-6744
E-mail: yohecky@gmail.com.

RMA Publicity LLC dba Sigma's Bookshelf, *(978-0-9987157; 978-0-9996577; 978-1-959538)* 13540 Knollway Dr. N, MINNETONKA, MN 55305 USA Tel 952-240-2513.

RMB Rocky Mountain Bks. (CAN) *(978-0-921102; 978-0-9690038; 978-1-894765; 978-1-897522; 978-1-926855; 978-1-927330; 978-1-77160) Dist. by* **Orca Bk Pub.**

RMB Rocky Mountain Bks. (CAN) *(978-0-921102; 978-0-9690038; 978-1-894765; 978-1-897522; 978-1-926855; 978-1-927330; 978-1-77160) Dist. by* **PerseuPGW.**

RNWC Media, LLC, *(978-1-937975)* P.O. Box 559, Pinehurst, TX 77362 USA Tel 281-506-2601; *Imprints:* Young Reader's Library (Young ReadL)
E-mail: gary@rnwcmedia.com
Web site: www.rnwcmedia.com.

Roach, Patricia, *(978-0-9817680)* 17 Hillside Ave., Winsted, CT 06098 USA.

Road Tunes Media, *(978-0-9721725)* Orders Addr.: 534 Hidden Way, Homer, AK 99603 USA (SAN 852-5188)
E-mail: roadtunes@gci.net
Web site: http://www.berniejones.com
Dist(s): **Follett School Solutions.**

Roadracing World Publishing, Inc., *(978-0-9749615)* P.O. Box 1428, Lake Elsinore, CA 92531 USA Tel 951-245-6411 Toll Free: 800-464-8336
E-mail: custsvc@roadracingworld.com
Web site: http://www.roadracingworld.com.

Roadrunner Pr., *(978-0-9636346)* Orders Addr.: 2815 Lake Shore Dr., Michigan City, IN 46360-1619 USA Tel 219-879-0133; 2815 Lake Shore Dr., Michigan City, IN 46360-1619
E-mail: roadrunnerpress@comcast.net
Web site: http://www.halhigdon.com.

RoadRunner Pr., *(978-1-937054; 978-1-950871)* P.O. Box 2564, Oklahoma City, OK 73101 USA Tel 405-524-6205
E-mail: jeanne@theroadrunnerpress.com
Web site: www.TheRoadRunnerPress.com
Dist(s): **Children's Plus, Inc.**

Roald Publishing, *(978-0-578-12595-4; 978-0-578-12602-9)* 1139 West Ave., J-9, Lancaster, CA 93534 USA.

Roane Ink LLC, *(978-0-9969750; 978-0-9976869)* 121 Arlette Dr, lafayette, LA 70503 USA Tel 337-278-0169
E-mail: GeorgeR728@aol.com.

Roane, Janice J. *See* **Roane Ink LLC**

Roaring Brook Pr., *(978-0-7613; 978-1-59643)* 115 West 18th Street, New York, NY 10011 USA Tel 212-886-1030; *Imprints:* First Second Books (First Second); Kingfisher (Kingfsh); Macaulay, David Studio (D Macaulay)
Web site: http://www.henryholt.com; http://us.macmillan.com/splash/publishers/roaring-brook-press.html
Dist(s): **Children's Plus, Inc.**
Follett School Solutions
Macmillan
MyiLibrary
Westminster John Knox Pr.

Roban, Whitney *See* **Chandler Publishing**

Robbie Dean Pr., *(978-0-9630608; 978-1-889743; 978-0-9892303; 978-0-9916017; 978-0-9982493; 978-0-9995842; 978-1-7327384; 978-1-7357470)* 2910 E. Eisenhower Pkwy., Ann Arbor, MI 48108 USA Tel 734-973-9511; Fax: 734-973-9475
E-mail: fairyha@aol.com.

Robe Communications, Inc., *(978-0-9817403; 978-1-935831)* 5138 S. Clifton Ave., Springfield, MO 65810 USA Tel 417-887-8793
E-mail: krobe@mchsi.com
Web site: http://www.robbietherabbit.com.

Roberson, Karen, *(978-0-578-42605-1)* 616 7th St., Peru, IL 61354 USA Tel 815-326-1369
E-mail: sweetpea-emt13@hotmail.com.

Robert L. Fouch *See* **Fouch, Robert L.**

Robert R. Gray, *(978-0-9994972)* 75 Glengarry Dr., Stratham, NH 03885 USA Tel 603-772-4971
E-mail: raygray@me.com.

Robert, Stephanie, *(978-1-7365608)* 403 Farley St., Mountain View, CA 94043 USA Tel 703-628-9187
E-mail: stephanie.lynn.robert@gmail.com.

Roberts & Ross Publishing *See* **Hugo House Publishers, Ltd.**

Roberts, Dallas P., *(978-0-9987695)* 1394 Highlands Rd., Sandpoint, ID 83864 USA Tel 208-290-9063
E-mail: dallas.kids@hotmail.com.

Roberts, Hebard D. Bks., *(978-0-692-05085-9)* 6769 Landover Cir., Tallahassee, FL 32317 USA Tel 850-878-1612
E-mail: gailroberts983@gmail.com.

Roberts, Laura, *(978-0-578-43509-1; 978-0-578-45472-6)* 4677 E. Donna Dr., Prescott, AZ 86301 USA Tel 916-202-0380
E-mail: LaRoberts163@gmail.com
Dist(s): **Independent Pub.**

Roberts, Michele, *(978-0-9760188)* P.O. Box 271611, Houston, TX 77277-1611 USA.

Roberts Publishing Co., *(978-0-931764)* 738 32nd St., S. E., Grand Rapids, MI 49548 USA Tel 616-245-1560; Fax: 616-245-1561 (orders can be sent by fax) Do not confuse with companies with the same or similar names in Sacramento, CA, San Marcos, CA, Great Lake, WI, Blaine, WA
E-mail: robertspublishingco@juno.com
Web site: http://www.scoliosishelp.com; http://www.scoliosishelp.org; http://www.robertsbookshelf.comw.

Robertson, Carra, *(978-1-7354435)* 3900 Camphor Ave, Newbury Park, CA 91320 USA Tel 310-529-3853
E-mail: carrarobertson@yahoo.com
Web site: www.SuperheroSocialSkills.com.

Robertson, Colin, *(978-0-9887049; 978-1-7322010)* 4375 Vinton Ave., Culver City, CA 90232 USA Tel 310-795-0824; *Imprints:* Gin & Tonic Press (Gin and Tonic)
E-mail: colin@espgraphics.com
Web site: http://www.gintonicpress.com.

Robertson, Deirdre, *(978-0-692-46152-5)* RT 5 Box 157, KEYSER, WV 26726 USA Tel 3048130345.

Robertson Publishing, *(978-0-9727721; 978-0-9796251; 978-0-9798633; 978-0-9801675; 978-1-935125; 978-1-61170)* 59 N. Santa Cruz Ave., Suite B, Los Gatos, CA 95030 USA Tel 408-354-5957 Toll Free: 888-354-5957
E-mail: alicia.r@robertsonpubblishing.com
Web site: http://www.RobertsonPublishing.com.

Robillard, Kristy, *(978-0-9800870)* 15110 S Oakleigh Ln., Prairieville, LA 70769 USA Fax: 225-744-3276
E-mail: robillard1@eatel.net.

Robin Corey Bks. *Imprint of* **Random Hse. Children's Bks.**

Robin Hood Tax On Wall Street *See* **WPR Bks.**

Robinbook, Ediciones S.L. (ESP) *(978-84-7927; 978-84-9917) Dist. by* **IPG Chicago.**

Robinbook, Ediciones S.L. (ESP) *(978-84-7927; 978-84-9917) Dist. by* **Lectorum Pubns.**

Robins Lane Pr. *Imprint of* **Gryphon Hse., Inc.**

Robinson, Beth, *(978-0-9799092)* P.O. Box 100, New Deal, TX 79350 USA (SAN 854-7378)
Web site: http://www.drbethrobinson.com.

Robinson, Consuelo, *(978-0-9786767)* P.O. Box 8662, Delray Beach, FL 33482 USA (SAN 851-2868)
E-mail: math1on1@math1on1.com
Web site: www.math1on1.com.

Robinson, Francesca *See* **Francesca Studios**

Robinson, Helen, *(978-0-692-93962-8)* 4102 Marbourne Dr., FT WASHINGTON, MD 20744 USA Tel 240-437-8490
E-mail: helen.rbnsn@gmail.com
Dist(s): **Ingram Content Group.**

Robinson, Julia, *(978-0-692-71414-0)* 28885 Fairway Dr, Buena Vista, CO 81211 USA Tel 717-395-2320
E-mail: georgejuliedt@hotmail.com.

Robinson- McLeod, Nichole *See* **Savoury Creations**

Robison Gamble Creative, *(978-1-933497)* 402B W Mt Vernon 272, Nixa, MO 65714 USA Tel 417-581-6008; Fax: 417-581-4542; Toll Free: 877-335-2735
E-mail: carrie@robisoncreative.com
Web site: http://www.robisoncreative.com.

Robot Playground, Inc., *(978-0-615-51355-3; 978-0-615-57232-1; 978-0-615-67487-2; 978-0-9862926)* 5110 LONG MEADOW DR, FRANKLIN, OH 45005 USA Tel 937-371-1240
E-mail: rita@ritajwebb.com
Dist(s): **CreateSpace Independent Publishing Platform.**

Robus, Debbie, *(978-0-9762034)* 31 Timberline Dr., Heber Springs, AR 72543-9417 USA
E-mail: firecrackerbaby57@yahoo.com
Web site: http://firecrackerbaby57.blogspot.com; http://www.workamper.com
Dist(s): **Workamper Bookstore.**

Robyn Z Moon Publishing, *(978-0-615-15292-9; 978-0-615-20370-6)* 3021 Eads Ave., Saint Lois, MO 63104 USA Toll Free: 877-544-0102
E-mail: robynzmoon@gmail.com
Dist(s): **Lulu Pr., Inc.**

Roc *Imprint of* **Penguin Publishing Group**

Roca Bolsillo (ESP) *(978-84-96940; 978-84-92833; 978-84-15729; 978-84-16240) Dist. by* **Spanish.**

Roca Editorial (ESP) *(978-84-96284; 978-84-96544; 978-84-96791; 978-84-9918; 978-84-92429; 978-84-16700; 978-84-16867; 978-84-17092) Dist. by* **Ediciones.**

Roca Editorial (ESP) *(978-84-96284; 978-84-96544; 978-84-96791; 978-84-9918; 978-84-92429; 978-84-16700; 978-84-16867; 978-84-17092) Dist. by* **Spanish.**

Rocco, Editora, Ltda (BRA) *(978-85-325; 978-85-62500) Dist. by* **Distribks Inc.**

Rock & Learn Educational Products *See* **Rock 'N Learn, Inc.**

Rock Cliff Media, *(978-0-9791384)* 553 Staci Ct., Ogden, UT 84404 USA
E-mail: info@rockcliffmedia.com
Web site: http://www.rockcliffmedia.com.

Rock Hse. Method, The *Imprint of* **Russell, Fred Publishing**

Rock Ink, *(978-0-9726979)* 2826 Cory Creek Rd., Oroville, CA 95965 USA Tel 530-894-7743; Fax: 530-892-8293
E-mail: mlrock@mariarock.com
Web site: http://www.mariarock.com.

Rock, James A. & Co. Pubs., *(978-0-918736; 978-1-59663)* 900 S. Irby St., #508, Florence, SC 29505-6357 USA (SAN 211-4690) Toll Free: 800-411-2230; 9710 Traville Gateway Dr., No. 305, Rockville, MD 20850; *Imprints:* Castle Keep Press (Castle Keep Pr); Sense of Wonder Press (Sense of Wonder); Mount Helicon Press (Mt Helicon MD)
E-mail: jarrock@sprintmail.com
Web site: http://www.rockpublishing.com; http://www.senseofwonderpress.com.

Rock 'N Learn, Inc., *(978-1-878489; 978-1-934312; 978-1-941722)* Orders Addr.: P.O. Box 3595, Conroe, TX 77305-3595 USA Tel 936-539-2731; Fax: 936-539-2659;

For full information on wholesalers and distributors, refer to the Wholesaler and Distributor Name Index

Toll Free Fax: 800-801-5481; Toll Free: 800-348-8445; Edit Addr.: 105 Commercial Cir., Conroe, TX 77304 USA
E-mail: info@rocknlearn.com
Web site: http://www.rocknlearn.com
Dist(s): **Big Kids Productions, Inc.**
Follett School Solutions
Rounder Kids Music Distribution.

Rock Paper Pen Pr., *(978-0-578-55349-8; 979-8-9886694)* 408 E 15TH ST, Yankton, SD 57078 USA Tel 402-860-1718
E-mail: mzandrews@mzandrews.com
Web site: www.mzanyandrews.com; www.mzandrews.com; www.rockpaperpenpress.com.

Rock Point Gift & Stationery *Imprint of* **Quarto Publishing Group USA**

Rock Point Pr., *(978-0-9912516)* 7 Avenida Vista Grande Suite B7-403, Santa Fe, NM 87508 USA Tel 267-304-8521
E-mail: joannavhill@gmail.com
Dist(s): **SCB Distributors.**

Rock Village Publishing, *(978-0-9674204; 978-0-9721389; 978-0-9766356; 978-1-934400)* 41 Walnut St., Middleborough, MA 02346 USA Tel 508-946-4738
E-mail: rockvillage@verizon.net.

Rock Wren Pr., *(978-0-692-96831-4)* 30 Lewis Mountain Ln., Durango, CO 81301 USA Tel 970-259-9179
E-mail: tiffmapel@yahoo.com.

Rockbott'm *See* **Spring Hollow Bks., LLC**

Rocket City Publishing, *(978-1-7325071; 978-1-7352475)* 990 Explorer Blvd. NW, HUNTSVILLE, AL 35811 USA Tel 256-453-4975
E-mail: rocketcitypublishing@gmail.com
Web site: www.rocketcitypublishing.com.

Rocket Press Books Inc. *See* **Rocket Press Publishing, LLC**

Rocket Press Publishing, LLC, *(978-0-9891732)* 139-B James Comeaux Rd. PMB No. 571, Lafayette, LA 70508 USA Tel 337-591-9845
E-mail: rocketpressbooks@gmail.com
Web site: www.rocketpressbooks.com.

Rocket Ride Bks., *(978-0-9823322)* P.O. Box 1223, Somerset, PA 15501 USA
E-mail: anthonyrotoolo@yahoo.com.

Rocket Science Productions, LLC, *(978-0-9821823; 978-0-9830725; 978-1-937121; 978-1-939954; 978-1-945355)* 5765-F Burke Centre Pkwy., No. 222, Burke, VA 22015 USA (SAN 857-4863) Tel 703-764-8000
E-mail: fmonahan@rsp-llc.com
Dist(s): **Smashwords.**

RockhopperBooks, *(978-0-615-72947-3; 978-0-615-87745-7; 978-0-692-27399-9; 978-0-692-45625-5; 978-0-9965424; 978-0-9986234)* 1944 Gibson Ave, Clovis, CA 93611 USA Tel 559-908-1654
Dist(s): **CreateSpace Independent Publishing Platform.**

Rocking Chair Kids *Imprint of* **Red Chair Pr.**

Rockit Pr., *(978-0-9908011; 978-0-9962160; 978-0-9981719)* 695 Nashville Pike, No. 200, Gallatin, TN 37066 USA Tel 818-850-3020
E-mail: shauna@rockitpress.com; david@rockitpress.com
Web site: http://www.rockitpress.com.

Rockland Press *See* **Peach Tree Pr.**

Rockmill Publishing Co., *(978-0-9764012)* Rockmill Management, Inc., 17360 Hunter Ct., Lake Oswego, OR 97035 USA (SAN 256-5722) Tel 503-989-2590 (phone/fax); 503-806-3970
E-mail: energiesinc@msn.com; tammystarnermotsch@msn.com.

Rockon Publishing, *(978-0-9726255)* 210 Hy Rd., Buda, TX 78610 USA Tel 512-295-4889
E-mail: wermundj@mail.utexas.edu.

Rockport Publishers *Imprint of* **Quarto Publishing Group USA**

Rockridge Pr. *Imprint of* **Callisto Media Inc.**

Rockridge University Press *See* **Callisto Media Inc.**

Rocksand, LLC, *(978-1-931552)* 238 Greenbrier Dr., Cape Girardeau, MO 63701 USA Tel 877-625-7263
E-mail: bethprints@ymail.com
Web site: http://www.rainbowindow.com.

Rockshow Comedy, Inc., *(978-0-9854699)* 130 Old Town Blvd. N., Argyle, TX 76226 USA Tel 817-915-4296
E-mail: todd@rockshowcomedy.com
Web site: www.rockshowcomedy.com.

RockTuff, *(978-0-9800754)* Orders Addr.: P.O. Box 133, Roscoe, SD 57471 USA (SAN 855-1308) Tel 605-287-4133; Fax: 605-287-4188; Edit Addr.: 34240 Hwy. 12, Roscoe, SD 57471 USA
E-mail: rocktuff@venturecomm.net
Web site: http://www.andreabeyers.com.

Rocky Mountain Bks., *(978-0-9605648; 978-0-692-12711-7)* P.O. Box 100663, Denver, CO 80210 USA (SAN 215-7047) Tel 303-850-9403; Fax: 303-771-6654 (call first)
E-mail: rockymountainbooks@yahoo.com
Web site: www.normasands.com
Dist(s): **Publishers Group West (PGW).**

Rocky Mountain Moonworks, *(978-0-9978271)* 845 Pine Dr. Hts., Orofino, ID 83544 USA Tel 208-553-2956
E-mail: shootingstar839@gmail.com.

Rocky Mountain Yeti *Imprint of* **Rocky Mountain Yeti**

Rocky Mountain Yeti, *(978-0-578-75931-9; 978-1-7359094)* P.O. Box 51, Eastlake, CO 80614 USA Tel 720-324-2860; *Imprints*: Rocky Mountain Yeti (MYID_K_ROCKY M)
E-mail: cme@ebizgrp.com.

Rocky Nook, *(978-1-933952; 978-1-937538; 978-1-68198; 979-8-88814)* 1010 B St. No. 350, San Rafael, CA 94901 USA (SAN 850-6906) Tel 415-419-6364; Toll Free: 866-687-1118
E-mail: ted@rockynook.com; scott@rockynook.com
Web site: http://www.rockynook.com
Dist(s): **Ingram Publisher Services**
MyiLibrary
O'Reilly Media, Inc.
ebrary, Inc.

Rocky Pond Bks. *Imprint of* **Penguin Young Readers Group**

Rod & Staff Pubs., Inc., *(978-0-7399)* P.O. Box 3, 14193 Hwy. 172, Crockett, KY 41413 USA (SAN 206-7633) Tel 606-522-4348; Fax: 606-522-4896; Toll Free Fax: 800-643-1244
Web site: http://www.rodstaff.com/.

Rodaian Pr., *(978-1-935436; 978-0-9847167; 978-0-9847986; 978-0-9893251)* P.O. Box 3128, Palm Springs, CA 92263 USA
Web site: http://www.rodaian.com.

Rodale Books *Imprint of* **Potter/Ten Speed/Harmony/Rodale**

Rodale Kids *Imprint of* **Random Hse. Children's Bks.**

†Rodale Pr., Inc., *(978-0-87596; 978-0-87857; 978-1-57954; 978-1-4050; 978-1-59486; 978-1-60529; 978-1-60961; 978-1-62336; 978-1-63565)* Orders Addr.: 16365 James Madison Hwy., Gordonsville, VA 22942-8501 USA Toll Free Fax: 800-672-2054; Toll Free: 888-330-8477; Edit Addr.: 400 S. Tenth St., Emmaus, PA 18098-0099 USA (SAN 200-2477) Tel 610-967-5171; Fax: 215-967-8961; Toll Free: 800-222-4997
E-mail: sara.cox@rodale.com
Web site: rodale.com
Dist(s): **Bilingual Pubns. Co., The**
Children's Plus, Inc.
Lectorum Pubns., Inc.
MBI Distribution Services/Quayside Distribution
Penguin Random Hse. Distribution
Penguin Random Hse. LLC
Send The Light Distribution LLC
St. Martin's Pr.
TNT Media Group, Inc.; *CIP.*

Rodgers, Alan Bks., *(978-1-59818; 978-1-60312; 978-1-60664; 978-1-4638)* 23511 Aliso Creek Rd., No. 120, Alsio Viejo, CA 92656-1341 USA
E-mail: AlanRodg@aol.com; amysterlingcasil@gmail.com; lmdegange@yahoo.com
Web site: http://www.aegypan.com; www.chameleonpublishers.com; http://www.chameleonmedia.co.

Rodgers & Nelsen Publishing Company *See* **Loveland Pr., LLC**

Rodrigue & Sons Company *See* **Rodrigue & Sons Co./Double R Books Publishing**

Rodrigue & Sons Co./Double R Books Publishing, *(978-0-9749026; 978-0-9833975; 978-1-938319)* Orders Addr.: 740 N. H St., Suite 170, Lompoc, CA 93436 USA Tel 805-735-7103 10am - 5pm PST; Fax: 805-737-9846; 740 N. H St., Suite 170, Lompoc, CA 93436 Tel 805-735-7103 10am - 5pm PST; Fax: 805-737-9846; *Imprints*: DOUBLE-R BOOKS (DOUBLE-R); DOUBLE R BOOKS (MYID_E_DOUBLE)
E-mail: publisher@doubleRbooks.com
Web site: http://DoubleRbooks.com
Dist(s): **INscribe Digital**
Independent Pubs. Group
Ingram Bk. Co.

Rodriguez, Estela, *(978-0-9772631)* Orders Addr.: 2050 NW 16th Terr., Apt. E111, Miami, FL 33125 USA Tel 305-549-3039; Edit Addr.: Jose Marti Stat. 27 & 4th St., Miami, FL 33135 USA
E-mail: colorama@bellsouth.net.

Rodriguez, Josue D., 34 Norwood Rd, NEW HAVEN, CT 06513 USA Tel 203-214-3981.

Rodriguez, Michelle, *(978-0-9900061)* 38-33 147th St., Flushing, NY 11354 USA Tel 646-217-9177
E-mail: maliperto1@gmail.com.

Rodriguez, Raul, *(978-0-9912750)* 9619 Judalon Ln, Houston, TX 77063 USA Tel 281-467-6992
E-mail: raul6992@yahoo.com.

Rodro, *(978-0-9744770; 978-1-7328579; 978-1-970056)* 52 Richmond Blvd., No. 3B, Ronkonkoma, NY 11779-3629 USA
Web site: http://www.rodro.com.

Roe, Gary, *(978-1-950382)* 4203 Cripple Creek Ct., College Station, TX 77845 USA Tel 425-422-2222
E-mail: garynroe@gmail.com.

Roedway Pr., *(978-0-9659650)* P.O. Box 903, La Quinta, CA 92253 USA Tel 760-771-9818; Fax: 760-771-9618; Toll Free: 888-694-2248.

Roehm, Nancy Jean, *(978-0-9745591)* 210 Stoney Ridge Dr., Alpharetta, GA 30022-7668 USA
E-mail: njroehm4116@aol.com.

Roger Dean Publishing Co., *(978-0-89328)* Div. of The Lorenz Corp., 501 E. Third St., Dayton, OH 45402-2118 USA Tel 937-228-6118; Toll Free: 800-444-1144
E-mail: order@lorenz.com
Web site: http://www.lorenz.com.

Rogers, Al M. Jr., *(978-0-9760159)* 48151 N. Laura Rogers Rd., Tickfaw, LA 70466 USA
Web site: http://www.lasttrumpgathering.com.

Rogers, Siobain K., *(978-0-615-13289-1)* 103 Harris Cir., Carthage, TX 75633 USA
Web site: http://www.lulu.com/siobainrogers
Dist(s): **Lulu Pr., Inc.**

Rogue Star Publishing LLC, *(978-1-7325362; 979-8-218-27730-7)* 37459 Ultima Plaza Blvd., Ste B 233, Prairieville, LA 70769 USA Tel 225-610-9170
E-mail: roguestarpublishing@gmail.com.

Rogue Wave Publishing *See* **Tonepoet Publishing**

Rohrer Design, *(978-0-9721138)* 725-17th St., Kenosha, WI 53140-1329 USA
Web site: http://www.rohrer-design.com.

Roisin Dubh Pubns., *(978-0-692-93065-6; 978-0-578-78510-3; 978-0-578-24120-3; 979-8-218-15675-6)* 1103 W Gardena Bl No. 237, Gardena, CA 90248 USA
E-mail: legacyofpacific@aol.com
Web site: www.alegacyofthepacific.com; www.dariabrooksbooks.com.

Roland & Eleanor Bergthold, *(978-0-9741193)* 9133 N. Stoneridge Ln., Fresno, CA 93720 USA Tel 559-434-4137
E-mail: rolbergthold@prodigy.net; embergthold@prodigy.net.

Roland Golf Services, *(978-0-9911293)* 8911 Shrockton St., Powell, OH 43065 USA Tel 614-264-0545
E-mail: Rolandgolfservices@gmail.com
Web site: Tonylema.com.

Rolemommy, *(978-0-9822974)* 36 Rutledge Rd., Scarsdale, NY 10583 USA
E-mail: beth@rolemommy.com; mail@plainwhitepress.com.

Rolest P. Inc., *(978-0-9786281; 978-0-9984275; 978-0-692-83116-8; 978-0-9986232)* 1503 Elberta Rd., No. 115, Warner Robins, GA 31093 USA Tel 478-442-6936
E-mail: rolest@juno.com.

Rolling Hills Pr., *(978-0-943978)* 17 Olive Ave., Novato, CA 94945-3428 USA (SAN 282-2601) Do not confuse with Rolling Hills Pr., in Alexandria, VA
E-mail: rhpressllc@aol.com.

Rolling Meadows Publishing, *(978-1-7349582)* W270N765 JOANNE DR, WAUKESHA, WI 53188 USA Tel 262-337-3646
E-mail: D.L.Siri999@gmail.com.

Rolling Through Life With TaLisha, *(978-0-578-55018-3; 978-0-578-61823-4; 978-0-9999013)* 9 Highland Blvd., New Castle, DE 19720 USA Tel 302-983-4038
E-mail: talishagrzyb@gmail.com.

Romain, Trevor Co., The, *(978-0-9762843; 978-0-9787783; 978-1-934365; 978-0-9819804; 978-1-936407)* 4412 Spicewood Springs Rd. Suite 705, Austin, TX 78759-8567 USA Toll Free: 877-876-6246
E-mail: sabrina@trevorromain.com
Web site: http://www.TrevorRomain.com; http://www.comicalsense.com.

Roman Candle Publishing, *(978-0-692-12039-2)* 1002 Faculty Dr., Columbus, OH 43221 USA Tel 415-816-5326
E-mail: dustinoverholser@gmail.com
Web site: www.imaginaryninjas.com.

Roman Catholic Bks., *(978-0-912141; 978-1-929291; 978-0-9793540; 978-1-934888)* Div. of Catholic Media Apostolate, Orders Addr.: P.O. Box 2286, Fort Collins, CO 80522 USA Fax: 970-493-8781; Edit Addr.: 1331 Red Cedar Cir., Fort Collins, CO 80524 USA
Web site: http://www.booksforcatholics.com.

Roman, Teresa, *(978-0-9961545; 979-8-9880311)* 5207 Arden Way, Carmichael, CA 95608 USA Tel 904-625-4310
E-mail: gayoba@gmail.com
Web site: teresaromanwrites.com.

Romancing Cathay, *(978-1-932592)* 10050 Montgomery Rd., No. 315, Cincinnati, OH 45242 USA Tel 513-290-7419; Fax: 949-266-8395
E-mail: business@romancingcathay.com
Web site: http://www.romancingcathay.com.

Romani, Gabriella *See* **BBM Bks.**

Romero Empire, *(978-0-578-19278-9)* 16 Blossom St., Leominster, MA 01453 USA.

Romita, Tom, *(978-0-9995928)* 29 Amherst Dr, Hastings on Hudson, NY 10706 USA Tel 914-693-4210
E-mail: tom@tomromita.com
Web site: www.tomromita.com.

Romoulous *Imprint of* **MIROGLYPHICS**

Romoulous Enterprises *See* **MIROGLYPHICS**

Ron Meyers Ministries, *(978-1-7334762)* 528 Brandi Ln., Gulfport, MS 39507 USA Tel 228-380-9336
E-mail: ron@thepromoter.org
Web site: www.thepromoter.org.

Ronald, George Pub., Ltd., *(978-0-85398)* 8325 17th St., N., Saint Petersburg, FL 33702-2843 USA (SAN 679-1859); 3 Rosecroft Ln. Oaklands, Welwyn, AL6 0UB
E-mail: sales@grbooks.com
Web site: www.grbooks.com
Dist(s): **Cambridge Univ. Pr.**

Ronan Enterprises, Inc., *(978-0-9821110)* P.O. Box 574, Richmond, MI 48062 USA.

Rondo Books *See* **Parrish, Fayrene**

Ronin Publishing, *(978-0-914171; 978-1-57951)* P.O. Box 22900, Oakland, CA 94609 USA (SAN 287-5365) Tel 510-420-3669; Fax: 510-420-3672; Toll Free: 800-858-2665 (orders) Do not confuse with Ronin Publishing in Cambridge, MA
E-mail: orders@roninpub.com
Web site: http://www.roninpub.com
Dist(s): **MyiLibrary**
New Leaf Distributing Co., Inc.
Publishers Group West (PGW)
ebrary, Inc.

RonJon Publishing, Incorporated *See* **Hewell Publishing**

Ronsdale Pr. (CAN) *(978-0-921870; 978-1-55380) Dist. by* **SPD-Small Pr Dist.**

Roost Books *Imprint of* **Shambhala Pubns., Inc.**

Rooster Pubns., *(978-0-9792135)* Orders Addr.: 101 S. Page St., Morrisonville, IL 62546-6746 USA; Edit Addr.: 101 S. Page St., Morrisonville, IL 62546-6746 USA
E-mail: grandmotherstewart@msn.com.

RoosterBugglePue Bks. *Imprint of* **Eupanapue-Auntella's Rooster Pubns.**

Roots & Wings, *(978-0-9703319)* 20114 Illinois Rte. 16, Nokomis, IL 62075 USA Tel 217-594-7300; Fax: 217-563-2111 Do not confuse with companies with the same name in Lake Forest, IL, New Paltz, NY, Boulder, CO
E-mail: beltpulley@ccipost.net.

Roots in Myth, *(978-1-949717)* 9223 Spicebrush Dr., Austin, TX 78759 USA Tel 512-797-6974
E-mail: triciajh@yahoo.com.

Roots, Robert, *(978-0-9715336)* 11820 Miramar Pkwy. No. 212, Miramar, FL 33025 USA
E-mail: rbroots22@yahoo.com; rr@robertroots.com
Web site: http://www.robertroots.com.

Rope Ferry Press *See* **Anemone Publishing**

Rope the Moon Publishing, *(978-0-9898800; 978-1-7336742)* 1230 Claude Jones Rd., Murfreesboro, TN 37129 USA Tel 615-663-0834
E-mail: katykat479@aol.com; ropethemoonpublishing@gmail.com.

Roque-Velasco, Dr. Ismael, *(978-0-9706319)* P.O. Box 432804, Miami, FL 3243 USA Tel 305-667-6230; 305-740-6724
E-mail: northernismael@aol.com
Web site: http://www.cubaforkids.com
Dist(s): **Lectorum Pubns., Inc.**

Rori Shay Author, *(978-1-7320479)* 3314 264th Ave. NE, REDMOND, WA 98053 USA Tel 571-213-6485
E-mail: ramkraut@gmail.com
Dist(s): **Ingram Content Group.**

RoRo, *(978-1-951187)* 848 N Rainbow Blvd, Las Vegas, NV 89107-1199 USA Tel 347-379-4049
E-mail: WolfORourc@Gmail.com
Web site: www.WolfORourc.com.

Rorschach Entertainment, *(978-0-9748654)* 15806 18th Ave W. Apt. F203, Lynnwood, WA 98087-8755 USA
E-mail: info@rorschachentertainment.com
Web site: http://www.rorschachentertainment.com.

Rosales, Irene, *(978-0-9824348)* PMB 154, 3118 FM 528, Webster, TX 77598 USA.

Rosalie Pr., *(978-1-7356752)* 8001 W. Gate Pk., West Chester, OH 45069 USA Tel 513-885-2080
E-mail: rjbrandell@gmail.com
Web site: rosaliepress.com.

Rosasharn Pr., *(978-0-615-96746-2; 978-0-9916496; 978-0-692-50595-3)* 1011 Serenity Cir., Auburn, AL 36830 USA Tel 334-750-6280
E-mail: info@pegathapress.com.

Rose, A., *(978-0-692-04963-1; 978-0-692-04964-8; 978-0-578-42827-7; 978-0-578-42828-4; 978-0-578-39476-3; 978-0-578-39477-0)* 1022 20th Ave. NE, Minneapolis, MN 55418 USA Tel 612 701 6262
E-mail: sadee.thompson@gmail.com
Dist(s): **Ingram Content Group.**

Rose Art Industries, Inc., *(978-1-57041)* 6 Regent St., Livingston, NJ 07039 USA Toll Free: 800-272-9667.

Rose Bud Publishing Co. LLC, *(978-0-9836913)* 8245 N. 27th Ave., Apt. 1048, Phoenix, AZ 85051 USA Tel 602-501-4533.

Rose Consultant *See* **Rose Consulting**

Rose Consulting, *(978-0-578-40200-0; 978-0-578-48402-0; 978-0-578-62948-3; 978-0-578-37618-9)* 8948 SW 211th Ln., Cutler Bay, FL 33189 USA Tel 786-209-4795
E-mail: drpattirose@gmail.com
Web site: https://drpattirose.wixsite.com/website.

Rose, Gary Publishing, *(978-0-9988777; 978-1-7348524; 978-1-7378736; 979-8-9886823)* 4065 River Woods, Auburn, CA 95602 USA Tel 530-885-3067
E-mail: grose1@pacbell.net.

Rose Gold Publishing, LLC, *(978-1-7332638; 978-0-578-62026-8; 978-1-952070)* 744 N. Gary Ave, Carol Stream, IL 60188 USA Tel 630-234-6421
E-mail: dolly@rosegoldpublishingllc.com
Web site: www.RoseGoldPublishingLLC.com.

Rose, Lisa Writes, *(978-0-692-06053-7)* 28860 Nottway, Farmington Hills, MI 48331 USA Tel 248-943-0742; Fax: 248-943-0742
E-mail: lchottiner@sbcglobal.net
Web site: www.LisaRoseWrites.com.

Rose Publishing, *(978-0-9655082; 978-1-890947; 978-1-59636; 978-1-62862; 978-1-64938)* Orders Addr.: 140 Summit St., Peabody, MA 01961 USA; Edit Addr.: 140 Summit St., Peabody, MA 01961-3473 USA (SAN 253-0120) Tel 800-358-3111; 978-573-3111; Fax: 978-573-8111 Do not confuse with companies with same or similar names in Flagtown, NJ, Arcadia, CA, Keystone Heights, FL, Salem, OR, Santa Cruz, CA, Tucson, AZ, Alameda, CA, Grand Rapids, MI, Little Rock, AR, Boulder, CO
Web site: http://www.rose-publishing.com; hendricksonrose.com
Dist(s): **Firebrand Technologies**
INscribe Digital
Spring Arbor Distributors, Inc.
Tyndale Hse. Pubs.

Rose River Publishing Co., *(978-0-9707976)* P.O. Box 19864, Alexandria, VA 22320 USA Tel 703-768-2380 (phone/fax)
E-mail: herbpuscheck@cs.com.

Rose, Susan Yoga, *(978-0-578-79563-8; 978-0-578-79674-1; 978-0-578-81168-0; 978-1-7367132)* 504 S. Florida Ave APT 211, TARPON SPRINGS, FL 34689 USA Tel 8122290134
E-mail: susrose@aol.com
Dist(s): **Ingram Content Group.**

Rose Valley Publishing, *(978-0-9765905)* 53762 Kristin Ct., Shelby Township, MI 48316 USA
E-mail: manitoumagic@aol.com
Web site: http://www.rosevalleypublishing.com.

Rose Water Cottage Pr., *(978-0-9853223; 978-0-9961393; 978-1-7352333)* 308 Stewart St., Franklin, TN 37064 USA Tel 615-476-6717
E-mail: tray296@att.net.

Rose Wind Pr., *(978-0-9631232)* Div. of Compass Rose Corp., 1701 Broadway, No. 345, Vancouver, WA 98663 USA Tel 360-693-7742; Fax: 360-693-0950
E-mail: galenahk@aol.com
Web site: http://www.compassart.

Roseann Miller & Linda Stephens-Hooe, *(978-0-9743964)* 11596 W. Sierra Dawn Blvd No. 3, Surprise, AZ 85378 USA Tel 207-338-8900
E-mail: backnphx@gmail.com.

Roseberg, Anders *See* **BaBk.y**

RoseDog Bks. *Imprint of* **Dorrance Publishing Co., Inc.**

RoseFountain Pr., LLC, *(978-0-9768051)* 65 High Ridge Rd., No. 163, Stamford, CT 06905-3814 USA (SAN 858-4664)
Dist(s): **BookBaby**
Enfield Publishing & Distribution Co., Inc.

RoseKnows, Inc., (*978-0-9755889*) P.O. Box 5448, McLean, VA 22103-5448 USA
Web site: http://www.playgeist.com.

Rosemaling & Crafts, (*978-0-9674583*) Orders Addr.: 3208 Snowbrush Pl., Fort Collings, CO 80521 USA Tel 970-229-9846; Fax: 970-229-5683
E-mail: diaedwards@cs.com
Web site: http://www.nordic-arts.com.

Rosemary Publishing, (*978-0-692-19340-2; 978-0-692-04304-2; 978-0-578-53544-9*) 1201 Dulles Ave. Apt. 2106, Stafford, TX 77477 USA Tel 832-763-0952
E-mail: theedonnamarie@gmail.com
Dist(s): **Ingram Content Group.**

Rosemont, Ltd., (*978-0-9635811*) 1620 Belmont St., Jackson, MS 39202-1203 USA Tel 601-355-1233.

Rosemount FARM Publishing, LLC, (*978-1-7324911*) 4822 S. 133 St., Omaha, NE 68137 USA Tel 402-884-5995
E-mail: rosemountfarm@conciergemarketing.com.

Rosen & Assocs., Inc., (*978-0-9746811; 978-0-9778973*) P.O. Box 17173, Chapel Hill, NC 27516 USA Tel 919-264-5976; Fax: 919-929-7119
E-mail: info@cashworkbooks.com
Web site: http://www.cashworkbooks.com.

Rosen Central *Imprint of* **Rosen Publishing Group, Inc., The**

Rosen Classroom *Imprint of* **Random Hse. Children's Bks.**

Rosen Classroom *Imprint of* **Rosen Publishing Group, Inc., The**

Rosen Classroom *Imprint of* **Penguin Young Readers Group**

Rosen Hse. Bks., (*978-1-7364973*) 3329 Mathern Trail, Lexington, KY 40509 USA Tel 513-225-5344
E-mail: rosenfamily06@yahoo.com.

†Rosen Publishing Group, Inc., The, (*978-0-8239; 978-1-56696; 978-1-4042; 978-1-59791; 978-1-4358; 978-1-60851; 978-1-60852; 978-1-60853; 978-1-60854; 978-1-61511; 978-1-61512; 978-1-61513; 978-1-61514; 978-1-61530; 978-1-61531; 978-1-61532; 978-1-61533; 978-1-4488; 978-1-4777; 978-1-4824; 978-1-4994; 978-1-68048; 978-1-5081; 978-1-68416; 978-1-5382; 978-1-5383; 978-1-64282; 978-1-64374; 978-1-7253) a/o Dept. C234561, 29 E. 21st St., New York, NY 10010 USA (SAN 203-3720) Tel 212-777-3017; Fax: 212-358-9588; Toll Free Fax: 888-436-4643; Toll Free: 800-237-9932; Imprints:* PowerKids Press (PowerKids Pr); Rosen Reference (RosenRef); Editorial Buenas Letras (EditBuenas); Powerstart Press (Powerstart Pr); Dance & Movement Press (Dance); Rosen Classroom (RosenClassrm); Britannica Educational Publishing (BritEducPub); Rosen Central (RosenCent); New York Times Educational Publishing (NewYork TEP); Windmill Books (WindmillBks); Rosen Young Adult (RosenYA)
E-mail: hollyc@rosenpub.com; info@rosenpub.com; customerservice@rosenpub.com; hollyc@rosen.pub
Web site: http://www.rosenpublishing.com; http://www.rosendigital.com; http://www.rosenclassroom.com
Dist(s): **Ebsco Publishing**
Encyclopaedia Britannica, Inc.
Follett School Solutions
Stevens, Gareth Publishing LLLP
Lectorum Pubns., Inc.
ebrary, Inc.; *CIP.*

Rosen Publishing Group, Incorporated, The *See* **Rosen Publishing Group, Inc., The**

Rosen Publishing, Inc., (*978-1-881930*) 3000 Chestnut Ave., Suite 300, Baltimore, MD 21211 USA Tel 800-237-9932; Fax: 410-889-1320.

Rosen Reference *Imprint of* **Rosen Publishing Group, Inc., The**

Rosen Young Adult *Imprint of* **Rosen Publishing Group, Inc., The**

Rosenberg, Harvey *See* **Go Jolly Bks.**

Rosenberger, Matthew, (*978-0-9760047; 978-0-9909415*) Div. of ABC Publishing for Kids, One Summit St., Philadelphia, PA 19118 USA (SAN 858-9887) Tel 215-242-4011; Fax: 215-242-9421
E-mail: mgr@kidstravelguides.com
Web site: http://www.kidstravelguides.com.

Roses Are READ Productions, (*978-0-9703489; 978-0-9755093*) P.O. Box 7844, Saint Paul, MN 55107 USA Tel 651-686-8418; Fax: 651-340-5333; *Imprints:* Little Petals (Little Petals)
E-mail: admin@rosesareread.cc.

Rosetta Stone Communications, (*978-0-9759331*) 1971 N. Nowak Ave., Thousand Oaks, CA 91360 USA (SAN 256-1549) Tel 805-370-0010; Fax: 805-435-1541
E-mail: johngriffith@maggio-associates.com
Web site: http://www.scientificgolfer.com.

Rosetta Stone Ltd., (*978-1-58022; 978-1-883972; 978-1-60391; 978-1-60717; 978-1-60829; 978-1-61716; 978-1-62821*) 135 W. Market St., Harrisonburg, VA 22801 USA Toll Free: 800-788-0822
E-mail: info@trstone.com; help@RosettaStone.com
Web site: http://www.rosettastone.com.

RosettaBooks, (*978-0-7953; 978-1-948122; 978-1-958657*) 845 Third Ave., 15th Flr., New York, NY 10022 USA Tel 212-751-4545; Fax: 212-755-2972
E-mail: ldwyer@rosettabooks.com
Web site: http://rosettabooks.com
Dist(s): **Ebsco Publishing**
INscribe Digital
Independent Pubs. Group
MyiLibrary
Open Road Integrated Media, Inc.
Simon & Schuster, Inc.
Two Rivers Distribution
ebrary, Inc.

Roslin Pr., (*978-1-946290*) 36-03 Stelton Terr., Fair Lawn, NJ 07410 USA Tel 484-557-1269
E-mail: haig@roslin.press.

Rosmen-Izdat (RUS) (*978-5-8451*) *Dist. by* **Distribks Inc.**

Ross, Alan Publications *See* **Ross Pubns.**

Ross & Perry, Inc., (*978-1-931641; 978-1-931839; 978-1-932080; 978-1-932109; 978-0-9849531*) 3 S. Haddon Ave., Suite 4, Haddonfield, NJ 08003 USA (SAN 253-8555) Tel 856 427-6135; Fax: 856-427-6136
E-mail: grfisheriii@gmail.com
Web site: http://www.rossperry.com; http://www.gporeprints.com
Dist(s): **TextStream.**

Ross, Cathy, (*978-0-9797832*) 1509 Cypress Rd., Olney, IL 62450 USA Tel 618-393-7732; Fax: 618-395-0123
E-mail: devspecinc@yahoo.com.

Ross, Jeanne, (*978-0-9850216*) PO Box 9011 PMB 308, Calexico, CA 92232 USA Tel 720-480-0121
E-mail: Raydiant1s@yahoo.com.

Ross, Keri, (*978-0-578-64265-9; 978-0-578-64266-6*) 37 Oakmont Dr., Falmouth, ME 04105 USA Tel 202-340-1701
E-mail: ross_consulting@yahoo.com
Web site: www.mystoryaboutpansandpandas.com.

Ross, Liesl, (*978-0-578-42456-9*) 3438 Nicklaus Dr., Rapid City, SD 57702 USA Tel 980-560-4743
E-mail: lieslross1985@yahoo.com
Dist(s): **Ingram Content Group.**

Ross Pubns., (*978-0-9617038*) 1438 W. Lantana Rd., No. 401, Lantana, FL 33462 USA (SAN 662-8230)
E-mail: alanross@aol.com
Web site: http://www.thegenuinejesus.com.

Rossi, Debra, (*978-0-9758982*) 813 Wentwood, Southlake, TX 76092 USA.

Rotaplast Pr., (*978-0-9706901*) Orders Addr.: P.O. Box 1100, Kennebunkport, ME 04046 USA Tel 207-967-0118; Edit Addr.: 4 East Ave., Kennebunkport, ME 04046 USA.

Rotenberg Consulting LLC, (*978-0-578-70324-4; 978-0-578-70326-8; 978-0-578-70327-5; 978-0-578-71253-6; 978-0-578-75415-4; 978-1-7356697; 978-1-7360824; 978-1-7367880; 978-1-7373238*) 305 Ivy Ct. 0, FRANKLIN LAKES, NJ 07417 USA Tel 2019814501
E-mail: rcrotenberg@gmail.com
Dist(s): **Ingram Content Group.**

Roth Pubs., (*978-0-9832102; 978-1-938428*) P.O. Box 1058, Monsey, NY 10952 USA Tel 845-474-0022; Fax: 845-770-3382
E-mail: solomon@rothpublishers.com
Web site: www.rothpublishers.com.

Roth Publishing *See* **HELORO Publishing Group**

Rothman Editions, (*978-0-692-50288-4; 978-0-692-53384-0; 978-0-692-58566-5; 978-0-692-64413-3; 978-0-692-71266-5; 978-0-692-75332-3; 978-0-692-76020-8; 978-0-692-76489-3; 978-0-692-91369-7; 978-0-692-15187-7*) P.O. Box 53, Cypress, TX 77410 USA Tel 281-382-1655
E-mail: ryvrsann@comcast.net
Web site: https://www.instagram.com/rothmaneditions/
Dist(s): **CreateSpace Independent Publishing Platform.**

Rothman, Suzanne, (*978-0-692-44502-0; 978-0-578-53348-3; 978-0-578-69623-2; 978-0-578-78000-9; 978-1-7361251; 979-8-9850896*) P.O. Box 53, Cypress, TX 77410 USA Tel 281-382-1655
Dist(s): **CreateSpace Independent Publishing Platform.**

Rothwell Digital Imagery, (*978-0-615-18912-3*) Orders Addr.: P.O. Box 383, Westfield, NY 14787 USA Tel 716-326-4319; 716-969-4088 (cell)
E-mail: tlroth@fairpoint.net; tlrothwell@gmail.com; lewisthedragon@live.com
Web site: http://lewisthedragon.com
Dist(s): **Not So Plain Jane Publishing.**

Rough Draft Printing, (*978-1-933998; 978-1-60386*) 1280 Queen St., Seaside, OR 97138 USA; *Imprints:* Merchant Books (Merchant Bks).

Round Cow Media Group, (*978-0-9745218*) Orders Addr.: P.O. Box 87, Alpharetta, GA 30009-0087 USA Tel 678-762-9053; Edit Addr.: 2822 Ashleigh Ln., Alpharetta, GA 30004 USA; *Imprints:* Biz4Kids (Biz4Kids)
E-mail: christian@biz4kids.com
Web site: http://www.biz4kids.com.

Round Tower Pr., (*978-0-9765964*) P.O. Box 2942, Paradise, CA 95969-2942 USA Tel 530-872-9705; Fax: 530-872-7732; Toll Free: 888-737-9705
E-mail: thor@roundtowerpress.com
Web site: http://www.roundtowerpress.com.

Rounder Bks., (*978-1-57940*) 29 Lancaster St., Cambridge, MA 02140 USA Tel 617-492-3799
Dist(s): **Leonard, Hal Corp.**

Roundsquare Pr., (*978-0-9717280*) 295 Marble St., Suite 303, Broomfield, CO 80020-2171 USA
E-mail: rs_press@msn.com.

Rourke Educational Media, (*978-0-86592; 978-0-86593; 978-0-86625; 978-1-55916; 978-1-57103; 978-1-58952; 978-1-59515; 978-1-60044; 978-1-60472; 978-1-60694; 978-1-61590; 978-1-61741; 978-1-61236; 978-1-61810; 978-1-62169; 978-1-62717; 978-1-63155; 978-1-63430; 978-1-68191; 978-1-68342; 978-1-64156; 978-1-64369; 978-1-7316) Div. of Carson-Dellosa Publishing, LLC, Orders Addr.: P.O. Box 643328, Vero Beach, FL 32964 USA (SAN 857-0825) Fax: 772-234-6622; Toll Free: 800-394-7055; Edit Addr.: 1701 Hwy. A1A S., Ste 300, Vero Beach, FL 32963 USA Toll Free Fax: 1-888-355-6270; Toll Free: 800-394-7055*
E-mail: rourke@rourkepublishing.com; rbrady@rourkepublishing.com; renee@roukeeducationalmedia.com
Web site: http://www.rourkeeducationalmedia.com
Dist(s): **Carson-Dellosa Publishing, LLC**
Children's Plus, Inc.
Findaway World, LLC
Follett School Solutions
Cengage Gale
Ideals Pubns.
MyiLibrary.

Rourke Enterprises, Inc., (*978-0-86592*) Div. of Rourke Publishing Group, P.O. Box 3328, Vero Beach, FL 32964-3328 USA Tel 561-234-6001; Fax: 561-234-6622
E-mail: rourke@sunet.net
Web site: http://www.rourkepublishing.com.

Rourke Publishing, LLC *See* **Rourke Educational Media**

Rourke, Ray Publishing Company, Incorporated *See* **Rourke Enterprises, Inc.**

Rousing Bks., (*978-0-578-45536-5; 978-0-578-57771-5; 978-1-7340594*) P.O. Box 90205, San Diego, CA 92169 USA Tel 858-866-4304
E-mail: cgrousing@gmail.com
Web site: https://www.cgrousing.com/.

Routledge *Imprint of* **CRC Pr. LLC**

Routledge *Imprint of* **Taylor & Francis Group**

†Routledge, (*978-0-04; 978-0-413; 978-0-415; 978-0-7100; 978-0-87830; 978-1-317; 978-1-003-16527-9*) Member of Taylor & Frances Group, Orders Addr.: 7625 Empire Dr., Florence, KY 41042 USA Toll Free Fax: 800-248-4724 (orders, customer serv.); Toll Free: 800-634-7064 (orders, customer serv.); Edit Addr.: 270 Madison Ave. # 3, New York, NY 10016-0601 USA (SAN 213-196X)
E-mail: cserve@routledge-ny.com; info@routledge-ny.com
Web site: http://www.routledge-ny.com
Dist(s): **CRC Pr. LLC**
Chicago Distribution Ctr.
Ebsco Publishing
MyiLibrary
National Bk. Network
Oxford Univ. Pr., Inc.
Pearson Education
Rowman & Littlefield Publishers, Inc.
Taylor & Francis Group
Women Ink; *CIP.*

Roux Publishing, (*978-0-9976979*) 17518 Amelia Dr, Baton rouge, LA 70810 USA Tel 225-281-3686
E-mail: Jbmoniotte@yahoo.com.

Rowan Mountain Pr., (*978-0-926487*) Orders Addr.: P.O. Box 10111, Blacksburg, VA 24062-0111 USA Tel 540-449-6178; Fax: 540-951-5214; Toll Free: 888-961-3315; Edit Addr.: 2010 Broken Oak Dr., Blacksburg, VA 24060-1448 USA Tel 540-449-6178
E-mail: faulkner@bev.net
Web site: http://www.rowanmountain.com.

Rowboat Pr., (*978-0-578-42401-9; 978-0-578-42676-1; 978-1-7339196*) 315 20th Ave NE, St. Pete, FL 33704 USA Tel 727-612-3444
E-mail: toriashleymcgee@gmail.com
Dist(s): **Independent Pub.**

Rowe, Kysha, (*978-0-9769339*) 605 Crested View Ct., Loganville, GA 30052-8926 USA
E-mail: kysha_r@yahoo.com
Web site: http://www.whatcreaturesteachus.com; http://www.focusontheyouth.com.

Rowe Publishing, (*978-0-9833971; 978-0-9851196; 978-1-939054; 978-1-64446*) 655 Old Lifsey Springs Rd, Molena, GA 30258 USA Tel 785-302-0451
E-mail: info@rowepublishingdesign.com
Web site: www.rowepub.com
Dist(s): **Smashwords.**

Rowe Publishing and Design *See* **Rowe Publishing**

Rowfant Pr., (*978-1-929731*) 845 N. Gow, Wichita, KS 67203 USA Tel 316-371-7254
E-mail: b_myers123@live.com
Web site: http://rowfantpress.org.

Rowles, Louis, (*978-0-9708748*) 204 12th Ave., N., Amory, MS 38821-1206 USA Tel 662-256-3865
E-mail: glrowles@network-one.com.

Rowman & Littlefield Education, (*978-0-8108; 978-1-56676; 978-1-57886; 978-1-60709; 978-1-61048; 978-1-4758*) Orders Addr.: 15200 NBN Way, Blue Ridge Summit, PA 17214 USA Tel 717-794-3800 (Sales, Customer Service, MIS, Royalties Inventory); Fax: 717-794-3803 (Customer Service & orders only); 717-794-3857 (Sales & MIS); 717-794-3856 (Royalties, Inventory Mgmt. & Distribution); Toll Free Fax: 800-338-4550 (Customer Service & orders); Toll Free: 800-462-6420 (Customer Service & orders); Edit Addr.: 4501 Forbes Blvd., Suite 200, Lanham, MD 20706 USA Tel 301-459-3366; Fax: 301-459-5748; Toll Free Fax: 800-338-4550; Toll Free: 800-462-6420; 4501 Forbes Blvd Suite 200, Lanham, MD 20706 Short Discount, contact ripgsales@rowman.com
E-mail: mmcmenamin@rowman.com; tkoerner@rowman.com
Web site: http://www.ripgbooks.com; http://www.scarecroweducation.com; http://www.rowman.com
Dist(s): **CreateSpace Independent Publishing Platform**
Ebsco Publishing
Follett School Solutions
MyiLibrary
National Bk. Network
Rowman & Littlefield Publishers, Inc.
Rowman & Littlefield Unlimited Model
ebrary, Inc.

†Rowman & Littlefield Publishers, Inc., (*978-0-8476; 978-0-87471; 978-0-9632978; 978-1-56699; 978-1-888052; 978-0-7425; 978-1-931890; 978-1-933494; 978-1-4422; 978-1-936283; 978-1-61281; 978-1-4616; 978-1-4617; 978-1-62093; 978-1-5381; 978-1-68475*) Mem. of Rowman & Littlefield Publishing Group, Inc., Orders Addr.: 15200 NBN Way, Blue Ridge Summit, PA 17214 USA Tel 717-794-3800 (Sales, Customer Service, MIS, Royalties, Inventory; Fax: 717-794-3803 (Customer Service & orders only); 717-794-3857 (Sales & MIS); 717-794-3856 (Royalties, Inventory Mgmt. & Distribution); Toll Free Fax: 800-338-4550 (Customer Service & orders); Toll Free: 800-462-6420 (Customer Service & orders); Edit Addr.: 4501 Forbes Blvd., Suite 200, Lanham, MD 20706 USA Tel 301-459-3366; Fax: 301-459-5749; Toll Free: 800-462-6420; *Imprints:* Gooseberry Patch (GooseberP) Short Discount, please contact ripgsales@rowman.com
E-mail: ripgsales@rowman.com; lweston@rowman.com
Web site: http://www.rowmanlittlefield.com; http://www.ripgbooks.com/bookseller/index.shtml
Dist(s): **Blackstone Audio, Inc.**
CreateSpace Independent Publishing Platform
Ebsco Publishing
Follett School Solutions
MyiLibrary
National Bk. Network
National Film Network LLC
Open Road Integrated Media, Inc.
Rowman & Littlefield Unlimited Model
Send The Light Distribution LLC
ebrary, Inc.; *CIP.*

Rowohlt Taschenbuch Verlag GmbH (DEU) (*978-3-499*) *Dist. by* **Distribks Inc.**

Rowohlt Taschenbuch Verlag GmbH (DEU) (*978-3-499*) *Dist. by* **Continental Bk.**

Roxbury Park Juvenile *Imprint of* **Lowell Hse. Juvenile**

Roxby Media Ltd. (GBR) (*978-1-900521; 978-0-9848539*) *Dist. by* **LaurusCo.**

Roxie Gibson Co., (*978-0-9763134; 978-0-578-66872-7; 978-0-578-77850-1; 978-0-578-33092-1; 978-0-578-33093-8*) 898 Ban Leer Dr., Nashville, TN 37220 USA Tel 615 383 7329; Fax: 615-298-9555.

Roy, Wendy, (*978-0-615-59502-3*) 18 Haviland St. No. 15, Boston, MA 02115 USA Tel 617-645-9018
E-mail: contactwendynow@yahoo.com
Web site: http://www.glamgranola.com.

Royal Botanic Gardens Edinburgh (GBR) (*978-1-872291; 978-1-900347; 978-0-9504270; 978-1-906129; 978-1-910877) Dist. by* **IPG Chicago.**

Royal British Columbia Museum (CAN) (*978-0-7718; 978-0-7726) Dist. by* **IPG Chicago.**

Royal Brown Publishing, (*978-0-9978541; 978-0-9979611*) 12138 Central Ave., Bowie, MD 20721 USA Tel 301-262-3472
E-mail: tdroyal@gmail.com
Web site: www.royalbrownpublishing.com.

Royal Caliber Pubns., (*978-0-9860785; 978-0-9860824*) 4043 Cypress Landing E., Winter Haven, FL 33884 USA
Dist(s): **Baker & Taylor Publisher Services (BTPS).**

Royal Collins Publishing Group Inc. (CAN) (*978-0-9918338; 978-1-4878; 978-1-927670; 978-1-987821) Dist. by* **IPG Chicago.**

Royal Council of the Real Fairyland, LLC, (*978-0-9841188*) 1332 Landfall Dr., Wilmington, NC 28405-2840 USA (SAN 858-4621)
Web site: http://www.therealtoothfairies.com.

Royal Financial Investment Group, (*978-0-578-16296-6; 978-0-578-16297-3; 978-0-578-16298-0; 978-0-9983860*) 1102-A Hwy 56 North, Waynesboro, GA 30830 USA
E-mail: info@royalfinancials.com
Web site: www.royalfinancials.com.

Royal Fireworks Publishing Co., (*978-0-88092; 978-0-89824*) Orders Addr.: P.O. Box 399, Unionville, NY 10988 USA (SAN 240-2394) Tel 845-726-4444; Fax: 845-726-3824; Edit Addr.: 1 First Ave., Unionville, NY 10988 USA
E-mail: rfpress@frontiernet.net
Web site: http://www.rfwp.com/
Dist(s): **Bridge Pubns., Inc.**

Royal Guard Dragon Society, The, (*978-0-9791733*) 706 Hall Ave., White Bear Lake, MN 55110 USA
E-mail: trgdspublications@trgds.com
Web site: http://trgds.com.

Royal Hse. Publishing, (*978-0-9772671*) 2315 Market Pl., Suite E, Huntsville, AL 35801 USA Tel 256-519-2291; Fax: 256-519-2292.

Royal Hues Designs, (*978-0-578-41614-4*) 1204 Village Market Pl. Suite 252, Morrisville, NC 27560 USA Tel 919-665-7691
E-mail: rhdrumgo@royalhuesdesigns.com
Dist(s): **Ingram Content Group.**

Royal Imprint Pr., Inc., (*978-0-9798624*) P.O. Box 342403, Austin, TX 78734 USA
Web site: http://http:www.TheRoyalYacht.net.

Royal Knight Inc., (*978-0-9777110*) 1204 Harbor Dr SE # 100, Rochester, MN 55904-5923 USA
Web site: http://www.royalknightresearch.com.

Royal Limited Partnership, (*978-0-9714798*) P.O. Box 448, Eugene, OR 97440-0448 USA
E-mail: fun@funnix.com
Web site: http://www.funnix.com.

Royal Peacock Publications *See* **Satin Finish Publishing**

Royal Penny Pr., The, (*978-0-9912370*) 9300 Colesville Rd., Silver Spring, MD 20901 USA Tel 240-372-1670
E-mail: sales@royalpennypress.com.

Royal Swan Enterprises, Inc., (*978-0-9793000; 978-0-9977720; 978-1-7336865; 979-8-9888406*) 201 Orchard Ln., Carrboro, NC 27510-2530 USA (SAN 853-0521); *Imprints:* Alazar Press (Alazar Pr)
E-mail: rse@nc.rr.com; alazar.press@gmail.com
Web site: http://www.royal-swan-enterprises.com; http://www.alazar-press.com
Dist(s): **Independent Pubs. Group**
MyiLibrary.

Royall World Productions, (*978-0-9768115*) 1608 N. 13th St., Kansas City, KS 66102 USA Toll Free: 800-331-7668
E-mail: royallworldproductions@unoi.org.

Royaltee Pr. LLC, (*978-1-7359437*) 537 LAKE KNOLL DR NW, LILBURN, GA 30047-8708 USA Tel 810-835-5172
E-mail: Royalteepress@gmail.com.

Royalti Virtue, (*978-0-692-18780-7; 978-0-578-48470-9*) 2444 Cole Branch Ct, 1, Indianapolis, IN 46239-7975 USA Tel 317-489-2496
E-mail: royaltivirtue@gmail.com
Web site: royaltivirtue.net.

For full information on wholesalers and distributors, refer to the Wholesaler and Distributor Name Index

Royalty Bks. International, Inc., *(978-0-9705458)* Orders Addr.: 2047 Gees Mill Rd. Suite 210, Conyers, GA 30013 USA
E-mail: royaltybooks@gmail.com
Web site: http://www.royaltybooksonline.com.

Royalty Company Two-Thousand, The *See* **Royalty Bks. International, Inc.**

Royalty Kingdom Publishing, *(978-1-7333167; 979-8-9876106)* 1135 Orange Arbour Trail, Ocoee, FL 34761 USA Tel 301-821-0456
E-mail: crawfordnicole@yahoo.com
Dist(s): **Ingram Bk. Co.**

Royalty Patrenia Turner Publications, *(978-0-578-15322-3; 978-0-578-18000-7; 978-0-578-18261-2; 978-0-578-19928-3)* 1532 N. Sedgewick Ave., Chicago, IL 60610 USA.

Royalty Pr., *(978-0-9795134)* 4835 Southmoor Rd., Richmond, VA 23234 USA Tel 804-201-7770.

Royalty Publishing Co., *(978-0-910487)* P.O. Box 2125, Bedford, IN 47421 USA (SAN 260-1265) Fax: 812-278-8785
E-mail: nitaspeaks@nitascoggan.com
Web site: http://www.the-maximum-zone.com.

Rozanski, Johnathan, *(978-0-9983327)* 471 E. Main St., Chicopee, MA 01020 USA Tel 413-594-3155
E-mail: mysteriousmisterenter@gmail.com.

RP Media, *(978-1-57545; 978-1-62716; 978-0-692-62456-2; 978-1-6660)* Div. of RP Bks., 300 Deschutes Way SW No. 304, Tumwater, WA 98501 USA; *Imprints*: Ruin Mist Publications (Ruin Mist Pubns); Reagent Press Signature Editions (Reagent Pr Sig Edns); Reagent Press Echo (Reagent Pr Echo); Reagent Press Books for Young Readers (RPBTR)
E-mail: sales@reagentpress.com; service@reagentpress.com; rights@reagentpress.com; emma.spring@reagentpress.com
Web site: http://www.reagentpress.com/; http://www.ruinmist.com/; http://www.williamrstanek.com/; http://www.robertstanek.com/; http://video.reagentpress.com/; http://graphics.reagentpress.com/; http://www.wizardsofskyhall.com/; http://www.ruinmistmovie.com/; http://www.themagiclands.com/; http://www.tvpress.com/; http://www.bugvillecritters.com/
Dist(s): **CreateSpace Independent Publishing Platform**
EBSCO Media
Ingram Content Group
MyiLibrary
OverDrive, Inc.
ebrary, Inc.

RPG Objects, *(978-0-9724826; 978-0-9743067; 978-1-935432)* 9275 Cedar Forest Rd., Eden Prairie, MN 55347 USA
E-mail: chris@rpgobjects.com
Web site: http://www.rpgobjects.com.

RPJ & Co., Inc., *(978-0-9761122; 978-0-615-27121-7; 978-0-9819980; 978-0-9828277; 978-1-937770)* 1080 Princewood Dr., Orlando, FL 32810-4542 USA Tel 407-617-3111; *Imprints*: SPC Books (SPCBks)
E-mail: kathy@rpjandco.com
Web site: http://www.rpjandco1417.com; http://www.rpjandco.com.
Dist(s): **Advocate Distribution Solutions**
Ingram Content Group Inc.
Send The Light Distribution LLC
Smashwords.

RPJ & Company, Incorporated *See* **RPJ & Co., Inc.**

RPKM Publishing, LLC, *(978-1-7347969)* 568 S 5 E, Vineyard, UT 84059 USA Tel 801-836-7023
E-mail: Author@Robertpkmooney.com
Web site: Robert-Mooney.com.

RPM Publishing *See* **RPM Publishing**

RPM Publishing, *(978-0-9764085; 978-0-9795126; 978-0-692-58325-8; 978-0-692-59412-4; 978-0-9992743; 978-1-7329503; 978-1-7342633; 978-1-7344407)* P.O. Box 841, Coeur d'Alene, ID 83814 USA Tel 425-890-3113
E-mail: sarahgerdesauthor@gmail.com
Web site: http://www.sarahgerdes.com
Dist(s): **CreateSpace Independent Publishing Platform**
Draft2Digital
Smashwords.

R.R Publishing Company *See* **Dara Publishing LLC**

RRJ Publishing, Inc., *(978-0-9857095)* 2073 SilverCrest Dr. unit C, Myrtle Beach, SC 29579 USA Tel 864-497-8392
E-mail: Mstnwright@yahoo.com.

RS Art Studio, *(978-0-9787729)* PO Box 64, Big Bear City, CA 92314 USA Tel 714-724-1480
E-mail: rsart@aol.com
Web site: http://www.rsartstudio.com.

R.S. Gallagher & Assocs. LLC, *(978-1-7366088)* P.O. Box PO Box 4023, Ithaca, NY 14852-4023 USA Tel 607-527-0283; Fax: 607-235-5003
E-mail: rich@rsgallagher.com
Web site: http://www.rsgallagher.com.

RS Publishing *See* **JD Entertainment**

RSMeans, *(978-1-940238; 978-1-943215; 978-1-946872; 978-1-950656; 978-1-955341; 978-1-961006)* 30 Patewood Dr. Suite 350, Greenville, SC 29615 USA Tel 781-422-5093
E-mail: dpanarelli@rsmeans.com.

RTC Publishing, *(978-1-939418; 978-1-947564)* P.O. Box 1603, Deerfield, IL 60015 USA Tel 833-750-5683; Fax: 833-750-5683.

RTE Media, LLC, *(978-0-692-80787-3)* 6 Westhill Rd., Saddle River, NJ 07458 USA Tel 201-934-9675
E-mail: aforment@optonline.net
Web site: www.alisonashleyformento.com.

RTI Publishing, LLC, *(978-0-9769086)* 5685 S. Topaz Pl., Chandler, AZ 85249-5804 USA (SAN 256-6338)
E-mail: rtipublishing@cox.net.

RTMC Organization, LLC, *(978-1-934316)* P.O. Box 15105, Baltimore, MD 21282 USA (SAN 852-6923) Tel 410-900-7834
E-mail: Sales@RTMC.org
Web site: http://www.rtmc.org.

RUACH PUBLISHING Co., *(978-0-692-11085-0; 978-0-692-14575-3; 978-0-578-71284-0; 978-0-578-72487-4; 978-1-7355819)* 6531 S Sepulveda Blvd., Los Angeles, CA 90045 USA.

Ruano, José A., *(978-0-9792972)* 8909 NW 189 TE, Miami, FL 33018 USA (SAN 853-0610) Tel 305-829-2683; Fax: 305-829-2094
E-mail: jaruano@bellsouth.net.

Rubber Ducky Pr., *(978-1-947141)* 2402 N Shadeland Ave. Ste. A Cardinal Publishers Group, INDIANAPOLIS, IN 46219-1746 USA Tel 317-352-8200; Fax: 317-352-8200
E-mail: tschmitt@cardinalpub.com; tdoherty@cardinalpub.com.

Rubicon Bks., *(978-0-9771676)* P.O. Box 1167, Silver City, NM 88062-1167 USA Tel 505-388-4585 Do not confuse with companies with the same name in Montrose, CA, Glendale, AZ
E-mail: badarmstrong@signalpeak.net.

Ruby Flower Publishing, *(978-0-615-79530-0; 978-0-615-83334-7; 978-0-615-83335-4; 978-0-615-84482-4; 978-0-615-85898-2; 978-0-615-87136-3; 978-0-9997172)* 527 E. Third Ave. No. 125, New York, NY 10016 USA Tel 2127261453
E-mail: belleusine@gmail.com
Dist(s): **CreateSpace Independent Publishing Platform.**

RUBY GULCH ENTERPRISES LLC, *(978-1-7325793)* P.O. Box 64, Craig, CO 81626 USA Tel 970-824-1908
E-mail: rubygulchenterprises@gmail.com
Dist(s): **Ingram Content Group.**

Ruby Tuesday Books Limited (GBR) *(978-1-909673; 978-1-910549; 978-1-911341; 978-1-78856)* *Dist. by* **Lerner Pub.**

Ruddick, Jessica Bks. LLC, *(978-1-946164)* 515 Miami Dr., Chesapeake, VA 23323 USA Tel 757-548-0468; Fax: 757-548-0468
E-mail: jmruddick@gmail.com.

Rugg's Recommendations, *(978-0-9608934; 978-1-883062)* P.O. Box 417, Fallbrook, CA 92088-0417 USA (SAN 237-9694) Tel 760-728-4558; Fax: 760-728-4467
E-mail: frugg@thegrid.net
Web site: http://www.ruggsrecommendations.com.

Ruin Mist Pubns. *Imprint of* **RP Media**

Ruiz, Katie Art, *(978-0-578-79625-3; 978-0-578-87729-7)* 2921 Via Ipanema, Carlsbad, CA 92009 USA Tel 760-505-6644
E-mail: Katieruizart@gmail.com
Web site: www.katieruizart.com.

Rule 2 Bks., *(978-0-9915511)* 2365 Rice Blvd, Houston, TX 77005 USA Tel 713-533-9300
E-mail: lchambers@brightskypress.com
Web site: www.rule2books.com
Dist(s): **Night Heron Media.**

Rules of a Big Boss LLC, The, *(978-0-578-83531-0; 978-0-578-83532-7; 978-0-578-87148-6; 978-0-578-87679-5; 978-1-7371907; 979-8-9856660; 979-8-9886962)* PO Box 545 0, KNIGHTDALE, NC 27545 USA Tel 9196797303
E-mail: DMoone@thebookofselflove.com.

Rummana Publishing Inc., *(978-0-9990610)* P.O. Box 354, Riverview, FL 33568 USA Tel 412-403-2577
E-mail: rummanapublishing@gmail.com.

Run to Win, LLC, *(978-1-943795)* 135 Maine St. Suite A No. 176, Brunswick, ME 04011 USA Tel 207-615-4819; *Imprints*: Trail Trotter Press (Trail Trotter Pr)
E-mail: blaine@trailtrotterpress.com.

Run With Me Publishing, *(978-0-9776835)* 15447 W. Monterey Ln., Kerman, CA 93630 USA Tel 559-846-6432
E-mail: runwithmepublishing@yahoo.com.

Runamuck Publishing, *(978-0-615-16220-1)* 221 Academy St., Mexico, NY 13114 USA
Dist(s): **Lulu Pr., Inc.**

Runestone Publishing, *(978-1-59648; 978-0-615-41705-9; 978-0-9881775)* 120 Ledgewood Dr. No. 10, Portsmouth, NH 03801 USA
E-mail: ajkitt@kripara.com.

Running Girl Productions *See* **Wheelhouse Publishing**

Running Horse Pr., *(978-0-9908979; 978-1-945087)* 700 Lavaca #1400 Pmb 90503, Austin, TX 78701 USA Tel 575-650-2246
E-mail: ecellenb@gmail.com
Web site: http://www.ellenbuikema.com.

Running Moose Publications, *(978-0-9777210)* 42400 Garfield Road, Clinton Township, MI 48038 USA
Dist(s): **Adventure Pubns.**

Running Pr. *Imprint of* **Running Pr.**

Running Pr. Kids *Imprint of* **Running Pr.**

Running Pr. Minature Editions *Imprint of* **Running Pr.**

†Running Pr., *(978-0-7624; 978-0-89471; 978-0-914294; 978-1-56138)* Div. of Perseus Books Group, 125 S. 22nd St., Philadelphia, PA 19103-4399 USA (SAN 204-5702) Tel 215-567-5080; Fax: 215-568-2919; Toll Free Fax: 800-453-2884; Toll Free: 800-345-5359 customer service; *Imprints*: Running Press (RunPr); Running Press Kids (RunningKids); Running Press Miniature Editions (RunMinEdns); Black Dog & Leventhal Publishers, Inc. (BlackDog Lev)
E-mail: support@runningpress.com
Web site: http://www.runningpress.com
Dist(s): **Blackstone Audio, Inc.**
Children's Plus, Inc.
Hachette Bk. Group
MyiLibrary
Open Road Integrated Media, Inc.
Zondervan
ebrary, Inc.; *CIP.*

Running Press Book Publishers *See* **Running Pr.**

Running the Goat, Bks. & Broadsides (CAN) *(978-0-9688712; 978-0-9737578; 978-0-9866113; 978-1-927917)* *Dist. by* **Orca Bk Pub.**

Runny Nose Press L.L.C., *(978-0-9788542)* 24111 Beierman, Warren, MI 48091-1714 USA
Web site: http://www.runnynosepress.com.

Rupa & Co. (IND) *(978-81-7167; 978-81-291)* *Dist. by* **S Asia.**

Rupanuga Vedic College, *(978-0-9650899; 978-0-9728372; 978-1-934405)* Div. of Iskcon Krishnafest, Inc., Orders Addr.: 5201 Paseo Blvd, Kansas City, MO 64110 USA Tel 224-558-8868; Edit Addr.: 5201 Paseo, Kansas City, MO 64110 USA Tel 816-924-5619; Fax: 816-924-5640
E-mail: eternityknowledgebliss@gmail.com; danavir.goswami@pamho.net
Web site: RVC.edu; DanavirGoswami.com; RVC.edu/RVC_BOOKS.html.

Rural Farm Productions, *(978-0-9753542)* 6538 Germanton Rd., Rural Hall, NC 27045 USA Tel 336-969-2202.

Rush, Hailey, *(978-0-692-99626-3)* 2704 Winslow Ridge Dr., Buford, GA 30519 USA Tel 662-871-7497
E-mail: hahumphr@gmail.com
Dist(s): **Ingram Content Group.**

Rush, Joy, *(978-1-7363475)* 4229 Saunders Tavern Trail, Henrico, VA 23233 USA Tel 804-332-7421
E-mail: yogajoyrva@gmail.com.

RUSH Pubns. & Educational Consultancy, LLC, *(978-0-9748222; 978-0-9748868; 978-0-9814958)* 1901 60th Pl. E., Suite L7432, Bradenton, FL 34203-5076 USA Tel 941-227-4444
E-mail: meylani@superonline.com
Web site: http://www.rushsociety.com
Dist(s): **Cardinal Pubs. Group.**

Rush, Ricki, *(978-0-9674292)* 123 Gregory Dr., Fairfax, CA 94930 USA Tel 415-457-6422; Fax: 415-456-4459
E-mail: rickicoach@aol.com
Web site: http://lifeworks-coaching.com.

Rushmore Pr. LLC, *(978-1-950818; 978-1-953223; 978-1-954345; 978-1-955156; 978-1-956010; 978-1-956696; 978-1-957220; 978-1-957943; 978-1-959182; 978-1-960546; 978-1-961227)* 7662 Balmoral Mills Ct, Las Vegas, NV 89113 USA Tel 888-733-9607
E-mail: daryl@rushmorepress.com
Web site: www.rushmorepress.com.

Russ Invision, *(978-0-9660122; 978-0-9720234; 978-0-9747064; 978-0-9799612; 978-0-9987090; 978-0-9987589; 978-1-958627)* 3219 Conquista Ave., Long Beach, CA 90808 USA (SAN 854-8315)
E-mail: rivision@aol.com
Web site: http://www.abridgeclub.com.

Russell, Fred Publishing, *(978-0-9764347; 978-0-9789832; 978-0-9796229)* 52 Collis St., West Haven, CT 06516 USA Tel 203-934-2501; Fax: 203-934-8723; Toll Free: 866-968-7685; *Imprints*: Rock House Method, The (The Rock)
E-mail: jp@rockhousemethod.com
Web site: http://www.rockhousemethod.com
Dist(s): **Leonard, Hal Corp.**
Music Sales Corp.

Russell, Hilary, *(978-0-578-50353-0; 978-0-578-51195-5)* 6600 Vanderbilt Ave., Dallas, TX 75214 USA Tel 817-937-4711
E-mail: hilaryrtx@yahoo.com.

Russet & Kensington Pr., *(978-1-940114)* 2066 Russet Dr. Suite 200, Troy, MI 48098 USA Tel 248-515-4247
E-mail: time4equilibrium@hotmail.com.

Russian Hill Pr., *(978-0-9911973; 978-0-9995162; 978-1-7341220; 978-1-7351763; 978-1-7378246; 979-8-9879285)* 166 Anna Maria St., Livermore, CA 94550 USA Tel 925-337-5983
E-mail: pchinick@russianhillpress.com
Web site: www.russianhillpress.com.

Rustik Haws LLC, *(978-0-578-51889-3; 978-0-578-51890-9; 978-0-578-53323-0; 978-0-578-53324-7; 978-1-951147; 978-1-952244; 978-1-952617; 978-1-64934)* 5221 Bon Vivant Dr. Apt. 208, TAMPA, FL 33603 USA Tel 813-467-7812
E-mail: services@rustikhaws.com
Dist(s): **Ingram Content Group.**

Rusu, Lacramioara, *(978-1-68501)* 1986 Pine St., Des Plaines, IL 60018 USA Tel 951-533-3348
E-mail: mimiandries94@gmail.com.

†Rutgers Univ. Pr., *(978-0-8135; 978-1-9788)* 106 Somerset St., Third Flr., New Brunswick, NJ 08901 USA (SAN 253-2115) Tel 848-445-7786
Web site: http://www.rutgersuniversitypress.org
Dist(s): **Chicago Distribution Ctr.**
De Gruyter, Inc.
Ebsco Publishing
Cengage Gale
JSTOR
Longleaf Services
MyiLibrary
Univ. of Chicago Pr.
Univ. of Chicago Pr. Distribution Clients
ebrary, Inc.; *CIP.*

Ruth, A. Creations, *(978-0-9656306; 978-0-9907390)* 1860 Wynnewood Ln., Cincinnati, OH 45237 USA Tel 513-821-9027; 513-512-2569
E-mail: aruthcreations@gmail.com
Web site: http://www.annieruth.com.

Rutigliano, Joe, *(978-0-9767769)* 178 Ramona Ave., Staten Island, NY 10312-2717 USA.

Rutledge Development, *(978-0-692-99491-7)* 815 Mission Trail, New Braunfels, TX 78130 USA Tel 830-660-1052
E-mail: Clint@clintrutledge.com
Dist(s): **Ingram Content Group.**

Rutledge, Susan *See* **Willow Bend Pr.**

Ruwanga Trading, *(978-0-9615102; 978-0-9701528)* P.O. Box 1027, Puunene, HI 96784 USA (SAN 694-2776)
Dist(s): **Booklines Hawaii, Ltd.**

Ruybal, Michael, *(978-0-9963959)* 4537 Azure Hills, Las Cruces, NM 88011 USA Tel 575-312-2581
E-mail: micru20@gmail.com.

RWP Bks. *Imprint of* **Redhawk Publishing**

Rx Humor, *(978-0-9639002; 978-1-892157)* 2272 Vistamont Dr., Decatur, GA 30033 USA Tel 404-321-0126; Fax: 404-633-9198
E-mail: nshulma@emory.edu.

Ryan Ave Publishing, *(978-0-9760759)* Div. of J. C. Melvin Seminars, Inc., 5738 Hedgeford Ct., Las Vegas, NV 89120 USA Tel 702-454-9822; Fax: 702-454-9821.

Ryan, Karlene Kay Author, *(978-0-9888843)* 5154 N. Woodson, Fresno, CA 93711 USA Tel 559-304-9737; Fax: 559-446-0565
E-mail: karleneryan@comcast.net
Web site: karleneryan.com.

Ryan, Shirley, *(978-0-9754196)* 6480 Havenside Dr., Sacramento, CA 95831-1504 USA
E-mail: shirleyryanphd@gmail.com
Web site: http://www.shirleyryan.net.

Ryan's World, *(978-0-615-49711-2)* 4620 N. Braeswood Blvd. - No 138, Houston, TX 77096 USA Tel 832-754-6700; Fax: 281-915-4505
E-mail: judy@judysworld.info.

Rye Grass Roots Publishing, *(978-0-9788713)* Orders Addr.: P.O. Box 291382, Port Orange, FL 32129-1382 USA (SAN 851-8289) Tel 386-212-1800
E-mail: jamesmhunt@ryegrassroots.com.

Ryherd, Tim Publishing, *(978-0-9749974)* 21479 FM 365, Beaumont, TX 77705 USA.

Ryken Augmented, *(978-0-692-90968-3; 978-0-578-46911-9; 978-0-578-82354-6)* 164 roosevelt, Buffalo, NY 14215 USA Tel 716-836-5034
E-mail: rykenworldcreator@gmail.com
Dist(s): **CreateSpace Independent Publishing Platform.**

Ryland, John B. Publishing *See* **DJ Blues Publishing**

Ryland Peters & Small (GBR) *(978-1-84172; 978-1-900518; 978-1-872536; 978-1-903116; 978-1-904991; 978-1-84597; 978-1-906094; 978-1-906525; 978-1-84975; 978-1-907563; 978-0-9571409; 978-1-909313; 978-1-78879; 978-1-912983; 978-1-913533; 978-1-907030)* *Dist. by* **S and S Inc.**

Ryland Peters & Small (GBR) *(978-1-84172; 978-1-900518; 978-1-872536; 978-1-903116; 978-1-904991; 978-1-84597; 978-1-906094; 978-1-906525; 978-1-907030; 978-1-84975; 978-1-907563; 978-0-9571409; 978-1-909313; 978-1-78879; 978-1-912983; 978-1-913533)* *Dist. by* **WIPRO.**

Rymer Bks., *(978-0-934723; 978-0-9600792)* P.O. Box 153, Tollhouse, CA 93667-0153 USA (SAN 207-1010) Tel 209-298-8845.

Ryu Cope *See* **D. W. Cope Pr.**

Ryzewski, Deborah, *(978-0-9765302)* 240 Crabapple Ln., Valparaiso, IN 46383 USA.

R.Z. Enterprises of Florida, *(978-0-9792031)* 7640 Prospect Hill Cir., New Port Richey, FL 34654-6376 USA
Web site: http://www.RobertzHicks.com.

S & S Pr., *(978-0-615-14271-5; 978-0-615-14642-3; 978-0-615-14930-1; 978-0-615-14931-8; 978-0-615-14954-7)* 35221 SE Kinsey, Suite 101, Snoqualmie, WA 98065 USA
Web site: http://www.gloriabond.com
Dist(s): **Lulu Pr., Inc.**

SMS Cos., Inc., *(978-0-9669595)* P.O. Box 1184, Smyrna, GA 30081 USA Tel 678-339-0626; Fax: 678-339-0726
E-mail: JMBryant@bellsouth.net
Web site: http://www.smsbooks.com
Dist(s): **Follett School Solutions.**

S.O.C.O. Pubns., *(978-0-910119)* 276 Ward Rd., Mohawk, NY 13407 USA (SAN 241-5720) Tel 315-866-7445
E-mail: copress@borg.com.

S P I E-International Society for Optical Engineering *See* **SPIE**

S. Swan, *(978-1-7342991)* 1143 Becky ln, Lancaster, TX 75134 USA Tel 405-905-0537
E-mail: i.nubes@me.com.

S V E & Churchill Media, *(978-0-7932; 978-0-89290; 978-1-56357)* 6465 N. Avondale Ave., Chicago, IL 60631-1909 USA (SAN 208-3930) Toll Free Fax: 800-624-1678; Toll Free: 800-829-1900
E-mail: custserv@svemedia.com
Web site: http://www.svemedia.com
Dist(s): **Video Project, The**
Weston Woods Studios, Inc.

†SYDA Foundation, *(978-0-911307; 978-0-914602; 978-1-930939)* 371 Brickman Rd., South Fallsburg, NY 12779 USA (SAN 206-5649) Tel 845-434-2000 Toll Free Fax: 888-422-2339 (ordering); Toll Free: 888-422-3334 (ordering); P.O. Box 600, South Fallsburg, NY 12779
Web site: http://www.siddhayoga.org
Dist(s): **Bookpeople**
Independent Pubs. Group
New Leaf Distributing Co., Inc.; *CIP.*

S2 Services, *(978-0-9770928; 978-1-953765)* Orders Addr.: 384 Russell Ave., Gaithersburg, MD 20877 USA; Edit Addr.: 384 Russell Ave., Gaithersburg, MD 20877 USA (SAN 257-3377) Tel 301-493-4982; 301-500-6973
E-mail: socrtwo@s2services.com
Web site: http://www.socrtwo.info/portfolio.htm; http://people.lulu.com/users/index.php?fHomepage=179563
Dist(s): **CafePress.com**
Lulu Pr., Inc.

S.A. Kokinos (ESP) *(978-84-88342; 978-84-96629)* *Dist. by* **Lectorum Pubns.**

Saar, Rachel *See* **Brookstone Pr.**

Sabeels Publishing, *(978-1-68376)* 40 E. Main St., Newark, DE 19711 USA Tel 902-457-9356
E-mail: isbn@speedy.partners.

Saberlee Bks., *(978-0-9815836; 978-0-9909606; 978-1-7340894)* 168 N. Catalina Ave. Apt. 103, Pasadena CA, CA 91106 USA
E-mail: saberleebooks@yahoo.com
Web site: http://www.lisettebrodey.com; http://facebook.com/BrodeyAuthor.

Publisher Name Index

Sable Creek Pr. LLC, *(978-0-9766823; 978-0-9828875; 978-0-9890667; 978-0-9974953; 978-0-9991157; 978-0-578-61507-3; 979-8-218-07283-4)*
E-mail: sablecreekpress@cox.net
Web site: http://www.sablecreekpress.com; http://janetclarkshay.com.

Sabledrake Enterprises, *(978-0-9702189; 978-0-9771005; 978-0-9844032)* P.O. Box 30751, Seattle, WA 98113 USA Tel 425-317-9241; Fax: 772-673-2381
E-mail: tim@sabledrake.com
Web site: http://www.sabledrake.com.

Sabre Publishing Hse., Inc., *(978-0-9746213)* 201 Huff Lake Ct., Ortonville, MI 48462 USA Tel 248-627-1112; Fax: 248-627-1113
E-mail: mikeatsabre@aol.com.

Sabyr Pr., *(978-0-9746463)* 2999 Allmon Ln., Missouri Vly, IA 51555-5057 USA
E-mail: info@sabyr.com
Web site: http://www.sabyr.com.

Sachedina, Dr. Shenin Medical Education Products, *(978-0-9778648)* 2200 Glenwood Dr., Winter Park, FL 32792 USA (SAN 850-4377) Tel 407-740-5127
E-mail: Metuandlee@aol.com
Web site: http://www.metuandlee.com.

Sacred Garden Fellowship, *(978-1-932746)* 293 Totem Lodge Rd., Averill Park, NY 12208 USA Tel 802-363-5579
E-mail: sacredgf@gmail.com
Web site: www.sacredgardenfellowship.org.

Sacred Life Publishers *See* **Sacred Life Pubs.**

Sacred Life Pubs., *(978-0-9822331; 978-0-9860270; 978-0-9896593; 978-0-9965785; 978-1-7330393; 978-1-7356932; 979-8-9868130)* P.O. Box P. O. Box 1127, Kihei, HI 96753 USA
E-mail: Sharon@SacredLife.com
Web site: htpp://www.SacredLife.com.

Sacred Structure Pr., *(978-0-692-07421-3)* 10129 E Elk Lake Dr., Rapid City, MI 49676 USA Tel 231-322-2159
E-mail: shawn@pollackfamily.org
Dist(s): **Ingram Content Group.**

Sacred Truth Publishing, *(978-1-56840)* Div. of Sacred Truth Ministries, Orders Addr.: P.O. Box 18, Mountain City, TN 37683 USA
E-mail: sacredtruthministries@mounet.com.

Saddle & Bridle, Inc., *(978-0-9655501)* 375 Jackson Ave., Saint Louis, MO 63130-4243 USA Tel 314-725-9115; Fax: 314-725-6440
E-mail: saddlebr@saddleandbridle.com
Web site: http://www.saddleandbridle.com.

Saddle Pal Creations, Inc., *(978-0-9663495; 978-1-931353)* Orders Addr.: P.O. Box 872127, Wasilla, AK 99687-2127 USA Tel 907-357-3235; Fax: 907-357-3446
Web site: http://www.alaskachildrensbooks.com
Dist(s): **Partners Bk. Distributing, Inc.**
Partners/West Book Distributors
Wizard Works.

Saddleback Educational Publishing *See* **Saddleback Educational Publishing, Inc.**

Saddleback Educational Publishing, Inc., *(978-1-56254; 978-1-59905; 978-1-60291; 978-1-61651; 978-1-61247; 978-1-62250; 978-1-62670; 978-1-63078; 978-1-68021; 978-1-64598; 978-1-63889)* 151 Kalmus Dr., J-1, Costa Mesa, CA 92626-4564 USA (SAN 860-0902) Toll Free Fax: 888-734-4010; Toll Free: 800-637-8715
E-mail: contact@saddleback.com; amchugh@sdlback.com; adormanesh@sdlback.com
Web site: http://www.sdlback.com
Dist(s): **Children's Plus, Inc.**
Findaway World, LLC
Follett School Solutions
ebrary, Inc.

Sade Harvison, *(978-0-578-28311-1; 978-0-578-28312-8; 979-8-218-15138-6; 979-8-218-15139-3)* 1910 Bruck St., Columbus, OH 43207 USA Tel 304-559-4996
E-mail: thelotuzbrand@gmail.com.

Sadie Bks., *(978-0-9816047; 978-0-615-55525-6; 978-0-615-74503-9)* 215 E. Camden Ave., H11, Moorestown, NJ 08057 USA (SAN 856-017X) Tel 856-234-2676; 856-313-0548
E-mail: info@sadie-books.com
Web site: http://www.sadie-books.com
Dist(s): **CreateSpace Independent Publishing Platform**
Dummy Record Do Not USE!!!!
Smashwords.

Sadlier *Imprint of* **Sadlier, William H. Inc.**

Sadlier, William H. Inc., *(978-0-8215; 978-0-87105; 978-1-4217)* 9 Pine St., New York, NY 10005-1002 USA (SAN 204-0948) Tel 212-227-2120; Fax: 212-267-8696; Toll Free: 800-221-5175; *Imprints:* Sadlier (Sadlier)
Web site: http://www.sadlier.com.

†SAE Intl., *(978-0-7680; 978-0-89883; 978-1-56091; 978-1-4686)* 400 Commonwealth Dr., Warrendale, PA 15096 USA (SAN 232-5721) Tel 724-776-4970; Fax: 724-776-0790
E-mail: customerservice@sae.org
Web site: http://www.sae.org; http://books.sae.org/; *CIP.*

Saeligstone, *(978-0-615-15984-3; 978-0-615-15985-0)* 13110 Moselle Forest, helotes, TX 78023 USA
E-mail: peirce1@saeligstone.com
Dist(s): **Lulu Pr., Inc.**

Safari, Ltd., *(978-1-881469)* Orders Addr.: P.O. Box 630685, Miami, FL 33163 USA Tel 305-621-1000; Fax: 305-621-6894; Toll Free: 800-554-5414; Edit Addr.: 1400 NW 159th St., Miami, FL 33169 USA
Web site: http://www.toydirectory.com.

Safari Pr., Inc., *(978-0-940143; 978-1-57157)* 15621 Chemical Ln., Suite B, Huntington Beach, CA 92649 USA (SAN 663-0723) Tel 714-894-9080; Fax: 714-894-4949; Toll Free: 800-451-4788 (orders only)
E-mail: info@safaripress.com
Web site: http://www.safaripress.com
Dist(s): **National Bk. Network.**

Safe Harbor Publications *See* **Family Christian Ctr.**

Safeblade, Evelyn Collins, *(978-0-9670655)* W8504 Jellen Rd., Spooner, WI 54801 USA Tel 715-635-7536.

SafePlans, *(978-0-9975811)* 3519 US Alt 19, Palm Harbor, FL 34683 USA Tel 573-636-5377
E-mail: heidi@safeplans.com; brad@safeplans.com
Web site: www.safeplans.com.

Safer Society Pr., *(978-1-884444; 978-1-940234)* Div. of Safer Society Foundation, Inc., Orders Addr.: P.O. Box 340, Brandon, VT 05733-0340 USA Tel 802-247-3132; Fax: 802-247-4233; Edit Addr.: 8-10 Conant Sq., Brandon, VT 05733-1121 USA
E-mail: Theream@saver.net
Web site: http://www.safersociety.org.

Safety Always Matters, Inc., *(978-0-9620584; 978-1-883994)* 222 Wildwood Ct., Bloomingdale, IL 60108 USA (SAN 248-9759) Tel 630-894-1229
Dist(s): **Syndistar, Inc.**

Safeworld Publishing Co., *(978-0-9655604; 978-0-578-15130-4; 978-0-692-31823-2; 978-0-692-31827-0; 978-0-692-31835-5; 978-1-954284)* 3 Greenshire Ln., Owings Mills, MD 21117-4813 USA Tel 410-356-7233
E-mail: janisraf4@aol.com
Web site: www.declineandfallofallevil.org.

SAGA Pr. *Imprint of* **Smocking Arts Guild of America**

SAGA Press *Imprint of* **Simon & Schuster Bks. For Young Readers**

Sagaponack Bks., *(978-0-9668845; 978-0-9801336; 978-0-9983526; 978-0-9985673; 978-0-9997045; 978-1-7339651; 978-1-7347374)* Orders Addr.: 101 South Walk Pl., Saint Augustine, FL 32086 USA Tel 904-429-7209
E-mail: fran@sagbooks.com
Web site: http://www.SagaponackBooks.com
Dist(s): **Follet Higher Education Grp**
Partners Bk. Distributing, Inc.

Sage, David, *(978-0-9894210; 978-1-7336402)* 67 N. Piney PO Box 208, Story, WY 82842 USA Tel 303-883-4148
E-mail: davesageinstory@gmail.com.

Sage Green Books *See* **SageGreenPr.**

Sage Hill Pubs., LLC, *(978-0-913205)* Orders Addr.: P.O. Box 866, Yerington, NV 89447 USA (SAN 283-0493) Tel 775-463-4188 (phone/fax)
E-mail: booksbysagehill@aol.com.

Sage Pr., *(978-0-9799972)* P.O. Box 981432, Park City, UT 84098 USA (SAN 854-9494) Tel 435-658-1238 Do not confuse with companies with similar name in Evergreen, CO, Phonenix, AZ, Murrieta, CA, Glenwood Springs, CO, San Diego, CA
E-mail: rudyandcoco@hotmail.com
Web site: http://www.rudyandcoco.com
Dist(s): **Itasca Bks.**

†SAGE Pubns., Inc., *(978-0-7619; 978-0-8039; 978-1-4129; 978-1-4522; 978-1-4462; 978-1-4833; 978-1-5063; 978-1-5443; 978-1-0718; 978-1-0719; 978-1-5297)* 2455 Teller Rd., Thousand Oaks, CA 91360 USA (SAN 204-7217) Tel 800-818-7243; Fax: 800-583-2665; 805-499-0871
E-mail: info@sagepub.com; deborah.vaughn@sagepub.com
Web site: http://www.sagepub.com; http://www.sagepub.co.uk; http://www.pineforge.com; http://sagepub.com
Dist(s): **Ambassador Bks. & Media**
Coutts Information Services
Cranbury International
Ebsco Publishing
Emery-Pratt Co.
Cengage Gale
MBS Textbook Exchange, Inc.
Midwest Library Service
MyiLibrary
Blackwell
Sage US Textbks.
Yankee Bk. Peddler, Inc.
ebrary, Inc.
; CIP.

SAGE Pubns., Ltd. (GBR) *(978-0-7619; 978-0-8039; 978-1-903300; 978-1-4129; 978-1-84445; 978-1-84641; 978-1-84860; 978-1-4462; 978-0-85725; 978-0-85702; 978-1-84787; 978-1-4739; 978-1-84920; 978-93-85985; 978-1-5264) Dist. by* **SAGE.**

Sagebrush Entertainment, Inc., *(978-0-9766557)* P.O. Box 261187, Encino, CA 91426-1187 USA Toll Free Fax: 800-881-4577; Toll Free: 800-711-4677
E-mail: info@hopalong.com
Web site: http://www.hopalong.com.

Sagebrush Writings, *(978-1-7322202)* 2900 Bosham Ln., Midlothian, VA 23113 USA Tel 804-937-7007
E-mail: libbymcnamee@yahoo.com
Web site: www.LibbyMcNamee.com.

SageGreenPr., *(978-1-7361182)* 12684 Willow Ln., Lakewood, CO 80215 USA Tel 720-280-2929
E-mail: ncarlisle01@gmail.com.

Sager Group, The, *(978-0-9831785; 978-0-9895241; 978-0-9916629; 978-0-9862679; 978-0-9964901; 978-0-9980793; 978-0-9996338; 978-1-950154; 978-1-958861)* 5996 La Jolla Corona Dr, La Jolla, CA 92037 USA Tel 619-218-2109
E-mail: info@mikesager.com
Web site: www.TheSagerGroup.net.

Sagis Pr., *(978-0-692-06119-0; 978-1-7321361)* 611 Grove Ave., Charlottesville, VA 22902 USA Tel 434-260-0290
E-mail: ottoerik@yahoo.com
Dist(s): **CreateSpace Independent Publishing Platform.**

Saguaro Bks,. LLC, *(978-0-615-98268-7; 978-0-615-98274-8; 978-0-615-99062-0; 978-0-692-20351-4; 978-0-692-24769-3; 978-0-692-27779-9; 978-0-692-83044-4; 978-0-692-06465-8; 978-0-578-43121-5; 978-0-578-45371-2; 978-0-578-67648-7; 978-0-578-69249-4; 978-1-7366967)* 16845 E. Ave. of the Fountains, Ste. 325, Fountain Hills, AZ 85268 USA Tel 602-309-7670; 480-372-1362
E-mail: mjnickum@saguarobooks.com
Web site: www.saguarobooks.com
Dist(s): **CreateSpace Independent Publishing Platform.**

Sahagian, Mark, *(978-0-578-40331-1)* 253A Lisa Ln., Nashville, TN 37210-2405 USA Tel 248-561-1013
E-mail: marksfreecomix@yahoo.com.

Sahaja Publishing, *(978-0-578-44421-5)* 12117 180th Ave. Ct. NW, Gig Harbor, WA 98329 USA Tel 253-884-2036
E-mail: sahaja@centurytel.net.

Sahtva, *(978-1-7327620)* 2 Northwood Dr, Downingtown, PA 19335-1757 USA Tel 484-784-7190
E-mail: H_mottaleb@yahoo.com
Web site: Www.bigworldlittleom.com.

Saint Andrew Pr., Ltd. (GBR) *(978-0-7152; 978-0-86153) Dist. by* **Westminster John Knox.**

Saint Anthony Messenger Press & Franciscan Communications *See* **Franciscan Media**

Saint Augustine Press *See* **Mary Jane Hayes**

St. Augustine's Pr., Inc., *(978-1-890318; 978-1-58731)* P.O. Box 2285, South Bend, IN 46680 USA Tel 574-291-3500; Fax: 574-291-3700; Toll Free: 888-997-4994
E-mail: bruce@staugustine.net
Web site: http://www.staugustine.net
Dist(s): **Chicago Distribution Ctr.**
Univ. of Chicago Pr.
Univ. of Chicago Pr. Distribution Clients.

St. Benedict Pr., LLC, *(978-0-89555; 978-0-9675978; 978-0-9770091; 978-1-935302; 978-1-61890; 978-1-5051)* 13315 Carowinds Blvd Suite Q, Charlotte, NC 28273 USA (SAN 760-789X) Tel 704-731-0651; Fax: 704-884-3262; Toll Free: 800-437-5876
Web site: http://www.saintbenedictpress.com; http://www.tanbooks.com; https://catholiccourses.benedictpress.com/index.php; https://neumann.benedictpress.com/
Dist(s): **Baker & Taylor Publisher Services (BTPS)**
Saint Benedict Pr.

St. Bob Pr., *(978-0-9796988)* 2095 Poplar Ave., Suite 54, Memphis, TN 38104 USA (SAN 854-1523) Tel 901-412-7362
E-mail: murff@saintbobpress.com
Web site: http://www.saintbobpress.com.

St. Clair Pubns., *(978-0-9801704; 978-0-9826302; 978-1-935786; 978-1-947514)* P.O. Box 727, Mc Minnville, TN 37111-0726 USA Tel 931-668-2860; Fax: 931-668-2861; Toll Free: 888-248-0192
E-mail: stan@stclair.net
Web site: http://stan.stclair.net/StClairPublications.html#books.

St. Clair Publishing, *(978-0-615-17629-1)* 3103 Fleece Flower, Austin, TX 78735 USA
Web site: http://www.richardshenderson.com.

St. Leo Pr., *(978-1-7341172; 978-1-7367189; 979-8-9852361)* 1037 E Vinedo Ln., Tempe, AZ 85284 USA Tel 480-838-7305
E-mail: bforbes@forbescompany.com
Web site: www.mysterysearchers.com.

Saint Mary's Press of Minnesota *See* **Saint Mary's Press of Minnesota**

Saint Mary's Press of Minnesota, *(978-0-88489; 978-1-59982; 978-1-64121)* 702 Terrace Heights, Winona, MN 55987-1320 USA (SAN 203-073X) Tel 507-457-7900; Fax: 507-457-7990; Toll Free Fax: 800-344-9225; Toll Free: 800-533-8095
E-mail: smpress@smp.org; hwilliams@smp.org
Web site: http://www.smp.org.

St. Nectarios Pr., *(978-0-913026)* 10300 Ashworth Ave., N., Seattle, WA 98133-9410 USA (SAN 203-3542) Tel 206-522-4471; Fax: 206-523-0550; Toll Free: 800-643-4233
E-mail: orders@stnectariospress.com; anneborozan@live.com
Web site: http://www.stnectariospress.com.

St. Nicholas Monastery, *(978-0-9773579)* 1340 Piney Rd., North Fort Myers, FL 33903-3822 USA.

St. Pancratius Pr., *(978-1-943835)* 4001 Pelham Rd. No. 82, Greer, SC 29650 USA Tel 864-320-8085
E-mail: saintpancratiuspress@gmail.com.

Saint Paul Books & Media *See* **Pauline Bks. & Media**

Saint Paul Brotherhood *See* **ACTS Pr.**

St. Vincent Archabbey Pubns., *(978-0-9708216; 978-0-9773909; 978-0-9906855)* 300 Fraser Purchase Rd., Latrobe, PA 15650-2690 USA Tel 724-805-2601; Fax: 724-805-2775
E-mail: kim.metzgar@email.stvincent.edu
Web site: http://www.stvincentstore.com
Dist(s): **Distributors, The.**

St. Vincent College Ctr. for Northern Appalachian Studies, *(978-1-885851)* 300 Fraser Purchase Rd., Latrobe, PA 15650 USA Tel 724-805-2316; Fax: 724-537-4554
E-mail: rwissolik@stvincent.edu
Web site: http://www.stvincent.edu/napp.

†St. Vladimir's Seminary Pr., *(978-0-88141; 978-0-913836; 978-0-9618545; 978-0-9622536; 978-1-879038; 978-1-891295)* 575 Scarsdale Rd., Yonkers, NY 10707 USA (SAN 204-6296) Tel 914-961-8313 x 348; Fax: 914-961-5456 Bookstore fax; 914-961-4507 Press fax; Toll Free: 800-204-2665 Bookstore
E-mail: benedict@svots.edu; ghatrak@svots.edu
Web site: http://www.svspress.com; *CIP.*

Saintly Lisle, *(978-1-7321396)* 5750 Buffington Rd, apt 2208, College Park, GA 30349 USA Tel 708-712-3594
E-mail: jonathan1989@sbcglobal.net.

Saints Of Glory Church, *(978-0-9673342)* Orders Addr.: P.O. Box 8957, Anaheim, CA 92812-0957 USA Tel 714-846-0401; Fax: 714-846-3395; Edit Addr.: 16102 Warmington Ln., Huntington Beach, CA 92649 USA
E-mail: sgcgow@aol.com.

Sakthi Bks., Inc., *(978-0-9752586)* Orders Addr.: 1507 Lone Oak Cir., Fairfield, IA 52556 USA
E-mail: pradheepkumar@hotmail.com
Web site: http://www.matrixjourney.com; http://www.rightawareness.com.

Sakura Pr., *(978-0-9660583)* Hesta Roach 227 Croatan Dr., Oriental, NC 28571 USA Tel 252-249-1929 (phone/fax) Do not confuse with Sakura Pr., Pleasant Hill, OR
E-mail: roachdj@hotmail.com.

Salaam Reads *Imprint of* **Simon & Schuster Bks. For Young Readers**

Salado Pr., LLC, *(978-0-9663870; 978-0-9835342; 978-0-9913118)* Orders Addr.: P.O. Box 470171, Fort Worth, TX 76147 USA Tel 972-215-6116
E-mail: lee@saladopress.com
Web site: http://www.saladopress.com.

SALAM Bk.,
Dist(s): **Consortium Bk. Sales & Distribution.**

Salamander Street Ltd. (GBR) *(978-1-913630) Dist. by* **Consort Bk Sales.**

Salani (ITA) *(978-88-7782; 978-88-8451) Dist. by* **Distribks Inc.**

Salariya Bk. Co. Ltd. (GBR) *(978-1-904194; 978-1-904642; 978-1-905087; 978-1-905638; 978-1-906370; 978-1-906714; 978-1-907184; 978-1-908759; 978-1-909645; 978-1-908177; 978-1-908973; 978-1-911242; 978-1-912006; 978-1-912537; 978-1-910706; 978-1-913337) Dist. by* **Sterling.**

Salaud Publishing, *(978-0-9713167)* P.O. Box 11681, Portland, OR 97211 USA Tel 919-963-9135
E-mail: jesse@hastardrecords.com; jesse@bastardrecords.com; jordan_lari@highcountrystudentpublishers.org
Web site: http://www.highcountrystudentpubishers.org; http://www.bastardrecords.com/salaud.htm.

Salazar, JC, *(978-0-9991496)* 805 Bomar No. 2, Houston, TX 77006 USA Tel 832-788-7858
E-mail: csal55@aol.com.

Salch, Megan F., *(978-0-9776154)* 3106 Lawrence St., Houston, TX 77018 USA Tel 713-864-1344.

Saleh, Salam, *(978-0-578-92062-7; 978-0-578-30583-7)* 3614 Dubonnet Ave, Rosemead, CA 91770 USA Tel 323-485-0742
E-mail: ssaleh@calstatela.edu.

Salem Academy & College, *(978-0-9789608)* P.O. Box 10548, Winston-Salem, NC 27108 USA
Web site: http://www.salem.edu.

Salem Author Services, *(978-1-931232; 978-1-59160; 978-0-9723806; 978-0-9740030; 978-1-59467; 978-0-9744668; 978-0-9754803; 978-1-59781; 978-0-9764981; 978-0-9769668; 978-1-60034; 978-1-934248; 978-1-60266; 978-0-9798246; 978-0-9798467; 978-1-60477; 978-0-9799120; 978-1-934937; 978-1-934938; 978-0-9802455; 978-0-9802456; 978-1-60647; 978-1-935097; 978-1-935098; 978-1-935204; 978-0-9820938; 978-1-60791; 978-1-935456; 978-1-61579; 978-1-936107; 978-1-936183; 978-0-9841965; 978-1-936198; 978-1-60957; 978-1-936400; 9) Div. of Salem Media Group, 2301 Lucien Way, Suite 415, Maitland, FL 32751 USA Tel 407-339-4217; Fax: 407-339-9898; Toll Free: 866-381-2665; Imprints:* Xulon Press (Xulon Prss); Mill City Press, Inc (Mill City); Two Harbors Press (TwoHarbors); Liberty Hill Publishing (Liberty Hill); North Loop Press (MYID_T_NORTH L)
Web site: http://www.salemauthorservices.com/; www.XulonPress.com; www.MyBookOrders.com; www.millcitypress.net; https://www.libertyhillpublishing.com/
Dist(s): **INscribe Digital**
Ingram Bk. Co.
Itasca Bks.
eBookit.com.

†Salem Pr., Inc., *(978-0-89356; 978-1-58765)* Div. of EBSCO Publishing, Orders Addr.: 10 Estes St, IPSWICH, MA 01938 USA (SAN 241-841X) Tel 800-758-5995; Fax: 201-968-1411; Toll Free: 800-221-1592
E-mail: csr@salempress.com
Web site: http://www.salempress.com; http://salempress.com/Store/pages/hwwilson.htm
Dist(s): **Ebsco Publishing**
Cengage Gale
Grey Hse. Publishing
MyiLibrary
ebrary, Inc.; *CIP.*

Salem Publishing Solutions, Incorporated *See* **Salem Author Services**

Salem Ridge Press LLC, *(978-0-9776786; 978-1-934671)* 4263 Salem Dr., Emmaus, PA 18049 USA
E-mail: customerservice@slaemridgepress.com.

Sales Effectiveness, Inc., *(978-0-9676255)* 221 Riverstone Way, GREER, SC 29651 USA Tel 770-842-8744; 770-552-6612
E-mail: carlos.quintero@gmail.com
Web site: http://www.saleseffectiveness.com.

Salih, Sara *See* **Harlan Rose Publishing**

Salina Bookshelf *See* **Salina Bookshelf Inc**

Salina Bookshelf Inc, *(978-0-9644189; 978-1-893354; 978-1-960830)* 1120 W. University Ave, Ste. 102, Flagstaff, AZ 86001 USA (SAN 253-0503) Tel 928-527-0070; Fax: 928-526-0386; Toll Free: 877-527-0070
E-mail: elockard@salinabookshelf.com; tmitchell@salinabookshelf.com
Web site: http://www.salinabookshelf.com.

Salisbury, Scott, *(978-1-7332680)* 6705 E. 134th Ave., Thornton, CO 80602 USA Tel 314-691-0334
E-mail: stlsalisbury@yahoo.com.

Salish Kootenia College Pr., *(978-1-934594)* Orders Addr.: P.O. Box 70, Pablo, MT 59855 USA Tel 406-275-4882; Fax: 406-275-4801; Edit Addr.: 52000 Hwy.93, Pablo, MT 59855 USA
E-mail: bob-bigant@skc.edu
Dist(s): **Stoneydale Pr. Publishing Co.**
Univ. of Nebraska Pr.

Sally Ride Science, *(978-0-9753920; 978-1-933798; 978-1-940073; 978-1-941094)* 9191 Towne Centre Dr. Ste. L101, San Diego, CA 92122-6204 USA Tel 858-638-1432; Fax: 858-638-1419; Toll Free: 800-561-5161
E-mail: tam@sallyridescience.com; bleck@sallyridescience.com
Web site: http://www.sallyridescience.com.

Sally Veillette, *(978-1-953501; 978-1-959832)* 15548 8th Ave NE, Shoreline, WA 98155 USA Tel 518-929-8049
E-mail: sally@ciaosally.com.

Salmon Hole Poetry Press *See* **Minimal Pr., The**

Salmon Run Pr., *(978-0-9634000; 978-1-887573)* Orders Addr.: P.O. Box 672130, Chugiak, AK 99567-2130 USA Tel 907-688-4268
E-mail: salmonrp@aol.com
Dist(s): **Partners/West Book Distributors**
SPD-Small Pr. Distribution
Todd Communications
Wizard Works.

Salmon Run Publishing Company *See* **Salmon Run Pr.**

Salt and Light Bks., *(978-0-692-67312-6; 978-0-692-67627-1; 978-0-692-67628-8; 978-1-946417)* P.O. Box 5, Hugoton, KS 67951 USA Tel 620-544-9042
Web site: www.saltandlightbooks.com
Dist(s): **CreateSpace Independent Publishing Platform.**

Salt City Books, *(978-0-9776332)* P.O. Box 6, Farmington, UT 84025-0006 USA (SAN 257-8522) Tel 801-309-7820; Fax: 801-485-2654
E-mail: saltcitybooks@msn.com.

Salt City Systems *See* **Salt Pubs.**

Salt of the Earth Pr., *(978-0-9816949; 978-0-9849183)* W. 4456 Hwy. 63, Springbrook, WI 54875 USA (SAN 856-2555) Fax: 715-318-6417
Web site: http://www.saltpress.com.

Salt Pubs., *(978-0-9709940; 978-0-9725804)* 6163 E. Molloy Rd., East Syracuse, NY 13057 USA Tel 315-437-1139; Fax: 315-463-2055; Toll Free: 800-324-2607
E-mail: salt@twcny.rr.com.

Salt Publishing (GBR) *(978-1-876857; 978-1-901994; 978-1-84471; 978-1-907773; 978-1-78463) Dist. by* **SPD-Small Pr Dist.**

Salty Dog, Inc., The, *(978-0-9793560)* Orders Addr.: a/o Mark Yarbrough, The Salty Dog Inc., 69 Arrow Rd., Hilton Head Island, SC 29928-2992 USA (SAN 853-2338)
Web site: http://www.saltydog.com.

Salty Doll Studios, *(978-0-692-12453-6; 978-0-578-41460-7; 978-0-578-67093-5; 978-0-578-67203-8)* P.O. Box 1392, Farmington, AR 72730 USA Tel 479-530-1586
E-mail: saltydollstudios@yahoo.com
Dist(s): **CreateSpace Independent Publishing Platform.**

Salty Paws Publishing, *(978-0-9986680)* 208 Mariela Ct., Ponte Vedra Beach, FL 32082 USA Tel 904-254-5763
E-mail: rigbym@bellsouth.net
Web site: saltypawspublishing.com.

Salty Pond Pubs., *(978-0-615-45705-5; 978-0-615-56089-2)* 10 Edward Kelly Rd., East Sandwich, MA 02537 USA Tel 781-715-5014; Fax: 508-833-8923
E-mail: jglinehan@comcast.net.

Salty Sea Publishing, *(978-0-692-78475-4)* 2400 NE 99th St., Vancouver, WA 98665 USA Tel 503-929-6941
E-mail: katebeeman@gmail.com
Web site: http://katebeeman.website.

Salvation Army, *(978-0-89216)* 440 W. Nyack Rd., West Nyack, NY 10994 USA (SAN 237-2649) Tel 845-620-7200 Do not confuse with Salvation Army Supplies, Southern, Des Plaines, IL (Southern Territory) or Salvation Army Supplies & Purchasing Dept., Des Plaines, IL or Salvation Army, Des Plaines, IL
Dist(s): **Baker & Taylor Publisher Services (BTPS).**

Salvatorelli, A. Michael, *(978-0-9992734)* 1002 Balcom Ave., Bronx, NY 10465 USA Tel 917-400-9729
E-mail: deaconsalvatorelli@gmail.com.

Salvo Pr. *Imprint of* **Start Publishing LLC**

Salzman Bks. LLC, *(978-0-9842632)* Orders Addr.: P.O. Box 189, Winfield, KS 67156 USA (SAN 858-8910) Tel 620-262-7280; Edit Addr.: 2106 Kickapoo, Winfield, KS 67156 USA
E-mail: jsalzman@salzmanbooks.com
Web site: http://www.salzmanbooks.com.

Saman Publishing, *(978-0-9728020)* 751 Lemonwood Ct., San Jose, CA 95120 USA.

Samantha's Stories Inc. *See* **Samantha's Stories Inc.**

Samantha's Stories Inc., 115 G st spc 14, arcata, CA 95521 USA Tel 707-999-7334
Web site: http://samanthastories.us; http://weilandenglishtutor.com.

Samara Pr., *(978-0-9577556)* c/o Trillium Hse., 241 Bonita, Los Trancos Woods, Portola Valley, CA 94028-8103 USA Tel 650-851-1847.

Sambodh Society, Inc., The, *(978-0-9785969)* 6363 N 24th St., Kalamazoo, MI 49004 USA (SAN 851-0849)
Web site: http://www.sambodh.us.

Same Old Story Productions, *(978-0-9845571; 978-1-945450)* 3993 Ivy Wood Dr., Amelia, OH 45102 USA.

Samhain Publishing, LTD, *(978-1-59998; 978-1-60504; 978-1-60928; 978-1-61921; 978-1-61922; 978-1-61923; 978-1-5139; 978-1-61923-400-0; 978-1-61923-300-3)* Orders Addr.: 11821 Mason Montgomery Rd. 4B, Cincinnati, OH 45249 USA; Edit Addr.: 11821 Mason Montgomery Rd. Suite 4b, Cincinnati, OH 45249 USA (SAN 257-7488) Tel 513-453-4688; Fax: 513-583-0191
E-mail: contracts@samhainpublishing.com
Web site: http://www.samhainpublishing.com.

Sami, Wafa *See* **Shami, Wafa**

Samizdat Express *See* **Seltzer Bks.**

Sammi Leigh Melville, *(978-0-578-40600-8)* 248 Maclay St., Harrisburg, PA 17110 USA Tel 508-243-2154
E-mail: Sammileighm@gmail.com
Dist(s): **Ingram Content Group.**

Sammy Bks., *(978-0-9984241)* 1845 Stinnett Rd., Huntingtown, MD 20639 USA Tel 410-535-2188
E-mail: bawilburn@comcast.net
Web site: www.sammybooks.com.

Sams, II, Carl R. Photography, Inc., *(978-0-9671748; 978-0-9770108; 978-0-9827625; 978-0-9989836)* 361 Whispering Pines, Milford, MI 48380-3807 USA (SAN 859-435X) Tel 248-685-2422; Fax: 248-685-1643; Toll Free: 800-552-1867
E-mail: carlsams@carlsams.com
Web site: http://www.carlsams.com; http://www.strangerinthewoods.com
Dist(s): **Follett School Solutions**
Partners Bk. Distributing, Inc.

Samuelson, Norma, *(978-1-7329192; 979-8-9863947)* 26862 Via Corta, San Juan Capistrano, CA 92675 USA Tel 949-291-7465
E-mail: normailu@cox.net.

San Diego Business Accounting Solutions a Non CPA Firm *See* **JA Pubns., Ltd.**

San Diego County Regional Airport Authority, *(978-0-9745294)* P.O. Box 82776, San Diego, CA 92138-2776 USA Tel 619-400-2400; Fax: 619-400-2866
Web site: http://www.san.org.

San Diego Museum of Man, *(978-0-937808)* 1350 El Prado, Balboa Pk., San Diego, CA 92101-1616 USA Tel 619-239-2001; Fax: 619- 239-2749
E-mail: khedges@museumofman.org
Web site: http://www.museumofman.org.

San Francisco Art Commission, The, *(978-1-888048)* 800 Chestnut St., San Francisco, CA 94133 USA Tel 415-771-7020; Fax: 415-252-2595; *Imprints:* WritersCorps Books (WrtrsCorps Bks)
Dist(s): **SPD-Small Pr. Distribution.**

San Francisco Story Works, *(978-0-9774227)* 386 Union St., San Francisco, CA 94133-3516 USA (SAN 257-5248)
Web site: http://www.pengey.com; http://www.sanfranciscostoryworks.com; TheGlassAlibi.com.

San Francisco Study Ctr., *(978-0-936434; 978-1-888956)* 1663 Mission St. Suite310, San Francisco, CA 94103 USA (SAN 214-4654) Tel 415-626-1650; Fax: 415-626-7276; Toll Free: 888-281-3757; *Imprints:* Study Center Press (Study Ctr Pr)
E-mail: marjorie@studycenter.org
Web site: http://www.studycenter.org
Dist(s): **Parent Services Project.**

San Juan Publishing, *(978-0-9707399; 978-0-9858897)* Orders Addr.: P.O. Box 923, Woodinville, WA 98072 USA
E-mail: sanjuanbooks@yahoo.com
Dist(s): **Partners Bk. Distributing, Inc.**

Sananda Publications *See* **Reverence for Life**

SanaOhio, *(978-0-692-91401-4)* 2323 Meadowpoint Dr, Troy, OH 45373 USA Tel 859-533-4905
E-mail: phash@sanaohio.com.

Sanchez, Shayla, *(978-0-9993636)* 38553 Blacow Rd., Fremont, CA 94536 USA Tel 510-797-4013
E-mail: shaylasanchez@att.net.

Sancho, Elizabeth, *(978-0-9980980)* P.O. Box 1889, kapaa, HI 96746 USA Tel 808-639-2090; Fax: 808-639-2090
E-mail: elizabethsancho227@gmail.com.

Sancho Storybooks *See* **Joseph Pubns.**

Sanctity Pubns., *(978-0-9983129)* 2732 Webber Ct., Steilacoom, WA 98388 USA Tel 253-292-1317
E-mail: Graciesmail@comcast.net.

Sanctuary Bks., *(978-0-9753334)* P.O. Box 1623, New York, NY 10028 USA Do not confuse with companies with the same or similar name in Mount Juliet, TN, Tampa, FL
E-mail: sanctuarybooks@earthlink.net
Web site: http://www.sanctuarybks.com.

Sanctuary Publishing, Inc., *(978-0-9746995; 978-0-9785334; 978-0-9843754; 978-0-9830018; 978-0-9840392)* 40 Red Butte Rd., Sedona, AZ 86351-7765 USA (SAN 920-1122) Tel 928-284-2269; 928-284-1154; Fax: 928-284-4782
Web site: http://www.SanctuaryPublications.com
Dist(s): **MyiLibrary.**

Sanctuary Publishing, Ltd. (GBR) *(978-1-86074; 978-1-898141) Dist. by* **H Leonard.**

Sand Dreams Pr., LLC, *(978-0-9798656)* P.O. Box 24, Whitehouse Station, NJ 08889-0024 USA (SAN 854-6134) Tel 908-256-4834
E-mail: imre@sanddreamspress.com
Web site: http://www.sanddreamspress.com.

Sand Hill Review Pr., *(978-1-937818; 978-1-949534)* Orders Addr.: One Baldwin, Suite 304, San Mateo, CA 94401 USA; Edit Addr.: One Baldwin, Suite 304, San Mateo, CA 94401 USA Tel 415-297-3571
E-mail: info@sandhillreviewpress.com; toryhartmann@hotmail.com
Web site: www.sandhillreviewpress.com
Dist(s): **BookBaby**
CreateSpace Independent Publishing Platform.

Sand Sage Pr., *(978-0-9793474)* Orders Addr.: P.O. Box 60812, Canyon, TX 79016 USA (SAN 853-1935) Toll Free: 888-655-0875 (phone/fax)
E-mail: psallison@earthlink.net
Web site: http://www.SandSagePress.com.

Sandbox Bks., *(978-0-9755184)* 6561 Portage Rd., DeForest, WI 53532-0000 USA
Web site: http://www.sandboxbooks.com.

Sandbridge Sons Publishing, *(978-0-9796039)* 2577 Sandpiper Rd., Virginia Beach, VA 23456 USA.

SandCastle *Imprint of* **ABDO Publishing Co.**

Sandcastle Publishing, *(978-0-9627756; 978-1-883995)* Orders Addr.: P.O. Box 3070, South Pasadena, CA 91031-6070 USA Fax: 323-255-3616; Edit Addr.: 1723 Hill Dr., South Pasadena, CA 91030 USA Tel 213-255-3616 Do not confuse with Sandcastle Publishing, Orleans, MA
E-mail: info@sandcastle-online.com; rwhatley@sandcastle-online.com
Web site: http://www.sandcastle-online.com
Dist(s): **Quality Bks., Inc.**
Unique Bks., Inc.

†Sandlapper Publishing Co., Inc., *(978-0-87844)* Orders Addr.: P.O. Box 730, Orangeburg, SC 29115 USA (SAN 203-2678) Toll Free Fax: 800-337-9420 (orders); Toll Free: 800-849-7263 (orders); Edit Addr.: 1281 Amelia St., NE., Orangeburg, SC 29116 USA Tel 803-533-1658; Fax: 803-534-5223
E-mail: agallman1@bellsouth.net
Web site: http://www.sandlapperpublishing.com
Dist(s): **Follet Higher Education Grp;** *CIP.*

Sandner-Petersen International Bks., *(978-0-9744852)* 5112 Coronado Pkwy., No.11, Cape Coral, FL 33904 USA Tel 739-549-3028; Fax: 239-549-5547.

Sandpiper *Imprint of* **Houghton Mifflin Harcourt Trade & Reference Pubs.**

Sandra Kitabjian, *(978-0-578-59816-1; 978-0-578-60451-0; 978-0-578-73626-6; 978-0-578-74338-7; 979-8-9855782)* 254 S. New Ardmore Ave., Broomall, PA 19008 USA Tel 610-864-6832
E-mail: bellask1@comcast.net.

Sandralena Hanley, *(978-1-7377398)* 969 S Signal Point Rd, Post Falls, ID 83854 USA Tel 208-415-0159
E-mail: slhanley44@gmail.com
Web site: www.sandralenahanley.com.

Sandramantos Publishing, *(978-0-9887848)* 1550 Alpine Trail, San Marcos, TX 78666 USA Tel 512-462-9670
E-mail: manager@Sandramantos.com
Web site: http://princessapril.com.

Sands, Monty, *(978-0-9788038; 978-0-615-25788-4; 978-0-578-15474-9)* P.O. Box 6463, Visalia, CA 93291 USA
E-mail: monger15@juno.com; montysands@yahoo.com.

Sands Pr. (CAN) *(978-0-9936753; 978-1-988281) Dist. by* **IPG Chicago.**

S&S Publishing LLC, *(978-0-9794710)* 1609 Dublin Dr., Silver Spring, MD 20902 USA Tel 301-681-8729
E-mail: xsalinas21@gmail.com.

Sandstein Kommunikation GmbH (DEU) *(978-3-95498) Dist. by* **ISD USA.**

Sandstone Pr. Ltd. (GBR) *(978-0-9546333; 978-1-905207; 978-1-908737; 978-1-910124; 978-1-912240; 978-1-910985; 978-1-913207) Dist. by* **Casemate Pubs.**

Sandvik Innovations, LLC, *(978-1-932915; 978-1-935868)* 460 E. Swedesford Rd., Suite 2030, Wayne, PA 19087 USA Tel 610-975-3585; Fax: 610-975-3587
Web site: http://www.sandvikinnovations.com.

Sandvik Publishing, *(978-1-58048; 978-1-881445)* Div. of Sandviks Bokforlag, Norway, 3729 Knights Rd., Bensalem, PA 19020-2908 USA Toll Free: 800-843-2445
E-mail: Nicole@sandvikpublishing.com; cust-serv@sandvikpublishing.com
Web site: http://www.sandviks.com.

Sandy Bay Publishing, *(978-0-9701285)* Orders Addr.: P.O. Box 580, Hatteras, NC 27943-0580 USA Tel 252-986-2195; Fax: 252-986-2372; Edit Addr.: 56187 Pamlico Dr., Hatteras, NC 27973-0580 USA Tel 252-986-2195
E-mail: joannewhale@earthlink.net.

Sandy Putter Pr., *(978-0-578-05153-6)* 9 Meadowview Rd., Asheville, NC 28804 USA.

Sandy's Shelf Bks., *(978-0-9980387; 978-1-7360742; 978-1-961153)* 4822 S 133 St, Ste 200, Omaha, NE 68137 USA Tel 402-884-5995
E-mail: sandysshelf@conciergemarketing.com.

SANE *See* **Sane**

Sane, *(978-0-692-15473-1; 978-0-578-44232-7; 978-0-578-44234-1; 978-0-578-45069-8; 978-0-578-45117-6; 978-0-578-55264-4; 979-8-218-26269-3)* 640 Eastern Pkwy. Unit 4c, Brooklyn, NY 11213 USA Tel 646-243-0842
E-mail: miriamyerushalmi18@gmail.com
Dist(s): **Ingram Content Group.**

SangFroid Pr., *(978-0-917939)* 34 Water St., Excelsior, MN 55331 USA (SAN 657-0178) Tel 952-474-6220; Fax: 952-474-6221 Do not confuse with Sang Froid in New York, NY.

Sanitaryum, *(978-0-9983352)* 414 Terr. Cir., Lamesa, TX 79331 USA Tel 505-362-6990; *Imprints:* Bookify by Sanitaryum (MYID_R_BKIFY B)
E-mail: nathantafoya@gmail.com
Web site: http://sanitaryum.com/bookify-publishing/; www.sanitaryum.com.

Sankofa Bks. *Imprint of* **Just Us Bks., Inc.**

Sankofa Pr., *(978-0-9654009)* Orders Addr.: P.O. Box 3144, Jacksonville, FL 32206 USA Tel 904-355-0126 (phone/fax); Edit Addr.: 239 W. 40th St., Jacksonville, FL 32206 USA
E-mail: sankofa@leading.net
Web site: http://www.users.southeast.net/~sankofa.

Sankofa Productions *See* **Sankofa Pr.**

Sankofa Project Productions, *(978-0-692-92878-3)* 1601 N Bryant No. 56, Little Rock, AR 72207 USA Tel 501-553-4460; Fax: 501-553-4460
E-mail: cindy@cindy-hurst.com.

SanPaul Group, LLC, The, *(978-0-9670875)* 209 Josephine St., Detroit, MI 48202-1811 USA (SAN 253-6013)
E-mail: SanPaulGroupQTP@gmail.com
Web site: http://www.qtpieworld.com.

Sanpitch Pr., *(978-0-9760607)* 141 S. Main, Manti, UT 84642 USA Tel 435-835-6271; Fax: 435-835-8431; Toll Free: 800-748-4660
E-mail: sanman@horseshoetrader.com.

Sans Soucie Studio, *(978-0-692-59323-3; 978-0-692-59522-0; 978-0-692-59523-7; 978-0-9977253; 979-8-9854579)* 8014 Nimrod Trail, Dallas, TX 75238 USA Tel 214-803-0169.

Santa Ana River Pr., *(978-0-9747638)* P.O. Box 5473, Norco, CA 92860 USA (SAN 255-7568)
E-mail: admin@santaanariverpress.com
Web site: http://www.santaanariverpress.com
Dist(s): **Sunbelt Pubns., Inc.**

Santa Barbara Pr. International, *(978-1-883102)* 329 San Ysidro Rd., Santa Barbara, CA 93108 USA Tel 805-969-3733 Do not confuse with Santa Barbara Pr. in Santa Barbara, CA.

Santa Fe Communications, Inc., *(978-1-933262)* 1126 S. 70th St. Suite N601, MILWAUKEE, WI 53214 USA
E-mail: bruno@heartofthenation.org; brunojohn2468@gmail.com
Web site: http://www.lightningbugflix.com.

Santa Fe Writers Project, *(978-0-9776799; 978-0-9819661; 978-0-9882252; 978-1-939650; 978-1-7337777; 978-1-951631)* No. 350, 369 Montezuma Ave., Santa Fe, NM 87501 USA (SAN 257-9588)
E-mail: agifford@sfwp.com
Web site: http://www.sfwp.com
Dist(s): **Ebsco Publishing**
Independent Pubs. Group
MyiLibrary
ebrary, Inc.

Santa Monica Pr., *(978-0-9639946; 978-1-891661; 978-1-59580)* Orders Addr.: P.O. Box 1076, Santa Monica, CA 90406 USA (SAN 298-1459) Tel 310-230-7759; Fax: 310-230-7761; Toll Free: 800-784-9553; Edit Addr.: 513 Wilshire Blvd., No. 321, Santa Monica, CA 90401 USA
E-mail: books@santamonicapress.com
Web site: http://www.santamonicapress.com
Dist(s): **Ebsco Publishing**
Legato Pubs. Group
MyiLibrary
Publishers Group West (PGW)
Perseus Bks. Group
ebrary, Inc.

Santa Sleigh, *(978-1-7332681)* 3505 s 107 st, Omaha, NE 68124 USA Tel 402-250-6838
E-mail: Santasworlds@gmail.com.

Santacroce, John, *(978-0-615-76887-8; 978-0-9899916)* 2066 Rivers Edge Dr., Rio Rancho, NM 87144 USA Tel 505-450-7096; *Imprints:* Four Oaks Publishing (Four Oaks Pub)
E-mail: johnpsantacroce@gmail.com.

Santiago, Claribel, *(978-0-9744726)* P.O. Box 25345, Tamarac, FL 33320 USA
E-mail: claribel_santiago@hotmail.com
Web site: http://www.claribelsantiago.com.

Santillana (COL) *(978-958-24) Dist. by* **Santillana.**

Santillana *Imprint of* **Santillana USA Publishing Co., Inc.**

Santillana Ecuador (ECU) *(978-9978-07; 978-9942-05; 978-9942-19; 978-9978-29) Dist. by* **Santillana.**

Santillana Ediciones Generales, S.A. de C.V. (MEX) *(978-607-11; 978-607-01) Dist. by* **Santillana.**

Santillana, Editorial, S.A. de C.V. (MEX) *(978-970-29; 978-968-430; 978-970-642) Dist. by* **Santillana.**

Santillana S. A. (URY) *(978-9974-590; 978-9974-671) Dist. by* **Santillana.**

Santillana Texto *Imprint of* **Santillana USA Publishing Co., Inc.**

Santillana USA Publishing Co., Inc., *(978-0-88272; 978-1-56014; 978-1-58105; 978-1-58986; 978-1-59437; 978-1-59820; 978-1-60396; 978-1-61605; 978-1-61435; 978-1-62263; 978-1-63113; 978-1-68292; 978-1-64101)* Div. of Grupo Santillana, 8333 NW 53rd St. Suite 402, Doral, FL 33166 USA (SAN 205-1133) Tel 617-351-4867; Av. Rio Mixcoac No. 274 Col. Acacias, C.P. 0324 Benito Juarez, Ciudad de Mexico, DF.; *Imprints:* Santillana (Santillana Imprint); Richmond (Richmond); Alfaguara (Alfaguara); Punto de Lectura (Punto de Lectura); Santillana Texto (SanTexto); Loqueleo (Loqueleo)
E-mail: dminella@vistahigherlearning.com; esanta@santillanausa.com; customerservice@santillanausa.com
Web site: http://www.loqueleo.com/us
Dist(s): **Barnes & Noble, Inc.**
Bilingual Pubns. Co., The
Children's Plus, Inc.
Continental Bk. Co., Inc.
CreateSpace Independent Publishing Platform
EMC/Paradigm Publishing
Follett School Solutions
Lectorum Pubns., Inc.
Libros Sin Fronteras.

Santoon Bks., *(978-0-9744905)* 13533 1/2 Village Dr., Cerritos, CA 90703 USA Tel 562-926-3361; Fax: 562-802-7680
E-mail: santoon@santoon.com.

Santoon Productions, Incorporated *See* **Santoon Bks.**

Santore, Marcia, *(978-0-692-05482-6; 978-0-692-06703-1; 978-0-692-03567-2)* 6 Texas Hill Rd, Plymouth, NH 03264-4226 USA; *Imprints:* Amalgamated Story (MYID_Y_AMALGAM)
E-mail: marcia@amalgamatedstory.com; mlsantore@gmail.com; info@amalgamatedstory.com
Web site: https://www.amalgamatedstory.com/; www.marciasantore.com
Dist(s): **CreateSpace Independent Publishing Platform.**

Sapati Ingera, *(978-0-9728549)*
E-mail: kenyawash@sbcglobal.net
Web site: www.kctaylorauthor.com.

Sapient Business Solutions *See* **Herobrine Publishing**

Sapling Bks., *(978-0-9650871)* 234 W. Concord Ln., Chicago, IL 60614 USA Tel 312-280-1058; Fax: 312-280-1013.

Sapphire Bks. Publishing, *(978-0-9828608; 978-1-939062; 978-1-943353; 978-1-948232; 978-1-952270; 978-1-959929)* P.O. Box 8142, Salinas, CA 93912 USA Tel 831-998-7145
E-mail: publisher@sapphirebooks.com; info@sapphirebooks.com
Web site: http://www.sapphirebooks.com.

Publisher Name Index

Saqi Bks. (GBR) *(978-0-86356; 978-1-84659; 978-1-908906; 978-1-84925) Dist. by* **Consort Bk Sales.**

Sara Anderson Children's Bks., *(978-0-9702784; 978-0-9911933; 978-1-943459)* 1522 Post Alley No. 206, Seattle, WA 98101 USA Tel 206-285-1520
E-mail: sara@saranderson.com
Web site: http://www.saranderson.com/
Dist(s): **BWI.**

Sarah & David LLC, *(978-0-9761648; 978-0-9796785)* P.O. Box 5894, Englewood, NJ 07631-5894 USA Fax: 201-221-7879
Web site: http://www.sarahdavid.com.

SarahRose Children's Bks. *Imprint of* **SarahRose Publishing**

SarahRose Publishing, *(978-0-9745865)* Orders Addr.: 12853 Dusty Willow RD, Manassas, VA 20112 USA Tel 253-232-9561; Edit Addr.: 14101 Parke Long Ct, Suite T, Chantilly, VA 20151 USA Tel 703-457-0429; *Imprints:* SarahRose Children's Books (SarahRose Child Bks)
E-mail: melodycurtiss@gmail.com
Web site: http://www.melodycurtiss.com; http://sarahrosepublishing.tumblr.com.

Sarah's Daughters Publishing *See* **Fidelity Heart Publishing**

Sarajames Poetry, Inc., *(978-0-9767395)* 88 Lawrence Ave., Brooklyn, NY 11230 USA Tel 718-972-2944
E-mail: jamestronan@yahoo.com.

Saranghay Studios, *(978-0-9887068)* 9 Brookside Dr., Foxboro, MA 02035 USA Tel 617-475-0563
E-mail: ray@saranghaystudios.com
Web site: www.saranghaystudios.com.

Saranjon Publishing, *(978-0-9665282)* Orders Addr.: P.O. Box 980, Homer, AK 99603-0980 USA Tel 907-235-8200; Fax: 907-235-8699; Edit Addr.: 385 E. Fairview St., Homer, AK 99603-0980 USA
E-mail: saranjon@alaska.net
Dist(s): **Wizard Works.**

Sari Karplus, *(978-0-578-80893-2; 978-0-578-80894-9; 978-0-578-96725-7; 979-8-9860297)*
E-mail: sari.karplus@gmail.com
Web site: https://www.robotasticbook.com.

Sarkisyan, Mary, *(978-0-692-15938-5; 978-0-692-15941-5)* 361 E 224th St., Carson, CA 90745 USA Tel 818-261-5956
E-mail: marysarkisyan@gmail.com
Dist(s): **Ingram Content Group.**

Sarvis, Barbara, *(978-0-9831346)* 1856 Trumbull Hill Rd., Shaftsbury, VT 05262 USA
E-mail: sarvisbarbara@gmail.com.

Saseen, Sharon, *(978-0-9748425)* 403 E. 46th St., Savannah, GA 31405 USA Tel 912-233-1341
E-mail: saseenart@aol.com
Web site: http://www.saseen.com.

Sasquatch Bks., *(978-0-912365; 978-1-57061; 978-0-9821188; 978-1-63217)* 1904 Third Avenue, Suite 710, Seattle, WA 98101 USA (SAN 289-0208) Toll Free: 800-775-0817; *Imprints:* Little Bigfoot (Little Bigfoot); Spruce Books (SpruceBooks)
E-mail: custserv@SasquatchBooks.com
Web site: http://www.sasquatchbooks.com
Dist(s): **Children's Plus, Inc.**
MyiLibrary
Penguin Random Hse. Distribution
Penguin Random Hse. LLC
Random Hse., Inc.

Sasscer, Abby, *(978-0-9854729)* 158 Nazareth Dr., Fort Valley, VA 22652 USA Tel 540-933-6496
E-mail: projectnazareth@yahoo.com.

sassyraspberry, *(978-1-7372478)* 1283 W MYRNA LN, TEMPE, AZ 85284-2842 USA Tel 480-907-8352
E-mail: lowemonica@hotmail.com
Web site: sassyraspberry.com.

Sastrugi Press *See* **Sastrugi Pr.**

Sastrugi Pr., *(978-0-9960206; 978-1-944986; 978-1-64922)* 335 W. Deloney St. No. E10, Jackson, WY 83001 USA Tel 619-363-5359
E-mail: aaron@sastrugipress.com; alinsdau@yahoo.com
Web site: www.sastrugipress.com.

Satellite Studio, *(978-0-9743968)* P.O. Box 32457, Knoxville, TN 37930-2457 USA Tel 865-691-1450; Fax: 865-691-2464
E-mail: dwilson@dannywilson.com.

Satin Finish Publishing, *(978-0-9764930; 978-0-9800209)* P.O. Box 481351, Kansas City, MO 64131 USA
E-mail: slfoster0826@kc.rr.com.

Saturn International, *(978-0-9764957)* 126 Herricks Rd., Mineola, NY 11501 USA Fax: 516-214-0154.

Saturn Music & Entertainment, *(978-0-692-82106-0; 978-0-692-83847-1; 978-0-692-84418-2; 978-0-692-88897-1; 978-0-692-93821-8; 978-0-692-15655-1; 978-0-578-40456-1)* 120 Madeira Dr. NE No. 220, Albuquerque, NM 91789 USA Tel 360-232-3022
E-mail: saturnmusicandentertainment@gmail.com
Dist(s): **CreateSpace Independent Publishing Platform.**

Satya Hse. Pubns., *(978-0-9729191; 978-0-9818720; 978-1-935874)* Orders Addr.: 22 Turkey St., Hardwick, MA 01037 USA; Edit Addr.: P.O. Box 122, Hardwick, MA 01037 USA
E-mail: julie@satyahouse.com
Web site: https://www.satyahouse.com; https://www.iseethesunbooks.com; https://lostvalleypress.com
Dist(s): **Independent Pubs. Group**
Midpoint Trade Bks., Inc.
OverDrive, Inc.
Smashwords.

Sauerlander AG (CHE) *(978-3-7941) Dist. by* **Distribks Inc.**

Saul, Robert, *(978-0-692-15368-0; 978-0-692-15369-7; 978-0-578-44407-9)* 108 Wimbledon Ct., GREENWOOD, SC 29646 USA Tel 864-980-8372
E-mail: robertsaul@me.com
Dist(s): **Ingram Content Group.**

Sauls, Lynn, *(978-0-615-74910-5; 978-0-615-78903-3; 978-0-9793216)* 14 Alexander St., Alexandria, VA 22314 USA Tel 703-549-5799
E-mail: lynnbsauls@aol.com.

Saunders Bk. Co. (CAN) *(978-1-895058; 978-1-897563; 978-1-926660; 978-1-926722; 978-1-926853; 978-1-77092; 978-1-77308; 978-1-77456) Dist. by* **Creative Co.**

Saunders Bk. Co. (CAN) *(978-1-895058; 978-1-897563; 978-1-926660; 978-1-926722; 978-1-926853; 978-1-77092; 978-1-77308; 978-1-77456) Dist. by* **RiverStream.**

Saur, Gregory, *(978-0-9964245; 978-0-692-80648-7; 978-1-949317)* 711 Old Wormley Creek Rd., Yorktown, VA 23692 USA Tel 757-898-1524
E-mail: imalepton@hotmail.com.

Sautrelle Publishing Co., *(978-1-947927)* 4100 W. 12th St., Lawrence, KS 66049 USA Tel 785-218-4046; Fax: 785-865-2966
E-mail: papahooge@gmail.com.

Sauvignon Pr., *(978-0-9889618)* 1459 Brookcliff Dr., Marietta, GA 30062 USA Tel 404-435-6507
E-mail: rewrites1@gmail.com.

Savage Books *See* **Blue Thunder Bks.**

Savage Pr., *(978-1-886028; 978-1-937706; 978-1-958211)* 14172 E Carlson Rd., Brule, WI 54820 USA Tel 218-391-3070 (phone/fax); 14172 E Carlson Rd., Brule, WI 54820 Tel 218-391-3070
E-mail: savpress@gmail.com; mail@savpress.com
Web site: http://www.savpress.com
Dist(s): **Baker & Taylor Bks.**
Partners Bk. Distributing, Inc.

Savanna Pr., *(978-0-9759440)* Orders Addr.: P.O. Box 777, Monte Vista, CO 81144 USA Tel 719-850-2255; Fax: 719-852-2211; Edit Addr.: 67 Gold Cir., Pagosa Springs, CO 81147 USA; P.O. Box 1806, Vryburg, 8600
E-mail: riovista@rmi.net.

Savannah College of Art & Design Exhibitions, *(978-0-9654682; 978-1-893974; 978-0-9797440; 978-0-615-22202-8)* Orders Addr.: P.O. Box 3146, Savannah, GA 31401-3146 USA Tel 912-525-5287; Fax: 912-525-4952; Edit Addr.: 212 W. Hall St., Garden Apt., Savannah, GA 31401 USA; *Imprints:* Design Press Books (Design Press Bks)
E-mail: asalgado@scad.edu
Web site: http://www.scadexhibitions.com
Dist(s): **D.A.P./Distributed Art Pubs.**

Savannah's Safe Publishing Co., *(978-0-692-73903-7; 978-1-7338884)* P.O. Box 972, Vallejo, CA 94590 USA Tel 415-574-1627
E-mail: optimalbf@gmail.com.

Savas, Bachtsoglou, *(978-0-9771020)* 139-02 97th Ave., Jamaica, NY 11435 USA Tel 718-793-0107
E-mail: avipremlall@gmail.com.

Savas Beatie, *(978-1-932714; 978-1-61121)* 989 Governor Dr., Suite 102, El Dorado Hills, CA 95762 USA Tel 916-941-6896; Fax: 916-941-6895
E-mail: sarahs@savasbeatie.com; editorial@savasbeatie.com
Web site: http://www.savasbeatie.com
Dist(s): **Casemate Pubs. & Bk. Distributors, LLC**
MBI Distribution Services/Quayside Distribution
MyiLibrary
Open Road Integrated Media, Inc.
ebrary, Inc.

Save Our Seas, Ltd., *(978-0-9800444)* 626 Elvira Ave., Redondo Beach, CA 90277-9027 USA Tel 310-792-0338; Fax: 310-792-9273
E-mail: jonr@jokarproductions.com
Web site: http://www.saveourseas.com
Dist(s): **National Bk. Network.**

Savino, Nicole, *(978-0-578-88697-8; 978-0-578-88698-5; 978-0-578-94508-8)* 3735 Thousand Oaks dr, San Jose, CA 95136 USA Tel 408-891-6659
E-mail: Savino.nicole@yahoo.com
Web site: Theveganvampire.info.

Savor Publishing Hse., Inc., *(978-0-9708296)* 6020 Broken Bow Dr., Citrus Heights, CA 95621 USA Tel 718-846-7277
E-mail: Smarties@SavorPublishing.com; SavorPubHouse@aol.com
Web site: http://www.savorpublishing.com
Dist(s): **Book Clearing Hse.**
Book Wholesalers, Inc.
Follett School Solutions.

Savory Palate, Inc., *(978-1-889374)* 8174 S. Holly, No. 404, Centennial, CO 80122-4004 USA Tel 303-741-5408; Fax: 303-741-0339; Toll Free: 800-741-5418
E-mail: info@savorypalate.com
Web site: http://www.savorypalate.com
Dist(s): **Brodart Co.**
New Leaf Distributing Co., Inc.
Quality Bks., Inc.
Royal Pubns., Inc.

Savory Words *See* **Savory Words Publishing**

Savory Words Publishing, *(978-0-9863552; 978-1-7377117)* P.O. Box 3941, Frederick, MD 21705 USA Tel 240-422-8540
E-mail: info@savorywords.com
Web site: http://www.savorywords.com/.

Savoury Creations, *(978-0-578-54590-5; 978-0-578-63468-5; 978-0-578-83776-5; 978-1-7367782)* 10731 Hellebore Rd., Charlotte, NC 28213 USA Tel 704-770-7947
E-mail: mcleodnrm@gmail.com.

Savvas Learning Co., *(978-1-59896; 978-1-60637)* 75 Arlington St., Boston, MA 02116 USA; *Imprints:* AGS Secondary (AGS Second); Dominie Elementary (Dominie Elem); FEARON (FEARON); GLOBE (GLOBPS); Celebration Press (Celebration); Dale Seymour Publications (Dale Seymo); Modern Curriculum Press (Mod Curriculu); Scott Foresman (Scott Fores); SILVER BURDETT (SilvBurd); Prentice Hall (PHall)
Dist(s): **Pearson Education.**

Savvy Cyber Kids, Inc., *(978-0-9827968)* 4780 Ashford Dunwoody Rd. Suite A 312, Atlanta, GA 30338 USA Tel 404-955-7233
E-mail: info@savvycyberkids.org
Web site: http://www.savvycyberkids.org.

Savvy Pr., *(978-0-9669877; 978-0-9826069; 978-0-9852115; 978-1-939113)* Orders Addr.: P.O. Box 63, Salem, NY 12865 USA Tel 518-633-4778; Fax: 815 346-2659
E-mail: info@savvypress.com; info@gowanusbooks.com
Web site: http://www.savvypress.com; http://www.sagasf.com; http://www.gowanusbooks.com
Dist(s): **Quality Bks., Inc.**

Sawatch Publishing, *(978-0-9989473)* 116 Wren Ct., Eagle, CO 81631 USA Tel 970-343-0470
E-mail: Jenniferalsever@gmail.com
Web site: www.trinityforestseries.com.

Sawmill Pr., 3326 Hollyberry Dr., VISTA, CA 92084 USA Tel 530-613-2817.

Sawmill Publishing, *(978-0-9749915)* 6444 E. Spring St., No. 215, Long Beach, CA 90815 USA
Web site: http://www.sawmillpublishing.com.

Sawmill Ridge Publishing, *(978-0-9761924)* 183 Post Oak Dr., Roanoke, VA 24019 USA Tel 540-966-5706.

Saxon Pubs., Inc., *(978-0-939798; 978-1-56577; 978-1-59141)* Div. of Houghton Mifflin Harcourt Supplemental Pubs., Orders Addr.: 6277 Sea Harbor Dr., 5th Flr., Orlando, FL 32887 USA Toll Free Fax: 877-578-2638; Toll Free: 888-363-4266; Edit Addr.: 10801 N. Mopac Expressway, Bldg. 3, Austin, TX 78759 USA (SAN 216-8960) Toll Free: 800-531-5015
Web site: http://www.saxonpublishers.com
Dist(s): **Follett School Solutions**
Houghton Mifflin Harcourt Publishing Co.

Say It Loud! Readers & Writers Series, *(978-0-9779499)* 1507 E. 53rd St., No. 841, Chicago, IL 60615 USA.

Say It Right, *(978-0-9723457; 978-0-9760490; 978-0-9770418; 978-1-934701)* Orders Addr.: P.O. Box 651, Tybee Island, GA 31328 USA Tel 912-228-4556; Fax: 912-480-4214; Toll Free: 888-811-0759
E-mail: jim@sayitright.org
Web site: http://www.sayitright.org.

Say Out Loud, LLC, *(978-0-9799127)* Orders Addr.: 885 Woodstock Rd. Suite 430-373, Roswell, GA 30075 USA (SAN 854-7483) Tel 404-428-7935; Fax: 404-506-9823
E-mail: author@wordstosayoutloud.com
Web site: http://www.wordstosayoutloud.com.

SB Home & World Inc., *(978-0-692-96820-8; 978-0-692-96985-4)* 1526 Locust Rd. NW, WASHINGTON, DC 20012 USA Tel 202-285-1841
E-mail: creative@legacyquiltsandart.com
Dist(s): **Ingram Content Group.**

S.B. McEwen, *(978-1-7375322; 979-8-9881462)* 1025 Sophia Ln., Mars, PA 16046 USA Tel 724-772-0225
E-mail: sherrimcewen@hotmail.com.

SBA Bks., LLC, *(978-0-9711404; 978-1-7326634; 978-1-956408)* Orders Addr.: P.O. Box 3019, Daphne, AL 36526 USA Tel 251-232-9927; Fax: 251-621-1834; Edit Addr.: 12655-a Dominion Dr., Fairhope, AL 36532 USA
E-mail: sheila@sbabooks.com
Web site: http://www.sbabooks.com
Dist(s): **Emerald Bk. Co.**
Greenleaf Book Group.

SC & FC Publications, *(978-0-9860794)* P.O. Box 124, Interlochen, MI 49643 USA.

S.C. TreeHouse LLC *See* **First Time Pr.**

S.C. TreeHouse LLC, *(978-0-692-87157-7; 978-0-578-46600-2; 978-0-578-47363-5; 978-0-578-50969-3; 978-0-578-56517-0; 978-0-578-56680-1)* 183 Parker RD, BENTON, TN 37307 USA Tel 423-715-4694
E-mail: jeffwcrawford5+LVP0003605@gmail.com; jeffwcrawford5+LVP0003605@gmail.com.

Scafe, Claire, *(978-0-9787695)* 7918 John Dr., Cheyenne, WY 82009 USA Tel 307-632-1702
E-mail: skir2@aol.com.

Scandinavia Publishing Hse. (DNK) *(978-87-7247; 978-87-87732; 978-87-7132; 978-87-7203) Dist. by* **Destiny Image Pubs.**

Scandora,

Scanlan, John M., *(978-0-9755405)* 5 Gumtree Rd., No. F-20, Hilton Head, SC 29926 USA (SAN 256-0771) Tel 843-342-2793; Fax: 419-281-6883 (orders); Toll Free: 800-247-6553 (orders)
E-mail: ping1@hargray.com; order@bookmasters.com
Web site: http://www.speedislife.us; http://www.atlasbooks.com.

Scanlan, John M. Literary Services *See* **Scanlan, John M.**

Scanlon, Helen, *(978-0-9894168)* 6 Kenyon Rd, Hampton, CT 06247 USA Tel 860-455-1965
E-mail: soundthebuglestudio@charter.net
Web site: www.soundthebuglestudio.com.

†Scarecrow Pr., Inc., *(978-0-8108; 978-1-57886)* Div. of Rowman & Littlefield Publishing Group, Orders Addr.: 15200 NBN Way, Blue Ridge Summit, PA 17214 USA Tel 717-794-3800 (Sales, Customer Service, MIS, Royalties, Inventory Mgmt., Dist., Credit & Collection); Fax: 717-794-3803 (Customer Service &/or orders); 717-794-3857 (Sales & MIS); 717-794-3856 (Royalties, Inventory Mgmt. & Dist.); Toll Free Fax: 800-338-4550 (Customer Service &/or orders); Toll Free: 800-462-6420 (Customer Service &/or orders); Edit Addr.: 4501 Forbes Blvd., Suite 200, Lanham, MD 20706-4310 USA Tel 301-459-3366; Fax: 301-429-5747 Short Discount, please contact rlpgsales@rowman.com
E-mail: custserv@rowman.com
Web site: http://www.scarecrowpress.com; http://www.rlpgbooks.com
Dist(s): **CreateSpace Independent Publishing Platform**
Ebsco Publishing
Follett School Solutions
Cengage Gale
MyiLibrary
National Bk. Network
Open Road Integrated Media, Inc.
Rowman & Littlefield Publishers, Inc.
Rowman & Littlefield Unlimited Model
ebrary, Inc.; *CIP.*

ScarecrowEducation *See* **Rowman & Littlefield Education**

Scarlet Primrose Pr., *(978-0-9851678)* 308 Blue Heron Cir., Simpsonville, SC 29680 USA Tel 585-545-0032
E-mail: andreacefalo4@gmail.com; scarletprimrosepress@gmail.com
Web site: http://www.andreacefalo.com
Dist(s): **CreateSpace Independent Publishing Platform**
Ingram Content Group
Smashwords.

Scarlett L Pr., *(978-0-615-60059-8; 978-0-9982452)* 7800 E Freeport Pl., Broken Arrow, OK 74014 USA Tel 918-520-5718
Dist(s): **CreateSpace Independent Publishing Platform.**

Scarletta *See* **Mighty Media Pr.**

Scars Pubns. & Design, *(978-1-891470)* 829 Brian Ct., Gurnee, IL 60031 USA
E-mail: Editor@scars.tv
Web site: http://scars.tv.

Scavenger's Pubns., *(978-0-9798792)* 3443 Remington Ct., Eau Claire, WI 54703 USA Tel 715-456-3909
E-mail: ggparadox@hotmail.com.

SCB Distributors, Orders Addr.: 15608 S. New Century Dr., Gardena, CA 90248-2129 USA (SAN 630-4818) Tel 310-532-9400; Fax: 310-532-7001; Toll Free: 800-729-6423 (orders only)
E-mail: info@scbdistributors.com
Web site: http://www.scbdistributors.com.

SCF Pr., *(978-0-9990337)* P.O. Box 329, Merrimac, MA 01860 USA Tel 617-852-2599
E-mail: schoolcounselingfiles@gmail.com.

Schachter, Madeleine Arts, *(978-1-7339003)* 300 Central Pk. W., New York, NY 10024 USA Tel 212-706-1914
E-mail: MadeleineSchachterArts@gmail.com
Web site: https://www.MadeleineSchachterArts.com.

Schadt, Susan Pr., LLC, *(978-0-9973559; 978-1-7336341; 979-8-9850713; 979-8-9874780)* 4728 Spottswood, Memphis, TN 38117 USA Tel 901-412-2334
E-mail: susan.schadt@sschadtpress.com
Web site: sschadtpress.com
Dist(s): **Ingram Publisher Services.**

Schafer-Post Entomology Pubns., *(978-0-9766855)* Entomology Dept. Hultz Hall, North Dakota State Univ., Fargo, ND 58105 USA Tel 701-231-7582; Fax: 701-231-8557
E-mail: david.rider@ndsu.edu.

Schallert, Ann, *(978-0-578-03425-6)* 10047 Hwy. 104, Tucumcari, NM 88401 USA
E-mail: crossann@shipleysystems.com.

Schaub, Stephen M. Photography *See* **Indian Hill Gallery of Fine Photography**

Scheck, Flora, *(978-1-7340616)* 38 Mountain Ct, Bedminster, NJ 07921 USA Tel 201-230-7327
E-mail: Florascheck22@gmail.com.

Scheer Delight Publishing, *(978-0-9671761)* 4030 E. Christy, Wichita, KS 67220-2540 USA (SAN 253-908X) Tel 316-683-2001; Fax: 316-636-1268
E-mail: schdelight@cox.net
Web site: http://scheerdelightpub.com.

Scheller, Debbie, *(978-0-9991885)* 13510 Smith Lake ln, houston, TX 77044 USA Tel 810-877-2852; Fax: 810-877-2852
E-mail: schellerdebbie@gmail.com.

Schermerhorn, Walters Co., *(978-0-9741746; 978-0-9824987)* 740 Purdue Dr., Claremont, CA 91711-3418 USA Tel 909-398-1228
E-mail: lilly.walters@verizon.net
Web site: http://www.motivational-keynote-speakers.com.

Scheuerman, Susan, *(978-0-692-12327-0; 978-0-692-12328-7)* 166 E. Genesee St., SKANEATELES, NY 13152 USA Tel 315-247-6096
E-mail: ryan@ryanzbartlett.com
Dist(s): **Ingram Content Group.**

Schiavi, Sherry *See* **Celltrition**

Schiffer Craft *Imprint of* **Schiffer Publishing, Ltd.**

Schiffer Military History *Imprint of* **Schiffer Publishing, Ltd.**

Schiffer Publishing, Ltd., *(978-0-7643; 978-0-87033; 978-0-88740; 978-0-89538; 978-0-916838; 978-0-9787278; 978-1-5073)* Orders Addr.: 4880 Lower Valley Rd., Atglen, PA 19310 USA (SAN 208-8428) Tel 610-593-1777; Fax: 610-593-2002; *Imprints:* Cornell Maritime Press/Tidewater Publishers (CornellTide); Schiffer Publishing Ltd (SCHIFFER PUBLI); Schiffer Military History (Schiffer Military History); Schiffer Craft (MYID_X_SCHIFFE); Red Feather (RedFeather)
E-mail: info@schifferbooks.com; karen@schifferbooks.com
Web site: http://www.schifferbooks.com.

Schiffer Publishing Ltd *Imprint of* **Schiffer Publishing, Ltd.**

Schiffner, Frederick A., *(978-0-9765782)* P.O. Box 1047, Spring Mt., PA 19478 USA Tel 610-287-5827
E-mail: fschiffner@fast.net.

Schiller Institute, Inc., *(978-0-9621095; 978-1-882985; 978-0-9997818)* Orders Addr.: P.O. Box 20244, Washington, DC 20041-0244 USA (SAN 250-4944) Tel 703-777-9451 ext 541; Fax: 703-771-3099
E-mail: SchillerInstitutePrinting@gmail.com; swelsh@schillerinstitute.org
Web site: http://www.schillerinstitute.org.

Schisler, Amy MacWilliams, *(978-0-615-93539-3; 978-0-692-40924-4; 978-0-692-49786-9; 978-0-692-77575-2; 978-0-692-83640-8; 978-0-692-94617-6; 978-0-692-94619-0; 978-0-692-94625-1; 978-0-692-98294-5; 978-1-7322242; 978-1-7346907; 979-8-9852232; 979-8-9883677)* 7604 Cooper Point Rd., Bozman, MD 21612 USA Tel 410-725-1693
E-mail: amyschisler@me.com
Web site: amyschislerauthor.com
Dist(s): **CreateSpace Independent Publishing Platform.**

Schl. of Life Pr., The (GBR) *(978-0-9935387; 978-0-9955736; 978-0-9957535; 978-1-9997471; 978-1-912891) Dist. by* **Consort Bk Sales.**

Schleich, James, *(978-0-615-12142-0)* 105 Woodland Dr., Zelienople, PA 16063-9316 USA
E-mail: james@the-soundman.org
Web site: http://www.the-soundman.org.

Schlessinger Media, *(978-1-57225; 978-1-879151)* Div. of Library Video Co., Orders Addr.: P.O. Box 580, Wynnewood, PA 19096 USA Tel 610-645-4000; Fax: 610-645-4050; Toll Free: 800-843-3620; Edit Addr.: 7 Wynnewood Rd., Wynnewood, PA 19096 USA
E-mail: sales@libraryvideo.com
Web site: http://www.libraryvideo.com
Dist(s): **Follett School Solutions Library Video Co. Video Project, The.**

Schlessinger Video Productions *See* **Schlessinger Media**

Schley, Michael, *(978-0-9759645)* 2 Oak Pk. Ave., Darien, CT 06820 USA
E-mail: mike_schley@yahoo.com.

Schmaus, Marcia L., *(978-0-692-94546-9; 978-0-692-97555-8)* 5401 34th St. S., Fargo, ND 58104 USA Tel 605-268-3303
E-mail: marsayam67@msn.com
Dist(s): **CreateSpace Independent Publishing Platform.**

Schmidt, Kimberly K, *(978-0-9864009)* 6507 Scottsville Rd., Scottsville, VA 24590 USA Tel 434-286-7226
E-mail: kkjschmidt@gmail.com.

Schmidt, M. Productions, *(978-0-692-09042-8; 978-0-692-09046-6; 978-0-692-09960-5; 978-0-692-09965-0; 978-0-692-11104-8; 978-0-692-12253-2; 978-0-692-15194-5; 978-0-692-15681-0; 978-0-692-15917-0; 978-0-692-15920-0; 978-0-692-17191-2; 978-0-692-17193-6; 978-0-692-17620-7; 978-0-692-17621-4; 978-0-578-44876-3; 978-0-578-44879-4; 978-0-578-45411-5; 978-0-578-45413-9; 978-0-578-51576-2; 978-0-578-51578-6; 978-0-578-59358-6; 978-0-578-64096-9; 978-0-578-64097-6; 978-0-578-73224-4; 978-0-578-73226-8; 978-0-578-77702-3) P.O. Box 371, Ellsworth, KS 67439 USA Tel 785-472-8665*
E-mail: dcountess.mary@gmail.com
Dist(s): **Ingram Content Group.**

Schmitt, Steven E. *See* **Global Partnership, LLC**

Schmul Publishing Co., Inc., *(978-0-88019)* Orders Addr.: P.O. Box 716, Salem, OH 44460-0716 USA (SAN 180-2771) Tel 330-222-2249; Fax: 330-222-0001; Toll Free: 800-772-6657; Edit Addr.: 3583 Newgarden Rd., Salem, OH 44460 USA
E-mail: spchale@valunet.com
Web site: http://www.wesleyanbooks.com.

Schnitzelbank Press *See* **BeerBooks.com**

Schnuerle, Angela, *(978-0-578-75789-6; 978-0-578-81028-7; 978-0-578-86493-8; 978-0-578-31875-2)* P.O. Box 728, Bonners Ferry, ID 83805 USA Tel 208-597-6307
E-mail: aibschnu@yahoo.com.

Schocken *Imprint of* **Knopf Doubleday Publishing Group**

Schoenberg & Assocs., *(978-0-9748208)* 8033 W. Sunset Blvd., No. 944, Los Angeles, CA 90046 USA
Web site: http://www.rdsphotos.com.

Schoenhof's Foreign Bks., Inc., *(978-0-87774)* 76a Mount Auburn St., Cambridge, MA 02138-5051 USA (SAN 212-0062)
E-mail: info@schoenhofs.com
Web site: http://www.schoenhofs.com.

Schofield, Lois E., *(978-0-692-12466-6; 978-0-578-74383-7)* 27 Wildwood Ln., South Hadley, MA 01075 USA Tel 413-887-8309
E-mail: geolo27@yahoo.com
Dist(s): **CreateSpace Independent Publishing Platform.**

Scholargy Custom Publishing, Incorporated *See* **Scholargy Publishing, Inc.**

Scholargy Publishing, Inc., *(978-1-58666; 978-1-59247)* 17855 N. Black Cnyon Hwy., Phoenix, AZ 85023 USA (SAN 254-7295) Tel 602-548-5833 (phone/fax); Fax: 602-353-0680
E-mail: stephanie@scholargy.com
Web site: http://www.scholargy.com.

Scholarly Hour, *(978-0-692-92871-4; 978-1-7325487)* 11260 Williams Ct., Carmel, IN 46033 USA Tel 317-440-7088
E-mail: jenny.bryant7@gmail.com.

Scholastic *Imprint of* **Scholastic, Inc.**

Scholastic Canada, Ltd. (CAN) *(978-0-439; 978-0-590; 978-0-7791; 978-1-4431) Dist. by* **PerseuPGW.**

Scholastic en Espanol *Imprint of* **Scholastic, Inc.**

Scholastic, Inc. *Imprint of* **Scholastic, Inc.**

†Scholastic, Inc., *(978-0-439; 978-0-590; 978-0-545; 978-1-338)* 557 Broadway, New York, NY 10012-3999 USA (SAN 202-5442) Fax: 212-343-6802; Toll Free: 800-325-6149 (customer service); *Imprints:* Cartwheel Books (Cartwheel); Scholastic Reference (Scholastic Ref); Blue Sky Press, The (Blue Sky Press); Scholastic (Scholastic); Levine, Arthur A. Books (A A Levine); Orchard Books (Orchard Bks); Scholastic Press (Scholastic Pr); Chicken House, The (Chick Hse); PUSH (PUSH); Scholastic en Espanol (Scholastic en Espanol); Scholastic Nonfiction (Schol Nonfic); Scholastic Paperbacks (Schol Pbk); Sidekicks TM (Sidekicks); Tangerine Press (Tang Pr Sch); Teaching Resources (Teach Res Sch); Graphix (Graphx); Scholastic Professional (ScholProf); Scholastic, Incorporated (Schlnc); Teaching Strategies (TeachStrategi); Theory & Practice (Theory & Prac); Little Shepherd (Little Shepard); Di Capua, Michael (Michael DiCapua); WestBow Press (WestBowPr)
E-mail: info@scholastic.com
Web site: http://www.scholastic.com
Dist(s): **Blackstone Audio, Inc. Brilliance Publishing, Inc. Children's Plus, Inc. Ebsco Publishing Follett School Solutions Hachette Bk. Group HarperCollins Pubs. INscribe Digital Lectorum Pubns., Inc. MyiLibrary Open Road Integrated Media, Inc. Perfection Learning Corp.;** *CIP.*

Scholastic Institute Chokyi Gyaltsen Univ., *(978-0-9973275; 978-0-9990141; 978-1-962750)* 3433 N Druid Hills Rd. Apt M, Decatur, GA 30033 USA Tel 404-825-8898
E-mail: office@sicgu.org
Web site: www.sicgu.org.

Scholastic Library Publishing, *(978-0-516; 978-0-531; 978-0-7172; 978-1-60631; 978-1-5461)* 90 Old Sherman Tpke., Danbury, CT 06816 USA (SAN 253-8865); *Imprints:* Orchard Books (Orchard Bks); Grolier Online (Grolier Online); Children's Press (Childrens Pr); Grolier (Grolier Schol); Watts, Franklin (Frank Watts)
E-mail: agraham@grolier.com; kbreen@scholastic.com
Web site: http://librarypublishing.scholastic.com
Dist(s): **Booksource, The Children's Plus, Inc. Hachette Bk. Group Lectorum Pubns., Inc.**

Scholastic Nonfiction *Imprint of* **Scholastic, Inc.**

Scholastic Paperbacks *Imprint of* **Scholastic, Inc.**

Scholastic Pr. *Imprint of* **Scholastic, Inc.**

Scholastic Professional *Imprint of* **Scholastic, Inc.**

Scholastic Reference *Imprint of* **Scholastic, Inc.**

Scholte, Sandra, *(978-0-692-16642-0; 978-0-692-18610-7)* 31960 Deerberry Ln., Murrieta, CA 92563 USA Tel 951-397-5144
E-mail: lostinnl@yahoo.com
Dist(s): **CreateSpace Independent Publishing Platform.**

Schonwalder, Helmut, *(978-0-9763267)* P.O. Box 1390, Monterey, CA 93940 USA Tel 831-375-7737
E-mail: helmut@schonwalder.org; helmut@schonwalder.com
Web site: http://www.schonwalder.com; http://www.gastronomical.net; http://www.kaufhouse.info.

School Age Notes *Imprint of* **Gryphon Hse., Inc.**

School Days, *(978-0-9744302)* Orders Addr.: P.O. Box 454, North Carrollton, MS 38947 USA
E-mail: schooldaysmemorybook@yahoo.com
Web site: http://www.schooldaysmemorybook.com
Dist(s): **Wimmer Cookbooks.**

†School for Advanced Research Pr./SAR Pr., *(978-0-933452; 978-1-930618; 978-1-934691; 978-1-938645)* P.O. Box 2188, Santa Fe, NM 87504-2188 USA (SAN 212-6222) Tel 505-954-7206; Fax: 505-954-7241; Toll Free: 888-390-6070
E-mail: press@sarsf.org
Web site: http://www.sarpress.sarweb.org
Dist(s): **Univ. of New Mexico Pr.;** *CIP.*

School Forest Publishing LLC, *(978-0-9996862)* 8906 W. RS Ave., Schoolcraft, MI 49087 USA Tel 269-217-6135
E-mail: davedevisser2@gmail.com.

School of American Research Press *See* **School for Advanced Research Pr./SAR Pr.**

School of Color Publishing, *(978-0-9679628; 978-1-931780)* Div. of The Michael Wilcox School of Color, Inc., P.O. Box 4793, Pinehurst, NC 28374 USA Toll Free: 888-794-5269
E-mail: wilcoxschool@earthlink.net; anne.m.gardner@worldnet.att.net
Web site: http://www.schoolofcolor.com
Dist(s): **F&W Media, Inc. Two Rivers Distribution.**

Schl. of Government, *(978-1-56011; 978-1-64238)* CB 3330 UNC Chapel Hill, Chapel Hill, NC 27599-3330 USA (SAN 204-8752) Tel 919-966-4119; Fax: 919-962-2707
E-mail: justice@sog.unc.edu; Twomey@sog.unc.edu; horton@sog.unc.edu
Web site: http://www.sog.unc.edu
Dist(s): **Univ. of North Carolina Pr. Univ. of Nebraska Pr.**

School of Music Publishing Hse. (RUS) *(978-5-9500) Dist. by* **Coronet Bks.**

Schl. Services of California, Inc., *(978-0-9708628; 978-0-9748487; 978-0-9848031)* 1121 L St., No. 1060, Sacramento, CA 95814 USA Tel 916-446-7517; Fax: 916-446-2011
E-mail: susanm@sscal.com
Web site: http://www.sscal.com.

School Specialty, Incorporated, P.O. Box 6031, Cambridge, MA 02139-9031 USA
Dist(s): **Children's Plus, Inc.**

School Street Bks., *(978-0-9845513)* 284 School St., Northboro, MA 01532 USA
Web site: http://www.writtenbyelizabethdougherty.com
Dist(s): **Smashwords.**

Schl. Tools, *(978-0-9754578)* 23418 28th Ave. W, Brier, WA 98036 USA.

School Zone Publishing Co., *(978-0-88743; 978-0-938256; 978-1-58947; 978-1-60041; 978-1-60159; 978-1-68147)* 1819 Industrial Dr., Grand Haven, MI 49417 USA (SAN 289-8314) Tel 616-846-5030; Fax: 616-846-6181; Toll Free: 800-253-0564
E-mail: christyf@schoolzone.com; sharonw@schoolzone.com
Web site: http://www.schoolzone.com.

Schoolhouse Partners *See* **Littleberry Pr. LLC**

Schoolhouse Publishing, *(978-0-9758543; 978-0-9845335; 978-0-9834657)* Orders Addr.: 659 Schoolhouse Rd., Telford, PA 18969-2449 USA Toll Free: 877-747-4711
Web site: http://www.shpublishing.com.

Schoolwide, Inc., *(978-0-9760421; 978-1-933552; 978-1-937694; 978-1-938508; 978-1-62621; 978-1-68341)* 4250 Veterans Memorial Hwy., Ste. 2000 W, Holbrook, NY 11741 USA Toll Free Fax: 866-333-1130; Toll Free: 800-261-9964
Web site: http://www.schoolwide.com.

Schooner Pubns., *(978-1-929234)* 1610-D Church St. Coastal Ctr., PMB 360, Conway, SC 29526 USA Tel 843-347-9792.

Schorb, Patricia, *(978-0-692-64126-2; 978-0-692-67740-7; 978-0-692-77548-6; 978-0-692-78684-0; 978-0-692-83356-8; 978-0-692-03402-6; 978-0-692-90525-8; 978-0-692-97774-3; 978-0-692-14998-0; 978-0-578-47471-7; 978-0-578-50478-0; 978-0-578-52906-6; 978-0-578-55975-9; 978-0-578-60136-6; 978-0-578-62611-6; 978-0-578-73906-9; 978-0-578-74470-4; 978-0-578-74471-1; 978-0-578-77900-3; 978-0-578-87618-4; 978-0-578-92463-2; 978-0-578-95498-1; 978-0-578-37506-9; 979-8-218-06886-8; 979-8-218-23080-7) P.O. Box 1461, MOORESVILLE, NC 28115 USA Tel 704-660-5453; 369 West Center Dr., Mooresville, NC 28115.*

Schott Music Corp., *(978-0-930448)* 35 E 21st ST., 8th Flr., New York, NY 10010 USA
E-mail: scott.wollschleger@eamdllc.com
Dist(s): **Leonard, Hal Corp.**

Schott Musik International GmbH & Co. KG (DEU) *(978-3-921729; 978-3-7957; 978-3-7877; 978-3-95983; 978-3-940105) Dist. by* **H Leonard.**

Schrader, Racheal, *(978-0-9815274)* P.O. Box 15603, Colorado Springs, CO 80935-5603 USA
E-mail: inspired-ink@hotmail.com
Web site: http://inspired-ink.net.

Schrauth, Ian, *(978-0-578-41273-3; 978-0-578-45875-5; 978-0-578-68343-0; 978-0-578-86345-0; 978-0-578-86485-3; 978-0-578-90597-6; 978-0-578-99916-6)* 6544 Towne Woods Dr., Saint Louis, MO 63129 USA Tel 314-660-8706
E-mail: ianthebookwriter@gmail.com
Dist(s): **Ingram Content Group.**

Schroeder, Patrick A. Publications: Civil War Books *See* **Schroeder Pubns.: Civil War Bks.**

Schroeder Pubns.: Civil War Bks., *(978-1-889246)* Orders Addr.: 131 Tanglewood Dr., Lynchburg, VA 24502 USA Tel 434-525-4431; Fax: 434-525-7293
E-mail: civilwarbooks@yahoo.com
Web site: http://www.civilwar-books.com.

Schue, Lori, *(978-0-692-11524-4; 978-0-692-11528-2; 978-0-692-12833-6; 978-0-692-15799-2; 978-0-578-40063-1)* 40377 Stonebrook Hamlet Pl., Waterford, VA 20197 USA Tel 540-882-3743
E-mail: lschue@comcast.net
Dist(s): **Ingram Content Group.**

Schultz, Ryan, *(978-0-9988918)* 19007 111 Pl SE, Snohomish, WA 98290 USA Tel 425-583-9523
E-mail: schultzry@hotmail.com.

Schulz, Debra, *(978-0-578-43687-6)* 106 SE 111th Ave., Portland, OR 97216 USA Tel 503-516-4367
E-mail: jdschulz@comcast.net.

Schumar Publishing, *(978-0-692-98181-8)* 1009 N Elbow Ln., Yardley, PA 19067 USA Tel 215-738-1670
E-mail: Sneakersgm@yahoo.com.

schurgin, arthur, *(978-0-692-10235-0)* 4629 E. Caron St., Phoenix, AZ 85028 USA Tel 480-213-8492
E-mail: arthur@schurgin.com
Dist(s): **CreateSpace Independent Publishing Platform.**

Schwarcz, Editora Ltda, Companhia das Letrinhas (BRA) *(978-85-7406) Dist. by* **Distribks Inc.**

Schwartau, Winn LLC, *(978-0-9628700; 978-0-9964019)* Orders Addr.: 545 Westport Dr., Old Hickory, TN 37138-1115 USA
E-mail: winn@securityexperts.com; winnschwartau@gmail.com
Web site: http://www.winnschwartau.com.

Schwartz & Wade Bks. *Imprint of* **Random Hse. Children's Bks.**

Schwartz, Arthur & Company, Incorporated/Woodstocker Books *See* **Woodstocker Books/Arthur Schwartz & Company**

Schwartz, Gary, *(978-0-9975860)* P.O. Box 1123, North Bend, WA 98045 USA Tel 425-831-5667
E-mail: gary@gary-schwartz.com
Web site: http://gary-schwartz.com.

Schwartz, Joel, *(978-0-9785885)* 1315 Cinnamon Dr., Fort Washington, PA 19034-2818 USA
E-mail: jshrink@comcast.net
Web site: http://www.stresslessshrink.com.

Schwartz Marketing, *(978-0-9893046)* 1234 Bloomfield St., Hoboken, NJ 07030 USA Tel 201-656-2223; Fax: 201-656-2223
E-mail: tomschwartz@earthlink.net.

Schwarz Pauper Pr., *(978-0-9621505)* 88 Winwood Dr., Barnstead, NH 03225 USA (SAN 251-4540) Tel 603-776-5680
E-mail: Granitesunset@aol.com.

Sci Fi-Arizona, Inc., *(978-1-929381)* 1931 E. Libra Dr., Tempe, AZ 85283 USA Tel 480-838-6558; *Imprints:* Third Millennium Publishing (Third Millen Pubng)
E-mail: mccollum@scifi-az.com
Web site: http://www.scifi-az.com; http://www.3mpub.com.

Science Academy Software, *(978-0-9623926)* 600 Baychester Ave., Apt 5B, Bronx, NY 10475-4457 USA Tel 718-561-4048.

Science & God, Inc., *(978-0-9745861)* P.O. Box 2036, Labelle, FL 33975-2036 USA Tel 239-218-4543.

Science & Humanities Pr., *(978-1-888725; 978-1-59630)* Subs. of Banis & Assocs., Orders Addr.: P.O. Box 7151, Chesterfield, MO 63006-7151 USA (SAN 299-8459) Tel 636-394-4950; Fax: 800-706-0585; P.O. Box 7151, Chesterfield, MO 63006-7151; Edit Addr.: 1023 Stuyvesant Ln., Manchester, MO 63011-3601 USA Tel 636-394-4950; Toll Free Fax: 800-706-0585; 1023 Stuyvesant Ln., Manchester, MO 63011-3601 Tel 636-394-4950; Toll Free Fax: 800-706-0585; *Imprints:* BeachHouse Books (BeachHouse Bks)
E-mail: banis@sciencehumanitiespress.com; banis@banis-associates.com
Web site: http://www.banis-associates.com; http://www.sciencehumanitiespress.com; http://www.macroprintbooks.com; http://www.stressmyth.com; http://www.normajeanebook.com; http://www.route66book.com; http://www.accessible-travel.com.

Science and Technology Concepts (STC) *Imprint of* **Smithsonian Science Education Ctr. (SSEC)**

Science Curriculum, Inc., *(978-1-882057)* Orders Addr.: 200 Union Blvd. Ste. G18, Lakewood, CO 80228-1845 USA (SAN 248-3637) Toll Free: 888-501-0957; 24 Stone Rd., Belmont, MA 04278
E-mail: marketing@sci-ips.com
Web site: http://www.sci-ips.com.

Science Education Online LLC, *(978-0-578-67698-2; 978-0-578-68884-8; 978-1-7351726)* 48 Lydia Dr, GUTTENBERG, NJ 07093 USA Tel 917-561-2753
E-mail: eduscienceonline@gmail.com
Web site: www.eduscienceonline.org.

Science Enterprises, Inc., *(978-0-930116)* 402 N. Blackford St., Indianapolis, IN 46202-3272 USA (SAN 210-6639).

Science, Naturally!, *(978-0-9678020; 978-0-9700106; 978-1-938492; 978-1-958629)* 725 Eighth St., SE., Washington, DC 20003 USA Tel 202-465-4798; Fax: 202-558-2132; Toll Free: 866-724-9876
E-mail: dia@sciencenaturally.com
Web site: http://www.sciencenaturally.com
Dist(s): **Children's Plus, Inc. MyiLibrary National Bk. Network ebrary, Inc.**

Science of Knowledge Pr., *(978-1-59620)* P.O. Box 324, Little Falls, NJ 07424 USA Fax: 973-272-1102
Web site: http://www.scienceok.com
Dist(s): **Majors, J. A. Co.**

Science of Mind Publishing *See* **Ctrs. for Spiritual Living**

Science of Mind Publishing *Imprint of* **Ctrs. for Spiritual Living**

Science Pubs., *(978-0-9700733; 978-0-9716445; 978-0-9749755; 978-1-938024)* Div. of BrainMind.com, 677 Elm St., San Jose, CA 95126 USA Do not confuse with companies with the same name in Hudson, WI, Flushing, NY, San Francisco, CA, Missoula, MT, Wolf City, TX
E-mail: RJoseph@BrainMind.com
Web site: http://BrainMind.com; http://Cosmology.com
Dist(s): **MyiLibrary.**

Science Square Publishing, *(978-0-9740861)* 2845 Bowen St., Graton, CA 95444-9347 USA
E-mail: info@sciencesquare.com
Web site: http://www.sciencesquare.com.

Science2Discover, Inc., *(978-0-9673811)* P.O. Box 2435, Del Mar, CA 92014-1735 USA Fax: 858-793-0410; Toll Free: 888-359-6075; 2015 Seaview Ave., Del Mar, CA 92014 Do not confuse with MetaMetrix, Inc., Norcross, GA
E-mail: info@science2discover.com
Web site: http://www.science2discover.com.

Sciencenter, *(978-0-578-00196-8; 978-0-578-00197-5)* 601 First St., Ithaca, NY 14850 USA Tel 607-272-0600
Dist(s): **Lulu Pr., Inc.**

Scientia Est Vox Pr., *(978-0-578-02353-3; 978-0-578-05385-1; 978-0-578-07089-6; 978-0-578-12511-4; 978-0-578-16302-4; 978-0-578-18130-1; 978-0-578-19361-8)* 2338 8th Ave., Terre Haute, IN 47804 USA Tel 812-917-4182; 812-917-4384
E-mail: magicianofoz@hotmail.com
Web site: http://www.magicianofoz.blogspot.com
Dist(s): **Lulu Pr., Inc.**

Scissortail Pr., *(978-1-955814)* 4500 E Burris Rd, Glencoe, OK 74032 USA Tel 907-764-6076
E-mail: bribri79@gmail.com
Web site: https://scissortailpress.com.

Scobre Pr. Corp., *(978-0-9708992; 978-0-9741695; 978-0-9741997; 978-0-9766240; 978-1-933423; 978-1-934713; 978-1-61570; 978-1-62920)* 2255 Calle Clara, La Jolla, CA 92037 USA Toll Free: 877-726-2734
E-mail: Scott@bookbuddyaudio.com
Web site: http://www.scobre.com
Dist(s): **Children's Plus, Inc. MyiLibrary.**

Scoggins, Sandi, *(978-0-578-75259-4)* 806 E. 10th St., Danville, AR 72833 USA Tel 479-495-9689; Fax: 479-495-7685
E-mail: pinkshellcreations@yahoo.com.

SCOJO ENTERTAINMENT, *(978-0-9651306; 978-0-9786488)* Orders Addr.: P.O. Box 1225, New York, NY 10008 USA
Web site: theportalinthepark.com.

SCOPE Pubns., *(978-0-9759955)* Orders Addr.: 100 Lawrence Ave., Smithtown, NY 11787 USA Tel 631-360-0800; Fax: 631-360-8489 Do not confuse with Scope Publications, Fairfax, OK
E-mail: bkauffman@scopeonline.us
Web site: http://www.scopeonline.us.

Scotland Gate, Inc., *(978-0-9830084; 978-0-9837523; 978-0-9839550; 978-0-9888972; 978-0-9888973)* 176 Edgecliff Dr., Highland Park, IL 60035 USA Tel 847-432-1947
E-mail: mskemp@sbcglobal.net.

Scotland Street Pr. (GBR) *(978-1-910895) Dist. by* **IPG Chicago.**

Scott, Cassandra Dr Ministries, *(978-0-9882936)* 3802 Hanberry, Pearland, TX 77584 USA Tel 713-550-3370
E-mail: cescott1@aol.com.

Scott, D.& F. Publishing, Inc., *(978-0-941037; 978-1-930566)* Orders Addr.: P.O. Box 821653, North Richland Hills, TX 76182-1653 USA (SAN 665-2875) Tel 817-788-2280; Fax: 817-788-9232; Toll Free: 888-788-2280; Edit Addr.:

Publisher Name Index

P.O. Box 821653, N Richlnd Hls, TX 76182-1653 USA; *Imprints:* WestWind Press (WstWind)
E-mail: info@dfscott.com
Web site: http://www.dfscott.com.

Scott Foresman *Imprint of* **Addison-Wesley Educational Pubs., Inc.**

Scott Foresman *Imprint of* **Addison-Wesley Educational Pubs., Inc.**

Scott Foresman *Imprint of* **Savvas Learning Co.**

Scott Foresman *Imprint of* **Addison Wesley Schl.**

Scott, J & N Pubs., *(978-0-9719868)* 10461 NW 20 St., Pembroke Pines, FL 33026 USA Tel 954-432-6578
E-mail: nscott2000@aol.com.

Scott, James *See* **Scott, J & N Pubs.**

Scott, Josephine, *(978-0-9718582; 978-0-9746600)* P.O. Box 55127, Bridgeport, CT 06610 USA
E-mail: jartist@optonline.net
Web site: http://www.ethnicitycards.com
Dist(s): **MyiLibrary**
ebrary, Inc.

Scott, Kirsti, *(978-0-9984995; 978-1-7377634)* 500 Brooktree Ranch Rd, Aptos, CA 95003 USA Tel 831-688-8246
E-mail: kirstiscott@me.com
Web site: http://www.etchedbythesea.com.

†Scott Pubns., Inc., *(978-0-916809; 978-1-893625; 978-0-9787419)* 2145 W. Sherman Blvd., Muskegon, MI 49441-3434 USA Toll Free: 866-733-9382 Do not confuse with Scott Pubns. in Indianapolis, IN
E-mail: contactus@scottpublications.com
Web site: http://www.scottpublications.com; *CIP.*

Scott Publishing Company *See* **Amos Media Co.**

Scott Publishing Co., *(978-0-9617626; 978-1-930043; 978-0-9908913; 978-0-9982386; 978-0-9991508; 978-0-9998884; 978-1-7328939; 978-1-7345637; 978-1-954463)* Orders Addr.: P.O. Box 9707, Kalispell, MT 59901 USA (SAN 664-6948) Tel 406-755-0099; Fax: 406-756-0098; Edit Addr.: 1845 Helena Flats Rd., Kalispell, MT 59901-6525 USA (SAN 664-6956) Do not confuse with companies with the same or similar name in Sidney, OH, Houston, TX, Edmonds, WA
E-mail: scott@scottcompnay.net.

Scott, Sue Ann, *(978-1-7329953)* 2010 Richard Garrett, Christiana, TN 37037 USA Tel 615-274-6264
E-mail: testimoniesbysue@comcast.net.

Scottish Children's Pr. (GBR) *(978-1-899218; 978-1-899827) Dist. by* **MYID_F_GATEWOO.**

Scottish Christmas, *(978-0-9726114)* 2369 Joslyn Ct., Lake Orion, MI 48360 USA.

Scottwall Assocs., *(978-0-942087; 978-0-9612790; 978-0-578-01245-2)* 95 Scott St., San Francisco, CA 94117 USA (SAN 289-8322) Tel 415-861-1956; Fax: 415-863-7273
E-mail: scotwall@pacbell.net
Web site: http://www.scottwallpub.com
Dist(s): **Sunbelt Pubns., Inc.**
Todd Communications.

Scott-Waters, Marilyn, *(978-0-9759864)* 1589 Baker St., Costa Mesa, CA 92626 USA
E-mail: msw@scottwatersdesign.com
Web site: http://www.thetoymaker.com.

Scout Comics, *(978-1-949514; 978-1-63969)* 80 Roland Ave., South Orange, NJ 07079 USA Tel 646-207-8960
E-mail: brendan.deneen@scoutcomics.com
Dist(s): **Simon & Schuster, Inc.**

SCPG Publishing Corp., *(978-1-938368; 978-1-63288)* 101 Lafayette Street, Suite No. 701, New York, NY 10013 USA Tel 212-334-1902
E-mail: SCPGLU@aol.com
Dist(s): **Independent Pubs. Group**
MyiLibrary.

SCR, Inc., *(978-0-9747582; 978-1-63227)* Orders Addr.: a/o Maximum Logistics, 93 S. JACKSON ST. -46673, SEATTLE, WA 98104 USA (SAN 256-6192)
E-mail: isbn@spamex.com
Web site: http://www.scrbooks.ocom
Dist(s): **Lulu Pr., Inc.**

SCR Publications *See* **SCR, Inc.**

Scramjet Bks., *(978-0-9887911)* P.O. Box 526, Spencer, IN 47460 USA Tel 812-361-5448
E-mail: kalynn.brower@gmail.com
Web site: www.khbrower.com.

S.C.R.A.P. Gallery, *(978-0-9708135)* 46-350 Arabia St., Indio, CA 92201 USA Tel 760-863-7777; Fax: 760-863-8973; Toll Free: 866-717-2727 (866-71-SCRAP)
E-mail: scrapgallery@earthlink.net
Web site: http://www.infoteam.com/nonprofit/scrapgallery.

Scrap Paper Pr., *(978-0-9745493)* 6 Manor Dr., Goldens Bridge, NY 10526 USA Tel 914-997-1692; Fax: 914-997-2253.

Screwy Ideas *Imprint of* **Hanke, Cheryl**

Scribble & Sons, *(978-0-615-93279-8; 978-0-615-93286-6; 978-0-615-93328-3; 978-0-615-93335-1; 978-0-615-93344-3; 978-0-9916352)* 720 W Idaho #28, Boise, ID 83702 USA Tel 970-556-3740
Web site: www.goodbookco.com
Dist(s): **CreateSpace Independent Publishing Platform**
Independent Pubs. Group.

Scribble Scholars, *(978-1-7348462)* 10756 Glacier Rapids Ct. 0, HENDERSON, NV 89052 USA Tel 7025210497
E-mail: sugarflare@gmail.com.

Scribbler's Sword, *(978-0-9761186)* 1640 Halfacre Rd., Newberry, SC 29108 USA.

Scribbles, *(978-0-615-18473-9)* 3852 Albright Ln., Orlando, FL 32828 USA Tel 321-287-7243; 407-312-3591
Web site: http://www.sunscribbles.com.

Scribbles 'n Lit, *(978-0-692-18937-5; 978-0-578-63459-3)* 102 Wye Way, Chocowinity, NC 27817 USA Tel 252-623-1975
E-mail: eileenlettick@gmail.com
Web site: www.eileenlettick.com.

Scribbulations LLC, *(978-0-9629311; 978-1-935751)* Orders Addr.: P.O. Box 3027TCB, W. Orange, NJ 07052 USA Tel 973-325-1648 Do not confuse with Bookcraft, Inc. in West Valley, UT
E-mail: info@scribbulations.com
Web site: http://www.scribbulations.com.

Scribe Publishing, *(978-0-9727077)* 842 S 2ND ST, Philadelphia, PA 19147 USA Do not confuse with companies with the same or similar name in King City, CA, Murray, UT, Welsh, LA, Seattle, WA, Redan, GA
E-mail: contact@scribenet.com
Web site: http://www.scribenet.com.

Scribe Publishing & Consulting Services, The, *(978-0-9793516)* Div. of TrueLight Ministries, P.O. Box 11013, Tacoma, WA 98411 USA Tel 253-312-9377; Fax: 253-238-6041; *Imprints:* Writing The Vision (Writing The Vision)
E-mail: missmillie59@yahoo.com
Web site: http://www.truelightmin.org.

Scribe Publishing Co., *(978-0-9859562; 978-1-940368; 978-0-9916021; 978-1-7353051)* 29488 Woodward Suite 426, Royal Oak, MI 48073 USA Tel 248-259-0090
E-mail: jennifer@scribe-publishing.com
Web site: http://scribe-publishing.com
Dist(s): **Independent Pubs. Group**
Midpoint Trade Bks., Inc.

Scribe Pubns. (AUS) *(978-0-908011; 978-1-920769; 978-1-921215; 978-1-921372; 978-1-921640; 978-1-921753; 978-1-921844; 978-1-921863; 978-1-921864; 978-1-921942; 978-1-922070; 978-1-922072; 978-1-922247; 978-1-925106; 978-1-925113; 978-1-925228; 978-1-925292; 978-1-925307; 978-1-925322; 978-1-925500; 978-1-947534; 978-1-925693; 978-1-911344; 978-1-925713; 978-1-925849; 978-1-950354; 978-1-925938; 978-1-922310; 978-1-922585; 978-1-922586; 978-1-957363; 978-1-76138; 978-1-925548; 978-1-925293; 978-1-925321) Dist. by* **Consort Bk Sales.**

Scribe Tribe, Inc., *(978-0-9986339)* 9594 Arbor View Dr N, Boynton Beach, FL 33437 USA Tel 305-206-4488
E-mail: arlene.hauben@gmail.com
Web site: http://scribetribe.com.

Scribe's Closet Pubns., The, *(978-0-9801269; 978-0-9832570; 978-0-9884125; 978-0-9912487; 978-1-943058)* 56 S. Rutherford, Macon, MO 63552 USA
E-mail: scribescloset@gmail.com
Web site: http://www.thescribesclosetpublications.com.

Scribez, Scarebz & Vibez, *(978-0-9853406)* 689 Macon St., Brooklyn, NY 11233 USA Tel 646-267-1459
E-mail: bedstuybelle1@gmail.com.

Scribner *Imprint of* **Scribner**

Scribner, *(978-0-684; 978-0-7432)* Orders Addr.: 100 Front St., Riverside, NJ 08075 USA; Edit Addr.: 1230 Ave. of the Americas, New York, NY 10020 USA; *Imprints:* Scribner (Scriblmp)
Dist(s): **Children's Plus, Inc.**
Simon & Schuster
Simon & Schuster, Inc.

Scribolin, *(978-0-9746226)* 10107 Copeland Dr., Manassas, VA 20109 USA Tel 703-257-7683
E-mail: books@scribolin.com
Web site: http://www.scribolin.com.

Scripto Love Pr., *(978-1-7377127)* 143 Old S. Plank Rd., Walden, NY 12586 USA Tel 914-213-3766
E-mail: georgemckeondesign@gmail.com.

Scriptorium, The *Imprint of* **Morelli, Laura**

Scripts Publishing, *(978-1-889826)* Orders Addr.: 638 Hennepin Ter., Mcdonough, GA 30253-5965 USA
E-mail: AtaxiaBooks@aol.com
Web site: http://www.hometown.aol.com/pathamilto/myhomepage/profile.html.

Scripture Mastery Resources!, *(978-1-933589)* 1814 Cranberry Way, Springville, UT 84663-3930 USA
E-mail: scripturemastery@kenalford.com
Web site: http://www.kenalford.com.

Scripture Memory Fellowship International, *(978-1-880960)* Orders Addr.: P.O. Box 411551, Saint Louis, MO 63141 USA Tel 314-569-0244; Fax: 314-569-0025; Toll Free: 888-569-2560; Edit Addr.: P.O. Box 568, Hannibal, MO 63401-0568 USA
E-mail: memorize@stlnet.com
Web site: http://www.scripturememory.com.

Scripture Union (GBR) *(978-0-85421; 978-0-86201; 978-1-85999; 978-1-873824; 978-1-84427; 978-1-78506) Dist. by* **STL Dist.**

Scripture Union (GBR) *(978-0-85421; 978-0-86201; 978-1-85999; 978-1-873824; 978-1-84427; 978-1-78506) Dist. by* **Gabriel Res.**

Scrivener Bks., *(978-0-9895523; 978-0-9986254; 978-1-949165)* 869 E. 2680 N., Provo, UT 84604 USA Tel 801-368-7374
E-mail: scrivenerbooks@gmail.com.

Scroll Group, The, *(978-0-692-76814-3; 978-0-692-04601-2)* 3 Bethesda Metro Ctr. Suite 700, Bethesda, MD 20814 USA Tel 202-748-6093.

†Scroll Pr., Inc., *(978-0-87592)* 2858 Valerie Ct., Merrick, NY 11566 USA (SAN 206-796X) Tel 516-379-4283; *CIP.*

Scroll Publishing Co., *(978-0-924722)* Orders Addr.: P.O. Box 4714, Tyler, TX 75712 USA; Edit Addr.: 22012 Indian Spring Tr., Amberson, PA 17210 USA Tel 717-349-7033; Fax: 717-349-7558
E-mail: customerservice@scrollpublishing.com
Web site: http://www.scrollpublishing.com.

Scrub Jay Journeys, *(978-0-9898122; 978-1-946253)* 205 Wiley Ln., Middleton, TN 38052 USA Tel 407-227-0540
E-mail: author@daviscrossing.com
Dist(s): **Whitaker Hse.**

Scruffy Pup Pr., *(978-1-7350697; 978-1-7372001)* 5 Chiswell Ct, Durham, NC 27705 USA Tel 512-698-2468
E-mail: alycia.washington@gmail.com.

Scrumps Entertainment, Inc., *(978-0-9672279)* 19320 NW. 47th Ave., Miami, FL 33055 USA Tel 305-624-7231
E-mail: climbcrick@aol.com.

Scuby's DogHse., *(978-0-578-45598-3)* 4013 Rubicon Peak Ct., Las Vegas, NV 89129 USA Tel 702-496-8511
E-mail: lovescuby2@gmail.com
Dist(s): **Ingram Content Group.**

Scuppernong Pr., The, *(978-0-9845529; 978-0-9898399; 978-1-942806)* P.O. Box 1724, Wake Forest, NC 27588 USA
E-mail: editor@scuppernongpress.com
Web site: http://www.scuppernongpress.com.

SD Mayer & Assocs. LLP, *(978-0-578-41354-9; 978-0-578-41355-6; 978-0-578-53696-5; 978-0-578-57070-9; 978-8-218-95148-1; 979-8-218-95183-2)* 235 Montgomery St. 30th Flr., San Francisco, CA 94104 USA Tel 415-691-4040; 415 867 2516
E-mail: info@sdmayer.com; info@5buckets.org
Web site: www.sdmayer.com
Dist(s): **Independent Pub.**

SDC Publishing, LLC, 221 Berry Ridge Rd., BUCHANAN, VA 24066 USA Tel 540-676-3279
E-mail: allenfmahon@gmail.com
Dist(s): **Ingram Content Group.**

SDH Publishing, *(978-0-9912363)* 134 N. Roosevelt Ave., Fort Collins, CO 80521 USA Tel 970-214-4079
E-mail: shealahenke@yahoo.com
Web site: IDEA33regeneration.com
Dist(s): **BookBaby.**

SDH Studio, LLC, *(978-0-578-46950-8)* 18200 NE 19th Ave., Suite 100, North Miami Beach, FL 33162 USA Tel 305-519-5731
E-mail: stephanie@sdhstudio.com.

SDP Publishing, *(978-0-9824461; 978-0-9829256; 978-0-9885157; 978-0-9889381; 978-0-9899723; 978-0-9911597; 978-0-9913167; 978-0-9905596; 978-0-9862896; 978-0-9964345; 978-0-9968426; 978-0-9972853; 978-0-9977224; 978-0-9981277; 978-0-9984240; 978-0-9986730; 978-0-9992839; 978-1-7321115; 978-1-7327933; 978-1-7338214; 978-1-7342402; 978-1-7343317; 978-1-7356973; 978-1-7361990; 978-1-7367204; 978-1-7378019; 979-8-9856475; 979-8-9862833; 979-8-9878348; 979-8-9882715; 979-8-9885439) Div. of SDP Publishing Solutions, LLC, Orders Addr.: P.O. Box 26, East Bridgewater, MA 02333 USA (SAN 858-1762)*
E-mail: lross@SDPPublishing.com
Web site: http://www.sdppublishingsolutions.com; http://www.PublishAtSweetDreams.com; http://www.sdppublishing.com
Dist(s): **Ingram Content Group.**

SDP Publishing Solutions *See* **SDP Publishing**

SE PrinTech, *(978-0-615-33647-3; 978-0-615-48019-0; 978-0-9847344)* 315 E. Banks St., Glennville, GA 30427 USA Tel 912-654-3610
E-mail: bill@welovetoprint.com.

Se7enth Swan Publishing Group, LLC, *(978-0-615-14849-6)* P.O. Box 16874, Chapel Hill, NC 27516 USA
Web site: http://www.se7enthswan.com
Dist(s): **Lulu Pr., Inc.**

Sea Blue Publishing, *(978-1-948458)* 220 Water St., Brooklyn, NY 11201 USA Tel 310-809-9633
E-mail: 1diannedain@gmail.com.

Sea Chest Bks., *(978-0-9742909)* 11573 Viking Ave., Northridge, CA 91326 USA
E-mail: info@beverlyhillsvideographer.com
Web site: http://www.seachestbooks.com.

Sea Keepers Publishing, *(978-0-9846251)* 936 N. Main St., Akron, OH 44310 USA.

Sea Lion Bks., *(978-0-578-06080-4; 978-0-9828186; 978-0-9836131; 978-0-9857691)* 6070 Autumn View Trail, Acworth, GA 30101 USA
E-mail: david@sealionbooks.com
Dist(s): **BookBaby**
Diamond Bk. Distributors.

Sea Oats Publishing, *(978-0-9798143)* 699-A Sterling Dr., James Island, SC 29412-9135 USA Tel 843-762-2606
E-mail: seaoatspublishing@yahoo.com.

Sea Raven Enterprises *See* **Sea Raven Pr.**

Sea Raven Pr., *(978-0-9768707; 978-0-9821899; 978-0-9827700; 978-0-9838185; 978-0-9858632; 978-0-9913779; 978-1-943737; 978-1-955351)* Orders Addr.: 223 Town Ctr. Pkwy No. 1484, Sprig Hill, TN 37174 USA Tel 615-241-1277; 223 Town Ctr. Pkwy. No. 1484, Spring Hill, TN 37174
E-mail: searavenpress@nii.net
Web site: https://www.searavenpress.com
Dist(s): **Ingram Content Group.**

Sea Spray Bks., *(978-1-7370062)* 1255 N. Ave Apt. C1U, New Rochelle, NY 10804 USA Tel 646-752-5463
E-mail: srussellspray@gmail.com.

Sea Turtle Press *See* **Sierra Muses Pr.**

Sea Wright Publishing, *(978-1-947702)* 1456 Operetta Ave. SE, Palm Bay, FL 32909 USA Tel 321-872-9190
E-mail: info@seawrightpublishing.com
Web site: seawrightpublishing.com.

Seachild, *(978-0-9787881)* P.O. Box 2600, Petaluma, CA 94952 USA (SAN 851-6499) Tel 707-762-7316
E-mail: jag@seachild.net
Web site: http://www.seachild.net.

Seacoast Publishing, Inc., *(978-1-878561; 978-1-59421)* P.O. Box 1504, Hartselle, AL 35640 USA Tel 256-367-4195; 256-318-6635; *Imprints:* Blackbirch Press, Incorporated (Blackbirch Pr) Do not confuse with companies with the same name in Monterey, CA, East Hampton, NY
E-mail: Seacoastpub@yahoo.com; Martinebates@charter.net
Web site: http://www.seacoastpublishing.org.

Seaforth Publishing, *(978-0-9725706)* 5818 Three Ponds Ct., West Bloomfield, MI 48324-3124 USA
Dist(s): **MyiLibrary.**

Seagrass *Imprint of* **Quarto Publishing Group USA**

Seagull Bks. (IND) *(978-81-7046) Dist. by* **Chicago Distribution Ctr.**

Seagull Books (GBR) *(978-1-905422; 978-1-906497; 978-0-85742) Dist. by* **Chicago Distribution Ctr.**

Seagull Pr., *(978-0-9753709)* 375-A Maxham Rd., No. 414, Austell, GA 30168 USA Fax: 770-944-3799 Do not confuse with companies with the same name in Oakland, CA, Owings, MD.

Seagull Pr., *(978-0-578-00924-7; 978-0-692-94200-0; 978-0-578-55479-2; 978-0-578-74729-3; 979-8-218-27930-1)* 2 Oakwood Rd., Springfiled, IL 62711 USA
E-mail: ken220@aol.com.

Seahorse Publishing, *(978-1-63897; 979-8-88735; 979-8-89042)* P.O. Box 771325, Coral Springs, FL 33077 USA Tel 772-559-0019
E-mail: rheakmwdesign@gmail.com.

Seal Pr. *Imprint of* **Basic Bks.**

Seal Publishing, LLC, *(978-0-9774062)* P.O. Box 435, Odessa, FL 33556 USA
Web site: http://www.sealswimschool.com.

Seal Rock Publishing, LLC, *(978-0-9763778)* 834 Marshall Rd., Boulder, CO 80305-7337 USA
E-mail: sealrockpub@yahoo.com.

Sealaska Heritage Institute, *(978-0-9825786; 978-0-9853129; 978-0-9963698; 978-1-946019; 978-1-956797)* 105 S. Seward St. Suite 201, Juneau, AK 99801 USA
E-mail: nobu.koch@sealaska.com.

Sealofters Pr., Inc., *(978-0-9821323; 978-0-9909113; 978-0-9968782; 978-0-9994562)* 32532 Hawks Lake Ln, Sorrento, FL 32776-7737 USA (SAN 857-345X)
E-mail: lori.chappel@hotmail.com.

Seaman, P. David, *(978-0-9755066)* 2645 E. Southern Ave. Apt. A679, Tempe, AZ 85282-7532 USA.

Sean Tigh Pr., *(978-0-9851200)* 1799 Ivy Oak Sq., Reston, VA 20190 USA Tel 321-446-1483
E-mail: kristen@kristenandjoe.com.

SeanBrown, *(978-0-578-89686-1)* 3147 W. springs dr, Ellicott City, MD 21043 USA Tel 240-644-8941
E-mail: brownsean234@gmail.com.

Search Pr., Ltd. (GBR) *(978-0-85532; 978-1-903975; 978-1-84448; 978-1-78126; 978-1-78221) Dist. by* **Peng Rand Hse.**

Searchlight Pr., *(978-0-9644609; 978-0-9824802; 978-1-936497)* Orders Addr.: 5634 Ledgestone Dr., Dallas, TX 75214-2026 USA Tel 214-662-5494
E-mail: searchlight@johncunyus.com; info@searchlight-press.com
Web site: http://www.johncunyus.com; http://www.searchlight-press.com.

SearlStudio Publishing, *(978-0-9883670; 978-0-9895062)* 5840 Red Bug Lake Rd No. 1654, Winter Springs, FL 32708-5011 USA Tel 407-821-7143
E-mail: searlstudio@me.com
Web site: http://www.searlstudio.com.

Sears, Brenda L., *(978-0-692-13305-7)* 5010 SW 19th St., West Park, FL 33023 USA Tel 305-308-8524
E-mail: truelcm@gmail.com.

Sears, M.A., *(978-0-9639785)* 16809 Superior, North Hills, CA 91343 USA; 555 W. Sierra Hwy., Acton, CA 93510 Tel 818-891-8632.

Sears, Stanley, *(978-0-9770067)* Rte. 1 Box 215, Hickman, NE 68372-9686 USA.

Seascape Pr., *(978-0-9769510)* P.O. Box 13132, Jekyll Island, GA 31527 USA Tel 912-635-3263; Fax: 912-635-3264 Do not confuse with Seascape Press, LLC in Santa Barbara, CA.

SeaScape Pr., Ltd., *(978-0-9669741; 978-0-9852381)* 5717 Tanner Ridge Ave., Westlake Vlg, CA 91362-5238 USA (SAN 299-8386) Tel 818-707-3080 Toll Free: 800-929-2906 do not confuse with Seascape Press in Jekyll Island, GA
E-mail: seapress@aol.com; llamensdor@aol.com
Web site: http://www.lenlamensdorf.com.

Seascay Productions, *(978-0-9764152)* 11 Ventnor Dr. Suite 906, Edison, NJ 08820 USA Tel 732-242-3902
E-mail: corporate@seascay.com
Web site: http://www.seascay.com.

Seashell Pr., The, *(978-0-9768866)* 28 Skytop Rd, Ipswich, MA 01938 USA
E-mail: mailbag@theseashellpress.com
Web site: http://www.theseashellpress.com.

Seaside Books *See* **Ladd, David Pr.**

Seasoning Quilting (Arts & Crafts), *(978-1-888413)* 806 Elvie St., Wilson, NC 27893-6116 USA Tel 919-291-7705.

Seasons of Preparation Publishing *See* **Tamara Taylor Edu Publishing LLC**

SeaSquirt Pubns. (GBR) *(978-1-905470) Dist. by* **Basic Dist.**

SeaStar Bks. *Imprint of* **Chronicle Bks. LLC**

Seastory Pr., *(978-0-9673704; 978-0-9768370; 978-0-9799474; 978-0-9821151; 978-1-936818)* 1508 Seminary St. #2, Key West, FL 33040 USA Tel 305-304-6090 mobile
E-mail: sheri@seastorypress.com; seastorypress@gmail.com
Web site: http://www.seastorypress.com
Dist(s): **MyiLibrary**
ebrary, Inc.

Sea-To-Sea Pubns., *(978-1-932889; 978-1-59771)* Div. of Creative Co., 2140 Howard Dr., W., North Mankato, MN 56003 USA
Dist(s): **Creative Co., The**
RiverStream Publishing.

Seattle Review Pr., *(978-0-692-34720-1)* 14232 221st Ave. NE, Woodinville, WA 98077 USA Tel 206-851-2286
Dist(s): **CreateSpace Independent Publishing Platform.**

Seawall Bks., Inc., *(978-0-615-34226-9; 978-0-615-34240-5; 978-0-615-37353-9; 978-0-615-75068-2; 978-0-9893324)* 7 Summit Dr., Hingham, MA 02043 USA Tel 781-749-4284; Fax: 781-749-0977
E-mail: donhussey@aol.com
Web site: http://donhussey.com.

SeaWorld Education Dept. *Imprint of* **SeaWorld, Inc.**

SeaWorld, Inc., *(978-1-893698)* Div. of Anheuser-Busch Adventure Parks, 500 SeaWorld Dr., San Diego, CA

92109 USA (SAN 255-576X) Tel 619-225-4275; Fax: 619-226-3634; Toll Free: 800-237-4268; *Imprints:* SeaWorld Education Department (SeaWorld Educ)
E-mail: swc.education@seaworld.com; debbie.nuzzolo@seaworld.com
Web site: http://www.seaworld.org
Dist(s): **Book Wholesalers, Inc.**
Brodart Co.
Carolina Biological Supply Co.

Second Ark Pubns., *(978-1-889667)* 2907 Kevin Ln., Houston, TX 77043 USA.

Second Base Publishing, *(978-0-9793562; 978-0-9981709)* 6197 Hinterlong Ct, Lisle, IL 60532 USA (SAN 853-2206)
Dist(s): **Ebsco Publishing**
Independent Pubs. Group
MyiLibrary
ebrary, Inc.

Second Sight Enterprises, Inc., *(978-0-9785222)* P.O. Box 251248, Plano, TX 75025 USA (SAN 850-7996)
Web site: http://www.asktheinventors.com.

Second Star Creations, *(978-0-9725977)* 12120 State Line Rd., No. 190, Leawood, KS 66209 USA Tel 913-681-2252
E-mail: jan@secondstar.us
Web site: http://www.secondstar.us.

Second Story Pr. (CAN) *(978-0-921299; 978-0-929005; 978-1-896764; 978-1-897187; 978-1-77260; 978-1-926739; 978-1-926920; 978-1-927583)* *Dist. by* **Orca Bk Pub.**

Second Time Media & Communications, *(978-0-9727498; 978-0-9815162; 978-0-9840660; 978-0-9831743)* P.O. Box 401367, Redford, MI 48240 USA Tel 800-377-7497
E-mail: secondtimemedia@yahoo.com
Web site: http://www.secondtimemedia.com.

Second Wind Publishing, LLC *See* **Indigo Sea Pr., LLC**

Secondary Worlds Pr., *(978-1-951108)* 2428 Dickens Ave, Manhattan, KS 66502 USA Tel 734-709-4632
E-mail: amity.l.thompson@gmail.com.

Secret Corners Publishing, *(978-0-615-24083-1; 978-0-615-24084-8)* 3613 ORANGEPOINTE RD, VALRICO, FL 33596 USA
E-mail: mhamlet@secret-corners.com
Web site: http://www.secret-corners.com.

Secret Garden Bookworks, *(978-0-9766283)* Orders Addr.: P.O. Box 1506, Oak Bluffs, MA 02557-1506 USA Tel 508-693-4759; Fax: 508-693-4867; Edit Addr.: 41 Circuit Ave., Oak Bluffs, MA 02557-1506 USA
E-mail: secretgardenmv@peoplepc.com
Web site: http://www.secretgardenbookworks.com.

Secret Hat, L.L.C., The, *(978-0-578-49629-0)* 2007 Columbia Rd., Berkley, MI 48072 USA Tel 248-632-3265
E-mail: peggylosey@gmail.com
Web site: www.thesecrethat.com.

Secret Mountain (CAN) *(978-2-923163; 978-2-924774; 978-2-924217; 978-2-89836)* *Dist. by* **IPG Chicago.**

Secret Passage Pr., *(978-1-888695)* 26 Tucker Hollow Rd., North Scituate, RI 02857 USA Tel 401-647-0440; Toll Free: 877-863-4622 (Orders Only)
E-mail: lucindalandon@verizon.net
Web site: http://www.megmackintosh.com
Dist(s): **Ebsco Publishing**
Enfield Publishing & Distribution Co., Inc.
Independent Pubs. Group
MyiLibrary.

Secret Staircase Bks., an imprint of Columbine Publishing Group, LLC *Imprint of* **Columbine Publishing Group, LLC**

Secret Staircase Books, an imprint of Columbine Publishing Group *See* **Columbine Publishing Group, LLC**

Secular Media Group *Imprint of* **Rare Bird Bks.**

Security Studies Pr., *(978-0-9797539)* 650 J St., Suite 405, Lincoln, NE 68508 USA
E-mail: rlund@securitystudies.us
Web site: http://www.securitystudies.us.

Sedell, Kirsten, *(978-0-9800838)* 3 John R's Bend, Berkley, MA 02779 USA
E-mail: ksedell@norton.k12.ma.us.

sedgewick eye Assocs., P.C., *(978-0-9968178)* 44121 harry byrd hwy, No. 175, ashburn, VA 20147 USA Tel 703-725-1698
E-mail: jrsedgewick@verizon.net
Web site: www.sedgewickeye.com.

Sedwick, Daniel Frank LLC, *(978-0-9820818)* P.O. Box 1964, Winter Park, FL 32790-1964 USA Tel 407-975-3325; Fax: 407-975-3327
E-mail: info@sedwickcoins.com
Web site: http://www.sedwickcoins.com.

See abc's LC, *(978-1-890566)* Orders Addr.: P.O. Box 276, Smithfield, UT 84335 USA; Edit Addr.: 9 S. 490 E., Smithfield, UT 84335 USA.

See Movement, *(978-0-9965398)* 415 W. Foothill Blvd. PH 1, Claremont, CA 91711 USA Tel 626-795-4500; Fax: 626-795-4545
E-mail: leatricel@earthlink.net
Web site: www.SeeMovement.com.

See Sharp Pr., *(978-0-9613289; 978-1-884365; 978-1-937276; 978-1-947071)* P.O. Box 1731, Tucson, AZ 85702-1731 USA (SAN 653-8134) Tel 520-628-8720 (phone/fax)
E-mail: info@seesharppress.com
Web site: http://www.seesharppress.com
Dist(s): **Ebsco Publishing**
Independent Pubs. Group
MyiLibrary
ebrary, Inc.

See The Wish, *(978-0-9822134; 978-0-9857676; 978-0-9886716)* 246 Main St., Cold Spring, NY 10516 USA Tel 845-797-9183
Web site: http://www.seethewish.com
Dist(s): **Follett School Solutions.**

Seed Faith Bks, *(978-1-60101)* P.O. Box 12227, Portland, OR 97212-0227 USA (SAN 850-6795)
Web site: http://seedfaithbooks.com.

SeeDEGA, *(978-0-9746586; 979-8-9859049; 979-8-9863131)* Orders Addr.: 46 Violet Pl., Rhinebeck, NY 12572 USA
E-mail: seedega@gmail.com
Web site: http://seedega.com.

Seeding Hearts, *(978-0-9998675)* 10441 Spring Green Blvd No. 805, KATY, TX 77494 USA Tel 713-545-9640
E-mail: divanwinkle@seedinghearts.com
Dist(s): **Ingram Content Group.**

Seedling Pubns. *Imprint of* **Continental Pr., Inc.**

Seeds of Fiction, *(978-0-578-35013-4; 979-8-9867946)* 415 Bohland Ave., Bellwood, IL 60104 USA Tel 312-402-3444
E-mail: writeremlacey@gmail.com; evangeline@emlacey.com
Web site: www.seedsoffiction.com.

Seeds of Imagination, *(978-0-9600253)* 2241 Hutchison St., Vista, CA 92084 USA
E-mail: lindaappo@sbcglobal.net
Dist(s): **Ingram Content Group.**

SeeHearDo Co., LLC, The, *(978-0-9788089)* 3011 E. 7145 S., Salt Lake City, UT 84121 USA.

Seelcraft Publishing, *(978-0-9728380)* 63 Church St., Suite 201, High Bridge, NJ 08829-1516 USA
Web site: http://www.seelcraft.com.

See-More's Workshop, *(978-1-882601)* Div. of Shadow Box Theatre, 325 West End Ave., New York, NY 10023 USA Tel 212-724-0677; Fax: 212-724-0767
E-mail: sbt@shadowboxtheatre.org
Web site: http://www.shadowboxtheatre.org
Dist(s): **Follett School Solutions**
Professional Media Service Corp.

See-Saw Publishing *Imprint of* **Peek-A-Boo Publishing**

Seff, Greg A. *See* **Fire Island Pr.**

Segal, Berty Inc., *(978-0-938395)* 1749 E. Eucalyptus St., Brea, CA 92821 USA (SAN 630-0553) Tel 714-529-5359; Fax: 714-529-3882
E-mail: bertytprsource@earthlink.net
Web site: http://www.tprsource.com
Dist(s): **Continental Bk. Co., Inc.**

Segal, Robin *See* **Murray Hill Bks., LLC**

Segarra, Angelo, *(978-0-9752664)* 422 Gregg Ave., Santa Fe, NM 87501-1600 USA
Dist(s): **Greenleaf Book Group.**

Seglie, Susan M., *(978-0-9747243)* 1 Deer Run Ln., Pittsburg, KS 66762 USA Fax: 620-232-5819.

Segue Pubs., *(978-0-9671796)* 527 arbor Rd., Cheltenham, PA 19012 USA Tel 215-277-5525 phone
E-mail: seguepublishing@aol.com; kbradford@seguepublishing.com
Web site: seguepublishing.com.

Seif, Daniel J., *(978-0-9983807)* 106 Kingfisher Ln., New Hartford, NY 13413 USA Tel 315-796-2751
E-mail: danseif@roadrunner.com.

Seigle Bks., *(978-0-9852819)* 235 County Rte. 627, Phillipsburg, NJ 08865 USA Tel 908-319-0384
E-mail: prepub@bookmasters.com.

Seitz, Nicole, *(978-0-9969402; 978-0-578-32072-4; 979-8-218-03618-8; 979-8-218-03619-5)* 451 Rice Hope Dr., Mount Pleasant, SC 29464 USA Tel 843-442-9759
E-mail: nicole@nicoleseitz.com.

Selah Publishing Group, LLC, *(978-0-9679371; 978-1-58930)* 162 Crescent Dr., Bristol, TN 37620 USA Toll Free Fax: 866-777-8909; Toll Free: 877-616-6451 Do not confuse with the same name in Kingston, NY, Berkley, MI
E-mail: garlen@selahbooks.com
Web site: http://www.selahbooks.com.

Selah Publishing, Incorporated *See* **Selah Publishing Group, LLC**

Selby Dean Ventures, Inc., *(978-0-9716479)* P.O. Box 246, Kure Beach, NC 28449 USA (SAN 852-7539) Tel 910-279-2486
E-mail: fishinstructor@aol.com
Web site: http://www.gullswatch.com; http://www.SelbyDeanVentures.com.

Selby, Kyle, *(978-1-7361816)* 5236 Kester Ave Apt No. 5, Sherman Oaks, CA 91411 USA Tel 951-722-0924
E-mail: Kylejselby@gmail.com.

Selective Mutism Anxiety Research & Treatment Ctr., *(978-0-9714800)* 1130 Herkness Dr., Meadowbrook, PA 19046 USA Tel 215 -887-5748; Fax: 215-827-5722
E-mail: dreshiponblum@aol.com
Web site: http://www.selectivemutismcenter.org.

Selector, S.A. de C.V. (MEX) *(978-968-403; 978-970-643; 978-607-453)* *Dist. by* **Spanish.**

Selenite Pr., *(978-0-9894685)* 377 Oliver Smith Rd, Flintville, TN 37335 USA Tel 931-492-3042
E-mail: kellymichaels@gmail.com
Web site: www.theliterarybrew.com.

self *See* **G.L. Sturdivant Pubs.**

Self, *(978-0-578-74273-1; 978-0-578-77767-2)* 10663 KATY LN, GRASS VALLEY, CA 95949-8146 USA Tel 626-827-2312
E-mail: amsav@att.net.

Self Discovery, Inc., *(978-0-692-92892-9; 978-0-9992696)* 5211 NE 27 Ave., Lighthouse Point, FL 33064 USA Tel 954-610-4816
E-mail: shivaliviviani@gmail.com
Dist(s): **Ingram Content Group.**

Self Pub., *(978-1-954850; 978-0-578-88040-2)* 819 Santee St, Los Angeles, CA 90014 USA Tel 626-283-5960.

Self-Discovery LLC, *(978-0-9974831)* 22200 W. Eleven Mile Rd. Unit No. 4232, Southfiled, MI 48037 USA Tel 248-705-9074
E-mail: Info@SelfDiscoverySolutions.com
Web site: http://www.selfdiscoverysolutions.com/.

Self-Esteem Adventures Pr., *(978-0-9747597)* P.O. Box 2145, Universal City, TX 78148 USA Tel 210-595-6952
E-mail: daddybooks@grandecom.net
Web site: http://www.daddybooks.com.

Self-Mastery Pr., *(978-0-9644765; 978-1-7357645)* W. Main St., Carrboro, NC 27510 USA Tel 855-706-4663; 661-904-2416
E-mail: Victoria@ManifestYourGood.com; lovelandcoen@gmail.com
Web site: http://www.ManifestYourGood.com; http://www.Breakthrough2.com
Dist(s): **New Leaf Distributing Co., Inc.**

Self-Pub., *(978-0-9912639)* 1417 Ray Rd., Hyattsville, MD 20782 USA Tel 202-276-4456
E-mail: oluaiafe@gmail.com.

Self-Realization Fellowship Pubs., *(978-0-87612; 978-1-68568)* Orders Addr.: 3208 Humboldt St., Los Angeles, CA 90031 USA (SAN 204-5788) Tel 323-276-6002; Fax: 323-276-6003; Toll Free: 888-773-8680; Edit Addr.: 3880 San Rafael Ave., Los Angeles, CA 90065 USA Tel 323-276 6000; 215 K. St., Encinitas, CA 92024 Tel 760-753-2888 ext 471; Fax: 323-276-6003
E-mail: sales@srfpublishers.org
Web site: http://www.srfpublishers.org
Dist(s): **Distributors, The**
TNT Media Group, Inc.

Sellers, Amy, *(978-0-9787632)* 5151 Round Lake Rd., Apopka, FL 32712 USA (SAN 851-5425)
E-mail: amycsellers@yahoo.com
Web site: http://www.amysellers.com.

Sellers Publishing, Inc., *(978-1-56906; 978-1-4162; 978-1-5319)* Orders Addr.: 161 John Roberts Rd, South Portland, ME 04106 USA (SAN 858-1258) Tel 207-772-6833; Fax: 207-772-6814; Toll Free: 800-625-3386 (800-MAKE-FUN); Edit Addr.: 161 John Roberts Rd., South Portland, ME 04106 USA
E-mail: rsp@rsvp.com
Web site: http://www.rsvp.com
Dist(s): **Bookazine Co., Inc.**
MBI Distribution Services/Quayside Distribution
New Leaf Distributing Co., Inc.
Partners Bk. Distributing, Inc.

Sellers, Ronnie Productions, Incorporated *See* **Sellers Publishing, Inc.**

Seltzer Bks., *(978-0-915232; 978-0-931968; 978-1-4553; 978-1-4554)* 33 Gould St., West Roxbury, MA 02132 USA (SAN 207-1037) Tel 617-469-2269
E-mail: seltzer@samizdat.com
Web site: http://www.samizdat.com/; http://store.yahoo.com/samizdat
Dist(s): **Smashwords.**

Sem Fronteiras Pr., Ltd., *(978-0-9642333)* 1530 Palisade Ave., Suite 2F, Fort Lee, NJ 07024 USA (SAN 253-4959) Toll Free Fax: 800-433-5193
E-mail: semfront@superlink.net.

Sem, Gilmore, *(978-0-9742299)* 1822 Carl St., Lauderdale, MN 55113-5203 USA.

Semele Bks., *(978-0-9764937)* 40 Cedar Ln., Princeton, NJ 08540 USA Tel 609-924-6481; Fax: 609-924-0549; Toll Free: 866-967-3835
E-mail: eva@evasiroka.com
Web site: http://www.evasiroka.com.

Semper Studio, *(978-0-9778420)* 4416 Rte. 47, Delmont, NJ 08314 USA (SAN 850-3885) Tel 609-501-3341
E-mail: Catherine@semperstudiosus.com
Web site: http://www.semperstudiosus.com.

Send The Light Distribution LLC, *(978-0-9835608; 978-1-939900)* Orders Addr.: 129 Mobilization Dr., Waynesboro, GA 30830 USA (SAN 631-8894) Tel 706-554-5827; Toll Free Fax: 877-323-4551; Toll Free: 877-323-4550; 100 Biblica Way, Elizabethton, TN 37643-6070 (SAN 630-7388) Tel 423-547-5131 editorial Toll Free Fax: 800-759-2779
E-mail: Customerservice@stl.org
Web site: http://www.stl-publisherservices.com.

Seneca Lake Pr., *(978-1-7321614)* P.O. Box 513, Ithaca, NY 14851 USA Tel 607-387-8425
E-mail: aileeneaster@gmail.com.

Seneca Mill Pr. LLC, *(978-0-9768986; 978-0-9899595)* P.O. Box 1423, Great Falls, VA 22066 USA
E-mail: senecamillpress@aol.com.

Sensational Bks., *(978-0-9770054)* P.O. Box 261085, Lakewood, CO 80226 USA (SAN 256-6265) Tel 303-238-4760; Fax: 303-205-0614
Web site: http://www.sensationalbooks.com.

Sensational Pubns., *(978-0-9888003; 978-0-9912808; 978-1-944948)* 1756 Cumberland Green Dr Unit 126, saint Charles, IL 60174 USA Tel 630-549-7226
E-mail: cindyjusino@ymail.com
Web site: www.cindyjusino.com; http://www.sensationalpublications.com.

Sensational Publishing *See* **Sensational Pubns.**

Sense of Wonder Pr. *Imprint of* **Rock, James A. & Co. Pubs.**

Senshu, Noriko *See* **Studio Cherry Publishing**

Sensory Resources, *(978-1-893601; 978-1-931615)* Div. of Future Horizons, Inc., P.O. Box 530790, Henderson, NV 89053-0790 USA (SAN 253-8288) Toll Free: 888-357-5867
E-mail: orders@sensoryresources.com
Web site: http://www.sensoryresources.com
Dist(s): **Ingram Publisher Services**
MyiLibrary.

Sentient Pubns., *(978-0-9710786; 978-1-59181)* 1113 Spruce St., Boulder, CO 80302 USA Tel 303-443-2188; Fax: 303-447-1511; Toll Free: 866-588-9846
E-mail: cshaw@sentientpublications.com; dialagzone@aol.com
Web site: http://www.sentientpublications.com/
Dist(s): **National Bk. Network**
Open Road Integrated Media, Inc.

Sentimental Bloke Holdings International, *(978-1-7328957)* 16373 SE 66th St., Bellevue, WA 98006 USA Tel 425-499-0735
E-mail: carol.eckersley@bigpond.com; publisher@sentimentalbloke.com
Web site: www.sentimentalbloke.com.

Sentinel *Imprint of* **Penguin Publishing Group**

Sentinel Publishing, *(978-0-9728291)* 1131 Rossiter Ln., Wayne, PA 19087-2812 USA Tel 610-687-5908; Fax: 610-687-5909 Do not confuse with Sentinel Publishing in Ogden, UT
E-mail: orchidman@snip.net
Web site: http://www.linenpostcards.com.

Sentry Bks. *Imprint of* **Great West Publishing**

Sentry Pr., Inc., *(978-1-889574)* 424 E. Call St., Tallahassee, FL 32301-7693 USA
E-mail: wwrogers@peoplepc.com
Web site: http://sentry-press.com/
Dist(s): **Polk County Historical Assn.**

Seoul Selection (KOR) *(978-89-91913; 978-89-953760; 978-89-97639; 979-11-89809)* *Dist. by* **UH Pr.**

Sephyrus *See* **Sephyrus Pr.**

Sephyrus Pr., *(978-0-615-23982-8; 978-0-9830137; 978-1-948728)* 192 Flicker Dr., Sandy, UT 84070 USA Tel 203-414-5694
E-mail: care@sephyrus.com; rachel@sephyrus.com
Web site: http://sephyruspress.com.

SepSha Publishing, *(978-0-9727885)* P.O. Box 462075, Aurora, CO 80046 USA (SAN 255-3007)
Web site: http://www.endtimebooks.com.

September Publishing, *(978-0-9629496)* 4139 Tujunga Ave., Studio City, CA 91604-3065 USA
Dist(s): **Consortium Bk. Sales & Distribution**
SCB Distributors.

September Twenty-One Productions *See* **September Publishing**

Sequent Media, Inc., *(978-0-9746531)* P.O. Box 126325, San Diego, CA 92112 USA
Web site: http://www.sequentmedia.com.

Sequoia Children's Bks., 8501 W. Higgins Road, Suite 790, Chicago, IL 60631 USA; *Imprints:* Sequoia Publishing & Media LLC (SequoiaPub); Sequoia Kids Media (SequoiaKM)
E-mail: cs@sequoiakidsbooks.com
Web site: https://sequoiakidsbooks.com/.

Sequoia Kids Media *Imprint of* **Phoenix International Publications, Inc.**

Sequoia Kids Media *Imprint of* **Sequoia Children's Bks.**

Sequoia Publishing & Media LLC *Imprint of* **Phoenix International Publications, Inc.**

Sequoia Publishing & Media LLC *Imprint of* **Sequoia Children's Bks.**

Seraph Publishing, *(978-1-934948)* 7660 Fay Ave., La Jolla, CA 92037-4843 USA
E-mail: info@markmlittle.com.

Seraphemera Bks *See* **Seraphemera Bks.**

Seraphemera Bks., *(978-0-9778989; 978-0-9815516; 978-0-9844441; 978-0-9846464; 978-0-9971384; 978-0-9978698; 978-1-947406)* 211 Greenwood Ave Suite 224, Bethel, CT 06801 USA Tel 832-515-9539
E-mail: three@seraphemera.org
Web site: http://www.seraphemera.org.

Seraphic Pr., *(978-0-9754382)* 1531 Cardiff Ave., Los Angeles, CA 90035 USA (SAN 256-0496) Tel 310-557-0132; Fax: 310-286-9534
E-mail: robert@seraphicpress.com; rjaprod@aol.com
Web site: http://www.seraphicpress.com
Dist(s): **David, Jonathan Pubs., Inc.**

Seraphim Pubns., *(978-0-615-21071-1)* 17641 Gilmore St., Van Nuys, CA 91406 USA
E-mail: toni@seraphimpublications.com
Web site: http://www.seraphimpublications.com.

Seraphina *Imprint of* **Bonita and Hodge Publishing Group**

Seren Bks. (GBR) *(978-0-907476; 978-1-85411; 978-1-78172)* *Dist. by* **IPG Chicago.**

Serena Bocchino/In His Perfect Time Collection, *(978-0-9767674; 978-0-9838660; 978-0-9961443)* 82 Haas Rd., Basking Ridge, NJ 07920 USA
E-mail: serena@serenabocchino.com; s_bocchino@msn.com
Web site: http://www.serenabocchino.com.

Serendib Pr., *(978-0-615-18889-8)* 1611 N. Bell, No. 3N, Chicago, IL 60647 USA
Dist(s): **Lulu Pr., Inc.**

Serendipity Art & Publishing *See* **Serendipity Art & Publishing**

Serendipity Art & Publishing, *(978-0-692-05369-0; 978-0-692-13288-3)* 2109 Pine Lake Dr., West Columbia, SC 29169 USA Tel 803-760-8445
E-mail: dkerlin50@yahoo.com
Dist(s): **CreateSpace Independent Publishing Platform.**

Serendipity Hse. *Imprint of* **Lifeway Christian Resources**

Serenity Pr., *(978-0-9787981)* 500 SW. 21st Terr., Fort Lauderdale, FL 33312 USA (SAN 851-6251)
E-mail: marty@mwpr.com
Web site: http://www.mwpr.com/Splash.html.

Serenity Pubs. *Imprint of* **Arc Manor**

Serey/Jones Pubs., *(978-1-881276)* 7413 W. Oraibi Dr., Glendale, AZ 85308 USA Tel 623-561-0240; Fax: 623-561-8441
E-mail: info@sereyjones.com.

Serpent's Tale Natural History Bk. Distributors, Inc., *(978-1-885209)* Orders Addr.: P.O. Box 405, Lanesboro, MN 55949-0405 USA (SAN 630-6101) Tel 507-467-8734; Fax: 507-467-8735
E-mail: zoobooks@acegroup.cc
Web site: http://www.zoobooksales.com.

Serprentress Publishing, *(978-0-578-15083-3; 978-0-9862022)* 14816 NE 23rd Ave, Vancouver, WA 98686 USA Tel 360-909-6168
E-mail: yauna.smith@icloud.com.

Serres, Ediciones, S. L. (ESP) *(978-84-88061; 978-84-95040; 978-84-8488)* *Dist. by* **Lectorum Pubns.**

Serve Man Pr., *(978-0-9768517)* P.O. Box 1445, Easthampton, MA 01027 USA Tel 413-209-1029
E-mail: rokaril@hotmail.com
Web site: http://www.seanwang.com; www.runnersuniverse.com.

Services, Atom LLC, *(978-1-956223; 978-1-960020)* 1309 Coffeen, Ave. STE 1200, Sheridan, WY 82801 USA Tel 646-726-0635
E-mail: atomserviceslimited@gmail.com.

Servilibro Ediciones, S.A. (ESP) *(978-84-7971) Dist. by* **Giron Bks.**

Serving Jesus Christ with Joy Ministries, *(978-0-9770078; 978-0-9774428)* Div. of Serving Jesus Christ with Joy, Orders Addr.: 316 E. Ajo, Tucson, AZ 85713 USA Tel 520-406-1674 (Publishing Phone) 520-889-0215 (Publishing Fax)
E-mail: pastorrandy@sjcwj.org; info@sjcwj.org
Web site: http://christianbooks1.com.

Serving One Lord Resources, *(978-0-9823137)* P.O. Box 98, Sewickley, PA 15143 USA
Web site: www.servingonelord.com.

Session Family, *(978-0-9658006)* Orders Addr.: P.O. Box 841, Florissant, MO 63032 USA Tel 314-972-7705 (phone/fax); Edit Addr.: 16856 Heather Moor Dr., Florissant, MO 63034 USA
E-mail: denise.session@att.net
Web site: http://www.sessionfamily.com.

Set in Stone Pr., *(978-1-7343336; 978-1-955227)* 5845 Pollard Dr, Westworth Village, TX 76114 USA Tel 817-655-2314
E-mail: skendall@setinstonepress.com
Web site: www.thebackyardtrio.com.

Set on a Hill, *(978-0-9971485)* 11152 Westheimer Rd No. 1115, Houston, TX 77042 USA Tel 832-900-9802
E-mail: info@setonahill.com
Web site: www.setonahill.com.

Seton Pr., *(978-1-60704)* 1350 Progress Dr., Front Royal, VA 22630 USA Tel 540-636-9990; Fax: 540-636-1602
Web site: http://setonhome.org.

Setubandh Pubns., *(978-0-9623674)* 1 Lawson Ln., Great Neck, NY 11023 USA Tel 516-482-6938
Web site: http://www.setubandh.com.

Seven Bears Publishing, *(978-1-7344259; 978-1-7361474; 979-8-9889368)* 5430 DAVIDS BEND DR, SUGAR LAND, TX 77479 USA Tel 281-433-5531
E-mail: priscilladoremus@gmail.com
Web site: www.sevenbearspublishing.com.

Seven C's Productions, Inc., *(978-0-9910345; 978-1-7338010)* Orders Addr.: 22050 Costanso St., Woodland Hills, CA 91364 USA; Edit Addr.: 22050 Costanso St., Woodland Hills, CA 91364 USA Tel 845-216-9884
E-mail: AuthorMarcClark@gmail.com
Web site: www.TheFablesKingdom.com.

Seven Footer Pr., *(978-0-9740439; 978-0-9788178; 978-1-934734)* 184 Kendrick Pl., Apt. 28, Gaithersburg, MD 20878-5662 USA; 247 W. 30th St., New York, NY 10001-2824
E-mail: david@wouldyourather.com; jnheimberg@aol.com
Web site: http://www.wouldyourather.com; http://www.movieplotgenerator.com
Dist(s): **Publishers Group West (PGW).**

Seven Guns Pr., *(978-0-615-70006-9; 978-0-9884259; 978-0-615-82838-1; 978-0-9899461; 978-0-9974474; 978-0-9982177)* 2405 Jennieville Dr., Davidsonville, MD 21035 USA Tel 4433066691
Dist(s): **CreateSpace Independent Publishing Platform.**

Seven Lions Publishing, *(978-0-615-82629-5; 978-0-615-91348-3; 978-0-615-99504-5; 978-0-692-29016-3; 978-0-692-42608-1; 978-0-692-71739-4; 978-0-9996879)* 3952 Lyndale Terr., North Chesterfield, VA 23235 USA Tel 8046775718
E-mail: martinctiller@gmail.com
Web site: martintillerauthor.com
Dist(s): **CreateSpace Independent Publishing Platform.**

†Seven Locks Pr., *(978-0-929765; 978-0-932020; 978-0-9615964; 978-1-931643; 978-0-9790950; 978-0-9795852; 978-0-9801270; 978-0-9822293; 978-0-9824957)* P.O. Box 25689, Santa Ana, CA 92799-5689 USA (SAN 211-9781) Toll Free: 800-354-5348
E-mail: sevenlocks@aol.com
Web site: http://www.sevenlockspublishing.com; *CIP.*

Seven Rivers Publishing, *(978-0-9728768; 978-0-615-63339-8; 978-1-7377173)* P.O. Box 682, Crowley, TX 76036-0682 USA
E-mail: seven-rivers@earthlink.net; trekkerdjls@gmail.com
Web site: http://www.sevenriverspublishing.com; http://www.smashwords.com/books/view/93148; https://www.amazon.com/Deborah-J-Lightfoot/e/B0065JZ0UA
Dist(s): **CreateSpace Independent Publishing Platform**
Hendrick-Long Publishing Co.
Independently Published
Ingram Content Group
Smashwords.

Seven Seas Entertainment, LLC, *(978-1-933164; 978-1-934876; 978-1-935934; 978-1-937867; 978-1-62692; 978-1-64275; 978-1-64505; 978-1-64827; 978-1-63858; 978-1-68579; 979-8-88843; 979-8-89160)*; *Imprints:* Airship (Airship)
Web site: http://www.gomanga.com
Dist(s): **Diamond Comic Distributors, Inc.**
Diamond Bk. Distributors
Macmillan
Penguin Random Hse. LLC.

Seven Seas Pr., *(978-0-578-06316-4; 978-0-578-06317-1; 978-0-578-06318-8; 978-0-578-06319-5; 978-0-578-06440-6; 978-0-578-06441-3; 978-0-578-06442-0; 978-0-578-06443-7; 978-0-9833381; 978-1-940654)* 2030 Castillo St, Santa Barbara, CA 93105 USA Tel 805-886-6548
E-mail: erikaromer@gmail.com
Web site: sevenseaspress.org.

Seven Stars Trading Co., *(978-0-9743999; 978-0-9863464)* 3543 Marvin St., Annandale, VA 22003 USA Tel 703-573-2939.

Seven Stories Pr., *(978-1-58322; 978-1-888363; 978-1-60980; 978-1-64421)* 140 Watts St., New York, NY 10013 USA Tel 212-226-8760; Fax: 212-226-1411; Toll Free: 800-596-7437; *Imprints:* Siete Cuentos Editorial (Siete Cuentos); Triangle Square (Triangle Sq)
E-mail: info@sevenstories.com
Web site: http://www.sevenstories.com
Dist(s): **Children's Plus, Inc.**
Independent Pubs. Group
MyiLibrary
Penguin Random Hse. Distribution
Penguin Random Hse. LLC
Random Hse., Inc.

SevenHorns Publishing *See* **Sevenhorns Publishing**

Sevenhorns Publishing, *(978-0-9838427; 978-0-9976846; 978-1-7323870; 978-0-9600817; 978-1-7349527; 978-1-7363887; 979-8-9852007)* Orders Addr.: 276 5th Avenue, Suite 704, New York, NY 10001 USA Tel 917-677-4540; Edit Addr.: 276 5th Ave Suite 704, New York, NY 10001 USA Tel 917-677-4540
E-mail: tasha.grant@sevenhornspublishing.com; admin@sevenhornspublishing.com
Web site: http://www.sonsofcaasi.com; http://www.sevenhornspublishing.com
Dist(s): **Ingram Content Group.**

Seventh Mind Publishing, *(978-0-9973547; 978-1-7330158; 978-1-7365898; 979-8-9862035)* 1096 Via Regina, Santa Barbara, CA 93111 USA Tel 805-964-6164
E-mail: britt.andreatta@gmail.com
Web site: www.SeventhMindPublishing.com.

Seventh Sense Publishing, *(978-1-7320813)* 8502 16th st APT 409, Rockville, MD 20850 USA Tel 803-840-6838
E-mail: iamjdixon@gmail.com.

Seventh Street Pr., Div. of Malone-Ballard Book Pubs., 2215 6th Ave. Apt D, Moline, IL 61265 USA
E-mail: bookwoman1110@hotmail.com.

Seward, Bernice, *(978-0-615-98377-6; 978-0-692-33409-6; 978-0-9862879; 978-0-692-71852-0; 978-0-9995378)* P.O. Box 2231, Lewiston, ID 83501 USA; *Imprints:* Seward Media (MYID_B_SEWARD)
Web site: www.berniceseward.com
Dist(s): **CreateSpace Independent Publishing Platform.**

Seward Media *Imprint of* **Seward, Bernice**

Sewell, Kelley, *(978-0-9996563; 978-1-7367095)* 15505 Bally View Ln., Redding, CA 96001 USA Tel 530-646-9551
E-mail: ksewell777@yahoo.com.

Seymour, Dale Pubns., *(978-0-201; 978-0-7690; 978-0-86651; 978-1-57232)* Div. of Pearson Learning, Orders Addr.: P.O. Box 2500, Lebanon, OH 43216 USA Toll Free Fax: 800-393-3156; Toll Free: 800-321-3106 (Customer Service); Edit Addr.: 10 Bank St., White Plains, NY 10602-5026 USA (SAN 200-9781) Toll Free Fax: 800-393-3156; Toll Free: 800-237-3142
E-mail: pearson_learning2@prenhall.com
Web site: http://www.pearsonlearning.com; http://www.pearsonlearning.com/rightsPerm.rtf
Dist(s): **Addison-Wesley Educational Pubs., Inc.**

Seymour Institute for Advanced Christian Studies, *(978-0-9765717)* 411 Washington St., Dorchester, MA 02124 USA Tel 617-373-7273; Fax: 617-373-7575
E-mail: erivers@ntlf.org.

Seymour Institute for the Advancement of Christian *See* **Seymour Institute for Advanced Christian Studies**

Seymour Reide, *(978-0-578-94566-8; 978-0-578-94568-2; 978-0-578-97666-2)* 2207 128th St. 0, COLLEGE POINT, NY 11356 USA Tel 2015545785
E-mail: anastasia.mota@yahoo.com
Dist(s): **Ingram Content Group.**

Seymour Science LLC *See* **Isabella Products, Inc.**

SF Publishing, *(978-0-578-40868-2; 978-0-578-43722-4; 978-0-578-44310-2; 978-1-7367459)* 1405 Dundalk Ave, Baltimore, MD 21222 USA Tel 443-537-0750
E-mail: victoriajhayes@gmail.com.

SFT Pubns., *(978-0-9724384)* Orders Addr.: 3915 S. Cramer Cir., Bloomington, IN 47403 USA (SAN 254-8283) Tel 812-333-8902
E-mail: leilarandle@sbcglobal.net.

Sgian Enterprises, *(978-0-9771197; 978-0-615-12814-6)* 4349 W. Tomahawk Dr., Beverly Hills, FL 34465-4871 USA.

Shaar Pr. *Imprint of* **Mesorah Pubns., Ltd.**

Shades of Me Publishing, *(978-0-9718307)* 3969 Strandhill Rd., Cleveland, OH 44128 USA
E-mail: marybury1927@msn.com.

Shades of White, *(978-0-9795834)* 301 Tenth Ave., Crystal City, MO 63019 USA Tel 314-740-0361; *Imprints:* Magical Child Books (Magical Child)
Web site: http://www.magicalchildbooks.com
Dist(s): **New Leaf Distributing Co., Inc.**

ShadeTree Publishing, LLC, *(978-0-9822632; 978-1-937331)* 1038 N. Eisenhower Dr., No. 274, Beckley, WV 25801 USA (SAN 857-6971)
E-mail: jennifer.minigh@shadetreepublishing.com
Web site: http://www.shadetreepublishing.com.

Shadow Canyon Graphics, *(978-0-9857420)* 454 Somerset Dr., Golden, CO 80401 USA Tel 303 278 0949; Fax: 303-279-5831
E-mail: dnshadow@earthlink.net.

Shadow Mountain *Imprint of* **Deseret Bk. Co.**

Shadow Mountain *Imprint of* **Shadow Mountain Publishing**

Shadow Mountain *Imprint of* **Shadow Mountain Publishing**

Shadow Mountain Publishing, *(978-0-87579; 978-1-57345; 978-1-59038; 978-1-60907)* Div. of Deseret Book Company, P.O. Box 30178, Salt Lake City, UT 84130 USA Tel 801-517-3223; *Imprints:* Shadow Mountain (ShadowMountain); Ensign Peak (EnsPeak); Shadow Mountain (ShadMtn)
E-mail: info@shadowmountain.com
Web site: http://www.shadowmountain.com
Dist(s): **Blackstone Audio, Inc.**
Deseret Bk. Co.

Shadow Pubns., *(978-0-9771424)* P.O. Box 1151, Valley Forge, PA 19482-1151 USA
Web site: http://www.olliedude.com.

ShadowPlay Pr., *(978-0-9638819)* P.O. Box 647, Forreston, IL 61030 USA Tel 815-938-3151; Fax: 815-371-1440
E-mail: sheilawelch@juno.com; ericwelch2@juno.com
Web site: http://www.shadowplay.userworld.com.

Shadowridge Pr., *(978-0-615-71838-5; 978-0-615-78251-5; 978-0-615-79586-7; 978-0-615-79587-4; 978-0-9897796; 978-0-615-94710-5; 978-0-692-37333-0; 978-0-692-37334-7; 978-1-946808)* 1447 Sycamore Dr, Simi Valley, CA 93065 USA Tel 8055017274
Web site: www.shadowridgepress.com
Dist(s): **CreateSpace Independent Publishing Platform.**

Shady Tree Productions, *(978-0-9747352)* 5383 Iron Pen Pl., Columbia, MD 21044 USA Tel 410-997-6337 (phone/fax)
E-mail: shadytreepro@hotmail.com; bigtree_75@msn.com; ronfullwood@returningsoldiers.us.

Shaffer, Dale E., *(978-0-915060)* 478 Jennings Ave., Salem, OH 44460-2732 USA (SAN 206-9067).

Shaffer, Earl Foundation, Inc., *(978-0-9795659)* 1635 Haft Dr., Reynoldsburg, OH 43068-3059 USA Tel 614-751-0029
E-mail: spur@mac.com
Web site: http://www.earlshaffer.org.

Shaffner, Randolph P. *See* **Faraway Publishing**

Shaggy Dog Pr., *(978-0-9722007; 978-0-578-89079-1)* P.O. Box 4436 Reeves Road, Ojai, CA 93023 USA Tel 805-646-1849
E-mail: shaggydogpress@gmail.com.

Shah, Meera, *(978-0-9774219)* 7003 Westminster Ln., Germantown, TN 38138 USA Tel 901-754-7197
E-mail: meeds_46@yahoo.com; merra.meeds46@gmail.com.

Shahine, Lora, *(978-0-9987146)* 1101 Madison St., Seattle, WA 98104 USA Tel 206-515-0000
E-mail: lshahine@pnwfertility.com.

Shahnawaz Khan *See* **Terra Blue Enterprises**

Shahriary, Cathlin, *(978-1-7328453)* 4301 Essex Ct., Flower Mound, TX 75028 USA
E-mail: cshahriary@gmail.com
Dist(s): **Ingram Content Group.**

Shakalot High Entertainment, *(978-0-9721067; 978-0-9796219; 978-1-7358905)* 20687 White Dove Ln., Bend, OR 97702 USA Tel 541-788-4011; 13019 SW 154th Ave., Tigard, OR 97223 Tel 503-548-3336; *Imprints:* Writing Wild & Crazy (Writing Wild)
E-mail: shakalothighentertainment@yahoo.com
Web site: http://www.shakalothigh.com
Dist(s): **Lulu Pr., Inc.**

Shake the Moon Bks., *(978-0-615-25125-7; 978-0-615-53638-5; 978-0-692-14333-9; 978-0-578-55965-0)* 431 N. Hidalgo Ave., ALHAMBRA, CA 91801 USA Tel 818-903-4112
E-mail: info@shakethemoonbooks.com; slangteau@gmail.com
Web site: http://www.shakethemoonbooks.com
Dist(s): **Baker & Taylor Publisher Services (BTPS).**

ShakeB Co., *(978-0-615-24232-3; 978-0-615-41353-2)* 1189 Masselin Ave., Los Angeles, CA 90019 USA.

Shaky Alien Pubns., *(978-1-7379463)* 650 Sun Valley Ct, GRANBURY, TX 76049 USA Tel 817-964-4076
E-mail: christenmariewatson@gmail.com.

Shalako Pr., *(978-0-9798898; 978-0-9830608; 978-0-9846811; 978-0-9892917; 978-0-9908878; 978-0-9964235; 978-0-9970679; 978-0-9990070; 978-1-7340795; 978-1-7351297; 979-8-9861870)* P.O. Box 371, Oakdale, CA 95361-0371 USA (SAN 854-6622)
E-mail: major@majormitchell.net
Web site: http://www.shalakopress.com
Dist(s): **Smashwords.**

Shalhout, Ahlam LLC *See* **Expressions Woven**

Shalom Secrets *See* **Socially Smarter**

Shalu Children's Series, The *Imprint of* **Penman Productions**

Shamber Pubns., *(978-0-9771326)* P.O. Box 470321, Lake Monroe, FL 32747-0321 USA
E-mail: unbrokencirclebymcghee@gmail.com.

Shambhala Publications, Incorporated *See* **Shambhala Pubns., Inc.**

†Shambhala Pubns., Inc., *(978-0-8348; 978-0-87773; 978-0-937938; 978-0-9627138; 978-1-55939; 978-1-56957; 978-1-57062; 978-1-930485; 978-1-59030; 978-1-61180; 978-1-64547)* 4720 Walnut St., Boulder, CO 80301 USA (SAN 203-2481) Tel 303-222-9598; 978-829-2599 (international); Toll Free: 888-424-2329 (orders); *Imprints:* Weatherhill, Incorporated (Weathill); Trumpeter (Trumpeter); Roost Books (Roost Bks); Snow Lion Publications, Incorporated (SnowLion); Bala Kids (Bala Kids)
E-mail: editors@shambhala.com; support@shambhala.com; customercare@shambhala.com
Web site: http://www.shambhala.com
Dist(s): **MyiLibrary**
Penguin Random Hse. Distribution
Penguin Random Hse. LLC
Random Hse., Inc.; *CIP.*

Shami, Wafa, *(978-0-9600147)* 1110 Nevada Ave., San Jose, CA 95125 USA Tel 626-628-7769
E-mail: wshami@gmail.com.

Shammah Ministries, *(978-0-9725944)* Orders Addr.: 1346 Oak Pk. Dr., Aransas Pass, TX 78336 USA Tel 361-226-4918
E-mail: tonia@shammah.org; twoolever@gmail.com
Web site: https://toniawoolever.com; http://www.shammah.org.

Shamrock Pr., *(978-0-9675410)* Orders Addr.: P.O. Box 58186, Charleston, WV 25358 USA Tel 304-744-4259 (phone/fax) Do not confuse with Shamrock Pr. in Chattanooga, TN
E-mail: shamrockpress@frontier.com
Web site: www.shamrockpress.com.

Shamrock Publishing, Inc., *(978-0-9743244; 978-0-9759703)* 400 Corey Ave., Wachovia Bldg., 2nd Flr., Saint Pete Beach, FL 33706 USA Tel 727-363-4747; Fax: 727-363-4848; 1220 S. State St., Chicago, IL 60605 Tel 312-212-1143; Fax: 708-371-9576 Do not confuse with Shamrock Publishing, Incorporated in New Orleans, LA
E-mail: tpmac@sprynet.com; bksemmer@blueshamrockpublishing.com.

Shamus B. Publishing, *(978-0-9753671)* 18533 Pond Dr., Abingdon, VA 24211 USA.

Shan Jen Publishing Co., Ltd. (TWN) *(978-986-7517; 978-957-2041; 978-957-8298; 978-957-9658; 978-957-99079) Dist. by* **Chinasprout.**

Shanahan, John Francis Publishing, *(978-0-9618275)* 6727 N. Lightfoot Ave., Chicago, IL 60646 USA (SAN 667-0490) Tel 773-631-6344; Fax: 773-631-6372
E-mail: REPSbooks@aol.com.

Shanbhag, Arun, *(978-0-9790081)* 32 Chatham St., Arlington, MA 02474-2008 USA
E-mail: arun@shanbhag.org.

Shanghai Pr.,
Dist(s): **Independent Pubs. Group.**

Shangri-La Pubns., *(978-0-9677201; 978-0-9714683; 978-0-9719496)* Orders Addr.: P.O. Box 65, Warren Center, PA 18851-0065 USA Toll Free: 866-966-6288; Edit Addr.: 3 Coburn Hill Rd., PMB 65, Warren Center, PA 18851 USA Tel 570-395-3423; Fax: 570-395-0146
E-mail: gosline@egypt.net; shangrila@egypt.net; shangri_la_book@hotmail.com
Web site: http://www.shangri-la.0catch.com/.

Shankopotamus Bks., *(978-1-7346378)* 10397 E. Rimrock Dr., Scottsdale, AZ 85255 USA Tel 319-759-0620
E-mail: heathervanfleet@hotmail.com
Web site: Shankopotamusbooks.com.

Shannon Road Pr., *(978-0-9788785; 978-0-9846101)* 16330 Shannon Rd., Los Gatos, CA 95032 USA
E-mail: info@shannonroadpress.com
Web site: http://www.shannonroadpress.com.

Shanti Publishing, *(978-0-615-86491-4; 978-0-615-88564-3; 978-0-615-93871-4; 978-0-692-32474-5; 978-0-692-35882-5; 978-0-692-36270-9; 978-0-692-38178-6; 978-0-692-38320-9; 978-0-692-44042-1; 978-0-692-47800-4; 978-0-9973754; 978-0-692-13178-7)* P.O. Box 6252, Pine Mountain Club, CA 93222 USA Tel 6613199977
Web site: www.ShantiPublishing.com
Dist(s): **CreateSpace Independent Publishing Platform.**

Shapato Publishing, LLC, *(978-0-9821058; 978-0-9826992; 978-0-9833526; 978-0-615-50457-5; 978-0-615-50918-1; 978-0-615-50920-4; 978-0-615-50921-1; 978-0-615-51306-5; 978-0-615-53431-2; 978-0-615-53435-0; 978-0-615-56643-6; 978-0-615-59791-1; 978-0-615-60650-7; 978-0-615-72638-0; 978-0-615-83271-5; 978-0-615-91943-0; 978-0-692-25479-0; 978-0-692-30027-5; 978-0-692-58092-9) Orders Addr.: P.O. Box 476, Everly, IA 51338 USA Tel 712-490-5165; Edit Addr.: 503 E 2nd St., Everly, IA 51338 USA*
E-mail: Jean@midwestwriter.com
Web site: http://www.shapatopublishing.com
Dist(s): **CreateSpace Independent Publishing Platform**
Smashwords.

Shaping Youth, *(978-1-954361)* 698 Port Dr., San Mateo, CA 94404 USA Tel 415-519-7000
E-mail: amy@amyjussel.com
Web site: shapingyouth.org.

Shar-Don & Associates, Incorporated *See* **Lovin Ovens, Inc.**

Share & Care Society Inc., *(978-0-9722025)* 3737 El Portal, C/o 57552 29 Palms Hwy. #52, 29 Palms, CA 92284 USA; *Imprints:* True Lightening (True Lght)
E-mail: london_pain@hotmail.com; elizabethbergman@shareandcaresociety.us
Web site: http://shareandcaresociety.us.

Share Publishing, *(978-0-9633705)* Orders Addr.: 313 Laurel Ave., Menlo Park, CA 94025 USA Tel 650-321-5947 (phone/fax)
E-mail: pamelalaw@sbcglobal.net
Web site: http://sharepublishing.com.

ShareInPrint, *(978-1-7330291; 978-1-7355501; 979-8-9874063; 979-8-218-12101-3)* 520 Mapleview Dr., University City, MO 63130 USA Tel 314-863-2476
E-mail: johnmramsay@mac.com
Web site: shareinprint.com; johnmramsay.com; https://www.amazon.com/s?k=John+Martin+Ramsay&crid=1ZT3FFLPTGZKM&sprefix=john+martin+ramsay%2Caps%2C97&ref=nb_sb_noss.

Sharif, Mboya *See* **Doses of Reality, Inc.**

Shark & Siren Pr., *(978-1-7328605)* 2317 Ebony St, Port Townsend, WA 98368 USA Tel 415-269-2587
E-mail: TRENOR@GMAIL.COM
Web site: www.umijoo.com.

Shark Press *See* **Lemon Shark Pr.**

†Sharp & Dunnigan, *(978-0-918495)* 2700 Richards Rd., Suite 110, Bellevue, WA 98005 USA (SAN 657-3029) Tel 425-467-6565; Fax: 425-467-6564
E-mail: ecovepress@aol.com
Web site: http://elfincovepress.com
Dist(s): **Elfin Cove Pr.**; *CIP.*

Sharp & Dunnigan, Publications, Incorporated *See* **Sharp & Dunnigan**

Sharp, Diana Consulting, *(978-0-9762626)* 5954 Fishhawk Crossing Blvd., Lithia, FL 33547-5878 USA.

SHARP Literacy, Inc., *(978-0-9770816; 978-0-9836222; 978-0-9986683)* 750 N. Lincoln Memorial Dr. Suite 311, Milwaukee, WI 53202 USA Tel 414-270-3388
Web site: http://www.sharpliteracy.org.

Sharp Pencil Pr., *(978-1-7367148)* 8302 Stoneybridge Cir., Highlands Ranch, CO 80126 USA Tel 303-809-0594
E-mail: ruthdenver@aol.com.

Sharpe, Jeannie W., (978-0-9763117) 373 Langford Rd., Blythewood, SC 29016 USA Fax: 803-786-4557 E-mail: jws415@aol.com.
Sharpe, Veronica C, (978-0-578-72645-8) 36 Harvest Brook Ct, O'fallon, MO 63366 USA Tel 314-913-5699 E-mail: sharpepictures@prodigy.net.
Sharpe Writings, (978-0-9997926) P.O. Box 194, Norwalk, IA 50211 USA Tel 515-802-7753 E-mail: jakesharpe@mchsi.com.
Shartec Systems, Incorporated See Mountcastle Co.
Shauger, Daniel, (978-0-9746114) 12438 Moorpark St., No. 241, Studio City, CA 91605 USA Tel 818-693-6231 E-mail: dan@aperfectswing.com Web site: http://www.aperfectswing.com.
Shaw, Dana, (978-0-9791091) Orders Addr.: P.O. Box 91, Franklin, ME 04634 USA (SAN 852-4815) Tel 207-565-4445; Edit Addr.: 206 Georges Pond Rd., Franklin, ME 04634 USA E-mail: myfriendzundel@yahoo.com Web site: http://myfriendzundel.com.
shaw, kiyana, (978-1-7374296) 2812 N. Calvert st., Baltimore, MD 21218 USA Tel 443-468-7009 E-mail: galaxy2418@yahoo.com.
Shawnee Pr., Inc., (978-0-8256; 978-0-9603394; 978-1-59235) Subs. of Music Sales Corp., Orders Addr.: P.O. Box 1250, Marshalls Creek, PA 18335 USA Toll Free Fax: 800-345-6842; Toll Free: 800-962-8584; Edit Addr.: 9 Dartmouth Dr., Bldg. 4, Marshalls Creek, PA 18335 USA (SAN 202-084X) Tel 212-254-2100 (copyright & licensing information); 570-476-0550; Fax: 570-476-5247 E-mail: shawnee-info@shawneepress.com Web site: http://www.shawneepress.com Dist(s): Leonard, Hal Corp. Music Sales Corp.
Shay, Marissa, (978-0-9899604) 575 Watchogue Rd., Staten Island, NY 10314 USA Tel 718-477-0026 E-mail: m.pessolano@yahoo.com.
Shayach Comics Imprint of Judaica Pr., Inc., The
Shaymaa Publishing Corp., (978-0-9719581) P.O. Box 501, Lodi, NJ 07644-0501 USA (SAN 255-738X) Fax: 973-237-0537 E-mail: elhewiemf@juno.com; todaysgy@todaysgym.com; elhewie@lift-4-life.com Web site: http://www.lift-4-life.com; http://www.todaysgym.com; http://www.shaymaa-publishing.com.
Shayne Publishing, (978-0-9771192) 4895 SE 40th St., Des Moines, IA 50320 USA (SAN 256-7997) Tel 515-263-2784 E-mail: dlhuston01@aol.com.
Shazak Productions Imprint of Torah Excel
She is Me, (978-0-578-41114-9) 5388 Chenin Blanc Pl., Vallejo, CA 94591 USA Tel 707-718-8832 E-mail: attorneyarmstrong@comcast.net Dist(s): Independent Pub.
She Soars LLC, (978-0-578-41577-2) 4407 Sweet Williams Ln., Wilson, NC 27896 USA Tel 252-991-7296 E-mail: hannahsheart7@gmail.com Dist(s): Independent Pub.
She Writes Pr., (978-1-938314; 978-1-63152; 978-1-64742) 1563 Solano Ave. No. 546, Berkeley, CA 94707 USA Tel 510-967-9333 E-mail: brooke@warnercoaching.com Dist(s): Ingram Publisher Services Publishers Group West (PGW) Seattle Bk. Co.
†Shearer Publishing, (978-0-940672) P.O. Box 2915, Fredericksburg, TX 78624 USA Tel 830-997-6529 E-mail: shearer@shearerpub.com Web site: http://www.shearerpub.com Dist(s): Texas A&M Univ. Pr.; CIP.
Shechinah Third Temple, Inc., (978-0-9723866; 978-0-9817212; 978-0-9895128) 11583 Pamplona Blvd., Boynton Beach, FL 33437 USA Tel 561-735-7958; Fax: 561-738-1535 E-mail: thirdtemple@bellsouth.net; jerrypollock@bellsouth.net Web site: http://www.shechinahthirdtemple.org.
Sheepdog Pr., (978-0-9742205) P.O. Box 60, Onancock, VA 23417 USA Tel 888-787-1951; Fax: 888-787-2675 E-mail: publisher@sheepdogpress.com Web site: http://www.sheepdogpress.com.
Sheepgate Pr., (978-1-7333733) 4590 Woodland Brook Dr. SE, Atlanta, GA 30339 USA Tel 770-639-1671 E-mail: emilyhjeffries@gmail.com Web site: www.emilyhjeffries.com.
Sheepscrot River Pr., (978-0-9964084) 147 Eddy Rd., Edgecomb, ME 04556 USA Tel 207-882-5569 E-mail: leawait@roadrunner.com Web site: www.leawait.com.
Sheets, Judy, (978-0-9726451) 2526 Brune Rd., Farmington, MO 63640 USA Tel 573-756-6254 E-mail: judys@i1.net.
Sheffield, Rhonda, (978-0-578-97435-4) 7570 Indigo St., Miramar, FL 33023 USA Tel 954-482-2349 E-mail: lamrhondasheffield@gmail.com Web site: www.rhondasheffield.com.
Shekinah Glory Publishing, (978-0-692-04329-5) 901 Wilson Rd., No. 121, Conroe, TX 77301 USA Tel 936-314-7458 E-mail: shekinahglorypublishing17@gmail.com Dist(s): Ingram Content Group.
Shekinah Productions, (978-0-9802250; 978-0-578-04316-6; 978-0-578-05243-4; 978-0-578-05610-4; 978-0-578-05834-4; 978-0-578-07417-7; 978-0-578-08092-5; 978-0-578-08093-2; 978-0-578-08094-9; 978-0-578-08182-3; 978-0-578-08415-2; 978-0-578-08869-3; 978-0-578-10324-2; 978-0-578-11645-7; 978-0-578-12000-3; 978-0-578-13210-5; 978-0-578-13328-7; 978-0-578-13499-4; 978-0-578-13962-3; 978-0-578-14057-5; 978-0-578-14114-5; 978-0-578-18040-3; 978-0-578-19525-4; 978-0-578-19715-9; 978-0-578-19716-6; 978-0-578-19838-5; 978-) 8111 Windersgate Drive, Olive Branch, MS 38654 USA Fax: 662-504-4234; P.O. Box 209, Olive Branch, MS 38654 E-mail: shekinah.productions@yahoo.com; shek.global@gmail.com Web site: http://www.skpseminars.com.
Shekinah Publishing Hse., (978-0-9700976; 978-1-940153) Orders Addr.: P.O. Box 1118811, Carrollton, TX 75011 USA Tel 877-538-1363; Edit Addr.: P.O. Box 118811, Carrollton, TX 75011 USA Fax: 877-538-1363; Imprints: Shekinah Publishing House (Shek Pub Hse) Do not confuse with companies with the same or similar names in Cameron, NC, Cameron, NC E-mail: lpbowk@thebwfg.com; author@shekinahpublishinghouse.com.
Shekinah Publishing Hse. Imprint of Shekinah Publishing Hse.
Shelby, Lloyd See Painted WORD Studios
Shelbykay Publishing Co., (978-0-9744407) 525 Greenhill Ln., Philadelphia, PA 19128 USA Tel 215-483-6688 E-mail: cdkae@aol.com.
Shelf Space Bks., (978-1-945713) 41 Poplar Ln., Indian Head, MD 20640 USA Tel 301-743-6009 E-mail: smrsaia@gmail.com Web site: www.shelfspacebooks.com.
Shelf-Life Bks., (978-1-880042) Div. of M.A.P.S., Inc., 2132 Fordem, Madison, WI 53704-0599 USA Tel 608-244-7767; Fax: 608-244-8394.
Shell Beach Publishing, LLC, (978-0-9706732) 677 Shell Beach Dr., Lake Charles, LA 70601-5732 USA Tel 433-439-2110 E-mail: kkblake@compuserve.com.
Shell Educational Publishing, (978-1-4258) 5301 Oceanus Dr., Huntington Beach, CA 92649 USA Tel 714-489-2080; Fax: 714-230-7070; Toll Free: 888-877-7606; 877-777-3450 E-mail: rkarnik@tcmpub.com; LShill@seppub.com Web site: http://www.seppub.com; http://www.tcmpub.com Dist(s): Follett School Solutions Lectorum Pubns., Inc. Teacher Created Materials, Inc.
Shella, Aaron, (978-0-578-44271-6; 978-0-578-48198-2) 1157 Waukegan Rd., Deerfield, IL 60015 USA Tel 847-945-6884; 847 309 2493 E-mail: aaron.shella@gmail.com Dist(s): Ingram Content Group.
Shelle, Carole Creative Arts, (978-0-9792641) P.O. Box 52972, Irvine, CA 92619 USA (SAN 852-9493) Toll Free: 800-929-1634.
Shelley Adina, (978-0-615-52095-7; 978-0-615-62675-8; 978-1-939087; 978-1-950854) P.O. Box 752, Redwood Estates, CA 95044 USA Tel 408-761-1195; Imprints: Moonshell Books, Inc. (MoonshellBks) Web site: http://www.shelleyadina.com Dist(s): Blackstone Audio, Inc. CreateSpace Independent Publishing Platform.
Shellymae, (978-0-578-57111-9) 5582 Yorkshire Pl., Lake Oswego, OR 97035 USA Tel 612-242-8393 E-mail: shellymae@msn.com.
Shelly's Adventures LLC, (978-0-9851845; 978-1-953768) P.O. Box 2632, Land O Lakes, FL 34639 USA Tel 352-219-7199 E-mail: kentrell@shellysadventuresllc.com; kentrell.martin15@gmail.com; kentrell@shellysadventures.com Web site: www.shellysadventuresllc.com; www.shellysadventures.com Dist(s): Partners Pubs. Group, Inc.
ShellyShines Bks., (978-0-9993131) 9134 Forest Willow Dr., Indianapolis, IN 46234 USA Tel 317-694-1409 E-mail: ShellyShines22@gmail.com Web site: www.ShellyShines.com.
ShellyShines22@gmail.com See ShellyShines Bks.
Shelter Harbor Pr., (978-0-9853230; 978-1-62795) 605 W. 115th St. Suite 163, New York, NY 10025 USA Tel 212-864-0427; Fax: 212-316-6496 E-mail: Jeanette.Limondjian@gmail.com; info@shelterharborpress.com; jeanette@shelterharborpress.com.
Shelter of Flint, Inc., (978-0-9740929) 902 E. 6th St., Flint, MI 48503-2787 USA E-mail: sof@shelterofflint.com Web site: http://www.shelterofflint.com.
†Shelter Pubns., Inc., (978-0-936070) Orders Addr.: P.O. Box 279, Bolinas, CA 94924 USA (SAN 122-8463) Tel 415-868-0280; Fax: 415-868-9053; Toll Free: 800-307-0131; Edit Addr.: 285 Dogwood Rd, Bolinas, CA 94924 USA E-mail: shelter@shelterpub.com Web site: http://www.shelterpub.com Dist(s): Bk. Express Bookmen, Inc. Distributors, The Koen Pacific Partners/West Book Distributors Publishers Group West (PGW); CIP.
shelterpetsink, (978-0-9740960) 16457 Gledhill St., North Hills, CA 91343 USA Fax: 818-892-2112 E-mail: shelterpetsink@shelterpetsink.com; remilove2002@yahoo.com Web site: http://www.shelterpetsink.com.
Shenandoah County Historical Society, Inc., (978-0-9795924) P.O. Box 506, Edinburg, VA 22824 USA Tel 540-465-5570 E-mail: adamsons@shentel.net.
Shenango River Bks., (978-1-888836) P.O. Box 631, Sharon, PA 16146 USA Tel 412-342-3811; Fax: 412-342-1583.
Shenanigan Bks., (978-0-9726614; 978-1-934860) 84 River Rd., Summit, NJ 07901-1443 USA (SAN 915-7085) Web site: http://www.shenaniganbooks.com Dist(s): Jobson, Oliver H.
Shenanigans Series,
Shenek, (978-0-692-08159-4; 978-1-7321464) 425 Zachary Way, Garner, NC 27529 USA Tel 919-834-3658 E-mail: shenek.alston@gmail.com.
Shenomenal Ink, (978-1-7321861) 17175 San Juan, Detroit, MI 48221 USA Tel 313-363-8824 E-mail: shenomenalink@gmail.com Web site: www.shenomenalink.com.
Shen's Bks. Imprint of Lee & Low Bks., Inc.
Shepard Pubns., (978-0-938497; 978-1-62035; 978-0-9849616; 978-0-9898649) P.O. Box 280, Friday Harbor, WA 98250 USA (SAN 661-0536); Imprints: Skyhook Press (Skyhook Pr) Web site: http://www.shepardpub.com Dist(s): Ingram Content Group.
Shepard's Ink See Shepard's Ink Publishing
Shepard's Ink Publishing, (978-0-9764645; 978-0-9799230; 978-1-7365449) 2201 Murfreesboro Pk., Nashville, TN 37211 USA; P.O. Box 78211, Nashville, TN 37207.
Shepherd Mountain Pr., (978-0-9749282) 21 Cargill Rd., Liberty, ME 04949 USA Tel 207-589-4772.
Shepherd Pr. Inc., (978-0-9663786; 978-0-9723046; 978-0-9767582; 978-0-9815400; 978-0-9824387; 978-0-9830990; 978-1-936908; 978-1-63342) Orders Addr.: P.O. Box 24, Wapwallopen, PA 18660 USA Tel 570-379-2101; Fax: 570-379-2071; Toll Free: 800-338-1445; Edit Addr.: 437 S. River St., Wapwallopen, PA 18660 USA Do not confuse with companies with the same or similar names in Tappan, NJ, S. Hackensack, NJ, Birmingham, AL, Amityville, NY E-mail: info@shepherdpress.com Web site: http://www.shepherdpress.com.
Shepherd's Workshop, LLC, The, (978-0-9752895) 8213 Otis Ct., Arvada, CO 80003 USA Toll Free: 888-257-4673 E-mail: info@tsworkshop.com Web site: http://www.tsworkshop.com.
Sheppard, Irma, (978-0-692-27047-9; 978-0-692-40904-6; 978-0-692-45901-0; 978-0-692-91638-4; 978-0-692-06424-5; 978-0-578-51412-3; 978-0-578-67871-9; 978-0-578-74390-5; 978-0-578-94456-2; 978-0-578-97203-9) 21 COUNTRY MEADOWS DR., ASHEVILLE, NC 28806 USA Tel 520-288-2185 E-mail: karl.moeller@me.com.
Sheppard Publishing, (978-0-9725286) 3371 Old Forge Rd., Kent, OH 44240 USA Tel 330-325-9658 E-mail: sheppardpublishing@neo.rr.com.
Sheptoski-Forbush, Faith, (978-0-9985228; 978-1-7340186) P.O. Box 74688, Romulus, MI 48174-0688 USA Tel 989-255-1326 E-mail: faithsf@yahoo.com.
Sher-A-Craft, (978-0-9670612) Div. of Bell Blueprint Co., Inc., 7888 Othello Ave., San Diego, CA 92111 USA Tel 619-278-4830; Fax: 619-278-6830; Toll Free: 877-235-5877.
Sheri McCulley Studio, (978-0-9981591) 5928 Hemlock St., Merriam, KS 66202 USA Tel 913-362-0560 E-mail: tseib@aol.com.
Sherian Publishing, (978-0-9795676) 2700 Braselton Hwy., Suite 10-390, Dacula, GA 30019-3207 USA Tel 888-276-6730; Fax: 888-209-8212; Toll Free: 888-276-6730 E-mail: sherri.sheusi@sherianinc.com Web site: http://www.sherianinc.com.
Sheridan Books See KEYGARD
Sheridan County Historical Society Pr., (978-0-9792871) Orders Addr.: 850 Sibley Cir., Sheridan, WY 82801-9626 USA Web site: http://www.sheridancountyhistory.org Dist(s): Greenleaf Book Group.
Sherman, Linda, (978-0-615-16017-7) 31557 W. 10 Mile Rd., Farmington, MI 48336 USA Tel 248-476-3433; Fax: 248-476-4307 E-mail: grandmalouie@hotmail.com Web site: http://grandmalouie.com.
Sheron Enterprises, Inc., (978-1-891877) 1035 S. Carley Ct., N Bellmore, NY 11710-2051 USA E-mail: sheron@concentric.net.
Sherrifmatt9 Publishing Company See Second Time Media & Communications
Sherry Chakrabarti, (978-0-578-38440-5) 712 Yorktown Ln., Moorestown, NJ 08057 USA Tel 267-408-7324 E-mail: sherry@pmc-group.com Web site: blueberryillustrations.com.
Sherry Gansle See Little Big Tomes
Sherwood, Jae Anne, (978-0-692-04564-0; 978-0-692-04621-0) 1002 Moss Haven Ct., Annapolis, MD 21403 USA Tel 703-581-4711 E-mail: toadsville@mac.com Dist(s): Ingram Content Group.
Sherwood Publishing LLC, (978-0-9987872) 16480 White Haven DR, Northville, MI 48168 USA Tel 734-420-6932 E-mail: jam@mipalmers.us.
Sheva, Marie, (978-0-9741736) 301 Main St., Apt. 8, East Greenwich, RI 02818 USA E-mail: mariesheva@yearofthedogs.com Web site: http://www.yearofthedogs.com.
ShiaGnosis, (978-0-9975945; 978-1-946737; 978-1-946737-00-7) 1115 Virginia Ave., Hagerstown, MD 21740 USA Tel 301-582-8743 E-mail: ddsodagar@gmail.com Web site: www.shiagnosis.com; https://heavenlywise.com.
Shields, Kathleen J. See Erin Go Bragh Publishing
Shiloh Children's Bks., (978-0-9777923; 978-0-615-81504-6) P.O. Box 954, Polson, MT 59860 USA Tel 406-531-2281 E-mail: cxman@blackfoot.net.
Shiloh Group See Shiloh Children's Bks.
Shiloh Kidz Imprint of Barbour Publishing, Inc.
'Shiloh Run Studios Imprint of Barbour Publishing, Inc.
Shine Bright Bks., (978-1-7375130) 5 High Sierra Dr., Alamogordo, NM 88310 USA Tel 619-403-0061 E-mail: Jnevin@protonmail.com.
Shine On Pubns., (978-0-9749806) 12325 Kosich Pl., Saratoga, CA 95070 USA; 12325 Kosich Pl., Saratoga, CA 95070-3575 Web site: http://www.shineonpublications.com.
Shine Publishing Hse., (978-0-9749467) 1811 Abbey Oak Dr., Suite 12879, Vienna, VA 22182 USA (SAN 255-9269) Tel 571-432-8922; Fax: 703-448-8443 E-mail: sales@shinepublishing.com Web site: http://www.shinepublishing.com Dist(s): CreateSpace Independent Publishing Platform Global Bk. Distributors.
Shine Time Records & Bks., (978-0-9712398) Orders Addr.: P.O. Box 331941, Nashville, TN 37203 USA Tel 615-242-9857 (phone/fax); Toll Free: 888-807-4463 (888-80-SHINE) E-mail: chucwhit@usit.net; info@shinetime.com; info@littlestar.com Web site: http://www.littlestar.com; http://www.shinetime.com.
Shine-A-Light Pr., (978-0-692-43551-9; 978-0-692-45864-8; 978-0-692-46053-5; 978-0-578-17880-6; 978-0-9976722; 978-1-953158) E-mail: chris@shinealightcorp.com Web site: www.shinealightpress.com.
Shining City Media, (978-1-7322512; 979-8-218-22419-6) 2101 No. Parish Place, Unit E, Burbank, CA 91504 USA Tel 818-843-3609 E-mail: geoffranya95@yahoo.com.
Shining Hall Imprint of Twelve Winters Pr.
Shining Tramp Pr., (978-0-9749352; 978-0-615-46043-7) 2114 Harbor View Dr., Rocky Hill, CT 06067 USA Tel 860-563-1899 E-mail: kjmurphy@sbcglobal.net Dist(s): CreateSpace Independent Publishing Platform.
Shinnery Publishing Co., (978-0-692-80660-9; 978-0-9990572) 102 W. 2nd St., Colorado City, TX 79512 USA Tel 325-436-1724 E-mail: sharongbarber@sbcglobal.net; sharongbarber@sbcglobal.net; sharongbarber@sbcglobal.net Dist(s): CreateSpace Independent Publishing Platform.
Shinobi Ent., Inc., 14622 Cypress Cottage Ct., Cypress, TX 77429 USA Tel 713-443-5774 E-mail: davewhitfield@comcast.net Web site: The NewRuleofThree.com Dist(s): Diamond Comic Distributors, Inc.
Shiny Red Ball Publishing, (978-0-9773608) 105 Lakeover Dr., Athens, GA 30607 USA Web site: http://www.shinyredball.com.
Shiptree Pubn., (978-0-615-77925-6; 978-0-692-20740-6; 978-0-9966682) 1040 Lunalilo St. Penthouse 2, Honolulu, HI 96822 USA Tel 808 599-3728 Web site: gardnermckay.net Dist(s): CreateSpace Independent Publishing Platform.
Shires Press Imprint of Northshire Pr.
Shirley's Girl Pubns., (978-0-578-06605-9) 2165 Silverado St., San Marcos, CA 92078 USA Tel 619-723-8492 E-mail: LVa2thpro@gmail.com.
Shirt Tales Imprint of Brookteam Corp.
Shively, Lisa Cookbooks, (978-0-9766756) P.O. Box 2123, Eden, NC 27289 USA E-mail: loopi3@earthlink.net; kitchenhelpers@earthlink.net Web site: http://www.fromourhometoyours.net; http://www.cookingwithlisa.com.
Shiver Hill Bks., (978-0-9747417) 1220 Tico Rd., Ojai, CA 93023 USA; 79 S Canyon Diablo Rd. Unit 11, Sedona, AZ 86351 Tel 805-908-1651 E-mail: geraldstanek@yahoo.com Dist(s): Lulu Pr., Inc.
Shivers, Frank Evangelistic Assn., (978-1-878127) Orders Addr.: P.O. Box 9991, Columbia, SC 29290 USA E-mail: fsea@juno.com Web site: http://FrankShivers.com.
Shnoozles, LLC, (978-0-9768852; 978-0-9770292) 8 Canyon Ridge, Irvine, CA 92603 USA Web site: http://www.shnoozles.com.
Shoestring Bk. Publishing, (978-0-615-90958-5; 978-0-9903893; 978-1-943974) 495 Penobscot Ave., Millinocket, ME 04462 USA Tel 207-731-6760 E-mail: shoestringpublishing4u@gmail.com Web site: www.shoestringbookpublishing.com.
Shoetree Publishers, Inc., (978-0-9755521) P.O. Box 2122, Chandler, AZ 85244 USA (SAN 850-9859) Fax: 480-812-0182 Web site: http://www.shoetreepublishers.com.
Shooting Star Edition Imprint of American Literary Pr.
Shooting Star Publishing, (978-0-9762835) 1305 E. Fort King St. # 100, Ocala, FL 34471-2443 USA Do not confuse with companies with the same name in Dearborn, MI, Moses Lake, WA Web site: http://www.shottingstarpublishing.com.
Shope, Diann, (978-0-9968988) 1222 20th Ave E., Seattle, WA 98112 USA Tel 206-329-1178 E-mail: eshope12@msn.com Web site: diannshope.com.
Shope, E. Raymond See Flutter-By Productions
Shophar So Good, (978-0-9970778) E-mail: Humbleentertainment@yahoo.com Web site: shopharsogood.com.
Shore Line Pr. Imprint of Pacific Bks.
Shorebird Media, (978-0-9745737) Orders Addr.: P.O. Box 372, Mukiltel, WA 98275-0372 USA (SAN 255-6359) E-mail: jeanie.james@verizon.net.
Shorefront N.F.P., (978-0-9765232; 978-1-946717) Orders Addr.: P.O. Box 1894, Evanston, IL 60204 USA Tel 847-864-7467; Edit Addr.: P.O. Box 1894, Evanston, IL 60204 USA Web site: http://shorefrontlegacy.org Dist(s): Lulu Pr., Inc.

Publisher Name Index

Shoreline Pr., *(978-1-887671)* P.O. Box 555, Jamestown, RI 02835 USA Do not confuse with Shoreline Press in Soquel, CA
E-mail: kennethproudfoot@hotmail.com.

Shore Publishing Co., *(978-0-9746846)* PMB 123, 7485 Rush River Dr., Suite 710, Sacramento, CA 95831-5260 USA Tel 916-442-4883; Fax: 916-428-9542.

Shorey Publications *See* **Shorey's Bookstore**

Shorey's Bookstore, *(978-0-8466)* P.O. Box 77316, Seattle, WA 98177-0316 USA (SAN 204-5958) Tel 206-633-2990
E-mail: shorey@serv.net
Web site: http://www.serv.net/shorey.

Short Books *See* **Half-Pint Kids, Inc.**

Short Power Press *See* **Bes Pr.**

Short Tales *Imprint of* **Magic Wagon**

Short Term Mission Language Program, *(978-0-9746182)* 3612 Mary Elizabeth Church Rd., Waxhaw, NC 28173-9273 USA
E-mail: info@missionlanguage.com
Web site: http://www.missionlanguage.com.

Shortbread Hill Bk. Co., *(978-0-9799162)* P.O. Box 1565, Veradale, WA 99037 USA (SAN 854-7599)
E-mail: shortbreadhill@hotmail.com.

Shortland Pubns. (U. S. A.) Inc., *(978-0-7699; 978-1-57257)* 19201 120th Ave NE Ste. 100, Bothell, WA 98011-9507 USA
Dist(s): **Heinemann-Raintree**
Wright Group/McGraw-Hill.

Shoshana Brand, *(978-0-9978213; 978-1-7378236)* 167 Stephanie Dr, Ozark, AL 36360 USA Tel 415-335-8595
E-mail: creativerosh@gmail.com
Web site: www.ajarbooks.com; www.theenglishteachercomics.com.

Shoshana Brand Ajar Books *See* **Shoshana Brand**

Shotwell, Sheila, *(978-0-9994225)* 54 Fitch Pl SE, Grand Rapids, MI 49503 USA Tel 616-451-4401
E-mail: sheilashotwell@aol.com.

Show N' Tell Publishing, *(978-0-615-19210-9; 978-0-9825700; 978-0-9968332; 978-0-9986498)* 56 Drakes Bay Dr., Corona Del Mar, CA 92625 USA Tel 946-644-2293
E-mail: dick@rate.com
Dist(s): **Publishers Services.**

Show What You KnowR Publishing, *(978-1-884183)* 6344 Nicholas Dr, Columbus, OH, OH 43235 USA.

Showcase Writers, *(978-0-9753340)* P.O. Box 13757, Richmond, VA 23225 USA Tel 804-398-1138
E-mail: editor@showcasewriters.com
Web site: http://www.showcasewriters.com.

Showdown Mesa, *(978-0-578-56096-0)* 829 E. Cedar Ct., Fruita, CO 81521 USA Tel 417-379-4685
E-mail: easy112233@gmail.com.

Showtime Bks., *(978-0-9911860)* 140 Sheldon Ave., Staten Island, NY 10312 USA Tel 718-356-2275
E-mail: bwshowtime@aol.com.

Shrewsbury Publishing, *(978-0-9673182)* 3624 Livingston, New Orleans, LA 70118 USA Tel 504-488-5249.

Shrimlife Pr., *(978-0-9997310)* 1 Ronwood Rd., Chestnut Ridge, NY 10977 USA Tel 845-371-2751
E-mail: susan@unlockyourchild.com
Web site: http://www.unlockyourchild.com.

Shulemite Christian Crusade, *(978-0-9714361)* 1420 Armstrong Valley Rd., Halifax, PA 17032-8383 USA (SAN 254-3931) Tel 717-896-8383; Fax: 717-896-8386
E-mail: sherrerd@epix.net
Web site: http://www.chrissherrerd.com.

Shulenberger Publishing, *(978-0-9767355)* 3912 NE 127th St., Seattle, WA 98125 USA (SAN 256-5935) Tel 206-367-5886
E-mail: ericshul@hotmail.com.

Shumpert, Sharon *See* **SYS Publishing**

Shun Watkins Productions, *(978-1-7353866)* 1961 Sandcreek Dr. SW, Atlanta, GA 30331 USA Tel 678-334-9244
E-mail: shunwatkinsproductions@gmail.com.

Shunday LLC *See* **Authorunit**

ShuNu Publishing, *(978-0-9742329)* P.O. Box 2031, Stafford, TX 77497 USA Tel 713-401-8479
E-mail: kmitchelithomas@aol.com.

Shurley Instructional Materials, Inc., *(978-1-881940; 978-1-58561)* 366 Sim Dr., Cabot, AR 72023 USA Tel 501-843-3869; Fax: 501-843-0583; Toll Free: 800-566-2966; Ballad Rd., Cabot, AR 72023
E-mail: shurley@shurley.com
Web site: http://www.shurley.com.

shuster books *See* **Roberts, Hebard D. Bks.**

Shy Cat Pubns., *(978-0-578-40488-2; 978-0-578-40882-8)* 2314 Roosevelt Ave., Redwood City, CA 94061 USA Tel 408-821-5635
E-mail: ashwinsunder@gmail.com
Dist(s): **Ingram Content Group.**

SIA Publishing, LLC, *(978-0-9787344; 978-1-936820)* 204 Wyndom Ct., Goodlettsvile, TN 37072-2176 USA
E-mail: donbloomquist@siapublishing.com
Web site: http://www.siapublishing.com
Dist(s): **Smashwords.**

SIA Software, LLC *See* **SIA Publishing, LLC**

Sibilant Pr., *(978-0-9987044)* 559 Ross Pl., Orlando, FL 32805 USA Tel 407-721-0589
E-mail: sibilantpublishing@gmail.com
Web site: www.sibilantpress.com.

Sibilant Press, LLC *See* **Sibilant Pr.**

Sibyl Merritt, *(978-0-9824565)* 25 Western Ledge Rd., Corea, ME 04624 USA (SAN 858-2157)
E-mail: bparks@maine.edu
Web site: http://sibylmerritt.com
Dist(s): **Ingram Content Group.**

Side FX Partners, LLC, *(978-0-692-82383-0; 978-0-692-83666-8; 978-0-692-83799-3)* 5875 Collins Ave No. 1801, MIAMI BEACH, FL 33140 USA Tel 443-570-4942
E-mail: jeffwcrawford5+LVP0003227@gmail.com; jeffwcrawford5+LVP0003227@gmail.com.

Sidedoor Publishing LLC, *(978-0-9770248)* P.O. Box 18271, San Jose, CA 95158-8271 USA
E-mail: isbn@sidedoorpublishing.com
Web site: http://www.sidedoorpublishing.com.

Sidekicks TM *Imprint of* **Scholastic, Inc.**

Sideline Ink Publishing, *(978-0-9992905; 978-1-7343909)* 2225 W. Berwyn Ave., Chicago, IL 60625 USA Tel 312-343-6273
E-mail: sidelineinkpublishing@gmail.com
Web site: www.creativeclassroomconsulting.com.

Siders, Autumn, *(978-0-578-43147-5; 978-0-578-67975-4; 978-0-578-76674-4)* P.O. Box 472, Wolfeboro Falls, NH 03896 USA Tel 603-393-4771
E-mail: espadadelanoche@gmail.com
Dist(s): **Ingram Content Group.**

Sidewalk Publishing, *(978-0-9766418)* Inform Design, 2809 Forest Hill Cir., SE, Olympia, WA 98501 USA Tel 360-570-9398
E-mail: informbarb@qwest.net
Web site: http://www.sidewalkpublishing.net.

Sidewalk Univ. Pr., *(978-0-9759962)* 1739 Springfield Ave., Maplewood, NJ 07040 USA Tel 973-885-0860
E-mail: sidewalku@msn.com
Web site: http://www.sidewalkuniversity.org.

Sidewinder Publishing LLC, *(978-0-914001)* 4609 Kinney St. SE, Albuquerque, NM 87105 USA Tel 505-998-8000
Web site: http://www.sidewinderpublishing.com/.

Sidran Institute Pr., *(978-0-9629164; 978-1-886968)* Div. of Sidran Institute, P.O. Box 436, Brooklandville, MD 21022 USA Tel 410-825-8888; Fax: 410-560-0134
E-mail: esther.giller@sidran.org
Web site: http://www.sidran.org
Dist(s): **New Leaf Distributing Co., Inc.**
Quality Bks., Inc.

Siebenaler, Sarina, *(978-0-578-60610-1; 978-1-7351996)* 6632 E. Calle De Las Estrellas, Cave Creek, AZ 85331 USA Tel 623-565-0199
E-mail: Sa30siebenaler@gmail.com
Dist(s): **Ingram Content Group.**

Siebold, Devin, *(978-0-578-25904-8; 978-0-578-26018-1)* 6315 Hidden Valley Ct., Orlando, FL 32819 USA
Web site: devincomedy.com.

Siegrist, Vicky, *(978-0-615-21676-8; 978-0-9820977; 978-0-9824444)* 1478 E. Buder Ave., Millington, MI 48529 USA
Web site: http://www.vicksiegrist.com
Dist(s): **Lulu Pr., Inc.**

Siemers, Robert, *(978-0-9744723)* P.O. Box 549, Koloa, HI 96756-0549 USA Tel 808-635-2905; Toll Free: 888-233-8365
Web site: http://www.teok.com.

Siems, D.R., *(978-0-9794483)* Orders Addr.: P.O. Box 83, Daniel, WY 83115 USA; Edit Addr.: 19 School House Ln., Daniel, WY 83115 USA.

Sienna Bay Pr., *(978-0-9898438; 978-1-945527)* 1409 Timber Ridge Cir., Nashville, TN 37211 USA Tel 615-693-1568
E-mail: shannonlbrown@yahoo.com.

Sierra Books *See* **VanLiss Publishing**

Sierra Club Bks. for Children, *(978-0-87156; 978-1-57805)* Div. of Sierra Club Bks., 85 Second Street, San Francisco, CA 94105 USA Tel 415-977-5500; Fax: 415-977-5792
E-mail: Books.Publishing@sierraclub.org
Web site: http://www.sierraclub.org/books
Dist(s): **Gibbs Smith, Publisher.**

Sierra Muses Pr., *(978-0-9912102)* P.O. Box 942, North San Juan, CA 95960 USA Tel 530-292-3610
E-mail: blisssearcher8@gmail.com.

Sierra Nevada Publishing Hse., *(978-0-9765697)* P.O. Box 50366, Henderson, NV 89016 USA Tel 702-991-1383; Fax: 702-953-8973; Toll Free: 800-254-6266
Web site: http://www.climbonsuccess.com.

Sierra Pr., *(978-0-939365; 978-0-9617651; 978-1-58071)* Div. of Panorama International Productions, Inc., Orders Addr.: 4988 Gold Leaf Dr., Mariposa, CA 95338 USA (SAN 662-6955) Tel 209-966-5071; Fax: 209-966-5073; Toll Free: 800-745-2631; *Imprints:* Wish You Were Here (Wish You Were Here)
E-mail: siepress@sti.net
Web site: http://www.nationalparksusa.com
Dist(s): **Smashwords.**

Sierra Raconteur Publishing, *(978-1-58365; 978-1-58582)* Orders Addr.: P.O. Box 97, Memphis, IN 47143 USA Tel 812-294-4693
E-mail: Lori_scard@yahoo.com.

Sierra Vista Junior High *See* **Sierra Vista Pubns.**

Sierra Vista Pubns., *(978-0-9711314; 978-0-615-11784-3)* Alpine Sports, Orders Addr.: P.O. Box 55391, Valencia, CA 91385 USA Fax: 661-259-8941; Toll Free: 800-330-7734; Edit Addr.: P.O. Box 186, Crystal Bay, NV 89402 USA (SAN 411-5961)
E-mail: alpinesport@earthlink.net
Web site: http://www.alpinebasketball.com
Dist(s): **American West Bks.**
Brigham Distribution.

Siete Cuentos Editorial *Imprint of* **Seven Stories Pr.**

Sigel Pr., *(978-1-905941)* Orders Addr.: 4403 Belmont Ct., Medina, OH 44256 USA (SAN 853-960X) Tel 330-722-2541 (phone/fax); 51a Victoria Rd., Cambridge, CB4 3BW Tel 01223 30 33 03
E-mail: tsigel@sigelpress.com
Web site: http://www.sigelpress.com
Dist(s): **MyiLibrary.**

SIGG ENTERPRISES, *(978-1-7361336)* 2863 Watercrest Dr NW, Concord, NC 28027 USA Tel 757-718-1841
E-mail: phiawatha3@gmail.com.

Sights Productions, *(978-0-9629978; 978-1-886366)* Orders Addr.: 15130 Black Ankle Rd., Mount Airy, MD 21771 USA Tel 410-795-4582; Fax: 410-795-5054
E-mail: eric@sights-productions.com
Web site: http://sights-productions.com
Dist(s): **Brodart Co.**
Follett School Solutions
Kamkyi Bks.
New Leaf Distributing Co., Inc.
Quality Bks., Inc.

Sigi & LuLu Productions, *(978-0-9829864; 978-1-937339)* 3733 Regina Royale Blvd, Sarasota, FL 34238 USA
Web site: www.theadventuresofsigi.com
Dist(s): **Ingram Content Group.**

Sigil Publishing, *(978-0-9728461; 978-0-9785642; 978-0-9846528; 978-0-9860323)* P.O. Box 824, Leland, MI 49654- USA (SAN 255-1667)
Web site: http://www.knightscares.com; www.realheroesread.com
Dist(s): **Partners Bk. Distributing, Inc.**
Quality Bks., Inc.

Sigler Printing & Publishing, Incorporated *See* **McMillen Publishing**

Sigmar (ARG) *(978-950-11) Dist. by* **Continental Bk.**

Sigmar (ARG) *(978-950-11) Dist. by* **AIMS Intl.**

Sigmar (ARG) *(978-950-11) Dist. by* **Mariuccia Iaconi Bk Imports.**

Sigmar (ARG) *(978-950-11) Dist. by* **Lectorum Pubns.**

Sign Up Learning, Incorporated *See* **Language Quest Corp.**

Sign2Me *Imprint of* **Sign2Me Early Learning / Northlight Communications, Inc.**

Sign2Me Early Learning / Northlight Communications, Inc., *(978-0-9668367; 978-1-932354)* Orders Addr.: 11112 47th Ave. W., Mukilteo, WA 98275 USA (SAN 850-7902) Tel 425-493-1903; Fax: 425-493-1904; Edit Addr.: 11112 4th Ave. W., Mukilteo, WA 98275 USA Tel 425-493-1903; Fax: 425-493-1904; Toll Free: 877-744-6263; *Imprints:* Sign2Me (Sign Two Me)
E-mail: btarcea@sign2me.com; acrain@sign2me.com
Web site: http://sign2me.com
Dist(s): **American Wholesale Bk. Co.**

Signal Fire Pr., *(978-0-9764128)* 25260 Terr. Grove Rd., Los Gatos, CA 95033 USA (SAN 256-4351)
Web site: http://www.signalfirepress.com.

Signator Publishing Group Inc., *(978-0-9728472)* 1725 I St. NW., Suite 300, Washington, DC 20006 USA Tel 202-349-3896; Fax: 202-349-3915
E-mail: info@signatorpublishing.com
Web site: http://www.signatorpublishing.com.

Signet *Imprint of* **Penguin Publishing Group**

SignificantFaith.com *See* **Sincerity Publishing**

Sigueme, Ediciones, S.A. (ESP) *(978-84-301) Dist. by* **1517Media.**

Sikes Sports Concepts *See* **Old Bay Publishing**

Sikh Research Institute, *(978-1-60411)* P.O. Box 690504, San Antonio, TX 78269 USA (SAN 854-0403)
E-mail: info@sikhri.org
Web site: http://www.sikhri.org.

Sikorski, Lorna D. & Associates *See* **LDS & Assocs.**

Silence Dogood Pr., *(978-0-9861967)* 4141 11th Ave SW, Naples, FL 34116 USA Tel 239-963-5063
E-mail: ronkezeske@gmail.com.

Silent Devil Productions, *(978-0-9752582; 978-0-9786451; 978-0-9789281; 978-0-9791192; 978-0-9796902)* 3777 Center Way, Fairfax, VA 22033 USA
E-mail: silentdevilproductions@hotmail.com
Web site: http://www.silentdevil.com.

Silent Moon Bks., *(978-0-9721457)* P.O. Box 1280, Seeley Lake, MT 59868 USA
E-mail: bschieber@yahoo.com.

Silent Thunder Publishing, *(978-1-938680)* 5663 Balboa Ave. No. 401, San Diego, CA 92111 USA Tel 619-925-0547
E-mail: teresa@teresaburrell.com.

Silhouette Pond Productions, *(978-0-9761169)* P.O. Box 778, Palm Harbor, FL 34682-0778 USA (SAN 256-3886) Tel 727-771-1691
E-mail: ceceenter@tampabay.rr.com
Web site: http://www.silhouettepond.com.

Silk Waters Mooney, *(978-0-9776608)* 316 E. El Paso St., Brackettville, TX 78832 USA Tel 830-563-3443; P.O. Box 393, Brackettville, TX 78832
E-mail: swmooney@pukathemoose.com.

Silky Sky Publishing, *(978-1-7365770; 978-1-958568)* 824 Lake Ave., LAKE WORTH BEACH, FL 33460-3754 USA Tel 573-268-1324
E-mail: info@susannahwelch.com
Web site: https://www.susannahwelch.com/.

Silly Goose Productions, LLC, *(978-0-9711500)* 525 Cutty Trl. Apt. A, Lakeway, TX 78734-4836 USA
E-mail: sallysue678@yahoo.com; sally@onmyown.com
Web site: http://www.starfishpublishing.com; http://www.onmyown.com
Dist(s): **Follett School Solutions.**

Silly Little Dog Productions, *(978-1-955048)* 1219 Rembrandt Dr., Sunnyvale, CA 94087 USA Tel 408-245-5213
E-mail: publisher@sillylittledog.com
Web site: sillylittledog.com.

Silly String Media, *(978-0-615-25193-6)* P.O. Box 884, Ross, CA 94957 USA
Web site: http://www.sillystringmedia.com
Dist(s): **Lulu Pr., Inc.**

Sillygeese Publishing, LLC, *(978-0-9987112; 978-1-951521)* P.O. Box 1434, Elgin, TX 78621 USA Tel 512-695-4048
E-mail: mydragonbubbles@gmail.com.

Siloam Pr. *Imprint of* **Charisma Media**

SILSNORRA LLC, *(978-1-951792; 978-1-955692; 978-1-962044)* 23 DANE CT, HAMPTON, VA 23666 USA Tel 757-969-9088
E-mail: ivryok@icloud.com.

Silver Bells Publishing Hse., *(978-0-9793517)* 19415 150th Ave., Tustin, MI 49688 USA Tel 231-829-3898
E-mail: dgbelleville@yahoo.com.

Silver Birch Ranch Pr., *(978-0-910421; 978-1-7328241)* Silver Birch Ranch, Star Rte., White Lake, WI 54491 USA (SAN 260-1354) Tel 715-484-8114.

SILVER BURDETT *Imprint of* **Savvas Learning Co.**

†Silver, Burdett & Ginn, Inc., *(978-0-382; 978-0-663; 978-1-4182)* Orders Addr.: P.O. Box 2500, Lebanon, IN 46052 USA Toll Free Fax: 800-841-8939; Toll Free: 800-552-2259; Edit Addr.: P.O. Box 480, Parsippany, NJ 07054 USA (SAN 204-5982); 108 Wilmot Rd., Suite 380, Midwest Div., Deerfield, IL 60015 (SAN 111-6517) Tel 708-945-1240
E-mail: customerservice@scottforesman.com
Web site: http://www.scottforesman.com/; *CIP.*

Silver Cloak Pubns., *(978-0-9777677)* P.O. Box 1027, Carpinteria, CA 93014-1027 USA
E-mail: SilverCloak@aol.com.

Silver Dagger Mysteries *Imprint of* **Overmountain Pr.**

Silver Dolphin Bks. *Imprint of* **Readerlink Distribution Services, LLC**

Silver Dolphin Bks. *Imprint of* **Printers Row Publishing Group**

Silver Dragon Bks. *Imprint of* **Zenescope Entertainment**

Silver Empire, *(978-1-949891)* 102 Wandering Ln, Harvest, AL 35749 USA Tel 256-503-0024
E-mail: russell@silverempire.org
Web site: https://silverempire.org/.

Silver Fire Publishing, *(978-0-9968168; 978-0-9976747; 978-1-7349929)* 701 Georgetown Ave, ELYRIA, OH 44035 USA Tel 440-366-6745
E-mail: theresalinden@oh.rr.com.

Silver Knight Publishing, LLC *See* **Black Forge**

Silver Lake Publishing, *(978-0-930868; 978-1-56343)* 1119 N. Broadway St., Aberdeen, WA 98520-2433 USA (SAN 203-8110) Toll Free: 800-663-3091 Do not confuse with Silver Lake Publishing, Morton, PA
E-mail: publisher@silverlakepublishing.com; SCRIBERE@aol.com; mthorpe@silverlakepub.com
Web site: http://www.silverlakepub.com
Dist(s): **SCB Distributors.**

Silver Leaf Bks., LLC, *(978-0-9744354; 978-0-9787782; 978-1-60975)* Orders Addr.: P.O. Box 6460, Holliston, MA 01746 USA Tel 508-740-6270; Toll Free: 888-823-6450; Edit Addr.: 13 Temi Rd., Holliston, MA 01746 USA
E-mail: Sales@SilverLeafBooks.com
Web site: http://www.silverleafbooks.com.

Silver Linden Pr., *(978-0-9981354)* 1094 37th Pl. NE No. 112, Salem, OR 97301 USA Tel 503-586-8696
E-mail: patti.bowman@msn.com.

Silver Maple Bks., *(978-0-692-76125-0; 978-1-7349008)* 31 Avenida Almendro NE, Albuquerque, NM 87123 USA Tel 505-298-8420
E-mail: rjulyan@comcast.net.

Silver Moon Pr., *(978-1-881889; 978-1-893110)* 400 E. 85th St. Apt. 15K, New York, NY 10028-6324 USA Toll Free: 800-874-3320
E-mail: mail@silvermoonpress.com
Web site: http://www.silvermoonpress.com.

Silver Print Pr., Inc., *(978-0-9628064; 978-0-9749890)* Div. of Peter Miller LLC, 20 Crossroad, Suite No. 1, Colbyville, VT 05676 USA (SAN 299-0350) Tel 802-272-8851
E-mail: peter@petermillerphotography.com
Web site: http://www.petermillerphotography.com.

Silver Rim Pr., *(978-1-878611)* 2759 Park Lake Dr., Boulder, CO 80301 USA Tel 303-666-4290 (phone/fax)
E-mail: Sybilset@aol.com.

Silver Rose Publishing, *(978-0-9778211)* P.O. Box 462174, Aurora, CO 80046 USA Tel 303-946-2183; Toll Free: 800-431-1579; *Imprints:* Raynestorm Books (Raynestorm Bks)
E-mail: contact@silverrosepublishing.com
Web site: http://www.silverrosepublishing.com; http://www.bookch.com
Dist(s): **BCH Fulfillment & Distribution.**

Silver Snowflake Publishing, *(978-0-9778476)* P.O. Box 1256, East Greenwich, RI 02818 USA (SAN 850-394X)
E-mail: exteriordesigner@cox.net
Web site: http://www.themagicsceptre.com; http://www.silversnowflakepublishing.com.

Silver Sprocket, *(978-1-945509; 979-8-88620)* 1057 Valencia St., San Francisco, CA 94110 USA Tel 408-391-2217
E-mail: avi@silversprocket.net
Web site: http://www.silversprocket.net
Dist(s): **SCB Distributors.**

Silver Thread Publishing, *(978-0-9844129; 978-0-9858326; 978-0-9861864; 978-0-9991794; 978-1-7353845; 978-0-578-32951-2)* 730 Vista Pacifica Cir., Pismo Beach, CA 93449 USA (SAN 859-3248)
E-mail: jeannie@asilverthread.com
Web site: http://www.asilverthread.com.

Silver Tree Communications, *(978-0-615-47364-2; 978-0-692-37842-7; 978-0-9990612; 978-0-9991491; 978-0-9994566; 978-1-948238)* 6121 108th Ave., Kenosha, WI 53142 USA Tel 262-891-3290
E-mail: kate@silvertreecomm.com.

Silver Whistle *Imprint of* **Harcourt Trade Pubs.**

Silver Wings Publishing *See* **Snowy Wings Publishing**

Silver Wreath, The, *(978-1-7321681; 978-1-7360230)* 3205 FAIRFOREST Pl., Raleigh, NC 27604 USA Tel 919-539-1914
E-mail: gale@woodsmanstories.com.

SilverBrown Bks., *(978-0-9840922)* 9355 54th Ave., S., Seattle, WA 98118 USA Tel 206-721-3794.

SilverhawkCorp., *(978-0-9772933)* 618 Draper Heights Way, Draper, UT 84020 USA.

Silverman, Toby, *(978-0-9793475)* 1611 Hemlock Farms, Lords Valley, PA 18428 USA
E-mail: tsilverman@noln.com.

SilverTip Books *Imprint of* **Bearport Publishing Co., Inc.**

Silverwood, Jennifer, *(978-0-692-09800-4)* P.O. Box 84, Milam, TX 75959 USA Tel 817-606-7366
E-mail: silverwoodj@gmail.com
Web site: http://jennifersilverwood.com.

Silvey Bk. Publishing, *(978-0-9762446)* P.O. Box 5171, Goodyear, AZ 85338-5171 USA Fax: 623-853-9172
E-mail: silveybooks@earthlink.net.

Simakan Group, The, *(978-0-9767812)* P.O. Box 492496, Atlanta, GA 30349 USA Fax: 770-981-1046
E-mail: info@playingyouragame.com
Web site: http://www.playingyourAgame.com.

imba Publishing Co., (*978-0-9765982*) 5413 Whistler Dr., Tallahassee, FL 32317 USA (SAN 256-4270) Tel 850-878-7741
E-mail: gladys_gikiri@simbapublishingcompany.com
Web site: http://www.simbapublishingcompany.com.

imba's Publishing, (*978-0-9765475*) P.O. Box 27634, Fresno, CA 93729-7634 USA.

imbosa Publishing, (*978-0-9996717*) 314 Vineyard Ln, Carlsbad, NM 88220 USA Tel 575-887-5858
E-mail: drlisas@hotmail.com.

Simcha Media Group, (*978-0-943706; 978-965-465; 978-1-930143; 978-1-932687; 978-1-934440; 978-1-936068*) 94 Dwight Pl., Englewood, NJ 07631 USA Tel 201-503-1151; Fax: 201-503-9761; *Imprints:* Devora Publishing (DevorPubng); Pitspopany Press (Pitspopany Pr)
Web site: http://www.pitspopany.com
Dist(s): **Coronet Bks.**
Lulu Pr., Inc.

Simmons, Kristina, (*978-0-9769843*) 40 Christopher Cir., Middletown, CT 06457 USA.

Simmons, Laura, (*978-0-692-16869-1*) P.O. Box 14, Richton Park, IL 60471 USA Tel 708-269-6928
E-mail: tgirl06@att.net
Dist(s): **CreateSpace Independent Publishing Platform.**

Simmons, Sukether Williams *See* **Shrewsbury Publishing**

Simms, Laura Storyteller, (*978-0-9911692*) 814 Broadway, New York, NY 10003 USA Tel 212-674-3479
E-mail: storymentor2010@gmail.com
Web site: http://www.laurasimms.com.

Simon & Barklee, Inc./ExplorerMedia, (*978-0-9704661; 978-0-9714502; 978-0-578-47400-7*) 2280 E. Whidbey Shores Rd., Langley, WA 98260 USA Tel 360-730-2360; Fax: 360-730-2355; *Imprints:* Explorer Media (Explorer Media)
E-mail: cwsch@whidbey.com
Web site: http://simonandbarklee.com
Dist(s): **Quality Bks., Inc.**

Simon & Brown, (*978-0-9814843; 978-1-936041; 978-1-61382; 978-1-7317*) 3140 N 52nd Ave, Hollywood, FL 33021 USA Tel 305-610-7128
E-mail: info@simonandbrown.com
Web site: http://www.simonandbrown.com.

Simon & Northrop of Cal, Incorporated *See* **Martell Publishing Co**

Simon & Schuster, (*978-0-671; 978-0-684; 978-0-689; 978-0-914676; 978-0-7432; 978-1-4165; 978-1-4391; 978-1-4516; 978-1-4767; 978-1-5011; 978-1-9821; 978-1-7214; 978-1-958698; 979-8-9866017*) Div. of Simon & Schuster, Inc., Orders Addr.: 100 Front St., Riverside, NJ 08075 USA (SAN 200-2442) Toll Free Fax: 800-943-9831; Toll Free: 800-223-2336 (ordering); 800-223-2348 (customer service); Edit Addr.: a/o Subsidiary Rights, 11th Flr., 1230 Avenue of the Americas, New York, NY 10020 USA (SAN 200-2450) Tel 212-698-7000; Fax: 212-698-7007; 212-632-8099 (Rights & Permissions); 212-698-1269 (Pocket Bks. Rights & Permissions); Toll Free: 800-897-7650 (customer financial services); 100 Front St., Riverside, NJ 08075 (SAN 852-5471) Tel 856-824-2115; *Imprints:* Atria Books (Atria); Beyond Words (BWords); North Star Way (NorthStarWay)
E-mail: ssonline_feedback@simonsays.com; consumer.customerservice@simonandschuster.com
Web site: http://www.simonsays.com; http://www.oasis.simonandschuster.com; http://www.simonandschuster.com/
Dist(s): **Cengage Gale**
Giron Bks.
Hachette Bk. Group
Libros Sin Fronteras
Simon & Schuster, Inc.
Studio Fun International
TextStream
Thorndike Pr.
Ulverscroft Large Print Bks., Ltd.

Simon & Schuster Audio, (*978-0-671; 978-0-7435; 978-1-4423*) Orders Addr.: 100 Front St., Riverside, NJ 08075 USA Toll Free Fax: 800-943-9831 (orders); Toll Free: 800-223-2336 (customer service); Edit Addr.: a/o Sub Rights Manager, 11th flr., 1230 Avenue of the Americas, New York, NY 10020 USA Tel 212-698-7000; Fax: 212-698-2370; 212-632-8091 (Rights & Permissions)
Web site: http://www.simonsays.com/subs/index.cfm?areaid=45
Dist(s): **Blackstone Audio, Inc.**
Follett School Solutions
Simon & Schuster
Simon & Schuster, Inc.

Simon & Schuster Bks. For Young Readers *Imprint of* **Simon & Schuster Bks. For Young Readers**

Simon & Schuster Bks. For Young Readers *Imprint of* **Simon & Schuster/Paula Wiseman Bks.**

Simon & Schuster Bks. For Young Readers, (*978-1-6659-0237-3*) Div. of Simon & Schuster Children's Publishing, 1230 Ave. of the Americas, New York, NY 10020 USA; *Imprints:* Simon & Schuster Books For Young Readers (S&SBFYng); Simon & Schuster/Paula Wiseman Books (S&SPaulaW); SAGA Press (SAGA Press); Salaam Reads (SalaamReads)
Dist(s): **Children's Plus, Inc.**
Simon & Schuster, Inc.

Simon & Schuster Canada (CAN) *Dist. by* **S and S Inc.**

Simon & Schuster Children's Publishing, (*978-0-02; 978-0-671; 978-0-684; 978-0-689; 978-0-7434; 978-1-4169; 978-1-4424; 978-0-85707*) Orders Addr.: 100 Front St., Riverside, NJ 08075 USA Toll Free Fax: 800-943-9831; Toll Free: 800-223-2336; Edit Addr.: a/o Subsidiary Rights, 4th floor, 1230 Avenue of the Americas, New York, NY 10020 USA Tel 212-698-7200; Fax: 212-698-2797 (Rights & Permissions); *Imprints:* Aladdin Library (AlaLib); Atheneum Books for Young Readers (AthenSS); Atheneum/Richard Jackson Books (Rich Jack); Simon Spotlight (SSpot); Simon & Schuster/Paula Wiseman Books (S&SPaulaW); Aladdin Paperbacks (AladdinPaperbcks); Atheneum/Caitlyn Dlouhy Books (Caitlyn Dlou); Aladdin (Aladdin)
Web site: http://www.simonsays.com
Dist(s): **Children's Plus, Inc.**
Follett School Solutions
Lectorum Pubns., Inc.
Simon & Schuster
Simon & Schuster, Inc.

†Simon & Schuster, Inc., (*978-0-02; 978-0-671; 978-0-684; 978-0-689; 978-0-88138; 978-0-914676; 978-0-937860; 978-1-55850; 978-1-58062; 978-0-7432; 978-0-7434; 978-0-7435; 978-1-59337; 978-1-4165; 978-1-4169; 978-1-59869; 978-1-60550; 978-1-4391; 978-1-4405; 978-1-4423; 978-1-4424; 978-1-4516; 978-0-85707; 978-1-4814; 978-1-5072; 978-1-5082; 978-1-5344; 978-1-7971; 978-1-6659; 978-1-6680; 978-1-6681; 978-1-6682; 978-1-970187; 978-1-970188) Div. of Viacom Co., Orders Addr.: 100 Front St., Riverside, NJ 08075 USA Toll Free Fax: 800-943-9831; Toll Free: 800-223-2336 (orders); 800-223-2348 (customer service); Edit Addr.: 1230 Ave. of the Americas, New York, NY 10020 USA Tel 212-698-7000*
E-mail: Consumer.CustomerService@simonandschuster.com
Web site: http://www.simonsays.com; http://www.simonandschuster.com
Dist(s): **Children's Plus, Inc.**
Follett School Solutions; *CIP.*

Simon & Schuster, Ltd. (GBR) (*978-0-671; 978-0-684; 978-0-689; 978-0-7432; 978-0-7434; 978-1-84738; 978-1-84737; 978-0-85720; 978-0-85707; 978-1-84983; 978-1-4711; 978-1-3985*) *Dist. by* **S and S Inc.**

Simon & Schuster Trade *See* **Simon & Schuster**

Simon & Schuster/Paula Wiseman Bks. *Imprint of* **Simon & Schuster Children's Publishing**

Simon & Schuster/Paula Wiseman Bks. *Imprint of* **Simon & Schuster Bks. For Young Readers**

Simon & Schuster/Paula Wiseman Bks. *Imprint of* **Simon & Schuster/Paula Wiseman Bks.**

Simon & Schuster/Paula Wiseman Bks., Div. of Simon & Schuster Children's Publishing, 1230 Ave. of the Americas, New York, NY 10020 USA; *Imprints:* Simon & Schuster Books For Young Readers (S&SBFYng); Simon & Schuster/Paula Wiseman Books (S&SPaulaW)
Dist(s): **Simon & Schuster, Inc.**

Simon & Simon, LLC *See* **Maestro Classics**

Simon & Son Publishing, (*978-0-9773665*) 4995 Paist Rd., Doylestown, PA 18901 USA; *Imprints:* Prophecy, The (Prophecy)
E-mail: frankfsp1@comcast.net
Web site: http://www.simonsonpublishing.com.

Simon, Les, (*978-0-9761914*) Orders Addr.: P.O. Box 57274, Washington, DC 20037-0274 USA Tel 202-659-3639; Fax: 202-457-1155; Edit Addr.: 1400 20th St., NW, No. 805, Washington, DC 20036 USA
E-mail: lessim2003@yahoo.com.

Simon Peter Pr., Inc., (*978-0-9761533; 978-0-9777430; 978-1-936159*) P.O. Box 2187, Oldsmar, FL 34677 USA Fax: 727-772-0368
E-mail: theaben@aol.com
Web site: http://www.simonpeterpress.com
Dist(s): **eBookit.com.**

Simon Publishing LLC, (*978-0-692-15702-2; 978-0-578-23587-5; 978-0-578-23588-2; 978-0-578-23589-9; 978-0-578-23590-5; 978-0-578-23591-2; 978-0-578-23592-9; 978-1-7361881; 978-1-7376246; 979-8-9861221; 979-8-9882937*) 1346 Mainsail Dr. No. 1323, Naples, FL 34145 USA Tel 239-784-2637
E-mail: joanne.tailele@gmail.com
Web site: www.joannetailele.com.

Simon Pulse *Imprint of* **Simon Pulse**

Simon Pulse, Div.of Simon & Schuster Children's Publishing, 1230 Ave. of the Americas, New York, NY 10020 USA; *Imprints:* Simon Pulse (SimonPulse)
Dist(s): **Children's Plus, Inc.**
Simon & Schuster, Inc.

Simon Pulse/Beyond Words, 1230 Avenue of the Americas, New York, NY 10020 USA
Dist(s): **Simon & Schuster, Inc.**

Simon Pulse/Mercury Ink *Imprint of* **Simon Pulse/Mercury Ink**

Simon Pulse/Mercury Ink, 1230 Avenue of the Americas, New York, NY 10020 USA; *Imprints:* Simon Pulse/Mercury Ink (SimoPulseMer)
Dist(s): **Simon & Schuster, Inc.**

Simon Scribbles *Imprint of* **Simon Scribbles**

Simon Scribbles, Div. of Simon & Schuster Children's Publishing, 1230 Ave. of the Americas, New York, NY 10020 USA; *Imprints:* Simon Scribbles (SScribbles)
Dist(s): **Children's Plus, Inc.**
Simon & Schuster, Inc.

Simon Spotlight *Imprint of* **Simon & Schuster Children's Publishing**

Simon Spotlight *Imprint of* **Simon Spotlight**

Simon Spotlight, Div. of Simon & Schuster Children's Publishing, 1230 Ave. of the Americas, New York, NY 10020 USA; *Imprints:* Simon Spotlight (SimonSpotlight)
Dist(s): **Simon & Schuster, Inc.**

Simon Spotlight/Nickelodeon *Imprint of* **Simon Spotlight/Nickelodeon**

Simon Spotlight/Nickelodeon, Div.of Simon & Schuster Children's Publishing, 1230 Ave. of the Americas, New York, NY 10020 USA; *Imprints:* Simon Spotlight/Nickelodeon (SSpotNick)
Dist(s): **Simon & Schuster, Inc.**

Simone, Julia, (*978-0-692-82697-3; 978-0-692-82698-0*)
E-mail: jeffwcrawford5+LVP0003217@gmail.com; jeffwcrawford5+LVP0003217@gmail.com.

simoneink, llc, (*978-0-692-98877-0*) P.O. Box 25723, Washington, DC 20007 USA Tel 703-534-8100
E-mail: simone@simoneink.com.

Simone's Bks., (*978-0-615-18719-8; 978-0-615-20614-1*) 65 Winding Wood Dr., Apt. 4A, Sayreville, NJ 08872 USA
Dist(s): **Lulu Pr., Inc.**

SIMONSAWYERPUB., (*978-1-7370609*) 130 E Oak St Apt 51B, Chicago, IL 60611 USA Tel 312-286-9226
E-mail: GWENLEVY51@GMAIL.COM.

Simpatico Bks., (*978-0-9771322*) P.O. Box 201, Heber Springs, AR 72543 USA Tel 501-362-2858
Web site: http://www.simpaticobooks.com.

Simple Faith Bks. *Imprint of* **Sunrise Mountain Bks.**

Simple Fish Bk. Co., LLC, (*978-0-9817598; 978-0-9837932*) 5500 Abercorn St., Suite 32, Savannah, GA 31405 USA
E-mail: bbrooks@simplefishbookco.com
Web site: http://www.simplefishbookco.com.

Simple Ink, LLC, (*978-0-9794167*) P.O. Box 1825, Hays, KS 67601 USA
E-mail: gmarconette@simpleink.net; gameck@gmail.com
Web site: http://www.simpleink.net.

Simple Procedure, A *See* **Pa-Pro-Vi Publishing**

Simple Productions *See* **Shepard Pubns.**

Simple Thoughts Pr., LLC, (*978-0-9768557*) Orders Addr.: P.O. Box 759, Northfield, MN 55057 USA; Edit Addr.: 14345 Falk Ave., Northfield, NJ 55057 USA
Web site: http://www.backandforthjournal.com.

Simple Truths *Imprint of* **Calvary Chapel Pasadena**

Simplemente Maria Pr., (*978-0-9766811; 978-1-7346768*)
E-mail: mary@maryheebner.com
Web site: http://www.maryheebnergallery.com; http://www.maryheebner.com.

Simpler Life Pr., (*978-0-9619806*) 1599 S. Uinta Way, Denver, CO 80231 USA (SAN 246-5809) Tel 303-751-2454; Fax: 303-671-5200
E-mail: avs@vansteenhouse.com
Web site: http://www.vansteenhouse.com.

Simplex Pubns., (*978-0-9623113; 978-1-929304*) Orders Addr.: 575 Larkspur Plaza Dr., Unit 4, Larkspur, CA 94939-1476 USA
E-mail: gosmith@pacbell.net
Web site: http://www.simplexpublications.com
Dist(s): **Bookpeople.**

SimpliFun Studios, (*978-1-932839*) 2070 Stratford Dr., Milpitas, CA 95035 USA Tel 408-946-8632; Toll Free: 800-850-4-FUN
E-mail: mail@simplifun.com
Web site: http://www.childrenspartygames.com.

Simply B *See* **Simply B, L.L.C.**

Simply B, L.L.C., (*978-0-9823900; 978-1-7331401; 978-1-7347930*) 3421 Hattie Ln., Columbia, TN 38401 USA (SAN 858-0294) Tel 615-609-5660
E-mail: B@SimplyBChanged.com
Web site: http://www.SimplyBChanged.com.

Simply Charlotte Mason, LLC, (*978-1-61634*) 930 New Hope Rd No. 11-892, Lawrenceville, GA 30045 USA
E-mail: contact@simplycharlottemason.com
Web site: http://https://simplycharlottemason.com/.

Simply Hooked, (*978-0-692-77545-5*) 12308 Marblehead Dr., Tampa, FL 33626 USA Tel 843-812-7686
E-mail: mwynnsc@hotmail.com
Web site: www.simplyhooked.co.

Simply Silly Stories, (*978-0-9838964*) 3603 Forsythia Dr., Wylie, TX 75098 USA Tel 214-597-8999
E-mail: bewilson@simplysillystories.com.

SimplyCMB,LLC, (*978-0-9980042*) 1958 S. Cherry Blossom Ln., Suttons Bay, MI 49682 USA
E-mail: yroehler@bookpublishing.com.

Simpson, Charles B., (*978-0-9703818*) 234 Faulkner Ave., Hazard, KY 41701 USA Tel 606-436-4652
E-mail: cngsimpson@earthlink.net
Web site: http://www.appalachianwriter.com.

Simpson Productions, (*978-1-946180*) 1423 W. Toledo St., Broken Arrow, OK 74012 USA Tel 918-258-1330
E-mail: transcriberls@cox.net
Web site: www.simpsonproductions.net.

Sims, Brianna V. *See* **Growsies**

Simsand Publishing, (*978-0-9765580*) 8 Huntington Pl. Dr., Atlanta, GA 30350 USA Tel 678-458-0759
E-mail: timsanders01@aol.com.

Sinanan, Cindy, (*978-0-9769004*) 10169 New Hampshire Ave., No. 155, Silver Spring, MD 20903 USA
E-mail: mybook@mris.com.

Sincerity Publishing, (*978-0-9848314; 978-1-945915*) 450 Pine Flower Ct., Highlands Ranch, CO 80126 USA
E-mail: hwhitmore12@icloud.com
Web site: http://www.HughWhitmore.com.

Sinclair, A. E., (*978-0-692-78356-6*) 8518 OAK VIEW DR, Chattanooga, TN 37421 USA Tel 423-693-3597
E-mail: aprilsinclair355@gmail.com.

Sinclair, Loretta, (*978-0-615-24452-5; 978-0-615-40432-5; 978-0-9916159; 978-0-9992025*) P.O. Box 2052, Rancho Cordova, CA 95741 USA
E-mail: lori@sinclairinkspot.com
Web site: http://www.sinclairinkspot.com.

Sinclair/Polk, (*978-0-615-20281-5*) 1717 W. Green Tree Rd., No. 204, Glendale, WI 53209 USA Tel 414-704-3207
E-mail: janpolk@janpolk.com; margerysinclair@juno.com
Web site: http://www.janpolk.com; http://www.margerysinclair.com; http://www.ayearofgoodmanners.com
Dist(s): **Signature Bks., LLC.**

Sine Qua Non, (*978-0-578-63151-6; 979-8-9851372*) 16012 N. 7th Dr., Phoenix, AZ 85023 USA Tel 602-843-1252
E-mail: Bibti1@yahoo.com.

SingaporeMath.com, Inc., (*978-0-9741573; 978-1-932906; 978-1-947226*) 19535 SW 129th Ave., Tualatin, OR 97062 USA (SAN 255-6510) Tel 503-557-8100; Fax: 503-557-8103
E-mail: accounting@singaporemath.com; dthomas@singaporemath.com; nicholle@singaporemath.com
Web site: http://www.singaporemath.com.

SingaporeMath.com, Incorporated *See* **SingaporeMath.com, Inc.**

singer, david, (*978-0-692-05439-0; 978-0-692-05478-9; 978-0-9998224; 978-0-692-15279-9; 978-0-692-16541-6; 978-0-692-17280-3; 978-1-7326875*) 19195 Mystic Pointe Dr. Apt. 2606, Aventura, FL 33180 USA Tel 786-525-1815
E-mail: drdsinger@gmail.com; drdsinger@hotmail.com
Web site: www.davidsingerauthor.com
Dist(s): **Ingram Content Group.**

Singing Magpies, (*978-0-692-16621-5*) 12500 Spring Creek Rd., Parker, CO 80138 USA Tel 720-270-3508
E-mail: jenmtaos@gmail.com.

Singing Moon Pr., (*978-0-9770497*) Singing Moon Press #239 2601 S. Minnesota Ave., Ste 105, Sioux Falls, SD 57105-4750 USA; *Imprints:* Itty Bitty Kitty (Itty Bitty Kitty)
E-mail: editor@singingmoonpress.com
Web site: http://www.singingmoonpress.com.

Singing River Pubns., (*978-0-9709575; 978-0-9759953; 978-0-9774831; 978-0-9789870; 978-0-9822596*) Orders Addr.: P.O. Box 72, Ely, MN 55731 USA (SAN 254-136X) Tel 218-365-3498; Fax: 218-365-5792; Edit Addr.: 3365 Wolf Lake Rd., Ely, MN 55731 USA
E-mail: cmoroni@singingriverpublications.com; info@singingriverpublications.com
Web site: http://www.singingriverpublications.com
Dist(s): **Adventure Pubns.**
Partners Bk. Distributing, Inc.

Singing Tree Pr., (*978-0-9708005*) P.O. Box 722, Auburn, CA 95604 USA (SAN 255-4011) Tel 530-823-9284
E-mail: editor@mail.singingtreepress.com; orders@singingtreepress.com
Web site: http://www.singingtreepress.com.

Singing Winds Pr., (*978-1-61955*) 1331 SE Ellis, Dallas, OR 97338 USA Tel 503-551-7241 (phone/fax)
E-mail: singingwindspress@gmail.com
Web site: www.singingwindspress.com.

Siniff Publishing *See* **Country Messenger Pr. Publishing Group, LLC**

Sinolingua (CHN) (*978-7-80052*) *Dist. by* **China Bks.**

Sinonexus Publishing Co., (*978-0-9787664*) 65 Wethersfield Rd., Bellingham, MA 02019-1045 USA Tel 508-966-4423
E-mail: sinonexus@yahoo.com
Web site: http://www.sinonexus.org.

Sinsinawa Dominicans, Inc., (*978-0-9774934*) 585 Cty. Rd., Z, Sinsinawa, WI 53824-9701 USA Tel 608-748-4411; Fax: 608-748-4491
E-mail: communication@sinsinawa.org
Web site: http://www.sinsinawa.org.

Sioux City Lewis & Clark Interpretive Ctr., The, (*978-0-9753860; 978-0-9785063*) 900 Larsen Pk. Rd., Sioux city, IA 51103 USA Tel 712-224-5242; Fax: 712-224-5244
E-mail: mpoole@siouxcitylcic.com
Web site: http://www.siouxcitylcic.com.

Sippel, Robert, (*978-0-692-84050-4*) 8745 Mcdowell Rd, Scottsdale, AZ 85257 USA Tel 928-254-0081
E-mail: rsippel@mail.com.

Sir Brody Bks., (*978-0-692-39979-8; 978-0-9978611; 978-1-951551*) 605 Sycamore Dr. NE, CLEVELAND, TN 37312 USA Tel 423-595-7005
Web site: sirbrody.com.

Sir King Products LLC, (*978-1-7362819*) 2128 Bishop Dr., Flower Mound, TX 75028 USA Tel 212-470-5452
E-mail: sirkingproducts@gmail.com.

Sir Pigglesworth Publishing, (*978-1-68055*) 1528 Savannah St., Mesquite, TX 75149 USA Tel 469-416-2501
E-mail: w_a_wagner@hotmail.com
Web site: www.sirpigglesworthpublishing.com.

Sir Pigglesworth Publishing, Incorporated *See* **Sir Pigglesworth Publishing**

Sir Wrinkles Pr., (*978-0-9766639*) 30692 Fox Run Ln., San Juan Capistrano, CA 92675 USA
Web site: http://www.sirwrinklesthebulldog.com.

Siren-BookStrand, Inc., (*978-1-933563; 978-1-60601; 978-1-61034; 978-1-61926; 978-1-62241; 978-1-62242; 978-1-62740; 978-1-62741; 978-1-63258; 978-1-63259; 978-1-68295; 978-1-64010; 978-1-64243; 978-1-64637*) 2500 S. Lamar Blvd., Austin, TX 78704 USA (SAN 256-6869) Toll Free: 866-887-4736
E-mail: diana.debalko@sirenpublishing.com
Web site: http://www.sirenpublishing.com; http://www.sirenbookstrand.com.

Sirius Entertainment, Inc., (*978-1-57989*) Orders Addr.: P.O. Box X, Unadilla, NY 13849 USA Tel 607-369-2620; Fax: 607-369-2623; Edit Addr.: P.O. Box X, Unadilla, NY 13849-0723 USA
E-mail: sirent@aol.com
Dist(s): **Diamond Comic Distributors, Inc.**
Diamond Bk. Distributors.

SIRS Mandarin *See* **SIRS Publishing, Inc.**

†SIRS Publishing, Inc., (*978-0-89777; 978-0-9678914*) Div. of ProQuest Information and Learning, 5201 Congress Ave., Suite 250, Boca Raton, FL 33487 USA (SAN 222-8920) Tel 561-994-0079; Fax: 561-995-4074; Toll Free: 800-521-0600
Web site: http://www.proquestK12.com; *CIP.*

Siruela, Ediciones S.A. (ESP) (*978-84-7844; 978-84-85876; 978-84-15937*) *Dist. by* **Lectorum Pubns.**

Sisco, John, (*978-0-578-99038-5; 978-0-578-30277-5*) 261 Firefly trace, Saint Augustine, FL 32092 USA Tel 904-806-3771
E-mail: john@booksbyjohnsisco.com.

Sistemas Tecnicos de Edicion, S.A. de C.V. (MEX) (*978-968-6579; 978-970-629; 978-968-6048; 978-968-6135; 978-968-6394*) *Dist. by* **AIMS Intl.**

Sisterhaus Publishing, (*978-0-578-05291-5*) 40555 La Colima Rd., Suite 100, Temecula, CA 92591 USA
E-mail: lisaharding4@yahoo.com.

Sisters of Providence, (*978-1-893789; 978-0-9897397*) a/o Ann Casper, SP, Sisters of Providence Owens Hall, Saint Mary-of-the-Woods, IN 47876 USA Tel 812-535-2800; Fax: 812-535-1009 Do not confuse with Sisters of Providence in Holyoke, MA
E-mail: acasper@spsmw.org
Web site: http://www.sistersofprovidence.org.

Sisters Three Publishing Inc., *(978-0-9787375)* 5026 SW. 94th Ave., Cooper City, FL 33328 USA Fax: 954-885-8007
Web site: http://www.sistersthreeseries.com.

Sisu Home Entertainment, Inc., *(978-1-56086; 978-1-884857)* 340 W. 39th St., 6th Flr., New York, NY 10018 USA Tel 212-779-1559; Fax: 212-779-7115; Toll Free Fax: 888-221-7478; Toll Free: 800-223-7478
E-mail: sisu@sisuent.com
Web site: http://www.sisuent.com
Dist(s): **Follett School Solutions.**

Sitare, Ltd., *(978-0-940178)* Orders Addr.: 1101 N. Rainbow Blvd., No. 52, Las Vegas, NV 89108 USA (SAN 217-0833) Tel 702-990-0688
E-mail: editor@dlvmagazine.com
Web site: http://www.dlvmagazine.com.

SitStayRead, *(978-0-9970312)* 2849 N. Clark St., Chicago, IL 60657 USA Tel 773-661-9251
E-mail: info@sitstayread.org
Web site: http://sitstayread.org.

SivART Gallery, The, *(978-0-692-94926-9; 978-0-578-50746-0; 978-1-7364337)* 9934 Gray Dove Ct., Charlotte, NC 28216 USA Tel 704-607-9728
E-mail: tathompson1987@yahoo.com
Dist(s): **Ingram Content Group.**

Six Foot Press *See* **Six Foot Pr., LLC**

Six Foot Pr., LLC, *(978-1-64442)* 4200 Montrose Blvd., Houston, TX 77006 USA Tel 323-612-8855
E-mail: coertv@6ft.com; charlesk@6ft.com
Dist(s): **Two Rivers Distribution.**

Six Seconds, *(978-0-9629123; 978-0-9716772; 978-0-9797343; 978-1-935667)* Orders Addr.: P.O. Box 1985, Freedom, CA 95019 USA Tel 831-763-1800
E-mail: staff@6seconds.org; jenny@6seconds.org
Web site: http://www.6seconds.org.

Six Suns Publishing, *(978-0-9654200)* P.O. Box 112852, Anchorage, AK 99511 USA Tel 907-344-2905
Dist(s): **Todd Communications**
Wizard Works.

Sixth Avenue Bks. *Imprint of* **Grand Central Publishing**

Sixth&Spring Bks., *(978-1-931543; 978-1-933027; 978-1-936096)* 233 Spring St., 3rd Flr., New York, NY 10013 USA; *Imprints:* Hart, Chris Books (Chris Hart)
E-mail: wendy@sohopublishing.com
Web site: http://sixthandspringbooks.com
Dist(s): **Sterling Publishing Co., Inc.**

Sizzle Pr. *Imprint of* **Little Bee Books Inc.**

SKALIUM Pr., *(978-0-9996836; 978-1-7355001)* 131 Overbrook, Irvine, CA 92620 USA Tel 949-903-9635
E-mail: bvukov71@gmail.com.

Skandisk, Inc., *(978-0-9615394; 978-1-57534)* 6667 W. Old Shakopee Rd., Suite 109, Bloomington, MN 55438-2622 USA (SAN 695-4405) Tel 952-829-8998; Fax: 952-829-8992; Toll Free: 800-468-2424 (orders)
E-mail: lhamnes@skandisk.com; tomten@skandisk.com
Web site: http://www.skandisk.com.

SkateRight Publishing, *(978-0-9798876)* 2913 Cummings, Berkley, MI 48072-4807 USA.

Skazka Publishing, *(978-0-9994522)* P.O. Box 661, Gaston, OR 97119 USA Tel 503-896-6680
E-mail: connect@ekaterinawalter.com.

Skeete, D., *(978-0-9769012)* P.O. Box 737, New York, NY 10030 USA
E-mail: msdss@aol.com
Web site: http://www.hiphopwordsearch.com.

Skeptical Guitarist Pubns., *(978-0-9665029; 978-0-9788609; 978-1-944210)* Orders Addr.: P.O. Box 5824, Raleigh, NC 27650-5824 USA Tel 919-834-2031; Edit Addr.: 714 Faircloth St., Raleigh, NC 27607-4013 USA
E-mail: bruceemery@mindspring.com
Web site: http://www.skepticalguitarist.com/.

Sketch Publishing, *(978-0-9726764)* 414 S. 43rd St, Philadelphia, PA 19104 USA Tel 215-243-0644
E-mail: msand227@aol.com.

Sketches From The Heart Publishing, *(978-0-9759300)* P.O. Box 3431, Boulder, CO 80307 USA
Web site: www.sketchesfromtheheart.com
Dist(s): **Bks. West**
Common Ground Distributors, Inc.
Partners/West Book Distributors
Quality Bks., Inc.

Ski, J. C., *(978-1-7340902)* 254 Dogwood Rd., Millersville, MD 21108 USA Tel 410-533-7035
E-mail: jcski254@yahoo.com
Web site: www.dogsrgoodpeople.com.

Skillful & Soulful Pr., *(978-0-9989520)* 3615 Elford Dr., Whittier, CA 90601 USA Tel 626-664-6471
E-mail: skillfulandsoulfulmovement@gmail.com
Web site: www.skillfulandsoulful.com.

Skillin Marketing/Advertising, Inc., *(978-0-578-40414-1; 978-0-578-40415-8)* 7560 St. Marlo CC Pkwy, Duluth, GA 30097 USA Tel 404-663-8837
E-mail: joe@skillinmarketing.com
Dist(s): **Ingram Content Group.**

Skinder-Strauss Assocs., *(978-1-57741)* Orders Addr.: P.O. Box 50, Newark, NJ 07101 USA Tel 973-642-1440; Fax: 973-242-1905; Toll Free: 800-444-4041; Edit Addr.: 240 Mulberry St., Newark, NJ 07101 USA
E-mail: ed@elaw.com
Web site: http://lawdiary.com; http://elaw.com.

Skinned Knee Publishing, *(978-0-9989580; 978-1-949633)* 902 Gardner Rd., Austin, TX 78721 USA Tel 512-203-7939
E-mail: gabgar30@yahoo.com.

Skinner, Emily, *(978-0-9994196; 978-1-7361911)* P.O. Box 8590, Seminole, FL 33775 USA Tel 727-409-6790
E-mail: eskinner@knology.net
Web site: www.emilyskinnerbooks.com.

Skinner Hse. Bks. *Imprint of* **Unitarian Universalist Assn.**

Skinner, Kerry L., *(978-0-9648743; 978-1-931080)* Div. of Think Life/Change, 50 YATES DR. HAMPTON, GA 30228 USA; *Imprints:* KLS LifeChange Ministries (KLS LifeChge)
E-mail: kerry@thinklifechange.com
Web site: http://www.thinklifechange.com.

Skinner, Lynn C., *(978-0-9991679; 978-1-7336531)* 402 W. College St., Ailey, GA 30410 USA Tel 912-583-4741
E-mail: skipandlynn@windstream.net.

Skinny On (tm), The *Imprint of* **Rand Media Co**

Skinulicious Services, *(978-0-9977601)* 5875 157th Ave N Apt. C, Clearwater, FL 33760 USA Tel 757-553-2593
E-mail: chocolatebitsthings@gmail.com.

Skira *Imprint of* **Rizzoli International Pubns., Inc.**

Skirvan, Pamela, *(978-0-9742943)* P.O. Box 484, New Harbor, ME 04554-0484 USA.

Skookum Bks., *(978-0-692-79518-7; 978-0-9983078; 978-0-9985225)* 1 Manatee Ct, Simpsonville, SC 29681 USA Tel 864-552-1055; Toll Free: 864-552-1055
Dist(s): **CreateSpace Independent Publishing Platform.**

Skoorbyland Studios, *(978-1-7376119)* 32838 The old Rd., Castaic, CA 91384 USA Tel 661-993-8797
E-mail: brooks@brookscampbell.com.

Skromovas, Andrea, *(978-1-7322796)* 5481 Grand Pk. Pl, Boca Raton, FL 33486 USA Tel 954-562-6702
E-mail: andrea.skromovas@hotmail.com.

Sky Blue Press *See* **Sky Blue Pr.**

Sky Blue Pr., *(978-0-9652364; 978-0-9774851; 978-0-9889170; 978-0-9987246; 978-1-7357459; 979-8-9855240)* 292 Ghaner Dr., State College, PA 16803 USA Tel 202-308-5588
E-mail: paulherron49@icloud.com
Web site: http://www.skybluepress.com
Dist(s): **Smashwords.**

Sky Carrier Pr., *(978-1-880589)* P.O. Box 442, Fayetteville, NY 13066 USA Tel 605-486-4310; 315-637-9511
E-mail: swagner711@aol.com.

Sky Pony Pr. *Imprint of* **Skyhorse Publishing Co., Inc.**

†Sky Publishing, *(978-0-933346; 978-1-931559; 978-0-615-38976-9)* Div. of New Track Media, 90 Sherman St. Ste. D, Cambridge, MA 02140-3264 USA (SAN 212-4556) Toll Free: 800-253-0245
E-mail: orders@SkyandTelescope.com
Web site: http://www.skyandtelescope.com
Dist(s): **F&W Media, Inc.**
Sterling Publishing Co., Inc.
Two Rivers Distribution; *CIP.*

Sky Publishing Corporation *See* **Sky Publishing**

Sky Rocket Pr., *(978-0-9724637)* Orders Addr.: 2104 Old York Dr., Keller, TX 76248-5497 USA Tel 817-498-4300; Fax: 757-299-3608
E-mail: robert@rocketvilletexas.com
Web site: http://www.rocketvilletexas.com.

Sky Sun Publishing, *(978-0-578-20088-0; 978-0-578-20247-1)* 12128 Lakeshore Drive, Clermont, FL 34711 USA.

Skybox Event Productions, *(978-0-692-02935-0; 978-0-692-03261-9)* 506 S. Meadows Rd., Covina, CA 91791 USA (SAN 860-4177).

Skybox Publishing *See* **Skybox Event Productions**

Skyd LLC, *(978-0-9963107)* 1543 NW 64th St., Seattle, WA 98107 USA Tel 412-414-6820
E-mail: dan@hellervogel.com
Web site: http://skydmagazine.com.

Skyhook Pr. *Imprint of* **Shepard Pubns.**

Skyhorse Publishing Co., Inc., *(978-0-934672; 978-0-941873; 978-1-56148; 978-1-892389; 978-1-59780; 978-1-60239; 978-1-61608; 978-1-61145; 978-1-936697; 978-1-61321; 978-1-62087; 978-1-62153; 978-1-62636; 978-1-62872; 978-1-62873; 978-1-62914; 978-1-940456; 978-1-63144; 978-1-63158; 978-1-63220; 978-1-63450; 978-1-68099; 978-1-5107; 978-1-68358) 307 W. 36th Street, Flr. 11, New York, NY 10018 USA Tel 212-643-6816; 212-643-6819; Imprints:* Arcade Publishing (ARCADE PUBLISH); Sky Pony Press (SKY PONY PRESS); Allworth Press (Allwrth Pr); Yucca Publishing (Yucca Pub); Good Books (GoodBksUSA); Racehorse Publishing (Racehorse Pub)
E-mail: skyhorsepublishing@gmail.com
Web site: http://www.skyhorsepublishing.com
Dist(s): **Children's Plus, Inc.**
Follett School Solutions
INscribe Digital
MBI Distribution Services/Quayside Distribution
MyiLibrary
National Bk. Network
Open Road Integrated Media, Inc.
Publishers Group West (PGW)
Random Hse., Inc.
Simon & Schuster, Inc.
Sterling Publishing Co., Inc.

Skylar Doreal, *(978-0-9667747; 978-0-578-49302-2; 978-0-578-49303-9)* 1304 N. Van Buren St., Allentown, PA 18109 USA.

Skylight Paths Publishing *Imprint of* **LongHill Partners, Inc.**

Skylight Publishing, *(978-0-9654853; 978-0-9727055; 978-0-9824775; 978-0-9972528)* Orders Addr.: 9 Bartlet St., Suite 70, Andover, MA 01810-3655 USA Tel 978-475-1431 (phone/fax); Toll Free: 888-476-1940
E-mail: support@skylit.com
Web site: http://www.skylit.com.

Skyline Pubn., *(978-0-9723493; 978-0-9815846; 978-0-9843602; 978-0-615-66773-7)* P.O. Box 295, Stormville, NY 12582-0295 USA; *Imprints:* Water Forest Press (Wtr Forest) Do not confuse with companies with the same or similar name in Lancaster, OH, Oakland Park, FL
E-mail: skylineeditor@aol.com
Web site: http://www.skylinemagazines.com
Dist(s): **CreateSpace Independent Publishing Platform.**

Skyline Publishing, *(978-0-918981)* Orders Addr.: P.O. Box 1118, Columbia Falls, MT 59912 USA (SAN 669-8662) Tel 406-892-5560; Fax: 406-892-1922; Edit Addr.: a/o Skyline Publishing, 3101 Hwy. 206, Columbia Falls, MT 59912 USA Do not confuse with companies with similar names in Londonderry, NH, Saint George, UT
E-mail: carolynj@rolandcheek.com
Web site: http://www.rolandcheek.com
Dist(s): **Partners/West Book Distributors.**

SkyMacSyd Publishing, *(978-0-9767244)* P.O. Box 56363, Little Rock, AR 72215 USA.

SkyMark Corp., *(978-0-9769873)* 7300 Penn Ave., Pittsburgh, PA 15208 USA Tel 412-371-0680; Fax: 412-371-0681
E-mail: marie.routledge@skymark.com
Web site: http://www.theseus.biz.

Skyrai Publishing, *(978-0-692-68252-4; 978-0-9978555)* 935 Carla Dr., Troy, IL 62294 USA Tel 309-338-7589
Dist(s): **CreateSpace Independent Publishing Platform.**

Skyscape *Imprint of* **Amazon Publishing**

Skyscraper Pr. (children's) *Imprint of* **Windy City Pubs.**

Skyward Bks., *(978-0-9777902)* Orders Addr.: P.O. Box 56734, Riverside, CA 92517 USA Tel 951-782-0711
E-mail: skywardbooks@msn.com.

Skyward Press *See* **Skyward Bks.**

Skyward Publishing Co., *(978-1-881554)* Div. of Paragon Media Corp., 813 Michael St., Kennett, MO 63857 USA (SAN 297-9705) Tel 573-888-5589
E-mail: nfo@skywardpublishing.com
Web site: http://www.skywardpublishing.com; http://www.bransonozarks.com; http://www.brandywineswar.com.

Skywater Publishing Co., *(978-0-9793081; 978-0-9818279; 978-1-938237)* Orders Addr.: 398 Goodrich Ave., Saint Paul, MN 55102 USA Tel 952-818-2178; *Imprints:* Flat Sole Studio (FlatSole)
E-mail: info@skywaterpublishing.com
Web site: http://www.solbooks.com
Dist(s): **Follett School Solutions**
Smashwords.

Skyway Pictures LLC., *(978-0-692-84306-2; 978-1-7379621)* 1700 ROBINSON DR N, SAINT PETERSBURG, FL 33710 USA Tel 321-578-0022; Fax: 727-201-2407
E-mail: tate_mcghee@yahoo.com.

Skyword Pr., *(978-0-9740202)* Orders Addr.: P.O. Box 1714, Hood River, OR 97031 USA; Edit Addr.: 555 Highline Rd., Hood River, OR 97031 USA.

SL Conradt, LLC, *(978-0-615-37381-2)* N1685 Amies Ln., Greenville, WI 54942 USA Tel 920-427-0512
E-mail: shanaleeconradt@gmail.com
Web site: http://www.getfitwithfood.com.

SL Resources, *(978-1-935040; 978-1-935808)* Orders Addr.: P.O. Box 36040, Birmingham, AL 35236 USA Tel 205-985-0760; Fax: 205-403-3969; Toll Free: 800-718-2267; Edit Addr.: 2183 Pkwy. Lake Dr., Hoover, AL 35242 USA
E-mail: products@studentlife.net; bradford@studentlife.net
Web site: http://www.studentlifestore.com.

SLABYPRESS, *(978-0-9774118; 978-0-9792622)* W25952 State Rd., 95, Arcadia, WI 54612 USA Tel 608-323-7335
E-mail: slabypress@yahoo.com
Web site: http://www.jsiwicki.com.

SLACK, Inc., *(978-0-913590; 978-0-943432; 978-1-55642; 978-1-61711; 978-1-63091; 978-1-63822)* 6900 Grove Rd., Thorofare, NJ 08086-9447 USA (SAN 201-8632) Tel 856-848-1000; Fax: 856-853-5991; Toll Free: 800-257-8290
E-mail: orders@slackinc.com
Web site: http://www.slackbooks.com
Dist(s): **Barnes & Noble Bks.-Imports**
Coutts Information Services
Ebsco Publishing
Emery-Pratt Co.
Holt, Henry & Co.
Majors, J. A. Co.
Macmillan
Matthews Medical Bk. Co.
Rittenhouse Bk. Distributors.

Slack Water Pr., *(978-0-9797613)*
E-mail: jon.adams@slackwaterpress.com
Web site: http://slackwaterpress.com
Dist(s): **Ingram Content Group**
Smashwords.

Slangman Publishing, *(978-1-891888; 978-1-947601)* Orders Addr.: 12206 Hillslope St., Studio City, CA 91604 USA Tel 323-481-9500; Fax: 213-769-6266
E-mail: info@slangman.com
Web site: http://www.slangman.com
Dist(s): **Delta Systems Company, Inc.**

Slant Bks., *(978-1-63982)* 19507 21st Pl. NW, Shoreline, WA 98177 USA Tel 206-799-3451
E-mail: gw@slantbooks.com
Web site: https://slantbooks.com/.

Slate Falls Pr., LLC, *(978-0-578-04697-6; 978-0-578-07199-2; 978-0-578-10560-4; 978-0-578-12468-1; 978-0-578-17224-8; 978-0-578-18544-6; 978-0-578-23865-4)* P.O. Box 7062, Loveland, CO 80537 USA; 1124 Harrison Ave., Loveland, CO 80537
Web site: http://www.slatefallspress.com.

Slater Software. Inc., *(978-0-9743149)* 351 Badger Ln., Guffey, CO 80820-9106 USA Tel 719-479-2255 Toll Free: 877-306-6968
E-mail: jim@slatersoftware.com
Web site: http://www.slatersoftware.com.

Slater-Milligan, Joey, *(978-0-9979619)* 184 Franklin Street, D17, Brooklyn, NY 11222 USA Tel 631-339-4411
E-mail: joeyslatermilligan@gmail.com.

Slave Labor Bks., *(978-0-943151; 978-1-59362)* 577 S. Market St., San Jose, CA 95113 USA (SAN 668-1204) Tel 408-971-8929; Fax: 408-279-0451; Toll Free: 800-866-8929; *Imprints:* Slave Labor Graphics (Slave Labor Graph)
E-mail: dan@slavelabor.com
Web site: http://www.slavelabor.com
Dist(s): **Diamond Comic Distributors, Inc.**
Diamond Bk. Distributors.

Slave Labor Graphics *Imprint of* **Slave Labor Bks.**

Slavens Enterprises & Marketing Services, LLP *See* **Slavens Enterprises, LLC.**

Slavens Enterprises, LLC., *(978-0-9740348)* 13335 SW Violet Ct., Beaverton, OR 97008-5015 USA Toll Free: 877-526-0904; *Imprints:* Special Editions — Customized Biographies (Special Edns)
E-mail: ricks@slavensmarketing.com.

Slavit, Norma, *(978-0-578-22043-7; 978-0-578-22494-7)* 1483 Fields Dr., San Jose, CA 95129 USA Tel 408-253-7200
E-mail: normaslavit86@gmail.com.

Sleek Publishing, *(978-0-9990479)* 5910 W Sumac Ave, Denver, CO 80123 USA Tel 303-562-6695
E-mail: Laura@sleekpublishing.com.

Sleep Garden, Inc., *(978-0-9752988)* P.O. Box 2365, Menlo Park, CA 94025-2365 USA Toll Free: 877-475-3376
E-mail: marykelley@amsiventures.com
Web site: http://www.zzonesleep.com.

Sleeping Bear Pr., *(978-1-57504; 978-1-886947; 978-1-58536)* Orders Addr.: P.O. Box 20, Chelsea, MI 48118 USA (SAN 253-8466) Tel 734-475-4411; Fax: 734-475-0787; Toll Free: 800-487-2323; Edit Addr.: 27500 Drake Rd., Farmington Hills, MI 48331 USA
E-mail: customerservice@sleepingbearpress.com
Web site: http://www.sleepingbearpress.com
Dist(s): **Booklines Hawaii, Ltd.**
Cherry Lake Publishing
Children's Plus, Inc.
Follett School Solutions
Keith Distributors
MyiLibrary
Partners Bk. Distributing, Inc.
Southern Bk. Service
Urban Land Institute.

The Sleeping Bear Pr., *(978-0-578-19814-9; 978-0-578-19815-6)* 2395 S. Huron Pkwy. Suite 200, Ann Arbor, MI 48104 USA Toll Free: 800-487-2323.

Sleeping Hse., LLC, *(979-8-9887903)* 2089 W 400 S, Lehi, UT 84043 USA Tel 480-695-5283
E-mail: welkerscott@yahoo.com.

Sleepless Warrior Publishing, *(978-0-9747707)* 14989 Grassy Knoll Ct., Woodbridge, VA 22193 USA (SAN 256-1069) Tel 703-897-9394; Fax: 703-897-0695
E-mail: cynthia.little@comcast.net
Web site: http://www.sleeplesswarrior.com.

Sleepy Cat Pr., *(978-1-890797)* 11107 NE. 60th St., Kirkland, WA 98033 USA (SAN 299-3422).

Sleepy Creek Music, *(978-0-9754633)* P.O. Box 2652, Bloomington, IN 47402-2652 USA Tel 812-334-9901
E-mail: grey@greylarsen.com
Web site: http://www.greylarsen.com.

Sleepy Dog Publishing, *(978-0-9842560)* P.O. Box 2033, Turlock, CA 95381 USA
E-mail: swolsen@sbcglobal.net
Web site: http://sleepydogpublishing.com.

Sleepytown Pr., *(978-0-9826344; 978-0-9831738; 978-1-937260)* 1709 Valley Creek Rd., Anniston, AL 36207 USA Tel 256-365-1416
E-mail: artnbooks73@yahoo.com
Web site: http://www.sleepytownpress.com.

Slezak, Will, *(978-1-7325280; 978-1-7368205)* 4820 E. Creek Ridge trail, Reno, NV 89519 USA Tel 775-313-6606
E-mail: willslezak@charter.net.

SLG, *(978-0-615-12907-5)* 128 C Main St., Agawam, MA 01001 USA
E-mail: slg_gallery@yahoo.com
Web site: http://geocities.com/slg_gallery/about.

Slhoetree Publishers, Incorporated *See* **Shoetree Publishers, Inc.**

S.L.Hollister, *(978-1-7328445)* 605 Talcottville Rd. 18, Vernon, CT 06066 USA Tel 860-454-4333
E-mail: s.hollister1@comcast.net
Dist(s): **Ingram Content Group.**

Slice of Lime Publishing, *(978-0-9789475)* 1415 Easy St., New Iberia, LA 70560 USA Tel 337-365-4136; Fax: 337-365-4137
E-mail: jady@sliceoflime.net
Web site: http://www.sliceoflime.net
Dist(s): **Partners Bk. Distributing, Inc.**

Slickcolors INC, *(978-1-7359741; 978-1-959284)* 13820 NE Airport Way, Portland, OR 97251-1158 USA Tel 815-799-4517
E-mail: leonid.tsvyetkov@gmail.com
Web site: aliciaortego.com.

Slim Goodbody Corp., *(978-1-887028; 978-0-9708230)* Orders Addr.: P.O. Box 242, Lincolnville, ME 04850 USA Tel 207-230-0399; Fax: 207-230-0795; Toll Free: 888-484-1100
E-mail: john@slimgoodbody.com
Web site: http://www.slimgoodbody.com
Dist(s): **INscribe Digital**
Independent Pubs. Group.

Slippers for Hannah (hardcover), *(978-0-692-31284-1; 978-0-692-34255-8)* 3650 N 3650 W, Moore, ID 83255 USA Tel 2084064777
E-mail: Littlelostcreations@gmail.com.

Slippery Slope Press *See* **Ideate Prairie**

SLM Bk. Publishing, *(978-0-9830039)* Orders Addr.: 21204 Pontiac Trail, No. 16, South Lyon, MI 48178 USA
E-mail: joanna@slmbookpublishing.com
Web site: http://www.slmbookpublishing.com.

Slow on the Draw Productions, *(978-0-615-48469-3; 978-0-615-74591-6)* 12826 Ironstone Way No. 304, Parker, CO 80134 USA Tel 720-838-5176
E-mail: swpaulding@msn.com
Web site: lifelessonsfromandywink.com.

Slugger International, *(978-1-7359235)* 7105 Pebble Gate Dr, Raleigh, NC 27612-7243 USA Tel 925-353-0789
E-mail: paul@paulrava.com
Web site: www.madalyou.com.

Slugger International, LLC *See* **Slugger International**

Sluser Publishing, *(978-0-578-03599-4; 978-0-578-03634-2; 978-0-578-04034-9; 978-0-578-06031-6; 978-0-578-08065-9; 978-0-578-10299-3; 978-0-578-10318-1; 978-0-578-12746-0;*

978-0-578-12986-0) 324 Stonegate Cir. N., Chambersburg, PA 17201 USA.
Slusser, Jan *See* **RiverCreek Bks., Inc.**
SM Ediciones (ESP) *(978-84-348; 978-84-404; 978-84-398; 978-84-675; 978-84-9107; 978-84-9182; 978-84-398-2663-7; 978-84-398-3219-5; 978-84-398-3531-8; 978-84-398-4146-3; 978-84-398-5547-7; 978-84-398-6213-0; 978-84-404-0085-7; 978-84-404-1546-2) Dist. by* **Continental Bk.**
SM Ediciones (ESP) *(978-84-348; 978-84-404; 978-84-398; 978-84-675; 978-84-9107; 978-84-9182; 978-84-398-2663-7; 978-84-398-3219-5; 978-84-398-3531-8; 978-84-398-4146-3; 978-84-398-5547-7; 978-84-398-6213-0; 978-84-404-0085-7; 978-84-404-1546-2) Dist. by* **AIMS Intl.**
SM Ediciones (ESP) *(978-84-348; 978-84-404; 978-84-398; 978-84-675; 978-84-9107; 978-84-9182; 978-84-398-2663-7; 978-84-398-3219-5; 978-84-398-3531-8; 978-84-398-4146-3; 978-84-398-5547-7; 978-84-398-6213-0; 978-84-404-0085-7; 978-84-404-1546-2) Dist. by* **Mariuccia Iaconi Bk Imports.**
SM Ediciones (ESP) *(978-84-348; 978-84-404; 978-84-398; 978-84-675; 978-84-9107; 978-84-9182; 978-84-398-2663-7; 978-84-398-3219-5; 978-84-398-3531-8; 978-84-398-4146-3; 978-84-398-5547-7; 978-84-398-6213-0; 978-84-404-0085-7; 978-84-404-1546-2) Dist. by* **IBD Ltd.**
SM Ediciones (ESP) *(978-84-348; 978-84-404; 978-84-398; 978-84-675; 978-84-9107; 978-84-9182; 978-84-398-2663-7; 978-84-398-3219-5; 978-84-398-3531-8; 978-84-398-4146-3; 978-84-398-5547-7; 978-84-398-6213-0; 978-84-404-0085-7; 978-84-404-1546-2) Dist. by* **Lectorum Pubns.**
Small Batch Bks., *(978-0-9829758; 978-1-937650; 978-1-951568)* 493 S. Pleasant St., Amherst, MA 01002 USA Tel 413-230-3943
E-mail: fred@smallbatchbooks.com
Web site: www.smallbatchbooks.com
Dist(s): **BookBaby**
Ingram Content Group.
Small Bear Publishing, *(978-0-9801662)* P.O. Box 842, Livingston, MT 59047 USA
E-mail: BarringtonBear@q.com
Web site: http://www.travelswithbarrington.com.
Small Beer Pr., *(978-1-931520; 978-1-61873)* 150 Pleasant St. #306, Easthampton, MA 01027 USA Fax: 413-203-1636; *Imprints*: Big Mouth House (BigMouthHse)
E-mail: info@smallbeerpress.com
Web site: http://www.smallbeerpress.com; http://www.weightlessbooks.com
Dist(s): **Children's Plus, Inc.**
Consortium Bk. Sales & Distribution
MyiLibrary
ebrary, Inc.
Small Fry Beginnings, *(978-0-9651690; 978-1-892703)* Affil. of LightVision Films, Inc., 6625 Hwy. 53 E. Suite No. 410-212, Dawsonville, GA 30534 USA Tel 770-451-7000
E-mail: dennis@smallfrybeginnings.com
Web site: http://www.smallfrybeginnings.com
Dist(s): **Follett School Solutions**
Ingram Entertainment, Inc.
VPD, Inc.
Valley Media, Inc.
Small Fry Productions *See* **Small Fry Beginnings**
Small Group, LLC, The, *(978-0-578-45676-8)* 108 King Sago Ct., Ponte Vedra Beach, FL 32082 USA Tel 843-384-9333
E-mail: briancsmall@gmail.com
Dist(s): **Ingram Content Group.**
Small New York LLC, *(978-0-578-16183-9; 978-0-9963985)* 676 Third Ave., New York, NY 10017 USA.
Small Press Distribution *See* **SPD-Small Pr. Distribution**
Small Pr., The, *(978-1-933651)* Div. of Brown Bks. Publishing Group, 16200 N. Dallay Pkwy., No. 170, Dallas, TX 75248 USA Tel 972-381-0009; Fax: 972-248-4336
Dist(s): **BookBaby**
Open Road Integrated Media, Inc.
Small Publishing, *(978-0-692-22459-5; 978-0-692-30147-0; 978-0-692-33282-5; 978-0-692-35425-4; 978-0-692-40481-2; 978-0-692-48561-3; 978-0-692-59717-0; 978-0-692-70869-9; 978-0-692-72714-0; 978-1-946257)* P.O. Box 800, Belleview, FL 34421 USA Do not confuse with Small Publishing in Monterey, CA
E-mail: smallpublishing1@gmail.com
Web site: http://smallpublishing.wordpress.com; facebook.com/SmallPublishing
Dist(s): **CreateSpace Independent Publishing Platform.**
Small Seed Pr., *(978-0-615-42484-2; 978-0-615-47783-1; 978-0-615-48922-3; 978-0-9895961; 978-0-9996061; 978-0-578-78882-1; 978-1-7373359)* P.O. Box 368, Miranda, CA 95553 USA Tel 707-206-7547
Dist(s): **CreateSpace Independent Publishing Platform.**
Small Waters Publishing, *(978-0-9765621)* 14251 75th Ave. SE, Atwater, MN 56209 USA Tel 320-894-7904; Fax: 320-235-6418
E-mail: markp@lakesideprintingandadvertising.com.
Small Wonder Publishing, *(978-0-9899964)* 130 Boniface Dr., Rochester, NY 14620 USA Tel 585-271-3492
E-mail: hdm@smallwonderpublishing.com.
Small Wonders Enterprises, *(978-0-9741888)* 12210 Fairfax Towne Ctr., PMB No. 901, Fairfax, VA 22033 USA Tel 703-352-0226 Do not confuse with Small Wonders Enterprises in Farmington, NM
E-mail: snickerdoodle@erols.com
Web site: http://www.snickerdoodleforkids.com.
Small World Toys, *(978-0-9774677; 978-0-9776034; 978-0-9795081)* P.O. Box 3620, Culver City, CA 90231-3620 USA
Web site: http://www.smallworldtoys.com.
Smallbag Bks., *(978-0-9761631)* Orders Addr.: 2000 Del Sol, Bowie, MD 20721 USA
E-mail: konaapub@yahoo.com
Web site: http://www.younganddebtfree.com.
SmallHorse Pr. *Imprint of* **Equine Graphics Publishing Group**
Smallwood, Edward, *(978-0-9741282)* 1609 Mountain Ashe Ct., Matthews, NC 28105 USA
Web site: http://www.jfrankles.com.
Smart & Smarter Publishing, *(978-0-9713530)* P.O. Box 1815, Zillah, WA 98953 USA (SAN 255-3104) Tel 877-807-3703 (phone/fax)
E-mail: daviddunham@smartandsmarter.com; services@smartandsmarter.com
Web site: http://www.smartandsmarter.com.
Smart Apple Media *Imprint of* **Black Rabbit Bks.**
Smart Data Processing, Inc., *(978-0-9718439)* 14 Molly Pitcher Dr., Manalapan, NJ 07726 USA Tel 732-598-4027; Fax: 732-409-1364
E-mail: info@smartdataprocessing.com
Web site: http://www.smartdataprocessing.com.
Smart Kids *Imprint of* **Penton Overseas, Inc.**
Smart Kids Publishing *See* **Smart Kidz Media, Inc.**
Smart Kidz Media, Inc., *(978-1-891100; 978-1-939658)* 2460 Hobbit Ln., Fallbrook, CA 92028 USA Tel 760-468-1891
Dist(s): **APG Sales & Distribution Services**
Whitaker Hse.
smart Life Ministries, Inc., The, *(978-0-9741091)* 1649 Springhill St., Chillicothe, MO 64601 USA.
Smart Love Pr., LLC, *(978-0-9838664; 978-1-7330897)* 400 E. Randolph St. Suite 1905, Chicago, IL 60601 USA Tel 312-970-9846; Fax: 312-278-0441
E-mail: smartlovepress@gmail.com; marthahpieper@smartlovepress.com
Web site: http://www.smartlovepress.com; http://www.jillysterribletempertantrums.com; http://www.mommydaddyihadabaddream.com
Dist(s): **Brigham Distributing.**
Smart Picks, Incorporated *See* **Smart Picks, LLC**
Smart Picks, LLC, *(978-0-9764785)*
E-mail: games@smartpicks.com
Smart Poodle Publishing, *(978-0-9800307)* 3436 Pierce St., Hollywood, FL 33021 USA
E-mail: debbie.glade@comcast.net
Web site: http://www.smartpoodlepublishing.com.
Smart Princess Bks. & More Publishing, *(978-0-692-08497-7; 978-0-578-44479-6; 978-0-578-50529-9; 978-1-7357141)* P.O. Box 2184, Davis, CA 95617 USA Tel 202-489-6098
E-mail: john@smartprincess.com
Dist(s): **CreateSpace Independent Publishing Platform.**
Smart Publishing, *(978-0-9761819)* P.O. Box 410894, Chicago, IL 60641 USA Tel 773-616-0267
E-mail: halfbakedsistas@aol.com
Web site: http://www.halfbakedsistas.com.
Smart Smiles Co., The, *(978-0-9722792; 978-0-9723727; 978-0-9762740; 978-0-9763328)* 380 S. Mizner Blvd., No. 1709, Boca Raton, FL 33432 USA Tel 561-347-3075; *Imprints*: Flat Kids (Flat Kids)
Web site: http://www.smartsmilescompany.com.
SmartBook Media, Inc., *(978-1-5105)* 350 5th Ave, 59th Floor, New York, NY 10118 USA Toll Free Fax: 866-449-3445; Toll Free: 866-649-3445
E-mail: linda@weigl.com; samantha.nugent@weigl.com
Web site: http://www.asmartbook.com.
SmartBooks Publishing, *(978-0-578-20283-9)* 29 Banbury Ln, Bloomfield, CT 06002 USA.
SmartCents, Inc., *(978-0-615-13730-8)* 2867 Humboldt Cir., Longmont, CO 80503-2339 USA
E-mail: janine@smartcentsinc.com
Web site: http://www.smartcentsinc.com
Dist(s): **Lulu Pr., Inc.**
Smartee Plate, *(978-0-9861787)* 2909 Woodwardia Dr., Los Angeles, CA 90077 USA Tel 310-474-7661
E-mail: jenng715@hotmail.com.
Smartinbooks, Inc., *(978-0-9761765)* Orders Addr.: P.O. Box 729, Paducah, KY 42002-0729 USA; Edit Addr.: 1441 HC Mathis Dr., Paducah, KY 42001 USA
E-mail: hmartin@paducah.com
Web site: http://www.smartinbooks.com.
Smartink Bks., LLC, *(978-1-932403)* 413 6th Ave., Brooklyn, NY 11215 USA Tel 718-768-3696; Fax: 718-369-0844
E-mail: publisher@smartinkbooks.com
Web site: http://www.smartinkbooks.com
Dist(s): **Hachette Bk. Group**
Ideals Pubns.
Penton Overseas, Inc.
SmartiPantz Publishing, *(978-0-9747563)* P.O. Box 24014, Minneapolis, MN 55424 USA (SAN 256-0720).
SmartLab *Imprint of* **becker&mayer! books**
SmartPop *Imprint of* **BenBella Bks.**
SMARTseeds Co., LLC, The, *(978-0-9790931)* P.O. Box 100028, Cudahy, WI 53110 USA (SAN 852-4068) Tel 414-433-0500
E-mail: carlos@thesmartseedscompany.com; info@thesmartseedscompany.com
Web site: http://www.thesmartseedscompany.com.
Smartypants Bks., *(978-0-9773550)* P.O. Box 1014, Logandale, NV 89021-1014 USA (SAN 257-3423)
Web site: http://www.smartypants-books.com.
Smartypants Publishing, *(978-0-9792897)* Orders Addr.: P.O. Box 1548, Buckley, WA 98321 USA Tel 253-278-6612
E-mail: christa@smartypantspublishing.com
Web site: http://smartypantspublishing.com.
Smashwords, *(978-1-4523; 978-1-4524; 978-1-4580; 978-1-4581; 978-1-4657; 978-1-4658; 978-1-4659; 978-1-4660; 978-1-4661; 978-1-4760; 978-1-4761; 978-1-4762; 978-1-4763; 978-1-4764; 978-1-301; 978-1-310; 978-1-311; 978-1-370; 978-0-463; 978-0-692-04063-8; 978-0-578-41339-6; 978-1-005; 978-0-578-87509-5; 978-0-578-87510-1)* *15951 Gatos Blvd., Suite 16, Los Gatos, CA 95032 USA Tel 408-358-1824; ziya gokalp mah. cimen sk. no:1/1 ikitelli koyu, basaksehir-istanbul, 34306 Tel 90 0538 8939727*
E-mail: bill@smashwords.com
Web site: http://www.smashwords.com
Dist(s): **Lulu Pr., Inc.**
SmatteringsBks., *(978-0-9800130)* P.O. Box 556, Clarence, NY 14031 USA (SAN 854-9931) Tel 716-818-0324
Web site: http://smatteringsbooks.com/books.html.
SMC Pubns., LLC, *(978-0-9729546)* P.O. Box 2684, Branchville, NJ 07826 USA Tel 973-948-7441 (phone/fax) Do not confuse with companies with the same name in Houston, TX, Garden Grove, CA, Corona, CA, West Long Branch, NJ
E-mail: smcpublications@embarqmail.com
Web site: http://www.magi-call.com.
SMC Publishing *See* **SMC Pubns., LLC**
SME Publishing, *(978-1-7360152)* 324 Rockmoor Trail, Marietta, GA 30066 USA Tel 678-951-7951
E-mail: jenn.h.scott@gmail.com
Web site: saltymermaidentertainment.com.
Smeagle the Beagle, *(978-1-7330354)* 339 Lodgepole Ln, Weippe, ID 83553 USA Tel 208-435-4558
E-mail: pkleinsmith@frontier.com.
Smeltzer, Micalea A. LLC, *(978-0-692-67369-0; 978-0-692-70392-2; 978-0-9976880; 978-0-692-83578-4; 979-8-218-06133-3; 979-8-218-06228-6; 979-8-218-06240-8; 979-8-218-10532-7; 979-8-218-10548-8; 979-8-218-10851-9; 979-8-218-10853-3; 979-8-218-15413-4; 979-8-218-16858-2; 979-8-218-16859-9; 979-8-218-17921-2; 979-8-218-17923-6; 979-8-218-18093-5; 979-8-218-18122-2; 979-8-218-18159-8; 979-8-218-20644-4) 306 Bedford Pl., Stephens City, VA 22655 USA Tel 540-931-4600*
E-mail: msmeltzer9793@gmail.com.
Smethwick Publishing LLC *See* **Oliver Pr. LLC**
Smile Time Publishing, *(978-0-9785961)* P.O. Box B, Del Mar, CA 92014 USA
E-mail: ps@peterstrunk.com
Web site: http://www.smile-time.com.
Smile-a-Lot, LLP, *(978-0-9785132)* 1050 Walnut St. #201, Boulder, CO 80302 USA Tel 303-443-2006; Fax: 303-443-9475; *Imprints*: Smiletown Books (Smiletown Bks)
E-mail: chris@smiletownbooks.com
Web site: http://smiletownbooks.com.
SmileInOut, *(978-0-578-68084-2; 978-0-578-77639-2; 978-1-7379522)* 9900 McNeil Dr., Austin, TX 78750 USA Tel 337-274-1370
E-mail: Rj.jackson05@gmail.com.
SMiles Productions (SMP), LLC, *(978-0-9768456)* 14241 NE Woodinville-Duvall Rd., Woodinville, WA 98072 USA Tel 425-481-8817; Fax: 425-481-8179
E-mail: language@smilesprod.com
Web site: http://www.smilesprod.com.
Smiletown Bks. *Imprint of* **Smile-a-Lot, LLP**
Smiley Co., *(978-0-9629001)* 401 Anglin St., Smiley, TX 78159-0099 USA (SAN 297-4045) Tel 830-587-6623; Fax: 830-587-6113; Toll Free: 800-584-3655
E-mail: npattesonsmiley@the-cia.net.
Smiley Originals *See* **Smiley Co.**
Smiley, Rhonda, *(978-0-9984492)* 1632 Royal Blvd, Glendale, CA 91207 USA Tel 818-545-8113
E-mail: rjsmiley@aol.com.
Smith & Assocs., *(978-0-9790817)* 70 Goodwin Cir., Hartford, CT 06105 USA (SAN 852-3886) Tel 860-543-0279; Fax: 860-586-8718
Web site: http://www.morningdovepress.com
Dist(s): **Connecticut River Pr.**
Smith & Daniel, *(978-0-9630463; 978-1-889668)* P.O. Box 8097, Jacksonville, FL 32239-0097 USA Toll Free: 800-330-1325.
Smith & Kraus Pubs., Inc., *(978-0-9622722; 978-1-57525; 978-1-880399; 978-1-936232; 978-1-937738; 978-1-943511; 978-1-970012; 978-1-68476)* Orders Addr.: P.O. Box 127, Lyme, NH 03768 USA (SAN 255-1454) Tel 603-643-6431; Toll Free: 877-866-8680; Edit Addr.: P.O. Box 564, Hanover, NH 03755 USA
E-mail: marisasmithkraus@gmail.com; boda@sover.net
Web site: http://www.smithandkraus.com.
Smith, Andrea Joy, *(978-0-9764396)* 2447 Mission Ave, Suite B, Carmichael, CA 95608 USA
E-mail: smithfamdent@aol.com
Web site: http://smileagainnow.com; http://inthechairwithdrsmith.com.
Smith, Barbara Maxine, *(978-0-578-11939-7; 978-0-615-85722-0)* 21103 Gary Dr., Apt 114, Castro Valley, CA 94546 USA.
Smith, Bill O., *(978-0-615-56972-7; 978-0-9895238)* 8489 Timbers Trail, Traverse City, MI 49685 USA Tel 313-515-4328
E-mail: bill@billosmith.com.
Smith, Brenda J. Few *See* **Tall Through Bks.**
Smith, C. Brandt, *(978-0-9768020)* 1910 Scenic Rd., Jonesboro, AR 72401-0220 USA Tel 870-933-1908
E-mail: brandt@walnutstreetbaptist.org.
Smith, Charmain, *(978-0-615-13989-0)* 1197 Eucalyptus Dr., El Cajon, CA 92020 USA
Dist(s): **Lulu Pr., Inc.**
Smith, David, *(978-0-692-97007-2; 978-0-692-15759-6)* 1025 Oakwood St. SE, North Canton, OH 44720 USA Tel 330-966-9734
E-mail: davidsmith0303@yahoo.com
Dist(s): **CreateSpace Independent Publishing Platform.**
Smith, Deanna *See* **Annade Publishing**
Smith, Debra, *(978-0-9747754)* 1934 Donna Dr., Coupeville, WA 98239 USA.
Smith, Donella, *(978-0-578-42129-2; 978-0-578-48347-4; 978-0-578-55940-7; 978-0-578-64810-1; 978-0-578-80185-8; 978-0-578-30291-1; 979-8-218-27963-9)* 474 Leaflet Ives Dr., Lawrenceville, GA 30045 USA Tel 404-438-7546
E-mail: msdonellas@yahoo.com
Dist(s): **Ingram Content Group.**
Smith, Ernest, *(978-0-9729154)* Orders Addr.: 3155 Sharpe Ave. Apt. 304, Memphis, TN 38111-3784 USA
E-mail: ernest725@Hotmail.com.
Smith, Florence B. *See* **Prickly Pr.**
Smith, George Publishing, *(978-0-9740434)* Orders Addr.: 11 Amberwinds Ct., Lakewood, NJ 08701 USA (SAN 255-3716)
E-mail: customer_support@georgesmithpublishing.com
Web site: http://www.georgesmithpublishing.com
Dist(s): **Mountain Bk. Co.**
Smith, Gibbs Publisher *See* **Gibbs Smith, Publisher**
Smith Island Foundation, *(978-0-9754170)* 44108 Bristow Cir., Ashburn, VA 20147 USA Tel 703-729-4462 Phone/Fax
E-mail: books@smithislandfoundation.org; heather@pneumabooks.com
Web site: http://www.smithislandfoundation.org.
Smith, Jennifer W. *See* **Apple House Publishing**
Smith, Joseph L., *(978-0-9754985)* 38118 Village 38, Camarillo, CA 93012 USA
E-mail: cayusekid@earthlink.net.
Smith, Kasper, *(978-0-9744519)* 4251 Fischer, Detroit, MI 48214 USA Tel 313-922-1728
E-mail: pastorsmith@dominionintl.org
Web site: http://www.dominionintl.org.
Smith, Keith Bks., *(978-0-9637682; 978-0-9740764)* 1115 E. Main St., Suite 219, Box 8, Rochester, NY 14609 USA Tel 585-473-6776; Fax: 585-482-2496
E-mail: keith@keithsmithbooks.com
Web site: http://www.keithsmithbooks.com.
Smith Kerr Assocs., *(978-0-9786899; 978-0-9830622; 978-0-692-33644-1)* 1 Government St No. 1, Kittery, ME 03904 USA Tel 207-703-2314; Fax: 207-703-2313; *Imprints*: Seapoint Books ()
E-mail: bizbks@aol.com
Dist(s): **National Bk. Network.**
smith, kia, *(978-0-692-85409-9)* 2202 paso rello, houston, TX 77077 USA Tel 281-995-0935
E-mail: janeenisfly@yahoo.com.
Smith Knutson Publishing, *(978-0-692-11869-6; 978-0-692-11877-1; 978-0-578-23099-3; 978-1-7367614)* 15414 McClamden Dr., Fishers, IN 46040 USA
Dist(s): **Ingram Content Group.**
Smith, Lindsay, *(978-0-692-05746-9; 978-0-692-05747-6)* 1143 3rd St NE, Washington, DC 20002 USA Tel 202-286-4999
E-mail: bohemienne@mac.com
Dist(s): **Ingram Content Group.**
Smith, Mason, *(978-0-692-02010-4)* 107 Southland Dr., Richmond, KY 40475-2413 USA Tel 859-582-5960
E-mail: mason.smith@eku.edu.
Smith, Melissa, *(978-0-578-24961-2; 978-0-578-97566-5)* 548 52nd St., #2B, Brooklyn, NY 11220 USA.
Smith, Michael *See* **East West Discovery Pr.**
Smith, Mildred C., *(978-0-9778641; 978-0-692-60783-1)* 4200 Cathedral Ave, NW, Apt. 610, Washington, DC 20016 USA Tel 202-363-5352
E-mail: mcs29@georgetown.edu.
Smith Novelty Co., Inc., *(978-0-938765; 978-1-59099; 978-1-934954)* Div. of Smith News Co., Inc., 460 Ninth St., San Francisco, CA 94103-4478 USA (SAN 216-2326) Tel 415-861-4900; Fax: 415-861-5683
E-mail: ken@smithnovelty.com; matt@smithnovelty.com
Web site: http://www.smithnovelty.com.
Smith, Peter Pub., Inc., *(978-0-8446)* Five Lexington Ave., Magnolia, MA 01930 USA (SAN 206-8885) Tel 978-525-3562; Fax: 978-525-3674.
Smith, Ronald *See* **Plenus Gratia Pubns.**
Smith, Ronald J. Sr., *(978-0-9749390)* JAYNORS Publishing, LLC, 4461 S. Four Mile Run Dr., Arlington, VA 22204-3640 USA Tel 571-212-1734
E-mail: Jaynors@outlook.com
Dist(s): **JAYNORS Publishing, LLC.**
Smith, S. Pubns., *(978-0-9769320)* P.O. Box 122, Severna Park, MD 21146 USA Tel 410-271-0837; Fax: 410-544-0059
E-mail: stew@stewsmith.com
Web site: http://www.stewsmith.com.
Smith, Sharon, *(978-0-9817615)* 13611 SW 285th Terr., Homestead, FL 33033 USA Tel 786-317-0267
E-mail: dexavior1@msn.com.
Smith Show Media Group, *(978-1-952524)* 515 emily, albany, GA 31701 USA Tel 229-439-2562
E-mail: kdmusic101@yahoo.com.
Smith, Tyjauna, *(978-0-9760112)* P.O. Box 2230 Misty Woods Rd., Lake Cormorant, MS 38641 USA
E-mail: tyjauna@bellsouth.net
Web site: http://www.authorsden.com/tyjaunalsmith.
Smith, Viveca Publishing, *(978-0-9740551; 978-1-7327568)* 550 N CENTRAL EXPY, McKinney, TX 75070-9998 USA Tel 214-793-0089; Fax: 214-261-2264
E-mail: vsp@vivecasmithpublishing.com
Web site: http://www.vivecasmithpublishing.com
Dist(s): **BookBaby**
ebrary, Inc.
Smithcraft Pr., *(978-0-9793935; 978-1-62927)* 1718 Ashcroft St., NW, Palm Bay, FL 32907-9474 USA
E-mail: smithcraftpress@gmail.com; questions@smithcraftpress.info; craig@smithcraft.org.
Smithfield Capital Corp., *(978-0-9764670)* 219 S. D. St., Hamilton, OH 45013 USA
E-mail: smithfieldcap@msn.com.
Smithfield Press *See* **Princeton Health Pr.**
Smithsonian Bks. *Imprint of* **Smithsonian Institution Scholarly Pr.**
†**Smithsonian Bks.,** *(978-0-87474; 978-1-56098; 978-1-58834)* Div. of Smithsonian Institution, Orders Addr.: 22883 Quicksilver Dr., Dulles, VA 20166 USA (SAN 253-3383); Edit Addr.: 600 Maryland Ave. SW,

Suite 6001, Washington, DC 20024 USA (SAN 206-8044)
E-mail: hugginsj2@si.edu
Web site: http://www.smithsonianbooks.com
Dist(s): **Children's Plus, Inc.**
CreateSpace Independent Publishing Platform
Ebsco Publishing
MyiLibrary
Penguin Random Hse. Distribution
Penguin Random Hse. LLC
Random Hse., Inc.
Rowman & Littlefield Publishers, Inc.
Wittenborn Art Bks.; *CIP.*

Smithsonian Institution Press *See* **Smithsonian Bks.**

Smithsonian Institution Scholarly Pr., *(978-0-9788460; 978-1-935623; 978-1-944466; 978-0-9992662; 978-0-9992663)* Orders Addr.: P.O. Box 37012, MRC 957, Washington, DC 20013 USA Tel 202-633-3017; Fax: 202-633-3017; *Imprints:* Smithsonian Books (SmithsonBks)
E-mail: schol.press@si.edu
Web site: http://www.scholarlypress.si.edu/
Dist(s): **MyiLibrary**
National Bk. Network
Penguin Random Hse. Distribution
Penguin Random Hse. LLC
Random Hse., Inc.
Rowman & Littlefield Publishers, Inc.

Smithsonian National Museum of the American Indian, *(978-0-9719163; 978-1-933565)* MRC 590 PO Box 37012, Washington, DC 20013-7012 USA; 4th St. & Independence Ave., SW, Washington, DC 20024
E-mail: nmai-pubs@si.edu
Web site: http://www.americanindian.si.edu
Dist(s): **Consortium Bk. Sales & Distribution**
D.A.P./Distributed Art Pubs.
Fulcrum Publishing.

Smithsonian Science Education Ctr. (SSEC), *(978-1-933008; 978-0-9985286; 978-0-9985287; 978-1-7324198; 978-1-7324199; 978-1-7324437; 978-1-7324438; 978-1-7357196; 978-1-7357197; 978-1-7368851; 978-1-7377876; 979-8-9855112; 979-8-9873364; 979-8-9873365)* 901 D St. SW, Suite 704B, Washington, DC 20024 USA Tel 202-633-2992; *Imprints:* Science and Technology Concepts (STC) (Sci & Tech)
E-mail: marohnp@si.edu
Web site: http://www.nsrconline.org; http://carolinacurriculum.com
Dist(s): **Carolina Biological Supply Co.**

SML Bks., *(978-0-578-05467-4)* 8149 calle Cataolonia, Carlsbad, CA 92009 USA
E-mail: mat@resultssource.com.

Smocking Arts Guild of America, *(978-0-9743959)* P.O. Box 214, Hathorne, MA 01937-0214 USA Tel 800-520-3101; Fax: 978-777-4329; *Imprints:* SAGA Press (SAGA Pr)
E-mail: sagahq@smocking.org
Web site: http://www.smocing.org.

Smokestack Bks. (GBR) *(978-0-9548691; 978-0-9551061; 978-0-9554028; 978-0-9575747; 978-0-9927409; 978-0-9560341; 978-0-9564175; 978-0-9568144; 978-0-9929581; 978-0-9571722) Dist. by* **Dufour.**

Smooth Sailing Press, LLC *See* **Mystic Harbor Pr., LLC**

Smore Bks., *(978-1-7329969)* 2880 Olympic View dr, Chino hills, CA 91709 USA Tel 626-264-2410; Fax: 626-264-2410
E-mail: hyerin.kang@gmail.com.

Smorgasbord Pubns., *(978-1-936954)* 22529 Downing St., Moreno Valley, CA 92553 USA
E-mail: juanita@juanitaray.com.

SMPR, *(978-0-9767898)* 4800 S. Westshore Blvd., Suite 411, Tampa, FL 33611 USA Tel 813-831-8206 (phone/fax); Toll Free Fax: 866-958-1323 (phone/fax)
E-mail: sonja.moffett@smpr.info
Web site: http://www.smpr.info.

†**Smyth & Helwys Publishing, Inc.,** *(978-0-9628455; 978-1-57312; 978-1-880837; 978-1-64173)* 6316 Peake Rd., Macon, GA 31210-3960 USA (SAN 298-7732) Tel 478-757-0564; Fax: 478-757-1305; Toll Free: 800-747-3016
E-mail: bowker@helwys.com
Web site: http://www.helwys.com
Dist(s): **CreateSpace Independent Publishing Platform**; *CIP.*

Snader Publishing Co., *(978-1-945871)* 218 CHESTNUT, HALSTEAD, KS 67056 USA Tel 316-217-4223
E-mail: billbush@usa.com
Web site: snaderpublishing.com.

Snake Country Publishing, *(978-0-9635828)* 16748 W. Linden St., Caldwell, ID 83607-9270 USA Tel 208-459-9233
E-mail: snakecountry@mindspring.com
Dist(s): **Caxton Pr.**

Snake Goddess Bks., *(978-0-9744910)* 11431/2 Gladys Ave., Long Beach, CA 90804 USA.

Snaptail Pr. *Imprint of* **Images Unlimited Publishing**

Snedecor, Cori, *(978-0-9973642)* 27 Glenhaven Cir., Saco, ME 04072 USA Tel 650-483-9655
E-mail: cori.snedecor@gmail.com.

Snelsonbks.com, *(978-0-9723935)* 355 N. Diamond Ave., Canon City, CO 81212 USA
E-mail: bs@ris.net
Web site: http://www.snelsonbooks.com.

Snipperdoomers Pr. *Imprint of* **Snipperdoomers Pr.**

Snipperdoomers Pr., *(978-0-578-77317-9; 978-1-7359496; 978-1-7377232; 979-8-9884201; 979-8-9891417)* 388 Solitaire Path, New Braunfels, TX 78130 USA Tel 830-252-2700; *Imprints:* Snipperdoomers Press (MYID_O_SNIPPER)
E-mail: therealjdbroyhill@gmail.com
Web site: www.authorjdbroyhill.com.

SNJ Enterprises, *(978-0-578-51015-6; 978-0-578-99228-0)* 4335 N. 28th St., Milwaukee, WI 53216 USA Tel 414-520-4959
E-mail: snjulie80@gmail.com
Dist(s): **Ingram Content Group.**

SNL Publishing, *(978-0-615-48221-7; 978-0-9848368)* 9 Spring Hill Ave., Norwalk, CT 06850 USA Tel 914-671-2252
E-mail: davidalara@aol.com; snlpublishing@aol.com.

Snodgrass, Ruth M., *(978-0-9754867)* 160 Polaris Dr., Dover, OH 44622 USA.

Snojoy Publishing, *(978-0-9743913)* 4509 14th St., Greeley, CO 80634 USA
E-mail: snojoy1@hotmail.com; gnojoy1@hotmail.com.

Snow In Sarasota Publishing, *(978-0-9663335; 978-0-9824611; 978-0-9830362; 978-0-9837685; 978-0-9893840; 978-0-9862979; 978-0-9977126; 978-0-9997415; 978-1-7333492)* 5170 Central Sarasota Pkwy., No.309, Sarasota, FL 34238 USA Tel 941-923-9201; Fax: 941-926-8739
E-mail: sarasota58@aol.com
Web site: http://www.snowinsarasota.com
Dist(s): **Follett School Solutions**
MyiLibrary
ebrary, Inc.

Snow Leopard Publishing, *(978-1-944361)* 171 Durham Rd., Dover, NH 03820 USA (SAN 990-1183) Tel 603-343-8107
E-mail: info@snowleopardpublishing.com
Web site: SnowLeopardPublishing.com.

Snow Lion Publications, Inc, *Imprint of* **Shambhala Pubns., Inc.**

Snow Publishing, *(978-0-692-83769-6; 978-0-692-08848-7; 978-0-578-92512-7)* 5641 High Tor Hill, Columbia, MD 21045 USA Tel 443-812-4240
E-mail: abby.snow@comcast.net; abby.snow@comcast.net; abby.snow@comcast.net
Web site: www.abbysnow.org
Dist(s): **CreateSpace Independent Publishing Platform.**

Snow Tree Bks., *(978-0-9749006)* Orders Addr.: P.O. Box 546, Peabody, MA 01960-7564 USA (SAN 255-965X) Tel 781-592-9866
E-mail: info@snowtreebooks.com
Web site: http://snowtreebooks.com.

Snowbound Bks., *(978-0-9722570)* Orders Addr.: P.O. Box 281327, Lamoille, NV 89828 USA; Edit Addr.: 1291 Country Ln., Lamoille, NV 89828 USA.

Snowbound Pr., Inc., *(978-1-932362)* P.O. Box 698, Littleton, CO 80160-0698 USA Tel 303-347-2869; Fax: 303-386-3232
E-mail: info@snowboundpress.com
Web site: http://www.snowboundpress.com
Dist(s): **Quality Bks., Inc.**

Snowman Learning Center, The, *(978-0-9674666)* 6 Carver St., Plymouth, MA 02360-3301 USA Tel 508-746-5993; Fax: 508-746-8097
E-mail: S.Snowmanph.d@worldnet.att.net.

Snowman Studios, Inc., *(978-0-9834244)* 25599 E. Middle Lake Rd., Canton, IL 61520 USA Tel 309-647-0569
E-mail: contact@snowmanstudios.com
Web site: snowmanstudios.com.

Snowpuppy, *(978-0-692-02600-7; 978-0-692-30007-7; 978-0-9963244; 979-8-9866562)* 494 riverside Dr., Burley, ID 83318 USA Tel 208 219 9056
Dist(s): **CreateSpace Independent Publishing Platform.**

Snowy Day Distribution & Publishing, A, *(978-0-9844681; 978-1-936615)* P.O. Box 2014, Merrimack, NH 03054 USA Tel 603-493-2276
E-mail: salspiritosr@asnowyday.com
Web site: http://www.asnowyday.com.

Snowy Night Pub., *(978-0-9860324)* 44240 Riverview Ridge Dr., Clinton Township, MI 48038 USA
E-mail: yroehler@bookpublishing.com.

Snowy Plains, *(978-0-9791367)* 270 Flodin Rd., Gwinn, MI 49841 USA
E-mail: jwsnowyplains@yahoo.com.

Snowy Wings Publishing, *(978-1-946202; 978-1-948661; 978-1-952667; 978-1-958051)* P.O. Box 1035, Turner, OR 97392 USA
E-mail: lyssa.chiavari@gmail.com.

Snuggle Up Bks., *(978-0-9655530)* 3145 Claremore Ave., Long Beach, CA 90808-4421 USA
E-mail: judybelshe@aol.com.

SnuggleBugzzz Pr., *(978-0-615-38169-5)* 21328 Independence Ave., Lakeville, MN 55044 USA Tel 612-910-0190; Fax: 952-985-4151
E-mail: kathylucilejohnson@att.net
Web site: http://www.snugglebugzzz.com
Dist(s): **West.**

Snyder Enterprises LLC, *(978-0-692-99640-9; 978-0-692-99661-4; 978-0-692-99918-9)* 468 N. Loafer Dr., Elk Ridge, UT 84651 USA Tel 801-687-0563
E-mail: amberley.snyder@hotmail.com
Dist(s): **Ingram Content Group.**

Snyder, Maria V., *(978-1-946381)* 200 Foreman Rd., Elizabethtown, PA 17022 USA Tel 717-475-8036
E-mail: mariavsnyder@gmail.com.

Snyder, Stacy, *(978-0-9600041)* P.O. Box 1411, Rancho Santa Fe, CA 92067 USA
E-mail: stacysnyder@mac.com; anne@wagdesign.be.

Snyder, Ted, *(978-0-9965019)* 8100 Valley Creek Dr., Choctaw, OK 73020 USA Tel 405-590-0794
E-mail: tedsnyder@reagan.com.

Snyder, Vicki, *(978-0-9773187)* 4349 Cimarron Ct., NW, Rochester, MN 55901 USA
E-mail: cctraining@prodigy.net.

Snyder-Winston Pr., *(978-0-9752749)* 23679 Calabasas Rd., No. 186, Calabasas, CA 91302 USA Tel 818-876-0188; Fax: 818-876-0133
E-mail: tedafed@earthlink.net
Web site: http://www.midaskids.com.

SNZ Publishing, *(978-0-9758815)* P.O. Box 32190, Cincinnati, OH 45232 USA (SAN 256-1255)
E-mail: doug@snzpublishing.com
Web site: http://www.snzpublishing.com.

So Pretty In Pink LLC *See* **King Production, A**

So Simple Learning, *(978-0-9772158)* 12463 Rancho Bernardo Rd., PMB 253, San Diego, CA 92128 USA Tel 858-530-5055
E-mail: info@sosimplelearning.com
Web site: http://www.sosimplelearning.com.

So So Little Reads, Inc., *(978-1-947302)* P.O. Box 136, New York, NY 10272 USA Tel 917-512-1706
E-mail: sosolittlereads@gmail.com
Web site: www.sosolittlereads.com.

So Squeaky LLC *See* **J.Y. Johnson-Garcia**

SOAR Pr., *(978-1-7356719)* 7431 E. State St. No. 259, Rockford, IL 61108 USA Tel 815-979-9038
E-mail: deannalc20@gmail.com.

Soar Publishing, LLC, *(978-0-9721142; 978-0-9825450; 978-0-9838220; 978-0-9888650; 978-0-9962052; 978-0-9992960; 978-1-7321782; 978-1-950269)* 16 Austree Ct., Columbia, SC 29229-7581 USA (SAN 255-4437) Tel 803-699-0633 phone; Fax: 803-699-0634 (phone/fax)
E-mail: smithser@bellsouth.net; smithser1@bellsouth.net
Web site: http://www.soarpublishing.com; http://www.titlewave.com; http://titletales.com
Dist(s): **Follett School Solutions.**

Soaring Sparrow Pr., *(978-1-891262)* 11795 SW Crater Loop, Beaverton, OR 97008 USA Tel 503-644-5960
E-mail: sparrowman@earthlink.net
Web site: www.marvinmallard.com.

Soccer Poet LLC, *(978-0-9896977)* 245 Falling Shoals Dr., Athens, GA 30605 USA Tel 706-201-3858
E-mail: soccerpoet@gmail.com
Web site: www.soccerpoet.com.

Soccertowns LLC *See* **LNG LLC**

Social Motion Publishing *Imprint of* **Social Motion Publishing**

Social Motion Publishing, *(978-0-9704379; 978-0-9968906; 978-0-578-41752-3)* Orders Addr.: P.O. Box 5301, Herndon, VA 20172-5301 USA; Edit Addr.: P.O. Box 5301, Herndon, VA 20172-5301 USA; *Imprints:* Social Motion Publishing (SocialMotion)
E-mail: andrew@socialmotionpublishing.com
Web site: http://www.JulyPublishing.com; http://www.SocialMotionPublishing.com.

Social Skill Builder, Inc., *(978-0-9819585)* P.O. Box 2430, Leesburg, VA 20177 USA.

Social Studies Schl. Service, *(978-1-56004; 978-1-57596)* Orders Addr.: 10200 Jefferson Blvd., P.O. Box 802, Culver City, CA 90232-0802 USA (SAN 168-9592) Tel 310-839-2436; Fax: 310-839-2249; Toll Free: 800-421-4246
E-mail: access@socialstudies.com
Web site: http://socialstudies.com
Dist(s): **Follett School Solutions.**

Social Success Central, LLC *Imprint of* **How to Make & Keep Friends, LLC**

Social-Emotional Learning Bks., *(978-0-692-93805-8; 979-8-9852939)* P.O. Box 184, Tolleson, AZ 85353 USA Tel 623-295-2806
E-mail: info@shymonsterstory.com.

Socially Smarter, *(978-1-930640)* 349 N. Detroit St., Los Angeles, CA 90036 USA Tel 323-549-0279
E-mail: info@sociallysmarter.com
Web site: sociallysmarter.com
Dist(s): **Feldheim Pubs.**

Sociedad de San Pablo (COL) *(978-958-607) Dist. by* **St Pauls Alba.**

Sociedad de San Pablo (ESP) *Dist. by* **St Pauls Alba.**

Sociedad General Espanola de Libreria (ESP) *(978-84-7143; 978-84-9778) Dist. by* **Distribks Inc.**

Sociedad General Espanola de Libreria (ESP) *(978-84-7143; 978-84-9778) Dist. by* **Continental Bk.**

Society for Developmental Education *See* **Staff Development for Educators**

Society For The Understanding Of Early Child Development, *(978-0-9762509)* 39741 Lynn St., Canton, MI 48187 USA (SAN 256-260X) Tel 734-416-0480; Fax: 734-459-5280
E-mail: rsawhney@infotreeservice.com.

Society for Visual Education, Incorporated *See* **S V E & Churchill Media**

Society of Automotive Engineers, Incorporated *See* **SAE Intl.**

Society of Young Inklings, *(978-0-615-42953-3; 978-0-9839568; 978-0-9910031; 978-0-9981849; 978-1-956380)* 16 Muller Pl., San Jose, CA 95126 USA Tel 650-861-0508
E-mail: naomi@younginklings.org; info@younginklings.org
Web site: www.younginklings.org
Dist(s): **Lulu Pr., Inc.**

Socrates Solutions Incorporated, *(978-0-692-00121-9; 978-0-615-52175-6; 978-0-9905501)* P.O. Box 18457, San Jose, CA 95158 USA Tel 408-448-4018
E-mail: joemessineo@yahoo.com.

Sofija Zlatanova, *(978-1-7338618)* 6 Clinton St., Cambridge, MA 02139 USA Tel 857-504-5591
E-mail: sofija.zlatanov@gmail.com.

Soft Saints, Inc., *(978-0-9769519)* 5753-G Santa Ana Canyon Rd., No. 378, Anaheim Hills, CA 92807 USA Tel 714-505-3127; Fax: 714-838-5857
E-mail: teri@softsaints.com
Web site: http://www.softsaints.com.

Soft Skull Pr. *Imprint of* **Counterpoint Pr.**

Softlight Pr. LLC, *(978-0-9983623)* P.O. Box 242, Wilton, CT 06897 USA Tel 203-554-8509
E-mail: abbymsmith@icloud.com.

SoftPlay, Inc., *(978-1-931312; 978-1-59292)* 3535 W. Peterson Ave., Chicago, IL 60659 USA (SAN 858-4982) Tel 773-509-0707; Fax: 773-509-0404
E-mail: sales@softplayforkids.com
Web site: http://www.softplayforkids.com.

SoGo Creation, *(978-0-9852052; 978-1-941006; 978-1-944425)* 6830 Via Marinero, Carlsbad, CA 92009 USA Tel 760-710-7144
E-mail: sogocreation@yahoo.com.

Soho Crime *Imprint of* **Soho Pr., Inc.**

Soho Pr., Inc., *(978-0-939149; 978-1-56947; 978-1-61695; 978-1-64129)* 853 Broadway Ste. 1402, New York, NY 10003 USA (SAN 662-5088) Tel 212-260-1900; Fax: 212-260-1902; *Imprints:* Soho Crime (Soho Crime); Soho Teen (Soho Teen)
E-mail: soho@sohopress.com
Web site: http://www.sohopress.com
Dist(s): **Children's Plus, Inc.**
MyiLibrary
Open Road Integrated Media, Inc.
Penguin Random Hse. Distribution
Penguin Random Hse. LLC
Random Hse., Inc.

Soho Publishing Company *See* **Sixth&Spring Bks.**

Soho Teen *Imprint of* **Soho Pr., Inc.**

Soil Science Society of America *See* **ASA-CSSA-SSSA**

SoJam Pr., *(978-0-9761477)* P.O. Box 25163, Woodbury, MN 55125-9998 USA (SAN 256-2359)
E-mail: sojam@comcast.net
Web site: http://www.sojampress.com.

Sojka, Allison, *(978-1-7361403)* 7319 S. 97th Cir., La Vista, NE 68128 USA Tel 402-699-5457
E-mail: LapisJayPress@gmail.com.

Sojourner Publishing, Inc., *(978-0-9701726; 978-0-9773156; 978-0-9824741)* Orders Addr.: 1208 Chilmark Av, Wake Forest, NC 27587 USA; Edit Addr.: 1208 Chilmark Ave., Wake Forest, NC 27587 USA Do not confuse with companies with the same name in Arlington, WA, Clarkston, MI
E-mail: wandam123@yahoo.com
Web site: http://www.thepaperjourney.com.

Sojourner Stories, *(978-0-9896660)* 4225 Piedmont Mesa Rd., Claremont, CA 91711 USA Tel 562-305-9119
E-mail: sojournerstories@gmail.com.

Sol de Oro Pubns., *(978-0-9754261)* 1004 S. Quinn Ct., Gilbert, AZ 85296-8818 USA Tel 480-892-0582
E-mail: SoldeOroPublications@yahoo.com
Web site: http://www.SoldeOroPublications.50megs.com.

Solar Publishing LLC, *(978-0-9785326)* P.O. Box 2116, Ellicott City, MD 21041 USA (SAN 850-8089) Tel 410-493-1872
E-mail: robyn@solarpub.com
Web site: http://www.solarpub.com
Dist(s): **BookBaby.**

Sole Bks., *(978-0-9844257; 978-1-938591)* P.O. Box 10445, Beverly Hills, CA 90213 USA Tel 424-283-4299
E-mail: yitzhak@wildsoccer.com; info@wildsoccer.com; sales@solebooks.com; taly@wildsoccer.com
Web site: http://www.wildsoccerbunch.com; http://www.solebooks.com.

Solebury Press *See* **Thompson Mill Pr.**

Solel Pubns., *(978-0-9748332)* 309 Concord Ave., Oceanside, NY 11572 USA Tel 516-678-9778.

Solemn Word Publishing *See* **Power In Words Publishing**

Soler, Michael, *(978-0-9795469)* 74 Sashington Heights Rd., Washington, NH 03280 USA (SAN 853-6996).

Solibros, *(978-0-9755945)* 2215 Peachtree N. Ct., Atlanta, GA 30338 USA
Web site: http://www.solibros.com.

Solid Ground Christian Bks., *(978-0-9710169; 978-1-932474; 978-1-59925)* Orders Addr.: P.O. Box 660132, Vestavia Hills, AL 35266 USA Tel 205-443-0311; Fax: 775-822-5917; Toll Free: 877-666-9469; Edit Addr.: 715 Oak Grove Rd., Birmingham, AL 35209-6503 USA
E-mail: solid-ground-books@juno.com; solid_ground_books@yahoo.com; sgcbclassics@juno.com; sgcb@charter.net
Web site: http://www.solid-ground-books.com.

Solid Rock Bks. *Imprint of* **Trumpet In Zion Publishing**

Solid Rock Publishing *See* **Trumpet In Zion Publishing**

SolidA, Inc., *(978-0-9677328)* 9339 Paradise Rd., Kewaskum, WI 53040 USA Tel 262-692-9609
E-mail: deanne@solida.net
Web site: http://www.solida.net.

Solitude Pr., *(978-1-928874)* 212 Brooks St., Williamsburg, VA 23185 USA Tel 757-564-1365
E-mail: zander67@cox.net.

Soliz, Jocelyn, *(978-1-7346844; 978-0-578-81237-3; 979-8-9885381)* 2001 Boxwood Path, Round Rock, TX 78664 USA Tel 254-316-2514
E-mail: jocsoliz@gmail.com
Web site: inspiredandrewired.com.

Soloman, Debra, *(978-0-578-20706-3)* 3814 N. 54th Ave., Omaha, NE 68104 USA.

Solomon & Makeda Publishing, *(978-0-9973104; 978-0-9987233; 978-1-7347318)* 914 Poplar Ln., Williamstown, NJ 08094 USA Tel 609-334-0643
E-mail: purityinstrength@gmail.com.

Solomon Schechter Day Schl. of Greater Boston, *(978-0-9836623)* 60 Stein Cir., Newton, MA 02459 USA Tel 617-964-7765
E-mail: amy.bardack@ssdsboston.org
Web site: www.ssdsboston.org.

Solomon's Bks., *(978-0-9763871; 978-0-9827949; 978-0-9838687; 978-0-615-67340-0)* 1100 Misty Meadows Way, Hampton, GA 30228 USA Tel 470-246-8075
E-mail: mrjquillings@gmail.com
Web site: solomonsbooks.org.

Solon Ctr. for Research & Publishing, *(978-1-882190; 978-1-959112)* Solon Center for Research and Publishing, Orders Addr.: 8 Brook St., Solon, ME 04979 USA (SAN 858-8902); Edit Addr.: 8 Brook St., Solon, ME 04979 USA
E-mail: paul@polarbearandco.com; solon@tds.net
Web site: http://www.polarbearandco.com; http://www.polarbearandco.org; https://soloncenter.org/; https://galleryfukurou.com/.

Solorzano, Laurel, *(978-1-7373974; 979-8-9884034)* 2712 Hope Diamond Ct, Raleigh, NC 27610-5996 USA Tel 919-710-7794
E-mail: laurelsolorzano@gmail.com
Web site: www.laurelsolorzano.com.

Solovisions *Imprint of* **Comic Library International**

Solsidan Hse., *(978-0-9741620)* Orders Addr.: 104 7th St., Colorado Springs, CO 80906 USA; Edit Addr.: 475 Sunnyside Ave., Eugene, OR 97404 USA
E-mail: solsidanhouse@yahoo.com
Web site: http://www.solsidanhouse.com.

Solution Hole Pr., *(978-0-9967031; 978-0-9981712; 978-1-954267)* 7450 S.W. 47 Ct., Miami, FL 33143 USA Tel 305-661-8401
E-mail: ricoy@bellsouth.net
Web site: solutionholepress.com.

Solutionary Stories Pr., *(978-0-692-79987-1)* 3761 Portland Ct., Carlsbad, CA 92010 USA Tel 760-729-7383
E-mail: writermeeg@gmail.com.

Solutions for Human Services, LLC, *(978-0-9764802)* 25 Vernon Dr., Warren, PA 16365 USA Tel 814-726-1228
E-mail: lindab@westpa.net.

Solving Light Bks., *(978-0-9705438; 978-0-692-26013-5)* 727 Mountalban Dr., Annapolis, MD 21409-4646 USA Tel 410-757-4630
E-mail: rbowiej@comcast.net; nancygjohnson@comcast.net
Web site: http://www.solvinglight.com; http://www.theparthenoncode.com
Dist(s): **BookBaby**
CreateSpace Independent Publishing Platform
Send The Light Distribution LLC.

Some Kids I Know, *(978-0-9768230)* Div. of Some Kids I Know, LLC, W323 N8164 Northcrest Dr., Hartland, WI 53029 USA Tel 262-966-2582
E-mail: thorst@wi.rr.com.

Some Kids I Know, LLC, *(978-0-9768230)* W323 N8164 Northcrest Dr., Hartland, WI 53029 USA.

Someday Ranch, *(978-0-9910180)* P.O. Box 414, Wauna, WA 98395 USA Tel 253-380-0663
E-mail: zookeeper99@comcast.net.

†Somerset Pubs., Inc., *(978-0-403)* 1532 State St., Santa Barbara, CA 93101 USA (SAN 204-6105) Toll Free: 800-937-7947
Dist(s): **North American Bk. Distributors**; *CIP.*

Somerspoint Pr., *(978-0-692-18941-2)* 9633 1/2 Red Pony Ln., El Cajon, CA 92021 USA Tel 619-204-7126
E-mail: arabiandaz@gmail.com
Dist(s): **Ingram Content Group.**

Somerville Hse. Bks., Ltd. (CAN) *(978-0-921051; 978-1-58184; 978-1-895897; 978-1-55286; 978-1-894042) Dist. by* **Penguin Grp USA.**

Something Or Other Publishing, *(978-0-9846938; 978-1-7324511; 978-1-954102)* 3537 Mammoth Trail, Madison, WI 53719 USA Tel 213-952-9557
E-mail: wfransson@gmail.com
Web site: soopllc.com.

Son of Thunder Pubns., *(978-1-7321638)* 155 Highland Way, Taylors, SC 29687 USA Tel 864-436-5898
E-mail: doberman9@juno.com
Web site: www.sonofthunderpublications.org.

Sona Bks. (GBR) *(978-1-912918) Dist. by* **IPG Chicago.**

Sonfire Media, LLC, *(978-0-9825773; 978-0-9891064)* 974 E. Stuart Dr. Suite D, PMB 232, Galax, VA 24333 USA; *Imprints:* Taberah Press (Taberah Pr)
Web site: http://www.sonfiremedia.com.

Song Revival Fellowship & Ministries *See* **Empower Pr.**

Songadh, Jain Swadhyay Mandir, *(978-0-9748681)* 304 Tall Oak Trail, Tarpon Springs, FL 34688 USA Tel 602-863-1073; 727-376-7290; Fax: 602-863-3557; 727-843-8157
E-mail: kahanguru@hotmail.com.

Songbird Pr., *(978-0-9720913)* Orders Addr.: P.O. Box 99, Freeport, ME 04032 USA Fax: 207-373-1128
Web site: http://www.songbirdpress.biz.

Songburd Music, *(978-1-7320252; 978-1-949670; 978-1-952680)* Orders Addr.: P.O. Box PO Box 5701, Bloomington IN, IN 47407 USA; Edit Addr.: PO Box 5701, Bloomington IN, IN 47407 USA; *Imprints:* Beginner Method Series (MYID_I_BEGINNE)
E-mail: brassincolor@gmail.com; admin@songburdmusic.com
Web site: www.brassincolor.com; songburdmusic.com.

Songpaint, *(978-1-7333488)* 201 Commons Pk. S., Stamford, CT 06902 USA Tel 718-413-8177
E-mail: byron.mccray@gmail.com.

Sonic Sword Productions, *(978-0-9797715)* 1089-A Alice Dr., Suite 327, Sumter, SC 29150 USA Tel 803-983-5084
E-mail: john@jhollandbooks.com
Web site: http://jhollandbooks.com; http://rjwargames.com.

Sonis, Gabriela, *(978-0-692-99275-3)* 2950 NE 188th St, Aventura, FL 33180 USA Tel 571-723-8817; *Imprints:* ML Networks (ML Networks)
E-mail: fs2005@gmail.com.

Sonnenschein Bks. *Imprint of* **Black Forest Pr.**

Sonny Evans, *(978-0-578-19464-6; 978-0-578-24259-0)* 969 Sheridan Rd., Glencoe, IL 60022 USA.

Sonny's Legacy Publishing, *(978-0-9990745; 978-1-7325686)* 3131 Harbinger Ln, Dallas, TX 75287 USA Tel 214-662-2782
E-mail: pcfoland4@pamela@folandtech.com; pamela@pamelafoland.com
Web site: www.meganswordbookseries.com.

Sono Nis Pr. (CAN) *(978-0-919203; 978-0-919462; 978-0-9690282; 978-1-55039) Dist. by* **Orca Bk Pub.**

SonoMagnetics *See* **RADIOIONICS RESEARCH**

Son-Rise Pubns. & Distribution Co., *(978-0-936369)* 51 Greenfield Rd., New Wilmington, PA 16142 USA (SAN 698-0031) Tel 724-946-9057; Fax: 724-946-8700; Toll Free: 800-358-0777
Web site: http://www.softspace.com/steelvalley; http://www.sonrisepublications.com.

Sonrise Publishing, *(978-0-9724458; 978-0-9845663; 978-0-9914347)* 131 Galleon St. # 2B, Marina Di Rey, CA 90292-5973 USA (SAN 254-8348) Do not confuse with companies with the same or similar names in Corte Madera, CA, Ashland, OH
E-mail: annsonrise@aol.com
Web site: http://www.sonrisepublishing.com; http://www.annhamiltonwallace.com
Dist(s): **Baker & Taylor Publisher Services (BTPS).**

Sonrise Stable Bks., *(978-0-9847242; 978-1-7333912)* 9451 Crottinger Rd, Plain City, OH 43064 USA Tel 937-644-1967
E-mail: vicki@vickiwatson.com
Web site: http://www.sonrisestable.com
Dist(s): **Follett School Solutions.**

Sonship Pr. *Imprint of* **21st Century Pr.**

Soothing Waterfalls Bks., *(978-0-692-06438-2; 978-0-692-13368-2; 978-0-692-14711-5; 979-8-218-22306-9)* 155 N Pearl Lake Causeway Unit 212, Altamonte Springs, FL 32714 USA Tel 786-267-4079
E-mail: info@soothingwaterfalls.com
Dist(s): **CreateSpace Independent Publishing Platform.**

†Sophia Institute Pr., *(978-0-918477; 978-0-928832; 978-1-933184; 978-1-62282; 978-1-64413; 979-8-88911)* Orders Addr.: P.O. Box 5284, Manchester, NH 03108 USA (SAN 657-7172) Tel 603-641-9344; Fax: 603-641-8108; Toll Free: 800-888-9344 Do not confuse with Sophia Pr., Durham, NH
E-mail: production@sophiainstitute.com
Web site: http://www.sophiainstitute.com
Dist(s): **eBookit.com**; *CIP.*

Sophie's Tales, LLC, *(978-0-578-03818-6; 978-0-9851575; 978-0-578-49615-3)* 665 S Skinker Blvd, Saint Louis, MO 63105 USA Tel 516-242-1466
E-mail: mpaticoff@sophiestales.com
Web site: www.sophiestales.com.

Sophisticated Unicorn, *(978-0-578-06935-7; 978-0-9897689)* 711 Bellaire Ave., Pittsburgh, PA 15226 USA
E-mail: catulathebook@gmail.com
Web site: http://www.catulathebook.com.

Sophrose Entertainment Inc., *(978-0-9800736)* P.O. Box 1989, Cape Canaveral, FL 32920-1989 USA (SAN 855-1286) Tel 321-459-3442 Toll Free: 888-599-7483
E-mail: mail@sophrose.com
Web site: http://www.sophrose.com.

Sopris West Educational Services *See* **Cambium Education, Inc.**

Sora Publishing, *(978-0-9765756)* 1800 Atlantic Blvd., A-405, Key West, FL 33040-5708 USA (SAN 256-4157) Tel 305-296-6699
E-mail: sorapublishing@comcast.net
Web site: http://www.sorapublishing.com.

Sorella Bks., *(978-0-9767351)* P.O. Box 454, Plantsville, CT 06479 USA
E-mail: sorellabooks@yahoo.com
Web site: http://www.sorellabooks.com.

Sorenson, E. Randy, *(978-0-615-16939-2)* 3053 Frederick Pl., West Valley City, UT 84119 USA
Web site: http://www.firstreindeer.com.

Sortis Publishing, *(978-0-9772025; 978-0-9827986)* 2193 E. Claxton Ave., Gilbert, AZ 85297 USA (SAN 256-923X) Tel 480-310-8316; Fax: 480-279-5851
E-mail: tradewebb@wydebeam.com
Web site: http://www.sortispublishing.com.

Sotina Publishing *See* **Joseph Reidhead & Co. Pubs.**

Soul Attitude Press, *(978-0-578-06870-1; 978-1-939181; 978-1-946338)* 6235 103rd Ave N, Pinellas Park, FL 33782 USA
Web site: http://www.johnrehg.com.

Soul Family Travels *See* **SFT Pubns.**

Soul Fire Press *Imprint of* **First Steps Publishing**

Soul Mate Publishing, *(978-1-61935; 978-1-68291; 978-1-64716)* P.O. Box 24, Macedon, NY 14502 USA Tel 315-986-4571
Web site: http://www.soulmatepublishing.com.

Soul Pubns., *(978-0-937327)* 232 Rockford St., Mt. Airy, NC 27030 USA (SAN 658-8050) Tel 336-786-4118 (phone/fax); 3220 Lazelle St. #114, STURGIS, SD 57785 Tel 605-720-0986
Dist(s): **Lulu Pr., Inc.**

Soul Vision Works Publishing, *(978-0-9659538; 978-0-9816254)* ; *Imprints:* Vision Works Publishing (Vis Wrks)
E-mail: mutiyaa@soulvisionworks.com
Web site: www.soulvisionworks.com.

Soulful Storytellers, Inc., *(978-0-9851628)* 3263 Ave. H, Brooklyn, NY 11210 USA Tel 718-781-7560
E-mail: soulmuze@gmail.com.

Soulo Communications, *(978-0-9778209; 978-0-9825607)* Div. of Soulo Communications, Orders Addr.: 2112 Broadway St., NE Suite 100, Minneapolis, MN 55413-3036 USA Tel 612-788-4341; Fax: 612-788-4347
E-mail: tomh@soulocommunications.com
Web site: http://www.soulocommunications.com
Dist(s): **Partners Pubs. Group, Inc.**

SoulRaye Publishing, *(978-0-578-41578-9)* 2370 Rising Glen Way No. 103, Carlsbad, CA 92008 USA Tel 212-316-3444
E-mail: soulraye@gmail.com
Dist(s): **Independent Pub.**

Soulshine Pr., LLC, *(978-0-578-40317-5; 978-1-7336496)* 1650 Red Sky Rd., Wimberley, TX 78676 USA Tel 832-964-4830
E-mail: mollybowen13@gmail.com
Web site: soulshinepress.com.

SoulSong Publishing, *(978-0-9793113)* Div. of SoulSong Enterprises, Orders Addr.: P.O. Box 715, Crestone, CO 81131 USA
E-mail: soulsongpublishing@yahoo.com
Web site: http://www.soulsong.org.

Sound Concepts, Incorporated *See* **Verb Technology, Inc.**

Sound Craft Designs, *(978-0-9771357)* P.O. Box 1563, Poway, CA 92074-1563 USA Tel 858-842-1985
E-mail: info@exploreguitar.com
Web site: http://www.exploreguitar.com.

Sound Library *Imprint of* **AudioGO**

Sound Reading *Imprint of* **Sound Reading Solutions**

Sound Reading Solutions, *(978-0-9704183; 978-0-9742485; 978-0-9743384)* 379 Turkey Hill Rd., Ithaca, NY 14850 USA Tel 607-273-1370 (phone/fax); Toll Free: 800-801-1954; *Imprints:* Sound Reading (Sound Read)
E-mail: info@soundreading.com
Web site: http://www.soundreading.com.

Sound Room Pubs., Inc., *(978-1-883049; 978-1-58472)* Orders Addr.: P.O. Box 3168, Falls Church, VA 22043 USA Tel 540-722-2535; Fax: 540-722-0903; Toll Free: 800-643-0295; Edit Addr.: 100 Weems Ln., Winchester, VA 22601 USA; *Imprints:* In Audio (In Aud)
E-mail: commuterslib@worldnet.att.net
Web site: http://www.inaudio.biz/
Dist(s): **Blackstone Audio, Inc.**
Distributors, The
Findaway World, LLC
Follett Media Distribution
Follett School Solutions.

Sound View Press *See* **Falk Art Reference**

Sound Volumes, *(978-0-9728919)* P.O. Box 828, Mercer Island, WA 98040-0828 USA Tel 425-894-9086
E-mail: sales@soundvolumes.com
Web site: http://www.soundvolumes.com.

Soundprints, *(978-0-924483; 978-1-56899; 978-1-931465; 978-1-59249; 978-1-60727)* Div. of Trudy Corp., 353 Main Ave., Norwalk, CT 06851 USA Fax: 203-846-1776; Toll Free: 800-228-7839; *Imprints:* Blackbirch Press, Incorporated (Blackbirch Pr); Little Soundprints (Little Sound)
Web site: http://www.soundprints.com
Dist(s): **Follett School Solutions**
Cengage Gale
Learning Connection, The.

Sounds Devine, *(978-0-9745249)* P.O. Box 251, Arabi, LA 70032 USA Do not confuse with Calliope Publishing in Steamboat Springs, CO
Web site: http://www.soundsdevine.com.

Sounds True, Inc., *(978-1-56455; 978-1-59179; 978-1-60407; 978-1-62203; 978-1-68364; 978-1-64963)* Orders Addr.: P.O. Box 8010, Boulder, CO 80306-8010 USA; Edit Addr.: 413 S. Arthur Ave., Louisville, CO 80027 USA (SAN 850-3532) Tel 303-665-3151; Fax: 303-665-5292; Toll Free: 800-333-9185
Web site: http://www.soundstrue.com
Dist(s): **Macmillan.**

Sounds Write Productions, Inc., *(978-0-9626286; 978-1-890161)* 6685 Norman Ln., San Diego, CA 92120 USA Tel 619-697-6120; Fax: 619-697-6124; Toll Free: 800-976-8639
E-mail: soundswrite@aol.com; info@soundswrite.com
Web site: http://www.soundswrite.com.

Sourcebook Project, The, *(978-0-915554; 978-0-9600712)* P.O. Box 107, Glen Arm, MD 21057 USA (SAN 201-7652) Tel 410-668-6047
Web site: http://www.science-frontiers.com.

Sourcebooks Casablanca *Imprint of* **Sourcebooks, Inc.**

†Sourcebooks, Inc., *(978-0-942061; 978-0-9629162; 978-0-9629803; 978-1-57071; 978-1-57248; 978-1-58182; 978-1-883518; 978-1-887166; 978-1-888952; 978-1-890208; 978-1-929345; 978-1-59058; 978-1-4022; 978-1-932783; 978-1-61595; 978-1-4642; 978-1-62047; 978-1-62886; 978-1-4926; 978-1-7282)* 1935 Brookdale Rd., Suite 139, Naperville, IL 60563 USA (SAN 666-7864) Tel 630-961-3900; Fax: 630-961-2168; Toll Free: 800-727-8866; *Imprints:* Sourcebooks Casablanca (Casablanca); Sourcebooks Landmark (Sourcebks Land); Sourcebooks MediaFusion (MediaFusion); Sourcebooks Jabberwocky (Srcbks Jabber); Marianne Richmond Studios, Incorporated (MarianneRich); Cumberland House (Cumberland); Hometown World (HometwnWrld); Poisoned Pen Press (Poisoned Press); Little Pickle Press (LittlePickle); Dawn Publications (DawnPubnsl); Bloom Books (BloomBooks)
E-mail: info@sourcebooks.com
Web site: http://www.sourcebooks.com/
Dist(s): **Children's Plus, Inc.**
Ebsco Publishing
Follett School Solutions
MyiLibrary
New Leaf Publishing Group
Source Bk. Pubns.; *CIP.*

Sourcebooks Jabberwocky *Imprint of* **Sourcebooks, Inc.**

Sourcebooks Landmark *Imprint of* **Sourcebooks, Inc.**

Sourcebooks MediaFusion *Imprint of* **Sourcebooks, Inc.**

Sourland Mountain Bks., *(978-1-7332865)* 2800 N Bismark Ln, Jupiter, FL 33458 USA Tel 561-762-8242
E-mail: kimgorey12@att.net
Web site: sourlandmountainbooks.com.

South Asia Bks., *(978-0-8364; 978-0-88386)* P.O. Box 502, Columbia, MO 65205 USA (SAN 207-4044) Tel 573-474-0116; Fax: 573-474-8124
E-mail: sabooks@juno.com
Web site: http://www.southasiabooks.com.

South Carolina Geographic Alliance, *(978-0-9768247)* Ctr. of Excellence for Geographic Education, Orders Addr.: Department of Geography, Univ. of S. C., Columbia, SC 29208 USA Toll Free: 888-895-2023
Web site: http://www.cas.sc.edu/cege/.

South Dakota Historical Society Pr., *(978-0-9622621; 978-0-9715171; 978-0-9749195; 978-0-9777955; 978-0-9798940; 978-0-9822749; 978-0-9845041; 978-0-9846505; 978-0-9852817; 978-0-9852905; 978-0-9860355; 978-1-941813)* 900 Governors Dr., Pierre, SD 57501 USA; *Imprints:* South Dakota State Historical Society Press (S Dak St Hist Soc Pr)
E-mail: jennifer.mcintyre@state.sd.us; orders@sdhspress.com; info@sdhspress.com; judy.uecker@state.sd.us
Web site: www.sdhspress.com
Dist(s): **BookBaby.**

South Dakota State Historical Society Pr. *Imprint of* **South Dakota Historical Society Pr.**

South Dakota State Historical Society Press *See* **South Dakota Historical Society Pr.**

South Florida Art Ctr., Inc., *(978-0-9719492)* 924 Lincoln Rd., Suite 205, Miami Beach, FL 33139-2609 USA
Web site: http://www.artcentersf.org.

South Hadley Publishing *See* **Moltiverse**

South Jersey Culture & History Ctr., *(978-0-9888731; 978-0-9976699; 978-1-947889)* 101 VKF Dr. ARHU / The Richard Stockton College of NJ, Galloway, NJ 08205 USA Tel 609-652-4505; Fax: 609-652-4550
E-mail: Thomas.Kinsella@stockton.edu.

South Main Media by Mindwatering, *(978-0-9909737)* 520 S. Main St., Wake Forest, NC 27587 USA Tel 919-556-3691
E-mail: nicki@southmainmedia.com
Web site: www.southmainmedia.com.

South River Pr., *(978-0-9770764)* P.O. Box 392, Indianola, IA 50125-5012 USA (SAN 256-6982) Tel 515-962-9375.

South Seas Family Publishing, *(978-1-7363754)* 21875 Riviera Ct., Mundelein, IL 60060 USA Tel 847-668-9135
E-mail: kafkas@comcast.net.

Southall, Twyla, *(978-0-9765501)* 5837 Karric Sq. Dr., Dublin, OH 43016 USA
E-mail: twyla@tsouthall.com
Web site: http://www.tsouthall.com.

Southampton Publishing, *(978-1-934483; 978-0-615-14312-5; 978-0-615-16736-7)* 22071 W. 866 Rd., Park Hill, OK 74451 USA (SAN 853-4772)
E-mail: Southamptonpublishing@gmail.com; wilcoxens@sbcglobal.net
Web site: http://www.eddiestuff.com
Dist(s): **Lulu Pr., Inc.**

Southeast Media, *(978-1-888141)* 87 Piedmont Dr., Palm Coast, FL 32164-7085 USA
E-mail: Reachment@msn.com
Web site: http://www-gout-haters.com.

Southern Acres Academy, *(978-0-615-17522-5)* 4955 Hwy. 4, Davenport, NE 68335ed USA
Dist(s): **Lulu Pr., Inc.**

Southern Girl Media, *(978-0-9744423)* PO BOX 510944, Punta Gorda, FL 33950 USA Tel 760-535-2640
Web site: http://www.masonweaver.com
Dist(s): **Tremendous Life Bks.**

Southern Lion Bks., *(978-0-9662454; 978-0-9794203; 978-1-935272)* 1070 Jordan Rd., Madison, GA 30650 USA Tel 706-474-1667 (Tel. & Fax)
E-mail: taniamcclain@yahoo.com; mcclain2@bellsouth.net
Web site: http://www.southernlionbooks.com.

Southern Living *Imprint of* **Time Inc. Bks.**

Southern Willow Publishing, *(978-1-956544)* 1114 Hwy. 96,, Kathleen, GA 31047 USA Tel 478-733-6502
E-mail: southernwillowpublishing@gmail.com
Web site: www.southernwillowpublishing.com.

Southern Yellow Pine (SYP) Publishing LLC, *(978-1-59616; 978-0-9857062; 978-1-940869)* 4351 Natural Bridge Rd., Tallahassee, FL 32305 USA Tel 850-933-0389; *Imprints:* SYP Kids (SYP Kids)
E-mail: tgerrell@syppublishing.com
Web site: www.syppublishing.com.

Southfarm Pr., *(978-0-913337)* Div. of Haan Graphic Publishing Services, Ltd., P.O. Box 1296, Middletown, CT 06457 USA (SAN 283-4146) Tel 860-346-8798
E-mail: southfar@ix.netcom.com
Web site: http://www.war-books.com; http://www.wandahaan.com.

Southgate Pubs. (GBR) *(978-1-85741) Dist. by* **Parkwest Pubns.**

Southpaw Books LLC, *(978-0-9777720)* Southpaw Books LLC, Maplewood, NJ 07040 USA (SAN 850-1017) Tel 973-313-0843; Fax: 973-313-0843
E-mail: info@southpawbooks.com
Web site: http://southpawbooks.com.

Southport Historical Society, Inc., *(978-1-892444)* P.O. Box 10014, Southport, NC 28461-0014 USA Tel 910-457-6940
E-mail: Furstenau@earthlink.net.

Southwest guns & stuff, *(978-0-9747407)* 4212 Lanshire Ct., Grand Prairie, TX 75052-3164 USA.

Southwest Legal Services, *(978-0-9644908; 978-0-9843383; 978-0-9980306)* Div. of Charlynn Publishing Co., Inc., Orders Addr.: P.O. Box 57091, Tucson, AZ 85732 USA Tel 520-795-1414; Edit Addr.: 4152 E. Fifth St., Tucson, AZ 85711 USA
E-mail: swlsorders@yahoo.com
Web site: http://www.southwestlegalservices.com; http://www.bustedbythefeds.com
Dist(s): **Charlynn Publishing Co., Inc.**

Southwest Parks & Monuments Association *See* **Western National Parks Assn.**

Southwestern Pr., Inc, *(978-0-923176)* Orders Addr.: P.O. Box 4297, Carlsbad, CA 92018-4297 USA (SAN 251-5601) Tel 760-434-8858; Fax: 760-434-8888
E-mail: sharon@southwesternpress.com
Web site: http://www.southwesternpress.com/.

Southwestern Publishing House *See* **Southwestern Publishing Hse., Inc.**

†Southwestern Publishing Hse., Inc., *(978-0-87197; 978-1-935442; 978-1-941800; 978-1-943198)* A member of the Southwestern Family of Companies, Orders Addr.: P.O. Box 305142, Nashville, TN 37230 USA (SAN 204-1197) Tel 615-391-2944; Fax: 615-391-2656; Toll Free: 800-798-1780; Edit Addr.: 2451 Atrium Way, Nashville, TN 37214 USA Fax: 615-391-2815; Toll Free:

Publisher Name Index

800-269-6839; *Imprints:* Beckon Books (BeckonBks) Do not confuse with Favorite Recipes in Vernal, UT
E-mail: info@frpbooks.com; kconnelly@swpublishinghouse.com
Web site: http://www.frpbooks.com; http://www.beckonbooks.com; http://www.swpublishinggroup.com; http://www.greenwichpublishing.com; http://quailridgepress.com; swphbooks.com; https://swphmarketplace.com/; http://southwesternbooks.com; http://frpbooks.com; HistoricHospitalityBooks.com; https://www.swphbooks.com/; bluesneakerpress.com; cookbookmarketplace.com; swpublishinghouse.com
Dist(s): **Blackstone Audio, Inc.**
Cookbook Marketplace, The
Simon & Schuster, Inc.; *CIP.*

Southworth, Nayla *See* **Prodigy Kids Pr.**

Souvenir Pr. Ltd. (GBR) *(978-0-285) Dist. by* **IPG Chicago.**

Souvenir Pr. Ltd. (GBR) *(978-0-285) Dist. by* **Consort Bk Sales.**

Sovereign Grace Pubs., Inc., *(978-1-878442; 978-1-58960)* P.O. Box 4998, Lafayette, IN 47903-4998 USA (SAN 299-6847) Toll Free: 800-447-9142 Do not confuse with Sovereign Grace Pubns., Lexington, KY
E-mail: jaygreenxx@iquest.net
Web site: http://www.sovgracepub.com.

Sovereign Press *See* **Margaret Weis Productions, Ltd.**

Sow Forth Publishing LLC, *(978-0-9822262)* P.O. Box 303, Lewis Center, OH 43035-9462 USA (SAN 857-7358)
E-mail: sowforth@insight.rr.com.

Sowash, Rick Publishing Co., *(978-0-9762412)* 338 Milton St. # 1, Cincinnati, OH 45202-0971 USA Toll Free: 888-255-2764
E-mail: rick@sowash.com
Web site: http://www.sowash.com.

Soxwings Publishing, *(978-0-615-20974-6)* 414 Executive Ctr. Blvd., Suite 105, El Paso, TX 79902 USA Tel 915-533-3827; Fax: 915-533-3745; Toll Free: 866-416-3827
E-mail: bobtjr@yahoo.com.

SP Family Productions, LLC, *(978-0-9773134)* 5 Knute Drive, Andover, NJ 07821-3912 USA Tel 973-479-6111
E-mail: seancanning@hotmail.com
Web site: http://www.seancanning.com.

Spalding, Brenda, *(978-0-692-25731-9; 978-0-692-92737-3; 978-0-692-97652-4)* 6109 55th Terr. E., Bradenton, FL 34203 USA Tel 941-739-0496
E-mail: bpspalding@msn.com.

Spalding Education International, *(978-1-935289; 978-1-952494)* 23335 N. 18th Dr., Suite 102, Phoenix, AZ 85027-6301 USA (SAN 857-0310) Tel 623-434-1204; Fax: 623-434-1208
E-mail: jsexton@spalding.org; kporter@spalding.org
Web site: http://www.spalding.org.

Spanish Language Texts, Inc., *(978-0-9710710)* Orders Addr.: P.O. Box 1088, New York, NY 10040 USA; Edit Addr.: 19 Seaman Ave. 2M, New York, NY 10034 USA
Web site: http://www.spanishlanguagetexts.com
Dist(s): **Lectorum Pubns., Inc.**

Spanish Pubs., LLC, 8871 SW 129 Terr., Miami, FL 33176 USA Tel 305-233-3365; Fax: 305-251-1310
E-mail: mariela@spanishpublishers.net
Web site: www.spanishpublishers.net.

Spanish-Live, *(978-0-9816973)* 1033 Imperial Dr., Morgantown, WV 26508 USA
E-mail: lorena@spanish-live.com
Web site: http://www.spanish-live.com.

Spann Productions, *(978-0-9772209)* P.O. Box 10412, Bakersfield, CA 93389 USA Tel 661-832-2135 (phone/fax)
E-mail: spannlake@aol.com.

SpanPress, Inc., *(978-1-58045; 978-1-887578)* 5722 S. Flamingo Rd., Suite 277, Cooper City, FL 33330 USA Tel 305-592-7913; Fax: 305-477-5632; Toll Free: 800-585-8384
Dist(s): **Continental Bk. Co., Inc.**
Lectorum Pubns., Inc.

Spark Hse., *(978-1-936174)* Div. of Augsburg Fortress, Pubs., 100 S. 5th St., Suite 600, Minneapolis, MN 55402 USA Tel 612-330-3305; Fax: 612-330-3514; Toll Free: 800-426-0115; *Imprints:* Sparkhouse Press (Sparkhouse)
E-mail: irene.crooks@augsburgfortress.org
Dist(s): **1517 Media.**

Spark Literary & Media Management, *(978-1-7356422)* 295 Madison Ave., New York, NY 10017 USA Tel 646-719-8002
E-mail: maggie.peterson@sparklm.com
Web site: www.sparklm.com.

Spark Notes *Imprint of* **Sterling Publishing Co., Inc.**

Spark Publishing Group *Imprint of* **Sterling Publishing Co., Inc.**

Sparkhouse Family *Imprint of* **1517 Media**

Sparkhouse Pr. *Imprint of* **Spark Hse.**

Sparkledoll Productions, *(978-0-9747832)* P.O. Box 56173, Virginia Beach, VA 23456 USA Tel 757-718-3095
E-mail: books@sparkledoll.com
Web site: http://www.sparkledoll.com/publishing.

Sparklesoup LLC, *(978-0-9714776; 978-1-932379; 978-1-59748; 978-1-61814)* 11700 W. Charleston Blvd., Ste. 170-95, Las Vegas, NV 89135 USA; *Imprints:* The Edge (TheEdge)
E-mail: sparklesoup@aol.com
Web site: http://www.sparklesoup.com; http://www.theedgebooks.com; http://www.kailingowbooks.com
Dist(s): **CreateSpace Independent Publishing Platform**
Independent Pubs. Group
Ingram Content Group.

Sparklesoup Studios, Incorporated *See* **Sparklesoup LLC**

Sparkling Bks. (GBR) *(978-1-907230) Dist. by* **LightSource CS.**

Sparkling Pr., *(978-0-9774855)* 137 E. Curtice St., St. Paul, MN 55107 USA Tel 651-227-5248.

SparkNotes *Imprint of* **Barnes & Noble, Inc.**

SparkPr. (a Bks.parks Imprint), *(978-1-940716; 978-1-943006; 978-1-68463)* 80 E. Rio Salado Pkwy., TEMPE, AZ 85281 USA Tel 480-275-4280; 480-650-1688
E-mail: Publishing@sparkpointstudio.com
Web site: gosparkpress.com; http://booksparkspr.com/
Dist(s): **Blackstone Audio, Inc.**
Ingram Publisher Services
Publishers Group West (PGW).

Sparks Fly, *(978-0-9789445)* 609 Myrtle Ave., Apt 3A, Brooklyn, NY 11205-1470 USA Toll Free: 866-556-2432
E-mail: info@sparksfly.org
Web site: http://www.sparksfly.org.

Sparrow Media Group, Inc., *(978-0-9719304; 978-0-9786018; 978-0-9829526)* P.O. Box 44272, Eden Prairie, MN 55344-4272 USA Tel 952-953-9166
Web site: http://www.sparrowmediagroup.com.

Sparrow's Nest Enterprises, LLC, The, *(978-0-578-41346-4; 978-0-578-60460-2; 978-0-578-97165-0)* 7535 Sparrow Rd., Hopedale, IL 61747 USA Tel 309-210-4758
E-mail: tomlbye@yahoo.com
Dist(s): **Independent Pub.**

Spatterdash Pr., *(978-0-9987565)* 1701 S Splitrock Blvd, Brandon, SD 57005 USA Tel 605-582-2266
E-mail: Tammy.osheim4@gmail.com.

Spatterlight Pr., *(978-1-61947)* 6383 Valley View Rd., Oakland, CA 94611-1226 USA Tel 510-502-1506; *Imprints:* Quantalore (MYID_R_QUANTAL)
E-mail: jhvance2@gmail.com
Web site: jackvance.com.

SPC Bks. *Imprint of* **RPJ & Co., Inc.**

SPCK Publishing (GBR) *(978-0-281; 978-0-7459; 978-0-85969; 978-1-902694) Dist. by* **Pilgrim OH.**

SPCK Publishing (GBR) *(978-0-281; 978-0-7459; 978-0-85969; 978-1-902694) Dist. by* **BTPS.**

SPD-Small Pr. Distribution, *(978-0-914068)* 1341 Seventh St., Berkeley, CA 94710-1409 USA (SAN 204-5826) Tel 510-524-1668; Fax: 510-524-0852; Toll Free: 800-869-7553 (orders)
E-mail: orders@spdbooks.org
Web site: http://www.spdbooks.org.

Speak *Imprint of* **Penguin Young Readers Group**

Speak Out Ministry, *(978-0-578-02848-4; 978-0-692-86807-2; 978-0-9993791; 978-0-578-88014-3)* 13844 Carter House Way, Silver Spring, MD 20904 USA Tel 202-412-7957
E-mail: aileencunningham15@gmail.com
Web site: http://www.alphathetaomega.com.

Speakeasy Comics (CAN) *(978-0-9737039; 978-0-9738388) Dist. by* **Diamond Book Dists.**

Speak-Easy Publishing, LLC, *(978-0-9714433; 978-0-9754977)* Orders Addr.: P.O. Box 11377, Takoma Park, MD 20913 USA Tel 202-723-1317
E-mail: jgduarte@speakeasypublishing.com; info@speakeasypublishing.com
Web site: http://www.speakeasypublishing.com
Dist(s): **Lyrical Liquor Productions.**

Speaking Volumes, LLC, *(978-1-935138; 978-1-61232; 978-1-62815; 978-1-64540; 979-8-89022)* 7820 Enchanted Hills Blvd. Suite A - No. 145, Rio Rancho, NM 87144 USA (SAN 856-5880) Tel 888-777-8204; 505-771-2251
E-mail: kurt@speaking-volumes.com
Web site: http://www.speaking-volumes.com/indexfish.asp; http://.www.speakingvolumes.us
Dist(s): **Follett School Solutions.**

SpeakToChange Enterprise, *(978-0-578-52851-9; 978-1-7353908)* 169 CR 381, Water Valley, MS 38965 USA Tel 662-801-6337
E-mail: speaktochange@yahoo.com.

Special Edition Studios, Inc., *(978-0-9759013)* P.O. Box 7216, Sebring, FL 33872-0104 USA
Web site: http://www.sestudios.com.

Special Editions — Customized Biographies *Imprint of* **Slavens Enterprises, LLC.**

Special Ideas, *(978-1-888547)* P.O. Box 9, Heltonville, IN 47436 USA Tel 812-834-5691 (phone/fax); Toll Free: 800-326-1197
E-mail: karen@special-ideas.com; justice@special-ideas.com
Web site: http://www.baheiresources.com; http://www.interfaithresources.com.

Special Kids Company, Incorporated *See* **Anythings Possible, Inc.**

Special Reads for Special Needs, *(978-0-9702698; 978-0-9795922)* 12025 Merganser Dr., Cincinnati, OH 45246-1542 USA Tel 513-541-7617; Fax: 513-541-2543; Toll Free: 866-553-2042
E-mail: specialreads@aol.com
Web site: http://www.specialreads.com.

Specialized Printing, LLC, *(978-0-615-38944-8)* 2430 NW Broadway St., Albany, OR 97321 USA Tel 800-282-6621
E-mail: ericbrunsvold@gmail.com.

Specialized Quality Pubns., *(978-0-9634906; 978-0-9789582)* 921 11th St., S., Wisconsin Rapids, WI 54494 USA (SAN 299-299X) Tel 715-423-7476; *Imprints:* SQP (SQP)
Web site: http://www.specializedqualitypublications.com/index.htm.

Specialty Educational Pubs., *(978-0-9718488)* P.O. Box 161, New Oxford, PA 17350 USA
E-mail: specialtypublishers@hotmail.com.

Specialty Greetings, *(978-0-9860024)* 2225 Grant St., Eugene, OR 97405 USA Tel 541-344-6400
E-mail: orders@specialtygreetings.com
Web site: http://www.SpecialtyGreetings.com.

Specialty Pr., Inc., *(978-0-9621629; 978-1-886941; 978-1-937761)* Orders Addr.: 3150 Willow Ln., Weston, FL 33331 USA; Edit Addr.: 300 NW 70th Ave., Suite 102, Plantation, FL 33317 USA (SAN 251-6977) Toll Free: 800-233-9273 Do not confuse with Specialty Pr., Inc., in Ocean, NJ
E-mail: sales@addwarehouse.com
Web site: http://www.addwarehouse.com
Dist(s): **Ebsco Publishing**
Independent Pubs. Group
MyiLibrary.

Specialty Publishing Co., *(978-0-9755199)* 135 E. Saint Charles Rd., Carol Stream, IL 60188 USA (SAN 256-0569) Tel 630-933-0844; Fax: 630-933-0845
Web site: http://www.specialtypub.com.

Species Spectrum LLC, *(978-1-7339209)* P.O. Box 32664, Santa Fe, NM 87594 USA Tel 505-231-2329
E-mail: contact@speciesspectrum.com
Web site: speciesspectrum.com.

Spectacle Films, Inc., *(978-0-9767771; 979-8-9888390)* 2021 Commonwealth Ave. #2, Boston, MA 02135 USA Tel 212-807-0290
E-mail: spectaclefilms@gmail.com; csoling@gmail.com
Web site: http://www.Rumpleville.com; http://www.SpectacleFilms.com.

Spectre Publishing, *(978-0-9709191)* 22316 Haig St., Taylor, MI 48180 USA
E-mail: publisher@spectrepublishing.com
Web site: http://www.spectrepublishing.com
Dist(s): **CreateSpace Independent Publishing Platform.**

Spectrum *Imprint of* **Carson-Dellosa Publishing, LLC**

Spectrum Films Inc., *(978-0-9760906)* 4319 Salisbury Rd., Suite 4, Jacksonville, FL 32216 USA
Web site: http://www.spectrumfilms.tv.

Spectrum Health Consulting, *(978-0-9835862)* 212 Mohegan St., New Britain, PA 18901 USA Tel 267-307-4224
E-mail: susiebeiler@hotmail.com.

SpeculativeFictionReview.com, *(978-0-9785232; 979-8-9892200)* 22281 Letur, Mission Viejo, CA 92691-1406 USA
Web site: http://www.speculativefictionreview.com.

Speech Bin, Inc., The, *(978-0-937857)* 1965 25th Ave., Vero Beach, FL 32960 USA (SAN 630-1657) Tel 772-770-0007; Fax: 772-770-0006
E-mail: info@speechbin.com
Web site: http://www.speechbin.com.

Speech Kids Texas Pr., *(978-1-933319)* 3802 Beaconsdale Dr., Austin, TX 78727-2951 USA (SAN 256-4122)
E-mail: info@speechkidstexaspress.com
Web site: http://www.speechkidstexaspress.com.

Speech Place Publishing, The, *(978-0-9794102)* 1810-A York Rd., No. 432, Lutherville, MD 21093 USA (SAN 853-3679) Tel 410-517-9026
E-mail: cs@thespeechplace.com
Web site: http://www.thespeechplace.com.

Speech Publishing Hse., *(978-0-9770483)* 1115 Cordova St., Suite 318, Pasadena, CA 91106-3013 USA Tel 626-372-1195
E-mail: jonandspeech@prodigy.net.

Speedwitch Media, *(978-0-9749508; 978-0-9987341)* 645 Tanner Marsh Rd., Guilford, CT 06437-2106 USA
Web site: http://www.speedwitchmedia.com.

Speedy Kids (Children's Fiction) *Imprint of* **Speedy Publishing LLC**

Speedy Publishing Books (General) *Imprint of* **Speedy Publishing LLC**

Speedy Publishing LLC, *(978-1-939643; 978-1-62884; 978-1-63022; 978-1-63187; 978-1-63287; 978-1-63383; 978-1-63428; 978-1-68032; 978-1-63501; 978-1-68127; 978-1-68145; 978-1-68185; 978-1-68212; 978-1-68260; 978-1-68280; 978-1-68305; 978-1-68326; 978-1-68368; 978-1-5419; 978-0-578-40177-5; 978-0-578-40278-9; 979-8-8694) 7914 Raven Creek Ln., Cypress, TX 77433 USA (SAN 920-6620) Tel 954-379-7796; Fax: 954-379-7796; 40 E. Main St., Newark, DE 19733; Imprints:* Dissected Lives (Auto Biographies) (Dissected Live); Speedy Kids (Children's Fiction) (Speedy Kids); Baby Professor (Education Kids) (Baby Profes); Jupiter Kids (Childrens & Kids Fiction) (Jupiter Kids); One True Faith (Religion & Spirituality) (One True Faith); Dot EDU (Educational & Textbooks) (Dot EDU); Biz Hub (Business & Investing) (Biz Hub); Universal Politics (Politics & Social Sciences) (Univ Politics); Speedy Publishing Books (General) (SpeedyPub); @ Journals & Notebooks (JournalsN); Professor Beaver (PrBeaver)
Web site: http://www.speedypublishing.com.

Speight, Theresa , L.L.C. *See* **Complete in Christ Ministries, Inc.**

Spellbound *Imprint of* **ABDO Publishing Co.**

Spellbound *Imprint of* **Magic Wagon**

Spellbound River Pr., *(978-0-9911914; 978-1-945017)* P.O. Box 161081, Austin, TX 78716 USA Tel 617 233 6143
E-mail: bondsam@hotmail.com.

†Speller, Robert & Sons, Pubs., Inc., *(978-0-8315)* Orders Addr.: P.O. Box 411, New York, NY 10159 USA (SAN 203-2295) Tel 646-334-8008; P.O. Box 461, New York, NY 10108 (SAN 203-2309); *CIP.*

Spence City *Imprint of* **Spencer Hill Pr.**

Spence Publishing Co., *(978-0-9653208; 978-1-890626)* 5646 Milton St. Ste. 314, Dallas, TX 75206-3923 USA (SAN 257-9383) Toll Free: 888-773-6782
E-mail: tspence@spencepublishing.com
Web site: http://www.spencepublishing.com
Dist(s): **Chicago Distribution Ctr.**
Vigilante, Richard Bks.

Spence, Stephen Mark, *(978-0-9705324)* 211 Moore Ave., Buffalo, NY 14223 USA Tel 716-836-5178
E-mail: spence@buffalo.edu
Web site: http://www.acsu.buffalo.edu/~spence/.

Spencer Hill Contemporary *Imprint of* **Spencer Hill Pr.**

Spencer Hill Middle Grade *Imprint of* **Spencer Hill Pr.**

Spencer Hill Pr., *(978-0-9845311; 978-0-9831572; 978-1-937053; 978-1-939392; 978-1-63392)* 27 W. 20th St., New York, NY 10011 USA (SAN 859-6573); *Imprints:* Spence City (Spence City); Spencer Hill Contemporary (SpencerHill); Spencer Hill Middle Grade (SpencHill Middl)
E-mail: karen@beaufortbooks.com
Web site: http://www.spencerhillpress.com; http://www.spencecity.com/
Dist(s): **INscribe Digital**
Independent Pubs. Group
Midpoint Trade Bks., Inc.

Spencer Pr., The, *(978-0-932270)* Div. of The Spencer Group, Nine Tudor Terr., Newton, MA 02466-1509 USA (SAN 205-5651) Tel 617-965-8388; Fax: 617-964-3971 Do not confuse with companies with similar names in Wells, ME, Portland, OR
E-mail: jacknusan@aol.com.

Spencer, Russell & Kathlynn, *(978-0-9664055)* Orders Addr.: 2484 Dewberry Ln., Oxnard, CA 93030 USA Tel 805-981-2820
E-mail: RSpencer@windshieldadventures.com
Web site: http://www.windshieldadventures.com
Dist(s): **Gem Guides Bk. Co.**

Spencer's Mill Pr., *(978-0-9771666)* 555 Church St. No. 1501, Nashville, TN 37219 USA (SAN 256-8225) Tel 615 477-2044
E-mail: trudychoices@aol.com
Web site: http://www.spencersmillpress.com
Dist(s): **BookBaby.**

Spending Solutions Pr., *(978-0-9729732)* 4347 W. NW Hwy., Suite 120, PMB 283, Dallas, TX 75220-3864 USA
Web site: http://www.spendingsolutions.com.

Sper, Emily *See* **Jump Pr.**

Speranza's Pr., *(978-0-9800327)* P.O. Box 2404, Glenview, IL 60025 USA.

Sphaira Publishing, *(978-0-692-60640-7; 978-1-7323585)* 1855 Tyler Trce, Lawrenceville, GA 30043 USA Tel 470-447-7251
Dist(s): **CreateSpace Independent Publishing Platform.**

Sphinx Publishing, *(978-0-9725951; 978-0-9762875; 978-0-9770912; 978-0-9776711; 978-1-934144; 978-1-935921)* 7400 Airport Dr., Macon, GA 31216 USA Toll Free: 866-311-9578; *Imprints:* Blue Marble Books (Blu Marble Bks)
E-mail: gpulliam@indigopublishing.us
Web site: http://www.indigopublishing.us
Dist(s): **American Wholesale Bk. Co.**
Parnassus Bk. Distributors.

SPI Bks., *(978-0-944007; 978-1-56171)* 99 Spring St., 3rd Flr., New York, NY 10012 USA Tel 212-431-5011; Fax: 212-431-8646
E-mail: ian@spibooks.com
Web site: http://www.spibooks.com
Dist(s): **APG Sales & Distribution Services.**

Spica Bks., *(978-0-9728531)* 9742 N. 105th Dr., Sun City, AZ 85351 USA Tel 623-583-6764 (phone/fax)
E-mail: marilyn@dreamlady.com
Web site: http://www.dreamlady.com.

Spicka, Jana Incorporated *See* **Tree of Life Pr.**

Spider Comics, *(978-0-9859884)* 1489 Wallace Dr., Springville, UT 84663 USA Tel 678-386-5550
E-mail: michael@spidercomics.com
Web site: www.spidercomics.com.

SPIE, *(978-0-8194; 978-0-89252; 978-1-62841; 978-1-5106)* Orders Addr.: P.O. Box 10, Bellingham, WA 98227-0010 USA (SAN 224-1706) Tel 360-676-3290; Fax: 360-647-1445; Edit Addr.: 1000 20th St., Bellingham, WA 98225 USA (SAN 669-1323) Tel 360-676-3290; Fax: 360-647-1445; Toll Free: 888-504-8171
E-mail: spie@spie.org; kerryg@spie.org; marysu@spie.org
Web site: http://www.spie.org/bookstore
Dist(s): **Wiley, John & Sons, Inc.**
ebrary, Inc.

Spineless Bks., *(978-0-9724244; 978-0-9801392; 978-0-9853578; 978-0-9998086)* P.O. Box 91, Urbana, IL 61803 USA Tel 217-722-1033
E-mail: william@spinelessbooks.com
Web site: http://www.spinelessbooks.com.

Spinelli, Patti, *(978-0-9742328)* 87 Portland Ave., Dover, NH 03820-3525 USA
E-mail: pasbug1010@aol.com.

Spinifex Pr. (AUS) *(978-1-875559; 978-0-908205; 978-1-876756; 978-1-74219; 978-0-646-04196-4; 978-1-925581; 978-1-925950; 978-1-922964) Dist. by* **IPG Chicago.**

Spinner Bks., *(978-1-59653)* 2030 Harrison St., San Francisco, CA 94110-1310 USA Tel 415-503-1600; Fax: 415-503-0085.

Spinner Pubns., Inc., *(978-0-932027)* 164 William St., New Bedford, MA 02740-6022 USA (SAN 686-0826) Tel 508-994-4564; Fax: 508-994-6925; Toll Free: 800-292-6062
E-mail: spinner@spinnerpub.com
Web site: http://www.spinnerpub.com.

Spinning Broom Bks. Publishing, LLC, *(978-0-692-61294-1; 978-0-9983244)* 1997 S. Meadows Dr., Kalispell, MT 59901 USA Tel 406-871-4292
E-mail: spinningbroombooks@gmail.com
Web site: http://www.spinningbroombookspublishing.com/
Dist(s): **CreateSpace Independent Publishing Platform.**

Spinning Horse Publishing, *(978-0-9842832)* 6320 Cty. Rd. K, Omro, WI 54963 USA Tel 920-685-2094.

SpinSmart Software, *(978-0-9743434)* Orders Addr.: 4717 S. Hydraulic, Wichita, KS 67216 USA
E-mail: support@spinsmart.com
Web site: http://www.spinsmart.com.

Spinsters Ink *See* **Spinsters Ink Bks.**

†Spinsters Ink Bks., *(978-1-883523; 978-1-935226)* Div. of Southern Belle Bks., P.O. Box 242, Midway, FL 32343

USA (SAN 212-6923) Tel 850-576-2370; Fax: 850-576-3498; Toll Free: 800-301-6860
E-mail: Linda@Spinstersink.com
Web site: http://www.spinstersink.com
Dist(s): **Bella Distribution**
SPD-Small Pr. Distribution
Two Rivers Distribution; *CIP*.

Spiny Woman LLC, *(978-1-950061)* 332 S. Michigan Ave. 1032-L483, Chicago, IL 60604 USA Tel 312-613-6225
E-mail: lisa@lisalilly.com.

Spirit & Life Productions, *(978-0-9788928)* Orders Addr.: 2260 Grand Ave., Baldwin, NY 11510 USA Tel 866-430-3801.

Spirit Pr. *Imprint of* **Bendon, Inc.**

Spirit Pr., LLC, *(978-1-893075)* Orders Addr.: 1520 NE 21st Ave. #101, Portland, OR 97232 USA Tel 503-954-0012 Do not confuse with companies with the same name in Santa Cruz, CA, Raleigh, NC
E-mail: suzannedeak@gmail.com; onespiritpress@gmail.com; spiritpresspublishing@gmail.com
Web site: http://www.onespiritpress.com
Dist(s): **CreateSpace Independent Publishing Platform**
Ingram Content Group.

Spirit Productions *See* **Personal Freedom Publishing**

Spirit Publishing LLC, *(978-0-9770967)* 819 Marcy Ave., Brooklyn, NY 11216 USA (SAN 256-7636) Tel 718-230-5605.

SpiritBooks *Imprint of* **Portal Ctr. Pr.**

Spiritbuilding *See* **Spiritbuilding Pubs.**

Spiritbuilding Pubs., *(978-0-9774754; 978-0-9821376; 978-0-9829811; 978-0-9990684; 978-1-7363224; 978-1-955285)* 9700 Ferry Rd., Waynesville, OH 45068 USA
E-mail: mhallen@spiritbuilding.com
Web site: http://www.spiritbuilding.com.

Spirited Presentations, *(978-0-9790017)* 4249 Peak Ln., Grand Rapids, MI 49525 USA
E-mail: Kathey@spiritedpresentations.com
Web site: http://Spiritedpresentations.com.

Spirited Publishing, LLC, *(978-0-9768513)* Orders Addr.: P.O. Box 1796, Appleton, WI 54912-1796 USA Tel 920-419-3340
E-mail: kris@spiritedpublishing.com
Web site: http://www.spiritedpublishing.com.

Spiritpoint Press *See* **Bitty Book Pr.**

Spiritual Hse. Pr., The, *(978-0-9656847)* 24 Old Milford Rd., Brookline, NH 03033 USA Tel 603-672-8550
E-mail: blueskies@myfairpoint.net
Web site: http://www.TheSpiritualHouse.com.

Spitzer, Lance, *(978-0-615-72525-3)* 226 Crestmoor Cir., Pacifica, CA 94044 USA Tel 650-922-8554
E-mail: lancesherwood@comcast.net.

Spizzirri Pr., Inc., *(978-0-86545)* P.O. Box 9397, Rapid City, SD 57709 USA (SAN 215-2851) Tel 605-348-2749; Fax: 605-348-6251 (orders); Toll Free: 800-325-9819; 800-322-9819
E-mail: spizzpub@aol.com; print@spipress.com
Web site: http://www.spizzirri.com; https://spipress.com.

Splash Designworks, *(978-0-692-87695-4; 978-0-578-42380-7; 978-0-578-42381-4)* 68 Shore Ln., Milford, DE 19963 USA Tel 302-399-7851
E-mail: info@splashdw.com
Web site: www.splashdw.com.

Splendid Benedict, *(978-0-615-90023-0; 978-0-9910809)* 5094 N Agave Trl, Flagstaff, AZ 86001 USA Tel 303-455-1835
Dist(s): **CreateSpace Independent Publishing Platform.**

Splendid Torch, *(978-0-9788027; 978-0-615-16717-6; 978-0-615-16784-8)* 2000 St. Regis Dr. #6d, Lombard, IL 60148 USA (SAN 851-6588)
Web site: http://www.puglish.com
Dist(s): **Lulu Pr., Inc.**

Splendors Publishing, *(978-0-9717228)* P.O. Box 1155, Soquel, CA 95073 USA Fax: 831-464-1854
E-mail: lalo@lalofiorelli.com
Web site: http://www.lalofiorelli.com.

Split Level of the Blessed Suburbs Publishing, *(978-0-9761515)* 56 Arbor St., Hartford, CT 06106-1201 USA Tel 860-586-8448 (phone/fax)
Web site: http://www.tedpaulsen.com.

Spoken Arts, Inc., *(978-0-8045)* Orders Addr.: 3901 Union Blvd Suite 160, St. Louis, MO 63115 USA (SAN 990-7734); Edit Addr.: 1517 Highland valley cir, wildwood, MO 63005 USA (SAN 205-079X) Fax: 845-878-9009; Toll Free: 800-326-4090
E-mail: sales@spokenartsinc.com
Web site: http://www.spokenartsinc.com
Dist(s): **AudioGO**
Follett Media Distribution
Follett School Solutions
Lectorum Pubns., Inc.
Weston Woods Studios, Inc.

Spoken Word, The, *(978-0-9637644)* 1031 Michigan Ave. NE, No. 205, Washington, DC 20017 USA Tel 202-832-2368 Do not confuse with Spoken Word, The, Arlington, TX.

SpokenVizions Entertainment Group, LLC, *(978-0-9773834)* P.O. Box 373, Florissant, MO 63032 USA Tel 314-517-8764
E-mail: info@spokenvizions.com
Web site: http://www.spokenvizions.com.

Spookatorium, The *See* **Spookatorium, The**

Spooky Hse., *(978-1-7340445; 978-1-959946)* 101 Pequot Ln., East Islip, NY 11730 USA Tel 631-804-9685
E-mail: rottone@lions.molloy.edu
Web site: www.spookyhousepress.com.

Spoon Publishing Hse., *(978-0-615-11213-8)* Div. of A Corpus Polymedia Monolith, 440 E. Broadway, Executive Suite 51, Salt Lake City, UT 84111-2651 USA
E-mail: spoonpublishing@corpuspolymedia.com
Web site: http://www.corpuspolymedia.com/spoonpublishing/; http://www.spoonpublishing.com.

Spoonbill, Patty Bks., *(978-1-7345570; 979-8-9860356)* 190 SW 203 Ave, Pembroke Pines, FL 33029 USA Tel 954-604-4438
E-mail: cl1129b@comcast.net.

Spooners Publishing, *(978-0-9766179)* 98 Onteora Ct., Shokan, NY 12481-5610 USA Tel 845-657-8737
E-mail: ecurtis@hvc.rr.com.

Spork *Imprint of* **Clear Fork Publishing**

Sport Workbooks, *(978-0-9787458)* P.O. Box 1623, Pacifica, CA 94044 USA (SAN 851-5093) Tel 650-270-3200
E-mail: baseballmath@hotmail.com.

Sport Your Stuff Corp., *(978-1-931746)* 5025 Longbrook Rd., Winston Salem, NC 27105 USA.

SportAmerica, *(978-1-879498; 978-1-955174)* P.O. Box 95030, South Jordan, UT 84095 USA Tel 801-253-3360; Fax: 801-253-3361; Toll Free: 800-467-7885
Web site: http://www.sportamerica.com.

Sportime International, *(978-0-9793506)* 3175 Northwoods Pkwy. # A, Norcross, GA 30071-1539 USA
E-mail: dkissel@sportime.com
Web site: http://www.sportime.com.

Sportiva Bks., *(978-0-692-11783-5; 978-0-692-13805-2; 978-0-9980307; 978-1-7342758)* 11435 Avondale Rd. NE, Redmond, WA 98052 USA Tel 425-405-8010
E-mail: info@acurcio.com; anthony@acurcio.com
Web site: www.sportivabooks.com.

Sports Challenge Network *See* **Toy Vey Toys**

Sports Illustrated Books *Imprint of* **Time Inc. Bks.**

Sports Illustrated For Kids, *(978-0-316; 978-0-553; 978-1-886749; 978-1-930623)* Div. of Time, Inc., 135 W. 50th St. , New York, NY 10020-1393 USA Tel 212-522-1212; Fax: 212-522-0926
E-mail: joe_nunziata@sikids.com
Web site: http://www.sikids.com
Dist(s): **Hachette Bk. Group**
Independent Pubs. Group.

Sports In Mind, *(978-0-9745066; 978-0-9765074)* 3603 Palm Harbor Blvd., Unit C, Palm Harbor, FL 34683 USA Fax: 727-942-3339
Web site: http://www.ravesystems.com.

Sports Marketing International, Inc., *(978-0-9743082)* 27 E. Housatonic St., Pittsfield, MA 01201-4121 USA Tel 413-499-1733; Fax: 413-499-3820; Toll Free: 800-320-1733; *Imprints*: Moscow Ballet (Moscow Ballet)
E-mail: smi@nutcracker.com
Web site: http://www.nutcracker.com.

Sports Masters, *(978-1-58382)* Div. of Sports Publishing, Inc., 804 N. Neil St., Champaign, IL 61820 USA Tel 217-363-2072; Fax: 217-363-2073; Toll Free: 877-424-2665
E-mail: choffman@sagamorepub.com
Dist(s): **Ingram Publisher Services.**

Sports Publishing, LLC, *(978-1-57167; 978-1-58261; 978-1-58382; 978-1-59670)* 804 N. Neil St., Champaign, IL 61820 USA Tel 217-363-2072; Fax: 217-353-2073; Toll Free: 877-424-2665 Do not confuse with Sports Publishing, Champaign, IL
E-mail: info@sportspublishingllc.com
Web site: http://www.sportspublishingllc.com
Dist(s): **Hachette Bk. Group**
MyiLibrary.

Sports Touch *See* **Sports Touch/Kate Montgomery**

Sports Touch/Kate Montgomery, *(978-1-878069)* 1625 E. Jackson Blvd., Elkhart, IN 46516 USA
E-mail: kate@sportstouch.com; katemontgomery@mac.com
Web site: http://www.lulu.com; http://www.sportstouch.com; http://www.createspace.com
Dist(s): **Lulu Pr., Inc.**

Sportsman's Connection, *(978-1-885010)* Div. of Sportsman's Marketing, Inc., Orders Addr.: P.O. Box 852, Lake Elmo, MN 55042 USA Tel 800-264-0474; Fax: 651-773-3320; Toll Free: 800-777-7461; Edit Addr.: 1810 N. 16th St. Ste. 1, Superior, WI 54880-2597 USA
E-mail: info@sportsmansconnection.com
Web site: http://www.sportsmansconnection.com
Dist(s): **Partners Bk. Distributing, Inc.**

SportsZone *Imprint of* **ABDO Publishing Co.**

Spotlight, *(978-1-59961)* Div. of ABDO Publishing Group, Orders Addr.: P.O. Box 398166, Edina, MN 55439-8166 USA Fax: 952-831-1632; Toll Free: 877-877-5939; Edit Addr.: 8000 W. 78th St., Suite 310, Edina, MN 55439 USA; *Imprints*: Chapter Books (ChapBooks); Graphic Novels (GraphicNovel); Picture Book (PicBook); Marvel Age (Marvel Age)
E-mail: info@abdopublishing.com
Web site: http://www.abdopublishing.com
Dist(s): **ABDO Publishing Co.**

Spotlight Books *See* **Hannacroix Creek Bks., Inc.**

Spotlight News Publications *See* **Autumn Hse. Publishing**

Spotted Dog Pr., Inc., *(978-0-9647530; 978-1-893343)* Orders Addr.: P.O. Box 1721, Bishop, CA 93515 USA (SAN 257-9936) Tel 760-872-1524; Fax: 800-872-0681; Toll Free: 800-417-2790 Do not confuse with Spotted Dog Pr., Ashland, OR
E-mail: wbenti@spotteddogpress.com; store@spotteddogpress.com
Web site: http://www.spotteddogpress.com
Dist(s): **Gem Guides Bk. Co.**
Partners/West Book Distributors
Treasure Chest Bks.

Sprangers, Peter, *(978-0-9970101)* 92 Brunson Ave, Columbus, OH 43203 USA Tel 6142605413; Toll Free: 6142605413
Web site: Please Select a Prefix
Dist(s): **CreateSpace Independent Publishing Platform.**

Spray, Misty *See* **DCT Ranch Pr.**

Spreeda Publishing, *(978-0-9748979)* Div. of SPREEDA, 14204 W. 72nd St., Shawnee, KS 66216 USA Do not confuse with Maple Leaf Publishing in Minneapolis, MN
E-mail: karen@spreeda.com
Web site: http://www.spreeda.com.

Spriitelee Enterprises, *(978-0-9773460)* P.O. Box 207, Westwood, MA 02090 USA.

Spring Creek Bk. Co., *(978-1-932898; 978-0-9960974; 978-1-944657)* P.O. Box 1013, Rexburg, ID 83440 USA Tel 801-669-4368
Web site: http://www.springcreekbooks.com
Dist(s): **Brigham Distribution.**

Spring Ducks Bks., LLC, *(978-0-9761076)* Orders Addr.: P.O. Box 44847, Madison, WI 53744-4847 USA Toll Free: 800-342-4404; Edit Addr.: 222 Carillon Dr., Madison, WI 53705 USA
E-mail: kathy@springducks.com
Web site: http://www.springducks.com.

Spring Harbor Pr., *(978-0-935891)* Div. of Spring Harbor, Ltd., Orders Addr.: P.O. Box 346, Delmar, NY 12054 USA (SAN 695-9768) Tel 518-478-7817 (phone/fax)
E-mail: springharbor@springharborpress.com; info@springharborpress.com
Web site: http://www.springharborpress.com.

Spring Hollow Bks., LLC, *(978-0-9665389)* P.O. Box 115, Cave Spring, GA 30124-0115 USA Tel 706-235-5113; Fax: 706-235-0742 Do not confuse with Spring Hollow Bks., Richfield, MN
E-mail: jbcjmc@aol.com.

Spring Song Pr., LLC, *(978-0-9891915; 978-1-954768)* 4311 Dubois St., Alexandria, VA 22310 USA Tel 979-220-9614; Fax: 979-220-9614
E-mail: ceciliacsells@gmail.com.

Spring Tide Publishing, *(978-0-9765578)* 1281 N. Ocean Dr. Suite 151, Singer Island, FL 33404 USA Tel 561-632-2278
E-mail: delores@springtidepublishing.com
Web site: www.springtidepublishing.com.

Spring Tree Pr., *(978-0-9785007)* P.O. Box 461, Atlantic Highlands, NJ 07716 USA (SAN 850-8429) Tel 732-872-8002; Fax: 732-872-6967
Web site: http://www.springtreepress.com
Dist(s): **New Leaf Distributing Co., Inc.**

Springboard Pr. *Imprint of* **Little Brown & Co.**

Springer *Imprint of* **Springer Berlin / Heidelberg**

†Springer, *(978-0-387; 978-0-8176; 978-3-211; 978-3-540; 978-3-7908; 978-4-431; 978-1-85233; 978-1-84628; 978-1-4419; 978-1-4612; 978-1-4613; 978-1-4614; 978-1-4615; 978-1-4684; 978-1-4757; 978-1-4899; 978-1-4939; 978-1-5041; 978-1-0716)* Subs. of Springer Science+Business Media, Orders Addr.: P.O. Box 2485, Secaucus, NJ 07096-2485 USA Tel 201-348-4033; Fax: 201-348-4505; Toll Free: 800-777-4643; Edit Addr.: a/o Springer Nature, 233 Spring St., New York, NY 10013-1578 USA (SAN 203-2228) Tel 212-815-0249; 212-460-1500; Fax: 212-460-1575; Toll Free: 800-777-4643 Thomson Delmar Learning Distributes Blanchard & Loeb Nursing Videos Only
E-mail: Slu@Springer-ny.com; service-ny@springer.com; customerservice@springernature.com.com
Web site: http://www.springeronline.com; http://www.springer.com
Dist(s): **Ebsco Publishing**
Cengage Gale
Metapress
MyiLibrary
Palgrave Macmillan
Rittenhouse Bk. Distributors
ebrary, Inc.; *CIP*.

Springer Berlin / Heidelberg,; *Imprints*: Springer (Springr SBH)
Dist(s): **Metapress**
MyiLibrary
Palgrave Macmillan
Springer
ebrary, Inc.

Springer Japan (JPN) *(978-4-431)* *Dist. by* **Spri.**

Springer, Mary Jane, *(978-0-578-22443-5; 978-0-578-67932-7)* 26029 S. Saddletree Dr., Sun Lakes, AZ 85248 USA Tel 815-985-4258
E-mail: maryspringer1109@gmail.com.

Springer Netherlands (NLD) *(978-0-85200; 978-0-89838; 978-1-55608; 978-90-247; 978-90-277; 978-0-7462; 978-90-6193; 978-90-286)* *Dist. by* **Spri.**

Springer New York, ., New York City, NY 10036 USA; *Imprints*: Humana (Humana NY)
Dist(s): **Ebsco Publishing**
Springer.

†Springer Publishing Co., Inc., *(978-0-8261; 978-0-939957; 978-1-888799; 978-1-932603; 978-0-9771597; 978-1-933864; 978-1-935281; 978-1-936287; 978-1-936303; 978-1-61705; 978-1-62070)* 11 W. 42nd St., 15th Fl., New York, NY 10036 USA (SAN 203-2236) Tel 212-431-4370; Fax: 212-941-7842; Toll Free: 877-687-7476
E-mail: Springer@springerpub.com; journals@springerpub.com; Editorial@springerpub.com; cs@springerpub.com
Web site: http://www.springerpub.com
Dist(s): **CreateSpace Independent Publishing Platform**
Ebsco Publishing
Independent Pubs. Group
Johns Hopkins Univ. Pr.
MyiLibrary
Rittenhouse Bk. Distributors
ebrary, Inc.; *CIP*.

Springer-Verlag New York, Incorporated *See* **Springer**

Springs Ink Publishing *See* **McCaid Paul Books**

SpringTree *Imprint of* **Forest Hill Publishing, LLC**

Sprite Pr., *(978-0-9706654; 978-0-9764295)* 2118 Sycamore Cove Cir., Miamisburg, OH 45343 USA Tel 740-767-2470
E-mail: spritepress@gmail.com
Web site: http://www.members.aol.com/spritepress.

Sproing Books *See* **Gripper Products**

Sproles, Clay books *See* **Cats Corner Publishing**

Sprouls, Bridget, *(978-0-692-09142-5; 978-0-692-11034-8; 978-0-578-31998-8)* 219 W. 18th St., SHIP BOTTOM, NJ 08008 USA Tel 609-576-6420
E-mail: BridgetSprouls@gmail.com
Dist(s): **Ingram Content Group.**

Sprout Printing, *(978-0-9863224)* P.O. Box 561, Manteno, IL 60950 USA Tel 847-875-4692
E-mail: kazman0@yahoo.com
Web site: richkazlausky.wix.com/richkazlausky.

Sprouting Peanut Pubs., *(978-0-615-22222-6; 978-0-578-66458-3; 978-0-578-66460-6; 979-8-9863373)* P.O. Box 2606, Gilroy, CA 95021 USA
Web site: http://www.whatsupwillie.com.

Spruce Bks. *Imprint of* **Sasquatch Bks.**

Spruce Box *See* **Fun Family Publishing**

Spruce Gulch Pr., *(978-0-9625714; 978-0-9841259)* Orders Addr.: P.O. Box 4347, Rome, NY 13442-4347 USA (SAN 297-3014) Tel 315-337-3626
E-mail: SprGulch@aol.com
Dist(s): **North Country Bks., Inc.**

Spuyten Duyvil Publishing, *(978-0-923389; 978-0-9661242; 978-1-881471; 978-0-9720662; 978-1-933132; 978-1-941550; 978-1-944682; 978-1-947980; 978-1-949966; 978-1-952419; 978-1-956005; 978-1-959556)* 223 Bedford Ave. No. 725, Brooklyn, NY 11211 USA (SAN 237-9481) Toll Free: 800-886-5304 (phone/fax)
E-mail: editors@spuytenduyvil.net
Web site: http://www.spuytenduyvil.net
Dist(s): **SPD-Small Pr. Distribution.**

SpyGirls Pr., *(978-0-9852273; 978-0-9979545)* P.O. Box 1537, Fairfax, VA 22038 USA Tel 571-213-1586
E-mail: melissamahle@verizon.net
Web site: www.anatoliasteppe.com.

Spyrou-Andriotis, Vicky, *(978-0-615-24795-3; 978-0-9821808)* 3919 Old Town Rd., Bridgeport, CT 06606 USA
E-mail: info@vickyandriotis.com
Web site: http://www.vickyandriotis.com.

SQP *Imprint of* **Specialized Quality Pubns.**

Square Circle Pr., LLC *See* **Square Circle Pr. LLC**

Square Circle Pr. LLC, *(978-0-9789066; 978-0-9833897; 978-0-9856926; 978-0-9989670)* P.O. Box 913, Schenectady, NY 12301 USA (SAN 851-9145) Tel 518-432-6657 Do not confuse with Square Circle Press in Corte Madera, CA
E-mail: bookinfo@squarecirclepress.com
Web site: http://www.squarecirclepress.com
Dist(s): **Ingram Content Group**
North Country Bks., Inc.

Square Deal Pr., *(978-0-9754941)* 368 S. McCaslin Blvd., Box 206, Louisville, CO 80027 USA.

Square Fish, *(978-0-312)* 175 Fifth Ave., New York, NY 10010 USA Tel 646-307-5770
E-mail: squarefish.market@hbpub.com
Web site: http://www.squarefishbooks.com
Dist(s): **Children's Plus, Inc.**
Macmillan
Westminster John Knox Pr.

Square Halo Bks., *(978-0-9658798; 978-0-9785097; 978-1-941106)* Orders Addr.: P.O. Box 18954, Baltimore, MD 21206 USA Tel 410-485-6227; Edit Addr.: 4310 Southern Ave., Baltimore, MD 21206 USA
E-mail: square_halo@yahoo.com; ned@squarehalobooks.com
Web site: http://www.squarehalobooks.com
Dist(s): **Baker & Taylor Publisher Services (BTPS).**

Square One Pubs., *(978-0-9664202; 978-0-7570; 978-0-9792746)* 115 Herricks Rd., Garden City Park, NY 11040 USA Tel 516-535-2010; Fax: 516-535-2014; *Imprints*: Vital Health Publishing (Vital Hlth)
E-mail: sq1info@aol.com
Web site: http://squareonepublishers.com
Dist(s): **Athena Productions, Inc.**

Square Tree *See* **Blast Cafe**

Square Tree Publishing, *(978-0-9903190; 978-0-9988328; 978-1-7329587; 978-1-7353859; 978-1-7369186; 978-1-957293; 979-8-218-20765-6)* 3221 St. Albans Dr., Los Alamitos, CA 90720 USA Tel 714-484-7000
E-mail: sherry@squaretreepublishing.com.

Squarey Head, Inc., *(978-0-9742003)* 6362 W. Cross Dr., Littleton, CO 80123 USA Tel 303-798-1877; Fax: 303-794-4639.

Squid Works, *(978-0-9755041; 978-0-9972813)* Orders Addr.: 2132 E. 97th Dr., Thornton, CO 80229 USA
E-mail: squidworkscomics@gmail.com
Web site: http://www.squidworkscomics.com
Dist(s): **Amplify Publishing Group.**

Squires Publishing, *(978-0-9816048)* 7224 S. Yates Blvd., Suite 3N, Chicago, IL 60649 USA Tel 773-667-0039
E-mail: tanyacloud@comcast.net.

SRA/McGraw-Hill, *(978-0-07; 978-0-383)* Div. of The McGraw-Hill Education Group, Orders Addr.: 220 E. Daniel Dale Rd., DeSoto, TX 75115-2490 USA Fax: 972-228-1982; Toll Free: 800-843-8855; Edit Addr.: 8787 Orion Pl., Columbus, OH 43240-4027 USA Tel 614-430-6600; Fax: 614-430-6621; Toll Free: 800-468-5850
E-mail: sra@mcgraw-hill.com
Web site: https://www.sraonline.com
Dist(s): **Libros Sin Fronteras**
Weston Woods Studios, Inc.

SRAtkinson, *(978-0-9964550)* 104 10th St 2E, Hoboken, NJ 07030 USA Tel 435-668-0225
E-mail: savvyatkinson@gmail.com
Web site: sratkinson.com.

SRattray, *(978-0-578-70599-6; 978-0-578-98551-0; 978-0-578-29374-5)* 3515 Corn Stream Rd, Randallstown, MD 21133 USA Tel 443-474-0271
E-mail: srattray11@gmail.com.

SRFPRTY, *(978-1-7342208)* 136 S. Navassa Rd., Leland, NC 28451 USA Tel 910-782-7934
E-mail: justicew095@gmail.com
Web site: FUDGEWILLI.COM.

Sri Ramakrishna Math (IND) *(978-81-7120; 978-81-86465; 978-81-7823) Dist. by* **Vedanta Pr.**

Sroda, George, *(978-0-9604486)* P.O. Box 97, Amherst Junction, WI 54407 USA (SAN 210-8607) Tel 715-824-3868; Fax: 715-824-5344.

SRT Publishing, *(978-0-9771248)* 530 Moon Clinton Rd., Moon Township, PA 15108 USA Tel 412-741-0581; Fax: 412-264-1103
E-mail: merch@silverringthing.com
Web site: http://www.silverringthing.com.

Sruvis Publishing, *(978-0-9889907)* 2219 Pear Blossom, San Antonio, TX 78247 USA Tel 210-219-2156; Fax: 210-494-1994
E-mail: lyndasdavis8@aol.com.

SS Publishing, *(978-1-7344347)* 4501 Lindell Blvd, St. Louis, MO 63108 USA Tel 314-531-1488
E-mail: sheilabader@sbcglobal.net.

SS Pubns., Ltd. (CAN) *(978-0-9699105; 978-0-9686803) Dist. by* **BTPS.**

Ssorgsoft, LLC, *(978-0-9765240)* P.O. Box 771192, Orlando, FL 32877 USA.

St. Aidan Pr., Inc., *(978-0-9719230)* 96 Dunlap Dr., Charles Town, WV 25414 USA
E-mail: michael_rabjohns@hotmail.com
Web site: http://www.staidanpress.com.

St. Augustine Academy Pr., *(978-1-936639; 978-1-64051)* 12050 Rambling Rd., Homer Glen, IL 60491 USA Tel 708-645-4691
E-mail: Lbergman2@sbcglobal.net
Web site: www.staugustineacademypress.com.

St Barts Publishing, *(978-1-7372778)* 129 St Barts Ave., St Augustine, FL 32082 USA Tel 860-558-9351
E-mail: jtmucci@comcast.net
Web site: stbartspublishings.com.

St. Bernard Publishing, LLC, *(978-0-9741269)* P.O. Box 2218, Bay City, MI 48707-2218 USA Tel 989-892-1348 (phone/fax)
E-mail: bcgirl@charter.net
Web site: http://www.lifeongrannysfarm.com/.

St. Cyr Pr., *(978-1-7339929)* 115 Grove Ave., Albany, NY 12208-3120 USA Tel 518-482-8816
E-mail: aliciastenard@yahoo.com
Web site: aliciastenard.com.

St. Hope Academy, *(978-0-9759548)* Orders Addr.: P.O. Box 5447, Sacramento, CA 95817 USA Tel 916-649-7900; Fax: 916-452-7177; Edit Addr.: 3400 3rd Ave., Sacramento, CA 95817 USA
Web site: http://40acresartgallery.org.

St. John's Pr., *(978-0-9710551; 978-0-615-83132-9; 978-0-9916014)* Orders Addr.: 5318 Torri Park Dr., Cottondale, AL 35453 USA Tel 205-242-4422; Fax: 205-553-9459 Do not confuse with Saint John's Press in Los Angeles, CA
E-mail: charleysix@gmail.com.

St. Leo Press *See* **St. Leo Pr.**

St. Martin's Griffin *Imprint of* **St. Martin's Pr.**

St. Martin's Paperbacks *Imprint of* **St. Martin's Pr.**

†St. Martin's Pr., *(978-0-312; 978-0-8050; 978-0-940687; 978-0-9603648; 978-1-55927; 978-1-58063; 978-1-58238; 978-1-4299; 978-1-250)* Div. of Holtzbrinck Pubs., Orders Addr.: 16365 James Madison Hwy., Gordonville, VA 22942 USA Tel 540-672-7600; Fax: 540-672-7540 (customer service); Toll Free Fax: 800-672-2054; Toll Free: 888-330-8477; Edit Addr.: 175 Fifth Ave., 20th Flr., New York, NY 10010 USA (SAN 200-2132) Tel 212-674-5151 (Trade Div.); 212-726-0200 (College Div.); Fax: 212-674-3179 (Trade Div.); 212-686-9491 (College Div.); Toll Free: 800-221-7945 (Trade Div.); 800-470-4767 (College Div.); *Imprints:* Saint Martin's Griffin (St Martin Griffin); Saint Martin's Paperbacks (St Martins Paperbacks); Dunne, Thomas Books (Thomas Dunne); Minotaur Books (Minotaur); Golden Books Adult Publishing Group (Golden Adult); Priddy Books (Priddy); Wednesday Books (Wednesday Bks); Odd Dot (Odd Dot); Neon Squid (Neon Squid)
E-mail: webmaster@stmartins.com; enquiries@stmartins.com
Web site: http://www.stmartins.com; http://www.smpcollege.com
Dist(s): **Blackstone Audio, Inc.**
Comag Marketing Group
Cambridge Univ. Pr.
Children's Plus, Inc.
CreateSpace Independent Publishing Platform
Ediciones Universal
Kaplan Publishing
Libros Sin Fronteras
Macmillan
MyiLibrary
Westminster John Knox Pr.
ebrary, Inc.; *CIP.*

St Mary's Church, *(978-0-9763902)* 429 Central Ave., Sandusky, OH 44870 USA Tel 419-625-7465
Web site: http://www.stmarysandusky.org.

St. Michael's Abbey, *(978-0-9742298)* 19292 El Toro Rd., Silverado, CA 92676-9710 USA
E-mail: fmorbertw@yahoo.com
Web site: http://www.abbeynews.com.

St. Nicholas Pr. *Imprint of* **CrossBearers Publishing**

St. Pauls *Imprint of* **St Pauls/Alba Hse. Pubs.**

St Pauls Pubns. (AUS) *(978-0-909986; 978-0-949080; 978-1-875570; 978-1-876295; 978-1-921032; 978-1-921472; 978-1-923033; 978-1-925494; 978-1-921963) Dist. by* **St Pauls Alba.**

†St Pauls/Alba Hse. Pubs., *(978-0-8189)* Div. of Society of St. Paul, 2187 Victory Blvd., Staten Island, NY 10314-6603 USA (SAN 201-2405) Tel 718-761-0047; Fax: 718-761-0057; 718-698-8390; Toll Free: 800-343-2522; *Imprints:* Saint Pauls (Saint Pauls)
E-mail: albabooks@aol.com
Web site: http://www.albahouse.org; *CIP.*

St. Roux Pr., *(978-0-9718433)* 308 Montmartre St., Folsom, LA 70437 USA
E-mail: faucheux@msn.com.

Stabenfeldt Inc., *(978-1-933343; 978-1-934983)* Orders Addr.: 225 N. Main St., Bristol, CT 06011 USA Toll Free: 800-410-4145; *Imprints:* PONY (Pny)
Web site: http://www.pony4kids.com.

Stacey Alysson Yoga, *(978-0-692-83320-9; 978-0-692-06023-0; 978-0-692-06025-4; 978-0-692-11213-7; 978-0-692-13589-1)* 234 s gale Dr. #109, BEVERLY HILLS, CA 90211 USA Tel 424-333-6771
E-mail: jeffwcrawford5+LVP0003257@gmail.com; jeffwcrawford5+LVP0003257@gmail.com.

Stacey, Emma *See* **Peer Leadership Advisory Network**

†Stackpole Bks., *(978-0-8117)* 5067 Ritter Rd., Mechanicsburg, PA 17055 USA (SAN 202-5396) Tel 717-796-0411; Fax: 717-796-0412; Toll Free: 800-732-3669
E-mail: ccraley@stackpolebooks.com
Web site: http://www.stackpolebooks.com/
Dist(s): **Blackstone Audio, Inc.**
MyiLibrary
National Bk. Network
Open Road Integrated Media, Inc.
Rowman & Littlefield Publishers, Inc.
Rowman & Littlefield Unlimited Model; *CIP.*

Stadium Adventure Series *See* **August in Au Train Press**

Staff Development for Educators, *(978-0-9627389; 978-1-884548; 978-1-934026; 978-1-935502; 978-1-63133)* Div. of Highlights for Children, Orders Addr.: P.O. Box 577, Peterborough, NH 03458 USA Tel 603-924-9621; Fax: 603-924-6688; Toll Free Fax: 800-337-9929; Toll Free: 800-321-0401; Edit Addr.: 10 Sharon Rd., Peterborough, NH 03458 USA; *Imprints:* Crystal Springs Books (Crystal Spgs)
E-mail: dfredericks@sde.com
Web site: http://www.sde.com; http://www.crystalsprings.com; http://www.barnesandnoble.com
Dist(s): **Follett School Solutions**
Stenhouse Pubs.

Stafford House, *(978-0-9822587; 978-0-9981070; 978-1-7344786; 978-1-7366220)* P.O. Box 291, Pacific Palisades, CA 90272 USA
Web site: http://www.abcyogaforkids.com; www.kidsyogaday.com.

Stagecast Software, Inc., *(978-1-929721)* 580 College Ave., Palo Alto, CA 94306 USA Tel 650-354-0735; Fax: 650-354-0739; Toll Free: 888-782-4322
E-mail: info@stagecast.com
Web site: http://www.stagecast.com.

Stahl Pubns., *(978-0-9755174)* P.O. Box 201, Ashley, IN 46705-0201 USA.

Stahlli Nation *See* **Bethany Stahl**

Staige Productions, *(978-0-9641375)* 290 Orrin St., Winona, MN 55987-2083 USA Tel 507-452-3627.

Stairway Pubns., *(978-0-9740061)* P.O. Box 518, Huntington, NY 11743-0518 USA (SAN 255-3422) Fax: 631-351-2142
E-mail: publisher@stairwaypub.com
Web site: http://www.stairwaypub.com
Dist(s): **Quality Bks., Inc.**

Stairway Publishing, *(978-0-9761953)* 1332 Anacapa St., Suite 200, Santa Barbara, CA 93101 USA; 230 E Pedregosa St., Santa Barbara, CA 93101 (SAN 256-761X) Tel 805-451-5070; Fax: 805-962-1404 Do not Confuse with Shoreline Publishing in Bayside, NY
E-mail: purnoff@seedmackall.com.

Stairwell Bks., *(978-0-9768730; 978-0-9833482; 978-1-939269)* 9 Carleton St., Greenwich, CT 06830 USA
E-mail: rose@stairwellbooks.com; argillott@gmail.com
Web site: http://www.dreamcatchermagazine.co.uk; http://www.stairwellbooks.co.uk; http://www.stairwellbooks.com.

Stampley, C. D. Enterprises, Inc., *(978-0-915741; 978-1-58087)* Orders Addr.: P.O. Box 33172, Charlotte, NC 28233 USA (SAN 294-1325) Tel 704-333-6631; Fax: 704-336-6932; Edit Addr.: 6100 Orr Rd., Charlotte, NC 28213 USA
E-mail: info@stampley.com; rick@stampley.com
Web site: http://www.stampley.com
Dist(s): **Follett School Solutions**
Giron Bks.

Stance Pubns., *(978-0-615-18108-0; 978-0-9821047)* 4510 Seashore Dr., #A, Newport Beach, CA 92663-2520 USA
E-mail: marcpent@msn.com
Web site: http://www.stancepublications.com
Dist(s): **Ingram Content Group.**

Stancofski, Hiba, *(978-0-578-79761-8)* 35948 Spinnaker Cir., Lewes, DE 19958 USA Tel 302-236-7798
E-mail: HibaStancofskiAuthor@gmail.com.

Stand up to Bullying *See* **Bks. by Tillie**

Standard International Print Group Inc., *(978-1-58279; 978-1-888777; 978-1-86091; 978-1-60081)* Orders Addr.: 9723 Acqua Ct. Unit 324, Naples, FL 34113 USA Tel 239-595-5516; Fax: 239-649-5832; Edit Addr.: 2614 Tamiami Trail N., Naples, FL 34103 USA Tel 239-248-5550
E-mail: sales@chefexpressmedia.com; sales@stndpub.com
Web site: https://www.chefexpressmedia.com/; http://stndpub.com/.

Standard Publications, Inc., *(978-0-9709788; 978-0-9722691; 978-1-59462; 978-1-60424; 978-1-60597; 978-1-4385; 978-1-61742)* P.O. Box 3204, Kirkland, WA 98083 USA (SAN 912-9251) Tel 708-669-4643; Fax: 630-214-0564; *Imprints:* Book Jungle (Book Jungle)
E-mail: spi@standardpublications.com
Dist(s): **MyiLibrary.**

†Standard Publishing, *(978-0-7847; 978-0-87239; 978-0-87403; 978-0-933657; 978-1-58170)* 8805 Governors Hill Dr. Ste. 400, Cincinnati, OH 45249-3319 USA (SAN 110-5515) Toll Free Fax: 877-867-5751 (customer service); Toll Free: 800-543-1301; 800-543-1353 (customer service); *Imprints:* Bean Sprouts (Bean Sprouts) Do not confuse with Standard Publishing Corp., Boston, MA
E-mail: customerservice@standardpub.com; trolfes@standardpub.com; dlewis@standardpub.com
Web site: http://www.standardpub.com
Dist(s): **B&H Publishing Group**
Cook, David C.; *CIP.*

Standard Publishing Company *See* **Standard Publishing**

Standing For Christ, Inc., *(978-0-9754834)* P.O. Box 28468, Cleveland, OH 44128 USA Tel 216-299-4523
E-mail: kelvinsfc@yahoo.com
Web site: http://www.standingforchrist.org.

Stanek, David, *(978-1-7351377)* 3398 Hickok Pl., Boulder, CO 80301 USA Tel 303-579-1580
E-mail: david.stanek37@gmail.com.

Stanek, Mary Beth, *(978-0-9747556)* 291 Lothrop Rd., Grosse Pointe, MI 48236 USA.

Stanfield, James Co., *(978-1-56304; 978-1-941264)* P.O. Box 41058, Santa Barbara, CA 93140 USA Tel 805-897-1185; Fax: 805-897-1187; Toll Free: 800-421-6534
E-mail: maindesk@stanfield.com
Web site: http://www.stanfield.com.

Stanford Center for Research in Disease Prevention (S C R D P) *See* **Stanford Prevention Research Ctr.**

Stanford Prevention Research Ctr., *(978-1-879552)* Div. of Stanford Univ. Schl. of Medicine, Hoover Pavilion, Rm. N 229 211 Quarry Rd., Stanford, CA 94305-5705 USA Tel 650-723-0003; Fax: 650-498-4828
E-mail: askhprc@med.stanford.edu
Web site: http://hprc.stanford.edu.

Stanger, Robert *See* **Club Pro Products**

Stanislaus, Justin, *(978-0-578-85592-9)* 112 Bear Oak Rd., Freehold, NJ 07728 USA Tel 732-642-9199
E-mail: justinstanislaus@gmail.com
Web site: www.iamjustinstan.com.

Stanley, Donna Lacy, *(978-0-9766894)* 244 Sunset Dr., Waynesboro, VA 22980 USA Tel 540-949-5474
E-mail: dlstanle@yahoo.com.

Stanley O. Williford Literary Agency, *(978-0-9651783; 978-0-9762730; 978-0-578-55930-8; 978-0-578-73343-2)* Do not confuse with companies with the same name in Sandy, UT, Huntsville, AL, Ramona, CA, Southfield, MI, Griffen, GA, Phoenix, MD, Detroit, MI
E-mail: Stanley O. Williford Literary Agency
Web site: http://www.visionpub@sbcglobal.net
Dist(s): **Send The Light Distribution LLC**
Smashwords.

Stanley Publishing Co., *(978-0-9790350; 978-0-615-55295-8; 978-0-9856495)* 810 Agua Caliente Dr., El Paso, TX 79912-1705 USA (SAN 852-257X)
E-mail: info@stanleypublishing.com
Web site: http://stanleypublishing.com.

Stanley, Shirley, *(978-0-9747318)* Orders Addr.: 1116 20th St. S., No. 216, Birmingham, AL 35205 USA Tel 205-663-6674.

Stansbury Publishing, *(978-0-9708922; 978-0-9766269; 978-1-935807)* Subs. of Heidelberg Graphics, Orders Addr.: 2 Stansbury Ct., Chico, CA 95928 USA
E-mail: spublishing@heidelberggraphics.com
Web site: http://www.heidelberggraphics.com.

Stanton & Harper Bks., *(978-0-9630151)* Orders Addr.: P.O. Box 21585, Greensboro, NC 27420 USA; Edit Addr.: 291 Buckhorn Trail, Reidsville, NC 27320 USA Tel 910-951-1234; Fax: 910-951-9966.

Stapled By Mom Publishing *Imprint of* **Baker, Adam**

Star Bible & Tract Corp., *(978-0-933672; 978-0-940999; 978-1-56794)* Orders Addr.: P.O. Box 821220, Fort Worth, TX 76182 USA (SAN 203-3518) Tel 817-416-5889; Fax: 817-251-0129; Toll Free: 800-433-7507; Edit Addr.: P.O. Box 821220, N Richlnd Hls, TX 76182-1220 USA (SAN 664-6247)
E-mail: starbible@starbible.com
Web site: http://www.starbible.com
Dist(s): **Twentieth Century Christian Bks.**

Star Bright Bks., Inc., *(978-1-887734; 978-1-932065; 978-1-59572; 978-1-64909)* 13 Landsdowne, Cambridge , MA 02139 USA (SAN 254-5225) Tel 617-354-1300; Fax: 617-354-1399; Toll Free: 800-788-4439
E-mail: info@starbrightbooks.com; r.s.lambert@starbrightbooks.com
Web site: http://www.starbrightbooks.com
Dist(s): **Children's Plus, Inc.**

Star Cross'd Destiny *Imprint of* **Bohemian Trash Studios**

Star Dome Publishing, LLC, *(978-0-9766662)* P.O. Box 411300, Melbourne, FL 32941 USA
E-mail: fcavalli@bellsouth.net
Web site: http://www.stardomepublishing.com.

Star Dust Dream, *(978-1-948060)* 4544 Dix, Luna Pier, MI 48157 USA Tel 734-317-7251; 3829 MI ST RD 151, Erie, MI 48133 Tel 734-317-7251
E-mail: mimmi92025@yahoo.com
Web site: prgarcia1.com.

Star Gem Publishing, *(978-0-615-54730-5; 978-0-9978384)* 4101 California Ave #44, Bakersfield, CA 93309 USA Tel 661-932-0573
Dist(s): **CreateSpace Independent Publishing Platform**
Dummy Record Do Not USE!!!!.

Star Light Pr., *(978-1-879817)* 1811 S. First St., Austin, TX 78704-4299 USA Tel 512-441-0588; 512-441-0062 (phone/fax); *Imprints:* Children (Children)
E-mail: info@starlightpress.com
Web site: http://www.starlightpress.com
Dist(s): **Book Wholesalers, Inc.**
iLeon.

Star Pr., The, *(978-0-9676189)* Div. of Indiana Newspapers, Inc., Orders Addr.: P.O. Box 2408, Muncie, IN 47307-0408 USA (SAN 169-2437) Tel 765-213-5799; Fax: 765-213-5703; Toll Free: 800-783-7827; Edit Addr.: 345 S. High St., Muncie, IN 47305 USA
E-mail: rfarmer@thestarpress.com
Web site: http://www.thestarpress.com.

Star Pubns., *(978-0-932356)* 1211 W. 60th Terr., Kansas City, MO 64113 USA (SAN 212-4564) Tel 816-523-8228 Do not confuse with companies with the same name in Rancho Palos Verdes, CA, Orange Park, FL, San Jose, CA, Colorado Springs, CO.

Star Publish LLC, *(978-1-932993; 978-1-935188)*
E-mail: starpublishinfo@gmail.com
Web site: http://www.starpublishllc.com
Dist(s): **Smashwords.**

Star Quest Publishing Phx, *(978-0-9767035)* 3030 E. Shangri-La Rd., Phoenix, AZ 85028 USA Tel 602-621-3431; Fax: 602-926-2484
E-mail: karen@starquestpublishingphx.com
Web site: http://www.starquestpublishing.com.

Star Tribe Publishing, *(978-0-9970554; 978-0-9996387)* 843 N. Calle De Pinos, Palm Springs, CA 92262 USA Tel 925-351-6717
E-mail: authorariellamoon@gmail.com
Web site: http://www.AriellaMoon.com.

Star Trilogy Publishing, *(978-1-7325372)* 1360 Riverside Ave., Boulder, CO 80304 USA Tel 303-440-9422
E-mail: thestartrilogy@aol.com
Web site: www.thedragonboy.com
Dist(s): **Independent Pubs. Group**
Midpoint Trade Bks., Inc.

Star Trilogy, The *See* **Star Trilogy Publishing**

Star Write Creations, *(978-0-9743851)* P.O. Box G, Birnamwood, WI 54414 USA Toll Free: 888-999-6609.

Starbell Bks., *(978-0-9747774)* 2507 LaBrecque Dr., Plainfield, IL 60544 USA Tel 815-254-9495
E-mail: starbellbooks@comcast.net
Web site: http://www.starbellbooks.com.

Starbound Bks. *Imprint of* **Wheatmark, Inc.**

Starbound Publishing Company *See* **Collectors Pr., Inc.**

Starbucks Coffee Co., *(978-0-9726394)* 2401 Utah Ave. S., Seattle, WA 98134 USA Tel 206-447-1575; Toll Free: 800-235-2883
E-mail: info@starbucks.com
Web site: http://www.starbuckscollectibles.com.

Starburns Industries Pr., *(978-0-9889363)* 23720 Canyon Rd, Battle Ground , WA 98604 USA Tel 360-431-4533
E-mail: Sbipress@starburnsind.com
Web site: starburnsindustries.com
Dist(s): **Diamond Comic Distributors, Inc.**
Diamond Bk. Distributors.

StarCastle Publishing *See* **ecEmedia, a Div. of The EC Corp.**

Starcatcher Pr., *(978-0-9700164; 978-0-9848455)* 256 Tudor Cir., Ashland, OR 97520 USA Tel 541-488-4230; Fax: 541-488-4354
E-mail: malcolm@wherewelive.com; starcatcherpress@aol.com
Web site: http://www.starcatcherpress.com.

Stardust Books *See* **Stardust Bks.**

Stardust Bks., *(978-0-692-85016-9; 978-0-692-16413-6)* 106 Standing Rock Dr., McMurray, PA 15317 USA Tel 412-736-3253
E-mail: sherri.laughner@gmail.com.

STAReviews *Imprint of* **N&N Publishing Co., Inc.**

Starfall Education, *(978-1-59577)* Starfall Education Foundation, P.O. Box 359, Boulder, CO 80306 USA Toll Free Fax: 800-943-6666; Toll Free: 888-857-8990
Web site: http://www.starfall.com
Dist(s): **Blue Mountain Arts Inc.**

Starfall Publications *See* **Starfall Education**

Starfish Aquatics Institute, *(978-0-9746613; 978-0-578-13105-4; 978-0-578-13448-2; 978-0-578-13449-9)* 10 Ramshorn Ct., Savannah, GA 31411 USA Tel 912-692-1173
E-mail: sara@sai-intl.org; jill@sai-intl.org
Web site: http://www.starfishaquatics.org.

Starfish Bay Publishing Pty Ltd. (AUS) *(978-1-76036) Dist. by* **BTPS.**

Stargazer Publishing Co., *(978-0-9643853; 978-0-9713756; 978-1-933277)* Orders Addr.: P.O. Box 77002, Corona, CA 92877-0100 USA (SAN 298-6566) Tel 951-898-4619; Fax: 951-898-4633; Toll Free: 800-606-7895; Edit Addr.: 958 Stanislaus Dr., Corona, CA 92881 USA Do not confuse with Stargazer Publishing in Neenah, WI
E-mail: stargazer@stargazerpub.com
Web site: http://www.stargazerpub.com.

Stark, Kate, *(978-1-7362913)* 4101 Volk Ct., Fort Worth, TX 76244 USA Tel 817-917-7348
E-mail: kateharris7@gmail.com.

Stark Productions Inc., *(978-1-936592)* 109 Orange Ave., St. Cloud, FL 34769 USA Tel 407-957-8502 (Tel/Fax) Do not confuse with Stark Productions Inc in OaklandCA
E-mail: stark109@hotmail.com
Web site: www.starkproductioninc.com.

Starks, Shirley *See* **Inspirational Hse. of America**

Starla Enterprises, Inc., *(978-1-938085; 978-0-692-94596-4; 978-0-692-96659-4; 978-0-692-97291-5; 978-0-692-97328-8; 978-0-692-97351-6; 978-0-692-07934-8; 978-0-692-08941-5; 978-0-692-08943-9; 978-0-692-08944-6; 978-0-692-12953-1; 978-0-578-40977-1; 978-0-578-40981-8; 978-0-578-40983-2; 978-0-578-40993-1; 978-0-578-40994-8; 978-0-578-40995-5; 978-0-578-48303-0; 978-0-578-48307-8; 978-0-578-52365-1) 9415 E. Harry St Ste 603, Wichita, KS 67207 USA Tel 316-393-8195*
E-mail: starla@starlakaye.com
Web site: www.starlacriser.com.

Starleights Press *See* **Snipperdoomers Pr.**

Starlight Pubns., *(978-0-9615667; 978-0-9936965-8-9)* 1438 Epping Forest Dr., Atlanta, GA 30319 USA (SAN 695-9644) Tel 404-237-7125.

StarLineage Pubns., *(978-1-885226)* P.O. Box 1630, McCloud, CA 96057-1630 USA Tel 530-964-2496.

Starling Publishing, *(978-0-9857394; 978-0-9976390; 978-1-954698)* 1011 Paintbrush Ave., Kimberly, ID 83341 USA Tel 435-881-4812
E-mail: amberargyle@yahoo.com.

Starlit Publishing LLC, *(978-0-9792946)* 1750 Powder Springs Rd. Suite 190, Marietta, GA 30064 USA.

Starlog Group, Incorporated *See* **Profile Entertainment, Inc.**

StarProse Corp., *(978-0-9721071)* 17445 Roosevelt Rd., Hemlock, MI 48626 USA
E-mail: webmaster@starprose.com
Web site: http://www.starprose.com.

STARR Publishing, *(978-0-9792333; 978-0-9882394)* Orders Addr.: 3340 SE Federal HWY No. 275, Stuart, FL 34997 USA Tel 786-693-4223
E-mail: joyce.starr@gmail.com
Web site: http://drjoycestarr.com; http://starrpublications.com; http://starrpublishing.com.

Starry Forest Bks. *Imprint of* **Starry Forest Bks., Inc.**

Starry Forest Bks., Inc., *(978-1-946000; 978-1-946260; 978-1-951784)* ; *Imprints:* Starry Forest Books (StrryFrstBk)
E-mail: robertagis@starryforestbooks.com
Dist(s): **Two Rivers Distribution.**

Starry Girl Publishing, *(978-0-9960737; 978-0-9986143)* 5553 W. 6th St. No. 2409, Los Angeles, CA 90036 USA Tel 323-931-4038
E-mail: jennifer.farwell@gmail.com
Web site: www.jenniferfarwell.com.

Starry Sky Publishing, *(978-0-9855899; 978-0-9961470; 978-0-9996399)* P.O. Box 419, Tampa, FL 33601 USA Tel 443-838-7228
E-mail: starryskypub@gmail.com.

StarryBks., *(978-0-9882113; 978-0-692-27075-2; 978-0-692-34543-6)* P.O. Box 1788, Yelm, WA 98597 USA Tel 360-894-3592
E-mail: dreamscapes@ywave.com
Dist(s): **CreateSpace Independent Publishing Platform.**

Starscape *Imprint of* **Doherty, Tom Assocs., LLC**

Starseed & Urantian Schools of Melchizedek Publishing *See* **Global Community Communications Publishing**

Starseed Universe Pr., *(978-0-9991251; 978-1-7362674)* 60 Overbrook Dr., Cherry Hill, NJ 08002 USA Tel 609-314-1750
E-mail: stefaniannmilanese@gmail.com.

Starshell Pr., Ltd., *(978-0-9707110)* 210 Ridge Rd., Watchung, NJ 07069 USA Tel 908-755-7050; Fax: 212-983-5271
E-mail: starshellpress@yahoo.com
Web site: http://www.starshellpress.com.

Starshow Pubns., *(978-0-9966665; 978-0-9989245)* 122 Woodland St., BURKESVILLE, KY 42717 USA Tel 6153069481.

Start Publishing LLC, *(978-0-939416; 978-0-9664520; 978-1-57344; 978-1-930486; 978-1-60977; 978-1-936740; 978-1-62558; 978-1-62778; 978-1-62793; 978-1-940550; 978-1-63228; 978-1-63355; 978-1-68146; 978-1-68299; 978-1-63596; 978-1-64506; 978-1-64593; 978-1-951273; 978-1-952438; 978-1-64974) 101 Hudson St. 37th Flr., Ste. 3705, Jersey City, NJ 07302 USA; Imprints:* Salvo Press (SalvoPr); Pyr (PyrBks); Cleis Press (CleisPr)
E-mail: weisfeld@start-media.com; start-publishing.com
Web site: http://www.start-publishing.com
Dist(s): **Blackstone Audio, Inc.**
MyiLibrary
National Bk. Network
Red Wheel/Weiser
Simon & Schuster, Inc.
SCB Distributors.

Starter Guides LLC, *(978-0-9995860)* 769 NW 10th St, Miami, FL 33136 USA Tel 520-413-8810
E-mail: info@starterguide.org
Web site: www.starterguide.org.

StarWalk Kids Media *Imprint of* **Isabella Products, Inc.**

Starward Publishing, *(978-0-9862099)* 18552 Ocean Mist Dr, Boca Raton, FL 33498 USA Tel 561-482-9812
E-mail: info@starwardpublishing.com.

Stash Bks. *Imprint of* **C & T Publishing**

State Historical Society of North Dakota, *(978-1-891419; 978-0-9796796; 978-0-9801993; 978-0-578-89980-0)* Orders Addr.: 612 E. Blvd. Ave., Bismarck, ND 58505-0830 USA Tel 701-205-7802; Fax: 701-328-3710
E-mail: nhowe@nd.gov
Web site: http://www.history.nd.gov.

State Historical Society of Wisconsin *See* **Wisconsin Historical Society**

State Hse. Pr., *(978-0-938349; 978-1-880510; 978-1-933337)* S. 14th & Sayles Blvd., Austin, TX 79697 USA (SAN 660-966X); McMurry University, Box 637, Abilene, TX 79697-0637 Tel 325-793-4697; Fax: 325-793-4754 Do not confuse with State House Publishing in Madison, WI
E-mail: ckahl@mcm.edu
Web site: http://www.mcwhiney.org
Dist(s): **Encino Pr.**
Texas A&M Univ. Pr.

State of Growth Publishing Co., *(978-0-9740289)* P.O. Box 38633, Colorado Springs, CO 80937 USA
Web site: http://www.stateofgrowth.com.

State Standards Publishing, LLC, *(978-1-935077; 978-1-935884; 978-1-938813; 978-1-946400)* P.O. Box 68, Athens, GA 30603 USA (SAN 856-292X) Tel 706-621-5225; Fax: 706-621-5226; Toll Free: 866-740-3056; *Imprints:* Everett Press (Everett Pr)
E-mail: jward@statestandardspublishing.com
Web site: http://www.statestandardspublishing.com.

State Street Pr. *Imprint of* **Borders Pr.**

†State Univ. of New York Pr., *(978-0-7914; 978-0-87395; 978-0-88706; 978-1-4384; 979-8-8558)* Orders Addr.: P.O. Box 960, Herndon, VA 20172-0960 USA (SAN 203-3496) Tel 703-661-1575; Fax: 703-996-1010; Toll Free Fax: 877-204-6074; Toll Free: 877-204-6073 (customer service); Edit Addr.: 22 Corporate Woods Blvd., 3rd Flr., Albany, NY 12211-2504 USA (SAN 658-1730) Tel 518-472-5000; Fax: 518-472-5038; Toll Free: 866-430-7869; 353 Broadway, State University Plaza, Albany, NY 12246 Tel 518-944-2803; *Imprints:* Suny Press (Suny Pr)
E-mail: info@sunypress.edu; suny@presswarehouse.com; sharla.clute@sunypress.edu aria.clute@sunypress.edu;
Web site: http://www.sunypress.edu
Dist(s): **Books International, Inc.**
CreateSpace Independent Publishing Platform
Ebsco Publishing
Pegasus Pr.
SPD-Small Pr. Distribution
TNT Media Group, Inc.
ebrary, Inc.; *CIP.*

Stationmaster Pr., *(978-0-692-11404-9)* 8907 Center St., Manassas, VA 20110 USA Tel 703-786-7798
E-mail: robbiekirby@yahoo.com
Dist(s): **Independent Pub.**

Staves Creations, *(978-0-9600739; 978-1-7333451; 978-1-951622)* 10745 Cather Ave, LAS VEGAS, NV 89166 USA
Dist(s): **Ingram Content Group.**

Staying Healthy Media, Inc., *(978-0-9763237)* 4409 Summer Grape Rd., Pikesville, MD 21208 USA Tel 410-484-0457
E-mail: healthy@stayinghealthymedia.com
Web site: http://www.stayinghealthymedia.com.

Steam Crow Pr., *(978-0-9774173)* 7233 W. Cottontail Ln., Peoria, AZ 85383 USA
E-mail: sales@steamcrow.com
Web site: http://www.steamcrow.com.

Steam, Karl *See* **Libro Studio LLC**

Steam Passages Pubns., *(978-0-9758584)* 508 Lakeview Ave., Wake Forest, NC 27587 USA
E-mail: sdegaetano@steampassages.com
Web site: http://www.dlrcad.com/book.

STEAM Publishing, LLC, *(978-0-9984337)* 2125 E STANFORD DR, TEMPE, AZ 85283 USA Tel 480-777-2621
E-mail: scolsen.writer@gmail.com.

†Steck-Vaughn, *(978-0-8114; 978-0-8172; 978-0-8393; 978-0-7398; 978-1-4190)* Div. of Houghton Mifflin Harcourt Supplemental Pubs., Orders Addr.: 6277 Sea Harbor Dr., 5th Flr., Orlando, FL 32887 USA Toll Free Fax: 877-578-2638; Toll Free: 888-363-4266; Edit Addr.: 10801 N. Mopac Expressway, Bldg. 3, Austin, TX 78759 USA (SAN 658-1757) Toll Free: 800-531-5015
E-mail: ecare@harcourt.com
Web site: http://www.harcourtachieve.com
Dist(s): **Children's Plus, Inc.**
Follett School Solutions
Houghton Mifflin Harcourt Publishing Co.
Houghton Mifflin Harcourt Supplemental Pubs.; *CIP.*

Stedjee Publishing *See* **Lawe Street Bks.**

Steel Bridge Pr., *(978-0-9764415)* 610 Briarcliff, Bardstown, KY 40004-8941 USA Tel 502-348-7447; Fax: 502-350-1126
E-mail: john@steelbridgepress.com.

Steel Inferno, The *See* **Chrysanthalix Pr.**

Steele, Eugene *See* **E-BookTime LLC**

Steele Studios, *(978-0-9716811)* Orders Addr.: P.O. Box 3093, Glenwood Springs, CO 81602 USA (SAN 254-3230); Edit Addr.: 125 Ctr. Dr., No.18, Glenwood Springs, CO 81601 USA.

Steenblik, Kyle J., *(978-0-692-97391-2)* 36 W. Burton Ln., KAYSVILLE, UT 84037 USA Tel 801-390-9519
E-mail: kyle.j.steenblik@gmail.com
Dist(s): **Ingram Content Group.**

Steerforth *Imprint of* **Steerforth Pr.**

Steerforth Pr., *(978-0-944072; 978-1-58195; 978-1-883642; 978-1-58642)* 45 Lyme Rd. # 208, Hanover, NH 03755-1219 USA; *Imprints:* Steerforth (Steerfor); Campfire (Campf); Pushkin Press (Pushkin P); Elsewhere Editions (ElsewhereEd); Pushkin Children's Books (PushkinChld); Pushkin Collection (PushkinColl)
E-mail: helga@steerforth.com; info@steerforth.com
Web site: http://www.steerforth.com
Dist(s): **Children's Plus, Inc.**
Consortium Bk. Sales & Distribution
MyiLibrary
Penguin Random Hse. Distribution
Penguin Random Hse. LLC
Random Hse., Inc.
Red Wheel/Weiser.

Stefanie Boggs-Johnson, *(978-0-578-91579-1)* 1731 Sapling Ct No. A, Concord, CA 94519 USA Tel 925-787-5817
E-mail: stefers143@gmail.com.

Steich, Brooke, *(978-0-578-54197-6; 978-1-7333882)* 12513 160th Ave SE, Renton, WA 98059 USA Tel 206-351-2474
E-mail: amaia.brooke@gmail.com.

†SteinerBooks, Inc., *(978-0-8334; 978-0-88010; 978-0-89345; 978-0-910142; 978-1-58420; 978-1-85584; 978-0-9701097; 978-0-9831984; 978-1-62148; 978-1-62151; 978-1-938685; 978-0-9969211; 978-1-7324613; 978-1-952166; 978-1-957569)* Orders Addr.: P.O. Box 960, Herndon, VA 20172-0960 USA Tel 703-661-1594 (orders); Fax: 702-661-1501; Toll Free Fax: 800-277-7947 (orders); Toll Free: 800-856-8664 (orders); Edit Addr.: 610 Main St., Suite 1, Great Barrington, MA 01230 USA Tel 413-528-8233; Fax: 413-528-8826; Fulfillment Addr.: 22883 Quicksilver Dr., Dulles, VA 20166 USA (SAN 253-9519) Tel 703-661-1529; Fax: 703-996-1010; *Imprints:* Bell Pond Books (Bell Pond); Lindisfarne Books (Lindisfarne)
E-mail: service@steinerbooks.org
Web site: http://www.steinerbooks.org
Dist(s): **NetRead, Inc.**
New Leaf Distributing Co., Inc.
Red Wheel/Weiser; *CIP.*

Steingart, Nathan Publishing, *(978-0-9769321)* 617 N. Kensington Dr., No. 1, Appleton, WI 54915 USA
E-mail: nathansteingart@new.rr.com
Web site: http://www.santastories.net.

Steinmark, Frances, *(978-0-9789272; 978-0-9977582)* 2374 NW 23rd Rd., Boca Raton, FL 33434-4368 USA
Web site: http://www.fransteinmark.com.

Steinschneider, Bernadetta, *(978-0-9790026)* 205 Georgetown Rd., Weston, CT 06883 USA Tel 203-454-8907; Fax: 203-227-0184
E-mail: swigutb@gmail.com.

Stejskal, Susan M., *(978-0-615-13395-9; 978-0-615-81867-2; 978-0-578-61240-9)* 15095 S. 18th St., Vicksburg, MI 49097 USA.

Stella Bks, Inc., *(978-0-9746932)* P.O. Box 4707, Edwards, CO 81632-4707 USA Tel 970-926-7827 (phone/fax)
E-mail: info@astellabook.com
Dist(s): **Partners/West Book Distributors.**

Stellar Learning, *(978-0-9763833)* P.O. Box 64, Guildrlnd Ctr, NY 12085-0064 USA
E-mail: admin@stellarleam.com
Web site: http://www.stellarleam.com.

Stellar Literary, *(978-1-7358010; 978-1-953904; 978-1-955243; 978-1-956741; 978-1-958518; 978-1-959173; 978-1-960159; 978-1-960684; 978-1-961507; 978-1-962110; 978-1-962569; 978-1-962730)* 1968 S. Coast Hwy No. 3880, Laguna Beach, CA 92651 USA Tel 650-666-8388; Fax: 650-460-8711
E-mail: admin@stellarliterary.com
Web site: stellarliterary.com.

Stellar Pubns., *(978-0-9761224)* 3767 Forest Ln., Suite 124 - MBX 1231, Dallas, TX 75244 USA Toll Free: 866-840-4378
E-mail: info@stellarpublishers.com; maymathis@msn.com
Web site: http://www.stellarpublishers.com.

Stellar Publishing, *(978-0-9703041; 978-0-9849660)* Div. of M & M Enterprises, Orders Addr.: 2114 S. Live Oak Pkwy., Wilmington, NC 28403 USA (SAN 860-2298) Tel 910-269-7444
E-mail: info@stellar-publishing.com
Web site: http://www.stellar-publishing.com
Dist(s): **Distributors, The.**

Stellinga, Mark, *(978-0-9762011; 978-0-9796421; 978-0-9817101)* 42 Lancester Pl., Iowa City, IA 52240 USA Tel 319-354-7287
E-mail: mark@writerofbooks.com
Web site: http://www.writerofbooks.com.

Stellium Pr., *(978-1-883376)* P.O. Box 82834, Portland, OR 97282-0834 USA.

Stelting, Kelsie Creative LLC, *(978-0-9998854; 978-1-956948)* 2470 Ptarmigan Ln., Colorado Springs, CO 80918 USA Tel 719-755-2099
E-mail: kelsie@kelsiestelting.com
Web site: www.kelsiestelting.com; https://www.kelsiehoss.com/.

Stelucan Pr., *(978-0-9601454)* 2129 State Hwy. 79 S., Wichita Falls, TX 76302 USA (SAN 221-3176).

Stelzer, Shifra, *(978-0-9992231)* 1827 New York Ave, Brooklyn, NY 11210-3941 USA Tel 718-692-2449
E-mail: ceo2.gye@gmail.com
Web site: www.EzequielStelzer.com.

†Stemmer Hse. Pubs., *(978-0-88045; 978-0-916144)* P.O. Box 89, Gilsum, NH 03448 USA (SAN 207-9623) Tel 603-357-0236; Fax: 603-357-2073; *Imprints:* NaturEncyclopedia (Naturencyclop)
E-mail: pbs@pathwaybook.com
Web site: http://stemmer.com
Dist(s): **Pathway Bk. Service**; *CIP.*

Stenhouse Pubs., *(978-1-57110; 978-1-62531)* Div. of Highlights for Children, Orders Addr.: P.O. Box 11020, Portland, ME 04104-7020 USA (SAN 298-1580) Tel 207-253-1600; Fax: 207-253-5121; Toll Free Fax: 800-833-9164; Toll Free: 800-988-9812 (orders)
E-mail: jkilburn@stenhouse.com
Web site: http://www.stenhouse.com
Dist(s): **Ebsco Publishing**
Follett School Solutions
MyiLibrary.

Stenquist, Cathy, *(978-1-7357680)* 322 Gorwin Dr., Holliston, MA 01746 USA Tel 774-217-3676
E-mail: cathy@stenquist.com.

Stensland Bks., *(978-0-9759456)* 6011 S. 102 St., Omaha, NE 68127 USA
E-mail: info@stenslandbooks.com
Web site: http://www.stenslandbooks.com.

Step One Publishing, *(978-0-615-84809-9; 978-0-9913224)* 5521 Scenic Brook Ln., Raleigh, NC 27616 USA Tel 9192107141
Dist(s): **CreateSpace Independent Publishing Platform.**

Stephanie J Studios, *(978-0-9986653)* 6005 Bermuda Dr., Fleming Island, FL 32003 USA Tel 904-635-1023; Fax: 904-635-1023
E-mail: stephanie.joy@live.com.

Stephen Steele Jackson, *(978-0-578-91534-0; 978-0-578-91535-7)* 2931 Cherokee Rd, Wisconsin Rapids, WI 54494 USA Tel 334-740-9870
E-mail: stephensteelejackson@gmail.com.

Stephi /Lee, *(978-0-578-11938-0)* 2884 Blairmont Dr., Danville, VA 24540 USA
Web site: http://www.wheredomyprayersgo.com; http://www.stephileebooks.com.

Stephnie Stewart, Inc., *(978-0-615-43619-7)* P.O. Box 25882, Tamarac, FL 33320 USA
E-mail: stephniestewart@aol.com.

Stepping Stone Pr. LLC, *(978-1-956582)* 4400 S Coltrane, Edmond, OK 73013 USA Tel 405-819-0152
E-mail: nhinjamichael@gmail.com.

Steps To Literacy, LLC, *(978-0-9728803; 978-1-59564; 978-1-60015; 978-1-60881; 978-1-60923; 978-1-61267; 978-1-62038; 978-1-63395; 978-1-63502; 978-1-68136; 978-1-68288; 978-1-68432; 978-1-64240; 978-1-64241)* Orders Addr.: P.O. Box 6737, Bridgewater, NJ 08807 USA (SAN 858-3005) Toll Free: 800-895-2804
E-mail: sales@stepstoliteracy.com
Web site: http://www.stepstoliteracy.com.

stepup strategies *See* **Stepup Strategies**

Stepup Strategies, *(978-0-9964109; 978-1-947276; 979-8-218-08917-7)* 116 Hazley Ave., Rochelle Park, NJ 07662 USA Tel 561-601-9871
E-mail: trevorscrane@gmail.com.

Sterli Publishing, *(978-0-9790014)* 986 Gable Cove, Collierville, TN 38017 USA (SAN 852-1638) Tel 352-753-4335 (sales office)
E-mail: admin@sterlipublishing.com
Web site: http://www.sterlipublishing.com.

Sterling & Ross Pubs., *(978-0-9766372; 978-0-9779545; 978-0-9787213; 978-0-9814535; 978-0-9814536; 978-0-9821391; 978-0-9821392; 978-0-9827588; 978-1-937802)* 1221 Ave. of the Americas Suite 4200, New York City, NY 10020 USA; *Imprints:* Cambridge House Press (CambridgeHse)
E-mail: contact@sterlingandross.com
Web site: http://www.sterlingandross.com.

Sterling, Bridgette, *(978-0-578-44760-5; 978-0-578-44761-2; 978-0-578-54355-0)* P.O. Box 190821, Hawi, HI 96719 USA Tel 808-731-6751
E-mail: alohasterlings@gmail.com
Dist(s): **Ingram Content Group.**

Sterling Education, *(978-0-9892925; 978-0-9977782; 978-1-947556; 978-1-954725; 979-8-88557)* 6 Liberty Sq. No. 11, Boston, MA 02109 USA Tel 617-777-5936
E-mail: info@onlinemcatprep.com
Web site: www.onlinemcatprep.com.

Sterling Epicure *Imprint of* **Sterling Publishing Co., Inc.**

Sterling Innovation *Imprint of* **Sterling Publishing Co., Inc.**

Sterling Investments I, LLC DBA Twins Magazine, *(978-0-9636745; 978-0-9655442; 978-1-891846)* 30799 Pinetree Rd., #256, Cleveland, OH 44124 USA Tel 855-758-9467; Fax: 855-758-9467; Toll Free: 855-758-9467; *Imprints:* Twins Books (Twins Bks)
E-mail: bill@twinsmagazine.com
Web site: http://www.twinsmagazine.com; http://www.twinsmagazine.com/theBookshelf.shtml.

Sterling Pr., Inc., *(978-0-9637735)* 6811 Old Canton Rd., Apt. 3802, Ridgeland, MS 39157-1248 USA Tel 602-957-9265 Do not confuse with companies with similar names in Bulverde, TX, Chicago, IL, Marysville, WA, Bedford, TX, Kihei,HI.

†Sterling Publishing Co., Inc., *(978-0-8069; 978-1-4027; 978-1-60582; 978-1-4549; 978-1-61837; 978-1-9847; 978-1-6697)* 1166 Avenue of the Americas, 17th Flr., New York, NY 10036 USA (SAN 211-6324) Tel 212-532-7160 212-213-2495; Toll Free Fax: 800-775-8736 (warehouse); Toll Free: 800-367-9692; 800-542-7567; 33 E. 17th St., 5th Flr., New York, NY 10003 Tel 212-532-7160; Toll Free Fax: 800-542-7567; Toll Free: 800-367-9692; *Imprints:* Sterling/Main Street (Sterling-Main St); Balloon Books (Balloon Books); Sterling Innovation (SterInnov); Puzzlewright (Puzzlewright); Sterling Epicure (Sterling Epicure); Spark Publishing Group (SparkPubng); Union Square Press (UnionSqPr); Spark Notes (Spark Notes) Do not confuse with companies with similar names in Falls Church, VA, Fallbrook, CA, Lewisville, TX
E-mail: custservice@sterlingpub.com; tradesales@sterlingpub.com
Web site: http://www.sterlingpublishing.com/
Dist(s): **Booklines Hawaii, Ltd.**
Children's Plus, Inc.
Follett School Solutions
Hachette Bk. Group
MBI Distribution Services/Quayside Distribution
Music Sales Corp.
MyiLibrary
Open Road Integrated Media, Inc.
Partners Bk. Distributing, Inc.; *CIP.*

Sterling Test Prep *See* **Sterling Education**

Sterling/Main St. *Imprint of* **Sterling Publishing Co., Inc.**

Stern, Frederick *See* **Stern Math, LLC**

Stern Math, LLC, *(978-0-9779132; 978-0-9845392)* 754 N. Hollow Rd., Box 172, Rochester, VT 05767 USA (SAN 850-6027) Tel 212-874-4530
E-mail: sternmath@gmail.com; fredstern@gmail.com; emilyalison@gmail.com
Web site: http://sternmath.com.

Sterner, Hilda, *(978-0-615-22164-9)* P.O. Box 713071, Santee, CA 92072-3071 USA
E-mail: hilda@momsauthenticassyrianrecipes.com
Web site: http://www.momsauthenticassyrianrecipes.com.

Steuben Pr., *(978-0-9823131; 978-1-935787; 978-1-940129; 978-1-947841; 978-1-949662; 978-1-950724; 978-1-951912; 978-0-578-23953-8)* 230 Primrose Ct. Unit No. 3, Longmont, CO 80501 USA Tel 303-482-2060; Fax: 303-557-6178
E-mail: sales@rrgraphics.com; noreply@steubenpress.com
Web site: www.steubenpress.com.

Stevans, Andrew, *(978-0-9848340)* 8409 Lee Hwy., Merrifield, VA 22116-0613 USA Tel 703-222-3790
E-mail: alstevans@cox.net.

Steve Diet Goedde, *(978-1-890836)* 2807 W. Sunset Blvd., Los Angeles, CA 90026 USA Tel 323-377-0235
E-mail: stevedg@gmail.com
Web site: http://www.stevedietgoedde.com.

Steveedee Publishing Co,

StevenMarksOnline *See* **Coburn Birge Publishing**

Stevens, Gareth Incorporated *See* **Stevens, Gareth Publishing LLLP**

†Stevens, Gareth Publishing LLLP, *(978-0-8368; 978-0-918831; 978-1-55532; 978-1-4339)* Orders Addr.: P.O. Box 360140, Strongsville, OH 44136-0140 USA Fax: 877-542-2596; Toll Free: 800-542-2595; Edit Addr.: 111 East 14th St., Suite 349, New York, NY 10003 USA (SAN 696-1592) Toll Free: 877-444-0210; *Imprints:* World Almanac Library (Wrld Almanac Lib); Weekly Reader (Weekly Reader); Weekly Reader Leveled Readers (Weekly Read); Gareth Stevens Secondary Library (G S

Sec Lib); Gareth Stevens Learning Library (G S Lrning Lib); Gareth Stevens Hi-Lo Must Reads (G S Hi-Lo)
E-mail: customerservice@gspub.com; hollyc@rosen.pub
Web site: http://www.garethstevens.com; http://www.garethstevensclassroom.com
Dist(s): **Bound to Stay Bound Bks.**
Davidson Titles, Inc.
Follett School Solutions
Lectorum Pubns., Inc.
Rosen Publishing Group, Inc., The; *CIP*.

Stevens Publishing, (*978-0-9632054; 978-1-885529*) Orders Addr.: P.O. Box 160, Kila, MT 59920 USA Tel 406-756-0307; Fax: 406-257-5051; Edit Addr.: 1550 Rogers Ln. Rd., Kila, MT 59920 USA Do not confuse with Stevens Publishing Corp. in Waco, TX.

Stevenson, Ian Author, (*978-0-9984836*) 2221 Eye St. NW, Washington, DC 20037 USA Tel 202-774-4596
E-mail: jim@getstyle.com
Web site: vocabularymoose.com.

Steward & Wise Publishing *See* **Acclaim Pr., Inc.**

Steward, Rebecca, (*978-0-578-58303-7; 979-8-218-04552-4*) 6061 S. Mack Ave., Gilbert, AZ 85298 USA Tel 480-650-0152
E-mail: 4stewsbus@gmail.com.

Stewart, Cathy L, (*978-0-692-06066-7; 978-0-692-06067-4; 978-0-692-06068-1; 978-0-692-06069-8; 978-0-692-06070-4; 978-0-692-06071-1; 978-0-692-06072-8; 978-0-692-06073-5*) 1910 NE Brown Dr, Madras, OR 97741 USA Tel 541-475-9371
E-mail: jimcath24@yahoo.com.

Stewart Education Services, (*978-0-9764154*) 3722 Bagely Ave., No. 19, Los Angeles, CA 90034-4113 USA Tel 310-838-6247; Fax: 310-838-6769
E-mail: info@stewarteducationservices.com
Web site: http://www.stewarteducationservices.com.

Stewart, H. K. Creative Services, Inc., (*978-0-9838992; 978-0-9972312; 978-1-7337964; 978-1-7353167; 979-8-9879632*) 2701 Kavanaugh Blvd. Suite 205, Little Rock, AR 72205 USA Tel 501-664-0500
E-mail: hks@hkstewart.com
Web site: www.hkstewart.com.

Stewart, Hannah, (*978-1-7377430*) 2746 36th Ave, Seattle, WA 98126 USA Tel 206-747-3132
E-mail: hvmsdoglover@gmail.com
Web site: www.hannahvstewart.weebly.com.

Stewart, Mary *See* **Rooster Pubns.**

Stewart, R. J. Bks., (*978-0-9791402; 978-0-9819246; 978-0-9856006; 979-8-9879381*) P.O. Box 239, Berkeley Springs, WV 25411 USA (SAN 852-5382)
E-mail: rjspeak@rjstewart.org
Web site: http://www.rjstewart.net.

†**Stewart, Tabori & Chang,** (*978-0-941434; 978-0-941807; 978-1-55670; 978-1-899791; 978-1-58479*) Div. of Harry N. Abrams, Inc., 115 W. 18th St., 5th Flr., New York, NY 10011 USA (SAN 293-4000) Tel 212-519-1200; Fax: 212-519-1210
E-mail: trudi@stcbooks.com
Web site: http://www.abramsbooks.com
Dist(s): **Abrams, Inc.**
Hachette Bk. Group
MyiLibrary
Open Road Integrated Media, Inc.; *CIP*.

Stewart, Talor *See* **Conscious Pubs.**

Stewart, Timothy, (*978-0-578-42711-9*) 1802 N. Union, Shawnee, OK 74804 USA Tel 405-250-9858
E-mail: timothyjstewart@att.net.

Stick & Poke Pr., (*979-8-9856118*) 89 Arden Rd. 0, BERKELEY, CA 94704 USA Tel 8186790693
E-mail: rcinlala@aol.com
Dist(s): **Ingram Content Group.**

Stickysoft Corp., (*978-0-9740384*) Orders Addr.: P.O. Box 7855, Buffalo Grove, IL 60089 USA Tel 847-229-9999; Fax: 847-808-8777; Toll Free: 800-366-8448; Edit Addr.: 620 Silver Rock Ln., Buffalo Grove, IL 60089 USA
E-mail: euclid@stickysoft.com
Web site: http://www.blackjack678.com.

Stiles, Alyssa, (*978-0-578-33208-6*) 949 McIntyre Rd, Shelocta, PA 15774 USA Tel 724-464-3138
E-mail: alyssamariestiles@gmail.com
Web site: www.pghomt.com.

Stiles, Ari, (*978-0-578-50664-7*) 2601 Princeton Dr., Austin, TX 78741 USA Tel 512-294-8696
E-mail: ari.stiles@gmail.com.

Still Water Publishing, (*978-0-9740855*) Orders Addr.: 1093 Kiva Cir., Windsor, CO 80550 USA
E-mail: chein8@attbi.com
Web site: http://www.stillwaterpublishing.com.

Stillman, Steve, (*978-0-9740508*) 251 Green St., Shrewsbury, MA 01545-4708 USA.

Stillwater River Pubns., (*978-0-615-87994-9; 978-0-615-94776-1; 978-0-615-95738-8; 978-0-692-23153-1; 978-0-692-23446-4; 978-0-692-24202-5; 978-0-692-28084-3; 978-0-692-29387-4; 978-0-692-31966-6; 978-0-692-33960-2; 978-0-692-34018-9; 978-0-692-35055-3; 978-0-692-37136-7; 978-0-692-42303-5; 978-0-692-45749-7; 978-0-692-47574-4; 978-0-692-47824-0; 978-0-692-47956-8; 978-0-692-48452-4; 978-0-692-49764-7; 978-0-692-50768-1; 978-0-692-51932-5; 978-0-692-55601-6; 978-0-692-56699-2; 978-0-692-56700-5; 978-0-692-56970-2;) 63 Sawmill Rd., Chepachet, RI 02814 USA Tel 401-949-5299*
E-mail: Info@StillwaterPress.com; steve@spimac.com
Web site: http://www.StillwaterPress.com
Dist(s): **CreateSpace Independent Publishing Platform.**

Stirred Creations, (*978-1-7348461*) 2960 Rolling Wood Loop, Colorado Springs, CO 80918 USA Tel 954-870-0251
E-mail: info@stirredcreations.com; jonathan.m.sud@gmail.com
Web site: https://www.stirredcreations.com.

Stitched Smile Pubns., (*978-0-692-60271-3; 978-0-692-64579-6; 978-0-692-65132-2; 978-0-692-67634-9; 978-1-945263*) 19607 twilight falls ln, Houston, TX 77084 USA Tel 281-902-7502
E-mail: Stitchedsmilespublications@gmail.com
Web site: Www.stitchedsmilepublications.com
Dist(s): **CreateSpace Independent Publishing Platform.**

STL Distribution North America *See* **Send The Light Distribution LLC**

Stockade Bks., (*978-0-9731570; 978-0-9863983; 978-0-9973879*) P.O. Box 30, Woodsville, NH 03785 USA Toll Free: 866-799-4500
E-mail: orders@stockadebooks.com
Web site: http://www.stockadebooks.com.

Stockcero, Inc., (*978-1-934768; 978-1-949938*) 3785 NW 82nd Ave. Suite 302, Doral, FL 33166 USA Tel 305-722-7628; Fax: 305-477-5794
E-mail: pagrest@stockcero.com; stockcero@stockcero.com
Web site: http://www.spanishbookpress.com; http://www.stockcero.com.

Stockman, Roger Theatricals, (*978-1-7348560*) 11365 82nd Pl. N., Maple Grove, MN 55369 USA Tel 612-616-2039
E-mail: roger.stockman83@gmail.com
Web site: www.rogerstockman.com.

Stockwell Publishing, (*978-0-9785594*) 84 State St. Suite 300, Boston, MA 02109 USA Tel 617-290-3039; Fax: 617-720-0761
E-mail: pel.stockwell@lpl.com
Web site: http://www.followthefox.com.

Stoddart, Beverly, (*978-1-7359282*) P.O. Box 502, Windham, NH 03087 USA Tel 603-289-9822
E-mail: mbstod@comcast.net
Web site: www.beverlystoddart.com.

Stogo, Malcolm Assocs., (*978-0-9712703; 978-0-615-28965-6; 978-0-9966586*) 79 Edgewood Ave., West Orange, NJ 07052 USA
Web site: www.icecreamuniversity.org.

Stoica, Dana, (*978-0-692-16913-1; 978-0-578-57564-3; 978-1-7344246*) 1593 Cipres Ct., Camarillo, CA 93010 USA Tel 805-402-6216
E-mail: danastoica7607@gmail.com.

Stoke Bks.,

Stone Acres Publishing Co., (*978-0-9765478; 978-1-937480*) P.O. Box 407, Waverly, PA 18471-0407 USA (SAN 850-0940) Fax: 570-319-1675
E-mail: gmiltony@yahoo.com
Web site: http://www.stoneacrespublishing.com.

Stone & Scott Pubs., (*978-0-9627031; 978-1-891135*) Orders Addr.: P.O. Box 56419, Sherman Oaks, CA 91413-1419 USA (SAN 297-3030) Tel 818-904-9088; Fax: 818-787-1431
E-mail: Friday@StoneandScott.com; BostonLesPaul@adelphia.net
Web site: http://www.stoneandscott.com.

Stone, Anne Publishing, (*978-0-9858811*) 1158 26th St. Suite 440, Santa Monica, CA 90403 USA Tel 310-418-4674; Fax: 310-828-8057
E-mail: JulieK.AnneStone@gmail.com
Web site: www.annestonepublishing.com.

Stone Arch Bks. *Imprint of* **Capstone**

Stone Arrow Bks., (*978-0-9825528*) P.o. Box 221, Draper, UT 84020 USA Tel 801-699-2844
E-mail: komarkris@gmail.com
Dist(s): **Coutts Information Services**
Ingram Content Group
Spring Arbor Distributors, Inc.

†**Stone Bridge Pr.,** (*978-0-9628137; 978-1-880656; 978-1-933330; 978-1-61172*) P.O. Box 8208, Berkeley, CA 94707 USA Tel 510-524-8732; Fax: 510-524-8711; Toll Free: 800-947-7271 (orders) Do not confuse with Stone Bridge Press in Naples, FL
Web site: http://www.stonebridge.com
Dist(s): **Art Media Resources, Inc.**
Consortium Bk. Sales & Distribution
MyiLibrary
SPD-Small Pr. Distribution; *CIP*.

Stone Castle Publishing, (*978-0-578-00171-5*) 2602 Skyline Dr., Sedalia, MO 65301 USA
Dist(s): **Lulu Pr., Inc.**

Stone Cottage Bks., (*978-0-9822503*) Orders Addr.: P.O. Box 962497, Riverdale, GA 30296 USA (SAN 857-6734)
E-mail: info@stonecottagebooks.com; orders@stonecottagebooks.com
Web site: http://www.stonecottagebooks.com; http://www.bigandgrown.com; http://www.bigandgrown.com.

Stone Guild Publishing, (*978-1-60532*) P.O. Box 860475, Plano, TX 75086-0475 USA.

Stone Hollow Pr., (*978-1-7341771; 979-8-9891563*) 37 Osborne Glen, Poughquag, NY 12570 USA Tel 845-476-4705
E-mail: dderobertis71@hotmail.com.

Stone Phoenix Pr., (*978-1-7370270*) 220 Lillards Ford Rd., Oak Park, VA 22730 USA
E-mail: missydegraff@gmail.com.

Stone Pier Pr., (*978-0-9988623; 978-1-7349011*) P.O. Box 170572, San Francisco, CA 94117 USA Tel 415-484-2821
E-mail: clare@stonepierpress.org
Web site: http://www.stonepierpress.org/
Dist(s): **Chelsea Green Publishing.**

Stone Pine Pr., (*978-0-9728929*) Orders Addr.: P.O. Box 585, Marcola, OR 97454-0585 USA; Edit Addr.: 92985 Marcola Rd., Marcola, OR 97454 USA.

Stone Publishing Co., (*978-1-880991*) Orders Addr.: P.O. Box 711, Mendocino, CA 95460 USA Tel 707-937-0239; Edit Addr.: 10491 Wheeler St., Mendocino, CA 95460 USA.

Stone Table Bks. *Imprint of* **Wipf & Stock Pubs.**

Stoneback, Paula, (*978-1-7325072*) 1827 Candlewyck Ln, Green Lane, PA 18054-2048 USA Tel 215-803-5000
E-mail: paulastoneback@yahoo.com.

Stonebridge Publications *See* **Rise Up**

Stonechester, Inc., (*978-0-9759014*) 4894 Lone Mountain Rd., No. 311, Las Vegas, NV 89130-2239 USA.

StoneGarden.net Publishing, (*978-0-9765426; 978-1-60076*) 3851 Cottonwood Dr., Danville, CA 94506 USA Tel 925-984-7867
E-mail: theshop@stonegarden.net
Web site: http://www.stonegarden.net.

Stonehorse Publishing, LLC, (*978-0-9764199*) Orders Addr.: 6528 E. 101st St. S., Ste D1 Rm. 296, Tulsa, OK 74133 USA (SAN 256-3797) Toll Free Fax: 888-867-1927; Toll Free: 888-867-1927
E-mail: generalinfo@stonehorsepublishing.com
Web site: http://www.stonehorsepublishing.com
Dist(s): **Educational Distribution Corp.**

StoneHouse Ink, (*978-0-9826078; 978-0-9827705; 978-0-615-52573-0; 978-0-615-52575-4; 978-0-615-53802-0; 978-0-615-54333-8; 978-0-615-54337-6; 978-0-615-54696-4; 978-0-615-54711-4; 978-0-615-54901-9; 978-0-615-56858-4; 978-0-615-56861-4; 978-0-615-56900-0; 978-0-615-57160-7; 978-0-615-57163-8; 978-0-615-57164-5; 978-0-615-57165-2; 978-0-615-57168-3; 978-0-615-57222-2; 978-0-615-57225-3; 978-0-615-57624-4; 978-0-615-58014-2; 978-0-615-61352-9; 978-0-615-61354-3; 978-0-615-61786-2; 978-1-938426; 978-0-615-626) 12235 W. Briarwood Dr, Boise, ID 83713 USA Tel 208-514-6631*
E-mail: Pattersonbooks@hotmail.com; stonehousepress@hotmail.com; StoneHouseMgr@gmail.com
Web site: http://www.stonegateink.com/; http://www.stonehouseink.net
Dist(s): **CreateSpace Independent Publishing Platform**
Smashwords
Wesscott Marketing, Inc.

Stoneledge Pr., (*978-0-615-55922-3; 978-0-9851799*) 251 Wax Myrtle Trail, Kitty Hawk, NC 27949 USA Tel 252-715-3621
E-mail: denine.phillips@charter.net.

StonesThrow Publishing, LLC, (*978-0-9793823*) P.O. Box 1898, Mount Dora, FL 32756 USA Tel 208-610-0431
Web site: http://stonesthrowpublishing.com.

Stonewell Pr., (*978-1-62730*) 965 BIRCHWOOD DR, Salt Lake City, UT 84121 USA Tel 801-269-1523
E-mail: jayparry84121@yahoo.com.

Stoneydale Pr. Publishing Co., (*978-0-912299; 978-1-931291; 978-1-938707*) Orders Addr.: P.O. Box 188, Stevensville, MT 59870 USA Tel 406-777-2729; Fax: 406-777-2521; Toll Free: 800-735-7006; Edit Addr.: 523 Main St., Stevensville, MT 59870 USA (SAN 265-3168)
E-mail: stoneydale@stoneydale.com; stoneydalepresspublishing@gmail.com; burklasvegas@aol.com
Web site: http://www.stoneydale.com
Dist(s): **Partners Bk. Distributing, Inc.**

Stony Meadow Publishing, (*978-0-9787925; 978-0-9834335; 978-0-9850290; 978-0-9885569; 978-0-9894090; 978-0-9962834*) 2440 WORLD Pkwy. BLVD APT 52, CLEARWATER, FL 33763 USA
E-mail: stonymeadowbooks@aol.com; darkmoondigest@gmail.com
Web site: http://www.stonymeadowpublishing.com; http://www.inspiration4songwriters.net; http://www.books4songwriters.com; http://htto://www.darkmoondigest.com.

Stop N Go Fitness, (*978-0-9800091*) 13518 L St., Omaha, NE 68137 USA Fax: 413-669-8870
E-mail: angelinsights@conciergemarketing.com
Web site: http://www.anangeltowatchover.com.

Storer, Mark *See* **Little River Bookshelf**

Storey Books *See* **Storey Publishing, LLC**

†**Storey Publishing, LLC,** (*978-0-88266; 978-1-58017; 978-0-9674717; 978-1-60342; 978-1-61212; 978-1-63586*) Subs. of Workman Publishing Co., Inc., Orders Addr.: 210 Mass Moca Way, North Adams, MA 01247 USA (SAN 203-4158) Fax: 413-346-2198; Toll Free Fax: 800-865-3429; Toll Free: 800-827-7444; c/o Workman Publishing, 225 Varick St., New York, NY 10014-4381 Tel 212-614-7700; Toll Free Fax: 800-521-1832; Toll Free: 800-722-7202
E-mail: info@storey.com; sales@storey.com
Web site: http://www.storey.com
Dist(s): **Blackstone Audio, Inc.**
Hachette Bk. Group
MBI Distribution Services/Quayside Distribution
Open Road Integrated Media, Inc.
Timber Pr., Inc.
Workman Publishing Co., Inc.; *CIP*.

Stori Tyme Huggggs, Inc., (*978-1-890925*) Div. of T.L.B. Publishing, 827 N. Hollywood, #202, Burbank, CA 91505 USA Tel 770-987-5547; 894 Roberts Way, Lawrenceville, GA 30043
E-mail: tenabrown@thejpak.com.

Storie Tree, Inc., The, (*978-0-9679014*) Orders Addr.: P.O. Box 441048, Aurora, CO 80044-1048 USA Tel 303-690-6493; Fax: 303-758-7792; Edit Addr.: 3952 S. Joplin Way, Aurora, CO 80044-1048 USA.

StoriePr. LLC, (*978-0-578-97634-1; 978-0-578-33316-8; 978-0-578-33320-5; 979-8-9871091*) 9921 Holly Ctr. Dr., Huntersville, NC 28078 USA Tel 407-969-6626
E-mail: miranda.clare.fair@gmail.com.

Stories By Mom, (*978-0-692-77347-5; 978-0-692-84555-4; 978-0-692-93774-7; 978-1-7339106*) 2314 E CAPRI AVE, Mesa, AZ 85204 USA Tel 480-293-4860
Web site: www.storiesbymom.com.

Stories From Four Publishing Co., (*978-0-9742288*) 558 N. Nash St., Hortonville, WI 54944 USA Tel 920-779-9995
E-mail: fourinspirations@aol.com
Web site: http://www.storiesfromfour.com.

Stories of Grandma, (*978-1-7333600*) 696 Heighland Avenew, Peekskill, NY 10566 USA Tel 914-434-0943
E-mail: mary.dortch@hotmail.com.

Stories of Life Productions, (*978-1-970032*) 1431 Reno Ridge Ln., Spring, TX 77373 USA Tel 832-914-4923
E-mail: rogerisi@icloud.com; contact@glsvb,org
Web site: www.glsvb.org.

Stories of My Life, The, (*978-0-9741215*) Div. of Frontsiders Marketing Strategists, P.O. Box 1478, Summerland, CA 93067 USA Tel 805-969-3597
Web site: http://www.thestoriesofmylife.com.

Storiez: Meagan Corrado, (*978-0-9970049; 978-1-7325813*) 4055 Ridge Ave Apt 4404, Philadelphia, PA 19129 USA Tel 267-418-6750
E-mail: storiezguide@gmail.com.

Storm Leaf, (*978-0-9858325*) 6041 S Valdai Way, Aurora, CO 80015 USA Tel 303-408-3838
E-mail: david@stormleaf.com
Web site: www.stormleaf.com.

Storm Moon Pr., LLC, (*978-0-9827008; 978-1-937058; 978-1-62757*) 5705 Fishermans Dr., Bradenton, FL 34209 USA
E-mail: editor@stormmoonpress.com
Web site: http://www.stormmoonpress.com
Dist(s): **Smashwords.**

Storm Mystery Pr., LLC, (*978-0-9987199*) 1212 1st St., Kirkland, WA 98033 USA Tel 425-736-6223; Fax: 425-739-7399
E-mail: dnj2@mac.com
Web site: www.JenniferLHotes.com.

Storm Peak Pr., (*978-0-9641357; 978-1-928990*) 2502 4th Ave N., Seattle, WA 98109-2149 USA.

Storm Praise Publishing, LLC, (*978-0-692-53485-4; 978-0-9995631; 978-1-7360559*) 5668 Fishhawk Crossing Blvd. Suite 130, Lithia, FL 33547 USA
E-mail: stormpraisepublishing@gmail.com
Web site: www.stormpraise.com.

Stormcave, (*978-0-9884512; 978-1-960357*) 6467 189th St., Chippewa Falls, WI 54729 USA Tel 919-714-0608
E-mail: jenelle.l.schmidt@gmail.com.

Stormcave Studios *See* **Stormcave**

Storms, Lorraine, (*978-1-7328492*) 106 Mayer St., Reading, PA 19606 USA Tel 610-370-5007
E-mail: lryanstorms@gmail.com
Dist(s): **Ingram Content Group.**

Story and Logic Media Group, (*978-0-615-72436-2; 978-0-615-74806-1; 978-0-9897549; 978-1-941622*) 12386 W. National Rd., New Carlisle, OH 45344 USA Tel 9374783002
E-mail: sharonalavy1@gmail.com
Web site: http://storyandlogic.blogspot.com/
Dist(s): **CreateSpace Independent Publishing Platform.**

Story & Seed, (*978-0-578-63976-5; 978-0-578-63996-3; 978-0-578-77623-1*) 1433 Rock View Ln. 0, LOGANVILLE, GA 30052 USA Tel 678-409-2368
E-mail: storyandseed@gmail.com
Dist(s): **Ingram Content Group.**

Story Direction, (*978-0-9675940*) 39650 Us Hwy. 19 N. Apt. 583, Tarpon Spgs, FL 34689-3950 USA Tel 727-939-8466
E-mail: angelface12@earthlink.net.

Story Merchant, (*978-0-9836058; 978-0-615-65754-7; 978-0-615-65947-3; 978-0-615-65967-1; 978-0-615-65969-5; 978-0-615-66089-9; 978-0-615-66180-3; 978-0-615-67581-7; 978-0-9897154; 978-0-9904216; 978-0-9909436; 978-0-9963689; 978-0-9969908; 978-0-9981628; 978-0-9991621; 978-1-7323411; 978-1-970157; 978-1-7340324) 400 S. Burnside Ave. 11B, Los Angeles, CA 90036 USA Tel 323-932-1685; Fax: 323-932-1220*
E-mail: lisacerasoli@gmail.com; DrK@storymerchant.com
Web site: www.storymerchant.com
Dist(s): **CreateSpace Independent Publishing Platform**
Lulu Pr., Inc.

Story Monsters LLC, (*978-0-9619853; 978-1-877749; 978-1-58985*) Orders Addr.: 4696 W Tyson St, Chandler, AZ 85226 USA (SAN 246-7429) Tel 480-940-8182; Fax: 480-940-8787; Edit Addr.: 4696 W. Tyson St., Chandler, AZ 85226-2903 USA; *Imprints*: Story Monsters Press (MYID_K_STORY M)
E-mail: Linda@storymonsters.com; Patti@storymonsters.com
Web site: http:www.storymonsters.com; http://www.DragonflyBookAwards.com; http://www.AuthorBookings.com
Dist(s): **Quality Bks., Inc.**
Unique Bks., Inc.
ebrary, Inc.

Story Monsters Pr. *Imprint of* **Story Monsters LLC**

Story Night Pr., (*978-0-692-45488-6; 978-0-692-45558-6; 978-0-692-48806-5; 978-0-692-65151-3; 978-0-9986699*) 21 Chestnut St. Apt. 603, Portland, ME 04101 USA Tel 207-761-5801
Dist(s): **CreateSpace Independent Publishing Platform.**

Story of Your Life Publishing Co., The, (*978-0-9771667*) 528 Palisades Dr., No. 711, Pacific Palisades, CA 90272 USA (SAN 256-8241) Tel 310-230-8510.

Story Plant, The, (*978-0-9816087; 978-0-9819568; 978-0-9841905; 978-1-61188*) P.O. Box 4331, Stamford, CT 06907 USA (SAN 856-0234)
Web site: http://www.thestoryplant.com
Dist(s): **MyiLibrary**
National Bk. Network
Open Road Integrated Media, Inc.

Story Pr. Africa *Imprint of* **Catalyst Pr. LLC**

Story Road Publishing, Inc., (*978-1-939898*) 16564 SW 47th Ter., Miami, FL 33185 USA Tel 818-590-3991
E-mail: zachary@zcbolger.com.

Story Store Collection Publishing, (*978-0-9764798*) 11040 Hickman Rd. # 226, Clive, IA 50325-3740 USA.

Story Stuff, Inc., *(978-1-928811)* P.O. Box 501372, Indianapolis, IN 46250-6372 USA Fax: 317-913-1777
E-mail: jmferrone@storystuff.com
Web site: http://www.storystuff.com.

Story Time Stories That Rhyme, *(978-1-56820)* P.O. Box 416, Denver, CO 80201-0416 USA Tel 303-575-5676; *Imprints*: folder leaf (folder leaf)
E-mail: emailstreet@gmail.com
Web site: http://www.storytimestoriesthatrhyme.net; http://www.storytimestoriesthatrhyme.com/; http://www.storytimestoriesthatrhyme.org; http://www.storiesforschools.com; http://www.kidsrhymenewsletter.com.

Story Trust Publishing, LLC, *(978-1-937228)* 36 Floral St., Newton, MA 02461 USA Tel 617-755-3283
E-mail: info@storytrust.com
Web site: www.storytrust.com.

Story Weaver Pr., *(978-0-9795580)* 155 Beech St., Frankfort, MI 49635 USA Tel 231-930-8722 Changed as of 09.13.22
E-mail: nedthebirder@gmail.com.

Storybook Acres, *(978-0-9761675)* 4309 Creek Rd., Conneaut, OH 44030 USA (SAN 256-2219) Tel 440-593-2780 (phone/fax)
E-mail: storybookacres@adelphia.net
Web site: http://storybookacres.org.

StoryBk. Genius, LLC, *(978-0-9910907; 978-1-941434; 978-1-949522; 978-1-952954)* Orders Addr.: 219 Jackson St., Augusta, MO 63332 USA; Edit Addr.: 219 Jackson St., Augusta, MO 63332 USA Tel 314-578-4341
E-mail: nwhartung@gmail.com
Web site: http://www.sbgpublishing.com.

Storybook Meadow Publishing, *(978-0-9704621; 978-0-9845236; 978-1-7321629)* 7700 Timbers Trail, Traverse City, MI 49684 USA; *Imprints*: Bower Books (Bower Bks)
E-mail: garybower@charter.net
Web site: http://www.bowerbooks.com
Dist(s): **Partners Bk. Distributing, Inc.**

Storybook Pr. & Productions, *(978-1-887683)* 467 Central Park W., Apt. 6E, New York, NY 10025 USA Tel 212-975-2473; 212-749-7178 (phone/fax); Fax: 212-975-2026; Toll Free: 800-779-4341
E-mail: storybookp@aol.com.

StoryBk. Story Publishing, *(978-1-7373053)* 220 E. Yanonali St., Santa Barbara, CA 93101 USA Tel 858-610-9744
E-mail: peter@petergmartin.com.

Storybook Theatre of Hawaii, *(978-0-9742224)* P.O. Box 820, Hanapepe, HI 96716 USA
Web site: http://www.storybook.org.

Storycraft Publishing, *(978-0-9638339)* Orders Addr.: P.O. Box 205, Masonville, CO 80541-0205 USA Tel 970-669-3755 (phone/fax); Edit Addr.: 8600 Firethorn Dr., Loveland, CO 80538 USA
E-mail: Vivian@storycraft.com
Web site: http://www.storycraft.com
Dist(s): **Book Wholesalers, Inc.**
Brodart Co.
Follett School Solutions
Quality Bks., Inc.
Unique Bks., Inc.

Storydog, Inc., *(978-0-9722690)* 3510 N. Bell Ave., Chicago, IL 60618 USA (SAN 254-9786) Tel 773-327-1588
Web site: http://www.storydog.com.

StoryGirl Productions, LLC, *(978-0-9762587)* 213 W. Montebello, Phoenix, AZ 85013 USA
E-mail: jaime@ding-a-lings.net
Web site: http://www.ding-a-lings.net.

Storyman Bks., *(978-1-7322282; 978-0-578-44792-6; 978-0-578-59587-0; 978-0-578-76817-5; 978-0-578-95708-1; 979-8-218-11040-6; 979-8-218-11041-3; 979-8-218-26761-2)* 19601 E 49th St. S., Broken Arrow, OK 74014 USA Tel 978-382-2379
E-mail: davidstoryman@gmail.com
Web site: www.healthylivingpublishing.net; www.storymanbooks.com.

StoryMaster Pr., *(978-0-9761179)* 15420 Memorial Dr., Suite M -141, Houston, TX 77079 USA Tel 281-920-0443; Fax: 281-920-1629
E-mail: info@storymasterpress.com
Web site: http://www.storymasterpress.com.

StoryRobin Co., *(978-1-937489)* 849 Durshire Way, Sunnyvale, CA 94087 USA Tel 408-905-7543
E-mail: suechen78@gmail.com
Web site: www.storyrobin.com.

StoryScapes, *(978-0-9975202; 978-0-9979283)* P.O. Box 116, Sebastopol, CA 95473 USA Tel 707-332-8100
E-mail: erik@permacultureartisans.com
Web site: storyscapes.us.

Storytime Ink International, *(978-0-9628769; 978-0-9897371)* P.O. Box 470505, Broadview Heights, OH 44147 USA Tel 440-584-0018; Fax: 270-573-4913; 10001 Gatewood Dr., Brecksville, OH 44141
E-mail: storytimeink@att.net
Web site: http://storytimeink.com.

Storytime Pr., Inc., *(978-0-9754942)* 427 W. Main, Suite D, Brighton, MI 48116 USA
E-mail: monroestudio@yahoo.com; mikemonroestudio@yahoo.com
Web site: http://www.michaelglennmonroe.com
Dist(s): **Ann Arbor Editions LLC.**

Storytime Works, *(978-0-9886984)* 904 Winter Dr., El Paso, TX 79912 USA Tel 915-248-9658
E-mail: storytimeworks@gmail.com
Web site: www.storytimeworks.com
Dist(s): **Greenleaf Book Group.**

StoryTime World Publishing Hse., *(978-0-9792800; 979-8-9879364)* Div. of The Pencil Pro, 202 Rollins Ave., Rockville, MD 20852 USA Tel 301-672-4296
Web site: http://roniorosenthal.com/.

StoryTyme Publishing, *(978-0-9753699)* 7909 Walergra Rd., Suite 112, PMB 178, Antelope, CA 95843 USA (SAN 256-0763)
Web site: http://www.storytymepublishing.com.

Stott, Darrel Ministry, *(978-0-9755564)* 1885 Nancy Ave., Central Point, OR 97502-1627 USA Tel 541-840-7171
E-mail: Dstottmin@yahoo.com
Web site: www.DarrelStott.com.

Stourbridge Distributors, Inc., *(978-0-9753758)* 812 Ct. St., Honesdale, PA 18431-1965 USA
E-mail: rich@stourbridgedist.com
Web site: http://www.stourbridgedist.com
Dist(s): **Phoenix Learning Resources, LLC.**

Stout, William Inc., *(978-0-9712716; 978-0-9743838)* 1468 Loma Vista St., Pasadena, CA 91104-4709 USA Tel 626-798-6490; Fax: 626-798-3756
E-mail: wmstout@altrionet.com
Web site: http://www.williamstout.com.

Stout-Castle Bks., *(978-0-578-77913-3; 978-0-578-93993-3; 979-8-218-12252-2)* 1509 Screechum Hollow Rd, Bedford, VA 24523 USA Tel 808-343-5621
E-mail: bdrutledge27@gmail.com
Web site: deannarutledge.com.

Stowe, Amber, *(978-1-7324237)* 8161 S. Estes St., Littleton, CO 80128 USA Tel 720-357-0398
E-mail: amber.stowe@gmail.com.

STR8*UP Productions *See* **Paved Roads Productions**

Strack, Beth, *(978-0-9898991)* 2594 Hastings Ave., Redwood City, CA 94061 USA Tel 650-368-6158
E-mail: hummingbirdhmmmm@aol.com.

Straight Edge Pr., The, *(978-1-883043)* Subs. of Straight Edge, Inc., 386 Clinton St., Brooklyn, NY 11231-3603 USA (SAN 254-9395) Toll Free: 800-732-3628
E-mail: info@straightedgeinc.com
Web site: http://www.straightedgeinc.com.

Straight Forward Technologies, *(978-0-9718515)* P.O. Box 102, Valley Center, KS 67147 USA Tel 316-207-3211; Toll Free Fax: 877-766-8566
E-mail: info@straightforwardtech.com
Web site: http://www.bakingwithmommy.com; http://www.straightforwardtech.com; http://www.gardeningwithmommy.com.

Straight From The Heart Publishing, *(978-0-692-78740-3)* 2600 W Ina Rd. Apt 135, Tucson, AZ 85741 USA Tel 310-739-9348
E-mail: Straight From The Heart Publishing jimmydanelli@aol.com.

Straight on till Morningside Prints *Imprint of* **Pitchford, D. L.**

Straight Paths Pr., *(978-0-9759871)* 17450 SW Viking St., Beaverton, OR 97007 USA (SAN 256-1468) Tel 503-259-9764 (phone/fax); Toll Free: 800-348-2346 ext. 23
E-mail: info@straightpathspress.com
Web site: http://www.straightpathspress.com.

Strang Communications Company *See* **Charisma Media**

Strange Jane Creations, *(978-0-9914211)* 1001 e alan ave, carrollton, TX 75006 USA Tel 214-893-4011
E-mail: Ash2b_me@hotmail.com; strange.jane.13@gmail.com.

StrangeDays Publishing, *(978-0-9747581)* P.O. Box 587, Merton, WI 53056 USA.

Stranger Comics, *(978-0-578-03139-2; 978-0-578-03140-8; 978-0-578-03141-5; 978-0-578-04111-7; 978-0-578-07612-6; 978-0-578-08000-0; 978-0-578-11087-5; 978-1-939834)* 4121 Redwood Ave. Suite 101, Los Angeles, CA 90066 USA
E-mail: sebjones3@gmail.com; stranger@strangercomics.com
Web site: http://www.strangercomics.com.

Strategic Bk. Publishing *Imprint of* **Strategic Book Publishing & Rights Agency (SBPRA)**

Strategic Book Publishing & Rights Agency (SBPRA), *(978-0-9795935; 978-1-934925; 978-1-60693; 978-1-60911; 978-1-60976; 978-1-61204; 978-1-61897; 978-1-62212; 978-1-62516; 978-1-62857; 978-1-63135; 978-1-63410; 978-1-943204; 978-1-68181; 978-1-946539; 978-1-946540; 978-1-948260; 978-1-948271; 978-1-948858; 978-1-949483; 978-1-950015; 978-1-950860; 978-1-951530; 978-1-952269) 2450 Louisiana St., Houston, TX 77006 USA (SAN 853-8492) Toll Free: 888-808-6187; Imprints:* Eloquent Books (Eloquent Bks); Strategic Book Publishing (Strat Bk)
E-mail: payroll@sbpra.net; support@sbpra.net; katie@sbpra.net
Web site: http://sbpra.net.

Strategic Destiny, LLC., *(978-0-9982566)* 175-60 Underhill Ave., Fresh Meadows, NY 11365 USA Tel 718-357-0064
E-mail: wyattstrategicdestiny@gmail.com.

Strategic Educational Tools, *(978-0-9842863)* 293 Center St., East Aurora, NY 14052 USA (SAN 858-9666) Tel 716-445-9609.

Strategic Media Group, *(978-0-9824157)* 9800 De Soto Ave., Chatsworth, CA 91311 USA (SAN 858-0979)
Web site: http://www.hospitalcritterz.com.

Strategic Partners Press *See* **Strategic Media Group**

Strategic Visions Inc., *(978-0-9769069)* Orders Addr.: 337 Turnberry Rd, Hoover, AL 35244 USA
E-mail: jom@strategicvisionsinc.com.

Strategies Publishing Co., *(978-0-9769662)* Orders Addr.: P.O. Box 5588, Cary, NC 27512 USA Do not confuse with companies with the same or similar name in Sahuarita, AZ, Tampa, FL, New Augusta, MS
E-mail: jjohnson0710@yahoo.com; strategiespublishing@nc.rr.com.

Stratford Road Pr., Ltd., *(978-0-9743221; 978-0-9835480; 978-0-9886853)* 128 S. Camden Dr., Suite 201, Beverly Hills, CA 90212-3232 USA Fax: 310-550-8926
E-mail: peasonions@aol.com; peasandonions@gmail.com.

Strathmoor *Imprint of* **Tabby Hse. Bks.**

Strathmoor Pr., *(978-0-9740718)* 1710 Tyler Pkwy., Louisville, KY 40204 USA Tel 502-479-3287.

Stratostream LLC, *(978-0-578-44486-4)* 372 Fifth Ave. 4E, New York, NY 10018 USA Tel 212-772-7109
E-mail: neonissima@gmail.com
Dist(s): **Ingram Content Group.**

Stratten, Lou, *(978-0-9747173)* Orders Addr.: 3144 S. Barrington Ave. #c, Los Angeles, CA 90066 USA; Edit Addr.: 3144 S. Barrington Ave. Apt. C, Los Angeles, CA 90066-1146 USA.

Stratton Pr., *(978-0-9624813; 978-0-692-86312-1; 978-0-692-86314-5)* Orders Addr.: P.O. Box 22391, San Francisco, CA 94122 USA (SAN 200-3457)
E-mail: sashley@strattonpress.com.

Straub, Rick, *(978-0-9793269; 978-0-9842209; 978-0-9913726)* Orders Addr.: 493 Ridgecrest Dr., Blairsville, GA 30512 USA Tel 706-781-6551
E-mail: csddata@windstream.net
Web site: http://www.straubpublishing.com/.

Strauberry Studios, *(978-0-9830321)* 11000 NE 10th St. No. 230, Bellevue, WA 98004 USA Tel 425-821-7007
E-mail: susan@strauberrystudios.com
Web site: http://www.strauberrystudios.com.

Straus, Jane, *(978-0-9667221)* Orders Addr.: P.O. Box 472, Mill Valley, CA 94942 USA (SAN 253-8202) Toll Free: 800-644-3222
E-mail: jane@grammarbook.com
Web site: http://www.grammarbook.com; http://www.thebluebooks.com.

Strauss Consultants, *(978-1-880559)* 48 W. 25th St., 11th Flr., New York, NY 10010-2708 USA Toll Free Fax: 888-528-8273; Toll Free: 800-236-7918
E-mail: strausscon@aol.com
Dist(s): **Smashwords.**

Strauss, Michael L., *(978-0-692-15559-2; 978-0-692-15562-2; 978-0-578-51104-7)* 2275 N. Legion Dr., Signal Hill, CA 90755 USA Tel 310-743-7339
E-mail: michaelstrauss44@yahoo.com
Dist(s): **Ingram Content Group.**

Stravard Lux Publishing Hse., *(978-0-578-45857-1; 978-0-578-55380-1; 978-1-7371440)* 3780 Old Norcross Rd., Duluth, GA 30096 USA Tel 678-979-6139
E-mail: yvettekendall.mail@gmail.com
Web site: www.stravardlux.com.

Strawbery Banke, Incorporated *See* **Strawbery Banke Museum**

Strawbery Banke Museum, *(978-0-9603896)* Orders Addr.: P.O. Box 300, Portsmouth, NH 03802-0300 USA (SAN 221-6515) Tel 603-433-1100; Fax: 603-433-1115; Edit Addr.: 454 Court St., Portsmouth, NH 03802-0300 USA
E-mail: deidre@perpublisher.com
Web site: http://www.strawberybanke.org
Dist(s): **Univ. Pr. of New England.**

Stray Dog Pr., LLC, *(978-0-9898831)* 1030 Bowen Creek Rd., Niangua, MO 65713 USA Tel 417-473-1136; *Imprints*: Fun 4 Kids Publishing (Fun four Kids)
E-mail: susankeenebooks@gmail.com.

Stray Letter Pr. LLC, The, *(978-0-9996709)* 17487 3rd Cir. S, Burien, WA 98148 USA Tel 253-880-7018; Fax: 253-880-7018
E-mail: LGMoriyama@gmail.com.

Straykat Productions, *(978-0-578-57161-4; 978-0-578-61612-4; 978-0-578-65172-9)* 27639 Kristin Ln., Santa Clarita, CA 91350 USA Tel 213-479-6620
E-mail: kat@connollyconsulting.com
Web site: adventuresofpj.com.

Streamline Brands, *(978-0-9855732; 978-0-692-86750-1; 978-1-7359613)* 80 So. Highland Ave. The Holyoke-Manhattan blg, Ossining, NY 10562 USA Tel 914-941-5668
E-mail: jacollen@collenip.com.

Streams Publishing Co., *(978-1-933358)* P.O. Box 260, Sidney, OH 45365-0260 USA Tel 937-492-4586; Fax: 937-492-7633
E-mail: budford@bright.net
Web site: http://www.cityreaching.net.

Strebor Bks. *Imprint of* **Strebor Bks.**

Strebor Bks., *(978-0-9674601; 978-0-9711953; 978-1-59309)* 1230 Ave. of the Americas, New York, NY 10020 USA; *Imprints*: Strebor Books (Strebor Imp)
Dist(s): **Simon & Schuster, Inc.**

Streetside Stories, Inc., *(978-0-9646977; 978-0-9710606)* 3130 20th St. Ste. 311, San Francisco, CA 94110-2700 USA
E-mail: contact@streetside.org
Web site: http://www.streetside.org.

StreetTalk Publishing Co., *(978-0-9770009)* 187 N. Garfield Ave., Columbus, OH 43203 USA; 1324 Cambrian Ct, Columbus, OH 43220
E-mail: amazingteistreet@gmail.com
Web site: www.amazingteistreet.com.

Streg, John Publishing, *(978-1-7326034)* 1023 N. William St., Ludington, MI 49431 USA Tel 231-852-0659
E-mail: jkg1950@hotmail.com.

Strelecky, John *See* **Aspen Light Publishing**

Strength Builders Publishing LLC, *(978-1-7368052; 979-8-9854028)* 1540 Swan Ct., Gretna, LA 70056 USA Tel 504-330-5627
E-mail: drevonasmith@strengthbuilderspublishing.com
Web site: https://www.strengthbuilderspublishing.com/.

Stress Free Kids, *(978-0-9708633; 978-0-9787781; 978-0-9800328; 978-0-9836256; 978-1-937985)* 2561 Chimney Springs Dr, Marietta, GA 30062 USA
E-mail: rick@StressFreeKids.com
Web site: www.stressfreekids.com
Dist(s): **Ingram Content Group.**

Stress Free Publishers *See* **Stress Free Kids**

Strickland, Wilton, *(978-0-9747035)* 618 Pk. Ave., Goldsboro, NC 27530 USA (SAN 255-8114) Tel 919-734-2830 (phone/fax)
E-mail: wilton@esn.net
Web site: http://www.wiltonstrickland.com.

Stride *Imprint of* **Child's World, Inc, The**

Strider Nolan Media, Incorporated *See* **Strider Nolan Publishing, Inc.**

Strider Nolan Publishing, Inc., *(978-1-932045)* Div. of Strider Nolan Media, Inc., 1990 Heritage Rd., Huntingdon Valley, PA 19006-7814 USA (SAN 255-0350); 702 Cricket Ave., Ardsley, PA 19038
E-mail: stridernolan13@yahoo.com
Web site: http://www.stridernolanmedia.com.

Striking Presence Pubns., *(978-0-9724935)* Orders Addr.: P.O. Box 475, Moorestown, NJ 08057 USA Tel 609-936-7278; Fax: 609-936-9651; Edit Addr.: 49-13 Quail Ridge Dr., Plainsboro, NJ 08536 USA
E-mail: jc@strikingpresence.com
Web site: http://www.strikingpresence.com.

String of Beads Pubns., *(978-0-9672012)* 9297 Avignon Pl., West Jordan, UT 84088 USA Fax: 801-566-0406
E-mail: jepp@fiber.net
Web site: http://www.stringofbeads.com.

Strive *See* **Staves Creations**

Strong Corner Publishing, LCC, *(978-0-9754755)* 5331 Talavero Pl., Parker, CO 80134-2799 USA
E-mail: spencerj@broncos.nfl.com.

Strong, Louise dev, *(978-0-9770950)* P.O. Box 197, Morristown, NY 13654 USA Tel 315-375-4238
E-mail: riverstrong@gisco.net.

Strother, Rosemarie, *(978-0-692-00131-8)* 4880 Coral Wood Dr., Naples, FL 34119 USA Tel 239-353-4919.

Structured Learning LLC, *(978-0-9787800; 978-0-9845881; 978-0-9893690; 978-1-942101)* 27062 Lost Colt Dr., Laguna Hills, CA 92653 USA
E-mail: askatechteacher@gmail.com
Web site: http://https://askatechteacher.com; http://https://www.structuredlearning.net.

Struggle Against the Odds, *(978-0-9778318)* 3929 Clay Pl., NE, Washington, DC 20019 USA Tel 202-397-5310 (phone/fax)
E-mail: satocommunications@rcn.com
Web site: http://www.satocommunication.com.

Struminger, Alexander, *(978-0-9915467)* 2985 Shiffletts Mill Rd, Crozet, VA 22932 USA Tel 434-974-7069; *Imprints*: Wren's Nest Productions LLC (WrensNestProd)
E-mail: astruminger@gmail.com.

Stryker Illustrations, *(978-0-9821038)* 18011 Biscayne Blvd. Apt. 1901, Aventura, FL 33160-5239 USA Toll Free: 888-710-2513
E-mail: strykercards@bellsouth.net.

Stryker, Laura Kirby, *(978-0-692-98556-4; 978-0-692-98557-1)* 3503 Langdale Dr., High Point, NC 27265 USA Tel 336-869-8377
E-mail: lkstryker@ymail.com.

STS Publishing, *(978-0-9798806)* 1125 E. Second St., Casper, WY 82601 USA Tel 307-577-4227.

Stuart & Weitz Publishing Group *See* **RJ Blackstone Ltd**

Stuart, Jesse Foundation, The, *(978-0-945084; 978-1-931672; 978-1-938471)* 1645 Winchester Ave., Ashland, KY 41101 USA (SAN 245-8845)
Web site: http://www.jsfbooks.com.

Stubblefield, Jean A, *(978-0-692-80292-2)* 2716 Inman Bend Rd, Morristown, TN 37814 USA Tel 423-307-3173
E-mail: craigjeanie@bellsouth.net.

Student Pr. Initiative, *(978-1-932948)* 509 W. 121st St., Suite 406, New York, NY 10027 USA Tel 212-678-8339; Fax: 212-678-3746
E-mail: epg10@columbia.edu.

Studio 37 Pubns., *(978-0-615-73166-7; 978-0-615-79740-3; 978-0-615-92329-1; 978-0-578-48087-9; 978-0-578-97663-1)* 3737 NE Alameda St, Portland, OR 97212 USA Tel 503-449-2821
Dist(s): **CreateSpace Independent Publishing Platform.**

Studio 403, *(978-0-9633943; 978-1-933129)* 399 Shoreland Dr., Lopez Island, WA 98261-8412 USA Tel 360-468-4347
E-mail: mark@studio403.com
Web site: http://www.studio403.com.

Studio 9 Bks. and Music, 162 Margaret St., Plattsburgh, NY 12901 USA Tel 518-298-8595
E-mail: studio9@rdppub.com.

Studio Cherry Publishing, *(978-0-9793360)* 3697 Rt.75, Huntington, WV 25704-9011 USA Tel 304-697-2051
E-mail: studio_cherry@verizon.net.

Studio Egg LLC, *(978-1-951669)* 3841 Third Ave. S., Minneapolis, MN 55409 USA Tel 612-520-1167
E-mail: Studioegglic@gmail.com
Web site: Studioegglic.com.

Studio Foglio, LLC, *(978-1-889061; 978-1-890856; 978-1-890856-65-6)* 2400 NW 80th St., Suite 129, Seattle, WA 98117-4449 USA (SAN 254-5128) Tel 206-782-8739; Fax: 206-783-3931
E-mail: foglio@studiofoglio.com; savannah@studiofoglio.com; foglio@xxxenophile.com
Web site: http://www.studiofoglio.com
Dist(s): **Berkeley Game Distributors**
Chessex
Cold Cut Comics Distribution
Diamond Comic Distributors, Inc.
Diamond Bk. Distributors
FM International
Rip Off Pr.
Syco Distribution.

Studio Fun International *Imprint of* **Printers Row Publishing Group**

Studio Fun International, *(978-0-276; 978-0-7621; 978-0-88705; 978-0-88850; 978-0-89577; 978-1-57584; 978-1-57619)* Subs. of Reader's Digest Assn., Inc., Reader's Digest Rd., Pleasantville, NY 10570-7000 USA (SAN 283-2143) Tel 914-244-4800; Fax: 914-244-4841; *Imprints*: Reader's Digest Children's Books (RD Childrens); Reader's Digest Young Families, Incorporated (RDYF)
Web site: http://www.readersdigestkids.com; http://www.studiofun.com/
Dist(s): **Children's Plus, Inc.**
Continental Bk. Co., Inc.
MyiLibrary
Simon & Schuster, Inc.
Simon & Schuster Children's Publishing
Simon & Schuster Children's Publishing.

Studio Indiana, *(978-0-9745186)* 430 N. Sewell Rd., Bloomington, IN 47408 USA Tel 812-223-5073 (phone/fax)
E-mail: john@studioindiana.com
Web site: http://www.studioindiana.com.

Studio Ironcat L.L.C. *See* **International Comics & Entertainment L.L.C.**

Studio Moonfall, (*978-0-9841746; 978-1-942811*) 5031 7th Ave., Kenosha, WI 53140 USA
Web site: http://www.fearandsunshine.com; http://www.ratatatgraphics.com
Dist(s): **Ingram Content Group.**

Studio Mouse LLC, (*978-1-59069*) 353 Main Ave., Norwalk, CT 06851 USA Tel 203-846-2274; Fax: 203-846-1776; Toll Free: 800-228-7839
E-mail: chelsea.shriver@soundprints.com
Dist(s): **Soundprints.**

Studio Pr., (*978-0-934420*) Orders Addr.: P.O. Box 407, Norfolk, NE 68702-0407 USA (SAN 214-400X) Tel 402-371-5040; Fax: 402-371-9382; Toll Free: 800-228-0629; Edit Addr.: 1500 Square Turn Blvd., Norfolk, NE 68702-0407 USA Do not confuse with companies with the same or similar names in Rome, NY, West Chazy, NY, Soulsbyville, CA, Elkton, MD, Tubac, AZ, Eureka Springs, AR
E-mail: contact@marathonpress.com
Web site: http://www.marathonpress.com
Dist(s): **Independent Pubs. Group.**

Studio See *See* **Studio See Publishing, LLC**

Studio See Publishing, LLC, (*978-0-9796974*) P.O. Box 7013, Sheridan, WY 82801 USA Tel 307-673-1207
E-mail: psee@fiberpipe.net
Web site: http://www.studiosee.com.

StudioLine Photo *Imprint of* **H&M Systems Software, Inc.**

Studios West Publications *See* **Ritchie Unlimited Pubns.**

Study Ctr. Pr. *Imprint of* **San Francisco Study Ctr.**

Stuff on Paper, (*978-0-578-01210-0; 978-0-578-05355-4; 978-0-578-13881-7*) 21849 Erdahl Ct. NE, Tenstrike, MN 56683 USA
Dist(s): **Aardvark Global Publishing.**

Stuhl, John, (*978-0-692-99808-3; 978-1-7321060*) 11318 Fords Cove Ln., Farragut, TN 37934 USA Tel 865-414-1639
E-mail: authorjohnstuhl@gmail.com
Dist(s): **Ingram Content Group.**

Stull, Judy, (*978-0-9765738*) 16401 96th St., Lexington, OK 73051-8208 USA Tel 405-527-7467
E-mail: puppetlady@valornet.com.

Stump, Christopher, (*978-0-692-92741-0*) 5144 Conroy Rd. Unit 1025, Orlando, FL 32811 USA Tel 321-279-8965
E-mail: ChristopherLStump@gmail.com
Dist(s): **Ingram Content Group.**

Stunt Publishing, (*978-0-9745930*) 22287 Mulholland Why, No. 281, Calabasas, CA 91302 USA Tel 818-312-5157
E-mail: stuntpublishing@earthlink.net.

Sturgeon, Cathy, (*978-1-947798*) 3105 Caroline Cres, Suffolk, VA 23435 USA Tel 503-703-6687
E-mail: catherinesturgeon@gmail.com.

Stuttering Foundation of America *See* **Stuttering Foundation, The**

Stuttering Foundation, The, (*978-0-933388; 978-1-930244*) Orders Addr.: P.O. Box 11749, Memphis, TN 38111-0749 USA (SAN 282-3330) Tel 901-452-7343; Fax: 901-452-3931; Toll Free: 800-992-9392
E-mail: stutter@stutteringhelp.org
Web site: http://www.stutteringhelp.org.

Stylewriter Pubns., (*978-0-9718288; 978-0-9721653; 978-0-9729411; 978-0-9748771*) Div. of Stylewriter, Inc., 4395 N. Windsor Dr., Provo, UT 84604-6301 USA Toll Free: 866-802-7888
E-mail: customerservice@spllc.rog
Web site: http://www.spllc.org.

Stylist B. & Creative Endeavors, (*978-0-615-28680-8; 978-0-9907554*) 7411 Dartmoor Dr., New Orleans, LA 70127 USA Tel 504-237-2464
E-mail: writerstylistb@gmail.com
Web site: www.stylistb.com.

Stylist B. & Stylistic Creations *See* **Stylist B. & Creative Endeavors**

Stylus Publishing, LLC, (*978-1-57922; 978-1-887208; 978-0-9729394; 978-1-62036; 978-1-64267*) Orders Addr.: P.O. Box 605, Herndon, VA 20172-0605 USA; Edit Addr.: 22883 Quicksilver Dr., Sterling, VA 20166-2012 USA (SAN 299-1853) Tel 703-661-1581; Fax: 703-661-1501 Do not confuse with companies with the same name in Sunnyvale, CA, Quakertown, PA
E-mail: stylusmail@presswarehouse.com; jean.westcott@styluspub.com
Web site: http://www.styluspub.com
Dist(s): **ebrary, Inc.**

Suarez, Reinhardt, (*978-1-7337106*) 3549 Girard Ave S, Minneapolis, MN 55408 USA Tel 312-451-6462
E-mail: the.reinhardt.conquest@gmail.com.

Subcomission Literature Christiana *See* **Libros Desafio**

Subterranean Pr., (*978-0-9649890; 978-1-892284; 978-1-931081; 978-1-59606; 978-1-64524*) P.O. Box 190106, Burton, MI 48519 USA Tel 810-232-1489; Fax: 810-232-1447 Do not confuse with Subterranean Pr., San Francisco, CA
E-mail: subpress@gmail.com; subpressgeralyn@gmail.com
Web site: http://www.subterraneanpress.com
Dist(s): **Diamond Comic Distributors, Inc.**
Diamond Bk. Distributors.

Subtopian, The *See* **Starburns Industries Pr.**

Success Empowering Techniques, Inc., (*978-0-9753415*) 5500 S. Eastern Ave., Las Vegas, NV 89119 USA Tel 702-893-0042
E-mail: set@setsuccess.com
Web site: http://www.setsuccess.com.

Success for All Foundation, (*978-0-9767850; 978-1-941010*) 300 E. Joppa Rd. 5th Flr., Baltimore, MD 21286 USA Tel 800-548-4998; Fax: 410-324-4458
E-mail: jworrell@successforall.org; tkoromah@successforall.org
Web site: http://www.successforall.org.

Success Hse. Publishing, (*978-0-578-60014-7*) 48 Bark Mill Terr., Montville, NJ 07045 USA Tel 201-286-3386
E-mail: marc@grandfatherlessons.com
Web site: www.marcdemetriou.com.

Sucharitkul, Somtow *See* **Diplodocus Pr.**

Suckerfish Bks., (*978-0-9764659; 978-1-7332801*) 23700 NW Skyline Blvd., North Plains, OR 97133 USA Tel 503-957-1554
Web site: http://www.suckerfishbooks.com.

Suerth, Renata, (*978-0-9882685*) 349 E. Crescent Ave., Elmhurst, IL 60126 USA Tel 773-793-6830
E-mail: renata98mc@yahoo.com.

Sugar Bean Publishing LLC, (*978-1-7363303*) 6376 W Fish Lake Dr, West Jordan, UT 84081 USA Tel 801-694-2181
E-mail: megarcia38@yahoo.com.

Sugar Creek Publishing, (*978-0-9712571*) 4126 N. London Rd., Fairland, IN 46126 USA Tel 727-399-0342.

Sugar Ducky Bks., Inc., (*978-0-9727388*) P.O. Box 56954, Jacksonville, FL 32241-6954 USA (SAN 255-1403)
E-mail: service@sugarduckybooks.com
Web site: http://www.sugarduckybooks.com.

Sugar Goblin LLC, The, (*978-0-9860859*) 2566 Delaware Ave., Sunfish Lake, MN 55118 USA.

Suits, Danial, (*978-0-615-42555-9; 978-0-692-95150-7; 978-0-692-97248-9; 978-0-692-06099-5*) 22660 I-30 Lot 33, Bryant, AR 72022 USA Tel 501-766-6011.

Suk, Amanda, (*978-0-692-19151-4*) 116 W Maple St No. 17, Glendale, CA 91204 USA Tel 314-593-0805
E-mail: amanda.suk@gmail.com.

Sulby Hall Publishing, (*978-0-615-84593-7; 978-0-615-86133-3; 978-0-615-89846-9*) P.O. Box 8687, Malibu, CA 90264 USA Tel 310-457-0439
Dist(s): **CreateSpace Independent Publishing Platform.**

Sullivan, Kayla , (*978-0-578-18078-6*) 2909 Springdale Ln, San Ramon, CA 94583 USA.

Sullivan, Kelley Enterprises, (*978-0-9728556*) c/o L. Leon, KSE, P.O. Box 1843, Lemon Grove, CA 91946-1843 USA
E-mail: ll@mykse.com
Web site: http://www.mykse.com.

Suma de Letras, S.L. (ESP) (*978-84-663; 978-84-95501; 978-84-96463*) *Dist. by* **Distribks Inc.**

Summa Bks., (*978-0-932423*) P.O. Box 2095, Darien, IL 60561-6895 USA (SAN 687-4096).

Summa Publishing Company *See* **Summa Bks.**

Summer Camp Stories LLC, (*978-0-9863743*) 35 Toilsome Brook Rd., Stamford, CT 06905 USA Tel 203-705-1600
E-mail: elliotsloyer@yahoo.com
Web site: www.summercampstories.com.

Summer Day Publishing, LLC, (*978-0-9768653*) 14747 San Marsala Ct., Tampa, FL 33626 USA Tel 727-224-9874; Fax: 813-926-8215
E-mail: baflorida@aol.com
Web site: http://www.thebreakawaykid.com.

Summer Storm Publishing, LLC, (*978-1-948657*)
E-mail: azettwoch@gmail.com.

Summer Street Pr., (*978-0-9766367; 978-0-9822541*) 460 Summer St., Stamford, CT 06901 USA Tel 203-325-2217; Fax: 203-325-2218 Do not confuse with Summer Street Press in Santa Barbara, CA
E-mail: Cathy@summerstreetpress.com
Web site: http://www.summerstreetpress.com.

Summerbook Co., (*978-1-933055*) 305 Lyndale Dr., Hartsville, SC 29550 USA Tel 843-383-5554 (phone/fax)
E-mail: angela@summerbookcompany.com
Web site: http://www.summerbookcompany.com.

Summerfield Publishing/New Plains Press, (*978-0-9794561; 978-0-9857703; 978-0-9986857; 978-1-7345719; 979-8-9874213*) Orders Addr.: P.O. Box 1946, Auburn, AL 36831-1946 USA (SAN 853-4845) Tel 334-728-2071; Edit Addr.: 833 Choctaw Ave., Auburn, AL 36830 USA
E-mail: summerfield_john@columbusstate.edu; publisher@newplainspress.com
Web site: http://newplainspress.com.

Summerhill Pr., (*978-0-9801861*) P.O. Box 79684, Fort Worth, TX 76179 USA; *Imprints:* Summertime Books (Summertime Bk) Do not confuse with Summerhill Pr., Naperville, IL
E-mail: summerhillpress@charter.net
Web site: http://www.summertimebooks.com.

Summerland Publishing, (*978-0-9794585; 978-0-9794863; 978-0-9795444; 978-0-9824870; 978-0-9837923; 978-0-9891121; 978-0-9893996; 978-0-9905886; 978-0-9963736; 978-0-9986451; 978-0-9995562; 978-1-7329072; 978-1-7375730; 979-8-9864312*) 3181 E. Elgin Dr., Salt Lake City, UT 84109 USA (SAN 853-4497) Tel 307-399-7744
E-mail: summerlandpublishing@gmail.com
Web site: http://www.SummerlandPublishing.com.

Summers, Christine, (*978-0-9987408*) 515 Ruxton Dr., Wilmington, DE 19809 USA Tel 302-545-2367
E-mail: organizedfitnesscoach@gmail.com
Web site: sketchowl.com.

Summers Island Pr., (*978-0-9964953; 978-1-944798; 978-1-957940*) P.O. Box 19293, Thorne Bay, AK 99919 USA Tel 907-419-0508
E-mail: wildernesschool@msn.com; ann@summersislandpress.com
Web site: http://www.SummersIslandPress.com; http://www.LightsmithPublishers.com.

Summerside Lane, (*978-0-9777570*) 179 Highlands Dr., Williston, VT 05495 USA (SAN 850-1793)
Web site: http://www.Summersidelane.com.

Summertime Bks. *Imprint of* **Summerhill Pr.**

Summertime Books *See* **Summerhill Pr.**

Summit Crossroads Press *See* **Summit Crossroads Pr./Amanita Bks.**

Summit Crossroads Pr./Amanita Bks., (*978-0-9614519; 978-0-9640558; 978-0-615-35670-9; 978-0-9834049; 978-0-9967142; 978-0-9991565; 978-1-7368214*) Orders Addr.: 9329 Angelina Cir., Columbia, MD 21045-5109 USA (SAN 689-5700) Tel 410-290-7058
E-mail: sumcross@aol.com; eileenmcintire@aol.com
Web site: http://www.parentsuccess.com; https://www.SecretPanels.net
Dist(s): **Follett School Solutions**
Ingram Content Group Inc.
Quality Bks., Inc.
Smashwords.

Summit Hse. Pubs., (*978-0-9746735; 978-0-9746735-5-4; 978-1-7356699*) Orders Addr.: P.O. Box 15478, Chicago, IL 60615 USA; *Imprints:* Ijiwola Press, Gregory (G Ijiwola Pr)
Web site: http://www.summitpublishers.com; http://thecitylight.org.

Summit Interactive, (*978-1-57458*) Orders Addr.: 302 Albany Ave., Shreveport, LA 71105 USA Tel 318-865-8232; Fax: 318-865-6227; Toll Free: 877-843-0277
E-mail: mhenry@sieducation.com; scavel@sieducation.com; kbriley@sieducation.com
Web site: http://www.sieducation.com; http://www.AscendEdu.com.

Summit Univ. Pr., (*978-0-916766; 978-0-922729; 978-0-9720402; 978-1-932890; 978-1-60988*) Orders Addr.: 63 Summit Way, Gardiner, MT 59030 USA Tel 406-848-9500; Fax: 406-848-9605; Toll Free: 800-245-5445
E-mail: info@summituniversitypress.com
Web site: http://www.summituniversitypress.com
Dist(s): **SCB Distributors.**

Sun Break Publishing, (*978-0-9815557; 978-1-60916*) 1037 NE 65th St., No. 164, Seattle, WA 98115 USA
Web site: http://sunbreakpublishing.com
Dist(s): **Smashwords.**

Sun Cycle Publishing, (*978-0-9794322*) Orders Addr.: 1415 Hwy 85 N Ste 310-439, Fayetteville, GA 30214 USA (SAN 853-4195)
E-mail: suncyclebooks@yahoo.com.

Sun on Earth Bks., (*978-1-883378*) P.O. Box 704, Heathsville, VA 22473 USA Tel 804-435-5195
E-mail: books@sunonearth.com
Web site: http://www.sunonearth.com.

Sun Pubns., (*978-0-9665932; 978-1-931034*) Div. of Success Unleashed, Inc., 300 Carlsbad Village Dr., Suite 108A-7B, Carlsbad, CA 92008 USA (SAN 253-4444) Tel 619-884-7505; Fax: 760-434-7076 Do not confuse with Sun Publications, Charlottesville, VA
E-mail: eagles10@pacbell.net
Dist(s): **Insight Publishing.**

Sun Rose Pubs., (*978-0-9712781*) P.O. Box 2314, East Orange, NJ 07019 USA
E-mail: carolineilo@yahoo.com; eph-ilogienboh@worldnet.att.net.

Sun Sings Pubns., (*978-0-9721429; 978-0-9832053*) 4144 Lafayette Pl., Culver City, CA 90232-2818 USA Tel 310-837-1313; Fax: 802-609-2959
E-mail: alan-alanlindgren@hotmail.com.

Sun Sprite Publishing, (*978-0-9745712*) 19 Milton Ave, Cranston, RI 02905 USA Toll Free: 877-883-4798
E-mail: kwanyin@ureach.com
Web site: http://www.mykwanyin.com/sunsprite.html.

Sunbelt Media, Incorporated *See* **Eakin Pr.**

†Sunbelt Pubns., Inc., (*978-0-916251; 978-0-932653; 978-0-9606704; 978-0-9620402; 978-1-941384*) 1250 Fayette St., El Cajon, CA 92020-1511 USA (SAN 630-0790) Tel 619-258-4911; Fax: 619-258-4916; Toll Free: 800-626-6579
E-mail: info@sunbeltpub.com; sales@sunbeltpub.com; dyoung@sunbeltpub.com; mail@sunbeltpub.com
Web site: http://www.sunbeltpub.com; http://www.sunbeltbooks.com; *CIP.*

Sunbird Books *Imprint of* **Phoenix International Publications, Inc.**

Sunbury Press, Inc., (*978-0-9760925; 978-1-934597; 978-1-62006; 979-8-88819*) PO Box, Boiling Springs, PA 17007-0548 USA Tel 1-855-338-8359
E-mail: orders@sunburypress.com
Web site: http://www.sunburypress.com
Dist(s): **Open Road Integrated Media, Inc.**

Suncoast Digital Pr., Inc., (*978-1-939237; 978-0-692-02053-1*) 8047 Royal Birkdale Cir., Lakewood Ranch, FL 34202 USA Tel 941-302-8600; Fax: 941-907-9340
E-mail: barbara@suncoastdigitalpress.com
Web site: http://www.suncoastdigitalpress.com.

SUNDADMOONMOM, (*978-1-7324860*) 667 Mcvey Ave., Lake Oswego, OR 97034 USA Tel 817-891-4809
E-mail: sundadmoonmom@gmail.com
Web site: sundadmoonmom.com.

Sundance Circle Publishing, (*978-0-9991179*) 540 E. Palm Ave., Burbank, CA 91501 USA Tel 818-679-8616
E-mail: driscoll.kevin1@gmail.com
Web site: www.sundancecircle.com.

Sundance Entertainment, (*978-0-9729847*) P.O. Box 418, New York, NY 10035 USA Tel 646-431-9334.

Sundance Media Group, Inc./VASST, (*978-0-9762380*) P.O. Box 3, Stockton, UT 84071 USA Tel 435-882-8494; Fax: 435-882-8508
E-mail: info@sundancemediagroup.com
Web site: http://www.vasst.com.

SunDance Press *See* **Bk. Pubs. of El Paso**

Sundance/Newbridge Educational Publishing, (*978-0-7608; 978-0-88741; 978-0-940146; 978-1-56784; 978-1-56801; 978-1-58273; 978-1-4007; 978-1-4207*) P.O. Box 740, Northborough, MA 01532 USA (SAN 169-3484) Tel 888-200-2720; Fax: 508-303-2015; Toll Free: 800-343-8204
E-mail: info@sundancepub.com; lroman@sundancepub.com
Web site: http://www.sundancepub.com; http://www.newbridgeonline.com.

Sunday School Board of the Southern Baptist Convention *See* **Lifeway Christian Resources**

Sunday School Publishing Board *See* **Townsend Pr. - Sunday Schl. Publishing Board**

SundaySchoolNetwork.com, (*978-0-9665124*) SA Keith of Creative Imaginations, 438 E. Ilex Dr., Lake Park, FL 33403-2606 USA Tel 561-281-5033
E-mail: info@sundayschoolnetwork.com; orders@SundaySchoolNetwork.com
Web site: http://sundayschoolnetwork.com; http://www.creativeimaginations.net.

Sundback, Ruth, (*978-0-9776850*) 10430 Perla Bello Ct., Las Vegas, NV 89135 USA (SAN 850-9719)
E-mail: ruthslv@earthlink.net.

Sundie Enterprises, (*978-0-9859811; 978-0-9991261*) P.O. Box 1274, Provo, UT 84603-1274 USA Tel 801-995-9342
E-mail: sundieents@gmail.com.

SunDog Enterprises, (*978-0-9854677*) 119 Persimmon Ridge Rd., Cleveland, SC 29635 USA Tel 864-836-2668
E-mail: gail.mcdiarmid@furman.edu.

Sundog, Ltd., (*978-1-932203; 978-1-59744*) Orders Addr.: 35 W. 92nd St., 5e, New York, NY 10025 USA.

Sunergos Bible Studies, (*978-1-932934*) 2485 Morse Rd., Sebastopol, CA 95472 USA Tel 707-829-2956
E-mail: rich@sunergosbible.org; jan@sunergosbible.org
Web site: http://www.sunergosbible.org.

sunflower, (*978-1-7373105*) 167 Pine St, AUBURN, CA 95603 USA Tel 916-595-4488
E-mail: karenlynnwaymire@gmail.com.

Sunflower Education, (*978-1-937166*) 15044 Haley Hollow, Austin, TX 78728 USA Tel 512-694-9380
E-mail: cynthia.hannon@gmail.com
Web site: sunflowereducation.net.

Sunflower Pr., (*978-0-9616586; 978-0-9768507; 978-0-9832659*) 104-40 Queens Blvd. (Apt. No. 20 B), Forest Hills, NY 11375 USA (SAN 659-7785)
E-mail: order@ckchutaichi.com
Web site: ckchutaichi.com.

Sunflower Pr., (*978-0-9896080*) 200 Viridian Dr., Muskegon, MI 49440 USA Tel 347-844-2149
E-mail: edzitron@edzitron.com.

Sunflower Publishing *See* **Growing Field Bks.**

Sunflower Seeds Pr., (*978-0-9743627; 978-0-9830089*) 9470 Hwy 96 W., Franklin, TN 37064 USA
E-mail: bill@rondafriend.com
Web site: http://www.sunflowerseedspress.com; http://www.downonfriendlyacres.com.

Sunflower Univ. Pr., (*978-0-89745*) Subs. of Journal of the West, Inc., 2961 Nevada St., Manhattan, KS 66502-2355 USA (SAN 218-5075) Toll Free: 800-258-1232 (orders)
E-mail: pub@sunflower-univ-press.org
Web site: http://www.sunflower-univ-press.org.

Sungi Bear LLC, (*978-0-692-61262-0; 978-0-692-71225-2; 978-0-9988483*) 11 Sager Pl, Irvington, NJ 07111 USA Tel 973-568-5256; 11 Sager Pl, Irvington, NJ 07111 Tel 973-568-5256.

Sungrazer Publishing, (*978-0-9994628*) 4070 Woodman Canyon, Sherman Oaks, CA 91423 USA Tel 310-924-2731
E-mail: albertleon@sungrazerpublishing.com.

SunHill Pubs., (*978-0-9673189; 978-1-956168*) Orders Addr.: 832 Commonwealth Ave Se, Atlanta, GA 30312 USA Do not confuse with Hill Publishing in Marina, CA
E-mail: ehill111@comcast.net; ericmhillauthor@yahoo.com.

Sunlight Publishing, (*978-0-9818190*) 339 E. Weller St., Ansonia, OH 45303 USA (SAN 924-7130) Tel 937-671-8511; 419-925-4121; *Imprints:* Candy Cane Books (CandyCane).

Sunny & The Chocolate Dog, LLC, (*978-0-9725945*) 5 Palm Row, Saint Augustine, FL 32084 USA Tel 904-808-7144; Fax: 904-808-7142
E-mail: josh@sunnyandthechocolatedog.com
Web site: http://www.sunnyandthechocolatedog.com.

Sunny Bks. *Imprint of* **J B Communications, Inc.**

Sunny Day Publishing, LLC, (*978-0-9825480; 978-0-9903823; 978-0-9978006; 978-1-948613*) 3365 Crestwood Cir., Cuyahoga Falls, OH 44223 USA (SAN 920-8232) Tel 330-414-2760 Do not confuse with Sunny Day Publishing in Richardson, TX
E-mail: sales@sunnydaypublishing.com; stacie@sunnydaypublishing.com
Web site: https://www.sunnydaypublishing.com.

Sunny Future Pr., (*978-0-9754980*) 890 Bruce Dr., Wantagh, NY 11793-1116 USA
E-mail: canivan@optonline.net
Web site: http://www.jc-solarhomes.com.

Sunny Hollow Pr., (*978-0-9755818*) 2517 N. 62nd St., Mesa, AZ 85215 USA Tel 480-830-7634; Toll Free: 800-442-0046
E-mail: rjvb@sunnyhollowpress.com
Web site: http://www.sunnyhollowpress.com.

Sunny Palms Pr., (*978-1-942073; 978-1-951314; 978-1-64778*) P.O. Box 230348, Encinitas, CA 92023 USA Tel 760-902-6502
E-mail: janmoran123@gmail.com.

Sunnycroft Bks., (*978-0-9904320*) 4110 SE Hawthorne Blvd. No. 749, Portland, OR 97214 USA Tel 503-867-3085
E-mail: sunnycroftbooks@gmail.com.

Sunnyfields Publishing, (*978-0-578-06095-8; 978-0-578-06541-0; 978-0-578-06574-8; 978-0-615-75133-7; 978-0-615-76128-2; 978-0-615-76235-7*) 1746 N. Gramercy Pl., No. 15, Los Angeles, CA 90028 USA Tel 323-960-2563
E-mail: Daviddayan666@aol.com.

Sunny's Light Books *See* **Sunny's Light Enterprises, LLC**

Sunny's Light Enterprises, LLC, (*978-1-7329989*) 1345 Towne Lake Hills South Dr. Unit 300-304 Unit 300-304, Woodstock, GA 30189 USA Tel 770-203-5003
E-mail: sunnyslightenterprises@gmail.com
Web site: sunnyslightllc.com.

Sunnyside Pr., (*978-0-9742566*) 902 E. 10th St., Jeffersonville, IN 47130 USA Tel 812-282-8832; Fax: 812-282-4057 Do not confuse with companies with the same or similar name in Saint Johnsville, NY, San Marcos, CA, Washington, DC
E-mail: bprintcenter@cs.com.

Sunphone, Ltd., (*978-0-9652458*) 427 Sippewissett Rd., Falmouth, MA 02540 USA Tel 508-540-6899; Fax: 508-540-8226
E-mail: sunfal@aol.com.

Sunraehealing, (*978-0-9896218; 978-0-9908374*) 3906 Cherrywood Rd., Austin, TX 78722 USA Tel 512-547-2454
E-mail: raedoman@hotmail.com.

SunRaSon Production Co., *(978-0-9677644)* 882 E. 57th St., Brooklyn, NY 11234 USA
E-mail: info@sunrason.com
Web site: http://www.sunrason.com.

Sunray Publishing, *(978-1-934478)* 25123 22nd Ave., Saint Cloud, MN 56301 USA Tel 320-253-8808; Fax: 320-253-9683; Toll Free: 888-253-8808
E-mail: jwindschitl@sunrayprinting.com
Web site: http://www.sunrayprinting.com
Dist(s): **Partners Bk. Distributing, Inc.**

Sunrise Bks., LLC *Imprint of* **Howard, Bob**

Sunrise Bks., *(978-0-940652)* P.O. Box 7003, Eureka, CA 95502-7003 USA (SAN 665-7893) Do not confuse with with companies with the same name in Lebanon, VA, Lake Bluff, IL
E-mail: Sunrise-2004@sbcglobal.net.

Sunrise Mountain Bks., *(978-0-9842362; 978-1-940728)* Div. of Sunrise Services Distributing, LLC, 13347 W. Tapatio Dr., Boise, ID 83713 USA (SAN 858-8139) Fax: 208-938-8338; *Imprints*: Simple Faith Books (SimpleFaith)
Web site: http://www.sunrisemountainbooks.com; http://www.sunrisedistrib.com; http://www.youcandoitart.com.

Sunrise Publications *See* **Prematurely Yours**

SunRise Publishing, *(978-0-9644552; 978-1-57636)* Orders Addr.: P.O. Box 1001, Orem, UT 84059 USA Tel 801-860-2665; Fax: 801-705-0124; Edit Addr.: P.O. Box 1001, Orem, UT 84059-1001 USA Do not confuse with companies with the same or similar names in Lake Forest, IL, Niagara Falls, NY, Lincoln City, OR, Santa Barbara, CA, Hatfield, PA, Maryland Heights, MD, Austinburg, OH, Inman, SC, Fort Lauderdale, FL, Albuquerque, NM
E-mail: brian@sunrisebooks.com
Web site: http://www.sunrisebooks.com
Dist(s): **Granite Publishing & Distribution Village Marketing.**

Sunrise Selections, *(978-0-9656307; 979-8-9861317)* Orders Addr.: 1102 N. Main St., Mapleton, UT 84664 USA Tel 801-319-3619; Fax: 801-489-9517; Edit Addr.: 1102 N. Main, Mapleton, UT 84664 USA
E-mail: betty-briggs@comcast.net
Web site: http://www.bettybriggs.com
Dist(s): **Granite Publishing & Distribution.**

SunriseHouse Pubs., *(978-0-9770783)* 5181 Blackpool Rd., Westminster, CA 92683 USA
E-mail: dawn@dawnwilliams.net
Web site: http://www.sunrisehousepublishers.com.

Sunseri, Heather, *(978-0-9887153; 978-1-943165)* P.O. Box 1264, Versailles, KY 40383 USA
E-mail: heather@heathersunseri.com.

Sunset Beach Music, *(978-0-9639279)* P.O. Box 159, Haleiwa, HI 96712 USA
E-mail: msmusic@hula.net.

Sunset Readers Publishing, *(978-0-9749333)* 220 W., 400 N., American Fork, UT 84003-1567 USA
E-mail: beb1@sisna.com
Web site: http://www.bennetthbracken.com.

Sunshine BlackRose Pubns., *(978-0-692-51205-0; 978-1-7321910)* 928 Shearwater Way, Warrenville, SC 29851 USA Tel 706-386-9525
Web site: www.sunshinebrpublications.com
Dist(s): **CreateSpace Independent Publishing Platform.**

Sunshine Bks. for Children, *(978-0-9745116)* 8127 E. Weldon Ave., Scottsdale, AZ 85251 USA.

Sunshine Center, Incorporated *See* **Prevention Through Puppetry, Inc.**

Sunshine In My Soul Publishing, *(978-1-68327)* 7380 Park Ridge Blvd. No. 124, San Diego, CA 92120 USA (SAN 990-0969) Tel 619-788-9612
E-mail: admin@speedypublishing.com; bowe@sunshineinmysoulpublishing.com.

Sunshine Publishing, *(978-0-9749844)* 1421 Washington St., Lincoln, NE 68502-2455 USA Do not confuse with companies with the same or similar names in Carthage, NY, Buffalo Grove, IL , Bristol, TN, Columbus, GA, Raleigh, NC, Ft Worth, TX.

Sunshine53 Pr., *(978-0-9855233)* 18008 NW Sylvania Ln., Portland, OR 97229 USA Tel 503-747-2658
E-mail: coryell5150@comcast.net.

Sunsprite Publishing, *(978-1-7358195)* 229 Ute Ln, Ventura, CA 93001 USA Tel 818-517-5726
E-mail: mona_c_lewis@yahoo.com.

Sunstar Publishing *Imprint of* **1st World Publishing, Inc.**

†Sunstone Pr., *(978-0-86534; 978-0-913270; 978-1-61139; 978-1-63293)* Div. of The Sunstone Corporation, Orders Addr.: 239 Johnson St., Santa Fe, NM 87504-2321 USA; Edit Addr.: P.O. Box 2321, Santa Fe, NM 87504-2321 USA (SAN 214-2090) Tel 505-988-4418; Fax: 505-988-1025; Toll Free: 800-243-5644 (Orders Only); *Imprints*: Blackbirch Press, Incorporated (Blackbirch Pr)
E-mail: jsmith@sunstonepress.com
Web site: http://www.sunstonepress.com
Dist(s): **Brodart Co.**
Ingram Content Group
New Leaf Distributing Co., Inc.
Quality Bks., Inc.
Rio Nuevo Pubs.; *CIP.*

Suny Pr. *Imprint of* **State Univ. of New York Pr.**

Super Dentists, The, *(978-0-9798506)* 2226 Otay Lakes Rd., Chula Vista, CA 91915 USA (SAN 854-5650)
Web site: http://www.thesuperdentists.com.

Super Duper Pubns., *(978-1-58650; 978-1-60723)* Div. of Super Duper, Inc., Orders Addr.: P.O. Box 24997, Greenville, SC 29616 USA Tel 864-288-3536; Fax: 864-288-3380; Toll Free: 800-277-8737; Edit Addr.: 5201 Pelham Rd., Greenville, SC 29615-5723 USA
E-mail: mdeShong@superduperinc.com; JWhitehead@superduperinc.com
Web site: http://www.superduperinc.com; http://www.handyhandouts.com; http://www.hearbuilder.com; http://www.superduperlearning.com.

Super, Jane, *(978-1-7351648)* 5305 Highstream Ct., GREENSBORO, NC 27407 USA Tel 336-772-1313
E-mail: janesuper2@gmail.com.

Super SandCastle *Imprint of* **ABDO Publishing Co.**

Super Smart Science Stuff, *(978-0-9843848; 978-0-9911472; 978-1-941775)* 5813 Anselm Ct, Austin, TX 78739-7873 USA Tel 512-203-6919; Fax: 512-288-0208
E-mail: april@supersmartsciencestuff.com.

SUPERI, LLC. *See* **Superi, LLC.**

Superi, LLC., *(978-0-9970364; 978-0-9974751; 978-1-7376058)* 16038 Eastcape Dr., Webster, TX 77598 USA Tel 832-738-7971
E-mail: cthurmon13@outlook.com
Web site: http://www.superiworld.com.

Superior Guidance, *(978-1-7366943)* 54 Victoria Heights pl, Dallas, GA 30132 USA Tel 404-547-2188
E-mail: Superiorguidance@gmail.com.

SuperKids Nutrition Inc., *(978-0-9801148; 978-1-7339692; 978-1-7373096)* 375 S. Grand Oaks Ave., Pasadena, CA 91107 USA (SAN 855-2436) Tel 626-818-6299
E-mail: melissa@superkidsnutrition.com
Web site: http://www.superkidsnutrition.com.

Supreme Art, *(978-1-942912)* 6425 Reseda Blvd., Reseda, CA 91335 USA Tel 818-438-9779
E-mail: info@supremeart.org
Web site: www.supremeArt.org

Supreme Design, LLC, *(978-0-9816170; 978-1-935721)* P.O. Box 10887, Atlanta, GA 30310 USA Tel 404-759-8799
E-mail: sujandass@ymail.com
Web site: http://www.supremedesignllc.com.

SuProCo, *(978-0-9906567)* 1300 Army Navy Dr. No. 1101, Arlington, VA 22202 USA Tel 703-271-8889
E-mail: SuProCo@aol.com.

Surber, Shawn-Michelle *See* **Mornin' Light Media**

Surface Communications LLC *See* **Books by Kids LLC**

Surfing Group, The, *(978-0-9770730)* Primedia, 236 Avenida Fabricante. Ste. 201, San Clemente, CA 92672-7557 USA
E-mail: ross.garrett@primedia.com.

Surfside Six Publishing, *(978-0-615-32262-9; 978-0-692-87258-1; 978-0-692-04632-6)* P.O. Box 545960, Surfside, FL 33154 USA
Dist(s): **CreateSpace Independent Publishing Platform.**

Sur-Mount Pubs., *(978-0-9673517; 978-0-9740107)* P.O. Box 99396, Emeryville, CA 94662-9396 USA Tel 510-559-8797
E-mail: cs@surmountpublishersincorporated.com; sales@surmountpublishersincorporated.com
Web site: http://www.surmountpublishersincorporated.com.

Suromex, Ediciones, S.A. (MEX) *(978-968-855) Dist. by* **Giron Bks.**

Susa Inc, *(978-1-7346078)* 9526 Linden Ave, Bethesda, MD 20814 USA Tel 617-803-1518
E-mail: nazilafp@gmail.com
Web site: www.susainc.org.

Susaeta Ediciones, S.A. (ESP) *(978-84-305; 978-84-677) Dist. by* **IPG Chicago.**

Susaeta Ediciones, S.A. (ESP) *(978-84-305; 978-84-677) Dist. by* **AIMS Intl.**

Susaeta Ediciones, S.A. (ESP) *(978-84-305; 978-84-677) Dist. by* **Lectorum Pubns.**

Susaeta Ediciones, S.A. (ESP) *(978-84-305; 978-84-677) Dist. by* **Giron Bks.**

Susan Palavics Publishing, *(978-0-692-78458-7)* 51760 Becker Rd., Bigfork, MN 56628 USA Tel 218-743-3458
E-mail: thewildernesslodge1@gmail.com.

Susanna Lagoon Bks. *Imprint of* **J. K. Eckert & Co., Inc.**

Susi B. Marketing, Inc., *(978-0-9773653)* 188 Wentworth St., Charleston, SC 29401 USA Tel 843-822-7676; Fax: 843-958-8444
Web site: http://www.angietheant.com.

Susquehanna Univ. Pr., *(978-0-941664; 978-0-945636; 978-1-57591)* Affil. of Associated Univ. Presses, Orders Addr.: 2010 Eastpark Blvd., Cranbury, NJ 08512 USA Tel 609-655-4770; Fax: 609-655-8366
Web site: http://www.susqu.edu/su_press
Dist(s): **Associated Univ. Presses**
Rowman & Littlefield Publishers, Inc.
ebrary, Inc.

Sussa Pr., *(978-0-615-93348-1)* 10 Ossipee Rd., Somerville, MA 02144 USA Tel 617-666-3278
E-mail: mark.schifferli@gmail.com.

Sussman Sales Co., *(978-0-9755367; 978-1-934211; 978-1-61717; 978-1-68265; 978-1-953038; 979-8-88634)* 250 E. 54th St. Suite 8A, New York, NY 10022 USA Toll Free Fax: 212-371-8882; Toll Free: 800-350-7180
E-mail: info@sussmansales.com
Web site: http://www.sussmansales.com.

Sussman, Valerie, *(978-1-7345971)* 7830 E. Roseland Dr., La Jolla, CA 92037 USA Tel 805-407-5635
E-mail: valsuss@me.com.

Susso, *(978-0-578-20339-3)* 315 Harrison Ave, Leadville, CO 80461 USA
E-mail: mountainsaintt@gmail.com; acsusso@hotmail.com
Web site: https://www.youtube.com/c/Susso.

Susso, Anthony *See* **Susso**

Susy Dorn Productions, LLC, *(978-0-9764010)* P.O. Box 111393, Campbell, CA 95011-1393 USA
Web site: http://www.juguemosenespanol.com.

Suteki Creative, *(978-1-948124; 978-1-63882)* 1715 Worthy Ct, Woodbridge, VA 22191-4538 USA
E-mail: editor@sutekicreative.com
Web site: http://www.SutekiCreative.com.

Sutherland, Charles, *(978-1-68419)* 8490 Metcalf Blvd., Manassas, VA 20110 USA Tel 540-287-7578
Dist(s): **Smashwords.**

suto, gyuszi, *(978-1-7366049)* 355 NE 49th Ave, Hillsboro, OR 97124-5096 USA Tel 503-640-0165
E-mail: suto.gyuszi@gmail.com.

Sutton, Robin, *(978-0-9755098)* P.O. Box 79174, Saginaw, TX 76179 USA
Web site: http://www.therobinsnestbooks.com.

Suzalooz Pr., *(978-0-9660350)* 139 S. Eighth St., Brooklyn, NY 11211 USA Tel 718-387-3384; Fax: 212-475-4442
E-mail: zhour@inx.net.

Suzeteo Enterprises *See* **Athanatos Publishing Group**

Suzeteo Enterprises *Imprint of* **Athanatos Publishing Group**

Suzuki *Imprint of* **Alfred Publishing Co., Inc.**

Susy & Livy Pubns., *(978-0-9727757)* Orders Addr.: P.O. Box 449, Virginia City, NV 89440 USA Tel 775-847-0454; Fax: 775-847-9010; Edit Addr.: 111 S. C St., Virginia City, NV 89440-0449 USA
E-mail: info@marktwainbooks.com
Web site: http://www.marktwainbooks.com.

Svoboda, David *See* **BooksbyDave Inc.**

Swafford, Bethany, P.O. Box 38, DENVER, IN 46926 USA Tel 765-633-3249
E-mail: bjswaff@gmail.com
Dist(s): **Ingram Content Group.**

Swallow Pr. *Imprint of* **Ohio Univ. Pr.**

Swampland Publishing Co., *(978-0-9754785)* P.O. Box 1311, Larose, LA 70373 USA
E-mail: alces@cajunswampland.com.

Swan Creek Pr., *(978-0-9753216; 978-1-7335341)* 3736 Linden Green Dr., Toledo, OH 43614 USA Tel 419-381-0115
E-mail: swancreekpress@buckeye-express.com
Dist(s): **Ingram Content Group.**

SwanCygnet Unlimited, *(978-0-9763081; 978-0-578-67756-9; 978-0-578-67789-7; 978-0-578-71766-1; 978-0-578-71768-5)* P.O. Box 564, Cedarburg, WI 53012 USA Toll Free: 888-360-3513
Web site: http://www.swancygnet.com.

Swan-Jones Production, *(978-1-882238)* 8362 San Cristobal Dr., Dallas, TX 75218 USA Tel 214-319-7049.

Swannee Rivers *See* **Rivers, Swannee**

Swanson, David, *(978-0-9830830; 978-0-9980859; 978-1-7347837; 979-8-9869811)* 707 Gillespie Ave., Charlottesville, VA 22902 USA Tel 434-296-4228
E-mail: david@davidswanson.org.

Swanson, Jennifer M, *(978-0-578-41021-0; 978-0-578-41067-8)* 1342A E. 28th St., Oakland, CA 94606 USA Tel 914-329-8376
E-mail: jenmyzel@gmail.com
Dist(s): **Ingram Content Group.**

SWC Editions *Imprint of* **Wayne, Steven Co.**

Sweden Trade, Inc., *(978-0-9744088)* 9-11 South Blvd. of Presidents, Sarasota, FL 34236 USA; *Imprints*: Sweden Trade Publishing (Sweden Trd Pub)
Web site: http://TheRoadToHappinessBook.com.

Sweden Trade Publishing *Imprint of* **Sweden Trade, Inc.**

Sweet 76 Bakery, *(978-0-615-80672-3)* 8709 58th Ave. SW Apt. D, Lakewood, WA 98499 USA Tel 253-205-1373
E-mail: dineensmith@yahoo.com.

Sweet, Charles *See* **Hesperia Publishing**

Sweet Cherry Publishing (GBR) *(978-1-78226; 978-1-80263) Dist. by* **BTPS.**

Sweet Dreams Pr. *Imprint of* **Bier Brothers, Inc.**

Sweet Grin Bks., *(978-0-9905402)* 1305 SE 3rd St., Cape Coral, FL 33990 USA Tel 239-478-0255
E-mail: befranz@yahoo.com.

Sweet, Joanne, *(978-0-9774881)* 228 Westin Hls., New Braunfels, TX 78132-2328 USA.

Sweet, Joanne, *(978-1-936660)* 228 Westin Hills, New Braunfels, TX 78132 USA Tel 830-624-4560
E-mail: store1@jhsweet.com
Web site: www.jhsweet.com.

Sweet Mama Bks., *(978-1-7330254)* 1838 3rd St, Kirkland, WA 98033 USA Tel 206-650-2250
E-mail: courtbcooke@gmail.com
Web site: sweetmamabooks.com.

Sweet Pea Bks., *(978-0-615-21845-8; 978-0-578-01706-8; 978-0-578-03074-6; 978-0-615-38010-0; 978-0-578-11547-4; 978-0-578-11548-1; 978-0-692-39897-5)* 601 Pelham Pwy. N., Suite 614, Bronx, NY 10467 USA (SAN 859-8983) Tel 914-843-1439; 347-341-6612
E-mail: sweetpeabooks@yahoo.com
Web site: http://sweetpeabooks.net.

Sweet Pea Productions, *(978-0-692-21374-2; 978-0-692-24407-4; 978-0-692-24410-4; 978-0-692-29778-0; 978-0-692-35306-6; 978-0-692-66546-6; 978-0-9981098; 978-1-7359187)* 16 lyndhurst Dr., bella vista, AR 72714 USA Tel 4796404312
Web site: www.jennybjones.com
Dist(s): **CreateSpace Independent Publishing Platform.**

Sweet Potato Brown, *(978-0-9788158)* Orders Addr.: 5208 S. Drexel Ave., 2w, Chicago, IL 60615 USA Tel 773-752-3521
E-mail: sofiapenelopebrown@sbcglobal.net
Web site: http://www.at3619.com
Dist(s): **Lulu Pr., Inc.**

Sweet Punkin Pr., *(978-0-9755078)* 43 Riverside Ave., No. 405, Medford, MA 02155-4605 USA Tel 781-389-0693; Fax: 781-396-8052
E-mail: cvenez@aol.com
Web site: http://www.sweetpunkinpress.com.

Sweet Sasifarsis Pubn., *(978-0-9837648)* 5828 Swanston Dr., Charlotte, NC 28269 USA Tel 704-340-3862
E-mail: nettark@aol.com.

Sweet Spot Publishing, *(978-0-9907739; 978-0-9863890)* 11370 Twelve Oaks Way, North Palm Beach, FL 33408 USA Tel 561-818-6700
E-mail: d.abis77@gmail.com.

Sweet Success Press *See* **Harmony Hse. Art Studio**

Sweetbeet Bks., *(978-0-9985362; 978-1-7336109; 978-1-7331539; 978-1-7376380)* P.O. Box 20817, Bethesda, MD 20015 USA
E-mail: almahammonddtc@gmail.com
Web site: http://www.sweetbeetbooks.com.

Sweetbriar Crafts & Pubns., *(978-0-9802015)* 3390 40th St., Mandan, ND 58554 USA Tel 701-663-6941
E-mail: swcandp@gmail.com.

Sweetbrier Pr., *(978-1-7347875)* 27582 Sweetbrier Ln., Mission Viejo, CA 92691 USA Tel 949-837-1134
E-mail: kallen43@cox.net.

Sweetgrass Bks. *Imprint of* **Farcountry Pr.**

Sweetwater Bks. *Imprint of* **Cedar Fort, Inc./CFI Distribution**

Sweetwater Distributing, *(978-0-9990943; 978-1-7323116; 978-1-960763)* 6612 Hwy. 17 N., DeMossville, KY 41033 USA Tel 859-472-5436
E-mail: lyndareesauthor@gmail.com
Web site: lyndareesauthor.com.

Sweetwater Pr., *(978-1-58173; 978-1-889372; 978-1-60196)* Div. of Books-A-Million, Orders Addr.: 3608 Clairmont Ave., Birmingham, AL 035222 USA Do not confuse with companies with the same name in Ault, CO, Raleigh, NC Miami FL, Little Rock AR .

Sweetwater Stagelines *Imprint of* **Old West Co., The**

Swell Thoughts, *(978-0-9995908)* 5716 Chicago Ave., Minneapolis, MN 55417 USA Tel 612-927-8018
E-mail: swellgaltalks@gmail.com.

Swift Learning Resources, *(978-0-944991; 978-1-56861)* Div. of Swift Printing Corp., 1520 N. State St., Lehi, UT 84043-1079 USA (SAN 245-6737) Toll Free: 800-292-2831
E-mail: swift@swift-net.com
Web site: http://www.swiftlearning.com.

Swingin' Bridge Bks. *Imprint of* **Keystone College Pr.**

Swingset Pr., LLC, *(978-0-9658167; 978-1-930680)* Orders Addr.: P.O. Box 18701, Encino, CA 91416-8701 USA Tel 818-779-1413; Fax: 818-779-1411; Toll Free: 888-543-9366; Edit Addr.: 5987 S. High Dr., Morrison, CO 80465-2608 USA
E-mail: info@swingsetpress.com
Web site: http://www.swingsetpress.com.

Swire Siegel, *(978-1-7359219)* 5166 Oakwood Ave. 0, LA CANADA FLINTRIDGE, CA 91011 USA Tel 8189528626
E-mail: ronnie@swiresiegel.com
Dist(s): **Ingram Content Group.**

Swiss Creek Pubns., *(978-0-9702276)* 10981 Willow Valley Ct, Las Vegas, NV 89135 USA Tel 650-741-5809
E-mail: bob@zeidman.net
Web site: http://www.zeidman.net; www.SwissCreek.com.

SwissRollz, *(978-0-578-99641-7; 978-0-578-32434-0)* 913 Navasota Tr., Mckinney, TX 75071 USA Tel 469-686-2118
E-mail: brookiesue9@gmail.com.

Switch Pr. *Imprint of* **Capstone**

Switzer Land Enterprises, *(978-0-9642663)* Orders Addr.: P.O. Box 3800, Estes Park, CO 80517 USA Tel 303-586-4624; Fax: 907-577-0775; Edit Addr.: 1236 Glacier View, Estes Park, CO 80517 USA
E-mail: philalpaca@aol.com.

Sword of the Lord Pubs., *(978-0-87398; 978-1-64942)* Orders Addr.: P.O. Box 1099, Murfreesboro, TN 37133 USA (SAN 203-5642) Tel 615-893-6700; Fax: 615-895-7447
E-mail: cpenland@swordofthelord.com
Web site: http://www.swordbooks.com/; http://www.swordofthelord.com/
Dist(s): **Dake Publishing.**

Sword of the Spirit Publishing, *(978-0-615-20617-2; 978-0-615-20810-7; 978-0-615-21223-4; 978-0-615-21437-5; 978-0-615-22183-0; 978-0-615-22348-3; 978-0-615-24292-7; 978-0-578-01560-6; 978-0-578-03282-5; 978-0-9825870; 978-0-9838836; 978-1-939219)* Orders Addr.: 219 Lakewood Dr., Crossville, TN 38558 USA Tel 931-287-0280
E-mail: scaramouche9999@yahoo.com
Web site: http://www.swordofspirit.net
Dist(s): **Lulu Pr., Inc.**
Send The Light Distribution LLC.

Swordfish Communications, LLC, *(978-0-9741955)* Orders Addr.: 1748 Ohlen Rd. #67, Austin, TX 78757 USA
E-mail: orders@swordfishcommunications.com
Web site: http://www.swordfishcommunications.com.

Sy Publishing, *(978-0-9761613)* 7720 E. Redfield Rd., Suite No. 7, Scottsdale, AZ 85260 USA Tel 480-596-9226; Fax: 480-967-8736
E-mail: devinsper@yahoo.com
Web site: http://www.devinsper.com.

Sybertooth, Inc. (CAN) *(978-0-9688024; 978-0-9739505; 978-0-9810244; 978-0-9864974; 978-1-927592) Dist. by* **LightSource CS.**

Sycuan Pr., *(978-0-9790951)* 5401 Sycuan Rd., El Cajon, CA 92019 USA Tel 619-445-6917; Fax: 619-445-5176
E-mail: jbathke@sycuan.org.

Sydney Pr., LLC, *(978-0-9724577)* Orders Addr.: 2035 Fanning Ct., Leland, NC 28451 USA Tel 910-632-7778
E-mail: buckaloha@gmail.com.

Sydnor, SonJoria, *(978-0-578-67635-7)* 2315 Noll Dr., Saint Louis, MO 63136 USA Tel 314-755-4372
E-mail: SydnorvilleBooks@gmail.com.

Syentek Books Company, Incorporated *See* **Syentek, Inc.**

Syentek, Inc., *(978-0-914082)* P.O. Box 26588, San Francisco, CA 94126 USA (SAN 202-7534) Tel 415-928-0471.

Sylables, *(978-0-9724394)* 2105 Sheldon Rd., Saint Albans, VT 05478 USA (SAN 255-1500) Tel 802-524-0262
E-mail: sylables@earthlink.net
Web site: http://www.sylables.com.

Syllabets, LLC, *(978-0-9794543)* 3740 30th Ave. S., Suite 307, Grand Forks, ND 58201-5820 USA (SAN 853-4632)
Web site: http://www.syllabets.com.

Syllogism Pr., *(978-0-9638001)* 875 Emory Shield Rd., Murphy, NC 28906 USA Tel 732-290-7901
E-mail: spress@dnet.net.

Sylph Pubns., *(978-0-9673004; 978-0-9760742)* 1248 E. Edison St., W., Tucson, AZ 85719 USA Tel 520-882-3794
E-mail: eliotbooks@aol.com
Web site: http://www.eliotbooks.com.

Sylvan Dell Publishing *See* **Arbordale Publishing**

Sylvan Learning Publishing *Imprint of* **Random Hse. Children's Bks.**

Sylvestre, Gibson Publishing, *(978-0-615-21166-4; 978-0-578-01878-2; 978-0-578-01879-9; 978-0-578-03784-4; 978-0-578-04150-6)* P.O. Box 934741, Margate, FL 33093 USA
E-mail: info@mylifeonpurpose.org
Web site: http://www.mylifeonpurpose.org.

Symmetry Learning Pr., *(978-1-58447)* Div. of Invariant Research Limited, 5 Bretton Rd., Dover, MA 02030 USA (SAN 299-7967)
E-mail: peter.bergethon@invariantresearch.com; peter.bergethon@symmetryresearch.org
Web site: http://www.symmetrylearning.com.

Symmetry Learning Systems *See* **Symmetry Learning Pr.**

Sympathetic Pr., *(978-0-578-12457-5; 978-0-578-54327-7; 978-0-578-64669-5; 978-0-578-86573-7; 978-0-578-86574-4)* 120 State Ave. N.E. No. 134, Olympia, WA 98501 USA Tel 360-943-0929
Dist(s): **SCB Distributors.**

Symtalk, Inc., *(978-1-932770; 978-1-933209)* 875 Montreal Way, Saint Paul, MN 55102-4245 USA Toll Free: 877-796-8255
E-mail: info@symtalk.com
Web site: http://www.symtalk.com.

Symtext Media, *(978-0-9768379)* 21538 N. 65th Ave., Glendale, AZ 85308-6410 USA Tel 623-362-1947
E-mail: fullschedule@symtextmedia.com
Web site: http://www.symtextmedia.com.

Synapse, Edition (JPN) *(978-4-901481; 978-4-931444; 978-4-86166) Dist. by* **Taylor and Fran.**

Synaptic Wammy Works *See* **Loose In The Lab**

Synaxis Pr., *(978-0-911523)* P.O. Box 689, Lynden, WA 98264 USA (SAN 685-4338) Tel 604-826-9336; Fax: 604-820-9758.

Synchrony Hse. Publishing, *(978-0-9993410)* 341 Spring Forest Dr., Simpsonville, SC 29681 USA Tel 864-313-4973
E-mail: elegantredneck@gmail.com.

Syncopation Pr., *(978-1-7360770)* 1017 Exeter Ave, Sheridan, WY 82801 USA Tel 307-752-9876
E-mail: Sheridanyoutharts@gmail.com.

Syndistar, Inc., *(978-1-56230)* P.O. Box 3027, Hammond, LA 70404-3027 USA (SAN 298-007X) Toll Free: 800-841-9532
E-mail: webmaster@syndistar.com
Web site: http://www.syndistar.com.

SynergEbooks *See* **CamCat Publishing**

Synergetic Pubns., Inc., *(978-0-9632248)* Orders Addr.: P.O. Box 1506, Hendersonville, TN 37075 USA (SAN 297-6129) Tel 615-264-3405; Edit Addr.: 205 Applewood Valley Dr., Hendersonville, TN 37075 USA.

Synergy-Bks. Publishing, *(978-1-936434)* 12702 Woodland Ln., Garden Grove, CA 92840 USA Tel 714-638-4813
E-mail: billw@synergy-books.com
Web site: http://synergy-books.com.

SYP Kids *Imprint of* **Southern Yellow Pine (SYP) Publishing LLC**

†Syracuse Univ. Pr., *(978-0-8156; 978-0-615-28768-3; 978-1-68445)* 621 Skytop Rd., Suite 110, Syracuse, NY 13244-5290 USA (SAN 206-9776) Tel 315-443-5534; Fax: 315-443-5545
E-mail: supress@syr.edu; arpfeiff@syr.edu
Web site: http://www.SyracuseUniversityPress.syr.edu
Dist(s): **Gryphon Hse., Inc.**
JSTOR
Longleaf Services
ebrary, Inc.; *CIP.*

Syren Bk. Co., *(978-0-929636)* Orders Addr.: 5120 Cedar Lake Rd., S., Minneapolis, MN 55416 USA (SAN 249-7719) Tel 763-398-0030; Fax: 763-398-0198; Toll Free: 800-901-3480 Do not confuse with BookMobile in Port Ludlow WA
E-mail: dleeper@bookmobile.com; jogren@bookmobile.com
Web site: http://www.itascabooks.com
Dist(s): **BookMobile**
Itasca Bks.

SYS Publishing, *(978-0-9794871)* P.O. Box 868, Montclair, NJ 07042 USA Tel 973-951-7490; 2142 Blackwolf Run Ln., Raleigh, NC 27604 Toll Free: 800-994-3683
E-mail: SYSPublishing@aol.com
Web site: http://www.sadieshero.com.

Systems Group, Inc., The, *(978-0-9847740)* 4618 Granite Rock Ct., Chantilly, VA 20151 USA Tel 703-378-4193
E-mail: Oliver.Franklin@verizon.net.

Sze-Wei Sylvia Chen, *(978-1-7369753)* 423 Mallorca Ln 0, BREA, CA 92823 USA Tel 6268411358
E-mail: sschen720@gmail.com.

Szydlowski, Mary Vigliante, *(978-0-9965622; 978-0-9983869; 978-1-7328815)* 37 Normanside Dr., Albany, NY 12208 USA Tel 518-453-3613
E-mail: maszyd@aol.com
Web site: http://www.maryvigliantеszydlowski.com/.

†TAB Bks., Div. of The McGraw-Hill Cos., 11 W. 19th St., New York, NY 10011 USA (SAN 202-568X)
E-mail: bookstore@mcgraw-hill.com; customer.service@mcgraw-hill.com
Web site: http://www.mcgraw-hill.com/; *CIP.*

T. A. S. Enterprises, Incorporated *See* **Lit Torch Publishing**

T & T Roberts Publishing, *(978-0-9723868; 978-0-578-69566-2; 979-8-218-01750-7)* 3105 S. Trenton Cir., Sioux Falls, SD 57103 USA
E-mail: tom.roberts@chssd.org
Web site: http://www.chssd.org/books.

TBM, Inc., *(978-0-9647096)* 280 N. Latah St., Boise, ID 83706 USA Tel 208-853-0555; Fax: 208-383-9010; 9295 Esterbrook, Boise, ID 83703
E-mail: realbows@aol.com
Web site: http://www.tradbow.com.

TCR Pr., *(978-0-9714465)* P.O. Box 12011, Raleigh, NC 27605 USA
E-mail: newplants@angelfire.com
Web site: http://www.tcrpress.com.

T. E. Publishing, Inc., *(978-0-9722036)* P.O. Box 823, Bath, NY 14810 USA Tel 607-76-1307
E-mail: pcarlton@tepublishing.com.

T. Fielding-Lowe Co., *(978-0-578-23207-2; 978-1-7350328; 978-1-7379915; 979-8-9865755; 979-8-9869194; 979-8-9869701; 979-8-9887677)* 140 George Eddy Dr., Pascoag, RI 02859 USA Tel 401-484-0893
E-mail: t.fieldinglowellc@gmail.com
Web site: www.T.FieldingLoweCompany.com.

THINC Corp., *(978-0-9655026)* Orders Addr.: P.O. Box 14, Batesville, MS 38606 USA Tel 601-563-1162; Fax: 601-563-6640; Toll Free: 888-837-7606; Edit Addr.: 150 Hwy. 35 N., Batesville, MS 38606 USA.

TM Photography, Inc., *(978-0-9660144)* 82 King St., Charleston, SC 29401 USA Tel 843-577-3237.

T Pubns. (GBR) *(978-0-9569434) Dist. by* **D C D.**

T.Y.M. Publishing, *(978-0-9641274)* 409 Melville Ave., Palo Alto, CA 94301 USA Tel 415-325-1130.

Tabby Hse. Bks., *(978-0-9627974; 978-1-881539)* Orders Addr.: P.O. Box 544, Mineral, VA 23117 USA Tel 540-895-9093 (phone/fax); Edit Addr.: 12004 Sycamore Shoals Dr. Bumpass, Va 23034, Bumpass, VA 23024 USA; *Imprints:* Strathmoor (Strathmoor); Atlantic Books (Atlantic Books)
E-mail: tabbyhouse@gmail.com; publisher@tabbyhouse.com
Web site: http://www.tabbyhouse.com
Dist(s): **Distributors, The.**

Taberah Pr. *Imprint of* **Sonfire Media, LLC**

Table Rock Bks., *(978-0-9726869)* 69 Woodland Ave., Smithfield, RI 02917 USA.

Tabloid Horrors *See* **Wild Ideas**

Tabor Pr., *(978-0-9745799)* Orders Addr.: P.O. Box 470842, Brookline Village, MA 02447 USA Tel 617-784-6561; Edit Addr.: 278 Warren St., Brookline, MA 02445 USA
E-mail: ephraim541@hotmail.com.

Tabron Publishing, *(978-0-9860593)* PO BOX 26553, OVERLAND PARK, KS 66225 USA Tel 913-908-0129; Fax: 913-945-1426
E-mail: tekobernard@yahoo.com
Web site: www.tekobernard.com.

Tachyon Pubns., *(978-0-9648320; 978-1-892391; 978-1-61696)* 1459 18th St., No. 139, San Francisco, CA 94107 USA Tel 415-285-5615
E-mail: tachyonsf@aol.com
Web site: http://www.tachyonpublications.com/
Dist(s): **Baker & Taylor Publisher Services (BTPS)**
Ebsco Publishing
Firebird Distributing, LLC
Follett School Solutions
Legato Pubs. Group
MyiLibrary
Publishers Group West (PGW)
ebrary, Inc.

Tackett, Melissa, *(978-0-578-45251-7; 978-0-578-45683-6)* 1200 W. Bartlett Ave., Las Vegas, NV 89106 USA Tel 702-824-0210
E-mail: Lyssaann43@gmail.com
Dist(s): **Ingram Content Group.**

Tackett, Viti, *(978-0-9769963)* 85 Pond St., Cabot, AR 72023-3741 USA Toll Free: 877-518-9575.

Tacoma Historical Society, *(978-0-9846234; 978-1-7336181)* P.O. Box 1865, Tacoma, WA 98401 USA Tel 253-472-3738
E-mail: info@tacomahistory.org
Web site: www.tacomahistory.org.

TA-DA! Language Productions, Inc., *(978-0-9988305; 978-1-952583)* 150 W Edith, Los Altos, CA 94022 USA Tel 669-264-6722
E-mail: michelle@tadalp.com; liz@tadalp.com; bert@tadalp.com
Web site: www.tadalp.com
Dist(s): **Two Rivers Distribution.**

Tadpole Pr. 4 Kids *Imprint of* **Mystic Harbor Pr., LLC**

Tadpole Pr., *(978-1-7328286)* 1802 Centaur Cir., Lafayette, CO 80026 USA Tel 303-668-8812
E-mail: amber@tadpolepress.com
Web site: www.tadpolepress.com.

TAE Nazca Resources, *(978-0-9749745)* P.O. Box 7592, Broomfield, CO 80021 USA
E-mail: anitajg5@aol.com
Web site: http://www.nazcaresources.com
Dist(s): **Mountain Bk. Co.**

Taffey Pop Kids Publishing, *(978-0-9771438)* Div. of Taffey Pop Kids Educational Services LLC, Orders Addr.: 6712 Longmeadow Dr., SACHSE, TX 75048 USA Tel 214-434-9024
E-mail: info@taffeyhpopkids.org
Web site: http://www.taffeypopkids.org.

TAG Publications *See* **Teachers Appreciation Guild**

TAG Publishing, LLC, *(978-1-934606)* Orders Addr.: P.O. Box 8975, Amarillo, TX 79109 USA (SAN 853-9251); Edit Addr.: 2618 Lipscomb, Amarillo, TX 79109 USA Do not confuse with companies with the same name in Hanover, VA, Camerillo, CA
E-mail: deaitra@suddenlink.net
Web site: www.tagbookpublishing.com.

Tague, Julie, *(978-1-7354161)* 3971 Foskett Rd 0, MEDINA, OH 44256 USA Tel 4405546909
E-mail: author.julialaporte@gmail.com
Dist(s): **Ingram Content Group.**

Tagus Pr., Div. of University of Massachusetts Dartmouth, 285 Old Westport Rd., North Dartmouth, MA 02747 USA
Web site: http://www.upne.com/distributed/dist_TPD.html; www.portstudies.umassd.edu
Dist(s): **Chicago Distribution Ctr.**
MyiLibrary
Univ. of Massachusetts Pr.

Tahrike Tarsile Quran, Inc., *(978-0-940368; 978-1-879402; 978-1-952290)* 80-08 51st Ave., Elmhurst, NY 11373 USA (SAN 658-1870) Tel 718-446-6472; Fax: 718-446-4370
E-mail: read@koranusa.org
Web site: http://www.koranusa.org
Dist(s): **BookBaby**
Publishers Group West (PGW).

Tai Chi Chuan Center of New York *See* **Sunflower Pr.**

Taiji Arts Publishing, *(978-0-9728192)* 50 Bates Rd., Hillsborough, CA 94010-7016 USA
E-mail: ben@TaijiArts.com
Web site: http://www.TaijiArts.com
Dist(s): **China Books & Periodicals, Inc.**

Tail Wagging Productions, *(978-0-9752887)* P.O. Box 1357, Brea, CA 92822-1357 USA
E-mail: contact@tailwaggingproductions.us
Web site: http://www.tailwaggingproductions.us.

Tailele, Joanne *See* **Simon Publishing LLC**

Tailgator Pr., *(978-1-7335015)* 17907 W Deer Creek Rd., Goodyear, AZ 85338 USA Tel 414-378-4208
E-mail: tailgatorpress@gmail.com
Web site: www.tailgatorpress.com.

Tailwind Press, *(978-0-9799473)* 58 Brookshire Dr., Warrenton, VA 20186-3033 USA
E-mail: loribakewell@gmail.com.

Taj Bks. International LLC, *(978-1-62732)* 219 Great Lake Dr., Cary, NC 27519 USA Tel 919-650-1719; *Imprints:* Bellagio Press (BellagioPr)
E-mail: suneel@tajbooks.com
Dist(s): **Casemate Pubs. & Bk. Distributors, LLC**
MyiLibrary.

Takahashi & Black, *(978-0-9723247)* Orders Addr.: 8725 Roswell Rd., Suite 0-129, Atlanta, GA 30350 USA; *Imprints:* PB&J OmniMedia (PB&J)
E-mail: orders@pbjomnimedia.com; credit@pbjomnimedia.com; returns@pbjomnimedia.com; domo@takahashiblack.com
Web site: http://www.pbjomnimedia.com
Dist(s): **Book Wholesalers, Inc.**
Brodart Co.

Takatuka (ESP) *(978-84-936766; 978-84-16003; 978-84-92696) Dist. by* **Lectorum Pubns.**

Take 2 Creative Storywriters, LLC, *(978-0-9982801; 978-1-7344913)* 2377 Gold Meadow Way Suite 100, Gold River, CA 95670 USA
E-mail: contact_us@take2creativestorywriters.com; r.rose@take2creativestorywriters.com; rcxyrvt@gmail.com
Web site: www.take2creativestorywriters.com.

Take Away Sleigh LLC, *(978-1-7351435)* 13471 E. Gold Dust Ave., Scottsdale, AZ 85259 USA Tel 513-236-5591
E-mail: yroehler@bookpublishing.com.

Take Charge Books *See* **Take Charge Bks.**

Take Charge Bks., *(978-0-9815818; 978-0-9883866; 978-0-9961589; 978-0-9982658; 978-1-7346068)* 392 Sunny Acre Ln., Brevard, NC 28712 USA Tel 828-883-5695
E-mail: kathleen@kathleenbarnes.com
Web site: http://www.kathleenbarnes.com
Dist(s): **BookBaby.**

Take Five Pubs., *(978-0-930099)* P.O. Box 1094, Arlington, IL 60006 USA (SAN 670-1884) Tel 847-253-4370
E-mail: m.shaughnessy@comcast.net.

Take Heart Press *See* **Skinned Knee Publishing**

Take Heart Pubns., *(978-0-916124; 978-1-878265; 978-1-883220; 978-1-58469)* 12402 Bitney Springs Rd., Nevada City, CA 95959 USA (SAN 856-8294) Tel 530-478-0111; Fax: 530-274-7778; Toll Free: 800-545-7475 Do not confuse with Dawn Pubns. in Pasadena, TX
E-mail: nature@dawnpub.com; info@dawnpub.com
Web site: http://www.dawnpub.com
Dist(s): **Brodart Co.**
Children's Plus, Inc.
Common Ground Distributors, Inc.
Follett School Solutions
Ingram Bk. Co.
Sourcebooks, Inc.
Territory Titles.

Take2CreativeStorywriters *See* **Take 2 Creative Storywriters, LLC**

Takeaway Press *See* **All About Learning Pr.**

Takhar's, Jodi Spilt Milk Collection, *(978-1-886000)* Orders Addr.: P.O. Box 1005, Bemidji, MN 56601 USA Tel 218-759-2089; Fax: 218-759-2088; Edit Addr.: 403 4th St., NW, No. 200, Bemidji, MN 56601 USA.

Taking Grades Publishing Co., *(978-1-934538)* 1110 4th St., Dr., S.E., Conover, NC 28613-1825 USA Tel 866-511-8378; Fax: 828-466-0025; Toll Free: 866-511-8378
E-mail: takinggrades@charter.net
Web site: http://www.takinggrades.com
Dist(s): **Follett School Solutions.**

TakingITGlobal, *(978-0-578-41496-6; 978-0-578-44580-9; 978-0-578-44608-0; 978-0-578-45153-4; 978-0-578-48869-1; 978-0-578-51229-7; 978-0-578-52184-8; 978-0-578-53028-4; 978-0-578-62032-9; 978-0-578-62839-4; 978-0-578-66957-1; 978-0-578-69230-2; 978-0-578-70762-4; 978-0-578-78140-2; 978-0-578-80089-9; 978-0-578-24343-6; 978-0-578-86066-4; 978-0-578-86731-1; 978-0-578-88055-6; 978-0-578-89643-4; 978-0-578-89644-1; 978-0-578-90761-1; 978-0-578-91704-7; 978-0-578-93419-8; 978-0-578-93981-0; 978-0-578-95232-1;) 540 President St. 3rd Flr., Brooklyn, NY 11215 USA Tel 416-301-5844*
E-mail: mfurdyk@takingitglobal.org
Web site: http://www.tigweb.org
Dist(s): **Independent Pub.**

Taku Graphics, *(978-0-9717820; 978-0-9772297; 978-0-9801616; 978-0-9823450; 978-0-9846318; 978-0-9899679)* 5763 Glacier Hwy., Juneau, AK 99801 USA Tel 907-780-6310; Fax: 907-780-6314; Toll Free: 800-278-3291
E-mail: adele@takugraphics.com
Web site: http://www.takugraphics.com.

Talaris Research Institute, *(978-0-9742761; 978-0-615-40953-5)* P.O. Box 45040, Seattle, WA 98145 USA Tel 206-859-5604; Fax: 206-859-5699
E-mail: tinam@talaris.org
Web site: http://www.talaris.org.

Ta-La-Vue Pub., *(978-0-9797521)* 316 Rowan Alley, Apt. 6, Pottstown, PA 19464 USA (SAN 854-2376).

Tale Wag Pr. *Imprint of* **Langson, Bridgett Bell**

Tale Weaver Pr., *(978-0-692-66880-1)* 10942 Canyon Mesa Ln., San Diego, CA 92126 USA Tel 619-200-3836
E-mail: lisadavis92127@gmail.com.

TALENT, *(978-1-7345039)* 3311 Caminito Eastbluff, La Jolla, CA 92037 USA Tel 858-452-2255
E-mail: sdtalent1@gmail.com
Web site: www.1talent1.com.

Talented *See* **Cantemos-bilingual bks. and music**

Tales Alive *See* **Words & Music**

Talicor, Inc., *(978-1-57057; 978-0-9674871)* 901 Lincoln Pkwy., Plainwell, MI 49080 USA (SAN 253-0406) Tel 269-685-2345; Fax: 269-685-6789; Toll Free: 800-433-4263
E-mail: webmaster@talicor.com; orders@talicor.com
Web site: http://www.talicor.com.

Taliesin Publishing LLC *See* **Hartwood Publishing Group, LLC, The**

Talisman Pr., *(978-0-9670848; 978-1-7363306)* 7036 Lyndale Cir., Elk Grove, CA 95758 USA Tel 916-683-1749
E-mail: talismanpress@aol.com.

TALK, *(978-0-9741182)* Orders Addr.: P.O. Box 9226, Peoria, IL 61612 USA Tel 309-224-9665; Edit Addr.: 5001 N. Big Hollow Rd., Peoria, IL 61615 USA Tel 309-694-5444
E-mail: dsymo92699@aol.com
Web site: http://www.doristalk.com.

TALKAIDS, Inc., *(978-0-9659046)* Orders Addr.: P.O. Box 112, New York, NY 10113 USA Tel 212-465-2646; Fax: 212-675-7291; Edit Addr.: 305 W. 13th St., 1K, New York, NY 10014 USA
E-mail: talkaids@aol.com.

Talking Crow Publishing, *(978-0-9860287)* P.O. Box 1356, Haines, AK 99827 USA.

Talking Drum Pr., Ltd., *(978-0-9662428)* Div. of Oversoul Theater Collective, Inc., P.O. Box 190028, Roxbury, MA 02119 USA
E-mail: talkingdrumpress@gmail.com.

Talking Drum Press/OTC, Incorporated *See* **Talking Drum Pr., Ltd.**

Talking Hands, Incorporated *See* **Time to Sign, Incorporated**

TalkTools/Innovative Therapists International, *(978-1-932460; 978-0-9979204)* 2209 Mechanic St., Charleston, SC 29405 USA Tel 843-789-3672; Fax: 843-206-0590; Toll Free: 888-529-2879
E-mail: info@talktools.com
Web site: http://www.talktools.com.

Tall Pine Bks., *(978-1-7353469; 978-1-955546; 979-8-218-25135-2)* 119 E Ctr. St. Suite B4A, Warsaw, IN 46580 USA Tel 574-551-2714
E-mail: npoe@tallpinebooks.com
Web site: tallpinebooks.com.

Tall Tails Publishing Hse., *(978-0-9823519)* 902 Arlington Box 113, Ada, OK 74820 USA (SAN 857-9288)
E-mail: talltailspublishing@gmail.com
Web site: http://www.talltailspublishing.com.

Tall Tales, *(978-0-9973641; 978-0-9979540; 978-1-947543)* P.O. Box 1262, Lynnwood, WA 98046 USA Tel 425-744-0580
E-mail: kizeliz@gmail.com
Web site: www.kizziejones.com.

Tall Through Bks., *(978-0-9744549)* P.O. Box 6723, Virginia Beach, VA 23456 USA Tel 757-635-6174; Fax: 757-563-8277
E-mail: tallthroughbooks@aol.com
Web site: http://www.tallthroughbooks.com.

Tallulah & Bear (GBR) *(978-0-9559752) Dist. by* **LuluCom.**

Talmage Publishing, *(978-0-9773010)* 4820 Strack Rd., Houston, TX 77069 USA (SAN 257-2370) Tel 281-440-1106.

Talonbooks, Ltd. (CAN) *(978-0-88922; 978-1-77201) Dist. by* **Consort Bk Sales.**

Tamaja Press *See* **Tamaja Pr. L.L.C.**

Tamaja Pr. L.L.C., *(978-0-9841260; 978-0-9863753)* Div. of Arteеs / Tamaja, 2476 Cty. RD. 59 2476. Cty. RD. 59, Prattville, AL 36067 USA
E-mail: tilmon.gloria@yahoo.com; gloriatillman23@yahoo.com; tam3artees@yahoo.com; Tillman.marlon3@yahoo.com.

Tamara Taylor Edu Publishing LLC, *(978-0-9970313)* P.O. Box PO Box 403, Frisco, TX 75034 USA
E-mail: print@ttayloredupublishing.com.

Tamara's Bks., *(978-0-9909379)* 1844 Colmar Rd., Gwynn Oak, MD 21207 USA Tel 888-503-1575
E-mail: tamarasbooks@gmail.com
Web site: tamarasbooks@gmail.com.

Tamarisk Tree Publishing House, *(978-0-578-18030-4; 978-1-948706)* 2208 Collier Dr., Franklin, TN 37064 USA.

Tameme, Inc., *(978-0-9674093)* 199 First St. Suite 335, Los Altos, CA 94022 USA Tel 650-941-2037; Fax: 650-941-5338
E-mail: Sales@tameme.org
Web site: http://www.tameme.org.

Tamerac Publishing, *(978-0-9621292)* 402 Conestoga Dr., Moscow, ID 83843 USA (SAN 250-9466) Tel 208-883-7761
Web site: www.tameracpub.com
Dist(s): **Ingram Content Group.**

Tamerac Publishing Company *See* **Tamerac Publishing**

Tamil Unlimited, *(978-0-9839087; 978-0-9839088; 978-0-692-51446-7; 978-0-692-51448-1; 979-8-9856875;*

979-8-9881619) 10 Maybelle Ct., Mechanicsburg, PA 17050 USA Tel 717-802-5889
E-mail: suganthi1068@gmail.com
Web site: http://www.tamilunltd.com/; https://suganthinadar.com
Dist(s): **Ingram Content Group.**

TAN Bks., *(978-0-89555; 978-0-911845; 978-0-9675978; 978-1-930873; 978-1-939094)* Div. of Saint Benedict Press, LLC, 13315 Carowinds Blvd Suite Q, Charlotte, NC 28273 USA; *Imprints*: Neumann Press (Neumann NC)
E-mail: rick@tanbooks.com; mara@tanbooks.com
Web site: https://tanbooks.com/; https://neumann.benedictpress.com/
Dist(s): **Baker & Taylor Publisher Services (BTPS)**
Saint Benedict Pr.

T&J Pubs., *(978-0-9962165; 978-0-692-68627-0; 978-0-692-74667-7; 978-0-692-75567-9; 978-0-9981621; 978-0-9994121; 978-0-9997806; 978-0-692-13503-7; 978-0-692-13531-0; 978-1-7324905; 978-1-7335470; 978-1-7345105; 978-1-7360003; 978-1-7376635; 979-8-218-15465-3; 979-8-218-17288-6)* 1104 Columns Dr., Lithia Springs, GA 30122 USA Tel 404-889-3684
E-mail: TJPublishers@gmail.com
Web site: www.TimothyFlemmingJr.com.

T&N Children's Publishing, *(978-1-55971; 978-1-58728)* Div. of Rowman & Littlefield Publishing Group, Orders Addr.: 8500 Normandale Lake Blvd., Minneapolis, MN 55437-3813 USA Toll Free: 888-255-9989; Fulfillment Addr.: SDS-12-2462, P.O. Box 86, Minneapolis, MN 55486-2462 USA; *Imprints*: NorthWord Books for Young Readers (NrthWrd Bks); Two-Can Publishing (TCan Pubng)
E-mail: sales@tnkidsbooks.com
Web site: http://www.tnkidsbooks.com
Dist(s): **Follett School Solutions**
National Bk. Network.

Tandora's Box Pr., *(978-0-9627337)* Orders Addr.: P.O. Box 8073, Vallejo, CA 94590 USA
E-mail: barbara@tangrammit.com
Web site: http://www.tangrammit.com.

Tangela Publishing, *(978-0-615-18297-1)* 8093 Miller Cir., Arvada, CO 80005 USA
E-mail: a.newell@comcast.net

Tangerine Pr. *Imprint of* **Scholastic, Inc.**

Tangerine Tide *Imprint of* **Orange Ocean Pr.**

TangleTown Media Inc., *(978-0-9724022)* 713 Minnehaha Ave. E. Suite 210, Saint Paul, MN 55106 USA (SAN 254-8054)
E-mail: todd.berntson@tangletownmedia.com
Web site: http://www.tangletownmedia.com.

Tanglewood Pr., *(978-0-9749303; 978-1-933718; 978-1-939100)* P.O. Box 3009, Terre Haute, IN 47803 USA Do not confuse with Tanglewood Press in Portland, OR, Raleigh, NC
E-mail: ptierney@tanglewoodbooks.com
Web site: http://www.tanglewoodbooks.com
Dist(s): **Children's Plus, Inc.**
Lectorum Pubns., Inc.
MyiLibrary
Publishers Group West (PGW)
Simon & Schuster, Inc.

Tango Bks. (GBR) *(978-1-85707)* *Dist. by* **IPG Chicago.**

Tango Latin, *(978-0-9663572)* 325 N. Maple Dr., Beverly Hills, CA 90209 USA Tel 213-381-5820; P.O. Box 16111, Beverly Hills, CA 90209
E-mail: tangomediagroup@yahoo.com.

Tango Publishing International, Incorporated *See* **Tango Latin**

TankerToys, *(978-0-615-16200-3)* 387 C Bergin Dr., Monterey, CA 93940 USA
E-mail: tanker@tankertoys.com
Web site: http://www.tankertoys.com
Dist(s): **Lulu Pr., Inc.**

Tanner, David, *(978-0-9767287; 978-0-578-00817-2)* P.O. Box 140, Avon, CT 06001-0140 USA; 3 David Dr., Simsbury, CT 06070
E-mail: collectiblesodacans@comcast.net
Web site: http://www.collectiblesodacans.com.

Tanner, Matt J., *(978-0-9885253)* 27 Amherst Dr., Basking Ridge, NJ 07920 USA Tel 908-581-9822
E-mail: mtanner07@msn.com.

Tanner, Ralph Assocs., Inc., *(978-0-942078)* P.O. Box 3400, Prescott, AZ 86302-3400 USA (SAN 239-9857).

TanosBooks Publishing, *(978-0-9764666; 978-0-9788520; 978-0-9815522; 978-0-9822543; 978-0-9844865; 978-0-9846540)* 1110 W. 5th St., Coffeyville, KS 67337 USA
Web site: http://www.tanosbookspublishing.com.

Tansaafl Press *See* **Tanstaafl Pr.**

Tanser, Julie, *(978-0-692-04586-2; 978-1-7336804; 978-1-7339244)* P.O. Box 26, NY, NY 10116 USA
E-mail: julie82146@gmail.com
Dist(s): **CreateSpace Independent Publishing Platform.**

Tanstaafl Pr., *(978-1-938124)* 891 PH 10, CASTLE ROCK, WA 98611 USA Tel 360-556-0149
E-mail: tgondolfi@tanstaaflpress.com.

TANTRUM, BARBARA Counseling LLC *See* **Comyn Publishing**

Tao of Golf *See* **DVTVFilm**

TAOC (AUS) *(978-0-9803455; 978-0-646-46214-1; 978-0-9808435)* *Dist. by* **Consort Bk Sales.**

TAOH Inspired Education, LLC *See* **Strategic Visions Inc.**

Taos Institute Pubns., *(978-0-9712312; 978-0-9819076; 978-0-9848656; 978-1-938552; 978-1-958170)* Orders Addr.: 63 Maple Hill Dr., Chagrin Falls, OH 44022 USA Tel 440-338-6733; Edit Addr.: 331 Rogers Ln., Wallingford, PA 19086 USA Toll Free: 888-999-8267
E-mail: info@taosinstitute.net; alex@taosinstitute.net
Web site: http://www.Taosinstitute.net.

Tapestry Productions, *(978-0-692-99114-5; 978-0-578-57750-0)* 6638 river springs dr. s, Salem, OR 97306 USA Tel 503-364-4787; Fax: 503-364-4787
E-mail: deirdradoan@gmail.com.

tapestrypublishing.com, *(978-0-692-86502-6; 978-0-692-91685-8)* 642 Corbin Lake Ct., SANDY SPRINGS, GA 30350 USA Tel 404-512-4542
E-mail: jeffwcrawford5+LVP0003519@gmail.com; jeffwcrawford5+LVP0003519@gmail.com.

Tapioca Stories, *(978-1-7347839; 979-8-9887499)* 55 Gerard St No. 455, Huntington, NY 11743 USA Tel 631-759-1517
E-mail: yberstein@tapiocastories.com
Web site: www.tapiocastories.com
Dist(s): **Baker & Taylor Publisher Services (BTPS).**

Tapis & Assocs., Inc., *(978-0-9729610; 978-0-9741172)* 1950 N. 6900 E., Croydon, UT 84018-9707 USA Tel 801-829-3295; Fax: 509-984-2718
E-mail: info@tapisinc.com
Web site: http://www.tapisinc.com.

Tapper Records Inc., *(978-0-9747465)* P.O. Box 5241, Hollywood, FL 33083-5241 USA Tel 954-483-5093; Fax: 954-961-9049
E-mail: thespeakingsax@juno.com
Web site: http://www.thespeakingsax.com.

Tapper Seminars *See* **Tapper Records Inc.**

Taqwa Images *See* **Early Rise Pubns.**

Tara Elsey Ackerman, *(978-0-578-35659-4; 978-0-578-36704-0)* 4871 E Kingwood Ct, Springfield, MO 65809 USA Tel 417-207-0539
E-mail: jameser84@yahoo.com.

Tara Publishing (IND) *(978-81-86211; 978-81-906756)* *Dist. by* **Consort Bk Sales.**

Tarbutton Pr., *(978-0-9714086; 978-1-933094)* 951 Snug Harbor St., Salinas, CA 93906 USA (SAN 254-4989) Tel 831-443-5694
E-mail: info@tarbuttonpress.com
Web site: http://www.tarbuttonpress.com
Dist(s): **CreateSpace Independent Publishing Platform**
Ingram Content Group.

TarcherPerigee *Imprint of* **Penguin Publishing Group**

targa 7 inc, *(978-0-692-84875-3; 978-0-692-84876-0; 979-8-218-26482-6)* 704 1st Ave. N., safety harbor, FL 34695 USA Tel 727-799-4891
E-mail: patriciastewart@tampabay.rr.com
Web site: www.patbrooksbooks.com.

Targum Pr., Inc., *(978-0-944070; 978-1-56871)* 22700 W. Eleven Mile Rd., Southfield, MI 48034 USA (SAN 242-8997) Tel 248-355-2266; Toll Free Fax: 888-298-9992
E-mail: targum@elronet.co.il
Web site: http://www.targum.com
Dist(s): **Feldheim Pubs.**
Lulu Pr., Inc.
SPD-Small Pr. Distribution.

Targum Press USA Incorporated *See* **Menucha Pubs. Inc.**

TARK Classic Fiction *Imprint of* **Arc Manor**

Tarquin Pubns. (GBR) *(978-0-906212; 978-1-899618; 978-1-907550; 978-1-911093; 978-1-913565)* *Dist. by* **IPG Chicago.**

Tarver, Monroe, *(978-0-9743568)* 7904 Calibre Crossing Dr. Apt. 205, Charlotte, NC 28227-6781 USA
E-mail: monroetarver@msn.com
Web site: http://www.worldoftarver.com.

TASCHEN (DEU) *(978-3-8228; 978-3-89450; 978-3-8365)* *Dist. by* **TwoRivers.**

T.A.S.K. Media/Divine Write Publishing, *(978-1-7378108)* 14643 222nd St., Springfield Gardens, NY 11413 USA Tel 347-262-9882
E-mail: wreachavoc@icloud.com
Web site: www.TheAmazinglySensationalKids.com.

Tasneem Sana Khan, *(978-0-578-87695-5)* 9330 Baseline Rd. Suite No. 204, Rancho Cucamonga, CA 91701 USA Tel 909-262-5216
E-mail: Sanakhanauthor277@gmail.com.

Taste Life Twice, *(978-0-9898506)* 320 NW Uptown Terr. No. 3B, Portland, OR 97210 USA Tel 805-550-4197
E-mail: mpinard2003@yahoo.com.

Tastica, Suanne Creations Inc., *(978-0-9769348)* 1621 25th St., PMB No. 337, San Pedro, CA 90732 USA.

Tasty Minstrel Games, *(978-0-9841558; 978-1-938146; 978-1-947941; 978-1-951531)* P.O. Box 64794, Tucson, AZ 85728 USA Tel 520-275-8913
E-mail: michael@playtmg.com; daniel@playtmg.com
Web site: http://playtmg.com.

Tate, Hakim, *(978-0-692-88171-2; 978-0-692-15282-9; 978-0-692-15286-7; 978-1-7350772)* 411 Millwoof Dr., capitol heights, MD 20743 USA Tel 202-577-7131
E-mail: hakimtate@gmail.com.

Tate Publishing, Ltd. (GBR) *(978-0-900874; 978-0-905005; 978-1-85437; 978-0-946590; 978-1-84976)* *Dist. by* **Abrams.**

Tate Publishing, Ltd. (GBR) *(978-0-900874; 978-0-905005; 978-1-85437; 978-0-946590; 978-1-84976)* *Dist. by* **HachBkGrp.**

Tathata Inc., *(978-0-578-21228-9)* 1104 Cornell Dr., Yardley, PA 19067 USA Tel 609-558-5696
E-mail: nickfels@gmail.com.

Tattered Essence Publishing LLC, *(978-0-9766130)* P.O. Box 290996, Nashville, TN 37229 USA Tel 615-360-6117
E-mail: info@cinderellasrebellion.com
Web site: http://www.tatteredessence.com.

Tattered Script Publishing, *(978-1-7375219)* P.O. Box P.O. Box 1704, Middleburg, VA 20117 USA Tel 207-522-2414
E-mail: tatteredscript@gmail.com
Web site: www.tatteredscript.com.

Tattersall Publishing, *(978-0-9640513; 978-0-9679775; 978-0-9835919; 978-0-9911515; 978-1-7320129)* 225 W Hickory Ste. 131, Denton, TX 76201 USA Tel 940-565-0804; Fax: 940-320-8604
E-mail: cwolfe@tattersallpub.com; cwood@tattersallpub.com
Web site: http://www.tattersallpub.com.

Tau Publishing *See* **Vesuvius Pr. Inc.**

Tau Publishing *Imprint of* **Vesuvius Pr. Inc.**

†Taunton Pr., Inc., *(978-0-918804; 978-0-942391; 978-1-56158; 978-1-60085; 978-1-62113; 978-1-62710; 978-1-63186; 978-1-64155)* 63 S. Main St., P. O. Box 5506, Newtown, CT 06470-5506 USA (SAN 210-5144) Tel 203-426-8171; Fax: 203-426-7184; Toll Free: 800-477-8727 (orders)
E-mail: tt@taunton.com; cmandarano@taunton.com
Web site: http://www.taunton.com
Dist(s): **Ingram Publisher Services**
Linden Publishing Co., Inc.
Simon & Schuster, Inc.
Two Rivers Distribution; *CIP.*

Taven Hill Studio, *(978-0-9765321)* 5214n 325w, LaPorte, IN 46350 USA
E-mail: mhill@mc123.com
Web site: http://www.tavenhill.com.

Tavine'ra Publishing, LLC, *(978-0-9713953; 978-1-7364879)* 270 Doug Baker Blvd Suite 700-316, Birmingham, AL 35242 USA Tel 205-218-7678; Toll Free: 888 234-7256
E-mail: tahiera@gmail.com
Web site: www.tahieramoniquebrown.com.

Tawa Productions, *(978-0-9718741)* Orders Addr.: 2186 Buffalo Dr., Grand Junction, CO 81503 USA
E-mail: information@peopal.com
Web site: http://www.poepal.com.

Tawnsy Publishing, *(978-0-9887612)* 1212 N. Wuthering Hills Dr., Janesville, WI 53546 USA Tel 608-754-2024
E-mail: tawnsy@charter.net.

Tayes Bks., *(978-0-9743207)* Orders Addr.: P.O. Box 50973, Fort Myers, FL 33994-0973 USA; Edit Addr.: 813 Dellena Ln., Fort Myers, FL 33905 USA
E-mail: tayesbooks@yahoo.com
Web site: http://www.tayesbooks.com.

Tayler Corp., The, *(978-0-9779074; 978-0-9835746; 978-1-945120)* Orders Addr.: 1066 N. 440 W., Orem, UT 84057 USA Tel 801-426-5714
Web site: http://www.schlockmercenary.com.

Taylor & Francis Group (GBR) *(978-0-389; 978-0-7484; 978-0-85066; 978-0-905273; 978-1-85000; 978-1-85728; 978-1-84142; 978-0-901286; 978-1-902653; 978-0-203; 978-1-904350; 978-1-907975; 978-1-84872; 978-1-134; 978-1-136; 978-1-910526; 978-0-367; 978-0-429; 978-1-000; 978-1-003; 978-1-032; 978-1-906540; 978-1-905981; 978-1-910887; 978-1-907747; 978-1-909662; 978-1-907625)* *Dist. by* **Taylor and Fran.**

†Taylor & Francis Group, *(978-0-335; 978-0-415; 978-0-8448; 978-0-85066; 978-0-89116; 978-0-903796; 978-0-905273; 978-1-56032; 978-1-85000; 978-1-59169; 978-1-315)* Orders Addr.: 7625 Empire Dr., Florence, KY 41042-2919 USA Toll Free Fax: 800-248-4724; Toll Free: 800-634-7064; 74 Rolark Dr., Scarborough, ON M1R 4G2 Tel 416-299-5388; Fax: 416-299-7531; Toll Free: 877-226-2237; Edit Addr.: 325 Chestnut St., Philadelphia, PA 19106 USA (SAN 241-9246) Tel 215-625-8900; Fax: 215-625-2940; 270 Madison Ave., 4th Flr., New York, NY 10016-0601; *Imprints*: Routledge (RtlgTnF)
Web site: http://www.routledge-ny.com; http://www.crcpress.com; http://www.garlandscience.com; http://www.taylorandfrancis.com
Dist(s): **CRC Pr. LLC**
Ebsco Publishing
LSC Communications Corp.
MyiLibrary
Norton, W. W. & Co., Inc.
Oxford Univ. Pr., Inc.
Pearson Education; *CIP.*

Taylor & Francis, Incorporated *See* **Taylor & Francis Group**

Taylor and Seale Publishing, *(978-0-9846558; 978-0-9887836; 978-1-940224; 978-1-943789; 978-1-950613)* 6241 S. Williamson Blvd. Unit 1006, Port Orange, FL 32118 USA Tel 386-481-0502
Web site: taylorandsealebooks.com.

Taylor, Ann, *(978-0-9800059)* 4319 Candlewood Ln., Ponce Inlet, FL 32127 USA
E-mail: taboka@aol.com; anntaylor@cfl.rr.com.

Taylor, Colleen, *(978-0-578-52021-6; 979-8-218-10341-5)* 816 W. Sycamore Ct., Litchfield Park, AZ 85340 USA Tel 602-647-0038
E-mail: viridianvisions@gmail.com
Web site: https://colleentaylorartist.com/.

Taylor, Dale *See* **Barton Publications**

Taylor, Del'Shawn, *(978-0-578-77954-6)* 2721 Deerskin Trl, South Bend, IN 46628 USA Tel 574-315-7164
E-mail: dtaylor19705@alumni.iu.edu.

Taylor, Dorothy Loring, *(978-0-9610640)* R. R. 2, Box 152, Virginia, IL 62691 USA (SAN 265-3567) Tel 217-458-2506.

Taylor Girl LLC *See* **TG8 LLC**

Taylor Productions *Imprint of* **G R M Assocs.**

Taylor Publishing Company *See* **Taylor Trade Publishing**

Taylor Publishing Grp., *(978-0-9762933)* 1605 E. Elizabeth St., Pasadena, CA 91104 USA Tel 626-398-2341
E-mail: tp@finishthetask.org
Web site: http://www.taylorpublishing.info.

Taylor, Sally & Friends, *(978-0-934101; 978-0-9604904)* 756 Kansas St., San Francisco, CA 94107-2699 USA (SAN 216-1990) Tel 415-824-1563; Fax: 415-648-5974.

Taylor Street Publishing LLC, *(978-0-9892854; 978-0-9911621)* 575 O'Farrell St. Suite 904, San Francisco, CA 94102 USA Tel 415-374-4846
E-mail: timhewtson@gmail.com
Web site: www.taylorstreetbooks.com.

Taylor, Tim P. *See* **Burkhart Bks.**

†Taylor Trade Publishing, *(978-0-87833; 978-0-925190; 978-1-57749; 978-1-58979; 978-1-63076)* Orders Addr.: 15200 NBN Way, Blue Ridge Summit, PA 17214 USA Tel 717-794-3800 (Sales, Customer Service, MIS, Royalties, Inventory Mgmt., Dist., Credit & Collections); Fax: 717-794-3803 (Customer Service &/or orders only); 717-794-3857 (Sales & MIS); 717-794-3856 (Royalties, Inventory Mgmt. & Dist.); Toll Free Fax: 800-338-4550 (Customer Service &/or orders); Toll Free: 800-462-6420 (Customer Service &/or orders); Edit Addr.: 4501 Forbes Blvd., Suite 200, Lanham, MD 20706 USA Tel 301-459-3366; Fax: 301-459-5743 Do not confuse with companies with the same or similar names in Rochester, MI, Bellingham, WA, St. Petersburg, FL, Owatonna, MN, Eureka, CA
Web site: http://www.rlpgbooks.com; http://www.taylortradepublishing.com
Dist(s): **Ebsco Publishing**
Follett School Solutions
MyiLibrary
National Bk. Network
Rowman & Littlefield Publishers, Inc.
Rowman & Littlefield Unlimited Model
Smashwords
ebrary, Inc.; *CIP.*

Taylor, Y. H., *(978-0-9788386)* P.O. Box 9618, Philadelphia, PA 19131-3315 USA.

Taylor-Dth Publishing, *(978-0-9712923; 978-0-9727583; 978-0-9747532; 978-0-9774431; 978-0-9834780; 978-0-9988935)* Orders Addr.: P.O. Box 216, Fairfax, CA 94978 USA Tel 415-299-1087
E-mail: ncardinali@taylor-dth.com
Web site: http://www.taylor-dth.com.

TaylorMade Publishing *See* **TaylorMade Publishing, LLC**

TaylorMade Publishing Inc., *(978-1-7354085; 979-8-9877470)* 1392 Madison Ave. Suite 220, New York, NY 10029 USA Tel 917-325-5300
E-mail: TaylorMadePublishingInc@gmail.com.

TaylorMade Publishing, LLC, *(978-0-9968123; 978-1-953526)* 590 Apple Creek Dr, Jacksonville, FL 32218 USA Tel 904-930-0531
E-mail: Frizella.donegan@gmail.com; info@taylormadepublishingfl.com
Web site: www.taylormadepublishingfl.com.

TAYLOR'S MOM LLC, *(978-1-7362189)* 1990 Royal Blvd, ELGIN, IL 60123 USA Tel 773-340-9367
E-mail: ambry.ivy@gmail.com.

Taylor's Production, *(978-0-9800468)* 126 Willowcrest Dr., Windsor, CT 06095 USA Tel 860-243-3196
E-mail: noproblem11@comcast.net.

TaySysCo Publishing, *(978-0-9773236)* 808 White Ivy Pl. NE, Cedar Rapids, IA 52402 USA
E-mail: taysysco@msn.com
Web site: http://taysysco.com.

TazTales, *(978-0-9742178)* P.O. Box 48031, Oak Park, MI 48237-5731 USA
E-mail: taztales@lycos.com
Web site: http://www.taztales.com.

TBCN Inc., *(978-0-938447)* 1680 Keylake Dr, Suwanee,, GA 30024 USA Tel 470-239-7375
E-mail: Fred@bookfunmagazine.com
Web site: http://www.bookfun.org.

TBG.LLC *See* **Gilliam, T. & Associates, LLC**

Tbooks Publishing Co., *(978-0-9789449)* 324 E. 2nd St., Benicia, CA 94510-3249 USA (SAN 852-0135) Tel 707-342-2280
E-mail: terrie@tbookspublishing.com
Web site: http://tbookspublishing.com.

TBSM Publishing, *(978-0-9860056)* P.O. Box 6314, Traverse City, MI 49686 USA.

T.C. McSears Publishing, *(978-0-9787015)* P.O. Box 341, Linconton, NC 28093 USA
E-mail: tryloc@tryloc.com
Web site: http://www.tryloc.com
Dist(s): **Big Tent Bks.**

TCB-Cafe Publishing, *(978-0-9674898; 978-0-9767682; 978-0-9798640; 978-0-9822200; 978-0-9911208; 979-8-9866612; 979-8-9875492)* Orders Addr.: P.O. Box 471706, San Francisco, CA 94147 USA Tel 415-263-6800
Web site: http://www.cafeandre.com; http://www.tastetv.com
Dist(s): **Quality Bks., Inc.**

TdB Pr. LLC, *(978-0-9740494)* P.O. Box 6348, Altadena, CA 91003-6348 USA (SAN 255-3147)
E-mail: mail@tdbpress.com
Web site: http://www.tdbpress.com.

TDG Communications, Inc., *(978-0-9793584)* 93 Sherman St., Deadwood, SD 57732-5773 USA (SAN 853-2478) Tel 605-722-7111; Fax: 605-722-7112
Web site: http://www.tdgcommunications.com.

TDH Publishing, *(978-0-9704566)* 783 Hunters Trail, Kikomo, IN 46901 USA (SAN 253-4460) Tel 765-457-6445; Fax: 765-459-4116
E-mail: tdhpublishing@insightbb.com; kellnikk@insightbb.com.

TDO Enterprises, *(978-0-9787624)* Orders Addr.: 92 N. Yale St., Nampa, ID 83651-2347 USA (SAN 851-6553)
E-mail: jscott@tdoent.com
Web site: http://www.tdoent.com; http://www.booksbyjeffscott.com.

TDR Brands *See* **TDR Brands Publishing**

TDR Brands Publishing, *(978-0-9907516; 978-0-9988804; 978-1-947574)* 4426 Hugh Howell Rd b No. 515, Tucker, GA 30084 USA Tel 888-353-0899
E-mail: tierradestinyreid@gmail.com
Web site: www.tierradestinyreid.com.

Te Herenga Waka University Press (NZL) *(978-0-86473; 978-1-77656; 978-1-77656-063-9; 978-1-77656-058-5; 978-1-77656-064-6; 978-1-77656-047-9; 978-1-77656-071-4; 978-1-77692)* *Dist. by* **IPG Chicago.**

Te Papa Pr. (NZL) *(978-0-909010; 978-0-908953; 978-0-9582371; 978-0-9582432; 978-1-877385; 978-0-9876686; 978-0-9941041; 978-0-9941362; 978-0-9941460; 978-0-9951031; 978-0-9951136; 978-0-9951384; 978-0-9951338; 978-1-9911509; 978-1-9911655; 978-1-991072)* *Dist. by* **IPG Chicago.**

Tea Party Pr., *(978-0-9749173)* P.O. Box 767425, Atlanta, GA 30076 USA Tel 770-649-4434 Do not confuse with Tea Party Press in Cincinnati, OH
E-mail: paula_taylor@bellsouth.net
Web site: http://www.teapartypress.com.

Tea Time Publishing, *(978-1-7324605)* P.O. Box 143, Troy, MO 63379 USA Tel 636-358-5020
E-mail: TeaTimePublishingllc@gmail.com
Web site: TeaTimePublishing.com.

Tea Time Socials, LLC *Imprint of* **Gunderson, Lisa M.**

Tea with Mrs. B, *(978-0-9863560)* 6703 Lumsden St., McLean, VA 22101 USA Tel 202-448-2930
E-mail: r@czfamily.com
Web site: www.TeawithMrsB.com.

Teach Me Tapes, Inc., *(978-0-934633; 978-1-59972)* P.O. Box 698, Mequon, WI 53092 USA (SAN 693-9309) Tel 262-518-6060; Toll Free: 800-456-4656
E-mail: renee@teachmetapes.com
Web site: http://www.teachmetapes.com
Dist(s): **Ingram Publisher Services.**

TEACH Ministries, *(978-0-9740326)* Orders Addr.: 891 Ted Ln., Elgin, IL 60120 USA
E-mail: marylou@empoweringdiversity.com
Web site: http://www.empoweringdiversity.com/anna.

Teach My Children Pubns., *(978-0-9668891)* 258 Bahia Ln., E., Litchfield Park, AZ 85340-4728 USA Tel 602-935-0386
E-mail: oldbaha@goodnet.com.

TEACH Services, Inc., *(978-0-945383; 978-1-57258; 978-1-4796)* 140 Industry Ln. Calhoun, Ga 3071, CALHOUN, GA 30701-7443 USA (SAN 246-9863) Tel 706-504-9192; Fax: 866-757-6023; Toll Free: 800-367-1844; 140 Industry Ln., Calhoun, GA 30701 Tel 800-367-1844; Fax: 866-757-6023; *Imprints:* Aspect Book (AspectBk)
E-mail: CMB@teachservices.com
Web site: http://www.teachservices.com; http://www.AspectBooks.com.

TEACH Services, Incorporated *See* **TEACH Services, Inc.**

Teacher Created Materials, Inc., *(978-0-87673; 978-0-7439; 978-1-4333; 978-1-60401; 978-1-4807; 978-1-4938; 978-1-5164; 978-1-64290; 978-1-64335; 978-1-64406; 978-1-64491; 978-1-0876; 979-8-7659)* 5301 Oceanus Dr., Huntington Beach, CA 92649 USA (SAN 665-5270) Tel 714-891-2273; Fax: 714-230-7070; Toll Free Fax: 888-877-7606; Toll Free: 800-858-7339
E-mail: sozbat@tcmpub.com; rkarnik@tcmpub.com; Support@tcmpub.com; pubops@tcmpub.com
Web site: http://www.tcmpub.com; www.teachercreatedmaterials.com
Dist(s): **Children's Plus, Inc.**
Ebsco Publishing
Follett School Solutions
Lectorum Pubns., Inc.
Shell Educational Publishing.

Teacher Created Resources, Inc., *(978-1-55734; 978-1-57690; 978-1-4206; 978-1-4570)* 12621 Western Ave., Garden Grove, CA 92841 USA Tel 714-891-1690; Fax: 800-525-1254; Toll Free: 800-662-4321
E-mail: custserv@teachercreated.com; lvenzon@teachercreated.com
Web site: http://www.teachercreated.com
Dist(s): **Austin & Company, Inc.**
Follett School Solutions
Partners Pubs. Group, Inc.

Teacher Press, Incorporated *See* **Teaching Point, Inc.**

Teachers Appreciation Guild, *(978-0-9752781)* 5320 Pocassett, ARLINGTON, TX 76018 USA Do not confuse with Press On Publishing in Port Huron, MI
E-mail: info@teachersappreciationguild.org
Web site: http://teacchersappreciationguild.org.

Teachers Change Brains Media, *(978-0-9963891; 978-1-7369889)* 7320 N. La Cholla 154613, Tucson, AZ 85741 USA Tel 520-850-3743
E-mail: teacherschangebrainsmedia@gmail.com
Web site: www.brainonschool.com; www.legendaryteacher.com.

†**Teachers College Pr., Teachers College, Columbia Univ.**, *(978-0-8077)* Div. of Teachers College, Columbia University, Orders Addr.: c/o AIDC, P.O. Box 20, Williston, VT 05495-0020 USA (SAN 248-3904) Fax: 802-864-7626; Toll Free: 800-575-6566; Edit Addr.: 1234 Amsterdam Ave., New York, NY 10027 USA (SAN 282-3985) Tel 212-678-3929; Fax: 212-678-4149
E-mail: tcpress@tc.columbia.edu
Web site: http://www.teacherscollegepress.com
Dist(s): **American International Distribution Corp.**
Ebsco Publishing
MyiLibrary; *CIP.*

Teachers College Press, Teachers College, Columbia University *See* **Teachers College Pr., Teachers College, Columbia Univ.**

Teachers' Curriculum Institute, *(978-1-58371; 978-1-934534; 978-1-68468)* 4009 Miranda Ave. Ste. 100, Palo Alto, CA 94304-1227 USA Toll Free: 800-497-6138; P.O. Box 1327, Rancho Cordova, CA 95741 Toll Free: 800-343-6828
E-mail: info@teachtci.com
Web site: http://www.teachtci.com.

Teacher's Discovery, *(978-1-884473; 978-0-7560)* Div. of American Eagle Co., Inc., 2741 Paldan Dr., Auburn Hills, MI 48326 USA (SAN 631-4570) Tel 248-340-7210; Fax: 248-340-7212; Toll Free: 800-832-2437
Web site: http://www.teachersdiscovery-science.com; http://www.teachersdiscovery-english.com; http://www.teachersdiscovery-social studies.com; http://www.teachersdiscovery-foreignlanguage.com; http://www.teachersdiscovery.com
Dist(s): **American Eagle Pubns., Inc.**
Follett School Solutions.

Teacher's Friend Pubns., Inc., *(978-0-943263; 978-1-57882)* Div. of Scholastic, Inc., 2155 Chicago Ave. Ste. 304, Riverside, CA 92507-2209 USA (SAN 668-3177) Toll Free Fax: 800-307-8176; Toll Free: 800-343-9680
E-mail: info@teachersfriend.com
Web site: http://www.teachersfriend.com
Dist(s): **Scholastic, Inc.**

Teachers' Handbooks, *(978-0-9634938)* P.O. Box 2778, San Rafael, CA 94912 USA (SAN 297-8326) Tel 415-461-0871; Fax: 415-461-5357.

Teacher's Treasure *See* **Perfect 4 Preschool**

Teaching & Learning Co., *(978-1-57310)* Div. of Lorenz Corp., 501 E. Third St., Dayton, OH 45401 USA Tel 937-228-6118; Fax: 937-223-2042; Toll Free: 800-444-1144
E-mail: customerservice@teachinglearning.com
Web site: http://www.teachinglearning.com
Dist(s): **Rainbow Horizons Publishing, Inc.**

Teaching Christ's Children Publishing, *(978-0-9855423; 978-0-615-80614-3; 978-0-692-20138-1; 978-0-692-20142-8; 978-0-692-20166-4; 978-0-692-61203-3; 978-1-948476)* 7404 Forrest Ave., Parkville, MD 21234 USA Tel 410-665-2655
E-mail: teachingchristschildren@yahoo.com
Web site: www.teachingchristschildren.com
Dist(s): **CreateSpace Independent Publishing Platform.**

Teaching Point, Inc., *(978-0-9629357; 978-1-931680; 978-1-59657)* Orders Addr.: 6950 Philips Hwy. Ste. 46, Jacksonville, FL 32216-6087 USA Toll Free: 877-494-0550; *Imprints:* Expert Systems for Teachers (Expert Systms Teach)
Web site: http://www.teaching-point.net.

Teaching Resources *Imprint of* **Scholastic, Inc.**

Teaching Strategies *Imprint of* **Scholastic, Inc.**

Teaching Strategies, Incorporated *See* **Teaching Strategies, LLC**

Teaching Strategies, LLC, *(978-0-9602892; 978-1-879537; 978-1-933021; 978-1-60617; 978-1-64553; 979-8-88820)* 4500 East W. Highway, Suite 300, Bethesda, MD 20814 USA (SAN 222-240X) Tel 301-634-0818; Fax: 301-657-0250; Toll Free: 800-637-3652
E-mail: Matt.M@teachingstrategies.com; jow@teachingstrategies.com; legal@teachingstrategies.com
Web site: http://www.teachingstrategies.com; http://www.EdPro.com; http://www.MindNurture.com
Dist(s): **Delmar Cengage Learning**
Gryphon Hse., Inc.

Teaching That Makes Sense, *(978-0-9972831)* 543 NE 84th St, Seattle, WA 98115 USA Tel 919-448-4332
E-mail: stevepeha@gmail.com
Web site: www.ttms.org.

Teacup Pr., *(978-1-881817)* Div. of Kettle, Inc., Orders Addr.: P.O. Box 613, Dover Plains, NY 12522-0613 USA; Edit Addr.: Berkshire Rd., Dover Plains, NY 12522-0613 USA Tel 914-832-6401 Do not confuse with Teacup Pr. in Charlotte, NC.

Teahouse of Danger, *(978-0-9801054)* P.O. Box 1361, Tucson, AZ 85702 USA (SAN 855-2193) Toll Free: 877-663-3324
E-mail: teahouseofdanger@gmail.com
Web site: http://www.teahouseofdanger.com.

Team B Creative LLC, *(978-0-9774119; 978-1-937665)* 9864 E. Grand River, Suite 110, No. 244, Brighton, MI 48116 USA
E-mail: mickmorrisinfo@yahoo.com; teambcreative@yahoo.com; karen@teambcreative.com
Web site: http://www.mickmorris.net; http://www.ghostboardposse.com; http://www.mickmorris.com; http://www.totallyunrehearsed.com
Dist(s): **Follett School Solutions**
Partners Bk. Distributing, Inc.

Team Dawg Productions, Inc., *(978-0-9749378)* Orders Addr.: P.O. Box 105, Nesconset, NY 11767 USA Tel 718-926-5984; Edit Addr.: 1 Mayfair Rd., Apt. 1, Nesconset, NY 11767 USA
E-mail: bobby@teamdawg.com
Web site: http://www.teamdawg.com.

Team EEK! *See* **This is RED**

Team Kidz, Inc., *(978-0-9793833; 978-1-7359021)* P.O. Box 2111, Voorhees, NJ 08043-8111 USA Tel 856-768-2181
E-mail: jgkeega@aol.com.

Team Luna Productions, Inc., *(978-0-692-10595-5)* 540 N. Central Ave., Glendale, CA 91203 USA Tel 310-721-2700
E-mail: molly@mollyannluna.com.

Team Publishing, *(978-0-9886287)* 828 E. Hermosa St., Santa Maria, CA 93454 USA Tel 805-878-5449
E-mail: jtianier@msn.com.

Team Reach, Inc., *(978-0-9767610)* 8448 Summit St., Lenexa, KS 66215-5388 USA Fax: 913-312-8872
E-mail: troy@krystal-planet.com; troy@troyhelming.com
Web site: http://www.troyhelming.com; http://www.teamreach.com.

Team Shonen Publishing, *(978-0-578-78435-9; 978-0-578-34732-5; 979-8-218-05328-4)* 8670 Camino Colegio, Rohnert Park, CA 94928 USA Tel 415-272-4240
E-mail: Kingofthewriters@gmail.com
Web site: BlackShonen.com.

TechArts International LLC, *(978-0-9726326)* 7638 S. Carroll Rd., Indianapolis, IN 46259 USA; P.O. Box 6983, Great Falls, MT 59405.

Technical Data Freeway, Inc., *(978-0-9841600)* P.O. Box 308, Poway, CA 92074 USA.

Technology & Imagination Pr., *(978-0-9798991; 978-1-944273)* 1970 Chalon Glen Ct., Livermore, CA 94550-8206 USA (SAN 854-7068) Tel 925-606-1285; Fax: 925-606-1297
E-mail: books@siliconmap.net.

Technology Education Concepts Inc., *(978-0-9740796; 978-0-9777525)* 32 Commercial St., Concord, NH 03301-5031 USA Tel 603-224-8324; Fax: 603-225-7766; Toll Free: 800-338-2238
E-mail: justyn@tecedu.com
Web site: http://www.tecedu.com.

Tecknì-Corp, Ltd., *(978-0-9724178)* P.O. Box 866, Bettendorf, IA 52722-1955 USA Tel 563-359-4388; Fax: 563-359-4671
E-mail: patrickm@studentsafe.com
Web site: http://www.studentsafe.com.

Tecolote, Ediciones, S.A. de C.V. (MEX) *(978-968-7381) Dist. by* **Mariuccia Iaconi Bk Imports.**

Tecolote, Ediciones, S.A. de C.V. (MEX) *(978-968-7381) Dist. by* **Lectorum Pubns.**

Tectum B.V.B.A. (BEL) *(978-90-76886; 978-90-79761) Dist. by* **InnovativeLog.**

Teddy Bear Pr., Inc., *(978-1-880017)* 5470 Van Ness, Bloomfield Hills, MI 48302 USA Tel 248-851-8607 Do not confuse with Teddy Bear Pr., Las Vegas, NV.

Teddy Traveler Co., *(978-0-9748954)* P.O. Box 3223, Manhattan Beach, CA 90266 USA
Web site: http://www.teddytraveler.com
Dist(s): **Beyda for Bks., LLC.**

Tedesco, James *See* **JBT Publishing**

Teen Alive, *(978-1-7337512; 978-1-955232)* 11844 Bandera Rd, Helotes, TX 78023 USA Tel 803-804-2990
E-mail: askdoctorlulu@gmail.com
Web site: www.teenalive.com.

Teen Town Pr. *Imprint of* **Youngs, Bettie Bks.**

Teen Town Pr. / Bettie Youngs Bks. *Imprint of* **Youngs, Bettie Bks.**

Teen Winners, LLC, *(978-0-9740356)* 19 Quail Run, Berlin, CT 06037 USA Tel 860-829-2067; Fax: 860-829-8067
E-mail: info@teenwinners.com
Web site: http://www.teenwinners.com.

Teens Can Dream LLC *See* **Inspired Imaginations, LLC**

Teeter, Diana, *(978-0-692-88078-4)* 6620 108th St Apt 1L, FOREST HILLS, NY 11375 USA Tel 248-895-9097
E-mail: jeffwcrawford5+LVP0003691@gmail.com; jeffwcrawford5+LVP0003691@gmail.com.

TEG Publishing, *(978-0-9707208; 978-0-9727410)* Orders Addr.: P.O. Box 12737, Tempe, AZ 85284 USA Tel 310-919-3013
E-mail: microlawyers@aol.com; tegpublishing@wwsws.com
Web site: http://www.tegpublishing.com.

Tegen, Katherine Bks *Imprint of* **HarperCollins Pubs.**

Tehabi Bks., *(978-1-887656; 978-1-931688)* 4920 Carroll Canyon Rd., Suite 200, San Diego, CA 92121 USA Tel 858-450-9100; Fax: 858-450-9146; Toll Free: 800-243-7259
E-mail: Emily.Henning@tehabi.com
Web site: http://www.tehabi.com.

Teigen, Madeline, *(978-1-7334255)* 708 Shea Ct, Evans, GA 30809-5311 USA Tel 706-231-5912
E-mail: booksbymadelineteigen@gmail.com
Web site: booksbymadelineteigen.com.

Teitelbaum, Robert Publishings, *(978-0-9993519; 978-1-7326485; 978-1-7337980; 978-1-7363675; 979-8-9869697)* 43585 Monterey Ave. No. 8, Palm Desert, CA 92260 USA Tel 818-278-2348
E-mail: rjtbaum@mac.com
Web site: Teitelbaumpublishing.com.

Telemachus Pr., LLC, *(978-0-9841083; 978-1-935670; 978-1-937387; 978-1-937698; 978-1-938135; 978-1-938701; 978-1-939337; 978-1-939927; 978-1-940745; 978-1-941536; 978-1-942899; 978-1-945330; 978-1-948046; 978-1-951744; 978-1-956867)* Orders Addr.: 7551 Ashlord Ct., Dublin, OH 43017 USA (SAN 858-4508) Tel 941-993-5816; 941-993-5987; Fax: 941-296-7873; 7551 Ashlord Ct., Dublin, OH 43017 (SAN 858-4508) Tel 941-993-5816; 941-993-5987; Fax: 941-296-7873
E-mail: Steve.himes@telemachuspress.com
Web site: http://www.telemachuspress.com
Dist(s): **Ingram Content Group**
Smashwords.

Tell Me Pr., LLC, *(978-0-9816453; 978-0-9819835; 978-0-9829421; 978-0-9906453)* 98 Mansfield St., New Haven, CT 06511 USA (SAN 857-8508) Tel 203-562-4215; Fax: 203-562-4225
E-mail: lisa@tellmepress.com
Web site: http://www.tellmepress.com
Dist(s): **Greenleaf Book Group.**

Tell My Story Publishing, LLC, *(978-0-9729363)* Orders Addr.: 898 Mahogany Dr., Kaysville, UT 84037-4409 USA
E-mail: tellmystory@msn.com.

Tella Tales LLC, *(978-1-7371809)* 235 Ponce de Leon Pl., Decatur, GA 30030 USA Tel 470-829-5680
E-mail: patricrayburn@gmail.com.

Tell-a-Vision Bks., *(978-0-9727706)* Orders Addr.: P.O. Box 396, Lexington, VA 24450 USA; Edit Addr.: 272 Dogwood Rise, Lexington, VA 24450 USA
Web site: http://www.tell-a-visionbooks.com.

Telling Family Tales, *(978-1-940379)* 12129 S. 2160 W., Riverton, UT 84065 USA Tel 801-787-5673
E-mail: raelyn@tellingfamilytales.com.

Telling Our Stories Pr., *(978-0-9829228; 978-0-9900081)* 185 AJK Blvd., No. 246, Lewisburg, PA 17837 USA Tel 570-795-9550; Fax: 570-246-4091
E-mail: cocoharris@gmail.com
Web site: www.TellingOurStoriesPress.com.

Temenos Pr., *(978-0-9701319)* Orders Addr.: P.O. Box 477, Ashfield, MA 01330 USA Tel 413-625-9148; Edit Addr.: 989 Apple Valley Rd., Ashfield, MA 01330 USA Do not confuse with Temenos Pr., in Cloverdale, CA.

Tempest Bk. Shop, *(978-0-9632484)* Orders Addr.: 5031 Main St., Waitsfield, VT 05673-7111 USA Tel 802-496-2022; Fax: 802-496-3299
E-mail: rayfieldvt@aol.com.

Tempest Pr., *(978-0-9790232)* P.O. Box 3504, New York, NY 10008-3504 USA (SAN 852-2340)
E-mail: info@tempestpress.com
Web site: http://www.tempestpress.com
Dist(s): **Greenfield Distribution, Inc.**

Templar *Imprint of* **Candlewick Pr.**

Temple Care: Body, Mind & Spirit, *(978-0-9773759)* P.O. Box 1221 Ring Bill Loop, Upper Marlboro, MD 20774-7170 USA Tel 301-218-5941; Fax: 719-218-5948
E-mail: templecare@verizon.com.

Temple Street Pr., *(978-0-9896231)* P.O. Box 7071, Halcyon, CA 93421 USA Tel 805-243-8144
E-mail: eva@templestreetpress.com
Web site: http://templestreetpress.com
Dist(s): **Children's Plus, Inc.**

†**Temple Univ. Pr.**, *(978-0-87722; 978-1-56639; 978-1-59213; 978-1-4399)* 1601 N. Broad St., Univ. Services Bldg., Rm. 305, Philadelphia, PA 19122-6099 USA (SAN 202-7666) Tel 215-204-3389; Fax: 215-204-4719; Toll Free: 800-447-1656
E-mail: charles.ault@temple.edu
Web site: http://www.temple.edu/tempress
Dist(s): **Chicago Distribution Ctr.**
Ebsco Publishing
Follett School Solutions
Fordham Univ. Pr.
JSTOR
MyiLibrary
Univ. of Chicago Pr.
ebrary, Inc.; *CIP.*

Templeton Foundation Press *See* **Templeton Pr.**

Templeton, Julia, *(978-0-9837367; 978-1-939863)* 601 NW 22nd St., Battle Ground, WA 98604 USA Tel 360-723-0654
E-mail: juliatempleton@comcast.net
Dist(s): **Smashwords.**

Templeton Pr., *(978-1-890151; 978-1-932031; 978-1-59947)* Div. of John Templeton Foundation, 300 Conshohocken State Rd., Conshohocken, PA 19428-3801 USA
E-mail: info@templetonpress.org; lbarrett@templeton.org
Web site: http://www.templetonpress.org
Dist(s): **Chicago Distribution Ctr.**
Ebsco Publishing
MyiLibrary
Rutgers Univ. Pr.
Univ. of Chicago Pr. Distribution Clients
ebrary, Inc.

Temporal Mechanical Pr., *(978-1-928878)* Div. of Enos Mills Cabin, Orders Addr.: 6760 Hwy. 7, Estes Park, CO 80517-6404 USA Tel 970-586-4706
E-mail: info@enosmills.com
Web site: http://www.enosmills.com.

Tempus (ESP) *(978-84-92567; 978-84-936181) Dist. by* **IPG Chicago.**

Tempus Pr., *(978-0-9620456)* Orders Addr.: P.O. Box 235, Tell City, IN 47586 USA (SAN 248-4609) Fax: 812-547-8144; Edit Addr.: 14904 Senator Way, Carmel, IN 46032-5111 USA (SAN 248-4617)
E-mail: philbalc@psci.net.

Ten Critters Pr., *(978-1-7335506)* 2506 Demere Rd, Saint Simons Island, GA 31522 USA Tel 678-772-9786
E-mail: cturtleatl@yahoo.com
Web site: cturtle.us.

Ten Gallon Pr., *(978-0-615-69261-6; 978-0-9883021; 978-0-9991217)* 2896 Bardy Rd., Santa Rosa, CA 95404 USA Tel 415-713-8386
E-mail: helen@helensedwick.com
Web site: www.tengallonpress.com
Dist(s): **CreateSpace Independent Publishing Platform.**

Ten Minas Publishing, *(978-0-9716786)* P.O. Box 8984, Reston, VA 20195 USA Fax: 703-834-1176
Web site: http://www.crowsofhiddencreek.

Ten Speed Pr. *Imprint of* **Potter/Ten Speed/Harmony/Rodale**

†**Ten Speed Pr.**, *(978-0-89815; 978-0-913668; 978-1-58008; 978-1-60774)* Div. of Crown Publishing Group, Orders Addr.: P.O. Box 7123, Berkeley, CA 94707 USA (SAN 202-7674) Fax: 510-559-1629 (orders); Toll Free: 800-841-2665; 555 Richmond St., W. Suite 405, Box 702, Toronto, ON M5V 3B1 Tel 416-703-7775; Fax: 416-703-9992; *Imprints:* Celestial Arts (CelestialArts); Tricycle Press (TricyclePress)
E-mail: order@tenspeed.com; alan@tenspeed.ca
Web site: http://www.tenspeed.com
Dist(s): **Fujii Assocs.**
MyiLibrary
Penguin Random Hse. LLC
Random Hse., Inc.; *CIP.*

Ten Story Bks., LLC, *(978-0-9916348; 978-1-945131)* P.O. Box 701561, Dallas, TX 75370 USA Tel 972-345-0734
E-mail: info@tenstorybooks.com.

TEN16 Pr. *Imprint of* **Orange Hat Publishing**

Tender Heart Pr., *(978-0-9741401)* 15448 S. Jasper, Bldg. G, Odessa, TX 79766 USA
Web site: http://www.tenderheartpress.com.

Tender Learning Concepts, *(978-0-9708796)* 5362 Rockledge Dr., Buena Pk., CA 90621 USA Tel 714 739 2145; 714-739-2145; Fax: 714-739-0593; Toll Free: 877 886-7091; *Imprints:* TLConcepts, Incorporated (TLCPTS)
E-mail: whm@iqboosters.com
Web site: http://www.iqboosters.com; http://tenderlearning.econgo.com.

Tendril Pr., LLC, *(978-0-9763706; 978-0-9802190; 978-0-9822394; 978-0-9841543; 978-0-9831587; 978-0-9858933)* Orders Addr.: P.O. Box 441110, Aurora, CO 80044 USA Tel 303-696-9227; Fax: 303-873-6766; 2215 S. Oakland Way, Aurora, CO 80014 Tel 720-275-8371 Direct
E-mail: publisher@tendrilpress.com
Web site: http://www.tendrilpress.com
Dist(s): **Brigham Distribution.**

teNeues Publishing Co., *(978-3-570; 978-3-8238; 978-3-929278; 978-3-8327; 978-1-933427; 978-1-60160; 978-1-62325; 978-3-96171)* 7 W. 18th St., New York, NY 10011 USA (SAN 245-176X) Tel 212-627-9090; Fax: 212-627-9511; Toll Free: 800-352-0305; 12 Ferndene Rd., London, SE24 0AQ
E-mail: tnp@teneues-usa.com
Web site: http://www.teneues.com
Dist(s): **National Bk. Network.**

Tengan, G. Shay Service Group, *(978-0-9883478)* 2229 Orange Grove Pl., Escondido, CA 92027 USA Tel 760-443-9069
E-mail: stengan@cox.net.

Teni & Tayo Creations LLC, *(978-1-7322315)* 14622 Ventura Blvd, Sherman Oaks, CA 91403 USA Tel 310-746-7579
E-mail: feyifayadventures@gmail.com.

Tenley Circle Pr., *(978-0-9773536)* Orders Addr.: P.O. Box 5625, Washington, DC 20016 USA.

Tennant, Sue, *(978-1-7351475)* 5015 NW 39TH TER, GAINESVILLE, FL 32606 USA Tel 352-281-4205
E-mail: Suet51@aol.com.

ennessee Valley Publishing, *(978-1-882194; 978-1-932604)* Orders Addr.: P.O. Box 52527, Knoxville, TN 37950-2527 USA Tel 865-584-5235; Fax: 865-584-0113; Toll Free: 800-762-7079; Edit Addr.: 5227 N. Middlebrook Pike., Knoxville, TN 37921-5963 USA
E-mail: info@tvp1.com
Web site: http://www.tvp1.com
Dist(s): **Chicago Distribution Ctr.**

Tenney, Bob Solutions, LLC, *(978-0-9763485)* 160 Hamburg Mountain Rd., Weaverville, NC 28787-9432 USA
E-mail: bobtenney@earthlink.net
Web site: http://www.tenneypubs.com.

Tensaw Pr., Inc., The, *(978-0-9746444)* 158 S. Jefferson St., Mobile, AL 36602-1119 USA Fax: 251-438-4545
E-mail: tensawpress@aol.com.

TEODOR 1 Inc., *(978-0-9769196)* Orders Addr.: 8221 Provident St., PHILADELPHIA, PA 19150 USA Tel 267-916-6442; Fax: 615-704-4422
E-mail: Contactjullenberlin@gmail.com.

Teora USA LLC, *(978-1-59496)* Orders Addr.: 505 Hampton Park Blvd. Ste. G, Capitol Hgts, MD 20743-3862 USA (SAN 256-1220)
E-mail: welcome@teora.com
Web site: http://www.teorausa.com.

TEPHRAMIRIAM Publishing, *(978-0-9996415)* 2 E. oak Street, 1406, Chicago, IL 60611-1249 USA Tel 505-615-4171; Fax: 505-615-4171
E-mail: dhyre505@gmail.com
Web site: tephramiriampublishing.com.

Terabyte Pr. LLC, *(978-0-9839877)* 223A S. Durkee Hill Ln., Southbury, CT 06488 USA Tel 203-448-8142
E-mail: cbaileysims@gmail.com.

Teresa Ann Winton, *(978-1-7344627)* 3618 Ian Dr, Johnson City, TN 37604 USA Tel 423-430-4801
E-mail: teresaann@zoho.com.

Teresa E Lavergne, *(978-0-9966237)* 721 W. Main St, New Iberia, LA 70560 USA Tel 337-321-2840
E-mail: teresa@nifreedom.com.

Terminal Pr., LLC, *(978-0-9753683)* 27 June Walk., Long Beach, NY 11561-2884 USA
E-mail: bferrara@terminalpress.com
Web site: http://www.terminalpress.com.

Termino Editorial, *(978-0-930549)* P.O. Box 8905, Cincinnati, OH 45208 USA (SAN 677-5756) Tel 513-891-4621; Fax: 513-791-1756
E-mail: rmadri7239@aol.com
Dist(s): **Ediciones Universal.**

Terra Blue Enterprises, *(978-1-928840)* 310 Lakefront Dr., Wylie, TX 75098 USA Tel 972-332-3880 land line; 469-774-7815 cell phone
E-mail: sheyuli325@yahoo.com; khashahnawaz@gmail.com
Web site: http://www.shwelumaung.org/.

Terra Denuo, Inc., *(978-1-933232)* P.O. Box 485, Rocklin, CA 95677 USA
E-mail: mark@terradenuo.com
Web site: http://www.terradenuo.com.

Terra Linda Publishing, *(978-0-9746710)* 593 Tamarack Dr., San Rafael, CA 94903 USA Tel 415-491-1042
E-mail: meolson@earthlink.net
Web site: http://www.terralindapublishing.com.

Terra Niños *See* **Solibros**

Terra Nova Press *See* **Across Ocean Bks.**

Terra Nova Publishing Company *See* **Dream Ship Publishing Co.**

Terra Tales, *(978-0-9771804)* 101 Lattice Ln., Collegeville, PA 19426-3374 USA.

Terran Empire Publishing, *(978-0-9990108; 978-0-9992022; 978-1-956584)* 1761 Hillside Ct, Placerville, CA 95667 USA Tel 530-333-7227
E-mail: terranempirepub@gmail.com.

Terrapin Pr., *(978-0-9753087)* 2094 Arthur St., Eugene, OR 97405-1519 USA Do not confuse with companies with the same name in Marina del Rey, CA, Aiken, SC.

Terrific Science Pr., *(978-1-883822)* Miami Univ. Middletown, 4200 E. University Blvd., Middletown, OH 45042 USA Fax: 513-727-3328
E-mail: cce@muohio.edu
Web site: http://www.terrificscience.org
Dist(s): **Carolina Biological Supply Co.**
Nasco Math Eighty-Six
Science Kit & Boreal Labs
Teacher's Discovery.

Terrific Twins LLC, *(978-0-9769910)* 659 Kensington Ave., Severna Park, MD 21146 USA Tel 410-647-8923 (phone/fax)
E-mail: carpenterzyla@hotmail.com
Web site: http://terrifictwins.com.

Terry Lowey's Children's Stories, LLC, *(978-0-9792695)* 1325 Airmotive Way, Suite 175, Reno, NV 89502 USA Tel 775-322-1924; Fax: 775-322-1937
Web site: http://www.lifeisamagicaljourney.com.

Tertulia Pubns., *(978-0-9785988)* P.O. Box 2450, Nevada City, CA 95959 USA (SAN 851-0962)
Web site: http://www.tertuliapress.com.

Terumah Publishing, *(978-0-9744277)* Orders Addr.: 5 Pipe Hill Ct., Unit C, Baltimore, MD 21209 USA Tel 410-486-0950
E-mail: info@terumah.com
Web site: http://www.terumah.com.

TESCH, GLORIA *See* **GOLDEN LIBERTY**

Tesoro Publishing, *(978-0-9797419; 978-1-941346)* P.O. Box 528, Fullerton, CA 92836 USA (SAN 854-2279)
E-mail: Info@Tesoropublishing.com
Web site: http://www.TesoroPublishing.com.

Tessellations, *(978-0-9802191; 978-0-9846042; 978-1-938664)* 3913 E. Bronco Tr., Phoenix, AZ 85044-2604 USA Tel 480-763-5440; Fax: 480-763-6948; Toll Free: 800-655-5341
E-mail: tessellations@cox.net
Web site: http://www.tessellations.com
Dist(s): **Parkwest Pubns., Inc.**

Testify Bks., Inc., *(978-0-9725920; 978-1-7320629)* 465 Greenwich St., No. 4, New York, NY 10013 USA
E-mail: extraclip@earthlink.net
Dist(s): **D.A.P./Distributed Art Pubs.**

TESTIMONY PUBLISHERS, LLC. *See* **Testimony Pubs., LLC.**

Testimony Pubs., LLC., *(978-1-7322956; 978-1-7331394; 978-1-7360187)* P.O. Box 2869, Jackson, WY 83001 USA Tel 410-746-5299
E-mail: admin@testimonypublishersllc.online
Web site: www.testimonypublishersllc.online.

Tetoca Pr., *(978-0-9788085)* P.O. Box 337, Puyallup, WA 98371 USA Tel 253-845-1256; 253-845-5090; Toll Free: 888-483-8622
E-mail: thhunter@earthlink.net; tetoca@tetocapress.net
Web site: http://www.tetocapress.net
Dist(s): **Pathway Bk. Service**
Quality Bks., Inc.

Tetrahedron, Incorporated *See* **Tetrahedron Publishing LLC**

Tetrahedron Publishing LLC, *(978-0-923550; 978-0-9609386)* Orders Addr.: c/o Healthy World Distributing, LLC, 206 N. Fourth Ave., Suite 147, Sandpoint, ID 83864 USA Tel 208-265-2575; Fax: 208-265-2775; Toll Free: 888-508-4787; Edit Addr.: P.O. Box 2033, Sandpoint, ID 83864-0906 USA (SAN 260-2717) Toll Free: 888-508-4787 (orders)
E-mail: tetra@tetrahedron.org
Web site: http://www.tetrahedron.org
Dist(s): **New Leaf Distributing Co., Inc.**

Tetreault, Donna, *(978-0-578-81236-6; 978-1-7364798; 979-8-218-18604-3; 979-8-218-18606-7; 979-8-218-18809-2)* 3882 Corbin Ave, TARZANA, CA 91356 USA Tel 818-481-1239
E-mail: dtetreault@gmail.com
Web site: donnatetreault.com.

Texas A&M AgriLife Extension Service, *(978-0-9672990; 978-0-9721049)* c/o Texas A & M University, 2112 TAMU, College Station, TX 77843-2112 USA Fax: 979-862-1202
E-mail: d-bowen@tamu.edu
Dist(s): **Texas A&M Univ. Pr.**

†Texas A&M Univ. Pr., *(978-0-89096; 978-1-58544; 978-1-60344; 978-1-62349; 978-1-64843)* 4354 TAMU John H. Lindsey Bldg., Lewis St., College Station, TX 77843-4354 USA (SAN 658-1919) Tel 979-458-3975; Fax: 979-847-8752; Toll Free Fax: 888-617-2421 (orders); Toll Free: 800-826-8911 (orders)
E-mail: katie.duelm@tamu.edu
Web site: http://www.tamupress.com
Dist(s): **Ebsco Publishing**
MyiLibrary
ebrary, Inc.; *CIP.*

Texas Bk. Pubs. Assn., *(978-0-87244; 978-0-9717667; 978-0-9798391; 978-0-9903714; 978-1-946182)* Orders Addr.: 11152 Westheimer Rd., #667, Houston, TX 77042 USA Tel 281-438-7500; Fax: 281-438-7501
E-mail: editor@texasbookpublishers.org; publisher@johnhardypublishing.com; sales@johnhardypublishing.com
Web site: http://www.johnmhardy.com; www.texasbookpublishers.org; www.texianpress.com; www.ironmtnpress.com; http://www.johnhardypublishing.com; http://www.calientexpress.com
Dist(s): **Ingram Content Group.**

Texas Cooperative Extension *See* **Texas A&M AgriLife Extension Service**

Texas Pride Publishing, *(978-0-9859601; 978-1-7349369; 978-1-7378854)* 5003 Walzem Rd Unit 326, San Antonio, TX 78218 USA Tel 214-326-4356
E-mail: theamazingcharity@gmail.com
Web site: http://charitymarie.com.

†Texas State Historical Assn., *(978-0-87611)* 2-306 Richardson Hall, University Sta., Austin, TX 78712 USA (SAN 202-7704) Tel 512-471-1525; Fax: 512-471-1551; Toll Free: 800-687-8132
Web site: http://www.tshaonline.org
Dist(s): **MyiLibrary**
Texas A&M Univ. Pr.
ebrary, Inc.; *CIP.*

†Texas Tech Univ. Pr., *(978-0-89672; 978-1-68283)* Affil. of Texas Tech Univ., P.O. Box 41037, Lubbock, TX 79409-1037 USA (SAN 218-5989) Tel 806-742-2982; Fax: 806-742-2979; Toll Free: 800-832-4042
E-mail: ttup@ttu.edu; barbara.brannon@ttu.edu
Web site: http://www.ttup.ttu.edu; http://www.ttupress.org
Dist(s): **Chicago Distribution Ctr.**
MyiLibrary; *CIP.*

†Texas Woman's Univ. Pr., *(978-0-9607488; 978-0-9712104)* Orders Addr.: P.O. Box 425858, Denton, TX 76204 USA (SAN 238-4833) Tel 940-898-3123; Fax: 940-898-3127; Edit Addr.: 1200 Frame St., Denton, TX 76205 USA
E-mail: wbenson@twu.edu; *CIP.*

Text 4m Publishing, *(978-0-9779207; 978-0-9795691)* P.O. Box 12586, Milwaukee, WI 53212-0586 USA (SAN 850-6299)
E-mail: info@text4mpublishing.com; teresarae@msn.com
Web site: http://www.text4mpublishing.com.

Text N Tone, Inc., *(978-0-9764429)* 1500 King William Woods Rd., Midlothian, VA 23113-9119 USA
E-mail: mchekel@dslextreme.com.

Textbook Pubs., *(978-0-7581; 978-1-60630; 978-1-62583)* Orders Addr.: 17853 Santiago Blvd. Suite 107-133, Villa Park, CA 92861 USA Fax: 951-767-0133
E-mail: reprintservices@gmail.com.

Textbooks On Demand *See* **Reprint Services Corp.**

Textorium Publishing, *(978-0-9988194)* P.O. Box 62385, Virginia Beach, VA 23466 USA Tel 757-270-5590
E-mail: textoriumpublishing@yahoo.com.

Texture Pr., *(978-0-9641837; 978-0-9712061; 978-0-9797573; 978-0-9850081; 978-0-615-69474-0; 978-0-615-71148-5; 978-0-615-71503-2; 978-0-615-75380-5; 978-0-615-77101-4; 978-0-615-78283-6; 978-0-615-81691-3; 978-0-615-82399-7; 978-0-615-85856-2; 978-0-615-87735-8; 978-0-615-90534-1; 978-0-615-95462-2; 978-0-615-95463-9; 978-0-692-21272-1; 978-0-692-30003-9; 978-0-692-30004-6; 978-0-692-31702-0; 978-0-692-35682-1; 978-0-692-35683-8; 978-0-692-36138-2; 978-0-692-39578-3; 978-0-692-40157-6; 978-0-692-52042-)* 1609 Oklahoma Ave., Norman, OK 73072 USA Tel 405-314-7730
E-mail: susan@beyondutopia.com; texturepress@beyondutopia.com
Web site: http://www.texturepress.org; http://beyondutopia.net/texturepress/
Dist(s): **SPD-Small Pr. Distribution.**

TF Pr., a Div. of Fezfam LLC, *(978-1-7358680)* 148 E. ROCKS RD, Norwalk, CT 06851 USA Tel 203-858-8751
E-mail: psfez@aol.com.

TF Press, Fezfam LLC *See* **TF Pr., a Div. of Fezfam LLC**

TFG, *(978-0-9884132)* P.O. Box 91452, Portland, OR 97291 USA Tel 503-629-5045; Fax: 503-531-9175
E-mail: kimball@kimballfisher.com; info@thefishergroup.com
Web site: www.kimballfisher.com; www.thefishergroup.com.

TFG Pr., *(978-0-9743521; 978-0-9748553)* 244 Madison Ave., No. 254, New York, NY 10016 USA Tel 877-822-2504 do nto confuse with TGF Press in New York, NY.

†TFH Pubns., Inc., *(978-0-7938; 978-0-86622; 978-0-87666; 978-1-85279)* Orders Addr.: One TFH Plaza, Third & Union Aves., Neptune City, NJ 07753 USA (SAN 202-7720) Tel 732-988-8400; Fax: 732-988-5466; Toll Free: 800-631-2188 (outside New Jersey); Edit Addr.: P.O. Box 427, Neptune, NJ 07753 USA (SAN 658-1862)
E-mail: info@tfh.com
Web site: http://www.tfh.com; *CIP.*

TFM Publishing Ltd. (GBR) *(978-0-9530052; 978-1-903378; 978-1-908986; 978-1-910079; 978-1-913755) Dist. by* **IngramPubServ.**

TG8 LLC, *(978-0-692-95819-3; 978-0-9997840)* 616 Rosarita Rd, Arlington, TX 76002 USA Tel 214-240-5511; Fax: 214-240-5511
E-mail: kendriatg@gmail.com
Web site: www.jaxandriley.com.

TGJS Publishing, *(978-0-578-54691-9; 978-0-578-54838-8; 978-0-578-55434-1; 978-0-578-56316-9; 978-0-578-56317-6; 978-0-578-56318-3; 978-0-578-58703-5; 978-0-578-58705-9; 978-0-578-58706-6; 978-0-578-59056-1; 978-0-578-59057-8; 978-0-578-59058-5; 978-0-578-63145-5; 978-0-578-63231-5; 978-0-578-64173-7; 978-0-578-64174-4; 978-0-578-64176-8; 978-0-578-66082-0; 978-0-578-66083-7; 978-0-578-66084-4; 978-0-578-67404-9; 978-0-578-67405-6; 978-0-578-67409-4; 978-0-578-68278-5; 978-0-578-68279-2; 978-0-578-68283-9;)*
E-mail: tgjsinfo@gmail.com
Dist(s): **Ingram Content Group.**

Th1nk Bks. *Imprint of* **NavPress Publishing Group**

Th3rd World Studios, *(978-0-9818694; 978-0-9832161; 978-0-9895744; 978-1-956694)* 290 Powell Cir., Berlin, MD 21811 USA
Web site: http://www.th3rdworld.com
Dist(s): **Diamond Comic Distributors, Inc.**
Diamond Bk. Distributors
Simon & Schuster, Inc.

Thacker Hse. Enterprises, *(978-0-9801919)* 1840 Thacker Ave., Jacksonville, FL 32207 USA Tel 904-398-8332
E-mail: 22dwebb@comcast.net
Web site: http://www.debrawebbrogers.com.

Thalian Bks., *(978-0-9884868; 978-0-9961317)* 271B Heritage Village, Southbury, CT 06488 USA Tel 203-262-1558
E-mail: becklean@gmail.com.

Thames & Hudson, *(978-0-500)* 500 Fifth Ave., New York, NY 10110 USA Tel 212-354-3763; Fax: 212-398-1252; Toll Free: 800-233-4830 (orders)
E-mail: bookinfo@thames.wwnorton.com
Web site: http://www.thamesandhudsonusa.com
Dist(s): **Hachette Bk. Group**
ISD
MyiLibrary
Norton, W. W. & Co., Inc.
Penguin Random Hse. Distribution
Penguin Random Hse. LLC.

Thameside Press *See* **Chrysalis Education**

Thandi's Place, A Billo Communication Company *See* **Youth Popular Culture Institute, Inc.**

Tharpa Pubns. USA, *(978-0-9789067; 978-0-9817277; 978-1-61606)* 47 Sweeney Rd., Glen Spey, NY 12737 USA Tel 845-856-5102; Fax: 845-856-2110; Toll Free: 888-741-3475
E-mail: sales.us@tharpa.com
Web site: http://www.tharpa.com
Dist(s): **Baker & Taylor Publisher Services (BTPS)**
Follett School Solutions
Ingram Publisher Services.

Tharpa Pubns. (GBR) *(978-0-948006; 978-1-899996; 978-0-9548790; 978-1-906665; 978-0-9558667; 978-84-15849-24-7) Dist. by* **BTPS.**

That Patchwork Place *Imprint of* **Martingale & Co.**

Thatch, Jaina, *(978-0-692-19830-8; 978-0-576-59280-0)* 111 Huron Ave, Tampa, FL 33606 USA Tel 215-356-7954
E-mail: jaina.thatch@gmail.com.

That's Life, Incorporated *See* **That's Life Publishing, Inc.**

That's Life Publishing, Inc., *(978-0-9722304)* 3431 Thunderbird Rd., No. 200, Phoenix,, AZ 85053 USA Toll Free: 877-896-9500; *Imprints:* ZZ Dogs Press (ZZ Dogs Pr)
Web site: http://www.zzdogs.com.

That's Love Publishing, *(978-1-953751)* 138 Woodford Ln., Canton, GA 30115 USA Tel 407-729-9789
E-mail: ebasora@yahoo.com
Web site: thatslovepublishing.com.

That's Me Publishing, LLC, *(978-1-933843)* Hc 62 Box 488., Salem, MO 65560-8819 USA
E-mail: mary@thatsmepublishing.com
Web site: http://www.thatsmepublishing.com.

ThatsMyLife Co., *(978-0-9760419)* 5516 Challis View Ln., Charlotte, NC 28226 USA Tel 704-752-0935; Toll Free: 866-752-0935
E-mail: customerservice@thatsmytale.com
Web site: http://www.thatsmytale.com.

The 101 Group, Inc., *(978-0-9772313; 978-0-9817033; 978-0-9848624; 978-1-7340727)* Orders Addr.: W358N5358 Crestview Dr., Oconomowoc, WI 53066 USA; Edit Addr.: P.O. Box 82, Okauchee, WI 53069 USA
Web site: http://www.the101group.com.

Adventures of Cordell, The, *(978-0-578-75490-1)* 13747 Falcon Way, McCordsville, IN 46055 USA Tel 317-417-5878
E-mail: deemichalowski@outlook.com
Web site: www.theadventuresofcordell.org.

The Adventures of Scuba Jack Publishers *See* **Adventures of Scuba Jack Pubs., The**

Adventures of Scuba Jack Pubs., The, *(978-0-9831123; 978-0-9834284; 978-0-578-14228-9; 978-0-692-24943-7; 978-0-692-25823-1; 978-0-692-26333-4; 978-0-692-26569-7; 978-0-692-26921-3; 978-0-692-27758-4; 978-0-692-50086-6; 978-0-692-72907-6; 978-0-578-47540-0; 978-0-578-52678-2; 978-0-578-57896-5; 978-0-578-59315-9) 16 Gibbs Hill Dr., Gloucester, MA 01930 USA Tel 978-491-0747*
Web site: www.adventuresofscubajack.com
Dist(s): **CreateSpace Independent Publishing Platform.**

Angelic Prince Publishing, The, *(978-0-9985145; 978-1-951428)* P.O. Box 33572, Tulsa, OK 74153 USA Tel 971-246-0160
E-mail: LantzdeContreras@gmail.com
Web site: LantzdeContreras.com.

The Arden Shakespeare *Imprint of* **Bloomsbury Publishing USA**

The Argonauts *See* **Argonauts, The**

The Art of Jessycka Drew, *(978-0-692-85164-7; 978-0-9987596)* 81 Westford St, HAVERHILL, MA 01832 USA.

August Publishing Co., The, *(978-1-7350696)* 1 Adrian Ave., Bronx, NY 10463 USA Tel 917-756-7693; Fax: 212-901-8587
E-mail: Sean.August@AugustWMG.com.

Bohemian Academic, The, *(978-1-7347796)* 12121 Quilt Patch Ln., Bowie, MD 20720 USA Tel 301-747-8712
E-mail: wendelynvega@gmail.com
Web site: wendelynvega.com.

The Bookworm of Edwards, *(978-0-692-81222-8; 978-0-692-86242-1; 978-0-692-09270-5; 978-0-578-48317-7; 978-0-578-70396-1; 978-0-578-91284-4; 978-0-578-29707-1; 979-8-218-20263-7)* 295 Main Street, C101, EDWARDS, CO 81632 USA Tel 970-926-7323
E-mail: nicole@bookwormofedwards.com; events@bookwormofedwards.com.

Children's Bible Project, The, *(978-1-7369361)* 5557 Baltimore Ave. Suite 500-1592, Upper Marlboro, MD 20781 USA Tel 215-290-7838
E-mail: audreyltaylor@hotmail.com
Web site: bigwonderworldofbooks.com.

The Child's World, Inc. *See* **Child's World, Inc, The**

†Child's World, Inc, The, *(978-0-89565; 978-0-913778; 978-1-56766; 978-1-59296; 978-1-60253; 978-1-60954; 978-1-60973; 978-1-61473; 978-1-62323; 978-1-62687; 978-1-63143; 978-1-63407; 978-1-5038)* Orders Addr.: 21735 E Idyllwilde Dr, Parker, CO 80138 USA (SAN 992-4981) Tel 800-599-7323; Fax: 888-320-2329; *Imprints:* Wonder Books(r) (Wonder Bks MN); MOMENTUM (MOMENTUMMN); First Steps (MYID_Y_FIRST S); Stride (MYID_U_STRIDE)
E-mail: info@childsworld.com
Web site: https://childsworld.com
Dist(s): **Peterson Publishing Co., Inc.;** *CIP.*

Circle Tales, The, *(979-8-9875276)* 828 6th St., Santa Monica, CA 90403 USA Tel 646-789-9134
E-mail: brigette@thecircletales.com
Web site: www.thecircletales.com.

The Crown Publishing Group *See* **Crown Publishing Group, The**

Dramatic Pen Pr., LLC, The, *(978-0-692-28380-6; 978-0-692-32954-2; 978-0-692-32958-0; 978-0-692-35487-2; 978-0-692-36604-2; 978-0-692-36728-5; 978-0-692-37996-7; 978-0-692-38986-7; 978-0-692-39163-1; 978-0-692-40865-0; 978-0-692-51342-2; 978-0-692-53385-7; 978-0-692-58038-7; 978-0-692-63114-0; 978-1-64157) 322 Cumberland St, Lolo, MT 59847 USA Tel 612-888-3722*
E-mail: susanethomas@juno.com
Web site: www.thedramaticpen.com
Dist(s): **CreateSpace Independent Publishing Platform.**

The Edge *Imprint of* **Sparklesoup LLC**

The Editorium, LLC, *(978-1-60096; 978-1-4341)* The Editorium 9198 Wild Acres Dr., West Jordan, UT 84081 USA Tel 385-775-4286 Cell; *Imprints:* Boomer Books (BoomerBks); Classic Books Library (ClassicBks); Waking Lion Press (WakingLion)
E-mail: lyon.jack@gmail.com
Web site: http://www.editorium.com; http://www.wakinglionpress.com; http://www.templehillbooks.com.

Emerald City Pr., The, *(978-0-578-65204-7; 978-0-578-70323-7; 978-0-578-81049-2; 978-1-7374610)* 1036 Savage St., Southington, CT 06489 USA Tel 860-621-8862
E-mail: theemeraldcity@netzero.net.

Beacon Hill Pr. of Kansas City, *(978-0-8341)* Div. of Nazarene Publishing Hse., 2345 Grand Blvd, Ste. 1900, Kansas City, MO 64108 USA (SAN 241-6328) Tel

Publisher Name Index

816-931-1900; Fax: 816-753-4071; Toll Free: 800-877-0700 (orders only)
E-mail: nphdirect@nph.com; orders@nph.com; inquiry@bhillkc.com
Web site: http://www.nph.com; http://www.bhillkc.com
Dist(s): **The Foundry Publishing.**

The Foundry Publishing, *(978-0-8341)* Orders Addr.: 2345 Grand Blvd., Suite 1900, Kansas City, MO 64108 USA (SAN 253-0902) Tel 816-931-1900; Edit Addr.: P.O. Box 419527, Kansas City, MO 64141 USA (SAN 202-9022) Tel 816-931-1900; Fax: 816-531-0923; Toll Free Fax: 800-849-9827; Toll Free: 800-877-0700
E-mail: heather@nph.com
Web site: http://www.bhillkc.com; http://www.nph.com
Dist(s): **Lifeway Christian Resources**
Lorenz Corp., The
Spring Arbor Distributors, Inc.

Golden Quill LLC, The, *(978-0-692-93298-8; 978-0-578-82953-1; 979-8-218-03126-8; 979-8-218-11955-3)* 19281 Rocky Summit Dr., Perris, CA 92570 USA Tel 310-818-3662
E-mail: sharon.judie@gmail.com.

The Gospel of Santa Claus *See* **Five Vines Pr.**

Harvest Ctr., The, *(978-1-7356183)* 1307 Denbright Rd., Catonsville, MD 21228 USA Tel 410-977-4454
E-mail: shuntley@som.umaryland.edu.

ICONS Foundation, The, *(978-1-7373659)* 1333 Burr Ridge Pkwy. - Suite 200, Burr Ridge, IL 60527 USA Tel 630-418-9102
E-mail: theiconsfoundation@gmail.com
Web site: www.theiconsfoundation.org.

The Ionian Press *See* **Paul Ferrante**

The Journey, *(978-0-692-78081-7; 978-0-692-78082-4; 978-0-692-18308-3; 978-0-578-43728-6)* 3171 E 129th Ave S., TULSA, OK 74134 USA Tel 918-576-8442.

Lab Comics, The, *(978-1-954080; 978-1-957793; 978-1-959190; 978-1-960893; 979-8-89158)* 914 Plaza St, Clearwater, FL 33755 USA Tel 646-599-5130
E-mail: thelabcomics@gmail.com.

Laurus Co., Inc., The, *(978-0-9841680; 978-0-9826957; 978-0-9847683; 978-1-938526; 978-1-943523; 978-1-957528)* P.O. Box 6173, Hickory, NC 28603 USA
E-mail: laurus@thelauruscompany.com; bookstore@thelauruscompany.com; nancywilliams@thelauruscompany.com; nanwills2@gmail.com
Web site: http://www.LaurusCompany.com; http://www.TheLaurusCompany.com; http://www.LaurusBooks.com; http://www.BookShelfDepot.com
Dist(s): **Laurus Co., The**
TLC Distributors.

LightHse. Bks., The, *(978-0-9994012; 978-1-950320)* 15600 E Caley Pl, Centennial, CO 80016 USA Tel 720-988-0850; 720-425-2300; 13721 E.Rice Pl, Aurora, CO 80015; *Imprints:* Lighthouse Press (MYID_F_LIGHTHO)
E-mail: agapeinc2@gmail.com
Web site: www.thelighthousebooks.com.

The Literary Brew *See* **Selenite Pr.**

Literary Revolutionary & Co., The, *(978-0-9968910; 978-1-950279)* 260 Peachtree St. NW Suite 2200, No. 9321, Atlanta, GA 30303 USA Tel 470-338-1637
E-mail: info@theliteraryrevolutionary.com
Web site: www.theliteraryrevolutionary.com.

Little Philosopher Group, The, *(978-1-942752)* 404 Miller Ave., Cape May, NJ 08204 USA Tel 609-675-0171
E-mail: andechris.family@gmail.com
Web site: www.thelittlephilosopher.com.

Magical World of AGAT Publishing, The, *(978-0-578-94223-0)* 109 Deerpath, Vernon hills, IL 60061 USA Tel 224-565-6166
E-mail: Krengauz@gmail.com.

Magnolia Gazette, The, *(978-0-692-19103-3)* 310 S. Cherry St., Magnolia, MS 39652 USA Tel 601-783-3006; Fax: 601-783-2441
E-mail: nancygazette@bellsouth.net.

Old West Co., The, *(978-0-9654341; 978-0-9801743; 978-0-9898004; 978-1-7320075)* Orders Addr.: 5118 Village Trail Dr., San Antonio, TX 78218-3831 USA; *Imprints:* Sweetwater Stagelines (Sweetwtr Stage)
E-mail: kirkwest@sbcglobal.net
Web site: theoldwestcompany.com; celebratethewest.com; lulu.com/spotlight/sweetwater; sweetwaterstagelines.com; aggieborifireflick.com; http://lulu.com/sweetwater.

Organic Study, The, *(978-1-7378846)* 3729 Sacramento St., San Francisco, CA 94118 USA Tel 917-449-6953
E-mail: layapayal@hotmail.com.

The Painted Word, Ltd., *(978-0-9846473; 978-0-692-03494-1)* P.O. Box 4132, Lutherville, MD 21094 USA.

Paper Posie Publishing Co., The, *(978-0-9707944; 978-0-9774763)* 315a Meigs Rd., No. 167, Santa Barbara, CA 93109 USA Tel 805-637-3194; Toll Free: 800-360-1761
Web site: http://www.paperposie.com; www.mothernaturenurseryrhymes.com.

Proud Brown Co., The, *(978-1-7379972)* 23131 MICHIGAN AVE No. 1077, Dearborn, MI 48124 USA Tel 313-330-0678
E-mail: theproudbrowncompany@gmail.com
Web site: Www.theproudbrowncompany.com.

The Publishing Place LLC, *(978-0-9754307; 978-0-9760129; 978-0-9763423; 978-0-9776554; 978-0-9788002; 978-0-9840555; 978-0-9845794; 978-0-9835095; 978-0-9849172)* 2330 Hickory Ridge, Ashland, KY 41101 USA Do not confuse with Avant-garde Publishing Company in Mableton, GA
E-mail: info@avantgardepublishing.com
Web site: http://www.avantgardepublishing.com
Dist(s): **Smashwords.**

The Reading Butterfly, INC., *(978-0-9993336)* 798 Rachel Dr., Franklinville, NJ 08322 USA Tel 609-703-3359; Fax: 856-422-0900
E-mail: gx3@comcast.net.

Regency Pubs., The, *(978-1-956074; 978-1-956515; 978-1-956736; 978-1-957054; 978-1-957724; 978-1-958517; 978-1-959434; 978-1-960113; 978-1-961096; 978-1-962313)* 521 5th Ave., New York, NY 10175 USA Tel 315-288-7938
E-mail: admin@theregencypublishers.com.

The Richard Janes Co., *(978-0-692-77834-0)* 12856 Walsh Ave, Los Angeles, CA 90066 USA Tel 310-801-2661
Dist(s): **Independent Pub.**

The Rolling Acorn Pr., *(978-0-692-31870-6; 978-0-692-37782-6; 978-0-692-79386-2; 978-0-692-10389-0; 978-0-692-14774-0)* 4730 Castle Rd, LA CANADA, CA 91011 USA Tel 818-434-2395.

Southern Babble, The, *(978-0-578-54130-3; 978-0-578-32129-5)* 267 Forest Lake Dr, Madison, MS 39110-9423 USA Tel 601-500-2290
E-mail: susannah@thesouthernbabble.com
Web site: www.thesouthernbabble.com.

Spookatorium, The, *(978-0-9966984)*
E-mail: Spookatorium.info@gmail.com
Web site: betsykatz.com.

The Svenson Group, Inc. *See* **Svenson Group, Inc., The**

Svenson Group, Inc., The, *(978-1-949436)* 2990 Northfied Dr., Tarpon Springs, FL 34688 USA Tel 727-945-7024
E-mail: svensona@aol.com
Web site: http://thehappyhollisters.com/.

The Tale of Noel: The Holiday Horse Angel, The, *(978-0-692-94230-7; 978-0-692-10176-6; 978-0-578-51603-5; 978-0-578-54889-0)* 14104 225th St., ELKADER, IA 52043 USA Tel 563-329-0806
E-mail: authorkristenhalverson@gmail.com
Dist(s): **Ingram Content Group.**

Teacshirt Co., The, *(978-1-7363656)* 1765 Sylvan St., Eugene, OR 97403 USA Tel 310-499-3906
E-mail: amazingnewlife5@gmail.com
Web site: Theteschshirtcompany.com.

Vision to Fruition Publishing Hse., The, *(978-0-692-25410-3; 978-0-692-30554-6; 978-0-692-32827-9; 978-0-692-34607-5; 978-0-692-42756-9; 978-0-692-48625-2; 978-0-692-56030-3; 978-0-692-99897-7; 978-1-7327674; 978-1-7339413; 978-0-578-72626-7; 978-1-7358359; 979-8-9869160)* 3261 Old Washington RD, STE 2020, Waldorf, MD 20602 USA Tel 301-659-2894
E-mail: info@thevtfgroup.com
Web site: www.vtfpublishing.com
Dist(s): **CreateSpace Independent Publishing Platform.**

The Wisdom Pages, Inc., *(978-0-9706482)* Div. of Bullies to Buddies, Inc., 65 Fraser St., Staten Island, NY 10314 USA (SAN 255-1217) Tel 718-983-1333; Fax: 718-983-3851
E-mail: miriam@bullies2buddies.com; izzy@bullies2buddies.com
Web site: http://www.bullies2buddies.com; http://www.thewisdompages.com.

Write Perspective, LLC, The, *(978-1-953962)* 7609 Bayhill Dr., Rowlett, TX 75088 USA Tel 469-684-8721
E-mail: authoraaronfields@gmail.com
Web site: thewriteperspective.net.

THEAQ LLC, *(978-0-9890723; 978-1-68189)* ; *Imprints:* THEAQ Publishing (THEAQPub)
E-mail: przcook2000@yahoo.com; rzeissler@yahoo.com.

THEAQ Publishing *Imprint of* **THEAQ LLC**

†Theatre Communications Group, Inc., *(978-0-88754; 978-0-913745; 978-0-930452; 978-1-55936; 978-1-84002; 978-1-85459; 978-1-870259; 978-1-899791; 978-1-63670)* 355 Lexington Ave., New York, NY 10017-6603 USA (SAN 210-9387) Tel 212-697-5230; Fax: 212-983-4847
Web site: http://www.tcg.org
Dist(s): **Abraham Assocs. Inc.**
Consortium Bk. Sales & Distribution
MyiLibrary
ebrary, Inc.; *CIP.*

Theatre of Innocence, A, L.L.C., *(978-0-9760283)* 1212 Hull St., No. 1, Louisville, KY 40204 USA.

TheCo.YouKeep.net, *(978-1-7370053)* 11270 Lamore Dr., Disputanta, VA 23842 USA Tel 804-536-1033
E-mail: ruthfrierson@outlook.com
Web site: www.thecompanyyoukeep.net.

Theee Hole Punch Publishing, *(978-0-9771678)* P.O. Box 4488, Midlothian, VA 23112 USA
E-mail: threeholepunchpublishing@verizon.net; vzentja9@verizon.net
Web site: http://threeholepunchpublishing.com.

TheFlashFictionPonder.com, *(978-0-578-21409-2)* 1427 Tully Rd. No. 8, Modesto, CA 95350 USA
Web site: www.theflashfictionponder.com.

Theisen, Patricia, *(978-0-9793076)* 10520 11th Ave. NW, Seattle, WA 98177 USA
E-mail: ptheisen@gmail.com.

Them Potatoes, *(978-0-9772564)* 7318 21st Ave NW, Seattle, WA 98117-5623 USA (SAN 257-1285)
E-mail: kbrown@thempotatoes.com
Web site: http://www.thempotatoes.com.

Theme Perks Incorporated *See* **Writing Academy Inc.**

Themm, Heather, *(978-0-578-79104-3; 978-0-578-88459-2)* 36029 capri dr, Winchester, CA 92596 USA Tel 951-239-9629
E-mail: Heatherthemm@gmail.com.

TheNetworkAdministrator.com, *(978-0-9744630; 978-1-937485)* Orders Addr.: 201 W. Cottesmore Cir., Longwood, FL 32779 USA
E-mail: douglaschick@thenetworkadministrator.com
Web site: http://www.thenetworkadministrator.com.

Theodore Berlin Publishing *See* **TEODOR 1 Inc.**

Theophany Pr., *(978-1-7339710; 979-8-9850527)* 2821 Rio Linda Dr., Bakersfield, CA 93305 USA Tel 661-477-6437
E-mail: theophanypress@gmail.com
Web site: jennylynnestes.com.

Theory & Practice *Imprint of* **Scholastic, Inc.**

†Theosophical Publishing Hse., *(978-0-8356; 978-81-7059; 978-0-7229)* Div. of Theosophical Society in America, 306 W. Geneva Rd., P.O. Box 270, Wheaton, IL 60189-0270 USA (SAN 202-5698) Tel 630-665-0130; Fax: 630-665-8791; Toll Free: 800-669-9425; *Imprints:* Quest Books (Quest)
E-mail: questbooks@aol.com; questoperations@theosmail.net; questbooks@theosophia.org; info@theosophical.org
Web site: http://www.theosophical.org
Dist(s): **MyiLibrary**
Red Wheel/Weiser; *CIP.*

Theotrope Publishing *See* **Theotrope Publishing**

Theotrope Publishing, *(978-1-7325935; 979-8-9851439)* P.O. Box 181, Bumpass, VA 23024 USA Tel 540-748-3908
E-mail: ktpistole@gmail.com
Web site: www.KatyPistole.com.

Theragogy.com, *(978-0-9749862)* 301 1/2 Crescent NE, Grand Rapids, MI 49503 USA
E-mail: drperkins@theragogy.com
Web site: http://www.theragogy.com.

Therapeutae Pr., *(978-0-9675575; 978-1-7335406)* P.O. Box 23542, Flagtaff, AZ 86002 USA
E-mail: nedwolf@rcia.com.

Therapy Art Theater LLC, *(978-0-9985790)* 1525 E Baseline Rd, 110 tempe AZ 85283, tempe, AZ 85283-1422 USA Tel 480-645-8845
E-mail: maryamnisajudan@gmail.com; nisajudan@yahoo.com.

TheWhippetyWood, *(978-0-9897216)* S9305 Slotty Rd., Prairie du Sac, WI 53578 USA Tel 608-544-2242
E-mail: pj.pixie1@gmail.com
Web site: www.theWhippetyWood.com.

Thewordverve, *(978-0-9857157; 978-0-9889264; 978-0-9896979; 978-1-941251; 978-0-9989052; 978-0-9992479; 978-1-948225; 978-1-956856)* 414 Pepperbush Bend, Canton, GA 30114 USA Tel 678-710-4353
E-mail: jan@thewordverve.com
Web site: www.thewordverve.com.

Theytus Bks., Ltd. (CAN) *(978-0-919441; 978-1-894778; 978-1-926886) Dist. by* **Orca Bk Pub.**

thierry, Ashley LLC, *(978-1-7369706)* 400 Forest Pk. Blvd apt 306, Oxnard, CA 93036 USA Tel 805-804-2542
E-mail: ashleythierryllc@gmail.com
Web site: www.ashleythierry.com.

Thies, Roberta A., *(978-0-692-93363-3; 978-0-578-47690-2)* 5278 Wolfpen Pleasant Hill Rd, MILFORD, OH 45150 USA Tel 513-218-2418
E-mail: thiesbobbi7@gmail.com
Dist(s): **Ingram Content Group.**

Thimble Mouse Publishing, Inc., *(978-0-9794522)* 1619 Saddle Creek Cir., No. 1312, Arlington, TX 76015 USA (SAN 853-4942).

Things That Matter LLC, *(978-0-692-85979-7)*
E-mail: thingsthatmatterllc@gmail.com
Dist(s): **Independent Pub.**

ThingsAsian Pr., *(978-0-9715940; 978-1-934159)* 3230 Scott St., San Francisco, CA 94123 USA Tel 415-921-1316; Fax: 415-921-3432
E-mail: info@thingsasian.com; albert@thingsasian.com
Web site: http://www.thingsasianpress.com; http://www.toasiawithlove.com; http://www.thingsasian.com
Dist(s): **Ingram Publisher Services.**

ThinkerBlox, LLC, *(978-1-7323299; 978-1-7326683)* 1655 Manitoba Dr., Sunnyvale, CA 94087 USA Tel 408-733-8973
E-mail: scurtis@laughingthunder.com.

Thinking Ink Pr., *(978-1-942480)* P.O. Box 1411, Campbell, CA 95009-1411 USA Tel 408-507-1990
E-mail: editorial@thinkinginkpress.com
Web site: www.thinkinginkpress.com.

Think-Outside-the-Book, Inc., *(978-0-9770751; 978-0-9896781; 978-0-9985471)* 2809 High Sail Ct., Las Vegas, NV 89117 USA
Web site: http://www.thinkoutsidethebook.com.

Think-Outside-the-Book Publishing, Inc. *See* **Think-Outside-the-Book, Inc.**

Thinkus Pubs., *(978-0-9818449)* Orders Addr.: 13109 SW 43rd St., Davie, FL 33330 USA
E-mail: loriflorido@aol.com
Web site: http://www.Dezzerthebook.com; http://www.HugothePunk.com
Dist(s): **Brodart Co.**
Follet Higher Education Grp
Quality Bks., Inc.

Third Axe Publishing, *(978-0-9765547)* 1150 McFarland, HR 26, Morristown, TN 37814 USA Tel 423-736-0884
E-mail: thirdaxepub@yahoo.com
Web site: http://www.brotherhoodofdwarves.com.

Third Dimension Publishing, *(978-0-9777041)* Div. of Third Dimension Group, Inc., Orders Addr.: P.O. Box 1845, Calhoun, GA 30703-1845 USA Tel 706-602-0398; Fax: 706-625-8712; Edit Addr.: 167 Richardson Rd., Calhoun, GA 30701 USA
E-mail: jeffcompton@msn.com
Web site: http://www.areyouawriter.com; http://www.thirddimensiongroup.com; http://www.thirddimensionpublishing.com.

Third Man Books, *(978-0-9913361; 978-0-9964016; 978-0-9974578; 978-1-7333501; 978-1-7348422; 978-1-7373829; 979-8-9866145)* 623 7th Ave. S., Nashville, TN 37203 USA (SAN 990-0071) Tel 615-720-6758
E-mail: chet@thirdmanrecords.com
Web site: www.thirdmanbooks.com
Dist(s): **Consortium Bk. Sales & Distribution.**

Third Man Records *See* **Third Man Books**

Third Millennium Pr., *(978-0-9795608; 978-0-9833308)* 1845 Avondale Dr., Baton Rouge, LA 70808-1913 USA (SAN 853-7496) Tel 805-217-3109; Toll Free: 800-891-0390
E-mail: ellenhbrown@gmail.com
Web site: http://www.webofdebt.com; http://www.forbiddenmedicine.org; http://www.ellenbrown.com
Dist(s): **Ingram Content Group.**

Third Millennium Pubns., *(978-1-932657; 978-1-934805; 978-1-947483)* Sci Fi - Arizona, Inc., 1931 E. Libra Dr., Tempe, AZ 85283-5117 USA Tel 602-740-0569
E-mail: mccollum@3mpub.com
Web site: http://www.3mpub.com; http://www.scifi-az.com
Dist(s): **Chicago Distribution Ctr.**

Third Millennium Publishing *Imprint of* **Sci Fi-Arizona, Inc.**

3rd Party Publishing Co., *(978-0-89914)* Div. of Third Party Assocs., Inc., P.O. Box 13306, Oakland, CA 94661-0306 USA (SAN 127-7294) Tel 510-339-2323; Fax: 510-339-6729; Toll Free: 888-339-2323
E-mail: paulmico@tpaserver.com
Web site: http://www.tpaserver.com.

Third Week Bks., *(978-0-9712816; 978-0-9829948)* 218 Birnamwood Dr., Burnsville, MN 55337-2975 USA Tel 612-990-6011
E-mail: caroleao@yahoo.com
Web site: http://ThirdWeekBooks.com.

Third World Games, Inc., *(978-0-9728526)* P.O. Box 667, Westminster, CA 92684-0667 USA Tel 714-357-2967
E-mail: companyisbn-dir@thirdworldgames.com
Web site: http://www.thirdworldgames.com.

Third World Press, *(978-0-88378)* P.O. Box 19730, Chicago, IL 60619 USA (SAN 202-778X) Tel 773-651-0700; Fax: 773-651-7286
E-mail: TWPress3@aol.com
Web site: http://www.thirdworldpressinc.com
Dist(s): **Austin & Company, Inc.**
Chicago Distribution Ctr.
Ingram Publisher Services.

Third-Career Pr., LLC, *(978-0-9988731)* 212 Magnolia Bluff Dr., COLUMBIA, SC 29229 USA Tel 516-398-2235
E-mail: HalinaSchafer@gmail.com.

Thirsty Horse LLC, *(978-0-9723127)* 1220 N. Market St., Suite 606, Wilmington, DE 19801-2598 USA (SAN 254-7767) Tel 302-428-1222
E-mail: orders@thirsty-horse.com
Web site: http://www.thirsty-horse-media.com.

Thirsty Sponge Publishing Co., *(978-0-9797960)* 898 Southgate Dr., Cookeville, TN 38501 USA.

Thirty-Three Hundred Pr., *(978-0-9646017)* 3300 Mission St., San Francisco, CA 94110 USA Tel 415-826-6886; 300 Vicksburg St., No. 5, San Francisco, CA 94114
Dist(s): **SPD-Small Pr. Distribution.**

This is RED, *(978-0-9767646)* 1 Furnace Rd., Hollidaysburg, PA 16648 USA
E-mail: gimmygum@gimmygum.com
Web site: http://www.gimmygum.com.

This Joy Bks., *(978-0-9821835; 978-0-9834546; 978-0-692-78357-3; 978-1-7323722)* 1111 Loyola Dr., Libertyville, IL 60048 USA Tel 847-401-7668
E-mail: mjvelotta@comcast.net.

This Little Light Productions, *(978-1-7324559)* 28 Balmoral Ct., Aberdeen, NJ 07747 USA Tel 646-320-4089
E-mail: suzvreeland@gmail.com.

Thistle Publishing, *(978-1-879403)* 11985 Cherokee Cir., Shelby Township, MI 48315 USA Tel 586-781-7039; Fax: 586-589-6011
Dist(s): **CreateSpace Independent Publishing Platform.**

Thistledown Pr., Ltd. (CAN) *(978-0-920066; 978-0-920633; 978-1-895449; 978-1-894345; 978-1-897235; 978-1-77187) Dist. by* **IngramPubServ.**

Thistlewood Publishing, *(978-0-9821507; 978-0-9853600)* 92 Wayside Ln., Apalachin, NY 13732 USA
E-mail: gnw@stny.rr.com; gwestover@thistlewoodpublishing.com
Web site: http://www.thistlewoodpublishing.com.

Thomas, Aisha, *(978-1-7330464)* 8101 Shin Oak Dr, Live Oak, TX 78233 USA Tel 240-691-6531
E-mail: aishamthomas@gmail.com
Web site: Aishathomas.org.

Thomas, Aldara, *(978-1-7368005)* 7131 Arlington Rd. No. 223, Bethesda, MD 20814 USA Tel 202-569-2227
E-mail: aldara.thomas@hotmail.com.

Thomas & Kay, LLC, *(978-0-9729505)* N37w26805 Kopmeier Dr., Pewaukee, WI 53072 USA (SAN 255-7576) Tel 414-581-0449
E-mail: susan@solutionsbysusan.com
Web site: http://www.solutionsbysusan.com.

Thomas & Mercer *Imprint of* **Amazon Publishing**

Thomas & Renae Barlow, *(978-0-578-29679-1)* 4143 Rte. 414, North Rose, NY 14516 USA Tel 315-960-4977
E-mail: thomasbarlow2580@gmail.com.

Thomas & Sons Bks., *(978-0-9758800)* 33 Greenwich Ave., Suite 7L, New York, NY 10014 USA
E-mail: willysthom@rcn.com.

Thomas, Angelo, *(978-0-692-16926-1)* 5505 W. Pages Ln., LOUISVILLE, KY 40258 USA Tel 502-889-6637
E-mail: imangelothomas@gmail.com
Dist(s): **Ingram Content Group.**

Thomas, Brandis, *(978-0-9792526)* P.O. Box 690162, Houston, TX 77269 USA.

†Thomas, Charles C. Pub., Ltd., *(978-0-398)* 2600 S. First St., Springfield, IL 62704 USA (SAN 201-9485) Tel 217-789-8980; Fax: 217-789-9130; Toll Free: 800-258-8980
E-mail: books@ccthomas.com; dmccarty@ccthomas.com; editorial@ccthomas.com
Web site: http://www.ccthomas.com
Dist(s): **Follett School Solutions**
MyiLibrary
ebrary, Inc.; *CIP.*

Thomas, Duerre, *(978-0-9793877; 978-0-9857798)* 23505 Ferndale Ave., Port Charlotte, FL 33980 USA
E-mail: d_jacel@yahoo.com; madpastor1@gmail.com
Web site: http://www.duerrethomas.com.

Thomas Expressions, Incorporated *See* **Thomas Expressions, LLC**
Thomas Expressions, LLC, *(978-0-9713573; 978-0-9771059)* Orders Addr.: 390 S. Tyndall Pkwy., #294, Panama City, FL 32404 USA Fax: 850-785-6408; Toll Free: 866-570-5560
E-mail: thomasexpressions@gmail.com
Web site: http://www.thomasexpressions.com; http://www.didyano.com
Dist(s): **Follett School Solutions.**
Thomas, Frederic Inc., *(978-0-9747133; 978-1-933443)* 5621 Strand Blvd. Ste. 301, Naples, FL 34110-7307 USA (SAN 255-8157); *Imprints:* Values to Live By Classic Stories (ValLiveByClass)
E-mail: freimer@fredericthomas.com; bmichalowski@fredericthomas.com
Web site: http://fredericthomas.com; http://www.healthylivingforkids.com; http://www.valuestoliveby.com.
Thomas, L.E., *(978-0-692-75690-4; 978-0-692-77301-7; 978-0-692-77357-4)* 2615 Crosswynd Terr., CUMMING, GA 30040 USA Tel 404-512-5836.
Thomas, L.J. *(978-1-7332610)* 356 Warren Ave, Zumbrota, MN 55992 USA Tel 605-270-1993
E-mail: laura.mokrzycki@gmail.com.
Thomas Max Publishing, *(978-0-9764052; 978-0-9788571; 978-0-9799950; 978-0-9822189; 978-0-9842626; 978-0-9846347; 978-0-9972920)* P.O. Box 250054, Atlanta, GA 30325-1054 USA Tel 404-794-6588
E-mail: LeeC@thomasmax.com; bee.ell.cee@comcast.net
Web site: http://www.thomasmax.com.
Thomas More Publishing, *(978-0-692-75285-2)*.
Thomas Pubns., *(978-0-939631; 978-1-57747)* 3245 Fairfield Rd., Gettysburg, PA 17325 USA (SAN 663-7213) Tel 717-642-6600; Fax: 717-642-5555; Toll Free: 800-840-6782 Do not confuse with companies with the same name in Austin, TX, La Crescenta, CA
E-mail: jim@horsesoldier.com
Web site: http://www.thomaspublications.com.
Thomas, R. E., *(978-0-9761077)* P.O. Box 53091, Houston, TX 77052 USA.
Thomas, Richard Kayeen *See* **MarWel Enterprises, Inc.**
Thomas, Sheldon Wade, *(978-0-9670539)* 1091 Thomas S. Boyland St., Brooklyn, NY 11236 USA Tel 718-495-6002 (phone/fax).
Thomas, Steve Art & Illustration, *(978-0-692-10564-1)* 22040 Iden Ave. N., Forest Lake, MN 55025 USA Tel 651-324-4511
E-mail: artist@stevethomasart.com
Dist(s): **Ingram Content Group.**
Thomas, Thomas C. II, *(978-0-692-80928-0; 978-0-692-84277-5)* 249 Santa Rita Ave., PALO ALTO, CA 94301 USA Tel 917-428-3322.
Thomastar Publishing, *(978-0-615-17087-9)* 14241 NE Wood-Duvall Rd Suite 406, Woodinville, WA 98072 USA Tel 425-703-8807
E-mail: thomastar.publishing@hotmail.com
Dist(s): **Lulu Pr., Inc.**
Thompkins, Valerie *See* **Visionary Pr. Publishing**
Thompson, Alyce C. Books, Inc., *(978-0-9746411)* Orders Addr.: 6105 W.master St., Philadelphia, PA 19151-0827 USA; Edit Addr.: P.O. Box 664, Havertown, PA 19083 USA
E-mail: emailalyce8@aol.com; msact@altarunstransportation.com
Web site: http://alycecthompsonbooksinc.com; http://www.myspace.com/alycecthompson; http://www.myspace.com/alycecthompsonbooksinc
Dist(s): **A & B Distributors & Pubs. Group**
Afrikan World Bk. Distributor
Culture Plus Bk. Distributors
Lushena Bks.
Thompson, Angela Bolden, *(978-0-615-14774-1)* 9501 W. 171st St. Ste. Q, Tinley Park, IL 60487 USA
Web site: http://angelathompson1.tripod.com/
Dist(s): **Lulu Pr., Inc.**
Thompson, Jeniffer, *(978-0-9798551; 978-0-9888882; 978-0-9974413; 978-1-959793)* 9880 Shadow Rd., La Mesa, CA 91941 USA Tel 619-955-8286; *Imprints:* MCM Publishing (MCMPubng)
E-mail: j@monkeycmedia.com
Web site: http://www.mcmpublishing.com
Dist(s): **Midpoint Trade Bks., Inc.**
Partners Pubs. Group, Inc.
Thompson, Marsha, *(978-0-692-89125-4; 978-0-692-94710-4; 978-0-578-45157-2)* 3130 E Lafayette St., Detroit, MI 48207 USA Tel 407-953-4869
E-mail: mdthomps21@yahoo.com
Web site: www.marshathompsonbooks.com.
Thompson Mill Pr., *(978-0-9883269; 978-0-9971239; 979-8-9862730)* 2110 S. Eagle Rd., No. 368, Newtown, PA 18940 USA
E-mail: bob.regan@thompsonmillpress.com
Web site: https://www.thompsonmillpress.com; https://www.KobeeManatee.com
Dist(s): **Independent Pubs. Group.**
Thompson Original Productions LLC, *(978-0-9799216; 978-1-954544)* 11997 Youngtree Ct., Bristow, VA 20136 USA (SAN 854-7203)
E-mail: tracyathompson@hotmail.com
Web site: https://www.worldoftheorb.com/; http://www.chickenboybooks.com; www.michaelthompsonbooks.com.
Thomsen, Keith Stuart II, *(978-0-692-55783-9; 978-0-692-79741-9)* 2417 Courtland Ave, HENDERSON, NV 89074 USA Tel 702-610-3662.
Thomson Custom Solutions *See* **CENGAGE Learning Custom Publishing**
Thomson, D.C. & Co., Ltd. (GBR) *(978-0-85116; 978-1-84535) Dist. by* **APG.**
Thomson Delmar Learning *See* **Delmar Cengage Learning**
Thomson ELT, *(978-1-4240; 978-1-4282)* 25 Thomson Pl., 5th Flr., Boston, MA 02210 USA Tel 617-289-7700 Toll Free: 800-237-0053
E-mail: reply@heinle.com
Web site: http://www.elt.thomson.com
Dist(s): **CENGAGE Learning.**
Thomson Gale *See* **Cengage Gale**
Thomson, J P, *(978-0-9754365)* P.O. Box 377, Exton, PA 19341 USA Tel 610-594-1707; Fax: 610-594-1866
E-mail: montanapino@comcast.net.
Thomson Learning *See* **CENGAGE Learning**
Thomson Peterson's *See* **Peterson's**
Thomson South-Western *See* **Cengage South-Western**
Thornapple Farms, LLC, *(978-0-9749728)* 13010 W. Darrow Rd., Vermilion, OH 44089 USA Tel 440-967-2680; Fax: 440-967-2696
E-mail: ashar@hbr.net
Web site: http://www.thornapplefarms.com.
Thorncrown Publishing *Imprint of* **Yorkshire Publishing Group**
†Thorndike Pr., *(978-0-7838; 978-0-7862; 978-0-8161; 978-0-89621; 978-1-56054; 978-1-4104)* Div. of Gale Group, 295 Kennedy Memorial Dr., Waterville, ME 04901 USA Tel 207-859-1053; 207-859-1020; 207-859-1000; Toll Free Fax: 800-558-4676; Toll Free: 800-223-1244 (ext. 15); 800-877-4253 (customer resource ctr.); *Imprints:* Large Print Press (Lrg Print Pr)
E-mail: jamie.knobloch@gale.com; barb.littfield@galegroup.com; Betsy.M.Brown@thomson.com; jamie.knobloch@cengage.com
Web site: http://www.gale.com/thorndike
Dist(s): **Cengage Gale;** *CIP.*
Thornton Publishing, *(978-1-882913)* 1504 Howard St., New Iberia, LA 70560 USA Tel 337-364-2752; Fax: 318-365-0316; Toll Free: 800-551-3076 Do not confuse with companies with the same or similar names in Littleton, CO, Forest Grove, OR, Burley, ID.
Thornton Publishing, Inc., *(978-0-9670242; 978-0-9719597; 978-0-9723309; 978-1-932344; 978-0-9774761; 978-0-9779960; 978-0-9801941; 978-0-9820838; 978-0-9824705; 978-0-9844838; 978-0-9845417; 978-0-9846342; 978-0-9856151; 978-0-9889816)* 17011 Lincoln Ave., No. 408, Parker, CO 80134 USA Tel 303-794-8888; Fax: 720-863-2013; *Imprints:* Profitable Publishing (Profitable Pubng); Books To Believe In (Bks To Believe In) Do not confuse with companies with the same or similar names in New Iberia, LA, Forest Grove, OR, Burley, ID
E-mail: publisher@bookstobelievein.com
Web site: http://bookstobelievein.com; http://www.getting-published.com
Dist(s): **Follett School Solutions.**
Thorogood (GBR) *(978-1-85418) Dist. by* **Stylus Pub VA.**
Thorpe, Betsy Literary Services, *(978-0-9909865; 978-0-9994302; 978-1-7329958; 978-1-7373746)* 824 Stargard Ct., Charlotte, NC 28270 USA Tel 704-840-8471
E-mail: bthorpe@mac.com
Web site: www.betsythorpe.com.
Thorpe, Sandy, *(978-0-9764147)* 20205 NE 3rd Ct., No. 3, N. Miami Beach, FL 33179 USA
E-mail: sthorpe@trekstuff.com.
Thotsup LLC, *(978-0-9883420)* Orders Addr.: 305 NE 6th St. Suite 588, Grants Pass, OR 97526 USA Tel 541-792-0212.
ThoughtRockets, Inc., *(978-0-9766793)* 2033 Ralston Ave., No. 114, Belmont, CA 94002 USA Tel 650-592-3169 (phone/fax)
E-mail: laura@thoughtrockets.com
Web site: http://www.thoughtrockets.com.
Thoughts 2 Print Pr., *(978-1-7374617)* P.O. Box P.O. Box 22211, Indianapolis, IN 46222 USA Tel 317-762-6136
E-mail: ohsodefined@gmail.com.
THP, *(978-1-7377836)* Apt. U7 308, Plus Park Blvd, TN 37217 USA Tel 079-569-2169
E-mail: kplushtv@gmail.com.
Thread, LLC, The, *(978-1-7332966; 978-1-954347)* 340 Sycamore Dr., Buellton, CA 93427 USA Tel 732-762-0336
E-mail: Thethread2018@gmail.com.
Threatt, Cedric L., *(978-0-9720543)* Div. of Ahava Publishing, LLC, 65 Twisted Oak Cir., Odenville, AL 35120 USA
E-mail: cl3tt@windstream.net
Web site: http://www.Ahavapublishing.org.
Three Angels Broadcasting Network, *(978-0-9718083; 978-0-9720888; 978-1-934869; 978-1-942455)* Orders Addr.: P.O. Box 220, West Frankfort, IL 62896 USA Tel 618-627-4651; Edit Addr.: 3391 Charley Good Rd., West Frankfort, IL 62896 USA
Web site: http://www.3abn.org
Dist(s): **Pacific Pr. Publishing Assn.**
Three Bean Pr., *(978-0-9767276; 978-0-9882212; 978-0-9903315)* P.O. Box 301711, Jamaica Plain, MA 02130 USA (SAN 256-5137) Tel 617-584-5759; 617-827-2042
E-mail: seneca@threebeanpress.com
Web site: http://www.threebeanpress.com
Dist(s): **Partners Bk. Distributing, Inc.**
Three Cents Publishing, *(978-0-9746697)* Orders Addr.: 177 Ocean St.: PO Box 339 Brant Rock Ma02020 Usa, Boston, MA 02020 USA.
Three Chucks, *(978-1-7320463)* 216 Juniper Dr., Lancaster, PA 17602 USA Tel 717-471-8278
E-mail: jj@thelandii.com
Web site: www.jjiandis.com.
Three Conditions Pr., *(978-0-9721241)* Drawer H, Baltimore, MD 21228 USA
Web site: http://www.marylandpoetry.org
Dist(s): **Independent Pubs. Group.**
Three Cord Pr., *(978-1-949785)* P.O. Box 260, Mc Lean, VA 22101 USA Tel 202-494-8072
E-mail: jb@jbsimmons.com
Web site: www.threecordpress.com.
Three Danes Publishing LLC, *(978-0-692-30930-8; 978-0-692-35972-3; 978-0-692-41545-0; 978-0-692-43367-6; 978-0-692-54420-4; 978-0-692-59099-7; 978-0-692-63312-0; 978-0-692-74548-9; 978-0-9983036; 978-0-9983037)* 62395 friendship church rd, Amite, LA 70380 USA Tel 985-507-3401
E-mail: author@dianamariedubois.com
Web site: www.dianamariedubois.com
Dist(s): **CreateSpace Independent Publishing Platform.**
Three Flower Farm Pr., *(978-0-615-67849-8)* 24 Brooks Rd, Wayland, MA 01778 USA Tel 508-653-9307
E-mail: kjlin306@gmail.com.
Three Four Three Publishing Co., *(978-0-9675286)* 3738 Victoria Dr., West Palm Beach, FL 33406 USA Tel 917-407-2270
E-mail: paulnison@mindspring.com
Web site: http://www.rawlife.com.
Three Gate Publishing, *(978-1-7334394)* 5285 Helene Pl., West Palm Beach, FL 33407 USA Tel 443-824-0671
E-mail: ewingate86@gmail.com.
Three Hermits Pr., *(978-0-9753906)* P.O. Box 99099, Bennington, VT 05201 USA
E-mail: threehermits@mail.com.
Three Kings Publishing, *(978-0-615-66434-7; 978-0-615-67293-9; 978-0-615-68737-7; 978-0-615-82080-4; 978-0-615-83943-1; 978-0-615-84331-5; 978-0-615-84662-0; 978-0-615-85067-2; 978-0-615-89442-3; 978-0-615-89444-7; 978-0-615-89445-4; 978-0-615-89492-8; 978-0-615-89944-2; 978-0-615-89996-1; 978-0-615-91430-5; 978-0-615-94295-7; 978-0-615-99659-2; 978-0-692-44805-2; 978-0-692-54999-5; 978-1-947018) 115 Canterbury Ct., Princeton, KY 42445 USA Tel 270.601.3401*
Dist(s): **CreateSpace Independent Publishing Platform.**
Three Knolls Publishing, *(978-0-9748059; 978-0-9817939; 978-1-941138; 978-1-953487)* 1770 N Camino Sabadell, Tucson, AZ 85715 USA (SAN 179-2709) Tel 520-603-2094
E-mail: editor@3knollspub.com
Web site: http://www.3knollspub.com.
Three Leaf Pr., *(978-0-9835033)* 97 Woodbridge Dr, Colorado Springs, CO 80906 USA Tel 719-352-5828 Do not confuse with Three Leaf Pr. in Grand Haven, MI
E-mail: 3leafpress@gmail.com.
Three Owls Creative, *(978-1-7331920; 978-1-955783)* 153 Timbercreek Pines Cir., Winter Garden, FL 34787 USA Tel 407-256-9089
E-mail: shay.shivecharan@gmail.com
Web site: http://threeowlspublishing.com/.
Three Part Harmony LLC, *(978-0-9800577)* Orders Addr.: 538 Eagle Blvd., Kingsland, GA 31548 USA (SAN 855-0972) Tel 386-717-4583; 912-882-7008
E-mail: threepartharmony@earthlink.net.
Three Pebble Pr., LLC, *(978-0-9799289; 978-0-9960219)* 10040 SW 25th Ave., Portland, OR 97219-6325 USA (SAN 854-7777) Tel 503-977-0944
E-mail: info@yogacalm.org
Web site: http://www.threepebblepress.com
Dist(s): **Follett School Solutions**
Independent Pubs. Group
MyiLibrary.
Three Pups Publishing & Creative Studio, *(978-0-692-99090-2; 978-0-692-13000-1)* 5126 Co Rd 40 NE, NEW LONDON, MN 56273 USA Tel 320-354-4103
E-mail: violetdauk@tds.net
Dist(s): **Ingram Content Group.**
Three Ring Circus Publishing Hse., Inc. *Imprint of* **405 Pubns.**
Three River Rambler, *(978-0-615-20131-3)* 422 W. Cumberland Ave., Knoxville, TN 37901 USA Tel 865-524-9411; Fax: 865-546-3717
E-mail: kac@gulfandohio.com
Web site: http://threeriversrambler.com.
Three Rivers Council, BSA, Incorporated *See* **Alchemy Creative, Inc.**
Three Rooms Pr., *(978-0-9840700; 978-0-9835813; 978-0-9884008; 978-0-9895125; 978-1-941110; 978-1-953103)*
E-mail: info@threeroomspress.com
Web site: http://threeroomspress.com
Dist(s): **MyiLibrary**
Publishers Group West (PGW).
Three Sisters Communication, LLC, *(978-0-9771204)* P.O. Box 280, Star, ID 83669-5015 USA (SAN 256-7970)
E-mail: sfunk624@heritagewifi.com.
Three Sisters Pr., *(978-0-9722999)* P.O. Box 17061, Golden, CO 80402 USA Tel 720-231-6540; Fax: 303-561-0626 Do not confuse with Three Sisters Pr., in Washington, DC
E-mail: violeta134@hotmail.com; sjbrehm@comcast.net.
Three Sisters Publishing Hse., Ltd., *(978-0-9785570)* 32104 Cty. Rd., 1, Saint Cloud, MN 56303 USA Tel 320-654-0001.
Three Sixteen Publishing, *(978-1-937212; 978-1-63664)* 17692 Cowan, Suite 200, Irvine, CA 92614 USA Tel 949-756-8400; Fax: 949-756-8484
E-mail: garyk@codra.com; diana@316publishing.com
Web site: www.316publishing.com
Dist(s): **Whitaker Hse.**
Three Socks Publishing, *(978-0-9789631)* 3351 Charlotte, Brighton, MI 48114 USA.
Three Spots Productions, *(978-0-9744509)* 67 Rutz St., Stamford, CT 06906 USA
E-mail: rarruzza@optonline.net; rarruzza@sparkyswalk.com
Web site: http://www.sparkyswalk.com.
Three Trees, Inc., *(978-0-9789426)* P.O. Box 92, Cottleville, MO 63368-6336 USA Tel 636-561-9184; Fax: 636-561-9184
Web site: http://Petalwinkthefairy.com.
Three Willows Pr., *(978-0-9770279)* 4680 S. 1000 W., Rensselaer, IN 47978 USA.
Three Wise Dogs Pr., *(978-1-7323227)* 3212 Storer Ave., Oakland, CA 94619 USA Tel 469-235-3048
E-mail: chrisgray4020@gmail.com
Web site: www.threewisedogspress.com.
Three Wishes Publishing Co., *(978-0-9796380)* 26500 W. Agoura Rd., Suite 102-754, Calabasas, CA 91302 USA Tel 818-878-0902; Fax: 818-878-1805
E-mail: alva710@aol.com
Web site: http://www.alvasachs.com; http://www.threewishespublishing.com.
Three-D Vision Productions *See* **Soul Vision Works Publishing**
Threshold Editions *Imprint of* **Threshold Editions**
Threshold Editions, Div. of Simon & Schuster, 1230 Ave. of the Americas, New York, NY 10020 USA; *Imprints:* Threshold Editions (ThresholdEdit)
Dist(s): **Simon & Schuster, Inc.**
Thriller Publishing Group, Inc., *(978-0-9819993; 978-1-937888; 978-1-954518)* 218 S. McIntyre Way, Golden, CO 80401 USA
E-mail: rjjagger@yahoo.com; hansenlawfirm@aol.com.
Thriller Publishing Group, Incorporated *See* **Thriller Publishing Group, Inc.**
Thrive Christian Pr., *(978-0-9800600; 978-0-615-70585-9; 978-0-615-80812-3; 978-0-615-83170-1; 978-0-692-02147-7; 978-0-692-32996-2; 978-0-692-35235-9; 978-0-692-37545-7; 978-0-692-38909-6; 978-0-692-55350-3; 978-0-692-67848-0; 978-1-945995)* 1095 Military Trail No. 8584, Jupiter, FL 33468 USA (SAN 855-1057)
Web site: www.thrivechristianpress.com; www.believersbyline.com
Dist(s): **CreateSpace Independent Publishing Platform.**
Thrive Services, *(978-0-578-92645-2)* 66 delsan Ct., Buffalo, NY 14216 USA Tel 716-939-5074
E-mail: thrivelifeskillsservices@gmail.com.
Thriving Churches International *See* **Pastorpreneur Ministries**
Through Their Eyes Bks., *(978-0-692-34424-8; 978-0-692-41922-9)* 5 Grossweiler Ln., Parlin, NJ 08859 USA Tel 732-439-6719
E-mail: info@throughtheireyesbooks.com; info@victoriannephoenix.com
Web site: www.throughtheireyesbooks.com; www.VictoriannePhoenix.com.
Throwback Publishing, *(978-0-9771630)*
Web site: http://www.throwbackpublishing.com.
Thule Ediciones, S. L. (ESP) *(978-84-933734; 978-84-96473) Dist. by* **IPG Chicago.**
Thumb Print Productions, *(978-0-692-97849-8)* 730 Indian springs rd, Georgetown, TX 78633 USA Tel 512-508-2922
E-mail: cat.davis226@gmail.com
Dist(s): **Ingram Content Group.**
Thumbprint Publishing, *(978-0-9741833)* P.O. Box 9972, Cincinnati, OH 45209 USA Tel 513-207-7550 Do not confuse with Thumbprint Publishing in Studio City, CA
E-mail: rdavis_art@fuse.net
Web site: http://www.connectionssp.org/.
Thumbs Up Pr., *(978-0-9772513)* 3731 Reed's Landing Cir., Midlothian, VA 23113 USA Tel 804-320-8331
E-mail: thumbsuppress@earthlink.net.
Thunder Bay Pr. *Imprint of* **Readerlink Distribution Services, LLC**
Thunder Bay Pr. *Imprint of* **Printers Row Publishing Group**
Thunder Bay Pr., *(978-1-882376; 978-1-933272; 978-1-62026)* 4503 S. M-76, West Branch, MI 48661 USA Tel 989-343-5213
E-mail: thunderbaypressmichigan@gmail.com
Web site: http://www.thunderpressmichigan.com
Dist(s): **Independent Pubs. Group**
Midpoint Trade Bks., Inc.
Partners Bk. Distributing, Inc.
Thunder Child Productions LLC *See* **Thunder Child Productions LLC. dba PuppyDucks Publishing**
Thunder Child Productions LLC. dba PuppyDucks Publishing, *(978-0-9967949)* 18 Old Stage Coach Rd., Newton, NJ 07860 USA
E-mail: rcruz@puppyducks.com
Web site: www.puppyducks.com.
Thunder Enlightening, *(978-0-9832491)* 11 Cherokee Camp Trail No. 20451, JASPER, GA 30143 USA Tel 706-692-2199
E-mail: chrisrumble@gmail.com
Web site: www.chrisrumble.com.
Thunder Mountain Bks., Co., *(978-0-9968565)* 7946 E. 35th Ave, Denver, CO 80238 USA Tel 303-506-1667
E-mail: anthony@aakerr.com
Web site: www.thundermountainbooks.com.
ThunderBolt Pubns., *(978-0-615-16040-5; 978-0-578-00692-5)* 14785 Kay Ln., Atlanta, GA 30306 USA
E-mail: medernach@bellsouth.net
Web site: http://www.kenmedernach.com
Dist(s): **Lulu Pr., Inc.**
Thunderbolt Publishing *See* **We Do Listen Foundation**
ThunderBolt Publishing, *(978-0-9799671)* 113 14th Ave. S., Nampa, ID 83651 USA Tel 208-466-0122; Fax: 208-466-5294
E-mail: arlette@thunder-bolt.com.
Thunderfly Productions, *(978-0-9997311; 978-1-7355408; 979-8-9856373)* 1031 Marcia Ln., Burleson, TX 76028 USA Tel 817-999-5435
E-mail: krissidallas@gmail.com
Web site: www.KrissiDallas.com.
ThunderHousePress *See* **ARK7EVEN Entertainment**
Thundermist Consulting and Research Co., *(978-0-9759494)* P.O. Box 7023, Cumberland, RI 02864-7023 USA
E-mail: book-sales@thundermist.com
Web site: http://www.thundermist.com; http://thundermist.blogspot.com.

ThunderStone Bks., *(978-1-63411)* 6575 Horse Dr., Las Vegas, NV 89131 USA Tel 801-471-9728
E-mail: rachellynchase@msn.com
Web site: www.thunderstonebooks.com.

Thureos Bks., *(978-1-7354856)* 7941 Katy Freeway 753, Houston, TX 77024 USA Tel 713-489-1240
E-mail: BOOKS@THUREOS.COM.

Thurman Hse., LLC, *(978-1-58989)* 5 Park Ctr. Ct., Suite 300, Owings Mills, MD 21117 USA Tel 410-902-9100; Fax: 410-902-7210
E-mail: thurmanhouse@ottenheimerpub.com.

Thurner, Annette, *(978-1-7360255)* 273 Stonecliffe Aisle, Irvine, CA 92603 USA Tel 949-233-0607
E-mail: contact@annettethurner.com
Web site: www.annettethurner.com.

Thurston, Dorothy Dawn, *(978-0-692-97524-4; 978-0-578-73563-4; 978-0-578-79526-3)* 2255 So Hill Rd No. 14, St. George, UT 84790 USA Tel 435-669-4359
E-mail: dorotthurst@aol.com
Dist(s): **Ingram Content Group.**

THV Pr., *(978-1-7334107)* 2213 Voorhees Ave., Redondo Beach, CA 90278 USA Tel 424-558-0778
E-mail: shawncbaker9@gmail.com
Web site: http://thehorrorvision.com/.

Thynne, Garry R. *See* **Garry & Donna, LLC**

Tia Chucha Pr., *(978-0-9624287; 978-1-882688)* Div. of Guild Complex, Orders Addr.: Northwestern University Press, Chicago Distribution Center, 11030 S. Langley Ave., Chicago, IL 60628 USA Tel 773-296-1108; Fax: 773-528-5452; Edit Addr.: c/o Arts Bridge, P.O. Box PO Box 328, San Fernando, CA 91341 USA
E-mail: SevenRabbit54@gmail.com
Web site: http://nupress.northwestern.edu/guild; https://www.tiachucha.org/tia_chucha_press
Dist(s): **Chicago Distribution Ctr.**
Northwestern Univ. Pr.
SPD-Small Pr. Distribution.

Tianjin Education Pr.,
Dist(s): **Chinasprout, Inc.**

Tiaanya Literature Pr., *(978-0-9768679; 978-1-60508)* 613 151st St. Pl., NE, Bellevue, WA 98007 USA
E-mail: tianyapress@hotmail.com
Web site: http://www.tianyapress.com.

Tiara Bks. LLC, *(978-0-9729846)* 62 Birchall Dr., Scarsdale, NY 10583-4503 USA Tel 914-723-9133.

Tickle Me Purple, LLC, *(978-0-9990536; 978-1-7341903)* 3120 Stone Arbor Ln., Glen Allen, VA 23059 USA Tel 803-410-0008
E-mail: tmpurple@yahoo.com
Web site: www.ticklemepurple.com.

Tickling Keys, Inc., *(978-0-9724258; 978-1-932802; 978-1-61547)* 13386 Judy Ave., NW, Uniontown, OH 44685 USA Tel 330-715-2875; Fax: 707-220-4510; *Imprints*: Holy Macro! Books (Holy Macro Bks)
E-mail: consult@mrexcel.com; pub@mrexcel.com
Web site: http://www.holymacrobooks.com
Dist(s): **Ebsco Publishing**
Independent Pubs. Group
MyiLibrary
ebrary, Inc.

TICO Publishing, *(978-0-9777688)* 25045 Jaclyn Ave., Moreno Valley, CA 92557 USA (SAN 850-167X) Tel 562-292-0796
E-mail: tijerin@yahoo.com; books@ticopublishing.com.

Tidal Press, Incorporated *See* **Mushgush Pr.**

Tidal Wave Bks., *(978-0-9724770)* 4476 Wedgewood Dr., Pleasant Grove, UT 84062 USA Tel 801-785-5555; Fax: 801-785-9676
E-mail: sgraham@tidalwavebooks.com
Web site: http://www.tidalwavebooks.com
Dist(s): **Send The Light Distribution LLC.**

Tidal Wave Productions *See* **Black, Judith Storyteller**

TidalWave *See* **TidalWave Productions**

TidalWave Productions, *(978-1-948724; 978-1-949738; 978-1-954044; 978-1-955686; 978-1-955712; 978-1-956841; 978-1-959998; 978-1-962404)* 10859 NW Laurinda Ct., Portland, OR 97229 USA
E-mail: ddavis@bluewaterprod.com
Web site: tidalwavecomics.com.

Tidball, Cynthia J, *(978-1-7338938)* 2496 Cty. Rd. C2 W., No. 210, Roseville, MN 55113 USA Tel 651-633-6697
E-mail: tidballs@gmail.com.

Tide-Mark Pr., Ltd, *(978-0-936846; 978-1-55949; 978-1-59490; 978-1-63114)* Orders Addr.: 22 Prestige Park Cir., East Hartford, CT 06108-1917 USA (SAN 222-1802) Tel 860-683-4499; Fax: 860-683-4055; Toll Free: 800-338-2508; Edit Addr.: 22 Prestige Park Cir., East Hartford, CT 06108-1917 USA (SAN 665-794X)
E-mail: carol@tide-press.com
Web site: http://www.tidemarkpress.com
Dist(s): **BookBaby.**

Ties That Bind Publishing, *(978-1-954608)* 9929 53rd Ct, Pleasant Prairie, WI 53158 USA Tel 847-445-7611
E-mail: Tiesthatbindpublishing@gmail.com
Web site: Tiesthatbindpublishing.com.

TiffanyJ, *(978-0-692-08394-9)* 536 Portchester Dr., COLUMBIA, SC 29203 USA Tel 803-380-8433
E-mail: tiffywill325@gmail.com
Web site: www.iamtiffanyj.com.

Tiffin Pr. of Maine, *(978-0-9646018)* Div. of Tiffin Pr., 110 Jones Point Rd., Brooksville, ME 04617-3570 USA Tel 207-326-0916
E-mail: tiffinpress@yahoo.com; joanmacc45@gmail.com
Dist(s): **Bilingual Pubns. Co., The.**

Tiffiney R. McDaniel, *(978-1-7354173)* 7730 Deer Trail, Trussville, AL 35173 USA Tel 205-705-8451; Fax: 205-655-2909
E-mail: TraVoris@att.net.

Tiger Iron Pr., *(978-0-9787263; 978-0-9851745; 979-8-9858829)* Orders Addr.: 4 Hopscotch Ln., Savannah, GA 31411 USA Tel 478-474-2323
E-mail: Sales@TigerIronPress.com
Web site: http://www.TigerIronPress.com; http://Http://www.TI-Holdings.com
Dist(s): **TI-Holdings Distribution Co.**

Tiger Lilia Publishing *See* **TA-DA! Language Productions, Inc.**

Tiger Lily Publishing, *(978-1-880883)* Six Swift Ct., Newport Beach, CA 92663 USA Tel 949-645-5907; Toll Free: 800-950-3237 (800-950-DADS)
E-mail: janedrew@home.com.

Tiger Publishing *See* **Tiger Tale Publishing Co.**

Tiger Stripe Publishing, *(978-0-9905895; 978-1-7355729)*
E-mail: jet@tigerstripepub.com.

Tiger Tale Publishing Co., *(978-0-9787533; 978-0-9859579)* 522 N. Grant Ave., Odessa, TX 79761 USA Tel 432-337-8511; Fax: 432-337-1035
E-mail: cynthia.l.clack@gmail.com
Dist(s): **BookBaby.**

Tiger Tales, *(978-1-58925; 978-1-68010; 978-1-944530; 978-1-6643)* ; *Imprints*: 360 Degrees (360 Degrees)
E-mail: barbknight@tigertalesbooks.com
Web site: http://www.tigertalesbooks.com
Dist(s): **Children's Plus, Inc.**
Midpoint National, Inc.
Penguin Random Hse. Distribution
Penguin Random Hse. LLC.

Tiger Tales Pubns., *(978-0-9610576)* 103 Monte Cresta, Oakland, CA 94611 USA (SAN 264-4347) Tel 510-653-8422.

Tigermoth Pubns., *(978-0-9844785)* P.O. Box 4367, Tulsa, OK 74159 USA (SAN 859-4953)
Web site: http://www.tigermothpublications.com.

TIGO & Co., *(978-0-9761167)* P.O. Box 210066, Dallas, TX 75211-0066 USA Tel 214-330-4420
E-mail: thekingskid1982@sbcglobal.net.

Tike Time, Inc., *(978-0-9729093)* Orders Addr.: 872 S. Milwaukee, No. 125, Libertyville, IL 60048 USA (SAN 255-3058)
E-mail: info@tiketime.com
Web site: http://www.tiketime.com.

Tiki Machine, LLC, *(978-0-615-39785-6; 978-0-615-49510-1; 978-0-615-54715-2; 978-0-615-65028-9; 978-0-9894507; 978-0-692-22851-7)* 160 W. Foothill Pkwy. Suite 105 No. 171, Corona, CA 92882 USA Tel 818-237-6325
Web site: www.tikimachine.blogspot.com; www.tikimachine.com.

Tiki Tales, *(978-0-9740582)* P.O. Box 1194, Haiku, HI 96708 USA
Dist(s): **Booklines Hawaii, Ltd.**

Tikva Corp., *(978-0-615-12595-4)* 40 W. 23rd St., New York, NY 10010-5215 USA
E-mail: emilyl@mkugodessa.org.

Tilbury Hse. Pubs., *(978-0-88448; 978-0-937966; 978-1-937644; 978-1-958394)* 12 Starr St., Thomaston, ME 04861 USA Toll Free: 800-582-1899 (orders)
E-mail: tilbury@tilburyhouse.com; mariellen@tilburyhouse.com
Web site: http://www.tilburyhouse.com
Dist(s): **Children's Plus, Inc.**
INscribe Digital
Lectorum Pubns., Inc.
Norton, W. W. & Co., Inc.
Rowman & Littlefield Publishers, Inc.
SPD-Small Pr. Distribution
Univ. Pr. of New England.

Tillinger, Theresa D., *(978-0-692-93617-7; 978-0-578-64581-0)* 5426 Old 96, FRANKLIN, TN 37064 USA Tel 203-526-6806
E-mail: Theresa.tillinger@gmail.com
Dist(s): **Ingram Content Group.**

†Timber Pr., Inc., *(978-0-88192; 978-0-917304; 978-0-931146; 978-0-931340; 978-1-60469; 978-1-64326)* Div. of Workman Publishing Co., Inc., 133 SW Second Ave., Suite 450, Portland, OR 97204-3527 USA (SAN 216-082X) Tel 503-227-2878; Fax: 503-227-3070; Toll Free: 800-327-5680; 20 Lonsdale Rd Swavesey, London, NW6 6RD Tel (01954) 232959; Fax: (01954) 206040
E-mail: info@timberpress.co.uk; publicity@timberpress.com
Web site: http://www.timberpress.com
Dist(s): **Blackstone Audio, Inc.**
Ebsco Publishing
Hachette Bk. Group
Meredith Bks.
Open Road Integrated Media, Inc.
Workman Publishing Co., Inc.; *CIP.*

Timberwood Pr., *(978-0-9745454)* 112 NW 156th St., Shoreline, WA 98177 USA Tel 206-295-6186
E-mail: kearney@timberwoodpress.com
Web site: http://www.timberwoodpress.com
Dist(s): **Partners Bk. Distributing, Inc.**

Time & Chance Publishing, *(978-0-9748274)* Orders Addr.: P.O. Box 488, New York, NY 10116 USA Tel 718-370-3655 [phone/fax]
E-mail: tandchpublishing@yahoo.com; timeandchancepublishing@yahoo.com
Dist(s): **Culture Plus Bks.**

Time & We *See* **Liberty Publishing Hse., Inc.**

Time Dancer Press *See* **5 Star Stories, Inc.**

Time For Kids *Imprint of* **Time Inc. Bks.**

Time Home Entertainment *Imprint of* **Time Inc. Bks.**

Time Home Entertainment, Incorporated *See* **Time Inc. Bks.**

Time Inc. Bks., *(978-1-883013; 978-1-929049; 978-1-931933; 978-1-932273; 978-1-932994; 978-1-933405; 978-1-933821; 978-1-60320; 978-1-61893; 978-1-68330; 978-1-5478)* Div. of Time, Inc., 1271 Avenue of the Americas, New York, NY 10020-1201 USA (SAN 227-3209); 225 Liberty St., New York, NY 10281; *Imprints*: Time Home Entertainment (TimeHomeEnt); Real Simple Books (RealSimpleBks); Sports Illustrated Books (SportsIllusBks); Liberty Street (LibertySt); Time For Kids (TimeForKids); Southern Living (SouthernLiving)
Dist(s): **Children's Plus, Inc.**
Hachette Bk. Group
Independent Pubs. Group
MyiLibrary
National Bk. Network
Rowman & Littlefield Publishers, Inc.
Rowman & Littlefield Unlimited Model.

Time to Organize, *(978-0-9786733)* 1414 Willow Creek Ln., Shoreview, MN 55126 USA Tel 651-717-1284
E-mail: sara@time2organize.net.

Time to Sign, Incorporated, *(978-0-9713666; 978-0-9765364)* Orders Addr.: P.O. Box 110308, Palm Bay, FL 32911 USA Tel 321-723-6997; Fax: 321-723-6896; Edit Addr.: 426 Olsmar St., Palm Bay, FL 32908 USA Do not confuse with Talking Hands, Inc., in Bangor, ME
E-mail: contact@timetosign.com
Web site: http://www.timetosign.com.

Time Warner Book Group *See* **Hachette Bk. Group**

Time Warner Custom Publishing, *(978-1-931722; 978-1-59995)* 1271 Ave. of the Americas, New York, NY 10020 USA Tel 212-522-7381
Dist(s): **Hachette Bk. Group.**

†Timeless Bks., *(978-0-931454; 978-1-932018)* Div. of Assn. for the Development of Human Potential, Orders Addr.: P.O. Box 3543, Spokane, WA 99220-3543 USA (SAN 211-6502) Fax: 509-838-6652; Toll Free: 800-251-9273; P.O. Box 9, Kootenay Bay, BC V0B 1X0 Tel 250-227-9224 (Business Office); Fax: 250-227-9494 (orders); Toll Free: 800-661-8711 (orders) Do not confuse with Timeless Books in Pickerington, OH
E-mail: info@timeless.org; orders@timeless.org; bookstore@timeless.org; Contact@timeless.org
Web site: http://timeless.org
Dist(s): **Lulu Pr., Inc.**
New Leaf Distributing Co., Inc.; *CIP.*

Timeless Voyager Pr., *(978-1-892264)* Orders Addr.: 249 Iris Ave., Goleta, CA 93117 USA; Edit Addr.: P.O. Box 6678, Santa Barbara, CA 93160 USA (SAN 253-9233) Tel 805-455-8895; Fax: 805-683-4456; Toll Free: 800-576-8463
E-mail: bsh@timelessvoyager.com
Web site: http://www.timelessvoyager.com.

Time-Life Education, Inc., *(978-0-7054; 978-0-7370; 978-0-7835; 978-0-8094)* Orders Addr.: P.O. Box 85026, Richmond, VA 23285-5026 USA Toll Free Fax: 800-449-2011; Edit Addr.: 2000 Duke St., Alexandria, VA 22314 USA Tel 703-838-7000; Fax: 703-518-4124; Toll Free: 800-449-2010
E-mail: education@timelifecs.com
Web site: http://www.timelifeedu.com/
Dist(s): **Hachette Bk. Group.**

†Time-Life, Inc., *(978-0-7835; 978-0-8094)* Div. of Time Warner Co., Orders Addr.: Three Center Plaza, Boston, MA 02108-2084 USA Toll Free Fax: 800-308-1083; 800-286-9471; Toll Free: 800-277-8844; 800-759-0190; Edit Addr.: 8280 Willow Oaks Corporate Dr., Fairfax, VA 22031-4511 USA (SAN 202-7836) Toll Free: 800-621-7026
Web site: http://www.timelifeedu.com
Dist(s): **Hachette Bk. Group**
Time-Life Publishing Warehouse
Worldwide Media Service, Inc.; *CIP.*

Timeout LLC, *(978-1-945034)* 531 77th St., West Des Moines, IA 50266 USA Tel 515-371-9710
E-mail: authorerinwatt@gmail.co.

Times Bks. *Imprint of* **Holt, Henry & Co.**

Times Square Church *See* **Petey, Rock & Roo Children's Pubns.**

Time-Together Pr., *(978-1-888384)* Orders Addr.: P.O. Box 11689, Saint Paul, MN 55111 USA Tel 612-827-1639; Fax: 612-823-6404.

T.I.M.M.-E. Co., Inc., *(978-0-9718232)* Div. of NYC Department of Education, 230 E. 25th St, Suite 2E, New York, NY 10010 USA
E-mail: tbellavia@weareallthesameinside.com; tools4tolerance@aol.com
Web site: http://www.weareallthesameinside.com
Dist(s): **Bookazine Co., Inc.**

Timothy Lane Pr., *(978-0-9744751)* 3211 Rosewood Dr., Hattiesburg, MS 39401-4517 USA
Web site: http://www.robynjackson.com.

Timshel Literature, *(978-0-9708317)* P.O. Box 751, Portsmouth, RI 02871 USA Tel 401-835-7156
E-mail: jkatz@timshelarts.com
Web site: http://www.timshelarts.com.

Timtu Ink., *(978-0-9742460)* 11 Via Acuatica, Rancho Santa Margarita, CA 92688-1482 USA (SAN 255-6146); 31441 Santa Margarita Pkwy., Suite A, No. 341, Rancho Santa Margarita, CA 92688
E-mail: timtuink@dslextreme.com
Web site: http://www.dragonopolis.com; http://www.dragonia.net.

Timun Mas, Editorial S.A. (ESP) *(978-84-480; 978-84-7176; 978-84-7722)* *Dist. by* **AIMS Intl.**

Timun Mas, Editorial S.A. (ESP) *(978-84-480; 978-84-7176; 978-84-7722)* *Dist. by* **Lectorum Pubns.**

Tin Hse. Bks., LLC, *(978-0-9773127; 978-0-9776989; 978-0-9794198; 978-0-9802436; 978-0-9820539; 978-0-9825030; 978-0-9825048; 978-0-9825691; 978-1-935639; 978-0-9850469; 978-0-9857869; 978-1-941040; 978-1-947793; 978-1-951142; 978-1-953534; 978-1-959030)* 2601 NW Thurman St., Portland, OR 97210 USA (SAN 257-2273) Tel 503-219-0622; Fax: 971-222-2548
E-mail: meg@tinhouse.com; beth@tinhouse.com
Web site: http://www.tinhouse.com
Dist(s): **MyiLibrary**
Norton, W. W. & Co., Inc.
Penguin Random Hse. Distribution
Penguin Random Hse. LLC.

TinaYoungPublishing *See* **Young Publishing**

TinBoxPr., *(978-0-9835546)* 550 E. Fourth No. 4f, Cincinnati, OH 45202 USA Tel 513-871-4205
E-mail: info@tinboxpress.com.

Tingley, Megan Bks. *Imprint of* **Little, Brown Bks. for Young Readers**

TINK INK Publishing, *(978-0-9840916)* 6817 W. Lariat Ln., Peoria, AZ 85383 USA Toll Free: 888-829-5117
Web site: http://www.tinkinkpublishing.com.

Tink Tales, LLC, *(978-1-7363113)* P.O. Box 191098, Boise, ID 83719 USA Tel 208-473-0898
E-mail: dtink2014@gmail.com.

Tinker Toddlers *Imprint of* **GenBeam LLC**

TinkerToddlers *See* **GenBeam LLC**

Tinkertown Museum, *(978-0-9793124)* Orders Addr.: P.O. Box 303, Sandia Park, NM 87047 USA (SAN 853-1161) Tel 505-281-5233; Edit Addr.: 121 Sandia Crest Rd., Sandia Park, NM 87047-0303 USA
E-mail: tinker4u@tinkertown.com
Web site: http://www.tinkertown.com.

Tinlizzy Publishing, *(978-1-7357363; 978-1-953814)* 5995 Fescue Dr., Colorado Springs, CO 80923 USA Tel 719-373-9702
E-mail: jonihmccoy@gmail.com
Web site: www.tinlizzypublishing.com.

Tino Turtle Travels, LLC, *(978-0-9793158; 978-0-9816297)* 8550 W. Charleston Blvd., Suite 102-398, Las Vegas, NV 89117 USA (SAN 853-0920) Tel 702-499-4477; Toll Free Fax: 800-656-4641
E-mail: info@tinoturtletravels.com
Web site: http://www.tinoturtletravels.com.

Tinsley Phelps, LLC *See* **Write Sing Work, Inc**

Tintagel Publications, *(978-0-9743718)* 45 Lapeer St., Lake Orion, MI 48362 USA.

Tintinatie Publishing Hse., *(978-0-9842625; 978-0-9830884; 978-0-9966540)* 32315 Corte Zamora, Temecula, CA 92592 USA Tel 888-998-4684
E-mail: natalie.tinti@tintinatie.com
Web site: http://tintinatiepublishing.com; http://www.sewingafriendship.com
Dist(s): **Ingram Content Group**
Smashwords.

Tiny Global Footprints, *(978-1-7334586; 978-1-7378577)* 2201 Ludlam Rd. Unit 312, Miami, FL 33155 USA Tel 612-730-0298
E-mail: haile.deborah@gmail.com
Web site: www.tinyglobalfootprints.com.

Tiny Owl Publishing Ltd. (GBR) *(978-1-910328)* *Dist. by* **Consort Bk Sales.**

Tiny Stachel Pr., *(978-0-9845318; 978-0-9849146)* 311 W. Seymour St., Philadelphia, PA 19144 USA Tel 215-266-9587
E-mail: TinySatchelPress@gmail.com
Web site: http://www.TinySatchelPress.com
Dist(s): **Two Rivers Distribution.**

Tiny Teal Bks., *(978-1-7364138)* 11295 Raging Brook Dr., BOWIE, MD 20720 USA Tel 3017686171
E-mail: srashad107@gmail.com; tinytealbooks@gmail.com
Web site: www.tinytealbooks.com
Dist(s): **Ingram Content Group.**

Tiny Tortoise Publishing, LLC, *(978-0-9787477)* Orders Addr.: P.O. Box 752123, Las Vegas, NV 89136 USA Tel 702-798-6646.

TinydragonBks., *(978-0-9906401)* 310 Springs Crossing, Canton, GA 30114 USA Tel 678-895-9689
E-mail: triphughes6@gmail.com
Web site: http://tinydragonbooks.wix.com/hornswoggle.

Tip Top Bks., *(978-0-9846830; 978-0-9904899; 978-1-954130)*
E-mail: karleen@karleent.com
Web site: http://tiptopbooks.us/; http://www.karleent.com/.

Tip-Of-The-Moon Publishing Co., *(978-0-9657047; 978-0-9746372; 978-0-9829121; 978-0-692-93276-6; 978-1-7326618)* Orders Addr.: 175 Crescent Rd., Farmville, VA 23901 USA; Edit Addr.: c/o Francis E. Wood, Jr., Rte. 2, Box 1725, Farmville, VA 23901 USA Tel 434-392-4195; Fax: 434-392-5724
E-mail: fewwords@moonstar.com
Web site: http://www.tipofthemoon.com.

Tippins, Karen, *(978-0-9861997)* 112 Fairway Ln., Pittsburgh, PA 15238 USA Tel 412-999-1211
E-mail: kat12345@verizon.net.

Tisdale, Edward W., *(978-0-9744166)* 3420 SW 1st Pl., Cape Coral, FL 33914 USA.

Tish & Co. LLC, *(978-0-9793419)* 10 Twin Pines Ln. No. 205, Belmont, CA 94002-3889 USA (SAN 853-182X)
Web site: http://www.tishandcompany.com
Dist(s): **Big Tent Bks.**
Music, Bks. & Business, Inc.

Tishomingo Tree Pr., The, *(978-0-9768861; 978-0-9986961)* 606 Bay St., Hattiesburg, MS 39401 USA
E-mail: info@tishomingotree.com
Web site: http://www.tishomingotree.com.

Titan Bks. Ltd. (GBR) *(978-0-907610; 978-1-84023; 978-1-85286; 978-1-900097; 978-1-84576; 978-1-84856; 978-0-85768; 978-1-78116; 978-1-78276; 978-1-78329; 978-1-78565; 978-1-78909; 978-1-80336)* *Dist. by* **Peng Rand Hse.**

Titan Publishing, *(978-0-9770680)* P.O. Box 2457, Glen Allen, VA 23058 USA (SAN 256-6737)
E-mail: sales@titan-media.com
Web site: http://www.titan-media.com.

Titletown Publishing, LLC, *(978-0-9820009; 978-0-9837547; 978-0-9888605; 978-0-9910699; 978-0-9911938; 978-1-955047)* Orders Addr.: P.O. Box 12093, Green Bay, WI 54304 USA Tel 920-737-8051; Edit Addr.: 1581 Forest Glen Dr., Green Bay, WI 54304 USA
E-mail: tracy@titletownpublishing.com
Web site: http://www.titletownpublishing.com
Dist(s): **Independent Pubs. Group**
Midpoint Trade Bks., Inc.
MyiLibrary.

Titlewaves Publishing, *(978-1-57077)* 1579 Kuhio Hwy., Suite 104, Kapaa, HI 96746 USA (SAN 152-1357) Tel 808-822-7449; Fax: 808-822-2312; Toll Free: 800-835-0583
E-mail: transform@hshawaii.com
Web site: http://www.bestbookshawaii.com; http://www.writersdirect.com.

Titus Institute of California *See* **ECF Bks.**

Tiville Press *See* **MiraQuest**

Publisher Name Index

ixlini Scriptorium, Inc., *(978-0-9723720)* 681 Grove St., San Luis Obispo, CA 93401 USA Tel 805-543-3540; Fax: 805-543-5195
E-mail: tixlini@yahoo.com.

izbit Books, LLC, *(978-0-9760553)* 304 Rte. 22 W., Springfield, NJ 07081 USA Tel 973-564-7200; Fax: 973-564-8895
E-mail: jill@tizbitbooks.com
Web site: http://www.tizbitbooks.com.

T.J. Publishing, *(978-0-9760811)* 1099 E. Champlain, Suite A, No. 152, Fresno, CA 93720 USA Tel 559-297-5559
E-mail: tjpub@aol.com.

TJG Management Publishing Services, Incorporated *See* **Gonsalves, Theresa Joyce**

TJMF Publishing, *(978-0-9759314; 978-0-9789705; 978-0-9801003; 978-0-9829447; 978-0-9910671)* P.O. Box 2923, Clarksville, IN 47131-2923 USA Tel 812-288-7597; Fax: 812-288-1329
E-mail: jimf@dialinn.com
Web site: http://www.tjmfpublishing.com.

TJMF Publishing Daylight Enterprises *See* **TJMF Publishing**

TK Enterprises, *(978-0-9977327; 978-1-7324354)* 5121 Corbina Way, Oxnard, CA 93035 USA Tel 310-591-2779
E-mail: tke@isle.net
Web site: www.archieartichoke.com.

TK SPP *See* **IIG Pub**

Tkac, John Enterprises LLC, *(978-0-9794454)* Orders Addr.: P.O. Box 7813, Delray Beach, FL 33482 USA Tel 954-632-6360; Fax: 561-330-6917; Edit Addr.: 1095 Hibiscus Ln., Delray Beach, FL 33444 USA
E-mail: adstkac@aol.com
Web site: http://www.jtack.com.

TLC, *(978-0-9853560)* 12 W. End Ave., Old Greenwich, CT 06870 USA Tel 203-344-9548
E-mail: tanyalceco@optonline.net.

TLC Information Services, *(978-0-9771594)* Orders Addr.: P.O. Box 944, Yorktown Heights, NY 10598 USA Tel 914-248-6770; Edit Addr.: 3 Louis Dr., Katonah, NY 10536-3122 USA
E-mail: ifaywanli@yahoo.com
Web site: http://www.mwsearch.com.

TLC Publishing, *(978-0-9721517)* c/o Tiller Lactation Consulting, 5221 Rushbrook Dr., Centreville, VA 20120 USA Tel 703-266-3823 Do not confuse with TLC Publishing in Paonia, CO
E-mail: stiller@breastfeeding101.com
Web site: http://www.breastfeeding101.com.

TLConcepts, Inc. *Imprint of* **Tender Learning Concepts**

TLK Pubns., *(978-0-9752558; 978-0-9970438)* Div. of TLK Enterprise, 762 Heather Ln., Easton, PA 18040 USA Tel 973-906-2814
E-mail: ugochuik@yahoo.com
Web site: http://www.tlkenterprise.com
Dist(s): **Lulu Pr., Inc.**

TLOV Publishing *Imprint of* **Kaloustian, Varak**

TLS Consulting *See* **TLS Publishing**

TLS Publishing, *(978-0-9716244)* P.O. Box 403, Dobbs Ferry, NY 10522 USA Tel 914-674-2257 Do not confuse with TLS Publishing in Irvine, CA
E-mail: tls@nvbb.net.

TMD Enterprises, *(978-0-9789297; 978-0-9842980)* 76 E. Blvd., Suite 11, Rochester, NY 14610-1536 USA (SAN 851-9617)
E-mail: dbeerse@tmd-enterprises.com
Web site: www.tmd-enterprises.com.

TNJ Ministries, *(978-0-9762770)* 8214 SW 52nd Ln., Gainesville, FL 32608 USA Tel 352-376-8930
E-mail: tnj_ministries@yahoo.com
Web site: http://www.wtswlg.bravehost.com.

TNMG Publishing, *(978-0-9768297)* P.O. Box 1032, Winter Park, FL 32790-1032 USA
Web site: http://www.tnmg.ws.

TNT Bks., *(978-1-885227)* Orders Addr.: 3657 Cree Dr., Salt Lake City, UT 84120-2867 USA
E-mail: twixom@msn.com.

TNT Publishing *See* **Reasor, Teresa J.**

TNT Publishing Co., *(978-0-9800860)* P.O. Box 456, Richmond, CA 94808-9991 USA (SAN 855-1634) Tel 510-334-2533
E-mail: tanithtyler@yahoo.com
Web site: http://tntpublishing.com.

To The Stars.., *(978-1-943272; 978-0-578-43460-5)* 1051 s. coast hwy 101, encinitas, CA 92024 USA Tel 760-645-1045
E-mail: kari@tothestarsinc.com
Web site: www.tothestarsinc.com
Dist(s): **INscribe Digital**
Independent Pubs. Group
Simon & Schuster, Inc.

Toasted Coconut Media LLC, *(978-1-934906)* 200 Second Ave 4th Flr., Suite 40, New York, NY 10003 USA (SAN 855-4862) Tel 917-658-6560
E-mail: donuts@toastedcoconutmedia.com; sales@toastedcoconutmedia.com
Web site: http://www.toastedcoconutmedia.com
Dist(s): **Diamond Comic Distributors, Inc.**
Diamond Bk. Distributors.

TOAT Venture LLC, *(978-0-9745386)* 2138 45th Ave. FL3, Long Island City, NY 07110 USA Tel 917-279-5920; *Imprints:* FancyCrazy Publishing (MYID_Z_FANCYCR)
E-mail: fch3000@yahoo.com; baltazarray@gmail.com
Web site: http://www.FancyCrazyHydrants.com.

Toby & Tutter Publishing, *(978-0-9847812)* 817 W. End Ave. No. 5E, New York, NY 10025-5319 USA (SAN 920-6868) Tel 212-663-8416; Fax: 212-663-8715
E-mail: laura@lauradwightphoto.com
Web site: http://www.tobyandtutter.com.

Toby Pr. LLC, The, *(978-1-902881; 978-1-59264; 978-965-301; 978-965-526; 978-1-61329; 978-0-9891520; 978-1-940516; 978-965-7765; 978-965-7760; 978-965-7766; 978-965-7766-25-5; 978-965-7766-63-7; 978-965-7766-23-1; 978-965-7766-35-4; 978-965-7767)* Orders Addr.: P.O. Box 8531, New Milford, CT 06776-8531 USA (SAN 253-9985) Fax: 203-830-8512 (questions & orders); Edit Addr.: P.O. Box 4044, Jerusalem, 91040 ISR Tel 972.2.633.0530; Fax: 972.2.673.9948; *Imprints:* Maggid (Maggid)
E-mail: laura@korenpub.com
Web site: http://www.tobypress.com; http://www.korenpub.com.

Todd Communications, *(978-1-57833; 978-1-878100)* 611 E. 12th Ave. Ste. 102, Anchorage, AK 99501-4663 USA (SAN 298-6280)
E-mail: editor@toddcom.com
Dist(s): **Chicago Distribution Ctr.**
Ingram Publisher Services
Wizard Works.

Toe The Line, *(978-0-9792820)* 7071 Warner Ave., Suite F-497, Huntington Beach, CA 92647-5495 USA
E-mail: toetheline@earthlink.net
Web site: http://Toetheline.org.

Tofte Literary Enterprises *See* **Creative Quill Publishing, Inc.**

Together in the Harvest Ministries, Incorporated *See* **Together in the Harvest Pubns./Productions**

Together in the Harvest Pubns./Productions, *(978-0-9637090; 978-1-892853)* Div. of Together In The Harvest Ministries, Inc., Orders Addr.: P.O. Box 612288, Dallas, TX 75261 USA Tel 817-849-8773; Fax: 888-800-1509
E-mail: contact@stevehill.org
Web site: http://www.stevehill.org.

Together, Inc., *(978-0-9764572; 978-1-933463)* 3205 Roosevelt St., NE, Saint Anthony, MN 55418 USA Tel 612-706-7836; Fax: 612-789-8008
E-mail: info@togetherinc.com; pesellors@minn.net
Web site: http://www.togetherinc.com.

Tognetti, Laurence, *(978-0-578-57502-5)* 4225 E McDowell Rd, Phoenix, AZ 85008 USA Tel 321-525-1531
E-mail: laurencetognetti@gmail.com.

Toki Productions, *(978-0-9729527)* P.O. Box 88216, Los Angeles, CA 90009-6888 USA
Web site: http://www.betteroffthan.com.

TokoBooks, LLC, *(978-0-9720436; 978-0-692-16778-6; 978-0-578-62519-5; 978-0-578-97416-3)* 1863c Brattleboro Ct., Kettering, OH 45440 USA (SAN 254-573X) Tel 937-231-4193.

Tokyopop Adult *Imprint of* **TOKYOPOP, Inc.**

TOKYOPOP, Inc., *(978-1-892213; 978-1-931514; 978-1-59182; 978-1-59532; 978-1-59816; 978-1-4278)* Div. of Mixx Entertainment, Inc., 9420 Reseda Blvd Suite 555, Northridge, CA 91324 USA Tel 323-920-5967; *Imprints:* TOKYOPOP Manga (Tokyopop Manga); Tokyopop Kids (TokyoKids); Tokyopop Adult (TokyoAdult)
Web site: http://www.tokyopop.com/
Dist(s): **Children's Plus, Inc.**
Independent Pubs. Group
MyiLibrary
Open Road Integrated Media, Inc.

Tokyopop Kids *Imprint of* **TOKYOPOP, Inc.**

TOKYOPOP Manga *Imprint of* **TOKYOPOP, Inc.**

Tokyopop Press *See* **TOKYOPOP, Inc.**

Tolana Publishing, *(978-0-9773912; 978-1-935208)* Orders Addr.: P.O. Box 719, Teaneck, NJ 07666 USA
E-mail: tolanapub@yahoo.com
Web site: http://www.tolanapublishing.com
Dist(s): **CreateSpace Independent Publishing Platform**
Ingram Content Group.

Tolbert, Kaydrie, *(978-1-7350974)* 37 E Meadow lark Ln., Elk Ridge, UT 84651 USA Tel 801-850-1063
E-mail: kaygirl24@gmail.com.

Toledo Zoo, The, *(978-0-9776974)* P.O. Box 140130, Toledo, OH 43614 USA Tel 419-385-5721; Fax: 419-724-0068
E-mail: tzgift@toledozoo.org
Web site: http://www.toledozoo.org.

Tolerance Project c/o CSS, *(978-1-942649)* P.O. Box 700, Cos Cob, CT 06807 USA Tel 203-861-4000
E-mail: amynewmark@me.com
Dist(s): **Simon & Schuster**
Simon & Schuster, Inc.

Tolstoy Dom Press, LLC *See* **Vernissage Pr., LLC**

Tolwis, *(978-1-944091)* 5211 S Cobble Creek Rd, Murray, UT 84117 USA Tel 972-522-8552
E-mail: gama@gamathewriter.com.

Tom & Susan Allen *See* **Dean's Bks., Inc.**

Tom Bird Retreats, Inc., *(978-1-62747; 978-0-578-43437-7)* 2220 Corral Rd, Sedona, AZ 86336 USA Tel 928-514-1616
E-mail: john@tombird.com
Web site: www.tombird.com.

Tom Bird Seminars, Inc. *See* **Tom Bird Retreats, Inc.**

Tom Icon, *(978-0-9987089; 978-0-9987089-4-2)* 902 Delrey, College Station, TX 77845 USA Tel 361-332-9104
E-mail: izzofzia@gmail.com
Web site: izzofzia.com.

Tomato Enterprises, *(978-0-9617357)* P.O. Box 73892, Davis, CA 95617 USA (SAN 664-0427) Tel 530-750-1832; Fax: 530-759-9741
E-mail: info@tomatoenterprises.com
Web site: http://www.tomatoenterprises.com.

Tomczak, Diane, *(978-0-578-33661-9)* 233 Jennison PL, Bay City, MI 48708-5699 USA Tel 989-225-3132
E-mail: bdtomczak@yahoo.com.

Tomlinson, Lauresa *See* **Young of Heart Publishing**

Tommy Bks. Pubng., *(978-0-9762690)* Div. of C4 Kids, 1220 N. Las Palmas, No. 201, Los Angeles, CA 90038 USA Tel 323-974-8249
E-mail: renegadepic@earthlink.net
Web site: http://www.tommybooks.net
Dist(s): **C4 Kids.**

Tommy Nelson *Imprint of* **Nelson, Thomas Inc.**

Tommye-music Corp. DBA Tom eMusic, *(978-1-62321; 979-8-89082)* 157-17 Willets Point Blvd., Whitestone, NY 11357 USA Tel 718-609-9420
E-mail: office@tommye-music.com.

Tomoka Pr., *(978-0-9657211)* Orders Addr.: 115 Coquina Ave., Ormond Beach, FL 32174 USA Tel 386-677-4219
E-mail: yvonnewpunnett@aol.com
Web site: http://www.tomokapress.com.

Tomorrow's Forefathers, Inc., *(978-0-9719405; 978-1-940793)* Orders Addr.: P.O. Box 11451, Cedar Rapids, IA 52410-1451 USA
E-mail: info@tomorrowsforefathers.com
Web site: http://www.tomorrowsforefathers.com
Dist(s): **Send The Light Distribution LLC.**

TOMY International, Inc., *(978-1-887327; 978-1-890647)* Orders Addr.: 2021 9th St., SE, Dyersville, IA 52040 USA Tel 563-875-5653; Fax: 563-875-5633; Edit Addr.: 1111 W. 22nd St., Oak Brook, IL 60523-1940 USA
E-mail: rcs@rc2corp.com; credit@rc2corp.com
Web site: http://www.learningcurve.com.

Tonepoet Publishing, *(978-0-922224)* 3069 Alamo Dr., Suite 146, Vacaville, CA 95687 USA (SAN 250-3654)
E-mail: tonepoet@jackshiner.com
Web site: http://www.jackshiner.com.

Tongue Untied Publishing, *(978-0-9745783)* Orders Addr.: P.O. Box 822, Jackson, GA 30233 USA; Edit Addr.: 2571 Hwy. 36 E., Jackson, GA 30233 USA
E-mail: maseyree2001@yahoo.com
Web site: http://www.tongueuntiedpublishing.com
Dist(s): **A & B Distributors & Pubs. Group**
Culture Plus Bk. Distributors.

Tony Franklin Cos., The, *(978-0-9714280)* 521 Ridge Rd., Lexington, KY 40503-1229 USA (SAN 254-2145)
E-mail: tf3c@aol.com; ed@crystalcommunications.biz
Web site: www.thetonyfranklin.com.

Tony Tales, *(978-0-9791362)* 6024 Cottontail Cove, Las Vegas, NV 89130 USA (SAN 852-5285) Tel 702-245-8624; Fax: 702-898-1359
E-mail: barbarites@aol.com
Web site: www.Tony.

Too Dang happy *See* **Too Dang Happy**

Too Dang Happy, *(978-1-7329877)* 111 Maggies Ln., Searcy, AR 72143 USA Tel 817-456-2966
E-mail: cynthia.anderson@onemomtoanother.com
Web site: onemomtoanother.com.

Too Fun Publishing, *(978-0-9773317)* P.O. Box 2098, Vashon Island, WA 98070 USA; 1055 SW 178th St., Vashon Island, WA 98070
E-mail: toofunpublishing@gmail.com.

Too Licky LLC, *(978-0-692-88872-8)* 937 Saratoga Dr., JACKSONVILLE, FL 32207 USA Tel 310-927-5345
Dist(s): **Ingram Content Group.**

Toobeez Project-Connect Joint Venture, *(978-0-9765670)* Div. of Connectable Color Tubes, LLC, Orders Addr.: Project Connect JV 1204 Thomas Rd., Wayne, PA 19087 USA Tel 610-975-0102 (phone/fax)
E-mail: jdonahue@toobeez.com
Web site: http://www.toobeez.com; http://www.project-connect.net.

Toodle-oo Innovative Products, *(978-0-9793145)* 2166 E. Wellington Ave., Santa Ana, CA 92701 USA (SAN 853-0890) Tel 714-558-9537
E-mail: w.kawamoto@cox.net; suszanales@adelphia.net
Web site: http://www.makebubblesgrow.com.

Tool Kits For Kids LLC, *(978-0-9819483)* Orders Addr.: P.O. Box 173, Glen Rock, NJ 07452 USA
Web site: http://www.toolkitsforkids.com.

Tools For Young Historians *Imprint of* **BrimWood Pr.**

Toolywoo Publishing, *(978-0-9600897)* 178 Water Oak Dr., Ponte Vedra Beach, FL 32082 USA Tel 904-504-3779
E-mail: sgoldmanart@bellsouth.net
Web site: sharongoldmanart.com.

TOON Books *Imprint of* **Astra Publishing Hse.**

Toon Books *Imprint of* **Astra Publishing Hse.**

Toon Books *Imprint of* **Candlewick Pr.**

TOON Books / RAW Junior, LLC, *(978-0-9799238; 978-1-935179; 978-1-943145; 978-1-954084)* 27 Greene St., New York, NY 10013 USA (SAN 854-7246) Tel 212-226-0146; Fax: 212-343-9296
E-mail: raw.junior@gmail.com
Web site: http://www.toon-books.com
Dist(s): **Children's Plus, Inc.**
Consortium Bk. Sales & Distribution
Diamond Comic Distributors, Inc.
Diamond Bk. Distributors.

Toonhound Studios, LLC, *(978-0-615-37908-1; 978-0-9833944)* 2761 Peach Dr., Little Elm, TX 75068 USA Tel 214-726-2875
E-mail: kurtz@pvponline.com
Web site: http://www.pvponline.com
Dist(s): **Diamond Comic Distributors, Inc.**

Tootle Time Publishing Co., *(978-0-9721706)* Orders Addr.: P.O. Box 62, Cade, LA 70519 USA Tel 337-364-6410; Fax: 337-364-6415; Edit Addr.: 1031 Mary Rd., New Iberia, LA 70560 USA
E-mail: marycelesteclement@yahoo.com.

Tootsiepup Pr., *(978-0-9970290)* 415 Camino de la Tierra, Corrales, NM 87048 USA Tel 505-440-3208
E-mail: liajesse@yahoo.com
Web site: tootsiesvision.org.

TOP *Imprint of* **Top Pubns., Ltd.**

Top5 Co., The, *(978-0-9746760)* Div. of Bucc Wild LLC, Orders Addr.: 785 E. Tibet Rd., Columbus, OH 43211 USA Tel 614-372-3367
E-mail: bzumfelde@hotmail.com.

Top Cat Publishing, *(978-0-9660839; 978-0-615-76812-0; 978-0-615-76816-8; 978-0-615-76817-5; 978-0-692-29330-0; 979-8-218-19808-4)* PO Box 972, Carlsborg, WA 98324 USA
E-mail: literiter@olypen.com
Web site: http://www.prostar.com/web/L-energy
Dist(s): **CreateSpace Independent Publishing Platform.**

Top Choice Pr., LLC., *(978-0-9761396)* 28 Worcester Sq., Unit No. 1, Boston, MA 02118-2943 USA Tel 617-424-9726; Fax: 617-262-0702
E-mail: tberkan@mindspring.com
Web site: http://topchoicebooks.com.

Top Drawer Ink Corp., *(978-0-9884095; 978-0-9861561; 978-1-948331)* Box 21 2659 NE 35th St., Ocala, FL 34479 USA Tel 352-564-1119
E-mail: editor@topdrawerinkcorp.com
Web site: www.topdrawerinkcorp.com.

Top Drawer Publishing, *(978-0-9887519; 978-0-9916564; 978-1-7347780)* 17888 Rd. 320, Springville, CA 93265 USA Tel 559-359-0568
E-mail: D.G.Stebbins@Azmerith.com
Web site: www.Azmerith.com.

Top Five Bks., *(978-0-9789270; 978-0-9852787; 978-1-938938)* 521 Home Ave., Oak Park, IL 60304 USA (SAN 851-9668) Tel 708-663-5133
E-mail: alex@topfivebooks.com
Web site: http://www.topfivebooks.com
Dist(s): **New Shelves Distribution.**

Top Pubns., Ltd., *(978-0-9666366; 978-1-929976; 978-1-935722; 978-1-7333283; 979-8-9784822)* Div. of Top Ventures, Ltd., Orders Addr.: P.O. Box 867564, Plano, TX 75086 USA Tel 972-960-2240; Fax: 972-233-0713; William Manchee 5101 Brouette Ct., Plano, TX 75023; *Imprints:* TOP (TOP USA)
E-mail: bill@topfiction.net; wm.manchee@gmail.com
Web site: http://toppub.com.

Top Quality Pubns., *(978-0-9726311)* Orders Addr.: 3925 Americana Dr., Tampa, FL 33634 USA
E-mail: parfisher@yahoo.com
Web site: http://www.topqualitypublications.org.

Top Shelf *Imprint of* **Jawbone Publishing Corp.**

Top Shelf Productions, *(978-1-891830; 978-1-60309)* Orders Addr.: P.O. Box 1282, Marietta, GA 30061 USA; Edit Addr.: 1150 Hungryneck Blvd. Ste C-348, Mount Pleasant, SC 29464 USA
E-mail: chris@topshelfcomix.com; crownelectric54@gmail.com
Web site: http://www.topshelfcomix.com
Dist(s): **Children's Plus, Inc.**
Consortium Bk. Sales & Distribution
Diamond Comic Distributors, Inc.
Diamond Bk. Distributors
Penguin Random Hse. Distribution
Penguin Random Hse. LLC.

Top Shelf Publishing, *(978-0-9770443)* 4124 W. Fremont Rd., Spokane, WA 99224 USA
Web site: http://www.melodramerica.com/html/grammar_keys.html.

Top That! Publishing PLC (GBR) *(978-1-902973; 978-1-84229; 978-1-84510; 978-1-904748; 978-1-905359; 978-1-84666; 978-1-84956; 978-1-78244; 978-1-78445)* *Dist. by* **IPG Chicago.**

Toplink Publishing, *(978-1-946801; 978-0-9991948; 978-1-947620; 978-1-947938; 978-1-948262; 978-1-948556; 978-1-948779; 978-1-948962; 978-1-949169; 978-1-949502; 978-1-949804; 978-1-970066; 978-1-950256; 978-1-950540; 978-1-7330557; 978-1-7330558; 978-1-7330559; 978-1-7330560; 978-1-7330561; 978-1-7331328; 978-1-7331329; 978-1-7331330; 978-1-7331331; 978-1-7331332; 978-1-7333368; 978-1-7333603; 978-1-7334214; 978-1-951464; 978-1-951518; 978-1-7340699; 978-1-7342919; 978-1-7342920)* 2227 Natmore Rd., Kelly, NC 28448 USA Tel 828-483-8791
E-mail: contact@toplinkpublishing.com
Web site: www.toplinkpublishing.com.

TopNotch Pr., *(978-0-930037; 978-1-959699)* P.O. Box 1185, Merchantville, NJ 08109 USA (SAN 669-7798) Tel 609-364-6902; Fax: 856-488-0291
E-mail: maryann@maryanndiorio.com
Web site: http://www.maryanndiorio.com.

Tor Bks. *Imprint of* **Doherty, Tom Assocs., LLC**

Tor Fantasy *Imprint of* **Doherty, Tom Assocs., LLC**

Tor Romance *Imprint of* **Doherty, Tom Assocs., LLC**

Tor Science Fiction *Imprint of* **Doherty, Tom Assocs., LLC**

Tor Teen *Imprint of* **Doherty, Tom Assocs., LLC**

†Torah Aura Productions, *(978-0-933873; 978-1-891662; 978-1-934527; 978-1-961607)* 1116 Grennell Ct., Lewisville, NC 90058 USA (SAN 692-7025) Fax: 323-585-0327; Toll Free: 800-238-6724
E-mail: jane@torahaura.com
Web site: http://torahaura.com; *CIP.*

Torah Excel, *(978-1-930925)* 6415 N. Sacramento, Chicago, IL 60645 USA Tel 773-743-7915; Fax: 773-508-9874; *Imprints:* Shazak Productions (Shazak Prods)
E-mail: torahxl@megsinet.com
Web site: http://torahxl.com.

Torah Institute of Baltimore, *(978-0-9767505)* 35 Rosewood Ln., Owings Mills, MD 21117-3704 USA Tel 410-654-3500 ext. 3; Fax: 443-394-5999
E-mail: tibexec@comcast.net
Web site: http://www.torahinstitute.org.

Torah Umesorah Pubns., *(978-0-914131; 978-1-878895)* 1090 Coney Island Ave. 3rd Flr., Brooklyn, NY 11230 USA (SAN 218-9992) Tel 718-259-1223; Fax: 718-259-1795.

Torch Flame Media, *(978-0-9988161)* 7162 Beverly Blvd, No. 225, Los Angeles, CA 90036 USA Tel 310-619-4251; Fax: 310-619-4251
E-mail: helena@girlunfiltered.com.

Torch Graphic Press *Imprint of* **Cherry Lake Publishing**

Torch Legacy Pubns., *(978-0-9763487; 978-0-9785333; 978-0-615-26544-5; 978-0-615-30182-2; 978-0-615-30191-4; 978-0-615-37024-8; 978-0-9830141; 978-0-9849441)* P.O. Box 165046, Irving, TX 75016 USA
E-mail: torchlegacypublications@msn.com
Web site: http://www.torchlegacy.com
Dist(s): **Send The Light Distribution LLC**
Smashwords.

Torchflame Bks. *Imprint of* **Light Messages Publishing**

Torchlight Publishing, *(978-1-887089; 978-0-9779785; 978-0-9817273; 978-1-937731)* Orders Addr.: P.O. Box 52, Badger, CA 93603 USA Tel 559-337-2200; Fax:

559-337-2354; Toll Free: 888-867-2458 Do not confuse with Torchlight Publishing in Colorado Springs, CO
E-mail: torchlightpublishing@yahoo.com
Web site: http://www.torchlight.com
Dist(s): **BookMasters**
Independent Pubs. Group.

Tor.com *Imprint of* **Doherty, Tom Assocs., LLC**

Torgerson Meadows Publishing, *(978-0-9767116)* 37492 Outpost Rd., NW, Grygla, MN 56727 USA Tel 218-294-6644
E-mail: sstorg@webtv.net
Web site: http://www.taolc.com.

Torgoff, Teresa, *(978-1-7342512)* 3601 5th St S, Arlington, VA 22204 USA Tel 702-981-4382
E-mail: Ttorgoff@gmail.com.

Torkavian, Devin, *(978-1-7352273)* General Delivery, Beaverton, OR 97005 USA Tel 609-703-8078
E-mail: Dtorkavian1687@gmail.com.

Tornado Creek Pubns., *(978-0-9652219; 978-0-9740881; 978-0-9821529)* P.O. Box 8625, Spokane, WA 99203-8625 USA Tel 509-838-7114; Fax: 509-455-6798; 1308 E. 29th Ave., Spokane, WA 99203 Tel 509-838-7114; Fax: 509-445-6798
E-mail: tcpoffice@comcast.net
Web site: http://www.tornadocreekpublications.com.

Torque Bks. *Imprint of* **Bellwether Media**

Torres, Eliseo & Sons, *(978-0-88303)* P.O. Box 2, Eastchester, NY 10709 USA (SAN 207-0235).

TortoiseBrand Bks., *(978-0-9847107)* 1810 S. El Camino Real Suite B101, Encinitas, CA 92024 USA Tel 760-213-3722 (phone/fax)
E-mail: lovely@AliciaPrevin.com
Web site: www.AliciaPrevin.com.

Tortuga Pr., *(978-1-889910)* Orders Addr.: PMB 181, 2777 Yulupa Ave., Santa Rosa, CA 95405 USA (SAN 299-1756) Tel 707-544-4720; Fax: 707-544-5609; Toll Free: 866-4 TORTUGA
E-mail: info@tortugapress.com
Web site: http://www.tortugapress.com
Dist(s): **Follett School Solutions**
Independent Pubs. Group.

Torty2 Publishing, *(978-0-9996326)* 1372 Trieste Ln., Carpinteria, CA 93013 USA Tel 805-722-7248
E-mail: Torty2@aol.com
Web site: Torty2Publishing.com.

Total 180 Pr., *(978-0-9744118)* Orders Addr.: P.O. Box 984, Monroe, WA 98272 USA Tel 360-794-9129; Edit Addr.: 18578 Rainier View Rd., Monroe, WA 98272 USA
E-mail: susan@howardcorp.com
Web site: http://www.total180.com.

Total Career Resources, *(978-0-615-24214-9; 978-0-9849970)* 2000 Bering Dr., Suite 460, Houston, TX 77057 USA Tel 713-784-3197.

Total Outreach for Christ Ministries, Inc., *(978-0-9745834)* 3411 Asher Ave., Little Rock, AR 72204 USA Tel 501-663-0362; Fax: 501-663-0390
E-mail: tofchristm@aol.com
Web site: http://theonenewman.org.

Total Publishing & Media *Imprint of* **Yorkshire Publishing Group**

Total Recall Learning, Inc., *(978-0-9716238)* 3944 Murphy Canyon Rd., Suite C203, San Diego, CA 92123 USA Tel 858-268-8875; *Imprints*: ExamWise (ExamWise)
E-mail: sales@totalrecallpress.com
Web site: http://www.totalrecalllearning.com
Dist(s): **Baker & Taylor Publisher Services (BTPS).**

Total Wellness *See* **Total Wellness Publishing**

Total Wellness Publishing, *(978-0-9744585)* 14545 Glenoak Pl., Fontana, CA 92337 USA
E-mail: micheleiqbal@netzero.net
Web site: http://www.Totalwellnesspublishing.com; http://www.micheleiqbal.com
Dist(s): **Distributors, The.**

Totally Outdoors Publishing, Inc., *(978-0-9726653)* 7284 Raccoon Rd., Manning, SC 29102 USA
Web site: http://www.totallyoutdoorspublishing.com.

TotalRecall Pubns., *(978-0-9704684; 978-1-59095; 978-1-64883)* Orders Addr.: 1103 Middlecreek, Friendswood, TX 77546 USA Tel 281-992-3131; Edit Addr.: 1103 Middlecreek, Friendswood, TX 77546 USA Tel 281-992-3131
E-mail: Sales@totalrecallpress.com; Bruce@totalrecallpress.com
Web site: http://www.mousegate.com; http://www.totalrecallpress.com
Dist(s): **Ingram Bk. Co.**
Ingram Content Group Inc.
MyiLibrary
ebrary, Inc.

Totem Tales Publishing, *(978-0-9843228)* 219 Salzedo St., Royal Palm Beach, FL 33411 USA Tel 561-537-2522
E-mail: books@totemtales.com; danbodenstein@yahoo.com
Web site: http://www.totemtales.com
Dist(s): **BookBaby.**

Toucan Pr., Inc., *(978-0-9744926)* 307 Sweet Bay Pl., Carrboro, NC 27510-2378 USA.

Toucan Valley Pubns., Inc., *(978-0-9634017; 978-1-884925)* Orders Addr.: P.O. Box 15520, Fremont, CA 94539-2620 USA Tel 510-498-1009; Fax: 510-498-1010; Toll Free Fax: 888-391-6943; Toll Free: 800-236-7946
E-mail: ben@toucanvalley.com; query@toucanvalley.com
Web site: http://www.toucanvalley.com
Dist(s): **Grey Hse. Publishing.**

Touch Books, Incorporated *See* **Minardi Photography**

Touch the Music, *(978-0-9837585)* 110 Konner Ave., Pine Brook, NJ 07058 USA (SAN 860-2794) Tel 973-220-9785
E-mail: Claudia@Touchthemusic.us
Web site: www.Touchthemusic.us.

TouchPoint Pr., *(978-0-615-97340-1; 978-0-615-97374-6; 978-0-615-97375-3; 978-0-615-97554-2; 978-0-615-97555-9; 978-0-615-97556-6; 978-0-615-97884-0; 978-0-615-97885-7; 978-0-615-98003-4; 978-0-615-98400-1; 978-0-615-98753-8; 978-0-615-99258-7; 978-0-615-99410-9; 978-0-692-20053-7; 978-0-692-02416-4; 978-0-692-02417-1; 978-0-692-24865-2; 978-0-692-24920-8; 978-0-692-25104-1; 978-0-692-25653-4; 978-0-692-25669-5; 978-0-692-27195-7; 978-0-692-28049-2; 978-0-692-28145-1; 978-0-692-28149-9; 978-0-692-28179-6;) Orders Addr.: 46 Brookland St, Ste 3, Brookland , AR 72417 USA Tel 662-595-4162; Fax: 870-200-6702; Edit Addr.: 46 Brookland St., Ste 3, Brookland, AR 72417 USA Tel 662-595-4162; Fax: 870-200-6702*
E-mail: info@touchpointpress.com; media@touchpointpress.com
Web site: http://www.touchpointpress.com
Dist(s): **CreateSpace Independent Publishing Platform.**

TouchSmart Publishing, LLC, *(978-0-9765060; 978-0-9787517)* 167 Old Richmond Rd., Swanzeyti, NH 03446 USA (SAN 256-3835) Tel 603-352-7282; a/o Touchsmart Publishing (Distributor), LLC, 6522 Waldorf Pl., Cincinnati, OH 45230 (SAN 631-8703) Tel 513-225-8765; Fax: 206-666-4856
E-mail: ccardine@touchsmart.net
Web site: http://www.touchsmart.net.

Touchstone *Imprint of* **Touchstone**

Touchstone, *(978-0-7432)* 1230 Avenue of the Americas, New York, NY 10020 USA; *Imprints*: Touchstone (TouchImp)
Dist(s): **Simon & Schuster, Inc.**

Touchstone Center for Children, Incorporated, The *See* **Touchstone Ctr. Pubns.**

Touchstone Ctr. Pubns., *(978-1-929299)* Div. of Touchstone Center for Children, Inc., Orders Addr.: 141 E. 88th St., New York, NY 10028 USA (SAN 265-3664) Tel 212-831-7717
E-mail: rlewis212@aol.com
Web site: http://www.touchstonecenter.net
Dist(s): **State Univ. of New York Pr.**

Touchstone Communications, *(978-0-9790775; 978-0-9973569)* Orders Addr.: P.O. Box 396, Oneonta, NY 13820-0396 USA (SAN 852-3835); 291 Chestnut St., Box 396, Oneonta, NY 13820
E-mail: Touchstonecom@stny.rr.com; bd@bookpublishguide.com
Web site: http://Touchstone-com.com.

Touchstones Discussion Project, *(978-1-878461; 978-1-937742; 978-1-958074)* PO Box 2329, Annapolis, MD 21404-2329 USA Toll Free: 800-456-6542
Web site: http://www.touchstones.org.

Toure, Khari, *(978-0-692-82465-8; 979-8-9856414)* .

Tower Pr., *(978-0-615-67490-2)* 7211 Brickyard Rd., Potomac, MD 20854 USA Tel 202 944 3810; Fax: 202 944 3826
Dist(s): **CreateSpace Independent Publishing Platform.**

Towers Maguire Publishing *Imprint of* **Local History Co., The**

Town & Country Reprographics, *(978-0-9725808; 978-0-9754383; 978-0-9771894; 978-0-9794860; 978-0-9801439; 978-0-9825067; 978-0-9835219; 978-0-9896702; 978-0-9968302; 978-0-692-16890-5)* 230 N. Main St., Concord, NH 03301 USA (SAN 254-959X)
Web site: http://www.reprographic.com
Dist(s): **Smashwords.**

Towne, Russ, *(978-0-692-56808-8; 978-0-692-56837-8; 978-0-692-57310-5; 978-0-692-57313-6; 978-0-692-57322-8; 978-0-692-57325-9; 978-0-692-57597-0; 978-0-692-57600-7; 978-0-692-57656-4; 978-0-692-57660-1; 978-0-692-57663-2; 978-0-692-60270-6; 978-0-692-70008-2; 978-0-692-70460-8; 978-0-692-70932-0; 978-0-692-72351-7; 978-0-692-74214-3; 978-0-692-77261-4; 978-0-692-80418-6; 978-0-692-80423-0; 978-0-692-81855-8; 978-0-692-90776-4; 978-0-692-94549-0; 978-1-948245; 978-0-578-51700-1) 1114 Bucknam Av, CAMPBELL, CA 95008 USA Tel 408-364-6987.*

Towne Woman Creations, *(978-0-9981499)* 2805 Mowrey Dr., Bloomington, IL 61704 USA Tel 360-485-8078
E-mail: Tammychewe@msn.com.

Townsend, Diana, *(978-0-615-15882-2; 978-0-615-16214-0)* 3432 Briaroaks Dr., Garland, TX 75044 USA Tel 214-703-9718
E-mail: dianatownsend@aol.com
Dist(s): **Lulu Pr., Inc.**

Townsend, J. N. Publishing *Imprint of* **PublishingWorks**

Townsend Pr., *(978-0-944210; 978-1-59194)* 439 Kelly Dr., West Berlin, NJ 08091-9284 USA (SAN 243-0444) Toll Free Fax: 800-225-8894; Toll Free: 800-772-6410
E-mail: townsendcs@aol.com; orderstp@aol.com; emily@townsend.press
Web site: http://www.townsendpress.com
Dist(s): **Children's Plus, Inc.**

Townsend Pr. - Sunday Schl. Publishing Board, *(978-0-910683; 978-1-932972; 978-1-939225; 978-1-945356; 978-1-949052; 978-1-957621)* 330 Charlotte Ave., Nashville, TN 37201-1188 USA (SAN 275-8598) Tel 615-256-2480; Fax: 615-242-4929; Toll Free: 800-359-9398
E-mail: bavant@sspbnbc.com.

Townsends, *(978-0-9997620; 978-0-9998644; 978-1-948837)* P.O. Box 415, Pierceton, IN 46562 USA Tel 574-594-3932
E-mail: jon.townsend1@gmail.com
Web site: townsends.us.

Toy Box Productions, *(978-1-887729; 978-1-932332)* Div. of CRT, Custom Products, Inc., 7532 Hickory Hills Ct., Whites Creek, TN 37189 USA Tel 615-299-0822; 615-876-5490; Fax: 615-876-3931; Toll Free: 800-750-1511
E-mail: leeann@crttoybox.com
Dist(s): **Christian Bk. Distributors.**

Toy Quest, *(978-0-9767325; 978-0-9786246)* Manley, 2229 Barry Ave., Los Angeles, CA 90064-1401 USA.

Toy Rocket Studios, LLC, *(978-0-615-23521-9; 978-0-578-15192-2)* Orders Addr.: 5410 Fallen Timbers Dr., West Chester, OH 45069 USA; Edit Addr.: 814 St.Clair Ave, Hamilton, OH 45015 USA
E-mail: ToyRocketLaunch@gmail.com
Web site: http://www.ToyRocketStudiosLLC.com; http://www.ToyRocketLaunch.com.

Toy Truck Publishing, *(978-0-9764983)* 4602 Lilac Ln., Lake Elmo, MN 55042 USA (SAN 256-3754) Tel 612-716-8383; Fax: 651-275-1279
E-mail: sales@toytruckpublishing.com
Web site: http://www.toytruckpublishing.com.

Toy Vey Toys, *(978-0-615-15195-3; 978-0-615-21091-9; 978-0-578-00861-5; 978-0-9819861; 978-1-935592)* Orders Addr.: 1420 Locust St., No. 10F, Philadelphia, PA 19102 USA (SAN 913-4190) Tel 1-267-847-9018
E-mail: elik@sportschallengenetwork.com
Web site: www.sportschallengenetwork.com.

Toys 'n Things Press *See* **Redleaf Pr.**

TPBMedia, *(978-0-692-95299-3)* 3212 Shoreview, Highland Village, TX 75077 USA Tel 214-995-0229
E-mail: tbevins@verizon.net
Dist(s): **Independent Pub.**

Tpprince Esquire *See* **Tpprince Esquire International**

Tpprince Esquire International, *(978-0-9790110; 978-0-692-22159-4; 978-1-63365)* 7840 Cassia Ct., Saint Louis, MO 63123 USA (SAN 852-2219) Tel 41794299891 (swiss portable); 41218821971 (swiss main office); Cretillon 9, Froideville, ch 1055 Fax: +41218821971
E-mail: dansekarski@gmail.com; tpprince_esq@yahoo.com; dan.sekarski@bluewin.ch; tpprince@tpprince-esquire.com; dan.sekarski@bluewin.ch; sheiwa@prontonmail.com
Web site: http://https://www.lulu.com/search?adult_audience_rating=00&contributorId=1393651&page=1&pageSize=10&q=tpprince; http://tpprince-esquire.com.

TPRS Publishing, Incorporated *See* **Fluency Matters**

TR Bks., *(978-0-9788969)* 2430 N. Penn Ave., Independence, KS 67301 USA (SAN 851-8882) Tel 620-331-4486; *Imprints*: Exhibit A (Exhibit A).

Tracepaper Bks. Inc., *(978-0-9792728)* 68 Ridgewood Ave., Selden, NY 11784 USA
Web site: http://www.tracepaper.net.

Trachtman, Joseph, *(978-0-9795170)* 5008 Pullman Ave. NE, Seattle, WA 98105 USA.

Traci A Patterson, *(978-0-578-58123-1; 978-0-578-71731-9; 978-0-578-71732-6)*
E-mail: amazinginfluence@gmail.com
Dist(s): **Ingram Content Group.**

Tracie T. Harden, *(978-0-578-95508-7; 978-0-578-36064-5)* 2320 HAFLINGER CIR, CONYERS, GA 30012 USA Tel 478-494-0571
E-mail: tracietharden@yahoo.com.

Tracks Publishing, *(978-1-884654; 978-1-935937)* 140 Brightwood Ave., Chula Vista, CA 91910 USA Tel 619-476-7125; Fax: 619-476-8173; Toll Free: 800-443-3570
E-mail: tracks@cox.net
Web site: http://www.startupsports.com
Dist(s): **Ebsco Publishing**
Independent Pubs. Group
MyiLibrary
ebrary, Inc.

Tractor Mac Inc., *(978-0-9788496; 978-0-9826870; 978-0-9888329)* 121 Transylvania Rd., Roxbury, CT 06783 USA Tel 860-210-9805; Fax: 260-210-9805
E-mail: bsteers@tractormac.com
Web site: http://tractormac.com.

Tracy, Jean A. *See* **KidsDiscuss.com**

tracy, maria, *(978-1-7355685)* 849 Ave. 'F', LANGHORNE, PA 19047 USA Tel 267-987-9612
E-mail: maria9tracy@aol.com.

TracyTrends, *(978-0-9708226; 978-0-9814737; 978-0-615-11462-0)* 7710-C Somerset Bay, Indianapolis, IN 46240-3336 USA Toll Free: 800-840-6118
E-mail: tracytrends@aol.com
Web site: http://www.tracytrends.com.

Tradewind Bks. (CAN) *(978-1-896580; 978-1-926890) Dist. by* **Orca Bk Pub.**

Tradition Publishing, *(978-0-9789969)* 1823 Hart Leonard Rd., Cornerville, TN 37047 USA (SAN 852-1603)
Web site: http://www.carouselcarving.com.

Trafalgar Square Bks., *(978-0-943955; 978-1-57076; 978-1-64601)* Orders Addr.: P.O. Box 257, North Pomfret, VT 05053 USA Tel 802-457-1911; Fax: 802-457-1913; Edit Addr.: Howe Hill Rd., North Pomfret, VT 05053 USA
E-mail: mcook@trafalgarbooks.com
Web site: http://www.horseandriderbooks.com; http://www.trafalgarbooks.com/
Dist(s): **Follett School Solutions**
Legato Pubs. Group
MyiLibrary
Publishers Group West (PGW)
Perseus Bks. Group.

Trafalgar Square Publishing, *(978-0-943955; 978-1-57076)* Orders Addr.: P.O. Box 257, North Pomfret, VT 05053-0257 USA (SAN 213-8859) Tel 802-457-1911; Fax 802-457-1913; Toll Free: 800-423-4525; Edit Addr.: 388 Howe Hill Rd., North Pomfret, VT 05053 USA Tel 802-423-4525; 802-457-1913
E-mail: tsquare@sover.net
Web site: http://www.trafalgarbooks.com; http://www.horseandriderbooks.com
Dist(s): **Independent Pubs. Group**
MyiLibrary.

Trafford Publishing, *(978-1-55212; 978-1-55369; 978-1-55395; 978-1-4120; 978-1-4122; 978-1-4251; 978-1-4269; 978-1-4669; 978-1-4907; 978-1-6987)* 1663 Liberty Dr., Suite 200, Bloomington, IN 47403 USA Tel 812-334-5345; 812-334-5223; 888-232-4444; Fax: 812-339-6554
E-mail: orders@trafford.com; info@trafford.com
Web site: http://www.trafford.com
Dist(s): **Author Solutions, LLC**
Baker & Taylor Publisher Services (BTPS)
CreateSpace Independent Publishing Platform
DecisionPro, Inc.
Ediciones Universal
Wizard Works
Zondervan.

Trahan, Virginia A. - Author *See* **CVTrahan Publishing**

Trail, George (GBR) *(978-0-9559927) Dist. by* **LuluCom.**

Trail Trotter Pr. *Imprint of* **Run to Win, LLC**

Trail Trotters Bk. Ranch, *(978-0-9763209)* 616 N. Aurelius Rd., Mason, MI 48854 USA Tel 517-244-0727
E-mail: rosewoodbouz@aol.com
Web site: http://www.ponypointers.com.

Trails Bks. *Imprint of* **Bower Hse.**

Trails of Discovery, *(978-0-9788926)* 31071 Marbella Vista, San Juan Capistrano, CA 92675 USA.

Train 4 Safety Pr., *(978-0-9987912; 978-1-947690)* 4691 Seabeck Holly Rd NW No. 902, Seabeck, WA 98380 USA Tel 808-371-2320
E-mail: heather_lynn_beal@yahoo.com
Web site: http://www.train4safety.com.

Training Grounds, *(978-0-9729057)* P.O. Box 5631, Tucson, KY 85703 USA
E-mail: sjrose@plantagriculture.org
Web site: http://www.plantagriculture.org.

Training Solutions, LLC, *(978-0-692-75590-7; 978-0-578-20525-0; 978-0-692-13028-5; 978-0-692-13029-2)* 3928 Ulu Alii St., Kalaheo, HI 96741 USA Tel 508-454-5096; P.O. Box 411387, Kalaheo, HI 96741
E-mail: davene13j@gmail.com
Web site: markjbooks.com.

Train-Up A Child, LLC, *(978-0-9703069)* P.O. Box 1122, Jenks, OK 74037 USA Tel 918-299-8178 (phone/fax)
E-mail: TrainUpStudies@aol.com
Web site: http://www.trainupstudies.com.

Trammel, Crystal, *(978-0-9746327)* 133 Montego Dr., Mesquite, TX 75149-1708 USA
E-mail: minc34@hotmail.com.

Tramuntana Editorial (ESP) *(978-84-16578; 978-84-17303; 978-84-939157; 978-84-940213; 978-84-940475; 978-84-941662; 978-84-941825; 978-84-942841; 978-84-942842) Dist. by* **Lectorum Pubns.**

Tranquility Hill Publishing, LLC., *(978-1-7369843)* 3717 Ballantrae Way, Flossmoor, IL 60422 USA Tel 708-816-4476
E-mail: TranquilityHill319@gmail.com.

Tranquility Publishing *See* **Tranquility Ranch Publishing**

Tranquility Ranch Publishing, *(978-0-9747425)* 25796 Tranquility Ln., Magnolia, TX 77355 USA
E-mail: gcadwalder@aol.com.

†Transaction Pubs., *(978-0-7658; 978-0-87855; 978-0-88738; 978-1-56000; 978-1-4128)* Div. of Taylor & Francis Group, Orders Addr.: Taylor & Francis Group LLC 7625 Empire Dr., Florence, KY 41042-2919 USA Toll Free Fax: 800-248-4724; Toll Free: 800-634-7064
E-mail: orders@transactionpub.com
Web site: http://www.transactionpub.com
Dist(s): **MyiLibrary**
ebrary, Inc.; *CIP.*

Transaltar Publishing, *(978-0-9771802; 978-0-615-20263-1; 978-0-615-20419-2; 978-0-615-20678-3; 978-0-615-20814-5)* 5517 E St., Sacramento, CA 95819 USA
E-mail: publisher@transaltar.com
Web site: http://www.transaltar.com; http://www.heathbuckmaster.com/
Dist(s): **CreateSpace Independent Publishing Platform**
Lulu Pr., Inc.

Transatlantic Arts, Inc., *(978-0-693)* P.O. Box 6086, Albuquerque, NM 87197 USA (SAN 202-7968) Tel 505-898-2289 Do not confuse with Trans-Atlantic Pubns., Inc., Philadelphia, PA.
E-mail: books@transatlantic.com
Web site: http://www.transatlantic.com/direct
Dist(s): **MyiLibrary.**

Trans-Atlantic Pubns., Inc., 33 Ashley Dr., Schwenksville, PA 19473 USA (SAN 694-0234) Tel 215-717-4655; Fax: 484-919-6486 Do not confuse with Transatlantic Arts, Inc., Albuquerque, NM
E-mail: order@transatlanticpub.com
Web site: http://www.transatlanticpub.com.

Transcontinental Education Inc., *(978-0-692-84805-0; 978-0-692-94946-7)* 11612 Brigit Ct, BOWIE, MD 20720 USA Tel 202-380-7738
E-mail: jeffwcrawford5+LVP0003383@gmail.com; jeffwcrawford5+LVP0003383@gmail.com.

Transcontinental Music Pubns., *(978-0-8074)* Div. of URJ, 633 Third Ave., 6th Flr., New York, NY 10017-6778 USA Tel 212-650-4101; Fax: 212-650-4109
E-mail: tmp@uahc.org
Web site: http://www.eTranscon.com
Dist(s): **Leonard, Hal Corp.**

Transfuzion Publishing *See* **Caliber Comics**

Trans-Galactic Pubns., *(978-0-9616078)* 20 Sunnyside Ave. Suite A134, Mill Valley, CA 94941 USA (SAN 698-0899)
E-mail: transpubls@aol.com.

Transitional Pr., *(978-0-9960369)* 8679 SW 51st St., Cooper City, FL 33328 USA Tel 954-298-8178
E-mail: Mortlaitner@bellsouth.net.

Transmundane Press *See* **Transmundane Pr., LLC**

Transmundane Pr., LLC, *(978-0-692-52614-9; 978-0-9984983; 978-1-948309)* Orders Addr.: 11150 Ana Ln., Guthrie, OK 73044 USA; Edit Addr.: 1332 Elysian Fields Ave, New Orleans, LA 70117 USA Tel 850-774-3366
Dist(s): **CreateSpace Independent Publishing Platform.**

For full information on wholesalers and distributors, refer to the Wholesaler and Distributor Name Index

Transworld Publishers Ltd. (GBR) *(978-0-552; 978-0-85752; 978-0-85750) Dist. by* **IPG Chicago.**

Transworld Publishers Ltd. (GBR) *(978-0-552; 978-0-85752; 978-0-85750) Dist. by* **Children Plus.**

Trapper Creek Museum Sluice Box Productions, *(978-0-9718302)* Orders Addr.: P.O. Box 13011, Trapper Creek, AK 99683 USA Tel 907-733-2555; Edit Addr.: Mile 3/4 Petersville Rd., Trapper Creek, AK 99683 USA
E-mail: info@trappercreekmuseum.com
Web site: http://www.trappercreekmuseum.com; http://www.sluiceboxproductions.com.

Trarina Washington Paige LLC, *(978-0-578-94410-4)* 301 W MONDAMIN UNIT 313, MINOOKA, IL 60447 USA Tel 779-230-8697
E-mail: INFO@TPAIGE.COM
Web site: HTTPS://WWW.TPAIGE.COM.

Trash, Steve Enterprises, *(978-0-9652542)* 975 Old Dirt Rd., Spruce Pine, AL 35585 USA.

Travel 4 Life !, *(978-0-9749441)* 2040 E. 22nd St., Box 911, Fremont, NE 68025 USA Tel 402-727-1559
E-mail: deanjcbs4u@yahoo.com
Web site: http://www.travel4life.org.

Travel America Bks., *(978-0-9795867)* 64 Vanderbilt Ave., Floral Park, NY 11001 USA Tel 516-354-2615
E-mail: shajovin@aol.com.

Travel With Me & See, *(978-0-9600423)* 1518 4th Ave N, Seattle, WA 98109 USA
E-mail: nancy@travelwithmeandsee.com
Web site: www.travelwithmeandsee.com.

TravelBrains, Inc., *(978-0-9705809; 978-1-933763)* 14 Tether Rd, Bedford, NH 03110-5660 USA
Web site: http://www.travelbrains.com.

Travelers' Tales, Incorporated *See* **Travelers' Tales/Solas House, Inc.**

Travelers' Tales/Solas House, Inc., *(978-1-885211; 978-1-932361; 978-1-60952)* 2320 Bowdoin St., Palo Alto, CA 94306 USA
Web site: http://www.travelerstales.com
Dist(s): **Baker & Taylor Publisher Services (BTPS)**
MyiLibrary
Publishers Group West (PGW)
ebrary, Inc.

Traveling Satchel, The, *(978-0-578-18660-3)* 1501 Oakwood Trail, Indianapolis, IN 46260 USA
E-mail: thetravelingsatchel@gmail.com.

Traveling Tales, *(978-0-578-40617-6)* 2526 W Perola Dr., Phoenix, AZ 85085 USA Tel 480-935-3221
E-mail: fin1640@aol.com.

Travis Parker Smith, *(978-1-7335837)* 1616 8th St. NW, Washington, DC 20001 USA Tel 206-465-4419
E-mail: travis.parker.smith@gmail.com.

Trawick, Gary E., *(978-0-615-66181-0)* 202 N. McNeil St., Burgaw, NC 28425 USA Tel 910-602-0993
E-mail: jenningstrawick@hotmail.com.

Traxler Marketing, *(978-0-9971788)* 11152 Westheimer Rd. No. 488, Houston, TX 77042 USA Tel 404-606-2116
E-mail: sonjatraxler@gmail.com.

Traylor, Waverley Publishing, *(978-0-9715068)* Div. of Waverley Traylor Photography, 3407 Longwood Dr., Smithfield, VA 23430 USA Tel 757-356-9119 (phone/fax)
E-mail: wtfoto@aol.com.

Tre, *(978-1-7332457)* 311 Ocean Ave, Spring Lake, NJ 07762 USA Tel 201-390-1813
E-mail: illana@etregirls.com
Web site: www.etregirls.com.

Tre H Publishing a division of Tre H Music, LLC *See* **Tre H Publishing a division of Tre H Productions, LLC**

Tre H Publishing a division of Tre H Productions, LLC, *(978-0-9987161; 978-1-954909)* 1615 Elysian St., HOUSTON, TX 77026 USA Tel 713-517-1129; Fax: 713-517-1129
E-mail: info@trehpublishing.com
Web site: www.TreHPublishing.com.

Treadle Pr., *(978-0-935143)* Div. of Binding & Printing Co., Box D, Sheperdstown, WV 25443 USA (SAN 695-2070) Tel 304-876-2557.

Treasure Bay, Inc., *(978-1-891327; 978-1-60115)* 5 Ash Ct., Novato, CA 94949 USA (SAN 859-0958)
E-mail: customerservice@webothread.com; donpanec@comcast.net
Web site: http://www.webothread.com
Dist(s): **Children's Plus, Inc.**

Treasure Chest Books *See* **Rio Nuevo Pubs.**

Treasure Hunt Adventures, Inc., *(978-0-9749809)* P.O. Box 1049, Carmel, NY 10512-9998 USA Tel 845-225-2539
E-mail: info@treasurehuntadventures.com
Web site: http://www.treasurehuntadventures.com.

Treasure Trove, Inc., *(978-0-9760618; 978-0-9772314)* P.O. Box 459, Pound Ridge, NY 10576 USA Fax: 203-801-0099
Web site: http://www.atreasuretrove.com.

Treasured Images, *(978-0-9728770)* P.O. Box 361, Milton, WA 98354-0361 USA
E-mail: snspubs@aol.com.

Treasured Legacies, *(978-0-9819217)* 1589 Althouse Rd., Cochranville, PA 19330 USA Tel 610-593-2053
E-mail: arjoy@epix.net.

Treasures Media Incorporated *See* **BroadStreet Publishing**

Treasures of Glory Ministries, *(978-0-9916112; 978-1-946162)* P.O. Box 23743, San Diego, CA 92193 USA Tel 858-254-1868
E-mail: treasuresofgloryministries@gmail.com.

Treble Heart Bks., *(978-0-9711882; 978-1-931742; 978-1-932695; 978-1-936127; 978-1-938370)* 1284 Overlook Dr., Sierra Vista, AZ 85635-5512 USA (SAN 254-7120) Tel 520-458-5602; Fax: 520-459-0162; *Imprints:* MountainView (MtnView)
Web site: http://www.trebleheartbooks.com
Dist(s): **Smashwords.**

Tree Branch Publishing, *(978-0-9772578)* Orders Addr.: P.O. Box 421004, Summerland Key, FL 33042 USA Tel 305-872-4600; Fax: 305-832-0156; Toll Free: 866-454-6525; Edit Addr.: 19769 Date Palm Dr., Summerland Key, FL 33042 USA
E-mail: info@treeoflifepublishing.com.

Tree Farm Pr., *(978-0-692-18141-6; 978-0-692-18142-3)* 326 N. Cir. Dr., Williamston, MI 48895 USA Tel 517-290-7768
E-mail: lizball@me.com
Dist(s): **Ingram Content Group.**

Tree Musketeers, Inc., *(978-0-9770196)* Orders Addr.: 136 Main St., El Segundo, CA 90245 USA
E-mail: gail@treemusketeers.org
Web site: http://www.treemusketeers.org.

Tree of Life Pr., *(978-0-9727103)* 8422 Woodbrook Dr., Knoxville, TN 37919-8828 USA
E-mail: jana@janaspicka.com
Web site: http://www.janaspicka.com.

Tree Of Life Publishing, *(978-0-9745052)* P.O. Box 421004, Summerland Key, FL 33042 USA Tel 305-744-0330; Fax: 305-744-0320; Toll Free: 866-454-6525; *Imprints:* Peeper & Friends (Peep & Friends)
E-mail: peeper@peeperandfriends.com
Web site: http://www.peeperandfriends.com.

Tree of Life Publishing Hse., *(978-0-9801357; 978-0-9822060)* 730 Gladstone St., La Verne, CA 91750 USA Tel 626-825-5539
E-mail: shaynah@treeoflifepublishinghouse.com
Web site: http://www.treeoflifepublishinghouse.com.

Tree Top Bks., *(978-1-7332492)* 2513 Ferdinand Dr., Knightdale, NC 27545 USA Tel 919-239-0613
E-mail: wearetreetopbooks@gmail.com.

Tree Tunnel Pr., *(978-0-9841037; 978-1-7375173)* P.O. Box 733, Capitola, CA 95010 USA (SAN 931-3931) Tel 831-427-5551; Toll Free: 800-213-1885
E-mail: contact@treetunnelpress.com
Web site: http://www.treetunnelpress.com.

Treecat Publishing, *(978-0-578-44699-8; 978-0-578-50989-1)* 1000 Wilsonville Rd., Newberg, OR 97132 USA Tel 765-662-3574
E-mail: dbhorine@gmail.com.

Treehaus Communications, Inc., *(978-0-929496; 978-1-886510)* Orders Addr.: P.O. Box 249, Loveland, OH 45140 USA (SAN 249-5325) Tel 513-683-5716; Fax: 513-683-2882; Toll Free: 800-638-4287; Edit Addr.: 906 W. Loveland Ave., Loveland, OH 45140 USA (SAN 249-5333)
E-mail: treehaus1@fuse.net
Dist(s): **ACTA Pubns.**

TreeHse. Publishing Group, *(978-0-9892079; 978-0-9963901; 978-1-7321391; 978-1-7363182)* Div. of Amphorae Publishing Group, 3963 Flora Pl., St. Louis, MO 63110 USA Tel 314-363-4546
E-mail: kbmakansi@blankslatecommunications.com
Web site: http://www.treehousepublishinggroup.com
Dist(s): **Independent Pubs. Group**
Midpoint Trade Bks., Inc.

TreeHse. Publishing Group, *(978-1-7360569; 979-8-9856021)* 136 Eastwind Ln., Jamestown, TN 38556 USA Tel 731-333-2400
E-mail: owl@treehousetoons.com
Web site: http://www.TreehouseToons.com.

Trefry, Deana, *(978-0-9798193)* 587 Essex St., Beverly, MA 01915 USA
E-mail: deanat@comcast.net.

Treherne, Annie S, *(978-0-578-72794-3; 978-0-578-73998-4; 978-0-578-96901-5; 978-0-578-98782-8)* 11560 227th St., Cambria Heights, NY 11411 USA Tel 347-650-9238
E-mail: scy.at4@gmail.com.

Trembath, Carol Consulting *See* **Lakeside Publishing MI**

Tremendous Leadership *Imprint of* **Tremendous Life Bks.**

Tremendous Life Bks., *(978-0-937539; 978-1-933715; 978-1-936354)* Div. of Life Management Services, Inc., 206 West Allen St., Mechanicsburg, PA 17055-6240 USA (SAN 156-5419) Tel 717-766-9499; Fax: 717-766-6565; Toll Free: 800-233-2665; *Imprints:* Tremendous Leadership (TremendLrdship)
E-mail: JLiller@TremendousLifeBooks.com
Web site: http://www.TremendousLifeBooks.com
Dist(s): **Send The Light Distribution LLC.**

Trend Enterprises, Inc., *(978-1-889319; 978-1-58792; 978-1-60912; 978-1-62807; 978-1-64488)* Orders Addr.: P.O. Box 64073, Saint Paul, MN 55164 USA Tel 651-631-2850; Fax: 651-582-3500; Toll Free Fax: 800-845-4832; Toll Free: 800-328-5540; Edit Addr.: 300 Ninth Ave., SW, New Brighton, MN 55112 USA
Web site: http://www.trendenterprises.com.

Trend Factor Pr., *(978-0-9818669; 978-1-7348534; 978-1-7356943)* 1530 P B Ln. No. M4819, Wichita Falls, TX 76302 USA (SAN 856-7468) Tel 571-723-5645
E-mail: Biz@trendpov.com
Web site: http://www.trendfactorpress.com
Dist(s): **Blu Sky Media Group.**

Trendwood Pr., *(978-1-947865)* 13729 Shirley St, Omaha, NE 68144-1240 USA Tel 402-915-9094
E-mail: danielkenneybooks@gmail.com.

Trenton Creative Enterprises, *(978-0-9754958)* 731 Springdale Dr., Spartanburg, SC 29302 USA
E-mail: trentoncreativeenterprises@charter.net
Web site: http://www.vintagegastonia.com.

Trent's Prints, *(978-0-9728872; 978-0-9762389; 978-0-9773723; 978-1-934035; 978-1-937000)* 3754 Willard Norris Rd., Pace, FL 32571 USA Tel 850-994-1421 Toll Free: 866-275-7124
Web site: http://www.trentsprints.com.

Treorca Pr., *(978-0-9766559)* 1718 W. 102nd St., Chicago, IL 60643-2147 USA
E-mail: joga9@aol.com
Web site: http://www.treorcapress.com.

Tres Canis Publishing Co., *(978-0-9659065)* P.O. Box 163, Nanticoke, PA 18634 USA Tel 570-735-0328
E-mail: rjanosov@verizon.net.

Tres Clavas Pr., *(978-0-615-37077-4; 978-0-9855731)*
E-mail: zackarmstrong@gmail.com
Web site: http://dexterandstray.com.

Trescott Research, *(978-0-916262)* 2503 Natalie Ln., Saintilacoum, WA 98388 USA (SAN 207-6535) Tel 253-217-1586
E-mail: trescott@umich.edu
Web site: http://www.trescottresearch.com.

Trevor Romain Company, The *See* **Romain, Trevor Co., The**

Tri House Bks., *(978-0-578-17752-6)* 35211 Buena Mesa, Calimesa, CA 92320 USA
Dist(s): **Outskirts Pr., Inc.**

Tri I Pubns., *(978-0-9793683; 978-0-9821674)* 100 Taylor Pl., Southport, CT 06890 USA Tel 203-254-7631; Fax: 203-254-7826
E-mail: thompson@triist.com; linda@lindasworlds.com
Web site: http://www.triist.com; http://www.lindasworlds.com; http://www.iammyowndragon.com.

TRI LIFE Press *See* **Life Works Pr.**

Tri Valley Children's Publishing, *(978-0-9790962)* 512 Briarwood Ct., Livermore, CA 94551 USA Tel 925-413-0546
E-mail: stephanierutledge@comcast.net.

†Triad Publishing Co., *(978-0-937404; 978-0-9600472)* Imprint of Triad Communications, Inc., Orders Addr.: P.O. Box 13355, Gainesville, FL 32604 USA (SAN 205-4574) Tel 352-373-5800 editorial office; Fax: 352-373-1488 editorial office; Toll Free Fax: 800-854-4947 orders & queries Do not confuse with companies with the same or similar name in Tujuga, CA, Sequim, WA, Parker, CO, Marlton, NJ, West Hartford, CT,Raleigh, NC , Sarasota, Fl
E-mail: lorna@triadpublishing.com
Web site: http://www.triadpublishing.com; *CIP.*

Tri-Ad veterans League, Inc., 31 Heath St., Jamaica Plain, MA 02130-1650 USA
E-mail: triadveterans@hotmail.com
Web site: http://www.triadveteransleague.org.

Trialtea USA, LLC, *(978-0-9741482; 978-0-9778295; 978-0-9796067; 978-0-9821418; 978-0-9841136; 978-0-9828388; 978-1-939645; 978-1-68165)* 7955 NW 12th St., Suite 115, Miami, FL 33126 USA Toll Free: 800-210-0344
E-mail: info@trialtea.com
Web site: http://www.trialtea.com
Dist(s): **INscribe Digital**
Independent Pubs. Group.

Triangle Square *Imprint of* **Seven Stories Pr.**

Triarchy Press (GBR) *(978-0-9550081; 978-1-909470; 978-1-911193) Dist. by* **IPG Chicago.**

Tribal Eye Productions, *(978-0-9800272; 978-0-692-78018-3; 978-0-692-95151-4; 978-0-692-95640-3; 978-0-692-16258-3; 978-0-578-49516-3; 978-1-7352003; 979-8-9887862)* P.O. Box 1123, Santa Ynez, CA 93460 USA
E-mail: garyd1123@gmail.com.

Tribute Bks., *(978-0-9765072; 978-0-9795045; 978-0-9814619; 978-0-9822565; 978-0-9837418; 978-0-9857922)* P.O. Box 95, Archbald, PA 18403 USA (SAN 256-4416) Tel 570-876-2416 (phone/fax)
E-mail: info@tribute-books.com
Web site: http://www.tribute-books.com
Dist(s): **Ingram Content Group.**

Tribute Publishing, *(978-0-9906001; 978-0-9982860; 978-0-9998358; 978-1-7337727)* 1624 Marble Falls Dr., Frisco, TX 75036 USA
E-mail: bonnie@TributePublishing.com.

Trice, B.E. Publishing, *(978-0-9631925; 978-1-890885)* 2727 Prytania St., New Orleans, LA 70130 USA Tel 504-895-0111
E-mail: betbooks@aol.com.

Trickle Creek Bks., *(978-0-9640742; 978-1-929432)* Orders Addr.: 500 Andersontown Rd., Mechanicsburg, PA 17055 USA Tel 717-766-2638; Fax: 717-766-1343; Toll Free: 800-353-2791
E-mail: tonialbert@aol.com
Web site: http://www.TrickleCreekBooks.com.

Tricolor Bks., *(978-0-9754641)* P.O. Box 24811, Tempe, AZ 85285 USA
E-mail: tricolorbrian@hotmail.com
Web site: http://www.mountainkingsnake.com.

Tricycle Pr. *Imprint of* **Ten Speed Pr.**

Tricycle Pr. *Imprint of* **Random Hse. Children's Bks.**

Triddias, *(978-0-9984231; 978-1-7379997; 978-1-957477)* 3021 Mill Ridge Dr, Plano, TX 75025 USA
E-mail: triddias@gmail.com.

Trident, Inc., *(978-1-887801; 978-1-58978)* Orders Addr.: 885 Pierce Butler Rte., Saint Paul, MN 55104 USA; *Imprints:* Atlas Games (Atlas Games)
E-mail: info@atlas-games.com
Web site: http://www.atlas-games.com
Dist(s): **PSI (Publisher Services, Inc.).**

Trident Press International *See* **Standard International Print Group Inc.**

TriEclipse, Inc., *(978-0-9704512; 978-0-9976342)* P.O. Box 7763, Jacksonville, FL 32238 USA Tel 904-778-0372
E-mail: vtaylor4@bellsouth.net
Web site: http://www.trieclipse.com.

Trifolium Bks., Inc. (CAN) *(978-1-55244; 978-1-895579) Dist. by* **Firefly Bks Limited.**

Trigger Memory Co., LLC, *(978-0-9762024; 978-0-9863000; 978-1-7352144)* P.O. Box 361, Pendleton, OR 97801 USA
E-mail: timestalesmj@msn.com
Web site: https://www.timestales.com.

Trigger Memory Systems *See* **Trigger Memory Co., LLC**

Trillas Editorial, S. A. (MEX) *(978-968-24) Dist. by* **Continental Bk.**

Trillas Editorial, S. A. (MEX) *(978-968-24) Dist. by* **Lectorum Pubns.**

Trilogy Christian Publishing, Inc., *(978-1-64088; 978-1-64773; 978-1-63769; 978-1-68556; 979-8-88738; 979-8-89041)* P.O. Box PO BOX A, Santa Ana, CA 92711 USA Tel 918-494-6868
E-mail: bryan@keymgc.com
Dist(s): **Destiny Image Pubs.**

Trilogy Pubns. LLC, *(978-0-9772799; 978-0-615-80854-3)* Orders Addr.: 560 Sylvan Ave. Suite 1240, Englewood Cliffs, NJ 07632 USA (SAN 257-2044) Tel 201-816-1211; Fax: 201-816-8424
Web site: http://www.trilogypublications.com.

Tri-M Media Marketing Maven LLC, *(978-1-7379791)* 2132 Glen Ellyn St., Oklahoma City, OK 73111 USA Tel 614-806-5857
E-mail: tonyamccleary@yahoo.com
Web site: Tri-M Media Marketing Maven LLC.

Trimark Pictures *See* **Lions Gate Home Entertainment**

Trimble Hollow Pr., The, *(978-0-615-20027-9; 978-0-615-26449-3; 978-0-9915614; 978-0-9861523; 978-1-946495)* 4944 Northside Dr., Acworth, GA 30101 USA; PO Box 251, Acworth, GA 30101
Dist(s): **Instant Pub.**

Trine, Greg, *(978-0-578-46407-7; 978-1-7339589; 979-8-218-16764-6; 979-8-218-18847-4)* 3742, Ventura, CA 93003 USA Tel 805-901-2310
E-mail: gjtrine@gmail.com
Web site: www.gregtrine.com.

Trinity Bks., *(978-0-9743669)* P.O. Box 401, Cascade, ID 83611 USA.

Trinity Hills Publishing, Orders Addr.: 855 Penal Rock Rd., Penal, 00000 TTO Tel 868-387-2744
E-mail: markdanielonline@gmail.com.

Trintiy Pr., *(978-0-9822113)* 303 Park Ave., New York, NY 10010 USA
E-mail: yroehker@bookoublishing.com.

†Trinity Univ. Pr., *(978-0-911536; 978-0-939980; 978-0-9651507; 978-1-893271; 978-1-59534)* One Trinity Pl., San Antonio, TX 78212 USA (SAN 205-4590) Tel 210-999-8881; Fax: 210-999-8182; *Imprints:* Maverick Books (MaverickBks) Do not confuse with Trinity University Press in Bannockburn, IL
E-mail: sarah.nawrocki@trinity.edu
Dist(s): **Bilingual Pr./Editorial Bilingue**
MyiLibrary
Publishers Group West (PGW); *CIP.*

Triple A Pr., *(978-0-692-72993-9; 978-0-9991181; 978-1-7372063; 978-1-962589)* P.O. Box 6561, Spartanburg, SC 29304 USA Tel 864-761-0952
E-mail: marymarj@aol.com.

Triple Ballerina Pr., *(978-1-7328429)* 115 Conifer Ct., MARKLE, IN 46770 USA Tel 260-602-5839
E-mail: BeverlyWriterAuthor@gmail.com
Web site: thetripletballerinas.com.

Triple Crown Pubns., *(978-0-9702472; 978-0-9747895; 978-0-9762349; 978-0-9767894; 978-0-9778804; 978-0-9799517; 978-0-9820996; 978-0-9825888; 978-0-9832095)* P.O. Box 247378, Columbus, OH 43219 USA (SAN 914-3815) Tel 614-478-9402
E-mail: editor@triplecrownpublications.com
Web site: http://www.triplecrownpublications.com
Dist(s): **Ambassador Bks. & Media**
Brodart Co.
MyiLibrary.

Triple Exposure Publishing, Incorporated *See* **T. E. Publishing, Inc.**

Triple Seven Pr., *(978-0-9710486)* P.O. Box 70552, Las Vegas, NV 89170-0552 USA Do not confuse with Triple Seven International, Gaston, IN
E-mail: wendy@777press.com
Web site: http://www.777press.com.

Triple Tail Publishing *See* **Farcountry Pr.**

Triple Tulip Pr., *(978-0-9754825; 978-0-615-11380-7)* Orders Addr.: P.O. Box 250, Sanbornville, NH 03872 USA Tel 603-522-3398; Fax: 603-218-6502; 2717 Wakefield Rd., Sanbornville, NH 03872 USA Tel 603-522-3398; Fax: 603-218-6502
E-mail: tripletulip@roadrunner.com
Web site: http://www.tripletulippress.com.

TripleCrown Pubns. *See* **Triple Crown Pubns.**

Tripod Pr., *(978-0-9673265)* P.O. Box 551, Fairfax, CA 94978-0551 USA
E-mail: Tripod@FrankMarrero.com
Web site: http://www.FrankMarrero.com
Dist(s): **Lulu Pr., Inc.**

Tripodi, Pina, *(978-1-7342116)* 1 Elide Rd., Katonah, NY 10536 USA Tel 914-715-3462
E-mail: peacefulbypina@gmail.com
Web site: peacefulbypina.com.

Tripping Light Pr., *(978-0-9795389)* P.O. Box 1107, Wheaton, IL 60189-1107 USA
Web site: http://www.trippinglightpress.com.

Trireme Studios, *(978-1-7321449)* P.O. Box 613, Caneadea, NY 14717 USA Tel 817-516-0018
E-mail: dlee.pe@gmail.com
Web site: triremestudios.com.

Trisar, Inc., *(978-1-886386)* 804 W. Town & Country Rd., Orange, CA 92868-4712 USA.

Mrs. Weisz Bks., *(978-0-9888338; 978-0-9985291; 978-0-9993886; 978-1-7363474)* 636 Elder Ln., Deerfield, IL 60015 USA Tel 847-602-5115
E-mail: erica@trismbooks.com
Web site: www.trismbooks.com
Dist(s): **Independent Pubs. Group.**

TRISTAN Publishing, Inc., *(978-0-931674; 978-0-9726504; 978-1-939881)* 2355 Louisiana Ave N. Ste. 2, Minneapolis, MN 55427-3646 USA Toll Free: 866-545-1383; *Imprints:* Waldman House Press (WaldmanHse)
E-mail: bwaldman@tristanpublishing.com; swaldman@tristanpublishing.com
Web site: http://www.tristanpublishing.com.

Tritium Pr., *(978-0-9761726)* 8690 Aero Dr., No. 339, San Diego, CA 92123 USA
E-mail: tritium@n2.net.

Triumph Bks., *(978-0-9624436; 978-1-57243; 978-1-880141; 978-1-60078; 978-1-61749)* Orders Addr.: 542 S. Dearborn St., Suite 750, Chicago, IL 60605 USA (SAN 852-6826) Tel 312-939-3330; Fax: 312-663-3557; Toll Free: 800-335-5323; Edit Addr.: c/o Kaplan Logistics, 901 Bilter Rd., Aurora, IL 60502 USA
E-mail: Ordering@TriumphBooks.com; J_Martini@triumphbooks.com; s_kaufman@triumphbooks.com;

Publisher Name Index

orders@triumphbooks.com; w.swanson@triumphbooks.com
Web site: http://www.triumphbooks.com
Dist(s): **Detroit Free Pr., Inc.**
Independent Pubs. Group
MyiLibrary.

Triumph Publishing, (*978-1-890430*) 10415 219th St., Queens Village, NY 11429-2020 USA Do not confuse with companies with a similar name in Omal, WA, College park, GA.

Triumphant Living Enterprises, Inc., (*978-0-9786681; 978-0-9852789; 979-8-9856827*) Orders Addr.: P.O. Box 691223, Orlando, FL 32869-1223 USA Tel 321-209-1980; Fax: 407-614-5200
E-mail: info@triumphantliving.org
Web site: http://www.triumphantliving.org; http://www.facebook.com/TriumphantLivingEnterprises; http://www.twitter.com/tlenterpriseinc; http://lorettafaithharris.com.

Triune Group, Inc., (*978-0-578-45332-3*) 1458 Sumter Dr. SW, Marietta, GA 30064 USA Tel 770-653-0160
E-mail: dickmcbain@gmail.com
Dist(s): **Ingram Content Group.**

Trivia Town Books LLC *See* **Beguile Media**

Trivium Pubns., (*978-0-9713671*) Orders Addr.: Dept. of Humanities & Human Sciences Point Park Univ., 201 Wood St., Pittsburgh, PA 15222 USA (SAN 254-5152) Tel 716-982-8591
E-mail: bdeanrob@janushead.org
Web site: http://www.janushead.org.

Trivium Pursuit, (*978-0-9743616; 978-1-933228*) 429 Lake Park Blvd., PMB 168, Muscatine, IA 52761 USA Tel 309-537-3641
E-mail: bluedorn@triviumpursuit.com
Web site: http://www.triviumpursuit.com
Dist(s): **Send The Light Distribution LLC.**

Troll Hetta Publishing Company *See* **SBA Bks., LLC**

Trolley (GBR) (*978-0-9542079; 978-0-9542648; 978-1-904563; 978-1-907112*) *Dist. by* **Dist Art Pubs.**

Trolley Press *See* **Ignite Reality**

Tronc, Muriel, (*978-1-7345593*) 1310 Whipple Ave., Redwood City, CA 94062 USA Tel 650-799-4585
E-mail: troncmuriel@gmail.com.

Trono-Calderon, Anne, 142 Whitney Ave., Los Gatos, CA 95030 USA Tel 408-677-6877
E-mail: atrocal@gmail.com.

Trotman, Charlie *See* **Iron Circus Comics**

Trotman, Kay L., (*978-0-615-13350-8*) P.O. Box 1501, Lake Elsinore, CA 92531 USA Tel 951-898-6094; Fax: 951-898-6094
E-mail: njeri@mac.com
Web site: www.onsafariwithkay.com.

Troublemaker Publishing, LP, (*978-1-933104*) P.O. Box 608, Spicewood, TX 78669 USA Tel 512-334-7777.

Troublemakers, (*978-0-692-10244-2*) 5130 E Pleasant Run Pkwy N. Dr, Indianapolis, IN 46219 USA Tel 317-354-6474
E-mail: kristinahulvershorn@gmail.com
Web site: www.secretofthetroublemakers.com.

Tru Publishing, (*978-0-9890985; 978-1-941420*) 2939 S Mayflower Way, Boise, ID 83709 USA Tel 612-423-1052; Fax: 888-854-7690
E-mail: Kevin@TruPublishing.com
Web site: www.TruPublishing.com.

truckerkidzPr., (*978-0-9856770*) 121 Overhill Rd., Warwick, RI 02818 USA Tel 401-480-3403
E-mail: ckmellor@cox.net
Web site: http://www.grandpaandthetruck.com.

Trudgian, Sherri *See* **Little Sprout Publishing Hse.**

True 2 Life Productions, (*978-0-9740610; 978-0-692-47282-8; 978-0-692-53315-4; 978-0-692-53329-1; 978-0-9971871*) 45 Academy St., Suite 309, Newark, NJ 07102 USA
E-mail: alsaadiqbanks@aol.com; alsaadigbanks@aol.com
Dist(s): **CreateSpace Independent Publishing Platform.**

True Beginnings Publishing, (*978-0-615-87592-7; 978-0-615-88705-0; 978-0-615-89298-6; 978-0-615-91710-8; 978-0-615-91711-5; 978-0-615-92382-6; 978-0-615-92815-9; 978-0-615-94325-1; 978-0-615-99079-8; 978-0-615-99134-4; 978-0-692-26679-3; 978-0-692-27317-3; 978-0-692-28121-5; 978-0-692-28436-0; 978-0-692-33830-8; 978-0-692-37980-6; 978-0-692-40891-9; 978-0-692-45875-4; 978-0-692-49473-8; 978-0-692-49594-0; 978-0-692-50791-9; 978-0-692-59441-4; 978-0-692-67290-7; 978-0-692-68342-2; 978-0-692-68562-4; 978-0-692-70221-5;) Orders Addr.: 79 Ballard Rd, Vilonia, AR 72173 USA*
E-mail: true_beginnings_publishing@yahoo.com
Web site: http://truebeginningspublishing.blogspot.com/; http://truebeginningspublishing.weebly.com
Dist(s): **Barnes & Noble Pr.**
CreateSpace Independent Publishing Platform
Ingram Bk. Co.

True Exposures Publishing, Inc., (*978-0-9642595; 978-0-9771762*) Orders Addr.: P.O. Box 5066, Brandon, MS 39047 USA Tel 601-829-1222; Fax: 601-829-1656; Toll Free: 800-323-3398; Edit Addr.: 106 Shenandoah Estates Cir., Brandon, MS 39047 USA
E-mail: trueexposures@bellsouth.net
Web site: http://www.trueexposures.com.

True Friends Bk. Club, LLC, (*978-0-9797165*) 3708 142nd Pl. NE, Bellevue, WA 98007 USA (SAN 854-1833) Tel 425-556-4319
E-mail: laurawreeves@yahoo.com
Web site: http://www.truefriendsbookclub.com.

True Gifts Publishing, (*978-0-9796701*) 14 Clark St., Belmont, MA 02478 USA (SAN 854-056X) Fax: 617-741-4013
Web site: http://truegifts.net.

True Horizon Publishing, (*978-0-9818396*) 12306 Fox Lake Pl., Fairfax, VA 22033 USA Toll Free: 866-601-4106 (phone/fax)
E-mail: montgomerylm@gmail.com
Web site: http://www.truehorizonpublishing.com.

True Light Publishing, (*978-0-9656670*) Orders Addr.: P.O. Box 1284, Boulder, CO 80308-0734 USA Tel 303-447-2547; Fax: 303-443-4373; Edit Addr.: 411 Wild Horse Cir., Boulder, CO 80304-0459 USA Do not confuse with True Light Publishing in Homewood, IL
E-mail: tlpub@ecentral.com; orders@truelightpub.com; amber@truelightmusic.com
Web site: http://www.truelightpub.com; http://www.truelightpublishing.com; http://www.truelightmusic.com
Dist(s): **New Leaf Distributing Co., Inc.**
Gangaji Foundation, The.

True Lightening *Imprint of* **Share & Care Society Inc.**

True Measure, (*978-0-578-42659-4; 978-0-578-42660-0*) 5902 Wishing Well Dr., Port Orange, FL 32127 USA Tel 386-589-2338
E-mail: truemeasureinspections@gmail.com
Dist(s): **Ingram Content Group.**

True North Studio, (*978-0-9845798*) 518 W. 8th St., Traverse City, MI 49684 USA.

True Path Pubs., (*978-0-9830978*) 9620 Smoot Ln., Argyle, TX 76226 USA Tel 817-879-8229
E-mail: ronda@ronda-ray.com.

True Perspective Publishing Hse., (*978-0-9832399; 978-0-9846672; 978-0-9852094; 978-0-9859892; 978-0-9894026; 978-0-9910561; 978-0-9904624; 978-0-9864305; 978-0-9975539; 978-0-9990755; 978-1-7340305; 978-1-7350275; 978-1-7357752; 979-8-9854594*) 2811 Imperial Point Terr., Clermont, FL 34711 USA Tel 407-383-3356; Fax: 352-394-4443
E-mail: seancort3839@yahoo.com
Web site: www.thepowerofperspective.net

True Vine Publishing Co., (*978-0-9760914; 978-0-9786088; 978-0-9822087; 978-0-9826694; 978-0-9894869; 978-0-9905326; 978-0-9989239; 978-1-7336315; 978-1-7357540; 978-1-7366672; 978-1-7375934; 978-1-956469*) P.O. Box 22448, Nashville, TN 37202 USA Tel 615-585-0143
E-mail: truevinepublishing@gmail.com
Web site: http://www.truevinepublishing.org.

True You Inc,

Trujillo, Gary M, (*978-0-578-43727-9; 978-0-578-62520-1; 978-0-578-35161-2*) 733 NE 204th St., Shoreline, WA 98198 USA Tel 206-353-1588
E-mail: smbizcs@hotmail.com.

Trujillo-Acosta, Katie, (*978-1-7377291*) 13149 Fencerow Rd, Fort Worth, TX 76244 USA Tel 806-335-0482
E-mail: mkmatthew@hotmail.com.

Truman Pr., Inc., (*978-0-9637846; 978-0-9798599*) 5 NW. Ave., Fayetteville, AR 72701 USA Tel 479-521-4999; Fax: 479-575-9393; *Imprints*: Hannover House (Hann Hse)
E-mail: hannoverhouse@aol.com
Web site: http://www.HannoverHouse.com
Dist(s): **Follett School Solutions**
National Bk. Network.

Truman State Univ. Pr., (*978-0-943549; 978-1-931112; 978-1-935503; 978-1-61248*) 100 E. Normal Ave., Kirksville, MO 63501-4221 USA (SAN 253-4231) Tel 660-785-7336; Fax: 660-785-4480; Toll Free: 800-916-6802
E-mail: tsup@truman.edu
Web site: http://tsup.truman.edu
Dist(s): **INscribe Digital**
ISD
Longleaf Services
Pennsylvania State Univ. Pr.

Trumpet In Zion Publishing, (*978-0-9716355*) Div. of Spring of Hope Church of God in Christ, P.O. Box 51163, Indian Orchard, MA 01151 USA Tel 413-733-1032; Fax: 413-241-6132; *Imprints*: Solid Rock Books (Solid Rock Bks).

Trumpeter *Imprint of* **Shambhala Pubns., Inc.**

Trunk Up Bks., (*978-1-7342129; 978-1-7349062; 979-8-9850227; 978-1-958368*) 659 Framingham Ct, Gurnee, IL 60031 USA Tel 815-603-8021
E-mail: vickyweber93@gmail.com
Web site: www.trunkupbooks.com.

Truth Bk. Pubs., (*978-0-9778261; 978-0-9794861; 978-0-9815203; 978-1-935298; 978-1-937089; 978-1-940725; 978-1-946598*) 824 Bills Rd., Franklin, IL 62638 USA (SAN 912-2834) Tel 217-243-8880
E-mail: faithprinting77@yahoo.com; truthbookpublishers@yahoo.com
Web site: http://www.faithprinting.net; http://www.itseasywithjesus-printing.com; http://www.truthbookpublishers.com
Dist(s): **BCH Fulfillment & Distribution**
BookBaby
eBooks2go Inc.

Truth For Eternity Ministries, (*978-1-889520*) Div. of Reformed Baptist Church of Grand Rapids, 860 Peachcrest Ct NE, Grand Rapids, MI 49505-6435 USA
E-mail: office@girbc.org
Web site: www.girbc.org.

Truth Pr., (*978-0-692-59377-6; 978-0-9974331*) 306 Hideaway Ln. Central, Hideaway Lakes, TX 75771 USA Tel 903-780-1236
Dist(s): **CreateSpace Independent Publishing Platform.**

Truth Publications, Inc., (*978-0-9620615; 978-1-58427*) Orders Addr.: 220 S. Marion St., Athens, AL 35611 USA Tel 855-492-6657 CEI Bookstore; Fax: 256-232-0913; Edit Addr.: 220 S. Marion St., Athens, AL 35611 USA (SAN 249-4221) Tel 346-216-1707
E-mail: sales@truthpublications.com; lance@truthpublications.com; kyle@truthpublications.com; mark@truthpublications.com
Web site: http://CEIbooks.com; http://www.truthbooks.com/; http://www.ceibooks.com/.

Truth Publishers *See* **Truth Bk. Pubs.**

Truthful Pr. Publishing, (*978-0-9799707*) P.O. Box 240, Statesville, NC 28687 USA Tel 704-287-8378; Fax: 704-878-8972
E-mail: author@daphinerobinson.com
Web site: http://www.daphinerobinson.com.

T.S. Poetry Pr., (*978-0-9845531; 978-0-692-01454-7; 978-0-9898542; 978-1-943120*) 21 Belleview Ave., Ossining, NY 10562 USA Tel 914-944-9036.

Tsaba Hse., (*978-0-9725486; 978-1-933853*) 2252 12th St., Reedly, CA 93654 USA (SAN 254-9441) Tel 559-643-8575; Fax: 559-638-2640
E-mail: ps@tsabahouse.com
Web site: http://www.tsabahouse.com
Dist(s): **Send The Light Distribution LLC.**

T.S.I. Strategies, LLC, (*978-0-9772609*) 140 SE 8th St., Cape Coral, FL 33990 USA Fax: 866-761-4233
E-mail: jim@jamesroach.com
Web site: http://www.producevideos.com.

TSM Publishing Group, LLC *See* **Autumn Publishing Group, LLC**

Tsui Wong-Avery, Sally, (*978-0-9798874; 978-0-9819358; 978-0-9855246*) 2618 W. Canyon Ave., San Diego, CA 92123 USA.

Tsunami Pr., (*978-1-7335000*) 6804 Quincy St. Apt. 1A, Philadelphia, PA 19119 USA Tel 610-564-1293
E-mail: mrues@me.com.

Tsvyetkov, Leonid *See* **Slickcolors INC**

TT Kreative Enterprise *See* **P A Reading Pr.**

Tu Bks. *Imprint of* **Lee & Low Bks., Inc.**

Tualen (GBR) (*978-0-9556798*) *Dist. by* **LuluCom.**

Tubbs, Stephen P., (*978-0-9659446; 978-0-9819753*) 1344 Firwood Dr., Pittsburgh, PA 15243-1861 USA Tel 412-279-4866
E-mail: electrpow@aol.com
Web site: http://www.members.aol.com/electrpow/power.htm.

Tubby & Coo's Mid-City Bk. Shop, (*978-1-7322794*) 432 N. Anthony St. Suite 305C, New Orleans, LA 70119 USA (SAN 920-8763) Tel 504-345-8491
E-mail: tubbyandcoos@gmail.com.

Tuck, Sarah Bks., (*978-0-578-43433-9; 978-0-578-43647-0; 978-0-578-47408-3; 978-0-578-48452-5; 978-0-578-68684-4; 978-0-578-68756-8; 978-0-578-79297-2; 978-0-578-79298-9*) 217 Stephens Hill Rd., Franklin, KY 42134 USA Tel 270-223-7371
E-mail: tuckproductions@yahoo.com
Dist(s): **Ingram Content Group.**

Tucker, Peggy *See* **Heritage Publishing**

Tucker, Peter E. *See* **PT Publishing**

Tucker, Terra, (*978-0-9794578*) P.O. Box 2792 Americus Dr, Thompson Station, TN 37179 USA (SAN 853-5027).

Tucson Botanical Gardens, (*978-0-9792253*) 2150 N. Alvernon Way, Tucson, AZ 85712 USA Tel 520-326-9686; Fax: 520-324-0166
E-mail: execdirector@tucsonbotanical.org
Web site: http://www.tucsonbotanical.org.

Tucu Pr., (*978-0-9766572*) Orders Addr.: P.O. Box 447, Bozeman, MT 59771-0447 USA Tel 406-586-5084 (phone/fax); Edit Addr.: 3150 Graf St., No. 8, Bozeman, MT 59715 USA
E-mail: anndiberardinis@msn.com.

Tudor Assocs. Pr., (*978-0-9760939*) P.O. Box 1804, Payson, AZ 85547-1804 USA Tel 928-978-5799
E-mail: press@tudorassociates.com
Web site: http://www.tudorassociates.com.

Tudor Hse. (GBR) (*978-0-9530676*) *Dist. by* **Orca Bk Pub.**

Tudor Pubs., Inc., (*978-0-936389; 978-0-9778026*) Orders Addr.: P.O. Box 38366, Greensboro, NC 27438 USA; Edit Addr.: 3109 Shady Lawn Dr., Greensboro, NC 27408 USA (SAN 697-3035) Tel 336-288-5395
E-mail: tudorpublishers@triad.rr.com
Dist(s): **Brodart Co.**

Tuesday's Child, (*978-0-9772795*) Orders Addr.: P.O. Box 2512, Cookeville, TN 38502-2512 USA (SAN 257-2060)
E-mail: tuesdayschildpub@charter.net
Web site: http://tuesdayschildpub.com.

Tuggle Publishing, (*978-0-9974722*) 5904 Meadows Dr., Fort Wayne, IN 46804 USA Tel 678-702-2139
E-mail: annieueber@yahoo.com
Web site: tugglepublishing.com.

Tughra Bks. *Imprint of* **Blue Dome, Inc.**

Tulika Pubs. (IND) (*978-81-86895; 978-81-8146*) *Dist. by* **IPG Chicago.**

Tulip & Petunia Publishing, (*978-0-692-82983-7*) 3800 Buchtel Blvd #103191, DENVER, CO 80250 USA Tel 720-474-0591
E-mail: jeffwcrawford5+LVP0003235@gmail.com; jeffwcrawford5+LVP0003235@gmail.com.

Tully, Jennifer Cahill, (*978-0-9980531*) 4550 Pearson st, Long Island city, NY 11101 USA Tel 860-810-5216; *Imprints*: Harvest Moon Books (MYID_D_HARVEST)
E-mail: Jncahill@gmail.com.

Tullycrine, LLC, (*978-0-9746554*) P.O. Box 178, Heisson, WA 98622-0178 USA
E-mail: tullycrineinc@aol.com; tullycrinellc@aol.com
Web site: http://www.tullycrine.com; http://www.book.traditionalcats.com.

Tumble Creek Pr., (*978-0-9800660; 978-1-953026*) P.O. Box P.O. Box 12639, Raleigh, NC 27605 USA (SAN 855-1197)
Web site: https://www.danidixonbooks.com; http://www.TUMBLECREEKPRESS.com.

Tumblehome Learning, (*978-0-9850008; 978-0-9897924; 978-0-9907829; 978-1-943431*) P.O. Box 171386, Boston, MA 02117-3225 USA Tel 781-924-5036
E-mail: info@tumblehomelearning.com
Web site: http://www.tumblehomelearning.com
Dist(s): **Independent Pubs. Group.**

Tumbleweed Press (CAN) (*978-1-7782017*) *Dist. by* **Orca Bk Pub.**

Tumbleweed Publishing, (*978-0-9720132*) P.O. Box 194, Valley City, OH 44280 USA Do not confuse with Tumbleweed Publishing Company in Eugene, OH
E-mail: tumbleweedbooks@aol.com.

Tundra Bks. (CAN) (*978-0-88776; 978-0-89541; 978-0-912766; 978-1-77049*) *Dist. by* **Random.**

Tundra Bks. (CAN) (*978-0-88776; 978-0-89541; 978-0-912766; 978-1-77049*) *Dist. by* **Peng Rand Hse.**

Tune, Riley, 10110 Strome Ave. 308, Raleigh, NC 27617 USA Tel 919-438-4780
E-mail: rtune86@gmail.com
Dist(s): **Ingram Content Group.**

Tuned in to Learning, (*978-0-9768881*) P.O. Box 221016, San Diego, CA 92192 USA (SAN 256-5803) Tel 858-453-0590; Fax: 858-777-3626
E-mail: mlazar@coastmusictherapy.com
Web site: http://www.tunedintolearning.com.

Turley, Sandy *See* **Helps4Teachers**

Turman, E., (*978-0-9753042*) 1321 Singingwood Ct., No. 1, Walnut Creek, CA 94595 USA Tel 925-944-5743
E-mail: shihtze1@msn.com.

Turman, Joe Garner, (*978-0-692-14181-6; 978-0-692-14226-4*) 164 Greenfield Ln, Alabaster, AL 35007 USA Tel 205-358-8782
E-mail: joegturman@gmail.com.

Turn the Page Publishing, (*978-0-9832148; 978-1-938501*) Memorial Sta., Upper Montclair, NJ 07043 USA (SAN 860-0864) Tel 973-202-8979
E-mail: rlentin@turnthepagepublishing.com
Web site: www.turnthepagepublishing.com
Dist(s): **Ingram Content Group.**

Turnapaige & Reed Moore, (*978-0-9725231*) P.O. Box 412, Scottsdale, AZ 85252 USA
E-mail: reedmoore@turnapaige.com
Web site: http://www.turnapaige.com.

Turnaround Bk. Publishing Corp., (*978-0-9753028*) 5047 W. Main St., Suite 212, Kalamazoo, MI 49001 USA.

Turnberry Pr., (*978-0-9971477*) 150 Crest Rd., Southern Pines, NC 28387 USA Tel 910-693-9906
E-mail: annieh@microcare.com
Web site: www.AnnabellesReadingCorner.com.

Turner, Barbara, (*978-0-9747019*) P.O. Box 893493, Temecula, CA 92589 USA Tel 951-699-3933
E-mail: adayinsanfrancisco@yahoo.com
Dist(s): **Lulu Pr., Inc.**

Turner, Blaine, (*978-0-615-25688-7; 978-0-578-00165-4; 978-0-578-00497-6; 978-0-578-09035-1; 978-0-578-12843-6; 978-0-578-14952-3*) 26626 Lily Lake Inn Rd., Webster, WI 54893 USA
E-mail: blaine_turner@tsco.org
Dist(s): **Lulu Pr., Inc.**

Turner Publishing Co., (*978-0-89793; 978-0-938021; 978-0-940069; 978-1-56311; 978-1-59652; 978-1-61858; 978-1-62045; 978-1-63026; 978-1-68162; 978-1-68336; 978-1-68442; 979-8-88798*) 200 4th Ave N. Ste. 950, Nashville, TN 37219-2145 USA; 424 Church St., Suite 2240, Nashville, TN 37209 Tel 615-255-2665; Fax: 615-255-5081; *Imprints*: Hunter House (HunterHse); Gurze Books (GurzeBks); Prospect Park Books (PrspctPkBks) Do not confuse with companies with the same or similar name in Atlanta, GA, Eastchester, NY, Houston, TX
E-mail: editorial@turnerpublishing.com
Web site: http://www.turnerpublishing.com
Dist(s): **Consortium Bk. Sales & Distribution**
MyiLibrary
Open Road Integrated Media, Inc.
Partners Bk. Distributing, Inc.
Two Rivers Distribution.

Turner, Rich Photographs, (*978-0-9762410*) 305 Fyffe Ave., Suite 158, Stockton, CA 95203 USA Tel 209-460-1050; Fax: 209-460-1051
E-mail: richt@turnerphoto.com
Web site: http://www.turnerphoto.com.

Turngroup Technologies, LLC, (*978-0-9794377*) 2811 Locust St., Saint Louis, MO 63103-1308 USA
Web site: http://www.hisforhopebooks.com
Dist(s): **Big River Distribution.**

Turning a New Page, (*978-0-9762030; 978-0-692-07658-3*) Orders Addr.: P.O. Box 91603, Tucson, AZ 85752-1603 USA Tel 520-579-7183; Fax: 520-407-6524
E-mail: rick4758@turninganewpage.com
Web site: http://www.turninganewpage.com.

Turning Point LLC, (*978-0-9745745*) 1339 Indiana Ave., Connersville, IN 47331 USA Tel 765-825-9835; 765-265-3207 (Mobile)
E-mail: lsfitzg@aol.com
Web site: http://www.stellarstar.biz.

Turning Point Pubns., LLC, (*978-0-9752742; 978-0-9840986*) Orders Addr.: 2822 Cashwell Dr., No. 233, Goldsboro, NC 27534 USA Tel 615-562-1540 Order books at www.turningpointstore.org Do not confuse with Turning Point Publications in Eureka, CA
E-mail: info@turningpointpublications.com
Web site: http://www.turningpointpublications.com.

Turning Tree Pr., (*978-1-7369405*) 7733 Stonehenge Farm Ln, Raleigh, NC 27613 USA Tel 919-491-7756
E-mail: shadmasen@gmail.com
Web site: www.turningtreepress.com.

Turnstyle, (*978-0-9668541*) Orders Addr.: P.O. Box 810, Portland, IN 47371 USA; Edit Addr.: 1601 W. 100 S., Portland, IN 47371 USA
E-mail: rogdomingo@gmail.com.

Turpin, Jill Lorraine, (*978-0-692-92451-8; 978-1-7320932*) 7311 Dogwood Dr, Fairview, TN 37062 USA Tel 615-509-3115
E-mail: jill.lorraine@gmail.com.

Turquoise Lake *See* **FireFly Lights**

Turquoise Morning Pr., (*978-1-935817; 978-1-937389; 978-1-62237*) PO Box 20, New Holland, OH 43145 USA Tel 859-940-6816
E-mail: kim@turquoisemorning.com; kim.tmpress@gmail.com
Web site: http://www.maddiejames.com
Dist(s): **Draft2Digital**
Smashwords.

Turquoise Rose Publishing, *(978-1-7334967)* 8117 Buckskin Trl., Snowflake, AZ 85937-5678 USA Tel 928-243-4163
E-mail: cliftonfoster@outlook.com
Web site: www.turquoiserosepublishing.com.
Turtle Bks. *Imprint of* **Jason & Nordic Pubs.**
Turtle Bks., *(978-1-890515)* 897 Boston Post Rd., Madison, CT 06443-3155 USA
E-mail: turtlebook@aol.com
Web site: http://www.turtlebooks.com
Dist(s): **Lectorum Pubns., Inc.**
Turtle Gallery Editions, *(978-0-9626935)* P.O. Box 219, Deer Isle, ME 04627-0219 USA Tel 207-348-9977 (phone/fax)
E-mail: person@turtlegallery.com
Web site: http://www.turtlegallery.com.
Turtle Point Pr., *(978-0-9627987; 978-1-885586; 978-1-885983; 978-1-933527; 978-1-885983-51-0; 978-1-7333680)* 233 Broadway, Rm. 946, New York, NY 10279 USA Tel 212-285-1019 (phone/fax)
E-mail: countomega@aol.com
Web site: http://www.turtlepoint.com
Dist(s): **Consortium Bk. Sales & Distribution**
Ingram Content Group
MyiLibrary
SPD-Small Pr. Distribution
Sprout, Inc.
Turtle Pr., *(978-1-880336; 978-1-934903; 978-1-938585; 978-0-9895971)* Orders Addr.: 500 N Washington St No. 1545, Rockville, MD 20849 USA Toll Free: 800-778-8785 (orders only)
E-mail: orders@turtlepress.com; turtlepress@gmail.com
Web site: http://www.turtlepress.com.
Turtle Press Corporation *See* **Turtle Pr.**
Turtle Shell Bks., *(978-0-578-70808-9)* 7057 28th St. N., Oakdale, MN 55128 USA Tel 651-592-6810
E-mail: TurtleShellBooks@outlook.com.
Turtle Time Bks., *(978-0-9770957)* P.O. Box 809, San Luis Obispo, CA 93406 USA.
Turtleback, 1000 North Second Ave., Logan, IA 51546-0500 USA.
Turtleback Books *See* **Turtleback Bks. Publishing, Ltd.**
Turtleback Bks. Publishing, Ltd., *(978-1-883385)* Orders Addr.: c/o Martel, P.O. Box 106, Anna Bay, NSW 2316 AUS Tel 0401 843 837; 0423 627 012 Do not confuse with Turtleback Bks., Madison, WI
E-mail: turtlebackbooks@australiamail.com; turtlebackbooks@usa.com
Web site: http://www.turtlebackbooks.net
Dist(s): **Partners/West Book Distributors.**
Tuscany Bay Bks., *(978-1-7335103; 979-8-9856708)* 10656 W Annafaye St, Star, ID 93063 USA Tel 805-795-3165
E-mail: JIMCHRISTINA@YAHOO.COM; richardpaolinelli@yahoo.com
Web site: www.tuscanybaybooks.com.
Tuscarora Publishing Company, *(978-0-9860321)* 3199 Sherman Rd, Mansfield, OH 44903 USA Tel 419-529-5596.
Tush People, The, *(978-0-9722514)* P.O. Box 950100, Mission Hills, CA 91395 USA Tel 661-298-2293; 818-897-1734; Fax: 818-899-4455
E-mail: dfav218@aol.com.
Tutortime4kidz, *(978-0-9986382)* 300 FOXBORO Ct., SAN RAMON, CA 94583 USA Tel 925-413-1071
E-mail: darienegrimm@sbcglobal.net.
Tuttle Publishing, *(978-0-8048; 978-1-4629; 978-1-955634)* Orders Addr.: 364 Innovation Dr., North Clarendon, VT 05759 USA (SAN 213-2621) Tel 802-773-8930; Fax: 802-773-6993; Toll Free Fax: 800-329-8885; Toll Free: 800-526-2778; *Imprints:* PeriplusEdition (PeriplEdns)
E-mail: info@tuttlepublishing.com
Web site: http://www.tuttlepublishing.com
Dist(s): **Cheng & Tsui Co.**
Children's Plus, Inc.
MyiLibrary
Publishers Group West (PGW)
Simon & Schuster
Simon & Schuster, Inc.
ebrary, Inc.
Tuva Publishing (TUR) *(978-605-5647) Dist. by* **IPG Chicago.**
Tuvott Publishing, *(978-0-9723974)* P.O. Box 18276, Erlanger, KY 41018 USA (SAN 255-3341) Tel 859-341-6004; Fax: 859-341-6033
E-mail: tuvott@fuse.net
Web site: http://www.trinityunveiled.com
Dist(s): **Book Clearing Hse.**
Spring Arbor Distributors, Inc.
Tuxbury Publishing LLC, *(978-0-9910680; 978-1-942444; 978-1-950155)* PO Box 264, Etna, NH 03750 USA Tel 603-643-2175
E-mail: sarinabowenwrites@gmail.com
Web site: www.sarinabowen.com.
Tuxedo Blue, LLC, *(978-0-9754056)* Orders Addr.: P.O. Box 2008, Lenox, MA 01240 USA Tel 413-637-2190; Edit Addr.: 455 W. 43rd St., No. 1A, New York, NY 10036 USA Tel 212-262-5113
E-mail: billiamsw@earthlink.net
Web site: http://www.spacenicks.com.
Tuxedo Pr., *(978-0-9774486; 978-1-936161)* 546 E. Springville Rd., Carlisle, PA 17015 USA
E-mail: info@Tuxedo-Press.com
Web site: http://Tuxedo-Press.com.
TV Acres Books *See* **Holst Bks.**
Twain, Mark Media, Inc. Pubs., *(978-1-58037)* 100 E. Main St., Lewistown, MO 63452 USA Tel 573-497-2202; Fax: 573-497-2507
Dist(s): **Carson-Dellosa Publishing, LLC.**
Tweed K LLC, *(978-0-9994843)* 21842 Old Bridge Trail, Boca Raton, FL 33428 USA Tel 561-302-2813
E-mail: foofyoofy@aol.com
Web site: www.spinoculars.com.
Tweener Pr. *Imprint of* **Baker Trittin Pr.**
Twelve Star Pr., *(978-0-9797232)* 1105 2nd Ave. NE, Clarion, IA 50525 USA Tel 515-689-9157
E-mail: duncalfj@goldfieldaccess.net.
Twelve Stones Publishing LLC, *(978-0-9712363; 978-0-692-30050-3; 978-0-692-65064-6; 978-1-7327071)* Orders Addr.: P.O. Box 921, Eufaula, AL 36072 USA Tel 334-687-4491 Do not confuse with Twelve Stones Publishing in Grandville, MI
E-mail: brittbooks@msn.com
Web site: http://www.poemsfromthefast.com
Dist(s): **CreateSpace Independent Publishing Platform.**
Twelve Twelve Productions, LLC, *(978-0-9890169; 978-1-7362311)* P.O. Box 22333, Santa Fe, NM 87502 USA
E-mail: alighthouse@mac.com.
Twelve Twelve Publishing, LLC *See* **Twelve Twelve Productions, LLC**
Twelve Winters Pr., *(978-0-9895151; 978-0-9861597; 978-0-9987057; 978-1-7331949; 979-8-9891086)* P.O. Box 414, Sherman, IL 62684 USA Tel 217-502-2570; *Imprints:* Shining Hall (ShiningHALL)
E-mail: xii.winters@gmail.com
Web site: twelvewinters.com; shininghall.com.
Twentieth Century Christian Bks., *(978-0-89098)* 2809 Granny White Pike, Nashville, TN 37204 USA (SAN 206-2550) Tel 615-383-3842.
Twenty First Century Bks., *(978-0-9636012; 978-1-893817)* P.O. Box 2001, 507 SCR 528, Breckenridge, CO 80424-2001 USA (SAN 298-248X) Tel 970-453-9293; Fax: 970-453-6692; Toll Free: 877-453-9293 Do not confuse with Twenty First Century Bks., Inc. in New York, NY
E-mail: order_desk03@tfcbooks.com; g.peterson@tfcbooks.com
Web site: http://www.tfcbooks.com; http://www.teslabooks.com
Dist(s): **MyiLibrary.**
Twenty-First Century Bks. *Imprint of* **Lerner Publishing Group**
Twenty-First Century Co., The, *(978-0-933451; 978-1-888264)* 2201 Rockbrook Dr., No. 1916, Lewisville, TX 75067-3830 USA Tel 972-459-6327 (phone/fax)
E-mail: t21cenco@flash.net
Web site: http://www.cleareducation.com.
Twenty-fourth Street Bks, LLC, *(978-0-9726939)* 215 E. 24th St., New York, NY 10010 USA
E-mail: cz@yiddishcat.com
Web site: http://www.yiddishcat.com.
Twenty-Third Pubns./Bayard, *(978-0-89622; 978-1-58595; 978-1-62785)* 1 Montauk Ave. No. 20, New London, CT 06320-4967 USA (SAN 658-2052) Toll Free Fax: 800-572-0788; Toll Free: 800-321-0411
E-mail: kerry.moriarty@bayard-inc.com
Web site: http://www.23rdpublications.com
Dist(s): **Forward Movement Pubns.**
Twenty-Three Publishing, *(978-0-692-25221-5; 978-0-692-25222-2; 978-0-692-25223-9; 978-0-692-25224-6; 978-0-9968131)* 2 Tether Moon Ln., Ladera Ranch, CA 92694 USA Tel 949 254-1011; Fax: (949) 388-0657
E-mail: cookingwithkids@cox.net
Dist(s): **CreateSpace Independent Publishing Platform.**
twhiteart, *(978-0-9639670)* 5290 Meadville St., Excelsior, MN 55331-8792 USA Tel 952-474-2083
E-mail: madonna@twhiteart.com
Web site: http://www.twhiteart.com.
Twianie Roberts Consulting, *(978-0-9718019; 978-0-9815629)* P.O. Box 70236, Rosedale, MD 21237 USA (SAN 855-8787) Fax: 301-965-8249
Web site: http://walkintheworddc.com/index.html.
Twice As Good Productions, LLC, *(978-0-9960696)* 1105 S. Rio Vista Blvd., Fort Lauderdale, FL 33316 USA Tel 305-778-2775
E-mail: johnathan@twiceasgoodshow.com
Web site: www.twiceasgoodshow.com
Dist(s): **Cookbook Marketplace, The.**
Twilight Tales, Inc., *(978-0-9711309; 978-0-9779856)* Orders Addr.: 331 Berkshire Terrace, Roselle, IL 60172 USA Tel 630-351-9311 Sales; Edit Addr.: 2339 N. Commonwealth, No. 4C, Chicago, IL 60614 USA (SAN 851-772X) Tel 773-472-8722
E-mail: sales@twilighttales.com
Web site: http://www.twilighttales.com.
Twilight Times Bks., *(978-1-931201; 978-1-933353; 978-1-60619)* Orders Addr.: P.O. Box 3340, Kingsport, TN 376643340 USA; *Imprints:* Paladin Timeless (PalaTimeless)
E-mail: publisher@twilighttimes.com
Web site: http://www.twilighttimesbooks.com
Dist(s): **Book Clearing Hse.**
Twilight Zones Pr., *(978-0-692-75328-6)*
Twim Publishing (The World is Mine), *(978-0-9773854)* Orders Addr.: P.O. Box 9414, Akron, OH 44305 USA Fax: 330-784-7603; Edit Addr.: 1229 Eastwood Ave., Akron, OH 44305 USA
E-mail: twimpublishing@hotmail.com
Web site: www.reallovedmc.com.
Twin 20 Publishing, *(978-1-7324014)* 3041 Saint Albans Dr., Los Alamitos, CA 90720 USA Tel 562-824-0760
E-mail: kristina@caseythecontainer.com.
Twin Flame Productions, *(978-1-880765; 978-0-692-24690-0; 978-1-68323; 979-8-88544)* 120 Sugarloaf St Unit B, Sedona, AZ 86351 USA (SAN 990-0934); *Imprints:* Harmony House (HarmonyHse)
E-mail: admin@twinflameproductions.us
Web site: https://aingealroseandahonu.com; https://twinflameproductions.us/
Dist(s): **CreateSpace Independent Publishing Platform.**
Twin Guardian Publishing, *(978-0-9858953)* 8821 W. Oklahoma Ave. No. 301, Milwaukee, WI 53227 USA Tel 414-477-5975
E-mail: debh1913@live.com
Web site: www.dperduehenderson.com.
Twin Lights Pubs., Inc., *(978-1-885435; 978-1-934907)* 8 Hale St., Rockport, MA 01966 USA (SAN 257-8867) Tel 978-546-7398; Fax: 978-546-5803; 6 Tide St., Boston, MA 02210
E-mail: info@twinlightspub.com; orders@twinlightspub.com
Web site: http://www.twinlightspub.com
Dist(s): **Strisik, Nancy**
Windhover Performing Arts Ctr.
Twin Monkeys Pr., *(978-0-9768602)* 146 First St., Dunellen, NJ 08812 USA Tel 732-752-3285
E-mail: storytellerjt@optonline.net
Web site: http://www.twinmonkeyspress.com.
Twin Peaks Publishing, Inc., *(978-0-9722259)* 4708 Mountain Vista Ct., Loveland, CO 80537 USA
E-mail: Twinpeakspublish@aol.com
Web site:
http://www.bookmasters.com/marktplc/rr00979.htm; http://www.atlasbooks.com/authorspotlight/asdmiller.htm; http://hometown.aol.com/TwinPeaksPublish/TwinPeaks.htm.
Twin Sisters IP, LLC, *(978-0-9632249; 978-1-57583; 978-1-882331; 978-1-59922; 978-1-61938; 978-1-62002; 978-1-62581; 978-1-64033; 978-1-64580)* Orders Addr.: 1653 Merriman Rd. Suite L-1, Akron, OH 44313 USA (SAN 859-8460) Toll Free: 800-248-8946; 800-480-8946
E-mail: doug.kline@twinsisters.com; melissa.chase@twinsisters.com
Dist(s): **Casemate Pubs. & Bk. Distributors, LLC.**
Twin Sisters Productions, LLC *See* **Twin Sisters IP, LLC**
Twin Sisters Publishing Co., *(978-0-615-23714-5; 978-0-615-24258-3; 978-0-578-00651-2)* 1805 Breckenridge Dr., Del City, OK 73115 USA Tel 405-882-9606
E-mail: twinsisterspublishing@yahoo.com
Web site: http://www.oklahomawriter/tripod.com
Dist(s): **Lulu Pr., Inc.**
TwinAtaa Studio, *(978-1-889926)* P.O. Box 1162, Stone Mountain, GA 30086 USA Tel 770-469-5138; Fax: 770-469-5139
E-mail: twinataa@twinataa.com; srw@twinataa.com
Web site: http://www.twinataa.com.
TwinAtaa/Sanaa Village Publications *See* **TwinAtaa Studio**
Twinbrook Publishing, *(978-0-9759086)* P.O. Box 355, Bedminster, NJ 07921 USA Tel 908-534-6799
Web site: http://www.pleasantdreaming.com/.
TwinDollicious Llc, *(978-0-692-35011-9; 978-0-578-75401-7; 978-0-578-75402-4)* 84 Fingerboard Rd., Staten Island, NY 10305 USA Tel 917-709-0118
E-mail: Marketing@twindollicious.com
Web site: Http://www.twindollicious.com.
Twinkle Bks., *(978-0-9792992)* 1415 Riverbank St., Lincoln Park, MI 48146-3880 USA (SAN 853-0483) Tel 313-381-2082
E-mail: Treasurecloud@msn.com
Web site: http://Twinkleblink.com.
Twinkle Twinkle Little Bks., *(978-0-9771447)* 131 E. Wilson St., Centre Hall, PA 16828-8703 USA Tel 814-364-2237
E-mail: nicole@twinkletwinklelittlebooks.com
Web site: http://www.twinkletwinklelittlebooks.com.
Twins Bks. *Imprint of* **Sterling Investments I, LLC DBA Twins Magazine**
TwinsBooks, *(978-0-615-35370-8; 978-0-615-60112-0)* 14590 Ludlow St., Oak Park, MI 48237 USA Tel 248-968-2135
E-mail: deanna41969@hotmail.com.
Twisted Key Publishing, LLC, *(978-1-947744; 978-1-63911)* 165 Bedford Rd., Lincoln, MA 01773 USA Tel 954-864-9405
E-mail: gimjarquin@gmail.com.
Twisted Spice *See* **Trio of Mermaids Publishing, A**
Twisted Tree Pr, *(978-0-9778865)* 1232 Grant Rd, Harlem, GA 30814 USA Tel 706-306-9503
E-mail: twisted_tree_press@hotmail.com.
Twister Publishing Company *See* **Twister Publishing LLC**
Twister Publishing LLC, *(978-0-9749744)* Orders Addr.: P.O. Box 123, Conover, WI 54519 USA; P.O. Box 123, Conover, WI 54519 Tel 715-479-9417
E-mail: donaldseltin@theministryofpanacea.org
Web site: http://www.theministryofpanacea.org.
Twizzlerbees Entertainment, *(978-1-7360151)* 11752 Chanceford Dr, Woodbridge, VA 22192 USA Tel 617-459-7944
E-mail: BKYoung80@gmail.com.
Two Bear Publishing *See* **Cracker the Crab LLC**
Two Chicks, *(978-0-9899544)* 2063 White Horse Rd, Berwyn, PA 19312 USA Tel 610-408-8688
E-mail: ayfriday@gmail.com.
Two Crabs & A Lion LLC, *(978-0-9895879; 978-1-7352666)* 4000 W 106th St. Ste 125-148, Carmel, IN 46032 USA Tel 317-853-9268; 317-249-0785; Fax: 317-708-4855
E-mail: nturner@raisingsupaman.com; naeemdreams@naeem.engineer; nate@nathanielaturner.com; lturner@2clconsultingllc.com; supaman627@gmail.com
Web site: www.raisingsupaman.com; www.nathanielturner.com; https://www.amazingworldofstem.com/.
Two Dogz, *(978-0-9767072)* Orders Addr.: 775 Lefort By Pass Rd., Thibodaux, LA 70301 USA
E-mail: zsagabby@yahoo.com
Web site: http://www.two-dogz.com.
Two Dolphins Publishing Group, *(978-0-615-47819-7; 978-0-9836920)* 28494 Westinghouse Pl. No. 201, Valencia, CA 91355 USA Tel 818-266-8210
E-mail: info@twodolphinspublishing.com
Web site: http://www.twodolphinspublishing.com; www.wendylewisbooks.com.
Two Girls and a Reading Corner, *(978-0-9994859; 978-1-7329685; 978-1-952879)* 311 Glenwood Dr., Madison, AL 35758 USA Tel 256-658-8794
E-mail: twogirlsandareadingcorner@gmail.com
Web site: www.twogirlsandareadingcorner.com.
Two Harbors Press *Imprint of* **Salem Author Services**
Two Lakes Pr., Inc., *(978-1-59885)* P.O. Box 384, Saint Joseph, MN 56374-0384 USA Tel 616-822-1865
E-mail: s@twolakespress.com
Web site: http://www.twolakespress.com.
Two Lands, *(978-1-933984)* 1631 Lakefield North Ct., Wellington, FL 33414-1066 USA
E-mail: twolandsoffice@yahoo.com.
Two Left Feet Books *See* **Two Left Feet Music**
Two Left Feet Music, *(978-1-7363891)* 1815 Northwood Dr., Knoxville, TN 37923 USA Tel 865-661-2411
E-mail: erickbakermusic@gmail.com
Web site: www.erickbaker.com.
Two Lines Pr.,
Dist(s): **MyiLibrary**
Publishers Group West (PGW).
Two Lions *Imprint of* **Amazon Publishing**
Two Little Birds Bks., *(978-0-9912935; 978-0-9995569)* 58 Cutts Rd., Kittery, ME 03904 USA Tel 603-828-7343
E-mail: birdie@twolittlebirdsbooks.com
Web site: www.twolittlebirdsbooks.com
Dist(s): **Ingram Publisher Services**
Univ. Pr. of New England.
Two Little Hands Productions LLC, *(978-1-933543; 978-1-936859)* Orders Addr.: 870 E. N. Union Ave., Midvale, UT 84047 USA
E-mail: rose@signingtime.com
Web site: http://www.signingtime.com.
Two Little Pubs., *(978-0-692-76235-6; 978-0-692-79163-9; 978-0-692-82284-5; 978-0-578-51981-4)* 2447 Stately Oaks Dr., Raleigh, NC 27614 USA Tel 803-622-0319
E-mail: globalpartners202@gmail.com.
Two Lives Publishing, *(978-0-9674468)* Orders Addr.: 2500 Painter Ct., Annapolis, MD 21401 USA; Edit Addr.: 2500 Painter Ct., Annapolis, MD 21401 USA
E-mail: bcombs@TwoLives.com
Web site: http://www.TwoLives.com
Dist(s): **Book Wholesalers, Inc.**
Brodart Co.
Two Oaks, LLC, *(978-0-692-92964-3; 978-0-692-92969-8; 978-0-692-93010-6; 978-0-692-93012-0; 978-0-692-10945-8; 978-0-692-10947-2)* 9417 Roosevelt Ave, CARR, CO 80612 USA Tel 970-231-7005
E-mail: monica.yoknis@gmail.com
Dist(s): **Ingram Content Group.**
Two Owls Press *See* **Indie Owl Pr.**
Two Paddles Pr., *(978-0-578-76840-3; 978-1-7364358)* PO Box 251, Oriental, NC 28571 USA Tel 252-639-1255
E-mail: jpriv2@gmail.com
Web site: www.jprivette.com.
Two Pens and a Grind Pubns., *(978-0-615-92288-1; 978-0-9978304)* 5915 Quantrell Ave, Alexandria, VA 22312 USA Tel 8509808678; Fax: 7039976332
Dist(s): **CreateSpace Independent Publishing Platform.**
Two Rivers Distribution, Div. of Ingram Content Group, Orders Addr.: 210 American Dr., Jackson, TN 38301 USA Toll Free Fax: 800-351-5073 (Customer Service); Toll Free: 866-400-5351 (Customer Service); 800-343-4499
E-mail: pd_orderentry@ingramcontent.com; ips@ingramcontent.com
Web site: http://www.tworiversdistribution.com/.
Two Saints Publishing, *(978-0-9625782)* 615 Mennonite Church Rd., Kalispell, MT 59901-7753 USA Tel 406-756-1959.
Two Seed Planters Inc., *(978-0-9755789)* 141 Tall Pines Dr., Leesburg, GA 31763-3143 USA
E-mail: twoseedplanters@aol.com
Web site: http://www.twoseedplanters.com.
Two Sees Inc., *(978-0-9983570)* 3811 Streamwood Dr., Hazel Crest, IL 60429 USA Tel 414-764-0206
E-mail: Two_Sees@yahoo.com.
Two Small Fish Pubns., *(978-0-9826582; 978-0-9971972)* 109 W. Market St., Freeburg, PA 17827 USA Tel 570-374-1363
E-mail: brendakhendricks@verizon.net
Web site: http://www.twosmallfish.org.
Two Sons Pr., Inc., *(978-0-9748995)* 14 Red Tail Dr., Highlands Ranch, CO 80126-5001 USA Tel 303-346-3003; Fax: 303-791-2226
E-mail: McAdamfam@aol.com.
Two Sweet Pea's Publishing *See* **Two Sweet Peas Publishing**
Two Sweet Peas Publishing, *(978-1-7378041; 979-8-9855605; 979-8-218-20656-7; 979-8-9885827)* 22111 Wood Island Ln., Huntington Beach, CA 92646 USA Tel 909-260-8228
E-mail: joanndickinson@hotmail.com
Web site: https://www.JoAnnDickinsonAuthor.com.
Two Sylvias Pr., *(978-0-615-95680-0; 978-0-615-96178-1; 978-0-615-96183-5; 978-0-692-27071-4; 978-0-692-33337-2; 978-0-692-35484-1; 978-0-692-37978-3; 978-0-692-44972-1; 978-0-692-45007-9; 978-0-692-45089-5; 978-0-692-49259-8; 978-0-692-49465-3; 978-0-692-57715-8; 978-0-692-62271-1; 978-0-692-64066-1; 978-0-692-65372-2; 978-0-692-66344-8; 978-0-692-72125-4; 978-0-692-76290-5; 978-0-9986314; 978-1-948767)* PO *Box 1524, Kingston, WA 98346 USA Tel 3608601213*
Dist(s): **CreateSpace Independent Publishing Platform.**
Two Tired Teachers Connection, Inc., The, *(978-0-9786835)* 151 Michael Ln., Aberdeen, NC 28315 USA (SAN 851-3090) Tel 910-944-8857
E-mail: bevlashley@nc.rr.com
Web site: http://www.twotiredteachers.com.
Two Way Bilingual, Inc., *(978-0-941911)* Cond The Falls, No. 405, Guaynabo, PR 00657 USA (SAN 666-0169).
Two-Can Publishing *Imprint of* **T&N Children's Publishing**
TwoDot *Imprint of* **Globe Pequot Pr., The**
TwoMorrows Publishing, *(978-1-893905; 978-1-60549)* TwoMorrows Inc., 10407 Bedfordtown Dr., Raleigh, NC 27614-8058 USA Tel 919-449-0344; Fax: 919-449-0327
E-mail: twomorrow@aol.com; john@twomorrows.com
Web site: http://www.twomorrows.com
Dist(s): **Diamond Comic Distributors, Inc.**
Diamond Bk. Distributors.

Publisher Name Index

TwoPenny Pubns., *(978-0-9755671)* 205 Rainbow Dr., No. 10503, Livingston, TX 77399-2005 USA
E-mail: samnalice@twopennytravels.com
Web site: http://www.79scenario.com.

Two's Company, *(978-0-9742862)* Div. of Threaded Images, 303 Wrenn Ave., New Paris, OH 45347 USA Tel 937-437-0095; 513-933-9207; Toll Free Fax: 877-217-0700; Toll Free: 800-487-0095
E-mail: sgray6@cinci.rr.com; timages@aol.com
Web site: http://www.twos-company.biz.

Two-Ten Book Press *See* **Two-Ten Bk. Pr., Inc.**

Two-Ten Bk. Pr., Inc., *(978-0-578-05661-6; 978-0-9827799; 978-0-9884642; 978-0-9896216; 978-1-941208; 978-1-946218; 978-1-956574)* 2522 Kay Ln., Charleston, WV 25302 USA; P.O. Box 4215, Charleston, WV 25364 Tel 304-419-4169
Web site: http://www.thedarkslayer.com; http://www.thedarkslayer.net
Dist(s): **Smashwords.**

TyBook, *(978-0-9779631)* 5504 Nieman Rd., Shawnee, KS 66203 USA Tel 503-407-1217
E-mail: clayme@claytonpixton.com
Web site: http://www.tybookinc.com.

Tyes, Raecine, *(978-0-578-59235-0)* 6118 Tracy Valley Dr, Norcross, GA 30093 USA Tel 678-791-8478
E-mail: 1rtyes@gmail.com
Dist(s): **Ingram Content Group.**

TYL Publishing, *(978-0-9753902)* 1902 Spillers Ln., Houston, TX 77043 USA Tel 713-647-9501; Fax: 713-647-9410
E-mail: tylnwt@gmail.com
Dist(s): **Partners/West Book Distributors**
Quality Bks., Inc.

Tyler, J. Publishing *See* **Crush Publishing**

Tyler Laws Pr., *(978-0-9992446)* 8344 Golf Links Rd., Oakland, CA 94605 USA Tel 510-423-1172
E-mail: enkaeconsulting@gmail.com.

Tyler's Field, *(978-0-9855870)* 4929 Turfway Trail, Harbor Springs, MI 49740 USA Tel 614-309-0048
E-mail: art@janicephelps.com.

Tyndale Entertainment *Imprint of* **Tyndale Hse. Pubs.**

Tyndale Fiction *Imprint of* **Tyndale Hse. Pubs.**

†Tyndale Hse. Pubs., *(978-0-8423; 978-1-4143; 978-1-4964; 978-1-7358909; 979-8-4005)* Orders Addr.: 351 Executive Dr., Carol Stream, IL 60188 USA; Edit Addr.: 351 Executive Dr., Carol Stream, IL 60188 USA (SAN 206-7749) Tel 630-668-8310; Fax: 630-668-3245; Toll Free: 800-323-9400; *Imprints:* Tyndale Kids (Tyndale Kids); Tyndale Entertainment (Tyndale Ent); Tyndale Fiction (TynFic); Tyndale Momentum (TyndaleMomentum); Wander (Wander); Happy Day (HappyDay); Faith that Sticks (FaiththatSticks)
E-mail: international@tyndale.com; permission@tyndale.com; mikeedelstein@tyndale.com
Web site: http://www.tyndale.com
Dist(s): **Anchor Distributors**
Brodart Co.
Christian Bk. Distributors
Cokesbury
CreateSpace Independent Publishing Platform
Editorial Unilit
Follett School Solutions
Ingram Entertainment, Inc.
Spring Arbor Distributors, Inc.; *CIP.*

Tyndale Kids *Imprint of* **Tyndale Hse. Pubs.**

Tyndale Momentum *Imprint of* **Tyndale Hse. Pubs.**

Type F, *(978-0-9768733)* P.O. Box 1045, Lodi, CA 95241-1045 USA
E-mail: info@enduranceguide.com
Web site: http://www.enduranceguide.com.

Tyr Publishing, *(978-0-9723473)* P.O. Box 19895, Fountain Hills, AZ 85269-9895 USA (SAN 254-7775) Tel 480-836-4261
E-mail: info@tyrpublishing.com
Web site: http://www.tyrpublishing.com
Dist(s): **Midpoint Trade Bks., Inc.**

Tyson, Sandi *See* **Christiangela Productions**

Tytam Publishing, *(978-0-9758602)* 111 Lincoln Ave., Suite A-9, Newark, NJ 07104-4607 USA
E-mail: Tygoode1@aol.com
Web site: http://www.tygoode.com.

Tzipora Pubns., Inc., *(978-0-9722595; 978-0-578-46157-1)* Orders Addr.: P.O. Box 115, New York, NY 10185 USA Tel 646-476-6115; Toll Free Fax: 775-414-2940
E-mail: ddg1096@gmail.com; tziporapub@msn.com
Web site: https://sites.google.com/view/dina=grossman; http://www.tziporapub.us.

U A H C Press *See* **URJ Pr.**

U H H Hale Kuamo'o Hawaiian Language Center *See* **Hale Kuamo'o Hawaiian Language Ctr. at UHH**

U. S. Capitol Historical Society, *(978-0-916200)* 200 Maryland Ave., NE, Washington, DC 20002 USA (SAN 226-6601) Tel 202-543-8919; Fax: 202-544-8244; Toll Free: 800-887-9318
E-mail: uschs@uschs.org
Web site: http://www.uschs.org
Dist(s): **University of Virginia Pr.**

U. S. Press & Graphics *See* **Three Knolls Publishing**

Ubaviel's Gifts, *(978-0-9713589)* 1550 Scenic View Dr., Loudon, TN 37774 USA
Web site: http://www.angelicgift.com.

UBUS Communications Systems, *(978-1-56411)* Div. of Khalifah's Booksellers & Associates, Orders Addr.: 26070 Barhams Hill Rd., Drewryville, VA Southhampton 23844 USA (SAN 630-6748) Tel 434-378-2140; 704-390-0663; *Imprints:* CB Publishing & Design (CB Pubng & Design)
E-mail: khabooksvirginia@yahoo.com
Web site: http://www.khabooks.com; http://www.khabooks.com; http://www.blackbooksaward.com; http://www.black-e-books.com; http://www.black-e-books.com
Dist(s): **Khalifah's Booksellers & Assocs.**

UCAN Publishing, LLC, *(978-0-9909310; 978-0-578-77103-8)* 8247 Forest Lake Dr., Conway, SC 29526 USA Tel 843-347-2382
E-mail: lowerycatherine@gmail.com
Web site: ucanpublishing.com.

Uccello Rosso, *(978-0-9819187)* 328 Windsor St., Reading, PA 19601-2124 USA (SAN 856-955X)
E-mail: mail@uccellorosso.com
Web site: http://uccellorosso.com.

UCLA Center for Labor Research & Education *See* **Center for Labor Research and Education, Univ. of California, Los Angeles**

UFO Photo Archives, *(978-0-934269; 978-0-9608558)* 27341 Stanford St., Hemet, CA 92544 USA (SAN 240-7949) Tel 520-907-0102
Web site: http://www.UFOPhotoArchives.com.

Ufodike, Ekwutosi, *(978-0-9800538)* 3987 Nemours Trail, Kennesaw, GA 30152 USA Tel 404-574-0193
E-mail: tosi.ufodike@ge.com.

Ufomadu Consulting & Publishing, *(978-0-9754197; 978-0-9790022; 978-1-7331255)* P.O. Box 746, Selma, AL 36702 USA Tel 334-418-0088
E-mail: info@ufomaduconsulting.com
Web site: http://www.ufomaduconsulting.com.

UglyTent, *(978-0-9995792)* 1154 Russell St, Ashland, KY 41101 USA Tel 606-232-2346
E-mail: uglytent@gmail.com
Web site: uglytent.com.

UI Wizards *See* **Deer Horn Pr.**

U-Impact Publishing LLC, *(978-0-692-38569-2; 978-0-692-38606-4; 978-0-692-39877-7; 978-0-692-45870-9; 978-0-692-49679-4; 978-0-692-49720-3; 978-0-692-50208-2; 978-0-692-52976-8; 978-0-692-57120-0; 978-0-692-57554-3; 978-0-692-65111-7; 978-0-692-65518-4; 978-0-692-65534-4; 978-0-692-69518-0; 978-0-692-72854-3; 978-0-692-72857-4)* 38 Ebbtide Ln., Willingboro, NJ 08046 USA Tel 6095262226
Dist(s): **CreateSpace Independent Publishing Platform.**

Uitti, Daniel, *(978-0-9708430; 978-0-9819478)* Div. of DaSum Company LLC, 223 Buckingham St., Oakville, CT 06779 USA Tel 860-274-9065; Fax: 860-417-0609
E-mail: dan@uitti.net
Web site: http://www.uitti.net/DaSum/.

UK Abrams Bks. for Young Readers,
Dist(s): **Abrams, Inc.**
Hachette Bk. Group.

Ullstein-Taschenbuch-Verlag (DEU) *(978-3-548) Dist. by* **Distribks Inc.**

Ultimacy Pr., *(978-0-9760205)* 11409 Parkside Pl., Bradenton, FL 34202 USA Tel 941-753-6560; Fax: 941-753-6561
E-mail: info@ultimatefinancialadvisor.com
Web site: http://www.ultimatefinancialadvisor.com.

Ultimate Bks., *(978-0-9725953; 978-0-9788430)* 104 Oakhill Key Ct., Valrico, FL 33594 USA Do not confuse with Ultimate Bks., in Glendale, CA
E-mail: info@opynyon.com
Web site: http://www.opynyon.com.

Ultimate Martial Arts CD, The *See* **Black Belt Training**

Ulverscroft Large Print Bks. (GBR) *(978-0-7089; 978-0-85456; 978-1-84395; 978-1-84617; 978-1-4448; 978-1-78541; 978-1-78782) Dist. by* **Ulverscroft US.**

Ulverscroft Large Print Bks., Ltd., *(978-0-7089; 978-1-84617)* Orders Addr.: P.O. Box 1230, West Seneca, NY 14224-1230 USA; Edit Addr.: 950 Union Rd., West Seneca, NY 14224-3438 USA (SAN 208-3035) Toll Free: 800-955-9659
E-mail: enquiries@ulverscroft.co.uk; sales@ulverscroft.com
Web site: http://www.ulverscroft.co.uk.

Ulysses Pr., *(978-0-915233; 978-1-56975; 978-1-61243; 978-1-64604)* Orders Addr.: P.O. Box 3440, Berkeley, CA 94703-3440 USA (SAN 289-8764) Tel 510-601-8301; Fax: 510-601-8307; Toll Free: 800-377-2542; Edit Addr.: 3286 Adeline St., Suite 1, Berkeley, CA 94703 USA (SAN 289-8772)
E-mail: ulysses@ulyssespress.com
Web site: http://www.ulyssespress.com
Dist(s): **MyiLibrary**
Open Road Integrated Media, Inc.
Publishers Group West (PGW)
Simon & Schuster, Inc.
Two Rivers Distribution
ebrary, Inc.

Ulyssian Pubns. *Imprint of* **Pine Orchard, Inc.**

Umbrelly Bks., *(978-0-9791127; 978-0-615-14064-3; 978-0-615-14065-0; 978-0-615-15448-0; 978-0-615-20654-7; 978-0-692-53594-3)* P.O. Box 2703, Saratoga, CA 95070-5608 USA
E-mail: umbrelly_books@yahoo.com
Web site: http://www.umbrellybooks.com
Dist(s): **Lulu Pr., Inc.**

UMI *Imprint of* **UMI (Urban Ministries, Inc.)**

UMI (Urban Ministries, Inc.), *(978-0-940955; 978-1-932715; 978-1-934056; 978-1-60352; 978-1-60997; 978-1-63038; 978-1-68353; 979-8-88976)* 1551 Regency Ct., Calumet City, IL 60409-5448 USA (SAN 665-2247) Fax: 708-868-7105; Toll Free: 800-860-8642; *Imprints:* UMI (UMI)
Web site: http://www.urbanministries.com
Dist(s): **Midpoint Trade Bks., Inc.**

Umina, Lisa M. *See* **Halo Publishing International**

Unaluna Ediciones (ARG) *(978-987-1296) Dist. by* **Lectorum Pubns.**

Unbridled Bks., *(978-1-932961; 978-1-936071; 978-1-60953)* 2000 Wadsworth Blvd., No. 195, Lakewood, CO 80214 USA Toll Free: 888-732-3822 (phone/fax)
E-mail: alexa@unbridledbooks.com; swallace@unbridledbooks.com
Web site: http://www.unbridledbooks.com
Dist(s): **Intrepid Group, Inc., The**
MyiLibrary
Publishers Group West (PGW).

Unchained Spirit Enterprises, *(978-0-9717790; 978-0-615-94962-8; 978-1-7342909)* 5432 Connecticut Ave NW No. 104, Washington, DC 20015 USA Tel 202-830-5115
Dist(s): **CreateSpace Independent Publishing Platform.**

Uncivilized Bks., *(978-0-9846814; 978-0-9889014; 978-1-941250)* 3336 30th Ave. S, Minneapolis, MN 55406 USA Tel 917-495-8637; *Imprints:* odod books (odod bks)
E-mail: chief@uncivilizedbooks.com
Web site: http://www.uncivilizedbooks.com/
Dist(s): **Consortium Bk. Sales & Distribution**
MyiLibrary.

Uncle Dave's Bks., *(978-0-692-68564-8; 978-0-692-84581-3; 978-0-9989598; 978-0-692-18597-1; 978-0-692-19848-3; 978-0-578-41013-5; 978-0-578-46788-7)* 4135 leechburg rd, new kensington, PA 15068 USA Tel 724-833-1289
Web site: www.uncledavesbooks.com; www.uncledavehoward.com
Dist(s): **Independent Pub.**

Uncle Henry Bks., *(978-1-932568)* P.O. Box 41310, Long Beach, CA 90853-1310 USA Tel 562-987-9165; Fax: 562-439-5924
E-mail: unclehenrybooks@aol.com.

Uncle Jim's Publishing, *(978-0-9800764)* Orders Addr.: c/o Potomac Adventist Bookstore, 12004 Cherry Hill Rd., Silver Spring, MD 20904 USA Tel 301-572-0700; Toll Free: 800-325-8492; P.O. Box 410, Chino Valley, AZ 86323 Tel 928-636-9419 (wholesale orders only); Fax: 928-636-1216 (wholesale orders only)
E-mail: soonchin@freezees.com
Web site: http://www.freezees.com; http://www.potomacabc.com.

Under the Green Umbrella, *(978-1-929701)* 5808 Westmont Dr., Austin, TX 78731-3836 USA Tel 512-454-2414
E-mail: janesbauld@aol.com
Web site: http://www.uts.cc.utexas.edu/~jbauld.

Under the Stars *Imprint of* **Disney Publishing Worldwide**

Underline Publishing LLC, *(978-1-949868; 978-1-962185)* P.O. Box 420790, Kissimmee, FL 34742 USA Tel 321-203-9874
E-mail: fcstarosa@gmail.com
Web site: www.underlinepublishing.com.

Underlined *Imprint of* **Random Hse. Children's Bks.**

Understanding For Life Ministries, Inc., *(978-0-9714584; 978-0-9721504; 978-0-9749019; 978-0-9797019; 978-0-9822938; 978-0-9833673; 978-0-9850813; 978-0-9904982; 978-0-9970699; 978-1-7343057)* 3665 Kirby Pkwy., Suite 6, Memphis, TN 38115 USA Tel 901-844-3962; Fax: 901-844-3944
E-mail: info@understandingforlife.org
Web site: http://www.understandingforlife.org
Dist(s): **BookBaby.**

Understanding Nutrition PC, *(978-0-9764002; 978-0-9800334)* Orders Addr.: 6240 E. Univ. Blvd., Dallas, TX 75214 USA Tel 214-503-7100
E-mail: jessica@understandingnutrition.com
Web site: http://www.understandingnutrition.com.

Underwood Books, *(978-0-88733; 978-0-934438; 978-1-887424; 978-1-59929)* Orders Addr.: P.O. Box 1919, Nevada City, CA 95945 USA Tel 530-470-9095; Fax: 530-470-9049; Edit Addr.: 12514 Cavanaugh Ln., Nevada City, CA 95959 USA
E-mail: tim@underwoodbooks.com; contact@underwoodbooks.com
Web site: http://www.underwoodbooks.com
Dist(s): **Publishers Group West (PGW).**

Undisciplined Pr., *(978-1-928539)* P.O. Box 8919, Portland, OR 97207-8919 USA Tel 503-224-8408; Fax: 503-224-8420.

Unicorn Castle Bks., *(978-0-615-56949-9; 978-0-9890340)* 1110 Pack Rd., White Bluff, TN 37187 USA Tel 615-477-4097; 509-999-4551
E-mail: unicorncastle@bellsouth.net
Web site: http://www.kerrydking.com.

Unicorn Pr., *(978-0-937004)* 3300 Chestnut St., Reading, PA 19605 USA Tel 610-929-8306 Do not confuse with Unicorn Pr. in Northville, MI
E-mail: kthynoll@aol.com
Web site: http://hometown.aol.com/kthynoll.

Unified Future, *(978-0-578-42197-1; 978-1-7334189)* 7612 Ecureil Dr., Austin, TX 78738 USA Tel 434-489-7684
E-mail: info@thebrothersepps.com
Dist(s): **Independent Pub.**

Uniformology, *(978-0-9815078; 978-1-935344)* 105 Coates Trail, Weatherford, TX 76087 USA Tel 817-629-9205
E-mail: uniformology@mac.com
Web site: http://www.uniformology.com.

Union Creek Communications, Inc., *(978-0-9721404)* P.O. Box 1811, Bryson City, NC 28713 USA Tel 828-488-3596; Fax: 828-488-1018
E-mail: info@researchpaperstation.com
Web site: http://researchpaperstation.com.

Union Square Pr. *Imprint of* **Sterling Publishing Co., Inc.**

Unique Artistic Creations Showcase, *(978-0-9892127; 978-0-9993142)* 4540 60th St., Ste.111, San Diego, CA 92115 USA Tel 619-955-8083
E-mail: ctpetate@gmail.com.

Unique Coloring, *(978-0-9787871; 978-1-935702; 978-1-63104)* P.O. Box 226, Williamstown, NY 13493 USA (SAN 851-6308)
Web site: http://www.uniquecoloring.com.

Unique Executive Pubs., *(978-0-9744978)* Div. of Unique Executive.com, 1653 Georgia Hwy. 257, Suite A, Cordele, GA 31015 USA Tel 229-273-8121; Fax: 229-273-7289; *Imprints:* Healthful Living Books (Living Books)
E-mail: harvardg@sowega.net
Web site: http://upublish.uniqueexecutive.com.

Uniquely You Resources, *(978-0-9627245; 978-1-888846)* P.O. Box 490, Blue Ridge, GA 30513 USA Tel 706 492 4709; 706-492-5490
E-mail: drmels@myuy.com
Web site: http://www.myuy.com; http://www.uyprofiler.com
Dist(s): **Send The Light Distribution LLC.**

Unisystems, Inc., *(978-0-7666; 978-0-87449; 978-1-56144)* 155 55th St., New York, NY 10022 USA Tel 212-826-0850; Fax: 212-758-4166
Web site: http://www.modernpublishing.com.

†Unitarian Universalist Assn., *(978-0-933840; 978-1-55896; 978-1-946169)* 25 Beacon St., Boston, MA 02108-2800 USA (SAN 225-4840) Tel 617-742-2100; Fax: 617-742-7025; Toll Free: 800-215-9076; *Imprints:* Skinner House Books (Skinner Hse)
Web site: http://www.uua.org
Dist(s): **Consortium Bk. Sales & Distribution**
Red Wheel/Weiser; *CIP.*

United Bible Societies Association Inc., *(978-1-57697; 978-1-930564; 978-1-931471; 978-1-931952; 978-1-932507; 978-1-933218; 978-1-59877; 979-8-88639)* 11401 SW 40TH ST Suite 201, MIAMI, FL 33165 USA Tel 305-702-1824; 305-593-0009; Fax: 305-702-1817 Do not confuse with United Bible Societies, New York, NY
E-mail: jhazbun@biblesocieties.org
Web site: http://www.unitedbiblesocieties.org
Dist(s): **American Bible Society.**

United Bible Societies/Americas Service Center *See* **United Bible Societies Association Inc.**

United Bks. Publishing, *(978-1-970052)* 473 Willow Rd., Macon, GA 31204 USA.

United Christian Fellowship of Chapel Hill, North Carolina *See* **Armour of Light Publishing**

United Comics, *(978-0-9743086)* Div. of Obsidian Entertainment, P.O. Box 401, Milford, CT 06460-0401 USA Toll Free: 800-546-3249 (phone/fax)
E-mail: unitedcomicworks@gmail.com
Web site: http://www.unitedcomicworks.com.

United Educators, Inc., *(978-0-87566)* 900 W. North Shore Dr. Ste. 279, Lake Bluff, IL 60044-2210 USA (SAN 204-8795).

UNITED Hse. Publishing, *(978-1-7327194; 978-1-952840)*
E-mail: info@unitedhousepublishing.com
Web site: http://unitedhousepublishing.com.

United InnoWorks Academy, *(978-0-9771380; 978-1-936478)* 9721 Conestoga Way, Potomac, MD 20854-4711 USA
E-mail: executive@innoworks.org; staff@innoworks.org
Web site: http://www.innoworks.org.

United Nation of Islam, The, *(978-0-9768502)* 1608 N. 13th St., Kansas City, KS 66102 USA Tel 913-342-0758; Fax: 913-342-0340; Toll Free: 800-331-7668
E-mail: unoi@unoi.org
Web site: http://www.unoi.org.

†United Nations Fund for Population Activities, *(978-0-89714; 978-1-61800)* 605 Third Ave, New York, NY 10158 USA (SAN 222-4429) Tel 212-297-4956; Fax: 212-370-0201
Web site: http://www.unfpa.org
Dist(s): **Casemate Pubs. & Bk. Distributors, LLC**
Rowman & Littlefield Publishers, Inc.
United Nations Pubns.; *CIP.*

United Network for Organ Sharing, *(978-1-886651)* Orders Addr.: P.O. Box 2484, Richmond, VA 23218 USA Tel 804-782-4800; Edit Addr.: 700 N. 4th St., Richmond, VA 23219 USA
Web site: http://www.unos.org.

United Optical Publishing Co., *(978-0-9764337)* 9147 Millbranch Rd., Southaven, MS 38671 USA
Web site: http://www.steelguitarbyhughjeffreys.com.

United Research Publishers, *(978-0-9614924; 978-1-887053)* Div. of Solor Products, Inc., 2233 Faraday Ave., Suite G, Carlsbad, CA 92008-7214 USA (SAN 693-5834) Tel 760-930-8937; Fax: 760-930-4291 Do not confuse with United Research, Black Mountain, NC
Web site: http://www.unitedresearchpubs.com.

†United States Government Printing Office, *(978-0-16; 978-0-18)* Orders Addr.: P.O. Box 371954, Pittsburgh, PA 15250-7954 USA (SAN 658-0785) Tel 202-512-1800; Fax: 202-512-2250; Toll Free: 866-512-1800; Edit Addr.: USGPO Stop SSMB, Washington, DC 20401 USA (SAN 206-152X) Tel 202-512-1705 (bibliographic information only); 202-512-2268 (book dealers only); Fax: 202-512-1655; *Imprints:* Defense Department (Defense Dept); Environmental Protection Agency (Envir Protect); Health and Human Services Department (Hlth & Human); Interior Department (Interior Dept); Copyright Office (Copyright Office); Defense Acquisition University (DefenseAcq U); Department of the Army (Dept Army); Federal Emergency Management Agency (F E M A); Food Safety & Inspection Service (F S I S); Forest Service (Forest Service); Joint Committee on Printing (Joint ComPrint); Joint Committee on Taxation (JointCommTaxation); National Defense University (National DefU); National Institute on Alcohol Abuse & Alcoholism (NIAAA); National Marine Fisheries Service (NMFS)
E-mail: orders@gpo.gov; rdavis@gpo.gov; ContactCenter@gpo.gov
Web site: http://bookstore.gpo.gov; https://www.gpo.gov
Dist(s): **Bernan Assocs.**
MyiLibrary
Rowman & Littlefield Publishers, Inc.
Trucatriche
ebrary, Inc.; *CIP.*

United States Judo Federation, Inc., *(978-0-9729790)* P.O. Box 338, Ontario, OR 97914-0338 USA Tel 541-889-8753; Fax: 541-889-5836
E-mail: natofc@usjf.com
Web site: http://www.usjf.com.

United States Power Squadrons, *(978-1-891148; 978-1-938405)* Orders Addr.: P.O. Box 30423, Raleigh, NC 27622 USA Tel 919-821-0281; Fax: 919-836-0813;

Toll Free: 888-367-8777; Edit Addr.: 1504 Blue Ridge Rd., Raleigh, NC 27607 USA
Web site: http://www.usps.org.

United States Trotting Association, *(978-0-9793891)* 750 Michigan Ave., Columbus, OH 43215 USA Tel 614-224-2291 Toll Free: 877-800-8782 (ext. 3260)
E-mail: jamie.rucker@ustrotting.com; HRCNews@ustrotting.com
Web site: http://www.ustrotting.com.

United Synagogue of America Bk. Service, *(978-0-8381)* Subs. of United Synagogue of America, 820 2nd Ave., New York, NY 10017-4504 USA (SAN 203-0551)
E-mail: booksvc@uscj.org
Web site: http://www.uscj.org/booksvc.
Dist(s): **Rowman & Littlefield Publishers, Inc.**

United Writers Pr., *(978-0-9725197; 978-0-9760824; 978-1-934216; 978-1-945338; 978-1-952248; 978-1-961813)* Orders Addr.: 17 Willow Tree Run, Asheville, NC 28803 USA
E-mail: vs@uwpnew.com
Web site: http://www.uwpnew.com.

Unitrust Design, *(978-0-9752775)* P.O. Box 653, Loma Linda, CA 92354 USA
E-mail: unitrustdesign@aol.com
Web site: http://www.unitrustdesign.com.

Unity Books & Multimedia Publishing (Unity School of Christianity) *See* **Unity Schl. of Christianity**

Unity Hse. *Imprint of* **Unity Schl. of Christianity**

Unity Project LLC, *(978-1-7355378)* 27454 Old School House Rd., Ardmore, AL 35739 USA Tel 334-657-4776
E-mail: admin@unityprojectllc.com.

Unity Schl. of Christianity, *(978-0-87159)* Orders Addr.: 1901 NW Blue Pkwy., Unity Village, MO 64065-0001 USA (SAN 204-8817) Tel 816-524-3550; 816 251-3571 (ordering); Fax: 816-251-3551; *Imprints:* Unity House (Unity Hse)
E-mail: unity@unityworldhq.org
Web site: http://www.unity.org
Dist(s): **BookBaby**
DeVorss & Co.
New Leaf Distributing Co., Inc.

Univ. of Alberta Pr. (CAN) *(978-0-88864; 978-0-919058; 978-1-55195; 978-1-896445; 978-1-77212) Dist. by* **Jhn Hpkn U Pr.**

Univ. of Buckingham Pr., The (GBR) *(978-0-9554642; 978-0-9560716; 978-0-9563952; 978-1-908684; 978-1-912500) Dist. by* **IPG Chicago.**

Univ. of Ottawa Pr./Presses de l'Universite d'Ottawa (CAN) *(978-0-7766; 978-2-7603) Dist. by* **TwoRivers.**

Univ. of Queensland Pr. (AUS) *(978-0-7022; 978-1-875491; 978-0-646-96356-3) Dist. by* **IPG Chicago.**

Univ. of the West Indies Pr. (JAM) *(978-976-640; 978-976-41-0029-4; 978-976-41-0044-7; 978-976-41-0068-3; 978-976-41-0109-3) Dist. by* **U of NC Pr.**

Universal Flag Publishing, *(978-1-933426)* Div. of Universal Flag Cos., 1440 W. Maple Ave., Suite 6B, Lisle, IL 60532 USA Tel 630-245-8500
E-mail: publishing@universalflag.com
Web site: www.universalflag.com.

Universal Handwriting *See* **Universal Publishing**

Universal Life Matters, Incorporated *See* **Quality of Life Publishing Co.**

Universal Marketing Media, Inc., *(978-0-9764272)* Orders Addr.: P.O. Box 7575, Pensacola, FL 32534-0575 USA Toll Free: 877-437-7811
E-mail: sales@universalmarketingmedia.com
Web site: http://www.universalmarketingmedia.com.

Universal Messengers Pubns., *(978-0-9768879)* P.O. Box 9039, Wilmington, DE 19809 USA Tel 302-764-4293; Toll Free: 866-207-9301
E-mail: phdfoxx@msn.com; phdfoxx@verizon.net
Web site: http://mysite.verizon.net/vze0488v.

Universal Politics (Politics & Social Sciences) *Imprint of* **Speedy Publishing LLC**

Universal Pubs., *(978-0-9658564; 978-1-58112; 978-1-59942; 978-1-61233; 978-1-62734)* Orders Addr.: 200 Spectrum Ctr. Dr. Ste 300, Irvine, CA 92618-5004 USA Tel 561-750-4344; 949-416-5590; Fax: 561-750-6797; Toll Free: 800-636-8329
E-mail: bookorders@upublish.com; bookorders@universal-publishers.com
Web site: http://www.dissertation.com; http://www.universal-publishers.com; http://www.BrownWalker.com.

Universal Publishing, *(978-1-883421; 978-1-931181; 978-1-934732; 978-1-63976)* Subs. of Gutenberg, Inc., 677 Roosevelt Hwy., Waymart, PA 18472 USA Tel 570-488-9820; Fax: 570-488-9750; Toll Free: 800-940-2270 Do not confuse with companies with the same or similar name in Ecino, CA, Egg Harbor Township, NJ, Gainesville, FL, Newport Beach, CA, Stoughton, MA, Pasadena, CA, Oak Park, IL, Jacksonville, FL
E-mail: tom@upub.net; larry@upub.net
Web site: http://www.upub.net; http://www.universalpublishing.net.

Universal Publishing LLC, *(978-0-9840456)* P.O. Box 99491, Emeryville, CA 94606 USA Tel 510-485-1183
E-mail: universalpublishingllc@gmail.com
Web site: www.universalpublishingllc@gmail.com.

Universal Reference Pubns. *Imprint of* **Grey Hse. Publishing**

Universal Values Media, LLC, *(978-0-9729821; 978-1-60210)* 3800 Powell Ln., No. 823, Falls Church, VA 22041 USA
Web site: http://www.onceandfuturebooks.com.

Universe Publishing, *(978-0-7893; 978-0-87663; 978-1-55550)* Div. of Rizzoli International Pubns., Inc., 300 Park Ave. S., 3rd Flr., New York, NY 10010 USA (SAN 202-537X) Tel 212-387-3400; Fax: 212-387-3444 Do not confuse with similar names in North Hollywood, CA, Englewood, NJ, Mendocino, CA
Dist(s): **Andrews McMeel Publishing**
Atlas Bks.
Ingram Publisher Services
MyiLibrary
Penguin Random Hse. Distribution
Penguin Random Hse. LLC
Random Hse., Inc.
Rizzoli International Pubns., Inc.

Univ. At Buffalo, Child Care Ctr., *(978-0-9712349)* Butler Annex A, 3435 Main St., Buffalo, NY 14214-3011 USA Tel 716-829-2226
E-mail: rorrange@buffalo.edu.

Univ. Editions, *(978-0-9711659; 978-0-615-11379-1; 978-0-692-63610-7; 978-0-578-48615-4; 978-1-7376511)* 1003 W. Centennial Dr., Peoria, IL 61614-2828 USA Tel 309-692-0621; Fax: 309-693-0628 Do not confuse with University Editions in Huntington, WV
E-mail: mikruc@aol.com
Web site: http://www.terrythetractor.com.

Univ. Games, *(978-0-935145; 978-1-57528)* 2030 Harrison St., San Francisco, CA 94110-1310 USA (SAN 695-2321) Tel 415-503-1600; Fax: 415-503-0085
E-mail: info@ugames.com
Web site: http://www.ugames.com.

Univ. of Alaska Pr., *(978-0-912006; 978-1-889963; 978-1-60223)* P.O. Box 756240, Fairbanks, AK 99775-6240 USA (SAN 203-3011) Tel 907-474-5831; Fax: 907-474-5502; Toll Free: 888-252-6657
E-mail: fypress@uaf.edu; sue.mitchell@alaska.edu
Web site: http://www.alaska.edu/uapress
Dist(s): **Chicago Distribution Ctr.**
Open Road Integrated Media, Inc.
Univ. of Chicago Pr. Distribution Clients
Wizard Works
ebrary, Inc.

Univ. of Arizona, Poetry Ctr., Arizona Board of Regents, *(978-0-9727635)* c/o Univ. of Arizona Poetry Ctr., 1216 N. Cherry Ave., Tucson, AZ 85719 USA Tel 520-626-3765; Fax: 520-621-5566
E-mail: poetry@u.arizona.edu
Web site: http://www.poetrycenter.arizona.edu.

†**University of Arizona Pr.,** *(978-0-8165; 978-1-941451)* 355 S. Euclid Ave., Suite 103, Tucson, AZ 85719 USA (SAN 205-468X) Tel 520-621-1441; Fax: 520-621-8899; Toll Free: 800-426-3797 (orders)
E-mail: orders@uapress.arizona.edu
Web site: http://www.uapress.arizona.edu
Dist(s): **Casemate Academic**
Chicago Distribution Ctr.
Continental Bk. Co., Inc.
JSTOR
Many Feathers Bks. & Maps
MyiLibrary
Univ. of Chicago Pr.
Univ of Arizona Critical Languages Program
ebrary, Inc.; *CIP.*

†**Univ. of Arkansas Pr.,** *(978-0-938626; 978-1-55728; 978-1-61075; 978-1-68226)* 105 N. McIlroy Ave., Fayetteville, AR 72701 USA (SAN 239-3972) Tel 479-575-7544; Fax: 479-575-6044; Toll Free: 800-626-0090
E-mail: info@uapress.com
Web site: http://www.uapress.com; http://www.uark.edu/~uaprinfo
Dist(s): **Chicago Distribution Ctr.**
JSTOR
MyiLibrary
Univ. of Chicago Pr. Distribution Clients
Yankee Peddler Bookshop
ebrary, Inc.; *CIP.*

Univ. of California, Agriculture and Natural Resources, *(978-0-931876; 978-1-879906; 978-1-60107; 978-1-62711)*
E-mail: anrcatalog@ucanr.edu; cckintigh@ucanr.edu
Web site: ucanr.edu; anrcatalog.ucanr.edu.

Univ. of California, Berkeley, Lawrence Hall of Science, *(978-0-912511; 978-0-924886; 978-1-931542)* U of CA, Lawrence Hall of Science, Berkeley, CA 94720-5200 USA (SAN 271-9754) Tel 510-642-7771; Fax: 510-643-0309; *Imprints:* GEMS (GEMS); EQUALS (EQUALS)
E-mail: gems@berkeley.edu
Web site: http://www.lhs.berkeley.edu; http://www.lhsgems.org
Dist(s): **Distributors, The.**

†**Univ. of California Pr.,** *(978-0-520; 978-1-7323203)* 155 Grand Ave., Suite 400, Oakland, CA 94612-3758 USA Tel 510-883-8232 (Books & Journals); Fax: 510-836-8910
E-mail: journals@ucpress.edu; orders@cpfsinc.com; askucp@ucpress.edu
Web site: http://www.ucpress.edu
Dist(s): **Ebsco Publishing**
JSTOR
MyiLibrary
Perseus Bks. Group
Ingram Academic
Two Rivers Distribution
ebrary, Inc.; *CIP.*

†**Univ. of Chicago Pr.,** *(978-0-226; 978-0-89065; 978-0-943056; 978-1-892850)* Orders Addr.: 11030 S. Langley Ave., Chicago, IL 60628 USA (SAN 202-5280) Tel 773-702-7000; Fax: 773-702-7212; Toll Free Fax: 800-621-8476 (US & Canada); Toll Free: 800-621-2736 (US & Canada); Edit Addr.: 1427 E. 60th St., Chicago, IL 60637 USA (SAN 202-5299) Tel 773-702-7700; 773-702-7748 (Marketing & Sales); Fax: 773-702-9756
E-mail: general@press.uchicago.edu; kh@press.uchicago.edu; custserv@press.uchicago.rdu; sales@press.uchicago.edu; marketing@press.uchicago.edu; publicity@press.uchicago.edu
Web site: http://www.press.uchicago.edu
Dist(s): **Chicago Distribution Ctr.**
CreateSpace Independent Publishing Platform
Ebsco Publishing
Giron Bks.
ISD
MyiLibrary
Oxford Univ. Pr., Inc.
Open Road Integrated Media, Inc.
TNT Media Group, Inc.
Univ. of Chicago Pr. Distribution Clients
Wiley, John & Sons, Inc.
ebrary, Inc.; *CIP.*

Univ. of Denver, Ctr. for Teaching International Relations Pubns., *(978-0-943804)* 2201 S. Gaylord St., Denver, CO 80208 USA (SAN 241-0877) Tel 303-871-2697; Fax: 303-871-2456
E-mail: ctir-press@du.edu; pubsinfo@du.edu
Web site: http://www.du.edu/ctir
Dist(s): **Ingram Content Group**
Social Studies Schl. Service
Teacher's Discovery.

†**Univ. of Georgia, Carl Vinson Institute of Government,** *(978-0-89854)* 201 N. Milledge Ave., Athens, GA 30602 USA (SAN 212-8012) Tel 706-542-2736; Fax: 706-542-6239
E-mail: pou@cviog.uga.edu
Web site: http://www.cviog.uga.edu; *CIP.*

†**Univ. of Georgia Pr.,** *(978-0-8203)* Orders Addr.: 4435 Atlanta Hwy. West Dock, Athens, GA 30602 USA; Edit Addr.: Main Library, Third Flr. 320 S. Jackson St., Athens, GA 30602 USA (SAN 203-3054) Fax: 706-542-2558; Toll Free: 800-266-5842
E-mail: books@uga.edu
Web site: http://www.ugapress.org
Dist(s): **Ebsco Publishing**
JSTOR
Longleaf Services
MyiLibrary
Open Road Integrated Media, Inc.
ebrary, Inc.; *CIP.*

Univ. of Guam, Micronesian Area Research Ctr., *(978-1-878453; 978-0-9800331; 978-1-935198; 978-1-961058)* 303 University Dr., UOG Sta., Mangilao, GU 96923 USA Tel 671-735-2150; Fax: 671-734-7403
Web site: http://www.uog.edu/marc
Dist(s): **Itasca Bks.**
Univ. of Hawaii Pr.

†**Univ. of Hawaii Pr.,** *(978-0-8248; 978-0-87022)* Orders Addr.: 2840 Kolowalu St., Honolulu, HI 96822-1888 USA (SAN 202-5353) Tel 808-956-8255; Fax: 808-988-6052; Toll Free Fax: 800-650-7811; Toll Free: 888-847-7377; *Imprints:* Latitude 20 (Latitude Twenty)
E-mail: uhpmkt@hawaii.edu; uhpbooks@hawaii.edu
Web site: http://www.uhpress.hawaii.edu
Dist(s): **Booklines Hawaii, Ltd.**
De Gruyter, Inc.
JSTOR
University of Hawaii Press Agrmt. 2; *CIP.*

†**Univ. of Iowa Pr.,** *(978-0-87745; 978-1-58729; 978-1-60938; 978-1-68597)* Div. of The University of Iowa, Orders Addr.: c/o Chicago Distribution Ctr. 11030 S. Langley Ave., Chicago, IL 60628 USA Toll Free Fax: 800-621-8476; Toll Free: 800-621-2736; Edit Addr.: 100 Kuhl Hse. 119 W. Park Rd., Iowa City, IA 52242-1000 USA (SAN 203-3070) Tel 319-335-2000; Fax: 319-335-2055 Do not confuse with Univ. of Iowa, Pubns. Dept. at same address
E-mail: uipress@uiowa.edu
Web site: http://www.uiowapress.org
Dist(s): **Chicago Distribution Ctr.**
Ebsco Publishing
JSTOR
Univ. of Chicago Pr.
Univ. of Chicago Pr. Distribution Clients
ebrary, Inc.; *CIP.*

University of Louisiana at Lafayette *See* **Univ. of Louisiana at Lafayette Pr.**

Univ. of Louisiana at Lafayette Pr., *(978-0-940984; 978-1-887366; 978-1-935754; 978-1-946160; 978-1-959569)* P.O. Box 43558, Lafayette, LA 70504 USA (SAN 630-9755) Tel 337-482-6027; Fax: 337-482-6028
E-mail: cls@louisiana.edu
Web site: http://www.ulpress.org
Dist(s): **Forest Sales & Distributing Co.**

†**Univ. of Michigan Pr.,** *(978-0-472; 978-1-6694)* Orders Addr.: c/o Chicago Distribution Center, Perseus Distribution 1094 Flex Dr., Jackson, TN 38301 USA (SAN 282-4884) Toll Free Fax: 800-351-5073; Toll Free: 800-343-4499 , ext. 165; Edit Addr.: 839 Greene St., Ann Arbor, MI 48104-3209 USA Tel 734-764-4388; Fax: 734-615-1540
E-mail: um.press@umich.edu
Web site: http://www.press.umich.edu/
Dist(s): **Chicago Distribution Ctr.**
Ebsco Publishing
JSTOR
MyiLibrary
Palgrave Macmillan
ebrary, Inc.; *CIP.*

†**Univ. of Minnesota Pr.,** *(978-0-8166; 978-1-4529; 978-1-5179)* Affil. of Univ. of Minnesota, 111 Third Ave. S., Suite 290, Minneapolis, MN 55401-2520 USA (SAN 213-2648) Tel 612-627-1970; Fax: 612-627-1980
E-mail: ump@umn.edu
Web site: http://www.upress.umn.edu
Dist(s): **Chicago Distribution Ctr.**
Ebsco Publishing
JSTOR
MyiLibrary
Univ. of Chicago Pr.
ebrary, Inc.; *CIP.*

Univ. of Missouri, Extension, *(978-0-933842)* a/o University of Missouri Extension, 506 Hitt St., 4 Whitten Hall, Columbia, MO 65211-6300 USA Tel 573-882-7216; 573-882-6845; Fax: 573-882-8007; Toll Free: 800-292-0969
E-mail: extpubs@missouri.edu; muextensionweb@missouri.edu; nexus@missouri.edu
Web site: http://https://extension.missouri.edu.

†**Univ. of Missouri Pr.,** *(978-0-8262)* 2910 LeMone Blvd., Columbia, MO 65201 USA (SAN 203-3143) Tel 573-882-7641; Fax: 573-884-4498; Toll Free: 800-828-1894 (orders only)
E-mail: rennerk@umsystem.edu; deandj@umsystem.edu
Web site: http://press.umsystem.edu
Dist(s): **Chicago Distribution Ctr.**
East-West Export Bks.
Ebsco Publishing
Lulu Pr., Inc.
Univ. of Chicago Pr.
ebrary, Inc.; *CIP.*

Univ. of Montana Pr., The, *(978-0-9754009; 978-0-9815760; 978-0-9837259; 978-0-9894031; 978-0-9909748; 978-0-9983438)* Div. of The Univ. of Montana, The University of Montana 32 Campus Dr. Todd Bldg., Lower Level, Missoula, MT 59812-0792 USA (SAN 255-9994) Tel 406-243-2711; Fax: 406-243-2615
E-mail: ken.price@umontana.edu
Web site: http://www.umt.edu/printingandgraphics.com.

†**Univ. of Nebraska Pr.,** *(978-0-8032; 978-1-4962; 978-1-64012)* Orders Addr.: 1111 Lincoln Mall, Lincoln, NE 68588-0630 USA Tel 402-472-3581; 402-472-7702; Fax: 402-472-6214; Toll Free Fax: 800-526-2617; Toll Free: 800-755-1105; Edit Addr.: P.O. Box 880630, Lincoln, NE 68588-0630 USA (SAN 202-5337); *Imprints:* Bison Books (Bison Books)
E-mail: pressmail@unl.edu
Web site: http://www.nebraskapress.unl.edu; http://www.bisonbooks.com
Dist(s): **Casemate Pubs. & Bk. Distributors, LLC**
Continental Bk. Co., Inc.
Ebsco Publishing
JSTOR
Longleaf Services
MyiLibrary
ebrary, Inc.; *CIP.*

Univ. of Nebraska-Lincoln, GPN, *(978-0-7941)* Orders Addr.: P.O. Box 80669, Lincoln, NE 68501-0669 USA (SAN 179-1699) Tel 402-472-2007; Fax: 402-472-4076; Toll Free: 800-228-4630; Edit Addr.: 1800 N. 33rd St., Lincoln, NE 68583 USA
E-mail: gpn@unl.edu
Web site: http://gpn.unl.edu; http://shopgpn.com/.

†**Univ. of New Mexico Pr.,** *(978-0-8263; 978-0-9766839)* Orders Addr.: 1312 Basehart Rd., SE, Albuquerque, NM 87106-4363 USA (SAN 213-9588) Tel 505-277-2346; 505-272-7777 (orders); Toll Free Fax: 800-622-8667; Toll Free: 800-249-7737 (orders)
E-mail: unmpress@unm.edu
Web site: http://www.unmpress.com
Dist(s): **Bks. West**
Casemate Academic
Children's Plus, Inc.
Continental Bk. Co., Inc.
D.A.P./Distributed Art Pubs.
MyiLibrary
Rio Nuevo Pubs.
ebrary, Inc.; *CIP.*

†**Univ. of North Carolina Pr.,** *(978-0-8078; 978-1-4696; 979-8-89084; 979-8-89085; 979-8-89086; 979-8-89087; 979-8-89088)* c/o Longleaf Services, 116 S. Boundary St., Chapel Hill, NC 27514-3808 USA (SAN 203-3151) Tel 919-966-3561; Fax: 919-966-3829; Toll Free Fax: 800-272-6817; Toll Free: 800-848-6224
E-mail: uncpress@unc.edu
Web site: www.uncpress.org
Dist(s): **CreateSpace Independent Publishing Platform**
D.A.P./Distributed Art Pubs.
Ebsco Publishing
Longleaf Services
Oxford Univ. Pr., Inc.
ebrary, Inc.; *CIP.*

†**Univ. of Oklahoma Pr.,** *(978-0-8061; 979-8-8559)* Orders Addr.: 2800 Venture Dr., Norman, OK 73069-8218 USA Tel 405-325-2000; Fax: 405-364-5798; Toll Free Fax: 800-735-0476; Toll Free: 800-627-7377
E-mail: pressc@ou.edu
Web site: http://www.oupress.com
Dist(s): **Ebsco Publishing**
Longleaf Services
ebrary, Inc.; *CIP.*

†**Univ. of Pennsylvania Pr.,** *(978-0-8122; 978-1-5128)* Orders Addr.: c/o Hopkins Fulfillment Srvc., Hopkins Fulfillment Service, Baltimore, MD 21211-4370 USA Tel 410-516-6948; Fax: 410-516-6998; Toll Free: 800-537-5487; Edit Addr.: 3905 Spruce St., Philadelphia, PA 19104-4112 USA (SAN 202-5345) Tel 215-898-6261; Fax: 215-898-0404; Toll Free: 800-537-5487 (book orders)
E-mail: custserv@pobox.upenn.edu
Web site: http://www.upenn.edu/pennpress
Dist(s): **De Gruyter, Inc.**
Hopkins Fulfillment Services
Ingram Publisher Services
JSTOR
MyiLibrary
TNT Media Group, Inc.
Two Rivers Distribution; *CIP.*

Univ. of Phoenix Bookstore, *(978-0-578-52063-6; 978-0-578-52064-3)* a/o University of Phoenix Bookstore, 4615 E. Elwood St., Phoenix, AZ 85040 USA Tel 602-966-7400 Ext. 2124; Fax: 602-920-9030.

Publisher Name Index

†**Univ. of Pittsburgh Pr.**, *(978-0-8229)* 3400 Forbes Ave., Eureka Bldg., Fifth Flr., Pittsburgh, PA 15260 USA (SAN 203-3216) Tel 412-383-2456; Fax: 412-383-2466
E-mail: press@pitt.edu
Web site: http://www.upress.pitt.edu
Dist(s): **Chicago Distribution Ctr.**
ISD
JSTOR
MyiLibrary; *CIP*.

†**Univ. of Puerto Rico Pr.**, *(978-0-8477)* Subs. of Univ. of Puerto Rico, Orders Addr.: P.O. Box 23322, Rio Piedras, PR 00931-3322 USA (SAN 208-1245) Tel 787-250-0435 Administrative Offices; 787-250-8996 Administrative Offices; 787-758-8345 Sales Office and Warehouse; 787-751-8251 Sales Office and Warehouse; 787-934-3400 Sales Office and Warehouse; Fax: 787-753-9116 Administrative Offices; 787-751-8785 Sales/Warehouse, Ordering fax
E-mail: info@laeditorialupr.com
Web site: http://www.laeditorialupr.com
Dist(s): **Ediciones Universal**
Lectorum Pubns., Inc.
Libros Sin Fronteras; *CIP*.

University of Regina Pr. (CAN) *(978-0-88977) Dist. by* **TwoRivers.**

Univ. of Rhode Island, Sea Grant Pubns. Unit, *(978-0-938412)* Narragansett Bay Campus, Narragansett, RI 02882-1197 USA (SAN 209-0708) Tel 401-874-6800
E-mail: tkennedy@mail.uri.edu
Web site: http://www.seagrant.gso.uri.edu/riseagrant
Dist(s): **Chicago Distribution Ctr.**

Univ. of Scranton Pr., *(978-0-940866; 978-1-58966)* Orders Addr.: c/o Univ. of Scranton Pr., St. Thomas Hall, Linden & Monroe Sts., Scranton, PA 18510 USA Toll Free Fax: 800-941-8804; Toll Free: 800-941-3081; Edit Addr.: Linden & Monroe Sts., Scranton, PA 18510 USA (SAN 688-4067) Tel 570-941-7955; Fax: 570-941-4309
E-mail: richard.rousseau@uofs.edu
Web site: http://www.scrantonpress.com
Dist(s): **Associated Univ. Presses**
Chicago Distribution Ctr.

†**Univ. of South Carolina Pr.**, *(978-0-87249; 978-1-57003; 978-1-61117; 978-1-64336)* Orders Addr.: 718 Devine St., Columbia, SC 29208 USA Tel 803-777-1774; Fax: 803-777-0026; Toll Free Fax: 800-868-0740; Toll Free: 800-768-2500; Edit Addr.: 1600 Hampton St., 5th Flr., Columbia, SC 29208 USA (SAN 203-3224) Tel 803-777-5243; Fax: 803-777-0160; Toll Free Fax: 800-868-0740; Toll Free: 800-768-2500
E-mail: jhaupt@sc.edu
Web site: http://www.sc.edu/uscpress/
Dist(s): **Ebsco Publishing**
JSTOR
MyiLibrary
Open Road Integrated Media, Inc.
ebrary, Inc.; *CIP*.

Univ. St. Mary of the Lake, Mundelein Seminary, *(978-0-9774733)* 1000 E. Maple Ave., Mundelein, IL 60060 USA Tel 847-566-6401; Fax: 847-566-7330
E-mail: info@usml.edu
Web site: http://www.usml.edu.

University of Tampa *See* **Univ. of Tampa Pr.**

Univ. of Tampa Pr., *(978-1-879852; 978-1-59732)* 401 W. Kennedy Blvd., Tampa, FL 33606 USA Tel 813-253-6266; Fax: 813-258-7593
E-mail: utpress@ut.edu
Web site: http://utpress.ut.edu.

Univ. of Temecula Pr., Inc., *(978-0-936283)* 42730 De Luz Ave., Murrieta, CA 92562-7214 USA (SAN 697-9793) Tel 951-698-0059; Fax: 951-698-3676; *Imprints*: UTP (UTP)
E-mail: mikeray@utem.com
Web site: http://www.utem.com.

Univ. of Texas, Harry Ransom Humanities Research Ctr., *(978-0-87959)* P.O. Box 7219, Austin, TX 78713 USA (SAN 203-1906) Tel 512-471-8944; Fax: 512-471-9646
E-mail: publications@hrc.utexas.edu
Web site: http://www.lib.texas.edu/libs/hrc/hrhrc.

†**Univ. of Texas Pr.**, *(978-0-292; 978-1-4773)* Orders Addr.: P.O. Box 7819, Austin, TX 78713-7819 USA (SAN 212-9876) Tel 512-471-7233; Fax: 512-232-7178; Toll Free: 800-252-3206; Edit Addr.: University of Texas at Austin 2100 Comal, Austin, TX 78722 USA
E-mail: info@utpress.utexas.edu
Web site: http://www.utexas.edu/utpress
Dist(s): **Chicago Distribution Ctr.**
Continental Bk. Co., Inc.
Ebsco Publishing
Cengage Gale
JSTOR
Open Road Integrated Media, Inc.
Urban Land Institute
ebrary, Inc.; *CIP*.

†**Univ. of Utah Pr.**, *(978-0-87480; 978-1-60781; 978-1-64769)* 295 S. 1500 E., Suite 5400, Salt Lake City, UT 84112-0860 USA (SAN 220-0023) Tel 801-585-0082; Fax: 801-581-3365; Toll Free: 800-773-6672
E-mail: info@upress.utah.edu
Web site: www.uofupress.com
Dist(s): **Casemate Academic**
Chicago Distribution Ctr.
Partners Bk. Distributing, Inc.
Rio Nuevo Pubs.
Univ. of Chicago Pr. Distribution Clients
ebrary, Inc.; *CIP*.

†**University of Virginia Pr.**, *(978-0-8139; 978-0-912759; 978-1-57814)* Orders Addr.: P.O. Box 400318, Charlottesville, VA 22904-4318 USA (SAN 202-5361) Tel 804-924-3468; Fax: 804-982-2655
E-mail: upress@virginia.edu
Web site: http://www.upress.virginia.edu
Dist(s): **Ediciones Universal**
Fordham Univ. Pr.
JSTOR
Longleaf Services
MyiLibrary; *CIP*.

†**Univ. of Washington Pr.**, *(978-0-295; 978-1-902716)* Orders Addr.: P.O. Box 50096, Seattle, WA 98145-5096 USA (SAN 212-2502) Tel 206-543-4050; Fax: 206-543-3932; Toll Free Fax: 800-669-7993; Edit Addr.: P.O. Box 50096, Seattle, WA 98145-5096 USA Toll Free Fax: 800-669-7993; 1126 N. 98th St., Seattle, WA 98103
E-mail: uwpord@u.washington.edu
Web site: http://www.washington.edu/uwpress
Dist(s): **Ebsco Publishing**
Hopkins Fulfillment Services
JSTOR
Johns Hopkins Univ. Pr.
MyiLibrary
Partners Bk. Distributing, Inc.
Urban Land Institute
ebrary, Inc.; *CIP*.

Univ. of West Florida Foundation, Inc., *(978-0-9659142; 978-0-9798292)* 11000 University Pkwy., Pensacola, FL 32514 USA
E-mail: cmarse@uwf.edu.

†**Univ. of Wisconsin Pr.**, *(978-0-299)* Orders Addr.: c/o Chicago Dist Ctr., 11030 S. Langley Ave., Chicago, IL 60628 USA Tel 773-568-1550; Fax: 773-660-2235; Toll Free Fax: 800-621-8476 (orders only); Toll Free: 800-621-2736 (orders only); Edit Addr.: 1930 Monroe St., 3rd Flr., Madison, WI 53711 USA Tel 608-263-1110; Fax: 608-263-1132
E-mail: uwiscpress@uwpress.wisc.edu
Web site: http://www.wisc.edu/wisconsinpress/
Dist(s): **Chicago Distribution Ctr.**
East-West Export Bks.
Ebsco Publishing
Follett School Solutions
JSTOR
MyiLibrary
ebrary, Inc.; *CIP*.

†**Univ. Pr. of America, Inc.**, *(978-0-7618; 978-0-8191; 978-1-879691)* Member of Rowman & Littlefield Publishing Group, Inc., Orders Addr.: 15200 NBN Way, Blue Ridge Summit, PA 17214-0190 USA Tel 717-794-3800 (Sales, Customer Service, MIS, Royalties, Inventory Mgmt, Dist., Credit & Collections); Fax: 717-794-3803 (Customer Service & orders); 717-794-3857 (Sales & MIS); 717-794-3856 (Royalties, Inventory Mgmt. & Dist.); Toll Free Fax: 800-338-4550 (Customer Service & /or orders); Toll Free: 800-462-6420 (Customer Service &/or orders); Edit Addr.: 4501 Forbes Blvd., Suite 200, Lanham, MD 20706 USA Tel 301-459-3366; Fax: 301-459-5748 Short Discount, please contact rlpgsales@rowman.com
E-mail: custserv@rowman.com
Web site: http://www.univpress.com; http://www.rlpgbooks.com
Dist(s): **CreateSpace Independent Publishing Platform**
Ebsco Publishing
MyiLibrary
National Bk. Network
Rowman & Littlefield Publishers, Inc.
Rowman & Littlefield Unlimited Model
Yale Univ. Pr.
ebrary, Inc.; *CIP*.

Univ. Pr. of Colorado, *(978-0-87081; 978-0-87421; 978-1-60732; 978-1-64642)* Orders Addr.: c/o Utah State University Press, 11030 S. Langley, Chicago, IL 60628 USA (SAN 202-9294) Toll Free: 800-621-2736 CDC; Edit Addr.: 245 Century Cir. Ste 202, Louisville, CO 80027 SUN (SAN 658-0343) Tel 720-406-8849 UPC; 3078 Old Main Hill, Logan, UT 84322 Toll Free: 720-406-8849 USUP
E-mail: beth@upcolorado.com
Web site: http://www.upcolorado.com; http://www.usupress.org
Dist(s): **Bks. West**
Chicago Distribution Ctr.
Ctr. for Literary Publishing, Colorado State Univ.
Ebsco Publishing
Follett School Solutions
JSTOR
MyiLibrary
O'Reilly Media, Inc.
Open Road Integrated Media, Inc.
Univ. of Oklahoma Pr.
Univ. of Chicago Pr. Distribution Clients
ebrary, Inc.

†**Univ. Pr. of Florida**, *(978-0-8130; 978-0-942084; 978-0-9760555; 978-1-61610; 978-1-942852; 978-1-68340)* Orders Addr.: 15 NW 15th St., Gainesville, FL 32611-0279 USA (SAN 207-9275) Tel 352-392-1351; Fax: 352-392-7302; Toll Free Fax: 800-680-1955; Toll Free: 800-226-3822; *Imprints*: Gatorbytes (Gatorbytes)
E-mail: press@upf.com; orders@upf.com
Web site: http://www.upf.com
Dist(s): **Casemate Academic**
Ebsco Publishing
JSTOR
MyiLibrary
Oxford Univ. Pr., Inc.
TNT Media Group, Inc.
ebrary, Inc.; *CIP*.

†**Univ. Pr. of Kentucky**, *(978-0-8131; 978-0-912839; 978-0-916968; 978-1-9859; 978-1-949668; 978-1-949669; 978-1-950564; 978-1-950690)* Orders Addr.: Hopkins Fulfillment Services, Baltimore, MD 21211-4370 USA Tel 800-537-5487; Fax: 410-516-6998; Toll Free: 800-839-6855; Edit Addr.: 663 S. Limestone St., Lexington, KY 40508-4008 USA (SAN 203-3275) Tel 859-257-5200; Fax: 859-323-4981; Toll Free Fax: 800-870-4981
E-mail: twell1@email.uky.edu
Web site: http://www.kentuckypress.com
Dist(s): **Ebsco Publishing**
JSTOR
MyiLibrary
Oxford Univ. Pr., Inc.
Open Road Integrated Media, Inc.
ebrary, Inc.; *CIP*.

†**Univ. Pr. of Mississippi**, *(978-0-87805; 978-1-57806; 978-1-934110; 978-1-60473; 978-1-61703; 978-1-62103; 978-1-62674; 978-1-62846; 978-1-4968)* 3825 Ridgewood Rd., Jackson, MS 39211-6492 USA (SAN 203-1914) Tel 601-432-6205; Fax: 601-432-6217; Toll Free: 800-737-7788 (orders only)
E-mail: kburgess@ihl.state.ms.us; press@mississippi.edu
Web site: http://www.upress.state.ms.us
Dist(s): **CreateSpace Independent Publishing Platform**
East-West Export Bks.
Ebsco Publishing
JSTOR
MyiLibrary
Oxford Univ. Pr., Inc.
ebrary, Inc.; *CIP*.

†**Univ. Pr. of New England**, *(978-0-87451; 978-0-915032; 978-1-58465; 978-1-61168; 978-1-5126; 978-1-68458)* Orders Addr.: One Court St., Suite 250, Lebanon, NH 03755 USA Tel 603-448-1533 (ext. 255); Fax: 603-448-9429; Toll Free: 800-421-1561; Edit Addr.: 415 South St., Waltham, MA 02453 USA
E-mail: University.Press@Dartmouth.edu
Web site: http://www.upne.com
Dist(s): **Casemate Academic**
Chicago Distribution Ctr.
Hopkins Fulfillment Services
JSTOR
MyiLibrary
Smashwords
Univ. of Chicago Pr. Distribution Clients
ebrary, Inc.; *CIP*.

Univ. Pr. of the Pacific, *(978-0-89875; 978-1-4102)* 4440 NW 73rd Ave., PTY 362, Miami, FL 33166-6437 USA Tel 407-650-2537 (phone/fax)
E-mail: bip@universitypressofthepacific.com
Web site: http://www.universitypressofthepacific.com.

University Publishing Associates, Incorporated *See* **National Film Network LLC**

Univ. Publishing Co., *(978-0-8346)* P.O. Box 80298, Lincoln, NE 68501 USA (SAN 206-0582) Tel 402-476-2761.

University Readers *See* **Cognella, Inc.**

Univ. Science Bks., *(978-0-935702; 978-1-891389; 978-1-938787; 978-1-940380)* 111 Prospect Pl., South Orange, NJ 07079 USA (SAN 213-8085); 111 Prospect Pl., South Orange, NJ 07079 Tel 973-378-3900
E-mail: jellis@aip.org; deskcopy@aip.org; fhenson@aip.org
Web site: uscibooks@aip.org
Dist(s): **RedShelf.**

UniversityPress.Info *See* **Science Pubs.**

Unland, Denise, *(978-0-9852748; 978-0-9983134; 978-1-949777)* 24954 S. Tryon, Channahon, IL 60410 USA Tel 815-715-4509
E-mail: Artemis279@aol.com.

Unleash Pr., *(978-1-7375194; 979-8-9862743)* 8072 Jonson Dr., Reynoldsburg, OH 43068 USA Tel 614-309-1795
E-mail: jenknox395@gmail.com
Web site: https://www.unleashcreatives.net/.

Unleashed Publishing, Inc, *(978-1-7333090; 978-1-7356913)* 975 Wayne Ave., No. 351, Chambersburg, PA 17201-3895 USA Tel 717-860-1848
E-mail: trinaolson@unleashedpublishing.net
Web site: unleashedpublishing.net; www.radicallaunch.org.

Unlimited Horizons, *(978-0-9753817)* 427 S. Fraser Dr., Mesa, AZ 85204-2605 USA.

Unlimited Possibilities Publishing, LLC, *(978-0-9724621; 978-0-615-31408-2; 978-0-615-32713-6; 978-0-615-32981-9; 978-0-615-33078-5; 978-0-615-33453-0; 978-0-9826543; 978-0-9828923; 978-0-9834311; 978-1-938442; 978-1-940574)* Orders Addr.: 110 Walter Way., No. 2635, Stockbridge, GA 30281 USA
E-mail: shawnaa@sastyl.com.

Unlimited Potential Publishing, *(978-0-9899212; 978-0-9979879)* 122 Camberley Ct., Columbia, SC 29223 USA Tel 706-399-4916; Fax: 803-865-9271
E-mail: will8149@bellsouth.net
Dist(s): **Ingram Content Group.**

Unlimited Publishing LLC, *(978-0-9677649; 978-1-58832)* P.O. Box 3007, Bloomington, IN 47402 USA Fax: 425-928-5465
E-mail: jaymasp@aol.com; paradoxofthesoul@aol.com
Web site: http://www.unlimitedpublishing.com
Dist(s): **CreateSpace Independent Publishing Platform**
TextStream.

Unlock A Bk. Pubs., LLC, *(978-0-9796456)* 225 S. Bishop, San Angelo, TX 76901 USA
Web site: http://unlockabook.com.

Unlockyourchild *See* **Shrimlife Pr.**

Unmistakably C K C, *(978-0-9742064)* 3244 Kingswood Glen, Decatur, GA 30034 USA Tel 404-244-8113; 404-242-2690; Fax: 678-418-3056
E-mail: info@billyzany.com
Web site: http://www.billyzany.com.

UnmistakablyCKC, *(978-0-692-19870-4; 978-0-578-94397-8)* 1740 Weatherstone Dr., Ann Arbor, MI 48108 USA Tel 323-326-8664; Fax: 323-326-8664
E-mail: yeswecanland@yahoo.com
Web site: allomothinmovie.com.

Unruly *Imprint of* **Enchanted Lion Bks., LLC**

Unseen Gallery, *(978-0-9795206)* Orders Addr.: P.O. Box 6065, Albuquerque, NM 87197 USA Tel 505-232-2161
E-mail: webmaster@unseengallery.com
Web site: http://www.unseengallery.com.

Unshackled Publishing, *(978-0-9708688)* Orders Addr.: P.O. Box 44216, Indianapolis, IN 46244 USA; P.O. Box 44216, Indianapolis, IN 46244
E-mail: lexthewriter@yahoo.com; treks-journey@yahoo.com
Web site: http://www.unshackledpublishing.com; http://www.alexusrhone.com.

Unspeakable Joy Pr., *(978-0-9761538)* Orders Addr.: 499 Adams St., #252, Milton, MA 02186 USA; Edit Addr.: 233 Eliot St., Milton, MA 02186 USA
E-mail: roybue@aol.com; adoptionis@aol.com
Web site: http://www.adoptionis.com.

Unspoken Knowledge Publishing, LLC, *(978-0-9986895)* P.O. Box 3, New Boston, MI 48164 USA Tel 313-570-5492
E-mail: rbey1124@gmail.com
Web site: www.unspokenknowledge.com.

Unspoken Words, *(978-0-9771358)* Orders Addr.: 11224 Mount Overlook, Cleveland, OH 44104 USA; Edit Addr.: 27600 Chardon Rd. Apt. 856, Wickliffe, OH 44092-2781 USA
E-mail: freespirit_publishing@yahoo.com.

Unstoppable Teen, Ltd. (GBR) *(978-0-9553488; 978-1-907189; 978-0-9956079) Dist. by* **Crown Hse.**

Untreed Reads Publishing, LLC, *(978-1-61187; 978-1-945447; 978-1-949135; 978-1-953601; 979-8-88860; 978-1-961689)* 506 Kansas St., San Francisco, CA 94107 USA Tel 415-621-0465; Toll Free Fax: 800-318-6037
E-mail: jhartman@untreedreads.com; kdsullivan@untreedreads.com
Web site: http://www.untreedreads.com.

Unveiled Media, LLC, *(978-0-9776385)* P.O. Box 930463, Verona, WI 53593 USA (SAN 257-8093); *Imprints*: Cotton Candy Press (CottonCandy Pr)
Web site: http://www.unveiledmedia.com
Dist(s): **Consortium Bk. Sales & Distribution**
CreateSpace Independent Publishing Platform
Ingram Content Group.

UP *See* **Infobus, Inc.**

Upcentral Publishing, *(978-0-9897466)* 29 Braeside Rd., Baldwinsville, NY 13027 USA Tel 315-720-4684
E-mail: garypluff@yahoo.com.

UPfirst.com Bks., *(978-0-9800222)* Div. of UPfirst.com, 2803 Us Hwy. 41 W. Suite 100, Marquette, MI 49855-2291 USA (SAN 855-0271)
E-mail: michaeleen@upfirst.com
Web site: http://www.upfirst.com.

UPfirst.com Picture Books for Children *See* **UPfirst.com Bks.**

upheaval dome, *(978-0-9988445; 979-8-218-26698-1; 979-8-218-26699-8)* 1475 Overlook Rd., Moab, UT 84532 USA Tel 435-260-0446; Fax: 435-260-0446
E-mail: sand@sandsheff.com.

Upheaval Media, Inc., *(978-0-615-19321-2; 978-0-578-03360-0; 978-0-615-36266-3; 978-0-9829610)* 100 Renaissance Ctr. No. 43233, Detroit, MI 48243 USA Tel 313-444-4885
E-mail: ida@upliftinc.org
Web site: http://www.upheavalmedia.net
Dist(s): **Lulu Pr., Inc.**

Upland Avenue Productions, *(978-0-578-10367-9; 978-0-615-92673-5; 978-0-9960401; 978-0-692-53123-5; 978-0-692-53124-2; 978-0-692-53125-9; 978-0-692-53127-3; 978-0-692-54731-1; 978-0-692-77111-2; 978-0-692-80419-3; 978-0-692-85300-9; 978-1-7324167)* 3201 Zafarano Dr. Suite C, No. 541, Santa Fe, NM 87507 USA
Web site: www.uplandavenueproductions.com
Dist(s): **CreateSpace Independent Publishing Platform**
Lulu Pr., Inc.

Upland Public Library Foundation *See* **Citrus Roots - Preserving Citrus Heritage Foundation**

Uplift Pr., *(978-0-9622834)* 295 Lenox Ave., #105, Oakland, CA 94610 USA Do not confuse with Uplift Pr. in Los Angeles, CA.

Upon Eagle's Wings, Malachi Ink, *(978-0-9982942)* 516 East Pk. Ave., Des MOines, IA 50315 USA Tel 515-344-1033
E-mail: authorsueraymond@gmail.com
Web site: sueraymondladylaindora.wordpress.com.

Upper Deck Co., LLC,The, *(978-1-931860; 978-1-932241; 978-1-932669; 978-1-932825; 978-1-932939; 978-1-933103; 978-1-933252; 978-1-933489; 978-1-59945; 978-1-60806)* 5909 Sea Otter Pl., Carlsbad, CA 92010 USA Tel 760-929-6500; Fax: 760-929-6548; Toll Free: 800-873-7332
Web site: http://www.upperdeck.com
Dist(s): **Diamond Bk. Distributors.**

Upper Room Bks. *Imprint of* **Upper Room Bks.**

Upper Room Bks., *(978-0-8358; 978-0-88177; 978-1-935205; 978-1-952421)* Div. of The Upper Room, 1908 Grand Ave., Nashville, TN 37212 USA (SAN 203-3364) Tel 615-340-7256; Toll Free: 800-972-0433 (customer service, orders); *Imprints*: Upper Room Books (UpperRmBks); Discipleship Resources (DiscipleshipRes) Do not confuse with Upper Room Education for Parenting, Inc. in Derry, NH
E-mail: jneely@gbod.org; lbruner@gbod.org; atrudel@gbod.org
Web site: http://www.upperroom.org; http://books.upperroom.org; http://bookstore.upperroom.org
Dist(s): **Smashwords.**

Upper Strata Ink, Incorporated *See* **Crowder, Jack L.**

Upside Down Tree Publishing, *(978-0-9802329)* 1605 N. Grand Ave., Maryville, MO 64468 USA.

Upstart Bks. *Imprint of* **Highsmith Inc.**

Upstart Pr. (NZL) *(978-1-927262; 978-1-927262-02-3; 978-1-927262-53-5; 978-1-988516; 978-1-990003; 978-1-77694) Dist. by* **IPG Chicago.**
UpTree Publishing, *(978-0-9787248)* P.O. Box 212863, Columbia, SC 29221 USA (SAN 851-447X) Toll Free: 800-905-2157 (phone/fax)
E-mail: sales@uptreepublishing.com; info@uptreepublishing.com
Web site: http://www.uptreepublishing.com.
Upublish.com *See* **Universal Pubs.**
Upword Pr., *(978-0-9654140)* Orders Addr.: P.O. Box 974, Atmore, AL 36504-0974 USA; 1879 Old Bratt Rd., Atmore, AL 36504 Tel 251-609-2918 Do not confuse with Upword Pr., Yelm, WA
Web site: http://www.scattersunshine.com
Dist(s): **American Wholesale Bk. Co.**
Urban Advocacy, *(978-0-9745122)* 917 Columbia Ave. Suite 123, Lancaster, PA 17603 USA Tel 717-490-6148
E-mail: vuuhu02@yahoo.com
Web site: http://www.urbanadvocacy.org.
Urban Edge Publishing Co., *(978-0-9743781)* 16209 Victory Blvd., Suite 207, Van Nuys, CA 91406 USA Tel 818-786-3700; Fax: 818-786-3737
E-mail: willcon@pacbell.net.
Urban, Keith Studios, *(978-0-9815370)* P.O. Box 4572, Wayne, NJ 07474 USA (SAN 855-8280)
Web site: http://www.keithurban.com.
Urban Leadership Institute *See* **Dare To Be King Project**
Urban Ministries, Incorporated *See* **UMI (Urban Ministries, Inc.)**
Urban Moon Productions, *(978-0-615-97108-7; 978-0-692-38027-7; 978-0-692-38990-4; 978-0-692-38992-8; 979-8-9870782)* P.O. Box 12394, Norfolk, VA 23541 USA Tel 757-228-4046
E-mail: Urbanmoonbooksandmore@gmail.com
Web site: www.urbanmoonbooks.net
Dist(s): **CreateSpace Independent Publishing Platform.**
Urban Moon Publishing, *(978-0-9787913; 978-0-9800101)* 931 Monroe Dr., Suite 276, Atlanta, GA 30308 USA Toll Free: 866-205-9228
E-mail: kinglistens@aol.com.
Urban Renaissance *Imprint of* **Kensington Publishing Corp.**
Urban Spirit!, *(978-0-9638127; 978-0-9845359; 978-0-9846480; 978-0-9881958; 978-0-9884572; 979-8-9853690; 978-1-958779)* 753 Walden Blvd., Atlanta, GA 30349 USA Tel 770-969-7891
E-mail: melbanks2002@yahoo.com; cpickenpack@sbcglobal.net
Web site: http://www.urbanspirit.biz.
Urbanik, Karen L., *(978-0-9759031)* 2285 Marsh Hawk Ln. Apt. 302, Orange Park, FL 32003-6366 USA.
Ure, Daylene, *(978-0-615-25326-8)* 160 E. 200 S., Washington, UT 84780 USA
Dist(s): **Lulu Pr., Inc.**
Urim Pubns. (ISR) *(978-965-7108; 978-965-524) Dist. by* **Lambda Pubs.**
Urim Pubns. (ISR) *(978-965-7108; 978-965-524) Dist. by* **Coronet Bks.**
†URJ Pr., *(978-0-8074)* 633 Third Ave., New York, NY 10017 USA (SAN 203-3291) Tel 212-650-4120; Fax: 212-650-4119; Toll Free: 888-489-8242
E-mail: press@urj.org
Web site: http://www.urjbooksandmusic.com
Dist(s): **Leonard, Hal Corp. MyiLibrary;** *CIP.*
URON Entertainment Corp. (CAN) *(978-0-9738652; 978-0-9781386; 978-1-897376; 978-1-926778; 978-1-927925; 978-1-77294) Dist. by* **D C D.**
Urquhart Design, *(978-0-615-35452-1)* 1109 Wandering Oaks Dr., Ormond Beach, FL 32174 USA Tel 386-673-3565
E-mail: urquhartdesign@gmail.com
Web site: http://www.urquhartdesign.com.
Ursie Wursie, *(978-1-949917)* PO Box 145, Wamego, KS 66547 USA Tel 775-397-7252
E-mail: wyo_mudpuddle@hotmail.com
Web site: www.ursiewursie.com.
Ursie Wursie World *See* **Ursie Wursie**
Ursu Pubns., *(978-0-9741634)* PMB 429, 5250 Grand Ave., Suite 14, Gurnee, IL 60031-1877 USA
E-mail: info@grandmaursu.com
Web site: http://www.grandmaursu.com.
Urtext, *(978-0-9790573; 978-1-940121)* 39 Longwood Dr., San Rafael, CA 94901-1026 USA (SAN 852-3061).
U.S. Games Systems, Inc., *(978-0-88079; 978-0-913866; 978-1-57281; 978-1-64671)* 179 Ludlow St., Stamford, CT 06902 USA (SAN 158-6483) Tel 203-353-8400; Fax: 203-353-8431; Toll Free: 800-544-2637
E-mail: usgames@aol.com
Web site: http://www.usgamesinc.com
Dist(s): **New Leaf Distributing Co., Inc.**
US Ghost Writing, *(979-8-9857885; 978-1-959484; 978-1-962381)* 1800 Century Pk. E Suite, No. 600, Los Angeles, CA 90067 USA Tel 844-200-1660
E-mail: logodesigncorps@gmail.com
Web site: https://usghostwriting.com.
Usborne *Imprint of* **EDC Publishing**
Usborne Publishing, Ltd. (GBR) *(978-0-7460; 978-0-86020; 978-1-85123; 978-1-4095; 978-1-4749; 978-1-78941) Dist. by* **HarperCollins Pubs.**
Usera, Christian, *(978-0-615-14618-8; 978-0-615-14645-4; 978-0-615-31319-1)* 7818 S. Zeno St., Centennial, CO 80016-1849 USA
Dist(s): **Lulu Pr., Inc.**
Utopia Pr., *(978-0-9661060)* 126 1/2 E. Front St., Traverse City, MI 49684 USA Tel 231-922-2234 editorial office
E-mail: pub@fimg.net.
Utopian Dreams Gifts, *(978-0-9997161)* P.O. Box 12, BLACK RIVER FALLS, WI 54615 USA Tel 715-299-4822
E-mail: UTOPIANDREAMSGIFTS@GMAIL.COM
Web site: Www.utopiandreamsgifts.webs.com.
UTP *Imprint of* **Univ. of Temecula Pr., Inc.**
Utterly Global, *(978-0-9891338)* 44 Lenhome Dr., Cranford, NJ 07016 USA Tel 908-272-0631
E-mail: info@antibullyingprograms.com
Web site: www.antibullyingprograms.com.
UWA Publishing (AUS) *(978-0-85564; 978-0-86422; 978-0-909751; 978-1-875560; 978-1-876268; 978-1-920694; 978-0-9802964; 978-0-9802965; 978-1-921401; 978-1-920964; 978-1-74258; 978-0-7316-0213-1; 978-0-7316-1196-6; 978-0-7316-1212-3; 978-0-7316-3945-8; 978-0-646-15226-4; 978-0-646-31692-5; 978-0-646-39116-8; 978-1-76080; 978-0-646-43446-9) Dist. by* **Inti Spec Bk.**
UXL *Imprint of* **Cengage Gale**
Uxor Pr., Inc., *(978-0-932555)* One Blackfield Dr. #174, Tiburon, CA 94920 USA Tel 415-383-8481
E-mail: bobzimmerman@usa.com.
V & R Editorial (ARG) *(978-987-612) Dist. by* **Lectorum Pubns.**
V Bks., *(978-0-9972031)* 7801 NW 37th St., Doral, FL 33166-6503 USA Tel 305-592-0839
E-mail: myarobarts@gmail.com
Web site: https://www.facebook.com/MyaRobartsBooks/.
V M I Publishers *See* **Deep River Bks.**
V V C Publishing *See* **Vic-Vincent Publishing**
Vabella Publishing, *(978-0-9712204; 978-0-9834332; 978-1-938230; 978-1-942766; 978-1-957479)* Orders Addr.: P.O. Box 1052, Carrollton, GA 30112 USA (SAN 920-1858) Tel 770-686-0181; Edit Addr.: 226 Shady Valley Dr, Carrollton, GA 30116 USA (SAN 860-1682) Tel 770-686-0181
E-mail: bellg@aol.com
Web site: www.vabella.com.
Vacation Spot Publishing, *(978-0-9637688; 978-1-893622)* Orders Addr.: P.O. Box 1723, Lorton, VA 22199-1723 USA Tel 703-684-8142; Fax: 703-684-7955; Toll Free: 800-441-1949; Edit Addr.: 1903 Duffield Ln., Alexandria, VA 22307 USA; *Imprints:* VSP Books (VSP Bks)
E-mail: mail@VSPBooks.com
Web site: http://www.vspbooks.com
Dist(s): **Follett School Solutions.**
Vadeboncoeur, Jim, *(978-0-9724697)* 3809 Laguna Ave., Palo Alto, CA 94306-2629 USA Fax: 650-493-1145
E-mail: images@bpib.com
Web site: http://www.bpib.com/images.htm.
Valancourt Bks., *(978-0-9766048; 978-0-9777841; 978-0-9792332; 978-1-934555; 978-1-939140; 978-1-941147; 978-1-943910; 978-1-948405; 978-1-954321; 978-1-960241)* PO Box 17642, Richmond, VA 23226 USA
E-mail: gothic@valancourtbooks.com
Web site: http://www.valancourtbooks.com
Dist(s): **Blackstone Audio, Inc.**
Valenti, Joseph, *(978-0-9700563)* Orders Addr.: P.O. Box 2763 nc highway 731 west, MOUNT GILEAD, NC 27306 USA Tel 914-628-9497; Edit Addr.: 2763 NC Hwy. 731 W., MOUNT GILEAD, NC 27306 USA
E-mail: jvalenti@nerolarp.com
Web site: http://www.nerolarp.com; http://nerolarponline.com.
Valenti, Robert A., *(978-0-9773119)* 3500 Galt Ocean Dr.2401, Fort Lauderdale, FL 33308-6809 USA Tel 954-563-0069; Fax: 954-563-4503
E-mail: rvalenti@bellsouth.net.
Valentine, Catherine, *(978-0-578-68664-6; 978-0-578-96359-4; 979-8-218-17221-3)* 8651 Nighthawk Rd., Neosho, MO 64850 USA Tel 417-658-9877
E-mail: catherinevalentinewriter@gmail.com.
Valerie Bendt, *(978-1-885814)* Orders Addr.: 333 W. Rio Vista Ct., Tampa, FL 33604 USA
E-mail: ValerieBendt@verizon.net; ValerieBendt@gmail.com
Web site: http://www.ValerieBendt.com
Dist(s): **Follett School Solutions.**
Valerie Seyforth Clayton, *(978-0-578-60466-4; 978-0-578-63630-6)* 127 Crane Dr., Port St. Joe, FL 32456 USA Tel 850-227-5557
E-mail: vksclayton@gmail.com.
Valiant Entertainment *See* **Valiant Entertainment LLC**
Valiant Entertainment LLC, *(978-0-9796409; 978-1-939346; 978-1-68215)* 424 W. 33rd St., New York, NY 10001 USA Tel 212-972-0361
E-mail: walterb@valiantentertainment.com; inquiries@valiantentertainment.com
Web site: http://www.valiantentertainment.com
Dist(s): **Diamond Comic Distributors, Inc. Diamond Bk. Distributors.**
Valiant Mouse, *(978-1-7370547)* P.O. Box 317, Franklin, TN 37065 USA Tel 615-289-7881
E-mail: thaddeusheffner@comcast.net.
Valknut Pr., *(978-0-9837520; 978-1-62411)* 1499 Amberley Dr., Clarksville, TN 37043 USA Tel 931-220-7758
E-mail: juliacrane@zoho.com
Web site: valknutpress.com
Dist(s): **Smashwords.**
Vallentine Mitchell Pubs. (GBR) *(978-0-85303; 978-1-910383; 978-1-912676; 978-1-80371) Dist. by* **IPG Chicago.**
Valley Pr., *(978-0-9748447)* P.O. Box 427, Vienna, VA 22183-1427 USA Fax: 703-281-2994 Do not confuse with companies with the same name in Bradenton, FL, Lyndhurst, NJ, GreenBay, WI, Mill Valley, CA.
Valley Publishing *See* **Karosa Publishing**
Values of America Co., *(978-0-9765868)* P.O. Box 1534, Merchantville, NJ 08109 USA Toll Free: 866-467-7304
E-mail: orders@quipman.com
Web site: http://www.quipman.com.
Values to Live By Classic Stories *Imprint of* **Thomas, Frederic Inc.**
Vample, Jessyca Publishing, *(978-0-9969817; 978-1-7323178; 978-1-7374279)* 1013 E Ellet St., Philadelphia, PA 19150 USA Tel 267-334-8423
E-mail: jbvample@yahoo.com.
Van der Westhuizen, Kevin Ministries International, Incorporated *See* **JMC Printing**
van der Zande, Irene, *(978-0-9796191)* P.O. Box 1212, Santa Cruz, CA 95061 USA Tel 831-426-4407 Toll Free: 800-467-6997
E-mail: safety@kidpower.org
Web site: http://www.kidpower.org
Dist(s): **Romeii LLC.**
Van Steenhouse, Andrea L. *See* **Simpler Life Pr.**
Vance Hardy Publishing, *(978-0-578-17187-6)* 2248 Grand Ave, Deland, FL 32720 USA.
V&A Publishing (GBR) *(978-0-905209; 978-1-85177; 978-0-901486; 978-0-948107; 978-0-9521209; 978-1-83851) Dist. by* **HachBkGrp.**
Vandalia Pr. *Imprint of* **West Virginia Univ. Pr.**
Vandam Pr., Inc., *(978-0-9702383; 978-1-937010)* P.O. Box 155, Brooklyn, NY 11230 USA Tel 212-969-0286; Fax: 212-858-5720
E-mail: publisher@vandampress.com
Web site: http://www.vandampress.com.
Vandamere Pr., *(978-0-918339)* Subs. of AB Assocs., Orders Addr.: P.O. Box 149, St. Petersburg, FL 33731 USA (SAN 657-3088) Tel 727-556-0950; Fax: 727-556-2560; Toll Free: 800-551-7776
Web site: www.vandamere.com.
V&R Editoras,
Dist(s): **Children's Plus, Inc. Lectorum Pubns., Inc.**
Vanessa Varela, *(978-1-7360365)* 1638 16th Ave., Grafton, WI 53024 USA Tel 281-704-3310
E-mail: vanessavarela4@hotmail.com.
Vangar Pubs./Baltimore, *(978-1-882788)* 2054 Kabletown Rd, Charles Town, WV 25414 USA Tel 304-728-2829
E-mail: robertgraf@aol.com.
Vanguard Pr., *(978-1-59315)* 425 Madison Ave., 3rd Flr., New York, NY 10017 USA Do not confuse with CDS Books in Paso Robles, CA Durham, NC
Dist(s): **Ebsco Publishing Hachette Bk. Group Open Road Integrated Media, Inc. ebrary, Inc.**
Vanguard Productions, *(978-1-887591; 978-1-934331)* 705 Rancho Dr, Mesquite, TX 75149 USA Tel 908-391-0937
E-mail: vanguardpub@att.net
Web site: http://vanguardpublishing.com
Dist(s): **Publishers Group West (PGW).**
Vanhoozer, Kari (askahomeSchl.mom.net), *(978-0-578-78399-4)* 1824 LEXINGTON PL, BEDFORD, TX 76022 USA Tel 817-508-8978
E-mail: klvanhoozer@yahoo.com.
Vanir Bks., *(978-0-615-28865-9)* 351 Salem St., No. 2, Glendale, CA 91203 USA Tel 818-669-4070
Web site: http://rickandbobo.com.
Vanishing Horizons, *(978-0-9823445; 978-1-7355602)* Orders Addr.: 1018 Cedarcrest Dr., Pueblo, CO 81005 USA Tel 719-561-0993
E-mail: vanishinghorizons1@me.com
Web site: http://www.vanishinghorizons.com.
Vanissery, Matthew, *(978-0-9759906)* P.O. Box 1056, Guasti, CA 91743-1056 USA; 175 Mountain View Ave., Scotch Plains, NJ 07076 Tel 908-889-7930; Fax: 908-889-6281
E-mail: chemplavil@aol.com.
VanLiss Publishing, *(978-0-578-47820-3)* 12675 NW 8 Trail, Miami, FL 33182 USA Tel 954-635-0234
E-mail: littleunicorns1111@yahoo.com.
Vansyckle, Elizabeth M., *(978-0-692-82343-9; 978-0-9986754)* 991 Abigail Way Apt 2202, Midlothian, TX 76065 USA Tel 214-422-0579
E-mail: velizabeth@me.com
Dist(s): **CreateSpace Independent Publishing Platform.**
VanVonderen, Susan, *(978-1-7333107)* 8815 Windsor Terr., Brooklyn Park, MN 55443 USA Tel 651-308-0419
E-mail: Sue1grohs@aol.com.
Vanwell Publishing, Ltd. (CAN) *(978-0-920277; 978-1-55068; 978-1-55125) Dist. by* **Casemate Pubs.**
Varas, Reny, *(978-0-9726946)* 918 Cortney Dr., Carpentersville, IL 60110 USA (SAN 255-3333) Tel 847-428-7852; Fax: 847-428-7880
E-mail: lionan2@msn.com.
Variance Author Services, *(978-1-935142)* P.O. Box 612, Cabot, AR 72023-7577 USA (SAN 856-6259) Tel 501-259-6102; *Imprints:* Breakneck Books (Breakneck)
E-mail: tpaulschulte@variancepublishing.com
Web site: http://www.variancepublishing.com
Dist(s): **Bookazine Co., Inc. Smashwords.**
Variance Publishing, LLC *See* **Variance Author Services**
Varida Publishing & Resources, *(978-1-937046)* P.O. Box 688, Woodinville, WA 98072 USA Tel 425-830-2909
E-mail: president@varida.com
Web site: varida.com.
Varnado, Chi, *(978-1-7341423)* 19529 Laurel Ln., Ramona, CA 92065 USA Tel 760-789-8532
E-mail: chivarnado@yahoo.com.
Vartan, Judith A., *(978-0-692-67697-4; 978-0-9986317; 978-0-578-60674-3)* 14 Atherton Ave., Atherton, CA 94027 USA Tel 650-322-9202
Vaughan, Christopher, *(978-0-9863101)* 203 Southbrook Pkwy., Kearney, MO 64060 USA Tel 816-728-5718
E-mail: Ljcv125@hotmail.com.
Vaughanworks *Imprint of* **Vaughanworks Publishing**
Vaughanworks Publishing, *(978-0-9771160)* Div. of Vaughanworks, Orders Addr.: P.O. Box 44224, West Allis, WI 53214 USA; *Imprints:* Vaughanworks (Vaughanworks)
E-mail: vaughanworks@sbcglobal.net
Web site: http://www.vaughanworks.com.
Vaughn, Dean Learning Systems, Inc., *(978-0-942168)* 631 Springhouse Ln., Hummelstown, PA 17036 USA (SAN 239-9911) Tel 717-433-7794
E-mail: mathaino@gmail.com
Web site: http://www.deanvaughnlearning.com
Dist(s): **Two Rivers Distribution.**
Vaughn, Jerry T., *(978-0-9772507)* 1921 Ashford Cir., Longmout, CO 80501 USA Tel 303-776-9134
E-mail: vaughn.jc@gmail.com.
Vault Comics *Imprint of* **Creative Mind Energy**
Vecchia Publishing, *(978-0-9860470; 978-1-944906)* 41 Grand Ave., Suite 101, River Edge, NJ 07661 USA.
Vedanta Pr., *(978-0-87481)* Div. of Vedanta Society of Southern California, Orders Addr.: 1946 Vedanta Pl., Hollywood, CA 90068-3996 USA (SAN 202-9340) Tel 323-960-1728 (general manager); 323-960-1727 (orders and customer service); Fax: 323-465-9568 (orders)
E-mail: bob@vedanta.com; vpress@vedanta.com
Web site: http://www.vedanta.com.
Veech, Alyssa, *(978-0-578-41555-0; 978-0-578-41558-1)* 71 Singer Dr., West Seneca, NY 14224 USA Tel 716-472-0403
E-mail: alyssajn18@gmail.com
Dist(s): **Ingram Content Group.**
Vega Dawn LLC, *(978-1-7359753)* 9722 Gaston Rd, KATY, TX 77494 USA Tel 346-313-8053
E-mail: psdixon@vegadawn.com.
Vegan Kids Pr., *(978-0-9980358)* 1835 Patricia Dr., Clarksville, TN 37040 USA Tel 916-261-2348
E-mail: kara@vegankidspress.com
Web site: vegankidspress.com.
Vegan Pubs., *(978-1-940184)* 6 Moore Cir., Danvers, MA 01923 USA (SAN 990-0683) Tel 617-872-3623
E-mail: veganpublishers@gmail.com
Web site: www.veganpublishers.com
Dist(s): **Blackstone Audio, Inc.**
Vegas Pub., LLC, A, *(978-0-9968437; 978-0-9969593; 978-0-9985574)* 115 Maple St., Henderson, NV 89015 USA Tel 702-277-8126
E-mail: avegaspublisher@yahoo.com
Web site: avegaspublisher.com.
vegaslocal.com, *(978-0-9752804)* 4329 Talofa Ave., Toluca Lake, CA 91602-2917 USA
E-mail: info@vegaslocal.com
Web site: http://www.vegaslocal.com.
Veglia, Peter, *(978-1-7345682)* 905 Newcastle Ct., Modesto, CA 95355 USA Tel 209-598-1742
E-mail: girlonthehill4peter@gmail.com.
Vegueta Ediciones S. L. (ESP) *(978-84-947237; 978-84-17137) Dist. by* **IPG Chicago.**
Veillette, Roseanne, *(978-0-9843705; 978-0-9977504)* Orders Addr.: 40 Tutherly Ave., Claremont, NH 03743 USA (SAN 859-2128) Tel 603-372-7390; *Imprints:* Little Paws Press (LittlePaws)
E-mail: roseanneveillette@comcast.net
Web site: http://www.buckandben.com.
Veillette, Sally *See* **Pop the Cork Publishing**
Velazquez de Leon, Mauricio *See* **Duo Pr. LLC**
Velesquious Studios, *(978-0-9754232)* P.O. Box 72, Blakeslee, PA 18610-0072 USA Tel 610-360-8946
E-mail: webmaster@velesquious.com
Web site: http://www.velesquious.com.
Velichko, Vera, *(978-0-9754433)* ; *Imprints:* Language Transformer Books (LangTransforBks)
E-mail: mail@kayky.net
Web site: http://kayky.net; http://exceptionalert.com; http://verakayky.com.
Velikanje, Kathryn *See* **Levity Pr.**
Vellum Books *Imprint of* **New Academia Publishing, LLC**
Veloce Publishing Ltd. (GBR) *(978-1-874105; 978-1-901295; 978-1-903706; 978-1-904788; 978-1-84584; 978-1-78711) Dist. by* **Natl Bk Netwk.**
Velvet Pony Stories, *(978-0-615-26652-7; 978-0-692-80080-5)*
Dist(s): **Independent Pub.**
Velázquez Pr., *(978-1-59495)* Div. of Academic Learning Co., LLC, 9682 Telstar Ave., Suite 110, El Monte, CA 91731-3009 USA (SAN 255-786X) Tel 626-448-3448; Fax: 626-602-3817
E-mail: info@academiclearningcompany.com
Web site: http://www.academiclearningcompany.com.
Vendera Publishing, *(978-0-9749411; 978-1-936307)* 61 Big Pete Rd., Franklin Furnace, OH 45629 USA Tel 740-531-2122; *Imprints:* 711Press (SevenElev)
E-mail: admin@venderapublishing.com
Web site: http://www.venderapublishing.com.
Vengco, Aletha Fulton, *(978-0-578-00613-0; 978-0-578-00778-6; 978-0-578-00890-5; 978-0-578-02728-9)* 2224 O St., Apt. 4, Sacramento, CA 95816 USA
Dist(s): **Lulu Pr., Inc.**
Venture Development Group, *(978-0-9748030)* 1114 Blue Lake Sq., Mountain View, CA 94040-4561 USA Tel 650-967-3403; Fax: 650-965-0320.
Venture Publishing, *(978-0-9761694)* 750 Tabor St., No. 64, Golden, CO 80401 USA Tel 303-239-6531 (phone/fax).
Venture Publishing, Inc., *(978-0-910251; 978-1-892132; 978-1-939476)* 1999 Cato Ave., State College, PA 16801 USA (SAN 240-897X) Tel 814-234-4561; Fax: 814-234-1651 Do not confuse with companies with the same name in Andover, MA, Ho-Ho-Kus, NJ
E-mail: vpublish@venturepublish.com
Web site: http://www.venturepublish.com.
Verb Technology, Inc., *(978-1-887938; 978-1-933057; 978-1-936631)* 782 S. Automall Dr. Unit A, American Fork, UT 84003 USA Tel 801-225-9520; Fax: 801-343-3301; Toll Free: 800-544-7044
E-mail: mjo@soundconcepts.com; jca@soundconcepts.com; jason@soundconcepts.com; vs@soundconcepts.com; edr@soundconcepts.com; jon@verb.tech; carley@verb.tech
Web site: http://www.soundconcepts.com; http://www.verb.tech.
Verbal Images Pr., *(978-0-9625136; 978-1-884281; 978-0-9821982)* 46 Duncott Rd., Fairport, NY 14450-3150 USA
Web site: http://www.verbalimagespress.com
Dist(s): **Gryphon Hse., Inc.**
Veritas Pr., Inc., *(978-1-930710; 978-1-932168; 978-1-936648; 978-1-950271; 978-1-951200; 978-1-956402)* 1805 Olde Homestead Ln, Lancaster, PA

Publisher Name Index

17601 USA (SAN 255-9617) Tel 717-519-1974; Fax: 717-519-1978; Toll Free: 800-922-5082 Do not confuse with companies with the same name in Santa Barbara CA, Santa Monica CA, Bronx NY, Clearwater Fl, Sioux Falls SD, West Hartford CT, West Allis, MI
E-mail: info@veritaspress.com
Web site: http://www.veritaspress.com.

Veritas Pubns. (IRL) *(978-1-85390; 978-0-901810; 978-0-905092; 978-0-86217; 978-1-84730) Dist. by* **Casemate Pubs.**

Verlag Wilhelm Heyne (DEU) *(978-3-453) Dist. by* **Distribks Inc.**

Verlin, Lily, *(978-0-578-26962-7)* 5940 Spruce Run Ct., Centreville, VA 20121 USA
E-mail: auhorlilyverlin@gmail.com
Web site: http://www.lilyverlin.com/.

Vermont Bookworks, *(978-0-9745931)* 12 Perry Ln., Rutland, VT 05701 USA
E-mail: digbysworld@comcast.net
Web site: http://www.digbysworld.com
Dist(s): **North Country Bks., Inc.**

Vermont Council on the Arts, Incorporated *See* **Vermont Folklife Ctr.**

†Vermont Folklife Ctr., *(978-0-916718; 978-0-692-00433-3)* Orders Addr.: 88 Main St., Middlebury, VT 05753 USA (SAN 208-9092) Tel 802-388-4964; Fax: 802-388-1844
E-mail: bbjorkman@vermontfolklifecenter.org
Web site: http://www.vermontfolklifecenter.org
Dist(s): **Thistle Hill Pubns.**; *CIP.*

†Vermont Life Magazine, *(978-0-936896; 978-1-931389; 978-1-941730)* Div. of State of Vermont, Agency on Development & Community Affairs, 1 National Life Drive, 6th fl, Montpelier, VT 05620-0501 USA (SAN 215-8213) Tel 802-828-3241; Fax: 802-828-3366; Toll Free: 800-455-3399
E-mail: info@vtlife.com; products@vtlife.com; subs@vtlife.com
Web site: http://www.vermontlife.com; http://www.VermontLifeCatalog.com
Dist(s): **Hood, Alan C. & Co., Inc.**
TNT Media Group, Inc.; *CIP.*

Vernacular Pr., *(978-0-9740266)* 197 Grand St. Ste. 2W, New York, NY 10013-3859 USA (SAN 255-3945)
E-mail: hthamann@vernacularpress.com; cvecoli@vernacularpress.com
Web site: http://www.vernacularpress.com.

Verney, Jeff *See* **JRV Publishing**

Vernier Software *See* **Vernier Software & Technology**

Vernier Software & Technology, *(978-0-918731; 978-1-929075; 978-1-948008)* 13979 SW Millikan Way, Beaverton, OR 97005-2886 USA (SAN 293-1753) Tel 503-277-2299; Fax: 503-277-2440
E-mail: info@vernier.com
Web site: http://www.vernier.com.

Vernissage Pr., LLC, *(978-0-9725027)* 2200 Central Ave., Boulder, CO 80301 USA Tel 303-440-8102; Toll Free: 888-849-8697
E-mail: info@vernissagepress.com
Web site: http://www.vernissagepress.com.

veromundo, *(978-1-7342399; 979-8-9852478)* 5126 solano ave, richmond, CA 94805 USA Tel 510-847-7263
E-mail: info@veromundo.com
Web site: veromundo.store.

Verona (Bk.) Publishing, Inc., *(978-0-9667037; 978-0-9769031)* P.O. Box 24071, Edina, MN 55426 USA
Web site: http://www.veronapublishing.com.

Versait Pr. LLC, *(978-0-9746810)* P.O. Box 644332, Vero Beach, FL 32964-4332 USA
E-mail: info@versaitpress.com
Web site: http://VersaitPress.com.

Versal Editorial Group *See* **Cambridge BrickHouse, Inc.**

Versal Technologies, Inc., *(978-0-9749460)* One Cranberry Hill, Suite 102, Lexington, MA 02421 USA.

Versary Pubns., *(978-0-9641429)* 984 Brownsville Rd., Wernersville, PA 19565 USA Tel 610-693-5920.

Versify *Imprint of* **HarperCollins Pubs.**

Verso Bks. (GBR) *(978-0-86091; 978-0-902308; 978-1-85984; 978-1-84467; 978-1-78168; 978-1-78478; 978-1-78663; 978-1-78873; 978-1-83976) Dist. by* **Peng Rand Hse.**

Vertel Publishing *Imprint of* **Nextone Inc.**

Vertical *Imprint of* **Kodansha America, Inc.**

Vertical *Imprint of* **Kodansha America, Inc.**

Vertical *Imprint of* **Vertical, Inc.**

Vertical Comics *Imprint of* **Vertical, Inc.**

Vertical Connect Pr., *(978-0-9769087)* 120 N. Magnolia St., Summerville, SC 29483-6836 USA; *Imprints:* Grand Kidz, The (Grand Kidz)
E-mail: kate@verticalconnectpress.com
Web site: http://www.verticalconnectpress.com.

Vertical, Inc., *(978-1-932234; 978-1-934287; 978-1-935654; 978-1-939130; 978-1-941220; 978-1-942993; 978-1-945054; 978-1-947194)* 451 Park Ave. S. 7th Flr., New York, NY 10016 USA; *Imprints:* Vertical Comics (Vertical Comics); Vertical (Vertical)
E-mail: info@vertical-inc.com
Web site: http://www.vertical-inc.com
Dist(s): **MyiLibrary**
Penguin Random Hse. Distribution
Penguin Random Hse. LLC
Random Hse., Inc.

Vertigo *Imprint of* **DC Comics**

Vertigo Publishing, *(978-0-9764463)* P.O. Box 2683, Dearborn, MI 48123 USA
E-mail: vertigopublish@cs.com
Web site: http://www.vertigopublishing.com.

Vertrees, Heidi, *(978-1-7328578)* P.O. Box 26, Sharpsburg, MD 21782 USA Tel 301-660-1341
E-mail: HMVertrees720@gmail.com.

Verum Publishing, *(978-0-9787476; 978-0-692-10816-1)* 1650 E. gonzales rd No. 187, oxnard, CA 93036 USA Toll Free: 866-600-4840
Web site: http://www.verumpress.com.

Vervante, *(978-0-9723559; 978-0-9854646; 978-1-938579; 978-1-939795; 978-1-940847; 978-1-942104; 978-1-943784; 978-1-946208; 978-1-948404; 978-1-949950; 978-1-950960; 978-1-64775)* 224 S. Main St., Suite 202, Springville, UT 84663 USA (SAN 631-8207) Tel 714-969-7243; Fax: 650-745-1215
E-mail: ctyler@vervante.com
Web site: http://www.vervante.com.

Vescori, Laura, *(978-0-9762965)* 28 Fir Tree Dr., Bradford, CT 06405 USA.

Vesper Enterprises, Inc., *(978-0-9663730)* Orders Addr.: P.O. Box 565, Hingham, MA 02043 USA Tel 781-749-5378; Fax: 781-740-2391; Edit Addr.: 102 Central St., Hingham, MA 02043 USA.

Vessel Ministries, *(978-0-9713345; 978-0-9816463; 978-0-615-11148-3)* 1974 E. Mcandrews Rd., Medford, OR 97504-5510 USA
E-mail: vesselmin@cox.net
Dist(s): **Todd Communications.**

Vessence, *(978-1-7362846)* 2001 MT VERNON Ave., ALEXANDRIA, VA 22301 USA Tel 703-519-4550
E-mail: nancy@vessence.com
Web site: www.vessence.com.

Vesta Bks., LLC, *(978-0-9791065)* 3624 Lone Wolf Trail, Saint Augustine, FL 32086-5316 USA.

Vesta Publishing, *(978-1-60481)* 3750 Priority Way S. Dr., Suite 114, Indianapolis, IN 46240 USA
E-mail: customerservice@vestapublishing.com
Web site: http://www.vestapublishing.com.

Vested Owl, *(978-0-9767926)* Div. of IRM, 3217 Wisconsin Ave., NW #5c, Washington, DC 20016 USA
E-mail: nino@irm360.com
Web site: http://www.vestedowl.com; http://www.kit4marketing.com.

Vesuvian Bks., *(978-1-944109; 978-1-64548)* 2817 W. End Ave. Ste. 126-283, Nashville, TN 37203 USA Tel 502-836-1201
E-mail: italia@vesuvianmedia.com
Web site: http://vesuvianbooks.com; http://VesuvianMediaGroup.com
Dist(s): **Independent Pubs. Group**
Pathway Bk. Service.

Vesuvius Pr. Inc., *(978-0-9719921; 978-0-9796766; 978-0-9815190; 978-1-935257; 978-1-61956)* Orders Addr.: 4727 N. 12th St., Phoenix, AZ 85014 USA (SAN 255-2981) Tel 602-651-1873; Fax: 602-651-1875; *Imprints:* Tau Publishing (TauPubng)
E-mail: jeffcampbell@vesuviuspress.com
Web site: http://www.taupublishing.com; http://Amordeus.com; http://http:/WellnessandEducation.com; http://Vesuviuspressincorporated.com; http://VesuviusPress.com.

VG Publishing, *(978-0-9785900)* 51613 Sass Rd., Chesterfield, MI 48047-5935 USA (SAN 851-0482)
Web site: http://www.voyagergrouplic.com.

Via Media, Incorporated *See* **Via Media, Pr.**

Via Media, Pr., *(978-0-9646362)* 3112 James St., San Diego, CA 92106 USA Tel 619-884-6440
E-mail: via_media_press@pacbell.net.

Viaduct Music, *(978-0-9831629)* 711 Broadway E. Apt. 9, Seattle, WA 98102-4680 USA Tel 206-322-3187
E-mail: theramster@gmail.com
Dist(s): **BookBaby.**

Vibatorium LLC, *(978-0-9742495)* 419 N. Larchmont Blvd., No. 3265, Los Angeles, CA 90004 USA Tel 323-460-4441; Fax: 323-935-0225
E-mail: info@backyardwonders.com
Web site: http://www.vibatorium.com; http://www.backyardwonders.com.

Vibrante Pr., *(978-0-935301)* P.O. Box 51853, Albuquerque, NM 87181-1853 USA (SAN 696-2351)
E-mail: Lonnie@vibrante.com
Web site: http://www.vibrante.com.

Vice Press Publishing Company *See* **Ascension Education**

Vicens-Vives, Editorial, S.A. (ESP) *(978-84-316) Dist. by* **Lectorum Pubns.**

Vickery Bks., *(978-1-928531)* 3012 Anchor Dr., Ormond Beach, FL 32176-2304 USA
E-mail: kvv145@gte.net.

Vic's Lab, LLC, *(978-1-942178)* P.O. Box 10865, Danville, VA 24543 USA Tel 512-842-7552
E-mail: vicslabpublishing@gmail.com
Web site: VicsLab.com.

Victoria Peace Green, *(978-0-692-85198-2)* 1155 Hillwood Loop, Lincoln, CA 95648 USA Tel 210-273-9012
E-mail: victoriapeace@att.net
Web site: www.victoriapeacegreen.com.

Victoria Tecken, *(978-0-9788850; 978-1-937363)* 1008 N Prairie St, Lake City, MN 55041 USA
E-mail: victoria.tecken@gmail.com; kastenkathy@gmail.com
Web site: https://victoriatecken.com/; www.lioncrestleadership.com.

Victorian Royalty, *(978-0-9998395)* 111 S. Morgan, Unit 817, Chicago, IL 60607 USA Tel 708-935-5001
E-mail: msvwatkins11914@gmail.com.

Victorious Publishing Group, *(978-0-9826609)* 2310 S. Green Bay Rd STe. C, No. 503 Ste. C, Racine, WI 53406 USA Tel 262-612-3070
E-mail: contactvwmag@gmail.com.

Victorious You *See* **Victorious You Pr.**

Victorious You Pr., *(978-1-7340609; 978-1-952756; 978-1-959719)* 725 Byrum Way St., Huntersville, NC 28027 USA Tel 703-967-2622
E-mail: joan@victoriousyoupress.com
Web site: VICTORIOUSYOUPRESS.COM.

Victor's Crown Publishing, *(978-0-9761188)* 3322 N. 900 E., Ogden, UT 84414 USA Fax: 801-782-3864
E-mail: steve@victorscrown.com
Web site: http://www.victorscrown.com.

Victory Belt Publishing, *(978-0-9777315; 978-0-9815044; 978-0-9825658; 978-1-936608; 978-1-62860)* 32245 Old Ranch Pk. Ln., Auberry, CA 93602 USA (SAN 850-0819) Tel 559-355-4188
Web site: http://www.victorybelt.com
Dist(s): **Penguin Random Hse. Distribution**
Penguin Random Hse. LLC
Simon & Schuster
Simon & Schuster, Inc.
Tuttle Publishing.

Victory by Any Means Games, *(978-0-9764048; 978-1-935074)* Orders Addr.: P.O. Box 329, Lusk, WY 82225-0329 USA Tel 307-334-3190; Edit Addr.: 315 S. Iron, Lusk, WY 82225-0329 USA
E-mail: tyrel@vbamgames.com
Web site: http://www.vbamgames.com.

Victory Graphics & Media *See* **Yorkshire Publishing Group**

Victory Hse. Pr., *(978-1-935571)* 3836 Tradition Dr., Fort Collins, CO 80526 USA Tel 970-226-1078.

Victory In Grace Ministries *See* **InGrace Pubns.**

Victory Pr., *(978-0-9753818)* P.O. Box 118, Massillon, OH 44648 USA Do not confuse with companies with the same name in Carlton OR, Chesterfield MO, Monterey CA
E-mail: rabteach2001@aol.com
Web site: http://www.ruthann.faithweb.com.

Victory Publishing Co., *(978-0-9778925)* 3797 N. Ashley Ct., Decatur, IL 62526 USA (SAN 850-4458) Do not confuse with companies with the same or similar name in Hampton, VA, Redwood City, CA, MOunt Pleasant, SC, Inglewood, CA, Banco, VA, Parma, ID, New Orleans, LA, Littleton, CO
E-mail: edmar84@aol.com.

Victory WW 2 Publishing Ltd., *(978-0-9700567)* 18140 Zane St. NW - 200, Elk River, MN 55330 USA (SAN 253-2476) Tel 763-753-5200; Fax: 763-753-2862
E-mail: victorypub@aol.com
Dist(s): **MyiLibrary**
ebrary, Inc.

Vic-Vincent Publishing, *(978-0-9646817)* Div. of Vic-Vincent Corp., Orders Addr.: 362 Gulf Breeze Pkwy., Suite 151, Gulf Breeze, FL 32561 USA (SAN 257-4039) Tel 850-476-7673; Toll Free: 800-772-3343
E-mail: inventorz@aol.com
Web site: http://www.inventorsfreehelp.com
Dist(s): **Distributors, The.**

Vida Life Publishers International *See* **Vida Pubs.**

Vida Pubs., *(978-0-8297)* 8410 NW 53rd Ter. Ste. 103, Miami, FL 33166-4510 USA Toll Free: 800-843-2548
E-mail: vidapubsales@harpercollins.com
Web site: http://www.editorialvida.com
Dist(s): **Follett School Solutions**
HarperCollins Christian Publishing
Zondervan.

Vidaurre, Edward, *(978-0-692-07752-8; 978-0-692-12827-5; 978-0-692-18350-2; 978-0-578-45506-8; 978-1-7338092; 978-1-7345617; 978-1-953447)* 1218 N 15th St, McAllen, TX 78501 USA Tel 956-739-2206
E-mail: info@flowersongpress.com
Web site: https://www.flowersongpress.com/
Dist(s): **Ingram Bk. Co.**
SPD-Small Pr. Distribution.

VIDENE Publications *See* **Red Poppy Pr.**

Vidro, Kenneth *See* **Gilbert Square Bks.**

Vidya Bks., *(978-1-878099)* P.O. Box 7788, Berkeley, CA 94707-0788 USA Tel 510-527-9932.

Vidyaranayam, *(978-0-692-71703-5; 978-0-578-47295-9; 978-1-7338088)* 3218 Sharpton Dr., DULUTH, GA 30096 USA Tel 617-899-9122.

Viet Baby, LLC, *(978-0-9776482)* Orders Addr.: P.O. Box 750074, Las Vegas, NV 89136-0074 USA Tel 702-234-5127
E-mail: an@viet-baby.com
Web site: http://www.viet-baby.com.

Vietnamese International Poetry Society, *(978-0-9746300)* Orders Addr.: P.O. Box 246958, Sacramento, CA 95824 USA; Edit Addr.: 3067 Harrison St., NW, Washington, DC 20015 USA.

Viewpoint Pr., *(978-0-943962)* Orders Addr.: P.O. Box 1090, Tehachapi, CA 93581 USA Tel 661-821-5110; Fax: 661-821-7515; Edit Addr.: 785 Tucker Rd., Apt. G400, Tehachapi, CA 93561 USA Do not confuse with companies with the same name in San Diego, CA, Portland, ME
E-mail: joie99@aol.com.

Viewpoints Research Institute, Inc., *(978-0-9743131)* 1209 Grand Central Ave., Glendale, CA 91201 USA
Web site: http://www.viewpointsresearch.org.

VIICCA LLC *See* **ColoringCrumbs LLC**

Viident Co., *(978-1-929266; 978-0-9841318; 978-1-937509; 978-1-942611; 978-1-63582)* 631 U.S. Hwy. 1 Suite 201 Suite 201, North Palm Beach, FL 33408 USA (SAN 858-5024) Tel 888-618-5253; *Imprints:* Little Sparrow (MYD_D_LITTLE) Do not confuse with Beacon Publishing in Theodore, AL, Brimfield, MA
E-mail: admin@bluesparrowbooks.org
Web site: https://www.matthewkelly.com/; http://www.beaconpublishinginc.com/; https://www.bluesparrowbooks.org/; https://www.wellspringbooks.org/
Dist(s): **BookBaby**
Follett School Solutions
Smashwords.

Vikasam, *(978-0-615-46456-5)* 23355 N. Empress Dr., Hawthorn Woods, IL 60047 USA Tel 847-815-1978
E-mail: dollysap@gmail.com.

VIKI Publishing, *(978-1-950263; 978-1-962083)* 5010 Barrenstar Way, San Ramon, CA 94582 USA Tel 408-726-4739
E-mail: vinaykiara@gmail.com
Web site: https://www.vikipublishing.com.

Viking *Imprint of* **Penguin Publishing Group**

Viking Adult *Imprint of* **Penguin Publishing Group**

Viking Books for Young Readers *Imprint of* **Penguin Young Readers Group**

VILA Group, Inc., The, *(978-0-9635047)* V2947 S. Atlantic Ave., Apt. 1906, Daytona Beach, FL 32118-6029 USA Tel 904-767-8245.

Vilasa Pr., *(978-0-9762809; 978-1-937927)* Orders Addr.: 2835 Long Valley Rd., Santa Ynez, CA 93460 USA (SAN 256-2995) Tel 805-688-6116; Fax: 805-456-3340
E-mail: vilasapress@gmail.com
Web site: http://www.vilasapress.com; http://sandynathan.com
Dist(s): **BookBaby**
Ingram Content Group
Smashwords.

Villa Serena Publishing, *(978-0-9753326)* 15657 Westbrook Rd., Livonia, MI 48154 USA.

Villa Wisteria Pubns., *(978-0-615-52506-8)* 6103 Hoochaneetsa Pl. N., Cochiti Lake, NM 87083 USA Tel 505-465-0361
E-mail: mlpbadarak@villawisteria.com
Web site: http://www.villawisteria.com.

Village Earth Pr. *Imprint of* **Harding Hse. Publishing Sebice Inc.**

Village Monkey LLC, The, *(978-0-9789633)* 7760 McWhorter Rd., Martinsville, IN 46151 USA Tel 765-352-1718
E-mail: zenmonkey@thevillagemonkey.com
Web site: http://www.thevillagemonkey.com.

Village Monkey, The *See* **Village Monkey LLC, The**

Village Museum, *(978-0-9740091)* Orders Addr.: 401 Pinckney St., McClellanville, SC 29458 USA Tel 843-887-3030; Edit Addr.: P.O. Box 595, McClellanville, SC 29458 USA Tel 843-887-3030
Web site: http://www.villagemuseum.com.

Village Publishing, *(978-0-9857741; 978-0-9981196-0-1)* 2924 W.132nd Pl., Gardena, CA 90249 USA Tel 310-922-6562
E-mail: wwilson150@gmail.com.

Village Tales Publishing, *(978-0-9753609; 978-0-9853625; 978-1-945408; 978-1-959580)* 662 Lookout Point, Lawrenceville, GA 30043 USA
E-mail: publisher@villagetalespublishing.com; villagetalespublishing@yahoo.com; villagetalespub@gmail.com
Web site: http://villagetalespublishing.com; http://www.villagetalespublishing.com.

Villager Bk. Publishing, *(978-1-934643)* Orders Addr.: P.O. Box 222 W. Las Colinas Blvd, Suite 1650, Irving, TX 75039 USA (SAN 854-0969)
E-mail: semerick@villagerdustbunnies.com; jbloom@villagerdustbunnies.com; lrinn@villagerdustbunnies.com; jfox@villagerdustbunnies.com
Web site: http://villagerpublishers.com; http://www.villagerdustbunnies.com.

Villard Bks. *Imprint of* **Random House Publishing Group**

Vilnius Pr., *(978-0-615-80054-7; 978-0-615-80223-7; 978-1-940136)* 152 Ct. St. Suite 2E, Portsmouth, NH 03801 USA Tel 8552607535
Web site: http://vilnius-press.com/
Dist(s): **CreateSpace Independent Publishing Platform.**

Vinay Shankar *See* **VIKI Publishing**

Vincent, Thomas J. Foundation Inc., *(978-0-9759284)* 44-447 Kaneohe Bay Dr., Kaneohe, HI 96744 USA
E-mail: vincentfoundation@yahoo.com.

Vincero Enterprises, *(978-0-9675329)* 490 Marin Oaks Dr., Novato, CA 94949 USA Tel 800-715-1492; Fax: 415-883-4115; Toll Free: 800-715-1492
E-mail: heritage1492@earthlink.net
Web site: http://www.italianheritage.net; http://www.hispaniclatino.net.

Vindof Publishing, *(978-0-9759310)* 410 N. 3rd St., Ft. Atkinson, WI 53538 USA.

Vine Publishing, *(978-1-931141)* P.O. Box 17912, Honolulu, HI 96817-9998 USA (SAN 253-3952) Tel 808-235-1730; Fax: 808-235-1735; Toll Free: 888-235-1630 Do not confuse with companies with the same or similar name in Exeter, NH, Girard, IL
E-mail: vine@hawaii-rr.com
Web site: http://www.vinepublishing.com
Dist(s): **Independent Pubs. Group.**

Vineyard Publishing, LLC *See* **Ampelon Publishing, LLC**

Vineyard Stories, *(978-0-9771384; 978-0-615-26606-0; 978-0-615-34267-2; 978-0-9827146; 978-0-9849136; 978-0-9915028; 978-0-692-40086-9; 978-0-692-73037-9; 978-0-692-86175-2; 978-0-692-07280-6; 978-0-692-17354-1; 978-0-578-50646-3)* Orders Addr.: RR 1, Box 65-B9, Edgartown, MA 02539 USA Tel 598-221-2338; Fax: 508-627-6909; Edit Addr.: 52 Bold Meadow Rd., Edgartown, MA 02539 USA
Web site: http://www.vineyardstories.com.

Vinland Pr., *(978-0-9721410)* P.O. Box 927, North Bend, OR 97459 USA Tel 541-751-1566
E-mail: s_coons@charter.net.

Vinland Publishing, *(978-0-9801601; 978-0-9889455)* 661 Tamarron Dr., Grand Jct, CO 81506-4911 USA (SAN 855-3564)
E-mail: jahunsinger@vinlandpublishing.com; info@vinlandpublishing.com
Web site: http://www.vinlandpublishing.com
Dist(s): **Follett School Solutions**
MyiLibrary
ebrary, Inc.

Vinny Tales, *(978-1-7325577)* 98-120 Queens Blvd. Apt. 4A, Rego Park, NY 11374 USA Tel 917-502-7593
E-mail: vinnychen@aol.com.

Vinspire Publishing LLC, *(978-0-9752868; 978-0-9770107; 978-0-9785368; 978-0-9793327; 978-0-9815592; 978-0-9819896; 978-0-9834198; 978-0-9851232; 978-0-9890632; 978-0-9903042; 978-0-9964423; 978-0-9971732; 978-1-7321348; 978-1-7327112; 978-1-7341507; 978-1-7363662; 979-8-9858530; 979-8-9880122)* P.O. Box 1165, Ladson, SC 29456 USA
Web site: http://www.vinspirepublishing.com.

Vintage *Imprint of* **Knopf Doubleday Publishing Group**

Vintage Bird Pr., *(978-0-9994793)* 2140 E. Hackamore St., Mesa, AZ 85213 USA Tel 480-593-4263
E-mail: lauraofgreen@aol.com
Web site: https://vintagebirdpressblog.wordpress.com/about/.

Vintage Romance Publishing, LLC *See* **Vinspire Publishing LLC**

Vintage Wild, *(978-0-9862627; 978-0-9986293; 978-1-7326900)* 10070 n.w. 9 St. Cir. 204, Miami, FL 33172 USA Tel 7863026680.

Vinvatar Publishing, *(978-1-945012; 978-1-63581)* P.O. Box 33, Lawrence, MI 49064 USA Tel 269-487-8184
E-mail: office@vinvatar.com
Web site: www.vinvatar.com.

Violet Bks., *(978-0-615-19128-7)* 306 Edgewater Dr., Anderson, SC 29626 USA
Dist(s): **Lulu Pr., Inc.**

Violette Editions (GBR) *(978-1-900828) Dist. by* **Dist Art Pubs.**

VIP INK Publishing Group, Inc., *(978-0-615-59125-4; 978-0-615-59946-5; 978-0-9886428; 978-0-9911719; 978-0-9861340; 978-0-9965701; 978-0-9970016; 978-0-9978116)* 4623 branch Ct., lithonia, GA 30038 USA
E-mail: AANDE46461@yahoo.com; Lenny@Printhousebooks.com
Web site: http://www.Printhousebooks.com
Dist(s): **Ingram Content Group eBookit.com.**

VIP Ink Publishing, L.L.C., *(978-1-939670)* 140 Belle Terre Blvd. Ste. D 211, LaPlace, LA 70068 USA Tel 985-359-2337
E-mail: info@vipinkpublishing.com
Web site: http://www.vipinkpublishing.com.

Viper Comics, *(978-0-9754193; 978-0-9777883; 978-0-9793680; 978-0-9802385; 978-0-9827117; 978-0-9833670)* Div. of Viper Entertainment Inc., 9400 N. MacArthur Blvd., Suite 124-215, Irving, TX 75063 USA Tel 214-638-1400; 469-682-9331; Fax: 817-741-3758
E-mail: jessie@vipercomics.com
Web site: http://www.vipercomics.com
Dist(s): **Diamond Comic Distributors, Inc.**

Virella, Mary, *(978-0-9993514; 978-1-7345618)* 289 Fox Bend Cir., Bolingbrook, 60440 SUN Tel 630-366-1171
E-mail: maainihi@gmail.com
Web site: mainihi.wordpress.com; https://ConcealedRealms.com.

Vireo Bks., A *Imprint of* **Rare Bird Bks.**

Virginia Museum of Natural History, *(978-0-9625801; 978-1-884549)* 21 Starling Ave., Martinsville, VA 24112-2921 USA
E-mail: dgreytak@vmnh.org.

Virginia Publishing Corporation *See* **Virginia Publishing Corp.**

Virginia Publishing Corp., *(978-0-9631448; 978-1-891442; 978-0-9914806)* P.O. Box 20586, Saint Louis, MO 63139 USA Tel 314-367-6612 (ext. 22); Fax: 314-367-0727 Do not confuse with Virginia Publishing Co. in Lynchburg, VA
E-mail: jeffl@stlprograms.com
Web site: http://www.stl-books.com; http://bluebirdbookpub.com; http://stlprograms.com
Dist(s): **Big River Distribution Partners Bk. Distributing, Inc.**

Virginian Pilot, *(978-0-9648308)* Div. of Landmark Communications, Inc., 150 W. Brambleton Ave., Norfolk, VA 23501 USA Tel 757-481-4777; Fax: 757-446-2963
E-mail: linda.hollingsworth@pilotonline.com; pam.smithrodden@pilotonline.com
Dist(s): **Parnassus Bk. Distributors.**

Virgo Rising Publishing Hse., *(978-1-7379711)* 5013 HOLLIS GOODWIN RD, DORA, AL 35062 USA Tel 205-617-7440
E-mail: info@virgorisingpublishing.com.

VirTru Powers, *(978-0-9778798; 978-0-9779497)* Orders Addr.: P.O. Box 9404, Tavernier, FL 33070 USA; Edit Addr.: 10S073 Clarendon Hills Rd., Willowbrook, IL 60527 USA (SAN 850-492X) Tel 630-986-5262; Fax: 630-986-5262
E-mail: nomorewast@aol.com.

Virtual Baby Nurse LLC, *(978-0-9755180)* P.O. Box 881296, Port Saint Lucie, FL 34988-1296 USA (SAN 256-1239)
Web site: http://www.virtualbabynurse.com.

Virtual Tales *See* **BRP Publishing Group**

Virtual Word Publishing, *(978-0-9787930)* 1660 Cathedral Dr., Margate, FL 33063 USA Tel 954-971-4025; Fax: 954-971-4025
E-mail: diana@virtualwordpublishing.com
Web site: http://www.virtualwordpublishing.com.

Virtualbookworm.com Publishing, Inc., *(978-0-9703682; 978-1-58939; 978-1-60264; 978-1-62137; 978-1-947532; 978-1-949756; 978-1-951985; 978-1-63868)* P.O. Box 9949, College Station, TX 77842 USA (SAN 852-6575) Toll Free: 877-376-4955 (phone/fax)
E-mail: info@virtualbookworm.com
Web site: http://www.virtualbookworm.com.

Virtue Bks., *(978-0-9746440)* Div. of Virtue Products, Inc., 197 Woodland Pkwy., No. 104-476, San Marcos, CA 92069 USA Tel 760-471-5511; Fax: 760-471-5515; Toll Free: 800-201-5200
E-mail: kenwilcox3@cox.net; ken@virtueproducts.com
Web site: http://www.virtueproducts.com.

Virtue Pr., *(978-0-615-57943-6; 978-0-615-57945-0; 978-0-615-58375-4; 978-0-615-60709-2; 978-0-615-60746-7; 978-0-615-61272-0)* P.O. Box 729, Kamuela, HI 96743 USA Tel 808-250-9235 Do not confuse with Virtue Press in Jacksonville, NC
Dist(s): **CreateSpace Independent Publishing Platform.**

Viselman, Kenn Presents.., *(978-0-9722361)* P.O. Box 195, New York, NY 10113 USA (SAN 254-7783) Tel 212-929-1234
E-mail: viselmanpresents@aol.com.

Visible Ink Pr., *(978-0-7876; 978-0-8103; 978-1-57859)* Orders Addr.: 1094 Flex Dr., Jackson, TN 38301-5070 USA Toll Free Fax: 800-351-5073; Toll Free: 800-343-4499; Edit Addr.: 43311 Joy Rd., Canton, MI 48187-2075 USA (SAN 860-2271) Tel 734-667-3211; Fax: 734-667-4311
E-mail: inquiries@visibleink.com
Web site: http://www.visibleink.com
Dist(s): **Ebsco Publishing Follett School Solutions Legato Pubs. Group Mint Pubs. Group MyiLibrary Publishers Group West (PGW) Perseus Bks. Group.**

Visikid Bks. *Imprint of* **GSVQ Publishing**

Vision *Imprint of* **Grand Central Publishing**

Vision & Voice Publishing LLC, *(978-0-692-77452-6)* 13102 Creek Bridge Ln., Alpharetta, GA 30004 USA Tel 718-598-3076; Fax: 800-387-9075
E-mail: traceyworthen@aol.com.

Vision Bks. LLC, *(978-0-9886402)* 14 Edith Ln., Douglasville, GA 30134 USA
E-mail: visionbooksga@gmail.com
Web site: www.facebook.com/VisionBooksGa.

Vision Chapters Publishing Co., *(978-0-9860169)* 932 Homestead Park Dr., Apex, NC 27502 USA.

Vision Forum, Inc., The, *(978-0-9665233; 978-1-929241; 978-0-9755263; 978-0-9787559; 978-1-934554)* 4719 Blanco Rd., San Antonio, TX 78212 USA Tel 210-340-5250; Fax: 210-340-8577; Toll Free: 800-440-0022
E-mail: orders@visionforum.com
Web site: http://www.visionforum.com
Dist(s): **Send The Light Distribution LLC.**

Vision Harmony Publishing, *(978-0-9748715)* 4195 Chino Hills Pkwy., #393, Chino Hills, CA 91709 USA Tel 951-505-2503; Toll Free Fax: 866-855-1476
E-mail: info@visionharmony.com
Web site: http://www.visionharmony.com.

Vision Pubns., *(978-0-9746161; 978-1-933260)* P.O. Box 71532, Marietta, GA 30007-1532 USA Fax: 770-973-9446; Toll Free: 800-862-5264 Do not confuse with companies with the same name in Southfield, MI, Saint Louis, MO, Boise, ID
E-mail: visionpublications@earthlink.net; dvandewalker@earlink.net.

Vision Publishers, Incorporated *See* **Vision Pubs., LLC**

Vision Pubs., LLC, *(978-0-9717054; 978-1-932676; 978-1-63100)* Orders Addr.: P.O. Box 190, Harrisonburg, VA 22803 USA Fax: 540-437-1969; Toll Free: 877-488-0901; Edit Addr.: 755 Cantrell Ave., Suite C, Harrisonburg, VA 22801 USA Do not confuse with Vision Publishers, Fort Lauderdale, FL
E-mail: visionpubl@ntelos.net
Web site: www.vision-publishers.com
Dist(s): **ebrary, Inc.**

Vision Publishing *See* **Stanley O. Williford Literary Agency**

Vision to Fruition Publishing *See* **Vision to Fruition Publishing Hse., The**

Vision Tree, Ltd., The, *(978-1-933334)* 216 Waterbury Cir., Lake Villa, IL 60046 USA (SAN 256-5072) Tel 847-833-2546; Fax: 847-356-3783
E-mail: jo@thevisiontree.com
Web site: http://www.thevisiontree.com.

Vision Unlimited Pr., *(978-0-9746385)* 3832 Radnor Ave., Long Beach, CA 90808 USA Tel 562-537-1397 Do not confuse with Vision Unlimited in Spartanburg, SC
E-mail: joachung@msn.com; susan@newhopegrief.org.

Vision Video, *(978-1-56364)* Orders Addr.: P.O. Box 540, Worcester, PA 19490 USA Tel 610-584-3500; Fax: 610-584-4610; Toll Free: 800-523-0226; Edit Addr.: 2030 Wentz Church Rd., Worcester, PA 19490 USA (SAN 298-7392)
E-mail: info@gatewayfilms.com; info@visionvideo.com
Web site: http://www.gatewayfilms.com
Dist(s): **BJU Pr. Christian Bk. Distributors Follett Media Distribution Follett School Solutions Midwest Tape Spring Arbor Distributors, Inc. Tapeworm Video Distributor, Inc.**

Vision Works Publishing *Imprint of* **Soul Vision Works Publishing**

Vision Writer Pubns., *(978-0-692-69848-8; 978-0-9991767)* 200 S. Wilcox St. #328, Castle Rock, CO 80104 USA Tel 303-525-8043
Web site: www.amberschamel.com
Dist(s): **CreateSpace Independent Publishing Platform.**

Vision Your Dreams, *(978-0-615-92446-5; 978-0-9969049)* 67 Curve St. 6, Millis, MA 02054 USA Tel 617-448-2504
E-mail: sandra@visionyourdreams.net
Web site: www.visionyourdreams.com.

Visionary Consulting Services, LLC, *(978-0-692-84351-2; 978-0-692-84352-9; 978-0-692-89967-0)* 9024 PENNINGTON PLACE, MONTGOMERY, AL 36117 USA Tel 334-277-8937
E-mail: jeffwcrawford5+LVP0003343@gmail.com; jeffwcrawford5+LVP0003343@gmail.com.

Visionary Play Pr., *(978-0-615-21946-2; 978-0-615-40324-3)* 5098 Reed Rd., Columbus, OH 43220 USA
Web site: http://www.InspiredFlying.com
Dist(s): **Ingram Content Group.**

Visionary Pr. Publishing, *(978-1-7361829; 979-8-9865221)* 11900 Edgewater 309, Lakewood, OH 44107 USA Tel 330-704-0893
E-mail: valerieterrell7@gmail.com.

VisionQuest Kids *Imprint of* **GSVQ Publishing**

Visions Given Life Publishing Co., *(978-0-9842468)* 1514 Parker Pointe Blvd., Odessa, FL 33556-4022 USA Tel 724-561-9426
E-mail: gdgregdixon@gmail.com.

Visions Of Nature, *(978-0-9656051; 978-0-9749570)* 460 E. 56th St., Suite A, Anchorage, AK 99518 USA Tel 907-561-4062
E-mail: robolson@gci.com
Web site: http://robertolson.com.

Visit to Hawaii, A, *(978-0-9772200)* 445 Kaiolu St., No. 807, Honolulu, HI 55303 USA Tel 808-921-2440
E-mail: hawaiiholm@aol.com
Dist(s): **Booklines Hawaii, Ltd.**

Visor Bks., *(978-0-9771994)* 62 W. Gaslight Pl., The Woodlands, TX 77382 USA (SAN 256-9752)
E-mail: rosszilla@sbcglobal.net
Web site: http://www.visorbooks.com.

Visor Libros (ESP) *(978-84-7522) Dist. by* **AIMS Intl.**

Vista Higher Learning, Inc., *(978-1-931100; 978-1-932000; 978-1-59334; 978-1-60007; 978-1-60576; 978-1-61767; 978-1-61857; 978-1-62680; 978-1-68004; 978-1-68005; 978-1-5433; 978-1-6699; 979-8-3847; 979-8-3848)* Orders Addr.: 500 Boylston St. Suite 620, Boston, MA 02116 USA (SAN 991-2002); Edit Addr.: 500 Boylston Street, Suite 620, Boston, MA 02116 USA (SAN 253-9586) Toll Free: 800-618-7375; 500 Boylston St. Suite 620, Boston, MA 02116 Toll Free: 800-618-7375.

Vista Italia, *(978-0-9820672)* P.O. Box 92, La Mirada, CA 90637 USA (SAN 857-1643).

Vista Press Ventures, Incorporated *See* **Eaglemont Pr.**

Vister Bks., *(978-0-9983337)* 429 Visser Dr., Blackwater, VA 24221 USA Tel 276-346-1650
E-mail: circlevisser@gmail.com.

Visual Adjectives, *(978-0-9833329; 978-1-941901)* 14280 Military Trail, No. 7501, Delray Beach, FL 33482 USA Tel 561-376-3130; *Imprints:* GoPublish (Gopublish)
E-mail: mlawrence@visadj.com; michelle@lawrence.net
Web site: www.visualadjectives.com.

Visual Education Productions, *(978-1-56918)* 1020 SE Loop 289, Lubbock, TX 79404 USA Tel 806-745-8820; Toll Free: 800-922-9965
E-mail: cev@cevmultimedia.com
Web site: http://www.cevmultimedia.com
Dist(s): **Follett School Solutions.**

Visual Manna, *(978-0-9677386; 978-0-9715970; 978-0-9816093)* Orders Addr.: P.O. Box 553, Salem, MO 65560 USA Tel 573-729-2100; Edit Addr.: 1403 Dent County Rd., 502A, Salem, MO 65560 USA
E-mail: visualmanna@gmail.com.

Visual Velocity, *(978-0-9884679)* 22106 Chesapeake Cir., Commerce Twp., MI 48390 USA Tel 248-345-0789
E-mail: visualvelocityllc@gmail.com.

Visualz, *(978-1-57175)* Orders Addr.: 845 Minnehaha Ave E, St. Paul, MN 55106 USA Tel 507-455-9076; Edit Addr.: 845 Minnehaha Ave E, St Paul, MN 55106 USA Tel 507-455-9076; Fax: 507-455-3380; Toll Free: 888-455-7003
E-mail: customerservice@learningzonexpress.com
Web site: http://www.learningzonexpress.com
Dist(s): **Follett School Solutions.**

Vital Health Publishing *Imprint of* **Square One Pubs.**

Vital Link Orange County, *(978-0-9765880)* Orders Addr.: P.O. Box 12064, Costa Mesa, CA 92627 USA Tel 949-646-2520; Fax: 949-646-2523; Edit Addr.: 1701 E. 16th St., Newport Beach, CA 92663 USA
E-mail: kathy@vitallinkoc.org
Web site: http://www.vitallinkoc.org.

Vital Links, *(978-0-9717653)* 6613 Seybold Rd., Suite E, Madison, WI 53719 USA Tel 608-270-5424; Fax: 608-278-9363; Toll Free: 866-829-6331
Web site: http://vitallinks.net.

Vital Narrative Pr., *(978-0-692-38692-7; 978-0-692-39642-1; 978-0-692-39747-3; 978-0-692-40643-4; 978-0-692-40899-5; 978-0-692-46199-0; 978-0-692-46406-9; 978-0-9983364; 978-0-578-44121-4; 978-0-578-46140-3; 978-0-578-46577-7; 978-0-578-59513-9; 978-0-578-64324-3; 978-0-578-64325-0; 978-0-578-71341-0; 978-0-578-78055-9; 978-0-578-89458-4) 1296 Sessions Ct S, Memphis, TN 38119 USA Tel 9196961665; Toll Free: 9196961665*
Dist(s): **CreateSpace Independent Publishing Platform.**

Vitale, Mary Ann, *(978-0-9981359; 978-0-9981359-1-5; 978-1-7341211)* 23550 Hall Rd., Woodhaven, MI 48183 USA Tel 734-675-7946; Fax: 734-675-7946
E-mail: nvitale1@comcast.net.

Vitality Pr., *(978-0-9905543; 979-8-9892103)* 45 Fernwood Dr., San Anselmo, CA 94960 USA Tel 415-459-3434
E-mail: voodee@sbcglobal.net.

Vitally Important,
Dist(s): **SPD-Small Pr. Distribution.**

Vitis Vera, LLC, *(978-0-615-73627-3; 978-0-9914009)* 12716 Cross Dale Dr., Huntersville, NC 28078 USA Tel 980-230-9625
E-mail: cwkinser@gmail.com.

Vivamorem Entertainment, Inc., *(978-1-7371651)* 757 Warwick Ave., Thousand Oaks, CA 91360 USA Tel 310-739-6160
E-mail: vivamorem@vivamorem.com.

Vives, Luis Editorial (Edelvives) (ESP) *(978-84-263; 978-84-140) Dist. by* **Lectorum Pubns.**

VivianLChilds *See* **VLChilds Publishing**

Vivid Kids Apparel, *(978-0-578-54182-2)* 245 W. Read St., Baltimore, MD 21201 USA Tel 410-762-8109
E-mail: info@vividkidsapparel.com
Web site: www.vividkidsapparel.com.

VivLiv Bks., *(978-1-7357147; 979-8-9866780)* 137 16th St., Brooklyn, NY 11215 USA Tel 516-655-8677
E-mail: justinearcher17@gmail.com.

Viz Comics *Imprint of* **Viz Media**

Viz Communications, Incorporated *See* **Viz Media**

Viz Media, *(978-0-929279; 978-1-56931; 978-1-59116; 978-1-4215; 978-1-9747)* Subs. of Shogakukan, Inc., 295 Bay St., San Francisco, CA 94133 USA (SAN 248-8604) Tel 415-546-7073; Fax: 415-546-7086; P.O. Box 77010, San Francisco, CA 94107 Fax: 415-546-7086; *Imprints:* Viz Comics (Viz Comics)
E-mail: scott@viz.com; info@info@viz.com
Web site: http://www.viz.com
Dist(s): **AAA Anime Distribution Children's Plus, Inc. Diamond Comic Distributors, Inc. Follett School Solutions Simon & Schuster, Inc. Simon & Schuster Children's Publishing.**

Vizione Productions Inc., *(978-0-9758863)* P.O. Box 54838, Atlanta, GA 30312 USA (SAN 256-1158) Tel 404-538-9424.

VK Pr., LLC, *(978-0-9982754; 979-8-218-08262-8)* 930 Prospect St Unit 206, Indianapolis, IN 46203 USA Tel 317-400-6883
E-mail: vkpressllc@gmail.com.

VK Publishing, Inc., *(978-0-9777171; 978-1-7352931; 979-8-9851651; 979-8-9856550)* 110 N. Milwaukee Ave. Apt.403, Wheeling, IL 60090 USA (SAN 850-0509)
E-mail: vkofman@stellaacademy.com.

VK Publishing, Incorporated *See* **VK Publishing, Inc.**

VL Publishing, *(978-0-692-60457-1; 978-0-692-90618-7; 978-1-959859)*
Dist(s): **CreateSpace Independent Publishing Platform.**

VLChilds Publishing, *(978-0-9799896)* Div. of V.L.Childs/UICF, LLC, P.O. Box 9334, Warner Robins, GA 31095 USA
E-mail: vlccreations@yahoo.com
Web site: http://www.vivianlchilds.com.

VMH Publishing, *(978-0-9984553; 978-0-9989653; 978-1-947928; 978-0-578-82335-5; 978-1-7378324; 979-8-9853349; 979-8-9865891; 979-8-9869758)* 3355 Lenox Rd. NE Suite 750, Atlanta, GA 30326 USA Tel 833-842-6657
E-mail: vikki.hankins@gmail.com; info@vikkihankins.net; info@vmhpublishing.com
Web site: http://www.vmhpublishing.com.

VMH Vikki M. Hankins Publishing *See* **VMH Publishing**

Vocal Power Inc., *(978-0-934419)* 2123 N. Topanga Canyon Blvd., Topanga, CA 90290 USA (SAN 693-4471) Toll Free: 800-829-7664
E-mail: info@vocalpowerinc.com
Web site: http://www.vocalpowerinc.com
Dist(s): **Alfred Publishing Co., Inc.**

Vocalis, Ltd., *(978-0-9665743; 978-0-9709948; 978-1-932653)* 100 Avalon Cir., Waterbury, CT 06710 USA Tel 203-753-5244; Fax: 203-574-5433
E-mail: vocalis@sbcglobal.net; info@VocalisESL.com
Web site: http://www.vocalisltd.com; http://www.vocalisesl.com; http://www.vocalis.com
Dist(s): **Follett School Solutions ebrary, Inc.**

Vogel, Robert, *(978-0-9768455)* P.O. Box 551, Chesterton, IN 46304 USA Tel 219-688-5895; Toll Free: 800-815-7685 (phone/fax) Do not confuse with Robert Vogel in South Burlington, VT
E-mail: contact@azarovmemories.com
Web site: http://www.garrythegroundhog.com.

Vogelsong, Mary *See* **BethBirdBks.**

Voice & Vision Pubns., *(978-1-888251)* 902 Fletcher Ave., Indianapolis, IN 46203 USA Tel 317-262-4030; Fax: 317-262-4029
E-mail: voicevision@apostolic.edu.

Voice Connection/Vendera Publishing, The *See* **Vendera Publishing**

Voice of Light Pubns., *(978-0-9785623)* P.O. Box 1437, Fair Oaks, CA 95628 USA (SAN 850-9905) Tel 916-965-3046
E-mail: voiceoflight@comcast.net.

Voice of Truths Publishing, *(978-0-9666777; 978-0-9742357; 978-0-9818992; 978-0-9916280)* P.O. Box 34, Donalds, SC 29638-9039 USA
E-mail: publishers@charter.net; robert@voiceoftruths.com
Web site: http://www.voiceoftruths.com.

Void Press *See* **Free Bird Pr.**

Voigt, J. M. Incorporated *See* **MindWare Holdings, Inc.**

Volare, LLC *See* **Dividion Group, LLC, The**

†Volcano pr., *(978-0-912078; 978-1-884244)* Orders Addr.: P.O. Box 270, Volcano, CA 95689 USA (SAN 220-0015) Tel 209-296-4991; Fax: 209-296-4995; Toll Free: 800-879-9636; Edit Addr.: 21496 National St., Volcano, CA 95689 USA
E-mail: info@volcanopress.com; sales@volcanopress.com; adam@volcanopress.com
Web site: http://www.volcanopress.com
Dist(s): **New Leaf Distributing Co., Inc. Quality Bks., Inc.;** *CIP.*

Volo *Imprint of* **Hyperion Bks. for Children**

Volunteers of the Colorado Historical Society, *(978-0-9770423)* 1560 Broadway, Ste. 400, Denver, CO 80202-5133 USA
E-mail: angela.caudill@chs.state.co.us.

†VOM Bks., *(978-0-88264)* Orders Addr.: P.O. Box 2273, Bartlesville, OK 74005-2273 USA (SAN 201-2731) Tel 918-337-8015; Fax: 918-338-0189; Toll Free: 800-747-0085; Edit Addr.: 200 E. Frank Phillips, Bartlesville, OK 74003 USA (SAN 244-7959)
E-mail: communications@vom-usa.org
Dist(s): **Whitaker Hse.;** *CIP.*

von Buchwald, Martin Farina, *(978-0-9777266)* 1158 5th Ave., New York, NY 10029 USA Tel 212-348-5580
E-mail: martin@farina.com.

Von Curtis Publishing, *(978-0-9749939)* 1278 Glenneyre, Suite 96, LaGuna Beach, CA 92651 USA Tel 800-459-4007; Fax: 949-497-7163
E-mail: info@beniceorelse.com
Web site: http://www.beniceorelse.com.

Von Hatten Pubns., *(978-1-7345386)* 30 Willington Ave., Stafford Springs, CT 06076 USA Tel 860-684-1508
E-mail: lhstevens@snet.net
Web site: LauraHanksStevens.com.

von Klan, Laurene, (*978-0-578-00322-1*) 4532 N. Albany, Chicago, IL 60625 USA
E-mail: chicagoriver@hotmail.com
Dist(s): **Lulu Pr., Inc.**

Vook Inc. *See* **Pronoun, Inc.**

Vorkapich, Rebecca, (*978-0-578-79338-2; 978-0-578-79339-9; 978-0-578-99017-0; 978-0-578-99018-7; 979-8-9872035*) 621 N 5th St 0, BURLINGTON, IA 52601 USA Tel 4802298017
E-mail: rlvorkapich@gmail.com
Dist(s): **Ingram Content Group.**

Vorndran, Judith Clay, (*978-0-9772439*) 6431 Antoinette Dr., Mentor, OH 44060-3431 USA
E-mail: jclayvorndran05@sbcglobal.net; jclayvorndran@aol.com
Web site: http://www.hometown.aol.com/jclayvorndran/myhomepage.

Vorpal Words, LLC, (*978-0-9881969*) 2840 W Hwy. 101, Wellsville, UT 84339 USA Tel 435-764-7052
E-mail: dcolemanbooks@gmail.com
Web site: www.dcolemanbooks.com.

Voss, Dawn L., (*978-0-615-15324-7; 978-0-615-15581-4*) 481 Hallman St., Berlin, WI 54923 USA
E-mail: wr1t3r@yahoo.com
Dist(s): **Lulu Pr., Inc.**

Votto, Maria, (*978-1-7357554*) 29 Brook Crossing Rd., BRENTWOOD, NH 03833 USA Tel 603-498-1909
E-mail: mevotto@icloud.com.

Vox Dei *Imprint of* **Booktrope**

Voyageur Pr. *Imprint of* **Quarto Publishing Group USA**

VRguy publishing *Imprint of* **LINX Corp.**

VSP Bks. *Imprint of* **Vacation Spot Publishing**

Vulpine Pr., (*978-1-939276; 978-1-910780-18-3*) 4208 Rebecca Ct., Quincy, IL 62305 USA
E-mail: olivia@oliviacunning.com.

WAMY International, Inc., (*978-1-882837*) P.O. Box 8096, Falls Church, VA 22041-8096 USA Tel 703-916-0924; Fax: 703-916-0925.

W & B Pubs., (*978-0-9767732; 978-0-9771971; 978-0-9788985*) Orders Addr.: 9001 Ridge Hill Dr, Kernersville, NC 27284 USA Tel 336-354-7173; 9001 Ridge Hill St., Kernersville, NC 27284
E-mail: argusenterprises@hotmail.com; a-argus@live.com; williamconnor@a-argusbooks.com
Web site: http://www.a-argusbooks.com.

WCS Corp., (*978-0-9639350*) Orders Addr.: P.O. Box 900, Lander, WY 82520 USA Tel 307-332-2881; Fax: 307-332-9332; Toll Free: 800-656-8762.

WGBH Boston Video, (*978-0-9636881; 978-1-57807; 978-1-884738; 978-1-59375*) Orders Addr.: P.O. Box 2284, South Burlington, VT 05407-2284 USA Fax: 802-864-9846; 617-300-1050; Toll Free: 800-255-9424
Web site: http://www.wgbh.org
Dist(s): **Follett School Solutions**
Midwest Tape.

W.J. Fantasy, Inc., (*978-1-56021*) 120 Long Hill Cross Rd., Shelton, CT 06484-6125 USA Toll Free Fax: 800-200-3000; Toll Free: 800-222-7529
E-mail: wjfantasy@erols.com.

WJH Publishing, (*978-0-9674864*) 1445 Ross St., Suite 5400, Dallas, TX 75202-2785 USA Tel 214-978-8520; Fax: 214-978-8526.

W M Books *See* **Sierra Raconteur Publishing**

W M C Publishing *See* **Milestone Pr., Inc.**

W MediaWorks, (*978-0-9981329*) 11124 66th ave, Forest Hills, NY 11375 USA Tel 646-477-8440
Web site: www.wmediaworks.com
Dist(s): **CreateSpace Independent Publishing Platform.**

WP Pr., Inc., (*978-0-9633019; 978-1-884837*) 525 N. Norris Ave., Tucson, AZ 85719-5239 USA.

W Q E D Multimedia, (*978-0-9713080; 978-0-9769936; 978-0-9816697*) 4802 Fifth Ave., Pittsburgh, PA 15213 USA
Web site: http://www.wqed.org.

W Q E D Pittsburgh *See* **W Q E D Multimedia**

WRE/ColorTech, (*978-1-892500*) Div. of Western Roto Engravers, Inc., 533 Banner Ave., Greensboro, NC 27401 USA Tel 336-275-9821; Fax: 336-275-1799
E-mail: johnc@wrecolor.com
Web site: http://www.wrecolor.com.

W S Publishing *See* **Oembe Publishing**

W. St. James Pr., (*978-0-9672818*) 2683 W. St. James Pkwy., Cleveland Heights, OH 44106 USA Tel 216-932-0290 (phone/fax)
E-mail: marcjaffe@aol.com.

WW West, Inc., (*978-0-9653924; 978-0-9727921; 978-0-9758960*) 20875 Sholes Rd., Bend, OR 97702 USA (SAN 299-2574) Tel 541-385-8911 (phone/fax)
E-mail: wwwest@bendbroadband.com
Web site: http://www.nationalparkspopup.com
Dist(s): **Farcountry Pr.**

W Y Publishing *See* **Bluewood Bks.**

W3 Publishing, (*978-0-9801322*) P.O. Box 1255, Suitland, MD 20752-2075 USA Tel 240-354-7077
E-mail: kellum_ent@verizon.net.

W5YI Group, Incorporated, The *See* **Master Publishing, Inc.**

Wachiye, Andolelye J., (*978-1-952426*) 12661 Luna Rd., Victorville, CA 92392 USA Tel 714-333-8378
E-mail: andoww@yahoo.com.

Wachob, Chuck , (*978-0-578-15467-1*) 311 Rigas Ct, Americas, GA 31709 USA.

Wack, Nancy, (*978-0-615-16634-6*) 600 Fairwick Dr., saint Louis, MO 63129 USA
Dist(s): **Lulu Pr., Inc.**

Wackophoto, (*978-0-9798532*) P.O. Box 14843, Richmond, VA 23221 USA (SAN 854-5529)
E-mail: info@coolingthesouth.com
Web site: http://www.wackophoto.com; http://www.coolingthesouth.com.

Wacky Bee Bks. (GBR) (*978-0-9931109; 978-0-9956972; 978-1-913292; 978-1-9999033*) *Dist. by* **IPG Chicago.**

Wacky World Studios LLC, (*978-0-9742997*) 148 E. Douglas Rd., Oldsmar, FL 34677-2939 USA Tel 813-818-8277; Fax: 813-818-8396; Toll Free: 877-429-2259
E-mail: info@wackyworld.tv
Web site: http://www.wackyworld.tv.

Wade & Kayak Fishing Bks., (*978-0-9742253*) 702 Balmoral Ct., Friendswood, TX 77546 USA
E-mail: flyfisher@ev1.net
Web site: http://www.texascoastalfishingbooks.com/pages/1/index.htm.

Wade, John Pub., (*978-0-9623934; 978-1-882425*) Orders Addr.: P.O. Box 303, Phillips, ME 04966 USA Tel 207-639-2501 (phone/fax); 1413 Hwy. 17 S., PMB 154, Surfside Beach, SC 29575 Tel 843-215-1097; Edit Addr.: 193 Weld Rd., Phillips, ME 04966 USA
E-mail: wadecjs@yahoo.com
Web site: http://www.johnwadepublisher.com.

Wade, T.K., (*978-0-692-04547-3; 978-0-692-04699-9*) 3016 Mandy Ln., Morehead City, NC 28557 USA Tel 252-725-1934
E-mail: tkwadeauthor@gmail.com
Dist(s): **Ingram Content Group.**

Wadhams! Pr., (*978-0-9754987*) c/o Cordelia Sand, P.O. Box 264, Essex, NY 12936 USA.

Wading River Bks., LLC., (*978-0-9791463*) P.O. Box 361, Calverton, NY 11933 USA Tel 516-527-6283
E-mail: robert@wrbooks.com
Web site: http://www.wrbooks.com.

†**Wadsworth,** (*978-0-15; 978-0-314; 978-0-534; 978-0-8185; 978-0-8273; 978-0-942728; 978-1-928916; 978-1-4163; 978-0-495*) Div. of CENGAGE Learning, Orders Addr.: 7625 Empire Dr., Florence, KY 41042-2978 USA (SAN 200-2663) Tel 859 525 2230; Toll Free Fax: 800-487-8488; Toll Free: 800 354 9706; 10650 Toebben Dr., Independence, KY 41051 Toll Free Fax: 800-487-8488; Toll Free: 800-354-9706; Edit Addr.: 10 Davis Dr., Belmont, CA 94002 USA Tel 650 595 2350; Fax: 606 592 9081
Web site: http://www.brookscole.com; http://www.wadsworth.com
Dist(s): **CENGAGE Learning**
Follett School Solutions
MyiLibrary; *CIP.*

Wadsworth Publishing *See* **Wadsworth**

Wagging Tails Publishing *See* **Wagging Tales Publishing**

Wagging Tales Publishing, (*978-0-9715224*) 727 Lincoln Ave., Carbondale, CO 81623 USA.

Wagner Entertainment, (*978-0-9754515*) Orders Addr.: 3640 Loadstone Dr., Sherman Oaks, CA 91403-4558 USA
Web site: http://www.wagnerentertainment.com.

Wahl, Leslea, (*978-1-7329037*) 5400 Preserve Pkwy. S., Greenwood Vlg., CO 80121-2146 USA Tel 303-346-5551
E-mail: Leslea.Wahl@gmail.com
Web site: www.LesleaWahl.com.

Waide Aaron Riddle, (*978-0-615-24430-3; 978-0-615-24648-2; 978-0-615-33363-2; 978-0-615-38560-0*) P.O. Box 691882, West Hollywood, CA 90069 USA
Web site: http://www.amazon.com/author/waideriddle
Dist(s): **Left Bank Bks.**
Tattered Cover Bookstore.

Waila Bks., (*978-0-578-42853-6; 978-0-578-43348-6*) 8008 Chapin Rd., Benbrook, TX 76116 USA Tel 541-633-3314
E-mail: dancedamnyou@gmail.com.

WainWave Media, (*978-0-9789319*) P.O. Box 11037, Lexington, KY 40512-1037 USA (SAN 853-6953) Tel 859-294-9033; Fax: 859-233-1999
E-mail: dougwain@earthlink.net
Web site: http://www.waragainstviolence.com.

WainWave Publishing *See* **WainWave Media**

Waiting Room to Heaven *Imprint of* **Loucks Studios Inc.**

Wajsbort, Rochel, (*978-0-9749491*) 1431 E9, Brooklyn, NY 11230 USA Tel 718-339-5070; Fax: 718-998-1615.

Wakefield Connection, The, (*978-0-9703632*) 5201 Kingston Pike, Suite 6-302, Knoxville, TN 37919-5026 USA Tel 304-624-3901
E-mail: richard@wakefieldconnection.com; wendy@wakefieldconnection.com
Web site: http://www.wakefieldconnection.com
Dist(s): **Independent Pubs. Group.**

Waking Lion Press *Imprint of* **The Editorium, LLC**

Wakinglion Studio, (*978-0-9767413*) P.O. Box 624, Bayfield, CO 81122 USA.

Walch Education, (*978-0-8251*) 40 Walch Dr., Portland, ME 04103 USA (SAN 669-6562) Fax: 207-828-8818; Toll Free Fax: 888-991-5755; Toll Free: 800-341-6094
E-mail: customerservice@walch.com
Web site: http://www.walch.com
Dist(s): **Follett School Solutions.**

Walch Publishing *See* **Walch Education**

Walden Pr., (*978-0-692-19471-3*) 1417 Pelican Way, Suisun City, CA 94585 USA Tel 707-372-3389
E-mail: annhamiltonshort@yahoo.com
Dist(s): **Ingram Content Group.**

Waldenhouse Pubs., Inc., (*978-0-9705214; 978-0-9761033; 978-0-9779189; 978-0-9793712; 978-0-9814996; 978-1-935186; 978-1-947589*) 100 Clegg St., Signal Mountain, TN 37377 USA (SAN 856-8111) Toll Free: 888-222-8228
E-mail: karenstone@waldenhouse.com
Web site: http://waldenhouse.com
Dist(s): **eBookit.com.**

Waldman House Pr. *Imprint of* **TRISTAN Publishing, Inc.**

Waldman Publishing Corp., (*978-0-86611; 978-1-59060; 978-1-60340*) P.O. Box 1587, New York, NY 10028-0013 USA (SAN 219-340X)
E-mail: info@waldmanbooks.com
Web site: http://www.waldmanbooks.com/.

Waldon Pond Pr. *Imprint of* **HarperCollins Pubs.**

Waldorf Early Childhood Assn. Of North America, (*978-0-9722238; 978-0-9796232; 978-0-9816159; 978-1-936849*) 285 Hungry Hollow Rd., Chestnut Ridge, NY 10977 USA Tel 845-352-1690
E-mail: mlyons@waldorfearlychildhood.org; publications@waldorfearlychildhood.org.

Waldorf Publications, (*978-0-9623978; 978-1-888365; 978-1-936367; 978-1-943582*) Div. of Research Institute for Waldorf Education, Orders Addr.: Publications Office 38 Main St., Chatham, NY 12037 USA Tel 303-545-9486; Edit Addr.: 575 Quail Cir., Boulder, CO 80304 USA
E-mail: ann_erwin@hotmail.com
Web site: http://www.whywaldorfworks.org; http://www.waldorfeducation.org; http://www.waldorfresearchinstitute.org
Dist(s): **Midpoint Trade Bks., Inc.**
SteinerBooks, Inc.

Waldorf Publishing, (*978-0-578-19693-0*) 2140 Hall Johnson Rd. 102-345, Grapevine, TX 76051 USA Tel 972-674-3131
E-mail: barbara@waldorfpublishing.com
Web site: http://www.waldorfpublishing.com.

Walford Pr., (*978-0-9787671; 978-0-615-35161-2; 978-0-9826629; 978-0-9826969*) 11693 San Vicente Blvd. Suite 393, Los Angeles, CA 90049 USA (SAN 851-4941) Tel 310-487-3552
E-mail: ericweinsteinl@walfordpress.com; sambabyhead@aol.com
Web site: http://www.walfordpress.com.

Walk Worthy Pr. *Imprint of* **Grand Central Publishing**

Walkabout Publishing, (*978-0-9802086; 978-0-9821799*) P.O. Box 151, Kansasville, WI 53139 USA Tel 262-878-0448
E-mail: publisher@walkaboutpublishing.com
Web site: http://www.walkaboutpublishing.com
Dist(s): **Smashwords.**

†**Walker & Co.,** (*978-0-8027*) 175 Fifth Ave., New York, NY 10010 USA (SAN 202-5213) Tel 646-438-6056; Fax: 212-780-0115 (orders); Toll Free Fax: 800-218-9367; Toll Free: 800-289-2553 (orders)
Web site: http://www.walkerbooks.com
Dist(s): **Children's Plus, Inc.**
Macmillan
Perfection Learning Corp.
Beeler, Thomas T. Pub.; *CIP.*

Walker Carter Publishing, LLC, (*978-1-947734*) 10945 SW Shad Rd, Terrebonne, OR 97760 USA Tel 402-806-1565
E-mail: carole14@walkercarter.com
Web site: www.walkercarter.com.

Walker, Esther, (*978-0-9716071*) 80-000 Ave. 48, Suite 131, Indio, CA 92201 USA Tel 760-347-4352
E-mail: strwalkr@easyfeed.com.

Walker, Fay Alice *See* **Favortwou Publishing**

Walker Hammond Pubs., (*978-0-615-62598-0; 978-0-615-62907-0; 978-0-615-67413-1; 978-0-615-72769-1; 978-0-692-36508-3; 978-0-692-52624-8; 978-0-692-61809-7; 978-0-9981054*) P.O. Box 192, Emmett, ID 83617 USA Tel 208-365-3733
Dist(s): **CreateSpace Independent Publishing Platform.**

Walker, J.W. Ministries *See* **LightHouse Pr.**

Walker Large Print *Imprint of* **Cengage Gale**

Walker Publishing Company *See* **Walker & Co.**

Walker, Sherry, (*978-0-578-19687-9*) 5280 Timucua Cir., Saint Augustine, FL 32086 USA.

Walking Elk Publications *See* **Runestone Publishing**

WALKING EVIL *See* **IRONSTREAM Pr.**

Walking Hare Press *See* **Red Raven Publishing**

Walking in The Truth Pr., (*978-0-9973741*) 210 Innsbruck Dr., Lehighton, PA 18235 USA Tel 610-377-6327
E-mail: acathers@foundchristcounsel.org.

Walking the Line Pubns., (*978-0-9714540; 978-0-9816247; 978-0-9846299*) 4638 W. Serendipity Way, South Jordan, UT 84009 USA Tel 801-558-2543
E-mail: kclawson@walkingthelinebooks.com; walkingthelinebooks@gmail.com
Web site: http://www.walkingthelinebooks.com.

Walking The Way, (*978-1-7378808*) 5012 W 56th St, Edina, MN 55436 USA Tel 952-239-4353
E-mail: kloberesidential@gmail.com
Web site: www.Anne-MarieKlobe.com.

Walking Tree, Inc., (*978-0-9749832*) P.O. Box 468, Crystal Beach, FL 34681 USA Tel 727-784-5016
E-mail: art@halstowers.com
Web site: http://www.halstowers.com; http://www.lifeblending.com.

Wall, Mary Joanne, (*978-0-9644283*) 601 Ingomar Rd., Pittsburgh, PA 15237-4983 USA Tel 412-364-2598; Fax: 412-314-0862.

Walling, Emma *See* **Emma's Pantry**

Wallis, Jared, (*978-1-7332665; 978-1-7344534; 978-1-953173*) 1125 Sheridan Ave., No. 38, Chico, CA 95926 USA Tel 530-966-8573
E-mail: zeusifer1315@gmail.com.

Walls Tumbling Down Publishing, (*978-0-9770098*) Manhhttanville Station, 871, New York, NY 10027-9998 USA Tel 212-865-6008
E-mail: antonioj365@aol.com
Web site: http://www.hometown.aol.com.

Wallworkshop, The, (*978-1-7328315*) 169 S. 2775 W., West Point, UT 84015 USA Tel 801-493-9655
E-mail: storyboarder@gmail.com
Web site: www.story-monster.com.

wallymeets, (*978-0-9843648*) Div. of wallymeets ltd., Orders Addr.: Hans Memlingdreef 50, LOMMEL, 3920 BEL
Web site: http://wallymeets.com/.

Walnut Springs Bks., (*978-1-933317; 978-1-59992; 978-1-934393; 978-1-935217*) 4110 Highland Dr. Ste. 300, Salt Lake Cty, UT 84124-2676 USA
E-mail: editorial@leatherwoodpress.com
Web site: http://www.leatherwoodpress.com
Dist(s): **Brigham Distribution**
Deseret Bk. Co.
Independent Pubs. Group.

Walnut Street Bks., (*978-1-947597*) 223 E. Walnut St., Lancaster, PA 17602 USA Tel 717-481-7518
E-mail: merlegood7@gmail.com
Dist(s): **Independent Pubs. Group.**

Walrus (FRA) (*978-2-36376*) *Dist. by* **Firefly Bks Limited.**

Walrus Publishing, Inc., (*978-0-9844857; 978-1-940442*) Div. of Amphorae Publishing Group, 4168 Hartford St., Saint Louis, MO 63116 USA (SAN 859-5305) Tel 314-606-7981
E-mail: lisa.miller@walruspublishing.com
Web site: www.walruspublishing.com
Dist(s): **Independent Pubs. Group**
Midpoint Trade Bks., Inc.

Walsh, Barbara, (*978-0-578-91532-6; 978-1-7374813*) 642 Memorial Dr. 642 Memorial Dr., Winthrop, ME 04364 USA Tel 207-462-4331
E-mail: mainescribe@gmail.com
Web site: https://www.barbarawalsh.net/.

Walsh, Joseph, (*978-0-9818019*) P.O. Box 34105, Granada Hills, CA 91394 USA
Web site: http://www.gamblerontheloose.com.

Walt Disney Home Video, 3333 N. Pagosa Ct., Indianapolis, IN 46226 USA Tel 317-890-3030; Fax: 818-560-1930
Web site: http://disney.go.com/DisneyVideos/
Dist(s): **Buena Vista Home Video**
Critics' Choice Video
Follett Media Distribution
Midwest Tape.

Walt Disney Records, (*978-0-7634; 978-1-55723*) Div. of Walt Disney Co., 3333 N. Pagosa Ct., Indianapolis, IN 46226 USA Tel 317-890-3030; Fax: 317-897-4614
Web site: http://disneymusic.disney.go.com/index.html
Dist(s): **Follett School Solutions**
Rounder Kids Music Distribution.

Walter Foster *Imprint of* **Quarto Publishing Group USA**

Walter Foster Jr *Imprint of* **Quarto Publishing Group USA**

Water Shoe Pr., (*978-0-9759499*) P.O. Box 928, Langley, WA 98260 USA.

Walter, Wendy D., (*978-0-9857147*) 301 Hillcrest Rd., San Carlos, CA 94070 USA Tel 650-598-0178; *Imprints:* Angry Bicycle (AngryBicycle)
Web site: ambrils-tale.com.

Walterick Pubs., Inc., (*978-0-937396; 978-1-884838*) Orders Addr.: P.O. Box 2216, Kansas City, KS 66110-0216 USA (SAN 211-9366) Tel 913-334-0100; Fax: 913-334-0153; Toll Free: 800-255-4097 (US only); Edit Addr.: 6549 State Ave., Kansas City, KS 66110 USA Toll Free: 800-648-0443 (Canada only).

walters, danna j. author, (*978-0-692-09629-1; 978-0-578-57249-9; 978-0-578-38573-0*) 506 Evergreen Dr., EULESS, TX 76040 USA Tel 817-688-6513
E-mail: dannawalters@yahoo.com
Dist(s): **Ingram Content Group.**

Walters, Jack C., (*978-0-9754658*) 2850 Airport Rd., No. 1, Carson City, NV 89706 USA Tel 775-882-0518
E-mail: waltersjc@charter.net.

Walters, Steve Ministries, (*978-0-9719767*) 3633 Corners Way, Norcross, GA 30092 USA Tel 770-409-1633; Fax: 770-300-9636; *Imprints:* Crowned Warrior Publishing (Crowned Warr)
E-mail: holyspiritinfo@stevewaltersministries.com
Web site: http://www.stevewaltersministries.com.

Waltham Publishing, LLC, (*978-0-9887524; 978-1-942781*) 15709 Brookview Dr., Urbandale, IA 50323 USA Tel 515-986-3626
E-mail: skhealthcomm@yahoo.com.

Waltower Publishing, (*978-0-9905422*) 6405 E. 129th Pl., Grandview, MO 64030 USA Tel 816-695-0541
E-mail: acwaltower@yahoo.com.

Wampum Bks., LLC, (*978-0-9842012*) 115a Pine St., Greenwich, CT 06830 USA (SAN 858-7116) Tel 203-531-8111
E-mail: sgalfas@itoinc.net.

Wan Lee Publishing, (*978-0-9858042*) 2860 Fenton Rd., Hartland, MI 48353 USA Tel 248-408-7103; Fax: 248-889-3647
E-mail: wayne@wanleepublishing.com
Web site: www.wanleepublishing.com.

Wanann, Inc., (*978-1-945352*) 2535 W. 237th St., STE 106, Torrance, CA 90505 USA Tel 310-415-5754
E-mail: publishing@wanann.com.

Wand, Dana Bks., (*978-0-9906659*) 69750 Holmes Rd., Sisters, OR 97759 USA Tel 541-588-6517
E-mail: dwredhatnana@gmail.com.

Wand In Magic, (*978-0-9761921*) P.O. Box 58068, Nashville, TN 37205 USA Fax: 615-269-6820.

W&D Parables, (*978-0-692-16936-0; 978-0-692-17831-7*) 4361 Baychester Ave., Bronx, NY 10466 USA Tel 917-841-3358
E-mail: whernandez4@aol.com.

Wander *Imprint of* **Tyndale Hse. Pubs.**

Wander Pr., (*978-0-9841320*) 16765 FishHawk Blvd., No. 319, Lithia, FL 33547 USA (SAN 858-5040)
E-mail: lisachavis@aol.com; chermacdonald@icloud.com
Web site: http://www.wanderpress.com; http://www.whatboundariestravel.com.

Wander Twins, The, (*978-0-9985434*) 2803 SE 87th Ave., Portland, OR 97266 USA Tel 707-267-1848
E-mail: wesleynickerman@gmail.com.

Wandering Sage Bookstore & More, LLC *See* **Wandering Sage Pubns., LLC**

Wandering Sage Pubns., LLC, (*978-0-9725230; 978-1-933300*) Orders Addr.: 614 Rivers Bend Estates Dr., Saint Charles, MO 63303 USA Tel 314-623-6647
E-mail: valkpub@yahoo.com
Web site: http://www.wanderingsagebooks.com
Dist(s): **Valkyrie Distribution.**

Wanderlust Publishing, (*978-0-9758933*) P.O. Box 1557, Eastsound, WA 98245-1557 USA
E-mail: info@sabinefinancialservices.com.

Wang, Cheng Sung, (*978-0-692-15607-0; 978-0-578-62599-7; 978-0-578-62819-6; 978-0-578-63057-1; 978-0-578-63640-5; 978-0-578-63685-6; 978-0-578-64052-5;*

For full information on wholesalers and distributors, refer to the Wholesaler and Distributor Name Index

978-0-578-65515-4; 978-0-578-67151-2) 2885 Sanford Ave. SW, Grandville, MI 49418 USA Tel 886-952-212750
E-mail: cswjohnni@gmail.com
Dist(s): **Ingram Content Group.**

WannaBees Media LLC, *(978-0-9767670)* 118 E. 25th St., Suite LL, New York, NY 10010 USA Tel 212-253-9874
E-mail: kdonovan@nvmagazine.com
Web site: http://www.theDobees.com.

Wanniarichchige, Somiruwan, *(978-0-615-17026-8)* 20700 San Jose Hills Rd., Suite 115, Walnut, CA 91789 USA
E-mail: ruwangotu@hotmail.com
Dist(s): **Lulu Pr., Inc.**

WAO Publishing *See* **Creatively Hue**

Waquis *See* **Black Ship Publishing**

War Monkey Pubns., LLC, *(978-1-7323662; 978-1-954043)* 573 E Heather Rd, Orem, UT 84097 USA Tel 801-680-5425
E-mail: warmonkeypublications@gmail.com
Web site: www.warmonkeypublications.com.

Warbelow, Willy Lou, *(978-0-9618314)* P.O. Box 252, Tok, AK 99780 USA (SAN 667-2639) Tel 907-883-2881.

Warbranch Pr., Inc., *(978-0-9667114; 978-0-692-52275-2)* 329 Warbranch Rd., Central, SC 29630 USA Tel 864-654-6180
E-mail: katesalleypalmer@gmail.com; jhpalmer42@gmail.com
Web site: http://www.warbranchpress.com
Dist(s): **Follett School Solutions**
Partners Bk. Distributing, Inc.

Ward, Amy M., *(978-0-692-05546-5; 978-0-692-11050-8; 978-0-692-18478-3)* 2101 Witcherville Rd., Greenwood, AR 72936 USA Tel 479-459-6928
E-mail: wardsarewriters@gmail.com
Dist(s): **Ingram Content Group.**

Ward Design, LLC DBA Teen Mystery Pr., *(978-0-9894143)* 1656 Hawksway Ct., Westlake Village, CA 91361 USA Tel 818-613-6389
E-mail: teendetectiveskylar@yahoo.com.

Ward, Jason E., *(978-0-9662366)* P.O. Box 719, Bronx, NY 10475 USA Tel 718-379-6285
E-mail: Jason@aiyahlevene.com.

Ward, John H., *(978-0-615-21017-9; 978-0-9834036)* 6606 Deerwood Dr., Crystal Lake, IL 60012 USA.

Ward Publishing, *(978-0-578-79873-8)* 4016 Grand Manor ct No. 307, Raleigh, NC 27612 USA Tel 919-631-7303
E-mail: leahwardauthor@yahoo.com.

Ward, Sierra, *(978-0-578-33723-4; 978-0-578-33724-1)* 3208 Cole ave, Richardson, TX 75082 USA Tel 972-210-9645
E-mail: sierrasmusic@gmail.com

Warde, Johanna, *(978-1-7372018)* 394 Bradford St., Orange, NJ 07050 USA Tel 973-444-7772
E-mail: johannawarde@hotmail.com.

Warden, Chris, *(978-1-7326741)* 6556 Wandermere Rd., MALIBU, CA 90265 USA Tel 310-457-3757
E-mail: zenwarden@yahoo.com.

Ware Resources, *(978-0-9844685; 978-0-9974404; 978-1-7360798; 979-8-9859685)* 147 Quigley Blvd. PO Box 13192, New Castle, DE 19720-9696 USA.

Warehousing & Fulfillment Specialists, LLC (WFS, LLC), *(978-1-57102; 978-1-58029; 978-1-59093)* 7344 Cockrill Bend Blvd., Nashville, TN 37209-1043 USA Toll Free Fax: 800-510-3650; Toll Free: 800-327-5113; *Imprints:* Eager Minds Press (Eager Minds)
E-mail: vhill@apgbooks.com
Web site: http://www.apgbooks.com
Dist(s): **APG Sales & Distribution Services.**

Warm, Hudson, *(978-1-7354098)* 40 Spring Ln., Chappaqua, NY 10514 USA Tel 914-602-3821
E-mail: hudsonpwarm@gmail.com.

Warne *Imprint of* **Penguin Publishing Group**

Warne *Imprint of* **Penguin Young Readers Group**

Warner Books, Incorporated *See* **Grand Central Publishing**

Warner Bros. Pubns. *Imprint of* **Alfred Publishing Co., Inc.**

Warner Brothers Records, *(978-1-880528)* Div. of Creative Enterprises, 3300 Warner Blvd., Burbank, CA 91505 USA Tel 818-953-3467; Fax: 818-953-3797.

Warner Coaching, Incorporated *See* **She Writes Pr.**

Warner, Debra Psy.D., *(978-0-692-13516-7; 978-0-692-13517-4; 978-0-578-53158-8; 978-0-578-63955-0; 978-0-578-71953-5; 978-0-578-71954-2; 978-0-578-87194-3; 978-0-578-91960-7; 978-0-578-94052-6; 979-8-218-02948-7; 979-8-218-03262-3; 979-8-218-22814-9)* 14450 Landon Rd., Moreno Valley, CA 92555 USA Tel 951-203-8415
E-mail: dwarner@mail.com
Dist(s): **Ingram Content Group.**

Warner Faith *See* **FaithWords**

†Warner Pr., Inc., *(978-0-87162; 978-1-59317; 978-1-68434)* Orders Addr.: P.O. Box 2499, Anderson, IN 46018-2499 USA (SAN 691-4241) Tel 765-648-2116; Fax: 765-622-9511; Toll Free: 800-848-2464; Edit Addr.: 2902 Enterprise Dr., Anderson, IN 46013 USA (SAN 111-8110) Tel 765-644-7721; Fax: 765-640-8005; Toll Free: 800-741-7721 (orders only)
E-mail: jallison@warnerpress.org; wporders@warnerpress.org; rjackson@warnerpress.org
Web site: http://www.warnerpress.org; http://www.francisasburypress.org
Dist(s): **Anchor Distributors**
Ingram Content Group
OverDrive, Inc.
Potter's House Book Service
SPD-Small Pr. Distribution
Send The Light Distribution LLC
Spring Arbor Distributors, Inc.; *CIP.*

Warner Press Publishers *See* **Warner Pr., Inc.**

Warren Machine Co., *(978-0-9729410; 978-1-934866)* 3 Taylor St., Portland, OR 04102 USA
E-mail: ari.meil@warren-machine.com
Web site: http://www.warren-machine.com.

Warren Publishing, Inc., *(978-1-886057; 978-0-9853094; 978-0-9884170; 978-0-9894814; 978-0-9960506; 978-0-9908136; 978-1-943258; 978-1-7323362; 978-1-7336158; 978-1-7337955; 978-1-7338973; 978-1-7339945; 978-1-7333252; 978-1-7341262; 978-1-7347075; 978-1-7350915; 978-1-7353023; 978-1-7355601; 978-1-7357280; 978-1-7358600; 978-1-7361714; 978-1-954614; 978-1-957723; 978-0-578-28610-5; 978-1-960146)* 8145 Ardrey Kell Rd. *Suite 207, CHARLOTTE, NC 28277 USA Tel 704-900-0236 Do not confuse with companies with the same or similar name in Indianapolis, IN, Pomona, CA, Washington, DC, Loomis, CA, Roseville, CA, , Chesterfield, VA*
E-mail: warrenpublish@gmail.com
Web site: http://warrenpublishing.net
Dist(s): **BookBaby.**

Warrington Pubns., *(978-0-9889698; 978-0-9890974; 978-0-9984331)* 11100 SE Petrovitsky Apt. A-104, Renton, WA 98055 USA Tel 425-793-9629; *Imprints:* Oceanus Books (Oceanus Bks)
E-mail: WarringtonPress@aol.com
Web site: WarringtonPublications.com.

Warrior Schl. Pr., *(978-0-9715289)* P.O. Box 768, Sonoita, AZ 85637 USA
E-mail: info@warriorschool.com
Web site: http://www.warriorschool.com.

WARTS etc., *(978-0-692-18181-2; 978-0-578-40722-7; 978-0-578-48969-8)* 3108 Taylor Ave., West Point, VA 23181 USA Tel 757-707-0909
E-mail: nayseyers@gmail.com
Dist(s): **CreateSpace Independent Publishing Platform**
Ingram Content Group.

Warwick Hse. Publishing, *(978-0-9638455; 978-1-890306; 978-0-9786369; 978-0-9790367; 978-0-9795258; 978-0-9801315; 978-0-9823004; 978-0-9842516; 978-0-9845166; 978-1-936553; 978-0-9978020; 978-0-9994023; 978-1-7349694; 978-1-7377606)* 720 Court St., Lynchburg, VA 24504 USA Tel 434-846-1200
E-mail: jwarem@aol.com
Web site: http://www.warwickpublishers.com.

Washington Bks., *(978-1-7331178)* 2699 Seville Blvd No. 203, Clearwater, FL 33764 USA Tel 202-390-8676
E-mail: lajarvik@icloud.com
Web site: https://washington-books.com; https://pennyapagepress.blogspot.com
Dist(s): **Ingram Bk. Co.**

Washington Pubs., *(978-0-9715721)* P.O. Box 12517, Tallahassee, FL 32317-2517 USA (SAN 254-2366) Do not confuse with Washington Publishers in Renton, WA
E-mail: info@washingtonpublishers.com
Web site: http://www.washingtonpublishers.com.

†Washington State Univ. Pr., *(978-0-87422; 978-1-63682; 978-1-63864)* P.O. Box 645910, Pullman, WA 99164-5910 USA (SAN 206-6688) Tel 509-335-7880; Toll Free: 800-354-7360
E-mail: wsupress@wsu.edu; lawton@wsu.edu
Web site: http://wsupress.wsu.edu
Dist(s): **Ebsco Publishing**
MyiLibrary
Partners Bk. Distributing, Inc.
Todd Communications; *CIP.*

Washington University, Gallery of Art *See* **Washington Univ., Mildred Lane Kemper Art Museum**

Washington Univ., Mildred Lane Kemper Art Museum, *(978-0-936316)* Campus Box 1214, 1 Brookings Dr., Saint Louis, MO 63130 USA (SAN 214-4859) Tel 314-935-7460; Fax: 314-935-7282
E-mail: Jane_Neidhardt@wustl.edu
Web site: http://www.kemperartmuseum.wustl.edu
Dist(s): **Chicago Distribution Ctr.**
D.A.P./Distributed Art Pubs.
Univ. of Chicago Pr.

WasiWorks Studio LLC, *(978-0-9845203)* 6109 Piping Rock Rd., Madison, WI 53711 USA Tel 608-239-2526
E-mail: odalo@wasiworks.com
Web site: http://www.wasiworks.com.

Waskey, Heather, *(978-0-692-16763-2; 978-0-578-90463-4)* 705 Estates Rd. SE, Roanoke, VA 24014 USA Tel 540-293-4536
E-mail: hwaskey@gmail.com.

Wasteland Pr., *(978-0-9715811; 978-0-9724289; 978-0-9729186; 978-0-9740725; 978-0-9742342; 978-0-9744368; 978-0-9746290; 978-0-9748230; 978-1-932852; 978-1-933265; 978-1-60047; 978-1-68111)* Orders Addr.: P.O. Box 5008, Waddy, KY 40076 USA; *Imprints:* Curio Creative (curcr).

Watch & Learn, Inc., *(978-1-893907; 978-1-940301)* 1882 Queens Way, Atlanta, GA 30341 USA Tel 404-762-7760; Fax: 770-457-2132; Toll Free: 800-416-7088
E-mail: bc@cvls.com
Web site: http://www.cvls.com
Dist(s): **Music, Bks. & Business, Inc.**

Watch Me Grow Kids, *(978-1-932555)* P.O. Box 4405, Carson, CA 90749 USA (SAN 255-5093) Fax: 310-532-4536
E-mail: panderson@watchmegrowkids.com
Web site: http://www.watchmegrowkids.com.

Watchmaker Publishing *Imprint of* **Wexford College Pr.**

Watchman Publishing, *(978-1-7325134)* 18520 NW 67th Ave. No. 131, Miami, FL 33015 USA Tel 901-517-8306
E-mail: tavares@innovopub.com.

Watchorn Motion, *(978-0-9990474)* 2430 E Dolphin Way, Cottonwood Heights, UT 84121 USA Tel 801-953-9449
E-mail: swatchster@gmail.com.

Water Daughter Publishing, *(978-0-9753089)* Orders Addr.: 108 Academy St., POUGHKEEPSIE, NY 12601 USA Tel 845-397-7157; Toll Free: 888-778-2928
E-mail: omikemi@hotmail.com
Web site: http://www.waterdaughter.com.

†Water Environment Federation, *(978-0-943244; 978-1-57278; 978-1-881369)* 601 Wythe St., Alexandria, VA 22314 USA (SAN 217-1406) Tel 703-684-2400; Fax: 703-684-2492; Toll Free: 800-666-0206
E-mail: pubs@wef.org
Web site: http://www.wef.org
Dist(s): **Independent Pubs. Group**; *CIP.*

Water for the Village Pr., *(978-0-578-52032-2)* 1439 Stonecutter, Hummelstown, PA 17036 USA Tel 717-343-5979
E-mail: nmikanatha@gmail.com.

Water Forest Pr. *Imprint of* **Skyline Pubn.**

Water Lily Pr., Inc., *(978-0-9772168; 978-0-9860394)* 17214 Hillview Ln., Spring, TX 77379 USA
E-mail: hfwynn@outlook.com
Web site: waterlilypress.com.

Water Wave Productions, *(978-0-9987104)* 4640 Waipahee Pl., Honolulu, HI 96821 USA Tel 808-233-9902; Fax: 808-233-9902
E-mail: lkemoto@gmail.com.

WaterBrook Pr. *Imprint of* **Crown Publishing Group, The**

Waterbrook Press *See* **Doubleday Religious Publishing Group, The**

Watercourse, The *See* **Project WET Foundation**

Waterfall Ridge, *(978-0-9725485)* 40497 Cty. Rd. 20, Saint Peter, MN 56082 USA.

Waterford Pr., Inc., *(978-1-62005)* 428 N. 24 St., Phoenix, AZ 85008-6014 USA Tel 602-681-3333
E-mail: jk@waterfordpress.com
Dist(s): **National Bk. Network**
Publishers Group West (PGW).

Waterfront Productions, *(978-0-9759185; 978-0-692-26375-4; 978-0-692-29262-4; 978-0-9976140; 979-8-218-00812-3; 979-8-9888005)* 3320 W. Foster Ave. No. 266, Chicago, IL 60625 USA
E-mail: jbchi@hotmail.com
Web site: http://bloodlinesdocumentary.com/; http://www.hhholmesthefilm.com; http://www.johnborowski.com; http://www.albertfishfilm.com; http://www.panzram.com; http://www.serialkillerculture.com
Dist(s): **MVD Entertainment Group.**

Waterhouse Press LLC, *(978-0-9897684; 978-0-9905056; 978-1-943893; 978-1-947222; 978-1-64263)* P.O. Box 2080, Conway, NH 03818 USA Tel 781-975-6191
E-mail: meredithwild@gmail.com
Dist(s): **Blackstone Audio, Inc.**
CreateSpace Independent Publishing Platform
Simon & Schuster
Simon & Schuster, Inc.

Waterhouse Publishing, *(978-0-9764082)* 40 Sheridan Ave., Congers, NY 10920 USA Tel 646-391-6669; Toll Free Fax: 877-260-5758 Do not confuse with Waterhouse Publishing in Scottsdale, AZ
E-mail: dfighter@msn.com
Web site: http://www.devonharris.com.

Watering Can, *(978-0-9759868; 978-0-9826416; 978-0-9984488)* 351 W. 19th St., New York, NY 10011 USA
E-mail: info@wateringcanpress.com
Web site: http://www.wateringcanpress.com.

Watering the Seed Productions *See* **Grace & Mercy Publishing**

Watermark Cruises, *(978-0-9754400)* P.O. Box 3350, Annapolis, MD 21403 USA
Web site: http://www.watermarkcruises.com.

WaterMark, Inc., *(978-1-882077)* 4720 Seminole Cir, Birmingham, AL 35243 USA (SAN 248-2010); P.O. Box 361243, Hoover, AL 35236 Do not confuse with Watermark Assocs. in New York, NY or Watermark Pr., Inc. in Wichita, KS
E-mail: amylgary@gmail.com; info@wmibooks.com
Web site: http://wmibooks.com/.

Watermark Pr., Inc., *(978-0-922820; 978-0-615-53794-8)* 149 N. Broadway, Wichita, KS 67202 USA (SAN 251-4265) Tel 316-263-3007 Do not confuse with companies with similar name in Owings Mill, MD, Seattle, WA.

Watermark Publishing, LLC, *(978-0-9631154; 978-0-9705787; 978-0-9720932; 978-0-9742672; 978-0-9753740; 978-0-9779143; 978-0-9790647; 978-0-9796769; 978-0-9815086; 978-0-9821698; 978-0-9844212; 978-1-935690; 978-1-948011; 978-1-958701)* Orders Addr.: 1000 Bishop St., Suite 806, Honolulu, HI 96813 USA (SAN 253-7427) Tel 808-587-7766; Fax: 808-521-3461; Toll Free: 866-900-2665 (866-900-BOOK) Do not confuse with confuse with companies with the same or similar names in San Diego, CA, Beverly Hills, CA, Seattle, WA
E-mail: info@bookshawaii.net
Web site: http://www.bookshawaii.net
Dist(s): **Booklines Hawaii, Ltd.**
Islander Group.

Watershed Bks. *Imprint of* **Pelican Ventures, LLC**

Waterside Pr., *(978-0-9627145; 978-1-939116; 978-1-941768; 978-1-943625; 978-1-945390; 978-1-945949; 978-1-947637; 978-1-949001; 978-1-949003; 978-1-951805; 978-1-954968; 978-1-956503; 978-1-957807; 978-1-958848; 978-1-960583)* 2055 Oxford Ave., Cardiff-by-the-Sea, CA 92007-1719 USA
Dist(s): **Blackstone Audio, Inc.**
INscribe Digital
Ingram Publisher Services
Midpoint Trade Bks., Inc.
Two Rivers Distribution.

Waterside Productions, Incorporated *See* **Waterside Pr.**

Waterside Publishing, *(978-0-9766801; 978-1-933754)* 2376 Oxford Ave., Cardiff-by-the-Sea, CA 92007 USA
E-mail: admin@waterside.com
Web site: http://www.waterside.com
Dist(s): **Ingram Publisher Services**
Two Rivers Distribution.

Watersprings Media House *See* **Watersprings Publishing**

Watersprings Publishing, *(978-0-692-51217-3; 978-0-9988249; 978-1-948877; 979-8-9859594)* PO Box 1284, Olive Branch, MS 38654 USA Tel 662-812-1568
E-mail: athena@waterspringsmedia.com
Dist(s): **Ingram Content Group.**

Waterton Publishing Co., *(978-0-615-68604-2; 978-0-9905249; 978-1-7336233; 978-1-7347632)* 1000 Elmhurst Dr. Unit A, Highlands Ranch, CO 80129 USA
Web site: http://watertonpublishing.com.

Waterwood Publishing Group, *(978-0-9769044)* Orders Addr.: P.O. Box 12540, Charlotte, NC 28220 USA (SAN 257-1072) Tel 704-477-0708
Web site: http://www.waterwoodpublishing.com.

WaterWords, *(978-0-9729599; 978-0-9833729; 978-0-692-13261-6; 978-0-578-46492-3)* 3244 NW Melville Dr, Bend, OR 97703 USA (SAN 255-4593) Tel 541-410-1478
E-mail: judysbend@gmail.com.

Watkins, Ariel, *(978-0-578-83460-3)* 2500 Shallowford Rd NE, ATLANTA, GA 30345 USA Tel 504-616-8356
E-mail: arielwtkns@yahoo.com
Web site: www.allaboutmovementdance.com.

Watkins Media Limited (GBR) *(978-1-900131; 978-1-903296; 978-1-84293; 978-1-904292; 978-1-84483; 978-1-906787; 978-0-85766; 978-1-907486; 978-1-78028; 978-1-84899; 978-1-914420; 978-1-915202)* *Dist. by* **Peng Rand Hse.**

Watling St., Ltd. (GBR) *(978-1-904153)* *Dist. by* **Trafalgar.**

Watling St., Ltd. (GBR) *(978-1-904153)* *Dist. by* **IPG Chicago.**

Watosh Publishing, *(978-0-9611954)* P.O. Box 11231, Las Vegas, NV 89111 USA (SAN 286-1976) Tel 702-896-4108
E-mail: gecfly@aol.com
Web site: http://www.watoshpublishing.com; http://www.angietheaviator.com.

Watson, Corinda, *(978-1-7336121; 978-1-7359452)* 651 Picketts Mill Dr., Shreveport, LA 71115 USA Tel 318-455-4761
E-mail: corindawatson@gmail.com
Web site: corindawatson.com
Dist(s): **Ingram Content Group.**

Watson Publishing, *(978-0-615-44576-2; 978-0-473-40077-4)* 8937 S Cornell Ave., Chicago, IL 60617 USA Tel 239-603-3121; Fax: 239-791-1260
E-mail: geraldcwatson@comcast.net.

Watson-Guptill *Imprint of* **Potter/Ten Speed/Harmony/Rodale**

†Watson-Guptill Pubns., Inc., *(978-0-8230; 978-1-60569)* Div. of Crown Publishing Grp., 575 Prospect St., Lakewood, NJ 08701 USA Tel 732-363-5679; Toll Free Fax: 877-227-6564; Edit Addr.: 1745 Broadway # 124, New York, NY 10019-4305 USA (SAN 282-5384)
E-mail: aalexander@watsonguptill.com
Web site: http://www.watsonguptill.com
Dist(s): **Children's Plus, Inc.**
Follett School Solutions
Leonard, Hal Corp.
MyiLibrary
Penguin Random Hse. Distribution
Penguin Random Hse. LLC
Random Hse., Inc.
ebrary, Inc.; *CIP.*

Wattpad Bks. (CAN) *(978-0-9936899; 978-1-989365; 978-1-7772900; 978-1-990259; 978-1-990778)* *Dist. by* **Macmillan.**

Watts, Erika, *(978-0-9980460)* 4277 Buford Cir., Lancaster, SC 29720 USA
E-mail: erikawatts83@gmail.com; dorkymomdoodles@gmail.com
Web site: www.dorkymomdoodles.com.

Watts, Franklin *Imprint of* **Scholastic Library Publishing**

Watts, Katherine (GBR) *(978-0-9556878)* *Dist. by* **LuluCom.**

Waugh Wright, *(978-0-9989586)* 919 Englewood Ave., Durham, NC 27701 USA Tel 215-715-8549
E-mail: waughwright@gmail.com.

Wave Blue World, A, *(978-0-9824539; 978-1-949518)* 399 W. St., New York, NY 10014 USA
Web site: http://www.awaveblueworld.com
Dist(s): **Diamond Comic Distributors, Inc.**

Wave Publishing, *(978-0-9642359; 978-0-9722430)* Div. of Caroy, Inc., 4 Yawl St., Venice, CA 90292 USA (SAN 298-3788) Tel 310-306-0699; Fax: 310-822-4921 Do not confusw with Wave Publishing in Virginia Beach, VA.

Wave Runner Publishing, *(978-1-7327170)* P.O. Box 7004, Springfield, OR 97475 USA Tel 541-515-1801
E-mail: kswarner@outlook.com.

WaveRider Pr., *(978-0-9968666; 978-1-7356890)* 2129 Central Pk. Ave., Evanston, IL 60201 USA Tel 847-475-4242
E-mail: cleopalex@gmail.com.

Waves of Bliss, *(978-0-9821302)* 6909 VT Rt. 15, Jeffersonville, VT 05464 USA
E-mail: nasrin@nasrinsafai.com
Web site: http://www.wavesofbliss.com.

Wawa Pr. *Imprint of* **Adisoft, Inc.**

Way Out Comics, *(978-0-9742386)* P.O. Box 642218, Los Angeles, CA 90064 USA
E-mail: julieyeh@sbcglobal.net
Web site: http://www.wayoutcomics.com.

Way With Words Publishing Company *See* **W3 Publishing**

WayaMedia, *(978-0-9765700)* 391 Watson Br. Rd., Cullowhee, NC 28723 USA (SAN 256-503X) Do not confuse with PPS Publishing Inc. in Lake in the Hills, IL
Web site: http://www.wayamedia.com.

Wayfarer Pr., LLC, *(978-0-9789965)* P.O. Box 948, Union Lake, MI 48387-0948 USA Do not confuse with Wayfarer Press in Plymouth, NH
E-mail: wayfarerpress@sbcglobal.net
Web site: http://www.wayfarerbooks.com.

Wayland Historical Society, *(978-0-9762756)* Orders Addr.: P.O. Box 56, Wayland, MA 01778 USA Tel 508-358-7959; Edit Addr.: 12 Cochituate Rd., Wayland, MA 01778 USA
E-mail: jane_sciacca@comcast.net
Web site: http://j.w.d.home.comcast.net/whs.

Wayne & Judith Rolfs, *(978-0-9799895)* P.O. Box 584, Fontana, WI 53125-5312 USA
E-mail: jwrolfs@charter.net
Web site: http://www.fantasticfamily.org.

†Wayne State Univ. Pr., *(978-0-8143)* Leonard N. Simons Bldg., 4809 Woodward Ave., Detroit, MI 48201-1309 USA (SAN 202-5221) Tel 313-577-6120; Fax:

Publisher Name Index

313-577-6131; Toll Free: 800-978-7323 (customer orders)
E-mail: theresa.martinelli@wayne.edu; Kristina.Stonehill@wayne.edu
Web site: http://wsupress.wayne.edu
Dist(s): **East-West Export Bks.**
INscribe Digital
Independent Pubs. Group
ebrary, Inc.; *CIP*.

Wayne, Steven Co., *(978-0-9713154; 978-0-9727696)* 3940 Laurel Canyon Blvd., No. 698, Studio City, CA 91604 USA Tel 323-654-9339; Fax: 323-656-7324; Toll Free: 866-446-1201; *Imprints*: SWC Editions (SWC Editions)
E-mail: wschoenfeld@stevenwaynecompany.com; schoenfeld@swceditions.com
Web site: http://www.stevenwaynecompany.com; http://www.swceditions.com.

Wayside Pubns., *(978-0-9749749)* P.O. Box 318, Goreville, IL 62939 USA (SAN 255-898X)
E-mail: belletrist.1@gmail.com.

Wayside Publishing, *(978-1-877653; 978-1-938026; 978-1-942400; 978-1-944876; 978-1-64159)* Orders Addr.: 262 US Rte 1, Ste 2, Freeport, ME 04032 USA Toll Free: 888-302-2519
E-mail: sales@waysidepublishing.com
Web site: http://www.waysidepublishing.com.

Waystone Pr., *(978-0-9988479; 978-1-7320873; 978-1-951536)* 2603 Jordanville Rd, Jordanville, NY 13361 USA Tel 315-219-0676
E-mail: nkotar@nicholaskotar.com
Web site: waystonepress.com.

Wayward Raven Media, *(978-0-615-77305-6; 978-0-692-29822-0; 978-0-692-91484-7; 978-0-692-91494-6; 978-0-692-94928-3; 978-0-578-54537-0; 979-8-9868513)* 121 Lynnbrook Rd, Fairfield, CT 06825 USA Tel 203-336-9559
Web site: http://waywardraven.com
Dist(s): **CreateSpace Independent Publishing Platform.**

Waywiser Pr., The (GBR) *(978-0-9532841; 978-1-904130; 978-1-911379) Dist. by* **SPD-Small Pr Dist.**

Wayword Pr. Bks., *(978-0-692-79523-1; 978-0-9990515)* 22925 Galaxy Ln., Lake Forest, CA 92630 USA Tel 406-369-0902.

WCI Pr., *(978-0-9745480)* 6161 7th Ave N., St Petersburg, FL 33710-7015 USA
E-mail: clauberfl@aol.com
Web site: http://www.SoccerDreamsBook.com.

WD/GBGM Bks. *Imprint of* **General Board of Global Ministries, The United Methodist Church**

We Do Listen *Imprint of* **We Do Listen Foundation**

We Do Listen Foundation, *(978-0-9715390; 978-0-9826165; 978-0-9910777; 978-0-578-39133-5)* 1750 Ben Franklin Dr. #11g, Sarasota, FL 34236 USA (SAN 254-8119); *Imprints*: We Do Listen (WE DO LISTEN)
E-mail: howardb@wedolisten.com
Web site: http://www.wedolisten.org
Dist(s): **Lerner Publishing Group.**

WE, LLC, *(978-0-9761322; 978-1-7323556)* P.O. Box 120804, Nashville, TN 37212 USA (SAN 256-257X) Tel 615-584-2071; Toll Free: 866-352-9263
E-mail: wanda.scott@live.com
Web site: www.WandaLScott.com.

Wealth of Wisdom LLC, A, *(978-0-9843125; 978-1-941635)* P.O. Box 390038, Keauhou, HI 96739 USA Tel 808-896-3950
Web site: http://www.awealthofwisdom.com.

Wealth Services *See* **Skylar Doreal**

Weapons of Mass Instruction, *(978-0-9766978; 978-0-9769266)* P.O. Box 1299, Freedom, CA 95019 USA Tel 831-728-0600
Web site: http://www.bilingualnation.com.

Weatherhill, Inc. *Imprint of* **Shambhala Pubns., Inc.**

Weatherstock, Inc., *(978-0-9728107)* P.O. Box 31808, Tucson, AZ 85751 USA.

Weaver *Imprint of* **Alpha Omega Pubns., Inc.**

Weaver, Jack R. Company, *(978-0-9773370)* 375 A. Donald Rd., Canton, GA 30114 USA Tel 770-479-1342
E-mail: jackweaver426@tds.net.

Web of Life Children's Bks., *(978-0-9773795; 978-0-9777539; 978-0-9883302; 978-0-9883303; 978-1-970039)* P.O. Box 2726, Berkeley, CA 94702-0726 USA
E-mail: mdunphy@weboflifebooks.com
Web site: http://www.weboflifebooks.com
Dist(s): **Publishers Group West (PGW).**

Web Wise Services, Inc., *(978-0-9748237; 978-1-933404)* 305 Woodstock Rd, Eastlake, OH 44095 USA Tel 440-953-2443; Toll Free: 866-232-7032
Web site: http://www.webwiseseniors.com.

Webb, Dirk E, *(978-0-578-01867-6; 978-0-578-05527-5)* 3367 E. 150 N., Anderson, IN 46012 USA Tel 765-378-7025
E-mail: dirk.webb@comcast.net
Web site: http://lulu.com/dirkwebb
Dist(s): **Lulu Pr., Inc.**

Webb, Genie, *(978-0-692-86133-2; 978-0-692-12959-3)* 1414 W. Lawn Ave, RACINE, WI 53405 USA Tel 262-497-0059
E-mail: jeffwcrawford5+LVP0003504@gmail.com; jeffwcrawford5+LVP0003504@gmail.com.

Webb, Jack, *(978-0-9640275; 978-0-9719906; 978-0-615-99047-7; 978-0-692-69771-9; 978-0-692-86917-8; 978-1-7320522; 978-0-578-49430-2)* Div. of San Diego State Univ. Research Foundation, Orders Addr.: 7618 Stevenson, San Diego, CA 92120 USA Tel 619-723-5371
E-mail: jackwebb1@cox.net
Web site: http://www.bordervoices.com.

Webb Ministries, Inc., *(978-0-9632226)* Orders Addr.: P.O. Box 520729, Longwood, FL 32752-0729 USA Tel 407-834-5233; Fax: 407-332-6277
E-mail: Webbministries@cfl.rr.com
Dist(s): **CreateSpace Independent Publishing Platform**
Spring Arbor Distributors, Inc.

WebbWorks, *(978-0-9791076)* P.O. Box 985, Semmes, AL 36575-0985 USA (SAN 852-4629)
E-mail: duet2sisters@bellsouth.net.

WebCartoons, LLC, *(978-0-9743215)* 3727 W. Magnilia Blvd., Suite No. 141, Burbank, CA 91510 USA Tel 818-620-4256; Fax: 818-598-1842
E-mail: jerryching@earthlink.net
Web site: http://www.thegreatestkingbok.com.

WeBeANS Corp., *(978-0-9740115)* 466 S. Spruce Ave., Galloway, NJ 08205 USA Tel 609-652-5778; Fax: 877-589-3184; Toll Free Fax: 877-589-3184; Toll Free: 888-867-8838
E-mail: john@webeans.net
Web site: http://www.webeans.net.

Webster Henrietta Publishing, *(978-0-9728222)* P.O. Box 50044, Myrtle Beach, SC 29579 USA Tel 843-251-8867; Fax: 843-236-0260
E-mail: mhetzer@websterhenrietta.com
Web site: http://www.websterhenrietta.com.

Webster House Publishing LLC, *(978-1-932635)* 309 Florida Hill Rd., Ridgefield, CT 06877 USA Tel 203-438-0345; Fax: 203-438-0379
E-mail: fred@websterhousepub.com
Web site: http://www.websterhousepub.com.

Webster Pr. LLC, *(978-0-9882261; 978-1-63558)* 57 Woodside Ave., Amherst, MA 01002 USA Tel 413-219-3966; Fax: 413-219-3966
E-mail: alexawh@gmail.com.

Wedding Solutions Publishing, Incorporated *See* **WS Publishing**

Wedgeworth, Anthony G., *(978-0-615-20879-4; 978-0-615-25816-4; 978-0-615-26007-5; 978-0-578-00695-6; 978-0-578-03617-5; 978-0-578-04710-2; 978-0-578-05827-6; 978-0-578-06337-9)* Orders Addr.: P.O. Box 621, Monona, IA 52159-0621ed USA; Edit Addr.: 104 N. Anderson St., Monona, IA 52159-0621 USA
E-mail: anthonywedgeworth@hotmail.com; thorik@alteredcreatures.com
Web site: http://www.anthonywedgeworth.com
Dist(s): **Lulu Pr., Inc.**
Smashwords.

Wedgeworth, Anthony G., *(978-0-9859159; 978-0-9989650; 978-0-578-71755-5; 978-1-7369704)* 1014 S. 6th St., Prairie du Chien, WI 53821 USA Tel 563-581-8353
E-mail: AnthonyWedgeworth@hotmail.com
Dist(s): **Ingram Bk. Co.**
Lulu Pr., Inc.
Smashwords.

WEDmiston Publishing, *(978-0-9993698)* 2236 kittiwake St., Arroyo Grande, CA 93420 USA Tel 805-481-7142; Fax: 805-481-7142
E-mail: wayneonespirit@charter.net
Web site: http://wedmiston.com; http://OneSpiritBeachWeddings.com.

Wednesday Bks. *Imprint of* **St. Martin's Pr.**

WeDream.com, *(978-0-9764351)* P.O. Box 6020, Dillon, CO 80435-6020 USA
E-mail: climbing@wedream.com
Web site: http://www.wedream.com; http://discgolfguides.com.

Wee Creek Pr. LLC, *(978-1-942922)* P.O. Box 51052, casper, WY 82605-1052 USA Tel 307-265-8585; Fax: 307-265-4640
E-mail: weecreekpress@gmail.com
Web site: www.weecreekpress.com.

Wee Read Publishing, *(978-0-9723122)* 2269 Ginger Hill Loop., Lincoln, CA 95648-8719 USA
E-mail: lindamarchus@yahoo.com; vmarchus@hotmail.com
Web site: http://www.weereadpublishing.com.

Weebie Publishing *See* **Susi B. Marketing, Inc.**

Weekly Reader *Imprint of* **Stevens, Gareth Publishing LLLP**

Weekly Reader Corp., *(978-0-8374)* Affil. of WRC Media, Orders Addr.: P.O. Box 120023, Stamford, CT 06912-0023 USA (SAN 207-060X) Tel 203-705-3569; Fax: 203-705-3483; Toll Free: 800-446-3355; 3001 Cindel Dr., Delran, NJ 08370 (SAN 207-0618); Edit Addr.: 1 Readers Digest Rd., Pleasantville, NY 10570-7000 USA
E-mail: cpekar@weeklyreader.com
Web site: http://www.weeklyreader.com.

Weekly Reader Leveled Readers *Imprint of* **Stevens, Gareth Publishing LLLP**

Weekly Reader Teacher's Pr *Imprint of* **iUniverse, Inc.**

Weeley Pr., *(978-0-692-84235-5)* 1500 Bay Area Blvd, Suite 324, Houston, TX 77058 USA Tel 832-805-1691; Fax: 832-805-1691
E-mail: phil.roiz@yahoo.com.

Weem, Nadia *See* **Weems, Madia**

Weems, Madia, *(978-0-615-19289-5)* 1343 Stevens Rd. SE, Washington, DC 20020 USA Tel 202-889-5239
E-mail: thewriter1115@yahoo.com.

Weeping Willow Publishing, *(978-0-9789227; 978-1-7322294)* 511 Mitchell Ryan, Wake Village, TX 75501 USA Tel 903-838-9062
E-mail: tomgreer1964@gmail.com
Web site: http://www.tomcgreer.com.

Wegeng, Pam, *(978-0-692-98663-9; 978-0-578-44306-5)* 2312 N Stoneybrook Ct, Wichita, KS 67226 USA Tel 316-636-9167
E-mail: pkwegeng@cox.net
Dist(s): **Ingram Content Group.**

Wehner, Adrienna, *(978-0-9653866)* P.O. Box 6196, San Jose, CA 95150-6196 USA
E-mail: Awehner408@hotmail.com.

Wehr Animations, *(978-0-9748093)* 3890 CloverLeaf Dr., Boulder, CO 80304 USA
Web site: http://www.wehranimations.com.

Wehrley, Susan K. & Associates, Incorporated *See* **Thomas & Kay, LLC**

Weight Loss Buddy, Inc., *(978-0-9754448)* P.O. Box 488, Tenafly, NJ 07670 USA Toll Free: 877-283-3987
Web site: http://www.weightlossbuddy.com.

Weight of Ink, The, *(978-1-7328987)* 305 Trilith Pkwy, Ste 300 No. 1596, Fayetteville, GA 30214 USA Tel 917-538-1596
E-mail: michael@theweightofink.com
Web site: www.theweightofink.com.

Weightman, Bud, *(978-0-9821035)* PMB#103, 5315 FM 1960 W., Suite B, Houston, TX 77069 USA (SAN 857-247X) Tel 281-444-4950; Fax: 281-966-1769
E-mail: budqsi@isoconsultants.com; piggytales.press@gmail.com
Web site: http://www.piggytalespress.com.

Weigl Pubs., Inc., *(978-1-930954; 978-1-59036; 978-1-60596; 978-1-61690; 978-1-61913; 978-1-62127; 978-1-4896; 978-1-7911; 979-8-8745)* Orders Addr.: 350 5th Ave. 59th Flr., New York, NY 10118 USA Tel 866-649-3445; Fax: 866-449-3445; 6325 Tenth St., SE, Calgary, AB T2H 2ZP Tel 403-233-7747; Fax: 403-233-7769; Edit Addr.: 276 5th Avenue Suite 704 #917, New York, NY 10001 USA; *Imprints*: AV2 by Weigl (AVTwo Weigl)
E-mail: editorial3@weigl.com
Web site: http://www.AV2books.com; http://www.weigl.com
Dist(s): **Follett School Solutions.**

Weimer, Brandon Publishing, *(978-0-692-14609-5)* 64 N Cameron St., Saratoga Springs, UT 84045 USA Tel 385-233-7811
E-mail: brandonweimersel@gmail.com
Dist(s): **Ingram Content Group.**

Weir, Kenneth, *(978-0-692-78593-5)* 125 Spring Dr, Marshall, TX 75672 USA Tel 903-746-4675
E-mail: kenweir@sehlah.com.

Wei's Publishing Co., *(978-0-9747284)* 116 W. Donald St., South Bend, IN 46613 USA
E-mail: liuwei82@hotmail.com
Web site: http://www.weispublishing.com.

Weisenbarger, Katie, *(978-0-692-10953-3; 978-0-692-10971-7)* 3624 Trebein Rd., FAIRBORN, OH 45324 USA Tel 937-902-2212
E-mail: katieweisenbarger@gmail.com
Dist(s): **Ingram Content Group.**

Weiser, Samuel Incorporated *See* **Red Wheel/Weiser**

Weiss, Janet Bruschetti, *(978-0-9747716)* P.O. Box 8411, Longboat Key, FL 34228 USA
E-mail: jentajean@aol.com.

Weit Pr., *(978-0-578-04365-4; 978-0-578-19298-7; 978-0-578-19299-4)* 8819 Lanier Dr., Suite 414, Silver Spring, MD 20910 USA
E-mail: weitpress@gmail.com
Web site: http://LiberalMandate.com.

Welbeck Publishing Group Ltd. (GBR) *(978-1-85906; 978-1-914317; 978-1-913519; 978-1-80338) Dist. by* **TwoRivers.**

Welch, Susannah *See* **Silky Sky Publishing**

Welcome Bks *Imprint of* **Rizzoli International Pubns., Inc.**

Weldon Owen, Inc., *(978-1-875137; 978-1-892374; 978-1-61628; 978-1-68188)* Div. of Bonnier Publishing USA, 1045 Sansome St. Suite 100, San Francisco, CA 94117 USA Tel 415-291-0111; *Imprints*: Bluestreak Books (Bluestreak Bk) Do not confuse with Weldon Owen Reference, Inc. also at the same address
E-mail: info@weldonowen.com; customer_service@weldonowen.info
Web site: http://www.weldonowen.com/
Dist(s): **Chain Sales Marketing, Inc.**
INscribe Digital
MyiLibrary
Open Road Integrated Media, Inc.
Simon & Schuster, Inc.

Weldon Pubns., Inc., *(978-0-9724175)* 432 Pennsylvania Ave., Waverly, NY 14892 USA
E-mail: weldon@cqservices.com; sales@cqservices.com
Web site: http://www.Marchintotheendlessmountains.com.

Well Fire Pubns., *(978-0-9701912; 978-0-615-11133-9; 978-0-615-11146-9)* Orders Addr.: 100 Markley St., Port Reading, NJ 07064-1897 USA Tel 732-636-2060; Fax: 732-636-2538
E-mail: sherryross@home.com
Web site: http://www.sherryross.com.

WellFire Publications *See* **Well Fire Pubns.**

Wellington, Charles, *(978-0-9972556; 979-8-88781)* 3300 Kauai Ct B-11, Reno, NV 89433 USA Tel 775-622-0986
E-mail: wellington.charles.2@gmail.com.

Wellington, Monica, *(978-0-578-41810-0)* 243 W. 70th St. No. 7F, New York, NY 10023 USA Tel 212-865-6588
E-mail: monicaaw@earthlink.net
Dist(s): **Ingram Content Group.**

Wellman, Patrick *See* **MrDuz.com**

Wellness & Lifestyle by Mel *See* **Our Blueprint-A Recipe for Wellness**

Wellness, Incorporated *See* **OrganWise Guys Inc., The**

Wellness Institute, Incorporated *See* **Wellness Institute/Self-Help Bks., LLC**

Wellness Institute/Self-Help Bks., LLC, *(978-0-9617202; 978-1-58741)* 515 W. N. St., Pass Christian, MS 39571 USA (SAN 663-382X) Tel 228-452-0770; Fax: 228-452-0775 YES NAME CHANGE CORRECT H DAWLEY
E-mail: publisher@selfhelpbooks.com
Web site: http://www.selfhelpbooks.com.

Wellness pH Productions, *(978-1-933559)* 510 United Cir. Apt B, Greer, SC 29651 USA (SAN 256-6753) Tel 864-608-7302
E-mail: stroblechristine@gmail.com
Web site: www.drchrismaria.com.

Wellness pH Publishing *See* **Wellness pH Productions**

Wellness Pubn., *(978-0-9701490; 978-0-9748581; 978-0-9906147)* 624 Marsat Ct., Chula Vista, CA 91911-4646 USA Toll Free: 800-755-4656; *Imprints*: Bayport Press (Bayport Pr) Do not confuse with companies with the same or similar name in Rockport, TX, Omaha, NE, Holland, MI, Ft. Lauderdale, FL, Santa Barbara, CA
E-mail: malan1208@sbcglobal.net; ted@soriano.com
Web site: http://www.drjwallach.com.

Well-Trained Mind Pr., *(978-0-9714129; 978-0-9728603; 978-1-933339; 978-1-942968; 978-1-945841; 978-1-952469)* 18021 The Glebe Ln., Charles City, VA 23030-3828 USA (SAN 254-1726)
E-mail: ptbuff@peacehillpress.net
Web site: http://www.peacehillpress.com
Dist(s): **Norton, W. W. & Co., Inc.**
Penguin Random Hse. Distribution
Penguin Random Hse. LLC.

Welt, Rich & Assocs., *(978-0-9706529)* 8401 Heron Cir., Huntington Beach, CA 92646 USA Tel 866-742-4935
E-mail: richwelt@aol.com
Web site: http://richwelt.com.

Wendelyn Vega *See* **Bohemian Academic, The**

Wendy Morris Jackson, *(978-0-578-87245-2)* 14452 Mattawoman Dr., Brandywine, MD 20613 USA Tel 301-514-8435
E-mail: Ateacupofinspirations@gmail.com.

Wenner Bks., *(978-1-932958)* 1290 Ave. of the Americas, 2nd Flr., New York, NY 10104 USA Tel 212-484-1696; Fax: 212-484-3433
E-mail: kate.rockland@wennermedia.com.

Wentworth Pr. *Imprint of* **Creative Media Partners, LLC**

We-Publish.com, *(978-1-931335)* 6311 Gulf Freeway #4201, Houston, TX 77023 USA Tel 713-448-0720 phone
E-mail: admin@banmex.com
Web site: http://www.we-publish.com.

Werner, L Marketing, *(978-1-7330062; 979-8-9890810)* 504 Leesburg St., Oswego, IL 60543-4086 USA Tel 630-538-2423
E-mail: ldisher27@live.com
Web site: www.illusionofagirl.com.

Werner, Tamra, *(978-0-692-94041-9; 978-0-692-94042-6; 978-0-692-94044-0; 978-0-578-52434-4; 978-0-578-52436-8; 978-0-578-35216-9)* 38 Crestview Dr., Pittsford, NY 14534 USA Tel 585-749-7043
E-mail: mytopaz39tw@gmail.com
Dist(s): **Ingram Content Group.**

WeShine Pr. Co., *(978-0-9818113)* 12 Lake Mist Dr., Sugar Land, TX 77479 USA
Web site: www.weshinepress.com.

Wesleyan Publishing Hse., *(978-0-89827; 978-1-63257; 978-0-692-88620-5; 978-0-692-92243-9; 978-0-578-98835-1)* Div. of The Wesleyan Church, P.O. Box 50434, Indianapolis, IN 46250-0434 USA (SAN 162-7104) Tel 317-774-3853; Fax: 317-774-3860; Toll Free Fax: 800-788-3535; Toll Free: 800-493-7539 (orders only)
E-mail: wph@wesleyan.org; lebarons@wesleyan.org
Web site: http://www.wesleyan.org/wph
Dist(s): **Faith Alive Christian Resources.**

West 44 Bks. *Imprint of* **Enslow Publishing, LLC**

West Alden Publishing, LLC, *(978-0-9976002)* 208 Biltmore Dr., Colonial Heights, VA 23834 USA Tel 804-520-8866
E-mail: scnorkus@gmail.com.

West Barnstable Pr., *(978-0-9816873; 978-0-9828122; 978-0-9978182; 978-1-7328701)* 21 Meadow Ln., West Barnstable, MA 02668 USA (SAN 856-2490)
Web site: http://www.westbarnstablepress.com.

West Coast Learning Development Center, *(978-0-615-19154-6; 978-0-615-19269-7; 978-0-578-12128-4)* P.O. Box 194, Torrance, CA 90507 USA
E-mail: westcoastlearningdevelopmentcenter@yahoo.com
Web site: http://www.westcoastlearningdevelopmentcenter.org
Dist(s): **Not So Plain Jane Publishing.**

West, Dave Corporation *See* **Aztec 5 Publishing**

West End Games *Imprint of* **Purgatory Publishing, Inc.**

West End Games, Inc., *(978-0-87431)* Subs. of Bucci Imports, R.D. 3, Box 2345, Honesdale, PA 18431 USA (SAN 687-8466) Tel 717-253-6990; Fax: 717-253-5104
E-mail: dspweg@hotmail.com
Web site: http://www.westendgames.net.

West Highland Pr., *(978-0-9721486)* P.O. Box 10040, Alexandria, VA 22310 USA
E-mail: westhighlandpress@earthlink.net
Web site: http://www.westhighlandpress.com.

West Margin Pr. *Imprint of* **West Margin Pr.**

West Margin Pr., *(978-0-944197; 978-1-941821; 978-1-943328; 978-1-5131; 978-1-5132; 978-1-5133)* P.O. Box 56118, Portland, OR 97238 USA Tel 503-254-5591; Fax: 503-254-5609; *Imprints*: Alaska Northwest Books (Alaska NW Bks); West Winds Press (West Winds Pr); West Margin Press (West Margin); Graphic Arts Books (Graphic Arts Bks)
Dist(s): **Independent Pubs. Group**
Ingram Publisher Services
MyiLibrary
Two Rivers Distribution.

West, Mary, *(978-0-578-02740-1)* 733 Avenida Tercera, Apt 109, Clermont, FL 34714 USA
E-mail: sales@hecalledianswered.com
Web site: http://www.hecalledianswered.com
Dist(s): **Lulu Pr., Inc.**

West Ridge Farm Publishing, *(978-0-9845582; 978-0-9892282)* 535 Glendale St., Hampden, MA 01036 USA Tel 413-566-5366
E-mail: luvfisk@yahoo.com; sanj535@charter.net
Web site: http://www.westridgefarmpublishing.com; http://www.angelsclubkids.com.

West Virginia Univ. Pr., *(978-0-937058; 978-1-933202; 978-1-935978; 978-1-938228; 978-1-940425; 978-1-943665; 978-1-946684; 978-1-949199; 978-1-952271; 978-1-959000)* Orders Addr.: P.O. Box 6295, Morgantown, WV 26506-6295 USA (SAN 205-5163) Tel 304-293-8400; Fax: 304-293-6585; Toll Free: 866-988-7737; *Imprints*: Vandalia Press (Vandalia Pr)
E-mail: fdowney2@wvu.edu
Web site: http://www.wvupress.com
Dist(s): **BookMobile**
Chicago Distribution Ctr.

MyiLibrary
ebrary, Inc.

West Wind Pr. *Imprint of* **First Steps Publishing**

West Winds Pr. *Imprint of* **West Margin Pr.**

West Woods Pr., *(978-0-9776837)* 3905 Westwood Cir., Flagstaff, AZ 86001 USA (SAN 257-9375)
Web site: http://www.WestWoodsPress.com.

WestBow Pr. *Imprint of* **Scholastic, Inc.**

WestBow Pr. *Imprint of* **Author Solutions, LLC**

Westchester Publishing, *(978-0-9891504)* 280 Mamaroneck Ave., White Plains, NY 10605 USA Tel 914-761-1894
E-mail: dhampton@newshelves.com.

Westcliffe Pubs. *Imprint of* **Bower Hse.**

Westcom Press *See* **Cathedrall Pr./Encycloware**

Western Images Pubns., Inc., *(978-0-9627600; 978-1-887302)* 2249 Marion St., Denver, CO 80205 USA.

Western Michigan University, New Issues Press *See* **New Issues Poetry & Prose, Western Michigan Univ.**

Western National Parks Assn., *(978-0-911408; 978-1-877856; 978-1-58369)* 12880 N. Vistoso Village Dr., Tucson, AZ 85755 USA (SAN 202-750X) Tel 520-622-1999; Fax: 520-623-9519
E-mail: abby@wnpa.org; derek@wnpa.org
Web site: http://www.wnpa.org
Dist(s): **Canyonlands Pubns.**
Rio Nuevo Pubs.
Sunbelt Pubns., Inc.

Western New York Wares, Inc., *(978-0-9620314; 978-1-879201)* Orders Addr.: P.O. Box 733, Buffalo, NY 14205 USA (SAN 248-6911) Tel 716-832-6088; Edit Addr.: 419 Parkside Ave., Buffalo, NY 14216 USA (SAN 248-692X) Tel 716-832-6088
E-mail: wnywares@gateway.net.

Western Psychological Services, *(978-0-87424)* Div. of Manson Western Corp., 12031 Wilshire Blvd., Los Angeles, CA 90025 USA (SAN 160-8002) Tel 310-478-2061; Fax: 310-478-7838; Toll Free: 800-648-8857
E-mail: weinberg@wpspublish.com
Web site: http://www.wpspublish.com.

Western Reflections Publishing Co., *(978-1-890437; 978-1-932738; 978-1-937851)* Orders Addr.: P.O. Box 1149, Lake City, CO 81235 USA Tel 970-944-0110 Toll Free: 800-993-4490
Web site: http://www.westernreflectionspub.com
Dist(s): **Bks. West**
Hinsdale County Historical Society
Lake City Downtown Improvement and Revitalization Team
Partners/West Book Distributors
Quality Bks., Inc.
Rio Nuevo Pubs.

Westie Pr., *(978-0-578-18653-5; 978-0-578-18956-7)* 26616 Pepperidge Cove, Millsboro, DE 19966 USA
Web site: www.customadultcoloring.com.

Westigan Review Press *See* **Ephemeron Pr.**

Westlake Pr. *Imprint of* **Book Publishing Co.**

†Westminster John Knox Pr., *(978-0-664; 978-0-8042; 978-1-61164; 978-1-947888; 978-1-64698)* Div. of Presbyterian Publishing Corp., Orders Addr.: 100 Witherspoon St., Louisville, KY 40202 USA (SAN 202-9669) Tel 502-569-5052 (outside U.S. for ordering); Fax: 502-569-5113 (outside U.S. for faxed orders); Toll Free Fax: 800-541-5113 (toll-free U.S. faxed orders); Toll Free: 800-227-2872 (customer service); *Imprints:* Flyaway Books (MYID_B_FLYAWAY)
E-mail: orders@wjkbooks.com
Web site: http://www.wjkbooks.com
Dist(s): **Faith Alive Christian Resources**
MyiLibrary
Presbyterian Publishing Corp.; *CIP.*

Weston Priory, *(978-0-9763005)* 58 Priory Hill Rd., Weston, VT 05161-6400 USA Tel 802-824-5409; Fax: 802-824-3573
E-mail: brjohn@westonpriory.org
Web site: http://www.westonpriory.org.

Weston Woods Studios, Inc., *(978-0-7882; 978-0-89719; 978-1-55592; 978-1-56008)* Div. of Scholastic, Inc., 143 Main St., Norwalk, CT 06851 USA (SAN 630-3838) Tel 203-845-0197; Fax: 203-845-0498; Toll Free: 800-243-5020
E-mail: questions@Scholastic.com
Web site: http://www.scholastic.com/westonwoods
Dist(s): **Findaway World, LLC**
Follett School Solutions.

Westphalia Press, *(978-0-918592; 978-0-944285; 978-1-935907; 978-1-941472; 978-1-941755; 978-1-63391; 978-1-63723)* 1527 New Hampshire Ave. NW, Washington, DC 20036 USA Tel 202-349-9282
E-mail: dgutierrezs@ipsonet.org
Web site: http://ipsonet.org.

Westphalia Thoroughbreds, LLC, *(978-0-9754103)* 1231 Latigo Ln., Flower Mound, TX 75022 USA Tel 817-368-6981
E-mail: arazielf@yahoo.com
Web site: http://www.westphaliathoroughbreds.com.

Westrim Crafts, *(978-0-9819053)* 7855 Hayvenhurst Ave., Van Nuys, CA 91406 USA Fax: 469-362-8016
E-mail: lisa.groshek@creativityinc.com
Web site: http://www.creativityinc.com.

Westry Wingate Group, Inc., *(978-1-935323)* 2708 Wet Stone Way Unit 108, Charlotte, NC 28208-4794 USA (SAN 857-183X)
E-mail: gabriel@westrywingate.com
Web site: http://www.westrywingate.com.

Westside Bks., *(978-1-934813)* Div. of Marco Bk. Co., 60 Industrial Rd., Lodi, NJ 07644 USA (SAN 855-0166) Tel 973-458-0485; Fax: 973-458-5289; Toll Free: 800-842-4234
Web site: http://www.westside-books.com
Dist(s): **Bks. & Media, Inc.**
Marco Bk. Co.
MyiLibrary.

Westside Press *See* **Wordsmith Pr.**

Westside Storybks., *(978-1-7354086)* 2034 Butler Way, Atlanta, GA 30318 USA Tel 404-421-7258
E-mail: kahamilton12@gmail.com.

Westside Studio, *(978-0-9786147)* P.O. Box 703, Trumansburg, NY 14886-0703 USA.

Westview Pr. *Imprint of* **Avalon Publishing**

Westview Publishing Co., Inc., *(978-0-9744322; 978-0-9748730; 978-0-9755646; 978-0-9764940; 978-0-9773179; 978-0-9776207; 978-1-933912; 978-0-9816172; 978-0-692-69338-4)* P.O. Box 210183, Nashville, TN 37221 USA
Web site: http://www.westviewpublishing.com.

Westview Publishing, Incorporated *See* **Westview Publishing Co., Inc.**

WestWind Pr. *Imprint of* **Scott, D.& F. Publishing, Inc.**

Westwood Bks. Publishing, *(978-1-949006; 978-1-64361; 978-0-578-41199-6; 978-0-578-41203-0; 978-0-578-41224-5; 978-0-578-41227-6; 978-0-578-41235-1; 978-1-64803; 978-1-68536; 979-8-88887)* 11416 SW Aventino Dr., Port Saint Lucie, FL 90064 USA Tel 888-420-8640
E-mail: admin@westwoodbookspublishing.com
Web site: www.westwoodbookspublishing.com.

Westwood Pr., Inc., *(978-0-936159)* 116 E. 16th St., New York, NY 10003-2112 USA (SAN 696-7183) Tel 212-420-8008 Do not confuse with Westwoods Press, Darien, CT.

Wever Books *See* **Red Engine Pr.**

WeWrite LLC, *(978-1-57635; 978-1-884987)* Orders Addr.: P.O. Box 593, Ben Lomond, CA 95005 USA Tel 831-336-3382; Fax: 831-336-8592; Toll Free: 800-295-9037; Edit Addr.: 11040 Alba Rd., Ben Lomond, CA 95005-9220 USA
E-mail: info@wewrite.net
Web site: http://www.wewrite.net.

Wexford College Pr., *(978-0-9709917; 978-0-9721786; 978-0-9726596)* P.O. Box 2839, Gearhart, OR 97138 USA; *Imprints:* Watchmaker Publishing (Watchmaker Pub)
E-mail: info@wexfordcollegepress.com; info@watchmakerpublishing.com
Web site: http://www.wexfordcollegepress.com; http://www.thenewsoutherngentleman.com/; http://merchantbooksonline.com/; http://www.roughdraftprinting.com/; http://www.watchmakerpublishing.com/index.html.

WGH Arts LLC, *(978-0-9776562)* P.O. Box 215, Lisbon, IA 52253-0215 USA
E-mail: bill@wgharts.com
Web site: http://www.wgharts.com.

WHA Publishing, *(978-0-9773228)* P.O. Box 20818, Wickenburg, AZ 85358 USA Tel 520-877-7860; Fax: 520-877-7869
E-mail: jerry@datssoftware.com.

Whale Pr. Bks., *(978-1-7325315; 979-8-88549)* 30 Jamaicaway, Apt 3, Boston, MA 02130 USA Tel 814-795-2552
E-mail: lukmitchell@gmail.com.

Whale Tale Pr., *(978-0-9824784)* 343 Hertford Cir., Decatur, GA 30030 USA
Web site: http://www.whaletalepress.com.

Whaleback Publishing, *(978-0-9725938)* 4 Captain's Way, Exeter, NH 03833 USA Fax: 603-772-5416; Toll Free: 800-207-2580
Web site: http://www.whalebackpublishing.com.

Whaler, Norman / Beneath Another Sky Bks., *(978-1-948131)* 2150 Ctr. Ave, Fort Lee, NJ 07024 USA Tel 201-927-0787
E-mail: normwhaler@gmail.com
Web site: normanwhaler.com.

Whale's Jaw Publishing, *(978-0-9740778)* 11 Dennison St., Gloucester, MA 01930 USA Tel 978-281-9684
E-mail: info@whalesjaw.com; chetbrig@comcast.net
Web site: http://www.whalesjaw.com.

Whale's Library, The *See* **Mindsong Math**

What If Pr., *(978-0-9977867)* 4102 S Little Valley Rd, St. George, UT 84790 USA Tel 408-460-7316
E-mail: karen@karenlynnbennett.com
Web site: karenlynnbennett.com.

What If? Publishing, *(978-0-692-81041-5; 978-0-692-90430-5; 978-0-9995878)* 133 E. 4th St., Loveland, CO 80537 USA Tel 970-667-0292
E-mail: liz@whatifideation.com
Web site: whatifpublishing.com.

What on Earth Books, The Black Barn Wickhurst Farm, Tonbridge Kent, TN11 8PS GBR; 6670 New Nashville Hwy Suite 120, Smyrna, TN 37167; *Imprints:* Britannica Books (BRTNCA)
Dist(s): **Encyclopaedia Britannica, Inc.**
Ingram Publisher Services.

What The Flux Media, Incorporated *See* **Ark Watch Holdings LLC**

WhatAboutABoo Productions, *(978-1-7328172)* 31 Olive Ct., Novato, CA 94945 USA Tel 415-235-9322
E-mail: buffypoet@gmail.com
Web site: buffyfordstewart.com.

Whatever is Lovely Publications LLC *See* **Whatever Is Lovely Pubns. LLC**

Whatever Is Lovely Pubns. LLC, *(978-0-615-67198-7; 978-1-948384)* 19 Eagle Rock Rd., Questa, NM 87556 USA Tel 575-404-1840
Dist(s): **CreateSpace Independent Publishing Platform.**

Whatever Publishing, Incorporated *See* **New World Library**

Wheat, Etoya, *(978-0-578-67610-4; 978-0-578-81539-8)* 209b ne main st, lees summit, MO 64063 USA Tel 816-778-6075
E-mail: el.miniwheat@gmail.com.

Wheat Penny Pr., *(978-1-7340901; 978-1-7362410; 978-1-7369497; 979-8-9868273)* P.O. Box 210, New Egypt, NJ 08533 USA Tel 917-355-4496
E-mail: rebekah.borucki@gmail.com
Dist(s): **Simon & Schuster, Inc.**

Wheat Publishing House *See* **Ken Bangs Writing**

Wheat State Media LLC, *(978-0-9882892)* 21606 W. 52nd St., Shawnee, KS 66226 USA Tel 816-668-8400
E-mail: bhowell@wheatstatemedia.com
Web site: http://www.wheatstatemedia.com
Dist(s): **Anchor Distributors.**

Wheatland Hse. publising, *(978-0-9963659; 978-0-692-13259-3)* 36969 53Rd St., Burlington, WI 53105 USA Tel 262-661-4546
E-mail: kbhumphrey@gmail.com.

Wheatland House publising *See* **Wheatland Hse. publising**

Wheatmark, Inc., *(978-1-58736; 978-1-60494; 978-1-62787; 979-8-88747)* 2030 E. Speedway Blvd., Suite 106, Tucson, AZ 85719 USA (SAN 253-1054) Tel 520-798-0888; Fax: 520-798-3394; Toll Free: 888-934-0888; *Imprints:* Starbound Books (Starbound Bks); Press Box Books (Pr Box Bks)
E-mail: sam@wheatmark.com; lori@wheatmark.com
Web site: http://www.wheatmark.com
Dist(s): **INscribe Digital.**

Wheaton-Smith, Simon, *(978-0-9765286)* 810 W. 6th St., Silver City, NM 88061 USA
E-mail: illustratingshadows@yahoo.com
Web site: http://www.illustratingshadows.com/.

WHEEL Council, Inc., The, *(978-0-9656732; 978-0-9728889)* P.O. Box 22517, Flagstaff, AZ 86002 USA Tel 928-214-0120
E-mail: info@wheelcouncil.org
Web site: http://www.wheelcouncil.org.

Wheeler Publishing, Inc. *Imprint of* **Cengage Gale**

Wheeler, Zachry, *(978-0-9982049; 978-1-9991027; 978-1-954153; 978-1-7771184)* 1037 NE 65th St No. 80852, Seattle, WA 98115 USA; *Imprints:* Mayhematic Press (MYID_N_MAYHEMA)
E-mail: zachrywheeler@gmail.com
Web site: http://www.zachrywheeler.com.

Wheelhouse Publishing, *(978-0-692-56894-1; 978-0-692-56905-4; 978-0-692-56909-2; 978-0-9977493; 978-1-947076)* 44519 N 10th St, New River, AZ 85087 USA Tel 425-891-8174
E-mail: villagiorello@gmail.com
Dist(s): **CreateSpace Independent Publishing Platform.**

When I Grow Up Publishing, Inc., *(978-0-9795117)* 3721 Chelton Rd., Shaker Hts., OH 44120 USA
E-mail: erinn@theblackcrayon.com
Web site: http://www.theblackcrayon.com.

When Miss Bluebird Died, L.L.C., *(978-0-692-92432-7)* P.O. Box 35454, PHOENIX, AZ 85069 USA Tel 831-917-1142
E-mail: jenreich1973@gmail.com
Dist(s): **Ingram Content Group.**

When We Read, *(978-1-7374202)* 11 Bentley Ln., Rome, GA 30165 USA Tel 423-400-1850
E-mail: anndvs33@gmail.com.

whenpigsjig *See* **Whenpigsjig**

Whenpigsjig, *(978-0-9989924)* 63 S. 1st E., Snowflake, AZ 85937 USA Tel 928-243-1441
E-mail: whenpigsjig@gmail.com.

Where Madi Goes, *(978-0-578-99471-0)* 2850 Delk Rd Apt 8A, Marietta, GA 30067 USA Tel 216-798-9626
E-mail: Miancawoodall@yahoo.com.

Where? Pr., Inc., *(978-0-9719144)* Orders Addr.: P.O. Box 154, Paintsville, KY 41240 USA Tel 606-789-9423; Edit Addr.: 830 Robin Ct., Paintsville, KY 41240 USA
E-mail: wherepress@mail.com
Web site: http://www.wherepress.netfirms.com.

Where-I-Live / Foster Pr., *(978-0-9764893)* 430 91st Ave., NE, Suite 3, Everett, WA 98205 USA Tel 425-334-9317; Fax: 425-334-8155
E-mail: vern@fosterpress.com
Web site: http://www.fosterpress.com.

Whimble Designs, *(978-0-9773523)* 1540/42 Monroe Dr., NE, Atlanta, GA 30324 USA.

WhipperSnapper Bks., *(978-0-9657218)* P.O. Box 3186, Los Altos, CA 94024 USA 925-249-0709 (orders/general); Toll Free: 800-910-4482.

Whipple, Natalie, *(978-0-9911785)* 1937 W. 800 N., Pleasant Grove, UT 84062 USA Tel 801-471-5169
E-mail: nataliewhipple@hotmail.com
Web site: nataliewhipple.com.

Whippoorwill, LLC, *(978-0-9741968)* 9601 Linden St., Overland Park, KS 66207 USA (SAN 255-6553) Tel 913-341-7104; Fax: 913-385-2453
E-mail: schase@mischomeloans.com.

Whipsaw Pr., *(978-0-9899005; 978-0-9970233; 978-1-946910)* 1131 NW Morgan Ln, Grants Pass, OR 97526 USA Tel 541-295-5662; Fax: 866-645-4232
E-mail: frank@frankmorin.org
Web site: www.frankmorin.org.

Whirling Dirvish Publishing, *(978-0-9768870)* 26895 Aliso Creek Rd., Suite B591, Aliso Viejo, CA 92656 USA Tel 949-643-1865; Fax: 949-606-7180; Toll Free: 800-993-1291
E-mail: info@whirlingdirvish.com
Web site: http://www.whirlingdirvish.com/.

Whirlwhim, *(978-0-9800274)* 12930 Ventura Blvd., Studio City, CA 91604 USA
E-mail: whirlwhim@yahoo.com
Web site: http://www.blunderbrothers.com.

Whirlwind Publishing Group, *(978-0-9882643)* 2506 Bridal Wreath Ln., Dallas, TX 75233 USA Tel 858-220-2917
E-mail: lolahawk@hotmail.com
Web site: www.whirlwindpublishinggroup.com
Dist(s): **CreateSpace Independent Publishing Platform.**

Whiskey & Willow Publishing, *(978-1-7325592)* 6335 Bismark, Colorado Springs, CO 80922 USA Tel 832-520-9035
E-mail: author@robindmahle.com
Web site: robindmahle.com.

Whiskey Creek Pr. *Imprint of* **Whiskey Creek Pr., LLC**

Whiskey Creek Pr., LLC, *(978-1-59374; 978-1-60313; 978-1-61160)* Orders Addr.: 609 Greenwich St. 6th Fl, New York, NY 10014 USA Tel 212-431-5455; Fax: 917-464-6394; *Imprints:* Whiskey Creek Press (Whisk Creek Pr)
E-mail: publishing@start-media.com
Web site: http://www.whiskeycreekpress.com; http://www.whiskeycreekpresstorrid.com
Dist(s): **All Romance Ebooks, LLC**
OverDrive, Inc.
Simon & Schuster, Inc.

Whiskey Creek Restorations, *(978-0-9625756)* 7205 68th Ave., S.W., Elgin, ND 58533 USA Tel 218-354-2253.

Whispering Pine Press, Incorporated *See* **Whispering Pine Pr. International, Inc.**

Whispering Pine Pr. International, Inc., *(978-0-9679368; 978-1-930948; 978-1-59210; 978-1-59434; 978-1-59649; 978-1-59808)* Orders Addr.: P.O. Box 70, Greenacres, WA 99016-0070 USA (SAN 253-200X) Tel 509-928-7888; Fax: 509-922-9949; Edit Addr.: 1710 N. Aladdin Rd., Liberty Lake, WA 99016 USA
E-mail: whisperingpinepress@outlook.com
Web site: http://www.whisperingpinepress.com; http://www.whisperingpinepressbookstore.com.

Whispering Wind Publishing Inc., *(978-0-9721640)* Orders Addr.: 11089 Utica Ct., Westminster, CO 80031-2057 USA Tel 303-717-6442
E-mail: KaKillam@cs.com; publisher@whisperingwind.org
Web site: http://www.whisperingwind.org
Dist(s): **Quality Bks., Inc.**

Whistle Pr., The, *(978-0-9624893)* P.O. Box 1006, Petal, MS 39465-8618 USA Tel 601-544-8486 (phone/fax)
E-mail: contact@whistlepress.com
Web site: www.whistlepress.com.

Whitaker Hse., *(978-0-88368; 978-1-60374; 978-1-62911; 978-1-64123; 979-8-88769)* Div. of Whitaker Corp., 1030 Hunt Valley Cir., New Kensington, PA 15068 USA (SAN 203-2104) Tel 724-334-7000 Whitaker House/Anchor Distributors; Fax: 724-334-1200 Anchor Distributors; Toll Free Fax: 866-773-7001 Whitaker House; 800-765-1960 Anchor Distributors; Toll Free: 877-793-9800 Whitaker House; 800-444-4484 Whitaker House/Anchor Distributors
E-mail: sales@whitakerhouse.com
Web site: http://www.whitakerhouse.com/; http://www.anchordistributors.com/; http://www.amazon.com/
Dist(s): **Anchor Distributors.**

Whitaker, Thurston Information Services, LLC, *(978-0-9758940; 978-0-9892525)* P.O. Box 271743, West Hartford, CT 06127-1743 USA Tel 860-922-4719
E-mail: gwhit@twisbiz.com
Web site: http://www.thurstonwhitaker.com.

Whitcombe, Renee *See* **Budding Family Publishing**

White Bird Pubns., *(978-0-9828024; 978-1-937690; 978-1-63363)* P.O. Box 90145, Austin, TX 78749 USA
E-mail: whitebirdpublications@gmail.com
Web site: http://www.whitebirdpublications.com.

White Cloud Pr., *(978-1-883991; 978-0-9745245; 978-0-9793840; 978-1-935952; 978-1-940468)* Orders Addr.: P.O. Box 3400, Ashland, OR 97520 USA; Edit Addr.: 300 E. Hersey St., #11, Ashland, OR 97520-6200 USA Fax: 541-482-7708; Toll Free: 800-380-8286 Do not confuse with White Cloud Pr. in Hobbs, NM
Web site: http://www.whitecloudpress.com
Dist(s): **MyiLibrary**
Publishers Group West (PGW).

White Dharma Ltd., *(978-0-9907781)* P.O. Box 390251, Cambridge, MA 02139 USA Tel 617-299-0883
E-mail: whitedharmaltd@gmail.com.

White Dog Pr., Ltd, *(978-0-9741027; 978-0-615-43844-3; 978-0-9855823; 978-0-615-93256-9; 978-0-692-48522-4)* 321 High School Rd., No. 393, Bainbridge Island, WA 98110-2977 USA Tel 206-661-5946
E-mail: whitedogpress@aol.com.

White Dog Studio, *(978-0-9667286; 978-0-9897882)* Orders Addr.: P.O. Box 189, Louisville, TN 37777 USA Tel 865-776-9886; Edit Addr.: 3825 Island Path, Louisville, TN 37777 USA
E-mail: jprince1@mac.com
Web site: http://www.newcooksinamerica.com; www.missjanetsglutenfreeamerica.

White Eagle Publishing Trust (GBR) *(978-0-85487) Dist. by* **DeVorss.**

White Falcon Publishing *Imprint of* **White Falcon Publishing**

White Falcon Publishing, *(978-1-943851; 978-1-947293; 978-1-63640; 979-8-89222)* 4637 Silvertide Dr., Union City, CA 94587 USA Tel 404-771-6653; *Imprints:* White Falcon Publishing (WhiteFalc Pub)
E-mail: whitefalconpublishing@gmail.com.

White Falcon Publishing Platform *See* **White Falcon Publishing**

White Feather Press, LLC *See* **White Feather Pr., LLC**

White Feather Pr., LLC, *(978-0-9766083; 978-0-9822487; 978-0-9831751; 978-1-61808)* 579 119th Ave, Martin, MI 49070 USA
E-mail: skipcoryell@hotmail.com
Web site: http://www.whitefeatherpress.com
Dist(s): **Smashwords.**

White Feather Publishing, *(978-0-9740413)* 5595 White Feather Way, Placerville, CA 95667 USA
E-mail: whitefeather@directcom.net.

White Flower Bks., *(978-0-578-77655-2)* 35 Rockland St, NATICK, MA 01760 USA Tel 614-961-9456
E-mail: andreakmarshall@gmail.com.

White Hare Publishing LLC, *(978-0-578-17267-5; 978-0-578-17268-2; 978-0-692-88819-3; 978-0-692-94388-5; 978-0-692-95475-1; 978-0-578-55881-3)* 8660 Fox Ridge Ln., Indianapolis, IN 46256 USA Tel 317-578-8356
E-mail: pbenages.whiteharepub@gmail.com.

White Hat Communications, *(978-0-9653653; 978-1-929109; 978-0-615-62872-1)* Orders Addr.: P.O. Box 5390, Harrisburg, PA 17110-0390 USA Tel

717-238-3787; Fax: 717-238-2090; Edit Addr.: 2793 Old Post Rd., Suite 13, Harrisburg, PA 17110 USA
E-mail: Linda.grobman@paonline.com; lindagrobman@gmail.com
Web site: http://www.whitehatcommunications.com; http://www.socialworker.com
Dist(s): **CreateSpace Independent Publishing Platform**
Smashwords.

White Heat Ltd., *(978-0-9740149; 978-0-9799108)* 901 N. Mcdonald St. Ste. 503, Mckinney, TX 75069-2166 USA
E-mail: info@whiteheatltd.com
Web site: http://www.whiteheatltd.com.

White Horse Bks., *(978-0-9744860; 978-0-9801406)* 1347 Glenmare St., Salt Lake City, UT 84105-2707 USA
Web site: http://www.whitehorsebooks.net.

White Horse Flying Pubns., *(978-0-615-28541-2; 978-0-615-41896-4; 978-0-9835647)* 24 N 28th St., Longport, NJ 08403 USA
E-mail: whitehorseflying@comcast.net.

White, Howard Ray *See* **Howard Ray White**

White, James C., *(978-0-9747752)* 7020 E. 28th Ter., Kansas City, MO 64129-1209 USA Do not confuse with James C. White in Ruston, LA
E-mail: jcwhite08@yahoo.com
Web site: http://www.jcwhite08.com.

White Kiser, Dolores, *(978-0-9766648)* 212 Quail Creek Rd., Durant, OK 74701-7543 USA
E-mail: wobblywh@yahoo.com.

White Knight Printing and Publishing, *(978-0-9725916)* 187 E. 670 S., Kamas, UT 84036 USA (SAN 853-3539) Tel 801-955-4504; Fax: 801-955-5324
E-mail: johnmsimmons@whiteknightpublish.com; brigdist@sisna.com; careenlancaster@whiteknightpublish.com
Web site: http://www.brighamdistributing.com; http://www.whiteknightpublish.com
Dist(s): **Brigham Distribution.**

White Line Productions Inc., *(978-0-9729965)* P.O. Box 248411, Coral Gables, FL 33124 USA Tel 305-663-3235
E-mail: lcoll@bewaretheunknown.com
Web site: http://www.bewaretheunknown.com.

White Lion Pr., *(978-0-9615707; 978-1-886942)* 225 E. Fifth St., No. 4D, New York, NY 10003 USA (SAN 695-7919) Tel 212-982-5518; Toll Free: 800-243-9642
Dist(s): **New Leaf Distributing Co., Inc.**

White Mane Kids *Imprint of* **White Mane Publishing Co., Inc.**

White Mane Publishing Co., Inc., *(978-0-942597; 978-1-57249)* Orders Addr.: P.O. Box 708, Shippensburg, PA 17257 USA (SAN 667-1926) Tel 717-532-2237; Fax: 717-532-6110; Toll Free: 888-948-6263; *Imprints:* White Mane Kids (WM Kids)
E-mail: marketing@whitemane.com
Web site: http://www.whitemane.com.

White Media Works, *(978-0-9905386; 978-1-64145)* 16496 Bernardo Ctr. Dr., San Diego, CA 92128 USA Tel 619-922-1579
E-mail: swhite@yinpop.com.

White Oak Creative, *(978-0-9763562)* 26415 W. Stonebriar Way, Channahon, IL 60410-8740 USA Tel 815-922-2890; Fax: 815-521-0042 Do not confuse with White Oak Publishing in Reed Springs, MO; Galena, MO; Sewickley, PA; Portland, OR
E-mail: kashmir37@aol.com.

White Owl Publishing, *(978-1-891691)* P.O. Box 1180, Redding, CA 96001 USA Tel 530-241-1921 Do not confuse with White Owl Publishing, Wellington, KS,
E-mail: editor@whiteowlweb.com
Web site: http://whiteowlweb.com
Dist(s): **Smashwords.**

White Parrot Pr. *Imprint of* **First Steps Publishing**

White Pelican Pr., *(978-0-9625544)* 1805 Cedar Ridge Dr., Austin, TX 78741 USA Tel 512-477-5211 Do not confuse with companies with the same name in Windsor, CO, Sharpsburg, GA.

White Phoenix, *(978-0-9886472)* 405 Litchfield Dr., Moore, SC 29369 USA Tel 847-848-6307
E-mail: ghallium50@yahoo.com.

White Rhino Pr., *(978-0-9704122)* Div. of The Patnaude Corp., Orders Addr.: 6068 Windsor Farm Rd., Summerfield, NC 273589053 USA Tel 336-253-8987; Fax: 336-644-7849
E-mail: joy@patnaude.com.

White Rhino Publishing *See* **White Rhino Pr.**

White, Russ, *(978-0-9742885)* 122 E. Oak Hill Dr., Florence, AL 35633 USA.

White Stag Pr., *(978-0-9792583; 978-0-9828216)* Div. of Publishers Design Group, Inc., P.O. Box 37, Roseville, CA 95678 USA (SAN 852-9353) Tel 916-784-0500; Fax: 916-773-7421; Toll Free: 800-587-6666
E-mail: orders@publishersdesign.com
Web site: http://www.publishersdesign.com.

White Star *Imprint of* **Rizzoli International Pubns., Inc.**

White Star Publishers (ITA) *(978-88-8095; 978-88-544; 978-88-7844; 978-88-540) Dist. by* **Random.**

White Star Publishers (ITA) *(978-88-8095; 978-88-544; 978-88-7844; 978-88-540) Dist. by* **Sterling.**

White Stone Bks., *(978-1-59379)* P.O. Box 35035, Tulsa, OK 74153 USA Toll Free: 866-253-8622 Do not confuse with White Stone Books in Atlanta, MI
E-mail: amandap@whitestonebooks.com
Web site: http://www.whitestonebooks.com
Dist(s): **Distributors, The**
Harrison House Pubs.

White Stone Publications *See* **Fair Havens Pubns.**

White Stone Publishing *See* **Matisse Studios**

White, T. *See* **twhiteart**

White, Terry, *(978-0-9755835)* P.O. Box 760399, Southfield, MI 48076-0399 USA.

White Tiger Pr. *Imprint of* **Homes for the Homeless Institute, Inc.**

White Tulip Publishing, *(978-0-9746890)* Orders Addr.: P.O. Box 645, Brewster, NY 10509 USA Tel 917-514-7701
E-mail: wtime2write@aol.com
Web site: http://www.whitetulippublishing.com
Dist(s): **Quality Bks., Inc.**

White Turtle Bks., *(978-1-933482)* P.O. Box 2113, North Mankato, MN 56003 USA Tel 605-770-5385
E-mail: info@whiteturtlebooks.com.

White Wolf Publishing, Inc., *(978-0-9627790; 978-1-56504; 978-1-58846)* 2075 W. Park Place Blvd. Ste. G, Stone Mtn, GA 30087-3542 USA (SAN 299-1349) Toll Free: 800-454-9653 Do not confuse with White Wolf Publishing, Cresson, TX
E-mail: dianez@white-wolf.com
Web site: http://www.white-wolf.com
Dist(s): **PSI (Publisher Services, Inc.).**

White Wolf Studio, Inc., *(978-0-9760654)* P.O. Box 490, Windermere, FL 34786 USA Tel 407-909-0889; Fax: 407-876-8462
E-mail: whitewolfstudio@aol.com
Web site: http://www.whitewolfstudio.com.

Whitecap Bks., Ltd. (CAN) *(978-0-920620; 978-0-921061; 978-0-921396; 978-1-55110; 978-1-895099; 978-1-55285; 978-1-77050) Dist. by* **IPG Chicago.**

Whitecap Bks., Ltd. (CAN) *(978-0-920620; 978-0-921061; 978-0-921396; 978-1-55110; 978-1-895099; 978-1-55285; 978-1-77050) Dist. by* **Firefly Bks Limited.**

Whitecap Bks., Ltd. (CAN) *(978-0-920620; 978-0-921061; 978-0-921396; 978-1-55110; 978-1-895099; 978-1-55285; 978-1-77050) Dist. by* **Wizard Works.**

Whitecaps Media, *(978-0-9758577; 978-0-9826353; 978-0-9836825; 978-0-9883628; 978-1-942732)* P.O. Box 680568, Houston, TX 77268-0568 USA
Web site: http://www.whitecapsmedia.com
Dist(s): **Partners Bk. Distributing, Inc.**

Whitedove Pr., *(978-0-9714908; 978-0-615-11118-6; 978-0-615-11600-6)* Orders Addr.: 401 Thornton Rd, Lithia Springs, GA 30112 USA Tel 800-326-2665; Edit Addr.: 2728 Davie Blvd. 226, Fort Lauderdale, FL 33312 USA Tel 954-981-2828; 954-981-2828; 2728 Davie Blvd No. 226, fort Lauderdale, FL 33312 Tel 954-981-2828
E-mail: mail@michelleWhitedove.com
Web site: http://www.michellewhitedove.com
Dist(s): **New Leaf Distributing Co., Inc.**

WhiteFire Printing & Design *See* **WhiteFire Publishing**

WhiteFire Publishing, *(978-0-9765444; 978-0-9834556; 978-1-939023; 978-1-946531; 979-8-88709)* Div. of WhiteFire Printing & Design, Inc., Orders Addr.: 13607 Bedford Rd., NE, Cumberland, MD 21502 USA (SAN 256-4238) Tel 443-321-3663; Fax: 443-321-3675; *Imprints:* WhiteSpark Publishing (MYID_T_WHITESP)
E-mail: info@whitefire-publishing.com
Web site: http://www.whitefireprinting.com
Dist(s): **eBookit.com.**

Whitegate Books *See* **Wild daisy art**

Whitehead, D. Literature, *(978-0-9972943)* 14854 depot Dr., Neosho, MO 64850 USA Tel 417-389-2773
E-mail: plantatree.doug@gmail.com
Web site: www.whiteheadliterature.com.

Whitehead, Judith, *(978-0-615-23987-3)* 5686 Fieldbrook Dr., East Amherst, NY 14051 USA Tel 716-238-5547
E-mail: juju8451@yahoo.com
Web site: http://myspace.com.

Whitehouse Publishing, *(978-0-9644171)* 6556 Mckenna Way, Alexandria, VA 22315-5571 USA Do not confuse with Whithouse Publishing in Corning, NY
E-mail: erw192@hotmail.com
Web site: http://users.starpower.net/whitee/bookcover/treasure.html

Whitehouse Publishing, *(978-1-933031)* P.O. Box 16, Corning, NY 14830 USA Toll Free: 800-784-0537 Do not confuse with Whitehouse Publishing in Alexandria, VA
E-mail: ew@compostinternational.org
Web site: http://www.whitehouse-publishing.com.

Whitepoint Pr., *(978-0-615-51020-0; 978-0-615-51021-7; 978-0-615-51022-4; 978-0-615-74499-5; 978-0-615-77099-4; 978-0-615-79369-6; 978-0-615-84585-2; 978-0-9898971; 978-1-944856)* 1809 S. Meyler St, San Pedro, CA 90731 USA Tel 310-940-1428
Web site: www.whitepointpress.com
Dist(s): **CreateSpace Independent Publishing Platform**
Dummy Record Do Not USE!!!!
Smashwords.

WhiteSpark Publishing *Imprint of* **WhiteFire Publishing**

Whiting, James Maxwell, *(978-0-692-94033-4; 979-8-218-05662-9)* 1262 Ruberta Ave., GLENDALE, CA 91201 USA Tel 818-406-3851
E-mail: jiamwfamily@gmail.com
Dist(s): **Ingram Content Group.**

Whitis, Cindy, *(978-0-615-17079-4)* 9018 Imperial Dr., Indianapolis, IN 46239 USA
E-mail: jim.whitis@sbcglobal.net.

Whitline Ink, Inc., *(978-1-930154)* Orders Addr.: P.O. Box 668, Boonville, NC 27011 USA Tel 336-367-6914; Fax: 336-367-6913; Edit Addr.: Hwy. 601 S., Boonville, NC 27011 USA
E-mail: whitlineink@yadtel.net
Dist(s): **Parnassus Bk. Distributors.**

Whitlock Publishing, *(978-0-9770956; 978-1-943115)* 16 High St, Alfred, NY 14802-1303 USA.

†**Whitman, Albert & Co.,** *(978-0-8075)* 250 S. Northwest Hwy. # 320, Park Ridge, IL 60068-4237 USA (SAN 201-2049) Toll Free: 800-255-7675; *Imprints:* AW Teen (AW Teen)
E-mail: mail@awhitmanco.com
Web site: http://www.albertwhitman.com
Dist(s): **Children's Plus, Inc.**
Follett School Solutions
MyiLibrary
Open Road Distribution
Perfection Learning Corp.; *CIP.*

Whitman Publishing LLC, *(978-0-937458; 978-1-930849; 978-0-7948)* Div. of Anderson Press Inc., Orders Addr.: 4001 Helton Dr., Florence, AL 35030 USA Tel 256-246-1166; Toll Free: 800-528-3992; Edit Addr.: 3101 Clairmont Rd., NE, Suite C, Atlanta, GA 30329 USA (SAN 253-522X) Tel 404-214-4300; Fax: 404-214-4391; Toll Free: 800-528-3992
E-mail: info@whitmanbooks.com
Web site: http://www.whitmanbooks.com.

†**Whitmore Publishing Co.,** *(978-0-87426)* 1144 Riverview Ln., West Conshohocken, PA 19428-2964 USA (SAN 203-2112)
E-mail: production@whitmorepublishing.com; *CIP.*

Whittet Bks., Ltd. (GBR) *(978-0-905483; 978-1-873580) Dist. by* **Diamond Farm Bk.**

Whike, Traudl, *(978-1-68377)* 40 Main St., Newark, DE 19711 USA Toll Free: 888-248-4521
E-mail: colinwfscott@gmail.com.

Who Am I Pr., *(978-0-9774174)* 4444 Hazeltine Ave., No. 229, Sherman Oaks, CA 91423 USA Tel 818-501-5908
E-mail: lea@godwhoami.com
Web site: http://www.godwhoami.com.

Who Chains You *See* **Who Chains You Bks.**

Who Chains You Bks., *(978-0-615-19983-2; 978-0-615-21952-3; 978-0-578-01626-9; 978-0-9842897; 978-0-692-71696-0; 978-0-692-74473-4; 978-1-946044; 978-1-954039)* 618 N. 12th St., Tyrone, PA 16686 USA Tel 757-474-5474
E-mail: tami@tamiracithayne.com
Web site: http://www.whochainsyou.com; http://www.wcyhumanepress.com; http://www.crescentrenewal.com; http://www.freedomchaserbooks.com
Dist(s): **CreateSpace Independent Publishing Platform.**

Who Would Win?, *(978-0-9852032; 978-0-9863487)* 25 Channel Ctr. St. No. 404, Boston, MA 02210 USA Tel 781-608-0626; Fax: 781-465-7999
E-mail: gpallotta@vzw.blackberry.net
Web site: www.jerrypallotta.com.

Whole Heart Ministries, *(978-1-888692)* P.O. Box 3445, Monument, CO 80132 USA; *Imprints:* Whole Heart Press (WholeHeart)
E-mail: whm@wholeheart.org; admin@wholeheart.org
Web site: http://www.wholeheart.org/
Dist(s): **BookBaby.**

Whole Heart Pr. *Imprint of* **Whole Heart Ministries**

Whole Spirit Pr., *(978-1-892857)* 1905 S. Clarkson St., Denver, CO 80210 USA Tel 303-979-5820; 303-246-9554; Fax: 303-979-6151; Toll Free: 877-488-3774
E-mail: sales@wholespiritpress.com
Web site: http://www.wholespiritpress.com.

Whole Systems Support *See* **WiseWoman Pr.**

Wholemovement Pubns., *(978-0-9766773)* 1802 24th AV s No. 4, Grand Forks, ND 58201 USA Tel 773-794-9764
E-mail: bradhs@interaccess.com
Web site: http://www.wholemovement.com.

Wholesome Pr., *(978-1-943449)* 892 Cabaniss Cres, Pensacola, FL 32508 USA
E-mail: hello@wholesome.press
Web site: wholesome.press.

Wholesome Puppy Tales, *(978-0-9762466)* 13432 San Pasqual Rd., Escondido, CA 92025-7834 USA
E-mail: cmodicagraphics@aol.com
Web site: http://www.wholesomepuppytales.com.

Wholistic Unity LLC, *(979-8-9864484; 978-1-960212)* 545 Majestic Oak Dr., Apopka, FL 32712 USA Tel 407-325-6973
E-mail: veenu@wholisticunity.com.

Whorl Bks., *(978-0-9778850; 978-0-615-70205-6; 978-0-615-71111-9; 978-0-615-72898-8; 978-0-615-99191-7; 978-0-692-21281-3; 978-0-692-30046-6; 978-0-692-37390-3; 978-0-692-47723-6)* 5658 NW Pioneer Cir., Norman, OK 73072 USA (SAN 850-5713); *Imprints:* Dark Passages (Dark Passages); WhorlBooks Thumbprints (WhorlBks)
E-mail: whorlbooks@gmail.com; marilynahudson@yahoo.com
Web site: http://www.freewebs.com/whorlbooks/
Dist(s): **CreateSpace Independent Publishing Platform.**

WhorlBooks Thumbprints *Imprint of* **Whorl Bks.**

Who's There, Incorporated *See* **KnockKnock LLC**

Who's Who In Sports *Imprint of* **Guidry Assocs., Inc.**

Why Mom Deserves a Diamond, Incorporated *See* **Moon Over Mountains Publishing (M.O.M.)**

Whyitsme Design, *(978-0-9905812)* 15303 SE 179th St., Renton, WA 98058 USA Tel 206-371-6278
E-mail: p.hevly@gmail.com
Dist(s): **Ingram Publisher Services.**

Wicked Cow Studios, *(978-0-692-91823-4; 978-0-692-07098-7)* 45 W 21st St., New York, NY 10010 USA Tel 212-699-1888
E-mail: mr@wickedcow.com
Dist(s): **Diamond Comic Distributors, Inc.**

Wicked Stepsister Productions, *(978-0-692-10358-6; 978-0-692-12319-5; 978-0-578-41493-5)* 506 Lee St, Murfreesboro, TN 37130 USA Tel 615-483-3833
E-mail: michelle@iwokeupwell.com.

Wicked Tree Pr., *(978-0-9995707; 979-8-9874301)* 990 Mayo St., Los Angeles, CA 90042 USA Tel 323-547-2359
E-mail: judd.jessi@gmail.com
Web site: www.wickedtreepress.com; www.jessicamaisonjudd.com.

Wickenburg Healthcare Alliance *See* **WHA Publishing**

Wicker Park Pr., Ltd., *(978-0-9789676; 978-1-936679)* 334 Hawthorn Ave., Glencoe, IL 60022 USA Tel 773-391-1199
E-mail: eric@3ibooks.com
Web site: http://www.wickerparkpress.us.

Wicks, Valerie, *(978-0-615-71556-8; 978-0-9912594)* 831 1/2 Silver Lake Blvd., Los Angeles, CA 90026 USA Tel 678 3613895
Web site: www.sevenspectral.com
Dist(s): **CreateSpace Independent Publishing Platform.**

Wide Awake Bks., *(978-0-692-58328-9; 978-0-692-62187-5; 978-0-692-69791-7; 978-0-692-70967-2; 978-0-9978609; 978-1-947987)* P.O. Box 950794, Oklahoma City, OK 73195 USA Tel 405-588-7948
E-mail: success@40daypublishing.com
Web site: https://www.goldstarpress.com/; https://www.40daypublishing.com/; https://www.wideawakebooks.com
Dist(s): **CreateSpace Independent Publishing Platform.**

Wide World Publishing/Tetra, *(978-0-933174; 978-1-884550)* Orders Addr.: P.O. Box 476, San Carlos, CA 94070 USA (SAN 211-1462) Tel 650-593-2839; Fax: 650-595-0802
E-mail: wwpbl@aol.com
Web site: http://www.wideworldpublishing.com
Dist(s): **Booklines Hawaii, Ltd.**
Islander Group
Publishers Group West (PGW).

WideThinker Bks., *(978-0-9728195)* P.O. Box 30144, Philadelphia, PA 19146 USA Tel 215-985-0322; Toll Free: 866-236-1077
E-mail: wtb@widethinker.com
Web site: http://www.widethinkerbooks.com.

WiDo Publishing, *(978-0-9796070; 978-0-9830238; 978-1-937178; 978-1-947966)* Orders Addr.: 840 S W. TEMPLE APT 2, Salt Lake City, UT 84101 USA (SAN 853-8786) Tel 801-935-4357
E-mail: information@widopublishing.com
Web site: http://www.widopublishing.com.

†**Wiener, Markus Pubs., Inc.,** *(978-0-910129; 978-0-945179; 978-1-55876)* 231 Nassau St., Princeton, NJ 08542 USA (SAN 282-5465) Tel 609-921-1141; Fax: 609-921-1140
E-mail: publisher@markuswiener.com
Web site: http://www.markuswiener.com; *CIP.*

Wiese, Michael Productions, *(978-0-941188; 978-1-932907; 978-1-61593)* 6049 37th Ave. NE, Seattle, WA 98115 USA (SAN 237-9716) Tel 206-283-2948; Fax: 206-283-2072; Toll Free: 800-833-5738 (24 hours); 800-379-8808
E-mail: mwpsales@earthlink.net; kenlee@mwp.com
Web site: http://www.mwp.com
Dist(s): **Consortium Bk. Sales & Distribution**
Follett School Solutions
Ingram Publisher Services
MyiLibrary
Elsevier Science & Technology Bks.

Wiggies, Piggy, *(978-1-939076)* 150 Ocean Pk. Blvd. Ste 418, Santa Monica, CA 90405 USA Tel 310-666-0069
E-mail: emma@emmalouisebooks.com.

Wiggles Pr., *(978-0-9823906; 978-1-935706)* Orders Addr.: 23 Athens St. Suite 2, Cambridge, MA 02138 USA Tel 617-895-7698; 617-981-0285
E-mail: rochelle.thorpe@yahoo.com.

Wighita Pr., *(978-0-9786648)* P.O. Box 30399, Little Rock, AR 72260-0399 USA
E-mail: info@wighitapress.com
Web site: www.wighitapress.com.

Wigu Publishing *Imprint of* **Wigu Publishing**

Wigu Publishing, *(978-1-939973)* 4327 N. Nines Ridge Ln., Boise, ID 83702 USA; *Imprints:* Wigu Publishing (WiguPubng)
E-mail: beressler59@gmail.com
Web site: www.wigupublishing.com; www.whenigrowupbooks.com.

Wigwam Publishing, *(978-0-9721022)* Orders Addr.: P.O. Box 574, Weyauwega, WI 54983 USA; Edit Addr.: 410 S. Harlon St., No. 2, Weyauwega, WI 54983 USA Do not confuse with companies with the same or similar names in Villa Park, IL, Cheyenne, WY.

WigWam Publishing Co., *(978-1-930076)* Orders Addr.: P.O. Box 6992, Villa Park, IL 60181 USA; *Imprints:* New Leaf Books (New Leaf Books) Do not confuse with companies with the same or similar names in Weyauwega, WI, Cheyenne, WY
E-mail: info@newleafbooks.net
Web site: http://www.newleafbooks.net.

Wilander Publishing Co., *(978-0-9628335)* Orders Addr.: P.O. Box 56121, Portland, OR 97238 USA.

Wild About Coloring, *(978-0-692-91040-5; 978-0-692-98064-4)* P.O. Box 94, KEELER, CA 93530 USA Tel 760-608-7245
E-mail: elmirafoley@gmail.com
Dist(s): **Ingram Content Group.**

Wild About Learning, Inc., *(978-0-9789880)* 964 John St., Joliet, IL 60435 USA Tel 815-740-1173; Fax: 815-740-1174
E-mail: info@wildaboutlearning.org
Web site: http://wildaboutlearning.org.

Wild Animal Publishing, *(978-0-9769555)* 246 Meridian St., Westerly, RI 02891 USA
E-mail: sciarrajb@aol.com; keith@wildanimalpublishing.com
Web site: http://www.wildanimalpublishing.com.

Wild Child Education Co., *(978-1-7342645)* 200 Stuart Ave, Hanover, PA 17331 USA Tel 717-521-7367
E-mail: wildchildeducation@yahoo.com
Web site: www.wildchildeducation.com.

Wild Child Publishing, *(978-0-9771314; 978-1-934069; 978-1-935013; 978-1-936222; 978-1-61798)* P.O. Box 4897, Culver City, CA 90231 USA
E-mail: mgbaun@wildchildpublishing.com; mbaun@freyasbower.com
Web site: http://www.wildchildpublishing.com; http://www.freyasbower.com/
Dist(s): **All Romance Ebooks, LLC.**

Wild daisy art, *(978-0-9767570)* The Appletree, P.O. Box 84, Cowley, WY 82420 USA
E-mail: Lyn@wilddaisyart.com
Web site: http://www.appletreedesigns.com.

Wild Earth, *(978-0-9719807)* P.O. Box 407, Charlottesville, VA 22902-0407 USA Tel 434-977-4615 Toll Free: 800-871-5647
Web site: http://www.animalessence.com/.

Wild Flower Pr. *Imprint of* **Granite Publishing, LLC**

Wild Flower USA, *(978-0-9646698)* 26614 Oak Ridge Dr., Suite 110, The Woodlands, TX 77380 USA Tel 281-363-2360; Fax: 281-367-4480.
E-mail: dgibbes@wildharepublishing.com
Wild Goose Publishing, *(978-0-9792657; 978-0-9799255)* Orders Addr.: P.O. Box 386, Charlotte, MI 48813 USA
E-mail: wildgoosepub@sbcglobal.net.
Wild Hare Collective, *(978-0-692-90631-6)* 1981 Deep Woods Trail, NASHVILLE, TN 37214 USA Tel 260-908-1908
E-mail: jandra@jandralee.com
Dist(s): **Ingram Content Group.**
Wild Hare Publishing, *(978-0-9772096)* P.O. Box 2144, Ridgeland, MS 39158-2144 USA (SAN 256-9639) Tel 601-853-8120; Fax: 601-853-8121
E-mail: dgibbes@wildharepublishing.com
Wild Heart Ranch, Inc., *(978-0-9761768)* 1385 Gulf Rd., Suite 102, Point Roberts, WA 98281 USA Toll Free Fax: 866-735-3518; Toll Free: 888-889-9215
E-mail: dawn@wildheartranch.com
Web site: http://www.wildheartranch.com; http://www.isaahorses.com.
Wild Horses Publishing Co., *(978-0-937148; 978-0-9601088)* Orders Addr.: P.O. Box 1373, Los Altos, CA 94022 USA (SAN 211-8289)
E-mail: pwalatka@earthlink.net
Dist(s): **TNT Media Group, Inc.**
Wild Hunt Pr., *(978-1-7323657; 978-1-7358054)* 266 Pennsylvania St., Buffalo, NY 14201 USA Tel 716-208-1738
E-mail: godofthunder85@gmail.com.
Wild Ideas, *(978-0-9620031; 979-8-9867998)* P.O. Box 458, Greenwood, SC 29648-0458 USA (SAN 247-5448) Do not confuse with Wild Ideas, West Brattleboro VT. .
Wild Meadow *Imprint of* **Perri, Jessica**
Wild, Meredith *See* **Waterhouse Press LLC**
Wild Mind Creations, *(978-0-615-15138-0)* P.O. Box 1935, Fairview, OR 97024-1806 USA
E-mail: jmm1965mionda_4@msn.com.
Wild Nature Institute, *(978-0-9898182; 978-1-7323234)* PO Box 44, Weaverville, NC 28787 USA Tel 415-763-0348
E-mail: monica@wildnatureinstitute.org
Web site: www.wildnatureinstitute.org.
Wild Plum Woods Bks., *(978-0-9745581)* 39042 Ruann Ct., Zephyrhills, FL 33540 USA.
Wild Quail Publishing, *(978-0-9909329; 978-0-9964350; 978-0-9968637; 978-0-9981950; 978-0-9982824; 978-0-9992448; 978-1-7327494; 978-0-9999009; 978-1-954325; 978-1-959529; 978-1-962452)* 2759 S. Perrault Way, Boise, ID 83716 USA Tel 678-591-4378
E-mail: keim.judy@gmail.com.
Wild Roots Pr., *(978-0-9996199)* P.O. Box 733, Narberth, PA 19072 USA Tel 484-844-3803
E-mail: maryam.moss.arts@gmail.com
Web site: www.maryammoss.com.
Wild Rose *Imprint of* **Mayhaven Publishing, Inc.**
Wild Rose Pr., Inc., The, *(978-1-60154; 978-1-61217; 978-1-62830; 978-1-5092)* P.O. Box 708, Adams Basin, NY 14410 USA Tel 585-880-0819
E-mail: info@thewildrosepress.com
Web site: http://www.thewildrosepress.com.
Wild Soccer USA Inc. *See* **Sole Bks.**
Wild Willow Pr., *(978-0-9995444)* 4713 Derbyshire Dr., Antioch, TN 37013 USA Tel 703-786-0948
Dist(s): **CreateSpace Independent Publishing Platform.**
Wilde Art, *(978-0-9974828)* 21807 el Coyote Dr., Sonora, CA 95370 USA Tel 209-533-1261
E-mail: kwilde55@gmail.com
Web site: wilde-art.com.
Wilder Pubns., Corp., *(978-0-9773040; 978-1-934451; 978-1-60459; 978-1-61720; 978-1-62755; 978-1-63384; 978-1-5154)* .
Wilder Publications, Limited *See* **Wilder Pubns., Corp.**
Wilderness Pr. *Imprint of* **AdventureKEEN**
Wilderness Visions Press *See* **Cloudland.net Publishing**
Wildfire Enterprises, *(978-0-9771969)* Orders Addr.: P.O. Box 402, Viola, AR 72583-0402 USA Tel 870-458-3600 (phone/fax); Edit Addr.: P O Box 402, Viola, AR 72583-0402 USA
E-mail: wfenterprises@hotmail.com
Web site: http://www.wildfireenterprises.iceryder.net.
Wildfire Publishing International Pty, Ltd. (AUS) *(978-0-9585365) Dist. by* **HachBkGrp.**
Wildflower Pr., The, *(978-0-9714343; 978-0-9779933)* P.O. Box 4757, Albuquerque, NM 87196-4757 USA Tel 505-296-0691; Fax: 505-296-6124 Do not confuse with companies with the same or similar name in Oceanside, CA ,Phoenix, AZ ,Littleton, CO
E-mail: jspoetry@aol.com
Dist(s): **Smashwords.**
Wildflower Run, *(978-0-9667086)* Orders Addr.: P.O. Box 9656, College Station, TX 77842 USA Tel 979-764-0166
E-mail: atmgold@aol.com
Web site: http://www.aggiegoose.com.
Wildlife Education, Limited *See* **National Wildlife Federation**
Wildlife Tales Publishing, *(978-0-9793207)* Div. of Ark R.A.I.N. Wildlife Sanctuary, Inc., P.O. Box 721, Brownsville, TN 38012-0721 USA Toll Free: 877-352-6657
E-mail: books@wildlifetalespublishing.com
Web site: http://www.wildlifetalespublishing.com.
Wildly Austin, *(978-0-9753990)* P.O. Box 161987, Austin, TX 78716-1987 USA
E-mail: vikki@wildlyaustin.com; vl@intersourcesearch.com
Web site: http://www.wildlyaustin.com.
Wildot Pr., *(978-0-9789043; 978-0-9797933)* 4402 W. Creedance Blvd., Glendale, AZ 85310-3921 USA Tel 623-434-2636
E-mail: wildotpress@cox.net
Web site: http://ww.wildotpress.com.
Wildside Pr., LLC, *(978-0-8095; 978-0-913960; 978-1-880448; 978-1-58715; 978-1-59224; 978-1-4344; 978-1-4794; 978-1-6676)* Orders Addr.: 7945 MacArthur Blvd., Suite 215, Cabin John, MD 20818 USA Tel 301-762-1305; Fax: 301-762-1306; Edit Addr.: 7945 MacArthur Blvd., Suite 215 Ste. 215, Cabin John, MD 20818 USA Tel 301-762-1305
E-mail: wildsidepress@gmail.com; wildsidepress@yahoo.com
Web site: http://www.wildsidepress.com; http://www.wildsidebooks.com; blackcatweekly.com
Dist(s): **Diamond Comic Distributors, Inc.**
Diamond Bk. Distributors
MyiLibrary
Wildstone Media, *(978-1-882467)* Orders Addr.: P.O. Box 511580, Saint Louis, MO 63151 USA Tel 314-482-8472; Fax: 314-487-1910; Toll Free: 800-296-1918
E-mail: wildstone@mlc.net
Web site: http://www.wildstonemedia.com
Dist(s): **Anderson News, LLC**
Big River Distribution
BookBaby.
Wildstorm *Imprint of* **DC Comics**
WildWest Publishing, *(978-0-9721800)* P.O. Box 11658, Olympia, WA 98508 USA
E-mail: clamityJan@aol.com
Web site: http://www.CalamityJan.com.
WildWing Pr., *(978-0-9798768; 978-0-9912715; 978-0-9976420; 978-0-9983149)* 3301 Brandywine Ct., Bellingham, WA 98226 USA
E-mail: editor@wildwingpress.com
Web site: http://www.wildwingpress.com
Dist(s): **Outskirts Pr., Inc.**
Smashwords.
Wiley *Imprint of* **Wiley, John & Sons, Inc.**
Wiley, Brandie, *(978-0-692-96976-2)* 5024 Waterford Dr., Fort Worth, TX 76179 USA Tel 682-559-9899
E-mail: brandiewiley@sbcglobal.net
Web site: HomeIsWhereTheAutismIs.com.
Wiley, John & Sons Canada, Ltd, (CAN) *(978-0-471; 978-0-939246) Dist. by* **TwoRivers.**
†Wiley, John & Sons, Inc., *(978-0-470; 978-0-471; 978-0-7645; 978-0-7821; 978-0-8260; 978-0-87605; 978-0-88422; 978-0-914993; 978-0-937721; 978-0-939246; 978-1-55828; 978-1-56217; 978-1-56561; 978-1-56884; 978-1-57313; 978-1-58245; 978-1-878058; 978-1-118; 978-1-119; 978-1-7994; 978-1-394; 979-8-203) Orders Addr.: c/o John Wiley & Sons, Inc., United States Distribution Ctr., 1 Wiley Dr., Somerset, NJ 08875-1272 USA Tel 732-469-4400; Fax: 732-302-2300; Toll Free Fax: 800-597-3299; Toll Free: 800-225-5945 (orders); Edit Addr.: 111 River St., Hoboken, NJ 07030 USA (SAN 200-2272) Tel 201-748-6000; 201-748-6276 (Retail and Wholesale); Fax: 201-748-6088; 201-748-8641 (Retail and Wholesale); Imprints:* Wiley-VCH (Wiley-VCH); Jossey-Bass (Jossey-Bass); For Dummies (For Dummies); Howell Book House (HBH); Capstone (CapstW); Wiley (JWiley); Wiley-Blackwell (WileyBlack)
E-mail: compbks@wiley.com; bookinfo@wiley.com; custserv@wiley.com
Web site: http://www.wiley.com/compbooks; http://www.interscience.wiley.com; http://www.wiley.com
Dist(s): **Casemate Pubs. & Bk. Distributors, LLC**
Ebsco Publishing
Follett School Solutions
Leonard, Hal Corp.
Ingram Content Group
Lippincott Williams & Wilkins
MBI Distribution Services/Quayside Distribution
Mastery Education
Mel Bay Pubns., Inc.
MyiLibrary
Open Road Integrated Media, Inc.
Pearson Education
TNT Media Group, Inc.
Urban Land Institute
ebrary, Inc.; *CIP.*
Wiley OBrien Worksapce *See* **OBrien, Wiley Workspace**
Wiley-Blackwell *Imprint of* **Wiley, John & Sons, Inc.**
Wiley-VCH *Imprint of* **Wiley, John & Sons, Inc.**
Wilfrid Laurier Univ. Pr. (CAN) *(978-0-88920; 978-0-921821; 978-1-55458; 978-1-77112) Dist. by* **TwoRivers.**
Wilkes Publishing Co., Inc., *(978-0-9747755)* P.O. Box 340, Washington, GA 30673 USA Tel 706-678-2636; Fax: 706-678-3857
E-mail: editor@news-reporter.com
Web site: http://www.news-reporter.com.
Wilkinson, Brittany, *(978-0-692-18822-4)* 12608 Richezza Dr., Venice, FL 34293 USA Tel 941-223-1694
E-mail: beginwithcompassion@yahoo.com
Dist(s): **Ingram Content Group.**
Wilkinson Publishing (AUS) *(978-0-9775457; 978-0-9802818; 978-1-921332; 978-1-921667; 978-1-921804; 978-1-922178; 978-1-925642; 978-1-925927; 978-1-922810; 978-1-925265) Dist. by* **IPG Chicago.**
Will Hall Bks., *(978-0-9630310; 978-0-9801257)* 611 Oliver Ave., Fayetteville, AR 72701 USA
E-mail: rharriso@uark.edu
Web site: http://www.willhallbooks.com.
Will Makes Bks., *(978-0-9983607; 978-0-692-88727-1; 978-0-9990158; 978-0-692-95759-2; 978-0-692-96547-4; 978-0-692-98058-3; 978-0-9996188; 978-1-7324130; 978-0-578-44255-6; 978-0-578-44259-4; 978-0-578-46713-9; 978-0-578-52476-4; 978-0-578-56816-4; 978-0-578-62676-5; 978-0-578-34763-9; 978-0-578-34764-6) 1504 Gemini St., Newberg, OR 97132 USA Tel 503-507-2712*
E-mail: willmakesbooks@gmail.com.
Will to Print Pr., *(978-0-9772985)* 234 Hyde St., San Francisco, CA 94102-3324 USA Tel 415-474-0508; Fax: 415-673-1027
E-mail: willtoprintpress@faithfulfools.org
Web site: http://www.faithfulfools.org.
WillGo Pr., *(978-0-9828231)* 2874 Arcade St., Maplewood, MN 55109 USA Tel 651-774-2558
E-mail: gdesigns@comcast.net.
William & William Publishing, *(978-0-615-29498-8; 978-0-615-53342-1; 978-0-615-58386-0; 978-0-9855110; 978-0-9890362; 978-0-9969259; 978-0-578-79157-9)* .
William Askel Art, *(978-0-9752528)* 21665 Wallace Dr., Southfield, MI 48075-7570 USA
E-mail: waksel@provide.net
Web site: http://fieldguidetomonsters.com.
William "Deek" Harris, *(978-0-578-21234-0; 978-0-578-45187-9; 978-0-578-70029-8; 978-0-578-38931-8; 979-8-218-10545-7)* 713 Bowfield Ct., Antioch, TN 37013 USA Tel 615-290-1818
E-mail: deekharrisbooks@gmail.com
Dist(s): **Independent Pub.**
William M. Gaines Agent, INC. *Imprint of* **Diamond Bk. Distributors**
William Morrow Paperbacks *Imprint of* **HarperCollins Pubs.**
William P Castor, *(978-0-578-42824-6)* 135 5th St. Apt. 1, Aspinwall, PA 15215 USA Tel 412-780-2331
E-mail: wpc1027@gmail.com
Dist(s): **Ingram Content Group.**
William Works, Inc., *(978-0-9745244)* P.O. Box 2709, Washington, DC 20013 USA Toll Free: 877-535-2057.
WilliamChristie Books *See* **Eclectry Bks.**
Williams and King Pubs., *(978-0-9983663; 978-0-9998406; 978-1-7332382; 979-8-9851466)* 1112 Climbing Rose Dr., Orlando, FL 32818 USA
E-mail: mwilliams@williamsandkingpublishers.com
Web site: WilliamsAndKingPublishers.com.
Williams, Angela Claudette, *(978-0-615-15833-4; 978-0-615-16052-8; 978-0-615-16098-6; 978-0-615-16138-9; 978-0-615-17571-3; 978-0-615-17889-9)* 3645 Watkins Ridge Ct., Raleigh, NC 27616 USA
E-mail: claudetteexpressiona@yahoo.com
Web site: http://www.claudetteexpressions.com
Dist(s): **Lulu Pr., Inc.**
Williams, Aspen *See* **Clair, Aspen**
Williams, Benjamin Publishing, *(978-0-9764945; 978-0-9796180; 978-0-9802398; 978-0-9850233; 978-0-9909650)* 18525 S. Torrence Ave. Suite D3, Lansing, IL 60438 USA Tel 1-888-757-0007
E-mail: ben@bwpublishing.com
Web site: http://www.bwpublishing.com.
Williams, Benny Publishing *See* **Williams, Benjamin Publishing**
Williams, C.H. Literary, *(978-1-7333569)* 10 Burns Way, Newark, DE 19702 USA Tel 302-319-2707
E-mail: chw@chwilliamsliterary.com
Web site: chwilliamsliterary.com.
Williams, Darnell *See* **Williams, Darnell L. Foundation, The**
Williams, Darnell L. Foundation, The, *(978-0-9747771)* 2402 Magnolia Dr., Harrisburg, PA 17104 USA Tel 717-233-1511
E-mail: WDam44243@aol.com.
Williams, Desiree, *(978-0-578-66330-2; 978-0-578-91793-1; 978-0-578-33695-4; 979-8-218-04365-0)* 4213 Capstone Cir., Williamsville, NY 14221 USA Tel 716-400-6865
E-mail: dlwilliams2@buffaloschools.org.
Williams, Dontez *See* **MySheri Enterprises, LLC**
Williams, Dr. Adrienne, *(978-0-578-53827-3)* 1303 Greentree Ct, Brandon, MS 39042 USA Tel 601-383-2655
E-mail: adriennefmw36@gmail.com.
Williams Enterprises, Inc., *(978-0-9755478)* 500 5th Ave., N., Greybull, WY 82426 USA.
Williams, Gary, *(978-0-9743000)* 574 Falcon Fork Way, Jacksonville, FL 32259 USA
Web site: http://www.fbcofmand.org.
Williams, Geoffrey T., *(978-0-9771381; 978-0-9801671)* 3119 Redwood St., San Diego, CA 92104 USA
Web site: http://wildvoices.com
Dist(s): **Audible.com**
Smashwords.
Williams International Publishing *See* **CreateBk.org**
Williams, James E., *(978-0-9746310)* P.O. Box 6921, Atlanta, GA 30315-0921 USA Fax: 404-691-0726.
Williams Jr, Kenneth E, *(978-1-7367355; 979-8-9879900)* 4613 Harvest Way, Montgomery, AL 36106 USA Tel 334-954-9577
E-mail: kjewilliams@hotmail.com.
Williams, Mary, *(978-0-9992773)* 2110 Garfias Dr., Pasadena, CA 91104 USA Tel 562-665-2447
E-mail: mronan1@gmail.com.
Williams, Michael, *(978-0-9761503)* 1324 Lake Grove Ln., Desoto, TX 75115-3326 USA.
Williams, Morgan, *(978-0-9762768)* 3243 Cloverwood Dr., Nashville, TN 37214-3428 USA
E-mail: mandj@magiclink.com
Web site: http://www.thestandards.com.
Williams, Reeva, *(978-0-578-91707-8)* 2205 Woodside Dr, Beaumont, TX 77707 USA Tel 409-499-8301
E-mail: reevawilliams2950@yahoo.com.
Williams, Rozalia *See* **Hidden Curriculum Education**
Williams, Tempestt *See* **ImaginAISHAn Media LLC**
Williams, Thomas, *(978-0-9763633)* 358 Homestead Rd., NW, Willis, VA 24380 USA Tel 540-789-4295
E-mail: tomwill@swva.net
Web site: http://www.santacares.org.
Williams, TJ, *(978-1-7349457)* 3712 Waterford Club Dr., Lithia Springs, GA 30122 USA Tel 678-613-9248
E-mail: tjwilliams326@gmail.com.
Williamson County Public Library, *(978-0-9911915; 978-0-9970690)* Williamson Cty. Public Library, Franklin, TN 37064 USA Tel 615-595-1240; *Imprints:* Academy Park Press (AcadParkPr)
E-mail: dgreenwald@williamson-tn.org
Web site: wcpltn.org.
Williamson, Leah, *(978-0-578-43572-5)* 511 Bertrand Dr. Apt. 2102, Lafayette, LA 70506 USA Tel 504-982-6211
E-mail: leahannwilliamson97@gmail.com
Dist(s): **Ingram Content Group.**
Williamspublishing, *(978-0-615-19121-8)* 317 E. Oakgrove, Kalamazoo, MI 49004 USA
E-mail: starowl1@hotmail.clm
Dist(s): **Lulu Pr., Inc.**
Williby-Walker, Debra June, *(978-0-692-70291-8; 978-0-692-85861-5)* 12018 Ingleside Rd., Oakvale, WV 24739 USA Tel 304-396-9105
E-mail: debbeejune@gmail.com.
Willie & Willie, *(978-0-9754126)* P.O. Box 26071, Saint Louis, MO 63136 USA.
Willis, E.B. Bks., *(978-0-9976634)* 209 Braxberry Way, Holly Springs, NC 27540 USA Tel 919-656-5893
E-mail: bethwillis@nc.rr.com
Web site: www.ebwillis.com.
Willis Music Co., *(978-0-87718)* Orders Addr.: P.O. Box 548, Florence, KY 41022-0548 USA (SAN 294-6947) Tel 606-283-2050 859; Fax: 606-283-1784; Toll Free: 800-354-9799; Edit Addr.: 7380 Industrial Rd., Florence, KY 41040 USA
E-mail: willis@willis-music.com; orderdpt@willis-music.com
Web site: http://www.willismusic.com
Dist(s): **Leonard, Hal Corp.**
Willoughby Arts, *(978-1-950285)* 1520 Festival Dr., Houston, TX 77062 USA Tel 713-815-0275
E-mail: trinawilloughby@yahoo.com.
Willow Bend Pr., *(978-0-9896564; 978-1-950019)* P.O. Box PO Box 247, Prosper, TX 75078 USA Tel 972-757-3787
E-mail: susanrutledge@mac.com.
Willow Bend Publishing, *(978-0-9709002; 978-0-9831138; 978-1-7337674)* P.O. Box 304, Goshen, MA 01032 USA Tel 413-230-1514 Do not confuse with Willow Bend Publishing in Lakeland, FL
E-mail: info@willowbendpublishing.com
Web site: http://www.willowbendpublishing.com.
Willow Bend Publishing Group, LLC, *(978-1-7347354)* 100 Gretta Ct., Warner Robins, GA 31088 USA Tel 478-733-6502
E-mail: willowbendpublishing@gmail.com.
Willow Breeze Publishing, *(978-1-7340039)* P.O. Box 700, Westminster, TX 75485-0700 USA Tel 909-544-1661
E-mail: fff@linkline.com
Web site: www.adogbling.com.
Willow Brook Publishing, *(978-0-9817636)* 19600 W. Shore Dr., Suite 101, Mundelein, IL 60060 USA (SAN 856-4914)
E-mail: Info@willowBrookPublishing.com
Web site: http://www.willowbrook-publishing.com/
Dist(s): **Pathway Bk. Service.**
†Willow Creek Pr., Inc., *(978-0-932558; 978-1-57223; 978-1-59543; 978-1-60755; 978-1-62343; 978-1-68234; 978-1-5492)* Orders Addr.: P.O. Box 147, Minocqua, WI 54548-0147 USA (SAN 255-4038) Tel 715-358-7010; Fax: 715-358-2807; Toll Free: 800-850-9453; P.O. Box 147 / EDI Orders, Minoqua, WI 54548 (SAN 920-8070) Tel 715-358-7010; Fax: 715-358-2807; Edit Addr.: 9931 Hwy 70 W, Minocqua, WI 54548 USA Toll Free: 800-850-9453 Do not confuse with Willowcreek Pr. in Aloha, OR
E-mail: info@willowcrewpress.com; info@wcpretail.com
Web site: http://www.wcpretail.com
Dist(s): **MyiLibrary**
Strauss Consultants; *CIP.*
Willow Creel Publishing Co., *(978-0-9729655)* 35 Willow Creek, 820 9th Ave. S., North Myrtle Beach, SC 29582 USA Tel 843-272-1096 Do not confuse with Willow Creek Publishing in Canton, MI, Pine River, MN
E-mail: grayfox.43@att.net
Web site: http://www.chinquawhere.com.
Willow Dance Pubns., *(978-0-9768750)* Orders Addr.: P.O. Box 71, Hillsdale, WY 82060 USA Tel 307-631-0236; Edit Addr.: 1370 CR 142, Hillsdale, WY 82060 USA
E-mail: willowdancepublishing@yahoo.com.
Willow Glen Pubns., *(978-0-9998090)* 12813 Willow Glen Ct., Oak Hill, VA 20171-1921 USA Tel 703-709-0188
E-mail: michaelquinn1@mac.com.
Willow Moon Publisher *See* **Willow Moon Publishing**
Willow Moon Publishing, *(978-1-948256)* 108 Saint Thomas Rd., Lancaster, PA 17601-4829 USA Tel 610-463-6614; Fax: 610-463-6614
E-mail: jodilstapler@gmail.com
Web site: willow-moon-publishing.com; WMPublishing.org; willowmoonpub.com.
Willow Point Press, LLC *See* **Grettler, Kelly**
Willow Publishing, *(978-0-9825212)* 1000 Kinsley Ave., No. 32, Winslow, AZ 86047 USA Toll Free Fax: 800-643-9527.
Willow River Pr. *Imprint of* **Between the Lines Publishing**
Willow Tree Bks. (GBR) *(978-0-9522921) Dist. by* **IPG Chicago.**
Willow Tree Books *See* **Apricot Pr.**
Willow Tree Press *See* **Little Willow Tree Bks.**
Willowgate Pr., *(978-1-930008)* P.O. Box 6529, Holliston, MA 01746 USA (SAN 253-0376); 120 Brook Rd., Port Jefferson, NY 11777-1665
E-mail: willowgatepress@yahoo.com
Web site: http://www.willowgatepress.com.
WillowSpring Downs, *(978-0-9648525; 978-0-9742716)* 1582 N. Falcon, Hillsboro, KS 67063 USA Tel 620-367-8432; Fax: 620-367-8218; Toll Free: 888-551-0973
E-mail: willowspringdowns@juno.com.
WillowTree Pr., L.L.C., *(978-0-9678221; 978-0-9794533; 978-1-937778)* Orders Addr.: 5501 Country Ln., High Ridge, MO 63049 USA; Edit Addr.: 5501 Country Ln., High Ridge, MO 63049 USA (SAN 253-1178); *Imprints:* Full Circle Press (Full Circle MO)
E-mail: info@willowtreepress.com
Web site: http://www.willowtreepress.com
Dist(s): **Smashwords.**
Willy Waw wees, LLC, *(978-0-9785103)* Orders Addr.: PO Box 390593, Deltona, FL 32739 USA
E-mail: artgallerymeris@aol.com
Web site: http://www.willywawwees.com.

Wilmer Bks., *(978-0-692-15591-2; 978-0-578-78093-1; 979-8-218-02470-3)* 730 Glenwood Ave SE Unit 251, Atlanta, GA 30312 USA Tel 443-421-6939
E-mail: wilmerbooks@gmail.com
Web site: www.danallwilmer.com.

Wilmer, Da'Nall *See* **Wilmer Bks.**

Wilmington Today LLC, *(978-0-9729573; 978-0-9916642)* 1213 Culbreth Dr., Wilmington, NC 28405 USA Tel 910-509-7195
E-mail: hwjones@wilmingtontoday.com
Web site: http://www.wilmingtontoday.com.

Wilshire House of Arkansas *See* **Ozark Publishing**

Wilson & Associates *See* **Gatewood Pr.**

Wilson, Bob, *(978-0-9908537)* 8061 W. Mesa Point Dr., Tucson, AZ 85281 USA Tel 480-710-0340
E-mail: bobwilson7711@gmail.com.

Wilson, Bob Solutions *See* **Wilson, Bob**

Wilson, Gerrard (IRL) *(978-0-9561553)* *Dist. by* **LuluCom.**

†Wilson, H.W., *(978-0-8242)* 950 University Ave., Bronx, NY 10452-4224 USA (SAN 203-2961) Tel 718-588-8400; Fax: 718-681-1511 (Outside of the U.S. & Canada); Toll Free: 800-367-6770 ext 2272
E-mail: custserv@hwwilson.com
Web site: http://www.hwwilson.com
Dist(s): **Ebsco Publishing**
Grey Hse. Publishing
MyiLibrary; *CIP.*

Wilson, Kristin, *(978-0-9998115)* 100 Tyler Gate Ln., Holly Springs, NC 27540 USA Tel 919-819-7152
E-mail: rookiewilson06@yahoo.com.

Wilson Language Training, *(978-1-56778)* 47 Old Webster Rd., Oxford, MA 01540-2705 USA Toll Free: 800-899-8454.

Wilson Place Comics, *(978-0-9744235)* P.O. Box 435, Oceanside, NY 11572 USA
E-mail: Wilplace@optonline.net
Web site: http://www.wjhc.com
Dist(s): **Brodart Co.**
Diamond Comic Distributors, Inc.
Diamond Bk. Distributors
Follett School Solutions
Mackin Library Media
Midwest Library Service.

Wilson Publishing, P.O. Box 754, Hilo, HI 96721 USA Tel 808-969-3674
E-mail: voltron_and_robots_collector@yahoo.com.

Wilson, Rebecca, *(978-0-9760569)* 450 Massachusetts Ave NW Apt. 1004, Washington, DC 20001-6222 USA
E-mail: info@sunfishmanuals.com
Web site: http://www.sunfishmanuals.com.

Wilson, Tom, *(978-1-7353376)* 15764 Amston Ct., Chino Hills, CA 91709 USA Tel 909-342-8250
E-mail: briarpins@gmail.com.

Wilson, W. Shane, *(978-0-578-00301-6; 978-0-578-00634-5; 978-0-578-00797-7; 978-0-578-01639-9; 978-0-578-02119-5; 978-0-578-02550-6; 978-0-578-03095-1; 978-0-578-03299-3)* 7600 NE 64th Cir., Vancouver, WA 98662 USA Tel 360-521-1584
E-mail: redtimberwolf67@yahoo.com
Web site: http://stores.lulu.com/shanesbooks
Dist(s): **Lulu Pr., Inc.**

Wilson-Barnett Publishing, *(978-1-888840)* P.O. Box 345, Tustin, CA 92781-0345 USA Tel 949-380-5748; Fax: 714-730-6140
E-mail: mrcalc@usa.net.

Wilson-Crawford & Co., *(978-0-9752948)* P.O. Box 809, Island Lake, IL 60042-0809 USA Fax: 847-487-1591
E-mail: freecellmax@aol.com
Web site: http://www.freecellsecrets.com.

Wilson-Jordan, Natashia, *(978-0-578-22011-6; 978-0-578-22204-2)* 4263 Sir Dixon Dr., Fairburn, GA 30213 USA Tel 646-423-1595
E-mail: Natashiawilsonjordan@yahoo.com
Web site: https://schoolisathome.com/.

Wilstonian, *(978-0-9772122)* 3603 Whitaker Dr., Melvindale, MI 48122 USA (SAN 257-0106)
Web site: http://www.wilstonian.com.

Wilt, Lisa, *(978-0-9770053)* Orders Addr.: 1072 Frye Rd., Jeannette, PA 15644-4717 USA
E-mail: thankyoumousie@comcast.net.

Wiltshire Bks., *(978-0-9831685; 978-0-9970240; 978-1-7365745)* 1924 Wiltshire Blvd., Huntington, WV 25701 USA Tel 304-730-0798
E-mail: WiltshireBookLLC@aol.com.

Wimabi Pr., *(978-0-578-02359-5; 978-0-578-03340-2; 978-0-578-05718-7)* 7102 Lakewood Dr., Richmond, VA 23229 USA
E-mail: inquiries@wimabi.com
Web site: http://www.wimabi.com
Dist(s): **Lulu Pr., Inc.**

Win Enterprises LLC, *(978-0-9826865)* 134R West St., Simsbury, CT 06070 USA Tel 860-651-6859; Fax: 203-413-4409
Dist(s): **Outskirts Pr., Inc.**

Win Publishing, LLC *See* **Win Enterprises LLC**

Winchester Pr., *(978-0-9745279)* P.O. Box 711, Hollis, NH 03049-0711 USA Tel 603-880-9559 Do not confuse with companies with the same or similar name in Southhampton, NY, Howell, NJ, LaFox, IL.

Wincik, Stephanie *See* **One Horse Pr.**

Wind & Rain Pr., *(978-1-7356287)* 810 Miguel Pedraza Sr Ct, Ysleta Sur, TX 79927 USA Tel 915-740-9023
E-mail: ajgurrola@gmail.com.

Wind Pubns., *(978-0-9636545; 978-1-893239; 978-1-936138)* Orders Addr.: 600 Overbrook Dr., Nicholasville, KY 40356 USA
E-mail: books@windpub.com
Web site: http://www.windpub.com.

Windbellows, *(978-0-578-59748-5)* 24909 W 41st St., Sand Springs, OK 74063 USA Tel 918-605-4704
E-mail: windbellowenterprises@gmail.com.

Windblown Enterprises, *(978-0-9752576)* 12207 243rd Pl NE, Redmond, WA 98053-5685 USA
E-mail: windblowne@msn.com.

Windblown Media, *(978-0-9647292; 978-1-935170; 978-1-61871)* 4680 Calle Norte, Newbury Park, CA 91320 USA Tel 805-498-2484; Fax: 805-499-4260
E-mail: office@windblownmedia.com
Web site: http://www.windblownmedia.com
Dist(s): **Hachette Bk. Group.**

Windcall Enterprises *See* **Windcall Publishing**

Windcall Publishing, *(978-0-9745884; 978-0-9845934; 978-0-9847607)* Div. of Windcall Enterprises, Orders Addr.: 75345 Rd. 317, Venango, NE 69168 USA Tel 308-447-5566 (phone/fax); Fax: 308-447-5566
E-mail: windcall@chase3000.com
Web site: http://www.windcallenterprises.com; http://www.windcallpublishing.com
Dist(s): **Smashwords.**

Windchimes Publishing, *(978-0-9763253)* P.O. Box 1433, Palm City, FL 34991-6433 USA Tel 772-285-5429
E-mail: wchimes@gate.net
Web site: http://www.wchimes.com.

Windfeather Pr., *(978-0-9620122)* 4545 W. Heart Rd., Bismarck, ND 58504-4257 USA (SAN 247-7246); 1203 N. 27th St., Bismarck, ND 58501 (SAN 247-7254) Tel 701-258-5047
Dist(s): **Duebbert, Harold F.**

Windham Pr., *(978-1-62845; 978-1-63775)* 11240 Plantation Oaks Ln, Lumberton, TX 77657 USA Tel 409-234-4533 Do not confuse with Windham Press in New Rochelle, NY, Miami, FL
E-mail: info@studyguideteam.com.

Windhill Bks. LLC, *(978-0-9844828; 978-1-944734)* 939 Windhill St., Onalaska, WI 54650-2081 USA (SAN 859-5135)
E-mail: jeanna@windhillbooks.com
Web site: http://www.windhillbooks.com.

Windhorse Bks., *(978-0-9973745)* 5429 SW 80 St., Gainesville, FL 32608 USA Tel 352-336-5888
E-mail: barbaragresbach@gmail.com
Web site: windhorsebooks.com.

Winding Hall Pubs., *(978-1-947035)* P.O. Box 2689, EUGENE, OR 97402 USA Tel 541-525-7888
E-mail: windinghall@gmail.com; editor@wordoutbooks.com
Web site: http://www.windinghall.com; www.wordoutbooks.com.

Winding Road Pubs., *(978-0-615-21989-9; 978-0-578-04819-2; 978-0-578-07274-6; 978-0-578-09900-2; 978-0-578-10413-3; 978-0-578-10703-5; 978-0-578-10929-9; 978-0-578-11074-5; 978-0-578-11693-8; 978-0-578-12821-4; 978-0-578-13843-5)* 2904 Giles St., West Des Moines, IA 50265 USA Tel 515-226-1179
Dist(s): **Lulu Pr., Inc.**

Windjammer Adventure Publishing, *(978-0-9768477; 978-0-615-29130-7; 978-0-615-33790-6; 978-0-615-36411-7; 978-0-615-38745-1; 978-0-9831300; 978-0-9898232; 978-0-99788807; 978-0-9994812; 978-1-7333668; 978-1-7362029)* 289 S. Franklin St., Chagrin Falls, OH 44022-3449 USA Tel 440-247-6610
E-mail: windjammerpub@mac.com
Web site: http://windjammerpublishing.com.

Windmill Bks. *Imprint of* **Rosen Publishing Group, Inc., The**

Windmill Bks. *Imprint of* **Windmill Bks.**

Windmill Bks., *(978-1-60754; 978-1-62275)* 303 Pk. Ave. S., Suite No. 1280, NEW YORK, NY 10010-3657 USA Tel 646-205-7415; *Imprints:* Windmill Books (WindmillBks)
Dist(s): **Rosen Publishing Group, Inc., The.**

Window Bks., *(978-1-889829)* Orders Addr.: 1425 Broadway #513, Seattle, WA 98122 USA Tel 206-351-9993
E-mail: orders@windowbooksonline.com
Web site: http://www.meetmarcadams.com; http://www.windowbooksonline.com.

Window Box Pr. LLC, *(978-0-9793738)* Orders Addr.: 13516 Fillmore Ct., Thornton, CO 80241-1330 USA (SAN 853-2958) Tel 303-255-9432
E-mail: windowboxpress@q.com
Web site: http://windowboxpress.com.

Window Seat Publishing, *(978-0-9721949)* 82 Marlborough Rd., West Hempstead, NY 11552 USA Tel 516-481-5969
E-mail: aferrant@optonline.net.

Windows of Discovery, *(978-0-9785399)* P.O. Box 9085, Spokane, WA 99209-9085 USA
Web site: http://theprofessorstelescope.com.

Windrad Press *See* **Pinwheel Bks.**

WinDruid Publishing, *(978-0-9758943)* Orders Addr.: 220 Walworth Dr., St. Louis, MO 63125-5008 USA; Edit Addr.: P.O. Box 25008, Saint Louis, MO 63125-5008 USA
E-mail: orders@LukeCarter.com; info@windruidpublishing.com; susan@windruidpublishing.com
Web site: http://www.LukeCarter.com; http://www.windruidpublishing.com
Dist(s): **Book Clearing Hse.**
Quality Bks., Inc.

Winds of Happiness, LLC, The, *(978-1-7320905)* 878 Marquette St, Menasha, WI 54952 USA Tel 920-831-3303
E-mail: TFieds5574@gmail.com.

Windsong Publishing Co., *(978-0-9655078)* P.O. Box 273, Monticello, UT 84535 USA Do not confuse with companies with the same or similar names in Eugene, OR, San Diego, CA, Staunton, VA, Lake Patagonia, AZ
Dist(s): **New Leaf Distributing Co., Inc.**

Windsor Heights Bks., *(978-0-9753566; 978-1-948204)* Orders Addr.: 8402 Hermosa Dr., Riverside, CA 92504 USA (SAN 255-9935)
E-mail: info@windsorheightsbooks.com
Web site: http://www.windsorheightsbooks.com.

Windsor Heights Publishing *See* **Windsor Heights Bks.**

Windsor Media Enterprises, Inc., *(978-0-9765304; 978-0-9777297; 978-1-934229)* 5412 Wolf St., Longmont, CO 80504-3432 USA Toll Free: 877-947-2665
E-mail: collins@wmebooks.com
Web site: http://www.wmebooks.com.

WindSpirit Publishing, *(978-0-9643407)* Orders Addr.: 220 Compass Ave., Beachwood, NJ 08722-2919 USA Fax: 732-240-7860
E-mail: windspiritpub@earthlink.net
Web site: http://www.windspiritpublishing.net.

Windsurf Publishing LLC, *(978-1-936509)* 14 Ctr. Dr., Old Greenwich, CT 06870 USA Tel 203-698-2975
E-mail: m.lagana@att.net.

Windswept Productions, *(978-0-9764825)* Orders Addr.: P.O. Box 167, Felton, PA 17322-0167 USA Tel 717-244-7700; Edit Addr.: 11525 High Point Rd., Felton, PA 17322 USA
E-mail: wpebs@earthlink.net.

Windswept Publishing, *(978-0-9893667; 978-0-9890280-0-4)* 318 Mathison Dr., Kerrville, TX 78028 USA Tel 830-353-1454
E-mail: ajzinger@gmail.com.

Windtree Pr., *(978-0-615-46251-6; 978-0-9835943; 978-1-940064; 978-1-942368; 978-1-943601; 978-1-944973; 978-1-947983; 978-1-950387; 978-1-952447; 978-1-957638; 978-1-962065)* 818 SW 3rd Ave. No. 221-2218, Portland, OR 97204-2405 USA
E-mail: windtreepress@gmail.com
Web site: https://windtreepress.com
Dist(s): **CreateSpace Independent Publishing Platform.**

Windwalker Pr., *(978-0-9993940)* P.O. Box 636, Dayton, WY 82836 USA
E-mail: rendallwriter@gmail.com
Web site: www.jaydinerendall.com; windwalkerpress.com.

Windward Publishing *Imprint of* **Finney Co., Inc.**

Windward Publishing, *(978-0-9758897)* 112 N. St., New Bedford, MA 02740-6513 USA Do not confuse with Windward Publishing in Minneapolis, MN
E-mail: windwardpublish@aol.com; josettefernandes@hotmail.com.

Windy City Pubs., *(978-0-9819505; 978-1-935766; 978-1-941478; 978-1-953294)* Box 89, South Haven, MI 49090 USA Tel 888-673-7126; *Imprints:* Skyscraper Press (children's) (Skyscraper Pr)
E-mail: dawn@windycitypublishers.com
Dist(s): **BookBaby.**

Windy City Publishing *See* **Windy City Pubs.**

Windy Hill Pr., *(978-0-9662983)* Orders Addr.: 22 Hilltop Ave., Barrington, RI 02806 USA Tel 401-247-2707 Do not confuse with Windy Hill Pr., in Menlo Park, CA
E-mail: windyhillpress@cox.net
Web site: http://www.windyhillpress.net.

Windy Hills Press *See* **Old Stone Pr.**

Windy Press International Publishing Hse., LLC, *(978-1-890568)* 29W 424 Tanglewood Ln, Warrenville, IL 60555-2663 USA; P.O. Box 5131, Wheaton, IL 60189-4383 Fax: 630-604-0490; Toll Free Fax: 888-508-5577; *Imprints:* A-BA-BA-HA-LA-MA-HA Publishers (A-BA-BA-HA-LA-MA-HA)
E-mail: interhouse@comcast.net
Web site: http://www.snowqueen.us.

Wineries by County, *(978-0-615-18047-2)* 3373 Silver Rapids Rd., Valley Spgs, CA 95252-9573 USA
E-mail: info@wineriesbycounty.com
Web site: http://www.wineriesbycounty.com.

Winestone *See* **Bed of Angels, Inc.**

Winfield Hse. Pr., *(978-1-7325814)* 610 Gibson Ln., Foster, KY 41043 USA Tel 606-756-2639
E-mail: peter@yourliteraryprose.com.

Winfrey Inc., *(978-0-9818526)* Orders Addr.: 14525 SW. Millikan Way #23515, Beaverton, OR 970052343 USA (SAN 856-7263) Tel 404-993-0532; 228 Pk. Ave. S. #23515, New York, NY 10003; Edit Addr.: 4480 S. Cobb Dr. Ste H Pmb 451, Smyrna, GA 30080 USA
E-mail: info@shakeetawinfrey.com
Web site: http://www.shakeetawinfrey.com
Dist(s): **APG Sales & Distribution Services**
BCH Fulfillment & Distribution
Bella Distribution
Book Hub, Inc.
Bks. Plus, U.S.A.
C & B Bk. Distribution
Cardinal Pubs. Group
Greenleaf Book Group
Independent Pubs. Group
Ingram Content Group
Midpoint Trade Bks., Inc.
Mint Pubs. Group
New Leaf Distributing Co., Inc.
Partners Bk. Distributing, Inc.
Penton Overseas, Inc.
Quality Bks., Inc.
SCB Distributors
SPD-Small Pr. Distribution
Send The Light Distribution LLC
Two Rivers Distribution.

Wing Books, *(978-0-9758719; 978-0-692-53294-2)* 1217 Sycamore St., Fort Collins, CO 80521 USA
E-mail: natashawing@gmail.com
Web site: http://www.natashawing.com.

Wing Dam Pr., *(978-0-9758615)* P.O. Box 200, Ferryville, WI 54628 USA Tel 608-734-3292 (phone/fax)
E-mail: nlichter@mwt.net.

Wing Lane Pr., *(978-0-9792430)* 19 Exeter Ln., Morristown, NJ 07960 USA
E-mail: tazni@optonline.net.

Wing, Natasha *See* **Wing Books**

Winged Lion Pr. Cooperative, *(978-0-692-69427-5; 978-0-692-99138-1; 978-0-692-08141-9)* 1385 Pinon Dr., Healdsburg, CA 95448 USA Tel 530-757-7576
Dist(s): **CreateSpace Independent Publishing Platform.**

Winged Lion Pr., LLC, *(978-1-935688)* 23 Julian Dr., Hamden, CT 06518 USA Tel 203-687-9385.

Winged Pubns., *(978-1-944203; 978-1-946939; 978-1-947523; 978-1-952661; 978-1-956654; 978-1-959788; 978-1-962168)* 16243 W. Statler St., Surprise, AZ 85374 USA Tel 623-910-4279
E-mail: cynthiahickey@outlook.com.

Winged Willow Pr., *(978-0-9664805)* Orders Addr.: P.O. Box 92, Carrboro, NC 27510 USA Tel 919-942-4689; Fax: 919-933-3555
E-mail: info@sudierakusin.com
Web site: http://www.sudierakusin.com
Dist(s): **Parnassus Bk. Distributors.**

Winger Publishing, P.O. Box 20991, Juneau, AK 99802 USA
E-mail: wingerpublishing@gmail.com.

Wings Above, *(978-0-9768403)* 1607 Market St., Galveston, TX 77550 USA Tel 409-750-9176.

Wings ePress, Inc., *(978-1-59088; 978-1-59705; 978-1-61309; 979-8-89197)* 113 Woodduck Ct., Winchester, KY 40391 USA; 3000 N. Rock Rd., Newton, KS 67114 Tel 316-283-0981 Do not confuse with companies with the same or similar name in Northhampton, MA, Union, ME, San Antonio, TX
E-mail: lindavoth@wingsepress.com; wingsbookkeeper@yahoo.com
Web site: http://www.wingsepress.com; http://
Dist(s): **CreateSpace Independent Publishing Platform**
Ingram Content Group
Smashwords.

Wings, Incorporated *See* **Rivertree Media**

Wings Pr., *(978-0-916727; 978-0-930324; 978-1-60940)* 627 E. Guenther, San Antonio, TX 78210 USA (SAN 209-4975) Tel 210-271-7805 Do not confuse with companies with the same or similar name in Northhampton, MA, UNion, ME, Lusk, WY
E-mail: milligan@wingspress.com
Web site: http://www.wingspress.com
Dist(s): **Brodart Co.**
Ebsco Publishing
Follett School Solutions
Independent Pubs. Group
MyiLibrary
SCB Distributors
ebrary, Inc.

Wings Press, Limited *See* **Wings ePress, Inc.**

Wings-on-Disk *Imprint of* **PassionQuest Technologies, LLC**

Wingspan Pr. *Imprint of* **WingSpan Publishing**

WingSpan Publishing, *(978-1-59594; 978-1-63683)* P.O. Box 2085, Livermore, CA 94551 USA Toll Free: 866-735-3782; *Imprints:* Wingspan Press (Wingspan Pr)
Web site: http://www.wingspanpress.com
Dist(s): **Draft2Digital**
Independently Published.

WingSpread Pubs. *Imprint of* **Moody Pubs.**

Wink Publishing, *(978-0-9702572)* P.O. Box 9957, Richmond, VA 23228 USA.

Winkelstein Studios, *(978-0-9824498; 978-0-578-77062-8)* 402 N. Fredericksburg Ave., Margate City, NJ 08402 USA
E-mail: stevenwinkelstein@gmail.com.

Winking Moon Pr., *(978-0-9764175)* 4130 S. Splendor Ct., Gilbert, AZ 85297 USA Do not confuse with Winking Moon Press in Cleveland OH.

Winn, Lynnette, *(978-0-9791884)* 2617 Claudia Dr., Leander, TX 78641 USA (SAN 852-7040)
Web site: http://www.butterpodjerome.com.

Winning Inc. of America, *(978-0-692-89096-7; 978-0-692-89097-4)* 1239 Golf Rd., Benton Harbor, MI 49022 USA Tel 269-934-7213; Fax: 269-934-7213
E-mail: miphilrose@ameritech.net.

Winning Proof, *(978-1-7346467)* 727 Cameron Woods Dr. 727 Cameron Woods Dr., Apex, NC 27523 USA (SAN 992-0234) Tel 714-797-3731
E-mail: winningproof@gmail.com
Web site: http://www.winningproof.com.

WinningwithCAS, *(978-1-7361539)* 1554 S ATLANTIC ST, SEATTLE, WA 98144 USA Tel 205-790-7530
E-mail: caugustus67@gmail.com
Web site: WinningwithCAS.

Winnow Pr., *(978-0-9764726)* 3505 El Dorado Trail, Suite A, Austin, TX 78739 USA (SAN 256-4017) Tel 512-280-4483
E-mail: publisher@winnowpress.com
Web site: http://winnowpress.com.

Winoca Bks. & Media, *(978-0-9755910; 978-0-9789736; 978-1-935619)* P.O. Box 515, Spur, TX 79370-0515 USA
E-mail: barbaralubbock@gmail.com
Web site: http://www.winocapress.com; http://www.Bookadelphia.com; http://www.winoca.com; http://www.BoldfaceBooks.com.

Winoca Press *See* **Winoca Bks. & Media**

Winslow's Art, *(978-0-9748505)* P.O. Box 2099, Avalon, CA 90704-2099 USA Tel 310-510-1613 (phone/fax)
E-mail: winslow@catalinaisp.com.

Winsor Corporation *See* **Winsor Learning, Inc.**

Winsor Learning, Inc., *(978-1-891602; 978-1-935450)* 3001 Metro Dr. Suite 480, Bloomington, MN 55425 USA Tel 800-321-7585; Fax: 651-222-3969; Toll Free: 800-321-7585
E-mail: info@winsorlearning.com
Web site: http://www.winsorlearning.com.

Winstead Pr., Ltd., *(978-0-940787)* 202 Slice Dr., Stamford, CT 06907 USA (SAN 664-6913) Tel 203-322-4941
E-mail: winstead.press@gte.net.

Winston Pr. Publishing, *(978-1-7362141)* 2275 Sophie Springer Ln., Sarasota, FL 34234 USA Tel 941-726-8160
E-mail: Myndelprincipal1@aol.com
Web site: winstonpresspublishing.com; myndelmiller.com.

Winter, David *See* **Rousing Bks.**

Winter Goose Publishing, *(978-0-9836764; 978-0-9851548; 978-0-9881845; 978-0-9889049; 978-0-9894792; 978-1-941058; 978-1-952909)* 45 Lafayette Rd. No. 114, North Hampton, NH 95835 USA Tel 530-771-7058
E-mail: jessica@wintergoosepublishing.com
Web site: http://wintergoosepublishing.com; http://hallwaypublishing.com
Dist(s): **Ingram Content Group.**

Winter Light Bks., Inc., *(978-0-9797372)* 734 Franklin Ave., No. 675, Garden City, NY 11530-4525 USA (SAN 854-2163)
Web site: http://www.winterlightbooks.com; http://www.winterlightbooks.org.

Winter Pr., *(978-0-578-06356-0)* 1237 Main St., Isleboro, ME 04848 USA
E-mail: eelliott246@aol.com.

Wintergreen Orchard Hse., *(978-1-933119; 978-1-936035; 978-1-945520)* Div. of Carnegie Communications, 2 Lan Dr., Suite 100, Westford, MA 01886 USA Tel 978-692-9708; Fax: 978-692-2304
E-mail: info@wintergreenorchardhouse.com; cglennon@carnegiecomm.com
Web site: http://www.wintergreenorchardhouse.com.

Winterhouse Editions, *(978-1-884381)* Orders Addr.: P.O. Box 159, Falls Village, CT 06031 USA Tel 860-824-5040; Fax: 860-824-1065
E-mail: desk@winterhouse.com
Web site: http://www.winterhouse.com
Dist(s): **Chicago Distribution Ctr.**
Columbia Univ. Pr.
SPD-Small Pr. Distribution
Univ. of Chicago Pr.

Wintermantel Group, LLC, The, *(978-0-9767418)* 316 Saddle Back Dr., Saint Louis, MO 63129-3449 USA
Web site: http://www.theangelchildren.com.

Winters Publishing, *(978-0-9625329; 978-1-883651; 978-1-954116)* Orders Addr.: P.O. Box 501, Greensburg, IN 47240 USA (SAN 298-1645) Tel 812-663-4948 (phone/fax); Toll Free: 800-457-3230; Edit Addr.: 705 E. Washington, Greensburg, IN 47240 USA Do not confuse with Winters Publishing, Wichita, KS
E-mail: tmwinters@juno.com
Web site: http://www.winterspublishing.com
Dist(s): **Partners Bk. Distributing, Inc.**
Partners/West Book Distributors
Send The Light Distribution LLC
Spring Arbor Distributors, Inc.

Winters Publishing Group, *(978-0-9976124; 978-1-947426)* 2448 E. 81st Street, Suite 5900, Tulsa, OK 74137 USA Tel 918-494-6868
E-mail: dboyd@wintersking.com
Dist(s): **Whitaker Hse.**

Winterwolf Publishing, *(978-0-9744831; 978-0-9752711; 978-0-9762471; 978-0-9772632)* Orders Addr.: P.O. Box 1373, Westerville, OH 43086-1373 USA; Edit Addr.: 5446 Highbrook Ct., Westerville, OH 43081 USA
Web site: http://www.winterwolfpublishing.com.

Wipf and Stock *Imprint of* **Wipf & Stock Pubs.**

Wipf & Stock Pubs., *(978-0-9653517; 978-1-55635; 978-1-57910; 978-1-59244; 978-1-59752; 978-1-60608; 978-1-60899; 978-1-61097; 978-1-62032; 978-1-62189; 978-1-62564; 978-1-63087; 978-1-4982; 978-1-5326; 978-1-7252; 978-1-6667; 979-8-3852)* Orders Addr.: 199 W 8th Ave Ste 3, Eugene, OR 97401 USA (SAN 990-3038) Tel 541-344-1528; Fax: 541-344-1506; Edit Addr.: 199 W 8th Ave Ste 3, Eugene, OR 97401 USA Tel 541-344-1528; Fax: 541-344-1506; *Imprints*: Resource Publications (OR) (Resource Pubcns); Wipf and Stock (Wipf and Stock); Stone Table Books (StneTbleBk)
E-mail: contentadmin@wipfandstock.com
Web site: http://wipfandstock.com/; http://stonetablebooks.com/
Dist(s): **Independently Published**
Ingram Bk. Co.
MyiLibrary
Spring Arbor Distributors, Inc.

WIPRO, 2 Christie Heights St., Leonia, NJ 07605 USA Tel 201-840-4755.

Wire Rim Bks., *(978-0-9802253; 978-0-615-15357-5; 978-1-935236)* 188 Spring Valley St., Hutto, TX 78634 USA (SAN 913-5960) Tel 512-740-1131
E-mail: hmelton@mac.com
Web site: http://www.wirerimbooks.com.

Wisconsin Dept. of Public Instruction, *(978-1-57337)* Orders Addr.: Drawer 179, Milwaukee, WI 53293-0179 USA Tel 608-266-2188; Fax: 608-267-9110; Toll Free: 800-243-8782; Edit Addr.: 125 S. Webster St., Box 7841, Madison, WI 53702 USA
Web site: http://www.dpi.state.wi.us.

†Wisconsin Historical Society, *(978-0-87020; 978-1-9766)* 816 State St., Madison, WI 53706 USA (SAN 203-350X) Tel 608-264-6584
E-mail: diane.drexler@wisconsinhistory.org; whspress@wisconsinhistory.org
Web site: http://www.wisconsinhistory.org
Dist(s): **Chicago Distribution Ctr.**
Hoover Institution Pr.
Univ. of Chicago Pr.; *CIP*.

Wisdom Audio-Books *Imprint of* **BloomingFields**

Wisdom Foundation Publishing, *(978-1-932590)* 796 Isenberg St., Suite 19E, Honolulu, HI 96826 USA Tel 808-944-3113; Fax: 808-988-4212
E-mail: wisdomfactors@hawaii.rr.com.

Wisdom Hse. Bks., NC Hwy. 54 W. #325, Carrboro, NC 27510 USA Tel 919-883-4669
E-mail: Ted@wisdomhousebooks.com
Web site: Wisdomhousebooks.com.

†Wisdom Pubns., *(978-0-86171; 978-1-61429; 978-1-949129; 979-8-89070)* 199 Elm St., Somerville, MA 02144 USA (SAN 246-022X) Tel 617-776-7416 ext 24; Fax: 617-776-7841; Toll Free Fax: 800-338-4550 (orders only); Toll Free: 800-462-6420 (orders only)
E-mail: tlulek@wisdompubs.org; admin@wisdompubs.org
Web site: http://www.wisdompubs.org
Dist(s): **MyiLibrary**
Simon & Schuster, Inc.; *CIP*.

Wisdom Tales *Imprint of* **World Wisdom, Inc.**

Wisdom Tree (IND) *(978-81-86685; 978-81-8328)* *Dist. by* **SCB Distributo.**

Wisdom Tree Records *See* **Rivertree Productions, Inc.**

Wisdon Hse. Bks., *(978-0-9984145; 978-0-9984145-1-5)* 412 Parker Rd., Mount Airy, NC 27030 USA Tel 336-786-4922; Fax: 336-786-4922
E-mail: dretjdt1987@gmail.com
Web site: www.wisdomhousebooks.com.

Wise Guides, LLC, *(978-0-9768772; 978-1-935237)* 1924 W. Montrose, PMB No. 206, Chicago, IL 60613 USA Toll Free: 866-262-3842
E-mail: info@wiseguidebooks.com
Web site: http://www.wiseguidebooks.com
Dist(s): **Zagat Survey.**

Wise Media Group, *(978-0-9822907; 978-1-935689; 978-1-62967)* 630 Quintana Rd. Suite 116, Morro Bay, CA 93442 USA
E-mail: support@selfpublish.org
Web site: https://www.50interviews.com; https://www.wisemediagroup.com.

Wise Owl Printing Plus, Incorporated *See* **Deziner Media International**

Wise Pubns. (GBR) *(978-0-7119; 978-0-86001)* *Dist. by* **Music Sales.**

Wise Wolf Bks., *(978-1-953944; 978-1-957548)* 9850 S. Maryland Pkwy. STE. A-5 No. 323, Las Vegas, NV 89183 USA Tel 702-689-3912
E-mail: admin@wisewolfbooks.com
Web site: www.wisewolfbooks.com.

Wise Wolf Books LLC *See* **Wise Wolf Bks.**

Wise Words Publications *See* **EPI Bks.**

Wise Writer Publishing, *(978-1-931627)* P.O. Box 564, Patton, CA 92346 USA Do not confuse with Pristine Publishing, Fairbanks, AK
E-mail: liliana630md@gmail.com
Web site: www.writerjulia@gmail.com.

Wisebison Pr., *(978-1-7344327)* 621 Altamont St., Ashland, OR 97520 USA Tel 541-301-0541
E-mail: doukat@pm.me.

Wisecracker Press, Inc., *(978-0-9752657)* 2735 April Hill Ln., Dallas, TX 75287 USA
Web site: http://www.wisecrackerpress.com.

Wisecraft Publishing, *(978-0-9976460; 978-1-953739)* 14505 Four Chimney Dr., Centreville, VA 20120 USA Tel 703-830-2704
E-mail: lampwright@gmail.com
Web site: http://www.ljagilamplighter.com/.

Wisehearted Warrior Enterprises, *(978-0-9972797)* 1606 Arrowhead Trail, Neptune Beach, FL 32266 USA Tel 904-307-1941
E-mail: deborajscott@aol.com.

WiseMind Educational Services LLC, *(978-0-692-78691-8; 978-0-692-78692-5; 978-0-692-18164-5; 979-8-9851249)* 1757 Schoolhouse Ct NW, SALEM, OR 97304 USA Tel 541-325-2195.

WiseWoman Pr., *(978-0-945385)* 1521 N. Jantzen Ave., No. 143, Portland, OR 97217 USA (SAN 247-0039) Tel 1-800-603-3005; 1408 NE 65th St., Vancouver, WA 98665 Tel 503 310-0105
E-mail: web@wisewomanpress.com
Web site: http://www.wisewomanpress.com
Dist(s): **DeVorss & Co.**
Lulu Pr., Inc.

Wish Publishing, *(978-1-930546; 978-0-9835754; 978-0-615-74522-0; 978-0-578-59227-5; 978-0-578-67115-4; 978-0-578-67716-3; 978-1-7351459; 978-1-7377612)* P.O. Box 10337, Terre Haute, IN 47801 USA (SAN 253-4320) Fax: 928-447-1836
E-mail: holly@wishpublishing.com
Web site: http://www.wishpublishing.com
Dist(s): **Cardinal Pubs. Group**
Ingram Content Group.

Wish You Were Here *Imprint of* **Sierra Pr.**

Wishful Penny Books *See* **See The Wish**

Wishing Star Children's Bks., *(978-0-615-16077-1; 978-0-615-16078-8; 978-0-615-16079-5)* 12755 Eureis Rd., Southgate, MI 48195 USA Tel 734-754-3168
E-mail: mgrazl@wowway.com
Web site: http://www.wishingstarchildrensbooks.com
Dist(s): **Lulu Pr., Inc.**

Wishing U Well Publishing, *(978-0-9769524)* 1560 Gulf Blvd., Unit 1202, Clearwater, FL 33767 USA.

Wishingstone Enterprises *See* **Wishingstone Publishing**

Wishingstone Publishing, *(978-0-9779701)* 1640 Hartley Ave., Henderson, NV 89052 USA Tel 702-612-7325
E-mail: dapwishingstone@earthlink.net.

Wispvine Publishing, *(978-1-939997)* Orders Addr.: PO BOX 777, Blaine, WA 98231 USA
E-mail: boyce@smboyce.com
Web site: http://smboyce.com.

Wit & Travesty, *(978-0-692-12532-8; 978-1-7355064)* 45 S. 900 E. No. 12, Provo, UT 84606 USA Tel 913-777-9385
E-mail: whit2ney@hotmail.com
Web site: http://witandtravesty.com.

Witcher Productions, *(978-0-925159; 978-1-55942)* Div. of Marsh Film Enterprises, Inc., P.O. Box 8082, Shawnee Mission, KS 66208 USA Tel 816-523-1059; Fax: 816-333-7421; Toll Free: 800-821-3303 (for orders/customer service only)
E-mail: info@marshmedia.com
Web site: http://www.marshmedia.com
Dist(s): **Follett School Solutions.**

With Little Salt, *(978-0-692-08793-0; 978-0-692-08799-2)* 2778 Kahana St No. C, Wahiawa, HI 96786 USA Tel 808-634-2287
E-mail: withlittlesalt@gmail.com
Dist(s): **Ingram Content Group.**

Witherspoon Pr. *Imprint of* **Curriculum Publishing, Presbyterian Church (U. S. A.)**

Within Reach, Inc., *(978-0-9718864)* P.O. Box 6217, Harrisburg, PA 17112 USA Tel 717-657-8689
E-mail: wreach@epix.net
Web site: http://www.boatingsidekicks.com.

WithinU Life Coaching LLC *See* **A Different Kind of Safari LLC**

Witness Productions, *(978-0-9627653; 978-1-891390)* Box 34, Church St., Marshall, IN 47859 USA Tel 765-597-2487.

Wits Univ. Pr. (ZAF) *(978-0-85494; 978-1-86814; 978-1-77614)* *Dist. by* **IngramPubServ.**

Wits Univ. Pr. (ZAF) *(978-0-85494; 978-1-86814; 978-1-77614)* *Dist. by* **TwoRivers.**

Witsil, Grace, *(978-0-578-47323-9)* 806 W. Brumback St., Boise, ID 83702 USA Tel 919-622-7198
E-mail: gwitsil@gmail.com.

Wittman, Natasha, *(978-0-9904091)* 708 Littler Pl., Edmond, OK 73034 USA Tel 405-432-8989
E-mail: natasha2036@gmail.com.

Witty Bit World, Inc., *(978-0-9770548)* 1009 Basil Dr., New Bern, NC 28562 USA
E-mail: deborah@wittybitworld.com
Web site: http://www.wittybitworld.com.

Witty Fools Productions, *(978-0-9745179)* 19 Le Grande Ave., No.14, Greenwich, CT 06830 USA Toll Free: 877-733-0528 (phone/fax)
E-mail: wittyfools@aol.com; flierlp@bww.com
Web site: http://www.wittyfools.com; http://www.prayerlaughterandbroccoli.com.

Witty Publishing, *(978-0-9785571)* 2875 F Northtowne, Box 232, Reno, NV 89512 USA Toll Free: 866-948-8948.

Witwer, Beverly *See* **Triple Ballerina Pr.**

Wiyd, Lewis, *(978-0-9650637)* 47 Glen Park Rd., East Orange, NJ 07017-1813 USA Tel 973-673-0094; Fax: 973-673-0095.

Wizard Academies, LLC, *(978-0-615-18398-5; 978-0-615-18505-7; 978-0-615-18594-1; 978-0-615-18712-9; 978-0-615-18713-6)* 57485 170th St., Ames, IA 50010-9425 USA
E-mail: rivals@interdrama.com
Web site: http://www.interdrama.com/wiz/
Dist(s): **Lulu Pr., Inc.**

Wizard Academy Pr., *(978-0-9714769; 978-1-932226; 978-0-9987523)* 16621 Crystal Hills Dr., Austin, TX 78737 USA Tel 512-295-5700; Fax: 512-295-5701; Toll Free: 800-425-4769
E-mail: publisher@wizardofads.com; sean@wizardofads.com
Web site: http://www.wizardacademypress.com
Dist(s): **BookBaby.**

Wizard Works, *(978-0-9621543; 978-1-890692)* Orders Addr.: P.O. Box 1125, Homer, AK 99603-1125 USA Toll Free: 877-210-2665
E-mail: wizard@xyz.net
Web site: http://www.xyz.net/~wizard.

Wizarding World Pr., *(978-0-9723936)* 8926 N. Greenwood Ave., Suite 133, Niles, IL 60714 USA
E-mail: wizardingworld@waycoolstuffonline.com
Web site: http://www.wizardingworldpress.com
Dist(s): **Children's Plus, Inc.**
SCB Distributors.

Wizard's Mark Pr., *(978-0-9915720)* 27 Ash Street, Dover, NH 03820 USA Tel 603-866-2466
E-mail: kerrydoherty001@gmail.com.

Wizards of the Coast *Imprint of* **Wizards of the Coast**

Wizards of the Coast, *(978-0-7869; 978-1-57530; 978-1-880992; 978-0-7430)* Subs. of Hasbro, Inc., Orders Addr.: P.O. Box 707, Renton, WA 98057-0709 USA Toll Free: 800-821-8028; Edit Addr.: 1801 Lind Ave., SW, Renton, WA 98055 USA (SAN 299-4410) Tel 425-226-6500; *Imprints*: Mirrorstone (Mirrorstone); Wizards of the Coast (Wiz Coast)
E-mail: angella@wizards.com; ben.glover@wizards.com
Web site: http://www.wizards.com
Dist(s): **Children's Plus, Inc.**
Diamond Bk. Distributors
MyiLibrary
Penguin Random Hse. Distribution
PSI (Publisher Services, Inc.)
Penguin Random Hse. LLC
Random Hse., Inc.
Doherty, Tom Assocs., LLC.

WizdomInc, *(978-0-9764829; 978-0-9767958; 978-0-9768053; 978-0-9778512; 978-0-9785170; 978-0-9786574; 978-0-9820173; 978-0-9840885)* 5438 Village Grn, Los Angeles, CA 90016 USA Tel 323-290-9012; Fax: 707-578-4978; Toll Free: 866-607-4510
E-mail: aswan@wizdominc.com
Web site: http://www.wizdominc.com.

WizKids, LLC, *(978-0-9703934; 978-1-931462; 978-1-59041)* Subs. of Topps Europe Ltd., 2002 156th Ave. NE, #300, Bellevue, WA 98007-3827 USA
E-mail: jenny@wizkidsgames.com; customerservice@wizkidsgames.com
Web site: http://www.mageknight.com
Dist(s): **Diamond Bk. Distributors.**

W.L. Everage U.D. Goines-Audrey, *(978-1-7372104)* 3225 Downan Point Dr., Land O' Lakes, FL 34638 USA Tel 808-753-2743
E-mail: ugoines001@gmail.com.

WMG Publishing, *(978-1-56146; 978-0-615-45856-4; 978-0-615-47789-3; 978-0-615-52179-4; 978-0-615-66540-5; 978-0-615-66719-5; 978-0-615-67595-4; 978-0-615-67930-3; 978-0-615-68516-8; 978-0-615-68580-9; 978-0-615-68615-8; 978-0-615-69013-1; 978-0-615-69847-2; 978-0-615-69928-8; 978-0-615-70162-2; 978-0-615-72423-2; 978-0-615-72618-2; 978-0-615-72684-7; 978-0-615-72699-1; 978-0-615-72735-6; 978-0-615-72785-1; 978-0-615-73028-8; 978-0-615-73043-1; 978-0-615-73363-0; 978-0-615-73684-6; 978-0-615-73725-6; 978-0-)* P.O. Box 269, Lincoln City, OR 97367 USA Tel 541-614-1400 Do not confuse with WMG Publishing in Riverside, CA
E-mail: publisher@wmgpublishing.com
Web site: www.wmgpublishing.com
Dist(s): **CreateSpace Independent Publishing Platform.**

Wms-Ashe, Marcella *See* **Allecram Publishing**

WND Bks, Inc., *(978-0-9746701; 978-0-9767269; 978-0-9778984; 978-0-9790451; 978-0-9792671; 978-1-935071; 978-1-936488; 978-1-938067; 978-1-942475; 978-1-944212; 978-1-944229; 978-1-946918; 978-1-7335841; 978-1-952256)* Orders Addr.: 845 Alder Creek, Medford, OR 97504 USA (SAN 255-7304) Tel 541-474-1776; Fax: 541-474-1770; Edit Addr.: 2020 Pennsylvania Ave., NW No. 351, Washington, DC 20006 USA Tel 571-612-8600; Fax: 571-612-8619; *Imprints*: Kids Ahead Books (Kids Ahead)
E-mail: marketing@wndbooks.com; gstone@wnd.com
Web site: http://www.wnd.com; http://www.wndbooks.com
Dist(s): **Follett School Solutions**
Independent Pubs. Group
McLemore, Hollern & Assocs.
Midpoint Trade Bks., Inc.
MyiLibrary
Quality Bks., Inc.
REKO
ebrary, Inc.

Wobble Hill Pr., *(978-0-9975892)* 2400 Johnson Ave., Bronx, NY 10463 USA Tel 347-907-2292
E-mail: estherk777@gmail.com
Web site: www.wobblehillpress.com.

Wobblefoot Ltd., *(978-0-9747149)* 1662 Mars Ave., Lakewood, OH 44107-3825 USA
E-mail: wblft1@sbcglobal.net
Web site: http://wobblefoot.com.

Wobbly Creek, LLC, *(978-1-7322989; 978-1-7331241; 978-1-953870)* 6579 SE 82nd Ave, Newberry, FL 32669 USA Tel 352-472-1992
E-mail: judithabarrettauthor@gmail.com; wcchick@gmail.com
Web site: wobblycreek.com.

Wobbly Creek, LLS *See* **Wobbly Creek, LLC**

Wocto Publishing, *(978-1-934867)* 7486 La Jolla Blvd., Pmb 559, La Jolla, CA 92037 USA (SAN 855-2754) Tel 858-551-5585; Fax: 858-731-4082; Toll Free: 888-551-5010
E-mail: lin@wocto.com; sales@wocto.com
Web site: http://www.wocto.com.

Wohlers Assocs., Inc., *(978-0-9754429; 978-0-9913332)* OakRidge Business Pk., 1511 River Oak Dr., Fort Collins, CO 80525-5537 USA
Web site: http://www.wohlersassociates.com.

Wojcik, Chelsea, *(978-0-692-32646-6; 978-0-692-99191-6)* 3467 Wainscott Pl., WOODBRIDGE, VA 22192 USA Tel 561-389-0033.

Woks Print *Imprint of* **Writers of the Apocalypse, The**

Wold Creative Group, *(978-0-615-24135-7)* 1392 S. 1100 E., Suite 201, Salt Lake City, UT 84105 USA Tel 801-783-4502
Web site: http://www.woldcreative.com
Dist(s): **Lulu Pr., Inc.**

Wold, Kelly, *(978-0-9768944)* 398 Ricketts Rd. Apt. D, Monterey, CA 93940-7420 USA
E-mail: kmwold@hotmail.com.

Wolf Clan LLC *See* **Wolf Clan LLC**

Wolf Clan LLC, *(978-0-9998710)* 349 W Commercial St. Suite 1100, East Rochester, NY 14445 USA Tel 585-775-7589
E-mail: tess@wolfclanllc.com
Web site: www.wolfclanllc.com.

Wolf Creek Publishing, *(978-0-9768983)* 193 Tenby Chase Dr., Apt. S-233, Delran, NJ 08075 USA
Web site: http://www.photosfromthewild.com.

Wolf Jump Publications, *(978-0-9820440)* 2217 Princess Anne St., Suite 101-1A c/o R.R.R., Fredericksburg, VA 22401 USA
E-mail: rrr@marstel-day.com.

Wolf Pirate Publishing, *(978-0-9798372; 978-0-9822343)* 337 Lost Lake Dr., Divide, CO 80814 USA
E-mail: cmrudy337@gmail.com
Web site: http://www.wolf-pirate.com.

Wolfenden, *(978-0-9642521; 978-0-9786951; 978-0-9973513)* 780-a Redwood Dr., Garberville, CA 95542 USA (SAN 298-4571)
E-mail: dai@asis.com
Web site: http://wolfendenpublishing.com
Dist(s): **Independent Pubs. Group.**

Wolfenden, Ingrid, *(978-0-692-73958-7; 978-0-692-87548-3; 978-0-578-41799-8; 978-0-578-41826-1; 978-0-578-44510-6; 978-0-578-75407-9)* 73 Paradise Cove Way, Felton, DE 19943 USA Tel 302-233-3595
Dist(s): **CreateSpace Independent Publishing Platform.**

Wolfhound Pr. (IRL) *(978-0-86327; 978-0-905473; 978-0-9503454)* *Dist. by* **Interlink Pub.**

Wolfhound Pr. (IRL) *(978-0-86327; 978-0-905473; 978-0-9503454)* *Dist. by* **Irish Amer Bk.**

Wolfhound Pr. (IRL) *(978-0-86327; 978-0-905473; 978-0-9503454)* *Dist. by* **Irish Bks Media.**

Wolfmont, LLC, *(978-0-9778402; 978-1-60364)* 238 Park Dr., NE, Ranger, GA 30734 USA Fax: 702-543-8386; P.O. Box 205, Ranger, GA 30734; *Imprints*: Honey Locust Press (Honey Locust)
E-mail: tony@wolfmont.com; editor@honeylocustpress.com
Web site: http://www.wolfmont.com; http://www.honeylocustpress.com
Dist(s): **Smashwords.**

Wolfmont Publishing *See* **Wolfmont, LLC**

Wolfpack Publishing, *(978-1-885339; 978-0-9895279; 978-1-62918; 978-1-64119; 978-1-64734; 978-1-63977)* 9850 S. Maryland Pkwy. STE. A-5 No. 323, Las Vegas, NV 89183 USA Tel 702-689-3912; *Imprints*: City Lights Press (City Lights P)
E-mail: admin@wolfpackpublishing.com
Web site: https://wolfpackpublishing.com.

Wolfs Corner Publishing, *(978-0-9779921)* 20 Primrose Ln., Sparta, NJ 07871 USA (SAN 856-4191) Tel 973-579-5305
E-mail: jmd_inc007@hotmail.com
Web site: http://www.wolfscornerpublishing.com.

Wolfy International Corp., *(978-1-7327901)* P.O.BOX 87061, College Park, GA 30337 USA Tel 678-368-1292
E-mail: cyapanther@gmail.com.

Wollaston Pr., *(978-0-9657005)* Div. of Ctr. for Learning Abilities, 4013 Coyte Ct., Marietta, GA 30062 USA Tel 678-318-3518; Fax: 208-474-9521
E-mail: morewords@comcast.net.
Wolter, Russel II, *(978-0-692-84564-6)* 7200 Carmel Valley Rd., Carmel, CA 93923 USA Tel 831-915-6798
E-mail: rwolterii@yahoo.com
Dist(s): **Independent Pub.**
Womack, Vanessa Consulting LLC, *(978-1-7348975)* 2123 Cedarhurst Dr., Richmond, VA 23225 USA Tel 804-307-7102
E-mail: vanessawomack@gmail.com
Web site: www.vanessawomack.com.
Womanhood in Color, LLC., *(978-0-578-62502-7)* 14121 bay vista dr apt 302, Woodbridge, VA 22191 USA Tel 434-272-9937
E-mail: kionnamyles@yahoo.com.
Woman's Missionary Union, *(978-0-936625; 978-1-62591)* Orders Addr.: c/o Carol Causey, P.O. Box 830010, Birmingham, AL 35283 USA (SAN 699-7015) Tel 205-991-8100; Fax: 205-995-4825; Toll Free: 800-968-7301; Edit Addr.: 100 Missionary Ridge, Birmingham, AL 35242 USA (SAN 699-7023)
E-mail: cwhite@wmu.org
Web site: http://www.wmu.com
Dist(s): **Send The Light Distribution LLC.**
Wombacher, Michael, *(978-0-9713033)* 2412 Valley St., Berkeley, CA 94702-2136 USA
E-mail: michael_wombacher@excite.com
Web site: http://www.doggonegood.org.
Women & Addiction Counseling & Educational Services, *(978-0-9663144)* 43522 Modena Dr., Temecula, CA 92592-9235 USA Tel 951-303-0235 (phone/fax)
E-mail: info@wacespublishing.com
Web site: http://www.wacespublishing.com.
Women in Aviation, International, *(978-0-9749190)* 3647 State Route 503 S., W Alexandria, OH 45381-9354 USA
Web site: http://www.wai.org.
Women's Pr., Ltd., The (GBR) *(978-0-7043) Dist. by* **Trafalgar.**
Womenspath, Inc., *(978-0-9748982; 978-1-7368226)* 12627 W. 143rd St., Homer Glen, IL 60491 USA Tel 708-645-0300; Fax: 708-645-0841
E-mail: womenspath@attglobal.com.
Wompetias Pr., *(978-0-9961142)* 448 Ocampo Dr., Pacific Palisades, CA 90272 USA Tel 310-454-3970
E-mail: JSharer@gibsondunn.com.
Wonder Books(r) *Imprint of* **Child's World, Inc, The**
Wonder Chess LLC, *(978-0-9771787)* 2622 10th Ave E., Seattle, WA 98102-3901 USA
E-mail: info@wonderchess.com
Web site: http://www.wonderchess.com.
Wonder Forge, Inc., *(978-0-9797123; 978-0-9819248; 978-1-935595)* 300 E. Pike St., Seattle, WA 98122 USA
E-mail: brant@thewonderforge.com
Web site: http://www.thewonderforge.com.
Wonder Forge LLC, The *See* **Wonder Forge, Inc.**
Wonder Mill Cosmos, *(978-1-949561; 978-1-958721)* 4013 Egypt Rd., WILLARD, OH 44890 USA Tel 256-318-1259
E-mail: fanning.lee@gmail.com
Web site: www.wondermillcosmos.com.
Wonder Storm Productions, LLC, *(978-0-578-41819-3; 978-0-578-41824-7; 978-0-578-43645-6)* 1321 Cty. Rd. 501, Bayfield, CO 81122 USA Tel 970-769-9638
E-mail: wonderstormproductions@gmail.com
Dist(s): **Ingram Content Group.**
Wonder Toast Arts, Incorporated *See* **WonderToast**
Wonder Workshop, *(978-1-56919)* Div. of Stephens Group, Inc., 1123 Brookstone Blvd., Mount Juliet, TN 37122-3274 USA Toll Free: 800-627-6874.
Wonderbooks Publishing, *(978-0-9773809)* P.O. Box 770741, Orlando, FL 32877 USA (SAN 257-4535)
Web site: http://www.wonderbookspublishing.com.
Wonderbound *Imprint of* **Creative Mind Energy**
Wonderful Publishing, *(978-0-9798421)* 150 Brewster Rd., Scarsdale, NY 10583 USA (SAN 854-5006)
Web site: http://www.madelineart.com
Dist(s): **Partners Pubs. Group, Inc.**
Wonderment Bks., *(978-0-578-32750-1)* 7836 Ward Pkwy., Kansas City, MO 64114 USA Tel 913-579-5477
E-mail: zachbsewell@gmail.com.
Wonderstrand Pr., *(978-0-9818295)* P.O. Box 156, North Eastham, MA 02651-0156 USA (SAN 856-6585)
E-mail: michael@successonyourownterms.com
Web site: http://www.wonderstrandpress.com.
Wonderstruck Bks. *Imprint of* **Crossroad Pr.**
WonderToast, *(978-0-9761606)* Orders Addr.: 3075 E. Bates Ave., Denver, CO 80210 USA Tel 303-330-4770
E-mail: anna@wondertoast.com
Web site: http://www.wondertoast.com.
Wonkybot Press *See* **Wonkybot Publishing**
Wonkybot Publishing, *(978-0-9830463)* 8583 Irvine Ctr. Dr. Suite No. 377, Irvine, CA 92618 USA
E-mail: hello@wonkybot.com; todd@wonkybot.com; stewart@wonkybot.com
Web site: https://www.wonkybot.com.
Wonnacott, Lee Anne, *(978-0-692-91628-5; 978-0-578-87823-2; 979-8-218-10613-3)* 4326 Avenida Lorenzo Apt A, OCEANSIDE, CA 92057 USA Tel 619-708-5913
E-mail: lwonnaco@gmail.com
Dist(s): **Ingram Content Group.**
Wood Designs, Inc., *(978-0-9729454)* P.O. Box 1790, New Waverly, TX 77358-1790 USA Toll Free Fax: 877-612-8306; Toll Free: 877-612-8306; *Imprints:* MomGeek.com (MomGeek.com)
E-mail: sales@pegrack.com
Web site: http://www.flamencoguide.com.
Wood, Ella Sue, *(978-0-9774937)* 3229 Regatta Pointe Ct., Midlothian, VA 23112 USA.
Wood, Katy Lynn, *(978-0-692-88033-3; 978-0-692-88034-0; 978-0-578-66828-4; 978-0-578-66832-1; 979-8-9861137)* 720 Melany Ln. APT 27 720 Melany Ln. APT 27, Colorado Springs, CO 80907 USA Tel 720-822-0598.
Wood Lake Publishing, Inc. (CAN) *(978-0-919599; 978-0-929032; 978-0-929599; 978-1-55145; 978-1-895562; 978-1-77343) Dist. by* **Westminster John Knox.**
Wood, Rachel, *(978-0-9998818)* 219 Chambers Dr., Lincoln, CA 95648 USA Tel 760-362-3356
E-mail: rcwauthor@gmail.com
Web site: rachelcherie.com.
Woodard, Kate, *(978-0-9979221)* 32 Harvard Sq., Woodridge, NY 12789 USA Tel 845-372-3886
E-mail: ladykatethegreat@hotmail.com.
Woodberry International Publishing, *(978-0-615-73339-5; 978-0-615-73423-1; 978-0-9916537; 979-8-9864744)* 3758 Riverchase way, Decatur, GA 30034 USA Tel 4042415864
Dist(s): **CreateSpace Independent Publishing Platform.**
†**Woodbine Hse.,** *(978-0-933149; 978-1-890627; 978-1-60613)* 6510 Bells Mill Rd., Bethesda, MD 20817 USA (SAN 630-4052) Tel 301-897-3570; Fax: 301-897-5838; Toll Free: 800-843-7323
E-mail: info@woodbinehouse.com
Web site: http://www.woodbinehouse.com; *CIP.*
Woodburn Graphics, Inc., *(978-0-9707547)* P.O. Box 490, Terre Haute, ID 47807 USA Tel 812-232-0323; Fax: 812-232-2733; Toll Free: 800-457-0674
E-mail: len@woodburngraphics.com
Web site: http://www.woodburngraphics.com.
Wooded Hill Productions, *(978-1-886635)* Orders Addr.: 7480 Esplin Way, Flagstaff, AZ 86004 USA Tel 928-522-0058 (phone/fax)
E-mail: sig@boloz.com; sigmund.boloz@nau.edu
Web site: http://www.boloz.com.
Wooded Isle Pr., LLC, *(978-0-9844898; 978-0-9916623)* 2400 NW 80th St., No. 272, Seattle, WA 98117-4449 USA (SAN 859-5534)
E-mail: jrdetering@comcast.net; editor@woodedislepress.com
Web site: http://www.woodedislepress.com.
Wooden Nickel Pr., *(978-0-615-25177-6; 978-0-9882891)* 2189 N. 55th St., Milwaukee, WI 53208 USA
Web site: http://www.woodennickelpress.com.
Wooden Roses Publishing!, *(978-1-7324627)* 1304 New York Ave Apt 5B, Brooklyn, NY 11203 USA Tel 646-707-7588
E-mail: nyeshadavis@gmail.com
Web site: woodenrosespublishing.com.
Wooden Shoe Pr., *(978-0-9762852)* N3566 Cty. Rd., GG, Hancock, WI 54943 USA Do not confuse with Wooden Shoe Press in Philadelphia, PA
E-mail: woodenshoepress@yahoo.com
Web site: http://www.woodenshoepress.com.
WoodenBoat Pubns., *(978-0-937822; 978-1-934982)* P.O. Box 78, Brooklin, ME 04616 USA Tel 207-359-4651; Fax: 207-359-2058; Toll Free: 800-273-7447
E-mail: books@woodenboat.com; wbstore@woodenboat.com
Web site: http://www.woodenboat.com.
Woodfrost Publishing, *(978-1-7320414)* 3944 Brown Bear Trail, Campbell, TX 75422 USA (SAN 990-9966) Tel 903-886-8999
E-mail: canzo2@gmail.com
Web site: davidcanzoneri.com.
Woodglen Publishing LLC, *(978-0-9827951)* P.O. Box 122, Califon, NJ 07830 USA Tel 908-638-5338; Fax: 908-638-0368
E-mail: stephanie@woodglenpublishing.com
Web site: http://www.woodglenpublishing.com.
Woodhall Pr., *(978-0-9975437; 978-1-949116; 978-1-954907; 978-1-960456)* 81 Main Street, Unit 25A, Branford, CT 06405 USA Tel 203-807-8321
E-mail: woodhallpress@gmail.com
Web site: woodhallpress.com
Dist(s): **Independent Pubs. Group.**
Woodland Health Books *See* **Woodland Publishing, Inc.**
Woodland Pr., *(978-0-9755822)* 605 Timber Ln., Lake Forest, IL 60045-3117 USA Tel 847-295-3514; 847-924-0324 Do not confuse with companies with the same name in Minneapolis, MN, Lapeer MI, Salt Lake City, UT.
Woodland Pr., LLC, *(978-0-9724867; 978-0-9793236; 978-0-9824939; 978-0-9829937; 978-0-9852640; 978-0-9912301)* 118 Woodland, Suite 1102, Chapmanville, WV 25508 USA (SAN 254-9999) Tel 304-752-7500; Fax: 304-752-9002 Do not confuse with companies with the same or similar names in Minneapolis, MN, Lapeer, MI, Salt Lake City, UT, Florance, AL, Moscow, ID
E-mail: info@woodlandpress.com; woodlandpressllc@mac.com; fkeithdavis@me.com
Web site: http://www.woodlandpress.com
Dist(s): **New Day Christian Distributors Gifts, Inc.**
Quality Bks., Inc.
West Virginia Book Co., The
Woodland Distribution.
Woodland Publishing, Inc., *(978-0-913923; 978-1-58054; 978-1-885670)* Orders Addr.: 1777 Sun Peak Dr., Park City, UT 84098 USA (SAN 286-9063)
Web site: http://www.woodlandpublishing.com
Dist(s): **Integral Yoga Pubns.**
New Leaf Distributing Co., Inc.
Nutri-Bks. Corp.
Royal Pubns., Inc.
Woodland Scenics, *(978-1-887436)* Div. of Osment Models, Inc., Orders Addr.: P.O. Box 98, Linn Creek, MO 65052 USA Tel 573-346-5555; Toll Free: 800-346-6642; Edit Addr.: 101 E. Valley Dr., Linn Creek, MO 65052 USA
E-mail: sales@woodlandscenics.com.
Woodruff, David Roberts, *(978-0-9716806)* 4075 Carmel View Rd., No.9, San Deigo, CA 92130 USA
E-mail: drbts@att.net.
Woodruff, Paul, *(978-0-9764327)* 58048 Inglewood Ln., Glenwood, IA 51534 USA.
Woods, Candace E., *(978-0-578-55878-3)* 11 Park Pl., New Rochelle, NY 10801 USA Tel 914-646-8481
Dist(s): **CreateSpace Independent Publishing Platform.**
Woods, Emmett L., *(978-0-615-12589-3)* 4016 Monterey Ct., Montgomery, AL 36116 USA Tel 334-288-1380.
Woods, James E, *(978-0-9973324; 978-1-947380)* P.O. Box PO Box 7414, Wilmington, DE 19803 USA Tel 267-446-4433
E-mail: woods2210@elsca.org.
Woods N' Water, Incorporated *See* **Woods N' Water Pr., Inc.**
Woods N' Water Pr., Inc., *(978-0-9707493; 978-0-9722804; 978-0-9769233; 978-0-9795131; 978-0-9820414; 978-0-9828228; 978-0-615-38124-4)* Orders Addr.: P.O. Box 10, South New Berlin, NY 13843 USA (SAN 254-3869) Tel 607-548-4011; Fax: 607-548-4013; Toll Free: 800-652-7527; Edit Addr.: 3312 State Hwy. 8, South New Berlin, NY 13843 USA Tel 607-548-4011; Fax: 607-548-4013; Toll Free: 800-652-7527
E-mail: kate@fiduccia.com
Web site: http://www.woodsnwaterpress.com; http://www.atabooks.com
Dist(s): **Cardinal Pubs. Group.**
Woodsmere Pr., LLC, *(978-0-9679600)* Orders Addr.: PO Box 726, Pendleton, SC 29670-0726 USA Tel 864-654-6833; Fax: 888-282-2320; Edit Addr.: P.O. Box 726, Pendleton, SC 29670 USA Tel 864-654-6833; Fax: 888-282-2320
E-mail: fredsias@woodsmerepress.com
Web site: http://www.woodsmerepress.com; http://www.woodsmere.com
Dist(s): **Euro Tool, Inc.**
Woodstocker Books/Arthur Schwartz & Company, *(978-1-879504)* 15 Meads Mountain Rd., Woodstock, NY 12498-1016 USA (SAN 630-0464) Tel 845-679-4024; Fax: 845-679-4093; Toll Free: 800-669-9080 (orders only)
E-mail: woodstockerbooks@woodstockerbooks.com
Web site: http://www.aschwartzbooks.com
Dist(s): **Antique Collectors' Club**
National Bk. Network.
Woodward, Stephanie Lynn, *(978-0-578-50075-1; 978-0-578-50076-8)* 4080 Riverlook Pkwy SE Unit 102, Marietta, GA 30067 USA Tel 817-637-0952
E-mail: Stephanielynnwoodward@gmail.com; boudreau619@gmail.com
Dist(s): **Ingram Content Group.**
Woody Norman LLC *See* **Archdeacon Bks.**
Woolfolk Publications *See* **Gye Nyame Hse.**
Woolley Family Studios, *(978-0-9909391)* 34 Hadley St., Cambridge, MA 02140 USA Tel 310-909-4329
E-mail: jakegpanda@gmail.com
Web site: www.endangeredfiles.com.
Wooster Bk. Co., The, *(978-1-888683; 978-1-59098)* 205 W. Liberty St., Wooster, OH 44691-4831 USA Tel 330-262-1688; Fax: 330-264-9753; Toll Free: 800-982-6651 (800-WUBook-1)
E-mail: mail@woosterbook.com
Web site: http://www.woosterbook.com.
W.O.P. Pr., *(978-0-615-95687-9; 978-0-615-97065-3; 978-0-692-71789-9; 978-0-692-05869-5)* 7237 Mountain Knoll Dr. SE, Caledonia, MI 49508 USA Tel 616-929-0697
E-mail: stephenstromp@gmail.com
Dist(s): **CreateSpace Independent Publishing Platform.**
Wo-Pila Publishing, *(978-1-886340)* Orders Addr.: P.O. Box 8966, Erie, PA 16505-0966 USA Tel 814-868-5331; Fax: 814-868-1711; Toll Free: 888-567-8267; Edit Addr.: 3324 Charlotte St., Erie, PA 16508-2224 USA
E-mail: WopilaPublishing@aol.com
Web site: http://www.MannyTwofeathers.com.
Word Aflame Pr., *(978-0-912315; 978-0-932581; 978-1-56722; 978-0-7577)* Subs. of Pentecostal Publishing Hse., 8855 Dunn Rd., Hazelwood, MO 63042 USA (SAN 212-0046) Tel 314-837-7300; Fax: 314-837-6574
E-mail: pph@upci.org
Web site: http://www.upci.org/pph.
Word Among Us Pr., *(978-0-932085; 978-1-59325)* 7115 Guilford Dr. Suite 100, Frederick, MD 21704 USA (SAN 686-4651) Tel 301-831-1262; Fax: 301-831-1188; Toll Free: 800-775-9673
E-mail: pmm@wall.org; april@wau.org
Web site: http://www.wau.org
Dist(s): **Spring Arbor Distributors, Inc.**
Word & Spirit Publishing, LLC., *(978-0-9842534; 978-1-936314; 978-1-939570; 978-1-949106; 978-1-68573)* 6604 S. 1st St., Broken Arrow, OK 74133 USA Tel 918-608-5858; Fax: 918-893-2656
Web site: http://www.wordandspiritresources.com
Dist(s): **Whitaker Hse.**
Word & Spirit Resources, LLC. *See* **Word & Spirit Publishing, LLC.**
Word Art Publishing, *(978-1-955070)* 9350 Wilshire Blvd, Suite 203, Beverly Hills, CA 90210 USA Tel 917-792-8190
E-mail: gelmelgar@gmail.com
Web site: www.wordartpublishing.com.
Word Assocs., Inc., *(978-0-939153; 978-1-57265)* 3226 Robincrest Dr., Northbrook, IL 60062 USA (SAN 679-7792) Tel 847-291-1101; Fax: 847-291-0931
E-mail: microlm@aol.com
Web site: http://www.wordassociates.com.
Word Association Pubs., *(978-1-891231; 978-1-932205; 978-1-59571; 978-1-63385)* 205 Fifth Ave., Tarentum, PA 15084 USA Tel 724-226-4526; Fax: 724-226-3974; Toll Free: 800-827-7903
E-mail: publish@wordassociation.com
Web site: http://www.wordassociation.com
Dist(s): **Chicago Distribution Ctr.**
Word Distribution *See* **Word Entertainment**
Word Entertainment, *(978-0-9644619; 978-1-933876)* 25 Music Sq. W., Nashville, TN 37203 USA Tel 615-726-7900; Toll Free Fax: 800-671-6601; Toll Free: 800-876-9673; *Imprints:* Word Music (Word Music)
E-mail: matt.taylor@wordentertainment.com
Web site: http://www.wordentertainment.com
Dist(s): **Christian Bk. Distributors.**
Word For Word Publishing Co., *(978-1-889732)* 144 Quincy St. Apt. 1, Brooklyn, NY 11216-1393 USA; *Imprints:* A & E Sivells Publications (A & E Sivells Pubns)
E-mail: word4wrd@aol.com.
Word Gift Pubns., *(978-0-9788381)* 6641 Cty. Rd. 912, Joshua, TX 76058 USA (SAN 851-7223)
E-mail: peregrina@wordgift.org
Web site: http://www.wordgift.org.
Word Music *Imprint of* **Word Entertainment**
Word of Life Fellowship, Inc., *(978-1-931235; 978-1-935475)* Orders Addr.: P.O. Box 600, Schroon Lake, NY 12870-0600 USA Fax: 518-494-6312; Toll Free: 888-932-5827; Edit Addr.: 71 Olmstedville Rd., Pottersville, NY 12860 USA Do not confuse with Word of Life Fellowship, Sand Springs, OK
E-mail: timf@wol.org; DReichard@wol.org
Web site: http://www.wol.org.
Word of Mouth Bks. *Imprint of* **KA Productions, LLC**
Word of Mouth Marketing, *(978-1-953448)* 9030 W. Sahara Suite 225, Las Vegas, NV 89117 USA Tel 702-243-8808
E-mail: terri@wordofmouthmarketinggroup.com
Web site: www.believeuniversity.org.
Word of Mouth Pr., *(978-0-615-24213-2; 978-0-578-03631-1; 978-0-578-05051-5; 978-0-578-05113-0; 978-0-578-12825-2; 978-0-578-93831-8; 978-0-578-93832-5)* 406 Shelby St., Kingsport, TN 37660 USA Tel 423-245-1199
E-mail: electragraphics@earthlink.net.
Word on Da Street Publishing, *(978-0-615-52643-0; 978-0-615-64869-9; 978-0-9885056)* 252 W. Westfield Ave. 252 W. Westfield Ave, Roselle Park, NJ 07204 USA Tel 973-445-1690
E-mail: llperry803@gmail.com.
Word Productions, *(978-0-9728590; 978-0-9765010; 978-0-9827998; 978-0-9909245; 978-0-9978373; 978-1-7356273; 979-8-9866629)* ; *Imprints:* Kid-E Books (KID-E Bks)
E-mail: media@wordproductions.org; wordproductions@aol.com
Web site: http://www.wordproductions.org
Dist(s): **Independently Published.**
Word Productions LLC *See* **Word Productions**
Word Prostitute, *(978-0-9728465)* 5016 SE. 33rd Pl., Portland, OR 97202 USA
E-mail: kalabjoster@wordprostitute.com
Web site: http://www.wordprostitute.com.
Word Riot Pr., *(978-0-9728200; 978-0-9779343)* P.O. Box 414, Middletown, NJ 07748 USA
E-mail: editor@wordriot.org
Web site: http://www.wordriot.org
Dist(s): **Pathway Bk. Service.**
Word Seed Publishing, *(978-0-9755232)* 650 NE 2nd St., Hermiston, OR 97838 USA Tel 541-567-0886; Fax: 541-481-7500
E-mail: hashcraftz1@charter.net.
Word Supremacy Pr., *(978-0-9747231)* 910 St., Paul St., No. C, Baltimore, MD 21202 USA Tel 443-414-4600; Fax: 877-504-3140
E-mail: taalam@aol.com
Web site: http://www.taalamacey.com.
Word To The Wise, A, *(978-0-9849321)* 2547 Dug Hill Rd., Brownsboro, AL 35741 USA Tel 256-541-4920
E-mail: edgoad@fastmail.fm.
Word Weaver Bks., Inc., *(978-0-9670600)* 9743 W. Bray Creek St., Star, ID 83669-5815 USA
E-mail: tidegirl32@aol.com
Web site: http://www.wordweaverbooks.com.
Word with You Pr., A, *(978-0-9843064; 978-0-9829094; 978-0-9884646; 978-1-7365480)* 802 S. Tremont St., Oceanside, CA 92054 USA Tel 760-500-5409; 310 E. A St. Suite B, Moscow, ID 83843 Tel 760-500-5409
E-mail: thom@awordwithyoupress.com
Web site: http://awordwithyoupress.com.
Word Wright International *See* **WordWright.biz, Inc.**
Wordclay *Imprint of* **Author Solutions, LLC**
Wordcraft of Oregon, LLC, *(978-1-877655; 978-0-9964371)* P.O. Box 3235, La Grande, OR 97850 USA Do not confuse with Wordcraft, Oakland, CA
E-mail: info@wordcraftoforegon.com
Web site: http://www.wordcraftoforegon.com.
Worden, Robin, *(978-1-7338803)* 2552 Big Oak Rd., Harrison, AR 72601 USA Tel 870-391-6352
E-mail: silvermustang2005@yahoo.com.
WordFire, Incorporated *See* **WordFire Pr.**
WordFire Pr. *Imprint of* **WordFire Pr.**
WordFire Pr., *(978-0-9673548; 978-1-61475; 978-1-68057)* P.O. Box 1840, Monument, CO 80132-1840 USA; *Imprints:* WordFire Press (WrdFire Pr)
E-mail: reb@wordfire.com
Web site: http://wordfire.com; http://wordfirepress.com
Dist(s): **Greenleaf Book Group**
Open Road Integrated Media, Inc.
WordHse., *(978-1-68547)* 101 Foundry Dr, West Lafayette, IN 47906 USA Tel 812-392-4053
E-mail: nicky.parker@wordhousebp.com
Web site: https://wordhousebp.com.
WordMaster Publishing, *(978-0-9740410)* 4317 W. Farrand Rd., Clio, MI 48420 USA (SAN 255-3325) Tel 810-686-2047; Fax: 810-564-9929
E-mail: wordmasterpub@aol.com.
Wordmeister Pr., *(978-0-9978925; 978-1-7351213)* 1101 Riverside Dr., Owosso, MI 48867 USA Tel 989-723-2084
E-mail: juliewenzlick@gmail.com.

Wordminder Pr., *(978-0-9729103)* Orders Addr.: 1008 Norview Ave., Norfolk, VA 23513-3410 USA Tel 757-853-4775
E-mail: sma@wordminderpress.com; wp@wordminderpress.com
Web site: http://www.wordminderpress.com
Dist(s): **CreateSpace Independent Publishing Platform.**

WordPlay Multimedia, LLC, *(978-0-9755444)* Orders Addr.: P.O. Box 9303, Jacksonville, FL 32208 USA Tel 904-683-8032
E-mail: jjfrederick98@aol.com
Web site: http://www.frederickpreston.com
Dist(s): **A & B Distributors & Pubs. Group.**

Words & Music, *(978-0-9800880; 978-0-615-15540-1)* 13967 Amber Pl., San Diego, CA 92130 USA Do not confuse with Words & Music, Gig Harbor, CA
E-mail: info@talesalive.com
Web site: http://www.talesalive.com.

Words & Pictures Publishing, Inc., *(978-0-9621280)* P.O. Box 61444, Honolulu, HI 96839 USA (SAN 250-9326) Tel 808-955-4742; Fax: 808-951-6541
E-mail: gecko@aloha.net
Web site: http://www.brucehale.com
Dist(s): **Booklines Hawaii, Ltd.**
Sunbelt Pubns., Inc.

Words From The Heart Publishing Co., *(978-1-7355012)* 99 Winslow Cir., Savannah, GA 31407 USA Tel 704-574-1650
E-mail: wordsfromtheheartpublishing@gmail.com
Web site: www.AuthorShabarbara.com.

Words In The Works, LLC, *(978-0-9910364; 978-0-9972284; 978-1-7320524)* P.O. Box 448, North Salem, NY 10560 USA Tel 914-841-0896; *Imprints:* Crystal Books (Crystal Bks)
E-mail: info@wordsintheworks.com.

Words of Essence Publishing, *(978-0-9768133)* P.O. Box 13182, Durham, NC 27709 USA Tel 919-624-4138
E-mail: godslove232@yahoo.com
Web site: http://www.wordsofessence.com.

Words of Wisdom, *(978-1-947211)* 803 Hadley Ave, Old Hickory, TN 37138 USA Tel 615-448-7304; Fax: 866-350-0669
E-mail: kpruittwow@gmail.com
Web site: www.woweducationalconsulting.com.

words4u, *(978-0-9740419)* P.O. Box 641257, San Francisco, CA 94164-1257 USA
E-mail: info@words4u.com
Web site: http://www.words4u.com.

WordsBright, *(978-1-940229)* 501-I S. Reino Rd, No. 365, Newbury Park, CA 91320 USA Tel 805-413-4525
E-mail: contactus@wordsbright.com
Web site: www.wordsbright.com
Dist(s): **Pathway Bk. Service.**

Wordshed, *(978-0-942684)* 5118 Glendale St., Duluth, MN 55804-1107 USA (SAN 239-6246) Tel 218-525-3266.

Wordsmith Bks., *(978-1-882646)* 107 SHERWOOD Cir., CROSSVILLE, TN 38558 USA Tel 931-287-0907 Do not confuse with Wordsmith Bks. in Auburn, AL
E-mail: catalano.tom@gmail.com.

Wordsmith Pr., *(978-1-893972)* 11462 East Ln., Whitmore Lake, MI 48189 USA Tel 810-231-5435
E-mail: info@thewordsmithpress.com
Web site: http://www.thewordsmithpress.com.

Wordsmiths, *(978-0-9632774; 978-1-886061)* 1355 Ferry Rd., Grants Pass, OR 97526 USA Tel 541-476-3080; Fax: 541-474-9756 Do not confuse with the Wordsmiths in Evergreen, CO
E-mail: frodej@chatlink.com
Web site: http://www.jsgrammar.com.

Wordsong *Imprint of* **Highlights Pr., c/o Highlights for Children, Inc.**

Wordsworth Editions, Ltd. (GBR) *(978-1-85326; 978-1-84022; 978-1-84870) Dist. by* **LBMayAssocs.**

WORDSWORTH Publishing Co., *(978-0-9672491; 978-0-9754351)* Orders Addr.: P.O. Box 7132, Santa Rosa, CA 95407 USA Tel 707-829-2316 (phone/fax); Edit Addr.: 2524 S. Edison St., Graton, CA 95444 USA
E-mail: wwinfo@getyourwordsworth.com
Web site: http://www.getyourwordsworth.com.

WordThunder Pubns., *(978-0-9745268; 978-1-59790)* P.O. Box 540931, Merritt Island, FL 32954 USA (SAN 256-3770)
E-mail: books@wordthunder.com
Web site: http://wordthunder.com/books/.

Wordwhittler Bks., *(978-0-9895487)* 3073 Cypress Creek Dr. N., Ponte Vedra Beach, FL 32082 USA Tel 904-285-8531
E-mail: sscalfee@aol.com.

Wordwindow LLC, *(978-0-9774484)* 2125 Jackson Bluff Rd. Apt. V-204, Tallahassee, FL 32304 USA Toll Free: 877-967-3946
Web site: http://www.thankheavenforart.com.

WordWorks Publishing, *(978-0-9831557)* 1081 Rosedale Dr., Atlanta, GA 30306 USA Tel 404-664-5256 Do not confuse with WordWorks Publishing in Austin, TX, Westfield, IN
E-mail: laurelannd@gmail.com
Dist(s): **BookBaby.**

Wordwright Communications, *(978-0-9718838)* 4900 Randall Pkwy. Ste. F, Wilmington, NC 28403-2831 USA Toll Free: 888-235-0248.

WordWright.biz, Inc., *(978-0-9700615; 978-0-9713832; 978-0-9717868; 978-1-932196; 978-1-934335)* P.O. Box 1785, Georgetown, TX 78627 USA Fax: 512-260-3080 (phone/fax); *Imprints:* Legacy (Lgcy TX); One Night Books (One Night Bks)
E-mail: joan@wordwright.biz; snwriter@earthlink.net; jnwriter@aol.com
Web site: http://www.wordwright.biz.

Work, Rare Bks., *(978-1-7367317; 978-1-7369312; 978-1-7369762)* 602 Cedar Swamp Ave., Watsonville, CA 95076 USA Tel 415-616-9372
E-mail: rareworkbooks@protonmail.com.

WorkBk. Pr., *(978-1-952754; 978-1-953839; 978-1-954753; 978-1-955459; 978-1-956017; 978-1-956876; 978-1-957618; 978-1-958176; 978-1-960752; 978-1-961845)* 187 E Warm Springs Rd, Suite B285, Las Vegas, NV 89119 USA Tel 888-818-4856
E-mail: admin@workbookpress.com
Web site: www.workbookpress.com.

Workhouse Road Productions *See* **DREAMTITLE PUBLISHING LLC**

Working Parents, LLC, *(978-0-9711040)* P.O. Box 715, Santa Clara, CA 95052-0715 USA Tel 408-554-0280 (phone/fax)
E-mail: info@workingparents.com
Web site: http://www.workingparents.com.

Working Title Publishing, *(978-1-59344; 978-0-9776440)* P.O. Box 384, Lodi, CA 95241 USA
Web site: http://www.workingtitlepublishing.com.

Working Words & Graphics *See* **Lockman, James Consulting**

†Workman Publishing Co., Inc., *(978-0-7611; 978-0-89480; 978-0-911104; 978-1-56305; 978-1-5235)* Orders Addr.: 225 Varick St., New York, NY 10014-4381 USA (SAN 203-2821) Tel 212-254-5900; Fax: 212-254-8098; Toll Free: 800-722-7202
E-mail: info@workman.com
Web site: http://www.workman.com
Dist(s): **Blackstone Audio, Inc.**
Children's Plus, Inc.
Experiment LLC, The
Hachette Bk. Group
Open Road Integrated Media, Inc.
Storey Publishing, LLC
Timber Pr., Inc.; *CIP.*

World Ahead Media *See* **WND Bks, Inc.**

World Almanac Library *Imprint of* **Stevens, Gareth Publishing LLLP**

World Audience Pubs., *(978-0-9788086; 978-1-934209; 978-0-9820540; 978-1-935444)* 303 Pk. Ave. S., Suite 1440, New York, NY 10010 USA
E-mail: worldaudience@gmail.com; mstefanstrozier@gmail.com
Web site: http://www.worldaudience.org; http://www.worldaudience.mobi; http://www.worldaudience.co.uk.

World Awake Bks., *(978-0-615-26795-1)* 15508 W. Bell Rd., Suite 101,, Surprise, AZ 85374 USA.

†World Bank Pubns., *(978-0-8213; 978-1-4648)* Orders Addr.: P.O. Box 960, Herndon, VA 20172-0960 USA Toll Free: 800-645-7247; Edit Addr.: 1818 H St., NW, Mail Stop: U11-1104, Washington, DC 20433 USA (SAN 219-0648) Tel 703-661-1580; 202-473-1000 (Head Office); Fax: 202-614-1237
E-mail: books@worldbank.org
Web site: http://www.worldbank.org/publications
Dist(s): **Bernan Assocs.**
Ebsco Publishing
Independent Pubs. Group
MyiLibrary
Oxford Univ. Pr., Inc.
Rowman & Littlefield Publishers, Inc.
ebrary, Inc.; *CIP.*

World Bk., Inc., *(978-0-7166)* Div. of Scott Fetzer Co., 180 N. LaSalle St., Suite 900, Chicago, IL 60601 USA (SAN 201-4815) Tel 312-729-5800; Fax: 312-729-5600; Toll Free Fax: 800-975-3250
Web site: http://www.worldbook.com
Dist(s): **MyiLibrary.**

World CARP, *(978-0-9722946)* 4 W. 43rd St., New York, NY 10036-7408 USA
E-mail: yyk21@worldcarp.org
Web site: http://www.worldcarp.org.

World Cycling Pr., *(978-0-9745842)* 3910 Chapman St., San Diego, CA 92110-5694 USA Tel 619-224-1050; Fax: 619-224-0530
E-mail: team_mallory@hotmail.com.

World Enough Writers, *(978-1-937797)* c/o Lana Ayers, P.O. Box 1808, Kingston, WA 98346 USA Tel 360-881-0880
E-mail: WorldEnoughWriters@yahoo.com
Web site: http://WorldEnoughWriters.com.

World Famous Children's Bks., *(978-0-9725398)* 4455 Torrance Blvd, No. 153, Torrance, CA 90503 USA
Web site: http://www.worldfamouschildrensbooks.com
Dist(s): **Quality Bks., Inc.**

World Forward Foundation, 5090 Easley Rd., Golden, CO 80403 USA Tel 720-545-6350
E-mail: shannon@worldforwardfoundation.org
Dist(s): **Ingram Content Group.**

World Health Organization, *(978-0-11)* Orders Addr.: 49 Sheridan Ave., Albany, NY 12210 USA (SAN 221-6310) Tel 518-436-9686; Fax: 518-436-7433; Edit Addr.: Av Appia, Geneva, 1211 CHE Tel 41-22) 7912111; Fax: 41-22) 7910746
E-mail: publications@who.int
Web site: http://www.who.ch
Dist(s): **Balogh International, Inc.**
Bernan Assocs.
MyiLibrary
Stylus Publishing, LLC
Women Ink.

World Is Mine Publishing LLC, *(978-0-692-83049-9; 978-0-578-99222-8; 979-8-218-15509-4)* 725 Schoolhouse Rd, San Jose, CA 95138 USA Tel 909-576-5542
E-mail: worldisminepublishing@outlook.com
Dist(s): **Independent Pub.**

World Leisure Marketing Ltd (GBR) *(978-1-84006; 978-1-899026) Dist. by* **Midpt Trade.**

World Library Pubns., *(978-0-937690; 978-1-58459; 978-1-64321)* Div. of J. S. Paluch Co., Inc., 3708 River Rd. Suite 400, Franklin Park, IL 60131-2158 USA (SAN 203-0306) Tel 847-233-2767; Toll Free Fax: 888-957-3291; Toll Free: 800-621-5197
E-mail: wlpcs@jspaluch.com
Web site: http://www.wlpmusic.com
Dist(s): **Ingram Publisher Services**
Spring Arbor Distributors, Inc.

World Nouveau, *(978-0-9828865; 978-1-938208)* P.O. Box 571, Torrance, CA 90508 USA Tel 310-776-5510
E-mail: WorldNouveau@Gmail.com
Web site: http://www.WorldNouveau.com.

World of Angels, A *See* **Roseann Miller & Linda Stephens-Hooe**

World of Empowerment *See* **Twin Flame Productions**

World of Imagination, *(978-0-9761228)* 200 N. Maryland Ave., Suite 101, Glendale, CA 91206 USA Tel 818-547-5541; Fax: 818-543-1889; Toll Free: 800-266-5255.

World of Learning Publishing *See* **Swift Learning Resources**

World of Reading, Ltd., P.O. Box 13092, Atlanta, GA 30324-0092 USA Tel 404-233-4042; Fax: 404-237-5511; Toll Free: 800-729-3703.

World of Whimsy Productions, LLC, *(978-0-9702675)* 409 N. Pacific Coast Hwy., No. 594, Redondo Beach, CA 90277 USA (SAN 256-1077) Fax: 310-542-9297; Toll Free: 1-888-4-WHIMSY
E-mail: info@worldofwhimsy.com
Web site: http://worldofwhimsy.com.

World Pubns. Group, Inc., *(978-0-7669; 978-0-9640034; 978-1-57215; 978-0-7429; 978-1-4132; 978-1-4279; 978-1-4376; 978-1-4513; 978-1-4643; 978-1-4785)* Orders Addr.: P.O. Box 509, East Bridgewater, MA 02333 USA (SAN 631-7014); *Imprints:* JG Press (JG Pr)
E-mail: sales@wrldpub.net
Web site: http://www.wrldpub.com
Dist(s): **Hachette Bk. Group.**

World Publications, Incorporated *See* **World Pubns. Group, Inc.**

World Quest Learning, *(978-1-933248)* P.O. Box 654, Lewis Center, OH 43035 USA Tel 740-548-3857; Toll Free Fax: 866-722-7521; Toll Free: 866-722-7520
E-mail: info@worldquestlearning.com
Web site: http://www.worldquestlearning.com.

World Thoughts Publishing, Co., *(978-0-9711018)* P.O. Box 3206, Saint Augustine, FL 32084-3206 USA
E-mail: beebes@aug.com
Web site: http://www.energeticawakening.com; http://www.worldthoughts.com.

World Tribune Pr., *(978-0-915678; 978-1-932911; 978-1-935523; 978-1-944604)* Orders Addr.: 8811 Aviation Blvd., Inglewood, CA 90301 USA Tel 310-337-0055; Fax: 310-642-4625; Toll Free: 800-626-1313; Edit Addr.: 606 Wilshire Blvd., Santa Monica, CA 90401 USA (SAN 683-230X) Tel 310-260-8900; Fax: 310-260-8910
E-mail: dmcneill@sgi-usa.org
Dist(s): **PCE International.**

World Wide Distributors, Limited *See* **Island Heritage Publishing**

World Wisdom, Inc., *(978-0-941532; 978-1-933316; 978-1-935493; 978-1-936597; 978-1-937786; 978-1-957670)* Orders Addr.: P.O. Box 2682, Bloomington, IN 47402-2682 USA (SAN 239-1406) Tel 812-330-3232; Fax: 812-333-1642; Toll Free: 888-992-6651; Edit Addr.: 1501 E. Hillside Dr., Bloomington, IN 47401 USA; *Imprints:* Wisdom Tales (WisdomTales)
Web site: http://www.worldwisdom.com
Dist(s): **Follett School Solutions**
MyiLibrary
National Bk. Network
New Leaf Distributing Co., Inc.
Send The Light Distribution LLC
ebrary, Inc.

Worlds In Ink *See* **Worlds In Ink Publishing, Inc.**

Worlds In Ink Publishing, Inc., *(978-0-9745568)* 4812 Ridgecrest Cir SE, Albuquerque, NM 87108-4435 USA
E-mail: info@WorldsInInk.com
Web site: http://www.WorldsInInk.com.

WorldTrek Publishing, *(978-1-936376)* 121 E. Vermijo, Colorado Springs, CO 80903 USA (SAN 859-7154).

Worldview Publishing, Inc., *(978-1-889995)* 521 Herchel Dr., Tampa, FL 33617 USA Tel 813-985-9344; Fax: 813-985-4505; Toll Free: 800-987-9444 Do not confuse with companies with same or similar names in Tiburon, CA, Colorado Springs, CO
E-mail: drlindahf@aol.com
Web site: http://www.worldviewpub.com.

Worldwide Publishing Group, *(978-0-692-20798-7; 978-0-692-21343-8; 978-0-692-23202-6; 978-0-692-26528-4; 978-0-692-28543-5; 978-0-692-33975-6; 978-0-692-34486-6; 978-0-692-34654-9; 978-0-692-35794-1; 978-0-692-35819-1; 978-0-692-36089-7; 978-0-692-38604-0; 978-0-692-40727-1; 978-0-692-41000-4; 978-0-692-41425-5; 978-0-692-41942-7; 978-0-692-46338-3; 978-0-692-47708-3; 978-0-692-49561-2; 978-0-692-49566-7; 978-0-692-49571-1; 978-0-692-50705-6; 978-0-692-50706-3; 978-0-692-50707-0; 978-0-692-50708-7; 978-0-692-50709-4;) P.O. Box 596, Litchfield, IL 62056 USA Tel 217-851-0361*
E-mail: rwgcontact@yahoo.com
Web site: http://www.worldwidepublishinggroup.com/
Dist(s): **CreateSpace Independent Publishing Platform.**

Worldwide United Publishing *See* **Pearl Publishing, LLC**

Worley, Kayla, *(978-0-578-43153-6; 978-0-578-63097-7; 978-0-578-63253-7)* 7411 N. Delaware Ave., Portland, OR 97217 USA Tel 503-887-5504
E-mail: thisissoyoudonotforget@hotmail.com
Dist(s): **Ingram Content Group.**

Worn Pants, *(978-0-9766621)* 19842 Needles St., Chatsworth, CA 91311 USA
E-mail: mbernal@aol.com.

Worthen, Olivia, *(978-0-9996833)* 9422 Heather Brae Ct., South Jordan, UT 84095 USA Tel 801-580-1465
E-mail: flower9422@comcast.net.

Worthwhile Bks. *Imprint of* **Idea & Design Works, LLC**

Worthy Kids/Ideals *Imprint of* **Worthy Publishing**

Worthy Publishing, 10 Cadillac Dr., Brentwood, TN 37027 USA Tel 615-221-0996; *Imprints:* F/S (FslashS); Ellie Claire (WEllieClaire); Ideals Publications (IdealsPub); Worthy Kids/Ideals (WKidsnIdeals)
Dist(s): **Blackstone Audio, Inc.**
Children's Plus, Inc.
Hachette Bk. Group
Tyndale Hse. Pubs.

Worthy Shorts, *(978-1-935340; 978-1-937503; 978-1-937504; 978-1-937505; 978-1-937506; 978-1-937507)* P.O. Box 177, Malden on Hudson, NY 12453 USA Tel 845-246-2336; 15 Bostan Rd., Malden on Hudson, NY 12453
Web site: http://www.worthyshorts.com
Dist(s): **Independent Pubs. Group**
Smashwords.

WoW! What a Trip!, *(978-0-9994314; 978-1-7331568; 979-8-9890112)* 10012, Sugar Mill Dr., Bradenton, FL 34212 USA Tel 813-943-1910; Fax: 813-943-1910
E-mail: sadlerfind@hotmail.com.

Wowza World LLC,

WowZee Works Inc, *(978-0-9778858)* 2217 Green Mountain Ct., Las Vegas, NV 89135 USA (SAN 850-5128).

WPR Bks., *(978-1-68089)* 2509 Capitol Ave., Ste. 100, Sacramento, CA 95816 USA Tel 916-446-6666; Fax: 916-446-2136; 624 Hillcrest Ln., Fallbrook, CA 92028
E-mail: campaigncoordinator@therobinhoodtaxonwallstreet.com; kirk@whisler.com
Web site: http://www.robinhoodtaxonwallstreet.com; wprbooks.com.

WPR Publishing, *(978-1-889379)* 624 Hillcrest Ln, Fallbrook, CA 92028 USA Tel 760-645-3455; Fax: 760-434-7476 Do not confuse with WPR Publishing, Dillon, MT
E-mail: kirk@whisler.com
Web site: http://www.WPRbooks.com
Dist(s): **Ingram Content Group.**

WRB Pub., *(978-0-9844198; 978-0-9838832; 978-0-9856762; 978-0-9896247; 978-0-9909040)* 1260 SW 25 LN, Palm City, FL 34990 USA Tel 772-463-0928; Fax: 267-220-1541
E-mail: wrb1174@att.net
Dist(s): **Smashwords.**

WRDSMTH Productions, *(978-0-9744562)* Orders Addr.: P.O. Box 1406, Lawton, OK 73502-1406 USA (SAN 255-7282) Tel 580-353-4710; Fax: 580-357-9787; Toll Free: 800-357-9854; Edit Addr.: 130 SW B Ave., Lawton, OK 73501 USA
E-mail: okteller@juno.com
Web site: http://www.stringfigurestore.com.

W.R.E.a.C Havoc Publishing, *(978-0-578-61255-3)* 14643 222nd St., Springfield Gardens, NY 11413 USA Tel 347-262-9882
E-mail: wreachavocwriter@gmail.com
Web site: www.wreachavoconline.com.

WREaC Havoc Publishing, *(978-0-615-48442-6; 978-0-615-94461-6; 978-0-692-61811-0; 978-0-692-62175-2; 978-0-578-36006-5; 978-0-578-36739-2; 978-0-578-37663-9; 978-0-578-28535-1; 979-8-218-01930-3; 979-8-218-16298-6; 979-8-218-17123-0; 979-8-218-22843-9; 979-8-218-22977-1; 979-8-218-22980-1) 1051 Schenectady Ave. #7, Brooklyn, NY 11203 USA Tel 347-262-9882*
Web site: www.wreachavoconline.com
Dist(s): **CreateSpace Independent Publishing Platform.**

Wren Song Pr., *(978-0-9769827)* 233 Poors Mill Rd., Belfast, ME 04915 USA Toll Free: 800-943-7664 Do not confuse with Wren Song Press in Ripton, VT
E-mail: jennifer@jenniferarmstrong.com
Web site: http://www.jenniferarmstrong.com.

Wren's Nest Productions LLC *Imprint of* **Struminger, Alexander**

Wren's Nest Publishing, Inc., *(978-0-9744111)* 177 Rabbit Farm Trail, Advance, NC 27006 USA Tel 336-998-2858
E-mail: rickyp@yadtel.net.

Wright Bk. Publishing, *(978-0-615-23176-1; 978-0-9822822)* 4188 Defoors Farm Dr., Powder Springs, GA 30127 USA
Web site: http://www.wrightbookpublishing.com; http://www.earthsavergirl.com.

Wright Bks., *(978-0-615-19564-3)* 3337 Manning Rd., Indianapolis, IN 46228 USA
E-mail: jbwright37@gmail.com
Web site: http://www.myspace.com/thewidowsjourney.

Wright, Dr. Author O., *(978-0-9679676)* 4524 Portland Ave., S., Minneapolis, MN 55407-3550 USA Tel 612-822-8032
E-mail: Awright@email.usps.gov.

Wright, Gladys, *(978-0-578-46190-8)* 1605 N. Houston School Rd., No. 3103, Lancaster, TX 75134 USA Tel 214-872-0838
E-mail: gladys_fuller@yahoo.com; gladyswrightauthor@yahoo.com
Dist(s): **Ingram Content Group.**

Wright Group/McGraw-Hill, *(978-0-322; 978-0-7802; 978-0-940156; 978-1-55624; 978-1-55911; 978-1-4045)* Div. of Mcgraw-Hill School Education Group, Orders Addr.: P.O. Box 545, Blacklick, OH 43004-0545 USA Tel 614-755-5645; Toll Free: 800-722-4726; 800-442-9685 (customer service)
Web site: http://www.wrightgroup.com/.

Wright Honey, *(978-0-578-84851-8)* 9030 Baker Rd, Gueydan, LA 70542 USA Tel 337-412-4752
E-mail: Timalaspeech@yahoo.com
Web site: Wrighthoney.com.

Wright, Lacie, *(978-0-615-20657-8; 978-0-615-20658-5)* 413 Acorn Grove Ln. Apt. C, Chesapeake, VA 23320-6561 USA
E-mail: paulndlacie@gmail.com
Dist(s): **Lulu Pr., Inc.**

Wright Publishing, Inc., *(978-0-935087; 978-0-9652368)* Orders Addr.: P.O. Box 1956, Fayetteville, GA 30214 USA Tel 770-460-5525; Fax: 770-460-8998; Edit Addr.: 320 Devilla Trace, Fayetteville, GA 30214 USA (SAN 695-0507) Do not confuse with companies with same or

Publisher Name Index

similar name in Los Angeles, CA, Virgina Beach, VA, West Seneca, NY, Torrance, CA, .

Wright, R. Inc., *(978-0-9718405; 978-0-9904955; 978-0-9862138; 978-0-9963713; 978-0-9971493; 978-0-9976850; 978-0-9994614)* 1140 W. Fulton, Chicago, IL 60607 USA Tel 312-563-0020; Fax: 312-563-0040
E-mail: mail@wright20.com
Web site: http://www.wright20.com.

Wright, Robert, *(978-0-9763223)* 272 Horse Hill Rd., Ashford, CT 06278 USA.

Wright, Sasha, *(978-0-578-41785-1)* 7829 Magellan Dr., North Charleston, SC 29420 USA Tel 843-343-3106
E-mail: skwright1922@gmail.com
Dist(s): **Ingram Content Group.**

Wright, Willie Etta, *(978-0-9703551)* 403 S. Raddant Rd., Batavia, IL 60510 USA Tel 630-406-1756
E-mail: wilwrite@chicago.avenew.com.

Wright's Way Inc., *(978-0-9767483)* 210 Henderson Dr., Jacksonville, NC 28540 USA Tel 910-989-0000 (phone/fax)
E-mail: sensei@bizec.rr.com
Web site: http://www.wrightskarate.com.

Write 211 LLC, *(978-1-952910)* P.O. Box 370502, West Hartford, CT 06137 USA Tel 860-830-6756
E-mail: crantzfv@gmail.com.

Write 4 Little Hearts *See* **Write For Kids**

Write & Release Publishing, *(979-8-9868798; 978-1-960764)* 1 Ingram Blvd., La Vergne, TN 37086 USA Tel 818-878-8195
E-mail: contact@writeandreleasepublishing.com
Web site: www.writeandreleasepublishing.com.

Write As Rain Bks., *(978-0-9897221; 978-1-7331168; 979-8-9853956)* 12131 SE 91st St., Newcastle, WA 98056 USA Tel 425-277-6585
E-mail: martinadalton@comcast.net.

Write Away, *(978-0-615-26181-2)* 242 Hyle Ave., Murfreesboro, TN 37128 USA Tel 615-848-0247.

Write Bloody Publishing, *(978-0-9789989; 978-0-9815213; 978-0-9821488; 978-0-9842515; 978-0-9845031; 978-1-935904; 978-1-938912; 978-1-949342)* 810 E. Santa Anita Ave., Burbank, CA 91501 USA; *Imprints:* Write Fuzzy (Write Fuzzy)
E-mail: writebloody@gmail.com
Web site: http://www.writebloody.com
Dist(s): **Ingram Bk. Co.**
Ingram Content Group
SCB Distributors.

Write Designs, Limited *See* **PricePoint+Publications**

Write 'em Cowgirl Publishing, *(978-1-959412)* 8931 Montezuma Rd., Jamestown, CA 95327 USA Tel 209-559-7366
E-mail: TRIGAR@MLODE.COM
Web site: www.triciagardella.com.

Write For Kids, *(978-1-7338697; 978-0-578-64748-7; 978-1-953913)* 8435 S Shepard Ave, Oak Creek, WI 53154 USA Tel 414-640-0908; Fax: 414-762-8765
E-mail: carriehyatt77@gmail.com.

Write Fuzzy *Imprint of* **Write Bloody Publishing**

Write Integrity Pr., *(978-0-9839485; 978-1-938092; 978-1-944120; 978-1-951602)* PO Box 702852, Dallas, TX 75370 USA (SAN 920-0673)
E-mail: writeintegrity@gmail.com; marji.laine@gmail.com
Web site: http://www.writeintegrity.com; http://MarjiLaine.com.

Write 'N Learn *Imprint of* **Zishka Publishing**

Write On!, *(978-0-9753870; 978-0-9825722; 978-0-9890688)* 644 Shadowbrook Dr, Columbia, TN 38401 USA Tel 615-415-9861 Do not confuse with companies with a similar name in Albuquerque, NM, Estes Park, CO
E-mail: writer@yvonneperry.net
Web site: http://weare1inspirit.com/.

Write One Publications *See* **Write One Pubns., Inc.**

Write One Pubns., Inc., *(978-0-9821484)* P.O. Box 20883, Chicago, IL 60620 USA
E-mail: snewell@writeonepublications.com
Web site: http://www.writeonepublications.com.

Write Place, *(978-0-9788507; 978-0-9968644)* 4310 S. Havana, Spokane, WA 99223 USA (SAN 851-7851) Tel 509-448-2901; *Imprints:* Bratcher Publishing (MYID_W_BRATCHE).

Write Sing Work, Inc, *(978-1-934195)* 4182 Clemmons Rd. Suite No. 125, Clemmons, NC 27012 USA Tel 888-212-6982
E-mail: info@writesingwork.com
Web site: http://www.writesingwork.com.

Write Spot, The, *(978-0-9895384)* 100 E. Cedar Ave., Coalinga, CA 93210 USA Tel 559-630-1922
E-mail: selwell549@aol.com.

Write Way Publishing, *(978-1-885173)* Orders Addr.: P.O. Box 441278, Aurora, CO 80044 USA Tel 303-617-0497; Fax: 303-617-1440; Toll Free: 800-680-1493 Do not confuse with Write Way Publishing, Charleston, WV
E-mail: staff@writewaypub.com; writewy@aol.com
Web site: http://www.writewaypub.com.

Write Way Publishing Co. LLC, *(978-0-9976076; 978-1-946425; 978-1-956543)* 322 Fox Hollow Dr, Clayton, NC 27527 USA Tel 919-606-2618; *Imprints:* Barnsley Ink (MYID_U_BARNSLE)
E-mail: kevin@writewaypublishingcompany.com; lee@writewaypublishing.com
Web site: writewaypublishing.com.

Write Words, Inc., *(978-0-9706152; 978-1-59431; 978-1-61386)* 2934 Old Rte. 50, Cambridge, MD 21613 USA (SAN 254-0304); *Imprints:* Cambridge Books (CB); Ebooks On The Net (Ebks on the net) Do not confuse with The Write Words Inc., in Arlington, VA
E-mail: arline@mail.com; ArlineChase@comcast.net
Web site: http://www.ebooksonthe.net; http://www.cambridgebooks.us
Dist(s): **CreateSpace Independent Publishing Platform.**

Write World, Inc., *(978-0-9722173)* 3839 McKinney Ave. No. 155-373, Dallas, TX 75204 USA (SAN 254-8445)
E-mail: writeworld@cs.com.

Write Your Way Through Publishing *See* **Urban Moon Publishing**

WriteGirl Pubns., *(978-0-9741251; 978-0-9837081; 978-0-692-88728-8; 978-0-578-49912-3)* 1330 Factory Pl. Unti 104, Los Angeles, CA 90013 USA Tel 213-253-2655
E-mail: info@writegirl.org
Web site: http://www.writegirl.org
Dist(s): **SPD-Small Pr. Distribution.**

WriteLife Publishing *Imprint of* **Boutique of Quality Books Publishing Co., Inc.**

WritePublishSell, *(978-0-9899347; 978-0-9861969; 978-0-9987779; 978-0-9994377; 978-1-948604; 978-1-955119)* P.O. Box 290041, Columbia, SC 29229 USA Tel 803-608-5138; *Imprints:* Purple Butterfly Press (MYID_M_PURPLE)
E-mail: info@writepublishsell.co
Web site: http://writepublishsell.com; http://katbiggiepress.com.

WRITER for HIRE!, *(978-0-9701356; 978-0-9854623; 978-1-950729)* 2425 Lawrenceville Hwy. No. C7, Decatur, GA 30033 USA Tel 404-358-0951 (9am-5pm EST); *Imprints:* Blue Room Books (MYID_O_BLUE RO)
E-mail: angeladurden@msn.com; angeladurden@gmail.com
Web site: https://www.angeladurden-books.com/books.

Writer's Coffee Bar Pr. *Imprint of* **Buddhapuss Ink LLC**

Writers Advantage Pr. *Imprint of* **iUniverse, Inc.**

Writers Apex, *(978-1-63950)* 8063 MADISON AVE No. 1252, INDIANAPOLIS, IN 46227 USA Tel 317-659-6889
E-mail: johnaguilar@writersapex.com
Web site: www.writersapex.com.

Writers Cafe Pr., The, *(978-1-934284)* 418 S. Brookfield Dr., Lafayette, IN 47905-7299 USA (SAN 852-5498)
E-mail: admin@thewriterscafe.com
Web site: http://www.thewriterscafe.com.

Writers Club Pr. *Imprint of* **iUniverse, Inc.**

Writer's Coffee Shop, The, *(978-1-61213)* P.O. Box 2116, Waxahachie, TX 75168 USA (SAN 860-0112)
E-mail: publishing@thewriterscoffeeshop.com; amhayward@thewriterscoffeeshop.com
Web site: http://www.thewriterscoffeeshop.com; http://ph.thewriterscoffeeshop.com/
Dist(s): **Lulu Pr., Inc.**
Penguin Random Hse. LLC
Sourcebooks, Inc.

Writers' Collective, The, *(978-0-9716734; 978-1-932133; 978-1-59411)* 780 Reservoir Ave., Suite 243, Cranston, RI 02910 USA Toll Free: 800-497-0037
E-mail: factotum@writerscollective.org
Web site: http://www.writerscollective.org
Dist(s): **Midpoint Trade Bks., Inc.**

Writer's Cramp, Inc., *(978-0-9645983)* 711 San Juan Dr., Coral Gables, FL 33143-6224 USA
E-mail: JandyPF@aol.com.

Writers in the Schools (WITS), *(978-0-9747704)* 1523 W. Main, Houston, TX 77006 USA
E-mail: mail@writersintheschools.org
Web site: http://www.writersintheschools.org.

Writer's Ink. Studios, Inc., *(978-0-9704460)* P.O. Box 952, Windermere, FL 34786 USA Tel 407-876-3399; Fax: 270-964-5984; Toll Free: 888-229-9200
E-mail: cat@brownbagbooks.com; writersinkstudios@cfl.rr.com
Web site: http://www.brownbagbooks.com.

Writers Marketplace:Consulting, Critiquing & Publishing, *(978-1-928632)* P.O. Box 21218, Carson City, NV 89721 USA Tel 775-544-0909; Fax: 775-884-3103.

Writers of the Apocalypse, The, *(978-1-944322; 978-0-692-56768-5)* 1117 N Carbon St PMB 208, Marion, IL 62959 USA Tel 618-715-5132; *Imprints:* Woks Print (Woks Print)
E-mail: B00mb00mp0p@apocalypsewriters.com
Web site: http://woksprint.com; http://www.apocalypsewriters.com
Dist(s): **Author's Republic**
BookBaby
CreateSpace Independent Publishing Platform
Ingram Bk. Co.
Smashwords.

Writer of the Round Table Pr., *(978-0-9814545; 978-0-9822206; 978-1-61066; 978-1-937443)* P.O. Box 511, Highland Park, IL 60035-0511 USA (SAN 855-6067)
Web site: www.roundtablecompanies.com; http://www.writersoftheroundtable.com
Dist(s): **Ingram Content Group.**

Writers on the Move Publishing, *(978-0-9992949; 979-8-9881233)* 3659 Bernard Dr. 3659 Bernard Dr., Wantagh, NY 11793 USA Tel 347-834-6700
E-mail: karencioffi@aol.com; kcioffiventrice@gmail.com
Web site: http://writersonthemove.com; http://karencioffiwritingforchildren.com.

Writer's Publishing Cooperative *Imprint of* **Beech River Bks.**

Writer's Showcase Pr. *Imprint of* **iUniverse, Inc.**

WritersCorps Bks. *Imprint of* **San Francisco Art Commission, The**

Writing Academy Inc., *(978-0-9729777)* 6488 Currin Dr., Orlando, FL 32835 USA (SAN 852-6435) Tel 407-296-5800; Fax: 407-296-5801
E-mail: salcom@alcom.com
Web site: http://www.themeperks.com
Dist(s): **Smashwords.**

Writing as a Ghost *See* **Jots & Tittles Publishing**

Writing Bench LLC., The, *(978-0-9818374)* P.O. Box 775037, Saint Louis, MO 63177-5037 USA
E-mail: backwardkingdom@yahoo.com.

Writing Center, The *See* **Full Court Pr.**

Writing etc. *See* **Etcetera Pr. LLC**

Writing for Children with Karen Cioffi *See* **Writers on the Move Publishing**

Writing for the Lord Ministries, *(978-0-9705902; 978-0-9883038; 978-0-9893188)* 6400 Shannon Ct., Clarksville, MD 21029 USA Tel 410-340-8633
E-mail: pastorkevinwaynejohnson@gmail.com; kgj27@aol.com
Web site: http://www.thejohnsonleadershipgroup.com; http://www.kevinwaynejohnson.com
Dist(s): **Ingram Bk. Co.**

Writing The Vision *Imprint of* **Scribe Publishing & Consulting Services, The**

Writing Times Publications *See* **Writing Times Publishing**

Writing Times Publishing, *(978-1-7337375)* Psc 3, Box 2177, APO, AE 96266 USA Tel 512-577-9341
E-mail: writingtimespub@gmail.com.

Writing Wild & Crazy *Imprint of* **Shakalot High Entertainment**

Writing-Right, *(978-0-9772196)* 27 Somerset Dr., Holbrook, NY 11741 USA
E-mail: lori@writing-right.org.

Written and Red, LLC *See* **Baxter The Dog Bks.**

Written & Spoken, *(978-1-7327212)* 7506 Blue Cedar Pl., Chesterfield, VA 23832 USA Tel 301-885-8309
E-mail: longcharlesm@gmail.com.

Written By Clark, Publishing, *(978-0-9795102)* Orders Addr.: P.O. Box 874023, Vancouver, WA 98687 USA Tel 323-447-9676
E-mail: jthomasclark@gmail.com; info@writtenbyclark.com
Web site: http://www.writtenbyclark.com
Dist(s): **Ingram Content Group.**

Written By Jess Publications *See* **Vample, Jessyca Publishing**

Written Images, Inc., *(978-0-9705721)* 1300 E. Lafayette, Suite 1104, Detroit, MI 48207 USA (SAN 253-7591) Tel 248-356-8310; Fax: 248-356-8311 Do not confuse with Written Image, The in Lancaster, NY
E-mail: writtenimages@aol.com
Web site: http://www.adiaryofjoseph.com.

Written in Black Publishing *See* **WordPlay Multimedia, LLC**

Written World Communications, *(978-0-9829377; 978-1-938679)* Orders Addr.: 4725 Splendid Cir. S., Colorado Springs, CO 80917 USA (SAN 859-9696) Tel 719-947-2181
E-mail: kristinepratt@gmail.com
Web site: http://www.writtenworldcommunications.com/.

WS Publishing, *(978-0-9639654; 978-1-887169; 978-1-934386; 978-1-936061; 978-1-61351)* 7290 Navajo Rd., Suite 207, San Diego, CA 92119 USA Tel 619-589-1919
E-mail: sarah@weddingsolutions.com; info@wspublishinggroup.com
Web site: http://wspublishinggroup.com
Dist(s): **Ingram Publisher Services**
Two Rivers Distribution.

WSB Publishing, Inc., *(978-1-64268)* 5264 Summerlin Commons Way, Fort Myers, FL 33907 USA Tel 850-971-6053
E-mail: w.bader@novumverlag.com.

Wu Li Turtle Corp., *(978-0-9741176)* 3885 S. Decatur Blvd., Suite 2010, Las Vegas, NV 89103 USA Tel 703-864-3769; Fax: 702-920-8118; Toll Free: 888-381-6864
E-mail: rbraye@wuliturtle.com
Web site: http://www.wuliturtle.com.

Wunderlannd Pr., *(978-0-615-62918-6; 978-0-9893166)* 3141 Elmer St., Sarasota, FL 34231 USA Tel 443-742-7039
E-mail: wunderlanndpress@hotmail.com.

Wunderlich, Jordan, *(978-0-578-44066-8; 978-0-578-44242-6)* 280 Hewlett Gulch Rd., Livermore, CO 80536 USA Tel 360-878-0684
E-mail: jwunder@votegoat.net
Dist(s): **Ingram Content Group.**

Wundermill *See* **WunderMill, Inc.**

WunderMill, Inc., *(978-1-943645; 978-1-943978)* 120A N. Salem St., Apex, NC 27502 USA Tel 919-303-3448; Fax: 919-303-3225; *Imprints:* Cornell Lab Publishing Group, The (CornellLab); Persnickety Press (PersnicketyPr)
E-mail: bsockin@cornelllabpg.com
Web site: www.cornelllabpgstore.com
Dist(s): **Baker & Taylor Publisher Services (BTPS)**
Publishers Group West (PGW).

Wutherwood Pr., *(978-0-578-21689-8; 978-0-578-23215-7; 978-0-578-24334-4; 978-0-578-25108-0; 978-0-578-25898-0; 978-0-578-27606-9; 978-0-578-27778-3)* 24227 NE 25th St., Sammamish, WA 98074 USA
E-mail: johnscannell1947@gmail.com
Dist(s): **Outskirts Pr., Inc.**

www.margaretmouse.com publishing co., *(978-0-9761326)* Orders Addr.: 41953 20th St., W., Palmdale, CA 93551-0000 USA Please allow four weeks for delivery. Shipments come direct from printer in China. Invoiced at order. Shipping free for all orders over 5000. Dolls are available as well. Please contact me direct at email Lparnold@verizon.net or call US 661-943-0275 with any questions or concerns or special orders.
E-mail: info@margaretmouse.com
Web site: http://www.margaretmouse.com
Dist(s): **Follett School Solutions.**

www.pmptools.com *See* **Project Management Excellence Ctr., Inc., The**

www.underdogpublishing.com, *(978-0-9754420)* 124 Titleist Cir., Savannah, GA 31419 USA; P.O. Box 638, Tybee Island, GA 31328 Tel 912-596-5532
Web site: http://www.underdogpublishing.com.

Wyatt Hse. Publishing, *(978-0-9882209; 978-0-9896119; 978-0-9915798; 978-0-9977422; 978-1-7326049; 978-1-7345398; 978-1-954798)* 399 Lakeview Dr. W., Mobile, AL 36695 USA Tel 251-421-1296
E-mail: editor@wyattpublishing.com
Web site: www.wyattpublishing.com.

Wyatt North, *(978-1-62278; 978-1-64798; 978-1-6673)* 5 Sylvia St. No. 1, Boston, MA 02130 USA Tel 978-460-1252
E-mail: WyattNorthPublishing@gmail.com
Web site: Www.WyattNorth.com.

Wyatt Pr., *(978-0-9718161)* 15005 W. 167th Terr., Olathe, KS 66062 USA Tel 913-768-1917; Fax: 913-768-4307.

Wyatt-MacKenzie Publishing, *(978-0-9673025; 978-1-932279; 978-0-9743832; 978-0-9820518; 978-1-936214; 978-1-939288; 978-1-942545; 978-1-948018; 978-1-954332; 979-8-218-16627-4)* 15115 Hwy. 36, Deadwood, OR 97430-9700 USA (SAN 990-1191) Tel 541-964-3314; Fax: 541-964-3315
E-mail: info@wymacpublishing.com; nancy@wyattmackenzie.com
Web site: http://www.wymacpublishing.com.

Wycliffe Bible Translators, *(978-0-938978)* P.O. Box 628200, Orlando, FL 32862-8200 USA (SAN 211-5484)
Web site: http://www.wycliffe.org.

Wyeast Career Pr., *(978-0-615-62120-3; 978-0-578-86351-1)* P.O. Box 20536, Portland, OR 97294 USA Tel 503-539-3954
Web site: www.pathfindercareers.com
Dist(s): **CreateSpace Independent Publishing Platform.**

Wyer Pearce Press *See* **SangFroid Pr.**

Wyland Galleries *See* **Wyland Worldwide, LLC**

Wyland Worldwide, LLC, *(978-0-9631793; 978-1-884840; 978-1-60586)* 6 Mason, Irvine, CA 92618 USA Tel 949-643-7070; Fax: 949-643-7082
E-mail: valeries@wyland.com
Web site: http://www.wyland.com
Dist(s): **Booklines Hawaii, Ltd.**

Wynden *Imprint of* **Canmore Pr.**

Wyoming Historical & Geological Society, *(978-0-937537)* 49 S. Franklin St., Wilkes-Barre, PA 18701 USA (SAN 281-2061) Tel 717-823-6244; Fax: 717-823-9011
E-mail: lchs@epix.net
Web site: http://www.luzernecountyhistory.com.

Wyrm Publishing, *(978-1-890464)* Orders Addr.: P.O. Box 172, Stirling, NJ 07980 USA Tel 908-626-1531 (phone/fax); Edit Addr.: 2461 Lanrell Dr., Tallahassee, FL 32303 USA
E-mail: wyrmpublishing@gmail.com
Dist(s): **Diamond Comic Distributors, Inc.**
Diamond Bk. Distributors.

Wyson, Dan, *(978-0-9771522)* 375 E. Riverside Dr. No. 201, Saint George, UT 84790 USA Tel 435-229-6714 Toll Free: 877-827-0710.

Wysteria, Limited *See* **Wysteria Publishing**

Wysteria Publishing, *(978-0-9651162; 978-0-9677839; 978-1-932412)* P.O. Box 1250, Bellmore, NY 11710 USA Toll Free Fax: 888-434-7979; Toll Free: 888-997-8300
E-mail: wysteria@wysteria.com
Web site: http://www.wysteria.com.

X, Y, & Me LLC, *(978-0-9755028; 978-0-9773441)* 21409 138th St., Webster, IA 52355-9079 USA
E-mail: customerservice@xyandme.com
Web site: http://www.xyandme.com.

Xanadu Metaphysical *See* **Xanadu New Age Products & Services, LLC**

Xanadu New Age Products & Services, LLC, *(978-0-9759752)* Orders Addr.: 1011 S. Lake St., Neenah, WI 54956 USA; Edit Addr.: 1011 S. Lake St., Neenah, WI 54956 USA
E-mail: parisdrake@parisdrake.com
Web site: http://www.parisdrake.com.

XanMaxBks., *(978-0-692-09280-4; 978-1-7326044)* 8842 Southern Orchard Rd N, DAVIE, FL 33328 USA Tel 954-547-4618
E-mail: chalenar@aol.com
Dist(s): **Ingram Content Group.**

XavierBks., *(978-0-578-95931-3; 978-0-578-32513-2)* 4341 Telfair BLVD, Camp Springs, MD 20746 USA Tel 202-422-3171
E-mail: ms.tiarracurrie@gmail.com.

xbks publishing, *(978-0-9626458)* c/o Arturo Watlington Station, P.O. Box 568, Saint Thomas, VI 00804 USA
E-mail: llrush@viaccess.net; mail@xbkspublishing.net
Web site: http://www.xbkspublising.net.

Xbooks *See* **xbks publishing**

Xeno Bks. *Imprint of* **Red Hen Pr.**

Xerces Society, The, *(978-0-9744475)* 4828 SE Hawthorne Blvd., Portland, OR 97215 USA Tel 503-232-6639; Fax: 503-233-6794
E-mail: mdshepherd@xerces.org
Web site: http://www.xerces.org.

Xist Classics *Imprint of* **Xist Publishing**

Xist Publishing, *(978-0-615-49153-0; 978-0-9838428; 978-1-62395; 978-1-68195; 978-1-5324)* 16604 Sonora St., Tustin, CA 92782 USA Tel 949-842-5296; 949-478-2568; P.O. Box 61593, Irvine, CA 92692; *Imprints:* Xist Classics (XistClassics)
E-mail: calee@xistpublishing.com; info@xistpublishing.com
Web site: http://xistpublishing.com
Dist(s): **Children's Plus, Inc.**
Follett School Solutions
Mackin Educational Resources
Open Road Integrated Media, Inc.

Xlibris, 1663 Liberty Dr., Bloomington, IN 47403 USA Tel 888-795-4274
E-mail: Johnnyline.Jagdon@xlibris.com
Web site: http://www2.xlibris.com/.

Xlibris Corporation *See* **Xlibris Corp.**

Xlibris Corp., *(978-0-7388; 978-0-9663501; 978-1-4010; 978-1-4134; 978-1-59926; 978-1-4257; 978-1-4363; 978-1-4415; 978-1-4500; 978-1-4535; 978-1-4568; 978-1-4628; 978-1-4653; 978-1-4691; 978-1-4771; 978-1-4797; 978-1-4836; 978-1-4931; 978-1-4990; 978-1-5035; 978-1-5144; 978-1-5245; 978-1-4990-9726-9; 978-1-4990-9725-2; 978-1-4990-9724-5; 978-1-5434; 978-1-9845; 978-1-7960; 978-1-6641; 978-1-6698; 979-8-3694) Orders Addr.: 1663 S. Liberty Dr. Suite 200, Bloomington, IN 47403 USA (SAN 299-5522) Tel*

812-334-5223; Fax: 812-334-5223; Toll Free: 888-795-4274
E-mail: info@xlibris.com
Web site: http://www2.xlibris.com
Dist(s): **Author Solutions, LLC**
Baker & Taylor Publisher Services (BTPS)
CreateSpace Independent Publishing Platform
International Pubns. Service
Lulu Pr., Inc.
Smashwords
TextStream.

Xophix, *(978-0-9754173)* P.O. Box 12081, Scottsdale, AZ 85267 USA Fax: 586-461-1712
E-mail: books@xophix.com
Web site: http://www.xophix.com.

X-treme Reviews *Imprint of* **N&N Publishing Co., Inc.**

Xulon Pr. *Imprint of* **Salem Author Services**

xyz *See* **EBk. Writing Hub**

XYZ Pr., *(978-0-9799269; 978-0-9885622; 978-0-9968745; 978-0-9993428; 978-1-7358315; 979-8-9890528)* 161 Miramar Dr, Prosper, TX 75078 USA Tel 214-549-6146
E-mail: tandreescu@gmail.com
Web site: http://www.awesomemath.org
Dist(s): **American Mathematical Society.**

Y Linh, *(978-0-9746135)* 6524 San Felipe, No. 110, Houston, TX 77057 USA Tel 713-271-4222
E-mail: ylinhdo@hotmail.com.

Y Lolfa (GBR) *(978-0-86243; 978-0-904864; 978-0-9500178; 978-0-9555272; 978-1-84771; 978-0-9567031; 978-0-9560125; 978-1-78461) Dist. by* **Casemate Pubs.**

Y Lolfa (GBR) *(978-0-86243; 978-0-904864; 978-0-9500178; 978-0-9555272; 978-1-84771; 978-0-9567031; 978-0-9560125; 978-1-78461) Dist. by* **Dufour.**

YA Angst *Imprint of* **Norilana Bks.**

YA Bks., *(978-0-615-72187-3; 978-0-615-79766-3; 978-0-9899934)* 211 Oxford St., Martin, TN 38237 USA Tel 7315875993
Web site: merrybrown.com
Dist(s): **CreateSpace Independent Publishing Platform.**

Yabitoon Bks., *(978-0-578-05342-4)* 1679 Bluffhill Dr., Monterey Park, CA 91754 USA.

Yacos Pubns., *(978-0-9653734)* Orders Addr.: 90-20 169th St., Apt. 4D, Jamaica, NY 11432 USA Tel 718-523-8911 (phone/fax)
E-mail: Drltgrant@yahoo.com
Web site: http://www.yacos.org.

Yad Vashem Pubns. (ISR) *(978-965-308) Dist. by* **Coronet Bks.**

Yadda Yadda Pr., *(978-0-9791387)* 1748 Donwell Dr., South Euclid, OH 44121-3734 USA
E-mail: williamecook@gmail.com
Web site: http://www.yaddayaddapress.com.

Yadeeda.com, *(978-0-9747122)* P.O. Box 38642, Colorado Springs, CO 80937 USA Tel 719-520-5125
E-mail: yadeeda@hotmail.com
Web site: http://www.yadeeda.com.

Yaipen, Natalie, *(978-0-578-64608-4; 978-0-578-93698-7)* 3749 98th ST, Corona, NY 11368 USA Tel 347-938-6557
E-mail: natalie.yaipen@gmail.com.

YALDAH Media, Incorporated *See* **Jewish Girls Unite**

†Yale Univ. Pr., *(978-0-300; 978-1-933789; 978-1-282)* Orders Addr.: c/o Trilteral LLC, 100 Maple Ridge Dr., Cumberland, RI 02864 USA Tel 401-531-2800; Fax: 401-531-2801; Toll Free Fax: 800-406-9145; Toll Free: 800-405-1619; Edit Addr.: 302 Temple St., New Haven, CT 06511 USA (SAN 203-2740) Tel 203-432-0960; Fax: 203-432-0948; *Imprints*: deCordova Sculpture Park and Museum (deCordova Scul)
E-mail: yupmkt@yale.edu
Web site: http://www.yale.edu/yup/; http://www.yale.edu/yup/index.html
Dist(s): **Casemate Academic**
Cheng & Tsui Co.
De Gruyter, Inc.
Ebsco Publishing
ISD
JSTOR
MyiLibrary
Oxford Univ. Pr., Inc.
Open Road Integrated Media, Inc.
TriLiteral, LLC
Wiley, John & Sons, Inc.
Yale Univ., Far Eastern Pubns.
ebrary, Inc.; *CIP.*

Yali Bks. *Imprint of* **Yali Publishing LLC**

Yali Books *See* **Yali Publishing LLC**

Yali Publishing LLC, *(978-0-9890615; 978-1-949528)* 43 Longwood Dr, Clifton Park, NY 12065 USA; *Imprints*: Yali Books (MYID_Z_YALI BK)
E-mail: editors@yalibooks.com; sales@yalibooks.com
Web site: www.yalibooks.com.

Yam Hill Publishing, *(978-0-692-50620-2; 978-0-692-83700-9; 978-0-692-84230-0)* 2926 NE Redwood Dr., McMinnville, OR 97128 USA Tel 503-857-5355
Web site: www.jim-gullo.com
Dist(s): **CreateSpace Independent Publishing Platform.**

Yana's Kitchen, *(978-0-9670982)* 5256 Pizzo Ranch Rd., La Canada, CA 91011 USA Tel 818-790-8381 (phone/fax)
E-mail: yana119@yahoo.com
Web site: http://yanasplace.com.

Yang, Jennifer, *(978-0-578-06384-3; 978-0-578-09356-7; 978-0-578-12358-5; 978-0-578-14107-7)* P.O. Box 22204, San Francisco, CA 94122 USA
E-mail: jenniyang@aol.com
Dist(s): **Lulu Pr., Inc.**

Yankee Cowboy, *(978-0-9708530; 978-0-9836149)* P.O. Box 123, Keller, TX 76244 USA Tel 800-557-8166; Toll Free: 800-557-8166
E-mail: publisher@yankeecowboy.com
Web site: http://www.amonplay.com; http://www.watchdognation.com; http://www.davelieber.org; https://www.PerotBook.com.

Yankee Publishing, Inc., *(978-0-89909; 978-1-57198)* Orders Addr.: P.O. Box 520, Dublin, NH 03444 USA Tel 603-563-8111; Fax: 603-563-8252; Edit Addr.: Main St., Dublin, NH 03444 USA; *Imprints*: Old Farmer's Almanac (OldFarmers) Do not confuse with Yankee Publishing, Saint Petersburg, FL
E-mail: almanac@yankeepub.com
Web site: http://www.almanac.com
Dist(s): **Houghton Mifflin Harcourt Publishing Co.**
Houghton Mifflin Harcourt Trade & Reference Pubs.
Hachette Bk. Group
HarperCollins Pubs.
MyiLibrary.

Yarbrough Hse. Publishing, *(978-0-9970132; 978-0-9995800)* 3596 Greensport Rd., Ashville, AL 35953 USA Tel 205-594-5338
E-mail: elizabethl.sorrell@gmail.com
Web site: www.elizabethleesorrell.com.

Yard Dog Pr., *(978-1-893687; 978-0-9824704; 978-1-937105; 978-1-945941)* 710 W. Redbud Ln., Alma, AR 72921 USA Tel 479-632-4693
Web site: http://www.yarddogpress.com
Dist(s): **Smashwords.**

Yari Publishing, *(978-0-578-06838-1)* P.O. Box 142624, Austin, TX 78714-2624 USA.

Yaroslavskaya, Lyudmila, *(978-0-9791248)* 600 W. Diversey Parkaway, Rm. 1410, Chicago, IL 60614 USA.

Yarrow Pr., *(978-0-9741562)* Orders Addr.: P.O. Box 665, Rainelle, WV 25962 USA Tel 304-438-1040 Do not confuse with Yarrow Press in Pelham, NY
E-mail: kate@yarrowpress.com
Web site: http://www.yarrowpress.com.

Yasram Global Industries, LLC, *(978-0-692-36502-1; 978-0-692-56482-0; 978-0-692-79807-2)* 2019 Fox Hill Glenn, Bldg. 18, Apt. 12, Grand Blanc, MI 48439 USA Tel 810-610-1040; Fax: 810-780-4268
Web site: www.keiraandme.info
Dist(s): **CreateSpace Independent Publishing Platform.**

YAV, *(978-0-9790221; 978-1-937449)* Orders Addr.: 1950 Hendersonville Rd. No. 243, Skyland, NC 28776 USA
E-mail: books@yav.com
Web site: http://InterestingWriting.com; http://ScienceOfWriting.com; http://YAVpublications.com.

Yawn Publishing LLC *Imprint of* **Yawn's Bks. & More, Inc.**

Yawn's Bks. & More, Inc., *(978-0-9818673; 978-0-9830190; 978-1-936815; 978-1-940395; 978-1-943529; 978-1-947773; 978-1-954617)* 2555 Marietta Hwy. Suite 103, Canton, GA 30114 USA (SAN 856-7476) Tel 678-880-1922; Fax: 678-880-1923; *Imprints*: Yawn Publishing LLC (MYID_Y_YAWN PU)
E-mail: fyawn@yawnsbooks.com
Web site: http://www.yawnspublishing.com.

Yay Learner LLC, *(978-0-578-40537-7; 978-0-578-99864-0)* 42993 Lago Stella Pl., Ashburn, VA 20148-7186 USA Tel 571-643-0833
E-mail: yaylearner@gmail.com
Dist(s): **Ingram Content Group.**

YBF Publishing LLC *See* **Literary Revolutionary & Co., The**

YBK Pubs., Inc., *(978-0-9703923; 978-0-9764359; 978-0-9790972; 978-0-9800508; 978-0-9824012; 978-1-936411)* 39 Crosby St. Apt. 2N, New York, NY 10013-3254 USA
E-mail: obarz@ybkpublishers.com
Web site: http://www.ybkpublishers.com.

Ye Hedge Schl., *(978-0-9723239; 978-0-9825521)* Orders Addr.: 24934 478 Ave., Garretson, SD 57030 USA
E-mail: mod61047@alliancecom.net
Web site: http://www.hedgeschool.com.

Ye Olde Dragon Bks., *(978-1-952345; 978-1-961129)* 6909 Ackley Rd., Parma, OH 44129 USA Tel 440-865-0909
E-mail: 2OldeDragons@gmail.com.

Ye Olde Font Shoppe, *(978-1-889289)* Orders Addr.: P.O. Box 8328, New Haven, CT 06708 USA Tel 203-575-9385; Edit Addr.: 35 Ferndale, Waterbury, CT 06708 USA Tel 860-870-9741
E-mail: varivas@yahoo.com
Web site: http://www.yeolde.org.

Yearling *Imprint of* **Random Hse. Children's Bks.**

Yearling *Imprint of* **Random Hse. Children's Bks.**

Yehuda, Ben Pr., *(978-0-9769862; 978-0-9789980; 978-1-934730; 978-1-953829)* 122 Ayers Ct. No. 1B, Teaneck, NJ 07666 USA Tel 201-833-5145; Fax: 201-917-1278
E-mail: yudel@benyehudapress.com
Web site: http://www.BenYehudaPress.com.

Yellow Brick Road Publishing, *(978-0-615-24159-3)* 35 Fiske St., No. 1, Waltham, MA 02451 USA.

Yellow Bricks & Rosie Lips, *(978-0-578-66480-4; 978-0-578-66793-5)* 70 Silverwood Dr. 0, NEWPORT NEWS, VA 23608 USA Tel 7572872938
E-mail: gilliamfamily5@live.com.

Yellow City Publishing, *(978-0-9991810; 978-1-7336241; 978-1-7354113)* 6500 Meister St., Amarillo, TX 79119 USA Tel 806-622-9093
E-mail: vickischoen@outlook.com
Web site: vickischoen.com.

Yellow Daffodil Pr., *(978-0-9824943)* 17939 Chatsworth St., No. 241, Granada Hills, CA 91344 USA
E-mail: mdesannoy@gmail.com.

Yellow Daisy Publishing, *(978-1-953556)* 10995 Timber Ridge Ln., Highlands Ranch, CO 80130 USA Tel 720-318-8696
E-mail: ajdreamchaser@hotmail.com
Web site: www.yellowdaisypub.com; www.ajkikumoto.com.

Yellow Hse. Pr., *(978-0-692-99794-9)* 4223 20th Ave S, Minneapolis, MN 55407 USA Tel 435-513-0057
E-mail: sarahholdenart@gmail.com
Dist(s): **CreateSpace Independent Publishing Platform.**

Yellow Jacket *Imprint of* **Bonnier Publishing USA**

Yellow Sun Bks., *(978-0-692-18165-2; 978-1-7327606)* 2919 S 93RD St., WEST ALLIS, WI 53227 USA Tel 414-232-8871
E-mail: yellowsunbooks@gmail.com
Web site: YellowSunBooks.com.

Yellowstone Association for Natural Science, History & Education, Incorporated *See* **Yellowstone Forever**

Yellowstone Forever, *(978-0-934948)* P.O. Box 117, Yellowstone National Park, WY 82190 USA (SAN 214-4921) Tel 406-848-2454; Fax: 406-848-2453
E-mail: dcollins@yellowstone.org
Web site: http://www.YellowstoneAssociation.org
Dist(s): **Outskirts Pr., Inc.**

Yen Pr. *Imprint of* **Yen Pr. LLC**

Yen Press *See* **Yen Pr. LLC**

Yen Pr. LLC, *(978-0-7595; 978-89-527; 978-1-9753; 979-8-8554)* Div. of Hachette Book Group, 150 W. 30th Street, 19th Flr., New York, NY 10001 USA; *Imprints*: Yen Press (YenOr); JY (JY)
E-mail: yenpress@yenpress.com
Web site: http://www.yenpress.com
Dist(s): **Children's Plus, Inc.**
Diamond Comic Distributors, Inc.
Hachette Bk. Group
MyiLibrary.

Yeoman Hse., *(978-0-9754676; 978-0-9822659; 978-0-9852537; 978-1-7363930; 979-8-9881943)* 10 Old Bulgarmarsh Rd., Tiverton, RI 02878 USA Tel 401-816-0061
E-mail: yeomanhouse@cox.net
Web site: www.jamesybartlett.com
Dist(s): **Ingram Content Group.**

YES - Your Emergency Safety, *(978-0-9740670)* 1302 W. Adams Ave., Saint Louis, MO 63122 USA Tel 314-822-8895; Fax: 775-458-7717
E-mail: info@youremergencysafety.org
Web site: http://www.youremergencysafety.org.

Yesterday's Classics, *(978-1-59915; 978-1-63334)* Orders Addr.: P.O. Box 3418, Chapel Hill, NC 27515 USA Tel 919-967-3119; Toll Free: 866-497-3729 (phone/fax); Edit Addr.: 1705 Audubon Rd., Chapel Hill, NC 27514 USA
Web site: http://www.yesterdaysclassics.com.

Yestermorrow, Inc., *(978-1-56723)* Orders Addr.: P.O. Box 700, Princess Anne, MD 21853 USA.

Yetta Nother Pr., *(978-0-9788367; 978-0-578-98901-3)* 17 Morrill St., Winthrop, ME 04364-1220 USA (SAN 851-7517)
E-mail: rossel@gwi.net.

Yetto Publishing Co., *(978-0-9666676; 978-0-9710470; 978-0-9741294; 978-0-9748591; 978-0-9760414; 978-0-9765369; 978-0-9776480; 978-0-9785934; 978-0-9791154; 978-1-934615; 978-1-939999)* 964 S. Highland Ave., Jackson, TN 38301 USA Fax: 731-225-8672; *Imprints*: MSP (MSP) Do not confuse with companies with same or similar names in Kingston, NJ, Shorewood, WI, Osage Beach MO
E-mail: editor@yettopublishing.com; sharibyetto@yahoo.com
Web site: http://www.yettopublishing.com.

Yewtree Pr. LLC, *(978-1-933029)* P.O. Box 110 671, Brooklyn, NY 11211 USA Toll Free: 800-939-7404
E-mail: info@yewtreepress.com
Web site: http://www.yewtreepress.com.

Yhabbut Publishing, *(978-0-9724292)* Orders Addr.: P.O. Box 23032, Seattle, WA 981 USA; Edit Addr.: 2111 15th Ave., S., Suite A, Seattle, WA 98144-4271 USA
E-mail: benthoven@qwest.net
Web site: http://www.1stbooks.com/bookview/20054.

Yiddishkayt Pr., *(978-0-692-92694-9; 978-0-9993365)* 11201 NW 1st Ct., Coral Springs, FL 33071 USA Tel 954-415-2730
E-mail: avihoffman33@gmail.com
Dist(s): **CreateSpace Independent Publishing Platform.**

Y-IREAD Publishing *See* **Sapati Ingera**

Yisrael, Sean Publishing Co., *(978-0-9772424)* 11769 Kenn Rd., Cincinnati, OH 45240 USA Tel 513-266-1158
E-mail: syisrael@dps.k12.oh.us.

YNR Media L.L.C., *(978-0-9753262)* 338 Streeter Dr., McCook Lake, SD 57049 USA Tel 310-422-1662.

Yo Puedo Publishing, *(978-0-9714533)* P.O. Box 940895, Houston, TX 77094 USA (SAN 254-3729) Tel 281-496-2015; 866-YO-PUEDO; Fax: 281-558-3773
E-mail: kathryn@yopuedo.com
Web site: http://www.yopuedo.com.

Yofi Bk. Publishing, Inc., *(978-1-931387; 978-1-60046; 978-1-7351868)* 199 Lee Ave. Unit #397, Brooklyn, NY 11211 USA Tel 718-694-9040; Fax: 718-694-9062
E-mail: yofi@yeshivanet.com.

Yoga Life *See* **Love Your Life**

Yoganathan, Anila, *(978-1-7334015)* 3555 Castleridge Dr., Tucker, GA 30084 USA Tel 404-989-5852
E-mail: anilayoganathan@gmail.com
Dist(s): **Ingram Content Group.**

Yogasaurus, *(978-0-9831418)* 137 Dewey Ave., Pittsfield, MA 01201 USA Tel 413-499-1350
E-mail: kenduncanduncan@yahoo.com.

Yoknapatawpha Pr., *(978-0-916242)* P.O. Box 248, Oxford, MS 38655 USA (SAN 213-7593) Tel 601-234-0909 (phone/fax)
E-mail: faulkner@watervalley.net
Web site: http://www.yoknapatawphapress.com.

YOLT Publishing, *(978-0-9982931)* 13518 L St., Omaha, NE 68137 USA Tel 402-884-5995
E-mail: yolt@conciergemarketing.com.

yomitobi, *(978-0-9799470)* 403 Knight Dr. Apt 9, Statesboro, GA 30458 USA
E-mail: yoko_6@hotmail.com
Web site: http://www.yomitobi.com.

Yonay, Shahar, *(978-0-927580; 978-0-9616783)* 126 Dover St., Brooklyn, NY 11235 USA (SAN 661-0544) Tel 718-615-0027.

Yoon-il Auh/Intrepid Pixels, *(978-1-882858)* 820 West End Ave., No. 9E, New York, NY 10025 USA Tel 212-662-6891.

Yoot Pr., *(978-0-9764611)* 17-47 Chandler Dr., Fair Lawn, NJ 07410 USA
Web site: http://www.yootpress.com.

York House Pr., Ltd., *(978-0-9791956; 978-0-9855508)* 1266 E. Main St, suite 700R., Stamford, CT 06902 USA Tel 203-539-6180; Fax: 914-764-5159
E-mail: pholt@yorkhousepress.com
Dist(s): **Ingram Content Group.**

Yorkshire Publishing Group, *(978-0-88144; 978-1-936750; 978-0-9883786; 978-0-9889281; 978-0-9896518; 978-1-942451; 978-1-946977; 978-1-947247; 978-1-947491; 978-1-947825; 978-1-948282; 978-1-949231; 978-1-950034; 978-1-952320; 978-1-954095; 978-1-957262; 978-1-960810)* 1425 E 41st Pl, Tulsa, OK 74105 USA (SAN 260-0285) Tel 918-394-2665; *Imprints*: Thorncrown Publishing (Thorncrown); Total Publishing & Media (Total Pubng)
Web site: http://www.yorkshirepublishing.com
Dist(s): **BookBaby**
INscribe Digital.

Yorkville Pr., *(978-0-9729427; 978-0-9767442)* Orders Addr.: 1202 Lexington Ave., No. 315, New York, NY 10028 USA (SAN 255-3139) Tel 212-650-9154; Fax: 212-650-9157; 1202 Lexington Ave. # 315, New York, NY 10028 Tel 212-650-9154
E-mail: editors@yorkvillepress.com
Web site: http://www.yorkvillepress.com.

Yoroson Publishing *See* **Young-Robinson, Christine**

Yosemite Association *See* **Yosemite Conservancy**

Yosemite Conservancy, *(978-0-939666; 978-1-930238; 978-1-951179)* Orders Addr.: P.O. Box 230, El Portal, CA 95318 USA (SAN 662-197X) Tel 209-379-2317; Edit Addr.: 5020 El Portal Rd., El Portal, CA 95318 USA
E-mail: nicolegeiger1@gmail.com; jedelbrock@yosemiteconservancy.org; kcoit@yosemiteconservancy.org
Web site: http://www.yosemiteconservancy.org
Dist(s): **MyiLibrary**
Publishers Group West (PGW)
Sunbelt Pubns., Inc.

Yosoy Publishing, *(978-0-9763503)* 4141 Linden Ave, Long Beach, CA 90807 USA Tel 714-271-7667; Fax: 562-989-2031
E-mail: goodbooks@yeomanhouse.com
Web site: http://www.ginaspoems.com; http://www.yosoypublishing.com.

Yost-Haynes, Melissa, *(978-0-9760909)* RR1, 115C, Ravenswood, WV 26164 USA.

You Are Here Bks. *Imprint of* **Bushel & Peck Bks.**

You Can Do It! Productions, *(978-0-9744306)* 106 Paradise Rd., Havana, FL 32333-4236 USA
E-mail: infinipede@juno.com
Web site: http://www.infinipede.com.

You Can Do It! ART Publications *See* **Sunrise Mountain Bks.**

You Come Too Publishing, *(978-0-9816836)* 3138 NW Colonial Dr., Bend, OR 97701 USA Tel 541-317-4912 (phone/fax)
E-mail: imkehoe@msn.com
Web site: http://youcometoo.com
Dist(s): **Smashwords.**

You Publishing Group, *(978-0-9764472)* 2500 S. Lamar Blvd., Austin, TX 78704 USA.

Young Advent Pilgrim's Bookshelf *See* **Barnes Printing**

Young, Beth, *(978-0-9760180)* 124 Chestnut St. Apt. 201, Englewood, OH 45322-1410 USA
E-mail: 369beth@bellsouth.net
Web site: http://www.saintlukespress.com.

Young Createers, *(978-0-9980893)* 4901 E. Kelton Ln, Scottsdale, AZ 85254 USA Tel 480-228-3988
E-mail: lisabenger@hotmail.com
Web site: youngcreateers.com.

Young, Estrell III, *(978-0-692-90306-3; 978-0-692-91185-3)* 2764 Pkwy. Cove, LITHONIA, GA 30058 USA Tel 678-485-8864
E-mail: just.estrell@gmail.com
Dist(s): **Ingram Content Group.**

young, monique, *(978-0-9993044)* 42 william St., Hempstead, NY 11550 USA Tel 516-808-2620
E-mail: jomoyoung@optonline.net.

Young of Heart Publishing, *(978-0-9995608; 978-1-950421)* P.O. Box 2274, McKinleyville, CA 95519 USA Tel 707-839-7061
E-mail: zjavanee@suddenlink.net.

Young Patronesses of the Opera, The, *(978-0-9785364; 978-0-9795725; 978-0-9993895)* P.O. Box 3471616, Miami, FL 33234-7616 USA Tel 305-665-3470; Fax: 305-667-9265
E-mail: education@YPO-Miami.org
Web site: www.ypo-miami.org.

Young Publishing, *(978-1-7343437)* 25 Rambling Ln., Aliso Viejo, CA 92656 USA Tel 714-316-9661
E-mail: Young4ever1960@gmail.com.

Young Reader's Library *Imprint of* **RNWC Media, LLC**

Young Readers Publications, *(978-0-9789525)* 47 W. Schuyler St., Oswego, NY 13126 USA
E-mail: guntherphotography@hotmail.com
Web site: http://jguntherphotography.com.

Young Scholars Pr., *(978-0-9787138)* 354 1/2 Calle Loma Norte, Santa Fe, NM 87501 USA Tel 505-989-7116; Fax: 505-820-2367
E-mail: MsAnnett1@aol.com
Web site: http://oneworldmanypeople.com.

Young Women Books *See* **Harper Kids Hse.**

Young Women Programming *Imprint of* **Harper Kids Hse.**

Young Writer's Contest Foundation *See* **Miracle Pr.**

Young, Zachary, *(978-1-7344311)* 65 Westbrook Ave., Daly City, CA 94015 USA Tel 415-613-3239
E-mail: aauzyoung@gmail.com.

Publisher Name Index

Youngheart Music, (*978-0-945267; 978-1-57471*) Affil. of Creative Teaching Pr., Orders Addr.: P.O. Box 2723, Huntington, CA 92647-0723 USA Tel 714-895-5047; Fax: 714-895-5087; Toll Free Fax: 800-229-9929; Toll Free: 800-444-4287; Edit Addr.: 15342 Graham St., Huntington Beach, CA 92649-1111 USA
E-mail: webmaster@creativeteaching.com; rebecca.cleland@creativeteaching.com
Web site: http://www.youngheartmusic.com; http://www.creativeteaching.com
Dist(s): **Creative Teaching Pr., Inc.**
Follett School Solutions
Rounder Kids Music Distribution.

Youngheart Records *See* **Youngheart Music**

Young-Robinson, Christine, (*978-0-9706985*) 1805 Clemson Road, 291333, Columbia, SC 29229 USA
E-mail: miraclewriter4u@aol.com
Web site: http://www.christineyoungrobinson.com.

Youngs, Bettie Bks., (*978-0-9843081; 978-1-936332; 978-0-9836045; 978-0-9882848; 978-1-940784*) Div. of Bettie Youngs Book Publishers, Box 735, Humboldt, IA 50548 USA Tel 702-467-0055; *Imprints:* Kendahl House Press (KendahlHse); Burres Books (BurresBks); Teen Town Press (Teen Town); Teen Town Press / Bettie Youngs Books (MYID_O_TEEN TO)
E-mail: Bettie@BettieYoungs.com
Web site: http://www.BettieYoungsBooks.com
Dist(s): **Brodart Co.**
Coutts Information Services
Independently Published
Ingram Content Group
Quality Bks., Inc.
Smashwords.

Youngs, C. R., (*978-0-9760451*) 11687 Sugar Creek Ave., Mount Carmel, IL 62863 USA
E-mail: ronyoungs@davidbook.com
Web site: http://www.davidbook.com/.

Your Culture Gifts, (*978-0-9797637*) P.O. Box 1245, Ellicott City, MD 21041 USA (SAN 854-3208) Tel 410-461-5799
E-mail: info@yourculturegifts.com
Web site: http://www.yourculturegifts.com.

Your Destiny Productions, (*978-0-9815332*) 276 Neuse Rd., Roanoke Rapids, NC 27870 USA Tel 252-676-7652
E-mail: yourdestinyproductions@gmail.com
Web site: http://angelaleemoody.wixsite.com/destinyproductions.

Your Shift Matters Publishing, (*978-1-7378234*) 9820 Rosewood Dr., Chardon, OH 44024 USA Tel 440-856-6859
E-mail: danazarcone@gmail.com.

Your Story Hour Recordings, P.O. Box 511, Medina, OH 44258 USA Tel 216-725-5767; 717 St. Jospeh Dr. #254, Saint Joseph, MI 49085 Tel 269-471-3701
Web site: http://www.yourstoryhour.org.

Your Vision LLC, (*978-0-9985032*) 1065 Dixwell Ave., Hamden, CT 06514 USA Tel 203-654-5519
E-mail: Tchtheauthor@gmail.com.

You're On!, Inc., (*978-0-9760280*) P.O. Box 101071, Fort Worth, TX 76185 USA.

Youth Communication - New York Center, (*978-0-9661256; 978-1-933939; 978-1-935552; 978-1-938970*) 244 W. 27th St., 2nd Flr., New York, NY 10001 USA Tel 212-279-0708 ext. 115; Fax: 212-279-8856
E-mail: khefner@youthcomm.org
Web site: http://www.youthcomm.org
Dist(s): **Follett School Solutions.**

Youth Cultural Publishing Co. (CHN) (*978-957-530; 978-957-574*) *Dist. by* **Chinasprout.**

Youth Development & Research Fund, (*978-0-9659130*) P.O. Box 2188, Germantown, MD 20875-2188 USA
E-mail: ed@ydrf.com
Web site: http://www.ydrf.com.

Youth Inkwell Publishing, (*978-0-9773451*) 155 S. El Molino Ave., Suite 102, Paadena, CA 91101 USA Tel 626-449-6884; Fax: 626-449-6885
E-mail: info@youthinkwell.org
Web site: http://youthinkwell.org; http://www.youthinkwell.org.

Youth Popular Culture Institute, Inc., (*978-1-887191*) 8906 Fox Park Rd., Clinton, MD 20735 USA Tel 301-877-1525.

Youth Quest Institute, (*978-0-9748994*) 5515 Azalea Trail Ln., Sugar Land, TX 77479 USA
Web site: http://youthquestinstitute.com; http://getagripbooks.com.

Youthleadership.com, (*978-0-9677981*) 5593 Golf Course Dr., Morrison, CO 80465 USA Tel 303-358-1563; Fax: 303-393-9066
E-mail: support@youthleadership.com; mariam@youthleadership.com
Web site: http://www.youthleadership.com.

Youthlight, Inc., (*978-1-889636; 978-1-59850*) Orders Addr.: P.O. Box 115, Chapin, SC 29036 USA (SAN 256-6400) Tel 803-345-1070; Fax: 803-345-0888; Toll Free: 800-209-9774; Edit Addr.: 105 Fairway Pond Dr., Chapin, SC 29036 USA
E-mail: yl@sc.rr.com; yl@youthlightbooks.com
Web site: http://www.youthlight.com; http://www.youthlightbooks.com.

YouthPlays, (*978-1-62088; 978-1-62088-584-0; 978-1-63932*) 7125 De Longpre Ave. No. 209, Los Angeles, CA 90046 USA Tel 424-703-5315
E-mail: info@youthplays.com
Web site: http://youthplays.com.

YoYo Bks. (BEL) (*978-90-5843; 978-90-8622; 978-94-6195; 978-94-6151; 978-94-6244*) *Dist. by* **S and S Inc.**

YP Publishing, (*978-0-692-16588-1; 978-0-578-56256-8; 978-0-578-70336-7; 978-0-578-90106-0; 978-0-578-93105-0; 979-8-218-15370-0*) 2219 Green House, Houston, TX 77084 USA Tel 281-608-9796
E-mail: yperry92@gmail.com.

Ysanti *See* **Lion's Crest Pr.**

Yucca Publishing *Imprint of* **Skyhorse Publishing Co., Inc.**

Yudcovitch, Lorne, (*978-0-9749781*) 6905 S.W. 7th Ave., Portland, OR 97219 USA Tel 503-293-6923
E-mail: yudcovil@pacificu.edu.

Yumcha Studios LLC, (*978-0-9881899*) 33-59 Farrington St., 2nd Flr., Flushing, NY 11354 USA Tel 917-332-8931; Fax: 917-332-8931
E-mail: yenyen@dimsumwarriors.com; colin@dimsumwarriors.com
Web site: www.dimsumwarriors.com
Dist(s): **Diamond Comic Distributors, Inc.**
Diamond Bk. Distributors.

Yunka Publishing, (*978-0-9989640; 978-1-7324236*) 18923 Camillo Ct, Houston, TX 77094 USA Tel 832-725-8787
E-mail: karayaka@msn.com.

Yuxu Taoism Inc., (*978-1-64894*) 1230 Madelena Ave., Winter Springs, FL 32708 USA Tel 863-666-0999
E-mail: GUANFRANK@YAHOO.COM
Web site: yuxutaoism.org.

YWAM Publishing, (*978-0-927545; 978-0-9615534; 978-1-57658; 978-1-64836*) Div. of Youth With A Mission International, P.O. Box 55787, Seattle, WA 98155 USA (SAN 248-4021)
E-mail: customerservice@ywampublishing.com
Web site: http://www.ywampublishing.com
Dist(s): **christianaudio.**

ZEM Pr., (*978-0-9634168*) 8220 Stone Trail Dr., Bethesda, MD 20817-4556 USA Tel 301-365-4585; Fax: 301-365-4586
E-mail: zem@wbh.com
Web site: http://www.wb4.com.

Z Health Bks. *Imprint of* **New Win Publishing**

Z Pr., (*978-0-615-14380-4*) P.O. Box 6556, Woodland Hills, CA 91365 USA Tel 717-337-9968
E-mail: amy@amyleecoy.com
Dist(s): **Lulu Pr., Inc.**

Z2 Comics, (*978-1-940878; 978-1-954928; 979-8-88656*)
E-mail: zipcomic@gmail.com
Web site: z2comics.com
Dist(s): **Diamond Comic Distributors, Inc.**
Diamond Bk. Distributors
Simon & Schuster, Inc.

Zaccheus Entertainment Co., (*978-0-692-53734-3; 978-0-9969964; 978-0-9981972; 978-0-9985191; 978-0-9994571; 978-0-9997854*) 136 Morrison Ave., Mt. Prospect, IL 60056 USA Tel 847-894-5574
E-mail: chiefcreta@att.net.

Zach Feuer Gallery, (*978-0-9768533*) 530 W 24th St., New York, NY 10011 USA Tel 212-989-7700
E-mail: zach@zachfeuer.com
Web site: http://www.zachfeuer.com
Dist(s): **D.A.P./Distributed Art Pubs.**

Zach, Jacob, (*978-0-692-93865-2*) 18233 Powers Creek Loop Rd NE, Silverton, OR 97381 USA Tel 541-216-0695
E-mail: jacobhzach@gmail.com.

Zach Zeis, (*978-1-7372550*) 17509 102nd Ave NE, Bothell, WA 98011 USA Tel 509-953-2381
E-mail: zachary.b.zeis@gmail.com.

Zachary James Novels, (*978-0-692-18648-0; 978-0-692-18793-7; 978-0-578-58271-9; 978-0-578-60205-9; 978-0-578-76237-1; 978-0-578-77572-2; 978-0-578-91457-2*) PO BOX 35 200 Rte. 94, BLAIRSTOWN, NJ 07825 USA Tel 9083627751
E-mail: zachjb2000@yahoo.com
Dist(s): **Ingram Content Group.**

Zachmeyer, Mary L., (*978-0-9646864*) 1008 County Road 105., Columbus, TX 78934-1606 USA.

Zack Geoffroy *See* **Jeffries Bks.**

Zack Zombie Publishing *Imprint of* **Herobrine Publishing**

Zadok Supply, LLC, (*978-0-9964727*) 1540 Keller Pkwy. Suite 108 No. 145, keller, TX 76248 USA Tel 800-582-5140; Fax: 800-582-7956
E-mail: info@zadoksupply.com
Web site: www.zadokpublishing.com.

Zadunajsky, Donna M., (*978-0-9842397; 978-1-938037*) Orders Addr.: 17344 S. Parker Rd., Homer Glen, IL 60491 USA (SAN 858-821X) Tel 708-548-9829
E-mail: dmzadunajsky@gmail.com; 72allshookup@gmail.com
Web site: http://www.donnazadunajskymalacina.blogspot.com; http://www.donnazadunajsky.com
Dist(s): **BookBaby**
MyiLibrary
ebrary, Inc.

Zafa Publishing, (*978-0-692-41055-4; 978-0-9967422*) 3918 Glendenning Rd., Downers Grove, IL 60515 USA Tel 630-964-1561
E-mail: mmludwig1@comcast.net.

Zagat Survey, (*978-0-943421; 978-0-9612574; 978-1-57006; 978-1-60478*) 4 Columbus Cir., New York, NY 10019 USA (SAN 289-4777) Tel 212-977-6000; Fax: 212-765-9438; Toll Free: 866-999-0991
E-mail: tradesales@justzagat.com; theinz@zagat.com
Web site: http://www.zagat.com
Dist(s): **Ingram Publisher Services**
Two Rivers Distribution.

Zagorski, Steve, (*978-0-578-05364-6*) Orders Addr.: P.O. Box 50196, Austin, TX 78763 USA Tel 517-789-3259; Edit Addr.: 1009 W. 6th St., Suite 206, Austin, TX 78703 USA
E-mail: swzagorski@gmail.com.

Zaharko, Mary, (*978-0-692-59295-3*) 70 Mohawk Dr., West Hartford, CT 06117 USA Tel 860-463-0700
E-mail: jmintonq@comcast.net.

Zahir Publishing, (*978-0-9741311; 978-0-9786041; 978-0-9831090; 978-0-623-7707*) 315 S. Coast Hwy. 101, Suite U8, Encinitas, CA 92024 USA
Web site: http://www.zahirtales.com.

Zahorí de Ideas (ESP) (*978-84-941150; 978-84-947135*) *Dist. by* **Lectorum Pubns.**

Zahrob Publishing Co., (*978-0-9753641*) Orders Addr.: P.O. Box 5825, Rochester, MN 55903-5825 USA; Edit Addr.: 1445 Valley High Dr., NW, Rochester, MN 55903-5825 USA.

Zaloli, LLC, (*978-0-9857047; 978-0-9897380*) 4065 Sleeping Indian Ln., Colorado Springs, CO 80904 USA Tel 719-685-6505
E-mail: goldflagstudios@gmail.com.

Zander Pubns., (*978-0-578-01907-9; 978-0-578-01908-6; 978-0-578-02012-9; 978-0-578-02076-1; 978-0-578-04264-0; 978-0-578-05322-6; 978-0-578-05695-1; 978-0-9834052*) 2351 Sunset Blvd., Suite 170-433, Rocklin, CA 95765 USA Tel 916-624-1578
E-mail: randall@ips.net; contact@zanderpublications.com
Web site: http://www.zanderpublications.com
Dist(s): **Lulu Pr., Inc.**

zandmsgma Bks., (*978-0-9989583*) 5130 Mayweed Ct, Colorado Springs, CO 80917 USA Tel 719-229-7189
E-mail: rhondaeclark56@gmail.com.

Zando, (*978-1-63893*) 88 Prospect Pl., Brooklyn, NY 11217 USA Tel 516-606-9445
E-mail: Alexander.czik@zandoprojects.com
Web site: www.zandoprojects.com
Dist(s): **Ingram Publisher Services**
Two Rivers Distribution.

Zaner-Bloser, Inc., (*978-0-7367; 978-0-88085; 978-0-88309; 978-1-4531*) Subs. of Highlights for Children, Orders Addr.: P.O. Box 16764, Columbus, OH 43216-6764 USA (SAN 282-5678) Tel 614-486-0221; Fax: 614-487-2263; Toll Free Fax: 800-992-6087; Toll Free: 800-421-3018; 1201 Dublin Rd., Columbus, OH 43215-1026
Web site: http://www.zaner-bloser.com/.

Zangadoo Entertainment, (*978-0-9847428*) 14101 19th Dr. SE, Mill Creek, WA 98012 USA Tel 206-234-8123
E-mail: dean@zangadoo.com
Web site: www.zangadoo.com.

Zangadoo LLC *See* **Zangadoo Entertainment**

Zany Angel Projects LLC, (*978-0-9769234*) P.O. Box 1411, New York, NY 10159 USA Tel 212-686-4206.

Zardoz Pr. *Imprint of* **Life Force Bks.**

Zarraonandia, Anne, (*978-0-9741070*) P.O. Box 151435, San Rafael, CA 94915 USA Tel 415-456-4070; Toll Free: 877-892-6974 (phone/fax)
E-mail: annezarra@aol.com
Web site: http://www.cowboyluke.com.

Zarrella, Sharon *See* **Lizzy Anne's Adventures**

Zarriello, Nancy, (*978-0-578-53204-2*) 1266 Ocean Ave., Sea Bright, NJ 07760 USA Tel 732-614-1403
E-mail: nancyzarriello12@gmail.com.

Zarrika, Ltd., (*978-0-9758663; 978-1-934252*) P.O. Box 488, Unionville, PA 19375 USA Fax: 610-486-6501; Toll Free: 888-369-3366
Web site: http://www.zarrika.com.

Zaster Publishing, (*978-0-578-19533-9*) 83 Rosewell Rd., Bedford, NH 03110 USA.

ZC Horses Series of Children's Bks., (*978-0-9721496; 978-0-9791719*) 8 Hokanson Ln., Salmon, ID 83467 USA Tel 208-756-7947
E-mail: zchorses@hotmail.com
Web site: http://www.zchorses.com.

ZCR Pr., (*978-0-9763926*) 4912 Woodman Ave., No. 3, Sherman Oaks, CA 91423 USA (SAN 256-3479) Tel 818-995-3032 (phone/fax)
E-mail: zaldy80@aol.com.

ZE Graphics Inc., (*978-0-692-98225-9; 978-0-692-15431-1; 978-0-692-04205-2; 978-0-578-45948-6; 978-0-578-48184-5; 978-0-578-53757-3; 978-0-578-57939-9*) 125 Radford St. No. 6E, YONKERS, NY 10705 USA Tel 914-457-5446
E-mail: ZEGraphicsinc@gmail.com
Dist(s): **Ingram Content Group.**

Zebra Ginkgo, (*978-0-9891510*) 310 Frieda Ave., Kirkwood, MO 63122 USA Tel 314-292-9452
E-mail: edchen7@zebraginkgo.com
Web site: www.zebraginkgo.com.

Zee Lacson, (*978-1-7351358*) 624 Dove Ct, Grayslake, IL 60030 USA Tel 847-912-3564
E-mail: zee@zshots.net
Web site: www.reveriethebook.com.

Zeezok Publishing *See* **Zeezok Publishing, LLC**

Zeezok Publishing, LLC, (*978-0-9746505; 978-1-933573; 978-1-61006*) P.O. Box 1960, Elyria, OH 44036 USA (SAN 179-4493) Fax: 440-323-9494; Toll Free: 800-749-1681
E-mail: info@zeezok.com
Web site: http://www.zeezok.com.

Zeidman Consulting *See* **Swiss Creek Pubns.**

Zeiger, J. Tod, (*978-1-928672*) 912 Kenilworth Cir., Maryville, TN 37804-5215 USA Tel 423-984-8531.

Zeiger, Jennifer M., (*978-0-692-99474-0; 978-1-7351226*) 185 Lakewood Dr., Sumter, SC 29150 USA Tel 719-235-8991
E-mail: jennifer.m.zeiger@gmail.com
Web site: jenniferzeiger.com
Dist(s): **Ingram Content Group.**

Zeke & Me Bks., (*978-0-9883042*) 2415 Outlook St., Kalamazoo, MI 49001 USA Tel 269-344-7757
E-mail: sstamm625@gmail.com.

Zellmann Publishing, LLC, (*978-0-9763325*) 420 Springwood Ct., Canton, GA 30115-8287 USA Tel 770-345-7265; Fax: 770-345-7265
E-mail: zellmann@zellmannpublishing.com.

Zelma's Farm, (*978-0-9989774; 979-8-9865433*) 1351 Fulton Rd., E. Corinth, VT 05040 USA Tel 802-439-5126
E-mail: zelmasfarm@gmail.com
Web site: zelmasfarm.com.

Zemek, Alan, (*978-0-9960921*) 1316 LaClair Ave., Pittsburgh, PA 15218 USA Tel 412-508-1491
E-mail: zemeka27@verizon.net.

Zemi Comics, (*978-0-9745825*) SDQ 17, 4440 NW, 73rd Ave., Miami, FL 33166 USA Tel 787-748-4567
E-mail: fans@zemicomics.com
Web site: http://www.zemicomics.com.

Zen Life Bks., (*978-0-578-42420-0; 978-1-7342391*) 782 Trail Ridge Dr., Louisville, CO 80027 USA Tel 209-736-7699
E-mail: alexandermilljr@gmail.com
Dist(s): **Independent Pub.**

Zendrera Zariquiey, Editorial (ESP) (*978-84-89675; 978-84-8418*) *Dist. by* **Mariuccia Iaconi Bk Imports.**

Zendrera Zariquiey, Editorial (ESP) (*978-84-89675; 978-84-8418*) *Dist. by* **Lectorum Pubns.**

Zenescope Entertainment, (*978-0-9786874; 978-0-9817550; 978-0-9823630; 978-0-9825826; 978-0-9827507; 978-0-615-40679-4; 978-0-9830404; 978-1-937068; 978-0-9853378; 978-1-939683; 978-1-942275; 978-1-951087*) 433 Caredean Dr Suite C, Horsham, PA 19044 USA (SAN 851-2760); *Imprints:* Silver Dragon Books (SilverDrag)
E-mail: jbrusha@zenscope.com
Web site: http://www.zenescope.com
Dist(s): **Diamond Comic Distributors, Inc.**
Diamond Bk. Distributors.

Zenga Publishing, (*978-0-9765484*) Orders Addr.: P.O. Box 461, Milton, NY 12547 USA
E-mail: mmaniatis@hvc.rr.com
Web site: http://www.agirlscourage.com; http://www.zengapublishing.com.

Zenith Pr. *Imprint of* **Quarto Publishing Group USA**

Zephyr Pr. *Imprint of* **Chicago Review Pr., Inc.**

Zephyr Pr., (*978-0-939010; 978-0-9815521; 978-0-9832970; 978-1-938890*) 50 Kenwood St., No. 2, Brookline, MA 02446 USA (SAN 239-7668) Do not confuse with companies with the same name in New York, NY, Tucson, AZ, Kansas City, MO, Canton, OH
E-mail: editors@zephyrpress.org
Web site: http://www.zephyrpress.org
Dist(s): **Consortium Bk. Sales & Distribution**
MyiLibrary
SPD-Small Pr. Distribution.

Zero To Three, (*978-0-943657; 978-1-934019; 978-1-938558; 978-1-956117*) Div. of Zero To Three: National Ctr. for Infants, Toddlers & Families, Orders Addr.: P.O. Box 960, Herndon, VA 20172 USA Toll Free: 800-899-4301; Edit Addr.: 1255 23RD St. NW, Suite 350, Washington, DC 20037 USA (SAN 242-5084) Tel 202-638-1144; Fax: 202-638-0851
E-mail: jenniferli@zerotothree.org
Web site: http://www.zerotothree.org.

Zero To Three Press *See* **Zero To Three**

Zeromayo Studios, LLP, (*978-0-9661985*) Orders Addr.: P.O. Box 417, Haydenville, MA 01039 USA Tel 413-584-9372; Fax: 413-665-2312; Edit Addr.: 16 Market St., Northampton, MA 01060 USA; *Imprints:* Empty Sky (Empty Sky)
E-mail: planetrace@aol.com
Web site: http://www.ninjaturtles.com
Dist(s): **Diamond Comic Distributors, Inc.**

Zest Bks. *Imprint of* **Lerner Publishing Group**

Zest Publishing, (*978-0-9758861*) Orders Addr.: P.O. Box 484, Edgar, NE 68935-0484 USA; Edit Addr.: R.R. 1, Edgar, NE 68935-0484 USA Do not confuse with Zest Publishing Company in Southfield, MI.

Zeus Media LLC, (*978-0-9765840*) 12900 Canterbury, Leawood, KS 66209 USA
Web site: http://www.wisdomofzeus.com.

Zeus Sports Florida LLC, (*978-0-9777437*) Orders Addr.: 2312 SE 23rd Rd., Homestead, FL 33035-1900 USA Tel 786-417-9197
E-mail: habbook@msn.com.

ZH, (*978-0-578-41269-6; 978-0-578-62393-1; 978-0-578-73277-0; 978-0-578-77691-0*) 609 Cordova Dept of Dermatology, Davis, CA 95616 USA Tel 555-555-5555
E-mail: spunky1000@aol.com
Dist(s): **Independent Pub.**

JYZ Bks., LLC, (*978-0-9743272; 978-0-9906905*) Orders Addr.: 5816 White Pebble Path, Clarksville, MD 21029 USA (SAN 990-1868) Tel 443-535-2541; Fax: 703-485-2970
E-mail: jianyi.zhang66@gmail.com.

Zhang, Shiyu, (*978-0-692-90983-6*) 888 O'Farrell St APT E509, San Francisco, CA 94109 USA Tel 612-636-7385
E-mail: fishjump_000ya@hotmail.com
Dist(s): **Ingram Content Group.**

Zhera Pubns., (*978-0-9618904*) Orders Addr.: 2605 E. Flora Pl., Denver, CO 80210-6827 USA (SAN 242-231X) Tel 303-753-0384
E-mail: Zhera@msn.com; zhera@msn.com.

Ziert, Paul Assocs., Inc., (*978-0-9666104*) Orders Addr.: P.O. Box 721020, Norman, OK 73070 USA Tel 405-447-9988; Fax: 405-447-5810; Edit Addr.: 3214 Bart Conner Dr., Norman, OK 73072 USA
E-mail: paul@intlgymnast.com; IGDwight@aol.com.

Zig the Pig, (*978-0-9761700*) 815 Poinsettia St., Columbia, SC 29205 USA.

Ziggy Owl Pr., (*978-0-9963747*) 24 Canal St., Medford, MA 02155 USA Tel 781-396-8470
E-mail: johngarp@aol.com.

Ziker, Andrew, (*978-0-9762147*) 1788 E. Indigo St., Gilbert, AZ 85298-3222 USA.

Zilber, Jeremy, (*978-0-9786688*) P.O. Box 5543, Madison, WI 53705 USA
E-mail: jzilber@littledemocrats.net
Web site: http://www.littledemocrats.net.

Zimmerman, W. Frederick *See* **Nimble Bks. LLC**

Zindel Publishing *See* **Graymalkin Media**

Zinka Pr., Inc., (*978-0-9647171*) 1480 Pulaski Ln., Wayne, PA 19087 USA Tel 610-688-2113; Fax: 610-688-0753
E-mail: zinkapress@aol.com
Web site: http://www.zinkapress.com.

Zino Pr. Children's Bks., (*978-1-55933*) Div. of Knowledge Unlimited, Inc., P.O. Box 52, Madison, WI 53701-0052 USA Tel 608-836-6660; Fax: 608-831-1570; Toll Free Fax: 800-618-1570; Toll Free: 800-356-2303
E-mail: madzino@zinopress.com
Web site: http://www.zinopress.com
Dist(s): **Brodart Co.**
Follett School Solutions.

Zion Publishing, (*978-0-9627147; 978-0-9979841; 978-0-9998819; 978-1-7333982; 978-1-7357958; 978-1-7368640; 979-8-9856705*) 1500 Crown Colony Ct., Suite 540, Des Moines, IA 50315 USA Tel 515-282-5940; Toll Free: 800-996-2777 Do not confuse with companies with the same name in Monarch Beach, CA, Vallejo, CA
E-mail: maryenilsen@aol.com
Web site: http://www.zionpublishing.org.

Zion Publishing, (*978-0-9714844*) 17 Harding Ln., Sumiton, AL 35148 USA Tel 205-648-6741
E-mail: driverdm@aol.com.

Zipporah J Productions, (*978-1-7379118*) 7727 LANKERSHIM BLVD APT 221, North Hollywood, CA 91605 USA Tel 916-715-8514
E-mail: missiraross@gmail.com.

Zishka Publishing, (*978-1-941691*) 242 B Keyser Ave. PMB 181, Natchitoches, LA 71457 USA Tel 318-228-8614; *Imprints:* Write 'N Learn (Write N Learn)
E-mail: chrism@chrismcmullen.com
Web site: engagenlearn.com.

Z-kai Inc. *See* **Z-kai USA Inc.**

Z-kai USA Inc., (*978-1-7373419*) 450 Massachusetts Ave., Arlington, MA 02474 USA
E-mail: info@zkai-usa.com.

Zo Publishing, (*978-0-938465*) Orders Addr.: P.O. Box 61335, Honolulu, HI 96839 USA (SAN 660-9864) Tel 808-988-7111; Edit Addr.: 2918 Manoa Rd., Honolulu, HI 96822 USA (SAN 660-9872)
E-mail: dyen@lava.net.

Zoe Life Christian Communications, (*978-0-9748251; 978-0-9779445; 978-1-934363; 978-1-938807; 978-0-9995405; 979-8-9855846*) 34232 Pembroke, LIVONIA, MI 48152 USA (SAN 256-1735) Tel 734-578-6703; 34232 Pembroke Ave, Livonia, MI, MI 48152
E-mail: info@zoelifepub.com
Web site: http://www.zoelifebooks.org
Dist(s): **Send The Light Distribution LLC.**

Zoe Life Publishing *See* **Zoe Life Christian Communications**

Zoey B, (*978-1-7357857*) 523 THUNDER TRL, FORNEY, TX 75126-4729 USA Tel 469-767-7964
E-mail: kirareicaro@yahoo.com.

Zolie Zi Empire, (*978-0-692-89897-0; 978-0-692-92967-4*) 200 S. Ryan Dr. #11207, RED OAK, TX 75154 USA Tel 469-892-8816
E-mail: zoliezi@yahoo.com; zoliezi@yahoo.com.

Zonderkidz, (*978-0-310*) Div. of Zondervan, 5300 Patterson Ave., SE, Grand Rapids, MI 49530 USA Tel 1-800-727-3480
E-mail: zprod@zondervan.com
Web site: http://www.zondervan.com
Dist(s): **Children's Plus, Inc.**
HarperCollins Christian Publishing
Nelson, Thomas Inc.
Zondervan.

†Zondervan, (*978-0-00; 978-0-310; 978-0-937336*) Div. of HarperCollins Christian Publishing, Orders Addr.: c/o Zondervan XNET Ordering Dept., 5249 Corporate Grove, Grand Rapids, MI 49512 USA (SAN 298-9107); Edit Addr.: 5300 Patterson Ave., SE, Grand Rapids, MI 49530 USA (SAN 203-2694) Tel 616-698-6900; Fax: 616-698-3439
Web site: http://www.zondervan.com
Dist(s): **Blackstone Audio, Inc.**
Brilliance Publishing, Inc.
Children's Plus, Inc.
Ebsco Publishing
Follett School Solutions
HarperCollins Christian Publishing
Open Road Integrated Media, Inc.
Send The Light Distribution LLC; *CIP.*

Zondervan bibles *See* **Zondervan Bibles**

Zondervan Bibles, (*978-0-310*) 5300 Patterson Ave., SE, Grand Rapids, MI 49530 USA Tel 800-727-3480
E-mail: zprod@zondervan.com
Web site: http://www.zondervan.com
Dist(s): **Zondervan.**

Zondervan Bks., (*978-0-310*) 5300 Patterson Ave., SE, Grand Rapids, MI 49530 USA Tel 1-800-727-3480
E-mail: zprod@zondervan.com
Web site: http://www.zondervan.com
Dist(s): **HarperCollins Christian Publishing**
Zondervan.

Zondervan Publishing House *See* **Zondervan**

Zonk Galleries *See* **Zonk Galleries and Pubns.**

Zonk Galleries and Pubns., (*978-0-9706537*) 2909 Hansen Rd., Hayward, CA 94541 USA (SAN 254-3443) Tel 510-530-2681
E-mail: davidhoobler@sbcglobal.net
Web site: http://zonktheturtle.com.

Zonneschijn Publishisn, (*978-0-692-10333-3*) 918 Park Ln., Pella, IA 50219 USA Tel 641-780-0714
E-mail: veenstrarosa22@gmail.com.

Zoo Bks. *Imprint of* **National Wildlife Federation**

Zoolook, (*978-0-9656228; 978-0-9830637; 978-0-9883950*) P.O. Box 640806, San Francisco, CA 94164 USA (SAN 254-0398) Tel 415-729-4709; *Imprints:* ComiXstand (ComiXstand)
E-mail: ndasilva@zoolook.com
Web site: http://https://www.zoolook.com; http://https://www.iriemag.com; http://www.dreadandalive.com; https://www.ninenight.com; http://https://www.comixstand.com.

Zoombird Bks., (*978-0-615-32691-7*) Orders Addr.: 2734 Carisbrook Dr., Oakland, CA 94611 USA Tel 510-530-2737
Web site: http://www.zoombirdbooks.com.

Zoo-phonics, Inc., (*978-0-9617342; 978-1-886441*) Orders Addr.: 20950 Ferretti Rd., Groveland, CA 95321 USA (SAN 663-8589) Tel 209-962-5030; Fax: 209-962-4320; Toll Free: 800-622-8104
E-mail: zoo-info@zoo-phonics.com; shirley@zoo-phonics.com
Web site: http://www.zoo-phonics.com.

Zora, (*978-0-9714039; 978-1-59898*) Orders Addr.: 450 Stedman Pl., Monrovia, CA 91016 USA Tel 626-536-0708
E-mail: emil@zorapubs.com.

Zottola Publishing, Inc., (*978-0-9725880; 978-0-9823907*) Orders Addr.: 4212 Boone Ave. N., New Hope, MN 55428-0001 USA
E-mail: zottolaj@comcast.net
Web site: http://www.zotpub.com.

Zou Zou Media Hse. Inc., (*978-1-7771895*) c/o Woolcock Patton, LLC, 88 Schoole's Mountain Rd., Bldg. 1A, Hackettstown, NJ 07840 USA Tel 647-448-4630; 3205 Colonial Dr., Mississauga, ON L5L 5K9 Tel 647-448-4630 Admin
E-mail: hello@valenecampbell.com.

zReyomi Publishing, (*978-0-9670712*) Div. of Reyomi Global Media Group, Inc., P.O. Box 51928, Durham, NC 27717 USA Tel 919-321-2573; Fax: 919-489-3913
E-mail: drtrevy@me.com
Dist(s): **Bk. Hse., The**
Brodart Co.

Zu Bks., (*978-0-615-15267-7*) 1813 Comet, Altus, OK 73521 USA Tel 580-477-0819
Web site: http://zuopolis.com
Dist(s): **Lulu Pr., Inc.**

Zuber Publishing, (*978-0-9785551*) 52180 Tammy Dr., Granger, IN 46530 USA Tel 574-272-8914
E-mail: admin@zuberpublishing.com
Web site: http://www.zuberpublishing.com
Dist(s): **Distributors, The.**

Zuiho, (*978-0-9743474*) 11628 82nd Ave. NE, Kirkland, WA 98034-3400 USA.

Zuiker Pr., (*978-1-947378; 978-1-7322612*) 16255 Ventura Blvd, Encino, CA 91436 USA Tel 917-847-4156
E-mail: dave@zuikerpress.com
Dist(s): **Simon & Schuster, Inc.**

Zulema Enterprises LLC, (*978-1-881223*) 7715 Yardley Dr., Tamarac, FL 33321 USA Tel 513-659-1753
E-mail: peopleteachers@aol.com
Web site: http://www.zulemabooks.com.

Zulema Enterprises Publishing *See* **Zulema Enterprises LLC**

Zulu Planet Pubs. (ZAF) (*978-1-920070; 978-1-920153*) *Dist. by* **APG.**

Zumaya Embraces *Imprint of* **Zumaya Pubns. LLC**

Zumaya Otherworlds *Imprint of* **Zumaya Pubns. LLC**

Zumaya Pubns. LLC, (*978-1-894869; 978-1-894942; 978-1-55410; 978-1-934135; 978-1-934841; 978-1-936144; 978-1-61271*) Orders Addr.: 3209 S. Interstate 35 APT 1086, Austin, TX 78741-6905 USA Tel 512-537-3145; 512-931-4594; Fax: 512-276-6745; *Imprints:* Zumaya Otherworlds (Zumaya Otherworlds); Zumaya Embraces (Zumaya Embraces); Zumaya Thresholds (ZumThresh)
E-mail: production@zumayapublishing.com; business@zumayapublishing.com
Web site: http://www.zumayapublications.com; http://www.zumayapublishing.com.

Zumaya Thresholds *Imprint of* **Zumaya Pubns. LLC**

Zuroam Media, (*978-0-578-48580-5; 978-1-7351455*) 5601 Windmier Cir., Dallas, TX 75252 USA Tel 703-772-7066
E-mail: chris.parsons88@gmail.com.

Zy Iman Pubng, (*978-0-9779130*) P.O. Box 367, Brooklyn, NY 11221 USA
Web site: http://www.ucanspeakup.com.

Zygote Games LLC, (*978-0-9770419*) 100 Venture Way, Flr. 3, Suite 4, Hadley, MA 01035 USA Tel 413-303-9031; Fax: 253-540-5054
E-mail: orders@zygotegames.com
Web site: http://www.zygotegames.com.

Zyia Consulting, (*978-0-578-89861-2*) 2033 Hidden Ivy Ln., Loganville, GA 30052 USA Tel 770-990-9428
E-mail: munchie28@gmail.com
Web site: www.Unbreakable-woman.com.

Zyrro, Roggen, (*978-0-9762580*) 5841 Wornall Rd., Kansas City, MO 64113 USA
Web site: http://www.bunsta.com.

ZZ Dogs Pr. *Imprint of* **That's Life Publishing, Inc.**

WHOLESALER & DISTRIBUTOR NAME INDEX

1517 Media, (*978-0-8006; 978-0-8066; 978-1-4514; 978-1-5064; 979-8-88983*) Orders Addr.: 411 Washington Ave N, FL 3, Minneapolis, MN 55401-1301 USA (SAN 169-4081) Toll Free Fax: 800-722-7766; Toll Free: 800-328-4648 (orders only); Edit Addr.: 411 Washington Ave N, FL 3, Minneapolis, MN 55401-1301 USA Tel 800-328-4648 800-722-7766
E-mail: customerservice@augsburgfortress.org; info@augsburgfortress.org; subscriptions@augsburgfortress.org; copyright@augsburgfortress.org; international@augsburgfortress.org
Web site: http://www.augsburgfortress.org.

1stBooks Library, *See* **AuthorHouse**

2Learn-English, (*978-0-9627878; 978-1-891077; 978-1-934637*) Div. of Authors & Editors, Orders Addr.: 10736 Jefferson Blvd., No. 604, Culver City, CA 90230-4969 USA Tel 310-251-3931 Arthur Rubin; 310-836-2014 General/Messages; Fax: 310-836-1845
E-mail: info@2learn-english.com
Web site: http://www.2learn-english.com.

3M Sportsman's Video Collection, 3M Ctr., Bldg. 223-4NE-05, Saint Paul, MN 55144-1000 USA (SAN 159-8929) Tel 612-733-7412; Fax: 612-736-7479; Toll Free: 800-940-8273 (orders only).

A & B Books, *See* **A & B Distributors & Pubs. Group**

A & B Distributors & Pubs. Group, (*978-1-881316; 978-1-886433*) Div. of A&B Distributors, 1000 Atlantic Ave., Brooklyn, NY 11238 USA (SAN 630-9216) Tel 718-783-7808; Fax: 718-783-7267; Toll Free: 877-542-6657; 146 Lawrence St., Brooklyn, NY 11201 (SAN 631-385X)
E-mail: maxtay@webspan.net.

A & M Church Supplies, 3535 Bay Rd., Saginaw, MI 48603-2464 USA (SAN 157-0145) Toll Free: 800-345-4694.

A B C-Clio Information Services, *See* **ABC-CLIO, LLC**

A B S Corporation, *See* **Budgetext**

A K J Educational Services, Incorporated, *See* **AKJ Bks.**

AAA Anime Distribution, 4509 Shirley Ave., Unit D, El Mone, CA 91731 USA Tel 626-575-8922
E-mail: vince@aaaanime.com.

Aardvark Global Publishing, (*978-0-9770328; 978-1-933570; 978-1-59971; 978-1-4276*) 9587 S. Grandview Dr., Sandy, UT 84092 USA Do not confuse with Aardvark Global Publishing, Atlanta, GA
E-mail: info@eckohousepublishing.com
Web site: http://eckohousepublishing.com/; http://aardvarkglobalpublishing.com/; http://eckobooks.com.

ABC-CLIO, LLC, (*978-0-275; 978-0-313; 978-0-8371; 978-0-86569; 978-0-87287; 978-0-87436; 978-0-89789; 978-0-89930; 978-0-903450; 978-0-938865; 978-1-56308; 978-1-56720; 978-1-57607; 978-1-85109; 978-1-58683; 978-1-59158; 978-0-9742537; 978-1-59884; 978-1-4408; 978-1-61069; 979-8-4006; 979-8-216) 147 Castilian Dr., Santa Barbara, CA 93117 USA (SAN 301-5467) Tel 805-968-1911; Fax: 805-685-9685; Toll Free: 800-368-6868; P.O. Box 93116, Goleta, CA 93116 (SAN 857-7099)*
E-mail: customerservice@abc-clio.com; service@abc-clio.com; salesuk@abc-clio.com
Web site: http://www.abc-clio.com.

ABC'S Bk. Supply, Inc., 7319 W. Flagler St., Miami, FL 33144 USA Toll Free: 877-383-4240
E-mail: abcbooks@abcbooks.com.

Abdo & Daughters Publishing, *See* **ABDO Publishing Co.**

ABDO Publishing Co., (*978-0-939179; 978-1-56239; 978-1-57765; 978-1-59197; 978-1-59679; 978-1-59928; 978-1-59961; 978-1-60270; 978-1-60453; 978-1-61613; 978-1-61714; 978-1-61758; 978-1-61783; 978-1-61784; 978-1-61785; 978-1-61786; 978-1-61787; 978-1-61478; 978-1-61479; 978-1-61480; 978-1-62401; 978-1-62402; 978-1-62403; 978-1-62968; 978-1-62969; 978-1-62970; 978-1-68076; 978-1-68077; 978-1-68078; 978-1-68079; 978-1-68080; 978-1-5321; 978-1-0982; 979-8-3849) Div. of ABDO Publishing Group, Orders Addr.: 8000 W. 78th St. Suite 310, Edina, MN 55439 USA (SAN 662-9172) Tel 952-831-2120; Fax: 952-831-1632; Toll Free Fax: 800-862-3480; Toll Free: 800-800-1312; Edit Addr.: P.O. Box 398166, Minneapolis, MN 55439 USA Tel 800-800-1312*
E-mail: info@abdopublishing.com
Web site: http://www.abdopublishing.com.

Abel Love, Inc., Orders Addr.: P.O. Box 2250, Newport News, VA 23609 USA (SAN 158-4081) Tel 757-877-2939; Toll Free: 800-520-2939; Edit Addr.: 935 Lucas Creek Rd., Newport News, VA 23608 USA Fax: 804-877-2939.

Abingdon Pr., (*978-0-687; 978-1-4267; 978-1-63088; 978-1-5018; 978-1-7910*) Div. of United Methodist Publishing House, Orders Addr.: 810 12th Ave. S., Nashville, TN 37203 USA Tel 615-749-6409; 615-749-6000; Fax: 615-749-6056; Toll Free: 800-627-1789; Edit Addr.: 810 12th Ave. S., Nashville, TN 37203 USA (SAN 699-9956) Tel 615-749-6000; Toll Free Fax: 800-445-8189; Toll Free: 800-672-1789
E-mail: rburgoyne@umpublishing.org; cokes_serv@cokesbury.com
Web site: http://www.abingdonpress.com/; http://www.umph.org.

Abraham Assocs. Inc., 5120-A Cedar Lake Rd., Minneapolis, MN 55416 USA Tel 952-927-7920; Fax: 952-927-8089; Toll Free: 800-701-2489
E-mail: stu@abrahamassociatesinc.com.

Abrams & Co. Pubs., Inc., (*978-0-7664*) Orders Addr.: 61 Mattatuck Heights, Waterbury, CT 06705 USA; Edit Addr.: P.O. Box 10025, Waterbury, CT 06725 USA (SAN 207-7078) Tel 203-756-6562; Fax: 203-756-2895; Toll Free: 800-874-0029
E-mail: custserve@abramsandcompany.com
Web site: http://www.abramsandcompany.com.

Abrams, Harry N. Incorporated, *See* **Abrams, Inc.**

Abrams, Inc., (*978-0-8109; 978-1-4197; 978-1-61769; 978-1-61312; 978-1-68335*) A Subsidiary of La Martinière Groupe, Orders Addr.: The Market Building Third Floor, 72-82 Rosebery Ave., London, EC1R 4RW GBR Tel 020 7713 2060; Fax: 020 7713 2061; Edit Addr.: 115 West 18th St., New York, NY 10011 USA (SAN 200-2434) Tel 212-206-7715; Fax: 212-519-1210
E-mail: webmaster@abramsbooks.com
Web site: http://www.abramsbooks.com.

Abrams Learning Trends, Orders Addr.: 16310 Bratton Ln., Suite 250, Austin, TX 78728 USA Tel 512-735-2863
E-mail: billt@abramslearningtrends.com.

Abyss Distribution, (*978-1-932548*) P.O. Box 48, Middlefield, MA 01243-0048 USA (SAN 630-9925) Tel 413-623-2155; Fax: 413-623-2156; Toll Free: 800-326-0804
E-mail: abyssdist@aol.com
Web site: http://www.azuregreen.om.

Academic Bk. Ctr., Inc., P.O. Box 1320, Lake Oswego, OR 97035-0320 USA (SAN 169-7145) Toll Free: 800-547-7704
E-mail: orders@acbc.com
Web site: http://www.abc.com.

Academic Bk. Services, Inc., 5490 Fulton Industrial Blvd., Atlanta, GA 30336 USA (SAN 631-0591) Tel 404-344-8317; Fax: 404-349-2127.

Academic Studies Pr., (*978-1-934843; 978-1-936235; 978-1-61811; 978-1-64469; 979-8-88719*) 28 Montfern Ave., Brighton, MA 02135 USA (SAN 855-1766)
E-mail: press@academicstudiespress.com; igor.nemirovsky@academicstudiespress.com
Web site: http://www.academicstudiespress.com.

Academi-Text Medical Wholesalers, P.O. Box 1080, Monroe, MI 48161-6080 USA (SAN 135-2415) Toll Free: 800-552-8398 (out of state)
E-mail: dyourist@academi-text.com.

ACCESS Pubs. Network, 6893 Sullivan Rd., Grawn, MI 49637 USA.

Acorn Alliance, 549 Old North Rd., Kingston, RI 02881-1220 USA Tel 401-783-5480; Fax: 401-284-0959; Fulfillment Addr.: Client Distribution Services 193 Edwards Dr., Jackson, TN 38301 USA Toll Free Fax: 800-351-5073; Toll Free: 800-343-4499
E-mail: moyerbellbooks@yahoo.com
Web site: http://www.moyerbellbooks.com.

ACTA Pubns., (*978-0-87946; 978-0-914070; 978-0-915388*) 5559 Howard St., Skokie, IL 60077-2621 USA (SAN 204-7489) Toll Free Fax: 800-397-0079; Toll Free: 800-397-2282; 4848 N. Clark St., Chicago, IL 60640
E-mail: actapublications@aol.com
Web site: http://www.actapublications.com.

Actar D, (*978-0-9893317; 978-1-940291; 978-1-945150; 978-1-948765; 978-1-63840*) 440 Pk. Ave. South, 17th FL, New York, NY 10016 USA Tel 212-966-2207; Fax: 212-966-2214
E-mail: brian@actar-d.com; ricardo.devesa@actar-d.com
Web site: www.actar-d.com.

Action Products International, Inc., 344 Cypress Rd., Ocala, FL 34472-3108 USA (SAN 630-8805) Tel 352-687-4961; Toll Free: 800-772-2846
E-mail: sales@apii.com.

Activated Ministries, P.O. Box 462805, Escondido, CA 92046-2805 USA Toll Free: 877-862-3228
E-mail: sales@activatedministries.org.

ACW Pr., (*978-0-9656749; 978-1-892525; 978-1-932124; 978-1-934668*) Orders Addr.: P.O. Box 110390, Nashville, TN 37222 USA Tel 615-834-0450; Toll Free: 800-219-7483; Edit Addr.: 4854 Aster Dr., Nashville, TN 37211 USA
E-mail: regaforder@aol.com.

Adams Bk. Co., Inc., LSC Communications, Attn: Receiving/Ellen Farrell 1 Pierson Parkway, Cranbury, NJ 08512 USA (SAN 107-7171) Tel 718-875-5464; Fax: 718-852-3212; Toll Free: 800-221-0909
E-mail: sales@adamsbook.com
Web site: http://www.adamsbook.com.

Adams News, 1555 W. Galer St., Seattle, WA 98119 USA (SAN 169-8842) Tel 206-284-7617; Fax: 206-284-7599; Toll Free: 800-533-7617.

Adams, Robert Henry Fine Art, (*978-0-9713010*) 2146 W. Sunnyside Ave., Chicago, IL 60625-1626 USA (SAN 159-6918)
E-mail: info@adamsfineart.com
Web site: http://www.adamsfineart.com.

Addicus Bks., (*978-1-886039; 978-1-936374; 978-1-938803; 978-1-940495; 978-1-943886; 978-0-692-67011-8; 978-1-950091*) Orders Addr.: P.O. Box 45327, Omaha, NE 68145 USA Tel 402-330-7493; Fax: 402 330-1707; Toll Free: 800-352-2873; Edit Addr.: 814 N. Franklin St., Chicago, IL 60610 USA
E-mail: addicusbks@aol.com; info@addicusbooks.com
Web site: http://www.AddicusBooks.com.

Addison-Wesley Educational Pubs., Inc., (*978-0-321; 978-0-328; 978-0-673*) Div. of Addison Wesley Longman, Inc., 75 Arlington St., Boston, MA 02116 USA Tel 617-848-7500; Toll Free: 800-447-2226
Web site: http://www.awl.com.

Addison-Wesley Longman, Inc., (*978-0-201; 978-0-321; 978-0-582; 978-0-673; 978-0-8013; 978-0-8053; 978-0-9654123*) Orders Addr.: 200 Old Tappan Rd., Old Tappan, NJ 07675 USA (SAN 299-4739) Toll Free: 800-922-0579; Edit Addr.: 75 Arlington St., Suite 300, Boston, MA 02116 USA (SAN 200-2000) Tel 617-848-7500; Toll Free: 800-447-2226
E-mail: pearsoned@eds.com; orderdeptnj@pearsoned.com
Web site: http://www.awl.com.

Addison-Wesley Publishing Company, Incorporated, *See* **Addison-Wesley Longman, Inc.**

Adelman, Joseph, 530 N. 40th St., Allentown, PA 18104-4558 USA (SAN 285-8002).

Adler, Leo, P.O. Box 10308, Eugene, OR 97440-2308 USA (SAN 169-7021).

Adler's Foreign Bks., Inc., (*978-0-8417*) 915 Foster St., Evanston, IL 60201 USA (SAN 111-3089) Tel 847-864-0664; Fax: 847-864-0804; Toll Free: 800-235-3771
E-mail: info@afb-adlers.com
Web site: http://www.afb-adlers.com.

Advanced Global Distribution Services, 5880 Oberlin Dr., San Diego, CA 32121 USA Toll Free Fax: 800-499-3822; Toll Free: 800-284-3580.

Adventures Unlimited Pr., (*978-0-932813; 978-1-931882; 978-1-935487; 978-1-939149; 978-1-948803*) Orders Addr.: P.O. Box 74, Kempton, IL 60946 USA (SAN 630-1126) Tel 815-253-6390; Fax: 815-253-6300; Edit Addr.: 303 Main St., Kempton, IL 60946 USA (SAN 250-3484)
E-mail: auphq@frontiernet.net
Web site: http://www.adventuresunlimitedpress.com.

Advertising Specialties, Inc., 4920 River Rd., Pascagoula, MS 39567 USA (SAN 108-6316) Tel 601-769-7904
Web site: http://www.advmkt.com; http://www.advantagebooksonline.com.

Advocate Distribution Solutions, Div. of Send The Light Distribution LLC, 100 Biblica Way, Elizabethton, TN 37643 USA Tel 423-767-1100; Fax: 423-547-5199; Toll Free Fax: 800-759-2779; Toll Free: 800-289-2772
Web site: http://www.stl-distribution.com; http://www.advocatedistribution.com.

Affiliated Bk. Distributor, Div. of North Shore Distributors, Inc., 1200 N. Branch St., Chicago, IL 60622 USA (SAN 169-2267).

Africa World Pr., (*978-0-86543; 978-1-59221*) 541 W. Ingham Ave., Suite B, Trenton, NJ 08638 USA (SAN 692-3925) Tel 609-695-3200; Fax: 609-695-6466
E-mail: customerservice@africaworldpressbooks.com
Web site: http://www.africaworldpressbooks.com.

African World Bks., 2217 Pennsylvania Ave., Baltimore, MD 21217 USA (SAN 631-3868) Tel 410-383-2006.

Afrikan World Bk. Distributor, Orders Addr.: P.O. Box 16447, Baltimore, MD 21217 USA; Edit Addr.: 2217 Pennsylvania Ave., Baltimore, MD 21217 USA (SAN 631-2020) Tel 410-383-2006.

Afro-American Bk. Distributor, 2537 Prospect, Houston, TX 77004 USA (SAN 169-8257).

Agencia de Publicaciones de Puerto Rico, GPO Box 4903, San Juan, PR 00936 USA (SAN 169-9296).

Agritech Publishing Group, Inc., Div. of Agritech Corp., 825 W. Samalayuca Dr., Tucson, AZ 85704-3912 USA (SAN 174-612X) Tel 520-544-2542.

AHA, Inc., (*978-0-918545*) P.O. Box 8405, Santa Cruz, CA 95061-8405 USA (SAN 295-5059) Tel 408-458-9119.

AIMS International Bks., Inc., (*978-0-922852*) 7709 Hamilton Ave., Cincinnati, OH 45231-3103 USA (SAN 630-270X) Tel 513-521-5590; Fax: 513-521-5592; Toll Free: 800-733-2067
E-mail: aimsbooks@fuse.net
Web site: http://www.aimsbooks.com.

A-K News Company, *See* **Aramark Magazine & Bk. Co.**

AK Pr. Distribution, (*978-1-873176; 978-1-902593; 978-0-9830597; 978-1-939202*) 370 Ryan Ave, Unit 100, Chico, CA 95973 USA (SAN 298-2234) Tel 510-208-1708; Fax: 510-208-1701
E-mail: akpress@akpress.org
Web site: http://www.akpress.org.

AKJ Bks., 2700 Hollins Ferry Road, Baltimore, MD 21230 USA (SAN 170-5431) Toll Free: 800-922-6066
E-mail: info@akjbooks.com
Web site: www.akjbooks.com; http://store.akjbooks.com; www.akjebooks.com.

Alabama Bookstore, Orders Addr.: P.O. Box 1279, Tuscaloosa, AL 35401-1626 USA Tel 205-758-4532; Fax: 205-758-5525; Toll Free: 800-382-2665 (orders only)
E-mail: ABS@AlabamaBook.com
Web site: http://www.AlabamaBook.com.

Alamo Square Distributors, P.O. Box 14543, San Francisco, CA 94114 USA Fax: 415-863-7456
E-mail: alamosqdist@earthlink.net.

Alba House, *See* **St Pauls/Alba Hse. Pubs.**

Alexander News Company, *See* **Blue Ridge News Co.**

Alfonsi Enterprises, 8621 Gavinton Ct., Dublin, OH 43017-9615 USA (SAN 169-4227).

Alfred Publishing Co., Inc., (*978-0-7390; 978-0-87487; 978-0-88284; 978-1-58951; 978-1-4574; 978-1-4706*) Orders Addr.: P.O. Box 10003, Van Nuys, CA 91410-0003 USA; Edit Addr.: 123 Dry Rd., Oriskany, NY 13424 USA Tel 315-736-1572; Fax: 315-736-7281
E-mail: customerservice@alfred.com; permissions@alfred.com; submissions@alfred.com
Web site: http://www.alfred.com.

Alibris, (*978-0-9702763*) 1250 45th St., Suite 100, Emeryville, CA 94608 USA Fax: 510-550-6052; Toll Free: 877-254-2747 (877-ALIBRIS, option 1)
E-mail: libraries@alibris.com
Web site: http://www.alibris.com/library.

Alive Books, *See* **Books Alive**

All Electronics Corp., 14928 Oxnard St., Van Nuys, CA 91411 USA.

All Romance Ebooks, LLC, (*978-1-936387; 978-1-943576; 978-1-945193; 978-1-946297*) 6252 Commercial Way No. 145, Weeki Wachee, FL 34613 USA
E-mail: info@allromanceebooks.com.

Allegro New Sound Distribution, Subs. of Allegro Distribution, 20048 NE San Rafael St., Portland, OR 97230-7459 USA.

Allentown News Agency, Inc., Orders Addr.: P.O. Box 446, Allentown, PA 18105 USA; Edit Addr.: 719-723 Liberty St., Allentown, PA 18105 USA (SAN 169-7226) Tel 610-432-4441; Fax: 610-432-2708.

Alliance Bk. Co., P.O. Box 7884, Hilton Head, SC 29938-7884 USA
E-mail: alliancebk@mindspring.com.

Alliance Game Distributors, Centennial Dr., Fort Wayne, IN 46808 USA Tel 260-482-5490 (ext. 253); Fax: 260-471-9539
E-mail: jjh@alliance-games.com
Web site: http://www.alliance-games.com.

Alliance Hse., Inc., (*978-0-9665234*) 220 Ferris Ave., Suite 201, White Plains, NY 10603 USA Tel 914-328-5456; Fax: 914-946-1929
E-mail: alliancehs@aol.com.

Alonso Bk. & Periodical Services, Inc., 2316 2nd St S., Arlington, VA 22204-2010 USA (SAN 170-7035).

Alpen Bks, 4602 Chennault Beach Rd. Ste. B1, Mukilteo, WA 98275-5016 USA.

Alpenbooks, *See* **Alpenbooks Pr. LLC**

Alpenbooks Pr. LLC, (*978-0-9669795*) 4602 Chennault Beach Rd. B1, Mukilteo, WA 98275 USA (SAN 113-5309) Tel 425-415-4560; Fax: 425-493-6381
E-mail: rkoch@alpenbooks.com
Web site: http://www.alpenbooks.com.

Alpha & Omega Distributor, P.O. Box 36640, Colorado Springs, CO 80936-3664 USA (SAN 169-0515).

Alpha Bks., (*978-0-02; 978-0-672; 978-0-7357; 978-0-7897; 978-1-56761; 978-1-57595; 978-0-7431; 978-1-59257; 978-1-61564*) Div. of Pearson Technology Group, 800 E 96th St., 3rd Flr., Indianapolis, IN 46290 USA (SAN 219-6298) Tel 317-581-3500 Toll Free: 800-571-5840 (orders)
Web site: http://www.idiotsguides.com.

Alpine News Distributors, Div. of Mountain States Distributors, 0105 Marand Rd., Glenwood Springs, CO 81601 USA Tel 970-945-2269; Fax: 970-945-2260.

Alta Book Center Publishers, *See* **Alta English Publishers**

Alta English Publishers, (*978-1-878598; 978-1-882483; 978-1-932383*) 1775 E. Palm Canyon Dr. Suite 110-275, Palm Springs, CA 92264 USA (SAN 630-9240) Tel 760-459-2603; Fax: 760-464-0588
E-mail: info@altaenglishpublishers.com
Web site: https://altaenglishpublishers.com; https://altaenglishonline.com.

AMACOM, (*978-0-7612; 978-0-8144*) Div. of Harpercollins Leadership, P.O. Box 141000, Nashville, TN 37214 USA (SAN 201-1670) Toll Free: 800-250-5308
E-mail: pubservice@amanet.org
Web site: http://www.amacombooks.org.

Amarillo Periodical Distributors, P.O. Box 3823, Lubbock, TX 70404 USA (SAN 156-4986) Tel 806-745-6000.

Amato, Frank Pubns., Inc., (*978-0-936608; 978-1-57188; 978-1-878175*) Orders Addr.: P.O. Box 82112, Portland, OR 97282 USA (SAN 214-3372) Tel 503-653-8108; Fax: 503-653-2766; Toll Free: 800-541-9498; Edit Addr.: 4040 SE Wister St., Milwaukie, OR 97222 USA (SAN 858-5741)
E-mail: wholesale@amatobooks.com; Lorraine@amatobooks.com
Web site: http://www.amatobooks.com.

Amazon Digital Services Inc., 440 Terry Ave. N., Seattle, WA 98109 USA.

Amazon.Com, (*978-1-58060*) 1200 12th Ave. S., Suite 1200, Seattle, WA 98144 USA (SAN 179-4205) Tel 206-266-6817; Orders Addr.: P.O. Box 80387, Seattle, WA 98108-0387 USA (SAN 156-143X) Tel 206-622-2335; Fax: 206-622-2405; 1 Centerpoint Blvd., non-carton, New Castle, DE 19720 (SAN 155-3992); 1 Centerpoint Blvd., carton, New Castle, DE 19720 (SAN 156-1405); 520 S. Brandon, non-carton, Seattle, WA 98108 (SAN 152-6642); 520 S. Brandon, carton, Seattle, WA 98108 (SAN 156-1383); 1600 E. Newlands Dr., carton, Fernley, NV 89408 (SAN 156-5982); 1600 E. Newlands Dr., non-carton, Fernley, NV 89408 (SAN 156-6008); Edit Addr.: 520 Pike St., Seattle, WA 98101 USA (SAN 155-3984); P.O. Box 81226, Seattle, WA 98108-1226; 705 Boulder Dr. Carton, Breinigsville, PA 18031
E-mail: catalog-dept@amazon.com
Web site: http://www.amazon.com.

Ambassador Bks. & Media, 42 Chasner St., Hempstead, NY 11550 USA Tel 516-489-4011; Fax: 516-489-5661; Toll Free: 800-431-8913
E-mail: ambassador@absbook.com
Web site: http://www.absbook.com.

Ambassador Book Service, *See* **Ambassador Bks. & Media**

America Hse. Bk. Pubs., (*978-1-893162; 978-1-58851; 978-1-59129*) Orders Addr.: P.O. Box 151, Frederick, MD 21705-0151 USA; Edit Addr.: 113 E. Church St., Frederick, MD 21701 USA
Web site: http://www.publishamerica.com.

American Assn. for Vocational Instructional Materials, (*978-0-89606; 978-0-914452*) 220 Smithonia Rd., Winterville, GA 30683 USA (SAN 225-8811) Tel 706-742-5355; Fax: 706-742-7005; Toll Free: 800-228-4689
E-mail: ksseab@aavim.com; sales@aavim.com
Web site: http://www.aavim.com.

American Bible Society, (*978-0-8267; 978-1-58516; 978-1-937628; 978-1-941448; 978-1-941449*) Orders Addr.: 6201 E. 43rd St., Tulsa, OK 74135-6562 USA (SAN 662-7129) Toll Free Fax: 866-570-2877; Edit Addr.: 1865 Broadway, New York, NY 10023-9980 USA (SAN 203-5189) Tel 212-408-1200; Fax: 212-408-1305; 700 Plaza Dr., 2nd Flr., Secaucus, NJ 07094
E-mail: info@americanbible.org
Web site: http://www.bibles.org; http://www.americanbible.org.

American Buddhist Shim Gum Do Assn., Inc., (*978-0-9614427*) 203 Chestnut Hill Ave., Brighton, MA 02135 USA (SAN 113-2873) Tel 617-787-1506; Fax: 617-787-2708
E-mail: marystackhouse@shimgumdo.org
Web site: http://www.shimgumdo.org.

American Business Systems, Inc., 315 Littleton Rd., Chelmsford, MA 01824 USA (SAN 264-8229) Tel 508-250-9600; Fax: 508-250-8027; Toll Free: 800-356-4034.

American Eagle Pubns., Inc., (*978-0-929408*) Orders Addr.: P.O. Box 5111, Sun City West, AZ 85376 USA (SAN 249-2415) Tel 623-556-2925; Fax: 623-556-2926; Toll Free: 866-764-2925; Edit Addr.: 12647 Crystal Lake Dr., Sun City West, AZ 85375 USA
E-mail: custservice@ameaglepubs.com
Web site: http://www.ameaglepubs.com.

American Education Corp., The, (*978-0-87570; 978-1-58636; 978-0-9841672; 978-0-9841972*) 7506 N. Broadway, Suite 505, Oklahoma City, OK 73116-9016 USA (SAN 654-6250) Tel 405-840-6031; Toll Free: 800-222-2811
E-mail: jamesr@amered.com
Web site: http://www.amered.com.

American Educational Computer, Incorporated, *See* **American Education Corp., The**

American Heritage Magazine, 90 Fifth Ave., New York, NY 10011 USA.

American International Distribution Corp., Orders Addr.: 82 Winter Sport Ln., Williston, VT 05495 USA (SAN 631-1083) Tel 802-488-2665; Edit Addr.: 82 Winter Sport Ln., Williston, VT 05495 USA (SAN 630-2238) Toll Free: 800-488-2665
E-mail: jmacon@aidcvt.com
Web site: http://www.aidcvt.com/Specialty/Home.asp.

American Kennel Club Museum of the Dog, (*978-0-9615072*) 1721 S. Mason Rd., Saint Louis, MO 63131 USA (SAN 110-8751) Tel 314-821-3647; Fax: 314-821-7381.

American Library Assn., (*978-0-8389; 978-1-937589*) 225 N. Michigan Ave. Suite 1300, chicago, IL 60601 USA (SAN 201-0062) Tel 312-280-2425; 312-944-8085; Fax: 770-280-4155 (Orders); Toll Free: 800-545-2433; 866-746-7252 (Orders)
E-mail: agwizdala@ala.org
Web site: http://www.ala.org; http://www.alastore.ala.org.

American Magazine Service, *See* **Prebound Periodicals**

American Marketing & Publishing Company, *See* **Christian Publishing Network**

American Mathematical Society, (*978-0-8218; 978-0-8284; 978-0-88385; 978-0-9835005; 978-1-61444; 978-1-4704; 978-1-939512*) Orders Addr.: 201 Charles St., Providence, RI 02904 USA (SAN 250-3263) Tel 401-455-4000; Fax: 401-331-3842; Toll Free: 800-321-4267
E-mail: las@ams.org
Web site: http://www.ams.org.

American Micro Media, 19 N. Broadway, Box 306, Red Hook, NY 12571 USA (SAN 653-9920) Tel 914-758-5567.

American News Company, 325 W. Potter Dr., Anchorage, AK 99518 USA (SAN 168-9274) Tel 907-563-3251; Fax: 907-261-8523 Do not confuse with companies with the same name in Winston-Salem, NC, Elizabeth, NC.

American Overseas Bk. Co., Inc., 550 Walnut St., Norwood, NJ 07648 USA (SAN 169-4863) Tel 201-767-7600; Fax: 201-784-0263
E-mail: books@aobc.com
Web site: http://www.aobc.com.

American Pharmacists Assn., (*978-0-914768; 978-0-917330; 978-1-58212*) 2215 Constitution Ave., NW, Washington, DC 20037-2907 USA (SAN 202-4446) Tel 202-628-4410; Fax: 202-783-2351; Toll Free: 800-878-0729
E-mail: kanderson@aphanet.org
Web site: http://www.pharmacist.com.

American Society of Agronomy, (*978-0-89118*) 5585 Guilford Rd., Fitchburg, WI 53711-5801 USA (SAN 107-5683)
Web site: http://www.agronomy.org.

American Society of Civil Engineers, (*978-0-7844; 978-0-87262*) 1801 Alexander Bell Dr., Reston, VA 20191-4400 USA (SAN 204-7594) Tel 703-295-6300; Fax: 703-295-6211; Toll Free: 800-548-2723
Web site: https://ascelibrary.org/; https://www.asce.org/publications-and-news.

American Technical Pubs., Inc., (*978-0-8269*) 10100 Orland Pkwy., Orland Park, IL 60467-5756 USA (SAN 206-8141) Toll Free: 800-323-3471
E-mail: service@americantech.net
Web site: http://www.americantech.net.

American West Bks., Orders Addr.: 14190 N. Washington Hwy., Ashland, VA 23005 USA (SAN 920-5233); Edit Addr.: 1254 Commerce Way, Sanger, CA 93657 USA (SAN 630-8570) Toll Free: 800-497-4909 Do not confuse with American West Bks., Albuquerque, NM
E-mail: JBM12@CSUFresno.edu.

American Wholesale Bk. Co., Subs. of Books-A-Million, Orders Addr.: 402 Industrial Ln., Birmingham, AL 35211-4465 USA (SAN 631-7391).

American Wholesale Booksellers Assn., (*978-0-9664715*) 702 S. Michigan St., South Bend, IN 46601 USA Tel 219-232-8500; Fax: 303-265-9292
E-mail: pwalsh@awba.com
Web site: http://www.awba.com.

Americana Publishing, Inc., (*978-1-58807; 978-1-58943*) 195 Us Highway 9. Ste. 204, Englishtown, NJ 07726-8294 USA Toll Free: 888-883-8203; 303 San Mateo Blvd, Ne, Albuquerque, NM 87108
E-mail: editor@americanabooks.com
Web site: http://www.americanabooks.com.

Americana Souvenirs & Gifts, (*978-1-890541*) 206 Hanover St., Gettysburg, PA 17325-1911 USA (SAN 169-7366) Toll Free: 800-692-7436.

America's Cycling Pubns., 6425 Capitol Ave., Suite F, Diamond Springs, CA 95619 USA.

America's Hobby Ctr., 146 W. 22nd St., New York, NY 10011 USA (SAN 111-0403) Tel 212-675-8922.

Ames News Agency, Inc., 2110 E. 13th St., Ames, IA 50010 USA (SAN 169-2550).

Amicus Learning, (*978-1-60753; 978-1-68151; 978-1-64549; 979-8-89200*) P.O. Box 227, Mankato, MN 56002 USA Tel 507-388-9357; Fax: 507-388-2746
E-mail: anna.erickson@amicuspublishing.us; rglaser@amicuspublishing.us; info@amicuspublishing.us
Web site: http://www.amicuspublishing.us.

Amicus Publishing, *See* **Amicus Learning**

Amigos Book Co., Orders Addr.: 5401 Bissonnet, Houston, TX 77081-6605 USA.

Amoskeag News Agency, 92 Allard Dr., Manchester, NH 03102 USA (SAN 169-4537) Tel 603-623-5343.

Amplify Publishing Group, (*978-0-9743442; 978-1-932888; 978-1-934878; 978-1-936319; 978-1-937406; 978-1-62086; 978-1-63177; 978-1-68401; 978-1-64307; 978-1-64543; 978-1-63755; 979-8-89138*) Orders Addr.: 620 Herndon Pkwy. Suite 220, Herndon, VA 20170 USA Tel 703-437-3584; Fax: 703-437-3554; Toll Free: 877-862-7568
E-mail: debbie@mascotbooks.com; naren@mascotbooks.com; kristin@mascotbooks.com; nina@mascotbooks.com
Web site: http://www.mascotbooks.com.

Analos Magazine, 475 Park Ave. S., New York, NY 10016 USA.

Anchor Distributors, 1030 Hunt Valley Cir., New Kensington, PA 15068 USA (SAN 631-077X) Tel 724-334-7000; Fax: 724-334-1200; Toll Free: 800-444-4484
E-mail: customerservice@anchordistributors.com
Web site: http://www.anchordistributors.com.

Anderson Merchandisers, 421 E. 34th St., Amarillo, TX 79103 USA (SAN 169-8028) Tel 806-376-6251
E-mail: hanleyg@amerch.com.

Anderson News - Tacoma, 9914 32nd Ave., S., Lakewood, WA 98499 USA (SAN 108-1322) Tel 253-581-1940; Fax: 253-584-5941; Toll Free: 800-552-2000 (in Washington).

Anderson News, LLC, 211 Industrial Dr., Roanoke, VA 24019 USA (SAN 168-9223); 6016 Brookvale Ln. Ste. 110B, Knoxville, TN 37919-4003 (SAN 168-9363); 2541 Westcott Blvd., Knoxville, TN 37931 Tel 423-966-7575; 3911 Volunteer Dr., Chattanooga, TN 37416 (SAN 169-7862) Tel 423-894-3945; 6301 Forbing Rd., Little Rock, AR 72219 Tel 501-562-7360; 1185a Commerce Blvd., Midway, FL 32343-6629; 1857 W. Grant Rd., Tucson, AZ 85745-1203; 5184 Sullivan Gardens Pkwy., Kingsport, TN 37660-8104 (SAN 241-6131); 390 Exchange St., Box 1624, New Haven, CT 06506 (SAN 241-6158) Tel 203-777-5545; 5000 Moline St., Denver, CO 80239-2622 Tel 303-321-1111; 1709 N. East St., Flagstaff, AZ 86002 (SAN 168-9290) Tel 520-774-6171; Fax: 520-779-1958; 6016 Brookvale Ln. Ste. 110B, Knoxville, TN 37919-4003; P.O. Box 22968, Chattanooga, TN 37422; P.O. Box 36003, Knoxville, TN 37930-6003; P.O. Box 280077, Memphis, TN 38168-0077; P.O. Box 6660, Pensacola, FL 32503 Do not confuse with Anderson News Company, Pinellas Park, FL.

Anderson-Austin News Co., LLC, 808 Newtown Cir., No. B, Lexington, KY 40511-1230 USA (SAN 169-2836) Tel 606-254-2765; Fax: 606-254-3328.

Andich Brothers News Company, *See* **Tobias News Co.**

Andrews McMeel Publishing, (*978-0-8362; 978-0-939251; 978-1-57939; 978-0-7407; 978-1-4494; 978-1-5248*) Orders Addr.: c/o Simon & Schuster, Inc., 100 Front St., Riverside, NJ 08075 USA Toll Free Fax: 800-943-9831; Toll Free: 800-943-9839 (Customer Service); 800-897-7650 (Credit Dept.); Edit Addr.: 1130 Walnut St., Kansas City, MO 64106-2109 USA (SAN 202-540X) Toll Free: 800-851-8923
Web site: http://www.AndrewsMcMeel.com.

Andrzejewski's Marian Church Supply, *See* **A & M Church Supplies**

Angel City Pr., (*978-1-883318; 978-1-62640*) 2118 Wilshire Blvd., PMB 880, Santa Monica, CA 90403-5784 USA (SAN 298-3370) Tel 310-395-9982; Fax: 310-395-3353; Toll Free: 800-949-8039 (orders)
E-mail: smcauley@angelcitypress.com
Web site: http://www.angelcitypress.com.

Angler's Bk. Supply, 1380 W. Second Ave., Eugene, OR 97402 USA (SAN 631-4546) Tel 541-342-8355; Fax: 541-342-1785; Toll Free: 800-260-3869.

Anglo-American Book Company, Limited (UK), *See* **Crown Hse. Publishing LLC**

Ann Arbor Editions LLC, (*978-1-58726*) 2500 S. State St., Ann Arbor, MI 48104 USA Tel 734-913-1302; Fax: 734-913-1249; 1094 Flex Dr., Jackson, TN 38301
E-mail: ljohnson@aaeditions.com
Web site: http://www.annarbormediagroup.com; http://www.mittenpress.com; http://www.aaeditions.com.

Ann Arbor Media Group, LLC, *See* **Ann Arbor Editions LLC**

answers period, inc., (*978-0-917875*) Orders Addr.: P.O. Box 427, Goliad, TX 77963 USA (SAN 112-6431) Tel 361-645-2268; Toll Free: 800-852-4752
Web site: http://www.answersbook.com.

Anthracite News Company, *See* **Great Northern Distributors, Inc.**

Anthroposophic Press, Incorporated, *See* **SteinerBooks, Inc.**

Antipodes Bks. & Beyond, 9707 Fairway Ave., Silver Spring, MD 20901-3001 USA Tel 301-602-9519; Fax: 301-565-0160
E-mail: Antipode@antipodesbooks.com
Web site: http://www.antipodesbooks.com.

Antiquarian Bookstore, The, 1070 Lafayette Rd., Portsmouth, NH 03801 USA (SAN 158-9938) Tel 603-436-7250.

Antique Collectors' Club, (*978-0-902028; 978-0-907462; 978-1-85149*) Orders Addr.: Eastworks, 116 Pleasant St., Easthampton, MA 01027 USA (SAN 630-7787) Tel 413-529-0861; Fax: 413-529-0862; Toll Free: 800-252-5231 (orders)
E-mail: info@antiquecc.com; sales@antiquecc.com
Web site: http://www.antiquecollectorsclub.com.

AOAC International, (*978-0-935584*) 481 N. Frederick Ave., Suite 500, Gaithersburg, MD 20877-2417 USA (SAN 260-3411) Tel 301-924-7077; Fax: 301-924-7089; Toll Free: 800-379-2622
E-mail: aoac@aoac.org
Web site: http://www.aoac.org.

A-One Bk. Distributors, Inc., 1555 Ocean Ave. Ste. D, Bohemia, NY 11716-1933 USA (SAN 630-7981).

APG Sales & Distribution Services, Div. of Warehousing and Fulfillment Specialists, LLC (WFS, LLC), 7344 Cockrill Bend Blvd., Nashville, TN 37209-1043 USA (SAN 630-818X) Toll Free: 800-327-5113
E-mail: sswift@agpbooks.com
Web site: http://www.apgbooks.com.

APG Sales & Fulfillment, *See* **APG Sales & Distribution Services**

Apollo Bks., (*978-0-938290*) 91 Market St., Wappingers Falls, NY 12590-2333 USA (SAN 170-0928).

Apollo Library Bk. Supplier, 865 Kent Ln., Philadelphia, PA 19115 USA (SAN 159-8031).

Appalachian Bible Co., (*978-1-889049*) Orders Addr.: 522 Princeton Rd., Johnson City, TN 37605 USA (SAN 169-7889) Tel 423-282-9475; Fax: 423-282-9110; Toll Free: 800-289-2772; Edit Addr.: P.O. Box 1573, Johnson City, TN 37601 USA
E-mail: appainc@aol.com.

Appalachian Bk. Distributors, Div. of Send The Light Distribution LLC, Orders Addr.: 100 Biblica Way, Elizabethton, TN 37643-6070 USA Toll Free Fax: 800-759-2779; Edit Addr.: 506 Princeton Rd., Johnson City, TN 37601 USA.

Appalachian, Incorporated, *See* **Appalachian Bible Co.**

Applause Learning Resources, (*978-0-9655052; 978-0-9786746; 978-0-9788527; 978-0-9790091; 978-1-60713*) 85 Fernwood Ln., Roslyn, NY 11576 USA Tel 516-625-1145; Fax: 516-625-7392; Toll Free Fax: 877-365-7484; Toll Free: 800-277-5287
E-mail: info@applauselearning.com
Web site: http://www.applauselearning.com.

Applause Productions, *See* **Applause Learning Resources**

Apple Bk. Co., Div. of Scholastic Bk. Fairs, Inc., Orders Addr.: P.O. Box 217156, Charlotte, NC 28221-0156 USA Tel 704-596-6641; Fax: 704-599-1738; Toll Free: 800-331-1993; Edit Addr.: 5901 N. Northwoods Business Pkwy., Charlotte, NC 28269 USA (SAN 108-4569).

Applewood Bks., (*978-0-918222; 978-1-55709; 978-1-889833; 978-1-933212; 978-1-4290; 978-0-9819430; 978-1-60889; 978-0-9844156; 978-0-9836416; 978-1-938700; 978-0-9882885; 978-1-941216; 978-1-5162; 978-1-944038; 978-1-945187; 978-1-64194*) 1 River Rd., Carlisle, MA 01741-1820 USA (SAN 210-3419) Toll Free: 800-277-5312; 1 Ingram Blvd., La Vergne, TN 37086
E-mail: applewood@awb.com; svec@awb.com
Web site: http://www.awb.com.

Aquarian Concepts Publishing & Distribution, (*978-0-9666593*) Orders Addr.: HC Box 81-L, Payson, AZ 85541 USA (SAN 299-7215) Tel 520-474-0816; Toll Free: 888-539-8069; Edit Addr.: 62 Switchman Ln., Payson, AZ 85541 USA
E-mail: concepts1@cybertrails.com.

Arabic & Islamic Univ. Pr., 4263 Fountain Ave., Los Angeles, CA 90029 USA (SAN 107-6299) Tel 323-665-1000; Fax: 323-665-3107.

Aramark, 18825 67th Ave., NE, Arlington, WA 98223-9656 USA (SAN 631-3507) Tel 360-435-2524; Fax: 360-435-6805 Do not confuse with Aramark, Albuquerque, NM.

Aramark Magazine & Bk. Co., P.O. Box 25489, Oklahoma City, OK 73125 USA (SAN 169-6971) Tel 405-843-9383; Fax: 405-843-0379 Do not confuse with Aramark Magazine & Bk. Services, Inc., Norfolk, VA.

Aramark Magazine & Bk. Services, Inc., P.O. Box 2240, Norfolk, VA 23501 USA (SAN 169-8680) Do not confuse with Aramark Magazine & Book Co., Oklahoma City, OK.

Arbit Bks., Inc., *(978-0-930038)* 8050 N. Port Washington Rd., Milwaukee, WI 53217 USA (SAN 169-913X) Tel 414-352-4404.

Arcadia Publishing, *(978-0-88289; 978-0-910462; 978-0-911116; 978-1-56554; 978-0-7385; 978-1-58973; 978-1-58980; 978-1-59629; 978-1-4396; 978-1-60949; 978-1-4556; 978-1-61423; 978-1-4671; 978-0-578-11080-6; 978-1-62584; 978-1-62585; 978-1-62619; 978-0-578-12310-3; -0-615-91258-5; 978-0-9903765; 978-1-944313; 978-1-5316; 978-1-5402; 978-0-578-19068-6; 978-0-578-59417-0; 978-0-578-59418-7) Orders Addr.: 420 Wando Pk. Blvd., Mount Pleasant, SC 29464 USA (SAN 255-268X) Tel 843-853-2070; Fax: 843-853-0044; Toll Free: 888-313-2665 Do not confuse with Arcadia Publishing in Greenwood Village, CO*
E-mail: sales@arcadiapublishing.com
Web site: http://www.arcadiapublishing.com.

Ardic Bk. Distributors, Inc., 331 High St., 2nd Flr., Burlington, NJ 08016-4411 USA (SAN 170-5415).

Argus International Corp., Subs. of ICS International Group, Skypark Business Pk., P.O. Box 4082, Irvine, CA 92716-4082 USA (SAN 681-9761) Tel 714-552-8494 (phone/fax).

Aries Pr., *(978-0-933646)* P.O. Box 30081, Chicago, IL 60630 USA (SAN 111-9168) Tel 312-725-8300.

Aries Productions, Inc., *(978-0-910035)* Orders Addr.: P.O. Box 29396, Sappington, MO 63126 USA (SAN 669-0009); Edit Addr.: 6935 Tholozan Ave., Saint Louis, MO 63109-1130 USA (SAN 241-2004)
E-mail: uspsisquad@aol.com
Web site: http://ww.ussisquad.com.

Arizona Periodicals, Inc., P.O. Box 5780, Yuma, AZ 85366-5780 USA Tel 520-782-1822.

Arkansas Bk. Co., 1207 E. Second St., Little Rock, AR 72202-2732 USA (SAN 168-9460) Tel 501-375-1184.

Arlington Card Co., Bk. Dept., 140 Gansett Ave., Cranston, RI 02910 USA (SAN 108-5794) Tel 401-942-3188.

Armstrong, J. B. News Agency, *See* **News Group, The**

Arrow, G. H. Co., P.O. Box 676, Bala Cynwyd, PA 19004 USA (SAN 111-3771) Tel 215-227-3211; Fax: 215-221-0631; Toll Free: 800-775-2776.

Arrowhead Magazine Co., Inc., P.O. Box 5947, San Bernardino, CA 92412 USA (SAN 169-0094) Tel 909-799-8294; Fax: 909-799-3774; 1055 Cooley Ave., San Bernardino, CA 92408 (SAN 249-2717) Tel 909-370-4420.

Ars Obscura, *(978-0-9623780)* P.O. Box 4424, Seattle, WA 98104-0424 USA (SAN 113-5368) Tel 206-324-9792.

Art Institute of Chicago, *(978-0-86559)* Orders Addr.: a/o Museum Shop Mail Order Dept., 950 N. North Branch St., Chicago, IL 60622-4276 USA; Edit Addr.: 111 S. Michigan Ave., Chicago, IL 60603-6110 USA (SAN 204-479X) Tel 312-443-3540; Fax: 312-443-1334
Web site: http://www.artic.edu.

Art Media Resources, Inc., *(978-1-878529; 978-1-58886)* 1507 S. Michigan Ave., Chicago, IL 60605 USA (SAN 253-8199) Tel 312-663-5351; Fax: 312-663-5177
E-mail: info@artmediaresources.com
Web site: http://www.artmediaresources.com.

ARVEST, P.O. Box 200248, Denver, CO 80220 USA (SAN 159-8694) Tel 303-388-8486; Fax: 303-355-4213; Toll Free: 800-739-0761
E-mail: copy@concentric.net.

Asia Bk. Corp. of America, *(978-0-940500)* 45-77 157th St., Flushing, NY 11355 USA (SAN 214-493X) Tel 718-762-7204; Fax: 718-460-5030.

ASM International, *(978-0-87170; 978-1-61503; 978-1-62708)* 9639 Kinsman Rd., Materials Park, OH 44073-0002 USA (SAN 204-7586) Tel 440-338-5151; Fax: 440-338-4634; Toll Free: 800-336-5152 Do not confuse with ASM International, Inc., Fort Lauderdale, FL
E-mail: karen.marken@asminternational.org; madrid.tramble@asminternational.org; scott.henry@asminternational.org; sue.sellers@asminternational.org; memberservicecenter@asminternational.org
Web site: http://www.asminternational.org.

ASP Wholesale, c/o A&A Quality Shipping Services 3623 Munster Ave, Unit B, Hayward, CA 94545 USA Tel 510-732-6521 (Voice).

Aspen Publishing, *(978-0-8080)* 130 Turner St, Waltham, MA 02453 USA.

Aspen West Publishing, *(978-0-9615390; 978-1-885348)* P.O. Box 522151, Salt Lake City, UT 84152-2151 USA (SAN 112-7993) Toll Free: 800-222-9133 (orders only)
E-mail: kent@aspenwest.com
Web site: http://www.aspenwest.com.

Assn. of Energy Engineers, Orders Addr.: P.O. Box 1026, Liburn, GA 30048 USA Tel 770-925-9558; Fax: 770-381-9865; Edit Addr.: 4025 Pleasantdale Rd., Suite 420, Atlanta, GA 30340 USA Tel 770-447-5083.

Associated Univ. Presses, *(978-0-8453)* 2010 Eastpark Blvd., Cranbury, NJ 08512 USA (SAN 281-2959) Tel 609-655-4770; Fax: 609-655-8366
E-mail: aup440@aol.com
Web site: http://www.aupresses.com.

Association of Official Analytical Chemists, *See* **AOAC International**

Astran, Inc., 6995 NW 82nd Ave. Ste. 40, Miami, FL 33166-2783 USA (SAN 169-1082) Toll Free: 800-431-4957
E-mail: sales@astranbooks.com
Web site: http://www.astranbooks.com.

ATEXINC, Corp., *(978-0-9702332; 978-1-60405)* Orders Addr.: 17738 Vintage Oak Dr., Glencoe, MO 63038-1478 USA (SAN 631-774X) Toll Free Fax: 866-346-9515 Do not confuse with Atex, Inc., Bedford, MA
E-mail: mail@atexinc.com
Web site: http://www.atexinc.com; http://www.thetextilekit.com; http://www.itextiles.com.

Athelstan Pubns., *(978-0-940753)* Orders Addr.: 5925 Kirby Dr. Suite E. 464, Houston, TX 77005 USA (SAN 663-5318) Tel 713-371-2107; Fax: 713-524-1159
E-mail: info@athel.com; barlow@athel.com
Web site: http://www.athel.com.

Athena Productions, Inc., 5500 Collins Ave., No. 901, Miami Beach, FL 33140 USA Tel 305-868-8482; Fax: 305-868-8891.

Atlas Bks., 2541 Ashland Rd., Ashland, OH 44905 USA.

Atlas News Co., Div. of Hudson News Co., P.O. Box 779, Boylston, MA 01505-0779 USA (SAN 169-3360).

Atlas Publishing Co., *(978-0-930575)* 1464 36th St., Ogden, UT 84403 USA (SAN 110-3873) Tel 801-627-1043.

Attainment Co., Inc., *(978-0-934731; 978-1-57861; 978-1-943148; 978-1-944315; 978-1-64856)* Orders Addr.: P.O. Box 930160, Verona, WI 53593 USA (SAN 694-1656) Tel 608-845-7880; Fax: 608-845-8040; Toll Free: 800-327-4269; Edit Addr.: 1158 Clarity St., Verona, WI 53593 USA (SAN 631-6174)
E-mail: info@attainmentcompany.com; ameyer@attainmentcompany.com
Web site: http://www.attainmentcompany.com/.

Audible.com, One Washington Pk., Newark, NJ 07102 USA Tel 973-820-0400 (International); Fax: 973-890-2442; Toll Free: 888-283-5051 (USA & Canada)
E-mail: content-requests@audible.com
Web site: http://www.audible.com.

Audio Bk. Co., *(978-0-89926)* 235 Bellefontaine St., Pasadena, CA 91105-2921 USA (SAN 158-1414) Toll Free: 800-423-8273
E-mail: sales@audiobookco.com
Web site: http://www.audiobookco.com.

AudioBks. Unleashed, *(978-1-953250; 978-1-63734)* 67A Old E. Neck Rd, Melville, NY 11747 USA Tel 631-560-9509
E-mail: info@audiobooksunleashed.com.

AudioGO, *(978-0-563; 978-0-7540; 978-0-7927; 978-0-89340; 978-1-55504; 978-1-60283; 978-1-60998; 978-1-62064; 978-1-62460; 978-1-4815; 978-1-4821)* Orders Addr.: c/o Perseus, 1094 Flex Dr., Jackson, TN 38301 USA; Edit Addr.: 42 Whitecap Dr., North Kingstown, RI 02852-7445 USA (SAN 858-7701) Toll Free: 800-621-0182
E-mail: laura.almeida@audiogo.com
Web site: http://www.audiogo.com/us/.

Audubon Prints & Bks., 9720 Spring Ridge Ln., Vienna, VA 22182 USA (SAN 111-820X).

Augsburg Fortress, Publishers, *See* **1517 Media**

Augusta News Co., 25 Second St., Apt. 124, Hallowell, ME 04347-1481 USA (SAN 169-3026).

Auromere, Inc., *(978-0-89744)* 2621 W. US Hwy. 12, Lodi, CA 95242-9200 USA (SAN 169-0043) Fax: 209-339-3715; Toll Free: 800-735-4691
E-mail: sasp@lodinet.com
Web site: http://www.auromere.com.

Austin & Company, Inc., *(978-0-9657153)* 104 S. Union St., Suite 202, Traverse City, MI 49684 USA (SAN 631-1466) Tel 231-933-4649; Fax: 231-933-4659
E-mail: aandn@aol.com
Web site: http://www.austinandcompanyinc.com.

Austin & Nelson Publishing, *See* **Austin & Company, Inc.**

Austin Management Group, Orders Addr.: P.O. Box 3206, Paducah, KY 42002-3206 USA (SAN 135-3349); Edit Addr.: P.O. Box 300, Paducah, KY 42002-0300 USA (SAN 249-6844).

Author Solutions, Incorporated, *See* **Author Solutions, LLC**

Author Solutions, LLC, *(978-1-5043; 978-1-9822; 979-8-7652)* Div. of Penguin Group (USA) Inc., 1663 Liberty Dr., Bloomington, IN 47403 USA Tel 812-334-5223; Toll Free: 877-655-1722
E-mail: sfurr@authorsolutions
Web site: http://www.authorsolutions.com.

AuthorHouse, *(978-1-58500; 978-0-9675669; 978-1-58721; 978-1-58820; 978-0-7596; 978-1-4033; 978-1-4107; 978-1-4140; 978-1-4184; 978-1-4208; 978-1-4259; 978-1-4343; 978-1-4389; 978-1-4490; 978-1-4520; 978-1-61764; 978-1-4567; 978-1-4582; 978-1-4624; 978-1-4633; 978-1-4634; 978-0-9846457; 978-1-4670; 978-1-4678; 978-1-4685; 978-1-4772; 978-1-4817; 978-1-4918; 978-1-4969; 978-1-5049; 978-1-5065; 978-1-5246; 978-1-5462; 978-1-7283; 978-1-6655; 979-8-8230) Div. of Author Solutions, Inc., 1663 Liberty Dr., Suite 200, Bloomington, IN 47403 USA (SAN 253-7605) Fax: 812-336-5449; Toll Free: 888-519-5121*
E-mail: authorsupport@authorhouse.com; sfurr@authorsolutions.com
Web site: http://www.authorhouse.com.

Authors & Editors, *See* **2Learn-English**

Author's Republic, *(978-1-943499; 978-1-5189; 978-0-9980029)* 2225 Kenmore Ave., Buffalo, NY 14207 USA Tel 905-634-7507
E-mail: michelle@authorsrepublic.com; info@authorsrepublic.com
Web site: www.authorsrepublic.com.

Auto-Bound, Inc., 909 Marina Village Pkwy., No. 67B, Alameda, CA 94501-1048 USA (SAN 170-0782) Tel 510-521-8655; Fax: 510-521-8755; Toll Free: 800-523-5833.

Avanti Enterprises, Inc., P.O. Box 3563, Hinsdale, IL 60522-3563 USA (SAN 158-3727) Toll Free: 800-799-6464.

Avenue Bks., 2270 Porter Way, Stockton, CA 95207-3339 USA (SAN 122-4158).

Avery BookStores, Inc., 516 Asharoken Ave., Northport, NY 11768-1176 USA (SAN 169-510X).

Avian Pubns., *(978-0-910335; 978-0-9585612)* 6380 Monroe St., NE, Minneapolis, MN 55432 USA (SAN 241-2691) Tel 763-571-8902
E-mail: bruce@avianpublications.com
Web site: http://www.avainpublications.com.

Aviation Bk. Co., *(978-0-911720; 978-0-911721; 978-0-916413)* 7201 Perimeter Rd., S., No. C, Seattle, WA 98108-3812 USA (SAN 120-1530) Tel 206-767-5232; Fax: 206-763-3428; Toll Free: 800-423-2708
E-mail: sales@aviationbook.com.

Avonlea Bks., Inc., Orders Addr.: P.O. Box 74, White Plains, NY 10602-0074 USA (SAN 680-4446) Tel 914-946-5923; Fax: 914-761-3119; Toll Free: 800-423-0622
E-mail: avonlea@bushkin.com
Web site: http://www.bushkin.com.

B. P. I. Communications, *See* **VNU**

B T P Distribution, 4135 Northgate Blvd., Suite 5, Sacramento, CA 95834-1226 USA (SAN 631-2489) Tel 916-567-2496; Fax: 916-441-6749.

Baggins Bks., 3560 Meridian St., Bellingham, WA 98225-1731 USA (SAN 156-501X).

Baha'i Distribution Service, *(978-0-87743)* Orders Addr.: P.O. Box 1759, Powder Springs, GA 30127-7522 USA (SAN 213-7496) Toll Free: 800-999-9019; Edit Addr.: 415 Linden Ave., Wilmette, IL 60091 USA Tel 847-251-1854; Fax: 847-251-3652
E-mail: bds@usbnc.org.

Baker & Taylor Bks., *(978-0-8480; 978-1-222; 978-1-223)* A Follett Company, Orders Addr.: Commerce Service Ctr., 251 Mt. Olive Church Rd., Commerce, GA 30599 USA (SAN 169-1503) Tel 404-335-5000; Toll Free: 800-775-1200 (customer service); 800-775-1800 (orders); Reno Service Ctr., 1160 Trademark Dr., Suite 111, Reno, NV 89511 (SAN 169-4464) Tel 775-850-3800; Fax: 775-850-3826 (customer service); Toll Free Fax: 800-775-1700 (orders); Edit Addr.: Bridgewater Service Ctr. 1120 US Hwy. 22 E., Bridgewater, NJ 08807 USA (SAN 169-4901) Toll Free: 800-775-1500 (customer service); Momence Service Ctr., 501W. Gladiolus St., Momence, IL 60954-1799 (SAN 169-2100) Tel 815-472-2444 (international customers); Fax: 815-472-9886 (international customers); Toll Free: 800-775-2300 (customer service, academic libraries)
E-mail: btinfo@btol.com
Web site: http://www.btol.com.

Baker & Taylor Fulfillment, Inc., 2550 W. Tyvola Rd., Suite 370, Charlotte, NC 28217 USA (SAN 760-8772) Tel 704-236-9553
E-mail: johnsod@btol.com.

Baker & Taylor International, 1120 US Hwy. 22 E., Box 6885, Bridgewater, NJ 08807 USA (SAN 200-6804) Tel 908-541-7000; Fax: 908-729-4037.

Baker & Taylor Publisher Services (BTPS), A Follett Company, Orders Addr.: 30 Amberwood Pkwy., Ashland, OH 44805 USA (SAN 631-936X) Fax: 419-281-6883; Toll Free: 800-537-6727; 30 Amberwood Pkwy., Ashland, OH 44805 (SAN 760-9264) Fax: 419-281-6883; Toll Free: 800-537-6727; 30 Amberwood Pkwy., Ashland, OH 44805 (SAN 760-6680) Fax: 419-281-6883; Toll Free: 800-537-6727
E-mail: orders@atlasbooks.com; MMG@btpubservices.com; eBooks@btpubservices.com
Web site: http://www.bookmasters.com/.

Baker & Taylor Publishing Group, *See* **Readerlink Distribution Services, LLC**

Baker Bks., *(978-0-8010; 978-0-913686; 978-0-8010-9491-0)* Div. of Baker Publishing Group, Orders Addr.: P.O. Box 6287, Grand Rapids, MI 49516-6287 USA (SAN 299-1500) Toll Free Fax: 800-398-3111 (orders only); Toll Free: 800-877-2665 (orders only); Edit Addr.: 6030 E. Fulton, Ada, MI 49301 USA (SAN 201-4041) Tel 616-676-9185; Fax: 616-676-9573
Web site: http://www.bakerpublishinggroup.com.

Baker Book House, Incorporated, *See* **Baker Publishing Group**

Baker Publishing Group, *(978-0-8007; 978-0-8010; 978-1-58743; 978-1-4412; 978-1-4934; 978-1-68196; 978-1-5409)* Orders Addr.: P.O. Box 6287, Grand Rapids, MI 49516-6287 USA Tel 616-676-9573; Toll Free Fax: 800-398-3111 (orders only); Toll Free: 800-877-2665 (orders only); Edit Addr.: 6030 E. Fulton, Ada, MI 49301 USA Tel 616-676-9185; Fax: 616-676-9573; Toll Free Fax: 800-398-3111; Toll Free: 800-877-2665
E-mail: webmaster@bakerpublishinggroup.com
Web site: http://www.bakerbooks.com; http://www.bakerpublishinggroup.com.

Balogh International, Inc., *(978-1-878762; 978-1-891770)* 1911 N. Duncan Rd., Champaign, IL 61822 USA (SAN 297-2344) Tel 217-355-9331; Fax: 217-355-9413
E-mail: balogh@balogh.com
Web site: http://www.balogh.com.

Balogh Scientific Books, *See* **Balogh International, Inc.**

Balzekas Museum of Lithuanian Culture, 6500 S. Pulaski Rd., Chicago, IL 60629 USA (SAN 110-8522) Tel 773-582-6500; Fax: 773-582-5133.

Banner of Truth, The, *(978-0-85151)* Orders Addr.: P.O. Box 621, Carlisle, PA 17013 USA Tel 717-249-5747; Fax: 717-249-0604; Toll Free: 800-263-8085; Edit Addr.: 63 E. Louther St., Carlisle, PA 17013 USA (SAN 112-1553)
E-mail: info@banneroftruth.org
Web site: http://www.banneroftruth.co.uk.

Banta Packaging & Fulfillment, 1071 Willow Spring Rd., Harrisonburg, VA 22801 USA (SAN 631-7731) Tel 540-442-1333; Fax: 540-434-3541; N9234 Lake Park Rd., Appleton, WI 54915 (SAN 631-8290) Tel 920-969-6400; Fax: 920-751-7794
E-mail: jfair@banta.com.

Barbour & Company, Incorporated, *See* **Barbour Publishing, Inc.**

Barbour Publishing, Inc., *(978-0-916441; 978-1-55748; 978-1-57748; 978-1-58660; 978-1-59310; 978-1-59789; 978-1-60260; 978-1-60742; 978-1-61626; 978-1-62029; 978-1-62416; 978-1-62836; 978-1-63058; 978-1-63409; 978-1-944836; 978-1-68322; 978-1-64352; 978-1-63609; 979-8-89151) Orders Addr.: P.O. Box 719, Uhrichsville, OH 44683 USA (SAN 295-7094) Fax: 740-922-5948; Toll Free Fax: 800-220-5948; Toll Free: 800-852-8010*
E-mail: info@barbourbooks.com
Web site: http://www.barbourbooks.com.

Barnes & Noble Bks.-Imports, *(978-0-389)* 4720 Boston Way, Lanham, MD 20706 USA (SAN 206-7803) Tel 301-459-3366; Toll Free: 800-462-6420.

Barnes & Noble, Inc., *(978-0-7607; 978-0-88029; 978-1-4028; 978-1-4114; 978-1-4351; 978-1-61551; 978-1-61552; 978-1-61553; 978-1-61554; 978-1-61555; 978-1-61556; 978-1-61557; 978-1-61558; 978-1-61559; 978-1-61560; 978-1-61679; 978-1-61680; 978-1-61681; 978-1-61682; 978-1-61683; 978-1-61684; 978-1-61685; 978-1-61686; 978-1-61687; 978-1-61688; 978-1-970008) 76 Ninth Ave., 9th Flr., New York, NY 10011 USA (SAN 141-3651) Tel 212-414-6385; 122 Fifth Ave., New York, NY 10011*
E-mail: smcculloch@bn.com.

Barnes & Noble Pr., *(978-1-68101; 978-1-5380; 978-1-9870; 978-1-0787; 978-1-6635; 978-1-6662; 978-0-578-90031-5; 978-1-6685; 979-8-7655; 979-8-218-02565-6; 979-8-8231; 979-8-3692; 979-8-8556)* 76 Ninth Ave, New York, NY 10011 USA; 1166 Avenue of the Americas 18th Flr., New York, NY 10036; 33 E. 17th St., New York, NY 10003
Web site: print.nookpress.com; press.barnesandnobel.com.

Barnes&Noble.com, *(978-1-4005; 978-1-4006)* c/o Merch Accounts Payable/NR Dept., 76 Ninth Ave., 9th Flr., New York, NY 10011 USA (SAN 192-6551) Tel 212-414-6000
Web site: http://www.bn.com.

Basic Crafts Co., 6001 66th Ave., No. 10, Riverdale, MD 20737-1717 USA (SAN 169-5622) Toll Free: 800-847-4127 (outside New York).

Basin News Co., P.O. Box 300, Paducah, KY 42002-0300 USA (SAN 169-2860).

Bassett Printing Corp., *(978-0-9632415)* Orders Addr.: P.O. Box 866, Bassett, VA 24055 USA Fax: 540-629-3416; Toll Free: 800-336-5102 (outside Virginia); Edit Addr.: 101 Main St., Bassett, VA 24055 USA Tel 540-629-2541.

Bay News, Inc., 3333 NW 35th Ave., Portland, OR 97210 USA Tel 503-219-3001; Fax: 503-241-1877.

Bayou Bks., 1005 Monroe St., Gretna, LA 70053 USA (SAN 120-1913) Tel 504-368-1171; Toll Free: 800-843-1724.

BBC Audiobooks America, *See* **AudioGO**

BCH Fulfillment & Distribution, 46 Purdy St., Harrison, NY 10528 USA
E-mail: info@bookch.com
Web site: http://www.bookch.com/.

Beagle Bay Bks., *(978-0-9679591; 978-0-9749610)* Div. of Beagle Bay, Inc., 2325 Homestead Pl., Reno, NV 89509-3657 USA
E-mail: info@beaglebay.com
Web site: http://www.beaglebay.com.

Beaver News Co., Inc., 230 W. Washington St., Rensselaer, IN 47978 USA (SAN 630-8864).

Beck's Bk. Store, 4520 N. Broadway, Chicago, IL 60640 USA (SAN 159-8139) Tel 773-784-7963; Fax: 773-784-0066
E-mail: rsvltrd@aol.com
Web site: http://www.aol.members/becks.html.

Beechwood Pubns., Inc., P.O. Box 1158, Kennett Square, PA 19348 USA (SAN 107-5853) Tel 610-444-5991; Fax: 215-566-4178.

Beekman Bks., Inc., *(978-0-8464)* 300 Old All Angels Hill Rd., Wappingers Falls, NY 12590 USA (SAN 170-1622) Tel 845-297-2690; Fax: 845-297-1002
E-mail: manager@beekmanbooks.com
Web site: http://www.beekmanbooks.com.

Beeler, Thomas T. Pub., *(978-1-57490)* Orders Addr.: P.O. Box 310, Rollinsford, NH 03869 USA Toll Free Fax: 888-222-3396; Toll Free: 800-818-7574; Edit Addr.: 710 Main St., Suite 300, Rollinsford, NH 03869 USA Tel 603-749-0392; Fax: 603-749-0395
E-mail: tombeeler@beelerpub.com
Web site: http://www.beelerpub.com.

Before Columbus Foundation, 655 13th St. Ste. 302, Oakland, CA 94612-1225 USA (SAN 159-2955).

Beijing Bk. Co., Inc., 701 E. Linden Ave., Linden, NJ 07036-2495 USA (SAN 169-5673) Tel 908-862-0909; Fax: 908-862-4201.

Bell Magazine, Orders Addr.: P.O. Box 1957, Monterey, CA 93940 USA (SAN 159-7221); Edit Addr.: 3 Justin Ct., Monterey, CA 93940 USA (SAN 169-0353) Tel 408-642-4668.

Bella Distribution, Orders Addr.: P.O. Box 10543, Tallahassee, FL 32302 USA; Edit Addr.: 1041 Aenon Church Rd., Tallahassee, FL 32304 USA Fax: 850-576-3498; Toll Free: 800-533-1973
E-mail: info@belladistribution.com
Web site: http://www.belladistribution.com.

Benchmark LLC, *(978-0-7834; 978-0-929591)* 559 San Ysidro Rd. Suite I, Santa Barbara, CA 93108 USA (SAN 249-7522) Tel 805-565-8911; Toll Free: 888-797-9377
E-mail: bridger@benchmarkmaps.com; teri@benchmarkmaps.com; curtis@benchmarkmaps.com
Web site: http://www.benchmarkmaps.com.

Benjamin News Group, Orders Addr.: 2131 International St., Columbus, OH 43228 USA (SAN 660-9406) Tel 614-777-9768; Fax: 7=614-777-9766; Edit Addr.: 1701 Rankin St., Missoula, MT 59808-1629 USA (SAN 169-4391) Tel 406-721-7801; Fax: 406-721-7802.

Bennett & Curran, Inc., *(978-1-879607)* 1280 Cherryville Rd., Greenwood Vlg, CO 80121-1222 USA
E-mail: Jeff@bennettandcurran.com.

Berkeley Educational Paperbacks, 2480 Bancroft Way, Berkeley, CA 94704 USA (SAN 168-9509) Tel 510-848-7907.

Berkeley Game Distributors, 5850 Hollis St., Emeryville, CA 94608-2016 USA (SAN 631-2934) Toll Free: 800-424-4263; 1164 E. Sandhill Ave., Carson, CA 90746
E-mail: bgdnorth@ix.netcom.com.

Bernan Assocs., *(978-0-400; 978-0-527; 978-0-89059; 978-1-59610; 978-1-59888; 978-1-60175; 978-1-60946; 978-1-63005; 978-1-64143; 978-1-63671; 979-8-89205)* Div. of Kraus Organization, The, Orders Addr.: 15200 NBN Way, P.O. Box 190, Blue Ridge Summit, PA 17214

USA (SAN 169-3182) Tel 301-459-7666; Fax: 301-459-6988; Toll Free Fax: 800-865-3450; Toll Free: 800-865-3457; Edit Addr.: 4501 Forbes Blvd., Suite 200, Lanham, MD 20706 USA (SAN 760-7253) Tel 301-459-2255; Fax: 301-459-0056; Toll Free: 800-416-4385; 15200 Nbn Way, Blue Ridge Summ, PA 17214
E-mail: query@bernan.com; order@bernan.com; info@bernan.com; jkemp@bernan.com; jculley@rowman.com
Web site: www.rowman.com.

Berrett-Koehler Pubs., Inc., *(978-1-57675; 978-1-58376; 978-1-881052; 978-1-60509; 978-1-60994; 978-1-62656; 978-1-5230; 979-8-89057; 979-8-89058)* Orders Addr.: c/o AIDC, P.O. Box 565, Williston, VT 05495 USA Fax: 802-864-7626 (orders); Toll Free: 800-929-2929 (orders); Edit Addr.: 1333 Broadway, Suite 1000, Oakland, CA 94612 USA Tel 510-817-2277; Fax: 415-362-2512
E-mail: bkpub@bkpub.com; awoodcock@bkpub.com
Web site: http://www.bkconnection.com.

Bess Pr., Inc., *(978-0-935848; 978-1-57306; 978-1-880188; 978-0-615-50460-5; 978-0-615-56510-1)* 3565 Harding Ave., Honolulu, HI 96816 USA (SAN 239-4111) Tel 808-734-7159; Fax: 808-732-3627
E-mail: kelly@besspress.com
Web site: http://www.besspress.com.

Best Bk. Ctr., Inc., 1016 Ave. Ponce De Leon, San Juan, PR 00926 USA (SAN 132-4403) Tel 809-727-7945; Fax: 809-268-5022.

Best Continental Bk. Co., Inc., P.O. Box 615, Merrifield, VA 22116 USA (SAN 107-3737) Tel 703-280-1400.

Bethany Hse. Pubs., *(978-0-7642; 978-0-87123; 978-1-55661; 978-1-56179; 978-1-57778; 978-1-880089; 978-1-59066)* Div. of Baker Publishing Group, Orders Addr.: P.O. Box 6287, Grand Rapids, MI 49516-6287 USA Toll Free Fax: 800-398-3111 (orders); Toll Free: 800-877-2665 (orders); Edit Addr.: 11400 Hampshire Ave., S., Bloomington, MN 55438-2455 USA (SAN 201-4416) Tel 952-829-2500; Fax: 952-996-1393
E-mail: orders@bakerbooks.com
Web site: http://www.bethanyhouse.com.

Better Homes & Gardens Books, *See* **Meredith Bks.**

Betty Segal, Inc., 1749 Eucalyptus St., Brea, CA 92621 USA Tel 714-529-5359; Fax: 714-529-3882
E-mail: BertySegal@aol.com
Web site: http://www.agoralang.com/trp-bertysegal.html.

Beyda & Associates, Incorporated, *See* **Beyda for Bks., LLC**

Beyda for Bks., LLC, P.O. Box 2535, Montclair, CA 91763-1035 USA (SAN 169-0426) Toll Free: 800-422-3932 (orders only)
E-mail: info@beydaforbooks.com
Web site: http://www.beydaforbooks.com.

B&H Publishing Group, *See* **B&H Publishing Group**

BHB Fulfillment, Div. of Weatherhill, Inc., 41 Monroe Tpke., Trumbull, CT 06611 USA.

BHB International, Incorporated, *See* **Continental Enterprises Group, Inc. (CEG)**

Bibliotech, Inc., P.O. Box 720459, Dallas, TX 75372-0459 USA (SAN 631-8312) Tel 214-221-0002; Fax: 214-221-1794
E-mail: metatron@airmail.net
Web site: http://www.bibliotechincorporated.com.

Biddy Bks., 1235 168 Model Rd., Manchester, TN 37355 USA (SAN 157-8561) Tel 931-728-6967.

Big Kids Productions, Inc., *(978-1-885627)* 2120 Oxford Ave., Austin, TX 78704-4014 USA (SAN 631-340X) Toll Free: 800-477-7811
E-mail: customerservice@bigkidsvideo.com
Web site: http://www.awardvids.com.

Big River Distribution, *(978-0-9795944; 978-0-9823575; 978-0-9845519)* Orders Addr.: 8214 Exchange Way, Saint Louis, MO 63144 USA (SAN 631-9114) Tel 314-918-9800; Fax: 314-918-9804
E-mail: info@bigriverdist.com; randy@bigriverdist.com
Web site: http://www.bigriverdist.com.

Big Tent Bks., *(978-1-60131; 978-0-578-47138-9; 978-0-578-66280-0)* 115 Bluebill Dr., Savannah, GA 31419 USA (SAN 851-1136)
E-mail: admin@dragonpencil.com; admin@bigtentbooks.com
Web site: http://www.bigtentbooks.com.

Bilingual Educational Services, Inc., *(978-0-86624; 978-0-89075)* 2514 S. Grand Ave., Los Angeles, CA 90007 USA (SAN 218-4680) Tel 213-749-6213; Fax: 213-749-1820; Toll Free: 800-448-6032
E-mail: sales@besbooks.com
Web site: http://www.besbooks.com.

Bilingual Pr./Editorial Bilingue, *(978-0-916950; 978-0-927534; 978-1-931010; 978-1-939743)* Orders Addr.: Hispanic Research Ctr. Arizona State Univ. P.O. Box 875303, Tempe, AZ 85287-5303 USA (SAN 208-5526) Fax: 480-965-8309; Toll Free: 800-965-2280; Edit Addr.: Bilingual Review Pr. Administration Bldg. Rm. B-255 Arizona State Univ., Tempe, AZ 85281 USA
E-mail: brp@asu.edu
Web site: http://www.asu.edu/brp.

Bilingual Pubns. Co., The, 270 Lafayette St., New York, NY 10012 USA (SAN 164-8993) Tel 212-431-3500; Fax: 212-431-3567 Do not confuse with Bilingual Pubns., in Denver, CO
E-mail: lindagoodman@juno.com; spanishbks@aol.com.

Birdlegs Christian Apparel, P.O. Box 189, Duluth, GA 30136-0189 USA (SAN 631-3280) Toll Free: 800-545-0790.

BJU Pr., *(978-0-89084; 978-1-57924; 978-1-59166; 978-1-60682; 978-1-62856; 978-1-64626)* 1430 Wade Hampton Blvd., Greenville, SC 29609 USA (SAN 223-7512) Tel 800-845-5731 Customer Service; Fax: 800-258-5853 Corporate Accounts; Toll Free: 864-370-1800 ext 3707, 4363 Content Development/Operations; 888-262-9914 Corporate Accounts-Pam Schaedel
E-mail: bjup@bjup.com
Web site: http://www.bjupress.com.

Bk. Box, Inc., 3126 Purdue Ave., Los Angeles, CA 90066 USA (SAN 243-2285) Tel 310-391-2313.

Bk. Buy Back, 5150 Candlewood St., No. 6, Lakewood, CA 90712 USA (SAN 631-7251) Tel 562-461-9355; Fax: 562-461-9445.

Bk. Co., The, 145 S. Glencoe St., Denver, CO 80222-1152 USA (SAN 200-2809).

Bk. Distribution Ctr., *(978-0-941722)* Div. of Free Islamic Literatures, Inc., Orders Addr.: P.O. Box 35844, Houston, TX 77235 USA (SAN 241-6395); Edit Addr.: P.O. Box 31669, Houston, TX 77231 USA (SAN 226-2770).

Bk. Distribution Ctr., Inc., Orders Addr.: P.O. Box 64631, Virginia Beach, VA 23467-6431 USA (SAN 134-8019) Tel 757-456-0005; Fax: 757-552-0837; Edit Addr.: 5321 Cleveland St., No. 203, Virginia Beach, VA 23462-6552 USA (SAN 169-8672)
E-mail: sales@bookdist.com
Web site: http://www.bookdist.com.

Bk. Dynamics, Inc., *(978-0-9612440)* 18 Kennedy Blvd., East Brunswick, NJ 08816 USA (SAN 169-5649) Tel 732-545-5151; Fax: 732-545-5959; Toll Free: 800-441-4510.

Bk. Express, *(978-0-9612322; 978-1-890308)* Orders Addr.: P.O. Box 1249, Bellflower, CA 90706 USA (SAN 289-1301) Tel 562-865-1226; Edit Addr.: 12122 E. 176th St., Artesia, CA 90701-4013 USA
E-mail: carbks4u@escapenet.net.

Bk. Home, The, 119 E. Dale St., Colorado Springs, CO 80903-4701 USA (SAN 249-3055) Tel 719-634-5885.

Bk. Hse., Inc., The, 208 W. Chicago St., Jonesville, MI 49250-0125 USA (SAN 169-3859) Tel 517-849-2117; Fax: 517-849-9716; Toll Free Fax: 800-858-9716; Toll Free: 800-248-1146
E-mail: bhinfo@thebookhouse.com.

Bk. Hse., The, 9719 Manchester Rd., Saint Louis, MO 63119 USA Toll Free: 800-513-4491.

Bk. Margins, Inc., 7100 Valley Green Rd., Fort Washington, PA 19034-2206 USA (SAN 106-7788) Tel 215-223-5300
E-mail: paul.gross@bookmargins.com
Web site: http://www.bookmargins.com.

Bk. Marketing Plus, 406 Post Oak Rd., Fredericksburg, TX 78624 USA (SAN 630-6543) Tel 830-997-4776; Fax: 830-997-9752; Toll Free: 800-356-2445.

Bk. Mart, The, 1153 E. Hyde Pk., Inglewood, CA 90302 USA (SAN 168-969X).

Bk. Service of Puerto Rico, 102 De Diego, Santurce, PR 00907 USA (SAN 169-9326) Tel 809-728-5000; Fax: 809-726-6131
E-mail: bellbook@coqui.net
Web site: http://home.coqui.net/bellbook.

Bk. Service Unlimited, P.O. Box 31108, Seattle, WA 98103-1108 USA (SAN 169-877X) Toll Free: 800-347-0042.

Bk. Services International, Orders Addr.: P.O. Box 1434-SMS, Fairfield, CT 06430 USA (SAN 157-9541) Tel 203-374-4939; Fax: 203-384-6099; Toll Free: 800-243-2790.

Bk. Shelf, The, 222 Crestview Dr., Fort Dodge, IA 50501-5708 USA (SAN 169-2658).

Bk. Warehouse, 5154 NW 165th St., Hialeah, FL 33014-6335 USA.

Bk. World, 311 Sagamore Pkwy., N., Lafayette, IN 47904 USA (SAN 135-4051) Tel 765-448-1131 Do not confuse with companies with the same or similar name in Sun Lakes, AZ, Roanoke, VA
E-mail: fsjinti@pworld.net.ph.

Bks. & Media, Inc., *(978-0-7848; 978-0-88483; 978-1-55744)* Div. of Marco Bk. Co., Orders Addr.: P.O. Box 695, Lodi, NY 07644 USA (SAN 206-3352) Tel 973-458-8153; Fax: 973-458-5289; Toll Free: 800-901-8150; Edit Addr.: 60 Industrail Rd., Lodi, NJ 07644 USA.

Bks. & Research, Inc., 145 Palisade St. Ste. 389, Dobbs Ferry, NY 10522-1628 USA (SAN 130-1101)
E-mail: brinc@ix.netcom.com
Web site: http://www.books-and-research.com.

Bks. Are Fun, Ltd., *(978-0-9649777; 978-1-58209; 978-1-890409; 978-1-59795; 978-1-60626)* 1 Readers Digest Rd., Pleasantville, NY 10570-7000 USA
E-mail: msmall@booksarefun.com
Web site: http://www.booksarefun.com.

Bks. Plus, U.S.A., 20171 Kelso Rd., Walnut, CA 91789-1922 USA (SAN 630-8473).

Bks. to Grow On, 826 S. Aiken Ave., Pittsburgh, PA 15232 USA (SAN 128-438X); 210 S. Highland Ave., Pittsburgh, PA 15206 Fax: 412-621-5324.

Bks. West, 11111 E. 53rd Ave., Unit D2, Boulder, CO 80239 USA (SAN 631-4724) Tel 303-449-5995; Fax: 303-449-5951; Toll Free: 800-378-4188; 6340 E. 58Th Ave, Commerce City, CO 80022 Do not confuse with Books West, San Diego, CA
E-mail: wnack@rmi.net
Web site: http://www.bookswest.net/.

Black Box Corp., 1000 Park Dr., Lawrence, PA 15055 USA (SAN 277-1985) Tel 412-746-5500; Fax: 412-746-0746.

Black Christian Bk. Distributors, 1169 North Burleson Blvd. Suite 107-246, Burleson, TX 76028 USA.

Black Magazine Agency, 4515 Fleur Dr. Ste. 301, Des Moines, IA 50321-2369 USA (SAN 107-0819) Toll Free: 800-782-9787.

Black Rabbit Bks., *(978-1-58340; 978-1-887068; 978-1-59920; 978-1-77092; 978-1-62310; 978-1-62588; 978-1-68071; 978-1-68072; 978-1-64466)* Orders Addr.: P.O. Box 227, Mankato, MN 56002 USA (SAN 925-4862); Edit Addr.: 2140 Howard Dr. W., North Mankato, MN 56003 USA (SAN 858-902X) Tel 507-388-6273
E-mail: info@blackrabbitbooks.com; info@thecreativecompany.us; rglaser@thecreativecompany.us
Web site: http://www.blackrabbitbooks.com.

Blackburn News Agency, P.O. Box 1039, Kingsport, TN 37662 USA (SAN 169-7900).

Blackstone Audio Books, Incorporated, *See* **Blackstone Audio, Inc.**

Blackstone Audio, Inc., *(978-0-7861; 978-1-4332; 978-1-4417; 978-1-4551; 978-1-4708; 978-1-4829; 978-1-4830; 978-1-5046; 978-1-5047; 978-1-5384; 978-1-5385; 978-1-9824; 978-1-9825; 978-1-9826; 978-1-7999; 978-1-0940; 978-1-0941; 978-1-6644; 978-1-6645; 978-1-6646; 978-1-6647; 978-1-6650; 978-1-6651; 978-1-6652; 979-8-200; 979-8-212) 31 Mistletoe Rd., Ashland, OR 97520 USA (SAN 173-2811) Fax: 800-482-9294; Toll Free Fax: 800-482-9294; Toll Free: 800-729-2665*
E-mail: Orders@blackstoneaudio.com; megan.wahrenbrock@blackstoneaudio.com; heather.johnson@blackstoneaudio.com
Web site: http://www.blackstoneaudio.com.

Blackwell, *(978-0-913262; 978-0-916472)* Orders Addr.: 6024 SW Jean Rd., Bldg. G, Lake Oswego, OR 97034 USA (SAN 169-7048) Tel 503-684-1140; Fax: 503-639-2481; Toll Free: 800-547-6426 (in Oregon); Edit Addr.: 100 University Ct., Blackwood, NJ 08012 USA (SAN 169-4596) Tel 856-228-8900; Toll Free: 800-257-7341
Web site: http://www.blackwell.com/.

Blackwell North America, *See* **Blackwell**

Bloomington News Agency, P.O. Box 3757, Bloomington, IL 61702-3757 USA (SAN 169-1732).

Bloomsbury Academic & Professional, *See* **Bloomsbury Academic & Professional**

Bloomsbury Publishing US Trade, Orders Addr.: 16365 James Madison Hwy., Gordonsville, VA 22942 USA.

Bloomsbury Publishing USA, *(978-1-58234; 978-1-59691; 978-1-59990; 978-1-60819; 978-1-84706; 978-1-61963; 978-1-62040; 978-1-62356; 978-1-62892; 978-1-63286; 978-1-5013; 978-1-68119; 978-1-63557; 978-1-5476; 978-1-63973; 979-8-7651)* Orders Addr.: 16365 James Madison Hwy., Gordonsville, VA 22942-8501 USA Tel 888-330-8477; Toll Free: 888-330-8477; Edit Addr.: 175 Fifth Ave., Suite 300, New York, NY 10010 USA Toll Free: 888-330-8477; 1385 Broadway, New York, NY 10018 Tel 212-419-5300
E-mail: bloomsbury.kids@bloomsburyusa.com; nathaniel.knaebel@bloomsbury.com; mike.o'connor@bloomsbury.com
Web site: https://www.bloomsbury.com/us/.

Blu Sky Media Group, P.O. Box 10069, Murfreesboro, TN 37129-0002 USA
Web site: http://www.bluskymediagroup.com.

Blue Cat, *(978-0-932679; 978-0-936200)* 469 Barbados, Walnut, CA 91789 USA (SAN 214-0322) Tel 909-594-3317.

Blue Mountain Arts Inc., *(978-0-88396; 978-1-58786; 978-1-59842; 978-1-68088)* Orders Addr.: P.O. Box 4549, Boulder, CO 80306 USA (SAN 299-9609) Tel 303-449-0536; Fax: 303-417-6434; 303-417-6496; Toll Free Fax: 800-943-6666; 800-545-8573; Toll Free: 800-525-0642
Web site: http://www.sps.com/.

Blue Mountain Arts (R) by SPS Studios, Incorporated, *See* **Blue Mountain Arts Inc.**

Blue Ridge News Co., 21 Westside Dr., No. B, Asheville, NC 28806-2846 USA (SAN 169-6335).

BMI Educational Services, *(978-0-922443; 978-1-60884; 978-1-60933; 978-1-63071; 978-1-5367)* Orders Addr.: 26 Haypress Rd., Cranbury, NJ 08512 USA (SAN 760-7032); Edit Addr.: P.O. Box 800, Dayton, NJ 08810-0800 USA (SAN 169-4669) Tel 732-329-6991; Fax: 732-329-6994; Toll Free Fax: 800-986-9393 (orders only); Toll Free: 800-222-8100 (orders only)
E-mail: info@bmionline.com
Web site: http://www.bmionline.com/.

Bolchazy-Carducci Pubs., *(978-0-86516; 978-1-61041)* 1570 Baskin Rd., Mundelein, IL 60060-4474 USA (SAN 219-7685) Toll Free: 800-392-6453
E-mail: jcull@bolchazy.com
Web site: http://www.bolchazy.com.

Boley International Subscription Agency, Inc., 1001 Fries Mill Rd., Blackwood, NJ 08012 USA (SAN 159-6225) Tel 609-629-2500.

Bolinda Publishing, Inc., Orders Addr.: 186 S. Long Swamp Rd., Jackson, ME 04921-3154 USA Toll Free Fax: 877-864-8307; Toll Free: 888-235-2019
E-mail: karen@bolinda.com
Web site: http://www.bolinda.com.

Bondcliff Bks., *(978-0-9657475; 978-1-931271)* Orders Addr.: P.O. Box 385, Littleton, NH 03561 USA Toll Free: 800-859-7581; Edit Addr.: 8 Bluejay Ln., Littleton, NH 03561 USA
E-mail: bondcliff@ncia.net.

Bonneville News Co., 965 Beardsley Pl., Salt Lake City, UT 84119 USA Tel 801-972-5454; Fax: 801-972-1075; Toll Free: 800-748-5453.

Book Clearing Hse., 46 Purdy St., Harrison, NY 10528 USA (SAN 125-5169) Tel 914-835-0015; Fax: 914-835-0398; Toll Free: 800-431-1579
E-mail: bookch@aol.com.

Book Gallery, *(978-1-878382)* 632 S. Quincy Ave., Apt. 1, Tulsa, OK 74120-4635 USA (SAN 630-9321).

Book Hub, Inc., 903 Pacific Ave., Suite 207A, Santa Cruz, CA 95060 USA Tel 831-466-0145; Fax: 831-515-5955.

Book Publishing Company, *See* **BPC**

Book Sales, Inc., *(978-0-7628; 978-0-7858; 978-0-89009; 978-1-55521; 978-1-57715; 978-1-4161)* Orders Addr.: 400 1st Ave N. Ste. 300, Minneapolis, MN 55401-1721 USA (SAN 169-488X) Toll Free: 800-526-7257; Edit Addr.: 276 Fifth Ave., Suite 206, New York, NY 10001 USA (SAN 299-4062) Tel 212-779-4972; Fax: 212-779-6058
E-mail: sales@booksalesusa.com
Web site: http://www.booksalesusa.com/.

Book Wholesalers, Inc., *(978-0-7587; 978-1-4046; 978-1-4131; 978-1-4155; 978-1-4156; 978-1-4287)* 1847 Mercer Rd., Lexington, KY 40511-1001 USA (SAN 135-5449) Toll Free: 800-888-4478
E-mail: jcarrico@bwibooks.com; lison@bwibooks.com
Web site: http://www.bwibooks.com.

Bookazine Co., Inc., 75 Hook Rd., Bayonne, NJ 07002 USA (SAN 169-5665) Tel 201-339-7777; Fax: 201-339-7778; Toll Free: 800-221-8112.

Bookazine Company, Incorporated, *See* **Bookazine Co., Inc.**

BookBaby, *(978-1-60984; 978-1-61792; 978-1-61842; 978-1-61927; 978-1-62095; 978-1-62309; 978-1-62488; 978-1-62675; 978-1-4835; 978-1-63192; 978-1-943612; 978-1-68222; 978-1-5439; 978-0-692-95466-9; 978-0-692-11235-9; 978-0-692-11236-6; 978-0-578-41517-8;-1-0983; 978-1-6678; 978-0-578-94766-2; 979-8-3509) 7905 N. Rt 130, Pennsauken, NJ 08110 USA Toll Free: 877-961-6878; 7905 N Crescent Blvd, Pennsauken, NJ 08110 Toll Free: 877-961-6878*
E-mail: info@bookbaby.com; support@bookbaby.com; jburton@bookbaby.com; jfoley@bookbaby.com
Web site: http://www.bookbaby.com.

BookHawkers Internet BookSeller, P.O. Box 2094, Wilkes-Barre, PA 18703 USA
Web site: http://www.bookhawkers.com.

Bookhouse, The, 10505 N. May Ave., Oklahoma City, OK 73120-2611 USA (SAN 200-8467) Tel 405-755-0020.

Booklegger, The, *(978-0-936421)* Orders Addr.: P.O. Box 2626, Grass Valley, CA 95945 USA (SAN 697-9548); Edit Addr.: 13100 Grass Valley Ave., Suite D, Grass Valley, CA 95945 USA (SAN 120-6125) Tel 530-272-1556; Fax: 530-272-2133; Toll Free Fax: 800-250-2199; Toll Free: 800-262-1556
E-mail: order@booklegger.com
Web site: http://www.booklegger.com/.

Bookline, Div. of Michiana News Service, Inc., 2232 S. 11th St., Niles, MI 49120 USA (SAN 169-3948) Tel 616-684-3013; Fax: 616-684-8740.

Booklines Hawaii, Ltd., *(978-1-929844; 978-1-58849; 978-1-60274)* Div. of Islander Group, 269 Pali'i St., Mililani, HI 96789 USA (SAN 630-6624) Tel 808-676-0116; Fax: 808-676-0634
E-mail: customerservice@booklines.com
Web site: http://www.booklineshawaii.com.

BookLink, *(978-0-9797436)* 465 Broad Ave., Leonia, NJ 07605-1637 USA (SAN 854-2473) Tel 201-947-3471; Fax: 201-947-6321
E-mail: booklink@es1booklink.com.

BookLink, Inc., 444 Broad St., Camden, SC 29020 USA (SAN 631-5291) Tel 803-432-5169; Fax: 803-424-8418
E-mail: sam@thebooklink.com
Web site: http://www.thebooklink.com.

Bookman Bks., 138 Elena St., Santa Fe, NM 87501 USA (SAN 630-933X) Tel 505-982-5964.

Bookmark, Inc., The, 1445 N. Winchester St., Olathe, KS 66061-5881 USA (SAN 131-4017) Toll Free: 800-642-1288.

Book$mart, Inc., *(978-1-885051)* Div. of Books-A-Million, 602 John Aldridge Dr., Tuscumbia, AL 35674-3002 USA Tel 256-314-4466 Do not confuse with Booksmart in Irondale, AZ
E-mail: brad@roses-4u.com.

BookSmiths, 6745 FM 2738, Burleson, TX 76028-1167 USA (SAN 630-8406) Do not confuse with BookMasters Inc., Ashland, OH.

Bookmasters Distribution, *See* **Baker & Taylor Publisher Services (BTPS)**

BookMasters, Inc., *(978-0-917889)* Orders Addr.: P.O. Box 388, Mansfield, OH 44903 USA (SAN 631-3566) Tel 419-281-1802; Fax: 419-281-6883; Toll Free: 800-247-6553; 30 Amberwood Pkwy., Ashland, OH 44805 Tel 419-281-1802; Fax: 419-281-6886
E-mail: info@bookmasters.com; order@bookmaster.com
Web site: http://www.bookmasters.com.

Bookmen, Inc., Orders Addr.: 2300 Louisiana Ave N. # B, Minneapolis, MN 55427-3631 USA (SAN 169-409X) Toll Free Fax: 800-266-5636; Toll Free: 800-328-8411 (customer service)
Web site: http://www.bookmen.com.

BookMobile, Orders Addr.: 5120 Cedar Lake Rd., Saint Louis Park, MN 55416 USA (SAN 760-7245) Fax: 763-398-0198
E-mail: dleeper@bookmobile.com
Web site: http://www.bookmobile.com.

BookPartners, Inc., *(978-0-9622269; 978-1-58151; 978-1-885221)* Orders Addr.: P.O. Box 345, Portland, OR 97205 USA; Edit Addr.: 620 SW Main, Portland, OR 97205 USA Tel 503-225-9900; Fax: 503-225-9901
Web site: http://www.amicapublishing.com.

Books Alive, *(978-0-920470; 978-1-55312)* Div. of Book Publishing Co., Orders Addr.: P.O. Box 99, Summertown, TN 38483 USA (SAN 115-7078) Tel 931-964-3571; Fax: 931-964-3518; Toll Free: 888-260-8458 (orders and customer service)
E-mail: Cynthia@bookpubco.com
Web site: http://www.bookpubco.com.

Books International, Inc., *(978-1-891078)* Orders Addr.: P.O. Box 605, Herndon, VA 20172-0605 USA (SAN 131-761X) Tel 703-661-1500; Fax: 703-661-1501
E-mail: bimail@presswarehouse.com.

Booksellers Order Service, 828 S. Broadway, Tarrytown, NY 10591-5112 USA (SAN 106-5181) Tel 914-591-2665; Fax: 914-591-2720; Toll Free: 800-637-0037.

Booksmith Promotional Co., 100 Paterson Plank Rd., Jersey City, NJ 07307 USA (SAN 664-5364) Tel 201-659-2768; Fax: 201-659-3631.

Booksource, The, *(978-0-7383; 978-0-8335; 978-0-911891; 978-0-9641084; 978-1-886379; 978-1-890760; 978-0-7568; 978-1-4117; 978-1-4178; 978-0-606; 978-1-60446; 978-1-4364; 979-8-3685)* Div. of GL group, Inc., Orders Addr.: 1230 Macklind Ave., Saint Louis, MO 63110-1432 USA (SAN 169-4324) Tel 314-647-0600 Toll Free Fax: 800-647-1923; Toll Free: 800-444-0435
E-mail: khostman@booksource.com; shankins@glgrp.com; shankins@booksource.com
Web site: http://www.booksource.com; http://www.goodluckgroup.com/.

BookWorksUSA, 385 Freeport Blvd., Suite 3, Sparks, NV 89431 USA
E-mail: bookworksusa@mac.com.

Bookworld Cos., P.O. Box 2260, Sarasota, FL 34230-2260 USA.

Bookworm, 14 Griffin St., Northport, ME 04849-4446 USA (SAN 170-8074).

Bookworm Bookfairs, P.O. Box 306, Simsbury, CT 06070-0306 USA (SAN 156-5621).

Bookworm, The, 417 Monmouth Dr., Cherry Hill, NJ 08002 USA (SAN 120-9531) Tel 609-667-5884.

Borchardt, G. Inc., 136 E. 57th St., New York, NY 10022 USA (SAN 285-8614) Tel 212-753-5785; Fax: 212-838-6518.

Borders, Inc., 9910 N. By NE Blvd., Bldg. 4, Fishers, IN 46038 USA (SAN 152-5352); Space 497, 1st Level 525 F D Roosevelt Ave. Plaza Las Americas, Hato Rey, PR 00917 (SAN 193-2314); 455 Industrial Blvd., Suite E, La Vergne, TN 37086 (SAN 156-6474); Edit Addr.: 100 Phoenix Dr., Ann Arbor, MI 48108 USA (SAN 152-3546) Tel 734-477-1100; Fulfillment Addr.: a/o Fulfillment Center, 100 Phoenix Dr., Ann Arbor, MI 48108-2202 USA (SAN 197-0917).

Bored Feet Pr., *(978-0-939431)* Orders Addr.: P.O. Box 1832, Mendocino, CA 95460 USA (SAN 661-6992) Tel 707-964-6629; Fax: 707-964-5953; Edit Addr.: 16630 Mitchell Creek Dr., Fort Bragg, CA 95437 USA (SAN 663-3226)
E-mail: Boredft@mcn.org.

Bored Feet Publications, *See* **Bored Feet Pr.**

Bottman Design, Inc., *(978-1-884741)* 1081 S. 300 W., No. A, Salt Lake City, UT 84101 USA (SAN 860-2166) Tel 801-487-1949; Fax: 801-973-6746; Toll Free: 800-365-5564.

Bottom Dog Pr., *(978-0-933087; 978-1-933964; 978-1-947504)* c/o Firelands College, P.O. Box 425, Huron, OH 44839 USA (SAN 689-5492) Tel 419-433-3573; Fax: 419-616-3966
E-mail: LSmithDog@aol.com; lsmithdog@smithdocs.net
Web site: https://www.facebook.com/BottomDogPress/?ref=bookmarks; http://smithdocs.net; http://smithdocs.net/recent_bottom_dog_press_titles.

Bound to Stay Bound Bks., *(978-0-9718238; 979-8-8550; 979-8-8551)* 1880 W. Morton Rd., Jacksonville, IL 62650 USA (SAN 169-1996) Toll Free Fax: 800-747-2872; Toll Free: 800-637-6586
Web site: http://www.btsb.com.

Bowers & Merena Galleries, Inc., *(978-0-943161)* Orders Addr.: P.O. Box 1224, Wolfeboro, NH 03894 USA (SAN 168-9746) Tel 603-569-5095; Fax: 603-569-5319; Toll Free: 800-222-5993; Edit Addr.: 18061 Fitch., Irvine, CA 92614-6018 USA (SAN 668-2561).

Bowker LLC, R. R., *(978-0-8352; 978-0-911255; 978-0-641; 978-0-9856945; 978-1-941808)* Subs. of Proquest LLC, Orders Addr.: P.O. Box 32, New Providence, NJ 07974 USA Tel 908-286-1090; Fax: 908-219-0098; Toll Free: 888-269-5372; Edit Addr.: 630 Central Ave., New Providence, NJ 07974 USA (SAN 214-1191); 630 Central Ave., B&T box, New Providence, NJ 07974 (SAN 857-8516)
E-mail: info@bowker.com; pad@bowker.com; customerservice@bowker.com; specialtytitles@bowker.com
Web site: http://www.bowker.com.

Bowling Green State University, Philosophy Documentation Center, *See* **Philosophy Documentation Ctr.**

Boydell & Brewer, Inc., *(978-0-85115; 978-0-85991; 978-0-907239; 978-0-938100; 978-1-57113; 978-1-58046; 978-1-85566; 978-1-870252; 978-1-878822; 978-1-879751; 978-1-900639; 978-1-84384; 978-1-84383; 978-1-64014; 978-1-64825)* Div. of Boydell & Brewer Group, Ltd., Orders Addr.: 668 Mount Hope Ave., Rochester, NY 14620-2731 USA (SAN 013-8479) Tel 585-275-0419; Fax: 585-271-8778
E-mail: boydell@boydellusa.net; boydell@boydell.co.uk
Web site: http://www.boydellandbrewer.com.

Boyds Mills Press, *See* **Highlights Pr., c/o Highlights for Children, Inc.**

BPC, *(978-0-913990; 978-1-57067; 978-0-9669317; 978-0-9673108; 978-0-9779183; 978-1-939053)* P.O. Box 99, Summertown, TN 38483 USA (SAN 202-439X) Tel 931-964-3571; Fax: 931-964-3518; Toll Free: 888-260-8458
E-mail: info@bookpubco.com
Web site: http://www.bookpubco.com.

BPDI, 1000 S. Lynndale Dr., Appleton, WI 54914 USA (SAN 631-6859) Tel 920-830-7897; Fax: 920-830-3857.

Brayshaw, R. C., *(978-0-578-27321-1)* P.O. Box 91, Warner, NH 03278 USA Tel 603-456-3101; 45 Waterloo St., Warner, NH 03278 Tel 603-456-3101
E-mail: general@rcbrayshaw.com
Web site: rcbrayshaw.com.

Bridge Pubns., Inc., *(978-0-88404; 978-1-57318; 978-1-4031; 978-1-61177; 978-1-4572; 978-1-0789)* Orders Addr.: 5600 E. Olympic Blvd., Commerce, CA 90022 USA (SAN 208-3884) Tel 323-888-6200; Fax: 323-888-6210; Toll Free: 800-722-1733; 800-334-5433; Edit Addr.: 4751_Fountain Ave., Los Angeles, CA 90029 USA
E-mail: annarnow@bridgepub.com; danielem@bridgepub.com; donarnow@bridgepub.com; purchaser@bridgepub.com
Web site: http://www.bridgepub.com; http://www.clearbodyclearmind.com; http://www.scientology.org; http://www.dianetics.org.

Bridge-Logos Foundation, *See* **Bridge-Logos, Inc.**

Bridge-Logos, Inc., *(978-0-88270; 978-0-912106; 978-0-9841034; 978-1-61036)* Orders Addr.: 14260 W. Newberry Rd, Newberry, FL 32669 USA (SAN 253-5254) Tel 352-727-9324; Toll Free: 800-935-6467 (orders only); 800-631-5802 (orders only)
E-mail: SWooldridge@bridgelogos.com
Web site: http://www.bridgelogos.com.

Brigham Distributing, *(978-0-578-09711-4; 978-0-578-14054-4)* 330 South 150 E., Burley, ID 83318 USA; 110 S 800 W., Brigham City, UT 84302.

Brigham Distribution, 110 S. 800 W., Brigham City, UT 84302 USA (SAN 760-7652) Tel 435-723-6611; Fax: 435-723-6644
E-mail: brigdist@sisna.com.

Brigham, Kay, Orders Addr.: 9500 Old Cutler Rd., Miami, FL 33156 USA Tel 305-666-3844; Fax: 305-661-4843
Web site: http://www.kaybrigham.com.

Brigham Young Univ. Print Services, *(978-0-578-64957-3)* 205 UPB, Provo, UT 84602 USA Tel 801-378-2809; Fax: 801-378-3374
E-mail: denise@upb.byu.edu
Web site: http://www.upb.byu.edu.

Bright Horizons Specialty Distributors, Inc., 206 Riva Ridge Dr., Fairview, NC 28730-9764 USA (SAN 110-4101) Toll Free: 800-437-3959 (orders only).

Bright Sky Publishing, *See* **Night Heron Media**

Brightpoint Literacy, 299 Market St., Saddle Brook, NJ 07663 USA Tel 201-708-6498.

Brill, E. J. U. S. A., Incorporated, *See* **Brill USA, Inc.**

Brill USA, Inc., *(978-0-916846)* Subs. of Brill Academic Publishing Co., The Netherlands, 2 Liberty Square, Eleventh Flr., Boston, MA 02109 USA (SAN 254-6922) Tel 617-263-2323; Fax: 617-263-2324; Toll Free: 800-962-4406
E-mail: cs@brillusa.com; brillonline@brillusa.com
Web site: http://www.brill.nl.

Brilliance Publishing, *See* **Brilliance Publishing, Inc.**

Brilliance Publishing, Inc., *(978-0-930435; 978-1-56100; 978-1-56740; 978-1-58788; 978-1-59086; 978-1-59355; 978-1-59600; 978-1-59710; 978-1-59737; 978-1-4233; 978-1-4418; 978-1-61106; 978-1-4558; 978-1-4692; 978-1-4805; 978-1-4915; 978-1-5012; 978-1-5113; 978-1-5226; 978-1-5318; 978-1-5366; 978-1-5436; 978-1-9786; 978-1-7213; 978-1-7997; 978-1-7135; 978-1-7136; 979-8-9850001; 979-8-4001) Orders Addr.: P.O. Box 887, Grand Haven, MI 49417 USA (SAN 690-1395) Tel 616-846-5256; Fax: 616-846-0630; Toll Free: 800-648-2312 x330 (phone/fax, retail & library orders); Edit Addr.: 1704 Eaton Dr., Grand Haven, MI 49417 USA (SAN 858-138X) Toll Free: 800-648-2312 x330*
E-mail: sales@brillianceaudio.com; customerservice@brillianceaudio.com; jcraig@brilliancepublishing.com
Web site: http://www.brilliancepublishing.com.

Brisco Pubns., *(978-0-9603576)* P.O. Box 2161, Palos Verdes Peninsula, CA 90274 USA (SAN 133-0268) Tel 310-534-4943; Fax: 310-534-8437.

Bristlecone Publishing Co., 2560 Brookridge Ave., Golden Valley, MN 55422 USA
E-mail: davej@jblcompanies.com.

Brodart Co., *(978-0-87272; 978-1-62844; 978-1-63546; 978-1-64838; 979-8-88880)* Orders Addr.: 500 Arch St., Williamsport, PA 17705 USA (SAN 169-7684) Tel 570-326-2461 (International); Fax: 570-326-1479; 717-326-2461; 519-759-1144 (Canada); Toll Free Fax: 800-999-6799; Toll Free: 800-233-8467 (US & Canada)
E-mail: bookinfo@brodart.com
Web site: http://www.brodart.com.

Brotherhood of Life, Inc., *(978-0-914732)* P.O. Box 46306, Las Vegas, NV 89114-6306 USA (SAN 111-3674) Fax: 702-319-5577
E-mail: brotherhoodoflife@hotmail.com
Web site: http://www.brotherhoodoflife.com.

Brown Bks., *(978-0-9668452; 978-0-9717197)* Div. of Personal Profiles, Inc., 16200 Dallas Pkwy., Suite 170, Dallas, TX 75248-2616 USA Do not confuse with companies with the same or similar names in Allen, TX, Redway, CA, Montrose, CO, Plano, TX
Web site: http://www.brownbooks.com.

Brown Books Publishing Group, *(978-0-9713265; 978-0-9744597; 978-0-9753907; 978-1-933285; 978-1-934812; 978-1-61254; 978-1-948307)* 16250 Knoll Trail Dr. Ste 205, Dallas, TX 75248 USA Tel 972-381-0009; Fax: 972-248-4336
E-mail: brittany.griffith@brownbooks.com
Web site: https://www.brownbookskids.com; https://www.brownbooks.com; https://www.thep3press.com.

Brown, David Book Company, The, *See* **Casemate Academic**

Brown Enterprises, Inc., *(978-0-9711451)* P.O. Box 11447, Durham, NC 27703 USA Tel 919-680-2288 Do not confuse with companies with the same or similar names in Pasadena, CA, Bellingham, WA
E-mail: brown.enterprisesinc@verizon.net.

Brunner News Agency, 217 Flanders Ave., P.O. Box 598, Lima, OH 45801 USA (SAN 169-6777) Tel 419-225-5826; Fax: 419-225-5537; Toll Free: 800-998-1727
E-mail: brunnews@aol.com
Web site: http://www.readmoreshallmark.com.

Bryan, R. L., *(978-0-934870)* P.O. Box 368, Columbia, SC 29202 USA Tel 803-779-3560.

Bryant Altman Map, Inc., Endicott St., Bldg. 26, Norwood, MA 02062 USA (SAN 630-2475) Tel 781-762-3339; Fax: 781-769-9080
E-mail: JPG63@aol.com.

Bryant-Altman Book & Map Distributors, *See* **Bryant Altman Map, Inc.**

Buckeye News Co., 6800 W. Central Ave., Suite F, Toledo, OH 43617-1157 USA (SAN 169-6874).

Budget Bk. Service, Inc., Div. of LDAP, Inc., 386 Park Ave. S., Suite 1913, New York, NY 10016-8804 USA (SAN 169-5762) Fax: 212-679-2247.

Budget Marketing, Inc., P.O. Box 1805, Des Moines, IA 50306 USA (SAN 285-8754).

Budgetext, Orders Addr.: P.O. Box 1487, Fayetteville, AR 72702 USA (SAN 111-3321) Tel 501-443-9205; Fax: 501-442-3064; Toll Free: 800-643-3432; Edit Addr.: 1936 N. Shiloh Dr., Fayetteville, AR 72704 USA (SAN 249-3330)
E-mail: wmorgan@absc.com; scaldwell@budgetext.com
Web site: http://www.budgetext.com.

Buena Vista Home Video, *(978-0-7888; 978-1-55890)* Div. of Walt Disney Studios, 500 S. Buena Vista St., Burbank, CA 91521-1120 USA (SAN 249-2342) Tel 818-295-4841; Fax: 818-972-2845; Toll Free: 800-723-4763
Web site: http://www.disney.com.

Burlington News Agency, 382 Hercules Dr., Colchester, VT 05446-5836 USA (SAN 169-8583).

Burns News Agency, P.O. Box 1211, Rochester, NY 14603-1211 USA (SAN 169-5320).

B.W. Bks. on Wings, Orders Addr.: 581 Market St., San Francisco, CA 94105-2847 USA.

BWI, 1340 Ridgeview Dr., Mchenry, IL 60050-7047 USA.

Byeway Bks., *(978-1-85997; 978-1-904586; 978-1-933581; 978-1-934004; 978-1-60176)* 15941 W. 65th St., Shawnee, KS 66217-9342 USA Toll Free Fax: 866-426-3929; Toll Free: 866-429-3929
E-mail: customerservice@byewaybooks.com
Web site: http://www.byewaybooks.com/how_to_order.html.

Byrrd Enterprises, Inc., *(978-1-886715)* 1302 Lafayette Dr., Alexandria, VA 22308 USA (SAN 169-8605) Tel 703-765-5626; Fax: 703-768-4086; Toll Free: 800-628-0901
E-mail: byrrdbooks@aol.com.

C & B Bk. Distribution, 65-77 160th St., Flushing, NY 11365 USA Tel 718-591-4525
Web site: http://www.cbbooksdistribution.com.

C & B Bk. Hse., 21 Oak Ridge Rd., Monroe, CT 06468 USA (SAN 159-8279).

C & H News Co., P.O. Box 2768, Corpus Christi, TX 78403-2768 USA (SAN 169-8249).

C & T Publishing, *(978-0-914881; 978-1-57120; 978-1-60705; 978-1-61745; 978-1-64403)* Orders Addr.: 1651 Challenge Dr., Concord, CA 94520 USA (SAN 289-0720) Tel 925-677-0377; Fax: 925-617-0374; Toll Free: 800-284-1114
E-mail: ctinfo@ctpub.com
Web site: http://www.ctpub.com.

C R C Publications, *See* **Faith Alive Christian Resources**

C4 Kids, Orders Addr.: 1220 N. Las Palmas, No. 201, Los Angeles, CA 90038 USA.

Cadmus Communications, a Cenveo Co., Publisher Services Group 136 Carlin Rd., Conklin, NY 13748 USA Tel 607-762-5555; Fax: 607-762-6774.

Cafepress, 127 Brockmoore Dr., East Amherst, NY 14051 USA.

CafePress.com, *(978-1-4148)* 1850 Gateway Dr. Ste. 300, Foster City, CA 94404-4061 USA Toll Free: 877-809-1659
E-mail: mystore@cafepress.com
Web site: http://www.cafepress.com.

Caldwell Letter Service, 4500 S. Kolin Ave., Chicago, IL 60632 USA.

Calico Subscription Co., P.O. Box 640337, San Jose, CA 95164-0337 USA (SAN 285-9173) Tel 408-432-8700; Fax: 408-432-8813; Toll Free: 800-952-2542.

California Princeton Fulfillment Services, 1445 Lower Ferry Rd., Ewing, NJ 08618 USA (SAN 630-639X) Tel 609-883-1759 ext 536; Toll Free: 800-777-4726
E-mail: donnaw@cpfs.pupress.princeton.edu.

Calliope Bks., *(978-0-9620187)* 2115 Chadbourne Ave., Madison, WI 53705 USA (SAN 247-9370) Tel 608-238-9258 Do not confuse with Calliope Books in Santa Barbara, CA
E-mail: wcoleman@facstaff.wisc.edu; calliopebooks@hotmail.com
Web site: http://www.execpc.com/~calliope.

Calvary Chapel Publishing, *(978-0-9676661; 978-0-9700218; 978-1-931667; 978-1-59751)* Div. of Calvary Chapel of Costa Mesa, 3232 W. MacArthur Blvd., Santa Ana, CA 92704 USA (SAN 631-7405) Tel 714-825-9673 (ext. 5501); Fax: 714-641-8201; Toll Free: 800-272-9673
E-mail: jesqueda@cccm.com
Web site: http://www.calvaryd.org; http://www.twft.com; http://www.backtobasicsradio.com.

Calvary Chapel Resources, *(978-0-936728; 978-1-931713; 978-1-932941; 978-1-59751)* Div. of Calvary Chapel Costa Mesa, Orders Addr.: P.O. Box 8000, Costa Mesa, CA 92628 USA (SAN 110-8379) Tel 714-825-9673 Toll Free: 800-272-9673; Edit Addr.: 3232 W. MacArthur Blvd., Santa Ana, CA 92704 USA (SAN 214-2260) Tel 714-825-9673 Toll Free: 800-272-9637
E-mail: cathyr@twft.com
Web site: http://www.twft.com; cccm.com.

Cambium Education, Inc., *(978-0-944584; 978-1-57035; 978-1-59318; 978-1-932282; 978-1-4168; 978-1-60218; 978-1-60697)* 4093 Specialty Pl., Longmont, CO 80504 USA (SAN 243-945X) Tel 303-651-2829; Fax: 303-907-8694; Toll Free: 800-547-6747 (orders only)
E-mail: publishing@sopriswest.com; customerservice@cambiumlearning.com
Web site: http://www.sopriswest.com.

Cambridge Bk. Co., *(978-0-8428)* Div. of Simon & Schuster, Inc., 4350 Equity Dr., Box 249, Columbus, OH 43216 USA (SAN 169-5703) Toll Free: 800-238-5833
Web site: http://www.simonsays.com/.

Cambridge Univ. Pr., *(978-0-521; 978-0-511)* Orders Addr.: 100 Brook Hill Dr., West Nyack, NY 10994-2133 USA (SAN 281-3769) Tel 845-353-7500; Fax: 845-353-4141; Toll Free: 800-872-7423 (orders, returns, credit & accounting); 800-937-9600; Edit Addr.: 32 Avenue of the Americas, New York, NY 10013-2473 USA (SAN 200-206X) Tel 212-924-3900; Fax: 212-691-3239
E-mail: customer_service@cup.org; orders@cup.org; information@cup.org
Web site: http://www.cambridge.org/.

Canyonlands Pubns., *(978-0-9702595)* Orders Addr.: P.O. Box 16175, Bellemont, AZ 86015-6175 USA (SAN 114-3824) Tel 520-779-3888; Fax: 520-779-3778; Toll Free: 800-283-1983; Edit Addr.: 4860 N. Ken Morey, Bellemont, AZ 86015 USA
E-mail: books@infomagic.com.

Cape Cod Scribe, 5 Camelot Ln., Bourne, MA 02532 USA Tel 508-415-1295.

Cape News Co., P.O. Box 568680, Rockledge, FL 32955 USA Tel 407-636-5909.

Capital Business Systems, Div. of Capital Business Service, Orders Addr.: P.O. Box 2088, Napa, CA 94558 USA (SAN 698-3146) Tel 707-252-8844; Fax: 707-252-6368; Edit Addr.: 2033 First St., Napa, CA 94558 USA.

Capital News Co., 961 Palmyra, Jackson, MS 39203 USA Tel 601-355-8341; Fax: 601-352-1343.

Capitol News Agency, P.O. Box 7886, Richmond, VA 23231 USA (SAN 249-2768); 5203 Hatcher St., Richmond, VA 23231-0271 Tel 804-222-7252.

Capper Pr., 1503 SW 42nd, Topeka, KS 66609 USA (SAN 285-8886) Tel 913-274-4324; Fax: 913-274-4305; Toll Free: 800-678-5779 (ext. 4324).

Capstone, *(978-0-7368; 978-0-929895; 978-1-56065; 978-0-7565; 978-1-4048; 978-1-59889; 978-1-4296; 978-1-934338; 978-1-4342; 978-1-936700; 978-1-937412; 978-1-62065; 978-1-4765; 978-1-62370; 978-1-4795; 978-1-62521; 978-1-4914; 978-1-63079; 978-1-4965; 978-1-4966; 978-1-5157; 978-1-5158; 978-1-68436; 978-1-5435; 978-1-9771; 978-1-68446; 978-1-6639; 978-1-6663; 978-1-6690) Div. of Coughlan Companies. LLC, 1905 Lookout Dr., North Mankato, MN 55033 USA Tel 507-385-8215; Fax: 507-388-3752; Orders Addr.: 1710 Roe Crest Dr., North Mankato, MN 56003 USA (SAN 254-1815) Toll Free Fax: 888-262-0705; Toll Free: 800-747-4992; Edit Addr.: 5050 Lincoln Dr Suite 200, Edina, MN 55436 USA Fax: 952-933-2410; Toll Free: 888-517-8977 Do not confuse with Capstone Pr., Inc. in Decatur, IL*
E-mail: customerservice@capstonepub.com
Web site: http://www.capstone-press.com; http://www.capstonepub.com; http://www.capstoneclassroom.com.

Capstone Press, Incorporated, *See* **Capstone**

Cardinal Publishing Group, 2402 N. Shadeland Ave., Suite A, Indianapolis, IN 46219 USA Tel 317-352-8200; Fax: 317-352-8202
E-mail: tdoherty@cardinalpub.com
Web site: http://ww.cardinalpub.com.

Cardinal Pubs. Group, 2402 N. Shadeland Ave. Ste. A, Indianapolis, IN 46219-1746 USA (SAN 631-7936)
E-mail: tdoherty@in.net.

Cards Bks. N Things, 1446 St., Rd. 2 West, La Porte, IN 46350 USA (SAN 159-8295).

Carlex, Orders Addr.: 1545 W. Hamlin, Rochester Hills, MI 48309 USA (SAN 631-5615) Tel 810-852-5422; Fax: 810-852-7142.

Carolina Biological Supply Co., *(978-0-89278; 978-1-4350)* 2700 York Rd., Burlington, NC 27215-3398 USA (SAN 249-2784) Tel 336-584-0381; Fax: 910-584-3399; Toll Free Fax: 800-222-7112; Toll Free: 800-334-5551
E-mail: carolina@carolina.com
Web site: http://www.carolina.com.

Carolina Cassette Distributors, Orders Addr.: P.O. Box 429, New Bern, NC 28560 USA (SAN 110-8395) Fax: 919-638-1291; Edit Addr.: 2600 Oaks Rd., New Bern, NC 28560 USA (SAN 659-2155) Tel 919-638-5583.

Carolina News Co., Orders Addr.: P.O. Box 10, Fayetteville, NC 28302 USA; Edit Addr.: 245 Tillinghast St., Fayetteville, NC 28301 USA Tel 910-483-4135.

Carson-Dellosa Publishing Company, Incorporated, *See* **Carson-Dellosa Publishing, LLC**

Carson-Dellosa Publishing, LLC, *(978-0-88724; 978-1-57156; 978-1-57332; 978-1-59441; 978-1-60022; 978-1-60418; 978-1-936022; 978-1-936023; 978-1-936024; 978-0-9823625; 978-0-9823626; 978-0-9823627; 978-0-692-00200-1; 978-1-60996; 978-1-62057; 978-1-62223; 978-1-62399; 978-1-62442; 978-1-62648; 978-1-4838) Orders Addr.: P.O. Box 35665, Greensboro, NC 27425 USA Tel 336-632-0084; Fax: 336-808-3249; Toll Free: 800-321-0943*
Web site: http://www.carsondellosa.com.

Carswell, Div. of The Thomson Corp., 28 Glen Ave., Millburn, NJ 07041 USA Toll Free Fax: 973-313-1245; Toll Free: 888-307-1355
E-mail: steve.roses@carswell.com.

Casa Del Libro, Orders Addr.: P.O. Box 3853, La Mesa, CA 91944-3853 USA.

Cascade News, Inc., 1055 Commerce Ave., Longview, WA 98632 USA (SAN 169-8761) Tel 360-425-2450; Fax: 360-425-2451.

Casemate Academic, *(978-0-9774094; 978-1-935488)* Orders Addr.: P.O. Box 511, Oakville, CT 06779 USA (SAN 630-9461) Tel 860-945-9329; Fax: 860-945-9468; Toll Free: 800-791-9354; Edit Addr.: 20 Main St., Oakville, CT 06779 USA
E-mail: queries@dbbconline.com
Web site: http://www.oxbowbooks.com.

Casemate Pubs. & Bk. Distributors, LLC, *(978-0-9711709; 978-1-932033; 978-1-935149; 978-1-61200;*

Wholesaler & Distributor Name Index

978-1-952715; 978-1-63624; 978-1-955041; 978-9-88857) Orders Addr.: 1950 Lawrence Rd., Havertown, PA 19083 USA; 22883 Quicksilver Dr., Herndon, VA 20166 (SAN 631-9386) Tel 703-661-1500; Edit Addr.: 180 Varick St. Suite 816, New York, NY 10014 USA
E-mail: casemate@casematepublishing.com
Web site: http://www.casematepublishing.com.

Casino Distributors, Orders Addr.: P.O. Box 849, Pleasantville, NJ 08232 USA (SAN 169-457X) Tel 609-646-4165; Fax: 609-645-0152; Edit Addr.: 10 Canale Dr., Pleasantville, NJ 08234 USA (SAN 249-3276).

Casper Magazine Agency, P.O. Box 2340, Casper, WY 82602 USA (SAN 159-8325).

Casscom Media, *(978-1-930034; 978-1-936081; 978-1-62758)* 6000 Industrial Dr., Greenville, TX 75402 USA Tel 903-455-2555; Fax: 903-455-4448; Toll Free: 800-974-1555
E-mail: sue@casscommedia.com; kathy@casscomedia.com
Web site: http://www.casscommedia.com.

Cassette Book Company, *See* **Audio Bk. Co.**

Cassette Communications, Incorporated, *See* **Casscom Media**

Castlebridge Distribution, 115 Bluebill Dr., Savannah, GA 31419 USA Toll Free: 888-300-1961 (phone/fax)
E-mail: orders@castlebridgedistribution.com.

Catholic Bk. Publishing Corp., *(978-0-89942; 978-0-9623410; 978-1-878718; 978-1-933066; 978-1-937913; 978-1-941243; 978-1-947070; 978-1-948843; 978-1-948844; 978-1-953152; 978-1-958237)* 77 West End Rd., Totowa, NJ 07512-1405 USA (SAN 204-3432) Tel 973-890-2400; Fax: 973-890-2410; Toll Free: 800-892-6657
E-mail: resurpress@aol.com
Web site: http://www.catholicbkpub.com.

Catholic Bookrack Service, 700 E. Elm St., La Grange, IL 60525 USA (SAN 169-2178) Tel 708-482-0044; Fax: 708-482-9644.

Catholic Literary Guild, Inc., 200 Hamilton Ave., White Plains, NY 10601 USA (SAN 285-8908) Tel 914-949-4444.

Catholic Univ. of America Pr., *(978-0-8132; 978-1-949822)* Orders Addr.: c/o Hopkins Fulfillment Services, P.O. Box 50370, Baltimore, MD 21211-4370 USA (SAN 203-6304) Tel 410-516-6953; Fax: 410-516-6998; Toll Free: 800-537-5487; Edit Addr.: 620 Michigan Ave., NE, Washington, DC 20064 USA (SAN 203-6290) Tel 202-319-5052; Fax: 202-319-4985
E-mail: cua-press@cua.edu
Web site: http://cuapress.cua.edu/.

Catweasel Productions, *See* **Ars Obscura**

Cave of the Winds, P.O. Box 826, Manitou Springs, CO 80829 USA Tel 719-685-5444
Web site: http://www.caveofthewinds.com.

Caxton Pr., *(978-0-87004)* Div. of Caxton Printers. Ltd., 312 Main St., Caldwell, ID 83605-3299 USA (SAN 201-9698) Tel 208-459-7421; Fax: 208-459-7450; Toll Free: 800-657-6465
E-mail: publish@caxtonprinters.com; sgipson@caxtonpress.com
Web site: http://www.caxtonpress.com.

Caxton Printers, Limited, *See* **Caxton Pr.**

CBLS Pubs., *(978-1-878907; 978-1-59529)* 119 Brentwood St., Marietta, OH 45750 USA (SAN 169-5517) Tel 740-374-9458; Fax: 740-374-8029
E-mail: cbls@cbls.com
Web site: http://www.cbls.com.

CD Baby, Orders Addr.: 5925 NE 80th Ave., Portland, OR 97218-2891 USA Tel 503-595-3000; Fax: 503-296-2370; Toll Free: 800-289-6923 (CD orders only)
E-mail: cdbaby@cdbaby.com
Web site: http://www.cdbaby.com.

CD Distributing, Inc., P.O. Box 4965, Missoula, MT 59806-4965 USA (SAN 169-4367) Fax: 406-454-0415.

Cedar Fort, Inc./CFI Distribution, *(978-0-88290; 978-0-934126; 978-1-55517; 978-1-59955; 978-1-4621)* 2373 West 700 South, Springville, UT 84663 USA (SAN 170-2858) Tel 801-489-4084; Fax: 801-489-1097; Toll Free: 800-759-2665
E-mail: skybook@cedarfort.com
Web site: http://www.cedarfort.com.

Cedar Graphics, *See* **Igram Pr.**

Cengage Gale, *(978-0-13; 978-0-7876; 978-0-8103; 978-0-936474; 978-1-57302; 978-1-878623; 978-1-59413; 978-1-59414; 978-1-59415; 978-1-4144; 978-1-4205; 978-1-59722; 978-1-4328; 978-1-5358)* Subs. of Cengage Learning, Orders Addr.: P.O. Box 9187, Farmington Hills, MI 48333-9187 USA Toll Free Fax: 800 414 5043; Toll Free: 800 877 4253; Edit Addr.: 27500 Drake Rd., Farmington Hills, MI 48331 USA (SAN 213-4373) Tel 248-699-8495 Toll Free: 800-877-4253; a/o Wheeler Publishing, 295 Kennedy Memorial Dr., Waterville, ME 04901 Toll Free: 800 223 1244
E-mail: gale.salesassistance@thomson.com
Web site: http://www.gale.com.

CENGAGE Learning, Orders Addr.: 10650 Toebben Dr., Independence, KY 41051 USA (SAN 200-2213) Tel 859-525-6620; Fax: 859-525-0978; Toll Free Fax: 800-487-8488; Toll Free: 800-354-9706
Web site: http://www.cengage.com/.

Centennial Pubns., 1400 Ash Dr., Fort Collins, CO 80521 USA (SAN 630-494X) Tel 970-493-2041 Do not confuse with Centennial Pubns., Grand Junction, CO.

Central Arizona Distributing, 4932 W. Pasadena Ave., Glendale, AZ 85301 USA (SAN 170-6128) Tel 602-939-6511.

Central Coast Bks., 1195 Al Sereno Ln., Los Osos, CA 93402-4413 USA Tel 805-534-0307 (phone/fax)
E-mail: ccbooks@charter.net.

Central European Univ. Pr., *(978-1-85866; 978-963-9116; 978-963-9241; 978-963-7326; 978-963-9776; 978-1-61055; 978-615-5053; 978-615-5225; 978-615-5211; 978-963-386)* Orders Addr.: 10335 Kensington Pkwy. Ste. A, Kensington, MD 20895 USA Tel 301-933-0607 All Inquiries & Orders; Toll Free Fax: 301-933-0615 Orders; c/o Books International, Russia Online Bookstore PO Box 558, Kensington, MD 20895; Edit Addr.: Október 6 utca 14, Budapest, 1051 HUN Tel 36-1-327-3000; Fax: 36-1-327-3183
E-mail: books@russia-on-line.com; ceupress@ceu.hu
Web site: http://www.ceupress.com; http://www.Russia-on-line.com.

Central Illinois Periodicals, P.O. Box 3757, Bloomington, IL 61701 USA (SAN 630-8945) Tel 309-829-9405.

Central Kentucky News Distributing Company, *See* **Anderson-Austin News Co., LLC**

Central News of Sandusky, 5716 McCartney Rd., Sandusky, OH 44870-1538 USA (SAN 169-684X).

Central Programs, 802 N. 41st St., Bethany, MO 64424 USA Tel 660-425-7777.

Central South Christian Distribution, 3730 Vulcan Dr., Nashville, TN 37211 USA (SAN 631-2543) Tel 615-833-5960; Toll Free Fax: 800-220-0194; Toll Free: 800-757-0856.

Centralia News Co., 232 E. Broadway, Centralia, IL 62801 USA (SAN 159-8341) Tel 618-532-5601.

CentroLibros de Puerto Rico, Inc., Santa Rosa Unit, Bayamon, PR 00960 USA (SAN 631-1245) Tel 787-275-0460; Fax: 787-275-0360.

Century Bk. Distribution, 814 Boon, Traverse City, MI 49686 USA Tel 231-933-6405 (phone/fax).

Century Pr., *(978-0-9659417)* Div. of Conservatory of American Letters, P.O. Box 298, Thomaston, ME 04861 USA Tel 207-354-0998; Fax: 207-354-8953 Do not confuse with companies with the same name in Arroyo Seco, NM, Oklahoma City, OK
E-mail: cal@americanletters.org
Web site: http://www.americanletters.org.

Ceramic Book & Literature Service, *See* **CBLS Pubs.**

Chain Sales Marketing, Inc., *(978-1-55836)* 149 Madison Ave., Suite 810, New York, NY 10016 USA (SAN 245-1328) Tel 212-696-4230; Fax: 212-696-4391.

Chambers Kingfisher Graham Publishers, Incorporated, *See* **Larousse Kingfisher Chambers, Inc.**

Champaign-Urbana News Agency, Orders Addr.: P.O. Box 793, Champaign, IL 61824 USA (SAN 630-8953) Tel 217-351-7047; Edit Addr.: 503 Kenyon, Champaign, IL 61820 USA.

Charisma Media, *(978-0-88419; 978-0-930525; 978-1-59185; 978-1-59979; 978-1-61638; 978-1-62136; 978-1-62998; 978-1-62999; 978-1-63641)* Div. of Creation House Pr., 600 Rinehart Rd., Lake Mary, FL 32746 USA (SAN 677-5640) Tel 407-333-0600; Fax: 407-333-7100; Toll Free: 800-283-8494
Web site: http://www.charismamedia.com/.

Charlynn Publishing Co., Inc., 4152 E. Fifth St., Tucson, AZ 85711 USA.

Checker Distributors, 400 W. Dussel Dr. Ste. B, Maumee, OH 43537-1636 USA (SAN 631-1431) Toll Free: 800-537-1060.

Chelsea Green Publishing, *(978-0-930031; 978-1-890132; 978-1-931498; 978-1-933392; 978-1-60358; 978-1-64502)* 85 N. Main St., Suite 120, White River Junction, VT 05001 USA
E-mail: info@chelseagreen.com
Web site: http://www.chelseagreen.com.

Cheng & Tsui Co., *(978-0-88727; 978-0-917056; 978-1-62291)* 25 W. St., Boston, MA 02111-1213 USA (SAN 169-3387)
E-mail: service@cheng-tsui.com
Web site: http://www.cheng-tsui.com.

Cherry Lake Publishing, *(978-1-60279; 978-1-61080; 978-1-62431; 978-1-62753; 978-1-63137; 978-1-63188; 978-1-63362; 978-1-63470; 978-1-63471; 978-1-63472; 978-1-5341; 978-1-6689)* 1215 Overidgeview Ct., Ann Arbor, MI 48103 USA Tel 248-705-2045; 1750 Northway Dr., Suite 101, North Mankato, MN 56003 (SAN 858-9275) Tel 866-918-3956; Toll Free Fax: 866-489-6490; 2395 S. Huron Prkwy Ste. 200, Ann Arbor, MI 48104
E-mail: customerservice@cherrylakepublishing.com; benmondloch@me.com; lois.hume@sleepingbearpress.com
Web site: http://cherrylakepublishing.com; www.sleepingbearpress.com.

Chesbro Music Co., 327 Broadway, Idaho Falls, ID 83403 USA (SAN 631-0850) Tel 208-522-8691.

Chicago Distribution Ctr., Orders Addr.: 11030 S. Langley Ave., Chicago, IL 60628 USA (SAN 630-6047) Tel 773-702-7000 (International); Fax: 773-702-7212 (International); Toll Free Fax: 800-621-8476 (USA/Canada); Toll Free: 800-621-2736 (USA/Canada); 800-621-8471 (credit & collections)
E-mail: custserv@press.uchicago.edu; orders@press.uchicago.edu
Web site: http://www.press.uchicago.edu; http://www.press.uchicago.edu/presswide/cdc/.

Chicago Review Pr., Inc., *(978-0-89733; 978-0-912777; 978-0-913705; 978-0-914090; 978-0-914091; 978-0-915864; 978-1-55652; 978-1-56976; 978-1-61373; 978-1-61374; 978-1-64160; 979-8-89068)* 814 N. Franklin St., Chicago, IL 60610 USA (SAN 213-5744) Tel 312-337-0747; Toll Free: 800-888-4741 (orders only)
E-mail: frontdesk@chicagoreviewpress.com; orders@ipgbook.com
Web site: http://www.ipgbook.com; http://www.chicagoreviewpress.com.

Chico News Agency, P.O. Box 690, Chico, CA 95927 USA (SAN 168-9533) Tel 530-895-1000; Fax: 530-895-0158.

Children's Bookfair Co., The, 700 E. Grand Ave., Chicago, IL 60611-3472 USA (SAN 630-6705) Tel 312-477-7323; 837 W. Altgeld St., Chicago, IL 60614 (SAN 630-6713).

Children's Plus, Inc., 1387 Dutch Ameican, Beecher, IL 60401 USA Tel 708-946-4100; Fax: 709-946-4199
E-mail: danw@childrensplusinc.com
Web site: http://www.childrensplusinc.com.

Child's World, Inc, The, *(978-0-89565; 978-0-913778; 978-1-56766; 978-1-59296; 978-1-60253; 978-1-60954; 978-1-60973; 978-1-61473; 978-1-62323; 978-1-62687; 978-1-63143; 978-1-63407; 978-1-5038)* Orders Addr.: 21735 E Idyllwilde Dr, Parker, CO 80138 USA (SAN 992-4981) Tel 800-599-7323; Fax: 888-320-2329
E-mail: info@childsworld.com
Web site: https://childsworld.com.

China Books & Periodicals, Inc., *(978-0-8351)* 360 Swift Ave., Suite 48, South San Francisco, CA 94080 USA (SAN 145-0557) Tel 650-872-7718; 650-872-7076; Fax: 650-872-7808
E-mail: chris@chinabooks.com
Web site: http://www.chinabooks.com.

China Cultural Ctr., 3535 Dunn Dr. Apt. 303, Los Angeles, CA 90034-4977 USA (SAN 111-8161).

China House Gallery, China Institute in America, *See* **China Institute Gallery, China Institute in America**

China Institute Gallery, China Institute in America, *(978-0-9654270; 978-0-9774054; 978-0-9893776; 978-0-692-93086-1; 979-8-218-13838-7)* Div. of China Institute in America, 100 Washington St., New York, NY 10006 USA (SAN 110-8743) Tel 212-744-8181; Fax: 212-628-4159
E-mail: gallery@chinainstitute.org
Web site: http://www.chinainstitute.org.

Chinasprout, Inc., *(978-0-9707332; 978-0-9747302; 978-0-9820227; 978-1-945947)* 110 W. 32nd St., Flr. 6, New York, NY 10001-3205 USA Toll Free: 800-644-2611
E-mail: info@chinasprout.com
Web site: http://www.chinasprout.com.

Chinese American Co., 44 Kneeland St., Boston, MA 02111 USA (SAN 159-7248) Fax: 617-451-2318.

Christian Bk. Distributors, Orders Addr.: P.O. Box 7000, Peabody, MA 01961 USA (SAN 630-5458) Tel 978-977-5000; Fax: 978-977-5010
Web site: http://www.christianbook.com.

Christian Literature Crusade, Incorporated, *See* **CLC Pubns.**

Christian Printing Service, 4861 Chino Ave., Chino, CA 91710-5132 USA (SAN 108-2647) Tel 714-871-5200.

Christian Publishing Network, *(978-0-9628406)* P.O. Box 405, Tulsa, OK 74101 USA (SAN 631-2756) Tel 918-296-4673 (918-296-HOPE); Toll Free: 888-688-8125
E-mail: vpsales@olp.net.

christianaudio, *(978-1-59644; 978-1-61045; 978-1-61843; 978-1-63389; 978-1-68366; 978-1-5459)* 6 Business Pk. Rd, Old Saybrook, CT 06475 USA
E-mail: amclaren@tantor.com
Web site: http://christianaudio.com.

Chronicle Bks. LLC, *(978-0-8118; 978-0-87701; 978-0-938491; 978-1-4521; 978-1-7972)* Div. of The McEvoy Group, Orders Addr.: 680 Second St., San Francisco, CA 94107 USA (SAN 202-165X) Tel 415-537-4200; Fax: 415-537-4460; Toll Free Fax: 800-286-9471; Toll Free: 800-759-0190 (orders only); Edit Addr.: 3 Center Plaza, Boston, MA 2108 USA
E-mail: order.desk@hbgusa.com; customer.service@hbgusa.com
Web site: http://www.chroniclebooks.com.

Chulain Publishing Corp., Orders Addr.: 8241 Sweet Water Rd., Lone Tree, CO 80124-3017 USA.

Church Hymnal Corporation, *See* **Church Publishing, Inc.**

Church of Scientology Information Service-Pubns., *(978-0-915598)* c/o Bridge Pubns., Inc., 1414 N. Catalina, Los Angeles, CA 90029 USA (SAN 268-9774).

Church Publishing, Inc., *(978-0-89869; 978-1-59627; 978-1-59628; 978-1-64065; 978-1-954184)* Orders Addr.: 19 E. 34th St., New York, NY 10016 USA (SAN 857-0140) Tel 212-592-1800; Fax: 212-779-3392; Toll Free: 800-242-1918; Edit Addr.: 19 East 34th st, New York, NY 10016 USA
E-mail: rmasteller@cpg.org; churchpublishingorders@pbd.com; lort@cpg.org; lsimonello@cpg.org
Web site: http://www.churchpublishing.org.

Church Richards Co., 1001 Roosevelt Rd., Westchester, IL 60154 USA (SAN 285-8975) Toll Free: 800-323-0227.

Circa Pubns., Inc., 415 Fifth Ave., Pelham, NY 10803-0408 USA (SAN 169-6122) Tel 914-738-5570; Toll Free: 800-582-5952 (orders only).

Circle Bk. Service, Inc., *(978-0-87397)* P.O. Box 626, Tomball, TX 77377 USA (SAN 158-2526) Tel 281-255-6824; Fax: 281-255-8158; Toll Free: 800-227-1591
E-mail: orders@circlebook.com
Web site: http://www.circlebook.com.

City News Agency, Orders Addr.: P.O. Box 561129, Charlotte, NC 28256-1129 USA (SAN 169-782X); Edit Addr.: P.O. Box 2069, Newark, OH 43055 USA (SAN 169-6947); 220 Cherry Ave., NE, Canton, OH 44702-1198 (SAN 169-6602); 303 E. Lasalle St., South Bend, IN 46617 (SAN 159-9992); 417 S. McKinnley, Harrisburg, IL 62946 (SAN 169-1961).

Clarks Out of Town News, 303 S. Andrews Ave., Fort Lauderdale, FL 33301 USA (SAN 159-8384) Tel 954-467-1543.

Class Pubns., Inc., *(978-0-913031)* 71 Bartholomew Ave., Hartford, CT 06106 USA (SAN 283-0302) Tel 860-951-9200.

Classroom Reading Service, P.O. Box 2708, Santa Fe Spgs, CA 90670-0708 USA (SAN 131-3959) Toll Free: 800-422-6657
E-mail: crsbooks@aol.com.

CLC Pubns., *(978-0-87508; 978-1-936143; 978-1-61958)* Div. of CLC Ministries International, Orders Addr.: P.O. Box 1449, Fort Washington, PA 19034-8449 USA Tel 215-542-1242; Fax: 215-542-7580; Toll Free: 800-659-1240; 701 Pennsylvania Ave., Fort Washington, PA 19034 (SAN 169-7358) Tel 215-542-1242; Fax: 215-542-7580; Toll Free: 800-659-1240
E-mail: orders@clcpublications.com; churd@clcpublications.com; dfessenden@clcpublications.com
Web site: http://www.clcusa.org; http://www.clcpublications.com.

CLEARVUE/eav, Inc., 6465 N. Avondale Ave., Chicago, IL 60631-1996 USA (SAN 204-1669) Tel 773-775-9433; Fax: 773-775-9855; Toll Free Fax: 800-444-9855 (24 Hours); Toll Free: 800-253-2788 (8:00 am to 4:30 pm Central Time M-F); P.O. Box 2284, S Burlington, VT 05407-2287
E-mail: custserv@clearvue.com
Web site: http://www.clearvue.com.

Closet Case Bks., P.O. Box 16116, Saint Paul, MN 55116 USA
Web site: http://www.closetcasebooks.com.

Clover Bk. Service, 1220 S. Monroe St., Covingtons, LA 70433-3639 USA (SAN 106-472X) Tel 504-875-0038.

Cobblestone Publishing Co., *(978-0-382; 978-0-942389; 978-0-9607638)* Div. of Cricket Magazine Group, 30 Grove St., Suite C, Peterborough, NH 03458 USA (SAN 237-9937) Tel 603-924-7209; Fax: 603-924-7380; Toll Free: 800-821-0115; P.O. Box 487, Effingham, IL 62401
E-mail: custsvc@cobblestone.mv.com
Web site: http://www.cobblestonepub.com.

Cogan Bks., *(978-0-940688)* P.O. Box 579, Hudson, OH 44236-0579 USA (SAN 168-9649) Toll Free: 800-733-3630.

Cokesbury, 2222 Rosa L. Parks Blvd., Nashville, TN 37228 USA (SAN 200-6863) Tel 615-749-6409; Toll Free: 800-672-1789
Web site: http://www.cokesbury.com.

Cold Cut Comics Distribution, 475-D Stockton Ave., San Jose, CA 95126 USA (SAN 631-6409) Tel 408-293-3844; Fax: 408-293-6645
E-mail: comics@coldcut.com
Web site: http://www.coldcut.com.

Cole, Bill Enterprises, Inc., P.O. Box 60, Randolph, MA 02368-0060 USA (SAN 685-6373) Tel 617-986-2653.

Collector Bks., *(978-0-89145; 978-1-57432; 978-1-60460)* Div. of Schroeder Publishing Co., Inc., Orders Addr.: P.O. Box 3009, Paducah, KY 42003 USA (SAN 157-5368) Tel 270-898-6211; 270-898-7903; Fax: 270-898-8890; 270-898-1173; Toll Free: 800-626-5420 (orders only); Edit Addr.: 5801 Kentucky Dam Rd., Paducah, KY 42003 USA (SAN 200-7479)
E-mail: Info@collectorbooks.com; info@AQSquilt.com
Web site: http://www.collectorbooks.com; http://www.americanquilter.com/.

College Bk. Co. of California, Inc., 181 W. Orangethorpe Ave. Ste. C, Placentia, CA 92870-6931 USA (SAN 269-0802).

Collegedale Distributors, *See* **Tree of Life Midwest**

Colonial Williamsburg Foundation, *(978-0-87935; 978-0-910412)* P.O. Box 3532, Williamsburg, VA 23187-3532 USA (SAN 128-4630) Fax: 757-565-8999 (orders only); Toll Free: 800-446-9240 (orders only)
Web site: http://www.colonialwilliamsburg.com.

Colorado Periodical Distributor, Inc., 1227 Pitkin St., Grand Junction, CO 81502 USA Tel 970-242-3865; Fax: 970-242-3760.

Colorado State University, Center for Literary Publishing, *See* **Ctr. for Literary Publishing, Colorado State Univ.**

Columbia County News Agency, Inc., 49 Bender Blvd., Ghent, NY 12075-3327 USA (SAN 169-5339).

Columbia Univ. Pr., *(978-0-231)* Orders Addr.: 61 W. 62nd St., New York, NY 10023-7015 USA (SAN 212-2480) Toll Free Fax: 800-944-1844; Toll Free: 800-944-8648 x 6240 (orders); Edit Addr.: 61 W. 62nd St., New York, NY 10023 USA (SAN 212-2472) Tel 212-459-0600; Fax: 212-459-3678; 387 Pk. Ave., S., New York, NY 10016; 1094 Flex Dr., Jackson, TN 38301
E-mail: cupbooks@columbia.edu
Web site: http://www.columbia.edu/cu/cup.

Comag Marketing Group, 1790 Broadway, Suite 401, New York, NY 10019 USA (SAN 169-5800) Tel 212-841-8365; Fax: 212-977-9401.

Comics Hawaii Distributors, *See* **Hobbies Hawaii Distributors**

Common Ground Distributors, Inc., Orders Addr.: P.O. Box 25249, Asheville, NC 28813-1249 USA Toll Free: 800-654-0626; Edit Addr.: 115 Fairview Rd., Asheville, NC 28803-2307 USA (SAN 113-8006) Tel 828-274-5575; Fax: 828-274-1955
E-mail: orders@comground.com.

Communication Service Corporation, *See* **Gryphon Hse., Inc.**

Communications Technology, Inc., *(978-0-918232)* P.O. Box 209, Rindge, NH 03461 USA (SAN 159-8198) Tel 603-899-6957.

Complete Book & Media Supply, 1200 Toro Grande Dr., Suite 200, Cedar Park, TX 78613 USA Fax: 512-616-0400; 512-616-0410; Toll Free: 800-986-1775
E-mail: books@completebook.com; bradm@completebook.com.

Computer & Technical Bks., 6338 Ranchview Ln., N., Osseo, MN 55311-3924 USA (SAN 630-8120).

Concordia Publishing Hse., *(978-0-570; 978-0-7586)* Subs. of Lutheran Church Missouri Synod, 3558 S. Jefferson Ave., Saint Louis, MO 63118-3968 USA (SAN 202-1781) Tel 314-268-1000; Fax: 314-268-1360; Toll Free Fax: 800-490-9889 (orders only); Toll Free: 800-325-3040 (orders only); 800-325-0191
E-mail: cphorder@cph.org
Web site: http://www.cph.org.

Conde Nast Pubns., Inc., *(978-1-878494)* Four Times Sq., 20th Flr., New York, NY 10036 USA (SAN 285-905X) Tel 212-880-8800; Fax: 212-880-8289.

Connecticut River Pr., *(978-0-9706573)* 111 Holmes Rd., Newington, CT 06111 USA Tel 860-666-1200; 203-254-0147; Fax: 860-594-6037
E-mail: wolftalk@ziplink.net.

Consortium Bk. Sales & Distribution, Div. of Ingram Content Group, Orders Addr.: 1094 Flex Dr., Jackson, TN 38301-5070 USA; Edit Addr.: 34 13th Ave NE, Suite 100, Minneapolis, MN 55413-1007 USA (SAN 200-6049) Toll Free: 800-283-3572 (orders)
E-mail: info@cbsd.com
Web site: http://www.cbsd.com/.

ConsuLogic Consulting Services, 276 Longhouse Ln., Slingerlands, NY 12159-3012 USA Tel 518-452-9228; Fax: 518-452-9216.

Contemporary Arts Pr., *(978-0-931818)* Div. of La Mamelle, Inc., P.O. Box 3123, San Francisco, CA 94119-3123 USA (SAN 170-5423) Tel 415-282-0286.

Continental Bk. Co., Inc., *(978-0-9626800)* Eastern Div., 80-00 Cooper Ave., Bldg. No. 29, Glendale, NY 11385 USA (SAN 169-5436) Tel 718-326-0560; Fax: 718-326-4276; Toll Free: 800-364-0350; Western Div., 625 E. 70th Ave., No. 5, Denver, CO 80229 (SAN 630-2882) Tel 303-289-1761; Fax: 303-289-1764
E-mail: hola@continentalbook.com; esl@continentalbook.com; bonjour@continentalbook.com; tag@continentalbook.com
Web site: http://www.continentalbook.com.

Continental Enterprises Group, Inc. (CEG), Orders Addr.: 108 Red Row St., Easley, SC 29640-2820 USA (SAN 631-0915)
E-mail: ContactUs@centerprisesgrp.com.

Continental Sales, 213 W. Main St., Barrington, IL 60010-0010 USA Tel 847-381-6530.

Cook, David C., *(978-0-7814; 978-0-88207; 978-0-89191; 978-0-89693; 978-0-912692; 978-1-55513; 978-1-56476; 978-1-4347)* 4050 Lee Vance View, Colorado Springs, CO 80918 USA (SAN 206-0981) Tel 719-536-0100; Fax: 719-536-3244; Toll Free: 800-708-5550; 800-323-7543 (Customer Service)
E-mail: wendi.lord@davidccook.com
Web site: http://www.davidccook.com.

Cook, David C. Publishing Company, *See* **Cook, David C.**

Cookbook Marketplace, The, Div. Southwestern Publishing Group, Inc, 2451 Atrium Way, Nashville, TN 37214 USA Fax: 615-391-2815; Toll Free: 800-269-6839
E-mail: info@frpbooks.com
Web site: http://www.cookbookmarketplace.com.

Coos Bay Distributors, 131 N. Schoneman St., Coos Bay, OR 97420 USA (SAN 169-7064) Tel 541-888-5912.

Copper Island News, 1010 Wright St., Marquette, MI 49855-1834 USA (SAN 169-3824).

Copyright Clearance Ctr., Inc., 222 Rosewood Dr, Danvers, MA 01923 USA Tel 978-750-8400; Fax: 978-750-4343
Web site: http://www.copyright.com.

Cornell Univ. Pr., *(978-0-8014; 978-0-87546; 978-1-5017)* Orders Addr.: P.O. Box 6525, Ithaca, NY 14851 USA (SAN 281-5680) Tel 607-277-2211; Toll Free Fax: 800-688-2877; Toll Free: 800-666-2211; Edit Addr.: Sage House, 512 E. State St., Ithaca, NY 14851 USA (SAN 202-1862) Tel 607-277-2338
E-mail: cupressinfo@cornell.edu; orders@nbninternational.com; cupress-sales@cornell.edu
Web site: http://www.cornellpress.cornell.edu.

Cornerstone Publishing & Distribution, Inc., *(978-1-929281)* P.O. Box 490, Bountiful, UT 84011-0490 USA Tel 801-295-9451; Fax: 801-295-0196; Toll Free: 800-453-0812
E-mail: rrhopkins@utah-inter.net.

Coronet Bks., *(978-0-89563)* 33 Ashley Dr., Schwenksville, PA 19473 USA (SAN 210-6043) Tel 484-919-6486; Fax: 215-717-4655 Do not confuse with Coronet Bks. & Pubns., Eagle Point, OR
E-mail: ronsmolin@earthlink.net; order@coronetbooks.com
Web site: http://www.coronetbooks.com.

Country News Distributors, Div. of Bakers, Inc., P.O. Box 1258, Brattleboro, VT 05302-1258 USA (SAN 169-8575).

Countryside Bks., *(978-0-88453)* 2430 Estancia Blvd. Ste. 100, Clearwater, FL 33761-2644 USA (SAN 107-4415).

Coutts Information Services, Div. of ProQuest LLC, Orders Addr.: 7309 Innovation BLVD, Fort Wayne, IN 46818 USA (SAN 920-6779); Edit Addr.: 7309 Innovation BLVD, Fort Wayne, IN 46818 USA (SAN 169-5401) Toll Free: 800-263-1686.

Coutts Library Service, Incorporated, *See* **Coutts Information Services**

Cove Distributors, 6325 Erdman Ave., Baltimore, MD 21205 USA (SAN 158-9814) Toll Free: 800-622-5656 (Orders).

Cowley Distributing, Inc., 732 Heisinger Rd., Jefferson City, MO 65109 USA (SAN 169-426X) Tel 573-636-6511; Fax: 573-636-6262; Toll Free: 800-346-5950 (orders).

Cox Subscriptions, Inc., 201 Village Rd., Shallotte, NC 28470 USA (SAN 107-0061) Tel 800-571-9554; Fax: 877-755-6274; Toll Free: 800-553-8088
E-mail: dknox@wtcox.com
Web site: http://www.wtcox.com.

CQ Products, 507 Industrial St., Waverly, IA 50677 USA (SAN 631-5216) Tel 319-352-2086; Fax: 319-352-5338
E-mail: gifts@cqproducts.com
Web site: http://www.cqproducts.com.

Crabtree Publishing, *(978-0-937070)* P.O. Box 3451, Federal Way, WA 98063 USA (SAN 214-3615) Tel 253-925-9300; 59Th Flr., New York, NY 10118 Do not confuse with Crabtree Publishing Co. in New York, NY.

Cram, George F. Co., Inc., *(978-0-87448)* 301 S. LaSalle St., P.O. Box 426, Indianapolis, IN 46201 USA (SAN 204-2630) Tel 317-635-5564; Fax: 317-635-2720; Toll Free: 800-227-4199
E-mail: cram-services@iquest.net.

Cranbury International, Orders Addr.: 7 Clarendon Ave., Suite 2, Montpelier, VT 05602 USA.

CRC Pr. LLC, *(978-0-8493; 978-0-87762; 978-0-87819; 978-0-935184; 978-1-56676; 978-1-57491; 978-1-58488; 978-1-58716; 978-1-4200; 978-1-4398; 978-1-4665; 978-1-4822; 978-1-4987; 978-1-351)* Subs. of Taylor & Francis, Inc., Orders Addr.: 6000 Broken Sound Pkwy., NW, Ste. 300, Boca Raton, FL 33487 USA Tel 800-272-7737 Toll Free Fax: 800-374-3401; Edit Addr.: 270 Madison Ave., New York, NY 10016 USA
E-mail: orders@crcpress.com; Theresa.Gutierrez@taylorandfrancis.com
Web site: http://www.crcpress.com; http://www.taylorandfrancis.com.

CreateSpace Independent Publishing Platform, *(978-1-58898; 978-1-5423; 978-1-59109; 978-1-59456; 978-1-59457; 978-1-4196; 978-1-4348; 978-1-4382; 978-1-4392; 978-1-4404; 978-1-4414; 978-1-4421; 978-1-61550; 978-1-4486; 978-1-4495; 978-1-4499; 978-1-4505; 978-1-4515; 978-1-4528; 978-1-4536; 978-1-4537; 978-1-4538; 978-1-4563; 978-1-4564; 978-1-4565; 978-1-61789; 978-1-4609; 978-1-4610; 978-1-4611; 978-1-61396; 978-1-61397; 978-1-4635; 978-1-4636; 978-1-4637; 978-1-4662; 978-1-4663; 978-1-4664; 978-1-61914; 978-1-61915; 978-1-61916; 978) Orders Addr.: 4900 LaCross Rd., North Charleston, SC 29406 USA (SAN 255-2132) Tel 843-225-4700 (Ask for ordering department); Fax: 843-577-7506; Toll Free: 866-308-6235; 4900 LaCross Rd., North Charleston, SC 29406*
E-mail: info@createspace.com
Web site: http://www.createspace.com.

Creative Co., The, *(978-0-87191; 978-0-88682; 978-0-89812; 978-1-56660; 978-1-56846; 978-1-58341; 978-1-60818; 978-1-62832; 978-1-68277; 978-1-64000; 978-1-64026; 979-8-88989)* 2140 Howard Drive West, North Mankato, MN 56003 USA Tel 507-388-6273; Fax: 507-388-4797; Toll Free: 800-445-6209 Do not confuse with The Creative Co., Lawrenceburg, IN
E-mail: info@thecreativecompany.us; rglaser@thecreativecompany.us
Web site: http://www.thecreativecompany.us.

Creative Homeowner, *(978-0-932944; 978-1-58011; 978-1-880029)* Div. of Courier Corporation, 24 Park Way, Upper Saddle River, NJ 07458-9960 USA (SAN 213-6627) Tel 201-934-7100; Fax: 201-934-8971; Toll Free: 800-631-7795
E-mail: info@creativehomeowner.com
Web site: http://www.creativehomeowner.com.

Creative Teaching Pr., Inc., *(978-0-88160; 978-0-916119; 978-1-57471; 978-1-59198; 978-1-60689; 978-1-61601; 978-1-62186; 978-1-63445; 978-1-68310; 978-1-64474)* Orders Addr.: P.O. Box 2723, Huntington Beach, CA 92647-0723 USA Tel 714-895-5047; Fax: 714-895-6547; Toll Free Fax: 800-444-4287; Edit Addr.: 6262 Katella Ave., Cypress, CA 90630 USA (SAN 294-9180) Tel 714-895-5047; Toll Free Fax: 800-229-9929; Toll Free: 800-444-4287
E-mail: toni.gardner@creativeteaching.com; webmaster@creativeteaching.com; we.listen@creativeteaching.com; emond.ling@creativeteaching.com; denise.clarke@creativeteaching.com
Web site: http://www.creativeteaching.com; http://www.thelearningworks.com; http://www.learntoreadkidsclub.com.

Crescent Imports & Pubns., *(978-0-933127)* P.O. Box 7827, Ann Arbor, MI 48107-7827 USA (SAN 111-3976) Tel 734-665-3492; Fax: 734-677-1717; Toll Free: 800-521-9744
E-mail: crescentus@aol.com
Web site: http://www.crescentimports.com.

Crescent International, Inc., 2238 Otranto Rd., Charleston, SC 29418 USA (SAN 110-0777) Tel 803-797-6363; Fax: 803-797-6367.

Critics' Choice, *See* **Critics' Choice Video**

Critics' Choice Video, *(978-1-932566; 978-1-933240)* 900 N. Rohlwing Rd., Itasca, IL 60143 USA Tel 630-775-3300; Fax: 603-775-3340
E-mail: rterry@ccvideo.com
Web site: http://www.ccvideo.com.

Cromland, 964 Marcon Blvd, Suite 190, Allentown, PA 18109 USA (SAN 254-6736) Tel 610-266-6610; Fax: 610-266-8987; Toll Free: 800-944-5554 (U.S. & Canada)
Web site: http://www.cromland.com.

CrossLife Expressions, *(978-0-9636049; 978-1-57838)* Div. of Exchanged Life Ministries, Inc., 10610 E. Bethany Dr., Suite A, Aurora, CO 80014 USA (SAN 169-0590) Tel 303-750-0440; Fax: 303-750-1228; Toll Free: 800-750-6818
E-mail: info@crosslifebooks.com
Web site: http://www.crosslifebooks.com.

Crowley Distributors, *See* **Sunburst Bks., Inc., Distributor of Florida Bks.**

Crowley, Inc., 16120 U.S. Hwy. 19 N., Suite 220, Clearwater, FL 34624-6862 USA (SAN 285-9130) Tel 813-531-5889.

Crown Agents Service, Ltd., 3100 Massachusetts Ave., NW, Washington, DC 20008 USA (SAN 285-919X).

Crown Hse. Publishing LLC, *(978-1-899836; 978-1-904424; 978-1-84590; 978-0-9823573; 978-1-935810; 978-1-78135; 978-1-78583)* Orders Addr.: P.O. Box 2223, Williston, VT 05495 USA Fax: 802-864-7626; Toll Free: 877-925-1213; Edit Addr.: Crown Bldg., Bancyfelin, Carmarthen, Dyfed SA33 5ND GBR Tel 01267 211345; 01267 211880; Fax: 01267 211882; 81 Brook Hills Dr., White Plains, NY 10605 Tel 914-946-3517; Toll Free: 866-272-8497
E-mail: books@crownhouse.co.uk; info@CHPUS.com
Web site: http://www.crownhouse.co.uk/; http://www.CHPUS.com; http://www.crownhousepublishing.com.

CSS Publishing Co., *(978-0-7880; 978-0-89536; 978-1-55673; 978-0-615-84860-0)* Orders Addr.: 5450 N. Dixie Hwy., Lima, OH 45807-9559 USA Tel 800-241-4056; 419-227-1818; Fax: 419-228-9184; Toll Free: 800-241-4056 Customer Service; 800-537-1030 Orders; Edit Addr.: P.O. Box 4503, Lima, OH 45802-4503 USA (SAN 207-0707) Tel 419-227-1818; Fax: 419-228-9184; Toll Free: 800-537-1030 (Orders); 800-241-4056 (Customer Service) Do not confuse with CSS Publishing in Tularosa, NM
E-mail: editor@csspub.com; csr@csspub.com; info@csspub.com; orders@csspub.com
Web site: http://www.csspub.com.

Ctr. for Literary Publishing, Colorado State Univ., *(978-1-885635)* Center for Literary Publishing, Department of English, Colorado State University, Fort Collins, CO 80523 USA Tel 970-491-5449; Fax: 970-491-0283
E-mail: creview@colostate.edu
Web site: http://coloradoreview.colostate.edu/.

Cultural Hispana/Ameriketako Liburuak, Orders Addr.: P.O. Box 7729, Silver Spring, MD 20907 USA (SAN 159-2823); Edit Addr.: 1413 Crestridge Dr., Silver Spring, MD 20910 USA (SAN 249-3063) Tel 301-585-0134
E-mail: mokordo@erols.com
Web site: http://www.coloquio.com/libros.html.

Culture Plus Bk. Distributors, 44 Willoughby St., Brooklyn, NY 11201-5200 USA.

Culture Plus Bks., 209 N. La Brea Ave., Inglewood, CA 90301-1247 USA (SAN 631-3876).

CUP Services, 750 Cascadilla St., Ithaca, NY 14851 USA (SAN 630-6519) Tel 607-277-2211; Fax: 607-277-6292; Toll Free: 800-666-2211.

Curran Assocs., Inc., *(978-1-60423; 978-1-60560; 978-1-61567; 978-1-61738; 978-1-61782; 978-1-61839; 978-1-62276; 978-1-62748; 978-1-62993; 978-1-63266; 978-1-63439; 978-1-5108; 978-1-7138)* 57 Morehouse Ln., Red Hook, NY 12571 USA Tel 845-758-0400; Fax: 845-758-2633
E-mail: curran@proceedings.com
Web site: https://www.proceedings.com.

Curreri, Michelle Morrow, 3 Eagle Ln., Beverly, MA 01915 USA Tel 978-921-8020; Fax: 978-921-7577
E-mail: michelle@curreriworldsvs.net.

Curtis, Ralph Books, *See* **Curtis, Ralph Publishing**

Curtis, Ralph Publishing, *(978-0-88359)* P.O. Box 349, Sanibel, FL 33957 USA (SAN 121-1323) Tel 239-454-0010; Fax: 239-395-2727; Toll Free: 888-454-0011
E-mail: rcurtisbks@yahoo.com
Web site: http://www.ralphcurtisbooks.com.

CustomFlix Labs, Inc., *(978-0-9774415)* 100 Enterprise Way Ste. A200, Scotts Valley, CA 95066-3266 USA.

Cybernetics Technology Corp., *(978-0-923458)* 1370 Port Washington Blvd., Port Washington, NY 11050-2628 USA (SAN 295-933X) Tel 516-883-7676.

Cypress Bk. Co., Inc., *(978-0-934643)* Subs. of China International Bk. Trading Corp., 360 Swift Ave. Ste. 42, S San Fran, CA 94080-6220 USA (SAN 112-1162) Toll Free: 800-383-1688
E-mail: sales@cypressbook.com; info@cypressbook.com; cypbook@pacbell.net
Web site: http://www.cypressbook.com.

Cypress Hse., *(978-1-879384; 978-0-9987864; 979-8-9854086)* 155 Cypress St., Fort Bragg, CA 95437 USA (SAN 297-9004) Tel 707-964-9520; Fax: 707-964-7531; Toll Free: 800-773-7782
E-mail: cypresshouse@cypresshouse.com; forms@cypresshouse.com
Web site: http://www.cypresshouse.com.

D & H News Co., Inc., 79 Albany Post Rd., Montrose, NY 10548 USA (SAN 169-5533) Tel 914-737-3152.

D & J Bk. Distributors, *(978-1-883080)* 229-21B Merrick Blvd., Laurelton, NY 11413 USA (SAN 630-5091) Tel 718-949-5400; Fax: 718-949-6161; Toll Free: 800-446-4707.

D K Publishing, Incorporated, *See* **Dorling Kindersley Publishing, Inc.**

Daedalus Bks., 9645 Gerwig Ln., Columbia, MD 21046-1520 USA (SAN 158-9202) Tel 410-309-2700
E-mail: tstock@daedalus-books.com; custserv@daedalus-books.com
Web site: http://www.daedalus-books.com.

Dahlstrom, Carol Field Inc., *(978-0-9679764; 978-0-9768446)* 7952 NE. Berwick Dr., Ankeny, IA 50021 USA Tel 515-964-1777; Fax: 515-964-1788
E-mail: braveink@aol.com
Web site: http://www.braveink.com.

Dake Bible Sales, *See* **Dake Publishing**

Dake Publishing, *(978-0-9655968; 978-1-55829)* Orders Addr.: P.O. Box 1050, Lawrenceville, GA 30046 USA (SAN 212-0828) Tel 770-963-1611; Fax: 770-963-7700; Toll Free: 800-241-1239; Edit Addr.: 764 Martins Chapel Rd., Lawrenceville, GA 30246 USA (SAN 243-2684)
E-mail: derrick@dake.com
Web site: http://www.dake.com.

Dakota News, Inc., 221 Petro Ave., Box 1310, Sioux Falls, SD 57101 USA (SAN 169-7854) Tel 605-336-3000; Fax: 605-336-7279; Toll Free: 800-658-5498.

Dakota West Bks., P.O. Box 9324, Rapid City, SD 57701 USA (SAN 630-351X) Tel 605-348-1075; Fax: 605-348-0615.

Danforth Bk. Distribution, Orders Addr.: 3220 228th St., S. E., Bothell, WA 98021 USA Tel 206-351-5872
E-mail: Danforthbookdist@gmail.com.

D.A.P./Distributed Art Pubs., *(978-1-881616; 978-1-891024; 978-1-933045; 978-1-935202; 978-1-938922; 978-1-942884; 978-1-63681)* Orders Addr.: 75 Broad St., Suite 630, New York, NY 10004 USA (SAN 630-6446) Tel 212-627-1999; Fax: 212-627-9484; Toll Free Fax: 800-478-3128; Toll Free: 800-338-2665
E-mail: dap@dapinc.com
Web site: http://www.artbook.com/.

Darr Subscription Agency, P.O. Box 575, Louisburg, KS 66053-0575 USA (SAN 285-9149) Toll Free: 800-850-3741
E-mail: lgriff@midusa.net.

David, Jonathan Pubs., Inc., *(978-0-8246)* 68-22 Eliot Ave., Middle Village, NY 11379 USA (SAN 169-5274) Tel 718-456-8611; Fax: 718-894-2818
E-mail: jondavpub@aol.com
Web site: http://www.jdbooks.com.

Davidson Titles, Inc., *(978-1-884756)* Orders Addr.: 2345 Dr. F.E. Wright Dr., Jackson, TN 38303 USA; Edit Addr.: P.O. Box 3538, Jackson, TN 38303-3538 USA (SAN 255-9129) Tel 731-988-5333; Fax: 731-988-5080; Toll Free Fax: 800-787-7935; Toll Free: 800-433-3903 Do not confuse with companies of the same name in Sugar Hill NH, Windsor CT, Redmond & Kirkland WA, Newark NJ, Fairfield & Reddick FL, East Lansing MI, Rocklin CA, Tolono IL, Missoula MT, Ann Arbor MI, Half Moon Bay CA
E-mail: brian@davidsontitles.com
Web site: http://www.davidsontitles.com.

Davis/Books Distribution, 215 W. Main, Cambridge City, IN 47357 USA Tel 765-478-5773.

Dawson Subscription Service, *See* **Faxon Illinois Service Ctr.**

Day School Magazine Service, P.O. Box 262, Brooklyn, NY 11219 USA (SAN 285-9157) Tel 718-871-1486; Fax: 718-435-2342
E-mail: Elciv@juno.com.

De Gruyter, Inc., *(978-0-89925; 978-1-56445; 978-1-934078; 978-1-61451; 978-1-5015; 978-1-5473; 978-1-5474)* Subs. of Walter de Gruyter & GmbH & Co. KG, Orders Addr.: P.O. Box 960, Herndon, VA 20172-0960 USA Tel 703-661-1589; Fax: 703-661-1501; Toll Free: 800-208-8144; Edit Addr.: 121 High St., Third Flr., Boston, MA 02110 USA Tel 857-284-7073; Fax: 857-284-7358
E-mail: info@deGruytemy.com; kruehle@degruytemy.com; USinfo@degruyter.com; info@degruyter.com
Web site: http://www.degruyter.com; http://www.mouton-publishers.com; http://www.mouton-online.com; www.degruyter.com.

De Gruyter, Walter Incorporated, *See* **De Gruyter, Inc.**

De Vore Group/Carla Bks. & More, Orders Addr.: P.O. Box 10276, San Juan, PR 00908 USA (SAN 159-8309) Tel 809-721-7645; Fax: 809-722-9216; Edit Addr.: 1409 Ave. Ponce De Leon, San Juan, PR 00907-4023 USA (SAN 249-2776).

Dearborn Financial Publishing, Inc., *(978-0-7931; 978-0-88462; 978-0-913864; 978-0-936894; 978-1-57410)* 30 South Wacker Dr., Chicago, IL 60606-1719 USA (SAN 201-3622) Tel 312-836-4400 ext 282429; Fax: 312-836-1021
Web site: http://www.dearborn.com.

Dearborn Trade, A Kaplan Professional Company, *See* **Kaplan Publishing**

DeBoer, Bernhard Inc., 113 E. Centre St., Nutley, NJ 07110 USA (SAN 282-1990) Tel 973-667-9300; Fax: 973-667-0086
E-mail: stout@javanet.com
Web site: http://www.javanet.com/-stout/pannus.

DecisionPro, Inc., 2452 General Potter Hwy., Centre Hall, PA 16828-9022 USA.

DeHoff Christian Bookstore, *(978-1-933965)* 749 N. W. Broad St., Murfreesboro, TN 37129-3797 USA (SAN 184-4202) Tel 615-893-8322; Fax: 615-896-7447; Toll Free: 800-695-5385
E-mail: dehoff@bellsouth.net; fakesb@yahoo.com
Web site: http://www.dehoffbooks.com.

Dehoff Publications, *See* **DeHoff Christian Bookstore**

Delmar Cengage Learning, *(978-0-314; 978-0-7668; 978-0-7693; 978-0-8273; 978-0-87350; 978-0-916032; 978-0-944132; 978-0-9653629; 978-1-56253; 978-1-56593; 978-1-56930; 978-1-4018; 978-1-4180; 978-1-4283; 978-1-4354; 978-1-7319)* Div. of Cengage Learning, Orders Addr.: c/o Thomson Learning Order Fulfillment, P.O. Box 6904, Florence, KY 41022 USA Toll Free Fax: 800 487 8488; Toll Free: 800 347 7707; c/o Thomson Delmar Learning Clinical Health Care Series, P.O. Box 3419, Scranton, PA 18505-0419 Fax: 570-347-9072; Toll Free: 888-427-5800; Edit Addr.: P.O. Box 15015, Albany, NY 12212-5015 USA (SAN 206-7544) Tel 518-348-2300; Fax: 518-373-6345; Toll Free: 800-998-7498; 5 Maxwell Dr., Clifton Park, NY 12065- (SAN 658-0440) Tel 518-348-2300; Fax: 518-881-1256; Toll Free: 800-998-7498
E-mail: matthew.grover@thomson.com; clinicalmanuals@thomson.com
Web site: http://www.delmarlearning.com; http://www.clinicalmanuals.com/.

Delmar News Agency, Inc., P.O. Box 7169, Newark, DE 19714-7169 USA (SAN 169-0892) Tel 302-455-9922; Toll Free: 800-441-7025.

DeLong Subscription Agency, P.O. Box 806, Lafayette, IN 47902 USA (SAN 285-9246) Toll Free: 800-992-2092.

Delphi Distribution Inc., Orders Addr.: 1263 SW Blvd., Kansas City, KS 66103 USA (SAN 760-7989) Tel 913-362-7400; Fax: 913-362-7401
E-mail: kent@delphidistribution.com; linda@midpt.com.

Delta Education, Incorporated, *See* **Delta Education, LLC**

Delta Education, LLC, *(978-0-87504; 978-1-58356; 978-1-59242; 978-1-59821; 978-1-60395; 978-1-60902; 978-1-62571; 978-1-64011; 978-1-68535)* 80 Northwest Blvd., Nashua, NH 03063 USA (SAN 630-1711) Toll Free: 800-442-5444
E-mail: ngosselin@delta-edu.com
Web site: http://www.delta-education.com.

Delta Systems Company, Inc., *(978-0-937354; 978-1-887744; 978-1-932748; 978-1-934960; 978-1-936299; 978-1-936402; 978-1-62167)* Orders Addr.: 1400 Miller Pkwy., McHenry, IL 60050-7030 USA

(SAN 220-0457) Tel 815-363-3582; Fax: 815-363-2948; Toll Free Fax: 800-909-9901; Toll Free: 800-323-8270
E-mail: d.patchin@DeltaPublishing.com; L.Bruell@DeltaPublishing.com; j.patchin@deltapublishing.com
Web site: http://www.deltapublishing.com; http://www.raventreepress.com.

Deltiologists of America, *(978-0-913782)* P.O. Box 8, Norwood, PA 19074 USA (SAN 170-3072) Tel 610-485-8572.

Derstine, Roy Bk. Co., 14 Birch Rd., Kinnelon, NJ 07405 USA (SAN 130-822X) Tel 973-838-1109.

DeRu's Fine Arts, *(978-0-939370)* 9100 E. Artesia Blvd., Bellflower, CA 90706 USA (SAN 159-3862) Tel 562-920-1312; Fax: 562-920-3077
E-mail: derusgal@aol.com
Web site: http://www.derusfinearts.com.

Deseret Bk. Co., *(978-0-87579; 978-0-87747; 978-1-57345; 978-1-59038; 978-1-60641; 978-1-60907; 978-1-60908; 978-1-62972; 978-1-62973; 978-1-64933; 978-1-63993)* Div. of Deseret Management Corp., P.O. Box 30178, Salt Lake City, UT 84130 USA (SAN 150-763X) Tel 801-517-3165 (Wholesale Dept.); 801-534-1515; Fax: 801-517-3338; Toll Free: 800-453-3876
E-mail: wholesale@deseretbook.com; dbwhsale@deseretbook.com
Web site: http://www.deseretbook.com; http://www.shadowmountain.com.

Destiny Image Pubs., *(978-0-7684; 978-0-914903; 978-1-56043; 978-0-9716036)* 167 Walnut Bottom Rd., Shippensburg, PA 17257 USA (SAN 253-4339) Tel 717-532-3040; Fax: 717-532-9291; Toll Free: 800-722-6774
E-mail: dnj@destinyimage.com; jinori@norimediagroup.com
Web site: http://www.destinyimage.com.

Detroit Free Pr., Inc., *(978-0-937247; 978-0-9605692)* Div. of Gannett, 615 W. Lafayette Blvd., Detroit, MI 48226 USA (SAN 239-6998) Tel 313-223-4575; Fax: 313-222-5982; Toll Free: 800-678-6400
E-mail: ajhartley@freepress.com; ldelves@freepress.com
Web site: http://www.freep.com.

Devin-Adair Pubs., Inc., *(978-0-8159)* P.O. Box A, Old Greenwich, CT 06870 USA (SAN 112-062X) Tel 203-531-7755; Fax: 718-359-8568.

DeVorss & Co., *(978-0-87516; 979-8-88774)* Orders Addr.: P.O. Box 1389, Camarillo, CA 93011-1389 USA (SAN 168-9886) Tel 805-322-9010; Fax: 805-322-9011; Toll Free: 800-843-5743; Edit Addr.: 1100 Flynn Rd., No. 104, Camarillo, CA 93012 USA
E-mail: service@devorss.com
Web site: http://www.devorss.com.

Diamond Bk. Distributors, *(978-1-64031)* Div. of Diamond Comic Distributors, Inc., Orders Addr.: 1966 Greenspring Dr., Suite 300, Timonium, MD 21093 USA (SAN 110-9502) Tel 410-560-7100; Fax: 410-560-2583; Toll Free: 800-452-6642
E-mail: books@diamondbookdistributors.com
Web site: http://www.diamondcomics.com; http://www.diamondbookdistributors.com/.

Diamond Book Distributors Inc., *See* **Diamond Comic Distributors, Inc.**

Diamond Comic Distributors, Inc., *(978-1-59396; 978-1-60584)* 1966 Greenspring Dr., Suite 300, Timonium, MD 21093 USA Tel 410-560-7100; Fax: 410-560-2583; Toll Free: 800-452-6642
E-mail: books@diamondbookdistributors.com
Web site: http://www.diamondbookdistributors.com/.

Diamond Distributors, Inc., Orders Addr.: 1966 Greenspring Dr., Suite 300, Timonium, MD 21093 USA Tel 410-560-7100.

Digital Manga Distribution, *See* **Digital Manga Publishing**

Digital Manga Publishing, *(978-1-56970)* Div. of Digital Manga, Inc., 1487 W. 178th St. Ste. 300, Gardena, CA 90248-3253 USA (SAN 111-817X) Toll Free: 866-897-7300
E-mail: contact@emanga.com
Web site: http://www.dmpbooks.com/.

Dillon Bk., Subs. of Harold Dillon, Inc., 460 S. Marion Pkwy., Apt. 851B, Denver, CO 80209-2508 USA (SAN 169-0493) Tel 303-442-5323; Toll Free: 800-525-0842.

Discount Bk. Distributors, 1854 Wallace School Rd., No. E, Charleston, SC 29407-4822 USA (SAN 107-2250) Tel 843-556-6582.

Disney Publishing Worldwide, *(978-1-892309; 978-1-931580; 978-1-4231; 978-1-4847; 978-1-368; 978-1-368-01377-2)* Subs. of Walt Disney Productions, 44 S. Broadway, 10th Flr., White Plains, NY 10601 USA Tel 914-288-4316; 1101 Flower St., Glendale, CA 91201
Web site: http://www.disney.go.com; http://www.hyperionbooksforchildren.com; books.disney.com.

Distribooks, Inc., Div. of MED, Inc., 8124 N. Ridgeway, Skokie, IL 60076 USA (SAN 630-9763) Tel 847-676-1596; Fax: 847-676-1195
E-mail: info@distribooks.com.

Distribuidora Escolar, Inc., 2250 SW 99th Ave., Miami, FL 00165-7569 USA (SAN 169-1104).

Distribuidora Norma, Inc., *(978-1-881700; 978-1-935164)* Div. of Carvajal International, Orders Addr.: P.O. Box 195040, San Juan, PR 00919-5040 USA Tel 787-788-5050; Fax: 787-788-7161; Edit Addr.: Carretera 869 Km 1.5 Barrio Palmas Royal Industrial, Catano, PR 00962 USA
Web site: http://www.norma.com.

Distribuidora Plaza Mayor, 1500 Ave. Ponce de Leon Local 2 El Cinco, San Juan, PR 1 USA.

Distribution Solutions Group, 1120 Rte. 22 E., Bridgewater, NJ 08807-0885 USA Toll Free: 866-374-4748.

Distributors International, Div. of Dennis-Landman Pubs., 1150 18th St., Santa Monica, CA 90403 USA (SAN 129-8089) Tel 310-828-0680
E-mail: info@moviecraft.com
Web site: http://www.moviecraft.com.

Distributors, The, *(978-0-942520)* 702 S. Michigan, South Bend, IN 46601 USA (SAN 169-2488) Tel 574-232-8500; Fax: 312-803-0887; Toll Free: 800-348-5200
E-mail: info@thedistributors.com
Web site: http://thedistributors.com/.

Diversion Books, *See* **Diversion Publishing Corp.**

Diversion Publishing Corp., *(978-0-9845151; 978-0-9829050; 978-0-9833371; 978-0-9838395; 978-0-9839885; 978-1-938120; 978-1-62681; 978-1-68230; 978-1-63576)* 443 Park Aveue S., Ste. 1008, New York, NY 10016 USA (SAN 990-6304) Tel 212-675-5556; 212-961-6390
E-mail: info@diversionbooks.com; charles@efit.com
Web site: http://www.diversionbooks.com.

Divine, Inc., *(978-0-87305)* 1600 Providence Hwy., Walpole, MA 02081-2553 USA (SAN 159-8619) Toll Free: 800-766-0039
E-mail: pubservices@faxon.com; helpdesk@faxon.com
Web site: http://www.faxon.com.

Dixie News Co., P.O. Box 561129, Charlotte, NC 28256-1129 USA (SAN 169-636X) Tel 704-376-0140; Fax: 704-335-8604; Toll Free: 800-532-1045.

DKE Toys, *(978-0-9915790)* 8563 Walnut Dr., Los Angeles, CA 90046 USA Tel 323-656-3262
E-mail: dkelemer@aol.com
Web site: dketoys.com.

Docustar, 1325 Glendale-Milford Rd., Cincinnati, OH 45215 USA Tel 513-772-5400; Fax: 513-772-5410.

Dog Museum, The, *See* **American Kennel Club Museum of the Dog**

Doherty, Tom Assocs., LLC, *(978-0-312; 978-0-7653; 978-0-8125)* Div. of Holtzbrinck Publishers, Orders Addr.: 16365 James Madison Hwy., Gordonsville, VA 22942-8501 USA Toll Free Fax: 800-672-2054; Toll Free: 888-330-8477; Edit Addr.: 175 Fifth Ave., New York, NY 10010 USA Tel 212-674-5151; Fax: 540-672-7540 (customer service)
E-mail: inquiries@tor.com
Web site: http://www.tor.com/.

Donars Spanish Bks., P.O. Box 808, Lafayette, CO 80026 USA (SAN 108-1586) Tel 303-666-9175; Toll Free: 800-552-3316
E-mail: donars@prolynx.com.

Dorling Kindersley Publishing, Inc., *(978-0-7894; 978-1-56458; 978-1-879431; 978-0-7566; 978-1-4654)* Div. of Penguin Publishing Group, 375 Hudson St., 2nd Flr., New York, NY 10014 USA (SAN 253-0791) Tel 212-213-4800; Fax: 212-213-5240; Toll Free: 877-342-5357 (orders only)
E-mail: Annemarie.Cancienne@dk.com; customer.service@dk.com
Web site: http://www.dk.com.

Dot Gibson Distribution, Div. of Dot Gibson Pubns., P.O. Box 117, Waycross, GA 31502 USA Tel 912-285-2848.

Dover Pubns., Inc., *(978-0-486; 978-1-60660)* Div. of Courier Corporation, 31 E. Second St., Mineola, NY 11501 USA (SAN 201-338X) Tel 516-294-7000; Fax: 516-873-1401 (orders only); Toll Free: 800-223-3130 (orders only)
E-mail: rights@doverpublications.com
Web site: http://www.doverdirect.com; http://www.doverpublications.com.

Downtown Bk. Ctr., Inc., *(978-0-941010)* 247 SE First St., Suites 236-237, Miami, FL 33131 USA (SAN 169-1112) Tel 305-377-9941
E-mail: raxdown@aol.com.

Draft2Digital, *(978-1-4977; 978-1-4989; 978-1-5014; 978-1-5022; 978-1-5070; 978-1-5130; 978-1-5163; 978-1-5199; 978-1-5242; 978-1-5337; 978-1-5365; 978-1-5401; 978-1-386; 978-1-393; 978-0-578-64452-3; 978-0-578-78856-2; 978-0-578-79287-3; 979-8-201; 979-8-215; 979-8-223) 9400 N. Broadway Ext. Ste. 410, Oklahoma City, OK 73114 USA Tel 866-336-5099; Toll Free Fax: 866-358-6413*
E-mail: support@draft2digital.com
Web site: www.draft2digital.com.

Dreams in Action Distribution, P.O. Box 1894, Sedona, AZ 86339 USA Tel 928-204-1560; 70 Yucca St., Sedona, AZ 86351
E-mail: sales@dreamsinaction.us; pamela@deamsinaction.us.

Drown News Agency, P.O. Box 2080, Folsom, CA 95763-2080 USA (SAN 169-0450).

Duebbert, Harold F., P.O.B. 629 E. Adolphus Ave., Fergus Falls, MN 56537 USA Tel 218-736-4312.

Dufour Editions, Inc., *(978-0-8023)* Orders Addr.: P.O. Box 7, Chester Springs, PA 19425-0007 USA (SAN 201-341X) Tel 610-458-5005; Fax: 610-458-7103; Toll Free: 800-869-5677
E-mail: info@dufoureditions.com
Web site: http://www.dufoureditions.com.

Dumont, Charles Son, Inc., *(978-1-61727)* 1085 Dumont Cir. PO Box 1017, Voorhees, NJ 08043 USA (SAN 631-0842) Tel 856-346-9100; Fax: 856-346-3452; Toll Free: 800-257-8283
E-mail: info@dumontmusic.com
Web site: http://www.dumontmusic.com.

Durst, Sanford J., *(978-0-915262; 978-0-942666; 978-1-886720)* 106 Woodcleft Ave., Freeport, NY 11520 USA (SAN 211-6987) Tel 516-867-3333; Fax: 516-867-3397
E-mail: sjdbooks@verizon.net.

Duval News Co., Orders Addr.: P.O. Box 61297, Jacksonville, FL 32203 USA (SAN 169-1015); Edit Addr.: 5638 Commonwealth Ave., Jacksonville, FL 32205 USA (SAN 249-2865) Tel 904-783-2350.

Duval-Bibb Publishing Co., *(978-0-937713)* Div. of Mareeco Enterprises, Inc., Orders Addr.: P.O. Box 24168, Tampa, FL 33623-4168 USA (SAN 111-8641) Tel 813-281-0091; Fax: 813-282-0220; 1808 B St. NW, Suite 140, Auburn, WA 98001 Toll Free Fax: 800-548-1169; Toll Free: 800-518-3541
E-mail: reese.cop@gte.net
Web site: http://lonepinepublishing.com/ordering.

E Learn Aid, Orders Addr.: P.O. Box 39545, Los Angeles, CA 90039-0545 USA Fax: 323-665-8875.

E M C Publishing, *See* **EMC/Paradigm Publishing**

Eagle Business Systems, *(978-0-928210)* P.O. Box 1240, El Toro, CA 92630-1240 USA (SAN 285-7510) Tel 714-859-9622.

Eagle Feather Trading Post, Inc., 168 W. 12th St., Ogden, UT 84404 USA (SAN 630-8996) Tel 801-393-3991; Fax: 801-745-0903; Toll Free: 800-547-3364 (orders only).

Eaglecrafts, Orders Addr.: 168 W. 12th St., Ogden, UT 84404 USA (SAN 630-6381) Tel 801-393-3991; Fax: 801-745-0903; Toll Free: 800-547-3364 (orders only)
E-mail: porsturbo@aol.com.

EAL Enterprises, Inc., Div. of Ambassador Bk. Service, 42 Chasner St., Hempstead, NY 11550 USA (SAN 169-6645) Toll Free: 800-431-8913.

East Kentucky News, Inc., 416 Teays Rd., Paintsville, KY 41240 USA (SAN 169-2879) Tel 606-789-8169.

East Texas Distributing, 7171 Grand Blvd., Houston, TX 77054 USA (SAN 169-8265) Tel 713-748-2520; Fax: 713-748-2504.

Eastern Bk. Co., Orders Addr.: P.O. Box 4540, Portland, ME 04112-4540 USA Fax: 207-774-0331; Toll Free Fax: 800-214-3895; Toll Free: 800-937-0331; Edit Addr.: 55 Bradley Dr., Westbrook, ME 04092-2013 USA (SAN 169-3050)
E-mail: info@ebc.com
Web site: http://www.ebc.com.

Eastern National, *(978-0-915992; 978-1-888213; 978-1-59091)* 470 Maryland Dr., Suite 1, Fort Washington, PA 19034 USA (SAN 630-4044)
E-mail: jasons@easternnational.org
Web site: http://www.easternnational.org.

Eastern National Park & Monument Association, *See* **Eastern National**

Eastern News Distributors, Subs. of Hearst Corp., 250 W. 55th St., New York, NY 10019 USA (SAN 169-5738) Tel 212-649-4484; Fax: 212-265-6239; Toll Free: 800-221-3148; 1 Media Way, 12406 Rte. 250, Milan, OH 44846-9705 (SAN 200-7711); 227 W. Trade St., Charlotte, NC 28202 (SAN 631-600X) Tel 704-348-8427
E-mail: enews@hearst.com.

Eastern Subscription Agency, 231 Moria Ct., Aston, PA 19014-1264 USA (SAN 285-9467).

Easton News Co., 2601 Dearborn St., Easton, PA 18042 USA (SAN 169-7315).

Eastview Editions, *(978-0-89860)* P.O. Box 247, Bernardsville, NJ 07924 USA (SAN 169-4952) Tel 908-204-0535.

East-West Export Bks., c/o Univ. of Hawaii Pr., 2840 Kolowalu St., Honolulu, HI 96822 USA Tel 808-956-8830; Fax: 808-988-6052
E-mail: royden@hawaii.edu
Web site: http://eastwestexportbooks.wordpress.com.

Eastwind Bks. & Arts, Inc., 1435-A Stockton St., San Francisco, CA 94133 USA (SAN 127-3159) Tel 415-772-5888; Fax: 415-772-5885
E-mail: info@eastwindsf.com
Web site: http://www.eastwindsf.com.

Eau Claire News Co., Inc., 8100 Partridge Rd., Eau Claire, WI 54703-9646 USA (SAN 169-9059) Tel 715-835-5437.

eBookit.com, *(978-1-4566)* Div. of Archieboy Holdings, LLC, 365 Boston Post Rd., No. 311, Sudbury, MA 01776 USA
Web site: http://www.ebookit.com.

eBooks2go, *See* **eBooks2go Inc**

eBooks2go Inc, *(978-1-61813; 978-1-5457)* 1111 N. Plaza Dr., Ste. 300, Schaumburg, IL 60173 USA Tel 847-598-1150
E-mail: ram@ebooks2go.net
Web site: www.gantecpublishing.com; http://www.ebooks2go.com/.

ebrary, Inc., Div. of Proquest LLC, 318 Cambridge Ave., Palo Alto, CA 94306 USA (SAN 760-7741) Tel 650-475-8700; Fax: 650-475-8881
E-mail: info@ebrary.com
Web site: http://www.ebrary.com.

ebrary.com, *See* **ebrary, Inc.**

EBS, Inc. Bk. Service, 290 Broadway, Lynbrook, NY 11563 USA (SAN 169-5487) Tel 516-593-1195; Fax: 516-596-2911.

EBSCO Media, *(978-1-885860)* Div. of EBSCO Industries, Inc., 801 Fifth Ave., S., Birmingham, AL 35233 USA Tel 205-323-1508; Fax: 205-226-8400; Toll Free: 800-765-0852
Web site: http://www.ebsco.com.

Ebsco Publishing, *(978-1-882248; 978-0-585; 978-1-4175; 978-1-4237; 978-1-4294; 978-1-4298; 978-1-4356; 978-1-4416; 978-1-4619)* Orders Addr.: 10 Estes St., Ipswich, MA 01938 USA (SAN 253-9497) Tel 978-356-6500; 800-653-2726; Fax: 978-356-6565
E-mail: information@ebscohost.com
Web site: http://www.ebscohost.com.

EBSCO Subscription Services, 5724 Hwy. 280 E., Birmingham, AL 35242-6818 USA (SAN 285-9394) Tel 205-991-6000; Fax: 205-991-1479
E-mail: jacomo@ebsco.com
Web site: http://www.ebsco.com.

Ecompass Business Ctr., 3125 Wellner Dr. NE, Rochester, MN 55906 USA Tel 507-280-0787.

Economical Wholesale Co., 6 King Philip Rd., Worcester, MA 01606 USA (SAN 169-3646).

EDC Publishing, *(978-0-7460; 978-0-86020; 978-0-88110; 978-1-58086; 978-0-7945; 978-1-60130)* Orders Addr.: P.O. Box 470663, Tulsa, OK 74147-0663 USA (SAN 658-0505); Edit Addr.: 10302 E. 55th Pl., Tulsa, OK 74146-6515 USA (SAN 107-5322) Tel 918-622-4522; Fax: 918-665-7919; Toll Free Fax: 800-747-4509; Toll Free: 800-475-4522
E-mail: edc@edcpub.com
Web site: http://www.edcpub.com.

Ediciones del Norte, *(978-0-910061)* P.O. Box 5130, Hanover, NH 03755 USA (SAN 241-2993).

Ediciones Enlace de PR, Inc., *(978-0-9904869)* 159 Calle Las Flores, San Juan, PR 00911-2223 USA Tel 787-725-7252; Fax: 787-725-7231
E-mail: info@edenlacepr.com; gramirez@edenlacepr.com
Web site: www.edenlacepr.com.

Ediciones Universal, *(978-0-89729; 978-1-59388)* Orders Addr.: P.O. Box 450353, Miami, FL 33245-0353 USA (SAN 658-0548); Edit Addr.: 3090 SW Eighth St., Miami, FL 33135 USA (SAN 207-2203) Tel 305-642-3355; Fax: 305-642-7978
E-mail: marta@ediciones.com; ediciones@ediciones.com
Web site: http://www.ediciones.com.

Editorial Betania, *See* **Grupo Nelson**

Editorial Cernuda, Inc., 1040 27th Ave., SW, Miami, FL 33135 USA (SAN 158-8850) Tel 305-264-9400.

Editorial Cultural, Inc., *(978-1-56758; 978-84-399)* Orders Addr.: P.O. Box 21056, San Juan, PR 00928 USA; Edit Addr.: Calle Robles, No. 51, San Juan, PR 00928 USA
E-mail: angiev@editorialculturalpr.com; alamo48@gmail.com
Web site: http://www.editorialculturalpr.com.

Editorial Unilit, *(978-0-7899; 978-0-945792; 978-1-56063)* Div. of Spanish Hse., Inc., 1360 NW 88th Ave., Miami, FL 33172-3093 USA (SAN 247-5979) Tel 305-592-6136; Fax: 305-592-0087; Toll Free: 800-767-7726
E-mail: sales1@unidial.com
Web site: http://www.editorialunilit.com/.

Educa Vision Inc., *(978-1-881839; 978-1-58432; 978-1-62632; 978-1-64382; 978-0-578-24509-6)* 7550 NW 47th Ave., Coconut Creek, FL 33073 USA (SAN 760-873X) Tel 954-968-7433; Fax: 954-970-0330; 2725 NW 19th St., Pompano Beach, FL 33069
E-mail: educa@aol.com
Web site: http://www.educavision.com; http://www.educabrazil.org; http://www.caribbeanstudiespress.com; www.educalanguage.com; https://www.educavision.org.

Education Guide, Inc., *(978-0-914880)* P.O. Box 421, Randolph, MA 02368 USA (SAN 201-4580) Tel 617-376-0066; Fax: 617-376-0067.

Educational Audio Visual, Incorporated, *See* **CLEARVUE/eav, Inc.**

Educational Bk. Distributors, P.O. Box 2510, Novato, CA 94948 USA (SAN 158-2259) Tel 415-883-3530; Fax: 415-883-4280; Toll Free: 800-761-5501
E-mail: PblshrSvcs@aol.com.

Educational Development Corporation, *See* **EDC Publishing**

Educational Distribution Corp., 10302 E. 55th Pl., Tulsa, OK 74146 USA Tel 918-622-4522.

Educational Media Corp., *(978-0-932796; 978-1-930572)* Orders Addr.: 1443 Old York Rd., Warminster, PA 18974 USA Fax: 215-956-9041; Toll Free: 800-448-2197; Edit Addr.: 4256 Central Ave. NE, Minneapolis, MN 55421-2920 USA (SAN 212-4203) Tel 763-781-0088; Fax: 763-781-7753; Toll Free: 800-966-3382
E-mail: emedia@educationalmedia.com
Web site: http://www.educationalmedia.com.

Educational Record Ctr., Inc., 3233 Burnt Mill Dr., Suite 100, Wilmington, NC 28403-2698 USA (SAN 630-592X) Tel 910-251-1235; Fax: 910-343-0311; Toll Free Fax: 888-438-1637; Toll Free: 800-438-1637
E-mail: info@erc-inc.com
Web site: http://www.erc-inc.com.

Educational Resources, 1550 Executive Dr., Elgin, IL 60123 USA (SAN 631-5674) Tel 847-888-8300; Toll Free: 800-624-2926 Do not confuse with companies with same or similar name in Shawnee Mission, Columbia, SC, Saint Paul, MN
E-mail: gmhardeman@aol.com.

Educational Showcase, 3571 Newgate Dr., Troy, MI 48084-1042 USA Toll Free: 800-213-3671.

Edumate-Educational Materials, Inc., P.O. Box 711174, San Diego, CA 92171-1174 USA (SAN 630-2955)
E-mail: GusBus@aol.com.

Edu-Tech Corp., The, 65 Bailey Rd., Fairfield, CT 06432 USA (SAN 157-5392) Tel 203-374-4212; Fax: 203-374-8050; Toll Free: 800-338-5463
E-mail: edutcorp@aoc.com.

Edward Weston Graphic, Incorporated, *See* **Weston, Edward Fine Arts**

El Qui-Jote Bk., Inc., 12651 Monarch, Houston, TX 77047 USA (SAN 107-8666) Tel 713-433-3388.

Elder's Bk. Store, 2115 Elliston Pl., Nashville, TN 37203 USA (SAN 112-6091) Tel 615-327-1867.

Elkins, C. J., 400 S. Beverly Dr. Suite 214, Beverly Hills, CA 90212 USA Toll Free: 800-769-2120
E-mail: sitare@aol.com; sitare@zwallet.com.

Ellis News Co., Affil. of L-S Distributors, 130 E. Grand Ave., South San Francisco, CA 94080 USA (SAN 169-0183) Tel 415-873-2094; Fax: 415-873-4222; Toll Free: 800-654-7040 (orders only).

ELS Educational Services, *(978-0-87789; 978-0-89285; 978-0-89318)* Orders Addr.: 200 Old Tappan Rd., Old Tappan, NJ 07675 USA; Edit Addr.: 1357 Second St., Santa Monica, CA 90401-1102 USA (SAN 281-6326).

Elsevier, *(978-0-444; 978-0-7204; 978-0-916086; 978-1-85617; 978-1-59278; 978-0-08; 978-1-4831; 978-1-4832; 978-1-4933)* Orders Addr.: P.O. Box 945, New York, NY 10159-0945 USA (SAN 251-2564) Tel Toll Free: 888-437-4636; P.O. Box 28430, Saint Louis, MO 63146-0930 Toll Free Fax: 800-535-9935; Toll Free: 800-460-3110 (Outside US); 800-545-2522; Edit Addr.: 360 Park Ave S. Flr. 11, New York, NY 10010-1710 USA

(SAN 200-2051); 525 B St., Suite 1800, San Diego, CA 92101-4475 Tel 800-894-3434; 1-619-231-6616
E-mail: usinfo-f@elsevier.com; custserv@elsevier.com; d.gomez@elsevier.com
Web site: http://www.elsevier.com.

Elsevier - Health Sciences Div., *(978-0-323; 978-0-443; 978-0-444; 978-0-7020; 978-0-7216; 978-0-7234; 978-0-7236; 978-0-7506; 978-0-8016; 978-0-8151; 978-0-920513; 978-0-932883; 978-1-55664; 978-1-56053; 978-1-898507; 978-1-932141; 978-1-4160; 978-1-4377; 978-1-4557)* Subs. of Elsevier Science, Orders Addr.: a/o Customer Service, 3251 Riverport Ln., Maryland Heights, MO 63043 USA Tel 314-453-7010; Fax: 314-447-8030; Toll Free Fax: 800-535-9935; Toll Free: 800-545-2522; 800-460-3110 (Customers Outside US); 1799 Highway 50, Linn, MO 65051 (SAN 200-2280); Edit Addr.: 1600 John F. Kennedy Blvd., Suite 1800, Philadelphia, PA 19103-2899 USA Tel 215-239-3900; Fax: 215-239-3990; Toll Free: 800-523-4069
E-mail: usbkinfo@elsevier.com
Web site: http://www.elsevier.com; http://www.us.elsevierhealth.com/.

Elsevier Science, *See* **Elsevier**

Elsevier Science - Health Sciences Division, *See* **Elsevier - Health Sciences Div.**

Elsevier Science & Technology Bks., Orders Addr.: P.O. Box 28430, Saint Louis, MO 63146-0930 USA Toll Free Fax: 800-535-9935; Toll Free: 800-545-2522; 800-460-3110 (Customers Outside US); Edit Addr.: 525 B St., Suite 1900, San Diego, CA 92101 USA Toll Free: 1-800-894-3434; 200 Wheeler Rd., 6th Flr., Burlington, MA 01803 Tel 781-313-4700
E-mail: bookstore.orders@elsevier.com
Web site: http://www.elsevier.com/; http://www.syngress.com.

EMC/Paradigm Publishing, *(978-0-7638; 978-0-8219; 978-0-88436; 978-0-912022; 978-1-56118; 978-1-5338)* Div. of EMC Corp., 875 Montreal Way, Saint Paul, MN 55102 USA (SAN 201-3800) Toll Free Fax: 800-328-4564; Toll Free: 800-328-1452
E-mail: publish@emcp.com; educate@emcp.com
Web site: http://www.emcp.com.

Emerald Bk. Co., *(978-1-934572; 978-1-937110)* Div. of Greenleaf Bk. Group, 4425 Mo Pac Expy., Suite 600, Austin, TX 78735 USA.

Emery-Pratt Co., Orders Addr.: 1966 W. M 21, Owosso, MI 48867-1397 USA (SAN 170-1401) Tel 989-723-5291; Fax: 989-723-4677; Toll Free Fax: 800-523-6379; Toll Free: 800-762-5683 (library orders only); 800-248-3887 (customer service only) Distributor to Libraries & Hospitals
E-mail: custserv@emery-pratt.com
Web site: http://www.emery-pratt.com.

Empire Comics, 375 Stone Rd., Rochester, NY 14616 USA (SAN 110-943X) Tel 716-442-0371; Fax: 716-442-7807
E-mail: empires@frontiernet.net.

Empire News of Jamestown, Foot Ave. & Extension St., Box 2029, Sta. A, Jamestown, NY 14702 USA (SAN 169-5371).

Empire Publishing Service, *(978-1-58690)* P.O. Box 1344, Studio City, CA 91614-0344 USA (SAN 630-5687) Tel 818-784-8918
E-mail: empirepubsvc@att.net.

Empire State News Corp., Orders Addr.: P.O. Box 1167, Buffalo, NY 14240-1167 USA Tel 716-681-1100; Fax: 716-681-1120; Toll Free: 800-414-6247; Edit Addr.: 316 Forestview Dr., Buffalo, NY 14221-1461 USA (SAN 169-5177)
Web site: http://www.esnc.com.

Empowerment Technologies, *See* **Empowerment Technologies/Neuro-Semantics Pubns.**

Empowerment Technologies/Neuro-Semantics Pubns., *(978-1-890001; 978-1-899836)* Orders Addr.: P.O. Box 8, Clifton, CO 81520 USA Tel 704-864-3585; Fax: 970-523-5790; Edit Addr.: P.O. Box 9231, Grand Junction, CO 81501 USA Tel 970-523-7877
E-mail: meta@acsol.net
Web site: http://www.neurosemantics.com.

Encino Pr., *(978-0-88426)* 510 Baylor St., Austin, TX 78703 USA (SAN 201-3843) Tel 512-476-6821; Fax: 512-476-9393.

Encyclopaedia Britannica, Inc., *(978-0-7826; 978-0-8347; 978-0-85229; 978-0-87827; 978-1-59339; 978-1-60835; 978-1-61535; 978-0-9823819; 978-0-9823820; 978-0-9823821; 978-0-9823822; 978-0-9823823; 978-0-9823824; 978-1-62513; 978-1-68382)* 325 N. La Salle St., Chicago, IL 60654 USA (SAN 204-1464) Toll Free Fax: 800-344-9624 (fax orders); Toll Free: 800-323-1229; 800-621-3900 (orders); 2nd Flr., Unity Wharf Mill St., London, SE1 2BH Tel 020 7500 7800; Fax: 020 7500 7878
E-mail: enquiries@britannica.co.uk; contact@eb.com
Web site: http://www.eb.com; http://www.britannica.co.uk.

Enfield Publishing & Distribution Co., Inc., *(978-0-9656184; 978-1-893598)* Orders Addr.: P.O. Box 699, Enfield, NH 03748 USA Tel 603-632-7377; Fax: 603-632-5611; Edit Addr.: 234 May St., Enfield, NH 03748 USA
E-mail: info@enfieldbooks.com
Web site: http://www.enfielddistribution.com; http://www.enfieldbooks.com.

Entrepreneur Media Inc/Entrepreneur Pr., *(978-0-916378; 978-1-55571; 978-1-891984; 978-1-932156; 978-1-932531; 978-1-59918; 978-1-61308; 978-1-64201)* 18061 Fitch, Irvine, CA 92614 USA Tel 949-622-7106; Fax: 949-622-7106; Toll Free: 800-864-6864
E-mail: vcampos@entrepreneur.com
Web site: http://www.entrepreneur.com; http://www.entrepreneurpress.com.

Entrepreneur Press, *See* **Entrepreneur Media Inc/Entrepreneur Pr.**

Entrepreneur Start a Business Store, 9114 River Look Ln., Fair Oaks, CA 95628-6565 USA (SAN 133-1485) Fax: 916-863-0361.

Epic Book Promotions, 914 Nolan Way, Chula Vista, CA 91911-2408 USA Tel 619-498-8547; Fax: 619-498-8540
E-mail: gvjack@pacbell.net.

Epicenter Pr., Inc., *(978-0-945397; 978-0-9708493; 978-0-9724944; 978-0-9745014; 978-0-9790470; 978-1-60381; 978-0-9800825; 978-1-935347; 978-1-941890)* Orders Addr.: 6524 NE 181st St., No. 2, Kenmore, WA 98028 USA (SAN 246-9405) Do not confuse with companies with similar names in Kanehoe, HI, Long Beach, CA, Oakland, CA
E-mail: info@epicenterpress.com; phil@epicenterpress.com; aubrey@epicenterpress.com
Web site: http://www.epicenterpress.com.

E-Pros DG, 32 N. Goodwin Ave., Elmsford, NY 10523 USA Toll Free: 866-377-6700
E-mail: sales@e-pros.ws.

Epson Mid-Atlantic, Subs. of Epson America, Inc., 8 Neshaminy Interplex, Suite 319, Trerose, PA 19053 USA (SAN 285-7243) Tel 215-245-2180.

Equinox, Ltd., 1307 Park Ave., Williamsport, PA 17701 USA.

Eriksson Enterprises, 126 Sunset Dr., Farmington, UT 84025-3426 USA (SAN 110-5892).

Erlbaum, Lawrence Assocs., Inc., *(978-0-8058; 978-0-86377; 978-0-89859; 978-1-880393; 978-1-4106)* 270 Madison Ave. Flr. 4, New York, NY 10016-0601 USA (SAN 213-960X) Toll Free: 800-926-6579 (orders only)
E-mail: orders@erlbaum.com
Web site: http://www.erlbaum.com.

ETA hand2mind, *See* **hand2mind**

ETD KroMar Temple, P.O. Box 535695, Grand Prairie, TX 75053-5625 USA (SAN 169-8435) Tel 254-778-5261; Fax: 254-778-5267.

Euro Tool, Inc., 14101 Botts Rd., Grandview, MO 64030 USA Toll Free: 800-552-3131
Web site: http://www.eurotool.com.

European Bk. Co., Inc., 925 Larkin St., San Francisco, CA 94109 USA (SAN 169-0191) Tel 415-474-0626; Fax: 415-474-0630; Toll Free: 877-746-3666
E-mail: info@europeanbook.com.

European Press Service - PBD America Wholesalers, 30 Edison Dr., Wayne, NJ 07470-4713 USA (SAN 630-7825).

Evans Bk. Distribution & Pubs., Inc., *(978-0-9654884; 978-1-56684)* 895 W. 1700 S., Salt Lake City, UT 84104 USA.

Evans Book, *See* **Evans Bk. Distribution & Pubs., Inc.**

Evanston Publishing, Inc., *(978-1-879260)* 4824 Brownsboro Ctr. Arcade, Louisville, KY 40207-2342 USA Tel 502-899-1919; Fax: 502-896-0246; Toll Free: 800-594-5190
E-mail: EvanstonPB@aol.com; info@evanstonpublishing.com
Web site: http://www.EvanstonPublishing.com.

Everbind/Marco Book Company, *See* **Marco Bk. Co.**

Excaliber Publishing Co., *(978-1-881353)* 7954 W. Bury Ave., San Diego, CA 92126 USA (SAN 297-6412) Tel 619-695-3091; Fax: 619-695-3095.

Exciting Times, 17430C Crenshaw Blvd., Torrance, CA 90504 USA (SAN 114-4642) Tel 310-515-2676; Fax: 310-515-1382.

Executive Books, *See* **Tremendous Life Bks.**

Experiment LLC, The, *(978-0-9620471; 978-1-891011; 978-1-61519)* 220 E. 23rd St. Suite 600, New York, NY 10010 USA (SAN 857-961X)
E-mail: info@theexperimentpublishing.com
Web site: http://www.theexperimentpublishing.com.

Exploration Films, P.O. Box 1069, Monument, CO 80132 USA Tel 719-481-4599; Fax: 719-481-1399; Toll Free: 800-964-0439
E-mail: jolene@explorationfilms.com
Web site: http://www.explorationfilms.com.

Explorations, 360 Interlocken Blvd., Suite 300, Broomfield, CO 80021 USA Toll Free Fax: 800-456-1139; Toll Free: 800-720-2114
E-mail: customerservice@gaiam.com
Web site: http://www.gaiam.com.

Express Media, *(978-0-9723163)* 127 Rankin Rd., Columbia, MS 37202 USA Tel 615-360-6400
Web site: http://www.authorsexpress.com.

Faber & Faber, Inc., *(978-0-571)* Affil. of Farrar, Straus & Giroux, LLC, Orders Addr.: c/o Van Holtzbrinck Publishing Services, 16365 James Madison Hwy., Gordonsville, VA 22942 USA Fax: 540-572-7540; Toll Free: 888-330-8477; Edit Addr.: 19 Union Sq., W, New York, NY 10003-3304 USA (SAN 218-7256) Tel 212-741-6900; Fax: 212-633-9385
E-mail: sales@fsgbooks.com
Web site: http://www.fsgbooks.com.

Fairfield Bk. Service Co., 150 Margherita Lawn, Stratford, CT 06615 USA (SAN 131-0976) Tel 203-375-7607.

Faith Alive Christian Resources, *(978-0-930265; 978-0-933140; 978-1-56212; 978-1-59255; 978-1-62025)* 2850 Kalamazoo Ave., SE, Grand Rapids, MI 49560 USA (SAN 212-727X) Tel 616-224-0784; Fax: 616-224-0834; Toll Free Fax: 888-642-8606; Toll Free: 800-333-8300; P.O. Box 5070, Burlington, ON L7R 3Y8 Toll Free Fax: 888-642-8606; Toll Free: 800-333-8300
E-mail: sales@faithaliveresources.org
Web site: http://www.faithaliveresources.org.

Falk Bks. Inc., W.E., 7491 N. Federal Hwy., PMB 267, Boca Raton, FL 33487 USA.

Falk, W. E., *See* **Falk Bks. Inc., W.E.**

Fall River News Co., Inc., 144 Robeson St., Fall River, MA 02720-4925 USA (SAN 169-3425) Tel 508-679-5266.

Family History World, P.O. Box 129, Tremonton, UT 84337 USA (SAN 159-673X) Fax: 801-250-6727; Toll Free: 800-377-6058
E-mail: genealogy@utahlinx.com
Web site: http://www.genealogical-institute.com.

Family Reading Service, 1601 N. Slappey Blvd., Albany, GA 31701-1431 USA (SAN 169-1376).

Fantaco Pubns., *(978-0-938782)* Affil. of Fantaco Enterprises, Inc., Orders Addr.: 1313 W. Gate Drive, Unit 408, Leland, NC 28451 USA; Edit Addr.: 1313 W. Gate Drive, Unit 408, Leland, NC 28451 USA (SAN 158-5134)
E-mail: sanchez.kaz@gmail.com; bluecheer1@yahoo.com
Web site: www.fantaco.net.

Far West Bk. Service, 3515 NE Hassalo, Portland, OR 97232 USA (SAN 107-6760) Tel 503-234-7664; Fax: 503-231-0573; Toll Free: 800-964-9378.

Farcountry Pr., *(978-0-938314; 978-1-56037; 978-1-59152)* Orders Addr.: P.O. Box 5630, Helena, MT 59604 USA (SAN 220-0732) Tel 406-422-1263; Fax: 406-443-5480; Toll Free: 800-821-3874; 2750 Broadwater, Helena, MT 59602
E-mail: books@farcountrypress.com
Web site: http://www.farcountrypress.com.

Farrar, Straus & Giroux, *(978-0-374; 978-0-571)* Div. of Holtzbrinck Publishers, Orders Addr.: c/o Holtzbrinck Publishers, 16365 James Madison Hwy., Gordonsville, VA 22942 USA Toll Free Fax: 800-672-2054; Toll Free: 888-330-8477; Edit Addr.: 18 W. 18th St., New York, NY 10011-4607 USA (SAN 206-782X)
E-mail: sales@fsgee.com; fsg.editorial@fsgee.com
Web site: http://www.fsgbooks.com/.

Faxon Company, The, *See* **Divine, Inc.**

Faxon Illinois Service Ctr., Affil. of Dawson Holdings PLC, 1600 Providence Hwy., Walpole, MA 02081-2553 USA (SAN 286-0147) Toll Free: 800-852-7404
E-mail: postmaster@dawson.com; sandy.nordman@dawson.com
Web site: http://www.faxon.com.

Fayette County News Agency, Orders Addr.: P.O. Box 993, Uniontown, PA 15401 USA Tel 724-437-1181; Edit Addr.: Cherry Tree Square 42 Matthew Dr., Uniontown, PA 15401 USA (SAN 169-765X).

FEC News Distributing, 2201 Fourth Ave., N., Lake Worth, FL 33461-3835 USA (SAN 169-1341) Tel 407-547-3000; Fax: 407-547-3080.

Feldheim, Philipp Incorporated, *See* **Feldheim Pubs.**

Feldheim Pubs., *(978-0-87306; 978-1-58330; 978-1-59826; 978-1-68025)* 208 Airport Executive Park., Nanuet, NY 10954-5262 USA (SAN 106-6307) Toll Free: 800-237-7149
E-mail: sales@feldheim.com; eli3@feldheim.com
Web site: http://www.feldheim.com.

Fell, Frederick Pubs., Inc., *(978-0-8119; 978-0-88391; 978-0-936320)* Orders Addr.: 1403 Shoreline Way, Hollywood, FL 33019-5007 USA (SAN 215-0670)
Web site: http://www.fellpub.com.

Fennell, Reginald F. Subscription Service, 1002 W. Michigan Ave., Jackson, MI 49202 USA (SAN 159-6071) Tel 517-782-3132; Fax: 517-782-1109.

FEP, A Booksource Co., 1230 Macklind Ave., Saint Louis, MO 63110 USA (SAN 169-1317) Tel 314-647-0600; Fax: 314-647-6850; Toll Free: 800-444-0435
Web site: http://www.booksource.com.

Fiddlecase Bks., HC 63 Box 104, East Alstead, NH 03602 USA (SAN 200-7495) Tel 603-835-7889.

Fiesta Bk. Co., *(978-0-88473)* P.O. Box 490641, Key Biscayne, FL 33149 USA (SAN 201-8470) Tel 305-858-4843.

Fiesta Publishing Corporation, *See* **Fiesta Bk. Co.**

Films for the Humanities & Sciences, *See* **Films Media Group**

Films Media Group, *(978-0-7365; 978-0-89113; 978-1-56950; 978-1-4213; 978-1-60467)* Div. of Infobase Learning, Orders Addr.: 132 W. 31st St., 17th Flr., New York, NY 10001 USA (SAN 653-2705) Toll Free Fax: 800-678-3633; Toll Free: 800-322-8755
E-mail: mgallo@infobaselearning.com
Web site: http://www.films.com.

Findaway Voices, 31999 Aurora Rd., Solon, OH 44139 USA
E-mail: support@findawayvoices.com
Web site: https://findawayvoices.com/.

Findaway World, LLC, *(978-1-59895; 978-1-60252; 978-1-60514; 978-1-60640; 978-1-60775; 978-1-60812; 978-1-60847; 978-1-61545; 978-1-61574; 978-1-61587; 978-1-61637; 978-1-61657; 978-1-61707; 978-1-4676; 978-1-5094; 978-1-9871; 978-1-0942; 978-1-6622; 978-1-6649; 978-1-6670; 978-1-6696; 979-8-8226; 979-8-3689; 979-8-8686; 979-8-8687) 31999 Aurora Rd., Solon, OH 44139 USA (SAN 853-8778) Tel 440-893-0808 x108; 4 World Trade Ctr., Fl. 62, New York, NY 10007*
Web site: http://www.findaway.com.

Fine Assocs., One Farragut Sq., S., Washington, DC 20006 USA (SAN 169-0914) Tel 202-628-2609.

Finn News Agency, Inc., 4415 State Rd. 327, Auburn, IN 46706-9542 USA (SAN 169-2356).

Finney Co., Inc., *(978-0-89317; 978-0-912486; 978-0-933855; 978-0-9617767; 978-0-9639705; 978-1-880654; 978-1-893272)* Orders Addr.: 8075 215th St. W., Lakeville, MN 55044 USA (SAN 206-412X) Tel 952-469-6699; Fax: 952-469-1968; Toll Free Fax: 800-330-6232; Toll Free: 800-846-7027
E-mail: feedback@finneyco.com
Web site: http://www.finneyco.com; http://www.ecopress.com; http://www.pogopress.com; http://www.astragalpress.com.

Fire Protection Publications, *See* **IFSTA**

Firebird Distributing, LLC, 1945 P St., Eureka, CA 95501-3007 USA (SAN 631-1229) Toll Free: 800-353-3575
E-mail: sales@firebirddistributing.com
Web site: http://www.firebirddistributing.com.

Firebrand Technologies, 44 Merrimac St., Newburyport, MA 01950 USA.

Firefly Bks., Ltd., *(978-0-920668; 978-1-55209; 978-1-895565; 978-1-896284; 978-1-55297; 978-1-55407)* Orders Addr.: c/o Frontier Distributing, 1000 Young St., Suite 160, Tonawanda, NY 14150 USA (SAN 630-611X) Tel 203-222-9700; Toll Free Fax: 800-565-6034; Toll Free: 800-387-5085; Edit Addr.: 8514 Long Canyon Dr., Austin, TX 78730-2813 USA
E-mail: service@fireflybooks.com
Web site: http://www.fireflybooks.com/.

Firenze Pr., *(978-0-9711236)* Orders Addr.: P.O. Box 6892, Wyomissing, PA 19610-0892 USA (SAN 254-315X); Edit Addr.: 612 Museum Rd., Reading, PA 19610-0892 USA Tel 610-374-7048 Do not confuse with Leonardo Pr., Camden, ME
E-mail: hailejohnjr@msn.com; HaileJohnJr@msn.com; InkPenCJH@msn.com
Web site: http://caroljhaile.com.

Fischer, Carl LLC, *(978-0-8258)* Orders Addr.: 588 N. Gulph Rd. Ste. B, King Of Prussa, PA 19406-2831 USA Toll Free: 800-762-2328; Edit Addr.: 65 Bleeker St., New York, NY 10012-2420 USA (SAN 107-4245) Tel 212-772-0900; Fax: 212-477-6996; Toll Free: 800-762-2328
E-mail: cf-info@carlfischer.com
Web site: http://www.carlfischer.com.

Fish, Enrica Medical Bks., 1208 W. Minnehaha Pkwy., Minneapolis, MN 55419-1163 USA (SAN 157-8588) Toll Free: 800-728-8398.

Fisher King Bks., 316 Mid Valley Ctr., #194, Carmel, CA 93923 USA Tel 831-238-7799; Toll Free: 800-228-9316 (Canada & US).

Flannery Co., 16430 Beaver Rd., Adelanto, CA 92301-3904 USA (SAN 168-9754) Toll Free: 800-456-3400.

Flannery, J. F. Company, *See* **Flannery Co.**

Fleming, Robert Hull Museum, *(978-0-934658)* Div. of Univ. of Vermont, Univ. of Vermont, 61 Colchester Ave., Burlington, VT 05405 USA (SAN 110-8824) Tel 802-656-0750; Fax: 802-656-8059
Web site: www.upne.com.

Flora & Fauna Bks., P.O. Box 15718, Gainesville, FL 32604 USA (SAN 133-1221) Tel 352-373-5630; Fax: 352-373-3249
E-mail: ffbks@aol.com
Web site: http://www.ffbooks.com.

Florida Academic Pr., *(978-1-890357)* P.O. Box 540, Gainesville, FL 32602-0540 USA (SAN 299-3643) Tel 352-332-5104; Fax: 352-331-6003
E-mail: fapress@worldnet.att.net.

Florida Classics Library, *(978-0-912451)* P.O. Drawer 1657, Port Salerno, FL 34992-1657 USA (SAN 265-2404) Tel 561-546-9380 (orders); Fax: 561-546-7545 (orders).

Florida Schl. Bk. Depository, 1125 N. Ellis Rd., Jacksonville, FL 32236 USA (SAN 161-8423) Tel 904-781-7191; Fax: 904-781-3486; Toll Free: 800-447-7957
Web site: http://www.fsbd.com.

Flury & Co., 322 First Ave S., Seattle, WA 98104 USA (SAN 107-5748) Tel 206-587-0260.

FM International, P.O. Box 91, Waunakee, WI 53597-0091 USA.

Fodor's Travel Guides, *See* **Fodor's Travel Pubns.**

Fodor's Travel Pubns., Div. of Random Hse., Information Group, Orders Addr.: 400 Hahn Rd., Westminster, MD 21157 USA Tel 410-848-1900; Toll Free: 800-726-0600; Edit Addr.: 1745 Broadway, New York, NY 10019 USA Tel 212-782-9000
Web site: http://www.fodors.com.

Follet Higher Education Grp, P.O. Box 3488, Oak Brook, IL 60522-3488 USA Tel 630-279-0123.

Follett Audiovisual Resources, *See* **Follett Media Distribution**

Follett Library Resources, *See* **Follett School Solutions**

Follett Media Distribution, 1847 Mercer Rd., Lexington, KY 40511-1001 USA (SAN 631-7316) Toll Free: 888-281-1216.

Follett School Solutions, *(978-0-329; 978-0-88153; 978-0-924917; 978-1-4898; 978-1-5160; 978-1-5181; 978-1-5379; 978-1-5444; 978-1-5490; 978-1-7254; 978-1-7137; 978-1-6688; 979-8-3687)* Div. of the Follett Corp., Orders Addr.: a/o McHenry Warehouse, 1340 Ridgeview Dr., McHenry, IL 60050 USA (SAN 169-1902) Toll Free: 888-511-5114; a/o Patti Hall: R & R Bindery Services, 499 Rachel Rd., Girard, IL 62640 (SAN 155-8412) Tel 815-759-1700; 160 Dulty's Lane, Suite 300, Burlington Township, NJ 08016 (SAN 991-1006); 2801 Alft Lane, Unit 100, Elgin, IL 60124 (SAN 991-1014); 2430 E. Arbrook Blvd, Suite 300, Arlington, TX 76014 (SAN 991-1022); a/o Formerly FES, 1433 Internationale Pkwy. DOCK Door 30, Woodridge, IL 60517 (SAN 631-7901) Tel 630-972-5600; Fax: 630-972-4673; Toll Free: 800-621-4272; a/o Russell Henning (Formerly FSC), 1391 Corporate Dr., McHenry, IL 60050-7041 (SAN 298-587X) Fax: 815-344-8774; 26682 Almond Avenue, Bldg 1, Suite 100, Redlands, CA 92374 (SAN 991-1030); a/o Formerly FLR, 1340 Ridgeview Dr., Suite EDI, McHenry, IL 60050-0000 (SAN 760-7164); 3057 Tradeport Drive, Suite 100, Orlando, FL 32824 (SAN 991-1049)
Web site: http://www.follett.com.

Fondo de Cultura Economica USA, 2293 Verus St., San Diego, CA 92154 USA (SAN 860-1380) Tel 619-429-0455; Fax: 619-651-9684; Toll Free: 800-532-3872
E-mail: orders@fceusa.com; drazo@fceusa.com; fondosales@fceusa.com
Web site: http://www.fceusa.com.

Fordham Univ. Pr., *(978-0-8232; 978-1-5315)* Joseph A. Martino Hall 45 Columbus Ave., New York, NY 10023 USA (SAN 201-6516) Tel 718-817-4795; Fax: 718-817-4785
E-mail: kasweeney@fordham.edu
Web site: http://www.fordhampress.com.

Forest Hse. Publishing Co., Inc., *(978-1-56674; 978-1-878363)* P.O. Box 738, Lake Forest, IL 60045 USA Tel 847-295-8287; Fax: 847-295-8201; Toll Free: 800-394-7323.

Forest Sales & Distributing Co., *(978-0-9712183)* 139 Jean Marie St., Reserve, LA 70084 USA (SAN 157-5511) Toll Free: 800-347-2106
E-mail: tbooks2@juno.com.

Forsa Editores, *(978-1-881714)* Orders Addr.: P.O. Box 11249, San Juan, PR 00922-1249 USA Tel 787-707-1792; Fax: 787-707-1797; Toll Free: 888-225-8984; Edit Addr.: No. 1594 J.T. Pinero Ave., Caparra Heights, PR 00920 USA
E-mail: forsa@forsaeditores.com
Web site: http://www.forsaeditores.com.

Forsyth Travel Library, Inc., *(978-0-9614539)* 1750 E. 131st St., P.O. Box 480800, Kansas City, MO 64148-0800 USA (SAN 169-2755) Tel 816-942-9050; Fax: 816-942-6969; Toll Free: 800-367-7984 (orders only)
E-mail: forsyth@gvi.net
Web site: http://www.forsyth.com.

Forward Movement Pubns., *(978-0-88028)* 300 West Fourth St., Cincinnati, OH 45202 USA (SAN 208-3841) Tel 513-721-6659; Fax: 513-721-0729; Toll Free: 800-543-1813 (orders only)
E-mail: Orders@forwarddaybyday.com
Web site: http://www.forwardmovement.org.

Foster, Walter Publishing, Incorporated, *See* **Quarto Publishing Group USA**

Four Winds Trading Co., *(978-0-9672393)* 6355 Joyce Dr., Golden, CO 80403-7568 USA (SAN 631-1989) Toll Free: 800-456-5444
E-mail: Paul@Fourwinds-trading.com; sales@fourwinds-trading.com
Web site: http://www.fourwinds-trading.com.

Fox Chapel Publishing Co., Inc., *(978-0-932944; 978-1-56523; 978-1-57421; 978-1-58011; 978-1-880029; 978-1-896980; 978-1-85974; 978-1-903366; 978-0-9777004; 978-1-905523; 978-1-60765; 978-1-906853; 978-1-4971; 978-1-4972; 978-1-5048; 978-1-908397; 978-1-910456; 978-1-64124; 978-1-64178; 978-1-63741; 978-1-63981; 979-8-89094) Orders Addr.: 1970 Broad St., East Petersburg, PA 17520 USA (SAN 920-8887) Tel 717-560-4703; Fax: 717-560-4702; Toll Free Fax: 888-369-2885; Toll Free: 800-457-9112 (orders); Edit Addr.: 903 Square St., Mount Joy, PA 17552 USA Fax: 888-369-2885; Toll Free: 1-800-457-9112*
E-mail: sales@carvingworld.com; alan@foxchapelpublishing.com; Younger@foxchapelpublishing.com; sales@foxchapelpublishing.com
Web site: http://www.foxchapelpublishing.com/; http://www.scrollsawer.com/; http://www.carvingworld.com; http://www.foxchapelpublishing.com; www.d-originals.com.

Franklin Bk. Co., Inc., P.O. Box 451, Newtown Sq, PA 19073-0451 USA (SAN 121-4160)
E-mail: service@franklinbook.com
Web site: http://www.franklinbook.com.

Franklin Readers Service, P.O. Box 662, Dunn Loring, VA 22027-0662 USA (SAN 285-9599).

Franklin Square Overseas, 17-19 Washington St., Tenafly, NJ 07670-2084 USA (SAN 285-9637) Tel 201-569-2500; Fax: 201-569-5141
E-mail: esstn@ebsco.com.

Free People Books, 10 Parker Cir., Salem, NH 03079 USA.

Freeman Family Ministries, Orders Addr.: P.O. Box 593, Waldo, FL 32694 USA Tel 352-468-2785
E-mail: freemanfamily9@msn.com.

Freihofer, A. G., 175 Fifth Ave., New York, NY 10010 USA (SAN 285-9602) Tel 272-460-7500; Fax: 272-473-6272.

French & European Pubns., Inc., *(978-0-320; 978-0-7859; 978-0-8288; 978-1-5479)* 425 E. 58th St., Suite 27D, New York, NY 10022-2379 USA (SAN 206-8109) Fax: 212-265-1094
E-mail: livresny@gmail.com; frenchbookstore@aol.com
Web site: http://www.frencheuropean.com.

Fresno Bk. Fairs, 1030 Bonita Ave., La Verne, CA 91750 USA (SAN 630-6225) Tel 909-593-0697; 1650 W. Orange Grove Ave., Pomona, CA 91768-2153 (SAN 299-2434)
Web site: http://www.mrsnelsons.com.

Friendly Hills Fellowship, *See* **Health and Growth Assocs.**

Fris News Co., 194 River Ave., Holland, MI 49423 USA (SAN 159-8643).

Frontline Communications, *See* **YWAM Publishing**

FRP Cookbook Marketplace, *See* **Cookbook Marketplace, The**

Fujii Assocs., 1400 W. 47th St. Ste. 4, La Grange, IL 60525-6148 USA (SAN 631-5305).

Fulcrum Publishing, *(978-0-912347; 978-1-55591; 978-1-56373; 978-1-936218; 978-1-938486; 978-1-68275)* Orders Addr.: 4690 Table Mountain Dr. Suite 100, Golden, CO 80403 USA (SAN 200-2825) Toll Free Fax: 800-726-7112; Toll Free: 800-992-2908
E-mail: info@fulcrumbooks.com
Web site: http://www.fulcrumbooks.com.

Fulmont News Co., Affil. of Rubin Periodical Group, P.O. Box 1211, Rochester, NY 14603-1211 USA (SAN 169-5029) Tel 518-843-2421.

Fultz News Agency, 2008 Woodbrook, Denton, TX 76205 USA (SAN 169-8168).

Futech Educational Products, Inc., *(978-0-9627001; 978-1-889192)* 2999 N. 44th St., Suite 225, Phoenix, AZ 85018-7248 USA Tel 602-808-8765; Fax: 602-278-5667; Toll Free: 800-597-6278.

G A M Printers & Grace Christian Bookstore, *See* **GAM Pubn.**

Gabriel Resources, Orders Addr.: P.O. Box 1047, Waynesboro, GA 30830 USA Tel 706-554-1594; Fax: 706-554-7444; Toll Free: 800-732-6657 (8MORE-BOOKS); Edit Addr.: 129 Mobilization Dr., Waynesboro, GA 30830 USA.

Galda Library Services, Inc., 33 Richdale Ave., Cambridge, MA 02140 USA (SAN 630-5806) Tel 617-864-8232.

Galesburg News Agency, Inc., Five E. Simmons St., Galesburg, IL 61401 USA (SAN 169-1945).

Galveston News Agency, P.O. Box 7608, San Antonio, TX 78207-0608 USA (SAN 169-8230).

GAM Pubn., P.O. Box 25, Sterling, VA 20167 USA (SAN 158-7218) Tel 703-450-4121; Fax: 703-450-5311.

Gamboge International, Inc., 18 Brittany Ave., Trumbull, CT 06611 USA (SAN 631-046X) Tel 203-261-2130; Fax: 203-452-0180
E-mail: gamboge@pcaet.com.

Gangaji Foundation, The, *(978-0-9632194; 978-1-887984)* P.O. Box 716, Ashland, OR 97520-0024 USA Toll Free: 800-267-9205
E-mail: order@Gangaji.org; info@gangaji.org
Web site: http://www.gangaji.org.

Gannon Distributing Co., *(978-0-88307)* 100 La Salle Cir., No. A, Santa Fe, NM 87505-6916 USA (SAN 201-5889).

Gardner's Book Service, *See* **Gardner's Bk. Service**

Garrett Educational Corp., *(978-0-944483; 978-1-56074)* Orders Addr.: P.O. Box 1588, Ada, OK 74820 USA (SAN 169-6955) Tel 580-332-6884; Fax: 580-332-1560; Toll Free: 800-654-9366; Edit Addr.: 130 E. 13th St., Ada, OK 74820 USA (SAN 243-2722)
E-mail: mail@garrettbooks.com
Web site: http://www.garrettbooks.com.

Gasman News Agency, 2211 Third Ave., S., Escanaba, MI 49829 USA (SAN 169-3794).

Gatewood Pr., *(978-0-9710427)* P.O. Box 356, Johnson City, TX 78636 USA Tel 832-723-7313 Do not confuse with Wilson & Associates, Gig Harbor, WA
E-mail: alvincoog@me.com.

Gaunt, Inc., *(978-0-912004; 978-1-56169; 978-1-60449)* 3011 Gulf Dr., Holmes Beach, FL 34217-2199 USA (SAN 202-9413) Tel 941-778-5211; Fax: 941-778-5252
E-mail: info@gaunt.com; sales@gaunt.com
Web site: http://www.gaunt.com.

Gaunt, William W. & Sons, Incorporated, *See* **Gaunt, Inc.**

GBGM Service Ctr., P.O. Box 691328, Cincinnati, OH 45269 USA.

Gefen Bks., *(978-0-86343)* 11 Edison Pl., Springfield, NJ 07081 USA (SAN 856-8065)
E-mail: gefenny@gefenpublishing.com
Web site: http://www.gefenpublishing.com.

Gem Guides Bk. Co., *(978-0-935182; 978-0-937799; 978-1-889786)* Orders Addr.: 1275 W. 9th St., Upland, CA 91786 USA (SAN 221-1637) Tel 626-855-1611; Fax: 626-855-1610
E-mail: info@gemguidesbooks.com
Web site: http://www.gemguidesbooks.com.

Gemini Enterprises, P.O. Box 8251, Stockton, CA 95208 USA (SAN 128-1402).

Genealogical Sources, Unlimited, *(978-0-913857)* 407 Ascot Ct., Knoxville, TN 37923-5807 USA (SAN 170-8058) Tel 865-690-7831.

Genealogy Digest, 960 N. 400 E., North Salt Lake, UT 84054-1920 USA (SAN 110-389X); 420 S. 425 W., Bountiful, UT 84010 (SAN 243-2439).

General Medical Pubs., *(978-0-935236)* P.O. Box 210, Venice, CA 90294-0210 USA (SAN 215-689X) Tel 310-392-4911.

Generic Computer Products, Inc., *(978-0-918611)* P.O. Box 790, Marquette, MI 49855 USA (SAN 284-8856) Tel 906-226-7600; Fax: 906-226-8309.

Geographia Map Co., Inc., *(978-0-88433)* 75 Moore St., Hackensack, NJ 07601-7107 USA (SAN 132-5566).

Gerold International Booksellers, Inc., 35-23 Utopia Pkwy., Flushing, NY 11358 USA (SAN 129-959X) Tel 718-358-4741; Fax: 718-358-3688.

Gibbs Smith, Publisher, *(978-0-87905; 978-0-941711; 978-1-58685; 978-1-4236)* Orders Addr.: P.O. Box 667, Layton, UT 84041 USA (SAN 201-9906) Tel 801-544-9800; Fax: 801-544-5582; Toll Free Fax: 800-213-3023 (orders); Toll Free: 800-748-5439 (orders); 800-835-4993 (Customer Service order only); Edit Addr.: 1877 E. Gentile St., Layton, UT 84040 USA Tel 801-544-9800; Fax: 801-546-8853
E-mail: info@gibbs-smith.com; tradeorders@gibbs-smith.com
Web site: http://www.gibbs-smith.com.

Gibson, Dot Pubns., *(978-0-941162)* Orders Addr.: P.O. Box 117, Waycross, GA 31502-0117 USA (SAN 200-4143) Tel 912-285-2848; Fax: 912-285-0349; Toll Free: 800-336-8095; Edit Addr.: 383 Bonneyman Rd., Blackshear, GA 31516 USA (SAN 200-9676)
E-mail: info@dotgibson.com
Web site: http://www.dotgibson.com.

Gilmore-Howard, P.O. Box 1268, Arlington, TX 76004-1268 USA (SAN 157-485X).

Giron Bks., *(978-0-9741393; 978-0-9915442)* 2141 W. 21st St., Chicago, IL 60608-2608 USA Tel 773-847-3000; Fax: 773-847-9197; Toll Free: 800-405-4276
E-mail: juanmanuel@gironbooks.com; carolina@gironbooks.com
Web site: http://www.gironbooks.com.

G-Jo Institute/DeerHaven Hills, *(978-0-916878)* P.O. Box 1460, Columbus, NC 28722-1460 USA (SAN 111-0004)
E-mail: officesupport@g-jo.com
Web site: http://www.g-jo.com.

G-Jo Institute/Falkyn, Incorporated, *See* **G-Jo Institute/DeerHaven Hills**

GL Services, 4588 Interstate Dr., Cincinnati, OH 45246 USA Tel 805-677-6815.

Global Bk. Distributors, P.O. Box 192629, Dallas, TX 75219 USA.

Global Engineering Documents-Latin America, 3909 NE 163rd St., Suite 110, North Miami Beach, FL 33160 USA (SAN 630-7868) Tel 305-944-1099; Fax: 305-944-1028
E-mail: global.csa@ihs.com.

Global Info Centres, *See* **Global Engineering Documents-Latin America**

Global Publishing Associates, Inc., *See* **Jobson, Oliver H.**

Globe Pequot Pr., The, *(978-0-7627; 978-0-87106; 978-0-88742; 978-0-914788; 978-0-933469; 978-0-934802; 978-0-941130; 978-1-56440; 978-1-57034; 978-1-57392; 978-1-58574; 978-1-59228; 978-1-59921; 978-1-4779; 978-1-4930)* Orders Addr.: P.O. Box 480, Guilford, CT 06437-0480 USA (SAN 201-9892) Tel 888-249-7586; Toll Free Fax: 800-820-2329 (in Connecticut); Toll Free: 800-243-0495 (24 hours); 800-336-8334; Edit Addr.: 246 Goose Ln., Guilford, CT 06437 USA Tel 203-458-4500; Fax: 203-458-4600; Toll Free Fax: 800-336-8334
E-mail: info@globepequot.com
Web site: http://www.globepequot.com.

Gluesing & Gluesing, *(978-0-9631357)* 10301 Bren Rd W. Ste. 165, Hopkins, MN 55343-9129 USA (SAN 630-0022) Toll Free: 800-747-0227.

GOBI Library Solutionis from EBSCO, 999 Maple St., Contocook, NH 03229 USA Tel 603-746-3102; Toll Free: 800-258-3774
Web site: http://www.gobi.ebsco.com.

Goldberg, Louis Library Bk. Supplier, 45 Belvidere St., Nazareth, PA 18064 USA (SAN 169-7536) Tel 610-759-9458; Fax: 610-759-8134.

Goldenrod Music, Inc., 1310 Turner Rd., Lansing, MI 48906-4342 USA (SAN 630-5962) Tel 517-484-1777
E-mail: music@goldenrod.com
Web site: http://www.goldenrod.com.

Goldenrod/Horizon Distribution, *See* **Goldenrod Music, Inc.**

Goldman, S. Otzar Hasefarim, Inc., 125 Ditmas Ave., Brooklyn, NY 11218 USA (SAN 169-5770) Tel 718-972-6200; Fax: 718-972-6204; Toll Free: 800-972-6201.

Good Bk. Publishing Co., *(978-1-881212)* P.O. Box 837, Kihei, HI 96753-0837 USA (SAN 297-9578) Tel 808-874-4876 (phone/fax)
E-mail: dickb@dickb.com
Web site: http://www.dickb.com/index.shtml.

Good News Magazine Distributors, 6332 Saunders St., Rego Park, NY 11374-2031 USA (SAN 113-7271) Toll Free: 800-624-7257.

Gopher News Co., 9000 10th Ave N., Minneapolis, MN 55427-4322 USA (SAN 169-4138).

Gopher News Company, *See* **St. Marie's Gopher News Co.**

Gospel Light Pubns., *(978-0-8307)* Orders Addr.: 1957 Eastman Ave., Ventura, CA 93003 USA (SAN 299-0873) Tel 805-644-9721; Fax: 805-289-0200; Toll Free: 800-446-7735 (orders only) Do not confuse with companies with similar names in Brooklyn, NY, Delight, AR
E-mail: info@gospellight.com; kyleloffelmacher@gospellight.com
Web site: http://www.gospellight.com.

Gospel Mission, Inc., *(978-1-62813)* Orders Addr.: P.O. Box 318, Choteau, MT 59422 USA (SAN 170-3196) Tel 406-466-2311; Edit Addr.: 316 First St., NW, Choteau, MT 59422 USA (SAN 243-2455).

Gospel Publishing Hse., *(978-0-88243; 978-1-60731)* Div. of General Council of the Assemblies of God, 1445 N. Boonville Ave., Springfield, MO 65802-1894 USA (SAN 206-8826) Tel 417-862-2781; Fax: 417-862-5881; Toll Free Fax: 800-328-0294; Toll Free: 800-641-4310 (orders only)
E-mail: webmaster@gph.com
Web site: http://www.gospelpublishing.com.

Goyescas Corp. of Florida, P.O. Box 524207, Miami, FL 33152-4207 USA (SAN 169-1120).

Graham Services, Inc., 180 James Dr., E., Saint Rose, LA 70087-9481 USA (SAN 169-2895) Tel 504-467-5863; Fax: 504-464-6196; Toll Free: 800-457-7323 (in Los Angeles only)
E-mail: gsi@aol.com.

Grand Central Publishing, *(978-0-445; 978-0-446; 978-0-7595; 978-1-4555; 978-1-5387; 978-1-5460)* Orders Addr.: c/o Little Brown & Co., 3 Center Plaza, Boston, MA 02108-2084 USA Toll Free Fax: 800-286-9471; Toll Free: 800-759-0190; Edit Addr.: 237 Park Ave., New York, NY 10017 USA (SAN 281-8892) Fax: 800-331-1664; Toll Free Fax: 800-759-0190; 1290 Avenue of the Americas, New York, NY 10104
E-mail: renee.supriano@twbg.com; customer.service@hbgusa.com
Web site: http://www.hbgusa.com.

Granite Publishing & Distribution, *(978-1-890558; 978-1-930980; 978-1-932280; 978-1-59936)* 868 N. 1430 W., Orem, UT 84057 USA (SAN 631-0605) Tel 801-229-9023; Fax: 801-229-1924; Toll Free: 800-574-5779 Do not confuse with companies with same or similar names in Madison, WI, Columbus, NC
E-mail: granite@granitepublishing.biz; gregg@granitepublishing.biz
Web site: http://granitepublishing.biz.

Great American Book Fairs, *See* **Scholastic Bk. Fairs**

Great Lakes Reader's Service, Inc., Orders Addr.: P.O. Box 1078, Detroit, MI 48231 USA (SAN 285-9912) Tel 313-965-4577; Fax: 313-965-2445.

Great Northern Distributors, Inc., 634 South Ave., Rochester, NY 14620-1316 USA (SAN 169-7676) Tel 717-342-8159.

Greathall Productions, Inc., *(978-1-882513; 978-1-940916)* Orders Addr.: P.O. Box 5061, Charlottesville, VA 22905-5061 USA Tel 434-296-4288; Fax: 434-296-4490; Toll Free: 800-477-6234
E-mail: greathall@greathall.com
Web site: http://www.greathall.com.

Green Dragon Bks., *(978-0-89334; 978-1-62386)* 2875 S. Ocean Blvd. Ste 200, Palm Beach, FL 33480 USA (SAN 658-0882) Toll Free Fax: 888-874-8844; Toll Free: 800-874-8844 Do not confuse with Humanics ErgoSystems, Inc., Reseda, CA
E-mail: info@greendragonbooks.com
Web site: http://www.greendragonbooks.com; http://www.humanicslearning.com; http://www.humanicsdealer.com.

Green Gate Bks., 6700 W. Chicago St., Chandler, AZ 85226 USA (SAN 169-6785) Tel 480-961-5176; Fax: 480-961-5256; Toll Free: 800-228-3816
E-mail: ggb@wcoil.com
Web site: http://www.greengatebooks.com.

Greenfield Distribution, Inc., Orders Addr.: c/o IDS, 400 Bedford St., Suite 322, Manchester, NH 03101 USA Tel 413-772-2976; Edit Addr.: 20 Blaine St., Manchester, NH 03102 USA
E-mail: Findikzade1@aol.com; Gdibooks@aol.com
Web site: http://www.gdibooks.com.

Greenleaf Book Group, *(978-0-9665319; 978-1-929774; 978-0-9790842; 978-1-60832; 978-1-61486; 978-1-62634; 979-8-88645)* Orders Addr.: 4005-B Banister Ln., Austin, TX 78704 USA Tel 512-891-6100; Fax: 512-891-6150; Toll Free: 800-932-5420; Edit Addr.: P.O. Box 91869, Austin, TX 78709 USA
E-mail: tanya@greenleafbookgroup.com
Web site: http://www.greenleafbookgroup.com.

Grey Hse. Publishing, *(978-0-939300; 978-1-891482; 978-1-930956; 978-1-59237; 978-1-61925; 978-1-68217; 978-1-64265; 978-1-63700; 979-8-89179)* 4919 Rte. 22 PO Box 56, Amenia, NY 12501 USA Tel 518-789-8700; Fax: 518-789-0556; Toll Free: 800-562-2139; 4919 Rte. 22 PO Box 56, Amenia, NY 12501 Tel 518-789-8700; Fax: 518-789-0556; Toll Free: 800-562-2139; 4919 Rte. 22 PO Box 56, Amenia, NY 12501 Tel 518-789-8700; Fax: 518-789-0556; Toll Free: 800-562-2139
E-mail: books@greyhouse.com
Web site: http://www.greyhouse.com.

Grey Owl Indian Craft Co., Inc., 132-05 Merrick Blvd., P.O. Box 468, Jamaica, NY 11434 USA (SAN 132-9979) Tel 718-341-4000.

Grolier Americana, 1111 Crandon Blvd., Apt. C501, Key Biscayne, FL 33149-2734 USA (SAN 108-1764) Tel 305-551-6711.

Grove/Atlantic, Inc., *(978-0-8021; 978-0-87113; 978-1-55584; 978-1-61185)* 841 Broadway, 4th Flr., New York, NY 10003-4793 USA (SAN 201-4890) Tel 212-614-7850; Fax: 212-614-7886; Toll Free: 800-521-0178
Web site: http://www.groveatlantic.com/.

Grupo Nelson, *(978-0-8499; 978-0-88113; 978-0-89922; 978-1-60255)* Div. of Thomas Nelson, Inc., 501 Nelson Pl., Nashville, TN 37217 USA (SAN 240-6349) Tel 615-889-9000; Fax: 615-883-9376; Toll Free: 800-251-4000
Web site: http://www.editorialcaribe.com.

Gryphon Hse., Inc., *(978-0-87659; 978-0-917505; 978-1-58904; 978-1-63650)* Orders Addr.: 6848 Leon's Way, Lewisville, NC 27023 USA (SAN 169-3190) Tel 800-638-0928; Fax: 800-638-7576; Toll Free: 800-638-0928
E-mail: info@ghbooks.com
Web site: http://www.gryphonhouse.com.

GSG & Assocs., *(978-0-945001; 978-1-933355)* Orders Addr.: P.O. Box 590, San Pedro, CA 90733 USA (SAN 245-7792) Tel 310-548-3455; Fax: 310-548-5802; Edit Addr.: 831 S. Palos Vereds St., San Pedro, CA 90731 USA
E-mail: gsgbooks@earthlink.net.

Guardian Bk. Co., P.O. Box 202, Ottawa Lake, MI 49267-0202 USA (SAN 163-7355).

Gulf States Book Fairs, *See* **Gulf States Educational Bks.**

Gulf States Educational Bks., Orders Addr.: 368 Laurel Dr., Satsuma, AL 36572 USA (SAN 158-7870) Toll Free: 800-533-1189.

Gumdrop Bks., Div. of Central Programs, Inc., Orders Addr.: P.O. Box 505, Bethany, MO 64424 USA (SAN 631-4988) Tel 660-425-3923; Fax: 660-425-3970; Toll Free: 800-821-7199; Edit Addr.: P.O. Box 505, Bethany, MO 64424-0505 USA (SAN 131-0860)
E-mail: wecare@gumdropbooks.com
Web site: http://www.gumdropbooks.com.

H & H Distribution, 1634 Stilesgate, Grand Rapids, MI 49508 USA Tel 616-248-7990; Fax: 616-248-0016.

Hachette Bk. Group, *(978-0-446; 978-1-60286; 978-1-60941; 978-1-61113; 978-1-61969; 978-1-4789; 978-1-64732; 978-1-63883; 979-8-88585; 979-8-88969)* Div. of Hachette Group Livre, Orders Addr.: 3 Center Plaza, Boston, MA 02108 USA (SAN 852-5463) Tel 617-263-1828; Toll Free Fax: 800-286-9471; Toll Free: 800-759-0190; Edit Addr.: P.O. Box 2146, Johannesburg, 2196 ZAF Tel 2711 783-7565; Fax: 2711 883-6866
Web site: http://www.hachettebookgroup.com.

Hagerstown News Distributors, *See* **Mid-States Distributors**

Haitiana Pubns., Inc., *(978-0-944987)* 3740 81st St. Apt. B3, Jackson Hts, NY 11372-6947 USA (SAN 245-7059)
E-mail: haitiana@idt.net
Web site: http://www.idtnet/haitiana/.com.

Halalco Bks., 108 E. Fairfax St., Falls Church, VA 22046 USA
E-mail: halalco@halalco.com.

Hale, Robert & Co., Inc., 1803 132nd Ave., NE, Suite 4, Bellevue, WA 98005 USA (SAN 200-6995) Tel 425-881-5212; Fax: 425-881-0731; Toll Free: 800-733-5330.

Half Halt Pr., *(978-0-939481)* Orders Addr.: P.O. Box 67, Boonsboro, MD 21713-0067 USA (SAN 663-270X) Tel 301-733-7119; Fax: 301-733-7408
E-mail: mail@halfhaltpress.com
Web site: http://www.halfhaltpress.com.

Ham Radio's Bookstore, *See* **Radio Bookstore**

Hamakor Judaica, Inc., 7777 Merrimac Ave., Niles, IL 60714 USA (SAN 169-1791) Tel 847-966-4040; Fax: 847-966-4033; Toll Free: 800-552-4088.

Hamel, Bernard H. Spanish Bk. Corp., 10977 Santa Monica Blvd., Los Angeles, CA 90025 USA (SAN 111-8862) Tel 310-475-0453; Fax: 310-473-6132
E-mail: spanish@primenet.com
Web site: http://www.BernardHamel.com; http://www.SpanishBooksUSA.com.

Hamilton News Co., Ltd., 41 Hamilton Ln., Glenmont, NY 12077 USA (SAN 169-5312) Tel 518-463-1135; Fax: 518-463-3154.

Hammond, Incorporated, *See* **Hammond World Atlas Corp.**

Hammond Publishing Co., Inc., *(978-1-883882)* P.O. Box 279, G7166 N. Saginaw St., Mount Morris, MI 48458 USA (SAN 185-142X) Tel 810-686-8881; Fax: 810-686-0561; Toll Free: 800-521-3440 (orders only) E-mail: hammondpub@juno.com.

Hammond World Atlas Corp., *(978-0-7230; 978-0-8437)* Subs. of Langenscheidt Pubs., Inc., 193 Morris Ave., Springfield, NJ 07081-1211 USA (SAN 202-2702) E-mail: rstrung@americanmap.com Web site: http://www.Hammondmap.com.

Hamon, Gerard Incorporated, *See* **Lafayette Bks.**

Hampton-Brown Books, *See* **National Geographic School Publishing, Inc.**

Hancock Hse. Pubs., *(978-0-88839; 978-0-919654; 978-1-55205)* No. 104- 4550 Birch Bay-Lynden Rd, Blaine, WA 98230-9436 USA (SAN 665-7079) Tel 604-538-1114; Fax: 604-538-2262; Toll Free Fax: 800-983-2262; Toll Free: 800-938-1114; 19313 Zero Ave., Surrey, BC V3S 9R9 (SAN 115-3730) E-mail: sales@hancockhouse.com Web site: http://www.hancockhouse.com.

hand2mind, *(978-0-7406; 978-0-914040; 978-0-923832; 978-0-938587; 978-1-57162; 978-1-57452; 978-1-63406)* 500 Greenview Ct., Vernon Hills, IL 60061 USA (SAN 285-7553) Tel 847-816-5050; Fax: 847-816-5066; Toll Free: 800-445-5985 E-mail: info@hand2mind.com Web site: http://www.hand2mind.com.

Handleman, 500 Kirts Blvd., Troy, MI 48084-5225 USA (SAN 106-4886).

Handler News Agency, P.O. Box 27007, Omaha, NE 68127-0007 USA (SAN 169-4405).

Hansen Hse., 1842 West Ave., Miami Beach, FL 33139 USA (SAN 200-7908) Tel 305-532-5461; Toll Free: 800-327-8202.

Harcourt Achieve, *See* **Houghton Mifflin Harcourt Supplemental Pubs.**

Harcourt Brace & Company, *See* **Harcourt Trade Pubs.**

Harcourt Trade Pubs., *(978-0-15)* Div. of Houghton Mifflin Harcourt Trade & Reference Pubs., Orders Addr.: 6277 Sea Harbor Dr., Orlando, FL 32887 USA (SAN 200-285X) Tel 619-699-6707; Toll Free Fax: 800-235-0256; Toll Free: 800-543-1918 (trade orders, inquiries, claims); Edit Addr.: 15 E. 26th St., New York, NY 10010 USA Tel 212-592-1000; Fax: 212-592-1011; 525 B St., Suite 1900, San Diego, CA 92101-4495 (SAN 200-2736) Tel 619-231-6616 E-mail: andrewporter@harcourt.com Web site: http://www.HarcourtBooks.com.

Harness, Miller, 750 Route 73 S. Ste. 110, Marlton, NJ 08053-4142 USA (SAN 169-5789) Toll Free: 800-526-6310.

HarperCollins Christian Publishing, Div. of HarperCollins Publishers, Orders Addr.: P.O. Box 141000, Nashville, TN 37214 USA Toll Free: 800-251-4000; Edit Addr.: 3900 Sparks Dr. SE, Grand Rapids, MI 49546 USA Toll Free: 800-226-1122 Web site: http://www.harpercollinschristian.com/.

HarperCollins Pubs., *(978-0-00; 978-0-06; 978-0-380; 978-0-688; 978-0-690; 978-0-694; 978-0-87795; 978-1-55710)* Div. of News Corp., Orders Addr.: 1000 Keystone Industrial Pk., Scranton, PA 18512-4621 USA (SAN 215-3742) Tel 570-941-1500; Toll Free Fax: 800-822-4090; Toll Free: 800-242-7737 (orders only); Edit Addr.: 10 E. 53rd St., New York, NY 10022-5299 USA (SAN 200-2086) Tel 212-207-7000 Web site: http://www.harpercollins.com; http://www.harpercollinschildrens.com.

Harrisburg News Co., 980 Briarsdale Rd., Harrisburg, PA 17109 USA (SAN 169-7420) Tel 717-561-8377; Fax: 717-561-1466 E-mail: jmurphy@harrisburgnewsco.com Web site: http://www.harrisburgnewsco.com.

Harrison House, Incorporated, *See* **Harrison House Pubs.**

Harrison House Pubs., *(978-0-89274; 978-1-57794; 978-1-60683; 978-1-68031; 978-1-6675; 979-8-218-01386-8)* Orders Addr.: P.O. Box 310, SHIPPENSBURG, PA 17257 USA (SAN 208-676X) Tel 717-532-3040; Toll Free Fax: 800-830-5688; Toll Free: 800-888-4126; Edit Addr.: 167 Walnut Bottom Rd., Shippensburg, PA 17257 USA Tel 717-532-3040; 717-532-9291; Toll Free Fax: 800-830-5688; 800-722-6774; Toll Free: 800-888-4126 E-mail: smckee@norimediagroup.com; jinori@norimediagroup.com; jinori@norimediagroup.com Web site: http://www.harrisonhouse.com.

Harry-Young Pubn. Services Agency, Inc., 6261 Manchester Blvd., Buena Park, CA 90621-2259 USA (SAN 110-8832).

Harvard Assocs., Inc., *(978-0-924346)* 10 Holworthy St., Cambridge, MA 02138 USA (SAN 170-2939) Tel 617-492-0660; Fax: 617-492-4610; Toll Free: 800-774-5646 E-mail: info@harvassoc.com Web site: http://www.harvassoc.com.

Harvard Business Review Pr., *(978-0-87584; 978-1-57851; 978-1-59139; 978-1-4221; 978-1-62527; 978-1-63369; 978-1-64782)* 60 Harvard Way, Boston, MA 02163 USA (SAN 202-277X) Tel 617-783-7400; Fax: 617 495 6181; Fax: 617-783-7492; Toll Free: 888-500-1016 6-19-01 faxed 2nd prefix app, charge, KC E-mail: corpcustserv@hbsp.harvard.edu Web site: http://www.hbsp.harvard.edu; http://www.harvardbusinessonline.com.

Harvard Business School Press, *See* **Harvard Business Review Pr.**

Harvard Univ. Art Museums Shop, 32 Quincy St., Cambridge, MA 02138 USA (SAN 111-3372) Tel 617-495-8286; Fax: 617-495-9985 E-mail: appleyar@fas.harvard.edu Web site: http://www.artmuseums.harvard.edu.

Harvard Univ. Pr., *(978-0-674; 978-0-916724; 978-0-935617; 978-0-674-26878-4)* Orders Addr.: c/o Triliteral LLC, 100 Maple Ridge Dr., Cumberland, RI 02864 USA Tel 401-531-2800; Fax: 401-531-2801; Toll Free Fax: 800-406-9145; Toll Free: 800-405-1619; 800-448-2242; Edit Addr.: 79 Garden St., Cambridge, MA 02138 USA (SAN 200-2043) Tel 617-495-2600; Fax: 617-495-5898 E-mail: contact_hup@harvard.edu Web site: http://www.hup.harvard.edu.

Harvest Distributors, *See* **ARVEST**

Hastings Bks., *(978-0-940846)* 116 N. Wayne Ave., Wayne, PA 19087 USA (SAN 205-048X).

Haven Distributors, 5456 N. Damen Ave., Chicago, IL 60625 USA.

Hawaiian Magazine Distributor, 3375 Koapaka St., No. D180, Honolulu, HI 98619-1865 USA (SAN 169-1619).

Hay Hse., Inc., *(978-0-937611; 978-0-945923; 978-1-56170; 978-1-891751; 978-1-58825; 978-1-4019)* Orders Addr.: P.O. Box 5100, Carlsbad, CA 92018-5100 USA (SAN 630-477X) Tel 760-431-7695 ext 112; Fax: 760-431-6948; Toll Free Fax: 800-650-5115 (orders only); Toll Free: 800-654-5126 (orders only); 2776 Loker Ave. W, Carlsbad, CA 92010 (SAN 257-3024) Tel 800-654-5126; Fax: 800-650-5115; 2776 Loker Ave. W., Carlsbad, CA 92010 E-mail: kjohnson@hayhouse.com; pcrowe@hayhouse.com Web site: http://www.hayhouse.com.

Hazelden, *(978-0-89486; 978-0-89638; 978-0-935908; 978-0-942421; 978-1-56246; 978-1-56838; 978-1-59285; 978-1-61649; 978-1-63634)* 15251 Pleasant Valley Rd., P.o. Box 176, Center City, MN 55012-0176 USA (SAN 209-4010) Fax: 651-213-4044; Toll Free: 800-328-9000; P.O. Box 176, RW4, Center City, MN 55012 Tel 651-213-4000; Toll Free: 800-328-9000 E-mail: bosterbauer@hazelden.org Web site: http://www.hazelden.org.

Hazelden Publishing & Educational Services, *See* **Hazelden**

Health and Growth Assocs., *(978-0-9630266)* Orders Addr.: 28195 Fairview Ave., Hemet, CA 92544 USA Tel 951-927-1768; Fax: 951-927-1548 E-mail: flloomis@earthlink.net.

Health Communications, Inc., *(978-0-932194; 978-1-55874; 978-0-7573; 978-0-9910732)* Orders Addr.: 3201 SW 15th St., Deerfield Beach, FL 33442-8190 USA (SAN 212-100X) Tel 954-360-0909; Fax: 954-360-0034; Toll Free: 800-441-5569 Do not confuse with Health Communications, Inc., Edison, NJ E-mail: terip@hcibooks.com; lorig@hcibooks.com Web site: http://www.hcibooks.com.

Hearst Distribution Group, Incorporated, Book Division, *See* **Comag Marketing Group**

Heartland Bk. Co., 10195 N. Lake Ave., Olathe, KS 66061 USA (SAN 631-2497) Tel 913-829-1784.

Heffernan Audio Visual, Orders Addr.: P.O. Box 5906, San Antonio, TX 78201-0906 USA Tel 210-732-4333; Fax: 210-732-5906; Edit Addr.: 435 Isom Rd. Ste. 210, San Antonio, TX 78216-5144 USA (SAN 166-8722) E-mail: sales@heffernanav.com Web site: http://www.heffernanav.com.

Heffernan School Supply, *See* **Heffernan Audio Visual**

Heinecken & Assoc., Ltd., 1733 N. Mohawk, Chicago, IL 60614 USA Toll Free Fax: 800-947-5694; Toll Free: 800-449-0138.

.Heinemann-Raintree, *See* **Heinemann-Raintree**

Heinemann-Raintree, *(978-0-431; 978-1-57572; 978-1-58810; 978-1-4034; 978-1-4109; 978-1-4329; 978-1-4846)* Div. of Capstone, Orders Addr.: 1710 Roe Crest Dr., North Mankato, MN 56003 USA; Halley Court Freepost PO Box 1125, Oxford, OX2 8YY.

Heirloom Bible Pubs., *(978-0-9817263)* Orders Addr.: P.O. Box 118, Wichita, KS 67201-0118 USA (SAN 630-2793) Fax: 316-267-1850; Toll Free: 800-676-2448; Edit Addr.: 9020 E. 35th St. N., Wichita, KS 67226-2017 USA.

Helix, 310 S. Racine St., Chicago, IL 60607 USA (SAN 111-915X) Tel 312-421-6000; Fax: 312-421-1586.

Hemed Books, Incorporated, *See* **Lambda Pubs., Inc.**

Hendrick-Long Publishing Co., *(978-0-937460; 978-1-885777)* Orders Addr.: 10635 Tower Oaks, Suite D, Houston, TX 77070 USA (SAN 281-7756) Toll Free: 800-544-3770; Edit Addr.: 10635 Tower Oaks Blvd., Houston, TX 77070-5927 USA (SAN 281-7748) E-mail: hendrick-long@worldnet.att.net Web site: http://www.hendricklongpublishing.com.

Herald Pr., *(978-0-8361; 978-1-5138)* Div. of MennoMedia, Inc., Orders Addr.: 1251 Virginia Ave., Harrisonburg, VA 22802 USA (SAN 202-2915) Fax: 1-316-283-0454; Toll Free: 1-800-245-7894; 800-631-6535 (Canada only) Do not confuse with Herald Pr., Charlotte, NC E-mail: info@mennomedia.org Web site: http://www.mennomedia.org.

Herald Publishing Hse., *(978-0-8309)* Orders Addr.: P.O. Box 390, Independence, MO 64051-0390 USA Tel 816-521-3015; Fax: 816-521-3066 (customer services); Toll Free: 800-767-8181; Edit Addr.: 1001W. Walnut St., Independence, MO 64051-0390 USA (SAN 111-7556) Tel 816-257-0200 E-mail: sales@HeraldHouse.org Web site: http://www.heraldhouse.org.

Heritage Bookstore, Orders Addr.: P.O. Box 6007, Springfield, MO 65801-6007 USA (SAN 111-7696).

Hertzberg-New Method Inc., 617 E. Vandalia Rd., Ebooks, Jacksonville, IL 62650 USA (SAN 780-0479) Tel 217-243-5451.

Hervey's Booklink & Cookbook Warehouse, P.O. Box 831870, Richardson, TX 75083 USA (SAN 630-9747).

Hesteria Records & Publishing Co., 124 Hagar Ct., Santa Cruz, CA 95064 USA Tel 831-459-2575; Fax: 831-457-2917 E-mail: alissa@aainnovators.com Web site: http://www.aainnovators.com.

Hi Jolly Library Service, 150 N. Gay St., Susanville, CA 96130-3902 USA (SAN 133-5944).

Hibel, Edna Studio, P.O. Box 9967, Riviera Beach, FL 33419 USA (SAN 111-1574) Tel 561-848-9640; Toll Free: 800-275-3426.

Hicks News Agency, Incorporated, *See* **NEWSouth Distributors**

High Peak Bks., *(978-1-884709)* Orders Addr.: P.O. Box 703, Wilson, WY 83014 USA (SAN 299-4232); Edit Addr.: 355 N. Bar Y Rd., Jackson, WY 83011 USA Tel 307-739-0147 Do not confuse with High Peak Pr. in Schenectady, NY.

Highlights Pr., c/o Highlights for Children, Inc., *(978-1-56397; 978-1-878093; 978-1-886910; 978-1-59078; 978-1-932425; 978-1-62091; 978-1-62979; 978-0-9961172; 978-0-9961173; 978-1-943283; 978-1-68238; 978-1-68329; 978-1-68437; 978-1-64472; 978-1-7922; 978-1-63962)* Div. of Highlights For Children, Inc., 815 Church St., Honesdale, PA 18431 USA (SAN 852-3177) Tel 570-251-4513; 570-251-4592.

Hill City News Agency, Inc., 3228 Odd Fellow Rd., Lynchburg, VA 24501 USA (SAN 169-8656) Tel 804-845-4231; Fax: 804-845-0864.

Hillsboro News, Orders Addr.: P.O. Box 25738, Tampa, FL 33622-5738 USA Tel 813-622-8087; Edit Addr.: 7002 Parke E. Blvd., Tampa, FL 33610 USA.

Himber Bks., Div. of F. C. Himber & Son's, Inc., 1380 W. Second Ave., Eugene, OR 97402 USA Tel 541-686-8003; Toll Free: 800-888-5904.

Himber, F. C., *See* **Himber Bks.**

Hinrichs, E. Louis, P.O. Box 1090, Lompoc, CA 93438-1090 USA (SAN 133-1493) Tel 805-736-7512 E-mail: booklompoc@aol.com.

Hinsdale County Historical Society, P.O. Box 353 130 N. Silver St., Lake City, CO 81235 USA Tel 970-944-2050.

Historic Aviation Bks., 121 Fifth Ave., Suite 300, New Brighton, MN 55112 USA (SAN 129-5284) Tel 651-635-0100; Fax: 651-635-0700.

Historic Cherry Hill, *(978-0-943366)* 523 1/2 S. Pearl St., Albany, NY 12202 USA (SAN 110-8859) Tel 518-434-4791; Fax: 518-434-4806.

Hobbies Hawaii Distributors, 4420 Lawehana St., No. 3, Honolulu, HI 96818 USA (SAN 630-8619) Tel 808-423-0265; Fax: 808-423-1635.

Holiday Enterprises, Inc., 3328 US Hwy. 123, Rochester Bldg., Greenville, SC 29611 USA (SAN 169-779X) Tel 864-220-3161; Fax: 864-295-9757.

Holt, Henry & Co., *(978-0-03; 978-0-8050)* Div. of Holtzbrinck Publishers, Orders Addr.: 16365 James Madison Hwy., Gordonsville, VA 22942-8501 USA Toll Free Fax: 800-672-2054; Toll Free: 888-330-8477; Edit Addr.: 115 W. 18th St., 5th Flr., New York, NY 10011 USA (SAN 200-6472) Tel 212-886-9200; Fax: 540-672-7540 (customer service) E-mail: info@hholt.com Web site: http://www.henryholt.com.

Holtzbrinck Publishers, *See* **Macmillan**

Holyoke News Co., Inc., 720 Main St., P.O. Box 990, Holyoke, MA 01041 USA (SAN 169-3468) Tel 413-534-4537; Fax: 413-538-7161; Toll Free: 800-628-8372 E-mail: sales@holyoke-news.com.

Homestead Book Co., *(978-0-930180)* Orders Addr.: P.O. Box 31608, Seattle, WA 98103 USA (SAN 662-037X); Edit Addr.: 6101 22nd Ave., NW, Seattle, WA 98107 USA (SAN 169-8796) Tel 206-782-4532; Fax: 206-784-9328; Toll Free: 800-426-6777 (orders only) E-mail: info@homesteadbook.com Web site: http://www.homesteadbook.com.

Homestead Book, Incorporated, *See* **Homestead Book Co.**

Hood, Alan C. & Co., Inc., *(978-0-911469)* P.O. Box 775, Chambersburg, PA 17201 USA (SAN 270-8221) Tel 717-267-0867; Fax: 717-267-0572; Toll Free Fax: 888-844-9433; 4501 Forbes Blvd., Lanham, MD 20706 E-mail: hoodbooks@pa.net Web site: http://www.hoodbooks.com.

Hoover Institution Pr., *(978-0-8179)* Stanford Univ., Stanford, CA 94305-6010 USA (SAN 202-3024) Tel 650-723-3373; Fax: 650-723-8626; Toll Free: 800-935-2882 E-mail: scott.harrison@stanford.edu Web site: http://www.hooverpress.org.

Hopkins Fulfillment Services, P.O. Box 50370, Baltimore, MD 21211-4370 USA Fax: 410-516-6998; Toll Free: 800-537-5487.

Hotho & Co., P.O. Box 9738, Fort Worth, TX 76147-2738 USA (SAN 169-8192).

Houghton Mifflin Company, *See* **Houghton Mifflin Harcourt Publishing Co.**

Houghton Mifflin Company Trade & Reference Division, *See* **Houghton Mifflin Harcourt Trade & Reference Pubs.**

Houghton Mifflin Harcourt Publishing Co., *(978-0-395; 978-0-87466; 978-0-9631591; 978-1-57630; 978-1-881527; 978-0-618; 978-0-544; 978-0-547; 978-1-328; 978-0-358; 979-8-202)* Orders Addr.: 9205 Southpark Ctr. Loop, Orlando, FL 32819 USA Toll Free: 800-225-3362; Edit Addr.: 222 Berkeley St., Boston, MA 02116 USA (SAN 215-3793) Tel 617-351-5000; 125 High St., Boston, MA 02110 Web site: http://www.hmco.com.

Houghton Mifflin Harcourt Supplemental Pubs., *(978-1-60032; 978-1-60277)* 10801 N. Mopac Expressway, Bldg. 3, Austin, TX 78759 USA Web site: www.harcourtachieve.com.

Houghton Mifflin Harcourt Trade & Reference Pubs., *(978-0-395; 978-0-89919; 978-0-618)* Orders Addr.: 9205 Southpark Ctr. Loop, Orlando, FL 32819 USA Tel 978-661-1300; Toll Free: 800-225-3362; Edit Addr.: 222 Berkeley St., Boston, MA 02116 USA (SAN 200-2388) Tel 617-351-5000; Fax: 617-227-5409; 215 Park Ave S., 12th Flr., New York, NY 10003-1621 E-mail: trade_sub_rights@hmco.com Web site: http://www.hmco.com/; http://www.houghtonmifflinbooks.com.

Houston Paperback Distributor, 4114 Gairloch Ln., Houston, TX 77025-2912 USA (SAN 169-8273).

Hovel Audio, Incorporated, *See* **christianaudio**

How-2 Bks., P.O. Box 5793, Denver, CO 80217 USA (SAN 631-1369) Tel 303-778-8383; Toll Free: 800-279-7323.

HPK Educational Resource Ctr., *(978-0-89895)* Div. of H. P. Koppelmann, Inc., 140 Van Block Ave., Hartford, CT 06141 USA (SAN 169-071X) Tel 860-549-6210; Toll Free: 800-243-7724.

Hubbard, P.O. Box 100, Defiance, OH 43512 USA (SAN 169-6726) Tel 419-784-4455; Fax: 419-782-1662; Toll Free: 800-582-0657 E-mail: hubbard@bright.net.

Hudson County News Co., 1305 Paterson Plank Rd., North Bergen, NJ 07047 USA (SAN 169-4782) Tel 201-867-3600.

Hudson Hills Pr. LLC, *(978-0-933920; 978-0-9646042; 978-1-55595)* Orders Addr.: P.O. Box 205, Manchester, VT 05254 USA; Edit Addr.: 74-2 Union St., Manchester, VT 05254 USA (SAN 213-0815) Tel 802-362-6450; Fax: 802-362-6459 E-mail: artbooks@hudsonhills.com Web site: http://www.hudsonhills.com/.

Hudson Hills Press, Incorporated, *See* **Hudson Hills Pr. LLC**

Hudson Valley News Distributors, P.O. Box 1236, Newburgh, NY 12550 USA (SAN 169-6084) Tel 914-562-3399; Fax: 914-562-6010.

Humanics Publishing Group, *See* **Green Dragon Bks.**

Hyperion Pr., *(978-0-7868; 978-1-56282; 978-1-4013)* Div. of Disney Bk. Publishing, Inc., A Walt Disney Co., Orders Addr.: c/o HarperCollins Publishers, 1000 Keystone Industrial Park, Scranton, PA 18512-4621 USA Toll Free: 800-242-7737; Edit Addr.: 114 Fifth Ave., New York, NY 110011 USA Tel 917-661-2000 Web site: http://www.hyperionbooks.com.

i. b. d., Ltd., *(978-0-88431)* 24 Hudson St., Kinderhook, NY 12106 USA (SAN 630-7779) Tel 518-758-1755; Fax: 518-758-6702 E-mail: lankhof@ibdltd.com Web site: http://www.ibdltd.com.

I S H K, *(978-0-86304; 978-0-900860; 978-1-883536; 978-1-933779; 978-1-942698; 978-1-944493; 978-1-946270; 978-1-948013; 978-1-949358; 978-1-953292; 978-1-958289; 978-1-959393; 978-1-960884)* Div. of Institute for the Study of Human Knowledge, Ishk-hoopoe-malor 548 Market St. No. 39187, San Francisco, CA 91404-5401 USA (SAN 226-4536) Tel 408-445-9639; Ishk-hoopoe-malor 548 Market St. No. 39187, San Francisco, CA 91404-5401 Tel 408-445-9639 E-mail: ishkadmin@ishk.net Web site: http://www.ishk.net; http://www.hoopoebooks.com; http://www.malorbooks.com.

Iaconi, Mariuccia Bk. Imports, *(978-0-9628720)* P.O. Box 77023, San Francisco, CA 94107-0023 USA (SAN 161-1364) Toll Free: 800-955-9577 E-mail: mibibook@ixnetcom.com Web site: http://www.mibibook.com.

ICG Muse, Inc., 420 W. 42nd St. Apt. 35B, New York, NY 10036-6863 USA (SAN 631-7200).

Icon Distribution, 3325 Donnell Dr., Forestville, MD 20747 USA.

ID International Bk. Service, 126 Old Ridgefield Rd., Wilton, CT 06897-3017 USA (SAN 630-8074) Tel 203-834-2272; Fax: 203-762-9725 E-mail: orders@idintl.com.

Idaho News Agency, 2710 Julia St., Coeur D'Alene, ID 83814 USA (SAN 169-1651) Tel 208-664-3444.

Ideal Foreign Bks., Inc., 132-10 Hillside Ave., Richmond Hill, NY 11418 USA (SAN 169-6173) Tel 718-297-7477; Fax: 718-297-7645; Toll Free: 800-284-2490 (orders only).

IFSTA, *(978-0-87939; 978-1-56916)* Orders Addr.: c/o Oklahoma State Univ., Fire Protection Pubns., 930 N. Willis, Stillwater, OK 74078-8045 USA Tel 405-744-5723; Fax: 405-744-8204; Toll Free: 800-654-4055 (orders only) Web site: http://www.ifsta.org/.

Ignatius Pr., *(978-0-89870; 978-1-58617; 978-1-62164; 978-1-68149; 978-1-64229)* Orders Addr.: P.O. Box 1339, Fort Collins, CO 80522-1339 USA (SAN 855-3556) Tel 970-221-3920; Fax: 970-221-3964; Toll Free Fax: 800-278-3566; Toll Free: 877-320-9276 (bookstore orders); 800-651-1531 (credit card orders, no minimum, individual orders); 1915 Astor Rd. Sycamore, Sycamore, IL 60178 (SAN 991-4595); 1915 Astor Rd., Sycamore, IL 60178 (SAN 991-4609); Edit Addr.: 1348 10th Ave., San Francisco, CA 94122 USA (SAN 214-3887) Toll Free: 800-651-1531 E-mail: info@ignatius.com Web site: http://www.ignatius.com.

Igram Pr., *(978-0-911119; 978-1-930279)* 311 Parsons Dr., Hiawatha, IA 52233 USA (SAN 263-1709) Tel 319-393-3600; Fax: 319-393-3934; Toll Free: 800-393-2399 E-mail: clabarr@cedargraphicsinc.com.

Illinois News Service, *See* **News Group - Illinois, The**

Ilmhouse Inc., P.O. Box 74, Haverford, PA 19041-0074 USA E-mail: admin@ilmhouse.com Web site: http://www.ilmhouse.com.

Image Processing Software, Inc., *(978-0-924507)* 6409 Appalachian Way, Madison, WI 53705 USA (SAN 265-5977) Tel 608-233-5033; 4414 Regent St., Madison, WI 53705 USA (SAN 249-3020).

Impact Photographics, *(978-0-918327; 978-1-56540; 978-1-60068)* 4961 Windplay Dr., Eldorado Hills, CA

95630 USA (SAN 657-3126) Tel 916-939-9333; Fax: 916-939-9334; Toll Free: 800-950-0110
E-mail: juliem@impactphotographics.com
Web site: http://www.impactphotographics.com.

Imperial News Co., Inc., 5131 Post Rd., Dublin, OH 43017-1160 USA (SAN 169-5509) Fax: 516-752-8515.

Imported Bks., Orders Addr.: St., Dallas, TX 75208 USA (SAN 169-8095) Tel 214-941-6497.

In Between Bks., *(978-0-935430; 978-0-9602007)* P.O. Box 790, Sausalito, CA 94966 USA (SAN 213-6236) Tel 415-383-8447; Fax: 415-381-1938; 415-381-3513
E-mail: inbetweenbooks@atthebutterflytree.com; karla@inbetweenbooks.com; juno@inbetweenbooks.com
Web site: http://www.atthebutterflytree.com.

Incor Periodicals, 32150 Hwy. 34, Tangent, OR 97389-9704 USA (SAN 169-7072) Tel 541-926-8889; Fax: 541-926-9553.

Independent Magazine Co., 2970 N. Ontario St., Burbank, CA 91504-2016 USA (SAN 159-8783).

Independent Pub., *(978-1-4243; 978-1-59975; 978-1-60402; 978-1-60461; 978-1-60530; 978-1-60585; 978-1-60643; 978-1-60702; 978-1-60725; 978-1-60743; 978-1-61539; 978-1-61584; 978-1-61623; 978-1-61658; 978-1-4507; 978-1-4675; 978-1-4951; 978-0-9927847; 978-1-5323;-1-7923; 978-0-578-33228-4; 978-0-578-33515-5; 978-0-578-33612-1; 978-0-578-35450-7; 979-8-3507; 979-8-218-21167-7; 979-8-218-21168-4; 979-8-218-28747-4; 979-8-218-28748-1) Div. of Bar Code Graphics, 875 N. Michigan Ave., Suite 2650, Chicago, IL 60615 USA Fax: 312-595-0725; Toll Free: 800-662-0701; 65 E. Wacker Pl., 18th Flr., Chicago, IL 60601 Tel 312-595-0600; Toll Free: 800-662-0703 Do not confuse with Independent Publishers in Bountiful, UT*
E-mail: pubserv@barcode-us.com
Web site: http://www.publisherservices-us.com; http://www.isbn-us.com.

Independent Pubs. Group, *(978-1-4956; 979-8-3688)* Subs. of Chicago Review Pr., 814 N. Franklin, Chicago, IL 60610 USA (SAN 201-2936) Tel 312-337-0747; Fax: 312-337-5985; Toll Free: 800-888-4741
E-mail: frontdesk@ipgbook.com
Web site: http://www.ipgbook.com; http://www.trafalgarsquarepublishing.com.

Independently published, *See* **Independently Published**

Indiana Periodicals, Inc., 2120 S. Meridian St., Indianapolis, IN 46225 USA (SAN 169-2380) Tel 317-786-1488; Fax: 317-782-4999.

Indiana Univ. Pr., *(978-0-253; 978-0-86196)* 601 N. Morton St., Bloomington, IN 47404-3797 USA (SAN 202-5647) Fax: 812-855-7931; Toll Free: 800-842-6796
E-mail: iuporder@indiana.edu
Web site: http://www.iupress.indiana.edu.

Indig, Stanley M. Specialty Pubn., *(978-0-945815; 978-1-57767)* 2173 E. 38th St., Brooklyn, NY 11234 USA (SAN 248-0719) Tel 718-692-0648; Fax: 718-677-9542
E-mail: indigpublishing@yahoo.com; indigpublishing@aol.com
Web site: http://www.indigpublishing.com.

Ingenix, Incorporated, *See* **OptumInsight, Inc.**

Ingham Publishing, Inc., *(978-0-9611804; 978-1-891130)* Orders Addr.: P.O. Box 12642, Saint Petersburg, FL 33733-2642 USA Tel 813-343-4811; Fax: 813-381-2807; Edit Addr.: 5650 First Ave., N., Saint Petersburg, FL 33710 USA (SAN 112-8930)
E-mail: ftreflex@concentric.net.

Ingram Academic, Div. of Ingram Content Group, Orders Addr.: c/o Perseus Books Group, 210 American Dr., Jackson, TN 38301 USA Toll Free Fax: 800-351-5073; Toll Free: 800-343-4499; c/o Publishers Group Canada, 76 Stafford St., Unit 300, Toronto, ON M6J 2S1 Tel 416-934-9900; Fax: 416-934-1410; Toll Free Fax: 800-565-3770; Toll Free: 800-663-5714
E-mail: academicorders@perseusbooks.com; client.info@perseusbooks.com
Web site: http://www.perseusacademic.com.

Ingram Bk. Co., *(978-1-61522; 978-1-60894)* Subs. of Ingram Industries, Inc., Orders Addr.: 1 Ingram Blvd., P.O. Box 3006, La Vergne, TN 37086-1986 USA (SAN 169-7978) Tel 615-213-5000; Fax: 615-213-3976 (Electronic Orders); Toll Free Fax: 800-285-3296 (fax inquiry US & Canada); 800-876-0186 (orders); 877-663-5367 (Canadian orders); Toll Free: 800-937-8000 (orders only); 800-937-8200 (customer service US & Canada); 800-289-0687 (Canadian orders only customer service); 800-234-6737 (electronic orders US & Canada)) Do not confuse with Ingram Pr., Sacramento, CA
E-mail: flashback@ingrambook.com; customerservice@ingrambook.com; ics-sales@ingrambook.com
Web site: http://www.ingrambook.com.

Ingram Content Group, Orders Addr.: 1246 Heil Quaker Blvd., LaVergne, TN 37086 USA (SAN 179-6976) Tel 615-213-4595; Fax: 615-213-4426; 860 Nestle Way - LSI Lightning Source, Breingsville, PA 18031 (SAN 920-4288); 4260 Port Union Rd. No. 100 - LSI Lightning Source, Fairfield, OH 45011 (SAN 920-4296); 150 Fieldcrest Ave - IBC Ingram Book - IBC, Edison, NJ 08837 (SAN 920-430X) Tel 615-413-4476; 4260 Port Union Rd. No. 100 - IBC Ingram Book - IBC, Fairfield, OH 45011 (SAN 920-4318); 150 Fieldcrest Ave - IPS Ingram Publisher Services, Edison, NJ 08837 (SAN 920-4431); 4260 Port Union Rd. No 100 - IPS Ingram Publisher Services, Fairfield, OH 45011 (SAN 920-444X); 860 Nestle Way - IBC, Breinigsville, PA 18031 (SAN 920-6264); 860 Nestle Way-IPS, Breinigsville, PA 18031 (SAN 920-6272); 3145 S. Northpointe Dr. - LSI N. Pointe Business Pk., Fresno, CA 93725 (SAN 920-6280); 3145 S Northpointe Dr - IPS, Fresno, CA 93725 (SAN 920-7937); 3145 S Northpointe Dr - IBC, Fresno, CA 93725 (SAN 920-7945); 210 American Dr. - IPS, Jackson, TN 3383017716 (SAN 991-1243) Tel 731-265-5943; 193 Edwards Dr. - LSI, Jackson , TN 3383017716 (SAN 991-1812); 1 Deltic Ave, IWUK Rooksley, Milton Keynes, MK13 8LD Tel 615-213-4514
E-mail: edi@ingramcontent.com.

Ingram Content Group Inc., Sub. of Ingram Industries Inc., 1 Ingram Blvd., La Vergne, TN 37086 USA Tel 615-793-5000; Toll Free: 800-937-8000 (option 3)
E-mail: inquiry@ingramcontent.com; customerservice@ingramcontent.com
Web site: http://www.ingramcontent.com.

Ingram Entertainment, Inc., Two Ingram Blvd. (Corp. Headquarters), La Vergne, TN 37089-7006 USA (SAN 630-6780) Tel 615-287-4000; Fax: 615-287-4995; Toll Free: 800-759-5000; 12000 Ridgemont Dr., Urbandale, IA 50323-2317 (SAN 630-6950); 26391 Curtiss Wright Pkwy. Ste. 106, Cleveland, OH 44143-4401 (SAN 630-6896) Toll Free: 800-621-1333; 15002 Sommermeyer, Houston, TX 77041-5333 (SAN 630-7000) Tel 713-937-3600; Fax: 713-466-4316; 382 E. Lies Rd., Carol Stream, IL 60188-9418 (SAN 630-690X) Toll Free: 800-621-1333; 7911 NE 33rd Dr., Suite 270, Portland, OR 97211-1920 (SAN 630-7116) Tel 503-281-2673; Fax: 503-284-6046; 23 Monte Vista Ave., Larkspur, CA 94939-2120 (SAN 630-6993) Toll Free: 800-621-1333; 2611 S. Roosevelt, Suite 102, Tempe, AZ 85282-2017 (SAN 630-7094) Tel 602-966-6691; Fax: 602-894-0329; 4703 Fulton Industrial Blvd., Atlanta, GA 30336-2017 (SAN 630-6845) Tel 404-691-6280; Fax: 404-696-3944; 400 Airport Executive Pk., Spring Valley, NY 10977-7404 (SAN 630-7078) Tel 914-425-3191; Fax: 914-425-7521; 7949 Woodley Blvd., Van Nuys, CA 91406 (SAN 630-7183) Tel 818-375-5027; Fax: 818-375-5001; 1293 Heil Quaker Blvd., Suite B, P.O. Box 7006, La Vergne, TN 37086-7006 (SAN 630-7051) Fax: 615-793-6196; Toll Free: 800-688-3110; 3675 Crestwood Pkwy NW Ste. 105, Duluth, GA 30096-5045 (SAN 630-6853) Toll Free: 800-876-0832; 3114 S. 24th St., Kansas City, KS 66106-4709 (SAN 630-7027) Tel 913-362-0391; Fax: 913-362-0605; Toll Free: 800-621-1333; 6635 NE 59th Pl., Portland, OR 97218-2709 (SAN 630-7124) Tel 503-284-3313; Fax: 503-284-3876; Toll Free: 800-876-0834; 7319 Innovation Blvd., Fort Wayne, IN 46818-1371 (SAN 630-6985) Fax: 219-489-8850; Toll Free: 800-759-5588; 8779 Greenwood Pl., Savage, MD 20763 (SAN 630-7019) Tel 301-490-1166; Fax: 301-490-0031; Toll Free: 800-621-1333; 1521 W. Copans Rd., Suite 105, Pompano Beach, FL 33064 (SAN 630-7108) Tel 954-971-5412; Fax: 954-971-3113; Toll Free: 800-888-3876; 20435 E. Business Pkwy., Walnut, CA 91789-2999 (SAN 630-7191) Tel 714-594-6569; Fax: 714-595-0735; Toll Free: 800-759-4422; 2 Ingram Blvd., La Vergne, TN 37086-3638 (SAN 630-6837) Toll Free: 800-621-1333; 1349 Charwood Rd., Hanover, MD 21076-3114 (SAN 630-6861) Tel 410-850-9191; Fax: 410-850-9229; 110 Shawmut Rd., Canton, MA 02021-1412 (SAN 630-687X) Tel 617-575-9585; Fax: 617-575-9586; 100 Dobbs Ln., Suite 206, Cherry Hill, NJ 08034-1435 (SAN 630-6888) Tel 609-428-8668; Fax: 609-428-8536; Toll Free: 800-288-7565; 11235 Knott Ave., Suite C, Cypress, CA 90630-5401 (SAN 630-6918) Tel 714-373-8855; Fax: 714-373-8858; Toll Free: 800-759-4422; 1430 Bradley Ln., No. 102, Carrollton, TX 75007-4855 (SAN 630-6926) Tel 214-245-6088; Fax: 214-323-3890; Toll Free: 800-621-1333; 2259 Merritt Dr., Garland, TX 75041-6138 (SAN 630-6934) Tel 214-840-6621; Fax: 214-840-3357; Toll Free: 800-727-0688; 10990 E. 55th Ave., Denver, CO 80239-2007 (SAN 630-6942) Tel 303-371-8372; Fax: 303-373-4583; 35245 Schoolcraft, Livonia, MI 48150-1209 (SAN 630-6969) Tel 313-422-9955; Fax: 313-422-1171; 3540 NW 56th St., Fort Lauderdale, FL 33309-2260 (SAN 630-6977) Tel 305-733-7440; Fax: 305-735-7752; 6733 S. Sepulveda, Suite 108, Los Angeles, CA 90045-1525 (SAN 630-7035) Tel 213-410-4067; Fax: 213-410-0919; Toll Free: 800-759-4422; 9549 Penn Ave S. Ste. 200, Minneapolis, MN 55431-2565 (SAN 630-7043) Toll Free: 800-825-3112; 25 Branca Rd., East Rutherford, NJ 07073-2121 (SAN 630-706X) Tel 201-933-9797; Fax: 201-933-5139; Toll Free: 800-621-1333; 5576 Inland Empire Blvd, Bldg. G, Suite A, Ontario, CA 91764-5117 (SAN 630-7086) Tel 714-948-7998; Fax: 714-948-9778; Freeport Ctr., Bldg. H-12 N., P.O. Box 1387, Clearfield, UT 84016-1387 (SAN 630-7132) Tel 801-775-0555; Fax: 801-773-8172; 2700 Merchantile Dr., Suite 100, Rancho Cordova, CA 95742-6574 (SAN 630-7140) Tel 916-638-8090; Fax: 916-638-8021; Toll Free: 800-866-1568; 4660 Viewridge Ave., Suite B, San Diego, CA 92123-1638 (SAN 630-7159) Tel 619-569-9816; Fax: 619-569-1542; Toll Free: 800-365-5229; 6411 S. 216th, Bldg. F, Kent, WA 98032-1392 (SAN 630-7167) Tel 206-395-3515; Fax: 206-395-0650; 445 W. Freedom Ave., Orange, CA 92865 (SAN 630-7175) Tel 714-282-1232; Fax: 714-282-2245; 201 Ingram Dr., Roseburg, OR 97470; 12600 SE Hwy. 212, Bldg. B, Clackamas, OR 97015-9081 Tel 615-287-4000
Web site: http://www.ingramentertainment.com.

Ingram Publisher Services, Orders Addr.: Customer Services, Box 512 1 Ingram Blvd., LaVergne, TN 37086 USA Toll Free Fax: 800-838-1149; Edit Addr.: 1 Ingram Blvd., LaVergne, TN 37086 USA (SAN 631-8630) Tel 615-793-5000; Fax: 615-213-5811
E-mail: customer.service@ingrampublisherservices.com; Publisher@ingrampublisherservices.com; Retailer@ingrampublisherservices.com
Web site: http://www.ingrampublisherservices.com.

Ingram Software, Subs. of Ingram Distribution Group, Inc., 1759 Wehrle, Williamsville, NY 14221 USA (SAN 285-760X) Toll Free: 800-828-7250; 900 W. Walnut Ave., Compton, CA 90220 (SAN 285-7073).

INgrooves, *See* **INscribe Digital**

Inland Empire Periodicals, *See* **Incor Periodicals**

Inner Traditions International, Ltd., *(978-0-89281; 978-0-905249; 978-1-899171; 978-0-906191; 978-0-9504268; 978-1-84409; 978-1-59477; 978-1-62055; 978-1-64411; 979-8-88850)* Orders Addr.: P.O. Box 388, Rochester, VT 05767-0388 USA Tel 802-767-3174; Fax: 802-767-3726; Toll Free Fax: 800-246-8648; Edit Addr.: One Park St., Rochester, VT 05767 USA (SAN 208-6948) Tel 802-767-3174; Fax: 802-767-3726
E-mail: customerservice@innertraditions.com; info@innertraditions.com
Web site: http://www.innertraditions.com.

Innovative Logistics, Orders Addr.: 575 Prospect St., Lakewood, NJ 08701 USA (SAN 760-6532) Tel 732-534-7001; 732-363-5679; Fax: 732-363-0338
E-mail: innlogorders@innlog.net
Web site: http://www.innlog.net.

INscribe Digital, *(978-1-61750; 978-1-62517)* Div. of Independent Publishers Group, 55 Francisco St. Suite 710, San Francisco, CA 94105 USA
E-mail: digitalpublishing@ingrooves.com
Web site: http://www.INscribeDigital.com.

Insight Guides, *(978-0-88729; 978-1-58573)* 46-35 54th Rd., Maspeth, NY 11378 USA Tel 718-784-0055; Fax: 718-784-1246
E-mail: customerservice@americanmap.com
Web site: http://www.americanmap.com.

Insight Publishing, *(978-0-9663550)* Orders Addr.: P.O. Box 32383, Jacksonville, FL 32237 USA Tel 904-262-9975; Fax: 904-262-3220; Edit Addr.: 5417 Autumnbrook Trail, N., Jacksonville, FL 32258 USA Do not confuse with companies with the same name in Yreka, CA, Parker, CO, Woodbridge, VA, Salt Lake City, UT, Tulsa, OK
E-mail: 102502.2561@compuserve.com.

Instant Pub., *(978-1-59196; 978-1-59872; 978-1-60458; 978-1-61422)* Orders Addr.: P.O. Box 985, Collierville, TN 38027 USA Tel 901-853-7070; Fax: 901-853-6196; Toll Free: 800-259-2592; Edit Addr.: 410 Hwy. 72 W., Collierville, TN 38017 USA
Web site: http://www.instantpublisher.com.

Instantpublisher.com, *See* **Instant Pub.**

Institute for Healthcare Advancement, *(978-0-9701245; 978-0-9720148; 978-0-9835976; 978-1-940874)* Orders Addr.: 501 S. Idaho St. Ste. 300, La Habra, CA 90631-6047 USA (SAN 860-3456) Tel 562-690-4001; Fax: 562-690-8988; Toll Free: 800-434-4633
E-mail: ESilvis@iha4health.org
Web site: http://www.iha4health.org; http://www.ihahealthliteracy.org.

Instructional Video, 2219 C St., Lincoln, NE 68502 USA (SAN 631-6115) Tel 402-475-6570; 402 475 6570; Fax: 402-475-6500; Toll Free: 800-228-0164 Do not confuse with Instructional Video in Golden, CO
E-mail: Kathy@insvideo.com
Web site: http://www.insvideo.com.

Integral Yoga Pubns., *(978-0-932040; 978-1-938477)* Satchidananda Ashram-Yogaville, 108 Yogaville Way, Buckingham, VA 23921 USA (SAN 285-0338) Tel 434-969-3121 ex 102; Fax: 434-969-1303; Toll Free: 800-262-1008 (orders)
Web site: http://www.yogaville.org.

Interlink Publishing Group, Inc., *(978-0-940793; 978-1-56656; 978-1-62371)* 46 Crosby St., Northampton, MA 01060-1804 USA (SAN 664-8908) Tel 413-582-7054; Fax: 413-582-6731; Toll Free: 800-238-5465
E-mail: info@interlinkbooks.com; editor@interlinkbooks.com
Web site: http://www.interlinkbooks.com.

InterMountain Periodical Distributors, *See* **Majic Enterprises**

International Bk. Ctr., Inc., *(978-0-86685; 978-0-917062)* 2007 Laurel Dr., P.O. Box 295, Troy, MI 48099 USA (SAN 169-4014) Tel 248-879-7920; 586-254-7230; Fax: 586-254-7230
E-mail: ibc@ibcbooks.com
Web site: http://www.ibcbooks.com.

International Magazine Service, Div. of Periodical Pubs. Service Bureau, 1 N. Superior St., Sandusky, OH 44870 USA (SAN 285-9955) Tel 419-626-0623.

International Networking Assn., 4130 Citrus Ave., Suite 5, Rocklin, CA 95677 USA (SAN 631-1857).

International Periodical Distributors, 674 Via de la Valle, Suite 204, Solana Beach, CA 92075 USA (SAN 250-5290) Tel 619-481-5928; Toll Free: 800-999-1170; 800-228-5144 (in Canada).

International Pubns. Service, *(978-0-8002)* Div. of Taylor & Francis, Inc., Orders Addr.: 325 Chestnut St., 8th Flr., Levittown, PA 19057-4700 USA Fax: 215-785-5515; Toll Free: 800-821-8312.

International Readers League, Div. of Periodical Pubs. Service Bureau, 1 N. Superior St., Sandusky, OH 44870 USA (SAN 285-9971) Tel 419-626-0633.

International Service Co., International Service Bldg., 333 Fourth Ave., Indialantic, FL 32903-4295 USA (SAN 169-5134) Tel 407-724-1443 (phone/fax).

International Specialized Book Services, *See* **ISBS Publisher Services**

International Thomson Computer Pr., *(978-1-85032)* Orders Addr.: 7625 Empire Dr., Florence, KY 41042-2978 USA Tel 606-525-6600; Fax: 606-525-7778; Toll Free: 800-842-3636; Edit Addr.: 20 Park Plaza, 13th Flr., Boston, MA 02116 USA Fax: 617-695-1615
E-mail: itcp@itp.thomson.com
Web site: http://www.itcpmedia.com.

Internet Systems, Inc., Subs. of Internet Systems, Inc., 20250 Century Blvd., Germantown, MD 20874 USA (SAN 129-9611) Tel 301-540-5100; Fax: 301-540-5522; Toll Free: 800-638-8725
Web site: http://www.pwl.com/Internet.

Interstate Distributors, 150 Blackstone River Rd. Ste. 4, Worcester, MA 01607-1455 USA (SAN 170-4885) Toll Free: 800-365-6430.

Interstate Periodical Distributors, 201 E. Badger Rd., Madison, WI 53713 USA (SAN 169-9105) Tel 608-277-2407; Fax: 608-277-2410; Toll Free: 800-752-3131.

Intertech Bk. Services, Inc., 25971 Sarazen Dr., South Riding, VA 20152-1741 USA (SAN 630-5253).

InterVarsity Pr., *(978-0-8308; 978-0-87784; 978-1-5140)* Div. of InterVarsity Christian Fellowship of the USA, Orders Addr.: P.O. Box 1400, Downers Grove, IL 60515 USA (SAN 202-7089) Tel 630-734-4000; Fax: 630-734-4200; Toll Free: 800-843-7225 (other depts.); 800-843-9487 (orders); 800-843-1019 (customer service); 800-873-0143 (electronic ordering)
E-mail: email@ivpress.com
Web site: http://www.ivpress.com.

Intrepid Group, Inc., The, 1331 Red Cedar Cir., Fort Collins, CO 80524 USA (SAN 631-5429) Tel 970-493-3793; Fax: 970-493-8781
E-mail: intrepid@frii.com.

Iowa & Illinois News, 8645 Northwest Blvd., Davenport, IA 52806-6418 USA (SAN 169-2607).

Irish American Bk. Co., Subs. of Roberts Rinehart Pubs., Inc., P.O. Box 666, Niwot, CO 80544-0666 USA Tel 303-652-2710; Fax: 303-652-2689; Toll Free: 800-452-7115
E-mail: irishbooks@aol.com
Web site: http://www.irishvillage.com.

Irish Bks. & Media, Inc., *(978-0-937702)* Orders Addr.: 2904 41st Ave S., Minneapolis, MN 55406-1814 USA (SAN 111-8870) Toll Free: 800-229-3505 Do not confuse with Irish Bks. in New York, NY
E-mail: Irishbook@aol.com
Web site: http://www.irishbook.com.

Iron Stream Media, *(978-1-56309; 978-1-59669)* 100 Missionary Ridge, Birmingham, AL 35242 USA Toll Free Fax: 888-811-9934.

Ironside International Pubs., Inc., *(978-0-935554)* Orders Addr.: P.O. Box 1050, Lorton, VA 22199-1050 USA (SAN 206-2380) Tel 703-493-9120; Fax: 703-493-9424; Edit Addr.: P.O. Box 1050, Lorton, VA 22199-1050 USA (SAN 663-656X)
E-mail: info@ironsidepub.com.

ISBS Publisher Services, 920 NE 58th Ave., Suite 300, Portland, OR 97213-3786 USA (SAN 169-7129) Tel 503-287-3093; Fax: 503-280-8832; Toll Free: 800-944-6190
E-mail: info@isbs.com
Web site: http://www.isbs.com.

ISD, 70 Enterprise Dr., Suite 2, Bristol, CT 06010 USA Tel 860-584-6546; Fax: 860-540-1001
E-mail: orders@isdistribution.com
Web site: https://www.isdistribution.com/.

Islamic Bk. Service, 1209 Cleburne, Houston, TX 77004 USA (SAN 169-2453) Tel 713-528-1440; Fax: 713-528-1085.

Island Heritage Publishing, *(978-0-89610; 978-0-931548; 978-1-59700)* Div. of The Madden Corp., 94-411 Koaki St., Waipahu, HI 96797 USA (SAN 211-1403) Tel 808-564-8800; Fax: 808-564-8888; Toll Free: 800-468-2800
E-mail: ihorders@welcometotheislands.com
Web site: http://www.welcometotheislands.com.

Islander Group, 269 Pali'i St., Mililani, HI 96789 USA Tel 808-676-0116
E-mail: customerservice@islandergroup.com
Web site: https://www.islandergroup.com/.

Israel Book Shop, *See* **Israel Bookshop Pubns.**

Israel Bookshop Pubns., *(978-0-9670705; 978-1-931681; 978-1-60091; 979-8-88673)* 501 Prospect St., No. 97, Lakewood, NJ 08701 USA Tel 732-901-3009; Fax: 732-901-4012; Toll Free: 888-536-7427
E-mail: sales@israelbookshoppublications.com
Web site: http://www.israelbookshoppublications.com.

Itasca Bks., *(978-0-9767054)* Orders Addr.: 5120 Cedar Lake Rd. S., Minneapolis, MN 55416 USA (SAN 855-3823) Tel 952-345-4488; Fax: 952-920-0541; Toll Free: 800-901-3480
E-mail: mjung@itascabooks.com
Web site: http://www.itascabooks.com.

iUniverse, Inc., *(978-0-9665514; 978-1-58348; 978-0-9668591; 978-1-893652; 978-0-595; 978-0-9795279; 978-1-60528; 978-1-4401; 978-1-936236; 978-1-4502; 978-1-4620; 978-1-4697; 978-1-4759; 978-1-4917; 978-1-5320; 978-1-6632)* Orders Addr.: 1663 Liberty Dr., Suite 300, Bloomington, IN 47403 USA (SAN 254-9425) Toll Free: 800-288-4677
Web site: http://www.iUniverse.com; http://iuniverse.com; www.balboapress.com.

iUniverse.com, Incorporated, *See* **iUniverse, Inc.**

J & H Bks., 6300 Wilshire Blvd., No. 130, Los Angeles, CA 90048 USA (SAN 631-8118) Tel 323-497-1089; Fax: 626-336-5700
E-mail: wcjiao@lycos.com.

J & J Bk. Sales, 24871 Pylos Way, Mission Viejo, CA 92691-4668 USA (SAN 253-8075)
E-mail: jacki@hydrasystems.com
Web site: http://www.divanet.com/matilda.

J & L Bk. Co., Orders Addr.: P.O. Box 13100, Spokane, WA 99213 USA (SAN 129-6817) Fax: 509-534-0152; 509-534-7713; Toll Free: 800-288-9756; Edit Addr.: 1710 Trent, Spokane, WA 99220 USA (SAN 243-2145).

J & N Creations, LLC, 48 First St., N., Sauk Centre, MN 56304 USA Tel 320-352-6260.

Jacobob Pr. Distributing, 11035 Ridge Forest Ct., Saint Louis, MO 63126 USA.

JAGCO & Associates Inc., Orders Addr.: 596 Indian Trail Rd. South #227, Indian Trail, NC 28079 USA Tel 802-223-6565.

Jalmar Pr., *(978-0-915190; 978-0-935266; 978-1-880396; 978-1-931061)* Subs. of B. L. Winch & Assocs., P.O. Box 370, Fawnskin, CA 92333-0370 USA (SAN 113-3640) Toll Free: 800-662-9662 (orders)
E-mail: jalmarpress@att.net
Web site: http://jalmarpress.com.

James & Law Co., Orders Addr.: P.O. Box 2468, Clarksburg, WV 26302-2468 USA (SAN 169-894X); Edit Addr.:

Middletown Mall I-79 & U. S. 250, Fairmont, WV 26554 USA (SAN 169-8966) Tel 304-624-7401.

James Trading Group, Limited, The, 13 Highview Ave., Orangeburg, NY 10962-2125 USA Toll Free: 800-541-5004
E-mail: sales@thejamestradinggroup.com.

Janway, 11 Academy Rd., Cogan Station, PA 17728 USA (SAN 108-3708) Tel 717-494-1239; Fax: 717-494-1350; Toll Free: 800-877-5242.

Jawbone Publishing Corp., *(978-0-9702959; 978-1-59094)* P.O. Box PO Box 3741, Costa Mesa, CA 92626 USA (SAN 253-5335)
E-mail: tara@taraballman.com
Web site: http://www.jawbonepublishing.com.

JAYNORS Publishing, LLC, 4461 S. Four Mile Run Dr. 0, ARLINGTON, VA 22204 USA Tel 5712121734
E-mail: Jaynors@outlook.com.

Jeanies Classics, *(978-0-9609672)* Orders Addr.: 2123 Oxford St., Rockford, IL 61103 USA (SAN 271-7409); Edit Addr.: 2123 Oxford St., Rockford, IL 61103 USA (SAN 271-7395) Tel 815-968-4544.

Jean's Dulcimer Shop & Crying Creek Pubs., P.O. Box 8, Hwy. 32, Cosby, TN 37722 USA (SAN 249-9282) Tel 423-487-5543.

Jech Distributors, 674 Via De La Valle, No. 204, Solana Beach, CA 92075-2462 USA (SAN 107-0258) Tel 619-452-7251.

Jellyroll Productions, *See* **Osborne Enterprises Publishing**

Jenkins Group, Inc., *(978-1-890587; 978-0-9860224)* 121 E. Front St., 4th Flr., Traverse City, MI 49684 USA Tel 231-933-0445; Fax: 231-933-0448; 1129 Woodmere Ave., Traverse City, MI 49686
Web site: http://www.bookpublishing.com.

JIST Publishing, *(978-0-942784; 978-1-56370; 978-1-57112; 978-1-59357; 978-1-63332)* Div. of EMC Publishing, 875 Montreal Way, Saint Paul, MN 55102 USA (SAN 240-2351) Tel 651-290-2800 Toll Free Fax: 800-547-8329
E-mail: info@jist.com
Web site: http://www.jist.com.

JIST Works, Incorporated, *See* **JIST Publishing**

JMS Distribution, 2017 San Mateo St., Richmond, CA 94804 USA.

Jobson, Oliver H., *(978-0-9764988)* 12171 SW 123rd Pl., Miami, FL 33186 USA (SAN 256-5463) Tel 954-260-4914
E-mail: ojobson@gmail.com
Web site: http://www.gpaonline.com.

Johns Hopkins Univ. Pr., *(978-0-8018; 978-1-4214)* Div. of Johns Hopkins Univ., Orders Addr.: P.O. Box 50370, Baltimore, MD 21211-4370 USA; Edit Addr.: 2715 N. Charles St., Baltimore, MD 21218-4319 USA (SAN 202-7348) Fax: 410-516-4189; Toll Free: 800-537-5487
E-mail: webmaster@press.jhu.edu
Web site: http://muse.jhu.edu/;
http://www.press.jhu.edu/books/.

Johnson News Agency, P.O. Box 9009, Moscow, ID 83843 USA (SAN 169-1678).

Johnson, Walter J. Inc., *(978-0-8472)* 1 New York Plaza 28th Flr., New York, NY 10004-1901 USA (SAN 209-1828).

Jones, Bob University Press, *See* **BJU Pr.**

Joseph Ruzicka, Incorporated, *See* **Southeast Library Bindery, Inc.**

Journey Pubns., LLC, *(978-0-9671696)* 6254 Wood Wren Dr., Baton Rouge, LA 70817 USA; 6254 Wood Wren Dr., Baton Rouge, LA 70817 Do not confuse with companies with the same or similar names in Woodstock, NY, Summerland, CA, Savannah, GA, Avon Park, FL, lacey, WA
E-mail: msl3393@yahoo.com;
mlewis@communiquellc.com.

Joyce Media, Inc., *(978-0-917002)* P.O. Box 57, Acton, CA 93510 USA (SAN 208-7197) Tel 805-269-1169; Fax: 805-269-2139
E-mail: joycemed@pacbell.net
Web site: http://joycemedia.com.

JPL Fulfillment, 3883 Linden Ave., Suite E, Wyoming, MI 49548 USA Toll Free: 877-683-6935
E-mail: orders@jplbooks.com
Web site: https://www.jplfulfillment.com/.

Jstor, *See* **JSTOR**

Julia Taylor Ebel, P.O. Box 11, Jamestown, NC 27282 USA
E-mail: ebel@northstate.net.

Junior League of Greensboro Pubns., *(978-0-9605788)* 3101 W. Friendly Ave., Greensboro, NC 27408-7801 USA (SAN 112-9597)
E-mail: Jlgso@aol.com.

Just Us Bks., Inc., *(978-0-940975; 978-1-933491)* 395 Pleasant Valley Way Suite B, West Orange, NJ 07052 USA (SAN 664-7413) Tel 973-672-7701
E-mail: justusbook@aol.com
Web site: http://www.justusbooks.com.

K. M. R. Enterprises, *(978-0-9656379)* 5731 Pony Express Trail, Pollock Pines, CA 95726 USA (SAN 299-237X) Tel 530-644-1410.

Kable Media Services, Subs. of AMREP Corp., 505 Park Ave. 7th Fl., New York, NY 10022 USA Tel 212-705-4600; Fax: 212-705-4666; Toll Free: 800-223-6640
E-mail: info@kable.com
Web site: http://www.kable.com/.

Kable News Company, Incorporated, *See* **Kable Media Services**

Kalispell News Agency, P.O. Box 4965, Missoula, MT 59806-4965 USA (SAN 169-4383) Toll Free: 800-955-1266.

Kamkin, Victor, P.O. Box 34583, Bethesda, MD 20827-0583 USA Toll Free: 800-852-6546; 925 Broadway, New York, NY 10010 (SAN 113-7395) Tel 212-673-0776; Fax: 212-673-2473.

Kamkyi Bks., *(978-0-9675031)* Div. of Source International Technology Corp., 939 E. 156th St., Bronx, NY 10455 USA (SAN 630-8392) Tel 718-378-3878 (phone/fax); Toll Free: 888-729-5117
E-mail: source.Intl.Tech@erols.com
Web site: http://www.kamkyibooks.

Kampmann, Kump & Bell, LLC, Orders Addr.: 27 W. 20th St., Suite 1102, New York, NY 10011 USA Tel 212-727-0190; Fax: 212-727-0195
E-mail: midpointny@aol.com.

Kane Miller, *(978-0-916291; 978-1-929132; 978-1-933605; 978-1-935279; 978-1-61067; 978-1-68464)* Div. of EDC Publishing, Orders Addr.: P.O. Box 470663, Tulsa, OK 74146 USA (SAN 295-8945) Tel 800-475-4522; 918-622-4522; Fax: 800-743-5660; Edit Addr.: P.O. Box 8515, La Jolla, CA 92038 USA Tel 858-456-0540
E-mail: info@kanemiller.com
Web site: http://www.kanemiller.com;
http://www.edcpub.com.

Kane/Miller#Book Publishers, Incorporated, *See* **Kane Miller**

Kansas City Periodical Distributing, Orders Addr.: P.O. Box 14948, Lenexa, KS 66285-4948 USA (SAN 107-9433); Edit Addr.: 9605 Dice Ln., Lenexa, KS 66215 USA Tel 913-541-8600.

Kansas State Reading Circle, 715 W. Tenth St., C-170, Topeka, KS 66601 USA (SAN 169-2771).

Kaplan Publishing, *(978-0-7931; 978-0-88462; 978-0-913864; 978-0-936894; 978-0-942103; 978-1-57410; 978-1-60714; 978-1-60978; 978-1-61865; 978-1-62523; 978-1-5062)* 395 Hudson St., New York, NY 10014 USA (SAN 211-2280); 395 Hudson St., New City, NY 10014
E-mail: deb.darrock@kaplan.com;
shayna.webb@kaplan.com;
alexander.noya@kaplan.com
Web site: http://www.kaplanpublishing.com;
http://www.kaplanprofessional.com.

Kaybee Montessori, Inc., 157 Lagrange Ave., Rochester, NY 14613-1511 USA (SAN 133-1256) Toll Free: 800-732-9304.

Kazi Pubns., Inc., *(978-0-933511; 978-0-935782; 978-1-56744; 978-1-871031; 978-1-930637)* 3023 W. Belmont Ave., Chicago, IL 60618 USA (SAN 162-3397) Tel 773-267-7001; Fax: 773-267-7002
E-mail: info@kazi.org
Web site: http://www.kazi.org.

Kehot Pubn. Society, *(978-0-8266)* Div. of Merkos L'Inyonei Chinuch, Orders Addr.: 291 Kingston Ave., Brooklyn, NY 11213 USA Tel 718-778-0226; Fax: 718-778-4148; Toll Free: 877-463-7567 (877-4MERKOS); Edit Addr.: 770 Eastern Pkwy., Brooklyn, NY 11213 USA (SAN 220-7060) Tel 718-604-2785
E-mail: orders@kehotonline.com; info@kehot.com
Web site: http://www.kehotonline.com.

Keith Distributors, 1230 Macklind Ave., Saint Louis, MO 63110-1432 USA (SAN 112-6377) Toll Free: 800-373-2366
E-mail: keithsbooks@juno.com.

Kensington Publishing Corp., *(978-0-7860; 978-0-8065; 978-0-8184; 978-0-8217; 978-1-55817; 978-1-57566; 978-0-7582; 978-1-4201; 978-1-59983; 978-1-60183; 978-0-9817144; 978-0-9818905; 978-0-9824170; 978-0-9841132; 978-1-61650; 978-1-61773; 978-1-4967; 978-1-5161; 978-1-63573; 978-1-64566) 119 W. 40th St., New York, NY 10018 USA Tel 212-407-1500; Fax: 212-935-0699; Toll Free: 800-221-2647; 499 North Canon Dr., Beverly Hills, CA 90210 Tel 310-887-7082*
E-mail: jmclean@kensingtonbooks.com;
melley@kensingtonbooks.com
Web site: http://www.kensingtonbooks.com.

Kent News Agency, Inc., P.O. Box 1828, Scottsbluff, NE 69363-1828 USA (SAN 169-4448) Tel 303-286-9694; 308-635-2225; Fax: 308-635-1563; Toll Free: 877-290-4740
E-mail: kentrob@prairieweb.com.

Keramos, P.O. Box 7500, Ann Arbor, MI 48107 USA (SAN 169-3670) Tel 313-439-1261.

Kerem Publishing, *(978-1-889727)* 723 N. Orange Dr., Los Angeles, CA 90038 USA (SAN 299-1209).

Kerhulas News Co., P.O. Box 751, Union, SC 29379 USA (SAN 169-7838).

Ketab Corp., *(978-1-883819; 978-1-59584)* 12701 Van Nuys blvd suite H, PACOIMA, CA 91331 USA (SAN 107-7791) Tel 310-477-7477; Fax: 818-908-1457; Toll Free: 800-367-4726
E-mail: ketab@ketab.com
Web site: http://www.ketab.com.

Key Bk. Service, Inc., *(978-0-934636)* P.O. Box 1434, Fairfield, CT 06430 USA (SAN 169-0671) Tel 203-374-4939; Fax: 203-384-6099.

Keystone Bks. & Media LLC, 12526 Cutten Rd., Suite C, Houston, TX 77066 USA (SAN 990-0160) Tel 281-893-2665; 888-670-2665; Fax: 281-549-2500; Toll Free: 888-670-2665
E-mail: books@keystonebooksmedia.com;
matthew@keystonebooksmedia.com
Web site: http://www.keystonebooksmedia.com/.

Khalifah's Booksellers & Assocs., Orders Addr.: 210 East Arrowhead Dr. #2, Charlotte, NC 28213 USA.

Kidsbooks, Inc., 220 Monroe Tpke., No. 560, Monroe, CT 06468-2247 USA (SAN 169-0795).

King Electronics Distributing, 1711 Southeastern Ave., Indianapolis, IN 46201-3990 USA (SAN 107-6795) Tel 317-639-1484; Fax: 317-639-4711.

Kingdom, Inc., P.O. Box 506, Mansfield, PA 16933 USA.

Kinokuniya Bookstores of America Co., Ltd., 1581 Webster St., San Francisco, CA 94115 USA (SAN 121-8441) Tel 415-567-7625; Fax: 415-567-4109.

Kinokuniya Pubns. Service of New York, 1075 Avenue Of The Americas., New York, NY 10018-3701 USA (SAN 157-5414)
E-mail: kinokuniya@kinokuniya.com
Web site: http://www.kinokuniya.com.

Kirkbride, B.B. Bible Co., Inc., *(978-0-88707; 978-0-934854)* P.O. Box 606, Indianapolis, IN 46206-0606 USA (SAN 169-2372) Tel 317-633-1900; Fax: 317-633-1444; Toll Free: 800-428-4385
E-mail: hyperbible@aol.com
Web site: http://www.kirkbride.com.

Kitrick Management Co., Ltd., P.O. Box 15523, Cincinnati, OH 45215 USA (SAN 132-6236) Tel 513-782-2930; Fax: 513-782-2936
E-mail: bachb@aol.com.

Klein's Booklein, Orders Addr.: P.O. Box 968, Fowlerville, MI 48836 USA (SAN 631-3329) Tel 517-223-3964; Fax: 517-223-1314; Toll Free: 800-266-5534; Edit Addr.: One Klein Dr., Fowlerville, MI 48836 USA (SAN 631-3337).

Knopf, Alfred A. Inc., *(978-0-394)* Div. of The Knopf Publishing Group, Orders Addr.: 400 Hahn Rd., Westminster, MD 21157 USA Tel 410-848-1900; Toll Free: 800-726-0600 (orders); Edit Addr.: 1745 Broadway, New York, NY 10019 USA (SAN 202-5825) Tel 212-782-9000; Toll Free: 800-726-0600
E-mail: customerservice@randomhouse.com
Web site: http://www.randomhouse.com/knopf.

Knox, John Press, *See* **Westminster John Knox Pr.**

KOCH Entertainment, LLC, *(978-0-9721700; 978-1-4172)* 740 Broadway, New York, NY 10003 USA Tel 212-353-8800; Fax: 212-505-3095; 22 Harbor Park Dr., Port Washington, NY 11050 Tel 516-484-1000; Fax: 516-484-4746; Toll Free: 800-332-7553
E-mail: nives@kochent.com; videosales@kochent.com
Web site: http://www.kochvision.com;
http://www.kochlorberfilms.com;
http://www.kochentertainment.com.

Kodansha America, Inc., *(978-0-87011; 978-1-56836; 978-1-935429; 978-1-61262; 978-1-63236; 978-1-64651; 979-8-88877)* 451 Park Ave S. Flr. 7, New York, NY 10016-7390 USA (SAN 201-0526) Toll Free: 800-451-7556
E-mail: t-sumi@kodansha-usa.com
Web site: www.kodansha.us.

Kodansha USA Publishing, *See* **Kodansha America, Inc.**

Koen Pacific, Orders Addr.: P.O. Box 600, Moorestown, NJ 08057-0600 USA (SAN 631-5593) Toll Free: 800-995-4840
E-mail: info@koenpacific.com.

Kraus Reprint, *See* **Periodicals Service Co.**

Kregel Pubns., *(978-0-8254)* Div. of Kregel, Inc., Orders Addr.: P.O. Box 2607, Grand Rapids, MI 49501-2607 USA (SAN 206-9792) Tel 616-451-4775; Fax: 616-451-9330; Toll Free: 800-733-2607; Edit Addr.: 733 Wealthy St., SE., Grand Rapids, MI 49503-5553 USA (SAN 298-9115)
E-mail: kregelbooks@kregel.com;
acquisitions@kregel.com
Web site: http://www.kregel.com.

Krullstone Distributing, LLC, 8751 Clayton Cove Rd., Springville, AL 35146 USA
E-mail: charlotte@krullstonepublishing.com
Web site: http://www.krullstonepublishing.com.

KSG Distributing, 1121 W. Flint Meadow Dr., Kaysville, UT 84037 USA.

Kurian, George Reference Bks., *(978-0-914746)* Orders Addr.: P.O. Box 519, Baldwin Place, NY 10505 USA (SAN 203-1981); Edit Addr.: 3689 Campbell Ct., Yorktown Heights, NY 10598 USA (SAN 110-6236) Tel 914-962-3287.

Kurtzman Bk. Sales Co., 17348 W. 12 Mile Rd., Southfield, MI 48076 USA (SAN 114-0787) Tel 248-557-7230; Fax: 248-557-8705; Toll Free: 800-869-0505.

Kuykendall's Pr., Bookstore Div., P.O. Box 627, Athens, AL 35612-0627 USA (SAN 168-9185) Tel 256-232-1754; Toll Free: 800-781-1754.

L I M Productions, LLC, *(978-1-929617)* 3553 Northdale St., NW, Uniontown, OH 44685-8004 USA Toll Free: 877-628-4532
E-mail: customerservice@limproductions.com
Web site: http://www.limproductions.com.

L L Co., *(978-0-937892)* 1647 Manning Ave., Los Angeles, CA 90024 USA (SAN 110-0009) Tel 310-615-0116; Fax: 310-640-6863; Toll Free: 800-473-3699
E-mail: wallacelab@aol.com.

L M C Source, P.O. Box 720400, San Jose, CA 95172-0400 USA (SAN 631-189X) Tel 408-630-0589; Fax: 408-634-1456; Toll Free: 800-873-3043
E-mail: lmcs@pacbell.net
Web site: http://www.csn.net/~david/.

L P C Group, c/o CDS, 193 Edwards Dr., Jackson, TN 38305 USA (SAN 630-5644) Fax: 731-423-1973; 731-935-7731; Toll Free Fax: 800-351-5073; Toll Free: 800-343-4499
E-mail: lpc-info@lpcgroup.com
Web site: http://www.lpcgroup.com.

La Belle News Agency, 814 University Blvd., Steubenville, OH 43952 USA (SAN 169-6858) Tel 740-282-9731.

La Cite French Bks., Div. of The La Cite Group, Inc., P.O. Box 64504, Los Angeles, CA 90064-0504 USA (SAN 168-9789)
E-mail: lacite@aol.com.

La Moderna Poesia, Inc., 5739 NW 7th St., Miami, FL 33126-3105 USA (SAN 169-1139).

Lafayette Bks., P.O. Box 758, Mamaroneck, NY 10543-0758 USA (SAN 135-292X) Tel 914-833-0248.

Lake City Downtown Improvement and Revitalization Team, P.O. Box 973 231 N. Silver St., Lake City, CO 81235 USA Tel 970-944-3478
E-mail: ed@lakecitydirt.com.

Lakeport Distributors, Inc., 139 W. 18th St., P.O. Box 6195, Erie, PA 16501 USA (SAN 169-734X).

Lambda Pubs., Inc., *(978-0-915361; 978-1-55774)* 3709 13th Ave., Brooklyn, NY 11218-3622 USA (SAN 291-0640) Tel 718-972-5449; Fax: 718-972-6307
E-mail: judaica@email.msn.com.

Lambert Bk. Hse., Inc., *(978-0-89315)* 4139 Parkway Dr., Florence, AL 35630-6347 USA (SAN 180-5169) Tel 256-764-4098; 256-764-4090; Fax: 256-766-9200; Toll Free: 800-551-8511
E-mail: Info@lambertbookhouse.com
Web site: http://www.lambertbookhouse.com.

Landmark Audiobooks, 4865 Sterling Dr., Boulder, CO 80301 USA Fax: 303-443-3775
Web site: http://www.landmarkaudio.com.

Landmark Bk. Co., *(978-0-929194)* 131 Hicks St., Brooklyn, NY 11201-2318 USA (SAN 169-5843).

Lang, Peter Publishing, Inc., *(978-0-8204; 978-1-4331; 978-1-4539; 978-1-4540; 978-1-4541; 978-1-4542; 978-1-63667)* Subs. of Verlag Peter Lang AG (SZ), 80 Broad St. 5th Flr., New York, NY 10004 USA (SAN 241-5534) Tel 212-647-7700; 212-647-7706 (Outside USA); Fax: 212-647-7707; Toll Free: 800-770-5264
E-mail: orders@peterlang.com
Web site: http://www.peterlang.com.

Langenscheidt Publishing Group, *(978-0-88729; 978-1-58573)* Subs. of Langenscheidt KG, Orders Addr.: 15 Tyger River Dr., Duncan, SC 29334 USA Fax: 888-773-7979; Toll Free: 800-432-6277; Edit Addr.: 36-36 33rd St., Long Island City, NY 11106 USA
Web site: http://www.americanmap.com;
http://www.langenscheidt.com.

Larousse Kingfisher Chambers, Inc., *(978-0-7534; 978-1-85697)* 215 Park Ave., S., New York, NY 10003 USA (SAN 297-7540); 181 Ballardvale St., Wilmington, MA 01887.

Las Vegas News Agency, 2312 Silver Bluff Ct., Las Vegas, NV 89134-6092 USA.

Lash Distributors, 7106 Geoffrey Way, Frederick, MD 21704 USA (SAN 169-3131).

Last Gasp Eco-Funnies, Incorporated, *See* **Last Gasp of San Francisco**

Last Gasp of San Francisco, *(978-0-86719)* Orders Addr.: 777 Florida St., San Francisco, CA 94110 USA (SAN 216-8308); Edit Addr.: 777 Florida St., San Francisco, CA 94110-2025 USA (SAN 170-3242) Tel 415-824-6636; Fax: 415-824-1836; Toll Free: 800-366-5121
E-mail: colin@lastgasp.com
Web site: http://www.lastgasp.com.

Laster, Larry D. Old & Rare Bks., Prints & Maps, 2416 Maplewood Ave., Winston-Salem, NC 27103 USA (SAN 112-9600) Tel 336-724-7544; Fax: 336-724-9055.

Latcorp, Ltd., 10 Norden Ln., Huntington Station, NY 11746 USA (SAN 159-8910) Tel 516-271-0548; Fax: 516-549-8849.

Latin American Book Source, Inc., 681 Anita St., Suit 102, Chula Vista, CA 91911-4663 USA
Web site: http://www.latambooks.com/.

Latin Trading Corp., 539 H St., Chula Vista, CA 91910 USA (SAN 630-2963) Tel 619-427-7867; Fax: 619-476-1817; Toll Free: 800-257-7248
E-mail: info@latintradingbooks.com
Web site: http://www.latintradingbooks.com.

Latta, J. S. Incorporated, *See* **Latta's**

Latta's, 1502 Fourth Ave., P.O. Box 2668, Huntington, WV 25726 USA (SAN 169-8982) Fax: 304-525-5038; Toll Free: 800-624-3501.

Laurus Co., The, Orders Addr.: 524 Guinevere Court, McDonough, GA 30252 USA (SAN 858-608X) Tel 678-814-4047; Fax: 678-272-7255; Toll Free: 800-596-7370
E-mail: thelaurusco@charter.net
Web site: http://www.thelauruscompany.com.

LD Bks., Inc., *(978-0-9772669; 978-0-9785897; 978-1-939048; 978-1-940281; 978-1-943387)* 8313 NW 68th St., Miami, FL 33166 USA (SAN 631-8088) Tel 305-406-2292; Fax: 305-406-2293
E-mail: vilmac@ldbooks.com; sales@ldbooks.com
Web site: http://www.sinlimites.net;
http://www.ldbooks.com.

LEA Bk. Distributors (Libros Espana y America), *(978-1-883110)* 170-23 83rd Ave., Jamaica Hills, NY 11432 USA (SAN 170-5407) Tel 718-291-9891; Fax: 718-291-9830
E-mail: leabook@idt.net
Web site: http://www.leabooks.com.

Learning Collection, The, 145 S. Glencoe St., Denver, CO 80246-1152 USA (SAN 630-8287).

Learning Connection, The, *(978-1-56831)* Orders Addr.: 4100 Silver Star Rd. Ste. D, Orlando, FL 32808-4618 USA Toll Free: 800-218-8489
Web site: http://www.tlconnection.com.

Learning Services, 2095 Laura St. Ste. H, Springfield, OR 97477-2285 USA Toll Free: 800-877-3278.

Lectorum Pubns., Inc., *(978-0-9625162; 978-1-880507; 978-1-930332; 978-1-933032; 978-1-941802; 978-1-63245; 978-1-64684)* Orders Addr.: 10 New Maple Ave. Suite 303, Pine Brook, NJ 07058 USA (SAN 990-0802) Tel 201-559-2232; Edit Addr.: 10 New Maple Ave. Suite 303, Pine Brook, NJ 07058 USA (SAN 860-0597) Tel 201-559-2200; Fax: 201-559-2201; Toll Free Fax: 877-532-8676; Toll Free: 800-345-5946
E-mail: acorrea@lectorum.com; ffebus@lectorum.com;
letiarry@verizon.net
Web site: http://www.lectorum.com;
http://www.librerialectorum.com.

Lee Bks., *(978-0-939818)* Div. of Lee S. Cole & Assocs., Inc., 524 San Anselmo Ave., No 215, San Anselmo, CA 94960-2614 USA (SAN 110-649X) Tel 415-456-4388; Fax: 415-456-7532; Toll Free: 800-828-3550 Do not confuse with other companies with the same or similar names in Jacksonville, FL, Columbia, SC
E-mail: lcs@lsc-associates.com
Web site: http://www.lsc-associates.com.

Left Bank Bks., 92 Pike St., Seattle, WA 98101 USA
Web site: http://www.leftbankbooks.com.

Left Bank Books Distribution & Publishing, *See* **Left Bank Distribution**

Wholesaler & Distributor Name Index

Left Bank Distribution, (978-0-939306) 92 Pike St., Seattle, WA 98101-2025 USA (SAN 216-5368) E-mail: leftbank@leftbankbooks.com Web site: http://www.leftbankbooks.com.

Legato Pubs. Group, Orders Addr.: 1700 4th St., Berkeley, CA 94710 USA Toll Free: 800-343-4499 Web site: http://www.legatopublishersgroup.com/.

Leman Pubns., Inc., (978-0-943721; 978-0-9602970) Div. of Rodale Pr. Co., Box 4100, 741 Corporate Cir., Suite A, Golden, CO 80401-5622 USA (SAN 213-3415) Fax: 303-277-0370; Toll Free: 800-877-3775.

Leonard, Hal Corp., *(978-0-634; 978-0-7935; 978-0-87910; 978-0-87930; 978-0-88188; 978-0-931340; 978-0-9607350; 978-1-56516; 978-1-57467; 978-1-4234; 978-1-936098; 978-1-61713; 978-1-61774; 978-1-61780; 978-1-4584; 978-1-4768; 978-1-4803; 978-1-62906; 978-1-4950; 978-1-5400; 978-1-7051; 979-8-3501) Orders Addr.: P.O. Box 13819, Milwaukee, WI 53213-0819 USA Tel 414-774-3630; Fax: 414-774-3259; Toll Free: 800-524-4425; Edit Addr.: 7777 W. Bluemound Rd., Milwaukee, WI 53213 USA (SAN 239-250X) Tel 414-777-3630; Fax: 414-774-4176* E-mail: halinfo@halleonard.com Web site: http://www.halleonard.com.

Leonardo Press, *See* **Firenze Pr.**

Lerner Publishing Group, *(978-0-7613; 978-0-8225; 978-0-87406; 978-0-87614; 978-0-929371; 978-0-930494; 978-1-57505; 978-1-58013; 978-1-58196; 978-1-4677; 978-1-5124; 978-1-5415; 978-1-7284; 979-8-7656)* Orders Addr.: 241 1ST AVE N, MINNEAPOLIS, MN 55401 USA (SAN 256-0283) Tel 612-332-3344; Fax: 612-204-9208; Edit Addr.: 241 First Ave., N., Minneapolis, MN 55401 USA (SAN 201-0828) Tel 612-332-3344; Fax: 612-215-6230; Toll Free Fax: 800-332-1132; Toll Free: 800-328-4929 E-mail: info@lernerbooks.com; custserve@lernerbooks.com Web site: http://www.lernerbooks.com; http://www.karben.com.

Levant Distributors, Incorporated, *See* **Levant USA, Inc.**

Levant USA, Inc., 145 Hook Creek Blvd. BLDG B6B3, Valley Stream, NY 11581-2223 USA (SAN 631-1970) E-mail: levantusa@cs.com.

Levine, J. Religious Supplies, Five W. 30th St., New York, NY 10001 USA (SAN 169-5878) Tel 212-695-6888; Fax: 212-643-1044 E-mail: sales@levine.judica.com.

Levy, Charles Company, *See* **Levy Home Entertainment, Ltd.**

Levy Home Entertainment, Ltd., Div. of Charles Levy Co., 1420 Kensington Rd. Ste. 300, Oak Brook, IL 60523-2164 USA (SAN 159-835X).

Lewis International, Inc., *(978-0-9666771; 978-1-930983)* 2201 NW 102nd Pl., No. 1, Miami, FL 33172 USA Tel 305-436-7984; Fax: 305-436-7985; Toll Free: 800-259-5962.

Lewis, John W. Enterprises, 168 Perez St. P.O. Box 3375, Santurce, PR 00936 USA (SAN 169-9334) Tel 809-722-0104.

Lexicon Pubns., Inc., P.O. Box 1737, Danbury, CT 06810 USA (SAN 205-664X) Tel 203-796-2540.

Liberation Distributors, *(978-0-89928)* P.O. Box 5341, Chicago, IL 60680 USA (SAN 169-880X) Tel 773-248-3442.

Library & Educational Services, P.O. Box 288, Berrien Springs, MI 49103 USA Tel 269-695-1800; Fax: 616-695-8500 E-mail: libraryanded@juno.com.

Library Bk. Selection Service, P.O. Box 277, Bloomington, IL 61702-0277 USA (SAN 169-1740).

Library Integrated Solutions & Assocs., P.O. Box 6189, Mckinney, TX 75071-5105 USA Web site: http://www.libs.com.

Library Sales of N.J., *(978-1-888032)* Orders Addr.: P.O. Box 335, Garwood, NJ 07027-0335 USA Tel 908-232-1446; Edit Addr.: 607 S. Chestnut St., Westfield, NJ 07090-1369 USA E-mail: Librarysalesofnj@aol.com.

Library Video Co., *(978-1-4171)* P.O. Box 580, Wynnewood, PA 19096 USA (SAN 631-3205) Fax: 610-645-4050; Toll Free: 800-843-3620 E-mail: cs@libraryvideo.com Web site: http://www.libraryvideo.com.

LibreDigital, 1835-B Kramer Ln. Suite 150, Austin, TX 78758 USA; 18 Soho Sq., London, W1D3QL E-mail: support@libredigital.com.

Libreria Bereana, 1825 San Alejandro, Urb San Ignacio, Rio Piedras, PR 00927-6819 USA (SAN 169-9288) Tel 809-764-6175.

Libreria Distribuidora Universal, 3090 SW 8th St., Miami, FL 33135 USA Tel 305-642-3234.

Libreria Universal, Inc., *(978-1-881375)* Orders Addr.: P.O. Box 1480, Mayaguez, PR 00680 USA; Edit Addr.: 55 N. Post St., Mayaguez, PR 00680 USA Tel 787-832-6041; Fax: 787-832-8477 E-mail: colom@coqui.net; nikkynicole2004@gmail.com.

Libros de Espana y America, *See* **LEA Bk. Distributors (Libros Espana y America)**

Libros Sin Fronteras, P.O. Box 2085, Olympia, WA 98507 USA Tel 360-357-4332; Fax: 360-357-4964 E-mail: info@librossinfronteras.com Web site: http://www.librossinfronteras.com.

Lifeway Christian Resources, *(978-0-7673; 978-0-633; 978-1-4158; 978-1-4300; 978-1-5359; 978-1-0877; 979-8-3845)* Div. of The Southern Baptist Convention, One Lifeway Plaza, Nashville, TN 37234 USA Tel 615-251-2000; Fax: 615-277-8221 (product info., ordering, order tracking); 615-251-2626 (shipping/transportation); Toll Free Fax: 800-296-4036; Toll Free: 800-458-2772 (product info., ordering); 800-251-3225; 200 Powell Pl., Suite 100, Brentwood, TN 37027 Tel 615-251-2000; 615-251-2657; Toll Free Fax: 800-296-4036; Toll Free: 800-458-2772 E-mail: customerservice@lifeway.com; support.lifeway.com Web site: http://www.lifewaystores.com; http://www.lifeway.com; http://www.bhpublishinggroup.com.

Light & Life Publishing Co., *(978-0-937032; 978-1-880971; 978-1-933654)* Orders Addr.: 4808 Park Glen Rd., Minneapolis, MN 55416 USA (SAN 213-8565) Tel 952-925-3888; Fax: 888-925-3918; Toll Free Fax: 888-925-3918 E-mail: ivy@light-n-life.com Web site: http://www.light-n-life.com.

Light Impressions Corp., *(978-0-87992)* Orders Addr.: P.O. Box 940, Rochester, NY 14603-0940 USA (SAN 169-619X) Toll Free Fax: 800-826-5539; Toll Free: 800-828-6216; Edit Addr.: P.O. Box 22708, Rochester, NY 14692-2708 USA Web site: http://www.lightimpresionsdirect.com.

Light Technology Publishing, *See* **Light Technology Publishing, LLC**

Light Technology Publishing, LLC, *(978-0-929385; 978-1-891824; 978-1-62233)* Orders Addr.: P.O. Box 3540, Flagstaff, AZ 86003 USA (SAN 249-1389) Tel 928-526-1345; Toll Free: 800-450-0985; Edit Addr.: 4030 E. Huntington Dr., Flagstaff, AZ 86004 USA (SAN 990-0101) E-mail: publishing@lighttechnology.net; art@lighttechnology.net; newmedia@lighttechnology.com; jon.campbell@lighttechnology.com Web site: http://www.sedonajournal.com; http://lighttechnology.com.

Lightning Source, LLC, *See* **Ingram Content Group**

Liguori Pubns., *(978-0-7648; 978-0-89243)* One Liguori Dr., Liguori, MO 63057-9999 USA (SAN 202-6783) Tel 636-464-2500; Fax: 636-464-8449; Toll Free Fax: 800-325-9526; Toll Free: 800-325-9521 (orders) E-mail: liguori@liguori.org Web site: http://www.liguori.org.

Likely Story Bookfairs, A, 7210 SW 57th Ave., Suite 207-A, South Miami, FL 33143 USA (SAN 631-1210) Tel 305-668-9183; Fax: 305-667-3323.

Lilly News Agency, P.O. Box 280077, Memphis, TN 38168-0077 USA (SAN 168-9452).

Limerock Bks., Inc., P.O. Box 57, New Canaan, CT 06840 USA (SAN 630-8708) Tel 203-322-5352; Fax: 203-322-2182 Do not confuse with Limerock Books, Thomaston, ME E-mail: limerockbk@aol.com Web site: http://www.netpocus.com/limerock.

Linden Publishing Co., Inc., *(978-0-941936; 978-1-933502; 978-1-61035)* 2006 S. Mary, Fresno, CA 93721 USA (SAN 238-6089) Tel 559-233-6633 (phone/fax); Toll Free: 800-345-4447 (orders only) Do not confuse with Linden Publishing in Avon, NY E-mail: richard@lindenpub.com Web site: http://www.lindenpub.com.

Linden Tree Children's Records & Bks., 265 State St., Los Altos, CA 94022 USA (SAN 131-744X) Tel 415-949-3390; Fax: 415-949-0346.

Linden Tree Children's Records & Books, *See* **Linden Tree Children's Records & Bks.**

Lindsay News & Photo Service, Inc., 868 Lockport Rd., Youngstown, NY 14174-1139 USA (SAN 169-6092).

Ling's International Bks., Orders Addr.: P.O. Box 82684, San Diego, CA 92138 USA (SAN 169-0116) Tel 619-292-8104; Fax: 619-292-8207; Edit Addr.: 3396 Via Cabo Verde., Escondido, CA 92029-7459 USA.

Linx Educational Publishing, Inc., *(978-1-891818; 978-0-9797510)* P.O. Box 50009, Jacksonville Beach, FL 32240 USA Tel 904-241-1861; Fax: 904-241-3279; Toll Free Fax: 888-546-9338; Toll Free: 800-717-5469 E-mail: mimi@lixedu.com; info@linxedu.com Web site: http://www.linxedu.com.

Lippincott Williams & Wilkins, *(978-0-316; 978-0-397; 978-0-683; 978-0-7817; 978-0-8067; 978-0-8121; 978-0-88167; 978-0-89004; 978-0-89313; 978-0-89640; 978-0-911216; 978-1-881063; 978-1-60547; 978-1-60831; 978-1-60929; 978-1-4698)* Orders Addr.: P.O. Box 1620, Hagerstown, MD 21741 USA Fax: 301-223-2400; Toll Free: 800-638-3030; Edit Addr.: 530 Walnut St., Philadelphia, PA 19106-3621 USA (SAN 201-0933) Tel 215-521-8300; Fax: 215-521-8902; Toll Free: 800-638-3030; 351 W. Camden St., Baltimore, MD 21201 Tel 410-528-4000; 410-528-4209; 345 Hudson St., 16th Flr., New York, NY 10014 Tel 212-886-1200; 16522 Hunters Green Pkwy., Hagerstown, MD 21740 Tel 301-223-2300; Fax: 301-223-2398; Toll Free: 800-638-3030 E-mail: custserv@lww.com; orders@lww.com Web site: http://www.lww.com.

Lippincott-Raven Publishers, *See* **Lippincott Williams & Wilkins**

Listen & Live Audio, Inc., *(978-1-885408; 978-1-931953; 978-1-59316; 979-8-88642)* Orders Addr.: P.O. Box 817, Roseland, NJ 07068 USA Tel 201-558-9000; Fax: 201-558-9800; Toll Free: 800-653-9400; Edit Addr.: 1700 Manhattan Ave., Union City, NJ 07087-5473 USA E-mail: Alfred@Listenandlive.com Web site: http://www.listenandlive.com.

Literal Bk. Distributors: Bks. in Spanish, Orders Addr.: P.O. Box 7113, Langley Park, MD 20787 USA; Edit Addr.: 7705 Georgia Ave. NW, Suite 102, Washington, DC 20012 USA (SAN 113-2784) Tel 202-723-8688; Fax: 202-882-6592; Toll Free: 800-366-8680.

Little Brown & Co., *(978-0-316; 978-0-8212; 978-0-7595)* Div. of Hachette Bk. Group, Orders Addr.: 3 Center Plaza, Boston, MA 02108-2084 USA (SAN 630-7248) Tel 617-227-0730; Toll Free Fax: 800-286-9471; Toll Free: 800-759-0190; Edit Addr.: 237 Park Ave., New York, NY 10017 USA (SAN 200-2205) Tel 212-364-0600; Fax: 212-364-0952 E-mail: customer.service@hbgusa.com Web site: http://www.hachettebookgroup.com.

Little Dania's Juvenile Promotions, Div. of Booksmith Promotional Co., 100 Paterson Plank Rd., Jersey City, NJ 07307 USA (SAN 169-5681) Tel 201-659-2317; Fax: 201-659-3631 E-mail: hochberga@aol.com.

Little Professor Bk. Ctrs., Inc., P.O. Box 3160, Ann Arbor, MI 48106-3160 USA (SAN 144-2503) Toll Free: 800-899-6232.

Llewellyn Pubns., *(978-0-7387; 978-0-87542; 978-1-56718)* Div. of Llewellyn Worldwide, Ltd., Orders Addr.: 2143 Wooddale Dr., Woodbury, MN 55125-2989 USA Tel 651-291-1970; Fax: 651-291-1908; Toll Free: 800-843-6666 E-mail: sales@llewellyn.com Web site: http://www.llewellyn.com; http://www.midnightinkbooks.com.

Llewellyn Worldwide Ltd., Orders Addr.: 2143 Wooddale Dr., Woodbury, MN 55125-2989 USA Tel 651-291-1970; Fax: 651-291-1908 E-mail: sales@llewellyn.com Web site: http://www.llewellyn.com.

Login Canada, Corporate Office & Distribution Centre 300 Saulteaux Crescent, Winnipeg, MB R3J 3T2 CAN Tel 1-800-665-1148 E-mail: custserv@lb.ca Web site: www.lb.ca.

Login Fulfillment Services, *See* **L P C Group**

Lone Pine Publishing USA, Orders Addr.: 1808 B St., NW Suite 140, Auburn, WA 98001 USA (SAN 859-0427) Tel 253-394-0400; Fax: 253-394-0405; Toll Free Fax: 800-548-1169; Toll Free: 800-518-3541 E-mail: mikec@lonepinepublishing.com Web site: http://www.lonepinepublishing.com; http://www.companyscoming.com/; http://overtimebooks.com; http://www.folklorepublishing.com/.

Lonely Planet Pubns., *(978-1-55992)* Orders Addr.: 124 Linden St., Oakland, CA 94607 USA (SAN 659-6541) Tel 510-893-8555; Fax: 510-893-8572; Toll Free: 800-275-8555 (orders, 9am - 5pm Pacific Time); 230 Franklin Rd., Bldg. 2B, Franklin, TN 37064; Edit Addr.: 315 W 36th St., 10th Flr., New York, NY 10018 USA E-mail: orders@lonelyplanet.com; lonelyplanet.kids@lonelyplanet.com; customerservice@lonelyplanet.com Web site: http://www.lonelyplanet.com.

Long Beach Bks., Inc., P.O. Box 179, Long Beach, NY 11561-0179 USA (SAN 164-632X) Tel 718-471-5934.

Longleaf Services, Orders Addr.: P.O. Box 8895, Chapel Hill, NC 27515-8895 USA Tel 800-848-6224; Fax: 800-272-6817; 919-962-2704 (24 hours) E-mail: customerservice@longleafservices.org; orders@longleafservices.org Web site: http://www.longleafservices.org/.

Longstreet Pr., Inc., *(978-0-929264; 978-1-56352)* Subs. of Cox Newspapers, Inc., 325 N. Milledge Ave., Athens, GA 30601-3805 USA (SAN 248-7640) E-mail: scottbard@gmail.com.

Looseleaf Law Pubns., Inc., *(978-0-930137; 978-1-889031; 978-1-932777; 978-1-60885)* Orders Addr.: P.O. Box 650042, Fresh Meadows, NY 11365-0042 USA Tel 718-359-5559; Fax: 718-539-0941; Toll Free: 800-647-5547 E-mail: info@looseleaflaw.com; lynette@looseleaflaw.com Web site: http://www.looseleaflaw.com.

Lord's Line, *(978-0-915952)* 1065 Lomita Blvd., No. 434, Harbor City, CA 90710-1944 USA (SAN 169-0051).

Lorenz Corp., The, *(978-0-7877; 978-0-88335; 978-0-89328; 978-1-55863; 978-1-57310; 978-1-885564; 978-1-4291)* 501 E. Third St., Dayton, OH 45401-0802 USA (SAN 208-7413) Tel 937-228-6118; Fax: 937-223-2042; Toll Free: 800-444-1144 E-mail: service@lorenz.com Web site: http://www.lorenz.com.

Los Angeles Mart, The, 1933 S. Broadway, Suite 665, Los Angeles, CA 90007 USA (SAN 168-9797) Tel 213-748-6449; Fax: 714-523-0796.

Lotus Lights Publications, *See* **Lotus Pr.**

Lotus Pr., *(978-0-910261; 978-0-914955; 978-0-940676; 978-0-940985; 978-0-941524; 978-1-60869)* Div. of Lotus Brands, Inc., P.O. Box 325, Twin Lakes, WI 53181 USA (SAN 239-1120) Tel 262-889-2461; Fax: 262-889-8591; Toll Free: 800-824-6396 Do not confuse with companies with the same or similar name in Lotus, CA, Westerville, OH, Bokeelia, FL, Brattleboro, VT, Detroit, MI, Tobyhanna, PA E-mail: lotuspress@lotuspress.com Web site: http://www.lotuspress.com.

Louisville Distributors, *See* **United Magazine**

Louisville News Co., P.O. Box 36, Columbia, KY 42728 USA (SAN 169-281X) Tel 502-384-3444; Fax: 502-384-9324.

LSC Communications Corp., Orders Addr.: 35 W. Wacker Dr., Chicago, IL 60601 USA (SAN 990-0403) E-mail: patricia.m.findlay@lsccom.com Web site: www.lsccom.com.

Lubrecht & Cramer, Ltd., *(978-0-934454; 978-0-945345)* P.O. Box 3110, Port Jervis, NY 12771-0176 USA; Orders Addr.: 2749 Albany Post Rd., Montgomery, NY 12549 USA (SAN 214-1256) Toll Free: 800-920-9334; Edit Addr.: 350 Fifth Ave., Suite 3304, New York, NY 10118-0069 USA E-mail: lubrecht@frontiernet.net; books@lubrechtcramer.com Web site: http://www.lubrechtcramer.com.

Luciano Bks., 13111 NW Le Jeune, Opa Locka, FL 33054 USA (SAN 631-2829) Tel 305-769-3103.

Ludington News Co., 1600 E. Grand Blvd., Detroit, MI 48211-3195 USA (SAN 169-3751) Tel 313-929-7600.

Lukeman Literary Management, Ltd., *(978-0-9829537; 978-0-9839778; 978-0-9849753; 978-1-939416; 978-1-63291; 978-1-64029; 978-1-0943; 978-0-578-36268-7)* 157 Bedford Ave., Brooklyn, NY 11211 USA Tel 718-599-8988; Fax: 775-264-2189 E-mail: noah@lukeman.com.

Lulu Enterprises Inc., *See* **Lulu Pr., Inc.**

Lulu Pr., Inc., *(978-1-4116; 978-1-84728; 978-1-4303; 978-1-4357; 978-1-60552; 978-0-557; 978-1-4583; 978-1-257; 978-1-105; 978-1-300; 978-1-4834; 978-1-304; 978-1-312; 978-1-326; 978-1-329; 978-1-365; 978-1-5342; 978-0-359; 978-0-578-42336-4; 978-1-68470; 978-1-68471; 978-1-68474; 978-1-716; 978-0-578-73052-3; 978-0-578-89171-2; 978-0-692-03785-0) 26-28 Hammersmith Grove, London, W6 7BA GBR; 700 Park Offices Dr #250, Research Traingle Park, NC 27709* E-mail: rbraynin@lulu.com; dliamas@lulu.com.

Lushena Bks., *(978-1-930097; 978-1-63182; 978-1-63923; 979-8-89096)* 607 Country Club Dr., Unit E, Bensenville, IL 60106 USA (SAN 630-5105) Tel 630-238-8708; Fax: 630-238-8824 E-mail: Lushenabks@yahoo.com Web site: http://www.lushenabks.com/.

Lyrical Liquor Productions, Orders Addr.: 7212 15th Ave., Takoma Park, MD 20912 USA Tel 202-723-1317 E-mail: llp@speakeasypublishing.com.

M & J Bk. Fair Service, 2307 Sherwood Cir., Minneapolis, MN 55431 USA (SAN 169-4030).

M & M News Agency, Orders Addr.: P.O. Box 1129, La Salle, IL 61301 USA (SAN 169-2062) Fax: 815-223-2828; Toll Free: 800-245-6247.

M L E S, *See* **Pathway Bk. Service**

Ma'ayan, *See* **WellSpring Bks.**

MacGregor News Agency, 1733 Industrial Park Dr., Mount Pleasant, MI 48858 USA (SAN 169-3921) Toll Free: 800-626-1982.

Mackin Bk. Co., 615 Travelers Trail W., Burnsville, MN 55337 USA (SAN 631-3442).

Mackin Educational Resources, *(978-1-62170; 978-1-62353)* 3505 CR 42 W., Burnsville, MN 55306 USA Tel 800-245-9540 E-mail: developers@mackin.com Web site: http://www.mackin.com/.

Mackin Library Media, 3505 County Rd. 42 W., Burnsville, MN 55306-3804 USA (SAN 134-8795) Toll Free: 800-245-9540 E-mail: mackin@mackin.com Web site: http://www.mackin.com.

Macmillan, *(978-0-374; 978-1-4668; 978-1-68274)* Div. of Holtzbrinck Publishing, Orders Addr.: 16365 James Madison Hwy., Gordonsville, VA 22942 USA (SAN 631-5011) Tel 540-672-7600; Fax: 540-672-7664; 540-672-7540 (Customer Service); Toll Free Fax: 800-672-2054 (Order Dept.); Toll Free: 888-330-8477; Edit Addr.: 175 Fifth Ave., 20th Flr., New York, NY 10010 USA Tel 212-674-5151; Fax: 212-677-6487; Toll Free Fax: 800-258-2769; Toll Free: 800-488-5233 E-mail: customerservice@mpsvirginia.com Web site: http://www.macmillan.com.

MacMillan Learning USA 1, Equitable Life Building 120 Broadway, New York, NY 10271 USA.

MacMillan Learning USA 2, Equitable Life Building 120 Broadway, New York, NY 10271 USA.

MacMillan Learning USA 3, Equitable Life Building 120 Broadway, New York, NY 10271 USA.

Macmillan USA, *See* **Alpha Bks.**

MacRae's Indian Bk. Distributor, 1605 Cole St., P.O. Box 652, Enumclaw, WA 98022 USA (SAN 157-5473) Tel 360-825-3737.

Madden Corp., The, *(978-1-61710)* 94-411 Koaki St., Waipahu, HI 96797 USA.

Madison Art Center, Incorporated, *See* **Madison Museum of Contemporary Art**

Madison Museum of Contemporary Art, *(978-0-913883)* 222 W. Washington Ave. Ste. 350, Madison, WI 53703-2719 USA E-mail: info@mmoca.org Web site: http://www.mmoca.org.

Magazine Distributors, Inc., 15 Sparks St., Plainville, CT 06062 USA (SAN 169-0817).

Magazines, Inc., 1135 Hammond St., Bangor, ME 04401 USA (SAN 169-3034) Tel 207-942-8237; Fax: 207-942-9226; Toll Free: 800-649-9224 (in Maine) E-mail: pam@mint.net.

Mahoning Valley Distributing Agency, Inc., 2556 Rush Blvd., Youngstown, OH 44507 USA Tel 330-788-6162; Fax: 330-788-9046.

Main Trail Productions, P.O. Box 365, Clearwater, MN 55320 USA.

Maine Writers & Pubs. Alliance, *(978-0-9618592)* P.O. Box 9301, Portland, ME 04104-9301 USA (SAN 224-2303).

Majic Enterprises, 2232 S. 11th St., Niles, MI 49120-4410 USA (SAN 169-8508).

Majors, J. A. Co., Orders Addr.: 1401 Lakeway Dr., Lewisville, TX 75057 USA (SAN 169-8117) Tel 972-353-1100; Fax: 972-353-1300; Toll Free: 800-633-1851 E-mail: dallas@majors.com Web site: http://www.majors.com.

Majors Scientific Bks., Inc., P.O. Box 35705, Dallas, TX 75235-0705 USA Toll Free: 800-633-1851 E-mail: dallas@majors.com Web site: http://www.majors.com.

Manchester News Co., Inc., P.O. Box 4838, Manchester, NH 03108-4838 USA (SAN 169-4480).

Manhattan Publishing Co., Div. of U.S. & Europe Bks., Inc., P.O. Box 850, Croton-on-Hudson, NY 10520 USA (SAN 113-7476) Tel 914-271-5194; Fax: 914-271-5856 Web site: http://www.manhattanpublishing.com.

Manitowoc News Agency, 907 S. Eighth St., Manitowoc, WI 54220 USA (SAN 159-9046).

Manning's Bks. & Prints, 580M Crespi Dr., Pacifica, CA 94044 USA (SAN 157-5384) Fax: 650-355-1851
E-mail: manningsbks@aol.com
Web site: http://www.printsoldandrare.com.

Many Feathers Bks. & Maps, 2626 W. Indian School Rd., Phoenix, AZ 85017 USA (SAN 158-8877) Tel 602-266-1043; Toll Free: 800-279-7652.

Map Link, *See* **Benchmark LLC**

Maple Press Co., 1000 Strickler Rd., Mount Joy, PA 17552 USA Tel 717-653-5483; Edit Addr.: P.O. Box 2695, York, PA 17406 USA Tel 717-764-5911; Fax: 717-764-4702; 480 Willow Springs Ln., York, PA 17406.

Marangio, Charles F. Distribution, Orders Addr.: P.O. Box 3643, Sonoro, CA 95370 USA (SAN 631-3965) Tel 209-533-0997; Edit Addr.: 659 Sanguinetti Rd., Sonoro, CA 95370 USA (SAN 631-3973).

Marco Bk. Co., *(978-0-9710756; 978-0-9729765)* 60 Industrail Rd., Lodi, NJ 07644 USA Tel 973-458-0485; Fax: 973-458-5289; Toll Free: 800-842-4234
E-mail: everbind5@aol.com

Marco Bk. Distributors, *(978-0-88298)* 60 Industrial Rd., Lodi, NJ 07644 USA (SAN 169-5142) Tel 973-458-0485; Fax: 973-458-5289; Toll Free: 800-842-4234
Web site: http://www.everbind.com.

MAR*CO Products, Inc., *(978-1-57543; 978-1-884063)* Orders Addr.: 1443 Old York Rd., Warminster, PA 18974 USA Tel 215-956-0313; Fax: 215-956-9041; Toll Free: 800-448-2197
E-mail: csfunk@marcoproducts.com; marcoproducts@comcast.net
Web site: http://www.store.yahoo.com/marcoproducts; http://www.marcoproducts.com.

Marcus Wholesale, P.O. Box 1618, R49 E. Hwy. 4, Murphys, CA 95247 USA (SAN 185-0296).

Mardelva News Co., Inc., 8999 Ocean Hwy., Delmar, MD 21875 USA (SAN 169-3247) Tel 410-742-8613; Fax: 410-742-2616.

Marshall Cavendish Corp., *(978-0-7614; 978-0-85685; 978-0-86307; 978-1-85435; 978-1-60870)* Member of Times Publishing Group, 99 White Plains Rd., Tarrytown, NY 10591-9001 USA (SAN 238-437X) Tel 914-332-8888; Fax: 914-332-8882; Toll Free: 800-821-9881
E-mail: mce@marshallcavendish.com
Web site: www.MCEducation.us.

Marshall-Mangold Distribution Co., Inc., 4805 Nelson Ave., Baltimore, MD 21215-2507 USA (SAN 169-3115) Toll Free: 800-972-2665.

Marvin Law Bk., 11020 27th Ave., S., Burnsville, MN 55337 USA (SAN 163-898X) Tel 612-644-2236.

Mascot Books, Incorporated, *See* **Amplify Publishing Group**

Master Communications, Inc., *(978-1-888194; 978-1-60480)* 2692 Madison Rd., Suite N1-307 N1-307, Cincinnati, OH 45208 USA (SAN 299-2140) Tel 513-563-3100; Fax: 513-563-3105; Toll Free: 800-765-5885
E-mail: sales@master-comm.com
Web site: http://www.worldculturemedia.com; http://www.master-comm.com.

Mastery Education, *(978-1-56256; 978-1-58984; 978-1-4138; 978-1-61526; 978-1-61527; 978-1-936025; 978-1-936026; 978-1-936027; 978-1-936028; 978-1-936029; 978-1-936030; 978-1-936031; 978-0-692-00207-0; 978-0-692-00208-7; 978-0-692-00209-4; 978-0-692-00210-0; 978-1-61602; 978-1-61734; 978-1-60979; 978-1-64090; 979-8-88711) Orders Addr.: P.O. Box 513, Saddle Brook, NJ 07633 USA Tel 201-712-0090; Fax: 201-712-1534; Toll Free: 800-822-1080; Edit Addr.: 299 Market St. Suite 240, Saddle Brook, NJ 07663 USA (SAN 857-9873)*
E-mail: solvier@peoplesed.com; sales@peoplesed.com; customersupport@peoplesed.com; editorial@peoplesed.com
Web site: http://www.masteryeducation.com/.

Matagiri Sri Aurobindo Ctr., *(978-0-89071)* 2288 Fulton St., No. 310, Berkeley, CA 94704-1449 USA (SAN 169-5541).

Matthews Medical Bk. Co., Orders Addr.: 10 Old Bloomfield Ave., Pine Brook, NJ 07058 USA; 11559 Rock Island Ct., Maryland Heights, MO 63043 (SAN 146-4655) Tel 314-432-1400; Fax: 314-432-7044
E-mail: mlc@mattmccoy.com
Web site: http://www.mattmccoy.com.

Maxwell Scientific International, Inc., *(978-0-8277)* Div. of Pergamon Pr., Inc., 1345 Ave. of the Americas, No. 1036C, New York, NY 10105-0302 USA (SAN 169-524X) Tel 914-592-9141.

May, L. B. & Assocs., 3517 Neal Dr., Knoxville, TN 37918 USA Tel 865-922-7490; Fax: 865-922-7492
E-mail: lbmay@aol.com.

MBI Distribution Services/Quayside Distribution, *(978-0-7603; 978-0-87938; 978-0-912612; 978-1-85010)* Div. of MBI Publishing Co. LLC, Orders Addr.: P.O. Box 1, Osceola, WI 54020-0001 USA (SAN 169-9164) Toll Free: 800-458-0454; Edit Addr.: 400 First Ave., N, Suite 300, Minneapolis, MN 55401 USA Toll Free: 800-328-0590
Web site: http://www.motorbooks.com.

MBS Textbook Exchange, Inc., Orders Addr.: 2711 W. Ash St., Columbia, MO 65203-4613 USA (SAN 140-7015) Tel 573-445-2243; Fax: 573-446-5254; Toll Free: 800-325-0929 (orders); 800-325-0530 (customer service); Edit Addr.: 2711 W. Ash St., Columbia, MO 65203 USA
E-mail: kyates@mbsbooks.com
Web site: http://www.mbsbooks.com.

McCaslin, Boyce, 3 Greenbriar Dr., Saint Louis, MO 63124-1819 USA (SAN 110-8298).

McCoy Church Goods, 1010 Howard Ave., San Mateo, CA 94401 USA (SAN 107-2315) Tel 415-342-0924.

McCrory's Books, *See* **McCrory's Wholesale Bks.**

McCrory's Wholesale Bks., Orders Addr.: P.O. Box 2032, Alexandria, LA 71301 USA (SAN 108-5999); Edit Addr.: 1808 Rapides Ave., Alexandria, LA 71301 USA.

McEvoy Group, The, 680 Second St., San Francisco, CA 94107 USA Tel 415-537-4300
E-mail: info@mcevoygroup.com
Web site: http://mcevoygroup.com.

McGraw-Hill Cos., The, *(978-0-07)* 6480 Jimmy Carter Blvd., Norcross, GA 30071-1701 USA (SAN 254-881X) Tel 614-755-5637; Fax: 614-755-5611; Orders Addr.: 860 Taylor Station Rd., Blacklick, OH 43004-0545 USA (SAN 200-254X) Fax: 614-755-5645; Toll Free: 800-722-4726 (orders & customer service); 800-338-3987 (college); 800-525-5003 (subscriptions); 800-352-3566 (books - US/Canada orders); P.O. Box 545, Blacklick, OH 43004-0545 Fax: 614-759-3759; Toll Free: 877-833-5524; a/o General Customer Service, P.O. Box 182604, Columbus, OH 43272 Fax: 614-759-3759; Toll Free: 877-833-5524
E-mail: customer.service@mcgraw-hill.com
Web site: http://www.mcgraw-hill.com; http://www.ebooks.mcgraw-hill.com/.

McGraw-Hill Create (TM), *(978-0-390)* Div. of McGraw-Hill Higher Education, 148 Princeton-Hightstown Rd., Hightstown, NJ 08520-1450 USA Tel 609-426-5721; Toll Free: 800-962-9342
Web site: http://www.mhhe.com.

McGraw-Hill Education, *(978-1-259; 978-1-260; 978-1-264; 978-1-265; 978-1-266; 979-8-219; 979-8-220; 979-8-221; 979-8-222)* Two Penn Plaza, New York, NY 10121-2298 USA Tel 212-904-2000; a/o The Mcgraw-Hill Companies, 8787 Orion Pl., Columbus, OH 43240 (SAN 256-3908) Tel 614-755-5637; Fax: 614-755-5611; Level 33, 680 George Street, Sydney, NSW 2000
E-mail: customer.service@mcgraw-hill.com
Web site: http://www.mheducation.com/custserv.html; http://www.mcgraw-hill.com.

McGraw-Hill Health Professions Division, *See* **McGraw-Hill Medical Publishing Div.**

McGraw-Hill Higher Education, *(978-0-07; 978-1-121)* Orders Addr.: P.O. Box 545, Blacklick, OH 43004-0545 USA Toll Free: 800-338-3987; Edit Addr.: 1333 Burr Ridge Pkwy., 3rd Flr., Burr Ridge, IL 60527 USA
E-mail: customer.service@mcgraw-hill.com
Web site: http://www.mhhe.com.

McGraw-Hill Medical Publishing Div., *(978-0-07)* Div. of The McGraw-Hill Cos., Orders Addr.: P.O. Box 545, Blacklick, OH 43004-0545 USA Fax: 614-755-5645 (customer service); Toll Free: 800-262-4729 (customer service); 800-722-4726 (bookstores & libraries)
E-mail: customerservice@mcgraw-hill.com
Web site: http://www.mghmedical.com.

McGraw-Hill Osborne, *(978-0-07; 978-0-88134; 978-0-931988)* Div. of The McGraw-Hill Professional, 160 Spear St. Flr. 7, San Francisco, CA 94105-1544 USA (SAN 274-3450) Toll Free: 800-227-0900
E-mail: customer.service@mcgraw-hill.com
Web site: http://www.osborne.com.

McGraw-Hill Primis Custom Publishing, *See* **McGraw-Hill Create (TM)**

McGraw-Hill Professional Publishing, *(978-0-07)* Div. of McGraw-Hill Higher Education, Orders Addr.: P.O. Box 545, Blacklick, OH 43004-0545 USA Fax: 614-755-5645; Toll Free: 800-722-4726; Edit Addr.: 2 Penn Plaza, New York, NY 10121-2298 USA Tel 212-904-2000.

McGraw-Hill Trade, *(978-0-07; 978-0-658; 978-0-8442)* Div. of McGraw-Hill Professional, Orders Addr.: P.O. Box 545, Blacklick, OH 43004-0545 USA Tel 800-722-4726; Fax: 614-755-5645; Edit Addr.: 2 Penn Plaza, New York, NY 10121 USA Tel 212-904-2000
E-mail: Jeffrey_Krames@mcgraw-hill.com
Web site: http://www.books.mcgraw-hill.com.

McGraw-Hill US Higher Ed ISE, *(978-1-260)* c/o McGraw-Hill, P.O. Box 182605, Columbus, OH 43218 USA Tel 800-338-3987; Fax: 800-953-8691
Web site: https://www.mheducation.com/highered/home-guest.html

McGraw-Hill US Higher Ed USE, P.O. Box 182605, Columbus, OH 43218 USA.

McGraw-Hill US Higher Ed USE Legacy, P.O. Box 182605, Columbus, OH 43218 USA.

McGraw-Hill/Contemporary, *(978-0-658; 978-0-8092; 978-0-8325; 978-0-8442; 978-0-88499; 978-0-89061; 978-0-913327; 978-0-940279; 978-0-941263; 978-0-9630646; 978-1-56626; 978-1-56943; 978-1-57028)* Div. of McGraw-Hill Higher Education, Orders Addr.: P.O. Box 545, Blacklick, OH 43004-0545 USA Toll Free Fax: 800-998-3103; Toll Free: 800-621-1918; Edit Addr.: 4255 W. Touhy Ave., Lincolnwood, IL 60712 USA (SAN 169-2208) Tel 847-679-5500; Fax: 847-679-2494; Toll Free Fax: 800-998-3103; Toll Free: 800-323-4900
E-mail: ntcpub@tribune.com
Web site: http://www.ntc-cb.com.

McKay, David Co., Inc., *(978-0-679; 978-0-88326; 978-0-89440)* Subs. of Random Hse., Inc., Orders Addr.: 400 Hahn Rd., Westminster, MD 21157 USA Tel 410-848-1900; Toll Free: 800-733-3000 (orders only); Edit Addr.: 201 E. 50th St., MD 4-6, New York, NY 10022 USA (SAN 200-240X) Tel 212-751-2600; Fax: 212-872-8026.

McKnight Sales Co., P.O. Box 4138, Pittsburgh, PA 15202 USA (SAN 169-7587) Tel 412-761-4443; Fax: 412-761-0122; Toll Free: 800-208-8078
E-mail: sales@mscmags.com
Web site: http://www.mscmags.com.

McLemore, Hollern & Assocs., 3538 Maple Park Dr., Kingwood, TX 77339 USA Tel 281-360-5204.

McMillen Bk. Distributors, 304 Main St., Ames, IA 50010 USA Fax: 515-232-0402; Toll Free: 866-385-2027.

MeadWestvaco, Orders Addr.: 4751 Hempstead Sta., Kettering, OH 45429 USA Tel 937-495-6323
Web site: http://us.meadwestvaco.com.

MediaTech Productions, *(978-0-9702309)* 917 E. Prospect Rd. Unit B, Fort Collins, CO 80525-1364 USA Toll Free: 800-816-7566 Do not confuse with companies with the same or similar name in Chicago, IL
E-mail: maury@mediatechproductions.com
Web site: http://mediatechproductions.com.

Medical Information Systems, Inc., 2 Seaview Blvd., Port Washington, NY 11050 USA (SAN 242-1720) Tel 516-621-7200 Do not confuse with Medical Information Systems, Inc., Stamford, CT.

Medicina Biologica, 2937 NE Flanders St., Portland, OR 97232 USA (SAN 113-0226) Tel 503-287-6775; Fax: 503-235-3520
E-mail: med_bio@imagina.com.

Mel Bay Pubns., Inc., *(978-0-7866; 978-0-87166; 978-1-56222; 978-1-60974; 978-1-61065; 978-1-61911; 978-1-5134)* 16 N Gore Ave Ste 203, Saint Louis, MO 63119-2315 USA (SAN 657-3630) Tel 636-257-3970; Fax: 636-257-5062; Toll Free: 800-863-5229
E-mail: email@melbay.com; sharon@melbay.com
Web site: http://www.melbay.com; www.melbaydealers.com.

Melton Book Company, Incorporated, *See* **Nelson Direct**

Mentor Bks., 5318 Lowell Blvd., Denver, CO 80221 USA Fax: 303-975-1936; Toll Free: 800-795-6198
E-mail: blair@mentorbooks.com.

Merced News Co., 1324 Coldwell Ave., Modesto, CA 95350-5702 USA (SAN 168-9894) Tel 209-722-5791.

Mercedes Book Distributors Corporation, *See* **Mercedes Distribution Ctr., Inc.**

Mercedes Distribution Ctr., Inc., Brooklyn Navy Yard, Bldg. No. 3, Brooklyn, NY 11205 USA (SAN 169-5150) Tel 718-534-3000; Fax: 718-935-9647; Toll Free: 800-339-4804
E-mail: contact@mdist.com.

Meredith Bks., *(978-0-696; 978-0-89721; 978-0-917102)* Div. of Meredith Corp., Orders Addr.: 1716 Locust St., LN-110, Des Moines, IA 50309-3023 USA (SAN 202-4055) Tel 515-284-2363; 515-284-2126 (sales); Fax: 515-284-3371; Toll Free: 800-678-8091 Do not confuse with Meredith Pr. in Skaneateles, NY
E-mail: John.OBannon@meredith.com
Web site: http://www.bhgstore.com.

Merkos Pubns., Div. of Merkos L'Inyonei Chinuch, 291 Kingston Ave., Brooklyn, NY 11213 USA (SAN 631-1040) Tel 718-778-0226; Fax: 718-778-4148.

Merry Thoughts, *(978-0-88230)* 364 Adams St., Bedford Hills, NY 10507 USA (SAN 169-5061) Tel 914-241-0447; Fax: 914-241-0247.

Messianic Jewish Resources International, Orders Addr.: P.O. Box 1539, Fort Lee, NJ 07024-1539 USA Fax: 201-840-7242; Toll Free: 800-410-7367.

Meta Co., LLC, P.O. Box 2667, Columbia, MD 21045 USA.

Metamorphosis Publishing Company, *See* **Metamorphous Pr., Inc.**

Metamorphous Pr., Inc., *(978-0-943920; 978-1-55552)* Orders Addr.: P.O. Box 10616, Portland, OR 97296-0616 USA (SAN 110-8786) Tel 503-228-4972; Fax: 503-223-9117; Toll Free: 800-937-7771 (orders only); Edit Addr.: P.O. Box 10616, Portland, OR 97296-0616 USA
E-mail: metabooks@metamodels.com
Web site: http://www.metamodels.com.

Metro Systems, 3381 Stevens Creek Blvd., Suite 209, San Jose, CA 95117 USA (SAN 631-1016) Tel 408-247-4050; Fax: 408-247-4236.

Metropolitan News Co., 47-25 34th, Long Island City, NY 11101 USA (SAN 159-9089) Do not confuse with Metropolitan News Co. in Los Angeles, CA.

Mi Lybro, 9775 Marconi Dr., Suite D, San Diego, CA 92154 USA Tel 619-900-7624
E-mail: sales@milybro.com.

Miami Bks., Inc., 17842 State Rd. 9, Miami, FL 33162 USA (SAN 106-8997) Tel 305-652-3231.

Miami Valley News Agency, 2127 Old Troy Pike, Dayton, OH 45404 USA (SAN 169-6718) Fax: 513-233-8544; Toll Free: 800-791-5137.

Michiana News Service, 2232 S. 11th St., Niles, MI 49120 USA (SAN 110-5051) Tel 616-684-3013; Fax: 616-684-8740.

Michigan Church Supply, P.O. Box 279, Mount Morris, MI 48458-0279 USA (SAN 184-413X) Toll Free: 800-521-3440.

Michigan State Univ. Pr., *(978-0-87013; 978-0-937191; 978-1-60917; 978-1-61186; 978-1-938065; 978-1-62895; 978-1-62896; 978-1-941258; 978-0-9967252; 978-1-68430; 978-1-941134; 978-1-948314)* Orders Addr.: 1405 S. Harrison Rd. Suite 25, East Lansing, MI 48823-5245 USA (SAN 202-6295) Tel 517-884-6901; Fax: 517-432-2611; Toll Free: 800-621-2736; 800-621-8476
E-mail: msupress@msupress.org
Web site: http://www.msupress.org.

Mickler's Bks., Inc., 61 Alafaya Woods Blvd., No. 197, Oviedo, FL 32765 USA Tel 407-365-8500; Toll Free Fax: 800-726-0585
E-mail: orders@micklers.com
Web site: http://www.micklers.com.

Micklers Floridiana, Incorporated, *See* **Mickler's Bks., Inc.**

Microdistributors International, Inc., *(978-0-918025)* Subs. of Medcomp Technologies, Inc., 34 Maple Ave., P.O. Box 8, Armonk, NY 10504 USA (SAN 296-158X) Tel 914-273-6480.

Mid Penn Magazine Agency, 100 Eck Cir., Williamsport, PA 17701 USA (SAN 169-7692).

Mid South Manufacturing Agency, Incorporated, *See* **Mid-South Magazine Agency, Inc.**

Mid-Cal Periodical Distributors, P.O. Box 245230, Sacramento, CA 95824-5230 USA (SAN 169-0078).

Midpoint National, Inc., 1263 Southwest Blvd., Kansas City, MO 66103-1901 USA (SAN 630-9860) Tel 913-831-2233; Fax: 913-362-7401; Toll Free: 800-228-4321.

Midpoint Trade Bks., Inc., *(978-1-940416)* Orders Addr.: 1263 Southwest Blvd., Kansas City, KS 66103 USA (SAN 631-3736) Tel 913-831-2233; Fax: 913-362-7401; Toll Free: 800-742-6139 (consumer orders); Edit Addr.: 27 W. 20th St., No. 1102, New York, NY 10011 USA (SAN 631-1075) Tel 212-727-0190; Fax: 212-727-0195
E-mail: info@midpointtrade.com
Web site: http://www.midpointtrade.com; http://www.midpointtradebooks.com/.

Mid-South Magazine Agency, Inc., P.O. Box 4585, Jackson, MS 39296-4585 USA (SAN 286-0163) Toll Free: 800-748-9444.

Mid-State Periodicals, Inc., P.O. Box 3455, Quincy, IL 62305-3455 USA Tel 217-222-0833; Fax: 217-222-1256.

Mid-States Distributors, P.O. Box 1374, Chambersburg, PA 17201-5374 USA (SAN 169-3166).

Midtown Auto Bks., 212 Burnet Ave., Syracuse, NY 13203 USA (SAN 169-6289).

Midwest European Pubns., 915 Foster St., Evanston, IL 60201 USA (SAN 169-1937) Tel 847-866-6289; Fax: 847-866-6290; Toll Free: 800-380-8919
E-mail: info@mep-eli.com
Web site: http://www.mep-eli.com.

Midwest Library Service, 11443 St. Charles Rock Rd., Bridgeton, MO 63044-2789 USA (SAN 169-4243) Tel 314-739-3100; Fax: 314-739-1326; Toll Free Fax: 800-962-1009; Toll Free: 800-325-8833
E-mail: hudson@midwestls.com.

Midwest Tape, Orders Addr.: P.O. Box 820, Holland, OH 43528-0820 USA (SAN 254-9913) Toll Free Fax: 800-444-6645; Toll Free: 800-875-2785
E-mail: randys@midwesttapes.com
Web site: http://www.midwesttapes.com.

MightyWords, Inc., *(978-1-58895; 978-0-7173; 978-1-4036)* 2850 Walsh Ave., Santa Clara, CA 95051 USA Tel 408-845-0100; Fax: 408-845-0425; Toll Free: 877-328-2724
Web site: http://www.mightywords.com.

Mightywords.com, *See* **MightyWords, Inc.**

Military History Assocs., 407B E. Sixth St., No. 200, Austin, TX 78701-3739 USA (SAN 111-7866).

Miller Educational Materials, *(978-1-934274)* Orders Addr.: P.O. Box 2428, Buena Park, CA 90621 USA Fax: 714-562-0237; Toll Free: 800-636-4375; Edit Addr.: 3294 Cherry Ave., Long Beach, CA 90807-5214 USA (SAN 631-5445)
E-mail: MillerEdu@aol.com
Web site: http://www.millereducational.com.

Miller Trade Bk. Marketing, 363 W. Erie St. Ste. 700E, Chicago, IL 60610-6996 USA (SAN 631-4287)
E-mail: millertrade@sbcglobal.net.

Milligan News Co., Inc., 150 N. Autumn St., San Jose, CA 95110 USA (SAN 169-0272) Tel 408-286-7604; Fax: 408-298-0235; Toll Free: 800-873-2387.

Millmark Education, *(978-1-4334; 978-1-61618)* Orders Addr.: 7272 Wisconsin Ave, Suite 300, Bethesda, MD 20814-2081 USA (SAN 852-4912) Tel 301-941-1974; Fax: 301-656-0183; Edit Addr.: 7272 Wisconsin Ave. Suite 300, Suite 300, Bethesda, MD 20814-2081 USA
E-mail: rachel.moir@millmarkeducation.com; info@millmarkeducation.com
Web site: http://www.millmarkeducation.com/.

Mind Trip Pr., P.O. Box 489, Georgetown, TX 78626 USA Tel 513-428-9278.

Minerva Science Bookseller, Inc., 175 Fifth Ave., New York, NY 10010 USA (SAN 286-0171).

Mint Pubs. Group, Orders Addr.: 62 June Rd., Suite 241, North Salem, NY 10560 USA Tel 914-276-6576; Fax: 914-276-6579; Edit Addr.: 1220 Nicholson Rd., Newmarket, ON I3Y 7V1 CAN Toll Free Fax: 800-363-2665; Toll Free: 800-399-6858
E-mail: info@mintpub.com
Web site: http://www.mintpub.com.

Mintright, Inc., *(978-1-4687)* 55 W. 26th St., Suite 36D, New York, NY 10010 USA (SAN 935-4840) Tel 646-368-8090; Fax: 646-368-8099
E-mail: content@mintright.com
Web site: http://mintright.com/.

Mission Resource Ctr., 1221 Profit Dr., Dallas, TX 75247 USA Toll Free: 800-305-9857.

Mississippi Library Media & Supply Co., P.O. Box 108, Brandon, MS 39043-0108 USA (SAN 169-4189) Tel 601-824-1900; Fax: 601-824-1999; Toll Free: 800-257-7566 (in Mississippi).

Mistco, Inc., P.O. Box 694854, Miami, FL 33269 USA (SAN 630-8384) Tel 305-653-2003; Fax: 305-653-2037; Toll Free: 800-552-0446
E-mail: mistco@worldnet.att.net
Web site: http://www.mistco.com.

Mobile News Co., 1118 14th St., Tuscaloosa, AL 35401-3318 USA (SAN 168-924X) Tel 334-479-1435.

Modern Curriculum Pr., *(978-0-7652; 978-0-8136; 978-0-87895)* Div. of Pearson Education, Orders Addr.: P.O. Box 2500, Lebanon, IN 46052-3009 USA (SAN 206-6572) Toll Free: 800-526-9907 (Customer Service)
Web site: http://www.pearsonlearning.com.

Modesto News Co., 1324 Coldwell Ave., Modesto, CA 95350-5702 USA (SAN 168-9908) Tel 209-577-5551.

Montfort Pubns., *(978-0-910984)* Div. of Montfort Missionaries, 26 S. Saxon Ave., Bay Shore, NY 11706-8993 USA (SAN 169-5053) Tel 631-665-0726; Fax: 631-665-4349
E-mail: info@montfortpublications.com
Web site: http://www.montfortmissionaries.com; http://www.montfortmissionaries.org; http://www.montfortpublications.com.

Mook & Blanchard, P.O. Box 4177, La Puente, CA 91747-4177 USA (SAN 168-9703) Toll Free: 800-875-9911
E-mail: mookbook@ix.netcom.com
Web site: http://www.mookandblanchard.com.

Moon Over the Mountain Publishing Company, *See* **Leman Pubns., Inc.**

More, Thomas Assn., 205 W. Monroe St., 5th Flr., Chicago, IL 60606-5097 USA (SAN 169-1880) Tel 312-609-8880; Toll Free: 800-835-8965.

Morgan James Publishing, *(978-0-9746133; 978-0-9758570; 978-0-9760901; 978-0-9768491; 978-1-933596; 978-1-60037; 978-0-9815058; 978-0-9817906; 978-0-9820750; 978-0-9823793; 978-0-9846170; 978-0-9828590; 978-0-9833715; 978-0-9835013; 978-1-61448; 978-0-9837125; 978-0-9840316; 978-1-938467; 978-1-63047; 978-1-63195; 978-1-68350; 978-0-9985823; 978-1-64279; 978-1-63698) Div. of Morgan James, LLC, 23rd Flr. 5 Penn Plaza, New York, NY 10001 USA* E-mail: kim@morganjamespublishing.com Web site: http://www.morganjamespublishing.com.

Morlock News Co., Inc., 496 Duanesburg Rd., Schenectady, NY 12306 USA (SAN 169-6246).

Morris Publishing, *(978-0-7392; 978-0-9631249; 978-1-57502; 978-1-885591; 978-0-9863567; 978-0-578-26187-4)* Orders Addr.: P.O. Box 2110, Kearney, NE 68847 USA Fax: 308-237-0263; Toll Free: 800-650-7888 Do not confuse with companies with the same Wesley Chapel, FL, Elkhart, IN E-mail: publish@morrispublishing.com Web site: http://www.morrispublishing.com.

Moshy Brothers, Inc., 127 W. 25th St., New York, NY 10001 USA (SAN 169-5886) Tel 212-255-0613.

Mother Lode Distributing, 17890 Lime Rock Dr., Sonora, CA 95370-8707 USA (SAN 169-0361).

Motorbooks International Wholesalers & Distributors, *See* **MBI Distribution Services/Quayside Distribution**

Mountain Bk. Co., P.O. Box 778, Broomfield, CO 80038-0778 USA Tel 303-436-1982; Fax: 917-386-2769 E-mail: wordguise@aol.com Web site: http://www.mountainbook.org.

Mountain n' Air Bks., *(978-1-879415)* Div. of Mountain n' Air Sports, Inc., Orders Addr.: P.O. Box 12540, La Crescenta, CA 91224 USA (SAN 630-5598) Tel 818-248-9345; Toll Free Fax: 800-303-5578; Toll Free: 800-446-9696; Edit Addr.: 2947-A Hololulu Ave., La Crescenta, CA 91214 USA (SAN 631-4198) E-mail: books@mountain-n-air.com Web site: http://mountain-n-air.com.

Mountain Pr. Publishing Co., Inc., *(978-0-87842)* Orders Addr.: P.O. Box 2399, Missoula, MT 59806-2399 USA (SAN 202-8832) Tel 406-728-1900; Fax: 406-728-1635; Toll Free: 800-234-5308; Edit Addr.: 1301 S. Third West, Missoula, MT 59801 USA (SAN 662-0868) E-mail: jrimel@mtnpress.com; info@mtnpress.com; anne@mtnpress.com Web site: http://www.mountain-press.com.

Mountain States News Distributor, P.O. Drawer P, Fort Collins, CO 80522 USA Tel 970-221-2330; Fax: 970-221-1251.

Mouse Works, *(978-0-7364; 978-1-57082)* Div. of Disney Bk. Publishing, Inc., A Walt Disney Co., 114 Fifth Ave., New York, NY 10011 USA (SAN 298-0797) Tel 212-633-4400; Fax: 212-633-4811 Web site: http://www.disneybooks.com.

MPS, 16365 James Madison Hwy., Gordonsville, VA 22942-8501 USA Toll Free Fax: 800-672-2054; Toll Free: 888-330-8477.

Mr. Paperback/Publishers News Co., 6030 Fostoria Ave., Findlay, OH 45840 USA (SAN 169-393X) Tel 419-424-6774; Fax: 419-420-1805; Toll Free: 800-872-0031.

M-S News Co., Inc., P.O. Box 13278, Wichita, KS 67213-0278 USA Fax: 316-267-5405.

Mullare News Agency, Inc., P.O. Box 578, Brockton, MA 02401 USA (SAN 169-3379) Tel 508-580-1000; Fax: 508-586-0968.

Multi-Cultural Bks. & Videos, Inc., *(978-0-9656274)* 30007 John R. Rd., Madison Hts, MI 48071-2526 USA (SAN 760-6796) Toll Free: 800-567-2220 E-mail: service@multiculbv.com Web site: http://www.multiculbv.com.

Multilingual Bks., Orders Addr.: P.O. Box 440632, Miami, FL 33144 USA (SAN 169-1155) Tel 305-471-9847 Do not confuse with Multilingual Bks., Seattle, WA.

Mumford Library Bks., Inc., 7847 Bayberry Rd., Jacksonville, FL 32256 USA (SAN 156-7721) Fax: 904-730-8913; Toll Free: 800-367-3927.

Mumford Library Book Sales, *See* **Mumford Library Bks., Inc.**

Murr's Library Service, 4045 E. Palm Ln., No. 5, Phoenix, AZ 85008-3116 USA (SAN 107-3222) Fax: 602-273-1217; Toll Free: 888-273-0279.

Music, Bks. & Business, Inc., Orders Addr.: 4305 32nd St W Suite A, Bradenton, FL 34205 USA (SAN 760-5986) Fax: 941-752-8994; Toll Free: 888-876-7716 E-mail: info@musicbooksbusiness.com Web site: http://www.musicbooksbusiness.com.

Music Design, Inc., 4650 N. Port Washington Rd., Milwaukee, WI 53212 USA (SAN 200-7649) Tel 414-961-8380; Fax: 414-961-8381; Toll Free: 800-862-7232 E-mail: order@musicdesign.com Web site: http://www.musicdesign.com.

Music in Motion, P.O. Box 869231, Plano, TX 75086-9231 USA (SAN 631-4589) Fax: 972-943-8906; Toll Free Fax: 866-943-8906; Toll Free: 800-445-0649 Do not confuse with Music In Motion, Ithaca, NY Web site: http://www.musicmotion.com.

Music is Elementary, *(978-0-9721085; 978-0-9910656; 978-0-9966913; 978-0-692-90589-0)* P.O. Box 24263, Cleveland, OH 44124 USA Tel 440-442-4475; Fax: 440-461-3631; Toll Free: 800-888-7502 E-mail: music@en.com Web site: http://www.musiciselementary.com.

Music Sales Corp., *(978-0-7119; 978-0-8256; 978-1-84609)* Orders Addr.: 445 Bellvale Rd., P.O. Box 572, Chester, NY 10918 USA (SAN 662-0876) Tel 845-469-2271; Fax: 845-469-7544; Toll Free Fax: 800-345-6842; Toll Free: 800-431-7187; Edit Addr.: 257 Park Ave., S., 20th Flr., New York, NY 10010 USA (SAN 282-0277) Tel 212-254-2100; Fax: 212-254-2103 E-mail: info@musicsales.com Web site: http://www.musicroom.com; http://www.musicsales.com.

Music Video Distributors, *See* **MVD Entertainment Group**

Musicart West, P.O. Box 1900, Orem, UT 84059-1900 USA (SAN 110-1250) Tel 801-225-0859; Toll Free: 800-950-1900 (orders only).

MVD Entertainment Group, Orders Addr.: 203 Windsor Rd., Limerick, PA 19464 USA (SAN 255-2663) Tel 610-650-8200; Fax: 610-650-9102; Toll Free: 800-888-0486 E-mail: musviddis@aol.com Web site: http://www.musicvideodistributors.com.

MVP Wholesales, 9301 W. Hwy. 290, No. D, Austin, TX 78736-7817 USA (SAN 630-9550) Tel 512-416-1452; Toll Free: 800-328-7931 (phone/fax).

MyiLibrary, *(978-1-280; 978-1-281; 978-1-282; 978-1-283; 978-1-299; 978-1-306; 978-1-322; 978-1-336)* Div. of Coutts Information Services, 14 Ingram Blvd., La Vergne, TN 37086 USA Tel 615-213-5400; Fax: 615-213-5111 E-mail: wendell.lotz@ingramcontent.com.

myON, 5050 Lincoln Dr., Suite 200, Edina, MN 55436 USA Toll Free: 800-864-3899.

NACSCORP, Incorporated, *See* .

Najarian Music Co., Inc., 236 Partridge Ln., Concord, MA 01742-2651 USA (SAN 169-3344).

Napa Book Company, *See* **Napa Children's Bk. Co.**

Napa Children's Bk. Co., 1239 First St., Napa, CA 94559 USA (SAN 122-2732) Tel 707-224-3893; Fax: 707-224-1212.

Nasco Math Eighty-Six, 901 Janesville Ave., Fort Atkinson, WI 53538 USA (SAN 679-7512).

National Academies Pr., *(978-0-309)* Orders Addr.: 8700 Spectrum Dr., Landover, MD 20785 USA; Edit Addr.: 500 Fifth St., NW Lockbox 285, Washington, DC 20001 USA (SAN 202-8891) Tel 202-334-3313; Fax: 202-334-2451; Toll Free: 888-624-7654 E-mail: zjones@nas.edu Web site: http://www.nap.edu.

National Academy Press, *See* **National Academies Pr.**

National Assn. of the Deaf, *(978-0-913072)* 8630 Fenton St. Ste. 820, Silver Spring, MD 20910-3819 USA (SAN 159-4974) E-mail: donna.morris@nad.org Web site: http://www.nad.org.

National Bk. Co., Keystone Industrial Pk., Scranton, PA 18512 USA Tel 717-346-2020; Toll Free: 800-233-4830 Do not confuse with National Book Company, Portland, OR.

National Bk. Network, Div. of Rowman & Littlefield Pubs., Inc., Orders Addr.: 15200 NBN Way, Blue Ridge Summit, PA 17214 USA (SAN 630-0065) Tel 717-794-3800; Fax: 717-794-3828; Toll Free Fax: 800-338-4550 (Customer Service); Toll Free: 800-462-6420 (Customer Service); a/o Les Petriw, 67 Mowat Ave., Suite 241, Toronto, ON M6P 3K3 Tel 416-534-1660; Fax: 416-534-3699 E-mail: custserv@nbnbooks.com Web site: http://www.nbnbooks.com.

National Catholic Reading Distributor, 997 Macarthur Blvd., Mahwah, NJ 07430 USA (SAN 169-4855) Tel 201-825-7300; Fax: 201-825-8345; Toll Free: 800-218-1903 E-mail: paulistp@pipeline.com.

National Educational Systems, Inc., *(978-1-893493)* P.O. Box 691450, San Antonio, TX 78269-1450 USA Toll Free: 800-442-2604.

National Film Network LLC, *(978-0-8026)* Orders Addr.: 4501 Forbes Blvd., Lanham, MD 20706 USA (SAN 630-1878) Tel 301-459-8020 ext 2066 E-mail: info@nationalfilmnetwork.com Web site: http://www.nationalfilmnetwork.com.

National Geographic School Publishing, Inc., *(978-0-7362; 978-0-917837; 978-1-56334)* Div. of CENGAGE Learning, Orders Addr.: 10650 Toebben Dr., Independence, KY 41051 USA Tel 859-282-5700; Toll Free Fax: 800-487-8488; Toll Free: 800-354-9706; 888-915-3276; Edit Addr.: 1 Lower Ragsdale Dr., Bldg. 1, Suite 200, Monterey, CA 93940 USA Web site: http://www.hampton-brown.com.

National Health Federation, Box 688, Monrovia, CA 91016 USA (SAN 227-9266) Tel 626-357-2181; Fax: 818-303-0642 E-mail: nhf@earthlink.net Web site: http://www.healthfreedom.net.

National Learning Corp., *(978-0-8293; 978-0-8373; 978-1-7318; 978-1-7993)* 212 Michael Dr., Syosset, NY 11791 USA (SAN 206-8869) Tel 516-921-8888; Fax: 516-921-8743; Toll Free: 800-645-6337 E-mail: sales@passbooks.com Web site: nlcpassbooks@aim.com.

National Magazine Service, Orders Addr.: P.O. Box 834, Mars, PA 16046 USA (SAN 169-7595); Edit Addr.: 535 Linden Way, Pittsburgh, PA 15202 USA Tel 412-898-0001.

National Organization Service, Inc., P.O. Box 2007, Birmingham, AL 35201-2007 USA (SAN 107-1548) Toll Free: 800-747-3032.

National Rifle Assn., *(978-0-935998)* a/c Office of the General Counsel, 11250 Waples Mill Rd., Fairfax, VA 22030 USA (SAN 213-859X) Tel 703-267-1250; Fax: 703-267-3985; Toll Free: 800-672-3888 E-mail: ndowd@nrahq.org.

National Sales, Inc., 1818 W. 2300 South, Salt Lake City, UT 84119 USA (SAN 159-9127) Tel 801-972-2300; Fax: 801-972-2883.

National Technical Information Service, U.S. Dept. of Commerce, *(978-0-934213; 978-1-935239)* Orders Addr.: 5285 Port Royal Rd., Springfield, VA 22161 USA (SAN 205-7255) Tel 703-605-6000; Fax: 703-605-6900; Toll Free: 800-553-6847 E-mail: orders@ntis.gov; info@ntis.gov Web site: http://www.ntis.gov; http://wnc.fedworld.gov.

Native Bks., P.O. Box 37095, Honolulu, HI 96837 USA (SAN 631-1121) Tel 808-845-8949; Fax: 808-847-6637; Toll Free: 800-887-7751.

Natural Math, 309 Silvercliff Trail, Cary, NC 27513 USA E-mail: reach.out@naturalmath.com.

Naval Institute Pr., *(978-0-87021; 978-1-55750; 978-1-59114; 978-1-61251; 978-1-68247; 978-1-68269)* Orders Addr.: 291 Wood Rd, Annapolis, MD 21402-5034 USA (SAN 662-0930) Tel 410-268-6110; Fax: 410-295-1084; Toll Free: 800-233-8764; Edit Addr.: 291 Wood Rd., Beach Hall, Annapolis, MD 21402-5034 USA (SAN 202-9006) E-mail: tskord@usni.org; books@usni.org Web site: http://www.usni.org.

Nazarene Publishing House, *See* **The Foundry Publishing**

Neal-Schuman Pubs., Inc., *(978-0-918212; 978-1-55570)* Div. of American Library Assn., 100 William St., Suite 2004, New York, NY 10038 USA (SAN 210-2455) Tel 212-925-8650; Fax: 212-219-8916; Toll Free Fax: 800-584-2414 E-mail: info@neal-schuman.com Web site: http://www.neal-schuman.com.

Neeland Media, LLC, 3921 Harvard Rd., Lawrence, KS 66049 USA Tel 913-548-6825.

Neighborhood Periodical Club, Inc., P.O. Box 830, Clementon, NJ 08021-0860 USA (SAN 285-9262).

Nelson Direct, P.O. Box 140300, Nashville, TN 37214 USA (SAN 169-8133) Toll Free: 800-441-0511 (sales); 800-933-9673 E-mail: csalazar@thomasnelson.com Web site: http://www.nelsondirect.com.

Nelson News, Inc., P.O. Box 27007, Omaha, NE 68127-0007 USA (SAN 169-443X) Tel 402-734-3333; Fax: 402-731-0516.

Nelson, Thomas Inc., *(978-0-529; 978-0-7852; 978-0-8407; 978-0-8499; 978-0-86605; 978-0-88113; 978-0-89840; 978-0-89922; 978-0-918956; 978-0-7180; 978-1-4002; 978-1-4003; 978-1-4016; 978-1-59145; 978-1-4041; 978-1-59554; 978-1-59555; 978-1-4185; 978-1-59951; 978-1-4261; 978-1-60255; 978-1-4845; 978-1-5000; 978-1-5314; 978-1-6623) Div. of HarperCollins Christian Publishing, Orders Addr.: P.O. Box 141000, Nashville, TN 37214-1000 USA (SAN 209-3820) Fax: 615-902-1866; Toll Free: 800-251-4000; Edit Addr.: 501 Nelson Pl., Nashville, TN 37214 USA* Web site: http://www.harpercollinschristian.com.

Nelson's Bks., *(978-0-9612188)* P.O. Box 2302, Santa Cruz, CA 95063 USA (SAN 289-4858) Tel 831-465-9148.

Ner Tamid Bk. Distributors, P.O. Box 10401, Riviera Beach, FL 33419-0401 USA (SAN 169-135X) Tel 561-686-9095.

Net Productions, 210 Elm Cir., Colorado Springs, CO 80906-3348 USA (SAN 159-9143).

NetLibrary, Incorporated, *See* **Ebsco Publishing**

NetRead, Inc., 2522 Great Hwy., San Francisco, CA 94116 USA (SAN 631-7863) Tel 415-566-5253 E-mail: graden@netread.com Web site: http://www.netread.com.

NetSource Distribution, Orders Addr.: 675 Dutchess Tpke., Poughkeepsie, NY 12603 USA Tel 845-463-1100 x314; Fax: 845-463-0018; Toll Free: 800-724-1100 Web site: http://www.hudsonhousepub.com.

New Alexandrian Bookstore, 110 N Cayuga St., Ithaca, NY 14850-4331 USA (SAN 159-4958) Tel 607-272-1163.

New Concepts Bks. & Tapes Distributors, Orders Addr.: P.O. Box 55068, Houston, TX 77255 USA (SAN 114-2682) Tel 713-465-7736; Fax: 713-465-7106; Toll Free: 800-842-4807; Edit Addr.: 9722 Pine Lake, Houston, TX 77055 USA (SAN 630-7531).

New Day Christian Distributors, *See* **New Day Christian Distributors Gifts, Inc.**

New Day Christian Distributors Gifts, Inc., *(978-0-692-10672-3)* 124 Shivel Dr., Hendersonville, TN 37075 USA (SAN 631-2551) Tel 615-822-3633; Fax: 615-822-5829; Toll Free: 800-251-3633; 126 Shivel Dr., Hendersonville, TN 37075 (SAN 920-6604).

New England Bk. Service, Inc., 7000 Vt Route 17 W., Vergennes, VT 05491-4408 USA (SAN 170-0952) Toll Free: 800-356-5772 E-mail: nebs@together.net.

New England Mobile Bk. Fair, 82 Needham St., P.O. Box 610159, Newton Highlands, MA 02461 USA (SAN 169-3530) Tel 617-527-5817; Fax: 617-527-0113.

New Jersey Bk. Agency, Orders Addr.: P.O. Box 144, Morris Plains, NJ 07950 USA (SAN 106-861X) Tel 973-267-7093; Fax: 973-292-3177; Edit Addr.: 7 Somerset Hills Ct. Apt. D, Bernardsville, NJ 07924-2619 USA (SAN 243-2307).

New Jersey Bks., Inc., 59 Market St., Newark, NJ 07102 USA Tel 973-624-8070; Toll Free: 800-772-3678.

New Leaf Distributing Co., Inc., *(978-0-9627209)* Div. of Al-Wali Corp., 401 Thornton Rd., Lithia Springs, GA 30122-1557 USA (SAN 169-1449) Tel 770-948-7845; Fax: 770-944-2313; Toll Free Fax: 800-326-1066; Toll Free: 800-326-2665 E-mail: santoshk@msn.com; alimt@bellsouth.net Web site: http://www.NewLeaf-dist.com.

New Leaf Press, Incorporated, *See* **New Leaf Publishing Group**

New Leaf Publishing Group, *(978-0-89051; 978-0-89221; 978-1-61458; 978-1-68344)* P.O. Box 726, Green Forest, AR 72638 USA (SAN 207-9518) Tel 870-438-5288; Fax: 870-438-5120 Toll Free: 800-643-9535; 800-999-3777 Do not confuse with companies with the same or similar name in Los Angeles, CAStone Mountain, GA E-mail: nlp@nlpg.com Web site: http://www.nlpg.com; http://www.masterbooks.com.

New Leaf Resources, 2102 Button Ln., Unit 2, Lagrange, KY 40031 USA Toll Free: 800-346-3087 E-mail: info@newleaf-resources.com Web site: http://www.www.newleaf-resources.com.

New Life Foundation, *(978-0-911203; 978-1-934162)* P.O. Box 2230, Pine, AZ 85544-2230 USA (SAN 170-3986) Tel 928-476-3224; Fax: 928-476-4743; Toll Free: 800-293-3377 (wholesale only) E-mail: info@anewlife.org Web site: http://www.anewlife.org.

New Shelves Distribution, 103 Remsen St., Cohoes, NY 12047 USA Tel 518-391-2300; Fax: 518-391-2365 Web site: http://www.newshelvesdistribution.com.

New Tradition Bks., *(978-0-9728473; 978-1-932420; 978-0-9845418)* 302 Maple Grove Ln, Apison, TN 37302 USA E-mail: newtraditionbooks@yahoo.com.

New World Library, *(978-0-931432; 978-0-945934; 978-1-57731; 978-1-880032; 978-1-60868; 978-1-955831)* 14 Pamaron Way, Novato, CA 94949 USA (SAN 211-8777) Tel 415-884-2100; Fax: 415-884-2199; Toll Free: 800-972-6657 (retail orders only) Do not confuse with New World Library Publishing Co., Los Altos, CA E-mail: escort@nwlib.com Web site: http://www.newworldlibrary.com.

New World Resource Ctr., P.O. Box 25310, Chicago, IL 60625-0310 USA (SAN 169-1848).

New York Periodical Distributors, P.O. Box 29, Massena, NY 13662-0029 USA (SAN 169-6149).

New York Univ. Pr., *(978-0-8147; 978-1-4798)* Div. of New York Univ., Orders Addr.: 838 Broadway, 3rd Flr., New York, NY 10003-4812 USA (SAN 658-1293) Tel 212-998-2575; Fax: 212-995-3833; Toll Free: 800-996-6987 (ordering) E-mail: orders@nyupress.org Web site: http://www.nyupress.org.

Newborn Enterprises, Inc., P.O. Box 1713, Altoona, PA 16603 USA (SAN 169-7242) Tel 814-944-3593; Fax: 814-944-1881; Toll Free: 800-227-0285 (in Pennsylvania).

NewLife Bk. Distributors, 2969 Spalding Dr., Suite 100, Atlanta, GA 30350 USA (SAN 169-121X) Tel 404-207-5280 E-mail: lifebooks@mindspring.com Web site: http://www.newlifebookdistributors.com.

News Group, 15 N. Spring St., #2, Bloomfield, NJ 07003 USA.

News Group - Illinois, The, 1301 SW Washington St., Peoria, IL 61602 USA (SAN 169-216X) Tel 309-673-4549; Fax: 309-673-8883.

News Group, The, 4070 Shirley Dr., Atlanta, GA 30336 USA Tel 404-691-2800 Web site: http://www.thenewsgroup.com.

News Supply Co., 216 S. La Huerta Cir., Carlsbad, NM 88220-9620 USA (SAN 159-9151).

Newsdealers Supply Co., Inc., P.O. Box 3516, Tallahassee, FL 32315-3516 USA.

NEWSouth Distributors, P.O. Box 61297, Jacksonville, FL 32236-1297 USA (SAN 159-8732).

Newsstand Distributors, 155 W. 14th St., Ogden, UT 84404 USA (SAN 169-8494) Fax: 810-621-7336; Toll Free: 800-283-6247; 800-231-4834 (in Utah).

Ng Hing Kee, 648 Jackson St., San Francisco, CA 94133 USA (SAN 107-1084) Tel 415-781-8330; Fax: 415-397-9766.

Niagara Collectibles, 3727 Lower River Rd., Youngstown, NY 14174 USA E-mail: nansimon@roadrunner.com.

Niagara County News, 70 Nicholls St., Lockport, NY 14094 USA (SAN 169-541X) Tel 716-433-6466.

Night Heron Media, *(978-0-9704729; 978-0-9709987; 978-1-931721; 978-1-933979; 978-1-936474; 978-1-939055; 978-1-942945)* Orders Addr.: 2365 Rice Blvd., Suite 202, Houston, TX 77005 USA Tel 713-533-9300; Fax: 713-528-2432 Do not confuse with Breakaway Bks., Halcottsville, NY E-mail: info@nightheronmedia.org Web site: www.nightheronmedia.org.

Noelke, Carl B., 529 Main, Box 563, La Crosse, WI 54602 USA (SAN 111-8315) Tel 608-782-8544.

Nonagon, 1556 Douglas Dr., El Cerrito, CA 94530 USA (SAN 654-0503) Tel 510-237-5290.

Nonetheless Pr., *(978-1-932053)* 20332 W. 98th St., Lenexa, KS 66220-2650 USA Tel 913-254-7266; Fax: 913-393-3245 E-mail: mschutte@nonethelesspress.com Web site: http://www.nonethelesspress.com; http://www.lookingglasspress.com.

NOOK Press, *See* **Barnes & Noble Pr.**

Nor-Cal News Co., 2040 Petaluma Blvd., P.O. Box 2508, Petaluma, CA 94953 USA (SAN 169-0035) Tel 707-763-2606; Fax: 707-763-3905.

Norfolk SPCA, 916 Ballentine Blvd., Norfolk, VA 23504 USA Tel 757-622-3319 Web site: http://www.norfolkspca.com.

Nori Media Group, 167 Walnut Bottom Rd., Shippensburg, PA 17257 USA Tel 717-532-3040 E-mail: marketing@norimediagroup.com Web site: https://norimediagroup.com/.

North American Bk. Distributors, P.O. Box 510, Hamburg, MI 48139 USA (SAN 630-4680) Tel 810-231-3728.

North Carolina News Co., P.O. Box 1051, Durham, NC 27702-1051 USA Tel 919-682-5779.

North Carolina Schl. Bk. Depository, Inc., P.O. Box 950, Raleigh, NC 27602-0950 USA (SAN 169-6467) Tel 919-833-6615.

North Central Bk. Distributors, N57 W13636 Carmen Ave., Menomonee Falls, WI 53051 USA (SAN 173-5195) Tel 414-781-3299; Fax: 414-781-4432; Toll Free: 800-966-3299.

North Country Bks., Inc., *(978-0-925168; 978-0-932052; 978-0-9601158; 978-1-59531)* 220 Lafayette Street, Utica, NY 13502 USA (SAN 110-828X) Tel 315-735-4877; Fax: (315) 738-4342 E-mail: ncbooks@verizon.net Web site: http://www.northcountrybooks.com.

North Shore Distributors, 1200 N. Branch, Chicago, IL 60622 USA (SAN 169-2275).

North Shore News Co., Inc., 150 Blossom St., Lynn, MA 01902 USA (SAN 169-3492).

North Star Editions, *(978-0-9848801; 978-0-9886491; 978-1-939967; 978-1-63163; 978-1-63517; 978-1-63583; 978-1-64185; 978-1-64493; 978-1-64494; 978-1-64619; 978-1-952455; 978-1-63738; 978-1-63739; 979-8-88998)* Subs. of Big Timber Media, 1600 Cliff Rd. E, Burnsville, MN 55337 USA (SAN 990-2325) Tel 952-446-7222 E-mail: info@northstareditions.com Web site: www.fluxnow.com; www.northstareditions.com; www.focusreaders.com.

North Texas Periodicals, Inc., Orders Addr.: P.O. Box 3823, Lubbock, TX 79452 USA Tel 806-745-6000; Fax: 806-745-7028; Edit Addr.: 118 E. 70th St., Lubbock, TX 79404 USA E-mail: ntp@hts-online.net.

Northern News Co., P.O. Box 467, Petoskey, MI 49770-0467 USA (SAN 169-3964) Toll Free: 800-632-7138 (Michigan only).

Northern Schl. Supply Co., P.O. Box 2627, Fargo, ND 58108 USA (SAN 169-6548) Fax: 800-891-5836.

Northern Sun, 2916 E. Lake St., Minneapolis, MN 55406 USA (SAN 249-9290) Tel 612-729-2001; Fax: 612-729-0149; Toll Free: 800-258-8579 Web site: http://www.northernsun.com/.

Northern Sun Merchandising, *See* **Northern Sun**

North-South Bks., Inc., *(978-0-7358; 978-1-55858; 978-1-58717)* 350 7th Ave. Rm. 1400, New York, NY 10001-5013 USA E-mail: mnavarro@northsouth.com Web site: http://www.northsouth.com.

Northwest News, 1560 NE First St., No. 13, Bend, OR 97701 USA (SAN 111-8587) Tel 541-382-6065; 3100 Merriman Rd., Medford, OR 97501 Tel 541-779-5225.

Northwest News Company, Incorporated, *See* **Benjamin News Group**

Northwest Textbook Depository, Orders Addr.: P.O. Box 5608, Portland, OR 97228 USA Toll Free: 800-676-6630; Edit Addr.: 17970 SW McEwan Rd., Portland, OR 97224 USA (SAN 631-4481) Tel 503-639-3193; Fax: 503-639-2559.

Northwestern Univ. Pr., *(978-0-8101)* Orders Addr.: c/o Univ. of Chicago Pr. Distribution Ctr., 11030 S. Langley Ave., Chicago, IL 60628 USA Tel 773-568-1550; Fax: 773-660-2235; Toll Free Fax: 800-621-8476; Toll Free: 800-621-2736; Edit Addr.: 629 Noyes St., Evanston, IL 60208-4210 USA (SAN 202-5787) Tel 847-491-5313; 847-491-2046; Fax: 847-491-8150 E-mail: nupress@northwestern.edu Web site: http://www.nupress.northwestern.edu.

Norton News Agency, 905 Kelly Ln., Dubuque, IA 52003-8526 USA (SAN 169-2631); 1467 Service Dr., Winona, MN 55987 (SAN 156-4889).

Norton, W. W. & Co., Inc., *(978-0-393; 978-0-88150; 978-0-914378; 978-0-936399; 978-0-942440; 978-1-58157; 978-1-324; 978-1-68268)* Orders Addr.: c/o National Book Company, 800 Keystone Industrial Pk., Scranton, PA 18512 USA (SAN 157-1869) Tel 570-346-2029; Fax: 570-346-1442; Toll Free Fax: 800-458-6515; Toll Free: 800-233-4830; Edit Addr.: 500 Fifth Ave., New York, NY 10110-0017 USA (SAN 202-5795) Tel 212-354-5500; Fax: 212-869-0856; Toll Free: 800-223-2584 Web site: http://www.wwnorton.com.

Not So Plain Jane Publishing, *(978-0-9700741; 978-1-59664)* 4322 Declaration Cir., Belcamp, MD 21017 USA Tel 443-866-9672; Fax: 212-681-8002 E-mail: steph.guzman@icloud.com Web site: http://www.olivertheclownfish.com.

Notions Marketing, 1500 Buchanan Ave., SW, Grand Rapids, MI 49507-1613 USA.

NTC/Contemporary Publishing Company, *See* **McGraw-Hill/Contemporary**

Nueces News Agency, 5130 Commerce Pkwy., San Antonio, TX 78218-5523 USA (SAN 169-8079).

Nueva Vida Distributors, 4300 Montana Ave., El Paso, TX 79903-4503 USA (SAN 107-8615) Tel 915-565-6215; Fax: 915-565-1722.

Nutri-Bks. Corp., Div. of Royal Pubns., Inc., 790 W. Tennessee Ave., P.O. Box 5793, Denver, CO 80223 USA Tel 303-778-8383; Fax: 303-744-9383; Toll Free: 800-279-2048 (orders only).

Oak Knoll Pr., *(978-0-938768; 978-1-884718; 978-1-58456; 978-1-872116)* 310 Delaware St., New Castle, DE 19720 USA (SAN 216-2776) Tel 302-328-7232; Fax: 302-328-7274; Toll Free: 800-996-2556 Do not confuse with Oak Knoll Press in Hardy, VA E-mail: oakknoll@oakknoll.com Web site: http://www.oakknoll.com.

Octagon Pr./ISHK Bk. Service, *See* **I S H K**

Ohio Periodical Distributors, P.O. Box 145449, Cincinnati, OH 45250-5449 USA (SAN 169-6904) Fax: 513-853-6245; Toll Free: 800-777-2216.

Ohio Univ. Pr., *(978-0-8214)* Orders Addr.: 11030 S. Langley Ave., Chicago, IL 60628 USA Tel 773-702-7000; Fax: 773-702-7212; Toll Free Fax: 800-621-8476; Toll Free: 800-621-2736; Edit Addr.: 19 Circle Dr. The Ridges, Athens, OH 45701 USA (SAN 282-0773) Tel 740-593-1154; Fax: 740-593-4536 Web site: https://www.ohioswallow.com/.

Oil City News Co., 112 Innis St., Oil City, PA 16301-2930 USA (SAN 169-7501).

Oleand Pubns., P.O. Box 375, Lyons, WI 53148 USA Tel 262-342-0018 (phone/fax) E-mail: wings@oleand.com.

Ollis Bk. Corp., Orders Addr.: P.O. Box 258, Steger, IL 60475 USA (SAN 658-1323); Edit Addr.: 28 E. 35th St., Steger, IL 60475 USA (SAN 169-2224) Tel 312-755-5151; Fax: 708-755-5153; Toll Free: 800-323-0343.

Olson, D & Company, *See* **Nelson's Bks.**

Olson News Agency, P.O. Box 129, Ishpeming, MI 49849 USA (SAN 169-3832).

Omega Pubns., Inc., *(978-0-930872; 978-1-941810)* 34 Amity Pl., Amherst, MA 01002-2255 USA (SAN 214-1493) Toll Free: 888-443-7107 (orders only) Do not confuse with companies with the same name in Medford, OR, Indianapolis, IN E-mail: sufibooks@omegapub.com Web site: http://www.omegapub.com.

Omnibooks, 456 Vista Del Mar Dr., Aptos, CA 95003-4832 USA (SAN 168-9487) Tel 408-688-4098; Toll Free: 800-626-6671.

Omnibus Pr., *(978-0-7119; 978-0-8256; 978-0-86001; 978-1-84449)* Div. of Music Sales Corp., Orders Addr.: 445 Bellvale Rd., Chester, NY 10918-0572 USA Tel 845-469-4699; Fax: 845-469-7544; Toll Free Fax: 800-345-6842; Toll Free: 800-431-7187; Edit Addr.: 257 Park Ave., S., 20th Flr., New York, NY 10010 USA Tel 212-254-2100; Fax: 212-254-2013 Do not confuse with Omnibus Pr., Menasha, WI E-mail: info@musicsales.com Web site: http://www.musicsales.com.

One Small Voice Foundation, P.O. Box 644, Elmhurst, IL 60126 USA Tel 630-620-6634 E-mail: onesmallvoice@earthlink.net Web site: http://www.onesmallvoicefoundation.org.

Onondaga News Agency, P.O. Box 6445, Syracuse, NY 13217-6445 USA (SAN 169-6297).

OPA Publishing & Distributing, Orders Addr.: P.O. Box 1764, Chandler, AZ 85244-1764 USA; Edit Addr.: 777 W. Chandler Blvd., Suite 1322, Chandler, AZ 85244-1764 USA.

Open Road Distribution, Div. of Open Road Integrated Media, Inc., 345 Hudson St., Suite 6C, New York, NY 10014 USA Tel 212-691-0900; Fax: 212-691-0901.

Open Road Integrated Media, Inc., *(978-1-58586; 978-0-7592; 978-1-936317; 978-1-4532; 978-1-61756; 978-0-9832929; 978-1-937624; 978-1-937957; 978-1-938582; 978-0-615-65097-5; 978-1-62467; 978-1-4804; 978-1-4976; 978-1-5040)* 180 Varick St. Suite 816, New York, NY 10014 USA Tel 212-691-0900; Fax: 212-691-0901; 345 Hudson St., Suite 6C, New York, NY 10014 Tel 212-691-0900; Fax: 212-691-0901 E-mail: acolvin@openroadmedia.com Web site: http://www.openroadmedia.com.

Options Unlimited, 550 Swan Creek Ct., Suwanee, GA 30174 USA (SAN 631-3949) Tel 770-237-3282 Do not confuse with Options Unlimited, Inc., Green Bay, WI.

OptumInsight, Inc., *(978-1-56329; 978-1-56337; 978-1-60151; 978-1-62254; 979-8-88952)* 2525 Lake Park Blvd., West Valley City, UT 84120 USA (SAN 630-5482) Tel 801-982-3000; Toll Free: 800-464-3649 (phone/fax) E-mail: jeni.smith@ingenix.com; chris.smith@ingenix.com; jean.parkinson@ingenix.com Web site: http://www.ingenix.com; http://www.IngenixOnline.com.

Orange News Company, *See* **Anderson News, LLC**

Orbit Bks. Corp., 43 Timberline Dr., Poughkeepsie, NY 12603 USA (SAN 169-6157) Tel 914-462-5653; Fax: 914-462-8409.

Orca Bk. Pubs. USA, *(978-0-920501; 978-1-55143; 978-1-55469)* Orders Addr.: P.O. Box 468, Custer, WA 98240-0468 USA (SAN 630-9674) Tel 250-380-1229; Fax: 250-380-1892; Toll Free: 800-210-5277 E-mail: orca@orcabook.com Web site: http://www.orcabook.com.

O'Reilly & Associates, Incorporated, *See* **O'Reilly Media, Inc.**

O'Reilly Media, Inc., *(978-0-937175; 978-1-56592; 978-3-89721; 978-3-930673; 978-4-900900; 978-0-596; 978-4-87311; 978-1-60033; 978-1-4493; 978-1-4919; 978-1-4920; 978-1-4571; 978-1-0981)* Orders Addr.: 1005 Gravenstein Hwy. N., Sebastopol, CA 95472 USA (SAN 658-5973) Fax: 707-829-0104; Toll Free: 800-998-9938; Edit Addr.: 10 Fawcett St. Ste. 4, Cambridge, MA 02138-1175 USA Toll Free: 800-775-7731; 4 Castle St, Farnham, GU9 7HR Tel 01252 71 17 76; Fax: 01252 73 42 11; c/o Madeleine Fakhoury Editions O'Reilly, 18, rue Seguier, Paris, F-75006 Tel 33 1 40 51 52 30; Fax: 33 1 40 51 52 31; c/o Michelle Chen, SIGMA Building, Suite B809 No. 49 Zhichun Rd. Haidian District, Beijing, 100080 Tel 86-10-88097476; 86-10-88097475; Fax: 86-10-88097463; c/o O'Reilly Verlag, Gerd Miske, Balthasarstr. 81, Köln, D-50670 Tel 49 221 973160 0; Fax: 49 221 973160 8; 1Fl, No. 21, Lane 295 Section 1, Fu-Shing South Rd., Taipei, Tel 886 2 27099669; Fax: 886 2 27038802; Intelligent Plaza Bldg. 1F 26 Banchi 27, Sakamachi, Shinjuku-ku, Tokyo, 160-0002 Tel 81 3 3356 5227; Fax: 81 3 3356 5261 E-mail: order@oreilly.com; information@oreilly.co.uk; nuts@ora.com; isbn-info@oreilly.com Web site: http://www.oreilly.com; http://www.editions-oreilly.fr; http://oreilly.co.uk; http://oreilly.com.tw; http://www.ora.com; http://www.oreilly.fr/; http://www.oreilly.com.cn/.

Original Pubns., *(978-0-942272)* Subs. of Maximo, Inc., 129 Forest Dr., Jericho, NY 11753-2324 USA (SAN 133-0225) Toll Free: 888-622-8581.

Osborne Enterprises Publishing, *(978-0-932117)* P.O. Box 255, Port Townsend, WA 98368 USA (SAN 242-7567) Tel 360-385-1200; Toll Free: 800-246-3255 (orders only) E-mail: jpo@olympus.net Web site: http://www.jerryosborne.com.

Osborne/McGraw-Hill, *See* **McGraw-Hill Osborne**

Osiander Bk. Trade, 7483H Candlewood Rd., Hanover, MD 21076-3102 USA (SAN 130-0970).

Outbooks, Incorporated, *See* **Vistabooks**

Outdoorsman, The, Orders Addr.: P.O. Box 268, Boston, MA 02134 USA (SAN 169-3352).

Outskirts Pr., Inc., *(978-0-9725874; 978-1-932672; 978-1-59800; 978-1-4327; 978-0-615-20388-1; 978-1-4787; 978-1-9772)* 10940 S. Parker Rd. - 515, Parker, CO 80134 USA (SAN 256-5420) Web site: http://www.OutskirtsPress.com.

Outskirts Press, Incorporation, *See* **Outskirts Pr., Inc.**

OverDrive, Inc., Valley Tech Ctr. 8555 Sweet Valley Dr., Cleveland, OH 44125-4210 USA (SAN 245-0658) Tel 216-573-6886; Fax: 216-573-6888 Web site: http://www.overdrive.com.

OverDrive Systems, Incorporated, *See* **OverDrive, Inc.**

Overmountain Pr., *(978-0-932807; 978-0-9644613; 978-1-57072; 978-1-935692)* P.O. Box 1261, Johnson City, TN 37605 USA (SAN 687-6641) Tel 423-926-2691; Fax: 423-232-1252; Toll Free: 800-992-2691 (orders only) E-mail: beth@overmtn.com Web site: http://www.silverdaggermysteries.com; http://www.overmountainpress.com.

Oxford Univ. Pr., Inc., *(978-0-19; 978-0-87893; 978-1-60535)* Orders Addr.: 2001 Evans Rd., Cary, NC 27513 USA (SAN 202-5892) Tel 919-677-0977 (general voice); Fax: 919-677-1303 (customer service); Toll Free: 800-445-9714 (customer service - inquiry); 800-451-7556 (customer service - orders); Edit Addr.: 198 Madison Ave., New York, NY 10016-4314 USA (SAN 202-5884) Tel 212-726-6000 (general voice); Fax: 212-726-6440 (general fax) E-mail: custserv@oup-usa.org; orders@oup-usa.org Web site: http://www.oup.com/us.

Oxford University Press USA - OSO, Orders Addr.: 2001 Evans Rd., Cary, NC 27513 USA Toll Free: 800-451-7556.

Oxmoor Hse., Inc., *(978-0-376; 978-0-8487)* Orders Addr.: Leisure Arts 5701 Ranch Dr., Little Rock, AR 72223 USA; Edit Addr.: 2100 Lakeshore Dr., Birmingham, AL 35209 USA Tel 205-445-6000; Fax: 205-445-6078; Toll Free: 800-633-4910 E-mail: allison_lowery@timeinc.com Web site: http://www.oxmoorhouse.com/.

Ozark Bk. Distributors, 1802 Van Buren Ave., Mountain Home, AR 72653 USA.

Ozark Magazine Distributing, Incorporated, *See* **Ozark News Distributor, Inc.**

Ozark News Agency, Inc., P.O. Box 1150, Fayetteville, AR 72702 USA.

Ozark News Distributor, Inc., 1630 N. Eldon Ave., Springfield, MO 65803 USA (SAN 169-4332) Tel 417-862-9224; Fax: 417-862-6642; Toll Free: 800-743-0380.

P & G Wholesale, P.O. Box 1548, Fargo, ND 58102 USA (SAN 156-4536).

P & R Publishing, *(978-0-87552; 978-1-59638; 978-1-62995)* Orders Addr.: 1102 Marble Hill Rd., Harmony, Phillipsburg, NJ 08865 USA (SAN 658-1463) Tel 908-454-0505; Fax: 908-859-2390; Toll Free: 800-631-0094 Do not confuse with P & R Publishing Co. in Sioux Center, IA E-mail: tara@prpbooks.com; jesse@prpbooks.com Web site: http://www.prpbooks.com.

P C I Education, *(978-1-884074; 978-1-58804; 978-1-61975)* 4560 Lockhill-Selma, Suite 100, San Antonio, TX 78265-4270 USA Tel 210-377-1999; Fax: 210-377-1121; Toll Free Fax: 888-259-8284; Toll Free: 800-594-4263 E-mail: lboulet@pcieducation.com Web site: http://www.pcieducation.com.

P C I Educational Publishing, *See* **P C I Education**

P. D. Music Headquarters, Inc., Orders Addr.: P.O. Box 252, New York, NY 10014 USA (SAN 282-5880) Tel 212-242-5322.

Pacific Island Bks., 2802 E. 132nd Cir., Thornton, CO 80241 USA Fax: 603-368-6628; Toll Free: 888-492-6657 (888-49-BOOKS) E-mail: pacificbks@aol.com Web site: http://www.pacificislandbooks.com.

Pacific Learning, Inc., *(978-1-59055; 978-1-60457; 978-1-61391; 978-1-59055-000-7; 978-1-958041; 978-1-962364)* Orders Addr.: P.O. Box 2723, Huntington Beach, CA 92647-0723 USA; Edit Addr.: 6262 Katella Ave., Cypress, CA 90630 USA Tel 800-279-0737; Toll Free: 800-279-0737 E-mail: customer.service@pacificlearning.com Web site: http://www.pacificlearning.com.

Pacific Magazine-Bk. Wholesaler, 1515 NW 51st St., Seattle, WA 98107 USA (SAN 274-3884) Tel 206-789-5333.

Pacific Periodical Services, LLC, *See* **Anderson News - Tacoma**

Pacific Pr. Publishing Assn., *(978-0-8163; 978-1-5180)* P.O. Box 5353, Nampa, ID 83653-5353 USA (SAN 202-8409) Tel 208-465-2500; Fax: 208-465-2531; Toll Free: 800-447-7377 E-mail: donlay@pacificpress.com Web site: http://www.AdventistBookCenter.com; http://www.pacificpress.com.

Pacific Trade Group, 68-309 Crozier Dr., Waialua, HI 96791 USA (SAN 169-1635) Tel 808-636-2300; Fax: 808-636-2301.

Paladin Pr., *(978-0-87364; 978-1-58160; 978-1-891268; 978-1-61004)* Orders Addr.: c/o Gunbarrel Tech Ctr., 7077 Winchester Cir., Boulder, CO 80301 USA (SAN 662-1066) Tel 303-443-7250; Fax: 303-442-8741; Toll Free: 800-392-2400 (Credit Card Orders Only) E-mail: sales@paladin-press.com; editorial@paladin-press.com; service@paladin-press.com Web site: http://www.paladin-press.com; http://www.flying-machines.com; http://www.sycamoreisland.com.

Palari Publishing LLP, *(978-1-928662)* Orders Addr.: P.O. Box 9288, Richmond, VA 23227-0288 USA Tel 804-355-1035; Toll Free Fax: 866-570-6724 (on demand); Toll Free: 866-570-6724 E-mail: dave@palaribooks.com Web site: http://www.palaribooks.com.

Palgrave, *See* **Palgrave Macmillan**

Palgrave Macmillan, *(978-0-312; 978-0-333; 978-1-4039; 978-0-230; 978-1-4472; 978-1-137; 978-1-349; 978-1-78632)* Orders Addr.: 16365 James Madison Hwy., Gordonsville, VA 22942-8501 USA Toll Free Fax: 800-672-2054; Toll Free: 888-330-8477; Edit Addr.: 175 Fifth Ave., New York, NY 10010 USA Tel 212-982-9300; Fax: 212-777-6359; Toll Free Fax: 800 672-2054 (Customer Service); Toll Free: 800-221-7945; 888-330-8477 (Customer Service) E-mail: customerservice@vhpsva.com Web site: http://www.palgrave.com.

PALH, *(978-0-9719458; 978-1-953716)* P.O. Box 5099, Santa Monica, CA 90409 USA E-mail: palh@aol.com Web site: http://www.palhbooks.com.

Palmer News Co., Inc., 534 S. Kansas Ave. Ste. 700, Topeka, KS 66603-3429 USA.

Palmer News, Inc., 9605 Dice Ln., Lenexa, KS 66215 USA Tel 913-541-8600; Fax: 913-541-9413 E-mail: palmerco@oni.com.

Palmetto News Co., 200 Sunbelt Ct., Greer, SC 29650-9349 USA.

Pan American Publishing, Inc., *(978-1-889867)* 420 E. Ohio St., Suite 4-F, Chicago, IL 60611-3355 USA (SAN 299-1977) Tel 773-404-7282.

Pan Asia Pubns. (USA), Inc., *(978-1-57227)* 29564 Union City Blvd., Union City, CA 94587 USA (SAN 173-685X) Tel 510-475-1185; Fax: 510-475-1489; Toll Free: 800-909-8088 E-mail: sales@panap.com; hchan@panap.com; info@panap.com Web site: http://www.panap.com; http://www.cjkv.com.

Pan De Vida Distributors, *(978-1-934811)* 5507 Brooks St., Montclair, CA 91763 USA (SAN 631-0753) Tel 909-510-5219; 909-510-5200; Fax: 909-510-5210 Web site: http://www.pandevida.com.

Panamericana Publishing LLC, 12902 SW 133 Ct., Suite D, Miami, FL 33186 USA (SAN 256-1409) Tel 305-278-2648; Fax: 305-436-7264 E-mail: operez@panamericana.com.co Web site: http://panamericanaeditorial.com.

Pantheon Bks., *(978-0-375; 978-0-394; 978-0-676; 978-0-679)* Orders Addr.: 400 Hahn Rd., Westminster, MD 21157 USA Toll Free: 800-733-3000 (orders); Edit Addr.: 299 Park Ave, New York, NY 10171 USA (SAN 202-862X).

Paperback Books, Incorporated, *See* **Bk. Distribution Ctr., Inc.**

Paperbacks for Educators, *(978-0-9702376; 978-1-59721)* 426 W. Front St., Washington, MO 63090 USA (SAN 103-3379) Tel 636-239-1999; Fax: 636-239-4515; Toll Free Fax: 800-514-7323; Toll Free: 800-227-2591 E-mail: paperbacks@usmo.com Web site: http://www.any-book-in-print.com.

Paradise Cay Pubns., *(978-0-939837; 978-1-937196)* P.O. Box 29, Arcata, CA 95518-0029 USA (SAN 663-690X) Tel 707-822-9063; Fax: 707-822-9163; Toll Free: 800-736-4509 (orders only) E-mail: jim@paracay.com Web site: http://www.paracay.com.

Parent Services Project, 79 Belvedere St., Suite 101, San Rafael, CA 94901 USA Tel 415-454-1870 E-mail: family@parentservices.org.

Parklane Publishing, *(978-1-59384)* Div. of Book Club of America, 100 Marcus Blvd. Ste. 8, Hauppauge, NY 11788-3749 USA E-mail: lbaumert@bookclubusa.com Web site: http://www.parklanepublishing.com.

Parkwest Pubns., Inc., *(978-0-88186)* P.O. Box 310251, Miami, FL 33231 USA (SAN 264-6846) Tel 305-256-7880; Fax: 305-256-7816 E-mail: parkwest@parkwestpubs.com; info@parkwestpubs.com Web site: http://www.parkwestpubs.com.

Parliament News Co., Inc., P.O. Box 910, Santa Clarita, CA 91380-9010 USA (SAN 168-9924).

Parnassus Bk. Distributors, 200 Academy Way, Columbia, SC 29206-1445 USA (SAN 631-0680) Tel 803-782-7748; Toll Free: 800-782-7760.

Partners Distributing, Orders Addr.: 13089 Root Rd., Columbia Station, OH 44028 USA Tel 216-236-3744.

Pathfinder Pr., *(978-0-87348; 978-0-913460; 978-1-60488)* Orders Addr.: P.O. Box 162767, Atlanta, GA 30321-2767 USA Tel 404-669-0600 (voice mail only); Fax: 707-667-1141; Pathfinder Books/Livres Pathfinder 6362 Fraser St. Suite 264, VANCOUVER, BC V5W 0A1 Tel 888-692-4939; Fax: 888-692-4939; 120 Bethnal Green Rd., London, E2 6DG; P.O. Box 10130,75723, Paris, Cedex 15 FRANCE Tel 014-010-2837; Fax: 014-010-2837; Australia Pathfinder Level 1, 3/281-287 Beamish St., Campsie, NSW, NSW 2194 Tel 029-718-9698; Fax: 029-718-9698; Unit 4, 125 Grafton Rd., Grafton, Auckland, none; Edit Addr.: 306 W. 37th St., 10th Flr., New York, NY 10018 USA (SAN 202-5906) Do not confuse with companies with the same or similar names in Alameda, CA, Battle Ground, WA, Elicott City, MD, Midland, MI E-mail: pathfinder@pathfinderpress.com; permissions@pathfinderpress.com; orders@pathfinderpress.com Web site: http://www.pathfinderpress.com.

Pathway Bk. Service, Div. of MLES, Inc., Orders Addr.: 4 White Brook Rd., Gilsum, NH 03448 USA (SAN 170-0545) Tel 603-357-0236; Fax: 603-357-2073; Toll Free: 800-345-6665; P.O. Box 89, Gilsum, NH 03448; Edit Addr.: 34 Production Ave., Keene, NH 03431 USA (SAN 991-2657) Tel 603-357-0236 E-mail: pbs@pathwaybook.com Web site: http://www.pathwaybook.com.

Pathway Bks., *(978-0-935538)* P.O. Box 27790, Golden Valley, MN 55427-0790 USA (SAN 213-4241) Tel.

612-694-9434; Toll Free: 800-958-3375 (Pin 32) Do not confuse with Pathway Books, Gilsum, NH
E-mail: shermjim@aol.com
Web site: http://www.caregiver911.com.

Paul & Co. Pubs. Consortium, Inc., Div. of Independent Publishers Group, Orders Addr.: 814 N. Franklin St., Chicago, IL 60610 USA Tel 312-337-0747; Fax: 312-337-5985; Toll Free: 800-888-4741
E-mail: frontdesk@ipgbook.com
Web site: http://www.ipgbook.com.

Paulsen, G. Co., 27 Sheep Davis Rd., Pembroke, NH 03275 USA (SAN 169-4499) Tel 603-225-9787.

PBD, Inc., *(978-0-9846038; 978-0-9837260; 978-1-62219)* 1650 Bluegrass Lakes Pkwy., Alpharetta, GA 30004 USA (SAN 126-6039) Tel 770-442-8633; Fax: 770-442-9742
Web site: http://www.pbd.com.

PCE International, 8811 Aviation Blvd., Inglewood, CA 90301 USA Tel 310-337-0055; Fax: 310-642-4625; Toll Free: 800-626-1313.

Pearson Education, *(978-0-13; 978-0-582; 978-0-7686; 978-1-5093)* Orders Addr.: 200 Old Tappan Rd., Old Tappan, NJ 07675 USA (SAN 200-2175) Tel 201-767-5000 (Receptionist); Toll Free Fax: 800-445-6991; Toll Free: 800-428-5331; 800-922-0579; Edit Addr.: One Lake St., Upper Saddle River, NJ 07458 USA Tel 201-236-7000; 201-236-5321; Fax: 201-236-6549; 800 E. 96th St., Suite 300, Indianapolis, IN 46240 Toll Free: 800-571-4580
E-mail: communications@pearsoned.com
Web site: http://www.pearsoned.com; www.pearson.com.

Pearson Learning, *(978-0-7652; 978-1-4284)* Div of Pearson Education, Orders Addr.: P.O. Box 2500, Lebanon, IN 46052 USA Toll Free Fax: 800-393-3156; Toll Free: 800-321-3106; Edit Addr.: 1 Lake St., U Saddle Riv, NJ 07458-1813 USA Toll Free: 800-526-9907 (Customer Service)
E-mail: jeff.hoitsma@pearsonlearning.com
Web site: http://www.pearsonlearning.com.

Pearson School, *See* **Savvas Learning Co.**

Pearson Technology Group, One Lake St., Upper Saddle River, NJ 07458 USA.

Pee Dee News Co., 2321 Lawrens Cir., Florence, SC 29501-9408 USA.

Pegasus Pr., *(978-1-889818)* 2641 S. Emerson St., Chandler, AZ 85248-3248 USA Do not confuse with companies with the same name in Vashon Island, WA, San Diego, CA, Kerrville, TX, Lake Forest, IL
E-mail: pegpress@hotmail.com
Web site: http://www.pegpress.org.

Pegram, Christine, 1901 Upper Cove Terr.. Sarasota, FL 33581 USA (SAN 110-0254) Tel 941-921-2467.

Pekin News Agency, 1637 Monroe St., Madison, WI 53711-2021 USA (SAN 169-2151).

Peller, A. W. & Assocs., 210 Sixth Ave., P.O. Box 106, Hawthorne, NJ 07507-0106 USA (SAN 631-1563) Tel 973-423-4666; Fax: 973-423-5569; Toll Free: 800-451-7450
E-mail: awpeller@worldnet.att.net
Web site: http://www.awpeller.com.

Pen Notes, Inc., *(978-0-939564)* 10111 NW 24th Pl. Apt. 201, Sunrise, FL 33322-6882 USA (SAN 107-3621)
E-mail: pennotes@worldnet.att.net.

Penguin Group (USA) Incorporated, *See* **Penguin Publishing Group**

Penguin Publishing Group, *(978-0-14; 978-0-399; 978-0-425; 978-0-452; 978-0-525; 978-0-698; 978-0-87477; 978-1-58542; 978-1-933438; 978-1-4295; 978-1-934511; 978-1-4362; 978-1-4406; 978-1-101; 978-1-937007)* Orders Addr.: 405 Murray Hill Pkwy., East Rutherford, NJ 07073-2136 USA (SAN 282-5074) Fax: 201-933-2903 (customer service); Toll Free Fax: 800-227-9604; Toll Free: 800-526-0275 (reseller sales); 800-631-8571 (reseller customer service); 800-788-6262 (individual consumer sales); Edit Addr.: 375 Hudson St., New York, NY 10014 USA Tel 212-366-2000; Fax: 212-366-2666; 405 Murray Hill Pkwy., East Rutherford, NJ 07073 (SAN 852-5455) Tel 201-933-9292
E-mail: customer.service@us.penguingroup.com
Web site: http://penguingroup.custhelp.com; http://booksellers.penguingroup.com; http://www.penguinputnam.com.

Penguin Random House LLC, *See* **Penguin Random Hse. Distribution**

Penguin Random House Publisher Services, Orders Addr.: 400 Hahn Rd., Westminster, MD 21157 USA; ., Crawfordsville, IN 11123
E-mail: distribution@penguinrandomhouse.com
Web site: http://www.penguinrandomhouse.biz/publisherservices/sales/index.html.

Penguin Random Hse. Distribution, *(978-0-593; 978-1-101; 978-1-9848)* 375 Hudson St. 3rd Fl., New York, NY 10014 USA.

Penguin Random Hse. LLC, *(978-0-593; 978-1-101; 978-1-9848; 979-8-217)* Orders Addr.: 400 Hahn Rd., Westminster, MD 21157 USA Toll Free Fax: 800-659-2436; Toll Free: 800-733-3000; Edit Addr.: 375 Hudson St. 3rd Flr., New York, NY 10014 USA Tel 212-366-2424
E-mail: brittany.wienke@us.penguingroup.com
Web site: http://www.PenguinRandomHouse.com.

Peniel Productions, 73 Smith Hill Rd., Monsey, NY 10952-4131 USA (SAN 631-2837).

Pen-Mar News Distributors, *See* **Americana Souvenirs & Gifts**

Penmarch Publishing, 3932 S. Willow Ave., Sioux Falls, SD 57105 USA Toll Free: 800-282-2399.

Penn News Co., 944 Franklin St., Johnstown, PA 15905 USA (SAN 169-7390).

Pennsylvania State Univ. Pr., *(978-0-271; 978-1-64602; 978-1-63779; 978-0-271-09566-0)* Orders Addr.: 820 N. University Dr., USB-1 Suite C, University Park, PA 16802 USA (SAN 213-5760) Tel 814-865-1327; Fax: 814-863-1408; Toll Free Fax: 877-778-2665 (orders only); Toll Free: 800-326-9180 (orders only)
E-mail: http://www.eisenbrauns.org; info@psupress.org; log-ins@press.psu.edu
Web site: http://www.psupress.org.

Pentecostal Publishing Hse., *(978-0-912315)* Subs. of United Pentecostal Church International, 8855 Dunn Rd., Hazelwood, MO 63042-2299 USA (SAN 219-3817) Tel 314-837-7300; (314) 837-7300; Fax: 314-837-4503
E-mail: PPHpublish@aol.com.

Penton Overseas, Inc., *(978-0-939001; 978-1-56015; 978-1-59125; 978-1-60379)* 1958 Kellogg Ave., Carlsbad, CA 92008 USA (SAN 631-0826) Tel 760-431-0060; Fax: 760-431-8110; Toll Free: 800-748-5804
E-mail: kellie@pentonoverseas.com; susan@pentonoverseas.com
Web site: http://www.pentonoverseas.com.

Peoples Education, *See* **Mastery Education**

Peregrine Outfitters, Orders Addr.: P.O. Box 1500, Williston, VT 05495 USA (SAN 631-1059) Tel 802-860-2977; Fax: 802-860-2978; Toll Free: 800-222-3088; Edit Addr.: 25 Omega Dr., Suite A, Williston, VT 05482 USA.

Perelandra, Ltd., *(978-0-927978; 978-0-9617713)* Orders Addr.: P.O. Box 3603, Warrenton, VA 20188 USA (SAN 665-0198) Tel 540-937-2153; Fax: 540-937-3360; Toll Free: 800-960-8806
E-mail: email@perelandra-ltd.com
Web site: http://www.perelandra-ltd.com.

Perfection Form Company, The, *See* **Perfection Learning Corp.**

Perfection Learning Corp., *(978-0-7807; 978-0-7891; 978-0-8124; 978-0-89598; 978-1-56312; 978-0-7569; 978-1-60686; 978-1-61563; 978-1-61383; 978-1-61384; 978-1-62299; 978-1-62359; 978-1-62765; 978-1-62766; 978-1-62974; 978-1-63419; 978-1-68064; 978-1-68065; 978-1-68240; 978-1-5311; 978-1-6903; 978-1-6636) 1000 N. 2nd Ave., Logan, IA 51546 USA (SAN 221-0010) Tel 712-644-2831; Fax: 712-644-2392; Toll Free Fax: 800-543-2745; Toll Free: 800-831-4190*
E-mail: orders@perfectionlearning.com
Web site: http://www.perfectionlearning.com.

Perfume River Pubns., 1420 2nd Ave., N., Suite 304, Sauk Rapids, MN 56379 USA Tel 320-761-1229.

Periodical Distributors, Incorporated, *See* **North Texas Periodicals, Inc.**

Periodical Marketing Services, 1065 Bloomfield Ave., Clifton, NJ 07012 USA (SAN 250-5304) Tel 201-342-6334.

Periodical Pubs. Service Bureau, One N. Superior St., Sandusky, OH 44870 USA (SAN 285-9351) Tel 419-626-0623.

Periodicals Service Co., *(978-0-527; 978-0-8115; 978-3-262; 978-3-601)* 11 Main St., Germantown, NY 12526 USA (SAN 164-8608) Tel 518-537-4700; Fax: 518-537-5899
E-mail: psc@periodicals.com
Web site: http://www.periodicals.com.

Perma-Bound Bks., *(978-0-605; 978-0-7804; 978-0-8000; 978-0-8479)* Div. of Hertzberg-New Method, Inc., 617 E. Vandalia Rd., Jacksonville, IL 62650 USA (SAN 169-202X) Tel 217-243-5451; Fax: 217-243-7505; Toll Free Fax: 800-551-1169; Toll Free: 800-637-6581 (customer service)
E-mail: books@permabound.com
Web site: http://www.perma-bound.com.

Perrone, Calle 11. #372-A Urb. Hill Brothers, San Juan, PR 00924 USA Tel 787-764-6112; Fax: 787-754-2374 Do not confuse with Perrone in Franklin, TN
E-mail: ecruz@perroneimporters.com
Web site: http://www.perroneimporters.com.

Perry Enterprises, *(978-0-941518)* 3907 N. Foothill Dr., Provo, UT 84604 USA (SAN 171-0281) Tel 801-226-1002.

Perseus Academic, *See* **Ingram Academic**

Perseus Bks. Group, *(978-0-7382; 978-0-938289; 978-1-58097; 978-1-882810; 978-1-903985; 978-1-78239)* Div. of Hachette Book Group, Orders Addr.: 2465 Central Ave., Suite 200, Boulder, CO 80301-5728 USA Toll Free: 800-343-4499 (customer service); Edit Addr.: 387 Park Ave., S., 12th Flr., New York, NY 10016-8810 USA Tel 212-340-8100; Fax: 212-340-8105
Web site: http://www.perseusbooksgroup.com.

Perseus Distribution, *See* **Two Rivers Distribution**

Perseus-PGW, *See* **Publishers Group West (PGW)**

Peterson Publishing Co., Inc., *(978-0-9709033)* 1660 Commerce Dr., Suite 1, North Mankato, MN 56003 USA Tel 507-625-4803 Do not confuse with Peterson Publishing Co. in Gunnison, CO.

Peterson's, *(978-0-7689; 978-0-87866; 978-1-56079)* Div. of Nelnet, Orders Addr.: P.O. Box 67005, Lawrenceville, NJ 08648-6105 USA (SAN 200-2167); Edit Addr.: 2000 Lenox Dr., 3rd Flr., Lawrenceville, NJ 08648 USA (SAN 297-5661) Tel 609-896-1800; Fax: 609-896-1811; Toll Free: 800-338-3282 X5660;Customer Service
E-mail: custsvc@petersons.com
Web site: http://www.petersons.com.

Petterson Antiques, 379 Clayton Dr., Charleston, SC 29414-5048 USA (SAN 114-2399).

Philippine American Literary House, *See* **PALH**

Philosophy Documentation Ctr., *(978-0-912632; 978-1-889680; 978-1-63435)* Orders Addr.: P.O. Box 7147, Charlottesville, VA 22906-7147 USA (SAN 218-6586) Tel 434-220-3300; Fax: 434-220-3301; Toll Free: 800-444-2419
E-mail: order@pdcnet.org
Web site: http://www.pdcnet.org.

Phoenix Distributors, Orders Addr.: P.O. Box 1589, Blaine, WA 98231 USA Toll Free Fax: 800-298-4422.

Phoenix Learning Resources, LLC, *(978-0-7915)* Orders Addr.: P.O. Box 510, Honesdale, PA 18431 USA (SAN 246-148X) Tel 570-251-6871; Fax: 570-253-3227; Toll Free: 800-228-9345
E-mail: rich@phoenixlr.com
Web site: http://www.phoenixlr.com.

Phoenix Rising Pr., *(978-0-9840521; 978-1-936429)* 157 Starling Pass, Asheville, NC 28804 USA (SAN 631-838X)
E-mail: lynnamesauthor@gmail.com
Web site: www.lynnames.com; http://www.phoenixrisingpress.com.

Pictorial Histories Distribution, *See* **West Virginia Book Co., The**

Pilgrim Pr., The/United Church Pr., *(978-0-8298)* Div. of United Church Board for Homeland Ministries, 700 Prospect Ave. E., Cleveland, OH 44115-1100 USA Tel 216-736-3848; Fax: 216-736-2207
E-mail: ucpress@ucc.org; pilgrim@ucc.org; bresnahana@ucc.org
Web site: http://www.ucpress.com; http://www.thepilgrimpress.com.

Pine Orchard, Inc., *(978-0-9645727; 978-1-930580)* Orders Addr.: 2850 Hwy 95 South. P.O. box 9184, Moscow, ID 83843 USA (SAN 253-4258) Tel 208-882-4838; Fax: 208-882-4845; Toll Free: 877-354-7433
E-mail: orders@pineorchard.com; pineorch@pineorchard.com
Web site: http://www.pineorchard.com.

Pine Orchard Press, *See* **Pine Orchard, Inc.**

Pioneer Enterprises, W10085 Pike Plain Rd., Dunbar, WI 54119 USA.

Pitsco Education, 1002 E. Adams St., Pittsburg, KS 66762-6050 USA Tel 620-231-0010.

Pittsfield News Co., Inc., 6 Westview Rd., Pittsfield, MA 01201 USA (SAN 124-2768) Tel 413-445-5682; Fax: 413-445-5683.

PixyJack Pr., Inc., *(978-0-9658098; 978-0-9773724; 978-1-936555)* Orders Addr.: P.O. Box 149, Masonville, CO 80541 USA Tel 303-810-2850; Toll Free Fax: 888-273-7499
E-mail: info@pixyjackpress.com
Web site: http://www.pixyjackpress.com.

Plains Distribution Service, P.O. Box 931, Moorhead, MN 56561 USA (SAN 169-6556).

Planeta Publishing Corp., *(978-0-9715256; 978-0-9719950; 978-0-9748724; 978-1-933169; 978-0-9795042)* 999 Ponce De Leon Blvd. Ste. 1045, Coral Gables, FL 33134-3047 USA
E-mail: mnorman@planetapublishing.com
Web site: http://www.planeta.es.

Plank Road Publishing, Orders Addr.: 3540 J N. 126 St., Brookfield, WI 53005 USA Tel 262-790-5210; Fax: 262-781-8818.

Players Pr., Inc., *(978-0-88734)* P.O. Box 1132, Studio City, CA 91614-0132 USA (SAN 239-0213) Tel 818-789-4980
E-mail: Playerspress@att.net.

Plough Publishing Hse., *(978-0-87486; 978-1-63608)* 151 Bowne Dr., Walden, NY 12586 USA (SAN 202-0092) Tel 845-572-3455; Fax: 845-572-3472; Toll Free: 800-521-8011
E-mail: info@plough.com; mariahine@ccimail.com
Web site: http://www.plough.com.

Plymouth Press, Limited, *See* **Plymouth Toy & Book**

Plymouth Toy & Book, *(978-1-882663)* 101 Panton Rd., Vergennes, VT 05491 USA Tel 802-877-2150; Fax: 802-877-2116; Toll Free: 800-350-1007 Do not confuse with Plymouth Pr. in Miami Beach, FL
E-mail: plymouth@together.net
Web site: http://www.plymouthtoyandbook.com.

PMG Bks. Ltd., P.O. Box 7608, San Antonio, TX 78207-0608 USA (SAN 631-3183).

Polk County Historical Assn., c/o UrbanDog Communications, Inc., P.O. Box 25474, Tampa, FL 33622 USA Tel 813-832-4538; Fax: 813-832-1759
E-mail: cbrownfl@earthlink.net.

Polybook Distributors, Orders Addr.: P.O. Box 109, Mount Vernon, NY 10550 USA Tel 914-664-1633; Fax: 904-428-3953; Edit Addr.: 501 Mamaroneck Ave., White Plains, NY 10605 USA (SAN 169-5568) Tel 914-328-6364
E-mail: mainstreetbook@gmail.com.

Pomona Valley News Agency, 10736 Fremont Ave., Ontario, CA 91762 USA (SAN 169-0019) Tel 909-591-3885.

Pop-M Company, *See* **Bk. Margins, Inc.**

Popular Subscription Service, P.O. Box 1566, Terre Haute, IN 47808 USA (SAN 285-9386) Tel 812-466-1258; Fax: 812-466-9443; Toll Free: 800-466-5038
E-mail: info@popularsubscriptionsvc.com
Web site: http://www.popularsubscriptionsvc.com.

Portland News Co., Orders Addr.: P.O. Box 6970, Scarborough, ME 04070-6970 USA (SAN 169-3093) Toll Free: 800-639-1708 (in Maine); Edit Addr.: 18 Hutcherson Dr., Gorham, ME 04038-2643 USA.

Postal Corner, 2240 Encinitas Blvd., Suite D, Encinitas, CA 92024 USA Tel 760-633-1100; Fax: 760-633-1486.

Potter's House Book Service, *(978-1-928717)* 1658 Columbia Rd., NW, Washington, DC 20009 USA Tel 202-232-5483; Fax: 202-328-7483
E-mail: pottershse@aol.com
Web site: http://www.pottershousebooks.com.

Potter's House Church, *See* **Potter's House Book Service**

Powells.com, Orders Addr.: 2720 NW 29th Ave., Portland, OR 97210 USA Tel 800-291-2676
Web site: http://www.powells.com/.

powerHouse Cultural Entertainment, Incorporated, *See* **powerHse. Bks.**

powerHse. Bks., *(978-1-57687; 978-1-64823)* 32 Adams St, Brooklyn, NY 11201 USA (SAN 850-5845)
E-mail: daniel@powerhousebooks.com
Web site: http://www.powerhousebooks.com; www.powkidsbooks.com; www.archways.us.

Practice Ring, *(978-0-929758)* Div. of Beeman Jorgensen, Inc., 7510 Allisonville Rd., Indianapolis, IN 46250 USA (SAN 630-6144) Tel 317-841-7677; Toll Free: 800-553-5319.

Pratz News Agency, Orders Addr.: P.O. Box 892, Deming, NM 88030 USA (SAN 159-9275).

Prebound Periodicals, 631 SW Jewell Ave., Topeka, KS 66606-1606 USA (SAN 285-8037).

Premier Pubs., Inc., *(978-0-915665)* P.O. Box 330309, Fort Worth, TX 76163 USA (SAN 292-5966) Tel 817-293-7030; Fax: 817-293-3410.

Presbyterian & Reformed Publishing Company, *See* **P & R Publishing**

Presbyterian Publishing Corp., *(978-0-664)* 100 Witherspoon St., Louisville, KY 40202-1396 USA Tel 502-569-5052; Fax: 502-569-8308; Toll Free Fax: 800-541-5113; Toll Free: 800-227-2872
E-mail: rpinotti@presbypub.com; customer_service@presbypub.com
Web site: http://www.ppcbooks.com.

Prestel Publishing, *(978-3-7913)* Orders Addr.: c/o VNU, 575 Prospect St., Lakewood, NJ 08701 USA Tel 732-363-5679; Fax: 732-363-0338; Toll Free Fax: 877-227-6564; Toll Free: 888-463-6110; Edit Addr.: 900 Broadway, Suite 603, New York, NY 10003 USA Tel 212-995-2720; Fax: 212-995-2733
E-mail: sales@prestel-usa.com
Web site: http://www.prestel.com; http://www.die-gestalten.de; http://www.scalo.com.

Princeton Bk. Co. Pubs., *(978-0-87127; 978-0-916622)* Orders Addr.: P.O. Box 831, Hightstown, NJ 08520-0831 USA (SAN 630-1568) Tel 609-426-0602; Fax: 609-426-1344; Toll Free: 800-220-7149; 614 Rte. 130, Hightstown, NJ 08520 (SAN 244-8076)
E-mail: pbc@dancehorizons.com; elysian@aosi.com
Web site: http://www.dancehorizons.com.

Princeton Univ. Pr., *(978-0-691)* Orders Addr.: California-Princeton Fulfillment Services, 1445 Lower Ferry Rd., Ewing, NJ 08618 USA Tel 800-777-4726; Fax: 800-999-1958; Edit Addr.: 41 William St., Princeton, NJ 08540 USA (SAN 202-0254) Tel 609-258-4900; Fax: 609-258-6305; 3 Market Place, Woodstock, OX20 1SY Tel (0) 1993 814501; Fax: (0) 1993 814504
E-mail: webmaster@pupress.princeton.edu
Web site: http://www.press.princeton.edu.

Princeton University Press_mupo, 41 William St., Princeton, NJ 08540 USA Tel 609-258-4900; Fax: 609-258-6305.

Print & Ship, 1412 Greenbrier Pkwy., Suite 145-B, Norfolk, VA 23320 USA Tel 757-424-5868.

Printed Matter, Inc., *(978-0-89439)* 195 10th Ave. FRNT, New York, NY 10011-4739 USA (SAN 169-5924)
E-mail: Keith@printedmatter.org; Max@printedmatter.org
Web site: http://www.printedmatter.org.

Productivity, Incorporated, *See* **Productivity Pr.**

Productivity Pr., *(978-0-527; 978-0-915299; 978-1-56327)* Orders Addr.: 7625 Empire Dr., Florence, KY 41042-2919 USA (SAN 290-036X) Toll Free Fax: 800-248-4724; Toll Free: 800-634-7064 (orders).

PRO-ED, Inc., *(978-0-88744; 978-0-89079; 978-0-933014; 978-0-936104; 978-0-944480; 978-1-4164)* Orders Addr.: 8700 Shoal Creek Blvd., Austin, TX 78757-6897 USA (SAN 222-1349) Tel 512-451-3246 Toll Free Fax: 800-397-7633; Toll Free: 800-897-3202; Edit Addr.: P.O. Box 679029, Dallas, TX 75267-9029 USA
E-mail: cheri@proedinc.com
Web site: http://www.proedinc.com.

Professional Book Distributors, Incorporated, *See* **PBD, Inc.**

Professional Media Service Corp., 1160 Trademark Dr., Suite 109, Reno, NV 89511 USA (SAN 630-5776) Toll Free Fax: 800-253-8853; Toll Free: 800-223-7672.

Project Patch, 2404 E. Mill Plain Blvd., Vancouver, WA 98661-4334 USA.

ProQuest Information and Learning, *See* **ProQuest LLC**

ProQuest LLC, *(978-0-14; 978-0-608; 978-0-7837; 978-0-8357; 978-0-88692; 978-0-89093; 978-0-912380; 978-1-55655; 978-0-591; 978-0-9702937; 978-0-599; 978-1-931694; 978-1-59399; 978-0-496; 978-0-542; 978-1-4247; 978-0-9778091; 978-1-60205; 978-1-4345; 978-0-549; 978-1-109; 978-1-124; 978-1-267; 978-1-303; 978-1-321; 978-1-339; 978-1-369; 978-0-355; 978-0-438; 978-1-392; 978-0-578-52671-3; 978-0-578-52672-0; 978-0-578-52673-7; 978-1-7331884; 978-1-7331885; 978-0-578-52675-1; 978-1-0732; 978-1-0739; 978-1-0) 5252 N. Edgewood Dr., Suite 125, Provo, UT 84604 USA Tel 801-765-1737; 789 Eisenhower Pkwy., Ann Arbor, MI 48108 Tel 734-761-4700; Toll Free: 800-521-0600; 7500 Old Georgetown Rd. Suite 1400, Bethesda, MD 20814*
E-mail: sales@csa.com
Web site: http://www.culturegrams.com; http://www.proquest.com/.

Prosperity Publishing Hse., 1405 Autumn Ridge Dr., Durham, NC 27712 USA Tel 919-767-9620.

Provident Music Distribution, 1 Maryland Farms, Brentwood, TN 37027 USA Tel 615-373-3950; Fax: 615-373-0386; Toll Free: 800-333-9000
E-mail: gmiller@pmgsonybmg
Web site: http://www.providentmusic.com.

PSI (Publisher Services, Inc.), 3095 Kingston Ct., Norcross, GA 30071-1231 USA Toll Free: 800-755-9653; 877-578-4774.

Public Lands Interpretive Assn., *(978-1-879343; 978-0-9863666)* 6501 Fourth St., NW, No. 1, Albuquerque, NM 87107-5800 USA (SAN 133-3119) Tel 505-345-9498; Fax: 505-344-1543.

Publication Consultants, *(978-0-9644809; 978-1-888125; 978-1-59433; 978-1-63747)* 8370 Eleusis Dr., Anchorage, AK 99502 USA Tel 907-349-2424; Fax: 907-349-2426
E-mail: evan@publicationconsultants.com
Web site: http://www.publicationconsultants.com.

Publications Unlimited, 7512 Coconut Dr., Lake Worth, FL 33467-6511 USA (SAN 285-9432) Tel 407-434-4688 Do not confuse with Publications Unlimited in Raleigh, NC.

Publishers Business Service, Inc., P.O. Box 25674, Chicago, IL 60625 USA (SAN 285-9459) Tel 312-561-5552.

Publishers Clearing Hse., 382 Channel Dr., Port Washington, NY 11050 USA (SAN 285-9440) Tel 516-883-5432.

Publishers Continental Sales Corp., 613 Franklin Sq., Michigan City, IN 46360 USA (SAN 285-9475) Tel 219-874-4245; Fax: 219-872-8961.

Publishers Group International, Inc., *(978-0-9633653)* 1506 27th St. NW, No. 1, Washington, DC 20007 USA Tel 202-342-0886; Fax: 202-338-1940 E-mail: issbooks@aol.com.

Publishers Group West (PGW), Div. of Ingram Content Group, Orders Addr.: 1094 Flex Dr., Jackson, TN 38301-5070 USA (SAN 631-7715) Tel 731-423-1973; Toll Free Fax: 800-351-5073; Toll Free: 800-343-4499; Edit Addr.: 387 Park Avenue South, New York, NY 10016 USA (SAN 631-760X) Tel 212-340-8100; Fax: 212-340-8195 E-mail: info@pgw.com Web site: http://www.pgw.com/home.

Publishers Media, *(978-0-934064)* 1447 Valley View Rd., Glendale, CA 91202-1716 USA (SAN 159-6683) Tel 818-548-1998.

Publishers News Company, *See* **Mr. Paperback/Publishers News Co.**

Publishers Services, Orders Addr.: P.O. Box 2510, Novato, CA 94948 USA (SAN 201-3037) Tel 415-883-3530; Fax: 415-883-4280.

Publishers Storage & Shipping, 46 Development Rd., Fitchburg, MA 01420 USA Tel 978-345-2121; 660 S. Mansfield Dr., Ypsilanti, MI 48197 Tel 734-487-9720 Web site: http://www.pssc.com.

Publishers Wholesale Assocs., Inc., Orders Addr.: P.O. Box 2078, Lancaster, PA 17608-2078 USA (SAN 630-7450) Fax: 717-397-9253; Edit Addr.: 231 N. Shippen St., Lancaster, PA 17608 USA.

Puerto Rico Postcard, P.O. Box 79710, Carolina, PR 00984-9710 USA.

Pulley Learning Assocs., 210 Alpine Meadow Rd., Winchester, VA 22602-6701 USA (SAN 133-1434).

Pura Vida Bks., Inc., P.O. Box 2002, Salinas, PR 00751 USA Tel 787-824-3763 E-mail: info@puravidabooks.com.

Purple Unicorn Bks., *(978-0-931998)* 1928 W. Kent Rd., Duluth, MN 55812-1154 USA (SAN 111-0071) Tel 218-525-4781 Do not confuse with Purple Unicorn in Augusta, ME.

Puzzle Piece Pubns., 846 36th Ave., N., Saint Cloud, MN 56303 USA Tel 320-656-5361.

Quality Bks., Inc., *(978-0-89196)* 1003 W. Pines Rd., Oregon, IL 61061-9680 USA (SAN 169-2127) Tel 815-732-4450; Fax: 815-732-4499; Toll Free: 800-323-4241 (libraries only) E-mail: info@quality-books.com.

Quality Book Fairs, 5787 Ryan Rd., Medina, OH 44256-8823 USA (SAN 630-7752).

Quality Schl. Plan, Inc., P.O. Box 10203, Des Moines, IA 50381-0001 USA (SAN 285-953X).

Quarto Publishing Group USA, *(978-0-7603; 978-0-86573; 978-0-89738; 978-0-912612; 978-0-929261; 978-0-9640392; 978-1-55832; 978-1-56010; 978-1-888608; 978-1-930604; 978-1-933662; 978-1-59186; 978-1-59233; 978-1-59253; 978-1-60058; 978-1-61673; 978-1-936309; 978-1-61058; 978-1-61059; 978-1-61060; 978-1-937994; 978-1-939581; 978-1-62788; 978-1-63106; 978-1-63159; 978-1-63322; 978-1-942875) Orders Addr.: Retail Order Dept., Quayside Publishing Group 18705 Lake Dr. E., Chanhassen, MN 55317 USA Tel 1-952-936-4700; Fax: 1-952-099-9101; Toll Free: 1-800-328-0590; Edit Addr.: 3 Wrigley Suite A, Irvine, CA 92618-2748 USA (SAN 249-051X) Toll Free: 800-426-0099* E-mail: rebecca.razo@quartous.com Web site: https://www.quartoknows.com/division/Quarto-Publishing-Group-USA/.

R & W Distribution, Inc., 87 Bright St., Jersey City, NJ 07302 USA (SAN 169-4723) Tel 201-333-1540; Fax: 201-333-1541 E-mail: rwmag@mail.idt.net.

R. C. Brayshaw, *See* **Brayshaw, R. C.**

R J Communications, LLC, *See* **Not So Plain Jane Publishing**

R T R Publishing Company, *See* **Red Toad Road Co.**

Radio Bookstore, P.O. Box 209, Rindge, NH 03461-0209 USA (SAN 111-3496) Tel 603-899-6957 Do not confuse with Radio Bookstore Pr., Bellevue, WA.

Raimond Graphics Inc., Orders Addr.: 360 Sylvan Ave., Englewd Clfs, NJ 07632-2712 USA.

Rainbow Bk. Co., *(978-1-932834; 978-1-60117; 978-1-60447)* 500 E. Main St., Lake Zurich, IL 60047 USA (SAN 920-2935) Tel 800-255-0965; Fax: 847-726-9935 Do not confuse with Rainbow Book Company in Mt. Mourne, NC E-mail: mike@rainbowbookcompany.com Web site: http://www.rainbowbookcompany.com.

Rainbow Horizons Publishing, Inc., *(978-1-55319)* Orders Addr.: P.O. Box 19729, San Diego, CA 92159 USA Toll Free Fax: 800-663-3608; Toll Free: 800-663-3609 E-mail: paul@classroomcompletepress.com Web site: http://www.ccpinteractive.com; http://www.rainbowhorizons.com; http://www.classroomcompletepress.com.

Rainbow Re-Source Ctr., P.O. Box 491, Kewanee, IL 61443 USA (SAN 631-4007) Tel 309-937-3385; Fax: 309-937-3382 E-mail: rainbowres@aol.com.

Rainier News, Inc., 3400-D Industry Dr., E., Fife, WA 98424-1853 USA (SAN 169-8745) Toll Free: 800-843-2995 (in Washington).

RAM Pubns. & Distribution, *(978-0-9630785; 978-0-9703860; 978-0-9897315)* Bergamot Sta., 2525 Michigan Ave., No. A2, Santa Monica, CA 90404 USA (SAN 298-2641) Tel 310-453-0043; Fax: 310-264-4888 E-mail: rampub@gte.net.

Rand McNally, *(978-0-528)* Orders Addr.: 9855 Woods Dr., Skokie, IL 60077-1074 USA Toll Free Fax: 800-934-3479 (Orders); Toll Free: 800-333-0136 (ext. 4771); 800-678-7263 (Orders); 8770 W Bryn Mawr Ave., Chicago, IL 60631 Tel 800-333-0136; Fax: 847-329-6139 E-mail: Education@randmcnally.com Web site: http://www.randmcnally.com.

Random House Adult Trade Publishing Group, *See* **Random House Publishing Group**

Random House, Incorporated, *See* **Random Hse., Inc.**

Random House Publishing Group, *(978-1-4070)* Orders Addr.: 400 Hahn Rd., Westminster, MD 21157 USA (SAN 852-5579) Tel 410-848-1900; 410-386-7560; Toll Free: 800-726-0600; Edit Addr.: 1745 Broadway, New York, NY 10019 USA Tel 212-751-2600; Fax: 212-572-4949; Toll Free: 800-726-0600 E-mail: lstark@randomhouse.com.

Random Hse. Bks. for Young Readers, *(978-0-375; 978-0-394; 978-0-517; 978-0-679; 978-1-4000)* Orders Addr.: 400 Hahn Rd., Westminster, MD 21157 USA; Edit Addr.: 1540 Broadway, New York, NY 10036 USA.

Random Hse., Inc., *(978-0-307; 978-0-345; 978-0-375; 978-0-385; 978-0-394; 978-0-440; 978-0-449; 978-0-517; 978-0-553; 978-0-593; 978-0-609; 978-0-676; 978-0-679; 978-0-7364; 978-0-7366; 978-0-7615; 978-0-7679; 978-0-7704; 978-0-8041; 978-0-8052; 978-0-8129; 978-0-8230; 978-0-87637; 978-0-87665; 978-0-87788; 978-0-88070; 978-0-913369; 978-0-914629; 978-0-930014; 978-0-945564; 978-1-57082; 978-1-57673; 978-1-57856; 978-1-878867; 978-1-884536; 978-1-885305; 978-1-58836; 978-1-4000; 978-1-59052; 978-1-4159; 978-) Div. of Penguin Random House LLC, Orders Addr.: 400 Hahn Rd., Westminster, MD 21157 USA (SAN 202-5515) Tel 410 848 1900; Toll Free Fax: 800 659 2436; Toll Free: 800 726 0600 (customer service/orders); Edit Addr.: 1745 Broadway, New York, NY 10019 USA (SAN 202-5507) Tel 212 782 9000; Fax: 212 302 7985* E-mail: customerservice@randomhouse.com Web site: http://www.randomhouse.com.

Raven West Coast Distribution, 767 W. 18th St., Costa Mesa, CA 92627 USA E-mail: ken@ravenwcd.com.

Read News Agency, 2501 Greensboro Ave., Tuscaloosa, AL 35401-5620 USA Tel 205-752-3515.

Readerlink Distribution Services, LLC, *(978-0-934429; 978-1-57145; 978-0-7944; 978-1-59223; 978-1-60710; 978-1-62686; 978-1-68412; 978-1-64147; 978-1-64517; 978-1-0785; 978-1-6672; 979-8-3690)* 9717 Pacific Heights Blvd Suite 100, San Diego, CA 92121 USA (SAN 630-8090) Toll Free: 800-284-3580 E-mail: lnordland@readerlink.com Web site: http://www.silverdolphinbooks.com; http://www.printersrowpublishinggroup.com; http://www.thunderbaybooks.com/; http://www.bathroomreader.com; http://www.readerlink.com.

Reader's Digest Assn., Inc., The, *(978-0-7621; 978-0-89577; 978-0-86438; 978-1-60652)* One Bedford Rd., Pleasantville, NY 10570 USA (SAN 282-2091) Toll Free: 800-463-8820; 800-334-9599; 800-635-5006 Web site: http://www.readersdigest.com; http://www.rd.com.

Reader's Digest Children's Publishing, Incorporated, *See* **Studio Fun International**

Readex Bk. Exchange, Box 1125, Carefree, AZ 85377 USA (SAN 159-9291).

Reading Circle, The, 7858 Industrial Pkwy., Plain City, OH 43064-9468 USA (SAN 169-670X).

Reading Matters, Inc., *(978-1-930654)* 806 Main St., Akron, PA 17501 USA Tel 717-859-5608; Fax: 717-859-3469; Toll Free: 888-255-6665 Do not confuse with companies with the same name in Brookline, MA, Denver, CO E-mail: office@readingmatters.net Web site: http://readingmatters.net.

Reading Peddler Bk. Fairs, 10580 3/4 W. Pico Blvd., Los Angeles, CA 90064 USA (SAN 157-9770) Tel 310-559-2665.

Reading's Fun/Books are Fun, Limited, *See* **Bks. Are Fun, Ltd.**

Readmor, Orders Addr.: P.O. Box 7264, Grand Rapids, MI 49508 USA (SAN 169-3875); Edit Addr.: 301 S. Rath Ave., Ludington, MI 49431 USA Tel 231-843-2537.

Readmore Academic Services, Orders Addr.: P.O. Box 1459, Blackwood, NJ 08012 USA (SAN 630-5741) Tel 609-227-1100; Fax: 609-227-8322; Toll Free: 800-645-6595; Edit Addr.: 700 Black Horse Pike, Suite 207, Blackwood, NJ 08012 USA.

Readmore, Inc., 22 Cortlandt St., New York, NY 10007 USA (SAN 159-9313) Tel 212-349-5540; Fax: 212-233-0746; Toll Free: 800-221-3306.

Recorded Bks., Inc., *(978-0-7887; 978-1-55690; 978-1-84197; 978-1-4025; 978-1-4193; 978-1-84505; 978-1-4281; 978-1-4361; 978-1-4407; 978-1-4498; 978-1-4561; 978-1-4618; 978-1-4640; 978-1-4703; 978-1-4906; 978-1-5019; 978-1-9800; 978-1-7050; 979-8-88956; 979-8-89059; 979-8-89178) Subs. of W. F. Howes Limited, Orders Addr.: 8400 Corporate Dr., Landover, MD 20785 USA (SAN 920-7414); Edit Addr.: 8400 Corporate Dr., Landover, MD 20785 USA (SAN 111-3984) Fax: 410-535-5499; Toll Free: 800-638-1304* E-mail: mmitchell@recordedbooks.com Web site: https://www.rbmediaglobal.com; https://rbmediaglobal.com/recorded-books/.

Recorded Books, LLC, *See* **Recorded Bks., Inc.**

Red Sea Pr., *(978-0-932415; 978-1-56902)* Affil. of Africa World Pr., 541 W. Ingham Ave., Suite B, Trenton, NJ 08638 USA (SAN 630-1983) Tel 609-695-3200; Fax: 609-695-6466 E-mail: awprsp@verizon.net Web site: http://www.africaworldpressbooks.com.

Red Toad Road Co., *(978-1-889287)* Orders Addr.: P.O. Box 642, Havre de Grace, MD 21078 USA Tel 410-939-4092; Fax: 410-939-5614; Edit Addr.: 223 Heather Way, Havre de Grace, MD 21078 USA E-mail: redtoadroad@aol.com Web site: http://www.amazon.com/shops/redtoadroad.

Red Wheel/Weiser, *(978-0-87728; 978-0-943233; 978-1-56414; 978-1-57324; 978-1-57863; 978-1-59003; 978-1-60163; 978-1-60925; 978-1-61283; 978-1-61852; 978-1-61940; 978-1-938875; 978-1-63265; 978-1-63341; 978-1-942785; 978-1-64297; 978-0-692-19811-7; 978-1-953650;-1-63748) Div. of Weiser Bks., Orders Addr.: 65 Parker St., Suite 7, Newburyport, MA 01950 USA (SAN 255-8610) Tel 978-465-0504; Fax: 978-465-0243; Toll Free Fax: 877-337-3309; Toll Free: 800-423-7087 (orders only)* E-mail: customerservice@redwheelweiser.com Web site: http://www.redwheelweiser.com.

RedShelf, Orders Addr.: 500 North Dearborn St., Suite 1200, Chicago, IL 60654 USA Tel 312-878-8586 E-mail: help@virdocs.com Web site: http://www.redshelf.com/.

Redwing Bk. Co., Orders Addr.: 202 Bendix Dr., Taos, NM 87571 USA Tel 505-758-7758; Fax: 505-758-7768; Toll Free: 800-873-3946 (USA); 888-873-3947 (Canada); Edit Addr.: P.O. Box 470688, Brookline Vlg, MA 02447-0688 USA (SAN 163-3597) Toll Free: 800-873-3946 E-mail: bob@redwingbooks.com Web site: http://www.redwingbooks.com.

Reference Bk. Ctr., 175 Fifth Ave., New York, NY 10010 USA (SAN 159-9356) Tel 212-677-2160; Fax: 212-533-0826.

Regent Bk. Co., Inc., Orders Addr.: P.O. Box 750, Lodi, NJ 07644-0750 USA Tel 973-574-7600; Fax: 973-574-7605; Toll Free: 800-999-9554; Edit Addr.: 101 E. Main St. BLDG 5, Little Falls, NJ 07424-1659 USA (SAN 169-4715) E-mail: info@regentbook.com Web site: http://www.regentbook.com.

REKO, P.O. Box 4005, Joplin, MO 64803 USA Tel 417-626-0402.

Renaissance News, 5232 Clairton Blvd., Pittsburgh, PA 15236 USA Tel 412-881-4848; Fax: 412-881-5422.

Replica Books, *See* **TextStream**

Representaciones Borinquenas, Inc., *(978-0-9727750; 978-0-9755107)* P.O. Box 139, Aguas Buenas, PR 00703-0139 USA Tel 787-309-9047; Fax: 787-780-5835 E-mail: rborinquenas@centennialpr.net.

Reprint Services Corp., *(978-0-7812; 978-0-932051; 978-1-4227)* P.O. Box 130, Murrieta, CA 92564-0130 USA (SAN 686-2640) Fax: 951-699-5065 E-mail: Reprintservices@gmail.com.

Research Bks., Inc., P.O. Box 555, Old Saybrook, CT 06475-0555 USA E-mail: info@researchbooks.com.

Resource Software International, Inc., *(978-0-87539)* Affil. of Datamatics Management, 330 New Brunswick Ave., Fords, NJ 08863 USA (SAN 264-8628) Tel 732-738-8500; Fax: 732-738-9603; Toll Free: 800-673-0366 E-mail: info@datamaticsinc.com Web site: http://www.tc-1.com.

Reveal Entertainment, Inc., *(978-0-9712633)* 1250 Petroleum Dr. Ste. B6, Abilene, TX 79602-7957 USA E-mail: revealgames@aol.com Web site: http://www.revealgames.com.

Review & Herald Publishing Assn., *(978-0-8127; 978-0-8280)* P.O. Box 2150, Hagerstown, MD 21742 USA (SAN 203-3798) Tel 301-393-3000 E-mail: mworden@rhpa.org Web site: http://www.reviewandherald.com/.

Revolution Booksellers, 60 Winter St., Exeter, NH 03833 USA Tel 603-772-7200; Fax: 603-772-7200; Toll Free: 800-738-6603.

Rhinelander News Agency, 314 Courtney, Crescent Lake, WI 54501 USA (SAN 159-9372) Tel 715-362-6397.

Rhino Entertainment Co, A Warner Music Group Co., *(978-0-7379; 978-0-930589; 978-1-56826; 978-0-9797278)* 3400 W. Olive Ave., Burbank, CA 91505 USA (SAN 677-5454) Tel 818-238-6110; Fax: 818-562-9239 E-mail: gladys.sanchez@wmg.com; tracie.bowers@wmg.com Web site: http://www.rhino.com.

Rhodes News Agency, *See* **Treasure Valley News**

Richardson's Bks., Inc., 2014 Lou Ellen Ln., Houston, TX 77018 USA (SAN 169-829X) Tel 713-688-2244; Fax: 713-688-8420; Toll Free: 800-392-8562.

Richardson's Educators, *See* **Richardson's Bks., Inc.**

Right Start, Inc., 5388 Sterling Center Dr., Suite C, Westlake Village, CA 91361-4687 USA (SAN 631-7022).

Rio Grande Bk. Co., P.O. Box 2795, McAllen, TX 78502-2795 USA (SAN 169-8354).

Rio Nuevo Pubs., *(978-0-918080; 978-1-887896; 978-0-9700750; 978-1-933855; 978-1-940322)* Orders Addr.: P.O. Box 5250, Tucson, AZ 85703-0250 USA (SAN 209-3251) Tel 520-623-9558; Fax: 520-624-5888; Toll Free Fax: 800-715-5888; Toll Free: 800-969-9558; Edit Addr.: 451 N. Bonita Ave., Tucson, AZ 85745 USA Tel 602-623-9558 E-mail: info@rionuevo.com; info@treasurechestbooks.com; aarond@rionuevo.com Web site: http://www.treasurechestbooks.com; http://www.rionuevo.com/.

Rip Off Pr., *(978-0-89620)* Orders Addr.: P.O. Box 4686, Auburn, CA 95604 USA (SAN 207-7671) Tel 530-885-8183; Toll Free: 800-468-2669 E-mail: authorkatee@gmail.com; mail@ripoffpress.com Web site: http://www.ripoffpress.com; http://www.kathetodd.com.

Rishor News Co., Inc., 109 Mountain Laurel Dr., Butler, PA 16001-3921 USA (SAN 159-9402).

Rittenhouse Bk. Distributors, *(978-0-87381)* Orders Addr.: P.O. Box 61565, Kng Of Prussa, PA 19406-0965 USA (SAN 213-4454) Toll Free Fax: 800-223-7488; Toll Free: 800-345-6425 E-mail: alan.yockey@rittenhouse.com; joan.townshend@rittenhouse.com Web site: http://www.rittenhouse.com.

Ritter Bk. Co., 7011 Foster Pl., Downers Grove, IL 60516-3446 USA (SAN 169-1856).

River Canyon Distributing, P.O. Box 70643, Eugene, OR 97401 USA.

River Road Recipes Cookbook, 9523 Fenway Dr., Baton Rouge, LA 70809 USA (SAN 132-7852) Tel 504-924-0300; Fax: 504-927-2547; Toll Free: 800-204-1726.

RiverStream Publishing, *(978-0-9834972; 978-1-62243)* Orders Addr.: P.O. Box 227, Mankato, MN 56002 USA; Edit Addr.: 2140 Howard Drive West, North Mankato, MN 56003 USA Tel 800-445-6209 E-mail: info@thecreativecompany.us Web site: https://riverstreampublishing.net.

Rizzoli International Pubns., Inc., *(978-0-8478; 978-0-88363; 978-0-941807; 978-1-932183; 978-1-59962)* Subs. of RCS Rizzoli Editore Corp., 300 Park Ave., S., 3rd Flr., New York, NY 10010 USA (SAN 111-9192) Tel 212-387-3400; Fax: 212-387-3535 Web site: http://www.rizzoliusa.com/.

Roadrunner Library Service, c/o Kerbs, 700 Highview Ave., Glen Ellyn, IL 60137-5504 USA.

Roberts, F.M. Enterprises, *(978-0-912746)* P.O. Box 608, Dana Point, CA 92629-0608 USA (SAN 201-4688) Tel 714-493-1977; Fax: 714-493-7124.

Rockbottom Bks., Pentagon Towers, P.O. Box 398166, Minneapolis, MN 55439 USA (SAN 108-4402) Tel 612-831-2120.

Rockland Catskill, Inc., 26 Church St., Spring Valley, NY 10977 USA (SAN 169-6254) Tel 914-356-1222; Fax: 914-356-8415; Toll Free: 800-966-6247.

Rocky Mount News Agency, Two Great State Ln., Rocky Mount, NC 27801 USA.

Rodale Institute Bookstore, *(978-0-9652477)* 611 Siegfriedale Rd., Kutztown, PA 19530 USA Tel 610-683-6009; Fax: 610-683-8548; Toll Free: 800-832-6285 E-mail: ribooks@fast.net Web site: http://www.rodaleinstitute.org.

Rogue Valley News Agency, Inc., 550 Airport Rd., Medford, OR 97504-4156 USA (SAN 169-7137).

Rohr, Hans E., 76 State St., Newburyport, MA 01950-6616 USA (SAN 113-8804).

Roig Spanish Bks., 146 W. 29th St., No. 3W, New York, NY 10001-5303 USA (SAN 165-1021) Fax: 212-695-6811.

Romeii LLC, *(978-0-9830484; 978-1-937391)* 1050 Sommers St. N, Hudson, WI 54016 USA Tel 651-204-3753 E-mail: steve@romeii.com Web site: Romeii.com.

Rosen Publishing Group, Inc., The, *(978-0-8239; 978-1-56696; 978-1-4042; 978-1-59791; 978-1-4358; 978-1-60851; 978-1-60852; 978-1-60853; 978-1-60854; 978-1-61511; 978-1-61512; 978-1-61513; 978-1-61514; 978-1-61530; 978-1-61531; 978-1-61532; 978-1-61533; 978-1-4488; 978-1-4777; 978-1-4824; 978-1-4994; 978-1-68048; 978-1-5081; 978-1-68416; 978-1-5382; 978-1-5383; 978-1-64282; 978-1-64374; 978-1-7253) a/o Dept. C234561, 29 E. 21st St., New York, NY 10010 USA (SAN 203-3720) Tel 212-777-3017; Fax: 212-358-9588; Toll Free Fax: 888-436-4643; Toll Free: 800-237-9932* E-mail: hollyc@rosenpub.com; info@rosenpub.com; customerservice@rosenpub.com; hollyc@rosen.pub Web site: http://www.rosenpublishing.com; http://www.rosendigital.com; http://www.rosenclassroom.com.

Rosen Publishing Group, Incorporated, The, *See* **Rosen Publishing Group, Inc., The**

Rosenblum's, *See* **Rosenblum's World of Judaica, Inc.**

Rosenblum's World of Judaica, Inc., 2906 W. Devon Ave., Chicago, IL 60659 USA (SAN 169-1864) Tel 773-262-1700; Fax: 773-262-1930; Toll Free: 800-626-6536.

Rosewood Foundation, The, Orders Addr.: P.O. Box 252, Archer, FL 32618 USA Tel 352-495-2197; Fax: 352-495-8313 E-mail: lizziePRJ@aol.com.

Rounder Kids Music Distribution, Orders Addr.: P.O. Box 516, Montpelier, VT 05602 USA (SAN 630-6675) Tel 802-223-5825; Fax: 802-223-5303; Toll Free: 800-223-6357; Edit Addr.: 80 W. Harvey Farm Rd., Waterbury Ctr, VT 05677-7132 USA E-mail: Pauls@rounder.com.

Routledge, *(978-0-04; 978-0-413; 978-0-415; 978-0-7100; 978-0-87830; 978-1-317; 978-1-003-16527-9)* Member of Taylor & Francis Group, Orders Addr.: 7625 Empire Dr., Florence, KY 41042 USA Toll Free Fax: 800-248-4724 (orders, customer serv.); Toll Free: 800-634-7064 (orders, customer serv.); Edit Addr.: 270 Madison Ave. # 3, New York, NY 10016-0601 USA (SAN 213-196X) E-mail: cserve@routledge-ny.com; info@routledge-ny.com Web site: http://www.routledge-ny.com.

Rowman & Littlefield Publishers, Inc., *(978-0-8476; 978-0-87471; 978-0-9632978; 978-1-56699; 978-1-888052; 978-0-7425; 978-1-931890; 978-1-933494; 978-1-4422; 978-1-936283; 978-1-61281; 978-1-4616; 978-1-4617; 978-1-62093; 978-1-5381; 978-1-68475)* Mem. of Rowman & Littlefield Publishing Group, Inc., Orders Addr.: 15200 NBN Way, Blue Ridge Summit, PA 17214 USA Tel 717-794-3800 (Sales, Customer Service, MIS, Royalties, Inventory; Fax: 717-794-3803 (Customer Service & orders only); 717-794-3857 (Sales & MIS); 717-794-3856 (Royalties, Inventory Mgmt. & Distribution); Toll Free Fax: 800-338-4550 (Customer Service & orders); Toll Free: 800-462-6420 (Customer Service & orders); Edit Addr.: 4501 Forbes Blvd., Suite 200, Lanham, MD 20706 USA Tel 301-459-3366; Fax: 301-459-5749; Toll Free:

800-462-6420 Short Discount, please contact rlpgsales@rowman.com
E-mail: rlpgsales@rowman.com; weston@rowman.com
Web site: http://www.rowmanlittlefield.com; http://www.rlpgbooks.com/bookseller/index.shtml.

Rowman & Littlefield Unlimited Model, Orders Addr.: 15200 NBN Way, Blue Ridge Summit, PA 17214-0190 USA; Edit Addr.: 4501 Forbes Blvd., Suite 200, Lanham, MD 20706 USA.

Royal Pubns., Inc., *(978-0-918738)* Orders Addr.: P.O. Box 5793, Denver, CO 80217 USA (SAN 244-7193) Tel 303-778-8383; Toll Free: 800-279-2048 (orders only); Edit Addr.: 790 W. Tennessee Ave., Denver, CO 80223 USA (SAN 169-054X).

Rumpf, Raymond & Son, Orders Addr.: P.O. Box 319, Sellersville, PA 18960 USA (SAN 631-5259).

Rushmore News, Inc., 924 East St. Andrew, Rapid City, SD 57701 USA (SAN 169-7846) Tel 605-342-2617; Fax: 605-342-9091; Toll Free: 800-423-0501
E-mail: afreese911@aol.com.

Russell News Agency, Inc., P.O. Box 158, Sarasota, FL 33578 USA (SAN 169-1287).

Russica Bk. & Art Shop, Inc., 799 Broadway, New York, NY 10003 USA (SAN 165-1072) Tel 212-473-7480; Fax: 212-473-7486.

Rutgers Univ. Pr., *(978-0-8135; 978-1-9788)* 106 Somerset St., Third Flr., New Brunswick, NJ 08901 USA (SAN 253-2115) Tel 848-445-7786
Web site: http://www.rutgersuniversitypress.org.

S & L Sales Co., Inc., Orders Addr.: P.O. Box 2067, Waycross, GA 31502 USA (SAN 107-413X) Tel 912-283-0210; Fax: 912-283-0261; Toll Free: 800-243-3699 (orders only).

S & S News & Greeting, 5304 15th Ave., S., Minneapolis, MN 55417-1812 USA (SAN 159-9453) Tel 612-224-8227; Toll Free: 800-346-9892.

S & W Distributors, Inc., 1600-H E. Wendover Ave., Greensboro, NC 27405 USA.

S. A. V. E. with Victor Hotho, *See* **S.A.V.E. Suzie & Vic Enterprises**

S V E & Churchill Media, *(978-0-7932; 978-0-89290; 978-1-56357)* 6465 N. Avondale Ave., Chicago, IL 60631-1909 USA (SAN 208-3930) Toll Free Fax: 800-624-1678; Toll Free: 800-829-1900
E-mail: custserv@svemedia.com
Web site: http://www.svemedia.com.

SAAN Corp., 189-01 Springfield Ave., Suite 201, Flossmoor, IL 60422 USA (SAN 631-0419) Tel 708-799-5225; Fax: 708-799-8713.

Saddleback Educational Publishing, *See* **Saddleback Educational Publishing, Inc.**

Saddleback Educational Publishing, Inc., *(978-1-56254; 978-1-59905; 978-1-60291; 978-1-61651; 978-1-61247; 978-1-62250; 978-1-62670; 978-1-63078; 978-1-68021; 978-1-64598; 978-1-63889)* 151 Kalmus Dr., J-1, Costa Mesa, CA 92626-4564 USA (SAN 860-0902) Toll Free Fax: 888-734-4010; Toll Free: 800-637-8715
E-mail: contact@saddleback.com; amchugh@sdlback.com; adormanesh@sdlback.com
Web site: http://www.sdlback.com.

Sadler, Dale, 209 Foster Dr., White House, TN 37188 USA.

Safari Museum Pr., 111 N. Lincoln Ave., Chanute, KS 66720 USA Tel 630-431-2730; Fax: 630-431-3848.

SAGE Pubns., Inc., *(978-0-7619; 978-0-8039; 978-1-4129; 978-1-4522; 978-1-4462; 978-1-4833; 978-1-5063; 978-1-5443; 978-1-0718; 978-1-0719; 978-1-5297)* 2455 Teller Rd., Thousand Oaks, CA 91360 USA (SAN 204-7217) Tel 800-818-7243; Fax: 800-583-2665; 805-499-0871
E-mail: info@sagepub.com; deborah.vaughn@sagepub.com
Web site: http://www.sagepub.com; http://www.sagepub.co.uk; http://www.pineforge.com; http://sagepub.com.

Sage US Textbks., 2455 Teller Rd., Thousand Oaks, CA 91360 USA.

Sagebrush Pr., *(978-0-930704)* P.O. Box 87, Morongo Valley, CA 92256 USA (SAN 113-387X) Tel 760-363-7398 Do not confuse with companies with same name in Cedarville, CA, Salt Lake City, UT.

Saint Benedict Pr., Div. of Saint Benedict Press, LLC, Orders Addr.: P.O. Box 410487, Charlotte, NC 28241 USA Toll Free: 800-437-5876
Web site: https://books.benedictpress.com/.

Saint George Book Service, Incorporated, *See* **Steiner, Rudolf College Pr./St. George Pubns.**

Saks News, Inc., P.O. Box 1857, Bismarck, ND 58502 USA (SAN 169-653X).

Sams Technical Publishing, LLC, *(978-0-7906; 978-0-578-12070-6)* 9850 E. 30th St., Indianapolis, IN 46229 USA Toll Free Fax: 800-552-3910; Toll Free: 800-428-7267
E-mail: samstech@samswebsite.com
Web site: http://www.samswebsite.com.

San Diego Historical Society, *(978-0-918740; 978-0-692-08840-1; 978-0-578-77315-5)* 1649 El Prado Suite 3, San Diego, CA 92101 USA (SAN 210-5438) Tel 619-232-6203; Fax: 619-232-6297
Web site: http://www.sandiegohistory.org.

San Diego Museum of Art, *(978-0-937108; 978-0-9845555)* Orders Addr.: P.O. Box 122107, San Diego, CA 92112-2107 USA Tel 619-696-1970; Fax: 619-232-9367
E-mail: sward@sdmart.org
Web site: http://www.sdmart.org.

San Franciscana, *(978-0-934715)* P.O. Box 590955, San Francisco, CA 94159 USA (SAN 161-1607) Tel 415-751-7222.

San Val, Incorporated, *See* **Turtleback Bks.**

Sandlapper Publishing Co., Inc., *(978-0-87844)* Orders Addr.: P.O. Box 730, Orangeburg, SC 29115 USA (SAN 203-2678) Toll Free Fax: 800-337-9420 (orders); Toll Free: 800-849-7263 (orders); Edit Addr.: 1281 Amelia St., NE., Orangeburg, SC 29116 USA Tel 803-533-1658; Fax: 803-534-5223
E-mail: agallman1@bellsouth.net
Web site: http://www.sandlapperpublishing.com.

Sandvik Publishing, *(978-1-58048; 978-1-881445)* Div. of Sandviks Bokforlag, Norway, 3729 Knights Rd., Bensalem, PA 19020-2908 USA Toll Free: 800-843-2445
E-mail: Nicole@sandvikpublishing.com; cust-serv@sandvikpublishing.com
Web site: http://www.sandviks.com.

Santa Barbara Botanic Garden, *(978-0-916436)* 1212 Mission Canyon Rd., Santa Barbara, CA 93105 USA (SAN 208-8398) Tel 805-682-4726; Fax: 805-563-0352
E-mail: info@sbbg.org
Web site: http://www.sbbg.org.

Santa Barbara News Agency, 725 S. Kellogg Ave., Goleta, CA 93117-3806 USA (SAN 168-9665) Tel 805-564-5200.

Santa Monica Software, Inc., 30018 Zenith Point Rd., Malibu, CA 90265-4264 USA (SAN 630-6764) Tel 310-457-8381; Fax: 310-395-7635.

Santillana USA Publishing Co., Inc., *(978-0-88272; 978-1-56014; 978-1-58105; 978-1-58986; 978-1-59437; 978-1-59820; 978-1-60396; 978-1-61605; 978-1-61435; 978-1-62263; 978-1-63113; 978-1-68292; 978-1-64101)* Div. of Grupo Santillana, 8333 NW 53rd St. Suite 402, Doral, FL 33166 USA (SAN 205-1133) Tel 617-351-4867; Av. Rio Mixcoac No. 274 Col. Acacias, C.P. 0324 Benito Juarez, Ciudad de Mexico, DF,
E-mail: dminella@vistahigherlearning.com; esanta@santillanausa.com; customerservice@santillanausa.com
Web site: http://www.loqueleo.com/us.

Saphrograph Corp., *(978-0-87557)* 5409 18th Ave., Brooklyn, NY 11204 USA (SAN 110-4128) Tel 718-331-1233; Fax: 718-331-8231
E-mail: saphrograph@verizon.net.

Sathya Sai Bk. Ctr. of America, *(978-1-57836)* 305 W. First St., Tustin, CA 92780 USA (SAN 111-3542) Tel 714-669-0522; Fax: 714-669-9138
Web site: http://www.sathyasaibooks.com.

Satsang Press, *See* **Gangaji Foundation, The**

Savant Bk. Distribution Co., 3107 E 62nd Ave., Spokane, WA 99223-6934 USA (SAN 631-9203) Tel 509-443-7057; Fax: 509-448-2191
E-mail: service@savant-books.com
Web site: http://www.savant-books.com.

S.A.V.E. Suzie & Vic Enterprises, 303 N. Main, P.O. Box 30, Schulenburg, TX 78956 USA (SAN 630-6365) Tel 409-743-4145; Fax: 409-743-4147.

Savvas Learning Co., *(978-1-59896; 978-1-60637)* 75 Arlington St., Boston, MA 02116 USA.

SCB Distributors, Orders Addr.: 15608 S. New Century Dr., Gardena, CA 90248-2129 USA (SAN 630-4818) Tel 310-532-9400; Fax: 310-532-7001; Toll Free: 800-729-6423 (orders only)
E-mail: info@scbdistributors.com
Web site: http://www.scbdistributors.com.

Schiffer Publishing, Ltd., *(978-0-7643; 978-0-87033; 978-0-88740; 978-0-89538; 978-0-916838; 978-0-9787278; 978-1-5073)* Orders Addr.: 4880 Lower Valley Rd., Atglen, PA 19310 USA (SAN 208-8428) Tel 610-593-1777; Fax: 610-593-2002
E-mail: info@schifferbooks.com; karen@schifferbooks.com
Web site: http://www.schifferbooks.com.

Schmul Publishing Co., Inc., *(978-0-88019)* Orders Addr.: P.O. Box 716, Salem, OH 44460-0716 USA (SAN 180-2771) Tel 330-222-2249; Fax: 330-222-0001; Toll Free: 800-772-6657; Edit Addr.: 3583 Newgarden Rd., Salem, OH 44460 USA
E-mail: spchale@valunet.com
Web site: http://www.wesleyanbooks.com.

Schoenhof's Foreign Bks., Inc., *(978-0-87774)* 76a Mount Auburn St., Cambridge, MA 02138-5051 USA (SAN 212-0062)
E-mail: info@schoenhofs.com
Web site: http://www.schoenhofs.com.

Scholar's Bookshelf, *(978-0-678; 978-0-945726; 978-1-60105)* Orders Addr.: 110 Melrick Rd., Cranbury, NJ 08512 USA (SAN 110-8360) Tel 609-395-6933; Fax: 609-395-0755
E-mail: books@scholarsbookshelf.com
Web site: http://www.scholarsbookshelf.com.

Scholastic Bk. Fairs, P.O. Box 958411, Lake Mary, FL 32795-8411 USA (SAN 173-7457) Tel 407-829-2600.

Scholastic, Inc., *(978-0-439; 978-0-590; 978-0-545; 978-1-338)* 557 Broadway, New York, NY 10012-3999 USA (SAN 202-5442) Fax: 212-343-6802; Toll Free: 800-325-6149 (customer service)
E-mail: info@scholastic.com
Web site: http://www.scholastic.com.

Scholium International, Inc., *(978-0-87936)* P.O. Box 1519, Port Washington, NY 11050-0306 USA (SAN 169-5282) Tel 516-767-7171; Fax: 516-944-9824
E-mail: info@scholium.com
Web site: http://www.scholium.com.

School Aid Co., *(978-0-87385)* 911 Colfax Dr., P.O. Box 123, Danville, IL 61832 USA (SAN 158-3719) Tel 217-442-6855; Toll Free: 800-447-2665.

School Aids, 9335 Interline Ave., Baton Rouge, LA 70809-1910 USA (SAN 169-2909) Tel 504-926-4498.

School Bk. Service, 3650 Coral Ridge Dr., Suite 112, Coral Springs, FL 33065-2559 USA (SAN 158-6963) Tel 954-341-7207; Fax: 954-341-7303; Toll Free: 800-228-7361
E-mail: compedge@ix.netcom.com.

School of Metaphysics, 163 Moonvalley Rd., Windyville, MO 65783 USA (SAN 159-5423) Tel 417-345-8411; Fax: 417-345-6668
E-mail: som@som.org
Web site: http://www.som.org.

Schroeder News Company, *See* **Merced News Co.**

Schroeder's Bk. Haven, 104 Michigan Ave., League City, TX 77573 USA (SAN 122-7998) Tel 281-332-5226; Fax: 281-332-1695; Toll Free: 800-894-5032
E-mail: schroedr@interloc.com.

Schulze News Co., 2451 Eastman Ave., Suite 13, Oxnard, CA 93030-5193 USA (SAN 169-0434) Tel 805-642-9759.

Schuylkill News Service, 1801 W. Market St., Pottsville, PA 17901-2001 USA (SAN 159-9518).

Schwartz, Arthur & Company, Incorporated/Woodstocker Books, *See* **Woodstocker Books/Arthur Schwartz & Company**

Schwartz Brothers, Inc., 822 Montgomery Ave., No. 204, Narberth, PA 19072-1937 USA (SAN 285-7529) Fax: 301-459-6418; Toll Free: 800-638-0243.

Science Kit & Boreal Labs, P.O. Box 5003, Tonawanda, NY 14151-5003 USA (SAN 631-2314)
E-mail: sk@sciencekit.com.

Scientific & Medical Pubns. of France, Inc., P.O. Box 3490, New York, NY 10163-3490 USA (SAN 169-5940).

SCPBooks, *See* **Phoenix Rising Pr.**

Seaboard Sub Agency, 215 S. Ott St., Allentown, PA 18104-6147 USA (SAN 285-9718).

Seaburn Bks., P.O. Box 2085, Long Island City, NY 11102 USA (SAN 631-2799) Tel 718-274-7040
E-mail: info@seaburn.com.

Seattle Bk. Co., Orders Addr.: P.O. Box 2222, Poulsbo, WA 98370 USA Tel 206-922-0418; Edit Addr.: 18864 Front St., Suite 200, Poulsbo, WA 98370 USA
E-mail: sales@seattlebookcompany.com.

Selective Bks., Inc., *(978-0-912584)* P.O. Box 1140, Clearwater, FL 34617 USA (SAN 204-577X) Tel 813-447-0100.

Selective Publishers, Incorporated, *See* **Selective Bks., Inc.**

Semler News Agency, Orders Addr.: P.O. Box 350, New Castle, PA 16101 USA (SAN 169-7471); Edit Addr.: P.O. Box 526, Morgantown, WV 26505 USA (SAN 169-8990).

Send The Light Distribution LLC, *(978-0-9835608; 978-1-939900)* Orders Addr.: 129 Mobilization Dr., Waynesboro, GA 30830 USA (SAN 631-8894) Tel 706-554-5827; Toll Free Fax: 877-323-4551; Toll Free: 877-323-4550; 100 Biblica Way, Elizabethton, TN 37643-6070 (SAN 630-7388) Tel 423-547-5131 editorial Toll Free Fax: 800-759-2779
E-mail: Customerservice@stl.org
Web site: http://www.stl-publisherservices.com.

Seneca News Agency, 800 Pre Emption Rd., Geneva, NY 14456-2010 USA (SAN 169-5304).

Sentai Distributors, 8839 Shirley Ave., Northridge, CA 91324 USA (SAN 168-9959) Tel 818-886-3113; Fax: 818-886-0423
Web site: http://www.plasticmodels.com.

Sepher-Hermon Pr., *(978-0-87203)* 1153 45th St., Brooklyn, NY 11219 USA (SAN 169-5959) Tel 718-972-9010; Fax: 718-972-6935.

Serendipity Couriers, Inc., P.O. Box 5897, Vallejo, CA 94591-5897 USA (SAN 169-0329) Toll Free: 800-459-4005 (Bay area only)
E-mail: dipity@14.netcom.com.

Serpent's Tale Natural History Bk. Distributors, Inc., *(978-1-885209)* Orders Addr.: P.O. Box 405, Lanesboro, MN 55949-0405 USA (SAN 630-6101) Tel 507-467-8734; Fax: 507-467-8735
E-mail: zoobooks@acegroup.cc
Web site: http://www.zoobooksales.com.

Service News Co., 1306 N. 23rd St., Wilmington, NC 28406 USA (SAN 169-6491) Tel 910-762-0837; Fax: 910-762-9539; Toll Free: 800-552-8238; P.O. Box 5027, Macon, GA 31208; Pope's Island, Box D-629, New Bedford, MA 02742 (SAN 169-3514).

Seven Locks Pr., *(978-0-929765; 978-0-932020; 978-0-9615964; 978-1-931643; 978-0-9790950; 978-0-9795852; 978-0-9801270; 978-0-9822293; 978-0-9824957)* P.O. Box 25689, Santa Ana, CA 92799-5689 USA (SAN 211-9781) Toll Free: 800-354-5348
E-mail: sevenlocks@aol.com
Web site: http://www.sevenlockspublishing.com.

Seymour, Dale Pubns., *(978-0-201; 978-0-7690; 978-0-86651; 978-1-57232)* Div. of Pearson Learning, Orders Addr.: P.O. Box 2500, Lebanon, OH 43216 USA Toll Free Fax: 800-393-3156; Toll Free: 800-321-3106 (Customer Service); Edit Addr.: 10 Bank St., White Plains, NY 10602-5026 USA (SAN 200-9781) Toll Free Fax: 800-393-3156; Toll Free: 800-237-3142
E-mail: pearson_learning2@prenhall.com
Web site: http://www.pearsonlearning.com; http://www.pearsonlearning.com/rightsPerm.rtf.

Shadow Mountain Publishing, *(978-0-87579; 978-1-57345; 978-1-59038; 978-1-60907)* Div. of Deseret Book Company, P.O. Box 30178, Salt Lake City, UT 84130 USA Tel 801-517-3223
E-mail: info@shadowmountain.com
Web site: http://www.shadowmountain.com.

Shambhala Publications, Incorporated, *See* **Shambhala Pubns., Inc.**

Shambhala Pubns., Inc., *(978-0-8348; 978-0-87773; 978-0-937938; 978-0-9627138; 978-1-55939; 978-1-56957; 978-1-57062; 978-1-930485; 978-1-59030; 978-1-61180; 978-1-64547)* 4720 Walnut St., Boulder, CO 80301 USA (SAN 203-2481) Tel 303-222-9598; 978-829-2599 (international); Toll Free: 888-424-2329 (orders)
E-mail: editors@shambhala.com; support@shambhala.com; customercare@shambhala.com
Web site: http://www.shambhala.com.

Sharon News Agency Co., 527 Silver St., Sharon, PA 16146 USA (SAN 169-7633).

Sharpe, M.E. Inc., *(978-0-7656; 978-0-87332; 978-1-56324)* 80 Business Park Dr., Armonk, NY 10504 USA (SAN 202-7100) Tel 914-273-1800; Fax: 914-273-2106; Toll Free: 800-541-6563
Web site: http://www.mesharpe.com.

Shea Bks., 1563 Solano Ave., Suite 206, Berkeley, CA 94707 USA (SAN 159-9720) Tel 510-528-5201; Fax: 510-528-4987.

Shell Educational Publishing, *(978-1-4258)* 5301 Oceanus Dr., Huntington Beach, CA 92649 USA Tel 714-489-2080; Fax: 714-230-7070; Toll Free: 888-877-7606; 877-777-3450
E-mail: rkarnik@tcmpub.com; LShill@seppub.com
Web site: http://www.seppub.com; http://www.tcmpub.com.

Shelter Pubns., Inc., *(978-0-936070)* Orders Addr.: P.O. Box 279, Bolinas, CA 94924 USA (SAN 122-8463) Tel 415-868-0280; Fax: 415-868-9053; Toll Free: 800-307-0131; Edit Addr.: 285 Dogwood Rd, Bolinas, CA 94924 USA
E-mail: shelter@shelterpub.com
Web site: http://www.shelterpub.com.

Shenanigan Bks., *(978-0-9726614; 978-1-934860)* 84 River Rd., Summit, NJ 07901-1443 USA (SAN 915-7085)
Web site: http://www.shenaniganbooks.com.

Shoppers Guide Pr., 706 N. Fifth, Alpine, TX 79830 USA (SAN 159-9550) Tel 915-837-7426.

Sierra News Co., 2136 Pony Express Ct., Stockton, CA 95215-7946 USA (SAN 169-4472).

Signature Bks., LLC, *(978-0-941214; 978-1-56085)* 564 W. 400 N., Salt Lake City, UT 84116-3411 USA (SAN 217-4391) Tel 801-531-1483; Fax: 801-531-1488; Toll Free: 800-356-5687 (orders only)
E-mail: people@signaturebooks.com
Web site: http://www.signaturebooks.com.

Silky Way, Inc., 1227 38th Ave., San Francisco, CA 94122-1334 USA (SAN 169-3328).

Silver Bow News Distributing Co., Inc., 219 E. Park St., Butte, MT 59701 USA (SAN 169-4359) Tel 406-782-6995.

Silver, Burdett & Ginn, Inc., *(978-0-382; 978-0-663; 978-1-4182)* Orders Addr.: P.O. Box 2500, Lebanon, IN 46052 USA Toll Free Fax: 800-841-8939; Toll Free: 800-552-2259; Edit Addr.: P.O. Box 480, Parsippany, NJ 07054 USA (SAN 204-5982); 108 Wilmot Rd., Suite 380, Midwest Div., Deerfield, IL 60015 (SAN 111-6517) Tel 708-945-1240; 1925 Century Blvd. NE, Suite 14, Southeast Div., Atlanta, GA 30345 (SAN 111-6509); 8445 Freeport Pkwy., Suite 400, South Div., Irving, TX 75063 (SAN 108-0458) Tel 214-915-4200; 2001 The Alameda, West Div., San Jose, CA 95126 (SAN 111-6525) Tel 408-248-6854; 160 Gould St., East Div., Needham Heights, MA 02194-2310; 1900 E. Lake Ave., Glenview, IL 60025
E-mail: customerservice@scottforesman.com
Web site: http://www.scottforesman.com/.

Simon & Schuster, *(978-0-671; 978-0-684; 978-0-689; 978-0-914676; 978-0-7432; 978-1-4165; 978-1-4391; 978-1-4516; 978-1-4767; 978-1-5011; 978-1-9821; 978-1-7214; 978-1-958698; 979-8-9866017)* Div. of Simon & Schuster, Inc., Orders Addr.: 100 Front St., Riverside, NJ 08075 USA (SAN 200-2442) Toll Free Fax: 800-943-9831; Toll Free: 800-223-2336 (ordering); 800-223-2348 (customer service); Edit Addr.: a/o Subsidiary Rights, 11th Flr., 1230 Avenue of the Americas, New York, NY 10020 USA (SAN 200-2450) Tel 212-698-7000; Fax: 212-698-7007; 212-632-8099 (Rights & Permissions); 212-698-1269 (Pocket Bks. Rights & Permissions); Toll Free: 800-897-7650 (customer financial services); 100 Front St., Riverside, NJ 08075 (SAN 852-5471) Tel 856-824-2115
E-mail: ssonline_feedback@simonsays.com; consumer.customerservice@simonandschuster.com
Web site: http://www.simonsays.com; http://www.oasis.simonandschuster.com; http://www.simonandschuster.com/.

Simon & Schuster Children's Publishing, *(978-0-02; 978-0-671; 978-0-684; 978-0-689; 978-0-7434; 978-1-4169; 978-1-4424; 978-0-85707)* Orders Addr.: 100 Front St., Riverside, NJ 08075 USA Toll Free Fax: 800-943-9831; Toll Free: 800-223-2336; Edit Addr.: a/o Subsidiary Rights, 4th floor, 1230 Avenue of the Americas, New York, NY 10020 USA Tel 212-698-7200; Fax: 212-698-2797 (Rights & Permissions)
Web site: http://www.simonsays.com.

Simon & Schuster, Inc., *(978-0-02; 978-0-671; 978-0-684; 978-0-689; 978-0-88138; 978-0-914676; 978-0-937860; 978-1-55850; 978-1-58062; 978-0-7432; 978-0-7434; 978-0-7435; 978-1-59337; 978-1-4165; 978-1-4169; 978-1-59869; 978-1-60550; 978-1-4391; 978-1-4405; 978-1-4423; 978-1-4424; 978-1-4516; 978-0-85707; 978-1-4814; 978-1-5072; 978-1-5082; 978-1-5344; 978-1-7971; 978-1-6659; 978-1-6680; 978-1-6681; 978-1-6682; 978-1-970187; 978-1-970188) Div. of Viacom Co., Orders Addr.: 100 Front St., Riverside, NJ 08075 USA Toll Free Fax: 800-943-9831; Toll Free: 800-223-2336 (orders); 800-223-2348 (customer service); Edit Addr.: 1230 Ave. of the Americas, New York, NY 10020 USA Tel 212-698-7000*
E-mail: Consumer.CustomerService@simonandschuster.com
Web site: http://www.simonsays.com; http://www.simonandschuster.com.

Simon & Schuster Trade, *See* **Simon & Schuster**

Skandisk, Inc., *(978-0-9615394; 978-1-57534)* 6667 W. Old Shakopee Rd., Suite 109, Bloomington, MN 55438-2622 USA (SAN 695-4405) Tel 952-829-8998; Fax: 952-829-8992; Toll Free: 800-468-2424 (orders)
E-mail: lhamnes@skandisk.com; tomten@skandisk.com
Web site: http://www.skandisk.com.

Sky Oaks Productions, Inc., *(978-0-940296; 978-1-56018)* P.O. Box 1102, Los Gatos, CA 95031 USA (SAN 217-5843) Tel 408-395-7600; Fax: 408-395-8440
E-mail: TRPWorld@aol.com
Web site: http://www.tpr-world.com.

Slatner, Thomas & Co., Inc., 193 Palisade Ave., 3rd Flr., Jersey City, NJ 07036-1112 USA (SAN 130-9862) Tel 201-420-6700; Fax: 201-420-6787.

Slavica Pubs., *(978-0-89357)* c/o Indiana University, 1430 N. Willis Dr., Bloomington, IN 47404 USA (SAN 208-8576) Tel 812-856-4186; Fax: 812-856-4187
E-mail: slavica@indiana.edu
Web site: http://www.slavica.indiana.edu.

Sleeper, Dick Distribution, 18680-B Langensand Rd., Sandy, OR 97055-6426 USA (SAN 631-0273) Tel 503-668-3454; Fax: 503-668-5314; Toll Free: 800-699-9911
E-mail: sleepydick@bigfoot.com.

Sleuth Pubns., Ltd., *(978-0-915341)* 3398 Washington, San Francisco, CA 94118 USA (SAN 130-9374) Tel 415-771-2689.

Small Pr. United, Div. of Independent Pubs. Group, 814 N. Franklin St., Chicago, IL 60610 USA Tel 312-337-0747 (ext. 274)
Web site: http://www.smallpressunited.com.

Small Press Distribution, *See* **SPD-Small Pr. Distribution**

Smashwords, *(978-1-4523; 978-1-4524; 978-1-4580; 978-1-4581; 978-1-4657; 978-1-4658; 978-1-4659; 978-1-4660; 978-1-4661; 978-1-4760; 978-1-4761; 978-1-4762; 978-1-4763; 978-1-4764; 978-1-301; 978-1-310; 978-1-311; 978-1-370; 978-0-463; 978-0-692-04063-8; 978-0-578-41339-6; 978-1-005; 978-0-578-87509-5; 978-0-578-87510-1) 15951 Gatos Blvd., Suite 16, Los Gatos, CA 95032 USA Tel 408-358-1824; ziya gokalp mah. cimen sk. no:1/1 ikitelli koyu, basaksehir-istanbul, 34306 Tel 90 0538 8939727*
E-mail: bill@smashwords.com
Web site: http://www.smashwords.com.

Smith, Gibbs Publisher, *See* **Gibbs Smith, Publisher**

Smith News Agency, 118 S. Mitchell St., Cadillac, MI 49601 USA (SAN 169-3727).

SMMA Distributors, 6609 Brooks Dr., Temple, TX 76502 USA Tel 254-773-4884.

Snyder Magazine Agency, 3050 S. 9th Terr., Kansas City, KS 66103-2629 USA (SAN 285-9750).

Social Studies Schl. Service, *(978-1-56004; 978-1-57596)* Orders Addr.: 10200 Jefferson Blvd., P.O. Box 802, Culver City, CA 90232-0802 USA (SAN 168-9592) Tel 310-839-2436; Fax: 310-839-2249; Toll Free: 800-421-4246
E-mail: access@socialstudies.com
Web site: http://socialstudies.com.

Sociedad Biblica de Puerto Rico, Orders Addr.: P.O. Box 2548, Bayamon, PR 00960-2548 USA; Edit Addr.: Carr. 167, Km 14.7 Bo, Bayamon, PR 00960-2548 USA.

Society for Visual Education, Incorporated, *See* **S V E & Churchill Media**

Sopris West Educational Services, *See* **Cambium Education, Inc.**

Sort Card Co., The, 400 S. Summit View Dr., Fort Collins, CO 80524-1424 USA (SAN 159-9607).

Soundprints, *(978-0-924483; 978-1-56899; 978-1-931465; 978-1-59249; 978-1-60727)* Div. of Trudy Corp., 353 Main Ave., Norwalk, CT 06851 USA Fax: 203-846-1776; Toll Free: 800-228-7839
Web site: http://www.soundprints.com.

Sounds True, Inc., *(978-1-56455; 978-1-59179; 978-1-60407; 978-1-62203; 978-1-68364; 978-1-64963)* Orders Addr.: P.O. Box 8010, Boulder, CO 80306-8010 USA; Edit Addr.: 413 S. Arthur Ave., Louisville, CO 80027 USA (SAN 850-3532) Tel 303-665-3151; Fax: 303-665-5292; Toll Free: 800-333-9185
Web site: http://www.soundstrue.com.

Source Bk. Pubns., *(978-1-887137)* 1814 Franklin St., Suite 820, Oakland, CA 94612 USA Tel 510-839-5471; Fax: 510-547-3245.

Source Bks., *(978-0-940147; 978-0-85650)* Orders Addr.: 204 E. Fourth St., Suite O, Santa Ana, CA 92701 USA (SAN 248-2231) Tel 714-558-8944 (phone/fax); Toll Free: 800-695-4237 Do not confuse with Source Bks., Nashville, TN
E-mail: studio185@earthlink.net.

Source International Technology Corporation, *See* **Kamkyi Bks.**

Sourcebooks, Inc., *(978-0-942061; 978-0-9629162; 978-0-9629803; 978-1-57071; 978-1-57248; 978-1-58182; 978-1-883518; 978-1-887166; 978-1-888952; 978-1-890208; 978-1-929345; 978-1-59058; 978-1-4022; 978-1-932783; 978-1-61595; 978-1-4642; 978-1-62047; 978-1-62886; 978-1-4926; 978-1-7282) 1935 Brookdale Rd., Suite 139, Naperville, IL 60563 USA (SAN 666-7864) Tel 630-961-3900; Fax: 630-961-2168; Toll Free: 800-727-8866*
E-mail: info@sourcebooks.com
Web site: http://www.sourcebooks.com/.

South Asia Bks., *(978-0-8364; 978-0-88386)* P.O. Box 502, Columbia, MO 65205 USA (SAN 207-4044) Tel 573-474-0116; Fax: 573-474-8124
E-mail: sabooks@juno.com
Web site: http://www.southasiabooks.com.

South Atlantic News, Orders Addr.: P.O. Box 61297, Jacksonville, FL 32236-1297 USA; Edit Addr.: 1426 NE Eighth Ave., Ocala, FL 32678 USA.

South Carolina Bookstore, Orders Addr.: P.O. Box 4767, West Columbia, SC 29171 USA (SAN 131-2294) Tel 803-796-8200; Fax: 803-794-6927; Toll Free: 800-845-8200; Edit Addr.: 523 Jasper St., West Columbia, SC 29169 USA (SAN 243-2390).

South Central Bks., Inc., 1106 S. Strong Blvd., McAlester, OK 74501-6952 USA (SAN 108-1144) Tel 405-275-4522; Toll Free: 800-548-9858.

South Eastern Bk. Co., Inc., 3333 Hwy. 641 N., P.O. Box 309, Murray, KY 42071 USA (SAN 630-4869) Tel 270-753-0732; Fax: 270-759-4742; Toll Free Fax: 800-433-6966 (orders); Toll Free: 800-626-3952 (orders)
E-mail: orders@sebook.com
Web site: http://www.sebook.com.

South Louisiana News Company, *See* **Southern Periodicals, Inc.**

Southeast Library Bindery, Inc., P.O. Box 35484, Greensboro, NC 27425-5484 USA (SAN 159-9445) Tel 336-931-0800
E-mail: 70304.3023@compuserve.com
Web site: http://www.webmasters.net/bookbinding/.

Southeast Periodical & Bk. Sales, Inc., 10100 NW 25th St., Box 520155-Biscayne Annex, Miami, FL 33152 USA.

Southeastern Educational Toy & Bk. Distributors, Orders Addr.: 3215 Wellington Court Suite 113, Raleigh, NC 27615 USA (SAN 630-8104) Tel 704-364-6988; Edit Addr.: 4217 Park Rd., Charlotte, NC 28209 USA Tel 704-527-1921; Fax: 704-527-1653.

Southeastern Library Service, Subs. of Haskins Hse., P.O. Box 44, Gainesville, FL 32602-0044 USA (SAN 159-9615) Tel 352-372-3823.

Southern Bk. Service, *(978-0-9663836)* 4360 NW 135th St, Opa Locka, FL 33054 USA (SAN 169-0981) Tel 305-624-4545; Fax: 305-621-0425; Toll Free: 800-766-3254.

Southern Cross Pubns., 1734 W. Roseberry Rd., P.O. Box 717, Donnelly, ID 83615 USA (SAN 110-8549) Tel 208-325-8606; Fax: 208-325-3400
E-mail: scp@cyberhighway.net
Web site: http://www.thoughtlines.com/southerncross/.

Southern Library Bindery Co., 2952 Sidco Dr., Nashville, TN 37204 USA (SAN 169-7986).

Southern Michigan News Co., 2571 Saradan, P.O. Box 908, Jackson, MI 49204 USA (SAN 169-3697) Tel 517-784-7163; Toll Free: 800-248-2213 (in Michigan); 800-828-2140.

Southern Periodicals, Inc., P.O. Box 407, Rayne, LA 70578-0407 USA (SAN 113-2520); 180 James Dr E., Saint Rose, LA 70087-4005.

Southern Tier News Co., P.O. Box 2128, Elmira Heights, NY 14903 USA (SAN 169-5223).

Southern Wisconsin News, 58 Artisan Dr., Edgerton, WI 53534 USA (SAN 169-9121) Tel 608-884-2600; Fax: 608-756-2357
E-mail: ndewar@southernwisconsinnews.com.

Southwest Cookbook Distributors, Orders Addr.: P.O. Box 707, Bonham, TX 75418 USA (SAN 200-4925) Tel 903-583-8898; Fax: 903-583-2522; Toll Free: 800-725-8898 (orders); Edit Addr.: P.O. Box 707, Bonham, TX 75418-0707 USA (SAN 630-8325).

Southwest Natural Cultural Heritage Association, *See* **Public Lands Interpretive Assn.**

Southwest News Co., Box 5465, Tucson, AZ 85704 USA (SAN 159-9631).

Southwestern Bk. Distributors, c/o Kerbs, 700 Highview Ave., Glen Ellyn, IL 60137-5504 USA (SAN 160-2373).

Sovereign News Company, *See* **Trans World News**

Spama, Inc., 78 Lake St., Jersey City, NJ 07306-3407 USA (SAN 169-5967).

Spanish & European Bookstore, Inc., 3102 Wilshire Blvd., Los Angeles, CA 90010 USA Tel 213-739-8899; Fax: 213-739-0087.

Spanish Bookstore-Wholesale, The, 10977 Santa Monica Blvd., Los Angeles, CA 90025-4538 USA (SAN 168-9835) Tel 310-475-0453; Fax: 310-473-6132
E-mail: BernardHamel@SpanishbooksUSA.com
Web site: http://www.BernardHamel.com.

Spanish Hse. Distributors, 1360 NW 88th Ave., Miami, FL 33172-3093 USA (SAN 169-1171) Tel 305-592-6136; Fax: 305-592-0087; Toll Free: 800-767-7726.

Spanish Language Bk. Services, Inc., Orders Addr.: 7855 N.W. 12th St., Suite 211, Miami, FL 33126 USA.

Spanish Pubs., LLC, 8871 SW 129 Terr., Miami, FL 33176 USA Tel 305-233-3365; Fax: 305-251-1310
E-mail: mariela@spanishpublishers.net
Web site: www.spanishpublishers.net.

Spanishtech, Inc., Div. of Editor's Bureau, Ltd., P.O. Box 68, Westport, CT 06881 USA (SAN 289-9620) Tel 203-452-7655.

SPD-Small Pr. Distribution, *(978-0-914068)* 1341 Seventh St., Berkeley, CA 94710-1409 USA (SAN 204-5826) Tel 510-524-1668; Fax: 510-524-0852; Toll Free: 800-869-7553 (orders)
E-mail: orders@spdbooks.org
Web site: http://www.spdbooks.org.

SpeakWare, 2836 Stephen Dr., Richmond, CA 94803 USA Tel 510-222-2455
E-mail: leds@speakware.com
Web site: http://www.speakware.com.

Specialized Bk. Service, Inc., 307 Autumn Ridge Rd., Fairfield, CT 06432-1003 USA (SAN 166-9788) Tel 203-377-6510; Fax: 203-377-4792.

Specialty Bk. Services, 1150 N. San Francisco, Flagstaff, AZ 86001 USA (SAN 130-8114) Tel 520-779-7843.

Specialty Promotions, 4516 S. Vincennes Ave. # 1S, Chicago, IL 60653-3470 USA (SAN 110-9987).

Speech Bin, Inc., The, *(978-0-937857)* 1965 25th Ave., Vero Beach, FL 32960 USA (SAN 630-1657) Tel 772-770-0007; Fax: 772-770-0006
E-mail: info@speechbin.com
Web site: http://www.speechbin.com.

Speedimpex U.S.A., Inc., 35-02 48th Ave., Long Island City, NY 11101-2421 USA (SAN 169-5479) Tel 718-392-7477; Fax: 718-361-0815
E-mail: nsalvatore@speedimpex.com
Web site: http://www.speedimpex.com.

Spencer Museum of Art, *(978-0-913689)* Affil. of Univ. of Kansas, Univ. of Kansas 1301 Mississippi St., Lawrence, KS 66045-7500 USA (SAN 111-347X) Tel 785-864-4710; Fax: 785-864-3112
E-mail: spencerart@ku.edu
Web site: http://www.spencerart.ku.edu.

SPI Bks., *(978-0-944007; 978-1-56171)* 99 Spring St., 3rd Flr., New York, NY 10012 USA Tel 212-431-5011; Fax: 212-431-8646
E-mail: ian@spibooks.com
Web site: http://www.spibooks.com.

Spirit Filled Pr., Inc., *(978-0-9656668)* 2549 Tallavana Trail, Havana, FL 32333 USA Tel 850-539-3843 (phone/fax)
E-mail: 2549@bellsouth.net
Web site: http://www.mindspring.com/~spiritfilled.

Spirit Rising, c/o Nicole Heyward, 1505 Hadley St., Houston, TX 77002 USA Tel 713-772-5175; Fax: 713-772-3034
E-mail: nicole.heyward@musicworldent.com.

Spring Arbor Distributors, Inc., Subs. of Ingram Industries Inc., 4271 Edison Ave., Chino, CA 91710 USA; 7315 Innovation Blvd., Fort Wayne, IN 46818-1371; 201 Ingram Dr., Roseburg, OR 97470-7148; Newbury Rd., East Windsor, CT 06088; 25420 Weakley Rd., Petersburg, VA 23803; 11333 E. 53rd Ave., Denver, CO 80239-2108; Edit Addr.: 1 Ingram Blvd., La Vergne, TN 37086-1976 USA Fax: 615-213-5192; Toll Free: 800-395-4340; 800-395-7234 (customer service)
E-mail: orders@springarbor.com.

Springer, *(978-0-387; 978-0-8176; 978-3-211; 978-3-540; 978-3-7908; 978-4-431; 978-1-85233; 978-1-84628; 978-1-4419; 978-1-4612; 978-1-4613; 978-1-4614; 978-1-4615; 978-1-4684; 978-1-4757; 978-1-4899; 978-1-58238; 978-1-4939; 978-1-5041; 978-1-0716)* Subs. of Springer Science+Business Media, Orders Addr.: P.O. Box 2485, Secaucus, NJ 07096-2485 USA Tel 201-348-4033; Fax: 201-348-4505; Toll Free: 800-777-4643; Edit Addr.: a/o Springer Nature, 233 Spring St., New York, NY 10013-1578 USA (SAN 203-2228) Tel 212-815-0249; 212-460-1500; Fax: 212-460-1575; Toll Free: 800-777-4643 Thomson Delmar Learning Distributes Blanchard & Loeb Nursing Videos Only
E-mail: Slu@Springer-ny.com; service-ny@springer.com; customerservice@springernature.com.com
Web site: http://www.springeronline.com; http://www.springer.com.

Springer-Verlag New York, Incorporated, *See* **Springer**

Springwater Bks., Orders Addr.: P.O. Box 194, Springwater, NY 14560-0194 USA (SAN 111-8900); Edit Addr.: Main St. & East Ave., Springwater, NY 14560-0194 USA (SAN 243-2412) Tel 716-669-2450.

Sprout, Inc., Orders Addr.: 430 Tenth St., NW, Suite 007, Atlanta, GA 30318 USA Tel 404-892-9600; Fax: 404-881-1383.

Square Deal Records, 303 Higuera St., San Luis Obispo, CA 93401-4209 USA (SAN 170-6799) Tel 805-543-3636; Fax: 805-543-3938; Toll Free: 800-253-4114
E-mail: sdrsslo@aol.com.

SRA/McGraw-Hill, *(978-0-07; 978-0-383)* Div. of The McGraw-Hill Education Group, Orders Addr.: 220 E. Daniel Dale Rd., DeSoto, TX 75115-2490 USA Fax: 972-228-1982; Toll Free: 800-843-8855; Edit Addr.: 8787 Orion Pl., Columbus, OH 43240-4027 USA Tel 614-430-6600; Fax: 614-430-6621; Toll Free: 800-468-5850
E-mail: sra@mcgraw-hill.com
Web site: https://www.sraonline.com.

Sri Aurobindo Association, Incorporated, *See* **Matagiri Sri Aurobindo Ctr.**

St. Marie's Gopher News Co., 9000 Tenth Ave., N., Minneapolis, MN 55427 USA (SAN 169-4103) Tel 612-546-5300; Fax: 612-546-1487.

St. Martin's Pr., *(978-0-312; 978-0-8050; 978-0-940687; 978-0-9603648; 978-1-55927; 978-1-58063; 978-1-58238; 978-1-4299; 978-1-250)* Div. of Holtzbrinck Pubs., Orders Addr.: 16365 James Madison Hwy., Gordonville, VA 22942 USA Tel 540-672-7600; Fax: 540-672-7540 (customer service); Toll Free Fax: 800-672-2054; Toll Free: 888-330-8477; Edit Addr.: 175 Fifth Ave., 20th Flr., New York, NY 10010 USA (SAN 200-2132) Tel 212-674-5151 (Trade Div.); 212-726-0200 (College Div.); Fax: 212-674-3179 (Trade Div.); 212-686-9491 (College Div.); Toll Free: 800-221-7945 (Trade Div.); 800-470-4767 (College Div.)
E-mail: webmaster@stmartins.com; enquiries@stmartins.com
Web site: http://www.stmartins.com; http://www.smpcollege.com.

St. Mary Seminary Bookstore, 28700 Euclid Ave., Wyckliffe, OH 44092 USA (SAN 169-667X) Tel 216-943-7600.

St Pauls/Alba Hse. Pubs., *(978-0-8189)* Div. of Society of St. Paul, 2187 Victory Blvd., Staten Island, NY 10314-6603 USA (SAN 201-2405) Tel 718-761-0047; Fax: 718-761-0057; 718-698-8390; Toll Free: 800-343-2522
E-mail: albabooks@aol.com
Web site: http://www.albahouse.org.

Stackpole Bks., *(978-0-8117)* 5067 Ritter Rd., Mechanicsburg, PA 17055 USA (SAN 202-5396) Tel 717-796-0411; Fax: 717-796-0412; Toll Free: 800-732-3669
E-mail: ccraley@stackpolebooks.com
Web site: http://www.stackpolebooks.com/.

Star Bright Bks., Inc., *(978-1-887734; 978-1-932065; 978-1-59572; 978-1-64909)* 13 Landsdowne, Cambridge , MA 02139 USA (SAN 254-5225) Tel 617-354-1300; Fax: 617-354-1399; Toll Free: 800-788-4439
E-mail: info@starbrightbooks.com; r.s.lambert@starbrightbooks.com
Web site: http://www.starbrightbooks.com.

StarCrossed Productions, *(978-0-9668483)* 14552 NW., 88 Pl., Miami, FL 33018 USA Tel 305-828-2619 Phone/Fax
E-mail: tinami@msn.com
Web site: http://www.cookiesisters.com.

Starkmann, Inc., 25-u Olympia Ave., Woburn, MA 01801 USA (SAN 126-6128) Tel 781-938-9643; Fax: 781-938 9647
E-mail: biggs@starkmann.co.uk.

Starmaster Co., 6911 Haverhill Dr., Knoxville, TN 37909 USA (SAN 108-1217) Tel 423-588-6661.

StarWalk Kids, 15 Cutter Mill Rd., Suite 242, Great Neck, NY 11021 USA.

State News Agency, 2750 Griffith Rd., Winston Salem, NC 27103-6418 USA (SAN 169-6424).

State Univ. of New York Pr., *(978-0-7914; 978-0-87395; 978-0-88706; 978-1-4384; 979-8-8558)* Orders Addr.: P.O. Box 960, Herndon, VA 20172-0960 USA (SAN 203-3496) Tel 703-661-1575; Fax: 703-996-1010; Toll Free Fax: 877-204-6074; Toll Free: 877-204-6073 (customer service); Edit Addr.: 22 Corporate Woods Blvd., 3rd Flr., Albany, NY 12211-2504 USA (SAN 658-1730) Tel 518-472-5000; Fax: 518-472-5038; Toll Free: 866-430-7869; 353 Broadway, State University Plaza, Albany, NY 12246 Tel 518-944-2803
E-mail: info@sunypress.edu; suny@presswarehouse.com; sharla.clute@sunypress.edu arla.clute@sunypress.edu;
Web site: http://www.sunypress.edu.

Steerforth Pr., *(978-0-944072; 978-1-58195; 978-1-883642; 978-1-58642)* 45 Lyme Rd. # 208, Hanover, NH 03755-1219 USA
E-mail: helga@steerforth.com; info@steerforth.com
Web site: http://www.steerforth.com.

Steiner, Rudolf College Pr/St. George Pubns., *(978-0-916786; 978-0-945803; 978-0-9818095)* 9200 Fair Oaks Blvd., Fair Oaks, CA 95628 USA (SAN 208-8371) Tel 916-961-3722; Fax: 916-961-3032
E-mail: claude.julien@steinercollege.edu; cbiatch@comcast.net
Web site: http://www.steinercollege.edu.

SteinerBooks, Inc., *(978-0-8334; 978-0-88010; 978-0-89345; 978-0-910142; 978-1-58420; 978-1-85584; 978-0-9701097; 978-0-9831984; 978-1-62148; 978-1-62151; 978-1-938685; 978-0-9969211; 978-1-7324613; 978-1-952166; 978-1-957569)* Orders Addr.: P.O. Box 960, Herndon, VA 20172-0960 USA Tel 703-661-1594 (orders); Fax: 702-661-1501; Toll Free Fax: 800-277-7947 (orders); Toll Free: 800-856-8664 (orders); Edit Addr.: 610 Main St., Suite 1, Great Barrington, MA 01230 USA Tel 413-528-8233; Fax: 413-528-8826; Fulfillment Addr.: 22883 Quicksilver Dr., Dulles, VA 20166 USA (SAN 253-9519) Tel 703-661-1529; Fax: 703-996-1010
E-mail: service@steinerbooks.org
Web site: http://www.steinerbooks.org.

Stenhouse Pubs., *(978-1-57110; 978-1-62531)* Div. of Highlights for Children, Orders Addr.: P.O. Box 11020, Portland, ME 04104-7020 USA (SAN 298-1580) Tel 207-253-1600; Fax: 207-253-5121; Toll Free Fax: 800-833-9164; Toll Free: 800-988-9812 (orders)
E-mail: jkilburn@stenhouse.com
Web site: http://www.stenhouse.com.

Sterling Publishing Co., Inc., *(978-0-8069; 978-1-4027; 978-1-60582; 978-1-4549; 978-1-61837; 978-1-9847; 978-1-6697)* 1166 Avenue of the Americas, 17th Flr., New York, NY 10036 USA (SAN 211-6324) Tel 212-532-7160 212-213-2495; Toll Free Fax: 800-775-8736 (warehouse); Toll Free: 800-367-9692; 800-542-7567; 33 E. 17th St., 5th Flr., New York, NY 10003 Tel 212-532-7160; Toll Free Fax: 800-542-7567; Toll Free: 800-367-9692 Do not confuse with companies with similar names in Falls Church, VA, Fallbrook, CA, Lewisville, TX
E-mail: custservice@sterlingpub.com; tradesales@sterlingpub.com
Web site: http://www.sterlingpublishing.com/.

Steuben Pr., 230 Primrose Ct. #3, Longmont, CO 80501 USA Tel 303-482-2060
E-mail: orders@steubenpress.com.

Stevens, Gareth Incorporated, *See* **Stevens, Gareth Publishing LLLP**

Stevens, Gareth Publishing LLLP, *(978-0-8368; 978-0-918831; 978-1-55532; 978-1-4339)* Orders Addr.: P.O. Box 360140, Strongsville, OH 44136-0140 USA Fax: 877-542-2596; Toll Free: 800-542-2595; Edit Addr.: 111 East 14th St., Suite 349, New York, NY 10003 USA (SAN 696-1592) Toll Free: 877-444-0210
E-mail: customerservice@gspub.com; hollyc@rosen.pub
Web site: http://www.garethstevens.com; http://www.garethstevensclassroom.com.

Stevens International, Orders Addr.: P.O. Box 126, Magnolia, NJ 08049 USA (SAN 631-3612) Tel 856-435-1555; Edit Addr.: 706 N. White Horse Pike, Magnolia, NJ 08049 USA
Web site: http://www.stevenshobby.com.

Stevens, Mark Industries, Div. of Christian World, Inc., 304 N. Meridian Ave., Suite 6, Oklahoma City, OK 73107 USA (SAN 631-127X) Toll Free: 800-654-6760.

STL Distribution North America, *See* **Send The Light Distribution LLC**

Stoneydale Pr. Publishing Co., *(978-0-912299; 978-1-931291; 978-1-938707)* Orders Addr.: P.O. Box 188, Stevensville, MT 59870 USA Tel 406-777-2729; Fax: 406-777-2521; Toll Free: 800-735-7006; Edit Addr.: 523 Main St., Stevensville, MT 59870 USA (SAN 265-3168)
E-mail: stoneydale@stoneydale.com; stoneydalepresspublishing@gmail.com; burklasvegas@aol.com
Web site: http://www.stoneydale.com.

Storey Books, *See* **Storey Publishing, LLC**

Storey Publishing, LLC, *(978-0-88266; 978-1-58017; 978-0-9674717; 978-1-60342; 978-1-61212; 978-1-63586)* Subs. of Workman Publishing Co., Inc., Orders Addr.: 210 Mass Moca Way, North Adams, MA 01247 USA (SAN 203-4158) Fax: 413-346-2198; Toll Free Fax: 800-865-3429; Toll Free: 800-827-7444; c/o Workman Publishing, 225 Varick St., New York, NY 10014-4381 Tel 212-614-7700; Toll Free Fax: 800-521-1832; Toll Free: 800-722-7202
E-mail: info@storey.com; sales@storey.com
Web site: http://www.storey.com.

Strang Communications Company, *See* **Charisma Media**

Strauss Consultants, 48 W. 25th St., 11th Flr., New York, NY 10010-2708 USA Toll Free Fax: 888-528-8273; Toll Free: 800-236-7918
E-mail: strausscon@aol.com.

Streamwood Distribution, P.O. Box 91011, Mobile, AL 36691 USA Tel 334-665-0022; Fax: 334-665-0570.

StreetLib USA, Inc., *(978-0-692-09834-9; 978-0-692-09835-6)* 65 30 Kissena Blvd., CEP Hall 2,

Tech Incubator, New York City, NY 11367 USA Tel 347-849-7672
E-mail: giacomo.dangelo@streetlib.com
Web site: https://streetlib.com.

Strelow, James C., 12588 Ivy Glen Ln., Garden Grove, CA 92841-4563 USA (SAN 132-4144).

Strisik, Nancy, 10 Main St., Rockport, MA 01966 USA Tel 978-546-7653.

Studio 2 Publishing, Inc., *(978-0-9763601; 978-0-9792455; 978-0-9815281; 978-0-9819874; 978-0-9826427; 978-0-9828175; 978-1-937013; 978-1-944413; 978-1-950082; 978-1-957159)* 2663 Byington Solway Rd., Knoxville, TN 37931 USA Tel 865-212-3797
E-mail: contact@studio2publishing.com
Web site: http://www.studio2publishing.com.

Studio Fun International, *(978-0-276; 978-0-7621; 978-0-88705; 978-0-88850; 978-0-89577; 978-1-57584; 978-1-57619)* Subs. of Reader's Digest Assn., Inc., Reader's Digest Rd., Pleasantville, NY 10570-7000 USA (SAN 283-2143) Tel 914-244-4800; Fax: 914-244-4841
Web site: http://www.readersdigestkids.com; http://www.studiofun.com/.

Stylus Publishing, LLC, *(978-1-57922; 978-1-887208; 978-0-9729394; 978-1-62036; 978-1-64267)* Orders Addr.: P.O. Box 605, Herndon, VA 20172-0605 USA; Edit Addr.: 22883 Quicksilver Dr., Sterling, VA 20166-2012 USA (SAN 299-1853) Tel 703-661-1581; Fax: 703-661-1501 Do not confuse with companies with the same name in Sunnyvale, CA, Quakertown, PA
E-mail: stylusmail@presswarehouse.com; jean.westcott@styluspub.com
Web site: http://www.styluspub.com.

Subscription Account, 84 Needham, Newton Highlands, MA 02161 USA (SAN 285-9424).

Subscription Hse., Inc., 209 Harvard St., Suite 407, Brookline, MA 02146-5005 USA (SAN 285-9343).

Subterranean Co., Orders Addr.: P.O. Box 160, Monroe, OR 97456 USA Fax: 541-847-6018
E-mail: subco@clipper.net.

Success Education Assn., Box 175, Roanoke, VA 24002 USA (SAN 159-9690).

Suite 3 Productions, 90 W. 100 N., Suite 13, Provo, UT 84501 USA Tel 801-472 — 6024.

Sun Life, *(978-0-937930)* 2399 Cool Springs Rd., Thaxton, VA 24174 USA (SAN 240-8333) Tel 540-586-4898.

Sunbelt Pubns., Inc., *(978-0-916251; 978-0-932653; 978-0-9606704; 978-0-9620402; 978-1-941384)* 1250 Fayette St., El Cajon, CA 92020-1511 USA (SAN 630-0790) Tel 619-258-4911; Fax: 619-258-4916; Toll Free: 800-626-6579
E-mail: info@sunbeltpub.com; sales@sunbeltpub.com; dyoung@sunbeltpub.com; mail@sunbeltpub.com
Web site: http://www.sunbeltpub.com; http://www.sunbeltbooks.com.

Sunburst Bks., Inc., Distributor of Florida Bks., 700 S. John Rodes Blvd., #D8, West Melbourne, FL 32904 USA Tel 321-409-0225; Fax: 321-728-2742
Web site: http://www.sunburstbooks.com.

Sunburst Communications, Inc., *(978-0-7805; 978-0-911831; 978-1-55636; 978-1-55826)* 400 Columbus Ave., Valhalla, NY 10595-1335 USA (SAN 213-5620) Toll Free: 800-431-1934
E-mail: webmaster@nysunburst.com
Web site: http://www.sunburst.com.

Sunburst Visual Media, *(978-1-59520)* Orders Addr.: P.O. Box 4455, Scottsdale, AZ 85261 USA Toll Free: 800-262-8837; Edit Addr.: P.O. Box 9120, Plainview, NY 11803-9020 USA
Web site: http://www.schoolspecialty.com.

Sunday School Board of the Southern Baptist Convention, *See* **Lifeway Christian Resources**

Sundaykool Bulletins, *(978-1-888824)* Div. of Griffin Publishing Co., 18022 Cowan, Suite 202, Irvine, CA 92614 USA (SAN 631-5046) Toll Free: 800-472-9741
E-mail: griffinbooks@earthlink.net
Web site: http://www.griffinpublishing.com.

Sunshine Harbor, 825 Glen Arden Way, Altamonte Springs, FL 32701 USA (SAN 159-6640) Tel 407-339-0401.

Swedenborg Foundation, Inc., *(978-0-87785)* 320 N. Church St., West Chester, PA 19380 USA (SAN 111-7920) Tel 610-430-3222; Fax: 610-430-7982
E-mail: editor@swedenborg.com
Web site: http://www.swedenborg.com.

Swenson, Jim, 2610 Riverside Ln., NE, Rochester, MN 55901 USA (SAN 285-9505).

Swift News Agency, Orders Addr.: P.O. Box 160, Poncha Springs, CO 81242 USA (SAN 282-3810); Edit Addr.: 338 E. Hwy. 50, Poncha Springs, CO 81242 USA (SAN 169-0639).

Syco Distribution, 9208A Venture Ct., Manassas, VA 20111-4804 USA.

Symmes Systems, *(978-0-916352; 978-0-9907312)* 3977 Briarcliff Rd., NE, Atlanta, GA 30345-2647 USA (SAN 169-1465) Tel 404-876-7260.

Syndistar, Inc., *(978-1-56230)* P.O. Box 3027, Hammond, LA 70404-3027 USA (SAN 298-007X) Toll Free: 800-841-9532
E-mail: webmaster@syndistar.com
Web site: http://www.syndistar.com.

Syracuse Univ. Pr., *(978-0-8156; 978-0-615-28768-3; 978-1-68445)* 621 Skytop Rd., Suite 110, Syracuse, NY 13244-5290 USA (SAN 206-9776) Tel 315-443-5534; Fax: 315-443-5545
E-mail: supress@syr.edu; arpfeiff@syr.edu
Web site: http://www.SyracuseUniversityPress.syr.edu.

T A Bookstore, *See* **Shea Bks.**

Taku Graphics, *(978-0-9717820; 978-0-9772297; 978-0-9801616; 978-0-9823450; 978-0-9846318; 978-0-9899679)* 5763 Glacier Hwy., Juneau, AK 99801 USA Tel 907-780-6310; Fax: 907-780-6314; Toll Free: 800-278-3291
E-mail: adele@takugraphics.com
Web site: http://www.takugraphics.com.

Tales of Wonder.com, 3037 Summer Oak Pl., Buford, GA 30518 USA (SAN 920-1246) Tel 770-904-2221; 770-904-2221; Toll Free: 866-796-6337
E-mail: service@towdistribution.com; rob@towdistribution.com
Web site: www.talesofwonder.com; http://www.towdistribution.com.

Tallahassee News Co., Inc., 3777 Hartsfield Rd., Tallahassee, FL 32303-1120 USA.

Tapeworm Video Distributor, Inc., 27833 Avenue Hopkins, Unit 6, Valencia, CA 91355-3407 USA (SAN 630-8767) Tel 805-257-4904; Fax: 805-257-4820; Toll Free: 800-367-8437
E-mail: sales@tapeworm.com
Web site: http://www.tapeworm.com.

Tatnuck BookSeller, The, 335 Chandler St., Worcester, MA 01602-3402 USA (SAN 169-3654) Tel 508-756-7644.

Tattered Cover Bookstore, 1628 16th St., Denver, CO 80202-1308 USA (SAN 631-0214) Toll Free: 800-833-9327 (ext. 250)
E-mail: roy@tatteredcover.com.

Taylor & Francis Group, *(978-0-335; 978-0-415; 978-0-8448; 978-0-85066; 978-0-89116; 978-0-903796; 978-0-905273; 978-1-56032; 978-1-85000; 978-1-59169; 978-1-315)* Orders Addr.: 7625 Empire Dr., Florence, KY 41042-2919 USA Toll Free Fax: 800-248-4724; Toll Free: 800-634-7064; 74 Rolark Dr., Scarborough, ON M1R 4G2 Tel 416-299-5388; Fax: 416-299-7531; Toll Free: 877-226-2237; Edit Addr.: 325 Chestnut St., Philadelphia, PA 19106 USA (SAN 241-9246) Tel 215-625-8900; Fax: 215-625-2940; 270 Madison Ave., 4th Flr., New York, NY 10016-0601
Web site: http://www.routledge-ny.com; http://www.crcpress.com; http://www.garlandscience.com; http://www.taylorandfrancis.com.

Taylor & Francis, Incorporated, *See* **Taylor & Francis Group**

TBN Enterprises, *See* **Ironside International Pubs., Inc.**

Teacher Created Materials, Inc., *(978-0-87673; 978-0-7439; 978-1-4333; 978-1-60401; 978-1-4807; 978-1-4938; 978-1-5164; 978-1-64290; 978-1-64335; 978-1-64406; 978-1-64491; 978-1-0876; 979-8-7659)* 5301 Oceanus Dr., Huntington Beach, CA 92649 USA (SAN 665-5270) Tel 714-891-2273; Fax: 714-230-7070; Toll Free Fax: 888-877-7606; Toll Free: 800-858-7339
E-mail: sozbat@tcmpub.com; rkarnik@tcmpub.com; Support@tcmpub.com; pubops@tcmpub.com
Web site: http://www.tcmpub.com; www.teachercreatedmaterials.com.

Teacher Created Resources, Inc., *(978-1-55734; 978-1-57690; 978-1-4206; 978-1-4570)* 12621 Western Ave., Garden Grove, CA 92841 USA Tel 714-891-1690; Fax: 800-525-1254; Toll Free: 800-662-4321
E-mail: custserv@teachercreated.com; lvenzon@teachercreated.com
Web site: http://www.teachercreated.com.

Teacher's Discovery, *(978-1-884473; 978-0-7560)* Div. of American Eagle Co., Inc., 2741 Paldan Dr., Auburn Hills, MI 48326 USA (SAN 631-4570) Tel 248-340-7210; Fax: 248-340-7212; Toll Free: 800-832-2437
Web site: http://www.teachersdiscovery-science.com; http://www.teachersdiscovery-english.com; http://www.teachersdiscovery-social studies.com; http://www.teachersdiscovery-foreignlanguage.com; http://www.teachersdiscovery.com.

Technical Bk. Co., P.O. Box 25934, Los Angeles, CA 90025-8994 USA (SAN 168-9851) Toll Free: 800-233-5150.

Techno Mecca, Inc., 4201 Wilshire Blvd., No. 620, Los Angeles, CA 90019 USA (SAN 631-7812) Tel 323-634-1650; Fax: 323-634-1655
E-mail: tjkim@tmecca.com
Web site: http://www.tmecca.com.

Temme Haus Pr., *(978-0-9727036)* 1784 Palm Ave., Stockton, CA 95205 USA (SAN 253-1925) Fax: 209-463-5527
E-mail: temmehaus1953@sbcglobal.net.

Temple News Agency, *See* **ETD KroMar Temple**

Tempo Bookstore, 4905 Wisconsin Ave., NW, Washington, DC 20016 USA Tel 202-363-6683; Fax: 202-363-6686
E-mail: Tempobookstore@usa.net; tempobookstore@usa.net.

Ten Speed Pr., *(978-0-89815; 978-0-913668; 978-1-58008; 978-1-60774)* Div. of Crown Publishing Group, Orders Addr.: P.O. Box 7123, Berkeley, CA 94707 USA (SAN 202-7674) Fax: 510-559-1629 (orders); Toll Free: 800-841-2665; 555 Richmond St., W. Suite 405, Box 702, Toronto, ON M5V 3B1 Tel 416-703-7775; Fax: 416-703-9992
E-mail: order@tenspeed.com; alan@tenspeed.ca
Web site: http://www.tenspeed.com.

teNeues Publishing Co., *(978-3-570; 978-3-8238; 978-3-929278; 978-3-8327; 978-1-933427; 978-1-60160; 978-1-62325; 978-3-96171)* 7 W. 18th St., New York, NY 10011 USA (SAN 245-176X) Tel 212-627-9090; Fax: 212-627-9511; Toll Free: 800-352-0305; 12 Ferndene Rd., London, SE24 0AQ
E-mail: tnp@teneues-usa.com
Web site: http://www.teneues.com.

Territory Titles, 22 Camino Real, Sandia Park, NM 87047 USA.

Tesla Bk. Co., *(978-0-914119; 978-0-9603536)* P.O. Box 121873, Chula Vista, CA 91912-6573 USA (SAN 241-8703) Tel 619-585-8487; Toll Free: 800-398-2056
E-mail: bfeuling@teslabook.com.

Teva Nature, 2344 Black Oak Ct., Sarasota, FL 34232 USA (SAN 631-4619) Tel 941-377-7414; Fax: 941-371-6237; Toll Free: 800-924-8382.

Texas A&M Univ. Pr., *(978-0-89096; 978-1-58544; 978-1-60344; 978-1-62349; 978-1-64843)* 4354 TAMU John H. Lindsey Bldg., Lewis St., College Station, TX 77843-4354 USA (SAN 658-1919) Tel 979-458-3975; Fax: 979-847-8752; Toll Free Fax: 888-617-2421 (orders); Toll Free: 800-826-8911 (orders)
E-mail: katie.duelm@tamu.edu
Web site: http://www.tamupress.com.

Texas Art Supply, 2001 Montrose Blvd., Houston, TX 77006 USA (SAN 169-8303) Tel 713-526-5221; Fax: 713-524-7474; Toll Free: 800-888-9278
E-mail: info@texasart.com
Web site: http://www.texasart.com.

Texas Bk. Co., Orders Addr.: 2601 King, Greenville, TX 75401 USA (SAN 103-4308) Tel 903-455-6969; Fax: 903-454-4775; US Naval Academy/TBC, 5th Wing Bancroft Hall/Textbook, 101 Wilson Rd., Anapolis, MD 21402 (SAN 920-8461) Tel 903-455-6969 ext 642; TBC-NWLTC Bookstore-810 8501 Technology Cir. - Unit 810, Greenville, TX 75402 (SAN 920-9050) Tel 903-455-6969; TBC - #820 Sowela Bookstore 3824 Sen. J. Bennett Johnston Ave., Lake Charles, LA 70615 (SAN 920-9069); TBC-Trenholm State Tech. Coll Bookstore-830 8501 Technology Circle-Unit 830, Greenville, TX 75402 (SAN 920-9077) Tel 903-455-6969; TBC-Drake State Tech College Bookstore-831 8501 Technology Circle-Unit 831, Greenville, TX 75402 (SAN 920-9085) Tel 903-455-6969; Edit Addr.: P.O. Box 212, Greenville, TX 75403 USA Fax: 903-454-2442; Toll Free: 800-527-1016
E-mail: monica@texasbook.com; diana@texasbook.com; molson@texasbook.com.

Texas Bookman, The, *(978-1-931040)* 2700 Lone Star Dr., Dallas, TX 75212-6209 USA (SAN 106-875X) Toll Free: 800-566-2665
E-mail: texas.bookman@halfpricebooks.com.

Texas Hill Country Cookbook, P.O. Box 126, Round Mountain, TX 78663 USA (SAN 110-831X) Tel 210-825-3242; Fax: 210-825-3244; Toll Free: 800-231-3553.

Texas Library Bk. Sales, 1408 West Koenig Lane, Austin, TX 78756 USA (SAN 169-8044) Tel 512-452-4140.

Textbooks On Demand, *See* **Reprint Services Corp.**

TextStream, *(978-0-7351)* Div. of Baker & Taylor Bks., Orders Addr.: c/o Baker & Taylor Digital Media Services, 1120 US Hwy., 22 E., Bridgewater, NJ 08807 USA Tel 908-541-7035; Toll Free Fax: 800-648-0541; Toll Free: 800-775-1800; Edit Addr.: P.O. Box 6885, Bridgewater, NJ 08807-0885 USA
E-mail: btinfo@baker-taylor.com
Web site: http://www.baker-taylor.com/textstream.

TFH Pubns., Inc., *(978-0-7938; 978-0-86622; 978-0-87666; 978-1-85279)* Orders Addr.: One TFH Plaza, Third & Union Aves., Neptune City, NJ 07753 USA (SAN 202-7720) Tel 732-988-8400; Fax: 732-988-5466; Toll Free: 800-631-2188 (outside New Jersey); Edit Addr.: P.O. Box 427, Neptune, NJ 07753 USA (SAN 658-1862)
E-mail: info@tfh.com
Web site: http://www.tfh.com.

Thames Bk. Co., 1 Quarry Rd., Mystic, CT 06355-3200 USA (SAN 169-0760).

Tharpa Pubns. USA, *(978-0-9789067; 978-0-9817277; 978-1-61606)* 47 Sweeney Rd., Glen Spey, NY 12737 USA Tel 845-856-5102; Fax: 845-856-2110; Toll Free: 888-741-3475
E-mail: sales.us@tharpa.com
Web site: http://www.tharpa.com.

The Child's World, Inc., *See* **Child's World, Inc, The**

The Foundry Publishing, *(978-0-8341)* Orders Addr.: 2345 Grand Blvd., Suite 1900, Kansas City, MO 64108 USA (SAN 253-0902) Tel 816-931-1900; Edit Addr.: P.O. Box 419527, Kansas City, MO 64141 USA (SAN 202-9022) Tel 816-931-1900; Fax: 816-531-0923; Toll Free Fax: 800-849-9827; Toll Free: 800-877-0700
E-mail: heather@nph.com
Web site: http://www.bhillkc.com; http://www.nph.com.

Theatre Communications Group, Inc., *(978-0-88754; 978-0-913745; 978-0-930452; 978-1-55936; 978-1-84002; 978-1-85459; 978-1-870259; 978-1-899791; 978-1-63670)* 355 Lexington Ave., New York, NY 10017-6603 USA (SAN 210-9387) Tel 212-697-5230; Fax: 212-983-4847
Web site: http://www.tcg.org.

Theme Stream, Inc., P.O. Box 142, Broomfield, CT 06002 USA Tel 860-243-5200
Web site: http://www.themestream.com.

Theological Bk. Service, P.O. Box 509, Barnhart, MO 63012 USA (SAN 631-6662) Tel 636-464-2500; Fax: 636-464-8449; Toll Free Fax: 800-325-9526; Toll Free: 877-484-1600
E-mail: tbs@execpc.com
Web site: http://www.theobooks.org.

Thieme Medical Pubs., Inc., *(978-0-86577; 978-0-913258; 978-1-58890; 978-1-60406; 978-1-62623; 978-1-68420; 978-1-63853; 979-8-88500)* Subs. of Georg Thieme Verlag Stuttgart, 333 Seventh Ave., 18th Flr., New York, NY 10001 USA (SAN 169-5983) Tel 212-760-0888; Fax: 212-947-1112; Toll Free: 800-782-3488 (orders only)
E-mail: customerservice@thieme.com
Web site: http://www.thieme.com.

Thieme-Stratton, Inc., *See* **Thieme Medical Pubs., Inc.**

Thinkers' Pr., Inc., *(978-0-938650; 978-1-888710)* Orders Addr.: P.O. Box 8, Davenport, IA 52805-0008 USA Tel 319-323-1226; Fax: 319-323-0511; Toll Free: 800-397-7117 (orders only); Edit Addr.: 1524 Leclaire St., Davenport, IA 52803-4428 USA (SAN 162-7759)
E-mail: tpi@chessco.com
Web site: http://www.chessco.com.

Thistle Hill Pubns., *(978-0-9705511)* 477 Thistle Hill Rd., North Pomfret, VT 05053-0307 USA Tel 802-457-2050; Fax: 802-457-3653; Fulfillment Addr.: P.O. Box 428, White River Junction, VT 05001 USA
E-mail: thp@together.net
Web site: http://www.thistlehillpub.com.

Thomas Brothers Maps, *(978-0-88130; 978-1-58174)* Div. of Rand McNally & Co., 17731 Cowan, Irvine, CA 92614 USA (SAN 158-8192) Fax: 949-757-1564; Toll Free: 800-899-6277
Web site: http://www.thomas.com.

Thompson Schl. Bk. Depository, Orders Addr.: P.O. Box 60160, Oklahoma City, OK 73146 USA (SAN 159-9747) Tel 405-525-9458; Fax: 405-524-5443; Edit Addr.: 39 NE 24th St., Oklahoma City, OK 73143 USA.

Thomson Delmar Learning, *See* **Delmar Cengage Learning**

Thomson Gale, *See* **Cengage Gale**

Thomson Learning, *See* **CENGAGE Learning**

Thomson, Linda, P.O. Box 1225, Orem, UT 84059-1225 USA (SAN 110-3881) Tel 801-226-0155; Fax: 801-226-0166; Toll Free: 800-226-0155.

Thomson Peterson's, *See* **Peterson's**

Thomson West, *See* **West**

Thorndike Pr., *(978-0-7838; 978-0-7862; 978-0-8161; 978-0-89621; 978-1-56054; 978-1-4104)* Div. of Gale Group, 295 Kennedy Memorial Dr., Waterville, ME 04901 USA Tel 207-859-1053; 207-859-1020; 207-859-1000; Toll Free Fax: 800-558-4676; Toll Free: 800-223-1244 (ext. 15); 800-877-4253 (customer resource ctr.)
E-mail: jamie.knobloch@gale.com; barb.littfield@galegroup.com; Betsy.M.Brown@thomson.com; jamie.knobloch@cengage.com
Web site: http://www.gale.com/thorndike.

Tiffin News Agency, 34 Kennat Blvd., Tiffin, OH 44883-4604 USA (SAN 169-6866).

Tiger Bk. Distributors, Ltd., 328 S. Jefferson, Chicago, IL 60661 USA (SAN 631-0672) Tel 312-382-1160; Fax: 312-382-0323.

TI-Holdings Distribution Co., 4 Hopscotch Ln., Savannah, GA 31411 USA.

Timber Pr., Inc., *(978-0-88192; 978-0-917304; 978-0-931146; 978-0-931340; 978-1-60469; 978-1-64326)* Div. of Workman Publishing Co., Inc., 133 SW Second Ave., Suite 450, Portland, OR 97204-3527 USA (SAN 216-082X) Tel 503-227-2878; Fax: 503-227-3070; Toll Free: 800-327-5680; 20 Lonsdale Rd Swavesey, London, NW6 6RD Tel (01954) 232959; Fax: (01954) 206040
E-mail: info@timberpress.co.uk; publicity@timberpress.com
Web site: http://www.timberpress.com.

Time Home Entertainment, Incorporated, *See* **Time Inc. Bks.**

Time Inc. Bks., *(978-1-883013; 978-1-929049; 978-1-931933; 978-1-932273; 978-1-932994; 978-1-933405; 978-1-933821; 978-1-60320; 978-1-61893; 978-1-68330; 978-1-5478)* Div. of Time, Inc., 1271 Avenue of the Americas, New York, NY 10020-1201 USA (SAN 227-3209); 225 Liberty St., New York, NY 10281.

Time Warner Book Group, *See* **Hachette Bk. Group**

Time-Life Publishing Warehouse, 5240 W. 76th, Indianapolis, IN 43268-4137 USA (SAN 631-1504) Fax: 717-348-6409; Toll Free: 800-277-8844
Web site: http://www.timelifecs.com; http://www.timelifeedu.com.

TIS, Inc., *(978-0-89917; 978-1-56581; 978-0-7421)* Orders Addr.: P.O. Box 669, Bloomington, IN 47402 USA Tel 812-332-3307; Fax: 812-331-7690; Toll Free: 800-367-4002; Edit Addr.: 5005 N. State Rd. 37 Business, Bloomington, IN 47404 USA.

Titan Bookstore, P.O. Box 34080, Fullerton, CA 92634-9480 USA (SAN 106-4851).

Title Bks., Inc., 3013 Second Ave. S, Birmingham, AL 35233 USA (SAN 168-9207) Tel 205-324-2596.

TLC Distributors, P.O. Box 434, Lake Dallas, TX 75065 USA.

Tobias News Co., 130 18th St., Rock Island, IL 61201 USA (SAN 169-2186) Tel 309-788-7517.

Todd Communications, *(978-1-57833; 978-1-878100)* 611 E. 12th Ave. Ste. 102, Anchorage, AK 99501-4663 USA (SAN 298-6280)
E-mail: editor@toddcom.com.

Topical Review Bk Co., Inc., *(978-1-929099; 978-1-939246; 978-1-962663)* P.O. Box 328, Onsted, MI 49265 USA Tel 517-547-8072; Fax: 517-547-7512
E-mail: topicalrbc@aol.com
Web site: www.topicalrbc.com.

Total Information, Inc., 844 Dewey Ave., Rochester, NY 14613 USA (SAN 123-7373) Tel 716-254-0621.

T.R. Bks., Orders Addr.: P.O. Box 310279, New Braunfels, TX 78131 USA (SAN 630-4885) Tel 830-625-2665; Fax: 830-620-0470; Toll Free: 800-659-4710; Edit Addr.: P.O. Box 310279, New Braunfels, TX 78131-0279 USA
E-mail: trbooks@trbooks.com
Web site: http://www.trbooks.com.

T.R. Trading Co., *See* **T.R. Bks.**

Tracor Technology Resources (TTR), Specialized Bk. Distributors, 1601 Research Blvd., Rockville, MD 20850 USA (SAN 169-3220) Tel 301-251-4970.

Trafalgar Square Publishing, *(978-0-943955; 978-1-57076)* Orders Addr.: P.O. Box 257, North Pomfret, VT 05053-0257 USA (SAN 213-8859) Tel 802-457-1911; Fax: 802-457-1913; Toll Free: 800-423-4525; Edit Addr.: 388 Howe Hill Rd., North Pomfret, VT 05053 USA Tel 802-423-4525; 802-457-1913
E-mail: tsquare@sover.net
Web site: http://www.trafalgarbooks.com; http://www.horseandriderbooks.com.

Trajectory, Inc., *(978-1-62028; 978-1-62665; 978-1-62978; 978-1-63209; 978-1-68100; 978-1-68124)* 50 Doaks Lane, Marblehead, MA 01945 USA Tel 781-476-2100
E-mail: info@trajectory.com; bob@trajectory.com
Web site: http://www.trajectory.com.

Trans World News, 3700 Kelley Ave., Cleveland, OH 44114-4533 USA (SAN 169-6688) Tel 216-391-4800; Fax: 216-391-9911; Toll Free: 800-321-9858.

Transaction Pubs., *(978-0-7658; 978-0-87855; 978-0-88738; 978-1-56000; 978-1-4128)* Div. of Taylor & Francis Group, Orders Addr.: Taylor & Francis Group LLC 7625 Empire

Dr., Florence, KY 41042-2919 USA Toll Free Fax: 800-248-4724; Toll Free: 800-634-7064
E-mail: orders@transactionpub.com
Web site: http://www.transactionpub.com.

Transamerican & Export News Co., 12345 World Trade Dr., San Diego, CA 92128-3743 USA (SAN 169-0140).

Trans-Atlantic Pubns., Inc., 33 Ashley Dr., Schwenksville, PA 19473 USA (SAN 694-0234) Tel 215-717-4655; Fax: 484-919-6486 Do not confuse with Transatlantic Arts, Inc., Albuquerque, NM
E-mail: order@transatlanticpub.com
Web site: http://www.transatlanticpub.com.

Traveler Restaurant, 741 Buckley Hwy., Union, CT 06076 USA (SAN 111-8218) Tel 860-684-4920.

Treasure Chest Bks., P.O. Box 5250, Tucson, AZ 85703-0250 USA Tel 520-623-9558; Fax: 520-624-5888; Toll Free Fax: 800-715-5888; Toll Free: 800-969-9558.

Treasure Chest Books, *See* **Rio Nuevo Pubs.**

Treasure Valley News, 4242 S. Eagleson Rd. Ste. 108B, Boise, ID 83705-4985 USA.

Tree Frog Trucking Co., 7983 SE 13th Ave., Portland, OR 97202-6665 USA (SAN 169-7188).

Tree Hse. Distribution, 1007 Perrywill Ave., Salt Lake City, UT 84124-2428 USA (SAN 631-6603) Fax: 801-262-2324; Toll Free: 888-299-7895.

Tree of Life Midwest, P.O. Box 2629, Bloomington, IN 47402-2629 USA (SAN 169-7994) Toll Free: 800-999-4200.

Tremendous Life Bks., *(978-0-937539; 978-1-933715; 978-1-936354)* Div. of Life Management Services, Inc., 206 West Allen St., Mechanicsburg, PA 17055-6240 USA (SAN 156-5419) Tel 717-766-9499; Fax: 717-766-6565; Toll Free: 800-233-2665
E-mail: JLiller@TremendousLifeBooks.com
Web site: http://www.TremendousLifeBooks.com.

Tres Americas Bks., Orders Addr.: 4336 N. Pulaski Rd., Chicago, IL 60641 USA Tel 773-481-9090.

T-Rex Products, 2391 Boswell Rd., Chula Vista, CA 91914-3509 USA.

Triangle News Co., Inc., 3498 Grand Ave., Pittsburgh, PA 15225 USA (SAN 169-7447).

Tri-County News Co., Inc., 1376 W. Main St., Santa Maria, CA 93458 USA (SAN 169-0345) Tel 805-925-6541; Fax: 805-925-3565
E-mail: trico2000@aol.com
Web site: http://tri-countynews.com.

TriLiteral, LLC, 100 Maple Ridge Dr., Cumberland, RI 02864-1796 USA (SAN 631-8126) Tel 401-531-2800; 401-531-2804 (Credit & Collections); 401-658-4226; Fax: 401-531-2801; 401-531-2803 (Credit & Collections); 401-658-4193; Toll Free Fax: 800-406-9145; Toll Free: 800-405-1619
E-mail: rich.swafford@triliteral.org; customer.care@Triliteral.org
Web site: http://www.triliteral.org/.

Triple Tail Publishing, *See* **Farcountry Pr.**

Tri-State News Agency, P.O. Box 778, Johnson City, TN 37601 USA (SAN 169-7897) Tel 423-926-8159; 604 Rolling Hills Dr., Johnson City, TN 37601 (SAN 282-4744).

Tri-State Periodicals, Inc., Orders Addr.: P.O. Box 1110, Evansville, IN 47706-1110 USA Tel 812-867-7416; Edit Addr.: 9844 Heddon Rd., Evansville, IN 47711 USA (SAN 241-7537) Tel 812-867-7419.

Trucatriche, Orders Addr.: 3800 Main St., Suite 8, Chula Vista, CA 91911 USA Tel 619-426-2690; Fax: 619-426-2695
E-mail: info@trucatriche.com
Web site: http://www.trucatriche.com.

Truth Pubns., Orders Addr.: 8105 NW 23rd Ave., Gainesville, FL 32606 USA Tel 352-376-6320; Fax: 352-376-7105 Do not confuse with companies with the same or similar name in Paris, TX, Lombard, IL, Philadelphia, PA, Springfield, MO, Woodstock, MO
E-mail: upgflorida@juno.com.

Tulare County News, 13595 El Nogal Ave., Visalia, CA 93292-9352 USA (SAN 169-0442) Toll Free: 800-479-6006.

Turner Subscription Agency, Subs. of Dawson Holdings PLC, 15 S. West Park., Westwood, MA 02090-1524 USA (SAN 107-7112) Toll Free: 800-847-4201
E-mail: postmaster@dawson.com.

Turtleback Bks., *(978-0-613; 978-0-7857; 978-0-8085; 978-0-8335; 978-0-88103; 978-1-4176; 978-1-4177; 978-1-4178)* Sub. of GL group, Inc., 1230 Macklind Ave., Saint Louis, MO 63110-1432 USA (SAN 159-947X) Tel 314-644-6100; Fax: 314-647-2845; Toll Free: 800-458-8438
E-mail: info@sanval.com; rheflin@turtleback.com
Web site: http://www.Turtleback.com.

Tuttle Publishing, *(978-0-8048; 978-1-4629; 978-1-955634)* Orders Addr.: 364 Innovation Dr., North Clarendon, VT 05759 USA (SAN 213-2621) Tel 802-773-8930; Fax: 802-773-6993; Toll Free Fax: 800-329-8885; Toll Free: 800-526-2778
E-mail: info@tuttlepublishing.com
Web site: http://www.tuttlepublishing.com.

Twentieth Century Christian Bks., *(978-0-89098)* 2809 Granny White Pike, Nashville, TN 37204 USA (SAN 206-2550) Tel 615-383-3842.

Twenty First Century Pubns., *(978-0-933278)* Orders Addr.: P.O. Box 702, Fairfield, IA 52556-0702 USA Tel 515-472-5105; Fax: 515-472-8443; Toll Free: 800-593-2665; Edit Addr.: 401 N. Fourth St., Fairfield, IA 52556 USA Do not confuse with Twenty First Century Pubns., Tolland, CT
E-mail: books21st@lisco.com
Web site: http://www.21stbooks.com.

Twenty-First Century Antiques, Orders Addr.: P.O. Box 70, Hatfield, MA 01038 USA (SAN 110-8085); Edit Addr.: 11 1/2 Main St., Hatfield, MA 01038 USA (SAN 243-248X) Tel 413-247-9396.

Twenty-Third Pubns./Bayard, *(978-0-89622; 978-1-58595; 978-1-62785)* 1 Montauk Ave. No. 20, New London, CT 06320-4967 USA (SAN 658-2052) Toll Free Fax: 800-572-0788; Toll Free: 800-321-0411
E-mail: kerry.moriarty@bayard-inc.com
Web site: http://www.23rdpublications.com.

Twin City News Agency, Inc., P.O. Box 466, Lafayette, IN 47902-0466 USA Tel 765-742-1051.

Two Rivers Distribution, Div. of Ingram Content Group, Orders Addr.: 210 American Dr., Jackson, TN 38301 USA Toll Free Fax: 800-351-5073 (Customer Service); Toll Free: 866-400-5351 (Customer Service); 800-343-4499
E-mail: pd_orderentry@ingramcontent.com; ips@ingramcontent.com
Web site: http://www.tworiversdistribution.com/.

Tyndale Hse. Pubs., *(978-0-8423; 978-1-4143; 978-1-4964; 978-1-7358909; 979-8-4005)* Orders Addr.: 351 Executive Dr., Carol Stream, IL 60188 USA; Edit Addr.: 351 Executive Dr., Carol Stream, IL 60188 USA (SAN 206-7749) Tel 630-668-8310; Fax: 630-668-3245; Toll Free: 800-323-9400
E-mail: international@tyndale.com; permission@tyndale.com; mikeedelstein@tyndale.com
Web site: http://www.tyndale.com.

Ubiquity Distributors, Inc., 607 Degraw St., Brooklyn, NY 11217 USA (SAN 200-7428) Tel 718-875-5491; Fax: 718-875-8047.

Ultra Bks., P.O. Box 945, Oakland, NJ 07436 USA (SAN 112-9074) Tel 201-337-8787.

Ulverscroft Large Print Bks., Ltd., *(978-0-7089; 978-1-84617)* Orders Addr.: P.O. Box 1230, West Seneca, NY 14224-1230 USA; Edit Addr.: 950 Union Rd., West Seneca, NY 14224-3438 USA (SAN 208-3035) Toll Free: 800-955-9659
E-mail: enquiries@ulverscroft.co.uk; sales@ulverscroft.com
Web site: http://www.ulverscroft.co.uk.

Unarius Academy of Science Pubns., *(978-0-932642; 978-0-935097)* Orders Addr.: 145 S. Magnolia Ave., El Cajon, CA 92020-4522 USA (SAN 168-9614) Tel 619-444-7062; Fax: 619-444-9637; Toll Free: 800-475-7062
E-mail: uriel@unarius.org
Web site: http://www.unarius.org.

Underground Railroad, The, 2769 Club House Rd., Mobile, AL 36605-4373 USA (SAN 630-7892) Tel 334-432-8811.

Unifacmanu International Trading Co., Inc., 22 Cross Ridge Rd., Chappaqua, NY 10514 USA (SAN 631-743X)
E-mail: unifacmanu@att.net
Web site: http://www.bookvariety.com.

Unique Bks., Inc., 5010 Kemper Ave., Saint Louis, MO 63139 USA (SAN 630-0472) Tel 314-776-6695; Fax: 314-776-0841; Toll Free: 800-533-5446.

United Magazine, Orders Addr.: P.O. Box 36, Columbia, KY 42728-0036 USA (SAN 169-2852) Tel 502-384-3444; Fax: 502-384-9324; Edit Addr.: 361 Industrial Park Rd., Louisville, KY 42728-0036 USA (SAN 250-3336).

United Methodist Publishing Hse., *(978-1-63088)* 201 Eighth Ave., S., Nashville, TN 37203 USA Tel 615-749-6000; Fax: 615-749-6079; Toll Free Fax: 800-836-7802; Toll Free: 800-672-1789 (orders only)
Web site: http://www.umph.org; http://www.abingdonpress.com.

United Nations Pubns., *(978-0-680; 978-0-89714; 978-92-1; 978-952-9520)* 300 E. 42nd St., 9th Flr., New York, NY 10017 USA (SAN 206-6718) Tel 212-963-8302; 212-963-7680 UN Bookshop; Fax: 212-963-3489; 212-963-4910 UN Bookshop; Toll Free: 800-253-9646 (bookshop orders); 800-553-3210 UN Bookshop
E-mail: publications@un.org
Web site: https://unp.un.org/.

United News Co., Inc., 111 Lake St., P.O. Box 3426, Bakersfield, CA 93305 USA (SAN 169-7579) Tel 805-323-7864.

United Society of Shakers, *(978-0-915836)* 707 Shaker Rd., New Gloucester, ME 04260 USA (SAN 158-619X) Tel 207-926-4597; Fax: 207-926-3559
E-mail: sdlshakers@aol.com
Web site: http://www.shaker.lib.me.us.

United States Government Printing Office, *(978-0-16; 978-0-18)* Orders Addr.: P.O. Box 371954, Pittsburgh, PA 15250-7954 USA (SAN 658-0785) Tel 202-512-1800; Fax: 202-512-2250; Toll Free: 866-512-1800; Edit Addr.: USGPO Stop SSMB, Washington, DC 20401 USA (SAN 206-152X) Tel 202-512-1705 (bibliographic information only); 202-512-2268 (book dealers only); Fax: 202-512-1655
E-mail: orders@gpo.gov; rdavis@gpo.gov; ContactCenter@gpo.gov
Web site: http://bookstore.gpo.gov; https://www.gpo.gov.

United Subscription Service, 527 Third Ave., No. 284, New York, NY 10016-4100 USA (SAN 286-0104).

Univ of Arizona Critical Languages Program, 1230 N. Park Ave., Suite 102, Tucson, AZ 85719 USA.

Univ. of Arkansas Pr., *(978-0-938626; 978-1-55728; 978-1-61075; 978-1-68226)* 105 N. McIlroy Ave., Fayetteville, AR 72701 USA (SAN 239-3972) Tel 479-575-7544; Fax: 479-575-6044; Toll Free: 800-626-0090
E-mail: info@uapress.com
Web site: http://www.uapress.com; http://www.uark.edu/~uaprinfo.

Univ. of California Pr., *(978-0-520; 978-1-7323203)* 155 Grand Ave., Suite 400, Oakland, CA 94612-3758 USA Tel 510-883-8232 (Books & Journals); Fax: 510-836-8910
E-mail: journals@ucpress.edu; orders@cpfsinc.com; askucp@ucpress.edu
Web site: http://www.ucpress.edu.

Univ. of Chicago Pr., *(978-0-226; 978-0-89065; 978-0-943056; 978-1-892850)* Orders Addr.: 11030 S. Langley Ave., Chicago, IL 60628 USA (SAN 202-5280) Tel 773-702-7000; Fax: 773-702-7212; Toll Free Fax: 800-621-8476 (US & Canada); Toll Free: 800-621-2736 (US & Canada); Edit Addr.: 1427 E. 60th St., Chicago, IL 60637 USA (SAN 202-5299) Tel 773-702-7700; 773-702-7748 (Marketing & Sales); Fax: 773-702-9756
E-mail: general@press.uchicago.edu; kh@press.uchicago.edu; custserv@press.uchicago.rdu; sales@press.uchicago.edu; marketing@press.uchicago.edu; publicity@press.uchicago.edu
Web site: http://www.press.uchicago.edu.

Univ. of Chicago Pr. Distribution Clients, 1427 East 60th Street, Chicago, IL 60637 USA
E-mail: tmcgraw@press.uchicago.edu.

Univ. of Georgia Pr., *(978-0-8203)* Orders Addr.: 4435 Atlanta Hwy. West Dock, Athens, GA 30602 USA; Edit Addr.: Main Library, Third Flr. 320 S. Jackson St., Athens, GA 30602 USA (SAN 203-3054) Fax: 706-542-2558; Toll Free: 800-266-5842
E-mail: books@uga.edu
Web site: http://www.ugapress.org.

Univ. of Hawaii Pr., *(978-0-8248; 978-0-87022)* Orders Addr.: 2840 Kolowalu St., Honolulu, HI 96822-1888 USA (SAN 202-5353) Tel 808-956-8255; Fax: 808-988-6052; Toll Free Fax: 800-650-7811; Toll Free: 888-847-7377
E-mail: uhpmkt@hawaii.edu; uhpbooks@hawaii.edu
Web site: http://www.uhpress.hawaii.edu.

Univ. of Massachusetts Pr., *(978-0-87023; 978-1-55849; 978-1-61376; 978-1-62534; 978-1-68575)* Orders Addr.: 180 Infirmary Way, 4th Fl, Amherst, MA 01003 USA (SAN 203-3089) Tel 413-545-2217 (editorial); Fax: 413-545-1226; Toll Free Fax: 800-537-5487
E-mail: info@umpress.umass.edu
Web site: www.umasspress.com.

Univ. of Michigan Library, *(978-1-125; 978-1-126; 978-1-127; 978-1-128; 978-1-129; 978-1-251; 978-1-252; 978-1-253; 978-1-254; 978-1-255; 978-1-4585)* 818 Hatcher St. S. University of Michigan, Ann Arbor, MI 48109-1205 USA Tel 734-764-9356; Fax: 734-763-5080
Web site: http://www.lib.umich.edu.

Univ. of Missouri Pr., *(978-0-8262)* 2910 LeMone Blvd., Columbia, MO 65201 USA (SAN 203-3143) Tel 573-882-7641; Fax: 573-884-4498; Toll Free: 800-828-1894 (orders only)
E-mail: rennerk@umsystem.edu; deandj@umsystem.edu
Web site: http://press.umsystem.edu.

Univ. of Nebraska Pr., *(978-0-8032; 978-1-4962; 978-1-64012)* Orders Addr.: 1111 Lincoln Mall, Lincoln, NE 68588-0630 USA Tel 402-472-3581; 402-472-7702; Fax: 402-472-6214; Toll Free Fax: 800-526-2617; Toll Free: 800-755-1105; Edit Addr.: P.O. Box 880630, Lincoln, NE 68588-0630 USA (SAN 202-5337)
E-mail: pressmail@unl.edu
Web site: http://www.nebraskapress.unl.edu; http://www.bisonbooks.com.

Univ. of New Mexico Pr., *(978-0-8263; 978-0-9766839)* Orders Addr.: 1312 Basehart Rd., SE, Albuquerque, NM 87106-4363 USA (SAN 213-9588) Tel 505-277-2346; 505-272-7777 (orders); Toll Free Fax: 800-622-8667; Toll Free: 800-249-7737 (orders)
E-mail: unmpress@unm.edu
Web site: http://www.unmpress.com.

Univ. of North Carolina Pr., *(978-0-8078; 978-1-4696; 979-8-89084; 979-8-89085; 979-8-89086; 979-8-89087; 979-8-89088)* c/o Longleaf Services, 116 S. Boundary St., Chapel Hill, NC 27514-3808 USA (SAN 203-3151) Tel 919-966-3561; Fax: 919-966-3829; Toll Free Fax: 800-272-6817; Toll Free: 800-848-6224
E-mail: uncpress@unc.edu
Web site: www.uncpress.org.

Univ. of Oklahoma Pr., *(978-0-8061; 979-8-8559)* Orders Addr.: 2800 Venture Dr., Norman, OK 73069-8218 USA Tel 405-325-2000; Fax: 405-364-5798; Toll Free Fax: 800-735-0476; Toll Free: 800-627-7377
E-mail: presscs@ou.edu
Web site: http://www.oupress.com.

Univ. of Pennsylvania Pr., *(978-0-8122; 978-1-5128)* Orders Addr.: c/o Hopkins Fulfillment Srvc., Hopkins Fulfillment Service, Baltimore, MD 21211-4370 USA Tel 410-516-6948; Fax: 410-516-6998; Toll Free: 800-537-5487; Edit Addr.: 3905 Spruce St., Philadelphia, PA 19104-4112 USA (SAN 202-5345) Tel 215-898-6261; Fax: 215-898-0404; Toll Free: 800-537-5487 (book orders)
E-mail: custserv@pobox.upenn.edu
Web site: http://www.upenn.edu/pennpress.

Univ. of Tennessee Pr., *(978-0-87049; 978-1-57233; 978-1-62190)* Div. of Univ. of Tennessee & Member of Assn. of American Univ. Presses, Orders Addr.: 11030 S. Langley, Chicago, IL 60628 USA Tel 773-568-1550; Toll Free Fax: 800-621-8471; Toll Free: 800-621-2736 (orders only); Edit Addr.: 110 Conference Ctr. Bldg., Knoxville, TN 37996-0325 USA (SAN 212-9930) Tel 865-974-3321; Fax: 865-974-3724
E-mail: tpost@utk.edu
Web site: http://www.utpress.org.

Univ. of Texas Pr., *(978-0-292; 978-1-4773)* Orders Addr.: P.O. Box 7819, Austin, TX 78713-7819 USA (SAN 212-9876) Tel 512-471-7233; Fax: 512-232-7178; Toll Free: 800-252-3206; Edit Addr.: University of Texas at Austin 2100 Comal, Austin, TX 78722 USA
E-mail: info@utpress.utexas.edu
Web site: http://www.utexas.edu/utpress.

Univ. of Washington Pr., *(978-0-295; 978-1-902716)* Orders Addr.: P.O. Box 50096, Seattle, WA 98145-5096 USA (SAN 212-2502) Tel 206-543-4050; Fax: 206-543-3932; Toll Free Fax: 800-669-7993; Edit Addr.: P.O. Box 50096, Seattle, WA 98145-5096 USA Toll Free Fax: 800-669-7993; 1126 N. 98th St., Seattle, WA 98103
E-mail: uwpord@u.washington.edu
Web site: http://www.washington.edu/uwpress.

Univ. of Wisconsin Pr., *(978-0-299)* Orders Addr.: c/o Chicago Dist Ctr., 11030 S. Langley Ave., Chicago, IL 60628 USA Tel 773-568-1550; Fax: 773-660-2235; Toll Free Fax: 800-621-8476 (orders only); Toll Free: 800-621-2736 (orders only); Edit Addr.: 1930 Monroe St., 3rd Flr., Madison, WI 53711 USA Tel 608-263-1110; Fax: 608-263-1132
E-mail: uwiscpress@uwpress.wisc.edu
Web site: http://www.wisc.edu/wisconsinpress/.

Univ. Pr. of Florida, *(978-0-8130; 978-0-942084; 978-0-9760555; 978-1-61610; 978-1-942852; 978-1-68340)* Orders Addr.: 15 NW 15th St., Gainesville, FL 32611-0279 USA (SAN 207-9275) Tel 352-392-1351; Fax: 352-392-7302; Toll Free Fax: 800-680-1955; Toll Free: 800-226-3822
E-mail: press@upf.com; orders@upf.com
Web site: http://www.upf.com.

Univ. Pr. of Kentucky, *(978-0-8131; 978-0-912839; 978-0-916968; 978-1-9859; 978-1-949668; 978-1-949669; 978-1-950564; 978-1-950690)* Orders Addr.: Hopkins Fulfillment Services, Baltimore, MD 21211-4370 USA Tel 800-537-5487; Fax: 410-516-6998; Toll Free: 800-839-6855; Edit Addr.: 663 S. Limestone St., Lexington, KY 40508-4008 USA (SAN 203-3275) Tel 859-257-5200; Fax: 859-323-4981; Toll Free Fax: 800-870-4981
E-mail: twell1@email.uky.edu
Web site: http://www.kentuckypress.com.

Univ. Pr. of Mississippi, *(978-0-87805; 978-1-57806; 978-1-934110; 978-1-60473; 978-1-61703; 978-1-62103; 978-1-62674; 978-1-62846; 978-1-4968)* 3825 Ridgewood Rd., Jackson, MS 39211-6492 USA (SAN 203-1914) Tel 601-432-6205; Fax: 601-432-6217; Toll Free: 800-737-7788 (orders only)
E-mail: kburgess@ihl.state.ms.us; press@mississippi.edu
Web site: http://www.upress.state.ms.us.

Univ. Pr. of New England, *(978-0-87451; 978-0-915032; 978-1-58465; 978-1-61168; 978-1-5126; 978-1-68458)* Orders Addr.: One Court St., Suite 250, Lebanon, NH 03755 USA Tel 603-448-1533 (ext. 255); Fax: 603-448-9429; Toll Free: 800-421-1561; Edit Addr.: 415 South St., Waltham, MA 02453 USA
E-mail: University.Press@Dartmouth.edu
Web site: http://www.upne.com.

Univelt, Inc., *(978-0-87703; 978-0-912183)* Orders Addr.: P.O. Box 28130, San Diego, CA 92198 USA; Edit Addr.: 740 Metcalf St., Suite 13, Escondido, CA 92025-1671 USA (SAN 658-2095)
E-mail: sales@univelt.com
Web site: http://www.univelt.com.

Universal Subscription Service, P.O. Box 35445, Houston, TX 77035 USA (SAN 287-4768).

Universe Publishing, *(978-0-7893; 978-0-87663; 978-1-55550)* Div. of Rizzoli International Pubns., Inc., 300 Park Ave. S., 3rd Flr., New York, NY 10010 USA (SAN 202-537X) Tel 212-387-3400; Fax: 212-387-3444 Do not confuse with similar names in North Hollywood, CA, Englewood, NJ, Mendocino, CA.

University Book Service, Orders Addr.: P.O. Box 608, Grove City, OH 43123 USA (SAN 169-6912); Edit Addr.: P.O. Box 607, Grove City, OH 43123-0607 USA (SAN 282-4841) Toll Free: 800-634-4272.

University of Arizona Pr., *(978-0-8165; 978-1-941451)* 355 S. Euclid Ave., Suite 103, Tucson, AZ 85719 USA (SAN 205-468X) Tel 520-621-1441; Fax: 520-621-8899; Toll Free: 800-426-3797 (orders)
E-mail: orders@uapress.arizona.edu
Web site: http://www.uapress.arizona.edu.

University of Hawaii Press Agrmt. 2, Orders Addr.: 2840 Kolowalu St., Honolulu, HI 96822 USA
E-mail: uhpbooks@hawaii.edu.

University of Nevada Pr., *(978-0-87417; 978-1-943859; 978-1-948908; 978-1-64779)* Orders Addr.: Mail Stop 166, Reno, NV 89557 USA (SAN 203-316X) Tel 775-784-6573; Fax: 775-784-6200; Toll Free: 877-682-6657 (orders only)
E-mail: vfontana@unpress.nevada.edu
Web site: http://www.unpress.nevada.edu.

University of Virginia Pr., *(978-0-8139; 978-0-912759; 978-1-57814)* Orders Addr.: P.O. Box 400318, Charlottesville, VA 22904-4318 USA (SAN 202-5361) Tel 804-924-3468; Fax: 804-982-2655
E-mail: upress@virginia.edu
Web site: http://www.upress.virginia.edu.

University Publishing Associates, Incorporated, *See* **National Film Network LLC**

Untreed Reads Publishing, LLC, *(978-1-61187; 978-1-945447; 978-1-949135; 978-1-953601; 979-8-88860; 978-1-961689)* 506 Kansas St., San Francisco, CA 94107 USA Tel 415-621-0465; Toll Free Fax: 800-318-6037
E-mail: jhartman@untreedreads.com; kdsullivan@untreedreads.com
Web site: http://www.untreedreads.com.

Upper Access, Inc., *(978-0-942679)* Orders Addr.: 87 Upper Access Rd., Hinesburg, VT 05461 USA (SAN 667-1195) Tel 802-482-2988 main office
E-mail: info@upperaccess.com
Web site: http://www.upperaccess.com.

Urban Land Institute, *(978-0-87420)* 1025 Thomas Jefferson St., NW, Suite 500 W., Washington, DC 20007-5201 USA (SAN 203-3399) Tel 202-624-7000; Fax: 202-624-7140; Toll Free: 800-321-5011
E-mail: bookstore@uli.org
Web site: http://www.uli.org/.

U.S. Games Systems, Inc., *(978-0-88079; 978-0-913866; 978-1-57281; 978-1-64671)* 179 Ludlow St., Stamford, CT 06902 USA (SAN 158-6483) Tel 203-353-8400; Fax: 203-353-8431; Toll Free: 800-544-2637
E-mail: usgames@aol.com
Web site: http://www.usgamesinc.com.

US PubRep, Inc., 5000 Jasmine Dr., Rockville, MD 20853 USA Tel 301-838-9276; Fax: 301-838-9278
E-mail: craigfalk@aya.yale.edu.

Val Publishing, 16 S. Terrace Ave., Mount Vernon, NY 10551 USA (SAN 107-6876) Tel 914-664-7077.
Valentine Publishing Group, Orders Addr.: P.O. Box 902582, Palmdale, CA 93590-2582 USA; Edit Addr.: 18543 Devonshire St., Northridge, CA 91324 USA Tel 818-831-0649; Fax: 818-831-6659
E-mail: sales@vpg.net.
Valiant International Multi-Media Corp., 55 Ruta Ct., South Hackensack, NJ 07606 USA (SAN 652-8813) Tel 201-229-9800; Fax: 201-814-0418.
Valjean Pr., 721 Shadowlawn Ct., Franklin, TN 37069 USA
E-mail: pastorforthemoment@gmail.com.
Valkyrie Distribution, 43 New Hope Ct., Florissant, MO 63033 USA Tel 314-623-6639
E-mail: valkpub@yahoo.com.
Valley Distributors, Inc., 2947 Felton Rd., Norristown, PA 19401 USA (SAN 169-7498) Tel 610-279-7650; Fax: 610-279-9093; Toll Free: 800-355-2665 (orders only).
Valley Media, Inc., 1276 Santa Anita Ct., Woodland, CA 95776 USA Tel 530-661-6600; Fax: 530-661-5472
E-mail: valley@valley-media.com
Web site: http://www.valsat.com.
Valley Record Distributors, *See* **Valley Media, Inc.**
Van Dyke News Agency, 2238 W. Pinedale Ave., Fresno, CA 93711-0453 USA (SAN 168-9630) Tel 209-291-7768; Fax: 209-291-7770.
Van Khoa Bks., 14601 Moran St., Westminster, CA 92683-5629 USA (SAN 110-7534)
E-mail: vankhoa@vinet.com.
Verham News Corp., 75 Main St., West Lebanon, NH 03784 USA (SAN 169-4561) Fax: 603-298-8843.
VHPS Distribution Center, *See* **MPS**
Victory Multimedia, *(978-0-9661850)* Div. of Victory Audio Video Services, Inc., 460 Hindry Ave., Suite D, Inglewood, CA 90301-2045 USA (SAN 631-4112)
E-mail: sbvictory@juno.com.
Vida Life Publishers International, *See* **Vida Pubs.**
Vida Pubs., *(978-0-8297)* 8410 NW 53rd Ter. Ste. 103, Miami, FL 33166-4510 USA Toll Free: 800-843-2548
E-mail: vidapubsales@harpercollins.com
Web site: http://www.editorialvida.com.
Video Project, The, 200 Estates Dr., Ben Lomond, CA 95005-9444 USA Toll Free: 800-475-2638
E-mail: videoproject@videoproject.org
Web site: http://www.videoproject.org.
Vigilante, Richard Bks., *(978-0-9800763; 978-0-9827163)* 7400 Metro Blvd. Suite 217, Minneapolis, MN 55439 USA.
Village Marketing, 145 W. 400 N., Richfield, UT 84701 USA (SAN 631-6751) Toll Free: 800-982-6683.
Vinabind, P.O. Box 340, Steelville, MO 65565 USA (SAN 159-9828).
Vincennes News Agency, P.O. Box 1110, Evansville, IN 47706-1110 USA (SAN 169-2518).
Virginia Periodical Distributors, *See* **Aramark Magazine & Bk. Services, Inc.**
Virginia Pubns., 16 W. Washington St., Lexington, VA 24450 USA Tel 540-462-3993
E-mail: vapublications@rockbridge.net.
Vision Distributors, *(978-0-9626732)* Div. of Infinite Creations, Inc., Orders Addr.: P.O. Box 9839, Santa Fe, NM 87504 USA Tel 505-986-8221.
Vision Press, *See* **Vision Distributors**
Vision Video, *(978-1-56364)* Orders Addr.: P.O. Box 540, Worcester, PA 19490 USA Tel 610-584-3500; Fax: 610-584-4610; Toll Free: 800-523-0226; Edit Addr.: 2030 Wentz Church Rd., Worcester, PA 19490 USA (SAN 298-7392)
E-mail: info@gatewayfilms.com; info@visionvideo.com
Web site: http://www.gatewayfilms.com.
Vistabooks, *(978-0-89646)* Orders Addr.: 637 Blue Ridge Rd., Silverthorne, CO 80498-8931 USA (SAN 211-0849) Tel 970-468-7673 (phone/fax)
E-mail: vistabooks@compuserve.com
Web site: http://www.vistabooks.com.
Vitality Distributors, 940 NW 51st Pl., Fort Lauderdale, FL 33309 USA (SAN 169-0973) Toll Free: 800-226-8482.
VNU, Div. of Prestel Publishing, 575 Prospect Ave., Lakewood, NJ 08701 USA (SAN 631-7758) Tel 732-363-5679; Fax: 732-363-0338; Toll Free: 888-463-6110.
volcano pr., *(978-0-912078; 978-1-884244)* Orders Addr.: P.O. Box 270, Volcano, CA 95689 USA (SAN 220-0015) Tel 209-296-4991; Fax: 209-296-4995; Toll Free: 800-879-9636; Edit Addr.: 21496 National St., Volcano, CA 95689 USA
E-mail: info@volcanopress.com; sales@volcanopress.com; adam@volcanopress.com
Web site: http://www.volcanopress.com.
VPD, Inc., 150 Parkshore Dr., Folsom, CA 95630-4710 USA (SAN 631-287X) Toll Free: 800-366-2111
Web site: http://www.vpdinc.com/.
Vroman's, A. C., *(978-0-9639197)* 695 E. Colorado Blvd., Pasadena, CA 91101 USA (SAN 169-0027) Tel 626-449-5320; Fax: 626-792-7308.
W5YI Group, Inc., P.O. Box 565101, Dallas, TX 75356 USA.
WA Bk. Service, P.O. Box 514, East Islip, NY 11730-0514 USA (SAN 107-2943).
Wabash Valley News Agency, 2200 N. Curry Pike, No. 2, Bloomington, IN 47404-1486 USA (SAN 169-250X).
Waffle, O. G. Bk. Co. (The Bookhouse), P.O. Box 586, Marion, IA 52302 USA (SAN 112-8817) Tel 319-373-1832.
Waldenbooks Company, Incorporated, *See* **Waldenbooks, Inc.**
Waldenbooks, Inc., *(978-0-681)* Div. of Borders Group, Inc., a/o Calendar Orders, 455 Industrial Blvd., Suite C, LaVergne, TN 37086 USA (SAN 179-3373); Orders Addr.: One Waldenbooks Dr., LaVergne, TN 37096 USA; 11625 Venture, Mira Loma, CA 91752 Tel 951-361-4025; Edit Addr.: 100 Phoenix Dr., Ann Arbor, MI 48108-2202 USA (SAN 200-8858) Tel 734-477-1100
E-mail: customerservice@waldenbooks.com
Web site: http://www.waldenbooks.com; http://www.preferredreader.com.
Walker Art Ctr., *(978-0-935640; 978-1-935963)* Orders Addr.: 1750 Hennepin Ave., Minneapolis, MN 55403 USA (SAN 206-1880) Tel 612-375-7638; Fax: 612-375-7565
E-mail: paul.schumacher@walkerart.org; lisa.middag@walkerart.org.
Wallace's College Bk. Co., P.O. Box 689, Nicholasville, KY 40340-0689 USA (SAN 169-2844) Tel 606-255-0886; Fax: 606-259-9892; Toll Free Fax: 800-433-9329 (orders only); Toll Free: 800-354-9590 (orders only); 800-354-9500
E-mail: orders@wallaces.com.
Walthers, William K. Inc., *(978-0-941952)* 5601 W. Florist Ave., Milwaukee, WI 53201-3039 USA (SAN 238-4868) Tel 414-527-0770; Fax: 414-527-4423; Toll Free: 800-877-7171.
Ware-Pak, Inc., Orders Addr.: 2427 Bond St., University Park, IL 60466 USA Tel 708-534-2600; Fax: 708-534-7803
E-mail: kshay@ware-pak.com
Web site: http://www.ware-pak.com.
Warner Books, Incorporated, *See* **Grand Central Publishing**
Warner Bros. Pubns., *(978-0-7604; 978-0-7692; 978-0-87487; 978-0-89724; 978-0-89898; 978-0-910957; 978-1-55122; 978-1-57623; 978-0-7579)* Div. of AOL Time Warner, 15800 NW 48th Ave., Miami, FL 33014-6422 USA (SAN 203-0586).
Warner Pr., Inc., *(978-0-87162; 978-1-59317; 978-1-68434)* Orders Addr.: P.O. Box 2499, Anderson, IN 46018-2499 USA (SAN 691-4241) Tel 765-648-2116; Fax: 765-622-9511; Toll Free: 800-848-2464; Edit Addr.: 2902 Enterprise Dr., Anderson, IN 46013 USA (SAN 111-8110) Tel 765-644-7721; Fax: 765-640-8005; Toll Free: 800-741-7721 (orders only)
E-mail: jallison@warnerpress.org; wporders@warnerpress.org; rjackson@warnerpress.org
Web site: http://www.warnerpress.org; http://www.francisasburypress.org.
Warner Press Publishers, *See* **Warner Pr., Inc.**
Washington Bk. Distributors, 4930A Eisenhower Ave., Alexandria, VA 22304 USA (SAN 631-0095) Tel 703-212-9113; Fax: 703-212-9114; Toll Free: 800-699-9113
E-mail: zacwbd@prodigy.net
Web site: http://www.washingtonbk.com.
Washington Toy Co., 2163 28th Ave., San Francisco, CA 94116-1732 USA (SAN 107-1718).
Watson, W. R. & Staff, 150 Mariner Green Ct., Corte Madera, CA 94925 USA (SAN 286-0155) Tel 510-524-6156; Fax: 510-526-5023.
Watson-Guptill Pubns., Inc., *(978-0-8230; 978-1-60569)* Div. of Crown Publishing Grp., 575 Prospect St., Lakewood, NJ 08701 USA Tel 732-363-5679; Toll Free Fax: 877-227-6564; Edit Addr.: 1745 Broadway # 124, New York, NY 10019-4305 USA (SAN 282-5384)
E-mail: aalexander@watsonguptill.com
Web site: http://www.watsonguptill.com.
Waverly News Co., 17 State St., Newburyport, MA 01950 USA (SAN 169-3522).
Wayland Audio-Visual, 210 E. 86th St., Suite 405, New York, NY 10028 USA Toll Free: 800-813-1271
E-mail: jm@waylandav.com.
Waymont Bk. Co., 136 Steuben St., Jersey City, NJ 07302 USA (SAN 630-768X) Tel 201-434-4268; Fax: 201-432-1293
E-mail: waymont@worldnet.att.net.
Wayne State Univ. Pr., *(978-0-8143)* Leonard N. Simons Bldg., 4809 Woodward Ave., Detroit, MI 48201-1309 USA (SAN 202-5221) Tel 313-577-6120; Fax: 313-577-6131; Toll Free: 800-978-7323 (customer orders)
E-mail: theresa.martinelli@wayne.edu; Kristina.Stonehill@wayne.edu
Web site: http://wsupress.wayne.edu.
Weiner News Co., 1011 N. Frio, P.O. Box 7608, San Antonio, TX 78207 USA (SAN 169-8427) Tel 210-226-9333; Fax: 210-226-8679.
Weiser, Samuel Incorporated, *See* **Red Wheel/Weiser**
WellSpring Bks., P.O. Box 2765, Woburn, MA 01888-1465 USA (SAN 111-3399) Do not confuse with companies with the same or similar names in Albuquerque, NM, Ukiah, CA, Adelphia, NJ, Woburn, MA, Groton, VT.
Wenatchee News Agency, 434 Rock Island Rd., East Wenatchee, WA 98802-5360 USA (SAN 169-8885) Tel 509-662-3511.
Wesscott Marketing, Inc., *(978-0-9764077)* P.O. Box 26144, Saint Louis Park, MN 55426 USA Fax: 952-541-4905; Toll Free: 800-375-3702.
West, *(978-0-314; 978-0-7620; 978-0-8321; 978-0-8366; 978-0-87632)* Orders Addr.: 610 Opperman Dr., Eagan, MN 55123-1396 USA Tel 657-687-6849; Fax: 651-687-6857; Toll Free: 800-328-2209; 800-328-9378 (Editorial) Do not confuse with The West Group in Prairie Village, KS
E-mail: west.bookstore@thomson.com; customer.service@westgroup.com; janet.linkert@thompson.com
Web site: http://west.thomson.com; http://westacademic.com.
West Music Co., 1212 Fifth St., Coralville, IA 52241 USA Toll Free: 800-397-9378.
West Texas News Co., Orders Addr.: 1214 Barranca, El Paso, TX 79935 USA; Edit Addr.: P.O. Box 26488, El Paso, TX 79926 USA (SAN 169-8184) Tel 915-594-7586; Fax: 915-594-7589.
West Virginia Book Co., The, 1125 Central Ave., Charleston, WV 25302 USA (SAN 920-9956) Tel 304-342-1848; Fax: 304-343-0594; Toll Free: 888-982-7472
E-mail: wvbooks@wvbookco.com.
Western Book Distributors/Booksource, *See* **Western Booksource, Inc.**
Western Booksource, Inc., 4935 Metart Shwayn, Tillamook, OR 97141 USA (SAN 158-4332) Toll Free: 800-825-0100; 230 Fifth Ave., No. 1104, New York, NY 10001 Tel 212-889-9339; Fax: 212-889-9572.
Western International, Inc., *(978-0-9665194)* 2220 Delaware St., Lawrence, KS 66046-3150 USA (SAN 631-1695) Toll Free: 800-634-6737.
Western Library Bks., 560 S. San Vicente Blvd., Los Angeles, CA 90048 USA (SAN 168-9878) Tel 213-653-8880.
Western Merchandisers, 2900 Airport Rd., Denton, TX 76207-2102 USA (SAN 156-4633).
Western Michigan News, *See* **Readmor**
Western Pubns. Service, 2128 Sun Valley Rd., San Marcos, CA 92069 USA (SAN 630-6241) Tel 760-295-2231; Fax: 760-295-3978.
Western Record Sales, 2991 Saint Andrews Rd., Fairfield, CA 94533-7839 USA (SAN 630-6667).
Western Reserve Historical Society, *(978-0-911704; 978-0-9967844)* 10825 East Blvd., Cleveland, OH 44106 USA (SAN 110-8387) Tel 216-721-5722; Fax: 216-721-0645.
Westminster John Knox Pr., *(978-0-664; 978-0-8042; 978-1-61164; 978-1-947888; 978-1-64698)* Div. of Presbyterian Publishing Corp., Orders Addr.: 100 Witherspoon St., Louisville, KY 40202 USA (SAN 202-9669) Tel 502-569-5052 (outside U.S. for ordering); Fax: 502-569-5113 (outside U.S. for faxed orders); Toll Free Fax: 800-541-5113 (toll-free U.S. faxed orders); Toll Free: 800-227-2872 (customer service)
E-mail: orders@wjkbooks.com
Web site: http://www.wjkbooks.com.
Weston, Edward Fine Arts, P.O. Box 3098, Chatsworth, CA 91313-3098 USA (SAN 168-9967) Tel 818-885-1044; Fax: 818-885-1021.
Weston Woods Studios, Inc., *(978-0-7882; 978-0-89719; 978-1-55592; 978-1-56008)* Div. of Scholastic, Inc., 143 Main St., Norwalk, CT 06851 USA (SAN 630-3838) Tel 203-845-0197; Fax: 203-845-0498; Toll Free: 800-243-5020
E-mail: questions@Scholastic.com
Web site: http://www.scholastic.com/westonwoods.
Westwater Bks., *(978-0-916370; 978-1-941406)* Div. of Belknap Photographic Services, Inc., P.O. Box 2560, Evergreen, CO 80437 USA (SAN 208-3698) Tel 303-674-5410; 303-378-2592; Fax: 303-670-0586; Toll Free: 800-628-1326.
WFiveYI Group, Inc., The, 7101 N. Ridgeway Ave., Lincolnwood, IL 60712 USA Tel 847-763-0916; Fax: 847-763-0918.
Whatever Publishing, Incorporated, *See* **New World Library**
Whitaker Distributors, *See* **Anchor Distributors**
Whitaker Hse., *(978-0-88368; 978-1-60374; 978-1-62911; 978-1-64123; 979-8-88769)* Div. of Whitaker Corp., 1030 Hunt Valley Cir., New Kensington, PA 15068 USA (SAN 203-2104) Tel 724-334-7000 Whitaker House/Anchor Distributors; Fax: 724-334-1200 Anchor Distributors; Toll Free Fax: 866-773-7001 Whitaker House; 800-765-1960 Anchor Distributors; Toll Free: 877-793-9800 Whitaker House; 800-444-4484 Whitaker House/Anchor Distributors
E-mail: sales@whitakerhouse.com
Web site: http://www.whitakerhouse.com/; http://www.anchordistributors.com/; http://www.amazon.com/.
Whitewing Pr., P.O. Box 1561, Hemphill, TX 75948 USA Tel 409-787-1526
E-mail: books@whitewingpress.com.
Whiting News Co., 1011 Azalea Dr., Munster, IN 46321-3501 USA (SAN 169-2542).
Whitlock & Co., 10001 Roosevelt Rd., Westchester, IL 60153 USA (SAN 285-9645).
Whitman Distribution Co., Orders Addr.: P.O. Box 513, Lebanon, NH 03766 USA (SAN 631-0540) Fax: 603-448-2576; Toll Free: 800-353-3730; Edit Addr.: 10 Water St., Lebanon, NH 03766 USA
E-mail: distribution@whitmancommunications.com.
Whitman Publishing & Distribution Company, *See* **Whitman Distribution Co.**
Wholesale Distributors, P.O. Box 126, Burlington, IA 52601 USA (SAN 145-8051) Tel 319-753-1683; Fax: 319-753-5988; Toll Free: 800-272-1556.
Wickel, W. W. Co., Inc., 520 N. Exchange Ct., Aurora, IL 60504 USA (SAN 135-1230) Tel 630-820-0044; Fax: 630-820-0057; Toll Free: 800-728-0708.
Wicker Park Pr., Ltd., *(978-0-9789676; 978-1-936679)* 334 Hawthorn Ave., Glencoe, IL 60022 USA Tel 773-391-1199
E-mail: eric@3ibooks.com
Web site: http://www.wickerparkpress.us.
Wilcor International Bk. Dept., 161 Drive In Rd., Frankfort, NY 13340-5238 USA (SAN 107-7023).
Wild Dog Bks., Orders Addr.: Seven Balsa Ct., Sante Fe, NM 87508 USA
E-mail: WildDogBooks@att.net.
Wiley, John & Sons, Inc., *(978-0-470; 978-0-471; 978-0-7645; 978-0-7821; 978-0-8260; 978-0-87605; 978-0-88422; 978-0-914993; 978-0-937721; 978-0-939246; 978-1-55828; 978-1-56217; 978-1-56561; 978-1-56884; 978-1-57313; 978-1-58245; 978-1-878058; 978-1-118; 978-1-119; 978-1-7994; 978-1-394; 979-8-203) Orders Addr.: c/o John Wiley & Sons, Inc., United States Distribution Ctr., 1 Wiley Dr., Somerset, NJ 08875-1272 USA Tel 732-469-4400; Fax: 732-302-2300; Toll Free Fax: 800-597-3299; Toll Free: 800-225-5945 (orders); Edit Addr.: 111 River St., Hoboken, NJ 07030 USA (SAN 200-2272) Tel 201-748-6000; 201-748-6276 (Retail and Wholesale); Fax: 201-748-6088; 201-748-8641 (Retail and Wholesale)*
E-mail: compbks@wiley.com; bookinfo@wiley.com; custserv@wiley.com
Web site: http://www.wiley.com/compbooks; http://www.interscience.wiley.com; http://www.wiley.com.
William Thomson, *See* **Thomson, Linda**
Williamson, Darcy, *See* **Southern Cross Pubns.**
Willman Productions, P.O. Box 272345, Fort Collins, CO 80527 USA Tel 970-224-5911; Toll Free: 800-816-7566.
Wilshire Bk. Co., *(978-0-87980)* 9731 Variel Ave., Chatsworth, CA 91311-4315 USA (SAN 168-9932)
E-mail: mpowers@mpowers.com
Web site: http://www.mpowers.com.
Wilson & Associates, *See* **Gatewood Pr.**
Wilson & Sons, P.O. Box 996, Bellevue, WA 98009 USA (SAN 129-0010) Tel 425-392-1965
E-mail: dchief@seanst.com.
Wimmer Companies, The, *See* **Wimmer Cookbooks**
Wimmer Cookbooks, *(978-0-918544; 978-0-939114; 978-1-879958)* 4650 Shelby Air Dr., Memphis, TN 38118 USA Tel 901-362-8900; 800-727-1034; Fax: 901-795-9806; Toll Free Fax: 800-794-9806; Toll Free: 800-727-1034 Do not confuse with Wimmer Cookbooks in Atlanta, GA
E-mail: wimmer@wimmerco.com
Web site: http://www.wimmerco.com.
Winch, B. L. & Assocs., *(978-0-935266)* P.O. Box 1185, Torrance, CA 90505 USA (SAN 247-2716) Tel 310-816-3085; Fax: 310-816-3092; Toll Free: 800-662-9662 (orders only)
E-mail: czippi@att.net
Web site: http://www.ierc.com.
Windham County News Co., P.O. Box 8127, Brattleboro, VT 05304 USA (SAN 159-9917) Tel 802-254-2373.
Windhover Performing Arts Ctr., 257 Granite St., Rockport, MA 01966 USA Tel 978-546-3611
Web site: http://www.windhover.org.
Wine Appreciation Guild, Ltd., *(978-0-932664; 978-1-891267; 978-1-934259; 978-1-935879)* 360 Swift Ave., Unit 30, South San Francisco, CA 94080-6220 USA (SAN 169-0264) Tel 650-866-3020; Fax: 650-866-3513; Toll Free: 800-242-9462 (orders only)
E-mail: Jim@wineappreciation.com; bryan.imelli@boardandbench.com
Web site: http://www.boardandbench.com.
Winebaum News, Inc., P.O. Box 1620, Raymond, NH 03077-3620 USA (SAN 169-4529).
Wing Aero, 545 Rowlett Rd., Suite A, Garland, TX 75043 USA (SAN 631-2659).
Wipf & Stock Pubs., *(978-0-9653517; 978-1-55635; 978-1-57910; 978-1-59244; 978-1-59752; 978-1-60608; 978-1-60899; 978-1-61097; 978-1-62032; 978-1-62189; 978-1-62564; 978-1-63087; 978-1-4982; 978-1-5326; 978-1-7252; 978-1-6667; 979-8-3852)* Orders Addr.: 199 W 8th Ave Ste 3, Eugene, OR 97401 USA (SAN 990-3038) Tel 541-344-1528; Fax: 541-344-1506; Edit Addr.: 199 W 8th Ave Ste 3, Eugene, OR 97401 USA Tel 541-344-1528; Fax: 541-344-1506
E-mail: contentadmin@wipfandstock.com
Web site: http://wipfandstock.com/; http://stonetablebooks.com/.
WIPRO, 2 Christie Heights St., Leonia, NJ 07605 USA Tel 201-840-4755.
Wisdom Pubns., *(978-0-86171; 978-1-61429; 978-1-949129; 979-8-89070)* 199 Elm St., Somerville, MA 02144 USA (SAN 246-022X) Tel 617-776-7416 ext 24; Fax: 617-776-7841; Toll Free Fax: 800-338-4550 (orders only); Toll Free: 800-462-6420 (orders only)
E-mail: tlulek@wisdompubs.org; admin@wisdompubs.org
Web site: http://www.wisdompubs.org.
Wittenborn Art Bks., *(978-0-8150; 978-0-89648)* Div. of Alan Wofsy Fine Arts, Orders Addr.: 1109 Geary Blvd., San Francisco, CA 94109 USA Tel 415-292-6500; Fax: 415-292-6594; Edit Addr.: P.O. Box 2210, San Francisco, CA 94126 USA Tel 510-482-3677; Toll Free: 800-660-6403
E-mail: editeur@eathlink.net; art-books.com@jps.net
Web site: http://www.art-books.com.
Wizard Works, *(978-0-9621543; 978-1-890692)* Orders Addr.: P.O. Box 1125, Homer, AK 99603-1125 USA Toll Free: 877-210-2665
E-mail: wizard@xyz.net
Web site: http://www.xyz.net/~wizard.
Wolper Sales Agency, Inc., 6 Centre Sq., Suite 302A, Easton, PA 18042-3606 USA (SAN 285-9785) Tel 610-559-9550; Fax: 610-559-9898.
Wolters Kluwer Legal & Regulatory US, *See* **Aspen Publishing**
Wolverine Distributing, Inc., *(978-0-941875)* P.O. Box 503, Powell, WY 82435 USA (SAN 666-1211) Tel 307-754-2948; Fax: 307-754-2968; Toll Free: 800-967-1633
E-mail: wolverine@tctwest.net.
Wolverine Gallery, *See* **Wolverine Distributing, Inc.**
Women Ink, 777 United Nations Plaza, New York, NY 10017 USA (SAN 630-8309) Tel 212-687-8633; Fax: 212-661-2704
E-mail: wink@womenink.org
Web site: http://www.womenink.org.
Woodbine Publishing Co., The, 15621 Chemical Ln., No. B, Huntington Beach, CA 92649 USA (SAN 114-4243) Tel 714-894-9080; Fax: 714-894-4949; Toll Free: 800-451-4788
Web site: http://www.safaripress.com.
Woodcrafters Lumber Sales, Inc., 212 NE Sixth Ave., Portland, OR 97232 USA (SAN 112-6075) Tel 503-231-0226; Toll Free: 800-777-3709.
Woodland Distribution, Orders Addr.: 118 Woodland Dr., Chapmanville, WV 25508 USA Tel 304-752-7152; Fax: 304-752-9002.

Woodstocker Books/Arthur Schwartz & Company, (*978-1-879504*) 15 Meads Mountain Rd., Woodstock, NY 12498-1016 USA (SAN 630-0464) Tel 845-679-4024; Fax: 845-679-4093; Toll Free: 800-669-9080 (orders only)
E-mail: woodstockerbooks@woodstockerbooks.com
Web site: http://www.aschwartzbooks.com.

Word Distribution, *See* **Word Entertainment**

Word Entertainment, (*978-0-9644619; 978-1-933876*) 25 Music Sq. W., Nashville, TN 37203 USA Tel 615-726-7900; Toll Free Fax: 800-671-6601; Toll Free: 800-876-9673
E-mail: matt.taylor@wordentertainment.com
Web site: http://www.wordentertainment.com.

Word For Today, The, *See* **Calvary Chapel Resources**

Word of Life Distributors, 2707 W. Olympic Blvd. Ste. 100, Los Angeles, CA 90006-2850 USA (SAN 108-433X) Toll Free: 800-347-7057.

WordWorks Publishing, (*978-1-887913*) Orders Addr.: 207 E. Pine Ridge Dr., Westfield, IN 46074 USA Tel 317-867-1879 (phone/fax) Do not confuse with Wordworks Publishing, Austin, TX
E-mail: joanetta.hendel@comcast.net.

Workamper Bookstore, 201 Hiram Rd., Heber Springs, AR 72543-8747 USA (SAN 631-547X) Tel 501-362-2637; Toll Free: 800-446-5627 (orders only)
Web site: http://www.workamper.com.

Workman Publishing Co., Inc., (*978-0-7611; 978-0-89480; 978-0-911104; 978-1-56305; 978-1-5235*) Orders Addr.: 225 Varick St., New York, NY 10014-4381 USA (SAN 203-2821) Tel 212-254-5900; Fax: 212-254-8098; Toll Free: 800-722-7202
E-mail: info@workman.com
Web site: http://www.workman.com.

World Bank Pubns., (*978-0-8213; 978-1-4648*) Orders Addr.: P.O. Box 960, Herndon, VA 20172-0960 USA Toll Free: 800-645-7247; Edit Addr.: 1818 H St., NW, Mail Stop: U11-1104, Washington, DC 20433 USA (SAN 219-0648) Tel 703-661-1580; 202-473-1000 (Head Office); Fax: 202-614-1237
E-mail: books@worldbank.org
Web site: http://www.worldbank.org/publications.

World of Reading, Ltd., P.O. Box 13092, Atlanta, GA 30324-0092 USA Tel 404-233-4042; Fax: 404-237-5511; Toll Free: 800-729-3703.

World Publications, Incorporated, *See* **World Pubns. Group, Inc.**

World Pubns. Group, Inc., (*978-0-7669; 978-0-9640034; 978-1-57215; 978-0-7429; 978-1-4132; 978-1-4279; 978-1-4376; 978-1-4513; 978-1-4643; 978-1-4785*) Orders Addr.: P.O. Box 509, East Bridgewater, MA 02333 USA (SAN 631-7014)
E-mail: sales@wrldpub.net
Web site: http://www.wrldpub.com.

World Scientific Textbook, Orders Addr.: 27 Warren St., Hackensack, NJ 07601 USA.

World Univ., (*978-0-941902*) P.O. Box 2470, Benson, AZ 85602 USA (SAN 239-7943) Tel 520-586-2985; Fax: 520-586-4764
E-mail: desertsanctuary@theriver.com
Web site: http://worlduniversity.org.

World Wide Distributors, Limited, *See* **Island Heritage Publishing**

World Wide Hunting Books, *See* **Woodbine Publishing Co., The**

World Wide Pubns., (*978-0-89066*) P.O. Box 668089, Charlotte, NC 28266-8089 USA (SAN 159-9941) Toll Free: 800-788-0442.

World Wisdom, Inc., (*978-0-941532; 978-1-933316; 978-1-935493; 978-1-936597; 978-1-937786; 978-1-957670*) Orders Addr.: P.O. Box 2682, Bloomington, IN 47402-2682 USA (SAN 239-1406) Tel 812-330-3232; Fax: 812-333-1642; Toll Free: 888-992-6651; Edit Addr.: 1501 E. Hillside Dr., Bloomington, IN 47401 USA
Web site: http://www.worldwisdom.com.

Worldwide Media Service, Inc., Affil. of Hudson County News Agency, 30 Montgomery St., Jersey City, NJ 07302-3821 USA (SAN 630-4826) Tel 201-332-7100; Fax: 201-332-0265; Toll Free: 800-345-6478
Web site: http://www.americanmagazine.com.

Wright Bk./Educational, 2195 Owendale Dr., Dayton, OH 45439 USA (SAN 159-9968).

Wright Group/McGraw-Hill, (*978-0-322; 978-0-7802; 978-0-940156; 978-1-55624; 978-1-55911; 978-1-4045*) Div. of Mcgraw-Hill School Education Group, Orders Addr.: P.O. Box 545, Blacklick, OH 43004-0545 USA Tel 614-755-5645; Toll Free: 800-722-4726; 800-442-9685 (customer service)
Web site: http://www.wrightgroup.com/.

Writers & Bks., (*978-0-9618487; 978-0-9863305*) 740 University Ave., Rochester, NY 14607-1259 USA (SAN 156-9678).

Wybel Marketing Group, Orders Addr.: 213 W. Main St., Barrington, IL 60010 USA Tel 847-382-0384.

Wyoming Periodical Distributor, P.O. Box 2340, Casper, WY 82601 USA (SAN 169-9245).

Xlibris Corp., (*978-0-7388; 978-0-9663501; 978-1-4010; 978-1-4134; 978-1-59926; 978-1-4257; 978-1-4363; 978-1-4415; 978-1-4500; 978-1-4535; 978-1-4568; 978-1-4628; 978-1-4653; 978-1-4691; 978-1-4771; 978-1-4797; 978-1-4836; 978-1-4931; 978-1-4990; 978-1-5035;-1-5144; 978-1-5245; 978-1-4990-9726-9; 978-1-4990-9725-2; 978-1-4990-9724-5; 978-1-5434; 978-1-9845; 978-1-7960; 978-1-6641; 978-1-6698; 979-8-3694) Orders Addr.: 1663 S. Liberty Dr. Suite 200, Bloomington, IN 47403 USA (SAN 299-5522) Tel 812-334-5223; Fax: 812-334-5223; Toll Free: 888-795-4274*
E-mail: info@xlibris.com
Web site: http://www2.xlibris.com.

Xlibris Corporation, *See* **Xlibris Corp.**

X-S Bks., Inc., 81 Brookside Ave., Amsterdam, NY 12010-0740 USA (SAN 169-4634).

Yale Univ., Far Eastern Pubns., (*978-0-88710*) 340 Edwards St., Box 208252, New Haven, CT 06520-8252 USA (SAN 219-0710) Tel 203-432-3109; Fax: 203-432-3111
Web site: http://www.yale.edu/fep.

Yale Univ. Pr., (*978-0-300; 978-1-933789; 978-1-282*) Orders Addr.: c/o Triliteral LLC, 100 Maple Ridge Dr., Cumberland, RI 02864 USA Tel 401-531-2800; Fax: 401-531-2801; Toll Free Fax: 800-406-9145; Toll Free: 800-405-1619; Edit Addr.: 302 Temple St., New Haven, CT 06511 USA (SAN 203-2740) Tel 203-432-0960; Fax: 203-432-0948
E-mail: yupmkt@yale.edu
Web site: http://www.yale.edu/yup/; http://www.yale.edu/yup/index.html.

Yankee Bk. Peddler, Inc., 999 Maple St., Contoocook, NH 03229 USA (SAN 169-4510) Tel 603-746-3102; Fax: 603-746-5628; Toll Free: 800-258-3774
E-mail: ybp@office.ybp.com
Web site: http://www.ybp.com.

Yankee Paperback & Textbook Co., P.O. Box 18880, Tucson, AZ 85731 USA (SAN 112-1073) Tel 520-325-7229 (phone/fax); Toll Free: 800-340-2665 (in Arizona, California, Nevada, Colorado, New Mexico and Utah only).

Yankee Paperback Distributors, *See* **Yankee Paperback & Textbook Co.**

Yankee Peddler Bookshop, (*978-0-918426*) 4299 Lake Rd., Williamson, NY 14589-9615 USA (SAN 209-925X)
E-mail: byankeep@rochester.rr.com
Web site: http://www.shoprochester.com//yankeepeddler-abc.

YBP Library Services, *See* **GOBI Library Solutionis from EBSCO**

Ye Olde Genealogie Shoppe, (*978-0-932924; 978-1-878311*) Orders Addr.: P.O. Box 39128, Indianapolis, IN 46239 USA (SAN 200-7010) Tel 317-862-3330; Toll Free: 800-419-0200 (orders)
E-mail: yogs@iquest.net
Web site: http://www.yogs.com.

Yosemite Association, *See* **Yosemite Conservancy**

Yosemite Conservancy, (*978-0-939666; 978-1-930238; 978-1-951179*) Orders Addr.: P.O. Box 230, El Portal, CA 95318 USA (SAN 662-197X) Tel 209-379-2317; Edit Addr.: 5020 El Portal Rd., El Portal, CA 95318 USA
E-mail: nicolegeiger1@gmail.com; jedelbrock@yosemiteconservancy.org; kcoit@yosemiteconservancy.org
Web site: http://www.yosemiteconservancy.org.

Young News, Inc., 1600 E. Grand Blvd., Detroit, MI 48211-3144 USA (SAN 169-3999) Fax: 517-753-7774.

Youthlight, Inc., (*978-1-889636; 978-1-59850*) Orders Addr.: P.O. Box 115, Chapin, SC 29036 USA (SAN 256-6400) Tel 803-345-1070; Fax: 803-345-0888; Toll Free: 800-209-9774; Edit Addr.: 105 Fairway Pond Dr., Chapin, SC 29036 USA
E-mail: yl@sc.rr.com; yl@youthlightbooks.com
Web site: http://www.youthlight.com; http://www.youthlightbooks.com.

Yuma News, Incorporated, *See* **Arizona Periodicals, Inc.**

YWAM Publishing, (*978-0-927545; 978-0-9615534; 978-1-57658; 978-1-64836*) Div. of Youth With A Mission International, P.O. Box 55787, Seattle, WA 98155 USA (SAN 248-4021)
E-mail: customerservice@ywampublishing.com
Web site: http://www.ywampublishing.com.

Zabel, C. & W. Co., Orders Addr.: P.O. Box 953, East Brunswick, NJ 08816-0953 USA (SAN 169-4731) Tel 732-254-1000; Fax: 732-254-0121; Edit Addr.: 76 Pennsbury Way, E Brunswick, NJ 08816-5278 USA (SAN 241-6441).

Zagat Survey, (*978-0-943421; 978-0-9612574; 978-1-57006; 978-1-60478*) 4 Columbus Cir., New York, NY 10019 USA (SAN 289-4777) Tel 212-977-6000; Fax: 212-765-9438; Toll Free: 866-999-0991
E-mail: tradesales@justzagat.com; theinz@zagat.com
Web site: http://www.zagat.com.

Zeitlin Periodicals Co., Inc., 7917 Lark Meadow Ave., Las Vegas, NV 89131-4710 USA (SAN 160-8088).

Zondervan, (*978-0-00; 978-0-310; 978-0-937336*) Div. of HarperCollins Christian Publishing, Orders Addr.: c/o Zondervan XNET Ordering Dept., 5249 Corporate Grove, Grand Rapids, MI 49512 USA (SAN 298-9107); Edit Addr.: 5300 Patterson Ave., SE, Grand Rapids, MI 49530 USA (SAN 203-2694) Tel 616-698-6900; Fax: 616-698-3439
Web site: http://www.zondervan.com.

Zondervan Publishing House, *See* **Zondervan**

Z-Twist Bks., 3312 Woodview Dr., Lafayette, CA 94549 USA Tel 916-570-3839.

Zubal, John T. Inc., (*978-0-939738*) 2969 W. 25th St., Cleveland, OH 44113 USA (SAN 165-5841) Tel 216-241-7640; Fax: 216-241-6966.

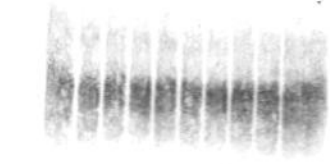